W9-CKS-286

38888033460712

Champion Hong Kong Auction August

Hyatt Regency 18 Hanoi Road Hong Kong

Champion Macau Auction Nov-26-2017

Consignment by 9/30

6/F Promenade, Sofitel Hotel Macau at Ponte 16

11/23-26 2017 Kam Pek Community Centre

Macau Numismatic Society 2017 International Show

12/3/2016 Champion Macau Auction Highlights **www.cghka.com**

Lot005 CHINA-ANHWEI 1898 50 Cents Silver (ASTC), L&M200, Y44.1, PCGS MS64. Charles Tanant Collection
Estimate: US $20,000
Realized:US $50,600

Lot084 CHINA-SZECHUAN ND (1902-11) One Rupee Silver, L&M360, Y3, PCGS MS65+. Charles Tanant Collection
Estimate: US $1,000
Realized:US $32,200

Lot165 CHINA-REPUBLIC ND (1927-28) 500 Cash Copper, Honan Mint, Hsu 445a, CCC559, NGC XF45BN. NC Collection
Estimate: US $10,000
Realized:US $46,000

Lot203 CHINA-KWEICHOW 1928 Auto Dollar Silver, with 3 blades of grass, L&M610, PCGS MS61. Highest graded coin by PCGS
Estimate: US $30,000
Realized:US $115,000

Lot220 CHINA-TAIWAN ND (1853) Ju-I Military Ration, with crossed lotus, L&M323, K2, NGC AU Details. NC Collection
Estimate: US $20,000
Realized:US $41,400

Lot253 CHINA-REPUBLIC ND Li Yuan Hung Commemorative Bronze Medal, Wuchang Mint Issue, NGC AU55BN. NC Collection
Estimate: US $3,000
Realized:US $27,600

Lot255 CHINA-HUPEH 1922 Wuchang Mint Director Guo Bronze Medal, NGC AU58BN. NC Collection
Estimate: US $3,000
Realized:US $34,500

Lot324 CHINA-MACAU 2016 Macau Numismatic Society 1000g .999 Silver Proof, diameter 120mm, Commemorative Show Panda, Serial number 01, Mintage 20
Estimate: US $1,000
Realized:US $6,900

Other Highlights

1898 Hunan Dollar Heaton Mint, NGC SP-67, NC Collection
12/1975 Paramount Auction
US$15,500
Realised: US $1,000,000+

Champion 15 (2011.8.26-28)
CHINA 1992 2000 Yuan 1 Kg Gold Proof Serial No. 06 Chinese, Invetions Discoveries Compass, NGC PF69 Ultra Cameo
Estimate US $750,000
Realised: US $1,298,000

Champion (2015.12.6)
Lot 185 CHINA-REPUBLIC 1912 Yuan Shi Kai Large Beard One Dollar Silver Pattern,Reeded Edge, NGC AU58
Estimate US $180,000
Realized： US $345,000

Champion (2016.8.23)
Lot 017 CHINA-CHIHLI 1896 One Dollar Silver,NGC MS63. Highest graded by grading service.
H.F.Bowker East Asia Collection
Estimate US $30,000
Realized： US $354,000

Champion Hong Kong
907 Silvercord Tower 2,30 Canton Rd,Tsim Sha Tsui,Kowloon Hong Kong
Tel：852-2150-5744
Fax：852-3007-4311
Email: championghka@gmail.com

iAsure Shanghai
Room 1808, Bao Hua Building, No.1211, Changde Road, Putuo District, Shanghai
Tel：86-21-62130771
Fax：86-21-62130773
Email: championghka@gmail.com

iAsure Taipei
Room 50-51, No.163 Nan King W.Rd Taipei
Tel: 886-2-25551761
Cell：886-920630566
Email: championghka@gmail.com

Follow me

2018 *Standard Catalog of®*

WORLD COINS

1901-2000

45th Edition

Thomas Michael, Senior Editor & Market Analyst

Tracy L. Schmidt, Editor

Richard Giedroyc, U.S. Market Analyst

Special Contributor

Michael Chou

Special Tribute

For years of service to Numismatics and coauthoring the Standard Catalog of® World Coins

Chester L. Krause

Bullion Value (BV) Market Valuations

Valuations for all platinum, gold, palladium and silver coins of the more common, basically bullion types, or those possessing only modest numismatic premiums are presented in this edition based on the market ranges of:

$975 - $1,050 per ounce for **platinum**
$750 - $775 per ounce for **palladium**
$1,225 - $1,275 per ounce for **gold**
$17.50 - $18.50 per ounce for **silver**

Published by

Krause Publications, a division of F+W Media, Inc.
700 East State Street • Iola, WI 54990-0001
715-445-2214 • 888-457-2873
www.krausebooks.com

To order books or other products call toll-free 1-800-258-0929
or visit us online at www.shopnumismaster.com

ISSN 1939-814X
ISBN-13: 978-1-4402-4797-2
ISBN-10: 1-4402-4797-8

Designed by Sandi Carpenter

Printed in the United States of America

10 9 8 7 6 5 4 3 2 1

INTRODUCTION

The *Standard Catalog of® World Coins* began its long and storied life as the brain child of authors Chester L. Krause and Clifford Mishler, known to hobbyists for half a century simply as "Chet and Cliff." The first edition, covering coinage from the "Mid-1800's To 1971," was published in 1971 and introduced the world to something quite different: a price guide with listings not only by type, but with each known date identified and valued. Initially most values were pretty well identical, but over the years date rarity and grade rarity have developed as I am certain Chet and Cliff knew they would.

This year marked the passing of Chet after a long and fulfilling life in many collecting fields. I will truly miss him. His collections had been dispersed over the last few years, but Chet's zeal for hobby pursuits never faded. His vision of providing formats for collectors and dealers to interact has led us from small groups in villages, towns, cities, states and countries to much broader spectrums. In the case of numismatics his aspirations helped evolve us into a true world hobby. I think we will all miss this man.

In tribute to Chet, I think none of this would have been possible without his vision. He pulled together a great group of people, both on staff and off sight. He gave us a forum in the form of a catalog and he encouraged us to expand. This is how we got here.

After that first edition in 1971 proved so very popular, Chet & Cliff set to work getting more expert assistance to broaden the scope of the catalog. Many dealers and collectors wrote in to comment on areas to improve and some offered to share their knowledge to help improve this new reference. A second edition, encompassing many improvements was published in 1973. It was named the 1974 edition, as is common in published to add shelf life to products. This 1974 edition, incidentally, was the first numismatic catalog I ever encountered. Prior to seeing the 1974 edition at a coin kiosk in a mall I had been using dictionaries and atlases to identify the coins I was ferreting out of junk boxes at flea markets!

Through the remainder of the 1970s several new and expanded editions of the *Standard Catalog of® World Coins* were published. Coin dealer Colin R. Bruce II arrived to help improve the China section and remained in Iola as editor, working with the essential coordinating editor, Marian S. Moe, who had been involved on the project from its inception. By 1979, the catalog became an annual production and has continued as such to this day. Every edition always offering updated values, more images and better descriptions all directed at improving the ease with which an average person can identify a coin and building out a base of knowledge for the world coin collecting community.

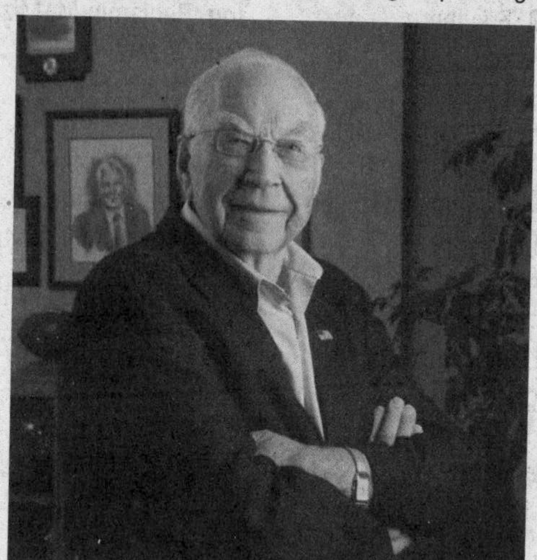

Chet Krause
1923-2016

In 1985 the first two volume Deluxe Library Edition was completed, pushing the boundaries back in time and offering more data than ever before. Two years later I arrived in Iola to find the core group brought together by Chet & Cliff had been joined by several others with the department of eight primary and support staff producing the annual catalog, as well as some of Krause Publications first specialized books. I jumped right in and began working on the U.S. based *Auction Prices Realized* with Robert Wilhite, while watching the other staff working on the *Standard Catalog of® World Coins* and the strange *Unusual World Coins*. My first *Standard Catalog of® World Coins*, the 1989 edition published in 1988, changed everything for me - Chet and Cliff had given me a calling.

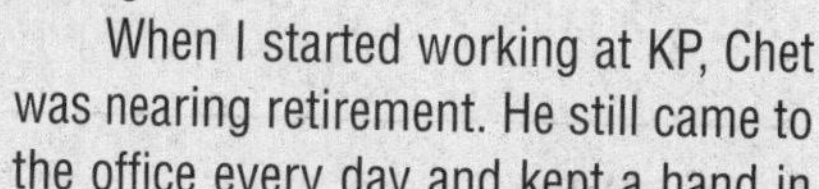

When I started working at KP, Chet was nearing retirement. He still came to the office every day and kept a hand in the decision making. He was the man who let me into the building that first wintery Sunday when I arrived for an interview, offering me coffee and saying the others would be there soon. It was with the blessing and support of Chet & Cliff that we developed more and more numismatic data, pushing back farther in time. This research produced a second two volume Deluxe ANA Centennial Edition in 1991, the 18th Century 1701-1800 Special Edition in 1993, the 19th Century 1801-1900 Special Edition and the 17th Century 1601-1700 Special Edition in 1996.

All of these Special Editions are in their 6th, 7th and 8th editions now. Each has expanded with more images, updated values and newly discovered varieties. Other special catalogs have been produced, like the *Standard Catalog of® German Coins 1501-Present* 3rd edition. On our website, www.shopNumisMaster.com, you can find all of our current products, including digital downloads and our most recent addition to the family, the *Standard Catalog of® World Coins 2001-Date*.

All of this has happened and is still developing because Chester L. Krause and Clifford Mishler had an idea that something better was possible - Thank you Chet & Cliff.

Best Wishes,
Thomas Michael
Senior Editor & Market Analyst
Standard Catalog of® World Coins

ACKNOWLEDGMENTS

Many individuals have contributed countless changes, which have been incorporated into this edition. While all may not be acknowledged, special appreciation is extended to the following individuals and organizations who have exhibited a special dedication – revising and verifying historical and technical data and coin listings, reviewing market valuations and sharing digital images - for this edition.

Esko Ahlroth
Stephen Album
Scott Annechino
Dr. Luis Alberto Asbun-Karmy
Jan Bendix
Richard Benson
Shamik Biswas
Joseph E. Boling
Richard Borek jun.
Klaus Bronny
Mahdi Bseiso
John T. Bucek
Chris Budesa
Juan Cayón
Adolfo Cayón
Henry K. H. Chan
Michael Chou
Mariano Cohen
Scott E. Cordry
Freeman Craig
Raymond E. Czahor
Howard Daniel
James R. Douglas
Wilhelm R. Eglseer
Andrzej Fischer
Joe Flores
Arthur M. Friedberg
Tom Galway
Dennis Gill
Ron Guth
Marcel Häberling
Flemming Lyngbeck Hansen
Emmanuel Henry
Serge Huard
Nelva G. Icaza
Hector Carlos Janson
Alex Kaglyan
Melvyn Kassenoff
Craig Keplinger
George Katsikis
Ronachai Krisadaolarn
Samson Kin Chiu Lai
Joseph E. Lang
Ma Tak Wo
Miguel Angel Pratt Mayans
Juozas Minikevicius
Ing. Benjamin M. Mizrachi R.
Paul Montz
Horst-Dieter Müller
Bill Noyes
Leonard Novotny
Alberto Paashaus
Sigurður Helgi Pálmason
Gastone Polacco
Yahya Qureshi
Dr. Dennis G. Rainey
Ivan Rakitin
Kavan Ratnatunga
Tony Raymond
Erwin Schäffer
Jacco Scheper
Gerhard Schön
Dale Seppa
Alexander Shapiro
Ole Sjoelund
Abu Shamim Mohammad Talha
Mehmet Tolga Taner
M. Louis Teller
Anthony Tumonis
Erik J. Van Loon
Carmen Viciedo
Wakim Wakim
Justin Wang
Paul Welz
J. Brix Westergaard
J. Hugh Witherow
Joseph Zaffern

AUCTION HOUSES

Aureo & Calicó
Daniel Frank Sedwick, LLC
Dix-Noonan-Webb
Gorny & Mosch
Heritage World Coin Auctions
Gerhard Hirsch
Fritz Rudolf Künker
Marudhar Arts
Morten & Eden Ltd.
Münz Zentrum Rheinland
Münzenhandlung Harald Möller, GmbH
MPO Auctions
Noble Numismatics, Pty. Ltd.
Stack's, Bowers and Ponterio
St James's Auctions
Stephen Album Rare Coins
Teutoburger Münzauktion & Handel GmbH
Varesi Numismatics
WAG Online oHG

WORLD MINTS, CENTRAL BANKS AND DISTRIBUTORS

Austrian Mint
Banco de Mexico
Banque Centrale Du Luxembourg
Bank du Liban
Black Mountain Coins
Casa de la Moneda de Cuba
Casa da Moeda do Brasil
Central Bank of D.P.R. Korea - Kumbyol Trading Corp.
Central Bank of the Russian Fed.
CIT
China Gold Coin Corporation
Czech National Bank
Educational Coin Company
Global Coins & Medals Ltd. - Official Sales Company of the Bulgarian Mint
Imprensa Nacional - Casa da Moeda, S.A.
Israel Coins & Medals Corp.
Istituto Poligrafico e Zecca dello Stato I.p.A.
Jablonex Group - Division of Czech Mint
Japan Mint
Kazakhstan Mint
KOMSCO - South Korea
Latvijas Banka
Lietuvos Bankas
Lithuanian Mint
Magyar Penzvero Zrt.
Mayer's Mint GmbH
MDM
Mennica Polska
Mincovna Kremnica
Mint of Finland, Ltd.
Mint of Norway
Monnaie de Paris
Moscow Mint
Naradowy Bank Polski
National Bank of the Republic of Belarus
National Bank of Ukraine
New Zealand Mint
Numiscom
Numistrade Gmbh & Co. kg.
PandaAmerica
Perth Mint
Pobjoy Mint
Real Casa de la Moneda – Spain
Romanian Mint
Royal Mint
Royal Australian Mint
Royal Belgian Mint
Royal Canadian Mint
Royal Dutch Mint
Royal Thai Mint
Servei D'Emissions Principat D'Andorra
Shanghai Mint
Singapore Mint
South African Mint
Staatliche Munze Berlin
Staatliche Munze Baden-Wurttemberg
Thailand Treasury Department
Ufficio Filatelico e Numismatico - Vatican
United States Mint

COUNTRY INDEX

HOW TO USE THIS CATALOG

This catalog is designed to serve the needs of both novice and advanced collectors. It provides a comprehensive guide to world coins struck in the 20th century (1901 thru 2000). It is arranged so that persons with a basic knowledge of world history and a casual acquaintance with coin collecting can consult it with confidence and ease. The following explanations summarize the general practices used in preparing the catalog listings. However, because of specialized requirements, which may vary by country and political era within a country, these should not be considered ironclad.

ARRANGEMENT

Countries are arranged alphabetically. Political changes within a country are arranged chronologically. In countries where Rulers are the single most significant political entity, a chronological arrangement by Ruler has been employed. Distinctive sub-geographic regions are listed alphabetically following the country's main listings. A few exceptions to these rules may exist. If a location is in question, please refer to the Country Index.

Diverse coinage types relating to fabrication methods, revaluations and change in denomination systems have been identified, separated and arranged in a logical fashion. Chronological arrangement is employed for most circulating coinage. Monetary system reforms will flow in order of their institution. Non-circulating types such as Essais, Piefort, Patterns, Trial Strikes, Mint and Proof sets follow at the end of the individual county's listings.

Within a coinage type coins will be listed by denomination, from smallest to largest. Numbered types within a denomination will be ordered by their first date of issue.

IDENTIFICATION

The most important step in the identification of a coin is the determination of the nation of origin. This is generally easily accomplished where the country name appears in easy to read characters; when in doubt, use of the country index is sometimes required. The coins of Great Britain do not have the county name, just the name and image of the ruler.

The coins of many countries beyond the English-language realm, such as those of French, Italian or Spanish heritage, are also quite easy to identify through reference to their legends, which appear in the national languages based on Western alphabets. In many instances the name is spelled exactly the same in English as in the national language, such as France; while in other cases it varies only slightly, like Italia for Italy, Belgique or Belgie for Belgium, Brasil for Brazil and Danmark for Denmark.

This is not always the case, however, as in Soumi for Finland, Norge for Norway, Espana for Spain, Slovensko for Slovakia, Sverige for Sweden and Helvetia for Switzerland. Some other examples include: Empire Cherifin Maroc for Morocco, Estados Unidos Mexicanos for United Mexican States (Mexico) and Etat du Grand Liban - State of Great Lebanon (Lebanon).

With the introduction of the Euro Coinage, some member nations have identified their coin with only country initials, such as BE for Belgium, IR for Italy, RF for France.

Thus it can be seen there are instances in which a little effort in the rudiments of foreign languages can be most helpful. In general, colonial possessions of countries using the Western alphabet are similarly identifiable as they often carry portraits of their current rulers, the familiar lettering, sometimes in combination with a companion designation in the local language.

Collectors have the greatest difficulty with coins that do not bear legends or dates in the Western systems. These include coins bearing Cyrillic lettering attributable to Bulgaria, Russia, the Slavic states and Mongolia; the Greek script peculiar to Greece, Crete and the Ionian Islands; the Amharic characters of Ethiopia; or Hebrew in the case of Israel. Dragons and sunbursts along with the distinctive word characters attribute a coin to the Oriental countries of China, Japan, Korea, Tibet, Viet Nam and their component parts.

The most difficult coins to identify are those bearing only Persian or Arabic script and its derivatives, found on the issues of nations stretching in a wide swath across North Africa and East Asia, from Morocco to Indonesia, and the Indian subcontinent coinages which surely are more confusing in their vast array of Nagari, Sanskrit, Ahom, Assamese and other local dialects found on the local issues of the Indian Princely States. Although the task of identification on the more modern issues of these lands is often eased by the added presence of Western alphabet legends, a feature sometimes adopted starting in the late 19th Century, for the earlier pieces it is often necessary if in doubt to laboriously seek and find.

Except for the cruder issues, however, it will be found that certain characteristics and symbols featured in addition to the predominant legends are typical on coins from a given country or group of countries. The *toughra* monogram, for instance, occurs on some of the coins of Afghanistan, Egypt, the Sudan, Pakistan, Turkey and other areas of the late Ottoman Empire. A predominant design feature on the coins of Nepal is the trident; while neighboring Tibet features a lotus blossom or lion on many of their issues.

To assist in identification of the more difficult coins, we have assembled the Instant Identifier and Monogram sections presented on the following pages. They are designed to provide a point of beginning for collectors by allowing them to compare unidentified coins with photographic details from typical issues.

We also suggest reference to the comprehensive Country Index.

DENOMINATIONS

The second basic consideration to be met in the attribution of a coin is the determination of denomination. Since denominations are usually expressed in numeric rather than word form on a coin, this is usually quite easily accomplished on coins from nations which use Western numerals, except in those instances where issues are devoid of any mention of face value, and denomination must be attributed by size, metallic composition or weight. Coins listed in this volume are generally illustrated in actual size. Where size is critical to proper attribution, the coin's millimeter size is indicated.

The sphere of countries stretching from North Africa through the Orient, on which numeric symbols generally unfamiliar to Westerners are employed, often provide the collector with a much greater challenge. This is particularly true on nearly all pre-20th Century issues. In many cases as the years progressed, Western-style numerals are often presented in combination with the local numeric systems on these coins.

Determination of a coin's currency system can also be valuable in attributing the issue to its country of origin. The table of Standard International Numeral Systems presents lists of the basic numeric designations found on coins of non-Western origin. Although denomination numerals are generally prominently displayed on coins, it must be remembered that these are general representations of characters, which individual coin designers may have rendered in widely varying styles. Where numeric or script denominations designation forms peculiar to a given coin or country apply, such as the script used on some Persian (Iranian) issues, they are so indicated or illustrated in conjunction with the appropriate listings.

DATING

Coin dating is the final basic attribution consideration. Here, the problem can be more difficult because the reading of a coin date is subject not only to the vagaries of numeric styling, but to calendar variations caused by the observance of various religious eras or regal periods from country to country, or even within a country. Here again, with the exception of the sphere from North Africa through the Orient, it will be found that most countries rely on Western date numerals and Christian (AD) era reckoning, although in a few instances, coin dating has been tied to the year of a reign or government. The Vatican, for example dates its coinage according to the year of reign of the current pope, in addition to the Christian-era date.

Countries in the Arabic sphere generally date their coins to the Muslim era (AH), which commenced on July 16, 622 AD (Julian calendar), when the prophet Mohammed fled from Mecca to Medina. As their calendar is reckoned by the lunar year of 354 days, which is about three percent (precisely 2.98%) shorter than the Christian year, a formula is required to convert AH dating to its Western equivalent. To convert an AH date to the approximate AD date, subtract three percent of the AH date (round to the closest whole number) from the AH date and add 622. A chart converting all AH years from 1010 (July 2, 1601) to 1450 (May 25, 2028) may be found elsewhere in this catalog under the name Hejira Date Chart.

The Muslim calendar is not always based on the lunar year (AH), however, causing some confusion, particularly in Afghanistan and Iran, where a calendar based on the solar year (SH) was introduced around 1920. These dates can be converted to AD by simply adding 621. In 1976 the government of Iran implemented a new solar calendar based on the foundation of the Iranian monarchy in 559 BC. The first year observed on the new calendar was 2535 (MS), which commenced March 20, 1976. A reversion to the traditional SH dating standard occurred a few years later.

Several different eras of reckoning, including Christian and Muslim (AH), have been used to date coins of the Indian subcontinent. The two basic systems are the Vikrama Samvat (VS), which dates from Oct. 18, 58 BC, and the Saka era, the origin of which is reckoned from March 3, 78 AD. Dating according to both eras appears on various coins of the area.

Coins of Thailand (Siam) are found dated by three different eras. The most predominant is the Buddhist era (BE), which originated in 543 BC. Next is the Bangkok or Ratanakosindsok (RS) era, dating from 1781 AD; followed by the Chula-Sakarat (CS) era, dating from 638 AD. The latter era originated in Burma and is used on that country's coins.

Other calendars include that of the Ethiopian era (EE), which commenced seven years, eight months after AD dating; and that of the Jewish people, which commenced on Oct. 7, 3761 BC. Korea claims a legendary dating from 2333 BC, which is acknowledged in some of its coin dating. Some coin issues of the Indonesian area carry dates determined by the Javanese Aji Saka era (AS), a calendar of 354 days (100 Javanese years equal 97 Christian or Gregorian calendar years), which can be matched to AD dating by comparing it to AH dating.

The following table indicates the year dating for the various eras, which correspond to 2016 in Christian calendar reckoning, but it must be remembered that there are overlaps between the eras in some instances.

Christian era (AD)	-	2017
Muslim era (AH)	-	AH1438
Solar year (SH)	-	SH1395
Monarchic Solar era (MS)	-	MS2576
Vikrama Samvat (VS)	-	VS2074
Saka era (SE)	-	SE1939
Buddhist era (BE)	-	BE2560
Bangkok era (RS)	-	RS236
Chula-Sakarat era (CS)	-	CS1379
Ethiopian era (EE)	-	EE2010
Korean era	-	4350
Javanese Aji Saka era (AS)	-	AS1950
Fasli era (FE)	-	FE1427
Jewish era (JE)	-	JE5777
Roman	-	MMXVII

Coins of Asian origin - principally Japan, Korea, China, Turkestan and Tibet and some modern gold issues of Turkey - are generally dated to the year of the government, dynasty, reign or cyclic eras, with the dates indicated in Asian characters which usually read from right to left. In recent years, however, some dating has been according to the Christian calendar and in Western numerals. In Japan, Asian character dating was reversed to read from left to right in Showa year 23 (1948 AD).

More detailed guides to less prevalent coin dating systems, which are strictly local in nature, are presented with the appropriate listings.

Some coins carry dates according to both locally observed and Christian eras. This is particularly true in the Arabic world, where the Hejira date may be indicated in Arabic numerals and the Christian date in Western numerals, or both dates in either form.

The date actually carried on a given coin is generally cataloged here in the first column (Date). If this date is in a non-Christian dating system, such as 'AH' (Muslim), the Christian equivalent date will appear in parentheses(), for example AH1336(1917). Dates listed alone in the date column which do not actually appear on a given coin, or dates which are known, but do not appear on the coin, are generally enclosed by parentheses with 'ND' at the left, for example ND(1926).

Timing differentials between some era of reckoning, particularly the 354-day Mohammedan and 365-day Christian years, cause situations whereby coins which carry dates for both eras exist bearing two year dates from one calendar combined with a single date from another.

Countermarked Coinage is presented with both 'Countermark Date' and 'Host Coin' date for each type. Actual date representation follows the rules outlined above.

For a more detailed information on coin dating see the *Illustrated Coin Dating Guide for the Eastern World* by Albert Galloway, Krause Publications, F+W Media, 2012.

NUMBERING SYSTEM

Some catalog numbers assigned in this volume are based on other established references. This practice has been observed for two reasons: First, when world coins are listed chronologically they are basically self-cataloging; second, there was no need to confuse collectors with totally new numeric designations where appropriate systems already existed. As time progressed we found many of these established systems incomplete and inadequate and many have now been replaced with KM numbers. If numbers have changed, appropriate cross-referencing has been provided.

Some of these references used in this catalog are (Y#) identified assigned by R.S. Yeoman, or slight adaptations thereof, in his *Modern World Coins*, and *Current Coins of the World*.

In some countries, listings are cross-referenced to Robert Friedberg's (FR#) *Gold Coins of the World* or *Coins of the British World*. Major Fred Pridmore's (P#) studies of British colonial coinage are also referenced, as are W.H. Valentine's (V#) references on the *Modern Copper Coins of the Mohammedan States*. Coins issued under the Chinese sphere of influence are assigned numbers from E. Kann's (K#) *Illustrated Catalog of Chinese Coins* and T.K. Hsu's (Su) work of similar title. In most cases, these cross-reference numbers are presented in the descriptive text for each type.

MINTAGES

Quantities minted of each date are indicated where that information is available, generally stated in millions or rounded off to the nearest 1,000 pieces when more exact figures are not available. On quantities of a few thousand or less, actual mintages are generally indicated. For combined mintage figures the abbreviation "Inc. Above" means Included Above, while "Inc. Below" means Included Below. "Est." beside a mintage figure indicates the number given is an estimate of the intended mintage or an advertised mintage limit when the final (actual) mintage is not known.

MINT AND PRIVY MARKS

The presence of distinctive, but frequently inconspicuously placed, mintmarks indicates the mint of issue for many of the coins listed in this catalog. An appropriate designation in the date listings notes the presence, if any, of a mint mark on a particular coin type by incorporating the letter or letters of the mint mark adjoining the date, i.e., 1950D or 1927R.

The presence of mint and/or mintmaster's privy marks on a coin in non-letter form is indicated by incorporating the a letter in lower case within parentheses adjoining the date; i.e. 1927(a). The corresponding mark is illustrated or identified in the introduction of the country.

In countries such as France and Mexico, where many mints may be producing like coinage in the same denomination during the same time period, divisions by mint have been employed. In these cases the mint mark may appear next to the individual date listings and/or the mint name or mint mark may be listed in the Note field of the type description.

Where listings incorporate mintmaster initials, they are always presented in capital letters separated from the date by one character space; i.e., 1850 MF. The different mintmark and mintmaster letters found on the coins of any country, state or city of issue are shown at the beginning of that country's listings.

METALS

Each numbered type listing will contain a description of the coins metallic content. The traditional coinage metals and their symbolic chemical abbreviations are:

Platinum - (PT)	Copper - (Cu)
Gold - (Au)	Silver - (Ag)
Copper-Nickel- (CN)	Lead - (Pb)
Nickel - (Ni)	Zinc - (Zn)
Tin - (Sn)	Bronze - (Ae)
Aluminum - (Al)	

During the 18th and 19th centuries, most of the world's coins were struck of copper or bronze, silver and gold. Commencing in the early years of the 20th century, however, numerous new coinage metals, primarily non-precious metal alloys, were introduced. Gold has not been widely used for circulation coinages since World War I, although silver remained a popular coinage metal in most parts of the world until after World War II. With the disappearance of silver for circulation coinage, numerous additional compositions were introduced to coinage applications.

Most recent is the development of clad or plated planchets in order to maintain circulation life and extend the life of a set of production dies as used in the production of the copper-nickel clad copper 50 centesimos of Panama or in the latter case to reduce production costs of the planchets and yet provide a coin quite similar in appearance to its predecessor as in the case of the copper plated zinc core United States 1983 cent.

Modern commemorative coins have employed still more unusual methods such as bimetallic coins, color applications and precious metal or gem inlays.

OFF-METAL STRIKES

Off-metal strikes previously designated by "OMS" which also included the wide range of error coinage struck in other than their officially authorized compositions have been incorporated into Pattern listings along with special issues, which were struck for presentation or other reasons.

Collectors of Germanic coinage may be familiar with the term *Abschlag* which quickly identifies similar types of coinage.

PRECIOUS METAL WEIGHTS

Listings of weight, fineness and actual silver (ASW), gold (AGW), platinum or palladium (APW) content of most machine-struck silver, gold, platinum and palladium coins are provided in this edition. This information will be found at the start of a type description, followed by other information related to the coin.

The ASW, AGW and APW figures were determined by multiplying the gross weight of a given coin by its officially known standard or tested fineness and converting the resulting gram or grain weight into troy ounces, rounded to the nearest hundreth of an ounce. A silver coin with a 24.25-gram weight and .875 fineness for example, would have a fine weight of approximately 21.22 grams, or a .6822 ASW, a factor that can be used to accurately determine the intrinsic value for multiple examples.

The ASW, AGW or APW figure can be multiplied by the spot price of each precious metal to determine the current intrinsic value of any coin accompanied by these designations.

Coin weights are indicated in grams (abbreviated "g") along with fineness where the information is of value in differentiating between types. These weights are based on 31.103 grams per troy (scientific) ounce, as opposed to the avoirdupois (commercial) standard of 28.35 grams. Actual coin weights are generally shown in hundredths of a gram; i.e., 0.500 SILVER 2.92g.

WEIGHTS AND FINENESSES

As the silver and gold bullion markets have advanced and declined sharply over the years, the fineness and total precious metal content of coins has become especially significant where bullion coins - issues which trade on the basis of their intrinsic metallic content rather than numismatic value - are concerned. In many instances, such issues have become worth more in bullion form than their nominal collector values or denominations indicate.

Establishing the weight of a coin can also be valuable for determining its denomination. Actual weight is also necessary to ascertain the specific gravity of the coin's metallic content, an important factor in determining authenticity.

TROY WEIGHT STANDARDS

24 Grains = 1 Pennyweight
480 Grains = 1 Ounce
31.103 Grams = 1 Ounce

UNIFORM WEIGHTS

15.432 Grains = 1 Gram
0.0648 Gram = 1 Grain

AVOIRDUPOIS STANDARDS

27-11/32 Grains = 11 Dram
437-1/2 Grains = 1 Ounce
28.350 Grams = 1 Ounce

BULLION VALUE

The simplest method for determining the bullion value of a precious metal coin is to multiply the actual precious metal weight by the current spot price for that metal. Using the example above, a silver coin with a .6822 actual silver weight (ASW) would have an intrinsic value of $12.25 when the spot price of silver is $17.95. If the spot price of silver rose to $22.50 that same coins intrinsic value would rise to $15.35.

HOMELAND TYPES

Homeland types are coins which colonial powers used in a colony, but do not bear that location's name. In some cases they were legal tender in the homeland, in others not. They are listed under the homeland and cross-referenced at the colony listing.

COUNTERMARKS/COUNTERSTAMPS

There is some confusion among collectors over the terms "countermark" and "counterstamp" when applied to a coin bearing an additional mark or change of design and/or denomination.

To clarify, a countermark might be considered similar to the "hall mark" applied to a piece of silverware, by which a silversmith assured the quality of the piece. In the same way, a countermark assures the quality of the coin on which it is placed, as, for example, when the royal crown of England was countermarked (punched into) on segmented Spanish reales, allowing them to circulate in commerce in the British West Indies. An additional countermark indicating the new denomination may also be encountered on these coins.

Countermarks are generally applied singularly and in most cases indiscriminately on either side of the "host" coin.

Counterstamped coins are more extensively altered. The counterstamping is done with a set of dies, rather than a hand punch. The coin being counterstamped is placed between the new dies and struck as if it were a blank planchet as found with the Manila 8 reales issue of the Philippines. A more unusual application, where the counterstamp dies were smaller than the host coin, can be seen in the revalidated 50 centimos and 1 colon of Costa Rica issued in 1923.

PHOTOGRAPHS

To assist the reader in coin identification, every effort has been made to use actual size images of each type listed. When available both sides are illustrated. When the coin has a diameter of 39mm or larger, usually the side required for identification of the type is illustrated. All coins up to 55mm are illustrated actual size, to the nearest 1/2mm up to 25mm, and to the nearest 1mm thereafter. Coins larger than 55mm diameter are illustrated in reduced size, with the actual size noted in the descriptive text block. Where slight change in size is important to coin type identification, actual millimeter measurements are stated in the listing. Moving forward, efforts are being made to include diameter measurements for all listed coin types. in the case where a coin is not machine made, and the size varies, the mm size range is stated when known.

TRADE COINS

From approximately 1750-1940, a number of nations, particularly European colonial powers and commercial traders, minted trade coins to facilitate commerce with the local populace of Africa, the Arab countries, the Indian subcontinent, Southeast Asia and the Far East. Such coins generally circulated at a value based on the weight and fineness of their silver or gold content, rather than their stated denomination. Examples include the sovereigns of Great Britain and the gold ducat issues of Austria, Hungary and the Netherlands. These coins will be segregated into a Trade coinage section near the end of the domestic issues.

VALUATIONS

Values quoted in this catalog represent the current retail market and are compiled from recommendations provided and verified through various source documents and specialized consultants. It should be stressed, however, that this book is intended to serve only as an aid for evaluating coins, actual market conditions are constantly changing and additional influences, such as particularly strong local demand for certain coin series, fluctuation of international exchange rates, changes in spot price of precious metals and worldwide collecting patterns must also be considered. Publication of this catalog is not intended as a solicitation by the publisher, editors or contributors to buy or sell the coins listed at the prices indicated.

All valuations are stated in U.S. dollars, based on careful assessment of the varied international collector markets. Valuations for coins priced below $100.00 are generally stated in full amounts, i.e. 37.50 or 95.00, while valuations at or above that $100.00 are rounded off in even dollars - i.e. $125.00 is expressed 125. A comma is added to indicate thousands of dollars in value (12,500.)

A dash (-) to the left of given values in a specific value field indicates a lack of a collectible premium. A coin in these lower grades would be worth only its face or intrinsic value. A dash (-) to the right of given values may mean very few or no examples of that grade exist for the type.

For coins which trade close to their bullion value (BV) autocalculations have been determined and instituted in this edition. These formulas will calculate a value based on the BV value of a coin, plus an acceptable premium. Unusual figures in the value column are an indication of this autocalculation function. To detremine a current BV value in shifting spot metal conditions, simply multiply the actual precious metal weight by the current spot metal price.

For the convenience of overseas collectors and for U.S. collectors doing business with overseas dealers, the exchange rate for current currencies is presented in the Foreign Exchange Table.

It should be noted that when particularly select uncirculated or proof-like examples of uncirculated coins become available they can be expected to command proportionately high premiums. Such examples in reference to choice Germanic Thalers are referred to as "erst schlage" or first strikes.

MEDALLIC ISSUES

Medallic issues are similar to coin-type issues and can generally be identified as commemoratives produced to the country's established coinage standards but without the usual indicator of denomination. These pieces sometimes feature designs adapted from the country's regular issue or commemorative coinage, and occassionally have been issued in conjunction with related coinage issues.

Medallic issues, though bearing these similarites to coinage issues, are not coins and therefore are not listed in this catalog, but can be found in the companion catalog *Unusual World Coins*. They are also listed on our searchable web catalog at www. NumisMaster.com.

RESTRIKES, COUNTERFEITS

Deceptive restrike and counterfeit (both contemporary and modern) examples exist of some coin issues. Where possible, the existence of official restrikes is noted. Warnings are also incorporated in instances where particularly deceptive counterfeits are known to exist. If you are uncertain about the authenticity of a coin held in your collection, or being offered for sale, one should take the precaution of having it authenticated by one of the recognized third party grading services. They are reasonably priced, and their products are widely accepted by collectors and dealers alike.

NON-CIRCULATING LEGAL TENDER COINS

Coins of non-circulating legal tender (NCLT) origin are individually listed and integrated by denomination into the regular listings for each country, excepting where large, established serialized categories exist. These coins fall outside the customary definitions of coin-of-the-realm issues, but where created and sold by, or under authorization of, agencies of sovereign governments expressly for collectors. These are primarily individual coins and sets of a commemorative nature, marketed at prices substantially in excess of both face and intrinsic value, and usually do not have counterparts released for circulation. If you are only interested in coins which circulate in commerce we offer a catalog titled *Collecting World Coins*, which lists only circulating world issues since 1901.

EDGE VARIETIES

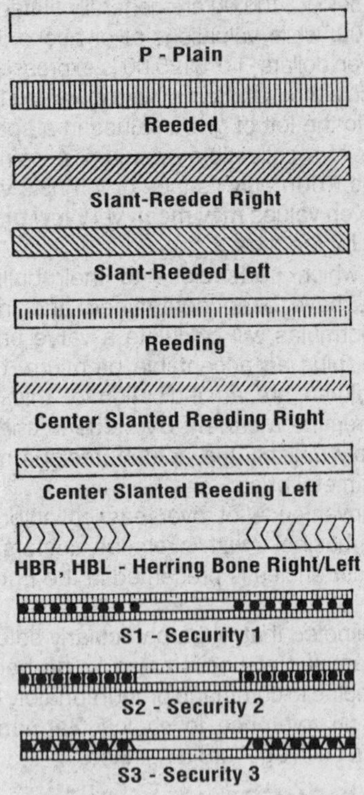

Scope of Listings

All coins dated from 1901 thru 2000 that have been physically observed by our staff or confirmed by our reliable sources have been incorporated into this edition. Exceptions exist in some countries where current date coin production lags far behind or information on current issues is less accessible.

SETS

Listings in this catalog for specimen, proof and mint sets are for official, government-produced sets. In many instances privately packaged sets also exist, these are not listed.

MINT SETS / FLEUR DE COIN SETS: Specially prepared by worldwide mints to provide banks, collectors and government dignitaries with examples of current coinage. Usually subjected to rigorous inspection to insure that top quality specimens of selected business strikes are provided. One of the most popular mint set is that given out by the monarch of Great Britain each year on Maunday Thursday. This set contains four special coins in denominations of 1, 2, 3 and 4 pence, struck in silver and contained in a little pouch. They have been given away in a special ceremony for the poor for more than two centuries.

The Paris Mint introduced polyvinyl plastic cases packed within a cardboard box for homeland and colonial Fleur de Coin sets of the 1960s. British colonial sets were issued in velvet-lined metal cases similar to those used for proof sets. For its client nations, the Franklin Mint introduced a sealed composition of cardboard and specially molded hard clear plastic protective container inserted in a soft plastic wallet. Discovery that soft polyvinyl packaging has proved hazardous to coins has resulted in a change to the use of hard, inert plastics for virtually all mint sets.

Some of the highest quality mint sets ever produced were those struck by the Franklin Mint during 1972-74. In many cases matte finish dies were used to strike a polished proof planchet. Later on, from 1975, sets contained highly polished, glassy-looking coins (similar to those struck by the Bombay Mint) for collectors over a period of twelve years.

SPECIMEN SETS: Forerunners of today's proof sets. In most cases the coins were specially struck, perhaps even double struck, to produce a very soft or matte finish on the effigies and fields, along with high, sharp, "wire" rims. The finish is rather dull to the naked eye.

The original purpose of these sets was to provide VIPs, monarchs and mintmasters around the world with samples of the highest quality workmanship of a particular mint. These were usually housed in elaborate velvet-lined leather and metal cases.

PROOF-LIKE SETS are relatively new to the field of numismatics. During the mid-1950s the Royal Canadian Mint furnished the hobby with specially selected early business strike coins that exhibited some qualities similar to proof coinage. However, the "proof-like" fields are generally flawed and the edges are rounded. These pieces are not double struck. These are commonly encountered in cardboard holders, later in soft plastic or pliofilm packaging. Of late, the Royal Canadian Mint packages such sets in rigid plastic cases.

Many worldwide officially issued proof sets would in reality fall into this category upon careful examination of the quality of the coin's finish.

Another term encountered in this category is "Special Select," used to describe the crowns of the Union of South Africa and 100-schilling coins produced for collectors in the late 1970s by the Austrian Mint.

PROOF SETS: This is undoubtedly among the most misused terms in the hobby, not only by collectors and dealers, but also by many of the world mints.

A true proof set must be comprised of coins which are at least double-struck on specially prepared polished planchets and struck using dies (which are also often polished) of the highest quality under greater than normal pressure.

Modern-day proof quality coins often consist of frosted portraits or design elements surrounded by absolute mirror-like fields. A reverse-proof has frosted portraits or design elements surrounded by frosted fields.

Listings for proof sets in this catalog are for officially issued proof sets so designated by the issuing authority, and may or may not possess what are considered modern proof quality standards.

It is necessary for collectors to acquire the knowledge to allow them to differentiate true proof sets from would-be proof sets and proof-like sets which may be encountered.

CONDITIONS / GRADING

Wherever possible, coin valuations are presented in five grades of preservation. In this catalog we have adopted the use of the 70-point numerical grading system employed in the United States. For modern commemoratives, which do not circulate, only Mint State prices are sufficient. Proof issues are indicated by the prefix PF-60, PF-63, PF-65, PF-67 or PF-69 next to the valuation following the mintage. Coins which are proof in quality but not yet priced, have the notation of Proof next to the date and no price information. For very recent circulating coins and coins of limited value only one, two or three grade values are presented with lower grade fields containing a dash (-) indicating no collector premium above face or intrinsic value.

There are almost no grading guides for world coins. What follows is an attempt to help bridge that gap until a detailed, illustrated guide becomes available.

In grading world coins, there are two elements to look for: 1) Overall wear, and 2) loss of design details, such as strands of hair, feathers on eagles, design elements on the coat-of-arms, etc.

The age, rarity or type of a coin should not be a consideration in grading.

Grade each coin by the weaker of the two sides. This method appears to give results most nearly consistent with the American Numismatic Association standards for U.S. coins. Split grades, i.e., F/VF for obverse and reverse, respectively, are normally no more than one grade apart. If the two sides are more than one grade apart, the series of coins probably wears differently on each side and should then be graded by the weaker side alone.

Grade by the amount of overall wear and loss of design detail evident on each side of the coin. On coins with a moderately small design element, which is prone to early wear, grade by that design alone. For example, the 5-ore (KM#554) of Sweden has a crown above the monogram on which the beads on the arches show wear most clearly. So, grade by the crown alone.

For **MS-66** grade full mint luster will be present with no visible signs of any wear or handling, even under strong magnification. An above average strike, with obvious and significant eye appeal are needed for assignment of this grade designation.

For **MS-65 (Gem Brilliant Uncirculated, GemBU)** grade there will be no visible signs of wear or handling, even under a 10-power loop. Full mint luster should be present, but is not a necessity of the grade. No detracting bag or adjustment marks will be present. Sharp rims and bold detail are characteristic of this grade.

For **MS-63 (Choice Brilliant Uncirculated, ChoiceBU)** grade there will be no visible signs of wear or handling, even under a 10-power loop. Mint luster will be present. Ideally no bags marks will be evident, light adjustment marks may be present.

For **MS-60 (Uncirculated, Unc.)** grade there will be no visible signs of wear or handling, even under a 10-power loop. Adjustment marks and bag marks may be present.

For **AU-50 (Almost Uncirculated, AU)** all details will be visible. There will be the slightest of wear only on the highest point of the coin. There will often be half or more of the original mint luster present.

On the **XF-40 (Extremely Fine, XF or EF)** coin, there will be about 95% of the original detail visible. Or, on a coin with a design with no inner detail to wear down, there will be a light wear over nearly all the coin. If a small design is used as the grading area, about 90% of the original detail will be visible. This latter rule stems from the logic that a smaller amount of detail needs to be present because a small area is being used to grade the whole coin.

The **VF-20 (Very Fine, VF)** coin will have about 75% of the original detail visible. Or, on a coin with no inner detail, there will be moderate wear over the entire coin. Corners of letters and numbers may be weak. A small grading area will have about 66% of the original detail.

For **F-12 (Fine, F)**, there will be about 50% of the original detail visible. Or, on a coin with no inner detail, there will be fairly heavy wear over all of the coin. Sides of letters will be weak. A coin which has not been cleaned will often appear as dirty or dull. A small amount of the grading area will have just about 50% of the original detail.

On the **VG-8 (Very Good, VG)** coin, there will be about 25% of the original detail visible. There will be heavy wear on all of the coin.

The **G-4 (Good, G)** coin's design will be clearly outlined but with substantial wear. Some of the larger detail may be visible. The rim may have a few weak spots of wear.

Strong or weak strikes, partially weak strikes, damage, corrosion, attractive or unattractive toning, rim bumps, dipping or cleaning should be described along with the above grades. These factors affect the quality of the coin just as do wear and loss of detail, but are easier to describe.

As the proof designation is a method of manufacture and not a grade, the price listings of PF-60, PF-63 and PF-65 are employed in these listings. At these levels, it is often the quality of strike and not actual wear, which is judged. In order to buy and sell proof coins at these designated grades, normally third-party grading and encapsulation is required. As the 21st century dawned, mints and distributors have employed special clean-room manufacturing processes which have virtually eliminated problems and imperfections in proof coins. The modern low mintage proof coin is often only available in sealed multi-coin sets, or encased within individual plastic holders within a larger fitted display case.

Coin Alignment

Medal Alignment

COIN vs MEDAL ALIGNMENT

Some coins are struck with obverse and reverse aligned at a rotation of 180° from each other. When a coin is held for vertical viewing with the obverse design aligned upright and the index finger and thumb at the top and bottom, upon rotation from left to right for viewing the reverse, the latter will be upside down. Such alignment is called "coin rotation." Other coins are struck with the obverse and reverse designs mated on an alignment of zero or 360°. If such an example is held and rotated as described, the reverse will appear upright. This is the alignment, which is generally observed in the striking of medals, and for that reason coins produced in this manner are considered struck in "medal rotation." In some instances, often through error, certain coin issues have been struck to both alignment standards, creating interesting collectible varieties, which will be found noted in some listings. In addition, some countries are now producing coins with other designated obverse to reverse alignments which are considered standard for this type.

STANDARD INTERNATIONAL GRADING TERMINOLOGY AND ABBREVIATIONS

U.S. and ENGLISH SPEAKING LANDS	UNCIRCULATED	EXTREMELY FINE	VERY FINE	FINE	VERY GOOD	GOOD	POOR
Abbreviation	UNC	EF or XF	VF	FF	VG	G	PR
BRAZIL	(1) DW	(3) S	(5) MBC	(7) BC	(8)	(9) R	UTGeG
DENMARK	O	01	1+	1	1÷	2	3
FINLAND	0·	01	1+	1	1?	2	3
FRANCE	NEUF	SUP	TTB or TB	TB or TB	B	TBC	BC
GERMANY	KFR	II / VZGL	III / SS	IV / S	V / S.g.E.	VI / G.e.	G.e.s.
ITALY	FdS	SPL	BB	MB	B	M	—
JAPAN	未使用	極美品	美品	並品	—	—	—
NETHERLANDS	FDC	Pr.	Z.F.	Fr.	Z.g.	G	—
NORWAY	0	01	1+	1	1÷	2	3
PORTUGAL	Novo	Soberbo	Muito bo	—	—	—	—
SPAIN	Lujo	SC, IC or EBC	MBC	BC	—	RC	MC
SWEDEN	0	01	1+	1	1?	2	—

BRAZIL

FE — Flor de Estampa
S — Soberba
MBC — Muito Bem Conservada
BC — Bem Conservada
R — Regular
UTGeG — Um Tanto Gasto e Gasto

DENMARK

O — Uncirkuleret
01 — Meget Paent Eksemplar
1+ — Paent Eksemplar
1 — Acceptabelt Eksemplar
1 —Noget Slidt Eksemplar
2 — Darlight Eksemplar
3 — Meget Darlight Eskemplar

FINLAND

00 — Kiiltolyönti
0 — Lyöntiveres
01 — Erittäin Hyvä
1+ — Hyvä
1? — Heikko
2 — Huono

FRANCE

NEUF — New
FDC — Fleur De Coin
SPL — Splendide
SUP — Superbe
TTB — Très Très Beau
TB — Très Beau
B — Beau
TBC — Tres Bien Conserve
BC — Bien Conserve

GERMANY

VZGL — Vorzüglich
SS — Sehr schön
S — Schön
S.g.E. — Sehr gut erhalten
G.e. — Gut erhalten
G.e.S. — Gering erhalten
Schlecht

ITALY

Fds — Fior di Stampa
SPL — Splendid
BB — Bellissimo
MB — Molto Bello
B — Bello
M — Mediocre

JAPAN

未使用 — Mishiyo
極美品 — Goku Bihin
美品 — Bihin
並品 — Futuhin

NETHERLANDS

Pr. — Prachtig
Z.F. — Zeer Fraai
Fr. — Fraai
Z.g. — Zeer Goed
G — Goed

NORWAY

0 — Usirkuleret eks
01 — Meget pent eks
1+ — Pent eks
1 — Fullgodt eks
1- — Ikke Fullgodt eks
2 — Darlig eks

ROMANIA

NC — Necirculata (UNC)
FF — Foarte Frumoasa (VF)
F — Frumoasa (F)
FBC — Foarte Bine Conservata (VG)
BC — Bine Conservata (G)
M — Mediocru Conservata (POOR)

SPAIN

EBC — Extraordinariamente Bien Conservada
SC — Sin Circular
IC — Incirculante
MBC — Muy Bien Conservada
BC — Bien Conservada
RC — Regular Conservada
MC — Mala Conservada

SWEDEN

0 — Ocirkulerat
01 — Mycket Vackert
1+ — Vackert
1 — Fullgott
1? — Ej Fullgott
2 — Dalight

STANDARD INTERNATIONAL NUMERAL SYSTEMS

Prepared especially for the *Standard Catalog of World Coins*© 2015 by Krause Publications

Western	0	½	1	2	3	4	5	6	7	8	9	10	50	100	500	1000
Roman			I	II	III	IV	V	VI	VII	VIII	IX	X	L	C	D	M
Arabic-Turkish	٠	١/٢	١	٢	٣	٤	٥	٦	٧	٨	٩	١٠	٥٠	١٠٠	٥٠٠	١٠٠٠
Malay-Persian	۰	۱/۲	۱	۲	۳	۴	۵	۶ or ۶	۷	۸	۹	۱۰	۵۰	۱۰۰	۵۰۰	۱۰۰۰
Eastern Arabic	۰	۱/۲	۱	۲	۳	۴	۵	۶	۷	۸	۹	۱۰	۵۰	۱۰۰	۵۰۰	۱۰۰۰
Hyderabad Arabic	۰	۱/۲	۱	۲	۳	۴	۵	۶	۷	۸	۹	۱۰	۵۰	۱۰۰	۵۰۰	۱۰۰۰
Indian (Sanskrit)	०	१/२	१	२	३	४	५	६	७	८	९	१०	५०	१००	५००	१०००
Assamese	০	১/২	১	২	৩	৪	৫	৬	৭	৮	৯	১০	৫০	১০০	৫০০	১০০০
Bengali	০	১/২	১	২	৩	৪	৫	৬	৭	৮	৯	১০	৫০	১০০	৫০০	১০০০
Gujarati	૦	૧/૨	૧	૨	૩	૪	૫	૬	૭	૮	૯	૧૦	૫૦	૧૦૦	૫૦૦	૧૦૦૦
Kutch	०	१/२	१	२	३	४	५	६	७	८	९	१०	५०	१००	५००	१०००
Devavnagri	०	१/२	१	२	३	४	५	६ or ६	७	८	९ or ९	१०	५०	१००	५००	१०००
Nepalese	०	१/२	१	२	३	४	५	६	७	८	९	१०	५०	१००	५००	१०००
Tibetan	༠	༡/༢	༡	༢	༣	༤	༥	༦	༧	༨	༩	༡༠	༥༠	༡༠༠	༥༠༠	༡༠༠༠
Mongolian	᠐	᠑/᠒	᠑	᠒	᠓	᠔	᠕	᠖	᠗	᠘	᠙	᠑᠐	᠕᠐	᠑᠐᠐	᠕᠐᠐	᠑᠐᠐᠐
Burmese	၀	၁/၂	၁	၂	၃	၄	၅	၆	၇	၈	၉	၁၀	၅၀	၁၀၀	၅၀၀	၁၀၀၀
Thai-Lao	๐	๑/๒	๑	๒	๓	๔	๕	๖	๗	๘	๙	๑๐	๕๐	๑๐๐	๕๐๐	๑๐๐๐
Lao-Laotian	໐		໑	໒	໓	໔	໕	໖	໗	໘	໙	໑໐				
Javanese	꧐		꧑	꧒	꧓	꧔	꧕	꧖	꧗	꧘	꧙	꧑꧐	꧕꧐	꧑꧐꧐	꧕꧐꧐	꧑꧐꧐꧐
Ordinary Chinese Japanese-Korean	零	半	一	二	三	四	五	六	七	八	九	十	十五	百	百五	千
Official Chinese			壹	貳	叁	肆	伍	陸	柒	捌	玖	拾	拾伍	佰	佰伍	仟
Commercial Chinese			〡	〢	〣	〤	〥	〦	〧	〨	〩	十	〥十	〡百	〥百	〡千
Korean		반	일	이	삼	사	오	육	칠	팔	구	십	오십	백	오백	천
Georgian			ა	ბ	გ	დ	ე	ვ	ზ	ჱ	თ	ი	ნ	რ	ფ	ჩ
			11 ია	20 კ	30 ლ	40 მ	60 ჲ	70 ო	80 პ	90 ჟ	200 ს	300 ტ	400 ჳ	600 ქ	700 ღ	800 ყ
Ethiopian	◆		፩	፪	፫	፬	፭	፮	፯	፰	፱	፲	፶	፻	፭፻	፲፻
				20 ፳	30 ፴	40 ፵	60 ፷	70 ፸	80 ፹	90 ፺						
Hebrew			א	ב	ג	ד	ה	ו	ז	ח	ט	י	נ	ק	תק	
				20 כ	30 ל	40 מ	60 ס	70 ע	80 פ	90 צ	200 ר	300 ש	400 ת	600 תר	700 תש	800 תת
Greek			Α	Β	Γ	Δ	Ε	Τ	Ζ	Η	Θ	Ι	Ν	Ρ	Φ	Α
				20 Κ	30 Λ	40 Μ	60 Ξ	70 Ο	80 Π		200 Σ	300 Τ	400 Υ	600 Χ	700 Ψ	800 Ω

INSTANT IDENTIFIER

Aachen (German States)

Albania

Austria

Baden (German States)

Brandenburg Ansbach (German States)

Finland

Jever (German States)

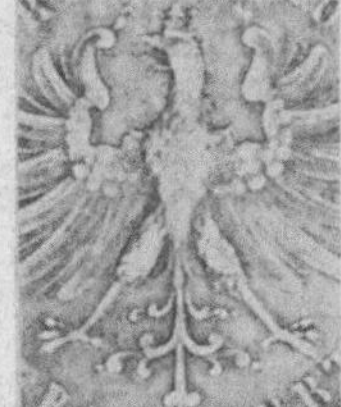
Frankfurt (German States)

Furstenberg (German States)

Geneva (Swiss Cantons)

German Empire

Montenegro (Yugoslavia)

Nürnberg (German States)

Milan (Italian States)

Prussia (German States)

Russia (Czarist) Russian Poland

Schwarzburg-Rudolstadt (German States)

Schwarzburg-Sondershausen (German States)

Serbia (Yugoslavia)

Teutonic Order (German States)

Genoa (Italian States)

Syrian Arab Republic

United Arab Republic (Egypt, Syria)

Arab Republic of Egypt Libya

Yemen Arab Republic

Bulgaria

Burma (Myanmar)

Ethiopia

Finland

Norway

Gorizia (Italian States)

Hannover (German States)

Hesse-Darmstadt (German States)

Hohenlohe-Neuenstein-Oehringen (German States)

Iran (Persia)

Morocco

Siberia

Tibet (China)

Nepal

Morocco (AH1371-1951AD)

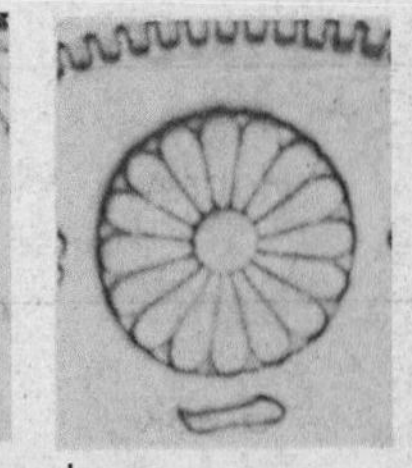
Manchoukuo (Puppet State-China)

Japan

INSTANT IDENTIFIER

Hanau-Munzenberg (German States)

Nassau (German States)

Hesse-Cassel (German States)

Sri Lanka (Ceylon)

Tibet (China)

Utrecht (Netherlands)

Venice (Italian States)

Neuchatel (Swiss Cantons)

China (Empire-Provincial)

China (Empire-Provincial)

Japan

Japan

African States

Bretzenheim (German States)

Hall in Swabia (German States)

Greenland

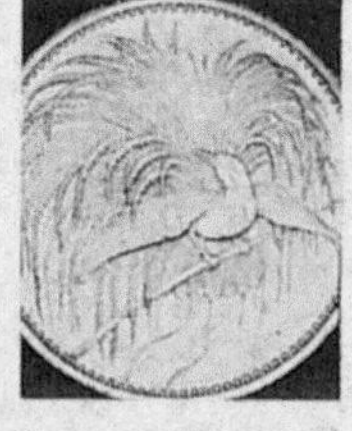
German New Guinea (Papua New Guinea)

Lithuania

Mongolia

Sudan

Algeria

Lowenstein-Wertheim (German States)

Maldive Islands

Afghanistan

Ireland

Israel

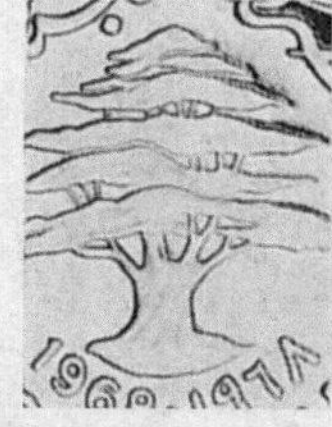
Lebanon

Papal States (Italian States)

Regensburg (German States)

Sweden

North Korea

CCCP-Russia

CCCP-Russia

Yugoslavia

Taiwan (Rep. of China)

Mainz (German States)

Solms-Laubach (German States)

Ticino (Swiss Cantons)

Fugger (German States)

Naples & Sicily (Italian States)

Saxe-Saalfeld (German States)

Stolberg-Stolberg (German States)

INSTANT IDENTIFIER

French Colonial

French Colonial

French Colonial

Bangladesh

Isle of Man
Sicily

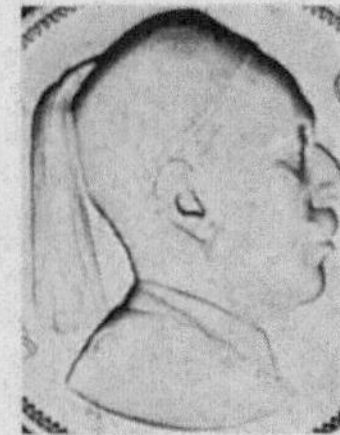
Libya

Anhalt-Bernburg
(German States)

Aargau
(Swiss Cantons)

Augsburg
(German States)

Basel
(Swiss Cantons)

Bavaria
(German States)

Brazil

Bremen
(German States)

Luzern
(Swiss Cantons)

Chur Pfalz
(German States)

Fulda
(German States)

Glarus
(Swiss Cantons)

Grand Duchy
of Warsaw
(Poland)

Graubunden
(Swiss Cantons)

Hamburg
(German States)

Lucca
(Italian States)

Hesse-Cassel
(German States)

Hesse-Homburg
(German States)

Hildesheim
(German States)

Hohenzollern-
Hechingen
(German States)

Hungary

Julich-Berg
(German States)

Gelderland
(Netherlands)

Lippe-Detmold
(German States)

Lübeck
(German States)

Mecklenburg-
Strelitz
(German States)

Oldenburg
(German States)

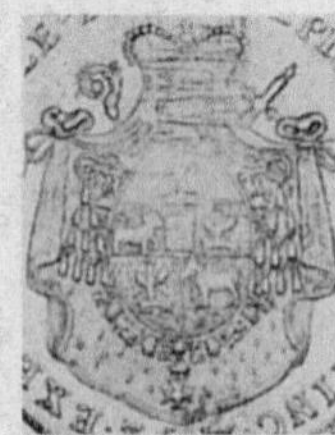
Passau
(German States)

Portugal

Vaud
(Swiss Cantons)

Anhalt
(Joint Coinage)
(German States)

Oldenburg
(German States)

Schwarzenberg
(German States)

Schaffhausen
(Swiss Cantons)

Paderborn
(German States)

Thurgau
(Swiss Cantons)

Westfrisia
(Netherlands)

INSTANT IDENTIFIER

Arenberg (German States)

Rhenish Confederation (German States)

Reuss-Greiz (German States)

Sardinia (Italian States)

Saxony (German States)

Schaumburg-Lippe (German States)

Schleswig-Holstein (German States)

St. Gall (Swiss Cantons)

Slovakia

Solothurn (Swiss Cantons)

Unterwalden (Nidwalden) (Swiss Cantons)

Württemberg (German States)

Würzburg (German States)

Zurich (Swiss Cantons)

Waldeck-Pyrmont (German States)

Iraq

Pakistan

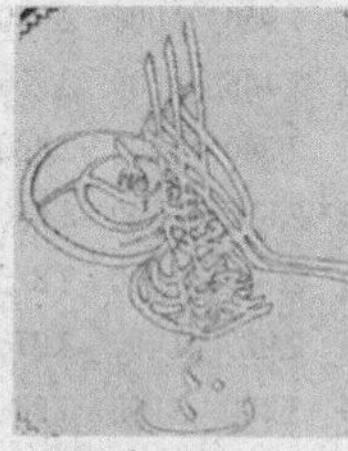
Turkey-Egypt Sudan, Algeria (Ottoman Empire)

Muscat & Oman, Oman

Saudi Arabia

Tunisia

Wismar (German States)

Order of Malta

Bamberg (German States)

Brunswick-Wolfenbüttel (German States)

Brunswick-Lüneburg (German States

Erfurt Mainz (German States)

Hannover (German States)

Eichstätt (German States)

Greece

Serbia

Switzerland

Albania

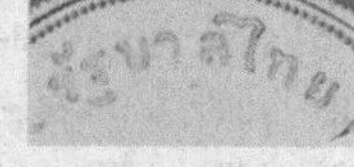
Thailand (Siam)

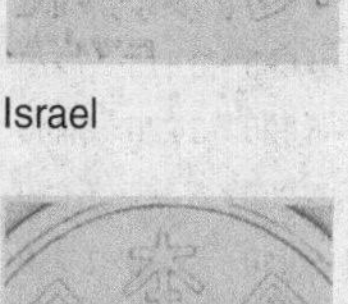
Israel

Japan (Dai Nippon)

South Korea

en
iss Cantons)

Rostock (German States)

Saint Alban (German States)

English East India Co. (Sumatra)

China, Japan, Annam, Korea
(All Holed 'cash' coins look quite similar.)

Japan

Korea

SILVER BULLION VALUE CHART $15 to $25

Oz.	15.00	15.50	16.00	16.50	17.00	17.50	18.00	18.50	19.00	19.50	20.00	20.50	21.00	21.50	22.00	22.50	23.00	23.50	24.00	24.50	25.00	Oz.
0.001	0.015	0.016	0.016	0.017	0.017	0.018	0.018	0.019	0.019	0.020	0.020	0.021	0.021	0.022	0.022	0.023	0.023	0.024	0.024	0.025	0.025	**0.001**
0.002	0.030	0.031	0.032	0.033	0.034	0.035	0.036	0.037	0.038	0.039	0.040	0.041	0.042	0.043	0.044	0.045	0.046	0.047	0.048	0.049	0.050	**0.002**
0.003	0.045	0.047	0.048	0.050	0.051	0.053	0.054	0.056	0.057	0.059	0.060	0.062	0.063	0.065	0.066	0.068	0.069	0.071	0.072	0.074	0.075	**0.003**
0.004	0.060	0.062	0.064	0.066	0.068	0.070	0.072	0.074	0.076	0.078	0.080	0.082	0.084	0.086	0.088	0.090	0.092	0.094	0.096	0.098	0.100	**0.004**
0.005	0.075	0.078	0.080	0.083	0.085	0.088	0.090	0.093	0.095	0.098	0.100	0.103	0.105	0.108	0.110	0.113	0.115	0.118	0.120	0.123	0.125	**0.005**
0.006	0.090	0.093	0.096	0.099	0.102	0.105	0.108	0.111	0.114	0.117	0.120	0.123	0.126	0.129	0.132	0.135	0.138	0.141	0.144	0.147	0.150	**0.006**
0.007	0.105	0.109	0.112	0.116	0.119	0.123	0.126	0.130	0.133	0.137	0.140	0.144	0.147	0.151	0.154	0.158	0.161	0.165	0.168	0.172	0.175	**0.007**
0.008	0.120	0.124	0.128	0.132	0.136	0.140	0.144	0.148	0.152	0.156	0.160	0.164	0.168	0.172	0.176	0.180	0.184	0.188	0.192	0.196	0.200	**0.008**
0.009	0.135	0.140	0.144	0.149	0.153	0.158	0.162	0.167	0.171	0.176	0.180	0.185	0.189	0.194	0.198	0.203	0.207	0.212	0.216	0.221	0.225	**0.009**
0.010	0.150	0.155	0.160	0.165	0.170	0.175	0.180	0.185	0.190	0.195	0.200	0.205	0.210	0.215	0.220	0.225	0.230	0.235	0.240	0.245	0.250	**0.010**
0.020	0.300	0.310	0.320	0.330	0.340	0.350	0.360	0.370	0.380	0.390	0.400	0.410	0.420	0.430	0.440	0.450	0.460	0.470	0.480	0.490	0.500	**0.020**
0.030	0.450	0.465	0.480	0.495	0.510	0.525	0.540	0.555	0.570	0.585	0.600	0.615	0.630	0.645	0.660	0.675	0.690	0.705	0.720	0.735	0.750	**0.030**
0.040	0.600	0.620	0.640	0.660	0.680	0.700	0.720	0.740	0.760	0.780	0.800	0.820	0.840	0.860	0.880	0.900	0.920	0.940	0.960	0.980	1.000	**0.040**
0.050	0.750	0.775	0.800	0.825	0.850	0.875	0.900	0.925	0.950	0.975	1.000	1.025	1.050	1.075	1.100	1.125	1.150	1.175	1.200	1.225	1.250	**0.050**
0.060	0.900	0.930	0.960	0.990	1.020	1.050	1.080	1.110	1.140	1.170	1.200	1.230	1.260	1.290	1.320	1.350	1.380	1.410	1.440	1.470	1.500	**0.060**
0.070	1.050	1.085	1.120	1.155	1.190	1.225	1.260	1.295	1.330	1.365	1.400	1.435	1.470	1.505	1.540	1.575	1.610	1.645	1.680	1.715	1.750	**0.070**
0.080	1.200	1.240	1.280	1.320	1.360	1.400	1.440	1.480	1.520	1.560	1.600	1.640	1.680	1.720	1.760	1.800	1.840	1.880	1.920	1.960	2.000	**0.080**
0.090	1.350	1.395	1.440	1.485	1.530	1.575	1.620	1.665	1.710	1.755	1.800	1.845	1.890	1.935	1.980	2.025	2.070	2.115	2.160	2.205	2.250	**0.090**
0.100	1.500	1.550	1.600	1.650	1.700	1.750	1.800	1.850	1.900	1.950	2.000	2.050	2.100	2.150	2.200	2.250	2.300	2.350	2.400	2.450	2.500	**0.100**
0.110	1.650	1.705	1.760	1.815	1.870	1.925	1.980	2.035	2.090	2.145	2.200	2.255	2.310	2.365	2.420	2.475	2.530	2.585	2.640	2.695	2.750	**0.110**
0.120	1.800	1.860	1.920	1.980	2.040	2.100	2.160	2.220	2.280	2.340	2.400	2.460	2.520	2.580	2.640	2.700	2.760	2.820	2.880	2.940	3.000	**0.120**
0.130	1.950	2.015	2.080	2.145	2.210	2.275	2.340	2.405	2.470	2.535	2.600	2.665	2.730	2.795	2.860	2.925	2.990	3.055	3.120	3.185	3.250	**0.130**
0.140	2.100	2.170	2.240	2.310	2.380	2.450	2.520	2.590	2.660	2.730	2.800	2.870	2.940	3.010	3.080	3.150	3.220	3.290	3.360	3.430	3.500	**0.140**
0.150	2.250	2.325	2.400	2.475	2.550	2.625	2.700	2.775	2.850	2.925	3.000	3.075	3.150	3.225	3.300	3.375	3.450	3.525	3.600	3.675	3.750	**0.150**
0.160	2.400	2.480	2.560	2.640	2.720	2.800	2.880	2.960	3.040	3.120	3.200	3.280	3.360	3.440	3.520	3.600	3.680	3.760	3.840	3.920	4.000	**0.160**
0.170	2.550	2.635	2.720	2.805	2.890	2.975	3.060	3.145	3.230	3.315	3.400	3.485	3.570	3.655	3.740	3.825	3.910	3.995	4.080	4.165	4.250	**0.170**
0.180	2.700	2.790	2.880	2.970	3.060	3.150	3.240	3.330	3.420	3.510	3.600	3.690	3.780	3.870	3.960	4.050	4.140	4.230	4.320	4.410	4.500	**0.180**
0.190	2.850	2.945	3.040	3.135	3.230	3.325	3.420	3.515	3.610	3.705	3.800	3.895	3.990	4.085	4.180	4.275	4.370	4.465	4.560	4.655	4.750	**0.190**
0.200	3.000	3.100	3.200	3.300	3.400	3.500	3.600	3.700	3.800	3.900	4.000	4.100	4.200	4.300	4.400	4.500	4.600	4.700	4.800	4.900	5.000	**0.200**
0.210	3.150	3.255	3.360	3.465	3.570	3.675	3.780	3.885	3.990	4.095	4.200	4.305	4.410	4.515	4.620	4.725	4.830	4.935	5.040	5.145	5.250	**0.210**
0.220	3.300	3.410	3.520	3.630	3.740	3.850	3.960	4.070	4.180	4.290	4.400	4.510	4.620	4.730	4.840	4.950	5.060	5.170	5.280	5.390	5.500	**0.220**
0.230	3.450	3.565	3.680	3.795	3.910	4.025	4.140	4.255	4.370	4.485	4.600	4.715	4.830	4.945	5.060	5.175	5.290	5.405	5.520	5.635	5.750	**0.230**
0.240	3.600	3.720	3.840	3.960	4.080	4.200	4.320	4.440	4.560	4.680	4.800	4.920	5.040	5.160	5.280	5.400	5.520	5.640	5.760	5.880	6.000	**0.240**
0.250	3.750	3.875	4.000	4.125	4.250	4.375	4.500	4.625	4.750	4.875	5.000	5.125	5.250	5.375	5.500	5.625	5.750	5.875	6.000	6.125	6.250	**0.250**
0.260	3.900	4.030	4.160	4.290	4.420	4.550	4.680	4.810	4.940	5.070	5.200	5.330	5.460	5.590	5.720	5.850	5.980	6.110	6.240	6.370	6.500	**0.260**
0.270	4.050	4.185	4.320	4.455	4.590	4.725	4.860	4.995	5.130	5.265	5.400	5.535	5.670	5.805	5.940	6.075	6.210	6.345	6.480	6.615	6.750	**0.270**
0.280	4.200	4.340	4.480	4.620	4.760	4.900	5.040	5.180	5.320	5.460	5.600	5.740	5.880	6.020	6.160	6.300	6.440	6.580	6.720	6.860	7.000	**0.280**
0.290	4.350	4.495	4.640	4.785	4.930	5.075	5.220	5.365	5.510	5.655	5.800	5.945	6.090	6.235	6.380	6.525	6.670	6.815	6.960	7.105	7.250	**0.290**
0.300	4.500	4.650	4.800	4.950	5.100	5.250	5.400	5.550	5.700	5.850	6.000	6.150	6.300	6.450	6.600	6.750	6.900	7.050	7.200	7.350	7.500	**0.300**
0.310	4.650	4.805	4.960	5.115	5.270	5.425	5.580	5.735	5.890	6.045	6.200	6.355	6.510	6.665	6.820	6.975	7.130	7.285	7.440	7.595	7.750	**0.310**
0.320	4.800	4.960	5.120	5.280	5.440	5.600	5.760	5.920	6.080	6.240	6.400	6.560	6.720	6.880	7.040	7.200	7.360	7.520	7.680	7.840	8.000	**0.320**
0.330	4.950	5.115	5.280	5.445	5.610	5.775	5.940	6.105	6.270	6.435	6.600	6.765	6.930	7.095	7.260	7.425	7.590	7.755	7.920	8.085	8.250	**0.330**
0.340	5.100	5.270	5.440	5.610	5.780	5.950	6.120	6.290	6.460	6.630	6.800	6.970	7.140	7.310	7.480	7.650	7.820	7.990	8.160	8.330	8.500	**0.340**
0.350	5.250	5.425	5.600	5.775	5.950	6.125	6.300	6.475	6.650	6.825	7.000	7.175	7.350	7.525	7.700	7.875	8.050	8.225	8.400	8.575	8.750	**0.350**
0.360	5.400	5.580	5.760	5.940	6.120	6.300	6.480	6.660	6.840	7.020	7.200	7.380	7.560	7.740	7.920	8.100	8.280	8.460	8.640	8.820	9.000	**0.360**
0.370	5.550	5.735	5.920	6.105	6.290	6.475	6.660	6.845	7.030	7.215	7.400	7.585	7.770	7.955	8.140	8.325	8.510	8.695	8.880	9.065	9.250	**0.370**
0.380	5.700	5.890	6.080	6.270	6.460	6.650	6.840	7.030	7.220	7.410	7.600	7.790	7.980	8.170	8.360	8.550	8.740	8.930	9.120	9.310	9.500	**0.380**
0.390	5.850	6.045	6.240	6.435	6.630	6.825	7.020	7.215	7.410	7.605	7.800	7.995	8.190	8.385	8.580	8.775	8.970	9.165	9.360	9.555	9.750	**0.390**
0.400	6.000	6.200	6.400	6.600	6.800	7.000	7.200	7.400	7.600	7.800	8.000	8.200	8.400	8.600	8.800	9.000	9.200	9.400	9.600	9.800	10.000	**0.400**
0.410	6.150	6.355	6.560	6.765	6.970	7.175	7.380	7.585	7.790	7.995	8.200	8.405	8.610	8.815	9.020	9.225	9.430	9.635	9.840	10.045	10.250	**0.410**
0.420	6.300	6.510	6.720	6.930	7.140	7.350	7.560	7.770	7.980	8.190	8.400	8.610	8.820	9.030	9.240	9.450	9.660	9.870	10.080	10.290	10.500	**0.420**
0.430	6.450	6.665	6.880	7.095	7.310	7.525	7.740	7.955	8.170	8.385	8.600	8.815	9.030	9.245	9.460	9.675	9.890	10.105	10.320	10.535	10.750	**0.430**
0.440	6.600	6.820	7.040	7.260	7.480	7.700	7.920	8.140	8.360	8.580	8.800	9.020	9.240	9.460	9.680	9.900	10.120	10.340	10.560	10.780	11.000	**0.440**
0.450	6.750	6.975	7.200	7.425	7.650	7.875	8.100	8.325	8.550	8.775	9.000	9.225	9.450	9.675	9.900	10.125	10.350	10.575	10.800	11.025	11.250	**0.450**
0.460	6.900	7.130	7.360	7.590	7.820	8.050	8.280	8.510	8.740	8.970	9.200	9.430	9.660	9.890	10.120	10.350	10.580	10.810	11.040	11.270	11.500	**0.460**

SILVER BULLION VALUE CHART $15 to $25

Oz.	15.00	15.50	16.00	16.50	17.00	17.50	18.00	18.50	19.00	19.50	20.00	20.50	21.00	21.50	22.00	22.50	23.00	23.50	24.00	24.50	25.00	Oz.
0.470	7.050	7.285	7.520	7.755	7.990	8.225	8.460	8.695	8.930	9.165	9.400	9.635	9.870	10.105	10.340	10.575	10.810	11.045	11.280	11.515	11.750	**0.470**
0.480	7.200	7.440	7.680	7.920	8.160	8.400	8.640	8.880	9.120	9.360	9.600	9.840	10.080	10.320	10.560	10.800	11.040	11.280	11.520	11.760	12.000	**0.480**
0.490	7.350	7.595	7.840	8.085	8.330	8.575	8.820	9.065	9.310	9.555	9.800	10.045	10.290	10.535	10.780	11.025	11.270	11.515	11.760	12.005	12.250	**0.490**
0.500	7.500	7.750	8.000	8.250	8.500	8.750	9.000	9.250	9.500	9.750	10.000	10.250	10.500	10.750	11.000	11.250	11.500	11.750	12.000	12.250	12.500	**0.500**
0.510	7.650	7.905	8.160	8.415	8.670	8.925	9.180	9.435	9.690	9.945	10.200	10.455	10.710	10.965	11.220	11.475	11.730	11.985	12.240	12.495	12.750	**0.510**
0.520	7.800	8.060	8.320	8.580	8.840	9.100	9.360	9.620	9.880	10.140	10.400	10.660	10.920	11.180	11.440	11.700	11.960	12.220	12.480	12.740	13.000	**0.520**
0.530	7.950	8.215	8.480	8.745	9.010	9.275	9.540	9.805	10.070	10.335	10.600	10.865	11.130	11.395	11.660	11.925	12.190	12.455	12.720	12.985	13.250	**0.530**
0.540	8.100	8.370	8.640	8.910	9.180	9.450	9.720	9.990	10.260	10.530	10.800	11.070	11.340	11.610	11.880	12.150	12.420	12.690	12.960	13.230	13.500	**0.540**
0.550	8.250	8.525	8.800	9.075	9.350	9.625	9.900	10.175	10.450	10.725	11.000	11.275	11.550	11.825	12.100	12.375	12.650	12.925	13.200	13.475	13.750	**0.550**
0.560	8.400	8.680	8.960	9.240	9.520	9.800	10.080	10.360	10.640	10.920	11.200	11.480	11.760	12.040	12.320	12.600	12.880	13.160	13.440	13.720	14.000	**0.560**
0.570	8.550	8.835	9.120	9.405	9.690	9.975	10.260	10.545	10.830	11.115	11.400	11.685	11.970	12.255	12.540	12.825	13.110	13.395	13.680	13.965	14.250	**0.570**
0.580	8.700	8.990	9.280	9.570	9.860	10.150	10.440	10.730	11.020	11.310	11.600	11.890	12.180	12.470	12.760	13.050	13.340	13.630	13.920	14.210	14.500	**0.580**
0.590	8.850	9.145	9.440	9.735	10.030	10.325	10.620	10.915	11.210	11.505	11.800	12.095	12.390	12.685	12.980	13.275	13.570	13.865	14.160	14.455	14.750	**0.590**
0.600	9.000	9.300	9.600	9.900	10.200	10.500	10.800	11.100	11.400	11.700	12.000	12.300	12.600	12.900	13.200	13.500	13.800	14.100	14.400	14.700	15.000	**0.600**
0.610	9.150	9.455	9.760	10.065	10.370	10.675	10.980	11.285	11.590	11.895	12.200	12.505	12.810	13.115	13.420	13.725	14.030	14.335	14.640	14.945	15.250	**0.610**
0.620	9.300	9.610	9.920	10.230	10.540	10.850	11.160	11.470	11.780	12.090	12.400	12.710	13.020	13.330	13.640	13.950	14.260	14.570	14.880	15.190	15.500	**0.620**
0.630	9.450	9.765	10.080	10.395	10.710	11.025	11.340	11.655	11.970	12.285	12.600	12.915	13.230	13.545	13.860	14.175	14.490	14.805	15.120	15.435	15.750	**0.630**
0.640	9.600	9.920	10.240	10.560	10.880	11.200	11.520	11.840	12.160	12.480	12.800	13.120	13.440	13.760	14.080	14.400	14.720	15.040	15.360	15.680	16.000	**0.640**
0.650	9.750	10.075	10.400	10.725	11.050	11.375	11.700	12.025	12.350	12.675	13.000	13.325	13.650	13.975	14.300	14.625	14.950	15.275	15.600	15.925	16.250	**0.650**
0.660	9.900	10.230	10.560	10.890	11.220	11.550	11.880	12.210	12.540	12.870	13.200	13.530	13.860	14.190	14.520	14.850	15.180	15.510	15.840	16.170	16.500	**0.660**
0.670	10.050	10.385	10.720	11.055	11.390	11.725	12.060	12.395	12.730	13.065	13.400	13.735	14.070	14.405	14.740	15.075	15.410	15.745	16.080	16.415	16.750	**0.670**
0.680	10.200	10.540	10.880	11.220	11.560	11.900	12.240	12.580	12.920	13.260	13.600	13.940	14.280	14.620	14.960	15.300	15.640	15.980	16.320	16.660	17.000	**0.680**
0.690	10.350	10.695	11.040	11.385	11.730	12.075	12.420	12.765	13.110	13.455	13.800	14.145	14.490	14.835	15.180	15.525	15.870	16.215	16.560	16.905	17.250	**0.690**
0.700	10.500	10.850	11.200	11.550	11.900	12.250	12.600	12.950	13.300	13.650	14.000	14.350	14.700	15.050	15.400	15.750	16.100	16.450	16.800	17.150	17.500	**0.700**
0.710	10.650	11.005	11.360	11.715	12.070	12.425	12.780	13.135	13.490	13.845	14.200	14.555	14.910	15.265	15.620	15.975	16.330	16.685	17.040	17.395	17.750	**0.710**
0.720	10.800	11.160	11.520	11.880	12.240	12.600	12.960	13.320	13.680	14.040	14.400	14.760	15.120	15.480	15.840	16.200	16.560	16.920	17.280	17.640	18.000	**0.720**
0.730	10.950	11.315	11.680	12.045	12.410	12.775	13.140	13.505	13.870	14.235	14.600	14.965	15.330	15.695	16.060	16.425	16.790	17.155	17.520	17.885	18.250	**0.730**
0.740	11.100	11.470	11.840	12.210	12.580	12.950	13.320	13.690	14.060	14.430	14.800	15.170	15.540	15.910	16.280	16.650	17.020	17.390	17.760	18.130	18.500	**0.740**
0.750	11.250	11.625	12.000	12.375	12.750	13.125	13.500	13.875	14.250	14.625	15.000	15.375	15.750	16.125	16.500	16.875	17.250	17.625	18.000	18.375	18.750	**0.750**
0.760	11.400	11.780	12.160	12.540	12.920	13.300	13.680	14.060	14.440	14.820	15.200	15.580	15.960	16.340	16.720	17.100	17.480	17.860	18.240	18.620	19.000	**0.760**
0.770	11.550	11.935	12.320	12.705	13.090	13.475	13.860	14.245	14.630	15.015	15.400	15.785	16.170	16.555	16.940	17.325	17.710	18.095	18.480	18.865	19.250	**0.770**
0.780	11.700	12.090	12.480	12.870	13.260	13.650	14.040	14.430	14.820	15.210	15.600	15.990	16.380	16.770	17.160	17.550	17.940	18.330	18.720	19.110	19.500	**0.780**
0.790	11.850	12.245	12.640	13.035	13.430	13.825	14.220	14.615	15.010	15.405	15.800	16.195	16.590	16.985	17.380	17.775	18.170	18.565	18.960	19.355	19.750	**0.790**
0.800	12.000	12.400	12.800	13.200	13.600	14.000	14.400	14.800	15.200	15.600	16.000	16.400	16.800	17.200	17.600	18.000	18.400	18.800	19.200	19.600	20.000	**0.800**
0.810	12.150	12.555	12.960	13.365	13.770	14.175	14.580	14.985	15.390	15.795	16.200	16.605	17.010	17.415	17.820	18.225	18.630	19.035	19.440	19.845	20.250	**0.810**
0.820	12.300	12.710	13.120	13.530	13.940	14.350	14.760	15.170	15.580	15.990	16.400	16.810	17.220	17.630	18.040	18.450	18.860	19.270	19.680	20.090	20.500	**0.820**
0.830	12.450	12.865	13.280	13.695	14.110	14.525	14.940	15.355	15.770	16.185	16.600	17.015	17.430	17.845	18.260	18.675	19.090	19.505	19.920	20.335	20.750	**0.830**
0.840	12.600	13.020	13.440	13.860	14.280	14.700	15.120	15.540	15.960	16.380	16.800	17.220	17.640	18.060	18.480	18.900	19.320	19.740	20.160	20.580	21.000	**0.840**
0.850	12.750	13.175	13.600	14.025	14.450	14.875	15.300	15.725	16.150	16.575	17.000	17.425	17.850	18.275	18.700	19.125	19.550	19.975	20.400	20.825	21.250	**0.850**
0.860	12.900	13.330	13.760	14.190	14.620	15.050	15.480	15.910	16.340	16.770	17.200	17.630	18.060	18.490	18.920	19.350	19.780	20.210	20.640	21.070	21.500	**0.860**
0.870	13.050	13.485	13.920	14.355	14.790	15.225	15.660	16.095	16.530	16.965	17.400	17.835	18.270	18.705	19.140	19.575	20.010	20.445	20.880	21.315	21.750	**0.870**
0.880	13.200	13.640	14.080	14.520	14.960	15.400	15.840	16.280	16.720	17.160	17.600	18.040	18.480	18.920	19.360	19.800	20.240	20.680	21.120	21.560	22.000	**0.880**
0.890	13.350	13.795	14.240	14.685	15.130	15.575	16.020	16.465	16.910	17.355	17.800	18.245	18.690	19.135	19.580	20.025	20.470	20.915	21.360	21.805	22.250	**0.890**
0.900	13.500	13.950	14.400	14.850	15.300	15.750	16.200	16.650	17.100	17.550	18.000	18.450	18.900	19.350	19.800	20.250	20.700	21.150	21.600	22.050	22.500	**0.900**
0.910	13.650	14.105	14.560	15.015	15.470	15.925	16.380	16.835	17.290	17.745	18.200	18.655	19.110	19.565	20.020	20.475	20.930	21.385	21.840	22.295	22.750	**0.910**
0.920	13.800	14.260	14.720	15.180	15.640	16.100	16.560	17.020	17.480	17.940	18.400	18.860	19.320	19.780	20.240	20.700	21.160	21.620	22.080	22.540	23.000	**0.920**
0.930	13.950	14.415	14.880	15.345	15.810	16.275	16.740	17.205	17.670	18.135	18.600	19.065	19.530	19.995	20.460	20.925	21.390	21.855	22.320	22.785	23.250	**0.930**
0.940	14.100	14.570	15.040	15.510	15.980	16.450	16.920	17.390	17.860	18.330	18.800	19.270	19.740	20.210	20.680	21.150	21.620	22.090	22.560	23.030	23.500	**0.940**
0.950	14.250	14.725	15.200	15.675	16.150	16.625	17.100	17.575	18.050	18.525	19.000	19.475	19.950	20.425	20.900	21.375	21.850	22.325	22.800	23.275	23.750	**0.950**
0.960	14.400	14.880	15.360	15.840	16.320	16.800	17.280	17.760	18.240	18.720	19.200	19.680	20.160	20.640	21.120	21.600	22.080	22.560	23.040	23.520	24.000	**0.960**
0.970	14.550	15.035	15.520	16.005	16.490	16.975	17.460	17.945	18.430	18.915	19.400	19.885	20.370	20.855	21.340	21.825	22.310	22.795	23.280	23.765	24.250	**0.970**
0.980	14.700	15.190	15.680	16.170	16.660	17.150	17.640	18.130	18.620	19.110	19.600	20.090	20.580	21.070	21.560	22.050	22.540	23.030	23.520	24.010	24.500	**0.980**
0.990	14.850	15.345	15.840	16.335	16.830	17.325	17.820	18.315	18.810	19.305	19.800	20.295	20.790	21.285	21.780	22.275	22.770	23.265	23.760	24.255	24.750	**0.990**
1.000	15.000	15.500	16.000	16.500	17.000	17.500	18.000	18.500	19.000	19.500	20.000	20.500	21.000	21.500	22.000	22.500	23.000	23.500	24.000	24.500	25.000	**1.000**

GOLD BULLION VALUE CHART $1160 to $1290

Oz.	1160.00	1170.00	1180.00	1190.00	1200.00	1210.00	1220.00	1230.00	1240.00	1250.00	1260.00	1270.00	1280.00	1290.00	Oz.
0.001	1.16	1.17	1.18	1.19	1.20	1.21	1.22	1.23	1.24	1.25	1.26	1.27	1.28	1.29	**0.001**
0.002	2.32	2.34	2.36	2.38	2.40	2.42	2.44	2.46	2.48	2.50	2.52	2.54	2.56	2.58	**0.002**
0.003	3.48	3.51	3.54	3.57	3.60	3.63	3.66	3.69	3.72	3.75	3.78	3.81	3.84	3.87	**0.003**
0.004	4.64	4.68	4.72	4.76	4.80	4.84	4.88	4.92	4.96	5.00	5.04	5.08	5.12	5.16	**0.004**
0.005	5.80	5.85	5.90	5.95	6.00	6.05	6.10	6.15	6.20	6.25	6.30	6.35	6.40	6.45	**0.005**
0.006	6.96	7.02	7.08	7.14	7.20	7.26	7.32	7.38	7.44	7.50	7.56	7.62	7.68	7.74	**0.006**
0.007	8.12	8.19	8.26	8.33	8.40	8.47	8.54	8.61	8.68	8.75	8.82	8.89	8.96	9.03	**0.007**
0.008	9.28	9.36	9.44	9.52	9.60	9.68	9.76	9.84	9.92	10.00	10.08	10.16	10.24	10.32	**0.008**
0.009	10.44	10.53	10.62	10.71	10.80	10.89	10.98	11.07	11.16	11.25	11.34	11.43	11.52	11.61	**0.009**
0.010	11.60	11.70	11.80	11.90	12.00	12.10	12.20	12.30	12.40	12.50	12.60	12.70	12.80	12.90	**0.010**
0.020	23.20	23.40	23.60	23.80	24.00	24.20	24.40	24.60	24.80	25.00	25.20	25.40	25.60	25.80	**0.020**
0.030	34.80	35.10	35.40	35.70	36.00	36.30	36.60	36.90	37.20	37.50	37.80	38.10	38.40	38.70	**0.030**
0.040	46.40	46.80	47.20	47.60	48.00	48.40	48.80	49.20	49.60	50.00	50.40	50.80	51.20	51.60	**0.040**
0.050	58.00	58.50	59.00	59.50	60.00	60.50	61.00	61.50	62.00	62.50	63.00	63.50	64.00	64.50	**0.050**
0.060	69.60	70.20	70.80	71.40	72.00	72.60	73.20	73.80	74.40	75.00	75.60	76.20	76.80	77.40	**0.060**
0.070	81.20	81.90	82.60	83.30	84.00	84.70	85.40	86.10	86.80	87.50	88.20	88.90	89.60	90.30	**0.070**
0.080	92.80	93.60	94.40	95.20	96.00	96.80	97.60	98.40	99.20	100.00	100.80	101.60	102.40	103.20	**0.080**
0.090	104.40	105.30	106.20	107.10	108.00	108.90	109.80	110.70	111.60	112.50	113.40	114.30	115.20	116.10	**0.090**
0.100	116.00	117.00	118.00	119.00	120.00	121.00	122.00	123.00	124.00	125.00	126.00	127.00	128.00	129.00	**0.100**
0.110	127.60	128.70	129.80	130.90	132.00	133.10	134.20	135.30	136.40	137.50	138.60	139.70	140.80	141.90	**0.110**
0.120	139.20	140.40	141.60	142.80	144.00	145.20	146.40	147.60	148.80	150.00	151.20	152.40	153.60	154.80	**0.120**
0.130	150.80	152.10	153.40	154.70	156.00	157.30	158.60	159.90	161.20	162.50	163.80	165.10	166.40	167.70	**0.130**
0.140	162.40	163.80	165.20	166.60	168.00	169.40	170.80	172.20	173.60	175.00	176.40	177.80	179.20	180.60	**0.140**
0.150	174.00	175.50	177.00	178.50	180.00	181.50	183.00	184.50	186.00	187.50	189.00	190.50	192.00	193.50	**0.150**
0.160	185.60	187.20	188.80	190.40	192.00	193.60	195.20	196.80	198.40	200.00	201.60	203.20	204.80	206.40	**0.160**
0.170	197.20	198.90	200.60	202.30	204.00	205.70	207.40	209.10	210.80	212.50	214.20	215.90	217.60	219.30	**0.170**
0.180	208.80	210.60	212.40	214.20	216.00	217.80	219.60	221.40	223.20	225.00	226.80	228.60	230.40	232.20	**0.180**
0.190	220.40	222.30	224.20	226.10	228.00	229.90	231.80	233.70	235.60	237.50	239.40	241.30	243.20	245.10	**0.190**
0.200	232.00	234.00	236.00	238.00	240.00	242.00	244.00	246.00	248.00	250.00	252.00	254.00	256.00	258.00	**0.200**
0.210	243.60	245.70	247.80	249.90	252.00	254.10	256.20	258.30	260.40	262.50	264.60	266.70	268.80	270.90	**0.210**
0.220	255.20	257.40	259.60	261.80	264.00	266.20	268.40	270.60	272.80	275.00	277.20	279.40	281.60	283.80	**0.220**
0.230	266.80	269.10	271.40	273.70	276.00	278.30	280.60	282.90	285.20	287.50	289.80	292.10	294.40	296.70	**0.230**
0.240	278.40	280.80	283.20	285.60	288.00	290.40	292.80	295.20	297.60	300.00	302.40	304.80	307.20	309.60	**0.240**
0.250	290.00	292.50	295.00	297.50	300.00	302.50	305.00	307.50	310.00	312.50	315.00	317.50	320.00	322.50	**0.250**
0.260	301.60	304.20	306.80	309.40	312.00	314.60	317.20	319.80	322.40	325.00	327.60	330.20	332.80	335.40	**0.260**
0.270	313.20	315.90	318.60	321.30	324.00	326.70	329.40	332.10	334.80	337.50	340.20	342.90	345.60	348.30	**0.270**
0.280	324.80	327.60	330.40	333.20	336.00	338.80	341.60	344.40	347.20	350.00	352.80	355.60	358.40	361.20	**0.280**
0.290	336.40	339.30	342.20	345.10	348.00	350.90	353.80	356.70	359.60	362.50	365.40	368.30	371.20	374.10	**0.290**
0.300	348.00	351.00	354.00	357.00	360.00	363.00	366.00	369.00	372.00	375.00	378.00	381.00	384.00	387.00	**0.300**
0.310	359.60	362.70	365.80	368.90	372.00	375.10	378.20	381.30	384.40	387.50	390.60	393.70	396.80	399.90	**0.310**
0.320	371.20	374.40	377.60	380.80	384.00	387.20	390.40	393.60	396.80	400.00	403.20	406.40	409.60	412.80	**0.320**
0.330	382.80	386.10	389.40	392.70	396.00	399.30	402.60	405.90	409.20	412.50	415.80	419.10	422.40	425.70	**0.330**
0.340	394.40	397.80	401.20	404.60	408.00	411.40	414.80	418.20	421.60	425.00	428.40	431.80	435.20	438.60	**0.340**
0.350	406.00	409.50	413.00	416.50	420.00	423.50	427.00	430.50	434.00	437.50	441.00	444.50	448.00	451.50	**0.350**
0.360	417.60	421.20	424.80	428.40	432.00	435.60	439.20	442.80	446.40	450.00	453.60	457.20	460.80	464.40	**0.360**
0.370	429.20	432.90	436.60	440.30	444.00	447.70	451.40	455.10	458.80	462.50	466.20	469.90	473.60	477.30	**0.370**
0.380	440.80	444.60	448.40	452.20	456.00	459.80	463.60	467.40	471.20	475.00	478.80	482.60	486.40	490.20	**0.380**
0.390	452.40	456.30	460.20	464.10	468.00	471.90	475.80	479.70	483.60	487.50	491.40	495.30	499.20	503.10	**0.390**
0.400	464.00	468.00	472.00	476.00	480.00	484.00	488.00	492.00	496.00	500.00	504.00	508.00	512.00	516.00	**0.400**
0.410	475.60	479.70	483.80	487.90	492.00	496.10	500.20	504.30	508.40	512.50	516.60	520.70	524.80	528.90	**0.410**
0.420	487.20	491.40	495.60	499.80	504.00	508.20	512.40	516.60	520.80	525.00	529.20	533.40	537.60	541.80	**0.420**
0.430	498.80	503.10	507.40	511.70	516.00	520.30	524.60	528.90	533.20	537.50	541.80	546.10	550.40	554.70	**0.430**
0.440	510.40	514.80	519.20	523.60	528.00	532.40	536.80	541.20	545.60	550.00	554.40	558.80	563.20	567.60	**0.440**
0.450	522.00	526.50	531.00	535.50	540.00	544.50	549.00	553.50	558.00	562.50	567.00	571.50	576.00	580.50	**0.450**
0.460	533.60	538.20	542.80	547.40	552.00	556.60	561.20	565.80	570.40	575.00	579.60	584.20	588.80	593.40	**0.460**

GOLD BULLION VALUE CHART $1160 to $1290

Oz.	1160.00	1170.00	1180.00	1190.00	1200.00	1210.00	1220.00	1230.00	1240.00	1250.00	1260.00	1270.00	1280.00	1290.00	Oz.
0.470	545.20	549.90	554.60	559.30	564.00	568.70	573.40	578.10	582.80	587.50	592.20	596.90	601.60	606.30	**0.470**
0.480	556.80	561.60	566.40	571.20	576.00	580.80	585.60	590.40	595.20	600.00	604.80	609.60	614.40	619.20	**0.480**
0.490	568.40	573.30	578.20	583.10	588.00	592.90	597.80	602.70	607.60	612.50	617.40	622.30	627.20	632.10	**0.490**
0.500	580.00	585.00	590.00	595.00	600.00	605.00	610.00	615.00	620.00	625.00	630.00	635.00	640.00	645.00	**0.500**
0.510	591.60	596.70	601.80	606.90	612.00	617.10	622.20	627.30	632.40	637.50	642.60	647.70	652.80	657.90	**0.510**
0.520	603.20	608.40	613.60	618.80	624.00	629.20	634.40	639.60	644.80	650.00	655.20	660.40	665.60	670.80	**0.520**
0.530	614.80	620.10	625.40	630.70	636.00	641.30	646.60	651.90	657.20	662.50	667.80	673.10	678.40	683.70	**0.530**
0.540	626.40	631.80	637.20	642.60	648.00	653.40	658.80	664.20	669.60	675.00	680.40	685.80	691.20	696.60	**0.540**
0.550	638.00	643.50	649.00	654.50	660.00	665.50	671.00	676.50	682.00	687.50	693.00	698.50	704.00	709.50	**0.550**
0.560	649.60	655.20	660.80	666.40	672.00	677.60	683.20	688.80	694.40	700.00	705.60	711.20	716.80	722.40	**0.560**
0.570	661.20	666.90	672.60	678.30	684.00	689.70	695.40	701.10	706.80	712.50	718.20	723.90	729.60	735.30	**0.570**
0.580	672.80	678.60	684.40	690.20	696.00	701.80	707.60	713.40	719.20	725.00	730.80	736.60	742.40	748.20	**0.580**
0.590	684.40	690.30	696.20	702.10	708.00	713.90	719.80	725.70	731.60	737.50	743.40	749.30	755.20	761.10	**0.590**
0.600	696.00	702.00	708.00	714.00	720.00	726.00	732.00	738.00	744.00	750.00	756.00	762.00	768.00	774.00	**0.600**
0.610	707.60	713.70	719.80	725.90	732.00	738.10	744.20	750.30	756.40	762.50	768.60	774.70	780.80	786.90	**0.610**
0.620	719.20	725.40	731.60	737.80	744.00	750.20	756.40	762.60	768.80	775.00	781.20	787.40	793.60	799.80	**0.620**
0.630	730.80	737.10	743.40	749.70	756.00	762.30	768.60	774.90	781.20	787.50	793.80	800.10	806.40	812.70	**0.630**
0.640	742.40	748.80	755.20	761.60	768.00	774.40	780.80	787.20	793.60	800.00	806.40	812.80	819.20	825.60	**0.640**
0.650	754.00	760.50	767.00	773.50	780.00	786.50	793.00	799.50	806.00	812.50	819.00	825.50	832.00	838.50	**0.650**
0.660	765.60	772.20	778.80	785.40	792.00	798.60	805.20	811.80	818.40	825.00	831.60	838.20	844.80	851.40	**0.660**
0.670	777.20	783.90	790.60	797.30	804.00	810.70	817.40	824.10	830.80	837.50	844.20	850.90	857.60	864.30	**0.670**
0.680	788.80	795.60	802.40	809.20	816.00	822.80	829.60	836.40	843.20	850.00	856.80	863.60	870.40	877.20	**0.680**
0.690	800.40	807.30	814.20	821.10	828.00	834.90	841.80	848.70	855.60	862.50	869.40	876.30	883.20	890.10	**0.690**
0.700	812.00	819.00	826.00	833.00	840.00	847.00	854.00	861.00	868.00	875.00	882.00	889.00	896.00	903.00	**0.700**
0.710	823.60	830.70	837.80	844.90	852.00	859.10	866.20	873.30	880.40	887.50	894.60	901.70	908.80	915.90	**0.710**
0.720	835.20	842.40	849.60	856.80	864.00	871.20	878.40	885.60	892.80	900.00	907.20	914.40	921.60	928.80	**0.720**
0.730	846.80	854.10	861.40	868.70	876.00	883.30	890.60	897.90	905.20	912.50	919.80	927.10	934.40	941.70	**0.730**
0.740	858.40	865.80	873.20	880.60	888.00	895.40	902.80	910.20	917.60	925.00	932.40	939.80	947.20	954.60	**0.740**
0.750	870.00	877.50	885.00	892.50	900.00	907.50	915.00	922.50	930.00	937.50	945.00	952.50	960.00	967.50	**0.750**
0.760	881.60	889.20	896.80	904.40	912.00	919.60	927.20	934.80	942.40	950.00	957.60	965.20	972.80	980.40	**0.760**
0.770	893.20	900.90	908.60	916.30	924.00	931.70	939.40	947.10	954.80	962.50	970.20	977.90	985.60	993.30	**0.770**
0.780	904.80	912.60	920.40	928.20	936.00	943.80	951.60	959.40	967.20	975.00	982.80	990.60	998.40	1006.20	**0.780**
0.790	916.40	924.30	932.20	940.10	948.00	955.90	963.80	971.70	979.60	987.50	995.40	1003.30	1011.20	1019.10	**0.790**
0.800	928.00	936.00	944.00	952.00	960.00	968.00	976.00	984.00	992.00	1000.00	1008.00	1016.00	1024.00	1032.00	**0.800**
0.810	939.60	947.70	955.80	963.90	972.00	980.10	988.20	996.30	1004.40	1012.50	1020.60	1028.70	1036.80	1044.90	**0.810**
0.820	951.20	959.40	967.60	975.80	984.00	992.20	1000.40	1008.60	1016.80	1025.00	1033.20	1041.40	1049.60	1057.80	**0.820**
0.830	962.80	971.10	979.40	987.70	996.00	1004.30	1012.60	1020.90	1029.20	1037.50	1045.80	1054.10	1062.40	1070.70	**0.830**
0.840	974.40	982.80	991.20	999.60	1008.00	1016.40	1024.80	1033.20	1041.60	1050.00	1058.40	1066.80	1075.20	1083.60	**0.840**
0.850	986.00	994.50	1003.00	1011.50	1020.00	1028.50	1037.00	1045.50	1054.00	1062.50	1071.00	1079.50	1088.00	1096.50	**0.850**
0.860	997.60	1006.20	1014.80	1023.40	1032.00	1040.60	1049.20	1057.80	1066.40	1075.00	1083.60	1092.20	1100.80	1109.40	**0.860**
0.870	1009.20	1017.90	1026.60	1035.30	1044.00	1052.70	1061.40	1070.10	1078.80	1087.50	1096.20	1104.90	1113.60	1122.30	**0.870**
0.880	1020.80	1029.60	1038.40	1047.20	1056.00	1064.80	1073.60	1082.40	1091.20	1100.00	1108.80	1117.60	1126.40	1135.20	**0.880**
0.890	1032.40	1041.30	1050.20	1059.10	1068.00	1076.90	1085.80	1094.70	1103.60	1112.50	1121.40	1130.30	1139.20	1148.10	**0.890**
0.900	1044.00	1053.00	1062.00	1071.00	1080.00	1089.00	1098.00	1107.00	1116.00	1125.00	1134.00	1143.00	1152.00	1161.00	**0.900**
0.910	1055.60	1064.70	1073.80	1082.90	1092.00	1101.10	1110.20	1119.30	1128.40	1137.50	1146.60	1155.70	1164.80	1173.90	**0.910**
0.920	1067.20	1076.40	1085.60	1094.80	1104.00	1113.20	1122.40	1131.60	1140.80	1150.00	1159.20	1168.40	1177.60	1186.80	**0.920**
0.930	1078.80	1088.10	1097.40	1106.70	1116.00	1125.30	1134.60	1143.90	1153.20	1162.50	1171.80	1181.10	1190.40	1199.70	**0.930**
0.940	1090.40	1099.80	1109.20	1118.60	1128.00	1137.40	1146.80	1156.20	1165.60	1175.00	1184.40	1193.80	1203.20	1212.60	**0.940**
0.950	1102.00	1111.50	1121.00	1130.50	1140.00	1149.50	1159.00	1168.50	1178.00	1187.50	1197.00	1206.50	1216.00	1225.50	**0.950**
0.960	1113.60	1123.20	1132.80	1142.40	1152.00	1161.60	1171.20	1180.80	1190.40	1200.00	1209.60	1219.20	1228.80	1238.40	**0.960**
0.970	1125.20	1134.90	1144.60	1154.30	1164.00	1173.70	1183.40	1193.10	1202.80	1212.50	1222.20	1231.90	1241.60	1251.30	**0.970**
0.980	1136.80	1146.60	1156.40	1166.20	1176.00	1185.80	1195.60	1205.40	1215.20	1225.00	1234.80	1244.60	1254.40	1264.20	**0.980**
0.990	1148.40	1158.30	1168.20	1178.10	1188.00	1197.90	1207.80	1217.70	1227.60	1237.50	1247.40	1257.30	1267.20	1277.10	**0.990**
1.000	1160.00	1170.00	1180.00	1190.00	1200.00	1210.00	1220.00	1230.00	1240.00	1250.00	1260.00	1270.00	1280.00	1290.00	**1.000**

GOLD BULLION VALUE CHART $1300 to $1420

Oz.	1300.00	1310.00	1320.00	1330.00	1340.00	1350.00	1360.00	1370.00	1380.00	1390.00	1400.00	1410.00	1420.00	Oz.
0.001	1.30	1.31	1.32	1.33	1.34	1.35	1.36	1.37	1.38	1.39	1.40	1.41	1.42	**0.001**
0.002	2.60	2.62	2.64	2.66	2.68	2.70	2.72	2.74	2.76	2.78	2.80	2.82	2.84	**0.002**
0.003	3.90	3.93	3.96	3.99	4.02	4.05	4.08	4.11	4.14	4.17	4.20	4.23	4.26	**0.003**
0.004	5.20	5.24	5.28	5.32	5.36	5.40	5.44	5.48	5.52	5.56	5.60	5.64	5.68	**0.004**
0.005	6.50	6.55	6.60	6.65	6.70	6.75	6.80	6.85	6.90	6.95	7.00	7.05	7.10	**0.005**
0.006	7.80	7.86	7.92	7.98	8.04	8.10	8.16	8.22	8.28	8.34	8.40	8.46	8.52	**0.006**
0.007	9.10	9.17	9.24	9.31	9.38	9.45	9.52	9.59	9.66	9.73	9.80	9.87	9.94	**0.007**
0.008	10.40	10.48	10.56	10.64	10.72	10.80	10.88	10.96	11.04	11.12	11.20	11.28	11.36	**0.008**
0.009	11.70	11.79	11.88	11.97	12.06	12.15	12.24	12.33	12.42	12.51	12.60	12.69	12.78	**0.009**
0.010	13.00	13.10	13.20	13.30	13.40	13.50	13.60	13.70	13.80	13.90	14.00	14.10	14.20	**0.010**
0.020	26.00	26.20	26.40	26.60	26.80	27.00	27.20	27.40	27.60	27.80	28.00	28.20	28.40	**0.020**
0.030	39.00	39.30	39.60	39.90	40.20	40.50	40.80	41.10	41.40	41.70	42.00	42.30	42.60	**0.030**
0.040	52.00	52.40	52.80	53.20	53.60	54.00	54.40	54.80	55.20	55.60	56.00	56.40	56.80	**0.040**
0.050	65.00	65.50	66.00	66.50	67.00	67.50	68.00	68.50	69.00	69.50	70.00	70.50	71.00	**0.050**
0.060	78.00	78.60	79.20	79.80	80.40	81.00	81.60	82.20	82.80	83.40	84.00	84.60	85.20	**0.060**
0.070	91.00	91.70	92.40	93.10	93.80	94.50	95.20	95.90	96.60	97.30	98.00	98.70	99.40	**0.070**
0.080	104.00	104.80	105.60	106.40	107.20	108.00	108.80	109.60	110.40	111.20	112.00	112.80	113.60	**0.080**
0.090	117.00	117.90	118.80	119.70	120.60	121.50	122.40	123.30	124.20	125.10	126.00	126.90	127.80	**0.090**
0.100	130.00	131.00	132.00	133.00	134.00	135.00	136.00	137.00	138.00	139.00	140.00	141.00	142.00	**0.100**
0.110	143.00	144.10	145.20	146.30	147.40	148.50	149.60	150.70	151.80	152.90	154.00	155.10	156.20	**0.110**
0.120	156.00	157.20	158.40	159.60	160.80	162.00	163.20	164.40	165.60	166.80	168.00	169.20	170.40	**0.120**
0.130	169.00	170.30	171.60	172.90	174.20	175.50	176.80	178.10	179.40	180.70	182.00	183.30	184.60	**0.130**
0.140	182.00	183.40	184.80	186.20	187.60	189.00	190.40	191.80	193.20	194.60	196.00	197.40	198.80	**0.140**
0.150	195.00	196.50	198.00	199.50	201.00	202.50	204.00	205.50	207.00	208.50	210.00	211.50	213.00	**0.150**
0.160	208.00	209.60	211.20	212.80	214.40	216.00	217.60	219.20	220.80	222.40	224.00	225.60	227.20	**0.160**
0.170	221.00	222.70	224.40	226.10	227.80	229.50	231.20	232.90	234.60	236.30	238.00	239.70	241.40	**0.170**
0.180	234.00	235.80	237.60	239.40	241.20	243.00	244.80	246.60	248.40	250.20	252.00	253.80	255.60	**0.180**
0.190	247.00	248.90	250.80	252.70	254.60	256.50	258.40	260.30	262.20	264.10	266.00	267.90	269.80	**0.190**
0.200	260.00	262.00	264.00	266.00	268.00	270.00	272.00	274.00	276.00	278.00	280.00	282.00	284.00	**0.200**
0.210	273.00	275.10	277.20	279.30	281.40	283.50	285.60	287.70	289.80	291.90	294.00	296.10	298.20	**0.210**
0.220	286.00	288.20	290.40	292.60	294.80	297.00	299.20	301.40	303.60	305.80	308.00	310.20	312.40	**0.220**
0.230	299.00	301.30	303.60	305.90	308.20	310.50	312.80	315.10	317.40	319.70	322.00	324.30	326.60	**0.230**
0.240	312.00	314.40	316.80	319.20	321.60	324.00	326.40	328.80	331.20	333.60	336.00	338.40	340.80	**0.240**
0.250	325.00	327.50	330.00	332.50	335.00	337.50	340.00	342.50	345.00	347.50	350.00	352.50	355.00	**0.250**
0.260	338.00	340.60	343.20	345.80	348.40	351.00	353.60	356.20	358.80	361.40	364.00	366.60	369.20	**0.260**
0.270	351.00	353.70	356.40	359.10	361.80	364.50	367.20	369.90	372.60	375.30	378.00	380.70	383.40	**0.270**
0.280	364.00	366.80	369.60	372.40	375.20	378.00	380.80	383.60	386.40	389.20	392.00	394.80	397.60	**0.280**
0.290	377.00	379.90	382.80	385.70	388.60	391.50	394.40	397.30	400.20	403.10	406.00	408.90	411.80	**0.290**
0.300	390.00	393.00	396.00	399.00	402.00	405.00	408.00	411.00	414.00	417.00	420.00	423.00	426.00	**0.300**
0.310	403.00	406.10	409.20	412.30	415.40	418.50	421.60	424.70	427.80	430.90	434.00	437.10	440.20	**0.310**
0.320	416.00	419.20	422.40	425.60	428.80	432.00	435.20	438.40	441.60	444.80	448.00	451.20	454.40	**0.320**
0.330	429.00	432.30	435.60	438.90	442.20	445.50	448.80	452.10	455.40	458.70	462.00	465.30	468.60	**0.330**
0.340	442.00	445.40	448.80	452.20	455.60	459.00	462.40	465.80	469.20	472.60	476.00	479.40	482.80	**0.340**
0.350	455.00	458.50	462.00	465.50	469.00	472.50	476.00	479.50	483.00	486.50	490.00	493.50	497.00	**0.350**
0.360	468.00	471.60	475.20	478.80	482.40	486.00	489.60	493.20	496.80	500.40	504.00	507.60	511.20	**0.360**
0.370	481.00	484.70	488.40	492.10	495.80	499.50	503.20	506.90	510.60	514.30	518.00	521.70	525.40	**0.370**
0.380	494.00	497.80	501.60	505.40	509.20	513.00	516.80	520.60	524.40	528.20	532.00	535.80	539.60	**0.380**
0.390	507.00	510.90	514.80	518.70	522.60	526.50	530.40	534.30	538.20	542.10	546.00	549.90	553.80	**0.390**
0.400	520.00	524.00	528.00	532.00	536.00	540.00	544.00	548.00	552.00	556.00	560.00	564.00	568.00	**0.400**
0.410	533.00	537.10	541.20	545.30	549.40	553.50	557.60	561.70	565.80	569.90	574.00	578.10	582.20	**0.410**
0.420	546.00	550.20	554.40	558.60	562.80	567.00	571.20	575.40	579.60	583.80	588.00	592.20	596.40	**0.420**
0.430	559.00	563.30	567.60	571.90	576.20	580.50	584.80	589.10	593.40	597.70	602.00	606.30	610.60	**0.430**
0.440	572.00	576.40	580.80	585.20	589.60	594.00	598.40	602.80	607.20	611.60	616.00	620.40	624.80	**0.440**
0.450	585.00	589.50	594.00	598.50	603.00	607.50	612.00	616.50	621.00	625.50	630.00	634.50	639.00	**0.450**
0.460	598.00	602.60	607.20	611.80	616.40	621.00	625.60	630.20	634.80	639.40	644.00	648.60	653.20	**0.460**

GOLD BULLION VALUE CHART $1300 to $1420

Oz.	1300.00	1310.00	1320.00	1330.00	1340.00	1350.00	1360.00	1370.00	1380.00	1390.00	1400.00	1410.00	1420.00	Oz.
0.470	611.00	615.70	620.40	625.10	629.80	634.50	639.20	643.90	648.60	653.30	658.00	662.70	667.40	**0.470**
0.480	624.00	628.80	633.60	638.40	643.20	648.00	652.80	657.60	662.40	667.20	672.00	676.80	681.60	**0.480**
0.490	637.00	641.90	646.80	651.70	656.60	661.50	666.40	671.30	676.20	681.10	686.00	690.90	695.80	**0.490**
0.500	650.00	655.00	660.00	665.00	670.00	675.00	680.00	685.00	690.00	695.00	700.00	705.00	710.00	**0.500**
0.510	663.00	668.10	673.20	678.30	683.40	688.50	693.60	698.70	703.80	708.90	714.00	719.10	724.20	**0.510**
0.520	676.00	681.20	686.40	691.60	696.80	702.00	707.20	712.40	717.60	722.80	728.00	733.20	738.40	**0.520**
0.530	689.00	694.30	699.60	704.90	710.20	715.50	720.80	726.10	731.40	736.70	742.00	747.30	752.60	**0.530**
0.540	702.00	707.40	712.80	718.20	723.60	729.00	734.40	739.80	745.20	750.60	756.00	761.40	766.80	**0.540**
0.550	715.00	720.50	726.00	731.50	737.00	742.50	748.00	753.50	759.00	764.50	770.00	775.50	781.00	**0.550**
0.560	728.00	733.60	739.20	744.80	750.40	756.00	761.60	767.20	772.80	778.40	784.00	789.60	795.20	**0.560**
0.570	741.00	746.70	752.40	758.10	763.80	769.50	775.20	780.90	786.60	792.30	798.00	803.70	809.40	**0.570**
0.580	754.00	759.80	765.60	771.40	777.20	783.00	788.80	794.60	800.40	806.20	812.00	817.80	823.60	**0.580**
0.590	767.00	772.90	778.80	784.70	790.60	796.50	802.40	808.30	814.20	820.10	826.00	831.90	837.80	**0.590**
0.600	780.00	786.00	792.00	798.00	804.00	810.00	816.00	822.00	828.00	834.00	840.00	846.00	852.00	**0.600**
0.610	793.00	799.10	805.20	811.30	817.40	823.50	829.60	835.70	841.80	847.90	854.00	860.10	866.20	**0.610**
0.620	806.00	812.20	818.40	824.60	830.80	837.00	843.20	849.40	855.60	861.80	868.00	874.20	880.40	**0.620**
0.630	819.00	825.30	831.60	837.90	844.20	850.50	856.80	863.10	869.40	875.70	882.00	888.30	894.60	**0.630**
0.640	832.00	838.40	844.80	851.20	857.60	864.00	870.40	876.80	883.20	889.60	896.00	902.40	908.80	**0.640**
0.650	845.00	851.50	858.00	864.50	871.00	877.50	884.00	890.50	897.00	903.50	910.00	916.50	923.00	**0.650**
0.660	858.00	864.60	871.20	877.80	884.40	891.00	897.60	904.20	910.80	917.40	924.00	930.60	937.20	**0.660**
0.670	871.00	877.70	884.40	891.10	897.80	904.50	911.20	917.90	924.60	931.30	938.00	944.70	951.40	**0.670**
0.680	884.00	890.80	897.60	904.40	911.20	918.00	924.80	931.60	938.40	945.20	952.00	958.80	965.60	**0.680**
0.690	897.00	903.90	910.80	917.70	924.60	931.50	938.40	945.30	952.20	959.10	966.00	972.90	979.80	**0.690**
0.700	910.00	917.00	924.00	931.00	938.00	945.00	952.00	959.00	966.00	973.00	980.00	987.00	994.00	**0.700**
0.710	923.00	930.10	937.20	944.30	951.40	958.50	965.60	972.70	979.80	986.90	994.00	1001.10	1008.20	**0.710**
0.720	936.00	943.20	950.40	957.60	964.80	972.00	979.20	986.40	993.60	1000.80	1008.00	1015.20	1022.40	**0.720**
0.730	949.00	956.30	963.60	970.90	978.20	985.50	992.80	1000.10	1007.40	1014.70	1022.00	1029.30	1036.60	**0.730**
0.740	962.00	969.40	976.80	984.20	991.60	999.00	1006.40	1013.80	1021.20	1028.60	1036.00	1043.40	1050.80	**0.740**
0.750	975.00	982.50	990.00	997.50	1005.00	1012.50	1020.00	1027.50	1035.00	1042.50	1050.00	1057.50	1065.00	**0.750**
0.760	988.00	995.60	1003.20	1010.80	1018.40	1026.00	1033.60	1041.20	1048.80	1056.40	1064.00	1071.60	1079.20	**0.760**
0.770	1001.00	1008.70	1016.40	1024.10	1031.80	1039.50	1047.20	1054.90	1062.60	1070.30	1078.00	1085.70	1093.40	**0.770**
0.780	1014.00	1021.80	1029.60	1037.40	1045.20	1053.00	1060.80	1068.60	1076.40	1084.20	1092.00	1099.80	1107.60	**0.780**
0.790	1027.00	1034.90	1042.80	1050.70	1058.60	1066.50	1074.40	1082.30	1090.20	1098.10	1106.00	1113.90	1121.80	**0.790**
0.800	1040.00	1048.00	1056.00	1064.00	1072.00	1080.00	1088.00	1096.00	1104.00	1112.00	1120.00	1128.00	1136.00	**0.800**
0.810	1053.00	1061.10	1069.20	1077.30	1085.40	1093.50	1101.60	1109.70	1117.80	1125.90	1134.00	1142.10	1150.20	**0.810**
0.820	1066.00	1074.20	1082.40	1090.60	1098.80	1107.00	1115.20	1123.40	1131.60	1139.80	1148.00	1156.20	1164.40	**0.820**
0.830	1079.00	1087.30	1095.60	1103.90	1112.20	1120.50	1128.80	1137.10	1145.40	1153.70	1162.00	1170.30	1178.60	**0.830**
0.840	1092.00	1100.40	1108.80	1117.20	1125.60	1134.00	1142.40	1150.80	1159.20	1167.60	1176.00	1184.40	1192.80	**0.840**
0.850	1105.00	1113.50	1122.00	1130.50	1139.00	1147.50	1156.00	1164.50	1173.00	1181.50	1190.00	1198.50	1207.00	**0.850**
0.860	1118.00	1126.60	1135.20	1143.80	1152.40	1161.00	1169.60	1178.20	1186.80	1195.40	1204.00	1212.60	1221.20	**0.860**
0.870	1131.00	1139.70	1148.40	1157.10	1165.80	1174.50	1183.20	1191.90	1200.60	1209.30	1218.00	1226.70	1235.40	**0.870**
0.880	1144.00	1152.80	1161.60	1170.40	1179.20	1188.00	1196.80	1205.60	1214.40	1223.20	1232.00	1240.80	1249.60	**0.880**
0.890	1157.00	1165.90	1174.80	1183.70	1192.60	1201.50	1210.40	1219.30	1228.20	1237.10	1246.00	1254.90	1263.80	**0.890**
0.900	1170.00	1179.00	1188.00	1197.00	1206.00	1215.00	1224.00	1233.00	1242.00	1251.00	1260.00	1269.00	1278.00	**0.900**
0.910	1183.00	1192.10	1201.20	1210.30	1219.40	1228.50	1237.60	1246.70	1255.80	1264.90	1274.00	1283.10	1292.20	**0.910**
0.920	1196.00	1205.20	1214.40	1223.60	1232.80	1242.00	1251.20	1260.40	1269.60	1278.80	1288.00	1297.20	1306.40	**0.920**
0.930	1209.00	1218.30	1227.60	1236.90	1246.20	1255.50	1264.80	1274.10	1283.40	1292.70	1302.00	1311.30	1320.60	**0.930**
0.940	1222.00	1231.40	1240.80	1250.20	1259.60	1269.00	1278.40	1287.80	1297.20	1306.60	1316.00	1325.40	1334.80	**0.940**
0.950	1235.00	1244.50	1254.00	1263.50	1273.00	1282.50	1292.00	1301.50	1311.00	1320.50	1330.00	1339.50	1349.00	**0.950**
0.960	1248.00	1257.60	1267.20	1276.80	1286.40	1296.00	1305.60	1315.20	1324.80	1334.40	1344.00	1353.60	1363.20	**0.960**
0.970	1261.00	1270.70	1280.40	1290.10	1299.80	1309.50	1319.20	1328.90	1338.60	1348.30	1358.00	1367.70	1377.40	**0.970**
0.980	1274.00	1283.80	1293.60	1303.40	1313.20	1323.00	1332.80	1342.60	1352.40	1362.20	1372.00	1381.80	1391.60	**0.980**
0.990	1287.00	1296.90	1306.80	1316.70	1326.60	1336.50	1346.40	1356.30	1366.20	1376.10	1386.00	1395.90	1405.80	**0.990**
1.000	1300.00	1310.00	1320.00	1330.00	1340.00	1350.00	1360.00	1370.00	1380.00	1390.00	1400.00	1410.00	1420.00	**1.000**

FOREIGN EXCHANGE TABLE

The latest foreign exchange rates below apply to trade with banks in the country of origin. The left column shows the number of units per U.S. dollar at the official rate. The right column shows the number of units per dollar at the free market rate. Rates recorded March 10, 2016.

COUNTRY	#/$	#/$
Afghanistan (New Afghani)	.68	–
Albania (Lek)	.123	–
Algeria (Dinar)	.108	–
Andorra uses Euro	0.910	–
Angola (Readjust Kwanza)	.158	–
Anguilla uses E.C. Dollar	2.70	–
Antigua uses E.C. Dollar	2.70	–
Argentina (Peso)	15.4	–
Armenia (Dram)	.491	–
Aruba (Florin)	1.79	–
Australia (Dollar)	1.34	–
Austria (Euro)	0.910	–
Azerbaijan (New Manat)	1.62	–
Bahamas (Dollar)	0.993	–
Bahrain Is. (Dinar)	0.374	–
Bangladesh (Taka)	.77	–
Barbados (Dollar)	2.00	–
Belarus (Ruble)	21,068	–
Belgium (Euro)	0.910	–
Belize (Dollar)	1.95	–
Benin uses CFA Franc West	.519	–
Bermuda (Dollar)	1.00	–
Bhutan (Ngultrum)	.67	–
Bolivia (Boliviano)	6.66	–
Bosnia-Herzegovina (Conv. marka)	1.78	–
Botswana (Pula)	11.0	–
British Virgin Islands uses U.S. Dollar	1.00	–
Brazil (Real)	3.73	–
Brunei (Dollar)	1.36	–
Bulgaria (Lev)	1.77	–
Burkina Faso uses CFA Franc West	.597	–
Burma (Kyat)	1,199	–
Burundi (Franc)	1,540	–
Cambodia (Riel)	3,912	–
Cameroon uses CFA Franc Central	.597	–
Canada (Dollar)	1.34	–
Cape Verde (Escudo)	.100	–
Cayman Islands (Dollar)	0.816	–
Central African Rep.	.597	–
CFA Franc Central	.597	–
CFA Franc West	.597	–
CFP Franc	.109	–
Chad uses CFA Franc Central	.597	–
Chile (Peso)	.669	–
China, P.R. (Renminbi Yuan)	6.52	–
Colombia (Peso)	3,110	–
Comoros (Franc)	.441	–
Congo uses CFA Franc Central	.597	–
Congo-Dem.Rep. (Congolese Franc)	.914	–
Cook Islands (Dollar)	1.48	–
Costa Rica (Colon)	.523	–
Croatia (Kuna)	6.85	–
Cuba (Peso)	.22	27
Cyprus (Euro)	0.910	–
Czech Republic (Koruna)	.24	–
Denmark (Danish Krone)	6.79	–
Djibouti (Franc)	.178	–
Dominica uses E.C. Dollar	2.70	–
Dominican Republic (Peso)	.45	–
East Caribbean (Dollar)	2.70	–
East Timor (U.S. Dollar)	1.00	–
Ecuador (U.S. Dollar)	1.00	–
Egypt (Pound)	7.81	–
El Salvador (U.S. Dollar)	1.00	–
Equatorial Guinea uses CFA Franc Central	.597	–
Eritrea (Nafka)	15.0	–
Estonia (Euro)	0.910	–
Ethiopia (Birr)	.21	–
Euro	0.910	–
Falkland Is. (Pound)	0.704	–
Faroe Islands (Krona)	6.79	–
Fiji Islands (Dollar)	2.08	–
Finland (Euro)	0.910	–
France (Euro)	0.910	–
French Polynesia uses CFP Franc	.108	–
Gabon (CFA Franc)	.597	–
Gambia (Dalasi)	.39	–
Georgia (Lari)	2.45	–
Germany (Euro)	0.910	–
Ghana (New Cedi)	3.84	–
Gibraltar (Pound)	0.704	–
Greece (Euro)	0.910	–
Greenland uses Danish Krone	6.79	–
Grenada uses E.C. Dollar	2.70	–
Guatemala (Quetzal)	7.52	–
Guernsey uses Sterling Pound	0.704	–
Guinea Bissau uses CFA Franc West	.597	–
Guinea Conakry (Franc)	7,571	–
Guyana (Dollar)	.198	–
Haiti (Gourde)	.61	–
Honduras (Lempira)	.22	–
Hong Kong (Dollar)	7.77	–
Hungary (Forint)	.282	–
Iceland (Krona)	.127	–
India (Rupee)	.62	–
Indonesia (Rupiah)	13,123	–
Iran (Rial)	30,195	–
Iraq (Dinar)	1,150	–
Ireland (Euro)	0.910	–
Isle of Man uses Sterling Pound	0.704	–
Israel (New Sheqel)	3.90	–
Italy (Euro)	0.910	–
Ivory Coast uses CFA Franc West	.597	–
Jamaica (Dollar)	.120	–
Japan (Yen)	.113	–
Jersey uses Sterling Pound	0.704	–
Jordan (Dinar)	0.706	–
Kazakhstan (Tenge)	.343	–
Kenya (Shilling)	.100	–
Kiribati uses Australian Dollar	1.34	–
Korea-PDR (Won)	.135	–
Korea-Rep. (Won)	1,211	–
Kuwait (Dinar)	0.300	–
Kyrgyzstan (Som)	.73	–
Laos (Kip)	7,910	–
Latvia (Lats)	0.640	–
Lebanon (Pound)	1,472	–
Lesotho (Maloti)	15.4	–
Liberia (Dollar)	.90	–
Libya (Dinar)	1.36	–
Liechtenstein uses Swiss Franc	0.998	–
Lithuania (Litas)	3.14	–
Luxembourg (Euro)	0.910	–
Macao (Pataca)	7.82	–
Macedonia (New Denar)	.55	–
Madagascar (Ariary)	3,170	–
Malawi (Kwacha)	.715	–
Malaysia (Ringgit)	4.11	–
Maldives (Rufiya)	14.9	–
Mali uses CFA Franc West	.597	–
Malta (Euro)	0.910	–
Marshall Islands uses U.S.Dollar	1.00	–
Mauritania (Ouguiya)	.337	–
Mauritius (Rupee)	.34	–
Mexico (Peso)	17.9	–
Moldova (Leu)	19.7	–
Monaco uses Euro	0.910	–
Mongolia (Tugrik)	2,038	–
Montenegro uses Euro	0.910	–
Montserrat uses E.C. Dollar	2.70	–
Morocco (Dirham)	9.82	–
Mozambique (New Metical)	.49	–
Namibia (Rand)	15.4	–
Nauru uses Australian Dollar	1.34	–
Nepal (Rupee)	.106	–
Netherlands (Euro)	0.910	–
Netherlands Antilles (Gulden)	2.00	–
New Caledonia uses CFP Franc	.109	–
New Zealand (Dollar)	1.48	–
Nicaragua (Cordoba Oro)	.28	–
Niger uses CFA Franc West	.597	–
Nigeria (Naira)	.197	–
Northern Ireland uses Sterling Pound	0.704	–
Norway (Krone)	8.56	–
Oman (Rial)	0.384	–
Pakistan (Rupee)	.103	–
Palau uses U.S.Dollar	1.00	–
Panama (Balboa) uses U.S.Dollar	1.00	–
Papua New Guinea (Kina)	2.98	–
Paraguay (Guarani)	5,591	–
Peru (Nuevo Sol)	3.39	–
Philippines (Peso)	.47	–
Poland (Zloty)	3.93	–
Portugal (Euro)	0.910	–
Qatar (Riyal)	3.64	–
Romania (New Leu)	4.06	–
Russia (Ruble)	.72	–
Rwanda (Franc)	.739	–
St. Helena (Pound)	0.624	–
St. Kitts uses E.C. Dollar	2.70	–
St. Lucia uses E.C. Dollar	2.70	–
St. Vincent uses E.C. Dollar	2.70	–
Samoa (Tala)	2.27	–
San Marino uses Euro	0.910	–
Sao Tome e Principe (Dobra)	22,298	–
Saudi Arabia (Riyal)	3.75	–
Scotland uses Sterling Pound	0.704	–
Senegal uses CFA Franc West	.597	–
Serbia (Dinar)	.112	–
Seychelles (Rupee)	11.8	–
Sierra Leone (Leone)	4,027	–
Singapore (Dollar)	1.38	–
Slovakia (Euro)	0.910	–
Slovenia (Euro)	0.910	–
Solomon Islands (Dollar)	8.10	–
Somalia (Shilling)	.579	–
Somaliland (Somali Shilling)	.579	4,000
South Africa (Rand)	15.4	–
Spain (Euro)	0.910	–
Sri Lanka (Rupee)	.142	–
Sudan (Pound)	6.06	–
Surinam (Dollar)	3.96	–
Swaziland (Lilangeni)	15.4	–
Sweden (Krona)	8.47	–
Switzerland (Franc)	0.998	–
Syria (Pound)	.220	–
Taiwan (NT Dollar)	.33	–
Tajikistan (Somoni)	7.87	–
Tanzania (Shilling)	2,143	–
Thailand (Baht)	.35	–
Togo uses CFA Franc West	.597	–
Tonga (Pa'anga)	2.30	–
Transdniestra (Ruble)	.72	–
Trinidad & Tobago (Dollar)	6.41	–
Tunisia (Dinar)	2.03	–
Turkey (New Lira)	2.91	–
Turkmenistan (Manat)	3.49	–
Turks & Caicos uses U.S. Dollar	1.00	–
Tuvalu uses Australian Dollar	1.34	–
Uganda (Shilling)	3,327	–
Ukraine (Hryvnia)	.26	–
United Arab Emirates (Dirham)	3.67	–
United Kingdom (Sterling Pound)	0.704	–
Uruguay (Peso Uruguayo)	.32	–
Uzbekistan (Sum)	2,846	–
Vanuatu (Vatu)	.111	–
Vatican City uses Euro	0.910	–
Venezuela (New Bolivar)	6.28	35
Vietnam (Dong)	22,003	–
Yemen (Rial)	.215	–
Zambia (Kwacha)	11.3	–
Zimbabwe (Dollar)	.373	–

A GUIDE TO INTERNATIONAL NUMERICS

	ENGLISH	CZECH	DANISH	DUTCH	ESPERANTO	FRENCH
1/4	quarter	jedna ctvrina	én kvart	een-kwart	unu-kvar'ono	quart
1/2	half	jedna polovinal	én halv	halve	unu-du'one	demi
1	one	jedna	én	een	unu	un
2	two	dve	to	twee	du	deux
3	three	tri	tre	drie	tri	trois
4	four	ctyri	fire	vier	kvar	quatre
5	five	pet	fem	vijf	kvin	cinq
6	six	sest	seks	zes	ses	six
7	seven	sedm	syv	zeven	sep	sept
8	eight	osm	otte	acht	ok	huit
9	nine	devet	ni	negen	nau	neuf
10	ten	deset	ti	tien	dek	dix
12	twelve	dvanáct	tolv	twaalf	dek du	douze
15	fifteen	patnáct	femten	vijftien	dek kvin	quinze
20	twenty	dvacet	tyve	twintig	du'dek	vingt
24	twenty-four	dvacetctyri	fireogtyve	vierentwintig	du'dek kvar	vingt-quatre
25	twenty-five	dvacetpet	femogtyve	vijfentwintig	du'dek kvin	vingt-cinq
30	thirty	tricet	tredive	dertig	tri'dek	trente
40	forty	ctyricet	fyrre	veertig	kvar'dek	quarante
50	fifty	padesát	halvtreds	vijftig	kvin'dek	cinquante
60	sixty	sedesát	tres	zestig	ses'dek	soixante
70	seventy	sedmdesát	halvfjerds	zeventig	sep'dek	soixante-dix
80	eighty	osemdesát	firs	tachtig	ok'dek	quatre-vingt
90	ninety	devadesát	halvfems	negentig	nau'dek	quatre-vingt-dix
100	one hundred	sto	hundrede	honderd	unu-cento	cent
1000	thousand	tis'c	tusind	duizend	mil	mille

	GERMAN	HUNGARIAN	INDONESIAN	ITALIAN	NORWEGIAN	POLISH
1/4	viertel	egy-negyed	satu per empat	quarto	en-fjeerdedel	jedna czwarta
1/2	halb	fél	satu per dua	mezzo	halv	podowa
1	ein	egy	satu	uno	en	jeden
2	zwei	kettö	dua	due	to	dwa
3	drei	három	tiga	tre	tre	trzy
4	vier	négy	empat	quattro	fire	cztery
5	fünf	öt	lima	cinque	fem	piec'
6	sechs	hat	enam	sei	seks	szes'c'
7	sieben	hét	tujuh	sette	sju	siedem
8	acht	nyolc	delapan	otto	atte	osiem
9	neun	kilenc	sembilan	nove	ni	dziewiec'
10	zehn	t'z	sepuluh	dieci	ti	dziesiec'
12	zwölf	tizenkettö	dua belas	dodici	tolv	dwanas' cie
15	fünfzehn	tizenöt	lima belas	quindici	femten	pietnas'cie
20	zwanzig	håsz	dua puluh	venti	tjue or tyve	dwadzies'cia
24	vierundzwanzig	håszonnégy	dua puluh empat	ventiquattro	tjue-fire or tyve-fire	dwadzies'cia-cztery
25	fünfundzwanzig	huszonöt	dua puluh lima	venticinque	tjue-fem or tyve-fem	dwadzies'cia-piec
30	dreissig	harminc	tiga puluh	trenta	tredve	trydzies'ci
40	vierzig	negyven	empat puluh	quaranta	forti	czterdries'ci
50	fünfzig	ötven	lima puluh	cinquanta	femti	piec'dziesiat
60	sechzig	hatvan	enam puluh	sessanta	seksti	szes'c'dziesiat
70	siebzig	hetven	tujuh pulu	settanta	sytti	siedemdziesiat
80	achtzig	nyolcyan	delapan puluh	ottonta	åttio	osiemdziesiat
90	neunzig	kilencven	sembilan puluh	novanta	nitti	dziewiec'dziesiat
100	hundert	száz	seratus	cento	hundre	jeden-sto
1000	tausend	ezer	seribu	mille	tusen	tysiac

	PORTUGUESE	ROMANIAN	SERBO-CROATIAN	SPANISH	SWEDISH	TURKISH
1/4	quarto	un-sfert	jedna ceturlina	carto	en-fjördedel	bir ceyrek
1/2	meio	o-jumatate	jedna polovina	medio	hölft	bir yarim
1	um	un	jedan	uno	en	bir
2	dois	doi	dva	dos	tva	iki
3	trÉs	trei	tri	tres	tre	üc
4	quatro	patru	cetiri	cuatro	fyra	dört
5	cinco	cinci	pet	cinco	fem	bes
6	seis	sase	sest	seis	sex	alti
7	sete	sapte	sedam	siete	sju	yedi
8	oito	opt	osam	ocho	åtta	sekiz
9	nove	noua	devet	nueve	nio	dokuz
10	dez	zece	deset	diez	tio	on
12	doze	doisprezece	dvanaest	doce	tolv	oniki
15	quinze	cincisprezece	petnaest	quince	femton	onbes
20	vinte	douazeci	dvadeset	veinte	tugu	yirmi
24	vinte-quatro	douacei si patru	dvadeset cetiri	veinticuatro	tjugu fyra	jirmidört
25	vinte-cinco	douacei si cinci	dvadeset pet	veinticinco	tjugu fem	yirmibes
30	trinta	treizeci	trideset	treinta	trettio	otuz
40	quarenta	patruzeci	cetrdeset	cuarenta	fyrtio	kirk
50	cinquenta	cincizeci	padeset	cincuenta	femtio	elli
60	sessenta	saizeci	sezdeset	sesenta	sextio	altmis
70	setenta	saptezeci	sedamdeset	setenta	sjuttio	yetmis
80	oitenta	optzeci	osamdeset	ochenta	åttio	seksen
90	noventa	nouazeci	devedeset	noventa	nittio	doksan
100	cem	suta	sto	cien	hundra	yüz
1000	mil	mie	Serbo hiljada	mil	tusen	bin

HEJIRA DATE CONVERSION CHART

HEJIRA (Hijira, Hegira), the name of the Muslim era (A.H. = Anno Hegirae) dates back to the Christian year 622 when Mohammed "fled" from Mecca, escaping to Medina to avoid persecution from the Koreish tribemen. Based on a lunar year the Muslim year is 11 days shorter.

*=Leap Year (Christian Calendar)

AH Hejira	AD Christian Date
1010	1601, July 2
1011	1602, June 21
1012	1603, June 11
1013	1604, May 30*
1014	1605, May 19
1015	1606, May 9
1016	1607, April 28
1017	1608, April 17*
1018	1609, April 6
1019	1610, March 26
1020	1611, March 16
1021	1612, March 4*
1022	1613, February 21
1023	1614, February 11
1024	1615, January 31
1025	1616, January 20*
1026	1617, January 9
1027	1617, December 29
1028	1618, December 19
1029	1619, December 8
1030	1620, November 26*
1031	1621, November 16
1032	1622, November 5
1033	1623, October 25
1034	1624, October 14*
1035	1625, October 3
1036	1626, September 22
1037	1627, September 12
1038	1628, August 31*
1039	1629, August 21
1040	1630, August 10
1041	1631, July 30
1042	1632, July 19*
1043	1633, July 8
1044	1634, June 27
1045	1635, June 17
1046	1636, June 5*
1047	1637, May 26
1048	1638, May 15
1049	1639, May 4
1050	1640, April 23*
1051	1641, April 12
1052	1642, April 1
1053	1643, March 22
1054	1644, March 10*
1055	1645, February 27
1056	1646, February 17
1057	1647, February 6
1058	1648, January 27*
1059	1649, January 15
1060	1650, January 4
1061	1650, December 25
1062	1651, December 14
1063	1652, December 2*
1064	1653, November 22
1065	1654, November 11
1066	1655, October 31
1067	1656, October 20*
1068	1657, October 9
1069	1658, September 29
1070	1659, September 18
1071	1660, September 6*
1072	1661, August 27
1073	1662, August 16
1074	1663, August 5
1075	1664, July 25*
1076	1665, July 14
1077	1666, July 4
1078	1667, June 23
1079	1668, June 11*
1080	1669, June 1
1081	1670, May 21
1082	1671, May 10
1083	1672, April 29*
1084	1673, April 18
1085	1674, April 7
1086	1675, March 28
1087	1676, March 16*
1088	1677, March 6
1089	1678, February 23

AH Hejira	AD Christian Date
1090	1679, February 12
1091	1680, February 2*
1092	1681, January 21
1093	1682, January 10
1094	1682, December 31
1095	1683, December 20
1096	1684, December 8*
1097	1685, November 28
1098	1686, November 17
1099	1687, November 7
1100	1688, October 26*
1101	1689, October 15
1102	1690, October 5
1103	1691, September 24
1104	1692, September 12*
1105	1693, September 2
1106	1694, August 22
1107	1695, August 12
1108	1696, July 31*
1109	1697, July 20
1110	1698, July 10
1111	1699, June 29
1112	1700, June 18
1113	1701, June 8
1114	1702, May 28
1115	1703, May 17
1116	1704, May 6*
1117	1705, April 25
1118	1706, April 15
1119	1707, April 4
1120	1708, March 23*
1121	1709, March 13
1122	1710, March 2
1123	1711, February 19
1124	1712, February 9*
1125	1713, January 28
1126	1714, January 17
1127	1715, January 7
1128	1715, December 27
1129	1716, December 16*
1130	1717, December 5
1131	1718, November 24
1132	1719, November 14
1133	1720, November 2*
1134	1721, October 22
1135	1722, October 12
1136	1723, October 1
1137	1724, September 19
1138	1725, September 9
1139	1726, August 29
1140	1727, August 19
1141	1728, August 7*
1142	1729, July 27
1143	1730, July 17
1144	1731, July 6
1145	1732, June 24*
1146	1733, June 14
1147	1734, June 3
1148	1735, May 24
1149	1736, May 12*
1150	1737, May 1
1151	1738, April 21
1152	1739, April 10
1153	1740, March 29*
1154	1741, March 19
1155	1742, March 8
1156	1743, February 25
1157	1744, February 15*
1158	1745, February 3
1159	1746, January 24
1160	1747, January 13
1161	1748, January 2
1162	1748, December 22*
1163	1749, December 11
1164	1750, November 30
1165	1751, November 20
1166	1752, November 8*
1167	1753, October 29
1168	1754, October 18
1169	1755, October 7
1170	1756, September 26*
1171	1757, September 15
1172	1758, September 4
1173	1759, August 25
1174	1760, August 13*
1175	1761, August 2
1176	1762, July 23
1177	1763, July 12
1178	1764, July 1*
1179	1765, June 20
1180	1766, June 9

AH Hejira	AD Christian Date
1181	1767, May 30
1182	1768, May 18*
1183	1769, May 7
1184	1770, April 27
1185	1771, April 16
1186	1772, April 4*
1187	1773, March 25
1188	1774, March 14
1189	1775, March 4
1190	1776, February 21*
1191	1777, February 1
1192	1778, January 30
1193	1779, January 19
1194	1780, January 8*
1195	1780, December 28*
1196	1781, December 17
1197	1782, December 7
1198	1783, November 26
1199	1784, November 14*
1200	1785, November 4
1201	1786, October 24
1202	1787, October 13
1203	1788, October 2*
1204	1789, September 21
1205	1790, September 10
1206	1791, August 31
1207	1792, August 19*
1208	1793, August 9
1209	1794, July 29
1210	1795, July 18
1211	1796, July 7*
1212	1797, June 26
1213	1798, June 15
1214	1799, June 5
1215	1800, May 25*
1216	1801, May 14
1217	1802, May 4
1218	1803, April 23
1219	1804, April 12*
1220	1805, April 1
1221	1806, March 21
1222	1807, March 11
1223	1808, February 28*
1224	1809, February 16
1225	1810, February 6
1226	1811, January 26
1227	1812, January 16*
1228	1813, January 6
1229	1813, December 24
1230	1814, December 14
1231	1815, December 3
1232	1816, November 21*
1233	1817, November 11
1234	1818, October 31
1235	1819, October 20
1236	1820, October 9*
1237	1821, September 28
1238	1822, September 18
1239	1823, September 8
1240	1824, August 26*
1241	1825, August 16
1242	1826, August 5
1243	1827, July 25
1244	1828, July 14*
1245	1829, July 3
1246	1830, June 22
1247	1831, June 12
1248	1832, May 31*
1249	1833, May 21
1250	1834, May 10
1251	1835, April 29
1252	1836, April 18*
1253	1837, April 7
1254	1838, March 27
1255	1839, March 17
1256	1840, March 5*
1257	1841, February 23
1258	1842, February 12
1259	1843, February 1
1260	1844, January 22*
1261	1845, January 10
1262	1845, December 30
1263	1846, December 20
1264	1847, December 9
1265	1848, November 27*
1266	1849, November 17
1267	1850, November 6
1268	1851, October 27
1269	1852, October 15*
1270	1853, October 4

AH Hejira	AD Christian Date
1271	1854, September 24
1272	1855, September 13
1273	1856, September 1*
1274	1857, August 22
1275	1858, August 11
1276	1859, July 31
1277	1860, July 20*
1278	1861, July 9
1279	1862, June 29
1280	1863, June 18
1281	1864, June 6*
1282	1865, May 27
1283	1866, May 16
1284	1867, May 5
1285	1868, April 24*
1286	1869, April 13
1287	1870, April 3
1288	1871, March 23
1289	1872, March 11*
1290	1873, March 1
1291	1874, February 18
1292	1875, February 7
1293	1876, January 28*
1294	1877, January 16
1295	1878, January 5
1296	1878, December 26
1297	1879, December 15
1298	1880, December 4*
1299	1881, November 23
1300	1882, November 12
1301	1883, November 2
1302	1884, October 21*
1303	1885, October 10
1304	1886, September 30
1305	1887, September 19
1306	1888, September 7*
1307	1889, August 28
1308	1890, August 17
1309	1891, August 7
1310	1892, July 26*
1311	1893, July 15
1312	1894, July 5
1313	1895, June 24
1314	1896, June 12*
1315	1897, June 2
1316	1898, May 22
1317	1899, May 12
1318	1900, May 1
1319	1901, April 20
1320	1902, April 10
1321	1903, March 30
1322	1904, March 18*
1323	1905, March 8
1324	1906, February 25
1325	1907, February 14
1326	1908, February 4*
1327	1909, January 23
1328	1910, January 13
1329	1911, January 2
1330	1911, December 22
1331	1912, December 11
1332	1913, November 30
1333	1914, November 19
1334	1915, November 9
1335	1916, October 28*
1336	1917, October 17
1337	1918, October 7
1338	1919, September 26
1339	1920, September 15*
1340	1921, September 4
1341	1922, August 24
1342	1923, August 14
1343	1924, August 2*
1344	1925, July 22
1345	1926, July 12
1346	1927, July 1
1347	1928, June 20*
1348	1929, June 9
1349	1930, May 29
1350	1931, May 19
1351	1932, May 7*
1352	1933, April 26
1353	1934, April 16
1354	1935, April 5
1355	1936, March 24*
1356	1937, March 14
1357	1938, March 3
1358	1939, February 21
1359	1940, February 10*
1360	1941, January 29

AH Hejira	AD Christian Date
1361	1942, January 19
1362	1943, January 8
1363	1943, December 28
1364	1944, December 17*
1365	1945, December 6
1366	1946, November 25
1367	1947, November 15
1368	1948, November 3*
1369	1949, October 24
1370	1950, October 13
1371	1951, October 2
1372	1952, September 21*
1373	1953, September 10
1374	1954, August 30
1375	1955, August 20
1376	1956, August 8*
1377	1957, July 29
1378	1958, July 18
1379	1959, July 7
1380	1960, June 25*
1381	1961, June 14
1382	1962, June 4
1383	1963, May 25
1384	1964, May 13*
1385	1965, May 2
1386	1966, April 22
1387	1967, April 11
1388	1968, March 31*
1389	1969, March 20
1390	1970, March 9
1391	1971, February 27
1392	1972, February 16*
1393	1973, February 4
1394	1974, January 25
1395	1975, January 14
1396	1976, January 3*
1397	1976, December 23*
1398	1977, December 12
1399	1978, December 2
1400	1979, November 21
1401	1980, November 9*
1402	1981, October 30
1403	1982, October 19
1404	1983, October 6
1405	1984, September 27*
1406	1985, September 16
1407	1986, September 6
1408	1987, August 26
1409	1988, August 14*
1410	1989, August 3
1411	1990, July 24
1412	1991, July 13
1413	1992, July 2*
1414	1993, June 21
1415	1994, June 10
1416	1995, May 31
1417	1996, May 19*
1418	1997, May 9
1419	1998, April 28
1420	1999, April 17
1421	2000, April 6*
1422	2001, March 26
1423	2002, March 15
1424	2003, March 5
1425	2004, February 22*
1426	2005, February 10
1427	2006, January 31
1428	2007, January 20
1429	2008, January 10*
1430	2008, December 29
1431	2009, December 18
1432	2010, December 8
1433	2011, November 27
1434	2012, November 15*
1435	2013, November 5
1436	2014, October 25
1437	2015, October 15
1438	2016, October 3*
1439	2017, September 22
1440	2018, September 12
1441	2019, September 1
1442	2020, August 20*
1443	2021, August 10
1444	2022, July 30
1445	2023, July 19
1446	2024, July 8*
1447	2025, June 27
1448	2026, June 17
1449	2027, June 6
1450	2028, May 25*

AFGHANISTAN

The Islamic State of Afghanistan, which occupies a mountainous region of Southwest Asia, has an area of 251,825 sq. mi. (652,090 sq. km.) and a population of 25.59 million. Presently, about a fifth of the total population lives in exile as refugees, (mostly in Pakistan). Capital: Kabul. It is bordered by Iran, Pakistan, Turkmenistan, Uzbekistan, Tajikistan, and China's Sinkiang Province. Agriculture and herding are the principal industries; textile mills and cement factories add to the industrial sector. Cotton, wool, fruits, nuts, oil, sheepskin coats and hand-woven carpets are normally exported but foreign trade has been interrupted since 1979.

On September 11, 2001, a terrorist attack on the United States, supported by the Taliban, led to retaliatory strikes by the U.S. Military in coalition with Afghans of a Northern Alliance. The Taliban regime was deposed. During a UN-sponsored conference on Afghanistan that was held in Bonn, Germany, in early November 2001, an agreement was reached for an Interim Authority, under the leadership of Hamid Karzai, to be installed in Afghanistan on December 22, 2001 and to hold power for the following four to six months. A "loya jirga" (Grand Council) then established a Transitional Authority with Hamid Karzai as president to prepare for general elections and a new constitution.

The national symbol on most coins of the kingdom is a stylized mosque, within which is seen the mihrab, a niche indicating the direction of Mecca, and the minbar, the pulpit, with a flight of steps leading up to it. Inscriptions in Pashtu were first used under the rebel Habibullah, but did not become standard until 1950.

Until 1919, coins were dated by the lunar Islamic Hejira calendar (AH), often with the king's regnal year as a second date. The solar Hejira (SH) calendar was introduced in 1919 (1337 AH, 1298 SH). The rebel Habibullah reinstated lunar Hejira dating (AH 1347-50), but the solar calendar was used thereafter. The solar Hejira year begins on the first day of spring, about March 21. Adding 621 to the SH year yields the AD year in which it begins.

RULERS

Names of rulers are shown in Perso-Arabic script in the style usually found on their coins; they are not always in a straight line.

BARAKZAI DYNASTY

حبيب الله

Habibullah, AH1319-1337/1901-1919AD

امان الله

Amanullah, AH1337, SH1298-1307/1919-1929AD

حبيب الله

Habibullah (rebel, known as Baccha-i-Saqao), AH1347-1348/1929AD

محمد نادر شاه

Muhammed Nadir Shah, AH1348-1350, SH1310-1312/1929-1933AD

محمد ظاهر شاه

Muhammad Zahir Shah, SH1312-1352/1933-1973AD

Republic, SH1352-1358/1973-1979AD
Democratic Republic, SH1358-1373/1979-1994 AD
Islamic Republic, SH1373-1381/1994-2002AD

MINT NAMES

Coins were struck at numerous mints in Afghanistan and adjacent lands. These are listed below, together with their honorific titles, and shown in the style ordinarily found on the coins.

افغانستان

Afghanistan

غزني

Ghazni

هراة هرات

Herat

كابل

Kabul

قندهار

Qandahar

MINT EPITHETS

دار الملك

"Dar ul-Mulk"
Abode of the King

دار النصرات

"Dar an-Nusrat"

KINGDOM

Abdur Rahman
AH1297-1319 / 1880-1901AD

MILLED COINAGE

10 Dinar = 1 Paisa; 5 Paise = 1 Shahi; 2 Shahi = 1 Sanar; 2 Sanar = 1 Abbasi; 1-1/2 Abbasi = 1 Qiran; 2 Qiran = 1 Kabuli Rupee; 1 Tilla = 10 Rupees

Afghanistan

KM# 831 1/2 RUPEE (Qiran)

4.65 g., 0.900 Silver 0.1346 oz. ASW **Obv:** Toughra **Rev:** Crossed cannons below mosque, wreath surrounds

Date	Mintage	VG8	F12	VF20	XF40	MS60
AH1319	—	25.00	45.00	85.00	140	—

Kabul

KM# 830 RUPEE

9.20 g., 0.900 Silver 0.2662 oz. ASW **Obv:** Date at right of toughra **Rev:** New style mosque

Date	Mintage	G4	VG8	F12	VF20	XF40
AH1318	—	—	8.00	16.00	27.00	55.00

Habibullah
AH1319-1337 / 1901-1919AD

LOCAL COINAGE

Ghazni

KM# 963 PAISA

Copper **Obv:** Text **Rev:** Star with five points within wreath **Note:** Struck over British East India Co., 1/4 Anna.

Date	Mintage	G4	VG8	F12	VF20	XF40
AH1322	—	20.00	35.00	60.00	100	—

Herat

KM# 956.1 PAISA

Copper **Note:** Round or irregular flan.

Date	Mintage	G4	VG8	F12	VF20	XF40
AH1322	—	6.00	10.00	18.00	30.00	—
AH1328	—	6.00	10.00	18.00	30.00	—
AH1329	—	6.00	10.00	18.00	30.00	—
AH1330	—	6.00	10.00	18.00	30.00	—
AH1331	—	6.00	10.00	18.00	30.00	—
AH1332	—	6.00	10.00	18.00	30.00	—
ND (1913)	—	3.00	4.00	7.00	12.00	—

Date off flan

KM# 956.2 PAISA

Copper **Rev:** In a rayed circle

Date	Mintage	G4	VG8	F12	VF20	XF40
AH1332	—	6.00	10.00	18.00	30.00	—

KM# 956.3 PAISA

Copper **Obv:** Scroll symbol

Date	Mintage	G4	VG8	F12	VF20	XF40
AH1325	—	8.00	13.00	25.00	45.00	—

KM# 957 PAISA

Copper **Note:** Counterstruck over Iran, 50 Dinars, Y#4.

Date	Mintage	G4	VG8	F12	VF20	XF40
AH1322	—	6.00	10.00	15.00	25.00	—
AH1328	—	7.00	12.00	20.00	35.00	—

KM# 958.1 PAISA

Copper **Obv:** Dar al-Nusrat added above date **Rev:** Mosque

Date	Mintage	G4	VG8	F12	VF20	XF40
AH1331	—	6.00	10.00	18.00	30.00	—

KM# 958.2 PAISA

Copper **Rev:** Date below mosque

Date	Mintage	G4	VG8	F12	VF20	XF40
AH1331	—	6.00	10.00	18.00	30.00	—

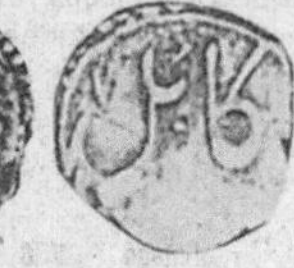

Kabul

KM# 973 PAISA

Copper

Date	Mintage	G4	VG8	F12	VF20	XF40
ND (1928)	—	15.00	25.00	45.00	75.00	—

Qandahar

KM# 960.1 PAISA

Copper **Rev:** Mosque **Note:** Dump.

Date	Mintage	G4	VG8	F12	VF20	XF40
AH1322	—	6.00	10.00	15.00	25.00	—

KM# 960.2 PAISA

Copper **Rev:** Mosque **Note:** Counterstruck on Iran 50 dinars, Y#4.

Date	Mintage	G4	VG8	F12	VF20	XF40
AH1321 year 1321 error-reading for 1322, does not exist	—	—	—	—	—	—
AH1322	—	6.00	10.00	18.00	30.00	—

KM# 960.3 PAISA

Copper **Rev:** Mosque **Note:** Counterstruck on Muscat and Oman, 1/4 Anna, KM#4.

Date	Mintage	G4	VG8	F12	VF20	XF40
AH1322	—	6.00	12.00	20.00	35.00	—

KM# 960.4 PAISA

Copper **Rev:** Mosque **Note:** Counterstruck on British East India Co., 1/4 Anna.

Date	Mintage	G4	VG8	F12	VF20	XF40
AH1322	—	6.00	12.00	20.00	35.00	—
AH1330 date not confirmed	—	—	—	—	—	—

KM# 960.5 PAISA

Copper **Rev:** Mosque **Note:** Overstruck on Oman, 1/4 Anna, KM#3.1.

Date	Mintage	G4	VG8	F12	VF20	XF40
AH1322	—	8.00	15.00	25.00	40.00	—

KM# 964 PAISA

Copper **Obv:** Text **Rev:** Mosque

Date	Mintage	G4	VG8	F12	VF20	XF40
AH1333	—	6.00	12.00	20.00	35.00	—
AH1334 date not confirmed	—	—	—	—	—	—

Without Mint Name

KM# 959 2 PAISE

Copper **Note:** Similar to Paisa, KM#965 but inscribed "Do Paisa" below mosque.

Date	Mintage	G4	VG8	F12	VF20	XF40
AH1329	—	12.00	20.00	30.00	50.00	—

MILLED COINAGE

10 Dinar = 1 Paisa; 5 Paise = 1 Shahi; 2 Shahi = 1 Sanar; 2 Sanar = 1 Abbasi; 1-1/2 Abbasi = 1 Qiran; 2 Qiran = 1 Kabuli Rupee; 1 Tilla = 10 Rupees

Afghanistan

KM# 848 PAISA

Brass or Bronze, 20 mm. **Obv:** Text within beaded circle **Rev:** Mosque

Date	Mintage	VG8	F12	VF20	XF40	MS60
AH1329/17	—	8.00	16.00	35.00	60.00	—

Note: On KM#828 obverse die

KM# 849 PAISA

Brass, 21 mm. **Obv:** Text **Rev:** Mosque within 8-pointed star

Date	Mintage	VG8	F12	VF20	XF40	MS60
AH1329	—	5.00	12.00	25.00	40.00	—
AH1331	—	5.00	12.00	25.00	40.00	—
AH1332	—	5.00	12.00	25.00	40.00	—

KM# 849a PAISA

Bronze, 21 mm. **Obv:** Text **Rev:** Mosque within 8-pointed star

Date	Mintage	VG8	F12	VF20	XF40	MS60
AH1334	—	8.00	18.00	35.00	60.00	—

KM# 854 PAISA

Brass or Bronze, 19 mm. **Obv:** Text within circle **Rev:** Mosque within 8-pointed star, circle surrounds **Note:** Thick flan, reduced size.

Date	Mintage	VG8	F12	VF20	XF40	MS60
AH1336	—	6.00	10.00	18.00	30.00	—

KM# 855 PAISA

Brass or Bronze **Note:** Thin flan.

Date	Mintage	VG8	F12	VF20	XF40	MS60
AH1336	—	7.00	14.00	27.00	45.00	—
AH1337	—	2.50	5.00	10.00	20.00	—

KM# 846 SANAR (10 Paisa)

1.55 g., 0.900 Silver 0.0449 oz. ASW, 13 mm. **Rev:** Mosque above crossed cannons and swords, wreath surrounds

Date	Mintage	VG8	F12	VF20	XF40	MS60
AH1325	—	25.00	55.00	100	—	—
AH1326	—	15.00	35.00	65.00	150	—
AH1328	—	15.00	35.00	65.00	150	—
AH1329	—	15.00	35.00	65.00	150	—

KM# 850 SANAR (10 Paisa)

1.55 g., 0.900 Silver 0.0449 oz. ASW, 13 mm. **Obv:** Text and date **Rev:** Mosque within 7-pointed star **Note:** Coins dated AH1333 and 1337 are known in two varieties.

Date	Mintage	VG8	F12	VF20	XF40	MS60
AH1329	—	15.00	25.00	40.00	75.00	—
AH1330	—	4.50	10.00	22.00	45.00	—
AH1331	—	4.50	10.00	22.00	45.00	—
AH1332	—	4.50	10.00	22.00	45.00	—
AH1333	—	4.00	9.00	20.00	35.00	—
AH1335	—	4.00	9.00	20.00	35.00	—
AH1337	—	4.50	10.00	25.00	50.00	—

KM# 837 ABBASI (20 Paisa)

3.11 g., 0.900 Silver 0.090 oz. ASW, 16 mm. **Obv:** Tughra within wreath **Rev:** Mosque above crossed cannons and swords, wreath surrounds

Date	Mintage	VG8	F12	VF20	XF40	MS60
AH1320	—	30.00	60.00	100	225	—

KM# 845 ABBASI (20 Paisa)

3.11 g., 0.900 Silver 0.090 oz. ASW, 17 mm. **Obv:** Tughra within wreath **Rev:** Mosque above crossed cannons and swords, wreath surrounds

Date	Mintage	VG8	F12	VF20	XF40	MS60
AH1324	—	35.00	70.00	125	250	—
AH1328	—	35.00	70.00	125	250	—
AH1329	—	50.00	100	175	300	—

KM# 851 ABBASI (20 Paisa)

3.11 g., 0.900 Silver 0.090 oz. ASW, 17 mm. **Obv:** Tughra within wreath **Rev:** Mosque above crossed cannons and swords, wreath surrounds

Date	Mintage	VG8	F12	VF20	XF40	MS60
AH1329	—	6.00	12.00	22.00	40.00	—
AH1330	—	6.00	12.00	22.00	40.00	—
AH1333	—	5.00	10.00	18.00	33.00	—
AH1334	—	5.00	10.00	18.00	33.00	—
AH1335	—	5.00	10.00	18.00	33.00	—
AH1337	—	5.00	10.00	18.00	33.00	—

KM# 838 1/2 RUPEE (Qiran)

4.65 g., 0.900 Silver 0.1346 oz. ASW, 19 mm. **Obv:** Toughra divides date **Rev:** Mosque above crossed cannons and swords, wreath surrounds

Date	Mintage	VG8	F12	VF20	XF40	MS60
AH1320	—	25.00	45.00	85.00	140	—
AH1325	—	20.00	40.00	75.00	125	—

Note: Two varieties of the AH1325 date are known

KM# 841 1/2 RUPEE (Qiran)

4.65 g., 0.900 Silver 0.1346 oz. ASW, 19 mm. **Obv:** Date at upper right of toughra **Rev:** Mosque above crossed cannons and swords, wreath surrounds, dated AH1320

Date	Mintage	VG8	F12	VF20	XF40	MS60
AH1321	—	25.00	45.00	85.00	140	—
AH1323	—	30.00	55.00	100	170	—

KM# 844.1 1/2 RUPEE (Qiran)

4.65 g., 0.900 Silver 0.1346 oz. ASW, 19 mm. **Obv:** Inscription and date within wreath **Rev:** Frozen date AH1320 split above mosque, crossed cannons and swords below, wreath surrounds

Date	Mintage	VG8	F12	VF20	XF40	MS60
AH1323	—	7.00	10.00	35.00	45.00	—
AH1324	—	6.00	9.00	18.00	30.00	—
AH1326	—	6.00	9.00	18.00	30.00	—
AH1327/6	—	6.00	9.00	18.00	30.00	—
AH1327	—	6.00	9.00	18.00	30.00	—
AH1328	—	7.00	10.00	22.00	40.00	—

KM# 844.2 1/2 RUPEE (Qiran)

4.65 g., 0.900 Silver 0.1346 oz. ASW, 19 mm. **Obv:** Inscription and date within wreath **Rev:** Mosque above crossed cannons and swords, wreath surrounds, actual date at top

Date	Mintage	VG8	F12	VF20	XF40	MS60
AH1326/3	—	25.00	45.00	75.00	135	—
Note: AH1326/0 for actual date on reverse						
AH1329	—	25.00	45.00	75.00	135	—

KM# 852 1/2 RUPEE (Qiran)

4.60 g., 0.900 Silver 0.1331 oz. ASW, 20 mm. **Obv:** Text within wreath **Rev:** Mosque within 8-pointed star, wreath surrounds

Date	Mintage	VG8	F12	VF20	XF40	MS60
AH1329	—	3.50	5.50	10.00	19.00	—
AH1333	—	3.50	5.50	10.00	19.00	—
AH1334	—	4.50	7.50	15.00	27.50	—
AH1335	—	4.50	7.50	15.00	27.50	—
AH1337	—	3.50	5.50	10.00	19.00	—

KM# 864 1/2 RUPEE (Qiran)

5.00 g., Silver **Obv. Legend:** Habibullah **Rev:** Star of Solomon

Date	Mintage	VG8	F12	VF20	XF40	MS60
AH1335	—	—	125	200	—	—

KM# 832 RUPEE

9.20 g., 0.900 Silver 0.2662 oz. ASW, 25 mm. **Obv:** Toughra of Habibullah in wreath, star above **Rev:** Mosque above crossed swords and cannons, wreath surrounds

Date	Mintage	VG8	F12	VF20	XF40	MS60
AH1319	—	10.00	14.00	30.00	85.00	—

Note: Two varieties are known

KM# 833.1 RUPEE

9.20 g., 0.900 Silver 0.2662 oz. ASW, 25 mm. **Obv:** Afghanistan above small toughra, star at right **Rev:** Mosque above crossed swords and cannons, large inverted pyramid dome

Date	Mintage	VG8	F12	VF20	XF40	MS60
AH1319	—	5.00	7.00	18.00	40.00	—
AH1320	—	5.00	7.00	15.00	30.00	—
AH1325	—	9.00	19.00	32.00	75.00	—

KM# 833.2 RUPEE

9.20 g., 0.900 Silver 0.2662 oz. ASW, 25 mm. **Obv:** Tughra within wreath, without star **Rev:** Swords and cannons crossed below mosque, wreath surrounds

Date	Mintage	VG8	F12	VF20	XF40	MS60
AH1319	—	5.00	7.00	13.00	32.00	—
AH1325	—	9.00	19.00	32.00	65.00	—

KM# 839 RUPEE

9.20 g., 0.900 Silver 0.2662 oz. ASW, 25 mm. **Obv:** Afghanistan divided by a star above large toughra **Rev:** Swords and cannons below mosque, wreath surrounds

Date	Mintage	VG8	F12	VF20	XF40	MS60
AH1320	—	6.00	10.00	20.00	40.00	—

KM# 840.1 RUPEE

9.20 g., 0.900 Silver 0.2662 oz. ASW, 25 mm. **Obv:** Tughra within wreath **Rev:** Small dome mosque above weapons within wreath

Date	Mintage	VG8	F12	VF20	XF40	MS60
AH1320	—	6.00	10.00	20.00	45.00	—

KM# 840.2 RUPEE

9.20 g., 0.900 Silver 0.2662 oz. ASW, 25 mm. **Obv:** Date in loop of toughra, wreath surrounds **Rev:** Mosque above weapons within wreath

Date	Mintage	VG8	F12	VF20	XF40	MS60
AH1321	—	13.00	20.00	35.00	75.00	—

KM# 842.1 RUPEE

9.20 g., 0.900 Silver 0.2662 oz. ASW, 25 mm. **Obv:** Text within wreath **Rev:** Afghanistan above mosque, crossed swords and cannons below, wreath surrounds

Date	Mintage	VG8	F12	VF20	XF40	MS60
AH1321	—	5.00	9.00	14.00	27.50	—
Note: Two varieties exist for AH1321 date						
AH1322	—	5.00	9.00	14.00	27.50	—

KM# 842.2 RUPEE

9.20 g., 0.900 Silver 0.2662 oz. ASW, 25 mm. **Obv:** Text within wreath **Rev:** Mosque above crossed cannons, wreath surrounds

Date	Mintage	VG8	F12	VF20	XF40	MS60
AH1322	—	5.00	6.00	11.00	25.00	—
AH1324	—	5.00	6.00	11.00	25.00	—
AH1325	—	6.00	10.00	15.00	32.00	—
AH1326//3	—	5.00	8.00	13.00	25.00	—
AH1327//6	—	8.00	10.00	19.00	37.50	—
AH1327	—	5.00	8.00	13.00	25.00	—
AH1328	—	8.00	10.00	19.00	37.50	—
Note: Two varieties exist for AH1328 date.						
AH1329	—	8.00	10.00	19.00	37.50	—

KM# 847.1 RUPEE

9.20 g., 0.900 Silver 0.2662 oz. ASW, 25 mm. **Obv:** Date divided 13 Arabic "j" 28 **Rev:** Large dome mosque without "Afghanistan"

Date	Mintage	VG8	F12	VF20	XF40	MS60
AH1328	—	12.00	25.00	45.00	75.00	—

KM# 847.2 RUPEE

9.20 g., 0.900 Silver 0.2662 oz. ASW, 25 mm. **Obv:** Date divided 132 Arabic "j" 8 **Rev:** Mosque above weapons, wreath surrounds

Date	Mintage	VG8	F12	VF20	XF40	MS60
AH1328	—	12.00	25.00	45.00	75.00	—

KM# 853 RUPEE

9.20 g., 0.900 Silver 0.2662 oz. ASW, 25 mm. **Obv:** Name and titles of Habibullah within wreath **Rev:** Mosque within 8-pointed star, wreath surrounds **Note:** Size varies. Two varieties exist for AH1330, 1331, and 1337 and three varieties exist for AH1333; thickness of obverse inscription and size of mosque dome on reverse vary.

Date	Mintage	VG8	F12	VF20	XF40	MS60
AH1329	—	5.00	8.00	13.00	25.00	—
AH1330	—	5.00	8.00	11.00	22.50	—
AH1331/0	—	5.00	8.00	11.00	22.50	—
AH1331	—	5.00	8.00	11.00	22.50	—
AH1332	—	5.00	8.00	11.00	22.50	—
AH1333	—	5.00	8.00	11.00	22.50	—
AH1334	—	5.00	8.00	11.00	22.50	—
AH1335	—	5.00	8.00	11.00	22.50	—
AH1337	—	5.00	8.00	13.00	25.00	—

Note: Two varieties of the AH1337 date exist, with either crossed cannons or a six-pointed star below the mosque

KM# 853a RUPEE

10.05 g., 0.900 Gold 0.2908 oz. AGW, 26 mm. **Obv:** Name and titles within wreath **Rev:** Mosque within 8-pointed star, wreath surrounds

Date	Mintage	F12	VF20	XF40	MS60	MS63
AH1334	—	—	—	2,500	—	—

Afghanistan

KM# 834.1 5 RUPEES

45.60 g., 0.900 Silver 1.3195 oz. ASW, 46 mm. **Obv:** Tughra divides date, wreath surrounds **Rev:** Similar to KM#826

Date	Mintage	VG8	F12	VF20	XF40	MS60
AH1319	—	50.00	70.00	135	265	—

KM# 834.2 5 RUPEES

45.60 g., 0.900 Silver 1.3195 oz. ASW, 46 mm. **Obv:** Date at left of tughra, wreath surrounds

Date	Mintage	VG8	F12	VF20	XF40	MS60
AH1319	—	50.00	70.00	135	265	—

KM# 843 5 RUPEES

45.60 g., 0.900 Silver 1.3195 oz. ASW, 45 mm. **Obv:** Wreath surrounds text **Rev:** Mosque within beaded circle, wreath surrounds **Note:** Most dates are recut dies. Two varieties are known for each date, AH1324 and 1327.

Date	Mintage	VG8	F12	VF20	XF40	MS60
AH1322	—	47.00	55.00	75.00	150	—
AH1324	—	47.00	50.00	70.00	135	—
AH1326	—	47.00	50.00	70.00	135	—
AH1327/6	—	47.00	50.00	70.00	135	—
AH1328	—	48.00	55.00	85.00	180	—
AH1329	—	47.00	60.00	105	220	—

KM# 835 TILLA (10 Rupees)

4.60 g., 0.900 Gold 0.1331 oz. AGW, 21 mm. **Obv:** Star above toughra within wreath **Rev:** Flags flank mosque above weapons, wreath surrounds

Date	Mintage	VG8	F12	VF20	XF40	MS60
AH1319	—	—	225	325	450	—

KM# 836.1 TILLA (10 Rupees)

4.60 g., 0.900 Gold 0.1331 oz. AGW, 21 mm. **Obv:** Legend divided by star above toughra, wreath surrounds **Obv. Legend:** Afghanistan **Rev:** Flags flank mosque above weapons, wreath surrounds

Date	Mintage	VG8	F12	VF20	XF40	MS60
AH1319	—	—	225	335	500	—

KM# 836.2 TILLA (10 Rupees)
4.60 g., 0.900 Gold 0.1331 oz. AGW, 21 mm. **Obv:** Legend above toughra with star to right, wreath surrounds **Obv. Legend:** Afghanistan **Rev:** Flags flank mosque above weapons, wreath surrounds

Date	Mintage	VG8	F12	VF20	XF40	MS60
AH1320	—	—	235	350	500	—

KM# A856 TILLA (10 Rupees)
4.60 g., 0.900 Gold 0.1331 oz. AGW, 21 mm. **Obv:** Date divided

Date	Mintage	VG8	F12	VF20	XF40	MS60
AH1325	—	—	550	1,000	1,400	—

KM# 856 TILLA (10 Rupees)
4.60 g., 0.900 Gold 0.1331 oz. AGW, 21 mm. **Obv. Legend:** Habibullah...

Date	Mintage	VG8	F12	VF20	XF40	MS60
AH1335	—	—	275	425	575	—
AH1336	—	—	225	295	400	—
AH1337	—	—	225	300	425	—

Amanullah
AH1337-1348 / 1919-1929AD

LOCAL COINAGE

Without Mint Name

KM# 965 PAISA
Copper, 20 mm. **Obv:** Denomination "Yek Paisa" **Note:** Crudely struck. Believed to be struck at Kabul.

Date	Mintage	G4	VG8	F12	VF20	XF40
SH1298	—	4.50	7.50	12.50	22.00	—
SH1299	—	4.50	7.50	12.50	22.00	—

KM# 966 PAISA
Copper **Note:** Crudely struck; without mint name, believed to be struck at Kabul.

Date	Mintage	G4	VG8	F12	VF20	XF40
SH1299	—	6.00	10.00	16.50	27.50	—

KM# 967 SHAHI (5 Paise)
Copper **Rev:** Both denominations **Note:** Crudely struck; without mint name, believed to be struck at Kabul.

Date	Mintage	G4	VG8	F12	VF20	XF40
AH1338 - SH1298	—	6.00	10.00	16.50	27.50	—
AH1338 - SH1299	—	7.50	12.50	20.00	35.00	—
AH1339 - SH1299	—	6.00	10.00	16.50	27.50	—

KM# A846 10 PAISE
Copper **Note:** Crudely struck; believed to be struck at Kabul.

Date	Mintage	G4	VG8	F12	VF20	XF40
SH1299	—	—	—	—	—	—

Note: Requires Confirmation

MILLED COINAGE

10 Dinar = 1 Paisa; 5 Paise = 1 Shahi; 2 Shahi = 1 Sanar; 2 Sanar = 1 Abbasi; 1-1/2 Abbasi = 1 Qiran; 2 Qiran = 1 Kabuli Rupee; 1 Tilla = 10 Rupees

Afghanistan

KM# 857 PAISA
Brass or Bronze, 20 mm. **Obv:** Text within wreath **Rev:** Mosque within 8-pointed star **Note:** Thin flan.

Date	Mintage	VG8	F12	VF20	XF40	MS60
AH1337	—	6.50	10.00	20.00	35.00	—

KM# 858 PAISA
Brass or Bronze, 19-20 mm. **Note:** Thin flan. Size varies.

Date	Mintage	VG8	F12	VF20	XF40	MS60
AH1337	—	3.00	6.00	10.00	20.00	—

Note: Three varieties are known dated AH1337

KM# 880 PAISA
Brass or Bronze, 20 mm.

Date	Mintage	VG8	F12	VF20	XF40	MS60
SH1299	—	2.50	5.50	12.00	22.50	—
SH1300	—	3.50	7.00	15.00	25.00	—
SH1301	—	3.50	7.00	15.00	25.00	—

Note: Two varieties are known dated SH1301

Date	Mintage	VG8	F12	VF20	XF40	MS60
SH1302	—	2.50	5.50	12.00	22.50	—
SH1303	—	2.50	5.50	12.00	22.50	—

KM# 859 SHAHI (5 Paise)
Copper or Brass, 25 mm. **Note:** Thick flan.

Date	Mintage	VG8	F12	VF20	XF40	MS60
AH1337	—	12.00	22.00	40.00	70.00	—

KM# 860 SHAHI (5 Paise)
Copper or Brass, 25 mm. **Note:** Thin flan.

Date	Mintage	VG8	F12	VF20	XF40	MS60
AH1337	—	10.00	20.00	35.00	55.00	—

KM# 861 SANAR (10 Paisa)
Copper or Brass, 29-30 mm. **Obv:** Text within inner circle, stars surround **Rev:** Mosque within 8-pointed star, within circle, stars surround **Note:** Thick flan. Size varies.

Date	Mintage	VG8	F12	VF20	XF40	MS60
AH1337	—	10.00	17.50	30.00	55.00	—

KM# 862 SANAR (10 Paisa)
Copper or Brass, 29-30 mm. **Note:** Thin flan. Size varies.

Date	Mintage	VG8	F12	VF20	XF40	MS60
AH1337	—	9.00	14.00	20.00	35.00	—

KM# 863 3 SHAHI (15 Paisa)
Copper, 32-33 mm. **Obv:** Without "Al-Ghazi" **Rev:** Mosque within 8-pointed star inside circle, stars surround **Note:** Size varies.

Date	Mintage	VG8	F12	VF20	XF40	MS60
AH1337	—	5.00	12.00	22.00	42.00	—

Note: Three varieties are known

KM# 869 3 SHAHI (15 Paisa)
Copper **Obv:** Shamsi left and below date **Rev:** Mosque within 8-pointed star within circle, stars surround

Date	Mintage	VG8	F12	VF20	XF40	MS60
SH1298	—	2.00	4.00	10.00	20.00	—

Note: Shamsi (Solar) is an additional word written on some of the coins dated SH1298, to show the change from a lunar to solar calendar

KM# 870 3 SHAHI (15 Paisa)
Copper, 33 mm. **Obv:** Al-Ghazi, without "Shamsi" by date **Rev:** Mosque within 8-pointed star, within circle, stars surround **Note:** Size varies.

Date	Mintage	VG8	F12	VF20	XF40	MS60
SH1298	—	3.00	5.00	10.00	20.00	—
SH1299	—	3.00	5.00	10.00	20.00	—

Note: 2 varieties of SH1299 exist

KM# 871.1 3 SHAHI (15 Paisa)
11.50 g., Copper, 33 mm. **Obv:** Al-Ghazi, Shamsi **Rev:** Mosque within 8-pointed star, within circle, stars surround **Note:** Thick flan.

Date	Mintage	VG8	F12	VF20	XF40	MS60
SH1298	—	10.00	15.00	22.00	42.00	—

KM# 871.2 3 SHAHI (15 Paisa)
9.00 g., Copper, 33 mm. **Obv:** Al-Ghazi, Shamsi **Rev:** Mosque within 8-pointed star, within circle, stars surround **Note:** Thin flan.

Date	Mintage	VG8	F12	VF20	XF40	MS60
SH1298	—	2.00	4.00	9.00	18.00	—

Note: Two reverse varieties with 10 or 11 circular stars exist

KM# 872 3 SHAHI (15 Paisa)
Copper, 33 mm. **Obv:** Shamsi **Rev:** Mosque in seven-pointed star

Date	Mintage	VG8	F12	VF20	XF40	MS60
SH1298	—	2.00	4.00	9.00	18.00	—

KM# 881 3 SHAHI (15 Paisa)
Copper, 33 mm. **Obv:** Stars surround inner circle, without "Shamsi" **Rev:** Mosque within 7-pointed star, within circle, stars surround **Note:** Four varieties for date SH1299 and three varieties for date SH1300 are known.

Date	Mintage	VG8	F12	VF20	XF40	MS60
SH1298	—	4.00	15.00	22.00	42.00	—
SH1299	—	1.50	3.50	8.00	17.00	—
SH1300	—	1.50	3.50	8.00	17.00	—

KM# 881a 3 SHAHI (15 Paisa)
Brass, 33 mm. **Obv:** Stars surround inner circle, without "Shamsi" **Rev:** Mosque within 7-pointed star, within circle, stars surround **Note:** Prev. KM#892.

Date	Mintage	VG8	F12	VF20	XF40	MS60
SH1300	—	4.00	8.00	15.00	30.00	—

KM# 891 3 SHAHI (15 Paisa)
Brass **Obv:** Eight stars around perimeter **Rev:** Eight stars around perimeter

Date	Mintage	VG8	F12	VF20	XF40	MS60
SH1300	—	—	—	—	—	—

KM# 893 3 SHAHI (15 Paisa)
Copper, 33 mm. **Obv:** Tughra, stars surround **Rev:** Mosque within 7-pointed star, within circle, stars surround

Date	Mintage	VG8	F12	VF20	XF40	MS60
SH1300	—	1.50	3.50	8.00	17.00	—
SH1301	—	1.50	3.50	8.00	17.00	—

Note: 2 varieties of SH1301 exist

Date	Mintage	VG8	F12	VF20	XF40	MS60
SH130x (error)	—	—	—	—	—	—
SH1303	—	1.50	3.50	8.00	17.00	—

KM# 874 ABBASI (20 Paisa)
Billon, 20 mm. **Obv:** Text within circle, stars surround **Rev:** Mosque within 8-pointed star, within circle, stars surround

Date	Mintage	VG8	F12	VF20	XF40	MS60
SH1298	—	50.00	80.00	120	200	—

KM# 882 ABBASI (20 Paisa)
Billon, 25 mm.

Date	Mintage	VG8	F12	VF20	XF40	MS60
SH1299	—	25.00	45.00	65.00	100	—

KM# 883 ABBASI (20 Paisa)
Billon, 25 mm. **Obv:** Tughra, stars surround **Rev:** Mosque within 7-pointed star, stars surround

Date	Mintage	VG8	F12	VF20	XF40	MS60
SH1299	—	2.00	6.00	15.00	30.00	—
SH1300	—	2.00	6.00	15.00	30.00	—
SH1301	—	2.00	6.00	15.00	30.00	—
Note: Two varieties for date SH1301 exist						
SH1302	—	2.00	6.00	15.00	30.00	—
SH2031 Error	—	7.00	15.00	30.00	50.00	—
SH1303	—	2.00	6.00	15.00	30.00	—

KM# 866 1/2 RUPEE (Qiran)
Silver, 25 mm. **Obv:** Legend within circle and wreath **Rev:** Mosque within 8-pointed star, wreath surrounds

Date	Mintage	VG8	F12	VF20	XF40	MS60
AH1337	—	150	300	500	725	—

KM# 865 1/2 RUPEE (Qiran)
Silver **Obv:** Uncircled inscription **Rev:** Mosque within 8-pointed star, wreath surrounds

Date	Mintage	VG8	F12	VF20	XF40	MS60
AH1337	—	5.00	11.00	18.00	30.00	—
Note: Five varieties are known						

KM# 875 1/2 RUPEE (Qiran)
4.75 g., 0.900 Silver 0.1374 oz. ASW, 20 mm. **Obv:** Star above inscription, "Shamsi" **Rev:** Mosque within 8-pointed star, wreath surrounds

Date	Mintage	VG8	F12	VF20	XF40	MS60
SH1298	—	4.00	7.00	12.00	25.00	—
Note: Two varieties are known						

KM# 876 1/2 RUPEE (Qiran)
4.75 g., 0.900 Silver 0.1374 oz. ASW, 20 mm. **Obv:** Al-Ghazi above inscription, "Shamsi" **Rev:** Mosque within 8-pointed star, wreath surrounds

Date	Mintage	VG8	F12	VF20	XF40	MS60
SH1298	—	17.00	33.00	55.00	85.00	—

KM# 884 1/2 RUPEE (Qiran)
4.75 g., 0.900 Silver 0.1374 oz. ASW, 20 mm. **Obv:** Without "Shamsi"

Date	Mintage	VG8	F12	VF20	XF40	MS60
SH1299	—	4.00	5.00	8.00	18.00	—
Note: Two varieties are known dated 1299						
SH1300	—	4.00	5.00	8.00	18.00	—

KM# 894 1/2 RUPEE (Qiran)
4.75 g., 0.900 Silver 0.1374 oz. ASW, 20 mm. **Obv:** Tughra within wreath **Rev:** Mosque within 7-pointed star, wreath surrounds

Date	Mintage	VG8	F12	VF20	XF40	MS60
SH1300	—	2.75	5.00	8.00	14.00	—
SH1301	—	2.75	5.00	8.00	14.00	—
SH1302	—	2.75	5.00	8.00	14.00	—
SH1303	—	2.75	5.00	8.00	14.00	—

KM# 867 RUPEE
9.20 g., 0.900 Silver 0.2662 oz. ASW, 25 mm. **Obv:** Name and titles of Amanullah, star above inscription **Rev:** Mosque within 8-pointed star, wreath surrounds

Date	Mintage	VG8	F12	VF20	XF40	MS60
AH1337	—	9.00	15.00	27.50	45.00	—
Note: Seven varieties are known						

KM# 877 RUPEE
9.00 g., 0.900 Silver 0.2604 oz. ASW, 25 mm. **Obv:** Al-Ghazi above inscription **Rev:** Mosque within 8-pointed star, wreath surrounds

Date	Mintage	VG8	F12	VF20	XF40	MS60
SH1298	—	9.00	11.00	15.00	27.50	—
Note: Four varieties are known for date SH1298						
SH1299	—	9.00	11.00	15.00	27.50	—
Note: Two varieties are known for date SH1299						

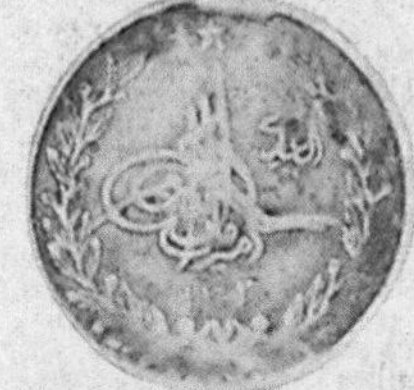

KM# 885 RUPEE
9.25 g., 0.900 Silver 0.2677 oz. ASW, 27 mm. **Obv:** Toughra of Amanullah **Rev:** Mosque within 7-pointed star, wreath surrounds

Date	Mintage	VG8	F12	VF20	XF40	MS60
SH1299	—	9.00	11.00	13.00	25.00	—
SH1300	—	9.00	11.00	13.00	25.00	—
SH1301	—	9.00	11.00	13.00	25.00	—
SH1302/1	—	9.00	11.00	13.00	25.00	—
SH1302	—	9.00	11.00	13.00	25.00	—
SH1303	—	9.00	11.00	13.00	25.00	—

KM# 878 2-1/2 RUPEES
22.92 g., 0.900 Silver 0.6632 oz. ASW, 34 mm. **Obv:** Tughra above date within wreath **Rev:** Mosque within 7-pointed star, wreath surrounds **Note:** Two varieties each are known for dates SH1298-1300.

Date	Mintage	VG8	F12	VF20	XF40	MS60
SH1298	—	15.00	23.00	35.00	85.00	—
SH1299	—	12.00	18.00	32.00	70.00	—
SH1300	—	12.00	18.00	32.00	70.00	—
SH1301	—	12.00	18.00	28.00	60.00	—
SH1302	—	12.00	18.00	28.00	60.00	—
SH1303	—	12.00	18.00	28.00	60.00	—

KM# 886 1/2 AMANI (5 Rupees)
2.30 g., 0.900 Gold 0.0666 oz. AGW, 16 mm. **Obv:** Tughra within wreath **Rev:** Mosque within 7-pointed star, wreath surrounds

Date	Mintage	VG8	F12	VF20	XF40	MS60
SH1299 (1920)	—	90.00	140	170	250	—

KM# 868.1 TILLA (10 Rupees)
4.60 g., 0.900 Gold 0.1331 oz. AGW, 21 mm. **Obv:** Text within wreath **Obv. Legend:** Amanullah... **Rev:** Mosque within 8-pointed star, crossed swords below mosque, wreath surrounds

Date	Mintage	VG8	F12	VF20	XF40	MS60
AH1337 (1918)	—	180	200	250	325	400

KM# 868.2 TILLA (10 Rupees)
4.60 g., 0.900 Gold 0.1331 oz. AGW, 21 mm. **Obv:** Text within wreath **Rev:** Mosque within 8-pointed star, 6-pointed star below mosque, wreath surrounds

Date	Mintage	VG8	F12	VF20	XF40	MS60
AH1337 (1918)	—	180	225	275	400	450

KM# 887 AMANI (10 Rupees)
4.60 g., 0.900 Gold 0.1331 oz. AGW, 22 mm. **Obv:** Tughra above date within wreath **Rev:** Mosque within 7-pointed star, wreath surrounds

Date	Mintage	VG8	F12	VF20	XF40	MS60
SH1299 (1920)	—	—	180	270	400	—

KM# 879 2 TILLAS (20 Rupees)
9.20 g., 0.900 Gold 0.2662 oz. AGW, 24 mm. **Obv:** Text above date, wreath surrounds **Rev:** Mosque within 8-pointed star, denomination above, wreath surrounds

Date	Mintage	F12	VF20	XF40	MS60	MS63
SH1298 (1919)	—	—	325	400	475	550

KM# 888 2 AMANI (20 Rupees)
9.20 g., 0.900 Gold 0.2662 oz. AGW, 24 mm. **Obv:** Tughra above date within wreath **Rev:** Mosque within 7-pointed star, wreath surrounds

Date	Mintage	VG8	F12	VF20	XF40	MS60
SH1299 (1920)	—	—	360	325	380	450
SH1300 (1921)	—	—	360	325	380	450
SH1301 (1922)	—	—	360	325	380	450
SH1302 (1923)	—	—	360	325	380	450
SH1303 (1924)	—	—	360	325	380	450

KM# 900 HABIBI (30 Rupees)
4.60 g., 0.900 Gold 0.1331 oz. AGW **Obv:** Small star replaces "30 Rupees" in legend **Rev:** Value stated as "Habibi"

Date	Mintage	VG8	F12	VF20	XF40	MS60
AH1347	—	180	225	400	600	900

Afghanistan

KM# 889 5 AMANI (50 Rupees)
23.00 g., 0.900 Gold 0.6655 oz. AGW, 34 mm. **Obv:** Tughra within wreath, Persian "5" above toughra; "Al Ghazi" at right **Rev:** Legend above mosque within 7-pointed star, wreath surrounds **Rev. Legend:** Amaniya

Date	Mintage	VG8	F12	VF20	XF40	MS60
SH1299 (1920)	—	900	850	1,250	1,800	3,000

KM# 890 5 AMANI (50 Rupees)
23.00 g., 0.900 Gold 0.6655 oz. AGW, 34 mm. **Obv:** Star above toughra within wreath **Rev:** Mosque within 7-pointed star, wreath surrounds, persian "5" above mosque

Date	Mintage	VG8	F12	VF20	XF40	MS60
SH1299	—	900	850	1,250	2,000	3,000

DECIMAL COINAGE

100 Pul = 1 Afghani; 20 Afghani = 1 Amani

KM# 905 2 PUL
2.00 g., Brass or Bronze, 18 mm. **Obv:** Tughra within inner circle, spray below **Rev:** Denomination within inner circle, spray below

Date	Mintage	F12	VF20	XF40	MS60	MS63
SH1304	—	3.00	5.00	9.00	15.00	—
SH1305	—	3.00	5.00	9.00	15.00	—

KM# 906 5 PUL
3.00 g., Brass or Bronze, 22 mm. **Obv:** Tughra within inner circle, spray below **Rev:** Denomination within inner circle, spray below

Date	Mintage	F12	VF20	XF40	MS60	MS63
SH1304	—	1.75	3.50	6.00	14.00	—
SH1305	—	1.50	3.00	5.50	14.00	—

KM# 907 10 PUL
6.00 g., Copper, 24 mm. **Obv:** Tughra within inner circle, spray below **Rev:** Denomination within inner circle, spray below

Date	Mintage	F12	VF20	XF40	MS60	MS63
SH1304	—	2.00	4.00	6.00	15.00	—
SH1305	—	2.50	4.50	7.00	20.00	—
SH1306	—	2.50	4.50	7.00	20.00	—

KM# 908 20 PUL
2.00 g., Billon, 19 mm. **Obv:** Tughra within inner circle, spray below **Rev:** Denomination within inner circle, spray below **Note:** Varieties exist.

Date	Mintage	F12	VF20	XF40	MS60	MS63
SH1304 (1925)	—	50.00	75.00	125	250	—
SH134 (1925) Error	—	—	—	—	—	—
SHND(1925)	—	—	100	175	—	—

KM# 909 1/2 AFGHANI (50 Pul)
5.00 g., 0.900 Silver 0.1447 oz. ASW, 25 mm. **Obv:** Tughra, date and spray below **Rev:** Mosque with flags flanking within wreath

Date	Mintage	F12	VF20	XF40	MS60	MS63
SH1304/7	—	2.75	4.00	8.00	15.00	25.00
Note: Two varieties are known dated SH1304						
SH1305/8	—	2.75	4.00	8.00	15.00	25.00
SH1306/9	—	2.75	4.00	8.00	15.00	25.00

KM# 915 1/2 AFGHANI (50 Pul)
5.00 g., 0.900 Silver 0.1447 oz. ASW, 25 mm. **Obv:** Date below mosque

Date	Mintage	F12	VF20	XF40	MS60	MS63
SH1307/10	—	4.00	7.00	14.00	42.00	—

KM# 910 AFGHANI (100 Pul)
10.00 g., 0.900 Silver 0.2894 oz. ASW, 29 mm. **Obv:** Date below toughra **Note:** Two varieties each are known for dates SH1305-06.

Date	Mintage	F12	VF20	XF40	MS60	MS63
SH1304/7	—	6.00	8.00	16.00	35.00	—
Note: Three varieties are known for date SH1304						
SH1305/8	—	6.00	8.00	16.00	25.00	50.00
SH1305/9	—	6.00	8.00	16.00	25.00	50.00
SH1306/9	—	6.00	8.00	16.00	25.00	50.00

KM# 913 2-1/2 AFGHANIS
25.00 g., 0.900 Silver 0.7234 oz. ASW, 38 mm. **Obv:** Tughra within wreath **Rev:** Mosque within wreath **Note:** Two varieties are known for each date.

Date	Mintage	F12	VF20	XF40	MS60	MS63
SH1305/8	—	18.00	30.00	70.00	175	—
SH1306/9	—	17.00	26.00	55.00	125	—

KM# 911 1/2 AMANI (5 Rupees)
3.00 g., 0.900 Gold 0.0868 oz. AGW, 18 mm.

Date	Mintage	F12	VF20	XF40	MS60	MS63
SH1304/7 (1925)	—	117	120	165	200	250
SH1305/8 (1926)	—	117	120	165	200	250
SH1306/9 (1927)	—	117	120	165	200	250

KM# 912 AMANI
6.00 g., 0.900 Gold 0.1736 oz. AGW, 23 mm.

Date	Mintage	F12	VF20	XF40	MS60	MS63
SH1304/7 (1925)	—	—	235	325	350	400
SH1305/8 (1926)	—	—	235	340	375	450
SH1306/9 (1927)	—	—	235	325	350	400

KM# 914 2-1/2 AMANI
15.00 g., 0.900 Gold 0.434 oz. AGW, 29 mm. **Obv:** Tughra above date within wreath **Rev:** Mosque within wreath

Date	Mintage	F12	VF20	XF40	MS60	MS63
SH1306/9 (1927)	—	—	—	8,500	11,500	—

Habibullah Ghazi

Rebel; AH1347-1348 / 1929AD; Struck in the name of Baccha-i-Saqao

LOCAL COINAGE

Herat

KM# 969 5 PAISE
Brass

Date	Mintage	G4	VG8	F12	VF20	XF40
AH1347	—	5.00	8.50	15.00	25.00	—

KM# 970.1 10 PAISE
Brass **Rev:** Denomination "Dah" written above "Paisa"

Date	Mintage	G4	VG8	F12	VF20	XF40
AH1347	—	6.00	10.00	16.50	27.50	—

KM# 970.2 10 PAISE
Brass **Rev:** Denomination "Dah" written at right of "Paisa"

Date	Mintage	G4	VG8	F12	VF20	XF40
AH1347	—	7.50	12.50	20.00	35.00	—

KM# 972 20 PAISE
Brass

Date	Mintage	G4	VG8	F12	VF20	XF40
AH1347	—	7.50	12.50	20.00	35.00	—
AH1348	—	10.00	15.00	25.00	40.00	—

MILLED COINAGE

10 Dinar = 1 Paisa; 5 Paise = 1 Shahi; 2 Shahi = 1 Sanar; 2 Sanar = 1 Abbasi; 1-1/2 Abbasi = 1 Qiran; 2 Qiran = 1 Kabuli Rupee; 1 Tilla = 10 Rupees

Afghanistan

KM# 901 10 PAISE

4.10 g., Copper, 22 mm. **Obv:** Text above spray **Rev:** Mosque within 8-pointed star, spray below

Date	Mintage	VG8	F12	VF20	XF40	MS60
AH1348	—	10.00	20.00	45.00	100	—

KM# 895 20 PAISE

5.70 g., Brass or Bronze, 25 mm. **Obv:** Text within wreath **Rev:** Mosque within 8-pointed star, wreath surrounds

Date	Mintage	VG8	F12	VF20	XF40	MS60
AH1347	—	3.00	5.00	7.50	18.00	—

KM# 896 1/2 RUPEE (Qiran)

4.70 g., 0.900 Silver 0.136 oz. ASW, 21 mm. **Obv:** Text within wreath **Rev:** Value (Qiran) above mosque within 8-pointed star, wreath surrounds

Date	Mintage	VG8	F12	VF20	XF40	MS60
AH1347	—	4.00	8.00	13.00	22.50	—

KM# 902 1/2 RUPEE (Qiran)

4.70 g., 0.900 Silver 0.136 oz. ASW, 21 mm. **Obv:** Text within wreath **Rev:** Value (Qiran) above mosque within 8-pointed star, wreath surrounds

Date	Mintage	VG8	F12	VF20	XF40	MS60
AH1348	—	13.00	22.50	35.00	55.00	—

KM# 897 RUPEE

9.10 g., 0.900 Silver 0.2633 oz. ASW, 25 mm. **Obv:** Name and titles of Amir Habibullah (The Usurper) **Rev:** Mosque within 8-pointed star, wreath surrounds

Date	Mintage	VG8	F12	VF20	XF40	MS60
AH1347	—	9.00	12.00	17.00	28.00	—

KM# 898 RUPEE

9.10 g., 0.900 Silver 0.2633 oz. ASW, 26 mm. **Obv:** Title in circle **Rev:** Mosque within 8-pointed star, wreath surrounds

Date	Mintage	VG8	F12	VF20	XF40	MS60
AH1347	—	27.50	38.50	60.00	100	—

KM# 899 HABIBI (30 Rupees)

4.60 g., 0.900 Gold 0.1331 oz. AGW, 21 mm. **Obv:** Value text within wreath **Rev:** Mosque within 8-pointed star, wreath surrounds, value stated as Habibi (2 values on coin)

Date	Mintage	VG8	F12	VF20	XF40	MS60
AH1347	—	—	215	245	450	650

Muhammed Nadir Shah

AH1348-1352 / 1929-1933AD

DECIMAL COINAGE

100 Pul = 1 Afghani; 20 Afghani = 1 Amani

KM# A922 PUL

1.00 g., Brass or Bronze, 15 mm. **Obv:** Text, stars surround **Rev:** Denomination within inner circle, stars surround

Date	Mintage	F12	VF20	XF40	MS60	MS63
AH1349	—	1.00	1.50	2.50	6.00	—

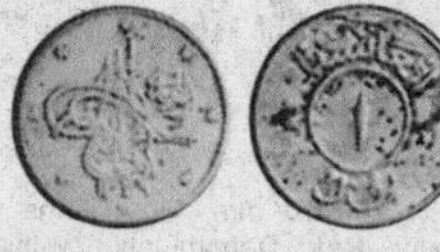

KM# 922 PUL

Brass or Bronze, 15 mm. **Obv:** Toughra **Rev:** Denomination within inner circle

Date	Mintage	F12	VF20	XF40	MS60	MS63
AH1349	—	100	250	300	550	—

KM# 917 2 PUL

2.00 g., Brass or Bronze, 18 mm. **Obv:** Tughra within inner circle **Rev:** Denomination within inner circle, spray below

Date	Mintage	F12	VF20	XF40	MS60	MS63
AH1348	—	1.25	2.50	5.00	16.00	—
AH1349/8	—	1.25	2.50	5.00	16.00	—

KM# 923 5 PUL

3.00 g., Brass or Bronze, 22 mm. **Obv:** Tughra within inner circle, wreath surrounds **Rev:** Denomination within inner circle, spray below

Date	Mintage	F12	VF20	XF40	MS60	MS63
AH1349	—	1.75	2.75	6.50	18.00	—
AH1350	—	1.25	2.25	6.00	18.00	—

Note: Two varieties are known dated AH1350

KM# 918 10 PUL

5.80 g., Copper or Brass, 25 mm. **Obv:** Tughra within circle **Rev:** Denomination within circle **Note:** Illustration shows an example struck off-center; prices are for properly struck specimens.

Date	Mintage	F12	VF20	XF40	MS60	MS63
AH1348	—	2.00	3.50	8.00	30.00	—
AH1349	—	2.25	4.00	10.00	30.00	—

Note: Small or large letters, weight varies: 5.8 or 5.3

KM# 919 20 PUL

5.56 g., Copper or Brass, 25 mm. **Obv:** Tughra within inner circle, wreath surrounds **Rev:** Denomination within circle, wreath surrounds

Date	Mintage	F12	VF20	XF40	MS60	MS63
AH1348	—	2.00	4.00	12.00	30.00	—
AH1349	—	3.00	5.00	14.00	35.00	—

KM# 924 25 PUL

6.00 g., Copper or Brass, 25 mm. **Obv:** Tughra within circle, wreath surrounds **Rev:** Denomination within circle, wreath surrounds **Note:** 2 varieties of letters

Date	Mintage	F12	VF20	XF40	MS60	MS63
AH1349	—	2.50	5.00	13.00	30.00	—
Note: Two varieties are known dated AH1349.						
134x	—	2.50	5.00	13.00	30.00	—

KM# 920 1/2 AFGHANI (50 Pul)

5.00 g., 0.900 Silver 0.1447 oz. ASW, 24 mm. **Obv:** Mosque above date within wreath **Note:** Prev. KM#919.

Date	Mintage	F12	VF20	XF40	MS60	MS63
AH1348/1	—	3.00	2.75	6.00	14.00	25.00
AH1349/2	—	3.00	2.75	6.00	14.00	25.00
AH1350/3	—	3.00	2.75	6.00	14.00	25.00

KM# 926 1/2 AFGHANI (50 Pul)

4.75 g., 0.900 Silver 0.1374 oz. ASW, 24 mm. **Obv:** Text within beaded circle, wreath surrounds **Rev:** Mosque within wreath

Date	Mintage	F12	VF20	XF40	MS60	MS63
SH1310	—	2.75	3.00	5.50	15.00	26.00
SH1311	—	2.75	2.50	4.50	12.50	25.00
Note: Two die varieties exist						
SH1312	—	2.75	3.00	5.50	15.00	26.00

Note: With and without diamond-shaped dot beneath the wreath on the obverse

KM# 921 AFGHANI (100 Pul)

9.95 g., 0.900 Silver 0.2879 oz. ASW, 30 mm. **Obv:** Tughra within wreath **Rev:** Mosque within wreath

Date	Mintage	F12	VF20	XF40	MS60	MS63
AH1348//1	—	5.75	10.00	12.00	22.50	—
AH1349//2	—	5.75	10.00	12.00	22.50	—
AH1350//3	—	5.75	10.00	12.00	22.50	—

KM# 927.1 AFGHANI (100 Pul)

10.00 g., 0.900 Silver 0.2894 oz. ASW, 27 mm. **Obv:** Text within beaded circle, wreath surrounds **Rev:** Mosque within wreath

Date	Mintage	F12	VF20	XF40	MS60	MS63
SH1310	—	—	—	—	180	250
SH1311 Unique	—	—	—	—	—	—

KM# 927.2 AFGHANI (100 Pul)

10.00 g., 0.900 Silver 0.2894 oz. ASW, 27 mm. **Obv:** Text within beaded circle, wreath surrounds **Rev:** Mosque within wreath **Note:** Thick flan - 2.8mm. Probable pattern.

Date	Mintage	F12	VF20	XF40	MS60	MS63
SH1310 Unique	—	—	—	—	—	—

KM# 925 20 AFGHANIS

6.00 g., 0.900 Gold 0.1736 oz. AGW, 22 mm.

Date	Mintage	F12	VF20	XF40	MS60	MS63
AH1348	—	—	240	320	400	475
AH1349	—	—	225	300	325	400
AH1350	—	—	225	300	325	400

Anonymous
SH1312 / 1933

KM# 928 2 PUL

2.00 g., Brass or Bronze, 18 mm. **Obv:** Text within beaded circle, wreath surrounds **Rev:** Denomination within beaded circle, wreath surrounds

Date	Mintage	F12	VF20	XF40	MS60	MS63
SH1311	—	2.00	3.00	4.00	12.00	—
SH1312	—	1.50	2.25	3.00	10.00	—
SH1313	—	1.75	2.75	3.75	12.00	—
SH1314	—	2.00	3.00	4.00	12.00	—

KM# 929 5 PUL

3.00 g., Brass or Bronze, 21 mm. **Obv:** Text within beaded circle, wreath surrounds **Rev:** Denomination within beaded circle, spray below

Date	Mintage	F12	VF20	XF40	MS60	MS63
SH1311	—	2.50	5.50	9.00	20.00	—
SH1312	—	2.50	5.50	9.00	20.00	—
SH1313	—	2.50	5.50	9.00	20.00	—
SH1314	—	2.50	5.50	9.00	20.00	—

KM# 930 10 PUL

Brass or Bronze, 23 mm. **Obv:** Text within beaded circle, spray below **Rev:** Denomination within small beaded circle, spray below

Date	Mintage	F12	VF20	XF40	MS60	MS63
SH1311	—	1.50	2.50	4.00	15.00	—
SH1312	—	1.50	2.50	4.00	15.00	—
SH1313	—	1.50	2.50	4.00	15.00	—
SH1314	—	1.50	2.50	4.00	15.00	—

Muhammed Zahir Shah
AH1352-1393 / SH1312-1352 / 1933-1973AD

KM# 936 2 PUL

2.00 g., Bronze, 15 mm. **Obv:** Arms within wreath, radiant background **Rev:** Denomination within inner circle, wreath surrounds, radiant background

Date	Mintage	F12	VF20	XF40	MS60	MS63
SH1316	—	—	—	0.50	1.00	1.40

KM# 937 3 PUL

2.50 g., Bronze, 16 mm. **Obv:** Arms within wreath, radiant background **Rev:** Denomination within inner circle, radiant background

Date	Mintage	F12	VF20	XF40	MS60	MS63
SH1316	—	—	—	0.50	1.00	1.40

KM# 938 5 PUL

3.03 g., Bronze, 17 mm. **Obv:** Arms within wreath, radiant background **Rev:** Denomination within inner circle, radiant background **Edge:** Reeded

Date	Mintage	F12	VF20	XF40	MS60	MS63
SH1316	—	—	—	0.50	1.00	1.40

KM# 939 10 PUL

2.50 g., Copper-Nickel, 18 mm. **Obv:** Arms within wreath, radiant background **Rev:** Denomination within inner circle, radiant background

Date	Mintage	F12	VF20	XF40	MS60	MS63
SH1316	—	—	—	0.50	1.00	2.00

KM# 931 25 PUL

7.00 g., Brass or Bronze, 24-25 mm. **Obv:** Text within beaded circle, wreath surrounds **Rev:** Denomination within inner circle, wreath surrounds **Note:** Size varies.

Date	Mintage	F12	VF20	XF40	MS60	MS63
SH1312	—	1.00	2.00	10.00	35.00	75.00
SH1313	—	1.00	2.00	10.00	35.00	75.00
SH1314	—	1.00	2.00	10.00	35.00	75.00
SH1316	—	1.00	2.00	10.00	35.00	75.00

KM# 940 25 PUL

2.90 g., Copper-Nickel, 20 mm. **Obv:** Text within inner circle, text surrounds **Rev:** Arms within wreath

Date	Mintage	F12	VF20	XF40	MS60	MS63
SH1316	—	—	—	0.75	1.25	2.50

KM# 941 25 PUL

3.00 g., Bronze, 20 mm. **Obv:** Text within inner circle, text surrounds **Rev:** Arms within wreath

Date	Mintage	F12	VF20	XF40	MS60	MS63
SH1330	—	—	0.50	0.65	1.00	1.50
SH1331	—	—	0.50	0.65	1.00	1.50
SH1332	—	—	0.50	0.65	1.00	1.50
SH1333 Requires Confirmation	—	—	—	—	—	—

KM# 943 25 PUL

3.00 g., Nickel Clad Steel **Edge:** Reeded

Date	Mintage	F12	VF20	XF40	MS60	MS63
SH1331	—	—	0.50	1.00	5.00	9.00
SH1332	—	—	0.50	1.00	7.00	10.00

KM# 944 25 PUL

3.00 g., Nickel Clad Steel **Edge:** Plain

Date	Mintage	F12	VF20	XF40	MS60	MS63
SH1331	—	—	0.50	0.85	2.00	3.00
SH1332	—	—	0.50	0.85	2.00	3.00
SH1333	—	—	0.50	0.85	2.00	3.00
SH1334/2	—	—	0.50	1.00	3.00	5.00
SH1334	—	—	0.50	0.85	2.00	3.00

KM# 945 25 PUL

Aluminum, 24 mm. **Obv:** Text within inner circle, text surrounds **Rev:** Arms within wreath **Note:** Struck on oversize 2 Afghani KM#949 planchets in 1970.

Date	Mintage	F12	VF20	XF40	MS60	MS63
SH1331	—	—	0.50	1.50	5.00	10.00

KM# 932.1 1/2 AFGHANI (50 Pul)

4.75 g., 0.900 Silver 0.1374 oz. ASW, 24 mm. **Obv:** Smaller dotted circle within wreath **Rev:** Arms within wreath

Date	Mintage	F12	VF20	XF40	MS60	MS63
SH1312 Rare	—	—	—	—	—	—

KM# 932.2 1/2 AFGHANI (50 Pul)

4.75 g., 0.900 Silver 0.1374 oz. ASW, 24 mm. **Obv:** Large dotted field in circle within wreath **Rev:** Arms within wreath

Date	Mintage	F12	VF20	XF40	MS60	MS63
SH1312	—	—	—	—	—	—
SH1313	—	2.75	3.50	4.50	9.00	15.00
Note: 60 dots in circle						
SH1314	—	2.75	3.50	4.50	9.00	15.00
Note: 60 dots in circle						
SH1315	—	2.75	3.50	4.50	9.00	15.00
Note: 40 dots in circle						
SH1316	—	2.75	3.50	4.50	9.00	15.00
Note: 40 dots in circle						

KM# 947 1/2 AFGHANI (50 Pul)

5.00 g., Nickel Clad Steel, 22.3 mm. **Obv:** Value on coin is "50 Pul" in Pashto. **Rev:** Arms within wreath

Date	Mintage	F12	VF20	XF40	MS60	MS63
SH1331	—	—	0.50	1.00	2.00	3.00
SH133x	—	—	1.00	3.00	10.00	20.00

KM# 942.1 50 PUL

4.80 g., Bronze, 22.5 mm. **Obv:** Denomination in numerals **Rev:** Arms within wreath

Date	Mintage	F12	VF20	XF40	MS60	MS63
SH1330	—	—	0.50	1.00	2.00	3.00
SH133x	—	—	1.00	3.00	10.00	20.00

KM# 942.2 50 PUL

Bronze, 24 mm. **Obv:** Denomination in numerals **Rev:** Arms within wreath

Date	Mintage	F12	VF20	XF40	MS60	MS63
SH1330	—	5.00	10.00	20.00	35.00	50.00

KM# 946 50 PUL
5.00 g., Nickel Clad Steel, 22.3 mm. **Obv:** Denomination within inner circle **Rev:** Arms within wreath

Date	Mintage	F12	VF20	XF40	MS60	MS63
SH1331	—	—	0.50	0.60	1.00	1.50
SH1332	—	—	0.50	0.60	1.00	1.50
SH1333	—	—	0.50	0.60	2.00	3.00
SH1334/2	—	—	0.50	0.60	1.00	1.50
SH1334	—	—	0.50	0.60	1.00	1.50

KM# 953 AFGHANI (100 Pul)
4.00 g., Nickel Clad Steel, 23 mm. **Obv:** Three wheat sprigs **Rev:** Denomination and stars **Edge:** Reeded

Date	Mintage	VF20	XF40	MS60	MS63	MS65
SH1340	—	—	0.50	0.70	1.00	1.25

KM# 949 2 AFGHANIS
2.50 g., Aluminum **Obv:** Arms within wreath, circle surrounds **Rev:** Denomination within inner circle **Note:** This issue was withdrawn and demonetized due to extensive counterfeiting.

Date	Mintage	VF20	XF40	MS60	MS63	MS65
SH1337	—	—	0.50	0.70	1.50	1.50

KM# 954.1 2 AFGHANIS
5.30 g., Nickel Clad Steel, 25.1 mm. **Obv:** Radiant eagle statue, with wings spread **Rev:** Wheat sprig left of denomination **Edge:** Plain **Note:** Coin turn.

Date	Mintage	VF20	XF40	MS60	MS63	MS65
SH1340	—	—	0.50	0.70	1.00	1.50

KM# 954.2 2 AFGHANIS
5.30 g., Nickel Clad Steel, 25.1 mm. **Obv:** Radiant eagle statue, with wings spread **Rev:** Wheat sprig left of denomination **Note:** Medallic die orientation.

Date	Mintage	VF20	XF40	MS60	MS63	MS65
SH1340	—	—	0.50	1.00	3.00	5.00

Note: Some evidence indicates that this variety was the first Republican issue struck in 1973

KM# 950 5 AFGHANIS
3.00 g., Aluminum **Obv:** Tughra within beaded circle **Rev:** Arms within beaded circle, denomination below **Note:** This issue was withdrawn and demonetized due to extensive counterfeiting.

Date	Mintage	VF20	XF40	MS60	MS63	MS65
SH1337	—	—	0.50	1.00	1.50	3.00

KM# 955 5 AFGHANIS
8.04 g., Nickel Clad Steel, 29 mm. **Obv:** Bust 3/4 right divides dates **Rev:** Wheat sprigs flank denomination **Edge:** Reeded

Date	Mintage	VF20	XF40	MS60	MS63	MS65
SH1340	—	—	0.25	0.50	1.00	3.00

KM# 948 10 AFGHANIS
Aluminum **Obv:** Tughra within beaded circle, denomination below **Rev:** Arms within wreath, date below, stars flank

Date	Mintage	VF20	XF40	MS60	MS63	MS65
SH1336	—	—	—	450	650	1,000

KM# 935 4 GRAMS
4.00 g., 0.900 Gold 0.1157 oz. AGW, 19 mm.

Date	Mintage	F12	VF20	XF40	MS60	MS63
SH1315 (1936)	—	—	157	215	245	335
SH1317 (1938)	—	—	157	215	245	335

KM# 933 TILLA
6.00 g., 0.900 Gold 0.1736 oz. AGW, 22 mm.

Date	Mintage	F12	VF20	XF40	MS60	MS63
SH1313 (1934)	—	235	320	340	450	600

KM# 934 8 GRAMS
8.00 g., 0.900 Gold 0.2315 oz. AGW, 22 mm.

Date	Mintage	F12	VF20	XF40	MS60	MS63
SH1314 (1935)	—	—	315	425	475	525
SH1315 (1936)	—	—	315	425	475	525
SH1317 (1938)	—	—	315	425	475	525

KM# 952 8 GRAMS
8.00 g., 0.900 Gold 0.2315 oz. AGW, 22 mm. **Obv:** Tughra **Rev:** Eagles divide date and flank figure above horse within cornucopias

Date	Mintage	F12	VF20	XF40	MS60	MS63
SH1339-AH1380	200	PF63 1,100				

Note: Struck for royal presentation purposes. Specimens struck with the same dies (including the "8 grams", the "8" having been effaced after striking), but on thin planchets weighing 3.9-4.0 grams, exist, they are regarded as "mint sports". Market value $550

REPUBLIC

SH1352-1357 / 1973-1978AD

STANDARD COINAGE

KM# 975 25 PUL
2.52 g., Brass Clad Steel **Obv:** National arms **Rev:** Denomination, six stars

Date	Mintage	VF20	XF40	MS60	MS63	MS65
SH1352(1973)	45,950,000	—	0.40	0.75	1.00	1.50

KM# 976 50 PUL
Copper Clad Steel, 21 mm. **Obv:** National arms **Rev:** Denomination, six stars **Edge:** Plain

Date	Mintage	VF20	XF40	MS60	MS63	MS65
SH1352(1973)	24,750,000	—	0.40	0.75	1.00	1.50

KM# 977 5 AFGHANIS
Copper-Nickel Clad Steel **Obv:** National arms **Rev:** Denomination within stylized grain sprig wreath

Date	Mintage	VF20	XF40	MS60	MS63	MS65
SH1352(1973)	34,750,000	—	0.50	1.00	1.50	2.50

KM# 978 250 AFGHANIS
28.57 g., 0.925 Silver 0.8497 oz. ASW, 38.5 mm. **Subject:** Conservation **Obv:** National arms **Rev:** Snow Leopard

Date	Mintage	VF20	XF40	MS60	MS63	MS65
1978	4,370	—	—	20.00	30.00	45.00

KM# 979 250 AFGHANIS
28.28 g., 0.925 Silver 0.841 oz. ASW **Subject:** Conservation **Obv:** National arms **Rev:** Snow Leopard

Date	Mintage	VF20	XF40	MS60	MS63	MS65
1978	4,387	PF63 35.00	PF65 45.00			

KM# 980 500 AFGHANIS
35.30 g., 0.925 Silver 1.0498 oz. ASW, 42 mm. **Subject:** Conservation **Obv:** National arms **Rev:** Siberian Crane

Date	Mintage	VF20	XF40	MS60	MS63	MS65
1978	4,374	—	—	22.00	32.00	47.00

KM# 981 500 AFGHANIS
35.00 g., 0.925 Silver 1.0409 oz. ASW **Series:** Conservation **Subject:** Siberian Crane **Obv:** National arms, date below **Rev:** Crane and denomination

Date	Mintage	VF20	XF40	MS60	MS63	MS65
1978	4,218	PF63 37.00	PF65 47.00			

KM# 982 10000 AFGHANIS
33.44 g., 0.900 Gold 0.9675 oz. AGW **Subject:** Conservation **Obv:** National arms **Rev:** Marco Polo Sheep

Date	Mintage	VF20	XF40	MS60	MS63	MS65
1978	694	—	—	—	2,250	2,750
1978	181	PF65 6,500				

DEMOCRATIC REPUBLIC

SH1358-1371 / 1979-1992AD

KM# 990 25 PUL
Aluminum-Bronze **Obv:** National arms **Rev:** Value at center

Date	Mintage	VF20	XF40	MS60	MS63	MS65
SH1357	—	—	0.40	0.75	1.00	1.50

KM# 996 25 PUL
2.30 g., Aluminum-Bronze, 19 mm. **Obv:** National arms **Rev:** Value at center

Date	Mintage	VF20	XF40	MS60	MS63	MS65
SH1359	—	—	0.40	0.75	1.00	1.50

KM# 992 50 PUL
3.10 g., Aluminum-Bronze, 20.9 mm. **Obv:** National arms **Rev:** Value at center

Date	Mintage	VF20	XF40	MS60	MS63	MS65
SH1357	—	—	0.40	0.75	1.00	1.50

KM# 997 50 PUL
3.16 g., Aluminum-Bronze, 21 mm. **Obv:** National arms **Rev:** Value at center

Date	Mintage	VF20	XF40	MS60	MS63	MS65
SH1359	—	—	0.40	0.75	1.00	1.50

KM# 993 AFGHANI
4.60 g., Copper-Nickel, 23 mm. **Obv:** National arms **Rev:** Value at center

Date	Mintage	VF20	XF40	MS60	MS63	MS65
SH1357	—	—	0.40	0.75	1.00	1.50

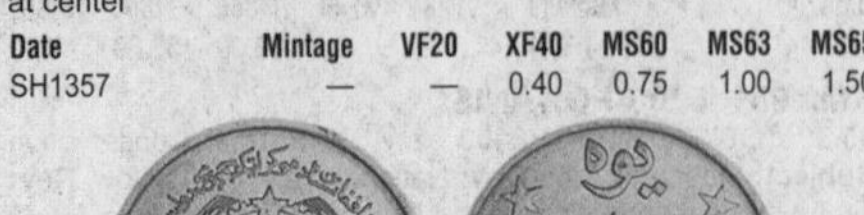

KM# 998 AFGHANI
6.18 g., Copper-Nickel **Obv:** National arms **Rev:** Value at center

Date	Mintage	VF20	XF40	MS60	MS63	MS65
SH1359	—	—	0.40	0.75	1.00	1.50

KM# 994 2 AFGHANIS
6.00 g., Copper-Nickel, 25 mm. **Obv:** National arms **Rev:** Value at center

Date	Mintage	VF20	XF40	MS60	MS63	MS65
SH1357	—	—	0.40	0.75	1.00	1.50
SH1358	—	—	0.40	0.75	1.00	1.50

KM# 999 2 AFGHANIS
6.21 g., Copper-Nickel **Obv:** Similar to 1 Afghani, KM#998

Date	Mintage	VF20	XF40	MS60	MS63	MS65
SH1359	—	—	0.40	1.00	1.50	2.00

KM# 995 5 AFGHANIS
7.40 g., Copper-Nickel **Obv:** National arms **Rev:** Value at center

Date	Mintage	VF20	XF40	MS60	MS63	MS65
SH1357	—	—	0.40	1.50	2.00	3.00

KM# 1000 5 AFGHANIS
7.40 g., Copper-Nickel

Date	Mintage	VF20	XF40	MS60	MS63	MS65
SH1359	—	—	0.50	1.00	1.50	2.00

KM# 1001 5 AFGHANIS
Brass **Series:** F.A.O. **Subject:** World Food Day **Obv:** National arms **Rev:** FAO logo

Date	Mintage	VF20	XF40	MS60	MS63	MS65
SH1360	—	—	0.40	0.65	0.75	1.00
SH1360	—	PF65 25.00				

KM# 1015 10 AFGHANIS
Brass **Subject:** 70th Anniversary of Independence **Obv:** Arch **Rev:** Bank logo

Date	Mintage	VF20	XF40	MS60	MS63	MS65
1989	—	—	—	1.00	2.50	3.50

KM# 1016 50 AFGHANIS
Copper-Nickel **Subject:** 100 Years of the Automobile **Obv:** National arms **Rev:** Ferrari

Date	Mintage	VF20	XF40	MS60	MS63	MS65
ND-1986	—	—	—	3.00	5.00	9.00

KM# 1006 50 AFGHANIS
Copper-Nickel **Subject:** World Wildlife Fund **Obv:** National arms **Rev:** Leopard

Date	Mintage	VF20	XF40	MS60	MS63	MS65
1987	28,000	—	—	2.00	4.00	7.00

KM# 1024 50 AFGHANIS
29.70 g., Copper, 38 mm. **Subject:** Prehistoric Animals **Obv:** National arms **Rev:** Deinotherium-Elephant

Date	Mintage	VF20	XF40	MS60	MS63	MS65
1993	—	—	—	6.00	9.00	12.00

KM# 1032 50 AFGHANIS
Copper **Subject:** Prehistoric Animals **Obv:** National arms **Rev:** Ankylosaurus

Date	Mintage	VF20	XF40	MS60	MS63	MS65
1995	Est. 100	PF60 25.00	PF63 35.00	PF65 55.00		

KM# 1014 100 AFGHANIS
15.10 g., Copper-Nickel, 31.1 mm. **Series:** World Soccer Championship **Subject:** Italy to U.S.A. **Obv:** Bank logo **Rev:** World Football Championship

Date	Mintage	VF20	XF40	MS60	MS63	MS65
1990	10,000	PF60 3.50	PF63 6.50	PF65 10.00		

KM# 1017 250 AFGHANIS
20.31 g., 0.925 Silver 0.604 oz. ASW **Subject:** Conservation **Obv:** National arms **Rev:** Snow Leopard

Date	Mintage	VF20	XF40	MS60	MS63	MS65
1978 4 known	—	—	—	—	550	—

KM# 1018 500 AFGHANIS
35.44 g., 0.925 Silver 1.054 oz. ASW **Subject:** Conservation **Obv:** National arms **Rev:** Siberian Crane

Date	Mintage	VF20	XF40	MS60	MS63	MS65
1978 4 known	—	—	—	—	550	—

KM# 1002 500 AFGHANIS
9.06 g., 0.900 Silver 0.2622 oz. ASW, 27 mm. **Series:** F.A.O. **Subject:** World Food Day **Obv:** National arms **Rev:** FAO

Date	Mintage	VF20	XF40	MS60	MS63	MS65
1981	—	PF60 7.00	PF63 12.00	PF65 18.00		

KM# 1003 500 AFGHANIS
12.00 g., 0.999 Silver 0.3854 oz. ASW **Series:** 100th Anniversary of the Automobile **Rev:** Ferrari

Date	Mintage	VF20	XF40	MS60	MS63	MS65
ND-1986	2,000	—	—	12.00	14.00	18.00

KM# 1004 500 AFGHANIS
12.00 g., 0.999 Silver 0.3854 oz. ASW **Subject:** 1988 Winter Games,Calgary **Obv:** National arms **Rev:** Ice dancers

Date	Mintage	VF20	XF40	MS60	MS63	MS65
ND-1986	10,000	—	—	10.00	12.00	16.00

KM# 1005 500 AFGHANIS
12.00 g., 0.999 Silver 0.3854 oz. ASW **Subject:** Wildlife Preservation **Obv:** National arms **Rev:** Leopard

Date	Mintage	VF20	XF40	MS60	MS63	MS65
1986	5,000	—	—	12.00	15.00	20.00

KM# 1010 500 AFGHANIS
12.00 g., 0.999 Silver 0.3854 oz. ASW **Series:** 1988 Summer Olympics **Subject:** Volleyball **Obv:** National arms above denomination

Date	Mintage	VF20	XF40	MS60	MS63	MS65
1987 (k)	10,000	—	—	10.00	12.00	16.00

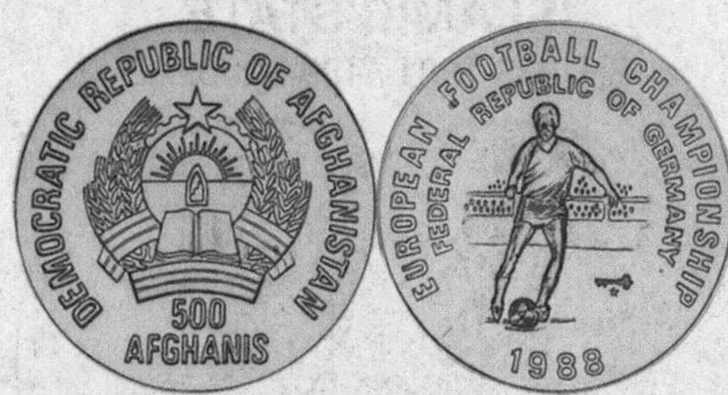

KM# 1007 500 AFGHANIS
12.00 g., 0.999 Silver 0.3854 oz. ASW **Subject:** European Soccer Championship - West Germany **Obv:** National Arms **Rev:** European Football Championship

Date	Mintage	VF20	XF40	MS60	MS63	MS65
1988 (k)	Est. 5000	—	—	12.00	15.00	20.00

KM# 1009 500 AFGHANIS
16.00 g., 0.999 Silver 0.5139 oz. ASW **Series:** 1986 World Soccer Championship - Mexico **Obv:** National Arms **Rev:** World Football Championship-Mexico 86

Date	Mintage	VF20	XF40	MS60	MS63	MS65
ND-1988	5,000	—	—	14.00	18.00	25.00

KM# 1008.1 500 AFGHANIS
16.00 g., 0.999 Silver 0.5139 oz. ASW **Series:** 1992 Winter Olympics **Subject:** Bobsledding **Obv:** National arms, short thick letters in legend. **Rev:** Bobsled between legends, date at right

Date	Mintage	VF20	XF40	MS60	MS63	MS65
1989	Est. 10000	PF60 11.00	PF63 18.00	PF65 26.00		

KM# 1008.2 500 AFGHANIS
16.00 g., 0.999 Silver 0.5139 oz. ASW **Series:** 1992 Winter Olympics **Subject:** Bobsledding **Obv:** National arms above denomination, tall thin letters **Rev:** Bobsled between legends, date at right

Date	Mintage	VF20	XF40	MS60	MS63	MS65
1989	Inc. above	PF60 12.00	PF63 22.00	PF65 32.00		

KM# 1011 500 AFGHANIS
16.00 g., 0.999 Silver 0.5139 oz. ASW **Series:** 1990 World Soccer Championship **Obv:** National Arms **Rev:** World Football Championship-Italy 1990

Date	Mintage	VF20	XF40	MS60	MS63	MS65
1989	10,000	PF60 12.00	PF63 22.00	PF65 32.00		

KM# 1012 500 AFGHANIS
16.00 g., 0.999 Silver 0.5139 oz. ASW **Series:** 1992 Summer Olympics **Subject:** Field Hockey **Obv:** National Arms **Rev:** XXV Olympic Games-Barcelona-Date, field hockey players between dates

Date	Mintage	VF20	XF40	MS60	MS63	MS65
1989	10,000	PF60 12.00	PF63 22.00	PF65 32.00		

KM# 1013 500 AFGHANIS
12.00 g., 0.999 Silver 0.3854 oz. ASW **Series:** 1994 World Cup Soccer Games U.S.A. **Obv:** National Arms **Rev:** XV World Cup across top - United States of America; date across bottom

Date	Mintage	VF20	XF40	MS60	MS63	MS65
1991	—	—	—	10.00	14.00	20.00

KM# 1022 500 AFGHANIS
20.00 g., 0.999 Silver 0.6424 oz. ASW **Series:** 1994 World Cup Soccer Games - U.S.A. **Obv:** National Arms **Rev:** XV World Cup across top-soccer player with date, USA in center

Date	Mintage	VF20	XF40	MS60	MS63	MS65
1992	—	PF60 15.00	PF63 20.00	PF65 30.00		

KM# 1020 500 AFGHANIS
16.00 g., 0.999 Silver 0.5139 oz. ASW **Subject:** Prehistoric Animals **Obv:** National Arms **Rev:** Deinotherium-Elephant

Date	Mintage	VF20	XF40	MS60	MS63	MS65
1993	—	PF60 15.00	PF63 20.00	PF65 30.00		

KM# 1021 500 AFGHANIS
16.00 g., 0.999 Silver 0.5139 oz. ASW **Subject:** Prehistoric Animals **Obv:** National Arms **Rev:** Styracosaurus

Date	Mintage	VF20	XF40	MS60	MS63	MS65
1994	—	PF60 15.00		PF63 20.00		PF65 30.00

KM# 1023 500 AFGHANIS
20.00 g., 0.999 Silver 0.6424 oz. ASW **Series:** 1996 Olympics **Obv:** National Arms **Rev:** Three runners and building, small date under building, large date under runners **Rev. Legend:** FROM ATHENS TO ATLANTA

Date	Mintage	VF20	XF40	MS60	MS63	MS65
1995	15,000	PF60 13.00		PF63 17.00		PF65 27.00

KM# 1035 500 AFGHANIS
16.00 g., 0.999 Silver 0.5139 oz. ASW **Subject:** Prehistoric Animals **Obv:** National arms **Rev:** Ankylosaurus

Date	Mintage	VF20	XF40	MS60	MS63	MS65
1995	—	PF60 15.00		PF63 20.00		PF65 30.00

KM# 1019 10000 AFGHANIS
33.66 g., 0.900 Gold 0.974 oz. AGW **Subject:** Conservation **Obv:** National Arms **Rev:** Marco Polo Sheep

Date	Mintage	VF20	XF40	MS60	MS63	MS65
1978 4 known	—	—	—	—	—	8,500

ISLAMIC STATE

SH1373-1381 / 1994-2002AD

KM# 1026 50 AFGHANIS
28.68 g., Copper-Nickel, 38.5 mm. **Series:** 50th Anniversary - United Nations **Obv:** National symbol, denomination below **Rev:** Meditating figure with three doves

Date	Mintage	VF20	XF40	MS60	MS63	MS65
ND-1995	—	—	—	2.50	3.50	5.00

KM# 1030 50 AFGHANIS
30.70 g., Copper-Nickel, 38 mm. **Subject:** World Food Summit **Obv:** National symbol, denomination below **Rev:** Gate of Zafar

Date	Mintage	VF20	XF40	MS60	MS63	MS65
1996	—	—	—	2.50	3.50	5.00

KM# 1037 50 AFGHANIS
Copper-Nickel **Series:** Sydney Olympics 2000 **Obv:** National symbol, denomination below **Rev:** Equestrian event

Date	Mintage	VF20	XF40	MS60	MS63	MS65
1999	10,000	—	—	2.50	3.50	5.00

KM# 1031 500 AFGHANIS
28.43 g., 0.925 Silver 0.8455 oz. ASW **Series:** 50th Anniversary United Nations **Obv:** National symbol, denomination below **Rev:** Meditating figure with three doves

Date	Mintage	VF20	XF40	MS60	MS63	MS65
ND-1995	—	PF60 18.00		PF63 22.00		PF65 28.00

KM# 1025 500 AFGHANIS
20.00 g., 0.999 Silver 0.6424 oz. ASW, 38 mm. **Obv:** National symbol, denomination below **Rev:** Multicolor Lynx

Date	Mintage	VF20	XF40	MS60	MS63	MS65
1996	—	PF60 20.00		PF63 25.00		PF65 32.00

KM# 1027 500 AFGHANIS
20.00 g., 0.999 Silver 0.6424 oz. ASW, 38 mm. **Subject:** XVI World Cup Soccer - France **Obv:** National symbol, denomination below **Rev:** Soccer player going for goal

Date	Mintage	VF20	XF40	MS60	MS63	MS65
1996	100	—	—	—	—	100
1996	10,000	PF60 15.00		PF63 17.00		PF65 20.00

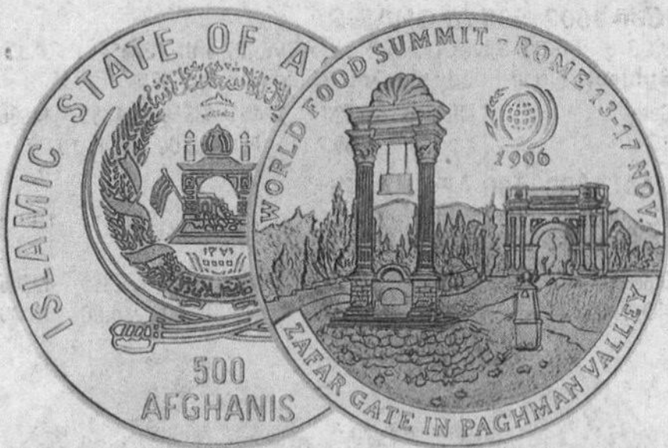

KM# 1028 500 AFGHANIS
20.00 g., 0.999 Silver 0.6424 oz. ASW, 38 mm. **Subject:** World Food Summit - Rome **Obv:** National symbol, denomination below **Rev:** Zafar Gate, F.A.O. logo, dates

Date	Mintage	VF20	XF40	MS60	MS63	MS65
1996	—	PF60 14.00		PF63 20.00		PF65 24.00

KM# 1029 500 AFGHANIS
15.00 g., 0.999 Silver 0.4818 oz. ASW **Subject:** World of Adventure - Charles A. Lindbergh **Obv:** National symbol, denomination below **Rev:** Multicolor enamel airplane and statue, cameo portrait **Note:** For this type weighing 30gr. See KM #P2.

Date	Mintage	VF20	XF40	MS60	MS63	MS65
1996	—	PF60 11.00		PF63 14.00		PF65 17.00

KM# 1036.1 500 AFGHANIS
20.00 g., 0.999 Silver 0.6424 oz. ASW **Subject:** Sydney Olympics 2000 **Obv:** National symbol, denomination below **Rev:** Winged goddess bearing torch, Greek temples behind

Date	Mintage	VF20	XF40	MS60	MS63	MS65
1996	Est. 500	PF60 20.00		PF63 30.00		PF65 42.00

KM# 1040 500 AFGHANIS
20.00 g., 0.999 Silver 0.6424 oz. ASW, 38 mm. **Subject:** World Cup Soccer **Obv:** National symbol, denomination below **Rev:** Multicolor soccer players, flags and ball **Edge:** Reeded

Date	Mintage	VF20	XF40	MS60	MS63	MS65
1996	—	PF60 12.00	PF63 15.00	PF65 18.00		

KM# 1033 500 AFGHANIS
15.00 g., 0.999 Silver 0.4818 oz. ASW, 35 mm. **Subject:** Sydney Olympics 2000 **Obv:** National symbol, denomination below **Rev:** Javelin thrower

Date	Mintage	VF20	XF40	MS60	MS63	MS65
1998	5,000	PF60 11.00	PF63 14.00	PF65 17.00		

KM# 1036.2 500 AFGHANIS
15.00 g., 0.999 Silver 0.4818 oz. ASW **Subject:** Sydney Olympics 2000 **Obv:** National symbol, denomination below **Rev:** Winged Goddess bearing torch, Greek temples behind

Date	Mintage	VF20	XF40	MS60	MS63	MS65
1998	—	PF60 12.00	PF63 15.00	PF65 18.00		

KM# 1039 500 AFGHANIS
15.00 g., 0.999 Silver 0.4818 oz. ASW, 35 mm. **Subject:** 16th World Cup - Soccer **Obv:** National symbol, denomination below **Rev:** Soccer player superimposed on ball **Edge:** Plain

Date	Mintage	VF20	XF40	MS60	MS63	MS65
1997	—	PF60 10.00	PF63 14.00	PF65 16.00		

KM# 1034 500 AFGHANIS
20.00 g., 0.999 Silver 0.6424 oz. ASW **Subject:** Fauna of Asia **Obv:** National symbol, denomination below **Rev:** Marco Polo Sheep

Date	Mintage	VF20	XF40	MS60	MS63	MS65
1998	Est. 100	PF63 70.00	PF65 95.00			

KM# 1038 500 AFGHANIS
20.00 g., 0.999 Silver 0.6424 oz. ASW **Subject:** Sydney Olympics - 2000 - XXVII Olympiad **Obv:** National symbol, denomination below **Rev:** Equestrian event

Date	Mintage	VF20	XF40	MS60	MS63	MS65
1999	5,000	PF60 14.00	PF63 16.00	PF65 20.00		

KM# 1041 500 AFGHANIS
14.90 g., 0.999 Silver 0.4786 oz. ASW, 35 mm. **Subject:** Third Millennium **Obv:** National symbol, denomination below **Rev:** Millennium change design **Edge:** Plain

Date	Mintage	VF20	XF40	MS60	MS63	MS65
ND(1999)	—	PF60 12.00	PF63 15.00	PF65 18.00		

KM# 1049 500 AFGHANIS
0.999 Silver, 25 mm. **Subject:** William Shakespeare **Obv:** National arms **Rev:** Bust at right, Globe Theater interior at left.

Date	Mintage	VF20	XF40	MS60	MS63	MS65
1999	—	PF60 10.00	PF63 12.00	PF65 15.00		

KM# 1042 500 AFGHANIS
15.00 g., 0.999 Silver 0.4818 oz. ASW, 35 mm. **Obv:** National symbol, denomination below **Rev:** Snow Leopard **Edge:** Plain

Date	Mintage	VF20	XF40	MS60	MS63	MS65
2000	—	PF60 12.00	PF63 15.00	PF65 18.00		

KM# 1047 5000 AFGHANIS
503.00 g., 0.999 Silver 16.1556 oz. ASW, 85 mm. **Subject:** XXVII Olympic Games - Sydney Olympics 2000 **Obv:** State emblem **Rev:** Wrestling, winged goddess bearing torch, 2 wrestlers

Date	Mintage	VF20	XF40	MS60	MS63	MS65
1999	—	PF63 365	PF65 410			

PATTERNS

Including off metal strikes

KM#	Date	Mintage	Identification	Mkt Val
Pn1	SH1310 (1931)	—	1/2 Afghani. Silver.	—
Pn2	SH1336 (1957)		5 Afghanis. Silver. Legend within off-center circle, denomination. National emblem with wreath, date.	375
Pn3	SH1336 (1957)	—	10 Afghanis. Silver. Toughra within off-center circle, denomination. National emblem with wreath, date.	375

PIEDFORT

KM#	Date	Mintage	Identification	Mkt Val
P1.1	1989	110	500 Afghanis. 0.999. Silver. National Arms. XVI Winter Olympic Games,bobsled 1989 in center,Albertville date at bottom. KM#1008.2.	125
P1.2	1989	—	500 Afghanis. 0.999. Silver. KM#1008.2, pine tree without needles.	160
P1.3	1989	—	500 Afghanis. 0.999. Silver. KM#1008.2, pine tree with sagging branches.	125
P1.4	1989	—	500 Afghanis. 0.999. Silver. KM#1008.2, pine tree with uplifted branches.	125
P2	1996	—	500 Afghanis. Silver. KM#1029.	100
P3	1998	—	500 Afghanis. Silver. KM#1033.	150
P4	1999	—	500 Afghanis. Silver. KM#1038.	110

AJMAN - U.A.E.

Ajman is the smallest and poorest of the emirates in the United Arab Emirates. It has an estimated area of 100sq. mi. (250 sq. km.) and a population of 6,000. Ajman's first act as an autonomous entity was entering into a treaty with Great Britain in 1820. On December 2, 1971 Ajman became one of the 6 original members of the United Arab Emirates.

TITLES

Ajman

RULERS
Abdul Aziz Bin Humaid al-Naimi, 1900-1908
Humaid Bin Abdul Aziz al-Naimi, 1908-1928
Rashid Bin Hamad al-Naimi, 1928-1981
Humaid Bin Rashid al-Naimi, 1981--

MONETARY SYSTEM
100 Dirhams = 1 Riyal

UNITED ARAB EMIRATE

NON-CIRCULATING LEGAL TENDER COINAGE

KM# 1.1 RIYAL
3.95 g., 0.640 Silver 0.0813 oz. ASW **Ruler:** Rashid Bin Hamad al-Naimi **Obv:** Denomination within circle **Rev:** Chicken below state emblem, two dates

Date	Mintage	VF20	XF40	MS60	MS63	MS65
AH1389 - 1969	20,000	—	—	10.00	15.00	20.00
AH1389 - 1969	1,200	PF65 60.00				

KM# 1.2 RIYAL
3.95 g., 0.640 Silver 0.0813 oz. ASW **Ruler:** Rashid Bin Hamad al-Naimi **Obv:** Denomination within circle **Rev:** Chicken below state emblem, three dates

Date	Mintage	VF20	XF40	MS60	MS63	MS65
AH1390 - 1970	—	—	—	12.00	22.00	30.00

KM# 2.1 2 RIYALS
6.45 g., 0.835 Silver 0.1732 oz. ASW **Ruler:** Rashid Bin Hamad al-Naimi **Obv:** Denomination within circle **Rev:** Chicken below state emblem, two dates

Date	Mintage	VF20	XF40	MS60	MS63	MS65
AH1389-1969	20,000	—	—	12.00	25.00	32.00
AH1389-1969	1,200	PF65 70.00				

KM# 2.2 2 RIYALS
6.45 g., 0.835 Silver 0.1732 oz. ASW **Ruler:** Rashid Bin Hamad al-Naimi **Obv:** Denomination within circle **Rev:** Chicken below state emblem, three dates

Date	Mintage	VF20	XF40	MS60	MS63	MS65
AH1390-1970	—	—	—	15.00	32.00	45.00

KM# 3.1 5 RIYALS
15.00 g., 0.835 Silver 0.4027 oz. ASW **Ruler:** Rashid Bin Hamad al-Naimi **Obv:** Denomination within circle **Rev:** Chicken below state emblem, two dates

Date	Mintage	VF20	XF40	MS60	MS63	MS65
AH1389-1969	10,000	—	—	25.00	38.00	50.00
AH1389-1969	1,200	PF65 80.00				

KM# 3.2 5 RIYALS
15.00 g., 0.835 Silver 0.4027 oz. ASW **Ruler:** Rashid Bin Hamad al-Naimi **Obv:** Denomination within circle **Rev:** Chicken below state emblem, three dates

Date	Mintage	VF20	XF40	MS60	MS63	MS65
AH1390-1970	—	—	—	28.00	50.00	60.00
AH1390-1970	—	PF65 100				

KM# 12 5 RIYALS
15.00 g., 0.925 Silver 0.4461 oz. ASW **Ruler:** Rashid Bin Hamad al-Naimi **Subject:** Death of Gamal Abdel Nassar **Obv:** State emblem divides denomination **Rev:** Head left divides dates

Date	Mintage	VF20	XF40	MS60	MS63	MS65
AH1390-1970	5,000	PF65 85.00				

KM# 17 5 RIYALS
15.00 g., 0.925 Silver 0.4461 oz. ASW **Ruler:** Rashid Bin Hamad al-Naimi **Obv:** State emblem, denomination above **Rev:** Head left, denomination below

Date	Mintage	VF20	XF40	MS60	MS63	MS65
ND-1970	1,175	PF65 225				

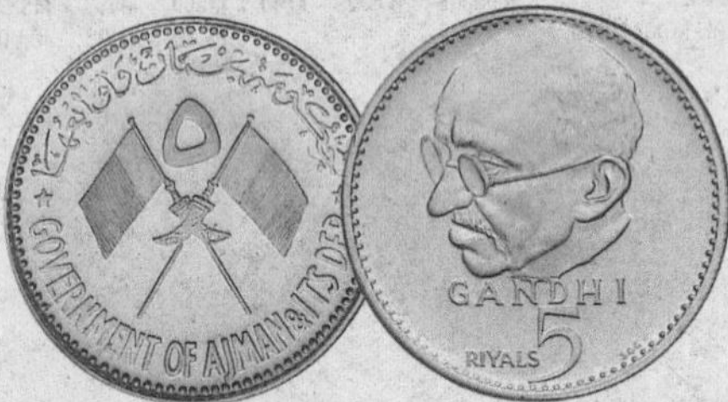

KM# 18 5 RIYALS
15.00 g., 0.925 Silver 0.4461 oz. ASW **Ruler:** Rashid Bin Hamad al-Naimi **Obv:** State emblem, denomination above **Rev:** Head left, denomination below

Date	Mintage	VF20	XF40	MS60	MS63	MS65
ND-1970	1,175	PF65 225				

KM# 19 5 RIYALS
15.00 g., 0.925 Silver 0.4461 oz. ASW **Ruler:** Rashid Bin Hamad al-Naimi **Obv:** State emblem, denomination above **Rev:** Head left, denomination below

Date	Mintage	VF20	XF40	MS60	MS63	MS65
ND-1970	1,175	PF65 225				

KM# 20 5 RIYALS
15.00 g., 0.925 Silver 0.4461 oz. ASW **Ruler:** Rashid Bin Hamad al-Naimi **Obv:** State emblem, denomination above **Rev:** Head left, denomination below

Date	Mintage	VF20	XF40	MS60	MS63	MS65
ND-1970	1,175	PF65 225				

KM# 21 5 RIYALS
15.00 g., 0.925 Silver 0.4461 oz. ASW **Ruler:** Rashid Bin Hamad al-Naimi **Obv:** State emblem, denomination above **Rev:** Head 3/4 left, denomination below

Date	Mintage	VF20	XF40	MS60	MS63	MS65
ND-1970	1,175	PF65 225				

KM# 22 5 RIYALS
15.00 g., 0.925 Silver 0.4461 oz. ASW **Ruler:** Rashid Bin Hamad al-Naimi **Obv:** State emblem, denomination above **Rev:** Head left, denomination below

Date	Mintage	VF20	XF40	MS60	MS63	MS65
ND-1970	1,175	PF65 225				

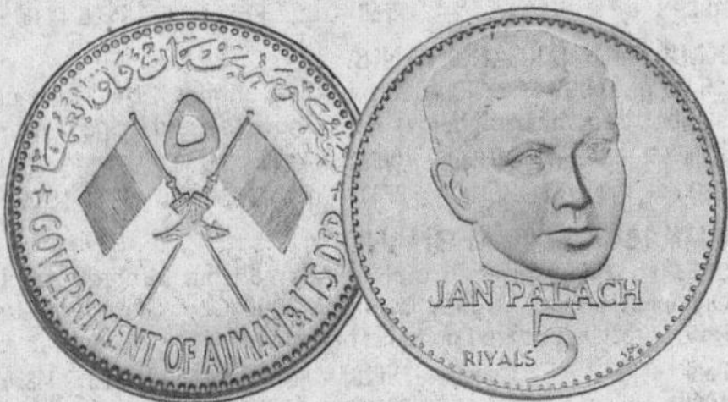

KM# 23 5 RIYALS
15.00 g., 0.925 Silver 0.4461 oz. ASW **Ruler:** Rashid Bin Hamad al-Naimi **Obv:** State emblem, denomination above **Rev:** Head 3/4 right, denomination below

Date	Mintage	VF20	XF40	MS60	MS63	MS65
ND-1970	1,175	PF65 225				

KM# 24 5 RIYALS
15.00 g., 0.925 Silver 0.4461 oz. ASW **Ruler:** Rashid Bin Hamad al-Naimi **Obv:** State emblem, denomination above **Rev:** Head 3/4 left, denomination below

Date	Mintage	VF20	XF40	MS60	MS63	MS65
ND-1970	1,175	PF65 225				

KM# 26 5 RIYALS
15.00 g., 0.925 Silver 0.4461 oz. ASW **Ruler:** Rashid Bin Hamad al-Naimi **Series:** F.A.O. **Obv:** State emblem, denomination above **Rev:** Open hands holding grain divide dates, F.A.O. below

Date	Mintage	VF20	XF40	MS60	MS63	MS65
AH1390-1970	2,000	PF65 275				

Note: This issue is not recognized by the F.A.O.

KM# 27 5 RIYALS
15.00 g., 0.925 Silver 0.4461 oz. ASW **Ruler:** Rashid Bin Hamad al-Naimi **Subject:** Save Venice **Obv:** State emblem, denomination above, bust below **Rev:** Denomination, symbols and legend

Date	Mintage	VF20	XF40	MS60	MS63	MS65
ND-1971	4,800	PF65 175				

KM# 5 7-1/2 RIYALS
23.00 g., 0.925 Silver 0.684 oz. ASW **Ruler:** Rashid Bin Hamad al-Naimi **Subject:** Rashid bin Humaid al-Naimi **Obv:** State emblem, denomination above, bust below **Rev:** Bonefish right, denomination below, circle surrounds

Date	Mintage	VF20	XF40	MS60	MS63	MS65
AH1389-1970	4,350	—	—	75.00	90.00	125
AH1389-1970	650	PF65 200				

KM# 6 7-1/2 RIYALS
23.00 g., 0.925 Silver 0.684 oz. ASW **Ruler:** Rashid Bin Hamad al-Naimi **Obv:** Bust facing divides dates, circle surrounds **Rev:** Barbary Falcon right, denomination above, circle

Date	Mintage	VF20	XF40	MS60	MS63	MS65
AH1389-1970	4,350	—	—	75.00	90.00	125
AH1389-1970	650	PF65 200				

KM# 7 7-1/2 RIYALS
23.00 g., 0.925 Silver 0.684 oz. ASW **Ruler:** Rashid Bin Hamad al-Naimi **Obv:** Bust facing divides dates, circle surrounds **Rev:** Gazelle left, denomination above within circle

Date	Mintage	VF20	XF40	MS60	MS63	MS65
AH1389-1970	4,350	—	—	75.00	90.00	125
AH1389-1970	650	PF65 200				

KM# 13 7-1/2 RIYALS
23.00 g., 0.835 Silver 0.6175 oz. ASW **Ruler:** Rashid Bin Hamad al-Naimi **Subject:** Death of Gamal Abdel Nassar **Obv:** State emblem divides denomination **Rev:** Head left divides dates

Date	Mintage	VF20	XF40	MS60	MS63	MS65
AH1390-1970	6,000	PF65 125				

KM# 9.1 10 RIYALS
30.00 g., 0.925 Silver 0.8922 oz. ASW **Ruler:** Rashid Bin Hamad al-Naimi **Obv:** State emblem, denomination above **Rev:** Head left, denomination at left

Date	Mintage	VF20	XF40	MS60	MS63	MS65
ND-1970	—	PF65 325				
ND-1970 Matte	—	—	—	—	—	325

KM# 9.2 10 RIYALS
30.00 g., 0.925 Silver 0.8922 oz. ASW **Ruler:** Rashid Bin Hamad al-Naimi **Obv:** State emblem, denomination above, PROOF added **Rev:** Head left, denomination at left

Date	Mintage	VF20	XF40	MS60	MS63	MS65
ND-1970	3,200	PF65 125				

KM# 15 25 RIYALS
5.18 g., 0.900 Gold 0.1497 oz. AGW **Ruler:** Rashid Bin Hamad al-Naimi **Subject:** Death of Gamal Abdel Nassar **Obv:** State emblem divides denomination **Rev:** Head left divides dates **Note:** Some examples have a serial number on the obverse below the bust.

Date	Mintage	VF20	XF40	MS60	MS63	MS65
AH1390-1970	1,100	PF65 400				

KM# 28 25 RIYALS
5.18 g., 0.900 Gold 0.1497 oz. AGW **Ruler:** Rashid Bin Hamad al-Naimi **Obv:** State emblem, denomination above **Rev:** Head left, denomination below

Date	Mintage	VF20	XF40	MS60	MS63	MS65
ND-1970	—	PF65 450				

KM# 29 25 RIYALS
5.18 g., 0.900 Gold 0.1497 oz. AGW **Ruler:** Rashid Bin Hamad al-Naimi **Obv:** State emblem, denomination above **Rev:** Head left, denomination below

Date	Mintage	VF20	XF40	MS60	MS63	MS65
ND-1970	—	PF65 450				

KM# 30 25 RIYALS
5.18 g., 0.900 Gold 0.1497 oz. AGW **Ruler:** Rashid Bin Hamad al-Naimi **Obv:** State emblem, denomination above **Rev:** Head left, denomination below

Date	Mintage	VF20	XF40	MS60	MS63	MS65
ND-1970	—	PF65 450				

KM# 31 25 RIYALS
5.18 g., 0.900 Gold 0.1497 oz. AGW **Ruler:** Rashid Bin Hamad al-Naimi **Obv:** State emblem, denomination above **Rev:** Head left, denomination below

Date	Mintage	VF20	XF40	MS60	MS63	MS65
ND-1970	—	PF65 450				

KM# 32 25 RIYALS
5.18 g., 0.900 Gold 0.1497 oz. AGW **Ruler:** Rashid Bin Hamad al-Naimi **Obv:** State emblem, denomination above **Rev:** Head 3/4 left, denomination below

Date	Mintage	VF20	XF40	MS60	MS63	MS65
ND-1970	—	PF65 450				

KM# 33 25 RIYALS
5.18 g., 0.900 Gold 0.1497 oz. AGW **Ruler:** Rashid Bin Hamad al-Naimi **Obv:** State emblem, denomination above **Rev:** Head left, denomination below

Date	Mintage	VF20	XF40	MS60	MS63	MS65
ND-1970	—	PF65 450				

KM# 34 25 RIYALS
5.18 g., 0.900 Gold 0.1497 oz. AGW **Ruler:** Rashid Bin Hamad al-Naimi **Obv:** State emblem, denomination above **Rev:** Head 3/4 right, denomination below

Date	Mintage	VF20	XF40	MS60	MS63	MS65
ND-1970	—	PF65 450				

KM# 35 25 RIYALS
5.18 g., 0.900 Gold 0.1497 oz. AGW **Ruler:** Rashid Bin Hamad al-Naimi **Obv:** State emblem, denomination above **Rev:** Head 3/4 left, denomination below

Date	Mintage	VF20	XF40	MS60	MS63	MS65
ND-1970	—	PF65 450				

KM# 36 25 RIYALS
5.18 g., 0.900 Gold 0.1497 oz. AGW **Ruler:** Rashid Bin Hamad al-Naimi **Rev:** Two men ringing large bell **Rev. Legend:** Save Venice

Date	Mintage	VF20	XF40	MS60	MS63	MS65
ND-1971	—	PF65 425				

KM# 16 50 RIYALS
10.35 g., 0.900 Gold 0.2995 oz. AGW **Ruler:** Rashid Bin Hamad al-Naimi **Subject:** Death of Gamal Abdel Nassar **Obv:** State emblem divides denomination **Rev:** Head left divides dates **Note:** Some examples have a serial number below the bust on the obverse

Date	Mintage	VF20	XF40	MS60	MS63	MS65
AH1390-1970	700	PF65 700				

KM# 39 50 RIYALS
10.35 g., 0.900 Gold 0.2995 oz. AGW **Ruler:** Rashid Bin Hamad al-Naimi **Subject:** Save Venice **Obv:** State emblem, denomination above, bust below **Rev:** Stallion divides denomination

Date	Mintage	VF20	XF40	MS60	MS63	MS65
ND-1971	—	PF65 750				

KM# 41 75 RIYALS
15.53 g., 0.900 Gold 0.4494 oz. AGW **Ruler:** Rashid Bin Hamad al-Naimi **Series:** F.A.O.

Date	Mintage	VF20	XF40	MS60	MS63	MS65
AH1389-1969	—	PF65 1,000				

KM# 10 100 RIYALS
20.70 g., 0.900 Gold 0.599 oz. AGW **Ruler:** Rashid Bin Hamad al-Naimi **Obv:** State emblem, denomination above **Rev:** Head left, denomination at left

Date	Mintage	VF20	XF40	MS60	MS63	MS65
ND-1970	1,000	PF65 1,300				

KM# 40 100 RIYALS
20.70 g., 0.900 Gold 0.599 oz. AGW **Ruler:** Rashid Bin Hamad al-Naimi **Subject:** Save Venice **Obv:** State emblem, denomination above, bust below **Rev:** Courthouse, denomination lower left

Date	Mintage	VF20	XF40	MS60	MS63	MS65
ND-1971	—	PF65 1,350				

ESSAIS

With Assay or Proof

KM#	Date	Mintage	Identification	Mkt Val
E1	1969	1,250	Riyal. Silver. Denomination within circle. Chicken below state emblem, two dates.	65.00
E2	1969	1,250	2 Riyals. Silver. Denomination within circle. Chicken below state emblem, two dates.	75.00
E3	1969	1,250	5 Riyals. Silver. Denomination within circle. Chicken below state emblem, two dates.	85.00
E4	1970	100	Riyal. Denomination within circle. Chicken below state emblem, three dates.	75.00
E5	1970	100	2 Riyals. Denoimination within circle. Chicken below state emblem, three dates.	85.00
E6	1970	100	5 Riyals. Denomination within circle. Chicken below state emblem, three dates.	110
E7	1970	—	5 Riyals. Aluminum. State emblem divides denomination. Head left divides dates.	80.00
E8	1970	—	7-1/2 Riyals. Silver. Denomination above state emblem, bust below divides dates. Fish above denomination, circle surrounds.	175
E9	1970	—	7-1/2 Riyals. Silver. Bust facing divides dates, circle surrounds. Barbary Falcon right, denomination above, circle surrounds.	175
E10	1970	—	7-1/2 Riyals. Aluminum. Bust facing divides dates, circle surrounds. Gazelle left divides denomination, circle surrounds.	145
E11	1970	—	7-1/2 Riyals. Aluminum. State emblem divides denomination. Head left divides dates.	145
E12	ND-1970	800	10 Riyals. KM#9.2.	125

PATTERNS

Including off metal strikes

KM#	Date	Mintage	Identification	Mkt Val
Pn1	1970	—	100 Dirhams. Copper-Nickel.	—

MINT SETS

KM#	Date	Mintage	Identification	Issue Price	Mkt Val
MS1	1969 (3)	—	KM#1.1-3.1	—	100
MS2	1970 (3)	4,350	KM#5-7	—	375

PROOF SETS

KM#	Date	Mintage	Identification	Issue Price	Mkt Val
PS1	1969 (3)	1,200	KM#1.1-3.1	11.22	180
PS2	1970 (8)	1,175	KM#17-24	—	1,800
PS3	1970 (8)	—	KM#28-35	—	2,450
PS4	1970 (4)	—	KM#12, 13, 15, 16	—	875
PS5	1970 (3)	100	KM#E4-6	—	275
PS6	1970 (3)	650	KM#5-7	19.50	600
PS7	1970 (3)	—	KM#E9, E7, 10	—	1,100
PS8	1970 (2)	800	KM#E7, 10	—	1,050
PS9	1970 (2)	5,000	KM#12, 13	9.50	200
PS10	1970 (3)	—	KM#12, 13, 15	—	400
PS11	1970 (3)	—	KM#9.1, 9.2, 10	—	1,200
PS12	1971 (4)	—	KM#27, 36, 39, 40	—	1,975

ALBANIA

MONTENEGRO
BULGARIA
Adriatic Sea
MACEDONIA
ITALY
GREECE
Ionian Sea
Aegean Sea

The Republic of Albania, a Balkan republic bounded by Macedonia, Greece, Montenegro, and the Adriatic Sea, has an area of 11,100 sq. mi. (28,748 sq. km.) and a population of 3.49 million. Capital: Tirane. The country is predominantly agricultural, although recent progress has been made in the manufacturing and mining sectors. Petroleum, chrome, iron, copper, cotton textiles, tobacco and wood products are exported.

Independence was re-established by revolt in 1912, and the present borders established in 1913 by a conference of European powers, which, in 1914, placed Prince William of Wied on the throne; popular discontent forced his abdication within months. In 1920, following World War I occupancy by several nations, a republic was set up. Ahmed Zogu seized the presidency in 1925, and in 1928 he proclaimed himself king with the title of Zog I. King Zog fled when Italy occupied Albania in 1939 and enthroned King Victor Emanuel of Italy. Upon the surrender of Italy to the Allies in 1943, German troops occupied the country. They withdrew in 1944, and communist partisans seized power, naming Gen. Enver Hoxha provisional president. In 1946, following a victory by the communist front in the 1945 elections, a new constitution modeled on that of the USSR was adopted. In accordance with the constitution of Dec. 28, 1976, the official name of Albania was changed from the Peoples Republic of Albania to the Peoples Socialist Republic of Albania.

Albania's former communists were routed in elections. March 1992, amid economic collapse and social unrest, Sali Berisha was elected as the first non-communist president since World War II. Rexhep Mejdani, elected president in 1997, succeeds him.

RULERS

Ahmed Bey Zogu - King Zog I, 1928-1939
Vittorio Emanuele III, 1939-1943

MINT MARKS

L – London
R - Rome
V – Vienna

MONETARY SYSTEM

100 Qindar Leku = 1 Lek
100 Qindar Ari = 1 Frang Ar = 5 Lek

KINGDOM

STANDARD COINAGE

KM# 1 5 QINDAR LEKU
Bronze **Ruler:** Zog I **Obv:** Lion head left **Rev:** Value above oak branch

Date	Mintage	VF20	XF40	MS60	MS63	MS65
1926 R	512,000	22.00	60.00	95.00	150	250

KM# 2 10 QINDAR LEKU
Bronze **Obv:** Eagle's head right **Rev:** Value between olive branches

Date	Mintage	VF20	XF40	MS60	MS63	MS65
1926 R	511,000	16.00	50.00	90.00	150	200

KM# 14 QINDAR AR
Bronze **Ruler:** Zog I **Obv:** Two headed Eagle **Rev:** Value above oak leaves and acorn

Date	Mintage	VF20	XF40	MS60	MS63	MS65
1935 R	2,000,000	2.50	8.00	18.00	30.00	45.00

KM# 15 2 QINDAR ARI
Bronze, 21 mm. **Ruler:** Zog I **Obv:** Two headed Eagle **Rev:** Value above oak leaves

Date	Mintage	VF20	XF40	MS60	MS63	MS65
1935 R	1,500,000	3.50	11.00	22.00	35.00	50.00

KM# 3 1/4 LEKU
4.00 g., Nickel, 21.5 mm. **Obv:** Lion advancing left **Rev:** Oak branch above value **Edge:** Reeded

Date	Mintage	VF20	XF40	MS60	MS63	MS65
1926 R	506,000	3.50	8.00	25.00	52.00	60.00
1927 R	756,000	3.50	8.00	18.00	40.00	55.00

KM# 4 1/2 LEK
6.00 g., Nickel, 24 mm. **Obv:** Two headed Eagle **Rev:** Hercules wrestling Nemean lion

Date	Mintage	VF20	XF40	MS60	MS63	MS65
1926 R	1,002,000	3.00	6.00	15.00	25.00	35.00

KM# 13 1/2 LEK
6.00 g., Nickel, 24 mm. **Ruler:** Zog I **Obv:** Kings arms **Rev:** Hercules wrestling Nemean lion

Date	Mintage	VF20	XF40	MS60	MS63	MS65
1930 V	500,000	3.00	6.00	19.00	25.00	35.00
1931 L	—	PF60 150	PF63 175	PF65 250		
1931 L	500,000	3.00	6.00	19.00	25.00	35.00

KM# 5 LEK
8.00 g., Nickel, 26.7 mm. **Obv:** Head right **Rev:** Caped man on horse right **Edge:** Reeded

Date	Mintage	VF20	XF40	MS60	MS63	MS65
1926 R	1,004,000	2.00	4.00	10.00	26.00	35.00
1927 R	506,000	3.00	7.00	18.00	38.00	45.00
1930 V	1,250,000	1.50	3.00	10.00	24.00	35.00
1931 L	1,000,000	2.00	4.00	10.00	26.00	35.00
1931 L	—	PF60 150	PF63 225	PF65 275		

KM# 6 FRANG AR
5.00 g., 0.835 Silver 0.1342 oz. ASW, 23 mm. **Obv:** Helmeted head right **Rev:** Prow of ancient ship

Date	Mintage	VF20	XF40	MS60	MS63	MS65
1927 R	100,000	70.00	150	200	350	500
1928 R	60,000	70.00	150	200	350	500

KM# 16 FRANG AR
5.00 g., 0.835 Silver 0.1342 oz. ASW, 23 mm. **Ruler:** Zog I **Obv:** Head right, date below **Rev:** King's Arms, value below

Date	Mintage	VF20	XF40	MS60	MS63	MS65
1935	700,000	5.00	10.00	30.00	50.00	75.00
1937	600,000	5.00	10.00	30.00	50.00	75.00

KM# 18 FRANG AR
5.00 g., 0.835 Silver 0.1342 oz. ASW, 23 mm. **Ruler:** Zog I **Subject:** 25th Anniversary of Independence **Obv:** Head right, date below **Rev:** Kings Arms

Date	Mintage	VF20	XF40	MS60	MS63	MS65
1937 R	50,000	8.00	20.00	45.00	75.00	150

KM# 7 2 FRANGA ARI
10.00 g., 0.835 Silver 0.2685 oz. ASW, 27 mm. **Obv:** Standing eagle with wings spread divides denomination **Rev:** Seed sower

Date	Mintage	VF20	XF40	MS60	MS63	MS65
1926	50,000	60.00	130	250	420	600
1927	50,000	60.00	130	250	420	600
1928 R	60,000	60.00	130	250	420	600

KM# 17 2 FRANGA ARI
10.00 g., 0.835 Silver 0.2685 oz. ASW, 27 mm. **Ruler:** Zog I **Obv:** Head right, date below **Rev:** Kings Arms, value below

Date	Mintage	VF20	XF40	MS60	MS63	MS65
1935 R	150,000	12.00	50.00	95.00	150	700

KM# 19 2 FRANGA ARI
10.00 g., 0.835 Silver 0.2685 oz. ASW, 27 mm. **Ruler:** Zog I **Subject:** 25th Anniversary of Independence **Obv:** Head right, date below **Rev:** Kings arms, value below

Date	Mintage	VF20	XF40	MS60	MS63	MS65
1937 R	25,000	15.00	50.00	100	150	300

KM# 8.1 5 FRANGA ARI
25.00 g., 0.900 Silver 0.7234 oz. ASW, 37 mm. **Ruler:** Zog I **Obv:** Head right **Rev:** Man with plow left, value below

Date	Mintage	VF20	XF40	MS60	MS63	MS65
1926	60,000	100	220	475	850	1,000
1927	Est. 40000	—	—	—	—	—

Note: Only exist as provas

KM# 8.2 5 FRANGA ARI

25.00 g., 0.900 Silver 0.7234 oz. ASW, 37 mm. **Ruler:** Zog I **Obv:** Head right, star below head **Rev:** Man with plow left, value below

Date	Mintage	VF20	XF40	MS60	MS63	MS65
1926	Inc. above	130	300	500	850	1,000

KM# 9 10 FRANGA ARI

3.23 g., 0.900 Gold 0.0933 oz. AGW **Ruler:** Zog I **Obv:** Head left **Rev:** Double imperial eagle divides denomination below

Date	Mintage	VF20	XF40	MS60	MS63	MS65
1927 R	6,000	185	230	450	550	—

KM# 10 20 FRANGA ARI

6.45 g., 0.900 Gold 0.1867 oz. AGW, 21 mm. **Ruler:** Zog I **Obv:** Head left **Rev:** Double imperial eagle divides denomination below

Date	Mintage	VF20	XF40	MS60	MS63	MS65
1926 R	—	250	325	425	500	800
1927 R	6,000	250	300	450	550	850

KM# 12 20 FRANGA ARI

6.45 g., 0.900 Gold 0.1867 oz. AGW, 21 mm. **Subject:** George Kastrioti "Skanderbeg" **Obv:** Lion of St. Mark right divides denomination, date below **Rev:** Bust right

Date	Mintage	VF20	XF40	MS60	MS63	MS65
1926 Fasces	100	—	—	4,600	7,300	—
Note: 90 pieces were reported melted						
1926 R	5,900	250	325	450	550	825
1927 V	5,053	250	300	425	500	750

KM# 20 20 FRANGA ARI

6.45 g., 0.900 Gold 0.1867 oz. AGW, 21 mm. **Ruler:** Zog I **Subject:** 25th Anniversary of Independence **Obv:** Head right, date below **Rev:** Kings arms, denomination below

Date	Mintage	VF20	XF40	MS60	MS63	MS65
1937 R	2,500	—	375	700	1,100	—

KM# 22 20 FRANGA ARI

6.45 g., 0.900 Gold 0.1867 oz. AGW, 21 mm. **Ruler:** Zog I **Subject:** Marriage of King Zog to Countess Geraldine Apponyi, April 27, 1938 **Obv:** Head right, date below **Rev:** Kings arms, denomination below

Date	Mintage	VF20	XF40	MS60	MS63	MS65
1938 R	2,500	—	325	675	1,000	1,500

KM# 24 20 FRANGA ARI

6.45 g., 0.900 Gold 0.1867 oz. AGW, 21 mm. **Ruler:** Zog I **Subject:** 10th Anniversary - Reign of King Zog **Obv:** Head right, date below **Rev:** Kings arms, denomination below

Date	Mintage	VF20	XF40	MS60	MS63	MS65
1938 R	1,000	—	500	900	1,250	—

Note: Pieces struck in 1969 from new dies

KM# 25 50 FRANGA ARI

16.13 g., 0.900 Gold 0.4667 oz. AGW **Ruler:** Zog I **Subject:** 10th Anniversary - Reign of King Zog **Obv:** Head right, date below **Rev:** Kings Arms, denomination below

Date	Mintage	VF20	XF40	MS60	MS63	MS65
1938 R	600	—	900	2,200	3,000	—

Note: Pieces struck in 1969 from new dies

KM# 11.1 100 FRANGA ARI

32.26 g., 0.900 Gold 0.9334 oz. AGW, 35 mm. **Ruler:** Zog I **Obv:** Head left **Rev:** Biga right, denomination below

Date	Mintage	VF20	XF40	MS60	MS63	MS65
1926 R	6,614	—	1,200	1,750	2,150	—

Note: Mintage figures includes provas, Pr14-16

KM# 11.2 100 FRANGA ARI

32.26 g., 0.900 Gold 0.9334 oz. AGW, 35 mm. **Ruler:** Zog I **Obv:** Head left, star below **Rev:** Biga right, denomination below

Date	Mintage	VF20	XF40	MS60	MS63	MS65
1926 R	Inc. above	—	1,750	1,950	3,350	—

KM# 11.3 100 FRANGA ARI

32.26 g., 0.900 Gold 0.9334 oz. AGW, 35 mm. **Ruler:** Zog I **Obv:** Head left, two stars below **Rev:** Biga right, denomination below

Date	Mintage	VF20	XF40	MS60	MS63	MS65
1926 R	Inc. above	—	1,600	1,800	2,850	—

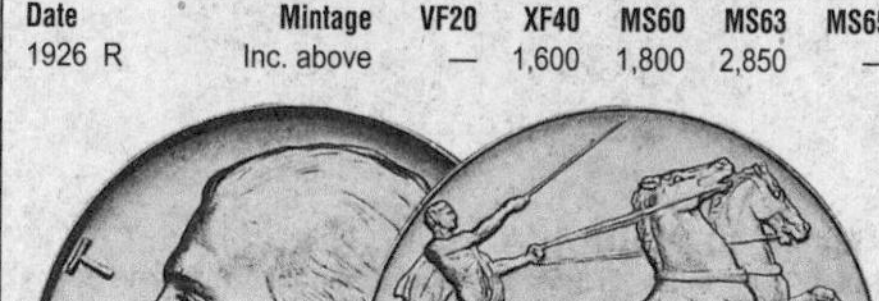

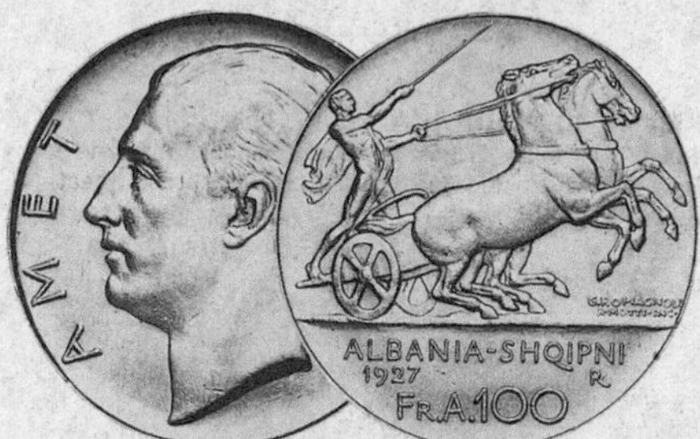

KM# 11a.1 100 FRANGA ARI

32.26 g., 0.900 Gold 0.9334 oz. AGW, 35 mm. **Ruler:** Zog I **Obv:** Head left **Rev:** Biga right, denomination below

Date	Mintage	VF20	XF40	MS60	MS63	MS65
1927 R	5,000	—	1,600	1,800	2,850	—

Note: Mintage figure includes provas, Pr17-19

KM# 11a.2 100 FRANGA ARI

32.26 g., 0.900 Gold 0.9334 oz. AGW **Ruler:** Zog I **Obv:** Head left, star below **Rev:** Biga right, denomination below

Date	Mintage	VF20	XF40	MS60	MS63	MS65
1927 R	Inc. above	—	1,700	1,900	3,250	—

KM# 11a.3 100 FRANGA ARI

32.26 g., 0.900 Gold 0.9334 oz. AGW **Ruler:** Zog I **Obv:** Head left, two stars below **Rev:** Biga right, denomination below

Date	Mintage	VF20	XF40	MS60	MS63	MS65
1927 R	Inc. above	—	1,700	1,900	3,250	—

KM# 21 100 FRANGA ARI

32.26 g., 0.900 Gold 0.9334 oz. AGW, 35 mm. **Ruler:** Zog I **Subject:** 25th Anniversary of Independence **Obv:** Head right, date below **Rev:** Kings arms divide denomination below

Date	Mintage	VF20	XF40	MS60	MS63	MS65
1937 R	500	—	1,800	2,650	5,250	—

KM# 23 100 FRANGA ARI

32.26 g., 0.900 Gold 0.9334 oz. AGW, 35 mm. **Ruler:** Zog I **Subject:** Marriage of King Zog to Countess Geraldine Apponyi, April 27, 1938 **Obv:** Head right, date below **Rev:** Kings Arms divide denomination below

Date	Mintage	VF20	XF40	MS60	MS63	MS65
1938 R	500	—	1,800	2,650	5,250	—

KM# 26 100 FRANGA ARI

32.26 g., 0.900 Gold 0.9334 oz. AGW, 35 mm. **Ruler:** Zog I **Subject:** 10th Anniversary - Reign of King Zog **Obv:** Head right, date below **Rev:** Kings Arms divide denomination below

Date	Mintage	VF20	XF40	MS60	MS63	MS65
1938 R	500	—	1,800	2,650	5,250	—

Note: Pieces restruck in 1969 from new dies

ITALIAN OCCUPATION WWII

KM# 27 0.05 LEK

Aluminum-Bronze, 20 mm. **Ruler:** Vittorio Emanuele III **Obv:** Head right **Rev:** Value below oak branch **Edge:** Plain

Date	Mintage	VF20	XF40	MS60	MS63	MS65
1940 R	1,400,000	3.00	6.00	16.00	32.00	—
1941 R Rare	200,000	75.00	100	200	350	—

KM# 28 0.10 LEK

Aluminum-Bronze **Ruler:** Vittorio Emanuele III **Obv:** Head left **Rev:** Value below olive branch

Date	Mintage	VF20	XF40	MS60	MS63	MS65
1940 R	550,000	4.00	8.00	22.00	38.00	—
1941 R	250,000	10.00	25.00	75.00	100	—

KM# 29 0.20 LEK

4.00 g., Stainless Steel, 21.7 mm. **Ruler:** Vittorio Emanuele III **Obv:** Helmeted head right **Rev:** Double eagle between fasces, value below

Date	Mintage	VF20	XF40	MS60	MS63	MS65
1939 R	900,000	1.00	4.00	8.00	15.00	—
Note: 1939 dated coins exist in 2 varieties, magnetic and non-magnetic						
1940 R	700,000	1.00	2.00	7.00	18.00	—
1941 R	1,400,000	1.00	2.00	5.00	14.00	—

KM# 30 0.50 LEK

Stainless Steel **Ruler:** Vittorio Emanuele III **Obv:** Helmeted head left **Rev:** Double eagle between fasces, value below

Date	Mintage	VF20	XF40	MS60	MS63	MS65
1939 R	100,000	2.00	5.00	12.00	30.00	—
Note: 1939 dated coins exist in two varieties, magnetic and non-magnetic						
1940 R	500,000	1.50	3.00	8.00	20.00	—
1941 R	—	1.50	3.00	8.00	20.00	—

KM# 31 LEK

8.00 g., Stainless Steel, 26.7 mm. **Ruler:** Vittorio Emanuele III **Obv:** Helmeted head right **Rev:** Double eagle between fasces, value below **Note:** Coins dated after 1939 were not struck for circulation.

Date	Mintage	VF20	XF40	MS60	MS63	MS65
1939 R	2,100,000	1.50	2.50	5.00	16.00	—
Note: 1939 dated coins exist in two varieties, magnetic and non-magnetic						
1940 R Rare	1,500,000	—	—	—	—	—
Note: The official mintage figure is large, but few examples are known						
1941 R Rare	1,000,000	—	—	—	—	—
Note: The official mintage figure is large, but few examples are known						

KM# 32 2 LEK

Stainless Steel **Ruler:** Vittorio Emanuele III **Obv:** Helmeted head left **Rev:** Double eagle between fasces, value below **Note:** Coins dated after 1939 were not struck for circulation.

Date	Mintage	VF20	XF40	MS60	MS63	MS65
1939 R	1,300,000	2.00	4.00	9.00	22.00	—
Note: 1939 dated coins exist in 2 varieties, magnetic and non-magnetic						
1940 R Rare	—	—	—	—	—	—
1941 R Rare	—	—	—	—	—	—

KM# 33 5 LEK

5.00 g., 0.835 Silver 0.1342 oz. ASW **Ruler:** Vittorio Emanuele III **Obv:** Head left **Rev:** Double eagle between fasces, value

Date	Mintage	VF20	XF40	MS60	MS63	MS65
1939 R	1,350,000	7.00	15.00	40.00	80.00	100

KM# 34 10 LEK

10.00 g., 0.835 Silver 0.2685 oz. ASW **Ruler:** Vittorio Emanuele III **Obv:** Head right **Rev:** Double eagle between fasces, value

Date	Mintage	VF20	XF40	MS60	MS63	MS65
1939 R	175,000	40.00	70.00	120	220	275

PEOPLE'S SOCIALIST REPUBLIC

1945 - 1990

KM# 39 5 QINDARKA

0.75 g., Aluminum, 18 mm. **Obv:** National Arms, date below **Rev:** Five stars across top, value in center of wheat

Date	Mintage	VF20	XF40	MS60	MS63	MS65
1964	—	0.10	0.25	0.50	1.25	1.50

KM# 44 5 QINDARKA

0.80 g., Aluminum, 18 mm. **Subject:** 25th Anniversary of Liberation **Obv:** National Arms, two dates below **Rev:** Five stars across top, value in center of wheat

Date	Mintage	VF20	XF40	MS60	MS63	MS65
ND (1969)	—	0.10	0.20	0.30	0.85	1.25

KM# 71 5 QINDARKA

Aluminum **Obv:** National Arms, date below **Rev:** Value between wheat **Edge:** Plain

Date	Mintage	VF20	XF40	MS60	MS63	MS65
1988	—	—	—	0.20	0.65	1.00

KM# 40 10 QINDARKA

1.09 g., Aluminum, 17.95 mm. **Obv:** National Arms, date below **Rev:** Five stars across top, value at center between wheat

Date	Mintage	VF20	XF40	MS60	MS63	MS65
1964	—	0.15	0.30	0.60	1.50	1.75

KM# 45 10 QINDARKA

1.20 g., Aluminum, 20 mm. **Subject:** 25th Anniversary of Liberation **Obv:** National Arms, two dates **Rev:** Five stars across top, value at center between wheat

Date	Mintage	VF20	XF40	MS60	MS63	MS65
ND (1969)	—	0.10	0.20	0.35	1.00	1.25

KM# 60 10 QINDARKA

Aluminum, 20 mm. **Obv:** National Arms, date below **Rev:** Value at center between wheat **Edge:** Plain

Date	Mintage	VF20	XF40	MS60	MS63	MS65
1988	—	—	—	0.30	0.80	1.25

KM# 41 20 QINDARKA

1.51 g., Aluminum, 22 mm. **Obv:** National Arms, date below **Rev:** Five stars across top, value at center between wheat

Date	Mintage	VF20	XF40	MS60	MS63	MS65
1964	—	0.20	0.40	0.60	1.75	2.00

KM# 46 20 QINDARKA

1.60 g., Aluminum, 22 mm. **Subject:** 25th Anniversary of Liberation **Obv:** National Arms, two dates **Rev:** Five stars across top, value at center between wheat

Date	Mintage	VF20	XF40	MS60	MS63	MS65
ND (1969)	—	0.15	0.30	0.50	1.25	1.50

KM# 65 20 QINDARKA

Aluminum **Obv:** National Arms, date below **Rev:** Value at center between wheat

Date	Mintage	VF20	XF40	MS60	MS63	MS65
1988	—	—	—	0.20	0.80	1.25

KM# 42 50 QINDARKA

2.00 g., Aluminum, 24.49 mm. **Obv:** National Arms, date below **Rev:** Five stars across top, value at center between wheat

Date	Mintage	VF20	XF40	MS60	MS63	MS65
1964	—	0.50	0.75	2.00	4.00	6.00

KM# 47 50 QINDARKA

2.00 g., Aluminum, 24.4 mm. **Subject:** 25th Anniversary of Liberation **Rev:** Two half-length figures holding torch aloft, value below

Date	Mintage	VF20	XF40	MS60	MS63	MS65
ND (1969)	—	0.30	0.50	1.00	2.00	3.00

KM# 72 50 QINDARKA

2.00 g., Aluminum, 24.1 mm. **Obv:** National Arms, date below **Rev:** Value at center between wheat, inside beaded circle **Edge:** Plain

Date	Mintage	VF20	XF40	MS60	MS63	MS65
1988	—	—	—	0.50	1.40	2.25

KM# 35 1/2 LEKU

2.10 g., Zinc **Obv:** National Arms inside 3/4 circle of stars **Rev:** Value inside circle of stars, date at bottom **Edge:** Plain

Date	Mintage	VF20	XF40	MS60	MS63	MS65
1947	—	0.80	2.00	5.00	7.00	—
1957	—	0.50	1.00	2.00	3.00	—

KM# 36 LEK

3.20 g., Zinc **Obv:** National Arms inside 3/4 circle of stars **Rev:** Value inside circle of stars, date at bottom **Edge:** Plain

Date	Mintage	VF20	XF40	MS60	MS63	MS65
1947	—	1.00	3.00	6.00	8.00	—
1957	—	0.75	1.50	3.00	4.00	—

KM# 43 LEK

2.30 g., Aluminum, 26.5 mm. **Obv:** National Arms between stars, date at bottom **Rev:** Five stars across top, value at center of wheat

Date	Mintage	VF20	XF40	MS60	MS63	MS65
1964	—	0.50	1.00	2.00	4.00	5.50

KM# 48 LEK

2.30 g., Aluminum, 26.5 mm. **Subject:** 25th Anniversary of Liberation **Obv:** National Arms between stars, two dates at bottom **Rev:** Armed man with knee on man on ground, value below

Date	Mintage	VF20	XF40	MS60	MS63	MS65
ND (1969)	—	0.35	0.75	1.25	3.00	5.00

KM# 66 LEK

Aluminum-Bronze **Obv:** National Arms inside legend, date below **Rev:** Large value above wheat inside beaded circle

Date	Mintage	VF20	XF40	MS60	MS63	MS65
1988	—	—	—	0.50	1.80	2.25

KM# 74 LEK

2.00 g., Aluminum, 24.2 mm. **Obv:** National Arms, date below **Rev:** Large value above wheat inside beaded circle

Date	Mintage	VF20	XF40	MS60	MS63	MS65
1988	—	—	—	0.40	1.60	2.00

KM# 37 2 LEKE

4.00 g., Zinc **Obv:** National Arms within 3/4 circle of stars, beaded edge **Rev:** Large value at center of circle stars, date below, beaded edge **Edge:** Plain

Date	Mintage	VF20	XF40	MS60	MS63	MS65
1947	—	1.25	3.00	6.00	8.00	—
1957	—	0.75	1.50	3.00	4.00	—

KM# 67 2 LEKE

7.60 g., Copper-Nickel, 26 mm. **Subject:** 45th Anniversary - WWII **Obv:** National Arms, date below **Rev:** Armed man standing inside star, right arm raised, value to right

Date	Mintage	VF20	XF40	MS60	MS63	MS65
1989	—	—	—	1.20	4.00	6.00

KM# 73 2 LEKE

Copper-Nickel **Obv:** National Arms, date below **Rev:** Large value above wheat within beaded circle **Edge:** Plain

Date	Mintage	VF20	XF40	MS60	MS63	MS65
1989	—	—	—	1.20	4.00	5.50

KM# 38 5 LEKE

6.20 g., Zinc, 26.6 mm. **Obv:** National Arms within 3/4 circle of stars **Rev:** Large value within circle of stars, date below **Edge:** Plain

Date	Mintage	VF20	XF40	MS60	MS63	MS65
1947	—	1.75	4.50	8.00	10.00	—
1957	—	1.00	2.00	3.50	5.00	—

KM# 49.1 5 LEKE

16.66 g., 0.999 Silver 0.5351 oz. ASW **Subject:** 500th Anniversary - Liga Lissi Skanderbeg's Victory Over the Turks **Obv:** Arms on shield, swords behind, flanking sides, cap on top, two dates below shield **Rev:** Arms above denomination, without date below, oval fineness countermark punched in

Date	Mintage	VF20	XF40	MS60	MS63	MS65
ND (1969)	8,540	PF65 14.00				

Note: Countermarks for 1968 and 1969 coins were hand positioned, then punched. The result is a variety of countermark positions, to the left and right of LEKE

KM# 49.2 5 LEKE

16.66 g., 0.999 Silver 0.5351 oz. ASW **Obv:** Arms on shield, cap above shield, swords behind, flanking sides, two dates below shield **Rev:** Denomination and date below arms

Date	Mintage	VF20	XF40	MS60	MS63	MS65
1969	1,500	PF65 35.00				

Note: Countermarks for 1968 and 1969 coins were hand positioned, then punched. The result is a variety of countermark positions, to the left and right of LEKE

KM# 49.3 5 LEKE

16.66 g., 0.999 Silver 0.5351 oz. ASW **Obv:** Arms on shield, cap above shield, swords behind flanking sides, two dates below **Rev:** Denomination and date below arms, oval fineness in relief

Date	Mintage	VF20	XF40	MS60	MS63	MS65
1970	500	PF65 55.00				

Note: For the 1970 issue the fineness marking has been incorporated in the dies

KM# 57 5 LEKE

28.20 g., Copper-Nickel, 38.7 mm. **Subject:** Seaport of Durazzo **Obv:** National Arms, date below **Rev:** Seaport left of sailing ship, denomination below

Date	Mintage	VF20	XF40	MS60	MS63	MS65
1987	Est. 50000	—	—	7.00	14.00	20.00

KM# 57a 5 LEKE

50.00 g., 0.900 Gold 1.4468 oz. AGW **Subject:** Seaport of Durazzo **Obv:** National arms, date below **Rev:** Seaport left of sailing ship, denomination below

Date	Mintage	VF20	XF40	MS60	MS63	MS65
1987	5	PF65 3,750				

KM# 61 5 LEKE

28.20 g., Copper-Nickel, 38.7 mm. **Subject:** 42nd Anniversary of First Railroad **Obv:** Steam locomotive and passenger train emerging from tunnel at left, date at lower left, denomination below **Rev:** Diesel locomotive and train emerging from tunnel on right, dates below **Edge:** Reeded

Date	Mintage	VF20	XF40	MS60	MS63	MS65
1988	20,000	—	—	7.00	15.00	22.00

KM# 50.1 10 LEKE

33.33 g., 0.999 Silver 1.0705 oz. ASW **Subject:** 500th Anniversary - Death of Prince Skanderbeg **Obv:** Figure on horseback right, divides dates **Rev:** Oval fineness countermark punched in, no date below; value below arms

Date	Mintage	VF20	XF40	MS60	MS63	MS65
ND (1968)	8,540	PF65 28.50				

Note: Countermark for 1968 and 1969 coins were hand positioned, then punched. The result is a variety of countermark positions, to the left and right of LEKE

KM# 50.2 10 LEKE

33.33 g., 0.999 Silver 1.0705 oz. ASW **Obv:** Figure on horseback right, divides dates **Rev:** Denomination and date below arms

Date	Mintage	VF20	XF40	MS60	MS63	MS65
1969	1,500	PF65 65.00				

Note: Countermark for 1968 and 1969 coins were hand positioned, then punched. The result is a variety of countermark positions, to the left and right of LEKE

KM# 50.3 10 LEKE

33.33 g., 0.999 Silver 1.0705 oz. ASW **Obv:** Figure on horseback right, divides dates **Rev:** Oval fineness is in relief, date and value below arms

Date	Mintage	VF20	XF40	MS60	MS63	MS65
1970	500	PF65 75.00				

Note: For the 1970 issues the fineness marking has been incorporated in the dies

KM# 50.4 10 LEKE

33.33 g., 0.999 Silver 1.0705 oz. ASW **Obv:** Figure on horseback right, divides dates **Rev:** Hallmark countermark left of LEKE, oval fineness countermark in relief, date and value below arms

Date	Mintage	VF20	XF40	MS60	MS63	MS65
1970	Inc. above	PF65 70.00				

Note: For the 1970 issues the fineness marking has been incorporated in the dies

KM# 51.1 20 LEKE

3.95 g., 0.900 Gold 0.1143 oz. AGW **Subject:** 500th Anniversary - Death of Prince Skanderbeg **Obv:** Skanderbeg helmet within wreath, scythe at left of helmet **Rev:** Arms, value below, oval fineness countermark punched in

Date	Mintage	VF20	XF40	MS60	MS63	MS65
1968	2,920	PF65 200				

Note: Countermark for 1968 and 1969 coins were hand positioned, then punched. The result is a variety of countermark positions, to the left and right of LEKE

KM# 51.2 20 LEKE

3.95 g., 0.900 Gold 0.1143 oz. AGW **Obv:** Skanderbeg helmet within wreath, scythe at left of helmet **Rev:** Without fineness countermark (error)

Date	Mintage	VF20	XF40	MS60	MS63	MS65
1968	Inc. above	PF65 200				

KM# 51.3 20 LEKE

3.95 g., 0.900 Gold 0.1143 oz. AGW **Obv:** Skanderbeg helmet within wreath, scythe at left of helmet **Rev:** Cornucopia countermark at right of LEKE **Note:** Variety of countermark positions.

Date	Mintage	VF20	XF40	MS60	MS63	MS65
1968 Paris	24	—	—	—	450	550

KM# 51.4 20 LEKE

3.95 g., 0.900 Gold 0.1143 oz. AGW **Obv:** Skanderbeg helmet within wreath, scythe at left **Rev:** Date added below arms **Note:** Variety of countermark positions.

Date	Mintage	VF20	XF40	MS60	MS63	MS65
1969	650	PF65 225				

KM# 51.5 20 LEKE

3.95 g., 0.900 Gold 0.1143 oz. AGW **Obv:** Skanderbeg helmet within wreath, scythe to left of helmet **Rev:** Date below arms, oval fineness in relief, incorporated in dies

Date	Mintage	VF20	XF40	MS60	MS63	MS65
1970	500	PF65 230				

KM# 51.6 20 LEKE

3.95 g., 0.900 Gold 0.1143 oz. AGW **Obv:** Skanderbeg helmet within wreath, scythe to left of helmet **Rev:** Sunken countermark 1 AR left of LEKE and raised oval fineness countermark on right incorporated into the dies

Date	Mintage	VF20	XF40	MS60	MS63	MS65
1970	—	PF65 265				

KM# 52.1 25 LEKE

83.33 g., 0.999 Silver 2.6764 oz. ASW, 60 mm. **Obv:** Dance with swords, date below **Rev:** Denomination below arms, oval fineness countermark

Date	Mintage	VF20	XF40	MS60	MS63	MS65
1968	8,540	PF65 69.00				

Note: Countermarks for 1968 and 1969 coins were hand positioned, then punched; the result is a variety of countermark positions, to the left and the right of LEKE

KM# 52.2 25 LEKE

83.33 g., 0.999 Silver 2.6764 oz. ASW, 60 mm. **Obv:** Dance with swords, date below **Rev:** Denomination below arms, oval fineness countermark

Date	Mintage	VF20	XF40	MS60	MS63	MS65
1969	1,500	PF65 100				

KM# 52.3 25 LEKE

83.33 g., 0.999 Silver 2.6764 oz. ASW, 60 mm. **Obv:** Dance with swords, without date **Rev:** Oval fineness countermark in relief **Note:** Illustration reduced.

Date	Mintage	VF20	XF40	MS60	MS63	MS65
1970	500	PF65 110				

Note: For the 1970 issue the fineness marking has been incorporated in the dies

KM# 53.1 50 LEKE

9.87 g., 0.900 Gold 0.2856 oz. AGW **Obv:** Argirocastrum Ruins, date below **Rev:** Oval fineness countermark

Date	Mintage	VF20	XF40	MS60	MS63	MS65
1968	3,120	PF65 475				

KM# 53.2 50 LEKE

9.87 g., 0.900 Gold 0.2856 oz. AGW **Obv:** Argirocastrum ruins, date below **Rev:** Date below arms, oval fineness countermark, value below date

Date	Mintage	VF20	XF40	MS60	MS63	MS65
1969	500	PF65 525				

KM# 53.3 50 LEKE

9.87 g., 0.900 Gold 0.2856 oz. AGW **Obv:** Ruins, without date **Rev:** Oval fineness countermark in relief

Date	Mintage	VF20	XF40	MS60	MS63	MS65
1970	100	PF65 550				

Note: For the 1970 issue the fineness marking has been incorporated in the dies

KM# 58 50 LEKE

168.15 g., 0.925 Silver 5.0007 oz. ASW, 65 mm. **Subject:** Seaport of Durazzo **Obv:** National arms, date below **Rev:** Seaport left of sailing ship, denomination below **Note:** Illustration reduced.

Date	Mintage	VF20	XF40	MS60	MS63	MS65
1987	Est. 15000	PF65 130				

KM# 58a 50 LEKE

155.50 g., 0.999 Gold 4.9944 oz. AGW **Subject:** Seaport of Durazzo **Obv:** National arms, date below **Rev:** Seaport left of sailing ship, denomination below

Date	Mintage	VF20	XF40	MS60	MS63	MS65
1987	5	PF65 9,500				

KM# 62 50 LEKE

168.15 g., 0.925 Silver 5.0007 oz. ASW, 65 mm. **Subject:** 42nd Anniversary - First Railroad **Obv:** Steam locomotive and passenger train emerging from tunnel at left, date at left, denomination below **Rev:** Diesel locomotive and passenger train emerging from tunnel at right, dates below **Note:** Tunnel is a hole in the coin.

Date	Mintage	VF20	XF40	MS60	MS63	MS65
1988	7,500	PF65 275				

KM# 54.1 100 LEKE

19.75 g., 0.900 Gold 0.5715 oz. AGW **Obv:** Peasant girl in national dress, date below **Rev:** Oval fineness countermark

Date	Mintage	VF20	XF40	MS60	MS63	MS65
1968	3,470	PF65 950				

KM# 54.2 100 LEKE

19.75 g., 0.900 Gold 0.5715 oz. AGW **Obv:** Peasant girl in national dress, date below **Rev:** Date below arms, oval fineness countermark

Date	Mintage	VF20	XF40	MS60	MS63	MS65
1969	450	PF65 1,050				

KM# 54.3 100 LEKE

19.75 g., 0.900 Gold 0.5715 oz. AGW **Obv:** Without date **Rev:** Oval fineness countermark in relief incorporated into the dies

Date	Mintage	VF20	XF40	MS60	MS63	MS65
1970	Inc. above	PF65 1,100				

KM# 59 100 LEKE

6.45 g., 0.900 Gold 0.1866 oz. AGW **Subject:** Seaport of Durazzo **Obv:** National arms, date below **Rev:** Seaport left of sailing ship, denomination below

Date	Mintage	VF20	XF40	MS60	MS63	MS65
1987	5,000	PF65 325				

KM# 63 100 LEKE

6.45 g., 0.900 Gold 0.1866 oz. AGW **Subject:** 42nd Anniversary - First Railroad **Obv:** Train engine emerging from tunnel **Rev:** Caboose entering tunnel **Note:** Without hole in coin

Date	Mintage	VF20	XF40	MS60	MS63	MS65
1988	2,000	PF65 375				

KM# 55.1 200 LEKE

39.49 g., 0.900 Gold 1.1427 oz. AGW **Subject:** Buthrotum Ruins **Obv:** Head right, date at left, ruins in background **Rev:** Arms above denomination

Date	Mintage	VF20	XF40	MS60	MS63	MS65
1968	2,170	PF65 1,950				

KM# 55.2 200 LEKE

39.49 g., 0.900 Gold 1.1427 oz. AGW **Obv:** Head right, date at left, ruins in background **Rev:** Date below arms, oval fineness countermark in a variety of positions

Date	Mintage	VF20	XF40	MS60	MS63	MS65
1969	200	PF65 2,150				

KM# 55.3 200 LEKE

39.49 g., 0.900 Gold 1.1427 oz. AGW **Obv:** Head right, ruins in background, without date **Rev:** Oval fineness countermark in relief incorporated into the die

Date	Mintage	VF20	XF40	MS60	MS63	MS65
1970	Inc. above	PF65 2,250				

KM# 56.1 500 LEKE

98.74 g., 0.900 Gold 2.8571 oz. AGW **Subject:** 500th Anniversary - Death of Prince Skanderbeg **Rev:** National arms above denomination

Date	Mintage	VF20	XF40	MS60	MS63	MS65
1968	1,520	PF65 4,900				

KM# 56.2 500 LEKE

98.74 g., 0.900 Gold 2.8571 oz. AGW **Rev:** Date below arms, oval fineness countermark in a variety of positions

Date	Mintage	VF20	XF40	MS60	MS63	MS65
1969	200	PF65 5,200				

KM# 56.3 500 LEKE

98.74 g., 0.900 Gold 2.8571 oz. AGW **Obv:** Without date **Rev:** Oval fineness countermark in relief incorporated into the die

Date	Mintage	VF20	XF40	MS60	MS63	MS65
1970	Inc. above	PF65 5,300				

KM# 64 7500 LEKE

483.75 g., 0.900 Gold 13.9976 oz. AGW **Subject:** 42nd Anniversary - First Railroad **Obv:** Engine emerging from tunnel **Rev:** Caboose entering tunnel **Note:** Similar to 50 Leke, KM#62.

Date	Mintage	VF20	XF40	MS60	MS63	MS65
1988	50	PF65 25,000				

REPUBLIC

KM# 75 LEK

3.00 g., Bronze, 18.1 mm. **Obv:** Dalmatian pelican **Rev:** Denomination **Edge:** Plain

Date	Mintage	VF20	XF40	MS60	MS63	MS65
1996	—	—	—	0.40	1.50	2.00

KM# 76 5 LEKE

3.12 g., Nickel Plated Steel, 20 mm. **Obv:** Imperial eagle **Rev:** Olive branch, denomination

Date	Mintage	VF20	XF40	MS60	MS63	MS65
1995	—	—	—	—	1.00	1.25
2000	—	—	—	—	1.00	1.25

KM# 68 10 LEKE

52.50 g., 0.925 Silver 1.5613 oz. ASW **Subject:** 1992 Summer Olympics - Equestrian **Rev:** Horse and rider right, incuse design

Date	Mintage	VF20	XF40	MS60	MS63	MS65
1991	980	—	—	150	200	240

KM# 69 10 LEKE

52.50 g., 0.925 Silver 1.5613 oz. ASW **Subject:** 1992 Summer Olympics - Equestrian **Obv:** National arms, value and date below **Rev:** Horse and rider left, relief design

Date	Mintage	VF20	XF40	MS60	MS63	MS65
1991	980	—	—	150	200	240

KM# 70 10 LEKE

28.46 g., 0.925 Silver 0.8464 oz. ASW **Subject:** 1992 Summer Olympics - Boxing **Obv:** National arms divide date **Rev:** Boxers left, value right center

Date	Mintage	VF20	XF40	MS60	MS63	MS65
1992	20,000	PF65 50.00				

KM# 77 10 LEKE

3.60 g., Aluminum-Bronze, 21.25 mm. **Obv:** Fortress **Rev:** Denomination above sprig with berries **Edge:** Reeded

Date	Mintage	VF20	XF40	MS60	MS63	MS65
1996	—	—	—	—	1.00	1.50
2000	—	—	—	—	1.00	1.50

KM# 78 20 LEKE

5.00 g., Aluminum-Bronze, 22.5 mm. **Obv:** Ancient sailing vessel **Rev:** Denomination **Edge:** Reeded

Date	Mintage	VF20	XF40	MS60	MS63	MS65
1996	—	—	—	—	1.25	1.75
2000	—	—	—	—	1.25	1.75

KM# 79 50 LEKE

5.50 g., Copper-Nickel, 24.25 mm. **Obv:** Ancient equestrian **Rev:** Denomination, tied oak sprigs **Edge:** Reeded

Date	Mintage	VF20	XF40	MS60	MS63	MS65
1996	—	—	—	—	1.50	2.50
2000	—	—	—	—	1.50	2.50

KM# 80 100 LEKE

6.70 g., Bi-Metallic Aluminum-Bronze center in Copper-Nickel ring, 24.75 mm. **Obv:** Teuta, Illyrian queen, stateswoman, reigned 231 BC **Rev:** Denomination in wreath. **Edge:** Reeded

Date	Mintage	VF20	XF40	MS60	MS63	MS65
2000	—	—	—	1.00	2.00	3.50

PATTERNS

Including off metal strikes

KM#	Date	Mintage	Identification	Mkt Val
Pn1	1926	—	5 Franga Ari. Brass. KM#8.1 (For type), no star below bust.	2,500

Note: Stack's sale 168, Lot #3040S, 10/8/2012 realized 2,500.

KM#	Date	Mintage	Identification	Mkt Val
Pn2	1926	—	5 Franga Ari. Copper. Km#8.2 (for type), one star below bust.	4,500

Note: Stack's sale 168. Lot #40406, 10/8/2012 realized $4,500.

KM#	Date	Mintage	Identification	Mkt Val
Pn3	1926	—	100 Franga Ari. Copper. Km#11.2 (for type), one star below bust.	3,250

Note: Stack's sale 168, Lot #40001, 10/8/2012 realized $3,100.

KM#	Date	Mintage	Identification	Mkt Val
Pn4	1927	—	Frang Ar. Silver. Plain. Prev. KM#Pn7.	550
Pn5	1927	—	5 Franga Ari. Copper. Prev. KM#Pn9.	—
Pn6	1928	—	2 Lek. Copper-Nickel. Prev. KM#Pn11.	—
Pn7	1968	—	10 Leke. 0.999. Silver. Like 10 Leke, KM#50. Blank except for MET in rectangle at 6 o'clock. Reeded.	—

ESSAIS

KM#	Date	Mintage	Identification	Mkt Val
E1	1926	—	5 Qindar Leku. Bronze.	—
E2	1926	—	10 Qindar Ari. Bronze. Prev. KM#Pn2.	—
E3	1926	—	1/2 Lek. Nickel. Prev. KM#Pn3.	—
E4	1926	50	2 Franga Ari. Silver. Prev. KM#Pn4.	550
E5	1927	—	Lek. Nickel. Prev. KM#Pn5.	—
E6	1927	—	Frang Ar. Silver. Prev. KM#Pn6.	550
E7	1927	50	2 Franga Ari. Silver. Prev. KM#Pn8.	700
E8	1927	—	100 Franga Ari. Silver. Prev. KM#Pn10.	—
E9	1928	—	2 Lek. Nickel. Prev. KM#Pn12.	—
E10	1928	50	Frang Ar. Silver. Prev. KM#Pn13.	550
E11	1928	50	2 Franga Ari. Silver. Prev. KM#Pn14.	700
E12	1938	—	100 Franga Ari. Gold. Without signature. Prev. KM#Pn15.	—
E13	1986	10	5 Leke. Copper-Nickel.	250
E14	1986	18	5 Leke. Palladium.	1,800

Note: Stack's sale 168, Lot#40005, 10/8/2012 realized $1,750.

PIEDFORT

KM#	Date	Mintage	Identification	Mkt Val
P1	1988	250	50 Leke. 0.925. Silver. KM#62 without tunnel hole.	600

PROVAS

Standard metals unless otherwise stated

KM#	Date	Mintage	Identification	Mkt Val
Pr1	1926R	50	5 Qindar Leku. Bronze. KM#1.	600
Pr2	1926R	50	10 Qindar Leku. Bronze. KM#2.	600
Pr3	1926R	50	1/4 Leku. Nickel. Male lion left. Oak leaf across top, value below. KM#3.	750
Pr4	1926	—	1/2 Lek. Nickel.	600
Pr5	1926R	—	1/2 Lek. Nickel. KM#4.	600
Pr6	1926R	50	Lek. Nickel. KM#5.	750
Pr7	1926R	—	2 Franga Ari. Silver. KM#7.	750
Pr8	1926R	—	5 Franga Ari. Silver. KM#8. Modern copy of 5 Franga Ari exist in copper and bronze.	1,200
Pr9	1926R	—	5 Franga Ari. Copper. KM#8. Modern copy of 5 Franga Ari exist in copper and bronze.	675
Pr10	1926R	—	5 Franga Ari. Silver. KM#8. Modern copy of 5 Franga Ari exist in copper and bronze.	825
Pr11	1926R	—	5 Franga Ari. Copper. KM#8. Modern copy of 5 Franga Ari exist in copper and bronze.	675
Pr12	1926R	50	20 Franga Ari. Gold. KM#12.	1,250
Pr13	1926	—	20 Franga Ari. Gold. KM#12.	8,250
Pr14	1926R	—	100 Franga Ari. Gold. KM#11.1.	4,000
Pr15	1926R	—	100 Franga Ari. Gold. Head left, star below. Biga right, denomination below.	4,250
Pr16	1926R	—	100 Franga Ari. Gold. Head left, two stars below. Biga right, denomination below.	4,250
Pr17	1927R	—	1/4 Leku. Nickel. Lion advancing left, date below. Oak branch above value.	750
Pr18	1927R	—	Lek. Nickel. Head right. Figure on horseback right, denomination below.	750
Pr19	1927R	50	Frang Ar. Silver. Helmeted head right. Prow of ancient ship, denomination above.	450
Pr20	1927V	—	Frang Ar. Silver. Helmeted head right. Prow of ancient ship, denomination above.	525
Pr21	1927R	—	2 Franga Ari. Silver. Standing eagle with wings spread divides denomination. Seed sower.	450
Pr22	1927V	—	5 Franga Ari. Silver.	675
Pr23	1927V	—	5 Franga Ari. Silver. Matte proof.	—
Pr24	1927	—	10 Franga Ari. Gold. Head left. Double eagle divides denomination below.	1,400
PrA25	1927R	—	Frang Ar. Silver. Head right. Double eagle, date and denomination below.	—
Pr25	1927R	50	10 Franga Ari. Gold. Head left. Double eagle, date and denomination below.	1,250
Pr26	1927	—	20 Franga Ari. Gold. Head left. Double eagle, date and denomination below.	1,250
Pr27	1927V	—	20 Franga Ari. Gold. Lion divides denomination, date below. Bust right.	1,250
Pr28	1927R	50	20 Franga Ari. Gold. Head left. Double eagle, date and denomination below.	1,250
Pr29	1927R	—	100 Franga Ari. Head left. Biga right, denomination below.	3,000
Pr30	1927R	—	100 Franga Ari. Gold. Head left, star below. Biga right, denomination below.	4,000
PrA31	1927V	—	100 Franga Ari. Silver. Head right. Man with oxen pulling plow left, denomination below.	2,500
Pr31	1927R	—	100 Franga Ari. Gold. Head left, two stars below. Biga right, denomination below.	4,000
Pr32	1928R	—	2 Lek. Copper-Nickel. Head left. Olive branch above denomination.	300
Pr33	1928R	—	2 Lek. Nickel. Head left. Olive branch above denomination.	—
PrA34	1928R	—	2 Lek. Nickel. Head right. Double eagle, date and denomination below.	450
Pr34	1928R	—	Frang Ar. Silver. Helmeted head right. Prow of ancient ship, denomination above.	300
Pr35	1928R	—	2 Franga Ari. Silver. Standing eagle with wings spread divides denomination. Seed sower.	375
PrA36	1928R	—	2 Franga Ari. Silver. Head right. Double eagle, denomination and date below.	525
Pr36	1928R	50	100 Franga Ari. Gold. Head left. Double eagle, cap on top, date bottom left. Bare head.	5,000
Pr37	1928R	50	100 Franga Ari. Gold. Head left within wreath left. Double eagle, cap on top, date at bottom left. Bare head, wreath.	5,750
Pr38	1928R	50	100 Franga Ari. Gold. Uniformed bust right. Double eagle, cap on top, date bottom left.	9,500
Pr39	1929R	50	100 Franga Ari. Gold. Head left within wreath. Double eagle, cap on top, date below tail. Bare head, wreath.	5,500
PrA40	1930	—	1/2 Leku. (No Composition).	—
Pr40	1935R	50	Qindar Ar. Bronze. Double eagle, date below. Value above oak leaves.	450
Pr41	1935R	50	2 Qindar Ari. Bronze. Double eagle, date below. Denomination above leaves.	450
Pr42	1935	50	Frang Ar. Silver.	1,400
Pr43	1935	50	2 Franga Ari. Silver.	1,500
Pr44	1935	—	5 Franga Ari. Silver. Pattern.	—
Pr45	1937R	50	Frang Ar. Silver. Head right. King's arms, denomination below.	1,450
Pr46	1937R	50	Frang Ar. Silver.	1,500
Pr47	1937R	50	2 Franga Ari. Silver.	1,600
Pr48	1937R	—	10 Franga Ari. Gold. Requires Confirmation.	—
Pr49	1937R	50	20 Franga Ari. Gold. Head right. King's arms, denomination below.	1,750
Pr50	1937R	50	100 Franga Ari. Gold. Head right, date below. King's arms, denomination below.	6,500
Pr51	1938R	50	20 Franga Ari. Gold. Head right, date below. King's arms, denomination below.	1,850
Pr52	1938R	50	20 Franga Ari. Gold. Head right, date below. King's arms, denomination below.	1,850
Pr53	1938R	50	50 Franga Ari.	3,000
Pr54	1938R	50	100 Franga Ari. Gold. Head right, date below. King's arms, denomination below.	5,500
Pr55	1938R	50	100 Franga Ari. Gold. Head right, d ate below. King's arms, denomination below.	5,500
Pr56	1939	—	0.05 Lek. Proof.	450
Pr57	1939	—	0.10 Lek. Proof.	450
Pr58	1939	—	0.20 Lek. Proof.	550
Pr59	1939	—	0.50 Lek. Proof.	550
Pr60	1939	—	Lek. Proof.	550
Pr61	1939	—	2 Lek. Proof.	600
Pr62	1939	—	5 Lek. Proof.	550
Pr63	1939	—	10 Lek. Silver. Proof.	700
Pr64	1947	—	10 Qindar Leku. Aluminum.	—
Pr65	1947	—	5 Qindar Leku. Tombac.	—
Pr66	1947	—	10 Qindar Leku. Aluminum.	—
Pr67	1947	—	10 Qindar Leku. Tombac.	—
Pr68	1947	—	20 Qindar Leku. Aluminum.	—
Pr69	1947	—	20 Qindar Leku. Tombac.	—
Pr70	1947	—	50 Qindar Leku. Aluminum.	—
Pr71	1947	—	50 Qindar Leku. Tombac.	—

TRIAL STRIKES

KM#	Date	Mintage	Identification	Mkt Val
TS1	1969	—	500 Leke. Goldine Brass. Blank with MET countermark. Like KM56.2.	225

MINT SETS

KM#	Date	Mintage	Identification	Issue Price	Mkt Val
MS1	1969 (5)	—	KM#44-48	6.00	25.00
MS2	2000 (5)	—	KM#76-80	—	15.00

PROOF SETS

KM#	Date	Mintage	Identification	Issue Price	Mkt Val
PS1	1968 (5)	1,500	KM#51.1, 53.1-56	470	8,750
PS2	1968 (8)	1,540	KM#49-56	—	8,950
PS3	1969 (5)	—	KM#51, 53-56	470	9,200
PS4	1969 (8)	—	KM#49-56	—	9,400
PS5	1970 (5)	—	KM#51.5, 53-56	516	9,450
PS6	1970 (3)	500	KM#49-50, 52	45.00	235
PS7	1991 (2)	980	KM#68-69	—	500
PSA2	1968 (3)	8,540	KM#49, 50, 52	44.00	125
PSA4	1969 (3)	1,500	KM#49, 50, 52	45.00	175

ALDERNEY

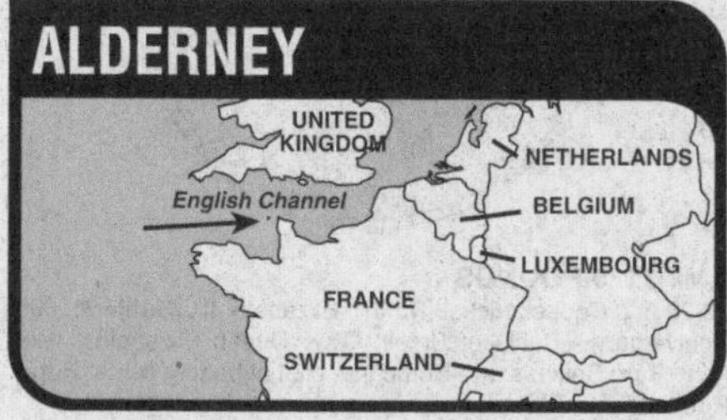

Alderney, the northernmost and third largest of the Channel Islands, separated from the coast of France by the dangerous 8-mile-wide tidal channel, has an area of 3 sq. mi. (8 km.) and a population of 1,686. It is a dependency of the British island of Guernsey, to the southwest. Capital: St. Anne. Principal industries are agriculture and raising cattle.

There is evidence of settlement in prehistoric times and Roman coins have been discovered on the island along with evidence of their buildings. Toward the close of the reign of Henry VIII, France began making plans to seize the Island of Sark. The English, realizing its strategic importance, began to build a defensive fort, which was abandoned some years later when Edward VI died. France constructed a large naval base at its northern tip, which incited the English into making Alderney the "Gibraltar of the Channel." Most of the Islanders were evacuated before the German occupation in 1940 but returned in 1945 when the Germans surrendered.

The Channel Islands have never been subject to the British Parliament and are self-governing units under the direct rule of the Crown acting through the Privy Council. Alderney is one of the nine Channel Islands, the only part of the Duchy of Normandy still belonging to the British Crown, and has been a British possession since the Norman Conquest of 1066. Legislation was only recently introduced for the issue of its own coinage, a right it now shares with Jersey and Guernsey.

RULER
British

MONETARY SYSTEM
100 Pence = 1 Pound Sterling

DEPENDENCY

STANDARD COINAGE

KM# 4 POUND

9.50 g., 0.925 Silver 0.2825 oz. ASW, 22.5 mm. **Ruler:** Elizabeth II **Subject:** 40th Anniversary - Coronation **Obv:** Crowned bust, right, date below **Rev:** Royal carriage

Date	Mintage	VF20	XF40	MS60	MS63	MS65
1993	Est. 20000	PF63 12.00	PF65 17.00			

KM# 12 POUND

9.50 g., 0.925 Silver 0.2825 oz. ASW, 22.5 mm. **Ruler:** Elizabeth II **Subject:** VE Day **Obv:** Crowned bust right **Rev:** VE Monogram and dove

Date	Mintage	VF20	XF40	MS60	MS63	MS65
ND-1995	Est. 20000	PF63 12.00	PF65 17.00			

KM# 12a POUND

15.80 g., 0.916 Gold 0.4653 oz. AGW, 22.5 mm. **Ruler:** Elizabeth II **Subject:** VE Day **Obv:** Crowned bust right **Rev:** VE Monogram and dove

Date	Mintage	VF20	XF40	MS60	MS63	MS65
ND-1995	500	PF65 750				

KM# 1 2 POUNDS

28.28 g., Copper-Nickel, 38.5 mm. **Ruler:** Elizabeth II **Subject:** Royal Visit **Obv:** Crowned bust, right, date below **Rev:** Arms surrounded by thrift plant

Date	Mintage	VF20	XF40	MS60	MS63	MS65
1989	—	—	—	—	6.00	8.00

KM# 1a 2 POUNDS

28.28 g., 0.925 Silver 0.841 oz. ASW, 38.6 mm. **Ruler:** Elizabeth II **Subject:** Royal Visit

Date	Mintage	VF20	XF40	MS60	MS63	MS65
1989	5,000	PF63 25.00	PF65 30.00			

KM# 1b 2 POUNDS

47.54 g., 0.917 Gold 1.4016 oz. AGW **Ruler:** Elizabeth II **Subject:** Royal Visit

Date	Mintage	VF20	XF40	MS60	MS63	MS65
1989	100	PF65 2,100				

KM# 2 2 POUNDS

28.28 g., Copper-Nickel, 38.5 mm. **Ruler:** Elizabeth II **Subject:** Queen Mother's 90th Birthday **Rev:** Queen Mother in cameo facing left, Glamis rose sprays flanking

Date	Mintage	VF20	XF40	MS60	MS63	MS65
1990	—	—	—	—	5.00	7.00

KM# 2a 2 POUNDS

28.28 g., 0.925 Silver 0.841 oz. ASW, 38.6 mm. **Ruler:** Elizabeth II **Subject:** Queen Mother's 90th Birthday **Edge:** Reeded

Date	Mintage	VF20	XF40	MS60	MS63	MS65
1990	5,000	PF63 20.00	PF65 25.00			

KM# 2b 2 POUNDS

47.54 g., 0.917 Gold 1.4016 oz. AGW **Ruler:** Elizabeth II **Subject:** Queen Mother's 90th Birthday

Date	Mintage	VF20	XF40	MS60	MS63	MS65
1990	90	PF65 2,100				

KM# 3 2 POUNDS

28.28 g., Copper-Nickel, 38.5 mm. **Ruler:** Elizabeth II **Subject:** 40th Anniversary - Queen's Reign **Rev:** Sailing ship on water, Crowned initials below within wreath

Date	Mintage	VF20	XF40	MS60	MS63	MS65
1992	—	—	—	—	5.00	7.00

KM# 3a 2 POUNDS

28.28 g., 0.925 Silver 0.841 oz. ASW, 38.6 mm. **Ruler:** Elizabeth II **Subject:** 40th Anniversary - Queen's Reign

Date	Mintage	VF20	XF40	MS60	MS63	MS65
1992	5,000	PF63 25.00	PF65 30.00			

KM# 3b 2 POUNDS

47.54 g., 0.917 Gold 1.4016 oz. AGW **Ruler:** Elizabeth II **Subject:** 40th Anniversary - Queen's Reign

Date	Mintage	VF20	XF40	MS60	MS63	MS65
1992	150	PF65 2,100				

KM# 5 2 POUNDS

28.28 g., Copper-Nickel, 38.8 mm. **Ruler:** Elizabeth II **Subject:** 40th Anniversary - Coronation **Rev:** Coronation coach, flags of the Union, Alderney of May 24 1989

Date	Mintage	VF20	XF40	MS60	MS63	MS65
1993	—	—	—	—	5.00	7.00

KM# 5a 2 POUNDS

28.28 g., 0.925 Silver 0.841 oz. ASW, 38.6 mm. **Ruler:** Elizabeth II **Subject:** 40th Anniversary - Coronation

Date	Mintage	VF20	XF40	MS60	MS63	MS65
1993	Est. 5000	PF63 25.00	PF65 30.00			

KM# 7 2 POUNDS

28.28 g., Copper-Nickel, 38.5 mm. **Ruler:** Elizabeth II **Subject:** Normandy Invasion **Rev:** Normandy beach landing scene

Date	Mintage	VF20	XF40	MS60	MS63	MS65
1994	Est. 5000000	—	—	—	6.00	8.00

KM# 7a 2 POUNDS

28.28 g., 0.925 Silver 0.841 oz. ASW, 38.6 mm. **Ruler:** Elizabeth II **Subject:** Normandy Invasion **Rev:** Normandy beach landing scene

Date	Mintage	VF20	XF40	MS60	MS63	MS65
1994	—	PF63 25.00	PF65 30.00			

KM# 13 2 POUNDS

28.28 g., Copper-Nickel, 38.5 mm. **Ruler:** Elizabeth II **Subject:** Islander's Return **Rev:** Steamship Autocarrier

Date	Mintage	VF20	XF40	MS60	MS63	MS65
ND-1995	—	—	—	—	8.00	10.00

KM# 13a 2 POUNDS

28.28 g., 0.925 Silver 0.841 oz. ASW, 38.6 mm. **Ruler:** Elizabeth II **Subject:** Islander's Return **Rev:** Steamship

Date	Mintage	VF20	XF40	MS60	MS63	MS65
ND-1995	10,000	PF63 25.00	PF65 30.00			

KM# 13b 2 POUNDS

47.54 g., 0.916 Gold 1.4001 oz. AGW **Ruler:** Elizabeth II **Subject:** Islander's Return **Rev:** Steamship

Date	Mintage	VF20	XF40	MS60	MS63	MS65
ND-1995	250	PF65 2,100				

KM# 16 2 POUNDS
28.28 g., Copper-Nickel, 38.5 mm. **Ruler:** Elizabeth II **Subject:** World Wildlife Fund **Obv:** Queen's portrait **Rev:** 2 Atlantic Puffin birds

Date	Mintage	VF20	XF40	MS60	MS63	MS65
1997	—	—	—	—	10.00	13.00

KM# 16a 2 POUNDS
28.28 g., 0.925 Silver 0.841 oz. ASW, 38.6 mm. **Ruler:** Elizabeth II **Subject:** World Wildlife Fund **Rev:** 2 Puffin birds

Date	Mintage	VF20	XF40	MS60	MS63	MS65
1997	—	PF63 25.00	PF65 30.00			

KM# 17 2 POUNDS
28.28 g., Copper-Nickel, 38.5 mm. **Ruler:** Elizabeth II **Subject:** Queen's Golden Wedding Anniversary **Obv:** Queen's portrait **Rev:** Queen crowning Prince Charles

Date	Mintage	VF20	XF40	MS60	MS63	MS65
ND-1997	—	—	—	—	6.00	8.00

KM# 18 2 POUNDS
28.28 g., Copper-Nickel, 38.5 mm. **Ruler:** Elizabeth II **Subject:** Total Eclipse of the Sun **Obv:** Queen's portrait **Rev:** 2 Northern Gannets and church

Date	Mintage	VF20	XF40	MS60	MS63	MS65
1999	—	—	—	—	13.00	15.00

KM# 18a 2 POUNDS
28.28 g., 0.925 Silver 0.841 oz. ASW, 38.6 mm. **Ruler:** Elizabeth II **Subject:** Total Eclipse of the Sun **Obv:** Queen's portrait **Rev:** 2 sea birds and church

Date	Mintage	VF20	XF40	MS60	MS63	MS65
1999	Est. 10000	PF63 25.00	PF65 30.00			

KM# 18b 2 POUNDS
47.54 g., 0.917 Gold 1.4016 oz. AGW **Ruler:** Elizabeth II **Subject:** Total Eclipse of the Sun **Obv:** Queen's portrait **Rev:** 2 sea birds and church

Date	Mintage	VF20	XF40	MS60	MS63	MS65
1999	Est. 100	PF65 2,150				

KM# 14 5 POUNDS
28.28 g., Copper-Nickel, 38.5 mm. **Ruler:** Elizabeth II **Subject:** Queen Mother - Children **Rev:** Queen Mother with children within circle

Date	Mintage	VF20	XF40	MS60	MS63	MS65
1995	—	—	—	—	8.00	10.00

KM# 14a 5 POUNDS
28.28 g., 0.925 Silver 0.841 oz. ASW, 38.6 mm. **Ruler:** Elizabeth II **Subject:** Queen Mother - Children

Date	Mintage	VF20	XF40	MS60	MS63	MS65
1995	10,000	PF63 25.00	PF65 30.00			

KM# 14b 5 POUNDS
47.54 g., 0.916 Gold 1.4001 oz. AGW **Ruler:** Elizabeth II **Subject:** Queen Mother - Children

Date	Mintage	VF20	XF40	MS60	MS63	MS65
1995	150	PF65 2,150				

KM# 15 5 POUNDS
28.28 g., Copper-Nickel, 38.5 mm. **Ruler:** Elizabeth II **Subject:** Queen Elizabeth's 70th Birthday - Flowers **Obv:** Crowned bust, right **Rev:** Rose, thistle, daffodil, clover representing the UK

Date	Mintage	VF20	XF40	MS60	MS63	MS65
1996	—	—	—	—	10.00	13.00

KM# 15a 5 POUNDS
28.28 g., 0.925 Silver 0.841 oz. ASW, 38.6 mm. **Ruler:** Elizabeth II **Subject:** Queen Elizabeth's 70th Birthday - Flowers

Date	Mintage	VF20	XF40	MS60	MS63	MS65
1996	Est. 10000	PF63 30.00	PF65 35.00			

KM# 15b 5 POUNDS
47.54 g., 0.917 Gold 1.4016 oz. AGW **Ruler:** Elizabeth II **Subject:** Queen Elizabeth's 70th Birthday - Flowers

Date	Mintage	VF20	XF40	MS60	MS63	MS65
1996	250	PF65 2,150				

KM# 19 5 POUNDS
28.28 g., Copper-Nickel, 38.61 mm. **Ruler:** Elizabeth II **Subject:** Total Eclipse of the Sun **Obv:** Queen's head right **Rev:** Map of Alderney; pre, post and actual phases of eclipse

Date	Mintage	VF20	XF40	MS60	MS63	MS65
1999	—	—	—	—	13.00	16.00

KM# 19a 5 POUNDS
28.28 g., 0.925 Silver 0.841 oz. ASW, 38.6 mm. **Ruler:** Elizabeth II **Subject:** Total Eclipse of the Sun **Obv:** Queen's bust right **Rev:** Map of Alderney; pre, post and actual phases of eclipse

Date	Mintage	VF20	XF40	MS60	MS63	MS65
1999	Est. 10000	PF63 30.00	PF65 35.00			

KM# 20 5 POUNDS
28.28 g., 0.925 Silver 0.841 oz. ASW **Ruler:** Elizabeth II **Subject:** Winston Churchill **Obv:** Queen's portrait **Rev:** Winston Churchill wearing hat **Edge Lettering:** And our dear Channel Islands are also to be freed today

Date	Mintage	VF20	XF40	MS60	MS63	MS65
1999	—	PF63 25.00	PF65 30.00			

KM# 20a 5 POUNDS
47.54 g., 0.9166 Gold 1.401 oz. AGW **Ruler:** Elizabeth II **Subject:** Winston Churchill **Obv:** Queen's portrait **Rev:** Winston Churchill wearing hat **Edge Lettering:** And our dear Channel Islands are also to be freed today

Date	Mintage	VF20	XF40	MS60	MS63	MS65
1999	125	PF65 2,150				

KM# 21 5 POUNDS
28.28 g., Copper-Nickel **Ruler:** Elizabeth II **Subject:** 60th Anniversary - Battle of Britain **Obv:** Queen Elizabeth's head right **Rev:** Spitfires and Hurricane, pilot at bottom center **Edge:** Reeded

Date	Mintage	VF20	XF40	MS60	MS63	MS65
2000	—	—	—	—	13.00	16.00

KM# 21a 5 POUNDS
28.28 g., 0.925 Silver 0.841 oz. ASW, 38.6 mm. **Ruler:** Elizabeth II **Subject:** 60th Anniversary - Battle of Britain **Obv:** Queen Elizabeth's head right **Rev:** Two spitfires in flight, pilot at bottom center **Edge:** Reeded

Date	Mintage	VF20	XF40	MS60	MS63	MS65
2000	—	PF63 25.00	PF65 30.00			

KM# 26 5 POUNDS
28.03 g., 0.925 Silver 0.8336 oz. ASW, 38.5 mm. **Ruler:** Elizabeth II **Subject:** Millennium **Obv:** Queen's portrait **Rev:** Radiant light house and birds **Edge:** Reeded

Date	Mintage	VF20	XF40	MS60	MS63	MS65
ND-2000	20,000	PF63 20.00	PF65 25.00			

KM# 52 5 POUNDS
28.28 g., 0.925 Silver 0.841 oz. ASW, 38.6 mm. **Ruler:** Elizabeth II **Subject:** Queen Mother's 100th Birthday **Obv:** Queen Elizabeth II **Rev:** Queen Mother above value **Edge:** Reeded

Date	Mintage	VF20	XF40	MS60	MS63	MS65
2000	—	PF63 25.00	PF65 32.00			

KM# 8 10 POUNDS
3.13 g., 0.999 Gold 0.1005 oz. AGW **Ruler:** Elizabeth II **Subject:** Normandy Invasion **Rev:** Paratroopers and Transport Plane

Date	Mintage	VF20	XF40	MS60	MS63	MS65
1994	Est. 1000	PF65 200				

KM# 90 10 POUNDS
155.50 g., 0.925 Silver 4.6245 oz. ASW, 65 mm. **Ruler:** Elizabeth II **Subject:** Royal family

Date	Mintage	VF20	XF40	MS60	MS63	MS65
2000	Est. 1000	PF63 150	PF65 175			

KM# 6 25 POUNDS
8.51 g., 0.917 Gold 0.251 oz. AGW **Ruler:** Elizabeth II **Subject:** 40th Anniversary - Coronation **Rev:** Royal carriage

Date	Mintage	VF20	XF40	MS60	MS63	MS65
1993	Est. 1000	PF65 450				

KM# 9 25 POUNDS
7.81 g., 0.999 Gold 0.2508 oz. AGW **Ruler:** Elizabeth II **Subject:** Normandy Invasion **Rev:** Fighter planes and tank

Date	Mintage	VF20	XF40	MS60	MS63	MS65
1994	Est. 1000	PF65 450				

KM# 57 25 POUNDS
7.81 g., 0.999 Gold 0.2508 oz. AGW **Ruler:** Elizabeth II **Subject:** Normandy Invasion **Rev:** Fighter planes and tank

Date	Mintage	VF20	XF40	MS60	MS63	MS65
1994	—	PF65 450				

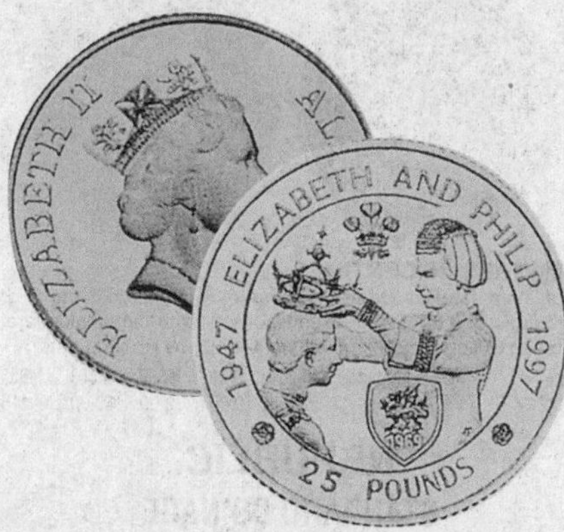

KM# 23 25 POUNDS
28.00 g., Copper-Nickel **Ruler:** Elizabeth II **Subject:** Golden Wedding Anniversary - Elizabeth and Philip **Obv:** Queen Elizabeth's head right **Rev:** Queen Elizabeth crowning Charles as Prince of Wales, date (1947-1997) in legend

Date	Mintage	VF20	XF40	MS60	MS63	MS65
ND(1997)	—	—	—	—	—	37.50

KM# 23a 25 POUNDS
28.28 g., 0.925 Silver 0.841 oz. ASW with Gold cameo. **Ruler:** Elizabeth II **Subject:** Golden Wedding Anniversary - Elizabeth and Philip **Obv:** Queen Elizabeth's head right **Rev:** Queen Elizabeth crowning Charles as Prince of Wales, date (1947-1997) in legend

Date	Mintage	VF20	XF40	MS60	MS63	MS65
ND(1997)	—	PF65 40.00				

KM# 23b 25 POUNDS
8.43 g., 0.916 Gold 0.2483 oz. AGW **Ruler:** Elizabeth II **Subject:** Golden Wedding Anniversary - Elizabeth and Philip **Obv:** Queen Elizabeth's head right **Rev:** Queen Elizabeth crowning Charles as Prince of Wales, date (1947-1997) in legend

Date	Mintage	VF20	XF40	MS60	MS63	MS65
ND(1997)	—	PF65 450				

KM# 71 25 POUNDS
7.81 g., 0.999 Gold 0.2508 oz. AGW **Ruler:** Elizabeth II **Subject:** Winston Churchill **Obv:** Crowned head right **Rev:** Churchill wearing hat

Date	Mintage	VF20	XF40	MS60	MS63	MS65
1999	2,500	PF65 900				

KM# 22 25 POUNDS
7.81 g., 0.916 Gold 0.230 oz. AGW **Ruler:** Elizabeth II **Subject:** 60th Anniversary - Battle of Britain **Obv:** Queen Elizabeth's head right **Rev:** Two spitfires in flight, pilot at bottom center **Edge:** Reeded

Date	Mintage	VF20	XF40	MS60	MS63	MS65
2000	—	PF65 400				

KM# 72 25 POUNDS
7.81 g., 0.999 Gold 0.2508 oz. AGW **Ruler:** Elizabeth II **Subject:** Queen Mother's 100th Birthday **Obv:** Crowned head right **Rev:** Bust of Queen Mother 3/4 left

Date	Mintage	VF20	XF40	MS60	MS63	MS65
2000	—	PF65 850				

KM# 217 25 POUNDS
7.81 g., 0.916 Gold 0.230 oz. AGW **Ruler:** Elizabeth II **Rev:** Queen Mother waving, surrounded by family

Date	Mintage	VF20	XF40	MS60	MS63	MS65
2000	—	PF65 425				

KM# 10 50 POUNDS
15.60 g., 0.999 Gold 0.501 oz. AGW **Ruler:** Elizabeth II **Subject:** Normandy Invasion **Rev:** British gliders

Date	Mintage	VF20	XF40	MS60	MS63	MS65
1994	Est. 1000	PF65 900				

KM# 11 100 POUNDS
31.21 g., 0.999 Gold 1.0024 oz. AGW **Ruler:** Elizabeth II **Subject:** Normandy Invasion **Obv:** Crowned bust, right, date below **Rev:** Normandy beach landing scene

Date	Mintage	VF20	XF40	MS60	MS63	MS65
1994	Est. 500	PF65 1,650				

PIEDFORT

KM#	Date	Mintage	Identification	Mkt Val
P1	1989	500	2 Pounds. 0.925. Silver. KM#1a.	80.00
P2	1990	500	2 Pounds. 0.925. Silver. KM#2a.	80.00
P3	1992	750	2 Pounds. 0.925. Silver. KM#3a.	50.00
P4	1993	500	2 Pounds. 0.925. Silver. KM#5a.	60.00
P5	1994	500	2 Pounds. 0.925. Silver. KM#7a.	60.00
P6	ND(1995)	500	2 Pounds. 0.925. Silver. KM#13a.	70.00
P7	1995	500	5 Pounds. 0.925. Silver. KM#14a.	65.00
P8	1996	500	5 Pounds. 0.925. Silver. KM#15a.	70.00

PROOF SETS

KM#	Date	Mintage	Identification	Issue Price	Mkt Val
PS1	1994 (5)	500	KM#7a, 8-11	—	3,500
PS2	1994 (4)	Inc. above	KM#8-11	—	3,450
PS3	1994 (4)	500	KM#7a, 8-10	—	1,650
PS4	1994 (3)	Inc. above	KM#8-10	—	1,600

ALGERIA

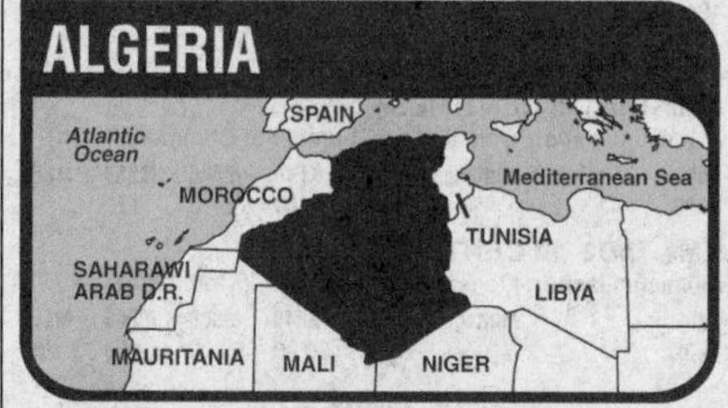

The People's Democratic Republic of Algeria, a North African country fronting on the Mediterranean Sea between Tunisia and Morocco, has an area of 919,595 sq. mi. (2,381,740 sq. km.) and a population of 31.6 million. Capital: Algiers (Alger). Most of the country's working population is engaged in agriculture although a recent industrial diversification, financed by oil revenues, is making steady progress. Wines, fruits, iron and zinc ores, phosphates, tobacco products, liquified natural gas, and petroleum are exported.

Following the armistice signed by France and Nazi Germany on June 22, 1940, Algeria fell under Vichy Government control until liberated by the Allied invasion forces under the command of Gen. D. D. Eisenhower on Nov. 8, 1942. The inability to obtain equal rights with Frenchmen led to an organized revolt which began on Nov. 1, 1954 and lasted until a ceasefire was signed on July l, 1962. Independence was proclaimed on July 5, 1962, following a self-determination referendum, and the Republic was declared on September 25, 1962.

MINT MARK
(a) – Paris, privy marks only

MONETARY SYSTEM
100 Centimes = 1 Franc

FRENCH OCCUPATION

COLONIAL COINAGE

KM# 91 20 FRANCS
Copper-Nickel, 23 mm. **Obv:** Head with laureled hood, right **Rev:** Value between columns of wheat, date at center

Date	Mintage	VF20	XF40	MS60	MS63	MS65
1949	25,556,000	1.00	2.00	5.00	10.00	15.00
1956	7,500,000	1.00	2.50	6.00	12.50	20.00

KM# 92 50 FRANCS
Copper-Nickel, 26.5 mm. **Obv:** Man with laureled hood, right **Rev:** Value between columns of wheat, date below

Date	Mintage	VF20	XF40	MS60	MS63	MS65
1949	18,000,000	1.50	3.00	9.00	18.00	27.00

KM# 93 100 FRANCS
Copper-Nickel, 29.8 mm. **Obv:** Man with laureled hood. right **Rev:** Value between wheat columns, date below **Edge:** Reeded **Note:** During World War II homeland coins were struck at the Paris Mint and the French 2 Francs, Y#89 were struck at the Philadelphia Mint for use in French African Territories.

Date	Mintage	VF20	XF40	MS60	MS63	MS65
1950	22,189,000	1.50	3.00	10.00	20.00	30.00
1952	12,000,000	2.00	4.00	12.00	25.00	45.00

TOKEN COINAGE

Alger

KM# TnA1 5 CENTIMES
Aluminum **Issuer:** Alger Chamber of Commerce **Obv:** Symbol between palm trees, beaded circle surrounding all **Rev:** Value above sprigs,with J. Bory

Date	Mintage	VF20	XF40	MS60	MS63	MS65
1916	—	5.00	10.00	20.00	35.00	60.00
1917	—	—	175	250	500	—
Note: The year 1917 is not a regular issue						
1919	—	4.00	6.00	12.00	18.00	35.00
1921	—	5.00	10.00	20.00	35.00	60.00

KM# TnA2 5 CENTIMES
Iron **Issuer:** Alger Chamber of Commerce

Date	Mintage	VF20	XF40	MS60	MS63	MS65
1916	—	30.00	50.00	100	200	—

KM# TnA3 5 CENTIMES
Zinc **Issuer:** Alger Chamber of Commerce

Date	Mintage	VF20	XF40	MS60	MS63	MS65
1917	—	3.50	10.00	20.00	40.00	—

Date	Mintage	VF20	XF40	MS60	MS63	MS65
1919	—	—	35.00	70.00	150	—

Note: The year 1919 is not a regular issue

KM# TnA4 5 CENTIMES
Brass **Issuer:** Alger Chamber of Commerce

Date	Mintage	VF20	XF40	MS60	MS63	MS65
1921	—	—	30.00	60.00	120	—

Note: Not a regular issue

KM# TnA5 10 CENTIMES
Aluminum **Issuer:** Alger Chamber of Commerce **Obv:** Symbol between palm trees, beaded circle surrounding all **Rev:** Value above sprigs,without J. Bory

Date	Mintage	VF20	XF40	MS60	MS63	MS65
1916 Without J. Bory	—	6.00	10.00	20.00	45.00	85.00
1918 with J. Bory	—	6.00	10.00	20.00	45.00	85.00
1918 Without J. Bory	—	6.00	10.00	15.00	32.00	85.00
1919 With J. Bory	—	4.00	6.00	12.00	25.00	75.00
1921 With J. Bory	—	3.00	6.00	12.00	25.00	75.00
1921 Without J. Bory	—	6.00	10.00	20.00	45.00	85.00

KM# TnA6 10 CENTIMES
Iron **Issuer:** Alger Chamber of Commerce **Rev:** Without J. Bory

Date	Mintage	VF20	XF40	MS60	MS63	MS65
1916	—	10.00	22.00	50.00	100	—

KM# TnA7 10 CENTIMES
Zinc **Issuer:** Alger Chamber of Commerce

Date	Mintage	VF20	XF40	MS60	MS63	MS65
1917	—	5.00	12.50	30.00	60.00	—
1918	—	—	40.00	100	160	—

Note: 1918 is not a regular issue

Date	Mintage	VF20	XF40	MS60	MS63	MS65
1919	—	—	40.00	100	160	—

Note: 1919 is not a regular issue

KM# TnA8 10 CENTIMES
Brass **Issuer:** Alger Chamber of Commerce **Note:** Not a regular issue.

Date	Mintage	VF20	XF40	MS60	MS63	MS65
1919	—	—	50.00	110	225	375
1921	—	—	65.00	125	245	—

Bone

KM# TnB1 5 CENTIMES
Aluminum **Issuer:** Bone Chamber of Commerce

Date	Mintage	VF20	XF40	MS60	MS63	MS65
1915	—	6.00	10.00	15.00	30.00	75.00
ND-1915	—	5.00	9.00	13.00	25.00	65.00

KM# TnB2 5 CENTIMES
Brass **Issuer:** Bone Chamber of Commerce **Note:** Not a regular issue.

Date	Mintage	VF20	XF40	MS60	MS63	MS65
ND-1915	—	—	30.00	60.00	120	—

KM# TnB3 10 CENTIMES
Aluminum **Issuer:** Bone Chamber of Commerce

Date	Mintage	VF20	XF40	MS60	MS63	MS65
1915	—	4.00	10.00	22.00	40.00	90.00
ND-1915	—	4.00	9.00	20.00	35.00	85.00

KM# TnB4 10 CENTIMES
Brass **Issuer:** Bone Chamber of Commerce **Note:** Not a regular issue.

Date	Mintage	VF20	XF40	MS60	MS63	MS65
ND-1915	—	—	30.00	60.00	120	—

KM# TnB5 50 CENTIMES
Brass **Issuer:** Bone Chamber of Commerce **Obv:** Head left, within wreath **Rev:** Value at center

Date	Mintage	VF20	XF40	MS60	MS63	MS65
ND-1915	—	15.00	30.00	50.00	75.00	150

KM# TnB6 50 CENTIMES
Copper-Nickel **Issuer:** Bone Chamber of Commerce **Note:** Not a regular issue.

Date	Mintage	VF20	XF40	MS60	MS63	MS65
ND-1915	—	—	20.00	45.00	75.00	150

KM# TnB7 FRANC
Brass **Issuer:** Bone Chamber of Commerce **Obv:** Head left, within wreath **Rev:** Value at center

Date	Mintage	VF20	XF40	MS60	MS63	MS65
ND-1915	—	25.00	40.00	65.00	120	—

KM# TnB8 FRANC
Copper-Nickel **Issuer:** Bone Chamber of Commerce **Note:** Not a regular issue.

Date	Mintage	VF20	XF40	MS60	MS63	MS65
ND-1915	—	—	30.00	60.00	90.00	175

KM# TnB9 FRANC
Copper **Issuer:** Bone Chamber of Commerce **Note:** Not a regular issue.

Date	Mintage	VF20	XF40	MS60	MS63	MS65
ND-1915	—	—	90.00	150	300	—

Bougie

KM# TnC1 5 CENTIMES
Aluminum **Issuer:** Bougie Chamber of Commerce **Obv:** Name of issuer, dots flank date **Rev:** Large value at center

Date	Mintage	VF20	XF40	MS60	MS63	MS65
1915	—	5.00	10.00	25.00	50.00	100

KM# TnC2.1 10 CENTIMES
Aluminum **Issuer:** Bougie Chamber of Commerce **Obv:** Name of issuer, dots flank date **Rev:** Large value at center

Date	Mintage	VF20	XF40	MS60	MS63	MS65
1915	—	6.00	12.00	28.00	60.00	120

KM# TnC2.2 10 CENTIMES
Aluminum **Issuer:** Bougie Chamber of Commerce **Obv:** Dot and triangle at right of date

Date	Mintage	VF20	XF40	MS60	MS63	MS65
1915	—	5.00	10.00	20.00	45.00	—

KM# TnC2a 10 CENTIMES
Zinc **Issuer:** Bougie Chamber of Commerce

Date	Mintage	VF20	XF40	MS60	MS63	MS65
1915	—	30.00	50.00	120	250	—

Constantine

KM# TnD1 5 CENTIMES
Aluminum **Issuer:** Constantine Chamber of Commerce

Date	Mintage	VF20	XF40	MS60	MS63	MS65
1922	—	25.00	35.00	60.00	120	—

KM# TnD2 10 CENTIMES
Aluminum **Issuer:** Constantine Chamber of Commerce

Date	Mintage	VF20	XF40	MS60	MS63	MS65
1922	—	20.00	30.00	50.00	100	200

Oran

KM# TnE1 5 CENTIMES
Aluminum **Issuer:** Oran Chamber of Commerce **Obv:** Small crowned shield, date below flanked by dots **Rev:** Large value left of spray

Date	Mintage	VF20	XF40	MS60	MS63	MS65
1921	—	4.50	9.00	25.00	50.00	100

KM# TnE2 10 CENTIMES
Aluminum **Issuer:** Oran Chamber of Commerce **Obv:** Small crowned shield, date below flanked by dots **Rev:** Large value left of tree

Date	Mintage	VF20	XF40	MS60	MS63	MS65
1921	—	3.00	6.00	12.00	25.00	35.00

KM# TnE2a 10 CENTIMES
Brass **Issuer:** Oran Chamber of Commerce

Date	Mintage	VF20	XF40	MS60	MS63	MS65
1921	—	—	75.00	150	300	—

KM# TnE3 25 CENTIMES
Aluminum **Issuer:** Oran Chamber of Commerce **Obv:** Similar to 10 Centimes, KM#TnE2 **Rev:** Similar to 25 Centimes, KM#TnE4

Date	Mintage	VF20	XF40	MS60	MS63	MS65
1921	—	4.00	8.50	25.00	50.00	—

KM# TnE4 25 CENTIMES
Aluminum **Issuer:** Oran Chamber of Commerce **Obv:** Small crowned shield, chains **Rev:** Large value within wreath

Date	Mintage	VF20	XF40	MS60	MS63	MS65
1921	—	5.00	10.00	30.00	60.00	—

KM# TnE5 25 CENTIMES
Aluminum **Issuer:** Oran Chamber of Commerce **Note:** For further listings of private token issues refer to the catalogue of "French Emergency Tokens of 1914-1922" by Robert Lamb.

Date	Mintage	VF20	XF40	MS60	MS63	MS65
1922	—	5.00	10.00	30.00	60.00	115

REPUBLIC

STANDARD COINAGE

KM# 94 CENTIME
0.50 g., Aluminum, 11.5 mm. **Obv:** National arms within wreath **Rev:** Value at center of scalloped circle **Edge:** Plain

Date	Mintage	VF20	XF40	MS60	MS63	MS65
AH1383-1964	35,000,000	—	0.20	0.40	1.00	2.00

KM# 95 2 CENTIMES
0.60 g., Aluminum, 18 mm. **Obv:** National arms within wreath **Rev:** Value at center of scalloped circle **Edge:** Plain

Date	Mintage	VF20	XF40	MS60	MS63	MS65
AH1383-1964	50,000,000	—	0.20	0.40	1.00	2.00

KM# 96 5 CENTIMES
0.85 g., Aluminum, 21.1 mm. **Obv:** National arms within wreath **Rev:** Value at center of scalloped circle

Date	Mintage	VF20	XF40	MS60	MS63	MS65
AH1383-1964	40,000,000	—	0.25	0.45	1.25	2.50

KM# 101 5 CENTIMES
1.50 g., Aluminum **Series:** F.A.O. **Subject:** 1st Four Year Plan **Obv:** Value at center **Rev:** Two dates center of circle, circle consists of gear teeth on left, sprays of grain on right **Note:** Varieties exist.

Date	Mintage	VF20	XF40	MS60	MS63	MS65
ND-1970	50,000,000	—	0.15	0.30	0.75	1.50

KM# 106 5 CENTIMES
1.50 g., Aluminum **Series:** F.A.O. **Subject:** 2nd Four Year Plan **Obv:** Large value at center **Rev:** Two dates at center of circle, circle consists of gear teeth on left, sprays of grain on right

Date	Mintage	VF20	XF40	MS60	MS63	MS65
ND-1974	10,000,000	—	0.15	0.30	0.75	1.50

KM# 113 5 CENTIMES
1.50 g., Aluminum **Series:** F.A.O. **Subject:** 1st Five Year Plan **Obv:** Large value at center **Rev:** Inscription within circle of gear teeth on left, grain spray on right

Date	Mintage	VF20	XF40	MS60	MS63	MS65
ND-1980	—	2.00	5.00	9.00	15.00	25.00

KM# 116 5 CENTIMES
1.50 g., Aluminum, 22 mm. **Series:** F.A.O. **Subject:** 2nd Five Year Plan **Obv:** Large value at center **Rev:** Two dates center of circle, circle consists of geared teeth on right, sprays of grain on left **Note:** Varieties exist in planchet thickness.

Date	Mintage	VF20	XF40	MS60	MS63	MS65
1985-1989	—	—	—	0.25	0.70	1.50
Note: 8 in dates have vertical sides						
1985-1989	—	—	—	0.25	0.70	1.50
Note: 8 in date have curved sides						

KM# 97 10 CENTIMES
2.50 g., Aluminum-Bronze **Obv:** Small arms within wreath **Rev:** Value in circle **Edge:** Plain

Date	Mintage	VF20	XF40	MS60	MS63	MS65
AH1383-1964	—	—	0.25	0.75	2.00	3.00

KM# 115 10 CENTIMES
Aluminum **Obv:** Large value in circle **Rev:** Palm tree flanked by rosettes, date below tree **Note:** Varieties exist.

Date	Mintage	VF20	XF40	MS60	MS63	MS65
1984	—	0.15	0.25	0.75	3.00	4.00
1989 Rare	—	—	—	—	—	—

KM# 98 20 CENTIMES
4.00 g., Aluminum-Bronze **Obv:** Arms within wreath **Rev:** Value in circle **Edge:** Plain

Date	Mintage	VF20	XF40	MS60	MS63	MS65
AH1383-1964	—	—	0.25	0.75	2.00	3.00

KM# 103 20 CENTIMES
4.00 g., Aluminum-Bronze **Series:** F.A.O. **Subject:** Agricultural Revolution **Obv:** Value in circle **Rev:** Cornucopia, date above **Edge:** Plain

Date	Mintage	VF20	XF40	MS60	MS63	MS65
1972	20,000,000	—	0.10	0.25	0.75	1.25

KM# 107.1 20 CENTIMES
4.00 g., Aluminum-Bronze **Series:** F.A.O. **Obv:** Value at center of circle **Rev:** Ram's head left, date below **Edge:** Plain

Date	Mintage	VF20	XF40	MS60	MS63	MS65
1975	50,000,000	—	0.20	0.45	1.75	2.00

KM# 107.2 20 CENTIMES
4.00 g., Aluminum-Bronze **Series:** F.A.O. **Obv:** Small flower above 20 **Rev:** Ram's head left, date below **Edge:** Plain

Date	Mintage	VF20	XF40	MS60	MS63	MS65
1975	Inc. above	—	0.15	0.30	1.50	2.00

KM# 118 20 CENTIMES
4.00 g., Aluminum-Bronze **Series:** F.A.O. **Obv:** Value in circle **Rev:** Rams head left, date below **Edge:** Plain

Date	Mintage	VF20	XF40	MS60	MS63	MS65
1987	60,000,000	0.50	1.00	2.00	8.00	12.00

KM# 99 50 CENTIMES
5.00 g., Aluminum-Bronze, 24 mm. **Obv:** Arms within wreath **Rev:** Value in circle **Edge:** Reeded

Date	Mintage	VF20	XF40	MS60	MS63	MS65
AH1383-1964	—	—	0.25	0.75	2.00	3.50

KM# 102 50 CENTIMES
5.00 g., Aluminum-Bronze, 24 mm. **Obv:** Book, divider on top, bottle at bottom **Rev:** Value in circle **Edge:** Reeded

Date	Mintage	VF20	XF40	MS60	MS63	MS65
AH1391-1971	10,000,000	0.25	0.50	1.50	3.00	5.00
AH1393-1973	10,000,000	0.25	0.50	1.50	3.00	5.00

KM# 109 50 CENTIMES
5.00 g., Aluminum-Bronze, 24 mm. **Subject:** 30th Anniversary French-Algerian Clash **Obv:** Value in circle **Rev:** Inscription **Edge:** Reeded

Date	Mintage	VF20	XF40	MS60	MS63	MS65
ND-1975	18,000,000	—	0.20	0.50	1.50	3.00

KM# 111 50 CENTIMES
5.00 g., Aluminum-Bronze, 24.5 mm. **Subject:** 1400th Anniversary of Mohammad's Flight **Obv:** Value in circle **Rev:** Value, outline of Mosque **Edge:** Reeded

Date	Mintage	VF20	XF40	MS60	MS63	MS65
AH1400-1980	—	0.15	0.25	0.50	2.50	4.50

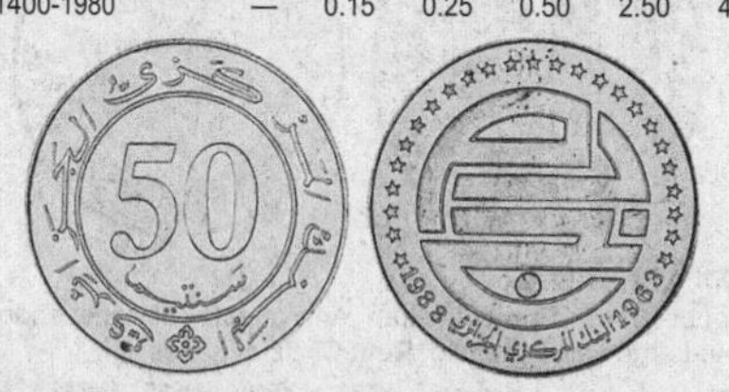

KM# 119 50 CENTIMES
5.00 g., Aluminum-Bronze, 24 mm. **Subject:** 25th Anniversary of Constitution **Obv:** Value in circle **Rev:** Stylized design **Edge:** Reeded

Date	Mintage	VF20	XF40	MS60	MS63	MS65
1988	40,000,000	0.15	0.25	0.75	3.00	6.00

KM# 127 1/4 DINAR
1.15 g., Aluminum, 16.5 mm. **Subject:** Fennec Fox **Obv:** Value in small circle **Rev:** Head facing

Date	Mintage	VF20	XF40	MS60	MS63	MS65
AH1413-1992	—	—	0.65	1.25	2.50	3.00
AH1413-1992	—	PF65 12.00				
AH1418-1998	—	—	0.65	1.25	2.50	3.00

KM# 128 1/2 DINAR
Stainless Steel **Subject:** Barbary Horse **Obv:** Value in small circle **Rev:** Encirled Barbary horse head dividing date at top, facing 3/4 left

Date	Mintage	VF20	XF40	MS60	MS63	MS65
AH1413-1992	—	PF65 12.00				
AH1413-1992	—	—	0.65	1.25	3.00	4.00

KM# 100 DINAR
Copper-Nickel **Obv:** Large arms within wreath **Rev:** Large value in circle

Date	Mintage	VF20	XF40	MS60	MS63	MS65
AH1383-1964	15,000,000	0.25	0.50	1.00	2.00	4.00
AH1383-1964	—	PF65 40.00				

KM# 104.1 DINAR
Copper-Nickel **Series:** F.A.O. **Obv:** Large value in circle, legend away from inner circle **Rev:** Hands grasped at top, man on tractor facing flanked by sprigs, date below

Date	Mintage	VF20	XF40	MS60	MS63	MS65
1972	20,000,000	0.25	0.50	1.00	2.50	3.50

KM# 104.2 DINAR
Copper-Nickel **Series:** F.A.O. **Obv:** Large value at center, legend touches inner circle **Rev:** Tractor

Date	Mintage	VF20	XF40	MS60	MS63	MS65
1972	Inc. above	0.20	0.45	0.85	2.00	3.00

KM# 112 DINAR
Copper-Nickel **Subject:** 20th Anniversary of Independence **Obv:** Large value in circle **Rev:** Circle of hands

Date	Mintage	VF20	XF40	MS60	MS63	MS65
ND-1983	—	0.35	0.75	1.50	3.50	5.50

KM# 117 DINAR
Copper-Nickel **Subject:** 25th Anniversary of Independence - Monument **Obv:** Large value in circle **Rev:** Monument within grain wreath

Date	Mintage	VF20	XF40	MS60	MS63	MS65
1987	—	0.35	0.75	1.50	3.50	5.50

KM# 120 DINAR
3.22 g., 0.920 Gold 0.0952 oz. AGW **Subject:** Historical Coin - 5 Aspers of Abd-el-Kader **Obv:** Old Islamic coin at center **Rev:** Old Islamic coin

Date	Mintage	VF20	XF40	MS60	MS63	MS65
AH1411-1991	—	—	—	—	250	300

KM# 129 DINAR
4.24 g., Stainless Steel, 20.6 mm. **Obv:** Value on silhouette of country, within circle **Rev:** African buffalo's head 3/4 left, ancient drawings above **Edge:** Plain

Date	Mintage	VF20	XF40	MS60	MS63	MS65
AH1413-1992	—	—	1.00	1.50	2.50	4.00
AH1413-1992	—	PF65 15.00				

Date	Mintage	VF20	XF40	MS60	MS63	MS65
AH1417-1997	—	—	1.00	1.50	2.50	4.00
AH1420-1999	—	—	1.00	1.50	2.50	4.00
AH1421-2000	—	—	1.00	1.50	2.50	4.00

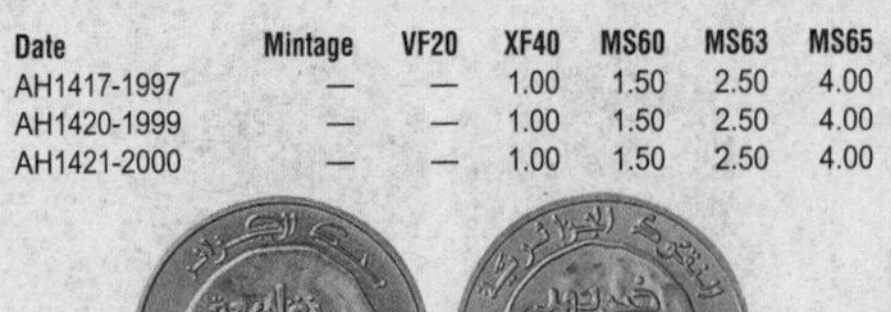

KM# 121 2 DINARS
6.45 g., 0.920 Gold 0.1908 oz. AGW **Subject:** Historical Coin - Dinar of 762 A.D. Rostomiden Dynasty

Date	Mintage	VF20	XF40	MS60	MS63	MS65
AH1411-1991	—	—	—	—	475	550

KM# 130 2 DINARS
5.13 g., Stainless Steel, 22.5 mm. **Obv:** Value on silhouette of country **Rev:** Dromedary camel's head right **Edge:** Plain

Date	Mintage	VF20	XF40	MS60	MS63	MS65
AH1413-1992	—	—	1.00	2.00	3.50	5.00
AH1413-1992	—	PF65 18.00				
AH1414-1993	—	—	1.00	2.00	3.50	5.00
AH1417-1996	—	—	—	—	—	—
AH1417-1997	—	—	1.00	2.00	3.50	5.00
AH1419-1999	—	—	1.00	2.00	3.50	5.00
AH1420-1999	—	—	1.00	2.00	3.50	5.00

KM# 133 2 DINARS
6.47 g., Gold **Subject:** Historical Coin - 2 Dinar of Abd Al-Qadir, AH1222-1300

Date	Mintage	VF20	XF40	MS60	MS63	MS65
AH1417-1996	—	—	—	—	550	650

KM# 105 5 DINARS
12.00 g., 0.750 Silver 0.2894 oz. ASW, 31 mm. **Series:** F.A.O. **Subject:** 10th Anniversary **Obv:** Large value flanked by small flowers within circle **Rev:** Tower with grain head at base dividing dates at bottom, Five stars flanking **Note:** Privy mark: owl.

Date	Mintage	VF20	XF40	MS60	MS63	MS65
ND-1972	5,000,000	—	10.00	14.00	20.00	—

KM# 105a.1 5 DINARS
12.00 g., Nickel, 31 mm. **Edge:** Reeded

Date	Mintage	VF20	XF40	MS60	MS63	MS65
ND-1972	10,000,000	—	7.00	10.00	18.00	—

KM# 105a.2 5 DINARS
12.00 g., Nickel, 31 mm. **Edge:** Reeded **Note:** Privy mark: dolphin.

Date	Mintage	VF20	XF40	MS60	MS63	MS65
ND-1972	10,000,000	—	7.00	10.00	18.00	—

KM# 108 5 DINARS
12.00 g., Nickel, 31 mm. **Subject:** 20th Anniversary of Revolution **Obv:** Large value in circle flanked by rosettes **Rev:** Armed revolutionary man leaning, right, two dates lower right **Edge:** Reeded

Date	Mintage	VF20	XF40	MS60	MS63	MS65
ND-1974	—	—	3.50	7.00	12.50	—

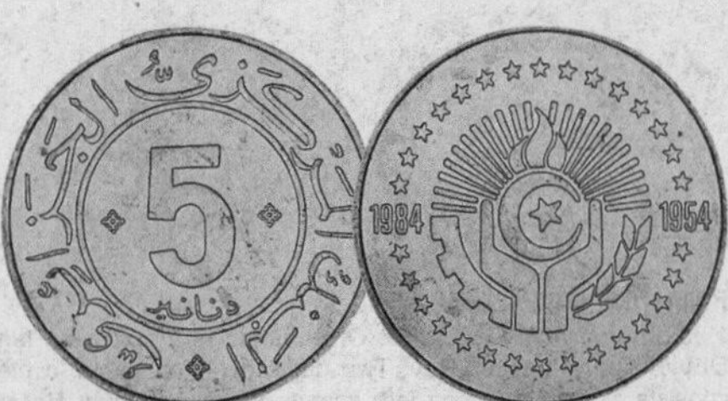

KM# 114 5 DINARS
12.00 g., Nickel, 31 mm. **Subject:** 30th Anniversary of Revolution **Obv:** Value flanked by small rosettes in circle **Rev:** Hands holding symbol, flanked by dates divided by stars **Edge:** Reeded

Date	Mintage	VF20	XF40	MS60	MS63	MS65
ND-1984	—	—	2.50	5.00	10.00	—

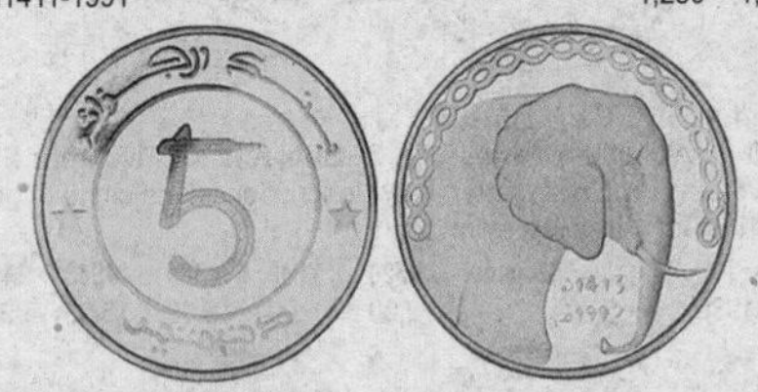

KM# 122 5 DINARS
16.12 g., 0.920 Gold 0.4768 oz. AGW **Subject:** Historical Coin - Denar of Numidian King Massinissa, 238-148 B.C. **Obv:** Standing elephant left, within circle flanked by value **Rev:** King,left within beaded circle

Date	Mintage	VF20	XF40	MS60	MS63	MS65
AH1411-1991	—	—	—	—	1,250	1,500

KM# 123 5 DINARS
6.20 g., Stainless Steel, 24.5 mm. **Obv:** Denomination within circle **Rev:** Forepart of African elephant right **Edge:** Plain

Date	Mintage	VF20	XF40	MS60	MS63	MS65
AH1413-1992	—	—	1.25	2.50	4.00	7.00
AH1413-1992	—	PF65 20.00				
AH1414-1993	—	—	1.25	2.50	4.00	7.00
AH1417-1997	—	—	1.25	2.50	4.00	7.00
AH1418-1997	—	—	1.25	2.50	4.00	7.00
AH1418-1998	—	—	1.25	2.50	4.00	7.00
AH1419-1998	—	—	1.25	2.50	4.00	7.00
AH1420-1999	—	—	1.25	2.50	4.00	7.00
AH1420-2000	—	—	1.25	2.50	4.00	7.00

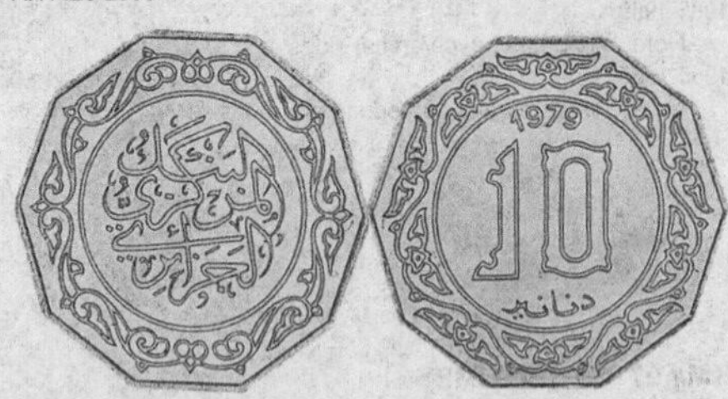

KM# 110 10 DINARS
11.37 g., Aluminum-Bronze **Obv:** Inscription within circle, wreath surrounds **Rev:** Large value within circle, date above **Shape:** 10-sided

Date	Mintage	VF20	XF40	MS60	MS63	MS65
1979	25,001,000	—	2.00	4.00	7.00	9.00
1981	40,000,000	—	2.00	4.00	7.00	9.00

KM# 110a 10 DINARS
14.60 g., 0.925 Silver 0.4342 oz. ASW

Date	Mintage	VF20	XF40	MS60	MS63	MS65
1979	1,000	—	—	—	35.00	45.00

KM# 110b 10 DINARS
24.50 g., 0.900 Gold 0.7089 oz. AGW

Date	Mintage	VF20	XF40	MS60	MS63	MS65
1979	100	—	—	—	1,400	1,600

KM# 124 10 DINARS

4.95 g., Bi-Metallic Aluminum center in Stainless Steel ring, 26.5 mm. **Obv:** Denomination **Rev:** Barbary falcon's head right **Edge:** Plain

Date	Mintage	VF20	XF40	MS60	MS63	MS65
AH1413-1992	—	—	2.00	4.00	7.00	10.00
AH1413-1992	—	PF65 22.00				
AH1414-1993	—	—	2.00	4.00	7.00	10.00
AH1417-1997	—	—	1.50	3.50	7.00	10.00
AH1418-1997	—	—	2.00	4.00	7.00	10.00
AH1421-2000	—	—	1.50	3.50	7.00	10.00

KM# 134 10 DINARS

14.60 g., 0.835 Silver 0.3919 oz. ASW, 31.5 mm. **Subject:** Jugurtha, King of Numidia (154-104BC) **Obv:** Denomination **Rev:** Head of Jugurtha left **Edge:** Reeded

Date	Mintage	VF20	XF40	MS60	MS63	MS65
AH1415	—	—	—	—	75.00	95.00

KM# 135 10 DINARS

14.60 g., 0.835 Silver 0.3919 oz. ASW, 31.5 mm. **Subject:** Abdelhamid Benbadis (1889-1940) **Obv:** Denomination **Rev:** 1/2 bust of Benbadis half left **Edge:** Reeded

Date	Mintage	VF20	XF40	MS60	MS63	MS65
AH1415	—	—	—	—	75.00	95.00

KM# 136 10 DINARS

14.60 g., 0.835 Silver 0.3919 oz. ASW, 31.5 mm. **Subject:** Houari Boumediene (1922-1978) **Obv:** Denomination **Rev:** Bust of Boumediene half left **Edge:** Reeded

Date	Mintage	VF20	XF40	MS60	MS63	MS65
AH1415	—	—	—	—	75.00	95.00

KM# 125 20 DINARS

8.62 g., Bi-Metallic Aluminum-Bronze center in Stainless Steel ring, 27.5 mm. **Subject:** Lion **Obv:** Denomination **Rev:** Head left

Date	Mintage	VF20	XF40	MS60	MS63	MS65
AH1413-1992	—	—	3.50	5.50	9.00	12.00
AH1413-1992	—	—	3.50	5.50	9.00	12.00

Note: Date doubled

Date	Mintage	VF20	XF40	MS60	MS63	MS65
AH1413-1992	—	PF65 30.00				
AH1414-1993	—	—	3.50	5.50	9.00	12.00
AH1416-1996	—	—	3.50	5.50	9.00	12.00
AH1417-1996	—	—	3.50	5.50	9.00	12.00
AH1417-1997	—	—	3.50	5.50	9.00	12.00
AH1418-1997	—	—	3.50	5.50	9.00	12.00
AH1420-1999	—	—	3.50	5.50	9.00	12.00
AH1421-2000	—	—	3.50	5.50	9.00	12.00

KM# 126 50 DINARS

9.27 g., Bi-Metallic Stainless Steel center in Aluminum-Bronze ring, 28.5 mm. **Obv:** Denomination **Rev:** Dama gazelle with head left

Date	Mintage	VF20	XF40	MS60	MS63	MS65
AH1413-1992	—	—	3.50	6.00	10.00	15.00
AH1413-1992	—	PF65 35.00				
AH1414-1993	—	—	3.50	6.00	10.00	15.00
AH1417-1996	—	—	3.50	6.00	10.00	15.00
AH1416-1996	—	—	3.50	6.00	10.00	15.00
AH1414-1996	—	—	3.50	6.00	10.00	15.00
AH1417-1997	—	—	3.50	6.00	10.00	15.00
AH1418-1998	—	—	3.50	6.00	10.00	15.00
AH1419-1999	—	—	3.50	6.00	10.00	15.00
AH1420-1999	—	—	3.50	6.00	10.00	15.00
AH1421-2000	—	—	3.50	6.00	10.00	15.00

KM# 131 50 DINARS

9.27 g., Bi-Metallic Stainless Steel center in Aluminum-Bronze ring, 28.5 mm. **Subject:** 40th Anniversary - Start of the Revolution **Obv:** Large value in circle **Rev:** Star dividing dates at right in circle

Date	Mintage	VF20	XF40	MS60	MS63	MS65
ND-1994	—	—	5.00	7.00	12.00	20.00
ND-1994	—	PF65 40.00				

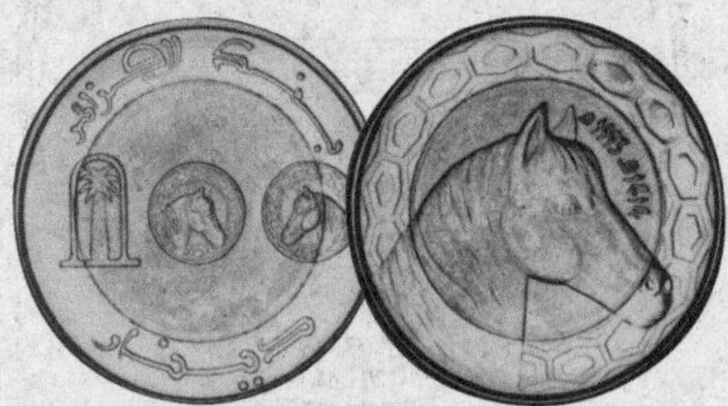

KM# 132 100 DINARS

11.00 g., Bi-Metallic Copper-Nickel center in Stainless Steel ring, 29.5 mm. **Obv:** Denomination stylized with reverse design **Rev:** Horse head right **Edge:** Reeded

Date	Mintage	VF20	XF40	MS60	MS63	MS65
AH1413-1992	—	—	5.00	8.00	14.00	22.00
AH1414-1993	—	—	5.00	8.00	14.00	22.00
AH1415-1994	—	—	5.00	8.00	14.00	22.00
AH1417-1997	—	—	5.00	8.00	14.00	22.00
AH1418-1998	—	—	5.00	8.00	14.00	22.00
AH1421-2000	—	—	5.00	8.00	14.00	22.00

ESSAIS

Standard metals unless otherwise noted

KM#	Date	Mintage	Identification	Mkt Val
E1	1949	1,500	20 Francs. Copper-Nickel. KM#91.	100
E2	1949	1,500	50 Francs. Copper-Nickel. KM#92.	115
E3	1950	1,500	100 Francs. Copper-Nickel. KM#93.	120
E4	ND-1972	2,250	5 Dinars. Silver. Value flanked by rosettes within circle. Tower with grain head at base dividing dates below, five stars flanking tower. KM#105.	60.00
E5	ND-1972	1,000	5 Dinars. Nickel. KM#105a.	100
E6	ND-1974	3,300	5 Dinars. Nickel. Large value flanked by rosettes within circle. Armed revolutionary man leaning, right,two dates bottom right. KM#108.	50.00
E7	1981	2,670	10 Dinars. Aluminum-Bronze. KM#110.	60.00

PIEDFORT WITH ESSAI

Double thickness -
Standard metals unless otherwise noted

KM#	Date	Mintage	Identification	Mkt Val
PE1	1949	104	20 Francs. Copper-Nickel. Head with laureated hood, right. Value, with date below, between columns of grain. KM#91.	225
PE2	1949	104	50 Francs. Copper-Nickel. Head with laureated hood, right. Value, with date below, between columns of grain. KM#92.	250
PE3	1950	104	100 Francs. Copper-Nickel. Head with laureated hood, right. Value, with date below, between columns of grain. KM#93.	275

PATTERNS

Including off metal strikes

KM#	Date	Mintage	Identification	Mkt Val
Pn4	1950	—	100 Francs. Silver. As KM#93.	1,500

AMERICAN SAMOA

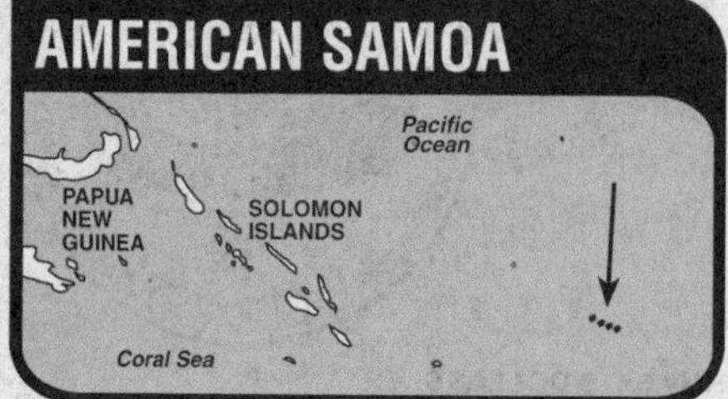

The Territory of American Samoa, with a population of 41,000, consists of seven major islands with a total land area of 76 sq. mi. (199 sq. km.) which are located about 2300 miles south-southwest of Hawaii. American Samoa was settled by the Polynesians around 600 BC. The capital is Pago Pago.

By 1900 the Samoan islands were being claimed by both Germany and the United States. Germany annexed several islands, which now comprise Western Samoa; the U.S. took Tutuila to use Pago Pago Bay as a coali ng station for naval ships.

As Japan began emerging as an international power in the mid-1930's, the U.S. Naval station on Tutuila began to acquire new strategic importance; and in 1940 the Samoan Islands became a training and staging area for the U.S. Marine Corps.

A. P. Lutali, Governor of American Samoa, signed a historic proclamation on May 23, 1988 that authorized the minting of the first numismatic issue for this unincorporated territory administered by the United States Department of the Interior.

MONETARY SYSTEM

100 Cents = 1 Dollar

U.S. TERRITORY

DECIMAL COINAGE

KM# 1.1 DOLLAR

31.10 g., Bronze 3mm Thick **Subject:** America's Cup **Obv:** Americas Cup **Rev:** Rope ornamentation at sides in legend gaps **Edge:** Reeded

Date	Mintage	VF20	XF40	MS60	MS63	MS65
1988	100,000	PF63 30.00	PF65 32.00			

Note: Mintage limit of 100,000

KM# 1.2 DOLLAR

31.10 g., Bronze 3mm Thick, Lighter in color than KM-1.1, 39 mm. **Obv:** Americas Cup **Rev:** 2 sailboats with crossed sails; Rope-like ornamentation at sides in legend gaps **Edge:** Plain **Note:** Currently being minted under the 100,000 mintage limit authorization of KM-1.1

Date	Mintage	VF20	XF40	MS60	MS63	MS65
1988	Inc. above	PF63 20.00	PF65 25.00			

KM# 2 5 DOLLARS
31.10 g., 0.999 Silver 0.9989 oz. ASW **Subject:** America's Cup **Obv:** Americas Cup

Date	Mintage	VF20	XF40	MS60	MS63	MS65
1988	1,000	PF63 60.00	PF65 95.00			

KM# 6.1 5 DOLLARS
31.10 g., 0.999 Silver 0.9989 oz. ASW **Subject:** XXIV Olympics **Obv:** Olympic logo above crossed symbol within circle, date below circle **Rev:** Olympic rings above Chamshil Stadium, value below **Note:** Coin die alignment.

Date	Mintage	VF20	XF40	MS60	MS63	MS65
1988	1,000	PF63 50.00	PF65 75.00			

KM# 6.2 5 DOLLARS
31.10 g., 0.999 Silver 0.9989 oz. ASW **Note:** Medallic die alignment.

Date	Mintage	VF20	XF40	MS60	MS63	MS65
1988	—	PF65 225				

KM# 3 25 DOLLARS
155.52 g., 0.999 Silver 4.9949 oz. ASW, 63 mm. **Subject:** America's Cup '88 **Obv:** America's Cup **Rev:** Sailboat

Date	Mintage	VF20	XF40	MS60	MS63	MS65
1988	100	PF63 175	PF65 245			

KM# 7 25 DOLLARS
155.52 g., 0.999 Silver 4.9949 oz. ASW, 63 mm. **Subject:** XXIV Olympics **Obv:** Bust of Gov. Lutali left **Rev:** Chamshil Stadium, large value below, five olympic rings above

Date	Mintage	VF20	XF40	MS60	MS63	MS65
ND-1988	100	PF63 225	PF65 325			

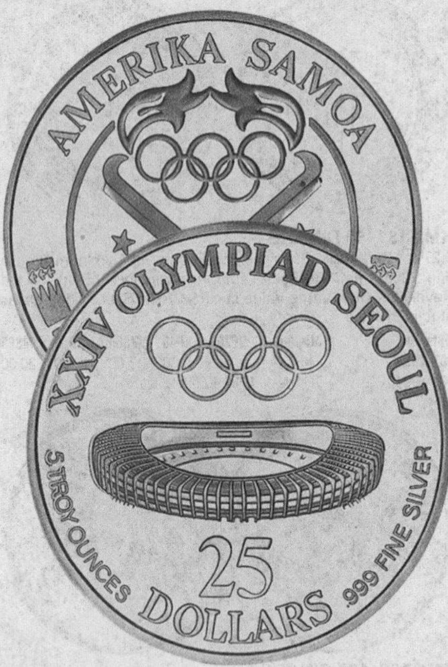

KM# 9 25 DOLLARS
155.52 g., 0.999 Silver 4.9949 oz. ASW, 63 mm. **Subject:** Olympics **Obv:** Olympic logo above symbol within circle, date below circle **Rev:** Olympic logo above Chamshil Stadium, value at bottom

Date	Mintage	VF20	XF40	MS60	MS63	MS65
1988	100	PF63 175	PF65 245			

KM# 10 25 DOLLARS
155.52 g., 0.999 Silver 4.9949 oz. ASW, 63 mm. **Subject:** XXIV Olympics **Rev:** Chamshil Stadium **Note:** Similar to KM#7 but denomination: TWENTY-FIVE.

Date	Mintage	VF20	XF40	MS60	MS63	MS65
1988	—	PF63 250	PF65 375			

KM# 4 50 DOLLARS
8.64 g., 0.900 Gold 0.250 oz. AGW **Subject:** America's Cup **Obv:** Olympic symbols **Rev:** Americas Cup

Date	Mintage	VF20	XF40	MS60	MS63	MS65
1988	100	PF65 550				

KM# 5 100 DOLLARS
31.10 g., 0.999 Gold 0.9989 oz. AGW **Subject:** America's Cup **Obv:** State seal **Rev:** USA's yacht passing New Zealand's yacht

Date	Mintage	VF20	XF40	MS60	MS63	MS65
1988	50	PF65 1,850				

KM# 8 100 DOLLARS
31.10 g., 0.999 Gold 0.9989 oz. AGW **Subject:** XXIV Olympics **Obv:** State seal **Rev:** Olympic rings and Chamshil Stadium above denomination

Date	Mintage	VF20	XF40	MS60	MS63	MS65
1988	50	PF65 2,000				

KM# 11 100 DOLLARS
31.10 g., 0.999 Gold 0.9989 oz. AGW **Obv:** USA's yacht passing New Zealand's yacht **Rev:** Olympic rings and Chamshil Stadium above denomination **Note:** Mule.

Date	Mintage	VF20	XF40	MS60	MS63	MS65
1988	5	PF65 3,200				

PROOF SETS

KM#	Date	Mintage	Identification	Issue Price	Mkt Val
PS1	1988 (3)	—	KM#2-4	315	900

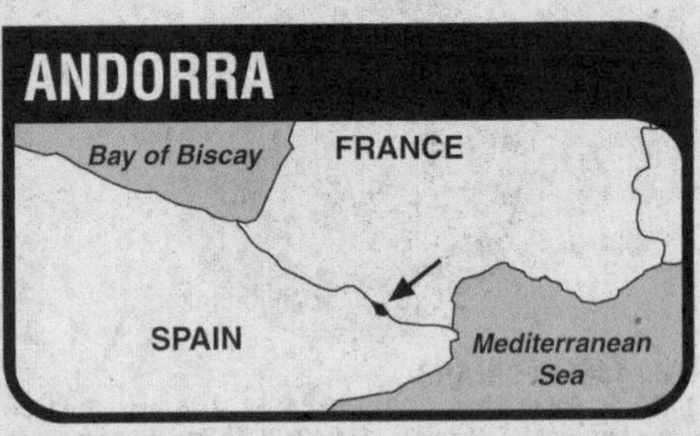

Principality of Andorra (Principat d'Andorra), situated on the southern slopes of the Pyrenees Mountains between France and Spain, has an area of 181 sq. mi. (453 sq. km.) and a population of 80,000. Capital: Andorra la Vella. Tourism is the chief source of income. Timber, cattle and derivatives, and furniture are exported.

According to tradition, the independence of Andorra derives from a charter Charlemagne granted the people of Andorra in 806 in recognition of their help in battling the Moors. An agreement between the Count of Foix (France) and the Bishop of Seo de Urgel (Spanish) in 1278 to recognize each other as Co-Princes of Andorra gave the state what has been its political form and territorial extent continuously to the present day. Over the years, the title on the French side passed to the Kings of Navarre, then to the Kings of France, and is now held by the President of France.

RULER
Joan D.M. Bisbe D'Urgell I

MONETARY SYSTEM
100 Centims = 1 Diner

NOTE: The Diners have been struck for collectors while the Euro is used in everyday commerce.

MINT MARK
Crowned M = Madrid

PRINCIPALITY

DECIMAL COINAGE

KM# 171 CENTIM
1.27 g., Aluminum, 22 mm. **Subject:** F.A.O. **Obv:** Denomination **Rev:** Winged figure carrying wheat **Edge:** Plain

Date	Mintage	VF20	XF40	MS60	MS63	MS65
1999	—	—	—	—	1.75	2.50

KM# 164 10 CENTIMS
6.81 g., Brass **Obv:** National arms **Rev:** Building and arms **Edge:** Plain

Date	Mintage	VF20	XF40	MS60	MS63	MS65
1997	—	—	—	—	4.00	5.00

KM# 33 25 CENTIMS
2.70 g., Bronze, 22 mm. **Obv:** Joan D. M. Bisbe D'Urgell I **Rev:** Crowned value within wreath **Edge:** Plain

Date	Mintage	VF20	XF40	MS60	MS63	MS65
1986	10,000	—	—	—	5.00	5.50

KM# 109 25 CENTIMS
Copper-Nickel, 30 mm. **Subject:** 50th Anniversary - F.A.O. **Obv:** Crowned arms to left of five line inscription, value below, date at bottom **Rev:** People on globe adoring F.A.O. logo

Date	Mintage	VF20	XF40	MS60	MS63	MS65
1995	50,000	—	—	—	7.00	10.00

KM# 382 25 CENTIMS
31.11 g., Copper-Nickel-Zinc, 38.61 mm. **Subject:** Year of the Tiger **Obv:** Tiger in color **Rev:** Crowned value in wreath

Date	Mintage	VF20	XF40	MS60	MS63	MS65
1998	—	—	—	—	—	25.00

KM# 134 50 CENTIMS
0.62 g., 0.999 Gold 0.020 oz. AGW **Obv:** Fleury cross **Rev:** Portrait of Queen Isabella I **Note:** Similar to 20 Diners, KM#137.

Date	Mintage	VF20	XF40	MS60	MS63	MS65
1997	Est. 50000	PF65 45.00				

KM# 14 DINER
6.50 g., Brass, 25 mm. **Obv:** Joan D.M. Bisbe D'Urgell I **Rev:** Arms within circle,lower circle divides value, date at bottom

Date	Mintage	VF20	XF40	MS60	MS63	MS65
1983	28,000	—	—	—	8.50	11.50

KM# 15 DINER
6.50 g., Copper and Zinc, 25 mm. **Obv:** Joan D.M.Bisbe D'Urgell I, left **Rev:** Crowned oval arms flanked by cherubs, value below **Note:** Cast.

Date	Mintage	VF20	XF40	MS60	MS63	MS65
1984	7,500	—	—	—	9.00	12.00

KM# 35 DINER
6.20 g., Brass, 25 mm. **Obv:** Bust of Joan D.M.Bisbe D'Urgell I, right **Rev:** Crowned value within wreath

Date	Mintage	VF20	XF40	MS60	MS63	MS65
1986	10,000	—	—	—	8.50	11.50

KM# 49 DINER
6.85 g., Copper-Nickel, 25 mm. **Subject:** Pont de la Margineda **Obv:** Bridge **Rev:** Large value, date to left

Date	Mintage	VF20	XF40	MS60	MS63	MS65
1988	5,000	—	—	—	10.00	12.00

KM# 127 DINER
10.00 g., 0.500 Silver 0.1608 oz. ASW **Subject:** Treaty of Rome **Obv:** Crowned arms **Rev:** Seated Europa placing laurel wreath on her head

Date	Mintage	VF20	XF40	MS60	MS63	MS65
1997	30,000	PF65 20.00				

KM# 135 DINER
1.24 g., 0.999 Gold 0.040 oz. AGW **Obv:** Fleury cross **Rev:** Portrait of Queen Isabella I **Note:** Similar to 20 Diners, KM#137.

Date	Mintage	VF20	XF40	MS60	MS63	MS65
1997	Est. 10000	PF65 75.00				

KM# 19 2 DINERS
15.00 g., Bi-Metallic Bronze center in Copper-Nickel ring, 32 mm. **Subject:** Wildlife **Obv:** Crowned shield divide value **Rev:** Brown bear left

Date	Mintage	VF20	XF40	MS60	MS63	MS65
1984	5,000	—	—	—	15.00	20.00

KM# 20 2 DINERS
15.00 g., Bi-Metallic Bronze center in Copper-Nickel ring, 32 mm. **Subject:** Wildlife **Obv:** Crowned shield divide value **Rev:** Red squirrel, facing

Date	Mintage	VF20	XF40	MS60	MS63	MS65
1984	5,000	—	—	—	15.00	20.00

KM# 21 2 DINERS
15.00 g., Bi-Metallic Bronze center in Copper-Nickel ring, 32 mm. **Subject:** Wildlife **Obv:** Crowned shield divide value **Rev:** Chamois facing

Date	Mintage	VF20	XF40	MS60	MS63	MS65
1984	5,000	—	—	—	15.00	20.00

KM# 27 2 DINERS
15.00 g., Bi-Metallic Bronze center in Copper-Nickel ring, 32 mm. **Subject:** 1988 Winter Olympics **Obv:** Arms in circle **Rev:** Skier, facing

Date	Mintage	VF20	XF40	MS60	MS63	MS65
1985	11,000	—	—	—	15.00	20.00

KM# 28 2 DINERS
15.00 g., Bi-Metallic Bronze center in Copper-Nickel ring, 32 mm. **Subject:** 1988 Summer Olympics **Obv:** Arms within circle **Rev:** High jumper

Date	Mintage	VF20	XF40	MS60	MS63	MS65
1985	11,000	—	—	—	15.00	20.00

KM# 36 2 DINERS
7.80 g., Brass, 28 mm. **Obv:** Joan D.M. Bisbe D'Urgell I, right **Rev:** Crowned value, date below within wreath

Date	Mintage	VF20	XF40	MS60	MS63	MS65
1986	10,000	—	—	—	8.00	10.00

KM# 40 2 DINERS
12.00 g., Copper-Nickel, 31.8 mm. **Subject:** 1988 Summer Olympics **Obv:** Arms on ornate shield divide value **Rev:** Tennis player facing, date bottom right

Date	Mintage	VF20	XF40	MS60	MS63	MS65
1987	20,000	—	—	—	8.00	10.00

KM# 46.1 2 DINERS
12.00 g., Copper-Nickel, 32 mm. **Subject:** 1992 Winter & Summer Olympics **Obv:** Small arms on shield, upper right, value at center, left **Rev:** Kayaker and skier **Note:** Prev. KM#46. Coin die rotation.

Date	Mintage	VF20	XF40	MS60	MS63	MS65
1987	20,000	—	—	—	8.00	10.00

KM# 46.2 2 DINERS
12.00 g., Copper-Nickel, 32 mm. **Subject:** 1992 Winter & Summer Olympics **Rev:** Kayaker and skier **Note:** Medallic die rotation.

Date	Mintage	VF20	XF40	MS60	MS63	MS65
1987	20,000	—	—	—	8.00	10.00

KM# 50 2 DINERS
9.50 g., Copper-Nickel, 28 mm. **Obv:** Church of Santa Coloma **Rev:** Large value, date to bottom right

Date	Mintage	VF20	XF40	MS60	MS63	MS65
1988	5,000	—	—	—	10.00	12.00

KM# 140 2 DINERS
20.00 g., 0.925 Silver 0.5948 oz. ASW **Subject:** 1998 Winter Olympics **Obv:** Crowned arms to left of five line inscription, value below, date at bottom **Rev:** Bobsled

Date	Mintage	VF20	XF40	MS60	MS63	MS65
1997 (1998) Proof	30,000	PF65 22.00				

KM# 16 5 DINERS
10.00 g., Cast Copper, 30 mm. **Obv:** Joan D.M. Bisbe D'Urgell I, left **Rev:** Crowned arms in oval flanked by cherubs, value below, date at bottom

Date	Mintage	VF20	XF40	MS60	MS63	MS65
1984	7,500	—	—	—	10.00	14.00

KM# 29 5 DINERS
16.00 g., Cast Copper, 35 mm. **Subject:** 2nd Congress of the Catalan Language **Obv:** Ornate arms **Rev:** Standing armored figure holding shield, rose stem below shield, figure divides value, date in legend

Date	Mintage	VF20	XF40	MS60	MS63	MS65
1986	6,000	—	—	—	14.00	18.00

KM# 37 5 DINERS
9.80 g., Bronze, 30 mm. **Obv:** Bust of Joan D.M. Bisbe D'Urgell I, right **Rev:** Crowned value, date below within wreath

Date	Mintage	VF20	XF40	MS60	MS63	MS65
1986	10,000	—	—	—	12.00	16.00

KM# 51 5 DINERS
13.75 g., Copper-Nickel, 31.5 mm. **Obv:** Church of St. Climent de Pal **Rev:** Large value, date

Date	Mintage	VF20	XF40	MS60	MS63	MS65
1988	5,000	—	—	—	13.00	17.00

KM# 80 5 DINERS
10.00 g., 0.500 Silver 0.1608 oz. ASW, 30 mm. **Subject:** 1994 Winter Olympics **Obv:** Crowned arms to left of five line inscription, value below, date at bottom **Rev:** Cross-country skier **Edge:** Reeded

Date	Mintage	VF20	XF40	MS60	MS63	MS65
1993	50,000	PF65 13.50				

KM# 102 5 DINERS
15.00 g., 0.925 Silver 0.4461 oz. ASW **Subject:** Andorran Circle of the Arts - 25th Anniversary **Obv:** Crowned arms to left of five line inscription, value below, date at bottom **Rev:** 3/4 Statue standing, left, tablet with quill on left of statue, figures in doorway on right

Date	Mintage	VF20	XF40	MS60	MS63	MS65
1993	3,000	PF65 28.00				

KM# 111 5 DINERS
1.56 g., 0.999 Gold 0.050 oz. AGW **Subject:** Wildlife **Obv:** Crowned arms to left of five line inscription, value below, date at bottom **Rev:** Red squirrel, left

Date	Mintage	VF20	XF40	MS60	MS63	MS65
1994	—	PF65 75.00				

KM# 112 5 DINERS
1.56 g., 0.9999 Gold 0.050 oz. AGW **Obv:** Defiant Golden Eagle **Rev:** Crowned denomination within wreath

Date	Mintage	VF20	XF40	MS60	MS63	MS65
1995	—	PF65 85.00				

KM# 116 5 DINERS
15.00 g., 0.925 Silver 0.4461 oz. ASW **Subject:** XXIII Photographers Federation Congress **Rev:** Hand on camera

Date	Mintage	VF20	XF40	MS60	MS63	MS65
1995	3,000	PF65 28.00				

KM# 117 5 DINERS
1.24 g., 0.999 Gold 0.040 oz. AGW **Subject:** Wildlife **Obv:** Crowned arms to left of five line inscription, value below, date at bottom **Rev:** Chamois, left

Date	Mintage	VF20	XF40	MS60	MS63	MS65
1996	Est. 100000	PF65 65.00				

KM# 118 5 DINERS
1.24 g., 0.999 Gold 0.040 oz. AGW **Subject:** Wildlife **Rev:** Brown bear and cub

Date	Mintage	VF20	XF40	MS60	MS63	MS65
1996	Est. 100000	PF65 65.00				

KM# 141 5 DINERS
3.11 g., 0.585 Gold 0.0585 oz. AGW **Subject:** 1998 Winter Olympics **Obv:** Crowned arms to left of five line inscription, value below, date at bottom **Rev:** Downhill skier

Date	Mintage	VF20	XF40	MS60	MS63	MS65
1997 (1998) Proof	5,000	PF65 110				

KM# 375 5 DINERS
31.11 g., 0.999 Silver 0.999 oz. ASW, 40 mm. **Obv:** Taipei Central Station **Rev:** Value in wreath

Date	Mintage	VF20	XF40	MS60	MS63	MS65
1997	—	PF65 45.00				

KM# 376 5 DINERS
31.11 g., 0.999 Silver 0.999 oz. ASW, 40 mm. **Obv:** Bridge in Danshui **Rev:** Value in weath

Date	Mintage	VF20	XF40	MS60	MS63	MS65
1997	—	PF65 45.00				

KM# 377 5 DINERS
31.11 g., 0.999 Silver 0.999 oz. ASW, 40 mm. **Obv:** Corn flower **Rev:** Value in wreath

Date	Mintage	VF20	XF40	MS60	MS63	MS65
1997	Est. 10000	PF65 45.00				

KM# 378 5 DINERS
31.11 g., 0.999 Silver 0.999 oz. ASW, 40 mm. **Obv:** Orchid in color **Rev:** Value in wreath

Date	Mintage	VF20	XF40	MS60	MS63	MS65
1997	Est. 10000	PF65 45.00				

KM# 379 5 DINERS
31.11 g., 0.999 Silver 0.999 oz. ASW, 40 mm. **Obv:** Chrysanthemum in color **Rev:** Value in wreath

Date	Mintage	VF20	XF40	MS60	MS63	MS65
1997	Est. 10000	PF65 45.00				

KM# 380 5 DINERS
31.11 g., 0.999 Silver 0.999 oz. ASW, 40 mm. **Obv:** Tulip in color **Rev:** Value in wreath

Date	Mintage	VF20	XF40	MS60	MS63	MS65
1997	Est. 10000	PF65 45.00				

KM# 381 5 DINERS
31.11 g., 0.999 Silver 0.999 oz. ASW, 40 mm. **Obv:** Rose in color **Rev:** Value in wreath

Date	Mintage	VF20	XF40	MS60	MS63	MS65
1997	Est. 10000	PF65 45.00				

KM# 384 5 DINERS
31.11 g., 0.999 Silver 0.999 oz. ASW, 40 mm. **Obv:** Rose in color **Rev:** Value in wreath

Date	Mintage	VF20	XF40	MS60	MS63	MS65
1998	Est. 10000	PF65 45.00				

KM# 385 5 DINERS
31.11 g., 0.999 Silver 0.999 oz. ASW, 40 mm. **Obv:** Violet in color **Rev:** Value in wreath

Date	Mintage	VF20	XF40	MS60	MS63	MS65
1998	Est. 10000	PF65 45.00				

KM# 386 5 DINERS
31.11 g., 0.999 Silver 0.999 oz. ASW, 40 mm. **Obv:** Chinese rose in color **Rev:** Value in wreath

Date	Mintage	VF20	XF40	MS60	MS63	MS65
1998	Est. 10000	PF65 45.00				

KM# 387 5 DINERS
31.11 g., 0.999 Silver 0.999 oz. ASW, 40 mm. **Obv:** Apple blossoms in color **Rev:** Value within wreath

Date	Mintage	VF20	XF40	MS60	MS63	MS65
1998	Est. 10000	PF65 45.00				

KM# 388 5 DINERS
31.11 g., 0.999 Silver 0.999 oz. ASW, 40 mm. **Obv:** Sunflowers in color **Rev:** Value within wreath

Date	Mintage	VF20	XF40	MS60	MS63	MS65
1998	Est. 10000	PF65 45.00				

KM# 390 5 DINERS
30.22 g., 0.925 Silver 0.8988 oz. ASW, 38 mm. **Subject:** Rossell's Manual Digest, 150th Anniversary **Obv:** National shield **Rev:** Ink drawing of an eagle

Date	Mintage	VF20	XF40	MS60	MS63	MS65
1998	Est. 10000	PF65 85.00				

KM# 155 5 DINERS
27.00 g., Bi-Metallic Silver center in Brass ring, 38.3 mm. **Obv:** World globe amid stars **Rev:** World globe with sun, planets and stars **Note:** Silver center and brass ring are within a silver ring.

Date	Mintage	VF20	XF40	MS60	MS63	MS65
1999	—	PF65 35.00				

KM# 393 5 DINERS
31.11 g., 0.999 Silver 0.999 oz. ASW, 40 mm. **Obv:** Peonies in color **Rev:** Value within wreath

Date	Mintage	VF20	XF40	MS60	MS63	MS65
1999	Est. 10000	PF65 45.00				

KM# 394 5 DINERS
31.11 g., 0.999 Silver 0.999 oz. ASW, 40 mm. **Obv:** Daffodils in color **Rev:** Value within wreath

Date	Mintage	VF20	XF40	MS60	MS63	MS65
1999	Est. 10000	PF65 45.00				

KM# 395 5 DINERS
31.11 g., 0.999 Silver 0.999 oz. ASW, 40 mm. **Obv:** Lotus flowers in color **Rev:** Value within wreath

Date	Mintage	VF20	XF40	MS60	MS63	MS65
1999	Est. 10000	PF65 45.00				

KM# 396 5 DINERS
31.11 g., 0.999 Silver 0.999 oz. ASW, 40 mm. **Obv:** Iris flower in color **Rev:** Value within wreath

Date	Mintage	VF20	XF40	MS60	MS63	MS65
1999	Est. 10000	PF65 45.00				

KM# 397 5 DINERS
31.11 g., 0.999 Silver 0.999 oz. ASW, 40 mm. **Obv:** Cherry blossom in color **Rev:** Value within wreath

Date	Mintage	VF20	XF40	MS60	MS63	MS65
1999	Est. 10000	PF65 45.00				

KM# 187 5 DINERS
15.55 g., 0.925 Silver 0.4624 oz. ASW **Obv:** National arms in wreath **Rev:** Nativity scene

Date	Mintage	VF20	XF40	MS60	MS63	MS65
2000	25,000	PF65 25.00				

KM# 401 5 DINERS
31.11 g., 0.999 Silver 0.999 oz. ASW, 38.61 mm. **Subject:** Year of the dragon **Obv:** Temple **Rev:** Dragon

Date	Mintage	VF20	XF40	MS60	MS63	MS65
2000	Est. 12000	PF65 40.00				

KM# 17 10 DINERS
8.00 g., 0.900 Cast Silver 0.2315 oz., 26 mm. **Obv:** Joan D.M. Bisbe D'Urgell I, left **Rev:** Crowned arms on oval shield flanked by cherubs, value below, date at bottom

Date	Mintage	VF20	XF40	MS60	MS63	MS65
1984	7,500	—	—	—	15.00	20.00

KM# 34 10 DINERS
8.00 g., 0.900 Cast Silver 0.2315 oz., 30 mm. **Subject:** 1988 World Cup Soccer Games **Obv:** Arms on shield within legend **Rev:** Soccer ball below, world globe above, ball and globe divide value, date in legend, bottom

Date	Mintage	VF20	XF40	MS60	MS63	MS65
1986 Prooflike	10,000	—	—	—	10.00	15.00

KM# 38 10 DINERS
8.00 g., 0.925 Silver 0.2379 oz. ASW, 28 mm. **Obv:** Joan D.M. Bisbe D'Urgell I, right **Rev:** Crowned value, date below within wreath

Date	Mintage	VF20	XF40	MS60	MS63	MS65
1986	10,000	—	—	—	10.00	15.00

KM# 52 10 DINERS
8.00 g., 0.925 Silver 0.2379 oz. ASW, 28 mm. **Obv:** Church of St. Joan de Caselles **Rev:** Large value, small vertical date to left

Date	Mintage	VF20	XF40	MS60	MS63	MS65
1988	5,000	—	—	—	12.00	18.00

KM# 53 10 DINERS
12.00 g., 0.925 Silver 0.3569 oz. ASW, 32 mm. **Subject:** 1990 World Cup Soccer Games **Obv:** Crowned arms to left of five line inscription, value below, date at bottom **Rev:** Figures on soccer field

Date	Mintage	VF20	XF40	MS60	MS63	MS65
1989	20,000	PF65 12.00				

KM# 55 10 DINERS
12.00 g., 0.925 Silver 0.3569 oz. ASW, 32 mm. **Subject:** 1992 Winter Olympics **Obv:** Crowned arms to left of five line inscription, value below, date at bottom **Rev:** Downhill skier

Date	Mintage	VF20	XF40	MS60	MS63	MS65
1989	15,000	PF65 12.00				

KM# 56 10 DINERS
12.00 g., 0.925 Silver 0.3569 oz. ASW, 32 mm. **Subject:** 1992 Summer Olympics **Obv:** Crowned arms to left of five line inscription, value below, date at bottom **Rev:** Soccer

Date	Mintage	VF20	XF40	MS60	MS63	MS65
1989	15,000	PF65 12.00				

KM# 60 10 DINERS
12.00 g., 0.925 Silver 0.3569 oz. ASW, 32 mm. **Subject:** 1990 World Cup Soccer Games **Obv:** Crowned arms to left of five line inscription, value below, date at bottom **Rev:** Map of Italy and soccer ball

Date	Mintage	VF20	XF40	MS60	MS63	MS65
1989	20,000	PF65 12.00				

KM# 71 10 DINERS
31.47 g., 0.925 Silver 0.9359 oz. ASW, 38.61 mm. **Subject:** ECU Customs Union **Obv:** Arms above "ECU", within circle of stars/beads **Rev:** Charlemagne

Date	Mintage	VF20	XF40	MS60	MS63	MS65
ND-1992	15,000	PF65 25.50				

KM# 74 10 DINERS
31.10 g., 0.925 Silver 0.925 oz. ASW, 38.7 mm. **Subject:** Wildlife **Obv:** Crowned arms to left of five line inscription, value below, date at bottom **Rev:** Red squirrel, left

Date	Mintage	VF20	XF40	MS60	MS63	MS65
1992	15,000	PF65 35.00				

KM# 75 10 DINERS
31.10 g., 0.925 Silver 0.925 oz. ASW, 38.7 mm. **Subject:** Wildlife **Obv:** Crowned arms to left of five line inscription, value below, date at bottom **Rev:** Chamois

Date	Mintage	VF20	XF40	MS60	MS63	MS65
1992	15,000	PF65 35.00				

KM# 76 10 DINERS
31.10 g., 0.925 Silver 0.925 oz. ASW, 38.7 mm. **Subject:** Wildlife **Obv:** Crowned arms to left of five line inscription, value below, date at bottom **Rev:** Brown bear and cub

Date	Mintage	VF20	XF40	MS60	MS63	MS65
1992	15,000	PF65 35.00				

KM# 78 10 DINERS
31.10 g., 0.925 Silver 0.925 oz. ASW, 38.7 mm. **Subject:** Discovery of the New World **Obv:** Crowned arms to left of five line inscription, value below, date at bottom **Rev:** Stylized ship on globe

Date	Mintage	VF20	XF40	MS60	MS63	MS65
1992	15,000	PF65 25.00				

KM# 84 10 DINERS
31.47 g., 0.925 Silver 0.9359 oz. ASW **Obv:** Crowned arms above denomination and date **Rev:** Stylized tree and birds

Date	Mintage	VF20	XF40	MS60	MS63	MS65
1993	15,000	PF65 25.50				

KM# 85 10 DINERS
31.47 g., 0.925 Silver 0.9359 oz. ASW **Subject:** Space Exploration **Obv:** Crowned arms to left of five line inscription, value below, date at bottom **Rev:** Tethered space walker Edward White

Date	Mintage	VF20	XF40	MS60	MS63	MS65
1993	15,000	PF65 27.50				

KM# 86 10 DINERS
31.47 g., 0.925 Silver 0.9359 oz. ASW **Subject:** 1994 World Cup Soccer **Obv:** Crowned arms to left of five line inscription, value below, date at bottom **Rev:** Player before world map

Date	Mintage	VF20	XF40	MS60	MS63	MS65
1993	20,000	PF65 27.50				

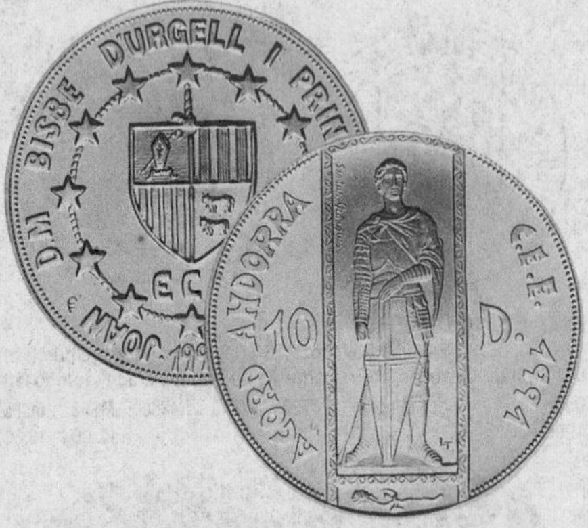

KM# 89 10 DINERS
31.47 g., 0.925 Silver 0.9359 oz. ASW **Subject:** ECU Customs Union **Obv:** Arms within circle of stars/beads **Rev:** St. George divides value,rose stem below feet

Date	Mintage	VF20	XF40	MS60	MS63	MS65
1993	25,000	PF65 25.50				

KM# 95 10 DINERS
31.47 g., 0.925 Silver 0.9359 oz. ASW **Subject:** 1996 Summer Olympic Games **Rev:** Cyclists

Date	Mintage	VF20	XF40	MS60	MS63	MS65
1994	50,000	PF65 25.50				

KM# 97 10 DINERS
31.47 g., 0.925 Silver 0.9359 oz. ASW **Subject:** Andorra U.N. Membership **Obv:** Crowned arms above "ECU" **Rev:** Woman kneeling, left hand on globe, globe symbol in wreath behind

Date	Mintage	VF20	XF40	MS60	MS63	MS65
1994	25,000	PF65 27.50				

KM# 98 10 DINERS
31.47 g., 0.925 Silver 0.9359 oz. ASW **Subject:** Discovery of the New World **Obv:** Crowned arms to left of five line legend, value below, date at bottom **Rev:** Sailing ship, small bust of cherub, top left, eight pointed star to right of ship

Date	Mintage	VF20	XF40	MS60	MS63	MS65
1994	20,000	PF65 30.50				

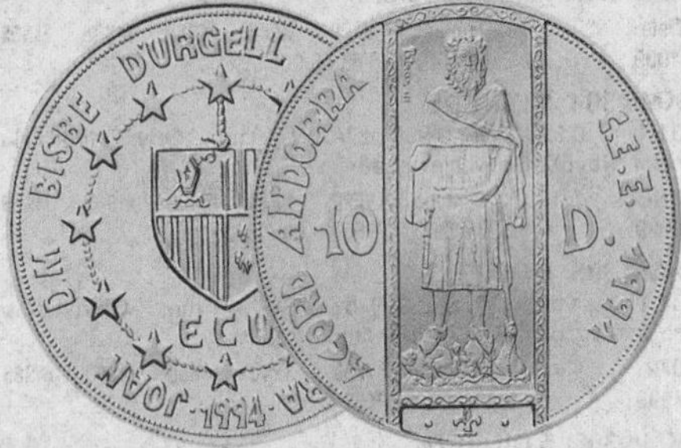

KM# 99 10 DINERS
31.47 g., 0.925 Silver 0.9359 oz. ASW **Subject:** ECU Customs Union **Obv:** Arms above "ECU", within circle of stars/beads **Rev:** Peter III of Catalonia and Aragon divides date, cross flanked by dots below feet

Date	Mintage	VF20	XF40	MS60	MS63	MS65
1994	25,000	PF65 25.50				

KM# 105 10 DINERS
31.47 g., 0.925 Silver 0.9359 oz. ASW **Subject:** ECU Customs Union **Rev:** Ramon Berenguer III

Date	Mintage	VF20	XF40	MS60	MS63	MS65
1995	30,000	PF65 25.50				

KM# 108 10 DINERS
31.60 g., 0.925 Silver 0.9398 oz. ASW **Subject:** Admission to the Council of Europe **Obv:** Arms above "ECU" **Rev:** Woman, left, walking through starred arch, arms forward, container in right hand

Date	Mintage	VF20	XF40	MS60	MS63	MS65
1995	35,000	PF65 25.50				

KM# 110 10 DINERS
31.10 g., 0.925 Silver 0.925 oz. ASW **Subject:** 50th Anniversary - F.A.O. **Obv:** Crowned arms to left of five line inscription, value below, date at bottom **Rev:** Ceres holding grain

Date	Mintage	VF20	XF40	MS60	MS63	MS65
1995	10,000	PF65 27.00				

KM# 113 10 DINERS
31.10 g., 0.925 Silver 0.925 oz. ASW **Subject:** Wildlife **Obv:** Crowned arms to left of five line inscription, value below, date at bottom **Rev:** Wolf, facing

Date	Mintage	VF20	XF40	MS60	MS63	MS65
1995	20,000	PF65 33.00				

KM# 114 10 DINERS
31.10 g., 0.925 Silver 0.925 oz. ASW **Subject:** Agnus Dei **Obv:** Crowned arms above "ECU" **Rev:** Lamb of God within circle, circle of stars surrounding

Date	Mintage	VF20	XF40	MS60	MS63	MS65
1995	Est. 35000	PF65 27.00				

KM# 119 10 DINERS
31.47 g., 0.925 Silver 0.9359 oz. ASW **Obv:** Arms above "ECU" **Rev:** Frederic II on throne

Date	Mintage	VF20	XF40	MS60	MS63	MS65
1996	—	PF65 27.50				

KM# 120 10 DINERS
31.47 g., 0.925 Silver 0.9359 oz. ASW **Obv:** Crowned Arms, date below **Rev:** Sailing ship

Date	Mintage	VF20	XF40	MS60	MS63	MS65
1996	Est. 20000	PF65 29.50				

KM# 121 10 DINERS
31.47 g., 0.925 Silver 0.9359 oz. ASW **Obv:** Crowned Arms above date **Rev:** Pope crowning Charlemagne

Date	Mintage	VF20	XF40	MS60	MS63	MS65
1996	Est. 30000	PF65 28.50				

KM# 125 10 DINERS
31.47 g., 0.925 Silver 0.9359 oz. ASW **Subject:** 25th Anniversary - Msgr. Alanis, Co-prince and Bishop of Andorra **Obv:** Crowned arms above "EURO" **Rev:** Enthroned prince, date

Date	Mintage	VF20	XF40	MS60	MS63	MS65
1996	30,000	PF65 28.50				

KM# A127 10 DINERS
31.47 g., 0.925 Silver 0.9359 oz. ASW **Subject:** Wildlife Protection **Obv:** Crowned arms **Rev:** Diving European Otter

Date	Mintage	VF20	XF40	MS60	MS63	MS65
1996	15,000	PF65 30.50				

KM# 130 10 DINERS
31.47 g., 0.925 Silver 0.9359 oz. ASW **Subject:** Treaty of Rome **Obv:** Crowned arms above "EURO" **Rev:** Seated Europa with olive branch and "EURO" shield, dates

Date	Mintage	VF20	XF40	MS60	MS63	MS65
1997	25,000	PF65 28.50				

KM# 131 10 DINERS
31.47 g., 0.925 Silver 0.9359 oz. ASW **Subject:** Wildlife **Obv:** Crowned arms, date below **Rev:** Red Fox vixen with kit

Date	Mintage	VF20	XF40	MS60	MS63	MS65
1997	15,000	PF65 35.50				

KM# 132 10 DINERS
31.47 g., 0.925 Silver 0.9359 oz. ASW **Obv:** Crowned arms above "ECU" **Rev:** Johan Sebastian Bach portrait, facing 3/4 right, dates

Date	Mintage	VF20	XF40	MS60	MS63	MS65
1997	Est. 25000	PF65 26.50				

KM# 133 10 DINERS
31.47 g., 0.925 Silver 0.9359 oz. ASW **Obv:** Crowned arms above "ECU" **Rev:** Antonio Vivaldi portrait, 3/4 left, dates

Date	Mintage	VF20	XF40	MS60	MS63	MS65
1997	Est. 25000	PF65 26.50				

KM# 136 10 DINERS
3.11 g., 0.999 Gold 0.0999 oz. AGW **Obv:** Fleury cross **Rev:** Bust of Queen Isabella I right **Note:** Similar to 20 Diners, KM#137.

Date	Mintage	VF20	XF40	MS60	MS63	MS65
1997	Est. 5000	PF65 175				

KM# 142 10 DINERS
31.47 g., 0.925 Silver 0.9359 oz. ASW **Subject:** 1998 World Cup Soccer **Obv:** Crowned arms and denomination **Rev:** Eiffel Tower and soccer ball

Date	Mintage	VF20	XF40	MS60	MS63	MS65
1997	15,000	PF65 29.50				

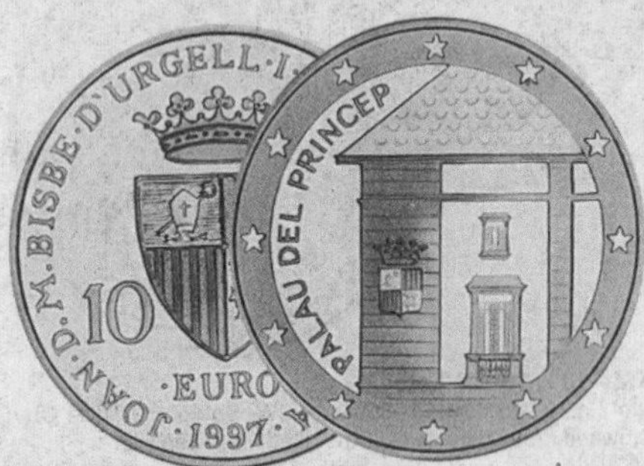

KM# 166 10 DINERS
31.47 g., 0.925 Silver 0.9359 oz. ASW **Subject:** Palau del Princep **Obv:** Crowned arms above "EURO" **Rev:** Crowned arms on house corner **Edge:** Reeded

Date	Mintage	VF20	XF40	MS60	MS63	MS65
1997	—	PF65 28.50				

KM# 143 10 DINERS
31.47 g., 0.925 Silver 0.9359 oz. ASW **Subject:** Human Rights **Obv:** Crowned arms above "EURO" **Rev:** Allegorical figure of Justice

Date	Mintage	VF20	XF40	MS60	MS63	MS65
1998	25,000	PF65 28.50				

KM# 146 10 DINERS
31.47 g., 0.925 Silver 0.9359 oz. ASW **Obv:** Crowned arms above "ECU" **Rev:** Portrait of Claudio Monteverdi,3/4 right, dates

Date	Mintage	VF20	XF40	MS60	MS63	MS65
1998	25,000	PF65 28.50				

KM# 147 10 DINERS
31.47 g., 0.925 Silver 0.9359 oz. ASW **Subject:** George Friedrich Handel **Obv:** Crowned arms above "ECU" **Rev:** Portrait, dates

Date	Mintage	VF20	XF40	MS60	MS63	MS65
1998	25,000	PF65 28.50				

KM# 150 10 DINERS
31.47 g., 0.925 Silver 0.9359 oz. ASW **Subject:** Europa **Obv:** Crowned arms above "EURO" **Rev:** Seated Europa

Date	Mintage	VF20	XF40	MS60	MS63	MS65
1998	25,000	PF65 28.50				

KM# 151 10 DINERS
31.47 g., 0.925 Silver 0.9359 oz. ASW **Subject:** Europa **Obv:** Crowned arms above "EURO" **Rev:** Europa driving quadriga

Date	Mintage	VF20	XF40	MS60	MS63	MS65
1998	25,000	PF65 35.00				

KM# 165 10 DINERS
31.11 g., 0.999 Silver 0.9992 oz. ASW **Subject:** Year of the Tiger **Obv:** Multicolored cartoon tiger and Chinese legend **Rev:** Crowned value within wreath **Edge:** Reeded

Date	Mintage	VF20	XF40	MS60	MS63	MS65
1998	—	PF65 32.00				

KM# 153 10 DINERS
31.47 g., 0.925 Silver 0.9359 oz. ASW **Subject:** 50th Anniversary - European Council **Obv:** Crowned arms above "EURO" **Rev:** Statue of Democracy

Date	Mintage	VF20	XF40	MS60	MS63	MS65
1999	15,000	PF65 25.50				

KM# 154 10 DINERS
31.47 g., 0.925 Silver 0.9359 oz. ASW **Subject:** 50th Anniversary - European Council **Obv:** Crowned arms above "EURO" **Rev:** Statue of Human Rights

Date	Mintage	VF20	XF40	MS60	MS63	MS65
1999	15,000	PF65 25.50				

KM# 156 10 DINERS
31.47 g., 0.925 Silver 0.9359 oz. ASW, 38.6 mm. **Subject:** Jubilee 2000 **Obv:** National arms **Rev:** Birth of Jesus **Edge:** Reeded

Date	Mintage	VF20	XF40	MS60	MS63	MS65
1999	15,000	PF65 25.50				

KM# 157 10 DINERS
31.47 g., 0.925 Silver 0.9359 oz. ASW **Subject:** Jubilee 2000 **Obv:** National arms **Rev:** Slaughter of the Innocents - Man with sword killing children

Date	Mintage	VF20	XF40	MS60	MS63	MS65
1999	15,000	PF65 25.50				

KM# 158 10 DINERS
31.47 g., 0.925 Silver 0.9359 oz. ASW **Subject:** Jubilee 2000 **Obv:** National arms **Rev:** John the Baptist baptizing Jesus

Date	Mintage	VF20	XF40	MS60	MS63	MS65
1999	15,000	PF65 25.50				

KM# 159 10 DINERS
31.47 g., 0.925 Silver 0.9359 oz. ASW **Subject:** Jubilee 2000 **Obv:** National arms **Rev:** Prodigal Son - Son kneeling before his father

Date	Mintage	VF20	XF40	MS60	MS63	MS65
1999	15,000	PF65 25.50				

KM# 160 10 DINERS
31.47 g., 0.925 Silver 0.9359 oz. ASW **Subject:** Jubilee 2000 **Obv:** National arms **Rev:** Jesus' entry into Jerusalem

Date	Mintage	VF20	XF40	MS60	MS63	MS65
1999	15,000	PF65 25.50				

KM# 161 10 DINERS
31.47 g., 0.925 Silver 0.9359 oz. ASW **Subject:** Jubilee 2000 **Obv:** National arms **Rev:** Last Supper scene

Date	Mintage	VF20	XF40	MS60	MS63	MS65
1999	15,000	PF65 25.50				

KM# 162 10 DINERS
31.47 g., 0.925 Silver 0.9359 oz. ASW **Subject:** Jubilee 2000 **Obv:** National arms **Rev:** Jesus on the cross

Date	Mintage	VF20	XF40	MS60	MS63	MS65
1999	15,000	PF65 25.50				

KM# 163 10 DINERS
31.47 g., 0.925 Silver 0.9359 oz. ASW **Subject:** Jubilee 2000 **Obv:** National arms **Rev:** Jesus standing in boat

Date	Mintage	VF20	XF40	MS60	MS63	MS65
1999	15,000	PF65 25.50				

KM# 398 10 DINERS
31.47 g., 0.925 Silver 0.9359 oz. ASW, 38.61 mm. **Subject:** 42nd Nordic Ski World Championships in Ramsau **Rev:** Skier

Date	Mintage	VF20	XF40	MS60	MS63	MS65
1999	Est. 15000	PF65 27.50				

KM# 399 10 DINERS
31.47 g., 0.925 Silver 0.9359 oz. ASW, 38.61 mm. **Subject:** 42nd Nordic Ski World Championships in Ramsau **Rev:** Cross-country skiers

Date	Mintage	VF20	XF40	MS60	MS63	MS65
1999	Est. 15000	PF65 27.50				

KM# 400 10 DINERS
31.47 g., 0.925 Silver 0.9359 oz. ASW, 38.61 mm. **Subject:** 63rd World Ice Hockey Championships in Herren, Norway **Obv:** Value flanking crowned shield **Rev:** Ice Hockey player and goalie

Date	Mintage	VF20	XF40	MS60	MS63	MS65
1999	Est. 15000	PF65 27.50				

KM# 402 10 DINERS
3.11 g., 0.999 Gold 0.0999 oz. AGW, 18 mm. **Subject:** Year of the Dragon **Obv:** Temple **Rev:** Dragon

Date	Mintage	VF20	XF40	MS60	MS63	MS65
2000	Est. 3000	PF65 200				

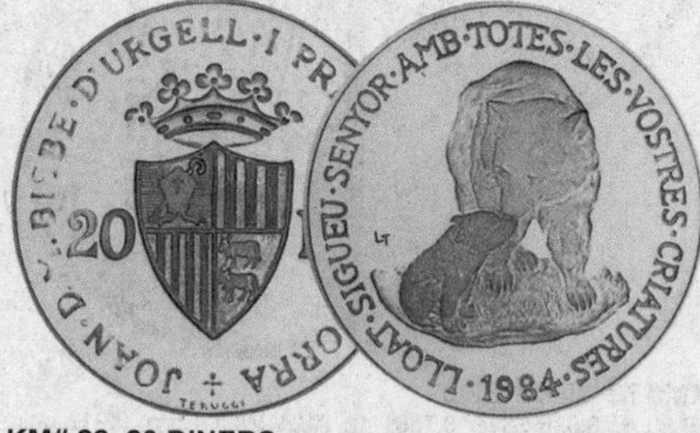

KM# 22 20 DINERS
16.00 g., 0.835 Silver 0.4295 oz. ASW, 35 mm. **Subject:** Wildlife **Obv:** Crowned arms **Rev:** Bear with cub

Date	Mintage	VF20	XF40	MS60	MS63	MS65
1984	5,000	PF65 35.00				

KM# 23 20 DINERS
16.00 g., 0.835 Silver 0.4295 oz. ASW, 35 mm. **Subject:** Wildlife **Obv:** Crowned arms **Rev:** Red squirrel

Date	Mintage	VF20	XF40	MS60	MS63	MS65
1984	5,000	PF65 35.00				

KM# 24 20 DINERS
16.00 g., 0.835 Silver 0.4295 oz. ASW, 35 mm. **Subject:** Wildlife **Obv:** Crowned arms **Rev:** Chamois

Date	Mintage	VF20	XF40	MS60	MS63	MS65
1984	5,000	PF65 35.00				

KM# 25 20 DINERS
16.00 g., 0.900 Silver 0.463 oz. ASW, 35 mm. **Subject:** 1984 Summer Olympics **Obv:** Crowned arms **Rev:** Shooter

Date	Mintage	VF20	XF40	MS60	MS63	MS65
1984	10,000	PF65 18.00				

KM# 26 20 DINERS
16.00 g., 0.900 Silver 0.463 oz. ASW, 35 mm. **Subject:** Christmas **Obv:** Ornate arms **Rev:** Madonna and child

Date	Mintage	VF20	XF40	MS60	MS63	MS65
1985	7,000	PF65 20.00				

KM# 39 20 DINERS
16.00 g., 0.900 Silver 0.463 oz. ASW, 35 mm. **Subject:** Olympic Tennis **Rev:** Tennis player, date lower right

Date	Mintage	VF20	XF40	MS60	MS63	MS65
1987	10,000	—	—	—	17.00	21.50

KM# 43 20 DINERS
16.00 g., 0.900 Silver 0.463 oz. ASW, 35 mm. **Subject:** 1988 Summer Olympics **Obv:** Crowned arms **Rev:** Chamshil Stadium

Date	Mintage	VF20	XF40	MS60	MS63	MS65
1988	12,000	—	—	—	17.00	21.50

KM# 47 20 DINERS
16.00 g., 0.925 Silver 0.4758 oz. ASW, 35 mm. **Subject:** 1992 Winter Olympics, Albertville **Obv:** Crowned arms to left of five line inscription, value below, date at bottom **Rev:** Pair of figure skaters

Date	Mintage	VF20	XF40	MS60	MS63	MS65
1988	15,000	PF63 16.50	PF65 20.00			

KM# 48 20 DINERS
16.00 g., 0.925 Silver 0.4758 oz. ASW, 35 mm. **Subject:** 1992 Summer Olympics **Obv:** Crowned arms to left of five line inscription, value below, date at bottom **Rev:** Gymnast on rings

Date	Mintage	VF20	XF40	MS60	MS63	MS65
1988	15,000	PF63 16.50	PF65 20.00			

KM# 54 20 DINERS
16.00 g., 0.925 Silver 0.4758 oz. ASW, 35 mm. **Subject:** 1992 Summer Olympics **Obv:** Crowned arms to left of five line inscription, value below, date at bottom **Rev:** Wind surfer

Date	Mintage	VF20	XF40	MS60	MS63	MS65
1989	15,000	PF63 16.50	PF65 20.00			

KM# 57 20 DINERS
16.00 g., 0.925 Silver 0.4758 oz. ASW, 35 mm. **Subject:** 1992 Summer Olympics **Obv:** Crowned arms to left of five line inscription, value below, date at bottom **Rev:** Kayaker

Date	Mintage	VF20	XF40	MS60	MS63	MS65
1989	15,000	PF63 17.50	PF65 21.00			

KM# 58 20 DINERS
16.00 g., 0.925 Silver 0.4758 oz. ASW, 35 mm. **Subject:** 1992 Summer Olympics, Barcelona **Obv:** Crowned arms to left of five line inscription, value below, date at bottom **Rev:** Hurdler

Date	Mintage	VF20	XF40	MS60	MS63	MS65
1990	15,000	PF63 17.50	PF65 21.00			

KM# 59 20 DINERS
16.00 g., 0.925 Silver 0.4758 oz. ASW, 35 mm. **Subject:** 1992 Summer Olympics **Obv:** Crowned arms to left of five line inscription, value below, date at bottom **Rev:** Equestrian

Date	Mintage	VF20	XF40	MS60	MS63	MS65
1990	15,000	PF63 17.50	PF65 21.00			

KM# 67 20 DINERS
21.00 g., 0.925 Silver 0.6245 oz. ASW, 34 mm. **Subject:** European Small States Games **Obv:** Crowned arms to left of five line inscription, value below, date at bottom **Rev:** Cyclist

Date	Mintage	VF20	XF40	MS60	MS63	MS65
1991	5,000	PF63 27.00	PF65 37.00			

KM# 72 20 DINERS
26.50 g., 0.925 Silver 0.7881 oz. ASW With 1.5 g. 0.917 gold inlay, 0.0442 oz. AGW., 38 mm. **Subject:** ECU Customs Union **Obv:** Similar to 10 Diners, KM#71 **Rev:** Charlemagne

Date	Mintage	VF20	XF40	MS60	MS63	MS65
ND-1992	5,000	—	—	—	70.00	80.00

KM# 90 20 DINERS
26.50 g., 0.925 Silver 0.7881 oz. ASW With 1.5 g. 0.917 gold inlay, 0.0442 oz. AGW. **Subject:** ECU Customs Union **Rev:** St. George

Date	Mintage	VF20	XF40	MS60	MS63	MS65
1993 Matte	5,000	—	—	—	95.00	110

KM# 100 20 DINERS
26.50 g., 0.925 Silver 0.7881 oz. ASW With 1.5 g. 0.917 gold inlay, 0.0442 oz. AGW. **Subject:** ECU Customs Union **Obv:** Arms above "ECU",within wreath of stars on rope **Rev:** Peter III of Catalonia and Aragon

Date	Mintage	VF20	XF40	MS60	MS63	MS65
1994	5,000	—	—	—	50.00	60.00

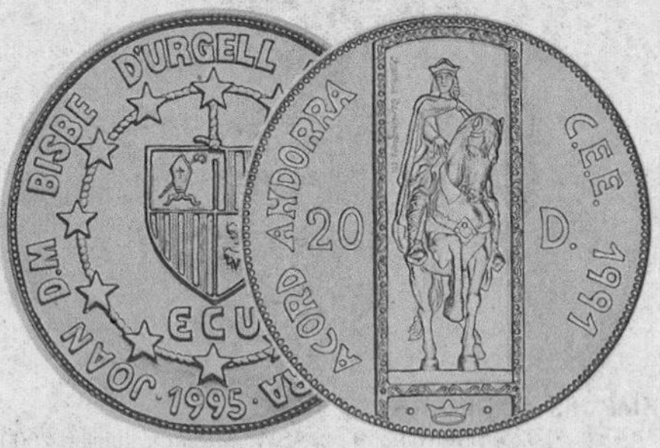

KM# 106 20 DINERS
25.00 g., 0.925 Silver 0.7435 oz. ASW With 1.6 g. 0.917 gold inlay, 0.0442 oz. AGW. **Subject:** ECU Customs Union **Obv:** Arms above "ECU", within wreath of stars on rope **Rev:** Ramon Berenger III, three pointed crown flanked by dots below horse hooves

Date	Mintage	VF20	XF40	MS60	MS63	MS65
1995	6,000	—	—	—	50.00	60.00

KM# 122 20 DINERS
25.00 g., 0.925 Silver 0.7435 oz. ASW With 1.6 g. 0.917 gold inlay, 0.0442 oz. AGW. **Obv:** Crowned arms and "ECU", date below arms **Rev:** Charlemagne being crowned

Date	Mintage	VF20	XF40	MS60	MS63	MS65
1996	Est. 5000	—	—	—	135	150

KM# 128 20 DINERS
25.00 g., 0.925 Silver 0.7435 oz. ASW With 1.6 g. 0.917 gold inlay, 0.0442 oz. AGW. **Subject:** Treaty at Rome **Obv:** Crowned arms above "EURO" **Rev:** Seated Europa with child holding "EURO" shield

Date	Mintage	VF20	XF40	MS60	MS63	MS65
1997	5,000	—	—	—	50.00	60.00

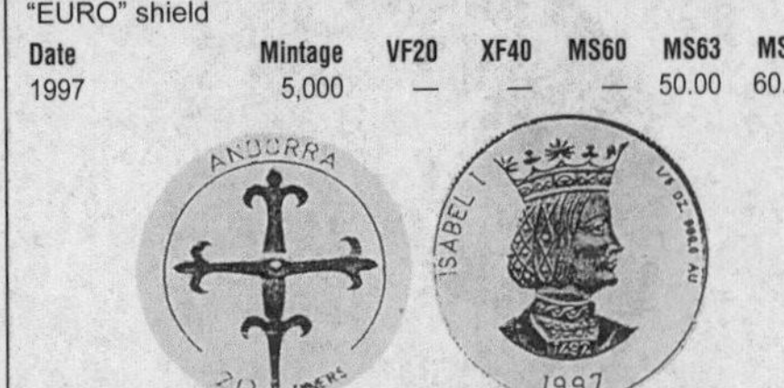

KM# 137 20 DINERS

6.22 g., 0.999 Gold 0.1998 oz. AGW **Obv:** Fleury cross **Rev:** Bust of Queen Isabella I right

Date	Mintage	VF20	XF40	MS60	MS63	MS65
1997	Est. 3500	PF65 335				

KM# 144 20 DINERS

25.00 g., 0.925 Silver 0.7435 oz. ASW with 1.5g, .917 gold inlay, .0442 oz. AGW **Subject:** Human Rights **Obv:** Crowned arms above "EURO" **Rev:** Young family and broken chain

Date	Mintage	VF20	XF40	MS60	MS63	MS65
1998	5,000	—	—	—	50.00	55.00

KM# 148 20 DINERS

25.00 g., 0.925 Silver 0.7435 oz. ASW With 1.5 g. 0.917 gold inlay, 0.0442 oz. AGW. **Subject:** XXVII Summer Olympics - Sydney 2000 **Obv:** Crowned arms above date **Rev:** Javelin thrower in gold inlay

Date	Mintage	VF20	XF40	MS60	MS63	MS65
1998	5,000	—	—	—	40.00	45.00

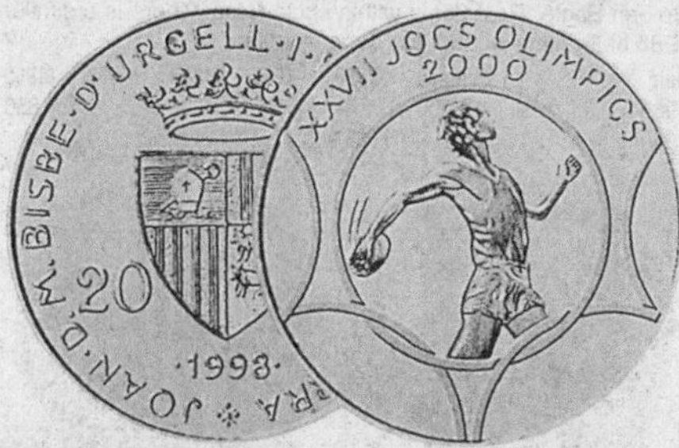

KM# 149 20 DINERS

25.00 g., 0.925 Silver 0.7435 oz. ASW With 1.5g 0.917 gold inlay, 0.0442 oz. AGW. **Subject:** XXVII Summer Olympics - Sydney 2000 **Obv:** Crowned arms above date **Rev:** Discus thrower in gold inlay

Date	Mintage	VF20	XF40	MS60	MS63	MS65
1998	5,000	—	—	—	40.00	45.00

KM# 225 20 DINERS

25.00 g., 0.925 Silver 0.7435 oz. ASW with 1.5g, .917 gold inlay, .0442 oz. AGW **Subject:** XXVII Summer Olympics - Sydney 2000 **Obv:** Crowned arms **Rev:** 1500 meter runner in gold inlay

Date	Mintage	VF20	XF40	MS60	MS63	MS65
1998	5,000	—	—	—	40.00	45.00

KM# 383 20 DINERS

15.55 g., 0.999 Gold 0.4994 oz. AGW, 28.4 mm. **Subject:** Year of the Tiger **Obv:** Tiger in color **Rev:** Crowned value in wreath

Date	Mintage	VF20	XF40	MS60	MS63	MS65
1998	Est. 3000	PF65 700				

KM# 389 20 DINERS

25.00 g., 0.925 Silver 0.7435 oz. ASW With 1.5g 0.917 gold inlay, 0.0442 oz. AGW., 38 mm. **Subject:** Year 2000 **Rev:** Child with peace doves, inlay

Date	Mintage	VF20	XF40	MS60	MS63	MS65
1998	Est. 10000	—	—	—	—	—

KM# 226 20 DINERS

25.00 g., 0.925 Silver 0.7435 oz. ASW With 1.5g 0.917 gold inlay, 0.0442 oz. AGW. **Subject:** XXVII Summer Olympics - Sydney 2000 **Obv:** Crowned arms **Rev:** Shot putter in gold inlay

Date	Mintage	VF20	XF40	MS60	MS63	MS65
1999	5,000	—	—	—	40.00	45.00

KM# 227 20 DINERS

25.00 g., 0.925 Silver 0.7435 oz. ASW With 1.5g 0.917 gold inlay, 0.0442 oz. AGW. **Subject:** XXVII Summer Olympics - Sydney 2000 **Obv:** Crowned arms **Rev:** 100 meter runner in gold inlay

Date	Mintage	VF20	XF40	MS60	MS63	MS65
1999	—	—	—	—	40.00	45.00

KM# 228 20 DINERS

25.00 g., 0.925 Silver 0.7435 oz. ASW With 1.5g 0.917 gold inlay, 0.0442 oz. AGW. **Subject:** XXVII Summer Olympics - Sydney 2000 **Obv:** Crowned arms **Rev:** Pole vaulter in gold inlay

Date	Mintage	VF20	XF40	MS60	MS63	MS65
1999	—	—	—	—	40.00	45.00

KM# 167 20 DINERS

25.00 g., 0.925 Silver 0.7435 oz. ASW with Gold inlay. **Subject:** XXVII Summer Olympics - Sydney 2000 **Obv:** Crowned arms, date and denomination **Rev:** Hurdler on gold inlay **Edge:** Plain

Date	Mintage	VF20	XF40	MS60	MS63	MS65
2000	6,000	—	—	—	40.00	45.00

KM# 168 20 DINERS

25.00 g., 0.925 Silver 0.7435 oz. ASW with Gold inlay. **Subject:** XXVII JOCS 2000 Olympics **Obv:** Crowned arms, date and denomination **Rev:** Runner on gold inlay **Edge:** Plain

Date	Mintage	VF20	XF40	MS60	MS63	MS65
2000	6,000	—	—	—	40.00	45.00

KM# 169 20 DINERS

25.00 g., 0.925 Silver 0.7435 oz. ASW with Gold inlay. **Subject:** XXVII JOCS 2000 Olympics **Obv:** Crowned arms, date and denomination **Rev:** Long jumper on gold inlay **Edge:** Plain

Date	Mintage	VF20	XF40	MS60	MS63	MS65
2000	6,000	—	—	—	40.00	45.00

KM# 170 20 DINERS

25.00 g., 0.925 Silver 0.7435 oz. ASW with Gold inlay. **Subject:** XXVII JOCS 2000 Olympics **Obv:** Crowned arms, date and denomination **Rev:** Pole vaulter on gold inlay **Edge:** Plain

Date	Mintage	VF20	XF40	MS60	MS63	MS65
2000	6,000	—	—	—	40.00	45.00

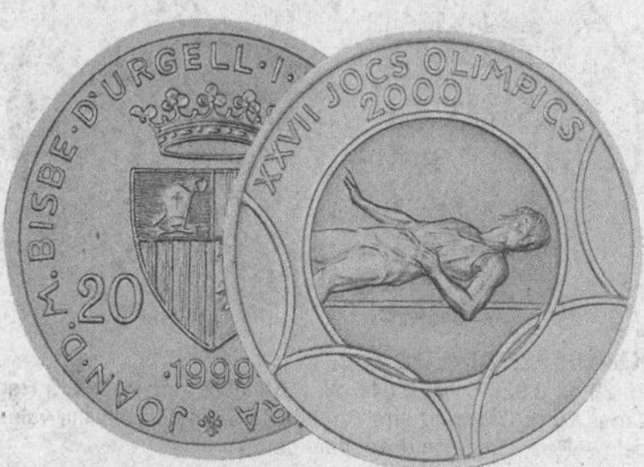

KM# 220 20 DINERS

26.50 g., Bi-Metallic .925 Silver 25g planchet with .917 Gold 1.5 g inlay, 38 mm. **Subject:** XXVII JOCS Olympics **Obv:** Crowned arms, value and date **Rev:** High jumper on gold inlay **Edge:** Plain

Date	Mintage	VF20	XF40	MS60	MS63	MS65
2000	6,000	—	—	—	40.00	45.00

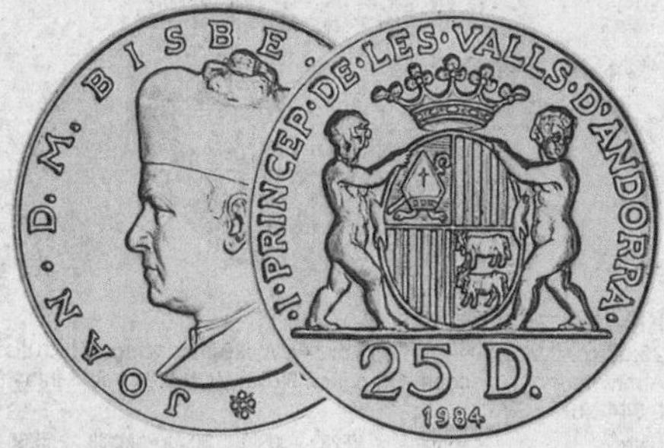

KM# 18 25 DINERS

20.00 g., 0.900 Silver 0.5787 oz. ASW, 38 mm. **Obv:** Joan D.M. Bisbe D'Urgell I, left **Rev:** Crowned oval arms flanked by cherubs, value below, date at bottom **Edge:** Reeded

Date	Mintage	VF20	XF40	MS60	MS63	MS65
1984	4,450	—	—	—	40.00	50.00
1984	550	PF65 120				

KM# 44.1 25 DINERS

20.00 g., 0.900 Silver 0.5787 oz. ASW, 38.5 mm. **Subject:** 700th Anniversary - Andorra's Governing Charter **Obv:** Fleury cross **Rev:** Grasped hands, right hand armored, left hand marked on back **Note:** Medallic die rotation.

Date	Mintage	VF20	XF40	MS60	MS63	MS65
ND-1988	20,000	—	—	—	20.00	25.00

KM# 44.2 25 DINERS

20.00 g., 0.900 Silver 0.5787 oz. ASW, 38.5 mm. **Subject:** 700th Anniversary - Andorra's Governing Charter **Note:** Medallic die rotation.

Date	Mintage	VF20	XF40	MS60	MS63	MS65
ND-1988	10,000	PF65 35.00				

KM# 61 25 DINERS

20.00 g., 0.900 Silver 0.5787 oz. ASW, 37 mm. **Subject:** Millenary of the Bishop of Sala **Obv:** Building within circle **Rev:** Bishop on horseback, value below

Date	Mintage	VF20	XF40	MS60	MS63	MS65
1989	Est. 5000	—	—	—	30.00	35.00

KM# 65 25 DINERS
28.28 g., 0.925 Silver 0.841 oz. ASW, 38.6 mm. **Subject:** Red Cross **Obv:** Crowned arms to left of five line inscription, value below **Rev:** Cross on dove, date below

Date	Mintage	VF20	XF40	MS60	MS63	MS65
1991	3,000	PF65 50.00				

KM# 69 25 DINERS
25.00 g., 0.925 Silver 0.7435 oz. ASW, 38 mm. **Subject:** 20th Anniversary - Episcopal Co-prince **Note:** With 0.917 gold inlay, 0.0442 oz. AGW.

Date	Mintage	VF20	XF40	MS60	MS63	MS65
1991	2,500	—	—	—	65.00	75.00

KM# 73 25 DINERS
7.77 g., 0.583 Gold 0.1456 oz. AGW, 25 mm. **Subject:** ECU Customs Union **Obv:** Arms with "ECU" below within circle of stars/beads **Rev:** St. Ermengol

Date	Mintage	VF20	XF40	MS60	MS63	MS65
1992	3,000	PF65 265				

KM# 81 25 DINERS
7.77 g., 0.583 Gold 0.1456 oz. AGW **Subject:** 1994 Winter Olympic Games, Lillehammer **Obv:** Crowned arms to left of five line inscription, value below, date at bottom **Rev:** Downhill skier

Date	Mintage	VF20	XF40	MS60	MS63	MS65
1993	6,000	PF65 285				

KM# 91 25 DINERS
7.77 g., 0.583 Gold 0.1456 oz. AGW **Subject:** ECU Customs Union **Obv:** Arms above "ECU" within circle of stars/beads **Rev:** Bishop riding a horse

Date	Mintage	VF20	XF40	MS60	MS63	MS65
1993	5,000	PF65 285				

KM# 92 25 DINERS
7.77 g., 0.583 Gold 0.1456 oz. AGW **Subject:** 1994 World Cup Soccer **Obv:** Crowned arms to left of five line inscription, value below, date at bottom **Rev:** Soccer player on right, outline of bird on top left

Date	Mintage	VF20	XF40	MS60	MS63	MS65
1993	5,000	PF65 300				

KM# 96 25 DINERS
7.77 g., 0.583 Gold 0.1456 oz. AGW **Subject:** 1994 Summer Olympic Games **Rev:** Tennis

Date	Mintage	VF20	XF40	MS60	MS63	MS65
1994	5,000	PF65 295				

KM# 101 25 DINERS
7.77 g., 0.583 Gold 0.1456 oz. AGW **Subject:** ECU Customs Union **Obv:** Coat of arms **Rev:** Bishop Pere D'Urg standing

Date	Mintage	VF20	XF40	MS60	MS63	MS65
1994	5,000	PF65 285				

KM# 107 25 DINERS
7.77 g., 0.583 Gold 0.1456 oz. AGW **Subject:** ECU Customs Union **Obv:** Coat of arms **Rev:** Bishop Pere D'Urg seated

Date	Mintage	VF20	XF40	MS60	MS63	MS65
1995	5,000	PF65 285				

KM# 123 25 DINERS
7.77 g., 0.583 Gold 0.1456 oz. AGW **Obv:** Arms and "ECU" **Rev:** Seated Europa

Date	Mintage	VF20	XF40	MS60	MS63	MS65
1996	Est. 5000	PF65 285				

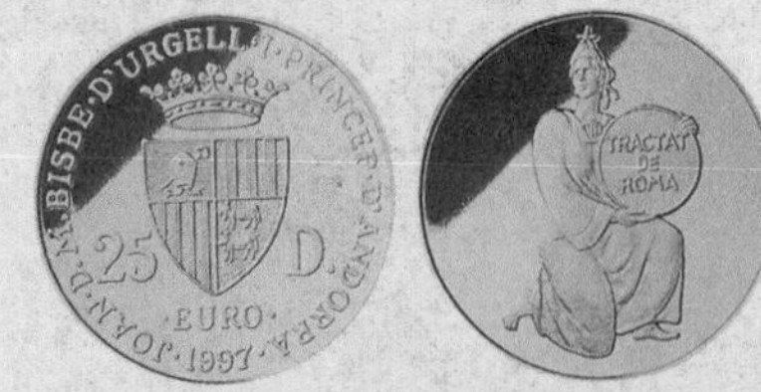

KM# 129 25 DINERS
7.77 g., 0.583 Gold 0.1456 oz. AGW **Subject:** Treaty of Rome **Obv:** Crowned arms **Rev:** Europa on knee, holding shield

Date	Mintage	VF20	XF40	MS60	MS63	MS65
1997	5,000	PF65 285				

KM# 139 25 DINERS
Bi-Metallic Gold center in Platinum ring **Obv:** Fleury cross **Rev:** Swan in water

Date	Mintage	VF20	XF40	MS60	MS63	MS65
1997	10,000	PF65 515				

KM# 145 25 DINERS
7.77 g., 0.585 Gold 0.1461 oz. AGW **Subject:** Human Rights **Obv:** Crowned arms **Rev:** Seated woman with quill

Date	Mintage	VF20	XF40	MS60	MS63	MS65
1998	5,000	PF65 285				

KM# 391 25 DINERS
17.14 g., 0.9167 Gold 0.505 oz. AGW, 29 mm. **Subject:** Rossell's Manual Digest, 150th Anniversary **Obv:** National shield **Rev:** Ink drawing of an eagle

Date	Mintage	VF20	XF40	MS60	MS63	MS65
1998	Est. 1000	PF65 850				

KM# 63 50 DINERS
15.55 g., 0.999 Gold 0.4994 oz. AGW, 30 mm. **Obv:** Defiant Golden Eagle **Rev:** Arms within circle **Note:** There is a similar 1988 half-ounce without the denomination.

Date	Mintage	VF20	XF40	MS60	MS63	MS65
1989	3,000	—	—	—	—	850
1989	—	PF65 900				

KM# 62 50 DINERS
17.03 g., 0.917 Gold 0.5019 oz. AGW, 29 mm. **Obv:** Arms within circle outlined with dots, value below **Rev:** Castle, Antoni Gaudi to left, two dates to right

Date	Mintage	VF20	XF40	MS60	MS63	MS65
1990	3,000	PF65 900				

KM# 64 50 DINERS
15.55 g., 0.999 Gold 0.4994 oz. AGW, 27 mm. **Subject:** Wildlife **Rev:** Red squirrel

Date	Mintage	VF20	XF40	MS60	MS63	MS65
1990	2,500	PF65 900				

KM# 68 50 DINERS
15.55 g., 0.999 Gold 0.4994 oz. AGW, 27 mm. **Subject:** Wildlife **Obv:** Crowned arms to left of five line inscription, value below, date below **Rev:** Chamois

Date	Mintage	VF20	XF40	MS60	MS63	MS65
1991	—	PF65 900				

KM# 70 50 DINERS
13.34 g., 0.585 Gold 0.2509 oz. AGW, 27.5 mm. **Subject:** 1992 Summer Olympic Games **Obv:** Crowned arms to left of five line inscription, value below, date at bottom **Rev:** Gymnast on rings

Date	Mintage	VF20	XF40	MS60	MS63	MS65
1991	3,000	PF65 425				

KM# 77 50 DINERS
15.55 g., 0.9999 Gold 0.500 oz. AGW, 27 mm. **Subject:** Wildlife **Obv:** Crowned arms to left of five line inscription, value below, date at bottom **Rev:** Brown Bears

Date	Mintage	VF20	XF40	MS60	MS63	MS65
1992	2,500	PF65 850				

KM# 82 50 DINERS
16.97 g., 0.916 Gold 0.4996 oz. AGW **Obv:** Crowned arms to left of five line inscription, value below, date at bottom **Rev:** Musician Pau Casals

Date	Mintage	VF20	XF40	MS60	MS63	MS65
1993	5,000	PF65 825				

KM# 104 50 DINERS
155.51 g., 0.925 Silver 4.6248 oz. ASW, 65 mm. **Subject:** 1st Anniversary - Andorran Constitution **Obv:** Arms above "ECU" **Rev:** Seated woman with open scroll, within large letter "C", date below, value to right **Note:** Illustration reduced.

Date	Mintage	VF20	XF40	MS60	MS63	MS65
1994	5,000	—	—	—	185	220

KM# 115 50 DINERS
155.51 g., 0.925 Silver 4.6248 oz. ASW, 65.8 mm. **Subject:** 1996 Olympic Games **Obv:** Arms above date **Rev:** Angel lighting Olympic flame

Date	Mintage	VF20	XF40	MS60	MS63	MS65
1995	5,000	—	—	—	200	230

KM# 124 50 DINERS
155.51 g., 0.925 Silver 4.6248 oz. ASW with insert of 2.5 g. 0.917 gold, 0.0737 AGW., 65 mm. **Subject:** Our Lady of Maritxell - Patroness of Andorra **Obv:** Crowned arms in inner circle **Rev:** Enthroned Madonna and child

Date	Mintage	VF20	XF40	MS60	MS63	MS65
1996	5,000	—	—	—	200	230

KM# 224 50 DINERS
15.55 g., 0.9999 Gold 0.4999 oz. AGW **Obv:** Fleury cross **Rev:** Bust of Queen Isabella right

Date	Mintage	VF20	XF40	MS60	MS63	MS65
1997	2,000	PF65 850				

KM# 152 50 DINERS
15.55 g., 0.916 Gold 0.458 oz. AGW **Subject:** 250th Anniversary - Synod Constitution **Obv:** Clerical arms **Rev:** Madonna and child

Date	Mintage	VF20	XF40	MS60	MS63	MS65
1998	1,998	PF65 850				

KM# 392 50 DINERS
34.24 g., 0.9167 Gold 1.0092 oz. AGW, 35 mm. **Subject:** Rossell's Manual Digest, 150th Anniversary **Obv:** National arms **Rev:** Ink drawing of an eagle

Date	Mintage	VF20	XF40	MS60	MS63	MS65
1998	Est. 1000	PF65 1,450				

KM# 403 50 DINERS
15.55 g., 0.999 Gold 0.4994 oz. AGW, 30 mm. **Subject:** Year of the Dragon **Obv:** Temple **Rev:** Dragon

Date	Mintage	VF20	XF40	MS60	MS63	MS65
2000	Est. 3000	PF65 750				

KM# 41 100 DINERS
5.00 g., 0.999 Gold 0.1606 oz. AGW, 22 mm. **Obv:** Joan D.M. Bisbe D'Urgell I, left **Rev:** Value, date below, within crowned wreath

Date	Mintage	VF20	XF40	MS60	MS63	MS65
1987	2,000	—	—	—	260	300

KM# 42 100 DINERS
5.00 g., 0.999 Gold 0.1606 oz. AGW **Obv:** Arms within circle **Rev:** Golden Eagle, mountains in background, date below

Date	Mintage	VF20	XF40	MS60	MS63	MS65
1988	2,000	—	—	—	260	300

KM# 45 250 DINERS
12.00 g., 0.999 Gold 0.3854 oz. AGW, 28.1 mm. **Subject:** 700th Anniversary - Andorra's Governing Charter **Obv:** Fleury cross, value at bottom **Rev:** Clasped hands, right hand armored, left hand in bishop's glove

Date	Mintage	VF20	XF40	MS60	MS63	MS65
ND-1988	3,000	—	—	—	570	620

KM# 30 SOVEREIGN
8.00 g., 0.918 Gold 0.2361 oz. AGW **Obv:** Joan D.M. Bisbe D'Urgell I, left **Rev:** Divided arms, value at top **Note:** Latin legend.

Date	Mintage	VF20	XF40	MS60	MS63	MS65
1982	1,500	—	—	—	400	430

KM# 31 SOVEREIGN
8.00 g., 0.918 Gold 0.2361 oz. AGW **Obv:** Joan D.M. Bisbe D'Urgell I, left **Rev:** Divided arms, value at top **Note:** Catalan legend.

Date	Mintage	VF20	XF40	MS60	MS63	MS65
1982	1,500	—	—	—	400	430

KM# 32 SOVEREIGN
8.00 g., 0.918 Gold 0.2361 oz. AGW **Obv:** Joan D.M. Bisbe D'Urgell I, right **Rev:** Crowned arms flanked by cherubs, value below **Note:** Latin legends.

Date	Mintage	VF20	XF40	MS60	MS63	MS65
1983	1,500	—	—	—	400	430

BULLION COINAGE

KM# 66 DINER
10.30 g., 0.999 Silver 0.3308 oz. ASW, 29.3 mm. **Obv:** Golden Eagle with wings open, value below **Rev:** Arms within circle

Date	Mintage	VF20	XF40	MS60	MS63	MS65
1990	6,000	—	—	—	27.50	32.50

KM# 79 100 DINERS
31.10 g., 0.999 Gold 0.999 oz. AGW, 35 mm. **Obv:** Defiant eagle above value **Note:** There is a similar 1988 one-ounce without the denomination.

Date	Mintage	VF20	XF40	MS60	MS63	MS65
1989	3,000	—	—	—	1,400	1,425

KM# 94 100 DINERS
31.10 g., 0.999 Gold 0.999 oz. AGW **Obv:** Defiant Golden Eagle, date below **Rev:** Value within crowned wreath

Date	Mintage	VF20	XF40	MS60	MS63	MS65
1992	—	—	—	—	1,400	1,425

PATTERNS

KM#	Date	Mintage	Identification	Mkt Val
Pn1	1987	—	2 Diners. Nickel Plated Bronze. KM#46.	150
Pn2	1992	2	50 Diners. 0.9999. Gold. Defiant eagle. Prev. KM#93.	—
Pn3	1994	2	5 Diners. 0.9999. Gold. Defiant eagle. KM# 112.	—
Pn4	1994	2	10 Diners. 0.9999. Gold. Defiant eagle.	—
Pn5	1994	2	25 Diners. 0.9999. Gold. Defiant eagle.	—
Pn6	1994	—	50 Diners. 0.9999. Gold. Defiant eagle.	—

MINT SETS

KM#	Date	Mintage	Identification	Issue Price	Mkt Val
MS1	1986 (5)	—	KM#33, 35-38	31.00	75.00

PROOF SETS

KM#	Date	Mintage	Identification	Issue Price	Mkt Val
PS1	1963 (2)	1,000	KM#M3, M4	51.00	80.00
PS2	1964 (2)	—	M5, M6	51.00	85.00
PS3	1964 (2)	4	X#M5a, M6a	—	2,400
PS4	1965 (2)	—	M7, M8	80.00	130
PS5	1965 (2)	—	X#M7a, M8a	—	2,400

ANGOLA

The Republic of Angola, a country on the west coast of southern Africa bounded by Congo Democratic Republic, Zambia, and Namibia (Southwest Africa), has an area of 481,351 sq. mi. (1,246,700 sq. km.) and a population of 12.78 million, predominantly Bantu in origin. Capital: Luanda. Most of the people are engaged in subsistence agriculture. However, important oil and mineral deposits make Angola potentially one of the richest countries in Africa. Iron and diamonds are exported.

The Portuguese navigator, Diogo Cao, discovered Angola in 1482 Angola. Portuguese settlers arrived in 1491, and established Angola as a major slaving center, which sent about 3 million slaves to the New World.

A revolt, characterized by guerrilla warfare, against Portuguese rule began in 1961 and continued until 1974, when a new regime in Portugal offered independence. The independence movement was actively supported by three groups; the National Front, based in Zaire, the Soviet-backed Popular Movement, and the moderate National Union. Independence was proclaimed on Nov. 11, 1975, and the Portuguese departed, leaving the Angolan people to work out their own political destiny. Within hours, each of the independence groups proclaimed itself Angola's sole ruler. A bloody intertribal civil war erupted in which the Communist Popular Movement, assisted by Soviet arms and Cuban mercenaries, was the eventual victor.

RULER
Portuguese until 1975

MINT MARK
KN - King's Norton

PORTUGUESE COLONY

DECIMAL COINAGE

1910-1975
100 Centavos = 20 Macutas = 1 Escudo
100 Centavos = 1 Escudo

KM# 60 CENTAVO
Bronze **Obv:** Value **Rev:** Arms, date below

Date	Mintage	VF20	XF40	MS60	MS63	MS65
1921	1,360,000	12.00	45.00	100	200	—

KM# 61 2 CENTAVOS
Bronze **Obv:** Value **Rev:** Arms, date below

Date	Mintage	VF20	XF40	MS60	MS63	MS65
1921	530,000	15.00	50.00	110	250	—

KM# 62 5 CENTAVOS
Bronze **Obv:** Value **Rev:** Arms, date below

Date	Mintage	VF20	XF40	MS60	MS63	MS65
1921	720,000	18.00	45.00	80.00	—	—
1922	5,680,000	10.00	25.00	45.00	90.00	—
1923	5,840,000	10.00	25.00	45.00	90.00	—
1924	—	35.00	70.00	140	225	—

KM# 66 5 CENTAVOS (1 Macuta)
Nickel-Bronze **Obv:** Head left **Rev:** Arms, value below

Date	Mintage	VF20	XF40	MS60	MS63	MS65
1927	2,001,999	3.00	12.00	25.00	45.00	75.00

KM# 63 10 CENTAVOS
Copper-Nickel **Obv:** Value **Rev:** Head, left

Date	Mintage	VF20	XF40	MS60	MS63	MS65
1921	160,000	20.00	50.00	125	225	—
1922	340,000	12.00	30.00	85.00	175	—
1923	2,960,000	5.00	15.00	45.00	100	150

KM# 70 10 CENTAVOS
Bronze, 17.8 mm. **Subject:** 300th Anniversary - Revolution of 1648 **Obv:** Value **Rev:** Five crowns above arms, date below **Edge:** Plain

Date	Mintage	VF20	XF40	MS60	MS63	MS65
1948	10,000,000	—	0.25	2.00	3.00	5.00
1949	10,000,000	—	0.25	2.00	3.00	5.00

KM# 82 10 CENTAVOS
Aluminum **Obv:** Value **Rev:** Five crowns above arms, date below

Date	Mintage	VF20	XF40	MS60	MS63	MS65
1974	4,000,000	—	—	8.00	15.00	20.00

Note: Not released for circulation, but relatively available

KM# 67 10 CENTAVOS (2 Macutas)
Copper-Nickel **Obv:** Head, left **Rev:** Arms, value below

Date	Mintage	VF20	XF40	MS60	MS63	MS65
1927	2,003,000	3.00	10.00	25.00	60.00	90.00
1928	1,000,000	3.00	10.00	25.00	60.00	90.00

KM# 64 20 CENTAVOS
Copper-Nickel **Obv:** Value **Rev:** Head left

Date	Mintage	VF20	XF40	MS60	MS63	MS65
1921	2,115,000	5.00	18.00	45.00	75.00	125
1922	1,730,000	10.00	25.00	65.00	100	150

KM# 71 20 CENTAVOS
2.84 g., Bronze, 20.5 mm. **Subject:** 300th Anniversary - Revolution of 1648 **Obv:** Value **Rev:** Five crowns above arms, date below **Edge:** Plain

Date	Mintage	VF20	XF40	MS60	MS63	MS65
1948	7,850,000	—	0.50	2.00	3.00	15.00
1949	2,150,000	—	10.00	40.00	60.00	100

KM# 78 20 CENTAVOS

Bronze, 18.2 mm. **Obv:** Value **Rev:** Five crowns above arms, date below **Edge:** Plain

Date	Mintage	VF20	XF40	MS60	MS63	MS65
1962	3,000,000	—	—	0.45	0.75	1.50

KM# 68 20 CENTAVOS (4 Macutas)

Copper-Nickel **Obv:** Laureled head, left **Rev:** Arms, value below

Date	Mintage	VF20	XF40	MS60	MS63	MS65
1927	2,001,000	3.00	10.00	25.00	50.00	75.00
1928	500,000	5.00	15.00	35.00	60.00	90.00

KM# 65 50 CENTAVOS

10.50 g., Nickel, 31 mm. **Obv:** Head left, date below **Rev:** Arms, value in legend

Date	Mintage	VF20	XF40	MS60	MS63	MS65
1922	6,000,000	5.00	20.00	35.00	50.00	—
1923	6,000,000	5.00	20.00	35.00	50.00	—
1923 KN	Inc. above	—	150	225	375	—

Note: Not released for circulation

KM# 69 50 CENTAVOS

9.81 g., Nickel-Bronze, 30.42 mm. **Obv:** Laureled, hooded bust with long hair, left **Rev:** Arms, value below

Date	Mintage	VF20	XF40	MS60	MS63	MS65
1927	1,608,000	10.00	25.00	50.00	90.00	150
1928/7	1,600,000	10.00	25.00	50.00	90.00	150
1928	Inc. above	10.00	25.00	50.00	90.00	150

KM# 72 50 CENTAVOS

Nickel-Bronze **Subject:** 300th Anniversary - Revolution of 1648 **Obv:** Value **Rev:** Five crowns above arms, date below

Date	Mintage	VF20	XF40	MS60	MS63	MS65
1948	4,000,000	—	0.25	6.00	10.00	20.00
1950	4,000,000	—	0.25	6.00	10.00	20.00

KM# 75 50 CENTAVOS

4.00 g., Bronze, 20 mm. **Obv:** Value **Rev:** Five crowns above arms, date below **Edge:** Plain

Date	Mintage	VF20	XF40	MS60	MS63	MS65
1953	5,000,000	—	0.50	1.50	3.00	9.00
1954	11,731,000	—	0.50	1.50	2.50	7.50
1955	1,126,000	—	1.00	10.00	25.00	60.00
1957	8,873,000	—	0.50	1.50	2.50	7.50
1958	17,520,000	—	0.50	1.50	2.50	7.50
1961	8,750,000	—	0.50	1.50	2.50	7.50

KM# 75a 50 CENTAVOS

Copper-Nickel

Date	Mintage	VF20	XF40	MS60	MS63	MS65
1974	150	—	—	125	200	250

Note: Not released for circulation

KM# 76 ESCUDO

8.00 g., Bronze, 26 mm. **Obv:** Value **Rev:** Five crowns above arms, date below

Date	Mintage	VF20	XF40	MS60	MS63	MS65
1953	2,001,000	—	2.50	7.50	15.00	50.00
1956	2,989,000	—	1.00	5.00	8.00	25.00
1963	5,000,000	—	1.00	2.50	5.00	15.00
1965	5,000,000	—	1.00	2.50	5.00	15.00
1972	10,000,000	—	1.00	2.50	5.00	15.00
1974	6,214,000	—	1.00	2.50	5.00	15.00

KM# 76a ESCUDO

Copper-Nickel **Note:** Not released for circulation.

Date	Mintage	VF20	XF40	MS60	MS63	MS65
1972 Rare	—	—	—	—	—	—
1974 Rare	—	—	—	—	—	—

KM# 77 2-1/2 ESCUDOS

3.40 g., Copper-Nickel, 20 mm. **Obv:** Arms, date below **Rev:** Five crowns above arms, value below **Edge:** Reeded

Date	Mintage	VF20	XF40	MS60	MS63	MS65
1953	6,008,000	—	1.00	7.00	12.00	25.00
1956	9,992,000	—	0.35	2.75	6.00	10.00
1967	6,000,000	—	0.35	2.75	6.00	10.00
1968	5,000,000	—	0.35	2.75	6.00	10.00
1969	5,000,000	—	0.35	2.75	6.00	10.00
1974	19,999,000	—	0.25	1.00	3.00	8.00

KM# 81 5 ESCUDOS

Copper-Nickel **Obv:** Arms, date below **Rev:** Five crowns above arms, value below

Date	Mintage	VF20	XF40	MS60	MS63	MS65
1972	8,000,000	—	5.00	12.00	25.00	50.00
1974	Est. 3343000	—	—	125	200	375

Note: Not released for circulation

KM# 73 10 ESCUDOS

5.00 g., 0.720 Silver 0.1157 oz. ASW, 24.0 mm. **Obv:** Arms, date below **Rev:** Five crowns above arms, value below

Date	Mintage	VF20	XF40	MS60	MS63	MS65
1952	2,023,000	2.25	5.00	10.00	15.00	25.00
1955	1,977,000	2.25	5.00	10.00	15.00	25.00

KM# 79 10 ESCUDOS

9.00 g., Copper-Nickel, 28.1 mm. **Obv:** Arms, date below **Rev:** Five crowns above arms, value below

Date	Mintage	VF20	XF40	MS60	MS63	MS65
1969	3,022,000	—	1.00	3.00	8.00	12.00
1970	978,000	—	1.00	5.00	10.00	15.00

KM# 74 20 ESCUDOS

10.00 g., 0.720 Silver 0.2315 oz. ASW **Obv:** Arms, date below **Rev:** Five crowns above arms, value below

Date	Mintage	VF20	XF40	MS60	MS63	MS65
1952	1,002,999	4.75	8.00	12.00	18.00	25.00
1955	997,000	4.75	7.00	10.00	15.00	20.00

KM# 80 20 ESCUDOS

12.06 g., Nickel, 30 mm. **Obv:** Arms on ornate shield, date below **Rev:** Arms, value below

Date	Mintage	VF20	XF40	MS60	MS63	MS65
1971	1,572,000	—	0.75	2.00	4.00	7.50
1972	428,000	—	1.50	3.00	7.00	15.00

PEOPLES REPUBLIC

DECIMAL COINAGE

1975 - 1998

100 Lwei = 1 Kwanza

KM# 90 50 LWEI

Copper-Nickel **Obv:** National arms **Rev:** Large value, dots near rim

Date	Mintage	VF20	XF40	MS60	MS63	MS65
ND1977	—	—	0.25	0.50	1.00	—
1979	—	—	—	0.35	0.50	1.00

KM# 83 KWANZA

3.91 g., Copper-Nickel, 20.9 mm. **Obv:** National arms **Rev:** Large value, dots near rim

Date	Mintage	VF20	XF40	MS60	MS63	MS65
ND1977	—	—	0.25	0.50	1.00	—
1978	—	—	—	0.35	0.50	1.00
1979	—	—	—	0.35	0.50	1.00

KM# 84 2 KWANZAS
5.00 g., Copper-Nickel, 23.2 mm. **Obv:** National arms **Rev:** Large value, dots near rim

Date	Mintage	VF20	XF40	MS60	MS63	MS65
ND-1977	—	—	0.25	0.75	1.00	—

KM# 85 5 KWANZAS
6.90 g., Copper-Nickel, 25.5 mm. **Obv:** National arms **Rev:** Large value, dots near rim

Date	Mintage	VF20	XF40	MS60	MS63	MS65
ND-1977	—	0.75	1.50	3.00	—	

KM# 86.1 10 KWANZAS
7.70 g., Copper-Nickel, 27.5 mm. **Obv:** National arms **Rev:** Small date, dots near rim, Large value

Date	Mintage	VF20	XF40	MS60	MS63	MS65
ND-1977	—	—	—	0.75	1.50	3.00
1978	—	—	—	0.75	1.50	3.00

KM# 86.2 10 KWANZAS
Copper-Nickel **Rev:** Large date, dots away from rim

Date	Mintage	VF20	XF40	MS60	MS63	MS65
1978	—	—	—	1.00	1.50	3.00

KM# 87 20 KWANZAS
10.00 g., Copper-Nickel, 29.1 mm. **Obv:** National arms **Rev:** Large value, dots near rim

Date	Mintage	VF20	XF40	MS60	MS63	MS65
1978	—	—	1.00	3.00	5.00	8.00

KM# 91 50 KWANZAS
Copper **Obv:** National arms **Rev:** Large value, dots near rim

Date	Mintage	VF20	XF40	MS60	MS63	MS65
ND-1978	—	—	1.00	4.00	6.00	12.00

KM# 101 50 KWANZAS
Copper Clad Steel, 23.3 mm. **Subject:** 15th Anniversary of the Angolan Kwanza Currency **Obv:** National arms within legend **Rev:** Value above anniversary date "8 Jan. 92" **Edge:** Reeded

Date	Mintage	VF20	XF40	MS60	MS63	MS65
ND-1992	—	—	10.00	18.00	30.00	50.00

KM# 92 100 KWANZAS
Copper **Obv:** National arms **Rev:** Large value, dots near rim

Date	Mintage	VF20	XF40	MS60	MS63	MS65
ND1991	—	1.00	3.00	7.00	12.00	—

REFORM COINAGE

1999 -

KM# 95 10 CENTIMOS
1.50 g., Copper Plated Steel, 15.04 mm. **Obv:** National arms, country name and date **Rev:** Denomination **Edge:** Plain

Date	Mintage	VF20	XF40	MS60	MS63	MS65
1999	—	—	—	0.50	1.00	2.00

KM# 96 50 CENTIMOS
3.00 g., Copper Plated Steel, 18 mm. **Obv:** National arms, country name and date **Rev:** Denomination **Edge:** Plain

Date	Mintage	VF20	XF40	MS60	MS63	MS65
1999	—	—	—	0.50	1.00	2.00

KM# 97 KWANZA
4.50 g., Nickel Plated Steel, 21 mm. **Obv:** National arms, country name and date **Rev:** Denomination **Edge:** Reeded

Date	Mintage	VF20	XF40	MS60	MS63	MS65
1999	—	—	—	0.50	1.00	2.00

KM# 98 2 KWANZAS
5.00 g., Nickel Plated Steel, 22 mm. **Obv:** National arms, country name and date **Rev:** Denomination **Edge:** Reeded

Date	Mintage	VF20	XF40	MS60	MS63	MS65
1999	—	—	—	0.75	1.50	3.00

KM# 99 5 KWANZAS
7.00 g., Nickel Plated Steel, 26 mm. **Obv:** National arms, country name and date **Rev:** Denomination **Edge:** Reeded

Date	Mintage	VF20	XF40	MS60	MS63	MS65
1999	—	—	—	0.75	1.50	3.00

KM# 93 10 KWANZAS
24.23 g., Copper-Nickel **Subject:** Olympics **Obv:** National arms **Rev:** Olympic logo and allegory **Edge:** Reeded

Date	Mintage	VF20	XF40	MS60	MS63	MS65
1999	—	PF60 9.00	PF63 12.00	PF65 15.00		

KM# 100 10 KWANZAS
23.05 g., Nickel Plated Steel **Subject:** Prince Henry the Navigator **Obv:** National arms **Rev:** Prince Henry in armor 3/4 left **Edge:** Reeded

Date	Mintage	VF20	XF40	MS60	MS63	MS65
1999	10,000	PF60 10.00	PF63 14.00	PF65 18.00		

KM# 94 100 KWANZAS
25.00 g., 0.925 Silver 0.7435 oz. ASW **Subject:** Olympics **Obv:** National arms **Rev:** Olympic logo and Allegory

Date	Mintage	VF20	XF40	MS60	MS63	MS65
1999	—	PF60 18.00	PF63 22.00	PF65 32.00		

KM# 102 100 KWANZAS
25.00 g., 0.925 Silver 0.7435 oz. ASW **Subject:** Prince Henry the Navigator **Obv:** National arms **Rev:** Bust of Prince Henry in armor 3/4 left **Edge:** Reeded

Date	Mintage	VF20	XF40	MS60	MS63	MS65
1999	10,000	PF60 20.00	PF63 25.00	PF65 35.00		

PATTERNS

Including off metal strikes

KM#	Date	Mintage	Identification	Mkt Val
Pn7	1972	—	50 Escudos. Silver. Shield within circle. Cross with winged arms and waves on top.	1,500

PROVAS

Raised or stamped "PROVA" in field

KM#	Date	Mintage	Identification	Mkt Val
Pr1	1921	—	Centavo. Bronze. KM#60.	220
Pr2	1921	—	2 Centavos. Bronze. KM#61.	285
Pr3	1921	—	5 Centavos. Bronze. KM#62.	180
Pr4	1921	—	10 Centavos. Copper-Nickel. KM#63.	240
Pr5	1921	—	20 Centavos. Copper-Nickel. KM#64.	100
Pr6	1922	—	5 Centavos. Bronze. KM#62.	125
Pr7	1922	—	10 Centavos. Copper-Nickel. KM#63.	180
Pr8	1922	—	20 Centavos. Copper-Nickel. KM#64.	150
Pr9	1923	—	5 Centavos. Bronze. KM#62.	125
Pr10	1923	—	10 Centavos. Copper-Nickel. KM#63.	110
Pr12	1924	—	5 Centavos. Bronze. KM#62.	285
Pr13	1927	—	5 Centavos. Nickel-Bronze. KM#66.	85.00
Pr14	1927	—	10 Centavos. Copper-Nickel. KM#67.	85.00
Pr15	1927	—	20 Centavos. Copper-Nickel. KM#68.	75.00
Pr16	1927	—	50 Centavos. Nickel-Bronze. KM#69.	150
Pr17	1928	—	10 Centavos. Copper-Nickel. KM#67.	100
Pr18	1928	—	20 Centavos. Copper-Nickel. KM#68.	100
Pr19	1928	—	50 Centavos. Nickel-Bronze. KM#69.	150
Pr20	1948	—	10 Centavos. Bronze. KM#70.	75.00
Pr21	1948	—	20 Centavos. Bronze. KM#71.	85.00
Pr22	1948	—	50 Centavos. Nickel-Bronze. KM#72.	90.00
Pr23	1949	—	10 Centavos. Bronze. KM#70.	85.00
Pr24	1949	—	20 Centavos. Bronze. KM#71.	95.00
Pr25	1949	—	50 Centavos. Nickel-Bronze. KM#72.	100
Pr26	1950	—	50 Centavos. Nickel-Bronze. KM#72.	75.00
Pr27	1952	—	10 Escudos. Silver. KM#73.	75.00
Pr28	1952	—	20 Escudos. Silver. KM#74.	110
Pr29	1953	—	50 Centavos. Bronze. KM#75.	65.00
Pr30	1953	—	Escudo. Bronze. KM#76.	75.00
Pr31	1953	—	2-1/2 Escudos. Copper-Nickel. KM#77.	85.00
Pr32	1954	—	50 Centavos. Bronze. KM#75.	65.00
Pr33	1954	—	Escudo. Bronze. KM#76.	75.00
Pr34	1954	—	2-1/2 Escudos. Copper-Nickel. KM#77.	85.00
Pr35	1955	—	50 Centavos. Bronze. KM#75.	65.00
Pr36	1955	—	Escudo. Bronze. KM#76.	75.00

Pr37	1955	—	2-1/2 Escudos. Copper-Nickel. KM#77.	85.00
Pr38	1955	—	10 Escudos. Silver. KM#73.	95.00
Pr39	1955	—	20 Escudos. Silver. KM#74.	110
Pr40	1956	—	50 Centavos. Bronze. KM#75.	45.00
Pr41	1956	—	Escudo. Bronze. KM#76.	55.00
Pr42	1956	—	2-1/2 Escudos. Copper-Nickel. KM#77.	65.00
Pr43	1957	—	50 Centavos. Bronze. KM#75.	45.00
Pr44	1957	—	Escudo. Bronze. KM#76.	55.00
Pr45	1957	—	2-1/2 Escudos. Copper-Nickel. KM#77.	65.00
Pr46	1958	—	50 Centavos. Bronze. KM#75.	45.00
Pr47	1958	—	Escudo. Bronze. KM#76.	55.00
Pr48	1958	—	2-1/2 Escudos. Copper-Nickel. KM#77.	65.00
Pr49	1959	—	50 Centavos. Bronze. KM#75.	45.00
Pr50	1959	—	Escudo. Bronze. KM#76.	55.00
Pr51	1959	—	2-1/2 Escudos. Copper-Nickel. KM#77.	65.00
Pr52	1960	—	50 Centavos. Bronze. KM#75.	45.00
Pr53	1960	—	Escudo. Bronze. KM#76.	55.00
Pr54	1960	—	2-1/2 Escudos. Copper-Nickel. KM#77.	65.00
Pr55	1961	—	50 Centavos. Bronze. KM#75.	45.00
Pr56	1961	—	Escudo. Bronze. KM#76.	55.00
Pr57	1961	—	2-1/2 Escudos. Copper-Nickel. KM#77.	65.00
Pr58	1962	—	20 Centavos. Bronze. KM#78.	45.00
Pr59	1962	—	Escudo. Bronze. KM#76.	55.00
Pr60	1962	—	2-1/2 Escudos. Copper-Nickel. KM#77.	65.00
Pr61	1963	—	Escudo. Bronze. KM#76.	55.00
Pr62	1963	—	2-1/2 Escudos. Copper-Nickel. KM#77.	65.00
Pr63	1964	—	Escudo. Bronze. KM#76.	55.00
Pr64	1964	—	2-1/2 Escudos. Copper-Nickel. KM#77.	65.00
Pr65	1965	—	Escudo. Bronze. KM#76.	55.00
Pr66	1965	—	2-1/2 Escudos. Copper-Nickel. KM#77.	65.00
Pr67	1966	—	Escudo. Bronze. KM#76.	55.00
Pr68	1966	—	2-1/2 Escudos. Copper-Nickel. KM#77.	65.00
Pr69	1967	—	Escudo. Bronze. KM#76.	55.00
Pr70	1967	—	2-1/2 Escudos. Copper-Nickel. KM#77.	65.00
Pr71	1968	—	Escudo. Bronze. KM#76.	55.00
Pr72	1968	—	2-1/2 Escudos. Copper-Nickel. KM#77.	65.00
Pr73	1969	—	Escudo. Bronze. KM#76.	55.00
Pr74	1969	—	2-1/2 Escudos. Copper-Nickel. KM#77.	65.00
Pr75	1969	—	10 Escudos. Copper-Nickel. KM#79.	75.00
Pr76	1970	—	Escudo. Bronze. KM#76.	55.00
Pr77	1970	—	2-1/2 Escudos. Copper-Nickel. KM#77.	65.00
Pr78	1970	—	10 Escudos. Copper-Nickel. KM#79.	75.00
Pr79	1971	—	Escudo. Bronze. KM#76.	55.00
Pr80	1971	—	2-1/2 Escudos. Copper-Nickel. KM#77.	65.00
Pr81	1971	—	20 Escudos. Nickel. KM#80.	85.00
Pr82	1972	—	Escudo. Bronze. KM#76.	55.00
Pr83	1972	—	2-1/2 Escudos. Copper-Nickel. KM#77.	65.00
Pr84	1972	—	5 Escudos. Copper-Nickel. KM#81.	75.00
Pr85	1972	—	20 Escudos. Nickel. KM#80.	85.00
Pr86	1974	—	Escudo. Bronze. KM#76.	65.00
Pr87	1974	—	2-1/2 Escudos. Copper-Nickel. KM#77.	95.00
Pr88	1974	—	5 Escudos. Copper-Nickel. KM#81.	275

MINT SETS

KM#	Date	Mintage	Identification	Issue Price	Mkt Val
MS1	ND (1979) (6)	—	KM#83, 84, 85, 86.2, 87, 90 This set was assembled by the National Bank of Angola in a folder which presents a brief monetary history of Angola including some banknote pictures.	20.00	22.50

The British dependency of Anguilla, a self-governing British territory situated in the east Caribbean Sea about 60 miles (100 km.) northwest of St. Kitts, has an area of 35 sq. mi. (91 sq. km.) and an approximate population of 12,000. Capital: The Valley. In recent years, tourism has replaced the traditional fishing, stock raising and salt production as the main industry.

Anguilla was discovered by Columbus in 1493 and became a British colony in 1650. As the other British areas in the West Indies did, Anguilla officially adapted to sterling beginning in 1825. From 1950 to 1965, Anguilla was a member of the British Caribbean Territories (Eastern Group) Currency Board, whose coinage it used. In March 1967, Anguilla was joined politically with St. Christopher (St. Kitts), as it had been for much of its colonial history, and Nevis to form a British associated state.

On June 16, 1967, the Provisional Government of Anguilla unilaterally declared its independence and seceded from the Federation. Later, on July 11, 1967, a vote of confidence was taken and the results favored independence. Britain refused to accept the declaration (nor did any other country recognize it) and appointed a British administrator whom Anguilla accepted. However, in Feb. 1969 Anguilla ousted the British emissary, voted to sever all ties with Britain, and established the Republic of Anguilla. The following month Britain landed a force of paratroopers and policemen. This bloodless counteraction ended the self-proclaimed republic and resulted in the installation of a governing commissioner. The troops were withdrawn in Sept. 1969, and the Anguilla Act of July 1971 placed Anguilla directly under British control. A new constitution in 1976 established Anguilla as a self-governing British dependant territory. Britain retains power over defense, police and civil service, and foreign affairs. Since 1981, Anguilla has employed the coinage of the East Caribbean States.

NOTE: There is no evidence that the issues of the self-proclaimed Provisional Government ever actually circulated. The c/s series most likely served as souvenirs of the "revolution" and can be found listed in our companion volume Unusual World Coins.

RULER

British

BRITISH DEPENDANT TERRITORY

DECIMAL COINAGE

KM# 15 1/2 DOLLAR

3.61 g., 0.999 Silver 0.1159 oz. ASW **Obv:** St. Mary's Church **Rev:** State arms

Date	Mintage	F12	VF20	XF40	MS60	MS63
ND	—	PF65 30.00				
1969	—	PF65 30.00				
1970	—	PF65 30.00				

KM# 16 DOLLAR

7.18 g., 0.999 Silver 0.2306 oz. ASW **Obv:** Map - Seahorse, Caribbean Silver Lobster, Shell **Rev:** State arms

Date	Mintage	F12	VF20	XF40	MS60	MS63
ND	—	PF65 40.00				
1969	—	PF65 40.00				
1970	—	PF65 40.00				

KM# 17 2 DOLLARS

14.14 g., 0.999 Silver 0.4542 oz. ASW **Obv:** National flag and map **Rev:** State arms

Date	Mintage	F12	VF20	XF40	MS60	MS63
ND	—	PF65 50.00				
1969	—	PF65 50.00				
1970	—	PF65 50.00				

KM# 18.1 4 DOLLARS

28.48 g., 0.999 Silver 0.9147 oz. ASW, 40 mm. **Obv:** Ship - Atlantic Star **Rev:** State arms, value at bottom

Date	Mintage	F12	VF20	XF40	MS60	MS63
ND	—	PF65 80.00				
1969	—	PF65 80.00				
1970	—	PF65 80.00				

KM# 18.2 4 DOLLARS

28.48 g., 0.999 Silver 0.9147 oz. ASW, 40 mm. **Obv:** Ship-Atlantic Star **Rev:** 2 hallmarks at 4 o'clock, state arms, value at bottom

Date	Mintage	F12	VF20	XF40	MS60	MS63
1970	—	PF65 100				

KM# 20 5 DOLLARS

2,46 g., 0.900 Gold 0.0712 oz. AGW **Obv:** Methodist Church of West End

Date	Mintage	F12	VF20	XF40	MS60	MS63
ND	1,925	PF65 145				
1969	—	PF65 145				
1970	—	PF65 145				

KM# 21 10 DOLLARS

4.93 g., 0.900 Gold 0.1427 oz. AGW **Obv:** Dolphin, Caribbean Silver Lobster, Starfish

Date	Mintage	F12	VF20	XF40	MS60	MS63
ND	1,615	PF65 275				
1969	—	PF65 275				
1970	—	PF65 275				

KM# 22 20 DOLLARS
9.87 g., 0.900 Gold 0.2856 oz. AGW **Obv:** Mermaids

Date	Mintage	F12	VF20	XF40	MS60	MS63
ND	1,395	PF65 525				
1969	—	PF65 525				
1970	—	PF65 525				

KM# 26 25 DOLLARS
31.00 g., 0.999 Silver 0.9957 oz. ASW **Subject:** 1st Year of Independence **Obv:** Three intertwined dolphins form circle **Rev:** President Ronald Webster bust left

Date	Mintage	F12	VF20	XF40	MS60	MS63
1968	—	PF65 125				

KM# 23 100 DOLLARS
49.37 g., 0.900 Gold 1.4286 oz. AGW **Subject:** Demonstrating Population **Obv:** People of Anguilla within beaded circle, grain spray below circle

Date	Mintage	F12	VF20	XF40	MS60	MS63
ND	—	PF65 2,750				
1969	—	PF65 2,750				
1970	—	PF65 2,750				

KM# 27 200 DOLLARS
38.00 g., 0.917 Gold 1.1203 oz. AGW **Subject:** 1st Year of Independence **Obv:** Three intertwined dolphins form circle **Rev:** President Ronald Webster bust left

Date	Mintage	F12	VF20	XF40	MS60	MS63
1968	—	PF65 2,150				

KM# 28 1500 DOLLARS
62.00 g., 0.999 Platinum 1.9914 oz. APW **Subject:** 1st Year of Independence **Obv:** Three intertwined dolphins form circle **Rev:** President Ronald Wester bust facing left

Date	Mintage	F12	VF20	XF40	MS60	MS63
1968	—	PF65 4,200				

TRIAL STRIKES

KM#	Date	Mintage	Identification	Mkt Val
TS1	ND (1969)	—	5 Dollars. Goldine Brass. Design of KM-20. Blank with MET countermark. Reeded. Uniface.	95.00
TS2	1969	—	100 Dollars. Goldine.	—
TS3	ND (1969)	—	5 Dollars. Goldine Brass. Design of KM-23. Blank with MET countermark. Reeded.	225

PROOF SETS

KM#	Date	Mintage	Identification	Issue Price	Mkt Val
PS1	1969 (8)	—	KM#15-18.1, 20-23	225	3,850
PS2	1969 (4)	—	KM#15-18.1	25.50	165
PS3	1969 (4)	—	KM#20-23	200	3,700
PS4	1970 (8)	—	KM#15-18.1, 20-23	225	3,850
PS5	1970 (4)	—	KM#15-18.1	25.50	165
PS6	1970 (4)	—	KM#20-23	200	3,700

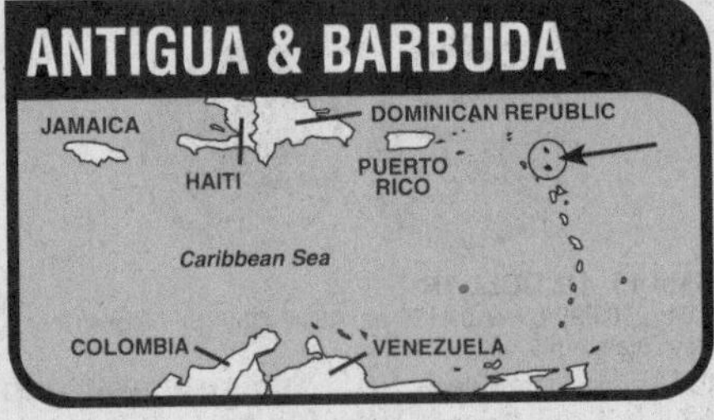

Antigua and Barbuda are located on the eastern edge of the Leeward Islands in the Caribbean Sea, have an area of 170 sq. mi. (440 sq. km.) and an estimated population of 68,000. Capital: St. John's. Prior to 1967, Antigua and its dependencies Barbuda and Redonda, comprised a presidency of the Leeward Islands. The mountainous island produces sugar, molasses, rum, cotton and fruit. Tourism is making an increasingly valuable contribution to the economy.

Antigua was discovered by Columbus in 1493, settled by British colonists from St. Kitts in 1632, occupied by the French in 1666, and ceded to Britain in 1667. It became an associated state with internal self-government on February 27, 1967. On November 1, 1981 it became independent as Antigua and Barbuda. As a constitutional monarchy, Elizabeth II is Queen of Antigua and Barbuda and Head of State.

Spanish silver coinage and French colonial "Black Dogs" were used throughout the islands' early history; however, late in the seventeenth century the introduction of British tin farthings was attempted with complete lack of success. In 1822, British colonial Anchor Money was introduced.

From 1825 to 1955, Antigua was on the sterling standard and used British coins. Coins of the British Caribbean Territories (Eastern Group) and East Caribbean States circulated from 1955, and banknotes of East Caribbean Currency Authority are now used on the island. The early coinage was augmented by that of the East Caribbean States in 1981.

RULER
British

ANTIGUA

BRITISH ADMINISTRATION

DECIMAL COINAGE

100 Cents = 1 Dollar

KM# 1 4 DOLLARS
28.30 g., Copper-Nickel, 38.5 mm. **Ruler:** Elizabeth II **Series:** F.A.O. **Obv:** Helmeted arms with supporters, date below **Rev:** Value at bottom divides sugar cane and banana tree branch **Edge:** Reeded

Date	Mintage	F12	VF20	XF40	MS60	MS63
1970	14,000	—	4.00	6.00	12.00	22.00
1970	2,000	PF60 22.00	PF63 35.00	PF65 50.00		

Note: For similar issues see Barbados, Dominica, Grenada, Montserrat, St. Kitts, St. Lucia and St. Vincent.

ANTIGUA & BARBUDA

BRITISH ADMINISTRATION

DECIMAL COINAGE

KM# 5 10 DOLLARS
Copper-Nickel, 38.8 mm. **Ruler:** Elizabeth II **Subject:** Royal Visit **Obv:** Crowned bust right **Rev:** Arms

Date	Mintage	VF20	XF40	MS60	MS63	MS65
1985	100,000	—	—	7.00	14.00	28.00

KM# 5a 10 DOLLARS
28.28 g., 0.925 Silver 0.841 oz. ASW **Ruler:** Elizabeth II **Subject:** Royal Visit **Obv:** Crowned bust right **Rev:** Arms

Date	Mintage	VF20	XF40	MS60	MS63	MS65
1985	5,000	PF63 25.00	PF65 40.00			

KM# 2 30 DOLLARS
31.10 g., 0.500 Silver 0.4999 oz. ASW **Ruler:** Elizabeth II **Subject:** George Washington - Yorktown, 1781 **Obv:** Helmeted arms, date below, value at bottom **Rev:** George Washington between two figures, lighting cannon

Date	Mintage	VF20	XF40	MS60	MS63	MS65
1982	1,200	PF63 35.00	PF65 55.00			

KM# 3 30 DOLLARS
31.10 g., 0.500 Silver 0.4999 oz. ASW **Ruler:** Elizabeth II **Subject:** George Washington - Inauguration, 1789 **Obv:** Helmeted arms, date below, value at bottom **Rev:** George Washington and men rowing across the Delaware

Date	Mintage	VF20	XF40	MS60	MS63	MS65
1982	1,125	PF63 35.00	PF65 55.00			

KM# 4 30 DOLLARS
31.10 g., 0.500 Silver 0.4999 oz. ASW **Ruler:** Elizabeth II **Subject:** George Washington - Verplanck's Point, 1790 **Obv:** Helmeted arms, date below, value at bottom **Rev:** George Washington standing next to horse, left

Date	Mintage	VF20	XF40	MS60	MS63	MS65
1982	675	PF63 85.00	PF65 110			

KM# 6 100 DOLLARS
129.60 g., 0.925 Silver 3.8542 oz. ASW, 63 mm. **Ruler:** Elizabeth II **Subject:** Tropical Birds **Obv:** Arms **Rev:** Cattle Egret

Date	Mintage	VF20	XF40	MS60	MS63	MS65
1988	10,000	PF63 95.00	PF65 120			

KM# 7 500 DOLLARS
47.54 g., 0.917 Gold 1.4016 oz. AGW **Ruler:** Elizabeth II **Subject:** Royal Visit **Obv:** Crowned bust right **Rev:** Arms

Date	Mintage	VF20	XF40	MS60	MS63	MS65
1985	250	PF65 2,000				

The Argentine Republic, located in southern South America, has an area of 1,073,518 sq. mi. (3,761,274 sq. km.) and an estimated population of 37.03 million. Capital: Buenos Aires. Its varied topography ranges from the subtropical lowlands of the north to the towering Andean Mountains in the west and the wind-swept Patagonian steppe in the south. The rolling, fertile pampas of central Argentina are ideal for agriculture and grazing, and support most of the republic's population. Meatpacking, flour milling, textiles, sugar refining and dairy products are the principal industries. Oil is found in Patagonia, but most mineral requirements must be imported.

Argentina was discovered in 1516 by the Spanish navigator Juan de Solis. A permanent Spanish colony was established at Buenos Aires in 1580, but the colony developed slowly. When Napoleon conquered Spain, the Argentines set up their own government on May 25, 1810. Independence was formally declared on July 9, 1816. A strong tendency toward local autonomy, fostered by difficult transportation, resulted in a federalized union with much authority left to the states or provinces, which resulted in the coinage of 1817-1867.

Internal conflict through the first half century of Argentine independence resulted in a provisional national coinage, chiefly of crown-sized silver. Provincial issues mainly of minor denominations supplemented this.

MINT MARKS
A = Korea
B = Great Britain
BA = Buenos Aires
C = France

MONETARY SYSTEM
100 Centavos = 1 Peso
10 Pesos = 1 Argentino
(Commencing 1970)
100 Old Pesos = 1 New Peso
(Commencing June 1983)
10,000 New Pesos = 1 Peso Argentino
1,000 Pesos Argentino = 1 Austral
(Commencing 1985)
1,000 Pesos Argentinos = 1 Austral
100 Centavos = 1 Austral
(Commencing 1992)
100 Centavos = 1 Peso

REPUBLIC

DECIMAL COINAGE

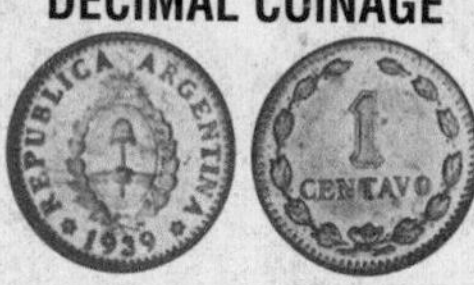

KM# 37 CENTAVO
1.94 g., Bronze, 16 mm. **Obv:** Argentine arms **Rev:** Value within wreath **Note:** Prev. KM#12.

Date	Mintage	VF20	XF40	MS60	MS63	MS65
1939	3,488,000	0.25	0.50	1.50	4.00	—
1940	3,140,000	0.15	0.35	1.00	2.00	—
1941	4,572,000	0.15	0.35	1.00	2.00	—
1942	495,000	0.30	0.75	1.50	7.50	—
1943	1,293,500	0.10	0.25	0.55	1.50	—
1944	3,102,743	0.20	0.50	1.00	2.75	—

KM# 37a CENTAVO
Copper, 16 mm. **Obv:** Argentine arms **Rev:** Value within wreath **Note:** Cruder diework. Prev. KM#12a.

Date	Mintage	VF20	XF40	MS60	MS63	MS65
1945	420,000	0.20	0.50	1.00	4.00	—
1946/6	4,450,000	0.15	0.35	0.50	2.00	3.00
1947	5,630,000	0.15	0.35	0.50	2.00	3.00
1948	4,419,545	0.15	0.35	0.50	2.00	3.00

KM# 38 2 CENTAVOS
3.40 g., Bronze, 20.5 mm. **Obv:** Argentine arms **Rev:** Value within wreath **Note:** Prev. KM#13.

Date	Mintage	VF20	XF40	MS60	MS63	MS65
1939	5,490,000	0.15	0.35	1.00	4.50	—
1940	4,625,000	0.15	0.35	1.00	5.00	—
1941	4,566,805	0.15	0.35	1.00	5.00	—
1942	2,082,492	0.15	0.35	1.00	5.50	—
1944	387,072	0.25	0.50	1.25	7.50	—
1945	4,585,000	0.15	0.35	1.00	5.00	—
1946/1946	3,395,000	0.15	0.35	1.00	5.00	—
1947	4,395,000	0.15	0.35	1.00	5.00	—

KM# 38a 2 CENTAVOS
3.40 g., Copper, 20.5 mm. **Obv:** Argentine arms **Rev:** Value within wreath **Note:** Cruder diework. Prev. KM#13a.

Date	Mintage	VF20	XF40	MS60	MS63	MS65
1947	Inc. above	0.15	0.35	1.00	5.50	—
1948	3,645,000	0.15	0.35	1.00	5.50	—
1949/9	7,290,000	0.15	0.35	1.00	3.50	5.00
1950	903,070	0.25	0.65	1.25	6.50	—

KM# 34 5 CENTAVOS
2.00 g., Copper-Nickel, 17.3 mm. **Obv:** Capped liberty head left **Rev:** Denomination within wreath **Edge:** Reeded **Note:** Prev. KM#9.

Date	Mintage	F12	VF20	XF40	MS60	MS63
1903	2,502,000	8.00	20.00	50.00	120	—
1904	2,518,000	6.00	15.00	30.00	80.00	—
1905	4,359,000	5.00	10.00	20.00	60.00	—
1906	3,939,000	6.00	12.00	25.00	60.00	—
1907	1,682,000	8.00	15.00	40.00	100	—
1908	1,693,000	6.00	12.00	30.00	80.00	—
1909	4,650,000	3.00	8.00	20.00	50.00	—
1910	1,469,000	6.00	12.00	40.00	100	—
1911	1,431,000	6.00	15.00	30.00	80.00	—
1912	2,377,000	5.00	10.00	25.00	60.00	—
1913	1,477,000	6.00	12.00	40.00	100	—
1914	1,097,000	8.00	15.00	40.00	100	—
1915	1,310,000	2.00	5.00	15.00	40.00	—
1916	1,310,000	5.00	10.00	20.00	60.00	—
1917	1,009,000	5.00	10.00	25.00	60.00	—
1918	2,287,000	1.00	3.00	8.00	20.00	—
1919	2,476,000	1.00	3.00	8.00	20.00	—
1920	5,235,000	1.00	2.00	6.00	15.00	—
1921	7,040,000	1.00	2.00	6.00	15.00	—
1922	9,427,000	1.00	2.00	5.00	10.00	—
1923	6,256,000	1.00	2.00	5.00	10.00	—
1924	6,355,000	1.00	2.00	5.00	10.00	—
1925	3,955,000	1.00	2.00	5.00	10.00	—
1926	3,560,000	1.00	2.00	5.00	10.00	—
1927	5,650,000	1.00	2.00	4.00	8.00	—
1928	6,380,000	1.00	2.00	4.00	8.00	—
1929	11,831,000	0.50	1.00	3.00	8.00	—
1930 round top 3	7,110,000	1.00	2.00	4.00	8.00	—
1931 flat top 3	506,000	5.00	10.00	20.00	60.00	—
1933 round top 3	5,537,000	0.50	1.00	3.00	8.00	—
1934 round top 3	1,288,000	1.00	2.00	20.00	10.00	—
1935	3,052,000	0.50	1.00	3.00	6.00	—
1936	7,175,000	0.50	1.00	3.00	6.00	—
1937	7,063,000	0.50	1.00	3.00	6.00	—
1938	10,252,000	0.50	1.00	3.00	6.00	—
1939	7,171,000	0.50	1.00	3.00	6.00	—
1940	10,191,000	0.50	1.00	3.00	6.00	—
1941	951,000	0.50	1.00	3.00	6.00	—
1942	8,692,000	0.50	1.00	3.00	6.00	—

KM# 40 5 CENTAVOS

2.00 g., Aluminum-Bronze, 17 mm. **Obv:** Value at center, grain spray on left, head of cow on right **Rev:** Grain sprig behind capped head, right **Note:** Prev. KM#15.

Date	Mintage	VF20	XF40	MS60	MS63	MS65
1942	2,130,000	0.50	1.50	5.00	—	—
1943	15,778,000	0.25	0.75	3.00	4.00	—
1944	21,081,000	0.25	0.75	3.00	4.00	—
1945	21,600,000	0.25	0.75	3.00	4.00	—
1946	20,460,000	0.25	0.75	3.00	4.00	—
1947	22,520,000	0.25	0.75	3.00	4.00	—
1948	42,790,000	0.25	0.50	2.00	3.00	—
1949	35,470,000	0.25	0.75	3.00	4.00	—
1950	13,500,000	0.25	0.75	3.00	4.00	—

KM# 43 5 CENTAVOS

2.00 g., Copper-Nickel, 17 mm. **Obv:** Value **Rev:** Jose de San Martin bust facing right **Edge:** Reeded **Note:** Prev. KM#18.

Date	Mintage	VF20	XF40	MS60	MS63	MS65
1950	3,460,000	0.40	0.60	2.00	3.00	—

KM# 46 5 CENTAVOS

2.00 g., Copper-Nickel, 17 mm. **Obv:** Value **Rev:** Jose de San Martin bust facing right **Edge:** Reeded **Note:** Prev. KM#21.

Date	Mintage	VF20	XF40	MS60	MS63	MS65
1951	34,994,000	0.20	0.30	0.50	0.75	—
1952	33,110,000	0.20	0.30	0.50	0.75	—
1953	20,129,000	0.20	0.30	0.50	0.75	—

KM# 46a 5 CENTAVOS

2.00 g., Copper-Nickel Clad Steel, 17 mm. **Obv:** Value **Rev:** Jose de San Martin bust facing right **Edge:** Plain **Note:** Prev. KM#21a.

Date	Mintage	VF20	XF40	MS60	MS63	MS65
1953	36,300,000	0.15	0.20	0.35	0.50	—

KM# 50 5 CENTAVOS

2.00 g., Copper-Nickel Clad Steel, 17 mm. **Obv:** Value **Rev:** Jose de San Martin bust facing right **Edge:** Plain **Note:** Bust slightly smaller than KM# 46a. Prev. KM#25.

Date	Mintage	VF20	XF40	MS60	MS63	MS65
1954	50,640,000	0.15	0.20	0.35	0.50	—
1955	42,200,000	0.15	0.20	0.35	0.50	—
1956	36,870,000	0.15	0.20	0.35	0.50	—

KM# 53 5 CENTAVOS

2.00 g., Copper-Nickel Clad Steel, 17 mm. **Obv:** Capped liberty head left **Rev:** Value within wreath **Edge:** Plain **Note:** Prev. KM#28.

Date	Mintage	VF20	XF40	MS60	MS63	MS65
1957	26,930,000	—	0.15	0.20	0.35	0.50
1958	13,108,000	—	0.15	0.20	0.35	0.50
1959	14,971,000	—	0.15	0.20	0.35	0.50

KM# 35 10 CENTAVOS

3.00 g., Copper-Nickel, 19.3 mm. **Obv:** Capped liberty head left **Rev:** Denomination within wreath **Edge:** Reeded **Note:** Prev. KM#10.

Date	Mintage	F12	VF20	XF40	MS60	MS63
1905	3,785,000	8.00	20.00	50.00	120	—
1906	3,854,000	6.00	15.00	40.00	120	—
1907	2,355,000	20.00	50.00	100	250	—
1908	2,280,000	10.00	25.00	60.00	150	—
1909	3,738,000	3.00	6.00	25.00	80.00	—
1910	3,026,000	5.00	10.00	40.00	100	—
1911	2,142,000	10.00	25.00	60.00	150	—
1912	2,993,000	5.00	10.00	30.00	100	—
1913 round top 3	1,828,000	10.00	25.00	60.00	150	—
1914	751,000	20.00	40.00	80.00	200	—
1915	2,607,000	2.00	5.00	20.00	50.00	—
1916	835,000	25.00	60.00	120	250	—
1918	3,897,000	1.00	3.00	15.00	40.00	—
1919	2,517,000	1.00	3.00	20.00	50.00	—
1920	7,509,000	1.00	2.00	6.00	25.00	—
1921	11,564,000	1.00	2.00	6.00	25.00	—
1922	6,542,000	1.00	2.00	6.00	25.00	—
1923	5,301,000	1.00	2.00	6.00	25.00	—
1924	3,489,000	1.00	2.00	6.00	25.00	—
1925	5,415,000	1.00	2.00	6.00	25.00	—
1926	5,055,000	1.00	2.00	6.00	25.00	—
1927	5,205,000	1.00	2.00	6.00	25.00	—
1928	8,255,000	1.00	2.00	5.00	20.00	—
1929	2,501,000	1.00	2.00	6.00	25.00	—
1930 round top 3	14,586,000	1.00	2.00	5.00	20.00	—
1931 flat top 3	893,000	3.00	6.00	20.00	80.00	—
1933	5,394,000	1.00	2.00	5.00	20.00	—
1934	3,319,000	1.00	2.00	5.00	20.00	—
1935	1,018,000	1.00	3.00	15.00	60.00	—
1936	3,000,000	1.00	2.00	4.00	15.00	—
1937	11,766,000	0.50	1.00	2.00	5.00	—
1938	10,494,000	0.50	1.00	2.00	5.00	—
1939	5,585,000	0.50	1.00	2.00	5.00	—
1940	3,955,000	0.50	1.00	2.00	5.00	—
1941	4,101,000	0.50	1.00	2.00	5.00	—
1942	2,962,000	0.50	1.00	2.00	5.00	—

KM# 41 10 CENTAVOS

3.00 g., Aluminum-Bronze, 19 mm. **Obv:** Value center, grain sprig on left, head of cow on right **Rev:** Grain sprig behind capped head facing right **Note:** Prev. KM#16.

Date	Mintage	VF20	XF40	MS60	MS63	MS65
1942	15,541,000	0.25	1.00	4.00	—	—
1943	13,916,000	0.35	1.25	6.00	—	—
1944	16,411,000	0.25	1.00	4.00	—	—
1945	12,500,000	0.50	2.00	7.00	—	—
1946	15,790,000	0.25	1.00	4.00	—	—
1947	36,430,000	0.25	1.00	2.50	3.50	—
1948	54,685,000	0.25	1.00	2.50	3.50	—
1949	57,740,000	0.25	1.00	2.50	3.50	—
1950	42,825,000	0.25	1.00	2.50	3.50	—

KM# 44 10 CENTAVOS

3.00 g., Copper-Nickel, 19 mm. **Subject:** San Martin, 100th Anniversary of Death **Obv:** Value **Rev:** Jose de San Martin bust facing right **Edge:** Reeded **Note:** Prev. KM#19.

Date	Mintage	VF20	XF40	MS60	MS63	MS65
1950	17,505,000	0.40	0.60	1.75	2.50	—

KM# 47 10 CENTAVOS

3.00 g., Copper-Nickel, 19 mm. **Obv:** Value **Rev:** Jose de San Martín bust right **Edge:** Reeded **Note:** Prev. KM#22.

Date	Mintage	VF20	XF40	MS60	MS63	MS65
1951	98,521,000	0.20	0.30	0.50	0.75	—
1952	67,328,000	0.20	0.30	0.50	0.75	—

KM# 47a 10 CENTAVOS

3.00 g., Nickel Clad Steel, 19 mm. **Obv:** Value **Rev:** Jose de San Martin bust right **Edge:** Plain **Note:** Prev. KM#22a.

Date	Mintage	VF20	XF40	MS60	MS63	MS65
1952	33,240,000	0.10	0.15	0.25	0.50	—
1953	106,685,000	0.10	0.15	0.25	0.50	—

KM# 51 10 CENTAVOS

3.00 g., Nickel Clad Steel, 19 mm. **Obv:** Value **Rev:** Jose de San Martin facing right **Edge:** Plain **Note:** Bust slightly smaller than KM# 47a. Prev. KM#26.

Date	Mintage	VF20	XF40	MS60	MS63	MS65
1954	117,200,000	0.10	0.15	0.25	0.50	—
1955	97,045,000	0.10	0.15	0.25	0.50	—
1956	122,630,000	0.10	0.15	0.25	0.50	—

KM# 54 10 CENTAVOS

3.00 g., Nickel Clad Steel, 19 mm. **Obv:** Capped liberty head facing left **Rev:** Value within wreath **Edge:** Plain **Note:** Prev. KM#29.

Date	Mintage	VF20	XF40	MS60	MS63	MS65
1957	52,810,000	—	0.10	0.15	0.25	0.50
1958	41,916,000	—	0.10	0.15	0.25	0.50
1959	29,183,000	—	0.10	0.15	0.25	0.50

KM# 36 20 CENTAVOS

4.00 g., Copper-Nickel, 21.5 mm. **Obv:** Capped liberty head left **Rev:** Denomination within wreath **Edge:** Reeded **Note:** Prev. KM#11.

Date	Mintage	F12	VF20	XF40	MS60	MS63
1905	4,455,000	5.00	15.00	50.00	150	—
1906	4,331,000	5.00	15.00	50.00	150	—
1907	3,730,000	10.00	30.00	80.00	200	—
1908	719,000	10.00	40.00	150	500	—
1909	1,329,000	5.00	15.00	50.00	150	—
1910	1,845,000	5.00	15.00	40.00	150	—
1911	1,110,000	10.00	30.00	80.00	200	—
1912	2,402,000	6.00	12.00	40.00	100	—
1913	1,579,000	5.00	15.00	60.00	150	—
1914	527,000	10.00	40.00	150	400	—
1915	1,921,000	3.00	8.00	20.00	50.00	—
1916	985,000	4.00	10.00	25.00	60.00	—
1918	1,638,000	2.00	5.00	20.00	50.00	—
1919	2,280,000	1.00	3.00	15.00	40.00	—
1920	7,572,000	1.00	2.00	6.00	25.00	—
1921	5,286,000	1.00	2.00	6.00	25.00	—
1922	2,324,000	1.00	2.00	6.00	25.00	—
1923	4,416,000	1.00	2.00	6.00	25.00	—
1924	3,676,000	1.00	2.00	6.00	25.00	—
1925	3,799,000	1.00	2.00	6.00	25.00	—
1926	3,250,000	1.00	2.00	6.00	25.00	—
1927	2,880,000	1.00	2.00	6.00	25.00	—
1928	2,886,000	1.00	2.00	6.00	25.00	—
1929	8,361,000	1.00	2.00	6.00	25.00	—
1930	8,281,000	1.00	2.00	6.00	25.00	—
1931	315,000	5.00	12.00	70.00	200	—
1935	1,127,000	1.00	2.00	5.00	20.00	—
1936	855,000	2.00	5.00	20.00	50.00	—
1937	3,314,000	0.50	1.00	2.00	5.00	—
1938	6,449,000	0.50	1.00	2.00	5.00	—
1939	3,555,000	0.50	1.00	2.00	5.00	—
1940	4,465,000	0.50	1.00	2.00	5.00	—
1941	600,000	1.00	2.00	5.00	10.00	—
1942	4,844,000	0.50	1.00	2.00	5.00	—

KM# 42 20 CENTAVOS

4.20 g., Aluminum-Bronze, 21.2 mm. **Obv:** Value at center, grain sprig to left, head of cow to right **Rev:** Grain sprig behind capped head right **Note:** Prev. KM#17.

Date	Mintage	VF20	XF40	MS60	MS63	MS65
1942	10,255,000	0.50	2.00	10.00	—	—
1943	13,775,000	0.35	1.50	7.00	—	—
1944	12,225,000	0.35	1.75	8.00	—	—

Date	Mintage	VF20	XF40	MS60	MS63	MS65
1945	13,340,000	0.35	1.50	7.00	—	—
1946	14,625,000	0.35	1.50	7.00	—	—
1947	23,165,000	0.25	1.25	6.00	7.50	—
1948	32,245,000	0.25	1.25	6.00	7.50	—
1949	67,115,000	0.25	1.25	6.00	7.50	—
1950	40,071,000	0.25	1.25	6.00	7.50	—

KM# 45 20 CENTAVOS

4.02 g., Copper-Nickel, 21.4 mm. **Obv:** Value **Rev:** Jose de San Martín portrait right **Edge:** Reeded **Note:** Prev. KM#20.

Date	Mintage	VF20	XF40	MS60	MS63	MS65
1950	86,770,000	0.15	0.25	0.60	1.50	2.00

KM# 48 20 CENTAVOS

3.90 g., Copper-Nickel, 21.3 mm. **Obv:** Value **Rev:** Jose de San Martín bust right **Edge:** Reeded **Note:** Prev. KM#23.

Date	Mintage	VF20	XF40	MS60	MS63	MS65
1951	85,782,000	0.10	0.20	0.30	0.50	0.75
1952	69,796,000	0.10	0.20	0.30	0.50	0.75

KM# 48a 20 CENTAVOS

4.00 g., Nickel Clad Steel, 21 mm. **Obv:** Value **Rev:** Jose de San Martín portrait right **Edge:** Plain **Note:** Prev. KM#23a.

Date	Mintage	VF20	XF40	MS60	MS63	MS65
1952	12,863,000	—	0.15	0.25	0.50	0.75
1953	36,893,000	—	0.15	0.40	1.00	1.50

KM# 52 20 CENTAVOS

4.00 g., Nickel Clad Steel, 21 mm. **Obv:** Value **Rev:** Jose de San Martin bust facing right **Note:** Head size reduced slightly. Prev. KM#27.

Date	Mintage	VF20	XF40	MS60	MS63	MS65
1954	52,563,000	—	0.15	0.20	0.25	0.50
1955	46,952,000	—	0.15	0.20	0.25	0.50
1956	35,995,000	—	0.15	0.20	0.25	0.50

KM# 55 20 CENTAVOS

4.00 g., Nickel Clad Steel, 19.59 mm. **Obv:** Capped liberty head left **Rev:** Value within wreath **Edge:** Plain **Note:** Prev. KM#30.

Date	Mintage	VF20	XF40	MS60	MS63	MS65
1957	89,365,000	—	0.15	0.20	0.25	0.50
1958	52,710,000	—	0.15	0.20	0.25	0.50
1959	56,585,000	—	0.15	0.20	0.25	0.50
1960	21,254,000	—	0.15	0.20	0.25	0.50
1961	2,083,000	—	0.25	0.50	1.50	2.00

KM# 39 50 CENTAVOS

6.00 g., Nickel, 24.5 mm. **Obv:** Capped liberty head, left **Rev:** Value within wreath **Edge:** Reeded **Note:** Prev. KM#14.

Date	Mintage	VF20	XF40	MS60	MS63	MS65
1941	1,000,000	0.40	1.00	2.00	3.50	6.00

KM# 49 50 CENTAVOS

5.12 g., Nickel Clad Steel, 21.3 mm. **Obv:** Value **Rev:** Jose de San Martín bust right **Edge:** Plain **Note:** Prev. KM#24.

Date	Mintage	VF20	XF40	MS60	MS63	MS65
1952	29,736,000	0.10	0.20	0.35	1.25	2.00
1953	62,814,000	0.10	0.20	0.35	1.25	2.00
1954	132,224,000	0.10	0.20	0.35	1.00	1.50
1955	75,490,000	0.10	0.20	0.35	1.25	2.00
1956	19,120,000	0.10	0.20	0.50	2.00	3.00

KM# 56 50 CENTAVOS

5.10 g., Nickel Clad Steel, 23.3 mm. **Obv:** Capped liberty head left **Rev:** Value within wreath **Edge:** Plain **Note:** Prev. KM#31.

Date	Mintage	VF20	XF40	MS60	MS63	MS65
1957	18,139,000	0.10	0.20	0.45	1.25	2.00
1958	51,750,000	0.10	0.20	0.35	1.00	1.50
1959	13,997,000	0.10	0.20	0.45	1.25	2.00
1960	26,038,000	0.10	0.20	0.35	1.00	1.50
1961	11,106,000	0.10	0.20	0.45	1.25	2.00

KM# 57 PESO

6.41 g., Nickel Clad Steel, 25.5 mm. **Obv:** Capped liberty head left **Rev:** Value within wreath **Note:** Prev. KM#32.

Date	Mintage	VF20	XF40	MS60	MS63	MS65
1957	118,118,000	0.10	0.20	0.40	2.00	3.00
1958	118,151,000	0.10	0.20	0.40	2.00	3.00
1959	237,733,000	0.10	0.20	0.30	1.50	2.50
1960	75,048,000	0.10	0.30	0.50	2.50	3.50
1961	76,897,000	0.10	0.30	0.50	2.50	3.50
1962	30,006,000	0.10	0.30	0.50	3.00	4.00

KM# 58 PESO

6.60 g., Nickel Clad Steel, 25.9 mm. **Subject:** 150th Anniversary - Removal of Spanish Viceroy **Obv:** Argentine arms, value at bottom **Rev:** Building, two dates below **Edge:** Reeded **Note:** Prev. KM#33.

Date	Mintage	VF20	XF40	MS60	MS63	MS65
ND-1960	98,751,000	0.20	0.50	0.75	1.00	1.50

KM# 59 5 PESOS

4.00 g., Nickel Clad Steel, 21.5 mm. **Obv:** Sailing ship-Fragata Sarmiento **Rev:** Value above date flanked by sprays **Edge:** Plain **Note:** Prev. KM#34.

Date	Mintage	VF20	XF40	MS60	MS63	MS65
1961	37,423,000	0.15	0.25	0.50	1.00	3.50
1962	42,362,000	0.15	0.25	0.50	1.00	3.50
1963	71,769,000	0.15	0.25	0.40	1.00	2.50
1964	12,302,000	0.20	0.35	0.60	1.00	4.00
1965	19,450,000	0.15	0.25	0.50	1.00	3.50
1966	17,259,000	0.15	0.25	0.50	1.00	3.50
1967	17,806,000	0.15	0.25	0.50	1.00	3.50
1968	12,634,000	0.20	0.35	0.60	1.00	4.00

KM# 60 10 PESOS

5.00 g., Nickel Clad Steel, 23.6 mm. **Obv:** Gaucho **Rev:** Laurel at left, value at right **Edge:** Plain **Note:** Prev. KM#35.

Date	Mintage	VF20	XF40	MS60	MS63	MS65
1962	57,401,000	0.15	0.25	0.50	1.00	3.50
1963	136,792,000	0.15	0.20	0.35	1.00	2.50
1964	46,576,000	0.15	0.25	0.50	1.00	3.50
1965	40,640,000	0.15	0.25	0.50	1.00	3.50
1966	50,733,000	0.15	0.20	0.40	1.00	3.00
1967	43,050,000	0.15	0.25	0.50	1.00	3.50
1968	36,588,000	0.15	0.25	0.50	1.00	3.50

KM# 62 10 PESOS

5.00 g., Nickel Clad Steel, 23.2 mm. **Subject:** 150th Anniversary - Declaration of Independence. **Rev:** Building facing right, two dates below **Note:** Prev. KM#37.

Date	Mintage	VF20	XF40	MS60	MS63	MS65
ND-1966	29,336,000	0.15	0.25	0.50	1.00	1.50

KM# 61 25 PESOS

6.45 g., Nickel Clad Steel, 26 mm. **Subject:** 1st issue of National Coinage in 1813. **Obv:** Radiant sunface within circle **Rev:** Argentine arms within circle **Edge:** Plain **Note:** Prev. KM#36.

Date	Mintage	VF20	XF40	MS60	MS63	MS65
1964	20,485,000	0.15	0.25	0.50	1.00	1.50
1965	14,884,000	0.15	0.25	0.50	1.00	1.50
1966	16,426,000	0.15	0.25	0.50	1.00	1.50
1967	15,734,000	0.15	0.25	0.50	1.00	1.50
1968	4,446,000	0.15	0.25	0.75	1.50	2.50

KM# 63 25 PESOS

6.46 g., Nickel Clad Steel, 26 mm. **Subject:** 80th Anniversary - Death of D. Faustino Sarmiento **Rev:** Head of Domingo Faustino Samiento, left, date below **Note:** Prev. KM#38.

Date	Mintage	VF20	XF40	MS60	MS63	MS65
1968	15,804,000	0.25	0.60	0.85	1.65	2.00

REFORM COINAGE

1970-1983

100 Old Pesos = 1 New Peso

KM# 64 CENTAVO

0.62 g., Aluminum, 15.74 mm. **Obv:** Capped Liberty head, left **Rev:** Value to left of grain sprig, date below **Edge:** Plain **Note:** Prev. KM#39.

Date	Mintage	VF20	XF40	MS60	MS63	MS65
1970	54,568,115	—	—	0.10	0.30	0.50
1971	44,644,000	—	—	0.10	0.30	0.50
1972	92,430,000	—	—	0.10	0.30	0.50
1973	29,515,000	—	—	0.10	0.30	0.50
1974	5,162,000	—	—	0.15	0.35	0.60
1975	3,840,000	—	0.10	0.20	0.50	0.75

KM# 65 5 CENTAVOS

0.98 g., Aluminum, 16.63 mm. **Obv:** Capped liberty head left **Rev:** Value with grain sprig to left **Edge:** Plain **Note:** Prev. KM#40.

Date	Mintage	VF20	XF40	MS60	MS63	MS65
1970	56,174,000	—	0.10	0.15	0.40	0.60
1971	3,798,000	0.10	0.20	0.35	0.65	0.90
1972	84,250,000	—	0.10	0.15	0.40	0.60
1973	113,912,000	—	0.10	0.15	0.40	0.60
1974	18,150,000	—	0.10	0.15	0.40	0.60
1975	6,940,000	0.10	0.20	0.35	0.65	0.90

KM# 66 10 CENTAVOS

2.00 g., Aluminum-Bronze **Obv:** Capped liberty head left **Rev:** Value with grain sprig to left **Note:** Prev. KM#41.

Date	Mintage	VF20	XF40	MS60	MS63	MS65
1970	64,585,300	—	0.10	0.15	0.35	0.55
1971	135,623,000	—	0.10	0.15	0.35	0.55
1973	19,930,000	—	0.10	0.15	0.35	0.55
1974	79,156,000	—	0.10	0.15	0.35	0.55
1975	31,270,000	—	0.10	0.15	0.35	0.55
1976	730,000	0.10	0.20	0.35	1.00	1.75

KM# 67 20 CENTAVOS

3.07 g., Aluminum-Bronze, 18.75 mm. **Obv:** Capped liberty head left **Rev:** Value with grain sprig to left **Edge:** Reeded **Note:** Prev. KM#42.

Date	Mintage	VF20	XF40	MS60	MS63	MS65
1970	27,029,000	—	0.10	0.15	0.35	0.55
1971	33,211,000	—	0.10	0.15	0.35	0.55
1972	220,000	1.00	2.00	4.00	8.00	10.00
1973	9,676,000	—	0.10	0.15	0.35	0.55
1974	41,024,000	—	0.10	0.15	0.35	0.55
1975	26,540,000	—	0.10	0.15	0.35	0.55
1976	960,000	—	0.10	0.15	0.35	0.55

KM# 68 50 CENTAVOS

4.35 g., Aluminum-Bronze, 21 mm. **Obv:** Capped liberty head left **Rev:** Value with grain sprig to left **Edge:** Reeded **Note:** Prev. KM#43.

Date	Mintage	VF20	XF40	MS60	MS63	MS65
1970	56,103,729	0.10	0.15	0.30	0.60	0.80
1971	34,947,000	0.10	0.15	0.30	0.60	0.80
1972	40,960,000	0.10	0.15	0.30	0.60	0.80
1973	59,472,124	0.10	0.15	0.30	0.60	0.80
1974	64,063,000	0.10	0.15	0.30	0.60	0.80
1975	64,859,000	0.10	0.15	0.30	0.60	0.80
1976	9,768,000	0.10	0.15	0.30	0.60	0.80

KM# 69 PESO

5.00 g., Aluminum-Bronze, 22 mm. **Obv:** Radiant sunface, grain sprays below **Rev:** Value with grain sprig to left **Edge:** Reeded **Note:** Wide rim variety on 1974-75 issues; narrow rim variety on 1975-76 issues. Prev. KM#44.

Date	Mintage	VF20	XF40	MS60	MS63	MS65
1974	77,292,000	—	0.10	0.25	0.75	1.00
1975 wide rim	423,000,000	—	0.10	0.20	0.50	0.75
1975 narrow rim	Inc. above	—	0.10	0.20	0.50	0.75
1976	100,075,000	—	0.10	0.20	0.50	0.75

KM# 71 5 PESOS

Aluminum-Bronze **Obv:** Radiant sunface, grain sprays below **Rev:** Value with grain sprig to left **Note:** Prev. KM#46.

Date	Mintage	VF20	XF40	MS60	MS63	MS65
1976	118,353,000	—	0.10	0.20	0.65	1.00
1977	66,765,684	—	0.10	0.20	0.65	1.00

KM# 73 5 PESOS

Aluminum-Bronze **Subject:** Admiral G. Brown Bicentennial **Obv:** Armored bust right divides dates **Rev:** Value with grain sprigs to left, date below **Note:** Prev. KM#48.

Date	Mintage	VF20	XF40	MS60	MS63	MS65
1977	11,297,808	0.10	0.15	0.30	0.75	1.00

KM# 72 10 PESOS

6.40 g., Aluminum-Bronze, 25.2 mm. **Obv:** Radiant sunface, grain sprays below **Rev:** Value with grain sprig to left **Edge:** Reeded **Note:** Prev. KM#47.

Date	Mintage	VF20	XF40	MS60	MS63	MS65
1976	130,216,724	0.10	0.15	0.35	1.00	1.50
1977	191,520,382	0.10	0.15	0.35	1.00	1.50
1978	259,424,310	0.10	0.15	0.35	1.00	1.50

KM# 74 10 PESOS

6.50 g., Aluminum-Bronze, 25.2 mm. **Subject:** Admiral G. Brown Bicentennial **Obv:** Armored bust right divides dates **Rev:** Value with grain sprigs to left, date below **Note:** Prev. KM#49.

Date	Mintage	VF20	XF40	MS60	MS63	MS65
1977	60,008,179	0.10	0.20	0.50	1.25	1.50

KM# 75 20 PESOS

Aluminum-Bronze **Subject:** 1978 World Soccer Championship **Obv:** Two soccer players, country above with two numbered year below country to right **Rev:** Soccer ball within symbol, top right, small mark to left, value below, date at bottom **Note:** Prev. KM#50.

Date	Mintage	VF20	XF40	MS60	MS63	MS65
1977	1,506,000	0.10	0.20	0.40	1.00	1.25
1978	2,000,000	0.10	0.20	0.40	1.00	1.25

KM# 76 50 PESOS

5.82 g., Aluminum-Bronze, 24.13 mm. **Subject:** 1978 World Soccer Championship **Obv:** Soccer player on lined globe, country name above with two numbered year below at right **Rev:** Soccer ball within symbol, top right, value below, date at bottom, small mark to left of symbol **Note:** Prev. KM#51.

Date	Mintage	VF20	XF40	MS60	MS63	MS65
1977	1,506,000	0.10	0.20	0.40	1.00	1.25
1978	2,000,000	0.10	0.20	0.40	1.00	1.25

KM# 81 50 PESOS

Aluminum-Bronze **Subject:** 200th Anniversary - Birth of Jose de San Martín **Obv:** Value, date below flanked by stars **Rev:** Armored bust of Jose de San Martin left, two dates at right **Note:** Prev. KM#56.

Date	Mintage	VF20	XF40	MS60	MS63	MS65
1978	40,601,000	0.20	0.50	1.00	2.00	2.50

KM# 83 50 PESOS

Aluminum-Bronze **Obv:** Value, date below **Rev:** Bust of Jose de San Martin left **Note:** Prev. KM#58.

Date	Mintage	VF20	XF40	MS60	MS63	MS65
1979	21,728,900	0.10	0.25	0.65	1.50	2.00
1980	—	0.10	0.25	0.65	1.50	2.00

Note: Mintage included with 1980 date of KM#83a

KM# 83a 50 PESOS

7.30 g., Brass Clad Steel, 26.3 mm. **Obv:** Value, date below **Rev:** Jose de San Martín portrait right **Edge:** Reeded **Note:** Prev. KM#58a.

Date	Mintage	VF20	XF40	MS60	MS63	MS65
1980	94,730,000	0.10	0.25	0.65	1.25	1.50
1981	26,507,500	0.10	0.25	0.65	1.25	1.50

KM# 84 50 PESOS

Aluminum-Bronze **Subject:** Conquest of Patagonia Centennial **Obv:** Value, date below **Rev:** Man on horse, lance in right hand, facing left **Note:** Prev. KM#59.

Date	Mintage	VF20	XF40	MS60	MS63	MS65
1979	34,761,829	0.10	0.25	0.65	1.00	1.50

KM# 77 100 PESOS

6.42 g., Aluminum-Bronze, 25.6 mm. **Subject:** 1978 World Soccer Championship **Obv:** Stadium on lined globe, country name above with two numbered year below at right **Rev:** Soccer ball within symbol, top right, value below, date at bottom, small mark at left of symbol **Note:** Prev. KM#52.

Date	Mintage	VF20	XF40	MS60	MS63	MS65
1977	1,506,000	0.15	0.30	0.75	1.50	2.00
1978	2,000,000	0.15	0.30	0.75	1.50	2.00

KM# 82 100 PESOS
7.90 g., Aluminum-Bronze, 27.3 mm. **Subject:** 200th Anniversary - Birth of Jose de San Martín **Obv:** Value at center, small mark at top, date at bottom **Rev:** Armored bust of Jose de San Martin, left **Note:** Prev. KM#57.

Date	Mintage	VF20	XF40	MS60	MS63	MS65
1978	113,826,000	—	0.25	0.50	1.00	1.50
1979	—	—	—	—	—	800

KM# 85 100 PESOS
7.90 g., Aluminum-Bronze, 27.3 mm. **Obv:** Value at center, small mark at top, date at bottom **Rev:** Jose de San Martín portrait left **Note:** Prev. KM#60.

Date	Mintage	VF20	XF40	MS60	MS63	MS65
1978	—	—	—	—	—	300
1979	43,389,383	0.15	0.30	0.75	1.25	1.50
1980	154,260,000	0.15	0.30	0.75	1.25	1.50

KM# 85a 100 PESOS
7.91 g., Brass Clad Steel **Obv:** Value at center, small mark at top, date at bottom **Rev:** Jose de San Martín portrait left **Note:** Prev. KM#60a.

Date	Mintage	VF20	XF40	MS60	MS63	MS65
1980	Inc. above	0.15	0.30	0.75	1.50	1.75
1981	99,512,000	0.15	0.30	0.75	1.25	1.50

KM# 86 100 PESOS
Aluminum-Bronze **Subject:** Conquest of Patagonia Centennial **Obv:** Value center, small mark at top, date below **Rev:** Man on horse holding lance in right, facing left **Note:** Prev. KM#61.

Date	Mintage	VF20	XF40	MS60	MS63	MS65
1979	34,132,135	0.15	0.30	0.75	1.00	1.50

KM# 78 1000 PESOS
10.00 g., 0.900 Silver 0.2894 oz. ASW **Subject:** 1978 World Soccer Championship **Obv:** Country name at top with two numbered year, below right, small radiant sunface to left of five line inscription **Note:** Prev. KM#53.

Date	Mintage	VF20	XF40	MS60	MS63	MS65
1977	98,837	—	—	7.75	10.00	12.50
1977	1,000	PF65 18.50				
1978	1,750	PF65 18.50				
1978	187,383	—	—	7.75	10.00	12.50

KM# 79 2000 PESOS
15.00 g., 0.900 Silver 0.434 oz. ASW **Subject:** 1978 World Soccer Championship **Obv:** Argentine arms beneath five sets of small arms, country name, year at bottom **Rev:** Soccer ball within symbol, top right, value below, date at bottom **Note:** Prev. KM#54.

Date	Mintage	VF20	XF40	MS60	MS63	MS65
1977	98,837	—	—	10.50	13.00	15.50
1977	1,000	PF65 25.00				
1978	187,383	—	—	10.50	13.00	15.50
1978	1,750	PF65 25.00				

KM# 80 3000 PESOS
25.00 g., 0.900 Silver 0.7234 oz. ASW **Subject:** 1978 World Soccer Championship **Obv:** Map of country on lined globe, grain sprigs below, country at top **Rev:** Soccer ball within symbol, top right, value below, date at bottom **Note:** Prev. KM#55.

Date	Mintage	VF20	XF40	MS60	MS63	MS65
1977	1,000	PF65 35.00				
1977	98,837	—	—	16.50	19.00	22.00
1978	1,750	PF65 35.00				
1978	187,383	—	—	16.50	19.00	22.00

REFORM COINAGE

1983-1985

10,000 Pesos = 1 Peso Argentino

100 Centavos = 1 Peso Argentino

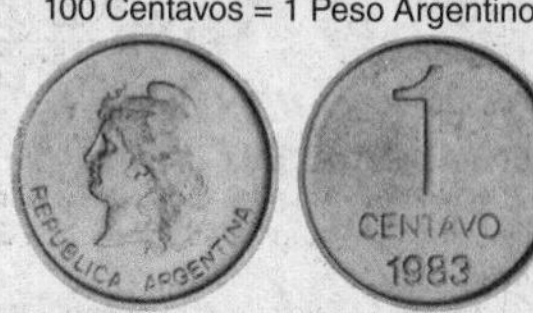

KM# 87 CENTAVO
Aluminum **Obv:** Capped liberty head, left **Rev:** Value, date below **Note:** Prev. KM#62.

Date	Mintage	VF20	XF40	MS60	MS63	MS65
1983	19,959,000	—	—	—	0.20	0.35

KM# 88 5 CENTAVOS
1.24 g., Aluminum **Obv:** Capped liberty head left **Rev:** Value, date below **Note:** Prev. KM#63.

Date	Mintage	VF20	XF40	MS60	MS63	MS65
1983	59,870,000	—	—	—	0.25	0.40

KM# 89 10 CENTAVOS
1.55 g., Aluminum, 20.08 mm. **Obv:** Capped liberty head, left **Rev:** Value, date below **Edge:** Plain **Note:** Prev. KM#64. Struck at the British Royal Mint.

Date	Mintage	VF20	XF40	MS60	MS63	MS65
1983	307,513,000	—	—	—	0.25	0.40

KM# 90 50 CENTAVOS
Aluminum **Obv:** Capped liberty head, left **Rev:** Value, date below **Note:** Prev. KM#65.

Date	Mintage	VF20	XF40	MS60	MS63	MS65
1983	243,909,000	—	—	—	0.45	0.60

KM# 91 PESO
Aluminum **Obv:** Capitol building **Rev:** Value, date below **Note:** National Congress. Prev. KM#66.

Date	Mintage	VF20	XF40	MS60	MS63	MS65
1984	184,691,379	—	—	—	0.50	0.65

KM# 92 5 PESOS
Brass **Obv:** Buenos Aires City Hall **Rev:** Value, date at bottom **Note:** Prev. KM#67.

Date	Mintage	VF20	XF40	MS60	MS63	MS65
1984	11,206,000	—	—	—	0.65	0.80
1985	14,168,000	—	—	—	0.65	0.80

KM# 93 10 PESOS
4.00 g., Brass **Obv:** Independence Hall at Tucuman **Rev:** Value, date at bottom **Note:** Prev. KM#68.

Date	Mintage	VF20	XF40	MS60	MS63	MS65
1984	16,528,000	—	—	—	0.85	1.00
1985	9,898,717	—	—	—	0.85	1.00

KM# 94 50 PESOS
4.83 g., Aluminum-Bronze **Subject:** 50th Anniversary of Central Bank **Obv:** Value, date at bottom **Rev:** Small capped liberty head within wreath, circle surrounding **Note:** Prev. KM#69.

Date	Mintage	VF20	XF40	MS60	MS63	MS65
1985	3,300,000	—	—	—	1.25	1.50

REFORM COINAGE

1985-1992

1,000 Pesos Argentinos = 1 Austral

100 Centavos = 1 Austral

KM# 95 1/2 CENTAVO
Brass **Obv:** Rufous Hornero Bird **Rev:** Value, date below **Note:** Prev. KM#70.

Date	Mintage	VF20	XF40	MS60	MS63	MS65
1985	7,490,000	—	—	—	0.75	1.50

KM# 96.1 CENTAVO
Brass, 20 mm, **Obv:** Common Rhea **Rev:** Value, date below **Note:** Thick flan. Prev. KM#71.1.

Date	Mintage	VF20	XF40	MS60	MS63	MS65
1985	76,082,000	—	—	—	1.00	2.00

KM# 96.2 CENTAVO
3.20 g., Brass, 20.6 mm. **Obv:** Common Rhea **Rev:** Value, date below **Edge:** Plain **Note:** Thin flan. Prev. KM#71.2.

Date	Mintage	VF20	XF40	MS60	MS63	MS65
1986	118,934,000	—	—	—	1.00	2.00
1987	87,315,000	—	—	—	1.00	2.00

KM# 97.1 5 CENTAVOS

Brass, 23 mm. **Obv:** Pampas Cat **Rev:** Value, date below **Edge:** Plain **Note:** Thick flan. Prev. KM#72.1.

Date	Mintage	VF20	XF40	MS60	MS63	MS65
1985	36,924,000	—	—	—	1.00	1.50

KM# 97.2 5 CENTAVOS

4.10 g., Brass, 23 mm. **Obv:** Pampas Cat **Rev:** Value, date below **Edge:** Plain **Note:** Thin flan. Prev. KM#72.2.

Date	Mintage	VF20	XF40	MS60	MS63	MS65
1986	66,414,000	—	—	—	1.00	1.50
1987	56,181,000	—	—	—	1.00	1.50
1988	23,895,000	—	—	—	1.00	1.50

KM# 98 10 CENTAVOS

4.45 g., Brass, 21.5 mm. **Obv:** Argentine arms **Rev:** Value, date below **Note:** Prev. KM#73.

Date	Mintage	VF20	XF40	MS60	MS63	MS65
1985	23,268,000	—	—	—	0.65	0.85
1986	158,427,000	—	—	—	0.65	0.85
1987	184,330,000	—	—	—	0.65	0.85
1988	174,003,000	—	—	—	0.65	0.85

KM# 99 50 CENTAVOS

5.40 g., Brass, 24.5 mm. **Obv:** Capped liberty head left **Rev:** Value, date below **Note:** Varieties exist. Previous KM#74.

Date	Mintage	VF20	XF40	MS60	MS63	MS65
1985	13,884,000	—	—	—	1.50	2.00
1986	59,074,000	—	—	—	1.45	1.85
1987	64,525,000	—	—	—	1.45	1.85
1988	62,388,000	—	—	—	1.45	1.85

KM# 100 AUSTRAL

1.55 g., Aluminum, 20.11 mm. **Obv:** Buenos Aires City Hall **Rev:** Large value in box at right, double lined "A" at top left, date below "A" **Edge:** Plain **Note:** Prev. KM#75.

Date	Mintage	VF20	XF40	MS60	MS63	MS65
1989	57,400,000	—	—	—	0.15	0.30

KM# 101 5 AUSTRALES

Aluminum, 21.6 mm. **Obv:** Independence Hall at Tucuman **Rev:** Large value in box at right, double lined "A" at left top, date below "A" **Edge:** Plain **Note:** Prev. KM#76.

Date	Mintage	VF20	XF40	MS60	MS63	MS65
1989	46,894,977	—	—	—	0.25	0.40

KM# 102 10 AUSTRALES

2.00 g., Aluminum, 23.2 mm. **Obv:** Casa del Acuerdo **Rev:** Large value in box at right, double lined "A" at top left, date below "A" **Edge:** Plain **Note:** Prev. KM#77.

Date	Mintage	VF20	XF40	MS60	MS63	MS65
1989	99,600,000	—	—	—	0.35	0.50

KM# 103 100 AUSTRALES

1.50 g., Aluminum, 19.52 mm. **Obv:** Argentine arms **Rev:** Large value in box, small double lined "A" at top, date below box **Edge:** Plain **Note:** Prev. KM#78.

Date	Mintage	VF20	XF40	MS60	MS63	MS65
1990	18,003,500	—	—	—	0.25	0.40
1991	31,996,500	—	—	—	0.25	0.40

KM# 104 500 AUSTRALES

Aluminum **Obv:** Argentine arms **Rev:** Large value in box, small double lined "A" at top, date below box **Note:** Prev. KM#79.

Date	Mintage	VF20	XF40	MS60	MS63	MS65
1990	29,312,000	—	—	—	0.35	0.50
1991	50,087,100	—	—	—	0.35	0.50

KM# 105 1000 AUSTRALES

Aluminum, 24.5 mm. **Obv:** Argentine arms **Rev:** Large value in box, small double lined "A" at top, date below box **Edge:** Plain **Note:** Prev. KM#80.

Date	Mintage	VF20	XF40	MS60	MS63	MS65
1990	8,282,000	—	—	—	0.60	0.75
1991	41,618,000	—	—	—	0.60	0.75

KM# 106 1000 AUSTRALES

27.00 g., 0.925 Silver 0.803 oz. ASW **Subject:** Ibero - American Series **Obv:** Argentine arms within legend and circle of arms **Rev:** Two globes, rising radiant sun above with four crowns above, flanked by columns within inner circle surrounded by legend **Note:** Prev. KM#81.

Date	Mintage	VF20	XF40	MS60	MS63	MS65
1991	—	PF63 45.00	PF65 60.00			

REFORM COINAGE

1992

100 Centavos = 1 Peso

KM# 108 CENTAVO

1.77 g., Aluminum-Bronze, 16.2 mm. **Obv:** Four line inscription within wreath **Rev:** Large value, date below **Edge:** Plain **Shape:** Octagonal **Note:** Prev. KM#83.

Date	Mintage	VF20	XF40	MS60	MS63	MS65
1992	30,000,000	—	—	—	0.25	0.40

KM# 113 CENTAVO

1.77 g., Aluminum-Bronze, 16.2 mm. **Obv:** Four line inscription within wreath **Rev:** Large value, date below **Edge:** Reeded **Shape:** Round **Note:** Prev. KM#88.

Date	Mintage	VF20	XF40	MS60	MS63	MS65
1992	30,000,000	—	—	—	0.25	0.40
1993	79,000,000	—	—	—	0.25	0.40

KM# 113a CENTAVO

2.00 g., Bronze, 16.2 mm. **Obv:** Four line inscription within wreath **Rev:** Large value, date below **Edge:** Reeded **Shape:** Round **Note:** Prev. KM#88a.

Date	Mintage	VF20	XF40	MS60	MS63	MS65
1993	48,000,000	—	—	—	0.25	0.40
1997	50,000,000	—	—	—	0.25	0.40
1998	50,000,000	—	—	—	0.25	0.40
1999	70,000,000	—	—	—	0.25	0.40
2000	37,000,000	—	—	—	0.25	0.40

KM# 109 5 CENTAVOS

2.02 g., Aluminum-Bronze, 17.2 mm. **Obv:** Radiant sunface **Rev:** Large value, date below **Edge:** Reeded **Note:** Prev. KM#84.

Date	Mintage	VF20	XF40	MS60	MS63	MS65
1992	230,000,000	—	—	—	0.45	0.60
1993	20,000,000	—	—	—	0.45	0.60

KM# 109a.1 5 CENTAVOS

2.25 g., Copper-Nickel, 17.2 mm. **Obv:** Radiant sunface, fine lettering **Rev:** Large value, date below **Edge:** Reeded **Note:** Prev. KM#84a.1.

Date	Mintage	VF20	XF40	MS60	MS63	MS65
1993	245,500,000	—	—	—	0.45	0.65
1994	—	—	—	—	0.45	0.65
1995	—	—	—	—	0.45	0.65

KM# 109a.2 5 CENTAVOS

2.25 g., Copper-Nickel, 17.2 mm. **Obv:** Radiant sunface. Bold lettering **Rev:** Large value, date below **Edge:** Reeded **Note:** Prev. KM#84a.2.

Date	Mintage	VF20	XF40	MS60	MS63	MS65
1993	—	—	—	—	0.45	0.65
1994	5,000,000	—	—	—	0.45	0.65
1995	25,000,000	—	—	—	0.45	0.60

KM# 107 10 CENTAVOS

2.25 g., Aluminum-Bronze, 18.2 mm. **Obv:** Argentine arms **Rev:** Value, date below **Edge:** Reeded **Note:** Prev. KM#82.

Date	Mintage	VF20	XF40	MS60	MS63	MS65
1992	805,000,000	—	—	—	0.65	0.85
1993	500,000,000	—	—	—	0.65	0.85
1994	80,000,000	—	—	—	0.65	0.85

KM# 110.1 25 CENTAVOS

5.40 g., Aluminum-Bronze, 24.2 mm. **Obv:** Buenos Aires City Hall, fine lettering **Rev:** Large value, date below **Edge:** Reeded **Note:** Prev. KM#85.1.

Date	Mintage	VF20	XF40	MS60	MS63	MS65
1992	150,000,000	—	—	—	0.50	1.00
1993	—	—	—	—	0.50	1.00

KM# 110.2 25 CENTAVOS

5.40 g., Aluminum-Bronze, 24.2 mm. **Obv:** Buenos Aires City Hall, bold lettering **Rev:** Large value, date below **Edge:** Reeded **Note:** Prev. KM#85.2.

Date	Mintage	VF20	XF40	MS60	MS63	MS65
1993	80,000,000	—	—	—	0.50	1.00

KM# 110a 25 CENTAVOS
6.10 g., Copper-Nickel, 24.2 mm. **Obv:** Buenos Aires City Hall, bold lettering **Rev:** Large value, date below **Edge:** Reeded **Note:** Prev. KM#85a.

Date	Mintage	VF20	XF40	MS60	MS63	MS65
1993	390,000,000	—	—	—	0.50	1.00
1994	200,000,000	—	—	—	0.50	1.00
1996	96,000,000	—	—	—	0.50	1.00

KM# 111.1 50 CENTAVOS
5.80 g., Aluminum-Bronze, 25.2 mm. **Obv:** Tucuman's house where the independence was signed; fine lettering **Rev:** Large value, date below **Edge:** Reeded **Note:** Prev. KM#86.1.

Date	Mintage	VF20	XF40	MS60	MS63	MS65
1992	290,000,000	—	—	—	1.00	1.50
1993	—	—	—	—	1.00	1.50
1994	—	—	—	—	1.00	1.50

KM# 111.2 50 CENTAVOS
5.80 g., Aluminum-Bronze, 25.2 mm. **Obv:** Tucuman's House where the independence was signed; bold lettering **Rev:** Large value, date below **Edge:** Reeded **Note:** Prev. KM#86.2.

Date	Mintage	VF20	XF40	MS60	MS63	MS65
1993	120,000,000	—	—	—	1.00	1.50
1994	304,000,000	—	—	—	1.00	1.50

KM# 119 50 CENTAVOS
5.80 g., Aluminum-Bronze, 25.2 mm. **Subject:** 50th Anniversary - UNICEF **Obv:** Girl with rag doll **Rev:** UNICEF logo above denomination **Edge:** Reeded **Note:** Prev. KM#94.

Date	Mintage	VF20	XF40	MS60	MS63	MS65
1996	1,000,000	—	—	—	1.00	1.50

KM# 121 50 CENTAVOS
5.80 g., Aluminum-Bronze, 25.2 mm. **Subject:** 50th Anniversary - Women's Right to Vote **Obv:** Bust of Eva Peron right **Rev:** Value with two dates above in circle, legend across top, date at bottom divides wreath **Edge:** Reeded **Note:** Prev. KM#96.

Date	Mintage	VF20	XF40	MS60	MS63	MS65
1997	2,000,000	—	—	—	1.00	1.50

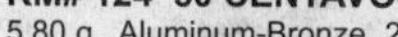

KM# 124 50 CENTAVOS
5.80 g., Aluminum-Bronze, 25.2 mm. **Subject:** Mercosur **Obv:** Southern Cross constellation **Rev:** Value in circle, date below circle **Edge:** Reeded **Note:** Prev. KM#99.

Date	Mintage	VF20	XF40	MS60	MS63	MS65
1998	1,000,000	—	—	—	1.00	1.50

KM# 129.1 50 CENTAVOS
5.80 g., Aluminum-Bronze, 25.2 mm. **Subject:** 179th Anniversary - Death of General Güemes **Obv:** Bearded portrait, right **Rev:** Value in circle **Edge:** Plain **Note:** Prev. KM#129

Date	Mintage	VF20	XF40	MS60	MS63	MS65
2000	1,695,000	—	—	—	1.00	1.50

KM# 129.2 50 CENTAVOS
5.80 g., Aluminum-Bronze, 25.2 mm. **Subject:** 179th Anniversary - Death of General Güemes **Obv:** Bearded portrait **Rev:** Denomination **Edge:** Reeded

Date	Mintage	VF20	XF40	MS60	MS63	MS65
2000	5,000	—	—	—	4.50	6.00

KM# 130.1 50 CENTAVOS
5.80 g., Aluminum-Bronze, 25.2 mm. **Subject:** 150th Anniversary - Death of General San Martin **Obv:** Bust facing **Rev:** Value to right of building **Edge:** Reeded **Note:** Previous KM#130

Date	Mintage	VF20	XF40	MS60	MS63	MS65
2000	995,000	—	—	—	1.00	1.50

KM# 130.2 50 CENTAVOS
5.80 g., Aluminum-Bronze, 25.2 mm. **Subject:** 150th Anniversary - Death of General San Martin **Obv:** Bust facing **Rev:** Denomination to right of building **Edge:** Plain

Date	Mintage	VF20	XF40	MS60	MS63	MS65
2000	5,000	—	—	—	4.50	6.00

KM# 112.1 PESO
6.35 g., Bi-Metallic Aluminum-Bronze center in Copper-Nickel ring, 23 mm. **Obv:** Argentine arms in circle **Rev:** Design of first Argentine coin in center **Edge:** Plain **Note:** Prev. KM#87.1.

Date	Mintage	VF20	XF40	MS60	MS63	MS65
1994 A	75,000,000	—	0.50	1.00	1.50	2.50
Note: Medal rotation						
1995 A	185,000,000	—	0.50	1.00	1.50	2.50
Note: Medal rotation						
1995 B	14,000,000	—	0.50	1.00	1.50	2.50
1996 A	30,000,000	—	0.50	1.00	1.50	2.50

KM# 112.2 PESO
6.35 g., Bi-Metallic Aluminum-Bronze center in Copper-Nickel ring, 23 mm. **Obv:** Smaller Argentine arms in circle **Rev:** Design of first Argentine coin in center **Note:** Prev. KM#87.2.

Date	Mintage	VF20	XF40	MS60	MS63	MS65
1995 C	90,000,000	—	—	—	1.50	2.50

KM# 112.3 PESO
6.35 g., Bi-Metallic Aluminum-Bronze center in Copper-Nickel ring, 23 mm. **Obv:** Argentine arms in circle **Rev:** Design of first Argentine coin in center, with error PROVINGIAS in legend **Note:** Prev. KM#87.3.

Date	Mintage	VF20	XF40	MS60	MS63	MS65
1995 B	56,000,000	—	—	—	2.00	3.00

KM# 126 PESO
25.00 g., 0.900 Silver 0.7234 oz. ASW **Subject:** 50th Anniversary - United Nations **Obv:** Stylized dove, national arms below **Rev:** UN logo, denomination **Rev. Legend:** ARGENTINA POR LA PAZ EN EL MUNDO **Note:** Prev. KM#101.

Date	Mintage	VF20	XF40	MS60	MS63	MS65
ND-1995	—	PF63	30.00	PF65	45.00	

KM# 120 PESO
6.35 g., Bi-Metallic Aluminum-Bronze center in Copper-Nickel ring, 23 mm. **Subject:** 50th Anniversary - UNICEF **Obv:** Girl with rag doll **Rev:** UNICEF logo above denomination **Note:** Prev. KM#95. Medal rotation.

Date	Mintage	VF20	XF40	MS60	MS63	MS65
1996	1,000,000	—	—	—	1.50	2.50

KM# 122 PESO
6.35 g., Bi-Metallic Aluminum-Bronze center in Copper-Nickel ring, 23 mm. **Subject:** 50th Anniversary - Women's Suffrage Law **Obv:** Bust of Eva Duarte de Peron right (social reformer) **Rev:** Denomination **Edge:** Reeded **Note:** Prev. KM#97. Medal rotation.

Date	Mintage	VF20	XF40	MS60	MS63	MS65
1997	1,000,000	—	—	—	2.50	4.00

KM# 125 PESO
6.35 g., Bi-Metallic Aluminum-Bronze center in Copper-Nickel ring, 23 mm. **Subject:** Mercosur **Obv:** Southern Cross constellation **Rev:** Denomination **Note:** Prev. KM#100. Medal rotation.

Date	Mintage	VF20	XF40	MS60	MS63	MS65
1998	496,715	—	—	—	3.00	4.50

KM# 127 PESO

25.00 g., 0.900 Silver 0.7234 oz. ASW, 37 mm. **Subject:** Jorge Luis Borges, 100th Anniversary of birth **Obv:** Profile of Borges left, dates **Rev:** Labyrinth, sundial, denomination and date **Note:** Prev. KM#102.

Date	Mintage	VF20	XF40	MS60	MS63	MS65
1999	—	PF65 95.00				

KM# 114 2 PESOS

10.50 g., Nickel, 30 mm. **Subject:** National Constitution Convention **Obv:** Argentine arms above two small arms **Rev:** Open book, ribbon across left page, five line inscription on right page, value below book **Note:** Prev. KM#89.

Date	Mintage	VF20	XF40	MS60	MS63	MS65
ND-1994	1,000,000	—	—	—	3.50	4.50
ND-1994	1,000	PF65 16.00				

KM# 114a 2 PESOS

12.50 g., 0.900 Silver 0.3617 oz. ASW, 30 mm. **Subject:** National Constitution Convention **Obv:** National arms **Rev:** Open book, ribbon across left page, five line inscription on right page, value below book **Note:** Prev. KM#89a.

Date	Mintage	VF20	XF40	MS60	MS63	MS65
ND (1994)	5,000	—	—	—	12.00	14.00
ND (1994)	1,500	PF65 28.00				

KM# 128 2 PESOS

10.40 g., Copper-Nickel, 30 mm. **Subject:** Jorge Luis Borges - 100th Anniversary of Birth **Obv:** Profile head of Borges left **Rev:** Labyrinth, sundial, denomination and date **Note:** Prev. KM#103.

Date	Mintage	VF20	XF40	MS60	MS63	MS65
1999	1,000,000	—	—	—	2.50	3.50

KM# 115 5 PESOS

21.50 g., Nickel, 35 mm. **Subject:** National Constitution Convention **Obv:** Argentine arms above two smaller arms **Rev:** Open book, ribbon across left page, five line inscription on right page, value below **Note:** Prev. KM#90.

Date	Mintage	VF20	XF40	MS60	MS63	MS65
ND (1994)	1,000,000	—	—	—	5.00	7.00
ND (1994)	1,000	PF65 25.00				

KM# 115a 5 PESOS

25.00 g., 0.900 Silver 0.7234 oz. ASW, 35 mm. **Subject:** National Constitution Convention **Obv:** Argentine arms above two smaller arms **Rev:** Open book, ribbon across left page, five line inscription on right page **Note:** Prev. KM#90a.

Date	Mintage	VF20	XF40	MS60	MS63	MS65
ND-1994	5,000	—	—	—	25.00	30.00
ND-1994	1,500	PF65 50.00				

KM# 136 5 PESOS

8.06 g., 0.900 Gold 0.2333 oz. AGW **Subject:** 50th Anniversary - United Nations **Obv:** Stylized dove, national arms below **Rev:** UN logo, denomination **Rev. Legend:** ARGENTINA POR LA PAZ EN EL MUNDO

Date	Mintage	VF20	XF40	MS60	MS63	MS65
ND-1995	—	PF65 1,200				

KM# 134 5 PESOS

8.06 g., 0.900 Gold 0.2333 oz. AGW, 22 mm. **Subject:** Jorge Luis Borges, 100th Anniversary of birth **Obv:** Head left **Rev:** Sundial within labyrinth **Edge:** Reeded

Date	Mintage	VF20	XF40	MS60	MS63	MS65
1999	2,000	PF65 500				

KM# 137 5 PESOS

8.06 g., 0.900 Gold 0.2333 oz. AGW, 22 mm. **Subject:** 150th Anniversary Death of San Martin **Obv:** Bust facing **Rev:** Building and value **Edge:** Reeded

Date	Mintage	VF20	XF40	MS60	MS63	MS65
2000	1,000	PF65 1,000				

KM# 148 5 PESOS

8.06 g., 0.900 Gold 0.2333 oz. AGW **Subject:** General Martin Miguel de Güemes **Obv:** Head right **Rev:** Value **Rev. Legend:** 17 de JUNO de 1821

Date	Mintage	VF20	XF40	MS60	MS63	MS65
2000	1,000	PF65 600				

KM# 116 25 PESOS

4.03 g., 0.900 Gold 0.1167 oz. AGW **Subject:** National Constitution Convention **Obv:** Argentine arms above two small arms **Rev:** Open book, ribbon across left page, five line inscription on right page **Note:** Prev. KM#91.

Date	Mintage	VF20	XF40	MS60	MS63	MS65
ND(1994)	5,000	—	—	—	225	250
ND-1994	1,000	PF65 350				

KM# 118 25 PESOS

27.00 g., 0.925 Silver 0.803 oz. ASW **Subject:** Environmental Protection **Rev:** Giant Armadillo **Note:** Prev. KM#93.

Date	Mintage	VF20	XF40	MS60	MS63	MS65
1997	—	PF63 35.00	PF65 55.00			

KM# 123 25 PESOS

27.00 g., 0.925 Silver 0.803 oz. ASW, 40 mm. **Subject:** Ibero-American Series - LaZamba **Obv:** Argentine arms within legend and circle of arms **Rev:** Zamba dancers **Note:** Prev. KM#98.

Date	Mintage	VF20	XF40	MS60	MS63	MS65
1997	—	PF63 25.00	PF65 40.00			

KM# 131 25 PESOS

27.00 g., 0.925 Silver 0.803 oz. ASW, 40 mm. **Subject:** Ibero-America Series **Obv:** Argentine arms within legend and circle of arms **Rev:** Bronco busting scene **Edge:** Reeded

Date	Mintage	VF20	XF40	MS60	MS63	MS65
2000	5,000	PF63 30.00	PF65 45.00			

KM# 117 50 PESOS

8.06 g., 0.900 Gold 0.2333 oz. AGW **Subject:** National Constitution Convention **Obv:** Argentine arms above two small arms **Rev:** Open book, ribbon across left page, five line inscription on right page **Note:** Prev. KM#92.

Date	Mintage	VF20	XF40	MS60	MS63	MS65
ND (1994)	5,000	—	—	—	475	500
ND (1994)	1,000	PF65 700				

PATTERNS

Including off metal strikes

KM#	Date	Mintage	Identification	Mkt Val
Pn35	19xx (1901)	—	Centavo. Copper.	—
Pn36	19xx (1902)	—	2 Centavos. Copper.	—
Pn37	1925	—	2 Centavos. Copper.	—
Pn38	1925	—	2 Centavos. Bronze.	—
Pn39	1932	—	Argentino. Copper.	—
Pn40	1932	—	Argentino. Bronze.	—
Pn41	1933	—	Argentino. Bronze.	—
Pn42	1934	—	Argentino. Copper.	—
Pn43	1935	—	Centavo. Copper.	400
Pn44	1935	—	2 Centavos. Copper.	400
Pn45	1936	—	50 Centavos. Bronze.	—
Pn46	1936	—	50 Centavos. Copper-Nickel.	600
Pn47	1936	—	Peso. Bronze.	—
Pn48	1936	—	Peso. Copper-Nickel.	475
Pn49	1937	—	Centavo. Copper. Argentine arms within wreath. Blank, post horn mint mark.	—
Pn50	1938	—	Centavo. Copper.	250
Pn51	1938	—	2 Centavos. Copper.	275
Pn52	1940	—	50 Centavos. Bronze.	225
Pn53	1940	—	50 Centavos. Copper-Nickel. Head by Oudine.	375

KM#	Date	Mintage	Identification	Mkt Val
Pn54	1940	—	50 Centavos. Nickel. Head by L. Bazor.	—
Pn55	1941	—	50 Centavos. Nickel.	—
Pn56	1943	—	Peso. Bronze.	—
Pn57	1943	—	Peso. Nickel.	—
Pn58	1943	—	Peso. Bronze. Condor.	—
Pn59	1945	—	Peso. Bronze.	—
Pn60	1945	—	Peso. Copper-Nickel.	—
Pn61	1946	—	Peso. Bronze.	—
Pn62	1946	—	Peso. Copper-Nickel.	550
Pn63	1971	—	50 Centavos. Aluminum. KM#43.	85.00
Pn64	1975	—	Peso. Aluminum-Bronze. KM#45.	145
Pn65	1976	—	5 Pesos. Aluminum-Bronze. KM#46.	—
Pn66	1977	—	10 Pesos. Aluminum-Bronze. KM#47.	—

MINT SETS

KM#	Date	Mintage	Identification	Issue Price	Mkt Val
MS2	1970 (5)	—	KM#64-68	—	3.25
MS3	1977 (6)	—	KM#75-80	—	65.00
MS4	1977 (3)	—	KM#75-77	—	4.75
MS5	1978 (6)	—	KM#75-80	—	65.00
MS6	1978 (3)	—	KM#75-77	—	4.75
MS7	1983 (4)	—	KM#87-90	—	2.00

PROOF SETS

KM#	Date	Mintage	Identification	Issue Price	Mkt Val
PS1	1977 (3)	1,000	KM#78-80	—	80.00
PS2	1978 (3)	1,750	KM#78-80	153	80.00
PS3	ND(1994) (2)	5,500	KM#114, 115	—	42.00
PS4	ND(1994) (2)	1,000	KM#114a, 115a	79.50	90.00
PS5	ND(1994) (2)	1,000	KM#116, 117	375	565

CATAMARCA

A province located in northwest Argentina having an area of 38,540 sq. mi. and a population of 309,130. Capital: Catamarca. Agriculture and mining are the main industries.

PROVINCE

TOKEN COINAGE

Stabilization Currency Unit

KM# Tn1 100000 AUSTRALES
15.00 g., 0.900 Silver 0.434 oz. ASW **Subject:** Fray Mamerto Esquiu **Obv:** Double-headed figure **Rev:** Head, 3/4 left, date below

Date	Mintage	VF20	XF40	MS60	MS63	MS65
1990	200,000	—	—	—	35.00	50.00

KM# Tn3 100000 AUSTRALES
14.85 g., 0.900 Silver 0.4297 oz. ASW **Subject:** 100th Anniversary - Coronation of Our Lady of the Valley **Obv:** Double-headed figure **Rev:** Imperial crown with cross on top dividing dates

Date	Mintage	VF20	XF40	MS60	MS63	MS65
1991	—	—	—	—	35.00	50.00

KM# Tn2 4000000 AUSTRALES
20.00 g., 0.750 Gold 0.4823 oz. AGW **Subject:** Fray Mamerto Esquiu **Note:** Denomination determined upon release.

Date	Mintage	VF20	XF40	MS60	MS63	MS65
1990	200	—	—	—	975	1,000

LA RIOJA

La Rioja (Rioxa), a city and province in northwest Argentina, directly to the south of Catamarca. More than one third of its population of 270,702 resides in the capital city of La Rioja. Total area of the province is 35,649 sq. mi. and the main industries are centered around agriculture and include olive trees, grapes and wine production.

PROVINCE

TOKEN COINAGE

Stabilization Currency Unit

KM# Tn1 100000 AUSTRALES
15.00 g., 0.900 Silver 0.434 oz. ASW **Subject:** 400th Anniversary - Foundation of La Rioja **Obv:** Mountains in oval within wreath, 1/2 radiant sunface at top **Rev:** Statue standing, divides dates

Date	Mintage	VF20	XF40	MS60	MS63	MS65
1991	200,000	—	—	—	45.00	60.00

KM# Tn2 4000000 AUSTRALES
20.00 g., 0.750 Gold 0.4823 oz. AGW **Subject:** 400th Anniversary - Foundation of La Rioja

Date	Mintage	VF20	XF40	MS60	MS63	MS65
1991	1,000	—	—	—	950	975

ARMENIA

The Republic of Armenia, formerly Armenian S.S.R., is bordered to the north by Georgia, the east by Azerbaijan and the south and west by Turkey and Iran. It has an area of 11,506 sq. mi. (29,800 sq. km) and an estimated population of 3.66 million. Capital: Yerevan. Agriculture including cotton, vineyards and orchards, hydroelectricity, chemicals - primarily synthetic rubber and fertilizers, vast mineral deposits of copper, zinc and aluminum, and production of steel and paper are major industries.

Russia occupied Armenia in 1801 until the Russo-Turkish war of 1878. British intervention excluded either side from remaining although the Armenians remained more loyal to the Ottoman Turks, but in 1894 the Ottoman Turks sent in an expeditionary force of Kurds fearing a revolutionary movement. Large massacres were followed by retaliations, then amnesty was proclaimed which led right into WW I and once again occupation by Russian forces in 1916. After the Russian revolution the Georgians, Armenians and Azerbaijanis formed the short-lived Transcaucasian Federal Republic on Sept. 20, 1917, which broke up into three independent republics on May 26, 1918. Communism developed and in Sept. 1920 the Turks attacked the Armenian Republic; the Russians soon followed suit from Azerbaijan routing the Turks. On Nov. 29, 1920 Armenia was proclaimed a Soviet Socialist Republic. On March 12, 1922, Armenia, Georgia and Azerbaijan were combined to form the Transcaucasian Soviet Federated Socialist Republic, which on Dec. 30, 1922, became a part of U.S.S.R. On Dec. 5, 1936, the Transcaucasian federation was dissolved and Armenia became a constituent Republic of the U.S.S.R. A new constitution was adopted in April 1978. Elections took place on May 20, 1990. The Supreme Soviet adopted a declaration of sovereignty in Aug. 1991, voting to unite Armenia with Nagorno - Karabakh. This newly constituted "Republic of Armenia" became fully independent by popular vote in Sept. 1991. It became a member of the CIS in Dec. 1991.

Fighting between Christians in Armenia and Muslim forces of Azerbaijan escalated in 1992 and continued through early 1994. Each country claimed the Nagorno-Karabakh, an Armenian ethnic enclave, in Azerbaijan. A temporary cease-fire was announced in May 1994.

MONETARY SYSTEM
100 Luma = 1 Dram

MINT NAME
Revan, (Erevan, now Yerevan)

REPUBLIC

STANDARD COINAGE

KM# 51 10 LUMA
0.59 g., Aluminum, 16 mm. **Obv:** National arms **Rev:** Value over date **Edge:** Plain

Date	Mintage	VF20	XF40	MS60	MS63	MS65
1994	—	—	—	—	0.40	0.50

KM# 52 20 LUMA
0.75 g., Aluminum, 18 mm. **Obv:** National arms **Rev:** Value over date **Edge:** Plain

Date	Mintage	VF20	XF40	MS60	MS63	MS65
1994	—	—	—	—	0.50	0.65

KM# 53 50 LUMA
0.93 g., Aluminum, 20 mm. **Obv:** National arms **Rev:** Value over date **Edge:** Plain

Date	Mintage	VF20	XF40	MS60	MS63	MS65
1994	—	—	—	—	0.60	0.75

KM# 54 DRAM
1.39 g., Aluminum, 22 mm. **Obv:** National arms **Rev:** Value over date in sprays **Edge:** Reeded

Date	Mintage	VF20	XF40	MS60	MS63	MS65
1994	—	—	—	—	0.75	1.00

KM# 55 3 DRAM
1.63 g., Aluminum, 24 mm. **Obv:** National arms **Rev:** Value over date within sprays **Edge:** Reeded

Date	Mintage	VF20	XF40	MS60	MS63	MS65
1994	—	—	—	—	1.00	1.25

KM# 56 5 DRAM
1.98 g., Aluminum, 26 mm. **Obv:** National arms **Rev:** Value over date within sprays **Edge:** Plain

Date	Mintage	VF20	XF40	MS60	MS63	MS65
1994	—	—	—	—	1.50	1.75

KM# 81 5 DRAM
31.37 g., 0.999 Silver 1.0076 oz. ASW, 38 mm. **Subject:** 5th Anniversary - Dram Currency, introduced on November 22, 1993 **Obv:** National arms **Rev:** 6 banknote designs

Date	Mintage	VF20	XF40	MS60	MS63	MS65
1998	500	PF65 60.00				

KM# 58 10 DRAM

2.30 g., Aluminum, 28 mm. **Obv:** National arms **Rev:** Value over date within sprays **Edge:** Plain

Date	Mintage	VF20	XF40	MS60	MS63	MS65
1994	—	—	—	—	2.00	2.50

KM# 82 10 DRAM

31.00 g., 0.999 Silver 0.9957 oz. ASW, 38 mm. **Subject:** 10th Anniversary - Earthquake, December 7, 1988 **Obv:** National arms **Rev:** Map and building

Date	Mintage	VF20	XF40	MS60	MS63	MS65
1998	1,000	PF65 40.00				

KM# 57 25 DRAM

31.10 g., 0.999 Silver 0.999 oz. ASW, 38 mm. **Subject:** 1918 Battle of Sardarapat **Obv:** National arms **Rev:** Symbolic design **Edge:** Numbered

Date	Mintage	VF20	XF40	MS60	MS63	MS65
1994	3,000	PF65 35.00				

KM# 59 25 DRAM

28.28 g., 0.925 Silver 0.841 oz. ASW, 38.61 mm. **Obv:** National arms above value **Rev:** Apricot

Date	Mintage	VF20	XF40	MS60	MS63	MS65
1994	10,000	PF65 40.00				

KM# 60 25 DRAM

31.10 g., 0.999 Silver 0.999 oz. ASW **Subject:** David of Sasun **Obv:** National arms above denomination **Rev:** Monument of David mounted on rearing horse with sword held with two hands **Edge:** Numbered

Date	Mintage	VF20	XF40	MS60	MS63	MS65
1994	5,000	PF65 45.00				

KM# 61 25 DRAM

31.10 g., 0.999 Silver 0.999 oz. ASW, 38 mm. **Subject:** Temple of Garni **Obv:** National arms over value and date **Rev:** Temple building **Edge:** Numbered

Date	Mintage	VF20	XF40	MS60	MS63	MS65
1994	5,000	PF65 45.00				

KM# 63 25 DRAM

31.10 g., 0.999 Silver 0.999 oz. ASW **Subject:** Artsakh **Obv:** National arms above denomination **Rev:** Symbolic artifacts, sword, eagle, church....

Date	Mintage	VF20	XF40	MS60	MS63	MS65
1994	5,000	PF65 45.00				

KM# 72 100 DRAM

28.28 g., 0.925 Silver 0.841 oz. ASW, 38.6 mm. **Subject:** 50th Anniversary - United Nations **Obv:** National arms **Rev:** Seated Madonna and child

Date	Mintage	VF20	XF40	MS60	MS63	MS65
1995	100,000	PF65 35.00				

KM# 64 100 DRAM

31.10 g., 0.999 Silver 0.999 oz. ASW, 38 mm. **Subject:** Chess Olympics in Yerevan **Obv:** National arms above value **Rev:** Symbolic chess board

Date	Mintage	VF20	XF40	MS60	MS63	MS65
1996	2,000	PF65 45.00				

KM# 69 100 DRAM

10.80 g., Copper-Nickel, 29.5 mm. **Subject:** XXXII Chess Olympiad in Yerevan **Obv:** Eagle and lion support arms **Rev:** Stylized stork and chessboard in inner circle

Date	Mintage	VF20	XF40	MS60	MS63	MS65
1996	—	—	—	3.00	5.00	7.00
1996	2,000	PF65 12.50				

KM# 70 100 DRAM

28.28 g., 0.925 Silver 0.841 oz. ASW, 38.61 mm. **Subject:** XXXII Chess Olympiad **Obv:** Eagle and lion support arms **Rev:** Stylized stork and chessboard

Date	Mintage	VF20	XF40	MS60	MS63	MS65
1996	10,000	PF65 40.00				

KM# 77 100 DRAM

31.15 g., 0.999 Silver 1.0005 oz. ASW, 38 mm. **Subject:** Marshal Bagramian, Centennial **Obv:** National arms **Rev:** Uniformed portrait

Date	Mintage	VF20	XF40	MS60	MS63	MS65
1996	—	PF65 275				
1997	1,200	PF65 45.00				

KM# 71 100 DRAM

28.28 g., Copper-Nickel, 38.61 mm. **Subject:** WWF Conserving Nature 1997 **Obv:** National emblem **Rev:** Caucasian otter

Date	Mintage	VF20	XF40	MS60	MS63	MS65
1997	—	—	—	—	12.00	15.00

KM# 71a 100 DRAM

28.28 g., 0.925 Silver 0.841 oz. ASW, 38.61 mm. **Subject:** WWF Conserving Nature **Obv:** National emblem **Rev:** Caucasian otter

Date	Mintage	VF20	XF40	MS60	MS63	MS65
1997	15,000	PF65 45.00				

KM# 76 100 DRAM
10.80 g., Copper-Nickel, 28.5 mm. **Subject:** Charents **Obv:** National emblem **Rev:** Facial portrait of poet, Yeghishe Charents, Centennial

Date	Mintage	VF20	XF40	MS60	MS63	MS65
1997	—	—	—	3.00	5.00	8.00

KM# 78 100 DRAM
Copper-Nickel, 38.61 mm. **Subject:** WWF Conserving Nature **Obv:** National arms **Rev:** Armenian silver seagull

Date	Mintage	VF20	XF40	MS60	MS63	MS65
1998	—	—	—	—	14.00	17.00

KM# 78a 100 DRAM
28.28 g., 0.925 Silver 0.841 oz. ASW, 38.61 mm. **Subject:** WWF Conserving Nature **Obv:** National arms **Rev:** Armenian silver seagull

Date	Mintage	VF20	XF40	MS60	MS63	MS65
1998	15,000	PF65 75.00				

KM# 79 100 DRAM
28.28 g., 0.925 Silver 0.841 oz. ASW, 38.61 mm. **Subject:** XVIII Olympic Winter Games **Obv:** Arms **Rev:** Downhill skiers

Date	Mintage	VF20	XF40	MS60	MS63	MS65
1998	10,000	PF65 80.00				

KM# 80 100 DRAM
28.28 g., 0.925 Silver 0.841 oz. ASW, 38.61 mm. **Subject:** 1998 World Cup Soccer **Obv:** Arms **Rev:** Soccer players, map of France

Date	Mintage	VF20	XF40	MS60	MS63	MS65
1998	10,000	PF65 95.00				

KM# 100 200 DRAM
31.10 g., 0.999 Silver 0.9989 oz. ASW, 38 mm. **Obv:** National arms **Rev:** A.S. Pushkin left, 200th Anniversary of birth June 6, 1799

Date	Mintage	VF20	XF40	MS60	MS63	MS65
1999	500	PF65 65.00				

KM# 65 500 DRAM
155.52 g., 0.999 Silver 4.995 oz. ASW, 63 mm. **Subject:** National Assembly Building **Obv:** National arms above value **Rev:** View of building **Edge:** 5TO .999 AG and serial number

Date	Mintage	VF20	XF40	MS60	MS63	MS65
1995	300	PF65 375				

KM# 66 500 DRAM
155.52 g., 0.999 Silver 4.995 oz. ASW, 63 mm. **Subject:** Historical Armenian Coat of Arms Series **Obv:** National arms **Rev:** Arms of the Kingdom of Cilicia

Date	Mintage	VF20	XF40	MS60	MS63	MS65
1995	300	PF65 375				

KM# 67 500 DRAM
155.52 g., 0.999 Silver 4.995 oz. ASW, 63 mm. **Subject:** Historical Armenian Coat of Arms Series **Obv:** National arms **Rev:** Arms of Arshakonni dynasty 66-428 AD

Date	Mintage	VF20	XF40	MS60	MS63	MS65
1995	300	PF65 375				

KM# 73 500 DRAM
155.52 g., 0.999 Silver 4.995 oz. ASW, 63 mm. **Subject:** Historical Armenian Coat of Arms - Lion **Obv:** National arms **Rev:** Arms of the Bagratourni dynasty **Edge:** With 5T0 .999 AG and serial number

Date	Mintage	VF20	XF40	MS60	MS63	MS65
1995	300	PF65 375				

KM# 74 500 DRAM
155.52 g., 0.999 Silver 4.995 oz. ASW, 63 mm. **Subject:** Historical Armenian Coat of Arms - Double Eagle **Obv:** National arms **Rev:** Arms of the Artashesyan Dynasty 189 BC to 1 AD

Date	Mintage	VF20	XF40	MS60	MS63	MS65
1995	300	PF65 375				

KM# 68 1000 DRAM
31.10 g., 0.999 Silver 0.999 oz. ASW **Subject:** Early Armenian Currency - Vignette from 100 Rouble Note **Obv:** National arms above value **Rev:** Vignette from 100 Rouble note

Date	Mintage	VF20	XF40	MS60	MS63	MS65
1994	5,000	PF65 45.00				

KM# 83 1000 DRAM
31.31 g., 0.999 Silver 1.0056 oz. ASW, 38 mm. **Subject:** 1700th Anniversary of the Adoption of Christianity in Armenia **Obv:** National arms **Rev:** Etchmiadzin church

Date	Mintage	VF20	XF40	MS60	MS63	MS65
1998	1,700	PF65 185				

KM# 84 1000 DRAM
31.31 g., 0.999 Silver 1.0056 oz. ASW, 38 mm. **Subject:** 1700th Anniversary of the Adoption of Christianity in Armenia **Obv:** National arms **Rev:** Ani church tower

Date	Mintage	VF20	XF40	MS60	MS63	MS65
1998	1,700	PF65 185				

KM# 85 1000 DRAM
31.10 g., 0.999 Silver 0.9989 oz. ASW, 38 mm. **Subject:** 1700th Anniversary of the Adoption of Christianity in Armenia **Obv:** National arms **Rev:** Haghpat carved stone cross, khachkar

Date	Mintage	VF20	XF40	MS60	MS63	MS65
1998	1,700	PF65 185				

KM# 88 2000 DRAM
28.28 g., 0.925 Silver 0.841 oz. ASW, 38.6 mm. **Subject:** Millennium **Obv:** National arms **Rev:** Mounted St. George slaying a dragon **Edge:** Plain **Shape:** 8-sided

Date	Mintage	VF20	XF40	MS60	MS63	MS65
2000	30,000	PF65 60.00				

KM# 89 5000 DRAM
31.10 g., 0.999 Silver 0.9989 oz. ASW, 38 mm. **Subject:** 1700th Anniversary of the adoption of Christianity in Armenia **Obv:** National arms **Rev:** Holy Cross Church (915) Aghtamar Island in Lake Van **Edge:** Plain with serial number

Date	Mintage	VF20	XF40	MS60	MS63	MS65
1999	1,700	PF65 225				

KM# 101 5000 DRAM
31.10 g., 0.999 Silver 0.9989 oz. ASW, 38 mm. **Obv:** National arms **Rev:** Chess Grand Master Tigran Petrosyan

Date	Mintage	VF20	XF40	MS60	MS63	MS65
1999	500	PF65 80.00				

KM# 103 5000 DRAM
31.10 g., 0.999 Silver 0.9989 oz. ASW, 38 mm. **Obv:** National arms **Rev:** First Pan-Armenian Games logo in Yerevan August 28 to September 15 1999

Date	Mintage	VF20	XF40	MS60	MS63	MS65
1999	500	PF65 80.00				

KM# 104 5000 DRAM
31.10 g., 0.999 Silver 0.9989 oz. ASW, 38 mm. **Obv:** National arms **Rev:** Large tree logo of the First Pan-Armenian Congress of the Armenian Diaspora September 22-23, 1999

Date	Mintage	VF20	XF40	MS60	MS63	MS65
1999	500	PF65 70.00				

KM# 90 10000 DRAM
8.64 g., 0.900 Gold 0.250 oz. AGW, 22 mm. **Subject:** Christian Armenia - Ani **Obv:** National arms **Rev:** Church tower **Edge:** Plain with serial number

Date	Mintage	VF20	XF40	MS60	MS63	MS65
1998	1,700	PF65 800				

KM# 91 10000 DRAM
8.64 g., 0.900 Gold 0.250 oz. AGW, 22 mm. **Subject:** 1700th Anniversary of the adoption of Christianity in Armenia **Obv:** National arms **Rev:** Multi-towered church **Edge:** Plain with serial number

Date	Mintage	VF20	XF40	MS60	MS63	MS65
1998	1,700	PF65 800				

KM# 75.1 25000 DRAM
4.30 g., 0.900 Gold 0.1244 oz. AGW, 18 mm. **Obv:** National arms **Rev:** Portrait of goddess Anahit **Edge:** Reeded

Date	Mintage	VF20	XF40	MS60	MS63	MS65
1997	—	PF65 285				

KM# 75.2 25000 DRAM
4.30 g., 0.900 Gold 0.1244 oz. AGW, 18 mm. **Obv:** National arms **Rev:** Portrait of goddess Anahit left **Edge:** Plain

Date	Mintage	VF20	XF40	MS60	MS63	MS65
1997	500	PF65 1,000				

KM# 92 50000 DRAM
8.64 g., 0.900 Gold 0.250 oz. AGW, 22 mm. **Subject:** 1700th Anniversary of the Adoption of Christianity in Armenia **Obv:** National arms **Rev:** Holy Cross Church (915) Aghtamar Island in Lake Van **Edge:** Plain with serial number

Date	Mintage	VF20	XF40	MS60	MS63	MS65
1999	1,700	PF65 800				

KM# 105 50000 DRAM
8.60 g., 0.900 Gold 0.2488 oz. AGW, 22 mm. **Obv:** National arms on an ancient coin design **Rev:** Ancient Armenian King Tigran the Great 95-55 BC

Date	Mintage	VF20	XF40	MS60	MS63	MS65
1999	500	PF65 1,200				

KM# 102 100000 DRAM
17.20 g., 0.900 Gold 0.4977 oz. AGW, 30 mm. **Obv:** National arms **Rev:** Noah's descent from Mt. Ararat

Date	Mintage	VF20	XF40	MS60	MS63	MS65
1999	1,000	PF65 1,900				

MINT SETS

KM#	Date	Mintage	Identification	Issue Price	Mkt Val
MS1	1994 (7)	—	KM#51-56, 58	30.00	12.00

ARUBA

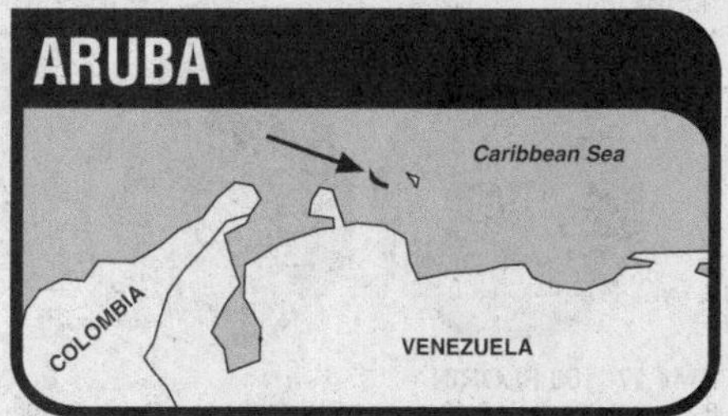

Aruba, formerly a part of the Netherlands Antilles, achieved on Jan. 1, 1986 a special status, "status aparte" as the third state under the Dutch crown, together with the Netherlands and the remaining five islands of the Netherlands Antilles. On Dec. 15, 1954 the Netherlands Antilles were given complete domestic autonomy and granted equality within the Kingdom of the Netherlands. The separate constitution put in place for Aruba in 1986 established it as an autonomous government within the Kingdom of the Netherlands. In 1990 Aruba opted to remain a part of the Kingdom without the promise of future independence. The rest of the Netherlands Antilles was dissolved on October 10, 2010, resulting in two new constituent countries, Curacao and Sint Maarten, while the other islands joining the Netherlands as "special municipalities".

The second largest island of the former Netherlands Antilles, Aruba is situated near the Venezuelan coast. The island has an area of 74-1/2 sq. mi. (193 sq. km.) and a population of 105,000. Capital: Oranjestad, named after the Dutch royal family. Aruba was important in the processing and transportation of petroleum products in the first part of the twentieth century, but today the chief industry is tourism.

For earlier issues see Curacao and the Netherlands Antilles.

RULER
Dutch

MINT MARKS
(u) Utrecht - Privy marks only
Anvil, 1986-1988
Bow and Arrow, 1989-1999
Bow and Arrow w/star, 2000

MONETARY SYSTEM
100 Cents = 1 Florin

DUTCH STATE

Status Aparte

DECIMAL COINAGE

KM# 1 5 CENTS
2.00 g., Nickel Bonded Steel, 16 mm. **Ruler:** Beatrix **Obv:** National arms **Rev:** Geometric design with value **Edge:** Plain

Date	Mintage	VF20	XF40	MS60	MS63	MS65
1986 (u)	276,220	—	0.10	0.25	0.50	1.00
1987 (u)	221,650	—	0.10	0.25	0.50	1.00
1988 (u)	656,500	—	0.10	0.25	0.50	1.00
1989 (u)	770,000	—	0.10	0.25	0.50	1.00
1990 (u)	612,000	—	0.10	0.25	0.50	1.00
1991 (u)	412,000	—	0.10	0.25	0.50	1.00
1992 (u)	810,500	—	0.10	0.25	0.50	1.00
1993 (u)	709,100	—	0.10	0.25	0.50	1.00
1994 (u)	709,100	—	0.10	0.25	0.50	1.00
1995 (u)	808,500	—	0.10	0.25	0.50	1.00
1996 (u)	587,500	—	0.10	0.25	0.50	1.00
1997 (u)	535,000	—	0.10	0.25	0.50	1.00
1998 (u)	919,000	—	0.10	0.25	0.50	1.00
1999 (u)	823,000	—	0.10	0.25	0.50	1.00
2000 (u)	886,500	—	0.10	0.25	0.50	1.00

KM# 2 10 CENTS
3.00 g., Nickel Bonded Steel, 18 mm. **Ruler:** Beatrix **Obv:** National arms **Rev:** Geometric design with value **Edge:** Reeded

Date	Mintage	VF20	XF40	MS60	MS63	MS65
1986 (u)	356,220	—	0.20	0.35	0.60	1.10
1987 (u)	221,650	—	0.20	0.35	0.60	1.10
1988 (u)	986,500	—	0.20	0.35	0.60	1.10
1989 (u)	610,000	—	0.20	0.35	0.60	1.10
1990 (u)	762,000	—	0.20	0.35	0.60	1.10
1991 (u)	512,000	—	0.20	0.35	0.60	1.10
1992 (u)	610,500	—	0.20	0.35	0.60	1.10
1993 (u)	1,009,100	—	0.20	0.35	0.60	1.10
1994 (u)	409,100	—	0.20	0.35	0.60	1.10
1995 (u)	918,500	—	0.20	0.35	0.60	1.10
1996 (u)	457,500	—	0.20	0.35	0.60	1.10
1997 (u) plain edge	416,000	—	0.40	0.75	1.25	2.00
1997 (u) reeded edge, sets only	7,500	PF65 3.00				
1998 (u)	953,000	—	0.20	0.35	0.60	1.10
1999 (u)	1,004,000	—	0.20	0.35	0.60	1.10
2000 (u)	759,500	—	0.20	0.35	0.60	1.10

KM# 3 25 CENTS
3.50 g., Nickel Bonded Steel, 20 mm. **Ruler:** Beatrix **Obv:** National arms **Rev:** Geometric design with value **Edge:** Plain

Date	Mintage	VF20	XF40	MS60	MS63	MS65
1986 (u)	356,220	—	0.20	0.40	0.75	1.50
1987 (u)	271,650	—	0.20	0.40	0.75	1.50
1988 (u)	116,500	—	0.20	0.40	0.75	1.50
1989 (u)	360,000	—	0.20	0.40	0.75	1.50
1990 (u)	512,000	—	0.20	0.40	0.75	1.50
1991 (u)	612,000	—	0.20	0.40	0.75	1.50
1992 (u)	460,500	—	0.20	0.40	0.75	1.50
1993 (u)	609,100	—	0.20	0.40	0.75	1.50
1994 (u)	109,100	—	0.20	0.40	0.75	1.50
1995 (u)	608,500	—	0.20	0.40	0.75	1.50
1996 (u)	287,500	—	0.20	0.40	0.75	1.50
1997 (u)	467,000	—	0.20	0.40	0.75	1.50
1998 (u)	640,000	—	0.20	0.40	0.75	1.50
1999 (u)	332,000	—	0.20	0.40	0.75	1.50
2000 (u)	330,500	—	0.20	0.40	0.75	1.50

KM# 4 50 CENTS
5.00 g., Nickel Bonded Steel, 20 mm. **Ruler:** Beatrix **Obv:** National arms **Rev:** Geometric design with value **Edge:** Plain **Shape:** 4-sided

Date	Mintage	VF20	XF40	MS60	MS63	MS65
1986 (u)	236,220	—	0.30	0.50	1.00	1.50
1987 (u)	121,651	—	0.30	0.50	1.00	1.50
1988 (u)	216,500	—	0.30	0.50	1.00	1.50
1989 (u)	110,000	—	0.30	0.60	1.25	2.25
1989 (u) medal struck	Inc. above	—	10.00	15.00	25.00	30.00
1990 (u)	262,000	—	0.30	0.50	1.00	1.50
1991 (u)	312,000	—	0.30	0.50	1.00	1.50
1992 (u)	310,500	—	0.30	0.50	1.00	1.50
1993 (u)	459,100	—	0.30	0.50	1.00	1.50
1994 (u)	309,100	—	0.30	0.50	1.00	1.50
1995 (u)	258,500	—	0.30	0.50	1.00	1.50
1996 (u)	392,500	—	0.30	0.50	1.00	1.50
1997 (u)	27,000	—	0.30	1.00	2.50	4.00
1998 (u)	196,000	—	0.30	0.50	1.00	1.50
1999 (u)	445,000	—	0.30	0.50	1.00	1.50
2000 (u)	54,500	—	0.30	1.00	1.00	1.50

KM# 5 FLORIN
8.50 g., Nickel Bonded Steel, 26 mm. **Ruler:** Beatrix **Obv:** Head left **Rev:** National arms and value **Edge:** Lettered **Edge Lettering:** GOD * ZIJ * MET * ONS *

Date	Mintage	VF20	XF40	MS60	MS63	MS65
1986 (u)	336,220	—	0.60	1.00	2.00	3.00
1987 (u)	221,650	—	0.60	1.00	2.00	3.00
1988 (u)	566,500	—	0.60	1.00	2.00	3.00
1989 (u)	410,000	—	0.60	1.00	2.00	3.00
1990 (u)	412,000	—	0.60	1.00	2.00	3.00
1991 (u)	162,000	—	0.60	1.00	2.00	3.00
1992 (u)	510,500	—	0.60	1.00	2.00	3.00
1993 (u)	409,100	—	0.60	1.00	2.00	3.00
1994 (u)	109,100	—	0.60	1.00	2.00	3.00
1995 (u)	208,500	—	0.60	1.00	2.00	3.00
1996 (u)	132,500	—	0.60	1.00	2.00	3.00
1997 (u)	415,000	—	0.60	1.00	2.00	3.00
1998 (u)	299,000	—	0.60	1.00	2.00	3.00
1999 (u)	430,000	—	0.60	1.00	2.00	3.00
2000 (u)	295,500	—	0.60	1.00	2.00	3.00

KM# 6 2-1/2 FLORIN
10.30 g., Nickel Bonded Steel, 30 mm. **Ruler:** Beatrix **Obv:** Head left **Rev:** National arms with value **Edge:** Lettered **Edge Lettering:** GOD * ZIJ * MET * ONS *

Date	Mintage	VF20	XF40	MS60	MS63	MS65
1986 (u)	56,220	—	—	1.75	2.50	5.00
1987 (u)	31,651	—	—	2.00	3.00	7.00
1988 (u)	27,500	—	—	2.00	3.00	7.00
1989 (u)	15,000	—	—	2.00	3.00	7.00
1990 (u)	17,000	—	—	2.00	3.00	7.00
1991 (u)	17,000	—	—	2.00	3.00	7.00
1991 (u) medal turn	Inc. above	—	7.50	10.00	20.00	30.00
1992 (u)	12,500	—	—	2.00	3.00	7.00
1993 (u)	11,100	—	—	2.00	3.00	7.00
1994 (u)	11,100	—	—	2.00	3.00	7.00
1995 (u)	10,500	—	—	2.00	3.00	7.00
1996 (u) Sets only	7,500	—	—	—	3.00	7.00
1997 (u) Sets only	7,500	—	—	—	3.00	7.00
1998 (u) Sets only	8,000	—	—	—	3.00	7.00
1999 (u) Sets only	7,000	—	—	—	3.00	7.00
2000 (u) Sets only	7,500	—	—	—	3.00	7.00

KM# 12 5 FLORIN
8.64 g., Nickel Bonded Steel, 26 mm. **Ruler:** Beatrix **Obv:** Head left **Rev:** National arms with value **Edge:** Plain **Shape:** 4-sided

Date	Mintage	VF20	XF40	MS60	MS63	MS65
1995 (u)	208,500	—	—	2.00	4.50	7.00
1996 (u)	357,500	—	—	2.00	4.50	7.00
1997 (u)	27,500	—	—	2.25	7.00	9.00
1998 (u)	162,000	—	—	2.00	4.50	7.00
1999 (u)	86,200	—	—	2.25	5.50	8.00
2000 (u) Sets only	7,500	—	—	3.00	7.00	9.00

KM# 7 25 FLORIN
25.00 g., 0.925 Silver 0.7435 oz. ASW, 38 mm. **Subject:** Independence **Obv:** Head of Queen Beatrix left **Rev:** Arms, treaty name, date, and value **Edge Lettering:** GOD * ZiJ * MET * ONS

Date	Mintage	VF20	XF40	MS60	MS63	MS65
ND(1986) (u)	5,000	—	—	15.00	20.00	22.00
ND(1986) (u)	10,250	PF65 25.00				

KM# 8 25 FLORIN
25.00 g., 0.925 Silver 0.7435 oz. ASW, 38 mm. **Subject:** 5 Years of Independence **Obv:** Head of Queen Beatrix left **Rev:** Triangular portion of flag, treaty name, date, value **Edge Lettering:** GOD * ZiJ * MET * ONS

Date	Mintage	VF20	XF40	MS60	MS63	MS65
ND(1991) (u)	2,500	—	—	15.00	20.00	25.00
ND(1991) (u)	4,600	PF65 30.00				

KM# 10 25 FLORIN
25.00 g., 0.925 Silver 0.7435 oz. ASW, 38 mm. **Series:** 1992 Olympics **Subject:** Windsurfing **Obv:** Head of Queen Beatrix left **Rev:** Windsurfer **Edge:** Plain

Date	Mintage	VF20	XF40	MS60	MS63	MS65
1992 (u)	2,000	—	—	17.00	22.00	25.00
1992 (u)	16,000	PF65 25.00				

KM# 11 25 FLORIN
25.00 g., 0.925 Silver 0.7435 oz. ASW, 38 mm. **Subject:** Oil for Peace (WWII) **Obv:** Head of Queen Beatrix left **Rev:** Freighter, tankers and refinery **Edge:** Plain

Date	Mintage	VF20	XF40	MS60	MS63	MS65
1994 (u)	1,500	—	—	20.00	30.00	35.00
1994 (u)	4,000	PF65 40.00				

KM# 13 25 FLORIN
25.00 g., 0.925 Silver 0.7435 oz. ASW, 38 mm. **Subject:** 100th Anniversary of the Olympics **Obv:** Head of Queen Beatrix left **Rev:** Cyclist and logo **Edge:** Plain

Date	Mintage	VF20	XF40	MS60	MS63	MS65
1995 (u)	1,000	—	—	20.00	30.00	35.00
1995 (u)	2,100	PF65 45.00				

KM# 14 25 FLORIN
25.00 g., 0.925 Silver 0.7435 oz. ASW, 38 mm. **Subject:** 100th Anniversary of the Olympics **Obv:** Head of Queen Beatrix left **Rev:** Cyclist, without logo **Edge:** Plain

Date	Mintage	VF20	XF40	MS60	MS63	MS65
1995 (u)	1,700	PF65 140				

KM# 15 25 FLORIN
25.00 g., 0.925 Silver 0.7435 oz. ASW, 38 mm. **Obv:** Head of Queen Beatrix left **Rev:** Sea turtles with pre-Columbian design **Edge:** Plain

Date	Mintage	VF20	XF40	MS60	MS63	MS65
1995 (u)	3,500	—	—	22.00	32.00	40.00
1995 (u)	2,000	PF65 45.00				

KM# 18 25 FLORIN
25.00 g., 0.925 Silver 0.7435 oz. ASW, 38 mm. **Subject:** Tradition With Vision - Discovery 1499 **Obv:** Portrait of Vespucci, sailing vessel, map **Rev:** Spanish fan and aboriginal design, dates **Edge:** Plain

Date	Mintage	VF20	XF40	MS60	MS63	MS65
ND-1999 (u)	1,850	PF65 50.00				

KM# 21 25 FLORIN
25.00 g., 0.925 Silver 0.7435 oz. ASW, 38 mm. **Subject:** Olympics **Obv:** Head of Queen Beatrix left **Rev:** Catamaran sailboat **Edge:** Plain

Date	Mintage	VF20	XF40	MS60	MS63	MS65
2000 (u)	3,500	PF65 35.00				

KM# 9 50 FLORIN
6.72 g., 0.900 Gold 0.1944 oz. AGW, 22.5 mm. **Subject:** Independence **Obv:** Head of Queen Beatrix left **Rev:** Triangular portion of flag, treaty name and date **Edge:** Grained

Date	Mintage	VF20	XF40	MS60	MS63	MS65
ND(1991) (u)	2,600	PF65 325				

KM# 16 50 FLORIN
25.00 g., 0.925 Silver 0.7435 oz. ASW, 38 mm. **Subject:** 10th Anniversary of Autonomy **Obv:** Head of Queen Beatrix left **Rev:** Portions of national flag and anthem score **Note:** Similar to 100 Florin, KM#17

Date	Mintage	VF20	XF40	MS60	MS63	MS65
ND(1996) (u)	500	—	—	—	45.00	55.00
ND(1996) (u)	2,000	PF65 50.00				

KM# 17 100 FLORIN
6.72 g., 0.900 Gold 0.1944 oz. AGW, 22.5 mm. **Subject:** 10th Anniversary of Autonomy **Obv:** Head of Queen Beatrix left **Rev:** Portions of national flag and anthem score **Edge:** Grained

Date	Mintage	VF20	XF40	MS60	MS63	MS65
ND(1996) (u)	535	PF65 475				

KM# 19 100 FLORIN
6.72 g., 0.900 Gold 0.1944 oz. AGW, 22.5 mm. **Subject:** Tradition With Vision - Discovery 1499 **Obv:** Portrait of Vespucci, sailing vessel, map **Rev:** Spanish fan and aboriginal design, dates **Edge:** Grained **Note:** Similar to 25 Florin, KM#18.

Date	Mintage	VF20	XF40	MS60	MS63	MS65
ND-1999 (u)	1,100	PF65 375				

MINT SETS

KM#	Date	Mintage	Identification	Issue Price	Mkt Val
MS1	1986 (6)	36,200	KM#1-6, with medal	8.95	10.00
MS2	1987 (6)	21,650	KM#1-6, with medal	9.95	12.00
MS3	1988 (6)	16,500	KM#1-6, with medal	12.95	12.00
MS4	1989 (6)	10,000	KM#1-6, with medal	12.00	12.00
MS5	1990 (6)	12,000	KM#1-6, with medal	—	12.00
MS6	1991 (6)	12,000	KM#1-6, with medal	14.50	12.00
MS7	1992 (6)	10,500	KM#1-6, with medal	—	12.00
MS8	1993 (6)	9,100	KM#1-6, with medal	—	12.00
MS9	1994 (6)	9,100	KM#1-6, with medal	14.50	12.00
MS10	1995 (1)	1,000	KM#12	—	16.00
MS11	1995 (6)	8,500	KM#1-6, with medal	17.50	16.00
MS12	1995 (1)	2,500	KM#15, 5 Florin banknote, with medal	56.50	65.00
MS13	1996 (7)	7,500	KM#1-6, 12, with medal	17.50	16.00
MS14	1997 (7)	8,000	KM#1-6, 12, with medal	17.50	22.00
MS15	1998 (7)	7,000	KM#1-6, 12, with medal	17.50	16.00
MS16	1999 (7)	7,000	KM#1-6, 12, with medal	17.50	16.00
MS17	2000 (7)	7,500	KM#1-6, 12	15.00	16.00

PROOF SETS

KM#	Date	Mintage	Identification	Issue Price	Mkt Val
PS1	1999 (2)	—	KM#18-19, with Netherlands Antilles KM#45-47 Tradition with Vision 1499-1999	580	1,450

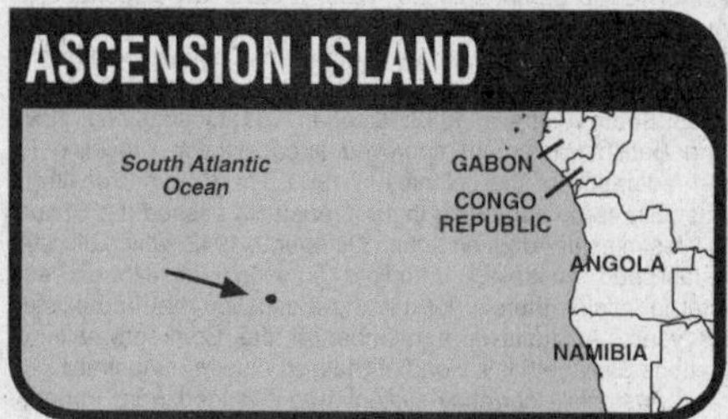

An island of volcanic origin, Ascension Island lies in the South Atlantic, 700 miles (1,100 km.) northwest of St. Helena. It has an area of 34 sq. mi. (88 sq. km.) on an island 9 miles (14 km.) long and 6 miles (10 km.) wide. Approximate population: 1,146. Although having little vegetation and scant rainfall, the island has a very healthy climate. The island is the nesting place for a large number of sea turtles and sooty terns. Phosphates and guano are the chief natural sources of income.

The island was discovered on Ascension Day, 1501, by Joao da Nova, a Portuguese navigator. It lay unoccupied until 1815, when occupied by the British. It was under Admiralty rule until 1922 when it was annexed as a dependency of St. Helena. During World War II an airfield was built that has been used as a fueling stop for Transatlantic flights to Southern Europe, North Africa and the Near-East.

RULER

British

MINT MARK

PM - Pobjoy Mint

BRITISH ADMINISTRATION

STANDARD COINAGE

KM# 1 25 PENCE (Crown)

Copper-Nickel, 38.5 mm. **Subject:** 25th Anniversary of Coronation **Obv:** Young bust of Queen Elizabeth right **Rev:** Lion left above sea turtle

Date	Mintage	VF20	XF40	MS60	MS63	MS65
1978 PM	—	—	—	3.00	5.00	10.00

KM# 1a 25 PENCE (Crown)

28.28 g., 0.925 Silver 0.841 oz. ASW, 38.5 mm. **Subject:** 25th Anniversary of Coronation **Obv:** Young bust of Queen Elizabeth II right **Rev:** Lion left above sea turtle

Date	Mintage	VF20	XF40	MS60	MS63	MS65
1978 PM	70,000	—	—	15.00	17.00	22.00
1978 PM	25,000	PF63 18.00	PF65 22.00			

KM# 2 25 PENCE (Crown)

28.28 g., 0.925 Silver 0.841 oz. ASW, 38.5 mm. **Subject:** 25th Anniversary of the Coronation **Obv:** Isle of Man,bust of young Elizabeth wearing crown, right **Rev:** Lion left above sea turtle **Note:** Error; mule.

Date	Mintage	VF20	XF40	MS60	MS63	MS65
ND-1978 PM	367	—	—	125	175	200

KM# 3 25 PENCE (Crown)

Copper-Nickel, 38.5 mm. **Subject:** Wedding of Prince Charles and Lady Diana **Obv:** Young bust of Queen Elizabeth II right **Rev:** 2 coats of arms

Date	Mintage	VF20	XF40	MS60	MS63	MS65
1981 PM	50,000	—	—	1.50	2.50	4.00

KM# 3a 25 PENCE (Crown)

28.28 g., 0.500 Silver 0.4546 oz. ASW, 38.5 mm. **Subject:** Wedding of Prince Charles and Lady Diana **Obv:** Young bust of Queen Elizabeth II right **Rev:** 2 coats of arms

Date	Mintage	VF20	XF40	MS60	MS63	MS65
1981	500	—	—	20.00	30.00	40.00

KM# 3b 25 PENCE (Crown)

28.28 g., 0.925 Silver 0.841 oz. ASW, 38.5 mm. **Subject:** Wedding of Prince Charles and Lady Diana **Obv:** Young bust of Queen Elizabeth II right **Rev:** 2 coats of arms

Date	Mintage	VF20	XF40	MS60	MS63	MS65
1981	30,000	PF65 22.00				

KM# 4 25 PENCE (Crown)

28.28 g., 0.925 Silver 0.841 oz. ASW, 38.5 mm. **Subject:** International Year of the Scout **Obv:** Bust of Queen Elizabeth II right **Rev:** Sir. Robert S. S. Baden-Powell, 3/4 left

Date	Mintage	VF20	XF40	MS60	MS63	MS65
ND-1983	10,000	—	—	15.00	17.00	22.00
ND-1983	10,000	PF63 18.00	PF65 22.00			

KM# 6 50 PENCE

Copper-Nickel, 38.5 mm. **Subject:** Royal Visit of Prince Andrew **Obv:** Young bust of Queen Elizabeth II, right **Rev:** Bust of Prince Andrew left

Date	Mintage	VF20	XF40	MS60	MS63	MS65
1984	125,000	—	—	1.00	1.50	2.50

KM# 6a 50 PENCE

28.28 g., 0.925 Silver 0.841 oz. ASW, 38.5 mm. **Subject:** Royal Visit of Prince Andrew **Obv:** Bust of young Queen Elizabeth II right **Rev:** Bust of Prince Andrew left

Date	Mintage	VF20	XF40	MS60	MS63	MS65
1984	5,000	PF65 22.00				

KM# 7 50 PENCE

Copper-Nickel, 38.5 mm. **Obv:** Bust of crowned Queen Elizabeth II, right **Rev:** Queen Mother fishing with waders and hat

Date	Mintage	VF20	XF40	MS60	MS63	MS65
1995	—	—	—	1.50	2.50	4.00

KM# 7a 50 PENCE

28.28 g., 0.925 Silver 0.841 oz. ASW, 38.5 mm. **Obv:** Crowned bust of Queen Elizabeth II right **Rev:** Queen Mother fishing in waders and hat

Date	Mintage	VF20	XF40	MS60	MS63	MS65
1995	—	PF63 18.00	PF65 22.00			

KM# 7b 50 PENCE

47.54 g., 0.916 Gold 1.4001 oz. AGW **Obv:** Crowned bust of Queen Elizabeth II right **Rev:** Queen Mother fishing with waders and hat

Date	Mintage	VF20	XF40	MS60	MS63	MS65
1995	150	PF65 2,000				

KM# 8 50 PENCE

Copper-Nickel, 38.5 mm. **Subject:** 70th Birthday - Queen Elizabeth II **Obv:** Crowned bust of Queen Elizabeth II, right **Rev:** 2 soldiers with standard

Date	Mintage	VF20	XF40	MS60	MS63	MS65
1996	—	—	—	2.00	4.00	6.00

KM# 8a 50 PENCE

28.28 g., 0.925 Silver 0.841 oz. ASW, 38.5 mm. **Subject:** 70th Birthday - Queen Elizabeth II **Obv:** Crowned bust of Queen Elizabeth II right **Rev:** 2 soldiers holding the standard

Date	Mintage	VF20	XF40	MS60	MS63	MS65
1996	5,000	PF65 28.00				

KM# 11 50 PENCE
Copper-Nickel, 38.5 mm. **Series:** Montreal Olympics **Subject:** Queen's portrait **Obv:** Bust of Queen Elizabeth II right **Rev:** Royal couple behind horse and rider jumping British arms

Date	Mintage	VF20	XF40	MS60	MS63	MS65
1997	—	—	—	1.50	2.50	4.00

KM# 9 50 PENCE
Copper-Nickel, 38.5 mm. **Subject:** World Wildlife Fund - Conserving Nature **Obv:** Crowned bust of Queen Elizabeth I, right **Rev:** Frigate birds

Date	Mintage	VF20	XF40	MS60	MS63	MS65
1998	—	—	—	2.00	4.00	6.00

KM# 9a 50 PENCE
28.28 g., 0.925 Silver 0.841 oz. ASW, 38.5 mm. **Subject:** World Wildlife Fund - Conserving Nature **Obv:** Crowned bust of Queen Elizabeth II right **Rev:** Frigate birds

Date	Mintage	VF20	XF40	MS60	MS63	MS65
1998	—	PF65 30.00				

KM# 10 50 PENCE
Copper-Nickel **Subject:** World Wildlife Fund - Conserving Nature **Obv:** Crowned bust of Queen Elizabeth II, right **Rev:** White-tailed tropicbird

Date	Mintage	VF20	XF40	MS60	MS63	MS65
1998	—	—	—	2.00	4.00	6.00

KM# 10a 50 PENCE
28.28 g., 0.925 Silver 0.841 oz. ASW **Subject:** World Wildlife Fund - Conserving Nature **Obv:** Crowned bust of Queen Elizabeth II right **Rev:** Long-tailed birds

Date	Mintage	VF20	XF40	MS60	MS63	MS65
1998	—	PF65 32.00				

KM# 12 50 PENCE
28.76 g., Copper-Nickel, 38.5 mm. **Subject:** 100th Birthday of the Queen Mother **Obv:** Crowned bust of Queen Elizabeth II, right **Rev:** Queen Mother's bust 3/4 facing half left **Edge:** Reeded

Date	Mintage	VF20	XF40	MS60	MS63	MS65
ND-2000	—	—	—	1.50	2.50	4.00

KM# 12a 50 PENCE
28.28 g., 0.925 Silver 0.841 oz. ASW, 38.6 mm. **Subject:** Queen Mother's 100th Birthday **Obv:** Crowned bust of Queen Elizabeth II right **Rev:** Queen Mother above dates 1900-2000 **Edge:** Reeded

Date	Mintage	VF20	XF40	MS60	MS63	MS65
ND(2000)	10,000	PF63 18.00	PF65 22.00			

KM# 12b 50 PENCE
47.54 g., 0.9166 Gold 1.401 oz. AGW, 38.6 mm. **Subject:** Queen Mother's 100th Birthday **Obv:** Crowned bust of Queen Elizabeth II, right **Rev:** Queen Mother above dates 1900-2000 **Edge:** Reeded

Date	Mintage	VF20	XF40	MS60	MS63	MS65
ND(2000)	100	PF65 2,100				

KM# 5 2 POUNDS
15.98 g., 0.917 Gold 0.4711 oz. AGW **Series:** International Year of the Scout **Rev:** Boy Scout

Date	Mintage	VF20	XF40	MS60	MS63	MS65
1983	2,000	—	—	—	—	825
1983	2,000	PF65 850				

PIEDFORT

KM#	Date	Mintage	Identification	Mkt Val
P1	1995	500	50 Pence. Silver. KM7a.	85.00

AUSTRALIA

The Commonwealth of Australia, the smallest continent in the world, is located south of Indonesia between the Indian and Pacific oceans. It has an area of 2,967,893 sq. mi. (7,686,850 sq. km.) and an estimated population of 18.84 million. Capital: Canberra. Due to its early and sustained isolation, Australia is the habitat of such curious and unique fauna as the kangaroo, koala, platypus, wombat, echidna and frilled-necked lizard. The continent possesses extensive mineral deposits, the most important of which are iron ore, coal, gold, silver, nickel, uranium, lead and zinc. Raising livestock, mining and manufacturing are the principal industries. Chief exports are wool, meat, wheat, iron ore, coal and nonferrous metals.

The first Caucasians to see Australia probably were Portuguese and Spanish navigators of the late 16th century. In 1770, Captain James Cook explored the east coast and annexed it for Great Britain. New South Wales was founded as a penal colony, following the loss of British North America, by Captain Arthur Phillip on January 26, 1788, a date now celebrated as Australia Day. Dates of creation of the six colonies that now comprise the states of the Australian Commonwealth are: New South Wales, 1823; Tasmania, 1825; Western Australia, 1838; South Australia, 1842; Victoria, 1851; Queensland, 1859. The British Parliament approved a constitution providing for the federation of the colonies in 1900. The Commonwealth of Australia came into being in 1901. Australia passed the Statute of Westminster Adoption Act on October 9, 1942, which officially established Australia's complete autonomy in external and internal affairs, thereby formalizing a situation that had existed for years. Australia is a member of the Commonwealth of Nations. Elizabeth II is Head of State as Queen of Australia.

Australia's currency system was changed from Pounds-Shillings-Pence to a decimal system of Dollars and Cents on Feb. 14, 1966.

RULER
British until 1942

MINT MARKS

Abbr.	Mint	Marks
A	Adelaide	-
(b)	Bombay	I below bust; dots before and after HALF PENNY, 1942-43
(b)	Bombay	I below bust dots before and after PENNY, 1942-43
B	Brisbane	-
(c)	Calcutta	I above date, 1916-18
(c)	Canberra	None, 1966 to date
C	Canberra	-
D	Denver	D above date 1/-& 2/-, below date on 3d
D	Denver	D below date on 6d
H	Heaton	H below date on silver coins, 1914-15
H	Heaton	H above date on bronze coins
(L)	London	1910-1915 (no marks), 1966
M	Melbourne	M below date on silver coins, 1916-20
M	Melbourne	M above date on the ground on gold coins w/St. George
M	Melbourne	-
(m)	Melbourne	Dot below scroll on penny, 1919-20
(m)	Melbourne	Two dots; below lower scroll and above upper, 1919-20
(m)	Melbourne	None, 1921-1964, 1966
P	Perth	P above date on the ground on gold coins w/St. George
(p)	Perth	Dot between KG (designer's initials), 1940-41
(p)	Perth	Dot after PENNY, 1941-51, 1954-64
(p)	Perth	Dot after AUSTRALIA, 1952-53
(p)	Perth	Dot before SHILLING, 1946
(p)	Perth	None, 1922 penny, 1966
P	Perth	Nuggets, 1986
PL	London	PL after PENNY in 1951
PL	London	PL on bottom folds of ribbon, 1951 threepence
PL	London	PL above date on sixpence
PL		1951
S	San Francisco	S above or below date, 1942-44, mm exists w/ and w/o bulbous serifs
S	Sydney	S above date on the ground on gold coins w/St. George
S	Sydney	-
(sy)	Sydney	Dot above bottom scroll on penny 1920
(sy)	Sydney	None, 1919-1926

Mint designations are shown in ( ). Ex. 1978(m).
Mint marks are shown after date. Ex. 1978M.

PRIVY MARKS

(ae) - American Eagle

(aa) - Adelaide Assay

(ba) - Basler Stab

(bg) - Brandenburg Gate

(d) – Ducat

(dp) – Dump

(e) – Emu

(ev) - Edward V

(f) – Fok

(f1) - Rev. 1 Florin, KM#31

(f3) - Rev. 1 Florin, KM#33

(f7) - Rev. 1 Florin, KM#47

(ge) - Golden Eagle

(gv) - George V, small head

(gV) - George V, large head

(h) – Hague

(hd) - Holey Dollar

(j) – Johanna

(jw) - Japanese Royal Wedding

(l) – Luk

(lh) - Liberty Head

(p) – Prospector

(qv) - Queen Victoria

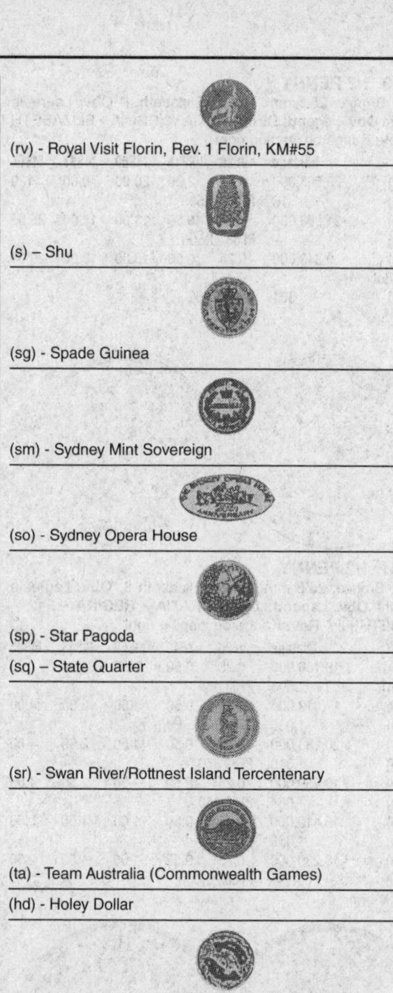

(rv) - Royal Visit Florin, Rev. 1 Florin, KM#55

(s) – Shu

(sg) - Spade Guinea

(sm) - Sydney Mint Sovereign

(so) - Sydney Opera House

(sp) - Star Pagoda

(sq) – State Quarter

(sr) - Swan River/Rottnest Island Tercentenary

(ta) - Team Australia (Commonwealth Games)

(hd) - Holey Dollar

(w) – Whales

(ww) - 50 Years Beyond WWII

MONETARY SYSTEM

Sterling Coinage (Until 1966)
12 Pence = 1 Shilling
2 Shillings = 1 Florin
5 Shillings = 1 Crown
20 Shillings = 1 Pound
1 Sovereign = 1 Pound

Decimal Coinage (Commencing 1966)
100 Cents = 1 Dollar

BRITISH COLONY

TRADE COINAGE

KM# 12 1/2 SOVEREIGN

3.99 g., 0.917 Gold 0.1178 oz. AGW, 19 mm. **Ruler:** Victoria **Obv:** Veiled head left **Rev:** St. George slaying dragon, mint mark above date

Date	Mintage	VF20	XF40	MS60	MS63	MS65
1901 M	—	**PF60** 77,000				
1901 P	—	**PF60** 104,500				

Note: Imperfect proofs worth substantially less.

KM# 13 SOVEREIGN

7.99 g., 0.917 Gold 0.2355 oz. AGW, 21 mm. **Ruler:** Victoria **Obv:** Older veiled head left **Rev:** St. George slaying the dragon

Date	Mintage	VF20	XF40	MS60	MS63	MS65
1901 S	3,012,000	—	335	500	800	—
1901 M	3,987,000	—	335	500	800	—
1901 M	—	**PF63** 60,500				
1901 P	2,889,000	—	335	500	1,000	—
1901 P	—	**PF63** 71,500				

COMMONWEALTH OF AUSTRALIA

STERLING COINAGE

KM# 22 1/2 PENNY

5.60 g., Bronze, 25.5 mm. **Ruler:** George V **Obv:** Crowned bust left **Rev:** Denomination within circle **Edge:** Plain

Date	Mintage	VF20	XF40	MS60	MS63	MS65
1911 (L)	2,832,000	3.50	16.00	160	280	420
1911 (L)	—	**PF63** 22,500				
1912 H	2,400,000	4.50	19.00	210	400	600
1912 H	—	**PF63** 22,500				
1913 (L) Wide date	2,160,000	5.00	35.00	455	720	1,100
1913 (L) Narrow date	Inc. above	4.50	30.00	420	720	1,100
1914 (L)	1,440,000	14.00	60.00	630	1,200	1,800
1914 H	1,200,000	14.00	60.00	560	960	1,450
1915 H	720,000	65.00	450	3,500	—	—
1916 (c) I	3,600,000	1.50	16.00	140	280	420
1916 (c) I	—	**PF63** 22,500				
1917 (c) I	5,760,000	1.50	15.00	140	280	420
1918 (c) I	1,440,000	20.00	200	2,100	—	—
1919 (sy)	3,326,000	1.00	14.00	150	240	360
1919 (sy)	—	**PF63** 25,000				
1920 (sy)	4,114,000	5.00	27.00	245	400	600
1920 (m)	—	**PF63** 30,000				
1921 (sy)	5,280,000	1.00	15.00	150	240	360
1922 (sy)	6,924,000	1.00	15.00	160	280	420
1923 (m)	Est. 1113000	2,300	9,000	31,500	—	—

Note: Dies dated 1922 were used for the majority of the calendar year 1923, leaving only a small portion of this mintage figure as 1923 dated coins.

Date	Mintage	VF20	XF40	MS60	MS63	MS65
1923 (m) Proof; Rare	—	—	—	—	—	—

Note: Noble Numismatics sale No. 62, 11-99, nearly FDC proof realized $56,745.

Date	Mintage	VF20	XF40	MS60	MS63	MS65
1924 (m)	682,000	11.00	65.00	700	1,200	1,800
1924 (m)	—	**PF63** 30,000				
1925 (m)	1,147,000	5.00	27.00	560	—	—
1925 (m)	—	**PF63** 45,000				
1926 (m & sy)	4,139,000	1.00	15.00	280	640	960
1926 (m)	—	**PF63** 22,500				
1927 (m)	3,072,000	1.00	14.00	160	280	420
1927 (m)	50	**PF63** 23,000				
1928 (m)	2,318,000	4.50	23.00	385	800	1,200
1928 (m)	—	**PF63** 23,000				
1929 (m)	2,635,000	1.00	14.00	175	360	550
1929 (m)	—	**PF63** 22,500				
1930 (m)	638,000	5.50	30.00	650	1,000	1,500
1930 (m)	—	**PF63** 60,000				
1931 (m)	370,000	5.50	30.00	850	1,285	1,950
1931 (m)	—	**PF63** 24,000				
1932 (m)	2,554,000	1.00	9.00	120	240	360
1932 (m)	—	**PF63** 24,000				
1933 (m)	4,608,000	1.00	8.00	85.00	160	240
1933 (m)	—	**PF63** 23,000				
1934 (m)	3,816,000	1.00	10.00	100	180	270
1934 (m)	100	**PF63** 27,500				
1935 (m)	2,916,000	1.00	10.00	100	180	270
1935 (m)	100	**PF63** 16,500				
1936 (m)	2,562,000	1.00	25.00	85.00	115	175
1936 (m)	—	**PF63** 22,500				

KM# 30 1/2 PENNY

Bronze, 25.5 mm. **Ruler:** George V **Obv:** India 1/4 Anna, KM#511 **Rev:** Value in inner circle **Note:** Mule.

Date	Mintage	VF20	XF40	MS60	MS63	MS65
1916 (c) I	Est. 10	85,000	—	—	—	—

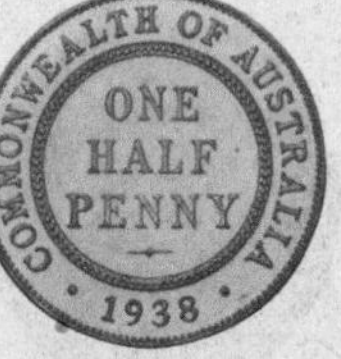

KM# 35 1/2 PENNY

5.60 g., Bronze, 25.5 mm. **Ruler:** George VI **Obv:** Head left

Rev: Value in inner circle **Edge:** Plain

Date	Mintage	VF20	XF40	MS60	MS63	MS65
1938 (m)	3,014,000	1.00	3.00	45.00	80.00	120
1938 (m)	250	PF63 10,000				
1939 (m)	4,382,000	1.00	3.50	85.00	140	210
1939 (m)	—	PF63 20,000				

KM# 41 1/2 PENNY

5.70 g., Bronze, 25.5 mm. **Ruler:** George VI **Obv:** Head left **Rev:** Kangaroo leaping right above value

Date	Mintage	VF20	XF40	MS60	MS63	MS65
1939 (m)	504,000	15.00	90.00	725	1,450	2,200
1939 (m)	100	PF63 16,500				
1940 (m)	2,294,000	1.00	7.50	120	180	270
1940 (m)	—	PF63 23,000				
1941 (m)	5,011,000	0.75	4.50	60.00	100	150
1941 (m)	—	PF63 23,000				
1942 (m)	720,000	4.00	22.00	160	320	480
1942 (m)	—	PF63 16,500				
1942 (p)	4,334,000	0.50	6.50	85.00	140	210
1942 (p)	—	PF63 16,000				
1942 (b) I Wide date	6,000,000	0.50	3.50	35.00	60.00	90.00
1942 (b) I Narrow date	Inc. above	0.50	3.50	35.00	60.00	90.00
1942 (b) I	—	PF63 16,000				
1943 (m)	33,989,000	0.25	2.50	16.00	28.00	42.00
1943 (p)	—	PF63 12,000				
1943 (b) I	6,000,000	0.30	3.00	28.00	45.00	70.00
1943 (b) I	—	PF63 16,000				
1944 (m)	720,000	4.50	35.00	175	400	600
1945 (p)	3,033,000	2.50	16.00	85.00	160	240
1945 (p)	—	PF63 17,500				
1945 (p) Without dot	Inc. above	3.00	16.00	85.00	160	240
1946 (p)	13,747,000	0.25	2.50	18.00	32.00	48.00
1946 (p)	—	PF63 17,500				
1947 (p)	9,293,000	0.25	3.00	20.00	40.00	60.00
1947 (p)	—	PF63 18,000				
1948 (m)	4,608,000	0.50	4.00	28.00	45.00	70.00
1948 (m)	—	PF63 18,000				
1948 (p)	25,553,000	0.25	2.50	18.00	32.00	48.00
1948 (p)	—	PF63 17,500				

KM# 42 1/2 PENNY

5.60 g., Bronze, 25.5 mm. **Ruler:** George VI **Obv:** Head left **Obv. Legend:** IND: IMP: dropped **Rev:** Kangaroo leaping right

Date	Mintage	VF20	XF40	MS60	MS63	MS65
1949 (m)	—	PF63 21,000				
Note: Some consider this a pattern						
1949 (p)	22,310,000	0.25	25.00	18.00	28.00	42.00
1949 (p)	—	PF63 17,500				
1950 (p)	12,014,000	0.25	2.50	32.00	45.00	70.00
1950 (p)	—	PF63 17,500				
1951 (p) With dot	—	0.25	2.50	18.00	28.00	42.00
1951 (p) With dot, Proof	—	PF63 18,000				
1951 (p) Without dot	29,422,000	0.50	4.00	20.00	35.00	55.00
1951 (p) Without dot; Proof	—	PF63 18,000				
1951 PL	17,040,000	0.25	0.75	6.00	10.00	15.00
Note: 5,040,000 struck at the Birmingham Mint.						
1951 PL	—	PF63 11,000				
1952 (p)	1,832,000	1.50	5.00	45.00	100	150
1952 (p)	—	PF63 11,500				

KM# 49 1/2 PENNY

5.67 g., Bronze, 25.5 mm. **Ruler:** Elizabeth II **Obv:** Laureate bust right **Obv. Legend:** DEI • GRATIA • REGINA + ELIZABETH • II • **Rev:** Kangaroo leaping right

Date	Mintage	VF20	XF40	MS60	MS63	MS65
1953 (p)	23,967,000	0.25	2.00	20.00	70.00	120
1953 (p)	16	PF63 11,500				
1954 (p)	21,963,000	0.25	0.50	13.00	18.00	25.00
1954 (p)	—	PF63 11,500				
1955 (p) Without dot	9,343,000	0.25	0.50	13.00	18.00	25.00
1955 (p) Without dot; Proof	301	PF63 6,000				

KM# 61 1/2 PENNY

5.90 g., Bronze, 25.5 mm. **Ruler:** Elizabeth II **Obv:** Laureate bust right **Obv. Legend:** DEI • GRATIA • REGINA • F:D: + ELIZABETH • II • **Rev:** Kangaroo leaping right

Date	Mintage	VF20	XF40	MS60	MS63	MS65
1959 (m)	10,166,000	0.25	0.50	2.00	4.00	7.00
1959 (m)	1,506	PF63 450				
1960 (p)	17,812,000	0.25	0.50	1.50	2.50	4.00
1960 (p)	1,030	PF63 350				
1961 (p)	20,183,000	0.25	0.50	1.50	2.50	4.00
1961 (p)	1,040	PF63 350				
1962 (p)	10,259,000	0.25	0.50	1.50	2.50	4.00
1962 (p)	1,064	PF63 350				
1963 (p)	16,410,000	0.25	0.50	1.00	1.50	2.50
1963 (p)	1,060	PF63 350				
1964 (p)	18,230,000	0.25	0.50	1.00	1.50	2.50
1964 (p) Proof; 1 known	—	PF63 25,000				

KM# 23 PENNY

9.40 g., Bronze, 30.8 mm. **Ruler:** George V **Obv:** Crowned bust left **Obv. Legend:** GEORGIVS V D.G. BRITT: OMN: REX F.D: IND: IMP **Rev:** Value in inner circle **Edge:** Plain

Date	Mintage	VF20	XF40	MS60	MS63	MS65
1911 (L)	3,768,000	4.00	40.00	280	5,500	8,500
1911 (L)	—	PF63 31,500				
1912 H	3,600,000	4.50	25.00	280	520	785
1912 H	—	PF63 31,500				
1913 (L) Narrow date	2,520,000	5.00	50.00	770	1,450	2,200
1913 (L) Wide date	Inc. above	5.00	50.00	770	1,450	2,200
1914 (L)	720,000	12.50	175	1,050	2,000	3,000
1915 (L)	960,000	10.00	200	1,250	2,240	3,350
1915 H	1,320,000	8.50	150	1,050	1,750	2,650
1916 (c) I	3,324,000	1.50	20.00	210	560	850
1916 (c) I	—	PF63 55,000				
1917 (c) I	6,240,000	1.50	22.00	175	450	650
1918 (c) I	1,200,000	10.00	225	1,450	2,100	3,150
1919 (m)	5,810,000	1.50	23.00	160	480	720
Note: Without dots						
1919 (m)	Inc. above	1.50	23.00	160	480	720
Note: Dot below bottom scroll						
1919 (m)	—	125	800	2,100	3,600	5,500
Note: Dots below bottom scroll and above upper						
1919 (m)	—	PF63 56,500				
1920 (m & sy)	9,041,000	125	700	4,550	9,600	14,500
Note: Without dots						
1920 (m)	Inc. above	10.00	125	980	1,520	2,280
Note: Dot below bottom scroll						
1920 (m)	—	PF63 52,500				
1920 (sy)	Inc. above	10.00	125	980	1,520	2,280
Note: Dot above bottom scroll						
1920	Inc. above	125	700	3,500	—	—
Note: Dots below bottom scroll and above upper						
1921 (m & sy)	7,438,000	6.00	40.00	490	960	1,450
1922 (m & p)	12,697,000	6.00	50.00	560	1,050	1,575
1923 (m)	5,654,000	6.00	50.00	560	1,050	1,575
1923 (m)	—	PF63 45,000				
1924 (m & sy)	4,656,000	5.00	35.00	420	800	1,200
1924 (m)	—	PF63 30,000				
1925 (m)	1,639,000	200	700	5,250	8,750	13,250
1925 (m)	—	PF63 150,000				
1926 (m & sy)	1,859,000	8.00	150	945	1,675	2,550
1926 (m)	—	PF63 29,000				
1927 (m)	4,922,000	2.25	35.00	210	400	600
1927 (m)	50	PF63 35,000				
1928 (m)	3,038,000	3.00	50.00	700	1,350	2,100
1928 (m)	—	PF63 28,000				
1929 (m)	2,599,000	3.00	55.00	825	1,675	2,550
1929 (m)	—	PF63 28,000				
1930 (m) Proof; Rare	Est. 6	PF63 450,000				
Note: Noble Numismatics sale No. 52, 7-97, nearly FDC proof realized $126,500. Noble Numismatics sale No. 62, 11-99, FDC proof realized $162,665.						
1930 (m)	Est. 3000	15,000	35,000	57,500	100,000	150,000
1931 (m) Normal date alignment	494,000	7.50	125	1,000	2,000	3,000
1931 (m) Fallen 1 in date	Inc. above	7.50	125	1,000	2,000	3,000
1931 (m)	—	PF63 55,000				
1932 (m)	2,117,000	3.00	60.00	245	525	785
1933/2 (m)	5,818,000	30.00	200	1,150	1,950	2,950
1933 (m)	Inc. above	1.50	24.00	120	200	300
1933 (m)	—	PF63 35,000				
1934 (m)	5,808,000	1.50	24.00	120	200	300
1934 (m)	100	PF63 23,000				
1935 (m)	3,725,000	1.50	24.00	125	240	360
1935 (m)	100	PF63 12,000				
1936 (m)	9,890,000	1.00	15.00	85.00	180	270
1936 (m)	—	PF63 30,000				

KM# 36 PENNY

9.40 g., Bronze, 30.8 mm. **Ruler:** George VI **Obv:** Head left **Obv. Legend:** GEORGIVS VI D:G:BR: OMN: REX F.D: IND: IMP **Rev:** Kangaroo leaping left **Edge:** Plain

Date	Mintage	VF20	XF40	MS60	MS63	MS65
1938 (m)	5,552,000	0.75	8.00	38.00	80.00	120
1938 (m)	250	PF63 26,000				
1939 (m)	6,240,000	0.75	8.00	45.00	100	150
1939 (m)	—	PF63 22,500				
1940 (m)	4,075,000	1.50	20.00	120	240	360
1940 (p) K.G.	1,114,000	7.00	75.00	550	1,280	1,950
1941 (m)	1,588,000	2.00	18.00	85.00	200	300
1941 (p) K.G.	12,794,000	5.00	60.00	280	480	725
1941 (p)	—	PF63 22,500				
1941 (p)	Inc. above	0.75	8.50	42.00	100	150
1941 (p) K.G. high dot after Y	Inc. above	10.00	125	950	—	—
1942 (p)	12,245,000	0.50	1.00	30.00	80.00	120
1942 (b) I	9,000,000	1.00	8.00	28.00	75.00	115
1942 (b) Without I	Inc. above	7.00	50.00	285	—	—
1942 (b)	—	PF63 14,500				
1943 (m)	11,112,000	2.00	15.00	42.00	80.00	120
1943 (p)	33,086,000	2.00	14.00	42.00	80.00	120
1943 (p)	—	PF63 19,000				
1943 (b) I	9,000,000	0.50	8.00	28.00	60.00	90.00
Note: Small and large denticle varieties exist.						
1943 (b) I Without I	Inc. above	4.00	25.00	110	—	—
1943 (b)	—	PF63 17,500				
1944 (m)	2,112,000	3.00	25.00	120	280	420
1944 (p)	27,830,000	0.50	7.00	28.00	55.00	85.00
1944 (p)	—	PF63 19,000				
1945 (p)	15,173,000	0.75	9.00	45.00	100	150
Note: With and without a large dot after the KG.						
1945 (p)	—	PF63 19,000				
1945 (b) I Rare	6	—	—	—	—	—
1945 (m) Rare	—	PF63 150,000				
Note: Considered by many to be a pattern						
1946 (m)	240,000	75.00	200	975	1,750	2,650
1947 (m)	6,864,000	0.50	4.50	20.00	35.00	55.00
1947 (p)	4,490,000	2.00	35.00	210	480	720
1947 (p)	—	PF63 19,000				
1948 (m)	26,616,000	0.50	3.50	17.50	28.00	42.00
1948 (p)	1,534,000	4.00	60.00	315	800	1,200
1948 (p)	—	PF63 22,500				

KM# 43 PENNY
9.41 g., Bronze, 31 mm. **Ruler:** George VI **Obv:** Head left **Obv. Legend:** IND: IMP. dropped **Rev:** Kangaroo leaping left **Edge:** Plain

Date	Mintage	VF20	XF40	MS60	MS63	MS65
1949 (m)	27,065,000	0.50	3.00	17.50	32.00	48.00
1949 (m)	—	PF63 24,000				
1950 (m)	36,359,000	0.50	2.50	14.00	32.00	48.00
1950 (m)	—	PF63 24,000				
1950 (p)	21,488,000	0.75	11.50	42.00	80.00	120
1950 (p)	—	PF63 24,000				
1951 (m)	21,240,000	0.50	1.00	12.00	24.00	36.00
1951 (p)	12,888,000	0.75	10.00	38.00	80.00	120
1951 (p)	—	PF63 22,500				
1951 PL	18,000,000	0.50	1.00	7.00	15.00	22.00
1951 PL	—	PF63 22,000				
1952 (m)	12,408,000	0.50	1.00	9.00	17.00	25.00
1952 (m)	—	PF63 18,000				
1952 (p)	45,514,000	0.50	1.00	7.00	15.00	22.00
Note: Two varieties of the 2 in the date.						
1952 (p)	—	PF63 18,000				

KM# 50 PENNY
9.44 g., Bronze, 31 mm. **Ruler:** Elizabeth II **Obv:** Laureate bust, right **Obv. Legend:** DEI • GRATIA • REGINA + ELIZABETH • II • **Rev:** Kangaroo leaping left **Edge:** Plain

Date	Mintage	VF20	XF40	MS60	MS63	MS65
1953 (m)	6,936,000	0.50	3.00	28.00	45.00	62.00
Note: Two varieties to the numeral 5.						
1953 (m)	—	PF63 16,000				
1953 (p)	6,203,000	1.00	3.00	28.00	45.00	62.00
1953 (p)	16	PF63 16,000				

KM# 56 PENNY
9.45 g., Bronze, 30.8 mm. **Ruler:** Elizabeth II **Obv:** Laureate bust right **Obv. Legend:** F:D: added **Rev:** Kangaroo leaping left **Edge:** Plain

Date	Mintage	VF20	XF40	MS60	MS63	MS65
1955 (m)	6,336,000	0.50	2.00	13.00	27.00	38.00
1955 (m)	1,200	PF63 500				
1955 (p)	11,110,000	0.75	2.00	17.00	35.00	50.00
1955 (p)	301	PF63 5,500				
1956 (m)	13,872,000	0.50	1.00	9.00	22.50	32.50
1956 (m)	1,500	PF63 500				
1956 (p)	12,121,000	0.50	1.00	9.00	22.50	32.50
1956 (p)	417	PF63 4,000				
1957 (p)	15,978,000	0.50	1.00	6.00	11.50	16.50
1957 (p)	1,112	PF63 1,000				
1958 (m)	10,012,000	0.50	1.00	6.00	11.50	16.50
1958 (m)	1,506	PF63 500				
1958 (p)	14,428,000	0.50	1.00	7.00	11.50	16.50
1958 (p)	1,028	PF63 700				
1959 (m)	1,617,000	1.50	8.00	55.00	115	155
1959 (m)	1,506	PF63 700				
1959 (p)	14,428,000	0.50	1.00	3.00	11.50	16.50
1959 (p)	1,030	PF63 700				
1960 (p)	20,515,000	0.50	1.00	2.00	8.00	11.50
1960 (p)	1,030	PF63 600				
1961 (p)	30,607,000	0.50	0.75	1.00	7.00	10.00
1961 (p)	1,040	PF63 600				
1962 (p)	34,851,000	0.50	0.75	1.00	6.00	9.00
1962 (p)	1,064	PF63 550				

Date	Mintage	VF20	XF40	MS60	MS63	MS65
1963 (p)	10,258,000	0.50	0.75	1.00	6.00	9.00
1963 (p)	1,100	PF63 600				
1964 (m)	49,130,000	0.50	0.75	1.00	6.00	9.00
1964 (p)	54,590,000	0.50	0.75	1.00	6.00	9.00
1964 (p)	—	PF63 19,000				
Proof; 1 known						

KM# 18 THREEPENCE
1.41 g., 0.925 Silver 0.0419 oz. ASW, 16 mm. **Ruler:** Edward VII **Obv:** Bust right **Rev:** Arms **Edge:** Plain

Date	Mintage	VF20	XF40	MS60	MS63	MS65
1910 (L)	4,000,000	5.00	13.50	45.00	80.00	120
1910 (L)	—	PF63 11,500				

KM# 24 THREEPENCE
1.32 g., 0.925 Silver 0.0393 oz. ASW, 16.1 mm. **Ruler:** George V **Obv:** Crowned bust left **Rev:** Arms **Edge:** Plain

Date	Mintage	VF20	XF40	MS60	MS63	MS65
1911 (L)	2,000,000	12.00	55.00	200	400	600
1911 (L)	—	PF63 22,000				
1911 (L)	—	PF63 67,500				
Note: Reeded edge						
1912 (L)	2,400,000	30.00	70.00	500	1,150	1,700
1914 (L)	1,600,000	35.00	160	775	1,750	2,650
1915 (L)	800,000	65.00	245	1,325	2,800	4,200
1916 M	25	PF63 12,000				
1916 M	1,913,000	12.00	70.00	450	950	1,450
1917 M	3,808,000	5.00	20.00	125	320	480
(1917) M	—	PF63 2,250				
1918 M	3,119,000	5.00	24.00	160	280	420
1918 M	—	PF63 52,500				
1919 M	3,201,000	5.00	35.00	210	450	675
1919 M	—	PF63 20,500				
1920 M	4,196,000	20.00	85.00	600	1,150	1,700
1920 M	—	PF63 21,000				
1921 (m)	Inc. above	25.00	125	575	1,000	1,500
1921 M	7,378,000	3.00	28.00	125	240	375
1921 M	—	PF63 21,000				
1922 (m)	5,531,000	5.00	35.00	210	450	675
1922/1 (m)	900	20,000	35,000	—	—	—
1922 (m)	—	PF63 21,000				
1923 (m)	815,000	35.00	125	825	1,750	2,750
1924 (m & sy)	2,013,999	18.50	100	700	1,600	2,400
1924 (m)	—	PF63 16,500				
1925 (m & sy)	4,347,000	2.75	32.00	160	360	550
1925 (m)	—	PF63 19,000				
1926 (m & sy)	6,158,000	2.75	19.50	120	240	365
1926 (m)	—	PF63 17,500				
1927 (m)	6,720,000	2.75	17.50	100	180	275
1927 (m)	50	PF63 17,500				
1928 (m)	5,000,000	2.75	17.50	100	240	365
1928 (m)	—	PF63 17,500				
1934/3 (m)	1,616,000	65.00	215	985	2,150	3,250
1934 (m)	100	PF63 9,000				
1934 (m)	Inc. above	2.75	22.00	120	200	300
1935 (m)	—	PF63 9,000				
1935 (m)	2,800,000	2.75	18.50	140	280	425
1936 (m)	3,600,000	1.50	8.50	65.00	140	215
1936 (m)	—	PF63 9,000				

KM# 37 THREEPENCE
1.41 g., 0.925 Silver 0.0419 oz. ASW, 16 mm. **Ruler:** George VI **Obv:** Head left **Rev:** Three wheat stalks divide date

Date	Mintage	VF20	XF40	MS60	MS63	MS65
1938 (m)	4,560,000	1.50	5.00	25.00	45.00	70.00
1938 (m)	250	PF63 7,500				
1939 (m)	3,856,000	1.50	10.00	42.00	100	150
1939 (m)	—	—	—	—	—	—
Proof						
1940 (m)	3,840,000	1.50	10.00	45.00	120	180
1941 (m)	7,584,000	1.50	10.00	28.00	60.00	90.00
1942 (m)	528,000	22.00	155	920	2,850	4,250
1942 D	16,000,000	0.80	1.50	8.50	14.50	22.00
1942 S	8,000,000	0.80	1.50	8.50	14.50	22.00
1943 (m)	24,912,000	0.80	1.50	8.50	14.50	22.00
1943 D	16,000,000	0.80	1.50	8.50	14.50	22.00
1943 S	8,000,000	0.80	1.50	8.50	14.50	22.00
1944 S	32,000,000	—	0.80	5.00	7.00	10.00
Note: Two varieties to the "S" mintmark.						

KM# 37a THREEPENCE
1.41 g., 0.500 Silver 0.0227 oz. ASW, 16 mm. **Ruler:** George VI **Obv:** Head left **Rev:** 3 wheat stalks divide date

Date	Mintage	VF20	XF40	MS60	MS63	MS65
1947 (m)	4,176,000	1.50	7.00	45.00	120	180
1948 (m)	26,208,000	0.50	0.75	6.50	13.50	20.00

KM# 44 THREEPENCE
1.41 g., 0.500 Silver 0.0227 oz. ASW, 16 mm. **Ruler:** George VI **Obv:** Head left **Obv. Legend:** IND: IMP. dropped **Rev:** Three wheat stalks divide date

Date	Mintage	VF20	XF40	MS60	MS63	MS65
1949 (m)	26,400,000	0.50	0.75	5.00	16.00	25.00
1949 (m)	—	—	—	—	—	—
Proof						
1950 (m)	35,456,000	0.50	0.70	5.25	13.60	20.00
1951 (m)	15,856,000	0.75	1.50	10.00	22.50	35.00
1951 PL	40,000,000	0.50	0.75	3.00	7.50	12.00
1951 PL	—	PF63 11,500				
1952 (m)	21,560,000	0.50	1.50	7.00	15.00	22.00

KM# 51 THREEPENCE
1.41 g., 0.500 Silver 0.0227 oz. ASW, 16 mm. **Ruler:** Elizabeth II **Obv:** Laureate bust, right **Rev:** Three wheat stalks divide date **Edge:** Plain

Date	Mintage	VF20	XF40	MS60	MS63	MS65
1953 (m)	7,664,000	1.50	3.50	20.00	48.00	75.00
1953 (m)	—	PF63 11,500				
1954 (m)	2,672,000	1.75	3.50	28.00	55.00	85.00
1954 (m)	—	PF63 11,500				

KM# 57 THREEPENCE
1.41 g., 0.500 Silver 0.0227 oz. ASW, 16 mm. **Ruler:** Elizabeth II **Obv:** Laureate bust right **Obv. Legend:** F:D: added **Rev:** Three wheat stalks divide date **Edge:** Plain

Date	Mintage	VF20	XF40	MS60	MS63	MS65
1955 (m)	27,088,000	—	0.50	5.00	12.00	18.00
1955 (m)	1,040	PF63 150				
1956 (m)	14,088,000	—	0.50	5.00	12.00	18.00
1956 (m)	1,500	PF63 100				
1957 (m)	26,704,000	—	0.50	3.00	7.00	10.00
1957 (m)	1,256	PF63 100				
1958 (m)	11,248,000	—	0.50	5.00	12.00	18.00
1958 (m)	1,506	PF63 100				
1959 (m)	19,888,000	—	0.50	3.00	7.00	10.00
1959 (m)	1,506	PF63 100				
1960 (m)	19,600,000	—	0.50	1.50	2.75	4.50
1960 (m)	1,509	PF63 100				
1961 (m)	33,840,000	—	0.50	1.50	2.75	4.50
1961 (m)	1,506	PF63 100				
1962 (m)	15,968,000	—	0.50	1.50	2.75	4.50
1962 (m)	2,016	PF63 90.00				
1963 (m)	44,016,000	—	0.50	1.50	2.75	4.50
1963 (m)	5,042	PF63 75.00				
1964 (m)	20,320,000	—	0.50	0.75	2.00	3.00

KM# 19 SIXPENCE
2.83 g., 0.925 Silver 0.0842 oz. ASW, 19.5 mm. **Ruler:** Edward VII **Obv:** Crowned bust right **Rev:** Arms **Edge:** Reeded

Date	Mintage	VF20	XF40	MS60	MS63	MS65
1910 (L)	3,046,000	13.00	40.00	125	400	600
1910 (L)	—	PF63 16,000				

KM# 25 SIXPENCE
2.82 g., 0.925 Silver 0.0839 oz. ASW, 19.3 mm. **Ruler:** George V **Obv:** Crowned bust left **Rev:** Arms **Edge:** Reeded

Date	Mintage	VF20	XF40	MS60	MS63	MS65
1911 (L)	1,000,000	18.00	90.00	490	1,200	1,800
1911 (L)	—	PF63 30,000				
1912 (L)	1,600,000	55.00	270	845	2,000	3,000
1914 (L)	1,800,000	16.50	90.00	490	1,120	1,700
1916 M	1,769,000	67.50	270	1,000	2,200	3,300
1916 M	25	PF63 19,000				
1917 M	1,632,000	32.00	115	385	2,000	3,000
1917 M	—	PF63 30,000				
1918 M	915,000	180	765	2,450	6,400	9,600
1918 M	—	PF63 90,000				
1919 M	1,521,000	36.00	135	800	1,680	2,550
1919 M	—	PF63 30,000				
1920 M	1,476,000	40.00	135	625	1,760	2,650
1920 M	—	PF63 30,000				
1921 (m & sy)	3,795,000	15.00	67.50	315	640	960
1921 (m)	—	PF63 30,000				
1922 (sy)	1,488,000	90.00	400	1,470	2,800	4,200
1922 (sy)	—	PF63 45,000				
1923 (m & sy)	1,458,000	45.00	270	1,050	2,400	3,600
1924 (m & sy)	1,038,000	45.00	270	1,100	2,800	4,200
1924 (m)	—	PF63 25,000				
1925 (m & sy)	3,266,000	12.50	50.00	210	640	960
1925 (m)	—	PF63 22,500				
1926 (m & sy)	3,609,000	16.50	55.00	280	600	900
1926 (m)	—	PF63 22,500				
1927 (m)	3,592,000	6.00	18.00	105	240	360
1927 (m)	50	PF63 22,500				
1928 (m)	2,721,000	13.50	45.00	280	680	1,020
1928 (m)	—	PF63 22,500				
1934 (m)	1,024,000	9.00	55.00	350	680	1,020
1934 (m)	100	PF63 10,000				
1935 (m)	392,000	20.00	115	665	1,520	2,280
1935 (m)	—	PF63 22,500				
1936 (m)	1,800,000	3.75	9.00	100	280	420
1936 (m)	—	PF63 22,500				

KM# 38 SIXPENCE
2.83 g., 0.925 Silver 0.0842 oz. ASW, 19.4 mm. **Ruler:** George VI **Obv:** Head left **Rev:** Arms **Edge:** Reeded

Date	Mintage	VF20	XF40	MS60	MS63	MS65
1938 (m)	2,864,000	1.70	6.50	35.00	68.00	110
1938 (m)	250	PF63 7,000				
1939 (m)	1,600,000	3.75	13.50	125	440	660
1940 (m)	1,600,000	1.70	9.00	65.00	140	210
1941 (m)	2,912,000	1.70	6.00	35.00	68.00	110
1942 (m)	8,968,000	1.70	3.50	25.00	45.00	70.00
1942 D	12,000,000	1.70	3.50	12.50	22.00	35.00
1942 S	4,000,000	1.70	3.50	16.00	28.00	42.00
1943 D	8,000,000	1.70	3.50	11.50	20.00	30.00
1943 S	4,000,000	1.70	3.50	16.00	28.00	42.00
1944 S	4,000,000	1.70	3.50	12.50	22.00	35.00
1945 (m)	10,096,000	1.70	3.50	16.00	28.00	42.00

KM# 38a SIXPENCE
2.83 g., 0.500 Silver 0.0455 oz. ASW, 19.5 mm. **Ruler:** George VI **Obv:** Head left **Rev:** Arms **Edge:** Reeded

Date	Mintage	VF20	XF40	MS60	MS63	MS65
1946 (m)	10,024,000	0.90	3.50	24.50	48.00	72.00
1946 (m)	—	PF63 15,000				
1948 (m)	1,584,000	0.90	3.50	35.00	55.00	85.00

KM# 45 SIXPENCE
2.83 g., 0.500 Silver 0.0455 oz. ASW, 19.5 mm. **Ruler:** George VI **Obv:** Head left **Obv. Legend:** IND: IMP. dropped **Rev:** Arms **Edge:** Reeded

Date	Mintage	VF20	XF40	MS60	MS63	MS65
1950 (m)	10,272,000	0.90	2.75	32.00	52.00	80.00
1951 (m)	13,760,000	0.90	2.75	22.00	42.00	65.00
1951 PL	20,024,000	0.90	2.75	6.50	13.00	20.00
1951 PL	—	PF63 13,500				
1952 (m)	2,112,000	4.50	27.00	175	440	660

KM# 52 SIXPENCE
2.83 g., 0.500 Silver 0.0455 oz. ASW, 19.5 mm. **Ruler:** Elizabeth II **Obv:** Laureate bust right **Rev:** Arms **Edge:** Reeded

Date	Mintage	VF20	XF40	MS60	MS63	MS65
1953 (m)	1,152,000	4.00	25.00	150	180	240
1953 (m)	—	PF63 11,500				
1954 (m)	7,672,000	0.90	4.00	7.00	13.50	18.00
1954 (m)	—	PF63 12,000				

KM# 58 SIXPENCE
2.83 g., 0.500 Silver 0.0455 oz. ASW, 19.4 mm. **Ruler:** Elizabeth II **Obv:** Laureate bust right **Obv. Legend:** F:D: added **Rev:** Arms **Edge:** Reeded

Date	Mintage	VF20	XF40	MS60	MS63	MS65
1955 (m)	14,248,000	0.90	2.50	14.00	22.50	30.00
1955 (m)	1,200	PF63 125				
1956 (m)	7,904,000	2.00	5.00	35.00	90.00	120
1956 (m)	1,500	PF63 125				
1957 (m)	13,752,000	—	0.90	4.00	9.00	12.00
1957 (m)	1,256	PF63 150				
1958 (m)	17,944,000	—	0.90	4.00	9.00	12.00
1958 (m)	1,506	PF63 125				
1959 (m)	11,728,000	—	0.90	6.50	10.00	14.00
1959 (m)	1,506	PF63 125				
1960 (m)	18,592,000	—	0.90	6.50	10.00	14.00
1960 (m)	1,509	PF63 125				
1961 (m)	9,152,000	—	0.90	3.00	5.50	7.50
1961 (m)	1,506	PF63 100				
1962 (m)	44,816,000	—	0.90	2.00	5.50	7.50
1962 (m)	2,016	PF63 100				
1963 (m)	25,056,000	—	0.90	2.00	5.50	7.50
1963 (m)	5,042	PF63 80.00				

KM# 20 SHILLING
5.65 g., 0.925 Silver 0.168 oz. ASW, 23.5 mm. **Ruler:** Edward VII **Obv:** Crowned bust right **Rev:** Arms **Edge:** Reeded

Date	Mintage	VF20	XF40	MS60	MS63	MS65
1910 (L)	2,536,000	26.00	90.00	200	300	—
1910 (L)	—	PF63 35,000				

KM# 26 SHILLING
5.45 g., 0.925 Silver 0.1621 oz. ASW, 24 mm. **Ruler:** George V **Obv:** Crowned bust left **Rev:** Arms **Edge:** Reeded

Date	Mintage	VF20	XF40	MS60	MS63	MS65
1911 (L)	1,700,000	40.00	135	280	1,600	2,400
1911 (L)	—	PF63 55,000				
1912 (L)	1,000,000	58.00	270	2,100	5,200	7,800
1913 (L)	1,200,000	40.00	200	1,900	4,000	6,000
1914 (L)	3,300,000	12.50	58.00	320	840	1,250
1915 (L)	800,000	135	585	3,500	7,200	11,000
1915 H	500,000	180	900	6,000	13,500	20,500
1915 H	—	PF63 85,000				
1916 M	5,141,000	13.50	45.00	210	440	675
1916 M	25	PF63 19,500				
1917 M	5,274,000	6.50	20.00	110	320	485
1918 M	3,761,000	13.50	55.00	215	485	725
1919 M	—	PF63 150,000				
Note: Some consider this to be a pattern.						
1920 M	520,000	36.00	225	910	1,850	2,750
1920 M	—	PF63 90,000				
Note: Some consider this to be a pattern						
1921 (sy) Star	1,641,000	155	725	4,200	9,200	13,800
1921 (m) Star; Proof	—	PF63 60,000				
1922 (m)	2,040,000	32.00	200	840	2,400	3,600
1922 (m)	—	PF63 35,000				
1924 (m & sy)	674,000	65.00	350	2,450	5,200	7,800
1924 (m)	—	PF63 45,000				
1925/3 (m & sy)	1,448,000	7.50	45.00	210	400	600
1925 (m)	—	PF63 35,000				
1926 (m & sy)	2,352,000	7.50	45.00	210	440	660
1926 (m)	—	PF63 35,000				
1927 (m)	1,146,000	32.00	180	495	—	—
1927 (m)	50	PF63 24,000				
1928 (m)	664,000	22.50	155	910	2,800	4,200
1928 (m)	—	PF63 40,000				
1931 (m)	1,000,000	6.50	36.00	175	800	1,200
1931 (m)	—	PF63 29,000				
1933 (m)	220,000	180	950	4,200	8,400	12,600
1933 (m)	—	PF63 75,000				
1934 (m)	480,000	16.00	80.00	320	650	960
1934 (m)	100	PF63 11,000				
1935 (m)	500,000	9.00	45.00	280	600	900
1935 (m)	—	PF63 13,500				
1936 (m)	2,000,000	6.50	16.00	120	150	220
1936 (m)	—	PF63 22,500				

KM# 39 SHILLING
5.65 g., 0.925 Silver 0.168 oz. ASW, 24 mm. **Ruler:** George VI **Obv:** Head left **Rev:** Ram's head left above value and date **Edge:** Reeded

Date	Mintage	VF20	XF40	MS60	MS63	MS65
1938 (m)	1,484,000	6.50	10.00	45.00	85.00	120
1938 (m)	250	PF63 8,000				
1939 (m)	1,520,000	22.50	90.00	140	240	360
1939 (m)	—	PF63 29,000				
1940 (m)	760,000	12.00	40.00	245	480	720
1941 (m)	3,040,000	3.25	7.20	38.00	80.00	120
1942 (m)	1,380,000	3.25	6.50	32.00	65.00	95.00
1942 S	4,000,000	3.25	6.50	20.00	35.00	55.00
1943 (m)	2,720,000	3.25	18.00	95.00	160	245
1943 S	16,000,000	3.25	6.50	10.00	20.00	30.00
1944 (m)	14,576,000	3.25	7.50	42.00	100	150
1944 S	8,000,000	3.25	5.50	14.00	24.00	36.00

KM# 39a SHILLING
5.65 g., 0.500 Silver 0.0908 oz. ASW, 24 mm. **Ruler:** George VI **Obv:** Head left **Rev:** Ram's head left above value **Edge:** Reeded

Date	Mintage	VF20	XF40	MS60	MS63	MS65
1946 (m)	10,072,000	1.80	3.50	20.00	35.00	55.00
1946 (p)	1,316,000	10.00	32.00	125	240	360
1948 (m)	4,131,999	3.50	5.00	20.00	40.00	60.00

KM# 46 SHILLING
5.65 g., 0.500 Silver 0.0908 oz. ASW, 24 mm. **Ruler:** George VI **Obv:** Head left **Obv. Legend:** IND: IMP. dropped **Rev:** Ram's head left above value, date **Edge:** Reeded

Date	Mintage	VF20	XF40	MS60	MS63	MS65
1950 (m)	7,188,000	3.50	5.00	20.00	40.00	60.00
1952 (m)	19,644,000	1.80	3.50	12.00	24.00	35.00

KM# 53 SHILLING
5.65 g., 0.500 Silver 0.0908 oz. ASW, 24 mm. **Ruler:** Elizabeth II **Obv:** Laureate bust right **Rev:** Ram's head left above value, date **Edge:** Reeded

Date	Mintage	VF20	XF40	MS60	MS63	MS65
1953 (m)	12,204,000	1.80	4.00	7.00	15.00	25.00
1953 (m)	—	PF63 11,500				
1954 (m)	16,187,999	1.80	4.00	7.00	15.00	25.00
1954 (m)	—	PF63 12,000				

KM# 59 SHILLING

5.65 g., 0.500 Silver 0.0908 oz. ASW, 24 mm. **Ruler:** Elizabeth II **Obv:** Laureate bust right **Obv. Legend:** F:D: added **Rev:** Ram's head left above value, date **Edge:** Reeded

Date	Mintage	VF20	XF40	MS60	MS63	MS65
1955 (m)	7,492,000	1.80	4.00	20.00	40.00	60.00
1955 (m)	1,200	PF63 150				
1956 (m)	6,064,000	1.80	5.00	30.00	65.00	125
1956 (m)	1,500	PF63 125				
1957 (m)	12,668,000	1.80	3.00	5.00	10.00	17.00
1957 (m)	1,256	PF63 175				
1958 (m)	7,412,000	1.80	3.00	5.00	10.00	17.00
1958 (m)	1,506	PF63 100				
1959 (m)	10,876,000	1.80	3.00	4.00	9.00	15.00
1959 (m)	1,506	PF63 125				
1960 (m)	14,512,000	—	1.80	4.00	8.50	15.00
1960 (m)	1,509	PF63 125				
1961 (m)	31,864,000	—	1.80	3.00	5.00	8.00
1961 (m)	1,506	PF63 125				
1962 (m)	6,592,000	—	1.80	3.00	5.00	10.00
1962 (m)	2,016	PF63 100				
1963 (m)	10,072,000	—	1.80	3.00	5.00	8.00
1963 (m)	5,042	PF63 95.00				

KM# 21 FLORIN

11.31 g., 0.925 Silver 0.3364 oz. ASW, 28.5 mm. **Ruler:** Edward VII **Obv:** Crowned bust right **Rev:** Arms **Edge:** Reeded

Date	Mintage	VF20	XF40	MS60	MS63	MS65
1910 (L)	1,259,000	50.00	250	750	1,500	3,500
1910 (L)	—	PF63 50,000				

KM# 27 FLORIN

11.31 g., 0.925 Silver 0.3364 oz. ASW, 28.5 mm. **Ruler:** George V **Obv:** Crowned bust left **Rev:** Arms **Edge:** Reeded

Date	Mintage	VF20	XF40	MS60	MS63	MS65
1911 (L)	950,000	175	700	2,250	3,750	8,000
1911 (L)	—	PF63 70,000				
1912 (L)	1,000,000	150	650	2,550	4,250	9,000
1913 (L)	1,200,000	175	875	3,300	5,500	11,500
1913 (L)	—	PF63 67,500				
1914 (L)	2,300,000	30.00	250	600	1,000	2,850
1914 H	500,000	225	875	3,300	5,500	11,500
1914 H	—	PF63 90,000				
Note: Noble Numismatics Sale Apr. 2008 Lot 2053 US $112,000						
1915 (L)	500,000	300	1,200	4,500	7,500	13,500
1915 H	750,000	200	550	1,800	3,000	7,000
1915 H	—	PF63 75,000				
1916 M	2,752,000	30.00	225	570	950	2,500
1916 M	25	PF63 22,500				
1917 M	4,305,000	22.00	200	420	700	1,250
1917 M	—	PF63 60,000				
1918 M	2,095,000	25.00	220	510	850	1,750
1918 M	—	PF63 60,000				
1919 M	1,677,000	150	550	1,350	2,250	4,500
1919 M	—	PF63 60,000				
1920 M Star; Proof	—	PF63 150,000				
1921 (m)	1,247,000	125	500	1,680	2,800	6,500
1921 (m)	—	PF63 60,000				
1922 (m)	2,057,999	125	450	1,200	2,000	4,250
1922 (m)	—	PF63 60,000				
1923 (m)	1,038,000	100	300	900	1,500	3,350
1923 (m)	—	PF63 60,000				
1924 (m & sy)	1,582,000	50.00	225	660	1,100	2,200
1924 (m)	—	PF63 67,500				
1925 (m & sy)	2,960,000	23.00	200	600	1,000	2,000
1925 (m)	—	PF63 45,000				
1926 (m & sy)	2,487,000	29.00	325	840	1,400	3,200
1926 (m)	—	PF63 45,000				
1927 (m)	3,420,000	25.00	70.00	225	375	750
1927 (m)	50	PF63 40,000				
1928 (m)	1,962,000	30.00	150	450	750	1,350
1928 (m)	—	PF63 45,000				
1931 (m)	3,129,000	20.00	40.00	135	225	475
1931 (m)	—	PF63 40,000				
1932 (m)	188,000	1,000	3,000	7,500	12,500	22,500
1933 (m)	488,000	250	800	4,500	7,500	16,500
1934 (m)	1,674,000	19.00	75.00	330	550	1,100
1934 (m)	100	PF63 15,000				
1935 (m)	915,000	25.00	70.00	300	500	1,000
1935 (m)	—	PF63 45,000				
1936 (m)	2,382,000	13.00	25.00	135	225	400
1936 (m)	—	PF63 40,000				

KM# 31 FLORIN

11.31 g., 0.925 Silver 0.3364 oz. ASW, 28.5 mm. **Ruler:** George V **Subject:** Opening of Parliament House, Canberra **Obv:** Crowned head left **Edge:** Reeded

Date	Mintage	VF20	XF40	MS60	MS63	MS65
1927 (m)	2,000,000	13.00	25.00	60.00	100	150
1927 (m)	400	PF63 22,500				

KM# 33 FLORIN

11.31 g., 0.925 Silver 0.3364 oz. ASW, 28.5 mm. **Ruler:** George V **Subject:** Centennial of Victoria and Melbourne **Obv:** Crowned bust left **Rev:** Horse prancing left with rider holding torch **Edge:** Reeded

Date	Mintage	VF20	XF40	MS60	MS63	MS65
ND-1934	—	225	250	285	500	950
Note: 21,000 pieces were melted						
ND-1934	—	PF63 25,000				

KM# 40 FLORIN

11.31 g., 0.925 Silver 0.3364 oz. ASW, 28.5 mm. **Ruler:** George VI **Obv:** Head left **Rev:** Arms **Edge:** Reeded

Date	Mintage	VF20	XF40	MS60	MS63	MS65
1938 (m)	2,990,000	6.75	30.00	60.00	100	200
1938 (m)	—	PF63 12,000				
1939 (m)	630,000	45.00	325	870	1,450	2,550
1940 (m)	8,410,000	6.75	13.00	27.00	45.00	65.00
1941 (m)	7,614,000	6.75	13.00	24.00	40.00	50.00
1942 (m)	17,986,000	6.75	13.00	18.00	30.00	45.00
1942 S	6,000,000	6.75	13.00	15.00	25.00	40.00
1943 (m)	12,762,000	6.75	13.00	13.20	22.00	35.00
1943 S	11,000,000	6.75	13.00	13.20	22.00	35.00
1944 (m)	22,440,000	6.75	13.00	13.20	22.00	35.00
1944 S	11,000,000	6.75	13.00	13.20	22.00	35.00
1945 (m)	11,970,000	6.75	17.00	36.00	60.00	100

KM# 40a FLORIN

11.31 g., 0.500 Silver 0.1818 oz. ASW, 28.6 mm. **Ruler:** George VI **Obv:** Head left **Rev:** Arms **Edge:** Reeded

Date	Mintage	VF20	XF40	MS60	MS63	MS65
1946 (m)	22,154,000	3.75	8.00	12.00	20.00	28.00
1946 (m)	—	PF63 19,500				
1947 (m)	39,292,000	3.75	8.00	12.00	20.00	28.00
1947 (m)	—	PF63 19,500				

KM# 47 FLORIN

11.31 g., 0.500 Silver 0.1818 oz. ASW, 28.5 mm. **Ruler:** George VI **Subject:** 50th Year Jubilee **Obv:** Head left **Rev:** Crowned crossed scepter and sword divide Jubilee dates **Edge:** Reeded

Date	Mintage	VF20	XF40	MS60	MS63	MS65
1951 (m)	2,000,000	3.75	8.00	14.00	19.00	28.00

KM# 47a FLORIN

Copper-Nickel, 28.5 mm. **Ruler:** George VI **Subject:** 50th Year Jubilee **Obv:** Head left **Rev:** Crowned crossed scepter and sword divide Jubilee dates **Edge:** Reeded

Date	Mintage	VF20	XF40	MS60	MS63	MS65
1951 (L)	—	PF63 27,000				
Note: Thought by many to be a trial strike or pattern						

KM# 48 FLORIN

11.31 g., 0.500 Silver 0.1818 oz. ASW, 28.5 mm. **Ruler:** George VI **Obv:** Head left **Obv. Legend:** IND: IMP. dropped **Rev:** Arms **Edge:** Reeded

Date	Mintage	VF20	XF40	MS60	MS63	MS65
1951 (m)	10,068,000	3.75	11.00	32.00	60.00	125
1952 (m)	10,044,000	3.75	11.00	32.00	60.00	125

KM# 54 FLORIN

11.31 g., 0.500 Silver 0.1818 oz. ASW, 28.5 mm. **Ruler:** Elizabeth II **Obv:** Laureate bust right **Rev:** Arms **Edge:** Reeded

Date	Mintage	VF20	XF40	MS60	MS63	MS65
1953 (m)	12,658,000	3.75	8.00	12.00	20.00	35.00
Note: Normal and large beads on the reverse.						
1953 (m)	—	PF63 12,000				
1954 (m)	15,366,000	3.75	8.00	20.00	35.00	65.00
1954 (m)	—	PF63 45,000				

KM# 55 FLORIN

11.31 g., 0.500 Silver 0.1818 oz. ASW, 28.5 mm. **Ruler:** Elizabeth II **Subject:** Royal Visit **Obv:** Laureate bust right **Rev:** Lion and kangaroo facing right **Edge:** Reeded

Date	Mintage	VF20	XF40	MS60	MS63	MS65
1954 (m)	4,000,000	3.75	11.00	18.00	30.00	46.00
1954 (m)	—	PF63 22,500				

KM# 60 FLORIN

11.31 g., 0.500 Silver 0.1818 oz. ASW, 28.5 mm. **Ruler:**

Elizabeth II **Obv:** Laureate bust right **Obv. Legend:** F:D: added **Rev:** Arms **Edge:** Reeded

Date	Mintage	VF20	XF40	MS60	MS63	MS65
1956 (m)	8,090,000	8.00	15.00	50.00	100	300
1956 (m)	1,500	PF63 175				
1957 (m)	9,278,000	3.75	6.00	7.50	11.00	16.00
1957 (m)	1,256	PF63 200				
1958 (m)	8,972,000	3.75	6.00	7.50	10.00	16.00
1958 (m)	1,506	PF63 175				
1959 (m)	3,500,000	3.75	6.00	7.50	9.00	14.00
1959 (m)	1,506	PF63 200				
1960 (m)	15,760,000	—	3.75	5.00	8.00	13.00
1960 (m)	1,509	PF63 200				
1961 (m)	9,452,000	—	3.75	5.00	8.00	13.00
1961 (m)	1,506	PF63 200				
1962 (m)	13,748,000	—	3.75	5.00	8.00	13.00
1962 (m)	2,016	PF63 150				
1963 (m)	12,002,000	—	3.75	5.00	8.00	13.00
1963 (m)	5,042	PF63 125				

KM# 34 CROWN

28.28 g., 0.925 Silver 0.841 oz. ASW, 38 mm. **Ruler:** George VI **Obv:** Head left **Rev:** Crown above date and value **Edge:** Reeded

Date	Mintage	VF20	XF40	MS60	MS63	MS65
1937 (m)	1,008,000	28.00	40.00	55.00	100	225
1937 (m)	100	PF63 26,000				
1938 (m)	102,000	120	175	225	375	1,650
1938 (m)	250	PF63 55,000				

TRADE COINAGE

KM# 14 1/2 SOVEREIGN

3.99 g., 0.917 Gold 0.1178 oz. AGW, 19 mm. **Ruler:** Edward VII **Obv:** Head right **Rev:** St. George slaying dragon

Date	Mintage	VF20	XF40	MS60	MS63	MS65
1902 S	84,000	210	225	600	825	975
1902 S	—	PF63 65,000				
1902 S	—	PF63 65,000				
Frosted, Proof						
1903 S	231,000	210	225	775	1,650	—
1904 P	60,000	255	1,450	5,500	—	—
1906 S	308,000	210	225	600	825	975
1906 M	82,000	225	1,000	3,300	5,500	—
1907 M	400,000	210	225	1,050	1,700	—
1908 S	538,000	210	225	500	650	785
1908 M	—	210	225	825	1,300	—
Note: Mintage included with 1907M						
1908 P	25,000	275	1,650	5,500	—	—
1909 M	186,000	210	275	1,100	1,650	—
1909 P	44,000	225	650	3,300	5,500	—
1910 S	474,000	210	225	450	650	785

KM# 28 1/2 SOVEREIGN

3.99 g., 0.917 Gold 0.1178 oz. AGW, 19 mm. **Ruler:** George V **Obv:** Head left **Rev:** St. George slaying dragon

Date	Mintage	VF20	XF40	MS60	MS63	MS65
1911 S	252,000	—	—	160	290	320
1911 S Matte Proof	—	PF63 65,000				
1911 P	130,000	—	160	350	375	400
1912 S	278,000	—	—	160	260	285
1914 S	322,000	—	—	160	260	285
1915 P	138,000	—	160	295	350	375
1915 S	892,000	—	—	160	260	285
1915 M	125,000	—	—	160	290	320
1916 S	448,000	—	—	160	260	285
1918 P	—	575	2,200	4,050	5,300	—
Note: Estimated 200-250 pieces minted						

KM# 15 SOVEREIGN

7.99 g., 0.917 Gold 0.2355 oz. AGW, 21 mm. **Ruler:** Edward VII **Obv:** Head right **Rev:** St. George on horseback with sword slaying the dragon

Date	Mintage	VF20	XF40	MS60	MS63	MS65
1902 S	2,813,000	—	—	320	525	550
1902 S	—	PF63 75,000				
1902 S	—	PF63 75,000				
Frosted proof						
1902 M	4,267,000	—	—	320	525	550
1902 P	4,289,000	—	—	320	575	600
1903 S	2,806,000	—	—	320	575	600
1903 M	3,521,000	—	—	320	525	550
1903 P	4,674,000	—	—	320	525	550
1904 S	2,986,000	—	—	320	525	550
1904 M	3,743,000	—	—	320	525	550
1904 M	—	PF63 65,000				
1904 P	4,506,000	—	—	320	525	550
1905 S	2,778,000	—	—	320	525	550
1905 M	3,633,000	—	—	320	525	550
1905 P	4,876,000	—	—	320	750	800
1906 S	2,792,000	—	—	320	525	550
1906 M	3,657,000	—	—	320	525	550
1906 P	4,829,000	—	—	320	575	600
1907 S	2,539,000	—	—	—	320	350
1907 M	3,332,000	—	—	—	320	350
1907 P	4,972,000	—	—	—	320	350
1908 S	2,017,000	—	—	—	320	350
1908 M	3,080,000	—	—	—	320	350
1908 P	4,875,000	—	—	—	320	350
1909 S	2,057,000	—	—	—	320	350
1909 M	3,029,000	—	—	—	320	350
1909 P	4,524,000	—	—	—	320	350
1910 S	2,135,000	—	—	—	320	350
1910 M	3,054,000	—	—	—	320	350
1910 M	—	PF63 60,000				
1910 P	4,690,000	—	—	320	525	550

KM# 29 SOVEREIGN

7.99 g., 0.917 Gold 0.2355 oz. AGW, 21 mm. **Ruler:** George V **Obv:** Head left **Rev:** St. George on horseback with sword slaying the dragon

Date	Mintage	VF20	XF40	MS60	MS63	MS65
1911 S	2,519,000	—	—	320	450	475
1911 S	—	PF63 65,000				
1911 M	2,851,000	—	—	320	450	475
1911 M	—	PF63 65,000				
1911 P	4,373,000	—	—	320	450	475
1912 S	2,227,000	—	—	320	450	475
1912 M	2,467,000	—	—	320	450	475
1912 P	4,278,000	—	—	320	450	475
1913 S	2,249,000	—	—	320	450	475
1913 M	2,323,000	—	—	320	450	475
1913 P	4,635,000	—	—	320	450	475
1914 S	1,774,000	—	—	320	450	475
1914 S	—	PF63 65,000				
1914 M	2,012,000	—	—	320	450	475
1914 P	4,815,000	—	—	320	450	475
1915 S	1,346,000	—	—	320	450	475
1915 M	1,637,000	—	—	320	450	475
1915 P	4,373,000	—	—	320	450	475
1916 S	1,242,000	—	—	320	450	475
1916 M	1,277,000	—	—	320	450	475
1916 P	4,906,000	—	—	320	450	475
1917 S	1,666,000	—	—	320	450	475
1917 M	934,000	—	—	320	450	475
1917 P	4,110,000	—	—	320	450	475
1918 S	3,716,000	—	—	320	450	475
1918 M	4,969,000	—	—	320	450	475
1918 P	3,812,000	—	—	320	450	475
1919 S	1,835,000	—	—	320	450	475
1919 M	514,000	—	450	500	550	575
1919 P	2,995,000	—	—	320	450	475
1920 S	360,000	75,000	150,000	275,000	—	—
1920 M	530,000	2,700	5,500	7,000	9,000	—
1920 P	2,421,000	—	—	320	450	475
1921 S	839,000	800	1,400	2,200	3,000	—
1921 M	240,000	8,000	12,000	16,000	18,500	—
1921 P	2,314,000	—	—	320	450	475
1922 S	578,000	8,500	12,500	17,000	19,500	—
1922 S	—	PF63 65,000				
1922 M	608,000	5,000	7,500	10,000	12,500	—
1922 P	2,298,000	—	—	320	450	475
1923 S	416,000	5,500	8,000	12,500	14,000	—
1923 S	—	PF63 65,000				
1923 M	510,000	—	—	—	—	—
1923 P	2,124,000	—	—	320	450	475
1924 S	394,000	800	1,400	2,300	2,800	—
1924 M	278,000	—	—	320	450	475
1924 P	1,464,000	—	—	320	450	475
1925 S	5,632,000	—	—	320	450	475
1925 M	3,311,000	—	—	320	450	475
1925 P	1,837,000	—	—	500	550	575
1926 S	1,030,999	10,000	15,000	20,000	22,500	—
1926 S	—	PF63 85,000				
1926 M	211,000	—	—	320	450	475
1926 P	1,131,000	1,000	1,500	3,000	3,500	—
1927 M	310,000	—	—	—	—	—
Note: None known.						
1927 P	1,383,000	320	450	500	700	850
1928 M	413,000	1,500	3,000	3,600	—	—
1928 P	1,333,000	—	—	320	450	475

KM# 32 SOVEREIGN

7.99 g., 0.917 Gold 0.2355 oz. AGW, 21 mm. **Ruler:** George V **Obv:** Head left **Rev:** St. George on horseback with sword slaying the dragon

Date	Mintage	VF20	XF40	MS60	MS63	MS65
1929 M	436,000	1,200	2,250	3,000	4,000	—
1929 M	—	PF63 65,000				
1929 P	1,606,000	—	—	320	450	475
1930 M	77,000	—	—	320	550	575
1930 M	—	PF63 65,000				
1930 P	1,915,000	—	—	320	450	475
1931 M	57,000	450	600	850	1,000	—
1931 M	—	PF63 65,000				
1931 P	1,173,000	—	—	320	450	475

KM# 16 2 POUNDS

15.98 g., 0.917 Gold 0.471 oz. AGW **Ruler:** Edward VII **Obv:** Head right **Rev:** St. George on horseback with sword slaying the dragon **Note:** Gilt lead electrotypes exist.

Date	Mintage	VF20	XF40	MS60	MS63	MS65
1902 S Matte Proof Rare	4	PF63 85,000				

KM# 17 5 POUNDS

39.94 g., 0.917 Gold 1.1775 oz. AGW **Ruler:** Edward VII **Obv:** Head right **Rev:** St. George on horseback with sword slaying the dragon **Note:** Gilt lead electrotypes exist.

Date	Mintage	VF20	XF40	MS60	MS63	MS65
1902 S Proof; Rare	Est. 3	PF63 150,000				
1902 S Matte Proof; Rare	Inc. above	PF63 150,000				
Note: Spink Australia Sale #30 11-89 nearly FDC realized $38,500						

DECIMAL COINAGE

KM# 62 CENT

2.60 g., Bronze, 17.65 mm. **Ruler:** Elizabeth II **Obv:** Young bust right **Rev:** Feather-tailed Glider and value **Edge:** Plain

Date	Mintage	VF20	XF40	MS60	MS63	MS65
1966 (c)	146,457,000	—	—	3.00	4.00	5.00
1966 (c)	18,000	PF65 15.00				
1966 (m)	238,990,000	—	—	3.00	4.00	5.00
Note: Blunted whisker on right						
1966 (p)	26,620,000	—	8.00	12.00	18.00	20.00
Note: Blunted 2nd whisker from right						
1967	110,055,000	—	—	5.00	6.00	7.00
1968	19,930,000	7.00	11.00	18.00	28.00	35.00
1969	87,680,000	—	—	4.00	5.00	6.00
1969	13,000	PF65 10.00				
1970	72,560,000	—	—	2.00	3.00	4.00
1970	15,000	PF65 10.00				
1971	102,455,000	—	—	2.00	3.00	4.00
1971	10,000	PF65 10.00				
1972	82,400,000	—	—	2.00	3.00	4.00
1972	10,000	PF65 10.00				
1973	140,710,000	—	—	2.00	3.00	4.00
1973	10,000	PF65 10.00				
1974	131,720,000	—	—	1.00	2.00	3.00
1974	11,000	PF65 10.00				
1975	134,775,000	—	—	1.00	2.00	3.00
1975	23,000	PF65 5.00				
1976	172,935,000	—	—	1.00	2.00	3.00
1976	21,000	PF65 7.00				
1977	153,430,000	—	—	1.00	2.00	3.00
1977	55,000	PF65 4.00				
1978	97,253,000	—	—	1.00	2.00	3.00
1978	39,000	PF65 4.00				
1979	130,339,000	—	—	1.00	2.00	3.00
1979	36,000	PF65 4.00				
1980	137,892,000	—	—	1.00	2.00	3.00
1980	68,000	PF65 4.00				
1981	223,900,000	—	—	1.00	2.00	3.00
1981	86,000	PF65 4.00				
1982	134,290,000	—	—	1.00	2.00	3.00
1982	100,000	PF65 4.00				
1983	205,625,000	—	—	1.00	2.00	3.00
1983	80,000	PF65 4.00				
1984	74,735,000	—	—	1.00	2.00	3.00
1984	61,000	PF65 4.00				

KM# 78 CENT

2.60 g., Bronze, 17.65 mm. **Ruler:** Elizabeth II **Obv:** Crowned head right **Rev:** Feather-tailed Glider and value

Date	Mintage	VF20	XF40	MS60	MS63	MS65
1985	38,300,000	—	—	2.00	3.00	4.00
1985	75,000	PF65 5.00				
1986 Sets only	180,000	—	—	—	—	8.00
1986	67,000	PF65 5.00				
1987	122,000,000	—	—	1.00	2.00	3.00
1987	70,000	PF65 5.00				
1988	105,900,000	—	—	1.00	2.00	3.00
1988	106,000	PF65 5.00				
1989	168,000,000	—	—	1.00	2.00	3.00
1989	67,000	PF65 5.00				
1990	52,900,000	—	—	2.00	3.00	4.00
1990	53,000	PF65 5.00				
	148,000	—	—	—	—	9.00
1991	41,000	PF65 5.00				

KM# 78a CENT

3.01 g., 0.925 Silver 0.0895 oz. ASW, 17.51 mm. **Ruler:** Elizabeth II **Obv:** Crowned head right **Rev:** Feather-tailed Glider and value

Date	Mintage	VF20	XF40	MS60	MS63	MS65
1991	25,000	PF65 5.00				
Note: In Proof sets only						

KM# 63 2 CENTS

5.20 g., Bronze, 21.6 mm. **Ruler:** Elizabeth II **Obv:** Young bust right **Rev:** Frill-necked lizard and value

Date	Mintage	VF20	XF40	MS60	MS63	MS65
1966 (c)	145,226,000	—	—	3.00	4.00	5.00
1966 (c)	18,000	PF65 15.00				
1966 (m)	66,575,000	—	—	6.00	7.00	8.00
Note: Blunted 3rd left claw						
1966 (p)	217,735,000	—	—	2.00	3.00	4.00
Note: Blunted 1st right claw						
1967	73,250,000	—	—	10.00	13.00	15.00
1967	Inc. above	—	—	80.00	100	110
Note: Without designer's initials on reverse						
1968	17,000,000	16.00	30.00	45.00	65.00	150
1969	12,940,000	—	—	6.00	7.00	8.00
1969	13,000	PF65 10.00				
1970	39,872,000	—	—	2.00	3.00	4.00
1970	15,000	PF65 10.00				
1971	60,735,000	—	—	2.00	3.00	4.00
1971	10,000	PF65 10.00				
1972	77,570,000	—	—	2.00	3.00	4.00
1972	10,000	PF65 10.00				
1973	94,058,000	—	—	2.00	3.00	4.00
1973	10,000	PF65 10.00				
1974	177,723,000	—	—	2.00	3.00	4.00
1974	11,000	PF65 10.00				
1975	100,045,000	—	—	2.00	3.00	4.00
1975	23,000	PF65 10.00				
1976	121,882,000	—	—	1.00	2.00	3.00
1976	21,000	PF65 7.00				
1977	102,000,000	—	—	1.00	2.00	3.00
1977	55,000	PF65 4.00				
1978	128,700,000	—	—	1.00	2.00	3.00
1978	39,000	PF65 4.00				
1979	69,705,000	—	—	1.00	2.00	3.00
1979	36,000	PF65 4.00				
1980	145,603,000	—	—	1.00	2.00	3.00
1980	68,000	PF65 4.00				
1981	247,300,000	—	—	1.00	2.00	3.00
1981	86,000	PF65 4.00				
1982	121,770,000	—	—	1.00	2.00	3.00
1982	100,000	PF65 4.00				
1983	177,227,000	—	—	1.00	2.00	3.00
1983	80,000	PF65 4.00				
1984	57,963,000	—	—	1.00	2.00	3.00
1984	61,000	PF65 4.00				

KM# 79 2 CENTS

5.20 g., Bronze, 21.6 mm. **Ruler:** Elizabeth II **Obv:** Crowned head right **Rev:** Frill-necked lizard and value **Edge:** Plain

Date	Mintage	VF20	XF40	MS60	MS63	MS65
1985	34,700,000	—	—	1.00	2.00	3.00
1985	75,000	PF65 5.00				
1986 Sets only	180,000	—	—	—	—	8.00
1986	67,000	PF65 5.00				
1987 Sets only	200,000	—	—	—	—	8.00
1987	70,000	PF65 5.00				
1988	28,905,000	—	—	1.00	2.00	3.00
1988	106,000	PF65 5.00				
1989	110,000,000	—	—	1.00	2.00	3.00
1989	67,000	PF65 5.00				
1990 Sets only	103,000	—	—	—	—	60.00
1990	53,000	PF65 25.00				
1991 Sets only	148,000	—	—	—	—	11.00
1991	41,000	PF65 5.00				

KM# 79a 2 CENTS

6.06 g., 0.925 Silver 0.1802 oz. ASW, 21.6 mm. **Ruler:** Elizabeth II **Obv:** Crowned head right **Rev:** Frill-necked lizard and value

Date	Mintage	VF20	XF40	MS60	MS63	MS65
1991	25,000	PF65 35.00				

KM# 64 5 CENTS

2.83 g., Copper-Nickel, 19.41 mm. **Ruler:** Elizabeth II **Obv:** Young bust right **Rev:** Echidna and value **Edge:** Reeded **Note:** For 1966 dated examples, the length of the whisker on top of the forward-most claw at left will indicate the mint: Canberra (less than .5mm) or London (greater than .6mm).

Date	Mintage	VF20	XF40	MS60	MS63	MS65
1966 (c)	45,427,000	—	—	5.00	7.00	9.00
1966 (c)	18,000	PF65 30.00				
1966 (L)	30,000,000	—	—	4.00	6.00	8.00
1967	62,144,000	—	—	5.00	7.00	9.00
1968	67,336,000	—	—	6.00	8.00	9.00
1969	38,170,000	—	—	4.00	6.00	7.00
1969	13,000	PF65 20.00				
1970	46,058,000	—	—	3.00	4.00	5.00
1970	15,000	PF65 15.00				
1971	39,516,000	—	—	3.00	4.00	5.00
1971	10,000	PF65 20.00				
1972	8,256,000	9.00	14.00	22.00	35.00	37.00
1972	10,000	PF65 20.00				
1973	48,816,000	—	—	3.00	4.00	5.00
1973	10,000	PF65 20.00				
1974	64,248,000	—	—	2.00	3.00	4.00
1974	11,000	PF65 15.00				
1975	44,256,000	—	—	1.00	2.00	3.00
1975	23,000	PF65 5.00				
1976	113,180,000	—	—	1.00	2.00	3.00
1976	21,000	PF65 7.00				
1977	108,800,000	—	—	1.00	2.00	3.00
1977	55,000	PF65 4.00				
1978	25,210,000	—	—	1.00	2.00	3.00
1978	39,000	PF65 5.00				
1979	44,533,000	—	—	1.00	2.00	3.00
1979	36,000	PF65 4.00				
1980	115,042,000	—	—	1.00	2.00	3.00
1980	68,000	PF65 4.00				
1981	162,264,000	—	—	1.00	2.00	3.00
1981	86,000	PF65 4.00				
1982	139,468,000	—	—	1.00	2.00	3.00
1982	100,000	PF65 4.00				
1983	131,568,000	—	—	1.00	2.00	3.00
1983	80,000	PF65 4.00				
1984	35,436,000	—	—	1.00	2.00	3.00
1984	61,000	PF65 4.00				

KM# 80 5 CENTS

2.83 g., Copper-Nickel, 19.41 mm. **Ruler:** Elizabeth II **Obv:** Crowned head right **Rev:** Echidna and value **Edge:** Reeded

Date	Mintage	VF20	XF40	MS60	MS63	MS65
1985 Sets only	170,000	—	—	—	—	30.00
1985	75,000	PF65 15.00				
1986 Sets only	180,000	—	—	—	—	7.00
1986	67,000	PF65 5.00				
1987	73,500,000	—	—	1.00	2.00	3.00
1987	70,000	PF65 5.00				
1988	106,100,000	—	—	1.00	2.00	3.00
1988	Inc. above	PF65 5.00				
1989	75,000,000	—	—	1.00	2.00	3.00
1989	67,000	PF65 5.00				
1990	33,200,000	—	—	1.00	2.00	3.00
1990	53,000	PF65 5.00				
1991	20,000,000	—	—	1.00	2.00	3.00
1991	41,000	PF65 5.00				
1992	51,200,000	—	—	1.00	2.00	3.00
1992	56,000	PF65 5.00				
1993	93,840,000	—	—	1.00	2.00	3.00
1993	46,000	PF65 5.00				
1994	146,669,000	—	—	1.00	2.00	3.00
1994	39,000	PF65 5.00				
1995	84,987,000	—	—	1.00	2.00	3.00
1995	48,000	PF65 5.00				
1996	79,210,000	—	—	1.00	2.00	3.00
1996	41,000	PF65 5.00				
1997	100,680,000	—	—	1.00	2.00	3.00
1997	32,000	PF65 10.00				
1998	88,532,000	—	—	1.00	2.00	3.00
1998	32,000	PF65 15.00				

KM# 80a 5 CENTS

3.27 g., 0.925 Silver 0.0972 oz. ASW, 19.4 mm. **Ruler:** Elizabeth II **Obv:** Crowned head right **Rev:** Echidna

Date	Mintage	VF20	XF40	MS60	MS63	MS65
1991	25,000	PF65 10.00				

KM# 401 5 CENTS

2.83 g., Copper-Nickel, 19.41 mm. **Ruler:** Elizabeth II **Obv:** Head with tiara right **Rev:** Echidna and value **Edge:** Reeded

Date	Mintage	VF20	XF40	MS60	MS63	MS65
1999	179,016,000	—	—	1.00	2.00	3.00
1999	28,000	PF65 15.00				
2000	97,422,000	—	—	1.00	2.00	3.00
2000	64,000	PF65 10.00				

KM# 481 5 CENTS

5.53 g., 0.999 Silver 0.1776 oz. ASW, 25 mm. **Ruler:** Elizabeth II **Series:** Masterpieces in Silver **Rev:** Half penny reverse design of KM#41 **Edge:** Reeded

Date	Mintage	VF20	XF40	MS60	MS63	MS65
1999 B	15,000	PF65 10.00				

KM# 65 10 CENTS

5.65 g., Copper-Nickel, 23.6 mm. **Ruler:** Elizabeth II **Obv:** Young bust right **Rev:** Lyrebird and vlaue **Edge:** Reeded **Note:** For 1966 dated examples, 11 spikes on the left Lyrebird indicates a strike from Canberra, 12 spikes indicate a London strike.

Date	Mintage	VF20	XF40	MS60	MS63	MS65
1966 (c)	10,984,000	—	—	6.00	9.00	11.00
1966 (c)	18,000	PF65 30.00				
1966 (L)	30,000,000	—	—	5.00	7.00	9.00
1967	51,032,000	—	—	7.00	10.00	14.00
1968	24,706,000	—	—	8.00	14.00	20.00
1969	54,634,000	—	—	6.00	9.00	11.00
1969	13,000	PF65 20.00				
1970	22,306,000	—	—	5.00	7.00	9.00
1970	15,000	PF65 15.00				
1971	20,726,000	—	—	9.00	11.00	13.00
1971	10,000	PF65 20.00				
1972	12,502,000	—	—	18.00	20.00	22.00
1972	10,000	PF65 20.00				
1973	27,320,000	—	—	6.00	8.00	10.00
1973	10,000	PF65 20.00				
1974	46,550,000	—	—	5.00	7.00	9.00
1974	11,000	PF65 15.00				
1975	50,900,000	—	—	2.00	3.00	4.00
1975	23,000	PF65 5.00				
1976	57,060,000	—	—	2.00	3.00	4.00
1976	21,000	PF65 7.00				
1977	10,940,000	—	—	2.00	3.00	4.00
1977	55,000	PF65 4.00				
1978	43,400,000	—	—	2.00	3.00	4.00
1978	39,000	PF65 4.00				
1979	36,950,000	—	—	1.00	2.00	3.00
1979	36,000	PF65 4.00				
1980	55,084,000	—	—	1.00	2.00	3.00
1980	68,000	PF65 4.00				
1981	116,060,000	—	—	1.00	2.00	3.00
Note: One 1981 coin was struck on a Sri Lanka 50 cents planchet, KM#135.1. It carries an approximate value of $600						
1981	86,000	PF65 4.00				
1982	61,492,000	—	—	1.00	2.00	3.00
1982	100,000	PF65 4.00				
1983	82,318,000	—	—	1.00	2.00	3.00
1983	80,000	PF65 4.00				
1984	25,728,000	—	—	1.00	2.00	3.00
1984	61,000	PF65 4.00				

KM# 81 10 CENTS

5.65 g., Copper-Nickel, 23.6 mm. **Ruler:** Elizabeth II **Obv:** Crowned head right **Rev:** Lyrebird and value **Edge:** Reeded

Date	Mintage	VF20	XF40	MS60	MS63	MS65
1985	2,100,000	—	—	7.00	9.00	10.00
1985	75,000	PF65 5.00				
1986 Sets only	180,000	—	—	—	—	9.00
1986	67,000	PF65 5.00				
1987 Sets only	200,000	—	—	—	—	9.00
1987	70,000	PF65 5.00				
1988	48,900,000	—	—	1.00	2.00	3.00
1988	106,000	PF65 5.00				
1989	43,000,000	—	—	1.00	2.00	3.00
1989	67,000	PF65 5.00				
1990	23,038,000	—	—	2.00	3.00	4.00
1990	53,000	PF65 5.00				
1991	3,174,000	—	—	5.00	6.00	7.00
1991	41,000	PF65 5.00				
1992	43,739,000	—	—	3.00	4.00	5.00
1992	56,000	PF65 5.00				
1993	23,100,000	—	—	3.00	4.00	5.00
1993	46,000	PF65 5.00				
1994	43,726,000	—	—	3.00	4.00	5.00
1994	39,000	PF65 5.00				
1995 Sets only	96,000	—	—	—	—	20.00
1995	41,000	PF65 10.00				
1996	108,000	—	—	15.00	20.00	25.00
1996	41,000	PF65 30.00				
1997	5,700,000	—	—	5.00	6.00	7.00
1997	32,000	PF65 40.00				
1998	47,989,000	—	—	2.00	3.00	4.00
1998	32,000	PF65 15.00				

KM# 81a 10 CENTS

6.52 g., 0.925 Silver 0.1939 oz. ASW, 23.6 mm. **Ruler:** Elizabeth II **Obv:** Crowned head right **Rev:** Lyrebird

Date	Mintage	VF20	XF40	MS60	MS63	MS65
1991	25,000	PF65 25.00				

KM# 402 10 CENTS

5.65 g., Copper-Nickel, 23.6 mm. **Ruler:** Elizabeth II **Obv:** Head with tiara right **Rev:** Lyrebird and value **Edge:** Reeded

Date	Mintage	VF20	XF40	MS60	MS63	MS65
1999	179,016,000	—	—	2.00	3.00	4.00
1999	28,000	PF65 15.00				
2000	51,117,000	—	—	2.00	3.00	4.00
2000	64,000	PF65 10.00				

KM# 482 10 CENTS

8.36 g., 0.999 Silver 0.2685 oz. ASW, 30 mm. **Ruler:** Elizabeth II **Series:** Masterpieces in Silver **Obv:** Head right **Rev:** Penny reverse design of KM#23 **Edge:** Reeded

Date	Mintage	VF20	XF40	MS60	MS63	MS65
1999 B	15,000	PF65 15.00				

KM# 66 20 CENTS

11.30 g., Copper-Nickel, 28.65 mm. **Ruler:** Elizabeth II **Obv:** Young bust right **Rev:** Duckbill Platypus **Edge:** Reeded **Note:** For 1966 dated examples, strikes from Canberra show a gap between sea line and right face of platypus

Date	Mintage	VF20	XF40	MS60	MS63	MS65
1966 (c)	28,223,000	—	—	35.00	45.00	50.00
1966 (c)	18,000	PF65 60.00				
1966 (L)	—	—	2,000	2,800	3,500	4,500
Note: Wave on base of 2						
1966 (L)	—	PF65 60.00				
1967	83,848,000	—	—	28.00	35.00	38.00
1968	40,537,000	—	—	24.00	30.00	60.00
1969	16,501,999	—	—	30.00	38.00	40.00
1969	13,000	PF65 50.00				
1970	23,271,000	—	—	17.00	22.00	24.00
1970	15,000	PF65 40.00				
1971	8,947,000	—	—	55.00	65.00	67.00
1971	10,000	PF65 40.00				
1972	16,643,000	—	—	17.00	22.00	26.00
1972	10,000	PF65 40.00				
1973	23,356,000	—	—	16.00	20.00	22.00
1973	10,000	PF65 40.00				
1974	33,548,000	—	—	16.00	20.00	22.00
1974	11,000	PF65 30.00				
1975	53,300,000	—	—	5.00	6.00	7.00
1975	23,000	PF65 10.00				
1976	59,774,000	—	—	4.00	5.00	6.00
1976	21,000	PF65 15.00				
1977	41,272,000	—	—	3.00	4.00	5.00
1977	55,000	PF65 7.00				
1978	37,400,000	—	—	2.00	3.00	4.00
1978	39,000	PF65 7.00				
1979	22,300,000	—	—	2.00	3.00	4.00
1979	36,000	PF65 7.00				
1980	84,400,000	—	—	2.00	3.00	4.00
1980	68,000	PF65 5.00				
1981	165,500,000	—	—	2.00	3.00	4.00
Note: Some 1981 dated coins were struck on a Hong Kong 2 Dollar planchet, KM#37. 6 pieces are reported. Each carries an approximate value of $7,500						
1981	86,000	PF65 5.00				
1982	76,600,000	—	—	2.00	3.00	4.00
1982	100,000	PF65 5.00				
1983	55,113,000	—	—	22.00	28.00	29.00
1983	80,000	PF65 25.00				
1984	27,820,000	—	—	28.00	35.00	45.00
1984	61,000	PF65 15.00				

KM# 82 20 CENTS

11.30 g., Copper-Nickel, 28.65 mm. **Ruler:** Elizabeth II **Obv:** Crowned head right **Rev:** Duckbill Platypus **Edge:** Reeded

Date	Mintage	VF20	XF40	MS60	MS63	MS65
1985	2,700,000	—	—	14.00	18.00	19.00
1985	75,000	PF65 10.00				
1986 Sets only	180,000	—	—	14.00	18.00	19.00
1986	67,000	PF65 10.00				
1987 Sets only	200,000	—	—	14.00	18.00	21.00
1987	70,000	PF65 10.00				
1988 Sets only	240,000	—	—	28.00	35.00	37.00
1988	106,000	PF65 10.00				
1989	150,000	—	—	20.00	25.00	30.00
1989	67,000	PF65 10.00				
1990	103,000	—	—	28.00	35.00	38.00
1990	53,000	PF65 15.00				
1991	148,000	—	—	14.00	18.00	20.00
1991	41,000	PF65 15.00				
1992	118,000	—	—	28.00	35.00	40.00
1992	56,000	PF65 15.00				
1993	84,000	—	—	32.00	40.00	42.00
1993	46,000	PF65 15.00				
1994	14,330,000	—	—	12.00	15.00	17.00
1994	39,000	PF65 15.00				
1995	4,840,000	—	—	50.00	60.00	65.00
1995	41,000	PF65 30.00				
1996	20,596,000	—	—	8.00	10.00	12.00
1996	41,000	PF65 20.00				
1997	16,730,000	—	—	12.00	15.00	18.00
1997	32,000	PF65 20.00				
1998	28,830,000	—	—	8.00	10.00	15.00
1998	32,000	PF65 25.00				

KM# 82a 20 CENTS

13.09 g., 0.925 Silver 0.3893 oz. ASW, 28.5 mm. **Ruler:** Elizabeth II **Obv:** Head right **Rev:** Duckbill Platypus

Date	Mintage	VF20	XF40	MS60	MS63	MS65
1991	25,000	PF65 30.00				

KM# 295 20 CENTS

11.30 g., Copper-Nickel, 28.65 mm. **Ruler:** Elizabeth II **Subject:** 50th Anniversary - United Nations **Obv:** Crowned head right **Rev:** UN logo over value **Rev. Legend:** UNITED NATIONS FIFTIETH ANNIVERSARY

Date	Mintage	VF20	XF40	MS60	MS63	MS65
1995	4,800,000	—	—	5.00	6.00	7.00

KM# 410 20 CENTS

13.36 g., 0.999 Silver 0.4291 oz. ASW, 28.52 mm. **Ruler:** Elizabeth II **Subject:** Coins of the 20th Century - Milestones **Obv:** Queens head right **Rev:** 1927 Parliament House Florin design

Date	Mintage	VF20	XF40	MS60	MS63	MS65
1998	15,000	PF65 30.00				

KM# 403 20 CENTS

11.30 g., Copper-Nickel, 28.65 mm. **Ruler:** Elizabeth II **Obv:** Head with tiara right **Rev:** Duckbill Platypus **Edge:** Reeded

Date	Mintage	VF20	XF40	MS60	MS63	MS65
1999	64,181,000	—	—	4.00	5.00	6.00

Date	Mintage	VF20	XF40	MS60	MS63	MS65
1999	28,000	PF65 25.00				
2000	35,584,000	—	—	4.00	5.00	6.00
2000	64,000	PF65 40.00				

KM# 483 20 CENTS
2.99 g., 0.999 Silver 0.096 oz. ASW, 17.5 mm. **Ruler:** Elizabeth II **Series:** Masterpieces in Silver **Obv:** Head right **Rev:** Threepence reverse design of KM#37 **Edge:** Reeded

Date	Mintage	VF20	XF40	MS60	MS63	MS65
1999 B	15,000	PF65 30.00				

KM# 496 20 CENTS
13.36 g., 0.999 Silver 0.4291 oz. ASW, 28.5 mm. **Ruler:** Elizabeth II **Series:** Masterpieces in Silver - 2000 Set **Obv:** Head with tiara right **Rev:** Crowned bust right **Edge:** Reeded

Date	Mintage	VF20	XF40	MS60	MS63	MS65
2000 B	15,000	PF65 30.00				

KM# 497 20 CENTS
13.36 g., 0.999 Silver 0.4291 oz. ASW, 28.5 mm. **Ruler:** Elizabeth II **Series:** Masterpieces in Silver - 2000 Set **Obv:** Head with tiara right **Rev:** Crowned bust left **Edge:** Reeded

Date	Mintage	VF20	XF40	MS60	MS63	MS65
2000 B	15,000	PF65 30.00				

KM# 498 20 CENTS
13.36 g., 0.999 Silver 0.4291 oz. ASW, 28.5 mm. **Ruler:** Elizabeth II **Series:** Masterpieces in Silver - 2000 Set **Obv:** Rank-Broadley head with tiara right **Rev:** Laureate bust right **Edge:** Reeded

Date	Mintage	VF20	XF40	MS60	MS63	MS65
2000 B	15,000	PF65 30.00				

KM# 113 25 CENTS
7.78 g., 0.999 Silver 0.2497 oz. ASW **Ruler:** Elizabeth II **Obv:** Crowned head right **Rev:** Aboriginal Culture **Note:** The center "plug" coin issued with 1 Dollar, KM#112.

Date	Mintage	VF20	XF40	MS60	MS63	MS65
1988	100,000	PF65 20.00				

KM# 132 25 CENTS
7.78 g., 0.999 Silver 0.2497 oz. ASW **Ruler:** Elizabeth II **Obv:** Crowned head right **Rev:** Wandjina of Aboriginal Mythology **Note:** The center "plug" coin issued with 1 Dollar, KM#131.

Date	Mintage	VF20	XF40	MS60	MS63	MS65
1989	45,000	PF65 25.00				

KM# 155 25 CENTS
7.78 g., 0.999 Silver 0.2497 oz. ASW **Ruler:** Elizabeth II **Obv:** Crowned head right **Rev:** 3 Mythological Creatures **Note:** The center "plug" coin issued with 1 Dollar, KM#154.

Date	Mintage	VF20	XF40	MS60	MS63	MS65
1990	30,000	PF65 28.00				

KM# 67 50 CENTS
13.28 g., 0.800 Silver 0.3416 oz. ASW, 31.5 mm. **Ruler:** Elizabeth II **Obv:** Young bust right **Rev:** Coat of arms with kangaroo and emu supporters

Date	Mintage	VF20	XF40	MS60	MS63	MS65
1966	36,454,000	—	6.75	9.00	12.00	14.00
Note: On reverse, two parallel horizontal bars behind Emu's head.						
1966	18,000	PF65 100				

KM# 68 50 CENTS
15.55 g., Copper-Nickel, 31.65 mm. **Ruler:** Elizabeth II **Obv:** Young bust right **Rev:** Coat of arms with kangaroo and emu supporters **Edge:** 12-sided

Date	Mintage	VF20	XF40	MS60	MS63	MS65
1969	14,015,000	—	—	20.00	25.00	28.00
1969	13,000	PF65 90.00				
1971	21,056,000	—	—	20.00	25.00	28.00
1971	10,000	PF65 60.00				
1972	5,586,000	—	—	45.00	55.00	58.00
1972	10,000	PF65 60.00				
1973	4,009,000	—	—	50.00	60.00	63.00
1973	10,000	PF65 60.00				
1974	8,962,000	—	—	28.00	35.00	38.00
1974	11,000	PF65 50.00				
1975	19,025,000	—	—	10.00	12.00	14.00
1975	23,000	PF65 15.00				
1976	27,280,000	—	—	10.00	12.00	14.00
1976	21,000	PF65 15.00				
1978	25,765,000	—	—	5.00	6.00	7.00
1978	39,000	PF65 10.00				
1979	24,886,000	—	—	4.00	5.00	6.00
1979	36,000	PF65 10.00				
1979	Inc. above	—	—	10.00	12.00	14.00
Note: On reverse, two parallel horizontal bars behind Emu's head						
1979	Inc. above	PF65 100				
1980	38,681,000	—	—	3.00	4.00	5.00
1980	Inc. above	—	—	8.00	10.00	12.00
Note: On reverse, two parallel horizontal bars behind Emu's head.						
1980	68,000	PF65 70.00				
1981	24,168,000	—	—	3.00	4.00	5.00
1981	86,000	PF65 7.00				
1983	48,923,000	—	—	3.00	4.00	5.00
1983	80,000	PF65 5.00				
1984	26,281,000	—	—	3.00	4.00	5.00
1984	61,000	PF65 6.00				

KM# 69 50 CENTS
15.55 g., Copper-Nickel, 31.65 mm. **Ruler:** Elizabeth II **Subject:** 200th Anniversary - Cook's Australian Voyage **Obv:** Young bust right **Rev:** Bust of Captain Cook at left, map of Australia at right **Shape:** 12-sided

Date	Mintage	VF20	XF40	MS60	MS63	MS65
1970	16,540,000	—	—	5.00	7.00	9.00
1970	15,000	PF65 60.00				

KM# 68a 50 CENTS
15.41 g., Copper-Nickel, 31.5 mm. **Ruler:** Elizabeth II **Obv:** Bust with tiara right **Rev:** Coat of arms with kangaroo and emu supporters **Shape:** 12-sided **Note:** Mule. Obv. of KM#70, rev. KM#68.

Date	Mintage	VF20	XF40	MS60	MS63	MS65
1977	—	—	—	—	—	17,350

KM# 70 50 CENTS
15.55 g., Copper-Nickel, 31.65 mm. **Ruler:** Elizabeth II **Subject:** Queen's Silver Jubilee **Obv:** Young bust right **Rev:** Circular geometric design **Shape:** 12-sided

Date	Mintage	VF20	XF40	MS60	MS63	MS65
1977	25,076,000	—	—	3.00	4.00	5.00
1977	55,000	PF65 10.00				

KM# A72 50 CENTS
15.55 g., Copper-Nickel, 31.65 mm. **Ruler:** Elizabeth II **Obv:** Young bust right **Rev:** Sailing canoe-Takia, denomination below **Note:** Mule

Date	Mintage	VF20	XF40	MS60	MS63	MS65
1978	—	PF65 2,000				

KM# 72 50 CENTS
15.55 g., Copper-Nickel, 31.65 mm. **Ruler:** Elizabeth II **Subject:** Wedding of Prince Charles and Lady Diana **Rev:** Conjoined heads of Prince Charles and Lady Diana, left

Date	Mintage	VF20	XF40	MS60	MS63	MS65
1981	44,100,000	—	—	4.00	6.00	7.00

KM# 74 50 CENTS
15.55 g., Copper-Nickel, 31.65 mm. **Ruler:** Elizabeth II

Subject: XII Commonwealth Games - Brisbane **Obv:** Young bust right **Rev:** Circle of images representing different sporting events **Shape:** 12-sided

Date	Mintage	VF20	XF40	MS60	MS63	MS65
1982	49,500,000	—	—	3.00	4.00	5.00
1982	100,000	PF65 8.00				

KM# 83 50 CENTS

15.55 g., Copper-Nickel, 31.65 mm. **Ruler:** Elizabeth II **Obv:** Young bust with tiara right **Rev:** Coat of arms with kangaroo and emu supporters **Shape:** 12-sided

Date	Mintage	VF20	XF40	MS60	MS63	MS65
1985	1,000,000	—	—	10.00	13.00	14.00
1985	75,000	PF65 10.00				
1986 Sets only	180,000	—	—	5.00	7.00	18.00
1986	67,000	PF65 15.00				
1987 Sets only	200,000	—	—	—	—	15.00
1987	70,000	PF65 12.00				
1989 Sets only	—	—	—	—	—	25.00
1989	—	PF65 10.00				
1990 Sets only	—	—	—	—	—	50.00
1990	—	PF65 20.00				
1992 Sets only	—	—	—	—	—	30.00
1992	47,000	PF65 15.00				
1993	980,000	—	—	18.00	22.00	25.00
1993	—	PF65 15.00				
1996	19,297,000	—	—	5.00	7.00	8.00
1996	—	PF65 20.00				
1997	4,340,000	—	—	25.00	30.00	32.00
1997	—	PF65 25.00				
1998	—	—	—	—	—	—
1998 Proof	—	—	—	—	—	—

KM# 99 50 CENTS

15.55 g., Copper-Nickel, 31.65 mm. **Ruler:** Elizabeth II **Subject:** Australian Bicentennial **Obv:** Crowned head right **Rev:** Ship sailing towards gridmarked map of Australia, compass at upper center **Rev. Legend:** AUSTRALIA - 1788-1988 **Shape:** 12-sided

Date	Mintage	VF20	XF40	MS60	MS63	MS65
1988	8,100,000	—	—	12.00	15.00	17.00
1988	106,000	PF65 10.00				

KM# 99a 50 CENTS

18.00 g., 0.925 Silver 0.5353 oz. ASW, 31.65 mm. **Ruler:** Elizabeth II **Subject:** Australian Bicentennial **Obv:** Crowned head right **Rev:** Ship sailing towards gridmarked map of Australia, compass at upper center

Date	Mintage	VF20	XF40	MS60	MS63	MS65
1988	25,000	PF65 30.00				
1989	25,000	PF65 30.00				

KM# 127 50 CENTS

18.00 g., 0.925 Silver 0.5353 oz. ASW, 31.5 mm. **Ruler:** Elizabeth II **Subject:** Cook Commemorative **Obv:** Crowned head right **Rev:** Bust of Captain Cook at left, map of Australia at right

Date	Mintage	VF20	XF40	MS60	MS63	MS65
1989	25,000	PF65 30.00				

KM# 128 50 CENTS

18.00 g., 0.925 Silver 0.5353 oz. ASW, 31.5 mm. **Ruler:** Elizabeth II **Subject:** Queen's Silver Jubilee **Obv:** Crowned head right **Rev:** Circular geometric design

Date	Mintage	VF20	XF40	MS60	MS63	MS65
1989	25,000	PF65 20.00				

KM# 129 50 CENTS

18.00 g., 0.925 Silver 0.5353 oz. ASW, 31.5 mm. **Ruler:** Elizabeth II **Subject:** Wedding of Prince Charles and Lady Diana **Obv:** Crowned head right **Rev:** Conjoined heads of Prince Charles and Lady Diana left

Date	Mintage	VF20	XF40	MS60	MS63	MS65
1989	25,000	PF65 30.00				

KM# 130 50 CENTS

18.00 g., 0.925 Silver 0.5353 oz. ASW, 31.5 mm. **Ruler:** Elizabeth II **Subject:** XII Commonwealth Games - Brisbane **Obv:** Crowned head right **Rev:** Circle of images representing different sporting events

Date	Mintage	VF20	XF40	MS60	MS63	MS65
1989	25,000	PF65 30.00				

KM# 139 50 CENTS

15.55 g., Copper-Nickel, 31.65 mm. **Ruler:** Elizabeth II **Subject:** 25th Anniversary of Decimal Currency **Obv:** Crowned head right **Rev:** Head of Merino ram

Date	Mintage	VF20	XF40	MS60	MS63	MS65
1991	4,364,000	—	7.00	8.00	10.00	18.00
1991	—	PF65 20.00				

KM# 139a 50 CENTS

18.00 g., 0.925 Silver 0.5353 oz. ASW, 31.65 mm. **Ruler:** Elizabeth II **Subject:** 25th Anniversary of Decimal Currency **Obv:** Crowned head right **Rev:** Head of Merino ram

Date	Mintage	VF20	XF40	MS60	MS63	MS65
1991	25,000	PF65 30.00				

KM# 257 50 CENTS

15.55 g., Copper-Nickel, 31.65 mm. **Ruler:** Elizabeth II **Subject:** International Year of the Family **Obv:** Crowned head right **Rev:** Crude drawings depicting a family

Date	Mintage	VF20	XF40	MS60	MS63	MS65
1994	21,200,000	—	—	9.00	12.00	14.00
1994	39,000	PF65 20.00				

KM# 294 50 CENTS

15.55 g., Copper-Nickel, 31.65 mm. **Ruler:** Elizabeth II **Subject:** Weary Dunlop **Obv:** Crowned head right **Rev:** Bust of Dunlop at center, value below

Date	Mintage	VF20	XF40	MS60	MS63	MS65
1995	15,860,000	—	—	5.00	7.00	8.00
1995	48,000	PF65 15.00				

KM# 364 50 CENTS

15.55 g., Copper-Nickel, 31.65 mm. **Ruler:** Elizabeth II **Subject:** Discovery of Bass Strait **Obv:** Crowned head right **Rev:** Busts of Bass and Flinders, map of mainland Australia and Tasmania at left

Date	Mintage	VF20	XF40	MS60	MS63	MS65
1998	22,390,000	—	—	5.00	7.00	8.00
1998	32,000	PF65 15.00				

KM# 411 50 CENTS

36.31 g., 0.999 Silver 1.1662 oz. ASW **Ruler:** Elizabeth II **Subject:** Masterpieces in Silver **Obv:** Crowned head right **Rev:** 1937 crown design

Date	Mintage	VF20	XF40	MS60	MS63	MS65
1998	15,000	PF65 47.00				

KM# 404 50 CENTS

15.55 g., Copper-Nickel, 31.65 mm. **Ruler:** Elizabeth II **Obv:** Head with tiara right **Rev:** Australian coat of arms with kangaroo and emu supporters **Edge:** Plain **Shape:** 12-sided

Date	Mintage	VF20	XF40	MS60	MS63	MS65
1999	20,318,000	—	—	6.00	8.00	9.00
1999	28,000	PF65 25.00				

KM# 484 50 CENTS

3.24 g., 0.999 Silver 0.1041 oz. ASW, 19.4 mm. **Ruler:** Elizabeth II **Series:** Masterpieces in Silver **Obv:** Bust right **Rev:** Coat of arms with kangaroo and emu supporters **Edge:** Reeded

Date	Mintage	VF20	XF40	MS60	MS63	MS65
1999 B	15,000	PF65 30.00				

KM# 437 50 CENTS

15.55 g., Copper-Nickel, 31.65 mm. **Ruler:** Elizabeth II **Subject:** Royal Visit **Obv:** Head with tiara right **Rev:** Australian flag above Canberra Parliament House, British crown at right **Edge:** Plain **Shape:** 12-sided

Date	Mintage	VF20	XF40	MS60	MS63	MS65
2000 B	5,000	—	—	7.00	9.00	10.00

KM# 437a 50 CENTS

18.24 g., 0.999 Silver 0.5858 oz. ASW, 31.65 mm. **Ruler:** Elizabeth II **Subject:** Royal Visit **Obv:** Head with tiara right **Rev:** Australian flag above Canberra Parliament House, British crown at right

Date	Mintage	VF20	XF40	MS60	MS63	MS65
2000 B	25,000	PF65 60.00				

KM# 488.1 50 CENTS

15.55 g., Copper-Nickel, 31.65 mm. **Ruler:** Elizabeth II **Subject:** Millennium **Obv:** Head with tiara right **Rev:** Australian flag **Edge:** Plain **Shape:** 12-sided **Note:** Prev. KM#488.

Date	Mintage	VF20	XF40	MS60	MS63	MS65
2000 B	16,600,000	—	—	5.00	7.00	8.00
2000 B	—	PF65 90.00				

KM# 488.2 50 CENTS

15.55 g., Copper-Nickel, 31.65 mm. **Ruler:** Elizabeth II **Subject:** Millennium **Obv:** Head with tiara right **Rev:** Multicolor Australian flag **Edge:** Plain **Shape:** 12-sided **Note:** Prev. KM#488.1.

Date	Mintage	VF20	XF40	MS60	MS63	MS65
2000 B	65,000	PF65 150				

KM# 499 50 CENTS

36.31 g., 0.999 Silver 1.1662 oz. ASW, 38.7 mm. **Ruler:** Elizabeth II **Series:** Masterpieces in Silver - 2000 Set **Obv:** Rank-Broadley head with tiara right **Rev:** Head left **Edge:** Reeded

Date	Mintage	VF20	XF40	MS60	MS63	MS65
2000 B	15,000	PF65 42.00				

KM# 77 DOLLAR

9.00 g., Aluminum-Bronze, 25 mm. **Ruler:** Elizabeth II **Obv:** Young bust right **Rev:** 5 kangaroos, denomination **Edge:** Segmented reeding

Date	Mintage	VF20	XF40	MS60	MS63	MS65
1984	159,000	PF65 9.00				
1984	185,985,000	—	2.00	3.00	4.00	5.00

KM# 84 DOLLAR

9.00 g., Aluminum-Bronze, 25 mm. **Ruler:** Elizabeth II **Obv:** Crowned head right **Rev:** 5 kangaroos, value **Edge:** Segmented reeding

Date	Mintage	VF20	XF40	MS60	MS63	MS65
1985	91,400,000	—	2.00	4.00	5.00	7.00
1985	75,000	PF65 12.00				
1987 Sets only	200,000	—	—	5.00	6.00	15.00
1987	70,000	PF65 14.00				
1989	—	—	—	9.00	12.00	20.00
1989	—	PF65 12.00				
1990	—	—	—	25.00	30.00	45.00
1990	—	PF65 22.00				
1991	—	—	—	28.00	35.00	50.00
1991	—	PF65 30.00				
1994	47,639,000	—	—	12.00	14.00	15.00
1994	—	PF65 13.00				
1995	21,412,000	—	—	8.00	10.00	12.00
1995	—	PF65 15.00				
1998	16,248,000	—	—	6.00	8.00	9.00
1998	—	PF65 25.00				

KM# 84a DOLLAR

11.49 g., 0.925 Silver 0.3417 oz. ASW, 25 mm. **Ruler:** Elizabeth II **Subject:** Masterpieces in Silver **Obv:** Crowned head right **Rev:** 5 kangaroos, value

Date	Mintage	VF20	XF40	MS60	MS63	MS65
1990	25,000	PF65 35.00				
1991	23,000	PF65 17.00				

KM# 87 DOLLAR

9.00 g., Aluminum-Bronze, 25 mm. **Ruler:** Elizabeth II **Subject:** International Year of Peace **Obv:** Crowned head right **Rev:** Dove above hands within wreath, value and legend below **Rev. Legend:** INTERNATIONAL YEAR OF PEACE **Edge:** Segmented reeding

Date	Mintage	VF20	XF40	MS60	MS63	MS65
1986	25,100,000	—	—	5.00	6.00	7.00
1986	67,000	PF65 20.00				

KM# 87a DOLLAR

11.49 g., 0.925 Silver 0.3417 oz. ASW, 25 mm. **Ruler:** Elizabeth II **Subject:** Masterpieces in Silver **Obv:** Crowned head right

Date	Mintage	VF20	XF40	MS60	MS63	MS65
1990	25,000	PF65 35.00				

KM# 100 DOLLAR

9.00 g., Aluminum-Bronze, 25 mm. **Ruler:** Elizabeth II **Subject:** First Fleet Bicentenary **Obv:** Crowned head right **Rev:** Kangaroo on aboriginal art patterned background, denomination below **Edge:** Segmented reeding

Date	Mintage	VF20	XF40	MS60	MS63	MS65
1988	20,294,000	—	—	4.00	5.00	6.00
1988	106,000	PF65 80.00				

KM# 100a DOLLAR

11.49 g., 0.925 Silver 0.3417 oz. ASW, 25 mm. **Ruler:** Elizabeth II **Subject:** First Fleet Bicentenary **Obv:** Crowned head right **Rev:** Kangaroo on aboriginal art patterned background, denomination below

Date	Mintage	VF20	XF40	MS60	MS63	MS65
1988	25,000	PF65 35.00				
1990	25,000	PF65 35.00				

KM# 112 DOLLAR

31.10 g., 0.999 Silver 0.9989 oz. ASW **Ruler:** Elizabeth II **Subject:** Aboriginal Culture **Obv:** Holey dollar with legend around **Rev:** Holey dollar with snake around eating its tail **Shape:** Round with hole in middle **Note:** The "outer ring" coin issued with the center "plug" 25 cents, KM#113.

Date	Mintage	VF20	XF40	MS60	MS63	MS65
1988	100,000	PF65 55.00				

KM# 131 DOLLAR

31.10 g., 0.999 Silver 0.9989 oz. ASW **Ruler:** Elizabeth II **Obv:** Holey dollar with small silhouette of crowned Queen at top dividing legend, value at bottom **Rev:** 2 crocodiles around hole **Shape:** Round with hole in middle **Note:** The "outer ring" coin issued with the center "plug" 25 cents, KM#132.

Date	Mintage	VF20	XF40	MS60	MS63	MS65
1989	45,000	PF65 42.00				

KM# 154 DOLLAR

31.10 g., 0.999 Silver 0.9989 oz. ASW **Ruler:** Elizabeth II **Rev:** Stylized Natives and Jungle **Note:** The "outer ring" coin issued with the center "plug" 25 cents, KM#155.

Date	Mintage	VF20	XF40	MS60	MS63	MS65
1990	30,000	PF65 45.00				

KM# 175 DOLLAR

9.00 g., Aluminum-Bronze, 25 mm. **Ruler:** Elizabeth II **Subject:** Barcelona - 25th Olympics **Obv:** Crowned head right **Rev:** Female javelin thrower **Edge:** Segmented reeding

Date	Mintage	VF20	XF40	MS60	MS63	MS65
1992	23,500	—	—	—	—	65.00
Note: Olympic card						
1992	16,996	—	—	—	—	85.00
Note: RAM wallet						
1992	Inc. above	—	—	—	—	150
Note: Olympic wallet						
1992	2,940	PF65 275				

KM# 175a.1 DOLLAR

11.49 g., 0.925 Silver 0.3417 oz. ASW, 25 mm. **Ruler:** Elizabeth II **Subject:** Barcelona - 25th Olympiad **Obv:** Crowned head right **Rev:** Female javelin thrower

Date	Mintage	VF20	XF40	MS60	MS63	MS65
1992	—	—	—	—	—	—
1992	12,500	PF65 175				

KM# 175a.2 DOLLAR

11.49 g., 0.925 Silver 0.3417 oz. ASW, 25 mm. **Ruler:** Elizabeth II **Subject:** Barcelona - 25th Olympiad **Obv:** Crowned head right **Rev:** Female javelin thrower **Edge:** Reeded

Date	Mintage	VF20	XF40	MS60	MS63	MS65
1992	2,500	PF65 295				

KM# 208 DOLLAR

9.00 g., Aluminum-Bronze, 25 mm. **Ruler:** Elizabeth II **Obv:** Crowned head right **Rev:** Stylized tree above value, 2 hands above Landcare Australia **Edge:** Segmented reeding **Note:** Visitors at mints and coin shows were allowed to strike a coin for a fee at the following C - Canberra, M - Royal Melbourne Show and S - Sydney Royal Easter Show.

Date	Mintage	VF20	XF40	MS60	MS63	MS65
1993	17,917,000	—	—	5.00	6.00	8.00
1993 M	—	PF65 55.00				
1993 C	91,993	—	—	6.00	8.00	10.00
1993 M	60,104	—	—	8.00	10.00	12.00
1993 S	87,939	—	—	6.00	8.00	10.00

KM# 208a.1 DOLLAR

Silver, 25 mm. **Ruler:** Elizabeth II **Obv:** Crowned head right **Rev:** Stylized tree, value below, hands above Landcare Australia **Edge:** Alternating reeded and plain sections

Date	Mintage	VF20	XF40	MS60	MS63	MS65
1993	20,000	PF65 110				

KM# 208a.2 DOLLAR

Silver, 25 mm. **Ruler:** Elizabeth II **Obv:** Crowned head right **Rev:** Stylized tree, value below, hands above Landcare Australia **Edge:** Reeded

Date	Mintage	VF20	XF40	MS60	MS63	MS65
1993	5,000	PF65 115				

KM# 258 DOLLAR

9.00 g., Aluminum-Bronze, 25 mm. **Ruler:** Elizabeth II **Subject:** 10th Anniversary - Introduction of Dollar Coin **Rev:** Paper money with coin design at left divides dates **Edge:** Segmented reeding **Note:** Visitors at mints and coin shows were allowed to strike a coin for a fee at the following C - Canberra, M - Royal Melbourne Show and S - Sydney Royal Easter Show.

Date	Mintage	VF20	XF40	MS60	MS63	MS65
1994 C	123,318	—	—	20.00	22.00	24.00
1994 M	65,440	—	—	21.00	23.00	25.00
1994 S	74,426	—	—	21.00	23.00	25.00

KM# 258a.1 DOLLAR

14.49 g., 0.925 Silver 0.4309 oz. ASW, 25 mm. **Ruler:** Elizabeth II **Subject:** 10th Anniversary - Introduction of Dollar Coin **Rev:** Paper money with coin design at left divides dates **Edge:** Reeded and plain sections

Date	Mintage	VF20	XF40	MS60	MS63	MS65
1994	20,000	PF65 68.00				

KM# 258a.2 DOLLAR

14.49 g., 0.925 Silver 0.4309 oz. ASW, 25 mm. **Ruler:** Elizabeth II **Subject:** 10th Anniversary - Introduction of Dollar Coin **Rev:** Paper money with coin design at left divides dates **Edge:** Reeded

Date	Mintage	VF20	XF40	MS60	MS63	MS65
1994	5,000	PF65 115				

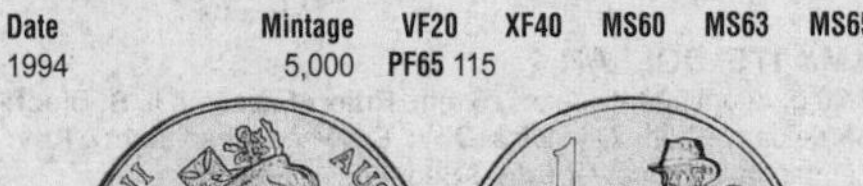

KM# 269 DOLLAR

9.00 g., Aluminum-Bronze, 25 mm. **Ruler:** Elizabeth II **Subject:** A.B. Banjo Paterson - Waltzing Matilda **Obv:** Crowned head right **Rev:** 3/4-length figure of Banjo Paterson on a walkabout with walking stick **Edge:** Segmented reeding **Note:** Mint visitors and at coin shows were allowed to strike a coin for a fee at the following C - Canberra, M - Royal Melbourne Show, S - Sydney Royal Easter Show and B - Brisbane Agricultural Show.

Date	Mintage	VF20	XF40	MS60	MS63	MS65
1995 B	74,353	—	—	35.00	45.00	50.00
1995 C	156,453	—	—	30.00	38.00	42.00
1995 M	74,255	—	—	35.00	45.00	50.00
1995 S	82,810	—	—	35.00	45.00	50.00

KM# 269a.1 DOLLAR

14.49 g., 0.925 Silver 0.4309 oz. ASW, 25 mm. **Ruler:** Elizabeth II **Subject:** A.B. Banjo Paterson - Waltzing Matilda **Obv:** Crowned head right **Rev:** 3/4-length figure of Banjo Paterson on a walkabout with walking stick **Edge:** Alternating reeded and plain sections

Date	Mintage	VF20	XF40	MS60	MS63	MS65
1995	20,000	PF65 90.00				

KM# 269a.2 DOLLAR

14.49 g., 0.925 Silver 0.4309 oz. ASW, 25 mm. **Ruler:** Elizabeth II **Subject:** A.B. Banjo Paterson - Waltzing Matilda **Obv:** Crowned head right **Rev:** 3/4-length figure of Banjo Paterson on a walkabout with walking stick **Edge:** Reeded

Date	Mintage	VF20	XF40	MS60	MS63	MS65
1995	2,500	PF65 160				

KM# 310 DOLLAR

9.00 g., Aluminum-Bronze, 25 mm. **Ruler:** Elizabeth II **Subject:** Sir Henry Parkes **Obv:** Crowned head right **Rev:** Large head of Sir Henry Parkes half facing right, legend around **Rev. Legend:** SIR HENRY PARKES 1815-1896, FATHER OF FEDERATION **Edge:** Segmented reeding **Note:** Visitors at mints and coin shows were allowed to strike a coin for a fee at the following C - Canberra, M - Royal Melbourne Show, S - Sydney Royal Easter Show, B - Brisbane Agricultural Show and A - Adelaide Show.

Date	Mintage	VF20	XF40	MS60	MS63	MS65
1996	26,200,000	—	—	5.00	7.00	9.00
1996	—	PF65 65.00				
1996 A	20,000	—	—	12.00	15.00	17.00
1996 B	30,000	—	—	12.00	15.00	17.00
1996 C	252,000	—	—	8.00	10.00	12.00
1996 M	20,110	—	—	12.00	15.00	17.00
1996 S	49,900	—	—	12.00	15.00	17.00

KM# 310a DOLLAR

11.49 g., 0.925 Silver 0.3417 oz. ASW, 25 mm. **Ruler:** Elizabeth II **Subject:** Sir Henry Parkes **Obv:** Crowned head right **Rev:** Large head of Sir Henry Parkes half facing right, legend around **Rev. Legend:** SIR HENRY PARKES 1815-1896, FATHER OF FEDERATION

Date	Mintage	VF20	XF40	MS60	MS63	MS65
1996	20,000	PF65 65.00				

KM# 326 DOLLAR

31.10 g., 0.999 Silver 0.999 oz. ASW **Ruler:** Elizabeth II **Subject:** 30th Anniversary - Decimal Coinage **Obv:** Crowned head right **Rev:** Map and seven different coin designs

Date	Mintage	VF20	XF40	MS60	MS63	MS65
1996	19,927	PF65 140				

KM# 327 DOLLAR

9.00 g., Aluminum-Bronze, 25 mm. **Ruler:** Elizabeth II **Subject:** Sir Charles Kingsford Smith **Obv:** Crowned head right **Rev:** Pilot above airplane, dates

Date	Mintage	VF20	XF40	MS60	MS63	MS65
1997	24,381,000	—	—	22.00	25.00	28.00

KM# 355 DOLLAR

9.00 g., Aluminum-Bronze, 25 mm. **Ruler:** Elizabeth II **Subject:** Sir Charles Kingsford Smith **Obv:** Crowned head right **Rev:** Head of Sir C. Kingsford Smith over airplane over world map **Note:** Visitors at mints and coin shows were allowed to strike a coin for a fee at the following C - Canberra, M - Royal Melbourne Show, S - Sydney Royal Easter Show, B - Brisbane Agricultural Show and A - Adelaide Show.

Date	Mintage	VF20	XF40	MS60	MS63	MS65
1997	28,616	—	—	22.00	25.00	28.00
1997 M	50,850	—	—	22.00	25.00	28.00
1997 A	25,400	—	—	18.00	20.00	22.00
1997 B	102,203	—	—	18.00	20.00	22.00
1997 C	27,430	—	—	22.00	25.00	28.00

KM# 355a DOLLAR

11.66 g., 0.999 Silver 0.3745 oz. ASW, 25 mm. **Ruler:** Elizabeth II **Subject:** Sir Charles Kingsford Smith **Obv:** Crowned head right **Rev:** Head of Sir C. Kingsford Smith over airplane over world map

Date	Mintage	VF20	XF40	MS60	MS63	MS65
1997	2,480	PF65 55.00				

KM# 721 DOLLAR

31.63 g., 0.999 Silver 1.0159 oz. ASW, 39.9 mm. **Ruler:** Elizabeth II **Obv:** Crowned head right **Rev:** Old Parliament building above 1927 one florin KM #31 coin design **Edge:** Reeded

Date	Mintage	VF20	XF40	MS60	MS63	MS65
1997	—	PF65 65.00				

KM# 366 DOLLAR

9.00 g., Aluminum-Bronze, 25 mm. **Ruler:** Elizabeth II **Obv:** Crowned head right **Rev:** Bust of Howard Florey facing **Note:** Visitors at mints and coin shows were allowed to strike a coin for a fee at the following C - Canberra, M - Royal Melbourne Show, S - Sydney Royal Easter Show, B - Brisbane Agricultural Show and A - Adelaide Show.

Date	Mintage	VF20	XF40	MS60	MS63	MS65
1998 A	21,120	—	—	14.00	18.00	20.00
1998 B	29,914	—	—	14.00	18.00	20.00
1998 C	77,035	—	—	10.00	12.00	15.00
1998 M	21,309	—	—	14.00	18.00	20.00
1998 S	44,080	—	—	14.00	18.00	20.00

KM# 366a DOLLAR

11.66 g., 0.999 Silver 0.3745 oz. ASW, 25 mm. **Ruler:** Elizabeth II **Obv:** Crowned head right **Rev:** Bust of Howard Florey facing

Date	Mintage	VF20	XF40	MS60	MS63	MS65
1998	20,000	PF65 60.00				

KM# 412 DOLLAR

31.10 g., 0.999 Silver 0.999 oz. ASW **Ruler:** Elizabeth II **Subject:** 10th Anniversary - New Parliament House **Obv:** Crowned head right **Rev:** Parliament building

Date	Mintage	VF20	XF40	MS60	MS63	MS65
1998	17,096	PF65 55.00				

KM# 722 DOLLAR

31.51 g., 0.999 Silver 1.0121 oz. ASW, 39.9 mm. **Ruler:** Elizabeth II **Obv:** Crowned head right **Rev:** Old Parliament building above 1988 5 dollar KM #102 coin design **Edge:** Reeded

Date	Mintage	VF20	XF40	MS60	MS63	MS65
1998	21,791	PF65 90.00				

KM# 400 DOLLAR

9.00 g., Aluminum-Bronze, 25 mm. **Ruler:** Elizabeth II **Obv:** Rank-Broadley head with tiara right **Rev:** Anzac soldier wearing slouch hat, 3/4 left **Note:** Visitors at mints and coin shows were allowed to strike a coin for a fee at the following C - Canberra, M - Royal Melbourne Show, S - Sydney Royal Easter Show, B - Brisbane Agricultural Show and A - Adelaide Show.

Date	Mintage	VF20	XF40	MS60	MS63	MS65
1999	53,286	—	—	25.00	30.00	35.00
1999 C	126,161	—	—	22.00	25.00	30.00
1999 B	33,634	—	—	28.00	35.00	40.00
1999 M	49,841	—	—	25.00	30.00	35.00
1999 A	28,681	—	—	28.00	35.00	40.00
2000	47,830	—	—	100	135	150

KM# 400a DOLLAR

11.66 g., 0.999 Silver 0.3745 oz. ASW, 25 mm. **Ruler:** Elizabeth II **Subject:** The Last of the Anzacs **Obv:** Rank-Broadley head with tiara right **Rev:** Anzac soldier wearing slouch hat **Edge:** Reeded and plain sections on edge

Date	Mintage	VF20	XF40	MS60	MS63	MS65
1999	25,000	PF65 35.00				

KM# 405 DOLLAR

9.00 g., Aluminum-Bronze, 25 mm. **Ruler:** Elizabeth II **Subject:** International Year of Older People **Obv:** Crowned head right **Rev:** IYOP logo **Rev. Legend:** TOWARDS A SOCIETY FOR ALL AGES - INTERNATIONAL YEAR OF OLDER PERSONS

Date	Mintage	VF20	XF40	MS60	MS63	MS65
1999	29,218,000	—	—	8.00	10.00	12.50
1999.	—	PF65 18.50				

KM# 476 DOLLAR

31.10 g., 0.999 Silver 0.999 oz. ASW **Ruler:** Elizabeth II

Subject: Majestic Images **Obv:** Head with tiara right **Rev:** Conjoined busts of Queen Elizabeth II **Edge:** Reeded

Date	Mintage	VF20	XF40	MS60	MS63	MS65
1999 B	17,000	PF65 80.00				

KM# 485 DOLLAR

6.57 g., 0.999 Silver 0.211 oz. ASW, 23.6 mm. **Ruler:** Elizabeth II **Series:** Masterpieces in Silver **Obv:** Head right **Rev:** Ram left above denomination and date **Edge:** Reeded

Date	Mintage	VF20	XF40	MS60	MS63	MS65
1999 B	15,000	PF65 18.00				

KM# 422 DOLLAR

9.00 g., Aluminum-Bronze, 25 mm. **Ruler:** Elizabeth II **Subject:** HMAS Sydney II **Obv:** Head with tiara right **Rev:** Ship above denomination **Edge:** Segmented reeding

Date	Mintage	VF20	XF40	MS60	MS63	MS65
2000 C	86,900	—	—	—	25.00	30.00
2000 S	52,000	—	—	—	30.00	35.00

KM# 422a DOLLAR

11.66 g., 0.999 Silver 0.3745 oz. ASW, 25 mm. **Ruler:** Elizabeth II **Obv:** Head with tiara right **Rev:** HMAS Sydney II above value

Date	Mintage	VF20	XF40	MS60	MS63	MS65
2000	20,000	PF65 70.00				

KM# 489 DOLLAR

9.00 g., Aluminum-Bronze, 25 mm. **Ruler:** Elizabeth II **Obv:** Head with tiara right **Rev:** Circle of 5 kangaroos **Edge:** Segmented reeding

Date	Mintage	VF20	XF40	MS60	MS63	MS65
2000 B	7,592,000	—	—	40.00	50.00	60.00
2000 B Proof	—	—	—	—	—	—

KM# 493 DOLLAR

9.00 g., Aluminum-Bronze, 25 mm. **Ruler:** Elizabeth II **Subject:** Victoria Cross **Obv:** Head with tiara right **Rev:** The Victoria Cross **Edge:** Segmented reeding

Date	Mintage	VF20	XF40	MS60	MS63	MS65
2000 B	49,877	—	—	—	295	315

KM# 509 DOLLAR

31.10 g., 0.999 Silver 0.999 oz. ASW, 40 mm. **Ruler:** Elizabeth II **Subject:** Proclamation Coins of Australia **Obv:** Head with tiara right **Rev:** The Cartwell Penny of 1797 **Edge:** Reeded

Date	Mintage	VF20	XF40	MS60	MS63	MS65
2000	18,400	PF65 65.00				

KM# 514 DOLLAR

31.10 g., 0.999 Silver 0.999 oz. ASW with Gold inlay., 40.4 mm. **Ruler:** Elizabeth II **Subject:** Millennium **Obv:** Head with tiara right **Rev:** Gold inlay earth and radiant sun as seen from the moon's surface **Edge:** Reeded

Date	Mintage	VF20	XF40	MS60	MS63	MS65
2000 Prooflike	30,000	—	—	—	—	37.50

KM# 529.1 DOLLAR

9.00 g., Aluminum-Bronze, 25 mm. **Ruler:** Elizabeth II **Subject:** Olymphilex Exhibition **Obv:** Head with tiara right **Rev:** Denomination and Olympic logo **Edge Lettering:** Incuse SYDNEY

Date	Mintage	VF20	XF40	MS60	MS63	MS65
2000 S	98,567	—	—	—	20.00	22.00

KM# 529.2 DOLLAR

9.00 g., Aluminum-Bronze, 25 mm. **Ruler:** Elizabeth II **Obv:** Head with tiara right **Rev:** Denomination and Olympic logo **Edge Lettering:** CANBERRA

Date	Mintage	VF20	XF40	MS60	MS63	MS65
2000 B	72,573	—	—	—	18.00	20.00

KM# 101 2 DOLLARS

6.60 g., Aluminum-Bronze, 20.5 mm. **Ruler:** Elizabeth II **Obv:** Crowned head right **Rev:** 1/2-length figure of Aboriginal man at left, 5 stars above value at right **Edge:** Segmented reeding

Date	Mintage	VF20	XF40	MS60	MS63	MS65
1988	160,700,000	—	—	4.00	5.00	6.00
1988	45,000	PF65 24.00				
1989	31,637,000	—	—	4.00	5.00	6.00
1989	—	PF65 8.00				
1990	10,330,500	—	—	6.00	8.00	9.00
1990	—	PF65 10.00				
1991 Sets only	—	—	—	—	120	125
1991	—	PF65 75.00				
1992	15,504,000	—	—	—	10.00	12.00
1992	47,000	PF65 10.00				
1993	4,870,000	—	—	—	15.00	17.00
1993	—	PF65 15.00				
1994	22,143,000	—	—	—	10.00	25.00
1994	—	PF65 20.00				
1995	13,929,000	—	—	—	8.00	10.00
1995	—	PF65 15.00				
1996	13,909,000	—	—	—	8.00	10.00
1996	—	PF65 20.00				
1997	19,039,000	—	—	—	10.00	12.00
1997	—	PF65 20.00				
1998	8,719,000	—	—	—	8.00	10.00
1998	—	PF65 25.00				

KM# 101a 2 DOLLARS

8.43 g., 0.925 Silver 0.2507 oz. ASW, 20.62 mm. **Ruler:** Elizabeth II **Obv:** Crowned head right **Rev:** Aboriginal Elder at left, 5 stars above value at right

Date	Mintage	VF20	XF40	MS60	MS63	MS65
1988	25,000	PF65 20.00				
1991	23,000	PF65 20.00				

KM# 406 2 DOLLARS

6.60 g., Aluminum-Bronze, 20.5 mm. **Ruler:** Elizabeth II **Obv:** Head with tiara right **Rev:** Aboriginal elder at left, stars above at right **Edge:** Segmented reeding

Date	Mintage	VF20	XF40	MS60	MS63	MS65
1999	35,718,000	—	—	—	20.00	22.00
1999	—	PF65 25.00				
2000	5,706,000	—	—	—	28.00	30.00
2000	—	PF65 50.00				

KM# 486 2 DOLLARS

13.36 g., 0.999 Silver 0.4291 oz. ASW, 28.5 mm. **Ruler:** Elizabeth II **Series:** Masterpieces in Silver **Obv:** Crowned head right **Rev:** St. George on horseback slaying the dragon **Edge:** Reeded

Date	Mintage	VF20	XF40	MS60	MS63	MS65
1999 B	15,000	PF65 25.00				

KM# 500 2 DOLLARS

8.55 g., 0.999 Silver 0.2746 oz. ASW, 20.5 mm. **Ruler:** Elizabeth II **Series:** Masterpieces in Silver - 2000 Set **Obv:** Head with tiara right **Rev:** Queen Victoria's bust, older with veiled head, left **Edge:** Reeded

Date	Mintage	VF20	XF40	MS60	MS63	MS65
2000 B	15,000	PF65 27.50				

KM# 102 5 DOLLARS

20.00 g., Aluminum-Bronze, 38.74 mm. **Ruler:** Elizabeth II **Obv:** Crowned head right **Rev:** Parliament House, Value below

Date	Mintage	VF20	XF40	MS60	MS63	MS65
1988	3,000,000	—	—	—	5.00	6.50
1988	80,000	PF65 12.00				

KM# 102a 5 DOLLARS

35.79 g., 0.925 Silver 1.0644 oz. ASW, 38.74 mm. **Ruler:** Elizabeth II **Obv:** Crowned head right **Rev:** Parliament House

Date	Mintage	VF20	XF40	MS60	MS63	MS65
1988	25,000	PF65 37.00				

KM# 134 5 DOLLARS

20.00 g., Aluminum-Bronze, 38.74 mm. **Ruler:** Elizabeth II

Subject: ANZAC Memorial **Obv:** Crowned head right **Rev:** Simpson and his donkey, value at top left

Date	Mintage	VF20	XF40	MS60	MS63	MS65
1990	774,349	—	—	—	5.50	7.00
1990	33,752	PF65 32.00				

KM# 190 5 DOLLARS

20.00 g., Aluminum-Bronze, 38.74 mm. **Ruler:** Elizabeth II **Subject:** Australian Role in Space Industry, value at bottom **Obv:** Crowned head right

Date	Mintage	VF20	XF40	MS60	MS63	MS65
1992	238,979	—	—	—	6.00	7.50
1992	25,006	PF65 17.00				

KM# 213 5 DOLLARS

35.79 g., 0.925 Silver 1.0644 oz. ASW **Ruler:** Elizabeth II **Subject:** Aboriginal Exploration, value bottom left **Obv:** Crowned head right **Rev:** Aborigine with spear in front of Australian geophysical map

Date	Mintage	VF20	XF40	MS60	MS63	MS65
1993	20,000	PF65 32.00				

KM# 214 5 DOLLARS

35.79 g., 0.925 Silver 1.0644 oz. ASW **Ruler:** Elizabeth II **Obv:** Crowned head right **Rev:** Bust of Abel Tasman in front of Australian map, value at top right

Date	Mintage	VF20	XF40	MS60	MS63	MS65
1993	20,000	PF65 32.00				

KM# 215 5 DOLLARS

35.79 g., 0.925 Silver 1.0644 oz. ASW **Ruler:** Elizabeth II **Obv:** Crowned head right **Rev:** Bust left in front of Australian map, large value to right of head

Date	Mintage	VF20	XF40	MS60	MS63	MS65
1993	20,000	PF65 32.00				

KM# 216 5 DOLLARS

35.79 g., 0.925 Silver 1.0644 oz. ASW **Ruler:** Elizabeth II **Obv:** Crowned head right **Rev:** Bust left in front of Australian map with value upper right

Date	Mintage	VF20	XF40	MS60	MS63	MS65
1993	20,000	PF65 32.00				

KM# 217 5 DOLLARS

35.79 g., 0.925 Silver 1.0644 oz. ASW **Ruler:** Elizabeth II **Obv:** Crowned head right **Rev:** Heads at left in front of Australian map with value upper right

Date	Mintage	VF20	XF40	MS60	MS63	MS65
1993	20,000	PF65 32.00				

KM# 224 5 DOLLARS

Bi-Metallic Aluminum-Bronze center in Stainless Steel ring, 28.12 mm. **Ruler:** Elizabeth II **Subject:** Women's Enfranchisement - 100-Year Anniversary of Women's Vote in South Australia **Obv:** Crowned head right within inner circle **Rev:** Head of Irish-born suffragist Mary Lee facing, within inner circle, value below circle **Note:** Non-magnetic.

Date	Mintage	VF20	XF40	MS60	MS63	MS65
1994	22,500	PF65 22.50				
1994	250,121	—	—	—	11.00	12.50

KM# 224a 5 DOLLARS

Aluminum-Bronze **Ruler:** Elizabeth II **Subject:** Women's Enfranchisement - 100 Year Anniversary of Women's Vote in South Australia **Obv:** Crowned head right within inner circle **Rev:** Head of Mary Lee facing, Irish-born suffragist

Date	Mintage	VF20	XF40	MS60	MS63	MS65
1994	2,500	PF65 42.00				

KM# 264 5 DOLLARS

31.10 g., 0.925 Silver 0.925 oz. ASW **Ruler:** Elizabeth II **Subject:** Australian Explorers **Obv:** Crowned head right **Rev:** Bust of Ludwig Leichhardt in front of route he explored, value bottom right

Date	Mintage	VF20	XF40	MS60	MS63	MS65
1994	Est. 20000	PF65 30.00				

KM# 265 5 DOLLARS

31.10 g., 0.925 Silver 0.925 oz. ASW **Ruler:** Elizabeth II **Subject:** Australian Explorers **Obv:** Crowned head right **Rev:** Bust 3/4 left, in front of route he explored on Australian map, value left of bust

Date	Mintage	VF20	XF40	MS60	MS63	MS65
1994	Est. 20000	PF65 30.00				

KM# 266 5 DOLLARS

31.10 g., 0.925 Silver 0.925 oz. ASW **Ruler:** Elizabeth II **Subject:** Australian Explorers **Obv:** Crowned head right **Rev:** Bust 3/4 right, to right of route he explored on map, value above map

Date	Mintage	VF20	XF40	MS60	MS63	MS65
1994	Est. 20000	PF65 30.00				

KM# 267 5 DOLLARS

31.10 g., 0.925 Silver 0.925 oz. ASW **Ruler:** Elizabeth II **Subject:** Australian Explorers **Obv:** Crowned head right **Rev:** Head 3/4 right, to right of map of exploration route at left, value right of beard

Date	Mintage	VF20	XF40	MS60	MS63	MS65
1994	Est. 20000	PF65 30.00				

KM# 268 5 DOLLARS
31.10 g., 0.925 Silver 0.925 oz. ASW **Ruler:** Elizabeth II **Subject:** Australian Explorers **Obv:** Crowned head right **Rev:** Bust left of route explored on map at right, value above map

Date	Mintage	VF20	XF40	MS60	MS63	MS65
1994	Est. 20000	PF65 30.00				

KM# 303 5 DOLLARS
35.79 g., 0.925 Silver 1.0644 oz. ASW **Ruler:** Elizabeth II **Subject:** The Gold Rush Era **Obv:** Crowned head right **Rev:** Two miners with supplies in front of mine, value at right

Date	Mintage	VF20	XF40	MS60	MS63	MS65
1995	20,000	PF65 35.00				

KM# 304 5 DOLLARS
35.79 g., 0.925 Silver 1.0644 oz. ASW **Ruler:** Elizabeth II **Subject:** Cobb and Co. 1853 **Obv:** Crowned head right **Rev:** Cobb & Co. Company stagecoach, value above

Date	Mintage	VF20	XF40	MS60	MS63	MS65
1995	20,000	PF65 35.00				

KM# 305 5 DOLLARS
35.79 g., 0.925 Silver 1.0644 oz. ASW **Ruler:** Elizabeth II **Subject:** Elizabeth MacArthur, 1766-1850 - Wool Merchant **Obv:** Crowned head right **Rev:** Head facing at lower right, flock of sheep above left, value below

Date	Mintage	VF20	XF40	MS60	MS63	MS65
1995	20,000	PF65 35.00				

KM# 306 5 DOLLARS
35.79 g., 0.925 Silver 1.0644 oz. ASW **Ruler:** Elizabeth II **Subject:** Col. William Light, 1786-1839 - City Plan **Obv:** Crowned head right **Rev:** Head of Col. Light at lower right half right, city plan at left, value below

Date	Mintage	VF20	XF40	MS60	MS63	MS65
1995	20,000	PF65 35.00				

KM# 307 5 DOLLARS
35.79 g., 0.925 Silver 1.0644 oz. ASW **Ruler:** Elizabeth II **Subject:** Charles Todd, 1827-1910 - Telegraph Line **Obv:** Crowned head right **Rev:** Head of Todd at lower right, telegraph line in background, value at lower left

Date	Mintage	VF20	XF40	MS60	MS63	MS65
1995	20,000	PF65 35.00				

KM# 311 5 DOLLARS
Bi-Metallic Aluminum-Bronze center in Stainless Steel ring, 28.12 mm. **Ruler:** Elizabeth II **Subject:** Sir Donald Bradman - Cricket Player **Obv:** Crowned head right **Rev:** 1/2-length figure holding bat within inner circle, value below, subject name above **Edge:** Smooth **Shape:** 24-sided **Note:** Non-magnetic.

Date	Mintage	VF20	XF40	MS60	MS63	MS65
1996	500,000	—	—	—	11.00	12.50
1997	—	—	—	—	11.00	12.50

KM# 312 5 DOLLARS
20.00 g., Aluminum-Bronze, 38.74 mm. **Ruler:** Elizabeth II **Subject:** Sir Donald Bradman, Cricket player, **Obv:** Crowned head right **Rev:** Standing figure in uniform within inner circle, value below

Date	Mintage	VF20	XF40	MS60	MS63	MS65
1996	22,500	PF65 37.50				

KM# 328 5 DOLLARS
35.79 g., 0.925 Silver 1.0644 oz. ASW **Ruler:** Elizabeth II **Subject:** Stockman **Obv:** Crowned head right **Rev:** Cowboy with whip, value top left

Date	Mintage	VF20	XF40	MS60	MS63	MS65
1996	20,000	PF65 37.50				

KM# 329 5 DOLLARS
35.79 g., 0.925 Silver 1.0644 oz. ASW **Ruler:** Elizabeth II **Subject:** Horse Racing **Obv:** Crowned head right **Rev:** Horse racing scene, denomination below

Date	Mintage	VF20	XF40	MS60	MS63	MS65
1996	20,000	PF65 37.50				

KM# 330 5 DOLLARS
35.79 g., 0.925 Silver 1.0644 oz. ASW **Ruler:** Elizabeth II **Obv:** Crowned head right **Rev:** Bust of soprano Dame Nellie Melba, with large hat, 3/4 facing, at right, drape, inscription and value at left

Date	Mintage	VF20	XF40	MS60	MS63	MS65
1996	20,000	PF65 37.50				

KM# 331 5 DOLLARS
35.79 g., 0.925 Silver 1.0644 oz. ASW **Ruler:** Elizabeth II **Subject:** Tom Roberts **Obv:** Crowned head right **Rev:** Half-length figure 3/4 facing, in front of painting, value at lower right

Date	Mintage	VF20	XF40	MS60	MS63	MS65
1996	20,000	PF65 37.50				

KM# 332 5 DOLLARS
35.79 g., 0.925 Silver 1.0644 oz. ASW **Ruler:** Elizabeth II **Subject:** Henry Lawson **Obv:** Crowned head right **Rev:** Author's portrait and letter to friends, value bottom left

Date	Mintage	VF20	XF40	MS60	MS63	MS65
1996	20,000	PF65 37.50				

KM# 356 5 DOLLARS

20.00 g., Aluminum-Bronze, 38.74 mm. **Ruler:** Elizabeth II **Subject:** Sydney 2000 **Obv:** Crowned head right **Rev:** Runner,left, Olympic logo below right elbow, value lower left

Date	Mintage	VF20	XF40	MS60	MS63	MS65
2000 (1997)	—	—	—	—	8.00	9.00

KM# 357 5 DOLLARS

20.00 g., Aluminum-Bronze, 38.74 mm. **Ruler:** Elizabeth II **Series:** Sydney 2000 Olympics **Obv:** Bust right **Rev:** Gymnast, value at right, Olympic logo bottom right

Date	Mintage	VF20	XF40	MS60	MS63	MS65
2000 (1997)	—	—	—	—	7.00	8.00

KM# 358 5 DOLLARS

20.00 g., Aluminum-Bronze, 38.74 mm. **Ruler:** Elizabeth II **Series:** Sydney 2000 Olympics **Obv:** Crowned head right **Rev:** Sailors, Olympic logo, upper right, value above rings

Date	Mintage	VF20	XF40	MS60	MS63	MS65
2000 (1997)	—	—	—	—	8.00	9.00

KM# 359 5 DOLLARS

20.00 g., Aluminum-Bronze **Ruler:** Elizabeth II **Subject:** Sydney 2000 **Obv:** Crowned head right **Rev:** Archer on left, Olympic logo at right, value above head

Date	Mintage	VF20	XF40	MS60	MS63	MS65
2000 (1997)	—	—	—	—	8.00	9.00

KM# 360 5 DOLLARS

20.00 g., Aluminum-Bronze, 38.74 mm. **Ruler:** Elizabeth II **Series:** Sydney 2000 Olympics **Obv:** Crowned head right **Rev:** Field hockey player Olympic logo lower right, value at upper right

Date	Mintage	VF20	XF40	MS60	MS63	MS65
2000 (1997)	—	—	—	—	7.00	8.00

KM# 361 5 DOLLARS

20.00 g., Aluminum-Bronze, 38.74 mm. **Ruler:** Elizabeth II **Series:** Sydney 2000 Olympics **Obv:** Crowned head right **Rev:** Power lifter, Olympic logo at lower right, value upper right

Date	Mintage	VF20	XF40	MS60	MS63	MS65
2000 (1997)	—	—	—	—	7.00	8.00

KM# 544 5 DOLLARS

35.79 g., 0.925 Silver 1.0644 oz. ASW, 38.9 mm. **Ruler:** Elizabeth II **Series:** Masterpieces of Transportation **Obv:** Crowned head right **Rev:** Camel pack train, value upper right **Edge:** Reeded

Date	Mintage	VF20	XF40	MS60	MS63	MS65
1997 B	10,000	PF65 38.00				

KM# 545 5 DOLLARS

35.79 g., 0.925 Silver 1.0644 oz. ASW, 38.9 mm. **Ruler:** Elizabeth II **Series:** Masterpieces of Transportation **Obv:** Crowned head right **Rev:** Riverboat, value below **Edge:** Reeded

Date	Mintage	VF20	XF40	MS60	MS63	MS65
1997 B	10,000	PF65 38.00				

KM# 546 5 DOLLARS

35.79 g., 0.925 Silver 1.0644 oz. ASW, 38.9 mm. **Ruler:** Elizabeth II **Series:** Masterpieces of Transportation **Obv:** Crowned head right **Rev:** Steam locomotive, value at top **Edge:** Reeded

Date	Mintage	VF20	XF40	MS60	MS63	MS65
1997 B	10,000	PF65 38.00				

KM# 547 5 DOLLARS

35.79 g., 0.925 Silver 1.0644 oz. ASW, 38.9 mm. **Ruler:** Elizabeth II **Series:** Masterpieces of Transportation **Obv:** Crowned head right **Rev:** Ox-drawn wagons, value below **Edge:** Reeded

Date	Mintage	VF20	XF40	MS60	MS63	MS65
1997	10,000	PF65 38.00				

KM# 548 5 DOLLARS

35.79 g., 0.925 Silver 1.0644 oz. ASW, 38.9 mm. **Ruler:** Elizabeth II **Series:** Masterpieces of Transportation **Obv:** Crowned head right **Rev:** Steam tractor, value below **Edge:** Reeded

Date	Mintage	VF20	XF40	MS60	MS63	MS65
1997 B	10,000	PF65 38.00				

KM# 368 5 DOLLARS

20.00 g., Aluminum-Bronze, 38.74 mm. **Ruler:** Elizabeth II **Series:** Sydney 2000 Olympics **Obv:** Crowned head right **Rev:** Cyclist, Olympic logo to right of head, value behind cyclist

Date	Mintage	VF20	XF40	MS60	MS63	MS65
2000 (1998)	—	—	—	—	8.00	9.00

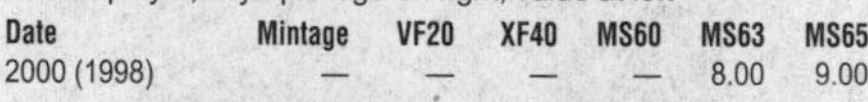

KM# 369 5 DOLLARS
20.00 g., Aluminum-Bronze, 38.74 mm. **Ruler:** Elizabeth II **Series:** Sydney 2000 Olympics **Obv:** Crowned head right **Rev:** Soccer player, Olympic logo on right, value at left

Date	Mintage	VF20	XF40	MS60	MS63	MS65
2000 (1998)	—	—	—	—	8.00	9.00

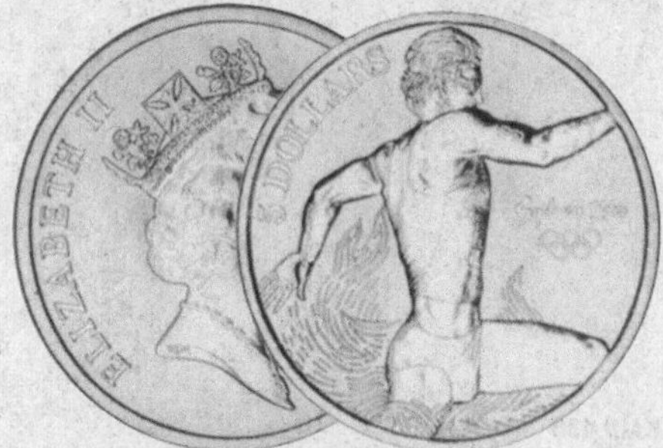

KM# 370 5 DOLLARS
20.00 g., Aluminum-Bronze, 38.74 mm. **Ruler:** Elizabeth II **Series:** Sydney 2000 Olympics **Obv:** Crowned head right **Rev:** Triathlon swimmer, Olympic logo on right, value upper left

Date	Mintage	VF20	XF40	MS60	MS63	MS65
2000 (1998)	—	—	—	—	8.00	9.00

KM# 371 5 DOLLARS
31.64 g., 0.999 Silver 1.0161 oz. ASW **Ruler:** Elizabeth II **Series:** Sydney 2000 Olympics **Obv:** Crowned head right **Rev:** Australian map above multicolor logo, Olympic logo at bottom

Date	Mintage	VF20	XF40	MS60	MS63	MS65
2000 (1998)	Est. 100000	PF65 45.00				

KM# 372 5 DOLLARS
31.64 g., 0.999 Silver 1.0161 oz. ASW **Ruler:** Elizabeth II **Series:** Sydney 2000 Olympics **Obv:** Crowned head right **Rev:** Two Great White sharks within wreath, Olympic logo at bottom

Date	Mintage	VF20	XF40	MS60	MS63	MS65
2000 (1998)	Est. 100000	PF65 55.00				

KM# 374 5 DOLLARS
Bi-Metallic Aluminum-Bronze center in Stainless Steel ring, 28.12 mm. **Ruler:** Elizabeth II **Subject:** 70 Years - Royal Flying Doctor Service **Obv:** Head with tiara right within inner circle **Rev:** Insignia above bi-plane, two dates below, within circle, value below circle

Date	Mintage	VF20	XF40	MS60	MS63	MS65
1998	—	—	—	—	10.00	12.00

KM# 375 5 DOLLARS
20.00 g., Aluminum-Bronze, 38.74 mm. **Ruler:** Elizabeth II **Series:** Sydney 2000 Summer Olympics **Obv:** Crowned head right **Rev:** Two netball players, Olympic logo at right, value on left

Date	Mintage	VF20	XF40	MS60	MS63	MS65
2000 (1998)	—	—	—	—	8.00	9.00

KM# 376 5 DOLLARS
20.00 g., Aluminum-Bronze, 38.74 mm. **Ruler:** Elizabeth II **Series:** Sydney 2000 Olympics **Obv:** Crowned head right **Rev:** Two wrestlers, Olympic logo to left, value at upper right

Date	Mintage	VF20	XF40	MS60	MS63	MS65
2000 (1998)	—	—	—	—	8.00	9.00

KM# 377 5 DOLLARS
20.00 g., Aluminum-Bronze, 38.74 mm. **Ruler:** Elizabeth II **Series:** Sydney 2000 Summer Olympics **Obv:** Crowned head right **Rev:** Canoeing event, Olympic logo at left, value at top

Date	Mintage	VF20	XF40	MS60	MS63	MS65
2000 (1998)	—	—	—	—	8.00	9.00

KM# 378 5 DOLLARS
20.00 g., Aluminum-Bronze, 38.74 mm. **Ruler:** Elizabeth II **Series:** Sydney 2000 Olympics **Obv:** Crowned head right **Rev:** Softball player swinging bat, Olympic logo at right, value at left

Date	Mintage	VF20	XF40	MS60	MS63	MS65
2000 (1998)	—	—	—	—	8.00	9.00

KM# 379 5 DOLLARS
31.64 g., 0.999 Silver 1.0161 oz. ASW **Ruler:** Elizabeth II **Series:** Sydney 2000 Olympics **Obv:** Crowned head right **Rev:** Frill-necked lizard within wreath, Olympic logo below

Date	Mintage	VF20	XF40	MS60	MS63	MS65
2000 (1998)	Est. 100000	PF65 55.00				

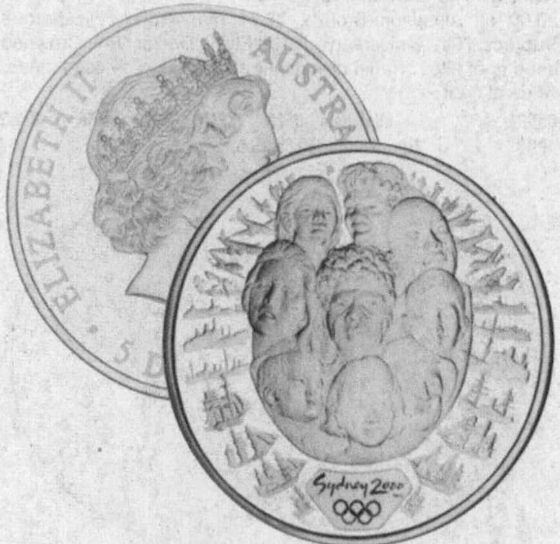

KM# 380 5 DOLLARS
31.64 g., 0.999 Silver 1.0161 oz. ASW **Ruler:** Elizabeth II **Series:** Sydney 2000 Olympics **Obv:** Crowned head right **Rev:** 9 Australian faces of different races, Olympic logo at bottom

Date	Mintage	VF20	XF40	MS60	MS63	MS65
2000 (1998)	Est. 100000	PF65 40.00				

KM# 381 5 DOLLARS
31.64 g., 0.999 Silver 1.0161 oz. ASW **Ruler:** Elizabeth II **Series:** Sydney 2000 Olympics **Obv:** Crowned head right **Rev:** Two dancing figures in dream circle, within circle of aquatic life, wreath encircling all, Olympic logo at bottom

Date	Mintage	VF20	XF40	MS60	MS63	MS65
2000 (1998)	Est. 100000	PF65 45.00				

KM# 382 5 DOLLARS
31.64 g., 0.999 Silver 1.0161 oz. ASW **Ruler:** Elizabeth II **Series:** Sydney 2000 Olympics **Obv:** Crowned head right **Rev:** Kangaroo in circle of grass trees, Olympic logo below, legend encircling all **Rev. Inscription:** Stuart Devlin

Date	Mintage	VF20	XF40	MS60	MS63	MS65
2000 (1998)	Est. 100000	PF65 55.00				

KM# 386 5 DOLLARS
20.00 g., Aluminum-Bronze, 38.74 mm. **Ruler:** Elizabeth II **Subject:** 70th Anniversary - Royal Flying Doctor **Obv:** Crowned head right **Rev:** Radio dispatcher and airplane divides legend, value at right

Date	Mintage	VF20	XF40	MS60	MS63	MS65
1998	Est. 20000	PF65 18.50				

KM# 407 5 DOLLARS
20.00 g., Aluminum-Bronze, 38.74 mm. **Ruler:** Elizabeth II **Series:** Sydney 2000 Olympics **Obv:** Crowned head right **Rev:** Two basketball players, value upper right, Olympic logo lower left

Date	Mintage	VF20	XF40	MS60	MS63	MS65
2000 (1999)	—	—	—	—	7.00	8.00

KM# 408 5 DOLLARS
20.00 g., Aluminum-Bronze, 38.74 mm. **Ruler:** Elizabeth II **Series:** Sydney 2000 Summer Olympics **Obv:** Crowned head right **Rev:** Tae Kwon Do competitor, Olympic logo at top, value on right

Date	Mintage	VF20	XF40	MS60	MS63	MS65
2000 (1999)	—	—	—	—	7.00	8.00

KM# 409 5 DOLLARS
20.00 g., Aluminum-Bronze, 38.74 mm. **Ruler:** Elizabeth II **Series:** Sydney 2000 Olympics **Obv:** Crowned head right **Rev:** Tennis player, value at left, Olympic logo below tennis ball

Date	Mintage	VF20	XF40	MS60	MS63	MS65
2000 (1999)	—	—	—	—	7.00	8.00

KM# 418 5 DOLLARS
20.00 g., Aluminum-Bronze, 38.74 mm. **Ruler:** Elizabeth II **Series:** Sydney 2000 Olympics **Obv:** Crowned head right **Rev:** Shooter with shotgun, Olympic logo above, value on right

Date	Mintage	VF20	XF40	MS60	MS63	MS65
2000 (1999)	—	—	—	—	7.00	8.00

KM# 419 5 DOLLARS
20.00 g., Aluminum-Bronze, 38.74 mm. **Ruler:** Elizabeth II **Series:** Sydney 2000 Olympics **Obv:** Crowned head right **Rev:** Table tennis player, Olympic logo upper left, value at top

Date	Mintage	VF20	XF40	MS60	MS63	MS65
2000 (1999)	—	—	—	—	7.00	8.00

KM# 420 5 DOLLARS
20.00 g., Aluminum-Bronze, 38.74 mm. **Ruler:** Elizabeth II **Series:** Sydney 2000 Olympics **Obv:** Crowned head right **Rev:** Fencer in action, Olympic logo below right arm, value at left

Date	Mintage	VF20	XF40	MS60	MS63	MS65
2000 (1999)	—	—	—	—	7.00	8.00

KM# 421 5 DOLLARS
20.00 g., Aluminum-Bronze, 38.74 mm. **Ruler:** Elizabeth II **Series:** Sydney 2000 Olympics **Obv:** Crowned head right **Rev:** Badminton player, Olympic logo above, value top right

Date	Mintage	VF20	XF40	MS60	MS63	MS65
2000 (1999)	—	—	—	—	8.00	9.00

KM# 438 5 DOLLARS
31.64 g., 0.999 Silver 1.0161 oz. ASW **Ruler:** Elizabeth II **Series:** Sydney 2000 Olympics **Obv:** Crowned head right **Rev:** Two emus with eggs and chicks within wreath, Olympic logo at bottom **Edge:** Reeded

Date	Mintage	VF20	XF40	MS60	MS63	MS65
2000 (1999)	100,000	PF65 50.00				

KM# 439 5 DOLLARS
31.64 g., 0.999 Silver 1.0161 oz. ASW **Ruler:** Elizabeth II **Series:** Sydney 2000 Olympics **Obv:** Crowned head right **Rev:** Koala in tree within wreath, Olympic logo below

Date	Mintage	VF20	XF40	MS60	MS63	MS65
2000 (1999)	100,000	PF65 45.00				

KM# 429 5 DOLLARS
20.00 g., Aluminum-Bronze, 38.74 mm. **Ruler:** Elizabeth II **Series:** Sydney 2000 Olympics **Obv:** Crowned head right **Rev:** Pentathlon events portrayed by 5 participants, Olympic logo at lower left, value at bottom

Date	Mintage	VF20	XF40	MS60	MS63	MS65
2000	—	—	—	—	8.00	9.00

KM# 430 5 DOLLARS
20.00 g., Aluminum-Bronze, 38.74 mm. **Ruler:** Elizabeth II **Obv:** Crowned head right **Rev:** Judo match, Olympic logo lower right, value at top

Date	Mintage	VF20	XF40	MS60	MS63	MS65
2000	—	—	—	—	7.00	8.00

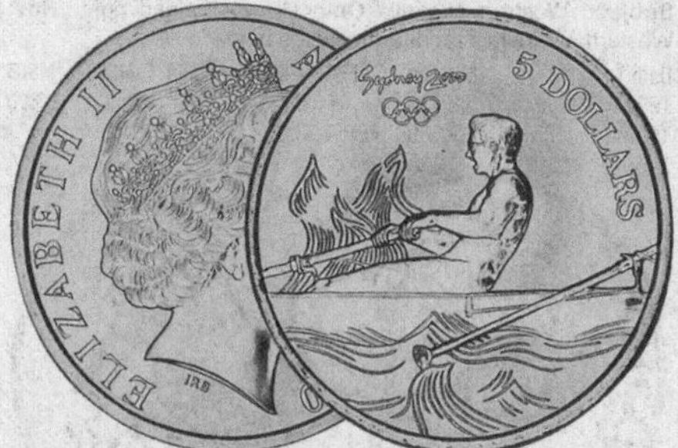

KM# 431 5 DOLLARS
20.00 g., Aluminum-Bronze, 38.74 mm. **Ruler:** Elizabeth II **Series:** Sydney 2000 Olympics **Obv:** Crowned head right **Rev:** Rower, Olympic logo upper left, value upper right

Date	Mintage	VF20	XF40	MS60	MS63	MS65
2000	—	—	—	—	8.00	9.00

KM# 432 5 DOLLARS
20.00 g., Aluminum-Bronze, 38.74 mm. **Ruler:** Elizabeth II **Series:** Sydney 2000 Olympics **Obv:** Crowned head right **Rev:** Two men boxing, value upper left, Olympic logo divides boxers at bottom

Date	Mintage	VF20	XF40	MS60	MS63	MS65
2000	—	—	—	—	8.00	9.00

KM# 433 5 DOLLARS
20.00 g., Aluminum-Bronze, 38.74 mm. **Ruler:** Elizabeth II **Series:** Sydney 2000 Olympics **Obv:** Crowned head right **Rev:** Volleyball player,Olympic logo below ball, value at left

Date	Mintage	VF20	XF40	MS60	MS63	MS65
2000	—	—	—	—	8.00	9.00

KM# 434 5 DOLLARS
20.00 g., Aluminum-Bronze, 38.74 mm. **Ruler:** Elizabeth II **Series:** Sydney 2000 Olympics **Obv:** Crowned head right **Rev:** Equestrian putting horse through jumps

Date	Mintage	VF20	XF40	MS60	MS63	MS65
2000	—	—	—	—	8.00	9.00

KM# 435 5 DOLLARS
20.00 g., Aluminum-Bronze, 38.74 mm. **Ruler:** Elizabeth II **Series:** Sydney 2000 Olympics **Obv:** Crowned head right **Rev:** Pitcher winding up

Date	Mintage	VF20	XF40	MS60	MS63	MS65
2000	—	—	—	—	8.00	9.00

KM# 436 5 DOLLARS
20.00 g., Aluminum-Bronze, 38.74 mm. **Ruler:** Elizabeth II **Series:** Sydney 2000 Olympics **Obv:** Crowned head right **Rev:** Swimmer, Olympic logo below, value above

Date	Mintage	VF20	XF40	MS60	MS63	MS65
2000	—	—	—	—	8.00	9.00

KM# 440 5 DOLLARS
31.64 g., 0.999 Silver 1.0161 oz. ASW **Ruler:** Elizabeth II **Series:** Sydney 2000 Olympics **Obv:** Crowned head right **Rev:** Three radiant circular views within circle of round maps Olympic logo at bottom

Date	Mintage	VF20	XF40	MS60	MS63	MS65
2000	100,000	**PF65** 37.50				

KM# 441 5 DOLLARS
31.64 g., 0.999 Silver 1.0161 oz. ASW **Ruler:** Elizabeth II **Series:** Sydney 2000 Olympics **Obv:** Crowned head right **Rev:** 7 figures positioned like spokes in a wheel, Olympic logo at bottom

Date	Mintage	VF20	XF40	MS60	MS63	MS65
2000	100,000	**PF65** 37.50				

KM# 478 5 DOLLARS
10.52 g., Bi-Metallic Aluminum-Bronze center in Stainless Steel ring, 28.12 mm. **Ruler:** Elizabeth II **Subject:** Phar Lap **Obv:** Head with tiara right within inner circle **Rev:** Jockey atop Phar Lap racing, right, within circle, divides date, value below circle **Edge:** Plain **Shape:** 24-sided

Date	Mintage	VF20	XF40	MS60	MS63	MS65
2000 B	—	—	—	—	10.00	12.00

KM# 510 5 DOLLARS
28.00 g., Aluminum-Bronze, 38.7 mm. **Ruler:** Elizabeth II **Subject:** Phar Lap **Obv:** Head with tiara right within inner circle **Rev:** Phar Lap and jockey facing right within horseshoe turned to left, value on bottom of shoe, subject name and date on top of shoe **Edge:** Reeded

Date	Mintage	VF20	XF40	MS60	MS63	MS65
2000	20,000	**PF65** 25.00				

KM# 515 5 DOLLARS
31.64 g., 0.999 Silver 1.0161 oz. ASW, 40.5 mm. **Ruler:** Elizabeth II **Series:** Olympics - Sydney Harbor Bridge **Obv:** Crowned head right **Rev:** Sydney suspension bridge within harbor wreath, Olympic logo at bottom **Edge Lettering:** GAMES OF THE XXVII OLYMPIAD twice

Date	Mintage	VF20	XF40	MS60	MS63	MS65
2000	100,000	**PF65** 45.00				

KM# 516 5 DOLLARS
31.64 g., 0.999 Silver 1.0161 oz. ASW, 40.5 mm. **Ruler:** Elizabeth II **Series:** Olympics - Kookaburra **Obv:** Crowned head right **Rev:** Kookaburra with Waratah leaves, within wreath, Olympic logo at bottom

Date	Mintage	VF20	XF40	MS60	MS63	MS65
2000	100,000	**PF65** 47.00				

KM# 517 5 DOLLARS
Aluminum-Bronze, 38.6 mm. **Ruler:** Elizabeth II **Subject:** Paralympics **Obv:** Crowned head right **Rev:** Wheelchair racer and multicolor logo, small value to right of chair **Edge:** Reeded

Date	Mintage	VF20	XF40	MS60	MS63	MS65
2000	Est. 30000	—	—	—	12.50	15.00

KM# 815 5 DOLLARS

31.64 g., 0.999 Silver 1.0161 oz. ASW, 40 mm. **Ruler:** Elizabeth II **Obv:** Queen's portrait **Rev:** Sydney Opera House

Date	Mintage	VF20	XF40	MS60	MS63	MS65
2000	100,000	PF65 40.00				

KM# 816 5 DOLLARS

31.64 g., 0.999 Silver 1.0161 oz. ASW, 40 mm. **Ruler:** Elizabeth II **Obv:** Queen's portrait **Rev:** Platypus duckbill in water

Date	Mintage	VF20	XF40	MS60	MS63	MS65
2000	100,000	PF65 42.00				

KM# 817 5 DOLLARS

31.64 g., 0.999 Silver 1.0161 oz. ASW, 40 mm. **Ruler:** Elizabeth II **Obv:** Queen's portrait **Rev:** Echidna

Date	Mintage	VF20	XF40	MS60	MS63	MS65
2000	100,000	PF65 42.00				

KM# 818 5 DOLLARS

31.64 g., 0.999 Silver 1.0161 oz. ASW, 40 mm. **Ruler:** Elizabeth II **Obv:** Queen's portrait **Rev:** Birds flying above Sydney Harbor

Date	Mintage	VF20	XF40	MS60	MS63	MS65
2000	100,000	PF65 40.00				

KM# 75 10 DOLLARS

20.00 g., 0.925 Silver 0.5948 oz. ASW **Ruler:** Elizabeth II **Subject:** XII Commonwealth Games - Brisbane **Obv:** Young bust right **Rev:** Outline of country with hurdles on top at center of shield of athletes, legend surrounds all

Date	Mintage	VF20	XF40	MS60	MS63	MS65
1982	125,700	—	—	—	20.00	22.00
1982	85,142	PF65 25.00				

KM# 85 10 DOLLARS

20.00 g., 0.925 Silver 0.5948 oz. ASW **Ruler:** Elizabeth II **Subject:** 150th Anniversary - State of Victoria **Obv:** Crowned head right **Rev:** Arms of Victoria, value at bottom, state name divides dates at top

Date	Mintage	VF20	XF40	MS60	MS63	MS65
1985	81,751	—	—	—	22.00	24.00
1985	55,806	PF65 27.00				

KM# 88 10 DOLLARS

20.00 g., 0.925 Silver 0.5948 oz. ASW **Ruler:** Elizabeth II **Subject:** 150th Anniversary - South Australia **Obv:** Crowned head right **Rev:** Arms of South Australia, value below, name divides dates at top

Date	Mintage	VF20	XF40	MS60	MS63	MS65
1986	78,100	—	—	—	22.00	24.00
1986	52,150	PF65 27.00				

KM# 93 10 DOLLARS

20.00 g., 0.925 Silver 0.5948 oz. ASW **Ruler:** Elizabeth II **Subject:** New South Wales **Obv:** Crowned head right **Rev:** Arms of New South Wales, value below

Date	Mintage	VF20	XF40	MS60	MS63	MS65
1987	55,000	—	—	—	22.00	24.00
1987	50,500	PF65 27.00				

KM# 103 10 DOLLARS

20.00 g., 0.925 Silver 0.5948 oz. ASW **Ruler:** Elizabeth II **Subject:** Landing of Governor Philip **Obv:** Crowned head right **Rev:** Large sailing ship to right, smaller ships behind and left, canoe with rowers in foreground, value at top left

Date	Mintage	VF20	XF40	MS60	MS63	MS65
1988	111,497	—	—	—	20.00	22.00
1988	80,099	PF65 25.00				

KM# 114 10 DOLLARS

20.00 g., 0.925 Silver 0.5948 oz. ASW **Ruler:** Elizabeth II **Subject:** Queensland **Obv:** Crowned head right **Rev:** Arms of Queensland, name of subject at top, value below arms

Date	Mintage	VF20	XF40	MS60	MS63	MS65
1989	48,929	—	—	—	22.00	24.00
1989	48,573	PF65 27.00				

KM# 133 10 DOLLARS

20.00 g., 0.925 Silver 0.5948 oz. ASW **Ruler:** Elizabeth II **Obv:** Crowned head right **Rev:** Kookaburras, value above

Date	Mintage	VF20	XF40	MS60	MS63	MS65
1989	50,000	PF65 45.00				

KM# 136 10 DOLLARS

20.00 g., 0.925 Silver 0.5948 oz. ASW **Ruler:** Elizabeth II **Obv:** Crowned head right **Rev:** Sulpher-crested cockatoo, value above

Date	Mintage	VF20	XF40	MS60	MS63	MS65
1990	49,801	PF65 50.00				

KM# 137 10 DOLLARS

20.00 g., 0.925 Silver 0.5948 oz. ASW **Ruler:** Elizabeth II **Subject:** Western Australia **Obv:** Crowned head right **Rev:** Western Australia coat of arms, value below

Date	Mintage	VF20	XF40	MS60	MS63	MS65
1990	28,133	—	—	—	24.00	26.00
1990	29,089	PF65 32.00				

KM# 153 10 DOLLARS

20.00 g., 0.925 Silver 0.5948 oz. ASW **Ruler:** Elizabeth II **Subject:** Tasmania **Obv:** Crowned head right **Rev:** Arms of Tasmania, value below, subject name above

Date	Mintage	VF20	XF40	MS60	MS63	MS65
1991	26,150	—	—	—	24.00	26.00
1991	27,664	PF65 32.00				

KM# 156 10 DOLLARS

20.00 g., 0.925 Silver 0.5948 oz. ASW **Ruler:** Elizabeth II **Obv:** Crowned head right **Rev:** Black-necked stork right, value above

Date	Mintage	VF20	XF40	MS60	MS63	MS65
1991	32,446	PF65 35.00				

KM# 188 10 DOLLARS

20.00 g., 0.925 Silver 0.5948 oz. ASW **Ruler:** Elizabeth II **Obv:** Crowned head right **Rev:** Northern Territory state arms, value below, subject name above

Date	Mintage	VF20	XF40	MS60	MS63	MS65
1992	24,164	—	—	—	24.00	26.00
1992	24,404	PF65 32.00				

KM# 199 10 DOLLARS
20.00 g., 0.925 Silver 0.5948 oz. ASW **Ruler:** Elizabeth II **Obv:** Crowned head right **Rev:** Emperor Penguins with chicks, value above

Date	Mintage	VF20	XF40	MS60	MS63	MS65
1992	Est. 25319	PF65 55.00				

KM# 210 10 DOLLARS
20.00 g., 0.925 Silver 0.5948 oz. ASW **Ruler:** Elizabeth II **Obv:** Crowned head right **Rev:** Australian Capital Territory state arms, value below

Date	Mintage	VF20	XF40	MS60	MS63	MS65
1993	19,288	—	—	—	24.00	26.00
1993	21,183	PF65 32.00				

KM# 221 10 DOLLARS
20.00 g., 0.925 Silver 0.5948 oz. ASW **Ruler:** Elizabeth II **Obv:** Crowned head right **Rev:** Palm cockatoo, value at right

Date	Mintage	VF20	XF40	MS60	MS63	MS65
1993	22,172	PF65 42.00				

KM# 317 10 DOLLARS
20.00 g., 0.925 Silver 0.5948 oz. ASW **Ruler:** Elizabeth II **Subject:** UNEP - Palm Cockatoo **Obv:** Crowned head right **Rev:** Palm cockatoo with UNEP logo at left, value at right

Date	Mintage	VF20	XF40	MS60	MS63	MS65
1993	—	PF65 42.00				

KM# 223 10 DOLLARS
20.00 g., 0.925 Silver 0.5948 oz. ASW **Ruler:** Elizabeth II **Obv:** Crowned head right **Rev:** Wedge-tailed eagle, left, value at left

Date	Mintage	VF20	XF40	MS60	MS63	MS65
1994	23,326	PF65 42.00				

KM# 225 10 DOLLARS
20.77 g., 0.999 Silver 0.6671 oz. ASW **Ruler:** Elizabeth II **Series:** Olympic Gold Medalists - Edwin Flack 1896 **Obv:** Crowned head right within circle **Rev:** Edwin Flack with Olympic Flame above wreath within circle, legend above, value below

Date	Mintage	VF20	XF40	MS60	MS63	MS65
1994 Matte Proof	21,484	PF65 22.00				

KM# 226 10 DOLLARS
20.77 g., 0.999 Silver 0.6671 oz. ASW **Ruler:** Elizabeth II **Series:** Olympic Gold Medalists - Sarah Durack 1912 **Obv:** Crowned head right within circle **Rev:** Circle surrounds swimmer within wreath above gold medal, denomination below

Date	Mintage	VF20	XF40	MS60	MS63	MS65
1994 Matte Proof	21,484	PF65 22.00				

KM# 296 10 DOLLARS
20.77 g., 0.999 Silver 0.6671 oz. ASW **Ruler:** Elizabeth II **Obv:** Crowned head right **Rev:** Numbat right, value at left

Date	Mintage	VF20	XF40	MS60	MS63	MS65
1995	25,000	PF65 45.00				

KM# 301 10 DOLLARS
20.77 g., 0.999 Silver 0.6671 oz. ASW **Ruler:** Elizabeth II **Series:** Olympic Gold Medalists - Dawn Fraser **Obv:** Crowned head right **Rev:** Half-length portrait

Date	Mintage	VF20	XF40	MS60	MS63	MS65
1995 Matte Proof	Est. 30000	PF65 28.00				

KM# 302 10 DOLLARS
20.77 g., 0.999 Silver 0.6671 oz. ASW **Ruler:** Elizabeth II **Series:** Olympic Gold Medalists - Murray Rose **Obv:** Crowned head right **Rev:** Murray Rose

Date	Mintage	VF20	XF40	MS60	MS63	MS65
1995 Matte Proof	Est. 30000	PF65 28.00				

KM# 314 10 DOLLARS
20.00 g., 0.925 Silver 0.5948 oz. ASW **Ruler:** Elizabeth II **Rev:** Southern right whale with baby, value below

Date	Mintage	VF20	XF40	MS60	MS63	MS65
1996	24,000	PF65 50.00				

KM# 315 10 DOLLARS
20.77 g., 0.999 Silver 0.6671 oz. ASW **Ruler:** Elizabeth II **Series:** Australia's Greatest Olympics - 1956 **Obv:** Crowned head right **Rev:** Betty Cuthbert, sprint champion 1956, born 1938 within circle, value below circle

Date	Mintage	VF20	XF40	MS60	MS63	MS65
1996 Matte Unc	15,300	—	—	—	55.00	60.00

KM# 316 10 DOLLARS
20.77 g., 0.999 Silver 0.6671 oz. ASW **Ruler:** Elizabeth II **Series:** Australia's Greatest Olympics - 1956 **Obv:** Crowned head right **Rev:** Shirley Strickland, hurdling champion, 1952 and 1956 within circle, value below circle

Date	Mintage	VF20	XF40	MS60	MS63	MS65
1996 Matte Unc	15,300	—	—	—	55.00	60.00

KM# 353 10 DOLLARS
20.77 g., 0.999 Silver 0.6671 oz. ASW **Ruler:** Elizabeth II **Subject:** Sydney Opera House **Obv:** Crowned head right **Rev:** Opera house and Sydney shoreline within circle, legend above circle, value below

Date	Mintage	VF20	XF40	MS60	MS63	MS65
1997 Matte Proof	20,000	PF65 32.50				

KM# 354 10 DOLLARS
20.77 g., 0.999 Silver 0.6671 oz. ASW **Ruler:** Elizabeth II **Subject:** Sydney Harbour Bridge **Obv:** Crowned head right **Rev:** Bridge over harbour within circle, value below circle, legend above

Date	Mintage	VF20	XF40	MS60	MS63	MS65
1997 Matte Proof	20,000	PF65 32.50				

KM# 367.1 10 DOLLARS
20.00 g., 0.999 Silver 0.6424 oz. ASW **Ruler:** Elizabeth II **Subject:** Red-tailed Black Cockatoo **Obv:** Crowned head right **Rev:** Cockatoo perched in dead tree, left, value to left

Date	Mintage	VF20	XF40	MS60	MS63	MS65
1997	24,000	PF65 40.00				

KM# 367.2 10 DOLLARS
40.00 g., 0.925 Silver 1.1896 oz. ASW **Ruler:** Elizabeth II **Subject:** Red-tailed Black Cockatoo **Obv:** Crowned head right **Rev:** Cockatoo perched in dead tree

Date	Mintage	VF20	XF40	MS60	MS63	MS65
1997	14,000	PF65 50.00				

KM# 387 10 DOLLARS
20.77 g., 0.999 Silver 0.6671 oz. ASW **Ruler:** Elizabeth II **Subject:** Melbourne **Obv:** Crowned head right **Rev:** Melbourne cricket grounds

Date	Mintage	VF20	XF40	MS60	MS63	MS65
1998 Matte Proof	20,000	PF65 32.50				

KM# 388 10 DOLLARS
20.77 g., 0.999 Silver 0.6671 oz. ASW **Ruler:** Elizabeth II **Subject:** Melbourne **Obv:** Crowned head right **Rev:** Street car

Date	Mintage	VF20	XF40	MS60	MS63	MS65
1998 Matte Proof	20,000	PF65 32.50				

KM# 397 10 DOLLARS
20.00 g., 0.925 Silver 0.5948 oz. ASW **Ruler:** Elizabeth II **Subject:** Northern Hairy-nosed Wombat **Obv:** Head with tiara right **Rev:** Wombat above denomination

Date	Mintage	VF20	XF40	MS60	MS63	MS65
1998	24,000	PF65 40.00				

KM# 414 10 DOLLARS
20.77 g., 0.999 Silver 0.6671 oz. ASW **Ruler:** Elizabeth II **Subject:** The Snowy Mountains Scheme **Obv:** Head with tiara right within inner circle **Rev:** Tunnel building scene within circle, value below, legend above

Date	Mintage	VF20	XF40	MS60	MS63	MS65
1999	20,000	—	—	—	28.00	32.00

KM# 415 10 DOLLARS
20.77 g., 0.999 Silver 0.6671 oz. ASW **Ruler:** Elizabeth II **Subject:** The Snowy Mountains Scheme **Obv:** Head with tiara right within inner circle **Rev:** Dam building scene within circle, value below, legend above

Date	Mintage	VF20	XF40	MS60	MS63	MS65
1999	20,000	—	—	—	28.00	32.00

KM# 423 10 DOLLARS
33.53 g., Bi-Metallic Copper center in .999 Silver ring **Ruler:** Elizabeth II **Subject:** Millennium Series, The Past **Obv:** Head with tiara right within circle **Rev:** Seedling on Australian map above denomination with rising sun background **Edge:** Reeded

Date	Mintage	VF20	XF40	MS60	MS63	MS65
1999 B	20,000	PF65 650				

KM# 511 10 DOLLARS
36.01 g., 0.999 Silver 1.1566 oz. ASW, 38.7 mm. **Ruler:** Elizabeth II **Series:** Millennium - The Present **Obv:** Head with tiara right within circle **Rev:** Australian map behind young tree, value at base of tree, all within circle, surrounded by circle of stick figures and ovals **Edge:** Reeded

Date	Mintage	VF20	XF40	MS60	MS63	MS65
2000	20,000	PF65 225				

KM# 518 10 DOLLARS
311.04 g., 0.999 Silver 9.990 oz. ASW, 75 mm. **Ruler:** Elizabeth II **Subject:** Paralympics **Obv:** Head with tiara right, denomination below **Rev:** Sydney Opera House and harbor bridge **Edge:** Lettering with logo **Edge Lettering:** GAMES OF THE XI PARALYMPIAD **Note:** Illustration reduced.

Date	Mintage	VF20	XF40	MS60	MS63	MS65
2000 Prooflike	3,000	—	—	—	—	425

KM# 218 20 DOLLARS
33.62 g., 0.925 Silver 0.9998 oz. ASW **Ruler:** Elizabeth II **Series:** Olympics **Subject:** Track Winners **Obv:** Crowned head right, denomination below **Rev:** Three athletes on podium, Olympic logo uppper right with two dates below **Edge Lettering:** CITIUS ALTIUS FORTIUS

Date	Mintage	VF20	XF40	MS60	MS63	MS65
1993	100,000	PF65 38.00				

KM# 219 20 DOLLARS
33.62 g., 0.925 Silver 0.9998 oz. ASW **Ruler:** Elizabeth II **Series:** Olympics **Subject:** Swimmers **Obv:** Crowned bust right, denomination below **Rev:** Four swimmers, Olympic logo upper right with two dates below **Edge Lettering:** CITIUS ALTIUS FORTIUS

Date	Mintage	VF20	XF40	MS60	MS63	MS65
1993	100,000	PF65 38.00				

KM# 519 20 DOLLARS
Bi-Metallic Gold center in Silver ring, 32 mm. **Ruler:** Elizabeth II **Subject:** Millennium **Obv:** Head with tiara right within circle, denomination below **Rev:** Earth view from space **Edge:** Reeded

Date	Mintage	VF20	XF40	MS60	MS63	MS65
2000 Prooflike	Est. 7500	—	—	—	—	575

KM# 200 25 DOLLARS
33.63 g., 0.925 Silver 1.0001 oz. ASW **Ruler:** Elizabeth II **Subject:** 40th Anniversary - Reign of Queen Elizabeth II - Queen Mother **Obv:** Queens portrait **Rev:** Bust of Queen Mother with tiara right, value below, within wreath of crowns

Date	Mintage	VF20	XF40	MS60	MS63	MS65
1992	—	PF65 32.50				

KM# 201 25 DOLLARS
33.63 g., 0.925 Silver 1.0001 oz. ASW **Ruler:** Elizabeth II **Subject:** 40th Anniversary - Reign of Queen Elizabeth II - Princess Diana **Obv:** Queens portrait **Rev:** Bust of Princess Diana with tiara right, value below, within wreath of crowns

Date	Mintage	VF20	XF40	MS60	MS63	MS65
1992	—	PF65 32.50				

KM# 202 25 DOLLARS
33.63 g., 0.925 Silver 1.0001 oz. ASW **Ruler:** Elizabeth II **Subject:** 40th Anniversary - Reign of Queen Elizabeth II - Princess Anne **Obv:** Queens portrait **Rev:** Bust of Princess Anne with tiara right, value below, within wreath of crowns

Date	Mintage	VF20	XF40	MS60	MS63	MS65
1992	—	PF65 32.50				

KM# 203 25 DOLLARS
33.63 g., 0.925 Silver 1.0001 oz. ASW **Ruler:** Elizabeth II **Subject:** 40th Anniversary - Reign of Queen Elizabeth II - Princess Margaret **Obv:** Queens portrait **Rev:** Bust of Princess Margaret with tiara left, value below, within wreath of crowns

Date	Mintage	VF20	XF40	MS60	MS63	MS65
1992	—	PF65 32.50				

KM# 520 30 DOLLARS
1002.50 g., 0.999 Silver 32.1989 oz. ASW, 100 mm. **Ruler:** Elizabeth II **Series:** Olympics **Obv:** Head with tiara right, denomination below **Rev:** Multicolor logo in center **Edge Lettering:** GAMES OF THE XXVII OLYMPIAD (logo) 1 KILO .999 SILVER **Note:** Illustration reduced.

Date	Mintage	VF20	XF40	MS60	MS63	MS65
2000	20,000	PF65 1,150				

KM# 313 40 DOLLARS
31.19 g., 0.9995 Palladium 1.0021 oz. APW **Ruler:** Elizabeth II **Obv:** Crowned head right, denomination below **Rev:** The Australian emu, left, date below

Date	Mintage	VF20	XF40	MS60	MS63	MS65
1995	—	—	—	—	—	850
1995	Est. 2500	PF65 890				

KM# 343 40 DOLLARS
31.19 g., 0.9995 Palladium 1.0021 oz. APW **Ruler:** Elizabeth II **Obv:** Crowned head right, denomination below **Rev:** Emu and chicks

Date	Mintage	VF20	XF40	MS60	MS63	MS65
1996	Est. 2500	PF65 890				

KM# 308 100 DOLLARS
10.37 g., 0.916 Gold 0.3053 oz. AGW, 25 mm. **Ruler:** Elizabeth II **Obv:** Queens portrait **Rev:** The Waratah Flower, value below

Date	Mintage	VF20	XF40	MS60	MS63	MS65
1995	3,000	—	—	—	—	545

KM# 308a 100 DOLLARS
10.37 g., 0.9999 Gold 0.3333 oz. AGW **Ruler:** Elizabeth II **Obv:** Queens portrait **Rev:** The Waratah flower

Date	Mintage	VF20	XF40	MS60	MS63	MS65
1995	2,500	PF65 595				

KM# 333 100 DOLLARS
10.37 g., 0.916 Gold 0.3053 oz. AGW **Ruler:** Elizabeth II **Subject:** Tasmanial Blue Gum Flower **Obv:** Queens portrait **Rev:** Flowering plant with long, droopy leaves

Date	Mintage	VF20	XF40	MS60	MS63	MS65
1996	—	—	—	—	—	545

KM# 333a 100 DOLLARS
10.37 g., 0.9999 Gold 0.3333 oz. AGW **Ruler:** Elizabeth II **Subject:** Tasmanial Blue Gum flower **Obv:** Queens portrait **Rev:** Flowering plant with long, droopy leaves

Date	Mintage	VF20	XF40	MS60	MS63	MS65
1996	—	PF65 595				

KM# 384 100 DOLLARS
10.37 g., 0.9167 Gold 0.3056 oz. AGW **Ruler:** Elizabeth II **Subject:** Mangles' Kangaroo Paw Flower, value below **Obv:** Queens portrait **Rev:** Flower

Date	Mintage	VF20	XF40	MS60	MS63	MS65
1997	3,000	—	—	—	—	545

KM# 373 100 DOLLARS
10.02 g., 0.9999 Gold 0.3222 oz. AGW **Ruler:** Elizabeth II **Series:** Sydney Olympics 2000 **Obv:** Crowned head right, denomination below **Rev:** Runner training in rain, Olympic logo above right foot

Date	Mintage	VF20	XF40	MS60	MS63	MS65
2000 (1998)	—	PF65 575				

KM# 383 100 DOLLARS
10.02 g., 0.9999 Gold 0.3222 oz. AGW **Ruler:** Elizabeth II **Series:** Sydney Olympics 2000 **Obv:** Crowned head right, denomination below **Rev:** Multicolor games logo within wreath

Date	Mintage	VF20	XF40	MS60	MS63	MS65
2000 (1998)	Est. 30000	PF65 575				

KM# 480 100 DOLLARS
10.37 g., 0.916 Gold 0.3053 oz. AGW, 25 mm. **Ruler:** Elizabeth II **Subject:** Stuart's Desert Pea **Obv:** Queens portrait **Rev:** Plant with pods **Edge:** Reeded

Date	Mintage	VF20	XF40	MS60	MS63	MS65
1998 B	3,000	—	—	—	—	545

KM# 480a 100 DOLLARS
10.37 g., 0.999 Gold 0.333 oz. AGW, 25 mm. **Ruler:** Elizabeth II **Subject:** Stuart's Desert Pea **Obv:** Queens portrait **Rev:** Plant with pods **Edge:** Reeded

Date	Mintage	VF20	XF40	MS60	MS63	MS65
1998 B	2,500	PF65 595				

KM# 442 100 DOLLARS
10.00 g., 0.999 Gold 0.3212 oz. AGW **Ruler:** Elizabeth II **Series:** Sydney Olympics 2000 **Obv:** Crowned head right **Rev:** 3 athletic workout scenes, Olympic logo at bottom **Edge:** Reeded

Date	Mintage	VF20	XF40	MS60	MS63	MS65
2000 (1999)	30,000	PF65 575				

KM# 443 100 DOLLARS
10.00 g., 0.999 Gold 0.3212 oz. AGW **Ruler:** Elizabeth II **Series:** Sydney Olympics 2000 **Obv:** Crowned head right **Rev:** Shot putter teaching seated children, Olympic logo below **Edge:** Reeded

Date	Mintage	VF20	XF40	MS60	MS63	MS65
2000 (1999)	30,000	PF65 575				

KM# 444 100 DOLLARS
10.00 g., 0.999 Gold 0.3212 oz. AGW **Ruler:** Elizabeth II **Series:** Sydney Olympics 2000 **Obv:** Crowned head right **Rev:** Sprinter being coached, Olympic logo at bottom **Edge:** Reeded

Date	Mintage	VF20	XF40	MS60	MS63	MS65
2000 (1999)	30,000	PF65 575				

KM# 474 100 DOLLARS
Bi-Metallic .2354 Gold center in .161 Silver ring **Ruler:** Elizabeth II **Subject:** Perth Mint Centennial Sovereign **Obv:** Head with tiara right within inner circle **Rev:** St. George with sword on horseback slaying dragon, circle surrounds all, dates below **Edge:** Reeded

Date	Mintage	VF20	XF40	MS60	MS63	MS65
ND-1999	7,500	PF65 750				

KM# 487 100 DOLLARS
10.37 g., 0.916 Gold 0.3053 oz. AGW, 25 mm. **Ruler:** Elizabeth II **Obv:** Queens portrait **Rev:** Common Heath flowers, value below **Edge:** Reeded

Date	Mintage	VF20	XF40	MS60	MS63	MS65
1999 B	3,000	—	—	—	—	545

KM# 487a 100 DOLLARS
10.37 g., 0.999 Gold 0.333 oz. AGW, 25 mm. **Ruler:** Elizabeth II **Obv:** Queens portrait **Rev:** Common Heath flowers **Edge:** Reeded

Date	Mintage	VF20	XF40	MS60	MS63	MS65
1999 B	2,500	PF65 595				

KM# 512 100 DOLLARS
10.37 g., 0.916 Gold 0.3053 oz. AGW, 25 mm. **Ruler:** Elizabeth II **Subject:** Cooktown Orchid **Obv:** Queens portrait **Rev:** Orchid and denomination **Edge:** Reeded

Date	Mintage	VF20	XF40	MS60	MS63	MS65
2000	3,000	—	—	—	—	550

KM# 512a 100 DOLLARS
10.37 g., 0.999 Gold 0.333 oz. AGW, 25 mm. **Ruler:** Elizabeth II **Subject:** Cooktown Orchid **Obv:** Queens portrait **Rev:** Orchid and denomination **Edge:** Reeded

Date	Mintage	VF20	XF40	MS60	MS63	MS65
2000	2,500	PF65 600				

KM# 521 100 DOLLARS
10.00 g., 0.999 Gold 0.3212 oz. AGW, 25 mm. **Ruler:** Elizabeth II **Series:** Olympics **Obv:** Head with tiara right, denomination below **Rev:** Multicolor torch flames within circle of figures **Edge:** Reeded

Date	Mintage	VF20	XF40	MS60	MS63	MS65
2000	20,000	PF65 565				

KM# 309 150 DOLLARS
15.55 g., 0.9999 Gold 0.4999 oz. AGW, 30 mm. **Ruler:** Elizabeth II **Obv:** Queens portrait **Rev:** The Waratah Flower above value

Date	Mintage	VF20	XF40	MS60	MS63	MS65
1995	1,500	PF65 900				

KM# 334 150 DOLLARS
15.55 g., 0.9999 Gold 0.4999 oz. AGW **Ruler:** Elizabeth II **Subject:** Tasmanian Blue Gum Flower **Obv:** Queens portrait **Rev:** Tasmanian Blue Gum Flower above value

Date	Mintage	VF20	XF40	MS60	MS63	MS65
1996	—	PF65 875				

KM# 413 150 DOLLARS
15.55 g., 0.9999 Gold 0.4999 oz. AGW **Ruler:** Elizabeth II **Obv:** Queens portrait **Rev:** Stuart's desert pea

Date	Mintage	VF20	XF40	MS60	MS63	MS65
1998	1,500	PF65 875				

KM# 475 150 DOLLARS
15.55 g., 0.9999 Gold 0.4999 oz. AGW **Ruler:** Elizabeth II **Subject:** Common Heath Flower **Obv:** Queens portrait **Rev:** Heath flowers above value **Edge:** Reeded

Date	Mintage	VF20	XF40	MS60	MS63	MS65
1999 B	1,500	PF65 875				

KM# 513 150 DOLLARS
15.55 g., 0.999 Gold 0.4995 oz. AGW, 30 mm. **Ruler:** Elizabeth II **Subject:** Cooktown Orchid **Obv:** Queens portrait **Rev:** Orchid above value **Edge:** Reeded

Date	Mintage	VF20	XF40	MS60	MS63	MS65
2000	1,500	PF65 875				

KM# 71 200 DOLLARS
10.00 g., 0.917 Gold 0.2948 oz. AGW **Ruler:** Elizabeth II **Obv:** Young bust right **Rev:** Koala in tree, value below

Date	Mintage	VF20	XF40	MS60	MS63	MS65
1980	207,500	—	—	—	500	525
1980	50,077	PF65 525				
1983	88,000	—	—	—	500	525
1983	15,889	PF65 525				
1984	49,200	—	—	—	500	525
1984	12,559	PF65 525				

KM# 73 200 DOLLARS
10.00 g., 0.917 Gold 0.2948 oz. AGW **Ruler:** Elizabeth II **Subject:** Wedding of Prince Charles and Lady Diana **Obv:** Young bust right **Rev:** Conjoined heads of Prince Charles and Lady Diana left

Date	Mintage	VF20	XF40	MS60	MS63	MS65
1981	77,890	—	—	—	500	525

KM# 76 200 DOLLARS
10.00 g., 0.917 Gold 0.2948 oz. AGW **Ruler:** Elizabeth II **Subject:** XII Commonwealth Games - Brisbane **Obv:** Young bust right **Rev:** Athlete running over hurdles, value below hurdler

Date	Mintage	VF20	XF40	MS60	MS63	MS65
1982	77,206	—	—	—	500	525
1982	30,032	PF65 525				

KM# 86 200 DOLLARS
10.00 g., 0.917 Gold 0.2948 oz. AGW **Ruler:** Elizabeth II **Obv:** Crowned head right **Rev:** Koala in tree, value below

Date	Mintage	VF20	XF40	MS60	MS63	MS65
1985	29,186	—	—	—	500	525
1985	16,691	PF65 525				
1986	15,298	—	—	—	500	525
1986	16,654	PF65 525				

KM# 94 200 DOLLARS
10.00 g., 0.917 Gold 0.2948 oz. AGW **Ruler:** Elizabeth II **Obv:** Crowned head right **Rev:** 1/2-length bust right, value below, 1787 above right shoulder

Date	Mintage	VF20	XF40	MS60	MS63	MS65
1987	20,800	—	—	—	500	525
1987	20,000	PF65 525				

KM# 115 200 DOLLARS
10.00 g., 0.917 Gold 0.2948 oz. AGW **Ruler:** Elizabeth II **Subject:** Bicentennial of Australia **Obv:** Crowned head right **Rev:** Early colonist standing in front of water in Sydney Cove, ship in background at right, value below

Date	Mintage	VF20	XF40	MS60	MS63	MS65
1988	11,000	—	—	—	500	525
1988	20,000	PF65 525				

KM# 135 200 DOLLARS
10.00 g., 0.917 Gold 0.2948 oz. AGW **Ruler:** Elizabeth II **Subject:** Pride of Australia **Obv:** Crowned head right **Rev:** Platypus above value

Date	Mintage	VF20	XF40	MS60	MS63	MS65
1990	8,340	—	—	—	500	525
1990	14,616	PF65 525				

KM# 160 200 DOLLARS
10.00 g., 0.917 Gold 0.2948 oz. AGW **Ruler:** Elizabeth II **Subject:** Pride of Australia **Obv:** Crowned head right **Rev:** Standing emu between tall grass, value below

Date	Mintage	VF20	XF40	MS60	MS63	MS65
1991	6,879	—	—	—	500	525
1991	9,560	PF65 525				

KM# 259 200 DOLLARS
10.00 g., 0.917 Gold 0.2948 oz. AGW **Ruler:** Elizabeth II **Subject:** Pride of Australia **Obv:** Crowned head right **Rev:** Echidna above value

Date	Mintage	VF20	XF40	MS60	MS63	MS65
1992	3,935	—	—	—	500	525
1992	5,921	PF65 525				

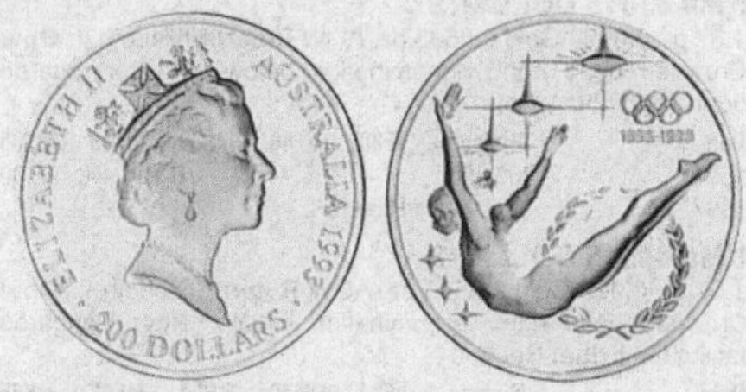

KM# 220 200 DOLLARS
16.82 g., 0.917 Gold 0.4959 oz. AGW **Ruler:** Elizabeth II **Series:** Olympic Centenary - 1896-1996 **Obv:** Crowned head right **Rev:** Gymnast in flight, Olympic logo top right **Edge Lettering:** CITIUS ALTIUS FORTIUS

Date	Mintage	VF20	XF40	MS60	MS63	MS65
1993	60,000	PF65 885				

KM# 222 200 DOLLARS
10.00 g., 0.917 Gold 0.2948 oz. AGW **Ruler:** Elizabeth II **Subject:** Pride of Australia **Obv:** Crowned head right **Rev:** Squirrel glider possum, value below

Date	Mintage	VF20	XF40	MS60	MS63	MS65
1993	3,014	—	—	—	500	525
1993	5,000	PF65 525				

KM# 262 200 DOLLARS
10.00 g., 0.917 Gold 0.2948 oz. AGW **Ruler:** Elizabeth II **Subject:** Pride of Australia **Obv:** Crowned head right **Rev:** Tasmanian devil, value below

Date	Mintage	VF20	XF40	MS60	MS63	MS65
1994	4,000	—	—	—	500	525
1994	5,000	PF65 525				

KM# 385 200 DOLLARS
15.55 g., 0.9999 Gold 0.4999 oz. AGW **Ruler:** Elizabeth II **Subject:** Mangles' Kangaroo Paw Flower **Obv:** Queens portrait **Rev:** Flower

Date	Mintage	VF20	XF40	MS60	MS63	MS65
1997	—	PF65 885				

KM# 204 250 DOLLARS
16.95 g., 0.917 Gold 0.4997 oz. AGW **Ruler:** Elizabeth II **Subject:** 40th Anniversary - Reign of Queen Elizabeth II - Queen Mother **Obv:** Queens portrait **Rev:** Portrait of Queen Mother right, within circle of crowns

Date	Mintage	VF20	XF40	MS60	MS63	MS65
1992	Est. 5000	PF65 825				

KM# 205 250 DOLLARS
16.95 g., 0.917 Gold 0.4997 oz. AGW **Ruler:** Elizabeth II **Subject:** 40th Anniversary - Reign of Queen Elizabeth II - Princess Diana **Obv:** Queens portrait **Rev:** Portrait of Princess Diana right, within circle of crowns

Date	Mintage	VF20	XF40	MS60	MS63	MS65
1992	Est. 5000	PF65 825				

KM# 206 250 DOLLARS
16.95 g., 0.917 Gold 0.4997 oz. AGW **Ruler:** Elizabeth II **Subject:** 40th Anniversary - Reign of Queen Elizabeth II - Princess Anne **Obv:** Queens portrait **Rev:** Portrait of Princess Anne right, within circle of crowns

Date	Mintage	VF20	XF40	MS60	MS63	MS65
1992	—	PF65 825				

KM# 207 250 DOLLARS
16.95 g., 0.917 Gold 0.4997 oz. AGW **Ruler:** Elizabeth II **Subject:** 40th Anniversary - Reign of Queen Elizabeth II - Princess Margaret **Obv:** Queens portrait **Rev:** Bust of Princess Margaret left, within circle of crowns

Date	Mintage	VF20	XF40	MS60	MS63	MS65
1992	—	PF65 825				

BULLION - KANGAROO

KM# 211.1 DOLLAR
31.57 g., 0.999 Silver 1.014 oz. ASW **Ruler:** Elizabeth II **Obv:** Crowned head right **Rev:** Kangaroo leaping right, value above **Edge:** Reeded

Date	Mintage	VF20	XF40	MS60	MS63	MS65
1993	73,000	—	—	—	35.00	40.00

KM# 211.2 DOLLAR
31.57 g., 0.999 Silver 1.014 oz. ASW **Ruler:** Elizabeth II **Obv:** Crowned head right **Rev:** Kangaroo leaping right **Edge:** Reeded and plain sections

Date	Mintage	VF20	XF40	MS60	MS63	MS65
1993 C	5,000	—	—	—	55.00	60.00

KM# 263.1 DOLLAR
31.64 g., 0.999 Silver 1.0161 oz. ASW **Ruler:** Elizabeth II **Obv:** Crowned head right **Rev:** Kangaroo leaping right, value above **Edge:** Reeded

Date	Mintage	VF20	XF40	MS60	MS63	MS65
1994 C	45,000	—	—	—	40.00	45.00

KM# 263.2 DOLLAR
31.64 g., 0.999 Silver 1.0161 oz. ASW **Ruler:** Elizabeth II **Obv:** Crowned head right **Rev:** Kangaroo leaping right **Edge:** Reeded and plain sections

Date	Mintage	VF20	XF40	MS60	MS63	MS65
1994 C	2,500	—	—	—	120	125

KM# 293.1 DOLLAR
31.64 g., 0.999 Silver 1.0161 oz. ASW **Ruler:** Elizabeth II **Obv:** Crowned head right **Rev:** Kangaroo head facing half left, value above **Edge:** Reeded

Date	Mintage	VF20	XF40	MS60	MS63	MS65
1995 C	73,000	—	—	—	37.00	40.00

KM# 293.2 DOLLAR
31.64 g., 0.999 Silver 1.0161 oz. ASW **Ruler:** Elizabeth II **Obv:** Crowned head right **Rev:** Kangaroo head facing half left **Edge:** Reeded and plain sections

Date	Mintage	VF20	XF40	MS60	MS63	MS65
1995 C	2,500	—	—	—	110	115

KM# 297 DOLLAR
31.64 g., 0.999 Silver 1.0161 oz. ASW **Ruler:** Elizabeth II **Obv:** Crowned head right **Rev:** Mother and baby kangaroo, value above

Date	Mintage	VF20	XF40	MS60	MS63	MS65
1996	—	—	—	—	35.00	40.00

KM# 325 DOLLAR
31.56 g., 0.999 Silver 1.0137 oz. ASW **Ruler:** Elizabeth II **Obv:** Crowned head right **Rev:** Kangaroo drinking water, reflection, value at bottom

Date	Mintage	VF20	XF40	MS60	MS63	MS65
1997 C	—	—	—	—	35.00	40.00

KM# 365 DOLLAR
32.00 g., 0.999 Silver 1.0278 oz. ASW **Ruler:** Elizabeth II **Obv:** Crowned head right **Rev:** Kangaroo bounding left, value above

Date	Mintage	VF20	XF40	MS60	MS63	MS65
1998	5,000	PF65 85.00				
1998 C	—	—	—	—	35.00	40.00

KM# 398 DOLLAR
32.25 g., 0.999 Silver 1.0358 oz. ASW **Ruler:** Elizabeth II **Obv:** Crowned head right **Rev:** Pair of kangaroos, value at right

Date	Mintage	VF20	XF40	MS60	MS63	MS65
1999	—	—	—	—	35.00	40.00
1999	—	PF65 90.00				

KM# 490.1 DOLLAR
31.10 g., 0.999 Silver 0.999 oz. ASW, 40 mm. **Ruler:** Elizabeth II **Obv:** Crowned head right **Rev:** Kangaroo with Australian map background, value top right **Edge:** Reeded

Date	Mintage	VF20	XF40	MS60	MS63	MS65
2000 B	—	—	—	—	35.00	40.00
2000 B	—	PF65 70.00				

KM# 490.2 DOLLAR
32.15 g., 0.999 Silver 1.0326 oz. ASW, 39.9 mm. **Ruler:** Elizabeth II **Obv:** Crowned head right **Rev:** Multicolor kangaroo on dark red map and green value **Edge:** Reeded

Date	Mintage	VF20	XF40	MS60	MS63	MS65
2000	—	—	—	—	35.00	40.00

KM# 117 5 DOLLARS
1.57 g., 0.999 Gold 0.0505 oz. AGW **Ruler:** Elizabeth II **Subject:** Red Kangaroo **Obv:** Crowned head right, denomination below **Rev:** Kangaroo leaping left, date below

Date	Mintage	VF20	XF40	MS60	MS63	MS65
1989	2,200	PF65 110				
1990	Est. 200000	—	—	—	—	92.00

KM# 140 5 DOLLARS
1.57 g., 0.999 Gold 0.0505 oz. AGW **Ruler:** Elizabeth II **Obv:** Crowned head right, denomination below **Rev:** Gray Kangaroo right, date below

Date	Mintage	VF20	XF40	MS60	MS63	MS65
1990	7,000	PF65 110				
1991	200,000	—	—	—	—	92.00
1991	—	PF65 110				

KM# 165 5 DOLLARS
1.57 g., 0.999 Gold 0.0505 oz. AGW **Ruler:** Elizabeth II **Subject:** Common Wallaroo **Obv:** Crowned head right, denomination below **Rev:** Kangaroo bounding left, date below **Note:** 1992 (ae) previously listed here is now KM#389.

Date	Mintage	VF20	XF40	MS60	MS63	MS65
1991	3,525	PF65 110				
1992	200,000	—	—	—	—	92.00
1992	—	PF65 110				

KM# 389 5 DOLLARS
1.57 g., 0.999 Gold 0.0505 oz. AGW **Ruler:** Elizabeth II **Obv:** Crowned head right, denomination below **Rev:** Nail-tailed Wallaby

Date	Mintage	VF20	XF40	MS60	MS63	MS65
1992 (ae)	500	PF65 115				

KM# 233 5 DOLLARS
1.57 g., 0.999 Gold 0.0505 oz. AGW **Ruler:** Elizabeth II **Obv:** Crowned head right, denomination below **Rev:** Whiptail Wallaby

Date	Mintage	VF20	XF40	MS60	MS63	MS65
1993	—	PF65 110				
1994	—	—	—	—	—	92.00

KM# 241 5 DOLLARS
1.57 g., 0.999 Gold 0.0505 oz. AGW **Ruler:** Elizabeth II **Obv:** Crowned head right, denomination below **Rev:** Red Kangaroo facing front, date below

Date	Mintage	VF20	XF40	MS60	MS63	MS65
1994	—	PF65 110				
1995	200,000	—	—	—	—	92.00

KM# 272 5 DOLLARS
1.57 g., 0.999 Gold 0.0505 oz. AGW **Ruler:** Elizabeth II **Obv:** Crowned head right, denomination below **Rev:** Two kangaroos standing, date below

Date	Mintage	VF20	XF40	MS60	MS63	MS65
1995	300	PF65 115				
1996	200,000	—	—	—	—	92.00

KM# 320 5 DOLLARS
1.57 g., 0.999 Gold 0.0505 oz. AGW **Ruler:** Elizabeth II **Obv:** Crowned head right, denomination below **Rev:** Kangaroo bounding right

Date	Mintage	VF20	XF40	MS60	MS63	MS65
1996 P	—	PF65 110				

Note: In proof sets only

KM# 338 5 DOLLARS
1.57 g., 0.9999 Gold 0.0505 oz. AGW **Ruler:** Elizabeth II **Obv:** Crowned head right, denomination below **Rev:** Kangaroo bounding right

Date	Mintage	VF20	XF40	MS60	MS63	MS65
1997	200,000	—	—	—	—	92.00
1997	—	PF65 110				

KM# 448 5 DOLLARS
1.57 g., 0.999 Gold 0.0505 oz. AGW **Ruler:** Elizabeth II **Obv:** Crowned head right, denomination below **Rev:** Kangaroo facing left **Edge:** Reeded

Date	Mintage	VF20	XF40	MS60	MS63	MS65
1999	200,000	—	—	—	—	99.00

KM# 464 5 DOLLARS
1.57 g., 0.999 Gold 0.0505 oz. AGW **Ruler:** Elizabeth II **Obv:** Crowned head right, denomination below **Rev:** Two kangaroos bounding left

Date	Mintage	VF20	XF40	MS60	MS63	MS65
2000	—	—	—	—	—	99.00

KM# 118 15 DOLLARS
3.11 g., 0.999 Gold 0.0999 oz. AGW **Ruler:** Elizabeth II **Obv:** Crowned head right, denomination below **Rev:** Red kangaroo leaping left, date below

Date	Mintage	VF20	XF40	MS60	MS63	MS65
1989	2,200	PF65 167				
1990	200,000	—	—	—	—	150

KM# 141 15 DOLLARS
3.11 g., 0.999 Gold 0.0999 oz. AGW **Ruler:** Elizabeth II **Obv:** Crowned head right, denomination below **Rev:** Gray kangaroo standing facing left, date below

Date	Mintage	VF20	XF40	MS60	MS63	MS65
1990	7,000	PF65 167				
1991	150,000	—	—	—	—	150
1991	—	PF65 200				

KM# 166 15 DOLLARS
3.11 g., 0.999 Gold 0.0999 oz. AGW **Ruler:** Elizabeth II **Subject:** Common Wallaroo **Obv:** Crowned head right, denomination below **Rev:** Radiant common walleroo facing right

Date	Mintage	VF20	XF40	MS60	MS63	MS65
1991	1,975	PF65 167				
1992	150,000	—	—	—	—	150
1992	—	PF65 172				

KM# 390 15 DOLLARS
3.11 g., 0.999 Gold 0.0999 oz. AGW **Ruler:** Elizabeth II **Obv:** Crowned head right, denomination below **Rev:** Nail-tailed wallaby

Date	Mintage	VF20	XF40	MS60	MS63	MS65
1992 (ae)	500	PF65 172				

KM# 234 15 DOLLARS
3.11 g., 0.999 Gold 0.0999 oz. AGW **Ruler:** Elizabeth II **Obv:** Crowned head right, denomination below **Rev:** Whiptail wallaby

Date	Mintage	VF20	XF40	MS60	MS63	MS65
1993	—	PF65 167				
1994	—	—	—	—	—	150

KM# 242 15 DOLLARS
3.11 g., 0.999 Gold 0.0999 oz. AGW **Ruler:** Elizabeth II **Obv:** Crowned head right, denomination below **Rev:** Red kangaroo standing facing forward, date below

Date	Mintage	VF20	XF40	MS60	MS63	MS65
1994	—	PF65 172				
1995	200,000	—	—	—	—	150

KM# 273 15 DOLLARS
3.11 g., 0.999 Gold 0.0999 oz. AGW **Ruler:** Elizabeth II **Obv:** Crowned head right, denomination below **Rev:** Two kangaroos, date below

Date	Mintage	VF20	XF40	MS60	MS63	MS65
1995	900	PF65 167				
1996	200,000	—	—	—	—	150

KM# 321 15 DOLLARS
3.11 g., 0.999 Gold 0.0999 oz. AGW **Ruler:** Elizabeth II **Obv:** Crowned head right, denomination below **Rev:** Kangaroo bounding right

Date	Mintage	VF20	XF40	MS60	MS63	MS65
1996 P	400	PF65 172				

KM# 339 15 DOLLARS
3.11 g., 0.999 Gold 0.0999 oz. AGW **Ruler:** Elizabeth II **Obv:** Crowned head right, denomination below **Rev:** Kangaroo bounding right

Date	Mintage	VF20	XF40	MS60	MS63	MS65
1997	200,000	—	—	—	—	150
1997	—	PF65 167				

KM# 449 15 DOLLARS
3.13 g., 0.999 Gold 0.1006 oz. AGW **Ruler:** Elizabeth II **Obv:** Crowned head right, denomination below **Rev:** Kangaroo facing left **Edge:** Reeded

Date	Mintage	VF20	XF40	MS60	MS63	MS65
1999	200,000	—	—	—	—	170

KM# 465 15 DOLLARS
3.13 g., 0.999 Gold 0.1006 oz. AGW **Ruler:** Elizabeth II **Obv:** Crowned head right, denomination below **Rev:** Two kangaroos bounding left **Edge:** Reeded

Date	Mintage	VF20	XF40	MS60	MS63	MS65
2000	—	—	—	—	—	170

KM# 119 25 DOLLARS
7.75 g., 0.999 Gold 0.2489 oz. AGW **Ruler:** Elizabeth II **Obv:** Crowned head right, denomination below **Rev:** Red kangaroo

Date	Mintage	VF20	XF40	MS60	MS63	MS65
1989	2,200	PF65 405				
1990	—	—	—	—	—	370

KM# 142 25 DOLLARS
7.75 g., 0.999 Gold 0.2489 oz. AGW **Ruler:** Elizabeth II **Obv:** Crowned head right, denomination below **Rev:** Gray kangaroo standing right, date below

Date	Mintage	VF20	XF40	MS60	MS63	MS65
1990	7,000	PF65 405				
1991	100,000	—	—	—	—	370
1991	—	PF65 415				

KM# 167 25 DOLLARS
7.75 g., 0.999 Gold 0.2489 oz. AGW **Ruler:** Elizabeth II **Subject:** Common Wallaroo **Obv:** Crowned head right, denomination below **Rev:** Radiant walleroo facing right

Date	Mintage	VF20	XF40	MS60	MS63	MS65
1991	1,991	PF65 415				
1992	100,000	—	—	—	—	370
1992	—	PF65 415				

KM# 391 25 DOLLARS
7.75 g., 0.999 Gold 0.2489 oz. AGW **Ruler:** Elizabeth II **Obv:** Crowned head right, denomination below **Rev:** Nail-tailed wallaby standing right, date below

Date	Mintage	VF20	XF40	MS60	MS63	MS65
1992 (ae)	500	PF65 420				

KM# 235 25 DOLLARS
7.75 g., 0.999 Gold 0.2489 oz. AGW **Ruler:** Elizabeth II **Obv:** Crowned head right, denomination below **Rev:** Whiptail wallaby

Date	Mintage	VF20	XF40	MS60	MS63	MS65
1993	—	PF65 415				
1993 (f)	200	PF65 425				
1994	—	—	—	—	—	370

KM# 243 25 DOLLARS
7.75 g., 0.999 Gold 0.2489 oz. AGW **Ruler:** Elizabeth II **Obv:** Crowned head right, denomination below **Rev:** Red kangaroo standing facing, date below

Date	Mintage	VF20	XF40	MS60	MS63	MS65
1994	—	PF65 405				
1995	150,000	—	—	—	—	370

KM# 274 25 DOLLARS
7.75 g., 0.999 Gold 0.2489 oz. AGW **Ruler:** Elizabeth II **Obv:** Crowned head right, denomination below **Rev:** Two kangaroos, date below

Date	Mintage	VF20	XF40	MS60	MS63	MS65
1995	650	PF65 405				
1996	150,000	—	—	—	—	370

KM# 322 25 DOLLARS
7.75 g., 0.999 Gold 0.2489 oz. AGW **Ruler:** Elizabeth II **Obv:** Crowned head right, denomination below **Rev:** Kangaroo bounding right

Date	Mintage	VF20	XF40	MS60	MS63	MS65
1996 (p)	400	PF65 500				

KM# 340 25 DOLLARS
7.75 g., 0.999 Gold 0.2489 oz. AGW **Ruler:** Elizabeth II **Obv:** Crowned head right, denomination below **Rev:** Kangaroo bounding right

Date	Mintage	VF20	XF40	MS60	MS63	MS65
1997	200,000	—	—	—	—	370
1997	—	PF65 405				

KM# 450 25 DOLLARS
7.81 g., 0.999 Gold 0.2507 oz. AGW **Ruler:** Elizabeth II **Obv:** Crowned head right, denomination below **Rev:** Kangaroo facing left **Edge:** Reeded

Date	Mintage	VF20	XF40	MS60	MS63	MS65
1999	150,000	—	—	—	—	370

KM# 466 25 DOLLARS
7.81 g., 0.999 Gold 0.2507 oz. AGW **Ruler:** Elizabeth II **Obv:** Crowned head right, denomination below **Rev:** Two kangaroos bounding left **Edge:** Reeded

Date	Mintage	VF20	XF40	MS60	MS63	MS65
2000	—	—	—	—	—	370

KM# 120 50 DOLLARS
15.50 g., 0.999 Gold 0.4979 oz. AGW **Ruler:** Elizabeth II **Obv:** Crowned head right, denomination below **Rev:** Red kangaroo leaping left, date below

Date	Mintage	VF20	XF40	MS60	MS63	MS65
1989	2,200	PF65 770				
1990	Est. 240000	—	—	—	—	720

KM# 143 50 DOLLARS
15.50 g., 0.999 Gold 0.4979 oz. AGW **Ruler:** Elizabeth II **Obv:** Crowned head right, denomination below **Rev:** Gray kangaroo facing right looking left, date below

Date	Mintage	VF20	XF40	MS60	MS63	MS65
1990	5,000	PF65 770				
1991	100,000	—	—	—	—	720
1991	—	PF65 780				

KM# 168 50 DOLLARS
15.50 g., 0.999 Gold 0.4979 oz. AGW **Ruler:** Elizabeth II **Subject:** Common wallaroo **Obv:** Crowned head right, denomination below **Rev:** Radiant common wallaroo facing right

Date	Mintage	VF20	XF40	MS60	MS63	MS65
1991	1,096	PF65 780				
1992	100,000	—	—	—	—	720
1992	—	PF65 790				

KM# 392 50 DOLLARS
15.50 g., 0.999 Gold 0.4979 oz. AGW **Ruler:** Elizabeth II **Obv:** Crowned head right, denomination below **Rev:** Nail-tailed wallaby

Date	Mintage	VF20	XF40	MS60	MS63	MS65
1992 (ae)	500	PF65 790				

KM# 236 50 DOLLARS
15.50 g., 0.999 Gold 0.4979 oz. AGW **Ruler:** Elizabeth II **Obv:** Crowned head right, denomination below **Rev:** Whiptail wallaby

Date	Mintage	VF20	XF40	MS60	MS63	MS65
1993	—	PF65 770				
1994	—	—	—	—	—	720

KM# 244 50 DOLLARS
15.50 g., 0.999 Gold 0.4979 oz. AGW **Ruler:** Elizabeth II **Obv:** Crowned head right, denomination below **Rev:** Red kangaroo standing facing front, date below

Date	Mintage	VF20	XF40	MS60	MS63	MS65
1994	—	PF65 780				
1995	30,000	—	—	—	—	720
1995 (f)	10,000	PF65 770				

KM# 275.1 50 DOLLARS
15.50 g., 0.999 Gold 0.4979 oz. AGW **Ruler:** Elizabeth II **Obv:** Crowned head right, denomination below **Rev:** Two kangaroos, date below

Date	Mintage	VF20	XF40	MS60	MS63	MS65
1995	300	PF65 780				
1996	100,000	—	—	—	—	720
1996 (s)	13,000	PF65 770				
1996 (l)	3,000	PF65 770				
1996 (f)	13,000	PF65 770				

KM# 275.2 50 DOLLARS

15.50 g., 0.999 Gold 0.4979 oz. AGW **Ruler:** Elizabeth II **Obv:** Crowned head right, denomination below **Rev:** Two kangaroos, date below **Edge:** Reeded and inscribed with date and serial number

Date	Mintage	VF20	XF40	MS60	MS63	MS65
1996	500	PF65 790				

KM# 341 50 DOLLARS

15.50 g., 0.999 Gold 0.4979 oz. AGW **Ruler:** Elizabeth II **Obv:** Crowned head right, denomination below **Rev:** Kangaroo bounding right

Date	Mintage	VF20	XF40	MS60	MS63	MS65
1996 (p)	400	PF65 800				
1997	100,000	—	—	—	—	720
1997	—	PF65 770				
1997 (f)	13,000	PF65 770				
1997 (l)	10,000	PF65 770				
1997 (s)	13,000	PF65 770				

KM# 451 50 DOLLARS

15.59 g., 0.999 Gold 0.5009 oz. AGW **Ruler:** Elizabeth II **Obv:** Crowned head right, denomination below **Rev:** Kangaroo facing left **Edge:** Reeded

Date	Mintage	VF20	XF40	MS60	MS63	MS65
1999	100,000	—	—	—	—	720

KM# 467 50 DOLLARS

15.59 g., 0.999 Gold 0.5009 oz. AGW **Ruler:** Elizabeth II **Obv:** Crowned head right, denomination below **Rev:** Two kangaroos bounding left **Edge:** Reeded

Date	Mintage	VF20	XF40	MS60	MS63	MS65
2000	—	—	—	—	—	720

KM# 121 100 DOLLARS

31.10 g., 0.999 Gold 0.999 oz. AGW **Ruler:** Elizabeth II **Obv:** Crowned head right, denomination below **Rev:** Red kangaroo bounding left, date below

Date	Mintage	VF20	XF40	MS60	MS63	MS65
1989	2,200	PF65 1,450				
1990	—	—	—	—	—	1,400

KM# 144 100 DOLLARS

31.10 g., 0.999 Gold 0.999 oz. AGW **Ruler:** Elizabeth II **Rev:** Gray kangaroo standing looking left, date below

Date	Mintage	VF20	XF40	MS60	MS63	MS65
1990	8,000	PF65 1,450				
1991	250,000	—	—	—	—	1,400
1991	—	PF65 1,450				

KM# 169 100 DOLLARS

31.10 g., 0.999 Gold 0.999 oz. AGW **Ruler:** Elizabeth II **Obv:** Crowned head right, denomination below **Rev:** Common wallaroo on all fours facing right, date below

Date	Mintage	VF20	XF40	MS60	MS63	MS65
1991	3,000	PF65 1,450				
1992	250,000	—	—	—	—	1,400

KM# 393 100 DOLLARS

31.10 g., 0.999 Gold 0.999 oz. AGW **Ruler:** Elizabeth II **Obv:** Crowned head right, denomination below **Rev:** Nail-tailed wallaby

Date	Mintage	VF20	XF40	MS60	MS63	MS65
1992	784	PF65 1,450				
1993	—	—	—	—	—	1,400

KM# 237 100 DOLLARS

31.10 g., 0.999 Gold 0.999 oz. AGW **Ruler:** Elizabeth II **Obv:** Crowned head right, denomination below **Rev:** Whiptail wallaby

Date	Mintage	VF20	XF40	MS60	MS63	MS65
1993	—	PF65 1,450				
1993 (f)	150	PF65 1,850				
1994	—	—	—	—	—	1,400

KM# 245 100 DOLLARS

31.10 g., 0.999 Gold 0.999 oz. AGW **Ruler:** Elizabeth II **Obv:** Crowned head right, denomination below **Rev:** Red kangaroo facing forward, date below

Date	Mintage	VF20	XF40	MS60	MS63	MS65
1994	—	PF65 1,450				
1995	350,000	—	—	—	—	1,400

KM# 276 100 DOLLARS

31.10 g., 0.999 Gold 0.999 oz. AGW **Ruler:** Elizabeth II **Obv:** Crowned head right, denomination below **Rev:** Two kangaroos

Date	Mintage	VF20	XF40	MS60	MS63	MS65
1995	300	PF65 1,475				
1995 (ww)	600	PF65 1,450				
1996	350,000	—	—	—	—	1,400

KM# 342 100 DOLLARS

31.10 g., 0.999 Gold 0.999 oz. AGW **Ruler:** Elizabeth II **Obv:** Crowned head right, denomination below **Rev:** Kangaroo bounding right

Date	Mintage	VF20	XF40	MS60	MS63	MS65
1996 (p)	—	PF65 1,450				
1997	350,000	—	—	—	—	1,400
1997	—	PF65 1,450				

KM# 452 100 DOLLARS

31.10 g., 0.999 Gold 0.999 oz. AGW **Ruler:** Elizabeth II **Obv:** Crowned head right, denomination below **Rev:** Kangaroo facing left **Edge:** Reeded

Date	Mintage	VF20	XF40	MS60	MS63	MS65
1999	350,000	—	—	—	—	1,400

KM# 468 100 DOLLARS

31.10 g., 0.999 Gold 0.999 oz. AGW **Ruler:** Elizabeth II **Obv:** Crowned head right, denomination below **Rev:** Two kangaroos bounding left, date below **Edge:** Reeded

Date	Mintage	VF20	XF40	MS60	MS63	MS65
2000	—	—	—	—	—	1,400

KM# 182 200 DOLLARS

62.21 g., 0.999 Gold 1.9982 oz. AGW **Ruler:** Elizabeth II **Obv:** Crowned head right, denomination below **Rev:** Red kangaroo leaping left, date below

Date	Mintage	VF20	XF40	MS60	MS63	MS65
1992	—	—	—	—	—	2,800
1994 Prooflike	—	—	—	—	—	2,800
1995	—	—	—	—	—	2,800
1996	—	—	—	—	—	2,800
1997	—	—	—	—	—	2,800

KM# 394 200 DOLLARS

62.21 g., 0.999 Gold 1.9982 oz. AGW **Ruler:** Elizabeth II **Obv:** Crowned head right, denomination below **Rev:** Nail-tailed wallaby

Date	Mintage	VF20	XF40	MS60	MS63	MS65
1992	152	PF65 3,650				

KM# 238 200 DOLLARS

62.21 g., 0.9999 Gold 2.000 oz. AGW **Ruler:** Elizabeth II **Obv:** Crowned head right, denomination below **Rev:** Whiptail wallaby

Date	Mintage	VF20	XF40	MS60	MS63	MS65
1993	—	PF65 3,650				

KM# 246 200 DOLLARS

62.21 g., 0.9999 Gold 2.000 oz. AGW **Ruler:** Elizabeth II **Obv:** Crowned head right, denomination below **Rev:** Red kangaroo

Date	Mintage	VF20	XF40	MS60	MS63	MS65
1994	325	PF65 3,650				

KM# 277 200 DOLLARS

62.21 g., 0.9999 Gold 2.000 oz. AGW **Ruler:** Elizabeth II **Obv:** Crowned head right, denomination below **Rev:** Two kangaroos, date below

Date	Mintage	VF20	XF40	MS60	MS63	MS65
1995	100	PF65 3,650				

KM# 150 500 DOLLARS

62.21 g., 0.999 Gold 1.9982 oz. AGW **Ruler:** Elizabeth II **Obv:** Crowned head right, denomination below **Rev:** Red kangaroo facing left

Date	Mintage	VF20	XF40	MS60	MS63	MS65
1991	—	—	—	—	—	2,800
1991	491	PF65 3,650				

KM# 395 1000 DOLLARS

311.07 g., 0.999 Gold 9.991 oz. AGW **Ruler:** Elizabeth II **Obv:** Crowned head right, denomination below **Rev:** Nail-tailed wallaby

Date	Mintage	VF20	XF40	MS60	MS63	MS65
1992	40	PF65 18,000				

KM# 239 1000 DOLLARS

311.07 g., 0.9999 Gold 10.000 oz. AGW **Ruler:** Elizabeth II **Obv:** Crowned head right, denomination below **Rev:** Red kangaroo

Date	Mintage	VF20	XF40	MS60	MS63	MS65
1993	—	PF65 18,000				

KM# 247 1000 DOLLARS

311.07 g., 0.9999 Gold 10.000 oz. AGW **Ruler:** Elizabeth II **Obv:** Crowned head right, denomination below **Rev:** Kangaroo in diamond shape

Date	Mintage	VF20	XF40	MS60	MS63	MS65
1994	—	PF65 18,000				

KM# 183 1000 DOLLARS

311.07 g., 0.9999 Gold 10.000 oz. AGW **Ruler:** Elizabeth II **Obv:** Crowned head right, denomination below **Rev:** Red kangaroo

Date	Mintage	VF20	XF40	MS60	MS63	MS65
1995	—	—	—	—	—	14,000
1996	—	—	—	—	—	14,000
1997	—	—	—	—	—	14,000

KM# 454 1000 DOLLARS

311.32 g., 0.999 Gold 9.9991 oz. AGW **Ruler:** Elizabeth II **Obv:** Crowned head right, denomination below **Rev:** Red kangaroo bounding left **Edge:** Reeded

Date	Mintage	VF20	XF40	MS60	MS63	MS65
1999	—	—	—	—	—	18,000

KM# 151 2500 DOLLARS

311.07 g., 0.999 Gold 9.991 oz. AGW **Ruler:** Elizabeth II **Obv:** Crowned head right, denomination below **Rev:** Red kangaroo

Date	Mintage	VF20	XF40	MS60	MS63	MS65
1991	—	—	—	—	—	14,000
1991	124	PF65 18,000				

KM# 184 3000 DOLLARS

1000.10 g., 0.9999 Gold 32.1507 oz. AGW **Ruler:** Elizabeth II **Obv:** Crowned head right, denomination below **Rev:** Red kangaroo

Date	Mintage	VF20	XF40	MS60	MS63	MS65
1992	—	—	—	—	—	44,500
1992	—	PF65 57,500				
1995	—	—	—	—	—	45,000
1996	—	—	—	—	—	44,500
1997	—	—	—	—	—	44,500

KM# 396 3000 DOLLARS

1000.10 g., 0.9999 Platinum 32.1507 oz. APW **Ruler:** Elizabeth II **Obv:** Crowned head right, denomination below **Rev:** Nail-tailed wallaby

Date	Mintage	VF20	XF40	MS60	MS63	MS65
1992	25	PF65 60,000				

KM# 240 3000 DOLLARS

1000.10 g., 0.9999 Gold 32.1507 oz. AGW **Ruler:** Elizabeth II **Obv:** Crowned head right, denomination below **Rev:** Whiptail wallaby

Date	Mintage	VF20	XF40	MS60	MS63	MS65
1993	—	PF65 57,500				

KM# 248 3000 DOLLARS

1000.10 g., 0.9999 Gold 32.1507 oz. AGW **Ruler:** Elizabeth II **Obv:** Crowned head right, denomination below **Rev:** Kangaroo in diamond shape

Date	Mintage	VF20	XF40	MS60	MS63	MS65
1994	—	PF65 57,500				

KM# 455 3000 DOLLARS

1000.35 g., 0.999 Gold 32.1298 oz. AGW **Ruler:** Elizabeth II **Obv:** Crowned head right, denomination below **Rev:** Red kangaroo bounding left **Edge:** Reeded

Date	Mintage	VF20	XF40	MS60	MS63	MS65
1999	—	—	—	—	—	57,500
2000	—	—	—	—	—	57,500

KM# 152 10000 DOLLARS

1000.10 g., 0.999 Gold 32.1218 oz. AGW **Ruler:** Elizabeth II **Obv:** Crowned head right, denomination below **Rev:** Red kangaroo leaping left, date below

Date	Mintage	VF20	XF40	MS60	MS63	MS65
1991	—	—	—	—	—	44,500
1991	95	PF65 57,500				

BULLION - KOOKABURRA

KM# 164 DOLLAR

31.10 g., 0.999 Silver 0.9989 oz. ASW **Ruler:** Elizabeth II **Obv:** Crowned head right, denomination below **Rev:** Australian Kookaburra in tree left, date below

Date	Mintage	VF20	XF40	MS60	MS63	MS65
1992	300,000	—	—	—	32.00	—

KM# 209 DOLLAR

31.10 g., 0.999 Silver 0.9989 oz. ASW **Ruler:** Elizabeth II **Obv:** Crowned head right **Rev:** Australian kookaburra feeding nestlings in tree, date below

Date	Mintage	VF20	XF40	MS60	MS63	MS65
1992	—	PF65 42.00				
1992 (ae)	750	PF65 185				
1993	Est. 300000	—	—	—	32.00	—

KM# 212.1 DOLLAR

31.10 g., 0.999 Silver 0.999 oz. ASW **Ruler:** Elizabeth II **Obv:** Crowned head right, denomination below **Rev:** Pair of Kookaburras, date below

Date	Mintage	VF20	XF40	MS60	MS63	MS65
1993 AE	—	PF65 35.00				
1993 AE	—	PF65 32.00				
1993 (ge)	500	PF65 75.00				
1993 (so)	13,000	PF65 42.00				
1994	2,500	PF65 37.00				
1994 (p) BU	—	—	—	—	32.00	—
1994 (ta)	15,000	—	—	—	32.00	—
Specimen						

KM# 212.2 DOLLAR

31.10 g., 0.999 Silver 0.999 oz. ASW **Ruler:** Elizabeth II **Obv:** Crowned head right, denomination below **Rev:** American Eagle privy mark above date below 2 kookaburras on tree branch

Date	Mintage	VF20	XF40	MS60	MS63	MS65
1993 AE	500	PF65 65.00				
1993 AE	—	PF65 75.00				

KM# 260 DOLLAR

31.10 g., 0.999 Silver 0.999 oz. ASW **Ruler:** Elizabeth II **Obv:** Crowned head right, denomination below **Rev:** Kookaburra on branch left, denmination below

Date	Mintage	VF20	XF40	MS60	MS63	MS65
1994	2,500	PF65 45.00				
1995	300,000	—	—	—	35.00	—

KM# 289.1 DOLLAR

31.64 g., 0.999 Silver 1.0161 oz. ASW **Ruler:** Elizabeth II **Obv:** Crowned head right **Rev:** Kookaburra in flight, date below

Date	Mintage	VF20	XF40	MS60	MS63	MS65
1995 P	4,900	PF65 35.00				
1996	300,000	—	—	—	32.00	—
1996 (bg)	5,000	—	—	—	45.00	—
1996 (ba)	2,500	—	—	—	47.00	—
1996 (sr)	5,000	—	—	—	45.00	—

KM# 289.2 DOLLAR

31.10 g., 0.999 Silver 0.999 oz. ASW **Ruler:** Elizabeth II **Obv:** Crowned head right **Rev:** Kookaburra in flight, date below **Edge:** Reeded and inscribed with date and serial

Date	Mintage	VF20	XF40	MS60	MS63	MS65
1996	1,500	—	—	—	52.00	—

KM# 701 DOLLAR

31.10 g., 0.999 Silver 0.999 oz. ASW **Ruler:** Elizabeth II **Obv:** Crowned head right **Rev:** Kookaburra

Date	Mintage	VF20	XF40	MS60	MS63	MS65
1996	—	PF65 40.00				
1997	—	—	—	—	—	—

KM# 1330 DOLLAR

31.62 g., 0.999 Silver 1.0156 oz. ASW, 40.3 mm. **Ruler:** Elizabeth II **Obv:** Head right **Rev:** Kookabara

Date	Mintage	VF20	XF40	MS60	MS63	MS65
1996 P	—	PF65 55.00				

KM# 318 DOLLAR

31.10 g., 0.999 Silver 0.999 oz. ASW **Ruler:** Elizabeth II **Obv:** Crowned head right within circle, denomination below **Rev:** Kookaburra and nestlings, mark at right of bird, date below **Note:** With Utrecht Coat of Arms privy mark.

Date	Mintage	VF20	XF40	MS60	MS63	MS65
1997 (u)	300,000	—	—	—	32.00	—
1997	—	—	—	—	32.00	—

KM# 362 DOLLAR

31.10 g., 0.999 Silver 0.999 oz. ASW **Ruler:** Elizabeth II **Obv:** Crowned head right, denomination below **Rev:** Kookaburra on fence right, date below

Date	Mintage	VF20	XF40	MS60	MS63	MS65
1997	2,000	PF65 40.00				
1998	—	—	—	—	35.00	—

KM# 399 DOLLAR

32.25 g., 0.999 Silver 1.0358 oz. ASW **Ruler:** Elizabeth II **Obv:** Head with tiara right within circle, denomination below **Rev:** Adult and chick kookaburras on branch left, date below

Date	Mintage	VF20	XF40	MS60	MS63	MS65
1999	—	—	—	—	37.00	—
1999	5,000	—	—	—	37.00	—
Note: Finnish 1 markka coin design privy mark						
1999	5,000	—	—	—	37.00	—
Note: French 5 francs coin design privy mark						
1999	5,000	—	—	—	37.00	—
Note: Belgian 50 frank coin design privy mark						
1999	5,000	—	—	—	37.00	—
Note: Netherlands 1 gulden coin design privy mark						
1999	5,000	—	—	—	37.00	—
Note: Irish 1 punt coin design privy mark						
1999	5,000	—	—	—	37.00	—
Note: Luxembourg 50 francs coin design privy mark						
1999	5,000	—	—	—	37.00	—
Note: Portuguese 50 escudo coin design privy mark						
1999	5,000	—	—	—	40.00	—
Note: Spanish 100 pesetas coin design privy mark						
1999	5,000	—	—	—	37.00	—
Note: German 1 mark coin design privy mark						
1999	5,000	—	—	—	37.00	—
Note: Austrian 20 schilling coin design privy mark						
1999	5,000	—	—	—	37.00	—
Note: Italian 1000 lire coin design privy mark						

KM# 416 DOLLAR

31.77 g., 0.999 Silver 1.0204 oz. ASW **Ruler:** Elizabeth II **Obv:** Queen's head with tiara, right, within circle, value below circle **Rev:** Kookaburra on branch, left, silver weight and date in legend

Date	Mintage	VF20	XF40	MS60	MS63	MS65
2000	—	—	—	—	32.00	—

KM# 604 DOLLAR

31.10 g., 0.999 Silver 0.999 oz. ASW, 40.4 mm. **Ruler:** Elizabeth II **Subject:** U.S. State Quarter - Delaware

Date	Mintage	VF20	XF40	MS60	MS63	MS65
1999	75,000	—	—	—	32.00	—

KM# 605 DOLLAR

31.10 g., 0.999 Silver 0.999 oz. ASW, 40.4 mm. **Ruler:** Elizabeth II **Subject:** U.S. State Quarter - Pennsylvania

Date	Mintage	VF20	XF40	MS60	MS63	MS65
1999	75,000	—	—	—	32.00	—

KM# 606 DOLLAR

31.10 g., 0.999 Silver 0.999 oz. ASW, 40.4 mm. **Ruler:** Elizabeth II **Subject:** U.S. State Quarter - New Jersey

Date	Mintage	VF20	XF40	MS60	MS63	MS65
1999	75,000	—	—	—	32.00	—

KM# 607 DOLLAR

31.10 g., 0.999 Silver 0.999 oz. ASW, 40.4 mm. **Ruler:** Elizabeth II **Subject:** U.S. State Quarter - Georgia

Date	Mintage	VF20	XF40	MS60	MS63	MS65
1999	75,000	—	—	—	32.00	—

KM# 608 DOLLAR

31.10 g., 0.999 Silver 0.999 oz. ASW, 40.4 mm. **Ruler:** Elizabeth II **Subject:** U.S. State Quarter - Connecticut

Date	Mintage	VF20	XF40	MS60	MS63	MS65
1999	75,000	—	—	—	32.00	—

KM# 611 DOLLAR

31.10 g., 0.999 Silver 0.999 oz. ASW, 40.4 mm. **Ruler:** Elizabeth II **Subject:** U.S. State Quarter - Massachusetts

Date	Mintage	VF20	XF40	MS60	MS63	MS65
2000	75,000	—	—	—	32.00	—

KM# 612 DOLLAR

31.10 g., 0.999 Silver 0.999 oz. ASW, 40.4 mm. **Ruler:** Elizabeth II **Subject:** U.S. State Quarter - Maryland

Date	Mintage	VF20	XF40	MS60	MS63	MS65
2000	75,000	—	—	—	32.00	—

KM# 613 DOLLAR

31.10 g., 0.999 Silver 0.999 oz. ASW, 40.4 mm. **Ruler:** Elizabeth II **Subject:** U.S. State Quarter - South Carolina

Date	Mintage	VF20	XF40	MS60	MS63	MS65
2000	75,000	—	—	—	32.00	—

KM# 614 DOLLAR

31.10 g., 0.999 Silver 0.999 oz. ASW, 40.4 mm. **Ruler:** Elizabeth II **Subject:** U.S. State Quarter - New Hampshire

Date	Mintage	VF20	XF40	MS60	MS63	MS65
2000	75,000	—	—	—	32.00	—

KM# 615 DOLLAR

31.10 g., 0.999 Silver 0.999 oz. ASW, 40.4 mm. **Ruler:** Elizabeth II **Subject:** U.S. State Quarter - Virginia

Date	Mintage	VF20	XF40	MS60	MS63	MS65
2000	75,000	—	—	—	32.00	—

KM# 176 2 DOLLARS

62.21 g., 0.999 Silver 1.998 oz. ASW, 50 mm. **Ruler:** Elizabeth II **Subject:** Kookaburra **Obv:** Elizabeth II **Rev:** Kookaburra on branch next to tree trunk **Edge:** Segmented reeding

Date	Mintage	VF20	XF40	MS60	MS63	MS65
1992 P	—	—	—	—	—	75.00

KM# 179 2 DOLLARS

62.21 g., 0.999 Silver 1.998 oz. ASW **Ruler:** Elizabeth II **Obv:** Crowned head right within inner circle, denomination below **Rev:** Australian Kookaburra on stump right within circle, date below

Date	Mintage	VF20	XF40	MS60	MS63	MS65
1992	—	—	—	—	—	75.00
1992	5,000	PF65 95.00				
1992 (gv)	500	PF65 175				
1992 (hd) Specimen	1,000	—	—	—	135	—
1993 (dp) Specimen	1,000	—	—	—	135	—
1993	—	—	—	—	125	—
1993 (w) Specimen	1,000	—	—	—	145	—
1993 (e) Specimen	1,000	—	—	—	125	—
1993 (ta) Specimen	1,000	—	—	—	125	—

KM# 227 2 DOLLARS

62.21 g., 0.999 Silver 1.998 oz. ASW **Ruler:** Elizabeth II **Obv:** Crowned head right, denomination below **Rev:** Kookaburra feeding nestling right, date below

Date	Mintage	VF20	XF40	MS60	MS63	MS65
1992	—	PF65 95.00				
1992 (aa)	500	PF65 375				
1993	—	—	—	—	—	75.00
1993	—	PF65 95.00				

KM# 230 2 DOLLARS

62.21 g., 0.999 Silver 1.998 oz. ASW **Ruler:** Elizabeth II **Obv:** Crowned head right, denomination below **Rev:** Pair of Kookaburras on branch, date below

Date	Mintage	VF20	XF40	MS60	MS63	MS65
1993	—	—	—	—	—	75.00
1993 (sm)	750	PF65 200				
1993	—	PF65 95.00				
1993 (ae)	500	PF65 300				
1994	—	PF65 95.00				
1994 (ev)	1,500	PF65 200				
1994	—	—	—	—	—	75.00
1994 (gv) Specimen	1,000	—	—	—	275	—
1994 (gv) Specimen	1,500	—	—	—	180	—

KM# 261 2 DOLLARS

62.21 g., 0.999 Silver 1.998 oz. ASW **Ruler:** Elizabeth II **Obv:** Crowned head right, denomination below **Rev:** Kookaburra on branch right, within circle, date below

Date	Mintage	VF20	XF40	MS60	MS63	MS65
1994 P	—	PF65 100				
1995	—	—	—	—	—	75.00
1995 (f1)	1,500	PF65 125				
1995 (f3)	1,500	PF65 135				
1995 (f7)	1,500	PF65 100				
1995 (rv)	1,500	PF65 95.00				

KM# 290 2 DOLLARS

62.21 g., 0.999 Silver 1.998 oz. ASW **Ruler:** Elizabeth II **Obv:** Crowned head right, denomination below **Rev:** Kookaburra in flight, date below **Note:** Privy marks on gold insert.

Date	Mintage	VF20	XF40	MS60	MS63	MS65
1995 P	650	PF65 85.00				
1995 P (ww)	1,300	PF65 135				
1995 (ge)	800	PF65 135				
1996	—	—	—	—	—	75.00
1996 (h)	1,500	PF65 90.00				
1996 (d)	1,500	PF65 115				
1996 (j)	1,500	PF65 120				
1996 (sg)	1,500	PF65 130				
1996 (sp)	1,500	PF65 135				

KM# 319 2 DOLLARS

62.21 g., 0.999 Silver 1.998 oz. ASW **Ruler:** Elizabeth II **Obv:** Crowned head right, denomination below **Rev:** Kookaburra and nestling within circle, date below

Date	Mintage	VF20	XF40	MS60	MS63	MS65
1997	—	—	—	—	—	75.00

KM# 363 2 DOLLARS

62.21 g., 0.999 Silver 1.998 oz. ASW **Ruler:** Elizabeth II **Obv:** Crowned head right, denomination below **Rev:** Kookaburra on fence, right, within circle, date below

Date	Mintage	VF20	XF40	MS60	MS63	MS65
1997	2,000	PF65 115				
1998	—	—	—	—	—	75.00

KM# 417.1 2 DOLLARS

62.85 g., 0.999 Silver 2.0187 oz. ASW, 49.83 mm. **Ruler:** Elizabeth II **Obv:** Crowned head right **Rev:** Kookaburra on branch left, within circle **Edge:** Segmented reeding

Date	Mintage	VF20	XF40	MS60	MS63	MS65
1999 Proof	—	—	—	—	—	—
2000	—	—	—	—	—	75.00

KM# 417.3 2 DOLLARS

62.85 g., 0.999 Silver 2.0187 oz. ASW, 49.83 mm. **Ruler:** Elizabeth II **Obv:** Crowned head right **Rev:** Kookaburra on branch **Edge:** Segmented reeding **Note:** Rev. with 1933 Shilling obv. & rev. design copper inserts.

Date	Mintage	VF20	XF40	MS60	MS63	MS65
1999	1,500	—	—	—	—	85.00

KM# 417.4 2 DOLLARS

62.85 g., 0.9999 Silver 2.0205 oz. ASW, 49.83 mm. **Ruler:** Elizabeth II **Obv:** Crowned head right **Rev:** Kookaburra perched on branch left **Edge:** Segmented reeding **Note:** Reverse with 1930 Penny obverse and reverse design copper inserts.

Date	Mintage	VF20	XF40	MS60	MS63	MS65
1999	—	PF65 100				

KM# 417.5 2 DOLLARS

62.85 g., 0.999 Silver 2.0187 oz. ASW, 49.83 mm. **Ruler:** Elizabeth II **Obv:** Crowned head right **Rev:** Kookaburra perched on branch left **Edge:** Segmented reeding **Note:** Reverse with 1932 Florin obverse and reverse design copper inserts.

Date	Mintage	VF20	XF40	MS60	MS63	MS65
1999	—	PF65 100				

KM# 445 2 DOLLARS

62.77 g., 0.999 Silver 2.0161 oz. ASW **Ruler:** Elizabeth II **Obv:** Crowned head right, denomination below **Rev:** Two kookaburras on branch **Edge:** Interrupted reeding on edge

Date	Mintage	VF20	XF40	MS60	MS63	MS65
1999	—	—	—	—	—	75.00
2000	—	PF65 110				

KM# 609 2 DOLLARS

62.21 g., 0.999 Silver 1.998 oz. ASW **Ruler:** Elizabeth II **Subject:** USA State Quarters - 1999 **Obv:** Crowned head right, denomination below **Rev:** Kookaburra on branch with five state quarter designs added below **Edge:** Reeded and plain sections

Date	Mintage	VF20	XF40	MS60	MS63	MS65
1999	10,000	—	—	—	—	80.00

KM# 616 2 DOLLARS

62.21 g., 0.999 Silver 1.998 oz. ASW, 49.83 mm. **Ruler:** Elizabeth II **Subject:** USA State Quarters - 2000 **Obv:** Crowned head right **Rev:** Kookaburra perched on branch left with five state quarter designs added below **Edge:** Segmented reeding **Note:** Prev. KM#417.2.

Date	Mintage	VF20	XF40	MS60	MS63	MS65
2000	10,000	—	—	—	—	80.00

KM# 138 5 DOLLARS

31.10 g., 0.999 Silver 0.999 oz. ASW **Ruler:** Elizabeth II **Obv:** Crowned head right, denomination below **Rev:** Australian Kookaburra sitting on branch facing right, date below **Note:** Special coin fair issues exist.

Date	Mintage	VF20	XF40	MS60	MS63	MS65
1990	22,000	PF65 40.00				
1991	300,000	—	—	—	—	37.50
1991	—	PF65 40.00				

KM# 189 5 DOLLARS

31.10 g., 0.999 Silver 0.999 oz. ASW **Ruler:** Elizabeth II **Obv:** Crowned head right, denomination below **Rev:** Australian Kookaburra sitting on stump right, date below

Date	Mintage	VF20	XF40	MS60	MS63	MS65
1990	300,000	—	—	—	—	37.50

KM# 161 10 DOLLARS
62.21 g., 0.999 Silver 1.9982 oz. ASW **Ruler:** Elizabeth II **Obv:** Crowned head right, denomination below **Rev:** Australian Kookaburra sitting on stump facing right, date below **Note:** Photo reduced.

Date	Mintage	VF20	XF40	MS60	MS63	MS65
1991	—	—	—	—	—	75.00
1991	5,000	PF65 85.00				
1992	—	—	—	—	—	75.00
1993	—	—	—	—	—	75.00

KM# 177 10 DOLLARS
311.04 g., 0.999 Silver 9.990 oz. ASW, 75 mm. **Ruler:** Elizabeth II **Subject:** Kookaburra **Obv:** Elizabeth II **Rev:** Kookaburra on branch next to tree **Edge:** Segmented reeding **Note:** Photo reduced.

Date	Mintage	VF20	XF40	MS60	MS63	MS65
1992 P	—	PF65 400				
1992 P	—	—	—	—	—	350

KM# 180 10 DOLLARS
311.07 g., 0.999 Silver 9.991 oz. ASW **Ruler:** Elizabeth II **Obv:** Crowned head right, denomination below **Rev:** Australian kookaburra sitting on branch facing right, date below

Date	Mintage	VF20	XF40	MS60	MS63	MS65
1992	—	—	—	—	—	350
1992	2,500	PF65 400				

KM# 228 10 DOLLARS
311.07 g., 0.999 Silver 9.991 oz. ASW **Ruler:** Elizabeth II **Obv:** Crowned head right, denomination below **Rev:** Kookaburra feeding nestling

Date	Mintage	VF20	XF40	MS60	MS63	MS65
1993	—	—	—	—	—	350
1993	—	PF65 650				

KM# 231 10 DOLLARS
311.04 g., 0.999 Silver 9.990 oz. ASW, 75 mm. **Ruler:** Elizabeth II **Subject:** The Australian Kookaburra **Obv:** Crowned head right, denomination below **Rev:** Pair of Kookaburras on branch, square mark above date below **Note:** Illustration reduced.

Date	Mintage	VF20	XF40	MS60	MS63	MS65
1993 (ae)	500	PF65 375				
1994	—	—	—	—	—	350
1994	—	PF65 400				

KM# 270 10 DOLLARS
311.07 g., 0.999 Silver 9.991 oz. ASW **Ruler:** Elizabeth II **Obv:** Crowned head right, denomination below **Rev:** Kookaburra on branch looking left, date below **Note:** Photo reduced.

Date	Mintage	VF20	XF40	MS60	MS63	MS65
1994 P	—	PF65 400				
1995	—	—	—	—	—	350
1995	—	PF65 400				

KM# 291 10 DOLLARS
311.07 g., 0.999 Silver 9.991 oz. ASW, 75.5 mm. **Ruler:** Elizabeth II **Obv:** Crowned head right, denomination below **Rev:** Kookaburra in flight right, date below, small "p" above bird's tail **Note:** Illustration reduced.

Date	Mintage	VF20	XF40	MS60	MS63	MS65
1995 P	1,300	PF65 375				
1995 (ge)	800	PF65 400				
Note: Privy mark on gold insert						
1996	—	—	—	—	—	350

KM# 351 10 DOLLARS
311.07 g., 0.999 Silver 9.991 oz. ASW **Ruler:** Elizabeth II **Subject:** Kookaburra and Nestling **Obv:** Crowned head right, denomination below **Rev:** Kookaburra looking right, nestling

Date	Mintage	VF20	XF40	MS60	MS63	MS65
1997	—	—	—	—	—	500

KM# 494 10 DOLLARS
311.04 g., 0.999 Silver 9.990 oz. ASW, 75 mm. **Ruler:** Elizabeth II **Subject:** Kookaburra Bullion **Obv:** Crowned head right, denomination below **Rev:** Kookaburra on fence right, date below **Edge:** Reeded and plain sections **Note:** Photo reduced.

Date	Mintage	VF20	XF40	MS60	MS63	MS65
1997 P	—	PF65 425				

KM# 446 10 DOLLARS
312.35 g., 0.999 Silver 10.0321 oz. ASW **Ruler:** Elizabeth II **Obv:** Crowned head right, denomination below **Rev:** Two kookaburras on branch **Edge:** Interrupted reeding **Note:** Photo reduced.

Date	Mintage	VF20	XF40	MS60	MS63	MS65
2000	—	—	—	—	—	350

KM# 178 30 DOLLARS
1000.00 g., 0.999 Silver 32.1186 oz. ASW, 100 mm. **Ruler:** Elizabeth II **Subject:** Kookaburra **Obv:** Elizabeth II **Rev:** Kookaburra on branch next to tree trunk **Edge:** Segmented reeding

Date	Mintage	VF20	XF40	MS60	MS63	MS65
1992 P	—	—	—	—	1,150	—
1992 P	—	PF65 1,175				

KM# 181 30 DOLLARS
1100.10 g., 0.999 Silver 35.3336 oz. ASW, 100 mm. **Ruler:** Elizabeth II **Obv:** Crowned head right within inner circle, denomination below **Rev:** Australian Kookaburra on stump facing right within circle, date below **Note:** Illustration reduced.

Date	Mintage	VF20	XF40	MS60	MS63	MS65
1992	—	—	—	—	1,250	—
1992	1,000	PF65 1,300				
1993	—	—	—	—	1,250	—
1993 (jw)	210	PF65 1,300				

KM# 229 30 DOLLARS
1000.21 g., 0.999 Silver 32.1253 oz. ASW **Ruler:** Elizabeth II **Obv:** Crowned head right, denomination below **Rev:** Kookaburra feeding nestling **Note:** Similar to 1 Dollar, KM#209.

Date	Mintage	VF20	XF40	MS60	MS63	MS65
1993	—	—	—	—	1,150	—
1993	—	PF65 1,200				

KM# 232 30 DOLLARS
1000.21 g., 0.999 Silver 32.1253 oz. ASW, 100 mm. **Ruler:** Elizabeth II **Obv:** Bust of Queen Elizabeth II, right **Rev:** Pair of kookaburras on branch within circle, silver weight and date in legend **Note:** Illustration reduced.

Date	Mintage	VF20	XF40	MS60	MS63	MS65
1994	—	—	—	—	1,150	—
1994	—	PF65 1,175				

KM# 271 30 DOLLARS
1000.21 g., 0.999 Silver 32.1253 oz. ASW **Ruler:** Elizabeth II **Obv:** Crowned head right, denomination below **Rev:** Kookaburra on branch looking left, date below **Note:** Illustration reduced.

Date	Mintage	VF20	XF40	MS60	MS63	MS65
1994 P	—	PF65 1,175				
1995	—	—	—	—	—	1,150
1995	—	PF65 1,175				

KM# 292 30 DOLLARS
1000.21 g., 0.999 Silver 32.1253 oz. ASW, 101 mm. **Ruler:** Elizabeth II **Obv:** Crowned head right, denomination below **Rev:** Kookaburra in flight, date below **Note:** Illustration reduced.

Date	Mintage	VF20	XF40	MS60	MS63	MS65
1995 (lh)	500	PF65 1,175				
1995 P	1,000	PF65 1,200				
1996	—	—	—	—	—	1,150

KM# 495 30 DOLLARS
1100.10 g., 0.999 Silver 35.3336 oz. ASW, 100 mm. **Ruler:** Elizabeth II **Subject:** Kookaburra Bullion **Obv:** Crowned head right, denomination below **Rev:** Kookaburra on fence facing right, date below **Edge:** Reeded and plain sections with serial number **Note:** Photo reduced.

Date	Mintage	VF20	XF40	MS60	MS63	MS65
1997 P	—	PF65 1,175				
1998 P	—	—	—	—	—	1,150

KM# 447 30 DOLLARS
1002.50 g., 0.999 Silver 32.1989 oz. ASW **Ruler:** Elizabeth II **Obv:** Crowned head right, denomination below **Rev:** Two kookaburras on branch, date below **Edge:** Reeded **Note:** Photo reduced.

Date	Mintage	VF20	XF40	MS60	MS63	MS65
1999	—	—	—	—	—	1,150
2000	—	PF65 1,175				

KM# 610 30 DOLLARS
1002.50 g., 0.999 Silver 32.1989 oz. ASW **Ruler:** Elizabeth II **Subject:** USA State Quarters - 1999 **Obv:** Crowned head right, denomination below **Rev:** Kookaburra on branch with five state quarter designs added below **Edge:** Reeded and plain sections

Date	Mintage	VF20	XF40	MS60	MS63	MS65
1999	1,000	—	—	—	—	1,150

KM# 617 30 DOLLARS
1002.50 g., 0.999 Silver 32.1989 oz. ASW **Ruler:** Elizabeth II **Subject:** USA State Quarters - 2000 **Obv:** Crowned head right, denomination below **Rev:** Kookaburra on branch with five state quarter designs added below **Edge:** Reeded and plain sections **Note:** Photo reduced.

Date	Mintage	VF20	XF40	MS60	MS63	MS65
2000	1,000	—	—	—	—	1,150

KM# 162 50 DOLLARS
311.07 g., 0.999 Silver 9.991 oz. ASW **Ruler:** Elizabeth II **Subject:** Australian Kookaburra **Obv:** Crowned head right, denomination below **Rev:** Kookaburra bird

Date	Mintage	VF20	XF40	MS60	MS63	MS65
1991	—	—	—	—	—	375
1991	2,500	PF65 400				

KM# 163 150 DOLLARS
1000.10 g., 0.999 Silver 32.1218 oz. ASW **Ruler:** Elizabeth II **Subject:** Australian Kookaburra **Obv:** Crowned head right, denomination below **Rev:** Kookaburra bird **Note:** Kilo

Date	Mintage	VF20	XF40	MS60	MS63	MS65
1991	—	—	—	—	—	1,150
1991	1,000	PF65 1,175				

BULLION - NUGGET

KM# 89 15 DOLLARS
3.11 g., 0.999 Gold 0.0999 oz. AGW **Ruler:** Elizabeth II **Obv:** Crowned head right, denomination below **Rev:** Little Hero, date below

Date	Mintage	VF20	XF40	MS60	MS63	MS65
1986 P	15,000	PF65 200				
1987	266,000	—	—	—	—	150
1988	104,000	—	—	—	—	150
1989	—	—	—	—	—	150

KM# 95 15 DOLLARS
3.11 g., 0.999 Gold 0.0999 oz. AGW **Ruler:** Elizabeth II **Obv:** Crowned head right, denomination below **Rev:** Golden Aussie, date below

Date	Mintage	VF20	XF40	MS60	MS63	MS65
1987 P	15,000	PF65 200				

KM# 104 15 DOLLARS
3.11 g., 0.999 Gold 0.0999 oz. AGW **Ruler:** Elizabeth II **Obv:** Crowned head right, denomination below **Rev:** Jubilee Nugget, date below

Date	Mintage	VF20	XF40	MS60	MS63	MS65
1988 P	Est. 10000	PF65 200				

KM# 90 25 DOLLARS
7.75 g., 0.999 Gold 0.2489 oz. AGW **Ruler:** Elizabeth II **Obv:** Crowned head right, denomination below **Rev:** Golden Eagle, date below

Date	Mintage	VF20	XF40	MS60	MS63	MS65
1986 P	15,000	PF65 475				
1987	233,000	—	—	—	—	370
1988	75,000	—	—	—	—	370
1989	—	—	—	—	—	370

KM# 96 25 DOLLARS
7.75 g., 0.999 Gold 0.2489 oz. AGW **Ruler:** Elizabeth II **Obv:** Crowned head right, denomination below **Rev:** Father's Day, date below

Date	Mintage	VF20	XF40	MS60	MS63	MS65
1987 P	15,000	PF65 475				

KM# 105 25 DOLLARS
7.75 g., 0.999 Gold 0.2489 oz. AGW **Ruler:** Elizabeth II **Obv:** Crowned head right, denomination below **Rev:** Ruby Well Nugget, date below

Date	Mintage	VF20	XF40	MS60	MS63	MS65
1988 P	Est. 10000	PF65 475				

KM# 91 50 DOLLARS
15.50 g., 0.999 Gold 0.4979 oz. AGW **Ruler:** Elizabeth II **Obv:** Crowned head right, denomination below **Rev:** Hand of Faith, date below

Date	Mintage	VF20	XF40	MS60	MS63	MS65
1986	15,000	PF65 925				
1987	188,000	—	—	—	—	720
1988	75,000	—	—	—	—	720
1989	100,000	—	—	—	—	720

KM# 97 50 DOLLARS
15.50 g., 0.999 Gold 0.4979 oz. AGW **Ruler:** Elizabeth II **Obv:** Crowned head right, denomination below **Rev:** Bobby Dazzler, date below

Date	Mintage	VF20	XF40	MS60	MS63	MS65
1987 P	15,000	PF65 925				

KM# 106 50 DOLLARS
15.50 g., 0.999 Gold 0.4979 oz. AGW **Ruler:** Elizabeth II **Obv:** Crowned head right, denomination below **Rev:** Welcome nugget, date below

Date	Mintage	VF20	XF40	MS60	MS63	MS65
1988 P	Est. 10000	PF65 925				

KM# 92 100 DOLLARS
31.10 g., 0.999 Gold 0.999 oz. AGW **Ruler:** Elizabeth II **Obv:** Crowned head right, denomination below **Rev:** Welcome Stranger, date below

Date	Mintage	VF20	XF40	MS60	MS63	MS65
1986 P	15,000	PF65 1,800				
1987	259,000	—	—	—	—	1,400
1988	116,000	—	—	—	—	1,400
1989	—	—	—	—	—	1,400

KM# 98 100 DOLLARS
31.10 g., 0.999 Gold 0.999 oz. AGW **Ruler:** Elizabeth II **Obv:** Crowned head right, denomination below **Rev:** Poseidon, date below

Date	Mintage	VF20	XF40	MS60	MS63	MS65
1987 P	15,000	PF65 1,800				

KM# 107 100 DOLLARS
31.10 g., 0.999 Gold 0.999 oz. AGW **Ruler:** Elizabeth II **Obv:** Crowned head right, denomination below **Rev:** Pride of Australia nugget

Date	Mintage	VF20	XF40	MS60	MS63	MS65
1988 P	Est. 10000	PF65 1,800				

BULLION - KOALA

KM# 122 5 DOLLARS
1.57 g., 0.999 Platinum 0.0505 oz. APW **Ruler:** Elizabeth II **Obv:** Crowned head right, denomination below **Rev:** Koala

Date	Mintage	VF20	XF40	MS60	MS63	MS65
1989	2,400	PF65 135				
1990	—	PF65 135				

KM# 145 5 DOLLARS
1.57 g., 0.999 Platinum 0.0505 oz. APW **Ruler:** Elizabeth II **Obv:** Crowned head right, denomination below **Rev:** Koala on tree limb facing right, date below

Date	Mintage	VF20	XF40	MS60	MS63	MS65
1990	2,500	PF65 135				
1991	20,000	—	—	—	—	75.00
1991	1,000	PF65 135				

KM# 170 5 DOLLARS
1.57 g., 0.999 Platinum 0.0505 oz. APW **Ruler:** Elizabeth II **Subject:** Koala **Obv:** Crowned head right, denomination below **Rev:** Koala sitting facing in crook of tree

Date	Mintage	VF20	XF40	MS60	MS63	MS65
1992	20,000	—	—	—	—	75.00

KM# 191 5 DOLLARS
1.57 g., 0.999 Platinum 0.0505 oz. APW **Ruler:** Elizabeth II **Obv:** Crowned head right, denomination below **Rev:** Koala facing left, sitting on branch, date below

Date	Mintage	VF20	XF40	MS60	MS63	MS65
1993	—	—	—	—	—	75.00

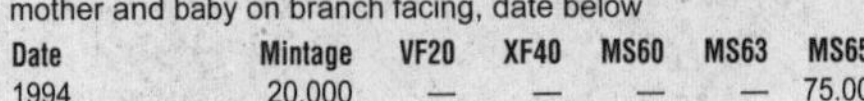

KM# 249 5 DOLLARS
1.57 g., 0.999 Platinum 0.0505 oz. APW **Ruler:** Elizabeth II **Obv:** Crowned head right, denomination below **Rev:** Koala mother and baby on branch facing, date below

Date	Mintage	VF20	XF40	MS60	MS63	MS65
1994	20,000	—	—	—	—	75.00

KM# 278 5 DOLLARS
1.57 g., 0.999 Platinum 0.0505 oz. APW **Ruler:** Elizabeth II **Obv:** Crowned head right, denomination below **Rev:** Koala in fork of tree facing, date below

Date	Mintage	VF20	XF40	MS60	MS63	MS65
1994	—	PF65 135				
1995	—	—	—	—	—	75.00

KM# 283 5 DOLLARS
1.57 g., 0.999 Platinum 0.0505 oz. APW **Ruler:** Elizabeth II **Obv:** Crowned head right, denomination below **Rev:** Baby koala on branch right, facing, date below

Date	Mintage	VF20	XF40	MS60	MS63	MS65
1995	200	PF65 135				
1996	20,000	—	—	—	—	75.00

KM# 344 5 DOLLARS
1.57 g., 0.9995 Platinum 0.0505 oz. APW **Ruler:** Elizabeth II **Subject:** Koala Bullion **Obv:** Crowned head right, denomination below **Rev:** Cuddling koalas

Date	Mintage	VF20	XF40	MS60	MS63	MS65
1997	20,000	—	—	—	—	75.00
1997	—	PF65 135				

KM# 456 5 DOLLARS
1.57 g., 0.999 Platinum 0.0505 oz. APW **Ruler:** Elizabeth II **Obv:** Crowned head right, denomination below **Rev:** Koala on log

Date	Mintage	VF20	XF40	MS60	MS63	MS65
1999	20,000	—	—	—	—	75.00

KM# 469 5 DOLLARS
1.57 g., 0.999 Platinum 0.0505 oz. APW **Ruler:** Elizabeth II **Obv:** Crowned head right, denomination below **Rev:** Seated koala

Date	Mintage	VF20	XF40	MS60	MS63	MS65
2000	—	—	—	—	—	75.00

KM# 108 15 DOLLARS
3.14 g., 0.999 Platinum 0.1008 oz. APW **Ruler:** Elizabeth II **Obv:** Crowned head right, denomination below **Rev:** Koala sitting facing

Date	Mintage	VF20	XF40	MS60	MS63	MS65
1988	—	—	—	—	—	127
1989	—	PF65 220				

KM# 123 15 DOLLARS
3.14 g., 0.999 Platinum 0.1008 oz. APW **Ruler:** Elizabeth II **Obv:** Crowned head right, denomination below **Rev:** Koala on tree branch with cub on her back

Date	Mintage	VF20	XF40	MS60	MS63	MS65
1989	2,400	PF65 225				
1990	—	PF65 225				

KM# 146 15 DOLLARS
3.14 g., 0.999 Platinum 0.1008 oz. APW **Ruler:** Elizabeth II **Subject:** Koala **Obv:** Crowned head right, denomination below **Rev:** Koala on branch facing left, looking right, date below

Date	Mintage	VF20	XF40	MS60	MS63	MS65
1990	2,500	PF65 225				
1991	20,000	—	—	—	—	127
1991	1,000	PF65 225				

KM# 171 15 DOLLARS
3.14 g., 0.999 Platinum 0.1008 oz. APW **Ruler:** Elizabeth II **Subject:** Koala Bullion **Obv:** Crowned head right, denomination below **Rev:** Koala in crook of tree facing

Date	Mintage	VF20	XF40	MS60	MS63	MS65
1992	20,000	—	—	—	—	127

KM# 192 15 DOLLARS
3.14 g., 0.999 Platinum 0.1008 oz. APW **Ruler:** Elizabeth II **Obv:** Crowned head right, denomination below **Rev:** Koala climbing tree

Date	Mintage	VF20	XF40	MS60	MS63	MS65
1993	—	—	—	—	—	127

KM# 250 15 DOLLARS

3.14 g., 0.999 Platinum 0.1008 oz. APW **Ruler:** Elizabeth II **Obv:** Crowned head right, denomination below **Rev:** Koala mother and baby facing forward, date below

Date	Mintage	VF20	XF40	MS60	MS63	MS65
1994	20,000	—	—	—	—	127

KM# 279 15 DOLLARS

3.14 g., 0.999 Platinum 0.1008 oz. APW **Ruler:** Elizabeth II **Obv:** Crowned head right, denomination below **Rev:** Koala in fork of tree facing forward, date below

Date	Mintage	VF20	XF40	MS60	MS63	MS65
1994	—	PF65 225				
1995	—	—	—	—	—	127

KM# 284 15 DOLLARS

3.14 g., 0.999 Platinum 0.1008 oz. APW **Ruler:** Elizabeth II **Obv:** Crowned head right, denomination below **Rev:** Baby koala on branch,right facing forward, date below

Date	Mintage	VF20	XF40	MS60	MS63	MS65
1995	800	PF65 225				
1996	20,000	—	—	—	—	127

KM# 345 15 DOLLARS

3.11 g., 0.9995 Platinum 0.0999 oz. APW **Ruler:** Elizabeth II **Subject:** Koalas **Obv:** Crowned head right, denomination below **Rev:** Cuddling koalas

Date	Mintage	VF20	XF40	MS60	MS63	MS65
1997	20,000	—	—	—	—	127
1997	—	PF65 225				

KM# 457 15 DOLLARS

3.14 g., 0.999 Platinum 0.1008 oz. APW **Ruler:** Elizabeth II **Obv:** Crowned head right, denomination below **Rev:** Koala on log facing forward, date below **Edge:** Reeded

Date	Mintage	VF20	XF40	MS60	MS63	MS65
1999	20,000	—	—	—	—	127

KM# 470 15 DOLLARS

3.14 g., 0.999 Platinum 0.1008 oz. APW **Ruler:** Elizabeth II **Obv:** Crowned head right, denomination below **Rev:** Seated koala **Edge:** Reeded

Date	Mintage	VF20	XF40	MS60	MS63	MS65
2000	—	—	—	—	—	127

KM# 109 25 DOLLARS

7.82 g., 0.999 Platinum 0.251 oz. APW **Ruler:** Elizabeth II **Obv:** Crowned head right, denomination below **Rev:** Seated koala facing

Date	Mintage	VF20	XF40	MS60	MS63	MS65
1988	—	—	—	—	—	305
1989	—	PF65 525				

KM# 124 25 DOLLARS

7.75 g., 0.999 Platinum 0.2489 oz. APW **Ruler:** Elizabeth II **Obv:** Crowned head right, denomination below **Rev:** Koala bear with cub on its back sitting on branch

Date	Mintage	VF20	XF40	MS60	MS63	MS65
1989	2,400	PF65 520				
1990	—	PF65 520				

KM# 147 25 DOLLARS

7.82 g., 0.999 Platinum 0.251 oz. APW **Ruler:** Elizabeth II **Obv:** Crowned head right, denomination below **Rev:** Koala on branch left facing right, date below

Date	Mintage	VF20	XF40	MS60	MS63	MS65
1990	2,500	PF65 525				
1991	20,000	—	—	—	—	305
1991	1,000	PF65 525				

KM# 172 25 DOLLARS

7.82 g., 0.999 Platinum 0.251 oz. APW **Ruler:** Elizabeth II **Subject:** Koala **Obv:** Crowned head right, denomination below **Rev:** Koala seated crook of tree

Date	Mintage	VF20	XF40	MS60	MS63	MS65
1992	20,000	—	—	—	—	305

KM# 193 25 DOLLARS

7.82 g., 0.999 Platinum 0.251 oz. APW **Ruler:** Elizabeth II **Obv:** Crowned head right, denomination below **Rev:** Koala sitting in tree right facing left, date below

Date	Mintage	VF20	XF40	MS60	MS63	MS65
1992 (ae)	750	PF65 525				
1993	Est. 20000	—	—	—	—	305

KM# 251 25 DOLLARS

7.82 g., 0.999 Platinum 0.251 oz. APW **Ruler:** Elizabeth II **Obv:** Crowned head right, denomination below **Rev:** Koala mother and baby on branch facing forward, date below

Date	Mintage	VF20	XF40	MS60	MS63	MS65
1994	20,000	—	—	—	—	305

KM# 280 25 DOLLARS

7.82 g., 0.999 Platinum 0.251 oz. APW **Ruler:** Elizabeth II **Obv:** Crowned head right, denomination below **Rev:** Koala in fork of tree facing forward, date below

Date	Mintage	VF20	XF40	MS60	MS63	MS65
1994	—	PF65 525				
1995	—	—	—	—	—	305

KM# 285 25 DOLLARS

7.82 g., 0.999 Platinum 0.251 oz. APW **Ruler:** Elizabeth II **Obv:** Crowned head right, denomination below **Rev:** Baby koala on branch right facing forward, date below

Date	Mintage	VF20	XF40	MS60	MS63	MS65
1995	200	PF65 525				
1996	20,000	—	—	—	—	305

KM# 346 25 DOLLARS

7.75 g., 0.9995 Platinum 0.2491 oz. APW **Ruler:** Elizabeth II **Subject:** Koala Bullion **Obv:** Crowned head right, denomination below **Rev:** Cuddling koalas

Date	Mintage	VF20	XF40	MS60	MS63	MS65
1997	20,000	—	—	—	—	300
1997	—	PF65 525				

KM# 458 25 DOLLARS

7.82 g., 0.999 Platinum 0.251 oz. APW **Ruler:** Elizabeth II **Obv:** Crowned head right, denomination below **Rev:** Koala on log facing forward, date below **Edge:** Reeded

Date	Mintage	VF20	XF40	MS60	MS63	MS65
1999	20,000	—	—	—	—	305

KM# 471 25 DOLLARS

7.82 g., 0.999 Platinum 0.251 oz. APW **Ruler:** Elizabeth II **Obv:** Crowned head right, denomination below **Rev:** Seated koala **Edge:** Reeded

Date	Mintage	VF20	XF40	MS60	MS63	MS65
2000	—	—	—	—	—	305

KM# 110 50 DOLLARS

15.61 g., 0.999 Platinum 0.5012 oz. APW **Ruler:** Elizabeth II **Obv:** Crowned head right, denomination below **Rev:** Koala bear on log facing forward, date below

Date	Mintage	VF20	XF40	MS60	MS63	MS65
1988	—	—	—	—	—	590
1988	12,000	PF65 1,000				
1989	—	PF65 1,000				

KM# 125 50 DOLLARS

15.61 g., 0.999 Platinum 0.5012 oz. APW **Ruler:** Elizabeth II **Obv:** Crowned head right, denomination below **Rev:** Koala bear on tree branch with cub on back

Date	Mintage	VF20	XF40	MS60	MS63	MS65
1989	2,400	PF65 1,000				
1990	8,000	PF65 1,000				

KM# 148 50 DOLLARS

15.61 g., 0.999 Platinum 0.5012 oz. APW **Ruler:** Elizabeth II **Obv:** Crowned head right, denomination below **Rev:** Koala bear in tree left facing right, date below

Date	Mintage	VF20	XF40	MS60	MS63	MS65
1990	5,500	PF65 1,000				
1991	20,000	—	—	—	—	590
1991	2,000	PF65 1,000				

KM# 173 50 DOLLARS

15.61 g., 0.999 Platinum 0.5012 oz. APW **Ruler:** Elizabeth II **Subject:** Koala **Obv:** Crowned head right, denomination below **Rev:** Koala in crook of tree facing

Date	Mintage	VF20	XF40	MS60	MS63	MS65
1992	20,000	—	—	—	—	590

KM# 194 50 DOLLARS

15.61 g., 0.999 Platinum 0.5012 oz. APW **Ruler:** Elizabeth II **Obv:** Crowned head right, denomination below **Rev:** Koala sitting in tree right, facing left, date below

Date	Mintage	VF20	XF40	MS60	MS63	MS65
1993	Est. 20000	—	—	—	—	590

KM# 252 50 DOLLARS

15.61 g., 0.999 Platinum 0.5012 oz. APW **Ruler:** Elizabeth II **Obv:** Crowned head right, denomination below **Rev:** Koala mother and baby in tree facing forward, date below

Date	Mintage	VF20	XF40	MS60	MS63	MS65
1994	5,000	—	—	—	—	590

KM# 281 50 DOLLARS
15.61 g., 0.999 Platinum 0.5012 oz. APW **Ruler:** Elizabeth II **Obv:** Crowned head right, denomination below **Rev:** Koala in fork of tree left, facing forward

Date	Mintage	VF20	XF40	MS60	MS63	MS65
1994	—	PF65 1,000				
1995	—	—	—	—	—	590

KM# 286 50 DOLLARS
15.61 g., 0.999 Platinum 0.5012 oz. APW **Ruler:** Elizabeth II **Obv:** Crowned head right, denomination below **Rev:** Baby koala on branch right, facing forward, date below

Date	Mintage	VF20	XF40	MS60	MS63	MS65
1995	450	PF65 1,000				
1995 (ww)	300	PF65 1,000				
1996	5,000	—	—	—	—	590

KM# 347 50 DOLLARS
15.55 g., 0.9995 Platinum 0.4998 oz. APW **Ruler:** Elizabeth II **Subject:** Koala Bullion **Obv:** Crowned head right, denomination below **Rev:** Cuddling koalas

Date	Mintage	VF20	XF40	MS60	MS63	MS65
1997	5,000	—	—	—	—	590
1997	—	PF65 1,000				

KM# 459 50 DOLLARS
15.61 g., 0.999 Platinum 0.5012 oz. APW **Ruler:** Elizabeth II **Obv:** Crowned head right, denomination below **Rev:** Koala on log left, facing forward **Edge:** Reeded

Date	Mintage	VF20	XF40	MS60	MS63	MS65
1999	5,000	—	—	—	—	590

KM# 472 50 DOLLARS
15.61 g., 0.999 Platinum 0.5012 oz. APW **Ruler:** Elizabeth II **Obv:** Crowned head right, denomination below **Rev:** Seated koala **Edge:** Reeded

Date	Mintage	VF20	XF40	MS60	MS63	MS65
2000	—	—	—	—	—	590

KM# 111 100 DOLLARS
31.19 g., 0.999 Platinum 1.0016 oz. APW **Ruler:** Elizabeth II **Obv:** Crowned head right, denomination below **Rev:** Seated Koala facing forward, date below

Date	Mintage	VF20	XF40	MS60	MS63	MS65
1988	—	—	—	—	—	1,150
1989	—	PF65 1,900				

KM# 126 100 DOLLARS
31.19 g., 0.999 Platinum 1.0016 oz. APW **Ruler:** Elizabeth II **Obv:** Crowned head right, denomination below **Rev:** Koala with baby on branch left, facing right

Date	Mintage	VF20	XF40	MS60	MS63	MS65
1989	2,400	PF65 1,900				
1990	—	PF65 1,900				

KM# 149 100 DOLLARS
31.19 g., 0.999 Platinum 1.0016 oz. APW **Ruler:** Elizabeth II **Obv:** Crowned head right, denomination below **Rev:** Koala bear in tree left, facing right

Date	Mintage	VF20	XF40	MS60	MS63	MS65
1990	3,500	PF65 1,900				
1991	75,000	—	—	—	—	1,150
1991	1,000	PF65 1,900				

KM# 174 100 DOLLARS
31.19 g., 0.999 Platinum 1.0016 oz. APW **Ruler:** Elizabeth II **Obv:** Crowned head right, denomination below **Rev:** Koala in fork of tree facing, date below

Date	Mintage	VF20	XF40	MS60	MS63	MS65
1992	75,000	—	—	—	—	1,150

KM# 195 100 DOLLARS
31.19 g., 0.999 Platinum 1.0016 oz. APW **Ruler:** Elizabeth II **Obv:** Crowned head right, denomination below **Rev:** Koala in fork of tree right, facing left, date below

Date	Mintage	VF20	XF40	MS60	MS63	MS65
1993	—	—	—	—	—	1,150

KM# 253 100 DOLLARS
31.19 g., 0.999 Platinum 1.0016 oz. APW **Ruler:** Elizabeth II **Obv:** Crowned head right, denomination below **Rev:** Koala mother and baby on branch facing forward. date below

Date	Mintage	VF20	XF40	MS60	MS63	MS65
1994 Prooflike	100,000	—	—	—	—	1,150

KM# 282 100 DOLLARS
31.19 g., 0.999 Platinum 1.0016 oz. APW **Ruler:** Elizabeth II **Obv:** Crowned head of Queen Elizabeth II, right **Rev:** Koala in fork of tree left, facing forward, date below

Date	Mintage	VF20	XF40	MS60	MS63	MS65
1994	—	PF65 1,900				
1995	—	—	—	—	—	1,150

KM# 287 100 DOLLARS
31.19 g., 0.999 Platinum 1.0016 oz. APW **Ruler:** Elizabeth II **Obv:** Crowned head right, denomination below **Rev:** Baby koala on branch right, date below

Date	Mintage	VF20	XF40	MS60	MS63	MS65
1995	200	PF65 1,900				
1996	100,000	—	—	—	—	1,150

KM# 348 100 DOLLARS
31.19 g., 0.999 Platinum 1.0016 oz. APW **Ruler:** Elizabeth II **Subject:** Koala Bullion **Obv:** Crowned head right, denomination below **Rev:** Cuddling koalas

Date	Mintage	VF20	XF40	MS60	MS63	MS65
1997	100,000	—	—	—	—	1,150
1997	—	PF65 1,900				

KM# 460 100 DOLLARS
31.19 g., 0.999 Platinum 1.0016 oz. APW **Ruler:** Elizabeth II **Obv:** Crowned head right, denomination below **Rev:** Koala on log left, date below **Edge:** Reeded

Date	Mintage	VF20	XF40	MS60	MS63	MS65
1999	100,000	—	—	—	—	1,150

KM# 473 100 DOLLARS
31.19 g., 0.999 Platinum 1.0016 oz. APW **Ruler:** Elizabeth II **Obv:** Crowned head right, denomination below **Rev:** Seated koala with branches left, date below **Edge:** Reeded

Date	Mintage	VF20	XF40	MS60	MS63	MS65
2000	—	—	—	—	—	1,150

KM# 185 200 DOLLARS
62.21 g., 0.9995 Platinum 1.9992 oz. APW **Ruler:** Elizabeth II **Obv:** Crowned head right, denomination below **Rev:** Koala bear in tree left, looking right, date below

Date	Mintage	VF20	XF40	MS60	MS63	MS65
1992	—	—	—	—	—	2,300
1992	—	PF65 3,750				
1996	—	—	—	—	—	2,300

KM# 196 200 DOLLARS
62.21 g., 0.9995 Platinum 1.9992 oz. APW **Ruler:** Elizabeth II **Obv:** Crowned head right, denomination below **Rev:** Koala bear in tree left, looking right, date below

Date	Mintage	VF20	XF40	MS60	MS63	MS65
1993	—	—	—	—	—	2,300
1994	—	—	—	—	—	2,300
1995	—	—	—	—	—	2,300
1997	—	—	—	—	—	2,300

KM# 254 200 DOLLARS
62.21 g., 0.9995 Platinum 1.9992 oz. APW **Ruler:** Elizabeth II **Obv:** Crowned head right, denomination below **Rev:** Koala with cub

Date	Mintage	VF20	XF40	MS60	MS63	MS65
1994	—	PF65 3,750				

KM# 288 200 DOLLARS
62.21 g., 0.9995 Platinum 1.9992 oz. APW, 41 mm. **Ruler:** Elizabeth II **Obv:** Crowned head right, denomination below **Rev:** Baby koala on branch right, date below

Date	Mintage	VF20	XF40	MS60	MS63	MS65
1995	100	PF65 3,750				

KM# 461 200 DOLLARS
62.31 g., 0.999 Platinum 2.0014 oz. APW, 41 mm. **Ruler:** Elizabeth II **Obv:** Crowned head right, denomination below **Rev:** Koala in tree left, looking right, date below **Edge:** Reeded

Date	Mintage	VF20	XF40	MS60	MS63	MS65
1999	—	—	—	—	—	2,300

KM# 157 500 DOLLARS
62.21 g., 0.999 Platinum 1.9982 oz. APW, 41 mm. **Ruler:** Elizabeth II **Subject:** Koala Bullion **Obv:** Crowned head right, denomination below **Rev:** Koala in tree

Date	Mintage	VF20	XF40	MS60	MS63	MS65
1991	—	—	—	—	—	2,300
1991	250	PF65 3,750				

KM# 186 1000 DOLLARS
311.07 g., 0.9995 Platinum 9.996 oz. APW **Ruler:** Elizabeth II **Obv:** Crowned head right, denomination below **Rev:** Koala

Date	Mintage	VF20	XF40	MS60	MS63	MS65
1992	—	—	—	—	—	11,500
1992	—	PF65 18,500				
1996	—	—	—	—	—	11,500

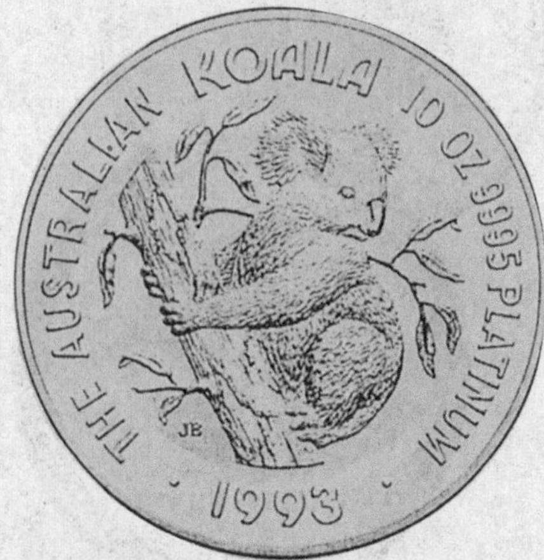

KM# 197 1000 DOLLARS
311.07 g., 0.9995 Platinum 9.996 oz. APW, 60.3 mm. **Ruler:** Elizabeth II **Obv:** Crowned head right, denomination below **Rev:** Koala on branch left, looking right, date below **Note:** Illustration reduced.

Date	Mintage	VF20	XF40	MS60	MS63	MS65
1993	—	—	—	—	—	11,500
1994	—	—	—	—	—	11,500
1995	—	—	—	—	—	11,500
1997	—	—	—	—	—	11,500

KM# 255 1000 DOLLARS
311.07 g., 0.9995 Platinum 9.996 oz. APW **Ruler:** Elizabeth II **Obv:** Crowned head right, denomination below **Rev:** Koala with cub

Date	Mintage	VF20	XF40	MS60	MS63	MS65
1994	—	—	—	—	—	11,500

KM# 462 1000 DOLLARS
311.69 g., 0.999 Platinum 10.0111 oz. APW **Ruler:** Elizabeth II **Obv:** Crowned head right, denomination below **Rev:** Koala in tree **Edge:** Reeded **Note:** Photo reduced.

Date	Mintage	VF20	XF40	MS60	MS63	MS65
1999	—	—	—	—	—	11,500

KM# 158 2500 DOLLARS
311.07 g., 0.999 Platinum 9.991 oz. APW **Ruler:** Elizabeth II **Subject:** Koala Bullion **Obv:** Crowned head right, denomination below **Rev:** Koala in tree

Date	Mintage	VF20	XF40	MS60	MS63	MS65
1991	—	—	—	—	—	11,500
1991	100	PF65 18,500				

KM# 187 3000 DOLLARS
1000.10 g., 0.9999 Platinum 32.1507 oz. APW **Ruler:** Elizabeth II **Obv:** Crowned head right, denomination below **Rev:** Koala in tree, date below

Date	Mintage	VF20	XF40	MS60	MS63	MS65
1992	—	—	—	—	—	36,500
1992	—	PF65 60,000				
1996	—	—	—	—	—	36,500

KM# 198 3000 DOLLARS
1000.10 g., 0.9999 Platinum 32.1507 oz. APW, 75.3 mm. **Ruler:** Elizabeth II **Obv:** Crowned head right, denomination below **Rev:** Koala on tree branch left, looking right, date below **Note:** Illustration reduced.

Date	Mintage	VF20	XF40	MS60	MS63	MS65
1993	—	—	—	—	—	36,500
1994	—	—	—	—	—	36,500
1995	—	—	—	—	—	36,500
1997	—	—	—	—	—	36,500

KM# 256 3000 DOLLARS
1000.10 g., 0.9995 Platinum 32.1379 oz. APW **Ruler:** Elizabeth II **Obv:** Crowned head right, denomination below **Rev:** Koala with cub

Date	Mintage	VF20	XF40	MS60	MS63	MS65
1994	—	—	—	—	—	36,500

KM# 463 3000 DOLLARS
1001.00 g., 0.999 Platinum 32.1507 oz. APW **Ruler:** Elizabeth II **Obv:** Crowned head right, denomination below **Rev:** Koala in tree **Edge:** Reeded **Note:** Photo reduced.

Date	Mintage	VF20	XF40	MS60	MS63	MS65
1999	—	—	—	—	—	36,500

KM# 159 10000 DOLLARS
1000.10 g., 0.999 Platinum 32.1218 oz. APW **Ruler:** Elizabeth II **Subject:** Koala Bullion **Obv:** Crowned head right, denomination below **Rev:** Koala

Date	Mintage	VF20	XF40	MS60	MS63	MS65
1991	—	—	—	—	—	36,500
1991	50	PF65 60,000				

BULLION - LUNAR YEAR

KM# 501 50 CENTS
16.89 g., 0.999 Silver 0.5424 oz. ASW, 32.1 mm. **Ruler:** Elizabeth II **Subject:** Year of the Rabbit **Obv:** Head with tiara right, denomination below **Rev:** Rabbit right, date at left **Edge:** Reeded

Date	Mintage	VF20	XF40	MS60	MS63	MS65
1999	—	—	—	—	20.00	22.00
1999	5,000	PF65 30.00				

KM# 522 50 CENTS
16.89 g., 0.999 Silver 0.5424 oz. ASW, 32.1 mm. **Ruler:** Elizabeth II **Series:** Dragons **Obv:** Head with tiara right **Rev:** Dragon **Edge:** Reeded

Date	Mintage	VF20	XF40	MS60	MS63	MS65
2000	5,000	PF65 50.00				

KM# 502 DOLLAR
31.64 g., 0.999 Silver 1.0161 oz. ASW, 40.6 mm. **Ruler:** Elizabeth II **Subject:** Year of the Rabbit **Obv:** Head with tiara right, denomination below **Rev:** Rabbit right, date at left **Edge:** Reeded

Date	Mintage	VF20	XF40	MS60	MS63	MS65
1999	—	—	—	—	60.00	80.00
1999	2,500	PF65 80.00				

KM# 502a DOLLAR
31.64 g., 0.999 Silver 1.0161 oz. ASW, 40.6 mm. **Ruler:** Elizabeth II **Subject:** Year of the Rabbit **Obv:** Head with tiara right, denomination below **Rev:** Rabbit right, date at left **Edge:** Reeded

Date	Mintage	VF20	XF40	MS60	MS63	MS65
1999	50,000	—	—	—	52.00	55.00

KM# 424 DOLLAR
31.10 g., 0.999 Silver 0.999 oz. ASW **Ruler:** Elizabeth II **Subject:** Year of the Dragon **Obv:** Head with tiara right within circle, denomination below **Rev:** Dragon, date at left

Date	Mintage	VF20	XF40	MS60	MS63	MS65
2000	—	—	—	—	100	120
2000	—	PF65 120				

KM# 424a DOLLAR
31.64 g., 0.999 Silver 1.0161 oz. ASW, 40.6 mm. **Ruler:** Elizabeth II **Subject:** Year of the Dragon **Obv:** Head with tiara right, denomination below **Rev:** Gold-plated dragon, date at left **Edge:** Reeded

Date	Mintage	VF20	XF40	MS60	MS63	MS65
2000	50,000	—	—	—	52.00	55.00

KM# 503 2 DOLLARS
62.77 g., 0.999 Silver 2.0161 oz. ASW, 49.9 mm. **Ruler:** Elizabeth II **Subject:** Year of the Rabbit **Obv:** Head with tiara right, denomination below **Rev:** Rabbit right, date at left **Edge:** Reeded and plain sections

Date	Mintage	VF20	XF40	MS60	MS63	MS65
1999	2,500	PF65 110				
1999	—	—	—	—	75.00	85.00

KM# 523 2 DOLLARS
62.21 g., 0.999 Silver 1.998 oz. ASW, 50.3 mm. **Ruler:** Elizabeth II **Series:** Dragons **Subject:** Year of the Dragon **Obv:** Head with tiara right, denomination below **Rev:** Dragon, date at left **Edge:** Segmented reeding

Date	Mintage	VF20	XF40	MS60	MS63	MS65
2000	—	PF65 115				

KM# 566 5 DOLLARS
1.56 g., 0.999 Gold 0.050 oz. AGW, 14.1 mm. **Ruler:** Elizabeth II **Subject:** Year of the Rat **Obv:** Crowned head right, denomination below **Rev:** Rat, right **Edge:** Reeded

Date	Mintage	VF20	XF40	MS60	MS63	MS65
1996 P	100,000	—	—	—	—	95.00

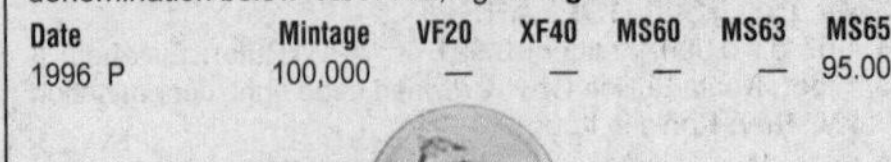

KM# 567 5 DOLLARS
1.56 g., 0.999 Gold 0.050 oz. AGW, 14.1 mm. **Ruler:** Elizabeth II **Subject:** Year of the Ox **Obv:** Crowned head right, denomination below **Rev:** Ox, left **Edge:** Reeded

Date	Mintage	VF20	XF40	MS60	MS63	MS65
1997 P	100,000	—	—	—	—	95.00

KM# 568 5 DOLLARS
1.56 g., 0.999 Gold 0.050 oz. AGW, 14.1 mm. **Ruler:** Elizabeth II **Subject:** Year of the Tiger **Obv:** Crowned head right, denomination below **Rev:** Tiger springing right **Edge:** Reeded

Date	Mintage	VF20	XF40	MS60	MS63	MS65
1998 P	100,000	—	—	—	—	95.00

KM# 425 5 DOLLARS
1.57 g., 0.9999 Gold 0.0505 oz. AGW **Ruler:** Elizabeth II **Subject:** Year of the Rabbit **Obv:** Crowned head right, denomination below **Rev:** Rabbit

Date	Mintage	VF20	XF40	MS60	MS63	MS65
1999	Est. 100000	—	—	—	—	95.00

KM# 569 5 DOLLARS
1.56 g., 0.999 Gold 0.050 oz. AGW, 14.1 mm. **Ruler:** Elizabeth II **Subject:** Year of the Dragon **Obv:** Crowned head right, denomination below **Rev:** Dragon **Edge:** Reeded

Date	Mintage	VF20	XF40	MS60	MS63	MS65
2000 P	100,000	—	—	—	—	95.00

KM# 504 10 DOLLARS
312.35 g., 0.999 Silver 10.0321 oz. ASW, 75.5 mm. **Ruler:** Elizabeth II **Subject:** Year of the Rabbit **Obv:** Head with tiara right, denomination below **Rev:** Rabbit right, date at left **Edge:** Reeded and plain sections **Note:** Illustration reduced.

Date	Mintage	VF20	XF40	MS60	MS63	MS65
1999	—	—	—	—	—	375
1999	2,500	PF65 400				

KM# 524 10 DOLLARS
311.04 g., 0.999 Silver 9.990 oz. ASW, 75.5 mm. **Ruler:** Elizabeth II **Series:** Dragons **Subject:** Year of the Dragon **Obv:** Head with tiara right, denomination below **Rev:** Dragon **Edge:** Segmented reeding

Date	Mintage	VF20	XF40	MS60	MS63	MS65
2000	—	—	—	—	—	375
2000	—	PF65 400				

KM# 298 15 DOLLARS
3.11 g., 0.999 Gold 0.0999 oz. AGW **Ruler:** Elizabeth II **Subject:** Year of the Rat **Obv:** Crowned head right, denomination below **Rev:** Rat facing right

Date	Mintage	VF20	XF40	MS60	MS63	MS65
1996	—	—	—	—	—	180
1996	—	PF65 190				

KM# 335 15 DOLLARS

3.11 g., 0.999 Gold 0.0999 oz. AGW **Ruler:** Elizabeth II **Subject:** Year of the Ox **Obv:** Crowned head right, denomination below **Rev:** Bull ox looking right

Date	Mintage	VF20	XF40	MS60	MS63	MS65
1997	—	—	—	—	—	180
1997	—	PF65 190				

KM# 506 15 DOLLARS

3.11 g., 0.999 Gold 0.0999 oz. AGW, 16.1 mm. **Ruler:** Elizabeth II **Subject:** Year of the Tiger **Obv:** Crowned head right, denomination below **Rev:** Tiger springing right **Edge:** Reeded

Date	Mintage	VF20	XF40	MS60	MS63	MS65
1998	—	—	—	—	—	180
1998 P	—	PF65 190				

KM# 426 15 DOLLARS

3.11 g., 0.9999 Gold 0.1001 oz. AGW **Ruler:** Elizabeth II **Subject:** Year of the Rabbit **Obv:** Crowned head right, denomination below **Rev:** Rabbit facing right

Date	Mintage	VF20	XF40	MS60	MS63	MS65
1999	—	PF65 190				
1999	Est. 80000	—	—	—	—	180

KM# 526 15 DOLLARS

3.11 g., 0.999 Gold 0.0999 oz. AGW, 16.1 mm. **Ruler:** Elizabeth II **Subject:** Year of the Dragon **Obv:** Crowned head right, denomination below **Rev:** Dragon **Edge:** Reeded

Date	Mintage	VF20	XF40	MS60	MS63	MS65
2000	—	—	—	—	—	180
2000	—	PF65 190				

KM# 299 25 DOLLARS

7.75 g., 0.999 Gold 0.2489 oz. AGW **Ruler:** Elizabeth II **Subject:** Year of the Rat **Obv:** Crowned head right, denomination below **Rev:** Rat facing right

Date	Mintage	VF20	XF40	MS60	MS63	MS65
1996	—	—	—	—	—	445
1996	—	PF65 470				

KM# 336 25 DOLLARS

7.75 g., 0.999 Gold 0.2489 oz. AGW **Ruler:** Elizabeth II **Subject:** Year of the Ox **Obv:** Crowned head right, denomination below **Rev:** Bull ox looking right

Date	Mintage	VF20	XF40	MS60	MS63	MS65
1997	—	—	—	—	—	445
1997	8,888	PF65 470				

KM# 507 25 DOLLARS

7.78 g., 0.999 Gold 0.2498 oz. AGW, 20.1 mm. **Ruler:** Elizabeth II **Subject:** Year of the Tiger **Obv:** Crowned head right, denomination below **Rev:** Tiger springing right **Edge:** Reeded

Date	Mintage	VF20	XF40	MS60	MS63	MS65
1998 P	—	—	—	—	—	445
1998 P	—	PF65 470				

KM# 427 25 DOLLARS

7.81 g., 0.9999 Gold 0.251 oz. AGW **Ruler:** Elizabeth II **Subject:** Year of the Rabbit **Obv:** Crowned head right, denomination below **Rev:** Rabbit facing right **Edge:** Reeded

Date	Mintage	VF20	XF40	MS60	MS63	MS65
1999	—	—	—	—	—	445
1999	—	PF65 470				

KM# 527 25 DOLLARS

7.75 g., 0.999 Gold 0.2489 oz. AGW, 20.1 mm. **Ruler:** Elizabeth II **Subject:** Year of the Dragon **Obv:** Crowned head right, denomination below **Rev:** Dragon **Edge:** Reeded

Date	Mintage	VF20	XF40	MS60	MS63	MS65
2000	—	—	—	—	—	445
2000	—	PF65 470				

KM# 505 30 DOLLARS

1002.50 g., 0.999 Silver 32.1989 oz. ASW, 101 mm. **Ruler:** Elizabeth II **Subject:** Year of the Rabbit **Obv:** Head with tiara right, denomination below **Rev:** Rabbit right, date at left **Edge:** Reeded and plain sections **Note:** Illustration reduced.

Date	Mintage	VF20	XF40	MS60	MS63	MS65
1999	2,500	PF65 1,200				
1999	—	—	—	—	—	1,150

KM# 525.1 30 DOLLARS

1002.50 g., 0.999 Silver 32.1989 oz. ASW, 101 mm. **Ruler:** Elizabeth II **Subject:** Year of the Dragon **Obv:** Head with tiara right, denomination below **Rev:** Dragon **Edge:** Segmented reeding **Note:** Prev. KM#525.

Date	Mintage	VF20	XF40	MS60	MS63	MS65
2000	—	—	—	—	—	1,150
2000	—	PF65 1,200				

KM# 525.2 30 DOLLARS

1000.00 g., 0.999 Silver 32.1186 oz. ASW, 101 mm. **Ruler:** Elizabeth II **Subject:** Year of the Dragon **Obv:** Head with tiara right, denomination below **Rev:** Dragon with diamonds for eyes and multicolor ornamentation

Date	Mintage	VF20	XF40	MS60	MS63	MS65
2000	5,000	PF65 1,250				

KM# 300 100 DOLLARS

31.10 g., 0.999 Gold 0.999 oz. AGW **Ruler:** Elizabeth II **Subject:** Year of the Rat **Obv:** Crowned head right, denomination below **Rev:** Rat facing right, date at left

Date	Mintage	VF20	XF40	MS60	MS63	MS65
1996	—	—	—	—	—	1,750
1996	—	PF65 1,800				

KM# 337 100 DOLLARS

31.10 g., 0.999 Gold 0.999 oz. AGW **Ruler:** Elizabeth II **Subject:** Year of the Ox **Obv:** Crowned head right, denomination below **Rev:** Ox left, looking right, date at left

Date	Mintage	VF20	XF40	MS60	MS63	MS65
1997	—	—	—	—	—	1,750
1997	8,888	PF65 1,800				

KM# 508 100 DOLLARS

31.10 g., 0.999 Gold 0.999 oz. AGW, 32.1 mm. **Ruler:** Elizabeth II **Subject:** Year of the Tiger **Obv:** Crowned head right, denomination below **Rev:** Tiger springing right, date at left **Edge:** Reeded

Date	Mintage	VF20	XF40	MS60	MS63	MS65
1998	—	—	—	—	—	1,750
1998 P	—	PF65 1,800				

KM# 428 100 DOLLARS

31.16 g., 0.9999 Gold 1.0018 oz. AGW **Ruler:** Elizabeth II **Subject:** Year of the Rabbit **Obv:** Crowned head right, denomination below **Rev:** Seated rabbit left, date at left **Edge:** Reeded

Date	Mintage	VF20	XF40	MS60	MS63	MS65
1999	Est. 30000	—	—	—	—	1,750
1999	—	PF65 1,800				

KM# 528 100 DOLLARS

31.10 g., 0.999 Gold 0.999 oz. AGW, 32.1 mm. **Ruler:** Elizabeth II **Subject:** Year of the Dragon **Obv:** Crowned head right, denomination below **Rev:** Dragon **Edge:** Reeded

Date	Mintage	VF20	XF40	MS60	MS63	MS65
2000	—	—	—	—	—	1,750
2000	—	PF65 1,800				

KM# 667 200 DOLLARS

62.21 g., 0.999 Gold 1.9982 oz. AGW, 40.6 mm. **Ruler:** Elizabeth II **Subject:** Year of the Dragon **Obv:** Crowned head right, denomination below **Rev:** Dragon **Edge:** Reeded

Date	Mintage	VF20	XF40	MS60	MS63	MS65
2000	—	—	—	—	—	3,500

KM# 702 1000 DOLLARS

311.05 g., 0.9999 Gold 9.9994 oz. AGW **Ruler:** Elizabeth II **Subject:** Year of the Dragon **Obv:** Crowned head right, denomination below **Rev:** Dragon

Date	Mintage	VF20	XF40	MS60	MS63	MS65
2000	—	—	—	—	—	18,000

KM# 1331 1000 DOLLARS

311.05 g., 0.999 Gold 9.9904 oz. AGW **Ruler:** Elizabeth II **Subject:** Year of the Dragon **Obv:** Head right

Date	Mintage	VF20	XF40	MS60	MS63	MS65
2000 P	—	—	—	—	—	18,000

KM# 703 3000 DOLLARS

1000.00 g., 0.9999 Gold 32.1475 oz. AGW **Ruler:** Elizabeth II **Subject:** Year of the Dragon **Obv:** Crowned head right, denomination below **Rev:** Dragon

Date	Mintage	VF20	XF40	MS60	MS63	MS65
2000	—	—	—	—	—	44,500

KM# 1332 3000 DOLLARS

1000.00 g., 0.999 Gold 32.1186 oz. AGW **Ruler:** Elizabeth II **Subject:** Year of the Dragon **Obv:** Head right

Date	Mintage	VF20	XF40	MS60	MS63	MS65
2000 P	—	—	—	—	—	44,500

TOKEN COINAGE

WWI Liverpool (NSW)

P.O.W.

KM# TnA1 THREEPENCE

Aluminum **Issuer:** WWI Liverpool (NSW) **Obv:** Double-headed eagle **Rev:** Large 3d **Shape:** Square

Date	Mintage	F12	VF20	XF40	MS60	MS63
ND (1918)	—	—	1,000	1,250	2,600	—

KM# TnB1 THREEPENCE
Aluminum **Issuer:** WWI Liverpool (NSW) **Obv:** Crown divides D - K **Rev:** Small 3d **Shape:** Oval

Date	Mintage	F12	VF20	XF40	MS60	MS63
ND (1918)	—	—	1,200	1,400	3,000	—

TOKEN COINAGE

WWII Internment Camp
P.O.W.

KM# Tn1.1 PENNY
Brass **Issuer:** WWII Internment Camp **Obv:** Center hole with beads and wreath around, legend above and below **Obv. Legend:** INTERNMENT / CAMPS **Rev:** Center hole with beads and wreath around, legend above and below **Rev. Legend:** ONE / PENNY

Date	Mintage	F12	VF20	XF40	MS60	MS63
ND (1943)	—	45.00	55.00	90.00	175	—

KM# Tn1.1a PENNY
Copper-Nickel **Issuer:** WWII Internment Camp **Obv:** Center hole with beads and wreath around, legend above and below **Obv. Legend:** INTERNMENT / CAMPS **Rev:** Center hole with beads and wreath around, legend above and below **Rev. Legend:** ONE / PENNY **Note:** Spink Australia Sale Nov. 1981. Lot 666A $600.

Date	Mintage	F12	VF20	XF40	MS60	MS63
ND (1943)	—	—	—	—	4,500	—

KM# Tn1.2 PENNY
Brass **Issuer:** WWII Internment Camp **Note:** Center hole misplaced (error).

Date	Mintage	F12	VF20	XF40	MS60	MS63
ND (1918)	—	75.00	100	150	—	—

KM# Tn1.3 PENNY
Brass **Issuer:** WWII Internment Camp **Note:** Without center hole (error).

Date	Mintage	F12	VF20	XF40	MS60	MS63
ND (1943)	—	—	400	600	1,000	—

KM# Tn2.1 THREEPENCE
Bronze **Issuer:** WWII Internment Camp **Obv:** Center hole with wreath around **Obv. Legend:** INTERNMENT CAMPS **Rev:** Center hole with wreath around **Rev. Legend:** THREE PENCE

Date	Mintage	F12	VF20	XF40	MS60	MS63
ND (1943)	—	55.00	75.00	100	225	—

KM# Tn2.2 THREEPENCE
Bronze **Issuer:** WWII Internment Camp **Obv:** Center hole with wreath around **Obv. Legend:** INTERNMENT CAMP **Rev. Legend:** THREE PENCE

Date	Mintage	F12	VF20	XF40	MS60	MS63
ND (1943) Rare	—	—	—	—	—	—

KM# Tn3 SHILLING
Bronze **Issuer:** WWII Internment Camp **Obv:** Center hole with wreath around **Obv. Legend:** INTERNMENT CAMPS **Rev:** Center hole with wreath around **Rev. Legend:** ONE SHILLING

Date	Mintage	F12	VF20	XF40	MS60	MS63
ND (1943)	—	200	250	300	800	—

KM# Tn4.1 2 SHILLING
Bronze **Issuer:** WWII Internment Camp **Obv:** Center hole with beads and wreath around **Obv. Legend:** INTERNMENT CAMPS **Rev:** Center hole with beads and wreath around **Rev. Legend:** TWO SHILLINGS

Date	Mintage	F12	VF20	XF40	MS60	MS63
ND (1943)	—	250	350	600	900	—

KM# Tn4.2 2 SHILLING
Bronze **Issuer:** WWII Internment Camp **Obv:** Beaded circle at center, wreath around **Obv. Legend:** INTERNMENT CAMPS **Rev:** Beaded circle at center, wreath around **Rev. Legend:** TWO SHILLINGS **Note:** Without center hole.

Date	Mintage	F12	VF20	XF40	MS60	MS63
ND (1943)	—	650	900	1,300	2,600	—

KM# Tn4.3 2 SHILLING
Bronze **Issuer:** WWII Internment Camp **Obv:** Off center hole partially within beaded circle, wreath surrounding **Obv. Legend:** Internment Camps **Rev:** Off center hole partially within beaded circle, wreath surrounding **Rev. Legend:** Two shillings **Note:** Center hole misplaced.

Date	Mintage	F12	VF20	XF40	MS60	MS63
ND (1943)	—	400	550	800	1,400	—

KM# Tn5.1 5 SHILLING
Bronze **Obv:** Center hole with beads and wreath around **Obv. Legend:** INTERNMENT CAMPS **Rev:** Center hole with beads and wreath around **Rev. Legend:** FIVE SHILLINGS

Date	Mintage	F12	VF20	XF40	MS60	MS63
ND (1943)	—	—	1,400	2,100	2,500	—

KM# Tn5.2 5 SHILLING
Bronze **Obv:** Center circle with beads and wreath around **Obv. Legend:** INTERNMENT CAMPS **Rev:** Center circle with beads and wreath around **Rev. Legend:** FIVE SHILLINGS **Note:** Without center hole.

Date	Mintage	F12	VF20	XF40	MS60	MS63
ND (1943)	—	—	2,500	4,000	7,000	—

KM# Tn5.3 5 SHILLING
Bronze **Obv:** Center circle with beads and wreath around **Obv. Legend:** INTERNMENT CAMPS **Rev:** Center circle with beads and wreath around **Rev. Legend:** FIVE SHILLINGS **Note:** Center hole misplaced,(hole at top of coin)

Date	Mintage	F12	VF20	XF40	MS60	MS63
ND (1943)	—	—	3,000	5,000	10,000	—

PATTERNS

Including off metal strikes

KM#	Date	Mintage	Identification	Mkt Val
Pn7	1909	—	Florin.	—
Pn8	1919	—	Penny. Copper-Nickel. T.3.	55,000
Pn8a	1919	—	Penny. Copper-Nickel. T.3.	60,000
Pn8b	1919	—	Penny. Copper-Nickel. T.3.	60,000
Pn9	1919	—	Penny. Copper-Nickel. T.4.	60,000
Pn9a	1919	—	Penny. 0.917. Silver. T.4.	110,000
Pn10	1919	—	Penny. Copper-Nickel. T.5.	60,000
Pn10a	1919	—	Penny. 0.917. Silver. T.5.	110,000
Pn11	1919	—	Penny. Copper-Nickel. T.6.	55,000
Pn11a	1919	—	Penny. 0.917. Silver. T.6.	100,000
Pn12	1919	—	Shilling. 0.625. Silver. KM#26.	120,000
Pn13	1920	—	1/2 Penny. Copper-Nickel. T.1.	—
Pn13a	1920	—	1/2 Penny. 0.917. Silver. T.1.	—
Pn14	1920	—	Penny. Copper-Nickel. T.7.	70,000
Pn14a	1920	—	Penny. Lead. T.7.	—
Pn15	1920	—	Penny. Copper-Nickel. T.8.	80,000
Pn16	1920	—	Penny. Copper-Nickel. T.9.	90,000
Pn17	1920	—	Penny. Copper-Nickel. T.10.	95,000
Pn18	1920	—	Florin. Silver. KM#27, star above date.	120,000
PnA18	1920	—	Shilling. Silver. KM#26, star above date.	70,000
Pn19	1921	—	1/2 Penny. Copper-Nickel. T.2.	90,000
Pn20	1921	—	Penny. Copper-Nickel. T.11.	40,000
Pn20a	1921	—	Penny. Copper-Nickel. T.11.	40,000
Pn20b	1921	—	Penny. Copper-Nickel. T.11.	45,000
Pn20c	1921	—	Penny. Nickel. T.11.	40,000
Pn21	1921	—	Penny. Copper-Nickel. T.12.	40,000
Pn21a	1921	—	Penny. Copper-Nickel. T.12.	45,000
Pn21b	1921	—	Penny. Copper-Nickel. T.12.	45,000
Pn22	1921	—	Penny. T.13.	45,000
Pn24	1937	12	Penny. Bronze. Head left. Kangaroo hopping, left, date below tail, value at bottom.	150,000
Pn25	1937	7	Threepence. Silver.	120,000
Pn26	1937	6	Shilling. Silver.	55,000
Pn28	1951	—	2 Shilling. Copper-Nickel. Jubilee.	30,000
Pn29	1967	—	50 Cents. Silver. KM#67.	—
Pn30	1968	—	50 Cents. Copper-Nickel. KM#68.	—

PIEDFORT

KM#	Date	Mintage	Identification	Mkt Val
P1	1989	15,000	10 Dollars. 0.925. Silver. Kookaburra, KM#133.	125
P2	1990	15,000	10 Dollars. 0.925. Silver. Cockatoo, KM#136.	150
P3	1991	17,000	10 Dollars. 0.925. Silver. Jabiru Stork, Proof, KM#156.	95.00
P4	1992	15,000	10 Dollars. 0.925. Silver. Penguins.	120
P5	1993	—	10 Dollars. 0.925. Silver. Palm cockatoo, KM#221.	125
P6	1994	15,000	10 Dollars. 0.925. Silver. Wedge tailed eagle, Proof, KM#223.	100
P7	1995	15,000	10 Dollars. 0.925. Silver. Numbat, KM#296.	100
P8	1996	14,000	10 Dollars. Silver. Whales, Proof, KM#314.	100
P9	1997	14,000	10 Dollars. Silver. Cockatoo, Proof, KM#367.	100
P10	1998	14,000	10 Dollars. Silver. Wombat, Proof, KM#397.	100

TRIAL STRIKES

KM#	Date	Mintage	Identification	Mkt Val
TS1	ND-1927	—	Shilling. Silver. Crowned head left. Uniface.	85,000
TS2	ND-1927	—	Florin. Silver. Crowned head left. Uniface. KM7.	—
TS3	1937	8	Penny. Bronze. Kangaroo hopping, left, date below tail, value at bottom. Uniface, reverse.	100,000
TS4	1937	15	Threepence. Silver. Uniface, reverse.	95,000

KM#	Date	Mintage	Identification	Mkt Val
TS5	1937	20	Shilling. Silver. Uniface, reverse.	85,000
TSA5	1937	—	Sixpence. Silver. Uniface, reverse.	—
TS6	1937	15	Florin. Silver. Uniface, reverse. Spink Remick Sale 9-06.	80,000

BABY MINT SETS

KM#	Date	Mintage	Identification	Issue Price	Mkt Val
BMS1	1993 (6)	17,000	KM#80-83, 101, 208	—	60.00
BMS2	1994 (6)	37,348	KM#80-82, 84, 101, 257	—	35.00
BMS3	1995 (6)	33,357	KM#80-82, 84, 101, 294 plus bronze medal	—	55.00
BMS4	1996 (6)	25,727	KM#80-83, 101, 310 plus bronze medal	—	135
BMS5	1997 (6)	27,421	KM#80-83, 101, 327 plus bronze medal	—	215
BMS6	1998 (6)	31,810	KM#80-82, 84, 101, 364 plus bronze medal	—	110
BMS7	1999 (6)	35,718	KM#401-406 Copper medal	—	50.00
BMS8	2000 (6)	39,120	KM#401-403, 406, 488.1, 489 plus bronze medal	—	115

BABY PROOF SETS

KM#	Date	Mintage	Identification	Issue Price	Mkt Val
BPS1	1995 (6)	3,624	KM#80-82, 84, 101, 294 plus silver medal	—	130
BPS2	1996 (6)	3,985	KM#80-83, 101, 310 plus silver medal	—	282
BPS3	1997 (6)	3,617	KM#80-83, 101, 327 plus silver medal	—	430
BPS4	1998 (6)	5,269	KM#80-82, 84, 101, 364 plus silver medal	—	265
BPS5	1999 (6)	6,707	KM#401-406 plus silver medal	—	230
BPS6	2000 (6)	15,287	KM#401-403, 406, 488.1, 489 plus silver medal	—	275

MINT SETS

KM#	Date	Mintage	Identification	Issue Price	Mkt Val
MS1	1966 (6)	16,359	KM62-67 (Card)	2.00	95.00
MS2	1969 (6)	31,176	KM62-66, 68	2.50	110
MS3	1970 (6)	40,230	KM62-66, 69	2.50	60.00
MS4	1971 (6)	28,572	KM62-66, 68	2.50	160
MS5	1972 (6)	39,068	KM62-66, 68	2.75	160
MS6	1973 (6)	30,928	KM62-66, 68	3.40	115
MS7	1974 (6)	25,948	KM62-66, 68	3.60	85.00
MS8	1975 (6)	30,121	KM62-66, 68	3.30	37.50
MS9	1976 (6)	40,004	KM62-66, 68	3.80	35.00
MS10	1977 (6)	128,000	KM62-66, 70	4.20	25.00
MS11	1978 (6)	70,000	KM62-66, 68	4.20	27.50
MS12	1979 (6)	70,000	KM62-66, 68	4.50	25.00
MS13	1980 (6)	100,000	KM62-66, 68	5.75	23.00
MS14	1981 (6)	120,010	KM62-66, 68	6.50	23.00
MS15	1982 (6)	195,950	KM62-66, 74	6.50	23.00
MS16	1983 (6)	155,700	KM62-66, 68	5.00	50.00
MS17	1984 (6)	150,014	KM62-66, 68	7.00	65.00
MS18	1985 (7)	170,000	KM78-84	4.00	95.00
MS19	1986 (7)	180,000	KM78-83, 87	5.50	80.00
MS20	1987 (7)	200,000	KM78-84	8.00	80.00
MS21	1988 (8)	240,000	KM78-82, 99-101	12.00	82.50
MS22	1989 (8)	—	KM78-84, 101	12.00	100
MS23	1990 (8)	—	KM78-84, 101	12.00	215
MS24	1991 (8)	25,000	KM78-82, 84, 101, 139	13.00	245
MS25	1992 (6)	104,000	KM80-83, 101, 175a.1	10.00	95.00
MS26	1993 (6)	—	KM80-83, 101, 208	10.00	110
MS27	1994 (6)	90,000	KM80-82, 84, 101, 257	11.25	85.00
MS29	1995 (6)	—	KM80-82, 84, 101, 294	—	125
MS30	1996 (6)	—	KM80-83, 101, 310	14.80	75.00
MS32	1997 (6)	—	KM80-83, 101, 327	—	105
MS33	1998 (6)	—	KM80-82, 83, 101, 364	12.75	45.00
MS34	1998 (6)	—	KM80-82, 84, 101, 364	16.60	55.00
MS35	1999 (6)	—	KM401-406	16.95	60.00
MS36	1999 (3)	—	KM#426-428	—	1,750
MS37	1999 (2)	—	KM400, 405	—	55.00
MS38	2000 (6)	—	KM401-403, 406, 488-489	10.60	115
MSA32	1997 (2)	—	KM327, 355	—	50.00
MSB36	1999 (5)	500	KM501-505	—	1,725
MSC36	1999 (3)	—	KM426-428	—	2,400

PROOF SETS

KM#	Date	Mintage	Identification	Issue Price	Mkt Val
PS1	1902S (4)	—	KM14-17 Rare	—	—
PS2	1911(L) (4)	—	KM24-27	—	177,500
PS3	1916M (4)	25	KM24-27	—	75,000
PS4	1925(m) (5)	—	KM22-26	—	272,000
PS5	1926(m) (6)	—	KM22-27	—	172,000
PS6	1927(m) (6)	50	KM22-27	—	162,000
PS7	1928(m) (6)	—	KM22-27	—	176,000
PS8	1929(m) (2)	—	KM22-23	—	50,500
PSA9	1930(m) (2)	—	KM22-23	—	510,000
PS9	1931(m) (4)	—	KM22-27	—	148,000
PS10	1933(m) (2)	—	KM22-23	—	58,000
PS11	1934(m) (6)	100	KM22-27	—	95,500
PS12	1935(m) (6)	100	KM22-27	—	120,000
PS13	1936(m) (6)	—	KM22-27	—	146,500
PS14	1938(m) (6)	250	KM35-40	—	70,500
PS15	1953(p) (2)	—	KM49-50	—	28,000
PS16	1955(m) (4)	1,200	KM56-59	—	5,950
PS17	1955(p) (2)	301	KM49, 56	—	11,500
PS18	1956(m) (5)	1,500	KM56-60	—	4,550
PS19	1957(m) (4)	1,256	KM57-60	—	650
PS20	1958(m) (5)	1,506	KM56-60	—	1,200
PS21	1959(m) (6)	1,506	KM56-61	—	1,700
PS22	1960(m) (4)	1,509	KM57-60	—	600
PS23	1960(p) (2)	1,030	KM56, 61	—	1,300
PS24	1961(m) (4)	1,506	KM57-60	—	525
PS25	1961(p) (2)	1,040	KM56, 61	—	1,100
PS26	1962(m) (4)	2,016	KM57-60	—	450
PS27	1962(p) (2)	1,064	KM56, 61	—	1,050
PS28	1963(m) (4)	5,042	KM57-60	—	450
PS29	1963(p) (2)	1,064	KM56, 61	—	1,650
PS30	1966 (6)	18,110	KM62-67	15.70	225
PS31	1969 (6)	12,696	KM62-66, 68	11.25	225
PS32	1970 (6)	15,112	KM62-66, 69	11.30	175
PS33	1971 (6)	10,066	KM62-66, 68	11.30	175
PS34	1972 (6)	10,272	KM62-66, 68	14.00	175
PS35	1973 (6)	10,090	KM62-66, 68	15.50	175
PS36	1974 (6)	11,103	KM62-66, 68	18.00	140
PS37	1975 (6)	23,021	KM62-66, 68	17.00	55.00
PS38	1976 (6)	21,200	KM62-66, 68	20.20	65.00
PS39	1977 (6)	55,000	KM62-66, 70	20.20	35.00
PS40	1978 (6)	38,513	KM62-66, 68	—	37.50
PS41	1979 (6)	36,000	KM62-66, 68	—	35.00
PS42	1980 (6)	68,000	KM62-66, 68	—	95.00
PS43	1981 (6)	86,008	KM62-66, 68	48.00	32.50
PS44	1982 (6)	100,000	KM62-66, 74	50.00	32.50
PS45	1983 (6)	80,000	KM62-66, 68	39.00	50.00
PS46	1984 (6)	61,398	KM62-66, 68	39.00	40.00
PS47	1985 (7)	74,809	KM78-84	27.50	65.00
PS48	1986 (7)	67,000	KM78-83, 87	40.00	70.00
PS49	1986P (4)	12,000	KM89-92	1,445	3,500
PS50	1986P (2)	3,000	KM89, 90	305	675
PS51	1987 (7)	69,684	KM78-84	40.00	60.00
PS52	1987 (4)	12,000	KM95-98	1,440	3,500
PS53	1987 (2)	3,000	KM95, 96	305	675
PS54	1988 (8)	101,000	KM78-82, 99-101	—	150
PS55	1988 (8)	5,000	KM78-82, 99-101, Coin Fair	—	150
PS56	1988 (4)	25,000	KM99a-102a	85.00	130
PS57	1988P (4)	9,000	KM104-107	—	3,500
PS58	1988 (2)	1,000	KM104-105	—	675
PS59	1988 (2)	—	KM112-113	50.00	75.00
PS60	1989 (8)	2,500	KM78-84, 101	—	65.00
PS61	1989 (8)	—	KM78-84, 101 Coin Fair	—	70.00
PS62	1989 (5)	2,200	KM117-121	1,595	3,500
PS63	1989 (5)	2,400	KM122-126	1,995	3,900
PS64	1989 (5)	25,000	KM99a, 127-130	—	145
PS65	1989 (2)	—	KM131-132	—	70.00
PS66	1990 (8)	—	KM78-84, 101	55.00	115
PS67	1990 (8)	—	KM78-84, 101 Coin Fair	—	115
PS68	1990 (5)	5,000	KM140-144	—	3,500
PS69	1990 (5)	2,500	KM145-149	—	3,900
PS70	1990 (3)	2,000	KM140-142	464	800
PS71	1990 (3)	1,000	KM138, 144, 149	1,900	3,750
PS72	1990 (2)	—	KM154-155	—	75.00
PS73	1990 (3)	25,000	KM84a, 87a, 100a. Sydney Coin Fair.	135	110
PS74	1991 (3)	1,000	KM140-142	—	815
PS75	1991 (8)	24,000	KM78-82, 84, 101, 139	55.00	165
PS76	1991 (8)	1,000	KM78-82, 84, 101a, 139	—	110
PS77	1991 (8)	23,000	KM78a-82a, 84a, 101a, 139a	—	180
PS78	1991 (5)	2,000	KM140-144	—	3,550
PS79	1991 (5)	1,000	PS145-149	—	3,900
PS80	1992 (6)	47,000	KM80-83, 101, 175.a1	40.00	230
PS81	1992 (4)	500	KM165-168	—	1,750
PS82	1992 (4)	—	KM200-203, plus medal	120	150
PS83	1992 (4)	5,000	KM204-207 plus medal	1,520	3,500
PSA84	1992 (3)	264	KM389-391	251	815
PSB84	1992 (5)	628	KM389-393	1,058	3,550
PSC84	1992 (4)	500	KM389-392 plus medal	758	1,750
PSD84	1992 (ae) (3)	750	KM193, 209, 391	—	1,200
PSE84	1993 (ae) (3)	500	KM212.2, 230, 231 plus silver bar	310	975
PS84	1993 (6)	—	KM80-83, 101, 208	—	115
PS85	1993 (5)	20,000	KM213-217	94.50	200
PS86	1994 (6)	45,000	KM80-82, 84, 101, 257	—	85.00
PS87	1994 (5)	20,000	KM264-268	101	165
PS88	1994 (3)	20,000	KM182, 232 (2), 253	—	7,750
PSA89	1994 (4)	—	KM#260, 261, 270, 271	—	1,725
PS89	1994 (3)	25	KM241, 260, 278	303	350
PSA90	1995 (6)	—	KM80-82, 84, 101, 294	—	95.00
PS90	1995 (5)	300	KM272-276	—	3,550
PSA91	1995 (3)	600	KM#289, 272, 283	—	350
PS91	1995 (5)	200	KM283-287	—	3,900
PSA92	1995 (3)	300	KM276, 286, 290	—	2,600
PS92	1995 (4)	1,000	KM289-292	—	1,675
PS93	1995 (3)	300	KM289-291	—	525
PS94	1995 (2)	600	KM289-290	—	125
PSA95	1995 (2)	800	KM290-291	—	485
PS95	1996 (3)	3,000	KM275, (f), (l), (s) privy marks	—	2,750
PS 97	1996 (6)	—	KM80-83, 101, 310, plus silver gumnut baby medal	59.25	175
PSA98	1996 (3)	400	KM321-322, 341	1,500	1,750
PSB98	1996 (6)	—	KM80-83, 101, 310	—	170
PS98	1997 (3)	3,888	KM335-337	914	2,500
PSA99	1997 (2)	20,000	KM#353, 354	—	65.00
PS99	1997 (3)	3,000	KM341 (f), (l), (s) privy marks	782	2,750
PS100	1998 (6)	—	KM80-82, 84, 101, 364	40.60	125
PS101	1998 (6)	—	KM80-82, 84, 101, 364. Baby set.	50.75	125
PS102	1999 (6)	—	KM401-406	—	125
PS103	1999 (3)	1,000	KM501-503	—	220
PS104	1999 (6)	15,000	KM481-486	66.25	130
PS105	2000 (5)	—	KM496-500 plus 20.5-gram silver ingot	—	170
PS106	2000 (6)	—	KM401-403, 406, 488.1, 489	34.35	260

The Republic of Austria, a parliamentary democracy located in mountainous central Europe, has an area of 32,374 sq. mi. (83,850 sq. km.) and a population of 8.08 million. Capital: Wien (Vienna). Austria is primarily an industrial country. Machinery, iron, steel, textiles, yarns and timber are exported.

The territories later to be known as Austria were overrun in pre-Roman times by various tribes, including the Celts. Upon the fall of the Roman Empire, the country became a margravate of Charlemagne's Empire. Premysl II of Otakar, King of Bohemia, gained possession in 1252, only to lose the territory to Rudolf of Habsburg in 1276. Thereafter, until World War I, the story of Austria was conducted by the ruling Habsburgs.

During the 17th century, Austrian coinage reflected the geo-political strife of three wars. From 1618-1648, the Thirty Years' War between northern Protestants and southern Catholics produced low quality, "kipperwhipper" strikes of 12, 24, 30, 60, 75 and 150 Kreuzer. Later, during the Austrian-Turkish War, 1660-1664, coinages used to maintain soldier's salaries also reported the steady division of Hungarian territories. Finally, between 1683 and 1699, during the second Austrian-Turkish conflict, new issues of 3, 6 and 15 Kreuzers were struck, being necessary to help defray mounting expenses of the war effort.

During World War I, the Austro-Hungarian Empire was one of the Central Powers with Germany, Bulgaria and Turkey. At the end of the war, the Empire was dismembered and Austria established as an independent republic. In March 1938, Austria was incorporated into Hitler's short-lived Greater German Reich. Allied forces of both East and West occupied Austria in April 1945, and subsequently divided it into 4 zones of military occupation. On May 15, 1955, the 4 powers formally recognized Austria as a sovereign independent democratic state.

NOTE: During the **GERMAN OCCUPATION** (1938-1945), the German Reichsmark coins and banknotes were circulated.

RULERS

Franz Joseph I, 1848-1916
Karl I, 1916-1918

AUSTRO-HUNGARIAN EMPIRE

REFORM COINAGE

100 Heller = 1 Corona

KM# 2800 HELLER

1.70 g., Bronze, 17 mm. **Ruler:** Franz Joseph I

Date	Mintage	F12	VF20	XF40	MS60	MS63
1901	52,096,000	0.20	2.00	6.00	12.00	25.00
1902	20,553,000	—	0.50	1.50	5.00	10.00
1903	13,779,000	—	0.50	3.00	8.00	15.00
1909	12,668,000	—	0.35	1.00	5.00	10.00
1910	21,941,000	—	0.35	1.00	5.00	10.00
1911	18,387,000	—	0.35	1.00	5.00	10.00
1912	27,053,000	—	0.35	1.00	5.00	10.00
1913	8,782,000	—	0.35	1.00	5.00	10.00
1914	9,906,000	—	0.35	1.00	5.00	10.00
1915	5,673,000	—	0.35	1.00	5.00	10.00
1916	12,484,000	—	0.50	3.00	8.00	15.00

KM# 2823 HELLER

Bronze, 17 mm. **Ruler:** Franz Joseph I **Obv:** Austrian shield on crowned double eagle's breast **Rev:** Value above sprays, date below, within shield

Date	Mintage	F12	VF20	XF40	MS60	MS63
1916	Inc. above	2.00	4.00	12.00	22.00	35.00

KM# 2801 2 HELLER

3.35 g., Bronze, 19 mm. **Ruler:** Franz Joseph I **Obv:** Crowned imperial double eagle **Rev:** Value above sprays, date below within shield **Edge:** Smooth

Date	Mintage	F12	VF20	XF40	MS60	MS63
1901	12,157,000	—	5.00	25.00	40.00	75.00
1902	18,760,000	—	1.00	5.00	10.00	15.00
1903	26,983,000	—	1.00	5.00	10.00	15.00
1904	12,863,000	—	3.00	10.00	20.00	35.00
1905	6,679,000	—	3.00	10.00	22.00	35.00
1906	20,104,000	—	1.00	3.00	8.00	15.00
1907	23,804,000	—	0.25	1.50	3.00	8.00
1908	21,984,000	—	0.25	1.50	3.00	8.00
1909	25,975,000	—	0.25	1.50	3.00	8.00
1910	28,406,000	—	0.25	1.50	5.00	10.00
1911	50,007,058	—	0.25	1.00	2.00	3.00
1912	74,234,000	—	0.20	1.00	2.00	3.00
1913	27,432,000	—	0.50	3.00	8.00	15.00
1914	60,674,000	—	0.20	1.00	2.00	3.00
1915	7,871,000	—	0.20	1.00	2.00	3.00

KM# 2824 2 HELLER

Iron **Ruler:** Karl I **Obv:** Austrian shield on crowned double eagle's breast **Rev:** Value above date, within wreath

Date	Mintage	F12	VF20	XF40	MS60	MS63
1916	61,909,000	—	0.50	1.25	12.00	24.00
1917	81,186,000	—	0.25	1.00	10.00	18.00
1918	66,352,999	—	0.25	1.00	6.00	12.00

KM# 2802 10 HELLER

3.00 g., Nickel **Ruler:** Franz Joseph I **Obv:** Crowned imperial double eagle **Rev:** Value above date at center of ornate shield **Edge:** Reeded

Date	Mintage	F12	VF20	XF40	MS60	MS63
1907	8,662,000	0.25	0.50	1.50	18.00	30.00
1908	7,772,000	—	0.50	1.25	12.50	25.00
1909	20,462,000	—	—	0.50	3.00	8.00
1910	10,164,000	—	—	0.50	3.00	8.00
1911	3,634,000	—	1.00	5.00	20.00	35.00

KM# 2822 10 HELLER

3.00 g., Copper-Nickel-Zinc, 19 mm. **Ruler:** Franz Joseph I **Obv:** Shield on crowned double eagle's breast **Rev:** Value within wreath, date below **Edge:** Reeded

Date	Mintage	F12	VF20	XF40	MS60	MS63
1915	18,366,000	—	—	0.50	3.00	10.00
1916	27,487,000	—	—	0.50	3.00	10.00

KM# 2825 10 HELLER

3.00 g., Copper-Nickel-Zinc, 19 mm. **Ruler:** Franz Joseph I **Obv:** Austrian shield on crowned double eagle's breast **Rev:** Value within wreath, date below **Edge:** Reeded

Date	Mintage	F12	VF20	XF40	MS60	MS63
1916	14,804,000	—	—	1.00	3.00	10.00

KM# 2803 20 HELLER

4.00 g., Nickel, 21 mm. **Ruler:** Franz Joseph I **Obv:** Crowned imperial double eagle **Rev:** Value above date at center of ornate shield **Edge:** Reeded

Date	Mintage	F12	VF20	XF40	MS60	MS63
1907	7,650,000	—	—	3.00	10.00	20.00
1908	7,469,000	—	—	3.00	10.00	20.00
1909	7,592,000	—	2.00	5.00	15.00	30.00
1911	19,560,000	—	—	1.00	3.00	8.00
1914	2,342,000	—	5.00	8.00	20.00	30.00

KM# 2826 20 HELLER

3.50 g., Iron **Ruler:** Karl I **Obv:** Austrian shield on crowned double eagle's breast **Rev:** Value within wreath, date below **Edge:** Reeded

Date	Mintage	F12	VF20	XF40	MS60	MS63
1916	130,770,000	—	0.25	1.00	3.00	15.00
1917	127,420,000	—	0.25	1.00	3.00	15.00
1918	48,985,000	—	0.25	1.00	3.00	15.00

KM# 2804 CORONA

5.00 g., 0.835 Silver 0.1342 oz. ASW, 23 mm. **Ruler:** Franz Joseph I **Obv:** Laureate head

Date	Mintage	F12	VF20	XF40	MS60	MS63
1901	10,387,000	2.75	5.00	6.00	12.00	20.00
1902	2,947,000	2.75	5.00	10.00	15.00	30.00
1903	2,198,000	2.75	5.00	15.00	25.00	45.00
1904	993,000	2.75	10.00	20.00	50.00	75.00
1905	505,000	5.00	20.00	35.00	75.00	100
1906	164,500	35.00	100	200	450	750
1907	244,000	10.00	60.00	125	225	400

KM# 2808 CORONA

5.00 g., 0.835 Silver 0.1342 oz. ASW **Ruler:** Franz Joseph I **Subject:** 60th Anniversary of Reign **Obv:** Head right **Rev:** Crown at top divides dates, FII on spray at center, value at bottom

Date	Mintage	F12	VF20	XF40	MS60	MS63
ND-1908	4,784,992	—	2.75	4.00	8.00	10.00

KM# 2820 CORONA

5.00 g., 0.835 Silver 0.1342 oz. ASW **Ruler:** Franz Joseph I **Obv:** Head right **Rev:** Crown above value, date at bottom, sprays flanking

Date	Mintage	F12	VF20	XF40	MS60	MS63
1912	8,457,000	—	—	2.75	5.00	12.00
1913	9,345,000	—	—	2.75	4.00	10.00
1914	37,897,000	—	—	2.75	3.50	5.00
1915	23,000,134	—	—	2.75	3.50	5.00
1916	12,415,404	—	—	2.75	3.50	5.00

KM# 2821 2 CORONA

10.00 g., 0.835 Silver 0.2685 oz. ASW, 27 mm. **Ruler:** Franz Joseph I **Obv:** Head right **Rev:** Crowned double eagle above date

Date	Mintage	F12	VF20	XF40	MS60	MS63
1912	10,244,500	—	—	5.25	8.00	10.00
1913	7,256,002	—	—	5.25	8.00	10.00

KM# 2807 5 CORONA

24.00 g., 0.900 Silver 0.6945 oz. ASW **Ruler:** Franz Joseph I **Obv:** Laureate, bearded head right **Rev:** Crowned imperial double eagle within circle surrounded by wreath of circled crowns and leaves

Date	Mintage	F12	VF20	XF40	MS60	MS63
1907	1,539,000	14.00	20.00	50.00	100	150
1907	—	PF63 650				

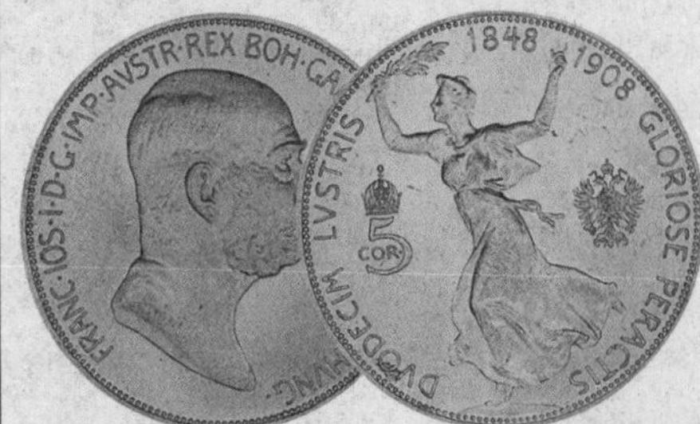

KM# 2809 5 CORONA

24.00 g., 0.900 Silver 0.6945 oz. ASW, 35 mm. **Ruler:** Franz Joseph I **Subject:** 60th Anniversary of Reign **Obv:** Head right **Rev:** Running figure of Fame

Date	Mintage	F12	VF20	XF40	MS60	MS63
ND-1908	5,089,700	14.00	20.00	35.00	65.00	100
ND-1908	—	PF63 650				
Restrike, Proof						

KM# 2813 5 CORONA
24.00 g., 0.900 Silver 0.6945 oz. ASW **Ruler:** Franz Joseph I **Obv:** Large head, right, continuous legend **Rev:** Crowned double eagle with shield on breast within circle, five crowns in circles and leaf sprays surrounding, date divides value at bottom

Date	Mintage	F12	VF20	XF40	MS60	MS63
1909	1,708,800	14.00	20.00	60.00	125	175

KM# 2814 5 CORONA
24.00 g., 0.900 Silver 0.6945 oz. ASW **Ruler:** Franz Joseph I **Obv:** Head right **Rev:** National arms, date below divides denomination

Date	Mintage	F12	VF20	XF40	MS60	MS63
1909	1,775,787	14.00	20.00	50.00	100	150

KM# 2805 10 CORONA
3.39 g., 0.900 Gold 0.098 oz. AGW, 19 mm. **Ruler:** Franz Joseph I **Obv:** Laureate, bearded head right **Rev:** Crowned imperial double eagle

Date	Mintage	F12	VF20	XF40	MS60	MS63
1905 - MDCCCCV	1,933,230	—	132	145	175	200
1906 - MDCCCCVI	1,081,161	—	132	145	175	200

KM# 2810 10 CORONA
3.39 g., 0.900 Gold 0.098 oz. AGW, 19 mm. **Ruler:** Franz Joseph I **Subject:** 60th Anniversary of Reign **Obv:** Small plain head right **Rev:** Crowned double eagle, tail divides two dates, value at bottom

Date	Mintage	F12	VF20	XF40	MS60	MS63
ND-1908	654,022	—	—	132	165	185

KM# 2815 10 CORONA
3.39 g., 0.900 Gold 0.098 oz. AGW, 19 mm. **Ruler:** Franz Joseph I **Obv:** Head right **Rev:** Crowned double eagle, date and value at bottom

Date	Mintage	F12	VF20	XF40	MS60	MS63
1909 - MDCCCCIX	2,319,872	—	—	132	160	180

KM# 2816 10 CORONA
3.39 g., 0.900 Gold 0.098 oz. AGW, 19 mm. **Ruler:** Franz Joseph I **Obv:** Large right **Rev:** Crowned double eagle, date and value at bottom

Date	Mintage	F12	VF20	XF40	MS60	MS63
1909 - MDCCCCIX	192,135	—	—	132	160	180
1910 - MDCCCCX	1,055,387	—	—	132	160	180
1911 - MDCCCCXI	1,285,667	—	—	132	160	180
1912 - MDCCCCXII Restrike	—	—	—	—	—	140

KM# 2806 20 CORONA
6.78 g., 0.900 Gold 0.196 oz. AGW, 21 mm. **Ruler:** Franz Joseph I **Obv:** Laureate, bearded head right **Rev:** Crowned imperial double eagle

Date	Mintage	F12	VF20	XF40	MS60	MS63
1901 - MDCCCCI	48,677	360	450	700	925	1,100
1902 - MDCCCCII	440,751	—	265	385	400	410
1903 - MDCCCCIII	322,679	—	—	265	325	345
1904 - MDCCCCIV	494,356	—	—	265	325	345
1905 - MDCCCCV	146,097	—	—	265	325	345

KM# 2811 20 CORONA
6.78 g., 0.900 Gold 0.196 oz. AGW, 21 mm. **Ruler:** Franz Joseph I **Subject:** 60th Anniversary of Reign **Obv:** Head right **Rev:** Crowned double eagle, crown divides two dates, value at bottom

Date	Mintage	F12	VF20	XF40	MS60	MS63
1908	188,000	265	350	400	425	500

KM# 2817 20 CORONA
6.78 g., 0.900 Gold 0.196 oz. AGW, 21 mm. **Ruler:** Franz Joseph I **Rev:** Crowned double eagle, value and date at bottom

Date	Mintage	F12	VF20	XF40	MS60	MS63
1909 - MDCCCCIX	227,754	475	775	1,450	1,850	2,200

KM# 2818 20 CORONA
6.78 g., 0.900 Gold 0.196 oz. AGW, 21 mm. **Ruler:** Franz Joseph I **Obv:** Head of Franz Joseph I, right

Date	Mintage	F12	VF20	XF40	MS60	MS63
MDCCCCIX (1909)	102,404	265	575	1,150	2,000	2,800
MDCCCCX (1910)	386,031	—	265	350	370	425
MDCCCCXI (1911)	59,313	265	375	625	800	975
MDCCCCXII (1912)	4,460	325	400	625	1,350	2,000
MDCCCCXIII (1913)	28,058	325	400	900	1,800	3,000
MDCCCCXIV (1914)	82,104	265	375	625	800	1,200
MDCCCCXV (1915) Restrike	—	—	—	—	—	280
MDCCCCXVI (1916)	71,763	1,200	2,500	3,500	5,500	7,500

KM# 2827 20 CORONA
6.78 g., 0.900 Gold 0.196 oz. AGW, 21 mm. **Ruler:** Franz Joseph I **Obv:** Head right **Rev:** Austrian shield on crowned double eagle, value and date at bottom

Date	Mintage	F12	VF20	XF40	MS60	MS63
1916 - MDCCCCXVI	Inc. above	265	450	750	900	1,250

KM# 2828 20 CORONA
6.78 g., 0.900 Gold 0.196 oz. AGW, 21 mm. **Ruler:** Karl I **Obv:** Head right **Rev:** Crowned national arms, date below divides denomination **Note:** 2000 pieces struck, all but one specimen were remelted.

Date	Mintage	F12	VF20	XF40	MS60	MS63
1918 - MDCCCCXVIII Unique	Est. 2000	—	—	—	—	—

KM# 2812 100 CORONA
33.88 g., 0.900 Gold 0.9802 oz. AGW, 37 mm. **Ruler:** Franz Joseph I **Subject:** 60th Anniversary of Reign **Obv:** Head right **Rev:** Resting figure of Fame

Date	Mintage	F12	VF20	XF40	MS60	MS63
ND-1908	16,000	1,325	1,650	1,750	1,950	3,500
ND-1908	—	**PF65** 3,750				

KM# 2819 100 CORONA
33.88 g., 0.900 Gold 0.9802 oz. AGW, 37 mm. **Ruler:** Franz Joseph I **Obv:** Head right **Rev:** Crowned double eagle, tail dividing value, date at bottom **Edge Lettering:** VNITIS VIRIBVS

Date	Mintage	F12	VF20	XF40	MS60	MS63
1909	3,203	—	1,325	1,600	1,800	2,200
1910	3,074	—	1,325	1,600	1,800	2,200
1911	11,165	—	1,325	1,600	1,800	2,200
1912	3,591	1,325	1,500	1,700	1,950	3,000
1913	2,696	—	1,325	1,600	1,800	2,450
1914	1,195	—	1,325	1,600	1,800	2,300
1915 Restrike	—	—	—	—	—	1,350
1915 Restrike, Proof	—	—	—	—	—	—

TRADE COINAGE

KM# 2267 DUCAT
3.49 g., 0.986 Gold 0.1107 oz. AGW **Ruler:** Franz Joseph I **Obv:** Laureate head right, heavy whiskers **Rev:** Crowned imperial double eagle **Note:** 996,721 pieces were struck from 1920-1936.

Date	Mintage	F12	VF20	XF40	MS60	MS63
1901	348,621	150	180	200	210	220
1902	311,471	150	180	200	210	220
1903	380,014	150	180	200	210	220
1904	517,118	150	180	200	210	220
1905	391,534	150	180	210	230	245

Date	Mintage	F12	VF20	XF40	MS60	MS63
1906	491,574	150	180	210	230	245
1907	554,205	150	180	225	290	310
1908	408,832	150	180	200	210	220
1909	366,318	150	180	200	210	220
1910	440,424	150	180	200	210	220
1911	590,826	—	150	180	210	220
1912	494,991	—	150	180	210	215
1913	319,926	—	150	180	210	215
1914	378,241	—	150	180	210	215
1915 Restrike	—	—	—	—	—	160
1915 Restrike, Proof	—	PF65 157				
1951 Error for 1915	—	150	180	210	250	275

KM# 2276 4 DUCAT
13.96 g., 0.986 Gold 0.4427 oz. AGW **Ruler:** Franz Joseph I **Obv:** Laureate, armored bust right **Rev:** Crowned imperial double eagle **Note:** without mint

Date	Mintage	F12	VF20	XF40	MS60	MS63
1901	51,597	600	750	1,000	1,600	2,000
1902	69,380	600	750	1,000	1,600	2,000
1903	72,658	600	750	1,000	1,600	2,000
1904	80,086	600	750	1,000	1,600	2,000
1905	90,906	600	750	1,000	1,600	2,000
1906	123,443	600	750	825	1,200	1,500
1907	104,295	600	750	825	1,200	1,500
1908	80,428	600	750	825	1,300	1,500
1909	83,852	600	750	825	1,050	1,250
1910	101,000	—	600	750	900	1,050
1911	141,857	—	600	750	825	950
1912	150,691	—	600	750	825	950
1913	119,133	—	600	750	825	950
1914	102,712	—	600	750	825	950
1915 (- 1936) Restrike	—	—	—	—	—	650

Note: 496,501 pieces were struck from 1920-1936

TRADE COINAGE

Restrikes

KM# T1 THALER
28.07 g., 0.833 Silver 0.7517 oz. ASW, 41 mm. **Obv:** Bust right **Rev:** Crowned imperial double eagle, heads in haloes **Note:** Many varieties exist. This type has been stuck by many different mints over the years, with some varieties commanding high premiums.

Date	Mintage	VF20	XF40	MS60	MS63	MS65
1780 SF	—	—	—	—	15.50	—
Note: Restrike; 1853 to present						
1780 SF	—	PF65 15.50				
Note: Restrike - 1853 to present						

KM# T2 20 DUCAT
72.75 g., Gold **Obv:** Bust of Maria Theresa, right **Rev:** Imperial Eagle **Mint:** London **Note:** Struck for Haile Selassie.

Date	Mintage	VF20	XF40	MS60	MS63	MS65
1780 SF	—	—	—	—	4,000	—
Note: Restrike - 1950s						

REPUBLIC

REFORM COINAGE

10,000 Kronen = 1 Schilling

KM# 2830 20 KRONEN
6.78 g., 0.900 Gold 0.196 oz. AGW **Obv:** Imperial Eagle, date below **Rev:** Value within wreath

Date	Mintage	F12	VF20	XF40	MS60	MS63
1923	6,988	300	650	1,400	1,850	2,750
1924	10,337	300	650	1,400	1,850	2,750

KM# 2831 100 KRONEN
33.88 g., 0.900 Gold 0.9802 oz. AGW **Obv:** Imperial Eagle, date below **Rev:** Value within wreath

Date	Mintage	F12	VF20	XF40	MS60	MS63
1923	617	—	1,800	1,900	2,750	5,000
1923	—	PF65 5,500				
1924	2,851	1,200	1,700	1,900	2,750	5,000
1924	—	PF65 5,500				

KM# 2832 100 KRONEN
1.67 g., Bronze, 17 mm. **Obv:** Eagle's head, right **Rev:** Value to right of leaf, date below

Date	Mintage	F12	VF20	XF40	MS60	MS63
1923	5,603,680	—	1.00	3.00	10.00	30.00
1924	43,813,820	—	—	0.25	1.50	3.00

KM# 2833 200 KRONEN
3.33 g., Bronze, 19 mm. **Obv:** Thick cross, date below **Rev:** Large value

Date	Mintage	F12	VF20	XF40	MS60	MS63
1924	57,160,000	—	—	1.00	3.00	5.00

KM# 2834 1000 KRONEN
4.50 g., Copper-Nickel, 22 mm. **Obv:** Woman of Tyrol, right **Rev:** Value within wreath

Date	Mintage	F12	VF20	XF40	MS60	MS63
1924	72,353,000	—	—	1.00	3.00	5.00

PRE WWII DECIMAL COINAGE

100 Groschen - 1 Schilling

KM# 2836 GROSCHEN
1.60 g., Bronze, 17 mm. **Obv:** Eagle's head right **Rev:** Large value, date below

Date	Mintage	F12	VF20	XF40	MS60	MS63
1925	31,798,000	—	—	0.50	1.00	2.00
1926	13,434,000	—	—	0.50	1.00	2.00
1927	15,900,000	—	—	0.50	1.00	2.00
1928	13,165,000	—	—	0.50	1.00	2.00
1929	10,364,000	—	—	0.50	1.00	2.00
1930	8,091,000	—	—	0.50	1.00	2.00
1931	1,026,000	3.00	5.00	15.00	40.00	60.00
1932	3,164,000	—	—	1.50	2.50	5.00
1933	3,079,000	—	—	0.50	1.50	3.00
1934	5,033,000	—	—	0.50	1.50	3.00
1935	4,443,000	—	—	0.50	1.50	3.00
1936	4,649,000	—	—	0.50	1.50	3.00
1937	5,522,000	—	—	2.00	1.50	3.00
1938	1,652,000	—	—	0.15	3.00	8.00

KM# 2837 2 GROSCHEN
3.30 g., Bronze, 19 mm. **Obv:** Thick cross, date below **Rev:** Large value **Edge:** Plain

Date	Mintage	F12	VF20	XF40	MS60	MS63
1925	30,292,000	—	—	0.50	1.50	3.00
1926	17,137,000	—	—	0.50	1.50	5.00
1927	8,722,000	—	—	0.50	1.50	5.00
1928	18,758,000	—	—	0.50	1.50	5.00
1929	16,184,000	—	—	0.50	1.50	5.00
1930	5,709,000	—	—	0.50	1.50	5.00
1934	812,000	1.00	3.00	5.00	10.00	20.00
1935	3,287,000	—	—	0.50	1.50	5.00
1936	4,657,000	—	—	0.50	1.50	5.00
1937	3,571,000	—	—	0.50	1.50	5.00
1938	864,000	—	—	1.50	5.00	8.00

KM# 2846 5 GROSCHEN
3.00 g., Copper-Nickel, 17 mm. **Obv:** Thick cross, date below **Rev:** Large value

Date	Mintage	F12	VF20	XF40	MS60	MS63
1931	17,389,000	—	—	—	1.50	2.00
1932	3,727,000	—	—	—	2.00	3.00
1934	3,426,000	—	—	0.50	1.50	3.00
1936	2,233,000	—	1.00	2.50	5.00	8.00
1937	923,000	3.00	5.00	25.00	45.00	75.00
1938	876,000	20.00	40.00	75.00	125	300

KM# 2838 10 GROSCHEN
4.50 g., Copper-Nickel, 22 mm. **Obv:** Woman of Tyrol right **Rev:** Value above date within wreath

Date	Mintage	F12	VF20	XF40	MS60	MS63
1925	73,563,000	—	—	0.50	1.50	2.00
1928	6,867,000	—	—	0.50	3.00	4.00
1929	10,607,000	—	—	0.50	1.50	2.00

KM# 2850 50 GROSCHEN

5.50 g., Copper-Nickel, 24 mm. **Obv:** Numeric value in box within circle, value at bottom **Rev:** Austrian shield on haloed double eagle's breast, tail dividing date

Date	Mintage	F12	VF20	XF40	MS60	MS63
1934	8,224,822	10.00	15.00	25.00	50.00	90.00
1934	Inc. above	PF65 250				

KM# 2854 50 GROSCHEN

5.50 g., Copper-Nickel, 24 mm. **Obv:** Austrian shield on haloed double eagle's breast, value at bottom **Rev:** Large value above date

Date	Mintage	F12	VF20	XF40	MS60	MS63
1935	12,635,000	—	—	1.00	3.00	5.00
1935	Inc. above	PF65 150				
1936	1,200,000	5.00	10.00	20.00	50.00	75.00
1936	Inc. above	PF65 250				

KM# 2839 1/2 SCHILLING

3.00 g., 0.640 Silver 0.0617 oz. ASW, 19 mm. **Obv:** Austrian shield at center **Rev:** Numeric value in diamond at center **Edge:** Reeded

Date	Mintage	F12	VF20	XF40	MS60	MS63
1925	22,763,000	—	1.20	150	3.00	5.00
1926	8,550,000	—	1.20	2.00	5.00	8.00

KM# 2835 SCHILLING

7.00 g., 0.800 Silver 0.180 oz. ASW, 26 mm. **Obv:** Parliament building in Vienna, date below **Rev:** Coat of arms on spray of edelweiss, value **Edge:** Reeded

Date	Mintage	F12	VF20	XF40	MS60	MS63
1924	11,086,000	—	3.50	5.00	8.00	10.00

KM# 2840 SCHILLING

6.00 g., 0.640 Silver 0.1235 oz. ASW, 25 mm. **Obv:** Parliament building in Vienna, date below **Rev:** Coat of arms on spray of edelweiss, value **Edge:** Reeded

Date	Mintage	F12	VF20	XF40	MS60	MS63
1925	40,009,000	—	2.50	3.00	5.00	8.00
1926	18,357,000	—	2.50	3.00	5.00	8.00
1932	700,000	15.00	20.00	50.00	90.00	150

KM# 2851 SCHILLING

7.00 g., Copper-Nickel, 26 mm. **Obv:** Two sprigs of grain in center with large numeric value on top **Rev:** Austrian shield on haloed double eagles breast, tail dividing date **Edge:** Reeded

Date	Mintage	F12	VF20	XF40	MS60	MS63
1934	42,826,000	—	—	1.00	2.00	3.50
1934	—	PF65 200				
1935	7,815,000	—	—	3.00	5.00	10.00

KM# 2843 2 SCHILLING

12.00 g., 0.640 Silver 0.2469 oz. ASW **Subject:** Centennial - Death of Franz Schubert **Obv:** Value within circle of shields **Rev:** Head of Franz Schubert, left, date at bottom left

Date	Mintage	F12	VF20	XF40	MS60	MS63
1928	6,900,000	—	5.00	8.00	10.00	15.00

KM# 2844 2 SCHILLING

12.00 g., 0.640 Silver 0.2469 oz. ASW **Subject:** 100th Anniversary - Birth of Dr. Theodor Billroth, Surgeon **Obv:** Value within circle of shields **Rev:** Head of Dr. Theodor Billroth, left, date below

Date	Mintage	F12	VF20	XF40	MS60	MS63
1929	2,000,000	—	5.00	8.00	10.00	15.00

KM# 2845 2 SCHILLING

12.00 g., 0.640 Silver 0.2469 oz. ASW **Subject:** 7th Centennial - Death of Walther von der Vogelweide, Minstrel **Obv:** Value within circle of shields **Rev:** Figure of Walther von der Vogelweide sitting, left, with doves, harp on lower left. date at bottom **Note:** Same reverse used on Germany, Weimar Republic 3 reichsmark.

Date	Mintage	F12	VF20	XF40	MS60	MS63
1930	500,000	—	5.00	8.00	10.00	15.00
1930	Inc. above	PF63 125				

KM# 2847 2 SCHILLING

12.00 g., 0.640 Silver 0.2469 oz. ASW **Subject:** 175th Anniversary - Birth of Wolfgang Mozart, Composer **Obv:** Value within circle of shields **Rev:** Head of Wolfgang Mozart, right, two dates at bottom

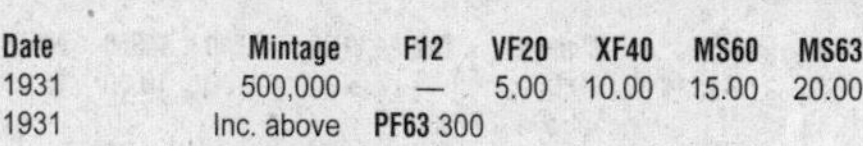

Date	Mintage	F12	VF20	XF40	MS60	MS63
1931	500,000	—	5.00	10.00	15.00	20.00
1931	Inc. above	PF63 300				

KM# 2848 2 SCHILLING

12.00 g., 0.640 Silver 0.2469 oz. ASW **Subject:** 200th Anniversary - Birth of Joseph Haydn, Composer **Obv:** Value within circle of shields **Rev:** Head of Joseph Haydn, left, date below

Date	Mintage	F12	VF20	XF40	MS60	MS63
1932	300,000	5.00	15.00	30.00	50.00	75.00
1932	Inc. above	PF63 550				

KM# 2849 2 SCHILLING

12.00 g., 0.640 Silver 0.2469 oz. ASW **Subject:** Death of Dr. Ignaz Seipel, Chancellor **Obv:** Value within circle of shields **Rev:** Head of Dr. Ignaz Seipel, right, two dates at bottom

Date	Mintage	F12	VF20	XF40	MS60	MS63
ND-1933	400,000	—	5.00	10.00	15.00	20.00
ND-1933	Inc. above	PF63 400				

KM# 2852 2 SCHILLING

12.00 g., 0.640 Silver 0.2469 oz. ASW **Subject:** Death of Dr. Engelbert Dollfuss, Chancellor **Obv:** Value within circle of shields **Rev:** Head of Dr. Engelbert Dollfuss, right, two dates at bottom

Date	Mintage	F12	VF20	XF40	MS60	MS63
1934	1,500,000	—	5.00	8.00	10.00	15.00
1934	Inc. above	PF63 275				

KM# 2855 2 SCHILLING

12.00 g., 0.640 Silver 0.2469 oz. ASW **Subject:** 25th Anniversary - Death of Dr. Karl Lueger, Politician, Social reformer **Obv:** Haloed double eagle with Austrian shield, date divides value at bottom **Rev:** Head of Dr. Karl Lueger, right

Date	Mintage	F12	VF20	XF40	MS60	MS63
1935	500,000	—	5.00	8.00	10.00	15.00
1935	Inc. above	PF63 285				

KM# 2858 2 SCHILLING

12.00 g., 0.640 Silver 0.2469 oz. ASW **Subject:** Bicentennial - Death of Prince Eugen of Savoy, Imperial Austrian Field Marshal **Obv:** Haloed double eagle with Austrian shield, date divides value below **Rev:** Head of Prince Eugen of Savoy, left

Date	Mintage	F12	VF20	XF40	MS60	MS63
1936	500,000	—	5.00	8.00	10.00	15.00
1936	Inc. above	PF63 225				

KM# 2859 2 SCHILLING

12.00 g., 0.640 Silver 0.2469 oz. ASW **Subject:** Bicentennial - Completion of St. Charles Church 1737 **Obv:** Haloed double eagle with Austrian shield, date divides value below **Rev:** St. Charles Church, date at bottom

Date	Mintage	F12	VF20	XF40	MS60	MS63
1937	500,000	—	5.00	8.00	10.00	15.00
1937	Inc. above	PF63 185				

KM# 2853 5 SCHILLING

15.00 g., 0.835 Silver 0.4027 oz. ASW, 31 mm. **Obv:** Haloed double eagle with Austrian shield, value **Rev:** Standing figure of Madonna of Mariazell, date below **Edge:** Lettered

Date	Mintage	F12	VF20	XF40	MS60	MS63
1934	3,285,400	8.00	12.00	18.00	25.00	50.00
1934	—	PF63 220				
1935	5,305,000	8.00	12.00	18.00	25.00	50.00
1936	1,409,000	12.00	20.00	40.00	65.00	100

KM# 2841 25 SCHILLING

5.88 g., 0.900 Gold 0.1702 oz. AGW **Obv:** Imperial Eagle with Austrian shield on breast, holding hammer and sickle, **Rev:** Value at top flanked by edelweiss sprays, date divided by sprigs at bottom

Date	Mintage	F12	VF20	XF40	MS60	MS63
1926 Prooflike	276,705	—	—	—	230	300
1927 Prooflike	72,672	—	—	—	230	300
1928 Prooflike	134,041	—	—	—	230	300
1929 Prooflike	243,269	—	—	—	230	300
1930 Prooflike	129,535	—	—	—	230	300
1931 Prooflike	169,002	—	—	—	230	300
1933 Prooflike	4,944	—	—	600	1,200	1,850
1934 Prooflike	11,000	—	—	300	400	600

KM# 2856 25 SCHILLING

5.88 g., 0.900 Gold 0.1702 oz. AGW **Obv:** Haloed double eagle with Austrian shield on breast, value below **Rev:** Half figure of St. Leopold, facing 3/4 forward, date at bottom

Date	Mintage	F12	VF20	XF40	MS60	MS63
1935 Prooflike	2,880	—	—	—	650	1,000
1936 Prooflike	7,260	—	—	—	600	850
1937 Prooflike	7,660	—	—	—	600	850
1938 Prooflike	1,360	—	—	5,000	15,000	25,000

KM# 2842 100 SCHILLING

23.52 g., 0.900 Gold 0.6807 oz. AGW **Obv:** Imperial Eagle with Austrian shield on breast holding hammer and sickle **Rev:** Value at top flanked by edelweiss sprays, date below, one star on either side

Date	Mintage	F12	VF20	XF40	MS60	MS63
1926 Prooflike	63,795	—	—	—	920	1,200
1927 Prooflike	68,746	—	—	—	920	1,200
1928 Prooflike	40,188	—	—	—	920	1,200
1929 Prooflike	74,849	—	—	—	920	1,200
1930 Prooflike	24,849	—	—	—	920	1,200
1931 Prooflike	101,935	—	—	—	920	1,200
1933 Prooflike	4,727	—	920	960	1,600	2,500
1934 Prooflike	9,383	—	—	—	920	1,200

KM# 2857 100 SCHILLING

23.52 g., 0.900 Gold 0.6807 oz. AGW **Obv:** Haloed eagle with Austrian shield on breast, value below **Rev:** Standing figure of Madonna of Mariazell, facing, date below

Date	Mintage	F12	VF20	XF40	MS60	MS63
1935 Prooflike	951	1,500	2,000	4,000	5,500	6,200
1936 Prooflike	12,000	—	920	1,200	1,650	2,300
1937 Prooflike	2,900	920	960	1,600	2,250	3,000
1938 Prooflike	1,400	2,500	5,000	10,000	25,000	—

POST WWII DECIMAL COINAGE

100 Groschen - 1 Schilling

KM# 2873 GROSCHEN

1.80 g., Zinc, 17 mm. **Obv:** Imperial Eagle with Austrian shield on breast **Rev:** Large value above date, spray of leaves below

Date	Mintage	VF20	XF40	MS60	MS63	MS65
1947	23,460,000	—	0.25	1.00	2.00	—

Note: Includes coins dated 1947, minted 1948-1950

KM# 2876 2 GROSCHEN

0.90 g., Aluminum, 18 mm. **Obv:** Imperial Eagle with Austrian shield on breast, holding hammer and sickle **Rev:** Large value in circle, date below circle **Edge:** Plain

Date	Mintage	VF20	XF40	MS60	MS63	MS65
1950	21,652,000	—	—	0.25	0.75	4.00
1950	—	PF65 10.00				
1951	7,377,000	—	—	—	0.50	3.00
1951	—	PF65 75.00				
1952	37,851,000	—	—	—	0.50	1.50
1952	—	PF65 10.00				
1954	46,167,000	—	—	—	0.50	1.50
1954	—	PF65 15.00				
1957	26,923,000	—	—	—	0.50	1.50
1957	—	PF65 20.00				
1962	6,692,000	—	—	—	1.00	1.50
1962	—	PF65 10.00				
1964	173,000	—	—	—	1.00	1.50
1964	—	PF65 1.00				
1965	14,475,000	—	—	—	—	0.50
1965	—	PF65 1.00				
1966	7,454,000	—	—	—	—	0.50
1966	—	PF65 1.00				
1967	13,000	PF65 20.00				
1968	1,803,400	—	—	—	0.50	0.75
1968	21,600	PF65 1.00				
1969	57,000	PF65 1.00				
1970	260,000	PF65 1.00				
1971	145,000	PF65 1.00				
1972	2,763,000	—	—	—	0.50	0.75
1972	132,000	PF65 1.00				
1973	5,883,000	—	—	—	0.50	0.75
1973 Proof	149,000	—	—	—	—	—
1974	1,387,000	—	—	—	0.50	0.75
1974	93,000	PF65 1.00				
1975	1,096,000	—	—	—	0.50	0.75
1975	52,000	PF65 1.00				
1976	2,755,000	—	—	—	0.50	0.75
1976	45,000	PF65 1.00				
1977	1,837,000	—	—	—	0.50	0.75
1977	47,000	PF65 1.00				
1978	1,527,000	—	—	—	0.50	0.75
1978	44,000	PF65 1.00				
1979	2,434,000	—	—	—	0.50	0.75
1979	44,000	PF65 1.00				
1980	1,893,000	—	—	—	0.50	0.75
1980	48,000	PF65 1.00				
1981	950,000	—	—	—	0.50	0.75
1981	49,000	PF65 1.00				
1982	3,950,000	—	—	—	0.50	0.75
1982	50,000	PF65 1.00				
1983	2,665,000	—	—	—	0.50	0.75
1983	65,000	PF65 1.00				
1984	500,000	—	—	—	0.50	0.75
1984	65,000	PF65 1.00				
1985	1,064,000	—	—	—	0.50	0.75
1985	45,000	PF65 1.00				
1986	1,798,000	—	—	—	0.50	0.75
1986	42,000	PF65 1.00				
1987	958,000	—	—	—	0.50	0.75
1987	42,000	PF65 1.00				
1988	1,061,000	—	—	—	0.50	0.75
1988	39,000	PF65 1.00				
1989	950,000	—	—	—	0.50	0.75
1989	38,000	PF65 1.00				
1990	35,000	PF65 1.00				
1991	2,600,000	—	—	—	0.50	0.75
1991	27,000	PF65 1.00				
1992 Special Unc	25,000	—	—	—	—	3.00
1993 Special Unc	28,000	—	—	—	—	3.00
1994 Special Unc	25,000	—	—	—	—	3.00

KM# 2875 5 GROSCHEN

2.50 g., Zinc, 19 mm. **Obv:** Eagle with Austrian shield on breast, holding hammer and sickle **Rev:** Large value **Edge:** Reeded

Date	Mintage	VF20	XF40	MS60	MS63	MS65
1948	17,269,000	—	—	3.00	5.00	—
1950	19,426,431	—	—	1.50	3.00	—
1950	—	PF65 75.00				
1951	12,454,569	—	—	3.00	5.00	—
1951	—	PF65 15.00				
1953	14,931,000	—	—	1.50	3.00	—
1955	12,288,000	—	—	3.00	5.00	—
1957	26,809,000	—	—	1.50	3.00	—
1957	—	PF65 20.00				
1961	3,429,000	—	—	1.50	3.00	—
1961	—	PF65 5.00				
1962	5,999,000	—	—	1.50	3.00	—
1963	13,293,000	—	—	1.50	3.00	—
1963	—	PF65 5.00				
1964	4,659,000	—	—	1.00	3.00	—
1964	—	PF65 1.00				
1965	13,293,000	—	—	0.50	1.50	—
1965	—	PF65 1.00				
1966	9,348,000	—	—	0.50	1.50	—
1966	—	PF65 8.00				
1967	4,404,000	—	—	0.50	1.50	—
1967	—	PF65 1.50				
1968	31,418,400	—	—	0.50	1.00	—
1968	15,600	PF65 1.50				
1969	44,000	PF65 1.50				
1970	144,000	PF65 1.00				
1971	125,000	PF65 1.00				
1972	10,979,000	—	—	0.25	0.50	—
1972	116,000	PF65 1.00				
1973	10,336,000	—	—	0.25	0.50	—
1973	120,000	PF65 1.00				
1974	2,911,000	—	—	0.25	0.50	—
1974	87,000	PF65 1.00				
1975	7,102,000	—	—	0.25	0.50	—
1975	51,000	PF65 1.00				
1976	8,079,000	—	—	0.25	0.50	—
1976	45,000	PF65 1.00				
1977	1,600,000	—	—	0.25	0.50	—
1977	45,000	PF65 1.00				
1978	2,657,000	—	—	0.25	0.50	—
1978	44,000	PF65 1.00				
1979	4,927,000	—	—	0.25	0.50	—
1979	44,000	PF65 1.00				
1980	3,100,000	—	—	0.25	0.50	—
1980	48,000	PF65 1.50				
1981	450,000	—	—	—	0.75	—
1981	49,000	PF65 1.50				
1982	3,950,000	—	—	—	0.75	—
1982	50,000	PF65 1.00				
1983	501,000	—	—	—	0.75	—

Date	Mintage	VF20	XF40	MS60	MS63	MS65
1983	65,000	PF65 1.00				
1984	988,000	—	—	—	0.75	—
1984	65,000	PF65 1.00				
1985	1,914,000	—	—	—	0.75	—
1985	45,000	PF65 1.50				
1986	100,800	—	—	—	2.00	—
1986	42,000	PF65 1.50				
1987	1,458,000	—	—	—	0.75	—
1987	42,000	PF65 1.50				
1988	1,261,000	—	—	—	0.75	—
1988	39,000	PF65 1.50				
1989	2,604,000	—	—	—	0.75	—
1989	38,000	PF65 1.00				
1990	2,608,000	—	—	—	0.75	—
1990	35,000	PF65 1.50				
1991	2,400,000	—	—	—	0.75	—
1991	27,000	PF65 1.50				
1992	671,000	—	—	—	0.75	—
1992 Special Unc	25,000	—	—	—	3.00	—
1993 Special Unc	28,000	—	—	—	3.00	—
1994 Special Unc	25,000	—	—	—	3.00	—

KM# 2874 10 GROSCHEN

3.50 g., Zinc, 21 mm. **Obv:** Imperial Eagle with Austrian shield on breast, holding hammer and sickle **Rev:** Large value above date, trumpet flower spray below **Edge:** Plain

Date	Mintage	VF20	XF40	MS60	MS63	MS65
1947	6,844,580	—	1.00	5.00	10.00	—
1947	—	PF65 15.00				
1948	66,205,000	—	0.50	1.50	3.00	—
1948	—	PF65 20.00				
1949	51,202,000	—	0.50	1.50	3.00	—
1949	—	PF65 25.00				

KM# 2878 10 GROSCHEN

1.10 g., Aluminum, 20 mm. **Obv:** Small Imperial Eagle with Austrian shield on breast, at top between numbers, scalloped rim, stylized inscription below **Rev:** Large value above date, scalloped rim **Edge:** Plain **Mint:** Vienna

Date	Mintage	VF20	XF40	MS60	MS63	MS65
1951	9,573,000	—	—	1.50	3.00	5.00
1951	—	PF65 85.00				
1952	45,911,400	—	—	0.75	1.00	2.00
1952	—	PF65 50.00				
1953	22,577,600	—	—	—	0.50	1.50
1953	—	PF65 175				
1955	51,707,000	—	—	—	0.50	1.50
1955	—	PF65 28.00				
1957	33,509,000	—	—	—	0.50	1.50
1957	—	PF65 150				
1959	80,719,000	—	—	—	0.50	1.50
1959	—	PF65 45.00				
1961	11,283,000	—	—	—	0.50	1.50
1961 Proof	—	—	—	—	—	—
1962	24,635,000	—	—	—	0.50	1.50
1962	—	PF65 40.00				
1963	38,062,000	—	—	—	0.50	1.50
1963	—	PF65 45.00				
1964	34,928,000	—	—	—	0.50	1.50
1964	—	PF65 1.50				
1965	40,615,000	—	—	—	0.50	1.50
1965	—	PF65 1.50				
1966	24,991,000	—	—	—	0.50	1.50
1966	—	PF65 6.00				
1967	32,552,999	—	—	—	0.50	1.50
1967	—	PF65 12.00				
1968	42,395,800	—	—	—	0.50	1.50
1968	16,000	PF65 2.00				
1969	19,953,000	—	—	—	—	0.50
1969	27,000	PF65 1.00				
1970	36,997,500	—	—	—	—	0.50
1970	102,000	PF65 0.50				
1971	57,450,000	—	—	—	—	0.50
1971	82,000	PF65 0.50				
1972	75,661,000	—	—	—	—	0.50
1972	81,000	PF65 0.50				
1973	60,244,000	—	—	—	—	0.50
1973	97,000	PF65 0.50				
1974	55,924,000	—	—	—	—	0.50
1974	78,000	PF65 0.50				

Date	Mintage	VF20	XF40	MS60	MS63	MS65
1975	60,576,000	—	—	—	—	0.50
1975	49,000	PF65 0.50				
1976	39,357,000	—	—	—	—	0.50
1976	44,000	PF65 0.50				
1977	53,610,000	—	—	—	—	0.50
1977	44,000	PF65 0.50				
1978	57,857,000	—	—	—	—	0.50
1978	43,000	PF65 0.50				
1979	103,686,000	—	—	—	—	0.50
1979	44,000	PF65 0.50				
1980	79,848,000	—	—	—	—	0.50
1980	48,000	PF65 0.50				
1981	92,268,000	—	—	—	—	0.50
1981	49,000	PF65 0.50				
1982	99,950,000	—	—	—	—	0.50
1982	50,000	PF65 0.50				
1983	93,768,000	—	—	—	—	0.50
1983	65,000	PF65 0.50				
1984	86,603,000	—	—	—	—	0.50
1984	65,000	PF65 0.50				
1985	86,304,000	—	—	—	—	0.50
1985	45,000	PF65 0.50				
1986	108,912,000	—	—	—	—	0.50
1986	42,000	PF65 0.50				
1987	114,058,000	—	—	—	—	0.50
1987	42,000	PF65 0.50				
1988	114,461,000	—	—	—	—	0.50
1988	39,000	PF65 0.50				
1989	127,784,000	—	—	—	—	0.50
1989	38,000	PF65 0.50				
1990	182,050,000	—	—	—	—	0.50
1990	35,000	PF65 0.50				
1991	145,000,000	—	—	—	—	0.50
1991	27,000	PF65 0.50				
1992	120,000,000	—	—	—	—	0.50
1992 Special Unc	25,000	—	—	—	—	1.00
1993	120,000,000	—	—	—	—	0.50
1993 Special Unc	28,000	—	—	—	—	1.00
1994	110,000,000	—	—	—	—	0.50
1994 Special Unc	25,000	—	—	—	—	1.00
1995	110,000,000	—	—	—	—	0.50
1995 Special Unc	27,000	—	—	—	—	—
1996	100,000,000	—	—	—	—	0.50
1996 Special Unc	25,000	—	—	—	—	1.50
1997	80,000,000	—	—	—	—	0.50
1997 Special Unc	25,000	—	—	—	—	1.50
1998	35,000,000	—	—	—	—	0.50
1998 Special Unc	25,000	—	—	—	—	1.50
1999 Special Unc	50,000	—	—	—	—	1.50
2000 Special Unc	75,000	—	—	—	—	1.50

KM# 2877 20 GROSCHEN

4.50 g., Aluminum-Bronze, 22 mm. **Obv:** Imperial Eagle with Austrian shield on breast, holding hammer and sickle **Rev:** Value at center above date **Edge:** Plain

Date	Mintage	VF20	XF40	MS60	MS63	MS65
1950	1,619,000	—	0.25	1.50	3.00	10.00
1950	—	PF65 20.00				
1951	7,781,000	—	0.25	0.75	1.50	3.00
1951	—	PF65 15.00				
1954	5,343,000	—	0.25	0.75	1.50	3.00
1954	—	PF65 150				

KM# 2870 50 GROSCHEN

1.40 g., Aluminum, 22 mm. **Obv:** Imperial Eagle with Austrian shield on breast holding hammer and sickle **Rev:** Numeric value on Austrian shield at center, date divided below shield **Edge:** Reeded

Date	Mintage	VF20	XF40	MS60	MS63	MS65
1946	13,058,000	—	0.50	1.50	3.00	5.00
1946	—	PF65 25.00				
1947	26,990,000	—	0.50	0.75	1.50	3.00
1947	—	PF65 10.00				

Date	Mintage	VF20	XF40	MS60	MS63	MS65
1952	7,455,000	—	0.50	1.25	2.50	4.00
1952	—	PF65 25.00				
1955	16,919,000	—	0.50	1.00	2.00	3.00
1955	—	PF65 25.00				

KM# 2885 50 GROSCHEN

3.00 g., Aluminum-Bronze, 19.5 mm. **Obv:** Austrian shield **Rev:** Large value above date **Edge:** Reeded

Date	Mintage	VF20	XF40	MS60	MS63	MS65
1959	14,122,000	—	0.50	2.00	8.00	15.00
1959	—	PF65 10.00				
1960	22,404,000	—	0.50	1.50	3.00	5.00
1960	—	PF65 25.00				
1961	19,891,000	—	0.50	1.50	3.00	5.00
1961	—	PF65 20.00				
1962	10,008,000	—	0.50	1.50	3.00	5.00
1962	—	PF65 40.00				
1963	9,483,000	—	0.50	1.50	3.00	5.00
1963	—	PF65 40.00				
1964	5,331,000	PF65 1.00				
1964	—	PF65 1.50				
1965	15,007,000	PF65 1.00				
1965	—	PF65 1.50				
1966	7,322,000	—	—	—	0.50	1.00
1966	—	PF65 10.00				
1967	8,237,000	PF65 1.00				
1967	—	PF65 15.00				
1968	7,726,200	—	—	—	0.50	1.00
1968	15,400	PF65 10.00				
1969	7,044,000	—	—	0.50	4.50	1.00
1969	26,000	PF65 0.75				
1970	2,865,200	—	—	0.50	0.65	1.00
1970	128,000	PF65 0.75				
1971	14,133,000	—	—	0.50	0.65	1.00
1971	84,000	PF65 0.75				
1972	17,287,000	—	—	0.50	0.65	1.00
1972	80,000	PF65 0.75				
1973	17,812,000	—	—	0.50	0.65	1.00
1973	90,000	PF65 0.75				
1974	15,776,000	—	—	0.50	0.65	1.00
1974	76,000	PF65 0.75				
1975	7,677,000	—	—	0.50	0.65	1.00
1975	49,000	PF65 0.75				
1976	11,106,000	—	—	0.50	0.65	1.00
1976	44,000	PF65 0.75				
1977	7,214,000	—	—	0.50	0.65	1.00
1977	44,000	PF65 0.75				
1978	12,364,000	—	—	0.50	0.65	1.00
1978	43,000	PF65 0.75				
1979	16,307,000	—	—	0.50	0.65	1.00
1979	44,000	PF65 0.75				
1980	29,836,000	—	—	0.50	0.65	1.00
1980	48,000	PF65 0.75				
1981	12,944,000	—	—	0.50	0.65	1.00
1981	49,000	PF65 0.75				
1982	9,900,000	—	—	0.50	0.65	1.00
1982	50,000	PF65 0.75				
1983	15,117,000	—	—	0.50	0.65	1.00
1983	65,000	PF65 0.75				
1984	20,677,000	—	—	0.50	0.65	1.00
1984	65,000	PF65 0.75				
1985	15,609,000	—	—	0.50	0.65	1.00
1985	45,000	PF65 0.75				
1986	16,974,000	—	—	0.50	0.65	1.00
1986	42,000	PF65 0.75				
1987	7,216,000	—	—	0.50	0.65	1.00
1987	42,000	PF65 0.75				
1988	16,222,000	—	—	0.50	0.65	1.00
1988	39,000	PF65 0.75				
1989	17,315,000	—	—	0.50	0.65	1.00
1989	38,000	PF65 0.75				
1990	29,618,000	—	—	0.50	0.65	1.00
1990	35,000	PF65 0.75				
1991	44,967,000	—	—	0.50	0.65	1.00
1991	27,000	PF65 0.75				
1992	1,975,000	—	—	—	0.25	0.50
1992 Special Unc	25,000	—	—	—	—	2.00
1993	14,972,000	—	—	—	0.25	0.50
1993 Special Unc	28,000	—	—	—	—	1.50
1994	9,975,000	—	—	—	0.25	0.50
1994 Special Unc	25,000	—	—	—	—	1.50
1995	19,973,000	—	—	—	0.25	0.50
1995 Special Unc	27,000	—	—	—	—	1.50
1996	14,975,000	—	—	—	0.25	0.50
1996 Special Unc	25,000	—	—	—	—	1.50
1997	9,975,000	—	—	—	0.25	0.50

Date	Mintage	VF20	XF40	MS60	MS63	MS65
1997 Special Unc	25,000	—	—	—	—	1.50
1998 Special Unc	25,000	—	—	—	—	1.50
1999 Special Unc	50,000	—	—	—	—	1.50
2000 Special Unc	75,000	—	—	—	—	1.50

KM# 2871 SCHILLING

2.00 g., Aluminum, 25 mm. **Obv:** Full figure with seedbag on left hip, dropping seed from right hand, divides value **Rev:** Eagle with Austrian shield, tail dividing date

Date	Mintage	VF20	XF40	MS60	MS63	MS65
1946	27,336,000	—	1.00	2.50	5.00	15.00
1946	—	PF65 175				
1947	35,838,000	—	0.50	1.00	2.00	3.00
1947	—	PF65 15.00				
1952	22,231,000	—	0.50	1.00	2.00	3.00
1952	—	PF65 20.00				
1957	28,649,000	—	0.50	1.00	2.00	3.00
1957	—	PF65 50.00				

KM# 2886 SCHILLING

4.20 g., Aluminum-Bronze, 22.5 mm. **Obv:** Large value above date **Rev:** Edelweiss flower **Edge:** Plain

Date	Mintage	VF20	XF40	MS60	MS63	MS65
1959	46,726,000	—	1.00	2.00	3.00	5.00
1959	—	PF65 5.00				
1960	46,111,000	—	1.00	2.00	3.00	5.00
1960	—	PF65 200				
1961	51,115,000	—	1.00	2.50	5.00	8.00
1961	—	PF65 400				
1962	9,303,000	—	1.00	2.50	5.00	—
1962	—	PF65 20.00				
1963	24,845,000	—	0.50	0.65	1.00	3.00
1963	—	PF65 10.00				
1964	11,709,000	—	0.50	0.60	0.75	1.50
1964	—	PF65 1.00				
1965	46,726,000	—	—	—	1.00	1.50
1965	27,900	PF65 3.00				
1966	23,925,000	—	—	—	1.00	1.50
1966	—	PF65 3.00				
1967	22,214,000	—	—	—	1.00	1.50
1967	—	PF65 3.00				
1968	30,860,000	—	—	—	1.00	1.50
1968	17,000	PF65 2.00				
1969	9,155,100	—	—	—	1.00	1.50
1969	28,000	PF65 1.00				
1970	10,678,600	—	—	—	1.00	1.50
1970	100,400	PF65 1.00				
1971	27,974,000	—	—	—	1.00	1.50
1971	82,000	PF65 1.00				
1972	54,577,000	—	—	—	0.50	1.00
1972	78,000	PF65 1.00				
1973	41,332,000	—	—	—	0.50	1.00
1973	90,000	PF65 1.00				
1974	43,712,000	—	—	—	0.50	1.00
1974	77,000	PF65 1.00				
1975	13,989,000	—	—	—	0.50	1.00
1975	49,000	PF65 1.00				
1976	28,748,000	—	—	—	0.50	1.00
1976	44,000	PF65 1.00				
1977	19,584,000	—	—	—	0.50	1.00
1977	44,000	PF65 1.00				
1978	35,632,000	—	—	—	0.50	1.00
1978	43,000	PF65 1.00				
1979	64,802,000	—	—	—	0.50	1.00
1979	44,000	PF65 1.00				
1980	49,855,000	—	—	—	0.50	1.00
1980	48,000	PF65 1.00				
1981	37,502,000	—	—	—	0.50	1.00
1981	49,000	PF65 1.00				
1982	29,950,000	—	—	—	0.50	1.00
1982	50,000	PF65 1.00				
1983	38,186,000	—	—	—	0.50	1.00
Note: Also exists with higher date						
1983	65,000	PF65 1.00				
1984	31,891,000	—	—	—	0.50	1.00
1984	65,000	PF65 1.00				

Date	Mintage	VF20	XF40	MS60	MS63	MS65
1985	49,154,000	—	—	—	0.50	1.00
1985	45,000	PF65 1.00				
1986	57,578,000	—	—	—	0.50	1.00
1986	42,000	PF65 1.00				
1987	44,158,000	—	—	—	0.50	1.00
1987	42,000	PF65 1.00				
1988	51,561,000	—	—	—	0.50	1.00
1988	39,000	PF65 1.00				
1989	62,821,000	—	—	—	0.50	1.00
1989	38,000	PF65 1.00				
1990	103,710,000	—	—	—	0.50	1.00
1990	35,000	PF65 1.00				
1991	117,700,000	—	—	—	0.50	1.00
1991	27,000	PF65 1.00				
1992	55,000,000	—	—	—	0.50	—
1992 Special Unc	25,000	—	—	—	—	1.00
1993	60,000,000	—	—	—	0.50	—
1993 Special Unc	28,000	—	—	—	—	1.00
1994	50,000,000	—	—	—	0.50	—
1994 Special Unc	25,000	—	—	—	—	1.00
1995	70,000,000	—	—	—	0.50	—
1995 Special Unc	27,000	—	—	—	—	1.00
1996	65,000,000	—	—	—	0.50	—
1996 Special Unc	25,000	—	—	—	—	1.00
1997	50,000,000	—	—	—	0.50	—
1997 Special Unc	25,000	—	—	—	—	1.00
1998	60,000,000	—	—	—	0.50	—
1998 Special Unc	25,000	—	—	—	—	1.00
1999 Special Unc	50,000	—	—	—	—	1.00
2000 Special Unc	75,000	—	—	—	—	1.00

KM# 2872 2 SCHILLING

2.80 g., Aluminum, 28 mm. **Obv:** Imperial Eagle with Austrian shield on breast, holding hammer and sickle **Rev:** Thick value above spray of leaves and berries, grain sprigs at top **Edge:** Plain

Date	Mintage	VF20	XF40	MS60	MS63	MS65
1946	13,423,000	—	1.00	5.00	10.00	15.00
1946	—	PF65 200				
1947	36,658,000	—	1.00	4.00	8.00	12.00
1947	—	PF65 15.00				
1952	577,000	50.00	75.00	85.00	110	175
1952	—	PF65 900				

KM# 2879 5 SCHILLING

4.00 g., Aluminum, 31 mm. **Obv:** Large value at center, geared rim **Rev:** Imperial Eagle with Austrian shield on breast, holding hammer and sickle **Edge:** Reeded

Date	Mintage	VF20	XF40	MS60	MS63	MS65
1952	43,231,000	0.25	0.50	1.25	2.50	3.00
1952	—	PF65 15.00				
1957	240,200	75.00	100	125	175	300
1957	—	PF65 475				

KM# 2889 5 SCHILLING

5.20 g., 0.640 Silver 0.107 oz. ASW, 23.5 mm. **Obv:** Lippizaner stallion with rider, rearing, left **Rev:** Austrian shield divides date, value above, sprays below **Edge:** Reeded

Date	Mintage	VF20	XF40	MS60	MS63	MS65
1960	12,618,000	—	2.25	2.50	3.00	3.50
1960	1,000	PF65 65.00				
1961	17,902,000	—	2.25	2.50	3.00	3.50
1961	—	PF65 25.00				
1962	6,771,000	—	2.25	2.50	3.00	3.50
1962	—	PF65 50.00				
1963	1,811,000	—	2.25	2.50	3.00	3.50
1963	—	PF65 120				
1964	4,030,000	—	2.25	2.50	3.00	3.50
1964	—	PF65 4.00				
1965	3,030,000	—	2.25	2.50	3.00	3.50
1965	—	PF65 4.00				
1966	4,481,000	—	2.25	2.50	3.00	3.50
1966	—	PF65 9.00				
1967	1,900,000	—	2.25	2.50	3.00	3.50
1967	—	PF65 15.00				
1968	4,812,000	—	2.25	2.50	3.00	3.50
1968	19,700	PF65 8.00				

KM# 2889a 5 SCHILLING

4.80 g., Copper-Nickel, 23.5 mm. **Obv:** Lippizaner stallion with rider, rearing left **Rev:** Austrian shield divides date, value above, sprays below **Edge:** Plain

Date	Mintage	VF20	XF40	MS60	MS63	MS65
1968	2,075,000	—	—	—	1.00	1.50
1969	41,222,000	—	—	—	1.00	1.50
1969	21,000	PF65 1.00				
1970	15,770,700	—	—	—	1.00	1.50
1970	92,300	PF65 1.00				
1971	21,422,000	—	—	—	1.00	1.50
1971	84,000	PF65 1.00				
1972	5,430,000	—	—	—	1.00	1.50
1972	75,000	PF65 1.00				
1973	8,259,000	—	—	—	1.00	1.50
1973	87,000	PF65 1.00				
1974	17,956,000	—	—	—	1.00	1.50
1974	76,000	PF65 1.00				
1975	6,849,000	—	—	—	1.00	1.50
1975	49,000	PF65 1.00				
1976	1,458,000	—	—	—	1.00	1.50
1976	44,000	PF65 1.00				
1977	6,423,000	—	—	—	1.00	1.50
1977	44,000	PF65 1.00				
1978	9,907,000	—	—	—	1.00	1.50
1978	43,000	PF65 1.00				
1979	11,607,000	—	—	—	1.00	1.50
1979	44,000	PF65 1.00				
1980	14,898,000	—	—	—	1.00	1.50
1980	48,000	PF65 1.00				
1981	13,837,000	—	—	—	1.00	1.50
1981	49,000	PF65 1.00				
1982	4,950,000	—	—	—	1.00	1.50
1982	50,000	PF65 1.00				
1983	9,268,000	—	—	—	1.00	1.50
1983	65,000	PF65 1.00				
1984	13,763,000	—	—	—	1.00	2.00
1984	65,000	PF65 1.00				
1985	12,754,000	—	—	—	1.00	2.00
1985	45,000	PF65 1.00				
1986	16,558,000	—	—	—	1.00	2.00
1986	42,000	PF65 1.00				
1987	6,758,000	—	—	—	1.00	2.00
1987	42,000	PF65 1.00				
1988	10,161,000	—	—	—	1.00	2.00
1988	39,000	PF65 1.00				
1989	24,045,000	—	—	—	1.00	2.00
1989	38,000	PF65 1.00				
1990	36,512,000	—	—	—	1.00	2.00
1990	35,000	PF65 1.00				
1991	24,000,000	—	—	—	1.00	2.00
1991	27,000	PF65 1.00				
1992	20,000,000	—	—	—	1.00	2.00
1992 Special Unc	25,000	—	—	—	—	2.50
1993	20,000,000	—	—	—	1.00	2.00
1993 Special Unc	28,000	—	—	—	—	2.50
1994	10,000,000	—	—	—	1.00	2.00
1994 Special Unc	25,000	—	—	—	—	3.50
1995	20,000,000	—	—	—	1.00	2.00
1995 Special Unc	27,000	—	—	—	—	2.50
1996	10,000,000	—	—	—	1.00	2.00
1996 Special Unc	25,000	—	—	—	—	3.50
1997	10,000,000	—	—	—	1.00	2.00
1997 Special Unc	25,000	—	—	—	—	4.00

Date	Mintage	VF20	XF40	MS60	MS63	MS65
1998	10,000,000	—	—	—	1.00	2.00
1998 Special Unc	25,000	—	—	—	—	1.50
1999 Special Unc	50,000	—	—	—	—	1.50
2000 Special Unc	75,000	—	—	—	—	1.50

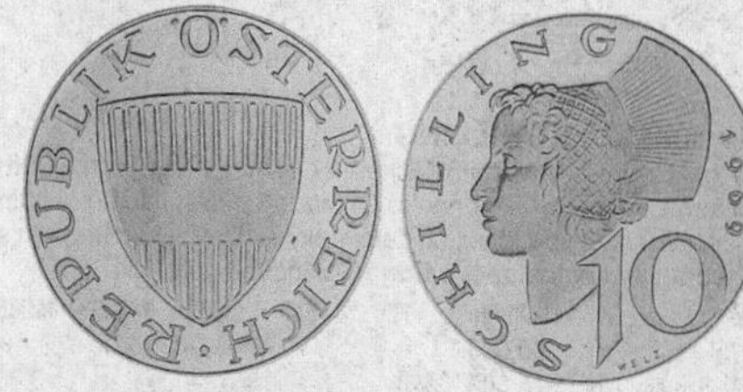

KM# 2882 10 SCHILLING
7.50 g., 0.640 Silver 0.1543 oz. ASW, 26 mm. **Obv:** Austrian shield **Rev:** Woman of Wachau, left, value at lower right, date to right of hat **Edge:** Reeded

Date	Mintage	VF20	XF40	MS60	MS63	MS65
1957	15,635,500	—	—	3.50	4.00	5.75
1957	—	PF65 20.50				
1958	27,280,000	—	—	3.50	4.00	5.75
1958	—	PF65 200				
1959	39,235,000	—	—	3.50	4.00	5.75
1959	—	PF65 10.50				
1964	195,000	3.00	4.00	5.75	15.50	25.50
1964	27,000	PF65 4.00				
1965	1,896,500	—	—	3.50	4.00	5.75
1965	—	PF65 4.00				
1966	3,392,000	—	—	3.50	4.00	5.75
1966	—	PF65 4.00				
1967	1,393,500	—	—	3.50	4.00	5.75
1967	—	PF65 4.00				
1968	1,525,000	—	—	3.50	4.00	5.75
1968	15,000	PF65 4.00				
1969	1,316,000	—	—	3.50	4.00	5.75
1969	20,000	PF65 4.00				
1970	4,493,000	—	—	—	—	3.50
1970	89,100	PF65 4.00				
1971	7,320,000	—	—	—	—	3.50
1971	80,000	PF65 4.00				
1972	14,210,000	—	—	—	—	3.50
1972	75,000	PF65 4.00				
1973	14,559,000	—	—	—	—	3.50
1973	80,000	PF65 4.00				

KM# 2918 10 SCHILLING
6.20 g., Copper-Nickel Plated Nickel, 26 mm. **Obv:** Imperial Eagle with Austrian shield on breast, holding hammer and sickle **Rev:** Woman of Wachau left, value and date right of hat **Edge:** Reeded

Date	Mintage	VF20	XF40	MS60	MS63	MS65
1974	59,877,000	—	—	—	1.00	2.00
1974	75,500	PF65 4.00				
1975	16,869,500	—	—	—	1.00	1.50
1975	49,000	PF65 3.00				
1976	13,459,500	—	—	—	1.00	1.50
1976	44,000	PF65 3.00				
1977	3,804,000	—	—	—	1.00	2.00
1977	44,000	PF65 3.00				
1978	6,813,000	—	—	—	1.00	2.00
1978	43,000	PF65 3.00				
1979	11,702,000	—	—	—	1.00	2.00
1979	44,000	PF65 2.50				
1980	10,884,000	—	—	—	1.00	2.00
1980	48,000	PF65 6.50				
1981	9,470,000	—	—	—	1.00	2.00
1981	49,000	PF65 6.50				
1982	4,950,000	—	—	—	1.00	2.00
1982	50,000	PF65 2.50				
1983	8,993,000	—	—	—	1.00	2.00
1983	65,000	PF65 2.50				
1984	7,939,000	—	—	—	1.00	1.50
1984	65,000	PF65 2.50				
1985	9,009,000	—	—	—	1.00	1.50
1985	45,000	PF65 2.50				
1986	8,819,000	—	—	—	1.00	1.50
1986	42,000	PF65 2.50				
1987	9,258,000	—	—	—	1.00	1.50
1987	42,000	PF65 2.50				
1988	9,011,000	—	—	—	1.00	1.50
1988	39,000	PF65 4.50				
1989	16,233,000	—	—	—	1.00	1.50
1989	38,000	PF65 2.50				
1990	27,150,000	—	—	—	1.00	1.50
1990	35,000	PF65 1.00				
1991	18,000,000	—	—	—	1.00	1.50
1991	27,000	PF65 1.00				
1992	10,952,000	—	—	—	1.00	1.50
1992 Special Unc	25,000	—	—	—	—	1.50
1993	12,500,000	—	—	—	1.00	—
1993 Special Unc	28,000	—	—	—	—	1.50
1994	15,000,000	—	—	—	1.00	—
1994 Special Unc	25,000	—	—	—	—	1.50
1995	12,500,000	—	—	—	1.00	—
1995 Special Unc	27,000	—	—	—	—	1.50
1996	12,500,000	—	—	—	1.00	—
1996 Special Unc	25,000	—	—	—	—	1.50
1997	11,000,000	—	—	—	1.00	—
1997 Special Unc	25,000	—	—	—	—	1.50
1998	5,000,000	—	—	—	1.00	—
1998 Special Unc	25,000	—	—	—	—	5.00
1999 Special Unc	50,000	—	—	—	—	1.50
2000 Special Unc	75,000	—	—	—	—	1.50

KM# 2946.1 20 SCHILLING
8.00 g., Copper-Aluminum-Nickel, 27.7 mm. **Obv:** Nine people standing (representing the nine Austrian provinces), center figure holding Austrian shield aloft **Rev:** Numeric value within shaded box within circle, date below box **Edge:** 19 incuse dots

Date	Mintage	VF20	XF40	MS60	MS63	MS65
1980	9,851,500	—	2.00	2.25	2.50	3.00
1980	48,000	PF65 3.00				
1981	450,500	—	2.00	2.25	2.50	3.00
1981	49,000	PF65 3.00				
1991	100,000	—	2.00	2.25	2.50	3.00

KM# 2955.1 20 SCHILLING
8.00 g., Copper-Aluminum-Nickel, 27.7 mm. **Subject:** 250th Anniversary - Birth of Joseph Haydn **Obv:** Value within box, small Austrian shield divides date below **Rev:** Bust of Joseph Haydn, 3/4 right, two dates to his left, his name to his right **Edge:** 19 incuse dots

Date	Mintage	VF20	XF40	MS60	MS63	MS65
1982	3,090,000	—	2.00	2.25	2.50	3.00
1982	50,000	PF65 3.00				
1991	100,000	—	2.00	2.25	2.50	3.00

KM# 2955.2 20 SCHILLING
8.00 g., Copper-Aluminum-Nickel, 27.7 mm. **Subject:** 20th Anniversary - Birth of Joseph Haydn **Obv:** Kurt Bodlak **Rev:** Bust of Joseph Haydn, 3/4 right, two dates to his left, his name to his right **Edge:** Plain

Date	Mintage	VF20	XF40	MS60	MS63	MS65
1992	100,000	—	2.00	2.25	2.50	3.00
1993	180,000	—	2.00	2.25	2.50	3.00

KM# 2960.1 20 SCHILLING
8.00 g., Copper-Aluminum-Nickel, 27.7 mm. **Obv:** Value within box, Austrian shield divides date below **Rev:** Hochosterwitz Castle **Edge:** 19 incuse dots

Date	Mintage	VF20	XF40	MS60	MS63	MS65
1983	1,002,000	—	2.00	2.25	2.50	3.00
1983	65,000	PF65 3.00				
1991	100,000	—	2.00	2.25	2.50	3.00

KM# 2965.1 20 SCHILLING
8.00 g., Copper-Aluminum-Nickel, 27.7 mm. **Obv:** Value within box, Austrian shield divides date below **Rev:** Grafenegg Palace, date at upper left **Edge:** 19 incuse dots

Date	Mintage	VF20	XF40	MS60	MS63	MS65
1984	1,203,000	—	2.00	2.25	2.50	3.00
1984	65,000	PF65 3.00				
1991	140,000	—	2.00	2.25	2.50	3.00

KM# 2970.1 20 SCHILLING
8.00 g., Copper-Aluminum-Nickel, 27.7 mm. **Subject:** 200th Anniversary - Diocese of Linz **Obv:** Value within box, Austrian shield divides date below **Rev:** Two shields on decorative background within circle, two dates below circle **Edge:** 19 incuse dots

Date	Mintage	VF20	XF40	MS60	MS63	MS65
1985	814,000	—	2.00	2.25	2.50	3.00
1985	45,000	PF65 3.00				
1991	100,000	—	2.00	2.25	2.50	3.00

KM# 2975.1 20 SCHILLING
8.00 g., Copper-Aluminum-Nickel, 27.7 mm. **Subject:** 800th Anniversary - Georgenberger Treaty **Obv:** Value within box, Austrian shield divides date below **Rev:** Ottakar IV of Steyr and Leopold V of Austria holding the secret treaty **Edge:** 19 incuse dots

Date	Mintage	VF20	XF40	MS60	MS63	MS65
1986	801,000	—	2.00	2.25	2.50	3.00
1986	42,000	PF65 3.00				
1991	100,000	—	2.00	2.25	2.50	3.00

KM# 2975.2 20 SCHILLING
8.00 g., Copper-Aluminum-Nickel, 27.7 mm. **Subject:** 800th Anniversary - Georgeberger Treaty **Obv:** Value within box, Austrian shield divides date below **Rev:** Ottakar IV of Steyr and Leopold V of Austria holding the secret treaty **Edge:** Plain

Date	Mintage	VF20	XF40	MS60	MS63	MS65
1993	180,000	—	2.00	2.25	2.50	3.00
1992	100,000	—	2.00	2.25	2.50	3.00

KM# 2980.1 20 SCHILLING
8.00 g., Copper-Aluminum-Nickel, 27.7 mm. **Subject:** 300th Anniversary - Birth of Salzburg's Archbishop Thun **Obv:** Value within box, Austrian shield divides date below **Rev:** Bishop's hat above supported arms, dates below supporters, subject name at bottom wth date below **Edge:** 19 incuse dots

Date	Mintage	VF20	XF40	MS60	MS63	MS65
1987	508,000	—	2.00	2.25	2.50	3.00
1987	42,000	PF65 3.00				
1991	100,000	—	2.00	2.25	2.50	3.00

KM# 2980.2 20 SCHILLING

8.00 g., Copper-Aluminum-Nickel, 27.7 mm. **Subject:** 300th Anniversary - Birth of Salzburg's Archbishop Thun **Obv:** Value within box, Austrian shield divides date below **Rev:** Bishop's hat above supported arms, dates below supporters, subject name at bottom with date below **Edge:** Plain

Date	Mintage	VF20	XF40	MS60	MS63	MS65
1992	100,000	—	2.00	2.25	2.50	3.00
1993	180,000	—	2.00	2.25	2.50	3.00

KM# 2988.1 20 SCHILLING

8.00 g., Copper-Aluminum-Nickel, 27.7 mm. **Subject:** Tyrol **Obv:** Value within box, Austrian shield divides date below **Rev:** Crowned eagle - Tyrol **Edge:** 19 incuse dots

Date	Mintage	VF20	XF40	MS60	MS63	MS65
1989	252,000	—	2.00	2.25	2.50	3.00
1989	38,000	PF65 3.00				
1991	100,000	—	2.00	2.25	2.50	3.00

KM# 2988.2 20 SCHILLING

8.00 g., Copper-Aluminum-Nickel, 27.7 mm. **Obv:** Value within box, Austrian shield divides date below **Rev:** Crowned eagle - Tyrol **Edge:** Plain

Date	Mintage	VF20	XF40	MS60	MS63	MS65
1992	100,000	—	2.00	2.25	2.50	3.00
1993	180,000	—	2.00	2.25	2.50	3.00

KM# 2993.1 20 SCHILLING

8.00 g., Copper-Aluminum-Nickel, 27.7 mm. **Obv:** Value within box, Austrian shield divides date below **Rev:** Martinsturm in Bregenz, small shield at upper left **Edge:** 19 incuse dots

Date	Mintage	VF20	XF40	MS60	MS63	MS65
1990	250,000	—	2.00	2.25	2.50	3.00
1990	35,000	PF65 3.00				
1991	100,000	—	2.00	2.25	2.50	3.00

KM# 2993.2 20 SCHILLING

8.00 g., Copper-Aluminum-Nickel, 27.7 mm. **Obv:** Value within box, Austrian shield divides date below **Rev:** Martinsturm in Bregenz, small shield at upper left **Edge:** Plain

Date	Mintage	VF20	XF40	MS60	MS63	MS65
1992	100,000	—	2.00	2.25	2.50	3.00
1993	180,000	—	2.00	2.25	2.50	3.00

KM# 2995.1 20 SCHILLING

8.00 g., Copper-Aluminum-Nickel, 27.7 mm. **Subject:** 200th Anniversary - Birth of Franz Grillparzer **Obv:** Value within shield, Austrian shield divides date below **Rev:** Bust of Franz Grillparzer on left, looking right, theater building on the right **Edge:** 19 incuse dots

Date	Mintage	VF20	XF40	MS60	MS63	MS65
1991	463,000	—	2.00	2.25	2.50	3.00
1991 Special Unc	10,000	—	—	—	—	3.00
1991	27,000	PF65 10.00				

KM# 2995.2 20 SCHILLING

8.00 g., Copper-Aluminum-Nickel, 27.7 mm. **Subject:** 200th Anniversary - Birth of Franz Grillparzer **Obv:** Value within shield, Austrian shield divides date below **Rev:** Bust of Franz Grillparzer on left, looking right, theater building on the right **Edge:** Plain

Date	Mintage	VF20	XF40	MS60	MS63	MS65
1992	100,000	—	2.00	2.25	2.50	3.00
1993	180,000	—	2.00	2.25	2.50	3.00

KM# 2946.2 20 SCHILLING

8.00 g., Copper-Aluminum-Nickel, 27.7 mm. **Obv:** Nine people standing (representing the nine Austrian provinces), center figure holding Austrian shield aloft **Rev:** Numeric value within shaded box within circle, date below box **Edge:** Plain

Date	Mintage	VF20	XF40	MS60	MS63	MS65
1992	100,000	—	2.00	2.25	2.50	3.00
1992 Special Unc	25,000	—	—	—	—	3.00
1993	180,000	—	2.00	2.25	2.50	3.00
1993 Special Unc	28,000	—	—	—	—	3.00

KM# 2960.2 20 SCHILLING

8.00 g., Copper-Aluminum-Nickel, 27.7 mm. **Obv:** Value within box, Austrian shield divides date below **Rev:** Hochosterwitz Castle **Edge:** Plain

Date	Mintage	VF20	XF40	MS60	MS63	MS65
1992	100,000	—	2.00	2.25	2.50	3.00
1993	180,000	—	2.00	2.25	2.50	3.00

KM# 2965.2 20 SCHILLING

8.00 g., Copper-Aluminum-Nickel, 27.7 mm. **Obv:** Value within box, Austrian shield divides date below **Rev:** Grafenegg Palace, date at upper left **Edge:** Plain

Date	Mintage	VF20	XF40	MS60	MS63	MS65
1992	100,000	—	2.00	2.25	2.50	3.00
1993	180,000	—	2.00	2.25	2.50	3.00

KM# 2970.2 20 SCHILLING

8.00 g., Copper-Aluminum-Nickel, 27.7 mm. **Subject:** 200th Anniversary - Diocese of Linz **Obv:** Value within box, Austrian shield divides date below **Rev:** Two shields on decorative background within circle, two dates below circle **Edge:** Plain

Date	Mintage	VF20	XF40	MS60	MS63	MS65
1992	100,000	—	—	—	2.00	2.50
1993	180,000	—	—	—	2.00	2.50

KM# 3016 20 SCHILLING

8.00 g., Copper-Aluminum-Nickel, 27.7 mm. **Subject:** 800th Anniversary - Vienna Mint **Obv:** Value within box, Austrian shield divides date below **Rev:** Vienna Mint, two dates below **Edge:** 19 incuse dots

Date	Mintage	VF20	XF40	MS60	MS63	MS65
1994	2,000,000	—	—	—	2.00	—
1994 Special Unc	37,000	—	—	—	—	3.00

KM# 3022 20 SCHILLING

8.00 g., Copper-Aluminum-Nickel, 27.7 mm. **Subject:** 1000th Anniversary - Krems **Obv:** Value within box, Austrian shield below **Rev:** Krems within box, dates flanking, legend at top **Edge:** 19 incuse dots

Date	Mintage	VF20	XF40	MS60	MS63	MS65
1995	2,000,000	—	—	—	2.00	—
1995 Special Unc	27,000	—	—	—	—	3.00

KM# 3033 20 SCHILLING

8.00 g., Copper-Aluminum-Nickel, 27.7 mm. **Obv:** Value within box, Austrian shield divides date at bottom **Rev:** Bust of Anton Bruckner, 3/4 facing, two dates below, name on the left, building on the right **Edge:** 19 incuse dots

Date	Mintage	VF20	XF40	MS60	MS63	MS65
1996	1,500,000	—	—	—	2.00	—
1996 Special Unc	35,000	—	—	—	—	3.00

KM# 3041 20 SCHILLING

8.00 g., Copper-Aluminum-Nickel, 27.7 mm. **Subject:** 850th Anniversary of St. Stephen's Cathedral **Obv:** Value within box, Austrian shield divides date below **Rev:** St. Stephen's Cathedral, two dates above **Edge:** 19 incuse dots

Date	Mintage	VF20	XF40	MS60	MS63	MS65
1997	700,000	—	—	—	2.00	—
1997 Special Unc	25,000	—	—	—	—	3.00

KM# 3048 20 SCHILLING

8.00 g., Copper-Aluminum-Nickel, 27.7 mm. **Subject:** 500th Anniversary of Michael Pacher's Death **Obv:** Value within box, Austrian shield divides date below **Rev:** Pacher's altar at St. Wolfgang **Edge:** 19 incuse dots

Date	Mintage	VF20	XF40	MS60	MS63	MS65
1998	200,000	—	—	—	2.00	—
1998 Special Unc	25,000	—	—	—	—	3.00

KM# 3056 20 SCHILLING

8.00 g., Copper-Aluminum-Nickel, 27.7 mm. **Obv:** Value within box, Austrian shield divides date below **Rev:** Hugo Von Hofmannsthal **Edge:** 19 incuse dots

Date	Mintage	VF20	XF40	MS60	MS63	MS65
1999	400,000	—	—	—	2.00	—
1999 Special Unc	50,000	—	—	—	—	3.00

KM# 3064 20 SCHILLING

8.00 g., Copper-Aluminum-Nickel, 27.7 mm. **Subject:** 150th Anniversary - First Austrian Postage Stamp **Obv:** Value within box, Austrian shield divides date below **Rev:** Canceled stamp design **Edge:** 19 incuse dots **Mint:** Vienna

Date	Mintage	VF20	XF40	MS60	MS63	MS65
2000	400,000	—	—	—	2.00	—
2000 Special Unc	85,000	—	—	—	—	3.00

KM# 2880 25 SCHILLING

13.00 g., 0.800 Silver 0.3344 oz. ASW, 30 mm. **Subject:** Reopening of the National Theater in Vienna **Obv:** Dragon within 3/4 circle of shields, larger Austrian shield at lower left, value to right of this **Rev:** Muse with mask and lyre **Edge:** Lettered

Date	Mintage	VF20	XF40	MS60	MS63	MS65
1955	1,499,000	—	—	—	6.75	8.00
1955	1,000	PF65 100				

KM# 2881 25 SCHILLING

13.00 g., 0.800 Silver 0.3344 oz. ASW, 30.2 mm. **Subject:** 200th Anniversary - Birth of Wolfgang Mozart **Obv:** Value within beaded circle, small spray of leaves below, surrounded by 3/4 circle of shields, **Rev:** Full length statue of Wolfgang Mozart, two dates below **Edge:** Lettered

Date	Mintage	VF20	XF40	MS60	MS63	MS65
1956	4,999,000	—	—	—	6.75	8.00
1956	1,000	PF65 100				

KM# 2883 25 SCHILLING

13.00 g., 0.800 Silver 0.3344 oz. ASW, 30 mm. **Subject:** 8th Centennial - Mariazell Basilica **Obv:** Value within beaded circle, small spray of leaves below, 3/4 circle of shields surrounding **Rev:** Mariazell Basilica, name below, two dates at bottom **Edge:** Lettered

Date	Mintage	VF20	XF40	MS60	MS63	MS65
1957	4,999,000	—	—	—	6.75	8.00
1957	1,000	PF65 100				

KM# 2884 25 SCHILLING

13.00 g., 0.800 Silver 0.3344 oz. ASW, 30 mm. **Subject:** 100th Anniversary - Birth of Auer von Welsbach, Chemist **Obv:** Value within beaded circle, small spray below, 3/4 circle of shields surrounds **Rev:** Head of Auer von Welsbach, right, date below **Edge:** Lettered

Date	Mintage	VF20	XF40	MS60	MS63	MS65
1958	4,999,000	—	—	—	6.75	8.00
1958	1,000	PF65 475				

KM# 2887 25 SCHILLING

13.00 g., 0.800 Silver 0.3344 oz. ASW, 30 mm. **Subject:** Archduke Johann, 100th Anniversary of Death **Obv:** Dragon within 3/4 circle of shields, larger Austrian shield lower left, value to right of this **Rev:** Collared head of Archduke Johann, right, collar divides date **Edge:** Lettered

Date	Mintage	VF20	XF40	MS60	MS63	MS65
1959	1,899,000	—	—	—	6.75	8.00
1959	1,000	PF65 100				

KM# 2890 25 SCHILLING

13.00 g., 0.800 Silver 0.3344 oz. ASW, 30 mm. **Subject:** Carinthian Plebiscite, 40th Anniversary **Obv:** Value within beaded circle above small spray of leaves, 3/4 circle of shields surrounds **Rev:** Large urn dividing two standing figures, shield below urn divides date **Edge:** Lettered

Date	Mintage	VF20	XF40	MS60	MS63	MS65
1960	1,599,000	—	—	—	6.75	8.00
1960	1,000	PF65 150				

KM# 2891 25 SCHILLING

13.00 g., 0.800 Silver 0.3344 oz. ASW, 30 mm. **Subject:** 40th Anniversary - Burgenland, Haydenkirche in Eisenstadt **Obv:** Value within beaded circle, small sprays below, 3/4 circle of shields surrounding **Rev:** Building, two dates lower left **Edge:** Lettered

Date	Mintage	VF20	XF40	MS60	MS63	MS65
1961	1,399,000	—	—	—	6.75	8.00
1961	1,000	PF65 75.00				

KM# 2892 25 SCHILLING

13.00 g., 0.800 Silver 0.3344 oz. ASW, 30 mm. **Obv:** Value within beaded circle, small spray of leaves below, 3/4 circle of shields surrounding **Rev:** Head of Anton Bruckner, right, Composer, date below **Edge:** Lettered

Date	Mintage	VF20	XF40	MS60	MS63	MS65
1962	2,399,000	—	—	—	6.75	8.00
1962	1,000	PF65 75.00				

KM# 2893 25 SCHILLING

13.00 g., 0.800 Silver 0.3344 oz. ASW, 30 mm. **Subject:** Prince Eugen, 300th Anniversary of Birth **Obv:** Value within beaded circle, small spray of leaves below, 3/4 circle of shields surrounding **Rev:** Half-length figure of Prince Eugen pointing, left, facing right, date below **Edge:** Lettered

Date	Mintage	VF20	XF40	MS60	MS63	MS65
1963	1,994,069	—	—	—	6.75	8.00
1963	5,931	PF65 25.00				

KM# 2895.1 25 SCHILLING

13.00 g., 0.800 Silver 0.3344 oz. ASW, 30 mm. **Obv:** Value within circle of shields **Rev:** Head of Franz Grillparzer, Poet, right, date below **Edge:** Lettering

Date	Mintage	VF20	XF40	MS60	MS63	MS65
1964	1,665,000	—	—	—	6.75	8.00
1964	35,000	PF65 7.25				

KM# 2895.2 25 SCHILLING

13.00 g., 0.800 Silver 0.3344 oz. ASW, 30 mm. **Obv:** Value within beaded circle, small spray of leaves below, surrounded by 3/4 circle of shields **Rev:** Head of Franz Grillparzer, right, date below **Edge:** Lettered **Note:** Obverse; Nine shields, (error)

Date	Mintage	VF20	XF40	MS60	MS63	MS65
1964	3,660	PF65 125				

KM# 2897 25 SCHILLING

13.00 g., 0.800 Silver 0.3344 oz. ASW, 30 mm. **Subject:** 150th Anniversary - Vienna Technical High School **Obv:** Value within circle of shields **Rev:** J.J. Ritter von Prechtl, technologist, director **Edge:** Lettered

Date	Mintage	VF20	XF40	MS60	MS63	MS65
1965	1,563,000	—	—	—	6.75	8.00
1965	37,000	PF65 7.25				

KM# 2899 25 SCHILLING

13.00 g., 0.800 Silver 0.3344 oz. ASW, 30 mm. **Subject:** Ferdinand Raimund, 130th Anniversary of Death **Obv:** Value within circle of shields **Rev:** 1/2-length figure of Ferdinand Raimund, arms crossed, 3/4 right, date on right **Edge:** Lettered

Date	Mintage	VF20	XF40	MS60	MS63	MS65
1966	1,388,200	—	—	—	6.75	8.00
1966	75,000					

KM# 2901 25 SCHILLING

13.00 g., 0.800 Silver 0.3344 oz. ASW, 30 mm. **Subject:** 250th Anniversary - Birth of Maria Theresa, Empress **Obv:** Value within circle of shields **Rev:** Bust of Maria Theresa, right, divides dates, date below right shoulder **Edge:** Lettered

Date	Mintage	VF20	XF40	MS60	MS63	MS65
1967	2,472,200	—	—	—	6.75	8.00
1967	27,800	PF65 7.25				

KM# 2903 25 SCHILLING

13.00 g., 0.800 Silver 0.3344 oz. ASW, 30 mm. **Subject:** Von

Hildebrandt, 300th Anniversary of Birth **Obv:** Value within circle of shields **Rev:** Main gateway to Belvedere Castle **Edge:** Lettered

Date	Mintage	VF20	XF40	MS60	MS63	MS65
1968	1,258,200	—	—	—	6.75	8.00
1968	41,800	PF65 7.25				

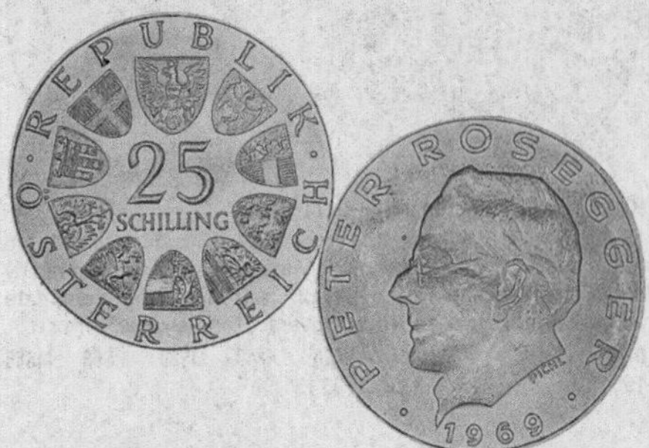

KM# 2905 25 SCHILLING

13.00 g., 0.800 Silver 0.3344 oz. ASW, 30 mm. **Obv:** Value within circle of shields **Rev:** Head of Peter Rosegger, poet, writer left, date below **Edge:** Lettered

Date	Mintage	VF20	XF40	MS60	MS63	MS65
1969	1,356,400	—	—	—	6.75	8.00
1969	43,600	PF65 7.25				

KM# 2907 25 SCHILLING

13.00 g., 0.800 Silver 0.3344 oz. ASW, 30 mm. **Subject:** 100th Anniversary - Birth of Franz Lehar, Composer **Obv:** Value within circle of shields **Rev:** Head of Franz Lehar, 3/4 left, date to the left, two dates below **Edge:** Lettered

Date	Mintage	VF20	XF40	MS60	MS63	MS65
1970	1,660,900	—	—	—	6.75	8.00
1970	139,100	PF65 7.25				

KM# 2910 25 SCHILLING

13.00 g., 0.800 Silver 0.3344 oz. ASW, 30 mm. **Subject:** 200th Anniversary - Vienna Bourse **Obv:** Value within circle of shields **Rev:** City building, two dates below, Austrian shield lower right **Edge:** Lettered

Date	Mintage	VF20	XF40	MS60	MS63	MS65
1971	1,804,000	—	—	—	6.75	8.00
1971	196,000	PF65 7.25				

KM# 2912 25 SCHILLING

13.00 g., 0.800 Silver 0.3344 oz. ASW, 30 mm. **Subject:** 50th Anniversary - Death of Carl M. Ziehrer, Composer **Obv:** Value within circle of shields **Rev:** Head of Carl M. Ziehrer, facing, three dates below **Edge:** Lettered

Date	Mintage	VF20	XF40	MS60	MS63	MS65
ND-1972	1,955,000	—	—	—	6.75	8.00
ND-1972	145,000	PF65 7.25				

KM# 2915 25 SCHILLING

13.00 g., 0.800 Silver 0.3344 oz. ASW, 30 mm. **Subject:** 100th Anniversary - Birth of Max Reinhardt, Producer, Theatrical manager **Obv:** Value within circle of shields **Rev:** Head of Max Reinhardt, left, three dates below **Edge:** Lettered

Date	Mintage	VF20	XF40	MS60	MS63	MS65
ND-1973	2,322,800	—	—	—	6.75	8.00
ND-1973	177,200	PF65 7.25				

KM# 2888 50 SCHILLING

20.00 g., 0.900 Silver 0.5787 oz. ASW, 34 mm. **Subject:** 150th Anniversary - Liberation of Tyrol **Obv:** Imperial Eagle within 3/4 circle of shields, wreath encircling head **Rev:** Andreas Hofer facing forward, two dates below **Edge:** Lettered

Date	Mintage	VF20	XF40	MS60	MS63	MS65
ND-1959	2,999,000	—	—	—	—	12.00
ND-1959	1,000	PF65 200				

KM# 2894 50 SCHILLING

20.00 g., 0.900 Silver 0.5787 oz. ASW, 34 mm. **Subject:** 600th Anniversary - Union with Tirol **Obv:** Value within beaded circle, small spray below, 3/4 circle of shields surrounding **Rev:** Arms of Tyrol and Austria above two dates **Edge:** Lettered

Date	Mintage	VF20	XF40	MS60	MS63	MS65
ND-1963	2,089,600	—	—	—	—	12.00
ND-1963	10,400	PF65 12.50				

KM# 2896 50 SCHILLING

20.00 g., 0.900 Silver 0.5787 oz. ASW, 34 mm. **Series:** Winter Olympics **Obv:** Value within beaded circle, small spray of leaves below, 3/4 circle of shields surrounding **Rev:** Innsbruck - Ski jumper, left, Olympic logo above **Edge:** Lettered

Date	Mintage	VF20	XF40	MS60	MS63	MS65
1964	2,832,050	—	—	—	—	12.00
1964	67,950	PF65 12.00				

KM# 2898 50 SCHILLING

20.00 g., 0.900 Silver 0.5787 oz. ASW, 34 mm. **Subject:** 600th Anniversary - Vienna University **Obv:** Value within circle of shields **Rev:** Crowned head, 3/4 right **Edge:** Lettered

Date	Mintage	VF20	XF40	MS60	MS63	MS65
ND-1965	2,163,000	—	—	—	—	12.00
ND-1965	37,000	PF65 12.00				

KM# 2900 50 SCHILLING

20.00 g., 0.900 Silver 0.5787 oz. ASW, 34 mm. **Subject:** National Bank, 150th Anniversary **Obv:** Value within circle of shields **Rev:** National Bank building above two line inscription, two dates below **Edge:** Lettered

Date	Mintage	VF20	XF40	MS60	MS63	MS65
ND-1966	1,782,600	—	—	—	—	12.00
ND-1966	17,400	PF65 12.50				

KM# 2902 50 SCHILLING

20.00 g., 0.900 Silver 0.5787 oz. ASW, 34 mm. **Subject:** Centennial of the Blue Danube Waltz **Rev:** Johann Strauss the Younger, playing the violin, date below **Edge:** Lettered

Date	Mintage	VF20	XF40	MS60	MS63	MS65
1967	2,973,900	—	—	—	—	12.00
1967	26,100	PF65 12.50				

KM# 2904.1 50 SCHILLING

20.00 g., 0.900 Silver 0.5787 oz. ASW, 34 mm. **Subject:** Republic - 50th Anniversary **Obv:** Value within circle of shields **Rev:** Parliament building in Vienna, matte surface between pillars, dates divided at bottom **Edge:** Lettered

Date	Mintage	VF20	XF40	MS60	MS63	MS65
ND-1968	1,660,200	—	—	—	—	12.00
ND-1968	39,800	PF65 12.00				

KM# 2904.2 50 SCHILLING

20.00 g., 0.900 Silver 0.5787 oz. ASW, 34 mm. **Subject:** Republic - 50th Anniversary **Obv:** Value within circle of shields **Rev:** Parliament building in Vienna, proof surface between pillars, dates divided at bottom **Edge:** Lettered

Date	Mintage	VF20	XF40	MS60	MS63	MS65
1968	—	PF65 35.00				

KM# 2904.3 50 SCHILLING

20.00 g., 0.900 Silver 0.5787 oz. ASW, 34 mm. **Subject:** Republic - 50th Anniversary **Obv:** Value within circle of shields **Rev:** Parliament building in Vienna, proof surface between pillars and below building wings, dates divided at bottom **Edge:** Lettered

Date	Mintage	VF20	XF40	MS60	MS63	MS65
1968	—	PF65 35.00				

KM# 2906 50 SCHILLING

20.00 g., 0.900 Silver 0.5787 oz. ASW, 34 mm. **Subject:** 450th Anniversary - Death of Maximilian I **Obv:** Value within circle of shields **Rev:** Bust of Maximillian I with hat, right, dates in legend **Edge:** Lettered

Date	Mintage	VF20	XF40	MS60	MS63	MS65
1969	2,045,000	—	—	—	—	12.00
1969	55,000	PF65 12.00				

KM# 2908 50 SCHILLING

20.00 g., 0.900 Silver 0.5787 oz. ASW, 34 mm. **Subject:** 300th Anniversary - Innsbruck University **Obv:** Value within circle of shields **Rev:** 1673 University seal, date at bottom **Edge:** Lettered

Date	Mintage	VF20	XF40	MS60	MS63	MS65
1970	2,087,300	—	—	—	—	12.00
1970	112,700	PF65 12.00				

KM# 2909 50 SCHILLING

20.00 g., 0.900 Silver 0.5787 oz. ASW, 34 mm. **Subject:** 100th Anniversary - Birth of Dr. Karl Renner, president **Obv:** Value within circle of shields **Rev:** Head of Dr. Karl Renner, right, date on left collar, two dates at left **Edge:** Lettered

Date	Mintage	VF20	XF40	MS60	MS63	MS65
1970	2,213,800	—	—	—	—	12.00
1970	286,200	PF65 12.00				

KM# 2911 50 SCHILLING

20.00 g., 0.900 Silver 0.5787 oz. ASW, 34 mm. **Subject:** 80th Anniversary - Birth of Julius Raab, chancellor **Obv:** Value within circle of shields **Rev:** Head of Julius Raab, right, date below, two dates at left **Edge:** Lettered

Date	Mintage	VF20	XF40	MS60	MS63	MS65
1971	2,317,000	—	—	—	—	12.00
1971	183,000	PF65 12.00				

KM# 2913 50 SCHILLING

20.00 g., 0.900 Silver 0.5787 oz. ASW, 34 mm. **Subject:** 350th Anniversary - Salzburg University **Obv:** Value within circle of shields **Rev:** Great seal of the University within circle, three dates below **Edge:** Lettered

Date	Mintage	VF20	XF40	MS60	MS63	MS65
ND-1972	2,864,000	—	—	—	—	12.00
ND-1972	136,000	PF65 12.00				

KM# 2914 50 SCHILLING

20.00 g., 0.900 Silver 0.5787 oz. ASW, 34 mm. **Subject:** 100th Anniversary - Institute of Agriculture **Obv:** Value within circle of shields **Rev:** Institute of Agriculture, shields flank inscription and dates below **Edge:** Lettered

Date	Mintage	VF20	XF40	MS60	MS63	MS65
ND-1972	1,891,000	—	—	—	—	12.00
ND-1972	109,000	PF65 12.00				

KM# 2916 50 SCHILLING

20.00 g., 0.900 Silver 0.5787 oz. ASW, 34 mm. **Subject:** 500th Anniversary - Bummerl House **Obv:** Value within circle of shields **Rev:** Bummerl House within circle, two shields flank date at top **Edge:** Lettered

Date	Mintage	VF20	XF40	MS60	MS63	MS65
1973	2,841,800	—	—	—	—	12.00
1973	158,200	PF65 12.00				

KM# 2917 50 SCHILLING

20.00 g., 0.900 Silver 0.5787 oz. ASW, 34 mm. **Subject:** 100th Anniversary - Birth of Dr. Theodor Korner, President **Obv:** Value within circle of shields **Rev:** Head of Dr. Theodor Korner, right, three dates below **Edge:** Lettered

Date	Mintage	VF20	XF40	MS60	MS63	MS65
ND-1973	2,868,400	—	—	—	—	12.00
ND-1973	131,600	PF65 12.00				

KM# 2919 50 SCHILLING

20.00 g., 0.640 Silver 0.4115 oz. ASW, 34 mm. **Subject:** Vienna International Flower show **Obv:** Value within circle of shields **Rev:** International Flower Show, date at bottom **Edge:** Lettered

Date	Mintage	VF20	XF40	MS60	MS63	MS65
1974	2,279,000	—	—	—	—	8.75
1974	221,000	PF65 8.75				

KM# 2920 50 SCHILLING

20.00 g., 0.640 Silver 0.4115 oz. ASW, 34 mm. **Subject:** 125th Anniversary - Austrian Police Force **Obv:** Value within circle of shields **Rev:** Imperial Eagle on shield, within wreath, within circle **Edge:** Lettered

Date	Mintage	VF20	XF40	MS60	MS63	MS65
ND-1974	2,258,600	—	—	—	—	8.75
ND-1974	241,400	PF65 8.75				

KM# 2921 50 SCHILLING

20.00 g., 0.640 Silver 0.4115 oz. ASW, 34 mm. **Subject:** 1200th Anniversary - Salzburg Cathedral **Obv:** Value within circle of shields **Rev:** St. Rupert and St. Vincent holding cathedral, date below **Edge:** Lettered

Date	Mintage	VF20	XF40	MS60	MS63	MS65
1974	2,292,600	—	—	—	—	8.75
1974	207,400	PF65 8.75				

KM# 2922 50 SCHILLING

20.00 g., 0.640 Silver 0.4115 oz. ASW, 34 mm. **Subject:** 50th Anniversary - Austrian Broadcasting **Obv:** Value within circle of shields **Rev:** Broadcasting symbol, two dates at top **Edge:** Lettered

Date	Mintage	VF20	XF40	MS60	MS63	MS65
1974	2,290,000	—	—	—	—	8.75
1974	210,000	PF65 8.75				

KM# 2937 50 SCHILLING
20.00 g., 0.640 Silver 0.4115 oz. ASW, 34 mm. **Subject:** 150th Anniversary - Death of Franz Schubert, Composer **Obv:** Value within circle of shields **Rev:** Bust of Franz Schubert, looking left, date below **Edge:** Lettered

Date	Mintage	VF20	XF40	MS60	MS63	MS65
1978	1,868,000	—	—	—	—	8.75
1978	132,000	PF65 8.75				

KM# 3038 50 SCHILLING
8.15 g., Bi-Metallic Copper-Nickel Clad Nickel center in Aluminum-Bronze ring, 26.5 mm. **Subject:** Austrian Millennium **Obv:** Circle of provincial arms around denomination **Rev:** Arms below Heinrich I as knight on horse back, within circle, two dates at right

Date	Mintage	VF20	XF40	MS60	MS63	MS65
ND-1996	900,000	—	—	—	5.00	—
ND-1996 Special Unc	100,000	—	—	—	—	5.00

KM# 3044 50 SCHILLING
8.15 g., Bi-Metallic Copper-Nickel Clad Nickel center in Aluminum-Bronze ring, 26.5 mm. **Subject:** 100th Anniversary - Wiener Secession **Obv:** Value within circle of provincial arms **Rev:** Vienna Secession building portal within circle, two dates at bottom, divided

Date	Mintage	VF20	XF40	MS60	MS63	MS65
ND-1997	1,500,000	—	—	—	5.00	—
ND-1997 Special Unc	100,000	—	—	—	—	5.00

KM# 3050 50 SCHILLING
8.15 g., Bi-Metallic Copper-Nickel Clad Nickel center in Aluminum-Bronze ring, 26.5 mm. **Subject:** Austrian Presidency of the European Union **Obv:** Value within circle of provincial arms **Rev:** New Hofburg palace with logo, within circle, date at bottom

Date	Mintage	VF20	XF40	MS60	MS63	MS65
1998	1,200,000	—	—	—	5.00	—
1998 Special Unc	100,000	—	—	—	—	5.00

KM# 3053 50 SCHILLING
8.15 g., Bi-Metallic Copper-Nickel Clad Nickel center in Aluminum-Bronze ring, 26.5 mm. **Obv:** Value within circle of provincial arms **Rev:** Head of Konrad Lorenz, looking right, with three Greylag geese on the right, within circle, two dates below circle

Date	Mintage	VF20	XF40	MS60	MS63	MS65
1998	1,200,000	—	—	—	5.00	—
1998 Special Unc	100,000	—	—	—	—	5.00

KM# 3057 50 SCHILLING
8.15 g., Bi-Metallic Copper-Nickel Clad Nickel center in Aluminum-Bronze ring, 26.5 mm. **Subject:** Euro Currency **Obv:** Value within circle of provincial arms **Rev:** Euro currency designs within circle, date below

Date	Mintage	VF20	XF40	MS60	MS63	MS65
1999	1,200,000	—	—	—	5.00	—
1999 Special Unc	100,000	—	—	—	—	5.00

KM# 3061 50 SCHILLING
8.15 g., Bi-Metallic Copper-Nickel clad Nickel center in Aluminum-Bronze ring, 26.5 mm. **Subject:** Centenary - Death of Johann Strauss **Obv:** Value within circle of provincial arms **Rev:** Bust of Johann Strauss, facing right, two dates to his right, two figures to his left, all within circle, music notes below circle **Mint:** Vienna

Date	Mintage	VF20	XF40	MS60	MS63	MS65
ND-1999	600,000	—	—	—	5.00	—
ND-1999 Special Unc	100,000	—	—	—	—	5.00

KM# 3066 50 SCHILLING
8.15 g., Bi-Metallic Copper-Nickel clad Nickel center in Aluminum-Bronze ring, 26.5 mm. **Obv:** Value within circle of provincial arms **Rev:** Bust of Sigmund Freud facing 1/4 left, two dates at upper right, all within circle **Edge:** Plain **Mint:** Vienna

Date	Mintage	VF20	XF40	MS60	MS63	MS65
ND-2000	600,000	—	—	—	5.00	—
ND-2000 Special Unc	90,000	—	—	—	—	5.00

KM# 3070 50 SCHILLING
8.15 g., Bi-Metallic Copper-Nickel clad Nickel center in Aluminum-Bronze ring, 26.5 mm. **Obv:** Value within circle of provincial arms **Rev:** Antique automobile on left and portrait of Ferdinand Porsche, facing, on right within circle, two dates lower right of circle **Edge:** Plain **Mint:** Vienna

Date	Mintage	VF20	XF40	MS60	MS63	MS65
2000	600,000	—	—	—	5.00	—
2000 Special Unc	100,000	—	—	—	—	5.00

KM# 2926 100 SCHILLING
24.00 g., 0.640 Silver 0.4938 oz. ASW, 36 mm. **Subject:** Winter Olympics - Innsbruck **Obv:** Value within circle of shields **Rev:** Emblem, Olympic logo above **Edge:** Lettered

Date	Mintage	VF20	XF40	MS60	MS63	MS65
ND-1974	2,256,400	—	—	—	10.00	10.50
ND-1974 Special Unc	300,000	—	—	—	—	10.50
ND-1974	373,600	PF65 10.50				

KM# 2923 100 SCHILLING
24.00 g., 0.640 Silver 0.4938 oz. ASW, 36 mm. **Subject:** 150th Anniversary - Birth of Johann Strauss the Younger, Composer **Obv:** Value within circle of shields **Rev:** Monument with standing statue of Strauss with violin, date below **Edge:** Lettered

Date	Mintage	VF20	XF40	MS60	MS63	MS65
1975	2,515,000	—	—	—	10.00	10.50
1975 Special Unc	131,400	—	—	—	—	10.50
1975	208,600	PF65 10.50				

KM# 2924 100 SCHILLING
24.00 g., 0.640 Silver 0.4938 oz. ASW, 36 mm. **Subject:** 20th Anniversary - State Treaty **Obv:** Box surrounds stylized Imperial Eagle, Austrian shield on breast, holding hammer and sickle, value below **Rev:** Round Austrian shield at center, date below **Edge:** Lettered

Date	Mintage	VF20	XF40	MS60	MS63	MS65
1975	3,015,000	—	—	—	10.00	10.50
1975 Special Unc	200,000	—	—	—	—	10.50
1975	225,000	PF65 10.50				

KM# 2925 100 SCHILLING
24.00 g., 0.640 Silver 0.4938 oz. ASW, 36 mm. **Subject:** 50th Anniversary - Schilling **Obv:** Box surrounds stylized Imperial Eagle, Austrian shield on breast, holding hammer and sickle, value below **Rev:** Sower, a plowed field **Edge:** Lettered

Date	Mintage	VF20	XF40	MS60	MS63	MS65
1975	3,018,000	—	—	—	10.00	10.50
1975 Special Unc	216,000	—	—	—	—	10.50
1975	201,000	PF65 10.50				

KM# 2927 100 SCHILLING
24.00 g., 0.640 Silver 0.4938 oz. ASW, 36 mm. **Subject:** Winter Olympics - Innsbruck **Obv:** Box surrounds stylized Imperial Eagle, Austrian shield on breast, holding hammer and sickle above value, small shield below box **Rev:** Buildings and Olympic logo **Edge:** Lettered

Date	Mintage	VF20	XF40	MS60	MS63	MS65
ND-1975 (h)	2,515,000	—	—	—	10.00	10.50
ND-1975 (h) Special Unc	177,000	—	—	—	—	10.50
ND-1975 (h)	223,000	PF65 10.50				
ND-1975 (v)	2,516,000	—	—	—	10.00	10.50
ND-1975 (v) Special Unc	202,000	—	—	—	—	10.50
ND-1975 (v)	232,000	PF65 10.50				

KM# 2928 100 SCHILLING
24.00 g., 0.640 Silver 0.4938 oz. ASW, 36 mm. **Subject:** Winter Olympics - Innsbruck **Obv:** Box surrounds stylized Imperial Eagle, Austrian shield on breast, holding hammer and sickle above value, small shield below box **Rev:** Skier **Edge:** Lettered

Date	Mintage	VF20	XF40	MS60	MS63	MS65
ND-1975 (h)	2,516,000	—	—	—	10.00	10.50
ND-1975 (h) Special Unc	120,000	—	—	—	—	10.50
ND-1975 (h)	179,000	PF65 10.50				
ND-1975 (v)	2,516,000	—	—	—	10.00	10.50
ND-1975 (v) Special Unc	124,800	—	—	—	—	10.50
ND-1975 (v)	184,200	PF65 10.50				

KM# 2929 100 SCHILLING
24.00 g., 0.640 Silver 0.4938 oz. ASW, 36 mm. **Subject:** Winter Olympics - Innsbruck **Obv:** Box surrounds stylized Imperial Eagle, Austrian shield on breast, above value, small shield below box **Rev:** Ski jump, Olympic logo upper left, circle surrounds, date lower right **Edge:** Lettered

Date	Mintage	VF20	XF40	MS60	MS63	MS65
ND-1976 (h)	2,505,000	—	—	—	10.00	—
ND-1976 (h) Special Unc	105,600	—	—	—	—	10.50
ND-1976 (h)	179,400	PF65 10.50				
ND-1976 (v)	2,508,000	—	—	—	10.00	10.50
ND-1976 (v) Special Unc	119,000	—	—	—	—	10.50
ND-1976 (v)	188,000	PF65 10.50				

KM# 2930 100 SCHILLING
24.00 g., 0.640 Silver 0.4938 oz. ASW, 36 mm. **Subject:** 200th Anniversary - Burgtheater **Obv:** Value within circle of shields **Rev:** Burgtheater, small crowned double eagle divides dates at top **Edge:** Lettered

Date	Mintage	VF20	XF40	MS60	MS63	MS65
ND-1976	1,518,600	—	—	—	10.00	10.50
ND-1976 Special Unc	111,400	—	—	—	—	10.50
ND-1976	220,000	PF65 10.50				

KM# 2931 100 SCHILLING
24.00 g., 0.640 Silver 0.4938 oz. ASW, 36 mm. **Subject:** 1000th Anniversary - Carinthia **Obv:** Box surrounds stylized Imperial Eagle, Austrian shield on breast, value below **Rev:** Monument, shield at lower right, two dates at bottom **Edge:** Lettered

Date	Mintage	VF20	XF40	MS60	MS63	MS65
ND-1976	1,529,000	—	—	—	10.00	10.50
ND-1976 Special Unc	103,000	—	—	—	—	10.50
ND-1976	168,000	PF65 10.50				

KM# 2932 100 SCHILLING
24.00 g., 0.640 Silver 0.4938 oz. ASW, 36 mm. **Subject:** 175th Anniversary - Birth of Johann Nestroy, Singer **Obv:** Value surrounds Imperial Eagle with Austrian shield on breast **Rev:** Head of Johann Nestroy, 3/4 left, two dates on the right, one date on left **Edge:** Lettered

Date	Mintage	VF20	XF40	MS60	MS63	MS65
1976	1,671,400°	—	—	—	10.00	10.50
1976 Special Unc	90,000	—	—	—	—	10.50
1976	138,600	PF65 10.50				

KM# 2934 100 SCHILLING
24.00 g., 0.640 Silver 0.4938 oz. ASW, 36 mm. **Subject:** 1200th Anniversary - Kremsmunster Monastery **Obv:** Value within circle of shields **Rev:** Chalice, divides dates at top **Edge:** Lettered

Date	Mintage	VF20	XF40	MS60	MS63	MS65
ND-1977	1,782,000	—	—	—	10.00	10.50
ND-1977 Select	83,000	—	—	—	—	10.50
ND-1977	135,000	PF65 10.50				

KM# 2935 100 SCHILLING
24.00 g., 0.640 Silver 0.4938 oz. ASW, 36 mm. **Subject:** 900th Anniversary - Hohensalzburg Fortress **Obv:** Box surrounds stylized Imperial Eagle, Austrian shield on breast, value below **Rev:** Hohensalzburg Fortress on right, dates divided by four line inscription on left **Edge:** Lettered

Date	Mintage	VF20	XF40	MS60	MS63	MS65
1977	1,802,400	—	—	—	10.00	10.50
1977 Special Unc	75,600	—	—	—	—	10.50
1977	122,000	PF65 10.50				

KM# 2936 100 SCHILLING
24.00 g., 0.640 Silver 0.4938 oz. ASW, 36 mm. **Subject:** 500th Anniversary - Hall Mint **Obv:** Value and three rows of shields within circle, two dates below circle **Rev:** Knight in full armor on armored horseback, right,and four shields, within circle,date in legend, two shields below circle **Edge:** Lettered

Date	Mintage	VF20	XF40	MS60	MS63	MS65
1977	1,794,000	—	—	—	10.00	10.50
1977 Special Unc	74,000	—	—	—	—	10.50
1977	132,000	PF65 10.50				

KM# 2938 100 SCHILLING
24.00 g., 0.640 Silver 0.4938 oz. ASW, 36 mm. **Subject:** 700th Anniversary - Gmunden **Obv:** Box surrounds stylized Imperial Eagle, Austrian shield on breast,holding hammer and sickle, value below **Rev:** Gmunden, building within circle, two dates at upper left **Edge:** Lettered

Date	Mintage	VF20	XF40	MS60	MS63	MS65
1978	1,794,000	—	—	—	10.00	10.50
1978 Special Unc	76,000	—	—	—	—	10.50
1978	130,000	PF65 10.50				

KM# 2939 100 SCHILLING
24.00 g., 0.640 Silver 0.4938 oz. ASW, 36 mm. **Subject:** 700th Anniversary - Battle of Durnkrut and Jedenspeigen **Obv:** Standing figures holding hands form a circle with an Austrian shield at center, value below, beaded circle surrounds all **Rev:** Bust of Rudolf I **Edge:** Lettered

Date	Mintage	VF20	XF40	MS60	MS63	MS65
1978	1,600,000	—	—	—	10.00	10.50
1978 Special Unc	77,000	—	—	—	—	10.50
1978	123,000	PF65 10.50				

KM# 2940 100 SCHILLING

24.00 g., 0.640 Silver 0.4938 oz. ASW, 36 mm. **Subject:** 1100th Anniversary - Founding of Villach **Obv:** Box surrounds stylized Imperial Eagle, Austrian shield on breast, holding hammer and sickle, value below **Rev:** Village divides shields with dates above **Edge:** Lettered

Date	Mintage	VF20	XF40	MS60	MS63	MS65
ND-1978	1,492,000	—	—	—	10.00	10.50
ND-1978 Select	77,000	—	—	—	—	10.50
ND-1978	131,000	PF65 10.50				

KM# 2941 100 SCHILLING

24.00 g., 0.640 Silver 0.4938 oz. ASW, 36 mm. **Subject:** Opening of Arlberg Tunnel **Obv:** Value and three rows of shields within circle, date below circle divided by small hammer and sickle emblem **Rev:** Sun above banner, mountains below, hands in front of mountains, circle surrounds all, two dates in legend, two shields below circle **Edge:** Lettered

Date	Mintage	VF20	XF40	MS60	MS63	MS65
1978	1,770,000	—	—	—	10.00	10.50
1978 Special Unc	74,000	—	—	—	—	10.50
1978	156,000	PF65 10.50				

KM# 2942 100 SCHILLING

24.00 g., 0.640 Silver 0.4938 oz. ASW, 36 mm. **Subject:** 700th Anniversary - Cathedral of Wiener Neustadt **Obv:** Imperial Eagle with Austrian shield on breast, holding hammer and sickle, value below **Rev:** Cathedral, date at bottom **Edge:** Lettered

Date	Mintage	VF20	XF40	MS60	MS63	MS65
1979	1,792,600	—	—	—	10.00	10.50
1979 Special Unc	73,000	—	—	—	—	10.50
1979	134,400	PF65 10.50				

KM# 2943 100 SCHILLING

24.00 g., 0.640 Silver 0.4938 oz. ASW, 36 mm. **Subject:** 200th Anniversary - Inn District **Obv:** Imperial eagle with shield on breast and value **Rev:** Buildings, inscriptions and date **Edge:** Lettered

Date	Mintage	VF20	XF40	MS60	MS63	MS65
1979	1,802,400	—	—	—	10.00	10.50
1979 Special Unc	68,000	—	—	—	—	10.50
1979	129,600	PF65 10.50				

KM# 2944 100 SCHILLING

24.00 g., 0.640 Silver 0.4938 oz. ASW, 36 mm. **Obv:** Value within circle of shields **Rev:** Vienna International center, date bottom right **Edge:** Lettered

Date	Mintage	VF20	XF40	MS60	MS63	MS65
1979	1,783,400	—	—	—	10.00	10.50
1979 Special Unc	72,000	—	—	—	—	10.50
1979	144,600	PF65 10.50				

KM# 2945 100 SCHILLING

24.00 g., 0.640 Silver 0.4938 oz. ASW, 36 mm. **Obv:** Value within circle of shields **Rev:** Festival and Congress Hall at Bregenz, date lower right **Edge:** Lettered

Date	Mintage	VF20	XF40	MS60	MS63	MS65
1979	1,500,000	—	—	—	10.00	10.50
1979 Special Unc	73,400	—	—	—	—	10.50
1979	161,600	PF65 10.50				

KM# 2996 100 SCHILLING

20.00 g., 0.900 Silver 0.5787 oz. ASW, 34 mm. **Obv:** Mozart-Salzburg, value below **Rev:** Mozart with violin and piano, right, two dates at left **Edge:** Reeded

Date	Mintage	VF20	XF40	MS60	MS63	MS65
1991	100,000	PF65 12.00				

KM# 2998 100 SCHILLING

20.00 g., 0.900 Silver 0.5787 oz. ASW, 34 mm. **Obv:** Mozart's Vienna Years- Burgtheater, value below **Rev:** Mozart seated at piano, left, two dates at right **Edge:** Reeded

Date	Mintage	VF20	XF40	MS60	MS63	MS65
1991	100,000	PF65 12.00				

KM# 3001 100 SCHILLING

20.00 g., 0.900 Silver 0.5787 oz. ASW, 34 mm. **Obv:** Rudolph I seated on throne flanked by figures kneeling, value at bottom **Rev:** Half-length figure of Rudolph I, facing **Edge:** Reeded

Date	Mintage	VF20	XF40	MS60	MS63	MS65
1991	75,000	PF65 12.00				

KM# 3003 100 SCHILLING

20.00 g., 0.900 Silver 0.5787 oz. ASW, 34 mm. **Obv:** Two seated figures facing each other, ribbon between heads, value at bottom **Rev:** Half-length figure of Maximillian I, with crown and armor, right **Edge:** Reeded

Date	Mintage	VF20	XF40	MS60	MS63	MS65
1992	75,000	PF65 12.00				

KM# 3005 100 SCHILLING

20.00 g., 0.900 Silver 0.5787 oz. ASW, 34 mm. **Obv:** Theater building, value below **Rev:** Bust of Otto Nicolai, 3/4 right **Edge:** Reeded

Date	Mintage	VF20	XF40	MS60	MS63	MS65
1992	75,000	PF65 12.00				

KM# 3007 100 SCHILLING

20.00 g., 0.900 Silver 0.5787 oz. ASW, 34 mm. **Obv:** Two half-length figures, 3/4 left, above inscription, value at bottom **Rev:** 3/4 length figure of Karl V in armor,facing 1/4 left, shield above each shoulder **Edge:** Reeded

Date	Mintage	VF20	XF40	MS60	MS63	MS65
1992	75,000	PF65 12.00				

KM# 3009 100 SCHILLING

20.00 g., 0.900 Silver 0.5787 oz. ASW, 34 mm. **Obv:** Armed figures on kneeling horses outside of city, value at bottom **Rev:** Kaiser Leopold I, in armor and robe, facing 1/4 right **Edge:** Reeded

Date	Mintage	VF20	XF40	MS60	MS63	MS65
1993	75,000	PF65 12.00				

KM# 3019 100 SCHILLING
20.00 g., 0.900 Silver 0.5787 oz. ASW, 34 mm. **Obv:** City buildings with water in foreground, date below, value at bottom **Rev:** Half-length figure of Franz Joseph I in uniform, 3/4 facing, two small crowns at left **Edge:** Reeded

Date	Mintage	VF20	XF40	MS60	MS63	MS65
1994	75,000	PF65 12.00				

KM# 3020 100 SCHILLING
20.00 g., 0.900 Silver 0.5787 oz. ASW, 34 mm. **Subject:** 1848 Revolution **Obv:** Armed figures and Bishop in front of church, value at bottom **Rev:** Seated half-length figure of Archduke Johann, 3/4 facing, looking right, two dates to right of left hand **Edge:** Reeded

Date	Mintage	VF20	XF40	MS60	MS63	MS65
1994	75,000	PF65 12.00				

KM# 3034 100 SCHILLING
20.00 g., 0.900 Silver 0.5787 oz. ASW, 34 mm. **Subject:** First Republic **Obv:** Columned buildings, statue at right, people in foreground, date below, value at bottom **Rev:** Coin, buildings and symbols, two dates lower right **Edge:** Reeded

Date	Mintage	VF20	XF40	MS60	MS63	MS65
1995	75,000	PF65 12.00				

KM# 3036 100 SCHILLING
20.00 g., 0.900 Silver 0.5787 oz. ASW, 34 mm. **Obv:** Four armored figures divide date, value at bottom **Rev:** Crowned half-length figure of Leopold III, facing, Austrian shield in left hand **Edge:** Reeded

Date	Mintage	VF20	XF40	MS60	MS63	MS65
1996	75,000	PF65 12.00				

KM# 3046 100 SCHILLING
20.00 g., 0.900 Silver 0.5787 oz. ASW, 34 mm. **Series:** Habsburg Tragedies **Obv:** Standing portrait in uniform of Emperor Maximilian of Mexico **Rev:** Miramar palace and the SMS Nowara

Date	Mintage	VF20	XF40	MS60	MS63	MS65
1997	65,000	PF65 12.00				

KM# 3051 100 SCHILLING
20.00 g., 0.900 Silver 0.5787 oz. ASW, 34 mm. **Series:** Habsburg Tragedies **Obv:** Standing portrait in uniform of Crown Prince Rudolf, 3/4 left **Rev:** Hearse with military honor guard

Date	Mintage	VF20	XF40	MS60	MS63	MS65
1998	50,000	PF65 12.00				

KM# 3059 100 SCHILLING
20.00 g., 0.900 Silver 0.5787 oz. ASW, 34 mm. **Series:** Habsburg Tragedies **Obv:** Archduke Franz Ferdinand and Sophie, 3/4 right **Rev:** The Royal couple getting into the car

Date	Mintage	VF20	XF40	MS60	MS63	MS65
1999	50,000	PF65 12.00				

KM# 3063 100 SCHILLING
13.70 g., Bi-Metallic Titanium center in 9.95g 0.900 Silver ring 0.2879 oz. ASW, 34 mm. **Subject:** Communications **Obv:** Computer chip design **Rev:** World map at center in ring **Edge:** Plain **Mint:** Vienna

Date	Mintage	VF20	XF40	MS60	MS63	MS65
2000	50,000					

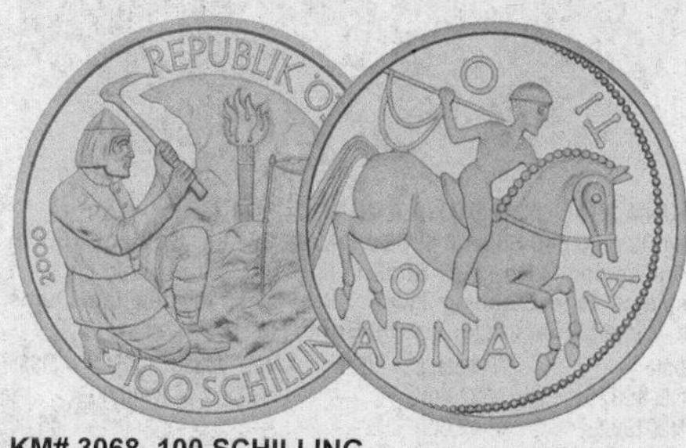

KM# 3068 100 SCHILLING
20.00 g., 0.900 Silver 0.5787 oz. ASW, 34 mm. **Obv:** Celtic salt miner **Rev:** Celtic coin design with mounted warrior **Edge:** Reeded **Mint:** Vienna

Date	Mintage	VF20	XF40	MS60	MS63	MS65
2000	50,000	PF65 12.00				

KM# 3069 100 SCHILLING
20.00 g., 0.900 Silver 0.5787 oz. ASW, 34 mm. **Obv:** Ancient Roman troops crossing pontoon bridge **Rev:** Bust of Marcus Aurelius right **Edge:** Reeded **Mint:** Vienna

Date	Mintage	VF20	XF40	MS60	MS63	MS65
2000	50,000	PF65 12.00				

KM# 3026 200 SCHILLING
33.63 g., 0.925 Silver 1.0001 oz. ASW, 40 mm. **Subject:** Olympic Centennial, 1896-1996 **Obv:** Male and Female figures standing with outstretched arms joined form a circle around Austrian shield, value and date at bottom **Rev:** Ribbon dancer on knees, left, looking up, Olympic logo upper right **Edge Lettering:** CITIUS ALTIUS FORTIUS

Date	Mintage	VF20	XF40	MS60	MS63	MS65
1995	100,000	PF65 21.00				

KM# 3027 200 SCHILLING
33.63 g., 0.925 Silver 1.0001 oz. ASW, 40 mm. **Series:** Olympics **Rev:** Skier **Edge Lettering:** CITIUS ALTIUS FORTIUS

Date	Mintage	VF20	XF40	MS60	MS63	MS65
1995	100,000	PF65 21.00				

KM# 2947 500 SCHILLING
24.00 g., 0.640 Silver 0.4938 oz. ASW, 38 mm. **Subject:** Millennium of Steyr **Obv:** Value within circle of shields **Rev:** City of Steyr **Edge:** Raised lettering

Date	Mintage	VF20	XF40	MS60	MS63	MS65
1980	825,800	—	—	—	40.00	—
1980 Special Unc	63,000	—	—	—	—	45.00
1980	111,200	PF65 42.00				

KM# 2948 500 SCHILLING

24.00 g., 0.640 Silver 0.4938 oz. ASW, 38 mm. **Subject:** 25th Anniversary - State Treaty **Obv:** Value within circle of shields **Rev:** Belvedere Castle, two dates below **Edge:** Raised lettering

Date	Mintage	VF20	XF40	MS60	MS63	MS65
ND-1980	787,000	—	—	—	40.00	—
ND-1980 Special Unc	79,000	—	—	—	—	45.00
ND-1980	134,000	PF65 42.00				

KM# 2949 500 SCHILLING

24.00 g., 0.640 Silver 0.4938 oz. ASW, 38 mm. **Subject:** Bicentennial - Death of Maria Theresa **Obv:** Value within circle of shields **Rev:** Bust of Maria Theresa, right, date at right **Edge:** Raised lettering

Date	Mintage	VF20	XF40	MS60	MS63	MS65
1980	842,000	—	—	—	40.00	—
1980 Special Unc	86,400	—	—	—	—	45.00
1980	171,600	PF65 42.00				

KM# 2950 500 SCHILLING

24.00 g., 0.640 Silver 0.4938 oz. ASW, 38 mm. **Subject:** Centennial - Austrian Red Cross **Obv:** Value within circle of shields **Rev:** Henri Dunant, Philanthropist, two dates at right **Edge:** Raised lettering

Date	Mintage	VF20	XF40	MS60	MS63	MS65
ND-1980	860,000	—	—	—	40.00	—
ND-1980 Special Unc	90,000	—	—	—	—	45.00
ND-1980	200,000	PF65 42.00				

KM# 2951 500 SCHILLING

24.00 g., 0.640 Silver 0.4938 oz. ASW, 38 mm. **Subject:** 800th Anniversary - Verdun Altar **Obv:** Value within circle of shields **Rev:** Man fighting lion in doorway divides dates, within circle **Edge:** Raised lettering

Date	Mintage	VF20	XF40	MS60	MS63	MS65
ND-1981	865,000	—	—	—	40.00	—
ND-1981 Special Unc	85,000	—	—	—	—	45.00
ND-1981	200,000	PF65 42.00				

KM# 2952 500 SCHILLING

24.00 g., 0.640 Silver 0.4938 oz. ASW, 38 mm. **Subject:** 100th Anniversary - Birth of Anton Wildgans, Writer **Obv:** Value within circle of shields **Rev:** Head of Anton Wildgans, left, within circle, three dates outside circle **Edge:** Raised lettering

Date	Mintage	VF20	XF40	MS60	MS63	MS65
1981	911,200	—	—	—	40.00	—
1981 Special Unc	72,000	—	—	—	—	45.00
1981	166,800	PF65 42.00				

KM# 2953 500 SCHILLING

24.00 g., 0.640 Silver 0.4938 oz. ASW, 38 mm. **Subject:** 100th Anniversary - Birth of Otto Bauer, Politician **Obv:** Value within circle of shields **Rev:** Head of Otto Bauer, 3/4 left, two dates at right **Edge:** Raised lettering

Date	Mintage	VF20	XF40	MS60	MS63	MS65
ND-1981	929,000	—	—	—	40.00	—
ND-1981 Special Unc	65,000	—	—	—	—	45.00
ND-1981	156,000	PF65 42.00				

KM# 2954 500 SCHILLING

24.00 g., 0.640 Silver 0.4938 oz. ASW, 38 mm. **Subject:** 200th Anniversary - Religious Tolerance **Obv:** Value within circle of shields **Rev:** Cross with religious symbols below, dates above, within circle **Edge:** Raised lettering

Date	Mintage	VF20	XF40	MS60	MS63	MS65
ND-1981	792,000	—	—	—	40.00	—
ND-1981 Special Unc	60,000	—	—	—	—	45.00
ND-1981	148,000	PF65 42.00				

KM# 2956 500 SCHILLING

24.00 g., 0.640 Silver 0.4938 oz. ASW, 38 mm. **Subject:** 1500th Anniversary - Death of St. Severin **Obv:** Value within circle of shields **Rev:** Standing figure of St. Severin divides dates, urns lower left, pillars at lower right **Edge:** Raised lettering

Date	Mintage	VF20	XF40	MS60	MS63	MS65
ND-1982	837,400	—	—	—	40.00	—
ND-1982 Special Unc	42,600	—	—	—	—	45.00
ND-1982	120,000	PF65 42.00				

KM# 2957 500 SCHILLING

24.00 g., 0.640 Silver 0.4938 oz. ASW, 38 mm. **Subject:** 500 Years of Austrian Printing **Obv:** Value within circle of shields **Rev:** Ancient printing system, date at bottom **Edge:** Raised lettering

Date	Mintage	VF20	XF40	MS60	MS63	MS65
1982	589,600	—	—	—	40.00	—
1982 Special Unc	42,200	—	—	—	—	45.00
1982	118,200	PF65 42.00				

KM# 2958 500 SCHILLING

24.00 g., 0.640 Silver 0.4938 oz. ASW, 38 mm. **Subject:** 825 Years of the Mariazell Shrine **Obv:** Value within circle of shields **Rev:** Standing figure of enshrined Madonna of Mariazell holding child, date below in leaves **Edge:** Raised lettering

Date	Mintage	VF20	XF40	MS60	MS63	MS65
1982	589,600	—	—	—	40.00	—
1982 Special Unc	41,600	—	—	—	—	45.00
1982	118,800	PF65 42.00				

KM# 2959 500 SCHILLING

24.00 g., 0.640 Silver 0.4938 oz. ASW, 38 mm. **Subject:** 80th Anniversary - Birth of Leopold Figl **Obv:** Value within circle of shields **Rev:** Bust of Leopold Figl, left **Edge:** Raised lettering

Date	Mintage	VF20	XF40	MS60	MS63	MS65
1982	344,000	—	—	—	40.00	—
1982 Special Unc	39,600	—	—	—	—	45.00
1982	116,400	PF65 42.00				

KM# 2961 500 SCHILLING

24.00 g., 0.925 Silver 0.7137 oz. ASW, 37 mm. **Subject:** World Cup Horse Jumping Championship **Obv:** Value within circle of shields **Rev:** Horse Jumper **Edge:** Lettered

Date	Mintage	VF20	XF40	MS60	MS63	MS65
1983	313,800	—	—	—	40.00	—
1983 Special Unc	53,800	—	—	—	—	45.00
1983	132,400	PF65 42.00				

KM# 2962 500 SCHILLING
24.00 g., 0.925 Silver 0.7137 oz. ASW, 37 mm. **Subject:** Centennial - Vienna City Hall **Obv:** Value within circle of shields **Rev:** Vienna City Hall, dates below **Edge:** Lettered

Date	Mintage	VF20	XF40	MS60	MS63	MS65
ND-1983	412,000	—	—	—	40.00	—
ND-1983 Special Unc	54,200	—	—	—	—	45.00
ND-1973	133,800	PF65 42.00				

KM# 2963 500 SCHILLING
24.00 g., 0.925 Silver 0.7137 oz. ASW, 37 mm. **Subject:** Catholic Day - Pope's Visit **Obv:** Value within circle of shields **Rev:** Pope Johannes Paul II, left, arms raised, cross with Jesus in left hand, cross dividing date behind head **Edge:** Lettered

Date	Mintage	VF20	XF40	MS60	MS63	MS65
1983	600,000	—	—	—	40.00	—
1983 Special Unc	60,000	—	—	—	—	45.00
1983	140,000	PF65 42.00				

KM# 2964 500 SCHILLING
24.00 g., 0.925 Silver 0.7137 oz. ASW, 37 mm. **Subject:** Centennial - Parliament Building **Obv:** Value within circle of shields **Rev:** Parliament Building, date upper left **Edge:** Lettered

Date	Mintage	VF20	XF40	MS60	MS63	MS65
1983	403,000	—	—	—	40.00	—
1983 Special Unc	59,600	—	—	—	—	45.00
1983	137,400	PF65 42.00				

KM# 2966 500 SCHILLING
24.00 g., 0.925 Silver 0.7137 oz. ASW, 37 mm. **Subject:** 175th Anniversary - Tirolean Revolution **Obv:** Value within circle of shields **Rev:** Statue of Tirolean Man standing, two dates lower left **Edge:** Lettered

Date	Mintage	VF20	XF40	MS60	MS63	MS65
ND-1984	392,200	—	—	—	40.00	—
ND-1984 Special Unc	63,200	—	—	—	—	45.00
ND-1984	144,600	PF65 42.00				

KM# 2967 500 SCHILLING
24.00 g., 0.925 Silver 0.7137 oz. ASW, 37 mm. **Subject:** 100th Anniversary - Commercial Shipping on Lake Constance **Obv:** Value within circle of shields **Rev:** Commercial ship on water, within 3/4 circle, date below, left of small shield **Edge:** Lettered

Date	Mintage	VF20	XF40	MS60	MS63	MS65
1984	394,800	—	—	—	40.00	—
1984 Special Unc	63,000	—	—	—	—	45.00
1984	142,200	PF65 42.00				

KM# 2968 500 SCHILLING
24.00 g., 0.925 Silver 0.7137 oz. ASW, 37 mm. **Subject:** 700th Anniversary - Stams Stift in Tirol **Obv:** Value within circle of shields **Rev:** Building, small shield below **Edge:** Lettered

Date	Mintage	VF20	XF40	MS60	MS63	MS65
1984	403,600	—	—	—	40.00	—
1984 Special Unc	58,400	—	—	—	—	45.00
1984	138,000	PF65 42.00				

KM# 2969 500 SCHILLING
24.00 g., 0.925 Silver 0.7137 oz. ASW, 37 mm. **Subject:** Fanny Elssler, 100th Anniversary of Death **Obv:** Value within circle of shields **Rev:** Full-length view of Fanny Elssler, 1810-1884, in inner circle **Edge:** Lettered

Date	Mintage	VF20	XF40	MS60	MS63	MS65
1984	407,200	—	—	—	40.00	—
1984 Special Unc	57,600	—	—	—	—	45.00
1984	135,200	PF65 42.00				

KM# 2971 500 SCHILLING
24.00 g., 0.925 Silver 0.7137 oz. ASW, 37 mm. **Subject:** 400th Anniversary - Graz University **Obv:** Value within circle of shields **Rev:** Bust of Archduke with ruffled collar, right, date below, within circle **Edge:** Lettered

Date	Mintage	VF20	XF40	MS60	MS63	MS65
1985	431,000	—	—	—	40.00	—
1985 Special Unc	50,000	—	—	—	—	45.00
1985	119,000	PF65 42.00				

KM# 2972 500 SCHILLING
24.00 g., 0.925 Silver 0.7137 oz. ASW, 37 mm. **Subject:** Peace in Austria, 40th Anniversary **Obv:** Value within circle of shields **Rev:** Woman standing in front of Austrian map holding branch of leaves **Edge:** Lettered

Date	Mintage	VF20	XF40	MS60	MS63	MS65
ND-1985	336,800	—	—	—	40.00	—
ND-1985 Special Unc	47,200	—	—	—	—	45.00
ND-1985	116,000	PF65 42.00				

KM# 2973 500 SCHILLING
24.00 g., 0.925 Silver 0.7137 oz. ASW, 37 mm. **Subject:** 500th Anniversary - Canonization of Leopold III **Obv:** Value within circle of shields **Rev:** Crowned standing figure of Leopold III, facing, holding model of church in left hand, divides dates **Edge:** Lettered

Date	Mintage	VF20	XF40	MS60	MS63	MS65
ND-1985	341,600	—	—	—	40.00	—
ND-1985 Special Unc	46,600	—	—	—	—	45.00
ND-1985	111,800	PF65 42.00				

KM# 2974 500 SCHILLING
24.00 g., 0.925 Silver 0.7137 oz. ASW, 37 mm. **Subject:** 2000th Anniversary - Bregenz **Obv:** Value within circle of shields **Rev:** Two coins on coin, left one with laureate head right, right one with shield of arms, date at bottom **Edge:** Lettered

Date	Mintage	VF20	XF40	MS60	MS63	MS65
1985	341,800	—	—	—	40.00	—
1985 Special Unc	46,000	—	—	—	—	45.00
1985	112,200	PF65 42.00				

KM# 2976 500 SCHILLING
24.00 g., 0.925 Silver 0.7137 oz. ASW, 37 mm. **Subject:** 300th Anniversary - St. Florian's Abbey **Obv:** Value within circle of shields **Rev:** St. Florian's Abbey, two dates below, small shield lower left **Edge:** Lettered

Date	Mintage	VF20	XF40	MS60	MS63	MS65
ND-1986	263,800	—	—	—	40.00	—

Date	Mintage	VF20	XF40	MS60	MS63	MS65
ND-1986 Special Unc	39,400	—	—	—	—	45.00
ND-1986	96,800	PF65 42.00				

KM# 2977 500 SCHILLING

24.00 g., 0.925 Silver 0.7137 oz. ASW, 37 mm. **Subject:** 500th Anniversary - First Thaler Coin Struck at Hall Mint **Obv:** Value within circle of shields **Rev:** Crowned figure with scepter, center, small eagle with shield at left, within inner circle, two dates below circle **Edge:** Lettered

Date	Mintage	VF20	XF40	MS60	MS63	MS65
ND-1986	359,800	—	—	—	40.00	—
ND-1986 Special Unc	41,200	—	—	—	—	45.00
ND-1986	99,000	PF65 42.00				

KM# 2978 500 SCHILLING

24.00 g., 0.925 Silver 0.7137 oz. ASW, 37 mm. **Subject:** 250th Anniversary - Birth of Prince Eugene of Savoy **Obv:** Value within circle of shields **Rev:** Man on rearing horse, three dates at bottom **Edge:** Lettered

Date	Mintage	VF20	XF40	MS60	MS63	MS65
1986	359,200	—	—	—	40.00	—
1986 Special Unc	41,200	—	—	—	—	45.00
1986	99,600	PF65 42.00				

KM# 2979 500 SCHILLING

24.00 g., 0.925 Silver 0.7137 oz. ASW, 37 mm. **Subject:** European Conference on Security and Cooperation **Obv:** Value within circle of shields **Rev:** Globe with map at top, inscription below, small shield at bottom with date to right **Edge:** Lettered

Date	Mintage	VF20	XF40	MS60	MS63	MS65
1986	162,000	—	—	—	40.00	—
1986 Special Unc	40,600	—	—	—	—	45.00
1986	97,400	PF65 42.00				

KM# 2981 500 SCHILLING

24.00 g., 0.925 Silver 0.7137 oz. ASW, 37 mm. **Subject:** 150th Anniversary - Austrian Railroad **Obv:** Value within circle of shields **Rev:** Trains, two dates to lower right **Edge:** Lettered

Date	Mintage	VF20	XF40	MS60	MS63	MS65
ND-1987	152,000	—	—	—	40.00	—
ND-1987 Special Unc	53,200	—	—	—	—	45.00
ND-1987	94,800	PF65 42.00				

KM# 2982 500 SCHILLING

24.00 g., 0.925 Silver 0.7137 oz. ASW, 37 mm. **Subject:** 400th Anniversary - Birth of Salzburg's Archbishop von Raitenau **Obv:** Value within circle of shields **Rev:** Bust of Archbishop von Raitenau, 3/4 left, two dates at left **Edge:** Lettered

Date	Mintage	VF20	XF40	MS60	MS63	MS65
ND-1987	157,600	—	—	—	40.00	—
ND-1987 Special Unc	48,800	—	—	—	—	45.00
ND-1987	93,600	PF65 42.00				

KM# 2983 500 SCHILLING

24.00 g., 0.925 Silver 0.7137 oz. ASW, 37 mm. **Subject:** 800th Anniversary - Holy Cross Church **Obv:** Value within circle of shields **Rev:** Holy Cross Church, date at upper left **Edge:** Lettered

Date	Mintage	VF20	XF40	MS60	MS63	MS65
1987	153,200	—	—	—	40.00	—
1987 Special Unc	52,000	—	—	—	—	45.00
1987	94,800	PF65 42.00				

KM# 2984 500 SCHILLING

24.00 g., 0.925 Silver 0.7137 oz. ASW, 37 mm. **Subject:** 850th Anniversary - St. Georgenberg Abbey **Obv:** Value within circle of shields **Rev:** St. Georgenberg Abbey, two dates at bottom **Edge:** Lettered

Date	Mintage	VF20	XF40	MS60	MS63	MS65
ND-1988	159,000	—	—	—	40.00	—
ND-1988 Special Unc	52,800	—	—	—	—	45.00
ND-1988	88,200	PF65 42.00				

KM# 2985 500 SCHILLING

24.00 g., 0.925 Silver 0.7137 oz. ASW, 37 mm. **Subject:** Pope's Visit to Austria **Obv:** Value within circle of shields **Rev:** Pope John Paul II, with high collar, right, date at bottom **Edge:** Lettered

Date	Mintage	VF20	XF40	MS60	MS63	MS65
1988	157,600	—	—	—	40.00	—
1988 Special Unc	53,600	—	—	—	—	45.00
1988	88,800	PF65 42.00				

KM# 2986 500 SCHILLING

24.00 g., 0.925 Silver 0.7137 oz. ASW, 37 mm. **Subject:** 100th Anniversary - Victor Adler and Christian Socialist Party **Obv:** Value within circle of shields **Rev:** Head of Victor Adler, facing, date below name at lower right **Edge:** Lettered

Date	Mintage	VF20	XF40	MS60	MS63	MS65
1988	160,800	—	—	—	40.00	—
1988 Special Unc	52,400	—	—	—	—	45.00
1988	86,800	PF65 42.00				

KM# 2987 500 SCHILLING

24.00 g., 0.925 Silver 0.7137 oz. ASW, 37 mm. **Obv:** Bust of Gustav Klimt, facing, value below **Rev:** Art Nouveau bust of woman facing forward **Edge:** Lettered

Date	Mintage	VF20	XF40	MS60	MS63	MS65
1989	183,600	—	—	—	40.00	—
1989 Special Unc	53,000	—	—	—	—	45.00
1989	88,000	PF65 42.00				

KM# 2991 500 SCHILLING

24.00 g., 0.925 Silver 0.7137 oz. ASW, 37 mm. **Obv:** Head of Koloman Moser, facing 3/4 left, value below **Rev:** Stained glass, winged figure standing at center **Edge:** Lettered

Date	Mintage	VF20	XF40	MS60	MS63	MS65
1989	176,000	—	—	—	40.00	—
1989 Special Unc	52,000	—	—	—	—	45.00
1989	88,000	PF65 42.00				

KM# 2992 500 SCHILLING

24.00 g., 0.925 Silver 0.7137 oz. ASW, 37 mm. **Obv:** Bust of Egon Schiele, 3/4 facing, value below **Rev:** Expressionism, mother with two children **Edge:** Lettered

Date	Mintage	VF20	XF40	MS60	MS63	MS65
1990	200,000	—	—	—	40.00	—
1990 Special Unc	46,600	—	—	—	—	45.00
1990	81,800	PF65 42.00				

KM# 2994 500 SCHILLING
24.00 g., 0.925 Silver 0.7137 oz. ASW, 37 mm. **Obv:** Head of Oskar Kokoschka, 3/4 left, value below **Rev:** Expressionism, woman figure facing right **Edge:** Lettered

Date	Mintage	VF20	XF40	MS60	MS63	MS65
1990	200,000	—	—	—	40.00	—
1990 Special Unc	45,200	—	—	—	—	45.00
1990	81,000	PF65 42.00				

KM# 2997 500 SCHILLING
8.11 g., 0.986 Gold 0.2572 oz. AGW, 22 mm. **Obv:** Bust of Mozart, 3/4 right, value at lower right **Rev:** Half-length figure of Don Giovanni playing instrument, facing, looking right **Edge:** Reeded

Date	Mintage	VF20	XF40	MS60	MS63	MS65
1991	50,000	PF65 400				

KM# 3000 500 SCHILLING
24.00 g., 0.925 Silver 0.7137 oz. ASW, 37 mm. **Obv:** Head of Herbert von Karajan facing left, right of artistic inscription **Rev:** Salzburg Festspielhaus **Edge Lettering:** Lettered

Date	Mintage	VF20	XF40	MS60	MS63	MS65
1991	85,600	—	—	—	40.00	—
1991 Special Unc	40,000	—	—	—	—	45.00
1991	74,400	PF65 42.00				

KM# 3002 500 SCHILLING
24.00 g., 0.925 Silver 0.7137 oz. ASW, 37 mm. **Obv:** Head of Karl Bohm facing at right, inscription at left **Rev:** Building, inscription below **Edge:** Lettered

Date	Mintage	VF20	XF40	MS60	MS63	MS65
1991	88,600	—	—	—	40.00	—
1991 Special Unc	40,000	—	—	—	—	45.00
1991	71,400	PF65 42.00				

KM# 3006 500 SCHILLING
8.11 g., 0.986 Gold 0.2572 oz. AGW, 22 mm. **Subject:** 150th Anniversary - Vienna Philharmonic **Obv:** Vienna Philharmonic Hall, date below, value at bottom **Rev:** Orchestra instruments, three violins and two horns **Edge:** Reeded

Date	Mintage	VF20	XF40	MS60	MS63	MS65
1992	50,000	PF65 400				

KM# 3010 500 SCHILLING
24.00 g., 0.925 Silver 0.7137 oz. ASW, 37 mm. **Obv:** Head of Gustav Mahler facing left at right, inscription at left **Rev:** Nude figure standing in center with harp at top, inscription below feet **Edge:** Lettered

Date	Mintage	VF20	XF40	MS60	MS63	MS65
1992	99,000	—	—	—	40.00	—
1992 Special Unc	37,000	—	—	—	—	45.00
1992	64,000	PF65 42.00				

KM# 3021 500 SCHILLING
24.00 g., 0.925 Silver 0.7137 oz. ASW, 37 mm. **Obv:** Head of Richard Strauss facing forward at right, inscription at left **Rev:** Man and woman standing, man slightly bent at waist **Edge:** Lettered

Date	Mintage	VF20	XF40	MS60	MS63	MS65
1992	101,100	—	—	—	40.00	—
1992 Special Unc	36,000	—	—	—	—	45.00
1992	62,900	PF65 42.00				

KM# 3011 500 SCHILLING
24.00 g., 0.925 Silver 0.7137 oz. ASW, 37 mm. **Obv:** Hallstatt and the Lakes Region, value below **Rev:** Boats on water **Edge:** Lettered

Date	Mintage	VF20	XF40	MS60	MS63	MS65
1993	180,000	—	—	—	40.00	—
1993 Special Unc	31,200	—	—	—	—	45.00
1993	60,000	PF65 42.00				

KM# 3012 500 SCHILLING
8.11 g., 0.986 Gold 0.2572 oz. AGW, 22 mm. **Obv:** City building, date at right, value at bottom **Rev:** Aligned heads of Emperors Rudolf II, Ferdinand II, and Archduke Leopold Wilhelm, right **Edge:** Reeded

Date	Mintage	VF20	XF40	MS60	MS63	MS65
1993	50,000	PF65 550				

KM# 3014 500 SCHILLING
24.00 g., 0.925 Silver 0.7137 oz. ASW **Obv:** Alpine Region, value at bottom **Rev:** Two Alpine dancers **Edge:** Lettered

Date	Mintage	VF20	XF40	MS60	MS63	MS65
1993	180,000	—	—	—	40.00	—
1993 Special Unc	30,600	—	—	—	—	45.00
1993	60,000	PF65 42.00				

KM# 3015 500 SCHILLING
8.11 g., 0.986 Gold 0.2572 oz. AGW, 22 mm. **Obv:** Congress of Vienna, value below **Rev:** Armored bust of Franz I, facing, looking left, small crown at left, two dates on right **Edge:** Reeded

Date	Mintage	VF20	XF40	MS60	MS63	MS65
1994	50,000	PF65 400				

KM# 3017 500 SCHILLING
24.00 g., 0.925 Silver 0.7137 oz. ASW, 37 mm. **Obv:** Pannonian Region, value below **Rev:** Dancers **Edge:** Lettered

Date	Mintage	VF20	XF40	MS60	MS63	MS65
1994	160,000	—	—	—	40.00	—
1994 Special Unc	28,800	—	—	—	—	45.00
1994	55,000	PF65 42.00				

KM# 3024 500 SCHILLING
24.00 g., 0.925 Silver 0.7137 oz. ASW, 37 mm. **Obv:** River Region, value below, date at bottom **Rev:** Folk paraders **Edge:** Lettered

Date	Mintage	VF20	XF40	MS60	MS63	MS65
1994	160,000	—	—	—	40.00	—
1994 Special Unc	27,800	—	—	—	—	45.00
1994	55,000	PF65 42.00				

KM# 3023 500 SCHILLING
13.45 g., Bi-Metallic 0.1542 ASW 5.333 g, .900 Silver center in 0.2572 AGW 8.113g, .986 Gold ring, 30 mm. **Subject:**

European Union - Austrian Membership **Obv:** Symbol with Austrian shield at right, value below, within circle **Rev:** Scene of city within circle **Note:** Stars in outer ring are completely punched through.

Date	Mintage	VF20	XF40	MS60	MS63	MS65
1995	50,000	PF65 425				

KM# 3025 500 SCHILLING
24.00 g., 0.925 Silver 0.7137 oz. ASW, 37 mm. **Obv:** Austrian Hill Country, value below, date at bottom **Rev:** Farm couple **Edge:** Lettered

Date	Mintage	VF20	XF40	MS60	MS63	MS65
1995	80,000	—	—	—	40.00	—
1995 Special Unc	25,000	—	—	—	—	45.00
1995	55,000	PF65 42.00				

KM# 3029 500 SCHILLING
24.00 g., 0.925 Silver 0.7137 oz. ASW, 37 mm. **Obv:** Alpine foothills, value below, date at bottom **Rev:** Lumberjack **Edge:** Lettered

Date	Mintage	VF20	XF40	MS60	MS63	MS65
1995	86,000	—	—	—	40.00	—
1995	24,000	—	—	—	—	45.00
1995	50,000	PF65 42.00				

KM# 3032 500 SCHILLING
8.11 g., 0.986 Gold 0.2572 oz. AGW **Obv:** Men on horseback, value below, date at lower right **Rev:** Half-length figure of Heinrich II Jasomirgott, sword in right hand, 3/4 facing **Edge:** Reeded

Date	Mintage	VF20	XF40	MS60	MS63	MS65
1996	50,000	PF65 400				

KM# 3035 500 SCHILLING
24.00 g., 0.925 Silver 0.7137 oz. ASW, 37 mm. **Obv:** The Mill Region, value below, date at bottom **Rev:** Man and woman with grain **Edge:** Lettered

Date	Mintage	VF20	XF40	MS60	MS63	MS65
1996	85,000	—	—	—	40.00	—
1996 Special Unc	25,000	—	—	—	—	45.00
1996	50,000	PF65 42.00				

KM# 3039 500 SCHILLING
24.00 g., 0.925 Silver 0.7137 oz. ASW **Series:** Town Series - Innsbruck Square **Obv:** View of town square, value below, date at bottom **Rev:** Outdoor market scene

Date	Mintage	VF20	XF40	MS60	MS63	MS65
1996	85,000	—	—	—	40.00	—
1996 Special Unc	25,000	—	—	—	—	45.00
1996	50,000	PF65 42.00				

KM# 3040 500 SCHILLING
8.04 g., 0.995 Gold 0.2572 oz. AGW, 22 mm. **Obv:** Franz Schubert at piano, S. M. Vogl in foreground, form a sepia sketch by Moritz von Schwind **Rev:** Bust of Franz Schubert, facing, two dates at left, line of musical score **Edge:** Reeded

Date	Mintage	VF20	XF40	MS60	MS63	MS65
1997	50,000	PF65 400				

KM# 3042 500 SCHILLING
24.00 g., 0.925 Silver 0.7137 oz. ASW, 37 mm. **Series:** Town Series - Bruck an der Mur **Obv:** Ornate pavilion on cobblestone street, value below, date at bottom **Rev:** Ironsmith at work **Edge:** Lettered

Date	Mintage	VF20	XF40	MS60	MS63	MS65
1997	55,000	—	—	—	40.00	—
1997 Special Unc	25,000	—	—	—	—	45.00
1997	45,000	PF65 42.00				

KM# 3045 500 SCHILLING
24.00 g., 0.925 Silver 0.7137 oz. ASW, 37 mm. **Obv:** Stone pulpit of St. Stephen's cathedral, value below **Rev:** Stone mason at work **Edge:** Lettered

Date	Mintage	VF20	XF40	MS60	MS63	MS65
1997	55,000	—	—	—	40.00	—
1997 Special Unc	25,000	—	—	—	—	45.00
1997	45,000	PF65 42.00				

KM# 3047 500 SCHILLING
8.04 g., 0.995 Gold 0.2572 oz. AGW, 22 mm. **Obv:** New York and Kyoto views, value at bottom **Rev:** Vienna Boy's Choir **Edge:** Reeded

Date	Mintage	VF20	XF40	MS60	MS63	MS65
ND-1998	50,000	PF65 400				

KM# 3049 500 SCHILLING
24.00 g., 0.925 Silver 0.7137 oz. ASW, 37 mm. **Obv:** Interior view of Adimont Abbey Library, value below legend, date at bottom **Edge:** Lettered **Note:** Book printing.

Date	Mintage	VF20	XF40	MS60	MS63	MS65
1998	68,000	—	—	—	40.00	—
1998 Special Unc	17,000	—	—	—	—	45.00
1998	40,000	PF65 45.00				

KM# 3054 500 SCHILLING
24.00 g., 0.925 Silver 0.7137 oz. ASW, 37 mm. **Obv:** Gold chalice and church, value left of chalice, date at bottom **Rev:** Goldsmith at work **Edge:** Lettered

Date	Mintage	VF20	XF40	MS60	MS63	MS65
1998	73,000	—	—	—	40.00	—
1998 Special Unc	17,000	—	—	—	—	45.00
1998	35,000	PF65 45.00				

KM# 3055 500 SCHILLING
8.04 g., 0.995 Gold 0.2572 oz. AGW, 22 mm. **Obv:** Waltzing couple and Strauss monument, value below **Rev:** Busts of Johann Strauss and son, Johann, 3/4 left, dates to left and right of busts **Edge:** Reeded

Date	Mintage	VF20	XF40	MS60	MS63	MS65
1999	50,000	PF65 400				

KM# 3058 500 SCHILLING
24.00 g., 0.925 Silver 0.7137 oz. ASW, 37 mm. **Obv:** Rosenburg Castle, falcon on perch in castle jousting court, value and date at bottom **Rev:** Jousting knights **Edge:** Lettered

Date	Mintage	VF20	XF40	MS60	MS63	MS65
1999	77,000	—	—	—	40.00	—
1999 Special Unc	15,000	—	—	—	—	45.00
1999	33,000	PF65 45.00				

KM# 3060 500 SCHILLING
24.00 g., 0.925 Silver 0.7137 oz. ASW, 37 mm. **Obv:** Burg Lockenhaus, value and date at bottom **Rev:** Two Templar knights on horseback, left **Edge:** Lettered

Date	Mintage	VF20	XF40	MS60	MS63	MS65
1999	77,000	—	—	—	40.00	—
1999 Special Unc	15,000	—	—	—	—	45.00
1999	33,000	PF65 45.00				

KM# 3065 500 SCHILLING
10.14 g., 0.986 Gold 0.3214 oz. AGW, 22 mm. **Subject:** 2000th Birthday of Jesus Christ **Obv:** Three wise men presenting gifts within circle, value below circle **Rev:** Portrait of Jesus, facing

Date	Mintage	VF20	XF40	MS60	MS63	MS65
2000	50,000	PF65 550				

KM# 3067 500 SCHILLING
24.00 g., 0.925 Silver 0.7137 oz. ASW, 37 mm. **Obv:** Hochosterwitz Castle, value lower left **Rev:** Walter von der Vogelweide and royal couple **Edge:** Lettered **Mint:** Vienna

Date	Mintage	VF20	XF40	MS60	MS63	MS65
2000	49,000	—	—	—	40.00	—
2000 Special Unc	15,000	—	—	—	—	45.00
2000	31,000	PF65 45.00				

KM# 3071 500 SCHILLING
24.00 g., 0.925 Silver 0.7137 oz. ASW, 37 mm. **Obv:** Burg Hohenwerfen Castle, value at bottom **Rev:** Medieval falcon training scene **Edge:** Plain with engraved lettering **Mint:** Vienna

Date	Mintage	VF20	XF40	MS60	MS63	MS65
2000	50,000	—	—	—	40.00	—
2000 Special Unç	15,000	—	—	—	—	45.00
2000	30,000	PF65 45.00				

KM# 2933 1000 SCHILLING
13.50 g., 0.900 Gold 0.3906 oz. AGW, 27 mm. **Subject:** Babenberg Dynasty Millennium **Obv:** Imperial Eagle with Austrian shield on breast, holding hammer and sickle, value below **Rev:** Seal of Duke Friedrich II within circle, dates above circle **Edge:** Reeded **Note:** Exists in shades of red to yellow gold.

Date	Mintage	VF20	XF40	MS60	MS63	MS65
ND-1976	1,800,000	—	—	—	—	600

KM# 2999 1000 SCHILLING
16.23 g., 0.986 Gold 0.5143 oz. AGW, 30 mm. **Obv:** Head of Mozart with high collar, left, date below collar, violin on right **Rev:** The Magic Flute Opera from a 1789 drawing by Dora Stode **Edge:** Reeded

Date	Mintage	VF20	XF40	MS60	MS63	MS65
1991	30,000	PF65 800				

KM# 3008 1000 SCHILLING
16.23 g., 0.986 Gold 0.5144 oz. AGW, 30 mm. **Obv:** City building, value below, date upper right **Rev:** 1/2-length figure of Johann Strauss playing violin looking forward **Edge:** Reeded

Date	Mintage	VF20	XF40	MS60	MS63	MS65
1992	50,000	PF65 800				

KM# 3013 1000 SCHILLING
16.23 g., 0.986 Gold 0.5144 oz. AGW, 30 mm. **Obv:** Buildings, date below, value at bottom **Rev:** 3/4 length torso of Maria Theresa holding scepter in right hand, half facing right **Edge:** Reeded

Date	Mintage	VF20	XF40	MS60	MS63	MS65
1993	50,000	PF65 800				

KM# 3018 1000 SCHILLING
39.80 g., Bi-Metallic 13.18g 0.4178 AGW, .986 Gold center in 26.67g 0.7717 oz. ASW, .900 Silver ring, 40 mm. **Subject:** 800th Anniversary of the Vienna Mint **Obv:** Symbol at center of three circles, two dates above **Rev:** Crowned figure on horseback in center of three circles surrounded by circle of laborers

Date	Mintage	VF20	XF40	MS60	MS63	MS65
ND-1994	50,000	PF65 650				

KM# 3028 1000 SCHILLING
16.97 g., 0.916 Gold 0.4998 oz. AGW, 28 mm. **Series:** Olympics **Obv:** Building, statue on right, date at base, shield on left, value above **Rev:** Head of Zeus on left, facing, Olympic logo, flame to the right **Edge Lettering:** CITIUS ALTIUS FORTIUS

Date	Mintage	VF20	XF40	MS60	MS63	MS65
1995	60,000	PF65 750				

KM# 3030 1000 SCHILLING
16.23 g., 0.986 Gold 0.5144 oz. AGW, 30 mm. **Subject:** 50th Anniversary - Second Republic **Obv:** Five men aligned behind railing, center man holding book, date below railing, value at bottom **Rev:** Stylized design **Edge:** Reeded

Date	Mintage	VF20	XF40	MS60	MS63	MS65
1995	50,000	PF65 750				

KM# 3037 1000 SCHILLING
16.23 g., 0.986 Gold 0.5144 oz. AGW, 30 mm. **Subject:** Millennium of the Name Osterreich **Obv:** Land grant within circle, dates at bottom, value below circle **Rev:** Seated, crowned figure of Otto III, facing **Edge:** Reeded

Date	Mintage	VF20	XF40	MS60	MS63	MS65
ND-1996	50,000	PF65 750				

KM# 3043 1000 SCHILLING
16.08 g., 0.995 Gold 0.5144 oz. AGW, 30 mm. **Subject:** Habsburg Tragedies - Marie Antoinette **Obv:** Half-length figure of Marie holding flowers, 3/4 right, value and date lower left **Rev:** Marie on trial **Edge:** Reeded

Date	Mintage	VF20	XF40	MS60	MS63	MS65
1997	50,000	PF65 750				

KM# 3052 1000 SCHILLING

16.08 g., 0.995 Gold 0.5144 oz. AGW, 30 mm. **Subject:** 100th Anniversary of Empress Elisabeth's Assassination by Luigi Luccheni in Geneva **Obv:** Bust of Empress Elisabeth, Queen of Hungary, 3/4 right **Rev:** Scene of Elisabeth's final moment **Edge:** Reeded

Date	Mintage	VF20	XF40	MS60	MS63	MS65
1998	50,000	PF65 750				

KM# 3062 1000 SCHILLING

16.08 g., 0.995 Gold 0.5144 oz. AGW, 30 mm. **Obv:** Emperor Karl I bust facing **Rev:** Interior view Habsburg crypt **Edge:** Reeded

Date	Mintage	VF20	XF40	MS60	MS63	MS65
1999	50,000	PF65 750				

KM# 3072 1000 SCHILLING

16.22 g., 0.986 Gold 0.5142 oz. AGW, 30 mm. **Obv:** Heidentor ancient gate and statue **Rev:** Constantius II portrait **Edge:** Reeded **Mint:** Vienna

Date	Mintage	VF20	XF40	MS60	MS63	MS65
2000	30,000	PF65 750				

BULLION COINAGE

Philharmonic Issues

KM# 3004 200 SCHILLING

3.12 g., 0.9999 Gold 0.1003 oz. AGW, 16 mm. **Series:** Vienna Philharmonic Orchestra **Obv:** The Golden Hall organ **Rev:** Wind and string instruments **Edge:** Reeded

Date	Mintage	VF20	XF40	MS60	MS63	MS65
1991	82,500	—	—	—	—	152
1992	99,000	—	—	—	—	152
1993	99,500	—	—	—	—	152
1994	112,000	—	—	—	—	152
1995	151,100	—	—	—	—	152
1996	128,300	—	—	—	—	152
1997	115,300	—	—	—	—	152
1998	102,800	—	—	—	—	152
1999	145,000	—	—	—	—	152
2000	32,600	—	—	—	—	152

KM# 2989 500 SCHILLING

7.78 g., 0.9999 Gold 0.250 oz. AGW, 22 mm. **Series:** Vienna Philharmonic Orchestra **Obv:** The Golden Hall organ **Rev:** Wind and string instruments **Edge:** Reeded

Date	Mintage	VF20	XF40	MS60	MS63	MS65
1989	272,000	—	—	—	—	370
1990	162,000	—	—	—	—	370
1991	146,000	—	—	—	—	370
1992	176,000	—	—	—	—	370
1993	126,000	—	—	—	—	370
1994	121,200	—	—	—	—	370
1995	156,000	—	—	—	—	370
1996	139,200	—	—	—	—	370
1997	100,700	—	—	—	—	370
1998	90,800	—	—	—	—	370
1999	81,600	—	—	—	—	370
2000	25,900	—	—	—	—	370

KM# 3031 1000 SCHILLING

15.55 g., 0.9999 Gold 0.500 oz. AGW, 28 mm. **Series:** Vienna Philharmonic Orchestra **Obv:** The Golden Hall organ **Rev:** Wind and string instruments **Edge:** Reeded

Date	Mintage	VF20	XF40	MS60	MS63	MS65
1994	57,400	—	—	—	—	730
1995	94,700	—	—	—	—	730
1996	88,000	—	—	—	—	730
1997	68,200	—	—	—	—	730
1998	47,300	—	—	—	—	730
1999	44,200	—	—	—	—	730
2000	20,500	—	—	—	—	730

KM# 2990 2000 SCHILLING

31.10 g., 0.9999 Gold 0.9999 oz. AGW, 37 mm. **Series:** Vienna Philharmonic Orchestra **Obv:** The Golden Hall organ **Rev:** Wind and string instruments **Edge:** Reeded

Date	Mintage	VF20	XF40	MS60	MS63	MS65
1989	351,000	—	—	—	—	1,400
1990	484,500	—	—	—	—	1,400
1991	233,500	—	—	—	—	1,400
1992	537,000	—	—	—	—	1,400
1993	234,000	—	—	—	—	1,400
1994	218,600	—	—	—	—	1,400
1995	645,500	—	—	—	—	1,400
1996	377,600	—	—	—	—	1,400
1997	408,300	—	—	—	—	1,400
1998	330,300	—	—	—	—	1,400
1999	230,700	—	—	—	—	1,400
2000	245,700	—	—	—	—	1,400

PROBA

KM#	Date	Mintage	Identification	Mkt Val
Pr3	1910	—	2 Corona. 0.835. Silver. KM#2821.	—
Pr4	1913	—	2 Corona. 835000. Silver. KM#2821.	—
Pr2	1914	—	Corona. 0.835. Silver. KM# 2820.	—
Pr1	1916	—	10 Heller. Aluminum. KM# 2825.	—

PATTERNS

Including off metal strikes

KM#	Date	Mintage	Identification	Mkt Val
Pn68	1908	—	100 Kronen. Without mint mark.	—
Pn69	1909	—	100 Kronen. Without mint mark.	—
Pn70	1910	—	2 Kronen. Silver. Similar to KM#2821.	2,600
Pn71	1913	—	Krone. Aluminum. KM#2820.	—
Pn72	1913	—	2 Corona. Aluminum. KM#2821.	220
Pn73	ND (1913)	—	50 Heller. Iron.	260
Pn74	1914	—	Heller. Copper. Privately produced by Karl Goetz in Munich, Germany.	165
Pn75	1914	—	Heller. Silver. Privately produced by Karl Goetz in Munich, Germany.	300
Pn76	1915	—	2 Heller. Bronze. KM#2801.	—
Pn77	1915	—	2 Heller. Iron. KM#2801.	—
Pn78	1915	—	20 Heller. Iron. KM#2826.	500
Pn79	1915	—	1/2 Krone. Silver.	—
Pn80	1915	—	Ducat. Aluminum. Plain.	110
Pn81	1915	—	Ducat. Copper. Reeded.	450
Pn82	1916	—	Heller. Iron. KM#2823.	300
Pn83	1916	—	2 Heller. Iron.	—
Pn84	1916	—	10 Heller. Aluminum. KM#2825.	300
Pn85	1916	—	Krone. Aluminum. KM#2820.	160
Pn86	1917	—	10 Heller. Steel. Plain. 10 in square, thick planchet.	—
Pn87	1917	—	10 Heller. Steel. Plain. 10 in square, thin planchet.	275
Pn88	1917	—	10 Heller. Steel. Milled.	—
Pn89	1918	—	20 Heller. Aluminum. 20 in square.	—
Pn90	1918	—	20 Heller. Aluminum. KM#2826.	275
Pn91	1918	—	5 Kronen. Brass.	—
Pn92	1918	—	20 Kronen. Copper.	—
Pn93	1918	1	20 Kronen. Gold.	—
Pn94	ND (1918)	—	10 Schilling. Nickel.	200
Pn95	ND (1918)	—	20 Schilling. Nickel.	450
Pn96	1924	—	1/2 Schilling. Silver. KM#2839.	1,400
Pn97	1924	—	Schilling. Silver. KM#2835.	900
Pn98	1924	—	Schilling. Silver. KM#2835. KM#2835. Octagonal planchets, 1 pair.	775
Pn99	1924	—	20 Kronen. Copper. Reeded. KM#2830.	1,650
Pn100	1924	—	20 Kronen. Silver. Reeded. Uniface, KM#2830.	775
Pn101	1930	—	100 Schilling. Silver. Plain. KM#2842.	2,200
Pn102	1931	—	5 Groschen. Copper-Nickel.	—
Pn103	1931	—	5 Groschen. Gold. KM#2846.	1,450
Pn104	1931	—	100 Schilling. Copper. KM#2842.	1,100
Pn105	1934	—	50 Groschen. Copper-Nickel. Uniface.	—
Pn106	1934	—	50 Groschen. Copper-Nickel. Uniface.	—
Pn107	1934	—	Schilling. Copper-Nickel. Uniface.	1,950
Pn108	1934	—	Schilling. Copper-Nickel. Uniface.	1,950
Pn109	1934	—	2 Schilling. Zinc. KM#2852.	1,100
Pn110	1934	—	2 Schilling. Zinc. One side struck on octagonal planchet, KM#2852.	650
Pn111	1935	1	25 Schilling. Gold. J. Prinz.	—
Pn112	1935	1	100 Schilling. Gold. J. Prinz.	—
Pn113	1937	—	2 Schilling. Copper. KM#2859.	220
Pn114	1938	1	5 Groschen. Gold. KM#2846.	1,450
Pn115	1947	—	Schilling. Copper-Nickel. KM#2871.	550
Pn116	1959	—	Schilling. Aluminum-Bronze. Similar to KM#2886.	925

TRIAL STRIKES

KM#	Date	Mintage	Identification	Mkt Val
TS1	1934	—	50 Groschen. Uniface.	—
TS2	1934	—	50 Groschen. Uniface.	—
TS3	ND-1973	—	5 Schilling. Nickel.	300
TS4	ND-1973	—	10 Schilling. Nickel.	220
TS5	ND-1973	—	20 Schilling. Nickel.	375
TS6	ND-1984	—	5 Groschen. Aluminum. Plain.	195

MINT SETS

KM#	Date	Mintage	Identification	Issue Price	Mkt Val
MS1	1992 (8)	25,000	KM#2875-2876, 2878, 2885-2886, 2889a, 2918, 2946.2	—	50.00
MS2	1993 (8)	28,000	KM#2875-2876, 2878, 2885-2886, 2889a, 2918, 2946.2	—	75.00
MS3	1994 (8)	25,000	KM#2875-2876, 2878, 2885-2886, 2889a, 2918, 3016	—	75.00
MS4	1995 (6)	27,000	KM#2878, 2885-2886, 2889a, 2918, 3022	—	45.00
MS5	1996 (6)	25,000	KM#2878, 2885-2886, 2889a, 2918, 3033	—	45.00
MS6	1997 (6)	25,000	KM#2878, 2885-2886, 2889a, 2918, 3041	—	45.00
MS7	1998 (6)	25,000	KM#2878, 2885-2886, 2889a, 2918, 3048	—	60.00
MS8	1999 (7)	50,000	KM#2878, 2885-2886, 2889a, 2918, 3056	22.00	35.00
MS9	2000 (6)	75,000	KM#2878, 2885-2886, 2889a, 2918, 3064	—	30.00

PROOF SETS

KM#	Date	Mintage	Identification	Issue Price	Mkt Val
PS1	1959 (2)	1,000	KM#2887-2888	—	750
PS2	1964 (9)	69,731	KM#2875-2876, 2878, 2882, 2885-2886, 2889, 2895.1, 2896	—	75.00
PS3	1964 (9)	2,700	KM#2875-2876, 2878, 2882, 2885-2886, 2889, 2895.2, 2896 (error set)	—	375
PS4	1964 (7)	—	KM#2875-2876, 2878, 2882, 2885-2886, 2889	—	37.50
PS5	1965 (7)	83,000	KM#2875-2876, 2878, 2882, 2885-2886, 2889	—	30.00
PS6	1965 (4)	38,000	KM#2882, 2889, 2897-2898	5.00	60.00
PS7	1966 (9)	1,765	KM#2875-2876, 2878, 2882, 2885-2886, 2889, 2899-2900	—	180
PS8	1966 (7)	—	KM#2875-2876, 2878, 2882, 2885-2886, 2889	—	65.00
PS9	1967 (9)	1,163	KM#2875-2876, 2878, 2882, 2885-2886, 2889, 2901-2902	5.50	300

PS10	1967 (7)	—	KM#2875-2876, 2878, 2882, 2885-2886, 2889	—	200
PS11	1968 (9)	15,200	KM#2875-2876, 2878, 2882, 2885-2886, 2889, 2903, 2904.1	5.75	115
PS12	1968 (7)	20,000	KM#2875-2876, 2878, 2882, 2885-2886, 2889	—	65.00
PS13	1969 (9)	20,000	KM#2875-2876, 2878, 2882, 2885-2886, 2889a, 2905-2906	7.50	100
PS14	1969 (7)	21,000	KM#2875-2876, 2878, 2882, 2885-2886, 2889a	—	55.00
PS15	1970 (9)	—	KM#2875-2876, 2878, 2882, 2885-2886, 2889a, 2907-2908	8.25	57.50
PS16	1970 (9)	—	KM#2875-2876, 2878, 2882, 2885-2886, 2889a, 2907, 2909	8.25	55.00
PS17	1970 (7)	92,000	KM#2875-2876, 2878, 2882, 2885-2886, 2889a	—	22.50
PS18	1970 (3)	—	KM#2907-2909	7.00	55.00
PS19	1971 (9)	50,000	KM#2875-2876, 2878, 2882, 2885-2886, 2889a, 2910-2911	8.25	55.00
PS20	1971 (7)	84,000	KM#2875-2876, 2878, 2882, 2885-2886, 2889a	—	22.50
PS21	1972 (9)	—	KM#2875-2876, 2878, 2882, 2885-2886, 2889a, 2912-2913	8.50	52.50
PS22	1972 (9)	—	KM#2875-2876, 2878, 2882, 2885-2886, 2889a, 2912, 2914	8.50	52.50
PS23	1972 (7)	75,000	KM#2875-2876, 2878, 2882, 2885-2886, 2889a	—	17.50
PS24	1972 (3)	—	KM#2912-2914	7.50	55.00
PS25	1972 (3)	—	KM#2912-2914	—	55.00
PS26	1973 (9)	—	KM#2875-2876, 2878, 2882, 2885-2886, 289a, 2915-2916	—	52.50
PS27	1973 (7)	87,000	KM#2875-2876, 2878, 2882, 2885-2886, 2889a	—	17.50
PS28	1974 (12)	—	KM#2875-2876, 2878, 2885-2886, 2889a, 2918-2922, 2926	29.70	95.00
PS29	1974 (8)	—	KM#2875-2876, 2878, 2885-2886, 2889a, 2918, 2921	—	30.00
PS30	1974 (7)	76,000	KM#2875-2876, 2878, 2885-2886, 2889a, 2918	—	15.00
PS31	1974 (5)	—	KM#2919-2922, 2926	27.00	80.00
PS32	1975 (10)	—	KM#2875-2876, 2878, 2885-2886, 289a, 2918, 2923-2925	30.00	65.00
PS33	1975 (7)	49,000	KM#2875-2876, 2878, 2885-2886, 2889a, 2918	—	14.00
PS34	1975 (3)	—	KM#2923-2925	27.00	55.00
PS35	1976 (7)	44,000	KM#2875-2876, 2878, 2885-2886, 2889a, 2918	3.00	15.00
PS37	1977 (7)	44,000	KM#2875-2876, 2878, 2885-2886, 2889a, 2918	3.15	14.00
PS38	1978 (7)	43,000	KM#2875-2876, 2878, 2885-2886, 2889a, 2918	—	14.00
PS39	1979 (7)	44,000	KM#2875-2876, 2878, 2885-2886, 2889a, 2918	—	14.00
PS40	1980 (8)	48,000	KM#2875-2876, 2878, 2885-2886, 2889a, 2918, 2946	—	60.00
PS42	1981 (8)	49,000	KM#2875-2876, 2878, 2885-2886, 2889a, 2918, 2946.1	—	62.50
PS43	1982 (8)	50,000	KM#2875-2876, 2878, 2885-2886, 2889a, 2918, 2955.1	—	27.50
PS44	1983 (8)	65,000	KM#2875-2876, 2878, 2885-2886, 2889a, 2918, 2960.1	—	25.00
PS45	1984 (8)	65,000	KM#2875-2876, 2878, 2885-2886, 2889a, 2918, 2965.1	—	25.00
PS46	1985 (8)	45,000	KM#2875-2876, 2878, 2885-2886, 2889a, 2918, 2970.1	—	35.00
PS47	1986 (8)	42,000	KM#2875-2876, 2878, 2885-2886, 2889a, 2918, 2975.1	—	50.00
PS48	1987 (8)	42,000	KM#2875-2876, 2878, 2885-2886, 2889a, 2918, 2980.1	—	35.00
PS49	1988 (7)	39,000	KM#2875-2876, 2878, 2885-2886, 2889a, 2918	—	20.00
PS50	1989 (8)	38,000	KM#2875-2876, 2878, 2885-2886, 2889a, 2918, 2988.1	—	25.00
PS51	1990 (8)	35,000	KM#2875-2876, 2878, 2885-2886, 2889a, 2918, 2993.1	—	55.00
PS52	1991 (8)	27,000	KM#2875-2876, 2878, 2885-2886, 2889a, 2918, 2995.1	—	35.00

The Republic of Azerbaijan (formerly Azerbaijan S.S.R.) includes the Nakhichevan Autonomous Republic. Situated in the eastern area of Transcaucasia, it is bordered in the west by Armenia, in the north by Georgia and Dagestan, to the east by the Caspian Sea and to the south by Iran. It has an area of 33,430 sq. mi. (86,600 sq. km.) and a population of 7.8 million. Capital: Baku. The area is rich in mineral deposits of aluminum, copper, iron, lead, salt and zinc, with oil as its leading industry. Agriculture and livestock follow in importance.

Until the Russian Revolution of 1905, there was no political life in Azerbaijan. A Mussavat (Equality) party was formed in 1911 by Mohammed Emin Rasulzade, a former Social Democrat. After the Russian Revolution of March 1917, the party started a campaign for independence. Baku, however, the capital with its mixed population, constituted an alien enclave in the country. While a national Azerbaijani government was established at Gandzha (Elizavetpol), a Communist controlled council assumed power at Baku with Stepan Shaumian, an Armenian, at its head. The Gandzha government joined first, on Sept. 20, 1917, a Transcaucasian federal republic, but on May 28, 1918, proclaimed the independence of Azerbaijan. On June 4, 1918, at Batum, a peace treaty was signed with Turkey. Turko-Azerbaijani forces started an offensive against Baku, occupied since Aug. 17, 1918 by 1,400 British troops coming by sea from Anzali, Persia. On Sept. 14 the British evacuated Baku, returning to Anzali, and three days later the Azerbaijan government, headed by Fath Khoysky, established itself at Baku.

After the collapse of the Ottoman Empire, the British returned to Baku, at first ignoring the Azerbaijan government. A general election with universal suffrage for the Azerbaijan constituent assembly took place on Dec. 7, 1918 and out of 120 members there were 84 Mussavat supporters. On Jan. 15, 1920, the Allied powers recognized Azerbaijan de facto, but on April 27 of the same year the Red army invaded the country, and a Soviet republic of Azerbaijan was proclaimed the next day. Later it became a member of the Transcaucasian Federation joining the U.S.S.R. on Dec. 30, 1922, it became a self-constituent republic in 1936.

The Azerbaijan Communist party held its first congress at Baku in Feb. 1920. From 1921 to 1925 its first secretary was a Russian, S.M. Kirov, who directed a mass deportation to Siberia of about 120,000 Azerbaijani "nationalist deviationists," among them the country's first two premiers.

In 1990 it adopted a declaration of republican sovereignty and in Aug. 1991 declared itself formally independent. This action was approved by a vote of referendum in Jan. 1992. It announced its intention of joining the CIS in Dec. 1991, but a parliamentary resolution of Oct. 1992 declined to confirm its involvement. On Sept. 20, 1993, Azerbaijan became a member of the CIS. Communist President Mutaibov was relieved of his office in May 1992. On June 7, in the first democratic election in the country's history, a National Council replaced Mutaibov with Abulfez Elchibey. Surat Huseynov led a military coup against Elchibey and seized power on June 30, 1993. Huseynov became prime minister with former communist Geidar Aliyev, president.

Fighting commenced between Muslim forces of Azerbaijan and Christian forces of Armenia in 1992 and continued through early 1994. Each faction claimed the Nagorno-Karabakh, an Armenian ethnic enclave, in Azerbaijan. A cease-fire was declared in May 1994.

MONETARY SYSTEM

100 Qapik = 1 Manat

REPUBLIC

DECIMAL COINAGE

KM# 1 5 QAPIK

Brass **Obv:** Value **Rev:** Three symbols above date at center of sun

Date	Mintage	VF20	XF40	MS60	MS63	MS65
1992	—	—	1.00	1.50	2.00	3.50

KM# 1a 5 QAPIK

0.85 g., Aluminum, 17.1 mm. **Obv:** Value **Rev:** Three symbols above date at center of sun **Edge:** Plain

Date	Mintage	VF20	XF40	MS60	MS63	MS65
1993	—	—	—	0.75	1.00	1.50

KM# 2 10 QAPIK

5.05 g., Aluminum, 22.23 mm. **Obv:** Denomination **Rev:** Star with date **Edge:** Plain

Date	Mintage	VF20	XF40	MS60	MS63	MS65
1992	—	—	0.50	0.75	1.00	1.75

KM# 3 20 QAPIK

Brass **Obv:** Moon and star at center **Rev:** Value above date within star **Edge:** Plain

Date	Mintage	VF20	XF40	MS60	MS63	MS65
1992	—	—	0.50	0.75	1.00	1.75
1993	—	—	0.50	0.75	1.00	1.75

KM# 3a 20 QAPIK

1.15 g., Aluminum, 20.1 mm. **Obv:** Moon and star at center **Rev:** Value above date within star **Edge:** Plain **Note:** Varieties in spelling of Respublikas exist.

Date	Mintage	VF20	XF40	MS60	MS63	MS65
1992	—	—	—	0.45	0.75	1.00
1993	—	—	—	0.45	0.75	1.00

Note: Two die varieties exist

KM# 4 50 QAPIK

Copper-Nickel **Obv:** Maiden tower ruins **Rev:** Value above date within ornate circle **Edge:** Plain

Date	Mintage	VF20	XF40	MS60	MS63	MS65
1992	—	—	0.75	1.25	1.75	3.50
1994	—	—	0.75	1.25	1.75	3.50

KM# 4a 50 QAPIK

1.45 g., Aluminum, 23 mm. **Obv:** Maiden tower ruins **Rev:** Value above date within ornate circle **Edge:** Plain

Date	Mintage	VF20	XF40	MS60	MS63	MS65
1992	—	—	—	1.00	1.25	1.50
1993	—	—	—	0.45	0.75	1.00

KM# 5 50 MANAT
28.28 g., 0.925 Silver 0.841 oz. ASW **Subject:** 500th Anniversary Mehemmed Fuzuli **Obv:** Deer by man comforting fallen comrade within circle, date below circle **Rev:** Portrait of Fuzuli bust, looking left

Date	Mintage	VF20	XF40	MS60	MS63	MS65
1996	—	—	—	—	50.00	60.00
1996	5,000	PF65 75.00				

KM# 38 50 MANAT
31.10 g., 0.925 Silver 0.9249 oz. ASW, 38.6 mm. **Subject:** 1300 Years of National Epic **Obv:** Musician riding horse within circle, date below circle **Rev:** Book title **Rev. Inscription:** KITABI / DÆDÆ / QORQUD / 1300 **Edge:** Reeded

Date	Mintage	VF20	XF40	MS60	MS63	MS65
1999	1,000	PF65 125				

KM# 6 100 MANAT
7.98 g., 0.9167 Gold 0.2352 oz. AGW **Subject:** 500th Anniversary Mehemmed Fuzuli **Obv:** Deer by man comforting fallen comrade **Rev:** Portrait of Fuzuli

Date	Mintage	VF20	XF40	MS60	MS63	MS65
1996	500	PF65 475				

KM# 45 100 MANAT
17.28 g., 0.900 Gold 0.500 oz. AGW, 25 mm. **Subject:** 1300 Years of National Epic **Obv:** Musician riding horse right **Rev:** Book title **Rev. Inscription:** KITABI / DÆDÆ / QORQUD / 1300

Date	Mintage	VF20	XF40	MS60	MS63	MS65
1999	150	PF65 975				

AZORES

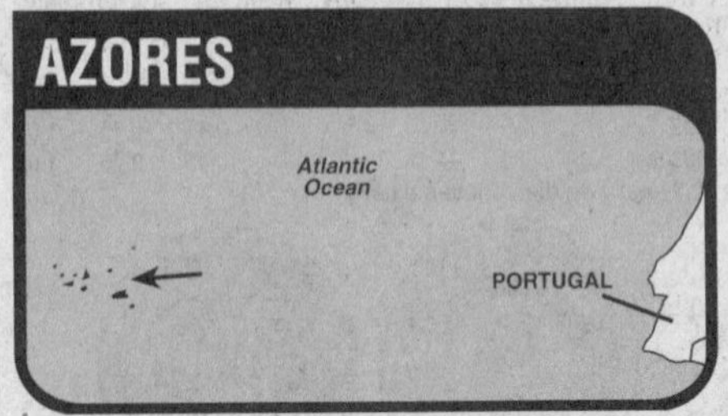

The Azores, an archipelago of nine islands of volcanic origin, are located in the Atlantic Ocean 740 miles (1,190 km.) west of Cape de Roca, Portugal. They are the westernmost region of Europe under the administration of Portugal and have an area of 902 sq. mi. (2,305 sq. km.) and a population of 236,000. Principal city: Ponta Delgada. The natives are mainly of Portuguese descent and earn their livelihood by fishing, wine making, basket weaving and the growing of fruit, grains and sugar cane. Pineapples are the chief item of export. The climate is particularly temperate, making the islands a favorite winter resort.

The Azores were discovered about 1427 by the Portuguese navigator Diogo de Sevill. Portugal secured the islands in the 15th century and established the first settlement on Santa Maria about 1439. From 1580 to 1640 the Azores were subject to Spain.

The Azores' first provincial coinage was ordered by law of August 19, 1750. Copper coins were struck for circulation in both the Azores and Madeira Islands, keeping the same technical specifications but with different designs. In 1795 a second provincial coinage was introduced but the weight was reduced by 50 percent.

Angra on Terceira Island became the capital of the captaincy-general of the Azores in 1766 and it was here in 1826 that the constitutionalists set up a pro-Pedro government in opposition to King Miguel in Lisbon. The whole Portuguese fleet attacked Terceira and was repelled at Praia, after which Azoreans, Brazilians and British mercenaries defeated Miguel in Portugal. Maria de Gloria, Pedro's daughter, was proclaimed queen of Portugal on Terceira in 1828.

A U.S. naval base was established at Ponta Delgada in 1917.

After World War II, the islands acquired a renewed importance as a refueling stop for transatlantic air transport. The United States maintains defense bases in the Azores as part of the collective security program of NATO.

In 1976 the archipelago became the Autonomous Region of Azores.

Note: Portuguese 50 Centavos and 1 Escudo pieces dated 1935 were issued for circulation in Azores. These are found under the appropriate listing in Portugal.

RULER
Portuguese

MONETARY SYSTEM
1000 Reis (Insulanos) = 1 Milreis

PORTUGUESE ADMINISTRATION

PROVINCIAL COINAGE

KM# 16 5 REIS
Copper, 25 mm. **Subject:** Carlos I **Obv:** Crowned arms **Rev:** Value within wreath, date below

Date	Mintage	F12	VF20	XF40	MS60	MS63
1901	800,000	1.75	3.50	9.00	25.00	35.00

KM# 17 10 REIS
Copper, 30 mm. **Subject:** Carlos I **Obv:** Crowned arms **Rev:** Value within wreath, date below

Date	Mintage	F12	VF20	XF40	MS60	MS63
1901	600,000	2.00	4.00	10.00	28.00	40.00

REPUBLIC

DECIMAL COINAGE

KM# 43 25 ESCUDOS
11.05 g., Copper-Nickel, 28.5 mm. **Subject:** Regional Autonomy **Obv:** Shields above denomination, stars below **Rev:** Supported arms **Edge:** Reeded

Date	Mintage	VF20	XF40	MS60	MS63	MS65
1980	770,000	—	1.00	2.50	4.50	6.50

KM# 43a 25 ESCUDOS
11.00 g., 0.925 Silver 0.3271 oz. ASW **Subject:** Regional Autonomy **Obv:** Shields above denomination, stars below **Rev:** Supported arms

Date	Mintage	VF20	XF40	MS60	MS63	MS65
1980	12,000	PF63 12.00	PF65 22.00			

KM# 44 100 ESCUDOS
Copper-Nickel **Subject:** Regional Autonomy **Obv:** Shields above denomination, stars below **Rev:** Supported arms

Date	Mintage	VF20	XF40	MS60	MS63	MS65
1980	270,000	—	1.50	3.50	6.50	11.50

KM# 44a 100 ESCUDOS
16.50 g., 0.925 Silver 0.4907 oz. ASW **Subject:** Regional Autonomy **Obv:** Shields above denomination, stars below **Rev:** Supported arms

Date	Mintage	VF20	XF40	MS60	MS63	MS65
1980	12,000	PF65 30.00				

KM# 45 100 ESCUDOS
16.50 g., Copper-Nickel, 34 mm. **Subject:** 10th Anniversary of Regional Autonomy **Obv:** Supported arms, value below **Rev:** Hydrangea plant, date below **Edge:** Reeded

Date	Mintage	VF20	XF40	MS60	MS63	MS65
1986	750,000	—	1.00	2.50	4.50	7.00

KM# 45a 100 ESCUDOS
16.50 g., 0.925 Silver 0.4907 oz. ASW **Subject:** 10th Anniversary of Regional Autonomy **Obv:** Supported arms **Rev:** Flower

Date	Mintage	VF20	XF40	MS60	MS63	MS65
1986	20,000	—	—	12.00	17.00	22.00
1986	10,000	PF65 28.00				

KM# 46 100 ESCUDOS
Copper-Nickel **Subject:** 100th Anniversary - Death of Poet Antero de Quental **Obv:** Offered hand with radiant sun behind, shield of arms below left, value at right **Rev:** Bust of Antero de Quental, facing, two dates at left

Date	Mintage	VF20	XF40	MS60	MS63	MS65
1991	750,000	—	—	1.50	3.50	6.00

KM# 46a 100 ESCUDOS
18.50 g., 0.925 Silver 0.5502 oz. ASW, 36 mm. **Subject:** 100th Anniversary - Death of Poet Antero de Quental **Obv:** Offered hand with radiant sun behind, shield of arms below left **Rev:** Bust of Antero de Quental facing

Date	Mintage	VF20	XF40	MS60	MS63	MS65
1991	20,000	—	—	—	16.00	22.00
1991	30,000	PF65 25.00				

KM# 47 100 ESCUDOS
Copper-Nickel **Subject:** Centennial of Azorean Autonomy **Obv:** Sun with star at center, over water, shield of arms below, value at bottom **Rev:** Goshawk with wings spread below dates, 1895 above 1995

Date	Mintage	VF20	XF40	MS60	MS63	MS65
ND-1995	500,000	—	—	1.50	2.50	4.50

KM# 47a 100 ESCUDOS
18.50 g., 0.925 Silver 0.5502 oz. ASW **Subject:** Centennial of Azorean Autonomy **Rev:** Goshawk with wings spread below dates, 1895 over 1995

Date	Mintage	VF20	XF40	MS60	MS63	MS65
ND-1995	5,000	—	—	—	18.00	25.00
ND-1995	10,000	PF65 28.00				

PATTERNS

Including off metal strikes

KM#	Date	Mintage	Identification	Mkt Val
Pn5	1901	—	5 Reis. Aluminum.	850
Pn6	1901	—	10 Reis. Aluminum.	850

PROVAS

KM#	Date	Mintage	Identification	Mkt Val
Pr1	1980	—	25 Escudos. Copper-Nickel. Incuse PROVA.	150

Pr2	1980	—	100 Escudos. Copper-Nickel. Shields above value, stars below. Supported arms. Incuse PROVA.	175
Pr3	1986	—	100 Escudos. Copper-Nickel. Incuse PROVA.	175

PROOF SETS

KM#	Date	Mintage	Identification	Issue Price	Mkt Val
PS1	1980 (2)	12,000	KM43a-44a	40.00	52.00

THE BAHAMAS

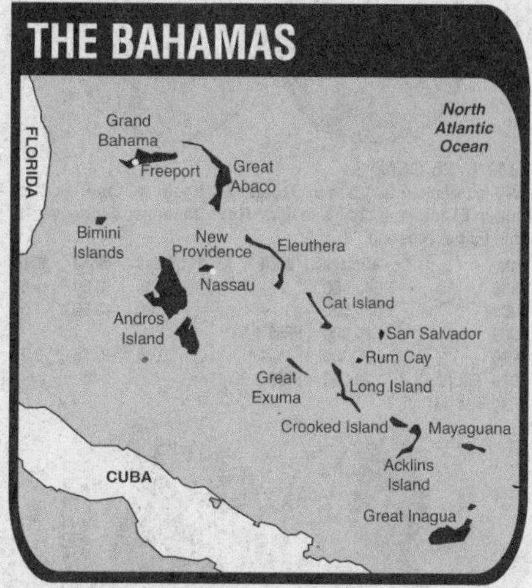

The Commonwealth of the Bahamas is an archipelago of about 3,000 islands, cays and rocks located in the Atlantic Ocean east of Florida and north of Cuba. The total land area of the 800 mile (1,287 km.) long chain of islands is 5,382 sq. mi. (13,935 sq. km.). They have a population of 302,000. Capital: Nassau. The Bahamas import most of their food and manufactured products and export cement, refined oil, pulpwood and lobsters. Tourism is the principal industry.

The Bahamas were discovered by Columbus October, 1492, upon his sighting of the island of San Salvador, but Spain made no attempt to settle them. British influence began in 1626 when Charles I granted them to the lord proprietors of Carolina, with settlements in 1629 at New Providence by colonists from the northern territory. Although the Bahamas were temporarily under Spanish control in 1641 and 1703, they continued under British proprietors until 1717, when, as the result of political and economic mismanagement, the civil and military governments were surrendered to the King and the islands designated a British Crown Colony. Full international agreement on British possession of the islands resulted from the Treaty of Versailles in 1783. The Bahamas obtained complete internal self-government under the constitution of Jan. 7, 1964. Full independence was achieved on July 10, 1973. The Bahamas is a member of the Commonwealth of Nations. Elizabeth II is Head of State as Queen of The Bahamas.

The coinage of Great Britain was legal tender in the Bahamas from 1825 to the issuing of a definitive coinage in 1966.

RULER

British

MINT MARKS

Through 1969 all decimal coinage of the Bahamas was executed at the Royal Mint in England. Since that time issues have been struck at both the Royal Mint and at the Franklin Mint (FM) in the U.S.A. While the mint mark of the latter appears on coins dated 1971 and subsequently, it is missing from the 1970 issues.

JP – John Pinches, London
None - Royal Mint
(t) - Tower of London
FM - Franklin Mint, U.S.A.

***NOTE**: From 1975-1985 the Franklin Mint produced coinage in up to 3 different qualities. Qualities of issue are designated in ( ) after each date and are defined as follows:

(M) MATTE - Normal circulation strike or a dull finish produced by sandblasting special uncirculated (polish finish) or proof quality dies.

(U) SPECIAL UNCIRCULATED - Polished or proof-like in appearance without any frosted features.

(P) PROOF - The highest quality obtainable having mirror-like fields and frosted features.

MONETARY SYSTEM

12 Pence = 1 Shilling

COMMONWEALTH

DECIMAL COINAGE

100 Cents = 1 Dollar

KM# 2 CENT

4.16 g., Nickel-Brass, 22.5 mm. **Ruler:** Elizabeth II **Obv:** Queen Elizabeth II right **Rev:** Starfish above date, value at top

Date	Mintage	VF20	XF40	MS60	MS63	MS65
1966	7,312,000	—	—	0.10	0.50	2.00
1968	800,000	—	—	0.25	0.75	2.25
1969	4,036,000	—	—	0.10	0.50	2.00
1969	10,000	PF65 1.50				

KM# 15 CENT

Bronze, 19 mm. **Ruler:** Elizabeth II **Obv:** Bust of Queen Elizabeth II right with tiara **Rev:** Starfish above date, value at top **Edge:** Plain **Note:** Proof specimens of this date are struck in "special brass" which looks like a pale bronze.

Date	Mintage	VF20	XF40	MS60	MS63	MS65
1970	125,000	—	0.10	0.25	0.50	1.50
1970	23,000	PF65 1.00				

KM# 16 CENT

3.13 g., Brass, 19.05 mm. **Ruler:** Elizabeth II **Obv:** Bust of Queen Elizabeth II right with tiara **Rev:** Starfish above date, value at top **Edge:** Plain

Date	Mintage	VF20	XF40	MS60	MS63	MS65
1971 FM	1,007,000	—	—	0.10	0.50	2.00
1971 FM (P)	31,000	PF65 1.50				
1972 FM	1,037,000	—	—	0.10	0.50	2.00
1972 FM (P)	35,000	PF65 1.50				
1973	7,000,000	—	—	0.20	0.50	2.00
1973 FM	1,040,000	—	—	0.10	0.50	2.00
1973 FM (P)	35,000	PF65 1.50				

KM# 59 CENT

3.16 g., Brass, 19.05 mm. **Ruler:** Elizabeth II **Obv:** National arms above date **Rev:** Starfish, value at top **Edge:** Plain

Date	Mintage	VF20	XF40	MS60	MS63	MS65
1974	11,000	—	—	0.20	0.50	1.50
1974 FM	71,000	—	—	0.10	0.25	1.00
1974 FM (P)	94,000	PF65 1.50				
1975 FM (M)	60,000	—	—	0.10	0.25	1.00
1975 FM (U)	3,845	—	—	0.10	0.50	1.50
1975 FM (P)	29,000	PF65 1.50				
1976 FM (M)	60,000	—	—	0.10	0.25	1.00
1976 FM (U)	1,453	—	—	0.10	0.50	1.50
1976 FM (P)	23,000	PF65 1.50				
1977	3,000,000	—	—	0.10	0.25	1.00
1977 FM (M)	60,000	—	—	0.10	0.25	1.00
1977 FM (U)	713	—	—	0.50	1.50	4.50
1977 FM (P)	11,000	PF65 1.50				
1978 FM (M)	60,000	—	—	0.10	0.25	1.00
1978 FM (U)	767	—	—	0.50	1.50	4.50
1978 FM (P)	6,931	PF65 1.50				
1979	—	—	—	0.10	0.25	1.00
1979 FM (P)	2,053	PF65 2.00				
1980	4,000,000	—	—	0.10	0.25	1.00
1980 FM (P)	2,084	PF65 2.00				
1981	5,000,000	—	—	0.10	0.25	1.00
1981 FM (M)	—	—	—	0.10	0.25	1.00
1981 FM (P)	1,980	PF65 2.00				
1982	5,000,000	—	—	0.10	0.25	1.00
1982 FM (M)	—	—	—	0.10	0.25	1.00
1982 FM (P)	1,217	PF65 2.00				
1983	8,000,000	—	—	0.10	0.25	1.00
1983 FM (P)	1,020	PF65 2.00				
1984	—	—	—	0.10	0.25	1.00
1984 FM (P)	7,500	PF65 1.50				
1985	12,000,000	—	—	0.10	0.25	1.00
1985 FM (P)	7,500	PF65 1.50				

KM# 59a CENT

2.50 g., Copper Plated Zinc, 19 mm. **Ruler:** Elizabeth II **Obv:** National arms above date **Obv. Legend:** COMMONWEALTH OF THE BAHAMAS **Rev:** Starfish, value at top **Edge:** Plain

Date	Mintage	VF20	XF40	MS60	MS63	MS65
1985	—	—	—	0.10	0.25	0.75
1987	12,000,000	—	—	0.10	0.25	0.75
1989	12,000,000	—	—	0.10	0.25	0.75
1989	—	PF65 2.00				
1990	—	—	—	0.10	0.25	0.75
1991	—	—	—	0.10	0.25	0.75
1992	—	—	—	0.10	0.25	0.75
1995	—	—	—	0.10	0.25	0.75
1996	—	—	—	0.10	0.25	0.75
1997	—	—	—	0.10	0.25	0.75
1998	—	—	—	0.10	0.25	0.75
1999	—	—	—	0.10	0.25	0.75
2000	—	—	—	0.10	0.25	0.75

KM# 3 5 CENTS

3.87 g., Copper-Nickel, 21 mm. **Ruler:** Elizabeth II **Obv:** Bust of Queen Elizabeth II right with tiara **Rev:** Pineapple above garland divides date and value **Edge:** Plain **Note:** The obverse of this coin also comes muled with the reverse of a New Zealand 2-cent piece, KM#32. The undated 1967 error is listed as New Zealand KM#33.

Date	Mintage	VF20	XF40	MS60	MS63	MS65
1966	2,571,000	—	—	0.10	0.25	0.75
1968	600,000	—	—	0.30	1.25	3.00
1969	2,026,000	—	—	0.10	0.25	0.75
1969	75,000	PF65 1.00				
1970	26,000	—	—	0.30	0.60	1.80
1970	23,000	PF65 1.50				

KM# 17 5 CENTS

Copper-Nickel, 21 mm. **Ruler:** Elizabeth II **Obv:** Bust of Queen Elizabeth II right with tiara **Rev:** Pineapple above garland divides date and value **Edge:** Plain

Date	Mintage	VF20	XF40	MS60	MS63	MS65
1971 FM	13,000	—	—	0.15	0.40	1.20
1971 FM (P)	31,000	PF65 1.00				
1972 FM	11,000	—	—	0.15	0.40	1.20
1972 FM (P)	35,000	PF65 1.00				
1973 FM	21,000	—	—	0.15	0.40	1.20
1973 FM (P)	35,000	PF65 1.00				

KM# 38 5 CENTS

3.90 g., Copper-Nickel, 21 mm. **Ruler:** Elizabeth II **Obv:** Bust right **Obv. Legend:** THE COMMONWEALTH OF THE BAHAMAS **Rev:** Pineapple **Edge:** Plain

Date	Mintage	VF20	XF40	MS60	MS63	MS65
1973	1,000,000	—	—	0.10	0.65	1.75

KM# 60 5 CENTS

3.94 g., Copper-Nickel, 21 mm. **Ruler:** Elizabeth II **Obv:** National arms above date **Obv. Legend:** COMMONWEALTH OF THE BAHAMAS **Rev:** Pineapple above garland divides value at top **Edge:** Plain

Date	Mintage	VF20	XF40	MS60	MS63	MS65
1974 FM	23,000	—	—	0.10	0.50	1.50
1974 FM (P)	94,000	PF65 1.00				
1975	—	—	—	0.10	0.30	0.90
1975 FM (M)	12,000	—	—	0.10	0.50	1.50

Date	Mintage	VF20	XF40	MS60	MS63	MS65
1975 FM (U)	3,845	—	—	0.15	0.75	2.25
1975 FM (P)	29,000	PF65 1.00				
1976 FM (M)	12,000	—	—	0.10	0.25	0.75
1976 FM (U)	1,453	—	—	0.50	1.00	3.00
1976 FM (P)	23,000	PF65 1.00				
1977 FM (M)	12,000	—	—	0.10	0.35	1.00
1977 FM (U)	713	—	—	0.50	1.50	4.50
1977 FM (P)	11,000	PF65 1.00				
1978 FM (M)	12,000	—	—	0.10	0.35	1.00
1978 FM (U)	767	—	—	0.50	1.50	4.50
1978 FM (P)	6,931	PF65 1.00				
1979 FM (P)	2,053	PF65 1.50				
1980 FM (P)	2,084	PF65 1.50				
1981	—	—	—	0.10	0.25	0.75
1981 FM (P)	1,980	PF65 1.50				
1982 FM (P)	1,217	PF65 1.50				
1983	2,000,000	—	—	0.10	0.25	0.75
1983 FM (P)	1,020	PF65 1.50				
1984	—	—	—	0.10	0.25	0.75
1984 FM (P)	1,036	PF65 1.50				
1985 FM (P)	7,500	PF65 1.50				
1987	4,000,000	—	—	0.10	0.25	0.75
1989	—	—	—	0.10	0.25	0.75
1989 (P)	—	PF65 1.50				
1991	—	—	—	0.10	0.25	0.75
1992	—	—	—	0.10	0.25	0.75
1996	—	—	—	0.10	0.25	0.75
1998	—	—	—	0.10	0.25	0.75
1999	—	—	—	0.10	0.25	0.75
2000	—	—	—	0.10	0.25	0.75

KM# 4 10 CENTS

5.54 g., Copper-Nickel, 23.5 mm. **Ruler:** Elizabeth II **Obv:** Bust of Queen Elizabeth II right with tiara, within beaded circle **Rev:** Two Bonefish between value and date **Shape:** Scallop

Date	Mintage	VF20	XF40	MS60	MS63	MS65
1966	2,198,000	—	—	0.10	0.50	1.50
1968	550,000	—	—	2.00	4.00	8.00
1969	2,026,000	—	—	0.10	0.50	1.50
1969	10,000	PF65 1.00				
1970	27,000	—	—	0.15	0.60	1.80
1970	23,000	PF65 1.00				

KM# 18 10 CENTS

Copper-Nickel, 23.5 mm. **Ruler:** Elizabeth II **Obv:** Bust of Queen Elizabeth II right with tiara, within beaded circle **Rev:** Two Bonefish between value and date **Edge:** Plain **Shape:** Scallop

Date	Mintage	VF20	XF40	MS60	MS63	MS65
1971 FM	13,000	—	—	0.15	0.50	1.50
1971 FM (P)	31,000	PF65 1.00				
1972 FM	11,000	—	—	0.15	0.50	1.50
1972 FM (P)	35,000	PF65 1.00				
1973 FM	15,000	—	—	0.15	0.50	1.50
1973 FM (P)	35,000	PF65 1.00				

KM# 39 10 CENTS

5.54 g., Copper-Nickel, 23.5 mm. **Ruler:** Elizabeth II **Obv. Legend:** THE COMMONWEALTH OF THE BAHAMAS **Rev:** Two Bonefish between value and date

Date	Mintage	VF20	XF40	MS60	MS63	MS65
1973	1,000,000	—	—	0.15	1.00	2.00

KM# 61 10 CENTS

5.13 g., Copper-Nickel, 23.5 mm. **Ruler:** Elizabeth II **Obv:** National arms, date below, within beaded circle **Rev:** Two bonefish above denomination **Edge:** Plain **Shape:** Scalloped

Date	Mintage	VF20	XF40	MS60	MS63	MS65
1974 FM	17,000	—	—	0.10	0.50	1.50
1974 FM (P)	94,000	PF65 1.50				
1975	3,000,000	—	—	0.10	0.50	1.50
1975 FM (M)	6,000	—	—	0.15	0.50	1.50
1975 FM (U)	3,845	—	—	0.15	0.50	1.50
1975 FM (P)	29,000	PF65 1.50				
1976 FM (M)	6,000	—	—	0.15	0.50	1.50
1976 FM (U)	1,453	—	—	0.25	1.00	3.00
1976 FM (P)	23,000	PF65 1.50				
1977 FM (M)	6,000	—	—	0.15	0.50	1.50
1977 FM (U)	713	—	—	0.50	1.50	3.00
1977 FM (P)	11,000	PF65 1.50				
1978 FM (M)	6,000	—	—	0.15	0.50	1.50

Date	Mintage	VF20	XF40	MS60	MS63	MS65
1978 FM (U)	767	—	—	0.50	1.50	3.00
1978 FM (P)	6,931	PF65 2.00				
1979 FM (P)	2,053	PF65 2.50				
1980	2,500,000	—	—	0.10	0.50	1.50
1980 FM (P)	2,084	PF65 2.50				
1981 FM (P)	1,980	PF65 2.50				
1982	2,000,000	—	—	0.10	0.50	1.50
1982 FM (P)	1,217	PF65 2.50				
1983 FM (P)	1,020	PF65 2.50				
1984 FM (P)	1,036	PF65 2.50				
1985	2,000,000	—	—	0.10	0.50	1.50
1985 FM (M)	—	—	—	0.15	0.50	1.50
1985 FM (P)	7,500	PF65 2.00				
1987	3,000,000	—	—	0.15	0.50	1.50
1989	—	—	—	0.15	0.50	1.50
1989	—	PF65 2.00				
1991	—	—	—	0.15	0.50	1.50
1992	—	—	—	0.15	0.50	1.50
1996	—	—	—	0.15	0.50	1.50
1998	—	—	—	0.15	0.50	1.50
2000	—	—	—	0.15	0.50	1.00

KM# 5 15 CENTS

6.50 g., Copper-Nickel, 25 mm. **Ruler:** Elizabeth II **Obv:** Bust of Queen Elizabeth II right with tiara **Rev:** Hibiscus, date divides value at bottom **Edge:** Plain **Shape:** 4-sided

Date	Mintage	VF20	XF40	MS60	MS63	MS65
1966	930,000	—	—	1.00	2.00	3.00
1969	1,026,000	—	—	0.20	0.75	2.25
1969	10,000	PF65 2.00				
1970	28,000	—	—	0.25	0.75	2.25
1970	23,000	PF65 1.50				

KM# 19 15 CENTS

6.50 g., Copper-Nickel, 25 mm. **Ruler:** Elizabeth II **Obv:** Bust of Queen Elizabeth II right with tiara **Rev:** Hibiscus, date divides value below **Edge:** Plain **Shape:** 4-sided

Date	Mintage	VF20	XF40	MS60	MS63	MS65
1971 FM	13,000	—	—	0.20	0.50	1.50
1971 FM	31,000	PF65 1.50				
1972 FM	11,000	—	—	0.20	0.50	1.50
1972 FM	35,000	PF65 1.50				
1973 FM	14,000	—	—	0.20	0.50	1.50
1973 FM	35,000	PF65 1.50				

KM# 62 15 CENTS

6.50 g., Copper-Nickel, 25 mm. **Ruler:** Elizabeth II **Obv:** National arms above date **Rev:** Hibiscus, value divided at bottom **Edge:** Plain **Shape:** 4-sided

Date	Mintage	VF20	XF40	MS60	MS63	MS65
1974 FM	15,000	—	—	0.20	0.50	1.50
1974 FM (P)	94,000	PF65 1.50				
1975 FM (M)	3,500	—	—	0.25	1.00	3.00
1975 FM (U)	3,845	—	—	0.25	1.00	3.00
1975 FM (P)	29,000	PF65 1.50				
1976 FM (M)	3,500	—	—	0.25	1.00	3.00
1976 FM (U)	1,453	—	—	0.30	1.50	4.50
1976 FM (P)	23,000	PF65 1.50				
1977 FM (M)	3,500	—	—	0.25	1.00	3.00
1977 FM (U)	713	—	—	0.50	2.00	6.00
1977 FM (P)	11,000	PF65 1.00				
1978 FM (M)	3,500	—	—	0.25	1.00	3.00
1978 FM (U)	767	—	—	0.50	2.00	6.00
1978 FM (P)	6,931	PF65 1.50				
1979 FM (P)	2,053	PF65 2.00				
1980 FM (P)	2,084	PF65 2.00				
1981 FM (P)	1,980	PF65 2.00				
1982 FM (P)	1,217	PF65 2.50				
1983 FM (P)	1,020	PF65 3.00				

Date	Mintage	VF20	XF40	MS60	MS63	MS65
1984 FM (P)	1,036	PF65 3.00				
1985 FM (P)	7,500	PF65 2.25				
1989	—	—	—	0.20	0.50	1.50
1989 (P)	—	PF65 3.00				
1991	—	—	—	0.20	0.50	1.50
1992	—	—	—	0.20	0.50	1.50
1996	—	—	—	0.20	0.50	1.50

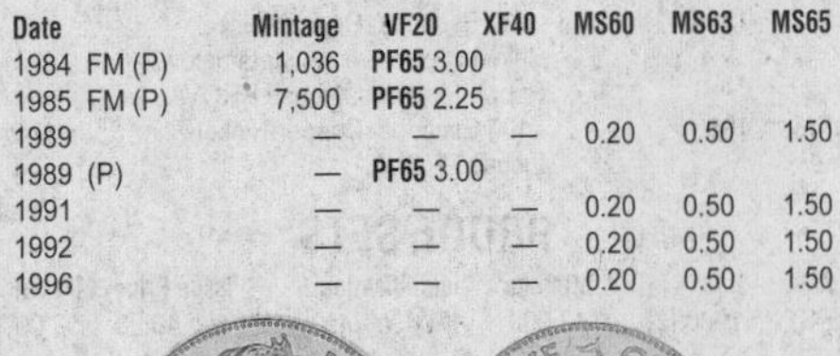

KM# 6 25 CENTS

6.90 g., Nickel, 24.26 mm. **Ruler:** Elizabeth II **Obv:** Bust of Queen Elizabeth II right with tiara **Rev:** Bahamian Sloop, value, date **Edge:** Reeded

Date	Mintage	VF20	XF40	MS60	MS63	MS65
1966	3,685,000	—	—	0.30	0.50	1.50
1969	1,026,000	—	—	0.30	0.50	1.50
1969	10,000	PF65 1.50				
1970	26,000	—	—	0.35	0.75	2.25
1970 FM (P)	23,000	PF65 2.00				
1970 FM (M)	—	—	—	—	—	—

KM# 20 25 CENTS

6.90 g., Nickel, 24.26 mm. **Ruler:** Elizabeth II **Obv:** Bust of Queen Elizabeth II right with tiara **Rev:** Bahamian Sloop, value, date **Edge:** Reeded

Date	Mintage	VF20	XF40	MS60	MS63	MS65
1971 FM	13,000	—	—	0.30	0.50	1.50
1971 FM (P)	31,000	PF65 1.50				
1972 FM	11,000	—	—	0.30	0.50	1.50
1972 FM (M)	—	—	—	0.30	0.50	1.50
1972 FM (P)	35,000	PF65 1.50				
1973 FM	12,000	—	—	0.30	0.50	1.50
1973 FM (P)	35,000	PF65 1.50				

KM# 63.1 25 CENTS

6.90 g., Nickel, 24.26 mm. **Ruler:** Elizabeth II **Obv:** National arms above date, beaded rim **Rev:** Bahamian Sloop, value above **Edge:** Reeded

Date	Mintage	VF20	XF40	MS60	MS63	MS65
1974 FM	13,000	—	—	0.30	0.50	1.50
1974 FM (P)	—	PF65 1.50				
1975 FM (M)	2,400	—	—	0.35	1.00	3.00
1975 FM (U)	3,845	—	—	0.35	1.00	3.00
1975 FM (P)	—	PF65 1.50				
1976 FM (M)	2,400	—	—	0.35	1.00	3.00
1976 FM (U)	1,453	—	—	0.35	1.25	3.75
1976 FM (P)	—	PF65 1.50				
1977	—	—	—	0.30	0.50	1.50
1977 FM (M)	2,400	—	—	0.35	1.00	3.00
1977 FM (U)	713	—	—	0.50	3.00	9.00
1977 FM (P)	11,000	PF65 1.50				
1978 FM	2,400	—	—	0.35	1.00	3.00
1978 FM (U)	767	—	—	0.50	3.00	9.00
1978 FM (P)	—	PF65 2.00				
1979	—	—	—	0.30	0.50	1.50
1979 FM (P)	—	PF65 3.00				
1980 FM (P)	—	PF65 3.00				
1981	1,600,000	—	—	0.30	0.50	1.50
1981 FM (P)	1,980	PF65 3.00				
1982 FM (P)	1,217	PF65 4.00				
1983 FM (P)	1,020	PF65 4.00				
1984 FM (P)	1,036	PF65 4.00				
1985	2,000,000	—	—	0.30	0.50	1.50
1985 FM (P)	—	PF65 2.00				
1987	—	—	—	0.30	0.50	1.50
1989	—	—	—	0.30	0.50	1.50
1989 (P)	—	PF65 3.00				

KM# 63.2 25 CENTS

5.75 g., Copper-Nickel, 24.26 mm. **Ruler:** Elizabeth II **Obv:** National arms, date below **Rev:** Bahamian Sloop, value above **Edge:** Reeded

Date	Mintage	VF20	XF40	MS60	MS63	MS65
1991	—	—	—	0.30	0.50	1.50
1992	—	—	—	0.30	0.50	1.50
1996	—	—	—	0.30	0.50	1.50
1997	—	—	—	0.30	0.50	1.50
1998	—	—	—	0.30	0.50	1.50
2000	—	—	—	0.30	0.50	1.50

KM# 7 50 CENTS

10.37 g., 0.800 Silver 0.2667 oz. ASW, 29 mm. **Ruler:** Elizabeth II **Obv:** Bust of Queen Elizabeth II right with tiara **Rev:** Blue Marlin, value and date at right

Date	Mintage	VF20	XF40	MS60	MS63	MS65
1966	701,000	—	—	5.25	6.00	8.00
1969	26,000	—	—	5.25	6.00	8.00
1969	10,000	**PF65** 11.00				
1970	25,000	—	—	5.25	6.00	8.00
1970	23,000	**PF65** 11.00				

KM# 21 50 CENTS

10.37 g., 0.800 Silver 0.2667 oz. ASW, 29 mm. **Ruler:** Elizabeth II **Obv:** Bust of Queen Elizabeth II right with tiara **Rev:** Blue Marlin, value and date at right

Date	Mintage	VF20	XF40	MS60	MS63	MS65
1971 FM	14,000	—	—	5.25	6.00	8.00
1971 FM (P)	31,000	**PF65** 11.00				
1972 FM	12,000	—	—	5.25	6.00	8.00
1972 FM (P)	35,000	**PF65** 11.00				
1973 FM	11,000	—	—	5.25	6.00	8.00
1973 FM (P)	35,000	**PF65** 11.00				

KM# 64 50 CENTS

Copper-Nickel, 29 mm. **Ruler:** Elizabeth II **Obv:** National arms, date below **Rev:** Blue Marlin, value at right

Date	Mintage	VF20	XF40	MS60	MS63	MS65
1974 FM	12,000	—	—	0.60	2.00	4.00
1975 FM (M)	1,200	—	—	1.00	6.00	12.00
1975 FM (U)	3,828	—	—	0.65	4.00	8.00
1976 FM (M)	1,200	—	—	0.75	5.00	10.00
1976 FM (U)	1,453	—	—	0.65	4.00	8.00
1977 FM (M)	1,200	—	—	0.75	5.00	10.00
1977 FM (U)	713	—	—	1.25	10.00	15.00
1978 FM (M)	1,200	—	—	1.00	8.00	12.00
1978 FM (U)	767	—	—	1.25	10.00	15.00
1981 FM (P)	1,980	**PF65** 6.00				
1982 FM (P)	1,217	**PF65** 7.00				
1983 FM (P)	1,020	**PF65** 7.00				
1984 FM (P)	1,036	**PF65** 7.00				
1985 FM (P)	7,500	**PF65** 5.00				
1989	—	—	—	0.75	2.25	3.00
1989	—	**PF65** 5.00				
1991	—	—	—	0.75	2.25	3.00
1992	—	—	—	0.75	2.25	3.00
1996	—	—	—	0.75	2.50	3.00

KM# 64a 50 CENTS

10.37 g., 0.800 Silver 0.2667 oz. ASW, 29 mm. **Ruler:** Elizabeth II **Obv:** National arms above date **Rev:** Blue Marlin to left of value

Date	Mintage	VF20	XF40	MS60	MS63	MS65
1974 FM (P)	94,000	**PF65** 8.00				
1975 FM (P)	29,000	**PF65** 8.00				
1976 FM (P)	23,000	**PF65** 8.00				
1977 FM (P)	11,000	**PF65** 8.00				
1978 FM (P)	6,931	**PF65** 10.00				
1979 FM (P)	2,053	**PF65** 17.00				
1980 FM (P)	2,084	**PF65** 17.00				

KM# 8 DOLLAR

18.14 g., 0.800 Silver 0.4666 oz. ASW, 34 mm. **Ruler:** Elizabeth II **Obv:** Bust of Queen Elizabeth II right with tiara **Rev:** Conch shell above garland, within 3/4 beaded circle, value and date above circle

Date	Mintage	VF20	XF40	MS60	MS63	MS65
1966	406,000	—	—	9.25	12.00	15.00
1969	26,000	—	—	9.25	12.00	15.00
1969	10,000	**PF65** 12.00				
1970	27,000	—	—	9.25	12.00	15.00
1970	23,000	**PF65** 12.00				

KM# 22 DOLLAR

18.14 g., 0.800 Silver 0.4666 oz. ASW, 34 mm. **Ruler:** Elizabeth II **Obv:** Bust of Queen Elizabeth II right with tiara **Rev:** Conch shell above garland within 3/4 beaded circle, value and date above

Date	Mintage	VF20	XF40	MS60	MS63	MS65
1971 FM	15,000	—	—	9.25	12.00	15.00
1971 FM (P)	31,000	**PF65** 12.00				
1972 FM	18,000	—	—	9.25	12.00	15.00
1972 FM (P)	35,000	**PF65** 12.00				
1973 FM	10,000	—	—	9.25	12.00	15.00
1973 FM (P)	35,000	**PF65** 12.00				

KM# 65 DOLLAR

Copper-Nickel, 34 mm. **Ruler:** Elizabeth II **Obv:** National arms above daate **Rev:** Conch shell above garland within 3/4 beaded circle, value at top

Date	Mintage	VF20	XF40	MS60	MS63	MS65
1974 FM	12,000	—	—	1.25	2.50	4.50
1975 FM (M)	600	—	—	7.50	25.00	—
1975 FM (U)	3,845	—	—	1.50	3.50	6.50
1976 FM (M)	600	—	—	7.50	25.00	—
1976 FM (U)	1,453	—	—	1.75	10.00	13.50
1977 FM (M)	600	—	—	7.50	25.00	—
1977 FM (U)	713	—	—	5.00	25.00	—
1978 FM (U)	1,367	—	—	2.00	10.00	13.50

KM# 65a DOLLAR

18.14 g., 0.800 Silver 0.4666 oz. ASW, 34 mm. **Ruler:** Elizabeth II **Obv:** National arms above date **Rev:** Conch shell above garland within 3/4 beaded circle below value

Date	Mintage	VF20	XF40	MS60	MS63	MS65
1974 FM (P)	94,000	**PF65** 12.00				
1975 FM (P)	29,000	**PF65** 12.00				
1976 FM (P)	23,000	**PF65** 12.00				
1977 FM (P)	11,000	**PF65** 14.00				
1978 FM (P)	6,931	**PF65** 14.00				
1979 FM (P)	2,053	**PF65** 18.00				
1980 FM (P)	2,084	**PF65** 18.00				

KM# 65b DOLLAR

Copper-Nickel, 32 mm. **Ruler:** Elizabeth II **Obv:** National arms above date **Rev:** Conch shell above garland within 3/4 beaded circle below value

Date	Mintage	VF20	XF40	MS60	MS63	MS65
1981 FM (P)	1,980	**PF65** 17.00				
1989	—	—	—	1.50	3.00	5.00
1989 (P)	—	**PF65** 17.00				
1991	—	—	—	1.50	3.00	5.00
1992	—	—	—	1.50	3.00	5.00
1996	—	—	—	1.50	3.00	5.00

KM# 89 DOLLAR

Copper-Nickel **Ruler:** Elizabeth II **Obv:** National arms, date below **Rev:** Poinciana flower, value above

Date	Mintage	VF20	XF40	MS60	MS63	MS65
1982 FM (P)	1,217	**PF65** 20.00				

KM# 93 DOLLAR

Copper-Nickel **Ruler:** Elizabeth II **Subject:** 10th Anniversary of Independence **Rev:** Allamanda flower, value above

Date	Mintage	VF20	XF40	MS60	MS63	MS65
1983 FM (P)	1,020	**PF65** 20.00				

KM# 104 DOLLAR

Copper-Nickel **Ruler:** Elizabeth II **Rev:** Bougainvillea flower, value above

Date	Mintage	VF20	XF40	MS60	MS63	MS65
1984 FM (P)	1,036	**PF65** 20.00				
1985 FM (P)	7,500	**PF65** 10.00				

KM# 154 DOLLAR

Copper-Nickel **Ruler:** Elizabeth II **Note:** Golf - Hole in One. Similar to 5 Dollars, KM#155.

Date	Mintage	VF20	XF40	MS60	MS63	MS65
1994	20,000	—	—	—	10.00	15.00

KM# 186 DOLLAR

1.24 g., 0.9999 Gold 0.040 oz. AGW **Ruler:** Elizabeth II **Rev:** Two flamingos **Note:** Similar to 5 Dollars, KM#188.

Date	Mintage	VF20	XF40	MS60	MS63	MS65
1995	—	**PF65** 75.00				

KM# 176 DOLLAR

31.18 g., 0.999 Silver 1.0015 oz. ASW **Ruler:** Elizabeth II **Subject:** Third Millennium - Year 2000 **Obv:** Crowned bust of Queen Elizabeth II right, date below **Rev:** Artistic map, value below

Date	Mintage	VF20	XF40	MS60	MS63	MS65
1996	50,000	PF65 28.00				

KM# 214 DOLLAR

Copper-Nickel **Ruler:** Elizabeth II **Subject:** 2000 Years of Christianity **Obv:** Crowned bust right

Date	Mintage	VF20	XF40	MS60	MS63	MS65
2000	—	—	—	—	6.00	9.00

KM# 9 2 DOLLARS

29.80 g., 0.925 Silver 0.8862 oz. ASW, 40 mm. **Ruler:** Elizabeth II **Obv:** Bust of Queen Elizabeth II right with tiara **Rev:** National bird - two flamingos, value and date at top

Date	Mintage	VF20	XF40	MS60	MS63	MS65
1966	104,000	—	—	17.50	20.50	24.50
1969	26,000	—	—	17.50	20.50	24.50
1969	10,000	PF65 23.50				
1970	32,000	—	—	17.50	20.50	24.50
1970	23,000	PF65 23.50				

KM# 23 2 DOLLARS

29.80 g., 0.925 Silver 0.8862 oz. ASW, 40 mm. **Ruler:** Elizabeth II **Obv:** Bust of Queen Elizabeth II right with tiara **Rev:** National bird-two flamingos, value and date at top

Date	Mintage	VF20	XF40	MS60	MS63	MS65
1971 FM	88,000	—	—	17.50	20.50	24.50
1971 FM (P)	60,000	PF65 23.50				
1972 FM	65,000	—	—	17.50	20.50	24.50
1972 FM (P)	59,000	PF65 23.50				
1973 FM	43,000	—	—	17.50	20.50	24.50
1973 FM (P)	50,000	PF65 23.50				

KM# 66 2 DOLLARS

Copper-Nickel, 40 mm. **Ruler:** Elizabeth II **Obv:** National arms, date below **Rev:** Two flamingos, value above **Edge:** Reeded

Date	Mintage	VF20	XF40	MS60	MS63	MS65
1974 FM	37,000	—	—	2.00	3.00	5.00
1975 FM (M)	300	—	—	9.00	25.00	—
1975 FM (U)	8,810	—	—	2.00	3.50	6.00
1976 FM (M)	300	—	—	9.00	25.00	—
1976 FM (U)	4,381	—	—	2.00	4.00	7.00
1977 FM (M)	300	—	—	9.00	25.00	—
1977 FM (U)	946	—	—	3.00	20.00	—
1978 FM (U)	1,067	—	—	3.00	15.00	—
1979 FM (U)	300	—	—	7.50	25.00	—
1980 FM (U)	—	—	—	—	75.00	—

KM# 66a 2 DOLLARS

29.80 g., 0.925 Silver 0.8862 oz. ASW, 40 mm. **Ruler:** Elizabeth II **Obv:** National arms above date **Rev:** Two flamingos, value above

Date	Mintage	VF20	XF40	MS60	MS63	MS65
1974 FM (P)	129,000	PF65 19.50				
1975 FM (P)	45,000	PF65 21.50				
1976 FM (P)	35,000	PF65 21.50				
1977 FM (P)	15,000	PF65 23.50				
1978 FM (P)	11,000	PF65 23.50				
1979 FM (P)	2,053	PF65 25.50				
1980 FM (P)	2,084	PF65 25.50				

KM# 66b 2 DOLLARS

Copper-Nickel, 40 mm. **Ruler:** Elizabeth II **Obv:** National arms above date **Rev:** Two flamingos, value above

Date	Mintage	VF20	XF40	MS60	MS63	MS65
1981 FM (P)	1,980	PF65 25.00				
1989	—	—	—	2.00	3.00	5.00

KM# 66c 2 DOLLARS

16.85 g., 0.925 Silver 0.5011 oz. ASW **Ruler:** Elizabeth II **Obv:** National arms above date **Rev:** Two flamingos, value above

Date	Mintage	VF20	XF40	MS60	MS63	MS65
1989	Est. 4000	PF65 20.00				
1991	600	—	—	—	50.00	75.00

KM# 90 2 DOLLARS

Copper-Nickel, 34 mm. **Ruler:** Elizabeth II **Obv:** National arms, date below **Rev:** Bahama swallows, value at top **Edge:** Reeded

Date	Mintage	VF20	XF40	MS60	MS63	MS65
1982 FM (P)	1,217	PF65 30.00				

KM# 94 2 DOLLARS

Copper-Nickel **Ruler:** Elizabeth II **Subject:** 10th Anniversary of Independence **Rev:** Honeycreepers, value at top

Date	Mintage	VF20	XF40	MS60	MS63	MS65
1983 FM (P)	1,020	PF65 30.00				

KM# 105 2 DOLLARS

Copper-Nickel **Ruler:** Elizabeth II **Rev:** Flamingos in flight, value at top

Date	Mintage	VF20	XF40	MS60	MS63	MS65
1984 FM (P)	1,036	PF65 25.00				
1985 FM (P)	7,500	PF65 12.50				

KM# 158 2 DOLLARS

28.28 g., 0.925 Silver 0.841 oz. ASW **Ruler:** Elizabeth II **Subject:** Royal Visit **Obv:** Coat of Arms **Rev:** Portraits and yacht, date at right

Date	Mintage	VF20	XF40	MS60	MS63	MS65
1994	10,000	PF65 22.00				

KM# 164 2 DOLLARS

31.10 g., 0.999 Silver 0.999 oz. ASW **Ruler:** Elizabeth II **Series:** Flora and Fauna **Obv:** National arms, date below **Rev:** Hibiscus flower and value within square, coin value below **Note:** Multicolor applique.

Date	Mintage	VF20	XF40	MS60	MS63	MS65
1995	25,000	PF65 26.00				

KM# 165 2 DOLLARS
28.28 g., 0.999 Silver 0.9083 oz. ASW, 38.61 mm. **Ruler:** Elizabeth II **Series:** Flora and Fauna **Rev:** Bahama Amazon Parrot on branch, value below **Note:** Multicolor applique.

Date	Mintage	VF20	XF40	MS60	MS63	MS65
1995	10,000	PF65 26.00				

KM# 166 2 DOLLARS
28.28 g., 0.999 Silver 0.9083 oz. ASW **Ruler:** Elizabeth II **Series:** Flora and Fauna **Rev:** Caribbean Monk Seal, value below **Note:** Multicolor applique.

Date	Mintage	VF20	XF40	MS60	MS63	MS65
1995	10,000	PF65 26.00				

KM# 183.1 2 DOLLARS
23.33 g., 0.925 Silver 0.6938 oz. ASW **Ruler:** Elizabeth II **Series:** Olympics **Subject:** Catamaran Sailing **Obv:** Crowned bust of Queen Elizabeth II right, date below **Rev:** Two figures on catamaran, sailing, value below **Rev. Legend:** OLIMPIC GAMES... **Note:** Reverse legend spelling error.

Date	Mintage	VF20	XF40	MS60	MS63	MS65
1995	30,000	PF65 21.50				

KM# 183.2 2 DOLLARS
23.33 g., 0.925 Silver 0.6938 oz. ASW **Ruler:** Elizabeth II **Series:** Olympics **Subject:** Catamaran Sailing **Rev:** Two figures on catamaran, sailing, value below **Rev. Legend:** OLYMPIC GAMES... **Note:** Corrected reverse legend.

Date	Mintage	VF20	XF40	MS60	MS63	MS65
1995	Inc. above	PF65 16.50				

KM# 187 2 DOLLARS
3.11 g., 0.9999 Gold 0.100 oz. AGW **Ruler:** Elizabeth II **Obv:** Crowned bust right, date below **Rev:** Two flamingos

Date	Mintage	VF20	XF40	MS60	MS63	MS65
1995	—	PF65 175				

KM# 177 2 DOLLARS
3.11 g., 0.9999 Gold 0.100 oz. AGW **Ruler:** Elizabeth II **Subject:** Third Millennium - Year 2000 **Obv:** Queen's portrait **Rev:** Sea shell shaped map **Note:** Similar to 1 Dollar, KM#176.

Date	Mintage	VF20	XF40	MS60	MS63	MS65
1996	10,000	PF65 175				

KM# 203 2 DOLLARS
23.33 g., 0.925 Silver 0.6938 oz. ASW, 38.6 mm. **Ruler:** Elizabeth II **Subject:** Protect Our World **Obv:** Queen's head right **Rev:** Flamingo and map, value below **Edge:** Reeded

Date	Mintage	VF20	XF40	MS60	MS63	MS65
1996	—	PF65 18.50				

KM# 198 2 DOLLARS
28.28 g., 0.925 Silver 0.841 oz. ASW **Ruler:** Elizabeth II **Subject:** WWF Conserving Nature **Obv:** Queen's portrait **Rev:** Spotfin Butterfly Fish and a Queen Angelfish, value below

Date	Mintage	VF20	XF40	MS60	MS63	MS65
1997	Est. 15000	PF65 22.00				

KM# 204 2 DOLLARS
23.32 g., 0.925 Silver 0.6935 oz. ASW, 38.5 mm. **Ruler:** Elizabeth II **Subject:** Queen Mother **Obv:** Crowned bust of Queen Elizabeth II right, date below **Rev:** Queen Mother's portrait circa 1908, within beaded circle, value below circle **Edge:** Reeded

Date	Mintage	VF20	XF40	MS60	MS63	MS65
1997	—	PF65 18.50				

KM# 206 2 DOLLARS
23.23 g., 0.925 Silver 0.6908 oz. ASW, 38.6 mm. **Ruler:** Elizabeth II **Subject:** UNICEF **Obv:** Bust of Queen Elizabeth II, right **Rev:** Two boys and a dolphin, value below **Edge:** Reeded

Date	Mintage	VF20	XF40	MS60	MS63	MS65
1997	25,000	PF65 18.50				

KM# 208 2 DOLLARS
23.33 g., 0.925 Silver 0.6937 oz. ASW **Ruler:** Elizabeth II **Subject:** FIFA - XVI World Championship Football - France 1998 **Obv:** Crowned bust right **Rev:** Ball being played

Date	Mintage	VF20	XF40	MS60	MS63	MS65
1997	—	PF65 18.50				

KM# 207 2 DOLLARS
28.20 g., 0.925 Silver 0.8387 oz. ASW with gilt outer ring, 38.5 mm. **Ruler:** Elizabeth II **Subject:** Queen Mother **Obv:** Queen's portrait **Rev:** Queen Mother with dog **Edge:** Reeded

Date	Mintage	VF20	XF40	MS60	MS63	MS65
2000	—	PF65 22.00				

KM# 215 2 DOLLARS
28.20 g., 0.925 Silver 0.8387 oz. ASW **Ruler:** Elizabeth II **Subject:** 2000 Years of Christianity **Obv:** Crowned bust right

Date	Mintage	VF20	XF40	MS60	MS63	MS65
2000	—	PF65 20.00				

KM# 10 5 DOLLARS
42.12 g., 0.925 Silver 1.2526 oz. ASW, 45 mm. **Ruler:** Elizabeth II **Obv:** Bust right with tiara **Rev:** Shield with crown at top, sailing ships below, banner below shield, garland above, date at right, value above

Date	Mintage	VF20	XF40	MS60	MS63	MS65
1966	100,000	—	—	25.00	29.50	34.00
1969	36,000	—	—	25.00	29.50	34.00
1969	10,000	PF65 35.00				
1970	43,000	—	—	25.00	29.50	34.00
1970	23,000	PF65 34.00				

KM# 24 5 DOLLARS
42.12 g., 0.925 Silver 1.2526 oz. ASW, 45 mm. **Ruler:** Elizabeth II **Obv:** Young bust of Queen Elizabeth II right **Rev:** National arms, date and value

Date	Mintage	VF20	XF40	MS60	MS63	MS65
1971 FM	29,000	—	—	25.00	29.50	34.00
1971 FM (P)	31,000	PF65 34.00				

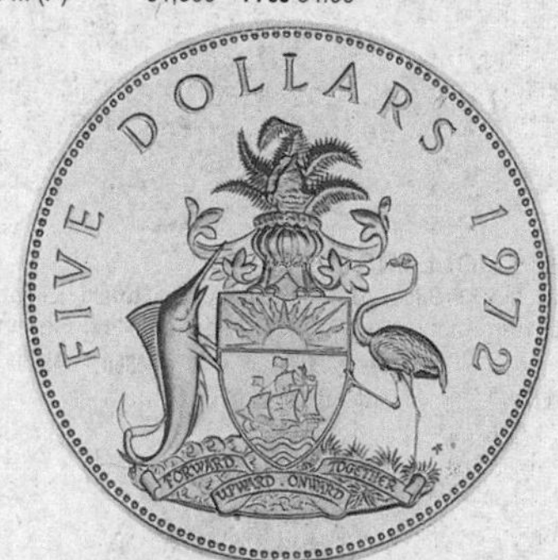

KM# 33 5 DOLLARS
42.12 g., 0.925 Silver 1.2526 oz. ASW, 45 mm. **Ruler:** Elizabeth II **Obv:** Young Queen Elizabeth II right **Rev:** National arms, value, date

Date	Mintage	VF20	XF40	MS60	MS63	MS65
1972 FM	32,000	—	—	25.00	29.50	34.00
1972 FM (P)	35,000	PF65 34.00				
1973 FM	32,000	—	—	25.00	29.50	34.00
1973 FM (P)	35,000	PF65 34.00				

KM# 67 5 DOLLARS

Copper-Nickel, 45 mm. **Ruler:** Elizabeth II **Obv:** National arms **Rev:** National flag, value above **Edge:** Reeded

Date	Mintage	VF20	XF40	MS60	MS63	MS65
1974 FM	32,000	—	—	3.50	6.00	7.50
1975 FM (M)	200	—	—	—	—	40.00
1975 FM (U)	7,058	—	—	—	7.00	9.00
1976 FM (M)	200	—	—	—	—	40.00
1976 FM (U)	2,591	—	—	—	8.00	10.00
1977 FM (M)	200	—	—	—	—	40.00
1977 FM (U)	801	—	—	—	—	30.00
1978 FM (U)	1,244	—	—	—	—	15.00

KM# 67a 5 DOLLARS

42.12 g., 0.925 Silver 1.2526 oz. ASW, 45 mm. **Ruler:** Elizabeth II **Obv:** National arms **Rev:** National flag, value above

Date	Mintage	VF20	XF40	MS60	MS63	MS65
1974 FM (P)	94,000	PF65 32.00				
1975 FM (P)	29,000	PF65 32.00				
1976 FM (P)	23,000	PF65 32.00				
1977 FM (P)	11,000	PF65 33.00				
1978 FM (P)	6,931	PF65 33.00				
1979 FM (P)	2,053	PF65 35.00				
1980 FM (P)	2,084	PF65 35.00				

KM# 67b 5 DOLLARS

42.12 g., 0.500 Silver 0.6771 oz. ASW **Ruler:** Elizabeth II **Obv:** National arms **Rev:** National flag, value above **Note:** Reduced diameter.

Date	Mintage	VF20	XF40	MS60	MS63	MS65
1981 FM (P)	1,980	PF65 21.50				

KM# 91 5 DOLLARS

42.12 g., 0.500 Silver 0.6771 oz. ASW **Ruler:** Elizabeth II **Obv:** National arms **Obv. Legend:** COMMONWEALTH OF THE BAHAMAS 1982 **Rev:** Columbus memorial, cross and ship, value above **Rev. Legend:** FIVE DOLLARS

Date	Mintage	VF20	XF40	MS60	MS63	MS65
1982 FM (P)	1,217	PF65 35.00				

KM# 95 5 DOLLARS

42.12 g., 0.500 Silver 0.6771 oz. ASW **Ruler:** Elizabeth II **Subject:** 10th Anniversary of Independence **Rev:** Flamingo

Date	Mintage	VF20	XF40	MS60	MS63	MS65
1983 FM (P)	1,020	PF65 40.00				

KM# 106 5 DOLLARS

42.12 g., 0.500 Silver 0.6771 oz. ASW **Ruler:** Elizabeth II **Rev:** Historical map, value above

Date	Mintage	VF20	XF40	MS60	MS63	MS65
1984 FM (P)	1,036	PF65 40.00				

KM# 107 5 DOLLARS

42.12 g., 0.500 Silver 0.6771 oz. ASW **Ruler:** Elizabeth II **Obv:** National arms, date below **Rev:** Half-length Christopher Columbus looking left, value above

Date	Mintage	VF20	XF40	MS60	MS63	MS65
1985 FM (P)	7,847	PF65 18.50				

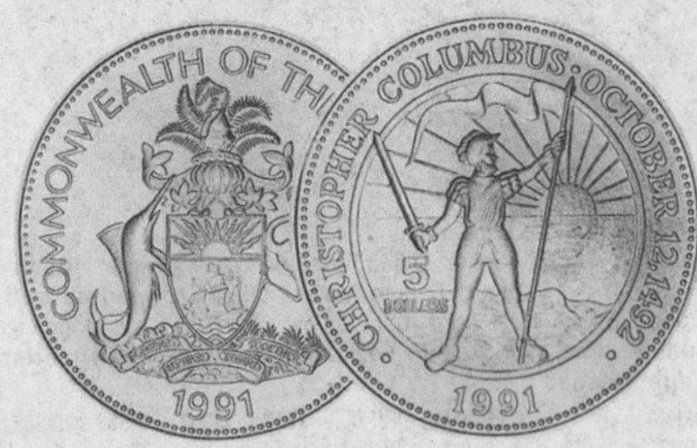

KM# 132 5 DOLLARS

19.44 g., 0.925 Silver 0.5781 oz. ASW **Ruler:** Elizabeth II **Obv:** National arms, date below **Rev:** Standing Christopher Columbus with sword and flag before radiant sun, value lower left, date below **Edge:** Reeded

Date	Mintage	VF20	XF40	MS60	MS63	MS65
1989	Est. 4000	PF65 16.00				
1991	750	—	—	—	—	55.00
1991	7,000	PF65 18.00				

KM# 139 5 DOLLARS

19.44 g., 0.925 Silver 0.5781 oz. ASW **Ruler:** Elizabeth II **Series:** 500th Anniversary of the Americas **Rev:** Bust of Columbus at left, standing Ferdinand and Isabella at right, value below

Date	Mintage	VF20	XF40	MS60	MS63	MS65
1991	Est. 25000	PF65 15.50				

KM# 140 5 DOLLARS

19.44 g., 0.925 Silver 0.5781 oz. ASW **Ruler:** Elizabeth II **Series:** 500th Anniversary of the Americas **Subject:** Columbus sighting land **Rev:** Columbus on ship, inset of picture at right, "1492" below inset, value at bottom

Date	Mintage	VF20	XF40	MS60	MS63	MS65
1991	—	PF65 15.50				

KM# 141 5 DOLLARS

19.44 g., 0.925 Silver 0.5781 oz. ASW **Ruler:** Elizabeth II **Series:** 500th Anniversary of the Americas **Subject:** Columbus claiming the land **Rev:** Columbus claiming the land, value at bottom

Date	Mintage	VF20	XF40	MS60	MS63	MS65
1991	—	PF65 15.50				

KM# 142 5 DOLLARS

19.44 g., 0.925 Silver 0.5781 oz. ASW **Ruler:** Elizabeth II **Series:** 500th Anniversary of the Americas **Rev:** Bust of Jacques Cartier, 3/4 right, and map, value at bottom

Date	Mintage	VF20	XF40	MS60	MS63	MS65
1991	Est. 25000	PF65 15.50				

KM# 143 5 DOLLARS

19.44 g., 0.925 Silver 0.5781 oz. ASW **Ruler:** Elizabeth II **Series:** 500th Anniversary of the Americas **Rev:** Bust of President Thomas Jefferson, facing, looking left, Independence Hall at left with date below, value at bottom

Date	Mintage	VF20	XF40	MS60	MS63	MS65
1991	Est. 25000	PF65 15.50				

KM# 138 5 DOLLARS

19.44 g., 0.925 Silver 0.5781 oz. ASW **Ruler:** Elizabeth II **Series:** Discovery of the New World **Obv:** Coat of arms **Rev:** Columbus' ships within circle, value below circle

Date	Mintage	VF20	XF40	MS60	MS63	MS65
1992	Est. 25000	PF65 15.50				

KM# 144 5 DOLLARS

19.44 g., 0.925 Silver 0.5781 oz. ASW **Ruler:** Elizabeth II **Series:** 500th Anniversary of the Americas **Rev:** Heads of Simon Bolivar and Jose San Martin on right, looking left, small statue of man on horseback at left, names at left, value at bottom

Date	Mintage	VF20	XF40	MS60	MS63	MS65
1992	Est. 25000	PF65 15.50				

KM# 145 5 DOLLARS

19.44 g., 0.925 Silver 0.5781 oz. ASW **Ruler:** Elizabeth II **Series:** 500th Anniversary of the Americas **Subject:** Abolition of slavery **Rev:** Bust of President Abraham Lincoln, 3/4 right, two figures at right, date at left, value at bottom

Date	Mintage	VF20	XF40	MS60	MS63	MS65
1992	Est. 25000	PF65 15.50				

KM# 146 5 DOLLARS

19.44 g., 0.925 Silver 0.5781 oz. ASW **Ruler:** Elizabeth II **Series:** 500th Anniversary of the Americas **Subject:** Electric light demonstration **Rev:** Bust of Thomas Edison with arms crossed, facing, light bulbs and inscription over left shoulder, people and name at right shoulder, value at bottom

Date	Mintage	VF20	XF40	MS60	MS63	MS65
1992	Est. 25000	PF65 15.50				

KM# 147 5 DOLLARS

19.44 g., 0.925 Silver 0.5781 oz. ASW **Ruler:** Elizabeth II **Series:** 500th Anniversary of the Americas **Subject:** Wright brothers' first airplane flight **Rev:** Two standing figures below plane, small date at right, words on lower left, value at bottom

Date	Mintage	VF20	XF40	MS60	MS63	MS65
1992	Est. 25000	PF65 15.50				

KM# 148 5 DOLLARS

19.44 g., 0.925 Silver 0.5781 oz. ASW **Ruler:** Elizabeth II **Series:** 500th Anniversary of the Americas **Rev:** Bust of Henry Ford on left facing right, automobiles at right with date and inscription, value at bottom

Date	Mintage	VF20	XF40	MS60	MS63	MS65
1992	Est. 25000	PF65 15.50				

KM# 149 5 DOLLARS

19.44 g., 0.925 Silver 0.5781 oz. ASW **Ruler:** Elizabeth II **Series:** 500th Anniversary of the Americas **Rev:** Bust of President Roosevelt on right looking left, Panama Canal on left, value at bottom

Date	Mintage	VF20	XF40	MS60	MS63	MS65
1992	Est. 25000	PF65 15.50				

KM# 150 5 DOLLARS

19.44 g., 0.925 Silver 0.5781 oz. ASW **Ruler:** Elizabeth II **Series:** 500th Anniversary of the Americas **Subject:** First manned moonlanding **Rev:** Astronaut on moon on left, planets in orbit and inscription on right, value at bottom

Date	Mintage	VF20	XF40	MS60	MS63	MS65
1992	Est. 25000	PF65 15.50				

KM# 192 5 DOLLARS

1.56 g., 0.500 Gold 0.025 oz. AGW **Ruler:** Elizabeth II **Obv:** Crowned bust of Queen Elizabeth II right, date below **Rev:** Facing pair of flamingos, value above

Date	Mintage	VF20	XF40	MS60	MS63	MS65
1992	—	PF65 65.00				

KM# 159 5 DOLLARS

23.33 g., 0.925 Silver 0.6938 oz. ASW **Ruler:** Elizabeth II **Obv:** Crowned bust of Queen Elizabeth II right, date below **Rev:** Pirate Captain Howell Davis, value below, within circle

Date	Mintage	VF20	XF40	MS60	MS63	MS65
1993	Est. 5000	PF65 18.50				

KM# 160 5 DOLLARS

23.33 g., 0.925 Silver 0.6938 oz. ASW **Ruler:** Elizabeth II **Obv:** Crowned bust of Queen Elizabeth II right, date below **Rev:** Pirate Captain Charles Vane, value at left foot, within circle

Date	Mintage	VF20	XF40	MS60	MS63	MS65
1993	Est. 5000	PF65 18.50				

KM# 161 5 DOLLARS

23.33 g., 0.925 Silver 0.6938 oz. ASW **Ruler:** Elizabeth II **Rev:** Pirate Captain Edward Teach, value lower left, within circle

Date	Mintage	VF20	XF40	MS60	MS63	MS65
1993	—	PF65 18.50				

KM# 169 5 DOLLARS

23.33 g., 0.925 Silver 0.6938 oz. ASW **Ruler:** Elizabeth II **Subject:** World Soccer Championship **Rev:** Soccer player kicking soccer ball value at lower left

Date	Mintage	VF20	XF40	MS60	MS63	MS65
1993	Est. 15000	PF65 18.50				

KM# 170 5 DOLLARS

23.33 g., 0.925 Silver 0.6938 oz. ASW **Ruler:** Elizabeth II **Rev:** Sailing ship, flamingo on right, Marlin on left, value at bottom

Date	Mintage	VF20	XF40	MS60	MS63	MS65
1993	—	PF65 18.50				

KM# 155 5 DOLLARS

31.10 g., 0.999 Silver 0.999 oz. ASW **Ruler:** Elizabeth II **Subject:** Golf - Hole in One **Obv:** National arms within 3/4 circle, legend around, date below **Obv. Legend:** COMMONWEALTH OF THE BAHAMAS **Rev:** Golf ball rolling towards cup **Note:** The cup is an actual hole in the coin.

Date	Mintage	VF20	XF40	MS60	MS63	MS65
1994	Est. 50000	PF65 55.00				

KM# 171 5 DOLLARS
31.10 g., 0.999 Silver 0.999 oz. ASW **Ruler:** Elizabeth II **Rev:** Space shuttle and satellite, value at upper left

Date	Mintage	VF20	XF40	MS60	MS63	MS65
1994	Est. 10000	PF65 36.00				

KM# 172 5 DOLLARS
23.33 g., 0.925 Silver 0.6938 oz. ASW **Ruler:** Elizabeth II **Obv:** Crowned bust of Queen Elizabeth II right, date below **Rev:** Two Black-billed whistling ducks in flight, value at bottom

Date	Mintage	VF20	XF40	MS60	MS63	MS65
1994	Est. 15000	PF65 27.50				

KM# 173 5 DOLLARS
31.47 g., 0.925 Silver 0.9359 oz. ASW **Ruler:** Elizabeth II **Obv:** Crowned bust of Queen Elizabeth II right, date below **Rev:** Ponce De Leon on horseback at right, small building at left, value below

Date	Mintage	VF20	XF40	MS60	MS63	MS65
1994	Est. 10000	PF65 32.50				

KM# 201 5 DOLLARS
3.11 g., 0.999 Gold 0.0999 oz. AGW **Ruler:** Elizabeth II **Subject:** Golf - Hole in One **Obv:** National arms within 3/4 circle, legend around, date below **Obv. Legend:** COMMONWEALTH OF THE BAHAMAS **Rev:** Golf ball rolling towards cup, value lower right

Date	Mintage	VF20	XF40	MS60	MS63	MS65
1994	250,000	PF65 180				

KM# 188 5 DOLLARS
6.22 g., 0.9999 Gold 0.200 oz. AGW **Ruler:** Elizabeth II **Obv:** Crowned bust of Queen Elizabeth II right, date below **Rev:** Two flamingos facing, value below

Date	Mintage	VF20	XF40	MS60	MS63	MS65
1995	—	PF65 325				

KM# 178 5 DOLLARS
7.78 g., 0.9999 Gold 0.250 oz. AGW **Ruler:** Elizabeth II **Subject:** Third Millennium - Year 2000 **Obv:** Bust of Queen Elizabeth II right **Rev:** Seashell-shaped world map

Date	Mintage	VF20	XF40	MS60	MS63	MS65
1996	5,000	PF65 400				

KM# 11 10 DOLLARS
3.99 g., 0.917 Gold 0.1178 oz. AGW **Ruler:** Elizabeth II **Subject:** Adoption of New Constitution **Obv:** Bust of Queen Elizabeth II right with tiara **Rev:** Fortress, date below, value above

Date	Mintage	VF20	XF40	MS60	MS63	MS65
1967	6,200	—	—	—	200	210
1967	850	PF65 230				

KM# 25 10 DOLLARS
3.99 g., 0.917 Gold 0.1178 oz. AGW **Ruler:** Elizabeth II **Obv:** Bust of Queen Elizabeth II right with tiara **Rev:** Fortress, date below, value above

Date	Mintage	VF20	XF40	MS60	MS63	MS65
1971	23,000	—	—	—	200	210
1971 (t)	1,250	PF65 240				

KM# 26.1 10 DOLLARS
3.99 g., 0.917 Gold 0.1178 oz. AGW **Ruler:** Elizabeth II **Obv:** Bust with tiara right **Rev:** Fortress between value and date, hallmark and fineness stamped right of date **Note:** Struck by the Gori and Zucchi Mint, Italy. Prev. KM#26.

Date	Mintage	VF20	XF40	MS60	MS63	MS65
1971	—	—	—	—	205	215

KM# 26.2 10 DOLLARS
3.99 g., 0.917 Gold 0.1178 oz. AGW **Ruler:** Elizabeth II **Obv:** Bust with tiara right **Rev:** Fortress between value & date, hallmark and fineness stamped left of date **Note:** Struck by the Gori and Zucchi Mint, Italy.

Date	Mintage	VF20	XF40	MS60	MS63	MS65
1971	—	—	—	—	205	215

KM# 34 10 DOLLARS
3.20 g., 0.917 Gold 0.0942 oz. AGW **Ruler:** Elizabeth II **Obv:** Bust of Queen Elizabeth II right **Rev:** Fortress, date below, value above

Date	Mintage	VF20	XF40	MS60	MS63	MS65
1972	11,000	—	—	—	155	160
1972	1,250	PF65 170				

KM# 40.1 10 DOLLARS
1.45 g., 0.750 Gold 0.035 oz. AGW, 15 mm. **Ruler:** Elizabeth II **Subject:** Independence Day - July 10 **Obv:** Bust of Queen Elizabeth II right with tiara, date below **Rev:** Tobacco Dove, value, without fineness and date

Date	Mintage	VF20	XF40	MS60	MS63	MS65
1973	—	—	—	—	60.00	65.00
1973	—	PF65 70.00				

KM# 40.2 10 DOLLARS
1.45 g., 0.750 Gold 0.035 oz. AGW, 15 mm. **Ruler:** Elizabeth II **Obv:** Bust of Queen Elizabeth II right with tiara, date below **Rev:** Tobacco Dove divides value, date at right, date without fineness

Date	Mintage	VF20	XF40	MS60	MS63	MS65
1973	—	—	—	—	60.00	65.00

KM# 41 10 DOLLARS
1.45 g., 0.585 Gold 0.0273 oz. AGW, 15 mm. **Ruler:** Elizabeth II **Obv:** Bust of Queen Elizabeth II right with tiara, date below **Rev:** Tobacco Dove divides value, date at right, .585 fineness and date

Date	Mintage	VF20	XF40	MS60	MS63	MS65
1973	9,960	—	—	—	60.00	65.00
1973	1,260	PF65 70.00				

KM# 42 10 DOLLARS
49.75 g., 0.925 Silver 1.4795 oz. ASW, 50 mm. **Ruler:** Elizabeth II **Subject:** Independence Day - July 10 **Obv:** Legend around queen's portrait **Rev:** Santa Maria with full sails, value below

Date	Mintage	VF20	XF40	MS60	MS63	MS65
1973 FM	28,000	—	—	—	38.50	45.50
1973 FM	63,000	PF65 49.00				

KM# 68 10 DOLLARS
Copper-Nickel, 50 mm. **Ruler:** Elizabeth II **Subject:** 1st Anniversary of Independence **Obv:** National arms, date below **Rev:** Head of Sir Milo B. Butler, Governor-General right, value above, legend below

Date	Mintage	VF20	XF40	MS60	MS63	MS65
1974 FM Proof	4,825	—	—	10.00	12.00	14.00

KM# 68a 10 DOLLARS
50.42 g., 0.925 Silver 1.4995 oz. ASW, 50 mm. **Ruler:** Elizabeth II **Subject:** 1st Anniversary of Independence **Obv:** National arms, date below **Rev:** Head of Sir Milo B. Butler, Governor-General right, value above, legend below **Edge:** Reeded

Date	Mintage	VF20	XF40	MS60	MS63	MS65
1974 FM	43,000	PF65 40.00				

KM# 76 10 DOLLARS

Copper-Nickel, 50 mm. **Ruler:** Elizabeth II **Subject:** Anniversary of Independence **Obv:** National arms with supporters, date below **Rev:** Yellow Elder, value at top

Date	Mintage	VF20	XF40	MS60	MS63	MS65
1975 FM (M)	100	—	—	—	60.00	90.00
1975 FM (U)	5,325	—	—	—	10.00	12.50
1976 FM (M)	100	—	—	—	60.00	90.00
1976 FM (U)	100	—	—	—	60.00	90.00
1977 FM (M)	100	—	—	—	60.00	90.00
1977 FM (U)	369	—	—	—	45.00	60.00

KM# 76a 10 DOLLARS

49.10 g., 0.925 Silver 1.4602 oz. ASW, 50 mm. **Ruler:** Elizabeth II

Date	Mintage	VF20	XF40	MS60	MS63	MS65
1975 FM (P)	63,000	PF63 34.00	PF65 39.00			
1976 FM (P)	10,000	PF63 35.00	PF65 40.00			
1977 FM (P)	4,424	PF63 35.00	PF65 40.00			

KM# 78.1 10 DOLLARS

45.36 g., 0.500 Silver 0.7292 oz. ASW, 50 mm. **Ruler:** Elizabeth II **Subject:** 5th Anniversary of Independence **Obv:** National arms, date below **Rev:** Head of Prince Charles, right, value at bottom

Date	Mintage	VF20	XF40	MS60	MS63	MS65
1978	50,000	PF65 19.50				

KM# 78.2 10 DOLLARS

45.36 g., 0.500 Silver 0.7292 oz. ASW, 50 mm. **Ruler:** Elizabeth II **Obv:** National arms, date below **Obv. Legend:** COMMONWEALTH OF THE BAHAMAS **Rev:** Head of Prince Charles, right, tower mint mark after DOLLARS **Rev. Legend:** FIFTH ANNIVERSARY OF INDEPENDENCE 10 JULY 1973 **Edge:** Reeded

Date	Mintage	VF20	XF40	MS60	MS63	MS65
1978 (t)	—	PF65 22.50				

KM# 79 10 DOLLARS

45.36 g., 0.500 Silver 0.7292 oz. ASW, 50 mm. **Ruler:** Elizabeth II **Subject:** 5th Anniversary of Independence **Obv:** National arms, date below **Rev:** Head of Sir Milo B. Butler, 3/4 left, value at bottom

Date	Mintage	VF20	XF40	MS60	MS63	MS65
1978	50,000	PF65 19.50				

KM# 84 10 DOLLARS

30.28 g., 0.500 Silver 0.4868 oz. ASW **Ruler:** Elizabeth II **Subject:** 10th Anniversary Caribbean Development Bank **Obv:** National arms **Rev:** Flag below globe, value at bottom

Date	Mintage	VF20	XF40	MS60	MS63	MS65
1980 FM	1,001	PF65 18.50				

KM# 85 10 DOLLARS

28.28 g., 0.925 Silver 0.841 oz. ASW **Ruler:** Elizabeth II **Subject:** Wedding of Prince Charles and Lady Diana **Obv:** Bust of Queen Elizabeth II right with tiara **Rev:** Conjoined busts of royal couple left

Date	Mintage	VF20	XF40	MS60	MS63	MS65
1981	39,000	PF65 22.00				

KM# 96 10 DOLLARS

30.28 g., 0.500 Silver 0.4868 oz. ASW **Ruler:** Elizabeth II **Subject:** 30th Anniversary - Coronation of Queen Elizabeth **Obv:** National arms, date below **Rev:** Royal symbols divided by sceptres, dates at either side, value at bottom

Date	Mintage	VF20	XF40	MS60	MS63	MS65
1983 FM	3,374	PF65 16.50				

KM# 97 10 DOLLARS

23.33 g., 0.925 Silver 0.6938 oz. ASW **Ruler:** Elizabeth II **Subject:** 10th Anniversary of Independence **Rev:** Standing figure in front of flag, value below

Date	Mintage	VF20	XF40	MS60	MS63	MS65
1983	800	PF65 21.50				

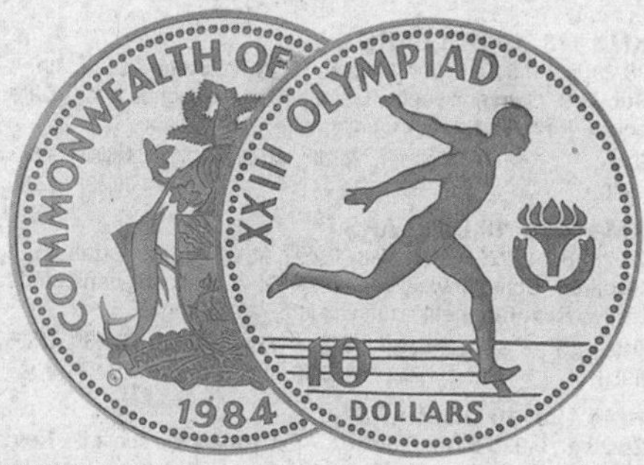

KM# 114 10 DOLLARS

23.33 g., 0.925 Silver 0.6938 oz. ASW **Ruler:** Elizabeth II **Subject:** Los Angeles Olympics **Obv:** National arms **Rev:** Sprinter, symbol at right, value at bottom

Date	Mintage	VF20	XF40	MS60	MS63	MS65
1984	2,100	PF65 21.50				

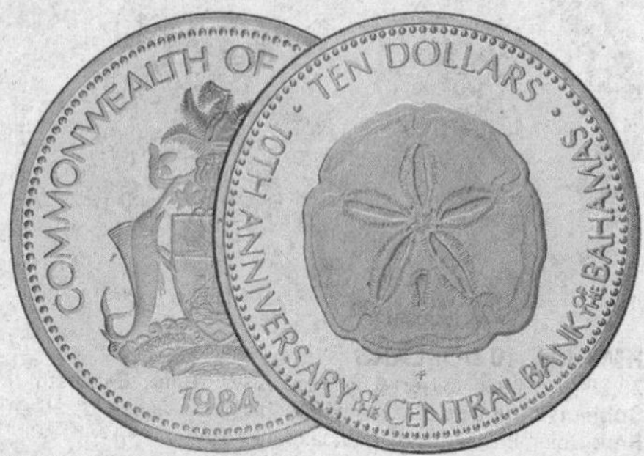

KM# 127 10 DOLLARS

29.17 g., 0.500 Silver 0.4689 oz. ASW **Ruler:** Elizabeth II **Subject:** 10th Anniversary of Central Bank **Obv:** National arms **Rev:** Sand dollar, value at top **Edge:** Reeded

Date	Mintage	VF20	XF40	MS60	MS63	MS65
1984 FM	1,001	PF65 22.00				

KM# 109 10 DOLLARS

28.28 g., 0.925 Silver 0.841 oz. ASW **Ruler:** Elizabeth II **Subject:** Royal Visit **Obv:** Bust right **Rev:** National arms, value below

Date	Mintage	VF20	XF40	MS60	MS63	MS65
1985	1,060	PF65 32.00				

KM# 109a 10 DOLLARS

47.54 g., 0.917 Gold 1.4016 oz. AGW **Ruler:** Elizabeth II **Subject:** Royal Visit **Obv:** Bust right **Rev:** National arms, value below

Date	Mintage	VF20	XF40	MS60	MS63	MS65
1985	—	PF65 2,500				

KM# 113 10 DOLLARS
28.28 g., 0.500 Silver 0.4546 oz. ASW **Ruler:** Elizabeth II **Subject:** Commonwealth Games **Obv:** National arms, date below **Rev:** Competitor running left, value at right

Date	Mintage	VF20	XF40	MS60	MS63	MS65
1986	899	—	—	—	30.00	32.50

KM# 113a 10 DOLLARS
28.28 g., 0.925 Silver 0.841 oz. ASW **Ruler:** Elizabeth II **Subject:** Commonwealth Games **Obv:** National arms, date below **Rev:** Competitor running left, value at right

Date	Mintage	VF20	XF40	MS60	MS63	MS65
1986	1,343	PF65 35.00				

KM# 120 10 DOLLARS
28.28 g., 0.925 Silver 0.841 oz. ASW **Ruler:** Elizabeth II **Rev:** Queen Isabella receiving Columbus

Date	Mintage	VF20	XF40	MS60	MS63	MS65
1987	1,800	PF65 35.00				

KM# 123 10 DOLLARS
28.28 g., 0.925 Silver 0.841 oz. ASW **Ruler:** Elizabeth II **Subject:** Columbus discovering America **Obv:** Queen Elizabeth **Rev:** Columbus sighting America, date below

Date	Mintage	VF20	XF40	MS60	MS63	MS65
1988	1,704	PF65 35.00				

KM# 128 10 DOLLARS
28.28 g., 0.925 Silver 0.841 oz. ASW **Ruler:** Elizabeth II **Obv:** Queen Elizabeth **Rev:** Columbus with flag and sword

Date	Mintage	VF20	XF40	MS60	MS63	MS65
1989	Est. 10000	PF65 24.00				

KM# 133 10 DOLLARS
28.28 g., 0.925 Silver 0.841 oz. ASW **Ruler:** Elizabeth II **Series:** Discovery of the New World **Obv:** Queen Elizabeth **Rev:** Bust of Columbus, left, within circle, value below

Date	Mintage	VF20	XF40	MS60	MS63	MS65
1990	550	—	—	—	—	110
1990	10,000	PF65 24.00				

KM# 196 10 DOLLARS
28.28 g., 0.925 Silver 0.841 oz. ASW **Ruler:** Elizabeth II **Series:** Discovery of the New World **Obv:** Queen's portrait **Rev:** 5 men rowing boat, Columbus' ships in background, all in inner circle, value below

Date	Mintage	VF20	XF40	MS60	MS63	MS65
1991	—	PF65 24.00				

KM# 193 10 DOLLARS
3.11 g., 0.500 Gold 0.050 oz. AGW **Ruler:** Elizabeth II **Obv:** Bust of Queen Elizabeth II right, date below **Rev:** Two flamingos facing, value above

Date	Mintage	VF20	XF40	MS60	MS63	MS65
1992	Est. 750	PF65 100				

KM# 197 10 DOLLARS
28.28 g., 0.925 Silver 0.841 oz. ASW **Ruler:** Elizabeth II **Series:** Discovery of the New World **Obv:** Crowned bust of Queen Elizabeth II right, date below **Rev:** Nina, Pinta, Santa Maria ships within circle, value below

Date	Mintage	VF20	XF40	MS60	MS63	MS65
1992	—	PF65 24.00				

KM# 162 10 DOLLARS
136.08 g., 0.925 Silver 4.0469 oz. ASW **Ruler:** Elizabeth II **Subject:** Expulsion of pirates **Obv:** Queen's portrait, legend around, date below **Obv. Legend:** • COMMONWEALTH OF THE BAHAMAS • **Rev:** Pirate ship, value below **Rev. Legend:** • EXPULSIS PIRATIS • RESTITUTA COMMERCIA •

Date	Mintage	VF20	XF40	MS60	MS63	MS65
1993	Est. 2000	PF65 112				

KM# 156 10 DOLLARS
7.78 g., 0.999 Gold 0.2498 oz. AGW **Ruler:** Elizabeth II **Subject:** Golf - Hole-in-One **Obv:** National arms **Rev:** Golfer making hole-in-one

Date	Mintage	VF20	XF40	MS60	MS63	MS65
1994	2,500	PF65 450				

KM# 167 10 DOLLARS
155.52 g., 0.999 Silver 4.995 oz. ASW **Ruler:** Elizabeth II **Obv:** Multicolor National arms **Rev:** Multicolor Bahama parrot on branch, value at bottom

Date	Mintage	VF20	XF40	MS60	MS63	MS65
1995	2,500	PF65 130				

KM# 168 10 DOLLARS
15.55 g., 0.999 Gold 0.4995 oz. AGW **Ruler:** Elizabeth II **Obv:** Queen's portrait **Rev:** Bahama Parrot

Date	Mintage	VF20	XF40	MS60	MS63	MS65
1995	2,000	PF65 850				

KM# 174 10 DOLLARS
28.28 g., 0.925 Silver 0.841 oz. ASW **Ruler:** Elizabeth II **Subject:** 25th Anniversary - Caribbean Development Bank **Obv:** National arms **Rev:** Globe within inscription, butterflies flanking, birds and flowers below

Date	Mintage	VF20	XF40	MS60	MS63	MS65
ND-1995	1,000	PF65 40.00				

KM# 189 10 DOLLARS
15.55 g., 0.9999 Gold 0.4999 oz. AGW **Ruler:** Elizabeth II **Obv:** Queen's portrait **Rev:** Two flamingos facing each other

Date	Mintage	VF20	XF40	MS60	MS63	MS65
1995	—	PF65 850				

KM# 179 10 DOLLARS
15.55 g., 0.9999 Gold 0.4999 oz. AGW **Ruler:** Elizabeth II **Subject:** Third Millennium - Year 2000 **Obv:** Queen's portrait **Rev:** Seashell-shaped world map

Date	Mintage	VF20	XF40	MS60	MS63	MS65
1996	5,000	PF65 850				

KM# 200 10 DOLLARS
31.10 g., 0.999 Silver 0.999 oz. ASW **Ruler:** Elizabeth II **Subject:** 50th Anniversary of the University of the West Indies **Obv:** National arms **Rev:** University arms, dates

Date	Mintage	VF20	XF40	MS60	MS63	MS65
1998	1,000	PF65 50.00				

KM# 212 10 DOLLARS
Silver **Ruler:** Elizabeth II **Subject:** XXVII Summer Olympics - Sydney 2000 **Obv:** National arms **Rev:** "The Golden Girls" - five relay runners, gilt

Date	Mintage	VF20	XF40	MS60	MS63	MS65
2000	—	PF65 125				

KM# 12 20 DOLLARS
7.99 g., 0.917 Gold 0.2355 oz. AGW **Ruler:** Elizabeth II **Subject:** Adoption of New Constitution **Obv:** Bust right **Rev:** Lighthouse, date below

Date	Mintage	VF20	XF40	MS60	MS63	MS65
1967	6,200	—	—	—	400	425
1967	850	PF65 450				

KM# 27 20 DOLLARS
7.99 g., 0.917 Gold 0.2355 oz. AGW **Ruler:** Elizabeth II **Obv:** Bust of Queen Elizabeth II with tiara right **Rev:** Lighthouse, value at top, date at bottom

Date	Mintage	VF20	XF40	MS60	MS63	MS65
1971	22,000	—	—	—	400	425
1971 (t)	1,250	PF65 450				

KM# 28 20 DOLLARS
7.99 g., 0.917 Gold 0.2355 oz. AGW **Ruler:** Elizabeth II **Obv:** Bust of Queen Elizabeth II right with tiara **Rev:** Lighthouse above date, value at top, hallmark and fineness stamped at bottom **Note:** Struck by the Gori and Zucchi Mint, Italy.

Date	Mintage	VF20	XF40	MS60	MS63	MS65
1971	—	PF65 400				

KM# 35 20 DOLLARS
6.48 g., 0.917 Gold 0.191 oz. AGW **Ruler:** Elizabeth II **Obv:** Bust of Queen Elizabeth II right **Rev:** Lighthouse above date, value at top

Date	Mintage	VF20	XF40	MS60	MS63	MS65
1972	10,000	—	—	—	320	350
1972	1,250	PF65 370				

KM# 43.1 20 DOLLARS
2.90 g., 0.750 Gold 0.0699 oz. AGW, 19 mm. **Ruler:** Elizabeth II **Subject:** Independence Day - July 10 **Obv:** Bust of Queen Elizabeth II right with tiara, date below **Rev:** Flamingos, without fineness and date, value at bottom

Date	Mintage	VF20	XF40	MS60	MS63	MS65
1973	—	—	—	—	120	130
1973	—	PF65 145				

KM# 43.2 20 DOLLARS
2.90 g., 0.750 Gold 0.0699 oz. AGW, 19 mm. **Ruler:** Elizabeth II **Subject:** Independence Day - July 10 **Obv:** Bust of Queen Elizabeth II right with tiara **Rev:** Flamingos, without fineness, high date

Date	Mintage	VF20	XF40	MS60	MS63	MS65
1973	—	—	—	—	120	130
1973	—	PF65 145				

KM# 44 20 DOLLARS
2.90 g., 0.585 Gold 0.0545 oz. AGW, 19 mm. **Ruler:** Elizabeth II **Obv:** Bust of Queen Elizabeth II right with tiara, date below **Rev:** Flamingos, .585 fineness, low date, value at bottom

Date	Mintage	VF20	XF40	MS60	MS63	MS65
1973	8,660	—	—	—	85.00	95.00
1973	1,260	PF65 100				

KM# 157 20 DOLLARS
15.55 g., 0.999 Gold 0.4995 oz. AGW **Ruler:** Elizabeth II **Obv:** Arms **Rev:** Golfer making hole-in-one

Date	Mintage	VF20	XF40	MS60	MS63	MS65
1994	2,500	PF65 850				

KM# 82 25 DOLLARS
37.38 g., 0.925 Silver 1.1117 oz. ASW **Ruler:** Elizabeth II **Subject:** 250th Anniversary of Parliament **Obv:** National arms, date below **Rev:** Royal sceptre divides dates, value at bottom

Date	Mintage	VF20	XF40	MS60	MS63	MS65
1979	3,002	PF65 33.00				

KM# 110 25 DOLLARS
120.00 g., 0.925 Silver 3.5687 oz. ASW, 63 mm. **Ruler:** Elizabeth II **Subject:** Columbus' Discovery of America **Obv:** National arms **Rev:** Columbus claiming the land by planting flag, crew with clergy holding cross behind, value above, date below

Date	Mintage	VF20	XF40	MS60	MS63	MS65
1985	1,950	PF65 91.00				

KM# 115 25 DOLLARS
129.60 g., 0.925 Silver 3.8542 oz. ASW, 63 mm. **Ruler:** Elizabeth II **Subject:** Bird Conservation **Obv:** National arms **Rev:** Flamingos, value at top

Date	Mintage	VF20	XF40	MS60	MS63	MS65
1985	1,060	PF65 110				

KM# 118 25 DOLLARS
129.60 g., 0.925 Silver 3.8542 oz. ASW **Ruler:** Elizabeth II **Obv:** Queen's portrait **Rev:** Queen Isabella receiving Columbus

Date	Mintage	VF20	XF40	MS60	MS63	MS65
1987	1,750	PF65 98.00				

KM# 124 25 DOLLARS
136.00 g., 0.925 Silver 4.0446 oz. ASW **Ruler:** Elizabeth II **Subject:** Columbus Discovering New World **Obv:** Queen's portrait **Rev:** Columbus on deck pointing towards land, date at bottom

Date	Mintage	VF20	XF40	MS60	MS63	MS65
1988	954	PF65 125				

KM# 129 25 DOLLARS
136.00 g., 0.925 Silver 4.0446 oz. ASW **Ruler:** Elizabeth II **Obv:** Queen Elizabeth **Rev:** Christopher Columbus, radiant sun and ocean in background, value below right hand, circle surrounds, date below circle

Date	Mintage	VF20	XF40	MS60	MS63	MS65
1989	1,572	PF65 105				

KM# 134 25 DOLLARS
124.00 g., 0.925 Silver 3.6877 oz. ASW **Ruler:** Elizabeth II **Series:** Discovery of the New World **Obv:** Queen Elizabeth **Rev:** Aborigine looking right, within circle, value below circle

Date	Mintage	VF20	XF40	MS60	MS63	MS65
1990	5,000	PF65 91.00				

KM# 153 25 DOLLARS
136.00 g., 0.925 Silver 4.0446 oz. ASW **Ruler:** Elizabeth II **Series:** Discovery of the New World **Obv:** Queen Elizabeth **Rev:** Facing half bust of Columbus holding map, ship at left, circle surrounds, value below circle

Date	Mintage	VF20	XF40	MS60	MS63	MS65
1991	Est. 500	PF65 105				

KM# 191 25 DOLLARS
136.00 g., 0.925 Silver 4.0446 oz. ASW, 63 mm. **Ruler:** Elizabeth II **Series:** Discovery of the New World **Obv:** Bust of Queen Elizabeth II right, date below **Rev:** Columbus meeting native Americans, within circle, value below circle **Note:** Illustration reduced.

Date	Mintage	VF20	XF40	MS60	MS63	MS65
1992	—	PF65 105				

KM# 194 25 DOLLARS
7.77 g., 0.500 Gold 0.1249 oz. AGW **Ruler:** Elizabeth II **Obv:** Bust of Queen Elizabeth II right, date below **Rev:** Pair of flamingos, value above

Date	Mintage	VF20	XF40	MS60	MS63	MS65
1992	Est. 750	PF65 215				

KM# 202 25 DOLLARS
31.10 g., 0.9999 Gold 0.9999 oz. AGW **Ruler:** Elizabeth II **Subject:** Golf - Hole-in-One **Obv:** National arms **Rev:** Golf ball rolling towards hole

Date	Mintage	VF20	XF40	MS60	MS63	MS65
1994	—	PF65 1,650				

KM# 190 25 DOLLARS
31.10 g., 0.9999 Gold 0.9999 oz. AGW **Ruler:** Elizabeth II **Obv:** Bust of Queen Elizabeth II right, date below **Rev:** Two flamingos, value at bottom

Date	Mintage	VF20	XF40	MS60	MS63	MS65
1995	—	PF65 1,650				

KM# 180 25 DOLLARS
31.10 g., 0.9999 Gold 0.9999 oz. AGW **Ruler:** Elizabeth II **Subject:** Third Millennium - Year 2000 **Obv:** Bust of Queen Elizabeth II right **Rev:** Seashell-shaped world map

Date	Mintage	VF20	XF40	MS60	MS63	MS65
1996	5,000	PF65 1,650				

KM# 209 25 DOLLARS
Silver **Ruler:** Elizabeth II **Subject:** 25th Anniversary College of the Bahamas **Obv:** Crowned bust right **Rev:** College facade

Date	Mintage	VF20	XF40	MS60	MS63	MS65
1998	—	PF65 95.00				

KM# 211 25 DOLLARS
Silver **Ruler:** Elizabeth II **Subject:** 25th Anniversary Central Bank **Obv:** Crowned bust right

Date	Mintage	VF20	XF40	MS60	MS63	MS65
1999	—	PF65 95.00				

KM# 13 50 DOLLARS
19.97 g., 0.917 Gold 0.5888 oz. AGW **Ruler:** Elizabeth II **Subject:** Adoption of New Constitution **Obv:** Bust of Queen Elizabeth II right with tiara **Rev:** Santa Maria in full sail, value and date above

Date	Mintage	VF20	XF40	MS60	MS63	MS65
1967	1,200	—	—	—	950	1,000
1967	850	PF65 1,050				

KM# 29 50 DOLLARS
19.97 g., 0.917 Gold 0.5888 oz. AGW **Ruler:** Elizabeth II **Obv:** Bust of Queen Elizabeth II right with tiara **Rev:** Santa Maria in full sail, value and date above

Date	Mintage	VF20	XF40	MS60	MS63	MS65
1971	6,800	—	—	—	950	1,000
1971 (t)	1,250	PF65 1,050				

KM# 30 50 DOLLARS
19.97 g., 0.917 Gold 0.5888 oz. AGW **Ruler:** Elizabeth II **Obv:** Bust of Queen Elizabeth II right with tiara **Rev:** Santa Maria in full sail, value and above, hallmark and fineness stamped at bottom **Note:** Struck by the Gori and Zucchi Mint, Italy.

Date	Mintage	VF20	XF40	MS60	MS63	MS65
1971	700	—	—	—	950	1,000

KM# 36 50 DOLLARS
15.97 g., 0.917 Gold 0.4708 oz. AGW **Ruler:** Elizabeth II **Obv:** Bust of Queen Elizabeth II right

Date	Mintage	VF20	XF40	MS60	MS63	MS65
1972	2,250	—	—	—	800	825
1972	1,250	PF65 875				

KM# 45 50 DOLLARS
7.27 g., 0.750 Gold 0.1753 oz. AGW, 22 mm. **Ruler:** Elizabeth II **Subject:** Independence Day - July 10 **Obv:** Bust of Queen Elizabeth II right, date below **Rev:** Spiny lobster, date below, value at bottom; without fineness

Date	Mintage	VF20	XF40	MS60	MS63	MS65
1973	—	—	—	—	290	300
1973	—	PF65 325				

KM# 46 50 DOLLARS
7.27 g., 0.585 Gold 0.1367 oz. AGW, 22 mm. **Ruler:** Elizabeth II **Obv:** Bust of Queen Elizabeth II right with tiara, date below **Rev:** Spiny lobster, .585 fineness to left, date to right, value at bottom

Date	Mintage	VF20	XF40	MS60	MS63	MS65
1973	5,160	—	—	—	215	225
1973	1,260	PF65 245				

KM# 47 50 DOLLARS
7.30 g., 0.750 Gold 0.176 oz. AGW, 22 mm. **Ruler:** Elizabeth II **Obv:** Bust of Queen Elizabeth II right with tiara, date below **Rev:** Spiny lobster, without date or fineness, value at bottom

Date	Mintage	VF20	XF40	MS60	MS63	MS65
1973	—	—	—	—	290	300

KM# 48 50 DOLLARS
15.64 g., 0.500 Gold 0.2515 oz. AGW, 29.2 mm. **Ruler:** Elizabeth II **Subject:** Independence Day - July 10 **Obv:** Bust of Queen Elizabeth II right with tiara **Rev:** Two flamingos, value below

Date	Mintage	VF20	XF40	MS60	MS63	MS65
1973 JP	23,000	—	—	—	410	430
1973 JP	18,000	PF65 475				

KM# 69 50 DOLLARS
2.73 g., 0.917 Gold 0.0805 oz. AGW, 17 mm. **Ruler:** Elizabeth II **Subject:** 1st Anniversary of Independence **Obv:** Bust of Queen Elizabeth II right with tiara, date below **Rev:** Tobacco Dove, value, date, without fineness

Date	Mintage	VF20	XF40	MS60	MS63	MS65
1974	34,000	—	—	—	130	140
1974	20,000	PF65 150				
1975	26,000	—	—	—	130	140
1975	15,000	PF65 150				
1976	2,207	—	—	—	—	145
1976	Inc. above	PF65 150				
1977	1,090	—	—	—	—	150
1977	—	PF65 160				

KM# 70 50 DOLLARS
2.73 g., 0.917 Gold 0.0805 oz. AGW **Ruler:** Elizabeth II **Obv:** Bust of Queen Elizabeth II right with tiara, date below **Rev:** Tobacco Dove, value date, .917 fineness

Date	Mintage	VF20	XF40	MS60	MS63	MS65
1974	—	—	—	—	—	130

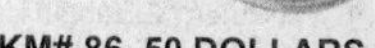

KM# 86 50 DOLLARS
2.68 g., 0.500 Gold 0.0431 oz. AGW **Ruler:** Elizabeth II **Obv:** National arms, date below **Rev:** Flamingos in flight

Date	Mintage	VF20	XF40	MS60	MS63	MS65
1981 FM	2,050	PF65 80.00				

KM# 92 50 DOLLARS
2.68 g., 0.500 Gold 0.0431 oz. AGW **Ruler:** Elizabeth II **Obv:** National arms, date below **Rev:** Marlin (Swordfish), value above

Date	Mintage	VF20	XF40	MS60	MS63	MS65
1982 FM	841	PF65 140				

KM# 98 50 DOLLARS
2.68 g., 0.500 Gold 0.0431 oz. AGW **Ruler:** Elizabeth II **Subject:** 10th Anniversary of Independence **Obv:** National arms, date below **Rev:** Flamingo, value above

Date	Mintage	VF20	XF40	MS60	MS63	MS65
1983 FM	962	PF65 110				

KM# 103 50 DOLLARS
2.68 g., 0.500 Gold 0.0431 oz. AGW **Ruler:** Elizabeth II **Obv:** National arms, date below **Rev:** Golden Allamanda, value above

Date	Mintage	VF20	XF40	MS60	MS63	MS65
1984 FM	3,716	PF65 80.00				

KM# 108 50 DOLLARS
2.68 g., 0.500 Gold 0.0431 oz. AGW **Ruler:** Elizabeth II **Obv:** National arms, date below **Rev:** Santa Maria, value above

Date	Mintage	VF20	XF40	MS60	MS63	MS65
1985 FM	1,575	PF65 85.00				

KM# 199 50 DOLLARS
6.48 g., 0.9167 Gold 0.191 oz. AGW **Ruler:** Elizabeth II **Subject:** Junkanoo Festival **Obv:** Crowned bust of Queen Elizabeth II right, date below **Rev:** Three costumed musicians, value below

Date	Mintage	VF20	XF40	MS60	MS63	MS65
1994	—	PF65 325				

KM# 181 50 DOLLARS
2000.00 g., 0.999 Silver 64.2371 oz. ASW **Ruler:** Elizabeth II **Subject:** Third Millennium - Year 2000 **Obv:** Bust of Queen Elizabeth II right **Rev:** Seashell-shaped world map

Date	Mintage	VF20	XF40	MS60	MS63	MS65
1996	2,000	PF65 1,450				

KM# 14 100 DOLLARS
39.94 g., 0.917 Gold 1.1775 oz. AGW **Ruler:** Elizabeth II **Subject:** Adoption of New Constitution **Obv:** Bust of Queen Elizabeth II right with tiara **Rev:** Columbus, date divides value at bottom

Date	Mintage	VF20	XF40	MS60	MS63	MS65
1967	1,200	—	—	—	1,650	1,750
1967	850	PF63 1,800	PF65 1,900			

KM# 31 100 DOLLARS
39.94 g., 0.917 Gold 1.1775 oz. AGW **Ruler:** Elizabeth II **Obv:** Bust of Queen Elizabeth II right with tiara **Rev:** Shield with crown at top, sailing ship at bottom, ribbon below shield, garland above, value, date

Date	Mintage	VF20	XF40	MS60	MS63	MS65
1971	6,800	—	—	—	1,650	1,750
1971 (t)	1,250	PF63 1,800	PF65 1,900			

KM# 32.1 100 DOLLARS
39.94 g., 0.917 Gold 1.1775 oz. AGW **Ruler:** Elizabeth II **Obv:** Bust of Queen Elizabeth II right with tiara **Rev:** Shield with crown at top, sailing ship at bottom, ribbon below shield, garland above, value, date; hallmark and fineness at bottom right

Date	Mintage	VF20	XF40	MS60	MS63	MS65
1971	—	—	—	—	1,650	1,750

KM# 32.2 100 DOLLARS
39.94 g., 0.917 Gold 1.1775 oz. AGW **Ruler:** Elizabeth II **Obv:** Bust of Queen Elizabeth II right with tiara **Rev:** Shield with crown at top, sailing ship at bottom, ribbon below shield, garland on top, value, date; hallmark at bottom right, without fineness

Date	Mintage	VF20	XF40	MS60	MS63	MS65
1971	—	—	—	—	1,650	1,750

KM# 32.3 100 DOLLARS
39.94 g., 0.917 Gold 1.1775 oz. AGW **Ruler:** Elizabeth II **Obv:** Bust of Queen Elizabeth II right with tiara **Rev:** Shield with crown at top, sailing ship at bottom, ribbon below shield, garland above, value, date; fineness at bottom right without hallmark **Note:** Struck by the Gori and Zucchi Mint, Italy.

Date	Mintage	VF20	XF40	MS60	MS63	MS65
1971	—	—	—	—	1,650	1,750

KM# 37 100 DOLLARS
31.95 g., 0.917 Gold 0.942 oz. AGW **Ruler:** Elizabeth II **Obv:** Bust of Queen Elizabeth II right **Note:** The 1972 proof $100 is serially numbered on the edge.

Date	Mintage	VF20	XF40	MS60	MS63	MS65
1972	2,250	—	—	—	1,350	1,400
1972	1,250	PF63 1,450	PF65 1,500			

KM# 49.1 100 DOLLARS
14.54 g., 0.750 Gold 0.3506 oz. AGW, 28 mm. **Ruler:** Elizabeth II **Subject:** Independence Day - July 10 **Obv:** Bust of Queen Elizabeth II right with tiara, date below **Rev:** National arms, value above, date below; without fineness

Date	Mintage	VF20	XF40	MS60	MS63	MS65
1973	—	—	—	—	575	600

KM# 49.2 100 DOLLARS
14.54 g., 0.750 Gold 0.3506 oz. AGW, 28 mm. **Ruler:** Elizabeth II **Subject:** Independence Day - July 10 **Obv:** Bust of Queen Elizabeth II right with tiara, date below **Rev:** National arms, value above; without date or fineness

Date	Mintage	VF20	XF40	MS60	MS63	MS65
1973	—	PF65 575				

KM# 50.1 100 DOLLARS
14.54 g., 0.585 Gold 0.2735 oz. AGW, 28 mm. **Ruler:** Elizabeth II **Obv:** Bust of Queen Elizabeth II right with tiara, date below **Rev:** National arms, value above, .585 fineness to left, date to right

Date	Mintage	VF20	XF40	MS60	MS63	MS65
1973	4,660	—	—	—	425	450
1973	1,260	PF65 475				

Note: Serial number on reverse

KM# 50.2 100 DOLLARS
14.54 g., 0.585 Gold 0.2735 oz. AGW, 28 mm. **Ruler:** Elizabeth II **Obv:** Bust of Queen Elizabeth II right, date below **Rev:** National arms, value above, date and fineness at right, serial number at left

Date	Mintage	VF20	XF40	MS60	MS63	MS65
1973	—	—	—	—	425	450

KM# 50.3 100 DOLLARS
14.54 g., 0.585 Gold 0.2735 oz. AGW, 28 mm. **Ruler:** Elizabeth II **Obv:** Bust of Queen Elizabeth II right with tiara, date below **Rev:** National arms, value above, serial number at left, fineness below, date at right

Date	Mintage	VF20	XF40	MS60	MS63	MS65
1973	—	—	—	—	425	450

KM# 71 100 DOLLARS
18.01 g., 0.500 Gold 0.2896 oz. AGW, 33 mm. **Ruler:** Elizabeth II **Subject:** 1st Anniversary of Independence **Obv:** National arms, date below **Rev:** Two flamingos, value at bottom, date at right

Date	Mintage	VF20	XF40	MS60	MS63	MS65
1974	4,486	—	—	—	450	460
1974	4,153	PF65 475				

KM# 72 100 DOLLARS
5.46 g., 0.917 Gold 0.161 oz. AGW, 21 mm. **Ruler:** Elizabeth II **Obv:** Bust of Queen Elizabeth II right with tiara, date below **Rev:** Broken waves behind flamingos' legs, value at bottom

Date	Mintage	VF20	XF40	MS60	MS63	MS65
1974	29,000	—	—	—	230	250
1975	—	—	—	—	240	260

KM# 73 100 DOLLARS
5.46 g., 0.917 Gold 0.161 oz. AGW, 21 mm. **Ruler:** Elizabeth II **Obv:** Bust of Queen Elizabeth II right with tiara, date below **Rev:** Unbroken waves behind flamingos' legs, value at bottom

Date	Mintage	VF20	XF40	MS60	MS63	MS65
1974	17,000	PF65 230				
1975	—	PF65 240				
1976	—	—	—	—	230	250
1976	—	PF65 240				
1977	—	—	—	—	240	260
1977	—	PF65 230				

KM# 74 100 DOLLARS
5.46 g., 0.917 Gold 0.161 oz. AGW, 21 mm. **Ruler:** Elizabeth II **Obv:** Bust of Queen Elizabeth II right with tiara, date below **Rev:** Unbroken waves behind flamingos legs, date at right, value at bottom; .917 fineness in oval

Date	Mintage	VF20	XF40	MS60	MS63	MS65
1974	—	—	—	—	230	250

KM# 77 100 DOLLARS
18.01 g., 0.500 Gold 0.2896 oz. AGW **Ruler:** Elizabeth II **Subject:** 2nd Anniversary of Independence **Obv:** National arms, date below **Rev:** Bahama Amazon Parrot, value at bottom

Date	Mintage	VF20	XF40	MS60	MS63	MS65
1974	—	PF65 475				
1975	3,694	—	—	—	450	460
1975	3,145	PF65 475				
1976	761	PF65 475				
1977	2,023	PF65 475				

KM# 80 100 DOLLARS
13.60 g., 0.963 Gold 0.4211 oz. AGW, 27 mm. **Ruler:** Elizabeth II **Subject:** 5th Anniversary of Independence **Obv:** National arms, date below **Rev:** Bust of H.R.H Prince Charles, right, value below

Date	Mintage	VF20	XF40	MS60	MS63	MS65
1978	3,275	PF65 680				

KM# 81 100 DOLLARS
13.60 g., 0.963 Gold 0.4211 oz. AGW **Ruler:** Elizabeth II **Subject:** 5th Anniversary of Independence **Obv:** National arms, date below **Rev:** Head of Sir Milo B. Butler, 1/2 left, value at bottom

Date	Mintage	VF20	XF40	MS60	MS63	MS65
1978	25,000	PF65 680				

KM# 87 100 DOLLARS
6.48 g., 0.900 Gold 0.1875 oz. AGW **Ruler:** Elizabeth II **Subject:** Wedding of Prince Charles and Lady Diana **Obv:** Bust of Queen Elizabeth II right with tiara **Rev:** Conjoined busts of royal couple left

Date	Mintage	VF20	XF40	MS60	MS63	MS65
1981	10,000	PF65 280				

KM# 99 100 DOLLARS
6.48 g., 0.900 Gold 0.1875 oz. AGW **Ruler:** Elizabeth II **Subject:** 10th Anniversary of Independence **Obv:** National arms, date below **Rev:** Bust of soldier left within unfurled flag, value at bottom

Date	Mintage	VF20	XF40	MS60	MS63	MS65
1983	400	PF65 300				

KM# 111 100 DOLLARS
6.48 g., 0.900 Gold 0.1875 oz. AGW **Ruler:** Elizabeth II **Subject:** Columbus' Discovery of America **Obv:** National arms **Rev:** Columbus with group of people, date at bottom, value at top

Date	Mintage	VF20	XF40	MS60	MS63	MS65
1985	450	PF65 300				

KM# 119 100 DOLLARS
6.48 g., 0.900 Gold 0.1875 oz. AGW **Ruler:** Elizabeth II **Obv:** Crowned bust of Queen Elizabeth II right **Rev:** Queen Isabella receiving Christopher Columbus, date below, value at top

Date	Mintage	VF20	XF40	MS60	MS63	MS65
1987	849	PF65 300				

KM# 125 100 DOLLARS
6.48 g., 0.900 Gold 0.1875 oz. AGW **Ruler:** Elizabeth II **Subject:** Columbus Discovering America **Obv:** Bust of Queen Elizabeth II right **Rev:** Columbus sighting America

Date	Mintage	VF20	XF40	MS60	MS63	MS65
1988	854	PF65 300				

KM# 130 100 DOLLARS
6.48 g., 0.900 Gold 0.1875 oz. AGW **Ruler:** Elizabeth II **Obv:** Queen Elizabeth **Rev:** Christopher Columbus, radiant sun and ocean in background within circle, date below, and at right of circle

Date	Mintage	VF20	XF40	MS60	MS63	MS65
1989	Est. 5000	PF65 300				

KM# 135 100 DOLLARS
6.48 g., 0.900 Gold 0.1875 oz. AGW **Ruler:** Elizabeth II **Subject:** Discovery of New World **Obv:** Queen Elizabeth II, date below **Rev:** Bust of Columbus left, value below circle

Date	Mintage	VF20	XF40	MS60	MS63	MS65
1990	500	—	—	—	—	300
1990	5,000	PF65 300				

KM# 151 100 DOLLARS
6.48 g., 0.900 Gold 0.1875 oz. AGW **Ruler:** Elizabeth II **Subject:** Discovery of New World **Obv:** Crowned bust of Queen Elizabeth II right, date below **Rev:** 5 men rowing boat, ships in background within inner circle, legend above, value below

Date	Mintage	VF20	XF40	MS60	MS63	MS65
1991	500	—	—	—	290	300

KM# 152 100 DOLLARS
6.48 g., 0.900 Gold 0.1875 oz. AGW **Ruler:** Elizabeth II **Subject:** Discovery of New World **Obv:** Crowned bust of Queen Elizabeth II right, date below **Rev:** Columbus' ships within circle, value below circle

Date	Mintage	VF20	XF40	MS60	MS63	MS65
1992	Est. 5000000	PF65 300				
1992 Matte	—	PF65 300				

KM# 195 100 DOLLARS
1000.00 g., 0.999 Silver 32.1186 oz. ASW **Ruler:** Elizabeth II **Subject:** Discovery of New World **Obv:** Bust of Queen Elizabeth II right, date below **Rev:** Columbus' three ships - the Niña, the Pinta, the Santa Maria, within circle, value below circle

Date	Mintage	VF20	XF40	MS60	MS63	MS65
1992	Est. 1500	PF65 780				

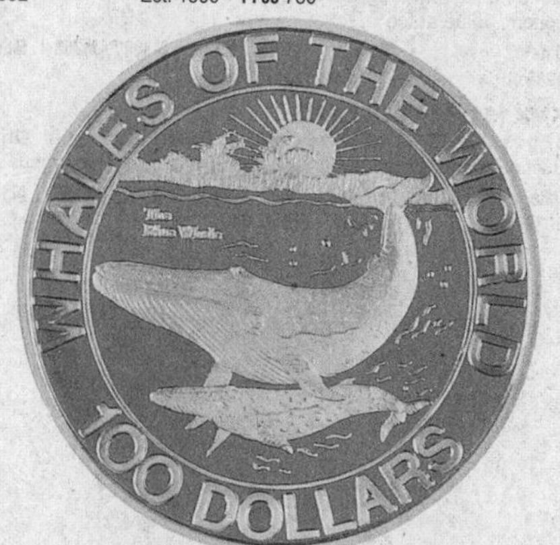

KM# 163 100 DOLLARS
999.98 g., 0.999 Silver 32.1178 oz. ASW **Ruler:** Elizabeth II **Series:** Whales of the World **Obv:** Bust of Queen Elizabeth II right, date below **Rev:** Blue Whale with baby, within circle, value below circle

Date	Mintage	VF20	XF40	MS60	MS63	MS65
1993	750	PF65 820				

KM# 184 100 DOLLARS
999.98 g., 0.999 Silver 32.1178 oz. ASW **Ruler:** Elizabeth II **Series:** Whales of the World **Obv:** Bust of Queen Elizabeth II right, date below **Rev:** Killer Whales in inner circle, value below

Date	Mintage	VF20	XF40	MS60	MS63	MS65
1994	750	PF65 840				

KM# 185 100 DOLLARS
999.98 g., 0.999 Silver 32.1178 oz. ASW **Ruler:** Elizabeth II **Series:** Whales of the World **Obv:** Bust of Queen Elizabeth II right, date below **Rev:** Humpback Whales within inner circle, value below

Date	Mintage	VF20	XF40	MS60	MS63	MS65
1995	750	PF65 820				

KM# 51 150 DOLLARS
8.19 g., 0.917 Gold 0.2415 oz. AGW, 24 mm. **Ruler:** Elizabeth II **Subject:** Independence Day - July 10 **Obv:** Bust of Queen Elizabeth II right with tiara, date below **Rev:** Spiny Lobster, value, small date at right

Date	Mintage	VF20	XF40	MS60	MS63	MS65
1973	—	—	—	—	375	385
1973	—	PF65 400				
1974	7,128	—	—	—	375	385
1974	4,787	PF65 400				
1975	3,141	—	—	—	375	385
1975	2,770	PF65 400				
1976	168	PF65 400				
1977	327	PF65 400				

KM# 52 150 DOLLARS
8.19 g., 0.917 Gold 0.2415 oz. AGW **Ruler:** Elizabeth II **Obv:** Bust of Queen Elizabeth II right with tiara, date below **Rev:** Spiny Lobster, value, small date at right

Date	Mintage	VF20	XF40	MS60	MS63	MS65
1974	—	PF65 400				

KM# 53 150 DOLLARS
8.19 g., 0.917 Gold 0.2415 oz. AGW **Ruler:** Elizabeth II **Obv:** Bust of Queen Elizabeth II right with tiara, date below **Rev:** Spiny Lobster, value, small date at right; .917 fineness in oval

Date	Mintage	VF20	XF40	MS60	MS63	MS65
1974	—	—	—	—	375	400

KM# 54 200 DOLLARS
10.92 g., 0.917 Gold 0.3219 oz. AGW, 28 mm. **Ruler:** Elizabeth II **Subject:** Independence Day - July 10 **Obv:** Bust of Queen Elizabeth II right with tiara, date below **Rev:** National arms, value above small date at right

Date	Mintage	VF20	XF40	MS60	MS63	MS65
1973	—	—	—	—	500	510
1973	—	PF65 520				
1974	5,528	—	—	—	500	510
1974	3,587	PF65 520				
1975	1,545	—	—	—	500	510
1975	1,570	PF65 520				
1976	168	PF65 550				
1977	321	PF65 530				

KM# 56 200 DOLLARS
10.92 g., 0.917 Gold 0.3219 oz. AGW **Ruler:** Elizabeth II **Obv:** Bust of Queen Elizabeth II right with tiara, date below **Rev:** National arms, value above, small date at right; .917 fineness in oval

Date	Mintage	VF20	XF40	MS60	MS63	MS65
1974	—	—	—	—	500	510

KM# 57 200 DOLLARS
10.92 g., 0.917 Gold 0.3219 oz. AGW **Ruler:** Elizabeth II **Obv:** Bust of Queen Elizabeth II right **Rev:** .916 fineness at left, serial number stamped below arms

Date	Mintage	VF20	XF40	MS60	MS63	MS65
1974	—	—	—	—	500	510

KM# 58 200 DOLLARS
Gold **Ruler:** Elizabeth II **Obv:** Bust right **Rev:** Without fineness, serial number to left

Date	Mintage	VF20	XF40	MS60	MS63	MS65
1974	—	PF65 525				
1974	—	—	—	—	—	—

KM# 83 250 DOLLARS
10.58 g., 0.900 Gold 0.3061 oz. AGW **Ruler:** Elizabeth II **Subject:** 250th Anniversary of Parliament **Obv:** Princess Anne's bust 1/2 left in inner circle, value below **Rev:** National arms, date below

Date	Mintage	VF20	XF40	MS60	MS63	MS65
1979	1,835	PF65 525				

KM# 117 250 DOLLARS
47.54 g., 0.917 Gold 1.4016 oz. AGW **Ruler:** Elizabeth II **Subject:** Commonwealth Games **Obv:** National arms **Rev:** Competitor running left, value at right, logo below

Date	Mintage	VF20	XF40	MS60	MS63	MS65
1985	101	PF65 2,100				

KM# 137 250 DOLLARS
47.54 g., 0.917 Gold 1.4016 oz. AGW **Ruler:** Elizabeth II **Subject:** Royal Visit **Obv:** Crowned bust of Queen Elizabeth II, right **Rev:** National arms, value below

Date	Mintage	VF20	XF40	MS60	MS63	MS65
1985	100	PF65 2,100				

KM# 121 250 DOLLARS
47.54 g., 0.917 Gold 1.4016 oz. AGW **Ruler:** Elizabeth II **Obv:** Bust of Queen Elizabeth II right **Rev:** Queen Isabella receiving Columbus, date at bottom, value at top

Date	Mintage	VF20	XF40	MS60	MS63	MS65
1987	100	PF65 2,100				

KM# 126 250 DOLLARS
47.54 g., 0.917 Gold 1.4016 oz. AGW **Ruler:** Elizabeth II **Subject:** Columbus Discovers the New World **Obv:** Bust of Queen Elizabeth II right **Rev:** Columbus sighting land, date at bottom, value at top

Date	Mintage	VF20	XF40	MS60	MS63	MS65
1988	53	PF65 2,200				

KM# 131 250 DOLLARS
47.54 g., 0.917 Gold 1.4016 oz. AGW **Ruler:** Elizabeth II **Obv:** Bust of Queen Elizabeth II right **Rev:** Christopher Columbus

Date	Mintage	VF20	XF40	MS60	MS63	MS65
1989	Est. 250	PF65 2,000				

KM# 136 250 DOLLARS
47.54 g., 0.917 Gold 1.4016 oz. AGW **Ruler:** Elizabeth II **Subject:** Discovery of New World **Obv:** Bust of Queen Elizabeth II right **Rev:** Native American facing right, within circle, value at bottom

Date	Mintage	VF20	XF40	MS60	MS63	MS65
1990	500	PF65 1,950				

KM# 175 250 DOLLARS
47.54 g., 0.917 Gold 1.4016 oz. AGW **Ruler:** Elizabeth II **Subject:** Discovery of the New World **Rev:** Columbus meeting native Americans, within circle, value below circle

Date	Mintage	VF20	XF40	MS60	MS63	MS65
1992	Est. 500	PF65 1,950				

KM# 182 250 DOLLARS
47.54 g., 0.917 Gold 1.4016 oz. AGW **Ruler:** Elizabeth II **Subject:** Royal Visit **Note:** Similar to 2 Dollars, KM#158.

Date	Mintage	VF20	XF40	MS60	MS63	MS65
1994	100	PF65 2,100				

KM# 210 250 DOLLARS
Gold **Ruler:** Elizabeth II **Subject:** 25th Anniversary College of the Bahamas **Obv:** Crowned bust right **Rev:** College facade

Date	Mintage	VF20	XF40	MS60	MS63	MS65
1998 Proof	—	—	—	—	—	—

KM# 213 250 DOLLARS
31.10 g., Gold, 38.61 mm. **Ruler:** Elizabeth II **Subject:** XXVII Summer Olympics - Sydney 2000 **Obv:** National arms **Rev:** "The Golden Girls" - five relay runners **Edge:** Reeded

Date	Mintage	VF20	XF40	MS60	MS63	MS65
2000	—	PF65 2,000				

KM# 88 500 DOLLARS
25.92 g., 0.900 Gold 0.750 oz. AGW **Ruler:** Elizabeth II **Subject:** Wedding of Prince Charles and Lady Diana **Obv:** Bust of Queen Elizabeth II right with tiara **Rev:** Conjoined busts of royal couple left

Date	Mintage	VF20	XF40	MS60	MS63	MS65
1981	5,000	PF63 950	PF65 1,100			

KM# 100 1000 DOLLARS
41.47 g., 0.900 Gold 1.200 oz. AGW **Ruler:** Elizabeth II **Subject:** America's Cup Challenge **Obv:** Bust right with tiara, date below **Rev:** Sailboat, value at left

Date	Mintage	VF20	XF40	MS60	MS63	MS65
1983	300	PF63 1,600	PF65 1,700			

KM# 75 2500 DOLLARS
407.26 g., 0.917 Gold 12.0069 oz. AGW, 72 mm. **Ruler:** Elizabeth II **Obv:** National arms **Rev:** Two flamingos, value above, date below **Note:** Illustration reduced.

Date	Mintage	VF20	XF40	MS60	MS63	MS65
1974	204	PF63 15,500	PF65 17,000			
1977	168	PF63 16,000	PF65 17,500			

KM# 101 2500 DOLLARS
407.26 g., 0.917 Gold 12.0069 oz. AGW, 72 mm. **Ruler:** Elizabeth II **Subject:** 10th Anniversary of Independence **Obv:** Bust right **Rev:** National arms, value below **Note:** Illustration reduced.

Date	Mintage	VF20	XF40	MS60	MS63	MS65
1983	55	PF65 18,000				

KM# 112 2500 DOLLARS
407.26 g., 0.917 Gold 12.0069 oz. AGW, 72 mm. **Ruler:** Elizabeth II **Subject:** Columbus' Discovery of America **Obv:** Bust of Queen Elizabeth II right **Rev:** Columbus with crew claiming land for Spain, planting flag, date below **Note:** Illustration reduced.

Date	Mintage	VF20	XF40	MS60	MS63	MS65
1985	37	PF65 18,500				

KM# 116 2500 DOLLARS
407.26 g., 0.917 Gold 12.0069 oz. AGW, 72 mm. **Ruler:** Elizabeth II **Rev:** Kneeling Columbus and Queen Isabella, date at bottom

Date	Mintage	VF20	XF40	MS60	MS63	MS65
1987	20	PF65 19,000				

KM# 122 2500 DOLLARS
407.26 g., 0.917 Gold 12.0069 oz. AGW **Ruler:** Elizabeth II **Obv:** Bust of Queen Elizabeth II right **Rev:** Columbus sighting "New World"

Date	Mintage	VF20	XF40	MS60	MS63	MS65
1988	32	PF65 18,500				

KM# 216 2500 DOLLARS
407.27 g., 0.9167 Gold 12.0032 oz. AGW **Ruler:** Elizabeth II **Subject:** Milllennium **Obv:** Crowned bust right **Rev:** Two flamingos standing facing each other, sunrise in backgound

Date	Mintage	VF20	XF40	MS60	MS63	MS65
2000	—	PF65 18,000				

MINT SETS

KM#	Date	Mintage	Identification	Issue Price	Mkt Val
MS1	1966 (9)	75,050	KM#2-10	16.00	85.00
MS2	1966 (7)	500,000	KM#2-8	5.25	40.00
MS3	1967 (4)	1,200	KM#11-14	180	3,750
MS4	1969 (9)	26,221	KM#2-10	20.25	85.00
MS5	1970 (9)	25,135	KM#3-10, 15	20.25	85.00
MS6	1971 (9)	12,895	KM#16-24	20.25	80.00
MS7	1971 (4)	6,800	KM#25, 27, 29, 31	185	3,750
MS8	1972 (9)	10,128	KM#16-23, 33	22.75	85.00
MS9	1972 (4)	2,250	KM#34-37	185	2,750
MS10	1973 (9)	9,853	KM#16-23, 33	23.75	80.00
MS11	1973 (4)	4,660	KM#40, 43, 47, 49.1	—	1,150
MS12	1973 (2)	—	KM#40, 43	—	200
MS13	1974 (9)	11,004	KM#59-67	22.50	32.00
MS14	1974 (4)	5,528	KM#51, 54, 69, 72	—	1,350
MS15	1974 (2)	—	KM#68, 71	—	475
MS16	1975 (9)	3,845	KM#59-67	27.00	70.00
MS17	1975 (4)	1,545	KM#51, 54, 69, 72	—	1,350
MS18	1976 (9)	1,453	KM#59-67	27.00	70.00
MS19	1977 (9)	731	KM#59-67	27.00	70.00
MS20	1978 (9)	767	KM#59-67	27.00	65.00
MS21	1989 (7)	—	KM#59a, 60-64, 65b	—	30.00
MS22	1991 (7)	5,000	KM#59a, 60-64, 65b	—	30.00
MS23	1992 (7)	—	KM#59a, 60-64, 65b	24.00	30.00

PROOF SETS

KM#	Date	Mintage	Identification	Issue Price	Mkt Val
PS1	1967 (4)	850	KM#11-14	252	4,000
PS2	1969 (8)	10,381	KM#2-10	35.00	85.00
PS3	1970 (9)	22,827	KM#3-10, 15	35.00	85.00
PS4	1971 (9)	30,507	KM#16-24	35.00	80.00
PS5A	1971 (4)	1,250	KM#25, 27, 29, 31	298	4,000
PS5B	1971 (4)	—	KM#26, 28, 30, 32.1	—	3,500
PS6	1972 (9)	34,789	KM#16-23, 33	35.00	85.00
PS7	1972 (4)	1,250	KM#34-37	565	3,200
PS8	1973 (9)	34,815	KM#16-23, 33	35.00	85.00
PS9	1973 (4)	1,260	KM#41, 44, 46, 50	402	950
PS10	1974 (9)	93,776	KM#59-63, 64a-67a	45.00	80.00
PS11	1974 (4)	3,587	KM#51, 54, 69, 73	1,000	1,350
PS12	1975 (9)	29,095	KM#59-63, 64a-67a	59.00	85.00
PS13	1975 (4)	1,570	KM#51, 54, 69, 73	1,000	1,375
PS14	1976 (9)	22,570	KM#59-63, 64a-67a	59.00	85.00
PS15	1976 (4)	—	KM#51, 54, 69, 73	1,000	1,400
PS16	1977 (9)	10,812	KM#59-63, 64a-67a	59.00	95.00
PS17	1977 (4)	—	KM#51, 54, 69, 73	—	1,500
PS18	1978 (9)	6,931	KM#59-63, 64a-67a	59.00	100
PS19	1979 (9)	2,053	KM#59-63, 64a-67a	115	150
PS20	1979 (2)	—	KM#82-83	445	600
PS21	1980 (9)	2,084	KM#59-63, 64a-67a	145	150
PS22	1981 (9)	1,980	KM#59-64, 65b-67b	62.00	70.00
PS23	1982 (9)	—	KM#59-64, 89-91	67.00	85.00
PS24	1983 (9)	1,009	KM#59-64, 93-95	67.00	85.00
PS25	1984 (9)	7,500	KM#59-64, 104-106	72.00	85.00
PS26	1985 (8)	1,576	KM#59-64, 104, 105, 107	—	65.00
PS27	1989 (9)	2,000	KM#59a, 60-64, 65b, 66c, 132	106	85.00
PS29	1992 (4)	750	KM#192-194 + gold-plated silver ingot	—	425

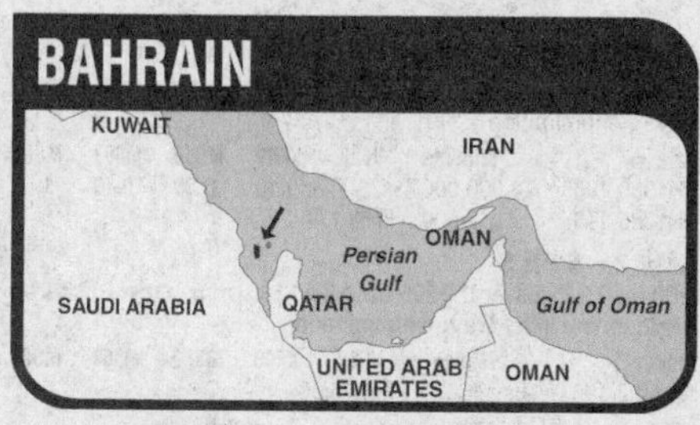

The State of Bahrain, a group of islands in the Persian Gulf off Saudi Arabia, has an area of 268 sq. mi. (622 sq. km.) and a population of 618,000. Capital: Manama. Prior to the depression of the 1930's, the economy was based on pearl fishing. Petroleum and aluminum industries and transit trade are the vital factors in the economy today.

The Portuguese occupied the islands in 1507 but were driven out in 1602 by Arab subjects of Persia. They in turn were ejected by Arabs of the Ataiba tribe from the Arabian mainland who have maintained possession up to the present time. The ruling sheikh of Bahrain entered into relations with Great Britain in 1805 and concluded a binding treaty of protection in 1861. In 1968 Great Britain decided to terminate treaty relations with the Persian Gulf sheikhdoms. Unable to agree on terms of union with the other sheikhdoms, Bahrain decided to seek independence as a separate entity and became fully independent on August 14, 1971.

Bahrain took part in the Arab oil embargo against the U.S. and other nations. The government bought controlling interest in the oil industry in 1975.

The coinage of the State of Bahrain was struck at the Royal Mint, London, England.

RULERS

Al Khalifa Dynasty
Isa Bin Ali, 1869-1932
Hamad Bin Isa, 1932-1942
Salman Bin Hamad, 1942-1961
Isa Bin Salman, 1961-1999
Hamed Bin Isa, 1999-

MINT MARKS

بحرين

Bahrain

البحرين

al-Bahrain = of the two seas

MONETARY SYSTEM

Falus, Fulus — Fals, Fils — Falsan

1000 Fils = 1 Dinar

KINGDOM

STANDARD COINAGE

KM# 1 FILS
1.50 g., Bronze, 15 mm. **Obv:** Palm tree within inner circle **Rev:** Denomination

Date	Mintage	VF20	XF40	MS60	MS63	MS65
AH1385-1965	1,500,000	—	0.10	0.20	0.40	1.50
AH1385-1965	12,000	PF65 1.00				
AH1386-1966	1,500,000	—	0.10	0.20	0.40	1.50
AH1386-1966	—	PF65 2.00				

KM# 1a FILS
1.50 g., 0.925 Silver 0.0446 oz. ASW **Obv:** Palm tree within inner circle **Rev:** Denomination

Date	Mintage	VF20	XF40	MS60	MS63	MS65
AH1403-1983	Est. 15000	PF65 5.00				

KM# 2 5 FILS
2.00 g., Bronze, 18.5 mm. **Obv:** Palm tree within inner circle **Rev:** Denomination

Date	Mintage	VF20	XF40	MS60	MS63	MS65
AH1385-1965	8,000,000	—	0.10	0.20	0.40	1.50
AH1385-1965	12,000	PF65 1.00				

KM# 2a 5 FILS
2.00 g., 0.925 Silver 0.0595 oz. ASW, 18.5 mm. **Obv:** Palm tree within inner circle **Rev:** Denomination

Date	Mintage	VF20	XF40	MS60	MS63	MS65
AH1403-1983	Est. 15000	PF65 5.00				

KM# 16 5 FILS
2.50 g., Brass, 19 mm. **Obv:** Palm tree within inner circle **Obv. Legend:** STATE OF BAHRAIN **Rev:** Numeric denomination back of boxed denomination within circle, chain border

Date	Mintage	VF20	XF40	MS60	MS63	MS65
AH1412-1991	—	—	—	0.50	0.75	1.25
AH1412-1992	—	—	—	0.50	0.75	1.25

KM# 3 10 FILS
4.75 g., Bronze, 23.5 mm. **Obv:** Palm tree within inner circle **Rev:** Denomination

Date	Mintage	VF20	XF40	MS60	MS63	MS65
AH1385-1965	8,500,000	—	0.25	0.50	1.00	4.00
AH1385-1965	12,000	PF65 1.50				

KM# 3a 10 FILS
4.75 g., 0.925 Silver 0.1413 oz. ASW, 23.5 mm. **Obv:** Palm tree within inner circle **Rev:** Denomination

Date	Mintage	VF20	XF40	MS60	MS63	MS65
AH1403-1983	Est. 15000	PF65 8.00				

KM# 17 10 FILS
3.35 g., Brass, 21 mm. **Obv:** Palm tree within inner circle **Rev:** Numeric denomination back of boxed denomination within circle, chain surrounds **Edge:** Plain

Date	Mintage	VF20	XF40	MS60	MS63	MS65
AH1412-1991	—	—	—	1.00	1.50	3.00
AH1412-1992	—	—	—	1.00	1.50	2.50
AH1420-2000	—	—	—	1.00	1.50	2.50

KM# 4 25 FILS
1.75 g., Copper-Nickel, 16.5 mm. **Obv:** Palm tree within inner circle **Rev:** Denomination **Edge:** Reeded

Date	Mintage	VF20	XF40	MS60	MS63	MS65
AH1385-1965	11,250,000	—	0.25	0.50	1.00	5.00
AH1385-1965	12,000	PF65 2.00				

KM# 4a 25 FILS
1.75 g., 0.925 Silver 0.052 oz. ASW, 16.5 mm. **Obv:** Palm tree within inner circle **Rev:** Denomination **Edge:** Reeded

Date	Mintage	VF20	XF40	MS60	MS63	MS65
AH1403-1983	Est. 15000	PF65 6.00				

KM# 18 25 FILS
3.50 g., Copper-Nickel, 20 mm. **Obv:** Ancient painting within circle **Rev:** Numeric denomination back of boxed denomination within circle, chain surrounds

Date	Mintage	VF20	XF40	MS60	MS63	MS65
AH1412-1992	—	—	—	1.00	2.00	3.00
AH1420-2000	—	—	—	1.00	2.00	3.00

KM# 5 50 FILS
3.10 g., Copper-Nickel, 20 mm. **Obv:** Palm tree within inner circle **Rev:** Denomination **Edge:** Reeded

Date	Mintage	VF20	XF40	MS60	MS63	MS65
AH1385-1965	6,909,000	—	0.35	0.75	1.25	6.00
AH1385-1965	12,000	PF65 2.50				

KM# 5a 50 FILS
3.10 g., 0.925 Silver 0.0922 oz. ASW, 20 mm. **Obv:** Palm tree within inner circle **Rev:** Denomination

Date	Mintage	VF20	XF40	MS60	MS63	MS65
AH1403-1983	Est. 15000	PF65 8.00				

KM# 19 50 FILS
4.50 g., Copper-Nickel, 22 mm. **Obv:** Stylized sailboat **Rev:** Numeric denomination back of boxed denomination within circle, chain surrounds

Date	Mintage	VF20	XF40	MS60	MS63	MS65
AH1412-1992	—	—	—	1.00	2.00	3.00
AH1420-2000	—	—	—	1.00	2.00	3.00

KM# 6 100 FILS
6.50 g., Copper-Nickel, 25 mm. **Obv:** Palm tree within inner circle **Rev:** Denomination **Edge:** Reeded

Date	Mintage	VF20	XF40	MS60	MS63	MS65
AH1385-1965	8,300,000	—	0.50	1.00	2.00	6.00
AH1385-1965	12,000	PF65 3.50				

KM# 6a 100 FILS
6.50 g., 0.925 Silver 0.1933 oz. ASW, 25 mm. **Obv:** Palm tree within inner circle **Rev:** Denomination **Edge:** Reeded

Date	Mintage	VF20	XF40	MS60	MS63	MS65
AH1403-1983	Est. 15000	PF65 10.00				

KM# 20 100 FILS
6.00 g., Bi-Metallic Copper-Nickel center in Brass ring, 24 mm. **Obv:** Coat of arms within circle, dates at either side **Obv. Legend:** STATE OF BAHRAIN **Rev:** Numeric denomination back of boxed denomination within circle, chain surrounds **Edge:** Reeded

Date	Mintage	VF20	XF40	MS60	MS63	MS65
AH1412-1992	—	—	—	1.50	2.50	5.00
AH1415-1995	—	—	—	1.50	2.50	5.00
AH1417-1997	—	—	—	1.50	2.50	5.00
AH1420-2000	—	—	—	1.50	2.50	5.00

KM# 7 250 FILS
15.55 g., Copper-Nickel, 32 mm. **Series:** F.A.O. **Obv:** Sailboat, palm tree at right **Rev:** F.A.O. logo divided by grain sprig

Date	Mintage	VF20	XF40	MS60	MS63	MS65
AH1389-1969	50,000	—	1.50	2.50	5.00	7.00
AH1389-1969	—	PF65 8.00				
AH1403-1983	3,000	—	2.50	5.00	10.00	15.00

KM# 7a 250 FILS
15.00 g., 0.925 Silver 0.4461 oz. ASW **Series:** F.A.O. **Obv:** Sailboat, palm tree at left **Rev:** F.A.O. logo divided by grain sprig

Date	Mintage	VF20	XF40	MS60	MS63	MS65
AH1403-1983	Est. 15000	PF65 18.00				

KM# 8 500 FILS
18.30 g., 0.800 Silver 0.4707 oz. ASW, 34.5 mm. **Ruler:** Isa Bin Salman **Obv:** Bust left **Rev:** Opening of Isa Town, crowned arms at center of octagon, dates appear in western and arabic script: 1368-1968

Date	Mintage	VF20	XF40	MS60	MS63	MS65
AH1368/1968	50,000	—	9.00	13.00	17.00	22.00
AH1368/1968	—	PF65 28.00				

KM# 8a 500 FILS
18.06 g., 0.925 Silver 0.5371 oz. ASW **Ruler:** Isa Bin Salman **Obv:** Bust left **Rev:** Opening of Isa Town, crowned arms at center of octagon

Date	Mintage	VF20	XF40	MS60	MS63	MS65
AH1403-1983	Est. 15000	PF65 35.00				

KM# 22 500 FILS
9.00 g., Bi-Metallic Brass center in Copper-Nickel ring, 27 mm. **Ruler:** Hamed Bin Isa **Obv:** Monument and inscription **Obv. Inscription:** STATE OF BAHRAIN **Rev:** Denomination **Edge:** Reeded

Date	Mintage	VF20	XF40	MS60	MS63	MS65
2000	—	—	—	3.00	5.00	9.00

KM# 13 5 DINARS
19.44 g., 0.925 Silver 0.5781 oz. ASW **Ruler:** Isa Bin Salman **Obv:** Bust left **Rev:** Goitered Gazelle running left **Edge Lettering:** World Wildlife Fund

Date	Mintage	VF20	XF40	MS60	MS63	MS65
AH1406-1986	Est. 25000	PF63 25.00	PF65 35.00			

KM# 14 5 DINARS
19.44 g., 0.925 Silver 0.5781 oz. ASW **Ruler:** Isa Bin Salman **Subject:** Save The Children **Obv:** Bust left **Rev:** Children playing

Date	Mintage	VF20	XF40	MS60	MS63	MS65
AH1410-1990	Est. 20000	PF63 22.00		PF65 32.00		

KM# 21 5 DINARS
28.23 g., 0.925 Silver 0.8395 oz. ASW **Ruler:** Isa Bin Salman **Subject:** 50th Anniversary - United Nations **Obv:** Bust left **Rev:** UN building, logo

Date	Mintage	VF20	XF40	MS60	MS63	MS65
ND-1995	—	PF63 30.00		PF65 40.00		

KM# 23 5 DINARS
19.40 g., 0.925 Silver 0.5769 oz. ASW, 35.9 mm. **Ruler:** Isa Bin Salman **Subject:** UNICEF **Obv:** Bust left **Rev:** Children within circle **Edge:** Reeded

Date	Mintage	VF20	XF40	MS60	MS63	MS65
AH1419-1998	—	PF63 25.00	PF65 35.00			

KM# 11 50 DINARS
15.98 g., 0.917 Gold 0.4711 oz. AGW **Ruler:** Isa Bin Salman **Subject:** 50th Anniversary of Bahrain Monetary Agency

Date	Mintage	VF20	XF40	MS60	MS63	MS65
AH1398-1978	5,000	PF60 750	PF63 850	PF65 1,000		

KM# 12 100 DINARS
31.96 g., 0.917 Gold 0.9423 oz. AGW **Ruler:** Isa Bin Salman **Subject:** 50th Anniversary of Bahrain Monetary Agency **Obv:** Bust left **Rev:** Coat of arms divides dates

Date	Mintage	VF20	XF40	MS60	MS63	MS65
AH1398-1978	5,000	PF60 1,350	PF63 1,450	PF65 1,600		

MINT SETS

KM#	Date	Mintage	Identification	Issue Price	Mkt Val
MS1	1992 (5)	—	KM#16-20	—	12.50

PROOF SETS

KM#	Date	Mintage	Identification	Issue Price	Mkt Val
PS1	1965 (7)	12,000	KM#1-6, 8	—	35.00
PS3	1983 (8)	15,000	KM#1a-8a	99.00	200

BANGLADESH

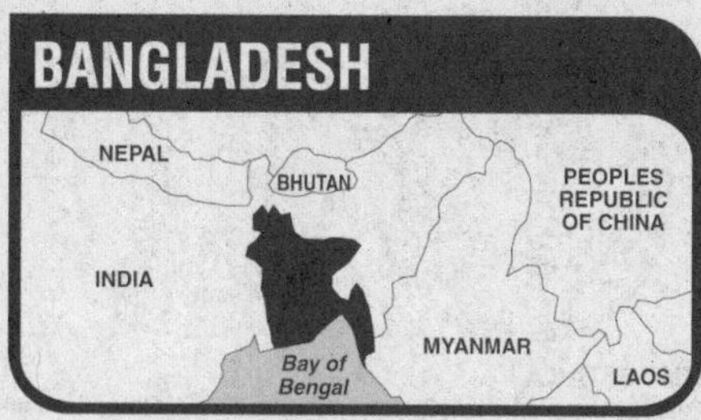

The Peoples Republic of Bangladesh (formerly East Pakistan), a parliamentary democracy located on the Bay of Bengal bordered by India and Burma, has an area of 55,598 sq. mi. (143,998 sq. km.) and a population of 128.1 million. Capital: Dhaka. The economy is predominantly agricultural. Jute products, jute and tea are exported.

British rule over the vast Indian sub-continent ended in 1947 when British India attained independence and was partitioned into the two successor states of India and Pakistan. Pakistan consisted of East and West Pakistan, two areas united by the Moslem religion but separated by culture and 1,000 miles of Indian territory. Restive under the de facto rule of the militant but fewer West Pakistanis, the East Pakistanis unsuccessfully demanded greater economic benefits and political reforms. The inability of the leaders of East and West Pakistan to resolve a political breakdown occasioned by the East Pakistan success in the general elections of 1970 precipitated massive civil disobedience in East Pakistan which West Pakistan sought to suppress militarily. East Pakistan seceded from Pakistan, March 26, 1971, and with the support of India declared an independent Peoples Republic of Bangladesh.

Bangladesh is a member of the Commonwealth of Nations. The president is the Head of State and the Government.

MONETARY SYSTEM
100 Poisha = 1 Taka

DATING
Christian era using Bengali numerals.

PEOPLES REPUBLIC

STANDARD COINAGE

KM# 5 POISHA
0.53 g., Aluminum, 16.03 mm. **Obv:** National emblem, Shapla (water lily) **Rev:** Vallue within decorative circle **Edge:** Plain

Date	Mintage	VF20	XF40	MS60	MS63	MS65
1974	300,000,000	—	0.60	1.00	—	—

KM# 1 5 POISHA
1.40 g., Aluminum, 22.4 mm. **Series:** F.A.O. **Obv:** National emblem, Shapla (water lily) **Rev:** Value and symbol within dentiled circle **Edge:** Plain **Shape:** 4-sided

Date	Mintage	VF20	XF40	MS60	MS63	MS65
1973	Est. 47088000	1.00	1.50	2.00	—	—
1974	—	1.00	1.50	2.00	—	—

KM# 6 5 POISHA
1.40 g., Aluminum, 22.46 mm. **Series:** F.A.O. **Obv:** National emblem, Shapla (water lily) **Rev:** Value and sumbol within dentiled circle **Edge:** Plain **Shape:** 4-sided

Date	Mintage	VF20	XF40	MS60	MS63	MS65
1974	5,000,000	1.25	1.50	2.00	—	—
1975	3,000,000	1.25	1.50	2.00	—	—
1976	3,000,000	1.25	1.50	2.00	—	—
1977	—	1.25	1.50	2.00	—	—
1978	—	1.25	1.50	2.00	—	—
1979	—	1.25	1.50	2.00	—	—

KM# 10 5 POISHA
1.43 g., Aluminum, 22.4 mm. **Series:** F.A.O. **Obv:** National emblem, Shapla (water lily) **Rev:** Value at right, 2/3 dentiled circle at left, symbol wihin **Edge:** Plain **Shape:** 4-sided square

Date	Mintage	VF20	XF40	MS60	MS63	MS65
1981	72,992,000	—	—	—	—	—
Note: Never issued in this year, mintage may represent fixed date striking of 1980 dies						
1977	90,000,000	—	0.75	1.25	—	—
1978	52,432,000	—	0.75	1.25	—	—
1979	120,096,000	—	0.50	1.00	—	—
1980	127,008,000	—	0.50	1.00	—	—
1994	—	—	0.50	1.25	—	—

KM# 2 10 POISHA
1.96 g., Aluminum, 24 mm. **Series:** F.A.O. **Obv:** National emblem, Shapla (water lily) **Rev:** Large leaf at center, stem divides value **Edge:** Plain **Shape:** Scalloped

Date	Mintage	VF20	XF40	MS60	MS63	MS65
1973	Est. 21500000	1.00	1.75	2.50	—	—
1974	—	1.00	1.75	2.50	—	—

KM# 7 10 POISHA
2.00 g., Aluminum, 24 mm. **Series:** F.A.O. **Obv:** National emblem, Shapla (water lily) **Rev:** Value at bottom, vehicle and plant at center **Edge:** Plain **Shape:** Scalloped

Date	Mintage	VF20	XF40	MS60	MS63	MS65
1974	5,000,000	1.25	1.75	2.25	—	—
1975	4,000,000	1.25	1.75	2.25	—	—
1976	4,000,000	1.25	1.75	2.25	—	—
1977	4,000,000	1.25	1.75	2.25	—	—
1978	141,744,000	1.25	1.75	2.25	—	—
1979	—	1.25	1.75	2.25	—	—

KM# 11.1 10 POISHA
2.00 g., Aluminum, 24 mm. **Series:** F.A.O. **Obv:** National emblem, Shapla (water lily) **Rev:** Family above value **Edge:** Plain **Shape:** Scalloped

Date	Mintage	VF20	XF40	MS60	MS63	MS65
1977	48,000,000	0.75	1.25	2.00	—	—
1978	77,518,000	0.75	1.25	2.00	—	—
1979	170,112,000	0.75	1.25	2.00	—	—
1980	200,000,000	0.75	1.25	2.00	—	—

KM# 11.2 10 POISHA
1.39 g., Aluminum, 22 mm. **Series:** F.A.O. **Obv:** National emblem, Shapla (water lily) within wreath above water **Rev:** Family, value below **Edge:** Plain **Shape:** Scalloped **Note:** Reduced size.

Date	Mintage	VF20	XF40	MS60	MS63	MS65
1981	—	—	—	—	—	—
1983	142,848,000	0.25	0.50	1.25	—	—
1984	—	—	—	—	—	—
1994	57,152,000	0.25	0.50	1.25	—	—

KM# 3 25 POISHA

2.65 g., Steel, 19 mm. **Series:** F.A.O. **Obv:** National emblem, Shapla (water lily) **Rev:** Rohu, right, value below **Edge:** Reeded

Date	Mintage	VF20	XF40	MS60	MS63	MS65
1973	Est. 25072000	1.50	2.50	3.50	—	—

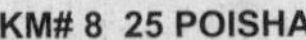

KM# 8 25 POISHA

2.66 g., Steel, 19 mm. **Series:** F.A.O. **Obv:** National emblem, Shapla (water lily) **Rev:** Carp, egg, banana, squash, value at bottom **Edge:** Reeded

Date	Mintage	VF20	XF40	MS60	MS63	MS65
1974	5,000,000	1.50	2.50	3.50	—	—
1975	6,000,000	1.50	2.50	3.50	—	—
1976	6,000,000	1.50	2.50	3.50	—	—
1977	51,300,000	1.50	2.50	3.50	—	—
1978	66,750,000	1.50	2.50	3.50	—	—
1979	—	1.50	2.50	3.50	—	—

KM# 12 25 POISHA

2.65 g., Steel, 19 mm. **Obv:** National emblem, Shapla (water lily) **Rev:** Tiger head left within inner circle **Edge:** Reeded

Date	Mintage	VF20	XF40	MS60	MS63	MS65
1977	45,300,000	0.50	1.25	1.50	—	—
1978	66,750,000	0.50	1.25	1.50	—	—
1979	56,704,000	0.50	1.25	1.50	—	—
1980	228,992,000	0.50	1.25	1.50	—	—
1981	50,002,000	—	—	—	—	—
Note: Never issued in this year, mintage may represent fixed date striking of 1980 dies						
1983	96,128,000	0.50	1.25	1.50	—	—
1984	203,872,000	0.50	1.25	1.50	—	—
1991	50,002,000	0.50	1.25	1.50	—	—
1994	—	0.50	1.25	1.50	—	—

KM# 4 50 POISHA

4.07 g., Steel, 22 mm. **Series:** F.A.O. **Obv:** National emblem, Shapla (water lily) **Rev:** Bird left, value below **Edge:** Reeded

Date	Mintage	VF20	XF40	MS60	MS63	MS65
1973	18,000,000	3.00	4.75	6.00	—	—

KM# 13 50 POISHA

4.00 g., Steel, 22 mm. **Series:** F.A.O. **Obv:** National emblem, Shapla (water lily) **Rev:** Symbols within inner ring, value at bottom **Edge:** Reeded

Date	Mintage	VF20	XF40	MS60	MS63	MS65
1977	12,700,000	0.50	1.25	1.75	—	—
1978	37,300,000	0.50	1.25	1.75	—	—
1979	2,208,000	0.50	1.25	1.75	—	—
1980	124,512,000	0.50	1.25	1.75	—	—
1981	36,680,000	—	—	—	—	—
Note: Never issued in this year, mintage may represent fixed date striking of 1980 dies						
1983	31,392,000	0.50	1.25	1.75	—	—
1984	168,608,000	0.50	1.25	1.75	—	—
1994	—	0.50	1.25	1.75	—	—

KM# 9 TAKA

6.05 g., Copper-Nickel, 26 mm. **Series:** F.A.O. **Obv:** National emblem, Shapla (water lily) **Rev:** Stylized family, value at right **Edge:** Reeded **Note:** Prev. KM # 9.1.

Date	Mintage	VF20	XF40	MS60	MS63	MS65
1975	4,000,000	2.00	3.00	4.00	—	—
1976	—	2.00	3.00	4.00	—	—
1977	—	2.00	3.00	4.00	—	—

KM# 17 TAKA

31.47 g., 0.925 Silver 0.9359 oz. ASW **Subject:** 20th Victory Day **Obv:** Inscribed with faces of 7 great heroes of Liberation War **Rev:** National memorial, value divides date below

Date	Mintage	VF20	XF40	MS60	MS63	MS65
1991	—	PF65 350				

KM# 9a TAKA

6.10 g., Steel, 25 mm. **Series:** F.A.O. **Obv:** National emblem, Shapla (water lily) **Rev:** Stylized family, value at right **Edge:** Reeded **Note:** Prev. KM # 9.2.

Date	Mintage	VF20	XF40	MS60	MS63	MS65
1992	—	1.00	1.50	2.00	—	—
1993	—	1.00	1.50	2.00	—	—
1995	—	1.00	1.50	2.00	—	—

KM# 14 TAKA

31.47 g., 0.925 Silver 0.9359 oz. ASW, 36.61 mm. **Subject:** Barcelona 1992 - 25th Summer Olympics **Obv:** Two athletes running with Olympic flame **Rev:** National emblem, Shapla (water lily) **Edge:** Reeded

Date	Mintage	VF20	XF40	MS60	MS63	MS65
1992	Est. 40000	PF65 40.00				

KM# 15 TAKA

31.47 g., 0.925 Silver 0.9359 oz. ASW **Subject:** Endangered Wildlife **Obv:** National emblem, Shapla (water lily) **Rev:** Deer **Edge:** Reeded **Note:** This coin does not have legal tender status as the Bangladesh Bank refused shipment from the mint who sold coins directly to distributors without permission.

Date	Mintage	VF20	XF40	MS60	MS63	MS65
1993	Est. 40000	PF65 50.00				

KM# 16 TAKA

31.47 g., 0.925 Silver 0.9359 oz. ASW **Subject:** World Cup Soccer, 1994 **Obv:** National emblem, Shapla (water lily) **Note:** This coin does not have legal tender status as the Bangladesh Bank refused shipment from the mint who sold coins directly to distributors without permission.

Date	Mintage	VF20	XF40	MS60	MS63	MS65
1993	40,000	PF65 65.00				

KM# 9b TAKA

4.00 g., Brass, 25 mm. **Series:** F.A.O. **Obv:** National emblem, Shapla (water lily) **Rev:** Stylized family, value at right **Edge:** Reeded **Note:** Prev. KM # 9.3.

Date	Mintage	VF20	XF40	MS60	MS63	MS65
1996	—	2.50	3.00	6.00	—	—
1999	—	2.50	3.00	6.00	—	—

KM# 18.1 5 TAKA

7.87 g., Steel, 27.7 mm. **Obv:** Shapla flower on waves within wreath **Rev:** Bridge, value below, weak clouds above **Edge:** Plain **Shape:** 12-sided **Note:** Varieties exist in the clouds.

Date	Mintage	VF20	XF40	MS60	MS63	MS65
1994	—	—	2.50	4.00	—	—

KM# 18.2 5 TAKA

7.87 g., Steel, 27.7 mm. **Obv:** Shapla flower on waves within wreath **Rev:** Bridge, value below, strong clouds above **Edge:** Plain **Shape:** 12-sided

Date	Mintage	VF20	XF40	MS60	MS63	MS65
1996	—	2.00	2.75	3.50	—	—

KM# 18.3 5 TAKA

8.17 g., Steel, 26.8 mm. **Obv:** Shapla flower on waves within wreath, thicker design **Rev:** Bridge, value, denomination at bottom, strong clouds above **Edge:** Plain **Shape:** 12-sided

Date	Mintage	VF20	XF40	MS60	MS63	MS65
1996	—	1.35	2.50	3.50	—	—

KM# 19 10 TAKA

31.47 g., 0.925 Silver 0.9359 oz. ASW, 38.61 mm. **Subject:** 25th Anniversary of Independence **Obv:** National monument in Savar **Rev:** Bust of Minister/President Mujibur Rahman, 1972-1975 left **Edge:** Reeded

Date	Mintage	VF20	XF40	MS60	MS63	MS65
1996	—	PF65 100				

KM# 20 10 TAKA

31.47 g., 0.925 Silver 0.9359 oz. ASW, 41.83 mm. **Subject:** 25th Anniversary Bangladesh Bank **Obv:** National arms **Rev:** Bangladesh Bank building in Dhaka **Edge:** Plain **Shape:** Octagonal

Date	Mintage	VF20	XF40	MS60	MS63	MS65
ND1996	—	PF65 100				

KM# 21 10 TAKA

25.00 g., Nickel, 35 mm. **Subject:** Opening of Bangabandhu Jamuna bridge **Obv:** Statues of three liberation fighters **Rev:** Bridge **Edge:** Reeded

Date	Mintage	VF20	XF40	MS60	MS63	MS65
1998	—	PF63 60.00	PF65 70.00			

KM# 22 20 TAKA

25.00 g., 0.999 Silver 0.803 oz. ASW, 38 mm. **Subject:** Opening of Bangabandhu Lamuna bridge **Obv:** Inscribed with the image of the Jamuna Bridge **Rev:** Portrait of Sheikh Mujibur Rahman **Edge:** Plain

Date	Mintage	VF20	XF40	MS60	MS63	MS65
1998	—	PF65 110				

KM# 23 20 TAKA

10.00 g., 0.9167 Gold 0.2947 oz. AGW, 25 mm. **Subject:** International Mother Language **Obv:** Central bank logo **Rev:** Shaheed Minar memorial **Edge:** Reeded

Date	Mintage	VF20	XF40	MS60	MS63	MS65
2000	—	PF63 650	PF65 700			

BARBADOS

DOMINICA
MARTINIQUE
ST. LUCIA
ST. VINCENT AND THE GRENADINES
GRENADA

Barbados, a Constitutional Monarchy within the Commonwealth of Nations, is located in the Windward Islands of the West Indies east of St. Vincent. The coral island has an area of 166 sq. mi. (430 sq. km.) and a population of 269,000. Capital: Bridgetown. The economy is based on sugar and tourism. Sugar, petroleum products, molasses, and rum are exported.

Barbados was named by the Portuguese who achieved the first landing on the island in 1563. British sailors landed at the site of present-day Holetown in 1624. Barbados was under uninterrupted British control from the time of the first British settlement in 1627 until it obtained independence on Nov. 30, 1966. It is a member of the Commonwealth of Nations. Elizabeth II is Head of State as Queen of Barbados.

The coinage and banknotes of the British Caribbean Territories (Eastern Group) were employed prior to 1973 when Barbados issued a decimal coinage.

RULER

British, until 1966

MINT MARKS

FM - Franklin Mint, U.S.A.*
(brm) – British Royal Mint
(O) – Ottawa Royal Canadian Mint
(v) - Valcambi
None - Royal Mint

***NOTE**: From 1973-1985 the Franklin Mint produced coinage in up to 3 different qualities. Qualities of issue are designated in ( ) after each date and are defined as follows:

(M) MATTE - Normal circulation strike or a dull finish produced by sandblasting special uncirculated (polish finish) or proof quality dies.

(U) SPECIAL UNCIRCULATED - Polished or proof-like in appearance without any frosted features.

(P) PROOF - The highest quality obtainable having mirror-like fields and frosted features.

MONETARY SYSTEM

100 Cents = 1 Dollar

COMMONWEALTH

DECIMAL COINAGE

KM# 10 CENT

3.11 g., Bronze, 19 mm. **Obv:** National arms **Rev:** Trident above value **Edge:** Plain

Date	Mintage	VF20	XF40	MS60	MS63	MS65
1973	5,000,000	—	—	0.10	0.25	0.75
1973 FM (M)	7,500	—	—	0.50	1.00	3.00
1973 FM (P)	97,454	PF65 1.00				
1974 FM (M)	8,708	—	—	0.50	1.00	3.00
1974 FM (P)	35,600	PF65 1.00				
1975 FM (M)	5,000	—	—	0.35	0.75	2.25
1975 FM (U)	1,360	—	—	0.50	1.00	3.00
1975 FM (P)	20,458	PF65 1.00				
1977 FM (M)	2,102	—	—	—	0.75	1.50
1977 FM (U)	468	—	—	1.50	3.00	6.00
1977 FM (P)	5,014	PF65 1.00				
1978	4,807,000	—	—	0.10	0.25	0.75
1978 FM (M)	2,000	—	—	0.50	1.00	3.00
1978 FM (U)	2,517	—	—	1.50	3.00	6.00
1978 FM (P)	4,436	PF65 1.50				
1979	5,606,000	—	—	0.10	0.25	0.75
1979 FM (M)	1,500	—	—	—	1.00	3.00
1979 FM (U)	523	—	—	1.50	3.00	6.00
1979 FM (P)	4,126	PF65 1.50				
1980	14,400,000	—	—	0.10	0.25	0.75
1980 FM (M)	1,500	—	—	0.50	1.00	3.00
1980 FM (U)	649	—	—	1.50	3.00	6.00
1980 FM (P)	2,111	PF65 3.00				
1981	10,160,000	—	—	0.10	0.25	0.75
1981 FM (M)	1,500	—	—	—	1.00	3.00
1981 FM (U)	327	—	—	1.50	3.00	6.00
1981 FM (P)	943	PF65 4.50				
1982	5,040,000	—	—	0.10	0.25	0.75
1982 FM (U)	1,500	—	—	—	1.25	3.75
1982 FM (P)	843	PF65 4.50				
1983 FM (M)	1,500	—	—	—	1.00	4.50
1983 FM (U)	—	—	—	—	1.25	3.75
1983 FM (P)	459	PF65 4.50				
1984	5,008,000	—	—	0.10	0.25	0.75
1984 FM (M)	868	—	—	—	1.25	4.50
1984 FM (P)	—	PF65 3.00				
1985	—	—	—	0.10	0.25	0.75
1986	—	—	—	0.10	0.25	0.75
1987	10,000,000	—	—	0.10	0.25	0.75
1988	12,136,000	—	—	0.10	0.25	0.75
1989	—	—	—	0.10	0.25	0.75
1990	—	—	—	0.10	0.25	0.75
1991	—	—	—	0.10	0.25	0.75

KM# 10a CENT

2.50 g., Copper Plated Zinc, 19 mm. **Obv:** National arms **Rev:** Trident above value **Edge:** Plain

Date	Mintage	VF20	XF40	MS60	MS63	MS65
1992	—	—	—	0.10	0.25	0.75
1993	—	—	—	0.10	0.25	0.75
1995	—	—	—	0.10	0.25	0.75
1996	—	—	—	0.10	0.25	0.75
1997	—	—	—	0.10	0.25	0.75
1997	—	PF65 2.00				
1998	—	—	—	0.10	0.25	0.75
1999	—	—	—	0.10	0.25	0.75
2000	—	—	—	0.10	0.25	0.75

KM# 19 CENT

3.11 g., Bronze, 19 mm. **Subject:** 10th Anniversary of Independence **Obv:** National arms **Rev:** Trident above value **Edge:** Plain

Date	Mintage	VF20	XF40	MS60	MS63	MS65
ND(1976)	6,406,000	—	—	0.10	0.20	0.60
ND(1976) FM (M)	5,000	—	—	—	0.50	1.50
ND(1976) FM (U)	996	—	—	—	1.00	3.00
ND-1976 FM (P)	11,929	PF65 1.00				

KM# 11 5 CENTS

3.75 g., Brass, 21 mm. **Obv:** National arms **Rev:** South Point Lighthouse, value below **Edge:** Plain

Date	Mintage	VF20	XF40	MS60	MS63	MS65
1973 FM (M)	7,500	—	—	—	1.25	3.75
1973	3,000,000	—	0.10	0.20	0.35	1.00
1973 FM (P)	97,454	PF65 1.50				
1974 FM (M)	8,708	—	—	—	1.25	3.75
1974 FM (P)	35,600	PF65 1.50				
1975 FM (M)	5,000	—	—	—	1.00	3.00
1975 FM (U)	1,360	—	—	—	1.25	3.75
1975 FM (P)	20,458	PF65 1.50				
1977 FM (M)	2,100	—	—	1.00	2.00	5.00
1977 FM (U)	468	—	—	1.50	3.00	6.00
1977 FM (P)	5,014	PF65 1.50				
1978 FM (M)	2,000	—	—	—	0.75	1.25
1978 FM (U)	2,517	—	—	1.25	2.75	5.00
1978 FM (P)	4,436	PF65 3.75				
1979	4,800,000	—	0.10	0.20	0.35	1.00
1979 FM (M)	1,500	—	—	—	0.75	1.50
1979 FM (U)	523	—	—	—	2.75	5.00
1979 FM (P)	4,126	PF65 3.75				
1980 FM (M)	1,500	—	—	—	1.00	3.00
1980 FM (U)	649	—	—	1.00	2.25	6.75
1980 FM (P)	2,111	PF65 4.25				
1981 FM (M)	1,500	—	—	—	1.00	3.00
1981 FM (U)	327	—	—	1.00	2.25	6.75
1981 FM (P)	943	PF65 4.25				
1982	2,100,000	—	0.10	0.20	0.35	1.00
1982 FM (U)	1,500	—	—	0.75	1.50	4.50
1982 FM (P)	843	PF65 4.25				
1983 FM (M)	1,500	—	—	0.75	1.50	4.50
1983 FM (U)	—	—	—	0.75	1.50	4.50
1983 FM (P)	459	PF65 4.25				
1984 FM	1,737	—	—	0.75	1.50	4.50
1984 FM (P)	—	PF65 4.25				
1985	—	—	—	0.10	0.25	0.75
1986	—	—	—	0.10	0.25	0.75
1988	4,200,000	—	—	0.10	0.25	0.75
1989	—	—	—	0.10	0.25	0.75
1991	—	—	—	0.10	0.25	0.75
1994	—	—	—	0.10	0.25	0.75
1995	—	—	—	0.10	0.25	0.75
1996	—	—	—	0.10	0.25	0.75
1997	—	—	—	0.10	0.25	0.75
1997	—	PF65 3.00				
1998	—	—	—	0.10	0.25	0.75
1999	—	—	—	0.10	0.25	0.75
2000	—	—	—	0.10	0.25	0.75

KM# 20 5 CENTS

3.75 g., Brass, 21 mm. **Subject:** 10th Anniversary of Independence **Obv:** National arms **Rev:** South Point Lighthouse, value below **Edge:** Plain

Date	Mintage	VF20	XF40	MS60	MS63	MS65
ND-1976 FM (M)	5,000	—	—	0.50	1.00	1.50
ND-1976 FM (U)	996	—	—	—	1.00	2.00
ND-1976 FM (P)	11,929	PF65 1.50				

KM# 12 10 CENTS

2.29 g., Copper-Nickel, 17.77 mm. **Obv:** National arms **Rev:** Tern flying left, value below **Edge:** Reeded

Date	Mintage	VF20	XF40	MS60	MS63	MS65
1973	4,000,000	—	0.10	0.25	0.50	1.00
1973 FM (M)	5,000	—	—	—	1.50	3.00
1973 FM (P)	97,454	PF65 2.00				
1974 FM (M)	6,208	—	—	—	1.25	2.50
1974 FM (P)	35,600	PF65 2.00				
1975 FM (M)	2,500	—	—	—	1.00	3.00
1975 FM (U)	1,360	—	—	—	1.50	3.00
1975 FM (P)	20,458	PF65 2.00				
1977 FM (M)	2,100	—	—	—	1.00	3.00
1977 FM (U)	468	—	—	2.50	4.00	8.00
1977 FM (P)	5,014	PF65 2.00				
1978 FM (M)	2,000	—	—	—	1.00	3.00
1978 FM (U)	2,517	—	—	—	3.00	6.00
1978 FM (P)	4,436	PF65 3.00				
1979	2,500,000	—	0.10	0.25	0.50	1.00
1979 FM (M)	1,500	—	—	1.00	2.50	5.00
1979 FM (U)	523	—	—	1.50	3.00	8.00
1979 FM (P)	4,126	PF65 3.00				
1980	3,500,000	—	0.10	0.25	0.50	1.00
1980 FM (M)	1,500	—	—	—	1.00	3.00
1980 FM (U)	649	—	—	1.00	2.50	7.00
1980 FM (P)	2,111	PF65 4.00				
1981 FM (M)	1,500	—	—	—	1.00	3.00
1981 FM (U)	327	—	—	—	2.50	7.00
1981 FM (P)	943	PF65 4.00				
1982 FM (M)	—	—	—	—	1.00	3.00
1982 FM (U)	1,500	—	—	—	1.75	4.25
1982 FM (P)	843	PF65 4.00				
1983 FM (M)	1,500	—	—	—	1.75	4.25
1983 FM (U)	—	—	—	—	1.75	4.25
1983 FM (P)	459	PF65 4.00				
1984	3,400,000	—	0.10	0.25	0.50	1.00
1984 FM (P)	—	PF65 4.50				
1985	—	—	0.10	0.25	0.50	1.50
1986	—	—	0.10	0.25	0.50	1.50
1987	3,500,000	—	0.10	0.25	0.50	1.00
1988	—	—	0.10	0.25	0.50	1.50
1989	—	—	0.10	0.25	0.50	1.50
1990	—	—	0.10	0.25	0.50	1.50
1992	—	—	0.10	0.25	0.50	1.50
1995	—	—	0.10	0.25	0.50	1.50
1996	—	—	0.10	0.25	0.50	1.50
1997	—	PF65 4.00				
1998	—	—	0.10	0.25	0.50	1.50
2000	—	—	0.10	0.25	0.50	1.50

KM# 21 10 CENTS

2.29 g., Copper-Nickel, 17.77 mm. **Subject:** 10th Anniversary of Independence **Obv:** National arms **Rev:** Tern flying left, value below **Edge:** Reeded

Date	Mintage	VF20	XF40	MS60	MS63	MS65
ND-1976 FM (M)	2,500	—	—	0.75	1.50	2.50

Date	Mintage	VF20	XF40	MS60	MS63	MS65
ND-1976 FM (P)	11,929	PF65 3.00				
ND-1976 FM (U)	996	—	—	—	1.75	5.00

KM# 13 25 CENTS

5.65 g., Copper-Nickel, 23.66 mm. **Obv:** National arms **Rev:** Morgan Lewis Windmill, value above **Edge:** Reeded

Date	Mintage	VF20	XF40	MS60	MS63	MS65
1973	6,000,000	—	0.15	0.30	0.60	1.00
1973 FM (M)	4,300	—	—	—	1.75	3.50
1973 FM (P)	97,454	PF65 2.50				
1974 FM (P)	35,600	PF65 2.50				
1974 FM (M)	5,508	—	—	—	1.00	2.00
1975 FM (U)	1,360	—	—	—	1.75	3.50
1975 FM (P)	20,458	PF65 2.50				
1975 FM (M)	1,800	—	—	—	1.25	3.00
1977 FM (P)	5,014	PF65 2.50				
1977 FM (M)	2,100	—	—	—	1.00	3.00
1977 FM (U)	468	—	—	—	4.25	10.00
1978	2,407,000	—	0.20	0.40	0.70	1.20
1978 FM (U)	2,517	—	—	—	3.25	9.00
1978 FM (P)	4,436	PF65 3.50				
1978 FM (M)	2,000	—	—	—	1.00	3.00
1979	1,200,000	—	0.20	0.40	0.70	1.20
1979 FM (P)	4,126,000	PF65 3.50				
1979 FM (U)	523	—	—	—	3.00	9.00
1979 FM (M)	1,500	—	—	—	1.00	3.00
1980	2,700,000	—	0.15	0.30	0.60	1.20
1980 FM (P)	2,111	PF65 3.50				
1980 FM (M)	1,500	—	—	0.75	3.00	8.00
1980 FM (U)	649	—	—	—	2.75	10.00
1981	4,365,000	—	0.15	0.30	0.60	1.20
1981 FM (M)	1,500	—	—	0.75	3.00	8.00
1981 FM (U)	327	—	—	—	2.75	10.00
1981 FM (P)	943	PF65 4.50				
1982 FM (P)	843	PF65 4.50				
1982 FM (U)	1,500	—	—	—	2.00	4.50
1983 FM (M)	1,500	—	—	—	2.00	4.50
1983 FM (P)	459	PF65 4.50				
1983 FM (U)	—	—	—	—	2.00	4.50
1984 FM (P)	—	PF65 5.00				
1984 FM	868	—	—	—	2.00	4.50
1985	—	—	0.15	0.30	0.60	1.60
1986	—	—	0.15	0.30	0.60	1.60
1987	3,150,000	—	—	—	1.00	2.00
1988	—	—	0.15	0.30	0.60	1.60
1989	—	—	0.15	0.30	0.60	1.60
1990	—	—	0.15	0.30	0.60	1.60
1994	—	—	0.15	0.30	0.60	1.60
1996	—	—	0.15	0.30	0.60	1.60
1997	—	PF65 4.50				
1998	—	—	0.15	0.30	0.60	1.60
2000	—	—	0.15	0.30	0.60	1.60

KM# 22 25 CENTS

5.65 g., Copper-Nickel, 23.66 mm. **Subject:** 10th Anniversary of Independence **Obv:** National arms **Rev:** Morgan Lewis Windmil, value above **Edge:** Reeded

Date	Mintage	VF20	XF40	MS60	MS63	MS65
ND-1976 FM (M)	1,800	—	—	1.00	2.00	4.00
ND-1976 FM (U)	996	—	—	1.00	2.00	6.00
ND-1976 FM (P)	11,929	PF65 2.00				

KM# 14.1 DOLLAR

6.32 g., Copper-Nickel, 28 mm. **Obv:** National arms **Rev:** Flying fish left, value below **Edge:** Plain **Shape:** 7-sided

Date	Mintage	VF20	XF40	MS60	MS63	MS65
1973	3,955,000	—	0.60	0.75	1.25	2.00
1973 FM (M)	3,000	—	—	—	2.00	6.00
1973 FM (P)	97,454	PF65 2.00				
1974 FM (M)	4,208	—	—	—	1.50	3.50
1974 FM (P)	35,600	PF65 3.00				
1975 FM (M)	500	—	—	1.25	3.50	9.00
1975 FM (U)	1,360	—	—	—	2.00	6.00
1975 FM (P)	20,458	PF65 3.00				
1977 FM (M)	600	—	—	1.75	5.00	9.00
1977 FM (U)	468	—	—	1.50	4.50	10.00
1977 FM (P)	5,014	PF65 5.00				
1978 FM (M)	—	—	—	—	—	—
Note: Requires Confirmation						
1978 FM (U)	1,017	—	—	1.25	3.50	6.00
1978 FM (P)	4,436	PF65 5.00				
1979	2,000,000	—	0.75	1.25	1.75	2.50
1979 FM (M)	600	—	—	1.50	3.00	9.00
1979 FM (U)	523	—	—	1.25	3.50	9.00
1979 FM (P)	4,126	PF65 5.00				
1980 FM (M)	600	—	—	1.50	3.50	9.00
1980 FM (U)	649	—	—	1.50	3.50	9.00
1980 FM (P)	2,111	PF65 5.00				
1981 FM (M)	600	—	—	1.25	3.00	9.00
1981 FM (U)	327	—	—	1.50	3.50	9.00
1981 FM (P)	943	PF65 6.00				
1982 FM (U)	600	—	—	1.25	3.00	9.00
1982 FM (P)	843	PF65 6.00				
1983 FM (M)	600	—	—	1.25	3.00	9.00
1983 FM (U)	—	—	—	1.25	3.00	9.00
1983 FM (P)	459	PF65 7.50				
1984 FM	469	—	—	—	3.50	9.00
1984 FM (P)	—	PF65 4.50				
1985	—	—	—	—	1.50	2.50
1986	—	—	—	—	1.50	2.50

KM# 14.2 DOLLAR

5.95 g., Copper-Nickel, 25.85 mm. **Obv:** National arms **Rev:** Flying fish left, value below **Shape:** 7-sided **Note:** Thinner planchet.

Date	Mintage	VF20	XF40	MS60	MS63	MS65
1988	3,145,000	—	—	0.75	1.50	2.50
1989	—	—	—	0.75	1.50	2.50
1994	—	—	—	0.75	1.50	2.50
1997	—	PF65 4.50				
1998	—	—	—	0.75	1.50	2.50
2000	—	—	—	0.75	1.50	2.50

KM# 23 DOLLAR

Copper-Nickel, 28 mm. **Subject:** 10th Anniversary of Independence **Obv:** National arms **Rev:** Flying fish left **Edge:** Plain **Shape:** Seven sided coin

Date	Mintage	VF20	XF40	MS60	MS63	MS65
ND-1976 (M)	500	—	—	2.00	4.00	9.00
ND-1976 (U)	996	—	—	2.00	3.50	8.00
ND-1976 (P)	11,929	PF65 4.00				

KM# 57 DOLLAR

10.00 g., 0.500 Silver 0.1608 oz. ASW **Subject:** Queen Elizabeth the Queen Mother **Obv:** National arms, date at bottom **Rev:** Bust facing

Date	Mintage	VF20	XF40	MS60	MS63	MS65
1994	Est. 50000	PF65 10.00				

KM# 65 DOLLAR

9.94 g., 0.925 Silver 0.2956 oz. ASW **Subject:** Queen Mother's 95th Birthday **Obv:** National arms **Rev:** Bust facing

Date	Mintage	VF20	XF40	MS60	MS63	MS65
1995	Est. 50000	PF65 12.00				

KM# 64 DOLLAR

10.24 g., 0.925 Silver 0.3045 oz. ASW, 30 mm. **Obv:** National arms **Rev:** Royal couple below gold inset monogrammed shield **Edge:** Reeded

Date	Mintage	VF20	XF40	MS60	MS63	MS65
1997	—	PF65 14.00				

KM# 15 2 DOLLARS

Copper-Nickel, 37 mm. **Obv:** National arms **Rev:** Staghorn coral **Edge:** Reeded

Date	Mintage	VF20	XF40	MS60	MS63	MS65
1973 FM (M)	3,000	—	—	1.25	2.50	5.00
1973 FM (P)	97,454	PF65 6.00				
1974 FM (M)	4,208	—	—	1.25	2.50	5.00
1974 FM (P)	35,600	PF65 6.00				
1975 FM (M)	500	—	—	1.25	5.00	9.00
1975 FM (U)	1,360	—	—	1.25	5.00	9.00
1975 FM (P)	20,458	PF65 5.00				
1977 FM (M)	600	—	—	1.25	5.00	9.00
1977 FM (U)	468	—	—	1.50	5.50	10.00
1977 FM (P)	5,014	PF65 5.00				
1978 FM (M)	—	—	—	—	—	—
Note: Requires Confirmation						
1978 FM (U)	1,017	—	—	1.25	5.00	9.00
1978 FM (P)	4,436	PF65 5.00				
1979 FM (M)	600	—	—	1.25	5.00	10.00
1979 FM (U)	523	—	—	1.25	5.00	10.00
1979 FM (P)	4,126	PF65 5.00				
1980 FM (M)	600	—	—	1.25	5.00	10.00
1980 FM (U)	649	—	—	1.25	5.00	10.00
1980 FM (P)	2,111	PF65 5.00				
1981 FM (M)	600	—	—	1.25	5.00	10.00
1981 FM (U)	327	—	—	1.25	5.00	10.00
1981 FM (P)	943	PF65 9.00				
1982 FM (U)	600	—	—	1.25	5.00	10.00
1982 FM (P)	843	PF65 9.00				
1983 FM (U)	—	—	—	1.25	5.00	10.00
1983 FM (P)	459	PF65 9.00				
1984 FM (U)	473	—	—	1.25	5.00	10.00
1984 FM (P)	—	PF65 9.00				

KM# 24 2 DOLLARS

Copper-Nickel, 37 mm. **Subject:** 10th Anniversary of Independence **Obv:** National arms **Rev:** Staghorn coral **Edge:** Reeded

Date	Mintage	VF20	XF40	MS60	MS63	MS65
ND-1976 FM (M)	500	—	—	3.00	7.00	10.00
ND-1976 FM (U)	996	—	—	2.00	6.00	9.00
ND-1976 FM (P)	11,929	PF65 10.00				

KM# A9 4 DOLLARS

Copper-Nickel, 38.5 mm. **Series:** F.A.O. **Obv:** National arms **Rev:** Sugarcane and banana tree branch **Edge:** Reeded

Date	Mintage	VF20	XF40	MS60	MS63	MS65
1970	30,000	—	5.00	8.00	20.00	30.00
1970	2,000	PF65 50.00				

KM# 16 5 DOLLARS

Copper-Nickel, 40 mm. **Obv:** National arms **Rev:** Shell Fountain in Bridgetown's Trafalgar Square **Edge:** Reeded

Date	Mintage	VF20	XF40	MS60	MS63	MS65
1974 FM (M)	3,958	—	—	2.50	5.00	7.50
1975 FM (M)	250	—	—	2.50	8.00	9.50
1975 FM (U)	1,360	—	—	2.50	5.00	7.50
1977 FM (U)	468	—	—	2.50	5.00	7.50
1977 FM (M)	600	—	—	2.50	5.00	7.50
1978 FM (U)	1,017	—	—	2.50	5.00	7.50
1979 FM (M)	600	—	—	2.50	5.00	7.50
1979 FM (U)	523	—	—	2.50	5.00	7.50
1980 FM (M)	600	—	—	2.50	5.00	7.50
1980 FM (U)	649	—	—	2.50	5.00	7.50
1981 FM (M)	600	—	—	2.50	5.00	7.50
1981 FM (U)	1,156	—	—	2.50	5.00	7.50
1982 FM (U)	600	—	—	2.50	5.00	7.50
1982 FM (P)	843	—	—	2.50	5.00	7.50
1983 FM (U)	261	—	—	2.50	5.00	7.50
1983 FM (M)	600	—	—	2.50	5.00	7.50
1984 FM	470	—	—	2.50	5.00	7.50

KM# 16a 5 DOLLARS

31.10 g., 0.800 Silver 0.7999 oz. ASW, 40 mm. **Obv:** National arms **Rev:** Shell Fountain in Bridgetown's Trafalgar Square **Edge:** Reeded

Date	Mintage	VF20	XF40	MS60	MS63	MS65
1973 FM (P)	97,454	PF65 18.00				
1973 FM (M)	2,750	—	—	—	22.00	28.00
1974 FM (P)	35,600	PF65 18.00				
1975 FM (P)	20,458	PF65 18.00				
1977 FM (P)	5,014	PF65 20.00				
1978 FM (P)	4,436	PF65 20.00				
1979 FM (P)	4,126	PF65 20.00				
1980 FM (P)	2,111	PF65 35.00				
1981 FM (P)	835	PF65 40.00				
1982 FM (P)	658	PF65 40.00				
1983 FM (P)	130	PF65 48.00				
1984 FM (P)	—	PF65 48.00				

KM# 25 5 DOLLARS

Copper-Nickel, 40 mm. **Subject:** 10th Anniversary of Independence **Obv:** National arms **Rev:** Shell Fountain **Edge:** Reeded

Date	Mintage	VF20	XF40	MS60	MS63	MS65
ND-1976 FM (M)	250	—	—	—	—	27.00
ND-1976 FM (U)	996	—	—	—	7.50	12.50

KM# 25a 5 DOLLARS

31.10 g., 0.800 Silver 0.7999 oz. ASW, 40 mm. **Subject:** 10th Anniversary of Independence **Obv:** National arms **Rev:** Shell Fountain **Edge:** Reeded

Date	Mintage	VF20	XF40	MS60	MS63	MS65
ND-1976 FM (P)	11,929	PF65 18.00				

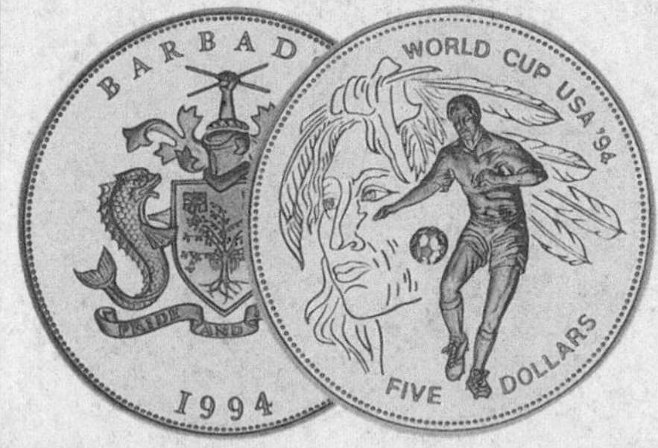

KM# 54 5 DOLLARS

28.28 g., 0.925 Silver 0.841 oz. ASW **Subject:** World Cup Soccer **Obv:** National arms **Rev:** Head of Native American with headdress left, soccer player in foreground

Date	Mintage	VF20	XF40	MS60	MS63	MS65
1994	Est. 10000	PF65 23.00				

KM# 55 5 DOLLARS

28.28 g., 0.925 Silver 0.841 oz. ASW, 38.61 mm. **Subject:** UN Global SIDS Conference **Obv:** National arms **Rev:** Stylized tropical island view

Date	Mintage	VF20	XF40	MS60	MS63	MS65
1994 (brm)	500	PF65 65.00				

KM# 58 5 DOLLARS

31.47 g., 0.925 Silver 0.9359 oz. ASW **Series:** Queen Elizabeth the Queen Mother **Subject:** Engagement **Obv:** National arms **Rev:** Bust right, spray below

Date	Mintage	VF20	XF40	MS60	MS63	MS65
1994	Est. 20000	PF65 28.50				

KM# 59 5 DOLLARS

28.28 g., 0.925 Silver 0.841 oz. ASW **Subject:** Pedro A. Campo **Obv:** National arms **Rev:** Seated figure at left facing right

Date	Mintage	VF20	XF40	MS60	MS63	MS65
1994	Est. 10000	PF65 23.00				

KM# 62 5 DOLLARS

Copper-Nickel **Subject:** 50th Anniversary - United Nations **Obv:** National arms **Rev:** Military figure raising flag, numbers at right signify years

Date	Mintage	VF20	XF40	MS60	MS63	MS65
1995	—	—	—	—	4.00	6.00

KM# 62a 5 DOLLARS

28.28 g., 0.925 Silver 0.841 oz. ASW **Subject:** 50th Anniversary - United Nations **Obv:** National arms **Rev:** Military figure raising flag, numbers at right signify years

Date	Mintage	VF20	XF40	MS60	MS63	MS65
1995	Est. 15000	PF65 23.00				

KM# 63 5 DOLLARS

28.28 g., 0.925 Silver 0.841 oz. ASW **Obv:** National arms **Rev:** First European settlers, 1625

Date	Mintage	VF20	XF40	MS60	MS63	MS65
1995	Est. 15000	PF65 22.00				

KM# 68 5 DOLLARS

28.28 g., 0.925 Silver 0.841 oz. ASW, 38.5 mm. **Subject:** Queen's 70th Birthday **Obv:** National arms **Rev:** Royal couple waving, two dates below **Edge:** Reeded

Date	Mintage	VF20	XF40	MS60	MS63	MS65
1996	—	PF65 23.00				

KM# 67 5 DOLLARS

28.28 g., 0.925 Silver 0.841 oz. ASW, 38.61 mm. **Subject:** Millennium **Obv:** National arms **Rev:** Eternal flame **Edge:** Reeded **Shape:** Octagonal

Date	Mintage	VF20	XF40	MS60	MS63	MS65
1999-2000 (brm)	Est. 50	PF65 100				

KM# 17 10 DOLLARS
Copper-Nickel, 42 mm. **Subject:** Neptune, God of the Sea **Obv:** National arms divide date **Rev:** Neptune at left looking right, whale under right hand **Edge:** Reeded

Date	Mintage	VF20	XF40	MS60	MS63	MS65
1974 FM (M)	3,958	—	—	5.00	10.00	12.00
1975 FM (M)	250	—	—	5.00	20.00	25.00
1975 FM (U)	1,360	—	—	5.00	12.50	14.00
1977 FM (M)	600	—	—	5.00	12.50	14.50
1977 FM (U)	468	—	—	5.00	12.50	14.50
1978 FM (U)	1,017	—	—	5.00	12.50	14.00
1979 FM (M)	600	—	—	5.00	12.50	14.50
1979 FM (U)	523	—	—	5.00	12.50	14.50
1980 FM (U)	649	—	—	5.00	12.50	14.50
1980 FM (M)	600	—	—	5.00	12.50	14.50
1981 FM (M)	600	—	—	5.00	12.50	14.50
1981 FM (U)	1,156	—	—	5.00	12.50	14.00

KM# 17a 10 DOLLARS
37.90 g., 0.925 Silver 1.1271 oz. ASW, 42 mm. **Subject:** Neptune, God of the Sea **Obv:** National arms **Rev:** Neptune at left looking right, whale under right hand **Edge:** Reeded

Date	Mintage	VF20	XF40	MS60	MS63	MS65
1973 FM (M)	2,750	—	—	—	—	26.00
1973 FM (P)	97,454	PF65 26.00				
1974 FM (P)	57,000	PF65 26.00				
1975 FM (P)	29,000	PF65 26.00				
1977 FM (P)	7,212	PF65 28.00				
1978 FM (P)	7,079	PF65 28.00				
1979 FM (P)	6,534	PF65 28.00				
1980 FM (P)	3,618	PF65 37.00				
1981 FM (P)	835	PF65 65.00				

KM# 26 10 DOLLARS
Copper-Nickel, 42 mm. **Subject:** 10th Anniversary of Independence **Obv:** National arms **Rev:** Neptune at left looking right, dolphin fish under right hand **Edge:** Reeded

Date	Mintage	VF20	XF40	MS60	MS63	MS65
ND-1976 FM (M)	250	—	—	—	—	35.00
ND-1976 FM (U)	996	—	—	7.50	15.00	17.50

KM# 26a 10 DOLLARS
37.90 g., 0.925 Silver 1.1271 oz. ASW, 42 mm. **Subject:** 10th Anniversary of Independence **Obv:** National arms **Rev:** Neptune at left looking right, whale under right hand **Edge:** Reeded

Date	Mintage	VF20	XF40	MS60	MS63	MS65
ND-1976 FM (P)	16,000	PF65 32.00				

KM# 34 10 DOLLARS
Copper-Nickel, 42mm mm. **Subject:** 10th Anniversary of the Central Bank of Barbados **Obv:** National arms **Rev:** Upright Blue Marlin divides date **Edge:** Reeded

Date	Mintage	VF20	XF40	MS60	MS63	MS65
1982 FM (U)	600	—	—	—	55.00	60.00

KM# 34a 10 DOLLARS
35.52 g., 0.925 Silver 1.0563 oz. ASW, 42 mm. **Obv:** National arms **Rev:** Upright dolphin-fish (mahi-mhai) divides date

Date	Mintage	VF20	XF40	MS60	MS63	MS65
1982 FM (P)	851	PF65 60.00				

KM# 36 10 DOLLARS
32.70 g., Copper-Nickel, 42 mm. **Subject:** Summer Olympics **Obv:** National arms **Rev:** Pelican with wings raised right

Date	Mintage	VF20	XF40	MS60	MS63	MS65
1983 FM (M)	600	—	—	—	120	—
1983 FM (U)	141	—	—	—	165	175

KM# 36a 10 DOLLARS
28.28 g., 0.925 Silver 0.841 oz. ASW, 42 mm. **Subject:** Pelican **Obv:** National arms **Rev:** Pelican with wings raised right

Date	Mintage	VF20	XF40	MS60	MS63	MS65
1983 FM (P)	679	PF65 115				

KM# 40 10 DOLLARS
28.28 g., 0.925 Silver 0.841 oz. ASW, 42 mm. **Subject:** Dolphins **Obv:** National arms **Rev:** Three dolphins left

Date	Mintage	VF20	XF40	MS60	MS63	MS65
1984 FM (M)	—	—	—	—	—	—
1984 FM (P)	469	PF65 200				

KM# 50 10 DOLLARS
28.28 g., 0.925 Silver 0.841 oz. ASW, 38.61 mm. **Subject:** International Cricket Belt Buckle **Obv:** National arms **Rev:** Belt buckle

Date	Mintage	VF20	XF40	MS60	MS63	MS65
1991 (brm)	100	PF65 75.00				

KM# 52 10 DOLLARS
23.33 g., 0.925 Silver 0.6938 oz. ASW **Subject:** Discovery of America **Obv:** Crowned bust right **Rev:** Columbus and Native American, ship and scroll

Date	Mintage	VF20	XF40	MS60	MS63	MS65
1991 Matte	750	PF65 65.00				
1991	Est. 25000	PF65 28.00				

KM# 53 10 DOLLARS
23.33 g., 0.925 Silver 0.6938 oz. ASW **Subject:** Discovery of America **Obv:** Crowned bust right **Rev:** Columbus and Tribal Chief with scroll

Date	Mintage	VF20	XF40	MS60	MS63	MS65
1992 Matte	500	PF65 65.00				
1992	Est. 25000	PF65 28.00				

KM# 61 10 DOLLARS
23.33 g., 0.925 Silver 0.6938 oz. ASW **Subject:** 1992 Summer Olympics **Obv:** Crowned bust right **Rev:** Sailboards

Date	Mintage	VF20	XF40	MS60	MS63	MS65
1992	10,000	PF65 17.50				

KM# 60 10 DOLLARS
7.78 g., 0.583 Gold 0.1458 oz. AGW **Subject:** Queen Mother's Engagement **Obv:** National arms **Rev:** Bust right, spray below

Date	Mintage	VF20	XF40	MS60	MS63	MS65
1995	Est. 5000	PF65 250				

KM# 66 10 DOLLARS
28.28 g., 0.925 Silver 0.841 oz. ASW **Subject:** 50th Anniversary of the University of the West Indies **Obv:** National arms **Rev:** University arms

Date	Mintage	VF20	XF40	MS60	MS63	MS65
1998 (brm)	800	PF65 55.00				

KM# 46 20 DOLLARS
23.33 g., 0.925 Silver 0.6938 oz. ASW **Subject:** Decade For Women **Obv:** National arms **Rev:** Teacher and class

Date	Mintage	VF20	XF40	MS60	MS63	MS65
1985	1,633	PF65 45.00				

KM# 49 20 DOLLARS
23.33 g., 0.925 Silver 0.6938 oz. ASW **Subject:** Summer Olympics **Obv:** National arms **Rev:** Men running hurdles

Date	Mintage	VF20	XF40	MS60	MS63	MS65
1988	15,000	—	—	14.00	15.50	18.50

KM# 27 25 DOLLARS
28.28 g., 0.925 Silver 0.841 oz. ASW **Subject:** Coronation Jubilee **Obv:** Young bust right **Rev:** Imperial Crown with supporters

Date	Mintage	VF20	XF40	MS60	MS63	MS65
1978 FM (M)	300	—	—	—	110	—
1978 FM (U)	69	—	—	—	265	275
1978 FM (P)	8,728	PF65 27.00				

KM# 30 25 DOLLARS
28.28 g., 0.500 Silver 0.4546 oz. ASW, 38.61 mm. **Subject:** 10th Anniversary of Caribbean Development Bank **Obv:** National arms **Rev:** Globe above flag

Date	Mintage	VF20	XF40	MS60	MS63	MS65
ND(1980) FM (P)	2,345	PF65 25.00				

KM# 31 25 DOLLARS
28.28 g., 0.500 Silver 0.4546 oz. ASW **Subject:** Caribbean Festival of Arts **Obv:** National arms **Rev:** Artistic design

Date	Mintage	VF20	XF40	MS60	MS63	MS65
1981 FM (P)	1,008	PF65 32.00				

KM# 37 25 DOLLARS
30.09 g., 0.500 Silver 0.4837 oz. ASW, 38.61 mm. **Subject:** 30th Anniversary Coronation of Queen Elizabeth II **Obv:** National arms **Rev:** Crossed sceptres divide royal symbols

Date	Mintage	VF20	XF40	MS60	MS63	MS65
1983 FM (P)	2,951	PF65 22.00				

KM# 43 25 DOLLARS
28.28 g., 0.925 Silver 0.841 oz. ASW **Subject:** Royal Visit **Obv:** Crowned bust right **Rev:** National arms

Date	Mintage	VF20	XF40	MS60	MS63	MS65
1985	Est. 5000	—	—	17.00	22.50	26.00

KM# 72 25 DOLLARS
23.33 g., 0.925 Silver 0.6938 oz. ASW, 38.61 mm. **Subject:** United Nations Decade for Women **Obv:** Coat of arms of Barabdos **Rev:** Woman teaching children about Barbados, legend, official symbol **Rev. Legend:** United Nations Decade for Women

Date	Mintage	VF20	XF40	MS60	MS63	MS65
1985	—	PF65 50.00				

KM# 44 25 DOLLARS
28.28 g., 0.500 Silver 0.4546 oz. ASW **Subject:** Commonwealth Games **Obv:** National arms **Rev:** Discus thrower right

Date	Mintage	VF20	XF40	MS60	MS63	MS65
1986	Est. 50000	—	—	9.00	10.00	13.00

KM# 44a 25 DOLLARS
28.28 g., 0.925 Silver 0.841 oz. ASW **Subject:** Commonwealth Games **Obv:** National arms **Rev:** Discus thrower right

Date	Mintage	VF20	XF40	MS60	MS63	MS65
1986	Est. 20000	PF65 28.00				

KM# 70 25 DOLLARS
31.39 g., 0.999 Silver 1.0082 oz. ASW, 37.85 mm. **Subject:** 25th Anniversary of the Central Bank **Obv:** National arms **Rev:** Upright Blue Marlin right divides dates **Edge:** Reeded

Date	Mintage	VF20	XF40	MS60	MS63	MS65
ND (1997) (brm)	500	PF65 65.00				

KM# 32 50 DOLLARS
27.35 g., 0.500 Silver 0.4397 oz. ASW **Subject:** World Food Day **Obv:** F.A.O. logo divided by grain sprig **Rev:** Black Belly Sheep right

Date	Mintage	VF20	XF40	MS60	MS63	MS65
1981 FM (U)	6,012	—	—	20.00	30.00	35.00

KM# 42 50 DOLLARS
16.85 g., 0.500 Silver 0.2709 oz. ASW **Series:** F.A.O. **Obv:** F.A.O. divided by grain sprig **Rev:** Fourwing flying fish **Edge:** Reeded

Date	Mintage	VF20	XF40	MS60	MS63	MS65
1984	3,600	—	—	25.00	35.00	40.00

KM# 47 50 DOLLARS
33.63 g., 0.925 Silver 1.000 oz. ASW, 38.61 mm. **Subject:** 350th Anniversary of Parliament **Obv:** National arms **Rev:** Parliament Building

Date	Mintage	VF20	XF40	MS60	MS63	MS65
ND-1989 (brm)	1,002	PF65 50.00				

KM# 51 50 DOLLARS

15.98 g., 0.917 Gold 0.4711 oz. AGW, 28.4 mm. **Subject:** International Cricket Belt Buckle **Obv:** National arms **Rev:** Belt buckle

Date	Mintage	VF20	XF40	MS60	MS63	MS65
1991 (brm)	50	**PF65** 900				

KM# 56 50 DOLLARS

15.98 g., 0.917 Gold 0.4711 oz. AGW, 38.4 mm. **Subject:** UN Global SIDS Conference **Obv:** National arms **Rev:** Small house and tree within hand design

Date	Mintage	VF20	XF40	MS60	MS63	MS65
1994 (brm)	500	**PF65** 850				

KM# 18 100 DOLLARS

6.21 g., 0.500 Gold 0.0998 oz. AGW **Subject:** 350th Anniversary - The English Ship **Obv:** National arms **Rev:** Olive Blossom with full sails

Date	Mintage	VF20	XF40	MS60	MS63	MS65
ND-1975 FM (M)	50	—	—	—	285	—
ND-1975 FM (U)	16,000	—	—	—	150	165
ND-1975 FM (P)	23,000	**PF65** 175				

KM# 28 100 DOLLARS

4.06 g., 0.900 Gold 0.1175 oz. AGW **Subject:** Human Rights **Obv:** National arms **Rev:** Praying hands beneath rolled scroll

Date	Mintage	VF20	XF40	MS60	MS63	MS65
1978	1,114	—	—	—	185	200

KM# 28a 100 DOLLARS

5.05 g., 0.900 Gold 0.1461 oz. AGW **Subject:** Human Rights **Obv:** National arms **Rev:** Praying hands beneath rolled scroll

Date	Mintage	VF20	XF40	MS60	MS63	MS65
1978	Inc. above	**PF65** 225				

KM# 38 100 DOLLARS

6.21 g., 0.500 Gold 0.0998 oz. AGW **Subject:** Neptune, God of the Sea **Obv:** National arms **Rev:** Standing figure looking right

Date	Mintage	VF20	XF40	MS60	MS63	MS65
1983 FM (U)	3	—	—	—	—	—
1983 FM (P)	484	**PF65** 220				

KM# 39 100 DOLLARS

6.21 g., 0.500 Gold 0.0998 oz. AGW **Subject:** Triton, Son of Neptune **Obv:** National arms **Rev:** Full figure left blowing horn

Date	Mintage	VF20	XF40	MS60	MS63	MS65
1984 FM (P)	1,103	**PF65** 185				

KM# 41 100 DOLLARS

6.21 g., 0.500 Gold 0.0998 oz. AGW **Subject:** Amphitrite, Wife of Neptune **Obv:** National arms **Rev:** Full figure facing looking left

Date	Mintage	VF20	XF40	MS60	MS63	MS65
1985 FM (P)	1,276	**PF65** 185				

KM# 48 100 DOLLARS

15.98 g., 0.917 Gold 0.471 oz. AGW, 28.4 mm. **Subject:** 350th Anniversary of Parliament **Obv:** Crowned bust right **Rev:** Parliament Building

Date	Mintage	VF20	XF40	MS60	MS63	MS65
ND-1989 (brm)	50	**PF65** 875				

KM# 33 150 DOLLARS

7.13 g., 0.500 Gold 0.1146 oz. AGW **Subject:** National Flower - Poinciana **Obv:** National arms **Rev:** Flower and map

Date	Mintage	VF20	XF40	MS60	MS63	MS65
1981 FM (U)	7	—	—	—	—	—
1981 FM (P)	1,140	**PF65** 185				

KM# 29 200 DOLLARS

8.12 g., 0.900 Gold 0.235 oz. AGW **Subject:** Year of the Child **Obv:** National arms **Rev:** Shaded circle above large shaded letter "Y" depicts child figure

Date	Mintage	VF20	XF40	MS60	MS63	MS65
1979	1,121	—	—	—	400	425

KM# 29a 200 DOLLARS

10.10 g., 0.900 Gold 0.2923 oz. AGW **Subject:** Year of the Child **Obv:** National arms **Rev:** Shaded circle above large shaded letter "Y" depicts child figure

Date	Mintage	VF20	XF40	MS60	MS63	MS65
1979	Inc. above	**PF65** 525				

KM# 35 250 DOLLARS

6.60 g., 0.900 Gold 0.191 oz. AGW, 24.25 mm. **Subject:** 250th Anniversary of Birth of George Washington **Obv:** National arms **Rev:** Small head left below building

Date	Mintage	VF20	XF40	MS60	MS63	MS65
1982 FM (P)	802	**PF65** 325				

KM# 45 250 DOLLARS

47.54 g., 0.917 Gold 1.4016 oz. AGW **Subject:** Commonwealth Games **Obv:** National arms **Rev:** Discus thrower right

Date	Mintage	VF20	XF40	MS60	MS63	MS65
1986	150	**PF65** 2,200				

KM# 71 500 DOLLARS

47.54 g., 0.917 Gold 1.4016 oz. AGW, 38.61 mm. **Subject:** Royal Visit **Obv:** Crowned bust right **Rev:** National arms

Date	Mintage	VF20	XF40	MS60	MS63	MS65
1985 (brm)	Est. 250	**PF65** 2,300				

MINT SETS

KM#	Date	Mintage	Identification	Issue Price	Mkt Val
MS1	1973 (8)	2,500	KM#10-15, 16a, 17a	25.00	65.00
MS2	1974 (7)	3,708	KM#10-17	25.00	50.00
MS3	1975 (8)	1,360	KM#10-17	27.50	55.00
MS4	1976 (8)	996	KM#19-26	27.50	55.00
MS5	1977 (8)	468	KM#10-17	27.50	58.00
MS6	1978 (8)	517	KM#10-17	29.00	55.00
MS7	1979 (8)	523	KM#10-17	29.00	55.00
MS8	1980 (8)	649	KM#10-17	30.00	60.00
MS9	1981 (8)	327	KM#10-17	30.00	65.00
MS10	1982 (8)	—	KM#10-16, 34	35.00	110
MS11	1983 (8)	141	KM#10-16, 36	35.50	225
MS12	1989 (5)	—	KM#10-13 & 14.2	17.00	15.00
MS13	1998 (5)	—	KM#10a, 11-13, 14.2	25.00	22.00

PROOF SETS

KM#	Date	Mintage	Identification	Issue Price	Mkt Val
PS1	1973 (8)	97,454	KM#10-15, 16a, 17a	37.50	55.00
PS2	1974 (8)	35,600	KM#10-15, 16a, 17a	50.00	60.00
PS3	1975 (8)	20,458	KM#10-15, 16a, 17a	55.00	60.00
PS4	1976 (8)	11,929	KM#19-24, 25a, 26a	55.00	50.00
PS5	1977 (8)	5,014	KM#10-15, 16a, 17a	55.00	55.00
PS6	1978 (8)	4,436	KM#10-15, 16a, 17a	58.00	60.00
PS7	1979 (8)	4,126	KM#10-15, 16a, 17a	60.00	60.00
PS8	1980 (8)	2,111	KM#10-15, 16a, 17a	117	110
PS9	1980 (2)	—	KM#16a, 17a	115	75.00
PS10	1981 (8)	943	KM#10-15, 16a, 17a	117	140
PS11	1982 (8)	843	KM#10-15, 16a, 34a	117	130
PS12	1983 (8)	459	KM#10-15, 16a, 36a	—	210
PS13	1984 (8)	—	KM#10-15, 16a, 40	132	285
PS14	1997 (6)	—	KM#10a, 11-13,14.2, 70	80.00	85.00

BELARUS

Belarus (Byelorussia, Belorussia, or White Russia-formerly the Belorussian S.S.R.) is situated along the western Dvina and Dnieper Rivers, bounded in the west by Poland, to the north by Latvia and Lithuania, to the east by Russia and the south by the Ukraine. It has an area of 80,154 sq. mi. (207,600 sq. km.) and a population of 4.8 million. Capital: Minsk. Chief products: peat, salt, and agricultural products including flax, fodder and grasses for cattle breeding and dairy products.

There never existed an independent state of Byelorussia. Until the partitions of Poland at the end of the 18th century, the history of Byelorussia is identified with that of Lithuania.

When Russia incorporated the whole of Byelorussia into its territories in 1795, it claimed to be recovering old Russian lands and denied that the Byelorussians were a separate nation. Significant efforts for independence did not occur until 1918 and were met by external antagonism from German, Polish, and Russian influences.

Soviet and anti-Communist sympathies continued to reflect the political and social unrest of the U.S.S.R. for Byelorussia. Finally, on August 25, 1991, following an unsuccessful coup, the Supreme Soviet adopted a declaration of independence, and the "Republic of Belarus" was proclaimed in September. In December, it became a founding member of the CIS.

MONETARY SYSTEM

100 Kapeek = 1 Rouble

REPUBLIC

STANDARD COINAGE

KM# 6 ROUBLE

28.28 g., Copper-Nickel, 38.61 mm. **Subject:** 50th Anniversary - United Nations **Obv:** National arms, date below **Rev:** Crane flying over map and UN logo **Edge:** Reeded

Date	Mintage	VF20	XF40	MS60	MS63	MS65
1996	40,000	—	—	—	—	20.00

KM# 6a ROUBLE

30.57 g., 0.925 Silver 0.9091 oz. ASW, 38.61 mm. **Subject:** United Nations, 50th Anniversary **Obv:** National arms **Rev:** Crane flying over map and UN logo **Edge:** Reeded

Date	Mintage	VF20	XF40	MS60	MS63	MS65
1996	20,000	PF65 200				

KM# 7 ROUBLE

13.16 g., Copper-Nickel, 32 mm. **Subject:** Olympics **Obv:** National arms and denomination **Rev:** Gymnast on the rings

Date	Mintage	VF20	XF40	MS60	MS63	MS65
1996	5,000	—	—	—	—	15.00

KM# 8 ROUBLE

13.16 g., Copper-Nickel, 32 mm. **Subject:** Olympics **Obv:** National arms **Rev:** Ribbon dancer

Date	Mintage	VF20	XF40	MS60	MS63	MS65
1996	5,000	—	—	—	—	15.00

KM# 31 ROUBLE

8.71 g., 0.9167 Gold 0.2567 oz. AGW, 22.05 mm. **Subject:** United Nations, 50th Anniversary **Obv:** National arms above date **Rev:** Crane flying over map and U.N. logo **Edge:** Reeded

Date	Mintage	VF20	XF40	MS60	MS63	MS65
1996	5,000	PF65 3,750				

KM# 9 ROUBLE

Copper-Nickel, 33 mm. **Subject:** Third Anniversary of Independence **Obv:** National arms, date below, circle surrounds **Rev:** Monument July 3

Date	Mintage	VF20	XF40	MS60	MS63	MS65
1997 Prooflike	5,000	—	—	—	—	18.00

KM# 34 ROUBLE

13.16 g., Copper-Nickel, 32 mm. **Subject:** Olympics **Obv:** National arms and denomination **Rev:** Biathalon skier with rifle

Date	Mintage	VF20	XF40	MS60	MS63	MS65
1997	5,000	—	—	—	—	15.00

KM# 36 ROUBLE

Copper-Nickel, 32 mm. **Subject:** Olympics **Obv:** National arms and denomination **Rev:** Two hockey players

Date	Mintage	VF20	XF40	MS60	MS63	MS65
1997 Prooflike	5,000	—	—	—	—	15.00

KM# 18 ROUBLE

Copper-Nickel, 32 mm. **Subject:** Architecture of Belarus **Obv:** National arms **Rev:** Castle at Mir

Date	Mintage	VF20	XF40	MS60	MS63	MS65
1998	2,000	PF65 75.00				

KM# 19 ROUBLE

Copper-Nickel, 32 mm. **Subject:** Cities of Belarus **Obv:** National arms **Rev:** Walled city of Polatsk with city arms

Date	Mintage	VF20	XF40	MS60	MS63	MS65
1998	2,000	PF65 70.00				

KM# 20 ROUBLE

Copper-Nickel, 33 mm. **Subject:** 200th Anniversary - Birth of A. Mitskevich - Poet **Obv:** National arms **Rev:** Head of Mitskevich, dates 1798-1855

Date	Mintage	VF20	XF40	MS60	MS63	MS65
1998	2,000	PF65 160				

KM# 21 ROUBLE

13.16 g., Copper-Nickel, 32 mm. **Subject:** Olympics **Obv:** National arms and denomination **Rev:** Hurdlers, Olympic crest

Date	Mintage	VF20	XF40	MS60	MS63	MS65
1998	5,000	—	—	—	—	15.00

KM# 22 ROUBLE

Copper-Nickel, 33 mm. **Subject:** Cities of Belarus **Obv:** National arms, date below, within circle **Rev:** Minsk view with city arms, within circle

Date	Mintage	VF20	XF40	MS60	MS63	MS65
1999 Prooflike	2,000	PF65 80.00				

KM# 23 ROUBLE

Copper-Nickel, 33 mm. **Subject:** 100th Anniversary - Birth of Mikhas Lynkou **Obv:** National arms **Rev:** Head of Lynkou facing right

Date	Mintage	VF20	XF40	MS60	MS63	MS65
1999 Prooflike	1,000	—	—	—	—	225

KM# 40 ROUBLE

14.50 g., Copper-Nickel, 33 mm. **Subject:** G.P. Glebov **Obv:** National arms **Rev:** Glebats portrait with two smaller portraits, dates 1899-1967 **Edge:** Reeded

Date	Mintage	VF20	XF40	MS60	MS63	MS65
1999 Prooflike	1,000	—	—	—	—	400

KM# 41 ROUBLE

Copper-Nickel, 33 mm. **Subject:** 2000 Years **Obv:** National arms **Rev:** Bethlehem view

Date	Mintage	VF20	XF40	MS60	MS63	MS65
1999 Prooflike	10,000	—	—	—	—	35.00

KM# 63 ROUBLE

14.36 g., Copper-Nickel, 33 mm. **Subject:** Jubilee 2000 **Obv:** National arms **Rev:** Logo and three churches of Pinsk, Grodna and Minsk **Edge:** Reeded

Date	Mintage	VF20	XF40	MS60	MS63	MS65
1999 Prooflike	10,000	—	—	—	—	35.00

KM# 65 ROUBLE
Copper-Nickel, 32 mm. **Subject:** Borisoglebsk Church **Obv:** National arms **Rev:** Borisoglebsk Church, seal

Date	Mintage	VF20	XF40	MS60	MS63	MS65
1999 Prooflike	2,000	—	—	—	—	60.00

KM# 48 ROUBLE
13.20 g., Copper-Nickel, 31.9 mm. **Subject:** Architecture **Obv:** National arms **Rev:** St. Boris and St. Gleb Church **Edge:** Reeded

Date	Mintage	VF20	XF40	MS60	MS63	MS65
2000 Prooflike	2,000	—	—	—	—	50.00

KM# 108 ROUBLE
Copper-Nickel, 33 mm. **Subject:** City Of Vitebsk **Obv:** National arms **Rev:** City coat of arms, Blagoveschenskaya Church, City Hall

Date	Mintage	VF20	XF40	MS60	MS63	MS65
2000 Prooflike	2,000	—	—	—	—	50.00

KM# 24 10 ROUBLES
16.96 g., 0.925 Silver 0.5044 oz. ASW, 33 mm. **Subject:** 200th Anniversary - Birth of A. Mitskevich **Obv:** National arms **Rev:** Portrait Mitskevich facing left, dates 1798-1855

Date	Mintage	VF20	XF40	MS60	MS63	MS65
1998	2,000	PF65 200				

KM# 25 10 ROUBLES
16.96 g., 0.925 Silver 0.5044 oz. ASW, 33 mm. **Subject:** G.P. Glebov - Theatre Artist **Obv:** National arms **Rev:** Glebats portrait with two smaller portraits, dates 1899-1967

Date	Mintage	VF20	XF40	MS60	MS63	MS65
1999	1,200	PF65 125				

KM# 26 10 ROUBLES
16.96 g., 0.925 Silver 0.5044 oz. ASW, 33 mm. **Subject:** 100th Anniversary - Birth of Mikhas Lynkou **Obv:** National arms **Rev:** Head of Lynkou facing right, dates 1899-1975

Date	Mintage	VF20	XF40	MS60	MS63	MS65
1999	1,200	PF65 125				

KM# 13 20 ROUBLES
33.84 g., 0.925 Silver 1.0064 oz. ASW, 39 mm. **Subject:** Olympics **Obv:** National arms and denomination **Rev:** Olympic crest, gymnast on rings

Date	Mintage	VF20	XF40	MS60	MS63	MS65
1996	1,000	PF65 225				

KM# 14 20 ROUBLES
33.84 g., 0.925 Silver 1.0064 oz. ASW, 39 mm. **Subject:** Olympics **Obv:** National arms and denomination **Rev:** Ribbon dancer

Date	Mintage	VF20	XF40	MS60	MS63	MS65
1996	1,000	PF65 225				

KM# 10 20 ROUBLES
34.56 g., 0.900 Silver 1.000 oz. ASW, 39 mm. **Subject:** Monument of Independence **Obv:** National arms and denomination **Rev:** Date July 3

Date	Mintage	VF20	XF40	MS60	MS63	MS65
1997	3,000	PF65 70.00				

KM# 11 20 ROUBLES
34.74 g., 0.900 Silver 1.0052 oz. ASW, 39 mm. **Subject:** Russia-Belarus State Treaty **Obv:** National arms **Rev:** 2 city views with respective national emblems and the date April 2 1996 at bottom

Date	Mintage	VF20	XF40	MS60	MS63	MS65
1997	5,000	PF65 70.00				

KM# 12 20 ROUBLES
31.48 g., 0.999 Silver 1.0111 oz. ASW, 39 mm. **Subject:** 75th Anniversary - Banking System **Obv:** National arms **Rev:** Bank building

Date	Mintage	VF20	XF40	MS60	MS63	MS65
1997	2,000	PF65 200				

KM# 15 20 ROUBLES
31.03 g., 0.925 Silver 0.9228 oz. ASW, 39 mm. **Subject:** Olympics **Obv:** National arms and denomination **Rev:** Biathlon skier

Date	Mintage	VF20	XF40	MS60	MS63	MS65
1997	Est. 1000	PF65 250				

KM# 16 20 ROUBLES
31.15 g., 0.925 Silver 0.9264 oz. ASW, 39 mm. **Subject:** Olympics **Obv:** National arms **Rev:** Two hockey players

Date	Mintage	VF20	XF40	MS60	MS63	MS65
1997	Est. 1000	PF65 250				

KM# 27 20 ROUBLES
33.52 g., 0.925 Silver 0.9969 oz. ASW, 38.61 mm. **Subject:** Architecture of Belarus **Obv:** National arms, date below, within circle **Rev:** Castle and Mir and seal

Date	Mintage	VF20	XF40	MS60	MS63	MS65
1998	2,000	PF65 185				

KM# 28 20 ROUBLES
33:52 g., 0.925 Silver 0.9969 oz. ASW **Subject:** Cities of Belarus **Obv:** National arms **Rev:** Polatsk with city arms above

Date	Mintage	VF20	XF40	MS60	MS63	MS65
1998	2,000	PF65 165				

KM# 29 20 ROUBLES
33.52 g., 0.925 Silver 0.9969 oz. ASW **Subject:** Olympics **Obv:** National arms and denomination **Rev:** Hurdlers, Olympic crest

Date	Mintage	VF20	XF40	MS60	MS63	MS65
1998	1,000	PF65 200				

KM# 17 20 ROUBLES
33.90 g., 0.925 Silver 1.0082 oz. ASW, 39 mm. **Subject:** 80th Anniversary - Financial System **Obv:** National arms, date below, within circle **Rev:** Anniversary logo

Date	Mintage	VF20	XF40	MS60	MS63	MS65
1999	1,000	PF65 450				

KM# 30 20 ROUBLES
33.52 g., 0.925 Silver 0.9969 oz. ASW, 39 mm. **Subject:** Cities of Belarus **Obv:** National arms, date below, within circle **Rev:** Minsk view with city arms

Date	Mintage	VF20	XF40	MS60	MS63	MS65
1999	2,000	PF65 200				

KM# 42 20 ROUBLES
33.86 g., 0.925 Silver 1.007 oz. ASW **Subject:** 2000 Years of Christianity **Obv:** National arms, date below, within circle **Rev:** Bethlehem view **Edge:** Reeded

Date	Mintage	VF20	XF40	MS60	MS63	MS65
1999	5,000	PF65 145				

KM# 43 20 ROUBLES
33.86 g., 0.925 Silver 1.007 oz. ASW **Subject:** Jubilee 2000 **Obv:** National arms **Rev:** Three churches of Pinsk, Grodno and Minsk

Date	Mintage	VF20	XF40	MS60	MS63	MS65
1999	5,000	PF65 145				

KM# 66 20 ROUBLES
33.85 g., 0.925 Silver 1.0067 oz. ASW, 38.5 mm. **Obv:** National arms **Rev:** Borisoglebsk church in Grodno **Edge:** Reeded

Date	Mintage	VF20	XF40	MS60	MS63	MS65
1999	2,000	PF65 120				

KM# 52 20 ROUBLES
31.45 g., 0.925 Silver 0.9353 oz. ASW, 38.6 mm. **Subject:** 2002 Winter Olympics **Obv:** National arms, date below, within circle **Rev:** Discus thrower **Edge:** Reeded

Date	Mintage	VF20	XF40	MS60	MS63	MS65
2000	20,000	PF65 175				

KM# 68 20 ROUBLES
33.85 g., 0.925 Silver 1.0067 oz. ASW, 38.5 mm. **Obv:** National arms **Rev:** Synkovichi church **Edge:** Reeded

Date	Mintage	VF20	XF40	MS60	MS63	MS65
2000	2,000	PF65 120				

KM# 109 20 ROUBLES
31.10 g., 0.925 Silver 0.9249 oz. ASW, 39 mm. **Subject:** City of Vitedsk **Obv:** National arms **Rev:** City coat of arms, Blagoveschenskaya Church, City Hall

Date	Mintage	VF20	XF40	MS60	MS63	MS65
2000	2,000	PF65 110				

KM# 32 50 ROUBLES
7.78 g., 0.999 Gold 0.2499 oz. AGW, 22 mm. **Subject:** Olympics **Obv:** National arms and denomination **Rev:** Ribbon dancer

Date	Mintage	VF20	XF40	MS60	MS63	MS65
1996	500	PF65 1,350				

KM# 33 50 ROUBLES
7.78 g., 0.999 Gold 0.2499 oz. AGW, 22 mm. **Obv:** National arms and denomination **Rev:** Gymnast on rings

Date	Mintage	VF20	XF40	MS60	MS63	MS65
1996	500	PF65 1,350				

KM# 35 50 ROUBLES
7.78 g., 0.999 Gold 0.2499 oz. AGW, 22 mm. **Obv:** National arms and denomination **Rev:** Biathalow skier with rifle

Date	Mintage	VF20	XF40	MS60	MS63	MS65
1997	500	PF65 1,350				

KM# 37 50 ROUBLES
7.78 g., 0.999 Gold 0.2499 oz. AGW, 22 mm. **Obv:** National arms and denomination **Rev:** Two hockey players

Date	Mintage	VF20	XF40	MS60	MS63	MS65
1997	500	PF65 1,350				

KM# 38 50 ROUBLES
7.78 g., 0.999 Gold 0.2499 oz. AGW **Obv:** National arms and denomination **Rev:** Two hurdlers

Date	Mintage	VF20	XF40	MS60	MS63	MS65
1997	500	PF65 1,200				

BELGIAN CONGO

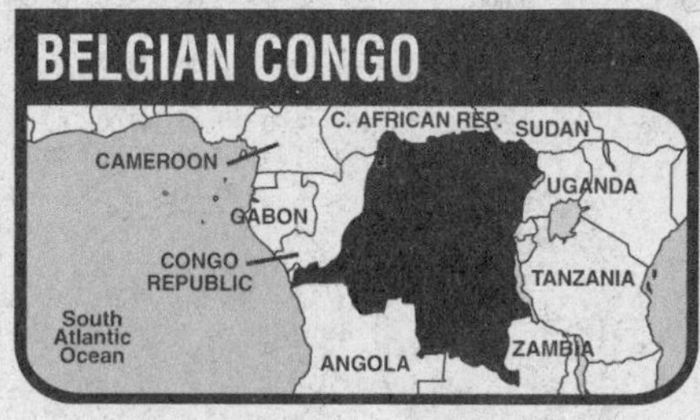

The Belgian Congo and Ruanda-Urundi were united administratively from 1925 to 1960. Ruanda-Urundi was made a U.N. Trust territory in 1946. Coins for these 2 areas were made jointly between 1952 and 1960. Ruanda-Urundi became the Republic of Rwanda on June 1, 1962.

MONETARY SYSTEM
100 Centimes = 1 Franc

RULER
Belgium

MINT MARK
(H) – Heaton, Birmingham – smaller, thicker “C” in denomination

COLONY

DECIMAL COINAGE

KM# 15 CENTIME
Copper **Obv:** Hole at center of crowned “A”s, circle surrounds **Rev:** Center hole within star, date below star, value above

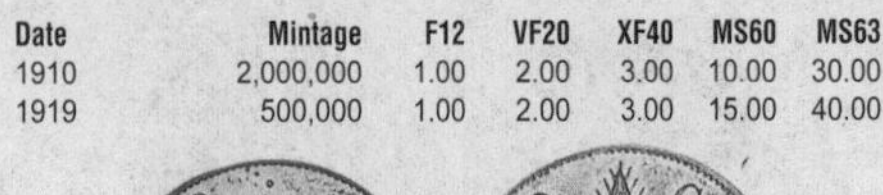

Date	Mintage	F12	VF20	XF40	MS60	MS63
1910	2,000,000	1.00	2.00	3.00	10.00	30.00
1919	500,000	1.00	2.00	3.00	15.00	40.00

KM# 16 2 CENTIMES

Copper **Obv:** Hole at center of crowned "A"s, circle surrounds **Rev:** Hole at center of star, date below star, value above

Date	Mintage	F12	VF20	XF40	MS60	MS63
1910	1,500,000	1.00	3.00	7.00	30.00	60.00
1919	500,000	1.50	3.50	10.00	35.00	75.00

KM# 12 5 CENTIMES

Copper-Nickel **Obv:** Hole at center of crowned "JL" circle surrounds **Rev:** Hole at center of star, date below star, value above

Date	Mintage	F12	VF20	XF40	MS60	MS63
1909	1,800,000	5.00	12.50	40.00	130	250

KM# 17 5 CENTIMES

2.50 g., Copper-Nickel, 19 mm. **Obv:** Hole at center of crowned "A"s, within circle **Rev:** Hole at center of star, date below star, value above **Note:** Coins struck at Heaton mint (H) have smaller dates than those produced elsewhere.

Date	Mintage	F12	VF20	XF40	MS60	MS63
1910	6,000,000	0.75	1.50	3.50	16.00	60.00
1911	5,000,000	0.75	1.50	3.50	16.00	50.00
1917	1,000,000	3.00	7.00	18.00	100	200
1917 (H)	—	PF60 1,000				
1919 (H)	3,000,000	1.50	3.00	7.00	35.00	70.00
1919	6,850,000	0.50	1.00	2.50	30.00	60.00
1920	2,740,000	0.50	1.00	3.50	30.00	60.00
1920/10	—	—	—	—	—	—
1921	17,260,000	0.25	0.75	1.50	15.00	35.00
1921 (H)	3,000,000	1.00	2.00	6.00	30.00	60.00
1925	11,000,000	0.25	0.75	2.00	30.00	60.00
1926/5	5,770,000	2.25	4.50	—	110	250
1926	Inc. above	0.25	1.00	2.00	20.00	40.00
1927	2,000,000	0.50	1.00	2.50	20.00	40.00
1928/6	1,500,000	2.00	4.00	8.00	40.00	80.00
1928	Inc. above	0.75	1.25	3.00	20.00	40.00

KM# 13 10 CENTIMES

Copper-Nickel **Obv:** Hole at center of crowned "L"s, backs touching, within circle **Rev:** Hole at center of star, date below star, value above

Date	Mintage	F12	VF20	XF40	MS60	MS63
1909	1,500,000	8.00	20.00	70.00	200	300

KM# 18 10 CENTIMES

Copper-Nickel **Obv:** Hole at center of crowned "A"s, within circle **Rev:** Hole at center of star, date below star, value above **Note:** Coins struck at Heaton mint (H) have smaller dates than those produced elsewhere.

Date	Mintage	F12	VF20	XF40	MS60	MS63
1910	5,000,000	0.50	1.00	3.00	15.00	50.00
1911	5,000,000	0.50	1.00	3.00	15.00	50.00
1917 (H)	500,000	5.00	10.00	25.00	75.00	220
1919	3,430,000	0.50	1.00	3.50	16.50	40.00
1919 (H)	1,500,000	0.75	1.25	4.00	22.00	45.00
1920	1,510,000	0.75	1.25	4.00	20.00	40.00
1921	13,540,000	0.25	0.75	2.00	10.00	35.00
1921 (H)	3,000,000	0.75	1.50	3.50	16.50	25.00
1922	14,950,000	0.25	1.00	2.50	10.00	25.00
1924	3,600,000	0.50	1.50	3.00	15.00	20.00
1925/4	4,800,000	2.00	4.00	8.00	50.00	100
1925	Inc. above	0.25	1.00	3.00	15.00	30.00
1927	2,020,000	0.25	1.00	3.00	12.00	25.00
1928/7	5,600,000	1.00	4.00	10.00	60.00	125
1928	Inc. above	0.25	1.00	3.00	12.00	25.00
1928/3	—	—	—	—	—	—
1928/5	—	—	—	—	60.00	125

KM# 14 20 CENTIMES

Copper-Nickel **Obv:** Hole at center of crowned "L"s, backs touching, within circle **Rev:** Hole at center of star, date below star, value above

Date	Mintage	F12	VF20	XF40	MS60	MS63
1909	300,000	10.00	25.00	65.00	195	300

KM# 19 20 CENTIMES

5.92 g., Copper-Nickel, 25.1 mm. **Obv:** Hole at center of crowned "A"s, within circle **Rev:** Hole at center of star, date below star, value above

Date	Mintage	F12	VF20	XF40	MS60	MS63
1910	1,000,000	2.00	5.00	12.00	40.00	120
1911	1,250,000	1.50	4.00	10.00	35.00	120

KM# 22 50 CENTIMES

6.46 g., Copper-Nickel, 24 mm. **Obv:** Laureate head left, French legend **Rev:** Oil palm divides denomination and date **Rev. Legend:** CONGO BELGE **Edge:** Reeded

Date	Mintage	F12	VF20	XF40	MS60	MS63
1921	4,000,000	0.60	2.00	8.00	40.00	80.00
1922	6,000,000	0.60	2.00	8.00	40.00	80.00
1923	7,200,000	0.60	2.00	8.00	40.00	80.00
1924	1,096,000	0.75	3.00	10.00	60.00	120
1925	16,104,000	0.60	2.00	7.00	40.00	80.00
1926/5	16,000,000	1.00	4.00	12.00	60.00	120
1926	Inc. above	0.60	2.00	8.00	40.00	80.00
1927	10,000,000	0.60	2.00	8.00	40.00	80.00
1929/7	7,504,000	0.60	2.00	9.00	60.00	120
1929/8	Inc. above	1.00	4.00	15.00	125	250
1929	Inc. above	0.60	2.00	7.00	40.00	80.00
1929/9	—	—	—	—	—	—

KM# 23 50 CENTIMES

6.50 g., Copper-Nickel, 24 mm. **Obv:** Laureate head left **Rev:** Oil palm divides denomination and date, Flemish legend **Rev. Legend:** BELGISCH CONGO

Date	Mintage	F12	VF20	XF40	MS60	MS63
1921	4,000,000	0.60	2.00	8.00	40.00	80.00
1922	5,592,000	0.60	2.00	7.00	40.00	80.00
1923/1	Inc. below	—	—	—	—	—
1923/2	Inc. below	25.00	45.00	80.00	175	350
1923	7,208,000	0.60	2.00	7.00	40.00	80.00
1924	7,000,000	0.60	2.00	8.00	40.00	80.00
1925/4	10,600,000	1.50	7.00	20.00	100	200
1925	Inc. above	0.60	2.00	7.00	40.00	80.00
1926	25,200,000	0.60	2.00	7.00	35.00	75.00
1927	4,800,000	0.60	2.00	8.00	40.00	80.00
1928	7,484,000	0.60	2.00	7.00	40.00	80.00
1929/8	116,000	25.00	50.00	75.00	130	260
1929	Inc. above	20.00	40.00	70.00	120	250

KM# 20 FRANC

10.00 g., Copper-Nickel, 28.8 mm. **Obv:** Laureate head left **Rev:** Oil palm divides denomination and date, French legend **Rev. Legend:** CONGO BELGE

Date	Mintage	F12	VF20	XF40	MS60	MS63
1920	4,000,000	0.85	2.75	10.00	50.00	100
1922	5,000,000	0.85	2.75	9.00	50.00	150
1923/2	5,000,000	2.00	7.00	16.00	60.00	120
1923	Inc. above	0.85	2.75	9.00	50.00	100
1924	6,030,000	0.85	2.75	9.00	45.00	90.00
1925	10,470,000	0.85	2.75	9.00	40.00	80.00
1926/5	12,500,000	2.00	7.00	16.50	50.00	100
1926	Inc. above	0.85	2.75	8.00	40.00	80.00
1927	15,250,000	0.85	2.75	8.00	40.00	80.00
1929	5,763,000	0.85	2.75	9.00	40.00	80.00
1930/29	Inc. below	15.00	30.00	60.00	125	300
1930	5,000,000	0.85	2.75	10.00	42.00	85.00

KM# 21 FRANC

10.00 g., Copper-Nickel, 28.9 mm. **Obv:** Laureate head left **Rev:** Oil palm divides denomination and date, Flemish legend **Rev. Legend:** BELGISCH CONGO

Date	Mintage	F12	VF20	XF40	MS60	MS63
1920	475,000	2.00	5.00	16.50	60.00	120
1921	3,525,000	0.85	3.00	9.00	50.00	100
1922	5,000,000	0.85	3.00	9.00	45.00	90.00
1923/2	7,362,000	2.00	5.00	17.00	55.00	110
1923	Inc. above	0.85	2.75	9.00	40.00	80.00
1924	4,608,000	0.85	3.00	10.00	45.00	90.00
1925	9,530,000	0.85	2.75	9.00	40.00	80.00
1925/3	—	—	—	—	—	—
1926/5	17,000,000	2.00	5.00	17.00	60.00	120
1926	Inc. above	0.85	2.75	9.00	40.00	80.00
1928	9,250,000	0.85	2.75	9.00	40.00	80.00
1929	4,250,000	0.85	3.00	10.00	45.00	92.00

KM# 31 FRANC

10.00 g., Nickel-Bronze **Obv:** KM 24 1936 **Rev:** KM 21 1922 **Note:** Mule. Probable pattern.

Date	Mintage	F12	VF20	XF40	MS60	MS63
1936	—	—	—	—	5,000	—

KM# 26 FRANC

2.48 g., Brass, 19.20 mm. **Obv:** Denomination, legend at top and bottom **Rev:** African elephant, date below

Date	Mintage	F12	VF20	XF40	MS60	MS63
1944	25,000,000	0.50	1.00	3.00	20.00	40.00
1946	15,000,000	0.75	1.50	3.50	25.00	45.00
1949	15,000,000	0.75	1.50	3.00	25.00	45.00

KM# 25 2 FRANCS
5.90 g., Brass, 25 mm. **Obv:** Denomination, stars flanking **Rev:** African elephant left, date below **Shape:** 6-sided

Date	Mintage	F12	VF20	XF40	MS60	MS63
1943	25,000,000	2.50	6.00	15.00	70.00	200

KM# 28 2 FRANCS
Brass **Obv:** Denomination, stars flanking, legend at top and bottom **Rev:** African elephant left, date below

Date	Mintage	F12	VF20	XF40	MS60	MS63
1946	13,000,000	1.00	2.00	4.00	25.00	60.00
1947	12,000,000	1.00	2.00	4.00	25.00	60.00

KM# 24 5 FRANCS
Nickel-Bronze **Obv:** Head of Leopold III, left **Rev:** Lion above denomination, star at left of denomination, legend surrounds

Date	Mintage	F12	VF20	XF40	MS60	MS63
1936	2,600,000	5.00	10.00	30.00	225	500
1937	11,400,000	4.00	12.00	35.00	250	525
1937 Specimen	—	PF60 2,500				

KM# 29 5 FRANCS
Brass **Obv:** Denomination at center, stars flanking, legend at top and bottom **Rev:** Africian elephant left, date below

Date	Mintage	F12	VF20	XF40	MS60	MS63
1947	10,000,000	3.00	7.00	15.00	50.00	90.00

KM# 27 50 FRANCS
17.50 g., 0.500 Silver 0.2813 oz. ASW, 35 mm. **Obv:** Denomination at center, stars flanking, legend at top and bottom **Rev:** African elephant left, date below

Date	Mintage	F12	VF20	XF40	MS60	MS63
1944	1,000,000	20.00	50.00	100	225	450

PATTERNS

Including off metal strikes

KM#	Date	Mintage	Identification	Mkt Val
Pn1	1930	—	Franc. Aluminum-Bronze. KM#20.	650
Pn2	1944	—	Franc. Brass. KM#26.	400
Pn3	1944	—	Franc. Steel. KM#26.	400
Pn4	1944	—	Franc. Copper.	400

TRIAL STRIKES

KM#	Date	Mintage	Identification	Mkt Val
TS30	1949	—	Franc. Copper. KM#26; Uniface.	600

RUANDA-URUNDI

U.N. TRUST TERRITORY

DECIMAL COINAGE

KM# 2 50 CENTIMES
0.67 g., Aluminum **Obv:** Crowned arms divide date **Rev:** Oil palm divides denomination

Date	Mintage	VF20	XF40	MS60	MS63	MS65
1954 DB	4,700,000	0.25	0.50	1.00	2.00	10.00
1955 DB	20,300,000	0.15	0.35	0.75	1.50	9.00

KM# 4 FRANC
1.40 g., Aluminum **Obv:** Crowned arms divide date **Rev:** Oil palm divides denomination

Date	Mintage	VF20	XF40	MS60	MS63	MS65
1957	10,000,000	0.45	0.75	1.50	3.00	10.00
1958	20,000,000	0.45	0.75	1.50	3.00	10.00
1959	20,000,000	0.45	0.75	1.50	3.00	10.00
1960	20,000,000	0.45	0.75	1.50	3.00	10.00

KM# 1 5 FRANCS
7.30 g., Brass

Date	Mintage	VF20	XF40	MS60	MS63	MS65
1952	10,000,000	0.75	1.25	5.00	10.00	30.00

KM# 3 5 FRANCS
2.20 g., Aluminum, 28 mm. **Obv:** Crowned arms divide date **Rev:** Oil palm divides denomination **Edge:** Reeded

Date	Mintage	VF20	XF40	MS60	MS63	MS65
1956 DB	10,000,000	—	1.00	2.00	4.00	20.00
1956 DB	—	PF60 50.00	PF63 85.00	PF65 125		
1958 DB	26,110,000	—	0.75	1.75	3.50	15.00
1959 DB	3,890,000	—	1.00	2.50	5.00	20.00

ESSAIS

KM#	Date	Mintage	Identification	Mkt Val
E1	1952	—	5 Francs. Value at center of star. Tree divides denomination and date.	75.00
E1a	1952	—	5 Francs. Silver.	300
E2	1954	—	50 Centimes.	200
E3	1954	—	50 Centimes. Silver.	220
E4	1956 DB	—	5 Francs. Crowned arms divide date. Tree divides denomination.	200
E5	1957	—	Franc. Crowned arms divides date. Tree divides denomination.	200
E6	1960	—	Franc. Bronze.	175

BELGIUM

The Kingdom of Belgium, a constitutional monarchy in northwest Europe, has an area of 11,780 sq. mi. (30,519 sq. km.) and a population of 10.1 million, chiefly Dutch-speaking Flemish and French-speaking Walloons. Capital: Brussels. Agriculture, dairy farming, and the processing of raw materials for re-export are the principal industries. Beurs voor Diamant in Antwerp is the world's largest diamond trading center. Iron and steel, machinery motor vehicles, chemicals, textile yarns and fabrics comprise the principal exports.

At the Congress of Vienna in 1815 the area was reunited with the Netherlands, but in 1830 independence was gained and the constitutional monarchy of Belgium was established. A large part of the Duchy of Luxembourg was incorporated into Belgium and the first king was Leopold I of Saxe-Coburg-Gotha. It was invaded by the German Army in August, 1914 and the German forces carried on a devastating occupation of most of the territory until the Armistice. Belgium joined the League of Nations. On May 10, 1940 it was invaded again by the German army. The Belgian and Allied forces were quickly overwhelmed and were evacuated through Dunkirk. Allied troops reached Belgium again in Sept. 1944. Prince Charles, Count of Flanders, assumed King Leopold's responsibilities until liberation by the U.S. Army in Austria on May 8, 1945. As of January 1, 1989, Belgium became a federal kingdom.

RULERS
Leopold II, 1865-1909
Albert I, 1909-1934
Leopold III, 1934-1950
Baudouin I, 1951-1993
Albert II, 1993-

MINT MARK
Angel head - Brussels

MINTMASTERS' INITIALS & PRIVY MARKS
(b) - bird - Vogelier
Lamb head – Lambret
NOTE: Beginning in 1987, the letters "qp" appear on the coins - (quality proof)

MONETARY SYSTEM
100 Centimes = 1 Franc
1 Euro = 100 Cents

LEGENDS
Belgian coins are usually inscribed either in Dutch, French or both. However some modern coins are being inscribed in Latin or German. The language used is best told by noting the spelling of the name of the country.
(Fr) French: BELGIQUE or BELGES
(Du) Dutch: BELGIE or BELGEN
(La) Latin: BELGICA
(Ge) German: BELGIEN
Many Belgian coins are collected by what is known as Position A and Position B edges. Some dates command a premium depending on the position which are as follows:
Position A: Coins with portrait side down having upright edge lettering.
Position B: Coins with portrait side up having upright edge lettering.

KINGDOM

DECIMAL COINAGE

KM# 33.1 CENTIME
2.00 g., Copper, 16.7 mm. **Ruler:** Leopold II **Obv:** Crowned monogram, legend in French **Obv. Legend:** DES BELGES **Rev:** Seated lion with tablet **Rev. Legend:** L'UNION FAIT LA FORCE **Edge:** Reeded

Date	Mintage	F12	VF20	XF40	MS60	MS63
1901/801 Near 1	3,743,000	0.50	2.50	5.00	18.00	40.00
1901/801 Far 1	Inc. above	0.50	2.50	5.00	18.00	40.00
1901	Inc. above	0.25	0.50	1.50	5.00	7.50
1902/802 Near 2	2,847,000	1.00	2.00	4.00	10.00	15.00
1902/802 Far 2	Inc. above	1.00	2.00	4.00	10.00	15.00
1902/801	Inc. above	1.00	2.00	4.00	10.00	15.00
1902/1	Inc. above	1.00	2.00	4.00	10.00	15.00
1902	Inc. above	0.20	0.50	1.50	5.00	7.50
1907	3,967,000	0.20	0.50	1.50	4.00	6.00

KM# 33.2 CENTIME

2.01 g., Copper **Ruler:** Leopold II **Obv:** Crowned monogram, legend in French **Obv. Legend:** DES BELGES **Rev:** Seated lion with tablet **Rev. Legend:** L'UNION FAIT LA FORCE **Note:** Thin flan.

Date	Mintage	F12	VF20	XF40	MS60	MS63
1901	Inc. above	1.00	1.50	3.50	7.50	12.50
1902	Inc. above	1.00	1.50	5.00	9.00	15.00

KM# 34.1 CENTIME

2.00 g., Copper, 16.5 mm. **Ruler:** Leopold II **Obv:** Crowned monogram, legend in Dutch **Obv. Legend:** DER BELGEN **Rev:** Seated lion with tablet **Rev. Legend:** EENDRACHT MAAKT MACHT

Date	Mintage	F12	VF20	XF40	MS60	MS63
1901/899	Inc. above	0.75	2.25	4.50	18.00	40.00
1901	Inc. above	0.25	0.50	1.50	5.00	7.50
1902/1	2,482,000	1.25	3.50	9.00	10.00	15.00
1902	Inc. above	0.25	0.50	1.50	5.00	7.50
1907	3,966,000	0.25	0.50	1.50	4.00	6.00

KM# 34.2 CENTIME

2.00 g., Copper, 16.5 mm. **Ruler:** Leopold II **Obv:** Crowned monogram legend in Dutch **Obv. Legend:** DER BELGEN **Rev:** Seated lion with tablet **Rev. Legend:** EENDRACHT MAAKT MACHT **Note:** Thin flan.

Date	Mintage	F12	VF20	XF40	MS60	MS63
1901	Inc. above	1.00	1.50	8.00	18.00	30.00
1902	Inc. above	1.00	1.50	8.00	18.00	30.00

KM# 33.3 CENTIME

2.00 g., Copper, 16.5 mm. **Ruler:** Leopold II **Obv:** Crowned monogram, legend in French **Obv. Legend:** DES BELGES **Rev:** Seated lion with tablet, additional stop in signature.. BRAEMT.F. **Rev. Legend:** L'UNION FAIT LA FORCE

Date	Mintage	F12	VF20	XF40	MS60	MS63
1902	Inc. above	1.00	2.00	10.00	20.00	40.00

KM# 76 CENTIME

2.00 g., Copper, 16.5 mm. **Obv:** Crowned letter "A", date below, legend in French **Obv. Legend:** DES BELGES **Rev:** Tablet at left of seated lion looking right, denomination below **Edge:** Reeded

Date	Mintage	F12	VF20	XF40	MS60	MS63
1912	2,540,000	0.20	0.50	2.50	5.00	7.50
1914	870,000	0.25	0.75	3.50	7.50	12.00

KM# 77 CENTIME

2.00 g., Copper, 16.5 mm. **Obv:** Crowned letter "A", date below, legend in Dutch **Obv. Legend:** DER BELGEN **Rev:** Tablet to left of seated lion looking right, denomination below **Edge:** Reeded

Date	Mintage	F12	VF20	XF40	MS60	MS63
1912	2,542,000	0.20	0.50	1.50	4.00	6.00

KM# 35.1 2 CENTIMES

4.00 g., Copper, 21.5 mm. **Ruler:** Leopold II **Obv:** Legend in French **Obv. Legend:** DES BELGES

Date	Mintage	F12	VF20	XF40	MS60	MS63
1902	2,490,000	0.15	0.50	2.00	5.00	15.00
1905	4,981,000	0.15	0.50	2.00	4.00	12.00
1909	Inc. above	0.15	0.50	2.00	4.00	12.00
1909/5	4,983,000	0.75	6.00	15.00	30.00	60.00
1909/1809	Inc. above	1.00	10.00	30.00	60.00	120

KM# 35.2 2 CENTIMES

Copper **Note:** Thin flan.

Date	Mintage	F12	VF20	XF40	MS60	MS63
1902	Inc. above	3.00	5.00	35.00	75.00	125

KM# 36 2 CENTIMES

4.00 g., Copper, 21.5 mm. **Obv:** Crowned design, date below, legend in Dutch **Obv. Legend:** DER BELGEN **Rev:** Tablet to left of seated lion looking right, denomination below

Date	Mintage	F12	VF20	XF40	MS60	MS63
1902	2,488,000	0.15	1.50	4.00	8.00	15.00
1905/2	4,986,000	1.50	3.00	20.00	45.00	60.00
1905	Inc. above	0.15	1.00	4.00	8.00	15.00
1909	565,000	0.50	2.00	20.00	45.00	60.00

KM# 65 2 CENTIMES

4.00 g., Copper, 21.5 mm. **Ruler:** Albert I **Obv:** Crowned letter "A", date below, legend in Dutch **Obv. Legend:** DER BELGEN **Rev:** Tablet to left of seated lion looking right, denomination below **Edge:** Reeded

Date	Mintage	F12	VF20	XF40	MS60	MS63
1910	1,248,000	0.25	0.50	3.00	10.00	15.00
1911 Large date	6,441,000	0.15	0.35	1.50	5.00	7.50
1911 Small date	Inc. above	0.15	0.35	1.50	5.00	7.50
1912	1,602,000	0.35	1.00	3.00	10.00	15.00
1919	4,998,000	0.15	0.35	0.75	3.00	5.00

KM# 64 2 CENTIMES

4.00 g., Copper, 21.5 mm. **Ruler:** Albert I **Obv:** Crowned letter "A", date below, legend in French **Obv. Legend:** DES BELGES **Rev:** Tablet to left of seated lion looking right, denomination below **Edge:** Reeded

Date	Mintage	F12	VF20	XF40	MS60	MS63
1911	645,000	1.50	3.00	15.00	30.00	45.00
1912/1	4,928,000	1.00	3.00	15.00	30.00	45.00
1912	Inc. above	0.15	0.50	2.00	5.00	7.50
1914	491,000	1.00	2.50	10.00	20.00	35.00
1919/4	5,000,000	0.75	1.00	3.00	5.00	7.50
1919	Inc. above	0.15	0.25	1.00	3.00	7.50

KM# 40 5 CENTIMES

3.00 g., Copper-Nickel, 19 mm. **Ruler:** Leopold II **Obv:** Legend in French **Obv. Legend:** DES BELGES

Date	Mintage	F12	VF20	XF40	MS60	MS63
1901	—	7.00	15.00	30.00	50.00	95.00

KM# 44 5 CENTIMES

3.00 g., Copper-Nickel, 19 mm. **Obv:** Denomination above star, circle surrounds **Rev:** Rampant lion left within circle, date below

Date	Mintage	F12	VF20	XF40	MS60	MS63
1901	2,494,000	3.00	7.00	15.00	30.00	50.00

KM# 45 5 CENTIMES

3.00 g., Copper-Nickel, 19 mm. **Obv:** Denomination above star, circle surrounds, legend in Dutch **Obv. Legend:** DER BELGEN **Rev:** Rampant lion left within circle, date below

Date	Mintage	F12	VF20	XF40	MS60	MS63
1901	2,491,000	3.00	7.00	15.00	30.00	50.00

KM# 46 5 CENTIMES

2.50 g., Copper-Nickel, 19 mm. **Obv:** Hole at center of crowned monogram, small date below, legend in French **Obv. Legend:** BELGIQUE **Rev:** Spray of leaves to left of center hole, denomination at right

Date	Mintage	F12	VF20	XF40	MS60	MS63
1901	202,000	15.00	35.00	75.00	145	245
1902/1	1,416,000	0.50	8.00	20.00	40.00	75.00
1902	Inc. above	0.25	3.00	12.00	25.00	50.00
1903	864,000	1.00	8.00	15.00	35.00	75.00

KM# 47 5 CENTIMES

2.50 g., Copper-Nickel, 19 mm. **Obv:** Center hole within crowned monogram, small date below, legend in Dutch **Obv. Legend:** BELGIE **Rev:** Spray of leaves to left of center hole, denomination to right

Date	Mintage	F12	VF20	XF40	MS60	MS63
1902/1	1,485,000	1.75	10.00	20.00	40.00	75.00
1902	Inc. above	0.15	3.00	12.00	25.00	50.00
1903	1,002,000	1.00	7.00	15.00	30.00	60.00

KM# 54 5 CENTIMES

2.50 g., Copper-Nickel, 19 mm. **Obv:** Center hole within crowned monogram, large date below, legend in French **Obv. Legend:** BELGIQUE **Rev:** Spray of leaves to left of center hole, denomination to right

Date	Mintage	F12	VF20	XF40	MS60	MS63
1904	5,814,000	0.15	0.35	2.50	5.00	10.00
1905/4	9,575,000	0.30	1.00	7.00	12.00	25.00
1905	Inc. above	0.15	0.35	2.50	5.00	10.00
1905 WICHAUX (error)	Inc. above	2.00	10.00	20.00	40.00	75.00
1905 A. MICHAUX	Inc. above	1.00	3.50	12.00	20.00	40.00
1906/5	8,463,000	0.30	1.50	3.50	7.00	15.00
1906	Inc. above	0.15	0.35	2.00	4.00	8.00
1907	993,000	1.00	6.00	12.00	20.00	40.00

KM# 55 5 CENTIMES

2.50 g., Copper-Nickel, 19 mm. **Obv:** Center hole within crowned monogram, large date below, legend in Dutch **Obv. Legend:** BELGIE **Rev:** Spray of leaves to left of center hole, denomination to right

Date	Mintage	F12	VF20	XF40	MS60	MS63
1904	5,812,000	0.15	0.35	2.50	5.00	10.00
1905/3	7,002,000	0.35	2.50	8.00	16.00	30.00
1905/4	Inc. above	0.30	1.50	7.00	12.00	25.00
1905	Inc. above	0.15	0.35	2.50	5.00	10.00
1905 Without cross	Inc. above	—	1.50	7.00	15.00	30.00
1906	11,016,000	0.15	0.35	2.00	4.00	8.00
1906 Without cross	Inc. above	0.30	1.50	4.00	7.00	15.00
1907	998,000	1.00	3.00	15.00	25.00	40.00

KM# 66 5 CENTIMES

2.50 g., Copper-Nickel, 19 mm. **Obv:** Center hole within crowned monogram, date below,legend in French **Obv. Legend:** BELGIQUE **Rev:** Spray of leaves to left of center hole, denomination to right

Date	Mintage	F12	VF20	XF40	MS60	MS63
1910	8,011,000	0.10	0.35	1.25	2.00	4.00
1913/0	5,005,000	0.20	0.75	2.25	7.00	15.00
1913	Inc. above	0.10	0.40	1.50	3.50	7.00
1914	1,004,000	1.00	3.00	8.00	20.00	35.00
1920/10	10,040,000	0.10	1.00	2.00	4.00	8.00
1920	Inc. above	0.10	0.35	1.25	2.00	4.00
1922/0	12,640,000	0.10	1.50	4.00	6.00	12.00
1922/1	Inc. above	0.10	1.50	3.50	5.00	10.00
1922	Inc. above	0.10	0.35	1.25	2.00	4.00
1923/13	9,000,000	0.10	0.75	2.50	4.00	8.00
1923	Inc. above	0.10	0.35	1.25	2.00	4.00

Date	Mintage	F12	VF20	XF40	MS60	MS63
1925/13	15,860,000	0.10	0.50	2.00	4.00	8.00
1925/23	Inc. above	0.10	0.50	2.00	4.00	8.00
1925	Inc. above	0.10	0.35	1.25	2.00	4.00
1926/5	7,000,000	0.10	1.00	2.50	4.00	8.00
1926	Inc. above	0.10	0.35	1.25	2.00	4.00
1927	2,000,000	0.10	1.00	2.50	6.00	12.00
1927 5 Cen	—	10.00	20.00	35.00	65.00	120
Note: Obverse of KM#66 in French paired with the reverse of KM#67 in Flemish						
1928	12,507,000	0.10	0.35	1.25	2.00	4.00
1932	—	7.00	25.00	70.00	120	200

KM# 67 5 CENTIMES

2.50 g., Copper-Nickel, 19 mm. **Obv:** Center hole within crowned monogram, date below, legend in Dutch **Obv. Legend:** BELGIE **Rev:** Spray of leaves to left of center hole, denomination to right, plain field above 5

Date	Mintage	F12	VF20	XF40	MS60	MS63
1910	8,033,000	0.10	0.35	1.25	2.00	4.00
1914	6,040,000	0.10	0.35	1.25	2.00	4.00
1920/10	10,030,000	0.10	0.35	1.25	3.00	6.00
1920	Inc. above	0.10	0.50	3.00	6.00	12.00
1921/11	4,200,000	0.10	1.00	2.50	6.00	12.00
1921	Inc. above	0.10	1.00	2.00	5.00	10.00
1922/12	13,180,000	0.10	1.00	2.50	4.00	8.00
1922/0	Inc. above	0.10	1.00	3.00	5.00	10.00
1922	Inc. above	0.10	0.35	1.25	2.00	4.00
1923/13	3,530,000	0.10	1.00	3.00	6.00	12.00
1923	Inc. above	0.10	0.75	2.00	5.00	10.00
1924/11	5,260,000	0.10	1.00	2.50	4.50	9.00
1924/14	Inc. above	0.10	0.50	1.75	4.00	9.00
1924	Inc. above	0.10	0.35	1.25	3.00	8.00
1925/13	13,000,000	0.10	1.00	2.00	4.00	8.00
1925/15 High 2	Inc. above	0.10	1.00	2.00	4.00	9.00
1925/15 Level 2	Inc. above	0.10	1.00	2.00	4.00	9.00
1925/3	Inc. above	0.10	0.60	2.00	4.00	9.00
1925	Inc. above	0.10	0.35	1.25	2.00	4.00
1927	6,938,000	0.10	0.35	1.25	2.00	4.00
1928/3	6,252,000	0.10	0.75	2.50	4.50	9.00
1928	Inc. above	0.10	0.35	1.25	2.00	4.00
1930	—	7.00	25.00	100	225	375
1931	—	10.00	30.00	60.00	125	225

KM# 80 5 CENTIMES

2.50 g., Zinc, 19 mm. **Obv:** Denomination within circle, date below circle, legend in French **Obv. Legend:** BELGIQUE-BELGIE **Rev:** Rampant lion, left, within circle **Note:** German Occupation WW I

Date	Mintage	F12	VF20	XF40	MS60	MS63
1915	10,199,000	0.15	2.00	4.00	15.00	—
1916	45,464,000	0.10	0.60	2.00	10.00	—

KM# 94 5 CENTIMES

2.50 g., Nickel-Brass, 19 mm. **Obv:** Center hole within crowned monogram, date below, legend in Dutch **Obv. Legend:** BELGIE **Rev:** Spray of leaves to left of center hole, denomination at right, star added above 5

Date	Mintage	F12	VF20	XF40	MS60	MS63
1930	3,000,000	0.10	0.20	0.35	1.50	3.00
1931	7,430,000	0.10	0.20	0.35	1.50	3.00

KM# 93 5 CENTIMES

2.50 g., Nickel-Brass, 19 mm. **Obv:** Legend in French **Obv. Legend:** BELGIQUE **Rev:** Star added above 5

Date	Mintage	F12	VF20	XF40	MS60	MS63
1932	5,520,000	0.10	0.20	0.35	1.50	3.00

KM# 110.1 5 CENTIMES

2.50 g., Nickel-Brass, 19 mm. **Obv:** Three shields above denomination, legend in French, hole at center **Obv. Legend:** BELGIQUE-BELGIE **Rev:** Hole at center of crowned design, date below

Date	Mintage	F12	VF20	XF40	MS60	MS63
1938	4,970,000	0.10	0.20	0.50	1.25	2.50
1939	—	—	—	—	—	—

Note: Struck at a later date

KM# 110.2 5 CENTIMES

2.50 g., Nickel-Brass, 19 mm. **Obv:** Three shields above denomination, legend in French, hole at center **Obv. Legend:** BELGIQUE-BELGIE **Rev:** Hole at center of crowned design, date below **Note:** Medal alignment.

Date	Mintage	F12	VF20	XF40	MS60	MS63
1938	Inc. above	4.00	7.00	12.00	20.00	40.00

KM# 111 5 CENTIMES

2.50 g., Nickel-Brass, 19 mm. **Obv:** Three shields above denomination, hole at center, legend in Dutch **Obv. Legend:** BELGIE-BELGIQUE **Rev:** Crowned design above date, hole at center

Date	Mintage	F12	VF20	XF40	MS60	MS63
1939	3,000,000	0.10	0.20	0.75	1.50	3.00
1940	1,970,000	0.20	0.50	1.25	2.50	5.00

KM# 123 5 CENTIMES

2.50 g., Zinc, 19 mm. **Obv:** Three shields above denomination, legend in French, hole at center **Obv. Legend:** BELGIQUE-BELGIE **Rev:** Hole at center of crowned design, date below **Note:** German Occupation WW II

Date	Mintage	F12	VF20	XF40	MS60	MS63
1941	10,000,000	0.10	0.20	1.00	4.00	—
1943	7,606,000	0.10	0.20	1.50	6.00	—

KM# 124 5 CENTIMES

2.50 g., Zinc, 19 mm. **Obv:** Three shields above denomination, hole at center, legend in Dutch **Obv. Legend:** BELGIE-BELGIQUE **Rev:** Crowned design above date, hole at center

Date	Mintage	F12	VF20	XF40	MS60	MS63
1941	4,000,000	0.15	0.75	3.00	17.00	40.00
1942	18,430,000	0.10	0.20	1.00	4.00	—

KM# 42 10 CENTIMES

4.50 g., Copper-Nickel, 21 mm. **Ruler:** Leopold II **Obv:** Denomination and star within shaded circle **Obv. Legend:** LEOPOLD II ROI DES BELGES **Rev:** Rampant lion left within circle **Rev. Legend:** L'UNION FAIT LA FORCE

Date	Mintage	F12	VF20	XF40	MS60	MS63
1901	551,000	25.00	45.00	125	200	325

KM# 43 10 CENTIMES

4.50 g., Copper-Nickel, 21 mm. **Ruler:** Leopold II **Obv:** Denomination above star, within circle, legend in Dutch **Obv. Legend:** LEOPOLD II KONING DER BELGEN **Rev:** Rampant lion left within circle **Rev. Legend:** EENDRACHT MAAKT MACHT

Date	Mintage	F12	VF20	XF40	MS60	MS63
1901	556,000	35.00	65.00	120	250	450

KM# 48 10 CENTIMES

4.00 g., Copper-Nickel, 22 mm. **Obv:** Center hole within crowned monogram, small date below, legend in French **Obv. Legend:** BELGIQUE **Rev:** Spray of leaves to left of center hole, denomination to right

Date	Mintage	F12	VF20	XF40	MS60	MS63
1901	582,000	6.00	12.00	25.00	45.00	75.00
1902/1	5,866,000	0.50	3.00	12.00	25.00	50.00
1902	Inc. above	0.15	1.00	3.00	5.00	10.00
1903	763,000	1.00	4.00	15.00	50.00	80.00

KM# 49 10 CENTIMES

4.00 g., Copper-Nickel, 22 mm. **Obv:** Center hole within crowned monogram, date below, legend in Dutch, **Obv. Legend:** BELGIE **Rev:** Spray of leaves to left of center hole, denomination to right

Date	Mintage	F12	VF20	XF40	MS60	MS63
1902	1,560,000	0.20	2.00	8.00	17.00	32.00
1903/2	—	0.50	1.25	7.00	12.00	22.00
1903	5,658,000	0.20	1.00	2.50	5.00	10.00

KM# 52 10 CENTIMES

4.00 g., Copper-Nickel, 22 mm. **Obv:** Center hole within crowned monogram, large date below, legend in French **Obv. Legend:** BELGIQUE **Rev:** Spray of leaves to left center hole, denomination to right

Date	Mintage	F12	VF20	XF40	MS60	MS63
1903	Inc. above	2.00	15.00	30.00	60.00	150
1904	16,354,000	0.15	1.00	3.00	5.00	10.00
1905/4	14,392,000	0.25	1.00	7.00	12.00	25.00
1905	Inc. above	0.15	0.60	2.00	4.50	9.00
1906/5	1,483,000	0.50	1.50	7.00	12.00	25.00
1906	Inc. above	0.25	0.75	7.00	15.00	30.00

KM# 53 10 CENTIMES

4.00 g., Copper-Nickel, 22 mm. **Obv:** Center hole within crowned monogram, large date below, legend in Dutch **Obv. Legend:** BELGIE **Rev:** Spray of leaves to left of center hole, denomination to right

Date	Mintage	F12	VF20	XF40	MS60	MS63
1903	Inc. above	1.00	4.00	12.00	25.00	45.00
1904	16,834,000	0.20	0.50	2.00	4.50	9.00
1905/3	13,758,000	0.35	1.00	3.00	7.00	15.00
1905/4	Inc. above	0.30	1.00	5.00	12.00	25.00
1905	Inc. above	0.20	0.50	2.00	4.50	9.00
1906/5	2,017,000	0.50	1.25	5.00	12.00	25.00
Note: Point above center of 6						
1906/5	Inc. above	0.50	1.25	5.00	12.00	25.00
Note: Point above right side of 6						
1906	Inc. above	0.10	0.75	7.00	15.00	30.00

KM# 81 10 CENTIMES

4.00 g., Zinc, 22 mm. **Obv:** Denomination within circle, date below, legend in French **Obv. Legend:** BELGIQUE-BELGIE **Rev:** Rampant lion, left, within circle **Note:** German Occupation. All of KM#81 have dots after the date. The 1916 is distinguished by a period after the date.

Date	Mintage	F12	VF20	XF40	MS60	MS63
1915	9,681,000	0.25	1.50	4.00	15.00	—
1916/15	37,382,000	20.00	30.00	70.00	125	—
.1916.	Inc. above	0.15	0.75	3.00	10.00	—
Note: With dots before and after date						
0.1916	Inc. above	7.00	15.00	50.00	100	—
Note: With dot before date only						
1916	Inc. above	10.00	25.00	100	200	—
Note: With dot after date only						
1917	1,447,000	17.50	25.00	85.00	200	—

KM# 85.1 10 CENTIMES

4.00 g., Copper-Nickel, 22 mm. **Obv:** Center hole within crowned monogram, date below, legend in French **Obv. Legend:** BELGIQUE **Rev:** Spray of leaves to left of center hole, denomination to right

Date	Mintage	F12	VF20	XF40	MS60	MS63
1920	6,520,000	0.15	0.40	1.50	2.50	5.00
1911	—	—	—	—	—	—
Note: Struck at a later date						
1921	7,215,000	0.15	0.20	1.00	2.00	4.00
1923	20,625,000	0.10	0.20	1.00	2.00	4.00
1926/5	Inc. above	0.20	0.75	3.00	6.00	12.00
1926	Inc. above	0.15	0.20	1.00	2.00	4.00
1926/3	6,916,000	0.20	0.75	3.00	6.00	12.00
1927	8,125,000	0.15	0.20	1.00	2.00	4.00
1928/3	6,895,000	0.20	1.00	4.00	7.00	14.00
1928/5	Inc. above	0.20	1.00	4.00	7.00	14.00
1928	Inc. above	0.15	0.20	1.00	2.00	4.00
1929	12,260,000	0.15	0.20	1.00	2.00	4.00

KM# 85.2 10 CENTIMES

4.00 g., Copper-Nickel, 22 mm. **Obv:** Center hole within crowned monogram, date below, legend in French **Obv. Legend:** BELGIQUE **Rev:** Spray of leaves to left of center hole, denomination to right, center line below ES of CES

Date	Mintage	F12	VF20	XF40	MS60	MS63
1920	Inc. above	0.50	3.00	7.00	15.00	30.00
1921	Inc. above	1.50	8.00	16.00	30.00	60.00

KM# 86 10 CENTIMES

4.00 g., Copper-Nickel, 22 mm. **Obv:** Center hole within crowned monogram, date below, legend in Dutch **Obv. Legend:** BELGIE **Rev:** Spray of leaves to left of center hole, denomination to right, plain field above 10 **Edge:** Plain

Date	Mintage	F12	VF20	XF40	MS60	MS63
1920	5,050,000	0.15	0.20	1.00	3.50	7.00
1921	7,580,000	0.15	0.20	1.00	2.00	4.00
1922	6,250,000	0.15	0.20	1.00	2.00	4.00
1924	5,825,000	0.15	0.20	1.00	3.00	6.00
1925/4	8,160,000	0.20	0.40	2.00	5.00	10.00
1925/3	Inc. above	0.20	0.40	2.00	5.00	10.00
1925	Inc. above	0.10	0.20	1.00	2.00	4.00
1926/5	6,250,000	0.20	0.40	2.00	5.00	10.00
1926/3	Inc. above	0.20	0.40	2.00	5.00	10.00
1926	Inc. above	0.15	0.20	1.00	2.00	4.00
1927	10,625,000	0.15	0.20	1.00	2.00	4.00
1928/5	6,750,000	0.20	0.40	2.00	5.00	10.00
1928/3	Inc. above	0.20	0.40	2.00	5.00	10.00
1928	Inc. above	0.15	0.20	1.00	2.00	4.00
1929	4,668,000	0.15	0.20	1.00	2.00	4.00
1930	—	15.00	30.00	75.00	125	250

KM# 95.1 10 CENTIMES

4.00 g., Nickel-Brass, 22 mm. **Obv:** Center hole within crowned monogram, date below, legend in French **Obv. Legend:** BELGIQUE **Rev:** Spray of leaves to left of center hole, denomination to right, star added above 10 **Edge:** Plain

Date	Mintage	F12	VF20	XF40	MS60	MS63
1930/20	2,000,000	50.00	120	250	325	525
1930	Inc. above	20.00	100	200	300	500
1931	6,270,000	5.00	10.00	20.00	30.00	50.00
1932	1,270,000	25.00	120	225	325	550
1932	Inc. above	50.00	150	275	360	600
Note: A instead of signature						

KM# 95.2 10 CENTIMES

4.00 g., Nickel-Brass, 22 mm. **Obv:** Legend in French **Obv. Legend:** BELGIQUE **Rev:** Single line below ES of CES, star added above 10

Date	Mintage	F12	VF20	XF40	MS60	MS63
1931	Inc. above	2.00	8.00	20.00	42.00	70.00
1932	Inc. above	45.00	150	275	360	600

KM# 96 10 CENTIMES

4.00 g., Nickel-Brass, 22 mm. **Obv:** Center hole within crowned monogram, date below, legend in Dutch **Obv. Legend:** BELGIE **Rev:** Spray of leaves to left of center hole, denomination to right, star added above 10

Date	Mintage	F12	VF20	XF40	MS60	MS63
1930	1,581,000	0.30	0.75	3.00	6.00	12.00
1931	5,000,000	25.00	75.00	150	240	400

KM# 112 10 CENTIMES

4.00 g., Nickel-Brass, 22 mm. **Obv:** Three shields above denomination, hole at center, legend in French **Obv. Legend:** BELGIQUE-BELGIE **Rev:** Crowned design above date, hole at center

Date	Mintage	F12	VF20	XF40	MS60	MS63
1938	6,000,000	0.10	0.25	0.50	1.00	2.00
1939	7,000,000	0.50	1.00	3.00	7.00	15.00

KM# 113.1 10 CENTIMES

4.00 g., Nickel-Brass, 22 mm. **Obv:** Three shields above denomination, hole at center, legend in Dutch **Obv. Legend:** BELGIE-BELGIQUE **Rev:** Crowned design above date, hole at center

Date	Mintage	F12	VF20	XF40	MS60	MS63
1939	8,425,000	0.10	0.25	0.50	0.90	1.50

KM# 113.2 10 CENTIMES

Nickel-Brass, 22 mm. **Obv:** Three shields above denomination, hole at center, legend in Dutch **Obv. Legend:** BELGIE-BELGIQUE **Rev:** Crowned design above date, hole at center **Note:** Thin flan.

Date	Mintage	F12	VF20	XF40	MS60	MS63
1939	Inc. above	1.25	3.00	9.00	20.00	35.00

KM# 125 10 CENTIMES

4.00 g., Zinc, 22 mm. **Obv:** Three shields above denomination, hole at center, legend in French **Obv. Legend:** BELGIQUE-BELGIE **Rev:** Crowned design above date, hole at center **Edge:** Plain **Note:** German Occupation WW II.

Date	Mintage	F12	VF20	XF40	MS60	MS63
1941	10,000,000	0.15	0.25	1.50	4.00	—
1942	17,000,000	0.15	0.25	1.50	4.00	—
1943	22,500,000	0.15	0.25	1.50	4.00	—
1945	—	—	—	—	—	—
Note: Struck at a later date						
1946	Est. 10370000	—	—	—	—	—
Note: Not released for circulation						

KM# 126 10 CENTIMES

4.00 g., Zinc, 22 mm. **Obv:** Three shields above denomination, hole at center, legend in Dutch **Obv. Legend:** BELGIE-BELGIQUE **Rev:** Crowned design above date, hole at center **Edge:** Plain

Date	Mintage	F12	VF20	XF40	MS60	MS63
1941	7,000,000	0.15	2.00	5.00	12.00	—
1942	21,000,000	0.15	0.25	1.50	4.00	—
1943	22,000,000	0.15	0.25	1.50	4.00	—
1944	28,140,000	0.15	0.25	1.50	4.00	—
1945	8,000,000	0.15	2.00	5.00	12.00	—
1946	5,370,000	0.15	1.00	3.00	10.00	—

KM# 146 20 CENTIMES

2.00 g., Bronze, 17 mm. **Obv:** Crowned denomination divides date, legend in French **Obv. Legend:** BELGIQUE **Rev:** Helmeted head, left, small miner's lamp at right **Edge:** Plain

Date	Mintage	VF20	XF40	MS60	MS63	MS65
1953	14,150,000	0.10	0.20	0.50	1.00	1.50
1953	—	0.10	0.65	1.25	2.50	4.00
Note: CENTIMES not touching rim						
1954	—	300	500	650	800	1,000
Note: Considered by some to be an Essai						
1957	13,300,000	—	0.10	0.35	1.00	1.50
1958	8,700,000	—	0.10	0.35	1.00	1.50
1959	19,670,000	—	0.10	0.35	1.00	1.50
1962	410,000	6.00	9.00	12.00	18.00	25.00
1963	2,550,000	0.20	0.50	1.00	2.00	3.00

KM# 147.1 20 CENTIMES

2.00 g., Bronze, 17 mm. **Obv:** Crowned denomination divides date, legend in Dutch **Obv. Legend:** BELGIE **Rev:** Helmeted head, left, small miner's lamp at right **Edge:** Plain

Date	Mintage	VF20	XF40	MS60	MS63	MS65
1954	50,130,000	—	0.10	0.35	1.00	1.50
1960	7,530,000	—	0.10	0.35	1.00	1.50

KM# 147.2 20 CENTIMES

2.00 g., Bronze, 17 mm. **Obv:** CENTIMES touching rim, crowned denomination divides date, legend in Dutch **Obv. Legend:** BELGIE **Rev:** Helmeted head, left, small miner's lamp at right **Edge:** Plain

Date	Mintage	VF20	XF40	MS60	MS63	MS65
1954	Inc. above	0.15	0.65	1.25	2.50	4.00
1960	Inc. above	0.15	0.65	1.25	2.50	4.00

KM# 62 25 CENTIMES

6.50 g., Copper-Nickel **Obv:** Center hole within crowned monogram, date below, legend in French **Obv. Legend:** BELGIQUE **Rev:** Spray of leaves to left of center hole, denomination to right

Date	Mintage	F12	VF20	XF40	MS60	MS63
1908	4,007,000	0.50	4.00	8.00	25.00	50.00
1909/8	1,998,000	4.00	7.00	45.00	175	350
1909	Inc. above	1.00	4.00	15.00	35.00	70.00

KM# 63 25 CENTIMES

6.50 g., Copper-Nickel **Obv:** Center hole within crowned monogram, date below, legend in Dutch **Obv. Legend:** BELGIE **Rev:** Spray of leaves to left of center hole, denomination to right

Date	Mintage	F12	VF20	XF40	MS60	MS63
1908	4,011,000	0.50	4.00	20.00	50.00	100

KM# 69 25 CENTIMES

6.50 g., Copper-Nickel, 26 mm. **Obv:** Center hole within crowned monogram, date below, legend in Dutch **Obv. Legend:** BELGIE **Rev:** Sprays to left of center hole, denomination to right

Date	Mintage	F12	VF20	XF40	MS60	MS63
1910	2,006,000	0.15	1.00	7.00	15.00	30.00
1911	—	—	—	—	—	—
Note: Struck at a later date						
1913	2,010,000	0.15	1.00	7.00	15.00	30.00
1921	11,173,000	0.15	0.25	2.00	4.00	7.00
1922/1	14,200,000	1.00	10.00	20.00	35.00	75.00

Date	Mintage	F12	VF20	XF40	MS60	MS63
1922	Inc. above	0.15	0.25	2.00	4.00	7.00
1926/3	6,400,000	0.35	3.00	7.00	12.00	25.00
1926	Inc. above	0.10	0.40	2.00	4.00	7.00
1927/3	3,799,000	0.35	3.00	7.00	12.00	25.00
1927	Inc. above	0.10	0.25	2.00	5.00	10.00
1928	9,200,000	0.10	0.25	1.50	3.00	6.00
1929	8,980,000	0.10	0.25	1.50	3.00	6.00

KM# 68.1 25 CENTIMES

6.40 g., Copper-Nickel, 26 mm. **Obv:** Center hole within crowned monogram, date below, legend in French **Obv. Legend:** BELGIQUE **Rev:** Spray of leaves to left of center hole, denomination to right

Date	Mintage	F12	VF20	XF40	MS60	MS63
1913	2,011,000	0.15	3.00	8.00	15.00	30.00
1920	2,844,000	0.15	2.00	7.00	12.00	25.00
1921	7,464,000	0.10	0.25	2.00	4.00	7.00
1922	7,600,000	0.10	0.25	2.00	4.00	7.00
1923	11,356,000	0.15	0.25	2.00	4.00	7.00
1926/3	1,300,000	1.00	4.00	9.00	12.00	25.00
1926	Inc. above	0.50	4.00	9.00	12.00	25.00
1927/3	8,800,000	1.00	10.00	20.00	35.00	75.00
1927	Inc. above	0.10	0.25	2.00	4.00	7.00
1928	4,351,000	0.10	1.00	2.00	5.00	10.00
1929	9,600,000	0.10	0.25	1.50	3.00	6.00

KM# 68.2 25 CENTIMES

6.50 g., Copper-Nickel, 26 mm. **Obv:** Center hole within crowned monogram, date below, legend in French **Obv. Legend:** BELGIQUE **Rev:** Single line below ES of CES, spray of leaves to left of center hole, denomination to right

Date	Mintage	F12	VF20	XF40	MS60	MS63
1920	Inc. above	0.50	2.00	7.00	12.00	25.00
1921	Inc. above	0.35	1.50	4.00	7.00	15.00

KM# 82 25 CENTIMES

6.50 g., Zinc, 26 mm. **Obv:** Denomination within beaded circle, stars flank date below, legend in French **Obv. Legend:** BELGIQUE-BELGIE **Rev:** Rampant lion left within beaded circle **Note:** German Occupation WW I

Date	Mintage	F12	VF20	XF40	MS60	MS63
1915	8,080,000	0.50	4.00	8.00	15.00	30.00
1916	10,671,000	0.50	3.00	7.00	12.00	20.00
1917	3,555,000	2.00	7.00	15.00	25.00	50.00
1918	5,489,000	1.00	6.00	12.00	20.00	40.00

KM# 114.1 25 CENTIMES

6.50 g., Nickel-Brass, 26 mm. **Obv:** Three shields above denomination, hole in center, legend in French **Obv. Legend:** BELGIQUE-BELGIE **Rev:** Crowned design above date, hole in center

Date	Mintage	F12	VF20	XF40	MS60	MS63
1938	7,200,000	—	0.25	1.00	2.00	4.00
1939	7,732,000	—	0.25	1.00	2.00	4.00

KM# 114.2 25 CENTIMES

6.50 g., Nickel-Brass, 26 mm. **Obv:** Three shields above denomination, hole in center, legend in French **Obv. Legend:** BELGIQUE-BELGIE **Rev:** Crowned design above date, hole in center **Note:** Medal alignment.

Date	Mintage	F12	VF20	XF40	MS60	MS63
1939	Inc. above	4.00	7.00	12.00	18.00	35.00

KM# 115.1 25 CENTIMES

6.50 g., Nickel-Brass, 26 mm. **Obv:** Three shields above denomination, hole at center, legend in Dutch **Obv. Legend:** BELGIE-BELGIQUE **Rev:** Crowned design above date, hole at center

Date	Mintage	F12	VF20	XF40	MS60	MS63
1938	14,932,000	—	0.25	0.75	1.50	3.00

KM# 115.2 25 CENTIMES

6.50 g., Nickel-Brass, 26 mm. **Obv:** Three shields above denomination, hole at center, legend in Dutch **Obv. Legend:** BELGIE-BELGIQUE **Rev:** Crowned design above date, hole at center **Note:** Medal alignment.

Date	Mintage	F12	VF20	XF40	MS60	MS63
1938	Inc. above	4.00	7.00	12.00	16.00	30.00

KM# 131 25 CENTIMES

6.50 g., Zinc, 26 mm. **Obv:** Three shields above denomination, hole at center, legend in French **Obv. Legend:** BELGIQUE-BELGIE **Rev:** Crowned design above date, hole at center **Note:** German Occupation WW II.

Date	Mintage	F12	VF20	XF40	MS60	MS63
1941 Rare	—	—	—	—	—	—
1942	14,400,000	—	0.20	0.75	5.00	—
1943	21,600,000	—	0.20	0.75	5.00	—
1945	—	—	—	—	—	—
Note: Struck at a later date						
1946	21,428,000	—	0.20	0.75	4.00	—
1947	—	—	—	—	—	—
Note: Not released for circulation						

KM# 132 25 CENTIMES

6.50 g., Zinc, 26 mm. **Obv:** Three shields above denomination, hole at center, legend in Dutch **Obv. Legend:** BELGIE-BELGIQUE **Rev:** Crowned design above date, hole at center **Edge:** Plain

Date	Mintage	F12	VF20	XF40	MS60	MS63
1942	14,400,000	—	1.00	2.00	8.00	—
1943	21,600,000	—	0.20	0.75	5.00	—
1944	25,960,000	—	0.20	0.75	5.00	—
1945	8,200,000	—	0.50	2.50	12.00	—
1946	11,652,000	—	0.50	2.50	10.00	—
1947	Est. 316000	—	—	—	—	—
Note: Not released for circulation						

KM# 153.1 25 CENTIMES

1.70 g., Copper-Nickel, 16 mm. **Obv:** Large denomination between mint marks, legend in French **Obv. Legend:** BELGIQUE **Rev:** Crowned "B" divides date **Edge:** Plain **Note:** Mint mark - Angel Head. Mintmaster Vogeleer's privy mark - Bird.

Date	Mintage	VF20	XF40	MS60	MS63	MS65
1964	21,770,000	—	—	0.10	0.15	0.25
1965	11,440,000	—	—	0.10	0.15	0.25
1966	19,990,000	—	—	0.10	0.15	0.25
1967	6,820,000	—	—	0.10	0.50	0.75
1968	25,250,000	—	—	0.10	0.15	0.25
1969	7,670,000	—	—	0.10	0.30	0.50
1970	27,000,000	—	—	0.10	0.15	0.25
1971	16,000,000	—	—	0.10	0.15	0.25
1972	20,000,000	—	—	0.10	0.15	0.25
1973	12,500,000	—	—	0.10	0.15	0.25
1974	20,000,000	—	—	0.10	0.15	0.25
1975	12,000,000	—	—	0.10	0.15	0.25

KM# 153.2 25 CENTIMES

2.00 g., Copper-Nickel, 16 mm. **Obv:** Large denomination between mint marks, legend in French **Obv. Legend:** BELGIQUE **Rev:** Crowned "B" divides date **Edge:** Plain **Note:** Medal alignment. Mint mark - Angel Head. Mintmaster Vogeleer's privy mark - Bird.

Date	Mintage	VF20	XF40	MS60	MS63	MS65
1964	Inc. above	—	3.00	5.00	7.00	12.00
1965	Inc. above	—	6.00	10.00	15.00	25.00
1967	Inc. above	—	6.00	10.00	15.00	25.00
1970	Inc. above	—	3.00	5.00	7.00	12.00
1971	Inc. above	—	3.00	5.00	7.00	12.00
1974	Inc. above	—	6.00	10.00	15.00	25.00

KM# 154.1 25 CENTIMES

2.00 g., Copper-Nickel, 16 mm. **Obv:** Large denomination between mint marks, legend in Dutch **Obv. Legend:** BELGIE **Rev:** Crowned "B" divides date **Edge:** Plain **Note:** Mint mark - Angel Head. Mintmaster Vogeleer's privy mark - Bird.

Date	Mintage	VF20	XF40	MS60	MS63	MS65
1964	21,300,000	—	—	0.10	0.15	0.25
1965	7,900,000	—	—	0.10	0.30	0.50
1966	23,420,000	—	—	0.10	0.15	0.25
1967	7,720,000	—	—	0.10	0.30	0.50
1968	22,750,000	—	—	0.10	0.15	0.25
1969	25,190,000	—	—	0.10	0.15	0.25
1970	12,000,000	—	—	0.10	0.15	0.25
1971	16,000,000	—	—	0.10	0.15	0.25
1972	20,000,000	—	—	0.10	0.15	0.25
1973	12,500,000	—	—	0.10	0.15	0.25
1974	20,000,000	—	—	0.10	0.15	0.25
1975	12,000,000	—	—	0.10	0.15	0.25

KM# 154.2 25 CENTIMES

2.00 g., Copper-Nickel, 16 mm. **Obv:** Large denomination between mint marks, legend in Dutch **Obv. Legend:** BELGIE **Rev:** Crowned "B" divides date **Edge:** Plain **Note:** Medal alignment. Mint mark - Angel Head. Mintmaster Vogeleer's privy mark - Bird.

Date	Mintage	VF20	XF40	MS60	MS63	MS65
1964	Inc. above	—	3.00	5.00	7.00	12.00
1965	Inc. above	—	3.00	5.00	8.00	15.00
1966	Inc. above	—	3.00	5.00	7.00	12.00
1967	Inc. above	—	4.00	6.00	8.00	15.00
1969	Inc. above	—	3.00	5.00	7.00	12.00
1971	Inc. above	—	4.00	6.00	8.00	15.00
1972	Inc. above	—	3.00	5.00	7.00	12.00

KM# 50 50 CENTIMES

2.50 g., 0.835 Silver 0.0671 oz. ASW **Obv:** Bearded head of Leopold II, left, legend in French **Obv. Legend:** DES BELGES **Rev:** Tablet to right of seated lion, looking left, denomination below, date to left of lion

Date	Mintage	F12	VF20	XF40	MS60	MS63
1901	3,000,000	4.00	10.00	20.00	50.00	80.00

KM# 51 50 CENTIMES

2.50 g., 0.835 Silver 0.0671 oz. ASW **Obv:** Legend in Dutch **Obv. Legend:** DER BELGEN

Date	Mintage	F12	VF20	XF40	MS60	MS63
1901	3,000,000	4.00	10.00	20.00	50.00	80.00

KM# 60.1 50 CENTIMES

2.50 g., 0.835 Silver 0.0671 oz. ASW **Obv:** Bearded head of Leopold II, left, legend in French **Obv. Legend:** DES BELGES **Rev:** Denomination above date within wreath

Date	Mintage	F12	VF20	XF40	MS60	MS63
1907	545,000	3.00	5.00	15.00	45.00	75.00
1909	2,503,000	2.00	3.00	7.50	25.00	40.00

KM# 60.2 50 CENTIMES

2.50 g., 0.835 Silver 0.0671 oz. ASW **Obv:** Bearded head of Leopold II, left, legend in French, without period in signature **Obv. Legend:** DES BELGES **Rev:** Denomination above date within wreath

Date	Mintage	F12	VF20	XF40	MS60	MS63
1907	Inc. above	3.50	7.50	25.00	100	175
1909	Inc. above	2.00	3.00	7.50	25.00	40.00

KM# 61.1 50 CENTIMES

2.50 g., 0.835 Silver 0.0671 oz. ASW, 18 mm. **Obv:** Bearded head of Leopold II, left, legend in Dutch **Obv. Legend:** DER BELGEN **Rev:** Denomination above date within wreath **Edge:** Reeded

Date	Mintage	F12	VF20	XF40	MS60	MS63
1907	545,000	3.00	6.00	15.00	45.00	85.00
1909	2,510,000	2.00	3.00	7.50	25.00	40.00

KM# 61.2 50 CENTIMES

2.50 g., 0.835 Silver 0.0671 oz. ASW **Obv:** Bearded head of Leopold II, left, legend in Dutch **Obv. Legend:** DER BELGEN **Rev:** Denomination above date within wreath **Note:** Medal alignment

Date	Mintage	F12	VF20	XF40	MS60	MS63
1909	Inc. above	15.00	18.00	55.00	160	215

KM# 70 50 CENTIMES

2.50 g., 0.835 Silver 0.0671 oz. ASW, 18 mm. **Obv:** Head of Albert, left, legend in French **Obv. Legend:** DES BELGES **Rev:** Denomination above date within wreath **Edge:** Reeded

Date	Mintage	VF20	XF40	MS60	MS63	MS65
1910	1,900,000	3.00	7.50	25.00	40.00	70.00
1911	2,063,000	6.00	15.00	45.00	65.00	120
1912	1,000,000	2.00	3.00	5.00	7.00	12.00
1914	240,000	3.00	7.50	25.00	50.00	100

KM# 71 50 CENTIMES

2.50 g., 0.835 Silver 0.0671 oz. ASW **Obv:** Head of Albert, left, legend in Dutch **Obv. Legend:** DER BELGEN **Rev:** Denomination above date within wreath

Date	Mintage	VF20	XF40	MS60	MS63	MS65
1910	1,900,000	5.00	10.00	30.00	60.00	120
1911	2,063,000	2.00	3.00	4.00	7.00	12.00
1912	1,000,000	2.00	3.00	4.00	7.00	12.00

KM# 83 50 CENTIMES

5.00 g., Zinc, 24 mm. **Obv:** Hole at center of star, tiny stars flank date below, legend in Dutch **Obv. Legend:** BELGIE-BELGIQUE **Rev:** Spray of leaves to left of center hole, denomination to right, small shield with rampant lion on spray **Note:** German Occupation WW I

Date	Mintage	F12	VF20	XF40	MS60	MS63
1918	7,394,000	0.50	6.00	10.00	35.00	70.00

KM# 87 50 CENTIMES

2.50 g., Nickel, 18 mm. **Obv:** Allegorically female figure of Belgium kneeling, wounded but recovering, legend in French **Obv. Legend:** BELGIQUE **Rev:** Caduceus divides denomination and dates **Edge:** Reeded

Date	Mintage	F12	VF20	XF40	MS60	MS63
1922	6,180,000	0.15	0.25	1.00	2.00	5.00
1923	8,820,000	0.15	0.25	1.00	2.00	5.00
1927	1,750,000	0.15	0.30	1.00	2.00	5.00
1928	3,000,000	0.15	0.35	2.00	4.00	7.00
1929	1,000,000	0.25	0.50	5.00	7.00	15.00
1930	1,000,000	0.25	0.50	5.00	7.00	15.00
1932/23	2,530,000	1.00	3.00	10.00	15.00	25.00
1932	Inc. above	0.15	0.50	1.00	2.00	5.00
1933	2,861,000	0.15	0.25	0.75	2.00	5.00

KM# 88 50 CENTIMES

2.50 g., Nickel, 18 mm. **Obv:** Allegorically female figure of Belgium kneeling, wounded but recovering **Obv. Legend:** BELGIE **Rev:** Caduceus divides denomination and date **Edge:** Reeded

Date	Mintage	F12	VF20	XF40	MS60	MS63
1922	—	—	—	—	—	—
Note: Struck at a later date						
1923	15,000,000	0.20	0.25	1.00	2.00	5.00
1928/3	10,000,000	0.25	0.50	5.00	7.00	12.00
1928	Inc. above	0.20	0.25	1.00	2.00	5.00
1930/20	2,252,000	0.50	2.00	3.50	8.00	16.00
1930	Inc. above	0.20	0.75	3.00	6.00	10.00
1932/22	—	0.25	3.00	5.00	12.00	20.00
1932	2,000,000	0.20	0.50	2.00	4.00	6.00
1933	1,189,000	1.00	5.00	9.00	15.00	25.00
1934	935,000	25.00	45.00	100	175	350

KM# 118 50 CENTIMES

2.50 g., Nickel, 18 mm. **Obv:** Legend in French **Obv. Legend:** BELGIQUE-BELGIE **Edge:** Reeded **Note:** Striking interrupted by the war. Very few coins have been officially released into circulation.

Date	Mintage	F12	VF20	XF40	MS60	MS63
1939	15,500,000	200	400	800	1,300	—

KM# 144 50 CENTIMES

2.75 g., Bronze, 19 mm. **Obv:** Crowned denomination divides date, legend in French **Obv. Legend:** BELGIQUE **Rev:** Helmeted mine worker, left, miner's lamp at r. Large head, tip of neck 1/2 mm from rim **Edge:** Plain

Date	Mintage	VF20	XF40	MS60	MS63	MS65
1952	3,520,000	0.10	0.25	0.50	1.50	3.50
1953	22,620,000	—	0.10	0.25	0.75	1.50
1955	29,160,000	—	0.10	0.25	0.75	1.50

KM# 145 50 CENTIMES

2.75 g., Bronze, 19 mm. **Obv:** Crowned denomination divides date, legend in Dutch **Obv. Legend:** BELGIE **Rev:** Helmeted mine worker left, miner's lamp at right, large head **Edge:** Plain

Date	Mintage	VF20	XF40	MS60	MS63	MS65
1952	5,830,000	0.10	0.25	0.50	1.50	3.00
1953	22,930,000	—	0.10	0.25	0.75	1.50
1954	15,730,000	—	0.10	0.25	0.75	1.50

KM# 148.2 50 CENTIMES

2.75 g., Bronze, 19 mm. **Ruler:** Baudouin I **Obv:** Crowned denomination divides date, legend in French **Obv. Legend:** BELGIQUE **Rev:** Helmeted mine worker left, miner's lamp at right, large head, tip of neck 1/2 mm from rim **Edge:** Plain **Note:** Medal alignment.

Date	Mintage	VF20	XF40	MS60	MS63	MS65
1953	Inc. above	—	—	—	15.00	30.00
1959	Inc. above	—	—	—	15.00	30.00
1965	Inc. above	—	—	—	15.00	30.00
1966	Inc. above	—	—	—	15.00	30.00
1969	Inc. above	—	—	—	15.00	30.00
1974	Inc. above	—	—	—	15.00	30.00
1976	Inc. above	—	—	—	15.00	30.00
1999	—	PF65 30.00				
2000	—	PF65 30.00				

KM# 149.1 50 CENTIMES

2.75 g., Bronze, 19 mm. **Ruler:** Baudouin I **Obv:** Crowned denomination divides date, legend in Dutch **Obv. Legend:** BELGIE **Rev:** Helmeted mine worker left, miner's lamp at right, large head **Edge:** Plain

Date	Mintage	VF20	XF40	MS60	MS63	MS65
1956	5,640,000	—	0.25	0.50	1.50	3.00
1957	13,800,000	—	0.10	0.25	0.75	1.50
1958	19,480,000	—	0.10	0.25	0.75	1.50
1962	4,150,000	—	0.25	0.50	1.50	3.00
1963	1,110,000	—	0.25	1.25	2.50	5.00
1964	10,340,000	—	0.10	0.25	0.75	1.50
1965	9,590,000	—	0.10	0.25	0.75	1.50
1966	6,930,000	—	0.10	0.25	0.75	1.50
1967	6,970,000	—	0.10	0.25	0.75	1.50
1968	2,000,000	—	0.50	1.00	1.75	3.50
1969	10,000,000	—	0.10	0.25	0.75	1.50
1970	12,000,000	—	0.10	0.25	0.75	1.50
1971	1,250,000	—	0.50	1.00	1.75	3.50
1972	7,000,000	—	0.10	0.25	0.75	1.50
1973	3,000,000	—	0.25	0.50	1.00	2.00
1974	5,000,000	—	0.10	0.25	0.75	1.50
1975	7,000,000	—	0.10	0.25	0.75	1.50
1976	8,000,000	—	0.10	0.25	0.75	1.50
1977	13,000,000	—	0.10	0.25	0.50	1.00
1978	2,500,000	—	0.25	0.50	1.00	2.00
1979	40,000,000	—	0.10	0.20	0.40	0.75
1980	20,000,000	—	0.10	0.20	0.40	0.75
1981	2,000,000	—	0.25	0.50	1.00	2.00
1982	7,000,000	—	0.10	0.25	0.75	1.50
1983	14,100,000	—	0.10	0.20	0.40	0.75
1985	6,000,000	—	0.10	0.20	0.40	0.75
1987	9,000,000	—	0.10	0.20	0.40	0.75
1988	9,000,000	—	0.10	0.25	0.50	1.00
1989 Sets only	60,000	—	—	—	1.50	3.00
1990 Sets only	60,000	—	—	—	1.50	3.00
1991	6,000,000	—	0.10	0.20	0.40	0.75
1992	7,060,000	—	0.10	0.20	0.40	0.75
1993	10,000,000	—	0.10	0.20	0.40	0.75
1994	10,000,000	—	—	0.15	0.25	0.50
1995 Sets only	60,000	—	—	—	1.00	2.00
1996	11,000,000	—	—	0.15	0.25	0.50
1997 Sets only	60,000	—	—	—	1.00	2.00
1998	30,000,000	—	—	0.15	0.25	0.50
1999 Sets only	60,000	—	—	—	1.00	2.00
2000 Sets only	60,000	—	—	—	1.00	2.00

KM# 149.2 50 CENTIMES

2.75 g., Bronze, 19 mm. **Ruler:** Baudouin I **Obv:** Crowned denomination divides date, legend in French **Obv. Legend:** BELGIQUE **Rev:** Helmeted mine worker left, miner's lamp at right, large head, tip of neck 1/2 mm from rim **Edge:** Plain **Note:** Medal alignment.

Date	Mintage	VF20	XF40	MS60	MS63	MS65
1953	Inc. above	—	—	—	15.00	30.00
1967	Inc. above	—	—	—	15.00	30.00
1969	Inc. above	—	—	—	15.00	30.00
1979	Inc. above	—	—	—	15.00	30.00
1988	Inc. above	—	—	—	15.00	30.00
1999	—	PF65 30.00				
2000	—	PF65 30.00				

KM# 148.1 50 CENTIMES

2.70 g., Bronze, 19 mm. **Ruler:** Baudouin I **Obv:** Crowned denomination divides date, legend in French **Obv. Legend:** BELGIQUE **Rev:** Helmeted mine worker left, miner's lamp at right, large head, tip of neck 1/2 mm from rim **Edge:** Plain

Date	Mintage	VF20	XF40	MS60	MS63	MS65
1958	9,750,000	—	0.25	0.50	1.00	2.00
1959	17,350,000	—	0.10	0.25	0.75	1.50
1962	6,160,000	—	0.25	0.75	1.50	3.00
1964	5,860,000	—	0.25	0.75	1.50	3.00
1965	10,320,000	—	0.10	0.25	0.75	1.50
1966	11,040,000	—	0.10	0.25	0.75	1.50
1967	7,200,000	—	0.10	0.25	0.75	1.50
1968	2,000,000	—	0.50	1.00	1.75	3.50
1969	10,000,000	—	0.10	0.25	0.75	1.50
1970	16,000,000	—	0.10	0.25	0.75	1.50
1971	1,250,000	—	0.50	1.00	1.75	3.50
1972	3,000,000	—	0.25	0.50	1.00	2.00
1973	3,000,000	—	0.25	0.50	1.00	2.00
1974	5,000,000	—	0.10	0.25	0.75	1.50
1974 Wide rim	Inc. above	—	0.10	0.25	0.75	1.50
1975	7,000,000	—	0.10	0.25	0.75	1.50
1976	8,000,000	—	0.10	0.25	0.75	1.50
1977	13,000,000	—	0.10	0.20	0.40	0.75
1978	2,500,000	—	0.25	0.50	1.00	2.00
1979	20,000,000	—	0.10	0.20	0.40	0.75
1980	20,000,000	—	0.10	0.20	0.40	0.75
1981	2,000,000	—	0.25	0.50	1.00	2.00
1982	7,000,000	—	0.10	0.25	0.75	1.50
1983	14,100,000	—	0.10	0.20	0.40	0.75
1985	6,000,000	—	0.10	0.20	0.40	0.75
1987	9,000,000	—	0.10	0.20	0.40	0.75

Date	Mintage	VF20	XF40	MS60	MS63	MS65
1988	4,500,000	—	0.10	0.25	0.50	1.00
1989 Sets only	60,000	—	—	—	1.50	3.00
1990 Sets only	60,000	—	—	—	1.50	3.00
1991	6,000,000	—	0.10	0.20	0.40	0.75
1992	7,060,000	—	0.10	0.20	0.40	0.75
1993	10,000,000	—	—	0.15	0.25	0.50
1994	10,000,000	—	—	0.15	0.25	0.50
1995 Sets only	60,000	—	—	—	1.00	2.00
1996	11,000,000	—	—	0.15	0.25	0.50
1997 Sets only	60,000	—	—	—	1.00	2.00
1998	30,000,000	—	—	0.15	0.25	0.50
1999 Sets only	60,000	—	—	—	1.00	2.00
2000 Sets only	60,000	—	—	—	1.00	2.00

KM# 56.1 FRANC

5.00 g., 0.835 Silver 0.1342 oz. ASW, 23 mm. **Obv:** Legend in French **Obv. Legend:** DES BELGES

Date	Mintage	F12	VF20	XF40	MS60	MS63
1904	803,000	5.00	14.00	25.00	60.00	150
1909	2,250,000	4.50	10.00	20.00	35.00	100

KM# 56.2 FRANC

5.00 g., 0.835 Silver 0.1342 oz. ASW, 22.9 mm. **Obv:** Without period in signature

Date	Mintage	F12	VF20	XF40	MS60	MS63
1904	Inc. above	6.00	35.00	100	270	350
1909	Inc. above	4.50	10.00	20.00	40.00	100

KM# 57.1 FRANC

5.00 g., 0.835 Silver 0.1342 oz. ASW **Obv:** Bearded head of Leopold II, left, legend in Dutch **Obv. Legend:** DER BELGEN **Rev:** Denomination above date within wreath

Date	Mintage	F12	VF20	XF40	MS60	MS63
1904	803,000	6.00	17.00	30.00	55.00	120
1909	2,250,000	5.00	12.00	30.00	55.00	110

KM# 57.2 FRANC

5.00 g., 0.835 Silver 0.1342 oz. ASW **Obv:** Bearded head of Leopold II, left, legend in Dutch, without period in signature **Obv. Legend:** DER BELGEN **Rev:** Denomination above date within wreath

Date	Mintage	F12	VF20	XF40	MS60	MS63
1909	Inc. above	5.00	11.00	25.00	36.00	90.00

KM# 72 FRANC

5.00 g., 0.835 Silver 0.1342 oz. ASW **Obv:** Legend in French **Obv. Legend:** DES BELGES **Note:** Prev. KM#72.1.

Date	Mintage	VF20	XF40	MS60	MS63	MS65
1910	2,190,000	7.00	9.00	16.00	32.00	85.00
1911	2,810,000	5.00	7.00	12.00	25.00	55.00
1912	3,250,000	—	—	3.00	5.00	7.00
1913	3,000,000	—	—	3.00	5.00	7.00
1914	10,563,000	—	—	3.00	5.00	7.00
1917	8,540,000	—	550	1,750	3,200	5,500
1918	1,469,000	—	450	1,350	3,000	5,000

KM# 73.1 FRANC

5.00 g., 0.835 Silver 0.1342 oz. ASW, 23 mm. **Obv:** Head of Albert, left, legend in Dutch **Obv. Legend:** DER BELGEN **Rev:** Denomination above date within wreath

Date	Mintage	VF20	XF40	MS60	MS63	MS65
1910	2,750,000	10.00	15.00	30.00	50.00	95.00
1911	2,250,000	—	6.00	12.00	20.00	35.00
1912	3,250,000	—	—	3.00	5.00	7.00
1913	3,000,000	—	—	3.00	5.00	7.00
1914	10,222,000	—	—	3.00	5.00	7.00
1918	—	—	450	1,350	3,000	5,000

KM# 73.2 FRANC

5.00 g., 0.835 Silver 0.1342 oz. ASW, 23 mm. **Obv:** Head of Albert, left, legend in Dutch **Obv. Legend:** DER BELGEN **Rev:** Denomination above date within wreath **Note:** Medal alignment.

Date	Mintage	VF20	XF40	MS60	MS63	MS65
1914	Inc. above	15.00	60.00	150	350	—

KM# 89 FRANC

5.00 g., Nickel, 23 mm. **Obv:** Kneeling figure, legend in French **Obv. Legend:** BELGIQUE **Rev:** Caduceus divides denomination and date **Edge:** Reeded

Date	Mintage	F12	VF20	XF40	MS60	MS63
1922	14,000,000	0.15	0.25	1.00	3.00	5.00
1923	22,500,000	0.15	0.25	1.00	3.00	5.00
1928/3	5,000,000	0.25	1.50	4.00	7.00	15.00
1928/7	Inc. above	0.25	1.50	4.00	7.00	15.00
1928	Inc. above	0.15	0.25	1.00	5.00	10.00
1929	7,415,000	0.15	0.25	1.00	3.50	7.50
1930	5,365,000	0.15	0.25	1.00	5.00	10.00
1931	—	250	650	950	1,300	2,000
1933	1,998,000	0.25	1.50	5.00	15.00	30.00
1934/24	10,263,000	0.25	1.50	4.00	7.00	15.00
1934	Inc. above	0.15	0.25	1.00	3.00	5.00

KM# 90 FRANC

5.00 g., Nickel, 23 mm. **Obv:** Kneeling figure, legend in Dutch **Obv. Legend:** BELGIE **Rev:** Caduceus divides denomination and date **Edge:** Reeded

Date	Mintage	F12	VF20	XF40	MS60	MS63
1922	19,000,000	0.15	0.25	1.00	3.00	5.00
1923/2	17,500,000	0.20	1.50	4.00	7.00	15.00
1923	Inc. above	0.15	0.25	1.00	3.00	5.00
1928/3	4,975,000	0.20	2.00	4.00	9.00	18.00
1928/7	Inc. above	0.20	2.00	4.00	9.00	18.00
1928	Inc. above	0.15	0.50	2.00	7.00	15.00
1929	10,365,000	0.15	0.25	1.00	3.50	7.50
1933	786,000	200	600	900	1,250	2,000
1934/24	8,025,000	0.35	2.50	4.50	7.50	15.00
1934	Inc. above	0.15	0.50	1.00	4.50	7.50
1935/23	2,238,000	1.50	4.00	12.00	22.00	45.00
1935	Inc. above	0.25	0.75	2.00	4.00	6.00

KM# 90.1 FRANC

5.00 g., Nickel, 23 mm. **Obv:** Kneeling figure, legend in Dutch **Obv. Legend:** BELGIE **Rev:** Caduceus divides denomination and date **Edge:** Reeded

Date	Mintage	F12	VF20	XF40	MS60	MS63
1934	Inc. above	25.00	40.00	60.00	100	200

KM# 119 FRANC

4.50 g., Nickel, 21.5 mm. **Obv:** Three shields, legend in French **Obv. Legend:** BELGIQUE-BELGIE **Rev:** Seated lion, right, facing left above date, denomination to right **Edge:** Reeded

Date	Mintage	F12	VF20	XF40	MS60	MS63
1939	46,865,000	0.15	0.25	0.50	1.00	2.00

KM# 120 FRANC

4.50 g., Nickel, 21.5 mm. **Obv:** Three shields, legend in Dutch **Obv. Legend:** BELGIE-BELGIQUE **Rev:** Seated lion, right, facing left above date, denomination at right **Edge:** Reeded

Date	Mintage	F12	VF20	XF40	MS60	MS63
1939	36,000,000	0.15	0.25	0.50	1.00	2.00
1940	10,865,000	0.20	0.40	0.75	2.00	4.00

KM# 127 FRANC

4.20 g., Zinc, 21.5 mm. **Obv:** Rampant lion, left on shield, legend in French **Obv. Legend:** BELGIQUE-BELGIE **Rev:** Crowned letter "L"s, backs touching, divide denomination, date below **Edge:** Reeded **Note:** German Occupation WW II.

Date	Mintage	F12	VF20	XF40	MS60	MS63
1941	16,000,000	0.20	0.75	1.50	15.00	25.00
1942	25,000,000	0.20	0.75	1.50	6.00	10.00
1943	28,000,000	0.20	0.75	1.50	6.00	10.00
1947	3,175,000	75.00	300	800	1,600	1,000

KM# 128 FRANC

4.30 g., Zinc, 21.7 mm. **Obv:** Rampant lion, left, on shield, legend in Dutch **Obv. Legend:** BELGIE-BELGIQUE **Rev:** Crowned "L"s, backs touching, divide denomination, date below **Edge:** Reeded

Date	Mintage	F12	VF20	XF40	MS60	MS63
1942	42,000,000	0.20	0.75	1.50	6.00	10.00
1943	28,000,000	0.20	0.75	1.50	6.00	10.00
1944	24,190,000	0.20	0.75	1.50	6.00	10.00
1945	15,930,000	0.20	1.00	4.00	15.00	25.00
1946	36,000,000	0.20	0.75	1.50	6.00	18.00
1947	3,000,000	25.00	40.00	100	200	350

KM# 142.1 FRANC

4.00 g., Copper-Nickel, 21 mm. **Obv:** Plant divides denomination , crown at top, legend in French **Obv. Legend:** BELGIQUE **Rev:** Laureate bust, left, small symbol at right, date at left **Edge:** Reeded

Date	Mintage	VF20	XF40	MS60	MS63	MS65
1950	13,630,000	—	0.10	2.50	5.00	8.00
1951	51,025,000	—	0.10	1.00	3.00	5.00
1952	53,205,000	—	0.10	2.00	4.50	7.00
1954	4,980,000	0.10	0.25	1.00	3.00	5.00
1955	3,960,000	0.10	0.25	0.50	1.00	2.50
1956	10,000,000	—	0.10	0.25	0.50	1.00
1958	31,750,000	—	0.10	0.25	0.50	1.00
1959	9,000,000	—	0.10	0.25	0.50	1.00
1960	10,000,000	—	0.10	0.25	0.50	1.00
1961	5,030,000	—	0.10	3.00	1.00	2.50
1962	12,250,000	—	0.10	0.25	0.50	1.00
1963	18,700,000	—	0.10	0.25	0.50	1.00
1964	10,110,000	—	0.10	0.25	0.50	1.00
1965	10,185,000	—	0.10	0.25	0.50	1.00
1966	16,430,000	—	0.10	0.25	0.50	1.00
1967	32,945,000	—	0.10	0.25	0.50	1.00
1968	8,000,000	—	0.10	0.25	0.50	1.00
1969	21,950,000	—	0.10	0.25	0.50	1.00
1970	35,500,000	—	0.10	0.15	0.25	0.50
1971	10,000,000	—	0.10	0.15	0.25	0.50
1972	35,000,000	—	0.10	0.15	0.25	0.50
1973	42,500,000	—	0.10	0.15	0.25	0.50
1974	30,000,000	—	0.10	0.15	0.25	0.50
1975	80,000,000	—	0.10	0.15	0.25	0.50
1976	18,000,000	—	0.10	0.15	0.25	0.50
1977	68,500,000	—	0.10	0.15	0.25	0.50
1978	47,500,000	—	0.10	0.15	0.25	0.50
1979	25,000,000	—	0.10	0.15	0.25	0.50
1980	66,500,000	—	0.10	0.15	0.25	0.50
1981	2,000,000	0.20	0.50	1.00	3.00	6.00
1988	17,500,000	—	0.10	0.15	0.25	0.50

KM# 142.2 FRANC

4.00 g., Copper-Nickel, 21 mm. **Obv:** Plant divides denomination, crown at top, legend in French **Obv. Legend:** BELGIQUE **Rev:** Laureate bust, left, date at left, small symbol at right **Edge:** Reeded **Note:** Medal alignment.

Date	Mintage	VF20	XF40	MS60	MS63	MS65
1952	Inc. above	—	—	10.00	30.00	60.00
1959	Inc. above	—	—	10.00	30.00	60.00
1963	Inc. above	—	—	10.00	30.00	60.00
1965	Inc. above	—	—	10.00	30.00	60.00
1970	Inc. above	—	—	10.00	30.00	60.00
1974	Inc. above	—	—	10.00	30.00	60.00
1977	Inc. above	—	—	10.00	30.00	60.00

Date	Mintage	VF20	XF40	MS60	MS63	MS65
1978	Inc. above	—	—	10.00	30.00	60.00
1979	Inc. above	—	—	10.00	30.00	60.00

KM# 143.1 FRANC

4.00 g., Copper-Nickel, 21 mm. **Obv:** Plant divides denomination, crown at top, legend in Dutch **Obv. Legend:** BELGIE **Rev:** Laureate bust, left, date at left, small symbol at right **Edge:** Reeded

Date	Mintage	VF20	XF40	MS60	MS63	MS65
1950	10,000,000	—	0.10	2.00	5.00	9.00
1951	53,750,000	—	0.10	1.00	3.00	5.00
1952	49,145,000	—	0.10	2.00	4.50	7.00
1953	9,915,000	—	0.10	0.50	1.50	3.00
1954	4,940,000	0.10	0.25	2.00	4.00	6.00
1955	3,960,000	0.10	0.25	2.50	5.00	8.00
1956	10,040,000	—	0.10	0.25	0.50	1.00
1957	18,315,000	—	0.10	0.25	0.50	1.00
1958	17,365,000	—	0.10	0.25	0.50	1.00
1959	5,830,000	—	0.10	0.50	1.00	2.00
1960	5,555,000	—	0.10	0.50	1.50	3.00
1961	9,350,000	—	0.10	0.25	0.50	1.00
1962	10,720,000	—	0.10	0.25	0.50	1.00
1963	23,460,000	—	0.10	0.25	0.50	1.00
1964	7,430,000	—	0.10	0.25	0.50	1.00
1965	11,190,000	—	0.10	0.25	0.50	1.00
1966	20,990,000	—	0.10	0.25	0.50	1.00
1967	27,470,000	—	0.10	0.25	0.50	1.00
1968	8,170,000	—	0.10	0.25	0.50	1.00
1969	21,730,000	—	0.10	0.25	0.50	1.00
1970	35,730,000	—	0.10	0.15	0.25	0.50
1971	10,000,000	—	0.10	0.15	0.25	0.50
1972	35,000,000	—	0.10	0.15	0.25	0.50
1973	42,500,000	—	0.10	0.15	0.25	0.50
1974	30,000,000	—	0.10	0.15	0.25	0.50
1975	80,000,000	—	0.10	0.15	0.25	0.50
1976	18,000,000	—	0.10	0.15	0.25	0.50
1977	68,500,000	—	0.10	0.15	0.25	0.50
1978	47,500,000	—	0.10	0.15	0.25	0.50
1979	50,000,000	—	0.10	0.15	0.25	0.50
1980	66,500,000	—	0.10	0.15	0.25	0.50
1981	2,000,000	0.10	0.25	2.00	4.00	6.00
1988	17,500,000	—	0.10	0.15	0.25	0.50

KM# 143.2 FRANC

4.00 g., Copper-Nickel, 21 mm. **Obv:** Plant divides denomination, crown at top, legend in Dutch **Obv. Legend:** BELGIE **Rev:** Laureate bust, left, date at left, small symbol at right **Edge:** Reeded **Note:** Medal alignment.

Date	Mintage	VF20	XF40	MS60	MS63	MS65
1952	Inc. above	—	—	10.00	30.00	60.00
1958	Inc. above	—	—	10.00	30.00	60.00
1970	Inc. above	—	—	10.00	30.00	60.00
1971	Inc. above	—	—	10.00	30.00	60.00
1973	Inc. above	—	—	10.00	30.00	60.00
1979	Inc. above	—	—	10.00	30.00	60.00

KM# 170 FRANC

2.77 g., Nickel Plated Iron, 18 mm. **Obv:** Head left, French legend **Obv. Legend:** BAUDOUIN I **Rev:** Center symbol divides Crown on left from denomination on right and dates, legend in French **Rev. Legend:** BELGIQUE

Date	Mintage	VF20	XF40	MS60	MS63	MS65
1989	200,060,000	—	—	—	—	0.35
1989 medal alignment	—	—	—	10.00	30.00	60.00
1990	200,060,000	—	—	—	—	0.35
1991	200,060,000	—	—	—	—	0.35
1991 medal alignment	—	—	—	10.00	30.00	60.00
1992 Sets only	60,000	—	—	—	—	18.00
1993	15,060,000	—	—	—	—	0.35

KM# 171 FRANC

2.75 g., Nickel Plated Iron, 18 mm. **Obv:** Head left, small mark lower right, legend in Dutch **Obv. Legend:** BOUDEWIJN I **Rev:** Center symbol divides Crown at left from denomination at right and dates, legend in Dutch **Rev. Legend:** BELGIE

Date	Mintage	VF20	XF40	MS60	MS63	MS65
1989	200,060,000	—	—	—	—	0.35
1989 medal alignment	—	—	—	10.00	30.00	60.00
1990	200,060,000	—	—	—	—	0.35
1990 medal alignment	—	—	—	10.00	30.00	60.00
1991	200,060,000	—	—	—	—	0.35
1991 medal alignment	—	—	—	10.00	30.00	60.00
1992 Sets only	60,000	—	—	—	—	18.00
1993	15,060,000	—	—	—	—	0.35

KM# 187 FRANC

2.75 g., Nickel Plated Iron, 18 mm. **Ruler:** Albert II **Obv:** Head left, outline around back of head **Rev:** Vertical line divides date and large denomination, legend in French **Rev. Legend:** BELGIQUE **Note:** Mint mark: angel head. Unknown mintmaster's privy mark: scales.

Date	Mintage	VF20	XF40	MS60	MS63	MS65
1994	75,060,000	—	—	—	—	0.30
1995	75,060,000	—	—	—	—	0.30
1996	75,060,000	—	—	—	—	0.30
1997	95,060,000	—	—	—	—	0.30
1998	75,060,000	—	—	—	—	0.30
1999 Sets only	60,000	—	—	—	—	3.00
1999	5,000	PF65 25.00				
Note: Medal alignment						
2000 Sets only	60,000	—	—	—	—	3.00
2000	5,000	PF65 25.00				
Note: Medal alignment						

KM# 188 FRANC

2.75 g., Nickel Plated Iron, 18 mm. **Ruler:** Albert II **Obv:** Head left, outline around back of head **Rev:** Vertical line divides date and large denomination, legend in Dutch **Rev. Legend:** BELGIE **Edge:** Plain

Date	Mintage	VF20	XF40	MS60	MS63	MS65
1994	75,060,000	—	—	—	—	0.30
1995	75,060,000	—	—	—	—	0.30
1996	95,060,000	—	—	—	—	0.30
1997	95,060,000	—	—	—	—	0.30
1998	75,060,000	—	—	—	—	0.30
1999 Sets only	60,000	—	—	—	—	3.00
1999	5,000	PF65 25.00				
Note: Medal alignment						
2000 Sets only	60,000	—	—	—	—	3.00
2000	5,000	PF65 25.00				
Note: Medal alignment						

KM# 58.1 2 FRANCS (2 Frank)

10.00 g., 0.835 Silver 0.2685 oz. ASW, 27.15 mm. **Obv:** Legend in French **Obv. Legend:** DES BELGES

Date	Mintage	F12	VF20	XF40	MS60	MS63
1904	400,000	11.00	25.00	90.00	155	325
1909	1,088,000	10.00	14.00	36.00	65.00	100

KM# 58.2 2 FRANCS (2 Frank)

10.00 g., 0.835 Silver 0.2685 oz. ASW **Obv:** Without period in signature, Legend in French **Obv. Legend:** DES BELGES

Date	Mintage	F12	VF20	XF40	MS60	MS63
1904	Inc. above	12.00	60.00	180	270	600

KM# 59 2 FRANCS (2 Frank)

10.00 g., 0.835 Silver 0.2685 oz. ASW **Obv:** Bearded head of Leopold II, left, legend in Dutch **Obv. Legend:** DER BELGEN **Rev:** Denomination above date within wreath

Date	Mintage	F12	VF20	XF40	MS60	MS63
1904	400,000	11.00	25.00	65.00	120	300
1909	1,088,000	10.00	14.00	36.00	65.00	100

KM# 74 2 FRANCS (2 Frank)

10.00 g., 0.835 Silver 0.2685 oz. ASW **Obv:** Head of Albert, left, legend in French **Obv. Legend:** DES BELGES **Rev:** Denomination above date within wreath

Date	Mintage	VF20	XF40	MS60	MS63	MS65
1910	800,000	14.00	48.00	85.00	120	—
1911	1,000,000	11.00	25.00	42.00	65.00	—
1912	375,000	18.00	48.00	70.00	115	—

KM# 75 2 FRANCS (2 Frank)

10.00 g., 0.835 Silver 0.2685 oz. ASW **Obv:** Head of Albert, left, legend in Dutch **Obv. Legend:** DER BELGEN **Rev:** Denomination above date within wreath

Date	Mintage	VF20	XF40	MS60	MS63	MS65
1911	1,775,000	10.00	14.00	30.00	48.00	—
1912	375,000	14.00	25.00	60.00	100	—

KM# 91.1 2 FRANCS (2 Frank)

10.00 g., Nickel, 27 mm. **Obv:** Kneeling figure, legend in French **Obv. Legend:** BELGIQUE **Rev:** Caduceus divides denomination and date **Edge:** Reeded

Date	Mintage	F12	VF20	XF40	MS60	MS63
1923	7,500,000	0.50	2.00	10.00	25.00	45.00
1930/20	1,250,000	12.00	60.00	140	250	500
1930	Inc. above	10.00	50.00	125	200	400

KM# 91.2 2 FRANCS (2 Frank)

10.00 g., Nickel, 27 mm. **Obv:** Kneeling figure, legend in French **Obv. Legend:** BELGIQUE **Rev:** Caduceus divides denomination and date **Edge:** Reeded **Note:** Medal alignment

Date	Mintage	F12	VF20	XF40	MS60	MS63
1923	Inc. above	5.00	8.00	45.00	110	200

KM# 92 2 FRANCS (2 Frank)

10.00 g., Nickel, 27 mm. **Obv:** Kneeling figure, legend in Dutch **Obv. Legend:** BELGIE **Rev:** Caduceus divides denomination and date **Edge:** Reeded

Date	Mintage	F12	VF20	XF40	MS60	MS63
1923	6,500,000	0.25	3.00	8.00	15.00	25.00
1924	1,000,000	5.00	10.00	25.00	60.00	90.00
1930/20	1,252,000	15.00	55.00	140	250	360
1930	Inc. above	8.00	45.00	125	200	300

KM# 133 2 FRANCS (2 Frank)

2.75 g., Zinc Coated Steel, 19 mm. **Obv:** Sprays below legend, small star at top, legend in French **Obv. Legend:** BELGIQUE-BELGIE **Rev:** Denomination flanked by sprays, date below **Edge:** Plain **Note:** Allied Occupation issue. Made in U.S.A. on blanks for 1943 cents.

Date	Mintage	F12	VF20	XF40	MS60	MS63
1944	25,000,000	0.25	0.50	1.50	5.00	10.00

KM# 133a 2 FRANCS (2 Frank)

3.58 g., Silver, 19 mm. **Note:** Made in error in U.S.A. on blanks for Netherlands 25 cents.

Date	Mintage	F12	VF20	XF40	MS60	MS63
1944	—	200	300	450	625	750

KM# 97.1 5 FRANCS (5 Frank)

13.80 g., Nickel, 31 mm. **Obv:** Head of Albert, left **Obv. Legend:** DES BELGES **Rev:** Wreath surrounds denomination and date, crown at top, value: UN BELGA **Note:** All dates exist in position A and B, values are the same.

Date	Mintage	F12	VF20	XF40	MS60	MS63
1930	1,600,000	1.50	6.00	8.00	50.00	80.00
1931	9,032,000	1.00	4.00	6.00	25.00	40.00
1932	3,600,000	1.50	7.00	10.00	60.00	90.00
1933	1,387,000	6.00	15.00	40.00	90.00	145
1934	1,000,000	30.00	75.00	250	425	900

KM# 97.2 5 FRANCS (5 Frank)

14.00 g., Nickel, 31 mm. **Obv:** Head of Albert, left **Obv. Legend:** DES BELGES **Rev:** Wreath surrounds denomination and date, crown at top,k value: UN BELGA **Note:** Medal alignment. Edge varieties exist.

Date	Mintage	F12	VF20	XF40	MS60	MS63
1930	Inc. above	17.50	30.00	50.00	150	350

KM# 98 5 FRANCS (5 Frank)

14.00 g., Nickel, 31 mm. **Obv:** Head of Albert, legend in Dutch **Obv. Legend:** DER BELGEN **Rev:** Denomination and date within wreath, Crown at top, value: EEN BELGA **Note:** All dates exist in position A and B, values are the same.

Date	Mintage	F12	VF20	XF40	MS60	MS63
1930	5,086,000	2.00	8.00	25.00	50.00	75.00
1931	5,336,000	1.50	6.00	15.00	30.00	50.00
1932	3,683,000	1.50	7.00	20.00	40.00	75.00
1933	2,514,000	8.00	20.00	75.00	150	300

KM# 108 5 FRANCS (5 Frank)

11.80 g., Nickel, 31 mm. **Rev:** Crown above denomination, sprays below **Rev. Legend:** BELGIQUE **Edge:** Lettered **Note:** Both dates exist in position A and B, values are the same. Prev. KM#108.1.

Date	Mintage	F12	VF20	XF40	MS60	MS63
1936	650,000	6.00	25.00	50.00	75.00	100
1937	1,848,000	6.00	20.00	40.00	60.00	90.00

KM# 109.1 5 FRANCS (5 Frank)

12.00 g., Nickel, 31 mm. **Obv:** Head of Leopold III, left, small date, lower right **Rev:** Crown above denomination, sprays below, legend in Dutch **Rev. Legend:** BELGIE **Note:** Both dates exist in position A and B, values are the same.

Date	Mintage	F12	VF20	XF40	MS60	MS63
1936	2,498,000	4.00	10.00	15.00	35.00	60.00

KM# 109.2 5 FRANCS (5 Frank)

21.00 g., Nickel, 31 mm. **Obv:** Head of Leopold III, left, small date, lower right **Rev:** Crown above denomination, sprays below, legend in Dutch **Rev. Legend:** BELGIE **Note:** Medal alignment. Edge varieties exist.

Date	Mintage	F12	VF20	XF40	MS60	MS63
1936	Inc. above	15.00	30.00	50.00	150	325

KM# 116.1 5 FRANCS (5 Frank)

9.00 g., Nickel, 25 mm. **Obv:** Three shields, legend in French **Obv. Legend:** BELGIQUE-BELGIE **Rev:** Seated lion, right, looking left, denomination at right, date below **Note:** Milled edge, lettering with crown.

Date	Mintage	F12	VF20	XF40	MS60	MS63
1938 Position A	11,419,000	0.20	1.50	3.50	7.00	15.00
1938 Position B	Inc. above	0.30	2.00	4.00	9.00	18.00

KM# 116.2 5 FRANCS (5 Frank)

9.00 g., Nickel, 25 mm. **Obv:** Three shields, legend in French **Obv. Legend:** BELGIQUE-BELGIE **Rev:** Seated lion, right, looking left, denomination at right, date below **Note:** Milled edge, lettering with star.

Date	Mintage	F12	VF20	XF40	MS60	MS63
1938 Position A	Inc. above	350	600	1,200	2,000	3,000
1939 Position B	Inc. above	350	600	1,200	2,000	3,000

KM# 116.3 5 FRANCS (5 Frank)

9.00 g., Nickel, 25 mm. **Obv:** Three shields, legend in French **Obv. Legend:** BELGIQUE-BELGIE **Rev:** Seated lion, right, looking left, denomination at right, date below **Note:** Milled edge, without lettering (error).

Date	Mintage	F12	VF20	XF40	MS60	MS63
1938	Inc. above	20.00	40.00	70.00	135	300

KM# 117.1 5 FRANCS (5 Frank)

9.00 g., Nickel, 25 mm. **Obv:** Three shields, legend in Dutch **Obv. Legend:** BELGIE-BELGIQUE **Rev:** Seated lion, right, looking left, date below, denomination at right **Note:** Milled edge, lettering with crown.

Date	Mintage	F12	VF20	XF40	MS60	MS63
1938 Position A	3,200,000	10.00	20.00	50.00	80.00	140
1938 Position B	Inc. above	10.00	20.00	50.00	80.00	140
1939 Position A	8,219,000	10.00	20.00	50.00	80.00	140
1939 Position B	Inc. above	10.00	20.00	50.00	80.00	140

KM# 117.2 5 FRANCS (5 Frank)

9.00 g., Nickel **Obv:** Three shields, legend in Dutch **Obv. Legend:** BELGIE-BELGIQUE **Rev:** Seated lion, right, looking left, date below, denomination at right **Note:** Milled edge, lettering with star.

Date	Mintage	F12	VF20	XF40	MS60	MS63
1938 Position B	Inc. above	12.00	25.00	60.00	90.00	160
1938 Position A	Inc. above	12.00	25.00	60.00	90.00	160
1939 Position A	Inc. above	0.15	0.50	2.00	3.00	7.50
1939 Position B	Inc. above	0.15	0.50	2.00	3.00	7.50

KM# 117.3 5 FRANCS (5 Frank)

9.00 g., Nickel, 25 mm. **Obv:** Three shields, legend in Dutch **Obv. Legend:** BELGIE-BELGIQUE **Rev:** Seated lion, right, looking left, date below, denomination at right **Note:** Milled edge, without lettering (error).

Date	Mintage	F12	VF20	XF40	MS60	MS63
1939	Inc. above	30.00	60.00	175	350	500

KM# 129.1 5 FRANCS (5 Frank)

6.00 g., Zinc, 25 mm. **Obv:** Head of Leopold III, right, legend in French **Obv. Legend:** DES BELGES **Rev:** Crown above large decorated denomination, flanked by symbols, date at bottom **Edge:** Reeded **Note:** German Occupation WW II.

Date	Mintage	F12	VF20	XF40	MS60	MS63
1941	15,200,000	1.00	2.50	4.00	8.00	15.00
1943	16,236,000	1.00	2.50	4.00	8.00	15.00
1944	1,868,000	6.00	17.00	25.00	40.00	75.00

Date	Mintage	F12	VF20	XF40	MS60	MS63
1945	3,200,000	2.00	5.00	8.00	15.00	30.00
1946	4,452,000	5.00	7.00	12.00	20.00	40.00
1947	3,100,000	30.00	50.00	80.00	150	240

KM# 129.2 5 FRANCS (5 Frank)

6.00 g., Zinc, 25 mm. **Obv:** Head of Leopold III, right, legend in Dutch **Obv. Legend:** DER BELGEN **Rev:** Crown above large decorated denomination flanked by symbols, date at bottom **Note:** Medal alignment.

Date	Mintage	F12	VF20	XF40	MS60	MS63
1943	Inc. above	5.00	12.00	25.00	50.00	130

KM# 130 5 FRANCS (5 Frank)

5.90 g., Zinc, 25 mm. **Obv:** Head of Leopold III, right, legend in Dutch **Obv. Legend:** DER BELGEN **Rev:** Crown above large decorated denomination flanked by symbols, date at bottom **Edge:** Reeded

Date	Mintage	F12	VF20	XF40	MS60	MS63
1941	27,544,000	0.75	1.50	3.00	6.00	12.00
1945	3,200,000	25.00	35.00	75.00	125	200
1946 Rare	4,000,000	—	—	—	—	—
1947	36,000	175	350	600	1,100	1,500

KM# 134.1 5 FRANCS (5 Frank)

6.00 g., Copper-Nickel, 24 mm. **Obv:** Plant divides denomination, Crown at top, legend in French **Obv. Legend:** BELGIQUE **Rev:** Laureate head, left, small diamonds flank date at left, symbol at right **Edge:** Reeded

Date	Mintage	VF20	XF40	MS60	MS63	MS65
1948	5,304,000	2.50	3.50	7.00	15.00	30.00
1949	38,752,000	—	1.00	1.50	3.00	7.50
1950	23,948,000	—	1.00	1.50	3.00	7.50
1958	9,088,000	—	0.50	1.00	2.00	5.00
1961	6,000,000	—	0.50	1.00	2.00	5.00
1962	6,576,000	—	0.50	1.00	2.00	5.00
1963	11,144,000	—	0.50	1.00	2.00	5.00
1964	3,520,000	0.50	1.00	2.00	3.00	7.50
1965	11,988,000	—	0.50	1.00	2.00	5.00
1966	6,772,000	—	0.50	1.00	2.00	5.00
1967	13,268,000	—	0.50	1.00	2.00	5.00
1968	5,192,000	0.35	0.75	1.25	2.50	6.00
1969	22,235,000	—	0.50	1.00	2.00	5.00
1969	Inc. above	2.00	3.00	5.00	10.00	20.00
Note: Without engraver's name						
1970	2,000,000	0.50	1.00	2.00	3.00	7.50
1971	15,000,000	—	—	0.25	0.50	1.00
1972	17,500,000	—	—	0.25	0.50	1.00
1973	10,000,000	—	—	0.25	0.50	1.00
1974	25,000,000	—	—	0.25	0.50	1.00
1975	34,000,000	—	—	0.25	0.50	1.00
1975	—	1.00	2.00	4.00	8.00	16.00
Note: Without engraver's name						
1976	7,500,000	—	—	0.25	0.50	1.00
1977	22,500,000	—	—	0.25	0.50	1.00
1978	27,500,000	—	—	0.25	0.50	1.00
1979	5,000,000	—	0.25	0.35	0.75	1.50
1980	11,000,000	—	—	0.25	0.50	1.00
1981	2,000,000	—	0.50	1.00	2.00	4.00

KM# 135.1 5 FRANCS (5 Frank)

6.00 g., Copper-Nickel, 24 mm. **Obv:** Plant divides denomination, Crown at top, legend in Dutch **Obv. Legend:** BELGIE **Rev:** Laureate head, left, small diamonds flank date at left, symbol at right **Edge:** Reeded

Date	Mintage	VF20	XF40	MS60	MS63	MS65
1948	4,800,000	—	4.00	9.00	16.00	30.00
1948	—	—	6.00	12.00	22.00	40.00
Note: Without engraver's name						
1949	31,500,000	0.50	1.00	2.00	3.00	7.50
1950	34,728,000	0.50	1.00	2.00	3.00	7.50
1958	2,672,000	—	1.50	3.00	6.00	10.00

Date	Mintage	VF20	XF40	MS60	MS63	MS65
1960	5,896,000	—	0.50	1.00	2.00	5.00
1961	4,120,000	0.50	1.00	2.00	3.00	7.50
1962	7,624,000	—	0.50	1.00	2.00	5.00
1963	6,136,000	—	0.50	1.00	2.00	5.00
1964	8,128,000	—	0.50	1.00	2.00	5.00
1965	9,956,000	—	0.50	1.00	2.00	5.00
1966	7,136,000	—	0.50	1.00	2.00	5.00
1966	—	—	4.00	6.00	12.00	20.00
Note: Without engraver's name						
1967	16,132,000	—	0.50	1.00	2.00	5.00
1968	3,200,000	0.50	1.00	2.00	3.00	7.50
1969	21,500,000	—	0.50	1.00	2.00	5.00
1970	2,000,000	0.50	1.00	2.00	3.00	7.50
1971	15,000,000	—	—	0.25	0.50	1.00
1972	17,500,000	—	—	0.25	0.50	1.00
1972	Inc. above	—	2.00	4.00	8.00	15.00
Note: Without engraver's name						
1973	10,000,000	—	—	0.25	0.50	1.00
1974	25,000,000	—	—	0.25	0.50	1.00
1974	—	—	2.00	4.00	8.00	15.00
Note: Without engraver's name						
1975	34,000,000	—	—	0.25	0.50	1.00
1976	7,500,000	—	—	0.25	0.50	1.00
1977	22,500,000	—	—	0.25	0.50	1.00
1978	27,500,000	—	—	0.25	0.50	1.00
1979	10,000,000	—	0.25	0.50	1.00	2.00
1980	11,000,000	—	—	0.25	0.50	1.00
1981	2,000,000	—	0.50	1.00	2.00	4.00

KM# 134.2 5 FRANCS (5 Frank)

6.00 g., Copper-Nickel, 24 mm. **Obv:** Plant divides denomination, Crown at top, legend in French **Obv. Legend:** BELGIQUE **Rev:** Laureate head, left, small diamonds flank date at left, symbol at right **Rev. Legend:** Rau **Edge:** Reeded **Note:** Medal alignment.

Date	Mintage	VF20	XF40	MS60	MS63	MS65
1949	Inc. above	—	4.00	9.00	16.00	30.00
1950	Inc. above	—	4.00	9.00	16.00	30.00
1963	Inc. above	—	4.00	9.00	16.00	30.00
1966	Inc. above	—	4.00	9.00	16.00	30.00
1969	Inc. above	—	4.00	9.00	16.00	30.00
1975	Inc. above	—	4.00	9.00	16.00	30.00

KM# 135.2 5 FRANCS (5 Frank)

6.00 g., Copper-Nickel, 24 mm. **Obv:** Plant divides denomination, Crown at top, legend in French **Obv. Legend:** BELGIQUE **Rev:** Laureate head, left, small diamonds flank date at left, symbol at right **Edge:** Reeded **Note:** Medal alignment.

Date	Mintage	VF20	XF40	MS60	MS63	MS65
1950	Inc. above	—	4.00	9.00	16.00	30.00
1962	Inc. above	—	4.00	9.00	16.00	30.00
1965	Inc. above	—	4.00	9.00	16.00	30.00
1974	Inc. above	—	4.00	9.00	16.00	30.00

KM# 163 5 FRANCS (5 Frank)

5.50 g., Brass or Aluminum-Bronze, 24 mm. **Obv:** Face, left, on divided coin **Rev:** Stylized denomination, date at bottom, legend in French **Rev. Legend:** BELGIQUE

Date	Mintage	VF20	XF40	MS60	MS63	MS65
1986	208,400,000	—	—	0.25	0.45	0.65
1987	22,500,000	—	—	0.25	0.50	1.00
1988	26,500,000	—	—	0.25	0.50	1.00
1989 Sets only	60,000	—	—	—	2.00	4.00
1990 Sets only	60,000	—	—	—	2.00	4.00
1991 Sets only	60,000	—	—	—	2.00	4.00
1992	5,060,000	—	0.25	0.50	1.00	2.00
1993	15,060,000	—	—	0.25	0.50	1.00

KM# 164 5 FRANCS (5 Frank)

5.50 g., Brass or Aluminum-Bronze, 24 mm. **Obv:** Face, left, on divided coin **Rev:** Stylized denomination, date at bottom, legend in Dutch **Rev. Legend:** BELGIE

Date	Mintage	VF20	XF40	MS60	MS63	MS65
1986	208,400,000	—	—	0.25	0.45	0.65
1987	22,500,000	—	—	0.25	0.50	1.00
1988	26,500,000	—	—	0.25	0.50	1.00
1989 Sets only	60,000	—	—	—	2.00	4.00
1990 Sets only	60,000	—	—	—	2.00	4.00
1991 Sets only	60,000	—	—	—	2.00	4.00
1992	5,060,000	—	0.25	0.50	1.00	2.00
1993	15,060,000	—	—	0.25	0.50	1.00

KM# 189 5 FRANCS (5 Frank)

5.50 g., Aluminum-Bronze, 24 mm. **Ruler:** Albert II **Obv:** Head left, outline around back of head **Rev:** Vertical line divides date and denomination, legend in French **Rev. Legend:** BELGIQUE **Note:** Mint mark: angel head. Mintmaster R. Coenen's privy mark: scale.

Date	Mintage	VF20	XF40	MS60	MS63	MS65
1994	15,060,000	—	—	—	0.25	0.50
1995 Sets only	60,000	—	—	—	2.00	4.00
1996	6,860,000	—	—	0.25	0.50	1.00
1997 Sets only	60,000	—	—	—	3.00	5.00
1998	32,560,000	—	—	—	0.25	0.50
1999 Sets only	60,000	—	—	—	2.00	4.00
1999	5,000	PF65 25.00				
Note: Medal alignment						
2000 Sets only	60,000	—	—	—	2.00	4.00
2000	5,000	PF65 25.00				
Note: Medal alignment						

KM# 190 5 FRANCS (5 Frank)

5.50 g., Aluminum-Bronze, 24 mm. **Ruler:** Albert II **Obv:** Head left, outline around back of head **Rev:** Vertical line divides date and large denomination, legend in Dutch **Rev. Legend:** BELGIE **Note:** Mint mark: angel head. Mintmaster R. Coenen's privy mark: scale.

Date	Mintage	VF20	XF40	MS60	MS63	MS65
1994	30,060,000	—	—	—	—	0.50
1995 Sets only	60,000	—	—	—	1.00	2.00
1996	3,133,000	—	—	—	—	1.00
1997 Sets only	60,000	—	—	—	3.00	5.00
1998	6,500,000	—	—	—	—	0.50
1999 Sets only	60,000	—	—	—	2.00	4.00
1999	5,000	PF65 20.00				
Note: Medal alignment						
2000 Sets only	60,000	—	—	—	2.00	4.00
2000	5,000	PF65 25.00				
Note: Medal alignment						

KM# 99 10 FRANCS-10 FRANK (Deux / Twee Belgas)

17.50 g., Nickel, 34 mm. **Subject:** Independence Centennial **Rev:** Legend in French **Rev. Legend:** BELGIQUE **Note:** Exists in position A or B, values are the same.

Date	Mintage	F12	VF20	XF40	MS60	MS63
1930	2,699,000	25.00	65.00	125	200	375

KM# 100 10 FRANCS-10 FRANK (Deux / Twee Belgas)

17.50 g., Nickel, 34 mm. **Obv:** Conjoined heads of Leopold I, Leopold II and Albert I, left, two dates at bottom **Rev:** Denomination flanked by sprays, legend in Dutch **Rev. Legend:** BELGIE **Note:** Exists in position A or B, values are the same.

Date	Mintage	F12	VF20	XF40	MS60	MS63
1930	3,000,000	30.00	70.00	150	250	450

KM# 155.1 10 FRANCS (10 Frank)

8.00 g., Nickel, 27 mm. **Obv:** Head, left **Rev:** Crowned arms divide denomination, date at bottom, legend in French **Rev. Legend:** BELGIQUE **Edge:** Plain **Note:** Mint mark - Angel head. Mintmaster Vogeleer's privy mark - Bird.

Date	Mintage	VF20	XF40	MS60	MS63	MS65
1969	22,235,000	—	—	0.25	0.40	0.70
1970	9,500,000	—	—	0.25	0.40	0.70
1971	15,000,000	—	—	0.25	0.40	0.70
1972	10,000,000	—	—	0.25	0.40	0.70
1973	10,000,000	—	—	0.25	0.40	0.70
1974	5,000,000	—	—	0.30	0.50	1.00
1975	5,000,000	—	—	0.30	0.50	1.00
1976	7,500,000	—	—	0.30	0.50	1.00
1977	7,000,000	—	—	0.30	0.50	1.00
1978	2,500,000	—	0.25	0.50	1.00	2.50
1979	5,000,000	—	—	0.40	0.60	1.50

KM# 155.2 10 FRANCS (10 Frank)

8.00 g., Nickel, 27 mm. **Obv:** Head, left **Rev:** Crowned arms divide denomination, date at bottom, legend in French **Rev. Legend:** BELGIQUE **Edge:** Plain **Note:** Medal alignment. Mint mark - Angel head. Mintmaster Vogeleer's privy mark - Bird.

Date	Mintage	VF20	XF40	MS60	MS63	MS65
1969	Inc. above	—	6.00	12.00	16.00	35.00
1974	Inc. above	—	6.00	12.00	16.00	35.00

KM# 156.1 10 FRANCS (10 Frank)

8.00 g., Nickel, 27 mm. **Obv:** Head, left **Rev:** Crowned arms divide denomination, date at bottom, legend in Dutch **Rev. Legend:** BELGIE **Edge:** Plain **Note:** Mint mark - Angel head. Mintmaster Vogeleer's privy mark - Bird.

Date	Mintage	VF20	XF40	MS60	MS63	MS65
1969	21,500,000	—	—	0.25	0.40	0.70
1970	10,000,000	—	—	0.25	0.40	0.70
1971	15,000,000	—	—	0.25	0.40	0.70
1972	10,000,000	—	—	0.25	0.40	0.70
1973	10,000,000	—	—	0.25	0.40	0.70
1974	5,000,000	—	—	0.30	0.50	1.00
1975	5,000,000	—	—	0.30	0.50	1.00
1976	7,500,000	—	—	0.30	0.50	1.00
1977	7,000,000	—	—	0.30	0.50	1.00
1978	2,500,000	—	0.25	0.50	1.00	2.50
1979	10,000,000	—	—	0.40	0.60	1.50

KM# 156.2 10 FRANCS (10 Frank)

8.00 g., Nickel, 27 mm. **Obv:** Head, left **Rev:** Crowned arms divide denomination, date at bottom, legend in French **Edge:** Plain **Note:** Medal alignment. Struck at Brussels Mint. Mint mark - Angel head. Mintmaster Vogeleer's privy mark - Bird.

Date	Mintage	VF20	XF40	MS60	MS63	MS65
1971	Inc. above	—	6.00	12.00	16.00	35.00
1976	Inc. above	—	6.00	12.00	16.00	35.00
1978	Inc. above	—	6.00	12.00	16.00	35.00

KM# 78 20 FRANCS (20 Frank)

6.45 g., 0.900 Gold 0.1867 oz. AGW **Obv:** Armored bust of Albert, left, legend in French **Obv. Legend:** DES BELGES **Rev:** Crowned arms divide denomination and date

Date	Mintage	F12	VF20	XF40	MS60	MS63
1914 Position A	125,000	—	—	250	350	475
1914 Position B	Inc. above	350	725	950	1,750	—

KM# 79 20 FRANCS (20 Frank)

6.45 g., 0.900 Gold 0.1867 oz. AGW **Obv:** Armored bust of Albert, left, legend in Dutch **Obv. Legend:** DER BELGEN **Rev:** Crowned arms divide denomination and date

Date	Mintage	F12	VF20	XF40	MS60	MS63
1914 Position A	125,000	—	—	250	325	400
1914 Position B	Inc. above	—	—	250	325	400

KM# 101.1 20 FRANCS (20 Frank)

20.00 g., Nickel, 37 mm. **Obv:** Head of Albert, left, legend in French **Obv. Legend:** DES BELGES **Rev:** Crowned arms divide denomination and date **Note:** All dates exist in position A and B, values are the same.

Date	Mintage	F12	VF20	XF40	MS60	MS63
1931	3,957,000	15.00	35.00	75.00	125	200
1932	5,472,000	15.00	35.00	75.00	125	200

KM# 101.2 20 FRANCS (20 Frank)

20.00 g., Nickel, 37 mm. **Obv:** Head of Albert, left, legend in French **Obv. Legend:** DES BELGES **Rev:** Crowned arms divide denomination and date **Note:** Medal alignment. Edge varieties exist.

Date	Mintage	F12	VF20	XF40	MS60	MS63
1932	Inc. above	65.00	125	225	425	650

KM# 102 20 FRANCS (20 Frank)

20.00 g., Nickel, 37 mm. **Obv:** Legend in Dutch **Obv. Legend:** DER BELGEN **Note:** All dates exist in position A and B, values are the same.

Date	Mintage	F12	VF20	XF40	MS60	MS63
1931	2,600,000	20.00	50.00	100	175	225
1932	6,950,000	15.00	35.00	75.00	100	175

KM# 103.1 20 FRANCS (20 Frank)

11.00 g., 0.680 Silver 0.2405 oz. ASW **Obv:** Head of Albert, left, legend in French **Obv. Legend:** DES BELGES **Rev:** Crowned arms divide denomination and date

Date	Mintage	F12	VF20	XF40	MS60	MS63
1933 Position A	200,000	25.00	70.00	120	190	215
1933 Position B	Inc. above	30.00	90.00	145	215	240
1934 Position A	12,300,000	—	8.00	12.00	25.00	42.00
1934 Position B	Inc. above	—	8.00	12.00	25.00	42.00

KM# 103.2 20 FRANCS (20 Frank)

11.00 g., 0.680 Silver 0.2405 oz. ASW **Obv:** Head of Albert, left, legend in French **Obv. Legend:** DES BELGES **Rev:** Crowned arms divide denomination and date **Note:** Medal alignment.

Date	Mintage	F12	VF20	XF40	MS60	MS63
1934	Inc. above	40.00	90.00	160	275	475

KM# 104.1 20 FRANCS (20 Frank)

11.00 g., 0.680 Silver 0.2405 oz. ASW **Obv:** Head of Albert, left, legend in Dutch **Obv. Legend:** DER BELGEN **Rev:** Crowned arms divide denomination and date

Date	Mintage	VF20	XF40	MS60	MS63	MS65
1933 Position B	Inc. above	48.00	95.00	145	240	—
1933 Position A	200,000	36.00	85.00	130	210	—
1934 Position A	12,300,000	4.75	8.00	12.00	18.00	—
1934 Position B	Inc. above	4.75	8.00	12.00	18.00	—

KM# 104.2 20 FRANCS (20 Frank)

11.00 g., 0.680 Silver 0.2405 oz. ASW **Obv:** Head of Albert, left, legend in Dutch **Obv. Legend:** DER BELGEN **Rev:** Crowned arms divide denomination and date **Note:** Medal alignment.

Date	Mintage	VF20	XF40	MS60	MS63	MS65
1934	Inc. above	85.00	150	225	425	650

KM# 105 20 FRANCS (20 Frank)

11.00 g., 0.680 Silver 0.2405 oz. ASW **Obv:** Head of Leopold II left, neck divides date **Rev:** Crown above sprig divides denomination **Note:** Both dates exist in position A and B, values are the same. Coins dated 1934 exist with and without umlauts above E in BELGIE.

Date	Mintage	F12	VF20	XF40	MS60	MS63
1934	1,250,000	4.75	10.00	14.00	25.00	45.00
1935	10,760,000	—	4.75	8.00	12.00	20.00

KM# 140.1 20 FRANCS (20 Frank)

8.00 g., 0.835 Silver 0.2148 oz. ASW, 27 mm. **Obv:** Rampant lion left with shield, denomination below, legend in French **Obv. Legend:** BELGIQUE **Rev:** Helmeted head right, small caduceus divides date at left **Edge:** Reeded

Date	Mintage	VF20	XF40	MS60	MS63	MS65
1949	4,600,000	4.25	7.00	10.00	17.00	25.00
1950	12,957,000	4.25	5.00	8.00	12.00	20.00
1953	3,953,000	4.25	7.00	10.00	17.00	25.00
1954	4,835,000	35.00	65.00	95.00	145	200
1955	1,730,000	650	800	1,000	1,350	1,800

KM# 140.2 20 FRANCS (20 Frank)

8.00 g., 0.835 Silver 0.2148 oz. ASW, 27 mm. **Obv:** Rampant lion left with shield, denomination below, legend in French **Obv. Legend:** BELGIQUE **Rev:** Helmeted head right, small caduceus divides date at left **Edge:** Reeded **Note:** Medal alignment.

Date	Mintage	VF20	XF40	MS60	MS63	MS65
1949	Inc. above	35.00	75.00	90.00	150	—
1950	Inc. above	35.00	75.00	90.00	150	—

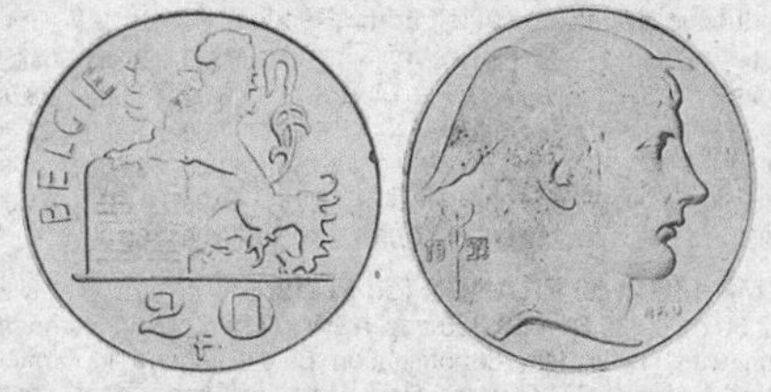

KM# 141.1 20 FRANCS (20 Frank)

8.00 g., 0.835 Silver 0.2148 oz. ASW, 27 mm. **Obv:** Rampant lion left with shield, denomination below, legend in Dutch **Obv. Legend:** BELGIE **Rev:** Helmeted head right, small caduceus divides date at left **Edge:** Reeded

Date	Mintage	VF20	XF40	MS60	MS63	MS65
1949	5,545,000	7.00	10.00	12.00	15.00	20.00
1950	—	350	650	850	1,150	1,500
1951	7,885,000	4.25	5.00	7.00	11.00	15.00
1953	6,625,000	4.25	6.00	8.00	12.00	15.00
1954	5,323,000	30.00	50.00	75.00	135	175
1955	3,760,000	75.00	125	200	250	350

KM# 141.2 20 FRANCS (20 Frank)

8.00 g., 0.835 Silver 0.2148 oz. ASW, 27 mm. **Obv:** Rampant lion left with shield, denomination below, legend in Dutch **Obv. Legend:** BELGIE **Rev:** Helmeted head right, small caduceus divides date at left **Edge:** Reeded **Note:** Medal alignment.

Date	Mintage	VF20	XF40	MS60	MS63	MS65
1949	Inc. above	40.00	60.00	110	160	—
1951	Inc. above	45.00	75.00	125	190	—

KM# 159 20 FRANCS (20 Frank)

8.40 g., Nickel-Bronze, 25.53 mm. **Obv:** Head, left **Rev:** Denomination at right above stylized spray, legend in French **Rev. Legend:** BELGIQUE

Date	Mintage	VF20	XF40	MS60	MS63	MS65
1980	60,000,000	—	0.50	0.75	1.00	2.00
1980	—	3.00	5.00	7.00	15.00	30.00
Note: Medal alignment						
1981	60,000,000	—	0.50	0.70	1.00	2.00
1982	54,000,000	—	0.50	0.70	1.00	2.00
1989 Sets only	60,000	—	—	—	4.00	6.00
1990 Sets only	60,000	—	—	—	4.00	6.00
1991 Sets only	60,000	—	—	—	4.00	6.00
1992	2,610,000	—	0.70	1.00	2.00	4.00
1993	7,540,000	—	0.50	0.75	1.50	3.00

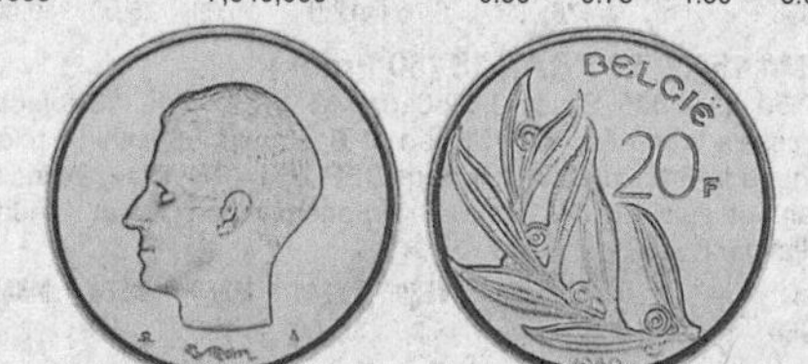

KM# 160 20 FRANCS (20 Frank)

8.56 g., Nickel-Bronze, 25.65 mm. **Obv:** Head, left **Rev:** Denomination at right above stylized spray, legend in Dutch **Rev. Legend:** BELGIE

Date	Mintage	VF20	XF40	MS60	MS63	MS65
1980	60,000,000	—	0.50	0.70	1.00	2.00
1980	—	4.00	8.00	10.00	15.00	30.00
Note: Medal alignment						
1981	60,000,000	—	0.50	0.70	1.00	2.00
1982	54,000,000	—	0.50	0.70	1.00	2.00
1989 Sets only	60,000	—	—	—	4.00	6.00
1990 Sets only	60,000	—	—	—	4.00	6.00
1991 Sets only	60,000	—	—	—	4.00	6.00
1992	2,610,000	—	0.70	1.00	2.00	4.00
1993	7,540,000	—	0.50	0.75	1.50	3.00

KM# 191 20 FRANCS (20 Frank)

8.50 g., Nickel-Bronze, 25.65 mm. **Ruler:** Albert II **Obv:** Head left, outline around back of head **Rev:** Vertical line divides date and large denomination, legend in French **Rev. Legend:** BELGIQUE **Note:** Mint mark: angel head. Mintmaster R. Coenen's privy mark: scale.

Date	Mintage	VF20	XF40	MS60	MS63	MS65
1994	12,560,000	—	0.50	0.75	1.00	1.00
1995 Sets only	60,000	—	—	—	3.00	5.00
1996	14,485,000	—	—	—	0.50	1.00
1997 Sets only	60,000	—	—	—	3.00	5.00
1998	6,500,000	—	—	0.75	1.50	3.00
1999 Sets only	60,000	—	—	—	3.00	5.00
1999	5,000	PF65 25.00				
Note: Medal alignment						
2000 Sets only	60,000	—	—	—	3.00	5.00
2000	5,000	PF65 25.00				
Note: Medal alignment						

KM# 192 20 FRANCS (20 Frank)

8.50 g., Nickel-Bronze, 25.7 mm. **Ruler:** Albert II **Obv:** Head left, outline around back of head **Rev:** Vertical line divides date and large denomination, legend in Dutch **Rev. Legend:** BELGIE **Note:** Mint mark: angel head. Mintmaster R. Coenen's privy mark: scale.

Date	Mintage	VF20	XF40	MS60	MS63	MS65
1994	12,560,000	—	—	—	0.50	1.00
1995 Sets only	60,000	—	—	—	2.50	5.00
1996	3,133,000	—	—	—	0.50	1.00
1997 Sets only	60,000	—	—	—	2.50	5.00
1998	6,500,000	—	—	0.75	1.50	3.00
1999 Sets only	60,000	—	—	—	2.50	5.00
1999	5,000	PF65 25.00				
Note: Medal alignment						
2000 Sets only	60,000	—	—	—	2.50	5.00
2000	5,000	PF65 25.00				
Note: Medal alignment						

KM# 106.1 50 FRANCS (50 Frank)

22.00 g., 0.680 Silver 0.481 oz. ASW, 35 mm. **Subject:** Brussels Exposition and Railway Centennial **Obv:** St. Michael slaying dragon (Brussels' patron saint) **Obv. Legend:** DE BELGIQUE **Rev:** Palais des Expositions, Heysel Park in Brussels. Two dates above, legend in French **Rev. Legend:** DE FER BELGES **Edge Lettering:** SOUS LE REGNE DE LEOPOLD III **Note:** Exists in positions A and B, values are the same.

Date	Mintage	VF20	XF40	MS60	MS63	MS65
1935	140,000	25.00	60.00	85.00	135	200

KM# 106.2 50 FRANCS (50 Frank)
22.00 g., 0.680 Silver 0.481 oz. ASW, 35 mm. **Subject:** Brussels Exposition and Railway Centenial **Obv:** St. Michael slaying dragon (Brussels' patron saint) **Obv. Legend:** DE BELGIQUE **Rev:** Palais des Expositions, Heysel Park in Brussels. Two dates above, legend in French **Rev. Legend:** DE FER BELGES **Edge Lettering:** SOUS LE REGNE DE LEOPOLD III **Note:** Medal alignment. Exists in positions A and B, values are the same.

Date	Mintage	VF20	XF40	MS60	MS63	MS65
1935	Inc. above	450	600	900	1,100	1,400

KM# 107.1 50 FRANCS (50 Frank)
22.00 g., 0.680 Silver 0.481 oz. ASW, 35 mm. **Obv:** St. Michael slaying dragon (Brussels' patron saint) **Obv. Legend:** BELGIE **Rev:** Palais des Expositions, Heysel Park in Brussels. Two dates above, legend in Dutch **Rev. Legend:** DER BELGISCHE **Edge Lettering:** ONDER DE REGEERING VAN KONIG LEOPOLD III **Note:** Exists in positions A and B, values are the same.

Date	Mintage	VF20	XF40	MS60	MS63	MS65
1935	140,000	35.00	75.00	120	165	225

KM# 107.2 50 FRANCS (50 Frank)
22.00 g., 0.680 Silver 0.481 oz. ASW, 35 mm. **Obv:** St. Michael slaying dragon (Brussels' patron saint) **Obv. Legend:** BELGIE **Rev:** Palais des Expositions, Heysel Park in Brussels. Two dates above, legend in Dutch **Rev. Legend:** DER BELGISCHE **Edge Lettering:** ONDER DE*REGEERING VAN KONIG LEOPOLD III **Note:** Medal alignment. Exists in positions A and B, values are the same.

Date	Mintage	VF20	XF40	MS60	MS63	MS65
1935	Inc. above	700	900	1,500	1,750	2,100

KM# 121 50 FRANCS (50 Frank)
20.00 g., 0.835 Silver 0.5369 oz. ASW, 33 mm. **Obv:** Head of Leopold III, left, date below **Rev:** Crown above nine shields dividing denomination, legend in French **Rev. Legend:** BELGIQUE: BELGIE **Note:** Both dates exist in positions A and B, values are the same.

Date	Mintage	F12	VF20	XF40	MS60	MS63
1939	1,000,000	—	10.50	19.00	27.50	48.00
1940	631,000	10.50	22.50	30.00	55.00	95.00

KM# 122.1 50 FRANCS (50 Frank)
20.00 g., 0.835 Silver 0.5369 oz. ASW, 33 mm. **Obv:** Head of Leopold III left, date below **Rev:** Crown above nine shields dividing denomination, legend in Dutch **Rev. Legend:** BELGIE: BELGIQUE **Note:** Both dates exist in positions A and B, values are the same.

Date	Mintage	F12	VF20	XF40	MS60	MS63
1939	1,000,000	—	10.50	19.00	27.50	48.00
1940	631,000	10.50	22.50	30.00	55.00	95.00

KM# 122.2 50 FRANCS (50 Frank)
20.00 g., 0.835 Silver 0.5369 oz. ASW, 33 mm. **Obv:** Head of Leopold III left, date below **Rev:** Crown above nine shields dividing denomination, legend in French, without cross on crown **Rev. Legend:** BELGIE: BELGIQUE **Note:** Both dates exist in positions A and B, values are the same.

Date	Mintage	F12	VF20	XF40	MS60	MS63
1939	Inc. above	19.00	36.00	48.00	70.00	120
1940	Inc. above	19.00	36.00	48.00	70.00	120

KM# 122.3 50 FRANCS (50 Frank)
20.00 g., 0.835 Silver 0.5369 oz. ASW, 33 mm. **Obv:** Head of Leopold III left, date below **Rev:** Triangle in third arms from left, cross on crown **Rev. Legend:** BELGIE: BELGIQUE **Note:** Both dates exist in positions A and B, values are the same.

Date	Mintage	F12	VF20	XF40	MS60	MS63
1940	Inc. above	22.50	42.00	70.00	120	170

KM# 122.4 50 FRANCS (50 Frank)
20.00 g., 0.835 Silver 0.5369 oz. ASW, 33 mm. **Obv:** Head of Leopold III, left, date below **Rev:** Without cross on crown and with triangle in third arms from left **Rev. Legend:** BEGIE: BELGIQUE **Note:** Both dates exist in positions A and B, values are the same.

Date	Mintage	F12	VF20	XF40	MS60	MS63
1940	Inc. above	30.00	90.00	140	225	400

KM# 136.1 50 FRANCS (50 Frank)
12.50 g., 0.835 Silver 0.3356 oz. ASW, 30 mm. **Obv:** Rampant lion with shield, left, denomination below, legend in French **Obv. Legend:** BELGIQUE **Rev:** Helmeted head, right, small caduceus divides date at left **Edge:** Reeded

Date	Mintage	VF20	XF40	MS60	MS63	MS65
1948	2,000,000	—	6.75	8.00	14.00	28.00
1949	4,354,000	—	6.75	7.00	12.00	24.00
1950	—	450	750	1,200	2,500	—
1951	2,904,000	—	6.75	7.00	12.00	24.00
1954	3,232,000	14.00	25.00	36.00	60.00	

KM# 136.2 50 FRANCS (50 Frank)
12.50 g., 0.835 Silver 0.3356 oz. ASW, 30 mm. **Obv:** Rampant lion with shield, left, denomination below, legend in French **Obv. Legend:** BELGIQUE **Rev:** Helmeted head, right, small caduceus divides date at left **Edge:** Reeded **Note:** Medal alignment.

Date	Mintage	VF20	XF40	MS60	MS63	MS65
1949	Inc. above	35.00	65.00	120	220	300

KM# 137 50 FRANCS (50 Frank)
12.50 g., 0.835 Silver 0.3356 oz. ASW, 30 mm. **Obv:** Rampant lion with shield left, denomination below, legend in Dutch **Obv. Legend:** BELGIE **Rev:** Helmeted head right, small caduceus divides date at left **Edge:** Reeded

Date	Mintage	VF20	XF40	MS60	MS63	MS65
1948	3,000,000	—	6.75	8.00	14.00	16.00
1950	4,110,000	—	6.75	7.00	12.00	15.00
1951	1,698,000	—	6.75	9.00	15.00	17.00
1954	2,978,000	—	6.75	7.00	12.00	15.00

KM# 150.1 50 FRANCS (50 Frank)
12.50 g., 0.835 Silver 0.3356 oz. ASW, 30 mm. **Subject:** Brussels World Fair **Obv:** Head of Baudouin, left, within circle, legend in French **Obv. Legend:** DES BELGES **Rev:** World's Fair, Steeple divides date from denomination

Date	Mintage	VF20	XF40	MS60	MS63	MS65
1958	476,000	6.75	12.00	15.00	25.00	40.00

KM# 150.2 50 FRANCS (50 Frank)
12.50 g., 0.835 Silver 0.3356 oz. ASW, 30 mm. **Subject:** Brussels World Fair **Obv:** Head of Baudouin left within circle, legend in French **Obv. Legend:** DES BELGES **Rev:** World's Fair, steeple divides date and denomination **Note:** Medal alignment.

Date	Mintage	VF20	XF40	MS60	MS63	MS65
1958	Inc. above	45.00	90.00	125	180	250

KM# 151.1 50 FRANCS (50 Frank)
12.50 g., 0.835 Silver 0.3356 oz. ASW, 29 mm. **Obv:** Head of Baudouin, left, within circle, legend in Dutch **Obv. Legend:** DER BELGEN **Rev:** World's Fair, Steeple divides date from denomination **Edge:** Reeded

Date	Mintage	VF20	XF40	MS60	MS63	MS65
1958	382,000	6.75	12.00	14.00	22.00	36.00

KM# 151.2 50 FRANCS (50 Frank)
12.50 g., 0.835 Silver 0.3356 oz. ASW, 29 mm. **Obv:** Head of Baudouin, left, within circle, legend in Dutch **Obv. Legend:** DER BELGEN **Rev:** World's Fair, Steeple divides date from denomination **Edge:** Reeded **Note:** Medal alignment.

Date	Mintage	VF20	XF40	MS60	MS63	MS65
1958	Inc. above	35.00	75.00	100	135	285

KM# 152.1 50 FRANCS (50 Frank)
12.50 g., 0.835 Silver 0.3356 oz. ASW, 29 mm. **Subject:** King Baudouin's marriage to Doña Fabiola de Mora y Aragon **Obv:** Conjoined heads of King Baudoin and Doña Fabiola de Mora y Aragon, left **Rev:** Arms flanked by sprays divide Crown and denomination

Date	Mintage	F12	VF20	XF40	MS60	MS63
1960	500,000	—	6.75	12.00	14.00	16.00

KM# 152.2 50 FRANCS (50 Frank)
12.50 g., 0.835 Silver 0.3356 oz. ASW, 29 mm. **Subject:** King Baudouin's marriage to Doña Fabiola de Mora y Aragon **Obv:** Conjoined heads of King Baudoin and Doña Fabiola de Mora y Aragon, left **Rev:** Arms flanked by sprays divide Crown and denomination **Note:** Medal alignment.

Date	Mintage	F12	VF20	XF40	MS60	MS63
1960	Inc. above	13.50	30.00	50.00	100	135

KM# 168 50 FRANCS (50 Frank)
7.00 g., Nickel, 22.75 mm. **Ruler:** Baudouin I **Obv:** Face left on divided coin **Rev:** Denomination, date at bottom, legend in French **Rev. Legend:** BELGIQUE **Edge:** Reeded

Date	Mintage	VF20	XF40	MS60	MS63	MS65
1987	30,000,000	—	—	2.00	3.00	5.00
1988	3,500,000	—	—	2.00	4.00	7.00
1989	15,060,000	—	—	2.00	3.00	5.00
1990	15,060,000	—	—	2.00	3.00	5.00
1991	3,500,000	—	—	2.00	3.50	6.00
1992	15,060,000	—	—	2.00	3.00	5.00
1993	15,060,000	—	—	2.00	3.00	5.00

KM# 169 50 FRANCS (50 Frank)
7.00 g., Nickel, 22.75 mm. **Ruler:** Baudouin I **Obv:** Face, left, on divided coin **Rev:** Denomination, date at bottom **Rev. Legend:** BELGIE

Date	Mintage	VF20	XF40	MS60	MS63	MS65
1987	30,000,000	—	—	2.00	3.00	5.00
1988	3,500,000	—	—	2.00	4.00	7.00
1989	15,060,000	—	—	2.00	3.00	5.00
1990	15,060,000	—	—	2.00	3.00	5.00
1991	3,500,000	—	—	2.00	3.50	6.00
1992	15,060,000	—	—	2.00	3.00	5.00
1993	15,060,000	—	—	2.00	3.00	5.00

KM# 193 50 FRANCS (50 Frank)

7.00 g., Nickel, 22.7 mm. **Ruler:** Albert II **Obv:** Head left, outline around back of head **Rev:** Vertical line divides large denomination and date, legend in French **Rev. Legend:** BELGIQUE **Note:** Mint mark: angel head. Mintmaster R. Coenen's privy mark: scale.

Date	Mintage	VF20	XF40	MS60	MS63	MS65
1994	5,060,000	—	—	2.00	3.00	5.00
1995 Sets only	60,000	—	—	—	—	8.00
1996 Sets only	60,000	—	—	—	—	8.00
1997 Sets only	60,000	—	—	—	—	8.00
1998	3,060,000	—	—	2.00	3.00	5.00
1999 Sets only	60,000	—	—	—	—	8.00
1999	5,000	PF65 20.00				
Note: Medal alignment						
2000 Sets only	60,000	—	—	—	—	8.00
2000	5,000	PF65 20.00				
Note: Medal alignment						

KM# 194 50 FRANCS (50 Frank)

7.00 g., Nickel, 22.75 mm. **Ruler:** Albert II **Obv:** Head left, outline around back of head **Rev:** Vertical line divides large denomination and date, legend in Dutch **Rev. Legend:** BELGIE **Note:** Mint mark: angel head. Mintmaster R. Coenen's privy mark: scale.

Date	Mintage	VF20	XF40	MS60	MS63	MS65
1994	5,060,000	—	—	2.00	3.00	5.00
1995 Sets only	60,000	—	—	—	—	8.00
1996 Sets only	60,000	—	—	—	—	8.00
1997 Sets only	60,000	—	—	—	—	8.00
1998	3,060,000	—	—	2.00	3.00	5.00
1999 Sets only	60,000	—	—	—	—	8.00
1999	5,000	PF65 25.00				
Note: Medal alignment						
2000 Sets only	60,000	—	—	—	—	8.00
2000	5,000	PF65 25.00				
Note: Medal alignment						

KM# 213.1 50 FRANCS (50 Frank)

7.00 g., Nickel, 22.75 mm. **Ruler:** Albert II **Subject:** European Soccer Championship **Obv:** Head of Albert II left **Rev:** Soccer ball, legend in French **Rev. Legend:** BELGIQUE **Edge:** Coarse reeding

Date	Mintage	VF20	XF40	MS60	MS63	MS65
2000	500,000	—	—	—	3.50	6.00

KM# 213.2 50 FRANCS (50 Frank)

7.00 g., Nickel, 22.75 mm. **Ruler:** Albert II **Subject:** Eurpoean Soccer Championship **Obv:** Head of Albert II left **Rev:** Soccer ball, legend in French **Rev. Legend:** BELGIQUE **Edge:** Coarse reeding **Note:** Medal alignment.

Date	Mintage	VF20	XF40	MS60	MS63	MS65
2000	20,000	PF65 20.00				
Note: In the "Euro 2000" sets only						

KM# 214.1 50 FRANCS (50 Frank)

7.00 g., Nickel, 22.75 mm. **Ruler:** Albert II **Subject:** European Soccer Championship **Obv:** Head of Albert II, left, rear of head outlined **Rev:** Soccer ball, legend in Dutch **Rev. Legend:** BELGIE **Edge:** Coarse reeding

Date	Mintage	VF20	XF40	MS60	MS63	MS65
2000	500,000	—	—	4.00	5.00	7.00

KM# 214.2 50 FRANCS (50 Frank)

7.00 g., Nickel, 22.75 mm. **Ruler:** Albert II **Subject:** European Soccer Championship **Obv:** Head of Albert II, left rear of head outlined **Rev:** Soccer ball, legend in Dutch **Rev. Legend:** BELGIE **Edge:** Coarse reeding **Note:** Medal alignment.

Date	Mintage	VF20	XF40	MS60	MS63	MS65
2000	20,000	PF65 20.00				
Note: In the "Euro 2000" sets only						

KM# 138.1 100 FRANCS (100 Frank)

18.00 g., 0.835 Silver 0.4832 oz. ASW, 33 mm. **Obv:** Crowned arms within wreath divide denomination, legend in French **Obv. Legend:** BELGIQUE **Rev:** Conjoined heads left of Leopold I, Leopold II, Albert I and Leopold III, left, Crown divides date at top, star at bottom

Date	Mintage	VF20	XF40	MS60	MS63	MS65
1948	1,000,000	9.75	18.00	20.00	30.00	48.00
1949	106,000	25.00	50.00	75.00	115	150
1950	2,807,000	9.75	18.00	20.00	27.00	36.00
1954	2,517,000	9.75	18.00	20.00	27.00	36.00

KM# 138.2 100 FRANCS (100 Frank)

18.00 g., 0.835 Silver 0.4832 oz. ASW, 33 mm. **Obv:** Crowned arms within wreath divide denomination, legend in French **Obv. Legend:** BELGIQUE **Rev:** Conjoined heads left of Leopold I, Leopold II, Albert I and Leopold III, left, Crown divides date at top, star at bottom **Note:** Medal alignment.

Date	Mintage	VF20	XF40	MS60	MS63	MS65
1948	Inc. above	45.00	100	240	450	800
1950	Inc. above	45.00	100	220	425	750

KM# 139.1 100 FRANCS (100 Frank)

18.00 g., 0.835 Silver 0.4832 oz. ASW, 33 mm. **Obv:** Crowned arms within wreath divide denomination, legend in Dutch **Obv. Legend:** BELGIE **Rev:** Conjoined heads left of Leopold I, Leopold II, Albert I and Leopold III, left, Crown divides date at top, star at bottom

Date	Mintage	VF20	XF40	MS60	MS63	MS65
1948	1,000,000	9.75	18.00	20.00	27.50	38.00
1949	2,271,000	9.75	18.00	20.00	25.00	35.00
1950	—	500	700	1,000	1,250	—
1951	4,691,000	9.75	18.00	20.00	25.00	35.00

KM# 139.2 100 FRANCS (100 Frank)

18.00 g., 0.835 Silver 0.4832 oz. ASW, 33 mm. **Obv:** Crowned arms within wreath divide denomination, legend in Dutch **Obv. Legend:** BELGIE **Rev:** Conjoined heads left of Leopold I, Leopold II, Albert I and Leopold III, left, Crown divides date at top, star at bottom **Note:** Medal alignment.

Date	Mintage	VF20	XF40	MS60	MS63	MS65
1948	Inc. above	44.00	100	220	425	—
1949	Inc. above	38.50	85.00	175	275	—

KM# 215 200 FRANCS (200 Frank)

18.75 g., 0.925 Silver 0.5576 oz. ASW, 33 mm. **Subject:** The Universe **Obv:** Legend in French **Obv. Legend:** BELGIQUE

Date	Mintage	VF20	XF40	MS60	MS63	MS65
2000	50,000	—	—	—	35.00	45.00
2000 (qp)	10,000	PF65 50.00				

KM# 216 200 FRANCS (200 Frank)

18.75 g., 0.925 Silver 0.5576 oz. ASW, 33 mm. **Subject:** The City **Obv:** Legend in Dutch **Obv. Legend:** BELGIE

Date	Mintage	VF20	XF40	MS60	MS63	MS65
2000	50,000	—	—	—	30.00	40.00
2000 (qp)	10,000	PF65 50.00				

KM# 217 200 FRANCS (200 Frank)

18.75 g., 0.925 Silver 0.5576 oz. ASW, 33 mm. **Subject:** The Nature **Obv:** Legend in German **Obv. Legend:** BELGIEN

Date	Mintage	VF20	XF40	MS60	MS63	MS65
2000	50,000	—	—	—	35.00	45.00
2000 (qp)	10,000	PF65 50.00				

KM# 157.1 250 FRANCS (250 Frank)

25.00 g., 0.835 Silver 0.6711 oz. ASW, 37 mm. **Subject:** Silver Jubilee of King Baudouin **Obv:** Head of Baudouin, left, legend in French **Obv. Legend:** ROI DES BELGES **Rev:** Crowned large "B", denomination below **Edge:** Reeded **Note:** Mint mark - Angel head. Mintmaster Vogeleer's privy mark - Bird.

Date	Mintage	VF20	XF40	MS60	MS63	MS65
ND(1976)	1,000,000	—	13.50	16.00	24.00	30.00
Note: Large B, slant 5						
ND(1976)	Inc. above	13.50	16.00	22.00	30.00	40.00
Note: Small B, upright 5						

KM# 157.2 250 FRANCS (250 Frank)

25.00 g., 0.835 Silver 0.6711 oz. ASW, 37 mm. **Subject:** Silver Jubilee of King Baudouin **Obv:** Head of Baudouin, left, legend in French **Obv. Legend:** ROIDES BELGES **Rev:** Crowned large "B", denomination below **Edge:** Stars **Note:** Mint mark - Angel head. Mintmaster Vogeleer's privy mark - Bird.

Date	Mintage	VF20	XF40	MS60	MS63	MS65
ND(1976)	100,000	—	—	16.00	24.00	40.00
Prooflike						

KM# 158.1 250 FRANCS (250 Frank)

25.00 g., 0.835 Silver 0.6711 oz. ASW, 37 mm. **Obv:** Head of Baudouin left, legend in Dutch **Obv. Legend:** KONING DER BELGEN **Rev:** Crowned large "B", denomination below **Edge:** Reeded **Note:** Mint mark - Angel head. Mintmaster Vogeleer's privy mark - Bird.

Date	Mintage	VF20	XF40	MS60	MS63	MS65
ND(1976)	1,000,000	—	13.50	15.00	22.00	25.00
Note: Large B, slant 5						
ND(1976)	Inc. above	24.00	28.00	30.00	37.00	42.00
Note: Small B, upright 5						

KM# 158.2 250 FRANCS (250 Frank)

25.00 g., 0.835 Silver 0.6711 oz. ASW, 37 mm. **Obv:** Head of Baudouin left, legend in Dutch **Obv. Legend:** KONING DER BELGEN **Rev:** Crowned large "B", denomination below **Edge:** Stars **Note:** Mint mark - Angel head. Mintmaster Vogeleer's privy mark - Bird.

Date	Mintage	VF20	XF40	MS60	MS63	MS65
ND(1976)	100,000	—	—	16.00	25.00	28.00
Prooflike						

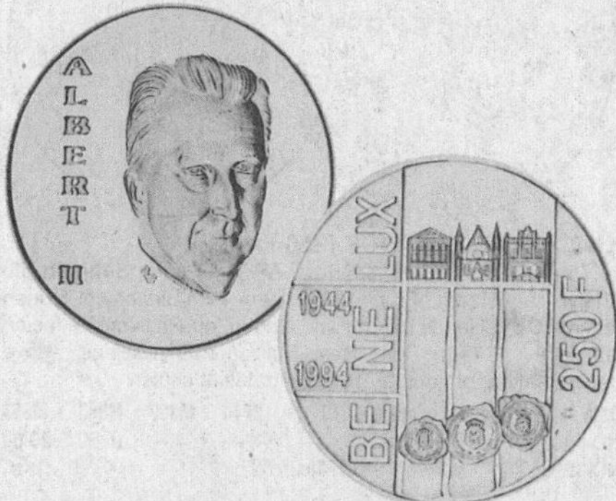

KM# 195 250 FRANCS (250 Frank)

18.75 g., 0.925 Silver 0.5576 oz. ASW, 33 mm. **Subject:** BE-NE-LUX Treaty **Obv:** Head of Albert II, 3/4 facing **Rev:** Three buildings, three sets of arms below, divide denomination and dates, legend on left **Note:** Mint mark - Angel head. Mintmaster R. Coenen's privy mark - Scale.

Date	Mintage	VF20	XF40	MS60	MS63	MS65
ND(1994)	90,000	—	—	15.00	22.00	25.00
ND(1994)	31,800	PF65 40.00				

KM# 199 250 FRANCS (250 Frank)
18.75 g., 0.925 Silver 0.5576 oz. ASW, 33 mm. **Subject:** 60th Anniversary - Death of Queen Astrid (car death) **Obv:** Crown above two sets of arms, denomination at bottom **Rev:** Bust of crowned Queen Astrid 1/4 facing right **Note:** Mint mark - Angel head. Mintmaster R. Coenen's privy mark - Scale.

Date	Mintage	VF20	XF40	MS60	MS63	MS65
ND(1995)	177,000	—	—	—	16.00	20.00
ND(1995)	25,000	PF65 40.00				

KM# 202 250 FRANCS (250 Frank)
18.75 g., 0.925 Silver 0.5576 oz. ASW, 33 mm. **Subject:** 20th Anniversary - King Baudouin Foundation **Obv:** Royal couple and monogram **Rev:** Denomination, stylized design and royal monogram

Date	Mintage	VF20	XF40	MS60	MS63	MS65
ND-1996	100,000	—	—	—	16.00	20.00
ND-1996	25,000	PF65 25.00				

KM# 207 250 FRANCS (250 Frank)
18.75 g., 0.925 Silver 0.5576 oz. ASW, 33 mm. **Subject:** 60th Birthday - Queen Paola **Obv:** Denomination **Rev:** Portrait, left **Note:** Mint mark - Angel head. Mintmaster R. Coenen's privy mark - Scale.

Date	Mintage	VF20	XF40	MS60	MS63	MS65
1997	100,000	—	—	—	16.00	20.00
1997	25,000	PF65 25.00				

KM# 208 250 FRANCS (250 Frank)
18.75 g., 0.925 Silver 0.5576 oz. ASW, 33 mm. **Subject:** 5th Anniversary Death of King Boudewijn - 70th Birthday of Queen Fabiola **Obv:** Heads of King and Queen, queen in profile facing left, king 1/4 facing left **Rev:** Pelican with nestlings, above denomination, at right, "F" dividing dates at center

Date	Mintage	VF20	XF40	MS60	MS63	MS65
ND-1998	100,000	—	—	—	16.00	20.00
ND-1998	—	PF65 25.00				

KM# 209 250 FRANCS (250 Frank)
18.75 g., 0.925 Silver 0.5576 oz. ASW, 33 mm. **Subject:** 40th Wedding Anniversary - King Albert and Queen Paola **Obv:** King and Queen's conjoining busts left **Rev:** St. Gudule Cathedral and city hall, dates at right, denomination at bottom **Edge:** Reeded

Date	Mintage	VF20	XF40	MS60	MS63	MS65
ND-1999	100,000	—	—	—	16.00	20.00
ND-1999	—	PF65 25.00				

KM# 218 250 FRANCS (250 Frank)
18.75 g., 0.925 Silver 0.5576 oz. ASW, 33 mm. **Subject:** Marriage of Prince Philip and Princess Mathilde **Rev:** Two hands joined on a rose

Date	Mintage	VF20	XF40	MS60	MS63	MS65
1999	200,000	—	—	—	16.00	20.00
1999	—	PF65 25.00				

KM# 161 500 FRANCS (500 Frank)
25.00 g., Silver Clad Copper-Nickel, 37 mm. **Subject:** 150th Anniversary of Independence **Obv:** Five heads within circles, legend and crown divide dates, French legend **Rev:** Legend on map of country, denomination below, French legend **Note:** Mint mark - Angel head. Mintmaster Vogeleer's privy mark - Bird.

Date	Mintage	VF20	XF40	MS60	MS63	MS65
ND(1980)	1,000,000	—	2.00	3.00	5.00	8.00

KM# 161a 500 FRANCS (500 Frank)
25.00 g., 0.510 Silver 0.4099 oz. ASW, 37 mm. **Subject:** 150th Anniversary of Independence **Obv:** Five heads within circles, legend and crown divide dates, French legend **Rev:** Legend on map of country, denomination below, French legend **Note:** Mint mark - Angel head. Mintmaster Vogeleer's privy mark - Bird.

Date	Mintage	VF20	XF40	MS60	MS63	MS65
ND(1980)	53,000	PF65 17.00				

KM# 162 500 FRANCS (500 Frank)
25.00 g., Silver Clad Copper-Nickel, 37 mm. **Obv:** Five heads within circles, legend with crown divides dates, Dutch legend **Rev:** Legend on map of country, denomination below, Dutch legend **Note:** Mint mark - Angel head. Mintmaster Vogeleer's privy mark - Bird.

Date	Mintage	VF20	XF40	MS60	MS63	MS65
ND(1980)	1,000,000	—	2.00	3.00	5.00	8.00

KM# 162a 500 FRANCS (500 Frank)
25.00 g., 0.510 Silver 0.4099 oz. ASW, 37 mm. **Obv:** Five heads within circles, legend with crown divides dates, Dutch legend **Rev:** Legend on map of country, denomination below, Dutch legend **Note:** Mint mark - Angel Head. Mintmaster Vogeleer's privy mark - Bird.

Date	Mintage	VF20	XF40	MS60	MS63	MS65
ND(1980)	52,000	PF65 17.00				

KM# 165 500 FRANCS (500 Frank)
25.00 g., 0.510 Silver 0.4099 oz. ASW **Obv:** Five heads within circles, legend with crown divides dates, French legend **Rev:** Legend on map of country, denomination below, Dutch legend **Note:** Mule. Mint mark - Angel head. Mintmaster Vogeleer's privy mark - Bird.

Date	Mintage	VF20	XF40	MS60	MS63	MS65
1980	—	—	—	—	—	1,500

KM# 178 500 FRANCS (500 Frank)
22.85 g., 0.833 Silver 0.612 oz. ASW, 37 mm. **Subject:** 60th Birthday of King Baudouin **Obv:** Head of King Baudouin, left, two dates below **Rev:** Denomination divides crown and date, Dutch legends

Date	Mintage	VF20	XF40	MS60	MS63	MS65
1990	475,000	—	—	—	12.00	16.00
1990	10,000	PF65 30.00				

KM# 179 500 FRANCS (500 Frank)
22.85 g., 0.833 Silver 0.612 oz. ASW, 37 mm. **Subject:** 60th Birthday of King Boudouin **Obv:** Head of King Boudouin, left, two dates below **Rev:** Denomination divides crown and date, French legends

Date	Mintage	VF20	XF40	MS60	MS63	MS65
1990	475,000	—	—	—	12.00	16.00
1990	10,000	PF65 30.00				

KM# 180 500 FRANCS (500 Frank)
22.85 g., 0.833 Silver 0.612 oz. ASW, 37 mm. **Subject:** 60th Birthday of King Baudouin **Obv:** Head of King Baudouin, left, two dates below **Rev:** Denomination divides crown and date, German legends

Date	Mintage	VF20	XF40	MS60	MS63	MS65
1990	50,000	—	—	—	16.00	20.00
1990	10,000	PF65 32.00				

KM# 196 500 FRANCS (500 Frank)
22.85 g., 0.833 Silver 0.612 oz. ASW, 37 mm. **Subject:** 40th Year of Reign **Obv:** Stylized design around **Rev:** Crown above, denomination, year below, Dutch legend

Date	Mintage	VF20	XF40	MS60	MS63	MS65
1991	250,000	—	—	—	16.00	20.00
1991	10,000	PF65 32.00				

KM# 197 500 FRANCS (500 Frank)
22.85 g., 0.833 Silver 0.612 oz. ASW, 37 mm. **Subject:** 40th Year of Reign **Obv:** Stylized design around **Rev:** Crown above, denomination, year below, French legend

Date	Mintage	VF20	XF40	MS60	MS63	MS65
1991	250,000	—	—	—	16.00	20.00
1991	10,000	PF65 32.00				

KM# 198 500 FRANCS (500 Frank)
22.85 g., 0.833 Silver 0.612 oz. ASW, 37 mm. **Subject:** 40th Year of Reign **Obv:** Stylized design around **Rev:** Crown above, denomination, year below, German legend

Date	Mintage	VF20	XF40	MS60	MS63	MS65
1991	250,000	—	—	—	16.00	20.00
1991	10,000	PF65 32.00				

KM# 186 500 FRANCS (500 Frank)
22.85 g., 0.833 Silver 0.612 oz. ASW, 37 mm. **Subject:** Europalaia - Mexico Exposition **Obv:** Design, legend and denomination within circle **Rev:** Mexico Exposition designs **Note:** Mint mark - Angel head. Mintmaster R. Coenen's privy mark - Scale.

Date	Mintage	VF20	XF40	MS60	MS63	MS65
ND(1993)	52,000	—	—	—	16.00	20.00
ND(1993)	8,000	PF65 32.00				

KM# 212 500 FRANCS (500 Frank)
22.85 g., 0.925 Silver 0.6795 oz. ASW, 37 mm. **Subject:** Brussels - European Culture Capital **Obv:** Denomination and European map **Rev:** Portraits of Albert and Elizabeth in ruffled collars **Edge:** Plain

Date	Mintage	VF20	XF40	MS60	MS63	MS65
ND-1999	200,000	—	—	—	16.00	20.00
ND-1999 (qp)	—	PF65 32.00				

KM# 219 500 FRANCS (500 Frank)
22.85 g., 0.925 Silver 0.6795 oz. ASW, 37 mm. **Subject:** Europe: Charles V **Obv:** Map and denomination **Rev:** Charles V of Spain and building **Edge:** Plain

Date	Mintage	VF20	XF40	MS60	MS63	MS65
ND-2000	100,000	PF65 35.00				
ND-2000 (qp)	20,000	PF65 40.00				

KM# 210 5000 FRANCS
15.55 g., 0.999 Gold 0.4994 oz. AGW, 29 mm. **Subject:** Brussels - European Culture Capital **Obv:** Denomination and European map **Rev:** Portraits of Albert and Elizabeth in ruffled collars **Edge:** Reeded

Date	Mintage	VF20	XF40	MS60	MS63	MS65
ND-1999 (qp)	—	PF65 950				
ND-1999 (qp)	—	PF65 1,700				

Note: Plain edge

KM# 220 5000 FRANCS
15.55 g., 0.999 Gold 0.4994 oz. AGW, 29 mm. **Subject:** Europe: Charles V **Obv:** Map and denomination **Rev:** Charles V of Spain with building **Edge:** Reeded

Date	Mintage	VF20	XF40	MS60	MS63	MS65
ND-2000 (qp)	—	PF65 1,200				
ND-2000 (qp)	—	PF65 950				

Note: Plain edge

TRADE COINAGE

European Currency Units

KM# 166 5 ECU
22.85 g., 0.833 Silver 0.612 oz. ASW, 37 mm. **Subject:** 30th Anniversary - Treaties of Rome **Obv:** Denomination, date and stars within circle **Rev:** Bust of Charles V, right

Date	Mintage	VF20	XF40	MS60	MS63	MS65
1987	985,000	—	—	—	25.00	55.00
1987 (qp)	15,000	PF65 70.00				
1988 (qp)	15,000	PF65 70.00				

KM# 183 5 ECU
22.85 g., 0.833 Silver 0.612 oz. ASW, 37 mm. **Obv:** Denomination, date and stars within circle **Rev:** Laureate head of Charlemagne, right

Date	Mintage	VF20	XF40	MS60	MS63	MS65
1991 (qp)	10,000	PF65 55.00				

KM# 185 5 ECU
22.85 g., 0.925 Silver 0.6795 oz. ASW, 37 mm. **Subject:** Belgian Presidency of the E.C. **Obv:** Head of King Baudouin, left **Rev:** Denomination, date and stars within circle

Date	Mintage	VF20	XF40	MS60	MS63	MS65
1993 (qp)	25,000	PF65 45.00				

KM# 200 5 ECU
22.85 g., 0.925 Silver 0.6795 oz. ASW, 37 mm. **Subject:** 50th Anniversary - United Nations **Obv:** Head of King Albert II, facing right, denomination and date **Rev:** UN logos with "50"

Date	Mintage	VF20	XF40	MS60	MS63	MS65
1995 (qp)	125,000	PF65 35.00				

KM# 203 5 ECU
22.85 g., 0.925 Silver 0.6795 oz. ASW, 37 mm. **Subject:** 50th Anniversary - UNICEF **Obv:** Royal couple, left **Rev:** UNICEF logo

Date	Mintage	VF20	XF40	MS60	MS63	MS65
1996 (qp)	Est. 40000	PF65 40.00				

KM# 205 5 ECU
22.85 g., 0.925 Silver 0.6795 oz. ASW, 37 mm. **Subject:** 40th Anniversary - Treaty of Rome **Obv:** Portraits of Albert II and Baudouin, left, date at bottom **Rev:** European Union map

Date	Mintage	VF20	XF40	MS60	MS63	MS65
1997 (qp)	—	PF65 45.00				

KM# 221 5 ECU
22.85 g., 0.925 Silver 0.6795 oz. ASW, 37 mm. **Subject:** 50th Anniversary - Human Rights Declaration **Obv:** Head of King Albert II, facing left, denomination and date **Rev:** Symbolic representation with "50"

Date	Mintage	VF20	XF40	MS60	MS63	MS65
1998 (qp)	—	PF65 45.00				

KM# 172 10 ECU
3.11 g., 0.999 Gold 0.0999 oz. AGW, 16 mm. **Rev:** Charles V bust right

Date	Mintage	VF20	XF40	MS60	MS63	MS65
1989 (qp)	2,000	PF65 200				
1990 (qp)	5,000	PF65 175				

KM# 176 10 ECU
Bi-Metallic 5.30g .900 Gold center, .100 oz AGW, .833 Silver ring, 22 mm. **Subject:** 60th Birthday of King Baudouin **Rev:** Denomination, date and stars within circle

Date	Mintage	VF20	XF40	MS60	MS63	MS65
1990 (qp)	42,000	PF65 175				

KM# 181 10 ECU
Bi-Metallic 5.30g .900 Gold center, .100 oz AGW, .833 Silver ring, 22 mm. **Subject:** 40th Year of Reign of King Baudouin **Obv:** Head of King Baudouin, left within circle, two dates below circle **Rev:** Denomination, date and stars within circle

Date	Mintage	VF20	XF40	MS60	MS63	MS65
1991 (qp)	15,738	PF65 175				

KM# 177 20 ECU
Bi-Metallic 10.50g .900 Gold center, .200 oz AGW, .833 Silver ring, 29 mm. **Subject:** 60th Birthday of King Baudouin **Obv:** Head of King Baudouin, left, within circle, two dates below circle **Rev:** Denomination, date and stars within circle

Date	Mintage	VF20	XF40	MS60	MS63	MS65
1990 (qp)	34,902	PF65 350				

KM# 182 20 ECU

10.50 g., 0.900 Bi-Metallic 0.3038 oz. Gold center in 0.200 oz AGW, .833 Silver ring **Subject:** 40th Year of Reign of King Baudouin **Obv:** Head of King Baudouin, left within circle, two dates below circle **Rev:** Denomination, date and stars within circle

Date	Mintage	VF20	XF40	MS60	MS63	MS65
1991 (qp)	13,082	PF65 375				

KM# 173 25 ECU

7.78 g., 0.999 Gold 0.250 oz. AGW, 21 mm. **Obv:** Denomination, date and stars within circle **Rev:** Laureate Diocletian bust, right

Date	Mintage	VF20	XF40	MS60	MS63	MS65
1989	30,000	—	—	—	—	440
1989 (qp)	2,000	PF65 460				
1990 (qp)	5,000	PF65 440				

KM# 167 50 ECU

17.28 g., 0.900 Gold 0.500 oz. AGW, 23 mm. **Subject:** 30th Anniversary - Treaties of Rome **Obv:** Denomination, date and stars within circle **Rev:** Bust of Charles V, right

Date	Mintage	VF20	XF40	MS60	MS63	MS65
1987	1,502,000	—	—	—	—	860
1987 (qp)	15,000	PF65 875				
1988 (qp)	15,000	PF65 875				

KM# 174 50 ECU

15.56 g., 0.999 Gold 0.4996 oz. AGW, 29 mm. **Obv:** Denomination, date and stars within circle **Rev:** Charlemagne seated on dais, facing

Date	Mintage	VF20	XF40	MS60	MS63	MS65
1989	60,000	—	—	—	—	860
1989 (qp)	2,000	PF65 875				
1990 (qp)	5,000	PF65 875				

KM# 184 50 ECU

15.56 g., 0.999 Gold 0.4996 oz. AGW, 29 mm. **Obv:** Denomination, date and stars within circle **Rev:** Laureate head of Charlemagne, right

Date	Mintage	VF20	XF40	MS60	MS63	MS65
1991 (qp)	4,000	PF65 860				

KM# 213 50 ECU

15.56 g., 0.999 Gold 0.4996 oz. AGW, 29 mm. **Subject:** Belgian Presidency of the E.C. **Obv:** Head of King Baudouin, left **Rev:** Denomination, date and stars within circle

Date	Mintage	VF20	XF40	MS60	MS63	MS65
1993 (qp)	10,000	PF65 860				

KM# 201 50 ECU

15.56 g., 0.999 Gold 0.4996 oz. AGW, 29 mm. **Subject:** 50th Anniversary - United Nations **Obv:** Head of King Albert II, facing right, denomination and date **Rev:** UN logo with "50"

Date	Mintage	VF20	XF40	MS60	MS63	MS65
1995 (qp)	2,500	PF65 860				

KM# 204 50 ECU

15.56 g., 0.999 Gold 0.4996 oz. AGW, 29 mm. **Subject:** 50th Anniversary - UNICEF **Obv:** Royal couple, left **Rev:** UNICEF logo

Date	Mintage	VF20	XF40	MS60	MS63	MS65
1996 (qp)	2,500	PF65 875				

KM# 206 50 ECU

15.56 g., 0.999 Gold 0.4996 oz. AGW, 29 mm. **Subject:** 40th Anniversary - Treaty of Rome **Obv:** Portraits of Albert II and Baudouin, left, date at bottom **Rev:** European Union map

Date	Mintage	VF20	XF40	MS60	MS63	MS65
1997 (qp)	2,500	PF65 875				

KM# 211 50 ECU

15.56 g., 0.999 Gold 0.4996 oz. AGW, 29 mm. **Subject:** 50th Anniversary - Human Rights Declaration **Obv:** Head of King Albert II, facing left, denomination and date **Rev:** Symbolic representation with "50"

Date	Mintage	VF20	XF40	MS60	MS63	MS65
1998 (qp)	2,500	PF65 875				

KM# 175 100 ECU

31.10 g., 0.999 Gold 0.999 oz. AGW, 37 mm. **Obv:** Denomination, date and stars within circle **Rev:** Bust of Maria Theresa, of Austria, right

Date	Mintage	VF20	XF40	MS60	MS63	MS65
1989	50,000	—	—	—	—	1,750
1989 (qp)	2,000	PF65 1,850				
1990 (qp)	5,000	PF65 1,800				

EURO COINAGE

European Union Issues

KM# 224 EURO CENT

2.30 g., Copper Plated Steel, 16.25 mm. **Ruler:** Albert II **Obv:** Head left within inner circle, stars 3/4 surround, date below **Rev:** Denomination and globe **Edge:** Plain

Date	Mintage	VF20	XF40	MS60	MS63	MS65
1999	235,240,000	—	0.30	0.50	0.75	1.00
1999	15,000	PF65 12.00				
2000 Sets only	40,000	—	—	—	27.50	40.00
2000	15,000	PF65 15.00				

KM# 225 2 EURO CENT

3.06 g., Copper Plated Steel, 18.75 mm. **Ruler:** Albert II **Obv:** Head left within circle, stars 3/4 surround, date below **Rev:** Denomination and globe **Edge:** Grooved

Date	Mintage	VF20	XF40	MS60	MS63	MS65
1999 Sets only	40,000	—	—	—	7.50	10.00
1999	15,000	PF65 15.00				
2000	373,040,000	—	0.30	0.50	0.75	1.00
2000	15,000	PF65 12.00				

KM# 226 5 EURO CENT

3.92 g., Copper Plated Steel, 21.25 mm. **Ruler:** Albert II **Obv:** Head left within circle, stars 3/4 surround, date below **Rev:** Denomination and globe **Edge:** Plain

Date	Mintage	VF20	XF40	MS60	MS63	MS65
1999	300,040,000	—	0.50	0.75	1.20	1.60
1999	15,000	PF65 12.00				
2000 Sets only	40,000	—	—	—	—	10.00
2000	15,000	PF65 15.00				

KM# 227 10 EURO CENT

4.10 g., Brass, 19.75 mm. **Ruler:** Albert II **Obv:** Head left within inner circle, stars 3/4 surround, date below **Rev:** Denomination and map **Edge:** Reeded

Date	Mintage	VF20	XF40	MS60	MS63	MS65
1999	180,990,000	—	—	—	0.75	1.25
1999	15,000	PF65 12.00				
2000 Sets only	40,000	—	—	—	7.50	10.00
2000	15,000	PF65 15.00				

KM# 228 20 EURO CENT

5.74 g., Brass, 22.25 mm. **Ruler:** Albert II **Obv:** Head left within circle, stars 3/4 surround, date below **Rev:** Denomination and map **Edge:** Notched

Date	Mintage	VF20	XF40	MS60	MS63	MS65
1999	40,000	—	—	—	7.50	10.00
1999	15,000	PF65 15.00				
2000	181,040,000	—	—	—	0.75	1.25
2000	15,000	PF65 12.00				

KM# 229 50 EURO CENT

7.80 g., Brass, 24.25 mm. **Ruler:** Albert II **Obv:** Head left within circle, stars 3/4 surround, date below **Rev:** Denomination and map **Edge:** Reeded

Date	Mintage	VF20	XF40	MS60	MS63	MS65
1999	197,040,000	—	—	—	0.75	1.25
1999	15,000	PF65 12.00				
2000 Sets only	40,000	—	—	—	7.50	10.00
2000	15,000	PF65 15.00				

KM# 230 EURO

7.50 g., Bi-Metallic Copper-Nickel center in Nickel-Brass ring, 23.25 mm. **Ruler:** Albert II **Obv:** Head left within circle, stars 3/4 surround, date below **Rev:** Denomination and map **Edge:** Segmented reeding

Date	Mintage	VF20	XF40	MS60	MS63	MS65
1999	160,040,000	—	—	—	2.50	4.50
1999	15,000	PF65 15.00				
2000 Sets only	40,000	—	—	—	—	12.50
2000	15,000	PF65 18.00				

KM# 231 2 EURO

8.50 g., Bi-Metallic Nickel-Brass center in Copper-Nickel ring, 25.75 mm. **Ruler:** Albert II **Obv:** Head left within circle, stars 3/4 surround, date below **Rev:** Denomination and map **Edge:** Reeded with 2's and stars

Date	Mintage	VF20	XF40	MS60	MS63	MS65
1999 Sets only	40,000	—	—	—	12.50	15.00
1999	15,000	PF65 20.00				
2000	120,040,000	—	—	—	3.50	5.50
2000	15,000	PF65 18.00				

PATTERNS

Including off metal strikes

KM#	Date	Mintage	Identification	Mkt Val
Pn93	1901	—	5 Centimes. Brass Plated Nickel.	260
Pn94	1901	—	5 Centimes. Copper-Iron Alloy. KM#45.	250
Pn95	1901	—	5 Centimes. Copper. Designer's initials as A.M.; KM#46.	300
Pn96	1901	—	5 Centimes. Copper. Thin flan, KM#46.	250
Pn97	1901	—	10 Centimes. Nickel. KM#48.	270
Pn98	1901	—	10 Centimes. Copper-Nickel.	275
Pn99	1901	—	50 Centimes. Copper. KM#50.	250
Pn100	1901	—	50 Centimes. Silver.	525
Pn101	1901	—	Franc. Silver.	600
Pn102	1901	—	Franc. Silver. Head left. Lion with constitution.	650
Pn103	1901	—	2 Francs. Silver.	825
Pn104	1901	—	2 Francs. Silver. Head left. Lion with constitution. Reeded.	1,000
Pn105	1902	—	5 Centimes. Nickel.	100
Pn106	1902	—	5 Centimes. Copper-Nickel. Without center hole; KM#47.	200
Pn107	19xx (1902)	—	Franc. Nickel-Brass.	250
Pn108	1902	—	Franc. Silver. Reeded. Small portrait, KM#56.1.	350
Pn109	1902	—	Franc. Silver. Plain. Small portrait, KM#56.1.	350
Pn110	1903	—	Franc. Silver. Reeded. Small portrait, KM#56.1.	350
Pn111	1903	—	Franc. Silver. Plain. Small portrait, KM#56.1.	350
Pn112	1903	—	Franc. Silver.	—
Pn113	1903	—	Franc. Silver.	—
Pn114	1903	—	Franc. Silver.	—
Pn115	1903	—	Franc. Silver.	—
Pn116	1903	—	Franc. Silver.	—
Pn117	1903	—	Franc. Silver.	—
Pn118	1903	—	Franc. Silver.	—
Pn119	1903	—	Franc. Silver.	—
Pn136	1904	—	50 Centimes. Silver. Plain. KM#60.1.	—
Pn137	1904	—	50 Centimes. Silver. Reeded. KM#60.1.	—
Pn138	1904	—	50 Centimes. Silver. Smaller designs, KM#60.1.	—
Pn139	1904	—	Franc. Silver. Reeded. Thin flan, KM#56.1.	400
Pn140	1904	—	Franc. Silver. Plain. Thick flan, KM#56.1.	500
Pn141	1904	—	2 Francs. Silver. Plain. KM#58.1.	—
Pn142	1904	—	2 Francs. Silver. Reeded. Thin flan, KM#58.1.	—
Pn143	1904	—	2 Francs. Silver. Plain. Thick flan, KM#58.1.	600
Pn144	1904	—	2 Francs. Silver. Plain. KM#59.1.	—
Pn145	1904	—	2 Francs. Silver. Reeded. Thin flan, KM#59.1.	—
Pn146	1904	—	2 Francs. Silver. Plain. Thick flan, KM#59.1.	600
Pn147	1906	—	5 Centimes. Nickel-Brass. Restrike, KM#93.	—
Pn148	1907	—	Centime. Copper. Reeded. Thick flan, KM#34.1.	300
Pn149	1907	—	25 Centimes. Copper-Nickel.	—
Pn150	1909	—	Franc. Silver. Reeded. KM#73.1.	400
Pn151	1910	—	5 Centimes. Gold. Not holed, KM#67.	1,400
Pn152	1910	—	5 Centimes. Silver. Not holed, KM#67.	450
Pn153	1910	—	5 Centimes. Bronze. Not holed, KM#67.	175
Pn154	1910	—	5 Centimes. Aluminum. Not holed, KM#67.	150
Pn155	1910	—	Franc. Silver. Reeded. KM#72.	350
Pn156	1910	—	Franc. Silver. Reeded. Thick planchet, KM#72.	450
Pn157	1910	—	Franc. Silver. Reeded. Thin planchet, KM#72.	400
Pn158	1910	—	Franc. Silver. Designer's name as Devreese, KM#72.	—
Pn159	1910	—	Franc. Silver. Plain. KM#73.1.	—
Pn160	1910	—	2 Francs. Silver. Plain. KM#74.	425
Pn161	1911	—	Centime. Copper. Restrike.	—
Pn162	1911	—	10 Centimes. Copper. Not holed.	—
Pn163	1911	—	10 Centimes. Brass. Holed.	—
Pn164	1911	—	10 Centimes. Copper-Nickel. Not holed.	—
Pn165	1911	—	10 Centimes. Gold. KM#85.1.	1,700
Pn166	1911	—	10 Centimes. Silver. KM#85.1.	600
Pn167	1911	—	10 Centimes. Bronze. KM#85.1.	—
Pn168	1911	—	10 Centimes. Copper. KM#85.1.	—
Pn169	1911	—	10 Centimes. Aluminum. KM#85.1.	—
Pn170	1911	—	10 Centimes. Gold. KM#86.	—
Pn171	1911	—	10 Centimes. Silver. KM#86.	—
Pn172	1911	—	10 Centimes. Bronze. KM#86.	—
Pn173	1911	—	10 Centimes. Copper. KM#86.	—
Pn174	1911	—	10 Centimes. Aluminum. KM#86.	—
Pn175	1911	—	Franc. Silver. Reeded. Designer's name as Devreese, KM#73.	—
Pn176	1911	—	Franc. Silver. Plain. Designer's name as Devreese, KM#73.	—
Pn177	1911	—	2 Francs. Copper. KM#74.	350
Pn178	1911	—	2 Francs. Gold.	1,650
Pn179	1911	—	10 Francs. Gold. Dutch legend.	2,250
Pn180	1911	—	10 Francs. Gold. French legend.	2,000
Pn181	1911	—	20 Francs. Brass Plated Copper.	—
Pn182	1911	—	20 Francs. Nickel.	—
Pn183	1911	—	20 Francs. Gold. Dutch legend.	2,400
Pn184	1911	—	20 Francs. Gold. French legend.	2,500
Pn185	1911	—	20 Francs. Pewter.	—
Pn186	1911	—	100 Francs. Aluminum-Nickel. Dutch legend.	—
Pn187	1911	—	100 Francs. Aluminum-Nickel. French legend.	—
Pn188	1911	—	100 Francs. Silver. Reeded.	—
Pn189	1912/1	—	Centime. Copper. Restrike, ESSAI.	400
Pn190	1912	—	10 Francs. Gold. Dutch legend.	2,200
Pn191	1912	—	10 Francs. Gold. French legend.	2,000
Pn192	1912	—	10 Francs. Gold. Reeded.	—
Pn193	1912	3	100 Francs. Gold. Dutch legend.	16,000
Pn194	1912	6	100 Francs. Gold. French legend.	12,500
Pn195	1914	—	2 Francs. Silver. Unadopted portrait. ESSAI/MONETAIRE/1914.	4,000
Pn196	ND-1915	—	Centime. Zinc.	—
Pn197	1915	—	5 Centimes. Copper-Iron Bi-Metal. Reeded. KM#66.	—
Pn198	1915	—	10 Centimes. Copper-Iron Bi-Metal. KM#681.	—
Pn199	1915	—	25 Centimes. Pot Metal.	—
Pn200	1916	—	10 Centimes. Copper-Iron Bi-Metal. KM#81.	—
Pn201	1917	—	10 Centimes. Silver. Plain. KM#81.	—
Pn202	1918	—	25 Centimes. Silver. Plain. KM#82.	—
Pn203	ND-1918	—	25 Centimes. Copper-Iron Bi-Metal. 2 branches around legend. Legend around 25 CES.	600
Pn204	ND-1918	—	25 Centimes. Zinc. Legend around 25 CENT. Lion, ESSAI.	350
Pn205	ND-1918	—	25 Centimes. Silver. 16 sided.	—
Pn206	1918	—	50 Centimes. Gold. KM#83.	1,650
Pn207	1918	—	50 Centimes. Silver. KM#83.	—
Pn208	1918	—	50 Centimes. Tan Bronze. KM#83.	—
Pn209	1918	—	50 Centimes. Red Bronze. KM#83.	—
Pn210	1918	—	50 Centimes. Aluminum. KM#83.	—
Pn211	1918	—	50 Centimes. Silver. Not holed.	—
Pn212	1918	—	50 Centimes. Nickel. Not holed.	—
Pn213	1918	—	50 Centimes. Copper-Nickel. Not holed.	—
Pn214	1920	—	5 Centimes. Nickel. Reeded. Not holed, KM#66.	400
PnA215	1920	—	20 Francs. Silver. Victory and Peace.	500
Pn216	1921	—	5 Centimes. Nickel. KM#69.	—
Pn217	1922	—	5 Centimes. Nickel-Brass. Restrike, KM#94.	—
Pn218	1922	—	50 Centimes. Bronze.	—
Pn219	1922	—	50 Centimes. Silver. Plain. KM#87.	—
Pn220	1922	—	50 Centimes. Bronze. Plain. KM#87.	—
Pn221	1922	—	50 Centimes. Aluminum. Plain. KM#87.	—
Pn222	1922	—	50 Centimes. Nickel. Plain. KM#87.	—
Pn223	1922	—	50 Centimes. Copper. Plain. KM#87.	—
Pn224	1922	—	50 Centimes. Copper-Tin. Plain. KM#87.	—
Pn225	1922	—	50 Centimes. Silver. Reeded. KM#87.	—
Pn226	1922	—	50 Centimes. Bronze. Reeded. KM#87.	—
Pn227	1922	—	50 Centimes. Aluminum. Reeded. KM#87.	—
Pn228	1922	—	50 Centimes. Nickel. Reeded. KM#87.	—
Pn229	1922	—	50 Centimes. Copper. Reeded. KM#87.	—
Pn230	1922	—	50 Centimes. Copper-Tin. Reeded. KM#87.	—
Pn231	1922	—	50 Centimes. Silver. Plain. KM#88.	—
Pn232	1922	—	50 Centimes. Bronze. Plain. KM#88.	—
Pn233	1922	—	50 Centimes. Aluminum. Plain. KM#88.	—
Pn234	1922	—	50 Centimes. Copper. Plain. KM#88.	—
Pn235	1922	—	50 Centimes. Copper-Tin. Plain. KM#88.	—
Pn236	1922	—	50 Centimes. Silver. Reeded. KM#88.	—
Pn237	1922	—	50 Centimes. Bronze. Reeded. KM#88.	—
Pn238	1922	—	50 Centimes. Aluminum. Reeded. KM#88.	—
Pn239	1922	—	50 Centimes. Copper. Reeded. KM#88.	—
Pn240	1922	—	50 Centimes. Copper-Tin. Reeded. KM#88.	—
Pn241	1922	—	Franc. Silver. Plain. KM#89.	800
Pn242	1922	—	Franc. Bronze. Plain. KM#89.	—
Pn243	1922	—	Franc. Aluminum. Plain. KM#89.	—
Pn244	1922	—	Franc. Copper. Plain. KM#89.	—
Pn245	1922	—	Franc. Copper-Tin. Plain. KM#89.	—
Pn246	1922	—	Franc. Silver. Reeded. KM#89.	750
Pn247	1922	—	Franc. Bronze. Reeded. KM#89.	—
Pn248	1922	—	Franc. Aluminum. Reeded. KM#89.	—
Pn249	1922	—	Franc. Copper. Reeded. KM#89.	—
Pn250	1922	—	Franc. Copper-Tin. Reeded. KM#89.	—
Pn251	1922	—	Franc. Silver. Plain. KM#90.	750
Pn252	1922	—	Franc. Bronze. Plain. KM#90.	—
Pn253	1922	—	Franc. Aluminum. Plain. KM#90.	—
Pn254	1922	—	Franc. Nickel. Plain. Irregular flan, KM#90.	—
Pn255	1922	—	Franc. Copper. Plain. KM#90.	—
Pn256	1922	—	Franc. Copper-Tin. Plain. KM#90.	—
Pn257	1922	—	Franc. Silver. Reeded. KM#90.	800
Pn258	1922	—	Franc. Bronze. Reeded. KM#90.	—
Pn259	1922	—	Franc. Aluminum. Reeded. KM#90.	—
Pn260	1922	—	Franc. Copper. Reeded. KM#90.	—
Pn261	1922	—	Franc. Copper-Tin. Reeded. KM#90.	—
Pn262	1922	—	Franc. Nickel. KM#89. KM#90.	—
Pn263	1923	—	2 Francs. Silver. ESSAI, KM#91.1.	—
Pn264	1923	—	2 Francs. Bronze. ESSAI, KM#91.1.	—
Pn265	1923	—	2 Francs. Aluminum. ESSAI, KM#91.1.	—
Pn266	1923	—	2 Francs. Copper-Tin. ESSAI, KM#91.1.	—
Pn267	1926	—	5 Francs. Red Bronze. ESSAI.	—
Pn268	1926	—	5 Francs. Silver. Head left. Wreath with 5 FR within.	—
Pn269	1926	—	5 Francs. Bronze. Head left. Wreath with 5 FR within.	—
Pn270	1926	—	5 Francs. Nickel. Head left. Wreath with 5 FR within.	—
Pn271	1926	—	5 Francs. Copper-Tin. Head left. Wreath with 5 FR within.	—
Pn272	1926	—	5 Francs. Silver. Crown above 5 Francs.	—
Pn273	1926	—	5 Francs. Bronze. Crown above 5 Francs.	—
Pn274	1926	—	5 Francs. Nickel. Crown above 5 Francs.	—
Pn275	1926	—	5 Francs. Copper-Tin. Crown above 5 Francs.	—
Pn276	1926	—	5 Francs. Silver. Crown above oak wreath, 5 Francs within.	—
Pn277	1926	—	5 Francs. Bronze. Crown above oak wreath, 5 Francs within.	—
Pn278	1926	—	5 Francs. Copper-Tin. Crown above oak wreath, 5 Francs within.	—
Pn279	1926	—	5 Francs. Gold. Wreath, UN BELGA CINQ FRANCS.	1,850
Pn280	1926	—	5 Francs. Silver. Wreath, UN BELGA CINQ FRANCS.	—
Pn281	1926	—	5 Francs. Bronze. Wreath, UN BELGA CINQ FRANCS.	—
Pn282	1926	—	5 Francs. Nickel. Wreath, UN BELGA CINQ FRANCS.	—
Pn283	1926	—	5 Francs. Copper-Tin. Wreath, UN BELGA CINQ FRANCS.	—

Pn284	1926	—	5 Francs. Gold. Lion in shield, SF flanking.	1,850
Pn285	1926	—	5 Francs. Silver. Lion in shield, SF flanking.	—
Pn286	1926	—	5 Francs. Bronze. Lion in shield, SF flanking.	—
Pn287	1926	—	5 Francs. Nickel. Lion in shield, SF flanking.	—
Pn288	1926	—	5 Francs. Copper-Tin. Lion in shield, SF flanking.	—
Pn289	1927	—	5 Francs. Silver. Head by Bonnetain. 2 laurel branches, UN BELGA/OU/5 FRANCS/ESSAI.	600
Pn290	1927	—	5 Francs. Copper. Head by Bonnetain. 2 laurel branches, UN BELGA/OU/5 FRANCS/ESSAI.	500
Pn291	1927	—	5 Francs. Copper-Tin. Head by Bonnetain. 2 laurel branches, UN BELGA/OU/5 FRANCS/ESSAI.	500
Pn292	1927	—	5 Francs. Nickel.	—
Pn293	1929	—	5 Centimes. Copper-Nickel. Not holed, KM#67.	—
Pn294	1929	—	10 Centimes. Nickel. Not holed, ESSAI, KM#85.1.	—
Pn295	1929	—	10 Centimes. Gold. KM#85.1.	1,200
Pn296	1929	—	10 Centimes. Silver. KM#85.1.	—
Pn297	1929	—	10 Centimes. Bronze. KM#85.1.	—
Pn298	1929	—	10 Centimes. Copper. KM#85.1.	—
Pn299	1929	—	10 Centimes. Aluminum. KM#85.1.	—
Pn300	1929	—	25 Centimes. Gold. ESSAI, KM#68.1.	1,400
Pn301	1929	—	25 Centimes. Silver. ESSAI, KM#68.1.	—
Pn302	1929	—	25 Centimes. Bronze. ESSAI, KM#68.1.	—
Pn303	1929	—	25 Centimes. Copper. ESSAI, KM#68.1.	—
Pn304	1929	—	25 Centimes. Aluminum. ESSAI, KM#68.1.	—
Pn305	1929	—	25 Centimes. Gold. ESSAI, KM#69.	1,400
Pn306	1929	—	25 Centimes. Silver. ESSAI, KM#69.	—
Pn307	1929	—	25 Centimes. Bronze. ESSAI, KM#69.	—
Pn308	1929	—	25 Centimes. Copper. ESSAI, KM#69.	—
Pn309	1929	—	25 Centimes. Aluminum. ESSAI, KM#69.	110
Pn310	1929	—	5 Francs. Nickel.	—
Pn311	1929	—	5 Francs. Bronze.	—
Pn312	1930	—	2 Francs. Copper. KM#92.	—
Pn313	1930	—	2 Francs. Bronze. KM#92.	—
Pn314	1930	—	10 Francs. Brass.	300
Pn315	1930	—	20 Francs. Silver.	—
Pn316	1931	—	Franc. Nickel.	—
Pn317	1931	—	20 Francs. Bronze. French legend.	275
Pn318	1931	—	20 Francs. Bronze. Dutch legend.	275
Pn319	1932	—	5 Centimes. Copper-Nickel.	—
Pn320	1932	—	5 Centimes. Dupriez's design.	—
Pn321	1932	—	5 Centimes. Copper. Not holed, KM#93.	—
Pn322	1932	—	50 Centimes. Nickel. KM#87. KM#88. Reeded.	—
Pn323	1932	—	50 Centimes. Nickel. KM#87. KM#88. Plain.	—
Pn324	1933	—	5 Francs. Silver.	—
Pn325	1933	—	10 Francs. Nickel.	—
Pn326	1933	—	10 Francs. Nickel. DEUX BELGAS/OU/10 FRANCS.	—
Pn327	1933	—	50 Francs. Silver. 10/ BELGAS/50/FRANCS within 2 oak branches. Plain.	—
Pn328	1933	—	50 Francs. Silver. Cross ornaments on edge.	—
Pn329	1933	—	50 Francs. Silver. Reeded.	—
Pn330	1933	—	50 Francs. Silver. Small head of Albert within pellet circle. Value within 2 laurel branches.	—
Pn331	1933	—	50 Francs. Silver. Bust by Bonnetain. Value within laurel branches.	—
Pn332	1933	—	100 Francs. Silver. Bust by Bonnetain. 20/BELGAS/100/ FRANCS within 2 laurel branches.	—
Pn333	1933	—	100 Francs. By Devreese.	—
Pn334	1933	—	100 Francs. L'UNION FAIT LA FORCE/100 FRS. By Devreese.	150
Pn335	1933	—	100 Francs. Bronze. 20/ BELGAS/100 FRANCS between 2 branches.	—
Pn336	1933	—	500 Francs. Bronze. 20/ BELGAS/500/FRANCS between laurel and oak branches.	250
Pn337	1933	—	500 Francs. Nickel.	300
Pn338	1934	—	5 Francs. Bronze.	130
Pn339	1934	—	20 Francs. Bronze.	140
Pn340	1935	—	Franc. Copper-Tin. Reeded.	—
Pn341	1935	—	Franc. Nickel. Reeded.	—
Pn342	1935	—	Franc. Silver. Allegory of Belgium kneeling left; BELGIQUE \ BELGIE at sides. Caduceus between IF and date. Plain.	—
Pn343	1935	—	Franc. Silver. Allegory of Belgium kneeling left. Plain.	—
Pn344	1935	—	Franc. Copper. Allegory of Belgium kneeling left. Plain.	—
Pn345	1935	—	Franc. Nickel. Allegory of Belgium kneeling left. Plain.	—
Pn346	1935	—	40 Francs. 0.680. Silver. Lettered.	14,000
Pn347	1935	—	40 Francs. Silver. Plain. Restrike.	—
Pn348	1935	—	40 Francs. Copper-Tin. Lettered. Expo commemorative.	—
Pn349	1935	—	40 Francs. Gold. Reeded. Expo commemorative.	—
Pn350	1935	—	40 Francs. Silver. Reeded. Expo commemorative.	—
Pn351	1935	—	40 Francs. Bronze. Reeded. Expo commemorative.	—
Pn352	1935	—	40 Francs. Copper. Reeded. Expo commemorative.	—
Pn353	1935	—	40 Francs. Copper-Tin. Reeded. Expo commemorative.	—
Pn354	1935	—	40 Francs. Nickel. Reeded. Expo commemorative.	—
Pn355	1935	—	40 Francs. Aluminum. Reeded. Expo commemorative.	—
Pn356	1935	—	40 Francs. Gold. Expo commemorative, thin planchet.	2,000
Pn357	1935	—	40 Francs. Silver. Expo commemorative, thin planchet.	800
Pn358	1935	—	40 Francs. Bronze. Expo commemorative, thin planchet.	400
Pn359	1935	—	40 Francs. Copper. Expo commemorative, thin planchet.	400
Pn360	1935	—	40 Francs. Copper-Tin. Expo commemorative.	400
Pn361	1935	—	40 Francs. Nickel. Expo commemorative, thin planchet.	450
Pn362	1935	—	40 Francs. Aluminum. Expo commemorative, thin planchet.	400
Pn363	1935	—	50 Francs. 0.680. Silver. Plain.	600
Pn364	1935	—	50 Francs. Silver. Plain. KM#106.1.	—
Pn365	1935	—	50 Francs. Copper. Plain. KM#106.1.	—
Pn366	1935	—	50 Francs. Copper-Tin. Plain. KM#106.1.	—
Pn367	1935	—	50 Francs. Copper-Tin. Edge inscription. KM#106.1.	—
Pn368	1935	—	50 Francs. Gold. Reeded. KM#106.1.	—
Pn369	1935	—	50 Francs. Silver. Reeded. KM#106.1.	—
Pn370	1935	—	50 Francs. Bronze. Reeded. KM#106.1.	—
Pn371	1935	—	50 Francs. Copper. Reeded. KM#106.1.	—
Pn372	1935	—	50 Francs. Copper-Tin. Reeded. KM#106.1.	—
Pn373	1935	—	50 Francs. Aluminum. Reeded. KM#106.1.	—
Pn374	1935	—	50 Francs. Silver. Plain. KM#107.1.	—
Pn375	1935	—	50 Francs. Copper-Tin. Plain. KM#107.1.	—
Pn376	1935	—	50 Francs. Bronze. Edge inscription, KM#107.1.	—
Pn377	1935	—	50 Francs. Copper-Tin. Reeded. KM#107.1.	—
Pn378	1936	—	5 Francs. Nickel.	185
Pn379	1938	—	5 Centimes. Copper-Tin. KM#110.1.	—
Pn380	1938	—	5 Centimes. Bronze. KM#110.1.	—
Pn381	1938	—	5 Centimes. Tin. Not holed, KM#110.1.	—
Pn382	1938	—	10 Centimes. Copper-Tin. Thin planchet, KM#112.	—
Pn383	1938	—	10 Centimes. Copper-Tin. Thick planchet, KM#112.	—
Pn384	1938	—	10 Centimes. Bronze. KM#112.	—
Pn385	1938	—	10 Centimes. Copper-Tin. Large letters, not holed.	—
Pn386	1938	—	25 Centimes. Nickel. Large shields.	—
Pn387	1938	—	25 Centimes. Copper-Tin. Not holed.	—
Pn388	1938	—	20 Francs. Silver.	—
Pn389	1938	—	20 Francs. Silver. Similar to KM#121.	—
Pn390	1938	—	20 Francs. Bronze. Similar to KM#121.	—
Pn391	1938	—	20 Francs. Copper. Similar to KM#121.	—
Pn392	1938	—	20 Francs. Copper-Tin. Similar to KM#121.	—
Pn393	1938	—	20 Francs. Nickel. Similar to KM#121.	—
Pn394	1938	—	20 Francs. Silver.	—
Pn395	1938	—	20 Francs. Copper-Tin.	—
Pn396	1938	—	20 Francs. Tin.	—
Pn397	1938	—	20 Francs. Silver. Thick planchet.	1,000
Pn398	1938	—	20 Francs. Copper-Tin. Thick planchet.	500
Pn399	1938	—	20 Francs. Tin. Thick planchet.	400
Pn400	1938	—	20 Francs. Silver. Small portrait.	—
Pn401	1938	—	20 Francs. Bronze. Small portrait.	—
Pn402	1938	—	20 Francs. Copper-Tin. Small portrait.	—
Pn403	1938	—	20 Francs. Tin. Small portrait.	—
Pn404	1938	—	50 Francs. Silver. Plain. KM#121.1.	—
Pn405	1938	—	50 Francs. Copper-Tin. Plain. KM#121.1.	—
Pn406	1938	—	50 Francs. Copper. Plain.	—
Pn407	1938	—	50 Francs. Copper. Plain. ESSAI.	—
Pn408	1939	—	25 Centimes. Copper-Tin. Not holed, KM#114.1.	—
Pn409	1939	—	25 Centimes. Bronze. KM#114.1.	—
Pn410	1939	—	Franc. Nickel. KM#120.	—
Pn411	1939	—	Franc. Bronze. Reeded. KM#120.	—
Pn412	1939	—	Franc. Copper-Tin. Reeded. KM#120.	—
Pn413	1939	—	50 Francs. Copper-Tin. Lettered. KM#121.1.	—
Pn414	1939	—	50 Francs. Bronze. Lettered. KM#121.1.	—
Pn415	1940	—	Franc. Nickel. Restrike, KM#119.	—
Pn416	1940	—	5 Francs. Copper-Tin. Portrait by Rau, Leopold III ROI DE BELGES. 5/FRANCS/1940 between oak and laurel branches.	—
Pn417	1940	—	5 Francs. Copper-Tin. Portrait by Rau. Thick planchet.	400
Pn418	1940	—	5 Francs. Copper-Tin. Portrait by Rau. KM#108.1.	—
Pn419	1940	—	5 Francs. Copper-Tin. Portrait by Rau. KM#108.1. Thick planchet.	400
Pn420	1940	—	5 Francs. Copper-Tin. Leopold III.	—
Pn421	1940	—	5 Francs. Copper-Tin. Leopold III. Thick planchet.	400
Pn422	1940	—	5 Francs. Nickel. Leopold III. Reeded.	—
Pn423	1940	—	5 Francs. Nickel. Leopold III. Reeded. Thick planchet.	400
Pn424	1940	—	5 Francs. Silver. Leopold III. KM#108.1.	—
Pn425	1940	—	5 Francs. Silver. Leopold III. KM#108.1. Thick planchet.	475
Pn426	1940	—	5 Francs. Copper-Tin. Leopold III, ROI DES BELGES. KM#108.1. Thick planchet.	400
Pn427	1941	—	10 Centimes. Silver. Reeded. KM#130.	—
Pn428	1941	—	5 Francs. Silver. Reeded. KM#130.	—
Pn429	1944	—	2 Francs. Silver. KM#133.	—
Pn430	1948	—	100 Francs. Copper. ESSAI, KM#138.	—
Pn431	1948	—	100 Francs. Copper. ESSAI, KM#139.1.	—
Pn432	1949	—	5 Francs. Copper. KM#134.1.	—
Pn433	1949	—	5 Francs. Copper. KM#135.1.	—
Pn434	1949	—	50 Francs. Bronze.	—
Pn435	1949	—	100 Francs. Silver.	—
Pn436	1949	—	100 Francs. Silver.	—
Pn437	1949	—	1000 Francs. Bronze. Plain.	—
Pn438	1949	—	1000 Francs. Silver.	900
Pn439	1949	—	1000 Francs. Gold. ESSAI.	10,920
Pn440	ND (1949)	—	1000 Francs. Bronze.	—
Pn441	1949	—	1000 Francs. Bronze. Milled.	—
Pn442	1951	—	20 Francs. Copper. ESSAI, KM#140.1.	—
Pn443	1951	—	20 Francs. Copper. ESSAI, KM#141.1.	—
Pn444	1951	—	20 Francs. Copper. ESSAI, KM#136.1.	—
Pn445	1951	—	50 Francs. Copper. ESSAI, KM#137.	—
Pn446	1952	—	Franc. Copper. KM#142.1.	—
Pn447	1952	—	Franc. Copper. KM#143.1.	—

PIEDFORT

KM#	Date	Mintage	Identification	Mkt Val
P4	1912	—	10 Francs. Gold. Plain.	2,700
P6	1918	—	50 Centimes. Zinc. Plain. Not holed, KM#83.	900
P7	1920	—	25 Centimes. Nickel. Plain. KM#68.1.	300
P8	1926	—	5 Centimes. Copper. Plain. Not holed, KM#66.	—
P9	1935	—	Franc. Silver.	1,000
P10	1935	—	Franc. Copper.	400
P11	1935	—	Franc. Nickel.	250
P12	1989	—	100 ECU. Gold. KM#175.	1,850

TRIAL STRIKES

KM#	Date	Mintage	Identification	Mkt Val
TS5	1903	—	Franc. Pewter. Uniface. Rectangle planchet.	1,000
TS6	1904	—	Franc. Pewter. Uniface. Rectangle planchet.	1,000
TS7	ND-1904	—	2 Francs. Lead. Uniface.	65.00
TS8	1910	—	2 Francs. Portrait, uniface.	—
TS9	1910	—	2 Francs. KM#74. Uniface.	—
TS10	1911	—	20 Francs. Gold. Error obverse.	1,550
TS11	1911	—	20 Francs. Aluminum. Error obverse.	600
TS12	1918	—	50 Centimes. Klippe.	1,000
TS13	1926	—	5 Francs. Nickel. Klippe.	1,000
TS14	1933	—	10 Francs. Silver. Legend within 2 branches.	—
TS15	1933	—	50 Francs. Silver. Irregular flan.	600
TS16	1949	—	1000 Francs. Red Copper. Klippe.	450
TS17	1949	—	1000 Francs. Yellow Copper. Klippe.	450
TS18	1949	—	1000 Francs. Red Copper. Klippe.	450
TS19	1949	—	1000 Francs. Yellow Copper. Klippe.	450
TS20	1949	—	1000 Francs. Silver. Klippe.	850

FDC SETS

KM#	Date	Mintage	Identification	Issue Price	Mkt Val
SS1	1970 (5)	5,000	KM#135.1, 143.1, 149.1, 154.1, 156.1 DU	0.60	225
SS2	1970 (5)	5,000	KM#134.1, 142.1, 148.1, 153.1, 155.1 FR	0.60	225
SS3	1971 (5)	10,000	KM#135.1, 143.1, 149.1, 154.1, 156.1 DU	0.63	75.00
SS4	1971 (5)	10,000	KM#134.1, 142.1, 148.1, 153.1, 155.1 FR	0.63	75.00
SS5	1972 (5)	10,000	KM#135.1, 143.1, 149.1, 154.1, 156.1 DU	0.70	85.00
SS6	1972 (5)	10,000	KM#134.1, 142.1, 148.1, 153.1, 155.1 FR	0.70	85.00
SS7	1973 (5)	16,778	KM#135.1, 143.1, 149.1, 154.1, 156.1 DU	0.80	40.00
SS8	1973 (5)	15,000	KM#134.1, 142.1, 148.1, 153.1, 155.1 FR	0.80	40.00
SS9	1974 (5)	20,608	KM#135.1, 143.1, 149,.1 154.1, 156.1 DU	1.10	22.00
SS10	1974 (5)	19,000	KM#134.1, 142.1, 148.1, 153.1, 155.1 FR	1.10	22.00
SS11	1975 (10)	45,752	KM#135.1, 143.1, 149.1, 154.1, 156.1 DU, 134.1, 142.1, 148.1, 153.1, 155.1 FR	2.50	10.00
SS12	1976 (10)	15,000	KM#135, 143, 149, 156, 158.1 DU, 134, 142, 148, 155, 157.1 FR	20.75	60.00
SS13	1977 (8)	45,938	KM#135, 143, 149, 156 DU, 134, 142, 148, 155 FR	2.65	6.00
SS14	1978 (8)	46,237	KM#135, 143, 149, 156 DU, 134, 142, 148, 155 FR	4.00	8.00
SS15	1979 (8)	49,997	KM#135, 143, 149, 156 DU, 134, 142, 148, 155 FR	4.00	6.00
SS16	1980 (8)	60,000	KM#135, 143, 149, 160 DU, 134, 142, 148, 159 FR	4.00	5.00
SS17	1981 (8)	54,331	KM#135, 143, 149, 160 DU, 134, 142, 148, 159 FR	3.25	8.00

MINT SETS

KM#	Date	Mintage	Identification	Issue Price	Mkt Val
MS1	1989 (10)	60,000	KM#149, 160, 164, 169, 171 DU; 148, 159, 163, 168, 170 FR	11.00	30.00
MS2	1990 (10)	60,000	KM#149, 160, 164, 169, 171 DU; 148, 159, 163, 168, 170 FR	13.00	25.00
MS3	1991 (8)	60,000	KM#149, 160, 164, 169, 171 DU; 148, 159, 163, 168, 170 FR	13.00	30.00
MS4	1991 (3)	—	KM#196-198	—	110
MS5	1992 (10)	60,000	KM#149, 160, 164, 169, 171 DU; 148, 159,	15.00	35.00
MS6	1993 (10)	40,000	KM#149, 160, 164, 169, 171 DU; 148, 159, 163, 168, 170 FR	15.00	10.00
MS7	1994 (10)	60,000	KM#148.1, 149.1, 187-194, medal	15.00	10.00
MS8	1995 (10)	60,000	KM#148.1, 149.1, 187-194, medal	15.00	35.00
MS9	1996 (10)	60,000	KM#148.1, 149.1, 187-194, medal	15.00	20.00
MS10	1997 (10)	60,000	KM#148.1, 149.1, 187-194, medal	—	40.00
MS11	1998 (10)	60,000	KM#148.1, 149.1, 187-194	15.00	15.00
MS12	1999 (10)	60,000	KM#148.1, 149.1, 187-194	15.00	45.00
MS13	2000 (9)	60,000	KM#148.1, 149.1, 187-194	15.00	40.00

PROOF SETS

KM#	Date	Mintage	Identification	Issue Price	Mkt Val
PS1	1987 (2)	15,000	KM#166-167	395	950
PS2	1988 (2)	15,000	KM#166-167	395	950
PS3	1989 (4)	2,000	KM#172-175	1,300	3,600
PS4	1990 (4)	5,000	KM#172-175	1,300	3,500
PS5	1990 (3)	10,000	KM#178-180	100	140
PS6	1991 (3)	10,000	KM#196-198	100	130
PS7	2000 (3)	10,000	KM#215-217	75.00	180
PS8	1999 (8)	15,000	KM#224-231	80.00	120
PS9	2000 (8)	15,000	KM#224-231	80.00	125

GHENT

GERMAN OCCUPATION WWI

TOKEN COINAGE

KM# Tn1 50 CENTIMES

Brass Plated Iron **Obv:** Rampant lion, left, within inner circle **Rev:** Denomination within inner circle, box surrounds **Shape:** Square **Note:** Similar to KM#Tn1a, thin "50".

Date	Mintage	F12	VF20	XF40	MS60	MS63
1915	512,000	7.00	12.00	22.00	55.00	150

KM# Tn1a 50 CENTIMES

Brass Plated Iron **Rev:** Thick "50"

Date	Mintage	F12	VF20	XF40	MS60	MS63
1915	Inc. above	7.00	12.00	22.00	55.00	150

KM# Tn2 FRANKEN

Brass Plated Iron **Obv:** Rampant lion, left, within inner circle **Rev:** Denomination within inner circle, box surrounds

Date	Mintage	F12	VF20	XF40	MS60	MS63
1915	370,000	7.00	12.00	22.00	65.00	200

KM# Tn2a FRANKEN

Brass Plated Iron **Rev:** 11. 1919 instead of 1.1. 1919

Date	Mintage	F12	VF20	XF40	MS60	MS63
1915	Inc. above	8.00	14.00	24.00	70.00	200

KM# Tn3 FRANKEN

Copper Gilt **Obv:** Lion in circle, STAD GENT VILLE DE GAND around **Rev:** 1915 1 FR in circle, UIT BETAALBAAR 1 JANUARI 1918 REMBOURSABLE 1 JANVIER 1920 along sides of square **Shape:** Square **Note:** This token was struck in 1920 for the benefit of charity.

Date	Mintage	F12	VF20	XF40	MS60	MS63
1915	—	50.00	200	350	600	1,100

KM# Tn4 2 FRANKEN

Brass Plated Iron **Obv:** Rampant lion, left, within inner circle **Rev:** Denomination within inner circle, box surrounds **Shape:** Square

Date	Mintage	F12	VF20	XF40	MS60	MS63
1915	314,000	10.00	22.00	35.00	75.00	200

KM# Tn5 2 FRANKEN

Copper Gilt **Obv:** Arms in circle, STAD GENT FIDES ET AMOR around **Rev:** 1928 2 FRANK in circle, UIT BETAAL BAAR JANUARI 1922 PAX ET LABOR around **Note:** This token was struck in 1920 for the benefit of charity.

Date	Mintage	F12	VF20	XF40	MS60	MS63
1918	—	45.00	175	300	550	900

KM# Tn6 5 FRANKEN

Brass Plated Iron **Obv:** Crowned shield within circle **Rev:** Denomination within inner circle, box surrounds

Date	Mintage	F12	VF20	XF40	MS60	MS63
1917	108,000	16.50	25.00	40.00	115	225

KM# Tn7 5 FRANKEN

Brass Plated Iron **Obv:** Crowned arms within circle **Rev:** Denomination below date, within circle

Date	Mintage	F12	VF20	XF40	MS60	MS63
1918	339,000	12.00	24.00	37.00	95.00	175

Belize, formerly British Honduras, but now a Constitutional Monarchy within the Commonwealth of Nations, is situated in Central America south of Mexico and east and north of Guatemala, with an area of 8,867 sq. mi. (22,960 sq. km.) and a population of *242,000. Capital: Belmopan. Tourism now augments Belize's economy, in addition to sugar, citrus fruits, chicle and hardwoods which are exported.

The area, site of the ancient Mayan civilization, was sighted by Columbus in 1502, and settled by shipwrecked English seamen in 1638. British buccaneers settled the former capital of Belize in the 17th century. Britain claimed administrative right over the area after the emancipation of Central America from Spain. In 1825, Imperial coins were introduced into the colony and were rated against the Spanish dollar and Honduran currency. It was declared a colony subordinate to Jamaica in 1862 and was established as the separate Crown Colony of British Honduras in 1884. In May, 1885 an order in Council authorized coins for the colony, with the first shipment arriving in July. While the Guatemalan peso was originally the standard of value, in 1894 the colony changed to the gold standard, based on the U.S. gold dollar. The anti-British Peoples United Party, which attained power in 1954, won a constitution, effective in 1964 which established self-government under a British appointed governor. British Honduras became Belize on June 1, 1973, following the passage of a surprise bill by the Peoples United Party, but the constitutional relationship with Britain remained unchanged.

In Dec. 1975, the U.N. General Assembly adopted a resolution supporting the right of the people of Belize to self-determination, and asking Britain and Guatemala to renew their negotiations on the future of Belize. Independence was obtained on Sept. 21, 1981. Elizabeth II is Head of State as Queen of Belize.

RULER

British, until 1981

MINT MARKS

H - Birmingham Mint
No mm - Royal Mint

***NOTE**: From 1975-1985 the Franklin Mint produced coinage in up to 3 different qualities. Qualities of issue are designated in ( ) after each date and are defined as follows:

(M) MATTE - Normal circulation strike or a dull finish produced by sandblasting special uncirculated (polish finish) or proof quality dies.

(U) SPECIAL UNCIRCULATED - Polished or proof-like in appearance without any frosted features.

(P) PROOF - The highest quality obtainable having mirror-like fields and frosted features.

MONETARY SYSTEM

Commencing 1864

100 Cents = 1 Dollar

COMMONWEALTH

DECIMAL COINAGE

KM# 33 CENT

2.70 g., Bronze, 19.5 mm. **Obv:** Bust of Queen Elizabeth right **Rev:** Denomination within circle, date lower right of circle **Edge:** Smooth **Shape:** Scalloped

Date	Mintage	VF20	XF40	MS60	MS63	MS65
1973	400,000	—	—	0.10	0.25	0.60
1974	2,000,000	—	—	0.10	0.20	0.50
1975	Inc. above	—	—	0.10	0.15	0.45
1976	3,000,000	—	—	0.10	0.15	0.45

KM# 33a CENT

0.80 g., Aluminum, 19.5 mm. **Obv:** Bust of Queen Elizabeth right **Rev:** Denomination within circle **Edge:** Smooth, scalloped

Date	Mintage	VF20	XF40	MS60	MS63	MS65
1976	2,049,999	—	—	0.10	0.25	0.60
1979	2,505,000	—	—	0.10	0.25	0.60
1980	1,505,000	—	—	0.10	0.25	0.60
1982	—	—	—	0.10	0.25	0.60
1983	—	—	—	0.10	0.25	0.60
1986	—	—	—	0.10	0.25	0.60
1987	—	—	—	0.10	0.25	0.60
1989	—	—	—	0.10	0.25	0.60
1990	—	—	—	0.10	0.25	0.60
1991	—	—	—	0.10	0.25	0.60
1992	—	—	—	0.10	0.25	0.60
1994	—	—	—	0.10	0.25	0.60
1996	—	—	—	0.10	0.20	0.50
1998	—	—	—	0.10	0.25	0.60
2000	—	—	—	0.10	0.25	0.60

KM# 38 CENT

2.67 g., Bronze **Obv:** National arms, date below, within wreath **Rev:** Swallow-tailed kite right, denomination above **Edge:** Smooth

Date	Mintage	VF20	XF40	MS60	MS63	MS65
1974 FM (M)	225,000	—	—	0.40	0.75	1.50
1974 FM (P)	21,000	PF65 1.25				

KM# 38a CENT

3.02 g., 0.925 Silver 0.0898 oz. ASW **Rev:** Swallow-tailed kite **Edge Lettering:** STERLING SILVER PROOF

Date	Mintage	VF20	XF40	MS60	MS63	MS65
1974 FM (P)	31,000	PF65 5.00				

KM# 46 CENT

Bronze **Obv:** National arms, date below, within wreath **Rev:** Swallow-tailed kite, right, denomination above **Edge:** Smooth **Shape:** Scalloped

Date	Mintage	VF20	XF40	MS60	MS63	MS65
1975 FM (M)	118,000	—	0.10	0.35	0.75	2.00
1975 FM (U)	1,095	—	—	0.50	1.00	2.25
1975 FM (P)	8,794	PF65 2.00				
1976 FM (M)	126,000	—	0.10	0.35	0.75	2.00
1976 FM (U)	759	—	—	0.50	1.00	2.25
1976 FM (P)	4,893	PF65 2.00				

KM# 46a CENT

3.02 g., 0.925 Silver 0.0898 oz. ASW, 19 mm. **Rev:** Swallow-tailed kite **Edge Lettering:** STERLING SILVER PROOF **Shape:** Scalloped

Date	Mintage	VF20	XF40	MS60	MS63	MS65
1975 FM (P)	13,000	PF65 5.00				
1976 FM (P)	5,897	PF65 5.00				
1977 FM (P)	3,197	PF65 5.00				
1978 FM (P)	3,342	PF65 5.00				
1979 FM (P)	2,445	PF65 5.00				
1980 FM (P)	1,826	PF65 5.00				
1981 FM (P)	615	PF65 5.00				

KM# 46a CENT

Aluminum **Obv:** National arms, date below, within wreath **Rev:** Swallow-tailed kite, right, denomination above **Edge:** Smooth **Shape:** Scalloped

Date	Mintage	VF20	XF40	MS60	MS63	MS65
1977 FM (U)	126,000	—	0.10	0.35	0.75	1.30
1977 FM (P)	2,107	PF65 2.00				
1978 FM (U)	125,000	—	0.10	0.35	0.75	1.30
1978 FM (P)	1,671	PF65 2.00				
1979 FM (U)	808	—	—	0.50	1.00	2.00
1979 FM (P)	1,287	PF65 2.00				
1980 FM (U)	761	—	0.15	0.40	0.75	1.00
1980 FM (P)	920	PF65 2.00				
1981 FM (U)	297	—	—	1.00	2.00	3.00
1981 FM (P)	643	PF65 2.00				

KM# 83 CENT

Aluminum **Rev:** Swallow-tailed kite **Edge:** Smooth **Shape:** Scalloped .

Date	Mintage	VF20	XF40	MS60	MS63	MS65
1982 FM (U)	—	0.15	0.25	0.65	1.50	1.75
1982 FM (P)	—	PF65 3.00				
1983 FM (U)	—	0.15	0.25	0.65	1.50	1.75
1983 FM (P)	—	PF65 3.00				

KM# 83a CENT

3.02 g., 0.925 Silver 0.0898 oz. ASW **Rev:** Swallow-tailed kite **Shape:** Scalloped

Date	Mintage	VF20	XF40	MS60	MS63	MS65
1982 FM (P)	381	PF65 9.00				
1983 FM (P)	336	PF65 9.00				

KM# 90 CENT

Aluminum **Rev:** Swallow-tailed kite, right, denomination above **Edge:** Smooth **Shape:** Scalloped

Date	Mintage	VF20	XF40	MS60	MS63	MS65
1984 FM (U)	—	0.15	0.25	0.65	1.50	1.75
1984 FM (P)	—	PF65 3.00				

KM# 90a CENT

3.02 g., 0.925 Silver 0.0898 oz. ASW **Rev:** Swallow-tailed kite **Shape:** Scalloped

Date	Mintage	VF20	XF40	MS60	MS63	MS65
1984 FM (P)	—	PF65 9.00				
1985	212	PF65 12.00				

KM# 34 5 CENTS

3.60 g., Nickel-Brass, 20.15 mm. **Obv:** Crowned bust of Queen Elizabeth II right **Rev:** Denomination within circle, date below circle **Edge:** Smooth

Date	Mintage	VF20	XF40	MS60	MS63	MS65
1973	210,000	—	—	0.50	1.00	2.00
1974	210,000	—	—	0.50	1.00	2.00
1975	420,000	—	—	0.20	0.40	1.00
1976	570,000	—	—	0.20	0.40	1.00
1979	—	—	—	0.20	0.40	1.00

KM# 34a 5 CENTS

1.04 g., Aluminum, 20.2 mm. **Obv:** Bust of Queen Elizabeth II right **Rev:** Denomination within circle **Edge:** Plain

Date	Mintage	VF20	XF40	MS60	MS63	MS65
1976	1,000,000	—	—	0.10	0.25	0.60
1979	960,000	—	—	0.10	0.25	0.75
1980	1,040,000	—	—	0.10	0.25	0.60
1986	—	—	—	0.10	0.25	0.60
1987	—	—	—	0.10	0.25	0.60
1989	—	—	—	0.10	0.25	0.60
1991	—	—	—	0.10	0.25	0.60
1992	—	—	—	0.10	0.25	0.60
1993	—	—	—	0.10	0.25	0.60
1994	—	—	—	0.10	0.25	0.60
2000	—	—	—	0.10	0.25	0.60

KM# 39 5 CENTS

Nickel-Brass, 20 mm. **Obv:** National arms, date below, within wreath **Rev:** Fork-tailed flycatchers, denomination above **Edge:** Smooth

Date	Mintage	VF20	XF40	MS60	MS63	MS65
1974 FM (M)	50,000	—	0.25	0.60	1.25	2.50
1974 FM (P)	21,000	PF65 2.00				

KM# 39a 5 CENTS

4.35 g., 0.925 Silver 0.1294 oz. ASW, 20 mm. **Rev:** Fork-tailed flycatcher

Date	Mintage	VF20	XF40	MS60	MS63	MS65
1974 FM (P)	31,000	PF65 6.00				

KM# 47 5 CENTS

3.60 g., Nickel-Brass, 20 mm. **Obv:** National arms, date below, within wreath **Rev:** Fork-tailed flycatchers, denomination above **Edge:** Smooth

Date	Mintage	VF20	XF40	MS60	MS63	MS65
1975 FM (M)	24,000	—	0.25	0.65	1.50	2.50
1975 FM (U)	1,095	—	—	0.50	1.00	2.50
1975 FM (P)	8,794	PF65 1.25				
1976 FM (M)	25,000	—	0.25	0.65	1.50	2.50
1976 FM (U)	759	—	0.25	0.65	1.50	2.50
1976 FM (P)	4,893	PF65 1.25				

KM# 47a 5 CENTS

4.35 g., 0.925 Silver 0.1294 oz. ASW, 20 mm. **Rev:** Fork-tailed flycatcher

Date	Mintage	VF20	XF40	MS60	MS63	MS65
1975 FM (P)	13,000	PF65 6.00				
1976 FM (P)	5,897	PF65 6.00				
1977 FM (P)	3,197	PF65 6.00				
1978 FM (P)	3,342	PF65 6.00				
1979 FM (P)	2,445	PF65 6.00				
1980 FM (P)	1,826	PF65 6.00				
1981 FM (P)	615	PF65 6.00				

KM# 47b 5 CENTS

Aluminum **Rev:** Fork-tailed flycatcher **Edge:** Smooth

Date	Mintage	VF20	XF40	MS60	MS63	MS65
1977 FM (U)	26,000	—	—	0.20	0.50	0.75
1977 FM (P)	2,107	PF65 2.00				
1978 FM (U)	25,000	—	—	0.20	0.50	0.75
1978 FM (P)	1,671	PF65 2.00				
1979 FM (U)	808	—	0.15	0.35	0.75	1.00
1979 FM (P)	1,287	—	0.25	0.50	1.00	1.50
1980 FM (U)	761	—	0.15	0.35	0.75	1.00
1980 FM (P)	920	PF65 2.00				
1981 FM (U)	297	—	0.15	0.35	0.75	1.00
1981 FM (P)	643	PF65 2.00				

KM# 64 5 CENTS

1.00 g., Aluminum, 20.15 mm. **Series:** World Food Day **Obv:** Crowned bust of Queen Elizabeth II, right **Rev:** Denomination, date upper right **Edge:** Smooth

Date	Mintage	VF20	XF40	MS60	MS63	MS65
1981	—	—	—	0.20	0.35	0.70

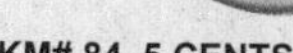

KM# 84 5 CENTS

Aluminum **Obv:** National arms within wreath, date below **Rev:** Fork-tailed flycatchers, denomination above **Edge:** Smooth

Date	Mintage	VF20	XF40	MS60	MS63	MS65
1982 FM (U)	—	0.15	0.25	0.65	1.50	2.00
1982 FM (P)	—	PF65 3.00				
1983 FM (U)	—	0.15	0.25	0.65	1.50	2.00
1983 FM (P)	—	PF65 3.00				

KM# 84a 5 CENTS

4.35 g., 0.925 Silver 0.1294 oz. ASW **Obv:** National arms within wreath, value below **Rev:** Fork-tailed flycatchers, denomination above

Date	Mintage	VF20	XF40	MS60	MS63	MS65
1982 FM (P)	381	PF65 14.00				
1983 FM (P)	479	PF65 14.00				

KM# 91 5 CENTS

Aluminum **Obv:** National arms within wreath, date below **Rev:** Fork-tailed flycatchers, denomination above

Date	Mintage	VF20	XF40	MS60	MS63	MS65
1984 FM (U)	—	0.25	0.45	0.75	1.75	2.25
1984 FM (P)	—	PF65 3.00				

KM# 91a 5 CENTS

4.35 g., 0.925 Silver 0.1294 oz. ASW **Obv:** National arms within wreath, date below **Rev:** Fork-tailed flycatchers, denomination above

Date	Mintage	VF20	XF40	MS60	MS63	MS65
1984 FM (P)	—	PF65 14.00				
1985	212	PF65 16.00				

KM# 115 5 CENTS

1.05 g., Aluminum, 20.2 mm.

Date	Mintage	VF20	XF40	MS60	MS63	MS65
1992	—	—	—	0.10	0.20	0.40
1993	—	—	—	0.10	0.20	0.40
1994	—	—	—	0.10	0.20	0.40
2000	—	—	—	0.10	0.20	0.40

KM# 35 10 CENTS

2.40 g., Copper-Nickel, 16.95 mm. **Obv:** Crowned bust of Queen Elizabeth, right **Rev:** Denomination within circle, date below **Edge:** Reeded

Date	Mintage	VF20	XF40	MS60	MS63	MS65
1974	100,000	—	0.15	0.35	0.60	1.25
1975	200,000	—	0.10	0.25	0.50	1.00
1976	700,000	—	0.10	0.25	0.45	0.85
1979	800,000	—	0.10	0.20	0.40	0.75
1980	—	—	0.10	0.20	0.40	0.75
1981	—	—	0.10	0.20	0.40	0.75
1992	—	—	0.10	0.20	0.40	0.75
2000	—	—	—	0.15	0.40	0.65

KM# 40 10 CENTS

2.40 g., Copper-Nickel, 16.95 mm. **Obv:** National arms, date below, within wreath **Rev:** Long-tailed hermit, right, denomination above **Edge:** Reeded

Date	Mintage	VF20	XF40	MS60	MS63	MS65
1974 FM (M)	27,000	—	—	1.00	2.00	4.00
1974 FM (P)	21,000	PF65 1.75				

KM# 40a 10 CENTS

2.79 g., 0.925 Silver 0.083 oz. ASW, 16.95 mm. **Rev:** Long-tailed hermit

Date	Mintage	VF20	XF40	MS60	MS63	MS65
1974 FM (P)	31,000	PF65 5.00				

KM# 48 10 CENTS

2.40 g., Copper-Nickel, 16.95 mm. **Obv:** National arms, date below, within wreath **Rev:** Long-tailed hermit, right, denomination above **Edge:** Reeded

Date	Mintage	VF20	XF40	MS60	MS63	MS65
1975 FM (M)	12,000	—	0.25	0.65	1.50	2.00
1975 FM (U)	1,095	—	—	1.00	2.00	4.00
1975 FM (P)	8,794	PF65 1.50				
1976 FM (M)	13,000	—	0.25	0.65	1.50	2.00
1976 FM (U)	759	—	—	1.00	2.00	4.00
1976 FM (P)	4,893	PF65 1.50				
1977 FM (U)	14,000	—	0.25	0.65	1.50	2.00
1977 FM (P)	2,107	PF65 2.00				
1978 FM (U)	13,000	—	0.25	0.65	1.50	1.75
1978 FM (P)	1,671	PF65 3.00				
1979 FM (U)	808	—	—	1.00	3.00	6.00
1979 FM (P)	1,287	PF65 3.00				
1980 FM (U)	761	—	—	1.00	3.00	6.00
1980 FM (P)	920	PF65 3.00				
1981 FM (U)	297	—	—	1.00	3.00	6.00
1981 FM (P)	643	PF65 4.00				

KM# 48a 10 CENTS

2.79 g., 0.925 Silver 0.083 oz. ASW, 16.95 mm. **Rev:** Long-tailed hermit

Date	Mintage	VF20	XF40	MS60	MS63	MS65
1975 FM (P)	13,000	PF65 5.00				
1976 FM (P)	5,897	PF65 5.00				
1977 FM (P)	3,197	PF65 5.00				
1978 FM (P)	3,342	PF65 5.00				
1979 FM (P)	2,445	PF65 5.00				
1980 FM (P)	1,826	PF65 5.00				
1981 FM (P)	615	PF65 6.00				

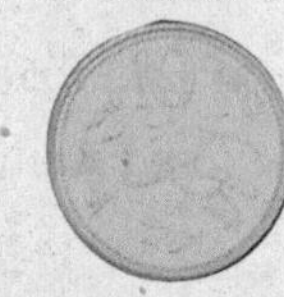

KM# 85 10 CENTS

2.40 g., Copper-Nickel, 16.95 mm. **Rev:** Long-tailed hermit **Edge:** Reeded

Date	Mintage	VF20	XF40	MS60	MS63	MS65
1982 FM (U)	—	—	0.25	1.00	2.50	3.50
1982 FM (P)	—	PF65 3.50				
1983 FM (U)	—	—	0.25	1.00	2.50	3.50
1983 FM (P)	—	PF65 3.50				

KM# 85a 10 CENTS

2.79 g., 0.925 Silver 0.083 oz. ASW, 16.95 mm. **Rev:** Long-tailed hermit

Date	Mintage	VF20	XF40	MS60	MS63	MS65
1982 FM (P)	381	PF65 16.00				
1983 FM (P)	312	PF65 16.00				

KM# 92 10 CENTS

2.40 g., Copper-Nickel, 16.95 mm. **Obv:** National arms within wreath, date below **Rev:** Long-tailed hermit, right, denomination above **Edge:** Reeded

Date	Mintage	VF20	XF40	MS60	MS63	MS65
1984 FM (U)	—	—	0.25	1.00	2.50	3.50
1984 FM (P)	—	PF65 3.50				

KM# 92a 10 CENTS

2.79 g., 0.925 Silver 0.083 oz. ASW, 16.95 mm. **Obv:** National arms within wreath, date below **Rev:** Long-tailed hermit, right, denomination above

Date	Mintage	VF20	XF40	MS60	MS63	MS65
1984 FM (P)	—	PF65 16.00				
1985	212	PF65 19.00				

KM# 36 25 CENTS

5.66 g., Copper-Nickel, 23.6 mm. **Obv:** Crowned bust of Queen Elizabeth II right **Rev:** Denomination within circle, date below **Edge:** Reeded

Date	Mintage	VF20	XF40	MS60	MS63	MS65
1974	100,000	—	0.35	0.65	1.25	2.50
1975	200,000	—	0.20	0.35	0.75	1.00
1976	790,000	—	0.20	0.35	0.75	1.00
1979	500,000	—	0.20	0.35	0.75	1.00
1980	—	—	0.20	0.35	0.75	1.00
1981	—	—	0.20	0.35	0.75	1.00
1986	—	—	0.20	0.35	0.75	1.00
1987	—	—	0.20	0.35	0.75	1.00
1988	—	—	0.20	0.35	0.75	1.00
1989	—	—	0.20	0.35	0.75	1.00
1991	—	—	0.20	0.35	0.75	1.00
1992	—	—	0.20	0.35	0.75	1.00
1993	—	—	0.20	0.35	0.75	1.00
1994	—	—	0.20	0.35	0.75	1.00
1998	—	—	0.20	0.35	0.75	1.00
2000	—	—	0.20	0.35	0.75	1.50

KM# 41 25 CENTS
Copper-Nickel, 23.6 mm. **Obv:** National arms, date below, within wreath **Rev:** Blue-crowned motmot, left, denomination above **Edge:** Reeded

Date	Mintage	VF20	XF40	MS60	MS63	MS65
1974 FM (M)	13,000	—	—	1.00	3.50	5.00
1974 FM (P)	21,000	PF65 3.00				

KM# 41a 25 CENTS
6.60 g., 0.925 Silver 0.1963 oz. ASW, 23.6 mm. **Rev:** Blue-crowned motmot

Date	Mintage	VF20	XF40	MS60	MS63	MS65
1974 FM (P)	31,000	PF65 9.00				

KM# 49 25 CENTS
Copper-Nickel, 23.6 mm. **Obv:** National arms above date within wreath **Rev:** Blue-crowned motmot left, denomination below **Edge:** Reeded

Date	Mintage	VF20	XF40	MS60	MS63	MS65
1975 FM (M)	4,716	—	0.35	1.00	3.00	4.00
1975 FM (U)	1,095	—	—	1.00	3.00	4.00
1975 FM (P)	8,794	PF65 2.50				
1976 FM (M)	5,000	—	0.50	2.00	4.00	5.00
1976 FM (U)	759	—	—	2.00	4.00	6.00
1976 FM (P)	4,893	PF65 2.50				
1977 FM (U)	5,520	—	0.30	1.00	3.00	4.00
1977 FM (P)	2,107	PF65 2.75				
1978 FM (U)	5,458	—	0.30	1.00	3.00	4.50
1978 FM (P)	1,671	PF65 2.75				
1979 FM (U)	808	—	—	2.00	4.00	6.00
1979 FM (P)	1,287	PF65 3.00				
1980 FM (U)	761	—	0.35	1.00	3.00	4.50
1980 FM (P)	920	PF65 3.00				
1981 FM (U)	297	—	0.35	1.25	3.50	6.00
1981 FM (P)	643	PF65 3.00				

KM# 49a 25 CENTS
6.60 g., 0.925 Silver 0.1963 oz. ASW, 23.6 mm. **Obv:** National arms above date within wreath **Rev:** Blue-crowned motmot

Date	Mintage	VF20	XF40	MS60	MS63	MS65
1975 FM (P)	13,000	PF65 10.00				
1976 FM (P)	5,897	PF65 10.00				
1977 FM (P)	3,197	PF65 10.00				
1978 FM (P)	3,342	PF65 10.00				
1979 FM (P)	2,445	PF65 10.00				
1980 FM (P)	1,826	PF65 10.00				
1981 FM (P)	615	PF65 12.00				

KM# 86 25 CENTS
Copper-Nickel, 23.6 mm. **Obv:** National arms within wreath, date below **Rev:** Blue-crowned motmot, right, denomination below

Date	Mintage	VF20	XF40	MS60	MS63	MS65
1982 FM (U)	—	—	0.50	1.50	4.00	5.00
1982 FM (P)	—	PF65 5.00				
1983 FM (U)	—	—	0.50	1.50	4.00	5.00
1983 FM (P)	—	PF65 5.00				

KM# 86a 25 CENTS
6.60 g., 0.925 Silver 0.1963 oz. ASW, 23.6 mm. **Obv:** National arms within wreath, date below **Rev:** Blue-crowned motmot

Date	Mintage	VF20	XF40	MS60	MS63	MS65
1982 FM (P)	381	PF65 22.50				
1983 FM (P)	314	PF65 22.50				

KM# 93 25 CENTS
Copper-Nickel, 23.6 mm. **Obv:** National arms within wreath, date below **Rev:** Blue-crowned motmot, right, denomination below **Edge:** Reeded

Date	Mintage	VF20	XF40	MS60	MS63	MS65
1984 FM (U)	—	—	0.50	1.50	4.00	5.00
1984 FM (P)	—	PF65 5.00				

KM# 93a 25 CENTS
6.60 g., 0.925 Silver 0.1963 oz. ASW, 23.6 mm. **Obv:** National arms within wreath, date below **Rev:** Blue-crowned motmot

Date	Mintage	VF20	XF40	MS60	MS63	MS65
1984 FM (P)	—	PF65 22.50				
1985	212	PF65 27.50				

KM# 77 25 CENTS
5.60 g., Copper-Nickel, 23.6 mm. **Subject:** World Forestry Congress **Obv:** Crowned bust of Queen Elizabeth right **Rev:** Denomination within circle, date below **Edge:** Reeded

Date	Mintage	VF20	XF40	MS60	MS63	MS65
1985	—	—	0.25	0.50	0.85	1.10

KM# 37 50 CENTS
9.07 g., Copper-Nickel, 27.74 mm. **Obv:** Crowned bust of Queen Elizabeth right **Rev:** Denomination within circle, date below **Edge:** Reeded

Date	Mintage	VF20	XF40	MS60	MS63	MS65
1974	123,000	—	0.50	1.50	3.00	4.50
1975	Inc. above	—	0.40	0.85	2.00	3.00
1976	312,000	—	0.40	0.85	2.00	3.00
1979	125,000	—	0.50	1.50	3.00	4.50
1980	—	—	0.35	0.75	1.75	2.75
1989	—	—	0.35	0.75	1.75	2.75
1991	—	—	0.50	1.00	2.00	3.00
1992	—	—	0.50	1.00	2.00	3.00
1993	—	—	0.50	1.00	2.00	3.00

KM# 42 50 CENTS
Copper-Nickel, 27.7 mm. **Rev:** Frigate bird **Edge:** Reeded

Date	Mintage	VF20	XF40	MS60	MS63	MS65
1974 FM (M)	8,806	—	0.40	2.00	4.50	—
1974 FM (P)	21,000	PF65 3.50				

KM# 42a 50 CENTS
9.94 g., 0.925 Silver 0.2956 oz. ASW, 27.7 mm. **Rev:** Frigate bird

Date	Mintage	VF20	XF40	MS60	MS63	MS65
1974 FM (P)	31,000	PF65 15.00				

KM# 50 50 CENTS
Copper-Nickel, 27.7 mm. **Obv:** National arms above date within wreath **Rev:** Frigate birds, denomination above **Edge:** Reeded

Date	Mintage	VF20	XF40	MS60	MS63	MS65
1975 FM (M)	2,358	—	0.65	3.00	6.00	7.00
1975 FM (U)	1,095	—	0.45	2.00	4.50	6.00
1975 FM (P)	8,794	PF65 4.00				
1976 FM (M)	3,259	—	0.50	2.00	5.00	6.00
1976 FM (U)	759	—	0.50	2.00	5.00	6.00
1976 FM (P)	4,893	PF65 6.00				
1977 FM (U)	3,540	—	0.45	2.00	4.50	6.00
1977 FM (P)	2,107	PF65 6.00				
1978 FM (U)	2,958	—	0.45	2.00	4.50	6.00
1978 FM (P)	1,671	PF65 6.00				
1979 FM (U)	808	—	0.50	2.00	5.00	7.50
1979 FM (P)	1,287	PF65 6.00				
1980 FM (U)	761	—	0.50	2.00	5.00	7.50
1980 FM (P)	920	PF65 6.50				
1981 FM (U)	297	—	0.50	2.00	5.00	7.50
1981 FM (P)	643	PF65 6.50				

KM# 50a 50 CENTS
9.94 g., 0.925 Silver 0.2956 oz. ASW, 27.7 mm. **Obv:** National arms above date within wreath **Rev:** Frigate bird **Edge Lettering:** STERLING SILVER PROOF and reeding

Date	Mintage	VF20	XF40	MS60	MS63	MS65
1975 FM (P)	13,000	PF65 8.00				
1976 FM (P)	5,897	PF65 10.00				
1977 FM (P)	3,197	PF65 10.00				

Date	Mintage	VF20	XF40	MS60	MS63	MS65
1978 FM (P)	3,342	PF65 10.00				
1979 FM (P)	2,445	PF65 11.00				
1980 FM (P)	1,826	PF65 13.00				
1981 FM (P)	615	PF65 16.00				

KM# 87 50 CENTS
Copper-Nickel, 27.7 mm. **Obv:** National arms within wreath, date below **Rev:** Frigate birds, denomination above **Edge:** Reeded

Date	Mintage	VF20	XF40	MS60	MS63	MS65
1982 FM (U)	—	0.75	1.50	3.00	6.50	7.00
1982 FM (P)	—	PF65 7.50				
1983 FM (U)	—	0.75	1.50	3.00	6.50	7.00
1983 FM (P)	—	PF65 7.50				

KM# 87a 50 CENTS
9.94 g., 0.925 Silver 0.2956 oz. ASW, 27.7 mm. **Obv:** National arms within wreath, date below **Rev:** Frigate bird

Date	Mintage	VF20	XF40	MS60	MS63	MS65
1982 FM (P)	381	PF65 33.00				
1983 FM (P)	312	PF65 33.00				

KM# 94 50 CENTS
Copper-Nickel, 27.7 mm. **Obv:** National arms within wreath, date below **Rev:** Frigate birds, denomination above **Edge:** Reeded

Date	Mintage	VF20	XF40	MS60	MS63	MS65
1984 FM (U)	—	0.75	1.50	3.00	6.50	7.00
1984 FM (P)	—	PF65 7.50				

KM# 94a 50 CENTS
9.94 g., 0.925 Silver 0.2956 oz. ASW, 27.7 mm. **Obv:** National arms within wreath, date below **Rev:** Frigate bird

Date	Mintage	VF20	XF40	MS60	MS63	MS65
1984 FM (P)	—	PF65 33.00				
1985	212	PF65 39.00				

KM# 118 50 CENTS
Copper-Nickel **Obv:** New portrait of Queen Elizabeth II **Rev:** Denomination within circle, date below

Date	Mintage	VF20	XF40	MS60	MS63	MS65
1992	—	—	—	1.00	2.00	3.50
1993	—	—	—	1.00	2.00	3.50

KM# 43 DOLLAR
Copper-Nickel, 35 mm. **Obv:** National arms above date within wreath **Rev:** Scarlet macaws, denomination above **Edge:** Reeded

Date	Mintage	VF20	XF40	MS60	MS63	MS65
1974 FM (M)	6,656	—	—	4.00	9.00	12.00
1974 FM (P)	21,000	PF65 6.00				
1975 FM (M)	1,182	—	1.50	4.50	10.00	12.50

Date	Mintage	VF20	XF40	MS60	MS63	MS65
1975 FM (U)	1,095	—	0.75	4.00	9.00	12.00
1975 FM (P)	8,794	PF65 6.00				
1976 FM (M)	1,250	—	1.50	4.50	10.00	12.50
1976 FM (U)	759	—	1.25	4.00	9.00	12.50
1976 FM (P)	4,893	PF65 6.00				
1977 FM (U)	1,770	—	1.00	3.50	9.00	12.00
1977 FM (P)	2,107	PF65 6.00				
1978 FM (U)	1,708	—	1.00	3.50	9.00	12.00
1978 FM (P)	1,671	PF65 6.00				
1979 FM (U)	808	—	1.25	3.75	9.00	12.00
1979 FM (P)	1,287	PF65 6.00				
1980 FM (U)	761	—	1.25	3.75	9.00	12.00
1980 FM (P)	920	PF65 6.00				
1981 FM (U)	297	—	1.50	4.00	10.00	12.50
1981 FM (P)	643	PF65 8.50				

KM# 43a DOLLAR

19.89 g., 0.925 Silver 0.5915 oz. ASW, 35 mm. **Obv:** National arms above date within wreath **Rev:** Scarlet macaw **Edge Lettering:** STERLING SILVER PROOF and reeding

Date	Mintage	VF20	XF40	MS60	MS63	MS65
1974 FM (P)	31,000	PF65 15.00				
1975 FM (P)	13,000	PF65 17.00				
1976 FM (P)	5,897	PF65 20.00				
1977 FM (P)	3,197	PF65 22.00				
1978 FM (P)	3,342	PF65 22.00				
1979 FM (P)	2,445	PF65 24.00				
1980 FM (P)	1,826	PF65 24.00				
1981 FM (P)	615	PF65 28.00				

KM# 88 DOLLAR

Copper-Nickel, 35 mm. **Obv:** National arms within wreath, date below **Rev:** Scarlet macaws, denomination above

Date	Mintage	VF20	XF40	MS60	MS63	MS65
1982 FM (U)	—	—	1.50	3.00	10.00	12.50
1982 FM (P)	—	PF65 8.50				
1983 FM (U)	—	—	1.50	3.00	10.00	12.50
1983 FM (P)	—	PF65 8.50				

KM# 88a DOLLAR

19.89 g., 0.925 Silver 0.5915 oz. ASW, 35 mm. **Obv:** National arms within wreath, date below **Rev:** Scarlet macaw

Date	Mintage	VF20	XF40	MS60	MS63	MS65
1982 FM (P)	381	PF65 45.00				
1983 FM (P)	1,589	PF65 45.00				

KM# 95 DOLLAR

Copper-Nickel, 35 mm. **Obv:** National arms within wreath, date below **Rev:** Scarlet macaws, denomination above

Date	Mintage	VF20	XF40	MS60	MS63	MS65
1984 FM (U)	—	—	1.50	3.00	10.00	12.50
1984 FM (P)	—	PF65 8.50				

KM# 95a DOLLAR

19.89 g., 0.925 Silver 0.5915 oz. ASW, 35 mm. **Obv:** National arms within wreath, date below **Rev:** Scarlet macaws, denomination above

Date	Mintage	VF20	XF40	MS60	MS63	MS65
1984 FM (P)	—	PF65 30.00				
1985	212	PF65 55.00				

KM# 99 DOLLAR

8.90 g., Nickel-Brass, 27 mm. **Obv:** Crowned bust of Queen Elizabeth II right **Rev:** Columbus' three ships, denomination above, date below **Edge:** Alternating reeded and plain **Shape:** 10-sided

Date	Mintage	VF20	XF40	MS60	MS63	MS65
1990	—	—	—	1.00	2.25	3.00
1991	—	—	—	1.00	2.25	3.00
1992	—	—	—	1.00	2.25	3.00
2000	—	—	—	1.00	2.25	3.00

KM# 99a DOLLAR

9.00 g., 0.925 Silver 0.2677 oz. ASW, 27 mm. **Obv:** Crowned Queen's portrait, right **Rev:** Columbus' three ships

Date	Mintage	VF20	XF40	MS60	MS63	MS65
1990	Est. 5000	PF65 25.00				

KM# 135 DOLLAR

15.95 g., Silver, 28.2 mm. **Subject:** Queen Elizabeth II - The Queen Mother - Summer in Balmoral Castle **Obv:** National arms **Rev:** Balmoral Castle **Edge:** Reeded

Date	Mintage	VF20	XF40	MS60	MS63	MS65
1997	—	—	—	—	—	20.00

KM# 100 2 DOLLARS

Copper-Nickel **Subject:** Queen Mother's 90th Birthday **Obv:** Crowned bust of Queen Elizabeth II right **Rev:** Crowned ornate "E"s, backs intertwined, sprays flanking, two dates below

Date	Mintage	VF20	XF40	MS60	MS63	MS65
ND-1990	—	—	—	—	3.00	5.00

KM# 100a 2 DOLLARS

28.28 g., 0.925 Silver 0.841 oz. ASW **Subject:** Queen Mother's 90th Birthday **Obv:** Crowned Queen's portrait, right **Rev:** Crowned ornate "E"s, backs intertwined, sprays flanking, two dates below

Date	Mintage	VF20	XF40	MS60	MS63	MS65
ND-1990	Est. 10000	PF63 25.00	PF65 32.00			

KM# 119 2 DOLLARS

28.28 g., 0.925 Silver 0.841 oz. ASW **Subject:** 40th Anniversary - Coronation of Queen Elizabeth II **Obv:** Crowned Queen's portrait, right **Rev:** Facing Queen Elizabeth II on horseback saluting, two dates at bottom

Date	Mintage	VF20	XF40	MS60	MS63	MS65
ND-1993	Est. 10000	PF63 25.00	PF65 32.00			

KM# 131 2 DOLLARS

8.00 g., Copper-Nickel, 28.4 mm. **Subject:** Battle of St. George's Caye **Obv:** National arms within wreath, denomination below **Rev:** Oar-powered landing craft shorebound, within circle, two dates below **Edge:** Reeded

Date	Mintage	VF20	XF40	MS60	MS63	MS65
ND-1998	5,000	—	—	—	5.00	7.00

KM# 132 2 DOLLARS

28.28 g., 0.925 Silver 0.841 oz. ASW, 38.6 mm. **Subject:** Heritage Protection **Obv:** National arms **Rev:** Large building, people, jaguar and arms, denomination below **Edge:** Reeded

Date	Mintage	VF20	XF40	MS60	MS63	MS65
1998	5,000	PF63 32.00	PF65 40.00			

KM# 44 5 DOLLARS

Copper-Nickel, 37.8 mm. **Obv:** National arms above date within wreath **Rev:** Keel-billed toucan, right, denomination above **Edge:** Reeded

Date	Mintage	VF20	XF40	MS60	MS63	MS65
1974 FM (M)	4,936	—	—	2.75	5.00	7.50
1974 FM (P)	21,000	PF65 6.50				
1975 FM (M)	237	—	—	7.00	15.00	25.00
1975 FM (U)	1,095	—	—	2.75	5.00	7.50
1975 FM (P)	8,794	PF65 6.50				
1976 FM (M)	250	—	—	7.00	15.00	25.00
1976 FM (U)	759	—	—	2.75	5.00	7.50
1976 FM (P)	4,893	PF65 6.50				
1977 FM (U)	720	—	—	2.75	5.00	7.50
1977 FM (P)	2,107	PF65 7.50				
1978 FM (U)	708	—	—	2.75	5.00	7.50
1978 FM (P)	1,671	PF65 7.50				
1979 FM (U)	808	—	—	2.75	5.00	7.50
1979 FM (P)	1,287	PF65 7.50				
1980 FM (U)	761	—	—	2.75	5.00	7.50
1980 FM (P)	920	PF65 7.50				
1981 FM (U)	297	—	—	2.75	5.00	7.50
1981 FM (P)	643	PF65 8.50				

KM# 44a 5 DOLLARS

26.40 g., 0.925 Silver 0.7851 oz. ASW, 37.8 mm. **Obv:** National arms above date within wreath **Rev:** Keel-billed toucan

Date	Mintage	VF20	XF40	MS60	MS63	MS65
1974 FM (P)	31,000	PF65 18.00				
1975 FM (P)	13,000	PF65 20.00				
1976 FM (P)	5,897	PF65 22.00				
1977 FM (P)	3,197	PF65 25.00				
1978 FM (P)	3,342	PF65 25.00				
1979 FM (P)	2,445	PF65 30.00				
1980 FM (P)	1,826	PF65 30.00				
1981 FM (P)	615	PF65 32.00				

KM# 89 5 DOLLARS

Copper-Nickel, 37.8 mm. **Obv:** National arms above date within wreath **Rev:** Keel-billed toucan

Date	Mintage	VF20	XF40	MS60	MS63	MS65
1982 FM (U)	—	—	2.00	4.00	10.00	12.00
1982 FM (P)	—	PF65 15.00				

Date	Mintage	VF20	XF40	MS60	MS63	MS65
1983 FM (U)	—	—	2.00	4.00	10.00	12.00
1983 FM (P)	—	PF65 15.00				

KM# 89a 5 DOLLARS
26.40 g., 0.925 Silver 0.7851 oz. ASW, 37.8 mm. **Obv:** National arms above date within wreath **Rev:** Keel-billed toucan

Date	Mintage	VF20	XF40	MS60	MS63	MS65
1982 FM (P)	381	PF65 75.00				
1983 FM (P)	311	PF65 75.00				

KM# 96 5 DOLLARS
Copper-Nickel, 37.8 mm. **Obv:** National arms within wreath, date below **Rev:** Keel-billed toucan, right, denomination above

Date	Mintage	VF20	XF40	MS60	MS63	MS65
1984 FM (U)	—	—	2.00	4.00	6.00	10.00
1984 FM (P)	—	PF65 12.50				

KM# 96a 5 DOLLARS
26.40 g., 0.925 Silver 0.7851 oz. ASW, 37.8 mm. **Obv:** National arms within wreath, date below **Rev:** Keel-billed toucan, right, denomination above

Date	Mintage	VF20	XF40	MS60	MS63	MS65
1984 FM (P)	—	PF65 50.00				
1985	212	PF65 65.00				

KM# 107 5 DOLLARS
28.28 g., 0.925 Silver 0.841 oz. ASW **Subject:** 50th Anniversary - Battle of El Alamein - Field Marshall Rommel **Obv:** Bust of Queen Elizabeth II right **Rev:** Field Marshall Rommel, right, in uniform, denomination lower right

Date	Mintage	VF20	XF40	MS60	MS63	MS65
1992	Est. 5000	PF65 45.00				

KM# 108 5 DOLLARS
28.28 g., 0.925 Silver 0.841 oz. ASW **Subject:** 50th Anniversary - Battle of El Alamein - Lt. Gen. Montgomery **Obv:** Bust of Queen Elizabeth II right **Rev:** Lt. Gen. Montgomery, denomination at bottom

Date	Mintage	VF20	XF40	MS60	MS63	MS65
1992	—	PF65 45.00				

KM# 126 5 DOLLARS
28.28 g., 0.925 Silver 0.841 oz. ASW **Subject:** Queen Mother - Balmoral Castle **Obv:** National arms within wreath, date below **Rev:** Balmoral Castle above date, denomination at bottom

Date	Mintage	VF20	XF40	MS60	MS63	MS65
1995	Est. 40000	PF65 25.00				

KM# 133 5 DOLLARS
28.50 g., 0.925 Silver 0.8476 oz. ASW, 38.5 mm. **Subject:** Queen Elizabeth II's Golden Wedding Anniversary **Obv:** National arms within wreath, date below **Rev:** Royal couple below gold inset shield, denomination at bottom **Edge:** Reeded

Date	Mintage	VF20	XF40	MS60	MS63	MS65
1997	—	PF65 35.00				

KM# 45 10 DOLLARS
Copper-Nickel, 40 mm. **Obv:** National arms above date within wreath **Rev:** Great curassow, right, denomination above **Edge:** Reeded

Date	Mintage	VF20	XF40	MS60	MS63	MS65
1974 FM (M)	4,726	—	—	3.50	9.00	12.00
1974 FM (P)	21,000	PF65 8.00				
1975 FM (M)	117	—	—	12.50	45.00	55.00
1975 FM (U)	1,095	—	—	3.50	10.00	12.50
1975 FM (P)	8,794	PF65 9.00				
1976 FM (M)	125	—	—	10.00	35.00	55.00
1976 FM (U)	759	—	—	3.50	10.00	12.50
1976 FM (P)	4,893	PF65 10.00				
1977 FM (U)	645	—	—	4.00	12.00	15.00
1977 FM (P)	2,107	PF65 12.50				
1978 FM (U)	583	—	—	5.00	12.00	15.00
1978 FM (P)	1,671	PF65 12.50				

KM# 45a 10 DOLLARS
29.80 g., 0.925 Silver 0.8862 oz. ASW, 40 mm. **Obv:** National arms above date within wreath **Rev:** Great curassow

Date	Mintage	VF20	XF40	MS60	MS63	MS65
1974 FM (P)	31,000	PF65 20.00				
1975 FM (P)	13,000	PF65 25.00				
1976 FM (P)	5,897	PF65 30.00				
1977 FM (P)	3,197	PF65 35.00				
1978 FM (P)	3,342	PF65 35.00				

KM# 57 10 DOLLARS
Copper-Nickel, 40 mm. **Obv:** National arms above date within wreath **Rev:** Flying jabirus, denomination above

Date	Mintage	VF20	XF40	MS60	MS63	MS65
1979 FM (U)	808	—	—	7.00	20.00	35.00
1979 FM (P)	1,287	PF65 30.00				

KM# 57a 10 DOLLARS
29.80 g., 0.925 Silver 0.8862 oz. ASW, 40 mm. **Obv:** National arms above date within wreath **Rev:** Flying jabirus

Date	Mintage	VF20	XF40	MS60	MS63	MS65
1979 FM (P)	2,445	PF65 40.00				

KM# 60 10 DOLLARS
Copper-Nickel, 40 mm. **Obv:** National arms above date within wreath **Rev:** Two Scarlet ibis, denomination above

Date	Mintage	VF20	XF40	MS60	MS63	MS65
1980 FM (U)	761	—	—	7.00	20.00	35.00
1980 FM (P)	920	PF65 35.00				

KM# 60a 10 DOLLARS
25.50 g., 0.925 Silver 0.7584 oz. ASW, 40 mm. **Obv:** National arms above date within wreath **Rev:** Scarlet ibis

Date	Mintage	VF20	XF40	MS60	MS63	MS65
1980 FM (P)	1,826	PF65 50.00				

KM# 65 10 DOLLARS
Copper-Nickel, 40 mm. **Obv:** National arms above date within wreath **Rev:** Roseate spoonbill, left, denomination above

Date	Mintage	VF20	XF40	MS60	MS63	MS65
1981 FM (U)	297	—	7.50	15.00	40.00	50.00
1981 FM (P)	643	PF65 50.00				

KM# 65a 10 DOLLARS
25.50 g., 0.925 Silver 0.7584 oz. ASW, 40 mm. **Obv:** National arms above date within wreath **Rev:** Roseate spoonbill

Date	Mintage	VF20	XF40	MS60	MS63	MS65
1981 FM (P)	615	PF65 75.00				

KM# 69 10 DOLLARS
Copper-Nickel, 40 mm. **Obv:** National arms above date within wreath **Rev:** Yellow-crowned Amazon parrot, right, denomination at bottom

Date	Mintage	VF20	XF40	MS60	MS63	MS65
1982 FM (U)	—	—	10.00	20.00	35.00	50.00
1982 FM (P)	—	PF65 65.00				

KM# 69a 10 DOLLARS
25.50 g., 0.925 Silver 0.7584 oz. ASW, 40 mm. **Obv:** National arms above date within wreath **Rev:** Yellow-crowned Amazon parrot

Date	Mintage	VF20	XF40	MS60	MS63	MS65
1982 FM (P)	381	PF65 120				

KM# 80 10 DOLLARS

Copper-Nickel, 40 mm. **Obv:** National arms within wreath, date below **Rev:** Great Curassow, right, denomination above **Note:** Mule.

Date	Mintage	VF20	XF40	MS60	MS63	MS65
1982 FM (U)	—	—	—	12.00	20.00	32.00

KM# 71 10 DOLLARS

Copper-Nickel, 40 mm. **Obv:** National arms above date within wreath **Rev:** Ringed Kingfisher, right, denomination above

Date	Mintage	VF20	XF40	MS60	MS63	MS65
1983 FM (U)	—	—	10.00	20.00	35.00	55.00
1983 FM (P)	—	PF65 60.00				

KM# 71a 10 DOLLARS

25.50 g., 0.925 Silver 0.7584 oz. ASW, 40 mm. **Obv:** National arms above date within wreath **Rev:** Ringed kingfisher

Date	Mintage	VF20	XF40	MS60	MS63	MS65
1983 FM (P)	334	PF65 135				

KM# 75 10 DOLLARS

Copper-Nickel, 40 mm. **Obv:** National arms within wreath, date below **Rev:** Laughing falcon, left, head divides denomination at top

Date	Mintage	VF20	XF40	MS60	MS63	MS65
1984 FM (U)	—	—	—	25.00	35.00	50.00
1984 FM (P)	—	PF65 60.00				

KM# 75a 10 DOLLARS

25.50 g., 0.925 Silver 0.7584 oz. ASW, 40 mm. **Obv:** National arms within wreath, date below **Rev:** Laughing falcon

Date	Mintage	VF20	XF40	MS60	MS63	MS65
1984 FM (P)	—	PF65 100				
1985	212	PF65 135				

KM# 102 10 DOLLARS

Copper-Nickel **Subject:** 10th Anniversary of Independence **Obv:** National arms within wreath, denomination below **Rev:** Building within circle, dates below

Date	Mintage	VF20	XF40	MS60	MS63	MS65
ND-1991	1,000,000	—	—	3.50	5.00	7.00

KM# 102a 10 DOLLARS

28.28 g., 0.925 Silver 0.841 oz. ASW **Subject:** 10th Anniversary of Independence **Obv:** National arms within wreath, denomination below **Rev:** Building within circle, dates below

Date	Mintage	VF20	XF40	MS60	MS63	MS65
ND-1991	Est. 1000	PF65 32.00				

KM# 104 10 DOLLARS

28.28 g., 0.925 Silver 0.841 oz. ASW **Subject:** 10th Anniversary of Central Bank **Obv:** National arms within wreath, denomination below **Rev:** Jabiru stork, left, within circle, two dates at bottom

Date	Mintage	VF20	XF40	MS60	MS63	MS65
1992	Est. 1000	PF65 37.00				

KM# 109 10 DOLLARS

155.60 g., 0.999 Silver 4.9976 oz. ASW **Subject:** 50th Anniversary - Battle of El Alamein - Lt. Gen. Montgomery **Obv:** Portrait of Queen Elizabeth II **Rev:** Similar to 250 Dollars, KM#113

Date	Mintage	VF20	XF40	MS60	MS63	MS65
1992	Est. 2500	PF65 145				

KM# 121 10 DOLLARS

28.28 g., 0.925 Silver 0.841 oz. ASW **Subject:** Royal visit **Obv:** Queen's portrait **Rev:** Cameo portraits above flowers

Date	Mintage	VF20	XF40	MS60	MS63	MS65
1994	—	PF65 35.00				

KM# 123 10 DOLLARS

28.28 g., 0.925 Silver 0.841 oz. ASW **Subject:** World Cup Soccer **Obv:** National arms within wreath, date below **Rev:** Soccer net and ball, denomination at bottom

Date	Mintage	VF20	XF40	MS60	MS63	MS65
1994	Est. 10000	PF65 35.00				

KM# 124 10 DOLLARS

28.28 g., 0.925 Silver 0.841 oz. ASW **Obv:** National arms within wreath, date at below **Rev:** Carrack sailing ship, denomination at bottom

Date	Mintage	VF20	XF40	MS60	MS63	MS65
1995	Est. 15000	PF65 28.00				

KM# 125 10 DOLLARS

28.28 g., 0.925 Silver 0.841 oz. ASW **Series:** Endangered Wildlife **Obv:** National arms within wreath, date below **Rev:** Howler monkey on branch, left, denomination below

Date	Mintage	VF20	XF40	MS60	MS63	MS65
1995	Est. 10000	PF65 35.00				

KM# 127 10 DOLLARS

28.28 g., 0.925 Silver 0.841 oz. ASW **Series:** Atlanta 1996 - 26th Summer Olympics **Obv:** National arms within wreath, date below **Rev:** Female softball player, denomination below

Date	Mintage	VF20	XF40	MS60	MS63	MS65
1996	Est. 10000	PF65 32.00				

KM# 128 10 DOLLARS

28.28 g., 0.925 Silver 0.841 oz. ASW **Subject:** Battle of St. George's Caye **Obv:** National arms within wreath, denomination below **Rev:** Oar-powered gunboats within circle, two dates below

Date	Mintage	VF20	XF40	MS60	MS63	MS65
ND-1998	—	PF65 40.00				

KM# 130 10 DOLLARS

28.28 g., 0.925 Silver 0.841 oz. ASW **Subject:** 50th Anniversary - University of the West Indies **Obv:** National arms within wreath, denomination below **Rev:** University arms, two dates below

Date	Mintage	VF20	XF40	MS60	MS63	MS65
ND-1999	1,000	PF65 60.00				

KM# 79 20 DOLLARS
23.33 g., 0.925 Silver 0.6938 oz. ASW **Series:** Los Angeles Olympics **Obv:** National arms within wreath, date below **Rev:** Bicyclist, Olympic torch at right, denomination lower left

Date	Mintage	VF20	XF40	MS60	MS63	MS65
1984	1,050	PF65 50.00				

KM# 82 20 DOLLARS
23.33 g., 0.925 Silver 0.6938 oz. ASW **Series:** Decade for Women **Obv:** National arms within wreath, date below **Rev:** Figures of women and trees, 3/4 surround legend and symbol at center, denomination at bottom

Date	Mintage	VF20	XF40	MS60	MS63	MS65
1985	Est. 20000	PF65 25.00				

KM# 54 25 DOLLARS
27.81 g., 0.925 Silver 0.8271 oz. ASW **Subject:** 25th Anniversary of Coronation **Obv:** Bust of Queen Elizabeth II, right, date below **Rev:** Crown with supporters, two dates below, denomination at bottom

Date	Mintage	VF20	XF40	MS60	MS63	MS65
1978 FM (U)	352	—	—	30.00	50.00	65.00
1978 FM (P)	8,438	PF65 25.00				

KM# 61 25 DOLLARS
30.28 g., 0.500 Silver 0.4868 oz. ASW **Subject:** 10th Anniversary - Caribbean Development Bank **Obv:** National arms **Rev:** Globe above flag, denomination below

Date	Mintage	VF20	XF40	MS60	MS63	MS65
ND(1980) FM (P)	2,647	PF65 22.00				

KM# 72 25 DOLLARS
30.28 g., 0.500 Silver 0.4868 oz. ASW **Subject:** 30th Anniversary of Coronation **Obv:** National arms within wreath, date below **Rev:** Crossed sceptres divide dates and royal symbols, denomination at bottom

Date	Mintage	VF20	XF40	MS60	MS63	MS65
1983 FM (P)	2,944	PF65 22.00				

KM# 78 25 DOLLARS
28.28 g., 0.925 Silver 0.841 oz. ASW **Subject:** Royal visit

Date	Mintage	VF20	XF40	MS60	MS63	MS65
1985	Est. 5000	PF65 25.00				

KM# 97 25 DOLLARS
28.28 g., 0.925 Silver 0.841 oz. ASW **Subject:** 500th Anniversary - Columbus Discovery of New World **Obv:** Crowned bust of Queen Elizabeth II right **Rev:** Ship in full sail, denomination at bottom

Date	Mintage	VF20	XF40	MS60	MS63	MS65
1989	Est. 5000	PF65 30.00				

KM# 106 25 DOLLARS
28.28 g., 0.925 Silver 0.841 oz. ASW **Subject:** Summer Olympics, Barcelona 1992 **Obv:** National arms within wreath, denomination below **Rev:** Hurdlers jumping large date

Date	Mintage	VF20	XF40	MS60	MS63	MS65
1992	30,000	PF65 20.00				

KM# 110 25 DOLLARS
3.13 g., 0.999 Gold 0.1005 oz. AGW **Subject:** 50th Anniversary - Battle of El Alamein **Obv:** Bust of Queen Elizabeth II right **Rev:** 4 tanks, denomination at bottom

Date	Mintage	VF20	XF40	MS60	MS63	MS65
1992	—	PF65 165				

KM# 66 50 DOLLARS
1.50 g., 0.500 Gold 0.0241 oz. AGW **Obv:** National arms, date below, 3/4 wreath surrounds **Rev:** White-necked Jacobin hummingbird, right, drinking from flower, date below

Date	Mintage	VF20	XF40	MS60	MS63	MS65
1981 FM (U)	200	—	—	—	65.00	70.00
1981 FM (P)	2,873	PF65 50.00				

KM# 81 50 DOLLARS
129.60 g., 0.925 Silver 3.8542 oz. ASW, 63 mm. **Subject:** Bird conservation **Obv:** National arms within wreath, date below **Rev:** Red-footed booby, left, denomination above

Date	Mintage	VF20	XF40	MS60	MS63	MS65
1985	Est. 10000	PF65 120				

KM# 111 50 DOLLARS
7.81 g., 0.999 Gold 0.2508 oz. AGW **Subject:** 50th Anniversary - Battle of El Alamein **Obv:** Bust of Queen Elizabeth II right **Rev:** Field Marshall Rommel, right, in uniform, denomination lower right

Date	Mintage	VF20	XF40	MS60	MS63	MS65
1992	Est. 500	PF65 425				

KM# 51 100 DOLLARS
6.21 g., 0.500 Gold 0.0998 oz. AGW **Subject:** 30th Anniversary of United Nations **Obv:** National arms above date within wreath **Rev:** Buildings, design above, denomination at top

Date	Mintage	VF20	XF40	MS60	MS63	MS65
1975 FM (M)	100	—	—	—	225	—
1975 FM (U)	2,028	—	—	—	185	—
1975 FM (P)	8,126	PF65 170				

KM# 52 100 DOLLARS
6.21 g., 0.500 Gold 0.0998 oz. AGW **Obv:** National arms above date, denomination below **Rev:** Ancient Mayan symbols representing numbers and days

Date	Mintage	VF20	XF40	MS60	MS63	MS65
1976 FM (M)	216	—	—	—	215	—
1976 FM (P)	11,000	PF65 170				

KM# 53 100 DOLLARS

6.21 g., 0.500 Gold 0.0998 oz. AGW **Obv:** National arms above date, denomination at bottom **Rev:** Kinich Ahau, Mayan sun god

Date	Mintage	VF20	XF40	MS60	MS63	MS65
1977 FM (M)	200	—	—	—	185	—
1977 FM (U)	51	—	—	—	375	—
1977 FM (P)	7,859	PF65 170				

KM# 55 100 DOLLARS

6.21 g., 0.500 Gold 0.0998 oz. AGW **Obv:** National arms above date, denomination below **Rev:** Itzamna Lord of Heaven, Ruler of the Gods

Date	Mintage	VF20	XF40	MS60	MS63	MS65
1978 FM (U)	351	—	—	—	200	—
1978 FM (P)	7,178	PF65 170				

KM# 58 100 DOLLARS

6.21 g., 0.500 Gold 0.0998 oz. AGW **Obv:** National arms, denomination below **Rev:** Queen angelfish, left, date below

Date	Mintage	VF20	XF40	MS60	MS63	MS65
1979 FM (U)	400	—	—	—	200	235
1979 FM (P)	4,465	PF65 175				

KM# 59 100 DOLLARS

6.47 g., 0.500 Gold 0.104 oz. AGW **Obv:** National arms, denomination below **Rev:** Star of Bethlehem, date below

Date	Mintage	VF20	XF40	MS60	MS63	MS65
1979 FM (U)	—	—	—	—	200	—
1979 FM (P)	—	PF65 175				

KM# 62 100 DOLLARS

6.21 g., 0.500 Gold 0.0998 oz. AGW **Obv:** National arms, denomination below **Rev:** Moorish idol reef fish, date below

Date	Mintage	VF20	XF40	MS60	MS63	MS65
1980 FM (U)	400	—	—	—	215	—
1980 FM (P)	3,993	PF65 185				

KM# 63 100 DOLLARS

6.21 g., 0.500 Gold 0.0998 oz. AGW **Obv:** National arms, denomination below **Rev:** Orchids, date below

Date	Mintage	VF20	XF40	MS60	MS63	MS65
1980 FM (U)	250	—	—	—	220	—
1980 FM (P)	2,454	PF65 190				

KM# 67 100 DOLLARS

6.21 g., 0.500 Gold 0.0998 oz. AGW **Obv:** National arms above denomination within circle **Rev:** Yellow swallowtail butterfly within circle, date below **Shape:** Five-sided coin

Date	Mintage	VF20	XF40	MS60	MS63	MS65
1981 FM (U)	200	—	—	—	250	—
1981 FM (P)	1,658	PF65 260				

KM# 68 100 DOLLARS

6.21 g., 0.500 Gold 0.0998 oz. AGW **Subject:** National independence **Rev:** Vertical date to left of map

Date	Mintage	VF20	XF40	MS60	MS63	MS65
1981 FM (U)	50	—	—	—	325	—
1981 FM (P)	1,401	PF65 200				

KM# 70 100 DOLLARS

6.21 g., 0.500 Gold 0.0998 oz. AGW **Obv:** National arms within wreath, denomination below **Rev:** Kinkajou, left, date below

Date	Mintage	VF20	XF40	MS60	MS63	MS65
1982 FM (U)	10	—	—	—	500	—
1982 FM (P)	586	PF65 215				

KM# 73 100 DOLLARS

6.21 g., 0.500 Gold 0.0998 oz. AGW **Obv:** National arms within wreath, denomination below **Rev:** Margay jungle cat, right, date below

Date	Mintage	VF20	XF40	MS60	MS63	MS65
1983 FM (U)	20	—	—	—	450	—
1983 FM (P)	494	PF65 240				

KM# 74 100 DOLLARS

6.21 g., 0.500 Gold 0.0998 oz. AGW **Obv:** National arms within wreath, denomination below **Rev:** White-tailed deer, facing, date lower right

Date	Mintage	VF20	XF40	MS60	MS63	MS65
1984 FM (P)	965	PF65 225				

KM# 76 100 DOLLARS

6.21 g., 0.500 Gold 0.0998 oz. AGW **Obv:** national arms within wreath, denomination below **Rev:** Ocelot, facing, date below

Date	Mintage	VF20	XF40	MS60	MS63	MS65
1985 FM (P)	899	PF65 260				

KM# 103 100 DOLLARS

15.98 g., 0.917 Gold 0.471 oz. AGW **Subject:** 10th Anniversary of Independence **Note:** Similar to 10 Dollars, KM#102.

Date	Mintage	VF20	XF40	MS60	MS63	MS65
1991	—	PF65 825				

KM# 112 100 DOLLARS

15.60 g., 0.999 Gold 0.501 oz. AGW **Subject:** 50th Anniversary - Battle of El Alamein **Obv:** Bust of Queen Elizabeth II right **Rev:** Infantry advancing, denomination below

Date	Mintage	VF20	XF40	MS60	MS63	MS65
1992	Est. 500	PF65 875				

KM# 129 100 DOLLARS

15.97 g., 0.917 Gold 0.4708 oz. AGW **Subject:** Battle of St. George's Caye **Note:** Similar to KM#128.

Date	Mintage	VF20	XF40	MS60	MS63	MS65
ND-1998	—	PF65 825				

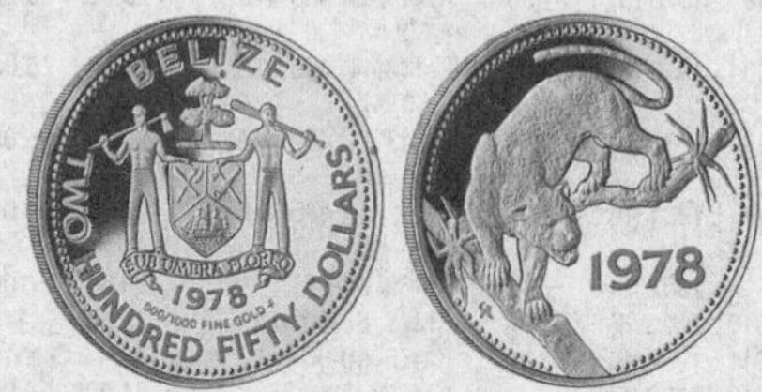

KM# 56 250 DOLLARS

8.81 g., 0.900 Gold 0.2549 oz. AGW **Obv:** National arms above date, denomination below **Rev:** Jaguar, date at right

Date	Mintage	VF20	XF40	MS60	MS63	MS65
1978 FM (U)	200	—	—	—	425	450
1978 FM (P)	—	PF65 465				

Note: 1,712 pieces were used in first-day covers

KM# 98 250 DOLLARS

15.98 g., 0.917 Gold 0.4711 oz. AGW **Subject:** 500th Anniversary of Columbus' Discovery of America

Date	Mintage	VF20	XF40	MS60	MS63	MS65
1989	Est. 500	PF63 675	PF65 750			

KM# 105 250 DOLLARS

15.98 g., 0.917 Gold 0.4711 oz. AGW **Subject:** 10th Anniversary of Central Bank **Rev:** Jabiru stork **Note:** Similar to KM#104.

Date	Mintage	VF20	XF40	MS60	MS63	MS65
1992	Est. 500	PF63 675	PF65 750			

KM# 113 250 DOLLARS

31.21 g., 0.999 Gold 1.0024 oz. AGW **Subject:** 50th Anniversary - Battle of El Alamein **Obv:** Bust of Queen Elizabeth II right **Rev:** Lt. Gen. Montgomery, denomination at bottom

Date	Mintage	VF20	XF40	MS60	MS63	MS65
1992	Est. 500	PF63 1,350	PF65 1,450			

KM# 101 500 DOLLARS

47.54 g., 0.917 Gold 1.4016 oz. AGW **Subject:** Royal Visit **Note:** Similar to KM#78.

Date	Mintage	VF20	XF40	MS60	MS63	MS65
1985	Est. 250	PF63 1,850	PF65 2,100			

KM# 120 500 DOLLARS

47.54 g., 0.917 Gold 1.4016 oz.. AGW **Subject:** 40th Anniversary - Coronation of Queen Elizabeth II

Date	Mintage	VF20	XF40	MS60	MS63	MS65
1993	Est. 100	PF63 2,000	PF65 2,150			

KM# 122 500 DOLLARS

47.54 g., 0.917 Gold 1.4016 oz. AGW **Subject:** Royal Visit **Rev:** Cameo portraits, flanked by roses, flowers above denomination

Date	Mintage	VF20	XF40	MS60	MS63	MS65
1994	—	PF63 2,100	PF65 2,250			

PIEDFORT

KM#	Date	Mintage	Identification	Mkt Val
PP1	1990	1,000	Dollar. 0.925. Silver. KM99a.	100

MINT SETS

KM#	Date	Mintage	Identification	Issue Price	Mkt Val
MS1	1974 (8)	4,506	KM38-45	20.00	30.00
MS2	1975 (8)	1,095	KM43-50	27.50	95.00
MS3	1976 (8)	759	KM43-50	27.50	50.00
MS4	1977 (8)	—	KM43-45, 46b -47b, 48-50	27.50	45.00
MS5	1978 (8)	458	KM43-45, 46b-47b, 48-50	28.50	45.00
MS6	1979 (8)	808	KM43-44, 46b-47b, 48-50, 57	28.50	75.00
MS7	1980 (8)	761	KM43-44, 46b-47b, 48-50, 60	29.50	65.00
MS8	1981 (8)	297	KM43-44, 46b-47b, 48-50, 65	29.50	95.00
MS9	1982 (8)	—	KM69, 83-89	29.50	100
MS10	1983 (8)	—	KM71, 83-89	29.50	110
MS11	1984 (8)	—	KM75, 90-96	—	110
MS12	1992 (5)	—	KM33a, 34a, 35-37, 99	24.00	24.00

PROOF SETS

KM#	Date	Mintage	Identification	Issue Price	Mkt Val
PS1	1974 (8)	21,470	KM38-45	35.00	28.00
PS2	1974 (8)	31,368	KM38a-45a	100	95.00
PS3	1975 (8)	8,794	KM43-50	37.50	30.00
PS4	1975 (8)	13,275	KM43a-50a	110	100
PS5	1976 (8)	4,893	KM43-50	37.50	30.00
PS6	1976 (8)	5,897	KM43a-50a	110	100
PS7	1977 (8)	2,107	KM43-45, 46b-47b, 48-50	37.50	50.00
PS8	1977 (8)	3,197	KM43a-50a	110	115
PS9	1978 (8)	1,671	KM43-45, 46b, 47b, 48-50	39.50	50.00
PS10	1978 (8)	3,342	KM43a-50a	110	115
PS11	1979 (8)	1,287	KM43-44, 46b-47b, 48-50, 57	41.50	62.50
PS12	1979 (8)	2,445	KM43a-44a, 46a-50a, 57a	112	120
PS13	1980 (8)	920	KM43-44, 46b-47b, 48-50, 60	41.50	85.00
PS14	1980 (8)	1,826	KM43a-44a, 46a-50a, 60a	222	135
PS15	1981 (8)	643	KM43-44, 46b-47b, 48-50, 65	41.50	85.00
PS16	1981 (8)	615	KM43a-44a, 46a-50a, 65a	—	185
PS17	1982 (8)	—	KM69, 83-89	49.50	115
PS18	1982 (8)	381	KM69a, 83a-89a	222	345
PS19	1983 (8)	306	KM71, 83-89	37.00	115
PS20	1983 (8)	241	KM71a, 83a-89a	197	360
PS21	1984 (8)	—	KM75, 90-96	37.00	110
PS22	1984 (8)	397	KM75a, 90a-96a	197	315
PS23	1985 (8)	212	KM75a, 90a-96a	—	375
PS24	1992 (4)	500	KM110-113	1,600	3,000
PS25	1992 (2)	—	KM107-108	100	110

BENIN

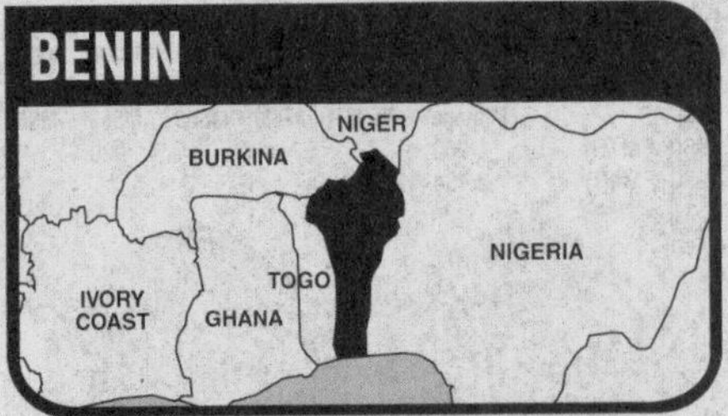

The Republic of Benin (formerly the Republic of Dahomey), located on the south side of the African bulge between Togo and Nigeria, has an area of 43,500 sq. mi. (112,620 sq. km.) and a population of 5.5 million. Capital: Porto-Novo. The principal industry of Benin, one of the poorest countries of West Africa, is the processing of palm oil products. Palm kernel oil, peanuts, cotton, and coffee are exported.

PEOPLES REPUBLIC

STANDARD COINAGE

KM# 10 200 FRANCS

Copper **Obv:** National arms, denomination below **Rev:** Sailing ship - Preussen, date below

Date	Mintage	VF20	XF40	MS60	MS63	MS65
1993	—	—	—	—	—	35.00
1993	100	PF65 75.00				

KM# 8 200 FRANCS

Copper-Nickel **Series:** Prehistoric Animals **Obv:** National arms, denomination below **Rev:** Dinosaurs - Acanthopholis, right, date lower right

Date	Mintage	VF20	XF40	MS60	MS63	MS65
1994	—	—	—	—	—	35.00

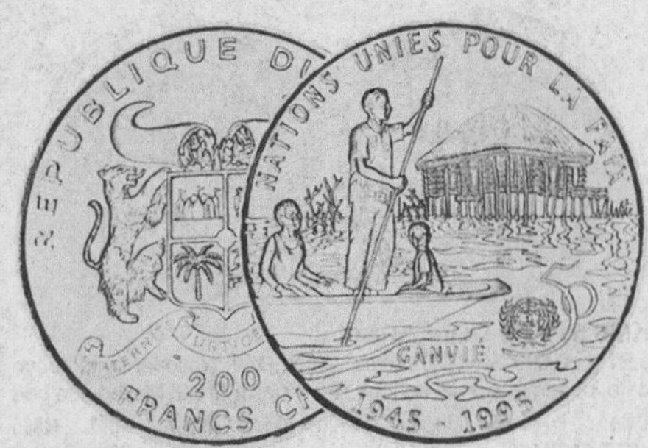

KM# 16 200 FRANCS

Copper-Nickel **Subject:** United Nations - 50 Years **Obv:** National arms, denomination below **Rev:** Family in boat, building in background, two dates at bottom

Date	Mintage	VF20	XF40	MS60	MS63	MS65
ND-1995	—	—	—	—	12.00	20.00

KM# 17 200 FRANCS

Nickel Bonded Steel with selective enameling **Rev:** WWI Austrian Hansa - Brandenburg D. I

Date	Mintage	VF20	XF40	MS60	MS63	MS65
1995	25,000	—	—	—	—	20.00

KM# 23 200 FRANCS

Copper **Series:** Prehistoric Animals **Obv:** National arms, denomination below **Rev:** Iguanodon, looking left, date at lower left

Date	Mintage	VF20	XF40	MS60	MS63	MS65
1995	100	PF65 75.00				

KM# 25 200 FRANCS

Copper-Nickel **Series:** Sydney 2000 **Obv:** National arms, denomination below **Rev:** Classic sculpture and racing scullcraft, date below

Date	Mintage	VF20	XF40	MS60	MS63	MS65
1999	10,000	—	—	—	7.00	9.00

KM# 3 500 FRANCS

12.00 g., 0.999 Silver 0.3854 oz. ASW **Subject:** 1992 World Cup Soccer **Obv:** National arms, denomination below **Rev:** Soccer goalie, large date in legend, small date at bottom

Date	Mintage	VF20	XF40	MS60	MS63	MS65
1992	Est. 10000	—	—	—	35.00	50.00

KM# 14 500 FRANCS
8.25 g., 0.999 Silver 0.265 oz. ASW **Rev:** Soccer - Eifel Tower, flag and ball, date below **Edge Lettering:** 1995 World Cup Soccer

Date	Mintage	VF20	XF40	MS60	MS63	MS65
1995	30,000	PF65 20.00				

KM# 31 500 FRANCS
8.25 g., 0.999 Silver 0.265 oz. ASW, 30.1 mm. **Obv:** National arms, denomination below **Rev:** Sailing ship, Gorch Fock **Edge:** Plain

Date	Mintage	VF20	XF40	MS60	MS63	MS65
1996	10,000	PF65 22.00				

KM# 1 1000 FRANCS
19.91 g., 0.999 Silver 0.6395 oz. ASW **Obv:** National arms, denomination below **Rev:** Five hands holding jar **Note:** Five hands holding jar

Date	Mintage	VF20	XF40	MS60	MS63	MS65
ND-1992	1,000	PF65 60.00				

KM# 2 1000 FRANCS
19.91 g., 0.999 Silver 0.6395 oz. ASW **Obv:** National arms, denomination below **Rev:** National map in radiant sun

Date	Mintage	VF20	XF40	MS60	MS63	MS65
ND-1992	1,000	PF65 70.00				

KM# 4 1000 FRANCS
20.00 g., 0.999 Silver 0.6424 oz. ASW **Series:** Barcelona 1992 - 25th Summer Olympics **Rev:** Gymnast, date at right

Date	Mintage	VF20	XF40	MS60	MS63	MS65
1992	Est. 5000	PF65 35.00				

KM# 5 1000 FRANCS
20.00 g., 0.999 Silver 0.6424 oz. ASW **Subject:** 1992 World Cup Soccer **Obv:** National arms, denomination below **Rev:** Player kicking ball, date at rght

Date	Mintage	VF20	XF40	MS60	MS63	MS65
1992	Est. 10000	PF65 35.00				

KM# 6 1000 FRANCS
20.00 g., 0.999 Silver 0.6424 oz. ASW **Subject:** Protection of Nature **Rev:** Elephant, within inner circle, elephants, (trunk to tail), form outer circle

Date	Mintage	VF20	XF40	MS60	MS63	MS65
1993	—	PF65 50.00				

KM# 7 1000 FRANCS
20.00 g., 0.999 Silver 0.6424 oz. ASW **Rev:** Sailing ship - Preussen, date below

Date	Mintage	VF20	XF40	MS60	MS63	MS65
1993	100	—	—	—	—	125
1993	10,000	PF65 30.00				

KM# 27 1000 FRANCS
20.00 g., 0.999 Silver 0.6424 oz. ASW **Series:** Protection of Nature **Rev:** Elephant, people, tree, map

Date	Mintage	VF20	XF40	MS60	MS63	MS65
1993	—	PF65 75.00				

KM# 9 1000 FRANCS
15.86 g., 0.994 Silver 0.5069 oz. ASW **Series:** Dinosaurs **Obv:** National arms, denomination below **Rev:** Tyrannosaurus Rex, left, date below tail

Date	Mintage	VF20	XF40	MS60	MS63	MS65
1994	—	PF65 45.00				

KM# 12 1000 FRANCS
20.00 g., 0.999 Silver 0.6424 oz. ASW **Series:** 1996 Olympics **Rev:** Three runners, large date below, small date at left

Date	Mintage	VF20	XF40	MS60	MS63	MS65
1995	15,000	PF65 28.00				

KM# 13 1000 FRANCS
20.00 g., 0.999 Silver 0.6424 oz. ASW **Subject:** 35 Years of Independence **Rev:** Woman stirring pot, hut at back left

Date	Mintage	VF20	XF40	MS60	MS63	MS65
1995	2,000	PF65 45.00				

KM# 18 1000 FRANCS
20.00 g., 0.999 Silver 0.6424 oz. ASW **Rev:** WWI Austrian Hansa - Brandenburg D. I, date lower right

Date	Mintage	VF20	XF40	MS60	MS63	MS65
1995	15,000	PF65 40.00				

KM# 28 1000 FRANCS
20.00 g., 0.999 Silver 0.6424 oz. ASW **Series:** Prehistoric Animals **Rev:** Iguanodon, looking left, date below tail **Edge:** Plain

Date	Mintage	VF20	XF40	MS60	MS63	MS65
1995	—	PF65 45.00				

KM# 19 1000 FRANCS

20.00 g., 0.999 Silver 0.6424 oz. ASW **Rev:** Head of Multicolor panther, 3/4 facing, date above

Date	Mintage	VF20	XF40	MS60	MS63	MS65
1996	—	PF65 50.00				

KM# 20 1000 FRANCS

15.00 g., 0.999 Silver 0.4818 oz. ASW, 35 mm. **Subject:** 1996 World Cup Soccer **Obv:** National arms, denomination below **Rev:** Two multicolor soccer players, small date at left

Date	Mintage	VF20	XF40	MS60	MS63	MS65
1996	—	PF65 35.00				

KM# 50 1000 FRANCS

15.00 g., 0.999 Silver 0.4818 oz. ASW, 35 mm. **Subject:** Graf von Zeplein **Rev:** Zeplein over Brandenberg gate, blue color sky

Date	Mintage	VF20	XF40	MS60	MS63	MS65
1996	—	PF65 40.00				

KM# 61 1000 FRANCS

Silver **Rev:** Multicolor Christopher Columbus and the Santa Maria

Date	Mintage	VF20	XF40	MS60	MS63	MS65
1996	—	PF65 27.00				

KM# 21 1000 FRANCS

15.00 g., 0.999 Silver 0.4818 oz. ASW **Series:** 2000 Summer Olympics **Obv:** National arms, denomination below **Rev:** Multicolored shot-putter and Olympic torch, date at right

Date	Mintage	VF20	XF40	MS60	MS63	MS65
1997	100	—	—	—	—	125
1997	—	PF65 35.00				

KM# 24 1000 FRANCS

20.00 g., 0.999 Silver 0.6424 oz. ASW **Subject:** 2000 Summer Olympics **Obv:** National arms, denomination below **Rev:** Two runners and statue

Date	Mintage	VF20	XF40	MS60	MS63	MS65
1997	100	—	—	—	—	125
1997	—	PF65 35.00				

KM# 43 1000 FRANCS

15.00 g., 0.999 Silver 0.4818 oz. ASW, 35 mm. **Obv:** National arms, denomination below **Rev:** Multicolor zebra **Edge:** Plain

Date	Mintage	VF20	XF40	MS60	MS63	MS65
1997	—	PF65 55.00				

KM# 48 1000 FRANCS

15.00 g., 0.999 Silver 0.4818 oz. ASW, 34 mm. **Subject:** Soccer **Obv:** National arms **Rev:** Multicolor Eiffel Tower and ball **Edge:** Plain

Date	Mintage	VF20	XF40	MS60	MS63	MS65
1997	—	PF65 27.00				

KM# 52 1000 FRANCS

19.99 g., Silver, 24.1 x 42.26 mm. **Obv:** Arms **Obv. Legend:** REPUBLIQUE **Rev:** German ocean liner Kaiser Wilhelm der Grosse **Edge:** Plain **Shape:** Rectangular

Date	Mintage	VF20	XF40	MS60	MS63	MS65
1998	—	—	—	—	—	85.00

KM# 26 1000 FRANCS

20.13 g., 0.999 Silver 0.6465 oz. ASW **Series:** 2000 Summer Olympics **Obv:** National arms, denomination below **Rev:** Classic statue and racing scullcraft, date below

Date	Mintage	VF20	XF40	MS60	MS63	MS65
1999	5,000	PF65 30.00				

KM# 39 1000 FRANCS

15.00 g., 0.999 Silver 0.4818 oz. ASW, 34.9 mm. **Subject:** Gutenberg **Obv:** National arms, denomination below **Rev:** Portrait and printing press, two dates lower right **Edge:** Plain

Date	Mintage	VF20	XF40	MS60	MS63	MS65
1999	7,000	PF65 30.00				

KM# 51 1000 FRANCS

Silver, 23 mm. **Subject:** Wildlife **Rev:** Elephant with calf

Date	Mintage	VF20	XF40	MS60	MS63	MS65
1999	—	PF65 40.00				

KM# 47 1000 FRANCS

14.96 g., 0.999 Silver 0.4805 oz. ASW, 35 mm. **Obv:** National arms **Rev:** Calipers, radiant sun and grid **Edge:** Plain

Date	Mintage	VF20	XF40	MS60	MS63	MS65
2000	—	PF65 35.00				

KM# 69 1000 FRANCS

Silver, 36 mm. **Obv:** National arms **Rev:** Wright flyer, globe below

Date	Mintage	VF20	XF40	MS60	MS63	MS65
2000	—	PF65 40.00				

KM# 70 1000 FRANCS

Silver, 36 mm. **Obv:** National arms **Rev:** Zeppelin above globe

Date	Mintage	VF20	XF40	MS60	MS63	MS65
2000	—	PF65 40.00				

KM# 11 6000 FRANCS

20.13 g., 0.999 Silver 0.6465 oz. ASW **Series:** Protection of Nature **Obv:** National arms, denomination below **Rev:** Elephant within inner circle, elephants, (trunk to tail), form outer circle

Date	Mintage	VF20	XF40	MS60	MS63	MS65
1993	5,000	PF65 65.00				

KM# 22 6000 FRANCS

28.34 g., 0.925 Silver 0.8428 oz. ASW **Subject:** 50th Anniversary U.N. **Obv:** National arms, denomination below **Rev:** Family in boat, two dates at bottom

Date	Mintage	VF20	XF40	MS60	MS63	MS65
ND-1995	—	PF65 45.00				

KM# 34 15000 FRANCS

500.00 g., 0.999 Silver 16.0593 oz. ASW, 84.8 mm. **Subject:** Wildlife Protection **Obv:** National arms, denomination below **Rev:** Multicolor crocodile, date at right **Edge:** Reeded **Note:** Illustration reduced.

Date	Mintage	VF20	XF40	MS60	MS63	MS65
1996	300	PF65 675				
1997	—	PF65 675				

KM# 36 20000 FRANCS

846.02 g., 0.999 Silver 27.1728 oz. ASW, 90.4 mm. **Subject:** African Fauna **Obv:** National arms, denomination below **Rev:** Multicolor zebra, date upper right **Edge:** Plain **Note:** Illustration reduced.

Date	Mintage	VF20	XF40	MS60	MS63	MS65
1997	—	PF65 850				

KM# 29 30000 FRANCS

15.55 g., 0.999 Gold 0.4994 oz. AGW **Obv:** National arms **Rev:** Map in radiant sun **Edge:** Reeded

Date	Mintage	VF20	XF40	MS60	MS63	MS65
ND-1992	Est. 100	PF65 750				

KM# 30 100000 FRANCS

31.10 g., 0.999 Gold 0.999 oz. AGW **Obv:** National arms **Rev:** President **Edge:** Reeded

Date	Mintage	VF20	XF40	MS60	MS63	MS65
1992 Rare	Est. 10	PF65 1,750				

PIEDFORT

KM#	Date	Mintage	Identification	Mkt Val
P1	1997	—	1000 Francs. Silver. KM#21.	200
P2	1997	—	1000 Francs. Silver. KM#24.	200
P3	1999	—	1000 Francs. Silver. KM#26.	200

BERMUDA

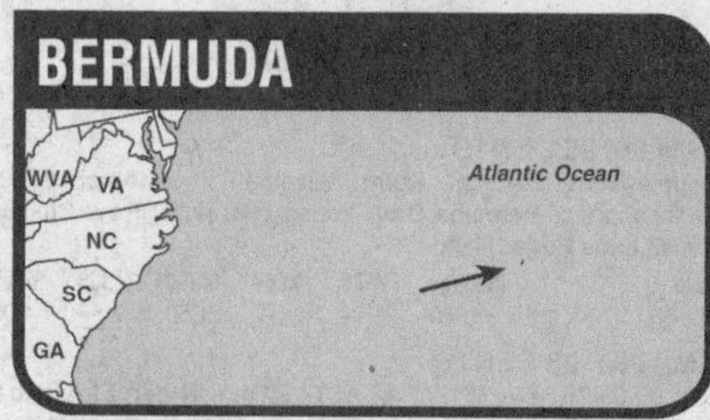

The Parliamentary British Colony of Bermuda, situated in the western Atlantic Ocean 660 miles (1,062 km.) east of North Carolina, has an area of 20.6 sq. mi. (53 sq. km.) and a population of 61,600. Capital: Hamilton. Concentrated essences, beauty preparations, and cut flowers are exported. Most Bermudians derive their livelihood from tourism. The British monarch is the head of state and is represented by a governor.

Bermuda was discovered by Juan de Bermudez, a Spanish navigator, in about 1503. British influence dates from 1609 when a group of Virginia-bound British colonists under the command of Sir George Somers was shipwrecked on the islands for 10 months. The islands were settled in 1612 by 60 British colonists from the Virginia Colony and became a crown colony in 1684. The earliest coins issued for the island were the "Hogge Money" series of 2, 3, 6 and 12 pence, the name derived from the pig in the obverse design, a recognition of the quantity of such animals then found there. The next issue for Bermuda was the Birmingham coppers of 1793; all locally circulating coinage was demonetized in 1842, when the currency of the United Kingdom became standard. Internal autonomy was obtained by the constitution of June 8, 1968.

In February, 1970, Bermuda converted from its former currency, which was sterling, to a decimal currency, the dollar unit which is equal to one U.S. dollar. On July 31, 1972, Bermuda severed its monetary link with the British pound sterling and pegged its dollar to be the same value as the U.S. dollar.

RULER

British

MINT MARKS

CHI - Valcambi, Switzerland

FM - Franklin Mint, U.S.A.*

***NOTE**: From 1975-1985 the Franklin Mint produced coinage in up to 3 different qualities. Qualities of issue are designated in ( ) after each date and are defined as follows:

(M) MATTE - Normal circulation strike or a dull finish produced by sandblasting special uncirculated (polish finish) or proof quality dies.

(U) SPECIAL UNCIRCULATED - Polished or proof-like in appearance without any frosted features.

(P) PROOF - The highest quality obtainable having mirror-like fields and frosted features.

MONETARY SYSTEM

12 Pence = 1 Shilling

20 Shillings = 1 Pound

BRITISH COLONY

POUND STERLING COINAGE

KM# 13 CROWN

28.28 g., 0.925 Silver 0.841 oz. ASW, 38 mm. **Ruler:** Elizabeth II **Subject:** 350th Anniversary - Colony Founding **Obv:** Crowned head right **Rev:** Map of islands with ships "Deliverance" and "Patience"

Date	Mintage	VF20	XF40	MS60	MS63	MS65
1959	100,000	—	17.00	19.00	22.00	25.00
1959 Matte proof	Est. 6-10	PF63 1,000				

KM# 14 CROWN

22.62 g., 0.500 Silver 0.3636 oz. ASW, 36 mm. **Ruler:** Elizabeth II **Obv:** Crowned head right **Rev:** Lion holding shield divides date **Edge:** Reeded

Date	Mintage	VF20	XF40	MS60	MS63	MS65
1964	470,000	—	—	7.25	9.25	11.50
1964	30,000	PF65 14.50				

DECIMAL COINAGE

100 Cents = 1 Dollar

KM# 15 CENT

3.11 g., Bronze, 19 mm. **Ruler:** Elizabeth II **Obv:** Young bust right **Rev:** Wild boar left **Edge:** Plain

Date	Mintage	VF20	XF40	MS60	MS63	MS65
1970	5,500,000	—	0.10	0.20	0.30	0.50
1970	11,000	PF65 0.50				
1971	4,256,000	—	0.10	0.20	0.30	0.50
1973	2,144,000	—	0.10	0.20	0.30	0.50
1974	856,000	—	0.10	0.25	0.35	0.60
1975	1,000,000	—	0.10	0.20	0.30	0.50
1976	1,000,000	—	0.10	0.20	0.30	0.50
1977	2,000,000	—	0.10	0.20	0.30	0.50
1978	3,160,000	—	0.10	0.20	0.30	0.50
1980	3,520,000	—	0.10	0.20	0.30	0.50
1981	3,200,000	—	0.10	0.20	0.30	0.50
1982	320,000	—	0.10	0.20	0.30	0.50
1983	800,000	—	0.10	0.20	0.30	0.50
1983	6,474	PF65 1.00				
1984	800,000	—	0.10	0.20	0.30	0.50
1985	800,000	—	0.10	0.20	0.30	0.50

KM# 44 CENT

3.11 g., Bronze, 19 mm. **Ruler:** Elizabeth II **Obv:** Crowned head right **Rev:** Wild boar left **Edge:** Plain

Date	Mintage	VF20	XF40	MS60	MS63	MS65
1986	1,360,000	—	0.10	0.20	0.30	0.50
1986	2,500	PF65 2.00				
1987	2,048,000	—	0.10	0.20	0.30	0.50
1990	1,500,000	—	0.10	0.20	0.30	0.50

KM# 44a CENT

2.80 g., Copper Plated Steel, 19 mm. **Ruler:** Elizabeth II **Obv:** Crowned head right **Rev:** Wild boar left **Edge:** Plain

Date	Mintage	VF20	XF40	MS60	MS63	MS65
1988	2,500,000	—	—	—	2.50	3.50

KM# 44b CENT

2.50 g., Copper Plated Zinc, 19 mm. **Ruler:** Elizabeth II **Obv:** Crowned head right **Rev:** Wild boar left **Edge:** Plain

Date	Mintage	VF20	XF40	MS60	MS63	MS65
1991	2,400,000	—	0.10	0.20	0.25	0.50
1993	1,600,000	—	0.10	0.20	0.25	0.50
1994	1,440,000	—	0.10	0.20	0.25	0.50
1995	1,920,000	—	0.10	0.20	0.25	0.50
1996	3,200,000	—	0.10	0.20	0.25	0.50
1997	3,400,000	—	0.10	0.20	0.25	0.50
1998	3,400,000	—	0.10	0.20	0.25	0.50

KM# 44c CENT

3.70 g., 0.925 Silver 0.110 oz. ASW, 19 mm. **Ruler:** Elizabeth II **Obv:** Crowned head right **Rev:** Wild boar left **Note:** In sets only.

Date	Mintage	VF20	XF40	MS60	MS63	MS65
1995	2,000	PF65 6.00				

KM# 44d CENT

6.20 g., 0.917 Gold 0.1828 oz. AGW, 19 mm. **Ruler:** Elizabeth II **Obv:** Crowned head right **Rev:** Wild boar left **Note:** In sets only.

Date	Mintage	VF20	XF40	MS60	MS63	MS65
1995	500	PF65 300				

KM# 107 CENT

2.50 g., Copper Plated Zinc, 19 mm. **Ruler:** Elizabeth II **Obv:** Head with tiara right **Rev:** Wild boar left **Edge:** Plain

Date	Mintage	VF20	XF40	MS60	MS63	MS65
1999	2,400,000	—	—	—	0.50	0.75
1999	2,500	PF65 2.50				
2000	—	—	—	—	0.50	0.75

KM# 16 5 CENTS

5.00 g., Copper-Nickel, 21.2 mm. **Ruler:** Elizabeth II **Obv:** Young bust right **Rev:** Queen angel fish left **Edge:** Plain

Date	Mintage	VF20	XF40	MS60	MS63	MS65
1970	2,190,000	—	0.10	0.25	0.50	0.75
1970	11,000	PF65 0.50				
1974	310,000	—	0.10	0.25	0.50	0.75
1975	500,000	—	0.10	0.25	0.50	0.75
1977	500,000	—	0.10	0.25	0.50	0.75
1979	500,000	—	0.10	0.25	0.50	0.75
1980	1,100,000	—	0.10	0.25	0.50	0.75
1981	900,000	—	0.10	0.25	0.50	0.75
1982	200,000	—	0.10	0.25	0.50	0.75
1983	800,000	—	0.10	0.25	0.50	0.75
1983	6,474	PF65 1.50				

Date	Mintage	VF20	XF40	MS60	MS63	MS65
1984	500,000	—	0.10	0.25	0.50	0.75
1985	500,000	—	0.10	0.25	0.50	0.75

KM# 45 5 CENTS

5.00 g., Copper-Nickel, 21.2 mm. **Ruler:** Elizabeth II **Obv:** Crowned head right **Rev:** Queen angel fish left **Edge:** Plain

Date	Mintage	VF20	XF40	MS60	MS63	MS65
1986	1,400,000	—	0.10	0.25	0.50	0.75
1986	2,500	PF65 2.50				
1987	1,050,000	—	0.10	0.25	0.50	0.75
1988	700,000	—	0.10	0.25	0.50	0.75
1990	700,000	—	0.10	0.25	0.50	0.75
1993	600,000	—	0.10	0.25	0.50	0.75
1994	1,100,000	—	0.10	0.25	0.50	0.75
1995	700,000	—	0.10	0.25	0.50	0.75
1996	1,500,000	—	0.10	0.25	0.50	0.75
1997	300,000	—	0.10	0.25	0.50	0.75
1998	300,000	—	0.10	0.25	0.50	0.75

KM# 45a 5 CENTS

5.70 g., 0.925 Silver 0.1695 oz. ASW, 21 mm. **Ruler:** Elizabeth II **Obv:** Crowned head right **Rev:** Queen angel fish left **Note:** In sets only.

Date	Mintage	VF20	XF40	MS60	MS63	MS65
1995	2,000	PF65 12.00				

KM# 45b 5 CENTS

5.70 g., 0.917 Gold 0.168 oz. AGW, 21 mm. **Ruler:** Elizabeth II **Obv:** Crowned head right **Rev:** Queen angel fish left **Note:** In sets only.

Date	Mintage	VF20	XF40	MS60	MS63	MS65
1995	500	PF65 300				

KM# 108 5 CENTS

5.00 g., Copper-Nickel, 21.2 mm. **Ruler:** Elizabeth II **Obv:** Head with tiara right **Rev:** Queen angel fish left **Edge:** Plain

Date	Mintage	VF20	XF40	MS60	MS63	MS65
1999	900,000	—	—	—	0.75	1.00
1999	2,500	PF65 3.50				
2000	1,000,000	—	—	—	0.75	1.00

KM# 17 10 CENTS

2.45 g., Copper-Nickel, 17.8 mm. **Ruler:** Elizabeth II **Obv:** Young bust right **Rev:** Bermuda lily **Edge:** Reeded

Date	Mintage	VF20	XF40	MS60	MS63	MS65
1970	2,500,000	—	0.10	0.20	0.35	0.50
1970	11,000	PF65 0.50				
1971	2,000,000	—	0.10	0.20	0.35	0.50
1978	500,000	—	0.10	0.20	0.40	0.60
1979	800,000	—	0.10	0.20	0.40	0.60
1980	1,100,000	—	0.10	0.20	0.35	0.50
1981	1,300,000	—	0.10	0.20	0.35	0.50
1982	400,000	—	0.10	0.20	0.40	0.60
1983	1,000,000	—	0.10	0.20	0.35	0.50
1983	6,474	PF65 2.00				
1984	500,000	—	0.10	0.20	0.40	0.60
1985	500,000	—	0.10	0.20	0.40	0.60

KM# 46 10 CENTS

2.45 g., Copper-Nickel, 17.9 mm. **Ruler:** Elizabeth II **Obv:** Crowned head right **Rev:** Bermuda lily **Edge:** Reeded

Date	Mintage	VF20	XF40	MS60	MS63	MS65
1986	750,000	—	0.10	0.20	0.40	0.60
1986	2,500	PF65 3.50				
1987	2,000,000	—	0.10	0.20	0.40	0.60
1988	720,000	—	0.10	0.20	0.40	0.60
1990	1,500,000	—	0.10	0.20	0.40	0.60
1993	15,000	—	—	—	3.00	4.00

Note: Sets only

Date	Mintage	VF20	XF40	MS60	MS63	MS65
1994	1,400,000	—	0.10	0.20	0.40	0.60
1995	1,400,000	—	0.10	0.20	0.40	0.60
1996	1,000,000	—	0.10	0.20	0.40	0.60
1997	800,000	—	0.10	0.20	0.40	0.60
1998	800,000	—	0.10	0.20	0.40	0.60

KM# 46a 10 CENTS

2.80 g., 0.925 Silver 0.0833 oz. ASW, 17.8 mm. **Ruler:** Elizabeth II **Obv:** Crowned head right **Rev:** Bermuda lily **Note:** In sets only.

Date	Mintage	VF20	XF40	MS60	MS63	MS65
1995	2,000	PF65 13.50				

KM# 46b 10 CENTS

4.75 g., 0.917 Gold 0.140 oz. AGW, 17.8 mm. **Ruler:** Elizabeth II **Obv:** Crowned head right **Rev:** Bermuda lily **Note:** In sets only.

Date	Mintage	VF20	XF40	MS60	MS63	MS65
1995	500	PF65 250				

KM# 109 10 CENTS

2.50 g., Copper-Nickel, 17.8 mm. **Ruler:** Elizabeth II **Obv:** Head with tiara right **Rev:** Bermuda lily **Edge:** Reeded

Date	Mintage	VF20	XF40	MS60	MS63	MS65
1999	1,400,000	—	—	—	0.85	1.00
1999	2,500	PF65 6.00				
2000	—	—	—	—	0.85	1.00

KM# 18 25 CENTS

5.92 g., Copper-Nickel, 24 mm. **Ruler:** Elizabeth II **Obv:** Young bust right **Rev:** White-tailed tropicbird **Edge:** Reeded

Date	Mintage	VF20	XF40	MS60	MS63	MS65
1970	1,500,000	—	0.30	0.60	1.25	1.50
1970	11,000	PF65 2.00				
1973	1,000,000	—	0.30	0.60	1.25	1.50
1979	570,000	—	0.30	0.60	1.25	1.50
1980	1,120,000	—	0.30	0.60	1.25	1.50
1981	2,200,000	—	0.30	0.60	1.25	1.50
1982	160,000	—	0.30	0.60	1.50	1.75
1983	600,000	—	0.30	0.60	1.25	1.50
1983	6,474	PF65 2.50				
1984	400,000	—	0.30	0.60	1.25	1.50
1985	412,500	—	0.30	0.60	1.25	1.50

KM# 32 25 CENTS

Copper-Nickel, 24 mm. **Ruler:** Elizabeth II **Subject:** 375th Anniversary of Bermuda **Obv:** Young bust right **Rev:** Arms of the Bermudas **Edge:** Reeded

Date	Mintage	VF20	XF40	MS60	MS63	MS65
1984	36,850	—	—	1.50	2.50	4.00

KM# 32a 25 CENTS

5.96 g., 0.925 Silver 0.1772 oz. ASW, 24 mm. **Ruler:** Elizabeth II **Subject:** 375th Anniversary of Bermuda **Obv:** Young bust right **Rev:** Arms of the Bermudas

Date	Mintage	VF20	XF40	MS60	MS63	MS65
1984	19,250	PF65 10.00				

KM# 33 25 CENTS

Copper-Nickel, 24 mm. **Ruler:** Elizabeth II **Subject:** 375th Anniversary of Bermuda **Obv:** Young bust right **Rev:** City of Hamilton arms **Edge:** Reeded

Date	Mintage	VF20	XF40	MS60	MS63	MS65
1984	36,850	—	—	1.50	2.50	4.00

KM# 33a 25 CENTS

5.96 g., 0.925 Silver 0.1772 oz. ASW, 24 mm. **Ruler:** Elizabeth II **Subject:** 375th Anniversary of Bermuda **Obv:** Young bust right **Rev:** City of Hamilton arms

Date	Mintage	VF20	XF40	MS60	MS63	MS65
1984	19,250	PF65 10.00				

KM# 34 25 CENTS

Copper-Nickel, 24 mm. **Ruler:** Elizabeth II **Subject:** 375th Anniversary of Bermuda **Obv:** Young bust right **Rev:** Town of St. George arms **Edge:** Reeded

Date	Mintage	VF20	XF40	MS60	MS63	MS65
1984	36,850	—	—	1.50	2.50	4.00

KM# 34a 25 CENTS

5.96 g., 0.925 Silver 0.1772 oz. ASW, 24 mm. **Ruler:** Elizabeth II **Subject:** 375th Anniversary of Bermuda **Obv:** Young bust right **Rev:** Town of St. George arms

Date	Mintage	VF20	XF40	MS60	MS63	MS65
1984	19,250	PF65 10.00				

KM# 35 25 CENTS

Copper-Nickel, 24 mm. **Ruler:** Elizabeth II **Subject:** 375th Anniversary of Bermuda **Obv:** Young bust right **Rev:** Warwick Parish arms **Edge:** Reeded

Date	Mintage	VF20	XF40	MS60	MS63	MS65
1984	36,850	—	—	1.50	2.50	4.00

KM# 35a 25 CENTS

5.96 g., 0.925 Silver 0.1772 oz. ASW, 24 mm. **Ruler:** Elizabeth II **Subject:** 375th Anniversary of Bermuda **Obv:** Young bust right **Rev:** Warwick Parish arms

Date	Mintage	VF20	XF40	MS60	MS63	MS65
1984	19,250	PF65 10.00				

KM# 36 25 CENTS

Copper-Nickel, 24 mm. **Ruler:** Elizabeth II **Subject:** 375th Anniversary of Bermuda **Obv:** Young bust right **Rev:** Smith's Parish arms **Edge:** Reeded

Date	Mintage	VF20	XF40	MS60	MS63	MS65
1984	36,850	—	—	1.50	2.50	4.00

KM# 36a 25 CENTS

5.96 g., 0.925 Silver 0.1772 oz. ASW, 24 mm. **Ruler:** Elizabeth II **Subject:** 375th Anniversary of Bermuda **Obv:** Young bust right **Rev:** Smith's Parish arms

Date	Mintage	VF20	XF40	MS60	MS63	MS65
1984	19,250	PF65 10.00				

KM# 37 25 CENTS

Copper-Nickel, 24 mm. **Ruler:** Elizabeth II **Subject:** 375th Anniversary of Bermuda **Obv:** Young bust right **Rev:** Devonshire Parish arms **Edge:** Reeded

Date	Mintage	VF20	XF40	MS60	MS63	MS65
1984	36,850	—	—	1.50	2.50	4.00

KM# 37a 25 CENTS

5.96 g., 0.925 Silver 0.1772 oz. ASW, 24 mm. **Ruler:** Elizabeth II **Subject:** 375th Anniversary of Bermuda **Obv:** Young bust right **Rev:** Devonshire Parish arms

Date	Mintage	VF20	XF40	MS60	MS63	MS65
1984	19,250	PF65 10.00				

KM# 38 25 CENTS

Copper-Nickel, 24 mm. **Ruler:** Elizabeth II **Subject:** 375th Anniversary of Bermuda **Obv:** Young bust right **Rev:** Sandy's Parish arms **Edge:** Reeded

Date	Mintage	VF20	XF40	MS60	MS63	MS65
1984	36,850	—	—	1.50	2.50	4.00

KM# 38a 25 CENTS

5.96 g., 0.925 Silver 0.1772 oz. ASW, 24 mm. **Ruler:** Elizabeth II **Subject:** 375th Anniversary of Bermuda **Obv:** Young bust right **Rev:** Sandy's Parish arms

Date	Mintage	VF20	XF40	MS60	MS63	MS65
1984	19,250	PF65 10.00				

KM# 39 25 CENTS

Copper-Nickel, 24 mm. **Ruler:** Elizabeth II **Subject:** 375th Anniversary of Bermuda **Obv:** Young bust right **Rev:** Hamilton Parish arms **Edge:** Reeded

Date	Mintage	VF20	XF40	MS60	MS63	MS65
1984	36,850	—	—	1.50	2.50	4.00

KM# 39a 25 CENTS

5.96 g., 0.925 Silver 0.1772 oz. ASW, 24 mm. **Ruler:** Elizabeth II **Subject:** 375th Anniversary of Bermuda **Obv:** Young bust right **Rev:** Hamilton Parish arms

Date	Mintage	VF20	XF40	MS60	MS63	MS65
1984	19,250	PF65 10.00				

KM# 40 25 CENTS

Copper-Nickel, 24 mm. **Ruler:** Elizabeth II **Subject:** 375th Anniversary of Bermuda **Obv:** Young bust right **Rev:** Southampton Parish arms **Edge:** Reeded

Date	Mintage	VF20	XF40	MS60	MS63	MS65
1984	36,850	—	—	1.50	2.50	4.00

KM# 40a 25 CENTS

5.96 g., 0.925 Silver 0.1772 oz. ASW, 24 mm. **Ruler:** Elizabeth II **Subject:** 375th Anniversary of Bermuda **Obv:** Young bust right **Rev:** Southampton Parish arms

Date	Mintage	VF20	XF40	MS60	MS63	MS65
1984	19,250	PF65 10.00				

KM# 41 25 CENTS

Copper-Nickel, 24 mm. **Ruler:** Elizabeth II **Subject:** 375th Anniversary of Bermuda **Obv:** Young bust right **Rev:** Pembroke Parish arms **Edge:** Reeded

Date	Mintage	VF20	XF40	MS60	MS63	MS65
1984	36,850	—	—	1.50	2.50	4.00

KM# 41a 25 CENTS

5.96 g., 0.925 Silver 0.1772 oz. ASW, 24 mm. **Ruler:** Elizabeth II **Subject:** 375th Anniversary of Bermuda **Obv:** Young bust right **Rev:** Pembroke Parish arms

Date	Mintage	VF20	XF40	MS60	MS63	MS65
1984	19,250	PF65 10.00				

KM# 42 25 CENTS

Copper-Nickel, 24 mm. **Ruler:** Elizabeth II **Subject:** 375th Anniversary of Bermuda **Obv:** Young bust right **Rev:** Paget Parish arms **Edge:** Reeded

Date	Mintage	VF20	XF40	MS60	MS63	MS65
1984	36,850	—	—	1.50	2.50	4.00

KM# 42a 25 CENTS

5.96 g., 0.925 Silver 0.1772 oz. ASW, 24 mm. **Ruler:** Elizabeth II **Subject:** 375th Anniversary of Bermuda **Obv:** Young bust right **Rev:** Paget Parish arms

Date	Mintage	VF20	XF40	MS60	MS63	MS65
1984	19,250	PF65 10.00				

KM# 47 25 CENTS

6.02 g., Copper-Nickel, 24.15 mm. **Ruler:** Elizabeth II **Obv:** Crowned head right **Rev:** White-tailed tropicbird right **Edge:** Reeded

Date	Mintage	VF20	XF40	MS60	MS63	MS65
1986	1,260,000	—	0.30	0.50	1.00	1.50
1986	2,500	PF65 6.00				
1987	600,000	—	0.30	0.50	1.00	1.50
1988	600,000	—	0.30	0.50	1.00	1.50
1993	480,000	—	0.30	0.50	1.00	1.50
1994	1,040,000	—	0.30	0.50	1.00	1.50
1995	960,000	—	0.30	0.50	1.00	1.50
1996	1,200,000	—	0.30	0.50	1.00	1.50
1997	1,200,000	—	0.30	0.50	1.00	1.50
1998	—	—	0.30	0.50	1.00	1.50

KM# 47a 25 CENTS

7.00 g., 0.925 Silver 0.2082 oz. ASW, 24 mm. **Ruler:** Elizabeth II **Obv:** Crowned head right **Rev:** Yellow-billed tropical bird right **Note:** In sets only.

Date	Mintage	VF20	XF40	MS60	MS63	MS65
1995	2,000	PF65 18.00				

KM# 47b 25 CENTS

11.70 g., 0.917 Gold 0.3449 oz. AGW, 24 mm. **Ruler:** Elizabeth II **Subject:** Yellow-billed tropical bird right **Obv:** Crowned head right **Note:** In sets only.

Date	Mintage	VF20	XF40	MS60	MS63	MS65
1995	500	PF65 600				

KM# 110 25 CENTS

Copper-Nickel, 24 mm. **Ruler:** Elizabeth II **Obv:** Head with tiara right **Rev:** Yellow-billed tropical bird right **Edge:** Reeded

Date	Mintage	VF20	XF40	MS60	MS63	MS65
1999	800,000	—	—	—	1.50	2.00
1999	2,500	PF65 10.00				
2000	800,000	—	—	—	1.50	2.00

KM# 19 50 CENTS

12.42 g., Copper-Nickel, 30.5 mm. **Ruler:** Elizabeth II **Obv:** Young bust right **Rev:** Arms **Edge:** Reeded

Date	Mintage	VF20	XF40	MS60	MS63	MS65
1970	1,000,000	—	0.60	0.75	1.00	1.50
1970	11,000	PF65 2.00				
1978	200,000	—	0.60	0.85	1.25	1.75
1980	60,000	—	0.60	0.85	1.50	2.00

Date	Mintage	VF20	XF40	MS60	MS63	MS65
1981	100,000	—	0.60	0.85	1.25	1.75
1982	80,000	—	0.60	0.85	1.50	2.00
1983	60,000	—	0.60	0.85	1.50	2.00
1983	6,474	PF65 4.50				
1984	40,000	—	0.60	0.85	1.50	2.00
1985	40,000	—	0.60	0.85	1.50	2.00

KM# 48 50 CENTS

12.60 g., Copper-Nickel, 30.5 mm. **Ruler:** Elizabeth II **Obv:** Crowned head right **Rev:** National arms **Edge:** Reeded

Date	Mintage	VF20	XF40	MS60	MS63	MS65
1986	120,000	—	0.60	0.85	1.50	2.00
1986	2,500	PF65 6.00				
1988	60,000	—	0.60	0.85	1.50	2.00

KM# 20 DOLLAR

28.28 g., 0.800 Silver 0.7274 oz. ASW, 38 mm. **Ruler:** Elizabeth II **Obv:** Young bust right **Rev:** Jugate heads right

Date	Mintage	VF20	XF40	MS60	MS63	MS65
1970	11,000	PF65 22.00				

KM# 22 DOLLAR

28.28 g., 0.500 Silver 0.4546 oz. ASW, 38 mm. **Ruler:** Elizabeth II **Subject:** Silver Wedding Anniversary **Obv:** Young bust right **Rev:** Crowned monograms divided by map

Date	Mintage	VF20	XF40	MS60	MS63	MS65
1972	65,074	—	—	—	12.00	14.00

KM# 22a DOLLAR

28.28 g., 0.925 Silver 0.841 oz. ASW, 38 mm. **Ruler:** Elizabeth II **Subject:** Silver Wedding Anniversary **Obv:** Young bust right **Rev:** Crowned monograms divided by map

Date	Mintage	VF20	XF40	MS60	MS63	MS65
1972	14,708	PF65 25.00				

KM# 28 DOLLAR

Copper-Nickel, 38.5 mm. **Ruler:** Elizabeth II **Subject:** Wedding of Prince Charles and Lady Diana **Obv:** Young bust right **Rev:** Jugate heads right **Edge:** Reeded

Date	Mintage	VF20	XF40	MS60	MS63	MS65
1981	65,004	—	—	—	5.00	7.00

KM# 28a DOLLAR

28.28 g., 0.925 Silver 0.841 oz. ASW, 38.5 mm. **Ruler:** Elizabeth II **Subject:** Wedding of Prince Charles and Lady Diana **Obv:** Young bust right **Rev:** Jugate heads right **Edge:** Reeded

Date	Mintage	VF20	XF40	MS60	MS63	MS65
1981	16,296	PF65 22.00				

KM# 30 DOLLAR

9.75 g., Copper-Nickel-Bronze, 22.75 mm. **Ruler:** Elizabeth II **Subject:** Cahow over Bermuda **Obv:** Young bust right **Rev:** Bird flying over map **Edge Lettering:** BERMUDA MONETARY AUTHORITY

Date	Mintage	VF20	XF40	MS60	MS63	MS65
1983	250,000	—	—	—	2.50	4.00
1983	6,474	PF65 6.50				

KM# 43 DOLLAR

Copper-Nickel, 38.5 mm. **Ruler:** Elizabeth II **Subject:** Cruise Ship Tourism **Obv:** Crowned bust right **Rev:** The Bermuda Buttery, an early refrigeration building and a cruise ship in the distance **Edge:** Reeded

Date	Mintage	VF20	XF40	MS60	MS63	MS65
1985	11,000	—	—	—	4.00	6.00

KM# 43a DOLLAR

28.28 g., 0.925 Silver 0.841 oz. ASW, 38.5 mm. **Ruler:** Elizabeth II **Subject:** Cruise Ship Tourism **Obv:** Young bust right **Rev:** The Bermuda Buttery, an early refrigeration building and a cruise ship in the distance **Edge:** Reeded

Date	Mintage	VF20	XF40	MS60	MS63	MS65
1985	2,500	—	—	—	30.00	32.50
1985	4,000	PF65 28.00				

KM# 49 DOLLAR

Copper-Nickel, 38.5 mm. **Ruler:** Elizabeth II **Series:** World Wildlife Fund **Obv:** Crowned head right **Rev:** Green Sea turtle, chelonia mydas **Edge:** Reeded

Date	Mintage	VF20	XF40	MS60	MS63	MS65
1986	33,320	—	—	—	10.00	12.00

KM# 49a DOLLAR

28.28 g., 0.925 Silver 0.841 oz. ASW, 38.61 mm. **Ruler:** Elizabeth II **Series:** World Wildlife Fund **Obv:** Crowned head right **Rev:** Green Sea Turtle **Edge:** Reeded

Date	Mintage	VF20	XF40	MS60	MS63	MS65
1986	10,000	—	—	—	28.00	32.00
1986	Est. 21872	PF65 35.00				

KM# 50 DOLLAR

9.75 g., Copper-Nickel-Zinc, 22.75 mm. **Ruler:** Elizabeth II **Obv:** Crowned head right **Rev:** Cahow over Bermuda **Edge Lettering:** BERMUDA MONETARY AUTHORITY

Date	Mintage	VF20	XF40	MS60	MS63	MS65
1986	2,500	PF65 12.50				

KM# 52 DOLLAR

28.28 g., Copper-Nickel, 38.5 mm. **Ruler:** Elizabeth II **Subject:** 50th Anniversary of Commercial Aviation **Obv:** Crowned head right **Rev:** Amphibious plane **Edge:** Reeded

Date	Mintage	VF20	XF40	MS60	MS63	MS65
1987	9,000	—	—	—	6.00	8.00

KM# 52a DOLLAR

28.28 g., 0.625 Silver 0.5683 oz. ASW, 38.61 mm. **Ruler:** Elizabeth II **Subject:** 50th Anniversary of Commercial Aviation **Obv:** Crowned head right **Rev:** Amphibious plane **Edge:** Reeded

Date	Mintage	VF20	XF40	MS60	MS63	MS65
1987	4,000	—	—	—	22.50	25.00
1987	5,000	PF65 25.00				

KM# 55 DOLLAR

28.28 g., Copper-Nickel, 38.5 mm. **Ruler:** Elizabeth II **Subject:** Railroad **Obv:** Crowned head right **Rev:** Train **Edge:** Reeded

Date	Mintage	VF20	XF40	MS60	MS63	MS65
1988	6,000	—	—	—	7.00	9.00

KM# 55a DOLLAR

28.28 g., 0.925 Silver 0.841 oz. ASW, 38.61 mm. **Ruler:** Elizabeth II **Subject:** Railroad **Obv:** Crowned head right **Rev:** Train

Date	Mintage	VF20	XF40	MS60	MS63	MS65
1988	5,000	—	—	—	28.00	30.00
1988	5,000	PF65 32.00				

KM# 56 DOLLAR

7.56 g., Nickel-Brass, 26 mm. **Ruler:** Elizabeth II **Obv:** Crowned head right **Rev:** Boat with full sails **Edge:** Alternating reeded and plain **Note:** Circulation type.

Date	Mintage	VF20	XF40	MS60	MS63	MS65
1988	2,000,000	—	—	—	2.00	3.00
1993	15,000	—	—	—	3.00	4.00
Note: Sets only.						
1996	300,000	—	—	—	2.00	3.00
1997	600,000	—	—	—	2.00	3.00

KM# 56a DOLLAR

9.20 g., 0.925 Silver 0.2736 oz. ASW, 26 mm. **Ruler:** Elizabeth II **Obv:** Crowned head right **Rev:** Boat with full sails

Date	Mintage	VF20	XF40	MS60	MS63	MS65
1988	Est. 3000	PF65 25.00				
1995	2,000	PF65 32.00				
Note: Sets only.						

KM# 56b DOLLAR

15.50 g., 0.917 Gold 0.457 oz. AGW, 26 mm. **Ruler:** Elizabeth II **Obv:** Crowned head right **Rev:** Boat with full sails

Date	Mintage	VF20	XF40	MS60	MS63	MS65
1995	500	PF65 750				
Note: Sets only.						

KM# 61 DOLLAR

28.28 g., Copper-Nickel, 38.5 mm. **Ruler:** Elizabeth II **Subject:** Monarch Conservation Project **Obv:** Crowned head right **Rev:** Monarch Butterflies within flower chain

Date	Mintage	VF20	XF40	MS60	MS63	MS65
1989	5,000	—	—	—	15.00	17.00

KM# 61a DOLLAR

28.28 g., 0.925 Silver 0.841 oz. ASW, 38.5 mm. **Ruler:** Elizabeth II **Subject:** Monarch Conservation Project **Obv:** Crowned head right **Rev:** Monarch butterflies within flower chain

Date	Mintage	VF20	XF40	MS60	MS63	MS65
1989	5,000	—	—	—	30.00	32.00
1989	5,000	PF65 35.00				

KM# 67 DOLLAR

28.28 g., Copper-Nickel, 38.5 mm. **Ruler:** Elizabeth II **Subject:** Queen Mother's 90th birthday **Obv:** Crowned head right **Rev:** Crowned monogram flanked by flowers **Edge:** Reeded

Date	Mintage	VF20	XF40	MS60	MS63	MS65
1990	5,000	—	—	—	4.00	5.00

KM# 67a DOLLAR

28.28 g., 0.925 Silver 0.841 oz. ASW, 38.5 mm. **Ruler:** Elizabeth II **Subject:** Queen Mother's 90th birthday **Obv:** Crowned head right **Rev:** Crowned monogram flanked by flowers **Edge:** Reeded

Date	Mintage	VF20	XF40	MS60	MS63	MS65
1990	5,000	PF65 40.00				

KM# 78 DOLLAR

28.28 g., Bronze, 38.61 mm. **Ruler:** Elizabeth II **Obv:** Crowned head right **Rev:** Olympic rings **Edge:** Reeded

Date	Mintage	VF20	XF40	MS60	MS63	MS65
1992	—	PF65 100				

KM# 85 DOLLAR

31.47 g., 0.925 Silver 0.9359 oz. ASW, 38.61 mm. **Ruler:** Elizabeth II **Series:** 1992 Olympics **Rev:** Sailboats **Edge:** Reeded

Date	Mintage	VF20	XF40	MS60	MS63	MS65
ND-1993	25,000	PF65 32.00				

KM# 91 DOLLAR

28.28 g., Copper-Nickel, 38.5 mm. **Ruler:** Elizabeth II **Subject:** International Senior Games **Obv:** Crowned head right **Rev:** Map divides monograms **Edge:** Reeded

Date	Mintage	VF20	XF40	MS60	MS63	MS65
1996	1,000	—	—	—	25.00	28.00

KM# 94 DOLLAR

28.28 g., Copper-Nickel, 38.5 mm. **Ruler:** Elizabeth II **Subject:** Queen Elizabeth II's 70th Birthday **Obv:** Crowned head right **Rev:** Horse-drawn carriage **Edge:** Reeded

Date	Mintage	VF20	XF40	MS60	MS63	MS65
ND-1996	5,000	—	—	—	8.00	10.00

KM# 105 DOLLAR

28.28 g., 0.925 Silver 0.841 oz. ASW, 38.61 mm. **Ruler:** Elizabeth II **Series:** Olympic Games **Obv:** Crowned head right **Rev:** Horse with rider jumping right **Edge:** Reeded

Date	Mintage	VF20	XF40	MS60	MS63	MS65
1996	30,000	PF65 32.00				

KM# 127 DOLLAR

28.28 g., Copper-Nickel, 38.6 mm. **Ruler:** Elizabeth II **Obv:** Crowned head right **Rev:** 1937 Coronation portrait **Edge:** Reeded

Date	Mintage	VF20	XF40	MS60	MS63	MS65
1996	10,000	—	—	—	7.00	9.00

KM# 127a DOLLAR

28.37 g., 0.925 Silver 0.8437 oz. ASW, 38.6 mm. **Ruler:** Elizabeth II **Obv:** Crowned head right **Rev:** 1937 Coronation portrait **Edge:** Reeded

Date	Mintage	VF20	XF40	MS60	MS63	MS65
1996	30,000	PF65 32.00				

KM# 135 DOLLAR

17.03 g., Copper-Nickel, 35 mm. **Ruler:** Elizabeth II **Obv:** Crowned head right **Rev:** Compass rose, map and ship **Edge:** Plain **Shape:** Triangular

Date	Mintage	VF20	XF40	MS60	MS63	MS65
1996	500	—	—	—	12.00	15.00

KM# 95 DOLLAR

Copper-Nickel, 35 mm. **Ruler:** Elizabeth II **Subject:** Wreck of the Sea Venture **Obv:** Crowned head right **Rev:** Shipwreck from Bermudan arms **Edge:** Smooth **Shape:** 3-sided

Date	Mintage	VF20	XF40	MS60	MS63	MS65
1997	—	—	—	—	13.00	16.00

KM# 119 DOLLAR

28.28 g., 0.925 Silver 0.841 oz. ASW, 39 mm. **Ruler:** Elizabeth II **Subject:** World Wildlife Fund - Conserving Nature **Obv:** Crowned head right **Rev:** Bermuda Rock Skink (Eumeces longirostris) on rock **Edge:** Reeded

Date	Mintage	VF20	XF40	MS60	MS63	MS65
1997	—	PF65 40.00				

KM# 126 DOLLAR

16.00 g., 0.925 Silver 0.4758 oz. ASW, 28.3 mm. **Ruler:** Elizabeth II **Subject:** Queen Mother **Obv:** Crowned head right **Rev:** 1937 Coronation portrait **Edge:** Reeded

Date	Mintage	VF20	XF40	MS60	MS63	MS65
1997	—	PF65 22.50				

KM# 104 DOLLAR

Copper-Nickel, 35 mm. **Ruler:** Elizabeth II **Obv:** Crowned head right **Rev:** Sailing ship Deliverance and map **Shape:** Triangular

Date	Mintage	VF20	XF40	MS60	MS63	MS65
1998	—	—	—	—	13.00	16.00

KM# 104a DOLLAR

20.00 g., 0.925 Silver 0.5948 oz. ASW, 35 mm. **Ruler:** Elizabeth II **Obv:** Crowned head right **Rev:** Ship on map **Edge:** Plain **Shape:** Triangular

Date	Mintage	VF20	XF40	MS60	MS63	MS65
1998	6,500	PF65 40.00				

KM# 111 DOLLAR

Nickel-Brass, 26 mm. **Ruler:** Elizabeth II **Obv:** Head with tiara right **Rev:** Sailboat

Date	Mintage	VF20	XF40	MS60	MS63	MS65
1999	12,000	—	—	—	3.00	3.50
1999	2,500	PF65 22.00				
2000	—	—	—	—	3.00	3.50

KM# 125 DOLLAR

28.28 g., Copper-Nickel, 38.6 mm. **Ruler:** Elizabeth II **Subject:** Millennium **Obv:** Crowned head right **Rev:** Radiant sun behind sailing ship **Shape:** Scalloped

Date	Mintage	VF20	XF40	MS60	MS63	MS65
1999-2000	—	—	—	—	20.00	22.00

KM# 117 DOLLAR

28.28 g., Copper-Nickel, 38.6 mm. **Ruler:** Elizabeth II **Subject:** Tall Ships **Obv:** Head with tiara right **Rev:** Three-masted sailing ship **Edge:** Reeded

Date	Mintage	VF20	XF40	MS60	MS63	MS65
2000	10,000	—	—	—	9.00	11.00

KM# 117a DOLLAR

28.28 g., 0.925 Silver 0.841 oz. ASW, 38.6 mm. **Ruler:** Elizabeth II **Subject:** Tall Ships **Obv:** Head with tiara right **Rev:** Three-masted sailing ship **Edge:** Reeded

Date	Mintage	VF20	XF40	MS60	MS63	MS65
2000	10,000	PF65 75.00				

KM# 122 DOLLAR

28.30 g., 0.925 Silver 0.8416 oz. ASW, 38.5 mm. **Ruler:** Elizabeth II **Subject:** Queen Mother **Obv:** Head with tiara right **Rev:** 1937 Coronation portrait **Edge:** Reeded

Date	Mintage	VF20	XF40	MS60	MS63	MS65
2000	—	PF65 37.00				

KM# 64 2 DOLLARS
28.28 g., 0.925 Silver 0.841 oz. ASW, 38.61 mm. **Ruler:** Elizabeth II **Obv:** Crowned head right **Rev:** Cicada insects **Edge:** Reeded

Date	Mintage	VF20	XF40	MS60	MS63	MS65
1990	3,000	PF65 32.50				

KM# 65 2 DOLLARS
28.28 g., 0.925 Silver 0.841 oz. ASW, 38.61 mm. **Ruler:** Elizabeth II **Subject:** Wildlife **Obv:** Crowned head right **Rev:** Tree frog **Edge:** Reeded

Date	Mintage	VF20	XF40	MS60	MS63	MS65
1990	3,000	PF65 32.50				

KM# 68 2 DOLLARS
28.28 g., 0.925 Silver 0.841 oz. ASW, 38.61 mm. **Ruler:** Elizabeth II **Obv:** Crowned head right **Rev:** Yellow-crowned night heron **Edge:** Reeded

Date	Mintage	VF20	XF40	MS60	MS63	MS65
1991	3,000	PF65 32.50				

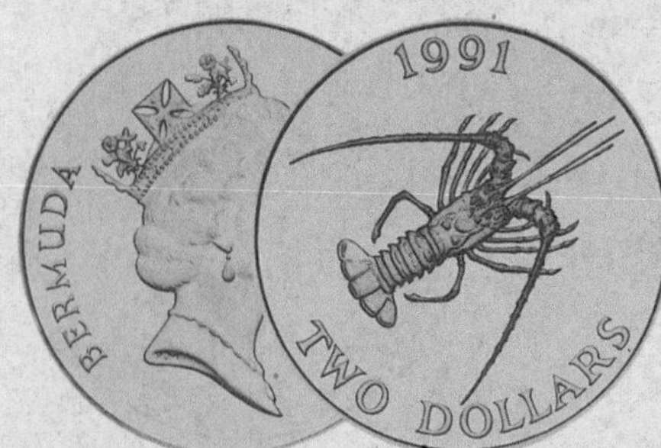

KM# 69 2 DOLLARS
28.28 g., 0.925 Silver 0.841 oz. ASW, 38.61 mm. **Ruler:** Elizabeth II **Obv:** Crowned head right **Rev:** Spiny lobster **Edge:** Reeded

Date	Mintage	VF20	XF40	MS60	MS63	MS65
1991	3,000	PF65 32.50				

KM# 71 2 DOLLARS
28.28 g., 0.925 Silver 0.841 oz. ASW, 38.61 mm. **Ruler:** Elizabeth II **Obv:** Crowned head right **Rev:** Eastern Bluebird feeding nestling **Edge:** Reeded

Date	Mintage	VF20	XF40	MS60	MS63	MS65
1992	2,500	PF65 32.50				

KM# 72 2 DOLLARS
28.28 g., 0.925 Silver 0.841 oz. ASW, 38.61 mm. **Ruler:** Elizabeth II **Obv:** Crowned head right **Rev:** Cedar tree **Edge:** Reeded

Date	Mintage	VF20	XF40	MS60	MS63	MS65
1992	2,500	PF65 32.50				

KM# 81 2 DOLLARS
23.00 g., 0.925 Silver 0.684 oz. ASW **Ruler:** Elizabeth II **Subject:** 200 Years of Bermudin Coinage **Obv:** Crowned head right **Rev:** 3-masted sailing ship

Date	Mintage	VF20	XF40	MS60	MS63	MS65
1993	5,000	PF65 30.00				

KM# 83 2 DOLLARS
28.28 g., 0.925 Silver 0.841 oz. ASW, 38.61 mm. **Ruler:** Elizabeth II **Obv:** Crowned head right **Rev:** Humpback whale leaping right **Edge:** Reeded

Date	Mintage	VF20	XF40	MS60	MS63	MS65
1993	2,000	PF65 35.00				

KM# 84 2 DOLLARS
28.28 g., 0.925 Silver 0.841 oz. ASW, 38.61 mm. **Ruler:** Elizabeth II **Obv:** Crowned head right **Rev:** White-tailed tropicbird **Edge:** Reeded

Date	Mintage	VF20	XF40	MS60	MS63	MS65
1993	2,000	PF65 35.00				

KM# 89 2 DOLLARS
28.28 g., 0.925 Silver 0.841 oz. ASW, 38.61 mm. **Ruler:** Elizabeth II **Subject:** City of Hamilton's 200th Anniversary **Obv:** Crowned head right **Rev:** Ship at dock within circle **Edge:** Reeded

Date	Mintage	VF20	XF40	MS60	MS63	MS65
1993	250	PF65 70.00				

KM# 86 2 DOLLARS
28.28 g., 0.925 Silver 0.841 oz. ASW, 38.61 mm. **Ruler:** Elizabeth II **Subject:** Royal visit **Obv:** Crowned head right **Rev:** Map divides conjoined heads of royal couple and royal emblem **Edge:** Reeded

Date	Mintage	VF20	XF40	MS60	MS63	MS65
1994	10,000	PF65 28.00				

KM# 87 2 DOLLARS
28.28 g., 0.925 Silver 0.841 oz. ASW, 38.61 mm. **Ruler:** Elizabeth II **Obv:** Crowned head right **Rev:** Long-snouted seahorse **Edge:** Reeded

Date	Mintage	VF20	XF40	MS60	MS63	MS65
1994	1,500	PF65 42.50				

KM# 88 2 DOLLARS
28.28 g., 0.925 Silver 0.841 oz. ASW, 38.61 mm. **Ruler:** Elizabeth II **Obv:** Crowned head right **Rev:** Lightbourn's Fisinus (seashell) **Edge:** Reeded

Date	Mintage	VF20	XF40	MS60	MS63	MS65
1994	1,500	PF65 42.50				

KM# 123 2 DOLLARS
28.20 g., 0.925 Silver 0.8387 oz. ASW, 38.6 mm. **Ruler:** Elizabeth II **Subject:** Queen's 70th Birthday **Obv:** Crowned head right **Rev:** Carriage and tree **Edge:** Reeded

Date	Mintage	VF20	XF40	MS60	MS63	MS65
1996	12,500	PF65 30.00				

KM# 121 2 DOLLARS
28.13 g., 0.925 Silver 0.8366 oz. ASW, 38.5 mm. **Ruler:** Elizabeth II **Subject:** Queen's Golden Wedding Anniversary **Obv:** Crowned head right **Rev:** Royal couple descending stairs with gold insert shield at right **Edge:** Reeded

Date	Mintage	VF20	XF40	MS60	MS63	MS65
ND-1997	—	PF65 40.00				

KM# 136 2 DOLLARS
28.14 g., 0.925 Silver 0.8369 oz. ASW, 38.6 mm. **Ruler:** Elizabeth II **Subject:** Town of St. George 200th Anniversary **Obv:** Crowned head right **Rev:** St. George slaying the dragon **Edge:** Reeded

Date	Mintage	VF20	XF40	MS60	MS63	MS65
1997	250	PF65 150				

KM# 116 2 DOLLARS
28.28 g., 0.925 Silver 0.841 oz. ASW, 38.6 mm. **Ruler:** Elizabeth II **Subject:** Millennium **Obv:** Crowned head right **Rev:** Radiant gilt sun behind sailing ship dividing dates 1999-2000 above map **Edge:** Plain **Shape:** Scalloped

Date	Mintage	VF20	XF40	MS60	MS63	MS65
ND-2000	30,000	PF65 35.00				

KM# 92 3 DOLLARS
20.00 g., 0.925 Silver 0.5948 oz. ASW, 35 mm. **Ruler:** Elizabeth II **Subject:** Bermuda Triangle **Obv:** Crowned head right **Rev:** Map, compass, and capsizing ship **Shape:** Three-sided coin

Date	Mintage	VF20	XF40	MS60	MS63	MS65
1996	5,000	PF65 50.00				

KM# 99 3 DOLLARS
20.25 g., 0.925 Silver 0.6022 oz. ASW, 35 mm. **Ruler:** Elizabeth II **Subject:** Wreck of the Sea Venture **Obv:** Crowned head right **Rev:** Shipwreck scene **Shape:** 3-sided

Date	Mintage	VF20	XF40	MS60	MS63	MS65
1997	—	PF65 50.00				

KM# 106 3 DOLLARS
20.00 g., 0.925 Silver 0.5948 oz. ASW, 35 mm. **Ruler:** Elizabeth II **Obv:** Crowned head right **Rev:** Sailing ship Deliverance and map **Shape:** Three-sided

Date	Mintage	VF20	XF40	MS60	MS63	MS65
1998	—	PF65 50.00				

KM# 106a 3 DOLLARS
31.49 g., 0.999 Gold 1.0114 oz. AGW, 35 mm. **Ruler:** Elizabeth II **Obv:** Crowned head right **Rev:** Ship on map **Edge:** Plain **Shape:** 3-sided

Date	Mintage	VF20	XF40	MS60	MS63	MS65
1998	—	—	—	—	—	1,700

KM# 163 3 DOLLARS
1.56 g., 0.999 Gold 0.0499 oz. AGW, 15 mm. **Ruler:** Elizabeth II **Obv:** Crowned bust right **Rev:** 17th century galleon, map grids, islands **Edge:** Plain **Shape:** Triangular

Date	Mintage	VF20	XF40	MS60	MS63	MS65
1998	—	PF65 85.00				

KM# 31 5 DOLLARS
12.40 g., Copper-Nickel-Zinc, 25.75 mm. **Ruler:** Elizabeth II **Obv:** Young bust right **Rev:** Onion superimposed over map **Edge Lettering:** BERMUDA MONETARY AUTHORITY

Date	Mintage	VF20	XF40	MS60	MS63	MS65
1983	100,000	—	—	—	6.50	8.50
1983	6,474	PF65 10.00				

KM# 51 5 DOLLARS
12.50 g., Copper-Nickel-Zinc, 25.75 mm. **Ruler:** Elizabeth II **Obv:** Young bust right **Rev:** Onion superimposed over Bermuda map **Edge Lettering:** BERMUDA MONETARY AUTHORITY

Date	Mintage	VF20	XF40	MS60	MS63	MS65
1986	2,500	PF65 12.50				

KM# 54 5 DOLLARS
155.52 g., 0.999 Silver 4.9949 oz. ASW, 65 mm. **Ruler:** Elizabeth II **Subject:** Sea Venture Wreck **Obv:** Crowned head right **Rev:** Sailing ship **Note:** Illustration reduced.

Date	Mintage	VF20	XF40	MS60	MS63	MS65
1987	6,800	PF65 165				

KM# 62 5 DOLLARS
155.52 g., 0.999 Silver 4.9949 oz. ASW, 65 mm. **Ruler:** Elizabeth II **Subject:** San Antonio **Obv:** Crowned head right **Rev:** Sailing ship **Note:** Illustration reduced.

Date	Mintage	VF20	XF40	MS60	MS63	MS65
1988	1,500	PF65 175				

KM# 79 5 DOLLARS
155.52 g., 0.999 Silver 4.9949 oz. ASW, 65 mm. **Ruler:** Elizabeth II **Series:** Olympics **Obv:** Crowned head right **Rev:** Various events depicted within Olympic rings **Note:** Illustration reduced.

Date	Mintage	VF20	XF40	MS60	MS63	MS65
1992	Est. 1250	PF65 180				

KM# 90 5 DOLLARS
56.56 g., 0.925 Silver 1.6821 oz. ASW **Ruler:** Elizabeth II **Subject:** 375th Anniversary of Bermudian Parliament **Obv:** Bust right **Rev:** Session House **Edge:** Reeded

Date	Mintage	VF20	XF40	MS60	MS63	MS65
1995	375	PF65 120				

KM# 96 9 DOLLARS

155.52 g., 0.999 Silver 4.995 oz. ASW, 65.27 mm. **Ruler:** Elizabeth II **Subject:** Bermuda Triangle **Obv:** Crowned head right **Rev:** Map of island, compass, early sailing ship listing **Edge:** Plain **Shape:** Triangular **Note:** Illustration reduced

Date	Mintage	VF20	XF40	MS60	MS63	MS65
1996	Est. 1000	PF65 200				

KM# 100 9 DOLLARS

155.52 g., 0.999 Silver 4.995 oz. ASW, 65.27 mm. **Ruler:** Elizabeth II **Subject:** Wreck of the Sea Venture **Obv:** Crowned head right **Rev:** Shipwreck scene **Edge:** Plain **Shape:** Triangular

Date	Mintage	VF20	XF40	MS60	MS63	MS65
1997	1,000	PF65 200				

KM# 112 9 DOLLARS

155.52 g., 0.999 Silver 4.9951 oz. ASW, 65.27 mm. **Ruler:** Elizabeth II **Subject:** Bermuda Triangle **Obv:** Crowned head right **Rev:** Sailing ship Deliverance, map in background **Edge:** Plain **Shape:** Triangular **Note:** Illustration reduced.

Date	Mintage	VF20	XF40	MS60	MS63	MS65
1998	1,000	PF65 200				

KM# 57 10 DOLLARS

3.13 g., 0.999 Gold 0.1007 oz. AGW, 16.5 mm. **Ruler:** Elizabeth II **Subject:** Hogge money **Obv:** Crowned head right **Rev:** Wild pig

Date	Mintage	VF20	XF40	MS60	MS63	MS65
1989	500	PF65 170				

KM# 66 10 DOLLARS

3.13 g., 0.999 Gold 0.1007 oz. AGW, 16.5 mm. **Ruler:** Elizabeth II **Subject:** Wildlife **Obv:** Crowned head right **Rev:** Tree frog **Edge:** Reeded

Date	Mintage	VF20	XF40	MS60	MS63	MS65
1990	1,000	PF65 170				

KM# 74 10 DOLLARS

3.13 g., 0.999 Gold 0.1007 oz. AGW, 16.5 mm. **Ruler:** Elizabeth II **Subject:** Hogge money **Obv:** Crowned head right **Rev:** Ship circle

Date	Mintage	VF20	XF40	MS60	MS63	MS65
1990	500	PF65 170				

KM# 70 10 DOLLARS

3.13 g., 0.999 Gold 0.1007 oz. AGW, 16.5 mm. **Ruler:** Elizabeth II **Obv:** Crowned head right **Rev:** Yellow-crowned night heron **Edge:** Reeded

Date	Mintage	VF20	XF40	MS60	MS63	MS65
1991	2,500	—	—	—	165	170

KM# 73 10 DOLLARS

3.13 g., 0.999 Gold 0.1007 oz. AGW, 16.5 mm. **Ruler:** Elizabeth II **Obv:** Crowned head right **Rev:** Eastern Bluebird feeding nestling **Edge:** Reeded

Date	Mintage	VF20	XF40	MS60	MS63	MS65
1992	2,500	—	—	—	165	170

KM# 132 10 DOLLARS

3.13 g., 0.999 Gold 0.1007 oz. AGW, 17 mm. **Ruler:** Elizabeth II **Obv:** Crowned head right **Rev:** White-tailed Tropic Bird **Edge:** Reeded

Date	Mintage	VF20	XF40	MS60	MS63	MS65
1993	1,501	—	—	—	165	170

KM# 133 10 DOLLARS

3.13 g., 0.999 Gold 0.1007 oz. AGW, 17 mm. **Ruler:** Elizabeth II **Obv:** Crowned head right **Rev:** Sea Horse **Edge:** Reeded

Date	Mintage	VF20	XF40	MS60	MS63	MS65
1994	1,000	—	—	—	170	180

KM# 138 10 DOLLARS

7.78 g., 0.583 Gold 0.1458 oz. AGW Alloyed with .417 Silver, 25 mm. **Ruler:** Elizabeth II **Obv:** Crowned head right **Rev:** 1937 Coronation portrait **Edge:** Reeded

Date	Mintage	VF20	XF40	MS60	MS63	MS65
1996	5,000	PF65 235				

KM# 118 15 DOLLARS

15.97 g., 0.999 Gold 0.5129 oz. AGW, 28.4 mm. **Ruler:** Elizabeth II **Subject:** Tall Ships **Obv:** Head with tiara right **Rev:** Three-masted sailing ship **Edge:** Reeded

Date	Mintage	VF20	XF40	MS60	MS63	MS65
2000	1,500	PF65 850				

KM# 21 20 DOLLARS

7.99 g., 0.917 Gold 0.2355 oz. AGW **Ruler:** Elizabeth II **Obv:** Young bust right **Rev:** Cahow in flight left

Date	Mintage	VF20	XF40	MS60	MS63	MS65
1970	1,000	PF65 400				

KM# 137 20 DOLLARS

7.98 g., 0.999 Gold 0.2563 oz. AGW, 22 mm. **Ruler:** Elizabeth II **Obv:** Head with tiara right **Rev:** New Millennium dawning over a ship at sea **Edge:** Plain **Shape:** Scalloped

Date	Mintage	VF20	XF40	MS60	MS63	MS65
2000	2,000	PF65 425				

KM# 23 25 DOLLARS

Copper-Nickel, 48 mm. **Ruler:** Elizabeth II **Subject:** Royal Visit **Obv:** Young bust right **Rev:** Scepter divides royal monograms **Edge:** Reeded

Date	Mintage	VF20	XF40	MS60	MS63	MS65
1975 FM (M)	100	—	—	—	45.00	—
1975 FM (U)	1,193	—	—	—	60.00	—

KM# 23a 25 DOLLARS

48.70 g., 0.925 Silver 1.4483 oz. ASW, 48 mm. **Ruler:** Elizabeth II **Subject:** Royal Visit **Obv:** Young bust right **Rev:** Scepter divides royal monograms **Edge:** Reeded

Date	Mintage	VF20	XF40	MS60	MS63	MS65
1975 FM (P)	14,708	PF65 65.00				

KM# 25 25 DOLLARS

54.75 g., 0.925 Silver 1.6282 oz. ASW, 50 mm. **Ruler:** Elizabeth II **Subject:** Queen's Silver Jubilee **Obv:** Young bust right **Rev:** Sailing ship

Date	Mintage	VF20	XF40	MS60	MS63	MS65
1977 CHI	6,225	—	—	—	55.00	—
1977 CHI	5,613	PF65 65.00				
1977	Est. 2312	—	—	—	100	—
Note: Struck at the Royal Canadian Mint						
1977	Est. 1887	PF65 120				
Note: Struck at the Royal Canadian Mint						

KM# 53 25 DOLLARS

31.10 g., 0.999 Palladium 0.9989 oz. APW, 34 mm. **Ruler:**

Elizabeth II **Subject:** Sea Venture **Obv:** Crowned head right **Rev:** Ship **Edge:** Reeded

Date	Mintage	VF20	XF40	MS60	MS63	MS65
1987	15,800	PF65 850				

KM# 63 25 DOLLARS
31.10 g., 0.999 Palladium 0.9989 oz. APW, 34 mm. **Ruler:** Elizabeth II **Subject:** Shipwreck of San Antonio **Obv:** Crowned head right **Rev:** Capsizing ship **Edge:** Reeded

Date	Mintage	VF20	XF40	MS60	MS63	MS65
1988	2,000	PF65 890				

KM# 58 25 DOLLARS
7.81 g., 0.999 Gold 0.251 oz. AGW, 22 mm. **Ruler:** Elizabeth II **Subject:** Hogge Money **Obv:** Crowned head right **Rev:** Ship

Date	Mintage	VF20	XF40	MS60	MS63	MS65
1989	500	PF65 425				

KM# 75 25 DOLLARS
7.81 g., 0.999 Gold 0.251 oz. AGW, 22 mm. **Ruler:** Elizabeth II **Subject:** Hogge Money **Obv:** Crowned head right **Rev:** Wild pig

Date	Mintage	VF20	XF40	MS60	MS63	MS65
1990	500	PF65 425				

KM# 97 30 DOLLARS
15.55 g., 0.999 Gold 0.4995 oz. AGW **Ruler:** Elizabeth II **Subject:** Bermuda Triangle **Obv:** Crowned head right **Rev:** Map, compass, capsizing ship

Date	Mintage	VF20	XF40	MS60	MS63	MS65
1996	Est. 1500	PF65 800				

KM# 101 30 DOLLARS
15.55 g., 0.999 Gold 0.4995 oz. AGW, 27 mm. **Ruler:** Elizabeth II **Subject:** Wreck of the Sea Venture **Obv:** Crowned head right **Rev:** Shipwreck scene **Shape:** 3-sided

Date	Mintage	VF20	XF40	MS60	MS63	MS65
1997	1,500	PF65 800				

KM# 113 30 DOLLARS
15.55 g., 0.999 Gold 0.4994 oz. AGW **Ruler:** Elizabeth II **Obv:** Crowned head right **Rev:** Sailing ship Deliverance and map

Date	Mintage	VF20	XF40	MS60	MS63	MS65
1998	1,500	PF65 800				

KM# 26 50 DOLLARS
4.05 g., 0.900 Gold 0.1172 oz. AGW, 19 mm. **Ruler:** Elizabeth II **Subject:** Queen's Silver Jubilee **Obv:** Young bust right **Rev:** Bermuda fitted dinghy **Edge:** Reeded

Date	Mintage	VF20	XF40	MS60	MS63	MS65
1977	3,950	—	—	—	180	—
1977 CHI	4,070	PF65 190				
1977	Est. 520	—	—	—	285	—
Note: Struck at the Royal Canadian Mint						
1977	Est. 580	PF65 300				
Note: Struck at the Royal Canadian Mint						

KM# 59 50 DOLLARS
15.61 g., 0.999 Gold 0.5013 oz. AGW, 27 mm. **Ruler:** Elizabeth II **Subject:** Hogge Money **Obv:** Crowned head right **Rev:** Wild pig

Date	Mintage	VF20	XF40	MS60	MS63	MS65
1989	500	PF65 825				

KM# 76 50 DOLLARS
15.61 g., 0.999 Gold 0.5013 oz. AGW, 27 mm. **Ruler:** Elizabeth II **Subject:** Hogge Money **Obv:** Crowned head right **Rev:** Ship

Date	Mintage	VF20	XF40	MS60	MS63	MS65
1990	500	PF65 825				

KM# 93 60 DOLLARS
31.49 g., 0.999 Gold 1.0114 oz. AGW, 35 mm. **Ruler:** Elizabeth II **Subject:** Bermuda Triangle **Obv:** Crowned head right **Rev:** Map, compass and capsizing ship **Shape:** 3-sided

Date	Mintage	VF20	XF40	MS60	MS63	MS65
1996	1,500	PF65 1,650				

KM# 102 60 DOLLARS
31.49 g., 0.999 Gold 1.0114 oz. AGW, 35 mm. **Ruler:** Elizabeth II **Subject:** Wreck of the Sea Venture **Obv:** Crowned head right **Rev:** Shipwreck scene **Shape:** Triangular

Date	Mintage	VF20	XF40	MS60	MS63	MS65
1997	1,500	PF65 1,650				

KM# 114 60 DOLLARS
31.48 g., 0.999 Gold 1.0111 oz. AGW, 35 mm. **Ruler:** Elizabeth II **Obv:** Crowned head right **Rev:** Sailing ship Deliverance and map **Shape:** Triangular

Date	Mintage	VF20	XF40	MS60	MS63	MS65
1998	1,500	PF65 1,650				

KM# 24 100 DOLLARS
7.03 g., 0.900 Gold 0.2034 oz. AGW, 24 mm. **Ruler:** Elizabeth II **Subject:** Royal Visit **Obv:** Young bust right **Rev:** Sceptre divides royal monograms

Date	Mintage	VF20	XF40	MS60	MS63	MS65
1975 FM (M)	25	—	—	—	450	—
Trial pieces						
1975 FM (M)	18,852	—	—	—	325	—
1975 FM (M)	27,270	PF65 325				

KM# 27 100 DOLLARS
8.10 g., 0.900 Gold 0.2344 oz. AGW, 25 mm. **Ruler:** Elizabeth II **Subject:** Queen's Silver Jubilee **Obv:** Young bust right **Rev:** Sailing ship Deliverance **Edge:** Reeded **Shape:** 3-sided

Date	Mintage	VF20	XF40	MS60	MS63	MS65
1977	6,225	—	—	—	400	—
1977 CHI	5,613	PF65 425				
1977	Est. 2312	—	—	—	425	—
Note: Struck at the Royal Canadian Mint						
1977	Est. 1887	PF65 425				
Note: Struck at the Royal Canadian Mint						

KM# 60 100 DOLLARS
31.21 g., 0.999 Gold 1.0024 oz. AGW, 32.69 mm. **Ruler:** Elizabeth II **Subject:** Hogge Money **Obv:** Crowned head right **Rev:** Ship

Date	Mintage	VF20	XF40	MS60	MS63	MS65
1989	500	PF65 170				

KM# 77 100 DOLLARS
31.21 g., 0.999 Gold 1.0024 oz. AGW, 32.69 mm. **Ruler:** Elizabeth II **Subject:** Hogge Money **Obv:** Crowned head right **Rev:** Wild pig

Date	Mintage	VF20	XF40	MS60	MS63	MS65
1990	500	PF65 1,700				

KM# 80 100 DOLLARS
47.54 g., 0.917 Gold 1.4016 oz. AGW, 38.61 mm. **Ruler:** Elizabeth II **Series:** Olympics **Subject:** Crowned head right **Rev:** Olympic rings

Date	Mintage	VF20	XF40	MS60	MS63	MS65
1992	Est. 250	PF65 2,250				

KM# 134 100 DOLLARS
47.54 g., 0.917 Gold 1.4016 oz. AGW, 38.6 mm. **Ruler:** Elizabeth II **Subject:** Royal Visit **Obv:** Crowned head right **Rev:** Royal couple above map **Edge:** Reeded

Date	Mintage	VF20	XF40	MS60	MS63	MS65
1994	250	PF65 2,250				

KM# 98 180 DOLLARS
155.52 g., 0.999 Gold 4.995 oz. AGW, 65 mm. **Ruler:** Elizabeth II **Subject:** Bermuda Triangle **Obv:** Crowned head right **Rev:** Map, compass, capsizing ship

Date	Mintage	VF20	XF40	MS60	MS63	MS65
1996	99	PF65 7,500				

KM# 103 180 DOLLARS
155.52 g., 0.999 Gold 4.995 oz. AGW, 65 mm. **Ruler:** Elizabeth II **Subject:** Wreck of the Sea Venture **Obv:** Crowned head right **Rev:** Shipwreck scene

Date	Mintage	VF20	XF40	MS60	MS63	MS65
1997	—	PF65 7,500				

KM# 115 180 DOLLARS
155.52 g., 0.999 Gold 4.9951 oz. AGW, 65 mm. **Ruler:** Elizabeth II **Obv:** Crowned head right **Rev:** Sailing ship Deliverance and map **Shape:** Triangular

Date	Mintage	VF20	XF40	MS60	MS63	MS65
1998	—	PF65 7,500				

KM# 82 200 DOLLARS
28.50 g., 0.999 Gold 0.9154 oz. AGW, 31 mm. **Ruler:** Elizabeth II **Subject:** 200 Years - Bermudian Coinage **Obv:** Crowned head right **Rev:** Sailing ship

Date	Mintage	VF20	XF40	MS60	MS63	MS65
1993	200	PF65 1,550				

KM# 29 250 DOLLARS
15.98 g., 0.917 Gold 0.471 oz. AGW, 28.4 mm. **Ruler:** Elizabeth II **Subject:** Wedding of Prince Charles and Lady Diana **Obv:** Crowned head right **Rev:** Jugate heads of the royal couple right **Edge:** Reeded

Date	Mintage	VF20	XF40	MS60	MS63	MS65
1981	217	—	—	—	800	825
1981	790	PF65 850				

PIEDFORT

KM#	Date	Mintage	Identification	Mkt Val
P1	1981	690	250 Dollars. KM29.	1,800
P2	1988	500	Dollar. 0.925. Silver. KM56a.	200

MINT SETS

KM#	Date	Mintage	Identification	Issue Price	Mkt Val
MS1	1970 (5)	360,000	KM15-19	3.25	5.25
MSA2	1977 (3)	—	KM25-27	—	825
MS2	1977Chi (3)	—	KM25-27	175	675
MS3	1977Chi (2)	—	KM26-27	150	625
MS4	1984 (11)	3,350	KM32-42	24.95	50.00
MS5	1993 (5)	15,000	KM44b, 45-47, 56	—	12.50
MS7	1999 (5)	5,000	KM107-111	15.00	20.00

PROOF SETS

KM#	Date	Mintage	Identification	Issue Price	Mkt Val
PS1	1970 (6)	10,000	KM15-20	24.00	25.00
PS2	1970 (7)	1,000	KM15-21	216	485
PSA3	1977 (3)	—	KM25-27	—	900
PS3	1977Chi (3)	—	KM25-27	245	725
PS4	1977Chi (2)	—	KM26-27	210	650
PS5	1981 (3)	500	KM28a, 29, (P1), numbered set	1,500	2,500
PS6	1983 (7)	6,474	KM15-19, 30, 31	30.00	30.00
PS7	1984 (11)	1,750	KM32a-42a	250	145
PS8	1986 (7)	2,500	KM44-48, 50-51	50.00	50.00
PS10	1989 (4)	500	KM57-60	1,495	3,350
PS11	1990 (4)	500	KM74-77	—	3,350
PS12	1992 (3)	250	KM78-80	1,075	2,700
PS13	1992 (2)	500	KM71-72	75.00	80.00
PSA14	1995 (5)	2,000	KM#44c, 45a, 46a, 47a, 56a	—	85.00
PS14	1995 (5)	500	KM44d, 45b-47b, 56b	1,100	2,250
PS15	1996 (2)	1,000	KM96-97	—	1,200
PS16	1999 (5)	2,500	KM107-111	50.00	50.00

BHUTAN

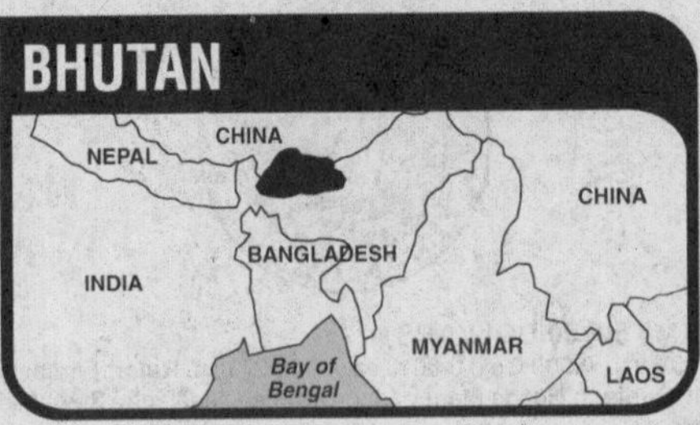

The Kingdom of Bhutan, a landlocked Himalayan country bordered by Tibet and India, has an area of 18,150 sq. mi. (38,394 sq. km.) and a population of 675,000. Capital: Thimphu. Virtually the entire population is engaged in agricultural and pastoral activities. Rice, wheat, barley, and yak butter are produced in sufficient quantity to make the country self-sufficient in food. The economy of Bhutan is primitive and many transactions are conducted on a barter basis.

Bhutan's early history is obscure, but is thought to have resembled that of rural medieval Europe. The country was conquered by Tibet in the 9th century, and a dual temporal and spiritual rule developed which operated until the mid-19th century, when the southern part of the country was occupied by the British and annexed to British India. Bhutan was established as a hereditary monarchy in 1907, and in 1910 agreed to British control of its external affairs. In 1949, India and Bhutan concluded a treaty whereby India assumed Britain's role in subsidizing Bhutan and guiding its foreign affairs. In 1971 Bhutan became a full member of the United Nations.

RULERS
Ugyen Wangchuk, 1907-1926
Jigme Wangchuk, 1926-1952
Jigme Dorji Wangchuk, 1952-1972
Jigme Singye Wangchuk, 1972-

CYCLICAL DATES

Earth-Dragon Iron-Tiger

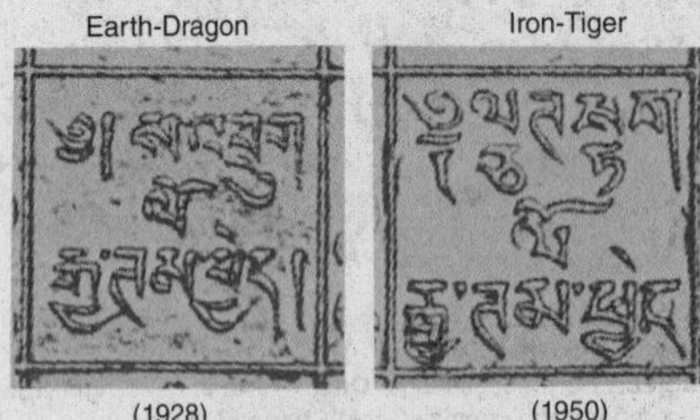

(1928) (1950)

OBVERSE LEGENDS

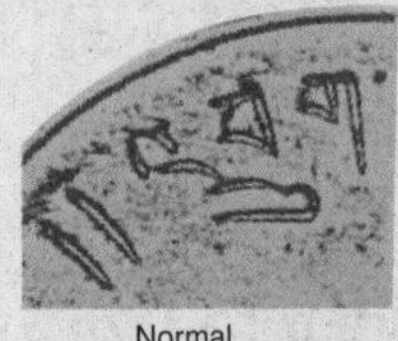
Normal

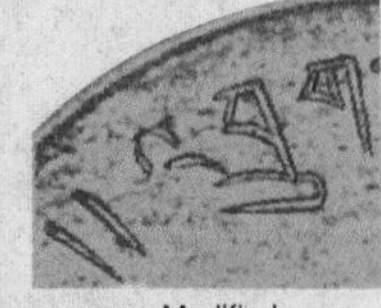
Modified

KINGDOM

HAMMERED COINAGE

Period III, 1835-1910AD

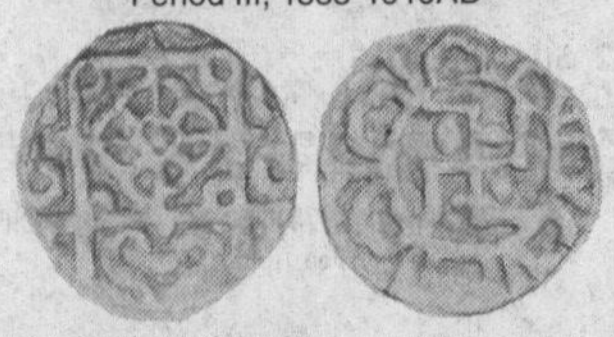

KM# 12 1/2 RUPEE (Deb)
Copper or Brass **Obv:** Double Dorje in a square **Rev:** Swastika counter-clockwise

Date	Mintage	G4	VG8	F12	VF20	XF40
ND(1885-1910)	—	—	—	8.00	15.00	30.00

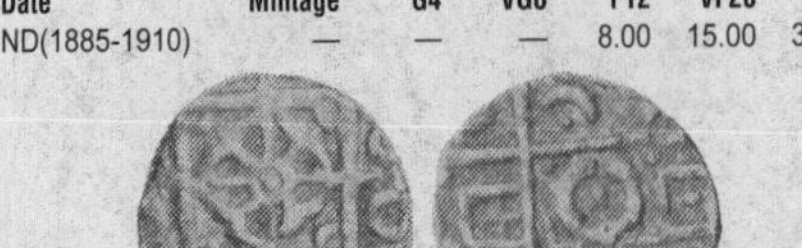

KM# 13 1/2 RUPEE (Deb)
Copper or Brass **Obv:** Double Dorje in a square **Rev:** Two fishes in center

Date	Mintage	G4	VG8	F12	VF20	XF40
ND(1885-1910)	—	—	—	8.00	20.00	25.00

KM# 14 1/2 RUPEE (Deb)
Copper or Brass **Obv:** Four dots above "ra" of syllable "ndra" **Rev:** Two fishes in center **Note:** Varieties exist.

Date	Mintage	G4	VG8	F12	VF20	XF40
ND(1885-1910)	—	—	—	5.00	16.00	22.00

KM# 15.1 1/2 RUPEE (Deb)
Copper or Brass **Obv:** Knot Syll. "ndra" (retro) to left side of the knot **Rev:** Conch shell

Date	Mintage	G4	VG8	F12	VF20	XF40
ND(1885-1910)	—	—	—	8.00	12.00	22.00

KM# 15.2 1/2 RUPEE (Deb)
Copper or Brass **Obv:** Knot Syll. "ndra" to right side of the knot **Rev:** Conch shell

Date	Mintage	G4	VG8	F12	VF20	XF40
ND(1885-1910)	—	—	—	8.00	12.00	22.00

KM# 15 1/2 RUPEE (Deb)
Copper or Brass **Obv:** Knot **Rev:** Conch shell

Date	Mintage	G4	VG8	F12	VF20	XF40
ND(1885-1910)	—	—	—	8.00	12.00	22.00

HAMMERED COINAGE

Period IV, 1910-1927AD

KM# A27 PICE
3.30 g., Bronze **Obv:** Mungo, head over bowl with jewelry **Rev:** Coin divided into nine sections, eight symbols, swastika clockwise with four dots at center **Edge:** Plain

Date	Mintage	F12	VF20	XF40	MS60	MS63
ND(1910-1926)	—	—	—	—	—	—

KM# 16 1/2 RUPEE (Deb)
Copper **Obv:** With five Buddh. symbols **Rev:** Square with knot, four Buddh. Symbols, varieties exist **Edge:** Plain

Date	Mintage	G4	VG8	F12	VF20	XF40
ND(1910-1926)	—	10.00	15.00	25.00	75.00	—

KM# 17 1/2 RUPEE (Deb)
Silver **Obv:** Syllable "ndra" retrograde, four Buddh. symbols **Rev:** Four squares with Buddh. symbols

Date	Mintage	G4	VG8	F12	VF20	XF40
ND(1910-1926)	—	10.00	15.00	25.00	75.00	—

KM# 17a 1/2 RUPEE (Deb)
Copper **Obv:** Obverse is similar to KM#17 **Rev:** Symbols on reverse are arranged differently **Note:** Varieties exist with and without syllable "ndra".

Date	Mintage	G4	VG8	F12	VF20	XF40
ND(1910-1926)	—	—	5.00	15.00	35.00	—

KM# 17a.1 1/2 RUPEE (Deb)

Copper **Obv:** Symbols "nd" and "ra" missing, four Buddh. Symbols **Rev:** Four squares with different Buddh. Symbols

Date	Mintage	G4	VG8	F12	VF20	XF40
ND(1910-1926)	—	—	15.00	25.00	45.00	—

KM# 17a.2 1/2 RUPEE (Deb)

Copper, 18.5 mm. **Obv:** Similar to KM#19 **Rev:** Similar to KM# 17

Date	Mintage	G4	VG8	F12	VF20	XF40
ND(1910-1926)	—	—	15.00	25.00	55.00	—

KM# 18 1/2 RUPEE (Deb)

Silver **Obv:** Syllable "ndra" and three Buddh. symbols **Rev:** Swastika in square counter-clockwise, with four Buddh. Symbols, three varieties exist

Date	Mintage	G4	VG8	F12	VF20	XF40
ND(1910-1926)	—	10.00	15.00	25.00	55.00	—

KM# 18a 1/2 RUPEE (Deb)

Copper **Obv:** Similar to KM# 18 **Rev:** Swastica clockwise, four squares with Buddh. Symbols **Note:** Obverse is similar to KM#18, but symbols on reverse are arranged differently.

Date	Mintage	G4	VG8	F12	VF20	XF40
ND(1910-1926)	—	—	5.00	15.00	35.00	—

KM# 18b 1/2 RUPEE (Deb)

Brass **Obv:** Syllable "ndra" retrograde, three Buddh. Symbols **Rev:** Similar to KM# 18 **Note:** Different obverse than KM#18, syllable "ndra" is retrograd

Date	Mintage	G4	VG8	F12	VF20	XF40
ND(1910-1926)	—	—	5.00	15.00	35.00	—

KM# 19 1/2 RUPEE (Deb)

Silver **Obv:** Three Buddh. Symbols and "sa" in four squares **Rev:** Four Buddh. Symbols in four squares **Note:** 30 different varieties are known, many involving placement of the "sa" characters.

Date	Mintage	G4	VG8	F12	VF20	XF40
ND(1910-1926)	—	10.00	15.00	25.00	55.00	—

KM# 19a 1/2 RUPEE (Deb)

Copper **Note:** Obverse is similar to KM#19, but symbols on reverse are arranged differently. 16 total varieties, including two struck in silver and a struck copper example worth about $50

Date	Mintage	G4	VG8	F12	VF20	XF40
ND(1910-1926)	—	6.00	12.00	15.00	20.00	—

KM# 19a.1 1/2 RUPEE (Deb)

Copper **Obv:** Square in center with large "sa" with "d'Bang" below **Rev:** Similar to KM# 19a

Date	Mintage	G4	VG8	F12	VF20	XF40
ND(1910-1926) Rare	—	—	—	—	—	—

KM# 20 1/2 RUPEE (Deb)

Silver **Obv:** Four Buddh. Symbols in squares **Rev:** Swastika counter-clockwise, four Buddh. symbols

Date	Mintage	G4	VG8	F12	VF20	XF40
ND(1910-1926)	—	—	—	—	—	—

KM# 20a 1/2 RUPEE (Deb)

Copper **Obv:** Three different swastika counter-clockwise with four different Buddh. Symbols **Rev:** Eight different reverses with four Buddh. Symbols in swastika counter-clockwise **Note:** Obverse is similar to KM#20, but symbols on reverse are arranged differently. Varieties exist

Date	Mintage	G4	VG8	F12	VF20	XF40
ND(1910-1926)	—	6.00	8.00	10.00	15.00	—

KM# 21 1/2 RUPEE (Deb)

Copper, 17 to 21 mm. **Obv:** Five different obverses with nine or more Buddh. symbols **Rev:** Buddh. Symbols, two varieties **Note:** Many varieties.

Date	Mintage	G4	VG8	F12	VF20	XF40
ND(1910-1926)	—	—	6.00	8.00	15.00	—

DECIMAL COINAGE

1966 - 100 Naya Paisa = 1 Rupee

KM# 23.1 PICE

7.00 g., Bronze, 26.5 mm. **Ruler:** Jigme Wangchuck **Obv:** Crowned bust, left, modified legend **Rev:** Nine sections: eight buddh, symbols, central square: EARTH-DRAGON-YEAR (1928)

Date	Mintage	F12	VF20	XF40	MS60	MS63
1928	—	—	—	—	—	—

Note: Actually struck in 1931.

KM# 23.2 PICE

4.90 g., Bronze, 25.1 mm. **Ruler:** Jigme Wangchuck **Obv:** Crowned bust, left **Rev:** Coin divided into nine sections, symbol on each section

Date	Mintage	F12	VF20	XF40	MS60	MS63
1928	10,000	20.00	45.00	80.00	120	200
Note: Actually struck in 1931.						
1928	—	PF63 250				
Note: Actually struck in 1931.						

KM# 27 PICE

2.90 g., Bronze, 21.28 mm. **Obv:** Nine sections: eight buddh, symbols central square: DRUK (Bhutan) **Rev:** Square in center, three sections with buddh, symbols, one with letter "sa" (earth) **Note:** Actually struck in 1951 and 1955. Later strikes of 1955 dates differ in detail because of recut dies.

Date	Mintage	F12	VF20	XF40	MS60	MS63
ND-1951	Est. 1260000	—	2.00	4.00	6.00	9.00

Note: No date, actually struck in 1951 and 1955. Later strikes of 1955 differ in detail because of recut dies (Fish with big eye).

KM# 29 25 NAYA PAISA

Copper-Nickel **Subject:** 40th Anniversary - Accession of Jigme Wangchuk **Obv:** Crowned bust, left **Rev:** Doubles-Dorje within circle

Date	Mintage	VF20	XF40	MS60	MS63	MS65
1966	10,000	—	1.00	1.75	2.50	5.00
1966	6,000	PF65 4.00				

KM# 30 50 NAYA PAISA

Copper-Nickel **Subject:** 40th Anniversary - Accession of Jigme Wangchuk **Obv:** Crowned bust, left, dates below **Rev:** Emblem withn circle, denomination below

Date	Mintage	VF20	XF40	MS60	MS63	MS65
1966	10,000	—	1.50	2.50	4.00	6.00
1966	6,000	PF65 7.00				

KM# 24 1/2 RUPEE

5.83 g., 0.917 Silver 0.1719 oz. ASW, 21.28 mm. **Ruler:** Jigme Wangchuck **Obv:** Crowned bust, left, first legend **Rev:** Nine sections: eight buddh, symbols, central square: EARTH-DRAGON-YEAR (1928) **Note:** Year written in Dzongkha characters. Weight varies: 5.83-5.85 grams.

Date	Mintage	F12	VF20	XF40	MS60	MS63
ND-1928	20,000	—	35.00	50.00	100	—
Note: Actually struck in 1929						
ND-1928	—	PF63 150				
Note: Actually struck in 1929						

KM# 25 1/2 RUPEE

5.83 g., 0.917 Silver 0.1719 oz. ASW **Ruler:** Jigme Wangchuck **Obv:** Crowned bust, left, modified legend **Rev:** Same die as KM# 24 **Note:** Year written in Dzongkha characters.

Date	Mintage	F12	VF20	XF40	MS60	MS63
ND-1928	30,000	—	35.00	50.00	100	—

Note: Actually struck in 1930. Legend modified.

KM# 26 1/2 RUPEE

5.72 g., Nickel, 24 mm. **Ruler:** Jigme Wangchuck **Obv:** Crowned bust, left, first legend **Rev:** Same die as KM# 24 **Note:** Year written in Dzongkha characters. Weight varies: 5.78-5.90 grams.

Date	Mintage	F12	VF20	XF40	MS60	MS63
ND-1928	20,000	—	45.00	60.00	120	—

Note: Actually struck in 1951

KM# 28.1 1/2 RUPEE

5.80 g., Nickel, 24 mm. **Ruler:** Jigme Wangchuck **Obv:** Crowned bust, left, first legend **Rev:** Central square: IRON-TIGER-Year (1950) **Note:** Year written in Dzongkha characters.

Date	Mintage	F12	VF20	XF40	MS60	MS63
1950	202,000	—	45.00	60.00	120	—

Note: Actually struck in 1955.

KM# 28.2 1/2 RUPEE

5.00 g., Nickel, 24 mm. **Ruler:** Jigme Wangchuck **Obv:** Crowned bust, left, first legend **Rev:** Central square: IRON-TIGER-Year (1950) **Note:** Year written in Dzongkha characters.

Date	Mintage	F12	VF20	XF40	MS60	MS63
1950	1,000,000	—	5.00	10.00	25.00	—

Note: Actually struck in 1967-68.

KM# 31 RUPEE

Copper-Nickel **Subject:** 40th Anniversary - Accession of Jigme Wangchuk **Obv:** Crowned bust, left, dates below **Rev:** Emblem divides date, denomination below

Date	Mintage	VF20	XF40	MS60	MS63	MS65
1966	10,000	—	2.00	3.50	5.00	9.00
1966	6,000	PF65 10.00				

KM# 32 3 RUPEE
Copper-Nickel, 38 mm. **Subject:** 40th Anniversary - Accession of Jigme Wangchuk **Obv:** Crowned bust, left, dates below **Rev:** Emblem divides date, denomination below

Date	Mintage	VF20	XF40	MS60	MS63	MS65
1966	5,826	—	—	7.50	12.50	22.50
1966	6,000	PF65 20.00				

KM# 32a 3 RUPEE
28.28 g., 0.925 Silver 0.841 oz. ASW, 38 mm. **Subject:** 40th Anniversary - Accession of Jigme Wangchuk

Date	Mintage	VF20	XF40	MS60	MS63	MS65
1966	—	—	—	—	—	375
1966	2,000	PF65 40.00				
1966 Matte proof	—	PF65 375				

KM# 33 SERTUM
7.98 g., 0.917 Gold 0.2353 oz. AGW **Subject:** 40th Anniversary - Accession of Jigme Wangchuk **Obv:** Crowned bust left, dates below **Rev:** Emblem divides date, denomination below

Date	Mintage	VF20	XF40	MS60	MS63	MS65
1966	2,300	—	—	—	—	425
1966	598	PF65 450				

KM# 33a SERTUM
9.84 g., 0.950 Platinum 0.3005 oz. APW **Subject:** 40th Anniversary - Accession of Jigme Wangchuk

Date	Mintage	VF20	XF40	MS60	MS63	MS65
1966	72	PF65 650				

KM# 36 SERTUM
7.98 g., 0.917 Gold 0.2353 oz. AGW **Obv:** Bust, right, date below

Date	Mintage	VF20	XF40	MS60	MS63	MS65
1970	3,111	—	—	—	425	450

KM# 34 2 SERTUMS
15.98 g., 0.917 Gold 0.4711 oz. AGW **Subject:** 40th Anniversary - Accession of Jigme Wangchuk **Obv:** Crowned bust, left, dates below **Rev:** Emblem divides date, denomination below

Date	Mintage	VF20	XF40	MS60	MS63	MS65
1966	800	—	—	—	825	850
1966	598	PF65 875				

KM# 34a 2 SERTUMS
19.67 g., 0.950 Platinum 0.6008 oz. APW **Subject:** 40th Anniversary - Accession of Jigme Wangchuk

Date	Mintage	VF20	XF40	MS60	MS63	MS65
1966	72	PF65 1,150				

KM# 35 5 SERTUMS
39.94 g., 0.917 Gold 1.1775 oz. AGW **Subject:** 40th Anniversary - Accession of Jigme Wangchuk **Obv:** Crowned bust, left, dates below **Rev:** Emblem divides date, denomination below

Date	Mintage	VF20	XF40	MS60	MS63	MS65
1966	800	—	—	—	2,100	2,250
1966	598	PF65 2,350				

KM# 35a 5 SERTUMS
49.18 g., 0.950 Platinum 1.5021 oz. APW **Subject:** 40th Anniversary - Accession of Jigme Wangchuk **Obv:** Crowned bust, left, dates below **Rev:** Emblem divides date, denomination below

Date	Mintage	VF20	XF40	MS60	MS63	MS65
1966	72	PF65 2,850				

REFORM COINAGE

1974 - 100 Chetrums (Paisa) = 1 Ngultrum (Rupee); 100 Ngultrums = 1 Sertum

KM# 37 5 CHETRUMS
1.48 g., Aluminum, 22 mm. **Obv:** Crowned bust left, date at left **Rev:** Emblem above denomination **Edge:** Plain **Shape:** 4-sided

Date	Mintage	VF20	XF40	MS60	MS63	MS65
1974	—	1.00	1.50	3.00	4.00	6.00
1974	1,000	PF63 8.00	PF65 10.00			
1975	—	1.00	1.50	3.00	4.00	6.00
1975	—	PF63 8.00	PF65 10.00			

KM# 45 5 CHETRUMS
1.90 g., Bronze, 17.15 mm. **Obv:** Symbols within circle, date below **Rev:** Symbols within circle, denomination below

Date	Mintage	VF20	XF40	MS60	MS63	MS65
1979	—	0.65	1.00	2.00	3.00	5.00
1979	—	PF63 6.00	PF65 8.00			

KM# 38 10 CHETRUMS
2.27 g., Aluminum, 26 mm. **Obv:** Crowned bust left, date at left **Rev:** Denomination below design **Shape:** Scalloped

Date	Mintage	VF20	XF40	MS60	MS63	MS65
1974	—	1.00	1.50	3.00	4.00	6.00
1974	1,000	PF63 8.00	PF65 10.00			

KM# 43 10 CHETRUMS
2.30 g., Aluminum, 26 mm. **Series:** F.A.O. and International Women's Year **Obv:** Emblem above denomination **Rev:** Half figure left, grain sprig on left, date below **Shape:** Scalloped

Date	Mintage	VF20	XF40	MS60	MS63	MS65
1975	4,000,000	0.65	1.00	2.50	3.50	5.00
1975	—	PF63 12.00	PF65 15.00			

KM# 46 10 CHHERTUM
3.60 g., Bronze, 20.35 mm. **Obv:** Shell and design within circle, date below **Rev:** Coin divided into nine sections, within circle, symbol in each section, denomination below

Date	Mintage	VF20	XF40	MS60	MS63	MS65
1979	—	0.50	0.75	2.00	3.00	5.00
1979	—	PF63 7.00	PF65 9.00			

KM# 39 20 CHETRUMS
Aluminum-Bronze, 22 mm. **Series:** F.A.O. **Obv:** Emblem above denomination **Rev:** Rice cultivation **Edge:** Reeded

Date	Mintage	VF20	XF40	MS60	MS63	MS65
1974	1,194,000	0.50	0.75	1.75	2.50	4.00
1974 Prooflike	—	—	—	—	4.00	—
Note: In mint sets only						
1974	1,000	PF63 5.00	PF65 7.00			

KM# 40.1 25 CHETRUMS
Copper-Nickel **Obv:** Crowned bust, left, date at left **Rev:** Fish above denomination, type I

Date	Mintage	VF20	XF40	MS60	MS63	MS65
1974	—	2.50	3.50	7.00	10.00	12.00

KM# 40.2 25 CHETRUMS
Copper-Nickel **Obv:** Crowned bust, left, date at left **Rev:** Fish above denomination, type II **Note:** Bottom of bust closer to rim; upper character at left revised.

Date	Mintage	VF20	XF40	MS60	MS63	MS65
1974	—	0.10	0.15	0.35	0.75	1.25
1974	—	PF65 3.00				
1975	—	0.10	0.15	0.35	0.75	1.25
1975	—	PF65 3.00				

KM# 47 25 CHHERTUM
4.60 g., Copper-Nickel, 21.95 mm. **Obv:** Fish within circle, date below **Rev:** Emblem within circle, denomination below

Date	Mintage	VF20	XF40	MS60	MS63	MS65
1979	—	1.50	2.00	4.00	6.00	8.00
1979	—	PF65 10.00				

KM# 47a 25 CHHERTUM
4.45 g., Aluminum-Bronze Plated Steel, 22 mm. **Obv:** Fish within circle, date below **Rev:** Emblem within circle, denomination below

Date	Mintage	VF20	XF40	MS60	MS63	MS65
1979	—	—	—	—	4.00	6.00

KM# 48 50 CHHERTUM
6.90 g., Copper-Nickel, 25.85 mm. **Obv:** Emblem within circle, date below **Rev:** Coin divided into nine sections within circle, symbol in each section, denomination below

Date	Mintage	VF20	XF40	MS60	MS63	MS65
1979	—	1.50	2.00	5.00	7.00	10.00
1979	—	PF65 12.00				

KM# 41 NGULTRUM
Copper-Nickel, 28 mm. **Obv:** Crowned bust, left, date at left **Rev:** Emblem above denomination **Edge:** Reeded security edge

Date	Mintage	VF20	XF40	MS60	MS63	MS65
1974	—	2.00	3.00	7.00	10.00	12.00
1974	1,000	PF65 20.00				
1975	—	4.00	6.00	15.00	20.00	25.00
1975	—	PF65 30.00				

KM# 49 NGULTRUM
8.20 g., Copper-Nickel, 27.95 mm. **Obv:** Emblem within circle, date below **Rev:** Coin divided into nine sections within circle, each has symbol, denomination below

Date	Mintage	VF20	XF40	MS60	MS63	MS65
1979	—	1.00	1.50	3.00	4.00	6.00
1979	—	PF65 7.50				

KM# 49a NGULTRUM
7.90 g., Copper-Nickel Clad Steel, 27.8 mm. **Obv:** Emblem within circle, date below **Rev:** Coin divided into nine sections within circle, each has symbol, denomination below **Note:** Magnetic

Date	Mintage	VF20	XF40	MS60	MS63	MS65
1979	—	—	—	—	6.00	9.00

KM# 50 3 NGULTRUMS
Copper-Nickel, 38.5 mm. **Obv:** Crowned head, left, date below **Rev:** National emblem within circle, denomination at right **Edge:** Reeded

Date	Mintage	VF20	XF40	MS60	MS63	MS65
1979	—	3.00	4.50	9.00	12.00	15.00
1979	—	PF65 18.00				

KM# 50a 3 NGULTRUMS
28.28 g., 0.925 Silver 0.841 oz. ASW **Obv:** Crowned head, left, date below **Rev:** National emblem within circle, denomination at right

Date	Mintage	VF20	XF40	MS60	MS63	MS65
1979	Est. 10000	PF65 30.00				

KM# 42 15 NGULTRUMS
22.30 g., 0.500 Silver 0.3585 oz. ASW, 39 mm. **Series:** F.A.O. **Obv:** Emblem above denomination **Rev:** Rice cultivation

Date	Mintage	VF20	XF40	MS60	MS63	MS65
1974	30,000	—	—	—	10.00	—
1974 Prooflike, sets only	24,000	—	—	—	—	12.00
1974	1,000	PF63 45.00	PF65 75.00			

KM# 44 30 NGULTRUMS
25.00 g., 0.500 Silver 0.4019 oz. ASW **Series:** F.A.O. and International Women's Year **Obv:** Emblem above denomination **Rev:** Half figure looking left, grain sprig on left, date at bottom

Date	Mintage	VF20	XF40	MS60	MS63	MS65
1975	14,000	—	—	—	12.00	14.00
1975	—	PF63 15.00	PF65 20.00			

KM# 54 50 NGULTRUMS
28.28 g., 0.925 Silver 0.841 oz. ASW **Series:** World Food Day **Obv:** Yak right, within circle, denomination below

Date	Mintage	VF20	XF40	MS60	MS63	MS65
1981	15,000	—	—	—	30.00	32.00
1981	5,000	PF63 35.00	PF65 40.00			

KM# 83 50 NGULTRUMS
Copper-Nickel **Subject:** 50 Years - United Nations **Obv:** National emblem within circle divides dates **Rev:** Bust, 3/4 right, symbol and dates at right, denomination below

Date	Mintage	VF20	XF40	MS60	MS63	MS65
1995	—	—	—	—	5.00	7.00

KM# 104 50 NGULTRUMS
16.00 g., 0.925 Silver 0.4758 oz. ASW, 28.3 mm. **Subject:** British Queen Mother **Obv:** National emblem within circle divides dates **Rev:** Home at St. Paul's Walden Bury, date and denomination below **Edge:** Reeded

Date	Mintage	VF20	XF40	MS60	MS63	MS65
1997	—	PF65 22.50				

KM# 58 100 NGULTRUMS
23.33 g., 0.925 Silver 0.6938 oz. ASW **Series:** Decade for Women **Obv:** National emblem within circle, date above, denomination below **Rev:** Women working

Date	Mintage	VF20	XF40	MS60	MS63	MS65
1984	1,050	PF63 35.00	PF65 50.00			

KM# 84 100 NGULTRUMS
Copper-Nickel **Subject:** St. Paul's Walden Bury Palace **Obv:** National emblem within circle divides dates **Rev:** Palace within circle, date and denomination below

Date	Mintage	VF20	XF40	MS60	MS63	MS65
1995	Est. 35000	—	—	—	6.00	9.00

KM# 103 100 NGULTRUMS
20.00 g., 0.925 Silver 0.5948 oz. ASW, 34 mm. **Subject:** Olympic Games 2000 **Obv:** National arms within circle divides dates **Rev:** Archer at left sighting in on target at right, denomination below **Edge:** Reeded

Date	Mintage	VF20	XF40	MS60	MS63	MS65
1998	—	PF63 14.00	PF65 18.00			

KM# 159 100 NGULTRUMS
28.28 g., Copper-Nickel, 38.61 mm. **Ruler:** Jigme Singye Wangchuck **Subject:** 25th Anniversary of Reign **Obv:** State seal **Rev:** Bust facing

Date	Mintage	VF20	XF40	MS60	MS63	MS65
1999	2,000	PF63 25.00	PF65 35.00			

KM# 57 200 NGULTRUMS
28.28 g., 0.925 Silver 0.841 oz. ASW **Series:** International Year of Disabled Persons **Obv:** Elephant carrying animals, tree and hills, date and denomination below **Rev:** Typist

Date	Mintage	VF20	XF40	MS60	MS63	MS65
1981	10,000	—	—	—	35.00	37.50
1981	10,000	PF65 40.00				

KM# 55 200 NGULTRUMS
28.28 g., 0.925 Silver 0.841 oz. ASW **Subject:** 75th Anniversary of Monarchy **Obv:** Crowned bust, facing, date below **Rev:** National emblem within circle **Note:** Issued in 1983.

Date	Mintage	VF20	XF40	MS60	MS63	MS65
1982	10,000	—	—	—	30.00	32.00
1982	5,000	PF65 45.00				

KM# 86 200 NGULTRUMS
10.00 g., 0.500 Silver 0.1608 oz. ASW **Series:** Olympics **Obv:** National emblem within circle divides dates **Rev:** Two basketball players, denomination below

Date	Mintage	VF20	XF40	MS60	MS63	MS65
1996 Proof	Est. 10000	—	—	—	15.00	17.50

KM# 87 200 NGULTRUMS
10.00 g., 0.500 Silver 0.1608 oz. ASW **Series:** Olympics **Obv:** National emblem divides dates **Rev:** Skiing scene, denomination at right

Date	Mintage	VF20	XF40	MS60	MS63	MS65
1996 Proof	—	—	—	—	12.00	15.00

KM# 61 300 NGULTRUMS
28.28 g., 0.925 Silver 0.841 oz. ASW **Subject:** World Championship Soccer, denomination below **Obv:** Crowned head, left, date below

Date	Mintage	VF20	XF40	MS60	MS63	MS65
1990	20,000	PF65 32.50				

KM# 65 300 NGULTRUMS
31.47 g., 0.925 Silver 0.9359 oz. ASW **Series:** Endangered wildlife **Rev:** Snow leopard, denomination below

Date	Mintage	VF20	XF40	MS60	MS63	MS65
1991	Est. 25000	PF65 32.50				

KM# 63 300 NGULTRUMS
28.28 g., 0.925 Silver 0.841 oz. ASW **Obv:** National emblem divides dates **Rev:** Solar system scene, denomination below

Date	Mintage	VF20	XF40	MS60	MS63	MS65
1992	—	PF65 32.50				

KM# 72 300 NGULTRUMS
31.47 g., 0.925 Silver 0.9359 oz. ASW **Subject:** World Cup Soccer **Obv:** National emblem within circle divides dates **Rev:** Two soccer players, radiant sunset behind, denomination below

Date	Mintage	VF20	XF40	MS60	MS63	MS65
1992	20,000	PF65 32.50				

KM# 74 300 NGULTRUMS
31.47 g., 0.925 Silver 0.9359 oz. ASW **Series:** Lillehammer 1994 - 17th Winter Olympic Games **Obv:** National emblem within circle divides dates **Rev:** Speed skating, denomination below

Date	Mintage	VF20	XF40	MS60	MS63	MS65
1992	40,000	PF65 28.00				

KM# 75 300 NGULTRUMS
31.47 g., 0.925 Silver 0.9359 oz. ASW **Series:** Endangered Wildlife **Obv:** National emblem within circle divides dates **Rev:** Golden langur monkey, denomination below

Date	Mintage	VF20	XF40	MS60	MS63	MS65
1992	—	PF65 35.00				

KM# 76 300 NGULTRUMS
31.47 g., 0.925 Silver 0.9359 oz. ASW **Series:** Barcelona 1992 - 25th Summer Olympics **Obv:** National emblem within circle divides dates **Rev:** Archery scene, denomination below

Date	Mintage	VF20	XF40	MS60	MS63	MS65
1992	20,000	PF65 28.00				

KM# 77 300 NGULTRUMS
31.47 g., 0.925 Silver 0.9359 oz. ASW **Series:** 1992 Olympic Games **Obv:** National emblem within circle divides dates **Rev:** Boxer, denomination below

Date	Mintage	VF20	XF40	MS60	MS63	MS65
1992	20,000	PF65 30.00				

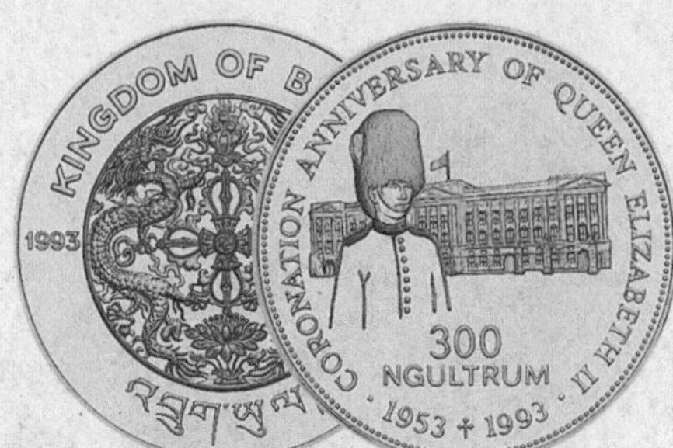

KM# 66 300 NGULTRUMS
31.47 g., 0.925 Silver 0.9359 oz. ASW **Subject:** 40th Anniversary - Coronation of Queen Elizabeth II **Obv:** National emblem within circle divides dates **Rev:** Royal Guard, palace in background, denomination and dates below

Date	Mintage	VF20	XF40	MS60	MS63	MS65
1993	Est. 10000	PF65 32.00				

KM# 67 300 NGULTRUMS
31.47 g., 0.925 Silver 0.9359 oz. ASW **Series:** Endangered Wildlife **Obv:** National emblem within circle divides dates **Rev:** Takin, denomination below

Date	Mintage	VF20	XF40	MS60	MS63	MS65
1993	Est. 10000	PF65 35.00				

KM# 68 300 NGULTRUMS
31.47 g., 0.925 Silver 0.9359 oz. ASW **Subject:** Protect Our World **Obv:** National emblem within circle divides dates **Rev:** Elephant, rhino, tree, and tiger, denomination below

Date	Mintage	VF20	XF40	MS60	MS63	MS65
1993	Est. 10000	PF65 45.00				

KM# 78 300 NGULTRUMS
31.32 g., 0.925 Silver 0.9314 oz. ASW **Subject:** World Championship Soccer **Obv:** National emblem within circle divides dates **Rev:** Ball in flight, denomination below

Date	Mintage	VF20	XF40	MS60	MS63	MS65
1993	30,000	PF65 37.00				

KM# 79 300 NGULTRUMS
31.32 g., 0.925 Silver 0.9314 oz. ASW **Series:** Olympic Games **Obv:** National emblem within inner circle **Rev:** Soccer, denomination below

Date	Mintage	VF20	XF40	MS60	MS63	MS65
1993	30,000	PF65 30.00				

KM# 89 300 NGULTRUMS
31.32 g., 0.925 Silver 0.9314 oz. ASW **Subject:** Maurice Ravel **Obv:** National emblem **Rev:** Portrait, musician, dancer, and dates, denomination below

Date	Mintage	VF20	XF40	MS60	MS63	MS65
1993	—	PF65 40.00				

KM# 118 300 NGULTRUMS
31.47 g., 0.925 Silver 0.9359 oz. ASW, 38.61 mm. **Ruler:** Jigme Singye Wangchuck **Rev:** François Marie Aroute Voltaire

Date	Mintage	VF20	XF40	MS60	MS63	MS65
1993	—	PF65 55.00				

KM# 69 300 NGULTRUMS
31.32 g., 0.925 Silver 0.9314 oz. ASW **Subject:** Protect Our World **Obv:** National emblem within inner circle **Rev:** Rain forest, denomination below

Date	Mintage	VF20	XF40	MS60	MS63	MS65
1994	Est. 10000	PF65 42.00				

KM# 73 300 NGULTRUMS
31.32 g., 0.925 Silver 0.9314 oz. ASW **Series:** 1996 Olympic Games **Obv:** National emblem within inner circle **Rev:** Basketball, denomination below

Date	Mintage	VF20	XF40	MS60	MS63	MS65
1994	30,000	PF65 30.00				

KM# 81 300 NGULTRUMS
31.45 g., 0.925 Silver 0.9353 oz. ASW **Subject:** Joao Cabral **Obv:** National emblem **Rev:** Two explorers, denomination below

Date	Mintage	VF20	XF40	MS60	MS63	MS65
1994	Est. 10000	PF65 40.00				

KM# 88 300 NGULTRUMS
31.45 g., 0.925 Silver 0.9353 oz. ASW **Series:** Endangered Wildlife **Obv:** National emblem within inner circle **Rev:** Kalij pheasant, denomination below

Date	Mintage	VF20	XF40	MS60	MS63	MS65
1994	—	PF65 37.00				

KM# 80 300 NGULTRUMS
28.28 g., 0.925 Silver 0.841 oz. ASW **Subject:** 50th Anniversary - United Nations **Obv:** National emblem within circle divides dates **Rev:** Bust, 3/4 right, symbol and dates at right, denomination below

Date	Mintage	VF20	XF40	MS60	MS63	MS65
1995	Est. 100000	PF65 25.00				

KM# 106 300 NGULTRUMS
31.77 g., 0.925 Silver 0.9448 oz. ASW, 38.55 mm. **Ruler:** Jigme Singye Wangchuck **Subject:** Queen Mother's parents home St. Paul's Walden Bury **Obv:** National arms **Rev. Legend:** QUEEN ELIZABETH THE QUEEN MOTHER **Edge:** Reeded

Date	Mintage	VF20	XF40	MS60	MS63	MS65
1995	25,000	PF65 37.00				

KM# 90 300 NGULTRUMS
31.50 g., 0.925 Silver 0.9368 oz. ASW **Subject:** Chinese Lunar

Year **Obv:** National emblem within circle divides dates **Rev:** Seated monkey within circle, denomination below

Date	Mintage	VF20	XF40	MS60	MS63	MS65
1996	—	PF65 40.00				

KM# 91 300 NGULTRUMS
31.50 g., 0.925 Silver 0.9368 oz. ASW **Subject:** Chinese Lunar Year **Obv:** National emblem **Rev:** Stylized rooster within circle, denomination below

Date	Mintage	VF20	XF40	MS60	MS63	MS65
1996	—	PF65 40.00				

KM# 92 300 NGULTRUMS
31.50 g., 0.925 Silver 0.9368 oz. ASW **Subject:** Chinese Lunar Year **Obv:** National emblem **Rev:** Stylized dog within circle, denomination below

Date	Mintage	VF20	XF40	MS60	MS63	MS65
1996	—	PF65 40.00				

KM# 93 300 NGULTRUMS
31.50 g., 0.925 Silver 0.9368 oz. ASW **Subject:** Chinese Lunar Year **Obv:** National emblem **Rev:** Stylized pig within circle, denomination below

Date	Mintage	VF20	XF40	MS60	MS63	MS65
1996	—	PF65 40.00				

KM# 94 300 NGULTRUMS
31.50 g., 0.925 Silver 0.9368 oz. ASW **Subject:** Chinese Lunar Year **Obv:** National emblem **Rev:** Stylized rat within circle, denomination below

Date	Mintage	VF20	XF40	MS60	MS63	MS65
1996	—	PF65 40.00				

KM# 95 300 NGULTRUMS
31.50 g., 0.925 Silver 0.9368 oz. ASW **Subject:** Chinese Lunar Year **Obv:** National emblem **Rev:** Stylized ox within circle, denomination below

Date	Mintage	VF20	XF40	MS60	MS63	MS65
1996	—	PF65 40.00				

KM# 96 300 NGULTRUMS
31.50 g., 0.925 Silver 0.9368 oz. ASW **Subject:** Chinese Lunar Year **Obv:** National emblem within circle divides dates **Rev:** Stylized tiger within circle, denomination below

Date	Mintage	VF20	XF40	MS60	MS63	MS65
1996	—	PF65 40.00				

KM# 97 300 NGULTRUMS
31.50 g., 0.925 Silver 0.9368 oz. ASW **Subject:** Chinese Lunar Year **Obv:** National emblem **Rev:** Stylized rabbit within circle, denomination below

Date	Mintage	VF20	XF40	MS60	MS63	MS65
1996	—	PF65 40.00				

KM# 98 300 NGULTRUMS
31.50 g., 0.925 Silver 0.9368 oz. ASW **Subject:** Chinese Lunar Year **Obv:** National emblem **Rev:** Stylized dragon within circle, denomination below

Date	Mintage	VF20	XF40	MS60	MS63	MS65
1996	—	PF65 40.00				

KM# 99 300 NGULTRUMS
31.50 g., 0.925 Silver 0.9368 oz. ASW **Subject:** Chinese Lunar Year **Obv:** National emblem **Rev:** Stylized snake within circle, denomination below

Date	Mintage	VF20	XF40	MS60	MS63	MS65
1996	—	PF65 40.00				

KM# 100 300 NGULTRUMS
31.50 g., 0.925 Silver 0.9368 oz. ASW **Subject:** Chinese Lunar Year **Obv:** National emblem **Rev:** Stylized horse within circle, denomination below

Date	Mintage	VF20	XF40	MS60	MS63	MS65
1996	—	PF65 40.00				

KM# 101 300 NGULTRUMS
31.50 g., 0.925 Silver 0.9368 oz. ASW **Subject:** Chinese Lunar Year **Obv:** National emblem **Rev:** Stylized ram within circle, denomination below

Date	Mintage	VF20	XF40	MS60	MS63	MS65
1996	—	PF65 40.00				

KM# 108 300 NGULTRUMS
1.24 g., 0.999 Gold 0.040 oz. AGW, 13.92 mm. **Ruler:** Jigme Singye Wangchuck **Obv:** National arms **Rev:** Statue of Bodhisattvas seated in lotus blossom **Edge:** Reeded

Date	Mintage	VF20	XF40	MS60	MS63	MS65
1996	50,000	PF65 75.00				

KM# 102 300 NGULTRUMS
1.24 g., 0.999 Gold 0.040 oz. AGW **Obv:** National emblem within circle divides dates **Rev:** Mask, facing, denomination at lower right

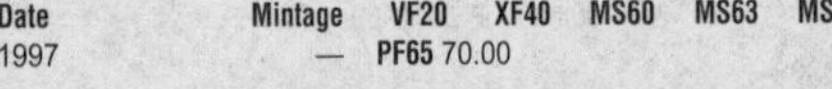

Date	Mintage	VF20	XF40	MS60	MS63	MS65
1997	—	PF65 70.00				

KM# 160 500 NGULTRUM
31.47 g., 0.999 Silver 1.0108 oz. ASW, 38.61 mm. **Ruler:** Jigme Singye Wangchuck **Subject:** 25th Anniversary of Reign **Obv:** State arms **Rev:** Bust faicng

Date	Mintage	VF20	XF40	MS60	MS63	MS65
1999	1,000	PF65 90.00				

KM# 120 1000 NGULTRUM
3.11 g., 0.999 Gold 0.0999 oz. AGW **Ruler:** Jigme Singye Wangchuck **Subject:** Year of the Rat

Date	Mintage	VF20	XF40	MS60	MS63	MS65
1996	Est. 25000	PF65 225				

KM# 121 1000 NGULTRUM
3.11 g., 0.999 Gold 0.0999 oz. AGW **Ruler:** Jigme Singye Wangchuck **Subject:** Year of the Ox

Date	Mintage	VF20	XF40	MS60	MS63	MS65
1996	Est. 25000	PF65 225				

KM# 122 1000 NGULTRUM
3.11 g., 0.999 Gold 0.0999 oz. AGW **Ruler:** Jigme Singye Wangchuck **Subject:** Year of the Tiger

Date	Mintage	VF20	XF40	MS60	MS63	MS65
1996	Est. 25000	PF65 225				

KM# 123 1000 NGULTRUM
3.11 g., 0.999 Gold 0.0999 oz. AGW **Ruler:** Jigme Singye Wangchuck **Subject:** Year of the Rabbit

Date	Mintage	VF20	XF40	MS60	MS63	MS65
1996	Est. 25000	PF65 225				

KM# 124 1000 NGULTRUM
3.11 g., 0.999 Gold 0.0999 oz. AGW **Ruler:** Jigme Singye Wangchuck **Subject:** Year of the Dragon

Date	Mintage	VF20	XF40	MS60	MS63	MS65
1996	Est. 25000	PF65 225				

KM# 125 1000 NGULTRUM
3.11 g., 0.999 Gold 0.0999 oz. AGW **Ruler:** Jigme Singye Wangchuck **Subject:** Year of the Snake

Date	Mintage	VF20	XF40	MS60	MS63	MS65
1996	—	PF65 225				

KM# 126 1000 NGULTRUM
3.11 g., 0.999 Gold 0.0999 oz. AGW **Ruler:** Jigme Singye Wangchuck **Subject:** Year of the Horse

Date	Mintage	VF20	XF40	MS60	MS63	MS65
1996	—	PF65 225				

KM# 127 1000 NGULTRUM
3.11 g., 0.999 Gold 0.0999 oz. AGW **Ruler:** Jigme Singye Wangchuck **Subject:** Year of the Goat

Date	Mintage	VF20	XF40	MS60	MS63	MS65
1996	Est. 25000	PF65 225				

KM# 128 1000 NGULTRUM
3.11 g., 0.999 Gold 0.0999 oz. AGW **Ruler:** Jigme Singye Wangchuck **Subject:** Year of the Monkey

Date	Mintage	VF20	XF40	MS60	MS63	MS65
1996	Est. 25000	PF65 225				

KM# 129 1000 NGULTRUM
3.11 g., 0.999 Gold 0.0999 oz. AGW **Ruler:** Jigme Singye Wangchuck **Subject:** Year of the rooster

Date	Mintage	VF20	XF40	MS60	MS63	MS65
1996	Est. 25000	PF65 225				

KM# 130 1000 NGULTRUM
3.11 g., 0.999 Gold 0.0999 oz. AGW **Ruler:** Jigme Singye Wangchuck **Subject:** Year of the dog

Date	Mintage	VF20	XF40	MS60	MS63	MS65
1996	Est. 25000	PF65 225				

KM# 131 1000 NGULTRUM
3.11 g., 0.999 Gold 0.0999 oz. AGW **Ruler:** Jigme Singye Wangchuck **Subject:** Year of the Pig

Date	Mintage	VF20	XF40	MS60	MS63	MS65
1996	Est. 25000	PF65 225				

KM# 162 1000 NGULTRUM
12.00 g., 0.999 Gold 0.3854 oz. AGW, 23.5 mm. **Ruler:** Jigme Singye Wangchuck **Subject:** Year of the Dragon

Date	Mintage	VF20	XF40	MS60	MS63	MS65
2000 Profo	—	PF65 800				

KM# 156 2000 NGULTRUMS
0.999 Silver **Ruler:** Jigme Singye Wangchuck **Rev:** Snow leopard

Date	Mintage	VF20	XF40	MS60	MS63	MS65
1996	—	PF65 1,500				

KM# 158 2000 NGULTRUMS
6.22 g., 0.999 Gold 0.1998 oz. AGW **Ruler:** Jigme Singye Wangchuck **Rev:** Budda on lotus flower

Date	Mintage	VF20	XF40	MS60	MS63	MS65
1996	—	PF65 400				

KM# 132 2500 NGULTRUM
7.78 g., 0.999 Gold 0.2499 oz. AGW **Ruler:** Jigme Singye Wangchuck **Subject:** Year of the Rat

Date	Mintage	VF20	XF40	MS60	MS63	MS65
1996	2,000	PF65 450				

KM# 133 2500 NGULTRUM
7.78 g., 0.999 Gold 0.2499 oz. AGW **Ruler:** Jigme Singye Wangchuck **Subject:** Year of the Ox

Date	Mintage	VF20	XF40	MS60	MS63	MS65
1996	2,000	PF65 450				

KM# 134 2500 NGULTRUM
7.78 g., 0.999 Gold 0.2499 oz. AGW **Ruler:** Jigme Singye Wangchuck **Subject:** Year of the tiger

Date	Mintage	VF20	XF40	MS60	MS63	MS65
1996	2,000	PF65 450				

KM# 135 2500 NGULTRUM
7.78 g., 0.999 Gold 0.2499 oz. AGW **Ruler:** Jigme Singye Wangchuck **Subject:** Year of the Rabbit

Date	Mintage	VF20	XF40	MS60	MS63	MS65
1996	2,000	PF65 450				

KM# 136 2500 NGULTRUM
7.78 g., 0.999 Gold 0.2499 oz. AGW **Ruler:** Jigme Singye Wangchuck **Subject:** Year of the Dragon

Date	Mintage	VF20	XF40	MS60	MS63	MS65
1996	2,000	PF65 450				

KM# 137 2500 NGULTRUM
7.78 g., 0.999 Gold 0.2499 oz. AGW **Ruler:** Jigme Singye Wangchuck **Subject:** Year of the Snake

Date	Mintage	VF20	XF40	MS60	MS63	MS65
1996	2,000	PF65 450				

KM# 138 2500 NGULTRUM
7.78 g., 0.999 Gold 0.2499 oz. AGW **Ruler:** Jigme Singye Wangchuck **Subject:** Year of the Horse

Date	Mintage	VF20	XF40	MS60	MS63	MS65
1996	2,000	PF65 450				

KM# 139 2500 NGULTRUM
7.78 g., 0.999 Gold 0.2499 oz. AGW **Ruler:** Jigme Singye Wangchuck **Subject:** Year of the Goat

Date	Mintage	VF20	XF40	MS60	MS63	MS65
1996	2,000	PF65 450				

KM# 140 2500 NGULTRUM
7.78 g., 0.999 Gold 0.2499 oz. AGW **Ruler:** Jigme Singye Wangchuck **Subject:** Year of the Monkey

Date	Mintage	VF20	XF40	MS60	MS63	MS65
1996	2,000	PF65 450				

KM# 141 2500 NGULTRUM
7.78 g., 0.999 Gold 0.2499 oz. AGW **Ruler:** Jigme Singye Wangchuck **Subject:** Year of the Rooster

Date	Mintage	VF20	XF40	MS60	MS63	MS65
1996	2,000	PF65 450				

KM# 142 2500 NGULTRUM
7.78 g., 0.999 Gold 0.2499 oz. AGW **Ruler:** Jigme Singye Wangchuck **Subject:** Year of the Dog

Date	Mintage	VF20	XF40	MS60	MS63	MS65
1996	Est. 2000	PF65 450				

KM# 143 2500 NGULTRUM
7.78 g., 0.999 Gold 0.2499 oz. AGW **Ruler:** Jigme Singye Wangchuck **Subject:** Year of the Pig

Date	Mintage	VF20	XF40	MS60	MS63	MS65
1996	2,000	PF65 450				

KM# 149 2500 NGULTRUM
15.55 g., 0.999 Gold 0.4994 oz. AGW **Ruler:** Jigme Singye Wangchuck **Subject:** Year of the Snake

Date	Mintage	VF20	XF40	MS60	MS63	MS65
1996	1,000	PF65 1,000				

KM# 163 3000 NGULTRUM
31.11 g., 0.999 Gold 0.999 oz. AGW, 38.61 mm. **Ruler:** Jigme Singye Wangchuck **Subject:** Year of the Dragon

Date	Mintage	VF20	XF40	MS60	MS63	MS65
2000	Est. 18888	PF65 1,800				

KM# 144 5000 NGULTRUM
15.55 g., 0.999 Gold 0.4994 oz. AGW **Ruler:** Jigme Singye Wangchuck **Subject:** Year of the rat

Date	Mintage	VF20	XF40	MS60	MS63	MS65
1996	1,000	PF65 900				

KM# 145 5000 NGULTRUM
15.55 g., 0.999 Gold 0.4994 oz. AGW **Ruler:** Jigme Singye Wangchuck **Subject:** Year of the Ox

Date	Mintage	VF20	XF40	MS60	MS63	MS65
1996	1,000	PF65 900				

KM# 146 5000 NGULTRUM
15.55 g., 0.999 Gold 0.4994 oz. AGW **Ruler:** Jigme Singye Wangchuck **Subject:** Year of the Tiger

Date	Mintage	VF20	XF40	MS60	MS63	MS65
1996	1,000	PF65 900				

KM# 147 5000 NGULTRUM
15.55 g., 0.999 Gold 0.4994 oz. AGW **Ruler:** Jigme Singye Wangchuck **Subject:** Year of the Rabbit

Date	Mintage	VF20	XF40	MS60	MS63	MS65
1996	1,000	PF65 900				

KM# 148 5000 NGULTRUM
15.55 g., 0.999 Gold 0.4994 oz. AGW **Ruler:** Jigme Singye Wangchuck **Subject:** Year of the Dragon

Date	Mintage	VF20	XF40	MS60	MS63	MS65
1996	1,000	PF65 900				

KM# 150 5000 NGULTRUM
15.55 g., 0.999 Gold 0.4994 oz. AGW **Ruler:** Jigme Singye Wangchuck **Subject:** Year of the Horse

Date	Mintage	VF20	XF40	MS60	MS63	MS65
1996	1,000	PF65 900				

KM# 151 5000 NGULTRUM
15.55 g., 0.999 Gold 0.4994 oz. AGW **Ruler:** Jigme Singye Wangchuck **Subject:** Year of the Goat

Date	Mintage	VF20	XF40	MS60	MS63	MS65
1996	1,000	PF65 900				

KM# 152 5000 NGULTRUM
15.55 g., 0.999 Gold 0.4994 oz. AGW **Ruler:** Jigme Singye Wangchuck **Subject:** Year of the Monkey

Date	Mintage	VF20	XF40	MS60	MS63	MS65
1996	1,000	PF65 900				

KM# 153 5000 NGULTRUM
15.55 g., 0.999 Gold 0.4994 oz. AGW **Ruler:** Jigme Singye Wangchuck **Subject:** Year of the Rooster

Date	Mintage	VF20	XF40	MS60	MS63	MS65
1996	1,000	PF65 900				

KM# 154 5000 NGULTRUM
15.55 g., 0.999 Gold 0.4994 oz. AGW **Ruler:** Jigme Singye Wangchuck **Subject:** Year of the Dog

Date	Mintage	VF20	XF40	MS60	MS63	MS65
1996	1,000	PF65 900				

KM# 155 5000 NGULTRUM
15.55 g., 0.999 Gold 0.4994 oz. AGW **Ruler:** Jigme Singye Wangchuck **Subject:** Year of the Pig

Date	Mintage	VF20	XF40	MS60	MS63	MS65
1996	1,000	PF65 900				

KM# 117 10000 NGULTRUMS
31.11 g., 0.999 Gold 0.999 oz. AGW **Ruler:** Jigme Singye Wangchuck **Subject:** Endangered wildlife **Obv:** National emblem **Rev:** Snow leopard **Edge:** Reeded

Date	Mintage	VF20	XF40	MS60	MS63	MS65
1996	500	PF65 1,800				

KM# 164 20000 NGULTRUM
155.52 g., 0.999 Gold 4.9951 oz. AGW, 65 mm. **Ruler:** Jigme Singye Wangchuck **Subject:** Year of the Dragon

Date	Mintage	VF20	XF40	MS60	MS63	MS65
2000	Est. 88	PF65 9,000				

KM# 157 50000 NGULTRUM
155.50 g., 0.999 Gold 4.9944 oz. AGW **Ruler:** Jigme Singye Wangchuck **Rev:** Snow leopard

Date	Mintage	VF20	XF40	MS60	MS63	MS65
1996	99	PF65 9,000				

KM# 51 SERTUM
7.98 g., 0.917 Gold 0.2353 oz. AGW **Obv:** Crowned bust, left, dates below **Rev:** Two dragons around inner circle

Date	Mintage	VF20	XF40	MS60	MS63	MS65
1979	1,000	—	—	—	400	—
1979	1,000	PF65 420				

KM# 51a SERTUM
9.85 g., 0.950 Platinum 0.3009 oz. APW **Obv:** Crowned bust left, dates below **Rev:** Two dragons around inner circle

Date	Mintage	VF20	XF40	MS60	MS63	MS65
1979	—	PF65 600				

KM# 56 SERTUM
7.99 g., 0.917 Gold 0.2356 oz. AGW **Subject:** 75th Anniversary of Monarchy

Date	Mintage	VF20	XF40	MS60	MS63	MS65
1982(1983)	1,000	—	—	—	400	—
1982(1983)	1,000	PF65 420				

KM# 85 SERTUM
1.24 g., 0.9999 Gold 0.040 oz. AGW **Subject:** 40th Anniversary - Queen Elizabeth II's Coronation **Obv:** National emblem within circle divides dates **Rev:** Royal Guard, palace in background, denomination and dates below

Date	Mintage	VF20	XF40	MS60	MS63	MS65
1995	Est. 250000	—	—	—	70.00	80.00

KM# 107 SERTUM
1.22 g., 0.999 Gold 0.0392 oz. AGW, 13.9 mm. **Ruler:** Jigme Singye Wangchuck **Obv:** National arms **Obv. Legend:** KINGDOM OF BHUTAN **Rev:** Solar System **Edge:** Reeded

Date	Mintage	VF20	XF40	MS60	MS63	MS65
1995	—	PF65 70.00				

KM# 52 2 SERTUMS
15.98 g., 0.917 Gold 0.4711 oz. AGW **Obv:** Crowned bust, left, dates below **Rev:** Two dragons around inner circle

Date	Mintage	VF20	XF40	MS60	MS63	MS65
1979	1,000	—	—	—	800	—
1979	1,000	PF65 825				

KM# 52a 2 SERTUMS
19.70 g., 0.950 Platinum 0.6017 oz. APW **Obv:** Crowned bust, left, dates below **Rev:** Two dragons around inner circle

Date	Mintage	VF20	XF40	MS60	MS63	MS65
1979	—	PF65 1,000				

KM# 60 2 SERTUMS
15.98 g., 0.917 Gold 0.4711 oz. AGW **Series:** International Year of Disabled Persons **Obv:** Dragon, date below, denomination at right **Rev:** Typist

Date	Mintage	VF20	XF40	MS60	MS63	MS65
1981	—	—	—	—	800	—
1981	—	PF65 925				

KM# 53 5 SERTUMS
39.94 g., 0.917 Gold 1.1775 oz. AGW **Obv:** Crowned bust, left, dates below **Rev:** Two dragons around inner circle

Date	Mintage	VF20	XF40	MS60	MS63	MS65
1979	1,000	—	—	—	1,850	—
1979	1,000	PF65 2,000				

KM# 53a 5 SERTUMS
49.20 g., 0.950 Platinum 1.5027 oz. APW **Obv:** Crowned bust, left, dates below **Rev:** Two dragons around inner circle

Date	Mintage	VF20	XF40	MS60	MS63	MS65
1979	—	PF65 2,750				

KM# 64 5 SERTRUMS
7.78 g., 0.5833 Gold 0.1458 oz. AGW **Series:** Endangered Wildlife **Obv:** National emblem within circle divides dates **Rev:** Black-necked crane, denomination below

Date	Mintage	VF20	XF40	MS60	MS63	MS65
1992	2,000	PF65 250				

KM# 70 5 SERTRUMS
7.78 g., 0.5833 Gold 0.1458 oz. AGW **Series:** 1992 Olympics **Obv:** National emblem within circle divides dates **Rev:** Archer, denomination below

Date	Mintage	VF20	XF40	MS60	MS63	MS65
1993	Est. 3000	PF65 250				

KM# 71 5 SERTRUMS
7.78 g., 0.5833 Gold 0.1458 oz. AGW **Subject:** World Cup '94 Soccer **Obv:** National emblem within circle divides dates **Rev:** Soccer players, denomination below

Date	Mintage	VF20	XF40	MS60	MS63	MS65
1993	Est. 2000	PF65 270				

KM# 82 5 SERTRUMS
7.78 g., 0.5833 Gold 0.1458 oz. AGW **Series:** Olympics **Subject:** Tae kwon do **Obv:** National emblem within circle divides dates **Rev:** Karate practitioner, denomination below

Date	Mintage	VF20	XF40	MS60	MS63	MS65
1994	Est. 3000	PF65 250				

KM# 119 5 SERTRUMS
7.78 g., 0.583 Gold 0.1458 oz. AGW, 25 mm. **Ruler:** Jigme Singye Wangchuck **Subject:** Queen Mother, 95th Birthday **Rev:** Buckingham Palace

Date	Mintage	VF20	XF40	MS60	MS63	MS65
1995	5,000	PF65 375				

KM# 161 10 SERTUM
31.11 g., 0.999 Gold 0.999 oz. AGW, 35 mm. **Ruler:** Jigme Singye Wangchuck **Subject:** 25th Anniversary of Reign **Obv:** State arms **Rev:** Bust facing

Date	Mintage	VF20	XF40	MS60	MS63	MS65
1999	500	PF65 1,650				

PIEDFORT

KM#	Date	Mintage	Identification	Mkt Val
P1	1981	—	2 Sertums. Gold. KM60.	1,350
P2	1981	Est. 1100	200 Ngultrums. Silver. KM57.	300

MINT SETS

KM#	Date	Mintage	Identification	Issue Price	Mkt Val
MS1	1966 (3)	300	KM33-35	175	3,350
MS2	1974 (2)	—	KM39, 42	4.00	17.50
MS3	1974 (4)	—	KM37-38, 40-41	6.00	5.25
MS4	1979 (3)	1,000	KM51-53	1,575	3,350

PROOF SETS

KM#	Date	Mintage	Identification	Issue Price	Mkt Val
PS1	1966 (4)	6,000	KM29-32	11.50	275
PS2	1966 (3)	598	KM33-35	300	3,525
PS3	1966 (3)	72	KM33a-35a	685	4,950
PS4	1974 (6)	1,000	KM37-42	18.00	125
PS5	1975 (5)	—	KM37, 40.2, 41, 43-44	—	150
PS6	1979 (5)	20,000	KM45-49	30.00	50.00
PS7	1979 (3)	1,000	KM51-53	2,100	3,450
PS8	1979 (3)	—	KM51a-53a	2,400	4,950

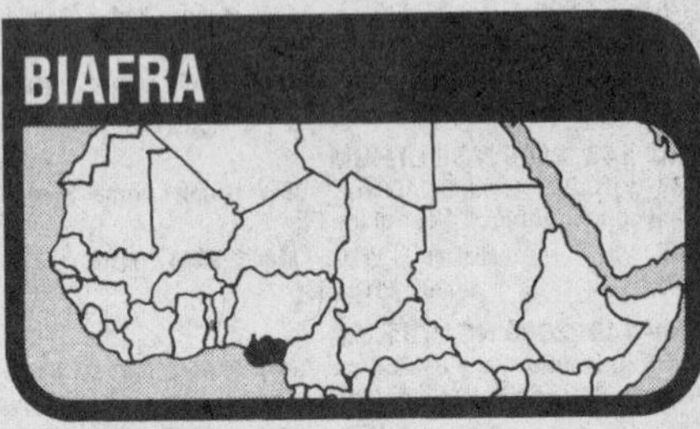

On May 30, 1967, the Eastern Region of the Republic of Nigeria, an area occupied principally by the proud and resourceful Ibo tribe, seceded from Nigeria and proclaimed itself the independent Republic of Biafra with Odumegwu Ojukwu as Chief of State. Civil war erupted and raged for 31 months. Casualties, including civilian, were about two million, the majority succumbing to malnutrition and disease. Biafra surrendered to the federal government on January 15, 1970.

MONETARY SYSTEM
12 Pence = 1 Shilling
20 Shillings = 1 Pound

INDEPENDENT REPUBLIC OF BIAFRA

STANDARD COINAGE

KM# 1 3 PENCE
Aluminum

Date	Mintage	VF20	XF40	MS60	MS63	MS65
1969	—	—	15.00	22.50	35.00	50.00

KM# 12 6 PENCE
Aluminum **Obv:** Denomination, date above **Rev:** Radiant sun rising behind tree, legend below horseshoe design

Date	Mintage	VF20	XF40	MS60	MS63	MS65
1969 5-10 pieces known	—	—	—	1,000	2,000	—

KM# 2 SHILLING
Aluminum, 23.5 mm. **Obv:** Eagle divides denomination and date **Rev:** Radiant sun rising behind tree, legend below horseshoe design

Date	Mintage	VF20	XF40	MS60	MS63	MS65
1969	—	—	12.00	25.00	40.00	70.00

KM# 3 SHILLING
Aluminum, 23.5 mm. **Obv:** Eagle divides date and denomination **Rev:** Radiant sun rising behind tree, legend below horseshoe design

Date	Mintage	VF20	XF40	MS60	MS63	MS65
1969	—	—	—	175	250	—

KM# 4 2-1/2 SHILLING
Aluminum **Obv:** Date and denomination below large cat **Rev:** Rising radiant sun behind tree, legend below horseshoe design

Date	Mintage	VF20	XF40	MS60	MS63	MS65
1969	—	—	15.00	30.00	45.00	75.00

KM# 5 CROWN
28.00 g., Silver **Subject:** Independence and Liberty **Obv:** Head right within circle **Rev:** Tree within circle, denomination below **Edge:** Plain

Date	Mintage	VF20	XF40	MS60	MS63	MS65
1969 Rare	—	—	—	—	—	—

Note: Stephen Album Rare Coins, Auction 18, 1-14, AU50 realized $13,000

KM# 6 POUND
25.60 g., 0.750 Silver 0.6173 oz. ASW **Obv:** National arms, date below **Rev:** Defiant eagle with scroll, wreathed shield at back, denomination below

Date	Mintage	VF20	XF40	MS60	MS63	MS65
1969	—	—	—	100	125	175

KM# 7 POUND
3.99 g., 0.917 Gold 0.1178 oz. AGW **Subject:** 2nd Anniversary of Independence **Obv:** National arms **Rev:** Defiant eagle with scroll, wreathed shield at back, denomination below

Date	Mintage	VF20	XF40	MS60	MS63	MS65
1969	3,000	**PF63** 187	**PF65** 195			

KM# 8 2 POUNDS
7.99 g., 0.917 Gold 0.2355 oz. AGW **Subject:** 2nd Anniversary of Independence **Obv:** National arms **Rev:** Defiant eagle with scroll, wreathed shield at back, denomination below

Date	Mintage	VF20	XF40	MS60	MS63	MS65
1969	3,000	**PF63** 365	**PF65** 380			

KM# 9 5 POUNDS
15.98 g., 0.917 Gold 0.471 oz. AGW **Subject:** 2nd Anniversary of Independence **Obv:** National arms **Rev:** Defiant eagle with scroll, wreathed shield at back, denomination below

Date	Mintage	VF20	XF40	MS60	MS63	MS65
1969	3,000	**PF63** 710	**PF65** 740			

KM# 10 10 POUNDS
39.94 g., 0.917 Gold 1.1775 oz. AGW **Subject:** 2nd Anniversary of Independence **Obv:** National arms **Rev:** Defiant eagle with scroll, wreathed shield at back, denomination below

Date	Mintage	VF20	XF40	MS60	MS63	MS65
1969	3,000	**PF63** 1,750	**PF65** 1,825			

KM# 11 25 POUNDS
79.88 g., 0.917 Gold 2.3551 oz. AGW **Subject:** 2nd Anniversary of Independence **Obv:** National arms **Rev:** Defiant eagle with scroll, wreathed shield at back, denomination below

Date	Mintage	VF20	XF40	MS60	MS63	MS65
1969	3,000	**PF63** 3,350	**PF65** 3,500			

PATTERNS

KM#	Date	Mintage	Identification	Mkt Val
Pn1	1968	—	Shilling. Aluminum. Plain. Similar to KM#3, without rope below eagle and textured palm trunk.	1,500

PROOF SETS

KM#	Date	Mintage	Identification	Issue Price	Mkt Val
PS1	1969 (5)	3,000	KM7-11	464	8,000

BOHEMIA & MORAVIA

Bohemia, a western province in the Czech Republic, was combined with the majority of Moravia in central Czechoslovakia (excluding parts of north and south Moravia which were joined with Silesia in 1938) to form the German protectorate in March, 1939, after the German invasion. Toward the end of war in 1945 the protectorate was dissolved and Bohemia and Moravia once again became part of Czechoslovakia.

MONETARY SYSTEM
100 Haleru = 1 Koruna

GERMAN PROTECTORATE

STANDARD COINAGE

KM# 1 10 HALERU
1.88 g., Zinc, 17 mm. **Obv:** Czech lion crowned left **Rev:** Charles bridge in Prague, denomination below **Edge:** Plain

Date	Mintage	F12	VF20	XF40	MS60	MS63
1940	82,114,000	0.35	0.75	1.50	10.00	13.50
1941	Inc. above	0.25	0.50	1.25	9.00	12.00
1942	Inc. above	0.25	0.50	1.25	9.00	12.00
1943	Inc. above	0.35	0.75	1.50	10.00	13.50
1944	Inc. above	0.75	1.50	3.00	14.00	17.50

KM# 2 20 HALERU
2.63 g., Zinc, 20 mm. **Obv:** Czech lion crowned left **Rev:** Wheat ears with sickle, denomination on left **Edge:** Plain

Date	Mintage	F12	VF20	XF40	MS60	MS63
1940	106,526,000	0.25	0.50	1.25	9.00	12.00
1941	Inc. above	0.25	0.50	1.25	9.00	12.00
1942	Inc. above	0.25	0.50	1.25	9.00	12.00
1943	Inc. above	0.50	0.75	1.50	10.00	13.50
1944	Inc. above	0.50	1.00	2.00	12.00	16.50

KM# 3 50 HALERU
3.70 g., Zinc, 22 mm. **Obv:** Czech lion crowned **Rev:** Value within linden branches, wheat ears below **Edge:** Milled

Date	Mintage	F12	VF20	XF40	MS60	MS63
1940	53,270,000	0.35	0.75	1.50	10.00	13.50
1941	Inc. above	0.35	0.75	1.50	10.00	13.50
1942	Inc. above	0.35	0.75	1.50	10.00	13.50
1943	Inc. above	0.75	1.50	3.00	15.00	20.00
1944	Inc. above	0.75	1.50	3.00	15.00	20.00

KM# 4 KORUNA
4.50 g., Zinc, 23 mm. **Obv:** Czech lion crowned left **Rev:** Linden branches divide denomination and date **Edge:** Milled

Date	Mintage	F12	VF20	XF40	MS60	MS63
1941	102,817,000	0.50	0.75	1.75	12.50	16.50
1942	Inc. above	0.50	0.75	1.75	12.50	16.50
1943	Inc. above	0.50	0.75	1.75	12.50	16.50
1944	Inc. above	0.50	0.75	1.75	12.50	16.50

PATTERNS

Including off metal strikes

KM#	Date	Mintage	Identification	Mkt Val
Pn1	1940	—	20 Haleru. Zinc. KM#2.	—
Pn2	1940	—	20 Haleru. Aluminum. KM#2.	—
Pn3	1940	—	50 Haleru. Aluminum. KM#3.	—
Pn4	1940	—	Koruna. Aluminum. KM#4.	—

BOLIVIA

The Republic of Bolivia, a landlocked country in west central South America, has an area of 424,165 sq. mi. (1,098,580 sq. km.) and a population of *8.33 million. Its capitals are: La Paz (administrative) and Sucre (constitutional). Principal exports are tin, zinc, antimony, tungsten, petroleum, natural gas, cotton and coffee.

Much of present day Bolivia was first dominated by the Tiahuanaco Culture ca.400 BC. It had in turn been incorporated into the Inca Empire by 1440AD prior to the arrival of the Spanish, in 1535, who reduced the Indian population to virtual slavery. When Joseph Napoleon was placed upon the throne of occupied Spain in 1809, a fervor of revolutionary activity quickened throughout Alto Peru - culminating in the 1809 Proclamation of Liberty. Sixteen bloody years of struggle ensued before the republic, named for the famed liberator Simon Bolivar, was established on August 6, 1825. Since then Bolivia has survived more than 16 constitutions, 78 Presidents, 3 military juntas and over 160 revolutions.

MINT MARKS
A - Paris
(a) - Paris, privy marks only
CHI - Valcambia
H - Heaton KN - Kings' Norton

REPUBLIC

REFORM COINAGE

1870 - 1951

KM# 173.1 5 CENTAVOS
Copper-Nickel, 20.5 mm. **Obv:** Arms without shield **Rev:** Caduceus above sprays divides denomination **Note:** Coins dated 1893, 1918 and 1919 medal rotation were struck at the Heaton Mint.

Date	Mintage	VF20	XF40	MS60	MS63	MS65
1909	4,000,000	1.00	6.00	12.00	20.00	—
1918	530,000	6.00	15.00	40.00	75.00	—
1919	4,370,000	5.00	10.00	20.00	45.00	—

KM# 173.3 5 CENTAVOS
Copper-Nickel, 20.5 mm. **Obv:** State arms within circle, stars below **Rev:** Cornucopia and torch flank date

Date	Mintage	VF20	XF40	MS60	MS63	MS65
1902	2,000,000	1.00	6.00	15.00	35.00	—
1907 (a)	2,000,000	1.00	6.00	15.00	35.00	—
1908	3,000,000	2.00	8.00	20.00	35.00	—
1909	—	3.00	10.00	30.00	60.00	—

KM# 178 5 CENTAVOS
Copper-Nickel, 18 mm. **Obv:** State emblem within circle, stars below **Rev:** Caduceus divides denomination, sprays below, date at bottom

Date	Mintage	VF20	XF40	MS60	MS63	MS65
1935	5,000,000	1.00	2.00	5.00	10.00	15.00

KM# 174.1 10 CENTAVOS
Copper-Nickel, 25.5 mm. **Obv:** State arms within circle, stars below **Obv. Legend:** REPUBLICA DE BOLIVIA **Rev:** Without privy marks **Note:** Coins dated 1893, 1918 and 1919 medal rotation were struck at the Heaton Mint.

Date	Mintage	VF20	XF40	MS60	MS63	MS65
1918	1,335,000	3.00	8.00	20.00	45.00	—
1919	6,165,000	2.00	6.00	15.00	35.00	—

KM# 174.3 10 CENTAVOS
Copper-Nickel, 25.5 mm. **Obv:** State emblem within circle, stars below **Rev:** Caduceus divides denomination, sprays below, date at bottom

Date	Mintage	VF20	XF40	MS60	MS63	MS65
1901	—	20.00	30.00	60.00	100	—
1902	8,500,000	2.00	5.00	12.00	30.00	—
1907/2	4,000,000	6.00	10.00	25.00	50.00	—
1907	Inc. above	2.00	5.00	12.00	30.00	—
1908	6,000,000	2.00	5.00	12.00	30.00	—
1909	8,000,000	2.00	5.00	12.00	30.00	—

KM# 179.1 10 CENTAVOS
Copper-Nickel **Obv:** State emblem within circle, stars below **Rev:** Caduceus divides denomination, sprays below, date at bottom

Date	Mintage	VF20	XF40	MS60	MS63	MS65
1935	10,000,000	0.50	1.00	2.50	6.00	12.00
1936	10,000,000	0.50	1.00	2.50	6.00	12.00

KM# 179.2 10 CENTAVOS
4.51 g., Copper-Nickel, 22.58 mm. **Obv:** State emblem within circle, stars below **Rev:** Caduceus divides denomination, sprays below, date at bottom

Date	Mintage	VF20	XF40	MS60	MS63	MS65
1939	—	0.50	1.00	2.50	6.00	12.00

KM# 179a 10 CENTAVOS
1.75 g., Zinc, 17.9 mm. **Obv:** State emblem within circle, stars below **Rev:** Caduceus divides denomination, sprays below, date at bottom

Date	Mintage	VF20	XF40	MS60	MS63	MS65
1942 (p)	10,000,000	0.50	1.00	3.00	7.00	—

KM# 180 10 CENTAVOS
4.50 g., Copper-Nickel, 22.5 mm. **Obv:** State emblem within circle, stars below **Rev:** Hand holding torch, date at bottom **Edge:** Plain

Date	Mintage	VF20	XF40	MS60	MS63	MS65
1937	20,000,000	0.50	1.00	2.50	5.00	10.00

KM# 159.2 20 CENTAVOS
4.60 g., 0.900 Silver 0.1331 oz. ASW, 22.5 mm. **Obv:** Crossed flags and weapons behind condor-topped oval arms, stars below **Obv. Legend:** REPUBLIC BOLIVIANA **Rev:** Denomination within wreath, date below **Note:** Reduced size dates and lettering, bar below CENTS. The small bar usually found below "S" in "9DS" is missing in the 1886-1888 and 1902 dates. Mint mark in monogram.

Date	Mintage	VG8	F12	VF20	XF40	MS60
1901 PTS MM	40,000	3.00	5.00	8.00	20.00	45.00
1901 PTS MM/.WM	—	3.00	5.00	8.00	25.00	50.00
1902 PTS MM	—	5.00	10.00	16.00	32.00	75.00
1903 PTS MM	10,000	7.00	16.00	22.00	42.00	110
1904 PTS MM	—	5.00	10.00	18.00	32.00	110
1907 PTS MM	—	20.00	50.00	100	175	325

KM# 176 20 CENTAVOS
4.00 g., 0.833 Silver 0.1071 oz. ASW, 22.5 mm. **Obv:** National arms, stars below **Rev:** Denomination within wreath, date below

Date	Mintage	F12	VF20	XF40	MS60	MS63
1909 H	1,500,000	—	4.00	8.00	22.50	45.00
1909 H	—	PF63 550				

KM# 183 20 CENTAVOS
3.25 g., Zinc, 21.7 mm. **Obv:** State emblem within circle, stars below **Rev:** Caduceus divides denomination, sprays below, date at bottom **Note:** Medal rotation strike.

Date	Mintage	VF20	XF40	MS60	MS63	MS65
1942 (p)	10,000,000	1.00	2.00	6.00	12.00	20.00

KM# 175.1 50 CENTAVOS (1/2 Boliviano)
11.50 g., 0.900 Silver 0.3328 oz. ASW, 30 mm. **Obv:** Crossed flags and weapons behind condor-topped oval arms, stars below **Obv. Legend:** REPUBLICA BOLIVIANA **Rev:** Denomination within wreath, date below **Note:** Mint mark in monogram.

Date	Mintage	VG8	F12	VF20	XF40	MS60
1901/0 PTS MM	—	—	7.25	15.00	32.00	50.00
1901 PTS MM	Inc. above	—	7.25	12.00	15.00	30.00
1902 PTS MM	1,530,000	—	7.25	12.00	15.00	30.00
1903/2 PTS MM	690,000	—	7.25	14.00	25.00	50.00
1903 PTS MM	Inc. above	—	7.25	12.00	15.00	30.00
1904 PTS MM	1,290,000	—	7.25	12.00	15.00	30.00
1905 PTS MM	1,690,000	—	7.25	12.00	15.00	30.00
1905 PTS AB	Inc. above	—	7.25	12.00	15.00	30.00
1906 PTS MM	630,000	—	7.25	12.00	20.00	42.00
1906 PTS AB	5,500,000	—	7.25	12.00	15.00	30.00
1907 PTS MM	50,000	—	7.25	14.00	20.00	42.00
1908 PTS MM	—	—	7.25	12.00	15.00	30.00
1908 PTS MM Inverted 8	—	—	7.25	20.00	42.00	70.00

KM# 177 50 CENTAVOS (1/2 Boliviano)
10.00 g., 0.833 Silver 0.2678 oz. ASW, 30 mm. **Obv:** National arms, stars below **Rev:** Denomination within wreath, date below

Date	Mintage	VG8	F12	VF20	XF40	MS60
1909 H	1,400,000	—	5.25	10.00	15.00	35.00
1909 H	—	PF63 400				

KM# 181 50 CENTAVOS (1/2 Boliviano)
7.00 g., Copper-Nickel, 25 mm. **Obv:** State emblem within circle, stars below **Rev:** Hand holding torch divides date and denomination **Note:** Most melted upon receipt in Bolivia. Medal rotation strike.

Date	Mintage	F12	VF20	XF40	MS60	MS63
1937	8,000,000	5.00	10.00	25.00	45.00	75.00

KM# 182 50 CENTAVOS (1/2 Boliviano)
8.45 g., Copper-Nickel, 29.05 mm. **Obv:** State emblem within circle, stars below **Rev:** Caduceus divides denomination, sprays below, date at bottom **Note:** Medal rotation strike.

Date	Mintage	VF20	XF40	MS60	MS63	MS65
1939	—	0.25	0.50	1.00	3.50	7.00

KM# 182a.1 50 CENTAVOS (1/2 Boliviano)
5.10 g., Bronze, 24.6 mm. **Obv:** State emblem within circle, stars below **Rev:** Caduceus divides denomination, sprays below, date at bottom **Note:** Medal rotation strike.

Date	Mintage	VF20	XF40	MS60	MS63	MS65
1942 (p)	10,000,000	0.35	0.60	1.25	4.00	8.00

KM# 182a.2 50 CENTAVOS (1/2 Boliviano)
5.12 g., Bronze, 24.5 mm. **Obv:** State emblem within circle, stars below **Rev:** Caduceus divides denomination, sprays below, date at bottom **Edge:** Reeded **Note:** Restrike - poor detail. Medal rotation strike.

Date	Mintage	VF20	XF40	MS60	MS63	MS65
1942	5,310,000	0.25	0.50	1.00	2.50	5.00

KM# 184 BOLIVIANO
3.00 g., Bronze, 18 mm. **Obv:** State emblem within circle, stars below **Rev:** Denomination within wreath, date below **Edge:** Reeded **Note:** Medal rotation strike.

Date	Mintage	VF20	XF40	MS60	MS63	MS65
1951	10,000,000	0.10	0.20	1.00	3.00	5.00
1951	10	PF63 200				
1951 H	15,000,000	0.10	0.20	1.00	3.00	5.00
1951 KN	15,000,000	0.25	0.50	1.50	4.00	6.00

KM# 185 5 BOLIVIANOS
Bronze **Obv:** National arms, stars below **Rev:** Denomination within wreath, date below **Note:** Medal rotation strike.

Date	Mintage	VF20	XF40	MS60	MS63	MS65
1951	7,000,000	0.25	0.50	1.00	3.50	5.50
1951	—	PF63 200				
1951 H	15,000,000	0.25	0.50	1.00	3.50	5.50
1951 KN	15,000,000	0.60	0.90	1.50	4.00	6.00

KM# 186 10 BOLIVIANOS (1 Bolivar)
Bronze, 26.5 mm. **Obv:** Armored bust, right **Rev:** Denomination within wreath, date below **Note:** Medal rotation strike.

Date	Mintage	VF20	XF40	MS60	MS63	MS65
1951	40,000,000	0.60	1.00	2.00	4.50	6.50
1951	—	PF63 200				

REFORM COINAGE

1965-1979; 100 Centavos = 1 Peso Boliviano

KM# 187 5 CENTAVOS
1.70 g., Copper Clad Steel, 16 mm. **Obv:** State emblem within circle, stars below **Rev:** Denomination, date below **Edge:** Plain **Note:** Medal rotation.

Date	Mintage	VF20	XF40	MS60	MS63	MS65
1965	10,000,000	0.20	0.30	0.65	2.00	2.50
1970	100,000	0.20	0.30	0.65	2.00	2.50

KM# 188 10 CENTAVOS
2.51 g., Copper Clad Steel, 19 mm. **Obv:** State emblem within circle, stars below **Rev:** Denomination, date below **Edge:** Plain **Note:** Medal rotation.

Date	Mintage	VF20	XF40	MS60	MS63	MS65
1965	10,000,000	0.10	0.25	0.50	1.50	2.00
1967	—	0.10	0.20	0.40	1.00	1.50
1969	5,700,000	0.10	0.20	0.40	1.00	1.50
1971	200,000	0.15	0.25	0.50	1.00	1.50
1972	100,000	0.20	0.40	0.80	1.50	2.00
1973	6,000,000	0.10	0.20	0.40	1.00	1.50

KM# 189 20 CENTAVOS
Nickel Clad Steel, 22 mm. **Obv:** State emblem within circle, stars below **Rev:** Denomination, date below **Note:** Medal rotation.

Date	Mintage	VF20	XF40	MS60	MS63	MS65
1965	5,000,000	0.20	0.40	0.70	2.00	2.50
1967	—	0.20	0.40	0.65	1.75	2.25
1970	400,000	0.20	0.40	0.80	2.50	3.50
1971	400,000	0.20	0.40	0.80	2.50	3.50
1973	5,000,000	0.20	0.40	0.60	1.50	2.00

KM# 193 25 CENTAVOS
Nickel Clad Steel **Obv:** State emblem within circle, stars below **Rev:** Denomination, date below **Note:** Medal rotation.

Date	Mintage	VF20	XF40	MS60	MS63	MS65
1971	—	0.15	0.30	0.60	1.00	1.50
1972	9,998,000	0.15	0.30	0.60	1.00	1.50

KM# 190 50 CENTAVOS
4.00 g., Nickel Clad Steel, 24 mm. **Obv:** State emblem within circle, stars below **Rev:** Denomination, date at bottom **Note:** Medal rotation.

Date	Mintage	VF20	XF40	MS60	MS63	MS65
1965	10,000,000	0.15	0.30	0.65	1.75	2.25
1967	—	0.15	0.30	0.65	1.25	1.75
1972	—	0.15	0.30	0.65	1.25	1.75
1973	5,000,000	0.15	0.30	0.65	1.25	1.75
1974	15,000,000	0.15	0.30	0.65	1.25	1.75
1978	5,000,000	0.15	0.30	0.65	1.25	1.75
1980	3,600,000	0.15	0.30	0.65	1.25	1.75

KM# 191 PESO BOLIVIANO
6.00 g., Nickel Clad Steel, 27 mm. **Series:** F.A.O. **Obv:** State emblem within circle, stars below **Rev:** Denomination **Note:** Medal rotation.

Date	Mintage	VF20	XF40	MS60	MS63	MS65
ND-1968	40,000	1.50	2.50	3.50	6.50	9.00

KM# 192 PESO BOLIVIANO
6.00 g., Nickel Clad Steel, 27 mm. **Series:** F.A.O. **Obv:** State emblem within circle, stars below **Rev:** Denomination, date below **Edge:** Reeded **Note:** Medal rotation.

Date	Mintage	VF20	XF40	MS60	MS63	MS65
1968	10,000,000	0.20	0.40	0.80	1.75	2.50
1969	—	0.20	0.40	0.80	1.75	2.50
1970	10,000,000	0.20	0.40	0.80	1.75	2.50
1972	—	0.20	0.40	0.80	1.75	2.50
1973	5,000,000	0.20	0.40	0.80	1.75	2.50
1974	15,000,000	0.20	0.40	0.80	1.75	2.50
1978	10,000,000	0.20	0.40	0.80	1.75	2.50
1980	2,993,000	0.20	0.40	0.80	1.75	2.50

KM# 197 5 PESOS BOLIVIANOS
8.50 g., Nickel Clad Steel, 30 mm. **Obv:** State arms within circle, stars below **Rev:** Denomination, date below **Edge:** Reeded **Note:** Medal rotation.

Date	Mintage	VF20	XF40	MS60	MS63	MS65
1976	20,000,000	0.65	1.25	2.50	5.00	6.50
1978	10,000,000	0.65	1.25	2.50	5.00	6.50
1980	5,231,000	0.65	1.25	2.50	5.00	6.50

KM# 194 100 PESOS BOLIVIANOS
10.00 g., 0.933 Silver 0.300 oz. ASW **Subject:** 150th Anniversary of Independence **Obv:** National arms divide dates **Rev:** Simon Bolivar and Hugo Banzer Suarez left, denomination below **Note:** Medal rotation.

Date	Mintage	VF20	XF40	MS60	MS63	MS65
ND-1975	160,000	—	6.00	7.75	12.00	16.00

KM# 198 200 PESOS BOLIVIANOS
23.33 g., 0.925 Silver 0.6938 oz. ASW **Subject:** International Year of the Child **Obv:** State emblem within circle, eagle at top, stars below **Rev:** Children divide small symbols, date at bottom, denomination at top **Note:** Medal rotation.

Date	Mintage	VF20	XF40	MS60	MS63	MS65
1979	15,000	PF65 25.00				

KM# 195 250 PESOS BOLIVIANOS
15.00 g., 0.933 Silver 0.4499 oz. ASW **Subject:** 150th Anniversary of Independence **Obv:** National arms divide dates **Rev:** Conjoined heads left with armored collars, denomination below **Note:** Medal rotation.

Date	Mintage	VF20	XF40	MS60	MS63	MS65
ND-1975	140,000	—	9.00	11.50	16.00	20.00

KM# 196 500 PESOS BOLIVIANOS
22.00 g., 0.933 Silver 0.6599 oz. ASW **Subject:** 150th Anniversary of Independence

Date	Mintage	VF20	XF40	MS60	MS63	MS65
ND-1975	100,000	—	13.00	16.50	22.00	30.00

KM# 199 4000 PESOS BOLIVIANOS
17.17 g., 0.900 Gold 0.4968 oz. AGW **Subject:** International Year of the Child **Obv:** State emblem within circle, eagle at top, stars below **Rev:** Child playing flute divides symbols, date below, denomination above

Date	Mintage	VF20	XF40	MS60	MS63	MS65
1979	6,315	PF65 875				

REFORM COINAGE

1987-; 1,000,000 Peso Bolivianos = 1 Boliviano; 100 Centavos = 1 Boliviano

KM# 200 2 CENTAVOS

1.00 g., Stainless Steel, 14.04 mm. **Obv:** National arms, star below **Rev:** Denomination within circle, date below **Edge:** Plain

Date	Mintage	VF20	XF40	MS60	MS63	MS65
1987	20,000,000	—	—	—	0.35	0.50

KM# 201 5 CENTAVOS

Stainless Steel **Obv:** National arms, star below **Rev:** Denomination within circle, date below

Date	Mintage	VF20	XF40	MS60	MS63	MS65
1987	20,000,000	—	—	—	0.50	0.65

KM# 202 10 CENTAVOS

1.85 g., Stainless Steel, 19 mm. **Obv:** National arms, star below **Rev:** Denomination within circle, date below

Date	Mintage	VF20	XF40	MS60	MS63	MS65
1987	20,000,000	—	—	0.25	0.60	0.80
1991	23,000,000	—	—	0.20	0.50	0.70
1995	14,000,000	—	—	0.20	0.50	0.70
1997	33,000,000	—	—	0.20	0.50	0.70

KM# 202a 10 CENTAVOS

1.85 g., Copper Clad Steel, 19 mm. **Obv:** National arms **Obv. Legend:** REPUBLICA DE BOLIVIA **Rev:** Denomination **Rev. Legend:** LA UNION ES LA FUERZA **Edge:** Plain

Date	Mintage	VF20	XF40	MS60	MS63	MS65
1997	—	—	—	0.20	0.50	0.65

KM# 203 20 CENTAVOS

3.25 g., Stainless Steel, 22 mm. **Obv:** National arms, star below **Obv. Legend:** REPUBLICA DE BOLIVIA **Rev:** Denomination within circle, date below **Rev. Legend:** LA UNION ES LA FUERZA **Edge:** Plain

Date	Mintage	VF20	XF40	MS60	MS63	MS65
1987	20,000,000	—	—	0.30	0.75	1.00
1991	20,000,000	—	—	0.25	0.60	0.80
1995	14,000,000	—	—	0.25	0.60	0.80
1997	19,000,000	—	—	0.25	0.60	0.80

KM# 204 50 CENTAVOS

3.75 g., Stainless Steel, 24 mm. **Obv:** National arms, star below **Obv. Legend:** REPUBLICA DE BOLIVIA **Rev:** Denomination within circle, date below **Rev. Legend:** LA UNION ES LA FUERZA **Edge:** Plain

Date	Mintage	VF20	XF40	MS60	MS63	MS65
1987	15,000,000	—	—	0.40	1.00	1.25
1991	20,000,000	—	—	0.30	0.75	1.00
1995	14,000,000	—	—	0.30	0.75	1.00
1997	15,000,000	—	—	0.30	0.75	1.00

KM# 205 BOLIVIANO

5.00 g., Stainless Steel, 27 mm. **Obv:** National arms, star below **Obv. Legend:** REPUBLICA DE BOLIVIA **Rev:** Denomination within circle, date below sprays **Rev. Legend:** LA UNION ES LA FUERZA **Edge:** Plain

Date	Mintage	VF20	XF40	MS60	MS63	MS65
1987	10,000,000	—	—	0.60	1.50	2.00
1991	20,000,000	—	—	0.35	0.90	1.20
1995	9,000,000	—	—	0.35	0.90	1.20
1997	17,000,000	—	—	0.35	0.90	1.20

KM# 210 BOLIVIANO

27.00 g., 0.925 Silver 0.803 oz. ASW **Subject:** 70th Anniversary - Bolivian Central Bank **Obv:** National arms above date, stars below **Rev:** Denomination above bank emblem, two dates below sprays

Date	Mintage	VF20	XF40	MS60	MS63	MS65
1998	1,000	PF65 75.00				

KM# 206.1 2 BOLIVIANOS

Stainless Steel **Obv:** National arms, star below **Rev:** Denomination within circle, date below **Shape:** 11-sided

Date	Mintage	VF20	XF40	MS60	MS63	MS65
1991	18,000,000	—	—	—	1.50	2.50

KM# 206.2 2 BOLIVIANOS

6.25 g., Stainless Steel, 27 mm. **Obv:** National arms, star below **Rev:** Denomination within circle, date below **Note:** Increased size.

Date	Mintage	VF20	XF40	MS60	MS63	MS65
1995	11,000,000	—	—	—	1.50	2.50
1997	—	—	—	—	1.50	2.50

KM# 207 10 BOLIVIANOS

27.00 g., 0.925 Silver 0.803 oz. ASW **Series:** Ibero - American **Obv:** National arms within legend, arms surrounding **Rev:** Radiant sun behind mountains, denomination, within circle, two dates below

Date	Mintage	VF20	XF40	MS60	MS63	MS65
1991	—	PF65 60.00				

KM# 209 10 BOLIVIANOS

27.13 g., 0.925 Silver 0.8068 oz. ASW **Series:** Ibero - American **Obv:** Bolivian arms within legend, arms surrounding **Rev:** Folk dancer, denomination within circle, date below

Date	Mintage	VF20	XF40	MS60	MS63	MS65
1997	33,000	PF65 60.00				

KM# 211 50 BOLIVIANOS

27.00 g., 0.925 Silver 0.803 oz. ASW **Subject:** 450th Anniversary of La Paz **Obv:** National arms, date below, stars at bottom **Rev:** City arms above church building, denomination, within circle, two dates below

Date	Mintage	VF20	XF40	MS60	MS63	MS65
1998	2,000	PF65 70.00				

PATTERNS

Including off metal strikes

KM#	Date	Mintage	Identification	Mkt Val
Pn54	1902 MM	—	20 Centavos. Brass. Struck at La Paz.	125
Pn55	1902 MM	—	20 Centavos. Brass. Struck at La Paz. 1/2 Medio Boliviano/20 Centavos error.	90.00
Pn56	1902 MM	—	50 Centavos. Brass.	125
Pn57	1942	—	50 Centavos. Silver. Struck at La Paz. KM#182a.1.	375

PIEDFORT

KM#	Date	Mintage	Identification	Mkt Val
P9	1979	90	200 Pesos. Silver. KM#198.	250
P10	1979	47	4000 Pesos. Gold. KM#199.	1,650

TRIAL STRIKES

KM#	Date	Mintage	Identification	Mkt Val
TS1	ND-1909	—	20 Centavos. Silver. Uniface.	—
TS2	1942	—	10 Centavos. Lead. KM179a, uniface.	150

BOSNIA - HERZEGOVINA

The Republic of Bosnia and Herzegovina borders Croatia to the north and west, Serbia to the east and Montenegro in the southeast with only 12.4 mi. of coastline. The total land area is 19,735 sq. mi. (51,129 sq. km.). They have a population of *4.34 million. Capital: Sarajevo. Electricity, mining and agriculture are leading industries.

After the defeat of Germany in WWII, during which Bosnia was under the control of Pavelic of Croatia, a new Socialist Republic was formed under Marshall Tito having six constituent republics, all subservient, quite similar to the constitution of the U.S.S.R. Military and civil loyalty was with Tito, not with Moscow. In Jan. 1990, the Yugoslav Government announced a rewriting of the Constitution, abolishing the Communist Party's monopoly of power. Opposition parties were legalized in July 1990. On Oct. 15, 1991 the National Assembly adopted a "Memorandum on Sovereignty", the envisaged Bosnian autonomy within a Yugoslav federation. In March 1992, an agreement was reached under EC auspices by Moslems, Serbs and Croats to set up 3 autonomous ethnic communities under a central Bosnian authority. Independence was declared on April 5, 1992. The 2 Serbian members of government resigned and fighting broke out between all 3 ethnic communities. The Dayton (Ohio) Peace Accord was signed in 1995, which recognized the Federation of Bosnia and Herzegovina and the Srpska (Serbian) Republic. Both governments maintain separate military forces, school systems, etc. The United Nations is currently providing humanitarian aid while a recent peace treaty allowed NATO "Peace Keeping" forces to be deployed in Dec. 1995 replacing the United Nations troops previously acting in a similar role.

MINT MARK

PM - Pobjoy Mint

MONETARY SYSTEM

1 Dinara = 100 Para, 1992-1998
1 Convertible Marka = 100 Convertible Feniga = 1 Deutschemark 1998-

NOTE: German Euros circulate freely.

REPUBLIC

DINARA COINAGE

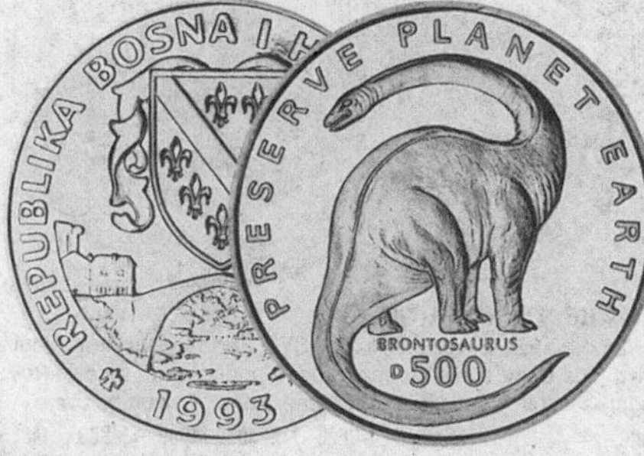

KM# 1 500 DINARA
Copper-Nickel **Series:** Preserve Planet Earth **Obv:** National arms above bridge, date at bottom **Rev:** Brontosaurus, facing back, looking left, denomination below

Date	Mintage	VF20	XF40	MS60	MS63	MS65
1993 Prooflike	—	—	—	—	8.00	12.00

KM# 4 500 DINARA
Copper-Nickel **Series:** Preserve Planet Earth **Obv:** National arms above bridge, date below **Rev:** Tyrannosaurus Rex, facing right, looking left, denomination below

Date	Mintage	VF20	XF40	MS60	MS63	MS65
1993 Prooflike	—	—	—	—	8.00	12.00

KM# 20 500 DINARA
Copper-Nickel **Series:** Preserve Planet Earth **Obv:** National arms above bridge, date below **Rev:** Eohippus

Date	Mintage	VF20	XF40	MS60	MS63	MS65
1994 Proof	—	—	—	—	8.00	12.00

KM# 23 500 DINARA
Copper-Nickel **Series:** Preserve Planet Earth **Obv:** National arms above bridge, date below **Rev:** Gray Wolf, right, above denomination

Date	Mintage	VF20	XF40	MS60	MS63	MS65
1994 Prooflike	—	—	—	—	8.00	12.00

KM# 24 500 DINARA
Copper-Nickel **Series:** Preserve Planet Earth **Obv:** National arms above bridge, date below **Rev:** Black Bear, left, with cub facing, denomination below

Date	Mintage	VF20	XF40	MS60	MS63	MS65
1994 Prooflike	—	—	—	—	8.00	12.00

KM# 25 500 DINARA
Copper-Nickel **Series:** Preserve Planet Earth **Obv:** National arms above bridge, date below **Rev:** River Kingfisher, left, fish in beak, denomination below

Date	Mintage	VF20	XF40	MS60	MS63	MS65
1994	—	—	—	—	8.00	12.00

KM# 39 500 DINARA
Copper-Nickel **Series:** Preserve Planet Earth **Obv:** National arms above bridge, date below **Rev:** Przewalskii Horses

Date	Mintage	VF20	XF40	MS60	MS63	MS65
1995	—	—	—	—	8.00	12.00

KM# 42 500 DINARA
Copper-Nickel **Series:** Preserve Planet Earth **Obv:** National arms above bridge, date below **Rev:** Hedgehogs

Date	Mintage	VF20	XF40	MS60	MS63	MS65
1995	—	—	—	—	9.00	13.00

KM# 64 500 DINARA
Copper-Nickel **Series:** European Youth Olympics **Obv:** National arms above bridge, date below **Rev:** Flame

Date	Mintage	VF20	XF40	MS60	MS63	MS65
1995	—	—	—	—	6.50	8.00

KM# 65 500 DINARA
Copper-Nickel **Series:** European Youth Olympics **Obv:** National arms above bridge, date below **Rev:** Rings

Date	Mintage	VF20	XF40	MS60	MS63	MS65
1995	—	—	—	—	6.50	8.00

KM# 52 500 DINARA
Copper-Nickel **Series:** Olympics **Obv:** National arms above bridge, date below **Rev:** Long jumper

Date	Mintage	VF20	XF40	MS60	MS63	MS65
1996	—	—	—	—	6.50	8.00

KM# 53 500 DINARA
Copper-Nickel **Series:** Olympics **Obv:** National arms above bridge, date below **Rev:** Sprinter

Date	Mintage	VF20	XF40	MS60	MS63	MS65
1996	—	—	—	—	6.50	8.00

KM# 54 500 DINARA
Copper-Nickel **Series:** Olympics **Obv:** National arms above bridge, date below **Rev:** Wrestlers

Date	Mintage	VF20	XF40	MS60	MS63	MS65
1996	—	—	—	—	6.50	8.00

KM# 55 500 DINARA
Copper-Nickel **Series:** Olympics **Obv:** National arms above bridge, date below **Rev:** Fencers

Date	Mintage	VF20	XF40	MS60	MS63	MS65
1996	—	—	—	—	6.50	8.00

KM# 76 500 DINARA
Copper-Nickel **Series:** Preserve Planet Earth **Obv:** National arms above bridge, date below **Rev:** Hoopoe Birds

Date	Mintage	VF20	XF40	MS60	MS63	MS65
1996	—	—	—	—	9.00	13.00

KM# 79 500 DINARA
Copper-Nickel **Series:** Preserve Planet Earth **Obv:** National arms above bridge, date below **Rev:** Goosander Birds

Date	Mintage	VF20	XF40	MS60	MS63	MS65
1996	—	—	—	—	12.00	16.00

KM# 95 500 DINARA
Copper-Nickel **Subject:** Jurassic Park **Obv:** National arms above bridge, date below **Rev:** Tyrannosaurus Rex, Jurassic Park logo

Date	Mintage	VF20	XF40	MS60	MS63	MS65
1997	—	—	—	—	12.00	16.00

KM# 2 750 DINARA
28.28 g., 0.925 Silver 0.841 oz. ASW **Series:** Preserve Planet

Earth **Obv:** National arms above bridge, date below **Rev:** Brontosaurus facing back, looking left, denomination below

Date	Mintage	VF20	XF40	MS60	MS63	MS65
1993	Est. 30000	PF65 32.50				

KM# 5 750 DINARA
28.28 g., 0.925 Silver 0.841 oz. ASW **Series:** Preserve Planet Earth **Obv:** National arms above bridge, date below **Rev:** Tyrannosaurus Rex, facing right, looking left, denomination below

Date	Mintage	VF20	XF40	MS60	MS63	MS65
1993	Est. 30000	PF65 32.50				

KM# 7 750 DINARA
28.28 g., 0.925 Silver 0.841 oz. ASW **Series:** Olympics **Obv:** National arms above bridge, date below **Rev:** 2 Bobsledders with sled, denomination below, within circle

Date	Mintage	VF20	XF40	MS60	MS63	MS65
1993	Est. 30000	PF65 35.00				

KM# 9 750 DINARA
28.28 g., 0.925 Silver 0.841 oz. ASW **Series:** Olympics **Obv:** National arms above bridge, date below **Rev:** Downhill skier above denomination, within circle

Date	Mintage	VF20	XF40	MS60	MS63	MS65
1993	Est. 30000	PF65 35.00				

KM# 11 750 DINARA
28.28 g., 0.925 Silver 0.841 oz. ASW **Series:** Olympics **Obv:** National arms above bridge, date below **Rev:** Cross-country skier above denomination, within circle

Date	Mintage	VF20	XF40	MS60	MS63	MS65
1993	Est. 30000	PF65 35.00				

KM# 13 750 DINARA
28.28 g., 0.925 Silver 0.841 oz. ASW **Series:** Lillehammer 1994 - 17th Winter Olympic Games **Obv:** National arms above bridge, date below **Rev:** Pairs Figure Skating above denomination, within circle

Date	Mintage	VF20	XF40	MS60	MS63	MS65
1993	Est. 30000	PF65 35.00				

KM# 21 750 DINARA
28.28 g., 0.925 Silver 0.841 oz. ASW **Series:** Preserve Planet Earth **Obv:** National arms above bridge, date below **Rev:** Eohippu **Note:** Similar to 10,000 Dinara, KM#22.

Date	Mintage	VF20	XF40	MS60	MS63	MS65
1994	Est. 30000	PF65 32.50				

KM# 26 750 DINARA
28.28 g., 0.925 Silver 0.841 oz. ASW **Series:** Preserve Planet Earth **Obv:** National arms above bridge, date below **Rev:** Wolf right, denomination below

Date	Mintage	VF20	XF40	MS60	MS63	MS65
1994	Est. 30000	PF65 40.00				

KM# 27 750 DINARA
28.28 g., 0.925 Silver 0.841 oz. ASW **Series:** Preserve Planet Earth **Obv:** National arms above bridge, date below **Rev:** Black bear left with cub facing, denomination below

Date	Mintage	VF20	XF40	MS60	MS63	MS65
1994	Est. 30000	PF65 40.00				

KM# 28 750 DINARA
28.28 g., 0.925 Silver 0.841 oz. ASW **Series:** Preserve Planet Earth **Obv:** National arms above bridge, date below **Rev:** River Kingfisher left, fish in beak, denomination below

Date	Mintage	VF20	XF40	MS60	MS63	MS65
1994	Est. 30000	PF65 35.00				

KM# 40 750 DINARA
28.28 g., 0.925 Silver 0.841 oz. ASW **Series:** Preserve Planet Earth **Obv:** National arms above bridge, date below **Rev:** Przewalskii horses right, denomination below

Date	Mintage	VF20	XF40	MS60	MS63	MS65
1995	Est. 30000	PF65 40.00				

KM# 43 750 DINARA
28.28 g., 0.925 Silver 0.841 oz. ASW **Series:** Preserve Planet Earth **Obv:** National arms above bridge, date below **Rev:** Hedgehog left with babies, denomination below

Date	Mintage	VF20	XF40	MS60	MS63	MS65
1995	Est. 30000	PF65 40.00				

KM# 66 750 DINARA
28.28 g., 0.925 Silver 0.841 oz. ASW **Series:** European Youth Olympics **Obv:** National arms above bridge, date below **Rev:** Figures within small circles on flame, denomination below

Date	Mintage	VF20	XF40	MS60	MS63	MS65
1995	—	PF65 32.50				

KM# 67 750 DINARA
28.28 g., 0.925 Silver 0.841 oz. ASW **Series:** European Youth Olympics **Obv:** National arms above bridge, date below **Rev:** Man on rings event, denomination below

Date	Mintage	VF20	XF40	MS60	MS63	MS65
1995	Est. 30000	PF65 32.50				

KM# 56 750 DINARA
28.28 g., 0.925 Silver 0.841 oz. ASW **Series:** Atlanta 1996 - 26th Summer Olympics **Obv:** National arms above bridge, date below **Rev:** Long jumper right, denomination below

Date	Mintage	VF20	XF40	MS60	MS63	MS65
1996	Est. 30000	PF65 30.00				

KM# 57 750 DINARA
28.28 g., 0.925 Silver 0.841 oz. ASW **Series:** Olympics **Obv:** National arms above bridge, date below **Rev:** Sprinter, right, denomination below

Date	Mintage	VF20	XF40	MS60	MS63	MS65
1996	Est. 30000	PF65 30.00				

KM# 58 750 DINARA
28.28 g., 0.925 Silver 0.841 oz. ASW **Series:** Olympics **Obv:** National arms above bridge, date below **Rev:** Wrestlers, denomination below

Date	Mintage	VF20	XF40	MS60	MS63	MS65
1996	Est. 30000	PF65 30.00				

KM# 59 750 DINARA
28.28 g., 0.925 Silver 0.841 oz. ASW **Series:** Olympics **Obv:** National arms above bridge, date below **Rev:** Fencers, denomination below

Date	Mintage	VF20	XF40	MS60	MS63	MS65
1996	—	PF65 30.00				

KM# 77 750 DINARA
28.28 g., 0.925 Silver 0.841 oz. ASW **Series:** Preserve Planet Earth **Obv:** National arms above bridge, date below **Rev:** Hoopoe birds, denomination below

Date	Mintage	VF20	XF40	MS60	MS63	MS65
1996	Est. 30000	PF65 32.50				

KM# 80 750 DINARA
28.28 g., 0.925 Silver 0.841 oz. ASW **Series:** Preserve Planet Earth **Obv:** National arms above bridge, date below **Rev:** Goosander birds, denomination below

Date	Mintage	VF20	XF40	MS60	MS63	MS65
1996	Est. 30000	PF65 32.50				

KM# 96 750 DINARA
28.28 g., 0.925 Silver 0.841 oz. ASW **Subject:** Jurassic Park **Obv:** National arms above bridge, date below **Rev:** Tyrannosaurus Rex, left, Jurassic Park logo, denomination at bottom

Date	Mintage	VF20	XF40	MS60	MS63	MS65
1997	Est. 10000	PF65 40.00				

KM# 3 10000 DINARA
6.22 g., 0.999 Gold 0.1998 oz. AGW **Series:** Preserve Planet Earth **Obv:** National arms above bridge, date below **Rev:** Brontosaurus, facing back, looking left, denomination below

Date	Mintage	VF20	XF40	MS60	MS63	MS65
1993	Est. 5000	PF65 350				

KM# 6 10000 DINARA
6.22 g., 0.999 Gold 0.1998 oz. AGW **Series:** Preserve Planet Earth **Obv:** National arms above bridge, date below **Rev:** Tyrannosaurus Rex, facing right, looking left, denomination below

Date	Mintage	VF20	XF40	MS60	MS63	MS65
1993	Est. 5000	PF65 350				

KM# 8 10000 DINARA
6.22 g., 0.999 Gold 0.1998 oz. AGW **Series:** Olympics **Obv:** National arms above bridge, date below **Rev:** Two bobsledders starting race

Date	Mintage	VF20	XF40	MS60	MS63	MS65
1993	Est. 5000	PF65 350				

KM# 10 10000 DINARA
6.22 g., 0.999 Gold 0.1998 oz. AGW **Series:** Olympics **Obv:** National arms above bridge, date below **Rev:** Downhill skier

Date	Mintage	VF20	XF40	MS60	MS63	MS65
1993	Est. 5000	PF65 350				

KM# 12 10000 DINARA
6.22 g., 0.999 Gold 0.1998 oz. AGW **Series:** Olympics **Obv:** National arms above bridge, date below **Rev:** Cross-country skier

Date	Mintage	VF20	XF40	MS60	MS63	MS65
1993	Est. 5000	PF65 350				

KM# 14 10000 DINARA
6.22 g., 0.999 Gold 0.1998 oz. AGW **Series:** Olympics **Obv:** National arms above bridge, date below **Rev:** Pair skating

Date	Mintage	VF20	XF40	MS60	MS63	MS65
1993	Est. 5000	PF65 350				

KM# 22 10000 DINARA
6.22 g., 0.999 Gold 0.1998 oz. AGW **Series:** Preserve Planet Earth **Obv:** National arms above bridge, date below **Rev:** Eohippu, right, denomination below

Date	Mintage	VF20	XF40	MS60	MS63	MS65
1994	Est. 5000	PF65 350				

KM# 29 10000 DINARA
6.22 g., 0.999 Gold 0.1998 oz. AGW **Series:** Preserve Planet Earth **Obv:** National arms above bridge, date below **Rev:** Wolf walking right

Date	Mintage	VF20	XF40	MS60	MS63	MS65
1994	5,000	PF65 350				

KM# 30 10000 DINARA
6.22 g., 0.999 Gold 0.1998 oz. AGW **Series:** Preserve Planet Earth **Obv:** National arms above bridge, date below **Rev:** Black bear and cub walking right

Date	Mintage	VF20	XF40	MS60	MS63	MS65
1994	5,000	PF65 350				

KM# 31 10000 DINARA
6.22 g., 0.999 Gold 0.1998 oz. AGW **Series:** Preserve Planet Earth **Obv:** National arms above bridge, date below **Rev:** Kingfisher left with fish in bill

Date	Mintage	VF20	XF40	MS60	MS63	MS65
1994	5,000	PF65 350				

KM# 41 10000 DINARA
6.22 g., 0.999 Gold 0.1998 oz. AGW **Series:** Preserve Planet Earth **Obv:** National arms above bridge, date below **Rev:** Przewalskii horses

Date	Mintage	VF20	XF40	MS60	MS63	MS65
1995	Est. 5000	PF65 350				

KM# 44 10000 DINARA
6.22 g., 0.999 Gold 0.1998 oz. AGW **Series:** Preserve Planet Earth **Obv:** National arms above bridge, date below **Rev:** Hedgehogs

Date	Mintage	VF20	XF40	MS60	MS63	MS65
1995	Est. 5000	PF65 350				

KM# 60 10000 DINARA
6.22 g., 0.999 Gold 0.1998 oz. AGW **Series:** Olympics **Obv:** National arms above bridge, date below **Rev:** Long jumper

Date	Mintage	VF20	XF40	MS60	MS63	MS65
1996	Est. 5000	PF65 350				

KM# 61 10000 DINARA
6.22 g., 0.999 Gold 0.1998 oz. AGW **Series:** Olympics **Obv:** National arms above bridge, date below **Rev:** Sprinter

Date	Mintage	VF20	XF40	MS60	MS63	MS65
1996	Est. 5000	PF65 350				

KM# 62 10000 DINARA
6.22 g., 0.999 Gold 0.1998 oz. AGW **Series:** Olympics **Obv:** National arms above bridge, date below **Rev:** Wrestlers

Date	Mintage	VF20	XF40	MS60	MS63	MS65
1996	Est. 5000	PF65 350				

KM# 63 10000 DINARA
6.22 g., 0.999 Gold 0.1998 oz. AGW **Series:** Olympics **Obv:** National arms above bridge, date below **Rev:** Fencers

Date	Mintage	VF20	XF40	MS60	MS63	MS65
1996	Est. 5000	PF65 350				

KM# 78 10000 DINARA
6.22 g., 0.999 Gold 0.1998 oz. AGW **Series:** Preserve Planet Earth **Obv:** National arms above bridge, date below **Rev:** Hoopoe birds

Date	Mintage	VF20	XF40	MS60	MS63	MS65
1996	Est. 5000	PF65 350				

KM# 81 10000 DINARA
6.22 g., 0.999 Gold 0.1998 oz. AGW **Series:** Preserve Planet Earth **Obv:** National arms above bridge, date below **Rev:** Goosander birds

Date	Mintage	VF20	XF40	MS60	MS63	MS65
1996	Est. 5000	PF65 350				

KM# 97 10000 DINARA
6.22 g., 0.999 Gold 0.1998 oz. AGW **Subject:** Jurassic Park **Obv:** National arms above bridge, date below **Rev:** Tyrannosaurus Rex, left, Jurassic Park logo above, denomination below

Date	Mintage	VF20	XF40	MS60	MS63	MS65
1997	Est. 2500	PF65 350				

MARKA / MARAKA COINAGE

KM# 98 5 MARKA

Copper-Nickel **Subject:** Princess Diana **Obv:** National arms above bridge, date below **Rev:** Portrait and map

Date	Mintage	VF20	XF40	MS60	MS63	MS65
1998	—	—	—	—	7.50	10.00

KM# 111 5 MARKA

Copper-Nickel **Subject:** Sydney 2000 - 27th Summer Olympics **Obv:** National arms above bridge, date below **Rev:** Javelin thrower

Date	Mintage	VF20	XF40	MS60	MS63	MS65
1998	—	—	—	—	6.50	8.00

KM# 99 10 MARKA

28.28 g., 0.925 Silver 0.841 oz. ASW **Subject:** Princess Diana **Obv:** National arms above bridge, date below **Rev:** Portrait and map divide dates, denomination at bottom

Date	Mintage	VF20	XF40	MS60	MS63	MS65
1998	Est. 10000	PF65 45.00				

KM# 112 10 MARKA

28.28 g., 0.925 Silver 0.841 oz. ASW **Subject:** Sydney 2000 - 27th Summer Olympics **Obv:** National arms above bridge, date below **Rev:** Javelin thrower, right, denomination lower left

Date	Mintage	VF20	XF40	MS60	MS63	MS65
1998	Est. 10000	PF65 40.00				

KM# 100 20 MARKA

1.24 g., 0.9999 Gold 0.040 oz. AGW **Subject:** Princess Diana **Obv:** National arms above bridge, date below **Rev:** Portrait and map

Date	Mintage	VF20	XF40	MS60	MS63	MS65
1998	Est. 10000	PF65 65.00				

KM# 101 50 MARKA

3.11 g., 0.9999 Gold 0.100 oz. AGW **Subject:** Princess Diana **Obv:** National arms above bridge, date below **Rev:** Portrait and map

Date	Mintage	VF20	XF40	MS60	MS63	MS65
1998	Est. 7500	PF65 165				

KM# 102 100 MARKA

6.22 g., 0.9999 Gold 0.200 oz. AGW **Subject:** Princess Diana **Obv:** National arms above bridge, date below **Rev:** Portrait and map

Date	Mintage	VF20	XF40	MS60	MS63	MS65
1998	Est. 5000	PF65 350				

KM# 113 100 MARKA

6.22 g., 0.9999 Gold 0.200 oz. AGW **Subject:** Sydney 2000 - 27th Summer Olympics **Obv:** National arms above bridge, date below **Rev:** Javelin thrower

Date	Mintage	VF20	XF40	MS60	MS63	MS65
1998	Est. 5000	PF65 350				

KM# 103 250 MARKA

15.55 g., 0.9999 Gold 0.4999 oz. AGW **Subject:** Princess Diana **Obv:** National arms above bridge, date below **Rev:** Portrait and map

Date	Mintage	VF20	XF40	MS60	MS63	MS65
1998	—	PF65 775				

TRADE COINAGE

KM# 15 1/25 DUKAT

1.24 g., 0.9999 Gold 0.040 oz. AGW **Subject:** Hajj - Kaaba in Mecca **Obv:** National arms above bridge, date below **Rev:** Building and denomination within circle

Date	Mintage	VF20	XF40	MS60	MS63	MS65
1993	Est. 25000	PF65 65.00				

KM# 16 1/10 DUKAT

3.11 g., 0.9999 Gold 0.100 oz. AGW **Subject:** Hajj - Kaaba in Mecca **Obv:** National arms above bridge, date below **Rev:** Building and denomination within circle

Date	Mintage	VF20	XF40	MS60	MS63	MS65
1993	Est. 20000	PF65 165				

KM# 17 1/5 DUKAT

6.22 g., 0.9999 Gold 0.200 oz. AGW **Subject:** Hajj - Kaaba in Mecca **Obv:** National arms above bridge, date below **Rev:** Building and denomination within circle

Date	Mintage	VF20	XF40	MS60	MS63	MS65
1993	Est. 5000	PF65 350				

KM# 18 1/2 DUKAT

15.55 g., 0.9999 Gold 0.4999 oz. AGW **Subject:** Hajj - Kaaba in Mecca **Obv:** National arms above bridge, date below **Rev:** Building and denomination within circle

Date	Mintage	VF20	XF40	MS60	MS63	MS65
1993	Est. 5000	PF65 775				

KM# 19 DUKAT

31.10 g., 0.9999 Gold 0.9999 oz. AGW **Subject:** Hajj - Kaaba in Mecca **Obv:** National arms above bridge, date below **Rev:** Building and denomination within circle

Date	Mintage	VF20	XF40	MS60	MS63	MS65
1993	—	PF65 1,450				
1994	—	PF65 1,450				

KM# 32 1/25 SUVERENA

1.24 g., 0.9999 Gold 0.040 oz. AGW **Subject:** Lipizzaner Stallion **Obv:** National arms above bridge, date below **Rev:** Horse rearing right, denomination below

Date	Mintage	VF20	XF40	MS60	MS63	MS65
1994	—	PF65 65.00				

KM# 45 1/25 SUVERENA

1.24 g., 0.9999 Gold 0.040 oz. AGW **Subject:** English Hack **Obv:** National arms above bridge, date below **Rev:** Horse running left, denomination below

Date	Mintage	VF20	XF40	MS60	MS63	MS65
1995	Est. 15000	PF65 65.00				

KM# 70 1/25 SUVERENA

1.24 g., 0.9999 Gold 0.040 oz. AGW **Subject:** Hanoverian Stallion **Obv:** National arms above bridge, date below **Rev:** Horse left, denomination below

Date	Mintage	VF20	XF40	MS60	MS63	MS65
1996	Est. 15000	PF65 65.00				

KM# 89 1/25 SUVERENA

1.24 g., 0.9999 Gold 0.040 oz. AGW **Subject:** The Arab **Obv:** National arms above bridge, date below **Rev:** Horse right, denomination below

Date	Mintage	VF20	XF40	MS60	MS63	MS65
1997	Est. 15000	PF65 65.00				

KM# 104 1/25 SUVERENA

1.24 g., 0.9999 Gold 0.040 oz. AGW **Subject:** Chinese Horse **Obv:** National arms above bridge, date below **Rev:** Horse, denomination below

Date	Mintage	VF20	XF40	MS60	MS63	MS65
1998	Est. 15000	PF65 65.00				

KM# 33 1/10 SUVERENA

3.11 g., 0.9999 Gold 0.100 oz. AGW **Subject:** Lipizzaner Stallion **Obv:** National arms above bridge, date below **Rev:** Horse rearing right, denomination below

Date	Mintage	VF20	XF40	MS60	MS63	MS65
1994	—	PF65 145				

KM# 46 1/10 SUVERENA

3.11 g., 0.9999 Gold 0.100 oz. AGW **Subject:** English Hack **Obv:** National arms above bridge, date below **Rev:** Horse running left, denomination below

Date	Mintage	VF20	XF40	MS60	MS63	MS65
1995	Est. 10000	PF65 145				

KM# 71 1/10 SUVERENA

3.11 g., 0.9999 Gold 0.100 oz. AGW **Subject:** Hanoverian Stallion **Obv:** National arms above bridge, date below **Rev:** Horse left, denomination below

Date	Mintage	VF20	XF40	MS60	MS63	MS65
1996	Est. 10000	PF65 145				

KM# 90 1/10 SUVERENA

3.11 g., 0.9999 Gold 0.100 oz. AGW **Subject:** The Arab **Obv:** National arms above bridge, date below **Rev:** Horse right, denomination below

Date	Mintage	VF20	XF40	MS60	MS63	MS65
1997	Est. 10000	PF65 145				

KM# 105 1/10 SUVERENA

3.11 g., 0.9999 Gold 0.100 oz. AGW **Subject:** Chinese Horse **Obv:** National arms above bridge, date below **Rev:** Horse left, denomination below

Date	Mintage	VF20	XF40	MS60	MS63	MS65
1998	Est. 10000	PF65 145				

KM# 34 1/5 SUVERENA

6.22 g., 0.9999 Gold 0.200 oz. AGW **Subject:** Lipizzaner Stallion **Obv:** National arms above bridge, date below **Rev:** Horse rearing right, denomination below

Date	Mintage	VF20	XF40	MS60	MS63	MS65
1994	—	PF65 310				

KM# 47 1/5 SUVERENA

6.22 g., 0.9999 Gold 0.200 oz. AGW **Subject:** English Hack **Obv:** National arms above bridge, date below **Rev:** Horse running left, denomination below

Date	Mintage	VF20	XF40	MS60	MS63	MS65
1995	Est. 5000	PF65 310				

KM# 72 1/5 SUVERENA

6.22 g., 0.9999 Gold 0.200 oz. AGW **Subject:** Hanoverian Stallion **Obv:** National arms above bridge, date below **Rev:** Horse left, denomination below

Date	Mintage	VF20	XF40	MS60	MS63	MS65
1996	—	PF65 310				

KM# 91 1/5 SUVERENA

6.22 g., 0.9999 Gold 0.200 oz. AGW **Subject:** The Arab **Obv:** National arms above bridge, date below **Rev:** Horse right, denomination below

Date	Mintage	VF20	XF40	MS60	MS63	MS65
1997	Est. 5000	PF65 310				

KM# 106 1/5 SUVERENA

6.22 g., 0.9999 Gold 0.200 oz. AGW **Subject:** Chinese Horse **Obv:** National arms above bridge, date below **Rev:** Horse left, denomination below

Date	Mintage	VF20	XF40	MS60	MS63	MS65
1998	Est. 5000	PF65 310				

KM# 35 1/2 SUVERENA

15.55 g., 0.9999 Gold 0.4999 oz. AGW **Subject:** Lipizzaner Stallion **Obv:** National arms above bridge, date below **Rev:** Horse rearing right, denomination below

Date	Mintage	VF20	XF40	MS60	MS63	MS65
1994	—	PF65 750				

KM# 48 1/2 SUVERENA

15.55 g., 0.9999 Gold 0.4999 oz. AGW **Subject:** English Hack **Obv:** National arms above bridge, date below **Rev:** Horse running left, denomination below

Date	Mintage	VF20	XF40	MS60	MS63	MS65
1995	Est. 2500	PF65 750				

KM# 73 1/2 SUVERENA

15.55 g., 0.9999 Gold 0.4999 oz. AGW **Subject:** Hanoverian Stallion **Obv:** National arms above bridge, date below **Rev:** Horse left, denomination below

Date	Mintage	VF20	XF40	MS60	MS63	MS65
1996	—	PF65 750				

KM# 92 1/2 SUVERENA

15.55 g., 0.9999 Gold 0.4999 oz. AGW **Subject:** The Arab **Obv:** National arms above bridge, date below **Rev:** Horse right, denomination below

Date	Mintage	VF20	XF40	MS60	MS63	MS65
1997	Est. 2500	PF65 750				

KM# 107 1/2 SUVERENA

15.55 g., 0.9999 Gold 0.4999 oz. AGW **Subject:** Chinese Horse **Obv:** National arms above bridge, date below **Rev:** Horse left, denomination below

Date	Mintage	VF20	XF40	MS60	MS63	MS65
1998	Est. 2500	PF65 750				

KM# 36 SUVERENA

Copper-Nickel **Subject:** Lipizzaner Stallion **Obv:** National arms above bridge, date below **Rev:** Horse rearing right, denomination below

Date	Mintage	VF20	XF40	MS60	MS63	MS65
1994	—	—	—	—	9.00	12.00

KM# 37 SUVERENA

31.10 g., 0.9999 Silver 0.9999 oz. ASW **Subject:** Lipizzaner Stallion **Obv:** National arms above bridge, date below **Rev:** Horse rearing right, denomination below

Date	Mintage	VF20	XF40	MS60	MS63	MS65
1994	—	PF65 40.00				

KM# 37a SUVERENA

31.10 g., 0.9999 Gold 0.9999 oz. AGW **Subject:** Lipizzaner Stallion **Obv:** National arms above bridge, date below **Rev:** Horse rearing right, denomination below

Date	Mintage	VF20	XF40	MS60	MS63	MS65
1994	—	PF65 1,600				

KM# 49 SUVERENA

Copper-Nickel **Subject:** English Hack **Obv:** National arms above bridge, date below **Rev:** Horse running left, denomination below

Date	Mintage	VF20	XF40	MS60	MS63	MS65
1995	—	—	—	—	7.50	9.50

KM# 50 SUVERENA

31.10 g., 0.9999 Silver 0.9999 oz. ASW **Subject:** English Hack **Obv:** National arms above bridge, date below **Rev:** Horse running left, denomination below

Date	Mintage	VF20	XF40	MS60	MS63	MS65
1995	—	PF65 40.00				

KM# 51 SUVERENA

31.10 g., 0.9999 Gold 0.9999 oz. AGW **Subject:** English Hack **Obv:** National arms above bridge, date below **Rev:** Horse running left, denomination below

Date	Mintage	VF20	XF40	MS60	MS63	MS65
1995	Est. 850	PF65 1,600				

KM# 74 SUVERENA

Copper-Nickel **Subject:** Hanoverian Stallion **Obv:** National arms above bridge, date below **Rev:** Horse left, denomination below

Date	Mintage	VF20	XF40	MS60	MS63	MS65
1996	—	—	—	—	7.50	9.50

KM# 75 SUVERENA

31.10 g., 0.9999 Silver 0.9999 oz. ASW **Subject:** Hanoverian Horse **Obv:** National arms above bridge, date below **Rev:** Horse left, denomination below

Date	Mintage	VF20	XF40	MS60	MS63	MS65
1996	Est. 30000	PF65 40.00				

KM# A76 SUVERENA

31.10 g., 0.9999 Gold 0.9999 oz. AGW **Subject:** Hanoverian Horse **Obv:** National arms above bridge, date below **Rev:** Horse left, denomination below

Date	Mintage	VF20	XF40	MS60	MS63	MS65
1996	850	PF65 1,600				

KM# 93 SUVERENA

Copper-Nickel **Subject:** The Arab **Obv:** National arms above bridge, date below **Rev:** Horse right, denomination below

Date	Mintage	VF20	XF40	MS60	MS63	MS65
1997	—	—	—	—	9.00	12.00

KM# 93a SUVERENA

31.10 g., 0.9999 Silver 0.9999 oz. ASW **Subject:** The Arab **Obv:** National arms above bridge, date below **Rev:** Horse right, denomination below

Date	Mintage	VF20	XF40	MS60	MS63	MS65
1997	—	PF65 40.00				

KM# 93b SUVERENA

31.10 g., 0.9999 Gold 0.9999 oz. AGW **Subject:** The Arab **Obv:** National arms above bridge, date below **Rev:** Horse right, denomination below

Date	Mintage	VF20	XF40	MS60	MS63	MS65
1997	850	PF65 1,600				

KM# 108 SUVERENA

Copper-Nickel **Subject:** Chinese Horse **Obv:** National arms above bridge, date below **Rev:** Horse left, denomination below

Date	Mintage	VF20	XF40	MS60	MS63	MS65
1998	—	—	—	—	9.00	12.00

KM# 108a SUVERENA

31.10 g., 0.9999 Silver 0.9999 oz. ASW **Subject:** Chinese Horse **Obv:** National arms above bridge, date below **Rev:** Horse left, denomination below

Date	Mintage	VF20	XF40	MS60	MS63	MS65
1998	—	PF65 40.00				

KM# 109 SUVERENA

31.10 g., 0.9999 Gold 0.9999 oz. AGW **Subject:** Chinese Horse **Obv:** National arms above bridge, date below **Rev:** Horse left, denomination below

Date	Mintage	VF20	XF40	MS60	MS63	MS65
1998	—	PF65 1,600				

KM# 82 14 ECUS

10.00 g., 0.925 Silver 0.2974 oz. ASW **Subject:** International Day of Peace **Obv:** National arms above bridge, date below **Rev:** Hands releasing bird of peace, symbol at center, denomination below

Date	Mintage	VF20	XF40	MS60	MS63	MS65
1993	Est. 20000	PF65 55.00				

KM# 83 14 ECUS

10.00 g., 0.925 Silver 0.2974 oz. ASW **Subject:** Peace - Teddy Bear **Obv:** National arms above bridge, date below **Rev:** Teddy bear above denomination

Date	Mintage	VF20	XF40	MS60	MS63	MS65
1994	20,000	PF65 50.00				

KM# 84 14 ECUS

10.10 g., 0.925 Silver 0.3004 oz. ASW **Subject:** Peace - Allegorical Europa **Obv:** National arms above bridge, date below **Rev:** Allegorical Europa, denomination below

Date	Mintage	VF20	XF40	MS60	MS63	MS65
1995	Est. 20000	PF65 50.00				

KM# 85 14 ECUS + 2 ECUS

9.97 g., 0.999 Silver 0.3202 oz. ASW **Subject:** War Relief Funding - Sarajevo Mosque **Obv:** National arms above bridge, date below **Rev:** Sarajevo Mosque, denomination below

Date	Mintage	VF20	XF40	MS60	MS63	MS65
1993	20,000	PF65 40.00				

KM# 86 21 ECUS + 3

15.56 g., 0.999 Silver 0.4998 oz. ASW **Subject:** War Relief Funding - Sarajevo Mosque

Date	Mintage	VF20	XF40	MS60	MS63	MS65
1993	Est. 15000	PF65 70.00				

KM# 87 70 ECUS + 10

6.22 g., 0.999 Gold 0.1998 oz. AGW **Subject:** War Relief Funding - Sarajevo Mosque **Obv:** National arms above bridge, date below **Rev:** Dove of Peace above Sarajevo Mosque

Date	Mintage	VF20	XF40	MS60	MS63	MS65
1993	Est. 5000	PF65 475				

KM# 88 14 EURO

10.00 g., 0.925 Silver 0.2974 oz. ASW **Subject:** Peace **Obv:** National arms above bridge, date below **Rev:** Rose and the word PEACE in many languages, denomination below

Date	Mintage	VF20	XF40	MS60	MS63	MS65
1996 PM	—	PF65 45.00				

KM# 110 14 EURO

10.00 g., 0.925 Silver 0.2974 oz. ASW **Subject:** Peace II **Obv:** National arms above bridge, date below **Rev:** Dove in flight with PEACE written in many different languages, denomination below

Date	Mintage	VF20	XF40	MS60	MS63	MS65
1998 PM	Est. 20000	PF65 50.00				

KM# 114 14 EURO
10.00 g., 0.925 Silver 0.2974 oz. ASW **Subject:** The Tree of Stability **Obv:** National arms above bridge, date below **Rev:** Woman planting oak tree, denomination below

Date	Mintage	VF20	XF40	MS60	MS63	MS65
1999 PM	Est. 20000	PF65 50.00				

REFORM COINAGE

1998-

KM# 115 10 FENINGA
3.90 g., Copper Plated Steel, 20 mm. **Obv:** Denomination on map within circle **Rev:** Triangle and stars, date at left within circle **Edge:** Plain

Date	Mintage	VF20	XF40	MS60	MS63	MS65
1998	30,000,000	—	—	0.25	0.50	0.75
2000 Sets only	10,000	—	—	—	—	2.00

KM# 116 20 FENINGA
4.50 g., Copper Plated Steel, 22 mm. **Obv:** Denomination on map within circle **Rev:** Triangle and stars, date at left within circle **Edge:** Reeded

Date	Mintage	VF20	XF40	MS60	MS63	MS65
1998	20,000,000	—	—	0.50	0.75	1.00
2000 Sets only	10,000	—	—	—	—	2.50

KM# 117 50 FENINGA
5.15 g., Copper Plated Steel, 24 mm. **Obv:** Denomination on map within circle **Rev:** Triangle and stars, date at left within circle

Date	Mintage	VF20	XF40	MS60	MS63	MS65
1998	20,000,000	—	—	1.00	1.50	2.00
2000 Sets only	10,000	—	—	—	—	4.00

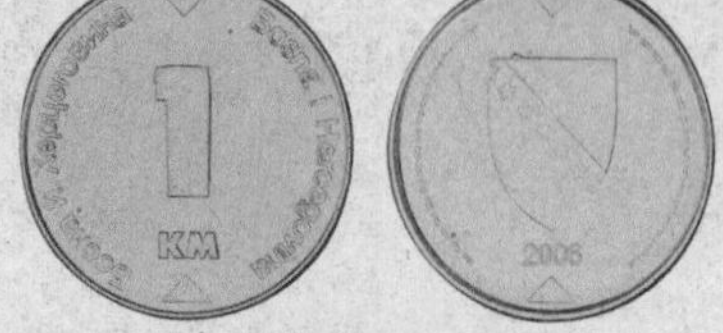

KM# 118 KONVERTIBLE MARKA
4.95 g., Nickel Plated Steel, 23.23 mm. **Obv:** Denomination **Rev:** Coat of arms above date **Edge:** Segmented reeding

Date	Mintage	VF20	XF40	MS60	MS63	MS65
2000	10,000,000	—	—	2.00	4.00	5.00

KM# 119 2 KONVERTIBLE MARKA
6.90 g., Bi-Metallic Copper-Nickel center in Nickel-Brass ring, 25.75 mm. **Obv:** Denomination within circle **Rev:** Dove of Peace, date at right within circle **Edge:** Segmented reeding

Date	Mintage	VF20	XF40	MS60	MS63	MS65
2000	5,000,000	—	—	2.50	4.50	6.00

MINT SETS

KM#	Date	Mintage	Identification	Issue Price	Mkt Val
MS1	2000 (5)	—	KM#115, 116, 117, 118, 119	20.00	27.50

PROOF SETS

KM#	Date	Mintage	Identification	Issue Price	Mkt Val
PS1	1996 (5)	500	KM#70-73, A76	—	3,350

BOTSWANA

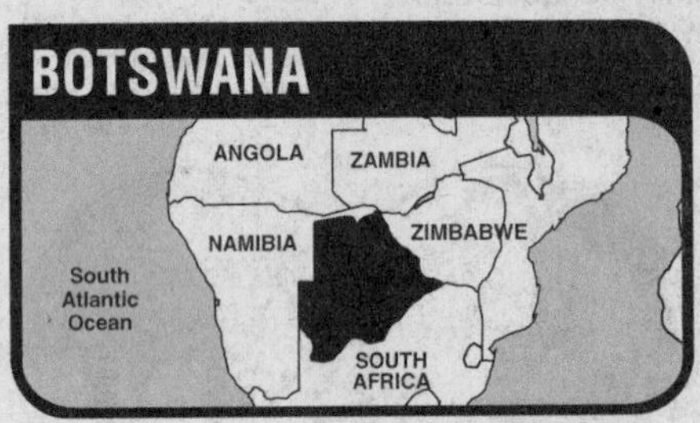

The Republic of Botswana (formerly Bechuanaland), located in south central Africa between Namibia and Zimbabwe, has an area of 224,607 sq. mi. (600,370 sq. km.) and a population of *1.62 million. Capital: Gaborone. Botswana is a member of a Customs Union with South Africa, Lesotho, and Swaziland. The economy is primarily pastoral with a rapidly developing mining industry, of which diamonds, copper and nickel are the chief elements. Meat products and diamonds comprise 85 percent of the exports.

Little is known of the origin of the peoples of Botswana. The early inhabitants, the Bushmen, did not develop a recorded history and are now dying out. The ancestors of the present Botswana residents probably arrived about 1600AD in Bantu migrations from the north and east. Bechuanaland was first united early in the 19th century under Chief Khama III to more effectively resist incursions by the Boer trekkers from Transvaal and by the neighboring Matabeles. As the Boer threat intensified, appeals for protection were made to the British Government, which proclaimed the whole of Bechuanaland a British protectorate in 1885. In 1895, the southern part of the protectorate was annexed to Cape Province. The northern part, known as the Bechuanaland Protectorate, remained under British administration until it became the independent Republic of Botswana on Sept. 30, 1966. Botswana is a member of the Commonwealth of Nations. The president is Chief of State and Head of government.

MINT MARK
B - Berne

MONETARY SYSTEM
100 Cents = 1 Thebe

REPUBLIC

STANDARD COINAGE

KM# 1 50 CENTS
10.00 g., 0.800 Silver 0.2572 oz. ASW, 27 mm. **Subject:** Independence Commemorative **Obv:** National arms with supporters, denomination below **Rev:** Sir Seretse Khama left

Date	Mintage	VF20	XF40	MS60	MS63	MS65
ND-1966 B	40,000	—	5.00	9.00	12.00	15.00
ND-1966 B	10,000	PF63 18.00	PF65 22.00			

KM# 2 10 THEBE
11.29 g., 0.900 Gold 0.3267 oz. AGW **Subject:** Independence Commemorative **Obv:** National arms with supporters, denomination below **Rev:** Sir Seretse Khama left

Date	Mintage	VF20	XF40	MS60	MS63	MS65
ND-1966 B	5,100	—	—	—	600	650

REFORM COINAGE

100 Thebe = 1 Pula

KM# 3 THEBE
0.80 g., Aluminum, 18.5 mm. **Obv:** National arms, date below **Rev:** Head of Turako, denomination upper right **Edge:** Reeded

Date	Mintage	VF20	XF40	MS60	MS63	MS65
1976	15,000,000	—	0.10	0.20	0.45	0.75
1976	26,000	PF65 0.75				
1981	10,000	PF65 1.00				
1983	5,000,000	—	0.10	0.20	0.45	1.00
1984	5,000,000	—	0.10	0.20	0.45	1.00
1985	—	—	0.10	0.20	0.45	1.00
1987	—	—	0.10	0.20	0.40	1.00
1988	—	—	0.10	0.20	0.40	1.00
1989	—	—	0.10	0.20	0.40	1.00
1991	—	—	0.10	0.20	0.40	1.00

KM# 14 2 THEBE
1.80 g., Bronze, 17.4 mm. **Subject:** World Food Day **Obv:** National arms above date **Rev:** Millet, denomination at top **Shape:** 12-sided

Date	Mintage	VF20	XF40	MS60	MS63	MS65
1981	9,990,000	—	0.15	0.25	0.50	1.00
1981	10,000	PF65 1.00				
1985	—	—	0.15	0.25	0.50	1.00

KM# 4 5 THEBE
2.66 g., Bronze, 19.5 mm. **Obv:** National arms above date **Rev:** Toko left, value above **Edge:** Reeded

Date	Mintage	VF20	XF40	MS60	MS63	MS65
1976	3,000,000	—	0.15	0.25	0.50	1.00
1976	26,000	PF65 1.25				
1977	250,000	—	0.15	0.25	0.50	1.00
1979	200,000	—	0.15	0.25	0.50	1.00
1980	1,000,000	—	0.15	0.25	0.50	1.00
1981	4,990,000	—	0.15	0.25	0.50	1.00
1981	10,000	PF65 1.50				
1984	2,000,000	—	0.15	0.25	0.50	1.00
1985	—	—	0.15	0.25	0.50	1.00
1988	—	—	0.15	0.25	0.50	1.00
1989	—	—	0.15	0.25	0.50	1.00

KM# 4a.1 5 THEBE
Copper Plated Steel, 19.5 mm. **Obv:** National arms above date **Rev:** Toko left, value above **Edge:** Plain

Date	Mintage	VF20	XF40	MS60	MS63	MS65
1991	—	—	0.15	0.25	0.50	1.00

KM# 4a.2 5 THEBE
Copper Plated Steel, 19.5 mm. **Obv:** National arms above date **Rev:** Toko left, value above **Edge:** Reeded **Note:** Modified design.

Date	Mintage	VF20	XF40	MS60	MS63	MS65
1996	—	—	0.15	0.25	0.50	1.00

KM# 26 5 THEBE
2.41 g., Copper Plated Steel, 16.9 mm. **Obv:** National arms, date below **Rev:** Toko bird left, value above **Edge:** Plain **Shape:** 7-sided

Date	Mintage	VF20	XF40	MS60	MS63	MS65
1998	—	—	—	0.25	0.50	1.00

KM# 5 10 THEBE
4.00 g., Copper-Nickel, 22 mm. **Obv:** National arms above date **Rev:** South African Oryx right, value above **Edge:** Reeded

Date	Mintage	VF20	XF40	MS60	MS63	MS65
1976	1,500,000	—	0.25	0.40	0.75	1.25
1976	26,000	PF65 1.50				
1977	500,000	—	0.25	0.40	0.75	1.25
1979	750,000	—	0.25	0.40	0.75	1.25
1980	—	—	0.25	0.40	0.75	1.25
1981	2,590,000	—	0.25	0.40	0.75	1.25
1981	10,000	PF65 1.75				
1984	4,000,000	—	0.20	0.30	0.60	1.00
1985	—	—	0.20	0.30	0.60	1.00
1989	—	—	0.20	0.30	0.60	1.00

KM# 5a 10 THEBE
3.80 g., Nickel Plated Steel; 22 mm. **Obv:** National arms above date **Rev:** South African Oryx right, value above **Edge:** Reeded

Date	Mintage	VF20	XF40	MS60	MS63	MS65
1991	—	—	0.20	0.30	0.60	1.00

KM# 27 10 THEBE
2.80 g., Nickel Plated Steel, 18 mm. **Obv:** National arms above date **Rev:** South African Oryx right, value above

Date	Mintage	VF20	XF40	MS60	MS63	MS65
1998	—	—	—	0.35	0.75	1.25

KM# 6 25 THEBE
5.80 g., Copper-Nickel, 25 mm. **Obv:** National arms, date below **Rev:** Zebu left, value above **Edge:** Reeded

Date	Mintage	VF20	XF40	MS60	MS63	MS65
1976	1,500,000	—	0.25	0.55	1.50	2.00
1976	26,000	PF65 2.50				
1977	265,000	—	0.25	0.60	1.75	2.25
1981	740,000	—	0.25	0.60	1.50	2.00
1981	10,000	PF65 2.50				
1982	400,000	—	0.25	0.60	1.75	2.25
1984	2,000,000	—	0.25	0.55	1.50	2.00
1985	—	—	0.30	0.60	1.50	2.00
1989	—	—	0.30	0.60	1.50	2.00

KM# 6a 25 THEBE
Nickel Plated Steel, 25 mm. **Obv:** National arms, date below **Rev:** Zebu left, value above

Date	Mintage	VF20	XF40	MS60	MS63	MS65
1991	—	—	0.30	0.60	1.50	2.00

KM# 28 25 THEBE
3.50 g., Nickel Plated Steel, 21 mm. **Obv:** National arms, date below **Rev:** Zebu left, value above **Shape:** 7-sided

Date	Mintage	VF20	XF40	MS60	MS63	MS65
1998	—	—	0.30	0.60	1.50	2.00
1999	—	—	0.30	0.60	1.50	2.00

KM# 7 50 THEBE
11.30 g., Copper-Nickel, 28.5 mm. **Obv:** National arms, date below **Rev:** African Fish Eagle left, value above

Date	Mintage	VF20	XF40	MS60	MS63	MS65
1976	266,000	—	0.65	1.35	2.25	2.75
1976	26,000	PF65 3.00				
1977	250,000	—	0.65	1.35	2.25	2.75
1980	—	—	0.65	1.35	2.25	2.75
1981	10,000	PF65 3.50				
1984	2,000,000	—	0.65	1.35	2.25	2.75
1985	—	—	0.65	1.35	2.25	2.75

KM# 7a 50 THEBE
11.17 g., Nickel Plated Steel, 28.5 mm. **Obv:** National arms, date below **Rev:** African Fish Eagle left, value above

Date	Mintage	VF20	XF40	MS60	MS63	MS65
1991	—	—	0.65	1.35	2.25	2.75

KM# 29 50 THEBE
4.82 g., Nickel Plated Steel, 21.5 mm. **Obv:** National arms, date below **Rev:** African Fish Eagle left, value above

Date	Mintage	VF20	XF40	MS60	MS63	MS65
1996	—	—	0.50	1.00	2.00	2.50
1998	—	—	0.50	1.00	2.00	2.50

KM# 8 PULA
16.40 g., Copper-Nickel, 29.5 mm. **Obv:** National arms, date below **Rev:** Zebra left, denomination above **Shape:** Scalloped

Date	Mintage	VF20	XF40	MS60	MS63	MS65
1976	166,000	—	1.50	2.50	5.00	7.50
1976	26,000	PF65 7.00				
1977	500,000	—	1.50	2.50	5.00	7.50
1981	—	—	1.50	2.50	5.00	7.50
1981	10,000	PF65 7.50				
1985	—	—	1.50	2.50	5.00	7.50
1987	—	—	1.50	2.50	5.00	7.50

KM# 24 PULA
8.70 g., Nickel-Brass, 23.5 mm. **Obv:** National arms, date below **Rev:** Zebra left, denomination above **Shape:** 7-sided

Date	Mintage	VF20	XF40	MS60	MS63	MS65
1991	—	—	1.00	1.75	3.50	6.00
1997	—	—	1.00	1.75	3.50	6.00

KM# 17 2 PULA
28.28 g., 0.500 Silver 0.4546 oz. ASW, 38.61 mm. **Subject:** Commonwealth Games **Obv:** National arms, date below **Rev:** Sprinter with flag, denomination below

Date	Mintage	VF20	XF40	MS60	MS63	MS65
1986	Est. 50000	—	—	—	12.50	15.00

KM# 17a 2 PULA
28.28 g., 0.925 Silver 0.841 oz. ASW **Obv:** National arms, date below **Rev:** Sprinter with flag, denomination below

Date	Mintage	VF20	XF40	MS60	MS63	MS65
1986	Est. 20000	PF65 25.00				

KM# 18 2 PULA
28.28 g., 0.925 Silver 0.841 oz. ASW **Subject:** Wildlife **Obv:** National arms, date below **Rev:** Slaty Egret, egretta vinaceiguia

Date	Mintage	VF20	XF40	MS60	MS63	MS65
1986	Est. 25000	PF65 32.50				

KM# 22 2 PULA
28.28 g., 0.925 Silver 0.841 oz. ASW **Subject:** Save The Children Fund **Obv:** National arms, date below **Rev:** Child milking goat, denomination below

Date	Mintage	VF20	XF40	MS60	MS63	MS65
1989	Est. 20000	PF65 35.00				

KM# 25 2 PULA
6.03 g., Nickel-Brass **Subject:** Wildlife **Obv:** National arms, date below **Rev:** Rhinoceros left, denomination above **Shape:** 7-sided

Date	Mintage	VF20	XF40	MS60	MS63	MS65
1994	—	—	1.25	2.50	5.00	7.00

KM# 9 5 PULA
28.28 g., 0.500 Silver 0.4546 oz. ASW **Subject:** 10th Anniversary of Independence **Obv:** Bust left **Rev:** National Assembly Building, denomination above

Date	Mintage	VF20	XF40	MS60	MS63	MS65
ND-1976	31,000	—	—	—	17.00	20.00

KM# 9a 5 PULA
28.28 g., 0.925 Silver 0.841 oz. ASW **Obv:** Bust left **Rev:** Buildings and flag, denomination above

Date	Mintage	VF20	XF40	MS60	MS63	MS65
ND-1976	22,000	PF65 32.50				

KM# 11 5 PULA

28.50 g., 0.500 Silver 0.4581 oz. ASW **Subject:** Wildlife **Obv:** National arms, date below **Rev:** Gemsbok left, denomination above

Date	Mintage	VF20	XF40	MS60	MS63	MS65
1978	4,026	—	—	—	22.00	25.00

KM# 11a 5 PULA

28.50 g., 0.925 Silver 0.8476 oz. ASW **Obv:** National arms, date below **Rev:** Gemsbok left, denomination below

Date	Mintage	VF20	XF40	MS60	MS63	MS65
1978	4,172	PF65 35.00				

KM# 15 5 PULA

28.50 g., 0.925 Silver 0.8476 oz. ASW **Subject:** International Year of Disabled Persons **Obv:** National arms, date below **Rev:** Figures at table, hut in background, denomination lower left

Date	Mintage	VF20	XF40	MS60	MS63	MS65
1981	13,000	—	—	—	27.00	30.00
1981	11,000	PF65 32.00				

KM# 19 5 PULA

15.98 g., 0.917 Gold 0.4711 oz. AGW **Subject:** Wildlife **Obv:** National arms, date below **Rev:** Red Lechwes (kobus leche leche) right, denomination above left

Date	Mintage	VF20	XF40	MS60	MS63	MS65
1986	Est. 5000	PF63 650	PF65 725			

KM# 20 5 PULA

Copper-Nickel **Subject:** Pope's Visit **Obv:** National arms, date below **Rev:** Bust left, denomination above

Date	Mintage	VF20	XF40	MS60	MS63	MS65
1988	Est. 50000	—	—	—	7.50	10.00

KM# 20a 5 PULA

28.28 g., 0.925 Silver 0.841 oz. ASW **Obv:** National arms, date below **Rev:** Bust left

Date	Mintage	VF20	XF40	MS60	MS63	MS65
1988	Est. 5000	PF65 40.00				

KM# 21 5 PULA

28.28 g., 0.925 Silver 0.841 oz. ASW **Subject:** 1988 Summer Olympics **Obv:** National arms, date below **Rev:** Runners

Date	Mintage	VF20	XF40	MS60	MS63	MS65
1988	25,000	PF65 30.00				

Note: A copper-nickel strike variety of this coin does not exist

KM# 23 5 PULA

10.00 g., 0.917 Gold 0.2948 oz. AGW **Subject:** Save the Children Fund **Obv:** National arms, date below **Rev:** Woman with child left, denomination on left

Date	Mintage	VF20	XF40	MS60	MS63	MS65
1989	—	PF63 400	PF65 450			

KM# 30 5 PULA

6.20 g., Bi-Metallic Copper-Nickel center in Brass ring, 23.4 mm. **Obv:** National arms, date below **Rev:** Mophane worm on a mophane leaf, denomination below within circle **Edge:** Reeded

Date	Mintage	VF20	XF40	MS60	MS63	MS65
2000	—	—	—	—	6.00	9.00

KM# 12 10 PULA

35.00 g., 0.500 Silver 0.5626 oz. ASW **Subject:** Wildlife **Obv:** National arms, date below **Rev:** Klipspringer left, denomination above

Date	Mintage	VF20	XF40	MS60	MS63	MS65
1978	4,088	—	—	—	32.00	37.00

KM# 12a 10 PULA

35.00 g., 0.925 Silver 1.0409 oz. ASW **Obv:** National arms, date below **Rev:** Klipspringer left, denomination above

Date	Mintage	VF20	XF40	MS60	MS63	MS65
1978	3,989	PF65 45.00				

KM# 10 150 PULA

15.98 g., 0.917 Gold 0.4711 oz. AGW **Subject:** 10th Anniversary of Independence **Obv:** National arms, date below **Rev:** Bust left

Date	Mintage	VF20	XF40	MS60	MS63	MS65
ND-1976	2,520	—	—	—	675	700
ND-1976	2,000	PF63 750	PF65 775			

KM# 13 150 PULA

33.44 g., 0.900 Gold 0.9675 oz. AGW **Subject:** Wildlife **Obv:** National arms, date below **Rev:** Brown Hyena facing, denomination above left

Date	Mintage	VF20	XF40	MS60	MS63	MS65
1978	664	—	—	—	1,450	1,550
1978	219	PF63 1,750	PF65 1,900			

KM# 16 150 PULA

15.98 g., 0.917 Gold 0.4711 oz. AGW **Subject:** International Year of Disabled Persons **Obv:** National arms, date below **Rev:** Figures with box, denomination lower right

Date	Mintage	VF20	XF40	MS60	MS63	MS65
1981	4,158	—	—	—	650	675
1981	4,155	PF63 700	PF65 750			

PIEDFORT

KM#	Date	Mintage	Identification	Mkt Val
P1	1981	1,000	5 Pula. Silver. KM#15.	80.00
P2	1981	510	150 Pula. Gold. KM#16.	1,800

MINT SETS

KM#	Date	Mintage	Identification	Issue Price	Mkt Val
MS1	1978 (2)	—	KM#11, 12	—	65.00

PROOF SETS

KM#	Date	Mintage	Identification	Issue Price	Mkt Val
PS1	1976 (6)	20,000	KM#3-8	18.00	17.50
PS2	1978 (2)	—	KM#11a, 12a	—	75.00
PS3	1981 (7)	10,000	KM#3-8, 14	33.00	20.00

The Federative Republic of Brazil, which comprises half the continent of South America and is the only Latin American country deriving its culture and language from Portugal, has an area of 3,286,488 sq. mi. (8,511,965 sq. km.) and a population of *169.2 million. Capital: Brasilia. The economy of Brazil is as varied and complex as any in the developing world. Agriculture is a mainstay of the economy, while only 4 percent of the area is under cultivation. Known mineral resources are almost unlimited in variety and size of reserves. A large, relatively sophisticated industry ranges from basic steel and chemical production to finished consumer goods. Coffee, cotton, iron ore and cocoa are the chief exports.

Brazil was discovered and claimed for Portugal by Admiral Pedro Alvares Cabral in 1500. Portugal established a settlement in 1532 and proclaimed the area a royal colony in 1549. During the Napoleonic Wars, Dom Joao VI established the seat of Portuguese government in Rio de Janeiro. When he returned to Portugal, his son Dom Pedro I declared Brazil's independence on Sept. 7, 1822, and became emperor of Brazil. The Empire of Brazil was maintained until 1889 when the federal republic was established. The Federative Republic was established in 1946 by terms of a constitution drawn up by a constituent assembly. Following a coup in 1964 the armed forces retained overall control under a dictatorship until civilian government was restored on March 15, 1985. The current constitution was adopted in 1988.

MINT MARKS

(a) - Paris, privy marks only
A - Berlin 1913
B - Bahia

MONETARY SYSTEM

(1833-1942)
1000 Reis = 1 Mil Reis
(1942-1967)
100 Centavos = 1 Cruzeiro

REPUBLIC

FIRST COINAGE - REIS

1889-1942

KM# 490 20 REIS

7.49 g., Bronze, 25 mm. **Obv:** Star with wreath in background **Rev:** Denomination

Date	Mintage	VF20	XF40	MS60	MS63	MS65
1901	713,000	5.00	10.00	18.00	22.00	35.00
1904	850,000	5.00	10.00	18.00	22.00	35.00
1905	1,075,000	8.00	17.00	35.00	50.00	65.00
1906	215,000	6.00	14.00	30.00	40.00	50.00
1908	4,558,000	5.00	10.00	18.00	22.00	35.00
1909	1,215,000	12.00	27.50	55.00	75.00	125
1910	828,000	5.00	10.00	18.00	22.00	35.00
1911	1,545,000	5.00	10.00	18.00	22.00	35.00
1912	480,000	5.00	10.00	18.00	22.00	35.00

KM# 516.1 20 REIS

Copper-Nickel, 15 mm. **Rev:** No dot between "2" and "0" in denomination

Date	Mintage	VF20	XF40	MS60	MS63	MS65
1918	—	0.50	1.00	3.50	4.50	7.50
1919	—	0.50	1.00	3.50	4.50	7.50
1920	—	0.50	1.25	4.00	6.00	8.00

KM# 516.2 20 REIS

Copper-Nickel, 15 mm. **Obv:** Denomination at center, dot between "2" and "0" in denomination **Rev:** Bust with cap, right, within 3/4 circle of stars

Date	Mintage	VF20	XF40	MS60	MS63	MS65
1918	—	0.50	1.00	2.00	3.00	5.00
1919	2,870,000	0.50	1.00	2.00	3.00	5.00
1920	825,000	0.75	1.25	2.50	5.00	7.50
1921	1,020,000	0.50	1.25	2.50	5.00	7.50
1927	53,000	10.00	25.00	50.00	80.00	100
1935	100	450	750	1,000	1,250	1,450

KM# 491 40 REIS

Bronze, 30 mm. **Obv:** Stars at center surrounded by circle of stars **Rev:** Denomination within circle

Date	Mintage	VF20	XF40	MS60	MS63	MS65
1901	525,000	2.50	4.00	12.00	20.00	30.00
1907	218,000	2.50	4.00	12.00	20.00	30.00
1908	4,639,000	2.50	4.00	12.00	20.00	30.00
1909	4,226,000	2.50	4.00	20.00	22.00	35.00
1910	848,000	2.50	5.00	20.00	25.00	45.00
1911	1,660,000	2.50	5.00	20.00	25.00	45.00
1912	819,000	3.00	6.00	22.00	27.00	48.00

KM# 517 50 REIS

3.08 g., Copper-Nickel, 17.3 mm. **Obv:** Denomination within circle, date flanked by stars below **Rev:** Liberty head right

Date	Mintage	VF20	XF40	MS60	MS63	MS65
1918	558,000	0.50	1.50	4.00	7.00	10.00
1919	558,000	0.50	1.50	4.00	7.00	10.00
1920	72,000	2.00	4.00	9.00	16.00	25.00
1921	682,000	0.50	1.50	4.00	7.00	10.00
1922	176,000	1.50	4.00	9.00	16.00	25.00
1925	128,000	1.50	4.00	12.00	20.00	35.00
1926	194,000	1.50	4.00	12.00	20.00	35.00
1931	20,000	12.00	35.00	65.00	85.00	125
1935	100	300	700	900	1,200	1,600

KM# 503 100 REIS

5.00 g., Copper-Nickel, 20.96 mm. **Obv:** National arms, denomination above **Rev:** Liberty bust right **Note:** Roman numeral date.

Date	Mintage	VF20	XF40	MS60	MS63	MS65
1901	15,775,000	1.50	3.25	10.00	12.00	20.00

KM# 518 100 REIS

4.95 g., Copper-Nickel, 21.3 mm. **Obv:** Denomination within circle, date below **Rev:** Liberty bust right

Date	Mintage	VF20	XF40	MS60	MS63	MS65
1918	600,000	1.50	3.25	12.00	15.00	25.00
1919	1,219,000	1.50	3.25	12.00	15.00	25.00
1920	1,251,000	1.50	3.25	12.00	15.00	25.00
1921	853,000	1.50	3.25	12.00	15.00	25.00
1922	347,000	2.00	5.00	13.00	16.00	27.00
1923	956,000	1.50	4.75	13.00	16.00	27.00
1924	1,478,000	2.50	6.50	18.00	25.00	35.00
1925	2,502,000	1.25	2.75	12.00	15.00	25.00
1926	1,807,000	1.50	4.75	20.00	35.00	—
1927	1,451,000	1.25	2.75	12.00	15.00	25.00
1928	1,514,000	1.25	2.75	12.00	15.00	25.00
1929	2,503,000	1.25	2.75	12.00	15.00	25.00
1930	2,398,000	1.25	2.75	12.00	15.00	25.00
1931	2,500,000	1.00	2.25	12.00	15.00	25.00
1932	948,000	1.00	2.25	12.00	15.00	25.00
1933	1,314,000	1.00	2.25	12.00	15.00	25.00
1934	3,614,000	1.00	2.25	12.00	15.00	25.00
1935	3,442,000	1.00	2.25	12.00	15.00	25.00

KM# 527 100 REIS

Copper-Nickel, 21 mm. **Subject:** 400th Anniversary of Colonization **Obv:** Cazique Tibirica **Rev:** Denomination below design **Edge:** Reeded **Note:** Medal rotation.

Date	Mintage	VF20	XF40	MS60	MS63	MS65
ND-1932	1,012,000	1.00	2.25	3.50	4.50	7.50

KM# 536 100 REIS

4.62 g., Copper-Nickel, 19 mm. **Obv:** Anchor divides denomination **Rev:** Admiral Marques Tamandare, founder of Brazilian Navy **Edge:** Plain **Note:** Medal rotation.

Date	Mintage	VF20	XF40	MS60	MS63	MS65
1936	3,928,000	0.50	1.00	1.50	2.50	4.00
1937	7,905,000	0.40	0.75	1.25	2.00	3.50
1938	8,618,000	0.40	0.75	1.25	2.00	3.50

KM# 544 100 REIS

2.53 g., Copper-Nickel, 16.87 mm. **Obv:** Denomination within wreath **Rev:** Dr. Getulio Vargas **Edge:** Fluted **Shape:** 16-sided

Date	Mintage	VF20	XF40	MS60	MS63	MS65
1938	8,106,000	0.40	0.75	1.25	2.00	3.50
1940	8,797,000	0.40	0.75	1.25	2.00	3.00
1942	1,285,000	0.75	1.25	1.75	2.75	4.50

Note: The 1942 issue has a deeper yellow cast due to higher copper content

KM# 504 200 REIS

8.02 g., Copper-Nickel, 25 mm. **Obv:** National arms, denomination above **Rev:** Liberty bust right **Edge:** Plain **Note:** Roman numeral date.

Date	Mintage	VF20	XF40	MS60	MS63	MS65
1901	12,625,000	1.00	6.00	12.00	15.00	25.00

KM# 519 200 REIS
7.80 g., Copper-Nickel, 25 mm. **Obv:** Denomination within circle, date below **Rev:** Liberty bust right

Date	Mintage	VF20	XF40	MS60	MS63	MS65
1918	625,000	1.25	2.50	5.00	10.00	18.00
1919	882,000	1.25	2.50	5.00	10.00	18.00
1920	1,657,000	1.00	2.00	5.00	10.00	18.00
1921	1,135,000	1.00	2.00	5.00	10.00	18.00
1922	678,000	1.25	2.50	5.00	10.00	18.00
1923	1,655,000	1.00	2.00	5.00	10.00	18.00
1924	1,750,000	1.00	2.00	5.00	10.00	18.00
1925	2,081,999	1.00	2.00	5.00	10.00	18.00
1926	324,000	3.00	7.00	12.00	22.00	32.00
1927	1,806,000	1.00	2.00	5.00	10.00	18.00
1928	782,000	1.00	2.00	5.00	10.00	18.00
1929	2,440,000	1.00	2.00	5.00	10.00	18.00
1930	1,697,000	1.00	2.00	5.00	10.00	18.00
1931	1,830,000	1.00	2.00	5.00	10.00	18.00
1932	761,000	1.25	2.50	5.00	10.00	18.00
1933	173,000	2.50	3.50	10.00	20.00	35.00
1934	612,000	1.25	2.50	8.00	12.00	22.00
1935	1,329,000	1.00	2.00	8.00	12.00	22.00

KM# 528 200 REIS
7.93 g., Copper-Nickel, 25 mm. **Subject:** 400th Anniversary of Colonization **Obv:** Globe with sash **Rev:** Ship, denomination below, two dates divided at top **Note:** Medal rotation.

Date	Mintage	VF20	XF40	MS60	MS63	MS65
ND-1932	596,000	1.75	3.50	10.00	14.50	17.50

KM# 537 200 REIS
6.00 g., Copper-Nickel, 23 mm. **Obv:** Steam engine, date above, denomination below **Rev:** Viscount de Maua, railway builder facing **Edge:** Plain **Note:** Medal rotation.

Date	Mintage	VF20	XF40	MS60	MS63	MS65
1936	2,256,000	0.75	2.00	4.00	6.50	10.00
1937	6,506,000	0.75	2.00	4.00	6.50	10.00
1938	5,787,000	0.75	2.00	4.00	6.50	10.00

KM# 545 200 REIS
3.44 g., Copper-Nickel, 18.8 mm. **Obv:** Denomination, date below, within wreath **Rev:** Dr. Getulio Vargas left **Edge:** Fluted **Shape:** 18-sided

Date	Mintage	VF20	XF40	MS60	MS63	MS65
1938	7,666,000	0.50	0.85	1.25	2.50	4.00
1940	10,161,000	0.40	0.60	1.00	2.00	3.50
1942	1,966,000	0.60	1.00	1.50	2.75	4.50

Note: The 1942 issue has a yellow cast due to higher copper content

KM# 538 300 REIS
8.00 g., Copper-Nickel, 25.2 mm. **Obv:** Harp divides denomination, date above **Rev:** Composer Antonio Carlos Gomes facing **Edge:** Plain **Note:** Medal rotation.

Date	Mintage	VF20	XF40	MS60	MS63	MS65
1936	3,029,000	1.25	3.50	5.00	8.00	12.50
1937	4,507,000	1.25	3.50	5.00	8.00	12.50
1938	3,753,000	1.25	3.50	5.00	8.00	12.50

KM# 546 300 REIS
4.40 g., Copper-Nickel, 20.8 mm. **Obv:** Denomination above date within wreath **Rev:** Dr. Getulio Vargas left **Edge:** Fluted **Shape:** 20-sided

Date	Mintage	VF20	XF40	MS60	MS63	MS65
1938	12,080,000	0.35	0.50	1.00	2.00	3.50
1940	8,124,000	0.35	0.50	1.00	2.00	3.50
1942	2,020,000	0.40	0.75	1.50	3.00	5.00

Note: The 1942 issue has a yellow cast due to higher copper content

KM# 505 400 REIS
11.73 g., Copper-Nickel, 30 mm. **Obv:** National arms, denomination above **Rev:** Liberty bust right, circle of stars surround **Edge:** Plain

Date	Mintage	VF20	XF40	MS60	MS63	MS65
MCMI (1901)	5,531,000	3.00	6.00	15.00	22.00	35.00

KM# 515 400 REIS
Copper-Nickel, 30 mm. **Obv:** National arms, denomination above within circle, date below **Rev:** Liberty bust left

Date	Mintage	VF20	XF40	MS60	MS63	MS65
1914	646,000	32.00	55.00	100	135	175

Note: This is considered a pattern by many authorities

KM# 520 400 REIS
11.70 g., Copper-Nickel, 30.2 mm. **Obv:** Denomination within circle, date below **Rev:** Liberty bust right

Date	Mintage	VF20	XF40	MS60	MS63	MS65
1918	491,000	2.00	4.00	7.00	12.00	20.00
1919	891,000	2.00	4.00	7.00	12.00	20.00
1920	1,521,000	2.00	4.00	7.00	12.00	20.00
1921	871,000	1.75	4.00	7.00	12.00	20.00
1922	1,275,000	1.75	4.00	7.00	12.00	20.00
1923	764,000	1.75	4.00	7.00	12.00	20.00
1925	2,048,000	1.75	4.00	7.00	12.00	20.00
1926	1,034,000	1.75	4.00	7.00	12.00	20.00
1927	738,000	1.75	4.00	7.00	12.00	20.00
1929	869,000	1.75	4.00	7.00	12.00	20.00
1930	1,030,999	1.75	4.00	7.00	12.00	20.00
1931	1,431,000	1.75	4.00	7.00	12.00	20.00
1932	588,000	1.75	4.00	7.00	12.00	20.00
1935	225,000	1.75	4.00	7.00	12.00	20.00

KM# 529 400 REIS
Copper-Nickel, 30 mm. **Subject:** 400th Anniversary of Colonization **Obv:** Map divides dates within circle **Rev:** Lusinian Cross **Note:** Medal rotation.

Date	Mintage	VF20	XF40	MS60	MS63	MS65
ND-1932	416,000	2.00	5.00	8.00	15.00	22.00

KM# 539 400 REIS
10.08 g., Copper-Nickel, 28.1 mm. **Obv:** Oil lamp, date above, denomination below **Rev:** Bust of Oswaldo Cruz, Microbiologist, 3/4 left **Note:** Medal rotation.

Date	Mintage	VF20	XF40	MS60	MS63	MS65
1936	2,079,000	1.00	1.75	3.00	5.00	8.00
1937	3,111,000	1.00	1.75	3.00	5.00	8.00
1938	2,681,000	1.00	1.75	3.00	5.00	8.00

KM# 547 400 REIS
5.44 g., Copper-Nickel, 23 mm. **Obv:** Denomination above date within wreath **Rev:** Bust of Dr. Getulio Vargas left **Edge:** Fluted **Shape:** 22-sided

Date	Mintage	VF20	XF40	MS60	MS63	MS65
1938	10,620,000	0.50	0.75	1.25	2.25	3.50
1940	7,312,000	0.50	0.75	1.25	2.25	3.50
1942	1,496,000	0.75	1.00	1.50	3.25	5.00

Note: The 1942 issue has a yellow cast due to higher copper content

KM# 506 500 REIS
5.00 g., 0.900 Silver 0.1447 oz. ASW, 22 mm. **Obv:** Liberty bust left, date below **Rev:** Denomination at center **Edge:** Reeded

Date	Mintage	VF20	XF40	MS60	MS63	MS65
1906	352,000	5.25	7.00	10.00	16.00	25.00
1907	1,282,000	5.25	7.00	10.00	16.00	25.00
1908	498,000	5.25	7.00	10.00	16.00	25.00
1911	8,000	70.00	120	275	450	—
1912	Est. 222000	60.00	90.00	200	325	—

KM# 509 500 REIS
5.00 g., 0.900 Silver 0.1447 oz. ASW, 22 mm. **Obv:** Liberty bust right within circle, date below **Rev:** Denomination within wreath, arms above

Date	Mintage	VF20	XF40	MS60	MS63	MS65
1912	—	7.50	14.00	20.00	28.00	45.00

KM# 512 500 REIS
5.00 g., 0.900 Silver 0.1447 oz. ASW, 22 mm. **Obv:** Liberty bust right within circle of stars, date below **Rev:** Denomination within wreath, arms above **Edge:** Reeded

Date	Mintage	VF20	XF40	MS60	MS63	MS65
1913 A	—	5.25	7.00	12.00	16.00	20.00

KM# 521.1 500 REIS
3.90 g., Aluminum-Bronze, 22.7 mm. **Subject:** Independence Centennial **Obv:** Dom Pedro and President Pessoa left **Rev:** Denomination at top, dates divided by centennial symbols **Edge:** Reeded

Date	Mintage	VF20	XF40	MS60	MS63	MS65
ND-1922	13,744,000	0.60	1.25	2.00	3.00	5.00

KM# 521.2 500 REIS
Aluminum-Bronze, 23 mm. **Obv:** Dom Pedro and President Pessoa left **Rev:** Denomination at top, dates divided by centennial symbols **Edge:** Reeded **Note:** Error: BBASIL instead of BRASIL.

Date	Mintage	VF20	XF40	MS60	MS63	MS65
ND-1922	Inc. above	32.00	45.00	75.00	100	135

KM# 524 500 REIS
3.95 g., Aluminum-Bronze, 22.73 mm. **Obv:** Denomination within wreath, date below **Rev:** Kneeling liberty figure right **Edge:** Reeded

Date	Mintage	VF20	XF40	MS60	MS63	MS65
1924	7,400,000	0.75	1.50	4.50	7.50	15.00
1927	2,725,000	1.00	2.00	5.00	8.00	16.00
1928	9,432,000	0.75	1.50	4.50	7.50	15.00
1930	146,000	2.50	4.00	8.00	12.50	25.00

KM# 530 500 REIS
Aluminum-Bronze, 23 mm. **Subject:** 400th Anniversary of Colonization **Obv:** Joao Ramalho, colonist, 3/4 right **Rev:** Clothing divides denomination **Edge:** Reeded **Note:** Medal rotation.

Date	Mintage	VF20	XF40	MS60	MS63	MS65
ND-1932	34,000	5.00	12.00	17.00	22.00	30.00

KM# 533 500 REIS
4.00 g., Aluminum-Bronze, 22 mm. **Obv:** Column divides denomination, date below **Rev:** Bust of Diego Antonio Feijo Regent of Brazil 1835-1837, 3/4 left **Note:** Medal rotation; wide rim.

Date	Mintage	VF20	XF40	MS60	MS63	MS65
1935	14,000	10.00	20.00	28.00	35.00	48.00

KM# 540 500 REIS
4.80 g., Aluminum-Bronze, 22.3 mm. **Obv:** Denomination divided by column, date below **Rev:** Bust of Diego Antonio Feijo 3/4 left **Edge:** Reeded **Note:** Medal rotation; thicker planchet.

Date	Mintage	VF20	XF40	MS60	MS63	MS65
1936	1,326,000	1.50	2.50	3.50	6.00	10.00
1937	Inc. above	1.50	2.50	3.50	6.00	10.00
1938	—	1.50	2.50	3.50	6.00	10.00

KM# 549 500 REIS
4.85 g., Aluminum-Bronze, 22.3 mm. **Obv:** Denomination above date within wreath **Rev:** Joaquim Machado de Assis, Author and Poet, 3/4 facing **Edge:** Reeded

Date	Mintage	VF20	XF40	MS60	MS63	MS65
1939	5,928,000	1.00	2.00	3.00	5.00	9.00

KM# 507 1000 REIS
10.00 g., 0.900 Silver 0.2894 oz. ASW **Obv:** Laureate liberty head left, date below flanked by stars **Rev:** Denomination at center **Edge:** Reeded

Date	Mintage	VF20	XF40	MS60	MS63	MS65
1906	420,000	6.50	8.00	15.00	22.00	35.00
1907	1,282,000	6.50	8.00	15.00	22.00	35.00
1908	1,624,000	6.50	8.00	15.00	22.00	35.00
1909	816,000	6.50	8.00	15.00	22.00	35.00
1910	2,354,000	6.50	8.00	15.00	22.00	35.00
1911	2,810,000	6.50	8.00	15.00	22.00	35.00
1912	1,570,000	6.50	8.00	15.00	22.00	35.00

KM# 510 1000 REIS
10.00 g., 0.900 Silver 0.2894 oz. ASW, 26.2 mm. **Obv:** Laureate head of Liberty right, circle surrounds, date below **Rev:** Denomination within wreath, arms above **Edge:** Reeded

Date	Mintage	VF20	XF40	MS60	MS63	MS65
1912	Inc. above	6.50	8.00	16.00	25.00	37.00
1913	2,525,000	6.50	8.00	16.00	25.00	37.00

KM# 513 1000 REIS
10.00 g., 0.900 Silver 0.2894 oz. ASW, 26 mm. **Obv:** Laureate liberty head right, star circle surrounds, date below **Rev:** Denomination within wreath, arms above **Edge:** Reeded

Date	Mintage	VF20	XF40	MS60	MS63	MS65
1913 A	—	5.25	8.00	15.00	20.00	30.00

KM# 522.1 1000 REIS
7.80 g., Aluminum-Bronze, 26.8 mm. **Subject:** Independence Centennial **Obv:** Dom Pedro and President Pessoa **Rev:** Denomination at top, dates divided by centennial symbols **Edge:** Reeded

Date	Mintage	VF20	XF40	MS60	MS63	MS65
ND-1922	16,698,000	0.60	2.00	3.50	7.00	10.00

KM# 522.2 1000 REIS
Aluminum-Bronze, 25 mm. **Obv:** Dom Pedro and President Pessoa left **Rev:** Denomination at top, dates divided by centennial symbols at center **Edge:** Reeded **Note:** Error: BBASIL instead of BRASIL.

Date	Mintage	VF20	XF40	MS60	MS63	MS65
ND-1922	Inc. above	5.00	7.00	12.00	18.00	30.00

KM# 525 1000 REIS
8.00 g., Aluminum-Bronze, 26.8 mm. **Obv:** Denomination within wreath, date below, monogram left of knot **Rev:** Kneeling liberty figure right **Edge:** Reeded

Date	Mintage	VF20	XF40	MS60	MS63	MS65
1924	9,354,000	1.00	2.25	5.00	8.00	15.00
1925	6,205,000	1.00	2.25	5.00	8.00	15.00
1927	35,817,000	1.00	2.25	5.00	8.00	15.00
1928	1,899,000	1.25	2.50	6.00	9.00	16.00
1929	83,000	15.00	45.00	75.00	115	145
1930	45,000	15.00	45.00	75.00	115	145
1931	200,000	6.00	10.00	12.00	15.00	25.00

KM# 531 1000 REIS
7.00 g., Aluminum-Bronze, 32 mm. **Subject:** 400th Anniversary of Colonization **Obv:** 3/4 figure of Martin Affonso da Sousa looking left **Rev:** Denomination encircles arms **Edge:** Reeded **Note:** Medal rotation.

Date	Mintage	VF20	XF40	MS60	MS63	MS65
ND-1932	56,000	5.00	8.00	10.00	12.00	20.00

KM# 534 1000 REIS
8.00 g., Aluminum-Bronze, 26 mm. **Obv:** Open bible, date above, denomination at top **Rev:** Head of Jose de Anchieta left **Note:** Medal rotation.

Date	Mintage	VF20	XF40	MS60	MS63	MS65
1935	138,000	2.50	4.00	7.50	10.00	15.00

KM# 541 1000 REIS

7.10 g., Aluminum-Bronze, 24.3 mm. **Obv:** Open bible, date above, denomination at top **Rev:** Head of Jose de Anchieta left **Edge:** Reeded **Note:** Size reduced. Medal rotation.

Date	Mintage	VF20	XF40	MS60	MS63	MS65
1936	926,000	1.00	2.00	4.00	6.00	10.00
1937	Inc. above	1.00	2.00	4.00	6.00	10.00
1938 LGCB under chin	—	1.00	2.00	4.00	6.00	10.00

KM# 550 1000 REIS

6.67 g., Aluminum-Bronze, 24.4 mm. **Obv:** Denomination above date within wreath **Rev:** Tobias Barreto de Menezes, Philosopher and Poet 3/4 right, BR monogram right of bust, two dates above right shoulder **Edge:** Reeded

Date	Mintage	VF20	XF40	MS60	MS63	MS65
1939	9,586,000	0.75	2.00	3.50	5.00	7.50

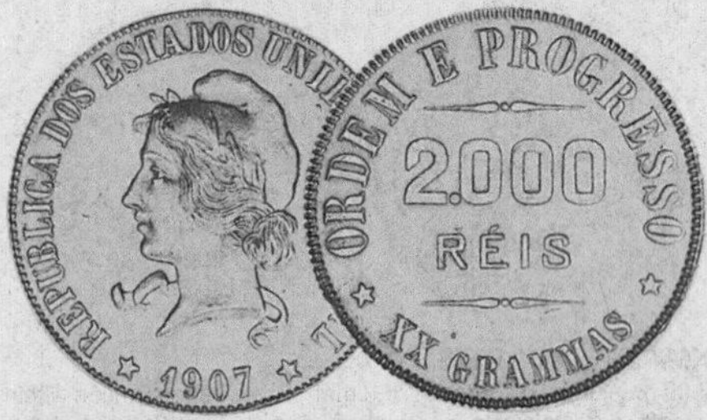

KM# 508 2000 REIS

20.00 g., 0.900 Silver 0.5787 oz. ASW **Obv:** Liberty head left, date below flanked by stars **Rev:** Denomination at center

Date	Mintage	VF20	XF40	MS60	MS63	MS65
1906	256,000	13.50	25.00	35.00	60.00	95.00
1907	2,863,000	13.00	20.00	25.00	35.00	60.00
1908	1,707,000	13.00	20.00	25.00	35.00	60.00
1910	585,000	13.50	25.00	35.00	60.00	95.00
1911	1,929,000	13.00	20.00	25.00	35.00	60.00
1912	741,000	13.50	25.00	35.00	60.00	95.00

KM# 511 2000 REIS

20.00 g., 0.900 Silver 0.5787 oz. ASW, 32.5 mm. **Obv:** Liberty head within circle, date below **Rev:** Denomination within wreath, national arms above

Date	Mintage	VF20	XF40	MS60	MS63	MS65
1912	Inc. above	13.00	22.00	30.00	55.00	90.00
1913	395,000	13.00	22.00	32.00	50.00	85.00

KM# 514 2000 REIS

20.00 g., 0.900 Silver 0.5787 oz. ASW, 32.5 mm. **Obv:** Laureate liberty head right within circle, date below **Rev:** Denomination within wreath, national arms above, continuous legend

Date	Mintage	VF20	XF40	MS60	MS63	MS65
1913 A	—	13.00	20.00	28.00	40.00	65.00

KM# 523 2000 REIS

7.90 g., 0.900 Silver 0.2286 oz. ASW, 26 mm. **Subject:** Independence Centennial **Obv:** Dom Pedro and President Pessoa left **Rev:** Two sets of arms, dates below, denomination at bottom **Edge:** Reeded

Date	Mintage	VF20	XF40	MS60	MS63	MS65
ND-1922	1,560,000	—	4.25	7.00	10.00	12.00

KM# 523a 2000 REIS

7.90 g., 0.500 Silver 0.127 oz. ASW, 26 mm. **Edge:** Reeded **Note:** Struck in both .900 and .500 fine silver, but can only be distinguished by analysis (and color), on worn specimens

Date	Mintage	VF20	XF40	MS60	MS63	MS65
ND-1922	Inc. above	2.25	5.00	8.00	12.00	14.00

KM# 526 2000 REIS

8.00 g., 0.500 Silver 0.1286 oz. ASW, 26 mm. **Obv:** Denomination within wreath, date below **Rev:** Laureate liberty head, right, within circle, stars surround

Date	Mintage	VF20	XF40	MS60	MS63	MS65
1924	9,147,000	2.50	5.00	8.00	12.00	14.00
1925	723,000	2.50	5.00	8.00	12.00	16.00
1926	1,787,000	2.50	5.00	8.00	12.00	14.00
1927	1,008,999	2.50	5.00	8.00	12.00	16.00
1928	1,250,000	2.50	5.00	8.00	12.00	14.00
1929	1,744,000	2.50	5.00	8.00	12.00	14.00
1930	1,240,000	2.50	5.00	8.00	12.00	14.00
1931	546,000	2.50	5.00	8.00	12.00	15.00
1934	938,000	2.50	5.00	8.00	12.00	15.00

KM# 532 2000 REIS

7.90 g., 0.500 Silver 0.127 oz. ASW, 26 mm. **Subject:** 400th Anniversary of Colonization **Obv:** Bust of John III 3/4 right **Rev:** Arms, denomination above **Note:** Medal rotation.

Date	Mintage	VF20	XF40	MS60	MS63	MS65
ND-1932	695,000	5.00	6.00	8.50	12.50	17.00

KM# 535 2000 REIS

8.00 g., 0.500 Silver 0.1286 oz. ASW, 26.2 mm. **Obv:** Sword divides denomination, date lower right **Rev:** Armored head of Duke of Caxias; left, CB below chin **Edge:** Reeded **Note:** Medal rotation.

Date	Mintage	VF20	XF40	MS60	MS63	MS65
1935	2,131,000	2.50	5.00	7.00	9.00	12.50

KM# 542 2000 REIS

8.62 g., Aluminum-Bronze, 26 mm. **Obv:** Hilt divides denomination, date upper right **Rev:** Armored bust of Duke of Caxias right, crown at left **Edge:** Reeded **Note:** Medal rotation.

Date	Mintage	VF20	XF40	MS60	MS63	MS65
1936	665,000	1.50	2.50	4.50	6.00	10.00
1937	Inc. above	1.50	2.50	4.50	6.00	10.00
1938	—	4.50	10.00	15.00	22.00	28.00

KM# 548 2000 REIS

Aluminum-Bronze, 26.3 mm. **Edge:** Plain **Note:** 24-sided planchet. Medal rotation.

Date	Mintage	VF20	XF40	MS60	MS63	MS65
1937	—	45.00	65.00	175	225	300
1938	—	1.50	3.00	4.50	6.00	10.00

KM# 551 2000 REIS

8.96 g., Aluminum-Bronze, 26.3 mm. **Obv:** Denomination above date within wreath **Rev:** Bust of President Floriano Peixoto facing **Edge:** Reeded

Date	Mintage	VF20	XF40	MS60	MS63	MS65
1939	5,048,000	1.00	2.00	3.50	4.50	8.00

KM# 543 5000 REIS

10.00 g., 0.600 Silver 0.1929 oz. ASW, 27.6 mm. **Obv:** Wing above denomination **Rev:** Head of aviation pioneer Alberto Santos Dumont left **Edge:** Reeded **Note:** Medal rotation.

Date	Mintage	VF20	XF40	MS60	MS63	MS65
1936	1,986,000	4.25	7.00	12.00	14.00	18.00
1937	414,000	4.25	7.00	12.00	14.00	18.00
1938	994,000	4.25	7.00	12.00	14.00	18.00

KM# 496 10000 REIS

8.96 g., 0.917 Gold 0.2643 oz. AGW **Obv:** Liberty head left within circle **Rev:** Star with wreath in background

Date	Mintage	F12	VF20	XF40	MS60	MS63
1901	111	1,000	2,000	3,000	7,000	10,000
1902 Unique	—	—	—	—	—	—
1903	391	1,000	2,000	3,000	7,000	10,000
1904	541	900	1,150	1,700	3,500	—
1906	572	900	1,150	1,700	3,500	—
1907	878	900	1,200	1,700	2,500	—
1908	689	900	1,200	1,700	2,500	3,000
1909	1,069	900	1,200	1,700	2,500	3,500
1911	137	1,000	2,000	3,000	7,000	10,000
1914	969	1,500	3,000	6,000	10,000	15,000
1915	4,314	1,000	1,200	2,000	4,000	—
1916	4,720	1,000	2,000	3,000	7,000	10,000
1919	526	1,000	2,000	3,000	7,000	10,000
1921	2,435	1,000	2,000	3,000	7,000	—
1922 Rare	6	—	—	—	—	—

KM# 497 20000 REIS

17.93 g., 0.917 Gold 0.5286 oz. AGW **Obv:** Liberty head left **Rev:** Stars at center surrounded by circle of stars

Date	Mintage	F12	VF20	XF40	MS60	MS63
1901	784	750	1,150	1,250	1,600	2,150
1902	884	1,000	1,150	1,250	1,600	2,000
1903	675	1,500	2,500	3,500	6,000	9,000
1904	444	1,500	2,500	3,500	6,000	9,000
1906	396	1,500	2,500	3,500	6,000	9,000
1907	3,310	850	1,100	1,400	1,900	2,700
1908	6,001,000	750	1,000	1,300	2,300	3,000
1909	4,427	750	1,000	1,300	2,300	3,000
1910	5,119	750	1,000	2,000	3,500	5,500
1911	8,467	750	1,000	1,300	2,300	3,000
1912	4,878	850	1,100	1,400	1,900	2,700
1913	5,182	850	1,100	1,400	1,900	2,700
1914	1,980	750	1,000	1,300	2,300	3,000
1917	2,269	750	1,000	2,000	3,500	5,500
1918	1,216	750	1,000	1,300	2,300	3,000
1921	5,924	750	1,000	2,000	3,500	5,500
1922	2,681	1,000	2,000	3,500	5,500	8,000

REFORM COINAGE

100 Centavos = 1 Cruzeiro

1942-1967

KM# 555 10 CENTAVOS

2.88 g., Copper-Nickel, 17.22 mm. **Obv:** Bust of Getulio Vargas 3/4 left **Rev:** Denomination above line, date below **Edge:** Plain **Note:** KM#555 has a very light yellowish appearance while KM#555a is a deeper yellow.

Date	Mintage	VF20	XF40	MS60	MS63	MS65
1942	3,826,000	0.35	0.50	0.75	1.00	1.50
1943	13,565,000	0.25	0.35	0.50	0.65	1.00

KM# 555a.1 10 CENTAVOS

2.97 g., Aluminum-Bronze, 17.2 mm. **Obv:** Bust left, initial after "Brasil" **Rev:** Denomination above line, date below, initial at end of line above date **Edge:** Plain **Note:** KM#555 has a very light yellowish appearance while KM#555a is a deeper yellow.

Date	Mintage	VF20	XF40	MS60	MS63	MS65
1943	Inc. above	0.25	0.35	0.50	0.65	1.00
1944	12,617,000	0.25	0.35	0.50	0.65	1.00
1945	24,674,000	0.25	0.35	0.50	0.65	1.00

KM# 555a.2 10 CENTAVOS

2.90 g., Aluminum-Bronze, 17.2 mm. **Obv:** Bust left **Rev:** Denomination above line, date below **Note:** Without initials.

Date	Mintage	VF20	XF40	MS60	MS63	MS65
1944	—	0.25	0.35	0.50	0.65	1.00
1945	—	0.25	0.35	0.50	0.65	1.00
1946	35,159,000	0.25	0.35	0.50	0.65	1.00
1947	20,664,000	0.25	0.35	0.50	0.65	1.00

KM# 561 10 CENTAVOS

3.00 g., Aluminum-Bronze, 17.3 mm. **Obv:** Jose Bonifacio de Andrada e Silva, Father of Independence left **Rev:** Denomination above line, date below

Date	Mintage	VF20	XF40	MS60	MS63	MS65
1947	Inc. above	0.15	0.20	0.35	0.50	1.00
1948	45,041,000	0.15	0.20	0.35	0.50	1.00
1949	21,763,000	0.15	0.20	0.35	0.50	1.00
1950	16,329,999	0.15	0.20	0.35	0.50	1.00
1951	15,561,000	0.10	0.15	0.35	0.50	1.00
1952	10,966,000	0.10	0.20	0.35	0.50	1.00
1953	25,883,000	0.10	0.15	0.35	0.50	1.00
1954	17,031,000	0.10	0.15	0.35	0.50	1.00
1955	25,172,000	0.10	0.15	0.35	0.50	1.00

KM# 564 10 CENTAVOS

1.10 g., Aluminum, 17.3 mm. **Obv:** National Arms **Rev:** Denomination above line, date below

Date	Mintage	VF20	XF40	MS60	MS63	MS65
1956	741,000	0.50	0.75	1.00	1.25	2.50
1957	25,311,000	0.10	0.15	0.25	0.50	1.00
1958	5,813,000	0.15	0.25	0.35	0.50	1.00
1959	2,611,000	0.15	0.25	0.35	0.50	1.00
1960	624,000	0.50	0.75	1.00	1.25	2.50
1961	951,000	0.50	0.75	1.00	1.25	2.50

KM# 556 20 CENTAVOS

Copper-Nickel, 20 mm. **Obv:** Bust of Getulio Vargas 3/4 left **Rev:** Denomination above line, date below **Edge:** Plain **Note:** KM#556 has a very light yellowish appearance while KM#556a is a deeper yellow.

Date	Mintage	VF20	XF40	MS60	MS63	MS65
1942	3,007,000	0.25	0.50	0.75	1.00	1.50
1943	13,392,000	0.15	0.35	0.50	0.75	1.00

KM# 556a 20 CENTAVOS

4.00 g., Aluminum-Bronze, 20 mm. **Obv:** Getulio Vargas bust left **Rev:** Denomination above line, date below **Edge:** Plain **Note:** KM#556 has a very light yellowish appearance while KM#556a is a deeper yellow.

Date	Mintage	VF20	XF40	MS60	MS63	MS65
1943	Inc. above	0.15	0.35	0.50	0.75	1.00
1944	12,673,000	0.15	0.35	0.50	0.75	1.00

Note: Coins dated 1944 exist with and without designer's initials and straight or curved-back 9 in date

Date	Mintage	VF20	XF40	MS60	MS63	MS65
1945	61,632,000	0.15	0.35	0.50	0.75	1.00
1946	31,526,000	0.15	0.35	0.50	0.75	1.00
1947	36,422,000	0.15	0.35	0.50	0.75	1.00
1948	39,671,000	0.15	0.35	0.50	0.75	1.00

KM# 562 20 CENTAVOS

4.00 g., Aluminum-Bronze, 19.26 mm. **Obv:** Bust of author and lawyer Ruy Barbosa left **Rev:** Denomination above line, date below

Date	Mintage	VF20	XF40	MS60	MS63	MS65
1948	Inc. above	0.15	0.25	0.50	0.75	1.00
1949	24,805,000	0.15	0.25	0.50	0.75	1.00
1950	15,145,000	0.15	0.25	0.50	0.75	1.00
1951	14,964,000	0.15	0.25	0.50	0.75	1.00
1952	10,942,000	0.15	0.25	0.50	0.75	1.00
1953	25,585,000	0.15	0.25	0.50	0.75	1.00
1954	16,477,000	0.15	0.25	0.50	0.75	1.00
1955	25,122,000	0.15	0.25	0.50	0.75	1.00
1956	6,716,000	0.15	0.25	0.50	0.75	1.00

KM# 565 20 CENTAVOS

Aluminum **Obv:** National arms **Rev:** Denomination above line, date below **Note:** Varieties exist in the thickness of the planchet for year 1956.

Date	Mintage	VF20	XF40	MS60	MS63	MS65
1956	Inc. above	0.10	0.25	0.50	0.75	1.00
1957	27,110,000	0.10	0.20	0.40	0.75	1.00
1958	8,552,000	0.10	0.20	0.40	0.75	1.00
1959	4,810,000	0.10	0.20	0.40	0.75	1.00
1960	510,000	0.25	0.50	0.65	0.85	1.25
1961	2,332,000	0.10	0.20	0.40	0.75	1.00

KM# 557 50 CENTAVOS

4.75 g., Copper-Nickel, 21 mm. **Obv:** Bust of Getulio Vargas 3/4 left **Rev:** Denomination above line, date below **Note:** KM#557 has a very light yellowish appearance while KM#557a is a deeper yellow.

Date	Mintage	VF20	XF40	MS60	MS63	MS65
1942	2,358,000	0.40	0.75	1.25	1.50	2.50
1943	13,392,000	0.35	0.65	0.85	1.25	1.50

KM# 557a 50 CENTAVOS

4.75 g., Aluminum-Bronze, 21.3 mm. **Obv:** Getulio Vargas bust left **Rev:** Denomination above line, date below **Edge:** Plain **Note:** KM#557 has a very light yellowish appearance while KM#557a is a deeper yellow.

Date	Mintage	VF20	XF40	MS60	MS63	MS65
1943	Inc. above	0.30	0.50	0.75	1.50	2.50
1944	12,102,000	0.30	0.50	0.75	1.50	2.50
1945	73,222,000	0.30	0.50	0.75	1.50	2.50
1946	13,941,000	0.30	0.50	0.75	1.50	2.50
1947	23,588,000	0.20	0.50	0.75	1.50	2.50

KM# 563 50 CENTAVOS

5.00 g., Aluminum-Bronze, 21.3 mm. **Obv:** Bust of General Eurico Gaspar Dutra left **Rev:** Denomination above line, date below

Date	Mintage	VF20	XF40	MS60	MS63	MS65
1948	32,023,000	0.15	0.25	0.45	0.65	1.00
1949	11,392,000	0.15	0.25	0.45	0.65	1.00
1950	7,804,000	0.15	0.35	0.50	0.75	1.25
1951	7,523,000	0.15	0.35	0.50	0.75	1.25
1952	6,863,000	0.15	0.35	0.50	0.75	1.25
1953	17,372,000	0.15	0.25	0.45	0.65	1.00
1954	11,353,000	0.15	0.25	0.45	0.65	1.00
1955	27,150,000	0.15	0.25	0.45	0.65	1.00
1956	32,130,000	0.15	0.25	0.45	0.65	1.00

KM# 566 50 CENTAVOS

3.00 g., Aluminum-Bronze, 17.04 mm. **Obv:** National arms **Rev:** Denomination above line, date below

Date	Mintage	VF20	XF40	MS60	MS63	MS65
1956	Inc. above	0.15	0.25	0.35	0.50	0.75

KM# 569 50 CENTAVOS

1.83 g., Aluminum, 21.07 mm. **Obv:** National arms **Rev:** Denomination above line, date below

Date	Mintage	VF20	XF40	MS60	MS63	MS65
1957	49,350,000	0.10	0.20	0.35	0.45	0.65
1958	59,815,000	0.10	0.20	0.35	0.45	0.65
1959	32,891,000	0.10	0.20	0.35	0.45	0.65
1960	15,997,000	0.10	0.20	0.35	0.45	0.65
1961	18,456,000	0.10	0.20	0.35	0.45	0.65

KM# 558 CRUZEIRO

6.92 g., Aluminum-Bronze, 22.9 mm. **Obv:** Topographical map **Rev:** Denomination, date at left **Edge:** Reeded

Date	Mintage	VF20	XF40	MS60	MS63	MS65
1942	381,000	0.50	1.00	2.50	7.00	15.00
1943	2,728,000	0.25	0.50	0.75	1.25	2.50

Date	Mintage	VF20	XF40	MS60	MS63	MS65
1944	3,820,000	0.25	0.50	0.75	1.25	2.50
1945	32,543,999	0.25	0.50	0.75	1.25	2.50
1946	49,794,000	0.25	0.50	0.75	1.25	2.50
1947	15,391,000	0.25	0.50	0.75	1.25	2.50
1949	7,889,000	0.25	0.50	0.75	1.25	2.50
1950	5,163,000	0.25	0.50	0.75	1.25	2.50
1951	3,757,000	0.25	0.50	0.75	1.25	2.50
1952	1,769,000	0.50	1.00	2.00	3.50	5.00
1953	5,195,000	0.25	0.50	0.75	1.25	2.50
1954	1,145,000	0.25	0.50	0.75	1.25	2.50
1955	1,758,000	0.25	0.50	0.75	1.25	2.50
1956	668,000	6.00	9.00	15.00	20.00	25.00

KM# 567 CRUZEIRO

4.03 g., Aluminum-Bronze, 19.03 mm. **Obv:** National arms **Rev:** Denomination above line, date below

Date	Mintage	VF20	XF40	MS60	MS63	MS65
1956	Inc. above	0.20	0.35	0.50	0.65	1.00

KM# 570 CRUZEIRO

2.38 g., Aluminum, 23.23 mm. **Obv:** National arms **Rev:** Denomination above line, date below **Edge:** Reeded

Date	Mintage	VF20	XF40	MS60	MS63	MS65
1957	11,849,000	0.20	0.50	0.75	1.25	2.50
1958	15,443,000	0.20	0.50	0.75	1.50	3.00
1959	25,010,000	0.20	0.50	0.75	1.25	2.50
1960	35,267,000	0.20	0.50	0.75	1.25	2.50
1961	22,181,000	0.20	0.50	0.75	1.50	3.00

KM# 559 2 CRUZEIROS

7.40 g., Aluminum-Bronze, 25 mm. **Obv:** Topographical map **Rev:** Denomination, date at left **Edge:** Reeded

Date	Mintage	VF20	XF40	MS60	MS63	MS65
1942	276,000	0.75	1.50	3.00	7.50	20.00
1943	1,929,000	0.25	0.50	1.00	1.50	3.00
1944	3,820,000	0.25	0.50	1.00	1.50	3.00
1945	32,543,999	0.20	0.40	1.00	1.50	3.00
1946	33,650,000	0.20	0.40	1.00	1.50	3.00
1947	9,908,000	0.20	0.40	1.00	1.50	3.00
1949	11,252,000	0.20	0.40	1.00	1.50	3.00
1950	7,754,000	0.25	0.50	1.00	1.50	3.00
1951	390,000	0.40	1.00	2.00	4.00	7.50
1952	1,456,000	1.00	2.00	3.00	5.00	8.50
1953	3,582,000	0.20	0.40	1.00	1.50	3.00
1954	1,197,000	0.25	1.00	2.00	3.00	5.00
1955	1,838,000	0.20	0.50	1.00	1.50	3.00
1956	253,000	2.00	4.00	6.00	10.00	15.00

KM# 568 2 CRUZEIROS

Aluminum-Bronze **Obv:** National arms **Rev:** Denomination above line, date below

Date	Mintage	VF20	XF40	MS60	MS63	MS65
1956	Inc. above	0.35	0.50	1.00	1.25	2.00

KM# 571 2 CRUZEIROS

2.76 g., Aluminum, 25.26 mm. **Obv:** National arms **Rev:** Denomination above line, date below **Edge:** Reeded

Date	Mintage	VF20	XF40	MS60	MS63	MS65
1957	194,000	0.50	0.75	1.25	2.00	3.00
1958	13,687,000	0.20	0.30	0.50	0.75	1.50
1959	20,894,000	0.20	0.30	0.50	0.75	1.50
1960	19,624,000	0.20	0.30	0.50	0.75	1.50
1961	24,924,000	0.20	0.30	0.50	0.75	1.50

KM# 560 5 CRUZEIROS

Aluminum-Bronze, 26 mm. **Obv:** Topographical map **Rev:** Denomination, date at left

Date	Mintage	VF20	XF40	MS60	MS63	MS65
1942	115,000	1.50	3.50	7.00	15.00	30.00
1943	222,000	1.00	2.50	5.00	10.00	25.00

KM# 572 10 CRUZEIROS

2.15 g., Aluminum, 23.5 mm. **Obv:** Topographical map **Rev:** Large denomination, date below

Date	Mintage	VF20	XF40	MS60	MS63	MS65
1965	46,057,000	0.10	0.20	0.35	0.50	0.75

KM# 573 20 CRUZEIROS

2.45 g., Aluminum, 25 mm. **Obv:** Topographical map **Rev:** Large denomination, date below

Date	Mintage	VF20	XF40	MS60	MS63	MS65
1965	52,026,000	0.15	0.25	0.40	0.60	0.80

KM# 574 50 CRUZEIROS

3.30 g., Nickel, 18 mm. **Obv:** Liberty head left **Rev:** Denomination above date

Date	Mintage	VF20	XF40	MS60	MS63	MS65
1965	28,213,000	0.20	0.40	0.60	0.75	1.25

REFORM COINAGE

1000 Old Cruzeiros = 1 Cruzeiro Novo (New);
100 Centavos = 1 (New) Cruzeiro
1967-1985

KM# 575.1 CENTAVO

2.63 g., Stainless Steel, 17 mm. **Obv:** Liberty head left **Rev:** Denomination above date

Date	Mintage	VF20	XF40	MS60	MS63	MS65
1967	100,246,000	—	—	0.15	0.25	0.35

KM# 575.2 CENTAVO

1.75 g., Stainless Steel, 17 mm. **Obv:** Liberty head left **Rev:** Denomination above date **Note:** Thinner planchet.

Date	Mintage	VF20	XF40	MS60	MS63	MS65
1969	243,966,303	—	—	0.15	0.25	0.35
Note: Mintage figure includes KM#575.1 coins struck in 1969 but dated 1967.						
1975	50,043,000	—	0.15	0.25	0.35	0.50

KM# 585 CENTAVO

1.75 g., Stainless Steel, 17 mm. **Series:** F.A.O. **Subject:** Sugar Cane **Obv:** Liberty head left **Rev:** Sugar cane, denomination and date to right **Edge:** Plain

Date	Mintage	VF20	XF40	MS60	MS63	MS65
1975	—	—	0.15	0.25	0.45	0.65
Note: Mintage included in KM#575.2						
1976	112,000	—	0.75	1.00	1.50	1.75
1977	100,000	—	0.75	1.00	1.50	1.75
1978	50,000	0.75	1.25	1.75	2.25	2.75

KM# 589 CENTAVO

1.58 g., Stainless Steel, 14 mm. **Series:** F.A.O. **Subject:** Soja **Obv:** Plants **Rev:** Denomination above date

Date	Mintage	VF20	XF40	MS60	MS63	MS65
1979	100,000	0.75	1.00	1.25	1.50	1.75
1980	60,000	1.00	1.50	2.00	2.50	2.75
1981	100,000	0.75	1.00	1.25	1.50	1.75
1982	100,000	0.75	1.00	1.25	1.50	1.75
1983	100,000	0.75	1.00	1.25	1.50	1.75

KM# 576.1 2 CENTAVOS

3.25 g., Stainless Steel, 19 mm. **Obv:** Liberty head left **Rev:** Denomination above date

Date	Mintage	VF20	XF40	MS60	MS63	MS65
1967	104,121,000	—	—	0.25	0.50	0.75

KM# 576.2 2 CENTAVOS

2.16 g., Stainless Steel, 19 mm. **Obv:** Liberty head left **Rev:** Denomination above date **Edge:** Plain **Note:** Thinner planchet.

Date	Mintage	VF20	XF40	MS60	MS63	MS65
1969	252,839,303	—	—	0.50	0.75	1.00
Note: Mintage figure includes KM#576.1 coins struck in 1969 dated 1967 and KM#576.2 coins struck through 1974 dated 1969						
1975	50,015,000	—	0.25	0.75	1.00	1.25

KM# 586 2 CENTAVOS

2.21 g., Stainless Steel, 19 mm. **Series:** F.A.O. **Subject:** Soja **Obv:** Liberty head left **Rev:** Denomination above date, plant at left

Date	Mintage	VF20	XF40	MS60	MS63	MS65
1975	—	—	0.15	0.25	0.45	0.65
Note: Mintage included with KM#576.2						
1976	136,000	—	0.75	1.00	1.50	1.75
1977	100,000	—	0.75	1.00	1.50	1.75
1978	50,000	0.75	1.25	1.75	2.25	2.75

KM# 577.1 5 CENTAVOS

3.97 g., Stainless Steel, 21 mm. **Obv:** Liberty head left **Rev:** Denomination above date

Date	Mintage	VF20	XF40	MS60	MS63	MS65
1967	98,532,000	—	0.20	0.50	0.75	1.00

KM# 577.2 5 CENTAVOS

2.70 g., Stainless Steel, 21 mm. **Obv:** Liberty head left **Rev:** Denomination above date **Note:** Thinner planchet.

Date	Mintage	VF20	XF40	MS60	MS63	MS65
1969	548,716,303	—	0.20	0.50	0.75	1.00

Note: Mintage figure includes KM#577.1 coins struck in 1969 dated 1967 and KM#577.2 coins struck through 1974 dated 1969

Date	Mintage	VF20	XF40	MS60	MS63	MS65
1975	85,123,000	—	0.20	0.50	0.75	1.00

KM# 587.1 5 CENTAVOS

2.64 g., Stainless Steel, 21 mm. **Series:** F.A.O. **Subject:** Zebu **Obv:** Liberty head left **Rev:** Denomination and date to right of Zebu **Edge:** Plain

Date	Mintage	VF20	XF40	MS60	MS63	MS65
1975	—	—	0.20	0.50	0.75	1.00

Note: Mintage included with KM#577.2

Date	Mintage	VF20	XF40	MS60	MS63	MS65
1976	93,644,000	—	0.20	0.50	0.75	1.00
1977	85,360,000	—	0.20	0.65	1.00	1.25
1978	34,090,000	—	0.20	0.65	1.00	1.25

KM# 587.2 5 CENTAVOS

2.69 g., Stainless Steel, 21 mm. **Obv:** Liberty head left **Rev:** Denomination and date to right of Zebu, "5" over wavy lines

Date	Mintage	VF20	XF40	MS60	MS63	MS65
1975	Inc. above	—	0.20	0.50	0.75	1.00
1976	Inc. above	—	0.20	0.50	0.75	1.00
1977	Inc. above	—	0.20	0.50	0.75	1.00
1978	Inc. above	—	0.20	0.65	1.00	1.25

KM# 578.1 10 CENTAVOS

5.52 g., Copper-Nickel, 23 mm. **Obv:** Liberty head left **Rev:** Oil refinery, denomination and date at right

Date	Mintage	VF20	XF40	MS60	MS63	MS65
1967	108,269,000	—	0.20	0.50	0.75	1.00

KM# 578.1a 10 CENTAVOS

4.22 g., Stainless Steel, 23 mm. **Obv:** Liberty head left **Rev:** Oil refinery, denomination and date at right

Date	Mintage	VF20	XF40	MS60	MS63	MS65
1974	114,598,153	—	0.20	0.35	0.50	0.65

Note: Mintage figure includes KM#578.2 coins struck in 1974 dated 1970.

Date	Mintage	VF20	XF40	MS60	MS63	MS65
1975	142,783,000	—	0.20	0.35	0.50	0.65
1976	129,060,000	—	0.20	0.35	0.50	0.65
1977	225,213,000	—	0.20	0.35	0.50	0.65
1978	225,000,000	—	0.20	0.35	0.50	0.65
1979	100,000,000	—	0.20	0.45	0.65	0.75

KM# 578.2 10 CENTAVOS

4.78 g., Copper-Nickel, 23 mm. **Obv:** Liberty head left **Rev:** Oil refinery, denomination and date at right **Note:** Thinner planchet.

Date	Mintage	VF20	XF40	MS60	MS63	MS65
1970	498,927,200	—	0.20	0.35	0.50	0.65

Note: Mintage figure includes KM#578.1 coins struck in 1970 dated 1967 and KM#578.2 coins struck through 1974 dated 1970

KM# 579.1 20 CENTAVOS

7.86 g., Copper-Nickel, 25 mm. **Obv:** Liberty head left **Rev:** Denomination above date, oil derrick at left **Note:** Thick planchet

Date	Mintage	VF20	XF40	MS60	MS63	MS65
1967	123,814,000	—	0.20	0.45	0.65	0.75

KM# 579.1a 20 CENTAVOS

5.67 g., Stainless Steel, 25 mm. **Obv:** Liberty head left **Rev:** Denomination above date, oil derrick at left

Date	Mintage	VF20	XF40	MS60	MS63	MS65
1975	102,386,000	—	0.20	0.45	0.65	0.75
1976	65,687,000	—	0.20	0.45	0.65	0.75
1977	240,001,000	—	0.20	0.45	0.65	0.75
1978	225,000,000	—	0.20	0.45	0.65	0.75
1979	116,000,000	—	0.25	0.50	0.65	1.00

KM# 579.2 20 CENTAVOS

6.55 g., Copper-Nickel, 25 mm. **Obv:** Liberty head left **Rev:** Denomination above date, oil derrick at left **Note:** Thinner planchet.

Date	Mintage	VF20	XF40	MS60	MS63	MS65
1970	634,780,353	—	0.20	0.50	0.65	0.85

Note: Mintage figure includes KM#579.1 coins struck in 1970 dated 1967 and KM#579.2 coins struck through 1974 dated 1970

KM# 580 50 CENTAVOS

8.74 g., Nickel, 27 mm. **Obv:** Liberty head left **Rev:** Freighter at pier divides date and denomination

Date	Mintage	VF20	XF40	MS60	MS63	MS65
1967	13,089,000	0.25	0.50	0.75	1.25	1.50

KM# 580a 50 CENTAVOS

7.71 g., Copper-Nickel, 27 mm. **Obv:** Liberty head left **Rev:** Freighter at pier divides date and denomination **Edge:** Reeded **Note:** Varieties of "7" in the date, with serif at top or bottom.

Date	Mintage	VF20	XF40	MS60	MS63	MS65
1970	440,643,353	0.20	0.35	0.50	1.00	1.25

Note: Mintage figure includes KM#580 coins struck in 1970 dated 1967.

Date	Mintage	VF20	XF40	MS60	MS63	MS65
1975	134,454,000	0.20	0.35	0.50	1.00	1.25

KM# 580b 50 CENTAVOS

6.65 g., Stainless Steel, 27 mm. **Obv:** Liberty head left **Rev:** Freighter at pier divides denomination and date **Edge:** Plain **Note:** Varieties of "7" in the date, with serif at top or bottom.

Date	Mintage	VF20	XF40	MS60	MS63	MS65
1975	—	0.20	0.35	0.50	1.00	1.25

Note: Mintage included in KM#580a

Date	Mintage	VF20	XF40	MS60	MS63	MS65
1976	135,781,000	0.20	0.35	0.50	1.00	1.25
1977	160,019,000	0.20	0.35	0.50	1.00	1.25
1978	200,000,000	0.20	0.35	0.50	1.00	1.25
1979	104,000,000	0.25	0.45	0.65	1.25	1.50

KM# 581 CRUZEIRO

10.08 g., Nickel, 29 mm. **Obv:** Liberty head left **Rev:** Denomination above date, spray at left

Date	Mintage	VF20	XF40	MS60	MS63	MS65
1970	18,000	**PF65** 3.50				
1970	53,271,200	0.20	0.45	0.75	1.00	1.25

Note: Mintage figure includes coins struck through 1972 dated 1970

KM# 581a CRUZEIRO

10.25 g., Copper-Nickel, 29 mm. **Obv:** Liberty head left **Rev:** Denomination above date, spray at left

Date	Mintage	VF20	XF40	MS60	MS63	MS65
1974	24,135,256	0.20	0.45	0.75	1.00	1.25
1975	21,613,000	0.20	0.45	0.75	1.00	1.25
1976	26,146,000	0.20	0.45	0.75	1.00	1.25
1977	98,000	1.00	1.50	2.00	3.00	5.00
1978	77,000	1.00	1.50	2.00	3.00	5.00

KM# 582 CRUZEIRO

10.08 g., Nickel, 29 mm. **Subject:** 150th Anniversary of Independence **Obv:** Pedro I and General Emilio Garrastazu Medici heads left, date below **Rev:** Map above denomination **Edge Lettering:** SESQUICENTENARIO DA INDEPENDENCIA

Date	Mintage	VF20	XF40	MS60	MS63	MS65
1972	19,999,800	0.40	0.75	1.25	1.65	2.00

Note: Lettered edge

Date	Mintage	VF20	XF40	MS60	MS63	MS65
1972	Inc. above	0.40	0.75	1.25	1.65	2.00

Note: Plain edge; Coins with plain edge are believed by some to be errors

Date	Mintage	VF20	XF40	MS60	MS63	MS65
1972	—	**PF65** 3.50				

Note: Lettered edge

Date	Mintage	VF20	XF40	MS60	MS63	MS65
1972	—	**PF65** 3.50				

Note: Plain edge; Coins with plain edge are believed by some to be errors

KM# 590 CRUZEIRO

3.23 g., Stainless Steel, 20 mm. **Obv:** Sugar cane **Rev:** Denomination above date, linear design **Edge:** Plain

Date	Mintage	VF20	XF40	MS60	MS63	MS65
1979	596,419,000	0.15	0.25	0.50	0.75	1.00
1980	690,497,000	0.15	0.25	0.50	0.65	0.85
1981	560,000,000	0.15	0.25	0.50	0.65	0.85
1982	300,000,000	0.15	0.25	0.50	0.65	0.85
1983	100,000	1.00	1.50	2.00	3.00	5.00
1984	62,100,000	0.15	0.25	0.45	0.65	0.85

KM# 598 CRUZEIRO

2.84 g., Stainless Steel, 20 mm. **Series:** F.A.O. **Obv:** Sugar cane **Rev:** Denomination above date, linear design

Date	Mintage	VF20	XF40	MS60	MS63	MS65
1985	10,000,000	—	0.20	0.35	0.50	0.75

KM# 591 5 CRUZEIROS

4.50 g., Stainless Steel, 22 mm. **Obv:** Coffee plant **Rev:** Denomination above date, linear design **Edge:** Plain

Date	Mintage	VF20	XF40	MS60	MS63	MS65
1980	388,250,000	0.20	0.35	0.50	0.75	1.00
1981	82,000,000	0.20	0.35	0.50	0.75	1.00
1982	108,000,000	0.20	0.35	0.50	0.75	1.00
1983	113,400,000	0.20	0.35	0.50	0.75	1.00
1984	243,400,000	0.20	0.35	0.50	0.75	1.00

KM# 599 5 CRUZEIROS

4.04 g., Stainless Steel, 22 mm. **Series:** F.A.O. **Obv:** Coffee plant **Rev:** Denomination above date, linear design

Date	Mintage	VF20	XF40	MS60	MS63	MS65
1985	10,000,000	0.20	0.40	0.60	0.85	1.25

KM# 588 10 CRUZEIROS

11.30 g., 0.800 Silver 0.2906 oz. ASW, 28 mm. **Subject:** 10th Anniversary of Central Bank **Obv:** Bust of Humberto de Alencar Castelo Branco left **Rev:** Denomination, design at upper right **Note:** Medal rotation.

Date	Mintage	VF20	XF40	MS60	MS63	MS65
1975	20,000	—	—	8.00	10.00	25.00

KM# 592.1 10 CRUZEIROS
5.35 g., Stainless Steel, 24 mm. **Obv:** Map of Brazil **Rev:** Denomination, value, date, linear design

Date	Mintage	VF20	XF40	MS60	MS63	MS65
1980	100,060,000	—	0.35	0.50	0.75	1.00
1981	200,000,000	—	0.35	0.50	0.75	1.00
1982	331,000,000	—	0.35	0.50	0.75	1.00
1983	390,000,000	—	0.35	0.50	0.75	1.00
1984	409,600,000	—	0.35	0.50	0.75	1.00

KM# 592.2 10 CRUZEIROS
4.78 g., Stainless Steel, 24 mm. **Obv:** Map of Brazil **Rev:** Value, date, linear design **Note:** Reduced weight.

Date	Mintage	VF20	XF40	MS60	MS63	MS65
1985	201,000,000	—	0.35	0.50	0.75	1.00
1986	39,109,000	—	0.50	0.75	1.00	1.25

KM# 583 20 CRUZEIROS
18.04 g., 0.900 Silver 0.522 oz. ASW, 34.1 mm. **Subject:** 150th Anniversary of Independence **Obv:** Pedro I and General Emilio Garrastazu Medici heads left, date below **Rev:** Map above denomination **Edge Lettering:** SESQUICENTENARIO DA INDEPENDENCIA

Date	Mintage	VF20	XF40	MS60	MS63	MS65
1972 (a)	502,000	—	9.75	10.50	13.50	17.50

KM# 593.1 20 CRUZEIROS
6.33 g., Stainless Steel, 26 mm. **Obv:** Francis of Assisi Church **Rev:** Denomination above date, linear design **Edge:** Plain

Date	Mintage	VF20	XF40	MS60	MS63	MS65
1981	88,297,000	—	0.25	0.50	0.85	1.20
1982	158,200,000	—	0.20	0.40	0.65	0.85
1983	312,000,000	—	0.20	0.40	0.65	0.85
1984	226,000,000	—	0.20	0.40	0.65	0.85

KM# 593.2 20 CRUZEIROS
5.60 g., Stainless Steel, 26 mm. **Obv:** Francis of Assisi Church **Rev:** Denomination above date, linear design **Edge:** Plain **Note:** Reduced weight.

Date	Mintage	VF20	XF40	MS60	MS63	MS65
1985	205,000,000	—	0.20	0.40	0.65	0.85
1986	26,840,000	—	0.25	0.50	0.75	1.00

KM# 594.1 50 CRUZEIROS
7.34 g., Stainless Steel, 28 mm. **Obv:** Map of Brasilia **Rev:** Denomination above date, linear design **Edge:** Plain

Date	Mintage	VF20	XF40	MS60	MS63	MS65
1981	57,000,000	—	0.35	0.60	1.00	1.50
1982	134,000,000	—	0.20	0.40	0.65	0.85
1983	181,800,000	—	0.20	0.40	0.65	0.85
1984	292,418,000	—	0.20	0.40	0.65	0.85

KM# 594.2 50 CRUZEIROS
6.49 g., Stainless Steel, 28 mm. **Obv:** Map **Rev:** Denomination above date, linear design **Note:** Reduced weight.

Date	Mintage	VF20	XF40	MS60	MS63	MS65
1985	180,000,000	—	0.20	0.40	0.65	0.85
1986	52,580,000	—	0.20	0.40	0.65	0.85

KM# 595 100 CRUZEIROS
2.05 g., Stainless Steel, 17 mm. **Obv:** National arms **Rev:** Denomination above date

Date	Mintage	VF20	XF40	MS60	MS63	MS65
1985	162,000,000	—	0.20	0.30	0.40	0.65
1986	97,169,000	—	0.20	0.30	0.40	0.65

KM# 596 200 CRUZEIROS
2.55 g., Stainless Steel, 19 mm. **Obv:** National arms **Rev:** Denomination above date

Date	Mintage	VF20	XF40	MS60	MS63	MS65
1985	55,000,000	—	0.25	0.35	0.50	0.75
1986	54,830,000	—	0.25	0.35	0.50	0.75

KM# 584 300 CRUZEIROS
16.65 g., 0.920 Gold 0.4925 oz. AGW, 27.5 mm. **Subject:** 150th Anniversary of Independence **Obv:** Pedro I and general Emilio Garrastazu Medici heads left, date below **Rev:** Denomination below map **Edge Lettering:** SESQUICENTENARIO DA INDEPENDENCIA

Date	Mintage	VF20	XF40	MS60	MS63	MS65
1972 (a)	50,000	—	630	690	750	820

KM# 597 500 CRUZEIROS
3.65 g., Stainless Steel, 21 mm. **Obv:** National arms **Rev:** Denomination above date

Date	Mintage	VF20	XF40	MS60	MS63	MS65
1985	74,000,000	—	0.35	0.75	1.00	1.25
1986	95,740,000	—	0.35	0.75	1.00	1.25

REFORM COINAGE

1000 Cruzeiros Novos = 1 Cruzado;
100 Centavos = 1 Cruzado
1986-1989

KM# 600 CENTAVO
1.60 g., Stainless Steel, 15 mm. **Obv:** National arms **Rev:** Denomination above date **Edge:** Plain

Date	Mintage	VF20	XF40	MS60	MS63	MS65
1986	100,000,000	—	—	0.15	0.25	0.35
1987	1,000,000	—	—	0.25	0.50	0.65
1988	1,000,000	—	—	0.25	0.50	0.65

KM# 601 5 CENTAVOS
1.85 g., Stainless Steel, 16 mm. **Obv:** National arms **Rev:** Denomination above date **Edge:** Plain

Date	Mintage	VF20	XF40	MS60	MS63	MS65
1986	99,282,000	—	—	0.15	0.25	0.35
1987	1,000,000	—	—	0.25	0.50	0.65
1988	1,000,000	—	—	0.25	0.50	0.65

KM# 602 10 CENTAVOS
2.05 g., Stainless Steel, 17 mm. **Obv:** National arms **Rev:** Denomination above date **Edge:** Plain

Date	Mintage	VF20	XF40	MS60	MS63	MS65
1986	200,000,000	—	—	0.15	0.25	0.35
1987	245,628,000	—	—	0.15	0.25	0.35
1988	21,293,000	—	—	0.20	0.35	0.50

KM# 603 20 CENTAVOS
2.55 g., Stainless Steel, 19 mm. **Obv:** National arms **Rev:** Denomination above date **Edge:** Plain

Date	Mintage	VF20	XF40	MS60	MS63	MS65
1986	140,000,000	—	—	0.20	0.30	0.50
1987	157,500,000	—	—	0.20	0.30	0.50
1988	16,000,000	—	—	0.25	0.40	0.60

KM# 604 50 CENTAVOS
3.65 g., Stainless Steel, 21 mm. **Obv:** National arms **Rev:** Denomination above date

Date	Mintage	VF20	XF40	MS60	MS63	MS65
1986	200,000,000	—	—	0.35	0.50	0.65
1987	201,884,000	—	—	0.35	0.50	0.65
1988	131,255,000	—	—	0.35	0.50	0.65

KM# 605 CRUZADO
4.38 g., Stainless Steel, 23 mm. **Obv:** National arms **Rev:** Date divides denomination **Edge:** Plain

Date	Mintage	VF20	XF40	MS60	MS63	MS65
1986	235,500,000	—	—	0.25	0.45	0.65
1987	403,600,000	—	—	0.25	0.45	0.65
1988	321,216,000	—	—	0.25	0.45	0.65

KM# 606 5 CRUZADOS
5.21 g., Stainless Steel, 25 mm. **Obv:** National arms **Rev:** Date divides denomination **Edge:** Plain

Date	Mintage	VF20	XF40	MS60	MS63	MS65
1986	97,263,000	—	—	0.45	0.65	0.85
1987	141,000,000	—	—	0.45	0.65	0.85
1988	291,906,000	—	—	0.45	0.65	0.85

KM# 607 10 CRUZADOS
6.06 g., Stainless Steel, 27 mm. **Obv:** National arms **Rev:** Date divides denomination **Edge:** Plain

Date	Mintage	VF20	XF40	MS60	MS63	MS65
1987	131,500,000	—	—	0.65	1.00	1.25
1988	608,736,000	—	—	0.45	0.85	1.00

KM# 608 100 CRUZADOS
9.95 g., Stainless Steel, 31 mm. **Subject:** Abolition of Slavery Centennial - Male **Obv:** Denomination **Rev:** Outline divides dates on left from head on right

Date	Mintage	VF20	XF40	MS60	MS63	MS65
1988	200,000	—	0.75	1.50	2.50	4.00

KM# 609 100 CRUZADOS
9.95 g., Stainless Steel, 31 mm. **Subject:** Abolition of Slavery Centennial - Female **Obv:** Denomination **Rev:** Outline divides dates on left from head on right

Date	Mintage	VF20	XF40	MS60	MS63	MS65
1988	200,000	—	0.75	1.50	2.50	4.00

KM# 610 100 CRUZADOS
9.95 g., Stainless Steel, 31 mm. **Subject:** Abolition of Slavery Centennial - Child **Obv:** Denomination **Rev:** Outline divides dates on left from head on right

Date	Mintage	VF20	XF40	MS60	MS63	MS65
1988	200,000	—	0.75	1.50	2.50	4.00

REFORM COINAGE

1000 Old Cruzados = 1 Cruzado Novo
1989-1990

KM# 611 CENTAVO
2.01 g., Stainless Steel, 16.5 mm. **Obv:** Outlined denomination **Rev:** Farmer, date divides cows at bottom **Edge:** Plain

Date	Mintage	VF20	XF40	MS60	MS63	MS65
1989	208,100,000	—	—	0.25	0.35	0.50
1990	1,000,000	—	—	0.50	1.00	1.50

KM# 612 5 CENTAVOS
2.26 g., Stainless Steel, 17.5 mm. **Obv:** Outlined denomination **Rev:** Fisherman, two fish above date at bottom **Edge:** Plain

Date	Mintage	VF20	XF40	MS60	MS63	MS65
1989	270,400,000	—	—	0.30	0.45	0.60
1990	934,000	—	—	0.50	1.00	1.50

KM# 613 10 CENTAVOS
2.54 g., Stainless Steel, 18.5 mm. **Obv:** Outlined denomination **Rev:** Miner, three diamonds above date at bottom **Edge:** Plain

Date	Mintage	VF20	XF40	MS60	MS63	MS65
1989	362,900,000	—	—	0.40	0.60	0.75
1990	136,000,000	—	—	0.40	0.60	0.75

KM# 614 50 CENTAVOS
2.85 g., Stainless Steel, 19.5 mm. **Obv:** Outlined denomination **Rev:** Figure above design, date at bottom **Edge:** Plain

Date	Mintage	VF20	XF40	MS60	MS63	MS65
1989	453,800,000	—	—	0.50	0.75	1.00
1990	216,644,000	—	—	0.50	0.75	1.00

KM# 615 NOVO CRUZADO
9.95 g., Stainless Steel, 31 mm. **Subject:** Centennial of the Republic **Obv:** Denomination **Rev:** Laureate liberty bust 3/4 left divides dates

Date	Mintage	VF20	XF40	MS60	MS63	MS65
ND-1989	10,000,000	—	—	1.00	1.50	2.50

KM# 616 200 NOVOS CRUZADOS
13.47 g., 0.999 Silver 0.4326 oz. ASW, 31 mm. **Subject:** Centennial of the Republic **Obv:** Denomination **Rev:** Laureate liberty bust 3/4 left divides dates

Date	Mintage	VF20	XF40	MS60	MS63	MS65
ND (1989)	30,000	PF63 20.00	PF65 25.00			

REFORM COINAGE

100 Centavos = 1 Cruzeiro; 1 Cruzado Novo = 1 Cruzeiro
1990-1993

KM# 617 CRUZEIRO
3.61 g., Stainless Steel, 20.5 mm. **Obv:** Outlined denomination **Rev:** Date lower right of design

Date	Mintage	VF20	XF40	MS60	MS63	MS65
1990	377,000,000	—	—	0.20	0.35	0.50

KM# 618.1 5 CRUZEIROS
3.97 g., Stainless Steel, 21.5 mm. **Obv:** Outlined denomination **Rev:** Laborer, date at bottom **Edge:** Plain

Date	Mintage	VF20	XF40	MS60	MS63	MS65
1990	517,000,000	—	—	0.25	0.45	0.60
1991	510,000,000	—	—	0.25	0.45	0.60
1991	510,000,000	—	—	0.25	0.45	0.60

KM# 618.2 5 CRUZEIROS
3.40 g., Stainless Steel, 21.5 mm. **Obv:** Outlined denomination **Rev:** Laborer at top, small village above date at bottom **Edge:** Plain **Note:** Thinner planchet.

Date	Mintage	VF20	XF40	MS60	MS63	MS65
1991	Inc. above	—	—	0.25	0.45	0.60
1992	19,881,000	—	—	0.35	0.60	0.75

KM# 619.1 10 CRUZEIROS
4.36 g., Stainless Steel, 22.5 mm. **Obv:** Outlined denomination **Rev:** Laborer at top, small village above date at bottom

Date	Mintage	VF20	XF40	MS60	MS63	MS65
1990	413,000,000	—	—	0.25	0.50	0.75
1991	947,909,000	—	—	0.25	0.50	0.75

KM# 619.2 10 CRUZEIROS
3.74 g., Stainless Steel, 22.5 mm. **Note:** Thinner planchet.

Date	Mintage	VF20	XF40	MS60	MS63	MS65
1991	Inc. above	—	—	0.25	0.50	0.75
1992	25,000,000	—	—	0.35	0.75	1.00

KM# 620.1 50 CRUZEIROS
4.78 g., Stainless Steel, 23.5 mm. **Obv:** Outlined denomination **Rev:** Farmer, fish above date below

Date	Mintage	VF20	XF40	MS60	MS63	MS65
1990	10,000,000	—	—	0.50	0.75	1.00
1991	74,945,000	—	—	0.35	0.65	0.80

KM# 620.2 50 CRUZEIROS
4.09 g., Stainless Steel, 23.5 mm. **Obv:** Outlined denomination **Rev:** Farmer, fish above date below **Edge:** Plain **Note:** Thinner planchet.

Date	Mintage	VF20	XF40	MS60	MS63	MS65
1991	Inc. above	—	—	0.35	0.65	0.80
1992	128,298,000	—	—	0.35	0.65	0.80

KM# 623 100 CRUZEIROS
2.38 g., Stainless Steel, 18 mm. **Obv:** Date left of denomination **Rev:** Manatee **Edge:** Plain

Date	Mintage	VF20	XF40	MS60	MS63	MS65
1992	500,000,000	—	—	0.30	0.65	1.00
1993	70,000,000	—	—	0.30	0.65	1.00

KM# 621 500 CRUZEIROS
27.00 g., 0.925 Silver 0.803 oz. ASW, 40 mm. **Obv:** National arms at center, denomination below, 13 sets of arms surround **Rev:** Ibero - American Series, two dates at bottom

Date	Mintage	VF20	XF40	MS60	MS63	MS65
1991	40,000	PF63 40.00	PF65 50.00			

KM# 624 500 CRUZEIROS
2.66 g., Stainless Steel, 19 mm. **Obv:** Date left of denomination **Rev:** Loggerhead Sea Turtle

Date	Mintage	VF20	XF40	MS60	MS63	MS65
1992	250,000,000	—	—	0.35	0.75	1.25
1993	105,000,000	—	—	0.35	0.75	1.25

KM# 626 1000 CRUZEIROS
2.96 g., Stainless Steel, 20 mm. **Obv:** Date to left of denomination **Rev:** Fish - Acara **Edge:** Plain

Date	Mintage	VF20	XF40	MS60	MS63	MS65
1992	30,000,000	—	—	0.50	1.00	1.50
1993	435,000,000	—	—	0.35	0.75	1.25

KM# 622 2000 CRUZEIROS
27.00 g., 0.925 Silver 0.803 oz. ASW, 40 mm. **Subject:** U.N. Conference on Environment and Development **Obv:** Hummingbird and flower, denomination above **Rev:** Ocean and mountains, date above

Date	Mintage	VF20	XF40	MS60	MS63	MS65
1992	30,000	PF63 35.00	PF65 45.00			

KM# 625 5000 CRUZEIROS
9.95 g., Stainless Steel, 31 mm. **Subject:** 200th Anniversary of Tiradentes' Death **Obv:** Denomination **Rev:** Bust left, two dates below

Date	Mintage	VF20	XF40	MS60	MS63	MS65
1992	10,000,000	—	—	0.65	1.25	1.75

REFORM COINAGE

1000 Cruzeiros = 1 Cruzeiro Real
1993-1994

KM# 627 5 CRUZEIROS REAIS
3.27 g., Stainless Steel, 21 mm. **Obv:** Date to left of denomination **Rev:** Macaw Parrots - Arara, left **Edge:** Plain

Date	Mintage	VF20	XF40	MS60	MS63	MS65
1993	250,000,000	—	—	0.35	0.75	1.25
1994	70,000,000	—	—	0.35	0.75	1.25

KM# 628 10 CRUZEIROS REAIS
3.59 g., Stainless Steel, 22 mm. **Obv:** Date to left of denomination **Rev:** Anteater - Tamandua, right **Edge:** Plain

Date	Mintage	VF20	XF40	MS60	MS63	MS65
1993	300,000,000	—	—	0.35	0.75	1.25
1994	150,252,000	—	—	0.35	0.75	1.25

KM# 629 50 CRUZEIROS REAIS
3.92 g., Stainless Steel, 23 mm. **Obv:** Date to left of denomination **Rev:** Mother jaguar and cub facing **Edge:** Plain

Date	Mintage	VF20	XF40	MS60	MS63	MS65
1993	50,000,000	—	—	0.50	0.85	1.50
1994	30,000,000	—	—	0.50	0.85	1.50

KM# 630 100 CRUZEIROS REAIS
4.27 g., Stainless Steel, 24 mm. **Obv:** Date to left of denomination **Rev:** Maned wolf right **Edge:** Plain

Date	Mintage	VF20	XF40	MS60	MS63	MS65
1993	50,000,000	—	—	0.50	0.85	1.50
1994	40,000,000	—	—	0.50	0.85	1.50

REFORM COINAGE

2750 Cruzeiros Reais = 1 Real; 100 Centavos = 1 Real
1994-present

KM# 631 CENTAVO
2.96 g., Stainless Steel, 20 mm. **Obv:** Laureate liberty head left, linear design **Rev:** Denomination above date **Edge:** Plain

Date	Mintage	VF20	XF40	MS60	MS63	MS65
1994	887,100,000	—	—	0.20	0.35	0.50
1995	283,799,000	—	—	0.20	0.35	0.50
1996	320,000,000	—	—	0.20	0.35	0.50
1997	500,000,000	—	—	0.20	0.35	0.50

KM# 647 CENTAVO
2.43 g., Copper Plated Steel, 17 mm. **Obv:** Cabral bust at right **Rev:** Denomination on linear design at left, 3/4 globe with sash on right, date below **Edge:** Plain

Date	Mintage	VF20	XF40	MS60	MS63	MS65
1998	185,250,000	—	—	0.20	0.35	0.50
1999	104,874,000	—	—	—	0.10	0.20
2000	88,256,000	—	—	—	0.10	0.20

KM# 632 5 CENTAVOS
3.27 g., Stainless Steel, 21 mm. **Obv:** Laureate liberty head left, linear design **Rev:** Denomination above date **Edge:** Plain

Date	Mintage	VF20	XF40	MS60	MS63	MS65
1994	732,980,000	—	—	0.25	0.45	0.65
1995	240,000,000	—	—	0.25	0.45	0.65
1996	111,600,000	—	—	0.25	0.45	0.65
1997	235,000,000	—	—	0.25	0.45	0.65

KM# 648 5 CENTAVOS
4.10 g., Copper Plated Steel, 22 mm. **Obv:** Tiradente bust at right, dove at left **Rev:** Denomination on linear design at left, 3/4 globe with sash on right, date below **Edge:** Plain

Date	Mintage	VF20	XF40	MS60	MS63	MS65
1998	116,324,000	—	—	0.25	0.45	0.65
1999	11,264,000	—	—	0.35	0.70	1.00
2000	28,416,000	—	—	0.30	0.60	0.80

KM# 633 10 CENTAVOS
3.59 g., Stainless Steel, 22 mm. **Obv:** Laureate liberty head, left, lined background **Rev:** Denomiation above date **Edge:** Plain

Date	Mintage	VF20	XF40	MS60	MS63	MS65
1994	640,682,000	—	—	0.30	0.60	0.80
1995	239,000,000	—	—	0.30	0.60	0.80
1996	255,000,000	—	—	0.30	0.60	0.80
1997	265,000,000	—	—	0.30	0.60	0.80

KM# 641 10 CENTAVOS
3.59 g., Stainless Steel, 22 mm. **Series:** F.A.O. **Obv:** Hands holding seedling **Rev:** Denomination above date

Date	Mintage	VF20	XF40	MS60	MS63	MS65
1995	1,000,000	—	—	0.35	0.70	1.00

KM# 649.1 10 CENTAVOS
4.80 g., Bronze Plated Steel, 20 mm. **Subject:** Pedro I **Obv:** Bust of Pedro, horseman with sword in left hand **Rev:** Denomination and date **Edge:** Reeded **Note:** Majority of mintage recalled and melted.

Date	Mintage	VF20	XF40	MS60	MS63	MS65
1997	—	—	—	—	—	—
1998	—	—	—	—	—	—

KM# 649.2 10 CENTAVOS
4.80 g., Bronze Plated Steel, 20 mm. **Obv:** Bust of Pedro at right, horseman with sword in right hand at left **Rev:** Denomination on linear design at left, 3/4 globe with sash on right, date below **Edge:** Reeded

Date	Mintage	VF20	XF40	MS60	MS63	MS65
1998	141,540,000	—	—	0.30	0.60	0.80
1999	9,620,000	—	—	0.50	1.00	1.25
2000	26,880,000	—	—	0.40	0.80	1.00

KM# 634 25 CENTAVOS
4.78 g., Stainless Steel, 23.5 mm. **Obv:** Stylized laureate liberty head left, date below **Rev:** Outlined denomination, linear design **Edge:** Plain

Date	Mintage	VF20	XF40	MS60	MS63	MS65
1994	285,000,000	—	—	0.35	0.75	1.00
1995	140,000,000	—	—	0.35	0.75	1.00

KM# 642 25 CENTAVOS
4.78 g., Stainless Steel, 23.5 mm. **Series:** F.A.O. **Obv:** Farmer working **Rev:** Outlined denomination, linear design

Date	Mintage	VF20	XF40	MS60	MS63	MS65
1995	1,000,000	—	—	0.50	1.00	1.50

KM# 650 25 CENTAVOS
7.55 g., Bronze Plated Steel, 25 mm. **Obv:** Deodoro bust at right, national arms at left **Rev:** Denomination on linear design at left, 3/4 globe with sash on right, date below **Edge:** Reeded

Date	Mintage	VF20	XF40	MS60	MS63	MS65
1998	43,238,000	—	—	0.35	0.75	1.00
1999	32,766,000	—	—	0.35	0.75	1.00
2000	25,312,000	—	—	0.35	0.75	1.00

KM# 635 50 CENTAVOS
3.92 g., Stainless Steel, 23 mm. **Obv:** Laureate liberty head left, linear design **Rev:** Denomination above date **Edge:** Plain

Date	Mintage	VF20	XF40	MS60	MS63	MS65
1994	421,898,000	—	—	0.65	1.25	1.50
1995	60,000,000	—	—	0.65	1.25	1.50

KM# 651 50 CENTAVOS
9.25 g., Copper-Nickel, 23 mm. **Obv:** Rio Branco bust at right, map at left **Rev:** Denomination on linear design at left, 3/4 globe with sash on right, date below **Edge Lettering:** BRASIL ORDEM E PROGRESSO

Date	Mintage	VF20	XF40	MS60	MS63	MS65
1998	24,900,000	—	—	0.75	1.50	1.75
1999 Proof	2,000	—	—	—	—	—
2000	14,912,000	—	—	0.75	1.50	1.75

KM# 636 REAL
4.27 g., Stainless Steel, 24 mm. **Obv:** Laureate liberty head left, linear design **Rev:** Denomination above date

Date	Mintage	VF20	XF40	MS60	MS63	MS65
1994	215,000,000	—	—	0.65	1.25	1.50

KM# 652 REAL
7.84 g., Bi-Metallic Copper-Nickel center in Nickel-Brass ring, 27 mm. **Obv:** Allegorical portrait left **Rev:** Denomination on linear design at left, 3/4 globe with sash on right, date below **Edge:** Segmented reeding

Date	Mintage	VF20	XF40	MS60	MS63	MS65
1998	18,000,000	—	—	0.75	1.35	1.75
1999	3,840,000	—	—	1.00	2.00	2.50

KM# 653 REAL
7.84 g., Bi-Metallic Copper-Nickel center in Nickel-Brass ring, 27 mm. **Subject:** Universal Declaration of Human Rights **Obv:** Globe **Rev:** Denomination left, globe with sash at right, date below, linear design **Edge:** Segmented reeding

Date	Mintage	VF20	XF40	MS60	MS63	MS65
1998	600,000	—	—	1.00	2.00	2.50

KM# 637 2 REAIS
27.00 g., 0.925 Silver 0.803 oz. ASW, 40 mm. **Subject:** 300th Anniversary - First Brazilian Mint **Obv:** Denomination to right of date, design in background **Rev:** 300th Anniversary year below inscription

Date	Mintage	VF20	XF40	MS60	MS63	MS65
1994	7,000	PF65 85.00				

KM# 643 2 REAIS
27.00 g., 0.925 Silver 0.803 oz. ASW, 40 mm. **Subject:** Ayrton Senna - Race Driver **Edge:** Reeded

Date	Mintage	VF20	XF40	MS60	MS63	MS65
1995	10,000	PF65 220				

KM# 640 3 REAIS
11.50 g., 0.925 Silver 0.342 oz. ASW, 28 mm. **Subject:** 30th Anniversary - Central Bank **Obv:** Bank logo **Rev:** Denomination, linear design **Edge:** Reeded

Date	Mintage	VF20	XF40	MS60	MS63	MS65
1995	5,000	PF65 80.00				

KM# 645 3 REAIS
11.50 g., 0.925 Silver 0.342 oz. ASW, 28 mm. **Subject:** Centennial of Belo Horizonte **Obv:** Denomination, date lower right **Rev:** Collage, name, dates **Edge Lettering:** Baneo Central De Brazil. 1965-1995 • 30 Anos

Date	Mintage	VF20	XF40	MS60	MS63	MS65
1997	20,000	PF65 70.00				

KM# 638 4 REAIS
27.00 g., 0.925 Silver 0.803 oz. ASW, 40 mm. **Subject:** World Cup Soccer **Obv:** Hands lofting trophy divides date at bottom **Rev:** Denomination, background is soccer net **Edge:** Reeded

Date	Mintage	VF20	XF40	MS60	MS63	MS65
1994	9,000	PF65 115				

KM# 654 5 REAIS
28.00 g., 0.999 Silver 0.8993 oz. ASW, 40 mm. **Subject:** 500 Years - Discovery of Brazil **Obv:** Partial compass face and feathers, anniversary inscription and dates at left **Rev:** Figure at left, ship at right, partial compass face and feathers at lower right **Edge:** Reeded

Date	Mintage	VF20	XF40	MS60	MS63	MS65
ND-2000	15,385	PF65 55.00				

KM# 639 20 REAIS
8.00 g., 0.900 Gold 0.2315 oz. AGW, 22 mm. **Subject:** World Cup Soccer **Obv:** Hand held trophy **Rev:** Denomination in net **Edge:** Reeded

Date	Mintage	VF20	XF40	MS60	MS63	MS65
1994	2,000	PF65 800				

KM# 644 20 REAIS
8.00 g., 0.900 Gold 0.2315 oz. AGW, 22 mm. **Subject:** Ayrton Senna - Race Driver **Edge:** Reeded

Date	Mintage	VF20	XF40	MS60	MS63	MS65
1995	5,000	PF65 625				

KM# 655 20 REAIS
8.00 g., 0.900 Gold 0.2315 oz. AGW, 22 mm. **Subject:** 500 Years - Discovery of Brazil **Obv:** Partial compass face and feathers at right, anniversary dates at left **Rev:** Ornamented map, denomination at left **Edge:** Reeded

Date	Mintage	VF20	XF40	MS60	MS63	MS65
ND-2000	6,558	PF65 500				

LEPROSARIUM COINAGE

KM# L1 100 REIS
Brass, 20 mm. **Issuer:** Colonia Santa Teresa **Obv:** Denomination **Rev:** C.S.T.

Date	Mintage	F12	VF20	XF40	MS60	MS63
ND1940	—	—	—	150	250	350

KM# L2 200 REIS
Brass, 23 mm. **Issuer:** Colonia Santa Teresa **Obv:** Denomination **Rev:** C.S.T.

Date	Mintage	F12	VF20	XF40	MS60	MS63
ND1940	—	—	—	200	300	400

KM# L3 300 REIS
Brass, 23 mm. **Issuer:** Colonia Santa Teresa **Obv:** Denomination **Rev:** C.S.T.

Date	Mintage	F12	VF20	XF40	MS60	MS63
ND1940	—	—	—	250	350	450

KM# L4 500 REIS
Brass, 25 mm. **Issuer:** Colonia Santa Teresa **Obv:** Denomination **Rev:** C.S.T.

Date	Mintage	F12	VF20	XF40	MS60	MS63
ND1940	—	—	—	300	400	500

KM# L5 1000 REIS
Brass, 25 mm. **Issuer:** Colonia Santa Teresa **Obv:** Denomination **Rev:** C.S.T.

Date	Mintage	F12	VF20	XF40	MS60	MS63
ND1940	—	—	—	350	450	550

KM# L6 1.00 REIS
Brass, 20 mm. **Issuer:** Santa Casa de Misericordia

Date	Mintage	F12	VF20	XF40	MS60	MS63
ND1920 Rare	—	—	—	—	—	—

KM# L7 2.00 REIS
Brass, 24 mm. **Issuer:** Santa Casa de Misericordia **Obv:** Issuer name **Rev:** Denomination within circle

Date	Mintage	F12	VF20	XF40	MS60	MS63
ND1920	—	—	250	450	—	—

KM# L8 5.00 REIS

Brass, 27.5 mm. **Issuer:** Santa Casa de Misericordia

Date	Mintage	F12	VF20	XF40	MS60	MS63
ND1920 Rare	—	—	—	—	—	—

KM# L9 1.000 REIS

Brass, 30 mm. **Issuer:** Santa Casa de Misericordia

Date	Mintage	F12	VF20	XF40	MS60	MS63
ND1920 Rare	—	—	—	—	—	—

KM# L10 5.000 REIS

Brass, 33.5 mm. **Issuer:** Santa Casa de Misericordia

Date	Mintage	F12	VF20	XF40	MS60	MS63
ND1920	—	—	550	750	—	—

PATTERNS

Including off metal strikes

KM#	Date	Mintage	Identification	Mkt Val
Pn179	1901	—	100 Reis. Nickel-Silver.	200
Pn180	1901	—	100 Reis. Nickel. Birmingham Mint.	200
Pn181	1901	—	100 Reis. Nickel. Hamburg Mint.	200
Pn182	1901	—	100 Reis. Silver.	325
Pn183	1901	—	100 Reis. Gold.	1,600
Pn184	1901	—	200 Reis. Nickel-Silver.	270
Pn185	1901	—	200 Reis. Nickel. Birmingham Mint.	270
Pn186	1901	—	200 Reis. Nickel. Hamburg Mint.	270
Pn187	1901	—	200 Reis. Silver.	325
Pn188	1901	—	200 Reis. Gold.	2,550
Pn189	1901	—	400 Reis. Nickel-Silver.	270
Pn190	1901	—	400 Reis. Nickel. Birmingham Mint.	270
Pn191	1901	—	400 Reis. Nickel. Hamburg Mint.	270
Pn192	1901	—	400 Reis. Silver.	650
Pn193	1901	—	400 Reis. Gold.	3,800
Pn194	1902	—	100 Reis. Nickel. MCMI. 1902.	425
Pn195	1907	—	100 Reis. Silver.	450
Pn196	1907	—	200 Reis. Silver.	650
Pn197	1907	—	500 Reis. Silver.	450
Pn198	1907	—	1000 Reis. Silver.	450
Pn199	1907	—	2000 Reis. Silver.	450
Pn200	1908	—	50 Reis. Silver.	450
Pn201	1908	—	500 Reis. Silver.	450
Pn202	1908	—	1000 Reis. Silver.	450
Pn203	1908	—	2000 Reis. Silver.	450
Pn204	1910	—	40 Reis. Silver.	450
Pn205	1910	—	1000 Reis. Silver.	450
Pn206	1910	—	2000 Reis. Silver.	500
Pn207	1912	—	2000 Reis. Copper.	350
Pn208	1913	—	1000 Reis. Copper.	350
Pn209	1914	—	50 Reis. Silver.	425
Pn210	1914	—	400 Reis. Nickel.	350
Pn211	1914	—	2000 Reis. Silver.	875
Pn212	1916	—	20 Reis. Silver.	325
Pn213	1916	—	200 Reis. Nickel.	325
Pn214	1916	—	200 Reis. Silver.	550
Pn215	1916	—	2000 Reis. Silver.	875
Pn216	1917	—	50 Reis. Nickel.	350
Pn217	1917	—	100 Reis. Nickel.	350
Pn218	1917	—	200 Reis. Nickel.	350
Pn219	1917	—	400 Reis. Nickel.	350
Pn220	1917	—	500 Reis. Nickel.	425
Pn221	1917	—	1000 Reis. Nickel.	350
Pn222	1917	—	2000 Reis. Nickel.	350
Pn223	1918	—	20 Reis. Nickel.	270
Pn224	1918	—	20 Reis. Nickel. Large planchet.	215
Pn225	1918	—	20 Reis. Silver.	375
Pn226	1918	—	2000 Reis. Nickel. Center hole.	325
Pn227	1921	—	1000 Reis.	230
Pn228	1921	—	2000 Reis.	450
Pn229	1921	—	10000 Reis. Gold.	1,450
Pn230	1921	—	20000 Reis. Gold.	1,450
Pn231	1922	—	50 Reis. Copper-Nickel.	325
Pn232	1922	—	50 Reis. Nickel-Silver.	220
Pn233	1922	—	500 Reis. Aluminum-Bronze.	220
Pn234	1922	—	500 Reis. Silver. Large planchet.	230
Pn235	1922	—	1000 Reis. Aluminum-Bronze.	220
Pn236	1922	—	2000 Reis. Silver.	325
Pn237	1922	—	2000 Reis. Silver.	300
Pn238	ND (1922)	—	2000 Reis. Silver.	300
Pn239	1922	—	2000 Reis. Silver.	300
Pn240	1922	—	2000 Reis. 0.650. Silver.	300
Pn241	1922	—	2000 Reis. 0.835. Silver.	300
Pn242	1922	—	2000 Reis. 0.900. Silver.	300
Pn243	1923	—	1000 Reis. Silver.	450
Pn244	1923	—	2000 Reis. Silver.	325
Pn245	1923	—	2000 Reis. Silver.	325
Pn246	1923	—	2000 Reis. Silver.	325
Pn247	1923	—	2000 Reis. Silver.	325
Pn248	1923	—	2000 Reis. Silver.	325
Pn249	1923	—	2000 Reis. Silver.	325
Pn250	1924	—	100 Reis. Nickel.	210
Pn251	1924	—	400 Reis. Nickel.	210
Pn252	1924	—	500 Reis. Nickel.	210
Pn253	1924	—	500 Reis. Silver.	230
Pn254	1924	—	1000 Reis. Silver.	230
Pn255	1924	—	1000 Reis. Silver.	230
Pn256	1924	—	1000 Reis. Silver.	130
Pn257	1924	—	1000 Reis. Silver.	130
Pn258	1927	—	Cruzeiro. Copper.	200
Pn259	1927	—	Cruzeiro. Silver.	275
Pn260	1927	—	Cruzeiro. Gold.	425
Pn261	1927	—	2 Cruzeiros. Gold.	450
Pn262	1928	—	Cruzeiro. Nickel.	270
Pn263	1928	—	2 Cruzeiros. Nickel.	270
Pn264	1928	—	4 Cruzeiros. Nickel.	270
Pn265	1928	—	5 Cruzeiros. Nickel.	270
Pn266	1928	—	10 Cruzeiros. Nickel.	450
Pn267	1931	—	10 Reis. Silver.	230
Pn268	1932	—	100 Reis. Nickel-Silver. St. Vincent.	230
Pn269	1932	—	100 Reis. Silver. St. Vincent.	450
Pn270	1932	—	200 Reis. Nickel-Silver.	270
Pn271	1932	—	200 Reis. Copper-Nickel. St. Vincent.	270
Pn272	1932	—	200 Reis. Silver. St. Vincent.	285
Pn273	1932	—	400 Reis. Nickel-Silver.	300
Pn274	1932	—	400 Reis. Silver. St. Vincent.	325
Pn275	1932	—	500 Reis. Copper. Large planchet.	300
Pn276	1932	—	1000 Reis. Copper. St. Vincent.	325
Pn277	1932	—	1000 Reis. Aluminum-Bronze. Arms.	325
Pn278	1932	—	1000 Reis. Silver.	325
Pn279	1932	—	1000 Reis. Silver. Large planchet.	450
Pn280	1932	—	2000 Reis. Silver. St. Vincent.	325
Pn281	1935	—	200 Reis. Nickel. Large planchet.	230
Pn282	1935	—	400 Reis. Silver.	260
Pn283	1935	—	500 Reis. Nickel.	425
Pn284	1935	—	500 Reis. Nickel-Silver.	425
Pn285	1935	—	1000 Reis. Copper.	230
Pn286	1935	—	1000 Reis. Nickel.	230
Pn287	1935	—	1000 Reis. Nickel-Silver.	425
Pn288	1935	—	1000 Reis. Silver.	450
Pn289	1935	—	2000 Reis. Zinc.	325
Pn290	1935	—	2000 Reis. Bronze.	300
Pn291	1935	—	2000 Reis. Copper.	300
Pn292	1935	—	2000 Reis. Nickel-Silver.	425
Pn293	1935	—	2000 Reis. Silver.	375
Pn294	1936	—	100 Reis. Nickel-Silver.	215
Pn295	1936	—	100 Reis. Silver.	375
Pn296	1936	—	200 Reis. Nickel-Silver.	120
Pn297	1936	—	200 Reis. Silver.	140
Pn298	1936	—	300 Reis. Nickel-Silver.	120
Pn299	1936	—	400 Reis. Nickel-Silver.	120
Pn300	1936	—	400 Reis. Silver.	140
Pn301	1936	—	500 Reis. Nickel-Silver.	120
Pn302	1936	—	500 Reis. Silver.	140
Pn303	1936	—	1000 Reis. Nickel-Silver.	120
Pn304	1936	—	1000 Reis. Silver.	140
Pn305	1936	—	2000 Reis. Nickel-Silver.	120
Pn306	1936	—	5000 Reis. Zinc.	120
Pn307	1936	—	5000 Reis. Nickel-Silver.	120
Pn308	1936	—	5000 Reis. Silver.	140
Pn309	1937	—	100 Reis. Nickel.	120
Pn310	1937	—	300 Reis. Nickel-Silver.	120
Pn311	1937	—	300 Reis. Nickel.	120
Pn312	1938	—	200 Reis. Nickel.	120
Pn313	1938	—	2000 Reis. Copper.	120
Pn314	1939	—	500 Reis. Nickel.	120
Pn315	1939	—	1000 Reis.	120
Pn316	1939	—	2000 Reis. Aluminum-Bronze.	120
Pn317	1939	—	2000 Reis. Aluminum-Bronze. Peixoto.	120
Pn318	1940	—	10 Centavos. Silver.	120
Pn319	1940	—	100 Reis. Copper-Nickel.	120
Pn320	1940	—	100 Reis. Nickel.	120
Pn321	1940	—	200 Reis. Copper-Nickel.	120
Pn322	1940	—	200 Reis. Nickel.	120
Pn323	1940	—	300 Reis. Copper-Nickel.	120
Pn324	1940	—	300 Reis. Nickel.	120
Pn325	1940	—	400 Reis. Copper-Nickel.	120
Pn326	1940	—	400 Reis. Nickel.	120
Pn327	1941	—	10 Centavos. Nickel.	120
Pn328	1941	—	10 Centavos. Nickel-Silver.	120
Pn329	1941	—	50 Centavos. Brass.	120
Pn330	1941	—	50 Centavos. Nickel.	120
Pn331	1941	—	50 Centavos. Nickel-Silver.	120
Pn332	1941	—	50 Centavos. Nickel-Silver.	120
Pn333	1941	—	50 Centavos. Silver.	120
Pn334	1941	—	50 Centavos. Silver.	120
Pn335	1941	—	Cruzeiro. Nickel-Silver.	120
Pn336	1941	—	2 Cruzeiros. Nickel.	120
Pn337	1941	—	2 Cruzeiros. Nickel-Silver.	70.00
Pn338	1941	—	2 Cruzeiros. Silver.	100
Pn339	1942	—	100 Reis. Nickel.	70.00
Pn340	1942	—	200 Reis. Nickel.	70.00
Pn341	1942	—	300 Reis. Nickel.	70.00
Pn342	1942	—	400 Reis. Nickel.	70.00
Pn343	1942	—	2 Cruzeiros. Nickel.	70.00
Pn344	1942	—	2 Cruzeiros. Nickel-Silver.	70.00
Pn345	1943	—	10 Centavos. Nickel-Silver.	70.00
Pn346	1943	—	20 Centavos. Nickel-Silver.	70.00
Pn347	1943	—	20 Centavos. Silver.	70.00
Pn348	1943	—	50 Centavos. Nickel-Silver.	70.00
Pn349	1943	—	Cruzeiro. Silver.	75.00
Pn350	1945	—	10 Centavos. Nickel-Silver.	70.00
Pn351	1945	—	10 Centavos. Silver.	70.00
Pn352	1945	—	50 Centavos. Nickel-Silver.	70.00
Pn353	1945	—	50 Centavos. Silver.	70.00
Pn354	1945	—	Cruzeiro. Nickel.	70.00
Pn355	1945	—	Cruzeiro. Nickel-Silver.	70.00
Pn356	1947	—	20 Centavos. Aluminum-Bronze.	70.00
Pn357	1947	—	50 Centavos. Aluminum-Bronze.	185
Pn358	1947	—	2 Cruzeiros. Aluminum-Bronze.	120
Pn360	1950	—	Cruzeiro. Silver.	85.00
Pn361	1950	—	Cruzeiro. Gold.	—
Pn362	1955	—	50 Centavos. Aluminum.	70.00
Pn363	1956	—	10 Centavos. Aluminum. Arms.	70.00
Pn364	1956	—	10 Centavos. Aluminum-Bronze. Arms.	70.00
Pn365	1956	—	10 Centavos. Aluminum-Bronze. Bonifacio.	70.00
Pn366	1956	—	20 Centavos. Aluminum-Bronze.	70.00
Pn367	1956	—	50 Centavos. Aluminum.	70.00
Pn368	1956	—	Cruzeiro. Aluminum.	70.00
Pn369	1961	—	2 Cruzeiros. Aluminum-Bronze.	120
Pn370	1962	—	5 Cruzeiros.	120
Pn371	1963	—	5 Cruzeiros. Aluminum. Map.	120
Pn372	1963	—	5 Cruzeiros. Aluminum. Arms.	120
Pn373	1963	—	5 Cruzeiros. Aluminum-Bronze. Arms.	120
Pn374	1964	—	5 Cruzeiros. Aluminum.	120
Pn375	1964	—	10 Cruzeiros. Aluminum.	120
Pn376	1964	—	20 Cruzeiros. Aluminum.	120
Pn377	1964	—	50 Cruzeiros. Nickel.	120
Pn378	1964	—	100 Cruzeiros. Nickel.	120
Pn379	1964	—	200 Cruzeiros. Nickel.	120
Pn380	1965	—	5 Cruzeiros. Aluminum. Map.	120
Pn381	1965	—	5 Cruzeiros. Aluminum. Arms.	120
Pn382	1966	—	Centavo. Stainless Steel.	120
Pn383	1966	—	2 Centavos. Stainless Steel.	120
Pn384	1966	—	5 Centavos. Stainless Steel.	120
Pn385	1966	—	5 Centavos. Nickel.	120
Pn386	1966	—	10 Centavos. Copper-Nickel.	120
Pn387	1966	—	20 Centavos. Copper-Nickel.	120
Pn388	1967	—	10 Centavos. Stainless Steel.	120
Pn389	1972	—	20 Cruzeiros. 0.900. Silver. KM#583.	130

PROVAS

KM#	Date	Mintage	Identification	Mkt Val
Pr1	1967	—	Cruzeiro. Nickel. PROVA.	70.00
Pr2	1967	—	Cruzeiro. Nickel. PROVA.	70.00
Pr3	1970	—	20 Centavos. Stainless Steel. KM#579.1.	70.00
Pr4	1970	—	50 Centavos. Stainless Steel.	70.00
Pr5	1972	—	Cruzeiro. Nickel. Y#94.	185
Pr6	1972	—	20 Cruzeiros. Silver. Pedro I and General Emilio Garrastazu Medici heads left, date below. Denomination below map. KM#583.	170
Pr7	1972	—	300 Cruzeiros. Brass. KM#584.	220
Pr8	1972	—	300 Cruzeiros. Gold. KM#584.	3,000
Pr9	1974	—	10 Centavos. Stainless Steel. KM#578.1a.	60.00
Pr10	1974	—	Cruzeiro. Nickel. KM#581.	60.00
Pr11	1975	—	Centavo. Stainless Steel. KM#585.	60.00
Pr12	1975	—	2 Centavos. Stainless Steel. KM#586.	60.00
Pr13	1975	—	5 Centavos. Stainless Steel. KM#587.1.	60.00
Pr14	1975	—	10 Centavos. Stainless Steel. KM#578.1a.	60.00
Pr15	1975	—	50 Centavos. Stainless Steel. KM#580b.	60.00
Pr16	1975	—	10 Cruzeiros. Silver. KM#588.	95.00
Pr17	1976	—	Centavo. Silver. KM#585.	95.00
Pr18	1976	—	2 Centavos. Stainless Steel. KM#586.	42.00
Pr19	1976	—	5 Centavos. Stainless Steel. KM#587.1.	60.00
Pr20	1980	5,000	Centavo. Steel. KM#589.	42.00
Pr21	1980	5,000	10 Centavos. Steel.	42.00
Pr22	1980	5,000	50 Centavos. Steel.	42.00
Pr23	1980	5,000	Cruzeiro. Steel. KM#590.	42.00
Pr24	1980	5,000	5 Cruzeiros. Steel. KM#591.	42.00
Pr25	1980	5,000	10 Cruzeiros. Steel. KM#592.	42.00
PrA26	1988	—	100 Cruzados. Stainless Steel. KM#608.	60.00
PrB26	1988	—	100 Cruzados. Stainless Steel. KM#609.	60.00
PrC26	1988	—	100 Cruzados. Stainless Steel. KM#610.	60.00
Pr26	1989	—	Centavo. Steel. KM#611.	55.00
Pr27	1989	—	5 Centavos. Steel. KM#612.	55.00
Pr28	1989	—	10 Centavos. Steel. KM#613.	60.00
Pr29	1989	—	50 Centavos. Steel. KM#614.	65.00
Pr30	ND (1989)	—	200 Novos Cruzados. 0.999. Silver. KM#616.	110
Pr31	1990	—	Cruzeiro. Steel. KM#617.	50.00
Pr32	1990	—	5 Cruzeiros. Steel. KM#618.	50.00
Pr33	1990	—	10 Cruzeiros. Steel. KM#619.	55.00
Pr34	1990	—	50 Cruzeiros. Steel. KM#620.	60.00
Pr35	1991	—	500 Cruzeiros. 0.925. Silver. KM#621.	150
Pr36	1992	—	2000 Cruzeiros. Silver. KM#622.	185
Pr37	ND (1992)	—	5000 Cruzeiros. Steel. KM#625.	90.00
Pr38	1994	—	4 Reais. 0.925. Silver. KM#638.	200

TRIAL STRIKES

KM#	Date	Mintage	Identification	Mkt Val
TS4	1948	—	1000 Cruzeiros. Uniface.	900

MINT SETS

KM#	Date	Mintage	Identification	Issue Price	Mkt Val
MS1	1972 (2)	—	KM#582-583	—	25.00

BRITISH GUIANA

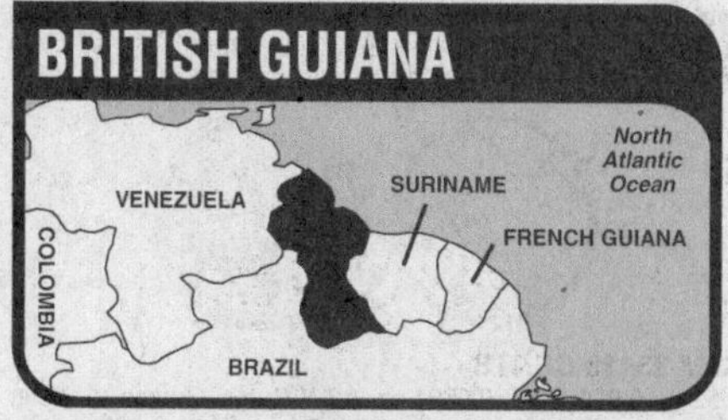

The first European settlement of this territory was made late in the 16th century by the Dutch, however, the region was claimed for the British by Sir Walter Raleigh during the reign of Elizabeth I. For the next 150 years, possession alternated between the Dutch and the British, with a short interval of French control. The British exercised de facto control after 1796 over the Dutch colonies of Essequibo, Demerary and Berbice. They were not ceded to them by the Dutch until 1814. From 1803 to 1831, Essequibo and Demerary were administered separately from Berbice. The three colonies were united in the British Crown Colony of British Guiana in 1831. British Guiana won internal self-government in 1952 and full independence, under the traditional name of Guyana, on May 26,1966.

BRITISH GUIANA AND WEST INDIES

STERLING COINAGE

KM# 26 4 PENCE
1.89 g., 0.925 Silver 0.0561 oz. ASW **Obv:** Head left **Rev:** Crowned denomination within wreath

Date	Mintage	F12	VF20	XF40	MS60	MS63
1901	60,000	5.00	10.00	22.50	55.00	70.00

KM# 27 4 PENCE
1.89 g., 0.925 Silver 0.0561 oz. ASW, 16 mm. **Obv:** Crowned bust right **Rev:** Crowned denomination within wreath **Edge:** Reeded

Date	Mintage	F12	VF20	XF40	MS60	MS63
1903	60,000	5.00	10.00	22.50	55.00	70.00
1903 Matte proof	—	PF63 450				
1908	30,000	5.00	12.50	40.00	90.00	100
1909	36,000	5.00	12.50	40.00	90.00	100
1910	66,000	5.00	10.00	40.00	85.00	100

KM# 28 4 PENCE
1.89 g., 0.925 Silver 0.0561 oz. ASW **Obv:** Crowned bust left **Rev:** Crowned denomination within wreath

Date	Mintage	F12	VF20	XF40	MS60	MS63
1911	30,000	8.00	25.00	70.00	115	130
1913	30,000	8.00	25.00	70.00	115	130
1916	30,000	8.00	25.00	70.00	115	130

BRITISH GUIANA

COLONIAL COINAGE

KM# 29 4 PENCE
1.89 g., 0.925 Silver 0.0561 oz. ASW **Obv:** Crowned bust left **Rev:** Crowned denomination within wreath

Date	Mintage	F12	VF20	XF40	MS60	MS63
1917	72,000	5.00	12.50	40.00	90.00	100
1917 Matte proof	—	PF63 450				
1918	210,000	2.00	3.50	15.00	55.00	65.00
1921	90,000	5.00	10.00	27.50	70.00	85.00
1923	12,000	20.00	45.00	85.00	160	180
1925	30,000	8.00	20.00	50.00	100	125
1926	30,000	8.00	20.00	50.00	100	125
1931	15,000	10.00	25.00	60.00	120	140
1931	—	PF63 175				
1935	36,000	3.00	12.50	50.00	175	200
1935	—	PF63 175				
1936	63,000	2.00	3.00	10.00	30.00	45.00
1936	—	PF63 225				

KM# 30 4 PENCE
1.89 g., 0.925 Silver 0.0561 oz. ASW **Obv:** Crowned head left **Rev:** Crowned denomination within wreath

Date	Mintage	F12	VF20	XF40	MS60	MS63
1938	30,000	8.00	20.00	50.00	100	125
1938	—	PF63 175				
1939	48,000	2.00	3.00	8.00	20.00	30.00
1939	—	PF63 175				
1940	90,000	2.00	3.00	7.00	18.50	25.00
1940	—	PF63 175				
1941	120,000	2.00	3.00	4.00	12.50	17.50
1941	—	PF63 175				
1942	180,000	2.00	3.00	4.00	12.50	17.50
1942	—	PF63 175				
1943	240,000	2.00	2.75	3.50	8.00	12.00
1943	—	PF63 400				

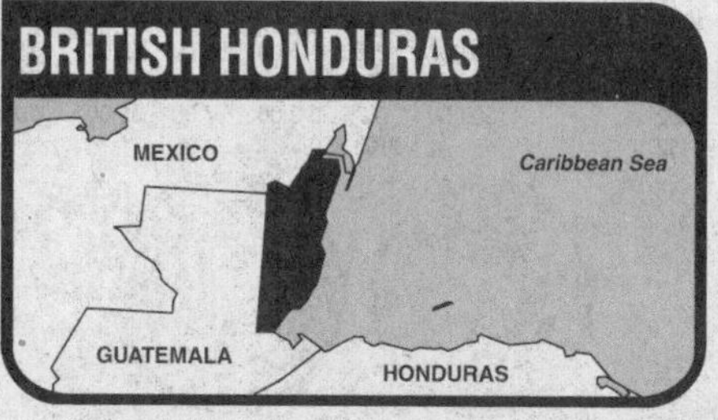

KM# 30a 4 PENCE
1.89 g., 0.500 Silver 0.0303 oz. ASW **Obv:** Head left **Rev:** Crowned denomination within wreath

Date	Mintage	F12	VF20	XF40	MS60	MS63
1944	90,000	1.25	2.00	6.50	18.50	25.00
1945	120,000	1.85	1.75	3.00	12.50	17.50
1945	—	PF63 200				

BRITISH HONDURAS

This area, site of the ancient Mayan civilization, was sighted by Columbus in 1502, and settled by shipwrecked English seamen in 1638. British buccaneers settled the former capital of Belize in the 17th century. Britain claimed administrative right over the area after the emancipation of Central America from Spain. In 1825, Imperial coins were introduced into the colony and were rated against the Spanish dollar and Honduran currency. It was declared a colony subordinate to Jamaica in 1862 and was established as the separate Crown Colony of British Honduras in 1884. In May, 1885 an order in Council authorized coins for the colony, with the first shipment arriving in July. While the Guatemalan peso was originally the standard of value, in 1894 the colony changed to the gold standard, based on the U.S. gold dollar. The anti-British Peoples United Party, which attained power in 1954, won a constitution, effective in 1964 which established self-government under a British appointed governor. British Honduras became Belize on June 1, 1973, following the passage of a surprise bill by the Peoples United Party, but the constitutional relationship with Britain remained unchanged. Full independence was achieved in 1981.

MONETARY SYSTEM
100 Cents = 1 Dollar

MINT MARKS
H - Heaton

BRITISH COLONY

DECIMAL COINAGE

KM# 11 CENT
Bronze **Ruler:** Edward VII **Obv:** Bust of King Edward VII right **Rev:** Numeric denomination within circle, denomination and date below

Date	Mintage	F12	VF20	XF40	MS60	MS63
1904	50,000	6.00	15.00	25.00	75.00	125
1904	—	PF63 400				
1904 Matte Proof	—	PF63 1,750				
1906	50,000	12.00	28.00	75.00	125	250
1906 Matte Proof	—	PF63 1,250				
1909	25,000	15.00	35.00	75.00	150	350

KM# 15 CENT
Bronze **Ruler:** George V **Obv:** Bust of King George V left **Rev:** Numeric denomination within circle, denomination and date below

Date	Mintage	F12	VF20	XF40	MS60	MS63
1911	50,000	20.00	50.00	100	250	650
1912 H	50,000	30.00	75.00	125	300	750
1913	25,000	40.00	90.00	150	450	850

KM# 19 CENT
Bronze **Ruler:** George V **Obv:** Bust of King George V left **Rev:** Numeric denomination within scalloped circle, denomination and date below

Date	Mintage	F12	VF20	XF40	MS60	MS63
1914	175,000	3.00	7.50	25.00	55.00	150
1916 H	125,000	3.50	8.50	28.00	65.00	175
1918	40,000	7.00	15.00	40.00	85.00	200
1919	50,000	7.00	15.00	40.00	85.00	200
1924	50,000	3.50	8.50	28.00	65.00	175
1924	—	PF63 350				
1926	50,000	5.00	12.00	35.00	70.00	185
1926	—	PF63 325				
1936	40,000	2.00	5.00	20.00	45.00	100
1936	50	PF63 500				

KM# 21 CENT
Bronze **Ruler:** George VI **Obv:** Bust of King George VI left **Rev:** Numeric denomination within scalloped circle, denomination and date below

Date	Mintage	F12	VF20	XF40	MS60	MS63
1937	80,000	0.75	4.00	12.00	75.00	—
1937	—	PF63 275				
1939	50,000	2.00	7.00	20.00	125	200
1939	—	PF63 200				
1942	50,000	2.00	7.00	20.00	150	—
1942	—	PF63 225				
1943	100,000	1.00	5.00	15.00	125	—
1943	—	PF63 250				
1944	100,000	2.00	7.00	20.00	150	—
1944	—	PF63 300				
1945	130,000	0.75	2.00	7.50	50.00	100
1945	—	PF63 225				
1947	100,000	0.75	2.50	10.00	75.00	150
1947	—	PF63 250				

KM# 24 CENT
Bronze **Ruler:** George VI **Obv:** Bust of King George VI left **Obv. Legend:** Without EMPEROR OF INDIA **Rev:** Numeric denomination within scalloped circle, denomination and date below

Date	Mintage	VF20	XF40	MS60	MS63	MS65
1949	100,000	0.60	1.50	8.00	12.00	18.00
1949	—	PF63 225				
1950	100,000	0.40	1.00	5.00	8.00	12.00
1950	—	PF63 225				
1951	100,000	0.60	1.50	8.00	12.00	18.00
1951	—	PF63 225				

KM# 27 CENT

Bronze **Ruler:** Elizabeth II **Obv:** Head right **Rev:** Numeric denomination within scalloped circle, date and denomination below **Edge:** Plain

Date	Mintage	VF20	XF40	MS60	MS63	MS65
1954	200,000	—	0.50	1.00	3.00	5.00
1954	—	PF63 175				

KM# 30 CENT

2.50 g., Bronze, 19.5 mm. **Ruler:** Elizabeth II **Obv:** Bust of Queen Elizabeth II right **Rev:** Numeric denomination within scalloped circle, date and denomination below **Edge:** Plain **Shape:** Scallop

Date	Mintage	VF20	XF40	MS60	MS63	MS65
1956	200,000	0.25	0.50	3.50	7.50	20.00
1956	—	PF63 85.00				
1958	400,000	2.00	9.00	60.00	100	—
1958	—	PF63 85.00				
1959	200,000	2.50	10.00	75.00	125	—
1959	—	PF63 110				
1961	800,000	—	0.15	0.25	0.50	1.50
1961	—	PF63 85.00				
1964	300,000	—	0.10	0.30	0.90	1.50
1965	400,000	—	—	0.10	0.50	1.50
1966	100,000	—	—	0.10	0.50	1.50
1967	400,000	—	—	0.10	0.50	1.50
1968	200,000	—	—	0.10	0.50	1.50
1969	520,000	—	—	0.10	0.40	1.50
1970	120,000	—	—	0.10	0.40	1.50
1971	800,000	—	—	0.10	0.40	1.50
1972	800,000	—	—	0.10	0.40	1.50
1973	400,000	—	—	0.10	0.40	1.50

KM# 14 5 CENTS

Copper-Nickel **Ruler:** Edward VII **Obv:** Bust of King Edward VII right within circle, date below **Rev:** Denomination within circle **Edge:** Plain

Date	Mintage	F12	VF20	XF40	MS60	MS63
1907	10,000	25.00	50.00	120	475	—
1909	10,000	25.00	60.00	150	1,450	—

KM# 16 5 CENTS

Copper-Nickel **Ruler:** George V **Obv:** Bust of King George V left within circle, date below **Rev:** Denomination within circle **Edge:** Plain

Date	Mintage	F12	VF20	XF40	MS60	MS63
1911	10,000	25.00	50.00	120	320	—
1912 H	20,000	10.00	25.00	60.00	260	—
1912 H	—	PF63 1,650				
1916 H	20,000	10.00	25.00	60.00	260	—
1918	20,000	10.00	25.00	60.00	260	—
1919	20,000	8.00	20.00	55.00	175	—
1936	60,000	2.50	5.00	25.00	135	200
1936	50	PF63 1,150				

KM# 22 5 CENTS

Copper-Nickel **Ruler:** George VI **Obv:** Head of King George VI left **Rev:** Denomination within circle, date below **Edge:** Plain

Date	Mintage	VF20	XF40	MS60	MS63	MS65
1939	20,000	6.00	20.00	60.00	100	125
1939	—	PF63 375				

KM# 22a 5 CENTS

Nickel-Brass **Ruler:** George VI **Obv:** Head of King George VI left **Rev:** Denomination within circle, date below

Date	Mintage	VF20	XF40	MS60	MS63	MS65
1942	30,000	15.00	65.00	300	—	—
1942	—	PF63 400				
1943	40,000	12.00	60.00	250	—	—
1944	50,000	10.00	50.00	225	—	—
1944	—	PF63 375				
1945	65,000	5.00	15.00	100	150	—
1945	—	PF63 250				
1947	40,000	5.00	15.00	125	175	—
1947	—	PF63 285				

KM# 25 5 CENTS

Nickel-Brass, 20 mm. **Ruler:** George VI **Obv:** Head of King George VI left **Obv. Legend:** Legend without EMPEROR OF INDIA **Rev:** Denomination within circle, date below **Edge:** Plain

Date	Mintage	VF20	XF40	MS60	MS63	MS65
1949	40,000	1.00	3.00	10.00	40.00	125
1949	—	PF63 250				
1950	225,000	1.50	5.00	15.00	50.00	150
1950	—	PF63 300				
1952	100,000	0.75	2.00	7.00	35.00	100
1952	—	PF63 350				

KM# 31 5 CENTS

3.60 g., Nickel-Brass, 20.26 mm. **Ruler:** Elizabeth II **Obv:** Bust of Queen Elizabeth II right **Rev:** Denomination within circle, date below **Edge:** Plain

Date	Mintage	VF20	XF40	MS60	MS63	MS65
1956	100,000	0.50	3.00	10.00	75.00	100
1956	—	PF63 150				
1957	100,000	0.75	1.50	5.00	10.00	15.00
1957	—	PF63 200				
1958	200,000	1.00	4.00	15.00	40.00	125
1958	—	PF63 150				
1959	100,000	2.00	6.00	25.00	75.00	200
1959	—	PF63 250				
1961	100,000	0.75	1.50	5.00	20.00	50.00
1961	—	PF63 150				
1962	200,000	0.25	0.50	0.75	1.25	2.00
1962	—	PF63 125				
1963	100,000	0.20	0.30	0.50	1.00	1.50
1963	—	PF63 200				
1964	100,000	0.15	0.25	0.35	0.65	1.00
1965	150,000	0.10	0.20	0.30	0.40	0.75
1966	150,000	0.10	0.20	0.25	0.35	0.60
1968	200,000	0.10	0.15	0.20	0.30	0.50
1969	540,000	0.10	0.15	0.20	0.30	0.50
1970	240,000	0.10	0.15	0.20	0.30	0.50
1971	450,000	0.10	0.15	0.20	0.30	0.50
1972	200,000	0.10	0.15	0.20	0.30	0.50
1973	210,000	0.10	0.15	0.25	0.40	0.75

KM# 20 10 CENTS

2.32 g., 0.925 Silver 0.0691 oz. ASW **Ruler:** George V **Obv:** Bust of King George V left **Rev:** Denomination within circle, date below **Edge:** Reeded

Date	Mintage	F12	VF20	XF40	MS60	MS63
1918	10,000	15.00	25.00	100	350	—
1919	10,000	15.00	25.00	100	350	—
1936	30,000	6.00	12.00	25.00	125	400
1936	50	PF63 1,150				

KM# 23 10 CENTS

2.32 g., 0.925 Silver 0.0691 oz. ASW **Ruler:** George VI **Obv:** Head of King George VI left **Rev:** Denomination within circle, date below **Edge:** Plain

Date	Mintage	F12	VF20	XF40	MS60	MS63
1939	20,000	3.00	7.00	20.00	60.00	120
1939	—	PF63 1,000				
1942	10,000	10.00	20.00	60.00	250	—
1943	20,000	3.00	6.00	45.00	250	—
1944	30,000	2.50	5.00	35.00	150	—
1944	—	PF63 600				
1946	10,000	5.00	12.00	45.00	200	—
1946	—	PF63 900				

KM# 32 10 CENTS

2.34 g., Copper-Nickel, 18 mm. **Ruler:** Elizabeth II **Obv:** Bust of Queen Elizabeth II right **Rev:** Denomination within circle, date below **Edge:** Plain

Date	Mintage	VF20	XF40	MS60	MS63	MS65
1956	100,000	0.75	1.25	3.00	7.50	10.00
1956	—	PF63 225				
1959	100,000	0.75	1.25	3.00	7.50	10.00
1959	—	PF63 150				
1961	50,000	0.35	0.75	1.50	3.00	5.00
1961	—	PF63 150				
1963	50,000	0.20	0.50	1.00	2.00	3.50
1963	—	PF63 150				
1964	60,000	0.15	0.25	0.75	1.00	3.00
1965/6	200,000	5.00	10.00	20.00	40.00	65.00
1965	Inc. above	—	0.10	0.25	0.50	1.00
1970	—	—	0.10	0.35	0.75	1.25

KM# 9 25 CENTS

5.81 g., 0.925 Silver 0.1728 oz. ASW **Ruler:** Victoria **Obv:** Head of Queen Victoria left **Rev:** Denomination within circle, date below **Edge:** Reeded

Date	Mintage	F12	VF20	XF40	MS60	MS63
1901	20,000	22.50	45.00	175	550	—
1901	30	PF63 2,000				

KM# 12 25 CENTS

5.81 g., 0.925 Silver 0.1728 oz. ASW **Ruler:** Edward VII **Obv:** Bust of King Edward VII right **Rev:** Denomination within circle, date below **Edge:** Reeded

Date	Mintage	F12	VF20	XF40	MS60	MS63
1906	30,000	15.00	30.00	110	375	—
1907	60,000	10.00	25.00	95.00	325	—

KM# 17 25 CENTS

5.81 g., 0.925 Silver 0.1728 oz. ASW, 23 mm. **Ruler:** George V **Obv:** Bust of King George V left **Rev:** Denomination within circle, date below **Edge:** Reede d

Date	Mintage	F12	VF20	XF40	MS60	MS63
1911	14,000	25.00	60.00	150	400	—
1919	40,000	8.00	17.50	75.00	250	1,200

KM# 26 25 CENTS
Copper-Nickel **Ruler:** George VI **Obv:** Head of King George VI left **Rev:** Denomination within circle, date below **Edge:** Reeded

Date	Mintage	F12	VF20	XF40	MS60	MS63
1952	75,000	2.00	5.00	50.00	150	250
1952	—	**PF63** 275				

KM# 29 25 CENTS
5.62 g., Copper-Nickel, 23.53 mm. **Ruler:** Elizabeth II **Obv:** Bust of Queen Elizabeth II right **Rev:** Denomination within circle, date below **Edge:** Reeded

Date	Mintage	VF20	XF40	MS60	MS63	MS65
1955	75,000	1.00	3.50	7.00	15.00	25.00
1955	—	**PF63** 175				
1960	75,000	1.00	5.00	15.00	100	175
1960	—	**PF63** 275				
1962	50,000	0.50	1.00	1.50	2.50	5.00
1962	—	**PF63** 175				
1963	50,000	0.50	1.25	3.50	7.50	10.00
1963	—	**PF63** 175				
1964	100,000	—	0.35	0.75	1.50	3.00
1965	75,000	0.25	0.40	1.00	2.00	5.00
1966	75,000	0.45	1.00	4.00	8.00	10.00
1968	125,000	0.25	0.35	1.00	2.00	3.00
1970	—	0.20	0.35	0.75	1.50	3.00
1971	150,000	0.20	0.35	0.75	1.50	3.00
1972	200,000	0.20	0.35	0.75	1.50	3.00
1973	100,000	0.30	0.50	1.00	1,75	3.00

KM# 10 50 CENTS
11.62 g., 0.925 Silver 0.3456 oz. ASW **Ruler:** Victoria **Obv:** Head of Queen Victoria left **Rev:** Denomination within circle, date below

Date	Mintage	F12	VF20	XF40	MS60	MS63
1901	10,000	45.00	100	450	1,100	—
1901	30	**PF63** 3,500	**PF65** 5,000			

KM# 13 50 CENTS
11.62 g., 0.925 Silver 0.3456 oz. ASW **Ruler:** Edward VII **Obv:** Bust of King Edward VII right **Rev:** Denomination within circle, date below

Date	Mintage	F12	VF20	XF40	MS60	MS63
1906	15,000	50.00	200	900	—	—
1907	19,000	40.00	150	800	3,000	—

KM# 18 50 CENTS
11.62 g., 0.925 Silver 0.3456 oz. ASW **Ruler:** George V **Obv:** Bust of King George V left **Rev:** Denomination within circle, date below

Date	Mintage	F12	VF20	XF40	MS60	MS63
1911	12,000	30.00	75.00	250	850	1,650
1919	40,000	20.00	40.00	150	450	1,350
1919	—	**PF63** 2,800				

KM# 28 50 CENTS
Copper-Nickel **Ruler:** Elizabeth II **Obv:** Bust of Queen Elizabeth II right **Rev:** Denomination within circle, date below

Date	Mintage	VF20	XF40	MS60	MS63	MS65
1954	75,000	0.30	0.50	2.00	4.00	10.00
1954	—	**PF63** 275				
1962	50,000	0.30	0.50	2.50	5.00	10.00
1962	—	**PF63** 300				
1964	50,000	0.30	0.50	2.50	3.50	8.00
1965	25,000	1.25	3.00	10.00	22.50	35.00
1966	25,000	1.00	2.00	6.00	15.00	25.00
1971	30,000	0.30	0.50	2.50	3.50	5.00

PROOF SETS

KM#	Date	Mintage	Identification	Issue Price	Mkt Val
PS2	1901 (2)	30	KM#9, 10	—	4,350
PS3	1936 (3)	50	KM#16, 19, 20	—	2,550
PS4	1939 (3)	—	KM#21-23	—	1,600
PS5	1949 (2)	—	KM#24, 25	—	475
PS6	1950 (2)	—	KM#24, 25	—	525
PS7	1954 (2)	—	KM#27, 28	—	450
PS8	1956 (3)	—	KM#30-32	—	475
PS9	1958 (2)	—	KM#30, 31	—	250

BRITISH NORTH BORNEO

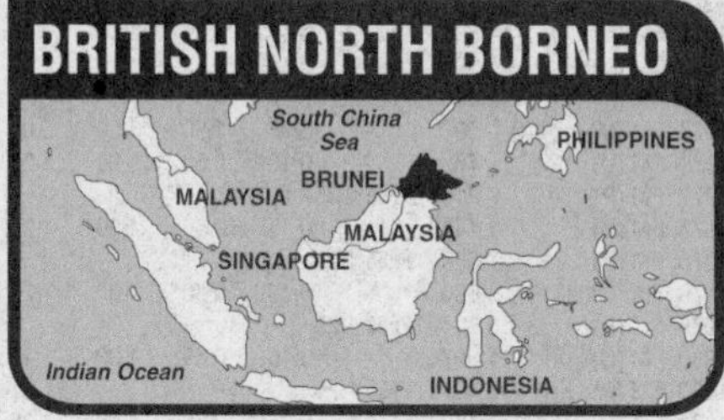

British North Borneo (now known as *Sabah*), a former British protectorate and crown colony, occupies the northern tip of the island of Borneo. The island of Labuan, which lies 6 miles off the northwest coast of the island of Borneo, was attached to Singapore settlement in 1907. It became an independent settlement of the Straits Colony in 1912 and was incorporated with British North Borneo in 1946. In 1963 it became part of Malaysia.

RULER
British

MINT MARKS
H - Heaton, Birmingham

MONETARY SYSTEM
100 Cents = 1 Straits Dollar

BRITISH PROTECTORATE

STANDARD COINAGE

KM# 1 1/2 CENT
Bronze **Obv:** Denomination within wreath **Rev:** National arms, date below

Date	Mintage	VF20	XF40	MS60	MS63	MS65
1907 H	1,000,000	55.00	200	350	500	800
1907 H	—	**PF60** 800	**PF63** 1,200			

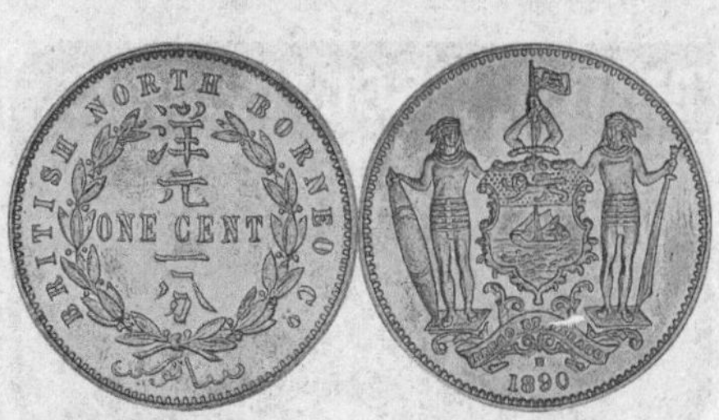

KM# 2 CENT
9.25 g., Bronze, 29.6 mm. **Obv:** Denomination within wreath **Rev:** National arms with supporters, date below

Date	Mintage	VF20	XF40	MS60	MS63	MS65
1907 H	1,000,000	65.00	175	300	500	800
1907 H	—	**PF60** 2,500	**PF63** 4,500			

KM# 3 CENT
Copper-Nickel **Obv:** Denomination within circle, date below **Rev:** National arms with supporters

Date	Mintage	VF20	XF40	MS60	MS63	MS65
1904 H	2,000,000	10.00	25.00	70.00	150	275
1921 H	1,000,000	10.00	25.00	70.00	150	275
1935 H	1,000,000	6.00	18.00	50.00	125	225
1938 H	1,000,000	6.00	18.00	50.00	125	225
1941 H	1,000,000	6.00	18.00	50.00	125	225

KM# 4 2-1/2 CENT
Copper-Nickel **Obv:** Denomination within circle, date below **Rev:** National arms with supporters

Date	Mintage	VF20	XF40	MS60	MS63	MS65
1903 H	2,000,000	35.00	75.00	125	185	300
1903 H	—	**PF60** 700	**PF63** 1,000			
1920 H	280,000	50.00	100	165	275	450

KM# 5 5 CENTS
Copper-Nickel, 28 mm. **Obv:** Denomination within circle, date below **Rev:** National arms with supporters

Date	Mintage	VF20	XF40	MS60	MS63	MS65
1903 H	1,000,000	16.00	25.00	50.00	100	175
1920 H	100,000	30.00	60.00	90.00	150	250
1921 H	500,000	12.00	20.00	45.00	90.00	135
1927 H	150,000	12.00	20.00	45.00	90.00	135
1928 H	150,000	7.00	15.00	35.00	75.00	125
1938 H	500,000	5.00	12.00	20.00	50.00	80.00
1940 H	500,000	5.00	12.00	20.00	50.00	80.00
1941 H	1,000,000	5.00	12.00	20.00	50.00	80.00

KM# 6 25 CENTS
2.83 g., 0.500 Silver 0.0455 oz. ASW **Obv:** Denomination within circle, date below **Rev:** National arms with supporters

Date	Mintage	VF20	XF40	MS60	MS63	MS65
1929 H	400,000	35.00	75.00	135	250	400
1929 H	—	**PF60** 700	**PF63** 1,000	**PF65** 1,500		

BRITISH VIRGIN ISLANDS

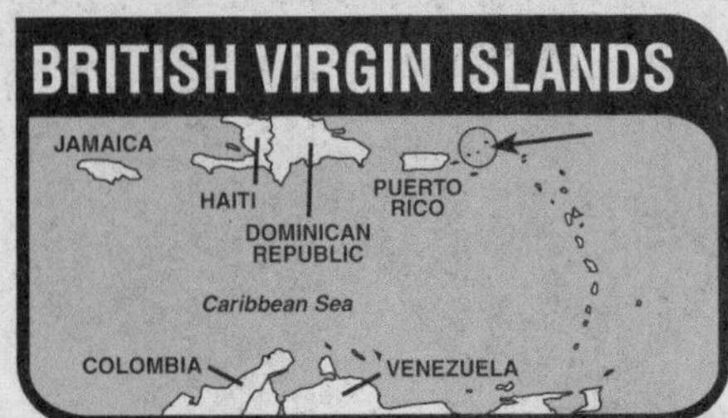

The Colony of the Virgin Islands, a British colony situated in the C aribbean Sea northeast of Puerto Rico and west of the Leeward Islands, has an area of 59 sq. mi. (155 sq. km.) and a population of 13,000. Capital: Road Town. The principal islands of the 36-island group are Tortola, Virgin Gorda, Anegada, and Jost Van Dyke. The chief industries are fishing and stock raising. Fish, livestock and bananas are exported.

The Virgin Islands were discovered by Columbus in 1493, and named by him, Las Virgienes, in honor of St. Ursula and her companions. The British Virgin Islands were formerly part of the administration of the Leeward Islands but received a separate administration as a Crown Colony in 1950. A new constitution promulgated in 1967 provided for a ministerial form of government headed by the Governor.

The Government of the British Virgin Islands issued the first official coinage in its history on June 30, 1973, in honor of 300 years of constitutional government in the islands. U.S. coins and currency continue to be the primary medium of exchange, though the coinage of the British Virgin Islands is legal tender.

***NOTE**: From 1975-1985 the Franklin Mint produced coinage in up to 3 different qualities. Qualities of issue are designated in ( ) after each date and are defined as follows:

(M) MATTE - Normal circulation strike or a dull finish produced by sandblasting special uncirculated (polish finish) or proof quality dies.

(U) SPECIAL UNCIRCULATED - Polished or proof-like in appearance without any frosted features.**(P) PROOF** - The highest quality obtainable having mirror-like fields and frosted features.

BRITISH COLONY

STANDARD COINAGE

KM# 1 CENT

1.50 g., Bronze **Ruler:** Elizabeth II **Obv:** Young bust right **Rev:** Green-throated Carib and Antillean Crested Hummingbird

Date	Mintage	VF20	XF40	MS60	MS63	MS65
1973 FM	53,000	—	0.10	0.30	0.50	1.00
1973 FM (P)	181,000	PF65 1.00				
1974 FM	22,000	—	0.10	0.30	0.50	1.00
1974 FM (P)	94,000	PF65 1.00				
1975 FM (M)	6,000	—	0.10	0.35	0.75	1.20
1975 FM (U)	2,351	—	0.10	0.30	0.50	1.00
1975 FM (P)	32,000	PF65 1.00				
1976 FM (M)	12,000	—	0.10	0.30	0.50	1.00
1976 FM (U)	996	—	0.10	0.30	0.50	1.00
1976 FM (P)	15,000	PF65 1.00				
1977 FM (M)	500	—	0.25	1.00	2.00	3.00
1977 FM (U)	782	—	0.10	0.30	0.50	1.00
1977 FM (P)	7,218	PF65 1.00				
1978 FM (U)	1,443	—	0.10	0.30	0.50	1.00
1978 FM (P)	7,059	PF65 1.00				
1979 FM (U)	680	—	0.10	0.30	0.50	1.00
1979 FM (P)	5,304	PF65 1.00				
1980 FM (U)	1,007	—	0.10	0.30	0.50	1.00
1980 FM (P)	3,421	PF65 1.00				
1981 FM (U)	472	—	0.10	0.30	0.50	1.00
1981 FM (P)	1,124	PF65 1.50				
1982 FM (U)	—	—	0.10	0.30	0.50	1.00
1982 FM (P)	—	PF65 1.50				
1983 FM (U)	—	—	0.10	0.30	0.50	1.00
1983 FM (P)	—	PF65 1.50				
1984 FM (P)	—	PF65 1.50				

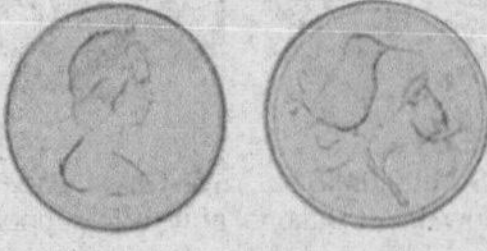

KM# 9 CENT

1.75 g., 0.925 Silver 0.052 oz. ASW **Ruler:** Elizabeth II **Subject:** Queen's Silver Jubilee **Obv:** Young bust right **Rev:** Green-throated Carib and Antillean Crested Hummingbird

Date	Mintage	VF20	XF40	MS60	MS63	MS65
1977 FM (P)	17,000	PF65 3.00				

KM# 16 CENT

1.75 g., 0.925 Silver 0.052 oz. ASW **Ruler:** Elizabeth II **Subject:** Coronation Jubilee **Obv:** Young bust right **Rev:** Hummingbird

Date	Mintage	VF20	XF40	MS60	MS63	MS65
1978 FM (P)	6,196	PF65 8.00				

KM# 42 CENT

Bronze **Ruler:** Elizabeth II **Obv:** Crowned head right **Rev:** Hawksbill Turtle left

Date	Mintage	VF20	XF40	MS60	MS63	MS65
1985 FM (P)	—	PF65 5.00				

KM# 42a CENT

1.75 g., 0.925 Silver 0.052 oz. ASW **Ruler:** Elizabeth II **Obv:** Crowned head right **Rev:** Hawksbill turtle left

Date	Mintage	VF20	XF40	MS60	MS63	MS65
1985 FM (P)	1,474	PF65 7.50				

KM# 2 5 CENTS

3.00 g., Copper-Nickel, 19.5 mm. **Ruler:** Elizabeth II **Obv:** Young bust right **Rev:** Zenaida Doves

Date	Mintage	VF20	XF40	MS60	MS63	MS65
1973 FM	26,000	—	0.15	0.40	0.75	1.00
1973 FM (P)	181,000	PF65 1.25				
1974 FM	18,000	—	0.15	0.40	0.75	1.00
1974 FM (P)	94,000	PF65 1.25				
1975 FM (M)	3,800	—	0.20	0.50	1.00	1.25
1975 FM (U)	2,351	—	0.15	0.40	0.75	1.00
1975 FM (P)	32,000	PF65 1.25				
1976 FM (M)	4,800	—	0.15	0.50	1.00	1.25
1976 FM (U)	996	—	0.15	0.65	1.25	1.50
1976 FM (P)	15,000	PF65 1.25				
1977 FM (M)	500	—	0.35	1.50	3.50	5.00
1977 FM (U)	782	—	0.15	0.50	1.00	1.25
1977 FM (P)	7,218	PF65 1.25				
1978 FM (U)	1,443	—	0.15	0.50	1.00	1.25
1978 FM (P)	7,059	PF65 1.25				
1979 FM (U)	680	—	0.15	0.50	1.00	1.25
1979 FM (P)	5,304	PF65 1.25				
1980 FM (U)	1,007	—	0.15	0.50	1.00	1.25
1980 FM (P)	3,421	PF65 1.25				
1981 FM (U)	472	—	0.15	0.50	1.00	1.25
1981 FM (P)	1,124	PF65 1.25				
1982 FM (U)	—	—	0.15	0.50	1.00	1.25
1982 FM (P)	—	PF65 1.25				
1983 FM (U)	—	—	0.15	0.50	1.00	1.25
1983 FM (P)	—	PF65 1.25				
1984 FM (P)	—	PF65 1.25				

KM# 10 5 CENTS

3.55 g., 0.925 Silver 0.1056 oz. ASW, 19.5 mm. **Ruler:** Elizabeth II **Subject:** Queen's Silver Jubilee **Obv:** Young bust right **Rev:** Zenaida Doves

Date	Mintage	VF20	XF40	MS60	MS63	MS65
1977 FM (P)	17,000	PF65 3.00				

KM# 17 5 CENTS

3.55 g., 0.925 Silver 0.1056 oz. ASW, 19.5 mm. **Ruler:** Elizabeth II **Subject:** Coronation Jubilee **Obv:** Young bust right divides dates **Rev:** Zenaida Doves

Date	Mintage	VF20	XF40	MS60	MS63	MS65
ND-1978 FM (P)	6,196	PF65 8.00				

KM# 43 5 CENTS

Copper-Nickel **Ruler:** Elizabeth II **Obv:** Crowned head right **Rev:** Bonito Fish left

Date	Mintage	VF20	XF40	MS60	MS63	MS65
1985 FM (P)	—	PF65 6.00				

KM# 43a 5 CENTS

3.56 g., 0.925 Silver 0.1057 oz. ASW **Ruler:** Elizabeth II **Obv:** Crowned head right **Rev:** Bonito fish left

Date	Mintage	VF20	XF40	MS60	MS63	MS65
1985 FM (P)	1,471	PF65 8.50				

KM# 3 10 CENTS

5.50 g., Copper-Nickel **Ruler:** Elizabeth II **Obv:** Young bust right **Rev:** Ringed Kingfisher right **Edge:** Reeded

Date	Mintage	VF20	XF40	MS60	MS63	MS65
1973 FM (U)	23,000	—	0.15	0.50	1.00	1.25
1973 FM (P)	181,000	PF65 2.00				
1974 FM (U)	13,000	—	0.15	0.50	1.00	1.25
1974 FM (P)	94,000	PF65 2.00				
1975 FM (M)	2,000	—	0.20	0.65	1.25	1.50
1975 FM (U)	2,351	—	0.15	0.50	1.00	1.25
1975 FM (P)	32,000	PF65 2.00				
1976 FM (M)	3,000	—	0.15	0.50	1.00	1.25
1976 FM (U)	996	—	0.20	0.65	1.25	1.50
1976 FM (P)	15,000	PF65 2.00				
1977 FM (M)	500	—	0.45	2.00	4.00	6.00
1977 FM (U)	782	—	0.20	0.75	1.50	2.00
1977 FM (P)	7,218	PF65 2.50				
1978 FM (U)	1,443	—	0.20	0.65	1.25	1.50
1978 FM (P)	7,059	PF65 2.00				
1979 FM (U)	680	—	0.20	0.75	1.50	2.00
1979 FM (P)	5,304	PF65 2.50				
1980 FM (U)	1,007	—	0.20	0.75	1.50	2.00
1980 FM (P)	3,421	PF65 2.50				
1981 FM (U)	472	—	0.25	1.00	2.00	2.50
1981 FM (P)	1,124	PF65 3.00				
1982 FM (U)	—	—	0.25	1.00	2.00	2.50
1982 FM (P)	—	PF65 3.00				
1983 FM (U)	—	—	0.25	1.00	2.00	2.50
1983 FM (P)	—	PF65 3.00				
1984 FM (P)	—	PF65 2.00				

KM# 11 10 CENTS

6.40 g., 0.925 Silver 0.1903 oz. ASW **Ruler:** Elizabeth II **Subject:** Queen's Silver Jubilee **Obv:** Young bust right **Rev:** Ringed Kingfisher left

Date	Mintage	VF20	XF40	MS60	MS63	MS65
1977 FM (P)	17,000	PF65 5.00				

KM# 18 10 CENTS

6.40 g., 0.925 Silver 0.1903 oz. ASW **Ruler:** Elizabeth II **Subject:** Coronation Jubilee **Obv:** Young bust right divides dates **Rev:** Ringed Kingfisher left

Date	Mintage	VF20	XF40	MS60	MS63	MS65
ND-1978 FM (P)	6,196	PF65 9.00				

KM# 44 10 CENTS
Copper-Nickel **Ruler:** Elizabeth II **Obv:** Crowned head right **Rev:** Great Barracuda right

Date	Mintage	VF20	XF40	MS60	MS63	MS65
1985 FM (P)	—	PF65 7.50				

KM# 44a 10 CENTS
6.40 g., 0.925 Silver 0.1903 oz. ASW **Ruler:** Elizabeth II **Obv:** Crowned head right **Rev:** Great Barracuda right

Date	Mintage	VF20	XF40	MS60	MS63	MS65
1985 FM (P)	1,474	PF65 10.00				

KM# 4 25 CENTS
7.50 g., Copper-Nickel **Ruler:** Elizabeth II **Obv:** Young bust right **Rev:** Mangrove Cuckoo **Edge:** Reeded

Date	Mintage	VF20	XF40	MS60	MS63	MS65
1973 FM	21,000	—	0.30	0.75	1.50	1.75
1973 FM (P)	181,000	PF65 1.50				
1974 FM	12,000	—	0.30	0.75	1.50	1.75
1974 FM (P)	94,000	PF65 2.00				
1975 FM (M)	1,000	—	0.35	1.50	3.00	4.00
1975 FM (U)	2,351	—	0.30	0.75	1.50	1.75
1975 FM (P)	32,000	PF65 2.00				
1976 FM (M)	2,000	—	0.30	1.00	2.00	3.00
1976 FM (U)	996	—	0.30	1.25	2.50	3.50
1976 FM (P)	15,000	PF65 2.00				
1977 FM (M)	500	—	0.50	2.50	5.00	7.00
1977 FM (U)	782	—	0.30	1.00	2.00	3.00
1977 FM (P)	7,218	PF65 2.00				
1978 FM (U)	1,443	—	0.30	0.75	1.75	2.25
1978 FM (P)	7,059	PF65 2.00				
1979 FM (U)	680	—	0.30	1.00	2.00	3.00
1979 FM (P)	5,304	PF65 2.00				
1980 FM (U)	1,007	—	0.30	1.00	2.00	3.00
1980 FM (P)	3,421	PF65 2.00				
1981 FM (U)	472	—	0.30	1.00	2.25	3.50
1981 FM (P)	1,124	PF65 2.00				
1982 FM (U)	—	—	0.30	1.00	2.25	3.50
1982 FM (P)	—	PF65 2.00				
1983 FM (U)	—	—	0.30	1.00	2.25	3.50
1983 FM (P)	—	PF65 2.00				
1984 FM (P)	—	PF65 2.00				

KM# 12 25 CENTS
8.81 g., 0.925 Silver 0.262 oz. ASW **Ruler:** Elizabeth II **Subject:** Queen's Silver Jubilee **Obv:** Young bust right

Date	Mintage	VF20	XF40	MS60	MS63	MS65
1977 FM (P)	17,000	PF65 7.50				

KM# 19 25 CENTS
8.81 g., 0.925 Silver 0.262 oz. ASW **Ruler:** Elizabeth II **Subject:** Coronation Jubilee **Obv:** Young bust right divides dates **Rev:** Mangrove Cuckoo

Date	Mintage	VF20	XF40	MS60	MS63	MS65
ND-1978 FM (P)	6,196	PF65 13.00				

KM# 45 25 CENTS
Copper-Nickel **Ruler:** Elizabeth II **Obv:** Crowned head right **Rev:** Blue Marlin jumping

Date	Mintage	VF20	XF40	MS60	MS63	MS65
1985 FM (P)	—	PF65 12.00				

KM# 45a 25 CENTS
8.81 g., 0.925 Silver 0.262 oz. ASW **Ruler:** Elizabeth II **Obv:** Crowned head right **Rev:** Blue Marlin jumping

Date	Mintage	VF20	XF40	MS60	MS63	MS65
1985 FM (P)	1,480	PF65 15.00				

KM# 5 50 CENTS
14.25 g., Copper-Nickel **Ruler:** Elizabeth II **Obv:** Young bust right **Rev:** Brown Pelican **Edge:** Reeded

Date	Mintage	VF20	XF40	MS60	MS63	MS65
1973 FM	20,000	—	0.50	1.00	2.00	3.00
1973 FM (P)	181,000	PF65 3.00				
1974 FM	12,000	—	0.50	1.00	2.00	3.00
1974 FM (P)	94,000	PF65 3.00				
1975 FM (M)	1,000	—	1.00	2.50	5.00	6.00
1975 FM (U)	2,351	—	0.75	1.25	2.50	3.00
1975 FM (P)	32,000	PF65 3.00				
1976 FM (M)	2,000	—	0.75	1.50	3.00	4.00
1976 FM (U)	996	—	0.75	1.75	3.50	4.50
1976 FM (P)	15,000	PF65 4.00				
1977 FM (M)	600	—	1.00	2.75	6.00	7.50
1977 FM (U)	782	—	0.75	1.75	3.50	4.50
1977 FM (P)	7,218	PF65 4.00				
1978 FM (U)	1,543	—	0.50	1.25	2.50	3.00
1978 FM (P)	7,059	PF65 3.00				
1979 FM (U)	680	—	0.75	1.75	3.50	4.50
1979 FM (P)	5,304	PF65 4.00				
1980 FM (U)	1,007	—	0.75	1.50	3.00	4.00
1980 FM (P)	3,421	PF65 4.00				
1981 FM (U)	472	—	0.75	1.75	3.50	5.00
1981 FM (P)	1,124	PF65 4.50				
1982 FM (U)	—	—	0.75	1.75	3.50	5.00
1982 FM (P)	—	PF65 4.50				
1983 FM (U)	—	—	0.75	1.75	3.50	5.00
1983 FM (P)	—	PF65 4.50				
1984 FM (P)	—	PF65 4.00				

KM# 13 50 CENTS
16.72 g., 0.925 Silver 0.4972 oz. ASW, 32 mm. **Ruler:** Elizabeth II **Subject:** Queen's Silver Jubilee **Obv:** Young bust right **Rev:** Brown Pelican **Edge:** Reeded

Date	Mintage	VF20	XF40	MS60	MS63	MS65
1977 FM (P)	17,000	PF65 10.00				

KM# 20 50 CENTS
16.72 g., 0.925 Silver 0.4972 oz. ASW **Ruler:** Elizabeth II **Subject:** Coronation Jubilee **Obv:** Young bust right divides dates **Rev:** Brown Pelican

Date	Mintage	VF20	XF40	MS60	MS63	MS65
ND-1978 FM (P)	6,196	PF65 22.00				

KM# 46 50 CENTS
Copper-Nickel **Ruler:** Elizabeth II **Obv:** Crowned head right **Rev:** Dolphin fish

Date	Mintage	VF20	XF40	MS60	MS63	MS65
1985 FM (P)	—	PF65 14.00				

KM# 46a 50 CENTS
16.72 g., 0.925 Silver 0.4972 oz. ASW, 32 mm. **Ruler:** Elizabeth II **Obv:** Crowned head right **Rev:** Dolphin fish **Edge:** Reeded

Date	Mintage	VF20	XF40	MS60	MS63	MS65
1985 FM (P)	1,406	PF65 25.00				

KM# 6 DOLLAR
Copper-Nickel, 39 mm. **Ruler:** Elizabeth II **Obv:** Young bust right **Rev:** Magnificent Frigate

Date	Mintage	VF20	XF40	MS60	MS63	MS65
1974 FM (M)	12,000	—	—	2.25	5.50	7.00
1974 FM (U)	—	—	—	—	—	—
1975 FM (M)	800	—	—	2.75	7.00	9.00
1975 FM (U)	2,351	—	—	2.50	6.50	7.00
1976 FM (M)	1,800	—	—	2.50	6.50	7.00
1976 FM (U)	996	—	—	2.75	7.00	9.00
1977 FM (M)	800	—	—	2.75	7.00	9.00
1977 FM (U)	782	—	—	2.75	7.00	9.00
1978 FM (U)	1,743	—	—	2.50	6.50	7.00
1979 FM (U)	680	—	—	2.75	7.00	9.00
1980 FM (U)	1,007	—	—	2.50	6.50	7.00
1981 FM (U)	472	—	—	3.75	9.00	11.50
1982 FM (U)	—	—	—	3.75	9.00	11.50
1983 FM (U)	—	—	—	3.75	9.00	11.50

KM# 6a DOLLAR
25.70 g., 0.925 Silver 0.7643 oz. ASW, 39 mm. **Ruler:** Elizabeth II **Obv:** Young bust right **Rev:** Magnificent Frigate

Date	Mintage	VF20	XF40	MS60	MS63	MS65
1973 FM (P)	181,000	PF65 22.00				
1973 FM (M)	20,000	—	17.00	22.00	25.00	—
1974 FM (P)	94,000	PF65 25.00				
1975 FM (P)	32,000	PF65 25.00				
1976 FM (P)	15,000	PF65 25.00				
1977 FM (P)	7,218	PF65 28.00				
1978 FM (P)	7,059	PF65 28.00				
1979 FM (P)	5,304	PF65 28.00				

Date	Mintage	VF20	XF40	MS60	MS63	MS65
1980 FM (P)	3,421	PF65 32.00				
1981 FM (P)	1,124	PF65 35.00				
1982 FM (P)	1,865	PF65 35.00				
1983 FM (P)	478	PF65 37.50				
1984 FM (P)	—	PF65 35.00				

KM# 14 DOLLAR
25.70 g., 0.925 Silver 0.7643 oz. ASW **Ruler:** Elizabeth II **Subject:** Queen's Silver Jubilee **Obv:** Young bust right **Rev:** Magnificent Frigate

Date	Mintage	VF20	XF40	MS60	MS63	MS65
1977 FM (P)	17,000	PF65 25.00				

KM# 21 DOLLAR
25.70 g., 0.925 Silver 0.7643 oz. ASW **Ruler:** Elizabeth II **Subject:** Coronation Jubilee **Obv:** Young bust right **Rev:** Magnificent Frigate

Date	Mintage	VF20	XF40	MS60	MS63	MS65
ND-1978 FM (P)	6,196	PF65 27.00				

KM# 47 DOLLAR
Copper-Nickel **Ruler:** Elizabeth II **Obv:** Crowned head right **Rev:** Butterfly Fish

Date	Mintage	VF20	XF40	MS60	MS63	MS65
1985 FM (P)	—	PF65 30.00				

KM# 47a DOLLAR
24.74 g., 0.925 Silver 0.7358 oz. ASW **Ruler:** Elizabeth II **Obv:** Crowned head right **Rev:** Butterfly fish

Date	Mintage	VF20	XF40	MS60	MS63	MS65
1985 FM (P)	1,372	PF65 35.00				

KM# 169 DOLLAR
Copper-Nickel **Ruler:** Elizabeth II **Subject:** 500th Anniversary - Columbus' First Voyage to America **Obv:** Crowned head right **Rev:** VIGILATE on banner below shield with woman and twelve lamps

Date	Mintage	VF20	XF40	MS60	MS63	MS65
ND-1992	—	PF65 12.00				

KM# 172 DOLLAR
Copper-Nickel, 38.6 mm. **Ruler:** Elizabeth II **Subject:** Queen Mother's 100th Birthday **Obv:** Crowned head right **Rev:** Bust facing divides dates **Edge:** Reeded

Date	Mintage	VF20	XF40	MS60	MS63	MS65
2000	100,000	—	—	—	5.50	7.50

KM# 175 DOLLAR
Copper-Nickel **Ruler:** Elizabeth II **Subject:** 1st Anniversary - Earl and Countess of Wessex **Obv:** Crowned head right **Rev:** Half figures facing, anniversary date below **Edge:** Reeded

Date	Mintage	VF20	XF40	MS60	MS63	MS65
2000	—	—	—	—	5.50	7.50

KM# 24 5 DOLLARS
Copper-Nickel **Ruler:** Elizabeth II **Obv:** Young bust right **Rev:** Snowy Egret left

Date	Mintage	VF20	XF40	MS60	MS63	MS65
1979 FM (U)	680	—	—	—	75.00	90.00

KM# 24a 5 DOLLARS
40.50 g., 0.925 Silver 1.2044 oz. ASW **Ruler:** Elizabeth II **Obv:** Young bust right **Rev:** Snowy Egret left

Date	Mintage	VF20	XF40	MS60	MS63	MS65
1979 FM (P)	5,304	PF65 42.50				

KM# 26 5 DOLLARS
Copper-Nickel **Ruler:** Elizabeth II **Obv:** Young bust right **Rev:** Great Blue Heron right

Date	Mintage	VF20	XF40	MS60	MS63	MS65
1980 FM (U)	1,007	—	—	—	50.00	75.00

KM# 26a 5 DOLLARS
40.50 g., 0.925 Silver 1.2044 oz. ASW **Ruler:** Elizabeth II **Obv:** Young bust right **Rev:** Great Blue Heron right

Date	Mintage	VF20	XF40	MS60	MS63	MS65
1980 FM (P)	3,421	PF65 50.00				

KM# 30 5 DOLLARS
Copper-Nickel **Ruler:** Elizabeth II **Subject:** Royal Tern left **Obv:** Young bust right

Date	Mintage	VF20	XF40	MS60	MS63	MS65
1981 FM (U)	472	—	—	—	75.00	90.00

KM# 30a 5 DOLLARS
40.50 g., 0.925 Silver 1.2044 oz. ASW **Ruler:** Elizabeth II **Obv:** Young bust right **Rev:** Royal Tern left

Date	Mintage	VF20	XF40	MS60	MS63	MS65
1981 FM (P)	1,124	PF65 50.00				

KM# 33 5 DOLLARS
Copper-Nickel **Ruler:** Elizabeth II **Obv:** Young bust right **Rev:** White-tailed tropic birds

Date	Mintage	VF20	XF40	MS60	MS63	MS65
1982 FM (U)	—	—	—	—	35.00	50.00

KM# 33a 5 DOLLARS
40.50 g., 0.925 Silver 1.2044 oz. ASW **Ruler:** Elizabeth II **Obv:** Young bust right **Rev:** White-tailed tropic birds

Date	Mintage	VF20	XF40	MS60	MS63	MS65
1982 FM (P)	1,865	PF65 50.00				

KM# 35 5 DOLLARS

Copper-Nickel **Ruler:** Elizabeth II **Obv:** Young bust right **Rev:** Yellow Warblers

Date	Mintage	VF20	XF40	MS60	MS63	MS65
1983 FM (U)	—	—	—	—	35.00	50.00

KM# 35a 5 DOLLARS

40.50 g., 0.925 Silver 1.2044 oz. ASW **Ruler:** Elizabeth II **Obv:** Young bust right **Rev:** Yellow Warblers

Date	Mintage	VF20	XF40	MS60	MS63	MS65
1983 FM (P)	478	PF63 50.00	PF65 75.00			
1984 FM (P)	—	PF63 50.00	PF65 75.00			

KM# 36 10 DOLLARS

30.28 g., 0.500 Silver 0.4868 oz. ASW **Ruler:** Elizabeth II **Subject:** 30th Anniversary - Coronation of Queen Elizabeth II **Obv:** Young bust right **Rev:** Sceptres divide dates and royal symbols

Date	Mintage	VF20	XF40	MS60	MS63	MS65
1983 FM (P)	2,957	PF63 20.00	PF65 25.00			

KM# 157 10 DOLLARS

Copper-Nickel **Ruler:** Elizabeth II **Subject:** Discovery of America **Obv:** Crowned head right **Rev:** Columbus landing

Date	Mintage	VF20	XF40	MS60	MS63	MS65
ND-1992 FM (P)	—	PF63 9.00	PF65 12.00			

KM# 173.1 10 DOLLARS

28.28 g., 0.925 Silver 0.841 oz. ASW, 38.6 mm. **Ruler:** Elizabeth II **Obv:** Crowned head right **Rev:** Bust facing divides dates **Edge:** Reeded

Date	Mintage	VF20	XF40	MS60	MS63	MS65
2000	10,000	PF63 20.00	PF65 25.00			

KM# 173.2 10 DOLLARS

28.28 g., 0.925 Silver 0.841 oz. ASW, 38.6 mm. **Ruler:** Elizabeth II **Subject:** Queen Mother **Obv:** Crowned head right **Rev:** Queen Mother's portrait with a tiny sapphire mounted on her broach **Edge:** Reeded

Date	Mintage	VF20	XF40	MS60	MS63	MS65
2000	1,000	PF63 50.00	PF65 60.00			

KM# 176 10 DOLLARS

28.28 g., 0.925 Silver 0.841 oz. ASW **Ruler:** Elizabeth II **Subject:** 1st Anniversary - Earl and Countess of Wessex **Obv:** Crowned head right **Rev:** Half figures facing, anniversary date below **Edge:** Reeded

Date	Mintage	VF20	XF40	MS60	MS63	MS65
2000	10,000	PF63 20.00	PF65 25.00			

KM# 48 20 DOLLARS

19.09 g., 0.925 Silver 0.5677 oz. ASW, 38 mm. **Ruler:** Elizabeth II **Obv:** Crowned head right **Rev:** Crossed cannons

Date	Mintage	VF20	XF40	MS60	MS63	MS65
1985 FM (P)	—	PF65 12.50				

KM# 49 20 DOLLARS

19.09 g., 0.925 Silver 0.5677 oz. ASW, 38 mm. **Ruler:** Elizabeth II **Obv:** Crowned head right **Rev:** Porcelain cup

Date	Mintage	VF20	XF40	MS60	MS63	MS65
1985 FM (P)	—	PF65 12.50				

KM# 50 20 DOLLARS

19.09 g., 0.925 Silver 0.5677 oz. ASW, 38 mm. **Ruler:** Elizabeth II **Obv:** Crowned head right **Rev:** Sextant

Date	Mintage	VF20	XF40	MS60	MS63	MS65
1985 FM (P)	—	PF65 12.50				

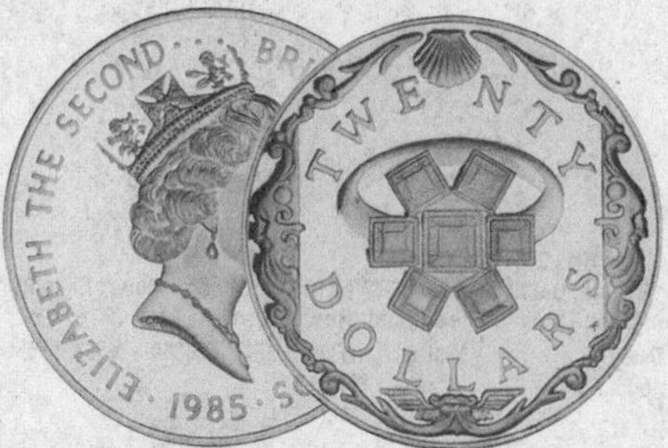

KM# 51 20 DOLLARS

19.09 g., 0.925 Silver 0.5677 oz. ASW, 38 mm. **Ruler:** Elizabeth II **Obv:** Crowned head right **Rev:** Emerald and gold ring

Date	Mintage	VF20	XF40	MS60	MS63	MS65
1985 FM (P)	—	PF65 12.50				

KM# 52 20 DOLLARS

19.09 g., 0.925 Silver 0.5677 oz. ASW, 38 mm. **Ruler:** Elizabeth II **Obv:** Crowned head right **Rev:** Gold doubloon of 1702

Date	Mintage	VF20	XF40	MS60	MS63	MS65
1985 FM (P)	—	PF65 12.50				

KM# 53 20 DOLLARS

19.09 g., 0.925 Silver 0.5677 oz. ASW, 38 mm. **Ruler:** Elizabeth II **Obv:** Crowned head right **Rev:** Anchor

Date	Mintage	VF20	XF40	MS60	MS63	MS65
1985 FM (P)	—	PF65 12.50				

KM# 54 20 DOLLARS
19.09 g., 0.925 Silver 0.5677 oz. ASW, 38 mm. **Ruler:** Elizabeth II **Obv:** Crowned head right **Rev:** Brass nocturnal

Date	Mintage	VF20	XF40	MS60	MS63	MS65
1985 FM (P)	—	PF65 12.50				

KM# 55 20 DOLLARS
19.09 g., 0.925 Silver 0.5677 oz. ASW, 38 mm. **Ruler:** Elizabeth II **Obv:** Crowned head right **Rev:** Sword guillon

Date	Mintage	VF20	XF40	MS60	MS63	MS65
1985 FM (P)	—	PF65 12.50				

KM# 56 20 DOLLARS
19.09 g., 0.925 Silver 0.5677 oz. ASW, 38 mm. **Ruler:** Elizabeth II **Obv:** Crowned head right **Rev:** Gold bar

Date	Mintage	VF20	XF40	MS60	MS63	MS65
1985 FM (P)	—	PF65 12.50				

KM# 57 20 DOLLARS
19.09 g., 0.925 Silver 0.5677 oz. ASW, 38 mm. **Ruler:** Elizabeth II **Subject:** Gold Escudo **Obv:** Crowned head right **Rev:** Obverse and reverse of gold 8 escudo of 1733

Date	Mintage	VF20	XF40	MS60	MS63	MS65
1985 FM (P)	—	PF65 12.50				

KM# 58 20 DOLLARS
19.09 g., 0.925 Silver 0.5677 oz. ASW, 38 mm. **Ruler:** Elizabeth II **Obv:** Crowned head right **Rev:** Ivory sundial

Date	Mintage	VF20	XF40	MS60	MS63	MS65
1985 FM (P)	—	PF65 12.50				

KM# 59 20 DOLLARS
19.09 g., 0.925 Silver 0.5677 oz. ASW, 38 mm. **Ruler:** Elizabeth II **Obv:** Crowned head right **Rev:** Gold monstrance, within square

Date	Mintage	VF20	XF40	MS60	MS63	MS65
1985 FM (P)	—	PF65 12.50				

KM# 60 20 DOLLARS
19.09 g., 0.925 Silver 0.5677 oz. ASW, 38 mm. **Ruler:** Elizabeth II **Obv:** Crowned head right **Rev:** Teapot

Date	Mintage	VF20	XF40	MS60	MS63	MS65
1985 FM (P)	—	PF65 12.50				

KM# 61 20 DOLLARS
19.09 g., 0.925 Silver 0.5677 oz. ASW, 38 mm. **Ruler:** Elizabeth II **Obv:** Crowned head right **Rev:** Brass religious medallion

Date	Mintage	VF20	XF40	MS60	MS63	MS65
1985 FM (P)	—	PF65 12.50				

KM# 62 20 DOLLARS
19.09 g., 0.925 Silver 0.5677 oz. ASW, 38 mm. **Ruler:** Elizabeth II **Obv:** Crowned head right **Rev:** Astrolabe

Date	Mintage	VF20	XF40	MS60	MS63	MS65
1985 FM (P)	—	PF65 12.50				

KM# 63.1 20 DOLLARS
19.09 g., 0.925 Silver 0.5677 oz. ASW, 38 mm. **Ruler:** Elizabeth II **Obv:** Crowned head right **Rev:** Bells **Note:** FM mint mark at right.

Date	Mintage	VF20	XF40	MS60	MS63	MS65
1985 FM (P)	—	PF65 12.50				

KM# 63.2 20 DOLLARS
19.09 g., 0.925 Silver 0.5677 oz. ASW, 38 mm. **Ruler:** Elizabeth II **Obv:** Crowned head right **Rev:** Bells **Note:** FM mint mark in center.

Date	Mintage	VF20	XF40	MS60	MS63	MS65
1985 FM (P)	—	PF65 12.50				

KM# 64 20 DOLLARS
19.09 g., 0.925 Silver 0.5677 oz. ASW, 38 mm. **Ruler:** Elizabeth II **Obv:** Crowned head right **Rev:** Porcelain bottle

Date	Mintage	VF20	XF40	MS60	MS63	MS65
1985 FM (P)	—	PF65 12.50				

KM# 65 20 DOLLARS
19.09 g., 0.925 Silver 0.5677 oz. ASW, 38 mm. **Ruler:** Elizabeth II **Obv:** Crowned head right **Rev:** Ship and Dutch cannons

Date	Mintage	VF20	XF40	MS60	MS63	MS65
1985 FM (P)	—	PF65 12.50				

KM# 66 20 DOLLARS
19.09 g., 0.925 Silver 0.5677 oz. ASW, 38 mm. **Ruler:** Elizabeth II **Obv:** Crowned head right **Rev:** Ancient coin **Note:** Spanish Colonial 8 Reales, Cob coin.

Date	Mintage	VF20	XF40	MS60	MS63	MS65
1985 FM (P)	—	PF65 12.50				

KM# 67 20 DOLLARS
19.09 g., 0.925 Silver 0.5677 oz. ASW, 38 mm. **Ruler:** Elizabeth II **Obv:** Crowned head right **Rev:** Ship's stern lantern

Date	Mintage	VF20	XF40	MS60	MS63	MS65
1985 FM (P)	—	PF65 12.50				

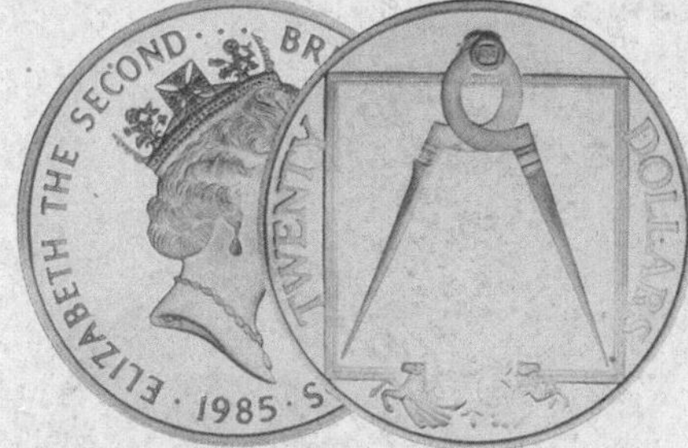

KM# 68 20 DOLLARS
19.09 g., 0.925 Silver 0.5677 oz. ASW, 38 mm. **Ruler:** Elizabeth II **Obv:** Crowned head right **Rev:** Brass dividers

Date	Mintage	VF20	XF40	MS60	MS63	MS65
1985 FM (P)	—	PF65 12.50				

KM# 69 20 DOLLARS
19.09 g., 0.925 Silver 0.5677 oz. ASW, 38 mm. **Ruler:** Elizabeth II **Obv:** Crowned head right **Rev:** Gold cross

Date	Mintage	VF20	XF40	MS60	MS63	MS65
1985 FM (P)	—	PF65 12.50				

KM# 70 20 DOLLARS
19.09 g., 0.925 Silver 0.5677 oz. ASW, 38 mm. **Ruler:** Elizabeth II **Obv:** Crowned head right **Rev:** Perfume bottle

Date	Mintage	VF20	XF40	MS60	MS63	MS65
1985 FM (P)	—	PF65 12.50				

KM# 71 20 DOLLARS
19.09 g., 0.925 Silver 0.5677 oz. ASW, 38 mm. **Ruler:** Elizabeth II **Obv:** Crowned head right **Rev:** Pocket watch

Date	Mintage	VF20	XF40	MS60	MS63	MS65
1985 FM (P)	—	PF65 12.50				

KM# 72 20 DOLLARS
19.09 g., 0.925 Silver 0.5677 oz. ASW, 38 mm. **Ruler:** Elizabeth II **Obv:** Crowned head right **Rev:** Gold bracelet and button

Date	Mintage	VF20	XF40	MS60	MS63	MS65
1985 FM (P)	—	PF65 12.50				

KM# 259 20 DOLLARS
19.11 g., 0.925 Silver 0.5683 oz. ASW, 37.9 mm. **Ruler:** Elizabeth II **Obv:** Crowned head right **Rev:** Ancient Egyptian reed sail boat **Edge:** Reeded

Date	Mintage	VF20	XF40	MS60	MS63	MS65
2000 FM	—	PF65 15.50				

KM# 260 20 DOLLARS
19.65 g., 0.925 Silver 0.5844 oz. ASW, 37.9 mm. **Ruler:** Elizabeth II **Obv:** Crowned head right **Rev:** Hansa Cog trading ship, 14th Century **Edge:** Reeded

Date	Mintage	VF20	XF40	MS60	MS63	MS65
2000 FM	—	PF65 16.00				

KM# 261 20 DOLLARS
18.93 g., 0.925 Silver 0.563 oz. ASW, 37.9 mm. **Ruler:** Elizabeth II **Obv:** Crowned head right **Rev:** Flag ship Santa Maria, 1492 **Edge:** Reeded

Date	Mintage	VF20	XF40	MS60	MS63	MS65
2000 FM	—	PF65 15.50				

KM# 262 20 DOLLARS
19.24 g., 0.925 Silver 0.5722 oz. ASW, 37.9 mm. **Ruler:** Elizabeth II **Obv:** Crowned head right **Rev:** The Ark Royal, 1588 **Edge:** Reeded

Date	Mintage	VF20	XF40	MS60	MS63	MS65
2000 FM	—	PF65 15.50				

KM# 263 20 DOLLARS
18.80 g., 0.925 Silver 0.5591 oz. ASW, 37.9 mm. **Ruler:** Elizabeth II **Obv:** Crowned head right **Rev:** Clipper ship Cutty Sark, 1869 **Edge:** Reeded

Date	Mintage	VF20	XF40	MS60	MS63	MS65
2000 FM	—	PF65 15.50				

KM# 264 20 DOLLARS
19.20 g., 0.925 Silver 0.571 oz. ASW, 37.9 mm. **Ruler:** Elizabeth II **Obv:** Crowned head right **Rev:** Training ship SMS Preussen **Edge:** Reeded

Date	Mintage	VF20	XF40	MS60	MS63	MS65
2000 FM	—	PF65 15.50				

KM# 22 25 DOLLARS
28.10 g., 0.925 Silver 0.8357 oz. ASW **Ruler:** Elizabeth II **Subject:** Coronation Jubilee **Obv:** Young bust right **Rev:** Imperial crown with supporters, dates below

Date	Mintage	VF20	XF40	MS60	MS63	MS65
1978 FM (P)	8,438	PF65 25.00				

KM# 27 25 DOLLARS
1.50 g., 0.500 Gold 0.0241 oz. AGW **Ruler:** Elizabeth II **Obv:** Young bust right **Rev:** Diving Osprey left

Date	Mintage	VF20	XF40	MS60	MS63	MS65
1980 FM (P)	11,000	PF65 45.00				

KM# 31.1 25 DOLLARS
1.50 g., 0.500 Gold 0.0241 oz. AGW **Ruler:** Elizabeth II **Obv:** Young bust right **Rev:** Caribbean Sparrow Hawk left

Date	Mintage	VF20	XF40	MS60	MS63	MS65
1981 FM (P)	2,513	PF65 55.00				

KM# 31.2 25 DOLLARS
1.50 g., 0.500 Gold 0.0241 oz. AGW **Ruler:** Elizabeth II **Obv:** Young bust right, error, without FM mint mark **Rev:** Caribbean Sparrow Hawk left

Date	Mintage	VF20	XF40	MS60	MS63	MS65
1981 (P)	—	PF65 60.00				

KM# 41 25 DOLLARS
1.50 g., 0.500 Gold 0.0241 oz. AGW **Ruler:** Elizabeth II **Obv:** Young bust right **Rev:** Red-tailed hawk in flight

Date	Mintage	VF20	XF40	MS60	MS63	MS65
1982 FM (FDC)	—	—	—	—	—	—
1982 FM (P)	3,819	PF65 55.00				

KM# 37 25 DOLLARS
1.50 g., 0.500 Gold 0.0241 oz. AGW **Ruler:** Elizabeth II **Obv:** Young bust right **Rev:** Merlin Hawk left

Date	Mintage	VF20	XF40	MS60	MS63	MS65
1983 FM (P)	5,949	PF65 50.00				

KM# 40 25 DOLLARS
1.50 g., 0.500 Gold 0.0241 oz. AGW **Ruler:** Elizabeth II **Obv:** Young bust right **Rev:** Peregrine Falcon

Date	Mintage	VF20	XF40	MS60	MS63	MS65
1984 FM (P)	97	PF65 110				

KM# 73 25 DOLLARS
1.50 g., 0.500 Gold 0.0241 oz. AGW **Ruler:** Elizabeth II **Obv:** Crowned head right **Rev:** Marsh Hawk

Date	Mintage	VF20	XF40	MS60	MS63	MS65
1985 FM (P)	1,294	PF65 75.00				

KM# 90 25 DOLLARS
20.09 g., 0.925 Silver 0.5975 oz. ASW **Ruler:** Elizabeth II **Series:** Sunken Ship Treasures **Obv:** Crowned head right **Rev:** Ornamental lock plate

Date	Mintage	VF20	XF40	MS60	MS63	MS65
1988 FM (P)	—	PF65 14.50				

KM# 91 25 DOLLARS

20.09 g., 0.925 Silver 0.5975 oz. ASW **Ruler:** Elizabeth II **Series:** Sunken Ship Treasures **Obv:** Crowned head right **Rev:** Royal coat of arms on bottle

Date	Mintage	VF20	XF40	MS60	MS63	MS65
1988 FM (P)	—	PF65 14.50				

KM# 92 25 DOLLARS

20.09 g., 0.925 Silver 0.5975 oz. ASW **Ruler:** Elizabeth II **Series:** Sunken Ship Treasures **Obv:** Crowned head right **Rev:** Finger ring

Date	Mintage	VF20	XF40	MS60	MS63	MS65
1988 FM (P)	—	PF65 14.50				

KM# 93 25 DOLLARS

20.09 g., 0.925 Silver 0.5975 oz. ASW **Ruler:** Elizabeth II **Series:** Sunken Ship Treasures **Obv:** Crowned head right **Rev:** Hour glass

Date	Mintage	VF20	XF40	MS60	MS63	MS65
1988 FM (P)	—	PF65 14.50				

KM# 94 25 DOLLARS

20.09 g., 0.925 Silver 0.5975 oz. ASW **Ruler:** Elizabeth II **Series:** Sunken Ship Treasures **Obv:** Crowned head right **Rev:** Dagger and scabbard

Date	Mintage	VF20	XF40	MS60	MS63	MS65
1988 FM (P)	—	PF65 14.50				

KM# 95 25 DOLLARS

20.09 g., 0.925 Silver 0.5975 oz. ASW **Ruler:** Elizabeth II **Series:** Sunken Ship Treasures **Obv:** Crowned head right **Rev:** Jewel-encrusted cross

Date	Mintage	VF20	XF40	MS60	MS63	MS65
1988 FM (P)	—	PF65 14.50				

KM# 96 25 DOLLARS

20.09 g., 0.925 Silver 0.5975 oz. ASW **Ruler:** Elizabeth II **Series:** Sunken Ship Treasures **Obv:** Crowned head right **Rev:** Crossed keys

Date	Mintage	VF20	XF40	MS60	MS63	MS65
1988 FM (P)	—	PF65 14.50				

KM# 97 25 DOLLARS

20.09 g., 0.925 Silver 0.5975 oz. ASW **Ruler:** Elizabeth II **Series:** Sunken Ship Treasures **Obv:** Crowned head right **Rev:** Belt buckle

Date	Mintage	VF20	XF40	MS60	MS63	MS65
1988 FM (P)	—	PF65 14.50				

KM# 98 25 DOLLARS

20.09 g., 0.925 Silver 0.5975 oz. ASW **Ruler:** Elizabeth II **Series:** Sunken Ship Treasures **Obv:** Crowned head right **Rev:** American bottle

Date	Mintage	VF20	XF40	MS60	MS63	MS65
1988 FM (P)	—	PF65 14.50				

KM# 99 25 DOLLARS

20.09 g., 0.925 Silver 0.5975 oz. ASW **Ruler:** Elizabeth II **Series:** Sunken Ship Treasures **Obv:** Crowned head right **Rev:** Religious medallion

Date	Mintage	VF20	XF40	MS60	MS63	MS65
1988 FM (P)	—	PF65 14.50				

KM# 100 25 DOLLARS

20.09 g., 0.925 Silver 0.5975 oz. ASW **Ruler:** Elizabeth II **Series:** Sunken Ship Treasures **Obv:** Crowned head right **Rev:** Baby figurines

Date	Mintage	VF20	XF40	MS60	MS63	MS65
1988 FM (P)	—	PF65 14.50				

KM# 101 25 DOLLARS

20.09 g., 0.925 Silver 0.5975 oz. ASW **Ruler:** Elizabeth II **Series:** Sunken Ship Treasures **Obv:** Crowned head right **Rev:** Insignia of the Royal French Marines

Date	Mintage	VF20	XF40	MS60	MS63	MS65
1988 FM (P)	—	PF65 14.50				

KM# 102 25 DOLLARS

20.09 g., 0.925 Silver 0.5975 oz. ASW **Ruler:** Elizabeth II **Series:** Sunken Ship Treasures **Obv:** Crowned head right **Rev:** Engraved printing block

Date	Mintage	VF20	XF40	MS60	MS63	MS65
1988 FM (P)	—	PF65 14.50				

KM# 103 25 DOLLARS
20.09 g., 0.925 Silver 0.5975 oz. ASW **Ruler:** Elizabeth II **Series:** Sunken Ship Treasures **Obv:** Crowned head right **Rev:** Antique clock

Date	Mintage	VF20	XF40	MS60	MS63	MS65
1988 FM (P)	—	PF65 14.50				

KM# 132 25 DOLLARS
20.09 g., 0.925 Silver 0.5975 oz. ASW **Ruler:** Elizabeth II **Obv:** Crowned head right **Rev:** Flintlock pistol

Date	Mintage	VF20	XF40	MS60	MS63	MS65
1988 FM (P)	—	PF65 14.50				

KM# 133 25 DOLLARS
20.09 g., 0.925 Silver 0.5975 oz. ASW **Ruler:** Elizabeth II **Obv:** Crowned head right **Rev:** Stylized fish statue

Date	Mintage	VF20	XF40	MS60	MS63	MS65
1988 FM (P)	—	PF65 14.50				

KM# 134 25 DOLLARS
20.09 g., 0.925 Silver 0.5975 oz. ASW **Ruler:** Elizabeth II **Obv:** Crowned head right **Rev:** Mortar and pestle

Date	Mintage	VF20	XF40	MS60	MS63	MS65
1988 FM (P)	—	PF65 14.50				

KM# 135 25 DOLLARS
20.09 g., 0.925 Silver 0.5975 oz. ASW **Ruler:** Elizabeth II **Obv:** Crowned head right **Rev:** Open-mouthed dragon head sculpture

Date	Mintage	VF20	XF40	MS60	MS63	MS65
1988 FM (P)	—	PF65 14.50				

KM# 136 25 DOLLARS
20.09 g., 0.925 Silver 0.5975 oz. ASW **Ruler:** Elizabeth II **Obv:** Crowned head right **Rev:** Military mortar

Date	Mintage	VF20	XF40	MS60	MS63	MS65
1988 FM (P)	—	PF65 14.50				

KM# 137 25 DOLLARS
20.09 g., 0.925 Silver 0.5975 oz. ASW **Ruler:** Elizabeth II **Obv:** Crowned head right **Rev:** Seated figure sculpture

Date	Mintage	VF20	XF40	MS60	MS63	MS65
1988 FM (P)	—	PF65 14.50				

KM# 138 25 DOLLARS
20.09 g., 0.925 Silver 0.5975 oz. ASW **Ruler:** Elizabeth II **Obv:** Crowned head right **Rev:** Lion sculpture

Date	Mintage	VF20	XF40	MS60	MS63	MS65
1988 FM (P)	—	PF65 14.50				

KM# 139 25 DOLLARS
20.09 g., 0.925 Silver 0.5975 oz. ASW **Ruler:** Elizabeth II **Obv:** Crowned head right **Rev:** Violin

Date	Mintage	VF20	XF40	MS60	MS63	MS65
1988 FM (P)	—	PF65 14.50				

KM# 140 25 DOLLARS
20.09 g., 0.925 Silver 0.5975 oz. ASW **Ruler:** Elizabeth II **Obv:** Crowned head right **Rev:** Chalice

Date	Mintage	VF20	XF40	MS60	MS63	MS65
1988 FM (P)	—	PF65 14.50				

KM# 141 25 DOLLARS
20.09 g., 0.925 Silver 0.5975 oz. ASW **Ruler:** Elizabeth II **Obv:** Crowned head right **Rev:** Pitcher

Date	Mintage	VF20	XF40	MS60	MS63	MS65
1988 FM (P)	—	PF65 14.50				

KM# 142 25 DOLLARS
20.09 g., 0.925 Silver 0.5975 oz. ASW **Ruler:** Elizabeth II **Obv:** Crowned head right **Rev:** Cannon

Date	Mintage	VF20	XF40	MS60	MS63	MS65
1988 FM (P)	—	PF65 14.50				

KM# 104 25 DOLLARS

21.54 g., 0.925 Silver 0.6406 oz. ASW **Ruler:** Elizabeth II **Series:** Discovery of America **Obv:** Crowned head right **Rev:** Columbus planning voyage

Date	Mintage	VF20	XF40	MS60	MS63	MS65
ND-1992 FM (P)	—	PF65 15.50				

KM# 105 25 DOLLARS

21.54 g., 0.925 Silver 0.6406 oz. ASW **Ruler:** Elizabeth II **Series:** Discovery of America **Obv:** Crowned head right **Rev:** Columbus lecturing

Date	Mintage	VF20	XF40	MS60	MS63	MS65
ND-1992 FM (P)	—	PF65 15.50				

KM# 106 25 DOLLARS

21.54 g., 0.925 Silver 0.6406 oz. ASW **Ruler:** Elizabeth II **Series:** Discovery of America **Obv:** Crowned head right **Rev:** Queen Isabella offering jewels

Date	Mintage	VF20	XF40	MS60	MS63	MS65
ND-1992 FM (P)	—	PF65 15.50				

KM# 107 25 DOLLARS

21.54 g., 0.925 Silver 0.6406 oz. ASW **Ruler:** Elizabeth II **Series:** Discovery of America **Obv:** Crowned head right **Rev:** Columbus aboard ship

Date	Mintage	VF20	XF40	MS60	MS63	MS65
ND-1992 FM (P)	—	PF65 15.50				

KM# 108 25 DOLLARS

21.54 g., 0.925 Silver 0.6406 oz. ASW **Ruler:** Elizabeth II **Series:** Discovery of America **Obv:** Crowned head right **Rev:** Columbus on horseback

Date	Mintage	VF20	XF40	MS60	MS63	MS65
ND-1992 FM (P)	—	PF65 15.50				

KM# 109 25 DOLLARS

21.54 g., 0.925 Silver 0.6406 oz. ASW **Ruler:** Elizabeth II **Series:** Discovery of America **Obv:** Crowned head right **Rev:** Ship under full sail

Date	Mintage	VF20	XF40	MS60	MS63	MS65
ND-1992 FM	—	PF65 15.50				

KM# 110 25 DOLLARS

21.54 g., 0.925 Silver 0.6406 oz. ASW **Ruler:** Elizabeth II **Series:** Discovery of America **Obv:** Crowned head right **Rev:** Ship at anchor

Date	Mintage	VF20	XF40	MS60	MS63	MS65
ND-1992 FM (P)	—	PF65 15.50				

KM# 111 25 DOLLARS

21.54 g., 0.925 Silver 0.6406 oz. ASW **Ruler:** Elizabeth II **Series:** Discovery of America **Obv:** Crowned head right **Rev:** Natives offering gifts

Date	Mintage	VF20	XF40	MS60	MS63	MS65
ND-1992 FM (P)	—	PF65 15.50				

KM# 112 25 DOLLARS

21.54 g., 0.925 Silver 0.6406 oz. ASW **Ruler:** Elizabeth II **Series:** Discovery of America **Obv:** Crowned head right **Rev:** Shipwreck

Date	Mintage	VF20	XF40	MS60	MS63	MS65
ND-1992 FM (P)	—	PF65 15.50				

KM# 113 25 DOLLARS

21.54 g., 0.925 Silver 0.6406 oz. ASW **Ruler:** Elizabeth II **Series:** Discovery of America **Obv:** Crowned head right **Rev:** Royal banquet

Date	Mintage	VF20	XF40	MS60	MS63	MS65
ND-1992 FM (P)	—	PF65 15.50				

KM# 114 25 DOLLARS

21.54 g., 0.925 Silver 0.6406 oz. ASW **Ruler:** Elizabeth II **Series:** Discovery of America **Obv:** Crowned head right **Rev:** Columbus predicting lunar eclipse to natives

Date	Mintage	VF20	XF40	MS60	MS63	MS65
ND-1992 FM (P)	—	PF65 15.50				

KM# 115 25 DOLLARS

21.54 g., 0.925 Silver 0.6406 oz. ASW **Ruler:** Elizabeth II **Series:** Discovery of America **Obv:** Crowned head right **Rev:** Columbus on shore

Date	Mintage	VF20	XF40	MS60	MS63	MS65
ND-1992 FM (P)	—	PF65 15.50				

KM# 116 25 DOLLARS
21.54 g., 0.925 Silver 0.6406 oz. ASW **Ruler:** Elizabeth II **Series:** Discovery of America **Obv:** Crowned head right **Rev:** Spanish figures

Date	Mintage	VF20	XF40	MS60	MS63	MS65
ND-1992 FM (P)	—	PF65 15.50				

KM# 117 25 DOLLARS
21.54 g., 0.925 Silver 0.6406 oz. ASW **Ruler:** Elizabeth II **Series:** Discovery of America **Obv:** Crowned head right **Rev:** Columbus with shore party

Date	Mintage	VF20	XF40	MS60	MS63	MS65
ND-1992 FM (P)	—	PF65 15.50				

KM# 118 25 DOLLARS
21.54 g., 0.925 Silver 0.6406 oz. ASW **Ruler:** Elizabeth II **Series:** Discovery of America **Obv:** Crowned head right **Rev:** Columbus on death bed

Date	Mintage	VF20	XF40	MS60	MS63	MS65
ND-1992 FM (P)	—	PF65 15.50				

KM# 122 25 DOLLARS
21.54 g., 0.925 Silver 0.6406 oz. ASW **Ruler:** Elizabeth II **Series:** Discovery of America **Obv:** Crowned head right **Rev:** Columbus bowing before King Ferdinand

Date	Mintage	VF20	XF40	MS60	MS63	MS65
ND-1992 FM (P)	—	PF65 15.50				

KM# 123 25 DOLLARS
21.54 g., 0.925 Silver 0.6406 oz. ASW **Ruler:** Elizabeth II **Series:** Discovery of America **Obv:** Crowned head right **Rev:** Columbus before Queen Isabella

Date	Mintage	VF20	XF40	MS60	MS63	MS65
ND-1992 FM (P)	—	PF65 15.50				

KM# 124 25 DOLLARS
21.54 g., 0.925 Silver 0.6406 oz. ASW **Ruler:** Elizabeth II **Series:** Discovery of America **Obv:** Crowned head right **Rev:** Columbus before King Ferdinand and Queen Isabella

Date	Mintage	VF20	XF40	MS60	MS63	MS65
ND-1992 FM (P)	—	PF65 15.50				

KM# 125 25 DOLLARS
21.54 g., 0.925 Silver 0.6406 oz. ASW **Ruler:** Elizabeth II **Series:** Discovery of America **Obv:** Crowned head right **Rev:** Columbus getting provisions for his ships

Date	Mintage	VF20	XF40	MS60	MS63	MS65
ND-1992 FM (P)	—	PF65 15.50				

KM# 126 25 DOLLARS
21.54 g., 0.925 Silver 0.6406 oz. ASW **Ruler:** Elizabeth II **Series:** Discovery of America **Obv:** Crowned head right **Rev:** Four sailing ships

Date	Mintage	VF20	XF40	MS60	MS63	MS65
ND-1992 FM (P)	—	PF65 15.50				

KM# 127 25 DOLLARS
21.54 g., 0.925 Silver 0.6406 oz. ASW **Series:** Discovery of America **Obv:** Head right, two dates below **Rev:** Columbus navigating by stars

Date	Mintage	VF20	XF40	MS60	MS63	MS65
ND-1992 FM (P)	—	PF65 15.50				

KM# 128 25 DOLLARS
21.54 g., 0.925 Silver 0.6406 oz. ASW **Series:** Discovery of America **Obv:** Head right, two dates below **Rev:** Sighting land, denomination upper left

Date	Mintage	VF20	XF40	MS60	MS63	MS65
ND-1992 FM (P)	—	PF65 15.50				

KM# 129 25 DOLLARS
21.54 g., 0.925 Silver 0.6406 oz. ASW **Ruler:** Elizabeth II **Series:** Discovery of America **Obv:** Crowned head right **Rev:** Columbus claiming the newly discovered land

Date	Mintage	VF20	XF40	MS60	MS63	MS65
ND-1992 FM (P)	—	PF65 15.50				

KM# 130 25 DOLLARS
21.54 g., 0.925 Silver 0.6406 oz. ASW **Ruler:** Elizabeth II **Series:** Discovery of America **Obv:** Crowned head right **Rev:** Columbus seated on shore with shipwreck offshore

Date	Mintage	VF20	XF40	MS60	MS63	MS65
ND-1992 FM (P)	—	PF65 17.00				

KM# 131 25 DOLLARS
21.54 g., 0.925 Silver 0.6406 oz. ASW **Ruler:** Elizabeth II **Series:** Discovery of America **Obv:** Crowned head right **Rev:** Columbus as prisoner

Date	Mintage	VF20	XF40	MS60	MS63	MS65
ND-1992 FM (P)	—	PF65 15.50				

KM# 186 25 DOLLARS
20.09 g., 0.925 Silver 0.5975 oz. ASW, 40 mm. **Ruler:** Elizabeth II **Obv:** Crowned head right, 1988 type of KM#90-103 **Rev:** Figure bowing to King, type of KM#122 originally minted in 1992 **Edge:** Reeded **Note:** Mint error; muled dies.

Date	Mintage	VF20	XF40	MS60	MS63	MS65
1988	—	—	—	—	—	800

KM# 143 25 DOLLARS
20.09 g., 0.925 Silver 0.5975 oz. ASW **Ruler:** Elizabeth II **Series:** Endangered Wildlife **Obv:** Crowned head right **Rev:** African elephants right, trunks raised

Date	Mintage	VF20	XF40	MS60	MS63	MS65
1993 FM (P)	—	PF65 25.50				

KM# 144 25 DOLLARS
20.09 g., 0.925 Silver 0.5975 oz. ASW **Ruler:** Elizabeth II **Series:** Endangered Wildlife **Obv:** Crowned head right **Rev:** Mountain gorilla left

Date	Mintage	VF20	XF40	MS60	MS63	MS65
1993 FM (P)	—	PF65 20.50				

KM# 145 25 DOLLARS
20.09 g., 0.925 Silver 0.5975 oz. ASW **Ruler:** Elizabeth II **Series:** Endangered Wildlife **Obv:** Crowned head right **Rev:** Cape mountain zebra right

Date	Mintage	VF20	XF40	MS60	MS63	MS65
1993 FM (P)	—	PF65 23.50				

KM# 146 25 DOLLARS
20.09 g., 0.925 Silver 0.5975 oz. ASW **Ruler:** Elizabeth II **Series:** Endangered Wildlife **Obv:** Crowned head right **Rev:** Polar bear right

Date	Mintage	VF20	XF40	MS60	MS63	MS65
1993 FM (P)	—	PF65 18.50				

KM# 147 25 DOLLARS
20.09 g., 0.925 Silver 0.5975 oz. ASW **Ruler:** Elizabeth II **Series:** Endangered Wildlife **Obv:** Crowned head right **Rev:** Bald Eagle, wings spread

Date	Mintage	VF20	XF40	MS60	MS63	MS65
1993 FM (P)	—	PF65 20.50				

KM# 148 25 DOLLARS
20.09 g., 0.925 Silver 0.5975 oz. ASW **Ruler:** Elizabeth II **Series:** Endangered Wildlife **Obv:** Crowned head right **Rev:** Snow Leopard right

Date	Mintage	VF20	XF40	MS60	MS63	MS65
1993 FM (P)	—	PF65 20.50				

KM# 149 25 DOLLARS
20.09 g., 0.925 Silver 0.5975 oz. ASW **Ruler:** Elizabeth II **Series:** Endangered Wildlife **Obv:** Crowned head right **Rev:** Javan Rhinoceros left

Date	Mintage	VF20	XF40	MS60	MS63	MS65
1993 FM (P)	—	PF65 18.50				

KM# 150 25 DOLLARS
20.09 g., 0.925 Silver 0.5975 oz. ASW **Ruler:** Elizabeth II **Series:** Endangered Wildlife **Obv:** Crowned head right **Rev:** Asian Lion left

Date	Mintage	VF20	XF40	MS60	MS63	MS65
1993 FM (P)	—	PF65 18.50				

KM# 151 25 DOLLARS
20.09 g., 0.925 Silver 0.5975 oz. ASW **Ruler:** Elizabeth II **Series:** Endangered Wildlife **Obv:** Crowned head right **Rev:** Seated Giant Panda right

Date	Mintage	VF20	XF40	MS60	MS63	MS65
1993 FM (P)	—	PF65 20.50				

KM# 152 25 DOLLARS
20.09 g., 0.925 Silver 0.5975 oz. ASW **Ruler:** Elizabeth II **Series:** Endangered Wildlife **Obv:** Crowned head right **Rev:** Golden Lion Tamarin

Date	Mintage	VF20	XF40	MS60	MS63	MS65
1993 FM (P)	—	PF65 23.50				

KM# 153 25 DOLLARS
20.09 g., 0.925 Silver 0.5975 oz. ASW **Ruler:** Elizabeth II **Series:** Endangered Wildlife **Obv:** Crowned head right **Rev:** Pere David's deer

Date	Mintage	VF20	XF40	MS60	MS63	MS65
1993 FM (P)	—	PF65 18.50				

KM# 154 25 DOLLARS
20.09 g., 0.925 Silver 0.5975 oz. ASW **Ruler:** Elizabeth II **Series:** Endangered Wildlife **Obv:** Crowned head right **Rev:** Spectacled bear standing

Date	Mintage	VF20	XF40	MS60	MS63	MS65
1993 FM (P)	—	PF65 28.50				

KM# 155 25 DOLLARS
20.09 g., 0.925 Silver 0.5975 oz. ASW, 40 mm. **Ruler:** Elizabeth II **Series:** Endangered Wildlife **Obv:** Crowned head right **Rev:** Imperial Parrot on tree branch **Edge:** Reeded

Date	Mintage	VF20	XF40	MS60	MS63	MS65
1993 FM (P)	—	PF65 25.50				

KM# 158 25 DOLLARS
21.59 g., 0.925 Silver 0.6421 oz. ASW **Ruler:** Elizabeth II **Series:** Endangered Wildlife **Obv:** Crowned head right **Rev:** Pair of black-footed ferrets, one standing

Date	Mintage	VF20	XF40	MS60	MS63	MS65
1993 FM	—	PF65 26.50				

KM# 159 25 DOLLARS
21.59 g., 0.925 Silver 0.6421 oz. ASW **Ruler:** Elizabeth II **Series:** Endangered Wildlife **Obv:** Crowned head right **Rev:** Large Anegada rock iguana right

Date	Mintage	VF20	XF40	MS60	MS63	MS65
1993 FM	—	PF65 29.50				

KM# 160 25 DOLLARS
21.59 g., 0.925 Silver 0.6421 oz. ASW **Ruler:** Elizabeth II **Series:** Endangered Wildlife **Obv:** Crowned head right **Rev:** Two Parma wallabies, one with offspring

Date	Mintage	VF20	XF40	MS60	MS63	MS65
1993 FM	—	PF65 24.50				

KM# 161 25 DOLLARS
21.59 g., 0.925 Silver 0.6421 oz. ASW **Ruler:** Elizabeth II **Series:** Endangered Wildlife **Obv:** Crowned head right **Rev:** Pair of leatherback sea turtles and Portuguese Man-o-War jelly fish

Date	Mintage	VF20	XF40	MS60	MS63	MS65
1993 FM	—	PF65 26.50				

KM# 170 25 DOLLARS
21.35 g., 0.925 Silver 0.6349 oz. ASW **Ruler:** Elizabeth II **Series:** Endangered Wildlife **Obv:** Crowned head right **Rev:** Cheetah running left

Date	Mintage	VF20	XF40	MS60	MS63	MS65
1993 FM (P)	—	PF65 19.00				

KM# 171 25 DOLLARS
21.35 g., 0.925 Silver 0.6349 oz. ASW **Ruler:** Elizabeth II **Series:** Endangered Wildlife **Obv:** Crowned head right **Rev:** European Bison in forest

Date	Mintage	VF20	XF40	MS60	MS63	MS65
1993 FM (P)	—	PF65 19.00				

KM# 178 25 DOLLARS
21.60 g., 0.925 Silver 0.6424 oz. ASW, 40 mm. **Ruler:** Elizabeth II **Series:** Endangered Wildlife **Obv:** Crowned head right **Rev:** Three flamingos and four nests **Edge:** Reeded

Date	Mintage	VF20	XF40	MS60	MS63	MS65
1993	—	PF65 19.50				

KM# 179 25 DOLLARS
20.90 g., 0.925 Silver 0.6216 oz. ASW, 40 mm. **Ruler:** Elizabeth II **Subject:** Endangered Wildlife **Obv:** Crowned head right **Rev:** Front half of tiger stalking left **Edge:** Reeded

Date	Mintage	VF20	XF40	MS60	MS63	MS65
1993 FM (P)	—	PF65 19.00				

KM# 165 25 DOLLARS
21.59 g., 0.925 Silver 0.6421 oz. ASW **Ruler:** Elizabeth II **Series:** Endangered Wildlife **Obv:** Crowned head right **Rev:** Two seals frolicking

Date	Mintage	VF20	XF40	MS60	MS63	MS65
1997	—	PF65 24.50				

KM# 166 25 DOLLARS
21.59 g., 0.925 Silver 0.6421 oz. ASW **Ruler:** Elizabeth II **Series:** Endangered Wildlife **Obv:** Crowned head right **Rev:** Sea otter holding a sea urchin

Date	Mintage	VF20	XF40	MS60	MS63	MS65
1997	—	PF65 24.50				

KM# 167 25 DOLLARS
21.59 g., 0.925 Silver 0.6421 oz. ASW **Ruler:** Elizabeth II **Series:** Endangered Wildlife **Obv:** Crowned head right **Rev:** Pair of sparring Arabian oryx

Date	Mintage	VF20	XF40	MS60	MS63	MS65
1997	—	PF65 26.50				

KM# 168 25 DOLLARS
21.59 g., 0.925 Silver 0.6421 oz. ASW **Ruler:** Elizabeth II **Series:** Endangered Wildlife **Obv:** Crowned head right **Rev:** Diving humpback whale

Date	Mintage	VF20	XF40	MS60	MS63	MS65
1997	—	PF65 24.50				

KM# 28 50 DOLLARS
2.68 g., 0.500 Gold 0.0431 oz. AGW **Ruler:** Elizabeth II **Obv:** Young bust right **Rev:** Golden Dove of Christmas

Date	Mintage	VF20	XF40	MS60	MS63	MS65
1980	6,379	PF65 80.00				

KM# 75 50 DOLLARS
2.07 g., 0.500 Gold 0.0333 oz. AGW **Ruler:** Elizabeth II **Obv:** Crowned head right **Rev:** Flute player

Date	Mintage	VF20	XF40	MS60	MS63	MS65
1988	—	PF65 60.00				

KM# 76 50 DOLLARS
2.07 g., 0.500 Gold 0.0333 oz. AGW **Ruler:** Elizabeth II **Obv:** Crowned head right **Rev:** Bird's-head staff

Date	Mintage	VF20	XF40	MS60	MS63	MS65
1988	—	PF65 60.00				

KM# 77 50 DOLLARS
2.07 g., 0.500 Gold 0.0333 oz. AGW **Ruler:** Elizabeth II **Obv:** Crowned head right **Rev:** Double-spouted vessel

Date	Mintage	VF20	XF40	MS60	MS63	MS65
1988	—	PF65 60.00				

KM# 78 50 DOLLARS
2.07 g., 0.500 Gold 0.0333 oz. AGW **Ruler:** Elizabeth II **Obv:** Crowned head right **Rev:** Deer-top bell

Date	Mintage	VF20	XF40	MS60	MS63	MS65
1988	—	PF65 60.00				

KM# 79 50 DOLLARS
2.07 g., 0.500 Gold 0.0333 oz. AGW **Ruler:** Elizabeth II **Obv:** Crowned head right **Rev:** Two-headed animal

Date	Mintage	VF20	XF40	MS60	MS63	MS65
1988	—	PF65 60.00				

KM# 80 50 DOLLARS
2.07 g., 0.500 Gold 0.0333 oz. AGW **Ruler:** Elizabeth II **Obv:** Crowned head right **Rev:** Turtle

Date	Mintage	VF20	XF40	MS60	MS63	MS65
1988	—	PF65 60.00				

KM# 81 50 DOLLARS
2.07 g., 0.500 Gold 0.0333 oz. AGW **Ruler:** Elizabeth II **Obv:** Crowned head right **Rev:** Frog

Date	Mintage	VF20	XF40	MS60	MS63	MS65
1988	—	PF65 60.00				

KM# 82 50 DOLLARS
2.07 g., 0.500 Gold 0.0333 oz. AGW **Ruler:** Elizabeth II **Obv:** Crowned head right **Rev:** Mixtec mask

Date	Mintage	VF20	XF40	MS60	MS63	MS65
1988	—	PF65 60.00				

KM# 83 50 DOLLARS
2.07 g., 0.500 Gold 0.0333 oz. AGW **Ruler:** Elizabeth II **Obv:** Crowned head right **Rev:** Chimu gold beaker

Date	Mintage	VF20	XF40	MS60	MS63	MS65
1988	—	PF65 60.00				

KM# 84 50 DOLLARS
2.07 g., 0.500 Gold 0.0333 oz. AGW **Ruler:** Elizabeth II **Obv:** Crowned head right **Rev:** Bird vessel

Date	Mintage	VF20	XF40	MS60	MS63	MS65
1988	—	PF65 60.00				

KM# 85 50 DOLLARS
2.07 g., 0.500 Gold 0.0333 oz. AGW **Ruler:** Elizabeth II **Obv:** Crowned head right **Rev:** Ceremonial headdress

Date	Mintage	VF20	XF40	MS60	MS63	MS65
1988	—	PF65 60.00				

KM# 86 50 DOLLARS
2.07 g., 0.500 Gold 0.0333 oz. AGW **Ruler:** Elizabeth II **Obv:** Crowned head right **Rev:** Sacrificial knife

Date	Mintage	VF20	XF40	MS60	MS63	MS65
1988	—	PF65 60.00				

KM# 87 50 DOLLARS
2.07 g., 0.500 Gold 0.0333 oz. AGW **Ruler:** Elizabeth II **Obv:** Crowned head right **Rev:** Ceremonial dancer

Date	Mintage	VF20	XF40	MS60	MS63	MS65
1988	—	PF65 60.00				

KM# 88 50 DOLLARS
2.07 g., 0.500 Gold 0.0333 oz. AGW **Ruler:** Elizabeth II **Obv:** Crowned head right **Rev:** Spanish Colonial gold coin

Date	Mintage	VF20	XF40	MS60	MS63	MS65
1988	—	PF65 60.00				

KM# 89 50 DOLLARS
2.07 g., 0.500 Gold 0.0333 oz. AGW **Ruler:** Elizabeth II **Obv:** Crowned head right **Rev:** Crossed hands

Date	Mintage	VF20	XF40	MS60	MS63	MS65
1988	—	PF65 60.00				

KM# 7 100 DOLLARS
7.10 g., 0.900 Gold 0.2054 oz. AGW **Ruler:** Elizabeth II **Obv:** Young bust right **Rev:** Royal Tern

Date	Mintage	VF20	XF40	MS60	MS63	MS65
1975 FM (M) Rare	10	—	—	—	—	—
1975 FM (U)	13,000	—	—	—	350	375
1975 FM (P)	—	PF65 400				

Note: Includes 8,754 in First Day Covers

KM# 8 100 DOLLARS
7.10 g., 0.900 Gold 0.2054 oz. AGW **Ruler:** Elizabeth II **Subject:** 50th Birthday of Queen Elizabeth II **Obv:** Young bust right **Rev:** Crowned monogram above shield with woman and twelve lamps, VIGILATE on banner below

Date	Mintage	VF20	XF40	MS60	MS63	MS65
1976 FM (M) Rare	10	—	—	—	—	—
1976 FM (U)	1,752	—	—	—	400	425
1976 FM (P)	12,000	PF65 435				

KM# 15 100 DOLLARS
7.10 g., 0.900 Gold 0.2054 oz. AGW **Ruler:** Elizabeth II **Subject:** Queen's Silver Jubilee **Obv:** Young bust right **Rev:** Imperial crown above two dates

Date	Mintage	VF20	XF40	MS60	MS63	MS65
1977 FM (U) Rare	10	—	—	—	—	—
1977 FM (P)	6,715	PF65 350				

KM# 23 100 DOLLARS
7.10 g., 0.900 Gold 0.2054 oz. AGW **Ruler:** Elizabeth II **Subject:** Coronation Jubilee **Obv:** Young bust right **Rev:** Crossed sceptres with royal orb at center **Shape:** 25-sided

Date	Mintage	VF20	XF40	MS60	MS63	MS65
1978 FM (P)	5,772	PF65 350				

KM# 25 100 DOLLARS
7.10 g., 0.900 Gold 0.2054 oz. AGW **Ruler:** Elizabeth II **Obv:** Young bust right **Rev:** Bust of Sir Francis Drake with ruffed collar right

Date	Mintage	VF20	XF40	MS60	MS63	MS65
1979 FM (P)	3,216	PF65 350				

KM# 29 100 DOLLARS
7.10 g., 0.900 Gold 0.2054 oz. AGW **Ruler:** Elizabeth II **Subject:** 400th Anniversary of Drake's Voyage **Obv:** Young bust right **Rev:** The Golden Hind

Date	Mintage	VF20	XF40	MS60	MS63	MS65
1980	5,412	PF65 350				

KM# 32 100 DOLLARS
7.10 g., 0.900 Gold 0.2054 oz. AGW **Ruler:** Elizabeth II **Subject:** Knighting of Sir Francis Drake **Obv:** Young bust right **Rev:** Queen with kneeling figure

Date	Mintage	VF20	XF40	MS60	MS63	MS65
1981 FM (P)	1,321	PF65 385				

KM# 34 100 DOLLARS
7.10 g., 0.900 Gold 0.2054 oz. AGW **Ruler:** Elizabeth II **Subject:** 30th Anniversary - Reign of Queen Elizabeth II **Obv:** Young bust right **Rev:** Crowned monogram **Shape:** 6-sided

Date	Mintage	VF20	XF40	MS60	MS63	MS65
1982 FM (P)	620	PF65 425				

KM# 38 100 DOLLARS
7.10 g., 0.900 Gold 0.2054 oz. AGW **Ruler:** Elizabeth II **Subject:** 30th Anniversary - Coronation of Queen Elizabeth II **Obv:** Young bust right **Rev:** Sceptres divide royal symbols and dates **Shape:** 6-sided

Date	Mintage	VF20	XF40	MS60	MS63	MS65
1983 FM (P)	624	PF65 425				

KM# 39 100 DOLLARS
7.10 g., 0.900 Gold 0.2054 oz. AGW **Ruler:** Elizabeth II **Subject:** Flora - Ginger Thomas **Obv:** Young bust right **Rev:** Flower

Date	Mintage	VF20	XF40	MS60	MS63	MS65
1984 FM (P)	25	PF65 575				

KM# 74 100 DOLLARS
7.10 g., 0.900 Gold 0.2054 oz. AGW **Ruler:** Elizabeth II **Subject:** Sir Francis Drake's West Indian Voyage **Obv:** Crowned head right **Rev:** Ship **Shape:** 6-sided

Date	Mintage	VF20	XF40	MS60	MS63	MS65
1985 FM (P)	772	PF65 400				

KM# 119 100 DOLLARS
4.12 g., 0.500 Gold 0.0662 oz. AGW **Subject:** Discovery of America - King Ferdinand of Spain **Obv:** Crowned head right **Rev:** Bust facing

Date	Mintage	VF20	XF40	MS60	MS63	MS65
ND-1991 FM (P)	—	PF65 120				

KM# 162 100 DOLLARS
4.12 g., 0.500 Gold 0.0662 oz. AGW **Ruler:** Elizabeth II **Obv:** Crowned head right **Rev:** The Pinta

Date	Mintage	VF20	XF40	MS60	MS63	MS65
ND-1994	—	PF65 120				

KM# 256 100 DOLLARS
4.31 g., 0.500 Gold 0.0693 oz. AGW, 20.75 mm. **Ruler:** Elizabeth II **Obv:** Crowned head right **Rev:** Columbus' landing scene **Edge:** Reeded

Date	Mintage	VF20	XF40	MS60	MS63	MS65
ND1996 FM	—	PF65 140				

KM# 174.1 100 DOLLARS
6.22 g., 0.999 Gold 0.1998 oz. AGW **Ruler:** Elizabeth II **Subject:** Queen Mother's 100th Birthday **Obv:** Crowned head right **Rev:** Bust facing divides dates **Edge:** Reeded

Date	Mintage	VF20	XF40	MS60	MS63	MS65
2000	5,000	PF65 325				

KM# 174.2 100 DOLLARS
6.22 g., 0.9999 Gold 0.200 oz. AGW, 22 mm. **Ruler:** Elizabeth II **Subject:** Queen Mother's 100th Birthday **Obv:** Crowned head right **Rev:** Bust facing, tiny black sapphire mounted on her broach **Edge:** Reeded

Date	Mintage	VF20	XF40	MS60	MS63	MS65
2000	1,000	PF65 350				

KM# 177 100 DOLLARS
6.22 g., 0.999 Gold 0.1998 oz. AGW **Ruler:** Elizabeth II **Subject:** 1st Anniversary - Earl and Countess of Wessex **Obv:** Crowned head right **Rev:** 1/2 figures facing, anniversary dates below **Edge:** Reeded

Date	Mintage	VF20	XF40	MS60	MS63	MS65
2000	5,000	PF65 325				

KM# 120 250 DOLLARS
8.05 g., 0.500 Gold 0.1294 oz. AGW **Ruler:** Elizabeth II **Subject:** Quincentennial - Discovery of America **Obv:** Crowned head right **Rev:** Bust of young Queen Isabella 3/4 left

Date	Mintage	VF20	XF40	MS60	MS63	MS65
ND-1991 FM (P)	—	PF65 275				

KM# 163 250 DOLLARS
8.05 g., 0.500 Gold 0.1294 oz. AGW **Ruler:** Elizabeth II **Subject:** The Nina **Obv:** Crowned head right **Rev:** Ship

Date	Mintage	VF20	XF40	MS60	MS63	MS65
ND-1994	—	PF65 275				

KM# 257 250 DOLLARS
8.17 g., 0.500 Gold 0.1313 oz. AGW, 26 mm. **Ruler:** Elizabeth II **Obv:** Crowned head right **Rev:** Columbus' personal coat of arms **Edge:** Reeded

Date	Mintage	VF20	XF40	MS60	MS63	MS65
ND(1996?) FM	—	PF65 250				

KM# 121 500 DOLLARS
19.81 g., 0.500 Gold 0.3185 oz. AGW **Ruler:** Elizabeth II **Subject:** Discovery of America **Obv:** Crowned head right **Rev:** Christopher Columbus 3/4 facing

Date	Mintage	VF20	XF40	MS60	MS63	MS65
ND-1991 FM (P)	—	PF65 550				

KM# 164 500 DOLLARS
19.81 g., 0.500 Gold 0.3185 oz. AGW **Ruler:** Elizabeth II **Subject:** The Santa Maria **Obv:** Crowned head right **Rev:** Ship sailing left, no gulls

Date	Mintage	VF20	XF40	MS60	MS63	MS65
ND-1994	—	PF65 550				

KM# 258 500 DOLLARS
20.22 g., 0.500 Gold 0.325 oz. AGW, 35.75 mm. **Ruler:** Elizabeth II **Obv:** Crowned head right **Rev:** Columbus' three ships crossing the Atlantic to America **Edge:** Reeded

Date	Mintage	VF20	XF40	MS60	MS63	MS65
ND(1996?) FM	—	PF65 575				

KM# 156 1000 DOLLARS
14.80 g., 0.999 Platinum 0.4754 oz. APW **Ruler:** Elizabeth II **Subject:** Discovery of America **Obv:** Crowned head right **Rev:** Three ships sailing

Date	Mintage	VF20	XF40	MS60	MS63	MS65
ND-1992	—	PF65 875				

MINT SETS

KM#	Date	Mintage	Identification	Issue Price	Mkt Val
MS1	1973 (6)	18,402	KM#1-5, 6a	11.50	25.00
MS2	1974 (6)	9,474	KM#1-6	10.00	12.00
MS3	1975 (6)	2,351	KM#1-6	12.50	10.00
MS4	1976 (6)	996	KM#1-6	13.50	25.00
MS5	1977 (6)	782	KM#1-6	12.50	25.00
MS6	1978 (6)	943	KM#1-6	13.00	25.00
MS7	1979 (7)	680	KM#1-6, 24	20.00	100
MS8	1980 (7)	1,007	KM#1-6, 26	21.00	85.00
MS9	1981 (7)	472	KM#1-6, 30	20.00	100
MS10	1982 (7)	—	KM#1-6, 33	28.50	100
MS11	1983 (7)	203	KM#1-6, 35	22.00	100

PROOF SETS

KM#	Date	Mintage	Identification	Issue Price	Mkt Val
PS1	1973 (6)	146,581	KM#1-5, 6a. Includes 34,418 proofs in First Day Covers	15.00	25.00
PS2	1974 (6)	93,555	KM#1-5, 6a	20.00	30.00
PS3	1975 (6)	32,244	KM#1-5, 6a	25.00	30.00
PS4	1976 (6)	15,003	KM#1-5, 6a	25.00	30.00
PS5	1977 (6)	7,218	KM#1-5, 6a	26.00	35.00
PS6	1977 (6)	17,366	KM#9-14	60.00	50.00
PS7	1978 (6)	7,059	KM#1-5, 6a	25.00	35.00
PS8	1978 (6)	6,196	KM#16-21	—	55.00
PS9	1979 (7)	5,304	KM#1-5, 6a, 24a	39.50	75.00
PS10	1980 (7)	3,421	KM#105, 6a, 26a	97.00	75.00
PS11	1981 (7)	1,124	KM#1-5, 6a, 30a	97.00	75.00
PS12	1982 (7)	—	KM#1-5, 6a, 33a	97.00	75.00
PS13	1983 (7)	478	KM#1-5, 6a, 35a	77.00	150
PS14	1984 (7)	5,000	KM#1-5, 6a, 35a	77.00	75.00
PS15	1985 (6)	—	KM#42-47	20.50	55.00
PS16	1985 (6)	—	KM#42a-47a	76.00	70.00
PS17	ND (1991) (3)	—	KM#119-121	975	950
PS18	ND (1994) (3)	—	KM#162-164	975	950
PS19	ND (1996) (3)	—	KM#256, 257, 258	—	950

BRITISH WEST AFRICA

SENEGAL
MALI
BURKINA
NIGER
TOGO
BENIN
CHAD
GUINEA
GUINEA BISSAU
IVORY COAST
LIBERIA
CAMEROON

British West Africa was an administrative grouping of the four former British West African colonies of Gambia, Sierra Leone, Nigeria and Gold Coast (now Ghana). All are now independent republics and members of the British Commonwealth of Nations. See separate entries for individual statistics and history.

The Bank of British West Africa became the banker to the Colonial Government in 1894 and held this status until 1912. As such they were responsible for maintaining a proper supply of silver coinage for the colonies.

Through the subsidiary efforts of the Governor of Lagos, Nigeria a specific British West African coinage was put into use between 1907 and 1911. These coins bear the inscription, NIGERIA-BRITISH WEST AFRICA.

The four colonies were supplied with a common coinage and banknotes by the West African Currency Board from 1912 through 1958. This coinage bore the inscription BRITISH WEST AFRICA. The coinage, which includes three denominations of 1936 bearing the name of Edward VIII, is obsolete.

For later coinage see Gambia, Ghana, Sierra Leone and Nigeria.

RULER
British, until 1958

MINT MARKS
G-J.R. Gaunt & Sons, Birmingham
H - Heaton Mint, Birmingham
K, KN - King's Norton, Birmingham
SA - Pretoria, South Africa
No mm - Royal Mint, London

MONETARY SYSTEM
12 Pence = 1 Shilling
20 Shillings = 1 Pound

BRITISH COLONIES

POUND COINAGE

KM# 1 1/10 PENNY
Aluminum **Ruler:** Edward VII **Obv:** Crown above center hole, denomination around hole in English, in Arabic beneath **Obv. Legend:** EDWARD VII KING & EMPEROR **Rev:** Hexagram divides date at bottom **Rev. Legend:** NIGERIA BRITISH WEST AFRICA

Date	Mintage	F12	VF20	XF40	MS60	MS63
1907	1,254,000	2.00	4.00	10.00	20.00	35.00
1908	8,363,000	1.00	3.00	6.00	15.00	25.00
1908	—	PF63 300				

KM# 3 1/10 PENNY
Copper-Nickel **Ruler:** Edward VII **Obv:** Crown above center hole, denomination around hole in English, in Arabic beneath **Obv. Legend:** EDWARD VII KING & EMPEROR **Rev:** Hexagram divides date at bottom **Rev. Legend:** NIGERIA BRITISH WEST AFRICA

Date	Mintage	F12	VF20	XF40	MS60	MS63
1908	9,600,000	0.30	0.50	1.00	2.00	3.50
1909	4,800,000	0.40	0.75	1.50	5.00	9.00
1910	7,200,000	0.50	1.00	2.00	7.50	12.50

KM# 4 1/10 PENNY
Copper-Nickel **Ruler:** George V **Obv:** Crown above center hole, denomination around hole in English, in Arabic beneath **Obv. Legend:** GEORGIVS V REX ET IND: IMP: **Rev:** Hexagram divides date at bottom **Rev. Legend:** NIGERIA BRITISH WEST AFRICA

Date	Mintage	F12	VF20	XF40	MS60	MS63
1911 H	7,200,000	1.50	3.50	7.50	15.00	28.00

KM# 7 1/10 PENNY
1.72 g., Copper-Nickel, 20.5 mm. **Ruler:** George V **Obv:** Crown above center hole, denomination around hole in English, in Arabic beneath **Obv. Legend:** GEORGIVS V REX ET IND: IMP: **Rev:** Hexagram divides date at bottom **Rev. Legend:** BRITISH WEST AFRICA **Edge:** Plain

Date	Mintage	F12	VF20	XF40	MS60	MS63
1912 H	10,800,000	0.30	0.75	1.50	3.50	7.00
1913	4,632,000	1.00	2.00	3.50	6.50	11.50
1913 H	1,080,000	0.30	0.75	1.50	3.50	7.00
1914	1,200,000	3.00	5.00	10.00	22.50	40.00
1914 H	20,088,000	0.50	1.25	2.00	5.00	9.00
1915 H	10,032,000	0.30	0.75	1.50	5.00	9.00
1916 H	480,000	25.00	40.00	60.00	100	125
1917 H	9,384,000	2.00	3.00	5.00	15.00	25.00
1919 H	912,000	1.25	2.00	4.00	7.50	13.50
1919 KN	480,000	10.00	25.00	50.00	75.00	100
1920 H	1,560,000	2.00	3.00	5.00	10.00	18.00
1920 KN	—	PF63 125				
1920 KN	12,996,000	0.40	1.00	3.00	5.00	9.00
1922 KN	7,265,000	1.00	1.75	4.50	12.00	20.00
1923 KN	12,000,000	0.30	0.75	1.50	5.00	9.00
1925	2,400,000	5.00	10.00	20.00	40.00	70.00
1925 H	12,000,000	2.00	3.00	5.00	12.00	20.00
1925 KN	12,000,000	0.75	1.50	3.00	8.00	15.00
1926	12,000,000	0.75	1.50	2.50	6.00	10.00
1927	3,984,000	0.20	0.50	1.50	3.00	6.00
1927	—	PF63 150				
1928	11,760,000	0.20	0.50	1.50	3.00	6.00
1928	—	PF63 150				
1928 H	2,964,000	0.20	0.50	1.50	3.00	6.00
1928 KN	3,151,000	2.00	3.00	6.00	15.00	25.00
1930	9,600,000	2.00	3.00	6.00	15.00	25.00
1930	—	PF63 150				
1931	9,840,000	0.20	0.50	1.00	3.00	6.00
1931	—	PF63 150				
1932	3,600,000	0.20	0.50	1.50	5.00	9.00
1932	—	PF63 150				
1933	7,200,000	0.20	0.50	1.50	3.50	7.00
1933	—	PF63 150				
1934	4,800,000	0.75	1.50	3.00	6.00	10.00
1934	—	PF63 150				
1935	13,200,000	0.75	1.50	3.00	7.50	12.50
1935	—	PF63 150				
1936	9,720,000	0.20	0.50	1.00	3.00	6.00
1936	—	PF63 150				

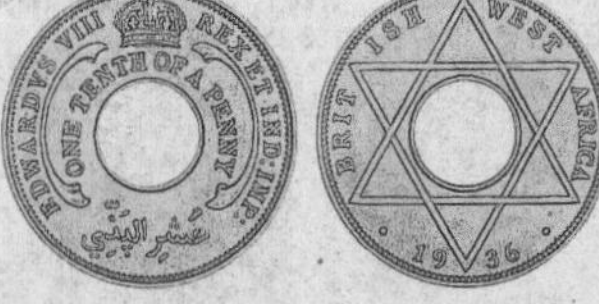

KM# 14 1/10 PENNY
1.90 g., Copper-Nickel, 20 mm. **Ruler:** Edward VIII **Obv:** Crown above center hole, denomination around hole in English, in Arabic beneath **Obv. Legend:** EDWARDVS VIII REX ET IND: IMP: **Rev:** Hexagram divides date at bottom **Rev. Legend:** BRITISH WEST AFRICA

Date	Mintage	F12	VF20	XF40	MS60	MS63
1936	5,880,000	0.25	0.50	1.00	2.50	4.50
1936	—	PF63 200				
1936 H	1,404,000	50.00	75.00	150	350	550
1936 H	—	PF63 300				
1936 KN	3,000,000	1.00	2.00	3.50	9.00	15.00
1936 KN	—	PF63 200				

KM# 20 1/10 PENNY
2.00 g., Copper-Nickel, 20 mm. **Ruler:** George VI **Obv:** Crown above center hole, denomination around hole in English, in Arabic beneath **Obv. Legend:** GEORGIVS VI REX ET IND: IMP: **Rev:** Hexagram divides date at bottom **Rev. Legend:** BRITISH WEST AFRICA

Date	Mintage	F12	VF20	XF40	MS60	MS63
1938	12,000,000	0.10	0.25	0.50	1.50	2.50
1938	—	PF63 125				
1938 H	1,596,000	5.00	8.00	12.00	22.50	40.00
1938 H	—	PF63 100				
1939	9,840,000	0.25	0.50	1.00	3.50	6.00
1939	—	PF63 200				
1940	13,920,000	0.25	0.50	1.00	2.00	3.50
1940	—	PF63 125				
1941	16,560,000	1.00	2.00	4.00	8.00	14.00
1941	—	PF63 125				
1942	12,360,000	1.00	2.50	4.50	10.00	18.00
1942	—	PF63 125				
1943	22,560,000	1.00	2.50	5.00	10.00	18.00
1944	10,440,000	1.00	2.50	5.00	10.00	18.00
1944	—	PF63 150				
1945	25,706,000	0.50	1.00	1.75	6.00	10.00
1945	—	PF63 125				
1946	2,803,000	1.00	2.00	4.00	9.00	15.00
1946	—	PF63 125				
1946 H	5,004,000	1.00	2.00	4.00	9.00	15.00
1946 KN	1,152,000	0.25	0.50	1.00	3.00	5.50
1946 KN	—	PF63 125				
1947	4,202,000	0.50	1.00	2.00	5.00	9.00
1947	—	PF63 125				
1947 KN	3,900,000	200	300	500	600	—

KM# 26 1/10 PENNY
Copper-Nickel, 20 mm. **Obv:** Crown above center hole, denomination around hole in English, in Arabic beneath **Obv. Legend:** GEORGIVS SEXTVS REX **Rev:** Hexagram divides date at bottom **Rev. Legend:** BRITISH WEST AFRICA

Date	Mintage	F12	VF20	XF40	MS60	MS63
1949 H	3,700,000	1.00	2.00	3.00	6.00	10.00
1949 KN	3,036,000	1.00	2.00	3.00	5.00	9.00
1950 KN	13,200,000	0.25	0.50	1.00	2.50	4.50
1950 KN	—	PF63 150				

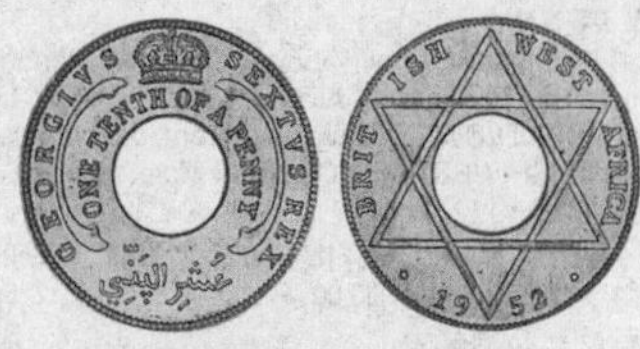

KM# 26a 1/10 PENNY

Bronze, 20 mm. **Obv:** Crown above center hole, denomination around hole in English, in Arabic beneath **Obv. Legend:** GEORGIVS SEXTVS REX **Rev:** Hexagram divides date at bottom **Rev. Legend:** BRITISH WEST AFRICA

Date	Mintage	F12	VF20	XF40	MS60	MS63
1952	15,060,000	0.50	1.00	2.00	6.00	10.00
1952	—	**PF60** 200	**PF63** 350	**PF65** 550		

KM# 32 1/10 PENNY

Bronze, 20 mm. **Ruler:** Elizabeth II **Obv:** Crown above center hole, denomination around hole in English, in Arabic beneath **Obv. Legend:** QUEEN ELIZABETH THE SECOND **Rev:** Hexagram divides date at bottom **Rev. Legend:** BRITISH WEST AFRICA

Date	Mintage	F12	VF20	XF40	MS60	MS63
1954	4,800,000	0.50	1.00	2.00	4.00	8.00
1954	—	**PF60** 150	**PF63** 200	**PF65** 350		
1956	2,400,000	100	200	400	700	—
1956	—	**PF60** 950	**PF63** 1,650	**PF65** 2,850		
1957	7,200,000	60.00	120	220	325	—
1957	—	**PF60** 600	**PF63** 750	**PF65** 1,350		

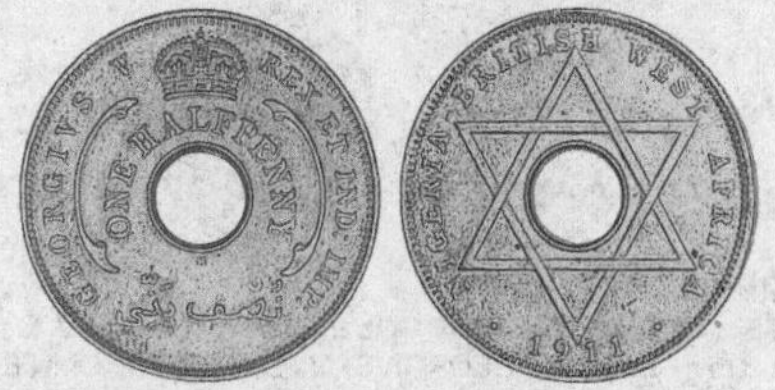

KM# 5 1/2 PENNY

Copper-Nickel **Ruler:** George V **Obv:** Crown above center hole, denomination around hole in English, in Arabic beneath **Obv. Legend:** GEORGIVS V REX ET IND: IMP: **Rev:** Hexagram divides date at bottom **Rev. Legend:** NIGERIA BRITISH WEST AFRICA

Date	Mintage	F12	VF20	XF40	MS60	MS63
1911 H	3,360,000	4.50	12.00	25.00	40.00	75.00

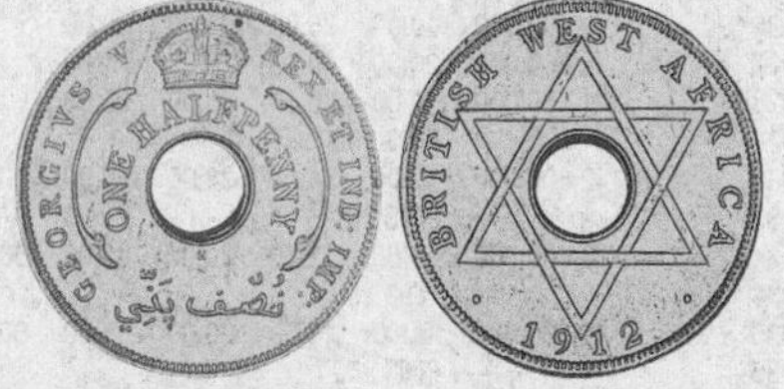

KM# 8 1/2 PENNY

Copper-Nickel, 25.2 mm. **Ruler:** George V **Obv:** Crown above center hole, denomination around hole in English, in Arabic beneath **Obv. Legend:** GEORGIVS V REX ET IND: IMP: **Rev:** Hexagram divides date at bottom **Rev. Legend:** BRITISH WEST AFRICA **Edge:** Plain

Date	Mintage	F12	VF20	XF40	MS60	MS63
1912 H	3,120,000	2.00	5.00	7.00	20.00	35.00
1913	1,382,000	150	250	325	500	—
1913 H	216,000	5.00	10.00	17.50	30.00	55.00
1914	240,000	10.00	20.00	35.00	60.00	110
1914 H	586,000	20.00	30.00	50.00	75.00	135
1914 K	3,360,000	3.00	6.00	17.50	30.00	55.00
1914 K	—	**PF63** 225				
Note: Issued with East Africa KM#11 in a double (4 pc.) specimen set						
1915 H	3,577,000	1.00	2.00	4.00	15.00	25.00
1916 H	4,046,000	1.00	3.00	5.00	15.00	25.00
1917 H	214,000	6.00	12.00	28.00	50.00	90.00
1918 H	490,000	2.50	5.00	10.00	30.00	55.00
1919 H	4,950,000	1.25	2.50	6.00	20.00	35.00
1919 KN	3,861,000	1.25	2.50	7.50	25.00	45.00
1920 H	26,285,000	1.50	3.00	7.50	15.00	25.00
1920 KN	13,844,000	0.50	3.00	8.50	16.50	30.00
1922 KN	5,817,000	300	500	750	1,200	—
1927	528,000	20.00	30.00	65.00	135	250
1927	—	**PF63** 225				
1929	336,000	6.00	22.00	47.50	95.00	165
1929	—	**PF63** 225				
1931	96,000	500	800	1,200	1,500	—
1931	—	**PF63** 225				
1932	960,000	2.50	15.00	35.00	55.00	100
1932	—	**PF63** 225				
1933	2,122,000	12.00	23.50	55.00	110	200
1933	—	**PF63** 225				
1934	1,694,000	2.50	15.00	35.00	75.00	135
1934	—	**PF63** 225				
1935	3,271,000	1.00	3.00	18.00	35.00	60.00
1935	—	**PF63** 225				
1936	5,400,000	2.50	5.00	18.00	32.00	55.00
1936	—	**PF63** 225				

KM# 15 1/2 PENNY

Copper-Nickel, 25.2 mm. **Ruler:** Edward VIII **Obv:** Crown above center hole, denomination around hole in English, in Arabic beneath **Obv. Legend:** EDWARDVS VIII REX • ET IND: IMP: **Rev:** Hexagram divides date at bottom **Rev. Legend:** BRITISH WEST AFRICA **Edge:** Plain

Date	Mintage	F12	VF20	XF40	MS60	MS63
1936	14,760,000	0.25	0.50	1.00	2.50	4.50
1936	—	**PF63** 400	**PF65** 550			
1936 H	2,400,000	1.00	2.00	5.00	12.50	20.00
1936 H	—	**PF63** 250				
1936 KN	2,298,000	0.65	1.25	2.25	4.00	7.00
1936 KN	—	**PF63** 250				

KM# 18 1/2 PENNY

5.30 g., Copper-Nickel, 25.9 mm. **Ruler:** George VI **Obv:** Crown above center hole, denomination around hole in English, in Arabic beneath **Obv. Legend:** GEORGIVS VI REX • ET IND: IMP: **Rev:** Hexagram divides date at bottom **Rev. Legend:** BRITISH WEST AFRICA

Date	Mintage	F12	VF20	XF40	MS60	MS63
1937 H	4,800,000	0.40	0.85	1.50	4.00	7.00
1937 H	—	**PF63** 125				
1937 KN	5,577,000	0.40	0.85	3.00	5.00	9.00
1940 KN	2,410,000	2.00	4.00	6.00	15.00	25.00
1940 KN	—	**PF63** 125				
1941 H	2,400,000	0.40	2.00	6.00	12.00	20.00
1942	4,800,000	0.40	0.85	4.00	8.50	15.00
1943	3,360,000	0.50	1.00	5.00	10.00	18.00
1944	3,600,000	1.00	3.00	7.00	20.00	35.00
1944	—	**PF63** 125				
1946	3,600,000	0.25	1.00	3.00	7.00	12.50
1946	—	**PF63** 125				
1947 H	15,218,000	0.35	0.75	1.25	5.00	9.00
1947 KN	12,000,000	0.40	0.85	2.00	6.00	10.00

KM# 27 1/2 PENNY

Copper-Nickel **Ruler:** Edward VII **Obv:** Crown above center hole, denomination around hole in English, in Arabic beneath **Obv. Legend:** GEORGIVS SEXTVS REX **Rev:** Hexagram divides date at bottom **Rev. Legend:** BRITISH WEST AFRICA

Date	Mintage	F12	VF20	XF40	MS60	MS63
1949 H	5,909,000	1.50	3.50	12.00	22.00	40.00
1949 KN	3,413,000	1.50	3.50	12.00	25.00	45.00
1951	3,468,000	1.50	3.50	12.00	25.00	45.00
1951	—	**PF63** 250				

KM# 27a 1/2 PENNY

5.60 g., Bronze, 25.9 mm. **Obv:** Crown above center hole, denomination around hole in English, in Arabic beneath **Obv. Legend:** GEORGIVS SEXTVS REX **Rev:** Denomination around hole in English, in Arabic beneath **Rev. Legend:** BRITISH WEST AFRICA

Date	Mintage	F12	VF20	XF40	MS60	MS63
1952	11,332,000	0.25	0.50	2.50	5.50	9.50
1952	—	**PF63** 150				
1952 H	27,603,000	0.20	0.35	0.75	2.00	3.50
1952 KN	4,800,000	0.50	2.00	5.00	10.00	18.00

KM# 2 PENNY

Copper-Nickel, 30.5 mm. **Ruler:** Edward VII **Obv:** Crown above center hole, denomination around hole in English, in Arabic beneath **Obv. Legend:** EDWARD VII KING & EMPEROR **Rev:** Hexagram, date beneath **Rev. Legend:** NIGERIA BRITISH WEST AFRICA

Date	Mintage	F12	VF20	XF40	MS60	MS63
1907	863,000	2.00	5.00	9.00	20.00	35.00
1908	3,217,000	2.00	4.00	8.00	17.50	30.00
1909	960,000	3.50	9.00	20.00	35.00	60.00
1910	2,520,000	2.75	7.00	12.00	25.00	45.00

KM# 6 PENNY

Copper-Nickel, 30.5 mm. **Ruler:** George V **Obv:** Crown above center hole, denomination around hole in English, in Arabic beneath **Obv. Legend:** GEORGIVS V REX ET IND: IMP: **Rev:** Hexagram, date beneath **Rev. Legend:** NIGERIA BRITISH WEST AFRICA

Date	Mintage	F12	VF20	XF40	MS60	MS63
1911 H	1,920,000	12.00	25.00	50.00	100	150

KM# 9 PENNY

Copper-Nickel, 30.5 mm. **Ruler:** George V **Obv:** Crown above center hole, denomination around hole in English, in Arabic beneath **Obv. Legend:** GEORGIVS V REX ET IND: IMP: **Rev:** Hexagram, date beneath **Rev. Legend:** BRITISH WEST AFRICA

Date	Mintage	F12	VF20	XF40	MS60	MS63
1912 H	1,560,000	1.50	3.00	10.00	22.50	40.00
1913	1,680,000	7.50	25.00	45.00	75.00	135
1913 H	144,000	5.00	10.00	17.50	35.00	60.00
1914	3,000,000	2.50	6.00	10.00	22.50	40.00
1914 H	72,000	35.00	50.00	120	200	—
1915 H	3,295,000	1.25	2.00	7.00	15.00	25.00
1916 H	3,461,000	1.25	2.00	10.00	20.00	35.00
1917 H	444,000	5.00	7.00	24.00	45.00	80.00
1918 H	994,000	7.50	15.00	45.00	75.00	135
1919 H	21,864,000	1.25	2.50	7.00	15.00	25.00
1919 KN	264,000	7.50	25.00	35.00	50.00	90.00
1920 H	37,870,000	1.00	1.75	5.50	12.50	22.50
1920 KN	20,685,000	1.00	2.00	8.00	17.50	30.00
1922 KN	3,971,000	400	750	1,000	1,500	—
1926	8,039,999	2.00	4.00	15.00	30.00	55.00
1927	792,000	25.00	45.00	125	200	—
1927	—	**PF63** 225				
1928	6,672,000	2.00	4.00	12.00	25.00	45.00
1928	—	**PF63** 225				
1929	636,000	20.00	35.00	65.00	100	—
1929	—	**PF63** 225				
1933	2,806,000	2.00	14.00	32.50	65.00	120
1933	—	**PF63** 225				
1934	2,640,000	3.50	15.00	35.00	75.00	135
1934	—	**PF63** 225				

Date	Mintage	F12	VF20	XF40	MS60	MS63
1935	8,551,000	1.25	12.50	27.50	45.00	80.00
1935	—	PF63 225				
1936	7,368,000	1.25	3.50	12.00	25.00	45.00
1936	—	PF63 225				

KM# 16 PENNY

9.37 g., Copper-Nickel, 30.5 mm. **Ruler:** Edward VIII **Obv:** Crown above center hole, denomination around hole in English, in Arabic beneath **Obv. Legend:** EDWARDVS VIII REX ET IND: IMP: **Rev:** Hexagram, date beneath **Rev. Legend:** BRITISH WEST AFRICA **Edge:** Plain

Date	Mintage	F12	VF20	XF40	MS60	MS63
1936	7,992,000	0.50	1.00	3.50	7.00	12.50
1936	—	PF63 400				
1936 H	12,600,000	0.35	0.75	1.00	2.25	4.00
1936 H	—	PF63 350				
1936 KN	12,512,000	0.35	0.75	1.00	2.25	4.00
1936 KN	—	PF63 300	PF65 500			

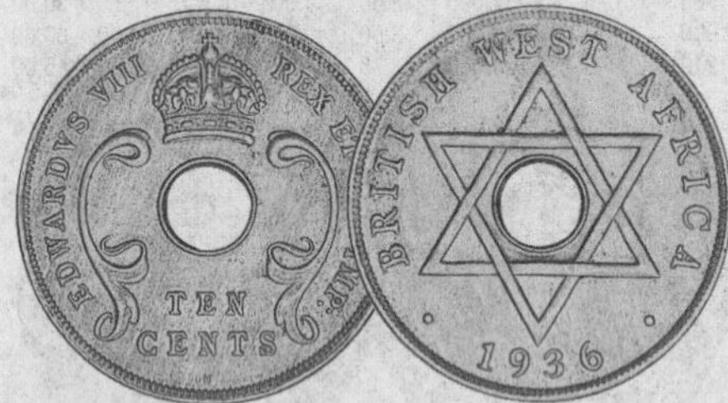

KM# 17 PENNY

Copper-Nickel, 30.5 mm. **Ruler:** Edward VIII **Obv:** Crown above center hole, denomination in English beneath **Obv. Legend:** EDWARDVS VIII REX ET IND: IMP: **Rev:** Hexagram, date beneath **Rev. Legend:** BRITISH WEST AFRICA **Note:** Mule.

Date	Mintage	F12	VF20	XF40	MS60	MS63
1936 H	—	125	165	275	650	850

KM# 19 PENNY

9.65 g., Copper-Nickel, 30.5 mm. **Ruler:** George VI **Obv:** Crown above center hole, denomination around hole in English, in Arabic beneath **Obv. Legend:** GEORGIVS VI REX • ET IND: IMP: **Rev:** Hexagram, date beneath **Rev. Legend:** BRITISH WEST AFRICA **Edge:** Plain

Date	Mintage	F12	VF20	XF40	MS60	MS63
1937 H	11,999,000	0.50	0.75	1.25	2.00	3.50
1937 H	—	PF63 200				
1937 KN	11,999,000	0.50	0.75	1.25	2.00	3.50
1937 KN	—	PF63 200				
1940	3,840,000	0.50	0.75	1.25	2.00	3.50
1940 Proof	—	—	—	—	—	—
1940 H	2,400,000	0.50	0.75	3.00	8.00	14.00
1940 KN	2,400,000	0.75	1.50	4.50	10.00	18.00
1941	6,960,000	0.35	0.75	1.25	3.50	6.00
1941 Proof	—	—	—	—	—	—
1942	18,840,000	0.30	0.60	1.00	3.00	5.00
1943	28,920,000	0.30	0.60	1.00	3.00	5.00
1943 H	7,140,000	2.00	5.00	10.00	20.00	35.00
1944	19,440,000	0.30	0.60	1.00	4.00	7.00
1945	6,072,000	0.45	0.90	1.75	5.00	9.00
1945	—	PF63 150				
1945 H	9,000,000	1.00	2.00	4.50	10.00	18.00
1945 KN	9,557,000	0.75	1.50	3.00	7.00	12.00
1946 H	10,446,000	0.85	1.75	3.75	8.00	14.00
1946 KN	11,976,000	0.30	0.60	1.00	5.00	9.00
1946 SA	1,020,000	250	500	750	1,150	—
1947 H	12,443,000	0.30	0.60	1.00	5.00	9.00
1947 KN	9,829,000	0.30	0.60	1.00	5.00	9.00
1947 SA	58,980,000	0.30	0.60	1.00	4.50	7.50

KM# 25 PENNY

Copper-Nickel, 30.5 mm. **Ruler:** George VI **Obv:** Crown above center hole, denomination around hole in English, in Arabic beneath **Obv. Legend:** GEORGIVS VI REX • ET IND: IMP: **Rev:** Hexagram, date beneath **Rev. Legend:** BRITISH WEST AFRICA **Note:** Mule, obverse KM#16, reverse KM#19.

Date	Mintage	F12	VF20	XF40	MS60	MS63
1945 H	—	1,000	2,000	3,500	5,500	—

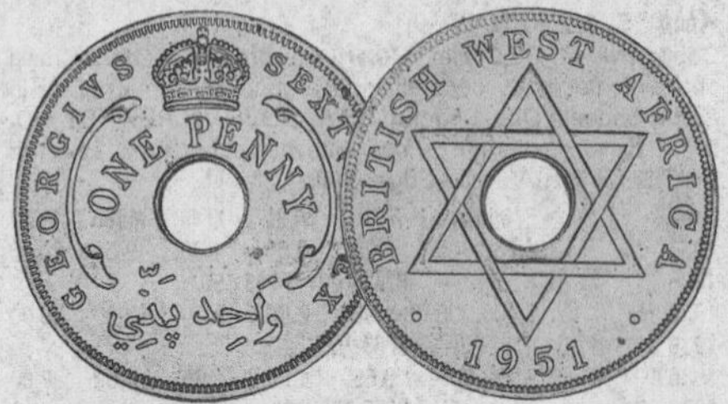

KM# 30 PENNY

Copper-Nickel, 30.5 mm. **Obv:** Crown above center hole, denomination around hole in English, in Arabic beneath **Obv. Legend:** GEORGIVS SEXTVS REX **Rev:** Hexagram, date beneath **Rev. Legend:** BRITISH WEST AFRICA

Date	Mintage	F12	VF20	XF40	MS60	MS63
1951	1,258,000	7.50	12.50	27.50	45.00	80.00
1951	—	PF63 250				
1951 KN	2,692,000	6.00	10.00	20.00	35.00	60.00

KM# 30a PENNY

Bronze, 30.5 mm. **Obv:** Crown above center hole, denomination around hole in English, in Arabic beneath **Obv. Legend:** GEORGIVS SEXTVS REX **Rev:** Hexagram, date beneath **Rev. Legend:** BRITISH WEST AFRICA

Date	Mintage	F12	VF20	XF40	MS60	MS63
1952	10,542,000	0.75	1.50	3.00	8.50	15.00
1952	—	PF63 175				
1952 H	30,794,000	0.20	0.40	0.60	3.00	5.00
1952 KN	45,398,000	0.20	0.40	0.60	3.00	5.00
1952 KN	—	PF63 175				

KM# 33 PENNY

Bronze, 30.5 mm. **Ruler:** Elizabeth II **Obv:** Crown above center hole, denomination around hole in English, in Arabic beneath **Obv. Legend:** QUEEN ELIZABETH THE SECOND **Rev:** Hexagram, date beneath **Rev. Legend:** BRITISH WEST AFRICA

Date	Mintage	F12	VF20	XF40	MS60	MS63
1956 H	13,503,000	0.75	1.50	3.50	9.00	16.00
1956 KN	13,500,000	0.30	0.60	2.50	8.00	14.00
1957	9,000,000	0.75	1.50	6.00	13.50	25.00
1957	—	PF63 150				
1957 H	5,340,000	1.00	2.50	10.00	20.00	35.00
1957 KN	5,600,000	1.00	2.50	8.00	16.00	28.00
1957 N	Inc. above	125	175	250	—	—
Note: Error strike missing the K						
1958	12,200,000	0.75	1.50	6.00	13.50	25.00
1958	—	PF63 125				
1958 KN	Inc. above	0.75	1.50	5.00	10.00	18.00

KM# 34 PENNY

Bronze, 30.5 mm. **Obv:** Crown above center hole, denomination around hole in English, in Arabic beneath **Obv. Legend:** GEORGIVS SEXTVS REX **Rev:** Hexagram, date beneath **Rev. Legend:** BRITISH WEST AFRICA **Note:** Mule, obverse KM#30, reverse KM#33.

Date	Mintage	F12	VF20	XF40	MS60	MS63
1956 H	—	50.00	100	185	225	350

KM# 10 3 PENCE

1.14 g., 0.925 Silver 0.034 oz. ASW **Ruler:** George V **Obv:** Bust of King George V left **Obv. Legend:** GEORGIVS V D.G.BRITT: OMN:REX F.D.IND:IMP: **Rev:** Denomination in wreath, date beneath **Rev. Legend:** BRITISH WEST AFRICA

Date	Mintage	F12	VF20	XF40	MS60	MS63
1913	240,000	3.50	7.50	35.00	65.00	90.00
1913	—	PF63 250				
1913 H	496,000	2.00	4.00	15.00	30.00	65.00
1914 H	1,560,000	1.25	2.50	12.50	25.00	45.00
1915 H	270,000	18.00	25.00	45.00	75.00	100
1916 H	820,000	10.00	15.00	25.00	50.00	75.00
1917 H	3,600,000	1.50	2.50	12.50	25.00	45.00
1918 H	1,722,000	1.75	3.50	10.00	20.00	35.00
1919 H	19,826,000	1.25	2.00	6.00	15.00	25.00
1919 H	—	PF63 200				

KM# 10a 3 PENCE

1.14 g., 0.500 Silver 0.0184 oz. ASW **Ruler:** George V **Obv:** Bust of George V facing left **Obv. Legend:** GEORGIVS V D.G.BRITT: OMN:REX F.D.IND:IMP: **Rev:** Denomination in wreath, date beneath **Rev. Legend:** BRITISH WEST AFRICA

Date	Mintage	F12	VF20	XF40	MS60	MS63
1920 H	3,616,000	25.00	50.00	125	185	—

KM# 10b 3 PENCE

Tin-Brass **Ruler:** George V **Obv:** Bust of George V facing left **Obv. Legend:** GEORGIVS V D.G.BRITT: OMN:REX F.D.IND:IMP: **Rev:** Denomination in wreath, date beneath **Rev. Legend:** BRITISH WEST AFRICA

Date	Mintage	F12	VF20	XF40	MS60	MS63
1920 KN	19,000,000	1.00	5.00	12.50	25.00	45.00
1920 KN	—	PF63 100				
1920 KN Unique	—	—	—	—	—	—
Note: Mint mark on obverse below bust						
1925	8,800,000	1.50	5.00	20.00	40.00	70.00
1926	1,600,000	10.00	25.00	35.00	60.00	125
1927	800,000	20.00	40.00	75.00	100	200
1928	1,760,000	10.00	30.00	45.00	75.00	150
1928	—	PF63 200				
1933	2,800,000	2.00	4.50	28.00	50.00	70.00
1933	—	PF63 250				
1934	6,400,000	1.00	12.50	20.00	35.00	60.00
1934	—	PF63 250				
1935	11,560,000	1.00	12.50	20.00	35.00	60.00
1935	—	PF63 250				
1936	17,160,000	1.00	3.50	15.00	28.00	50.00
1936	—	PF63 250				
1936 H	1,000,000	15.00	25.00	35.00	75.00	125
1936 H	—	PF63 250				
1936 KN	2,037,999	10.00	15.00	35.00	65.00	110

KM# 21 3 PENCE

5.10 g., Copper-Nickel, 21.45 mm. **Ruler:** George VI **Obv:** Bust of George VI left **Obv. Legend:** GEORGIVS VI D.G.BRITT: OMN:REX F.D.IND:IMP: **Rev:** Denomination in wreath, date beneath **Rev. Legend:** BRITISH WEST AFRICA

Date	Mintage	F12	VF20	XF40	MS60	MS63
1938 H	7,000,000	0.30	0.60	2.50	7.50	12.50
1938 H	—	PF63 200				
1938 KN	9,056,000	0.35	0.75	2.50	8.00	14.00
1938 KN	—	PF63 250				
1939 H	16,500,000	0.30	0.60	2.00	5.00	9.00
1939 H	—	PF63 300				
1939 KN	15,500,000	0.30	0.60	2.00	8.00	14.00
1939 KN	—	PF63 200				
1940 H	3,862,000	0.50	1.00	2.50	7.50	13.50
1940 KN	10,000,000	0.30	0.60	2.00	5.00	9.00
1941 H	5,032,000	0.40	0.85	3.50	9.00	16.00
1943 H	5,106,000	0.40	0.85	6.00	15.00	25.00

Date	Mintage	F12	VF20	XF40	MS60	MS63
1943 KN	9,502,000	0.40	0.85	3.50	9.00	16.00
1944 KN	2,536,000	0.40	0.85	6.50	15.00	25.00
1945 H	998,000	3.00	5.00	12.00	20.00	35.00
1945 KN	3,000,000	0.40	0.85	5.00	12.50	22.00
1946 KN	7,488,000	0.40	0.85	3.50	9.00	16.00
1947 H	10,000,000	0.35	0.75	3.50	8.00	14.00
1947 KN	11,248,000	0.40	0.85	3.50	8.00	14.00

KM# 35 3 PENCE

Copper-Nickel **Ruler:** Elizabeth II **Obv:** Bust of Queen Elizabeth II facing right **Obv. Legend:** QUEEN ELIZABETH THE SECOND **Rev:** Denomination in wreath, date beneath **Rev. Legend:** BRITISH WEST AFRICA

Date	Mintage	F12	VF20	XF40	MS60	MS63
1957 H	800,000	35.00	60.00	125	175	300

KM# 11 6 PENCE

2.83 g., 0.925 Silver 0.0841 oz. ASW **Ruler:** George V **Obv:** Bust of King George V facing left **Obv. Legend:** GEORGIVS V D.G.BRITT: OMN:REX F.D.IND:IMP: **Rev:** Denomination in wreath, date beneath **Rev. Legend:** BRITISH WEST AFRICA

Date	Mintage	F12	VF20	XF40	MS60	MS63
1913	560,000	4.00	7.00	20.00	35.00	60.00
1913	—	PF63 350				
1913 H	400,000	4.00	7.00	20.00	37.50	65.00
1914 H	952,000	3.00	7.00	25.00	40.00	70.00
1916 H	400,000	5.00	10.00	25.00	50.00	85.00
1917 H	2,400,000	4.00	7.00	20.00	37.50	65.00
1918 H	1,160,000	3.00	7.00	20.00	37.50	65.00
1919 H	8,676,000	3.00	5.00	11.50	22.00	40.00
1919 H	—	PF63 200				

KM# 11a 6 PENCE

2.83 g., 0.500 Silver 0.0455 oz. ASW **Ruler:** George V **Obv:** Bust of George V facing left **Obv. Legend:** GEORGIVS V D.G.BRITT: OMN:REX F.D.IND:IMP: **Rev:** Denomination in wreath, date beneath **Rev. Legend:** BRITISH WEST AFRICA

Date	Mintage	F12	VF20	XF40	MS60	MS63
1920 H	2,948,000	12.50	30.00	100	185	—
1920 H	—	PF63 275				

KM# 11b 6 PENCE

Tin-Brass **Ruler:** George V **Obv:** Bust of George V facing left **Obv. Legend:** GEORGIVS V D.G.BRITT: OMN:REX F.D.IND:IMP: **Rev:** Denomination in wreath, date beneath **Rev. Legend:** BRITISH WEST AFRICA

Date	Mintage	F12	VF20	XF40	MS60	MS63
1920 KN	12,000,000	1.00	5.00	20.00	37.50	65.00
1920 KN	—	PF63 125	PF65 175			
1923 H	2,000,000	5.00	22.50	35.00	75.00	100
1924	1,000,000	15.00	30.00	50.00	100	175
1924 H	1,000,000	15.00	30.00	50.00	100	175
1924 KN	1,000,000	15.00	30.00	50.00	100	175
1925	2,800,000	3.50	7.00	35.00	60.00	100
1928	400,000	25.00	50.00	100	200	350
1928	—	PF63 200	PF65 250			
1933	1,000,000	20.00	40.00	90.00	150	250
1933	—	PF63 225	PF65 285			
1935	4,000,000	5.00	12.50	25.00	50.00	90.00
1935	—	PF63 225	PF65 285			
1936	10,400,000	7.50	15.00	25.00	50.00	90.00
1936	—	PF63 225	PF65 285			
1936 H	480,000	25.00	50.00	100	150	250
1936 H	—	PF63 225	PF65 285			
1936 KN	2,696,000	15.00	25.00	35.00	70.00	125
1936 KN	—	PF63 225	PF65 285			

KM# 22 6 PENCE

3.49 g., Nickel-Brass, 19.34 mm. **Ruler:** George VI **Obv:** Bust of King George VI left **Obv. Legend:** GEORGIVS VI D.G.BRITT: OMN:REX F.D.IND:IMP: **Rev:** Denomination in wreath, date beneath **Rev. Legend:** BRITISH WEST AFRICA

Date	Mintage	F12	VF20	XF40	MS60	MS63
1938	12,114,000	0.50	1.00	2.00	8.00	14.00
1938	—	PF63 200				
1940	17,829,000	0.75	1.50	3.00	10.00	18.00
1940	—	PF63 200				
1942	1,600,000	2.50	4.00	10.00	20.00	35.00
1943	10,586,000	0.75	1.75	5.00	11.00	20.00
1944	1,814,000	2.00	3.00	15.00	30.00	55.00
1945	4,000,000	1.00	2.00	12.50	25.00	45.00
1945	—	PF63 200				
1946	4,000,000	2.50	5.00	25.00	50.00	90.00
1946	—	PF63 225				
1947	6,120,000	0.50	1.50	5.00	15.00	25.00
1947	—	PF63 175				

KM# 31 6 PENCE

Nickel-Brass **Ruler:** George VI **Obv:** Bust of King George VI facing left **Obv. Legend:** GEORGIVS VI DIE GRA. BRITT. OMN: REX FID: DEF: **Rev:** Denomination in wreath, date beneath **Rev. Legend:** BRITISH WEST AFRICA

Date	Mintage	F12	VF20	XF40	MS60	MS63
1952	2,544,000	—	—	—	120	200
1952	—	PF60 500	PF63 750		PF65 1,000	

Note: This type was never released into circulation and the majority of the mintage was melted down at Riverside Metal Company in New Jersey; Approximately 167 pieces avoided the furnace and found their way into the numismatic market

KM# 12 SHILLING

5.66 g., 0.925 Silver 0.1682 oz. ASW **Ruler:** George V **Obv:** Bust of King George V facing left **Obv. Legend:** GEORGIVS V D.G.BRITT: OMN:REX F.D.IND:IMP: **Rev:** Palm tree divides date in circular frame **Rev. Legend:** BRITISH WEST AFRICA

Date	Mintage	F12	VF20	XF40	MS60	MS63
1913	8,800,000	6.00	7.00	12.50	22.50	45.00
1913	—	PF63 400				
1913 H	3,540,000	10.00	20.00	55.00	100	150
1914	3,000,000	6.00	7.00	15.00	35.00	65.00
1914 H	11,292,000	6.00	7.00	12.50	30.00	55.00
1915 H	254,000	20.00	40.00	100	165	—
1916 H	11,838,000	6.00	8.00	18.50	35.00	65.00
1917 H	15,018,000	6.00	8.00	18.50	35.00	65.00
1918 H	9,486,000	6.00	8.00	20.00	40.00	70.00
1918 H	—	PF63 200				
1919	2,000,000	10.00	15.00	30.00	55.00	95.00
1919 H	992,000	15.00	30.00	65.00	100	150
1919 H	—	PF63 200				
1920	828,000	22.50	40.00	100	165	200

KM# 12a SHILLING

5.70 g., Tin-Brass, 23.6 mm. **Ruler:** George V **Obv:** Bust of George V facing left **Obv. Legend:** GEORGIVS V D.G.BRITT: OMN:REX F.D.IND:IMP: **Rev:** Palm tree divides date in circular frame **Rev. Legend:** BRITISH WEST AFRICA

Date	Mintage	F12	VF20	XF40	MS60	MS63
1920 G	16,000	1,000	2,000	2,500	3,000	—
1920 KN	38,800,000	1.50	5.00	12.50	32.50	55.00
1920 KN	—	PF63 200				
1920 KN Unique	—	—	—	—	—	—

Note: Mint mark on obverse below bust

Date	Mintage	F12	VF20	XF40	MS60	MS63
1922 KN	32,324,000	2.00	6.50	35.00	70.00	125
1923 H	24,384,000	4.00	7.50	25.00	45.00	80.00
1923 KN	5,000,000	8.00	15.00	50.00	90.00	150
1924	17,000,000	2.00	6.50	35.00	60.00	110
1924 H	9,567,000	10.00	20.00	70.00	125	175
1924 KN	7,000,000	7.50	15.00	45.00	80.00	135
1925	19,800,000	4.00	8.00	22.00	45.00	80.00
1926	19,952,000	2.00	5.00	20.00	40.00	70.00
1927	22,248,000	1.50	4.00	18.50	35.00	60.00
1927	—	PF63 250				
1928	10,000,000	10.00	20.00	45.00	100	225
1928	—	PF63 300				
1936	70,200,000	3.00	6.50	18.00	32.50	55.00
1936	—	PF63 225				
1936 H	10,920,000	5.00	10.00	35.00	60.00	90.00
1936 KN	14,962,000	2.00	5.00	25.00	42.50	75.00
1936 KN	—	PF63 200				

KM# 23 SHILLING

5.63 g., Nickel-Brass, 23.6 mm. **Ruler:** George VI **Obv:** Bust of King George VI left **Obv. Legend:** GEORGIVS VI D.G.BRITT: OMN:REX F.D.IND:IMP: **Rev:** Palm tree divides date in circular frame **Rev. Legend:** BRITISH WEST AFRICA

Date	Mintage	F12	VF20	XF40	MS60	MS63
1938	57,806,000	0.50	1.25	4.50	12.00	20.00
1938	—	PF63 200				
1939	55,472,000	0.50	1.25	6.50	18.00	30.00
1939	—	PF63 200				
1940	40,311,000	0.50	1.25	5.50	15.00	25.00
1940	—	PF63 200				
1942	42,000,000	0.50	1.25	6.50	18.00	30.00
1943	133,600,000	0.50	1.25	5.50	15.00	25.00
1945	8,010,000	1.00	1.50	12.00	25.00	42.00
1945	—	PF63 200				
1945 H	12,864,000	2.00	3.50	18.00	35.00	60.00
1945 KN	11,120,000	1.00	2.00	12.00	25.00	42.00
1946	37,350,000	1.00	2.00	18.00	35.00	60.00
1946	—	PF63 200				
1946 H	—	750	1,000	2,000	4,000	—
1947	99,200,000	0.50	1.00	4.50	12.00	20.00
1947	—	PF63 200				
1947 H	10,000,000	1.50	3.00	17.50	30.00	50.00
1947 KN	10,384,000	0.50	1.00	6.50	16.50	28.00

KM# 28 SHILLING

Tin-Brass **Ruler:** George VI **Obv:** Bust of King George VI facing left **Obv. Legend:** GEORGIVS VI DIE GRA. BRITT. OMN: REX FID: DEF: **Rev:** Palm tree divides date in circular frame **Rev. Legend:** BRITISH WEST AFRICA

Date	Mintage	F12	VF20	XF40	MS60	MS63
1949	70,000,000	0.50	2.50	12.00	25.00	42.00
1949	—	PF63 175				
1949 H	10,000,000	1.25	4.00	12.50	27.50	47.50
1949 KN	10,016,000	1.25	4.00	12.50	27.50	47.50
1949 KN	—	PF63 200				
1951	35,346,000	1.25	5.00	15.00	30.00	50.00
1951	—	PF63 175				
1951 H	10,000,000	1.25	5.00	15.00	30.00	50.00
1951 KN	16,832,000	1.25	5.00	15.00	30.00	50.00
1952	98,654,000	0.50	1.00	3.00	9.00	15.00
1952	—	PF63 200				
1952 KN	41,653,000	0.50	1.00	2.00	6.00	10.00
1952 H	44,096,000	0.50	1.00	2.00	7.50	12.50
1952 KN	—	PF63 175				

KM# 13 2 SHILLINGS

11.31 g., 0.925 Silver 0.3364 oz. ASW **Ruler:** George V **Obv:** Bust of King George V facing left **Obv. Legend:** GEORGIVS V D.G.BRITT: OMN:REX F.D.IND:IMP: **Rev:** Palm tree divides date in circular frame **Rev. Legend:** BRITISH WEST AFRICA

Date	Mintage	F12	VF20	XF40	MS60	MS63
1913	2,100,000	11.00	13.00	17.50	45.00	80.00
1913	—	PF63 500				
1913 H	1,176,000	12.00	15.00	27.50	55.00	95.00
1914	330,000	15.00	50.00	100	150	250
1914 H	637,000	12.00	25.00	45.00	75.00	135
1915 H	66,000	25.00	60.00	120	180	300

Date	Mintage	F12	VF20	XF40	MS60	MS63
1916 H	9,824,000	11.00	15.00	30.00	60.00	110
1917 H	1,059,000	15.00	35.00	70.00	100	175
1917 H	—	PF63 300				
1918 H	7,294,000	11.00	15.00	30.00	55.00	95.00
1919	2,000,000	12.00	20.00	50.00	85.00	150
1919 H	10,866,000	11.00	15.00	40.00	65.00	115
1919 H	—	PF63 200				
1920	683,000	30.00	60.00	120	180	275

KM# 13a 2 SHILLINGS

11.31 g., 0.500 Silver 0.1818 oz. ASW **Ruler:** George V **Obv:** Bust of George V facing left **Obv. Legend:** GEORGIVS V D.G.BRITT: OMN:REX F.D.IND:IMP: **Rev:** Palm tree divides date in circular frame **Rev. Legend:** BRITISH WEST AFRICA

Date	Mintage	F12	VF20	XF40	MS60	MS63
1920 H	1,926,000	30.00	55.00	175	275	450

KM# 13b 2 SHILLINGS

Tin-Brass **Ruler:** George V **Obv:** Bust of George V facing left **Obv. Legend:** GEORGIVS V D.G.BRITT: OMN:REX F.D.IND:IMP: **Rev:** Palm tree divides date in circular frame **Rev. Legend:** BRITISH WEST AFRICA

Date	Mintage	F12	VF20	XF40	MS60	MS63
1920 KN	15,856,000	2.50	5.00	20.00	40.00	70.00
1920 KN	—	PF63 250				
1922	10,000,000	3.00	9.00	27.50	55.00	95.00
1922 KN	5,500,000	6.00	15.00	45.00	75.00	135
1922 KN	—	PF63 250				
1923 H	12,696,000	4.00	12.00	37.50	65.00	115
1924	1,500,000	8.00	20.00	55.00	90.00	160
1925	3,700,000	4.00	12.00	40.00	70.00	125
1926	11,500,000	4.50	15.00	50.00	80.00	140
1927	11,100,000	6.00	20.00	65.00	100	185
1927	—	PF63 250				
1928	7,900,000	1,500	2,000	3,000	5,000	—
1928	—	PF63 3,000				
1936	32,939,999	5.00	12.00	35.00	60.00	100
1936	—	PF63 250				
1936 H	8,703,000	6.00	18.00	45.00	75.00	130
1936 KN	8,794,000	6.00	18.00	45.00	75.00	130

KM# 24 2 SHILLINGS

11.37 g., Nickel-Brass, 28.51 mm. **Ruler:** George VI **Obv:** Bust of King George VI left **Obv. Legend:** GEORGIVS VI D.G.BRITT: OMN:REX F.D.IND:IMP: **Rev:** Palm tree divides date in circular frame **Rev. Legend:** BRITISH WEST AFRICA

Date	Mintage	F12	VF20	XF40	MS60	MS63
1938 H	32,000,000	1.00	2.00	6.50	15.00	28.00
1938 KN	27,852,000	1.00	2.00	6.50	15.00	28.00
Note: Grained edge variety exists, valued at $325						
1939 H	5,750,000	2.00	5.00	20.00	35.00	65.00
1939 KN	6,250,000	1.00	4.00	16.50	30.00	55.00
1939 KN	—	PF63 200				
1942 KN	10,000,000	1.25	4.50	17.00	30.00	55.00
1946 H	10,500,000	1.25	4.00	12.00	27.50	50.00
1946 KN	4,800,000	1.25	7.00	27.00	42.50	80.00
1947 H	5,055,000	1.00	6.00	25.00	40.00	75.00
1947 KN	4,200,000	1.25	7.00	27.00	42.50	80.00

KM# 29 2 SHILLINGS

Nickel-Brass **Ruler:** George VI **Obv:** Bust of King George VI facing left **Obv. Legend:** GEORGIVS VI DIE GRA. BRITT. OMN: REX FID: DEF: **Rev:** Palm tree divides date in circular frame **Rev. Legend:** BRITISH WEST AFRICA

Date	Mintage	F12	VF20	XF40	MS60	MS63
1949 H	7,500,000	1.25	7.00	22.00	40.00	75.00
1949 KN	7,576,000	1.25	6.00	20.00	35.00	65.00
1951 H	—	PF63 250				
1951 H	6,566,000	1.25	7.00	22.00	40.00	75.00
1952 H	4,410,000	2.00	8.00	22.50	42.00	80.00
1952 KN	1,236,000	8.00	20.00	50.00	75.00	145

PATTERNS

Including off metal strikes

KM#	Date	Mintage	Identification	Mkt Val
Pn1	1906	4	1/10 Penny. Aluminum. Crown above center hole, denomination around hole in English, in Arabic beneath. Hexagram divides date at bottom.	3,750
Pn2	1906	—	Penny. Copper-Nickel. Two varieties known, thick and thin flan.	3,750
Pn3	1920G	—	Shilling. Silver.	1,800
PnA4	1920	—	Penny. Brass. #KM9.	2,150
Pn4	1920KN	—	2 Shillings. Silver. Uniface.	300
Pn5	1925	—	Shilling. Nickel-Brass. Bare headed. ROYAL MINT 1925.	2,400
PnA6	1936	—	Shilling. Nickel-Brass. Security. Raised word SPECIMEN in field above date.	—
Pn6	1936H	—	Shilling. Nickel-Brass. King's bust, left. Palm tree divides date in circular frame. Security. Raised word SPECIMEN in field above date.	750
Pn7	1936KN	—	Shilling. Nickel-Brass. Fine reeded. Word SPECIMEN in field above date.	550
Pn8	1936KN	—	Shilling. Nickel-Brass. Security. Raised word SPECIMEN in field above date.	650
Pn9	1936KN	—	Shilling. Nickel-Brass. Coarser reeded. Without word SPECIMEN.	1,800
PnA10	1937H	—	Penny. Bronze. KM#19.	1,200
Pn10	1938KN	—	2 Shillings. Nickel-Brass. Security. Raised word SPECIMEN in field.	950
PnA11	1949KN	—	2 Shillings. Copper-Nickel.	175
Pn11	1952KN	—	2 Shillings. Nickel-Brass. Raised word SPECIMEN in field below date.	650
Pn12	ND (1952)	—	Shilling. Nickel-Brass. KM#13b. Raised word MODEL.	1,000

TRIAL STRIKES

KM#	Date	Mintage	Identification	Mkt Val
TS1	1952	—	Shilling. Steel. King's head, left. Palm tree divides date within circular frame. Raised word TRIAL vertical in field on both sides.	225
TS2	1952	—	Shilling. Nickel. Raised word TRIAL vertical in field on both sides.	175
TS3	1952	—	Shilling. Steel. Palm tree divides date, raised word TRIAL vertical. King's head, raised word TRIAL horizontal.	250
TS4	1952	—	Shilling. Nickel. Raised word TRIAL vertical. Raised word TRIAL horizontal.	150

SPECIMEN SETS (SS)

KM#	Date	Mintage	Identification	Issue Price	Mkt Val
SS1	1913 (8)	14	KM10-13 Double set	—	1,250
SS2	1913 (4)	200	KM10-13	—	550
SS3	1919H (8)	2	KM10-13 Double set	—	1,500
SS4	1920KN (8)	36	KM10b-11b, 12a, 13b Double set	—	1,150
SSA5	1920KN (4)	4	KM10b-11b, 12a, 13b	—	700
SS5	1928 (4)	—	KM10b-11b, 12a, 13b	—	6,000
SS6	1936H (3)	—	KM14-16	—	450
SS7	1952 (4)	—	KM26a-27a, 30a, 31	—	750

BRUNEI

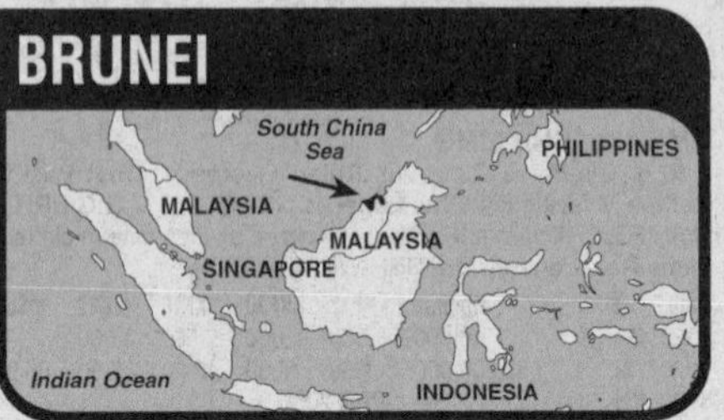

Negara Brunei Darussalam (State of Brunei Haven of Peace), an independent sultanate on the northwest coast of the island of Borneo, has an area of 2,226 sq. mi. (5,765 sq. km.) and a population of *326,000. Capital: Bandar Seri Begawan. Crude oil and rubber are exported.

Magellan was the first European to visit Brunei in 1521. It was a powerful state, ruling over northern Borneo and adjacent islands from the 16th to the 19th century. Brunei became a British protectorate in 1888 and a British dependency in 1905. The Constitution of 1959 restored control over internal affairs to the sultan, while delegating responsibility for defense and foreign affairs to Britain. On January 1, 1984 it became independent and is a member of the Commonwealth of Nations.

TITLE

Negri Brunei

RULERS

Sultan Hashim Jalal, 1885-1906
Sultan Mukammad Jamalul Alam II, 1906-1924
Sultan Almad Tajuddin, 1924-1950
Sultan Sir Omar Ali Saifuddin III, 1950-1967
Sultan Hassanal Bolkiah, 1967-

SULTANATE

DECIMAL COINAGE

100 Sen = 1 Dollar (Ringgit)

KM# 4 SEN

Bronze, 17.7 mm. **Ruler:** Sultan Sir Omar Ali Saifuddin III **Obv:** Uniformed head left **Rev:** Native design, denomination below, date at right

Date	Mintage	VF20	XF40	MS60	MS63	MS65
1967	1,000,000	0.20	0.75	1.25	1.50	2.00

KM# 9 SEN

Bronze, 17.7 mm. **Ruler:** Sultan Hassanal Bolkiah **Obv:** Head right **Rev:** Native design, denomination below, date at right

Date	Mintage	VF20	XF40	MS60	MS63	MS65
1968	60,000	0.30	1.50	2.75	3.50	4.00
1970	4,000	PF65 6.00				
1970	140,000	0.20	0.50	0.75	1.00	1.50
1971	400,000	0.10	0.20	0.60	0.80	1.25
1973	120,000	0.20	0.75	1.25	2.50	3.00
1974	640,000	—	0.20	0.60	0.80	1.25
1976	140,000	—	0.20	0.60	0.80	1.25
1977	140,000	—	0.20	0.60	0.80	1.25

KM# 15 SEN

Bronze, 17.7 mm. **Ruler:** Sultan Hassanal Bolkiah **Obv:** Head right **Rev:** Native design, denomination below, date at right, legend without numeral 'I' in title

Date	Mintage	VF20	XF40	MS60	MS63	MS65
1977	280,000	—	0.20	0.50	0.70	1.50
1978	269,000	—	0.20	0.50	0.70	1.50
1979	10,000	PF65 5.00				
1979	250,000	0.10	0.40	0.75	1.00	2.00
1980	260,000	—	0.25	0.50	0.70	1.50
1981	540,000	—	0.25	0.50	0.70	1.50
1982	100,000	—	1.50	2.50	3.00	5.00
1983	500,000	—	—	0.25	0.50	1.00
1984	400,000	—	—	0.25	0.50	1.00
1984	3,000	PF65 4.00				
1985	200,000	—	—	0.25	0.50	1.00
1985	—	PF65 4.00				
1986	101,000	—	—	0.25	0.50	1.00
1986	7,000	PF65 4.00				

KM# 15a SEN

Copper Clad Steel, 17.7 mm. **Ruler:** Sultan Hassanal Bolkiah **Obv:** Head right **Rev:** Native design, denomination below, date at right, legend without numeral 'I' in title

Date	Mintage	VF20	XF40	MS60	MS63	MS65
1986	102,000	—	—	0.25	0.50	1.00
1987	390,000	—	—	0.25	0.50	1.00
1988	500,000	—	—	0.25	0.50	1.00
1989	601,000	—	—	0.25	0.50	1.00
1990	680,000	—	—	0.25	0.50	1.00
1991	680,000	—	—	0.25	0.50	1.00
1992	887,000	—	—	0.25	0.50	1.00
1993	948,000	—	—	0.25	0.50	1.00

KM# 15b SEN

2.92 g., 0.925 Silver 0.0868 oz. ASW, 17.7 mm. **Ruler:** Sultan Hassanal Bolkiah **Obv:** Head right **Rev:** Native design, denomination below, date at right, legend without numeral 'I' in title

Date	Mintage	VF20	XF40	MS60	MS63	MS65
1987	2,000	PF65 4.00				
1988	2,000	PF65 4.00				
1989	2,000	PF65 4.00				
1990	2,000	PF65 4.00				
1991	2,000	PF65 4.00				
1992	2,000	PF65 4.00				
1993	2,000	PF65 4.00				

KM# 42 SEN

3.10 g., 0.925 Silver 0.0922 oz. ASW, 17.7 mm. **Subject:** 25 Years - Currency Board **Obv:** Sultan's portrait **Rev:** Mosque **Edge:** Reeded

Date	Mintage	VF20	XF40	MS60	MS63	MS65
1992	2,000	PF65 6.50				

KM# 34 SEN

1.75 g., Copper Clad Steel, 17.7 mm. **Ruler:** Sultan Hassanal Bolkiah **Obv:** Uniformed bust facing **Rev:** Native design, denomination below, date at right **Edge:** Plain

Date	Mintage	VF20	XF40	MS60	MS63	MS65
1993	680,000	—	—	0.50	0.75	1.00
1994	1,900,000	—	—	0.50	0.75	1.00
1995	—	—	—	0.50	0.75	1.00
1996	3,044,000	—	—	0.50	0.75	1.00
2000	—	—	—	0.50	0.75	1.00

KM# 34a SEN

2.92 g., 0.925 Silver 0.0868 oz. ASW, 17.7 mm. **Ruler:** Sultan Hassanal Bolkiah **Obv:** Uniformed bust facing **Rev:** Native design denomination below, date at right **Edge:** Plain

Date	Mintage	VF20	XF40	MS60	MS63	MS65
1993	—	PF65 4.00				
1994	—	PF65 4.00				

KM# 54 SEN

Copper Clad Steel, 17.7 mm. **Ruler:** Sultan Hassanal Bolkiah **Subject:** 10 Years of Independence **Obv:** Sultan's portrait **Rev:** National arms

Date	Mintage	VF20	XF40	MS60	MS63	MS65
ND-1994	—	—	—	0.75	1.00	1.50

KM# 54a SEN

3.10 g., 0.925 Silver 0.0922 oz. ASW, 17.7 mm. **Ruler:** Sultan Hassanal Bolkiah **Subject:** 10 Years of Independence **Obv:** Sultan's portrait **Rev:** National arms

Date	Mintage	VF20	XF40	MS60	MS63	MS65
ND-1994	1,980	PF65 9.00				

KM# 5 5 SEN

1.41 g., Copper-Nickel, 16.26 mm. **Ruler:** Sultan Sir Omar Ali Saifuddin III **Obv:** Uniformed head left **Rev:** Native design, denomination below, date at right **Edge:** Reeded

Date	Mintage	VF20	XF40	MS60	MS63	MS65
1967	1,500,000	0.20	0.30	1.20	2.00	2.50

KM# 10 5 SEN

1.41 g., Copper-Nickel, 16.26 mm. **Ruler:** Sultan Hassanal Bolkiah **Obv:** Head right **Rev:** Native design, denomination below, date at right **Edge:** Reeded

Date	Mintage	VF20	XF40	MS60	MS63	MS65
1968	320,000	0.15	0.25	0.75	1.50	2.00
1970	4,000	PF65 6.00				
1970	760,000	0.15	0.25	0.75	1.50	2.00
1971	320,000	0.15	0.25	0.75	1.50	2.00
1973	128,000	0.25	0.50	1.50	2.50	3.00
1974	576,000	0.15	0.25	0.50	1.25	2.00
1976	384,000	0.15	0.25	0.75	1.50	2.00
1977	384,000	0.15	0.25	0.75	1.50	2.00

KM# 16 5 SEN

1.41 g., Copper-Nickel, 16.26 mm. **Ruler:** Sultan Hassanal Bolkiah **Obv:** Head right, legend without numeral 'I' in title **Rev:** Native design denomination below, date at right **Edge:** Reeded

Date	Mintage	VF20	XF40	MS60	MS63	MS65
1977	920,000	0.10	0.15	0.30	0.60	1.00
1978	640,000	0.10	0.15	0.30	0.60	1.00
1979	650,000	0.15	0.20	0.50	0.80	1.25
1979	10,000	PF65 7.50				
1980	640,000	0.10	0.15	0.35	0.50	0.75
1981	960,000	0.10	0.15	0.35	0.50	0.75
1982	240,000	0.50	0.75	1.25	2.25	3.00
1983	1,280,000	—	0.10	0.25	0.35	0.50
1984	3,000	PF65 6.00				
1984	800,000	—	0.10	0.25	0.35	0.50
1985	—	PF65 6.00				
1985	800,000	—	0.10	0.25	0.35	0.50
1986	7,000	PF65 6.00				
1986	189,000	—	—	0.25	0.35	0.50
1987	960,000	—	—	0.25	0.35	0.50
1988	820,000	—	—	0.25	0.35	0.50
1989	1,504,000	—	—	0.25	0.35	0.50
1990	1,340,000	—	—	0.25	0.35	0.50
1991	1,340,000	—	—	0.25	0.35	0.50
1992	1,900,000	—	—	0.25	0.35	0.50
1993	1,951,000	—	—	0.25	0.35	0.50

KM# 16a 5 SEN

1.65 g., 0.925 Silver 0.0491 oz. ASW **Ruler:** Sultan Hassanal Bolkiah **Obv:** Head right, legend without numeral "1" in title **Rev:** Native design denomination below, date at right

Date	Mintage	VF20	XF40	MS60	MS63	MS65
1987	2,000	PF65 4.00				
1988	2,000	PF65 4.00				
1989	2,000	PF65 4.00				
1990	2,000	PF65 4.00				
1991	2,000	PF65 4.00				
1992	2,000	PF65 4.00				
1993	2,000	PF65 4.00				

KM# 43 5 SEN

1.90 g., 0.925 Silver 0.0565 oz. ASW **Subject:** 25 Years - Currency Board **Obv:** Sultan's portrait **Rev:** Mosque **Edge:** Reeded

Date	Mintage	VF20	XF40	MS60	MS63	MS65
1992	2,000	PF65 9.00				

KM# 35 5 SEN

1.41 g., Copper-Nickel, 16.26 mm. **Ruler:** Sultan Hassanal Bolkiah **Obv:** Uniformed bust facing **Rev:** Native design, denomination below, date at right **Edge:** Reeded

Date	Mintage	VF20	XF40	MS60	MS63	MS65
1993	1,340,000	—	0.40	1.00	1.25	1.75
1994	2,600,000	—	0.40	1.00	1.25	1.75
1996	3,571,000	—	0.40	1.00	1.25	1.75
2000	—	—	0.40	1.00	1.25	1.75

KM# 35a 5 SEN

1.65 g., 0.925 Silver 0.0491 oz. ASW, 16.26 mm. **Ruler:** Sultan Hassanal Bolkiah **Obv:** Uniformed bust facing **Rev:** Native design **Edge:** Reeded

Date	Mintage	VF20	XF40	MS60	MS63	MS65
1993	—	PF65 4.00				
1994	—	PF65 4.00				

KM# 55 5 SEN

1.41 g., Copper-Nickel, 16.26 mm. **Ruler:** Sultan Hassanal Bolkiah **Subject:** 10 Years of Independence **Obv:** Sultan's portrait **Rev:** National arms **Edge:** Reeded

Date	Mintage	VF20	XF40	MS60	MS63	MS65
ND-1994	3,000	—	—	1.00	1.50	2.00

KM# 55a 5 SEN

1.90 g., 0.925 Silver 0.0565 oz. ASW **Ruler:** Sultan Hassanal Bolkiah **Subject:** 10 Years of Independence **Obv:** Sultan's portrait **Rev:** National arms

Date	Mintage	VF20	XF40	MS60	MS63	MS65
ND-1994	1,980	PF65 12.00				

KM# 6 10 SEN

2.82 g., Copper-Nickel, 19.4 mm. **Ruler:** Sultan Sir Omar Ali Saifuddin III **Obv:** Military head left **Rev:** Native design, denomination below, date at right **Edge:** Reeded

Date	Mintage	VF20	XF40	MS60	MS63	MS65
1967	3,510,000	—	0.25	1.25	2.00	3.00

KM# 11 10 SEN

2.82 g., Copper-Nickel, 19.4 mm. **Ruler:** Sultan Hassanal Bolkiah **Obv:** Head right **Rev:** Native design, value below, date at right **Edge:** Reeded

Date	Mintage	VF20	XF40	MS60	MS63	MS65
1968	580,000	—	0.25	1.00	1.50	2.00
1970	1,360,000	—	0.25	1.00	1.50	2.00
1970	4,000	PF65 6.00				
1971	420,000	—	0.25	0.75	1.30	2.00
1973	300,000	—	0.25	0.75	1.30	2.00
1974	1,410,000	—	0.15	0.50	1.00	1.50
1976	920,000	—	0.15	0.50	1.00	1.50
1977	920,000	—	0.15	0.50	1.00	1.50

KM# 17 10 SEN

2.82 g., Copper-Nickel, 19.4 mm. **Ruler:** Sultan Hassanal Bolkiah **Obv:** Head right, legend without numeral 'I' in title **Rev:** Native design, denomination below, date at right **Edge:** Reeded

Date	Mintage	VF20	XF40	MS60	MS63	MS65
1977	1,800,000	—	0.10	0.40	0.80	1.25
1978	1,080,000	—	0.10	0.40	0.80	1.25
1979	10,000	PF65 10.00				
1979	2,050,000	—	0.10	0.40	0.80	1.25
1980	2,840,000	—	0.10	0.30	0.40	0.65
1981	976,000	—	0.10	0.30	0.40	0.65
1983	1,080,000	—	0.10	0.30	0.40	0.65
1984	1,400,000	—	0.10	0.30	0.40	0.65
1984	3,000	PF65 8.50				
1985	1,540,000	—	0.10	0.25	0.35	0.50
1985	—	PF65 8.50				
1986	7,000	PF65 8.50				
1986	2,181,000	—	—	0.25	0.35	0.50
1987	2,560,000	—	—	0.25	0.35	0.50
1988	960,000	—	—	0.25	0.35	0.50
1989	1,000,000	—	—	0.25	0.35	0.50
1990	1,800,000	—	—	0.25	0.35	0.50
1991	1,800,000	—	—	0.25	0.35	0.50
1992	3,839,000	—	—	0.25	0.35	0.50
1993	3,973,000	—	—	0.25	0.35	0.50

KM# 17a 10 SEN

3.35 g., 0.925 Silver 0.0996 oz. ASW **Ruler:** Sultan Hassanal Bolkiah **Obv:** Head right, legend without numeral 'I' in title **Rev:** Native design, denomination below, date at right

Date	Mintage	VF20	XF40	MS60	MS63	MS65
1987	2,000	PF65 7.00				
1988	2,000	PF65 7.00				
1989	2,000	PF65 7.00				
1990	2,000	PF65 7.00				
1991	2,000	PF65 7.00				
1992	2,000	PF65 7.00				
1993	2,000	PF65 7.00				

KM# 44 10 SEN

3.50 g., 0.925 Silver 0.1041 oz. ASW **Obv:** Sultan's portrait **Rev:** Mosque **Edge:** Reeded

Date	Mintage	VF20	XF40	MS60	MS63	MS65
1992	2,000	PF65 12.00				

KM# 36 10 SEN

2.82 g., Copper-Nickel, 19.4 mm. **Ruler:** Sultan Hassanal Bolkiah **Obv:** Uniformed bust facing **Rev:** Native design, denomination below, date at right **Edge:** Reeded

Date	Mintage	VF20	XF40	MS60	MS63	MS65
1993	1,800,000	—	0.50	1.00	1.25	1.75
1994	2,200,000	—	0.50	1.00	1.25	1.75
1996	3,618,000	—	0.50	1.00	1.25	1.75

KM# 36a 10 SEN

3.35 g., 0.925 Silver 0.0996 oz. ASW, 19.4 mm. **Ruler:** Sultan Hassanal Bolkiah **Obv:** Uniformed portrait **Rev:** Native design **Edge:** Reeded

Date	Mintage	VF20	XF40	MS60	MS63	MS65
1993	—	PF65 6.00				
1994	—	PF65 6.00				

KM# 56 10 SEN

2.82 g., Copper-Nickel, 19.4 mm. **Ruler:** Sultan Hassanal Bolkiah **Subject:** 10 Years of Independence **Obv:** Sultan's portrait **Rev:** National arms **Edge:** Reeded

Date	Mintage	VF20	XF40	MS60	MS63	MS65
ND-1994	3,000	—	—	—	2.00	3.00

KM# 56a 10 SEN

3.50 g., 0.925 Silver 0.1041 oz. ASW **Subject:** 10 Years of Independence **Obv:** Sultan's portrait **Rev:** National arms

Date	Mintage	VF20	XF40	MS60	MS63	MS65
ND-1994	1,980	PF65 15.00				

KM# 7 20 SEN

5.65 g., Copper-Nickel, 23.5 mm. **Ruler:** Sultan Sir Omar Ali Saifuddin III **Obv:** Uniformed head left **Rev:** Native design, denomination below, date at right **Edge:** Reeded

Date	Mintage	VF20	XF40	MS60	MS63	MS65
1967	2,130,000	0.35	0.75	2.00	4.00	6.00

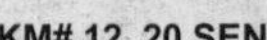

KM# 12 20 SEN

5.65 g., Copper-Nickel, 23.5 mm. **Ruler:** Sultan Hassanal Bolkiah **Obv:** Head right **Rev:** Native design, denomination below, date at right **Edge:** Reeded

Date	Mintage	VF20	XF40	MS60	MS63	MS65
1968	510,000	0.20	0.50	1.50	3.00	3.50
1970	850,000	0.15	0.45	1.50	3.00	3.50
1970	4,000	PF65 6.00				
1971	450,000	0.20	0.50	1.25	2.00	2.50
1973	450,000	0.20	0.75	3.00	4.00	4.50
1974	700,000	0.15	0.25	1.25	2.00	2.50
1976	640,000	0.15	0.25	1.25	2.00	2.50
1977	640,000	0.15	0.25	1.25	2.00	2.50

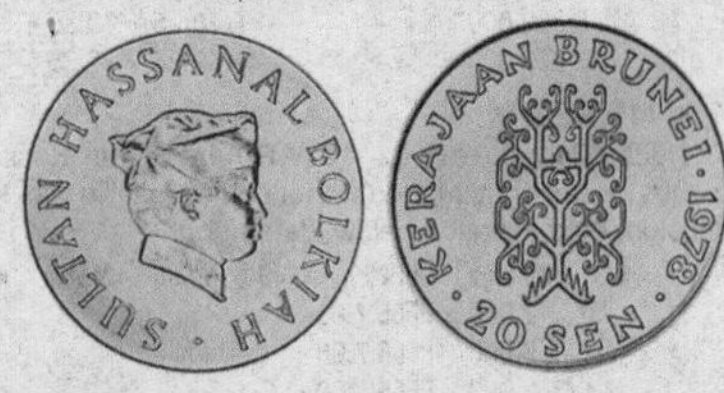

KM# 18 20 SEN

5.65 g., Copper-Nickel, 23.5 mm. **Ruler:** Sultan Hassanal Bolkiah **Obv:** Head right, legend without numeral 'I' in title **Rev:** Native design, denomination below, date at right **Edge:** Reeded

Date	Mintage	VF20	XF40	MS60	MS63	MS65
1977	1,200,000	0.15	0.25	1.25	2.00	3.00
1978	720,000	0.20	0.50	1.50	2.25	3.50
1979	10,000	PF65 11.50				
1979	1,060,000	0.20	0.50	1.50	2.25	3.50
1980	1,540,000	0.15	0.35	1.25	2.00	3.00
1981	2,140,000	0.10	0.25	1.20	2.00	3.00
1982	120,000	2.00	4.00	8.00	12.00	16.00
1983	1,350,000	0.10	0.35	0.75	1.20	2.00
1984	750,000	0.10	0.35	0.75	1.20	2.00
1984	3,000	PF65 9.50				
1985	1,000,000	0.10	0.35	0.75	1.20	2.00
1985	—	PF65 9.50				
1986	7,000	PF65 9.50				
1986	2,639,000	—	—	0.75	1.20	2.00
1987	2,400,000	—	—	0.75	1.20	2.00
1988	560,000	—	—	0.50	1.00	1.50
1989	500,000	—	—	0.50	1.00	1.50
1990	720,000	—	—	0.50	1.00	1.50
1991	725,000	—	—	0.50	1.00	1.50
1992	2,432,000	—	—	0.50	1.00	1.50
1993	2,521,000	—	—	0.50	1.00	1.50

KM# 18a 20 SEN

6.51 g., 0.925 Silver 0.1936 oz. ASW **Ruler:** Sultan Hassanal Bolkiah **Obv:** Head right, legend without numeral 'I' in title **Rev:** Native design, denomination below, date at right

Date	Mintage	VF20	XF40	MS60	MS63	MS65
1987	2,000	PF65 12.00				
1988	2,000	PF65 12.00				
1989	2,000	PF65 12.00				
1990	2,000	PF65 12.00				
1991	2,000	PF65 12.00				
1992	2,000	PF65 12.00				
1993	2,000	PF65 12.00				

KM# 45 20 SEN

6.70 g., 0.925 Silver 0.1993 oz. ASW **Subject:** 25 Years - Currency Board **Obv:** Sultan's portrait **Rev:** Mosque **Edge:** Reeded

Date	Mintage	VF20	XF40	MS60	MS63	MS65
1992	2,000	PF65 16.00				

KM# 37 20 SEN

5.65 g., Copper-Nickel, 23.5 mm. **Ruler:** Sultan Hassanal Bolkiah **Obv:** Uniformed bust facing **Rev:** Native design, denomination below, date at right **Edge:** Reeded

Date	Mintage	VF20	XF40	MS60	MS63	MS65
1993	720,000	—	0.45	1.00	1.20	1.50
1994	2,000,000	—	0.45	1.00	1.20	1.50
1996	2,767,000	—	0.45	1.00	1.20	1.50
2000	—	—	0.45	1.00	1.20	1.50

KM# 37a 20 SEN

6.51 g., 0.925 Silver 0.1936 oz. ASW, 23.5 mm. **Ruler:** Sultan Hassanal Bolkiah **Obv:** Uniformed portrait **Rev:** Native design **Edge:** Reeded

Date	Mintage	VF20	XF40	MS60	MS63	MS65
1993	—	PF65 10.00				
1994	—	PF65 10.00				

KM# 57 20 SEN

5.65 g., Copper-Nickel, 23.5 mm. **Ruler:** Sultan Hassanal Bolkiah **Subject:** 10 Years of Independence **Obv:** Sultan's portrait **Rev:** National arms **Edge:** Reeded

Date	Mintage	VF20	XF40	MS60	MS63	MS65
ND-1994	3,000	—	—	1.25	2.50	3.50

KM# 57a 20 SEN

6.70 g., 0.925 Silver 0.1993 oz. ASW **Subject:** 10 Years of Independence **Obv:** Sultan's portrait **Rev:** National arms

Date	Mintage	VF20	XF40	MS60	MS63	MS65
ND-1994	1,980	PF65 18.00				

KM# 8 50 SEN

9.33 g., Copper-Nickel, 27.7 mm. **Ruler:** Sultan Sir Omar Ali Saifuddin III **Obv:** Uniformed head left within circle **Rev:** National arms, denomination below, date at right **Edge:** Security

Date	Mintage	VF20	XF40	MS60	MS63	MS65
1967	788,000	0.75	1.50	3.00	5.00	7.00

KM# 13 50 SEN

9.33 g., Copper-Nickel, 27.7 mm. **Ruler:** Sultan Hassanal Bolkiah **Obv:** Head right **Rev:** National arms within circle, denomination below, date at right **Edge:** Security

Date	Mintage	VF20	XF40	MS60	MS63	MS65
1968	212,000	0.50	1.00	2.00	3.00	3.50
1970	300,000	0.50	1.00	2.00	3.00	3.50
1970	4,000	PF65 10.00				
1971	320,000	0.45	1.00	2.00	3.00	3.50
1973	140,000	—	2.00	4.00	6.00	9.00
1974	244,000	0.45	1.00	2.00	3.00	3.50
1976	240,000	0.45	1.00	2.00	3.00	3.50
1977	240,000	0.45	1.00	2.00	3.00	3.50

KM# 19 50 SEN

9.33 g., Copper-Nickel, 27.7 mm. **Ruler:** Sultan Hassanal Bolkiah **Obv:** Head right, legend without numeral 'I' in title **Rev:** National arms within circle, denomination below, date at right **Edge:** Security

Date	Mintage	VF20	XF40	MS60	MS63	MS65
1977	499,000	0.30	0.65	1.25	2.00	3.00
1978	264,000	0.30	0.65	1.25	2.00	3.00
1979	730,000	0.30	0.65	1.25	2.00	3.00
1979	10,000	PF65 16.50				
1980	536,000	0.30	0.65	1.25	2.00	3.00
1981	960,000	0.30	0.50	1.00	1.50	2.50
1982	136,000	2.00	5.00	9.00	12.00	15.00
1983	408,000	0.30	0.75	1.25	1.50	2.50
1984	3,000	PF65 13.50				
1984	320,000	0.30	0.75	1.25	1.50	2.50
1985	—	PF65 13.50				
1985	450,000	0.30	0.75	1.25	1.50	2.50
1986	7,000	PF65 13.50				
1986	1,067,000	—	—	1.25	1.50	2.50
1987	1,120,000	—	—	1.25	1.50	2.50
1988	250,000	—	—	1.25	1.50	2.50
1989	500,000	—	—	1.25	1.50	2.50
1990	472,000	—	—	1.25	1.50	2.50
1991	508,000	—	—	1.25	1.50	2.50
1992	1,072,000	—	—	1.25	1.50	2.50
1993	1,102,000	—	—	1.25	1.50	2.50

KM# 19a 50 SEN

10.82 g., 0.925 Silver 0.3218 oz. ASW **Ruler:** Sultan Hassanal Bolkiah **Obv:** Head right, legend without numeral 'I' in title **Rev:** National arms within circle, denomination below, date at right

Date	Mintage	VF20	XF40	MS60	MS63	MS65
1987	2,000	PF65 17.00				
1988	2,000	PF65 17.00				
1989	2,000	PF65 17.00				
1990	2,000	PF65 17.00				
1991	2,000	PF65 17.00				
1992	2,000	PF65 17.00				
1993	2,000	PF65 17.00				

KM# 46 50 SEN

11.10 g., 0.925 Silver 0.3301 oz. ASW **Subject:** 25 Years - Currency Board **Obv:** Sultan's portrait **Rev:** Mosque

Date	Mintage	VF20	XF40	MS60	MS63	MS65
1992	2,000	PF65 25.00				

KM# 38 50 SEN

9.33 g., Copper-Nickel, 27.7 mm. **Ruler:** Sultan Hassanal Bolkiah **Obv:** Uniformed bust facing **Rev:** National arms within circle, denomination below, date at right **Edge:** Security

Date	Mintage	VF20	XF40	MS60	MS63	MS65
1993	472,000	—	1.00	1.75	3.50	5.00
1994	600,000	—	1.00	1.75	2.00	3.50
1996	458,000	—	1.00	1.75	2.50	3.50
2000	—	—	1.00	1.75	2.50	3.50

KM# 38a 50 SEN

10.82 g., 0.925 Silver 0.3218 oz. ASW, 27.7 mm. **Ruler:** Sultan Hassanal Bolkiah **Obv:** Uniformed bust facing **Rev:** National arms within circle, denomination below, date at right **Edge:** Reeded

Date	Mintage	VF20	XF40	MS60	MS63	MS65
1993	—	PF65 16.00				
1994	—	PF65 16.00				

KM# 58 50 SEN

9.33 g., Copper-Nickel, 27.7 mm. **Ruler:** Sultan Hassanal Bolkiah **Subject:** 10 Years of Independence **Obv:** Sultan's portrait **Rev:** National arms **Edge:** Security

Date	Mintage	VF20	XF40	MS60	MS63	MS65
ND-1994	3,000	—	—	—	4.50	6.00

KM# 58a 50 SEN

11.10 g., 0.925 Silver 0.3301 oz. ASW **Subject:** 10 Years of Independence **Obv:** Sultan's portrait **Rev:** National arms

Date	Mintage	VF20	XF40	MS60	MS63	MS65
ND-1994	1,980	PF65 25.00				

KM# 64 50 SEN

9.33 g., Copper-Nickel, 27.7 mm. **Subject:** Sultan's 50th Birthday **Obv:** Sultan's portrait **Rev:** Waterfront building **Edge:** Security

Date	Mintage	VF20	XF40	MS60	MS63	MS65
ND-1996	500	PF65 25.00				

KM# 14 DOLLAR
Copper-Nickel **Ruler:** Sultan Hassanal Bolkiah **Obv:** Head right **Rev:** Antique cannon, date above, denomination below

Date	Mintage	VF20	XF40	MS60	MS63	MS65
1970	5,000	PF65 80.00				

KM# 20 DOLLAR
Copper-Nickel **Obv:** Legend without numeral 'I' in title

Date	Mintage	VF20	XF40	MS60	MS63	MS65
1979	10,000	PF65 50.00				
1984	5,000	—	—	—	16.00	20.00
1984	3,000	PF65 45.00				
1985	15,000	—	—	—	15.00	18.00
1985	10,000	PF65 45.00				
1986	10,000	—	—	—	15.00	18.00
1986	7,000	PF65 45.00				
1987	3,000	—	—	—	16.50	22.50
1988	2,000	—	—	—	16.50	22.50
1989	2,000	—	—	—	16.50	22.50
1990	3,000	—	—	—	16.50	22.50
1991	3,000	—	—	—	16.50	22.50
1992	—	—	—	—	16.50	22.50

KM# 20a DOLLAR
18.05 g., 0.925 Silver 0.5368 oz. ASW **Obv:** Legend without numeral 'I' in title

Date	Mintage	VF20	XF40	MS60	MS63	MS65
1987	2,000	PF65 40.00				
1988	2,000	PF65 40.00				
1989	2,000	PF65 40.00				
1990	2,000	PF65 40.00				
1991	2,000	PF65 40.00				
1992	2,000	PF65 40.00				
1993	2,000	PF65 40.00				

KM# 47 DOLLAR
18.20 g., 0.925 Silver 0.5413 oz. ASW **Ruler:** Sultan Hassanal Bolkiah **Subject:** 25th Anniversary of Brunei Currency Board **Obv:** Sultan Hassanal Bolkiah **Rev:** Mosque

Date	Mintage	VF20	XF40	MS60	MS63	MS65
1992	2,000	PF65 50.00				

KM# 47a DOLLAR
0.917 Gold **Ruler:** Sultan Hassanal Bolkiah **Subject:** 25th Anniversary of Brunei Currency Board **Obv:** Sultan Hassanal Bolkiah **Rev:** Mosque

Date	Mintage	VF20	XF40	MS60	MS63	MS65
1992	1,000	PF65 650				

KM# 76 DOLLAR
16.80 g., Copper-Nickel, 33.3 mm. **Ruler:** Sultan Hassanal Bolkiah **Obv:** Uniformed bust facing **Rev:** Antique cannon **Edge:** Reeded

Date	Mintage	VF20	XF40	MS60	MS63	MS65
1993	—	—	—	—	10.00	12.50

KM# 76a DOLLAR
18.05 g., 0.925 Silver 0.5368 oz. ASW, 33.3 mm. **Ruler:** Sultan Hassanal Bolkiah **Obv:** Uniformed bust facing **Rev:** Antique cannon **Edge:** Reeded

Date	Mintage	VF20	XF40	MS60	MS63	MS65
1993	2,000	PF65 40.00				

KM# 59 DOLLAR
Copper-Nickel **Subject:** 10 Years of Independence **Obv:** Sultan's portrait **Rev:** National arms

Date	Mintage	VF20	XF40	MS60	MS63	MS65
ND-1994	3,000	—	—	—	8.00	10.00

KM# 59a DOLLAR
18.20 g., 0.925 Silver 0.5413 oz. ASW **Subject:** 10 Years of Independence **Obv:** Sultan's portrait **Rev:** National arms

Date	Mintage	VF20	XF40	MS60	MS63	MS65
ND-1994	1,980	PF65 35.00				

KM# 71 2 DOLLARS
9.30 g., Copper-Nickel **Subject:** 20th SEA Games **Obv:** Sultan's multicolor portrait **Rev:** Multicolor logo above stadium **Edge:** Reeded

Date	Mintage	VF20	XF40	MS60	MS63	MS65
1999	1,350	PF65 35.00				

KM# 74 2 DOLLARS
9.80 g., Copper-Nickel, 27.3 mm. **Ruler:** Sultan Hassanal Bolkiah **Subject:** APEC **Obv:** Multicolor bust of Sultan 3/4 left, facing **Obv. Legend:** SULTAN HAJI HASSANAL BOLKIAH **Rev:** Multicolor flower and APEC initials above date below world map, denomination at bottom **Rev. Legend:** ASIA PACIFIC ECONOMIC COOPERATION NEGARA BRUNEI DARUSSALAM **Edge:** Reeded

Date	Mintage	VF20	XF40	MS60	MS63	MS65
2000	3,000	PF65 60.00				

KM# 68 3 DOLLARS
10.00 g., Copper-Nickel **Subject:** 30 Years ASEAN **Obv:** Sultan's portrait **Rev:** Map and sailboat **Edge:** Reeded

Date	Mintage	VF20	XF40	MS60	MS63	MS65
1997	750	PF63 40.00	PF65 45.00			

KM# 23 5 DOLLARS
Copper-Nickel **Ruler:** Sultan Hassanal Bolkiah **Subject:** Year of Hejira 1400 **Obv:** Head right, legend without numeral 'I' in title **Rev:** Denomination below design

Date	Mintage	VF20	XF40	MS60	MS63	MS65
AH1400	10,000	—	7.00	20.00	35.00	50.00

KM# 48 5 DOLLARS
0.917 Gold **Ruler:** Sultan Hassanal Bolkiah **Subject:** 25th Anniversary of Brunei Currency Board **Obv:** Sultan Hassanal Bolkiah **Rev:** Mosque

Date	Mintage	VF20	XF40	MS60	MS63	MS65
1992	1,000	PF65 700				

KM# 60 5 DOLLARS
Copper-Nickel **Subject:** 10 Years of Independence **Obv:** Sultan's portrait **Rev:** National arms

Date	Mintage	VF20	XF40	MS60	MS63	MS65
ND-1994	3,000	—	—	—	16.00	18.00

KM# 60a 5 DOLLARS
28.28 g., 0.925 Silver 0.841 oz. ASW **Subject:** 10 Years of Independence **Obv:** Sultan's portrait **Rev:** National arms

Date	Mintage	VF20	XF40	MS60	MS63	MS65
ND-1994	1,980	PF65 45.00				

KM# 21 10 DOLLARS
28.28 g., 0.925 Silver 0.841 oz. ASW **Ruler:** Sultan Hassanal Bolkiah **Subject:** 10th Anniversary of Brunei Currency Board **Obv:** Head right, legend without numeral 'I' in title **Rev:** Mosque above denomination

Date	Mintage	VF20	XF40	MS60	MS63	MS65
1977	10,000	PF63 30.00	PF65 40.00			

KM# 26 10 DOLLARS
Copper-Nickel **Ruler:** Sultan Hassanal Bolkiah **Subject:** Independence Day **Obv:** Uniformed bust 3/4 right **Rev:** Building within circle, denomination below

Date	Mintage	VF20	XF40	MS60	MS63	MS65
1984	15,000	—	—	—	25.00	30.00
1984	5,000	PF65 65.00				

KM# 49 10 DOLLARS
0.917 Gold **Ruler:** Sultan Hassanal Bolkiah **Subject:** 25th Anniversary of Brunei Currency Board **Obv:** Bust right **Rev:** Mosque

Date	Mintage	VF20	XF40	MS60	MS63	MS65
1992	1,000	PF65 800				

KM# 61 10 DOLLARS
Copper-Nickel **Subject:** 10 Years of Independence **Obv:** Sultan's portrait **Rev:** National arms

Date	Mintage	VF20	XF40	MS60	MS63	MS65
1994	3,000	—	—	—	18.00	20.00

KM# 61a 10 DOLLARS
30.70 g., 0.925 Silver 0.913 oz. ASW **Subject:** 10 Years of Independence **Obv:** Sultan's portrait **Rev:** National arms

Date	Mintage	VF20	XF40	MS60	MS63	MS65
ND-1994	2,500	—	—	—	45.00	50.00
ND-1994	2,480	PF65 90.00				

KM# 32 20 DOLLARS
28.28 g., 0.925 Silver 0.841 oz. ASW **Ruler:** Sultan Hassanal Bolkiah **Subject:** 20th Anniversary of Brunei Currency Board **Obv:** Uniformed bust 3/4 right **Rev:** Mosque above denomination

Date	Mintage	VF20	XF40	MS60	MS63	MS65
1987	3,000	PF65 85.00				

KM# 29 20 DOLLARS
28.28 g., 0.925 Silver 0.841 oz. ASW **Ruler:** Sultan Hassanal Bolkiah **Subject:** 20th Anniversary of Coronation **Obv:** Uniformed bust 3/4 right **Rev:** Arms within wreath divides dates at top, denomination below wreath

Date	Mintage	VF20	XF40	MS60	MS63	MS65
ND-1988	5,000	—	—	—	30.00	35.00
ND-1988	1,000	PF65 60.00				

KM# 72 20 DOLLARS
62.20 g., 0.999 Silver 1.9978 oz. ASW **Subject:** 20th SEA Games **Obv:** Sultan's multicolor portrait **Rev:** Multicolor logo above stadium **Edge:** Reeded

Date	Mintage	VF20	XF40	MS60	MS63	MS65
1999	500	PF65 185				

KM# 79 20 DOLLARS
62.20 g., 0.999 Silver 1.9978 oz. ASW **Ruler:** Sultan Hassanal Bolkiah **Subject:** APEC **Obv:** Multicolor flower at left, bust of Sultan 3/4 left, facing at right **Obv. Legend:** Sultan Haji Hassanal Bolkiah **Rev:** Elliptical globe at center **Rev. Legend:** ASIA PACIFIC ECONOMIC COOPERATION **Shape:** Rectangular, 65 x 31 mm

Date	Mintage	VF20	XF40	MS60	MS63	MS65
2000	400	PF65 250				

KM# 39 25 DOLLARS
Copper-Nickel **Subject:** 25th Anniversary of Accession

Date	Mintage	VF20	XF40	MS60	MS63	MS65
ND-1992	7,500	PF65 50.00				

KM# 39a 25 DOLLARS
0.917 Gold **Subject:** 25th Anniversary of Accession

Date	Mintage	VF20	XF40	MS60	MS63	MS65
ND-1992	—	PF65 1,000				

KM# 50 25 DOLLARS

31.10 g., 0.925 Silver 0.9249 oz. ASW, 38.7 mm. **Ruler:** Sultan Hassanal Bolkiah **Subject:** 25th Anniversary of Brunei Currency Board **Obv:** Sultan Hassanal Bolkiah **Rev:** Mosque

Date	Mintage	VF20	XF40	MS60	MS63	MS65
1992	2,000	PF65 95.00				

KM# 50a 25 DOLLARS

Gold **Ruler:** Sultan Hassanal Bolkiah **Subject:** 25th Anniversary of Brunei Currency Board **Obv:** Sultan Hassanal Bolkiah **Rev:** Mosque

Date	Mintage	VF20	XF40	MS60	MS63	MS65
1992 Proof	1,000	—	—	—	—	—

KM# 69 30 DOLLARS

62.21 g., 0.999 Silver 1.998 oz. ASW **Ruler:** Sultan Hassanal Bolkiah **Subject:** 30 Years - ASEAN **Obv:** Sultan Hassanal Bolkiah **Rev:** Seven multicolor flags

Date	Mintage	VF20	XF40	MS60	MS63	MS65
1997	500	PF65 200				

KM# 70 30 DOLLARS

31.10 g., 0.917 Gold 0.9169 oz. AGW **Subject:** 30 Years - ASEAN **Obv:** Sultan Hassanal Bolkiah **Rev:** ASEAN logo

Date	Mintage	VF20	XF40	MS60	MS63	MS65
1997	300	PF65 1,650				

KM# 24 50 DOLLARS

28.28 g., 0.925 Silver 0.841 oz. ASW **Ruler:** Sultan Hassanal Bolkiah **Subject:** Year of Hejira 1400 **Obv:** Head right, legend without numeral 'I' in title **Rev:** Design above denomination

Date	Mintage	VF20	XF40	MS60	MS63	MS65
AH1400	3,000	PF65 150				

KM# 40 50 DOLLARS

30.70 g., 0.925 Silver 0.913 oz. ASW, 42 mm. **Ruler:** Sultan Hassanal Bolkiah **Subject:** 25th Anniversary of Accession **Obv:** Sultan Hassanal Bolkiah **Rev:** Royal procession **Edge:** Reeded

Date	Mintage	VF20	XF40	MS60	MS63	MS65
ND-1992	3,500	PF65 150				

KM# 40a 50 DOLLARS

0.917 Gold **Ruler:** Sultan Hassanal Bolkiah **Subject:** 25th Anniversary of Accession **Obv:** Sultan Hassanal Bolkiah **Rev:** Royal procession

Date	Mintage	VF20	XF40	MS60	MS63	MS65
ND-1992	—	—	—	—	—	—

KM# 51 50 DOLLARS

0.917 Gold **Ruler:** Sultan Hassanal Bolkiah **Subject:** 25th Anniversary of Brunei Currency Board **Obv:** Sultan Hassanal Bolkiah **Rev:** Mosque

Date	Mintage	VF20	XF40	MS60	MS63	MS65
1992	1,000	PF65 900				

KM# 65 50 DOLLARS

62.21 g., 0.999 Silver 1.998 oz. ASW **Ruler:** Sultan Hassanal Bolkiah **Subject:** 50th Birthday - Sultan Hassanal Bolkiah **Obv:** Sultan Hassanal Bolkiah's multicolor portrait **Rev:** Buildings on waterfront

Date	Mintage	VF20	XF40	MS60	MS63	MS65
ND-1996	1,100	PF65 300				

KM# 66 50 DOLLARS

62.21 g., 0.999 Silver 1.998 oz. ASW **Ruler:** Sultan Hassanal Bolkiah **Subject:** 50th Birthday - Sultan Hassanal Bolkiah **Obv:** Sultan Bolkiah arms **Rev:** Building

Date	Mintage	VF20	XF40	MS60	MS63	MS65
ND-1996	1,000	PF65 300				

KM# 67 50 DOLLARS

31.10 g., 0.917 Gold 0.917 oz. AGW **Ruler:** Sultan Hassanal Bolkiah **Subject:** 50th Birthday - Sultan Hassanal Bolkiah **Obv:** Sultan Hassanal Bolkiah **Rev:** Mosque

Date	Mintage	VF20	XF40	MS60	MS63	MS65
ND-1996	500	PF65 1,600				

KM# 27 100 DOLLARS

28.28 g., 0.925 Silver 0.841 oz. ASW **Ruler:** Sultan Hassanal Bolkiah **Subject:** Independence Day **Obv:** Uniformed bust 3/4 right **Rev:** Mosque within circle, denomination below

Date	Mintage	VF20	XF40	MS60	MS63	MS65
1984	5,000	—	—	—	150	180
1984	2,000	PF65 200				

KM# 33 100 DOLLARS

13.50 g., 0.917 Gold 0.398 oz. AGW **Ruler:** Sultan Hassanal Bolkiah **Subject:** 20th Anniversary of Brunei Currency Board **Obv:** Uniformed bust 3/4 right **Rev:** Mosque above denomination

Date	Mintage	VF20	XF40	MS60	MS63	MS65
1987	1,000	PF65 725				

KM# 30 100 DOLLARS

31.10 g., 0.925 Silver 0.9249 oz. ASW **Ruler:** Sultan Hassanal Bolkiah **Subject:** 20th Anniversary of Coronation **Obv:** Uniformed bust 3/4 right **Rev:** Arms within wreath divides dates at top, denomination below wreath

Date	Mintage	VF20	XF40	MS60	MS63	MS65
ND-1988	2,000	PF65 200				

KM# 52 100 DOLLARS

0.917 Gold **Ruler:** Sultan Hassanal Bolkiah **Subject:** 25th Anniversary of Brunei Currency Board **Obv:** Sultan Hassanal Bolkiah **Rev:** Mosque

Date	Mintage	VF20	XF40	MS60	MS63	MS65
1992	1,000	PF65 1,350				

KM# 62 100 DOLLARS

0.917 White Gold **Ruler:** Sultan Hassanal Bolkiah **Subject:** 10th Year of Independence **Obv:** Sultan Hassanal Bolkiah I **Rev:** National arms

Date	Mintage	VF20	XF40	MS60	MS63	MS65
ND-1994	1,480	—	—	—	—	1,100
ND-1994	1,500	PF65 1,200				

KM# 73 200 DOLLARS

31.10 g., 0.917 Gold 0.9169 oz. AGW **Ruler:** Sultan Hassanal Bolkiah **Subject:** 20th SEA Games **Obv:** Sultan Hassanal Bolkiah I **Rev:** Multicolor logo above stadium

Date	Mintage	VF20	XF40	MS60	MS63	MS65
1999	100	PF65 1,650				

KM# 53 250 DOLLARS

0.917 Gold **Ruler:** Sultan Hassanal Bolkiah **Subject:** 25th Anniversary of Brunei Currency Board **Obv:** Sultan Hassanal Bolkiah I **Rev:** Mosque

Date	Mintage	VF20	XF40	MS60	MS63	MS65
1992	1,000	PF65 1,650				

KM# 41 500 DOLLARS

50.00 g., 0.917 Gold 1.4741 oz. AGW **Ruler:** Sultan Hassanal Bolkiah **Subject:** 25th Anniversary of Accession **Obv:** Sultan's portrait **Rev:** Other portrait

Date	Mintage	VF20	XF40	MS60	MS63	MS65
MS-1992	1,500	PF65 2,650				

KM# 25 750 DOLLARS

15.98 g., 0.917 Gold 0.4711 oz. AGW **Ruler:** Sultan Hassanal Bolkiah **Subject:** Year of Hejira 1400 **Obv:** Head right **Rev:** Design above denomination

Date	Mintage	VF20	XF40	MS60	MS63	MS65
AH1400	1,000	PF65 875				

KM# 22 1000 DOLLARS

50.00 g., 0.917 Gold 1.4741 oz. AGW **Ruler:** Sultan Hassanal Bolkiah **Subject:** 10th Anniversary of Sultan's Coronation **Obv:** Head right **Rev:** Coronation design above denomination, date at right

Date	Mintage	VF20	XF40	MS60	MS63	MS65
ND-1978	1,000	PF65 2,750				

KM# 28 1000 DOLLARS

50.00 g., 0.917 Gold 1.4741 oz. AGW **Ruler:** Sultan Hassanal Bolkiah **Subject:** Independence Day **Obv:** Bust half right **Rev:** Off-shore oil rig, denomination below

Date	Mintage	VF20	XF40	MS60	MS63	MS65
1984	4,000	—	—	—	2,550	2,650
1984	1,000	PF65 2,750				

KM# 31 1000 DOLLARS

50.00 g., 0.917 Gold 1.4741 oz. AGW **Ruler:** Sultan Hassanal Bolkiah **Subject:** 20th Anniversary of Coronation **Obv:** Uniformed bust 3/4 right **Rev:** Arms within wreath divide dates at top, denomination below

Date	Mintage	VF20	XF40	MS60	MS63	MS65
ND-1988	1,000	PF65 2,800				

KM# 63 1000 DOLLARS

0.999 Gold **Ruler:** Sultan Hassanal Bolkiah **Subject:** 10 Years of Independence **Obv:** Sultan Hassanal Bolkiah I **Rev:** National arms

Date	Mintage	VF20	XF40	MS60	MS63	MS65
ND-1994	500	—	—	—	2,650	2,750
ND-1994	480	PF65 2,850				

PROOF SETS

KM#	Date	Mintage	Identification	Issue Price	Mkt Val
PSA1	1970 (5)	—	KM9-13	—	35.00
PS1	1979 (6)	10,000	KM15-20	30.00	85.00
PS2	1984 (6)	3,000	MS15-20	—	90.00
PS3	1984 (3)	500	KM26-28	—	3,100
PS4	1985 (6)	10,000	KM15-20	30.00	90.00
PS5	1986 (6)	5,000	KM15-20	30.00	90.00
PS6	1987 (6)	2,000	KM15b, 16a-20a	52.00	90.00
PS7	1988 (6)	2,000	KM15b, 16a-20a	—	90.00
PS8	1989 (6)	2,000	KM15b, 16a-20a	—	90.00
PS9	1990 (6)	2,000	KM15b, 16a-20a	—	90.00
PS10	1991 (6)	2,000	KM15b, 16a-20a	—	90.00
PS11	1992 (6)	2,000	KM15b, 16a-20a	—	90.00
PS12	1992 (7)	2,000	KM42-47, 50	—	220
PS13	1992 (7)	1,000	KM47a, 48-53	—	6,200
PS14	1993 (6)	2,000	KM15b, 16a-20a	—	90.00
PS15	1994 (8)	1,980	KM54a-61a	—	250
PS16	1996 (4)	500	KM64-67	—	2,250
PS17	1997 (3)	500	KM68-70	—	1,900
PS18	1999 (3)	350	KM71-73	—	1,875
PS19	2000 (2)	400	KM#74, 79	—	320

SPECIMEN SETS (SS)

KM#	Date	Mintage	Identification	Issue Price	Mkt Val
MS2	1984 (6)	5,000	KM15-20	—	30.00
MS3	1984 (3)	500	KM26-28	—	2,900
MS4	1985 (6)	15,000	KM15-20	10.00	22.00
MS5	1986 (6)	10,000	KM15-20	10.00	22.00
MS6	1987 (6)	3,000	KM15a, 16-20	15.60	35.00
MS7	1988 (6)	2,000	KM15a, 16-20	15.60	35.00
MS8	1989 (6)	2,000	KM15a, 16-20	—	35.00
MS9	1990 (6)	3,000	KM15a, 16-20	—	35.00
MS10	1991 (6)	3,000	KM15a, 16-20	—	35.00
MS11	1994 (8)	—	KM54-61	—	65.00

BULGARIA

The Republic of Bulgaria, formerly the Peoples Republic of Bulgaria, a Balkan country on the Black Sea in southeastern Europe, has an area of 42,855 sq. mi. (110,910 sq. km.) and a population of *8.31 million. Capital: Sofia. Agriculture remains a key component of the economy but industrialization, particularly heavy industry, has been emphasized since the late 1940s. Machinery, tobacco and cigarettes, wines and spirits, clothing and metals are the chief exports.

The area now occupied by Bulgaria was conquered by the Bulgars, an Asiatic tribe, in the 7th century. Bulgarian kingdoms continued to exist on the Bulgarian peninsula until it came under Turkish rule in 1395. In 1878, after nearly 500 years of Turkish rule, Bulgaria was made a principality under Turkish suzerainty. Union seven years later with Eastern Rumelia created a Balkan state with borders approximating those of present-day Bulgaria. A Bulgarian kingdom, fully independent of Turkey, was proclaimed Sept. 22, 1908. During WWI Bulgaria had been aligned with Germany. After the Armistice certain land concessions were given to Greece and Romania. In 1934 King Boris III suspended all political parties and established a dictatorial monarchy. In 1938 the military began rearming through the aide of the Anglo-French loan. As WW II developed, Bulgaria again supported the Germans but protected their Jewish community. Boris died mysteriously in 1943 and Simeon II became King at the age of six. The country was then ruled by a pro-Nazi regency until it was liberated by Soviet forces in 1944.

The monarchy was abolished and Simeon was ousted by plebiscite in 1946 and Bulgaria became a Peoples Republic on the Soviet pattern. After democratic reforms in 1989 the name was changed to the Republic of Bulgaria.

Coinage of the Peoples Republic features a number of politically oriented commemoratives.

RULERS
Ferdinand I, as Prince, 1887-1908
As King, 1908-1918
Boris III, 1918-1943

MINT MARKS
A - Berlin
(a) Cornucopia & torch - Paris
BP - Budapest
H - Heaton Mint, Birmingham
KB - Kormoczbanya
(p) Poissy - Thunderbolt

MONETARY SYSTEM
100 Stotinki = 1 Lev

PRINCIPALITY

Under Turkish Suzerainty

STANDARD COINAGE

KM# 22.1 STOTINKA
Bronze, 15 mm. **Ruler:** Ferdinand I **Obv:** Crowned arms within circle **Rev:** Denomination and date within wreath, privy mark and designer's name below

Date	Mintage	F12	VF20	XF40	MS60	MS63
1901	20,000,000	1.25	2.50	9.00	15.00	25.00

KM# 22.2 STOTINKA
Bronze **Ruler:** Ferdinand I **Obv:** Crowned arms within circle **Rev:** Denomination above date within wreath, without privy marks and designer name

Date	Mintage	F12	VF20	XF40	MS60	MS63
1912	20,000,000	0.75	2.00	7.00	10.00	20.00

KM# 23.1 2 STOTINKI
2.01 g., Bronze, 20.14 mm. **Ruler:** Ferdinand I **Obv:** Crowned arms within circle **Rev:** Denomination above date within wreath, privy marks and designer name below denomination

Date	Mintage	F12	VF20	XF40	MS60	MS63
1901 (a)	40,000,000	1.00	2.00	5.00	8.00	15.00

KM# 24 5 STOTINKI
3.00 g., Copper-Nickel, 17 mm. **Ruler:** Ferdinand I **Obv:** Crowned arms within circle **Rev:** Denomination above date within wreath

Date	Mintage	F12	VF20	XF40	MS60	MS63
1906	14,000,000	0.20	0.60	3.00	6.00	10.00
1912	14,000,000	0.20	0.40	2.00	4.00	7.50
1913	20,000,000	0.20	0.40	1.50	3.00	6.00
1913	—	PF63 120				

KM# 24a 5 STOTINKI
Zinc **Ruler:** Ferdinand I **Obv:** Crowned arms within circle **Rev:** Denomination above date within wreath

Date	Mintage	F12	VF20	XF40	MS60	MS63
1917	53,200,000	0.60	1.00	3.00	8.00	—

KM# 25 10 STOTINKI
4.00 g., Copper-Nickel **Ruler:** Ferdinand I **Obv:** Crowned arms within circle **Rev:** Denomination above date within wreath

Date	Mintage	F12	VF20	XF40	MS60	MS63
1906	13,000,000	0.50	1.00	3.00	6.00	10.00
1912	13,000,000	0.20	0.40	1.75	3.00	5.00
1912	—	PF63 110				
1913	20,000,000	0.20	0.40	1.00	2.00	3.50

KM# 25a 10 STOTINKI
Zinc **Ruler:** Ferdinand I **Obv:** Crowned arms within circle **Rev:** Denomination above date within wreath

Date	Mintage	F12	VF20	XF40	MS60	MS63
1917	59,100,000	0.40	1.00	2.50	6.50	—
1917	—	PF63 135				

KM# 26 20 STOTINKI
5.00 g., Copper-Nickel **Ruler:** Ferdinand I **Obv:** Crowned arms within circle **Rev:** Denomination above date within wreath

Date	Mintage	F12	VF20	XF40	MS60	MS63
1906	10,000,000	0.50	1.50	5.00	9.00	15.00
1912	10,000,000	0.20	0.50	2.00	6.00	10.00
1913	5,000,000	0.20	1.50	3.00	7.50	12.00

KM# 26a 20 STOTINKI
3.90 g., Zinc, 21.14 mm. **Ruler:** Ferdinand I **Obv:** Crowned arms within circle **Rev:** Denomination above date within wreath

Date	Mintage	F12	VF20	XF40	MS60	MS63
1917	40,000,000	0.50	1.75	6.00	12.00	—
1917	—	PF63 130				

KINGDOM

KM# 23.2 2 STOTINKI
Bronze **Ruler:** Ferdinand I **Obv:** Crowned arms within circle **Rev:** Denomination above date within wreath, without privy marks and designer name

Date	Mintage	F12	VF20	XF40	MS60	MS63
1912	40,000,000	0.50	1.00	2.00	3.50	7.50

KM# 27 50 STOTINKI
2.50 g., 0.835 Silver 0.0671 oz. ASW **Ruler:** Ferdinand I **Obv:** Head right **Rev:** Denomination above date within wreath

Date	Mintage	F12	VF20	XF40	MS60	MS63
1910	400,000	2.50	4.00	12.00	20.00	35.00

KM# 30 50 STOTINKI
2.50 g., 0.835 Silver 0.0671 oz. ASW, 18.06 mm. **Ruler:** Ferdinand I **Obv:** Head left **Rev:** Denomination above date within wreath

Date	Mintage	F12	VF20	XF40	MS60	MS63
1912	2,000,000	2.25	4.40	8.00	12.00	20.00
1913	3,000,000	2.25	3.30	4.40	7.50	15.00
1916	4,562,000	—	—	150	350	600

Note: The 1916 date was withdrawn from circulation and destroyed. An uncertain quality remain, but beware of possible counterfeits

KM# 46 50 STOTINKI
Aluminum-Bronze **Ruler:** Boris III **Obv:** Crowned arms with supporters **Rev:** Denomination above date within wreath

Date	Mintage	F12	VF20	XF40	MS60	MS63
1937	60,200,000	0.25	0.50	1.25	4.50	10.00

KM# 28 LEV
5.00 g., 0.835 Silver 0.1342 oz. ASW, 23 mm. **Ruler:** Ferdinand I **Obv:** Head right **Rev:** Denomination above date within wreath

Date	Mintage	F12	VF20	XF40	MS60	MS63
1910	3,000,000	5.00	6.00	10.00	15.00	25.00

KM# 31 LEV
5.00 g., 0.835 Silver 0.1342 oz. ASW **Ruler:** Ferdinand I **Obv:** Head left **Rev:** Denomination above date within wreath

Date	Mintage	F12	VF20	XF40	MS60	MS63
1912	2,000,000	4.50	6.00	9.00	15.00	25.00
1913	3,500,000	4.50	6.00	9.00	15.00	25.00
1916	4,569,000	—	—	350	700	1,300

Date	Mintage	F12	VF20	XF40	MS60	MS63

Note: The 1916 date was withdrawn from circulation and destroyed. An uncertain quality remain, but beware of possible counterfeits

KM# 35 LEV

Aluminum **Ruler:** Boris III **Obv:** Crowned arms with supporters on ornate shield **Rev:** Denomination above date within wreath

Date	Mintage	F12	VF20	XF40	MS60	MS63
1923	40,000,000	—	3.00	7.50	15.00	35.00

KM# 37 LEV

2.99 g., Copper-Nickel, 19.7 mm. **Ruler:** Boris III **Obv:** Crowned arms with supporters on ornate shield **Rev:** Denomination above date within wreath **Edge:** Reeded

Date	Mintage	F12	VF20	XF40	MS60	MS63
1925	35,000,000	0.30	0.60	1.50	3.50	7.50
1925 (p)	34,982,000	0.25	0.60	1.50	3.50	7.50

Note: The Poissy issue bears the thunderbolt mint mark

KM# 37a LEV

Iron **Ruler:** Boris III **Obv:** Crowned arms with supporters on ornate shield **Rev:** Denomination above date within wreath

Date	Mintage	F12	VF20	XF40	MS60	MS63
1941	10,000,000	3.00	8.00	22.00	55.00	—

KM# 29 2 LEVA

10.00 g., 0.835 Silver 0.2685 oz. ASW **Ruler:** Ferdinand I **Obv:** Head right **Rev:** Denomination above date within wreath

Date	Mintage	F12	VF20	XF40	MS60	MS63
1910	400,000	9.00	12.00	22.00	35.00	60.00

KM# 32 2 LEVA

10.00 g., 0.835 Silver 0.2685 oz. ASW **Ruler:** Ferdinand I **Obv:** Head left **Rev:** Denomination above date within wreath

Date	Mintage	F12	VF20	XF40	MS60	MS63
1912	1,000,000	9.00	11.00	14.00	20.00	35.00
1913	500,000	9.00	11.00	17.50	25.00	40.00
1916 Rare	2,286,000	—	—	—	—	—

Note: The 1916 date was withdrawn from circulation and destroyed. An uncertain quality remain, but beware of possible counterfeits

KM# 36 2 LEVA

Aluminum **Ruler:** Ferdinand I **Obv:** Crowned arms with supporters on ornate shield **Rev:** Denomination above date within wreath

Date	Mintage	F12	VF20	XF40	MS60	MS63
1923	20,000,000	—	3.00	10.00	25.00	40.00

KM# 38 2 LEVA

4.97 g., Copper-Nickel, 22.95 mm. **Ruler:** Boris III **Obv:** Crowned arms with supporters on ornate shield **Rev:** Denomination above date within wreath

Date	Mintage	F12	VF20	XF40	MS60	MS63
1925	20,000,000	0.60	1.00	1.50	3.00	7.50
1925 (p)	20,000,000	0.50	1.00	1.50	3.00	7.50

Note: The Poissy issue bears the thunderbolt privy mark

KM# 38a 2 LEVA

5.00 g., Iron, 23.1 mm. **Ruler:** Boris III **Obv:** Crowned arms with supporters on ornate shield **Rev:** Denomination above date within wreath

Date	Mintage	F12	VF20	XF40	MS60	MS63
1941	15,000,000	0.75	1.50	8.00	30.00	—

KM# 49 2 LEVA

Iron **Ruler:** Boris III **Obv:** Crowned arms with supporters **Rev:** Denomination above date within wreath

Date	Mintage	F12	VF20	XF40	MS60	MS63
1943	35,000,000	0.75	2.00	14.00	40.00	—

KM# 39 5 LEVA

7.75 g., Copper-Nickel, 26.13 mm. **Ruler:** Boris III **Obv:** Denomination above date within wreath **Rev:** Figure on horseback, animals below

Date	Mintage	F12	VF20	XF40	MS60	MS63
1930	20,001,000	0.60	1.50	3.00	5.00	15.00

KM# 39a 5 LEVA

8.00 g., Iron, 26 mm. **Ruler:** Boris III **Obv:** Denomination above date within wreath **Rev:** Figure on horseback, animals below

Date	Mintage	F12	VF20	XF40	MS60	MS63
1941	15,000,000	1.00	3.00	8.50	30.00	—

KM# 39b 5 LEVA

Nickel Plated Steel **Ruler:** Boris III **Obv:** Denomination above date within wreath **Rev:** Figure on horseback, animals below

Date	Mintage	F12	VF20	XF40	MS60	MS63
1943	36,000,000	0.50	1.00	3.50	7.50	15.00

KM# 40 10 LEVA

10.90 g., Copper-Nickel, 30 mm. **Ruler:** Boris III **Obv:** Denomination above date within wreath **Rev:** Figure on horseback, animals below **Edge:** Reeded

Date	Mintage	F12	VF20	XF40	MS60	MS63
1930	15,001,000	0.75	2.20	5.00	9.00	18.00

KM# 40a 10 LEVA

Iron **Obv:** Denomination above date within wreath **Rev:** Figure on horseback, animals below

Date	Mintage	F12	VF20	XF40	MS60	MS63
1941	2,200,000	6.00	12.00	26.00	70.00	—

KM# 40b 10 LEVA

10.90 g., Nickel Plated Steel, 30 mm. **Ruler:** Boris III **Obv:** Denomination above date within wreath **Rev:** Figure on horseback, animals below

Date	Mintage	F12	VF20	XF40	MS60	MS63
1943	25,000,000	0.60	1.25	3.00	5.00	10.00

KM# 33 20 LEVA

6.45 g., 0.900 Gold 0.1867 oz. AGW, 21 mm. **Ruler:** Ferdinand I **Subject:** Declaration of Independence **Obv:** Head left **Rev:** Crowned arms, denomination and date below

Date	Mintage	F12	VF20	XF40	MS60	MS63
1912	75,000	237	285	325	400	750
1912	Inc. above	PF63 5,000				
1912 Proof; restrike	2,950	PF63 600				

Note: Official restrikes of this type were produced at the Bulgarian Mint in Sophia from 1967-68 and released prior to 2002; These pieces can be distinguished by their thicker more widely spaced edge legends

KM# 41 20 LEVA

4.00 g., 0.500 Silver 0.0643 oz. ASW **Ruler:** Boris III **Obv:** Head left **Rev:** Denomination above date within wreath

Date	Mintage	F12	VF20	XF40	MS60	MS63
1930 BP	10,016,000	2.50	3.50	5.00	10.00	15.00

KM# 47 20 LEVA

Copper-Nickel **Ruler:** Boris III **Obv:** Head left **Rev:** Denomination above date within wreath

Date	Mintage	F12	VF20	XF40	MS60	MS63
1940 A	6,650,000	0.50	1.00	2.50	5.00	10.00

KM# 42 50 LEVA

10.00 g., 0.500 Silver 0.1608 oz. ASW **Ruler:** Boris III **Obv:** Head left **Rev:** Denomination above date within wreath

Date	Mintage	F12	VF20	XF40	MS60	MS63
1930 BP	9,028,000	4.00	6.00	10.00	15.00	25.00

KM# 44 50 LEVA

10.00 g., 0.500 Silver 0.1608 oz. ASW **Ruler:** Boris III **Obv:** Head left **Rev:** Denomination at top, date below, flower at bottom, grain sprigs flank

Date	Mintage	F12	VF20	XF40	MS60	MS63
1934	3,001,000	4.00	6.00	10.00	15.00	25.00
1934 Proof	—	—	—	—	—	—

KM# 48 50 LEVA
10.00 g., Copper-Nickel **Ruler:** Boris III **Obv:** Head left **Rev:** Denomination above date within wreath

Date	Mintage	F12	VF20	XF40	MS60	MS63
1940 A	12,340,000	0.75	1.75	2.50	5.00	12.00

KM# 48a 50 LEVA
9.87 g., Nickel Plated Steel **Ruler:** Boris III **Obv:** Head left **Rev:** Denomination above date within wreath

Date	Mintage	F12	VF20	XF40	MS60	MS63
1943 A	15,000,000	1.00	2.50	5.50	10.00	15.00

KM# 34 100 LEVA
32.26 g., 0.900 Gold 0.9334 oz. AGW, 35 mm. **Ruler:** Ferdinand I **Subject:** Declaration of Independence **Obv:** Head left **Rev:** Crowned arms divide denomination, date below

Date	Mintage	F12	VF20	XF40	MS60	MS63
1912	5,000	1,300	1,600	1,750	2,250	3,750
1912	Inc. above	PF63 7,000				
1912 Proof; restrike	1,000	PF63 2,500				

Note: Official restrikes of this type were produced at the Bulgarian Mint in Sophia from 1967-68 and released prior to 2002; These pieces can be distinguished by their thicker more widely spaced edge legends

KM# 43 100 LEVA
20.00 g., 0.500 Silver 0.3215 oz. ASW **Ruler:** Boris III **Obv:** Head, left **Rev:** Denomination above date within wreath

Date	Mintage	F12	VF20	XF40	MS60	MS63
1930 BP	1,556,000	6.00	9.00	15.00	25.00	40.00

KM# 45 100 LEVA
20.00 g., 0.500 Silver 0.3215 oz. ASW **Ruler:** Boris III **Obv:** Head left **Rev:** Denomination at top, date below, flower at bottom, grain sprigs flank

Date	Mintage	F12	VF20	XF40	MS60	MS63
1934	2,506,000	6.00	9.00	15.00	25.00	40.00
1934 Proof	—	—	—	—	—	—
1937	2,207,000	6.00	9.00	15.00	25.00	40.00

MEDALLIC COINAGE

Originally produced as a jewelry item.
A similar piece with Russian legends also exists.

KM# M1 4 DUKAT
13.96 g., 0.986 Gold 0.4425 oz. AGW **Ruler:** Ferdinand I **Obv:** Military bust right **Obv. Legend:** ФЕРДИНАНДЪ I ЦАРЬ НА БЪЛГАРИТЪ **Rev:** Crowned supported arms **Countermark:** Crown and government mark

CM Date	Host Date	F12	VF20	XF40	MS60	MS63
ND	1910	560	620	765	800	1,000
ND	1911	560	620	785	825	1,050
ND	1912	560	620	765	800	1,000
ND	1914	560	620	825	975	1,550
ND	1917	560	620	825	975	1,550
ND	1918	560	620	785	825	1,050
ND	1919	560	620	825	975	1,550

Note: Values above are for holed or holed and plugged specimens; unholed specimens command 5 times the values indicated

KM# M2 4 DUKAT
13.96 g., 0.986 Gold 0.4425 oz. AGW **Ruler:** Boris III **Obv:** Military bust left **Obv. Legend:** ВОРИСЪ Ш ЦАРЪ НА БЪЛГАРИТЪ **Rev:** Crowned supported arms **Countermark:** Crown and government mark

CM Date	Host Date	F12	VF20	XF40	MS60	MS63
ND0	1921	620	800	900	1,450	2,350
ND	1926	620	800	900	1,450	2,350

Note: Values above are for holed or holed and plugged specimens; unholed specimens command 5 times the values indicated

PEOPLES REPUBLIC

STANDARD COINAGE

KM# 50 STOTINKA
1.00 g., Brass, 15.2 mm. **Obv:** National arms within circle **Rev:** Denomination above date at right, grain sprig at left **Edge:** Reeded

Date	Mintage	VF20	XF40	MS60	MS63	MS65
1951	—	—	0.10	0.25	0.50	1.00

KM# 59 STOTINKA
1.00 g., Brass, 15 mm. **Obv:** National arms within circle, date 9 / IX / 1944 on ribbon **Rev:** Denomination above date, grain sprigs flank **Edge:** Reeded

Date	Mintage	VF20	XF40	MS60	MS63	MS65
1962	—	—	0.10	0.25	0.50	1.00
1970	—	0.25	0.50	1.00	1.50	3.00

KM# 84 STOTINKA
1.00 g., Brass, 15 mm. **Obv:** National arms within circle, dates 681-1944 on ribbon **Rev:** Denomination above date within wreath **Edge:** Reeded **Note:** Reeded and security edge varieties exist.

Date	Mintage	VF20	XF40	MS60	MS63	MS65
1974	—	—	0.10	0.15	0.50	1.00
1979	2,000	PF65 1.50				
1980	2,000	PF65 1.50				
1981	137	—	—	22.00	—	—
1988	—	—	0.10	0.15	0.50	1.00
1989	—	—	0.10	0.15	0.50	1.00
1990	—	—	0.10	0.15	0.50	1.00

KM# 111 STOTINKA
1.00 g., Brass, 15 mm. **Subject:** 1300th Anniversary of Bulgaria **Obv:** National arms within circle **Rev:** Denomination above date within wreath **Edge:** Reeded

Date	Mintage	VF20	XF40	MS60	MS63	MS65
1981	—	0.10	0.20	0.30	0.50	1.00
1981	—	PF65 2.00				

KM# 60 2 STOTINKI
2.00 g., Brass, 18.16 mm. **Obv:** National arms within circle, date 9*IX*1944 on ribbon **Rev:** Denomination above date, grain sprigs flank **Edge:** Reeded

Date	Mintage	VF20	XF40	MS60	MS63	MS65
1962	—	—	0.10	0.15	0.25	1.00

KM# 85 2 STOTINKI
2.00 g., Brass, 18 mm. **Obv:** National arms within circle, dates 681-1944 on ribbon **Rev:** Denomination above date within wreath **Edge:** Reeded

Date	Mintage	VF20	XF40	MS60	MS63	MS65
1974	—	—	0.10	0.15	0.25	1.00
1979	2,000	PF65 2.00				
1980	2,000	PF65 2.00				
1981 Rare	20	—	—	—	—	—
1988	—	—	0.10	0.15	0.25	1.00
1989	—	—	0.10	0.15	0.25	1.00
1990	—	—	0.10	0.15	0.25	1.00

KM# 112 2 STOTINKI
2.00 g., Brass, 18 mm. **Subject:** 1300th Anniversary of Bulgaria **Obv:** National arms within circle **Rev:** Denomination above date within wreath **Edge:** Reeded

Date	Mintage	VF20	XF40	MS60	MS63	MS65
1981	—	0.10	0.20	0.30	0.60	1.20
1981	—	PF65 2.50				

KM# 51 3 STOTINKI
2.24 g., Brass, 19.66 mm. **Obv:** National arms within circle **Rev:** Denomination above date at right, grain sprig at left **Edge:** Reeded

Date	Mintage	VF20	XF40	MS60	MS63	MS65
1951	—	0.10	0.25	0.40	0.75	1.50

KM# 52 5 STOTINKI
2.97 g., Brass, 22.16 mm. **Obv:** National arms within circle **Rev:** Denomination above date at right, grain sprig at left **Edge:** Reeded

Date	Mintage	VF20	XF40	MS60	MS63	MS65
1951	—	0.15	0.25	0.40	0.75	1.50

KM# 61 5 STOTINKI
2.86 g., Brass, 22 mm. **Obv:** National arms within circle, date 9 • IX • 1944 on ribbon **Rev:** Denomination above date, grain sprigs flank **Edge:** Reeded

Date	Mintage	VF20	XF40	MS60	MS63	MS65
1962	—	0.10	0.15	0.25	0.50	1.00

KM# 86 5 STOTINKI
3.00 g., Brass, 22 mm. **Obv:** National arms within circle, dates 681-1944 on ribbon **Rev:** Denomination above date within wreath **Edge:** Reeded

Date	Mintage	VF20	XF40	MS60	MS63	MS65
1974	—	0.10	0.15	0.25	0.50	1.00
1979	2,000	PF65 2.00				
1980	2,000	PF65 2.00				
1988	—	—	0.15	0.25	0.50	1.00
1989	—	—	0.15	0.25	0.50	1.00
1990	—	—	0.15	0.25	0.50	1.00

KM# 113 5 STOTINKI
3.00 g., Brass, 22 mm. **Subject:** 1300th Anniversary of Bulgaria **Obv:** National arms within circle **Rev:** Denomination above date within wreath **Edge:** Reeded

Date	Mintage	VF20	XF40	MS60	MS63	MS65
1981	—	0.10	0.25	0.35	0.65	1.25
1981	—	PF65 2.50				

KM# 53 10 STOTINKI
1.80 g., Copper-Nickel, 16.59 mm. **Obv:** National arms within circle **Rev:** Denomination above date at right, grain sprig at left **Edge:** Reeded

Date	Mintage	VF20	XF40	MS60	MS63	MS65
1951	—	0.10	0.20	0.30	0.50	1.00

KM# 62 10 STOTINKI
1.60 g., Nickel-Brass, 16 mm. **Obv:** National arms within circle, date 9 • IX • 1944 on ribbon **Rev:** Denomination above date within wreath **Edge:** Reeded

Date	Mintage	VF20	XF40	MS60	MS63	MS65
1962	—	0.10	0.20	0.30	0.50	1.00

KM# 87 10 STOTINKI
1.60 g., Nickel-Brass, 16 mm. **Obv:** National arms within circle, dates 681-1944 on ribbon **Rev:** Denomination above date within wreath **Edge:** Reeded

Date	Mintage	VF20	XF40	MS60	MS63	MS65
1974	—	0.10	0.15	0.25	0.50	1.00
1979	2,000	PF65 3.50				
1980	2,000	PF65 3.50				
1988	—	—	0.15	0.25	0.50	1.00
1989	—	—	0.15	0.25	0.50	1.00
1990	—	—	0.15	0.25	0.50	1.00

KM# 114 10 STOTINKI
1.60 g., Copper-Nickel, 16 mm. **Subject:** 1300th Anniversary of Bulgaria **Obv:** National arms within circle **Rev:** Denomination above date within wreath **Edge:** Reeded

Date	Mintage	VF20	XF40	MS60	MS63	MS65
1981	—	0.15	0.25	0.50	1.00	1.50
1981	—	PF65 3.50				

KM# 55 20 STOTINKI
3.20 g., Copper-Nickel, 21 mm. **Obv:** National arms within circle **Rev:** Denomination above date at right, grain sprig at left **Edge:** Reeded

Date	Mintage	VF20	XF40	MS60	MS63	MS65
1952	—	2.50	6.50	9.00	12.00	16.00
1954	—	0.25	0.50	0.75	1.00	1.50

KM# 63 20 STOTINKI
3.20 g., Nickel-Brass, 21 mm. **Obv:** Date 9 • IX • 1944 on ribbon **Edge:** Reeded

Date	Mintage	VF20	XF40	MS60	MS63	MS65
1962	—	0.20	0.30	0.50	0.75	1.25

KM# 88 20 STOTINKI
3.20 g., Nickel-Brass, 21 mm. **Obv:** National arms within circle, dates 681-1944 on ribbon **Rev:** Denomination above date within wreath **Edge:** Reeded

Date	Mintage	VF20	XF40	MS60	MS63	MS65
1974	—	0.20	0.30	0.60	0.75	1.25
1979	2,000	PF65 3.50				
1980	2,000	PF65 3.50				
1988	—	—	0.30	0.60	0.75	1.25
Note: Large date (7mm) and small date (5mm) exist						
1989	—	—	0.30	0.60	0.75	1.25
1990	—	—	0.30	0.60	0.75	1.25

KM# 115 20 STOTINKI
3.20 g., Copper-Nickel, 21 mm. **Subject:** 1300th Anniversary of Bulgaria **Obv:** National arms within circle **Rev:** Denomination above date within wreath **Edge:** Reeded

Date	Mintage	VF20	XF40	MS60	MS63	MS65
1981	—	0.25	0.50	0.75	1.00	1.50
1981	—	PF65 4.00				

KM# 54 25 STOTINKI
3.50 g., Copper-Nickel **Obv:** National arms within circle **Rev:** Denomination above date at right, grain sprig at left **Edge:** Reeded

Date	Mintage	VF20	XF40	MS60	MS63	MS65
1951	—	0.20	0.50	0.75	1.20	2.00

KM# 56 50 STOTINKI
4.00 g., Copper-Nickel, 23 mm. **Obv:** National arms within circle **Rev:** Denomination above date at right, grain sprig at left

Date	Mintage	VF20	XF40	MS60	MS63	MS65
1959	—	0.20	0.40	0.75	1.00	1.50

KM# 64 50 STOTINKI
4.00 g., Nickel-Brass, 23 mm. **Obv:** National arms within circle, date 9 • IX • 1944 on ribbon **Rev:** Denomination above date within wreath **Edge:** Reeded

Date	Mintage	VF20	XF40	MS60	MS63	MS65
1962	—	0.40	0.65	1.00	1.25	2.00

KM# 89 50 STOTINKI
4.00 g., Nickel-Brass, 23 mm. **Obv:** National arms within circle, dates 681-1944 on ribbon **Rev:** Denomination above date within wreath **Edge:** Reeded

Date	Mintage	VF20	XF40	MS60	MS63	MS65
1974	—	—	0.50	0.75	1.00	1.50
1979	2,000	PF65 4.00				
1980	2,000	PF65 4.00				
1988	—	—	0.50	0.75	1.00	1.50
1989	—	—	0.50	0.75	1.00	1.50
1990	—	—	0.50	0.75	1.00	1.50

KM# 98 50 STOTINKI
Copper-Nickel **Subject:** University Games at Sofia **Obv:** Runner with torch, left, date at lower left **Rev:** Denomination divides arms and date

Date	Mintage	VF20	XF40	MS60	MS63	MS65
1977	2,000,000	0.30	0.65	1.00	1.25	2.00

KM# 116 50 STOTINKI
4.00 g., Copper-Nickel, 23 mm. **Subject:** 1300th Anniversary of Bulgaria **Obv:** National arms within circle **Rev:** Denomination above date within wreath **Edge:** Reeded

Date	Mintage	VF20	XF40	MS60	MS63	MS65
1981	—	0.25	0.50	0.75	1.00	1.50
1981	—	PF65 4.00				

KM# 57 LEV
Copper-Nickel **Obv:** National arms within circle, date 9 • IX • 1944 on ribbon **Rev:** Denomination above date within wreath

Date	Mintage	VF20	XF40	MS60	MS63	MS65
1960	—	0.25	0.60	1.00	1.25	2.00

KM# 58 LEV
Nickel-Brass **Obv:** National arms within circle **Rev:** Denomination above date, grain sprigs flank

Date	Mintage	VF20	XF40	MS60	MS63	MS65
1962	—	0.50	1.00	1.50	2.00	2.50

KM# 74 LEV
7.70 g., Nickel-Brass, 27 mm. **Subject:** 25th Anniversary of Socialist Revolution **Obv:** Wide denomination above date, grain sprigs flanking **Rev:** Monument to the fighters of the resistance

Date	Mintage	VF20	XF40	MS60	MS63	MS65
1969	2,410,196	0.50	1.00	1.25	1.75	2.50

KM# 76 LEV
Nickel-Brass, 27 mm. **Subject:** 90th Anniversary Liberation From Turks **Obv:** Denomination within wreath, date below **Rev:** Equestrian statue of Alexander II, Czar of Russia, dates flank

Date	Mintage	VF20	XF40	MS60	MS63	MS65
1969	1,290,373	0.60	1.25	1.50	2.00	3.00

KM# 94 LEV
Bronze, 27 mm. **Subject:** 100th Anniversary of the "April Uprising" Against the Turks **Obv:** Lion above denomination, date at left, circle surrounds **Rev:** Weapons above date within circle

Date	Mintage	VF20	XF40	MS60	MS63	MS65
1976	300,000	0.50	0.75	1.25	1.75	3.00
1976	—	PF65 4.00				

KM# 90 LEV
4.20 g., Nickel-Brass, 27 mm. **Obv:** National arms within circle, dates 681-1944 on ribbon **Rev:** Denomination above date, grain sprigs flank **Edge:** Reeded

Date	Mintage	VF20	XF40	MS60	MS63	MS65
1979	2,000	PF65 6.00				
1980	2,000	PF65 6.00				
1988	—	—	0.45	0.75	1.00	1.50
1989	—	—	0.45	0.75	1.00	1.50
1990	—	—	0.45	0.75	1.00	1.50

KM# 107 LEV
6.90 g., Copper-Nickel, 27.2 mm. **Subject:** World Cup Soccer Games in Spain **Obv:** Arms divide date above denomination **Rev:** World Cup trophy **Edge:** Plain

Date	Mintage	VF20	XF40	MS60	MS63	MS65
1980	220,000	—	0.60	1.00	1.75	3.00
1980	30,000	PF65 4.00				

KM# 117 LEV
4.20 g., Copper-Nickel, 27 mm. **Subject:** 1300th Anniversary of Bulgaria **Obv:** National arms within circle **Rev:** Denomination above date within wreath **Edge:** Reeded

Date	Mintage	VF20	XF40	MS60	MS63	MS65
1981	—	—	0.60	1.00	1.50	2.50
1981	—	PF65 3.00				

KM# 118 LEV
Copper-Nickel, 27 mm. **Subject:** International Hunting Exposition **Obv:** Arms above denomination, grain sprigs flank, date at bottom left **Rev:** Antlered deer head, left, inscription at right

Date	Mintage	VF20	XF40	MS60	MS63	MS65
1981	250,000	—	0.60	1.00	1.50	2.50
1981	50,000	PF65 4.00				

KM# 119 LEV
Copper-Nickel, 31 mm. **Subject:** Russo-Bulgarian Friendship **Obv:** Arms above denomination **Rev:** Flags at top, hands grasped at center, date at bottom **Note:** The same reverse die was used for both Bulgaria 1 Lev, KM#119 and Russia 1 Rouble, KM#189.

Date	Mintage	VF20	XF40	MS60	MS63	MS65
1981	220,800	—	0.60	1.00	1.50	2.50
1981	50,000	PF65 4.00				

KM# 175 LEV
Copper-Nickel, 27 mm. **Series:** 1980 Winter Olympics **Obv:** National arms **Rev:** Hockey player, denomination and date at bottom **Edge:** Reeded

Date	Mintage	VF20	XF40	MS60	MS63	MS65
1987	—	—	—	1.00	1.50	2.50
1987	300,000	PF65 4.00				

KM# 176 LEV
Copper-Nickel, 27 mm. **Series:** Summer Olympics **Obv:** National arms **Rev:** Sprinters, denomination and date below **Edge:** Reeded

Date	Mintage	VF20	XF40	MS60	MS63	MS65
1988	—	—	—	1.00	1.50	2.50
1988	300,000	PF65 4.00				

KM# 65 2 LEVA
8.89 g., 0.900 Silver 0.2572 oz. ASW **Subject:** 1100th Anniversary - Slovanic Alphabet **Obv:** Denomination above shield **Rev:** St. Cyril and St. Methodias, dates at bottom

Date	Mintage	VF20	XF40	MS60	MS63	MS65
ND-1963	10,000	PF65 12.00				

KM# 69 2 LEVA
8.89 g., 0.900 Silver 0.2572 oz. ASW **Subject:** 20th Anniversary Peoples Republic **Obv:** Flag above denomination, two dates at bottom **Rev:** Head left, two dates below

Date	Mintage	VF20	XF40	MS60	MS63	MS65
ND-1964	20,000	PF65 12.00				

KM# 73 2 LEVA
Copper-Nickel, 30 mm. **Subject:** 1050th Anniversary - Death of Ochridsky, Founder of the First European University **Obv:** Denomination between columns **Rev:** Figure divides dates

Date	Mintage	VF20	XF40	MS60	MS63	MS65
ND-1966	506,000	0.75	1.50	2.50	4.00	6.00

KM# 75 2 LEVA
10.80 g., Copper-Nickel, 30 mm. **Subject:** 25th Anniversary of Socialist Revolution, September 9, 1944 **Obv:** Large denomination between grain sprigs, date at bottom **Rev:** Monument to the Soviet Soldiers in Plovdiv

Date	Mintage	VF20	XF40	MS60	MS63	MS65
1969	1,082,210	—	0.75	1.25	2.00	4.00

KM# 77 2 LEVA
11.70 g., Copper-Nickel, 30 mm. **Subject:** 90th Anniversary - Liberation from Turks **Obv:** Denomination within wreath, date below **Rev:** The Battle on the Orlovo Enesdo (Eagle's nest) by the Russian painter Popov, two dates below

Date	Mintage	VF20	XF40	MS60	MS63	MS65
1969	756,759	—	0.75	1.25	2.00	4.00

KM# 80 2 LEVA
Nickel-Brass, 30 mm. **Subject:** 150th Anniversary - Birth of Dobri Chintulov **Obv:** Denomination above date **Rev:** Head facing, two dates below

Date	Mintage	VF20	XF40	MS60	MS63	MS65
1972	100,000	1.00	1.50	2.25	3.50	5.50

KM# 95.1 2 LEVA
11.00 g., Copper-Nickel, 30 mm. **Subject:** 100th Anniversary of the "April Uprising" Against the Turks **Obv:** Wreath above denomination, date at left, circle surrounds **Rev:** Figure with cannon, date at left, within circle

Date	Mintage	VF20	XF40	MS60	MS63	MS65
1976	224,800	—	0.75	1.00	1.50	2.50
1976	—	PF65 4.00				

KM# 95.2 2 LEVA
Copper-Nickel, 30 mm. **Obv:** Wreath above denomination, date at left, circle surrounds **Rev:** Figure with cannon, date at left, within circle **Edge:** Lettered

Date	Mintage	VF20	XF40	MS60	MS63	MS65
1976	138	—	—	—	—	—

KM# 108 2 LEVA
11.00 g., Copper-Nickel, 30 mm. **Subject:** World Cup Soccer Games in Spain **Obv:** Soccer logo **Rev:** National arms within circle divides dates above denomination, grain sprigs flank **Edge:** Plain

Date	Mintage	VF20	XF40	MS60	MS63	MS65
1980	220,000	0.60	0.75	1.00	1.50	2.50
1980	30,000	PF63 3.00	PF65 4.50			

KM# 110 2 LEVA
Copper-Nickel, 30 mm. **Subject:** 100th Anniversary - Birth of Yordan Yovkov, Writer **Obv:** Denomination above date **Rev:** Head facing, two dates below **Edge:** Plain

Date	Mintage	VF20	XF40	MS60	MS63	MS65
1980	200,000	—	0.75	1.25	2.00	4.00

KM# 120 2 LEVA
Copper-Nickel, 30 mm. **Subject:** International Hunting Exposition **Obv:** National arms above denomination, date bottom left **Rev:** Half figure of hunter with hawk, left

Date	Mintage	VF20	XF40	MS60	MS63	MS65
1981	250,000	—	0.75	1.00	1.50	2.50
1981	50,000	PF63 3.50	PF65 5.00			

KM# 121 2 LEVA
Copper-Nickel, 30 mm. **Subject:** 1300th Anniversary of Nationhood **Obv:** Line divides anniversary years and denomination, circle surrounds **Rev:** Equestrian figure, right, animal below **Edge:** Reeded

Date	Mintage	VF20	XF40	MS60	MS63	MS65
1981	—	—	—	1.00	1.50	2.50
1981	—	PF63 3.00	PF65 4.50			

KM# 122 2 LEVA
Copper-Nickel, 30 mm. **Subject:** 1300th Anniversary of Nationhood **Obv:** Wreath divides arms and denomination, date at bottom left **Rev:** Mother and child, radiant sun in background **Edge:** Reeded

Date	Mintage	VF20	XF40	MS60	MS63	MS65
1981	—	PF63 3.00	PF65 4.50			

KM# 123 2 LEVA
11.10 g., Copper-Nickel, 30 mm. **Subject:** 1300th Anniversary of Nationhood **Obv:** Line divides left facing head, date at right and denomination, circle surrounds **Rev:** Dimitrov **Edge:** Reeded

Date	Mintage	VF20	XF40	MS60	MS63	MS65
1981	—	—	—	1.00	1.50	2.50
1981	—	PF63 3.50	PF65 5.50			

KM# 124 2 LEVA
Copper-Nickel, 30 mm. **Subject:** 1300th Anniversary of Nationhood **Obv:** Buildings above denomination, date lower right **Rev:** King and saint **Edge:** Reeded

Date	Mintage	VF20	XF40	MS60	MS63	MS65
1981	—	—	—	1.00	1.50	2.50
1981	—	PF63 3.00	PF65 4.50			

KM# 125 2 LEVA
Copper-Nickel, 30 mm. **Subject:** 1300th Anniversary of Nationhood **Obv:** Line divides weapons on oak leaf, date at right and denomination within circle **Rev:** Soldier **Edge:** Reeded

Date	Mintage	VF20	XF40	MS60	MS63	MS65
1981	—	—	—	1.00	1.50	2.50
1981	—	PF63 3.00	PF65 4.50			

KM# 126 2 LEVA
Copper-Nickel, 30 mm. **Subject:** 1300th Anniversary of Nationhood **Obv:** Line divides flower, date at right and denomination within circle **Rev:** Clandestine meeting **Edge:** Reeded

Date	Mintage	VF20	XF40	MS60	MS63	MS65
1981	—	PF63 3.50	PF65 5.00			

KM# 127 2 LEVA
Copper-Nickel, 30 mm. **Subject:** 1300th Anniversary of Nationhood **Obv:** Decorative arms with supporters above denomination, date at left **Rev:** Cyrillic alphabet **Edge:** Reeded

Date	Mintage	VF20	XF40	MS60	MS63	MS65
1981	—	—	—	1.00	1.50	2.50
1981	—	PF63 3.00	PF65 4.50			

KM# 128 2 LEVA
Copper-Nickel, 30 mm. **Subject:** 1300th Anniversary of Nationhood **Obv:** Arms within circle, denomination below flanked by symbols, date at lower left **Rev:** Rila Monastary **Edge:** Reeded

Date	Mintage	VF20	XF40	MS60	MS63	MS65
1981	—	—	—	1.00	1.50	2.50
1981	—	PF63 3.00	PF65 4.50			

KM# 129 2 LEVA
Copper-Nickel, 30 mm. **Subject:** 1300th Anniversary of Nationhood **Obv:** Line divides weapons on shield flanked by flags, date at right and denomination below **Rev:** Russky monument **Edge:** Reeded

Date	Mintage	VF20	XF40	MS60	MS63	MS65
1981	—	PF63 3.50	PF65 5.00			

KM# 130 2 LEVA

Copper-Nickel, 30 mm. **Subject:** 1300th Anniversary of Nationhood **Obv:** Sevastokratoritza Desislava - Founder of Bojana Church. denomination, date below **Rev:** Bojana church **Edge:** Reeded

Date	Mintage	VF20	XF40	MS60	MS63	MS65
1981	300,000	PF63 3.50	PF65 5.00			

KM# 161 2 LEVA

Copper-Nickel, 30 mm. **Subject:** 1300th Anniversary of Nationhood - Oboriste Assembly **Obv:** National arms within circle at top, denomination below flanked by weapons, date at bottom left **Rev:** Inscription on monument within wreath **Edge:** Reeded

Date	Mintage	VF20	XF40	MS60	MS63	MS65
1981	300,000	PF63 3.50	PF65 5.00			

KM# 162 2 LEVA

Copper-Nickel, 30 mm. **Subject:** 1300th Anniversary of Nationhood - Uprising of Assen and Peter **Obv:** Building above denomination and date **Rev:** Soldiers with weapons on horseback **Edge:** Reeded

Date	Mintage	VF20	XF40	MS60	MS63	MS65
1981	300,000	PF63 3.50	PF65 5.00			

KM# 163 2 LEVA

Copper-Nickel, 30 mm. **Subject:** 1300th Anniversary of Nationhood - 100th Anniversary of Serbo-Bulgarian War **Obv:** Inscription within wreath above denomination and date **Rev:** Warrior women, facing, with shields and swords, rampant lion at left **Edge:** Reeded

Date	Mintage	VF20	XF40	MS60	MS63	MS65
1981	—	PF63 3.50	PF65 5.00			

KM# 155 2 LEVA

Copper-Nickel, 30 mm. **Subject:** Soccer **Obv:** National arms **Rev:** Outstretched soccer figure, date at right, denomination below **Edge:** Reeded

Date	Mintage	VF20	XF40	MS60	MS63	MS65
1986	100,000	PF63 3.50	PF65 5.00			

KM# 158 2 LEVA

Copper-Nickel, 30 mm. **Subject:** 13th World Eurythmic Championships - Varna 1987 **Obv:** Arena below map, denomination at bottom, date lower left **Rev:** Ribbon Dancer, left **Edge:** Reeded

Date	Mintage	VF20	XF40	MS60	MS63	MS65
1987	300,000	PF63 3.00	PF65 4.00			

KM# 159 2 LEVA

Copper-Nickel, 30 mm. **Series:** Winter Olympics **Obv:** National arms **Rev:** Skier, denomination and date below **Edge:** Reeded

Date	Mintage	VF20	XF40	MS60	MS63	MS65
1987	300,000	PF63 3.50	PF65 5.00			

KM# 165 2 LEVA

Copper-Nickel, 30 mm. **Subject:** 100th Anniversary of Sophia University **Obv:** University building, denomination and date at bottom **Rev:** Half figure with open book, two dates over left shoulder **Edge:** Reeded

Date	Mintage	VF20	XF40	MS60	MS63	MS65
1988	—	PF63 3.50	PF65 5.00			

KM# 166 2 LEVA

Copper-Nickel, 30 mm. **Subject:** Soviet-Bulgarian Space Flight **Obv:** Denomination and date within wreath, arms above **Rev:** Space flight within diamond **Edge:** Reeded

Date	Mintage	VF20	XF40	MS60	MS63	MS65
1988	300,000	PF63 3.00	PF65 4.00			

KM# 177 2 LEVA

Copper-Nickel, 30 mm. **Series:** Seoul 1988 - 24th Summer Olympic Games **Obv:** National arms **Rev:** High jumper, denomination and date below **Edge:** Reeded

Date	Mintage	VF20	XF40	MS60	MS63	MS65
1988	300,000	PF63 3.00	PF65 4.00			

KM# 178 2 LEVA

Copper-Nickel, 30 mm. **Subject:** Sports **Obv:** National arms above denomination and date **Rev:** Rowers **Edge:** Reeded

Date	Mintage	VF20	XF40	MS60	MS63	MS65
1989	300,000	PF63 3.00	PF65 4.00			

KM# 66 5 LEVA

16.67 g., 0.900 Silver 0.4823 oz. ASW **Subject:** 1100th Anniversary Slavic Alphabet **Obv:** Denomination above shield **Rev:** St. Cyril and St. Medhodius standing, two dates below

Date	Mintage	VF20	XF40	MS60	MS63	MS65
ND-1963	5,000	PF65 20.00				

KM# 70 5 LEVA

16.67 g., 0.900 Silver 0.4823 oz. ASW **Subject:** 20th Anniversary Peoples Republic, Georgi Dimitrov **Obv:** Flag above denomination, two dates below **Rev:** Head left, two dates below

Date	Mintage	VF20	XF40	MS60	MS63	MS65
ND-1964	10,000	PF65 18.00				

KM# 78 5 LEVA

20.50 g., 0.900 Silver 0.5932 oz. ASW, 36 mm. **Subject:** 120th Anniversary - Birth of Ivan Vazov, Poet **Obv:** National above date and denomination **Rev:** Head right, two dates at bottom

Date	Mintage	VF20	XF40	MS60	MS63	MS65
1970	370,000	—	11.00	11.50	12.00	13.00
1970	109,700	PF65 18.50				

KM# 79 5 LEVA

20.50 g., 0.900 Silver 0.5932 oz. ASW, 36 mm. **Subject:** 150th Anniversary - Birth of Georgi S. Rakovski, Constitution Author **Obv:** National arms above date, denomination below **Rev:** Bust 3/4 left, two dates below

Date	Mintage	VF20	XF40	MS60	MS63	MS65
1971 Prooflike	300,000	—	—	11.50	14.00	16.00

KM# 81 5 LEVA
20.50 g., 0.900 Silver 0.5932 oz. ASW, 36 mm. **Subject:** 250th Anniversary - Birth of Paisi Hilendarski, Historian **Obv:** National arms above denomination, date at left **Rev:** Figure with open book looking left, two dates below

Date	Mintage	VF20	XF40	MS60	MS63	MS65
1972	200,000	PF65 13.00				

KM# 82 5 LEVA
20.50 g., 0.900 Silver 0.5932 oz. ASW, 36 mm. **Subject:** Centennial - Death of Vasil Levski, Revolutionary **Obv:** National arms above denomination, date at left **Rev:** Head facing, divides dates

Date	Mintage	VF20	XF40	MS60	MS63	MS65
1973	200,000	PF65 13.00				

KM# 83 5 LEVA
20.50 g., 0.900 Silver 0.5932 oz. ASW, 36 mm. **Subject:** 50th Anniversary - Anti-fascist Uprising of September 9, 1923 **Obv:** National arms, date below **Rev:** Soldiers with flag, date below

Date	Mintage	VF20	XF40	MS60	MS63	MS65
1973	200,000	PF65 13.00				

KM# 91 5 LEVA
20.50 g., 0.900 Silver 0.5932 oz. ASW, 36 mm. **Subject:** 50th Anniversary - Death of Alexander Stamboliiski, Politician **Obv:** National arms, date and denomination below **Rev:** Head left, two dates below

Date	Mintage	VF20	XF40	MS60	MS63	MS65
1974	200,000	PF65 13.00				

KM# 92 5 LEVA
20.50 g., 0.900 Silver 0.5932 oz. ASW, 36 mm. **Subject:** 30th Anniversary - Liberation from Fascism September 9, 1944 **Obv:** National arms above denomination, date at left **Rev:** 2 soldiers and factory, two dates at right

Date	Mintage	VF20	XF40	MS60	MS63	MS65
1974	200,000	PF65 13.00				

KM# 96 5 LEVA
20.50 g., 0.900 Silver 0.5932 oz. ASW, 36 mm. **Subject:** Centennial - Death of Khristo Botev **Obv:** National arms above date and denomination **Rev:** Head 3/4 left, two dates upper right

Date	Mintage	VF20	XF40	MS60	MS63	MS65
1976	196,660	PF65 13.00				

KM# 97 5 LEVA
20.50 g., 0.500 Silver 0.3295 oz. ASW, 36 mm. **Subject:** 100th Anniversary of the "April Uprising" against the Turks **Obv:** Woman with sword divides dates, circle surrounds **Rev:** National arms above denomination, date at left

Date	Mintage	VF20	XF40	MS60	MS63	MS65
1976	200,000	PF65 9.25				

KM# 99 5 LEVA
20.50 g., 0.500 Silver 0.3295 oz. ASW, 36 mm. **Subject:** 150th Anniversary - Birth of Petko Slaveykov, Poet **Obv:** National arms above denomination, date at left **Rev:** Bust 3/4 left, two dates below

Date	Mintage	VF20	XF40	MS60	MS63	MS65
1977	200,000	PF65 9.25				

KM# 100 5 LEVA
20.50 g., 0.500 Silver 0.3295 oz. ASW, 36 mm. **Subject:** 100th Anniversary - Birth of Peio Javoroff, Poet and Actor **Obv:** National arms above denomination, date bottom left **Rev:** Bust left, looking forward, two dates at right

Date	Mintage	VF20	XF40	MS60	MS63	MS65
1978	200,000	PF65 9.25				

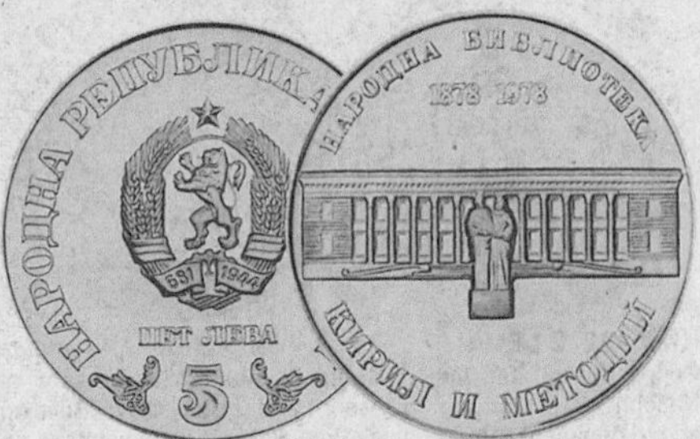

KM# 101 5 LEVA
20.50 g., 0.500 Silver 0.3295 oz. ASW, 36 mm. **Subject:** 100th Anniversary - National Library **Obv:** National arms, denomination below **Rev:** Statue in front of library, two dates above

Date	Mintage	VF20	XF40	MS60	MS63	MS65
ND-1978	200,000	PF65 9.25				

KM# 103 5 LEVA
20.50 g., 0.500 Silver 0.3295 oz. ASW, 103 mm. **Subject:** 100th Anniversary - Communication Systems **Obv:** National arms above denomination, date at left **Rev:** Radio tower within soundwaves, horn below divides dates

Date	Mintage	VF20	XF40	MS60	MS63	MS65
1979	35,000	—	—	6.50	8.75	10.50
1979	15,000	PF65 12.50				

KM# 109 5 LEVA
Copper-Nickel, 34 mm. **Subject:** World Cup Soccer Games in Spain **Obv:** National arms divides date above denomination flanked by grain sprigs **Rev:** Soccer players, date at bottom right **Edge:** Plain

Date	Mintage	VF20	XF40	MS60	MS63	MS65
1980	220,000	—	—	2.00	3.00	5.00
1980	30,000	PF65 7.00				

KM# 131 5 LEVA
Copper-Nickel **Subject:** International Hunting Exposition **Obv:** National arms above denomination, date at bottom left **Rev:** Antlered deer head, facing, date between antlers

Date	Mintage	VF20	XF40	MS60	MS63	MS65
1981	250,000	—	—	2.00	3.00	5.00
1981	50,000	PF65 7.00				

KM# 132 5 LEVA
Copper-Nickel **Subject:** 1300th Anniversary of Nationhood - Friendship with Hungary **Obv:** National arms above denomination, date below, grain sprigs flank **Rev:** Quill and sword handle divide heads

Date	Mintage	VF20	XF40	MS60	MS63	MS65
1981	140,000	—	—	2.50	4.00	6.00
1981	—	PF65 8.00				

KM# 140 5 LEVA
Copper-Nickel **Subject:** 100th Anniversary - Birth of Vladimir Dimitrov **Obv:** Denomination, date below **Rev:** Bust 3/4 left

Date	Mintage	VF20	XF40	MS60	MS63	MS65
1982	283,050	PF65 6.50				

KM# 141 5 LEVA
Copper-Nickel, 34 mm. **Subject:** 40th Anniversary - Birth of Lyudmila Zhivkova **Obv:** Arms above denomination, date at lower left **Rev:** Head left, two dates at right

Date	Mintage	VF20	XF40	MS60	MS63	MS65
1982	20,000	PF65 7.00				

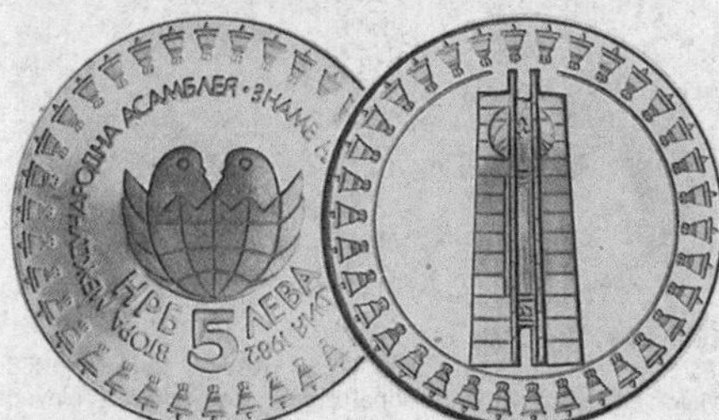

KM# 142 5 LEVA
Copper-Nickel **Subject:** 2nd International Children's Assembly **Obv:** Assembly logo above denomination, bells encircle outer edge **Rev:** Tower within circle, bells encircle edge

Date	Mintage	VF20	XF40	MS60	MS63	MS65
1982	200,000	PF65 4.00				

KM# 151 5 LEVA
Copper-Nickel, 34.5 mm. **Subject:** 3rd International Children's Assembly **Obv:** Assembly logo at top, denomination devides bells below, date lower left, child figures encircle edge **Rev:** Mosaic girl and boy with flowers, child figures encircle edge

Date	Mintage	VF20	XF40	MS60	MS63	MS65
1985	100,000	PF65 5.00				

KM# 152 5 LEVA
Copper-Nickel **Subject:** 90th Anniversary of Tourism Movement - Konstantinov **Obv:** National arms above denomination, date lower left **Rev:** Head left within circle, two dates below

Date	Mintage	VF20	XF40	MS60	MS63	MS65
1985	100,000	PF65 5.00				

KM# 153 5 LEVA
Copper-Nickel **Subject:** 4th Anniversary of UNESCO **Obv:** National arms above, bigas flank, denomination below, date lower left **Rev:** Logo above building

Date	Mintage	VF20	XF40	MS60	MS63	MS65
1985	100,000	PF65 5.00				

KM# 154 5 LEVA
Copper-Nickel **Subject:** Young Inventors' Exposition **Obv:** Rose on globe, denomination and date below **Rev:** Expo design

Date	Mintage	VF20	XF40	MS60	MS63	MS65
1985	100,000	PF65 5.00				

KM# 167.1 5 LEVA
Copper-Nickel **Subject:** Chiprovo Uprising **Obv:** National arms, date and denomination below **Rev:** Activists **Edge:** Plain

Date	Mintage	VF20	XF40	MS60	MS63	MS65
1988	100,000	PF65 5.00				

KM# 167.2 5 LEVA
Copper-Nickel **Subject:** Chiprovo Uprising **Obv:** National arms, date and denomination below **Rev:** Activists **Edge:** Reeded

Date	Mintage	VF20	XF40	MS60	MS63	MS65
1988	—	PF65 5.00				

KM# 168 5 LEVA
Copper-Nickel **Subject:** 120th Anniversary - Dimitar and Karadzha **Obv:** National arms above denomination and date, oak leaves flank **Rev:** Conjoined busts above dates

Date	Mintage	VF20	XF40	MS60	MS63	MS65
1988	100,000	PF65 5.00				

KM# 169 5 LEVA
Copper-Nickel **Obv:** National arms above denomination, date to left **Rev:** Steel factory worker from Kremikovtzi facing

Date	Mintage	VF20	XF40	MS60	MS63	MS65
1988	148,000	PF65 4.50				

KM# 170 5 LEVA
Copper-Nickel, 34 mm. **Subject:** Childrens' Assembly **Obv:** Denomination and date divides bell and logo within inner circle **Rev:** Child with birds within circle

Date	Mintage	VF20	XF40	MS60	MS63	MS65
1988	100,000	PF65 5.00				

KM# 179 5 LEVA
Copper-Nickel **Subject:** 200th Birthday of Aprilov **Obv:** Building above denomination and date **Rev:** Bust 3/4 left, two dates below

Date	Mintage	VF20	XF40	MS60	MS63	MS65
1989	100,000	PF65 5.00				

KM# 180 5 LEVA
Copper-Nickel **Subject:** 250th Anniversary - Birth of Vrachanski **Obv:** National arms within wreath, denomination below, date at bottom **Rev:** Half figure facing divides dates

Date	Mintage	VF20	XF40	MS60	MS63	MS65
1989	100,000	PF65 5.00				

KM# 67 10 LEVA
8.44 g., 0.900 Gold 0.2443 oz. AGW **Subject:** 1100th Anniversary - Slavic Alphabet **Obv:** Denomination above shield **Rev:** Two figures above dates

Date	Mintage	VF20	XF40	MS60	MS63	MS65
ND-1963	7,000	PF63 345	PF65 390			

KM# 71 10 LEVA
8.44 g., 0.900 Gold 0.2443 oz. AGW **Subject:** 20th Anniversary - Peoples Republic **Obv:** Flag above denomination, two dates below **Rev:** Head of Georgi Dimitrov, left, two dates below

Date	Mintage	VF20	XF40	MS60	MS63	MS65
ND-1964	10,000	PF63 345	PF65 390			

KM# 93.1 10 LEVA
29.95 g., 0.900 Silver 0.8666 oz. ASW **Subject:** 10th Olympic Congress **Obv:** National arms above date and denomination **Rev:** Old coin above Olympic rings **Edge:** Inscription in Latin

Date	Mintage	VF20	XF40	MS60	MS63	MS65
1975	50,000	PF65 20.00				

KM# 93.2 10 LEVA
29.95 g., 0.900 Silver 0.8666 oz. ASW **Obv:** National arms above date and denomination **Rev:** Old coin above Olympic rings **Edge:** Inscription in Cyrillic

Date	Mintage	VF20	XF40	MS60	MS63	MS65
1975	50,000	PF65 20.00				

KM# 102 10 LEVA
29.85 g., 0.500 Silver 0.4798 oz. ASW **Subject:** 100th Anniversary - Liberation from Turks **Obv:** National arms **Rev:** Monument above dates

Date	Mintage	VF20	XF40	MS60	MS63	MS65
ND-1978	200,000	PF65 13.00				

KM# 104 10 LEVA
23.33 g., 0.925 Silver 0.6938 oz. ASW **Series:** International Year of the Child **Obv:** Arms divide date above denomination **Rev:** Children divide symbols, date below

Date	Mintage	VF20	XF40	MS60	MS63	MS65
1979	16,906	PF65 19.00				

KM# 105 10 LEVA
14.00 g., 0.500 Silver 0.2251 oz. ASW **Subject:** Bulgarian-Soviet Cosmonaut Flight **Obv:** National arms above denomination and date **Rev:** Cosmonaut flight; space shuttle

Date	Mintage	VF20	XF40	MS60	MS63	MS65
1979	35,000	PF65 10.00				

KM# 105a 10 LEVA
23.85 g., 0.900 Silver 0.6901 oz. ASW **Obv:** National arms above denomination and date **Rev:** Cosmonaut flight; space shuttle

Date	Mintage	VF20	XF40	MS60	MS63	MS65
1979	15,000	PF65 19.00				

KM# 143 10 LEVA
18.88 g., 0.500 Silver 0.3035 oz. ASW **Subject:** Soccer Games **Obv:** National arms divide date above denomination **Rev:** Ball and net

Date	Mintage	VF20	XF40	MS60	MS63	MS65
1982	7,800	PF65 12.00				

KM# 144 10 LEVA
18.88 g., 0.500 Silver 0.3035 oz. ASW **Subject:** Soccer Games **Obv:** National arms within circle divide date, wreathed denomination below **Rev:** Soccer players

Date	Mintage	VF20	XF40	MS60	MS63	MS65
1982	7,200	PF65 12.00				

KM# 146 10 LEVA
23.33 g., 0.925 Silver 0.6938 oz. ASW **Series:** Winter Olympics **Obv:** National arms above denomination, date at bottom left **Rev:** Downhill skier

Date	Mintage	VF20	XF40	MS60	MS63	MS65
1984	8,464	PF65 18.00				

KM# 147 10 LEVA
Copper-Nickel **Subject:** Summer Olympics **Obv:** Arms over value **Rev:** Gymnast executing ribbon dance

Date	Mintage	VF20	XF40	MS60	MS63	MS65
1984	2,000	PF65 475				

KM# 147a 10 LEVA
23.33 g., 0.925 Silver 0.6938 oz. ASW **Subject:** Summer Olympics **Obv:** Arms over value **Rev:** Gymnast executing the ribbon dance event

Date	Mintage	VF20	XF40	MS60	MS63	MS65
1984	300	PF65 675				

KM# 149 10 LEVA
23.33 g., 0.925 Silver 0.6938 oz. ASW **Subject:** International Decade for Women **Obv:** National arms within wreath of roses, denomination and date below **Rev:** Woman carrying baskets of flowers, dates above

Date	Mintage	VF20	XF40	MS60	MS63	MS65
1984	5,572	PF65 32.00				

KM# 157 10 LEVA
18.75 g., 0.640 Silver 0.3858 oz. ASW **Obv:** Design above denomination, date at left **Rev:** Cosmonauts

Date	Mintage	VF20	XF40	MS60	MS63	MS65
1985	7,501	PF65 30.00				

KM# 184 10 LEVA
18.75 g., 0.640 Silver 0.3858 oz. ASW **Series:** 1988 Winter Olympics **Obv:** National arms **Rev:** Hockey player, denomination and date below

Date	Mintage	VF20	XF40	MS60	MS63	MS65
1987	15,000	PF65 15.00				

KM# 185 10 LEVA
18.75 g., 0.640 Silver 0.3858 oz. ASW **Series:** Summer Olympics **Obv:** National arms **Rev:** Sprinters, denomination and date below

Date	Mintage	VF20	XF40	MS60	MS63	MS65
1988	22,650	PF65 14.00				

KM# 68 20 LEVA
16.89 g., 0.900 Gold 0.4887 oz. AGW **Subject:** 100th Anniversary - Slavic Alphabet **Obv:** Denomination above shield **Rev:** Two figures above dates

Date	Mintage	VF20	XF40	MS60	MS63	MS65
ND-1963	3,000	PF63 690	PF65 780			

KM# 72 20 LEVA
16.89 g., 0.900 Gold 0.4887 oz. AGW **Subject:** 20th Anniversary - Peoples Republic **Obv:** Flag above denomination, dates at bottom **Rev:** Head of Georgi Dimitrov, left, two dates below

Date	Mintage	VF20	XF40	MS60	MS63	MS65
ND-1964	5,000	PF63 690	PF65 780			

KM# 106 20 LEVA
21.80 g., 0.500 Silver 0.3504 oz. ASW **Subject:** Centennial of Sofia as Capital **Obv:** National arms above ribbon, denomination and date at bottom **Rev:** Crowned head left, two dates bottom right

Date	Mintage	VF20	XF40	MS60	MS63	MS65
1979	35,000	—	—	10.00	12.00	15.00

KM# 106a 20 LEVA
32.00 g., 0.900 Silver 0.9259 oz. ASW **Subject:** Centennial of Sofia as Capital **Obv:** National arms above ribbon, denomination and date at bottom **Rev:** Crowned head left, two dates lower right

Date	Mintage	VF20	XF40	MS60	MS63	MS65
1979	15,000	PF65 25.00				

KM# 133.1 20 LEVA
14.00 g., 0.500 Silver 0.2251 oz. ASW **Subject:** 40th Anniversary - Birth of Lyudmila Zhivkova **Obv:** Denomination with date to left **Rev:** Head of Lyudmila Zhivkova left

Date	Mintage	VF20	XF40	MS60	MS63	MS65
1982	10,000	PF65 11.00				

KM# 133.2 20 LEVA
14.00 g., 0.500 Silver 0.2251 oz. ASW **Obv:** Denomination between emblems of Children's Assembly and Year of the Child **Rev:** Head of Lyudmila Zhivkova, left, two dates at right

Date	Mintage	VF20	XF40	MS60	MS63	MS65
1982	—	PF65 300				

KM# 164 20 LEVA
11.22 g., 0.500 Silver 0.1804 oz. ASW **Obv:** National arms, date and denomination below **Rev:** Bust of Vasil Levsky facing

Date	Mintage	VF20	XF40	MS60	MS63	MS65
1987	100,000	PF65 7.25				

KM# 171 20 LEVA
11.39 g., 0.500 Silver 0.1831 oz. ASW **Subject:** Bulgarian Railways **Obv:** National arms within circle, denomination and date below **Rev:** Train engines, old and new, within circle

Date	Mintage	VF20	XF40	MS60	MS63	MS65
1988	93,000	PF65 7.25				

KM# 172 20 LEVA
11.22 g., 0.500 Silver 0.1804 oz. ASW **Subject:** 110th Anniversary of Liberation **Obv:** Monument above denomination, date at right **Rev:** Liberation celebration, date below

Date	Mintage	VF20	XF40	MS60	MS63	MS65
1988	100,000	PF65 7.25				

KM# 173 20 LEVA
11.55 g., 0.500 Silver 0.1857 oz. ASW **Subject:** 100th Anniversary of Sophia University **Obv:** University above spray, denomination and date below **Rev:** Man, moth and kite, dates at left

Date	Mintage	VF20	XF40	MS60	MS63	MS65
1988	100,000	PF65 7.25				

KM# 174 20 LEVA
11.19 g., 0.500 Silver 0.1799 oz. ASW **Subject:** Soviet-Bulgarian Space Flight **Obv:** National arms above denomination, date at left **Rev:** Astronauts

Date	Mintage	VF20	XF40	MS60	MS63	MS65
1988	100,000	PF65 7.25				

KM# 181 20 LEVA
Copper-Nickel-Zinc **Obv:** National arms within circle **Rev:** Denomination above date, grain sprigs flank

Date	Mintage	VF20	XF40	MS60	MS63	MS65
1989	—	PF63 2.00	PF65 4,00			

KM# 183 20 LEVA
12.13 g., 0.500 Silver 0.195 oz. ASW **Subject:** Academy of Science **Obv:** National arms within pegged circle **Rev:** Academy building, two dates above, denomination and date below within pegged circle

Date	Mintage	VF20	XF40	MS60	MS63	MS65
1989	58,000	PF65 7.50				

KM# 134 25 LEVA
14.00 g., 0.500 Silver 0.2251 oz. ASW **Subject:** 1300th Anniversary of Nationhood **Obv:** National arms within wreath above denomination and date **Rev:** Woman and child, radiant sun in background

Date	Mintage	VF20	XF40	MS60	MS63	MS65
1981	Est. 100000	PF65 8.25				

KM# 145 25 LEVA
14.00 g., 0.500 Silver 0.2251 oz. ASW **Subject:** 100th Anniversary - Birth of Georgi Dimitrov **Obv:** National arms, denomination below, date at right **Rev:** Head left, two dates lower right

Date	Mintage	VF20	XF40	MS60	MS63	MS65
1982	15,000	PF65 8.25				

KM# 148 25 LEVA
14.00 g., 0.500 Silver 0.2251 oz. ASW **Subject:** 40th Anniversary of Peoples Republic **Obv:** National arms at top, denomination below divides dates **Rev:** Flowers on design

Date	Mintage	VF20	XF40	MS60	MS63	MS65
ND-1984	91,000	PF65 8.25				

KM# 156.1 25 LEVA
23.33 g., 0.925 Silver 0.6938 oz. ASW **Subject:** Soccer **Obv:** National arms **Rev:** Stylized eagle with soccer ball, denomination and date at left

Date	Mintage	VF20	XF40	MS60	MS63	MS65
1986	12,902	PF65 20.00				

KM# 156.2 25 LEVA
23.33 g., 0.925 Silver 0.6938 oz. ASW **Obv:** National arms **Rev:** Stylized eagle with soccer ball, denomination at left, without date in field above eagle's head

Date	Mintage	VF20	XF40	MS60	MS63	MS65
1986	Inc. above	PF65 22.00				

KM# 194 25 LEVA
23.33 g., 0.925 Silver 0.6938 oz. ASW **Subject:** Soccer **Obv:** National arms **Rev:** Soccer player, vertical date above, denomination at right

Date	Mintage	VF20	XF40	MS60	MS63	MS65
1986	12,250	PF65 20.00				

KM# 160 25 LEVA
23.33 g., 0.925 Silver 0.6938 oz. ASW **Series:** Winter Olympics **Obv:** National arms **Rev:** Skier, date and denomination below

Date	Mintage	VF20	XF40	MS60	MS63	MS65
1987	15,000	PF65 20.00				

KM# 186 25 LEVA
23.33 g., 0.925 Silver 0.6938 oz. ASW **Series:** Seoul 1988 - Summer Olympic Games **Subject:** High Jump **Obv:** National arms **Rev:** High jumper, date and denomination below

Date	Mintage	VF20	XF40	MS60	MS63	MS65
1988	20,000	PF65 20.00				

KM# 187 25 LEVA
23.33 g., 0.925 Silver 0.6938 oz. ASW **Subject:** Soccer **Obv:** Denomination above date **Rev:** Two players, date below

Date	Mintage	VF20	XF40	MS60	MS63	MS65
1989	17,600	PF65 20.00				

KM# 189 25 LEVA
23.38 g., 0.925 Silver 0.6953 oz. ASW **Series:** 1992 Summer Olympics **Obv:** National arms, date and denomination below **Rev:** Two rowers, date upper left

Date	Mintage	VF20	XF40	MS60	MS63	MS65
1989	57,560	PF65 18.00				

KM# 190 25 LEVA
23.38 g., 0.925 Silver 0.6953 oz. ASW **Series:** Albertville 1992 - 16th Winter Olympic Games **Obv:** National arms, date and denomination below **Rev:** Figure skating pairs competition, date at right

Date	Mintage	VF20	XF40	MS60	MS63	MS65
1989	48,449	PF65 18.00				

KM# 193 25 LEVA
23.38 g., 0.925 Silver 0.6953 oz. ASW **Subject:** Wildlife **Obv:** National arms, denomination and date below **Rev:** Mother bear and cubs

Date	Mintage	VF20	XF40	MS60	MS63	MS65
1989	15,000	PF65 32.00				

KM# 191 25 LEVA
23.38 g., 0.925 Silver 0.6953 oz. ASW **Subject:** Soccer **Obv:** National arms, denomination and date below **Rev:** Globe, net, and shoe

Date	Mintage	VF20	XF40	MS60	MS63	MS65
1990	15,600	PF65 30.00				

KM# 192 25 LEVA
23.38 g., 0.925 Silver 0.6953 oz. ASW **Subject:** Soccer **Obv:** National arms, date and denomination below **Rev:** Ball design, date

Date	Mintage	VF20	XF40	MS60	MS63	MS65
1990	14,900	PF65 25.00				

KM# 195 25 LEVA
23.38 g., 0.925 Silver 0.6953 oz. ASW **Series:** Winter Olympics **Obv:** National arms, date and denomination below **Rev:** Cross-country skiers, date at right

Date	Mintage	VF20	XF40	MS60	MS63	MS65
1990	46,400	PF65 19.00				

KM# 196 25 LEVA
23.38 g., 0.925 Silver 0.6953 oz. ASW **Series:** Summer Olympics **Obv:** National arms, date and denomination below **Rev:** Runners, date below

Date	Mintage	VF20	XF40	MS60	MS63	MS65
1990	50,235	PF65 18.00				

KM# 197 25 LEVA
23.38 g., 0.925 Silver 0.6953 oz. ASW **Subject:** Wildlife **Obv:** National arms, date and denomination below **Rev:** Two lynx

Date	Mintage	VF20	XF40	MS60	MS63	MS65
1990	14,840	PF65 28.00				

KM# 135 50 LEVA
20.50 g., 0.900 Silver 0.5932 oz. ASW **Subject:** 1300th Anniversary of Nationhood **Obv:** Dates above denomination **Rev:** Equestrian figure right, animal below

Date	Mintage	VF20	XF40	MS60	MS63	MS65
1981	Est. 10000	PF65 25.00				

KM# 136 50 LEVA
20.50 g., 0.900 Silver 0.5932 oz. ASW **Subject:** 1300th Anniversary of Nationhood **Obv:** Head of Georgi Dimitrov left, denomination below line **Rev:** Woman striding left

Date	Mintage	VF20	XF40	MS60	MS63	MS65
1981	1,000	PF65 42.00				

KM# 137 50 LEVA
20.50 g., 0.900 Silver 0.5932 oz. ASW **Subject:** 1300th Anniversary of Nationhood **Obv:** National arms above sprays, date and denomination below **Rev:** Mother and child in front of radiant sun

Date	Mintage	VF20	XF40	MS60	MS63	MS65
1981	1,000	PF65 42.00				

KM# 138 50 LEVA
20.50 g., 0.900 Silver 0.5932 oz. ASW **Subject:** 1300th Anniversary of Nationhood **Obv:** Buildings above date and denomination **Rev:** Warrior figures

Date	Mintage	VF20	XF40	MS60	MS63	MS65
1981	Est. 10000	PF65 22.00				

KM# 182 50 LEVA
Copper-Nickel-Zinc **Obv:** National arms within circle **Rev:** Denomination above date, grain sprays flank

Date	Mintage	VF20	XF40	MS60	MS63	MS65
1989	—	PF63 3.00	PF65 5.00			

KM# 150 100 LEVA
8.44 g., 0.900 Gold 0.2443 oz. AGW **Subject:** International Womens Decade **Obv:** National arms within wreath, date and denomination below **Rev:** Woman with child divides dates **Note:** .076 Silver, .024 Copper

Date	Mintage	VF20	XF40	MS60	MS63	MS65
1984	500	PF65 400				

KM# 150a 100 LEVA
8.44 g., 0.900 Gold 0.2443 oz. AGW **Subject:** International Womens Decade **Obv:** National arms within wreath, date and denomination below **Rev:** Woman with child divides date **Note:** .100 Copper

Date	Mintage	VF20	XF40	MS60	MS63	MS65
1984	2,032	PF65 375				

KM# 139 1000 LEVA
16.88 g., 0.900 Gold 0.4884 oz. AGW **Subject:** 1300th Anniversary of Nationhood **Obv:** National arms above denomination and date **Rev:** Mother and child in front of radiant sun

Date	Mintage	VF20	XF40	MS60	MS63	MS65
1981	2,000	PF65 750				

REPUBLIC

KM# 199 10 STOTINKI
1.60 g., Nickel-Brass, 17.2 mm. **Obv:** Ancient lion sculpture left within circle **Rev:** Denomination divides date **Edge:** Reeded

Date	Mintage	VF20	XF40	MS60	MS63	MS65
1992	—	—	—	—	0.25	0.35

KM# 200 20 STOTINKI
2.00 g., Nickel-Brass, 19.2 mm. **Obv:** Ancient lion sculpture left within circle **Rev:** Denomination divides date **Edge:** Reeded

Date	Mintage	VF20	XF40	MS60	MS63	MS65
1992	—	—	—	—	0.35	0.50

KM# 201 50 STOTINKI
3.00 g., Nickel-Brass, 21.2 mm. **Obv:** Ancient lion sculpture left within circle **Rev:** Denomination divides date **Edge:** Reeded

Date	Mintage	VF20	XF40	MS60	MS63	MS65
1992	—	—	—	—	0.50	0.75

KM# 202 LEV
4.00 g., Nickel-Brass, 23.2 mm. **Obv:** Madara horseman right within circle **Rev:** Denomination divides symbols, date below **Edge:** Reeded

Date	Mintage	VF20	XF40	MS60	MS63	MS65
1992	—	—	—	—	0.75	1.00

KM# 203 2 LEVA
5.00 g., Nickel-Brass, 25.2 mm. **Obv:** Madara horseman right

within circle **Rev:** Denomination divides symbols, date below **Edge:** Reeded

Date	Mintage	VF20	XF40	MS60	MS63	MS65
1992	—	—	—	—	1.25	1.50

KM# 204 5 LEVA
6.00 g., Nickel-Brass, 27.2 mm. **Obv:** Madara horseman right within circle **Rev:** Denomination divides symbols, date below **Edge:** Reeded

Date	Mintage	VF20	XF40	MS60	MS63	MS65
1992	—	—	—	—	1.75	2.00

KM# 205 10 LEVA
9.00 g., Copper-Nickel-Zinc, 30.2 mm. **Obv:** Madara horseman right within circle **Rev:** Denomination divides symbols, date below **Edge:** Reeded

Date	Mintage	VF20	XF40	MS60	MS63	MS65
1992	—	—	—	—	2.50	3.00

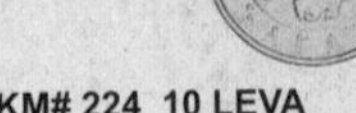

KM# 224 10 LEVA
1.50 g., Brass, 15.5 mm. **Obv:** Madara horseman right within circle **Rev:** Denomination divides symbols, date below **Edge:** Reeded **Note:** Reduced size and metal change.

Date	Mintage	VF20	XF40	MS60	MS63	MS65
1997	—	—	—	—	1.25	1.50

KM# 228 20 LEVA
2.50 g., Brass, 17.5 mm. **Obv:** Madara horseman right within circle **Rev:** Denomination divides symbols, date below **Edge:** Reeded

Date	Mintage	VF20	XF40	MS60	MS63	MS65
1997	—	—	—	—	1.50	1.75

KM# 198 50 LEVA
10.07 g., 0.925 Silver 0.2995 oz. ASW **Series:** Olympics **Obv:** Denomination above date within wreath **Rev:** Downhill skier, date below

Date	Mintage	VF20	XF40	MS60	MS63	MS65
1992	52,390	PF65 8.75				

KM# 213 50 LEVA
Copper-Nickel **Subject:** Centennial of Olympics in Bulgaria **Obv:** Denomination above date within wreath **Rev:** Gymnasts divide dates

Date	Mintage	VF20	XF40	MS60	MS63	MS65
1994	19,210	PF63 3.00	PF65 5.00			

KM# 225 50 LEVA
3.50 g., Brass, 19.5 mm. **Obv:** Madara horseman right within circle **Rev:** Denomination divides symbols, date below **Edge:** Reeded

Date	Mintage	VF20	XF40	MS60	MS63	MS65
1997	—	—	—	—	1.75	2.00

KM# 212 100 LEVA
23.23 g., 0.925 Silver 0.6908 oz. ASW **Obv:** Denomination above date within wreath **Rev:** Old Ship Radetsky, date at right

Date	Mintage	VF20	XF40	MS60	MS63	MS65
1992	28,765	PF65 20.00				

KM# 226 100 LEVA
23.23 g., 0.925 Silver 0.6908 oz. ASW **Obv:** Denomination above date within wreath **Rev:** Eagle descending on prey

Date	Mintage	VF20	XF40	MS60	MS63	MS65
1992	27,651	PF65 23.00				

KM# 209 100 LEVA
23.33 g., 0.925 Silver 0.6938 oz. ASW **Series:** 1994 Olympics **Obv:** Denomination above date within wreath **Rev:** Bobsled, date upper right

Date	Mintage	VF20	XF40	MS60	MS63	MS65
1993	33,690	PF65 19.00				

KM# 210 100 LEVA
23.33 g., 0.925 Silver 0.6938 oz. ASW **Subject:** 1994 World Cup Soccer **Obv:** Denomination above date within wreath **Rev:** Soccer player and buildings, within circle

Date	Mintage	VF20	XF40	MS60	MS63	MS65
1993	27,840	PF65 20.00				

KM# 227 100 LEVA
23.33 g., 0.925 Silver 0.6938 oz. ASW **Obv:** Denomination above date within wreath **Rev:** Chamois left

Date	Mintage	VF20	XF40	MS60	MS63	MS65
1993	20,000	PF65 28.00				

KM# 231 100 LEVA
23.33 g., 0.925 Silver 0.6938 oz. ASW **Obv:** Denomination above date within wreath **Rev:** Parliament building

Date	Mintage	VF20	XF40	MS60	MS63	MS65
1993	15,000	PF65 26.00				

KM# 206 500 LEVA
33.63 g., 0.925 Silver 1.000 oz. ASW **Subject:** European Community - St. Theodor Stratilat **Obv:** ECU monogram and date in circle of stars **Rev:** Face within design, denomination at right

Date	Mintage	VF20	XF40	MS60	MS63	MS65
1993	51,031	PF65 24.00				

KM# 211 500 LEVA
23.00 g., 0.925 Silver 0.684 oz. ASW **Subject:** World Cup Soccer **Obv:** Denomination above date within wreath **Rev:** Soccer ball and net, date below

Date	Mintage	VF20	XF40	MS60	MS63	MS65
1994	24,351	PF65 21.00				

KM# 219 500 LEVA
10.00 g., 0.925 Silver 0.2974 oz. ASW **Subject:** Soccer **Obv:** Denomination above date within wreath **Rev:** Two soccer players

Date	Mintage	VF20	XF40	MS60	MS63	MS65
1996	60,000	PF65 20.00				

KM# 223 500 LEVA
10.00 g., 0.925 Silver 0.2974 oz. ASW, 30 mm. **Subject:** 100th Anniversary - National Art Academy **Obv:** Denomination above date within wreath **Rev:** Academy on paint palette **Edge:** Plain

Date	Mintage	VF20	XF40	MS60	MS63	MS65
1996	30,000	PF65 35.00				

KM# 229 500 LEVA
Copper-Nickel-Zinc **Subject:** NATO **Obv:** Denomination above date within wreath **Rev:** City arms and NATO flag

Date	Mintage	VF20	XF40	MS60	MS63	MS65
1997	30,000	—	—	2.00	3.00	5.00

KM# 214 1000 LEVA
23.33 g., 0.925 Silver 0.6938 oz. ASW **Series:** 50 Years - F.A.O. **Obv:** Denomination above date within wreath **Rev:** Wheat and globe within circle, two dates below

Date	Mintage	VF20	XF40	MS60	MS63	MS65
1995	12,000	PF65 21.00				

KM# 215 1000 LEVA
23.33 g., 0.925 Silver 0.6938 oz. ASW **Subject:** 100 Years of Olympic Games **Obv:** Denomination above date within wreath **Rev:** Equestrian, left

Date	Mintage	VF20	XF40	MS60	MS63	MS65
1995	28,713	PF65 21.00				

KM# 216 1000 LEVA
23.33 g., 0.925 Silver 0.6938 oz. ASW **Subject:** 110 Years - Union of Eastern Rumelia with the Bulgarian Principality **Obv:** Denomination above date within wreath **Rev:** Map behind figure with flag, two dates upper left

Date	Mintage	VF20	XF40	MS60	MS63	MS65
1995	15,000	PF65 21.00				

KM# 217 1000 LEVA
33.63 g., 0.925 Silver 1.000 oz. ASW **Subject:** Rozhen Peak Astronomical Observatory **Obv:** ECU monogram and date within circle of stars **Rev:** Observatory, circle of stars above, denomination below

Date	Mintage	VF20	XF40	MS60	MS63	MS65
1995	32,796	PF65 28.00				

KM# 220 1000 LEVA
23.33 g., 0.925 Silver 0.6938 oz. ASW **Obv:** Denomination above date within wreath **Rev:** Sailing Ship Kaliakra

Date	Mintage	VF20	XF40	MS60	MS63	MS65
1996	23,052	PF65 22.00				

KM# 221 1000 LEVA
23.33 g., 0.925 Silver 0.6938 oz. ASW **Series:** Olympics **Obv:** Denomination above date within wreath **Rev:** Speed skater

Date	Mintage	VF20	XF40	MS60	MS63	MS65
1996	22,602	PF65 18.00				

KM# 222 1000 LEVA
33.63 g., 0.925 Silver 1.000 oz. ASW **Subject:** St. Ivan of Rila **Obv:** ECU monogram and date within circle of stars **Rev:** Standing saint, church, and denomination

Date	Mintage	VF20	XF40	MS60	MS63	MS65
1996	42,445	PF65 29.00				

KM# 232 1000 LEVA
23.33 g., 0.925 Silver 0.6938 oz. ASW **Subject:** UNICEF **Obv:** Denomination above date within wreath **Rev:** Singing child, UNICEF logo

Date	Mintage	VF20	XF40	MS60	MS63	MS65
1997	6,001	PF65 35.00				

KM# 233 1000 LEVA
23.33 g., 0.925 Silver 0.6938 oz. ASW **Subject:** World Cup Soccer - France 1998 **Obv:** Denomination above date within wreath **Rev:** Three soccer players

Date	Mintage	VF20	XF40	MS60	MS63	MS65
1997	22,606	PF65 30.00				

KM# 230 1000 LEVA
Copper-Nickel-Zinc **Subject:** Bulgarian Telegraphic Agency Centennial **Obv:** Crowned arms **Rev:** World map and logo **Note:** Prev. KM#239.

Date	Mintage	VF20	XF40	MS60	MS63	MS65
1998	—	PF63 3.00	PF65 5.00			

KM# 207 5000 LEVA
8.64 g., 0.900 Gold 0.250 oz. AGW **Subject:** European Community - Slavonic Alphabet **Obv:** ECU monogram and date within circle of stars **Rev:** Denomination to left of design

Date	Mintage	VF20	XF40	MS60	MS63	MS65
1993	Est. 2500	PF65 425				

KM# 243 5000 LEVA
10.00 g., 0.925 Silver 0.2974 oz. ASW **Obv:** National arms, date and denomination below **Rev:** Building above "EURO"

Date	Mintage	VF20	XF40	MS60	MS63	MS65
1998	—	PF65 11.00				

KM# 208 10000 LEVA
15.57 g., 0.999 Platinum 0.500 oz. APW **Rev:** Bust of Sevastokratoritza Desislava 1/2 right, founder of Boyana church, denomination at right

Date	Mintage	VF20	XF40	MS60	MS63	MS65
1993	Est. 2500	PF65 1,000				

KM# 218 10000 LEVA
8.64 g., 0.900 Gold 0.250 oz. AGW **Obv:** Denomination above date within wreath **Rev:** St. Alexander Nevski Cathedral

Date	Mintage	VF20	XF40	MS60	MS63	MS65
1994	30,000	PF65 400				

KM# 234 10000 LEVA
23.33 g., 0.925 Silver 0.6938 oz. ASW **Subject:** 120th Anniversary of Liberation **Obv:** National arms above date, denomination below **Rev:** Decorated soldier with flag

Date	Mintage	VF20	XF40	MS60	MS63	MS65
1998	15,000	PF65 37.00				

KM# 235 10000 LEVA
23.33 g., 0.925 Silver 0.6938 oz. ASW **Subject:** United Europe **Obv:** Rider of Madara over dead lion **Rev:** Ancient cup and map

Date	Mintage	VF20	XF40	MS60	MS63	MS65
1998	18,152	PF65 32.00				

KM# 236 20000 LEVA
1.56 g., 0.999 Gold 0.050 oz. AGW **Subject:** Czar Ivan Alexander **Obv:** Stylized lion, left, date and denomination below **Rev:** Four human figure sculptures

Date	Mintage	VF20	XF40	MS60	MS63	MS65
1998	—	PF65 75.00				

REFORM COINAGE

KM# 237 STOTINKA
1.80 g., Aluminum-Bronze, 16 mm. **Obv:** Madara horseman right, animal below **Rev:** Denomination above date **Edge:** Plain

Date	Mintage	VF20	XF40	MS60	MS63	MS65
1999	1,277,500	—	—	0.15	0.25	0.35
2000	—	—	—	0.15	0.25	0.35

KM# 237a STOTINKA
1.80 g., Brass Plated Steel, 16 mm. **Obv:** Madara horseman right **Rev:** Denomination above date

Date	Mintage	VF20	XF40	MS60	MS63	MS65
2000	1,277,500	—	—	0.15	0.25	0.35

KM# 238 2 STOTINKI
2.50 g., Aluminum-Bronze, 18 mm. **Obv:** Madara horseman right, animal below **Rev:** Denomination above date **Edge:** Plain

Date	Mintage	VF20	XF40	MS60	MS63	MS65
1999	2,048,900	—	—	0.20	0.35	0.50
2000	—	—	—	0.20	0.35	0.50

KM# 238a 2 STOTINKI
2.50 g., Brass Plated Steel, 18 mm. **Obv:** Madara horseman right **Rev:** Denomination above date

Date	Mintage	VF20	XF40	MS60	MS63	MS65
2000	—	—	—	0.20	0.35	0.50

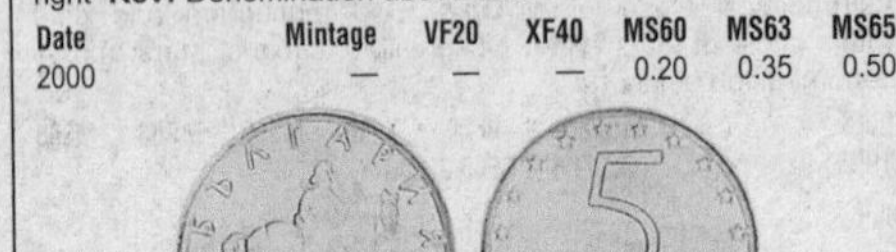

KM# 239 5 STOTINKI
3.50 g., Aluminum-Bronze, 20 mm. **Obv:** Madara horseman right, animal below **Rev:** Denomination above date **Edge:** Plain **Note:** Prev. KM#A239.

Date	Mintage	VF20	XF40	MS60	MS63	MS65
1999	3,453,025	—	—	0.25	0.50	0.65
2000	—	—	—	0.25	0.50	0.65

KM# 239a 5 STOTINKI
3.50 g., Brass Plated Steel, 20 mm. **Obv:** Madara horseman right **Rev:** Denomination above date

Date	Mintage	VF20	XF40	MS60	MS63	MS65
2000	—	—	—	0.25	0.50	0.65

KM# 240 10 STOTINKI
3.00 g., Copper-Nickel-Zinc, 18.5 mm. **Obv:** Madara horseman right, animal below **Rev:** Denomination above date **Edge:** Reeded

Date	Mintage	VF20	XF40	MS60	MS63	MS65
1999	8,231,400	—	—	0.30	0.65	0.85

KM# 241 20 STOTINKI
4.00 g., Copper-Nickel-Zinc, 20.5 mm. **Obv:** Madara horseman right, animal below **Rev:** Denomination above date **Edge:** Reeded

Date	Mintage	VF20	XF40	MS60	MS63	MS65
1999	11,967,500	—	—	0.40	0.85	1.00

KM# 242 50 STOTINKI
5.00 g., Copper-Nickel-Zinc, 22.5 mm. **Obv:** Madara horseman right, animal below **Rev:** Denomination above date **Edge:** Reeded

Date	Mintage	VF20	XF40	MS60	MS63	MS65
1999	15,607,000	—	—	0.60	1.25	1.50

KM# 245 10 LEVA
23.35 g., 0.925 Silver 0.6944 oz. ASW, 38.5 mm. **Obv:** National arms **Rev:** Mediterranean Monk Seal, denomination above, date at left **Edge:** Plain

Date	Mintage	VF20	XF40	MS60	MS63	MS65
1999 Proof	15,000	—	—	—	28.00	32.00

KM# 248 10 LEVA
23.33 g., 0.925 Silver 0.6938 oz. ASW, 38.5 mm. **Obv:** Bust of Theodor Burmov 3/4 left, denomination and date below **Rev:** "EURO" map in circle of stars **Edge:** Plain

Date	Mintage	VF20	XF40	MS60	MS63	MS65
1999	20,000	PF63 30.00	PF65 32.00			

KM# 249 10 LEVA
23.33 g., 0.925 Silver 0.6938 oz. ASW, 38.5 mm. **Subject:** Euro Integration **Obv:** National arms, date and denomination below **Rev:** Plovdiv old town street view **Edge:** Plain

Date	Mintage	VF20	XF40	MS60	MS63	MS65
1999	20,000	PF63 30.00	PF65 32.00			

KM# 250 10 LEVA
23.33 g., 0.925 Silver 0.6938 oz. ASW, 38.5 mm. **Subject:** Summer Olympic Games **Obv:** National arms **Rev:** High jumper divides date and denomination **Edge:** Plain

Date	Mintage	VF20	XF40	MS60	MS63	MS65
1999	20,000	PF63 30.00	PF65 32.00			

KM# 244 10 LEVA
10.35 g., 0.800 Silver 0.2662 oz. ASW, 33.9 mm. **Subject:** The Year 2000 **Obv:** National arms above date with pierced zeros, denomination below **Rev:** Bell above date with pierced zeros **Edge:** Plain

Date	Mintage	VF20	XF40	MS60	MS63	MS65
2000	—	PF65 55.00				

KM# 251 10 LEVA
23.33 g., 0.925 Silver 0.6938 oz. ASW, 38.5 mm. **Subject:** Summer Olympics **Obv:** National arms, date and denomination below **Rev:** Weight lifter **Edge:** Plain

Date	Mintage	VF20	XF40	MS60	MS63	MS65
2000	20,000	PF63 30.00	PF65 32.00			

KM# 252 10 LEVA
23.33 g., 0.925 Silver 0.6938 oz. ASW, 38.5 mm. **Subject:** Christianity **Obv:** National arms **Rev:** Church patriarch **Edge:** Plain

Date	Mintage	VF20	XF40	MS60	MS63	MS65
2000	—	PF65 35.00				

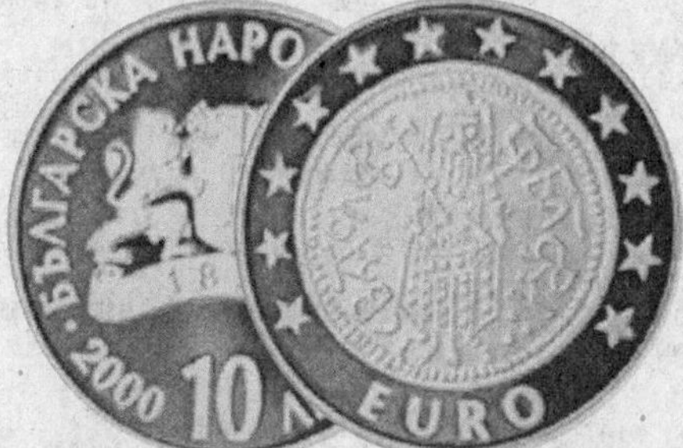

KM# 253 10 LEVA
23.33 g., 0.925 Silver 0.6938 oz. ASW, 38.5 mm. **Subject:** Bulgarian Association with the European Union **Obv:** National arms, date and denomination below **Rev:** Bulgarian coin design of the Middle Ages featuring Czar Theodor Svetoslav **Edge:** Plain

Date	Mintage	VF20	XF40	MS60	MS63	MS65
2000	20,000	PF65 35.00				

KM# 278 20 LEVA
1.55 g., 0.999 Gold 0.0498 oz. AGW, 13.93 mm. **Obv:** National arms **Rev:** Busts of Mother Mary and Jesus at left **Edge:** Reeded

Date	Mintage	VF20	XF40	MS60	MS63	MS65
1999	—	PF65 80.00				

KM# 255 100 LEVA
16.00 g., 0.900 Gold 0.463 oz. AGW, 30 mm. **Subject:** Todor Burmov **Obv:** Bust 3/4 facing, date and denomination below **Rev:** "EURO" and map **Edge:** Plain

Date	Mintage	VF20	XF40	MS60	MS63	MS65
1999	5,000	PF65 750				

KM# 256 20000 LEVA
1.55 g., 0.999 Gold 0.0498 oz. AGW **Obv:** National arms **Rev:** National Bank building, date and denomination below **Edge:** Plain

Date	Mintage	VF20	XF40	MS60	MS63	MS65
1999	30,000	PF65 80.00				

ESSAIS

KM#	Date	Mintage	Identification	Mkt Val
E9	1925(a)	—	2 Leva. Copper-Nickel.	300

PIEDFORT

KM#	Date	Mintage	Identification	Mkt Val
P3	1979	2,000	10 Leva. Silver. KM#104.	85.00

TRIAL STRIKES

KM#	Date	Mintage	Identification	Mkt Val
TS1	1901	—	2 Stotinki. Bronze. Uniface.	—
TS2	1901	—	2 Stotinki. Bronze. Uniface.	—

PATTERNS

Including off metal strikes

KM#	Date	Mintage	Identification	Mkt Val
PnA6	1923H	—	Lev. Aluminum. Similar to KM#35.	—
Pn6	1923H	—	Lev. Aluminum-Bronze.	—
Pn7	1923H	—	2 Leva. Aluminum.	285
PnA8	1923H	—	2 Leva. Aluminum. Similar to KM#36.	—
Pn8	1923H	—	2 Leva. Aluminum-Bronze.	—
Pn9	1928	2	5 Leva.	—
Pn10	1930	2	5 Leva.	—
Pn11	1930	2	10 Leva.	—
Pn12	1950	—	2 Leva. Nickel Alloy. 20.17 mm.	—
Pn13	1950	—	5 Leva. Nickel Alloy. 21.45 mm.	—
Pn14	1952	—	2 Stotinki. Copper-Nickel. 16mm.	—
Pn15	1952	—	20 Stotinki. Copper-Nickel. 21mm.	—
Pn16	1960	—	Lev. Copper-Nickel. 24mm.	—
Pn17	1960	—	Lev. Copper-Nickel. 24mm.	—
Pn18	1960	—	Lev. Aluminum. 25mm.	—
Pn19	1960	—	Lev. Aluminum. 20mm.	—
Pn20	1960	—	Lev. Copper. 20mm.	—
Pn21	1962	—	Lev. Copper-Nickel. 24mm.	—
Pn22	1962	—	Lev. Copper-Nickel. 24mm.	—
Pn23	1964	—	20 Leva. Copper. KM#72, 27mm.	—
Pn24	1966	—	Lev. Copper-Nickel. 24mm.	—
Pn25	1984	1,500	10 Leva. Copper-Nickel. Reeded. PROBA I; KM#146.	50.00
Pn26	1984	250	10 Leva. 0.640. Silver. Plain. PROBA II; KM#146a.	125
Pn27	1984	50	10 Leva. 0.925. Silver. Lettered. SPECIMEN; KM#146a.	245
Pn28	1984	2,000	10 Leva. Copper-Nickel. Reeded. PROBA I; KM#147.	65.00
Pn29	1984	300	10 Leva. 0.640. Silver. Plain. PROBA II; KM#147a.	165
Pn30	1984	50	10 Leva. 0.925. Silver. Lettered. SPECIMEN; KM#147a.	295

MINT SETS

KM#	Date	Mintage	Identification	Issue Price	Mkt Val
MSA1	1962 (7)	—	KM#58-64, either restrikes or leftovers marketed post 2000	—	5.00
MS1	1981 (3)	—	KM#118, 120, 131	—	20.00
MS2	1992 (7)	—	KM#199-205	—	10.00
MS3	1999 (6)	—	KM#237-242, plus medal	—	12.00

PROOF SETS

KM#	Date	Mintage	Identification	Issue Price	Mkt Val
PS1	1912 (2)	—	KM#33-34. Official restrikes of these types were made in the 1960's.	—	12,000
PS2	1962/66 (8)	—	KM#58-64 (1962), 73 (1966) Issued after these types were demonetized in 1995 and 1997.	—	12.50
PS3	1963 (2)	5,000	KM#65-66	—	35.00
PS4	1963/73 (8)	—	KM#65-66, 69-70, 78-79, 80-81 mixed date set, REPUBLIQUE DE BULGARIE	—	155
PS5	1964 (2)	10,000	KM#69-70	—	32.00
PS6	1979 (7)	2,000	KM#84-90	—	22.50
PS7	1980 (7)	2,000	KM#84-90	—	22.50

BURUNDI

The Republic of Burundi, a landlocked country in central Africa, was a kingdom with a feudalistic society, caste system and Mwami (king) for more than 400 years before independence. It has an area of 10,740 sq. mi. (27,830 sq. km.) and a population of 6.3 million. Capital: Bujumbura. Plagued by poor soil, irregular rainfall and a single-crop economy, coffee, Burundi is barely able to feed itself. Coffee and tea are exported.

Although the area was visited by European explorers and missionaries in the latter half of the 19th century, it wasn't until the 1890s that it, together with Rwanda, fell under European domination as part of German East Africa. Following World War I, the territory was mandated to Belgium by the League of Nations and administered with the Belgian Congo. After World War II it became a U.N. Trust Territory. Limited self-government was established by U.N.-supervised elections in 1961. Burundi gained independence as a kingdom under Mwami Mwambutsa IV on July 1, 1962. The republic was established by military coup in 1966.

NOTE: For earlier coinage see Belgian Congo, and Rwanda and Burundi. For previously listed coinage dated 1966, coins of Mwambutsa IV and Ntare V, refer to UNUSUAL WORLD COINS, 6th edition, Krause Publications, 2011.

RULERS
Mwambutsa IV, 1962-1966
Ntare V, 1966

MINT MARKS
PM - Pobjoy Mint
(b) - Privy Marks, Brussels

MONETARY SYSTEM
100 Centimes = 1 Franc

KINGDOM

STANDARD COINAGE

KM# 6 FRANC
Brass, 23 mm. **Obv:** Denomination within circle, circle with monogram below **Rev:** Arms above date **Edge:** Reeded

Date	Mintage	VF20	XF40	MS60	MS63	MS65
1965	10,000,000	—	0.75	1.75	3.00	5.00

KM# 1 5 FRANCS
Copper-Nickel **Ruler:** Mwambutsa IV **Subject:** Burundi Independence **Obv:** Uniformed bust left **Rev:** Arms, date and denomination below

Date	Mintage	VF20	XF40	MS60	MS63	MS65
1962	—	—	—	—	—	—
1962	—	PF65 2,550				

KM# 1a 5 FRANCS
24.11 g., 0.900 Silver 0.6976 oz. ASW **Ruler:** Mwambutsa IV **Subject:** Burundi Independence **Obv:** Uniformed bust left **Rev:** Arms, date and denomination below

Date	Mintage	VF20	XF40	MS60	MS63	MS65
1962 Proof	—	—	—	—	—	—

KM# 2 10 FRANCS
3.20 g., 0.900 Gold 0.0926 oz. AGW **Ruler:** Mwambutsa IV **Subject:** Burundi Independence **Obv:** Uniformed bust left, beaded rim **Rev:** Arms, date and denomination below, beaded rim

Date	Mintage	VF20	XF40	MS60	MS63	MS65
1962	7,500	PF65 165				

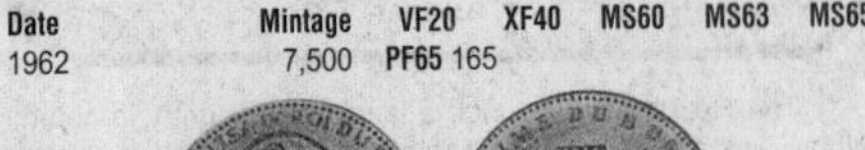

KM# 7 10 FRANCS
3.00 g., 0.900 Gold 0.0868 oz. AGW **Ruler:** Mwambutsa IV **Subject:** 50th Anniversary - Reign of Mwambutsa IV **Obv:** Uniformed bust 3/4 facing divides dates, beaded rim **Rev:** Arms, denomination below, beaded rim

Date	Mintage	VF20	XF40	MS60	MS63	MS65
ND-1965	—	—	—	—	135	155
ND-1965	5,000	PF65 160				

KM# 3 25 FRANCS
8.00 g., 0.900 Gold 0.2315 oz. AGW **Ruler:** Mwambutsa IV **Subject:** Burundi Independence **Obv:** Uniformed bust left, beaded rim **Rev:** Arms, denomination and date below, beaded rim

Date	Mintage	VF20	XF40	MS60	MS63	MS65
1962	15,000	PF65 400				

KM# 8 25 FRANCS
7.50 g., 0.900 Gold 0.217 oz. AGW **Ruler:** Mwambutsa IV **Subject:** 50th Anniversary - Reign of Mwambutsa IV **Obv:** Uniformed bust 3/4 facing divides dates, beaded rim **Rev:** Arms, denomination below, beaded rim

Date	Mintage	VF20	XF40	MS60	MS63	MS65
ND-1965	—	—	—	—	325	375
ND-1965	5,000	PF65 395				

KM# 4 50 FRANCS
16.00 g., 0.900 Gold 0.463 oz. AGW **Ruler:** Mwambutsa IV **Subject:** Burundi Independence **Obv:** Uniformed bust left, beaded rim **Rev:** Arms, denomination and date below, beaded rim

Date	Mintage	VF20	XF40	MS60	MS63	MS65
1962	3,500	PF65 800				

KM# 9 50 FRANCS
15.00 g., 0.900 Gold 0.434 oz. AGW **Ruler:** Mwambutsa IV **Subject:** 50th Anniversary - Reign of Mwambutsa IV **Obv:** Uniformed bust 3/4 facing divides dates, beaded rim **Rev:** Arms, denomination below, beaded rim

Date	Mintage	VF20	XF40	MS60	MS63	MS65
ND-1965	—	—	—	—	650	750
ND-1965	5,000	PF65 770				

KM# 5 100 FRANCS
32.00 g., 0.900 Gold 0.9259 oz. AGW **Ruler:** Mwambutsa IV **Subject:** Burundi Independence **Obv:** Uniformed bust left, beaded rim **Rev:** Arms, denomination and date below, beaded rim

Date	Mintage	VF20	XF40	MS60	MS63	MS65
1962	2,500	PF65 1,600				

KM# 10 100 FRANCS
30.00 g., 0.900 Gold 0.8681 oz. AGW **Ruler:** Mwambutsa IV **Subject:** 50th Anniversary - Reign of Mwambutsa IV **Obv:** Uniformed bust 3/4 facing divides dates, beaded rim **Rev:** Arms, denomination below, beaded rim

Date	Mintage	VF20	XF40	MS60	MS63	MS65
ND-1965	—	—	—	—	1,300	1,500
ND-1965	5,000	PF65 1,550				

REPUBLIC

1966-

KM# 18 FRANC
0.84 g., Aluminum, 19.2 mm. **Obv:** Rising sun above date **Rev:** Denomination

Date	Mintage	VF20	XF40	MS60	MS63	MS65
1970	10,000,000	4.50	7.50	12.00	17.50	20.00

KM# 19 FRANC
0.87 g., Aluminum, 18.91 mm. **Obv:** Denomination **Rev:** Arms above date **Edge:** Reeded

Date	Mintage	VF20	XF40	MS60	MS63	MS65
1976	5,000,000	0.30	0.75	1.25	1.75	2.50
1980	—	0.20	0.65	1.25	1.75	2.50
1990	—	0.15	0.50	1.00	1.50	2.00
1993 PM	—	0.15	0.50	1.00	1.50	2.00

KM# 16 5 FRANCS
Aluminum **Obv:** Three stars at center, date below leaves **Rev:** Denomination within wreath

Date	Mintage	VF20	XF40	MS60	MS63	MS65
1968 (b)	2,000,000	0.25	0.85	1.50	2.00	2.75
1969 (b)	2,000,000	0.25	0.85	1.50	2.00	2.75
1971 (b)	2,000,000	0.25	0.85	1.50	2.00	2.75

KM# 20 5 FRANCS
2.20 g., Aluminum, 25 mm. **Obv:** Arms above date **Rev:** Denomination

Date	Mintage	VF20	XF40	MS60	MS63	MS65
1976	2,000,000	0.25	0.65	1.25	1.75	2.50
1980	—	0.25	0.65	1.25	1.75	2.50

KM# 11 10 FRANCS
3.20 g., 0.900 Gold 0.0926 oz. AGW **Subject:** First Anniversary of Republic

Date	Mintage	VF20	XF40	MS60	MS63	MS65
1967	—	PF65 170				

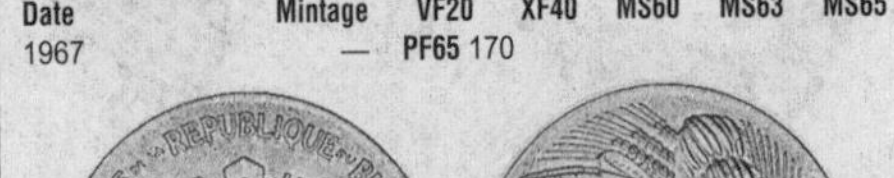

KM# 17 10 FRANCS
7.85 g., Copper-Nickel, 28 mm. **Series:** F.A.O. **Subject:** First Anniversary of Republic **Obv:** Date at center **Rev:** Denomination at center **Edge:** Reeded

Date	Mintage	VF20	XF40	MS60	MS63	MS65
1968	2,000,000	0.65	1.25	2.00	3.00	4.00
1971	2,000,000	0.65	1.25	2.00	3.00	4.00

KM# 12 20 FRANCS
6.40 g., 0.900 Gold 0.1852 oz. AGW **Subject:** First Anniversary of Republic

Date	Mintage	VF20	XF40	MS60	MS63	MS65
ND-1967	—	PF65 340				

KM# 13 25 FRANCS
8.00 g., 0.900 Gold 0.2315 oz. AGW **Subject:** First Anniversary of Republic

Date	Mintage	VF20	XF40	MS60	MS63	MS65
ND-1967	—	PF65 410				

KM# 14 50 FRANCS
16.00 g., 0.900 Gold 0.463 oz. AGW **Subject:** First Anniversary

of Republic **Obv:** Bust, facing **Rev:** Arms above denomination

Date	Mintage	VF20	XF40	MS60	MS63	MS65
ND-1967	—	PF65 800				

KM# 15 100 FRANCS
32.00 g., 0.900 Gold 0.9259 oz. AGW **Subject:** First Anniversary of Republic

Date	Mintage	VF20	XF40	MS60	MS63	MS65
ND-1967	—	PF65 1,600				

PROOF SETS

KM#	Date	Mintage	Identification	Issue Price	Mkt Val
PS1	1962 (4)	2,500	KM2-5	—	2,975
PS2	1965 (4)	5,000	KM7-10	—	2,875
PS3	1967 (5)	—	KM11-15	—	3,325

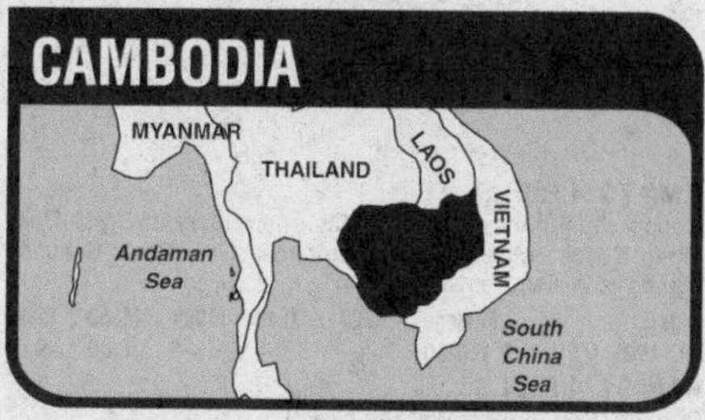

The State of Cambodia, formerly Democratic Kampuchea and the Khmer Republic, a land of paddy fields and forest-clad hills located on the Indo-Chinese peninsula, fronting on the Gulf of Thailand, has an area of 70,238 sq. mi. (181,040 sq. km.) and a population of *11.21 million. Capital: Phnom Penh. Agriculture is the basis of the economy, with rice the chief crop. Native industries include cattle breeding, weaving and rice milling. Rubber, cattle, corn, and timber are exported.

The region was the nucleus of the Khmer empire which flourished from the 5th to the 12th century and attained an excellence in art and architecture still evident in the magnificent ruins at Angkor. The Khmer empire once ruled over much of Southeast Asia, but began to decline in the 13th century as the Thai and Vietnamese invaded the region and attached its territories. At the request of the Cambodian king, a French protectorate attached to Cochin-China was established over the country in 1863, saving it from dissolution, and in 1885, Cambodia was included in the French Union of Indo-China.

France established a constitutional monarchy for Cambodia within the French Union in 1949. The 1954 Geneva Convention resulted in full independence for the Kingdom of Cambodia. King Sihanouk abdicated to his father and won the office of Prime Minister.

Prince Sihanouk was toppled by a bloodless coup led by Lon Nol in March of 1970. Sihanouk moved to Peking to head a government-in-exile. On Oct. 9, 1970, Cambodia became the Khmer Republic, and Lon Nol its President. The government of Lon Nol was in turn toppled, April 17, 1975, by the Khmer Rouge insurgents who took control of the government and renamed the country Democratic Kampuchea.

The Khmer Rouge completely eliminated the economy and created a state without money, exchange or barter while exterminating about 2 million Cambodians. These atrocities were finally halted at the beginning of 1979 when the Vietnamese regulars and Cambodian rebels launched an offensive that drove the Khmer Rouge out of Phnom Penh and the country acquired another new title - The Peoples Republic of Kampuchea.

In 1993 Prince Norodom Sihanouk returned to Kampuchea to lead the Supreme National Council.

RULERS
Kings of Cambodia
Norodom I, 1859-1904
Sisowath, 1904-1927
Sisowath Monivong, 1927-1941
Norodom Sihanouk, 1941-1955
Norodom Suramarit, 1955-1960
Heng Samrin, 1979-1985
Hun Sen, 1985-1991
Norodom Sihanouk, 1991-1993
Chairman, Supreme National Council
King, 1993-2012

MINT MARKS
(a) - Paris, privy marks only
(k) - Key, Havana, Cuba

MONETARY SYSTEM
(Commencing 1860)
100 Centimes = 1 Franc

KINGDOM
TICAL COINAGE

KM# 26 2 PE (1/2 Fuang)
Billon, 13-15 mm. **Obv:** Garuda bird facing left within denticles **Note:** Weight varies: 1.00-2.00 grams. Size varies.

Date	Mintage	VG8	F12	VF20	XF40	MS60
ND	—	3.00	6.00	10.00	15.00	—

Note: Varieties exist in style of denticles

KM# 30 2 PE (1/2 Fuang)
Brass or Copper **Obv:** Garuda bird facing left but without border around bird **Rev:** 3-line legend

Date	Mintage	VG8	F12	VF20	XF40	MS60
ND(1880)	—	40.00	75.00	120	175	—

KM# 30a 2 PE (1/2 Fuang)
1.46 g., Billon

Date	Mintage	VG8	F12	VF20	XF40	MS60
ND(1880)	—	—	50.00	70.00	90.00	—

Note: The precise status is undetermined. It is probably a token issue

TOKEN COINAGE

KM# Tn1 CENTIME
Brass, 26 mm. **Issuer:** Panom Penh Royal Palace **Obv:** Hole in center square **Obv. Legend:** SOMDACH PREA NÒRÒDOM... **Rev:** Hole in center square, denomination below

Date	Mintage	F12	VF20	XF40	MS60	MS63
ND(1875-1904)	—	—	175	220	325	550

KM# Tn2 10 CENTIMES
Brass, 26 mm. **Issuer:** Panom Penh Royal Palace **Obv. Legend:** SOMDACH PREA NÒRÒDOM...

Date	Mintage	F12	VF20	XF40	MS60	MS63
ND(1875-1904)	—	—	250	300	425	600

KM# Tn3 20 CENTIMES
Brass, 26 mm. **Issuer:** Panom Penh Royal Palace **Obv:** Monogram within circle **Obv. Legend:** SOMDACH PREA NÒRÒDOM... **Rev:** Denomination within circle

Date	Mintage	F12	VF20	XF40	MS60	MS63
ND(1875-1904)	—	—	250	300	425	600

KM# Tn4 25 CENTIMES
Brass, 26 mm. **Issuer:** Panom Penh Royal Palace **Obv:** Monogram within circle **Obv. Legend:** SOMDACH PREA NÒRÒDOM... **Rev:** Denomination

Date	Mintage	F12	VF20	XF40	MS60	MS63
ND(1875-1904)	—	—	275	350	475	700

INDEPENDENT KINGDOM
DECIMAL COINAGE

KM# 51 10 CENTIMES
Aluminum **Obv:** Bird statue left **Rev:** Denomination within wreath

Date	Mintage	VF20	XF40	MS60	MS63	MS65
1953 (a)	4,000,000	0.45	0.85	2.00	4.50	6.00

KM# 52 20 CENTIMES
Aluminum **Obv:** Two ceremonial bowls **Rev:** Denomination within wreath

Date	Mintage	VF20	XF40	MS60	MS63	MS65
1953 (a)	3,000,000	0.65	1.50	3.00	4.00	5.50

KM# 53 50 CENTIMES
Aluminum **Obv:** Royal emblem **Rev:** Denomination within wreath

Date	Mintage	VF20	XF40	MS60	MS63	MS65
1953 (a)	4,200,000	0.85	2.00	4.00	5.00	7.00

KM# 54 10 SEN
1.30 g., Aluminum, 23 mm. **Obv:** Bird statue left **Rev:** Denomination within wreath

Date	Mintage	VF20	XF40	MS60	MS63	MS65
1959 (a)	1,000,000	0.20	0.35	1.00	1.50	2.00

KM# 55 20 SEN
Aluminum, 27 mm. **Obv:** Two ceremonial bowls **Rev:** Denomination within wreath

Date	Mintage	VF20	XF40	MS60	MS63	MS65
1959 (a)	1,004,000	0.25	0.60	1.00	1.25	1.50

KM# 56 50 SEN
Aluminum **Obv:** Royal emblem **Rev:** Denomination within wreath

Date	Mintage	VF20	XF40	MS60	MS63	MS65
1959 (a)	3,399,000	0.35	0.75	1.50	2.00	2.50

KHMER REPUBLIC
1970 - 1975

KM# 59 RIEL
2.85 g., Copper-Nickel, 19.42 mm. **Series:** F.A.O. **Obv:** Temple of Angkor Wat **Rev:** Grain bouquet, denomination **Edge:** Reeded

Date	Mintage	VF20	XF40	MS60	MS63	MS65
1970	5,000,000	—	3.50	6.00	10.00	15.00

Note: According to the Royal Mint of Great Britain, this coin was minted at the Llantrissant Branch Mint in 1972 but dated 1969. According to the FAO, the coin was to have been dated 1971, but was "not minted" due to the fall of the Cambodian government in 1970. However, this coin was released in limited numbers in 1983. The photograph of the coin, supplied by the FAO, is dated 1970. This type is currently available from many sources in the numismatic market

KM# 60 5000 RIELS
19.01 g., 0.925 Silver 0.5653 oz. ASW **Obv:** Temple of Angkor Wat **Rev:** Royal emblem above denomination

Date	Mintage	VF20	XF40	MS60	MS63	MS65
1974	500	—	—	—	50.00	70.00
1974	800	PF63 50.00	PF65 70.00			

KM# 61 5000 RIELS
19.01 g., 0.925 Silver 0.5653 oz. ASW **Obv:** Cambodian dancers **Rev:** Similar to KM#60, (royal emblem above denomination)

Date	Mintage	VF20	XF40	MS60	MS63	MS65
1974	500	—	—	—	70.00	90.00
1974	800	PF63 70.00	PF65 90.00			

KM# 62 10000 RIELS
38.03 g., 0.925 Silver 1.131 oz. ASW **Obv:** Bust of President Lon Nol left **Rev:** Royal emblem above denomination

Date	Mintage	VF20	XF40	MS60	MS63	MS65
1974	500	—	—	—	90.00	120
1974	800	PF63 90.00	PF65 120			

KM# 63 10000 RIELS
38.03 g., 0.925 Silver 1.131 oz. ASW **Obv:** Celestial dancer **Rev:** Royal emblem above denomination

Date	Mintage	VF20	XF40	MS60	MS63	MS65
1974	500	—	—	—	110	150
1974	800	PF63 110	PF65 150			

KM# 64 50000 RIELS
6.71 g., 0.900 Gold 0.1942 oz. AGW **Obv:** Cambodian dancers **Rev:** Royal emblem above denomination

Date	Mintage	VF20	XF40	MS60	MS63	MS65
1974	3,250	—	—	—	345	355
1974	2,300	PF65 370				

KM# 65 50000 RIELS
6.71 g., 0.900 Gold 0.1942 oz. AGW **Obv:** Celestial dancer **Rev:** Royal emblem above denomination

Date	Mintage	VF20	XF40	MS60	MS63	MS65
1974	300	PF65 435				
1974	450	—	—	—	360	385

KM# 66 100000 RIELS
13.42 g., 0.900 Gold 0.3883 oz. AGW **Obv:** Bust of President Lon Nol left **Rev:** Royal emblem above denomination

Date	Mintage	VF20	XF40	MS60	MS63	MS65
1974	100	PF65 825				
1974	250	—	—	—	675	700

PEOPLE'S REPUBLIC OF KAMPUCHEA

1979 - 1990

KM# 69 5 SEN
2.49 g., Aluminum, 20.39 mm. **Obv:** Royal emblem **Rev:** Denomination, date at bottom **Edge:** Plain

Date	Mintage	VF20	XF40	MS60	MS63	MS65
1979	—	0.60	1.25	2.00	3.00	5.00

KM# 71 4 RIELS
Copper-Nickel **Subject:** Cambodian Transportation **Obv:** Royal emblem above denomination **Rev:** Old sailing ship, date at right

Date	Mintage	VF20	XF40	MS60	MS63	MS65
1988	1,500	—	—	—	7.00	10.00

KM# 75 4 RIELS
Copper, 38.5 mm. **Subject:** 700th Anniversary of Swiss Unity **Obv:** Royal emblem above denomination **Rev:** Standing figures of William Tell and his son

Date	Mintage	VF20	XF40	MS60	MS63	MS65
ND-1988	15,000	—	—	—	6.00	9.00

KM# 91 4 RIELS
Copper **Rev:** Angkor Wat Temples

Date	Mintage	VF20	XF40	MS60	MS63	MS65
ND-1988	—	—	—	—	7.00	10.00

KM# 74 4 RIELS
Copper-Nickel **Subject:** World Championship Soccer - Italy **Obv:** Royal emblem above denomination **Rev:** Soccer ball with country names and dates, Italy at center

Date	Mintage	VF20	XF40	MS60	MS63	MS65
1989	2,000	—	—	—	4.00	6.00

KM# 90 4 RIELS
Copper **Obv:** Royal emblem above denomination **Rev:** Angkor Wat Temples

Date	Mintage	VF20	XF40	MS60	MS63	MS65
1989	—	—	—	—	6.00	9.00

KM# 70 20 RIELS
12.06 g., 0.999 Silver 0.3873 oz. ASW **Subject:** Cambodian Transportation **Obv:** Royal emblem above denomination **Rev:** Old sailing ship

Date	Mintage	VF20	XF40	MS60	MS63	MS65
1988	3,000	—	—	—	25.00	28.00

KM# 72 20 RIELS
12.06 g., 0.999 Silver 0.3873 oz. ASW **Subject:** World Championship Soccer - Mexico **Obv:** Royal emblem above denomination **Rev:** Soccer goalie, country name and date below

Date	Mintage	VF20	XF40	MS60	MS63	MS65
1988	5,000	—	—	—	25.00	28.00

KM# 73 20 RIELS
16.00 g., 0.999 Silver 0.5139 oz. ASW **Subject:** 700th Anniversary of Swiss Unity - 1991 **Obv:** Royal emblem above denomination **Rev:** Standing figures of man and boy

Date	Mintage	VF20	XF40	MS60	MS63	MS65
ND-1988	2,000	PF63 30.00	PF65 35.00			

KM# 78 20 RIELS
12.00 g., 0.999 Silver 0.3854 oz. ASW **Subject:** European Soccer Championship - Germany **Obv:** Royal emblem above denomination **Rev:** Soccer players, date below

Date	Mintage	VF20	XF40	MS60	MS63	MS65
1988	5,000	—	—	—	25.00	28.00

KM# 76 20 RIELS
16.00 g., 0.999 Silver 0.5139 oz. ASW **Obv:** Royal emblem above denomination **Rev:** Angkor Wat Temples

Date	Mintage	VF20	XF40	MS60	MS63	MS65
1989	2,000	PF63 35.00	PF65 40.00			

KM# 79 20 RIELS
16.00 g., 0.999 Silver 0.5139 oz. ASW **Subject:** World Championship Soccer - Italy **Obv:** Royal emblem above denomination **Rev:** Soccer ball with country names and dates, Italy at center

Date	Mintage	VF20	XF40	MS60	MS63	MS65
1989	10,000	PF65 25.00				

KM# 80 20 RIELS
16.00 g., 0.999 Silver 0.5139 oz. ASW **Subject:** Summer Olympics **Obv:** Royal emblem above denomination **Rev:** Fencers, date at right

Date	Mintage	VF20	XF40	MS60	MS63	MS65
1989	10,000	PF65 25.00				

KM# 81 20 RIELS
16.00 g., 0.999 Silver 0.5139 oz. ASW **Subject:** Winter Olympics **Obv:** Royal emblem above denomination **Rev:** Skier, date at lower left

Date	Mintage	VF20	XF40	MS60	MS63	MS65
1989	5,000	PF65 30.00				

KM# 77 40 RIELS
3.15 g., 0.999 Gold 0.1012 oz. AGW **Obv:** Royal emblem above denomination **Rev:** Angkor Wat Temples

Date	Mintage	VF20	XF40	MS60	MS63	MS65
1989	500	—	—	—	175	195

KM# 82 40 RIELS
3.15 g., 0.999 Gold 0.1012 oz. AGW **Obv:** Royal emblem above denomination **Rev:** Folklore dance, date lower left

Date	Mintage	VF20	XF40	MS60	MS63	MS65
1990	500	PF65 200				

STATE OF CAMBODIA

1990 - 1993

KM# 83 4 RIELS
Nickel Plated Steel **Subject:** Barcelona 1992 - 25th Summer Olympic Games **Obv:** National flag above denomination **Rev:** Tennis player, date below

Date	Mintage	VF20	XF40	MS60	MS63	MS65
1991	5,000	—	—	—	10.00	12.00

KM# 86 4 RIELS
Copper-Nickel **Series:** Prehistoric animals, date at left **Obv:** National flag above denomination **Rev:** Cryptocleidus

Date	Mintage	VF20	XF40	MS60	MS63	MS65
1993	—	—	—	—	17.00	23.00

KM# 89 4 RIELS
Copper-Nickel **Series:** Prehistoric Animals **Obv:** National flag above denomination **Rev:** Anatosaurus, date at right

Date	Mintage	VF20	XF40	MS60	MS63	MS65
1994	—	—	—	—	17.00	23.00

KM# 84 20 RIELS
11.96 g., 0.999 Silver 0.3841 oz. ASW **Subject:** World Cup Soccer - 1994 **Obv:** National flag above denomination **Rev:** Player kicking ball, date at left

Date	Mintage	VF20	XF40	MS60	MS63	MS65
1991	30,000	—	—	—	20.00	25.00

KM# 88 20 RIELS
11.96 g., 0.999 Silver 0.3841 oz. ASW **Subject:** World Cup Soccer - 1994 **Obv:** National flag above denomination **Rev:** 2 players kicking ball, date below

Date	Mintage	VF20	XF40	MS60	MS63	MS65
1992	—	PF65 35.00				

KM# 85 20 RIELS
19.95 g., 0.999 Silver 0.6408 oz. ASW **Subject:** Protection

of Nature **Obv:** National flag above denomination **Rev:** Asian elephants, date at right

Date	Mintage	VF20	XF40	MS60	MS63	MS65
1993	—	PF65 40.00				

KM# 87 20 RIELS
16.06 g., 0.999 Silver 0.5158 oz. ASW **Series:** Prehistoric Animals **Obv:** National flag above denomination **Rev:** Indricotherium, date lower right

Date	Mintage	VF20	XF40	MS60	MS63	MS65
1993	—	PF65 32.00				

KM# 96 20 RIELS
16.10 g., 0.999 Silver 0.5171 oz. ASW **Series:** Prehistoric Animals **Obv:** National flag above denomination **Rev:** Nothosaurus at water's edge, date lower right **Edge:** Plain

Date	Mintage	VF20	XF40	MS60	MS63	MS65
1994	—	PF65 37.00				

KM# 97 20 RIELS
16.10 g., 0.999 Silver 0.5171 oz. ASW, 37.9 mm. **Subject:** Prehistoric Animals **Obv:** National flag above denomination **Rev:** Monoclonius, date lower left **Edge:** Plain

Date	Mintage	VF20	XF40	MS60	MS63	MS65
1994	—	PF65 40.00				

KINGDOM

1993 -

KM# 92 50 RIELS
1.60 g., Steel, 15.9 mm. **Obv:** Single towered building **Rev:** Denomination within wreath **Edge:** Plain

Date	Mintage	VF20	XF40	MS60	MS63	MS65
BE2538-1994	—	—	—	—	0.25	0.45

KM# 93 100 RIELS
2.00 g., Steel, 17.9 mm. **Obv:** Three-towered building **Rev:** Denomination within wreath

Date	Mintage	VF20	XF40	MS60	MS63	MS65
BE2538-1994	—	—	—	—	0.50	0.85

KM# 94 200 RIELS
2.40 g., Steel, 19.9 mm. **Obv:** 2 Ceremonial bowls **Rev:** Denomination within wreath

Date	Mintage	VF20	XF40	MS60	MS63	MS65
BE2538-1994	—	—	—	—	1.00	1.50

KM# 95 500 RIELS
6.50 g., Bi-Metallic Steel center in Brass ring, 25.8 mm. **Obv:** Royal emblem **Rev:** Denomination within wreath **Edge:** Plain and reeded sections

Date	Mintage	VF20	XF40	MS60	MS63	MS65
BE2538-1994	—	—	—	—	2.00	3.50

ESSAIS

KM#	Date	Mintage	Identification	Mkt Val
E9	1953	1,200	10 Centimes.	45.00
E10	1953	1,200	20 Centimes.	45.00
E11	1953	1,200	50 Centimes.	50.00

PATTERNS

Including off metal strikes

KM#	Date	Mintage	Identification	Mkt Val
Pn15	1902	—	4 Francs. Silver. Palace at Phnom Penh.	375
Pn16	1970	—	Riel. Copper-Nickel. KM59.	—

PIEDFORT WITH ESSAI

Double thickness

KM#	Date	Mintage	Identification	Mkt Val
PE9	1953	104	10 Centimes.	250
PE10	1953	104	20 Centimes.	250
PE11	1953	104	50 Centimes.	300

PIEDFORT

KM#	Date	Mintage	Identification	Mkt Val
P12	1989	110	20 Riels. 0.999. Silver. KM80.	125
P13	1989	110	20 Riels. 0.999. Silver. KM76.	125

MINT SETS

KM#	Date	Mintage	Identification	Issue Price	Mkt Val
MS1	1953 (3)	—	KM51-53	—	17.50
MS2	1974 (7)	250	KM60-66	—	1,850
MS3	1974 (4)	500	KM60-63	—	500

PROOF SETS

KM#	Date	Mintage	Identification	Issue Price	Mkt Val
PS1	1974 (7)	100	KM60-66	—	2,100
PS2	1974 (4)	800	KM60-63	—	500

CAMEROON

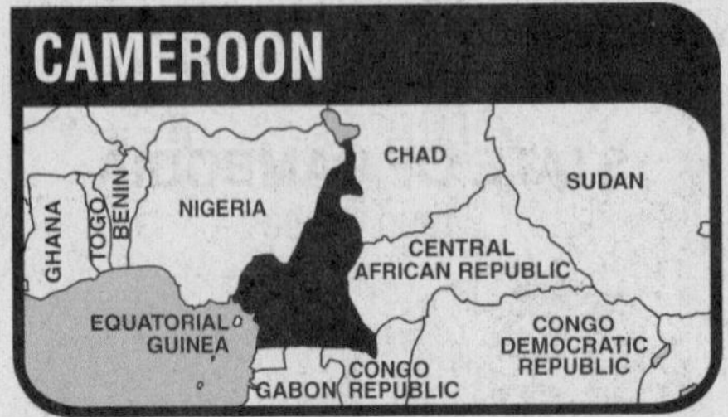

The Republic of Cameroon, located in west-central Africa on the Gulf of Guinea, has an area of 183,569 sq. mi. (475,445 sq. km.) and a population of *15.13 million. Capital: Yaounde. About 90 percent of the labor force is employed on the land; cash crops account for 80 percent of the country's export revenue. Cocoa, coffee, aluminum, cotton, rubber, and timber are exported.

European contact with what is now the United Republic of Cameroon began in the 16th century with the voyage of Portuguese navigator Fernando Po. The following three centuries saw continuous activity by Spanish, Dutch, and British traders and missionaries. The land was spared colonial rule until 1884, when treaties with tribal chiefs brought German domination. In 1919, the League of Nations divided the Cameroons between Great Britain and France, with the larger eastern area going to France. The French and British mandates were converted into United Nations trusteeships in 1946. French Cameroon became the independent Cameroon Republic on Jan. 1, 1960. The federation of East (French) and West (British) Cameroon was established in 1961 when the southern part of British Cameroon voted for reunification with the Cameroon Republic, and the northern part for union with Nigeria Cameroon joined the Commonwealth of Nations in November 1995.

Coins of French Equatorial Africa and of the monetary unions identified as the Equatorial African States and Central African States are also current in Cameroon.

MINT MARKS
(a) - Paris, privy marks only
SA - Pretoria, 1943

MONETARY SYSTEM
100 Centimes = 1 Franc

FRENCH MANDATE

STANDARD COINAGE

KM# 1 50 CENTIMES
2.53 g., Aluminum-Bronze, 17.5 mm. **Obv:** Laureate head left, date below **Rev:** Spray of branches below denomination

Date	Mintage	F12	VF20	XF40	MS60	MS63
1924 (a)	4,000,000	1.50	3.50	45.00	100	250
1925 (a)	2,500,000	2.00	5.00	50.00	110	275
1926 (a)	7,800,000	1.00	2.00	30.00	85.00	200

KM# 4 50 CENTIMES
2.76 g., Bronze, 20.2 mm. **Obv:** Rooster left, monogramed shield top right **Rev:** Cross of Lorraine divides denomination below, date at bottom

Date	Mintage	F12	VF20	XF40	MS60	MS63
1943 SA	4,000,000	2.00	3.50	12.00	30.00	60.00

KM# 6 50 CENTIMES
Bronze **Obv:** Rooster left, monogramed shield at top right, LIBRE added to legend **Rev:** Cross of Lorraine divides denomination below, date at bottom

Date	Mintage	F12	VF20	XF40	MS60	MS63
1943 SA	4,000,000	2.50	5.50	12.00	25.00	40.00

KM# 2 FRANC
5.10 g., Aluminum-Bronze, 23 mm. **Obv:** Laureate head left, date below **Rev:** Denomination above three branched spray **Edge:** Reeded

Date	Mintage	F12	VF20	XF40	MS60	MS63
1924 (a)	3,000,000	2.00	4.00	45.00	100	260
1925 (a)	1,722,000	3.00	6.00	60.00	125	285
1926 (a)	12,928,000	1.00	2.00	25.00	60.00	150

KM# 5 FRANC
Bronze, 25 mm. **Obv:** Rooster left, monogrammed shield top right **Rev:** Cross of Lorraine divides denomination below, date at bottom

Date	Mintage	F12	VF20	XF40	MS60	MS63
1943 SA	3,000,000	2.50	4.50	17.50	35.00	50.00

KM# 7 FRANC
Bronze, 25 mm. **Obv:** Rooster left, monogrammed shield at top right, LIBRE added to legend **Rev:** Cross of Lorraine divides denomination below, date at bottom

Date	Mintage	F12	VF20	XF40	MS60	MS63
1943 SA	3,000,000	3.50	7.50	20.00	40.00	50.00

KM# 8 FRANC
Aluminum, 23 mm. **Obv:** Winged bust left, date below **Rev:** Gazelle (gazella Leptoceros), antlers divide denomination

Date	Mintage	F12	VF20	XF40	MS60	MS63
1948 (a)	8,000,000	0.15	0.35	0.85	1.50	2.00

KM# 3 2 FRANCS
9.80 g., Aluminum-Bronze, 27 mm. **Obv:** Laureate head left, date below **Rev:** Denomination above three branch spray **Edge:** Reeded

Date	Mintage	F12	VF20	XF40	MS60	MS63
1924 (a)	500,000	5.00	15.00	100	185	300
1925 (a)	100,000	8.00	25.00	160	300	500

KM# 9 2 FRANCS
2.21 g., Aluminum, 27 mm. **Obv:** Winged bust left, date bilow **Rev:** Gazelle (gazella leptoceros), antlers divide denomination **Edge:** reeded

Date	Mintage	F12	VF20	XF40	MS60	MS63
1948 (a)	5,000,000	0.65	1.25	2.00	3.50	6.00

FRENCH EQUATORIAL AFRICA - CAMEROON

KM# 10 5 FRANCS
Aluminum-Bronze **Obv:** Three giant eland **Rev:** Denomination

Date	Mintage	F12	VF20	XF40	MS60	MS63
1958 (a)	30,000,000	0.25	0.50	1.00	3.00	5.00

KM# 11 10 FRANCS
Aluminum-Bronze **Obv:** Three giant eland left, date below **Rev:** Denomination within wreath

Date	Mintage	F12	VF20	XF40	MS60	MS63
1958 (a)	25,000,000	0.25	0.50	1.50	3.00	5.00

KM# 12 25 FRANCS
7.56 g., Aluminum-Bronze, 27.2 mm. **Obv:** Three giant eland left, date below **Rev:** Denomination within wreath

Date	Mintage	F12	VF20	XF40	MS60	MS63
1958 (a)	12,000,000	0.50	1.00	2.00	3.50	6.00

REPUBLIC

KM# 13 50 FRANCS
11.90 g., Copper-Nickel, 30 mm. **Subject:** Independence Commemorative **Obv:** Three giant eland left, date above **Rev:** Denomination within wreath **Edge:** Reeded

Date	Mintage	VF20	XF40	MS60	MS63	MS65
1960 (a)	9,000,000	3.50	5.50	7.50	11.50	16.00

KM# 14 100 FRANCS
12.00 g., Nickel, 25.5 mm. **Obv:** Three giant eland left **Rev:** Denomination, date above **Edge:** Reeded **Note:** KM#14 was issued double thick and should not be considered a piefort.

Date	Mintage	VF20	XF40	MS60	MS63	MS65
1966 (a)	4,000,000	2.00	4.50	10.00	12.50	—
1967 (a)	4,000,000	2.00	4.50	10.00	12.50	—
1968 (a)	5,000,000	2.00	4.50	10.00	12.50	—

KM# 15 100 FRANCS
7.00 g., Nickel, 25.5 mm. **Obv:** Three giant eland left **Rev:** Denomination within circle, date below **Edge:** Reeded **Note:** Refer also to Equatorial African States and Central African States.

Date	Mintage	VF20	XF40	MS60	MS63	MS65
1971 (a)	9,000,000	2.00	3.00	7.00	12.50	—
1972 (a)	3,000,000	2.00	3.00	7.00	12.50	—

KM# 16 100 FRANCS
7.00 g., Nickel, 25.5 mm. **Obv:** Three giant eland left **Rev:** Denomination within circle, date below **Edge:** Reeded **Note:** Mule

Date	Mintage	VF20	XF40	MS60	MS63	MS65
1972 (a)	4,000,000	12.50	22.50	45.00	80.00	—

KM# 17 100 FRANCS
7.00 g., Nickel, 25.5 mm. **Obv:** Three giant eland left **Rev:** Denomination above date, within circle **Edge:** Reeded

Date	Mintage	VF20	XF40	MS60	MS63	MS65
1975 (a)	—	2.00	3.00	5.50	7.00	—
1980 (a)	—	2.00	3.00	5.50	7.00	—
1982 (a)	—	1.50	2.50	4.50	6.00	—
1983 (a)	—	1.50	2.50	4.50	6.00	—
1984 (a)	—	1.50	2.50	4.50	6.00	—
1986 (a)	—	1.50	2.50	4.50	6.00	—

KM# 23 500 FRANCS
10.89 g., Copper-Nickel, 30.04 mm. **Obv:** Plants divide denomination and date **Rev:** Head 3/4 left

Date	Mintage	VF20	XF40	MS60	MS63	MS65
1985 (a)	—	2.00	3.50	7.50	10.00	18.00
1986 (a)	—	2.00	3.50	7.50	10.00	18.00
1988	—	2.00	3.50	7.50	10.00	18.00

KM# 18 1000 FRANCS
3.50 g., 0.900 Gold 0.1013 oz. AGW **Subject:** 10th Anniversary of Independence **Obv:** Head of President El Hajj Ahmadou Ahidjo left **Rev:** Design at center, denomination below, arms above

Date	Mintage	VF20	XF40	MS60	MS63	MS65
1970	4,000	PF65 185				

KM# 19 3000 FRANCS
10.50 g., 0.900 Gold 0.3038 oz. AGW **Subject:** 10th Anniversary of Independence **Obv:** Head of President El Hajj Ahmadou Ahidjo left **Rev:** Design at center, denomination below, arms above

Date	Mintage	VF20	XF40	MS60	MS63	MS65
1970	4,000	PF65 550				

Note: With or without cornucopia mint mark on reverse

KM# 20 5000 FRANCS
17.50 g., 0.900 Gold 0.5064 oz. AGW **Subject:** 10th Anniversary of Independence **Obv:** Head of President El Hajj Ahmadou Ahidjo left **Rev:** Head, left, within center circle, denomination below, arms above

Date	Mintage	VF20	XF40	MS60	MS63	MS65
1970	4,000	PF65 875				

KM# 21 10000 FRANCS
35.00 g., 0.900 Gold 1.0127 oz. AGW **Subject:** 10th Anniversary of Independence **Obv:** President El Hajj Ahmadou Ahidjo left **Rev:** Elands facing center, denomination below, arms above

Date	Mintage	VF20	XF40	MS60	MS63	MS65
1970	4,000	PF65 2,000				

KM# 22 20000 FRANCS
70.00 g., 0.900 Gold 2.0255 oz. AGW **Subject:** 10th Anniversary of Independence **Obv:** Head of President El Hajj Ahmadou Ahidjo left **Rev:** Arms, denomination below

Date	Mintage	VF20	XF40	MS60	MS63	MS65
1970	4,000	PF65 4,000				

TOKEN COINAGE

KM# Tn3 50 CENTIMES
Brass **Issuer:** Societe Nationale **Obv:** SOCIETE NATIONALE DU CAMEROUN in legend **Rev:** 50c

Date	Mintage	VG8	F12	VF20	XF40	MS60
ND(1962)	—	40.00	100	175	350	650

KM# Tn4 FRANC
Brass **Rev:** 50c **Note:** Similar to KM#TN3.

Date	Mintage	VG8	F12	VF20	XF40	MS60
ND(1962)	—	50.00	120	220	400	725

ESSAIS

Standard metals unless otherwise noted

KM#	Date	Mintage	Identification	Mkt Val
E1	1924(a)	—	50 Centimes. Aluminum-Bronze. KM1.	200
E2	1924(a)	—	Franc. Aluminum-Bronze. KM2.	240
E3	1924(a)	—	2 Francs. Aluminum-Bronze. Laureate head left, date below. Denomination above three branch spray. KM3.	350
E4	1943	—	1/2 Franc.	725
E5	1948(a)	2,000	Franc. Copper-Nickel. KM8.	30.00
E6	1948(a)	2,000	2 Francs. Copper-Nickel. KM9.	45.00
E7	1958(a)	2,030	5 Francs. Aluminum-Bronze. KM24.	30.00
E8	1958(a)	2,030	10 Francs. Aluminum-Bronze. KM25.	20.00
E9	1958(a)	2,030	25 Francs. Aluminum-Bronze. KM26.	25.00
E10	1960(a)	1,500	50 Francs. Copper-Nickel. Three giant eland left, date above. Denomination within wreath. KM13.	40.00
E11	1966(a)	1,200	100 Francs. Nickel. KM14.	45.00
E12	1970(a)	—	1000 Francs. Bronze. KM18.	125
E13	1971(a)	1,550	100 Francs. Nickel. KM15.	30.00
E14	1971	6	100 Francs. Gold. KM15.	2,625
E15	1972	1,550	100 Francs. Nickel. KM16.	40.00
E16	1975	1,700	100 Francs. Nickel. KM17.	30.00
E17	1985	—	500 Francs. Copper-Nickel. Plants divide denomination and date. KM23.	40.00

PIEDFORT WITH ESSAI

Double thickness -
Standard metals unless otherwise noted

KM#	Date	Mintage	Identification	Mkt Val
PE1	1948(a)	104	Franc. Aluminum. KM8.	250
PE2	1948(a)	104	2 Francs. Aluminum. KM9.	250
PE3	1948(a)	—	2 Francs. Aluminum. KM9, double piefort.	550
PE4	1948(a)	—	2 Francs. Copper-Nickel. KM9.	250

PROOF SETS

KM#	Date	Mintage	Identification	Issue Price	Mkt Val
PS1	1970 (5)	4,000	KM18-22	—	7,650

CANADA

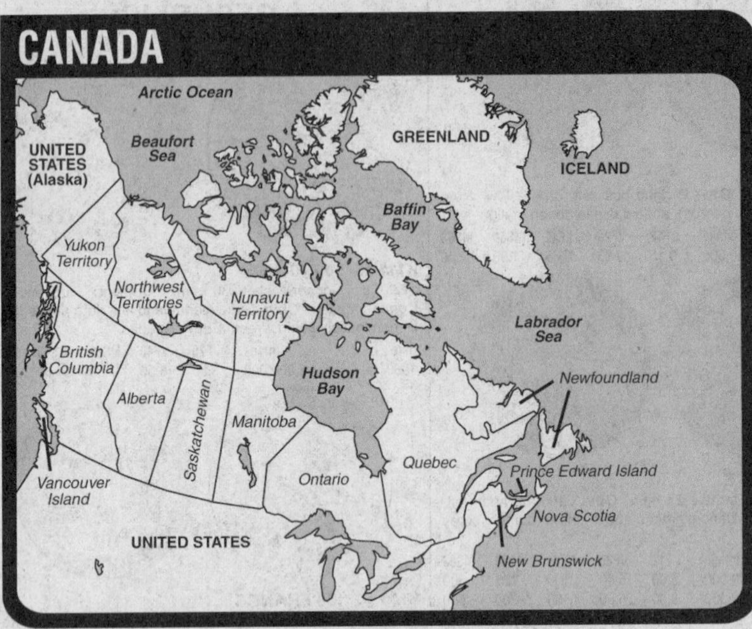

Canada is located to the north of the United States, and spans the full breadth of the northern portion of North America from Atlantic to Pacific oceans, except for the State of Alaska. It has a total area of 3,850,000 sq. mi. (9,971,550 sq. km.) and a population of 30.29 million. Capital: Ottawa.

Jacques Cartier, a French explorer, took possession of Canada for France in 1534, and for more than a century the history of Canada was that of a French colony. Samuel de Champlain helped to establish the first permanent colony in North America, in 1604 at Port Royal, Acadia – now Annapolis Royal, Nova Scotia. Four years later he founded the settlement in Quebec.

The British settled along the coast to the south while the French, motivated by a grand design, pushed into the interior. France's plan for a great American empire was to occupy the Mississippi heartland of the country, and from there to press in upon the narrow strip of English coastal settlements from the west. Inevitably, armed conflict erupted between the French and the British; consequently, Britain acquired Hudson Bay, Newfoundland and Nova Scotia from the French in 1713. British control of the rest of New France was secured in 1763, largely because of James Wolfe's great victory over Montcalm near Quebec in 1759.

During the American Revolution, Canada became a refuge for great numbers of American Royalists, most of whom settled in Ontario, thereby creating an English majority west of the Ottawa River. The ethnic imbalance contravened the effectiveness of the prevailing French type of government, and in 1791 the Constitutional act was passed by the British parliament, dividing Canada at the Ottawa River into two parts, each with its own government: Upper Canada, chiefly English and consisting of the southern section of what is now Ontario; and Lower Canada, chiefly French and consisting principally of the southern section of Quebec. Subsequent revolt by dissidents in both sections caused the British government to pass the Union Act, July 23, 1840, which united Lower and Upper Canada (as Canada East and Canada West) to form the Province of Canada, with one council and one assembly in which the two sections had equal numbers.

The union of the two provinces did not encourage political stability; the equal strength of the French and British made the task of government all but impossible. A further change was made with the passage of the British North American Act, which took effect on July 1, 1867, and established Canada as the first federal union in the British Empire. Four provinces entered the union at first: Upper Canada as Ontario, Lower Canada as Quebec, Nova Scotia and New Brunswick. The Hudson Bay Company's territories were acquired in 1869 out of which were formed the provinces of Manitoba, Saskatchewan and Alberta. British Columbia joined in 1871 and Prince Edward Island in 1873. Canada took over the Arctic Archipelago in 1895. In 1949 Newfoundland came into the confederation.

In the early years, Canada's coins were struck in England at the Royal Mint in London or at the Heaton Mint in Birmingham. Issues struck at the Royal Mint do not bear a mint mark, but those produced by Heaton carry an "H". All Canadian coins have been struck since January 2, 1908, at the Royal Canadian Mints at Ottawa and recently at Winnipeg except for some 1968 pure nickel dimes struck at the U.S. Mint in Philadelphia, and do not bear mint marks. Ottawa's mint mark (C) does not appear on some 20th Century Newfoundland issues, however, as it does on English type sovereigns struck there from 1908 through 1918.

Canada is a member of the Commonwealth of Nations. Elizabeth II is Head of State as Queen of Canada.

RULER
British 1763-

MONETARY SYSTEM
1 Dollar = 100 Cents

CONFEDERATION

CIRCULATION COINAGE

KM# 7 CENT

5.67 g., Bronze, 25.5 mm. **Ruler:** Victoria **Obv:** Crowned head left within beaded circle **Obv. Legend:** VICTORIA DEI GRATIA REGINA. CANADA **Rev:** Denomination and date within beaded circle, chain of leaves surrounds **Edge:** Plain

Date	Mintage	VG8	F12	VF20	XF40	AU50	MS60	MS63	MS65
1901	4,100,000	3.00	4.00	6.00	10.00	22.00	45.00	100	650

KM# 8 CENT

5.67 g., Bronze, 25.5 mm. **Ruler:** Edward VII **Obv:** Kings bust right within beaded circle **Rev:** Denomination above date within circle, chain of leaves surrounds **Edge:** Plain

Date	Mintage	VG8	F12	VF20	XF40	AU50	MS60	MS63	MS65
1902	3,000,000	2.25	3.00	4.00	8.00	13.50	27.00	70.00	300
1903	4,000,000	2.25	3.00	4.00	8.00	15.00	30.00	90.00	450
1904	2,500,000	2.50	4.00	6.00	10.00	22.00	45.00	100	700
1905	2,000,000	4.00	6.00	9.00	13.00	27.00	55.00	125	700
1906	4,100,000	2.25	3.00	4.00	8.00	18.00	40.00	150	1,200
1907	2,400,000	2.50	3.00	5.00	10.00	19.50	40.00	150	1,400
1907 H	800,000	13.00	20.00	30.00	50.00	90.00	175	550	—
1908	2,401,506	3.00	4.00	6.00	10.00	22.00	40.00	100	750
1908	—	**PF60** 85.00 **PF63** 175 **PF65** 700							
1909	3,973,339	2.00	2.50	4.00	7.00	15.00	30.00	100	850
1910	5,146,487	1.50	2.00	3.00	6.00	13.50	30.00	80.00	1,000

KM# 15 CENT

5.67 g., Bronze, 25.5 mm. **Ruler:** George V **Obv:** King's bust left **Rev:** Denomination above date within beaded circle, chain of leaves surrounds **Edge:** Plain

Date	Mintage	VG8	F12	VF20	XF40	AU50	MS60	MS63	MS65
1911	4,663,486	0.80	1.50	2.25	3.50	13.50	25.00	65.00	350
1911	—	**PF60** 125 **PF63** 250 **PF65** 900							

KM# 21 CENT

5.67 g., Bronze, 25.5 mm. **Ruler:** George V **Obv:** King's bust left **Rev:** Denomination above date within beaded circle, chain of leaves surrounds **Edge:** Plain

Date	Mintage	VG8	F12	VF20	XF40	AU50	MS60	MS63	MS65
1912	5,107,642	0.90	1.75	2.50	4.00	13.00	30.00	70.00	450
1913	5,735,405	0.90	1.75	2.50	5.00	13.00	27.00	90.00	800
1914	3,405,958	1.25	1.75	3.00	5.00	18.00	40.00	100	700
1915	4,932,134	0.90	1.50	2.50	5.00	13.00	35.00	90.00	700
1916	11,022,367	0.60	0.80	1.75	3.00	9.00	19.00	60.00	400
1917	11,899,254	0.60	0.80	1.75	2.50	5.00	16.00	50.00	450
1918	12,970,798	0.60	0.80	1.75	2.50	5.00	14.00	50.00	400
1919	11,279,634	0.60	0.80	1.75	2.50	5.00	14.00	50.00	400
1920	6,762,247	0.70	0.90	1.75	2.50	8.00	22.00	80.00	1,100

Dot below date

KM# 28 CENT

3.24 g., Bronze, 19.10 mm. **Ruler:** George V **Obv:** King's bust left **Rev:** Denomination above date, leaves flank **Edge:** Plain

Date	Mintage	VG8	F12	VF20	XF40	AU50	MS60	MS63	MS65
1920	15,483,923	0.20	0.45	0.90	1.75	5.00	15.00	50.00	650
1921	7,601,627	0.45	0.75	1.75	5.00	13.00	35.00	250	—
1922	1,243,635	13.00	16.00	25.00	45.00	100	200	1,200	—
1923	1,019,002	29.00	35.00	40.00	60.00	150	300	2,000	—
1924	1,593,195	6.00	7.00	12.00	20.00	55.00	125	850	—
1925	1,000,622	22.00	25.00	30.00	50.00	100	200	1,100	—
1926	2,143,372	4.00	5.00	7.00	16.00	45.00	90.00	600	—
1927	3,553,928	1.25	1.75	3.50	8.00	22.00	40.00	225	3,000
1928	9,144,860	0.15	0.30	0.65	1.50	8.00	20.00	90.00	2,200
1929	12,159,840	0.15	0.30	0.65	1.50	9.00	20.00	80.00	1,600
1930	2,538,613	2.00	2.50	4.50	9.00	27.00	50.00	225	2,200
1931	3,842,776	0.65	1.00	2.50	6.00	22.00	40.00	200	1,800
1932	21,316,190	0.15	0.20	0.50	1.50	5.00	16.00	60.00	1,000
1933	12,079,310	0.15	0.30	0.50	1.50	5.00	16.00	50.00	550
1934	7,042,358	0.20	0.30	0.75	1.50	5.00	16.00	60.00	900
1935	7,526,400	0.20	0.30	0.75	1.50	5.00	16.00	50.00	700
1936	8,768,769	0.15	0.30	0.75	1.50	5.00	14.00	45.00	250
1936 dot below date; Rare	678,823	—	—	—	—	—	—	—	250,000
Note: Only one possible business strike is known to exist. No other examples (or possible business strikes) have ever surfaced.									
1936 dot below date, specimen, 3 known	—	—	—	—	—	—	—	—	—
Note: At the David Akers auction of the John Jay Pittman collection (Part 1, 10-97), a gem specimen realized $121,000. At the David Akers auction of the John Jay Pittman collection (Part 3, 10-99), a near choice specimen realized $115,000.									

Maple leaf

KM# 32 CENT

3.24 g., Bronze, 19.10 mm. **Ruler:** George VI **Obv:** Head left **Rev:** Maple leaf divides date and denomination **Edge:** Plain

Date	Mintage	VG8	F12	VF20	XF40	AU50	MS60	MS63	MS65
1937	10,040,231	0.35	0.45	0.65	0.90	1.50	2.50	12.00	55.00
1938	18,365,608	0.10	0.20	0.30	0.70	1.50	2.50	13.00	55.00
1939	21,600,319	0.10	0.20	0.30	0.65	1.25	2.00	8.00	35.00
1940	85,740,532	—	0.10	0.25	0.50	0.90	2.50	8.00	45.00
1941	56,336,011	—	0.10	0.25	0.50	2.25	8.00	50.00	450
1942	76,113,708	—	0.10	0.25	0.50	1.75	7.00	50.00	500
1943	89,111,969	—	0.10	0.25	0.45	1.25	3.50	22.00	225
1944	44,131,216	—	0.10	0.30	0.60	2.25	10.00	65.00	1,800
1945	77,268,591	—	0.10	0.20	0.35	0.90	2.50	20.00	450
1946	56,662,071	—	0.10	0.20	0.35	0.90	2.50	12.00	90.00
1947	31,093,901	—	0.10	0.20	0.35	0.90	2.50	9.00	50.00
1947 maple leaf	47,855,448	—	0.10	0.20	0.35	0.90	2.50	9.00	100

KM# 41 CENT

3.24 g., Bronze, 19.10 mm. **Ruler:** George VI **Obv:** Modified legend **Edge:** Plain

Date	Mintage	VG8	F12	VF20	XF40	AU50	MS60	MS63	MS65
1948	25,767,779	—	0.15	0.25	0.70	1.25	4.00	27.00	450
1949	33,128,933	—	—	0.15	0.35	0.90	2.50	9.00	45.00
1950	60,444,992	—	—	0.15	0.25	0.65	1.75	9.00	50.00
1951	80,430,379	—	—	0.15	0.20	0.45	1.75	14.00	125
1952	67,631,736	—	—	0.15	0.20	0.45	1.25	9.00	50.00

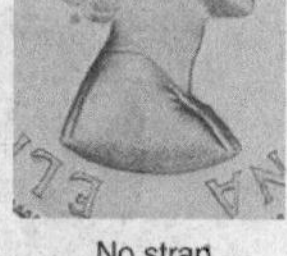
No strap

KM# 49 CENT

3.24 g., Bronze, 19.10 mm. **Ruler:** Elizabeth II **Obv:** Laureate bust right **Rev:** Maple leaf divides date and denomination

Date	Mintage	VG8	F12	VF20	XF40	AU50	MS60	MS63	MS65
1953	67,806,016	—	—	—	0.25	0.45	0.80	2.50	35.00
Note: Without strap									
1953	Inc. above	0.50	1.00	1.50	2.50	7.00	12.00	60.00	1,000
Note: With strap									
1954	22,181,760	—	—	0.10	0.40	0.90	1.75	6.00	125
Note: With strap									
1954 Prooflike only	Inc. above	—	—	—	—	—	550	800	1,800
Note: Without strap									
1955	56,403,193	—	—	—	0.15	0.20	0.45	3.00	35.00
Note: With strap									
1955	Inc. above	100	150	175	250	400	600	2,000	—
Note: Without strap									
1956	78,658,535	—	—	—	0.15	0.20	0.30	2.00	30.00
1957	100,601,792	—	—	—	—	—	0.10	1.00	27.00
1958	59,385,679	—	—	—	—	—	0.10	1.00	27.00
1959	83,615,343	—	—	—	—	—	—	0.60	18.00
1960	75,772,775	—	—	—	—	—	—	0.60	18.00
1961	139,598,404	—	—	—	—	—	—	0.60	18.00
1962	227,244,069	—	—	—	—	—	—	0.40	18.00
1963	279,076,334	—	—	—	—	—	—	0.40	15.00
1964	484,655,322	—	—	—	—	—	—	0.40	15.00

KM# 59.1 CENT

3.24 g., Bronze, 19.10 mm. **Ruler:** Elizabeth II **Obv:** Queens bust right **Rev:** Maple leaf divides date and denomination **Edge:** Plain

Date	Mintage	VG8	F12	VF20	XF40	AU50	MS60	MS63	MS65
1965	304,441,082	—	0.10	0.20	0.40	0.70	1.00	5.00	60.00
Note: Small beads, pointed 5									
1965	Inc. above	—	—	—	—	—	—	0.40	15.00
Note: Small beads, blunt 5									
1965	Inc. above	1.75	3.00	4.50	7.00	12.50	18.00	45.00	250
Note: Large beads, pointed 5									
1965	Inc. above	—	—	—	—	—	—	0.40	15.00
Note: Large beads, blunt 5									
1966	184,151,087	—	—	—	—	—	—	0.40	18.00
1968	329,695,772	—	—	—	—	—	—	0.40	18.00
1969	335,240,929	—	—	—	—	—	—	0.40	18.00
1970	311,145,010	—	—	—	—	—	—	0.40	18.00
1971	298,228,936	—	—	—	—	—	—	0.40	18.00
1972	451,304,591	—	—	—	—	—	—	0.40	18.00
1973	457,059,852	—	—	—	—	—	—	0.40	18.00
1974	692,058,489	—	—	—	—	—	—	0.40	18.00
1975	642,318,000	—	—	—	—	—	—	0.40	18.00
1976	701,122,890	—	—	—	—	—	—	0.40	18.00
1977	453,762,670	—	—	—	—	—	—	0.40	18.00

KM# 65 CENT

3.24 g., Bronze, 19.10 mm. **Ruler:** Elizabeth II **Subject:** Confederation Centennial **Obv:** Queen's bust right **Rev:** Dove with wings spread, denomination above, two dates below

Date	Mintage	VF20	XF40	MS60	MS63	MS65
1967	345,140,645	—	—	—	0.40	18.00
1967 Specimen	—	PF60 2.25	PF63 4.50	PF65 22.00		

KM# 59.2 CENT

3.24 g., Bronze, 19.10 mm. **Ruler:** Elizabeth II **Obv:** Queen's bust right **Rev:** Maple leaves **Edge:** Plain **Note:** Thin planchet.

Date	Mintage	VF20	XF40	MS60	MS63	MS65
1978	911,170,647	—	—	—	0.30	18.00
1979	754,394,064	—	—	—	0.30	18.00

KM# 127 CENT

2.80 g., Bronze, 19.10 mm. **Ruler:** Elizabeth II **Obv:** Queen's bust right **Edge:** Plain **Note:** Reduced weight.

Date	Mintage	VF20	XF40	MS60	MS63	MS65
1980	912,052,318	—	—	—	0.30	18.00
1981	1,209,468,500	—	—	—	0.30	22.00
1981	199,000	PF65 2.25				

KM# 132 CENT

2.50 g., Bronze, 19.10 mm. **Ruler:** Elizabeth II **Obv:** Queen's bust right **Rev:** Maple leaf divides date and denomination **Edge:** Plain **Shape:** 10-sided **Note:** Reduced weight.

Date	Mintage	VF20	XF40	MS60	MS63	MS65
1982	911,001,000	—	—	—	0.30	22.00
1982	180,908	PF65 1.75				
1983	975,510,000	—	—	—	0.30	18.00
1983	168,000	PF65 1.75				
1984	838,225,000	—	—	—	0.30	22.00
1984	161,602	PF65 3.00				
1985	771,772,500	2.50	3.50	10.00	19.00	50.00
Note: Pointed 5						
1985	Inc. above	—	—	—	0.30	27.00
Note: Blunt 5						
1985	157,037	PF65 3.00				
Note: Blunt 5						
1986	740,335,000	—	—	—	0.30	22.00
1986	175,745	PF65 3.00				
1987	774,549,000	—	—	—	0.30	27.00
1987	179,004	PF65 3.00				
1988	482,676,752	—	—	—	0.30	35.00
1988	175,259	PF65 3.00				
1989	1,077,347,200	—	—	—	0.30	22.00
1989	170,928	PF65 3.00				

KM# 181 CENT

2.50 g., Bronze, 19.10 mm. **Ruler:** Elizabeth II **Obv:** Crowned Queen's head right **Rev:** Maple leaf divides date and denomination **Edge:** Plain

Date	Mintage	VF20	XF40	MS60	MS63	MS65
1990	218,035,000	—	—	—	0.30	22.00
1990	140,649	PF65 4.50				
1991	831,001,000	—	—	—	0.30	18.00
1991	131,888	PF65 7.00				
1993	752,034,000	—	—	—	0.30	18.00
1993	145,065	PF65 3.50				
1994	639,516,000	—	—	—	0.30	18.00
1994	146,424	PF65 4.50				
1995	624,983,000	—	—	—	0.30	18.00
1995	—	PF65 4.50				
1996	445,746,000	—	—	—	0.30	18.00
1996	—	PF65 7.00				

KM# 204 CENT

Bronze, 19.10 mm. **Ruler:** Elizabeth II **Subject:** Confederation 125 **Obv:** Crowned Queen's head right **Rev:** Maple leaf divides date and denomination

Date	Mintage	VF20	XF40	MS60	MS63	MS65
1992	673,512,000	—	—	—	0.30	18.00
1992	147,061	PF65 3.00				

KM# 289 CENT

2.25 g., Copper Plated Steel, 19.05 mm. **Ruler:** Elizabeth II **Obv:** Crowned head right **Rev:** Maple twig design **Edge:** Round and plain

Date	Mintage	VF20	XF40	MS60	MS63	MS65
1997	549,868,000	—	—	—	0.30	18.00
1997	—	PF65 5.00				
1998	999,578,000	—	—	—	0.30	22.00
1998	—	PF65 5.00				
1998 W PL	—	—	—	—	—	1.00
1999 P PL	—	—	—	—	13.00	—
1999	1,089,625,000	—	—	—	0.30	18.00
1999	—	PF65 8.00				
1999 W	—	—	—	—	—	—
2000	771,908,206	—	—	—	0.30	18.00
2000	—	PF65 5.00				
2000 W	—	—	—	—	2.50	—

KM# 289a CENT

Bronze, 19.10 mm.

Date	Mintage	VF20	XF40	MS60	MS63	MS65
1998	—	—	—	—	—	7.00

Note: In Specimen sets only

KM# 309 CENT

5.67 g., 0.925 Copper Plated Silver 0.1686 oz. **Ruler:** Elizabeth II **Subject:** 90th Anniversary Royal Canadian Mint - 1908-1998

Date	Mintage	VF20	XF40	MS60	MS63	MS65
1908-1998	25,000	—	—	—	16.00	—
Note: Antique finish						
1908-1998 Proof	—	—	—	—	—	—

KM# 332 CENT

5.67 g., 0.925 Silver 0.1686 oz. ASW **Ruler:** Elizabeth II **Subject:** 90th Anniversary Royal Canadian Mint - 1908-1998 **Obv:** Crowned Queen's head right, with "Canada" added to head **Rev:** Denomination above dates withn beaded circle, chain of leaves surrounds

Date	Mintage	VF20	XF40	MS60	MS63	MS65
1908-1998	—	PF65 16.00				
Note: Mirror finish						

Round O's

KM# 2 5 CENTS

1.16 g., 0.925 Silver 0.0346 oz. ASW **Ruler:** Victoria **Obv:** Head left **Obv. Legend:** VICTORIA DEI GRATIA REGINA. CANADA **Rev:** Denomination and date within wreath, crown above

Date	Mintage	VG8	F12	VF20	XF40	AU50	MS60	MS63	MS65
1901	2,000,000	6.00	8.00	16.00	35.00	80.00	175	500	1,300

KM# 9 5 CENTS

1.16 g., 0.925 Silver 0.0346 oz. ASW, 15.5 mm. **Ruler:** Edward VII

Date	Mintage	VG8	F12	VF20	XF40	AU50	MS60	MS63	MS65
1902	2,120,000	2.00	3.00	5.00	9.00	19.50	45.00	65.00	200
1902	2,200,000	2.00	4.00	7.00	14.00	27.00	45.00	80.00	400
Note: Large broad H									
1902	Inc. above	10.00	17.00	30.00	50.00	85.00	125	225	750
Note: Small narrow H									

KM# 13 5 CENTS

1.16 g., 0.925 Silver 0.0346 oz. ASW, 15.5 mm. **Ruler:** Edward VII **Obv:** King's bust right **Rev:** Denomination and date within wreath, crown at top

Date	Mintage	VG8	F12	VF20	XF40	AU50	MS60	MS63	MS65
1903	1,000,000	5.00	9.00	22.00	45.00	100	200	450	1,100
1903 H	2,640,000	2.50	4.50	10.00	22.00	65.00	125	400	2,900
1904	2,400,000	4.00	5.00	9.00	30.00	90.00	225	650	2,700
1905	2,600,000	2.50	4.00	10.00	20.00	50.00	125	300	1,100
1906	3,100,000	2.50	3.00	7.00	16.00	45.00	100	250	1,800
1907	5,200,000	2.50	3.00	5.00	12.00	30.00	70.00	175	650
1908	1,220,524	7.00	13.00	30.00	50.00	85.00	125	225	700
1909 Round leaves	1,983,725	4.00	8.00	13.00	40.00	95.00	250	700	2,200
1909 Pointed leaves	Inc. above	16.00	24.00	55.00	125	250	700	1,700	—
1910 Pointed leaves	3,850,325	2.50	3.00	6.00	12.00	27.00	65.00	125	500
1910 Round leaves	Inc. above	18.00	24.00	45.00	100	225	550	1,700	—

KM# 16 5 CENTS

1.16 g., 0.925 Silver 0.0346 oz. ASW **Ruler:** George V **Obv:** King's bust left **Rev:** Denomination and date within wreath, crown above

Date	Mintage	VG8	F12	VF20	XF40	AU50	MS60	MS63	MS65
1911	3,692,350	2.50	4.00	7.00	12.00	40.00	80.00	125	300

KM# 22 5 CENTS

1.13 g., 0.925 Silver 0.0336 oz. ASW, 15.5 mm. **Ruler:** George V **Obv:** King's bust left **Rev:** Denomination and date within wreath, crown above

Date	Mintage	VG8	F12	VF20	XF40	AU50	MS60	MS63	MS65
1912	5,863,170	2.50	3.00	6.00	10.00	30.00	70.00	200	1,100
1913	5,488,048	2.50	3.00	5.00	8.00	18.00	35.00	70.00	250
1914	4,202,179	2.50	3.00	6.00	10.00	30.00	65.00	200	1,100
1915	1,172,258	14.00	20.00	35.00	65.00	175	350	750	2,500
1916	2,481,675	4.00	7.00	12.00	27.00	65.00	125	300	1,500
1917	5,521,373	2.25	3.00	4.00	9.00	22.00	40.00	100	400
1918	6,052,298	2.25	3.00	4.00	8.00	18.00	40.00	85.00	400
1919	7,835,400	2.25	3.00	4.00	8.00	18.00	35.00	80.00	450

KM# 22a 5 CENTS

1.17 g., 0.800 Silver 0.030 oz. ASW, 15.48 mm. **Ruler:** George V

Date	Mintage	VG8	F12	VF20	XF40	AU50	MS60	MS63	MS65
1920	10,649,851	2.00	2.50	3.00	6.50	17.00	28.00	65.00	300
1921	2,582,495	4,500	6,000	7,000	9,000	12,500	16,000	28,000	—

Note: Approximately 460 known; balance remelted. Stack's A.G. Carter Jr. Sale (12-89) choice BU, finest known, realized $57,200

Far 6

KM# 29 5 CENTS

4.60 g., Nickel, 21.2 mm. **Ruler:** George V **Obv:** King's bust left **Rev:** Maple leaves divide denomination and date

Date	Mintage	VG8	F12	VF20	XF40	AU50	MS60	MS63	MS65
1922	4,794,119	0.30	0.90	1.75	7.00	30.00	60.00	125	900
1923	2,502,279	0.40	1.25	5.50	16.00	60.00	150	350	—
1924	3,105,839	0.30	1.00	4.00	10.00	40.00	100	250	—
1925	201,921	70.00	90.00	125	300	700	1,600	5,000	—
1926 Near 6	938,162	3.00	7.00	16.00	75.00	225	450	1,600	—
1926 Far 6	Inc. above	150	175	300	600	1,100	2,000	6,000	—
1927	5,285,627	0.30	0.65	3.00	13.00	35.00	75.00	175	1,800
1928	4,577,712	0.30	0.65	3.00	13.00	35.00	65.00	125	1,000
1929	5,611,911	0.30	0.65	3.00	13.00	35.00	80.00	200	1,800
1930	3,704,673	0.30	1.25	3.00	15.00	45.00	100	250	—
1931	5,100,830	0.30	1.25	3.50	18.00	70.00	175	650	—
1932	3,198,566	0.30	1.00	3.50	16.00	50.00	150	500	—
1933	2,597,867	0.40	1.50	6.00	18.00	80.00	200	800	—
1934	3,827,304	0.30	1.00	3.00	16.00	50.00	150	500	—
1935	3,900,000	0.30	1.00	3.00	11.00	50.00	125	350	1,800
1936	4,400,450	0.30	0.65	1.75	9.00	30.00	60.00	150	1,100

KM# 33 5 CENTS

4.50 g., Nickel, 21.2 mm. **Ruler:** George VI **Obv:** Head left **Rev:** Beaver on rock divides denomination and date

Date	Mintage	VG8	F12	VF20	XF40	AU50	MS60	MS63	MS65
1937 Dot	4,593,263	0.20	0.30	1.25	2.50	5.00	12.00	24.00	27.00
1938	3,898,974	0.30	0.90	2.50	10.00	40.00	80.00	175	7,000
1939	5,661,123	0.20	0.35	1.25	5.00	22.00	55.00	90.00	500
1940	13,920,197	0.20	0.30	1.00	2.25	9.00	20.00	55.00	900
1941	8,681,785	0.20	0.30	1.00	3.00	13.00	28.00	70.00	2,000
1942 Round	6,847,544	0.20	0.30	1.00	2.50	9.00	20.00	50.00	500

KM# 39 5 CENTS

Tombac Brass, 21.2 mm. **Ruler:** George VI **Obv:** Head left **Rev:** Beaver on rock divides denomination and date **Shape:** 12-sided

Date	Mintage	VG8	F12	VF20	XF40	AU50	MS60	MS63	MS65
1942	3,396,234	0.40	0.65	1.25	1.75	2.50	4.00	16.00	175

KM# 40 5 CENTS

Tombac Brass, 21.2 mm. **Ruler:** George VI **Subject:** Victory **Obv:** Head left **Rev:** Torch on "V" divides date

Date	Mintage	VG8	F12	VF20	XF40	AU50	MS60	MS63	MS65
1943	24,760,256	0.20	0.30	0.40	0.80	1.75	3.50	12.00	150
1944	8,000	—	—	80,000	—	—	—	—	—
Note: 1 known									

KM# 40a 5 CENTS

4.40 g., Chrome Plated Steel, 21.2 mm. **Ruler:** George VI **Obv:** Head left **Rev:** Torch on "V" divides date

Date	Mintage	VG8	F12	VF20	XF40	AU50	MS60	MS63	MS65
1944	11,532,784	0.15	0.20	0.45	0.90	1.25	2.50	6.00	50.00
1945	18,893,216	0.10	0.20	0.40	0.80	1.25	2.50	6.00	80.00

Maple leaf

KM# 39a 5 CENTS

4.50 g., Nickel, 21.2 mm. **Ruler:** George VI **Obv:** Head left **Rev:** Beaver on rock divides denomination and date

Date	Mintage	VG8	F12	VF20	XF40	AU50	MS60	MS63	MS65
1946	6,952,684	0.10	0.25	0.50	2.00	8.00	16.00	40.00	1,100
1947	7,603,724	0.20	0.25	0.50	1.25	5.00	12.00	28.00	650
1947 Dot	Inc. above	18.00	22.00	35.00	75.00	125	200	400	1,800
1947 Maple leaf	9,595,124	0.20	0.25	0.45	1.25	5.00	12.00	25.00	225

KM# 42 5 CENTS

4.54 g., Nickel, 21.2 mm. **Ruler:** George VI **Obv:** Head left, modified legend **Rev:** Beaver on rock divides date and denomination

Date	Mintage	VG8	F12	VF20	XF40	AU50	MS60	MS63	MS65
1948	1,810,789	0.40	0.70	1.00	3.00	10.50	20.00	40.00	225
1949	13,037,090	0.15	0.25	0.45	1.00	3.50	7.00	16.00	125
1950	11,970,521	0.15	0.25	0.45	1.00	3.50	7.00	16.00	300

KM# 42a 5 CENTS

Chromium and Nickel Plated Steel, 21.2 mm. **Ruler:** George VI **Obv:** Head left **Rev:** Beaver on rock divides date and denomination

Date	Mintage	VG8	F12	VF20	XF40	AU50	MS60	MS63	MS65
1951	4,313,410	0.15	0.20	0.45	0.80	1.75	3.50	10.00	125
Note: Low relief; Second "A" in GRATIA points between denticles									
1951	Inc. above	400	550	750	1,200	1,800	2,400	3,500	4,500
Note: High relief; Second "A" in GRATIA points to a denticle									
1952	10,891,148	0.15	0.20	0.45	0.80	1.75	3.50	8.00	90.00

KM# 48 5 CENTS

4.55 g., Nickel, 21.2 mm. **Ruler:** George VI **Subject:** Nickel Bicentennial **Obv:** Head left **Rev:** Buildings with center tower divide dates and denomination **Shape:** 12-sided

Date	Mintage	VG8	F12	VF20	XF40	AU50	MS60	MS63	MS65
1951	9,028,507	0.15	0.25	0.30	0.45	0.90	1.75	8.00	125

KM# 50 5 CENTS

Chromium and Nickel Plated Steel, 21.2 mm. **Ruler:** Elizabeth II **Obv:** Laureate queen's bust, right **Rev:** Beaver on rock divides date and denomination **Shape:** 12-sided

Date	Mintage	VG8	F12	VF20	XF40	AU50	MS60	MS63	MS65
1953	16,635,552	—	0.20	0.40	0.90	1.75	3.00	7.00	60.00
Note: Without strap									
1953	Inc. above	175	250	350	550	900	1,500	3,500	—
Note: With strap, far leaf									
1953	Inc. above	300	450	650	900	1,100	1,300	3,500	—
Note: Without strap, near leaf									
1953	Inc. above	—	0.20	0.40	0.90	2.25	5.00	8.00	60.00
Note: With strap									
1954	6,998,662	—	0.25	0.50	1.00	2.50	6.00	12.00	80.00

KM# 50a 5 CENTS

4.59 g., Nickel, 21.2 mm. **Ruler:** Elizabeth II **Obv:** Laureate queen's bust right **Rev:** Beaver on rock divides date and denomination

Date	Mintage	VG8	F12	VF20	XF40	AU50	MS60	MS63	MS65
1955	5,355,028	—	0.15	0.40	0.75	1.75	3.50	6.50	70.00
1956	9,399,854	—	0.15	0.30	0.45	1.25	2.50	5.00	60.00
1957	7,387,703	—	0.15	0.25	0.30	0.65	1.25	3.50	45.00
1958	7,607,521	—	0.15	0.25	0.30	0.65	1.25	3.50	45.00
1959	11,552,523	—	—	0.15	0.20	0.25	0.45	1.75	45.00
1960	37,157,433	—	—	0.15	0.20	0.25	0.45	1.75	45.00
1961	47,889,051	—	—	0.15	0.20	0.25	0.40	1.25	45.00
1962	46,307,305	—	—	—	—	0.20	0.40	1.25	60.00

KM# 57 5 CENTS

Nickel, 21.2 mm. **Ruler:** Elizabeth II **Obv:** Laureate queen's bust right **Rev:** Beaver on rock divides date and denomination **Shape:** Round

Date	Mintage	VG8	F12	VF20	XF40	AU50	MS60	MS63	MS65
1963	43,970,320	—	—	—	—	0.15	0.30	0.80	100
1964	78,075,068	—	—	—	—	0.15	0.30	0.80	90.00
1964	—	18.00	20.00	21.00	24.00	30.00	40.00	125	—
Note: Extra water line									

KM# 60.1 5 CENTS

4.54 g., Nickel, 21.2 mm. **Ruler:** Elizabeth II **Obv:** Queen's bust right **Rev:** Beaver on rock divides date and denomination

Date	Mintage	VF20	XF40	MS60	MS63	MS65
1965	84,876,018	—	—	0.30	0.80	90.00
1966	27,976,648	—	—	0.30	0.80	300
1968	101,930,379	—	—	0.30	0.80	35.00
1969	27,830,229	—	—	0.30	0.80	50.00
1970	5,726,010	—	0.25	0.50	1.75	35.00
1971	27,312,609	—	—	0.30	0.80	35.00
1972	62,417,387	—	—	0.30	0.80	35.00
1973	53,507,435	—	—	0.30	0.80	27.00
1974	94,704,645	—	—	0.30	0.80	45.00
1975	138,882,000	—	—	0.30	0.80	35.00
1976	55,140,213	—	—	0.30	0.80	35.00
1977	89,120,791	—	—	—	0.80	45.00
1978	137,079,273	—	—	—	0.80	22.00

KM# 66 5 CENTS

Nickel, 21.2 mm. **Ruler:** Elizabeth II **Subject:** Confederation Centennial **Obv:** Queen's bust right **Rev:** Snowshoe rabbit bounding left divides dates and denomination

Date	Mintage	VF20	XF40	MS60	MS63	MS65
1867-1967	36,876,574	PF65 2.00				

KM# 60.2 5 CENTS

Nickel, 21.2 mm. **Ruler:** Elizabeth II **Obv:** Queen's bust right **Rev:** Beaver on rock divides date and denomination

Date	Mintage	VF20	XF40	MS60	MS63	MS65
1979	186,295,825	—	—	—	0.60	22.00
1980	134,878,000	—	—	—	0.60	45.00
1981	99,107,900	—	—	—	0.60	175
1981	199,000	PF65 2.00				

KM# 60.2a 5 CENTS

4.60 g., Copper-Nickel, 21.2 mm. **Ruler:** Elizabeth II **Obv:** Queen's bust right **Rev:** Beaver on rock divides date and denomination

Date	Mintage	VF20	XF40	MS60	MS63	MS65
1982	64,924,400	—	—	—	0.60	90.00
1982	180,908	PF65 2.00				
1983	72,596,000	—	—	—	0.60	175
1983	168,000	PF65 2.00				
1984	84,088,000	—	—	—	0.60	100
1984	161,602	PF65 2.00				
1985	126,618,000	—	—	—	0.60	125
1985	157,037	PF65 2.00				
1986	156,104,000	—	—	—	0.60	125
1986	175,745	PF65 2.00				
1987	106,299,000	—	—	—	0.60	40.00
1987	179,004	PF65 2.00				
1988	75,025,000	—	—	—	0.60	100
1988	175,259	PF65 2.00				
1989	141,570,538	—	—	—	0.70	40.00
1989	170,928	PF65 2.00				

KM# 182 5 CENTS

4.60 g., Copper-Nickel, 19.55 mm. **Ruler:** Elizabeth II **Obv:** Crowned head right **Rev:** Beaver on rock divides dates and denomination **Edge:** Plain

Date	Mintage	VF20	XF40	MS60	MS63	MS65
1990	42,537,000	—	—	—	0.60	55.00
1990	140,649	PF65 3.50				
1991	10,931,000	—	—	0.45	0.95	35.00
1991	131,888	PF65 7.00				
1993	86,877,000	—	—	—	0.60	40.00
1993	143,065	PF65 2.50				
1994	99,352,000	—	—	—	0.60	27.00
1994	146,424	PF65 3.00				
1995	78,528,000	—	—	—	0.60	55.00
1995	—	PF65 2.50				
1996 Far 6	36,686,000	—	—	—	1.75	225
1996 Near 6	Inc. above	—	—	—	0.90	27.00
1996	—	PF65 6.00				
1997	27,354,000	—	—	—	0.60	22.00
1997	—	PF65 5.00				
1998	156,873,000	—	—	—	0.60	22.00
1998 W PL	—	—	—	—	—	2.25
1998	—	PF65 5.00				
1999	124,861,000	—	—	—	0.60	18.00
1999 W	—	—	—	—	—	—
1999	—	PF65 9.00				
2000	108,514,000	—	—	—	0.60	22.00
2000 W PL	—	—	—	—	—	2.25
2000	—	PF65 5.00				

KM# 205 5 CENTS

4.60 g., Copper-Nickel, 21.2 mm. **Ruler:** Elizabeth II **Subject:** Confederation 125 **Obv:** Crowned head right **Rev:** Beaver on rock divides date and denomination

Date	Mintage	VF20	XF40	MS60	MS63	MS65
1992	53,732,000	—	—	—	0.60	27.00
1992	147,061	PF65 2.50				

KM# 182a 5 CENTS

5.35 g., 0.925 Silver 0.1591 oz. ASW, 21.2 mm. **Ruler:** Elizabeth II **Obv:** Crowned head right **Rev:** Beaver on rock divides date and denomination

Date	Mintage	VF20	XF40	MS60	MS63	MS65
1996	—	PF65 8.00				
1997	—	PF65 8.00				
1998	—	PF65 8.00				
1998 O	—	PF65 8.00				
1999	—	PF65 8.00				
2000	—	PF65 8.00				

KM# 182b 5 CENTS

3.90 g., Nickel Plated Steel, 21.2 mm. **Ruler:** Elizabeth II **Obv:** Crowned head right **Rev:** Beaver on rock divides date and denomination **Edge:** Plain

Date	Mintage	VF20	XF40	MS60	MS63	MS65
1999 P PL	Est. 20000	—	—	—	—	13.00
2000 P	Est. 2300000	—	—	—	0.90	22.00

KM# 310 5 CENTS

1.17 g., 0.925 Silver 0.0347 oz. ASW **Ruler:** Elizabeth II **Subject:** 90th Anniversary Royal Canadian Mint **Obv:** Crowned head right **Rev:** Denomination and date within wreath, crown above

Date	Mintage	VF20	XF40	MS60	MS63	MS65
1908-1998	25,000	—	—	—	12.00	—
1908-1998	25,000	PF65 12.00				

KM# 400 5 CENTS

0.925 Silver, 21.2 mm. **Ruler:** Elizabeth II **Subject:** First French-Canadian Regiment **Obv:** Crowned head right **Rev:** Regimental drums, sash and baton, denomination above, date at right **Edge:** Plain

Date	Mintage	VF20	XF40	MS60	MS63	MS65
2000	—	PF65 7.00				

KM# 3 10 CENTS

2.32 g., 0.925 Silver 0.0691 oz. ASW, 18.03 mm. **Ruler:** Victoria **Obv:** Head left **Obv. Legend:** VICTORIA DEI GRATIA REGINA. CANADA **Rev:** Denomination and date within wreath, crown above **Edge:** Reeded

Date	Mintage	VG8	F12	VF20	XF40	AU50	MS60	MS63	MS65
1901	1,200,000	13.00	24.00	50.00	100	150	250	850	1,800

KM# 10 10 CENTS

2.32 g., 0.925 Silver 0.0691 oz. ASW, 18.03 mm. **Ruler:** Edward VII **Obv:** Crowned bust right **Rev:** Denomination and date within wreath, crown above **Edge:** Reeded

Date	Mintage	VG8	F12	VF20	XF40	AU50	MS60	MS63	MS65
1902	720,000	9.00	18.00	35.00	100	200	450	1,200	4,500
1902 H	1,100,000	6.00	9.00	20.00	45.00	90.00	150	350	1,100
1903	500,000	15.00	35.00	90.00	250	600	1,200	2,300	8,000
1903 H	1,320,000	8.00	18.00	35.00	90.00	150	350	800	2,700
1904	1,000,000	12.00	27.50	50.00	125	225	400	1,000	3,500
1905	1,000,000	7.00	27.50	60.00	150	300	600	1,400	5,000
1906	1,700,000	7.00	13.00	35.00	80.00	150	350	900	2,600
1907	2,620,000	5.00	12.00	25.00	45.00	125	300	600	2,100
1908	776,666	9.00	27.50	60.00	150	200	300	600	1,300
1909	1,697,200	7.00	20.00	45.00	125	225	500	1,200	5,000
Note: Victorian leaves, similar to 1902-08 coins									
1909	Inc. above	11.00	30.00	60.00	150	350	750	1,800	5,500
Note: Broad leaves, similar to 1910-12 coins									
1910	4,468,331	4.00	9.00	20.00	40.00	80.00	150	400	1,200

KM# 17 10 CENTS

2.32 g., 0.925 Silver 0.0691 oz. ASW, 23.5 mm. **Ruler:** George V **Obv:** Crowned bust left **Rev:** Denomination and date within wreath, crown above **Edge:** Reeded

Date	Mintage	VG8	F12	VF20	XF40	AU50	MS60	MS63	MS65
1911	2,737,584	5.00	12.00	20.00	45.00	80.00	150	300	700

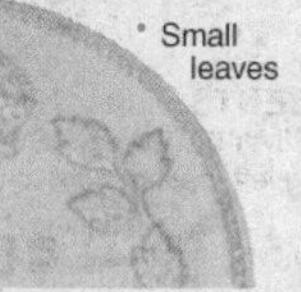

KM# 23 10 CENTS

2.32 g., 0.925 Silver 0.0691 oz. ASW, 17.8 mm. **Ruler:** George V **Obv:** Crowned bust left **Rev:** Denomination and date within wreath, crown above **Edge:** Reeded

Date	Mintage	VG8	F12	VF20	XF40	AU50	MS60	MS63	MS65
1912	3,235,557	2.50	5.00	10.00	35.00	90.00	250	650	1,900
1913	3,613,937	2.50	3.50	9.00	30.00	80.00	200	500	1,300
Note: Small leaves									
1913	Inc. above	125	225	450	1,200	3,000	8,000	27,500	—
Note: Large leaves									
1914	2,549,811	2.00	4.00	9.00	30.00	75.00	175	500	1,700
1915	688,057	7.00	16.00	40.00	125	225	500	950	2,600
1916	4,218,114	2.00	3.50	6.00	20.00	45.00	100	200	800
1917	5,011,988	2.00	3.50	4.00	12.00	40.00	70.00	125	400
1918	5,133,602	2.00	3.50	4.00	10.00	35.00	60.00	100	350
1919	7,877,722	2.00	3.50	4.00	10.00	35.00	60.00	100	250

KM# 23a 10 CENTS

2.33 g., 0.800 Silver 0.060 oz. ASW, 17.9 mm. **Ruler:** George V **Obv:** Crowned bust left **Rev:** Denomination and date within wreath, crown above **Edge:** Reeded

Date	Mintage	VG8	F12	VF20	XF40	AU50	MS60	MS63	MS65
1920	6,305,345	2.00	2.75	3.50	12.00	40.00	75.00	125	400
1921	2,469,562	2.00	2.75	6.00	20.00	50.00	90.00	225	900
1928	2,458,602	2.00	2.75	4.00	12.00	40.00	80.00	150	600
1929	3,253,888	2.00	3.00	3.50	12.00	40.00	75.00	125	400
1930	1,831,043	2.00	3.50	4.50	14.00	45.00	80.00	175	500
1931	2,067,421	2.50	3.50	4.00	12.00	40.00	70.00	125	400
1932	1,154,317	2.00	3.00	9.00	23.00	60.00	125	250	600
1933	672,368	2.50	5.00	12.00	35.00	90.00	200	400	1,300
1934	409,067	4.00	7.00	22.00	60.00	150	350	650	1,800
1935	384,056	4.50	7.00	19.00	60.00	150	350	600	1,600
1936	2,460,871	2.00	2.50	3.00	9.00	30.00	60.00	100	250
1936 Specimen	—	—	—	—	—	—	—	125,000	200,000

Note: Dot on reverse. Specimen, 4 known; David Akers sale of John Jay Pittman collection, Part 1, 10-97, a gem specimen realized $120,000

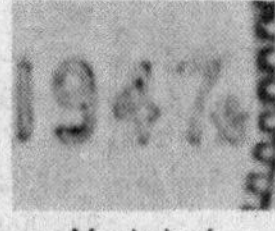

Maple leaf

KM# 34 10 CENTS

2.33 g., 0.800 Silver 0.060 oz. ASW, 18.03 mm. **Ruler:** George VI **Obv:** Head left **Rev:** Bluenose sailing left, date at right, denomination below **Edge:** Reeded

Date	Mintage	VG8	F12	VF20	XF40	AU50	MS60	MS63	MS65
1937	2,500,095	1.10	3.00	3.50	4.00	8.00	16.00	24.00	175
1938	4,197,323	1.10	3.00	4.50	10.00	30.00	60.00	100	800
1939	5,501,748	1.10	3.00	3.50	6.00	22.00	50.00	85.00	500
1940	16,526,470	—	1.10	3.00	4.00	9.00	20.00	40.00	225
1941	8,716,386	—	1.10	3.00	7.00	22.00	50.00	100	500
1942	10,214,011	—	1.10	3.00	5.00	18.00	40.00	60.00	600
1943	21,143,229	—	1.10	3.00	4.00	9.00	20.00	35.00	225
1944	9,383,582	—	1.10	3.00	5.00	12.00	28.00	45.00	250
1945	10,979,570	—	1.10	3.00	4.00	9.00	20.00	35.00	225
1946	6,300,066	1.10	2.00	4.00	5.00	15.00	30.00	45.00	225
1947	4,431,926	1.10	2.00	3.00	7.00	18.00	40.00	60.00	400
1947	9,638,793	—	1.10	3.00	4.00	7.00	15.00	20.00	125
Note: Maple leaf									

KM# 43 10 CENTS

2.33 g., 0.800 Silver 0.060 oz. ASW, 18.03 mm. **Ruler:** George VI **Obv:** Head left, modified legend **Rev:** Bluenose sailing left, date at right, denomination below

Date	Mintage	VG8	F12	VF20	XF40	AU50	MS60	MS63	MS65
1948	422,741	2.50	3.50	7.50	13.00	35.00	60.00	80.00	650
1949	11,336,172	—	1.10	2.00	2.50	6.00	12.00	18.00	150
1950	17,823,075	—	1.10	2.00	2.50	5.00	10.00	15.00	250
1951	15,079,265	—	—	1.10	2.50	4.00	7.00	12.00	175
1951	—	—	6.00	8.00	12.00	18.00	40.00	65.00	350
Note: Doubled die									
1952	10,474,455	—	—	1.10	2.50	4.00	6.00	10.00	90.00

KM# 51 10 CENTS

2.31 g., 0.800 Silver 0.0594 oz. ASW, 18 mm. **Ruler:** Elizabeth II **Obv:** Laureate bust right **Rev:** Bluenose sailing left, date at right, denomination below

Date	Mintage	VG8	F12	VF20	XF40	AU50	MS60	MS63	MS65
1953	Inc. above	—	1.10	2.00	3.00	3.50	4.00	8.00	125
Note: With straps									
1953	17,706,395	—	—	1.10	3.00	3.50	4.50	9.00	50.00
Note: Without straps									
1954	4,493,150	—	1.10	2.00	3.00	7.00	12.00	20.00	125
1955	12,237,294	—	—	1.10	2.00	3.00	4.50	8.00	55.00
1956	Inc. above	1.10	3.50	4.00	7.00	9.50	15.00	24.00	125
Note: Dot below date									
1956	16,732,844	—	—	—	1.10	2.00	3.00	6.00	45.00
1957	16,110,229	—	—	—	1.10	2.25	3.50	4.00	35.00
1958	10,621,236	—	—	—	1.10	2.25	3.50	4.00	35.00
1959	19,691,433	—	—	—	1.10	1.20	3.00	4.00	35.00
1960	45,446,835	—	—	—	1.10	1.20	3.00	4.00	45.00
1961	26,850,859	—	—	—	1.10	1.20	3.00	4.00	45.00
1962	41,864,335	—	—	—	1.10	1.20	2.00	2.50	22.00
1963	41,916,208	—	—	—	1.10	1.20	2.00	2.50	22.00
1964	49,518,549	—	—	—	1.10	1.20	2.00	2.50	22.00

KM# 61 10 CENTS

2.33 g., 0.800 Silver 0.060 oz. ASW, 18.03 mm. **Ruler:** Elizabeth II **Obv:** Young bust right **Rev:** Bluenose sailing left, date at right, denomination below

Date	Mintage	VF20	XF40	MS60	MS63	MS65
1965	56,965,392	—	—	1.20	2.50	18.00
1966	34,567,898	—	—	1.20	2.50	27.00

KM# 67 10 CENTS

2.33 g., 0.800 Silver 0.060 oz. ASW, 18.03 mm. **Ruler:** Elizabeth II **Subject:** Confederation Centennial **Obv:** Bust right **Rev:** Atlantic mackeral left, denomination above, dates below

Date	Mintage	VF20	XF40	MS60	MS63	MS65
1867-1967	62,998,215	—	—	1.20	2.50	27.00
ND1867-1967	—	PF65 18.00				

KM# 67a 10 CENTS

2.33 g., 0.500 Silver 0.0375 oz. ASW, 18.03 mm. **Ruler:** Elizabeth II **Subject:** Confederation Centennial **Obv:** Young bust right **Rev:** Atlantic mackeral left, denomination above, dates below

Date	Mintage	VF20	XF40	MS60	MS63	MS65
1867-1967	Inc. above	—	—	0.70	2.00	27.00

Ottawa

KM# 72 10 CENTS

2.33 g., 0.500 Silver 0.0375 oz. ASW, 18.03 mm. **Ruler:** Elizabeth II **Obv:** Bust right **Rev:** Bluenose sailing left, date at right, denomination below **Note:** Ottawa Mint reeding has pointed deep areas in the edge reeding.

Date	Mintage	VF20	XF40	MS60	MS63	MS65
1968	70,460,000	—	—	0.70	1.50	18.00

Ottawa

KM# 72a 10 CENTS

Nickel, 18.03 mm. **Ruler:** Elizabeth II **Obv:** Young bust right **Rev:** Bluenose sailing left, date at right, denomination below **Note:** Ottawa Mint reeding has pointed deep areas in the edge reeding.

Date	Mintage	VF20	XF40	MS60	MS63	MS65
1968	87,412,930	—	—	—	0.40	90.00

KM# 73 10 CENTS

2.33 g., Nickel, 18.03 mm. **Ruler:** Elizabeth II **Obv:** Young bust right **Rev:** Bluenose sailing left, date at right, denomination below **Note:** Philadelphia Mint reeding has flat deep areas in the edge reeding.

Date	Mintage	VF20	XF40	MS60	MS63	MS65
1968	85,170,000	—	—	—	0.40	40.00
1969	—	12,000	16,000	25,000	—	—

Note: Large date, large ship, 10-20 known

KM# 77.1 10 CENTS

2.07 g., Nickel, 18.03 mm. **Ruler:** Elizabeth II **Obv:** Young bust right **Rev:** Redesigned smaller Bluenose sailing left, date at right, denomination below **Edge:** Reeded

Date	Mintage	VF20	XF40	MS60	MS63	MS65
1969	55,833,929	—	—	0.25	0.70	30.00
1970	5,249,296	—	—	0.40	1.25	27.00
1971	41,016,968	—	—	0.20	0.70	27.00
1972	60,169,387	—	—	0.20	0.70	30.00
1973	167,715,435	—	—	0.20	0.70	45.00
1974	201,566,565	—	—	0.20	0.70	45.00
1975	207,680,000	—	—	0.20	0.70	45.00
1976	95,018,533	—	—	0.20	0.70	45.00
1977	128,452,206	—	—	—	0.70	35.00
1978	170,366,431	—	—	—	0.70	45.00

KM# 77.2 10 CENTS

2.07 g., Nickel, 18.03 mm. **Ruler:** Elizabeth II **Obv:** Smaller young bust right **Rev:** Redesigned smaller Bluenose sailing left, denomination below, date at right **Edge:** Reeded

Date	Mintage	VF20	XF40	MS60	MS63	MS65
1979	237,321,321	—	—	—	0.60	30.00
1980	170,111,533	—	—	—	2.25	45.00
1981	123,912,900	—	—	—	0.60	85.00
1981	199,000	PF65 1.50				
1982	93,475,000	—	—	—	0.60	45.00
1982	180,908	PF65 1.50				
1983	111,065,000	—	—	—	0.60	45.00
1983	168,000	PF65 1.50				
1984	121,690,000	—	—	—	0.60	65.00
1984	161,602	PF65 2.00				
1985	143,025,000	—	—	—	0.60	40.00
1985	157,037	PF65 2.00				
1986	168,620,000	—	—	—	0.60	45.00
1986	175,745	PF65 2.00				
1987	147,309,000	—	—	—	0.60	40.00
1987	179,004	PF65 2.00				
1988	162,998,558	—	—	—	0.60	40.00
1988	175,259	PF65 2.00				
1989	199,104,414	—	—	—	0.70	35.00
1989	170,528	PF65 2.00				

KM# 183 10 CENTS

2.14 g., Nickel, 18.03 mm. **Ruler:** Elizabeth II **Obv:** Crowned head right **Rev:** Bluenose sailing left, date at right, denomination below **Edge:** Reeded

Date	Mintage	VF20	XF40	MS60	MS63	MS65
1990	65,023,000	—	—	—	0.60	30.00
1990	140,649	PF65 2.50				
1991	50,397,000	—	—	0.65	0.90	27.00
1991	131,888	PF65 4.00				
1993	135,569,000	—	—	—	0.60	27.00
1993	143,065	PF65 2.00				
1994	145,800,000	—	—	—	0.60	30.00
1994	146,424	PF65 2.50				
1995	123,875,000	—	—	—	0.60	27.00
1995	—	PF65 2.50				
1996	51,814,000	—	—	—	0.60	30.00
1996	—	PF65 3.50				
1997	43,126,000	—	—	—	0.60	27.00
1997	—	PF65 3.50				
1998	203,514,000	—	—	—	0.60	30.00
1998	—	PF65 4.50				
1998 W PL	—	PF60 2.50				
1999	258,462,000	—	—	—	0.60	30.00
1999	—	PF65 6.00				
2000	159,125,000	—	—	—	0.50	30.00
2000	—	PF65 4.00				
2000 W PL	—	—	—	—	—	1.75

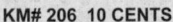

KM# 206 10 CENTS

Nickel, 18.03 mm. **Ruler:** Elizabeth II **Subject:** Confederation 125 **Obv:** Crowned head right **Rev:** Bluenose sailing left, date at right, denomination below

Date	Mintage	VF20	XF40	MS60	MS63	MS65
1867-1992	174,476,000	—	—	—	0.60	27.00
1867-1992	147,061	PF65 2.50				

KM# 183a 10 CENTS

2.40 g., 0.925 Silver 0.0714 oz. ASW, 18.03 mm. **Ruler:** Elizabeth II **Obv:** Crowned head right **Rev:** Bluenose sailing left, date at right, denomination below

Date	Mintage	VF20	XF40	MS60	MS63	MS65
1996	—	PF65 5.50				
1997	—	PF65 5.50				
1998	—	PF65 4.00				
1998 O	—	PF65 4.00				
1999	—	PF65 5.00				
2000	—	PF65 5.00				

KM# 299 10 CENTS

2.40 g., 0.925 Silver 0.0714 oz. ASW, 18.03 mm. **Ruler:** Elizabeth II **Subject:** John Cabot **Obv:** Crowned head right **Rev:** Ship with full sails divides dates, denomination below

Date	Mintage	VF20	XF40	MS60	MS63	MS65
1997	—	PF65 13.50				

KM# 311 10 CENTS

2.32 g., 0.925 Silver 0.069 oz. ASW, 18.03 mm. **Ruler:** Elizabeth II **Subject:** 90th Anniversary Royal Canadian Mint **Obv:** Crowned head right **Rev:** Denomination and date within wreath, crown above

Date	Mintage	VF20	XF40	MS60	MS63	MS65
1908-1998 Matte	—	PF65 10.00				
1908-1998	—	PF65 10.00				

KM# 183b 10 CENTS

1.77 g., Nickel Plated Steel, 18.03 mm. **Ruler:** Elizabeth II **Obv:** Crowned head right **Rev:** Bluenose sailing left, date at right, denomination below **Edge:** Reeded

Date	Mintage	VF20	XF40	MS60	MS63	MS65
1999 P PL	Est. 20000	—	—	—	—	10.00
2000 P	Est. 200	—	—	600	1,000	2,000

KM# 409 10 CENTS

2.40 g., 0.925 Silver 0.0714 oz. ASW, 18.03 mm. **Ruler:** Elizabeth II **Subject:** First Canadian Credit Union **Obv:** Crowned head right **Rev:** Alphonse Desjardins' house (founder of the first credit union in Canada), dates at right, denomination below **Edge:** Reeded

Date	Mintage	VF20	XF40	MS60	MS63	MS65
2000	—	PF65 7.00				

KM# 5 25 CENTS

5.81 g., 0.925 Silver 0.1728 oz. ASW, 23.88 mm. **Ruler:** Victoria **Obv:** Crowned head left **Obv. Legend:** VICTORIA DEI GRATIA REGINA / CANADA **Rev:** Denomination and date within wreath, crown above

Date	Mintage	VG8	F12	VF20	XF40	AU50	MS60	MS63	MS65
1901	640,000	15.00	24.00	65.00	200	350	650	1,400	2,600

KM# 11 25 CENTS

5.81 g., 0.925 Silver 0.1728 oz. ASW, 23.4 mm. **Ruler:** Edward VII **Obv:** Crowned bust right **Rev:** Denomination and date within wreath, crown above

Date	Mintage	VG8	F12	VF20	XF40	AU50	MS60	MS63	MS65
1902	464,000	16.00	35.00	85.00	250	450	1,000	2,500	7,500
1902 H	800,000	11.00	22.50	65.00	125	225	350	650	2,100
1903	846,150	20.00	40.00	100	300	500	1,000	2,600	9,500
1904	400,000	30.00	75.00	200	500	950	2,250	7,000	—
1905	800,000	20.00	45.00	150	350	800	2,000	5,500	—
1906 Large crown	1,237,843	14.00	30.00	75.00	250	450	800	2,200	11,000
1906 Small crown, Rare	Inc. above	3,500	5,500	10,000	18,000	24,000	30,000	40,000	—
1907	2,088,000	11.00	22.50	65.00	175	300	600	1,600	5,000
1908	495,016	27.00	50.00	100	250	400	550	1,000	1,900
1909	1,335,929	15.00	40.00	100	250	450	850	2,000	8,000

KM# 11a 25 CENTS

5.83 g., 0.925 Silver 0.1734 oz. ASW **Ruler:** Edward VII **Obv:** Crowned bust right **Rev:** Denomination and date within wreath, crown above

Date	Mintage	VG8	F12	VF20	XF40	AU50	MS60	MS63	MS65
1910	3,577,569	10.00	22.50	50.00	100	200	350	850	3,500

KM# 18 25 CENTS

5.83 g., 0.925 Silver 0.1734 oz. ASW **Ruler:** George V **Obv:** Crowned bust left **Obv. Legend:** GEORGIVS V REX ET IND IMP **Rev:** Denomination and date within wreath, crown above

Date	Mintage	VG8	F12	VF20	XF40	AU50	MS60	MS63	MS65
1911	1,721,341	12.00	20.00	50.00	100	175	350	650	1,600

KM# 24 25 CENTS

5.83 g., 0.925 Silver 0.1734 oz. ASW, 23.5 mm. **Ruler:** George V **Obv:** Crowned bust left **Obv. Legend:** GEORGIVS V DEI GRA REX ET IND IMP **Rev:** Denomination and date within wreath, crown above

Date	Mintage	VG8	F12	VF20	XF40	AU50	MS60	MS63	MS65
1912	2,544,199	9.00	14.00	30.00	70.00	200	400	1,500	4,500
1913	2,213,595	8.00	14.00	30.00	65.00	175	350	1,250	4,000
1914	1,215,397	9.00	16.00	40.00	80.00	250	650	2,000	7,000
1915	242,382	28.00	70.00	225	600	1,500	3,500	8,000	25,000
1916	1,462,566	7.00	11.00	25.00	50.00	100	250	800	3,500
1917	3,365,644	7.00	9.00	18.00	40.00	65.00	150	300	900
1918	4,175,649	6.00	9.00	13.00	35.00	55.00	100	225	850
1919	5,852,262	6.00	9.00	13.00	35.00	50.00	125	225	950

Dot below wreath

KM# 24a 25 CENTS

5.83 g., 0.800 Silver 0.150 oz. ASW **Ruler:** George V **Obv:** Crowned bust left **Rev:** Denomination and date within wreath, crown below

Date	Mintage	VG8	F12	VF20	XF40	AU50	MS60	MS63	MS65
1920	1,975,278	5.00	9.00	18.00	40.00	90.00	200	500	1,600
1921	597,337	17.00	35.00	125	300	750	1,450	3,500	12,000
1927	468,096	40.00	65.00	125	250	650	1,000	2,100	7,000
1928	2,114,178	5.00	9.00	18.00	50.00	90.00	175	450	1,600
1929	2,690,562	5.00	9.00	18.00	45.00	90.00	150	400	1,200
1930	968,748	5.00	9.00	27.00	50.00	95.00	250	600	1,800
1931	537,815	5.00	10.00	30.00	65.00	100	250	650	2,300
1932	537,994	5.00	10.00	30.00	65.00	100	250	650	2,100
1933	421,282	5.00	10.00	35.00	85.00	125	250	450	1,300
1934	384,350	5.00	12.00	45.00	90.00	150	350	650	2,300
1935	537,772	5.00	10.00	35.00	65.00	125	200	350	1,200
1936	972,094	5.00	8.00	13.00	28.00	55.00	100	225	800
1936 Dot below wreath	153,322	40.00	95.00	225	450	750	1,050	2,400	9,500

Note: David Akers John Jay Pittman sale Part Three, 10-99, nearly Choice Unc. realized $6,900; considered a possible specimen example

Maple leaf after date

KM# 35 25 CENTS

5.83 g., 0.800 Silver 0.150 oz. ASW, 23.5 mm. **Ruler:** George VI **Obv:** Head left **Rev:** Caribou left, denomination above, date at right

Date	Mintage	VG8	F12	VF20	XF40	AU50	MS60	MS63	MS65
1937	2,690,176	2.75	5.00	7.00	7.50	13.00	20.00	40.00	250
1938	3,149,245	2.75	5.00	8.00	15.00	35.00	75.00	150	1,000
1939	3,532,495	2.75	5.00	8.00	11.00	27.00	60.00	125	400
1940	9,583,650	—	2.75	4.00	5.00	10.00	20.00	40.00	250
1941	6,654,672	—	2.75	4.00	6.00	10.00	23.00	45.00	250
1942	6,935,871	—	2.75	4.00	6.00	10.00	24.00	45.00	350

Date	Mintage	VG8	F12	VF20	XF40	AU50	MS60	MS63	MS65
1943	13,559,575	—	2.75	4.00	6.00	10.00	23.00	45.00	350
1944	7,216,237	2.75	4.00	5.00	6.00	15.00	30.00	60.00	400
1945	5,296,495	—	2.75	4.00	6.00	10.00	23.00	50.00	350
1946	2,210,810	2.75	4.00	6.00	12.00	30.00	50.00	100	400
1947	1,524,554	2.75	4.00	6.00	12.00	35.00	60.00	100	1,000
1947 Dot after 7	Inc. above	65.00	90.00	125	225	300	450	900	8,500
1947 Maple leaf after 7	4,393,938	—	2.75	4.00	6.00	11.00	20.00	30.00	250

KM# 44 25 CENTS

5.83 g., 0.800 Silver 0.150 oz. ASW, 23.5 mm. **Ruler:** George VI **Obv:** Head left, modified legend **Rev:** Caribou left, denomination above, date at right

Date	Mintage	VG8	F12	VF20	XF40	AU50	MS60	MS63	MS65
1948	2,564,424	2.75	4.00	6.00	11.00	30.00	65.00	125	500
1949	7,988,830	—	2.75	4.00	8.00	10.50	14.00	30.00	500
1950	9,673,335	—	2.75	4.00	8.00	10.00	12.00	23.00	350
1951	8,290,719	—	2.75	4.00	7.00	9.00	10.00	18.00	350
1952	8,859,642	—	2.75	4.00	7.00	8.50	10.00	17.00	500

KM# 52 25 CENTS

5.83 g., 0.800 Silver 0.150 oz. ASW, 23.8 mm. **Ruler:** Elizabeth II **Obv:** Laureate bust right **Rev:** Caribou left, denomination above, date at right

Date	Mintage	VG8	F12	VF20	XF40	AU50	MS60	MS63	MS65
1953 Without strap	10,546,769	—	—	2.75	4.00	6.00	8.00	14.00	100
1953 With strap	Inc. above	—	2.75	4.00	6.00	8.50	11.00	27.00	350
1954	2,318,891	2.75	4.00	5.00	10.00	18.00	30.00	55.00	450
1955	9,552,505	—	—	2.75	6.00	7.50	9.00	16.00	225
1956	11,269,353	—	—	—	2.75	5.50	8.00	12.00	100
1957	12,770,190	—	—	—	2.75	5.50	8.00	10.00	75.00
1958	9,336,910	—	—	—	2.75	5.50	8.00	10.00	65.00
1959	13,503,461	—	—	—	2.75	3.25	5.50	8.00	125
1960	22,835,327	—	—	—	2.75	3.25	5.50	8.00	72.00
1961	18,164,368	—	—	—	2.75	3.25	5.50	8.00	72.00
1962	29,559,266	—	—	—	2.75	3.25	5.50	8.00	62.00
1963	21,180,652	—	—	—	—	2.75	3.25	8.00	47.00
1964	36,479,343	—	—	—	—	2.75	3.25	8.00	42.00

KM# 62 25 CENTS

5.83 g., 0.800 Silver 0.150 oz. ASW, 23.8 mm. **Ruler:** Elizabeth II **Obv:** Young bust right **Rev:** Caribou left, denomination above, date at right

Date	Mintage	VF20	XF40	MS60	MS63	MS65
1965	44,708,869	—	—	3.00	8.00	42.00
1966	25,626,315	—	—	3.00	8.00	42.00

KM# 68 25 CENTS

5.83 g., 0.800 Silver 0.150 oz. ASW, 23.8 mm. **Ruler:** Elizabeth II **Subject:** Confederation Centennial **Obv:** Young bust right **Rev:** Lynx striding left divides dates and denomination

Date	Mintage	VF20	XF40	MS60	MS63	MS65
1867-1967	48,855,500	—	—	3.00	6.00	27.00

KM# 68a 25 CENTS

5.83 g., 0.500 Silver 0.0937 oz. ASW, 23.8 mm. **Ruler:** Elizabeth II **Subject:** Confederation Centennial **Obv:** Young bust right **Rev:** Lynx striding left divides dates and denomination

Date	Mintage	VF20	XF40	MS60	MS63	MS65
1867-1967	Inc. above	—	—	1.80	4.50	27.00

KM# 62a 25 CENTS

5.83 g., 0.500 Silver 0.0937 oz. ASW, 23.8 mm. **Ruler:** Elizabeth II **Obv:** Young bust right **Rev:** Caribou left, denomination above, date at right

Date	Mintage	VF20	XF40	MS60	MS63	MS65
1968	71,464,000	—	—	1.80	4.50	27.00

KM# 62b 25 CENTS

5.06 g., Nickel, 23.8 mm. **Ruler:** Elizabeth II **Obv:** Young bust right **Rev:** Caribou left, denomination above, date at right

Date	Mintage	VF20	XF40	MS60	MS63	MS65
1968	88,686,931	—	—	0.45	0.80	42.00
1969	133,037,929	—	—	0.45	0.80	42.00
1970	10,302,010	—	—	1.00	2.00	42.00
1971	48,170,428	—	—	0.45	0.80	32.00
1972	43,743,387	—	—	0.45	0.80	32.00
1974	192,360,598	—	—	0.45	0.80	32.00
1975	141,148,000	—	—	0.45	0.80	42.00
1976	86,898,261	—	—	0.45	0.80	42.00
1977	99,634,555	—	—	0.45	0.80	27.00
1978	176,475,408	—	—	0.45	0.80	62.00

KM# 81.1 25 CENTS

Nickel, 23.8 mm. **Ruler:** Elizabeth II **Subject:** Royal Candian Mounted Police Centennial **Obv:** Young bust right **Rev:** Mountie divides dates, denomination above **Note:** 120 beads.

Date	Mintage	VF20	XF40	MS60	MS63	MS65
1873-1973	134,958,587	—	—	0.55	1.25	32.00

KM# 81.2 25 CENTS

Nickel, 23.8 mm. **Ruler:** Elizabeth II **Subject:** RCMP Centennial **Obv:** Young bust right **Rev:** Mountie divides dates, denomination above **Note:** Large bust, 132 beads.

Date	Mintage	VF20	XF40	MS60	MS63	MS65
1873-1973	Inc. above	125	150	300	700	3,000

KM# 74 25 CENTS

5.07 g., Nickel, 23.88 mm. **Ruler:** Elizabeth II **Obv:** Small young bust right

Date	Mintage	VF20	XF40	MS60	MS63	MS65
1979	131,042,905	—	—	0.45	0.75	27.00
1980	76,178,000	—	—	0.45	1.00	120
1981	131,580,272	—	—	0.45	1.00	57.00
1981	—	PF65 2.00				
1982	171,926,000	—	—	0.45	1.00	57.00
1982	180,908	PF65 2.00				
1983	13,162,000	—	—	1.00	2.00	62.00
1983	168,000	PF65 3.00				
1984	121,668,000	—	—	0.45	1.00	57.00
1984	161,602	PF65 2.00				
1985	158,734,000	—	—	0.45	1.00	87.00
1985	157,037	PF65 2.00				
1986	132,220,000	—	—	0.45	1.00	62.00
1986	175,745	PF65 2.00				
1987	53,408,000	—	—	0.60	1.25	47.00
1987	179,004	PF65 2.00				
1988	80,368,473	—	—	0.45	0.95	57.00
1988	175,259	PF65 2.00				
1989	119,796,307	—	—	0.45	1.00	57.00
1989	170,928	PF65 2.50				

KM# 184 25 CENTS

5.07 g., Nickel, 23.88 mm. **Ruler:** Elizabeth II **Obv:** Crowned head right **Rev:** Caribou left, denomination above, date at right

Date	Mintage	VF20	XF40	MS60	MS63	MS65
1990	31,258,000	—	—	0.45	0.90	50.00
1990	140,649	PF65 3.50				

Date	Mintage	VF20	XF40	MS60	MS63	MS65
1991	459,000	—	—	6.00	12.00	65.00
1991	131,888	PF65 20.00				
1993	73,758,000	—	—	0.50	0.70	60.00
1993	143,065	PF65 2.50				
1994	77,670,000	—	—	0.50	0.70	50.00
1994	146,424	PF65 3.00				
1995	89,210,000	—	—	0.50	0.70	35.00
1995	—	PF65 3.00				
1996	28,106,000	—	—	0.50	0.70	35.00
1996	—	PF65 6.00				
1997 PL	—	—	—	—	—	4.50
1997	—	PF65 6.00				
1998 W PL	—	—	—	—	—	10.00
1999 PL	258,888,000	—	—	—	—	5.00
1999	—	PF65 9.50				
2000 PL	434,087,000	—	—	—	—	5.00
2000	—	PF65 6.00				
2000 W PL	—	—	—	—	—	5.00

KM# 203 25 CENTS

5.00 g., Nickel, 23.9 mm. **Ruler:** Elizabeth II **Series:** 125th Anniversary of Confederation **Subject:** New Brunswick **Obv:** Crowned head right **Rev:** Covered bridge in Newton, denomination below

Date	Mintage	VF20	XF40	MS60	MS63	MS65
1992	12,174,000	—	—	0.50	1.00	45.00

KM# 203a 25 CENTS

5.83 g., 0.925 Silver 0.1734 oz. ASW, 23.8 mm. **Ruler:** Elizabeth II **Series:** 125th Anniversary of Confederation **Subject:** New Brunswick **Obv:** Crowned head right **Rev:** Covered bridge in Newton, denomination below

Date	Mintage	VF20	XF40	MS60	MS63	MS65
1992	149,579	PF65 8.50				

KM# 207 25 CENTS

Nickel, 23.8 mm. **Ruler:** Elizabeth II **Subject:** Confederation 125 **Obv:** Crowned head right **Rev:** Caribou left, denomination above, date at right

Date	Mintage	VF20	XF40	MS60	MS63	MS65
1867-1992	147,061	PF65 16.00				
1867-1992 PL	442,986	—	—	—	—	13.00

KM# 212 25 CENTS

Nickel, 23.8 mm. **Ruler:** Elizabeth II **Series:** 125th Anniversary of Confederation **Subject:** Northwest Territories **Obv:** Crowned head right

Date	Mintage	VF20	XF40	MS60	MS63	MS65
1992	12,582,000	—	—	0.50	1.00	45.00

KM# 212a 25 CENTS

5.83 g., 0.925 Silver 0.1734 oz. ASW, 23.8 mm. **Ruler:** Elizabeth II **Series:** 125th Anniversary of Confederation **Subject:** Northwest Territories **Obv:** Crowned head right

Date	Mintage	VF20	XF40	MS60	MS63	MS65
1992	149,579	PF65 8.50				

KM# 213 25 CENTS

Nickel, 23.8 mm. **Ruler:** Elizabeth II **Series:** 125th Anniversary of Confederation **Subject:** Newfoundland **Rev:** Fisherman rowing a dory, denomination below

Date	Mintage	VF20	XF40	MS60	MS63	MS65
1992	11,405,000	—	—	0.50	1.00	45.00

KM# 213a 25 CENTS

5.83 g., 0.925 Silver 0.1734 oz. ASW, 23.8 mm. **Ruler:** Elizabeth II **Series:** 125th Anniversary of Confederation **Subject:** Newfoundland **Rev:** Fisherman rowing a dory, denomination below

Date	Mintage	VF20	XF40	MS60	MS63	MS65
1992	149,579	PF65 8.50				

KM# 214 25 CENTS

Nickel, 23.8 mm. **Ruler:** Elizabeth II **Series:** 125th Anniversary of Confederation **Subject:** Manitoba **Obv:** Crowned head right

Date	Mintage	VF20	XF40	MS60	MS63	MS65
1992	11,349,000	—	—	0.50	1.00	45.00

KM# 214a 25 CENTS

5.83 g., 0.925 Silver 0.1734 oz. ASW, 23.8 mm. **Ruler:** Elizabeth II **Series:** 125th Anniversary of Confederation **Subject:** Manitoba **Obv:** Crowned head right

Date	Mintage	VF20	XF40	MS60	MS63	MS65
1992	149,579	PF65 8.50				

KM# 220 25 CENTS

Nickel, 23.8 mm. **Ruler:** Elizabeth II **Series:** 125th Anniversary of Confederation **Subject:** Yukon **Obv:** Crowned head right

Date	Mintage	VF20	XF40	MS60	MS63	MS65
1992	10,388,000	—	—	0.50	1.00	45.00

KM# 220a 25 CENTS

5.83 g., 0.925 Silver 0.1734 oz. ASW, 23.8 mm. **Ruler:** Elizabeth II **Series:** 125th Anniversary of Confederation **Subject:** Yukon **Obv:** Crowned head right

Date	Mintage	VF20	XF40	MS60	MS63	MS65
1992	149,579	PF65 8.50				

KM# 221 25 CENTS

Nickel, 23.8 mm. **Ruler:** Elizabeth II **Series:** 125th Anniversary of Confederation **Subject:** Alberta **Obv:** Crowned head right **Rev:** Rock formations in the badlands near Drumhelter, denomination below

Date	Mintage	VF20	XF40	MS60	MS63	MS65
1992	12,133,000	—	—	0.50	1.00	45.00

KM# 221a 25 CENTS

5.83 g., 0.925 Silver 0.1734 oz. ASW, 23.8 mm. **Ruler:** Elizabeth II **Series:** 125th Anniversary of Confederation **Subject:** Alberta **Obv:** Crowned head right **Rev:** Rock formations in the badlands near Drumhelter, denomination below

Date	Mintage	VF20	XF40	MS60	MS63	MS65
1992	—	PF65 8.50				

KM# 222 25 CENTS

Nickel, 23.8 mm. **Ruler:** Elizabeth II **Series:** 125th Anniversary of Confederation **Subject:** Prince Edward Island **Obv:** Crowned head right

Date	Mintage	VF20	XF40	MS60	MS63	MS65
1992	13,001,000	—	—	0.50	1.00	60.00

KM# 222a 25 CENTS

5.83 g., 0.925 Silver 0.1734 oz. ASW, 23.8 mm. **Ruler:** Elizabeth II **Series:** 125th Anniversary of Confederation **Subject:** Prince Edward Island **Obv:** Crowned head right

Date	Mintage	VF20	XF40	MS60	MS63	MS65
1992	149,579	PF65 8.50				

KM# 223 25 CENTS

Nickel, 23.8 mm. **Ruler:** Elizabeth II **Series:** 125th Anniversary of Confederation **Subject:** Ontario **Obv:** Crowned head right **Rev:** Jack pine, denomination below

Date	Mintage	VF20	XF40	MS60	MS63	MS65
1992	14,263,000	—	—	0.50	1.00	60.00

KM# 223a 25 CENTS

5.83 g., 0.925 Silver 0.1734 oz. ASW, 23.8 mm. **Ruler:** Elizabeth II **Series:** 125th Anniversary of Confederation **Subject:** Ontario **Obv:** Crowned head right **Rev:** Jack pine, denomination below

Date	Mintage	VF20	XF40	MS60	MS63	MS65
1992	149,579	PF65 8.50				

KM# 231 25 CENTS
5.03 g., Nickel, 23.8 mm. **Ruler:** Elizabeth II **Series:** 125th Anniversary of Confederation **Subject:** Nova Scotia **Obv:** Crowned head right **Rev:** Lighthouse, denomination below

Date	Mintage	VF20	XF40	MS60	MS63	MS65
1992	13,600,000	—	—	0.50	1.00	45.00

KM# 231a 25 CENTS
5.83 g., 0.925 Silver 0.1734 oz. ASW, 23.8 mm. **Ruler:** Elizabeth II **Series:** 125th Anniversary of Confederation **Subject:** Nova Scotia **Obv:** Crowned head right **Rev:** Lighthouse, denomination below

Date	Mintage	VF20	XF40	MS60	MS63	MS65
1992	149,579	PF65 8.50				

KM# 232 25 CENTS
Nickel, 23.8 mm. **Ruler:** Elizabeth II **Series:** 125th Anniversary of Confederation **Subject:** British Columbia **Obv:** Crowned head right, dates below **Rev:** Large rock, whales, denomination below

Date	Mintage	VF20	XF40	MS60	MS63	MS65
1992	14,001,000	—	—	0.50	1.00	60.00

KM# 232a 25 CENTS
5.83 g., 0.925 Silver 0.1734 oz. ASW, 23.8 mm. **Ruler:** Elizabeth II **Series:** 125th Anniversary of Confederation **Subject:** British Columbia **Obv:** Crowned head right, dates below **Rev:** Large rock, whales, denomination below

Date	Mintage	VF20	XF40	MS60	MS63	MS65
1992	149,579	PF65 8.50				

KM# 233 25 CENTS
Nickel, 23.8 mm. **Ruler:** Elizabeth II **Series:** 125th Anniversary of Confederation **Subject:** Saskatchewan **Obv:** Crowned head right **Rev:** Buildings behind wall, grain stalks on right, denomination below

Date	Mintage	VF20	XF40	MS60	MS63	MS65
1992	14,165,000	—	—	0.50	1.00	75.00

KM# 233a 25 CENTS
5.83 g., 0.925 Silver 0.1734 oz. ASW, 23.8 mm. **Ruler:** Elizabeth II **Series:** 125th Anniversary of Confederation **Subject:** Saskatchewan **Obv:** Crowned head right **Rev:** Buildings behind wall, grain stalks on right, denomination below

Date	Mintage	VF20	XF40	MS60	MS63	MS65
1992	149,579	PF65 8.50				

KM# 234 25 CENTS
Nickel, 23.8 mm. **Ruler:** Elizabeth II **Series:** 125th Anniversary of Confederation **Subject:** Quebec **Obv:** Crowned head right **Rev:** Boats on water, large rocks in background, denomination below

Date	Mintage	VF20	XF40	MS60	MS63	MS65
1992	13,607,000	—	—	0.50	1.00	60.00

KM# 234a 25 CENTS
5.83 g., 0.925 Silver 0.1734 oz. ASW, 23.8 mm. **Ruler:** Elizabeth II **Series:** 125th Anniversary of Confederation **Subject:** Quebec **Obv:** Crowned head right **Rev:** Boats on water, large rocks in background, denomination below

Date	Mintage	VF20	XF40	MS60	MS63	MS65
1992	149,579	PF65 8.50				

KM# 184a 25 CENTS
5.90 g., 0.925 Silver 0.1755 oz. ASW, 23.88 mm. **Ruler:** Elizabeth II **Obv:** Crowned head right **Rev:** Caribou left, denomination above, date at right

Date	Mintage	VF20	XF40	MS60	MS63	MS65
1996	—	PF65 9.50				
1997	—	PF65 9.50				
1998	—	PF65 8.50				
1998 O	—	PF65 8.50				
1999	—	PF65 8.50				

KM# 312 25 CENTS
0.925 Silver, 23.88 mm. **Ruler:** Elizabeth II **Subject:** 90th Anniversary Royal Canadian Mint **Obv:** Crowned head right **Rev:** Denomination and date within wreath, crown above

Date	Mintage	VF20	XF40	MS60	MS63	MS65
1998 Matte	—	PF65 15.00				
1998	—	PF65 15.00				

KM# 184b 25 CENTS
4.40 g., Nickel Plated Steel, 23.88 mm. **Ruler:** Elizabeth II **Obv:** Crowned head right **Rev:** Caribou left, denomination above, date at right

Date	Mintage	VF20	XF40	MS60	MS63	MS65
1999 P	Est. 20000	—	—	—	—	14.00
2000 P	—	—	—	3,500	5,500	—

Note: 3-5 known

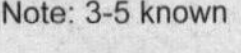

KM# 342 25 CENTS
5.07 g., Nickel, 23.8 mm. **Ruler:** Elizabeth II **Series:** Millennium **Subject:** January - A Country Unfolds **Obv:** Crowned head right **Rev:** Totem pole, portraits

Date	Mintage	VF20	XF40	MS60	MS63	MS65
1999	12,181,200	—	—	—	1.00	32.00

KM# 342a 25 CENTS
5.83 g., 0.925 Silver 0.1734 oz. ASW, 23.8 mm. **Ruler:** Elizabeth II **Series:** Millennium **Subject:** January **Obv:** Crowned head right **Rev:** Totem pole, portraits

Date	Mintage	VF20	XF40	MS60	MS63	MS65
1999	113,645	PF65 9.00				

KM# 343 25 CENTS
5.09 g., Nickel, 23.8 mm. **Ruler:** Elizabeth II **Series:** Millennium **Subject:** February - Etched in Stone **Obv:** Crowned head right **Rev:** Native petroglyphs

Date	Mintage	VF20	XF40	MS60	MS63	MS65
1999	14,469,250	—	—	—	0.65	32.00

KM# 343a 25 CENTS
5.83 g., 0.925 Silver 0.1734 oz. ASW, 23.8 mm. **Ruler:** Elizabeth II **Series:** Millennium **Subject:** February **Obv:** Crowned head right **Rev:** Native petroglyphs

Date	Mintage	VF20	XF40	MS60	MS63	MS65
1999	—	PF65 9.00				

KM# 344 25 CENTS
5.07 g., Nickel, 23.8 mm. **Ruler:** Elizabeth II **Series:** Millennium **Subject:** March - The Log Drive **Obv:** Crowned head right **Rev:** Lumberjack

Date	Mintage	VF20	XF40	MS60	MS63	MS65
1999	15,033,500	—	—	—	0.65	32,00

KM# 344a 25 CENTS
5.83 g., 0.925 Silver 0.1734 oz. ASW, 23.8 mm. **Ruler:** Elizabeth II **Series:** Millennium **Subject:** March **Obv:** Crowned head right **Rev:** Lumberjack

Date	Mintage	VF20	XF40	MS60	MS63	MS65
1999	113,645	PF65 9.00				

KM# 345 25 CENTS

5.07 g., Nickel, 23.8 mm. **Ruler:** Elizabeth II **Series:** Millennium **Subject:** April - Our Northern Heritage **Obv:** Crowned head right **Rev:** Owl, polar bear

Date	Mintage	VF20	XF40	MS60	MS63	MS65
1999	15,446,000	—	—	—	0.65	32.00

KM# 345a 25 CENTS

5.83 g., 0.925 Silver 0.1734 oz. ASW, 23.8 mm. **Ruler:** Elizabeth II **Series:** Millennium **Subject:** April **Obv:** Crowned head right **Rev:** Owl, polar bear

Date	Mintage	VF20	XF40	MS60	MS63	MS65
1999	113,645	PF65 9.00				

KM# 346 25 CENTS

5.07 g., Nickel, 23.8 mm. **Ruler:** Elizabeth II **Series:** Millennium **Subject:** May - The Voyageures **Obv:** Crowned head right **Rev:** Voyageurs in canoe

Date	Mintage	VF20	XF40	MS60	MS63	MS65
1999	15,566,100	—	—	—	0.65	32.00

KM# 346a 25 CENTS

5.83 g., 0.925 Silver 0.1734 oz. ASW, 23.8 mm. **Ruler:** Elizabeth II **Series:** Millennium **Subject:** May **Obv:** Crowned head right **Rev:** Voyageurs in canoe

Date	Mintage	VF20	XF40	MS60	MS63	MS65
1999	113,645	PF65 9.00				

KM# 347 25 CENTS

5.03 g., Nickel, 23.8 mm. **Ruler:** Elizabeth II **Series:** Millennium **Subject:** June - From Coast to Coast **Obv:** Crowned head right **Rev:** 19th-century locomotive **Edge:** Reeded

Date	Mintage	VF20	XF40	MS60	MS63	MS65
1999	20,432,750	—	—	—	0.65	32.00

KM# 347a 25 CENTS

5.83 g., 0.925 Silver 0.1734 oz. ASW, 23.8 mm. **Ruler:** Elizabeth II **Series:** Millennium **Subject:** June **Obv:** Crowned head right **Rev:** 19th-century locomotive **Edge:** Reeded

Date	Mintage	VF20	XF40	MS60	MS63	MS65
1999	113,645	PF65 9.00				

KM# 348 25 CENTS

5.07 g., Nickel, 23.8 mm. **Ruler:** Elizabeth II **Series:** Millennium **Subject:** July - A Nation of People **Obv:** Crowned head right **Rev:** 6 stylized portraits

Date	Mintage	VF20	XF40	MS60	MS63	MS65
1999	17,321,000	—	—	—	0.65	32.00

KM# 348a 25 CENTS

5.83 g., 0.925 Silver 0.1734 oz. ASW, 23.8 mm. **Ruler:** Elizabeth II **Series:** Millennium **Subject:** July **Obv:** Crowned head right **Rev:** 6 stylized portraits

Date	Mintage	VF20	XF40	MS60	MS63	MS65
1999	113,645	PF65 9.00				

KM# 349 25 CENTS

5.07 g., Nickel, 23.8 mm. **Ruler:** Elizabeth II **Series:** Millennium **Subject:** August - The Pioneer Spirit **Obv:** Crowned head right **Rev:** Hay harvesting

Date	Mintage	VF20	XF40	MS60	MS63	MS65
1999	18,153,700	—	—	—	0.65	32.00

KM# 349a 25 CENTS

5.83 g., 0.925 Silver 0.1734 oz. ASW, 23.8 mm. **Ruler:** Elizabeth II **Series:** Millennium **Subject:** August **Obv:** Crowned head right **Rev:** Hay harvesting

Date	Mintage	VF20	XF40	MS60	MS63	MS65
1999	113,645	PF65 9.00				

KM# 350 25 CENTS

5.07 g., Nickel, 23.8 mm. **Ruler:** Elizabeth II **Series:** Millennium **Subject:** September - Canada Through a Child's Eye **Obv:** Crowned head right **Rev:** Childlike artwork

Date	Mintage	VF20	XF40	MS60	MS63	MS65
1999	31,539,350	—	—	—	0.65	32.00

KM# 350a 25 CENTS

5.83 g., 0.925 Silver 0.1734 oz. ASW, 23.8 mm. **Ruler:** Elizabeth II **Series:** Millennium **Subject:** September **Obv:** Crowned head right **Rev:** Childlike artwork

Date	Mintage	VF20	XF40	MS60	MS63	MS65
1999	113,645	PF65 9.00				

KM# 351 25 CENTS

5.07 g., Nickel, 23.8 mm. **Ruler:** Elizabeth II **Series:** Millennium **Subject:** October - Tribute to the First Nations **Obv:** Crowned head right **Rev:** Aboriginal artwork

Date	Mintage	VF20	XF40	MS60	MS63	MS65
1999	32,136,650	—	—	—	0.65	32.00

KM# 351a 25 CENTS

5.83 g., 0.925 Silver 0.1734 oz. ASW, 23.8 mm. **Ruler:** Elizabeth II **Series:** Millennium **Subject:** October **Obv:** Crowned head right **Rev:** Aboriginal artwork

Date	Mintage	VF20	XF40	MS60	MS63	MS65
1999	113,645	PF65 9.00				

KM# 352 25 CENTS

5.07 g., Nickel, 23.8 mm. **Ruler:** Elizabeth II **Series:** Millennium **Subject:** November - The Airplane Opens the North **Obv:** Crowned head right **Rev:** Bush plane with landing skis

Date	Mintage	VF20	XF40	MS60	MS63	MS65
1999	27,162,800	—	—	—	0.65	32.00

KM# 352a 25 CENTS

5.83 g., 0.925 Silver 0.1734 oz. ASW, 23.8 mm. **Ruler:** Elizabeth II **Series:** Millennium **Subject:** November **Obv:** Crowned head right **Rev:** Bush plane with landing skis

Date	Mintage	VF20	XF40	MS60	MS63	MS65
1999	113,645	PF65 9.00				

KM# 353 25 CENTS

5.07 g., Nickel, 23.8 mm. **Ruler:** Elizabeth II **Series:** Millennium **Subject:** December - This is Canada **Obv:** Crowned head right **Rev:** Eclectic geometric design

Date	Mintage	VF20	XF40	MS60	MS63	MS65
1999	43,339,200	—	—	—	0.65	32.00

KM# 353a 25 CENTS

5.10 g., 0.925 Silver 0.1517 oz. ASW, 23.8 mm. **Ruler:** Elizabeth II **Series:** Millennium **Subject:** December **Obv:** Crowned head right **Rev:** Eclectic geometric design

Date	Mintage	VF20	XF40	MS60	MS63	MS65
1999	113,645	PF65 9.00				

KM# 373 25 CENTS

Nickel, 23.8 mm. **Ruler:** Elizabeth II **Subject:** Health **Obv:** Crowned head right, denomination below **Rev:** Ribbon and caduceus, date above

Date	Mintage	VF20	XF40	MS60	MS63	MS65
2000	35,470,900	—	—	—	0.65	32.00

KM# 373a 25 CENTS
0.925 Silver, 23.8 mm. **Ruler:** Elizabeth II **Subject:** Health **Obv:** Crowned head right, denomination below **Rev:** Ribbon and caduceus, date above

Date	Mintage	VF20	XF40	MS60	MS63	MS65
2000	—	PF65 9.00				

KM# 374 25 CENTS
5.10 g., Nickel, 23.85 mm. **Ruler:** Elizabeth II **Subject:** Freedom **Obv:** Crowned head right, denomination below **Rev:** 2 children on maple leaf and rising sun, date above

Date	Mintage	VF20	XF40	MS60	MS63	MS65
2000	35,188,900	—	—	—	0.65	32.00

KM# 374a 25 CENTS
0.925 Silver, 23.8 mm. **Ruler:** Elizabeth II **Subject:** Freedom **Obv:** Crowned head right, denomination below **Rev:** 2 children on maple leaf and rising sun, date above

Date	Mintage	VF20	XF40	MS60	MS63	MS65
2000	—	PF65 9.00				

KM# 375 25 CENTS
Nickel, 23.8 mm. **Ruler:** Elizabeth II **Subject:** Family **Obv:** Crowned head right, denomination below **Rev:** Wreath of native carvings, date above

Date	Mintage	VF20	XF40	MS60	MS63	MS65
2000	35,107,700	—	—	—	0.65	32.00

KM# 375a 25 CENTS
0.925 Silver, 23.8 mm. **Ruler:** Elizabeth II **Subject:** Family **Obv:** Crowned head right, denomination below **Rev:** Wreath of native carvings, date above

Date	Mintage	VF20	XF40	MS60	MS63	MS65
2000	—	PF65 9.00				

KM# 376 25 CENTS
5.08 g., Nickel, 23.8 mm. **Ruler:** Elizabeth II **Subject:** Community **Obv:** Crowned head right, denomination below **Rev:** Map on globe, symbols surround, date above

Date	Mintage	VF20	XF40	MS60	MS63	MS65
2000	35,155,400	—	—	—	0.65	32.00

KM# 376a 25 CENTS
0.925 Silver, 23.8 mm. **Ruler:** Elizabeth II **Subject:** Community **Obv:** Crowned head right, denomination below **Rev:** Map on globe, symbols surround, date above

Date	Mintage	VF20	XF40	MS60	MS63	MS65
2000	—	PF65 9.00				

KM# 377 25 CENTS
Nickel, 23.8 mm. **Ruler:** Elizabeth II **Subject:** Harmony **Obv:** Crowned **Rev:** Maple leaf, date above

Date	Mintage	VF20	XF40	MS60	MS63	MS65
2000	35,184,200	—	—	—	0.65	32.00

KM# 377a 25 CENTS
0.925 Silver, 23.8 mm. **Ruler:** Elizabeth II **Subject:** Harmony **Obv:** Crowned head right, denomination below **Rev:** Maple leaf

Date	Mintage	VF20	XF40	MS60	MS63	MS65
2000	—	PF65 9.00				

KM# 378 25 CENTS
Nickel, 23.8 mm. **Ruler:** Elizabeth II **Subject:** Wisdom **Obv:** Crowned head right, denomination below **Rev:** Man with young child, date above

Date	Mintage	VF20	XF40	MS60	MS63	MS65
2000	35,123,950	—	—	—	0.65	32.00

KM# 378a 25 CENTS
0.925 Silver, 23.8 mm. **Ruler:** Elizabeth II **Subject:** Wisdom **Obv:** Crowned head right, denomination below **Rev:** Man with young child

Date	Mintage	VF20	XF40	MS60	MS63	MS65
2000	—	PF65 9.00				

KM# 379 25 CENTS
Nickel, 23.8 mm. **Ruler:** Elizabeth II **Subject:** Creativity **Obv:** Crowned head right, denomination below **Rev:** Canoe full of children, date above

Date	Mintage	VF20	XF40	MS60	MS63	MS65
2000	35,316,770	—	—	—	0.65	32.00

KM# 379a 25 CENTS
0.925 Silver, 23.8 mm. **Ruler:** Elizabeth II **Subject:** Creativity **Obv:** Crowned head right, denomination below **Rev:** Canoe full of children

Date	Mintage	VF20	XF40	MS60	MS63	MS65
2000	—	PF65 9.00				

KM# 380 25 CENTS
Nickel, 23.8 mm. **Ruler:** Elizabeth II **Subject:** Ingenuity **Obv:** Crowned head right, denomination below **Rev:** Crescent-shaped city views, date above

Date	Mintage	VF20	XF40	MS60	MS63	MS65
2000	36,078,360	—	—	—	0.65	32.00

KM# 380a 25 CENTS
0.925 Silver, 23.8 mm. **Ruler:** Elizabeth II **Subject:** Ingenuity **Obv:** Crowned head right, denomination below **Rev:** Crescent-shaped city views

Date	Mintage	VF20	XF40	MS60	MS63	MS65
2000	—	PF65 9.00				

KM# 381 25 CENTS
Nickel, 23.8 mm. **Ruler:** Elizabeth II **Subject:** Achievement **Obv:** Crowned head right, denomination below **Rev:** Rocket above jagged design, date above

Date	Mintage	VF20	XF40	MS60	MS63	MS65
2000	35,312,750	—	—	—	0.65	32.00

KM# 381a 25 CENTS
0.925 Silver, 23.8 mm. **Ruler:** Elizabeth II **Subject:** Achievement **Obv:** Crowned head right, denomination below **Rev:** Rocket above jagged design

Date	Mintage	VF20	XF40	MS60	MS63	MS65
2000	—	PF65 9.00				

KM# 382 25 CENTS
Nickel, 23.8 mm. **Ruler:** Elizabeth II **Subject:** Natural legacy **Obv:** Crowned head right, denomination below **Rev:** Environmental elements, date above

Date	Mintage	VF20	XF40	MS60	MS63	MS65
2000	36,236,900	—	—	—	0.65	32.00

KM# 382a 25 CENTS
0.925 Silver, 23.8 mm. **Ruler:** Elizabeth II **Subject:** Natural legacy **Obv:** Crowned head right, denomination below **Rev:** Environmental elements

Date	Mintage	VF20	XF40	MS60	MS63	MS65
2000	—	PF65 9.00				

KM# 383 25 CENTS
Nickel, 23.8 mm. **Ruler:** Elizabeth II **Subject:** Celebration **Obv:** Crowned head right, denomination below **Rev:** Fireworks, children behind flag, date above

Date	Mintage	VF20	XF40	MS60	MS63	MS65
2000	35,144,100	—	—	—	0.65	32.00

KM# 383a 25 CENTS

0.925 Silver, 23.8 mm. **Ruler:** Elizabeth II **Subject:** Celebration **Obv:** Crowned head right, denomination below **Rev:** Fireworks, children behind flag

Date	Mintage	VF20	XF40	MS60	MS63	MS65
2000	—	PF65 9.00				

KM# 384.1 25 CENTS

Nickel, 23.8 mm. **Ruler:** Elizabeth II **Subject:** Pride **Obv:** Crowned head right, denomination below **Rev:** Large ribbon 2 in red with 3 small red maple leaves on large maple leaf, date above **Edge:** Reeded **Note:** Colorized version.

Date	Mintage	VF20	XF40	MS60	MS63	MS65
2000 PL	49,399	—	—	—	—	18.00

KM# 384.2 25 CENTS

Nickel, 23.8 mm. **Ruler:** Elizabeth II **Subject:** Pride **Obv:** Crowned head right, denomination below **Rev:** Large ribbon 2 with three small maple leaves on large maple leaf, date above

Date	Mintage	VF20	XF40	MS60	MS63	MS65
2000	50,666,800	—	—	—	0.65	32.00

KM# 384.2a 25 CENTS

0.925 Silver, 23.8 mm. **Ruler:** Elizabeth II **Subject:** Pride **Obv:** Crowned head right, denomination below **Rev:** Ribbon 2 with 3 small maple leaves on large maple leaf

Date	Mintage	VF20	XF40	MS60	MS63	MS65
2000	—	PF65 9.00				

KM# 6 50 CENTS

11.62 g., 0.925 Silver 0.3456 oz. ASW, 29.72 mm. **Ruler:** Victoria **Obv:** VICTORIA DEI GRATIA REGINA. CANADA **Rev:** Denomination and date within wreath, crown above **Edge:** Reeded

Date	Mintage	VG8	F12	VF20	XF40	AU50	MS60	MS63	MS65
1901	80,000	80.00	150	300	750	2,000	7,000	16,000	26,000

Victorian leaves

KM# 12 50 CENTS

11.62 g., 0.925 Silver 0.3456 oz. ASW, 29.72 mm. **Ruler:** Edward VII **Obv:** Crowned bust right **Rev:** Denomination and date within wreath, crown above **Edge:** Reeded

Date	Mintage	VG8	F12	VF20	XF40	AU50	MS60	MS63	MS65
1902	120,000	28.00	55.00	150	350	650	1,800	4,500	7,500
1903 H	140,000	35.00	70.00	225	550	850	2,000	5,000	8,500
1904	60,000	175	350	750	1,500	2,700	5,000	14,500	25,000
1905	40,000	225	450	1,000	2,100	4,000	9,000	18,000	—
1906	350,000	24.00	45.00	150	400	800	1,800	4,500	7,500
1907	300,000	24.00	50.00	125	350	700	1,800	5,000	8,500
1908	128,119	40.00	90.00	250	550	850	1,400	2,700	4,500
1909	302,118	30.00	90.00	250	700	1,600	3,000	11,000	20,000
1910 Victoria leaves	649,521	35.00	65.00	175	500	1,050	2,200	7,000	12,000

Edwardian leaves

KM# 12a 50 CENTS

11.62 g., 0.925 Silver 0.3456 oz. ASW, 29.72 mm. **Ruler:** Edward VII **Obv:** Crowned bust right **Rev:** Denomination and date within wreath **Edge:** Reeded

Date	Mintage	VG8	F12	VF20	XF40	AU50	MS60	MS63	MS65
1910 Edwardian leaves	Inc. above	22.00	40.00	100	350	650	1,550	4,500	7,500

KM# 19 50 CENTS

11.62 g., 0.925 Silver 0.3456 oz. ASW, 29.72 mm. **Ruler:** George V **Obv:** Crowned bust left **Rev:** Denomination and date within wreath, crown above **Edge:** Reeded

Date	Mintage	VG8	F12	VF20	XF40	AU50	MS60	MS63	MS65
1911	209,972	25.00	100	350	750	1,100	1,950	4,000	10,000

KM# 25 50 CENTS

11.62 g., 0.925 Silver 0.3456 oz. ASW, 29.72 mm. **Ruler:** George V **Obv:** Crowned bust left, modified legend **Rev:** Denomination and date within wreath, crown above **Edge:** Reeded

Date	Mintage	VG8	F12	VF20	XF40	AU50	MS60	MS63	MS65
1912	285,867	16.00	40.00	150	350	650	1,500	4,000	12,000
1913	265,889	16.00	40.00	175	400	800	1,800	6,000	20,000
1914	160,128	40.00	100	300	750	1,800	4,000	10,000	—
1916	459,070	15.00	24.00	75.00	200	400	900	2,700	9,500
1917	752,213	13.00	22.00	50.00	150	300	650	1,600	3,500
1918	754,989	13.00	20.00	40.00	125	250	500	1,300	4,000
1919	1,113,429	13.00	20.00	40.00	125	225	500	1,300	4,000

KM# 25a 50 CENTS

11.66 g., 0.800 Silver 0.300 oz. ASW, 29.72 mm. **Ruler:** George V **Obv:** Crowned bust left **Rev:** Denomination and date within wreath, crown below **Edge:** Reeded

Date	Mintage	VG8	F12	VF20	XF40	AU50	MS60	MS63	MS65
1920	584,691	17.00	22.00	55.00	200	400	800	2,000	4,500
1921	—	30,000	40,000	50,000	55,000	60,000	65,000	125,000	—

Note: 75 to 100 known; David Akers John Jay Pittman sale, Part Three, 10-99, Gem Unc. realized $63,250

Date	Mintage	VG8	F12	VF20	XF40	AU50	MS60	MS63	MS65
1929	228,328	13.00	22.00	50.00	150	300	650	1,500	4,000
1931	57,581	25.00	45.00	100	300	600	1,100	2,200	5,500
1932	19,213	150	250	500	1,000	2,200	5,000	9,500	—
1934	39,539	30.00	50.00	100	300	550	900	1,800	4,500
1936	38,550	24.00	45.00	100	300	450	700	1,300	3,500

KM# 36 50 CENTS

11.66 g., 0.800 Silver 0.300 oz. ASW, 29.72 mm. **Ruler:** George VI **Obv:** Head left **Rev:** Crowned arms with supporters, denomination above, date below **Edge:** Reeded

Date	Mintage	VG8	F12	VF20	XF40	AU50	MS60	MS63	MS65
1937	192,016	5.50	12.00	14.00	18.00	25.00	40.00	90.00	1,800
1938	192,018	5.50	15.00	20.00	40.00	85.00	175	450	4,500
1939	287,976	5.50	13.00	15.00	28.00	60.00	100	300	2,500
1940	1,996,566	—	—	5.50	14.00	19.00	35.00	75.00	1,000
1941	1,714,874	—	—	5.50	14.00	19.00	35.00	75.00	1,300
1942	1,974,164	—	—	5.50	14.00	19.00	35.00	75.00	1,300
1943	3,109,583	—	—	5.50	14.00	19.00	35.00	75.00	1,300
1944	2,460,205	—	—	5.50	14.00	19.00	35.00	75.00	1,300
1945	1,959,528	—	—	5.50	14.00	19.00	35.00	90.00	2,700
1946	950,235	—	5.50	13.00	18.00	35.00	75.00	175	3,500
1946 hoof in 6	Inc. above	30.00	40.00	60.00	225	600	1,650	4,500	—
1947 straight 7	424,885	—	5.50	13.00	20.00	45.00	90.00	250	—
1947 curved 7	Inc. above	—	5.50	13.00	29.00	65.00	125	350	3,500
1947 maple leaf, straight 7	38,433	28.00	40.00	50.00	100	150	250	400	3,500
1947 maple leaf, curved 7	Inc. above	1,500	1,950	2,300	3,000	4,000	6,000	13,000	—

KM# 45 50 CENTS

11.66 g., 0.800 Silver 0.300 oz. ASW, 29.72 mm. **Ruler:** George VI **Obv:** Head left, modified legend **Rev:** Crowned arms with supporters, denomination above, date below **Edge:** Reeded

Date	Mintage	VG8	F12	VF20	XF40	AU50	MS60	MS63	MS65
1948	37,784	90.00	125	150	175	225	300	450	2,200
1949	858,991	—	—	5.50	13.00	22.00	50.00	125	1,300
1949 hoof over 9	Inc. above	20.00	22.50	45.00	90.00	200	500	1,150	—
1950 no lines in 0	2,384,179	14.00	16.00	18.00	45.00	90.00	175	300	2,700
1950 lines in 0	Inc. above	—	—	5.50	12.00	14.50	16.00	45.00	900
1951	2,421,730	—	—	—	5.50	10.00	14.00	30.00	250
1952	2,596,465	—	—	—	5.50	10.00	14.00	22.00	150

KM# 53 50 CENTS

11.66 g., 0.800 Silver 0.300 oz. ASW, 29.72 mm. **Ruler:** Elizabeth II **Obv:** Laureate bust right **Rev:** Crowned arms with supporters, denomination above, date below **Edge:** Reeded

Date	Mintage	VG8	F12	VF20	XF40	AU50	MS60	MS63	MS65
1953	1,630,429	—	—	—	5.50	9.50	13.00	22.50	225
Note: small date									
1953	Inc. above	—	—	5.50	12.00	15.00	27.00	50.00	800
Note: large date, straps									
1953	Inc. above	—	5.50	12.00	20.00	45.00	90.00	225	3,500
Note: large date without straps									
1954	506,305	—	—	5.50	14.00	19.50	28.00	50.00	350
1955	753,511	—	—	5.50	12.00	15.00	18.00	30.00	250
1956	1,379,499	—	—	—	5.50	6.50	12.00	20.00	225
1957	2,171,689	—	—	—	5.50	6.50	12.00	13.00	150
1958	2,957,266	—	—	—	5.50	6.50	12.00	13.00	200

KM# 56 50 CENTS

11.66 g., 0.800 Silver 0.300 oz. ASW, 29.7 mm. **Ruler:** Elizabeth II **Obv:** Luareate bust right **Rev:** Crown divides date above arms with supporters, denomination at right **Edge:** Reeded

Date	Mintage	VF20	XF40	MS60	MS63	MS65
1959	3,095,535	—	—	5.75	12.00	175
Note: horizontal shading						
1960	3,488,897	—	—	5.75	12.00	175
1961	3,584,417	—	—	5.75	12.00	100
1962	5,208,030	—	—	5.75	12.00	80.00
1963	8,348,871	—	—	5.75	12.00	100
1964	9,377,676	—	—	5.75	12.00	80.00

KM# 63 50 CENTS

11.66 g., 0.800 Silver 0.300 oz. ASW, 29.72 mm. **Ruler:** Elizabeth II **Obv:** Young bust right **Rev:** Crown divides date above arms with supporters, denomination at right **Edge:** Reeded

Date	Mintage	VF20	XF40	MS60	MS63	MS65
1965	12,629,974	—	—	5.75	12.00	80.00
1966	7,920,496	—	—	5.75	12.00	100

KM# 69 50 CENTS

11.66 g., 0.800 Silver 0.300 oz. ASW, 29.72 mm. **Ruler:** Elizabeth II **Subject:** Confederation Centennial **Obv:** Young bust right **Rev:** Seated wolf howling divides denomination at top, dates at bottom **Edge:** Reeded

Date	Mintage	VF20	XF40	MS60	MS63	MS65
1867-1967	4,211,392	PF65 14.00				
1867-1967	—	PF63 14.00				

KM# 75.1 50 CENTS

8.10 g., Nickel, 27.13 mm. **Ruler:** Elizabeth II **Obv:** Young bust right **Rev:** Crown divides date above arms with supporters, denomination at right **Edge:** Reeded

Date	Mintage	VF20	XF40	MS60	MS63	MS65
1968	3,966,932	—	—	0.80	1.25	62.00
1969	7,113,929	—	—	0.80	1.25	62.00
1970	2,429,526	—	—	0.80	1.25	42.00
1971	2,166,444	—	—	0.80	1.25	62.00
1972	2,515,632	—	—	0.80	1.25	62.00
1973	2,546,096	—	—	0.80	1.25	62.00
1974	3,436,650	—	—	0.80	1.25	42.00
1975	3,710,000	—	—	0.80	1.25	85.00
1976	2,940,719	—	—	0.80	1.25	175

KM# 75.2 50 CENTS

8.10 g., Nickel, 27.13 mm. **Ruler:** Elizabeth II **Obv:** Small young bust right **Rev:** Crown divides date above arms with supporters, denomination at right **Edge:** Reeded

Date	Mintage	VF20	XF40	MS60	MS63	MS65
1977	709,839	—	—	1.25	2.00	80.00

KM# 75.3 50 CENTS

8.10 g., Nickel, 27.13 mm. **Ruler:** Elizabeth II **Obv:** Young bust right **Rev:** Crown divides date above arms with supporters, denomination at right, redesigned arms **Edge:** Reeded

Date	Mintage	VF20	XF40	MS60	MS63	MS65
1978	3,341,892	—	—	0.65	1.25	85.00
Note: square jewels						
1978	Inc. above	1.00	2.50	4.50	6.00	95.00
Note: round jewels						
1979	3,425,000	—	—	0.65	1.25	40.00
1980	1,574,000	—	—	0.65	1.25	40.00
1981	2,690,272	—	—	0.65	1.25	55.00
1981	199,000	PF65 3.00				
1982	2,236,674	—	22.00	35.00	55.00	250
Note: small beads						
1982	180,908	PF65 3.00				
Note: small beads						
1982	Inc. above	—	—	0.65	1.25	35.00
Note: large beads						
1983	1,177,000	—	—	0.65	1.25	60.00
1983	168,000	PF65 3.00				
1984	1,502,989	—	—	0.65	1.25	40.00
1984	161,602	PF65 3.00				
1985	2,188,374	—	—	0.65	1.25	65.00
1985	157,037	PF65 3.00				
1986	781,400		—	0.80	1.25	40.00
1986	175,745	PF65 3.00				
1987	373,000	—	—	0.80	1.50	40.00

Date	Mintage	VF20	XF40	MS60	MS63	MS65
1987	179,004	PF65 3.50				
1988	220,000	—	—	1.75	2.25	40.00
1988	175,259	PF65 4.00				
1989	266,419	—	—	0.80	1.25	40.00
1989	170,928	PF65 4.00				

KM# 185 50 CENTS

8.10 g., Nickel, 27.13 mm. **Ruler:** Elizabeth II **Obv:** Crowned head right **Rev:** Crown divides date above arms with supporters, denomination at right **Edge:** Reeded

Date	Mintage	VF20	XF40	MS60	MS63	MS65
1990	207,000	—	—	1.75	2.50	40.00
1990	140,649	PF65 5.00				
1991	490,000	—	—	0.85	1.25	27.00
1991	131,888	PF65 7.00				
1993	393,000	—	—	0.85	1.25	27.00
1993	143,065	PF65 4.00				
1994	987,000	—	—	0.75	1.25	27.00
1994	146,424	PF65 4.00				
1995	626,000	—	—	0.75	1.25	27.00
1995	—	PF65 4.00				
1996	458,000	—	—	0.65	1.25	27.00
1996	—	PF65 7.00				

KM# 208 50 CENTS

8.10 g., Nickel, 27.1 mm. **Ruler:** Elizabeth II **Subject:** Confederation 125 **Obv:** Crowned head right **Rev:** Crown divides date above arms with supporters, denomination at right **Edge:** Reeded

Date	Mintage	VF20	XF40	MS60	MS63	MS65
1992	445,000	—	—	1.50	2.50	40.00
1992	147,061	PF65 5.00				

KM# 261 50 CENTS

9.34 g., 0.925 Silver 0.2778 oz. ASW **Ruler:** Elizabeth II **Obv:** Crowned head right **Rev:** Atlantic Puffin, denomination and date at right

Date	Mintage	VF20	XF40	MS60	MS63	MS65
1995	—	PF65 12.00				

KM# 262 50 CENTS

9.34 g., 0.925 Silver 0.2778 oz. ASW **Ruler:** Elizabeth II **Obv:** Crowned head right **Rev:** Whooping crane left, denomination and date at right

Date	Mintage	VF20	XF40	MS60	MS63	MS65
1995	—	PF65 12.00				

KM# 263 50 CENTS

9.34 g., 0.925 Silver 0.2778 oz. ASW **Ruler:** Elizabeth II **Obv:** Crowned head right **Rev:** Gray Jays, denomination and date at right

Date	Mintage	VF20	XF40	MS60	MS63	MS65
1995	—	PF65 12.00				

KM# 264 50 CENTS

9.34 g., 0.925 Silver 0.2778 oz. ASW **Ruler:** Elizabeth II **Obv:** Crowned head right **Rev:** White-tailed ptarmigans, date and denomination at right

Date	Mintage	VF20	XF40	MS60	MS63	MS65
1995	—	PF65 12.00				

KM# 185a 50 CENTS

11.64 g., 0.925 Silver 0.3461 oz. ASW **Ruler:** Elizabeth II **Obv:** Crowned head right **Rev:** Crown divides date above arms with supporters, denomination at right

Date	Mintage	VF20	XF40	MS60	MS63	MS65
1996	—	PF65 13.00				

KM# 283 50 CENTS

9.34 g., 0.925 Silver 0.2778 oz. ASW, 27 mm. **Ruler:** Elizabeth II **Obv:** Crowned head right **Rev:** Moose calf left, denomination and date at right

Date	Mintage	VF20	XF40	MS60	MS63	MS65
1996	—	PF65 17.00				

KM# 284 50 CENTS

9.34 g., 0.925 Silver 0.2778 oz. ASW, 27 mm. **Ruler:** Elizabeth II **Obv:** Crowned head right **Rev:** Wood ducklings, date and denomination at right

Date	Mintage	VF20	XF40	MS60	MS63	MS65
1996	—	PF65 17.00				

KM# 285 50 CENTS

9.34 g., 0.925 Silver 0.2778 oz. ASW, 27 mm. **Ruler:** Elizabeth II **Obv:** Crowned head right **Rev:** Cougar kittens, date and denomination at right

Date	Mintage	VF20	XF40	MS60	MS63	MS65
1996	—	PF65 17.00				

KM# 286 50 CENTS

9.34 g., 0.925 Silver 0.2778 oz. ASW, 27 mm. **Ruler:** Elizabeth II **Obv:** Crowned head right **Rev:** Bear cubs standing, date and denomination at right

Date	Mintage	VF20	XF40	MS60	MS63	MS65
1996	—	PF65 17.00				

KM# 290 50 CENTS

8.10 g., Nickel, 27.1 mm. **Ruler:** Elizabeth II **Obv:** Crowned head right **Rev:** Redesigned arms **Edge:** Reeded

Date	Mintage	VF20	XF40	MS60	MS63	MS65
1997	387,000	—	—	0.70	1.25	30.00
1997	—	PF65 7.50				
1998	308,000	—	—	0.70	1.25	60.00
1998	—	PF65 13.00				
1998 W PL	—	—	—	—	—	3.50
1999	496,000	—	—	0.70	1.25	40.00
1999	—	PF65 9.00				
2000	559,000	—	—	0.70	1.25	35.00
2000	—	PF65 8.00				
2000 W	—	—	—	—	—	1.50

KM# 290a 50 CENTS

11.66 g., 0.925 Silver 0.3469 oz. ASW, 27.13 mm. **Ruler:** Elizabeth II **Obv:** Crowned head right **Rev:** Redesigned arms **Edge:** Reeded

Date	Mintage	VF20	XF40	MS60	MS63	MS65
1997	—	PF65 10.00				
1998	—	PF65 13.00				
1999	—	PF65 13.00				
2000	—	PF65 12.00				

KM# 292 50 CENTS

9.34 g., 0.925 Silver 0.2778 oz. ASW, 27 mm. **Ruler:** Elizabeth II **Obv:** Crowned head right **Rev:** Duck Toling Retriever, date and denomination at right

Date	Mintage	VF20	XF40	MS60	MS63	MS65
1997	—	PF65 16.00				

KM# 293 50 CENTS

9.34 g., 0.925 Silver 0.2778 oz. ASW **Ruler:** Elizabeth II **Obv:** Crowned head right **Rev:** Labrador leaping left, date and denomination at right

Date	Mintage	VF20	XF40	MS60	MS63	MS65
1997	—	PF65 16.00				

KM# 294 50 CENTS

9.34 g., 0.925 Silver 0.2778 oz. ASW **Ruler:** Elizabeth II **Obv:** Crowned head right **Rev:** Newfoundland right, date and denomination at right

Date	Mintage	VF20	XF40	MS60	MS63	MS65
1997	—	PF65 16.00				

KM# 295 50 CENTS

9.34 g., 0.925 Silver 0.2778 oz. ASW, 27.1 mm. **Ruler:** Elizabeth II **Obv:** Crowned head right **Rev:** Eskimo dog leaping forward, date and denomination at right

Date	Mintage	VF20	XF40	MS60	MS63	MS65
1997	—	PF65 16.00				

KM# 313 50 CENTS

11.66 g., 0.925 Silver 0.3469 oz. ASW **Ruler:** Elizabeth II **Subject:** 90th Anniversary Royal Canadian Mint **Obv:** Crowned head right **Rev:** Denomination and date within wreath, crown above

Date	Mintage	VF20	XF40	MS60	MS63	MS65
1908-1998 Matte	—	PF65 14.00				
1908-1998	—	PF65 14.00				

KM# 314 50 CENTS

9.34 g., 0.925 Silver 0.2778 oz. ASW **Ruler:** Elizabeth II **Subject:** 110 Years Canadian Speed and Figure Skating **Obv:** Crowned head right **Rev:** Speed skaters, dates below, denomination above

Date	Mintage	VF20	XF40	MS60	MS63	MS65
1998	—	PF65 12.00				

KM# 315 50 CENTS

9.34 g., 0.925 Silver 0.2778 oz. ASW **Ruler:** Elizabeth II **Subject:** 100 Years Canadian Ski Racing **Obv:** Crowned head right **Rev:** Skiers, dates below, denomination upper left

Date	Mintage	VF20	XF40	MS60	MS63	MS65
1998	—	PF65 12.00				

KM# 318 50 CENTS

9.34 g., 0.925 Silver 0.2778 oz. ASW **Ruler:** Elizabeth II **Obv:** Crowned head right **Rev:** Killer Whales, date and denomination at right

Date	Mintage	VF20	XF40	MS60	MS63	MS65
1998	—	PF65 16.00				

KM# 319 50 CENTS

9.34 g., 0.925 Silver 0.2778 oz. ASW, 27 mm. **Ruler:** Elizabeth II **Obv:** Crowned head right **Rev:** Humpback whale, date and denomination at right

Date	Mintage	VF20	XF40	MS60	MS63	MS65
1998	—	PF65 16.00				

KM# 320 50 CENTS

9.34 g., 0.925 Silver 0.2778 oz. ASW **Ruler:** Elizabeth II **Obv:** Crowned head right **Rev:** Beluga whales, date and denomination at right

Date	Mintage	VF20	XF40	MS60	MS63	MS65
1998	—	PF65 16.00				

KM# 321 50 CENTS
9.34 g., 0.925 Silver 0.2778 oz. ASW, 27 mm. **Ruler:** Elizabeth II **Obv:** Crowned head right **Rev:** Blue whale, date and denomination at right

Date	Mintage	VF20	XF40	MS60	MS63	MS65
1998	—	PF65 16.00				

KM# 327 50 CENTS
9.34 g., 0.925 Silver 0.2778 oz. ASW **Ruler:** Elizabeth II **Subject:** 110 Years Canadian Soccer **Obv:** Crowned head right **Rev:** Soccer players, dates above, denomination at right

Date	Mintage	VF20	XF40	MS60	MS63	MS65
1998	—	PF65 12.00				

KM# 328 50 CENTS
9.34 g., 0.925 Silver 0.2778 oz. ASW **Ruler:** Elizabeth II **Subject:** 20 Years Canadian Auto Racing **Obv:** Crowned head right **Rev:** Race car divides date and denomination

Date	Mintage	VF20	XF40	MS60	MS63	MS65
1998	—	PF65 12.00				

KM# 290b 50 CENTS
6.90 g., Nickel Plated Steel, 27.13 mm. **Ruler:** Elizabeth II **Obv:** Crowned head right **Rev:** Redesigned arms **Edge:** Reeded

Date	Mintage	VF20	XF40	MS60	MS63	MS65
1999 P	Est. 20000	—	—	—	—	10.00
2000 P	Est. 50	—	—	—	—	3,500

Note: Available only in RCM presentation coin clocks

KM# 333 50 CENTS
9.34 g., 0.925 Silver 0.2778 oz. ASW **Ruler:** Elizabeth II **Subject:** 1904 Canadian Open **Obv:** Crowned head right **Rev:** Golfers, date at right, denomination below

Date	Mintage	VF20	XF40	MS60	MS63	MS65
1999	—	PF65 14.00				

KM# 334 50 CENTS
9.34 g., 0.925 Silver 0.2778 oz. ASW **Ruler:** Elizabeth II **Subject:** First U.S.-Canadian Yacht Race **Obv:** Crowned head right **Rev:** Yachts, dates at left, denomination below

Date	Mintage	VF20	XF40	MS60	MS63	MS65
1999	—	PF65 12.00				

KM# 335 50 CENTS
9.34 g., 0.925 Silver 0.2778 oz. ASW **Ruler:** Elizabeth II **Series:** Canadian Cats **Obv:** Crowned head right **Rev:** Cymric cat, date below, denomination at bottom

Date	Mintage	VF20	XF40	MS60	MS63	MS65
1999	—	PF65 20.00				

KM# 336 50 CENTS
9.34 g., 0.925 Silver 0.2778 oz. ASW **Ruler:** Elizabeth II **Series:** Canadian Cats **Obv:** Crowned head right **Rev:** Tonkinese cat, date below, denomination at bottom

Date	Mintage	VF20	XF40	MS60	MS63	MS65
1999	—	PF65 20.00				

KM# 337 50 CENTS
9.34 g., 0.925 Silver 0.2778 oz. ASW **Ruler:** Elizabeth II **Series:** Canadian Cats **Obv:** Crowned head right **Rev:** Cougar, date and denomination below

Date	Mintage	VF20	XF40	MS60	MS63	MS65
1999	—	PF65 20.00				

KM# 338 50 CENTS
9.34 g., 0.925 Silver 0.2778 oz. ASW **Ruler:** Elizabeth II **Series:** Canadian Cats **Obv:** Crowned head right **Rev:** Lynx, date and denomination below

Date	Mintage	VF20	XF40	MS60	MS63	MS65
1999	—	PF65 20.00				

KM# 371 50 CENTS
9.36 g., 0.925 Silver 0.2784 oz. ASW, 27.1 mm. **Ruler:** Elizabeth II **Subject:** Basketball **Obv:** Crowned head right **Rev:** Basketball players **Edge:** Reeded

Date	Mintage	VF20	XF40	MS60	MS63	MS65
1999	—	PF65 10.00				

KM# 372 50 CENTS
9.36 g., 0.925 Silver 0.2784 oz. ASW, 27.1 mm. **Ruler:** Elizabeth II **Obv:** Crowned head right **Rev:** Football players **Edge:** Reeded

Date	Mintage	VF20	XF40	MS60	MS63	MS65
1999	—	PF65 11.00				

KM# 385 50 CENTS
9.35 g., 0.925 Silver 0.2781 oz. ASW **Ruler:** Elizabeth II **Subject:** Ice Hockey **Obv:** Crowned head right **Rev:** 4 hockey players

Date	Mintage	VF20	XF40	MS60	MS63	MS65
2000	—	PF65 11.00				

KM# 386 50 CENTS
9.35 g., 0.925 Silver 0.2781 oz. ASW **Ruler:** Elizabeth II **Subject:** Curling **Obv:** Crowned head right **Rev:** Motion study of curlers, dates and denomination below

Date	Mintage	VF20	XF40	MS60	MS63	MS65
1910-2000	—	PF65 11.00				

KM# 389 50 CENTS

9.35 g., 0.925 Silver 0.2781 oz. ASW **Ruler:** Elizabeth II **Obv:** Crowned head right **Rev:** Great horned owl, facing, date and denomination at right

Date	Mintage	VF20	XF40	MS60	MS63	MS65
2000	—	PF65 17.00				

KM# 390 50 CENTS

9.35 g., 0.925 Silver 0.2781 oz. ASW **Ruler:** Elizabeth II **Obv:** Crowned head right **Rev:** Red-tailed hawk, dates and denomination at right

Date	Mintage	VF20	XF40	MS60	MS63	MS65
2000	—	PF65 17.00				

KM# 391 50 CENTS

9.35 g., 0.925 Silver 0.2781 oz. ASW **Ruler:** Elizabeth II **Obv:** Crowned head right **Rev:** Osprey, dates and denomination at right

Date	Mintage	VF20	XF40	MS60	MS63	MS65
2000	—	PF65 17.00				

KM# 392 50 CENTS

9.35 g., 0.925 Silver 0.2781 oz. ASW **Ruler:** Elizabeth II **Obv:** Crowned head right **Rev:** Bald eagle, dates and denomination at right

Date	Mintage	VF20	XF40	MS60	MS63	MS65
2000	—	PF65 17.00				

KM# 393 50 CENTS

9.35 g., 0.925 Silver 0.2781 oz. ASW **Ruler:** Elizabeth II **Subject:** Steeplechase **Obv:** Crowned head right **Rev:** Steeplechase, dates and denomination below

Date	Mintage	VF20	XF40	MS60	MS63	MS65
1840-2000	—	PF65 11.00				

KM# 394 50 CENTS

9.35 g., 0.925 Silver 0.2781 oz. ASW **Ruler:** Elizabeth II **Subject:** Bowling **Obv:** Crowned head right

Date	Mintage	VF20	XF40	MS60	MS63	MS65
2000	—	PF65 11.00				

KM# 30 DOLLAR

23.33 g., 0.800 Silver 0.600 oz. ASW, 36 mm. **Ruler:** George V **Subject:** Silver Jubilee **Obv:** Bust left **Rev:** Voyager, date and denomination below

Date	Mintage	VG8	F12	VF20	XF40	AU50	MS60	MS63	MS65
1935	428,707	—	22.00	27.00	30.00	35.00	40.00	65.00	300
1935 Specimen	—	—	—	—	—	—	—	1,800	6,000

KM# 31 DOLLAR

23.33 g., 0.800 Silver 0.600 oz. ASW, 36 mm. **Ruler:** George V **Obv:** Crowned bust left **Rev:** Voyageur, date and denomination below

Date	Mintage	VG8	F12	VF20	XF40	AU50	MS60	MS63	MS65
1936	339,600	—	24.00	28.00	30.00	35.00	50.00	100	750
1936 Specimen	—	—	—	—	—	—	—	2,200	9,000

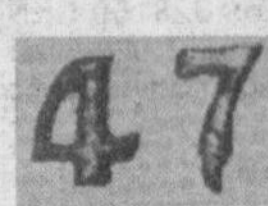

Pointed 7

KM# 37 DOLLAR

23.33 g., 0.800 Silver 0.600 oz. ASW, 36 mm. **Ruler:** George VI **Obv:** Head left **Rev:** Voyageur, date and denomination below

Date	Mintage	VG8	F12	VF20	XF40	AU50	MS60	MS63	MS65
1937	207,406	—	24.00	28.00	30.00	35.00	45.00	90.00	—
1937 Mirror Specimen	1,295	—	—	—	—	—	—	650	1,300
1937 Matte Specimen	—	—	—	—	—	—	—	225	450
1938	90,304	—	32.00	45.00	65.00	80.00	100	250	4,500
1938 Specimen	—	—	—	—	—	—	—	5,000	9,000
1945	38,391	—	125	175	225	250	350	750	13,000
1945 Specimen	—	—	—	—	—	—	—	1,300	5,000
1946	93,055	—	25.00	40.00	55.00	75.00	100	400	9,000
1946 Specimen	—	—	—	—	—	—	—	1,300	5,000
1947 Pointed 7	Inc. below	—	80.00	125	175	225	400	2,000	—
1947 Pointed 7, Specimen	—	—	—	—	—	—	—	2,700	5,000
1947 Blunt 7	65,595	—	60.00	90.00	125	150	175	400	7,000
1947 Blunt 7, Specimen	—	—	—	—	—	—	—	2,700	5,000
1947 Maple leaf	21,135	—	150	200	225	300	400	800	7,000
1947 Maple leaf, Specimen	—	—	—	—	—	—	—	2,200	6,000

KM# 38 DOLLAR

23.33 g., 0.800 Silver 0.600 oz. ASW, 36 mm. **Ruler:** George VI **Subject:** Royal Visit **Obv:** Head left **Rev:** Tower at center of building, date and denomination below

Date	Mintage	VG8	F12	VF20	XF40	AU50	MS60	MS63	MS65
1939	1,363,816	—	—	11.00	16.00	20.00	24.00	35.00	500
1939 Matte specimen	—	—	—	—	—	—	—	450	900
1939 Mirror specimen	—	—	—	—	—	—	—	650	1,300

KM# 46 DOLLAR

23.33 g., 0.800 Silver 0.600 oz. ASW, 36 mm. **Ruler:** George VI **Obv:** Head left, modified left legend **Rev:** Voyageur, date and denomination below

Date	Mintage	VG8	F12	VF20	XF40	AU50	MS60	MS63	MS65
1948	18,780	—	750	950	1,200	1,300	1,600	2,900	15,000
1948 Specimen	—	—	—	—	—	—	—	4,500	9,000
1950	261,002	—	11.00	20.00	24.00	25.00	30.00	60.00	250
Note: With 3 water lines									
1950 Specimen	—	—	—	—	—	—	—	1,000	1,800
Note: With 3 water lines									
1950 Matte Proof	—	PF65 18,000							
Note: With 4 water lines, 1 known									
1950	Inc. above	—	22.00	28.00	35.00	40.00	50.00	125	2,200
Note: Arnprior with 2-1/2 water lines									
1950 Specimen	—	—	—	—	—	—	—	1,300	3,000
Note: Arnprior with 2-1/2 water lines									
1951	416,395	—	—	11.00	18.00	22.00	25.00	40.00	650
Note: With 3 water lines									
1951 Specimen	—	—	—	—	—	—	—	900	1,800
Note: With 3 water lines									
1951	Inc. above	—	40.00	55.00	90.00	125	225	450	6,500
Note: Arnprior with 1-1/2 water lines									
1951 Specimen	—	—	—	—	—	—	—	1,300	3,500
Note: Arnprior with 1-1/2 water lines									
1952	406,148	—	—	—	11.00	22.00	24.00	35.00	500
Note: With 3 water lines									
1952 Specimen	—	—	—	—	—	—	—	650	1,800
Note: With 3 water lines									
1952	Inc. above	—	11.00	25.00	27.00	35.00	50.00	100	—
Note: Short water links									
1952 Specimen	—	—	—	—	—	—	—	650	1,800
Note: Short water lines									
1952	Inc. above	—	11.00	18.00	22.00	24.00	26.00	55.00	900
Note: Without water lines									
1952 Specimen	—	—	—	—	—	—	—	650	1,800
Note: Without water lines									

KM# 47 DOLLAR

23.33 g., 0.800 Silver 0.600 oz. ASW, 36 mm. **Ruler:** George VI **Subject:** Newfoundland **Obv:** Head left **Rev:** "The Matthew", John Cabot's ship, date and denomination below

Date	Mintage	VG8	F12	VF20	XF40	AU50	MS60	MS63	MS65
1949	672,218	—	11.00	20.00	23.00	27.00	30.00	35.00	90.00
1949 Specimen	—	—	—	—	—	—	—	700	1,800
1949	—	PF60 2,600							

KM# 54 DOLLAR

23.33 g., 0.800 Silver 0.600 oz. ASW, 36 mm. **Ruler:** Elizabeth II **Obv:** Laureate bust right **Rev:** Voyageur, date and denomination below **Note:** All genuine circulation strike 1955 Arnprior dollars have a die break running along the top of TI in the word GRATIA on the obverse.

Date	Mintage	VG8	F12	VF20	XF40	AU50	MS60	MS63	MS65
1953	1,074,578	—	—	—	—	11.00	23.00	30.00	500
Note: Without strap, wire rim									
1953 Specimen	Inc. above	—	—	—	—	—	—	800	2,200
Note: Without strap, wire rim									
1953	Inc. above	PF60 1,600							
Note: Without strap, wire rim									
1953	Inc. above	—	—	—	—	11.00	23.00	30.00	550
Note: With strap, flat rim									
1953 Specimen	—	—	—	—	—	—	—	900	2,300
Note: With strap, flat rim									
1954	246,606	—	17.00	18.00	20.00	25.00	29.00	50.00	1,300
1955	268,105	—	14.00	16.00	18.00	24.00	29.00	50.00	1,100
Note: With 3 water lines									
1955	Inc. above	—	85.00	90.00	100	125	150	250	2,900
Note: Arnprior with 1-1/2 water lines* and die break									
1956	209,092	—	20.00	22.00	24.00	26.00	35.00	80.00	3,500
1957	496,389	—	—	—	11.00	21.00	23.00	26.00	2,700
Note: With 3 water lines									
1957	Inc. above	—	20.00	22.00	24.00	26.00	28.00	50.00	3,000
Note: With 1 water line									
1959	1,443,502	—	—	—	11.00	16.00	20.00	24.00	2,000
1960	1,420,486	—	—	—	—	11.00	18.00	24.00	1,000
1961	1,262,231	—	—	—	—	11.00	12.50	24.00	1,800
1962	1,884,789	—	—	—	—	11.00	18.00	24.00	900
1963	4,179,981	—	—	—	—	11.00	12.50	24.00	1,300

KM# 55 DOLLAR

23.33 g., 0.800 Silver 0.600 oz. ASW, 36 mm. **Ruler:** Elizabeth II **Subject:** British Columbia **Obv:** Laureate bust right **Rev:** Totem Pole, dates at left, denomination below

Date	Mintage	VG8	F12	VF20	XF40	AU50	MS60	MS63	MS65
1858-1958	3,039,630	—	—	11.00	18.00	21.00	23.00	26.00	450

KM# 58 DOLLAR

23.33 g., 0.800 Silver 0.600 oz. ASW, 36 mm. **Ruler:** Elizabeth II **Subject:** Charlottetown **Obv:** Laureate bust right **Rev:** Design at center, dates at outer edges, denomination below

Date	Mintage	VG8	F12	VF20	XF40	AU50	MS60	MS63	MS65
1864-1964	7,296,832	—	—	—	—	11.00	12.50	27.00	1,300
1864-1964 Specimen	—	—	—	—	—	—	—	225	450

Small beads

KM# 64.1 DOLLAR

23.33 g., 0.800 Silver 0.600 oz. ASW, 36 mm. **Ruler:** Elizabeth II **Obv:** Young bust right **Rev:** Voyageur, date and denomination below

Date	Mintage	VG8	F12	VF20	XF40	AU50	MS60	MS63	MS65
1965	10,768,569	—	—	—	—	11.00	13.00	25.00	750
Note: Small beads, pointed 5									
1965	—	PF63 400							
Note: Small beads, pointed 5									
(1965) Specimen	—	—	—	—	—	—	—	250	900
Note: Small beads, pointed 5									
1965	Inc. above	—	—	—	—	11.00	13.00	25.00	1,400
Note: Small beads, blunt 5									
1965	—	PF63 400							
Note: Small beads, blunt 5									
1965 Specimen	—	—	—	—	—	—	—	250	650
Note: Small beads, blunt 5									
1965	Inc. above	—	—	—	—	11.00	13.00	25.00	650
Note: Large beads, blunt 5									
1965 Specimen	—	—	—	—	—	—	—	225	500
Note: Large beads, blunt 5									
1965	Inc. above	—	—	—	—	12.00	24.00	28.00	650
Note: Large beads, pointed 5									
1965 Specimen	—	—	—	—	—	—	—	450	900
Note: Large beads, pointed 5									
1965	Inc. above	—	—	11.00	22.00	25.00	29.00	45.00	1,800
Note: Medium beads, pointed 5									

Date	Mintage	VG8	F12	VF20	XF40	AU50	MS60	MS63	MS65
1966	9,912,178	—	—	—	—	11.00	13.00	25.00	550
Note: Large beads									
1966 Specimen	—	—	—	—	—	—	—	250	900
Note: Large beads									
1966	485	—	—	—	2,300	2,600	3,000	4,000	—
Note: Small beads									

KM# 70 DOLLAR

23.33 g., 0.800 Silver 0.600 oz. ASW, 36 mm. **Ruler:** Elizabeth II **Subject:** Confederation Centennial **Obv:** Young bust right **Rev:** Goose left, dates below, denomination above

Date	Mintage	VF20	XF40	MS60	MS63	MS65
1867-1967	6,767,496	—	—	18.00	23.00	400
1867-1967 Specimen	—	—	—	—	30.00	45.00

KM# 76.1 DOLLAR

15.64 g., Nickel, 32 mm. **Ruler:** Elizabeth II **Obv:** Young bust right **Rev:** Voyageur, date and denomination below

Date	Mintage	VF20	XF40	MS60	MS63	MS65
1968	5,579,714	—	—	1.75	2.50	45.00
1968 Prooflike	1,408,143	—	—	—	—	2.50
1968 Small island	—	—	—	5.00	10.00	100
1968 Prooflike	—	—	—	—	—	10.00
Note: Small island						
1968 No Island	—	—	—	5.00	12.00	65.00
1968 Prooflike	—	—	—	—	—	4.50
Note: No island						
1968	Prooflike	—	—	22.00	30.00	70.00
Note: Doubled die; exhibits extra water lines						
1969	4,809,313	—	—	2.25	3.50	225
1969 Prooflike	594,258	—	—	—	2.00	—
1965 Specimen	—	—	—	—	—	500
1972	2,676,041	—	—	2.25	3.50	225
1972 Prooflike	405,865	—	—	—	—	2.25

KM# 78 DOLLAR

15.60 g., Nickel, 32 mm. **Ruler:** Elizabeth II **Subject:** Manitoba **Obv:** Young bust right **Rev:** Pasque flower divides dates and denomination

Date	Mintage	VF20	XF40	MS60	MS63	MS65
1870-1970	4,140,058	—	—	2.25	3.50	150
1870-1970 Prooflike	645,869	—	—	—	—	2.25
1870-1970 Specimen	—	—	—	—	—	40.00

KM# 79 DOLLAR

15.70 g., Nickel, 32.1 mm. **Ruler:** Elizabeth II **Subject:** British Columbia **Obv:** Young bust right **Rev:** Shield divides dates, denomination below, flowers above

Date	Mintage	VF20	XF40	MS60	MS63	MS65
1871-1971	4,260,781	—	—	2.25	3.50	175

Date	Mintage	VF20	XF40	MS60	MS63	MS65
1871-1971 Prooflike	468,729	—	—	—	—	2.25
1871-1971 Specimen	—	—	—	—	—	40.00

KM# 80 DOLLAR

23.33 g., 0.500 Silver 0.375 oz. ASW, 36 mm. **Ruler:** Elizabeth II **Subject:** British Columbia **Obv:** Young bust right **Rev:** Crowned arms with supporters divide dates, maple at top divides denomination, crowned lion atop crown on shield

Date	Mintage	VF20	XF40	MS60	MS63	MS65
1871-1971 Specimen	585,674	—	—	—	—	12.00

KM# 64.2a DOLLAR

23.33 g., 0.500 Silver 0.375 oz. ASW, 36 mm. **Ruler:** Elizabeth II **Obv:** Smaller young bust right **Rev:** Voyageur

Date	Mintage	VF20	XF40	MS60	MS63	MS65
1972 Specimen	341,598	—	—	—	—	13.00
1972 Proof	Inc. above	—	—	—	—	—
Note: doesn't exist						

KM# 82 DOLLAR

Nickel, 32 mm. **Ruler:** Elizabeth II **Subject:** Prince Edward Island **Obv:** Young bust right **Rev:** Building, inscription below divides dates, denomination above

Date	Mintage	VF20	XF40	MS60	MS63	MS65
1873-1973	3,196,452	—	—	2.25	3.00	65.00
1873-1973 (c) Prooflike	—	—	—	—	—	2.25

KM# 83 DOLLAR

23.33 g., 0.500 Silver 0.375 oz. ASW, 36 mm. **Ruler:** Elizabeth II **Obv:** Young bust right **Rev:** Mountie left, dates below, denomination at right

Date	Mintage	VF20	XF40	MS60	MS63	MS65
1873-1973 Specimen	1,031,271	—	—	—	—	12.00
1873-1973 Specimen	—	—	—	—	20.00	—
Note: Dollar housed in special blue case with RCMP crest.						

KM# 88 DOLLAR

Nickel, 32 mm. **Ruler:** Elizabeth II **Subject:** Winnipeg Centennial **Obv:** Young bust right **Rev:** Zeros frame pictures, dates below, denomination at bottom

Date	Mintage	VF20	XF40	MS60	MS63	MS65
1874-1974	2,799,363	—	—	2.50	3.50	90.00
1874-1974 (c) Prooflike	—	—	—	—	—	2.50

KM# 88a DOLLAR

23.33 g., 0.500 Silver 0.375 oz. ASW, 36 mm. **Ruler:** Elizabeth II **Subject:** Winnipeg Centennial **Obv:** Young bust right **Rev:** Zeros frame pictures, dates below, denomination at bottom

Date	Mintage	VF20	XF40	MS60	MS63	MS65
1974-1974 Specimen	728,947	—	—	—	—	12.00

KM# 76.2 DOLLAR

15.62 g., Nickel, 32 mm. **Ruler:** Elizabeth II **Obv:** Smaller young bust right **Rev:** Voyageur

Date	Mintage	VF20	XF40	MS60	MS63	MS65
1975	3,256,000	—	—	2.25	2.50	90.00
1975 Prooflike	322,325	—	—	—	—	2.50
1976	2,498,204	—	—	2.25	2.50	90.00
1976 Prooflike	274,106	—	—	—	—	2.50

KM# 76.3 DOLLAR

Nickel, 32 mm. **Ruler:** Elizabeth II **Obv:** Young bust right **Rev:** Voyageur **Note:** Only known in prooflike sets with 1976 obverse slightly modified.

Date	Mintage	VF20	XF40	MS60	MS63	MS65
1975	Inc. above	—	—	—	3.00	—

Note: mule with 1976 obv.

KM# 97 DOLLAR

23.33 g., 0.500 Silver 0.375 oz. ASW, 36 mm. **Ruler:** Elizabeth II **Subject:** Calgary **Obv:** Youmg bust right **Rev:** Figure on bucking horse, dates divided below, denomination above

Date	Mintage	VF20	XF40	MS60	MS63	MS65
1875-1975 Specimen	930,956	—	—	—	—	12.00

KM# 106 DOLLAR

23.33 g., 0.500 Silver 0.375 oz. ASW, 36 mm. **Ruler:** Elizabeth II **Subject:** Parliament Library **Obv:** Young bust right **Rev:** Library building, dates below, denomination above

Date	Mintage	VF20	XF40	MS60	MS63	MS65
1876-1976 Specimen	578,708	—	—	—	—	12.00
1876-1976	—	PF65 22.00				

Note: Blue VIP case

KM# 117 DOLLAR

Nickel, 32 mm. **Ruler:** Elizabeth II **Obv:** Young bust right **Rev:** Voyageur modified

Date	Mintage	VF20	XF40	MS60	MS63	MS65
1977	1,393,745	—	—	2.50	3.50	90.00
1977 Prooflike	—	—	—	—	—	2.50

KM# 118 DOLLAR

23.33 g., 0.500 Silver 0.375 oz. ASW, 36 mm. **Ruler:** Elizabeth II **Subject:** Silver Jubilee **Obv:** Young bust right, dates below **Rev:** Throne, denomination below

Date	Mintage	VF20	XF40	MS60	MS63	MS65
1952-1977 Specimen	744,848	—	—	—	—	12.00
1952-1977 Specimen	—	—	—	—	—	30.00

Note: Red VIP case

KM# 120.1 DOLLAR

15.50 g., Nickel, 32.1 mm. **Ruler:** Elizabeth II **Obv:** Young bust right **Rev:** Voyageur, date and denomination below **Note:** Modified design.

Date	Mintage	VF20	XF40	MS60	MS63	MS65
1978	2,948,488	—	—	2.25	2.50	100
1979	2,954,842	—	—	2.25	2.50	175
1980	3,291,221	—	—	2.50	3.00	90.00
1981	2,778,900	—	—	2.50	3.00	125
1981	—	PF65 5.00				
1982	1,098,500	—	—	2.50	3.00	90.00
1982	180,908	PF65 5.00				
1983	2,267,525	—	—	2.50	4.00	100
1983	166,779	PF65 5.00				
1984	1,223,486	—	—	2.50	3.00	100
1984	161,602	PF65 6.00				
1985	3,104,092	—	—	2.50	3.50	—
1985	153,950	PF65 7.00				
1986	3,089,225	—	—	2.50	4.00	90.00
1986	176,224	PF65 7.00				
1987 PL	287,330	—	—	—	—	5.00
1987	175,686	PF65 7.50				

KM# 121 DOLLAR

23.33 g., 0.500 Silver 0.375 oz. ASW, 36 mm. **Ruler:** Elizabeth II **Subject:** XI Commonwealth Games **Obv:** Young bust right **Rev:** Commonwealth games, logo at center

Date	Mintage	VF20	XF40	MS60	MS63	MS65
1978 Specimen	709,602	—	—	—	—	12.00

KM# 124 DOLLAR
23.33 g., 0.500 Silver 0.375 oz. ASW, 36 mm. **Ruler:** Elizabeth II **Subject:** Griffon **Obv:** Young bust right **Rev:** Ship, dates below, denomination above

Date	Mintage	VF20	XF40	MS60	MS63	MS65
1979 Specimen	826,695	—	—	—	—	12.00

KM# 128 DOLLAR
23.33 g., 0.500 Silver 0.375 oz. ASW, 36 mm. **Ruler:** Elizabeth II **Subject:** Arctic Territories **Obv:** Young bust right **Rev:** Bear right, date below, denomination above

Date	Mintage	VF20	XF40	MS60	MS63	MS65
1980 Specimen	539,617	—	—	—	—	17.00

KM# 130 DOLLAR
23.33 g., 0.500 Silver 0.375 oz. ASW, 36 mm. **Ruler:** Elizabeth II **Subject:** Transcontinental Railroad **Obv:** Young bust right **Rev:** Train engine and map, date below, denomination above

Date	Mintage	VF20	XF40	MS60	MS63	MS65
1981	699,494	—	—	—	—	10.00
1981	—	PF65 14.00				

KM# 133 DOLLAR
23.33 g., 0.500 Silver 0.375 oz. ASW, 36 mm. **Ruler:** Elizabeth II **Subject:** Regina **Obv:** Young bust right **Rev:** Cattle skull divides dates and denomination below

Date	Mintage	VF20	XF40	MS60	MS63	MS65
1882-1982	144,930	—	—	—	—	10.00
1882-1982	—	PF65 14.00				

KM# 134 DOLLAR
15.42 g., Nickel, 32 mm. **Ruler:** Elizabeth II **Subject:** Constitution **Obv:** Young bust right **Rev:** Meeting of Government

Date	Mintage	VF20	XF40	MS60	MS63	MS65
1867-1982	9,709,422	—	—	1.75	2.50	65.00

KM# 138 DOLLAR
23.33 g., 0.500 Silver 0.375 oz. ASW, 36 mm. **Ruler:** Elizabeth II **Subject:** Edmonton University Games **Obv:** Young bust right **Rev:** Athlete within game logo, date and denomination below

Date	Mintage	VF20	XF40	MS60	MS63	MS65
1983	159,450	—	—	—	—	10.00
1983	—	PF65 14.00				

KM# 140 DOLLAR
23.33 g., 0.500 Silver 0.375 oz. ASW, 36 mm. **Ruler:** Elizabeth II **Subject:** Toronto Sesquicentennial **Obv:** Young bust right

Date	Mintage	VF20	XF40	MS60	MS63	MS65
1984	133,610	—	—	—	—	10.00
1984	—	PF65 14.00				

KM# 141 DOLLAR
15.50 g., Nickel, 32 mm. **Ruler:** Elizabeth II **Subject:** Jacques Cartier **Obv:** Young bust right **Rev:** Cross with shield above figures

Date	Mintage	VF20	XF40	MS60	MS63	MS65
1534-1984	7,009,323	—	—	1.75	3.50	90.00
1534-1984	—	PF65 6.00				

KM# 120.2 DOLLAR
Nickel, 32.13 mm. **Ruler:** Elizabeth II **Obv:** Young bust right **Rev:** Voyageur **Note:** Mule with New Zealand 50 cent, KM-37 obverse.

Date	Mintage	VF20	XF40	MS60	MS63	MS65
1985	—	—	—	3,000	10,000	—

KM# 143 DOLLAR
23.33 g., 0.500 Silver 0.375 oz. ASW, 36 mm. **Ruler:** Elizabeth II **Subject:** National Parks **Obv:** Young bust right **Rev:** Moose right, dates above, denomination below

Date	Mintage	VF20	XF40	MS60	MS63	MS65
1885-1985	163,314	—	—	—	—	10.00
1885-1985	733,354	PF65 14.00				

KM# 149 DOLLAR

23.33 g., 0.500 Silver 0.375 oz. ASW, 36 mm. **Ruler:** Elizabeth II **Subject:** Vancouver **Obv:** Young bust right **Rev:** Train left, dates divided below, denomination above

Date	Mintage	VF20	XF40	MS60	MS63	MS65
1886-1986	125,949	—	—	—	—	10.00
1886-1986	—	PF65 14.00				

KM# 154 DOLLAR

23.33 g., 0.500 Silver 0.375 oz. ASW, 36 mm. **Ruler:** Elizabeth II **Subject:** John Davis **Obv:** Young bust right **Rev:** Ship "John Davis" with masts, rock in background, dates below, denomination at bottom

Date	Mintage	VF20	XF40	MS60	MS63	MS65
1587-1987	118,722	—	—	—	—	10.00
1587-1987	—	PF65 14.00				

KM# 157 DOLLAR

7.00 g., Aureate-Bronze Plated Nickel, 26.5 mm. **Ruler:** Elizabeth II **Obv:** Young bust right **Rev:** Loon right, date and denomination below **Shape:** 11-sided

Date	Mintage	VF20	XF40	MS60	MS63	MS65
1987	205,405,000	—	—	—	2.25	35.00
1987	178,120	PF65 8.00				
1988	138,893,539	—	—	—	3.50	50.00
1988	175,259	PF65 6.50				
1989	184,773,902	—	—	—	4.00	65.00
1989	170,928	PF65 6.50				

KM# 161 DOLLAR

23.33 g., 0.500 Silver 0.375 oz. ASW, 36 mm. **Ruler:** Elizabeth II **Subject:** Ironworks **Obv:** Young bust right **Rev:** Ironworkers, date and denomination below

Date	Mintage	VF20	XF40	MS60	MS63	MS65
1988	106,872	—	—	—	—	10.00
1988	—	PF65 15.00				

KM# 168 DOLLAR

23.33 g., 0.500 Silver 0.375 oz. ASW, 36 mm. **Ruler:** Elizabeth II **Subject:** MacKenzie River **Obv:** Young bust right **Rev:** People in canoe, date above, denomination below

Date	Mintage	VF20	XF40	MS60	MS63	MS65
1989	99,774	—	—	—	—	13.00
1989	—	PF65 17.50				

KM# 170 DOLLAR

23.33 g., 0.500 Silver 0.375 oz. ASW, 36 mm. **Ruler:** Elizabeth II **Subject:** Henry Kelsey **Obv:** Crowned head right **Rev:** Kelsey with natives, dates below, denomination above

Date	Mintage	VF20	XF40	MS60	MS63	MS65
1690-1990	99,455	—	—	—	—	12.00
1690-1990	—	PF65 20.00				

KM# 186 DOLLAR

7.00 g., Aureate-Bronze Plated Nickel, 26.5 mm. **Ruler:** Elizabeth II **Obv:** Crowned head right **Rev:** Loon right, date and denomination **Shape:** 11-sided

Date	Mintage	VF20	XF40	MS60	MS63	MS65
1990	68,402,000	—	—	—	3.50	63.00
1990	140,649	PF65 7.00				
1991	23,156,000	—	—	—	3.50	63.00
1991	131,888	PF65 13.00				
1993	33,662,000	—	—	—	3.00	63.00
1993	143,065	PF65 6.00				
1994	16,232,530	—	—	—	3.50	32.00
1994	104,485	PF65 7.00				
1995	27,492,630	—	—	—	3.50	42.00
1995	101,560	PF65 7.00				
1996	17,101,000	—	—	—	3.50	32.00
1996	112,835	PF65 7.50				
1997 PL		—	—	—	—	13.00
1997	113,647	PF65 8.00				
1998 PL	—	—	—	—	—	6.00
1998 W Prooflike	—	—	—	—	—	10.00
1998	93,632	PF65 10.00				
1999 PL	—	—	—	—	—	6.00
1999	95,113	PF65 13.00				
2000 PL	—	—	—	—	—	6.00
2000 W Prooflike	—	—	—	—	—	9.00
2000	90,921	PF65 8.00				

KM# 179 DOLLAR

23.33 g., 0.500 Silver 0.375 oz. ASW, 36 mm. **Ruler:** Elizabeth II **Subject:** S.S. Frontenac **Obv:** Crowned head right **Rev:** Ship, "Frontenac," date and denomination below,

Date	Mintage	VF20	XF40	MS60	MS63	MS65
1991	73,843	—	—	—	—	12.00
1991	195,424	PF65 23.00				

KM# 209 DOLLAR
Aureate, 26.5 mm. **Ruler:** Elizabeth II **Subject:** Loon right, dates and denomination **Obv:** Crowned head right

Date	Mintage	VF20	XF40	MS60	MS63	MS65
1867-1992	4,242,085	—	—	—	3.50	45.00
1867-1992	147,061	PF65 8.00				

KM# 210 DOLLAR
25.18 g., 0.925 Silver 0.7487 oz. ASW, 36 mm. **Ruler:** Elizabeth II **Subject:** Stagecoach service **Obv:** Crowned head right **Rev:** Stagecoach, date and denomination below

Date	Mintage	VF20	XF40	MS60	MS63	MS65
1992	78,160	—	—	—	—	17.00
1992	187,612	PF65 25.00				

KM# 218 DOLLAR
Aureate, 26 mm. **Ruler:** Elizabeth II **Subject:** Parliament **Obv:** Crowned head right, dates below **Rev:** Backs of three seated figures in front of building, denomination below

Date	Mintage	VF20	XF40	MS60	MS63	MS65
1867-1992	23,915,000	—	—	—	3.50	35.00
1867-1992	—	PF65 9.00				

KM# 235 DOLLAR
25.18 g., 0.925 Silver 0.7487 oz. ASW, 36 mm. **Ruler:** Elizabeth II **Subject:** Stanley Cup hockey **Obv:** Crowned head right **Rev:** Hockey players between cups, dates below, denomination above

Date	Mintage	VF20	XF40	MS60	MS63	MS65
1993	88,150	—	—	—	—	20.00
1993	—	PF65 25.00				

KM# 248 DOLLAR
7.00 g., Aureate-Bronze Plated Nickel, 26 mm. **Ruler:** Elizabeth II **Subject:** War Memorial **Obv:** Crowned head right, date below **Rev:** Memorial, denomination at right

Date	Mintage	VF20	XF40	MS60	MS63	MS65
1994	20,004,830	—	—	—	2.25	35.00
1994	—	PF65 10.00				

KM# 251 DOLLAR
25.18 g., 0.925 Silver 0.7487 oz. ASW, 36 mm. **Ruler:** Elizabeth II **Subject:** Last RCMP sled-dog patrol **Obv:** Crowned head right **Rev:** Dogsled, denomination divides dates below

Date	Mintage	VF20	XF40	MS60	MS63	MS65
1969-1994	61,561	—	—	—	—	22.00
1969-1994	170,374	PF65 25.00				

KM# 258 DOLLAR
7.00 g., Aureate Bronze, 26 mm. **Ruler:** Elizabeth II **Subject:** Peacekeeping Monument in Ottawa **Obv:** Crowned head right, date below **Rev:** Monument, denomination above right **Note:** Mintage included with KM#186.

Date	Mintage	VF20	XF40	MS60	MS63	MS65
1995	18,502,750	—	—	—	2.25	35.00
1995	—	PF65 10.00				

KM# 259 DOLLAR
25.18 g., 0.925 Silver 0.7487 oz. ASW, 36 mm. **Ruler:** Elizabeth II **Subject:** Hudson Bay Company **Obv:** Crowned head right **Rev:** Explorers and ship, date and denomination below

Date	Mintage	VF20	XF40	MS60	MS63	MS65
1995	61,819	—	—	—	—	17.00
1995	166,259	PF65 29.00				

KM# 274 DOLLAR
25.18 g., 0.925 Silver 0.7487 oz. ASW, 36 mm. **Ruler:** Elizabeth II **Subject:** McIntosh Apple **Obv:** Crowned head right **Rev:** Apple, dates and denomination below

Date	Mintage	VF20	XF40	MS60	MS63	MS65
1796-1996	58,834	—	—	—	—	17.00
1796-1996	133,779	PF65 25.00				

KM# 282 DOLLAR
25.18 g., 0.925 Silver 0.7487 oz. ASW, 36 mm. **Ruler:** Elizabeth II **Subject:** 25th Anniversary Hockey Victory **Obv:** Crowned head right **Rev:** The winning goal by Paul Aenderson. Based on a painting by Andre l'Archeveque, dates at right, denomination at bottom

Date	Mintage	VF20	XF40	MS60	MS63	MS65
1972-1997	155,252	—	—	—	—	20.00
1972-1997	184,965	PF65 29.00				

KM# 291 DOLLAR

7.00 g., Aureate-Bronze Plated Nickel, 26 mm. **Ruler:** Elizabeth II **Subject:** Loon Dollar 10th Anniversary **Obv:** Crowned head right **Rev:** Loon in flight left, dates above, denomination below

Date	Mintage	VF20	XF40	MS60	MS63	MS65
1987-1997 Prooflike	—	—	—	—	—	22.00

KM# 296 DOLLAR

25.18 g., 0.925 Silver 0.7487 oz. ASW, 36 mm. **Ruler:** Elizabeth II **Subject:** Loon Dollar 10th Anniversary **Obv:** Crowned head right **Rev:** Loon in flight left, dates above, denomination below

Date	Mintage	VF20	XF40	MS60	MS63	MS65
1987-1997	—	PF65 95.00				

KM# 306 DOLLAR

25.18 g., 0.925 Silver 0.7487 oz. ASW, 36 mm. **Ruler:** Elizabeth II **Subject:** 120th Anniversary Royal Canadian Mounted Police **Obv:** Crowned head right **Rev:** Mountie on horseback, dates at left, denomination above **Note:** Individually cased prooflikes, proofs or specimens are from broken-up prooflike or specimen sets.

Date	Mintage	VF20	XF40	MS60	MS63	MS65
1873-1998	79,777	—	—	—	—	17.00
1873-1998	120,172	PF65 29.00				

KM# 355 DOLLAR

25.18 g., 0.925 Silver 0.7487 oz. ASW, 36 mm. **Ruler:** Elizabeth II **Subject:** International Year of Old Persons **Obv:** Crowned head right **Rev:** Figures amid trees, date and denomination below

Date	Mintage	VF20	XF40	MS60	MS63	MS65
1999	—	PF65 40.00				

KM# 356 DOLLAR

25.18 g., 0.925 Silver 0.7487 oz. ASW, 36 mm. **Ruler:** Elizabeth II **Subject:** Discovery of Queen Charlotte Isle **Obv:** Crowned head right **Rev:** Ship and three boats, dates at right, denomination below

Date	Mintage	VF20	XF40	MS60	MS63	MS65
1999	67,655	—	—	—	—	22.00
1999	126,435	PF65 30.00				

KM# 401 DOLLAR

25.18 g., 0.925 Silver 0.7487 oz. ASW, 36 mm. **Ruler:** Elizabeth II **Subject:** Voyage of Discovery **Obv:** Crowned head right **Rev:** Human and space shuttle, date above, denomination below

Date	Mintage	VF20	XF40	MS60	MS63	MS65
2000	60,100	—	—	—	—	21.00
2000	114,130	PF65 29.00				

KM# 270 2 DOLLARS

7.30 g., Bi-Metallic Aluminum-Bronze center in Nickel ring, 28 mm. **Ruler:** Elizabeth II **Obv:** Crowned head right within circle, date below **Rev:** Polar bear right within circle, denomination below **Edge:** Segmented reeding

Date	Mintage	VF20	XF40	MS60	MS63	MS65
1996	375,483,000	—	—	2.50	5.00	45.00
1996	—	PF65 10.00				
1997	16,942,000	—	—	—	3.50	90.00
1998 PL	4,926,000	—	—	—	—	7.00
1998 W PL	Inc. above	—	—	—	—	7.00
1999 PL	25,130,000	—	—	—	—	7.00
2000 PL	29,847,000	—	—	—	—	5.00
2000 W PL	Inc. above	—	—	—	—	5.00

KM# 270a 2 DOLLARS

11.32 g., Bi-Metallic .916 Gold 6.2679g center in .999 Silver 5.0958g ring, 28 mm. **Ruler:** Elizabeth II **Obv:** Crowned head right within circle, date below **Rev:** Polar bear right within circle, denomination below

Date	Mintage	VF20	XF40	MS60	MS63	MS65
1996	—	PF60 375				

KM# 270b 2 DOLLARS

25.00 g., 0.925 Bi-Metallic 0.7435 oz. Gold plated silver center on Silver planchet, 28 mm. **Ruler:** Elizabeth II **Obv:** Crowned head right within circle, date below **Rev:** Polar bear right within circle, denomination below **Edge:** 4.5mm thick

Date	Mintage	VF20	XF40	MS60	MS63	MS65
1996	10,000	PF60 55.00				
1998 Proof	—	—	—	—	—	—

KM# 270c 2 DOLLARS

8.83 g., 0.925 Silver 0.2626 oz. ASW gold plated center, 28 mm. **Ruler:** Elizabeth II **Obv:** Crowned head right within circle, date below **Rev:** Polar bear right within circle, denomination below **Note:** 1.9mm thick.

Date	Mintage	VF20	XF40	MS60	MS63	MS65
1996	10,000	PF65 12.00				
1997	—	PF65 10.00				
1998 O	—	PF65 12.00				
1999	—	PF65 12.00				
2000	—	PF65 12.00				

KM# 357 2 DOLLARS

7.30 g., Bi-Metallic Aluminum-Bronze center in Nickel ring, 28 mm. **Ruler:** Elizabeth II **Subject:** Nunavut **Obv:** Crowned head right **Rev:** Inuit person with drum, denomination below **Edge:** Segmented reeding

Date	Mintage	VF20	XF40	MS60	MS63	MS65
1999	—	—	—	2.50	4.00	30.00

KM# 357a 2 DOLLARS

8.52 g., 0.925 Silver 0.2534 oz. ASW gold plated center, 28 mm. **Ruler:** Elizabeth II **Subject:** Nunavut **Obv:** Crowned head right **Rev:** Drum dancer **Edge:** Interrupted reeding

Date	Mintage	VF20	XF40	MS60	MS63	MS65
1999	39,873	PF65 15.00				

KM# 357b 2 DOLLARS

Gold Yellow gold center in White Gold ring **Ruler:** Elizabeth II **Subject:** Nunavut **Obv:** Crowned head right **Rev:** Drum dancer

Date	Mintage	VF20	XF40	MS60	MS63	MS65
1999	4,298	PF60 400				

KM# 399 2 DOLLARS

7.30 g., Bi-Metallic Aluminum-Bronze center in Nickel ring, 28 mm. **Ruler:** Elizabeth II **Subject:** Knowledge **Obv:** Crowned head right within circle, denomination below **Rev:** Polar bear and 2 cubs right within circle, date above **Edge:** Segmented reeding

Date	Mintage	VF20	XF40	MS60	MS63	MS65
2000 Specimen	1,500	—	—	2.50	5.00	30.00

KM# 399a 2 DOLLARS

8.52 g., 0.925 Silver 0.2534 oz. ASW gold plated center. **Ruler:** Elizabeth II **Subject:** Knowledge **Obv:** Crowned head right within circle, denomination below **Rev:** Polar bear and 2 cubs within circle, date above

Date	Mintage	VF20	XF40	MS60	MS63	MS65
2000	39,768	PF65 15.00				

KM# 399b 2 DOLLARS

6.31 g., 0.916 Gold 0.1858 oz. AGW Yellow gold center in White Gold ring **Ruler:** Elizabeth II **Subject:** Knowledge **Obv:** Crowned head right within circle, denomination below **Rev:** Polar bear and two cubs right within circle, date above

Date	Mintage	VF20	XF40	MS60	MS63	MS65
2000	5,881	PF60 350				

KM# 14 SOVEREIGN

7.99 g., 0.917 Gold 0.2355 oz. AGW **Ruler:** Edward VII **Rev:** St. George slaying dragon, mint mark below horse's rear hooves

Date	Mintage	VG8	F12	VF20	XF40	AU50	MS60	MS63	MS65
1908 C	636	—	1,800	2,500	3,500	4,000	4,500	5,500	8,000
1909 C	16,273	—	300	350	400	450	650	2,200	7,000
1910 C	28,012	—	300	350	400	450	650	2,700	9,500

KM# 20 SOVEREIGN

7.99 g., 0.917 Gold 0.2355 oz. AGW **Ruler:** George V **Rev:** St. George slaying dragon, mint mark below horse's rear hooves

Date	Mintage	VG8	F12	VF20	XF40	AU50	MS60	MS63	MS65
1911 C	256,946	—	—	300	350	400	450	500	550
1911 C Specimen	—	—	—	—	—	—	—	3,000	8,000
1913 C	3,715	—	650	800	1,050	1,400	1,800	3,500	—
1914 C	14,871	—	300	400	450	500	650	1,150	3,500
1916 C About 20 known	—	—	16,000	17,000	18,000	22,000	24,000	40,000	100,000
Note: Stacks' A.G. Carter Jr. Sale 12-89 Gem BU realized $82,500									
1917 C	58,845	—	—	300	350	400	450	650	2,000
1918 C	106,514	—	—	300	350	400	450	1,000	—
1919 C	135,889	—	—	300	350	400	450	800	—

KM# 26 5 DOLLARS

8.36 g., 0.900 Gold 0.2419 oz. AGW **Ruler:** George V **Obv:** Crowned bust left **Rev:** Arms within wreath, date and denomination below

Date	Mintage	VG8	F12	VF20	XF40	AU50	MS60	MS63	MS65
1912	165,680	—	—	310	350	400	450	650	2,200
1913	98,832	—	—	310	350	400	450	800	2,800
1914	31,122	—	—	310	450	600	900	3,000	15,000

KM# 84 5 DOLLARS

24.30 g., 0.925 Silver 0.7227 oz. ASW, 38 mm. **Ruler:** Elizabeth II **Subject:** 1976 Montreal Olympics **Obv:** Young bust right, small maple below, date at right **Rev:** Sailboat "Kingston", date at left, denomination below **Note:** Series I.

Date	Mintage	VF20	XF40	MS60	MS63	MS65
1973	—	—	—	—	20.00	—
1973	165,203	PF63 20.00				

KM# 85 5 DOLLARS

24.30 g., 0.925 Silver 0.7227 oz. ASW, 38 mm. **Ruler:** Elizabeth II **Subject:** 1976 Montreal Olympics **Obv:** Young bust right, small maple leaf below, date at right **Rev:** North American map, denominaton below **Note:** Series I.

Date	Mintage	VF20	XF40	MS60	MS63	MS65
1973	—	—	—	—	20.00	—
1973	165,203	PF63 20.00				

KM# 89 5 DOLLARS

24.30 g., 0.925 Silver 0.7227 oz. ASW, 38 mm. **Ruler:** Elizabeth II **Subject:** 1976 Montreal Olympics **Obv:** Young bust right, small maple leaf below, date at right **Rev:** Olympic rings, denomination below **Note:** Series II.

Date	Mintage	VF20	XF40	MS60	MS63	MS65
1974	—	—	—	—	20.00	—
1974	—	PF63 20.00				

KM# 90 5 DOLLARS

24.30 g., 0.925 Silver 0.7227 oz. ASW, 38 mm. **Ruler:** Elizabeth II **Subject:** 1976 Montreal Olympics **Obv:** Young bust right, small maple leaf below, date at right **Rev:** Athlete with torch, denomination below **Note:** Series II.

Date	Mintage	VF20	XF40	MS60	MS63	MS65
1974	—	—	—	—	20.00	—
1974	—	PF63 20.00				

KM# 91 5 DOLLARS

24.30 g., 0.925 Silver 0.7227 oz. ASW, 38 mm. **Ruler:** Elizabeth II **Subject:** 1976 Montreal Olympics **Obv:** Young bust right, small maple leaf below, date at right **Rev:** Rower, denomination below **Note:** Series III.

Date	Mintage	VF20	XF40	MS60	MS63	MS65
1974	—	—	—	—	20.00	—
1974	104,684	PF63 20.00				

KM# 92 5 DOLLARS

24.30 g., 0.925 Silver 0.7227 oz. ASW, 38 mm. **Ruler:** Elizabeth II **Subject:** 1976 Montreal Olympics **Obv:** Young bust right, small maple leaf below, date at right **Rev:** Canoeing, denomination below **Note:** Series III.

Date	Mintage	VF20	XF40	MS60	MS63	MS65
1974	—	—	—	—	20.00	—
1974	104,684	PF63 20.00				

KM# 98 5 DOLLARS

24.30 g., 0.925 Silver 0.7227 oz. ASW, 38 mm. **Ruler:** Elizabeth II **Subject:** 1976 Montreal Olympics **Obv:** Young bust right, small maple leaf below, date at right **Rev:** Marathon, denomination below **Note:** Series IV.

Date	Mintage	VF20	XF40	MS60	MS63	MS65
1975	—	—	—	—	20.00	—
1975	—	PF63 20.00				

KM# 99 5 DOLLARS

24.30 g., 0.925 Silver 0.7227 oz. ASW, 38 mm. **Ruler:** Elizabeth II **Subject:** Montreal 1976 - 21st Summer Olympic Games **Obv:** Young bust right, small maple leaf below, date at right **Rev:** Women's javelin event, denomination below **Note:** Series IV.

Date	Mintage	VF20	XF40	MS60	MS63	MS65
1975	—	—	—	—	20.00	—
1975	—	PF63 20.00				

KM# 100 5 DOLLARS

24.30 g., 0.925 Silver 0.7227 oz. ASW, 38 mm. **Ruler:** Elizabeth II **Subject:** 1976 Montreal Olympics **Obv:** Young bust right, small maple leaf below, date at right **Rev:** Swimmer, denomination below **Note:** Series V.

Date	Mintage	VF20	XF40	MS60	MS63	MS65
1975	—	—	—	—	20.00	—
1975	—	PF63 20.00				

KM# 101 5 DOLLARS

24.30 g., 0.925 Silver 0.7227 oz. ASW, 38 mm. **Ruler:** Elizabeth II **Subject:** Montreal 1976 - 21st Summer Olympic Games **Obv:** Young bust right, small maple leaf below, date at right **Rev:** Platform Diver, denomination below **Note:** Series V.

Date	Mintage	VF20	XF40	MS60	MS63	MS65
1975	—	—	—	—	20.00	—
1975	—	PF63 20.00				

KM# 107 5 DOLLARS

24.30 g., 0.925 Silver 0.7227 oz. ASW, 38 mm. **Ruler:** Elizabeth II **Subject:** 1976 Montreal Olympics **Obv:** Young bust right, small maple leaf below, date at right **Rev:** Fencing, denomination below **Note:** Series VI.

Date	Mintage	VF20	XF40	MS60	MS63	MS65
1976	—	—	—	—	20.00	—
1976	—	PF63 20.00				

KM# 108 5 DOLLARS

24.30 g., 0.925 Silver 0.7227 oz. ASW, 38 mm. **Ruler:** Elizabeth II **Subject:** 1976 Montreal Olympics **Obv:** Young bust right, small maple leaf below, date at right **Obv. Legend:** Boxing **Rev:** Boxers, denomination below **Note:** Series VI.

Date	Mintage	VF20	XF40	MS60	MS63	MS65
1976	—	—	—	—	20.00	—
1976	82,302	PF63 20.00				

KM# 109 5 DOLLARS

24.30 g., 0.925 Silver 0.7227 oz. ASW, 38 mm. **Ruler:** Elizabeth II **Subject:** 1976 Montreal Olympics **Obv:** Young bust right, small maple leaf below, date at right **Rev:** Olympic village, denomination below **Note:** Series VII.

Date	Mintage	VF20	XF40	MS60	MS63	MS65
1976	—	—	—	—	20.00	—
1976	—	PF63 20.00				

KM# 110 5 DOLLARS

24.30 g., 0.925 Silver 0.7227 oz. ASW, 38 mm. **Ruler:** Elizabeth II **Subject:** 1976 Montreal Olympics **Obv:** Young bust right, maple leaf below, date at right **Rev:** Olympic flame, denomination below **Note:** Series VII.

Date	Mintage	VF20	XF40	MS60	MS63	MS65
1976	—	—	—	—	20.00	—
1976	—	PF63 20.00				

KM# 316 5 DOLLARS

31.39 g., 0.9999 Silver 1.0091 oz. ASW **Ruler:** Elizabeth II **Subject:** Dr. Norman Bethune **Obv:** Young bust right **Rev:** Bethune and party, date at upper right

Date	Mintage	VF20	XF40	MS60	MS63	MS65
1998	—	PF60 40.00				

KM# 398 5 DOLLARS

Copper-Nickel-Zinc **Ruler:** Elizabeth II **Obv:** Young bust right **Rev:** Viking ship under sail **Note:** Sold in sets with Norway 20 kroner, KM#465.

Date	Mintage	VF20	XF40	MS60	MS63	MS65
1999	28,450	PF60 18.50				

KM# 27 10 DOLLARS

16.72 g., 0.900 Gold 0.4838 oz. AGW, 26.92 mm. **Ruler:** George V **Obv:** Crowned bust left **Rev:** Arms within wreath, date and denomination below

Date	Mintage	VG8	F12	VF20	XF40	AU50	MS60	MS63	MS65
1912	74,759	—	—	700	750	800	900	2,500	7,500
1912 Specimen	—	—	—	—	—	—	—	7,000	135,000
1913	149,232	—	—	700	750	800	900	3,000	13,000
1912 Specimen	—	—	—	—	—	—	—	—	—
1914	140,068	—	—	750	800	850	1,100	3,000	13,000
1914 Specimen	—	—	—	—	—	—	—	—	—

KM# 86.1 10 DOLLARS

48.60 g., 0.925 Silver 1.4453 oz. ASW, 45 mm. **Ruler:** Elizabeth II **Subject:** 1976 Montreal Olympics **Obv:** Young bust right, maple leaf below, date at right **Rev:** World map, denomination below **Note:** Series I.

Date	Mintage	VF20	XF40	MS60	MS63	MS65
1973	103,426	—	—	—	40.00	—
1973	165,203	PF63 40.00				

KM# 87 10 DOLLARS

48.60 g., 0.925 Silver 1.4453 oz. ASW, 45 mm. **Ruler:** Elizabeth II **Subject:** 1976 Montreal Olympics **Obv:** Young bust right, small maple leaf below, date at right **Rev:** Montreal skyline, denomination below **Note:** Series I.

Date	Mintage	VF20	XF40	MS60	MS63	MS65
1973	165,203	PF63 40.00				
1973	—	—	—	—	40.00	—

KM# 86.2 10 DOLLARS

48.60 g., 0.925 Silver 1.4453 oz. ASW, 45 mm. **Ruler:** Elizabeth II **Subject:** 1976 Montreal Olympics **Obv:** Young bust right, small maple leaf below, date at right **Rev:** World map **Note:** Series I.

Date	Mintage	VF20	XF40	MS60	MS63	MS65
1974	320	—	—	—	325	—

Note: Error: mule

KM# 93 10 DOLLARS

48.60 g., 0.925 Silver 1.4453 oz. ASW, 45 mm. **Ruler:** Elizabeth II **Subject:** 1976 Montreal Olympics **Obv:** Young bust right, small maple leaf below, date at right **Rev:** Head of Zeus, denomination below **Note:** Series II.

Date	Mintage	VF20	XF40	MS60	MS63	MS65
1974	104,684	PF63 40.00				
1974	—	—	—	—	40.00	—

KM# 94 10 DOLLARS
48.60 g., 0.925 Silver 1.4453 oz. ASW, 45 mm. **Ruler:** Elizabeth II **Subject:** 1976 Montreal Olympics **Obv:** Young bust right, small maple leaf below, date at right **Rev:** Temple of Zeus, denomination below **Note:** Series II.

Date	Mintage	VF20	XF40	MS60	MS63	MS65
1974	—	—	—	—	40.00	—
1974	104,684	PF63 40.00				

KM# 95 10 DOLLARS
48.60 g., 0.925 Silver 1.4453 oz. ASW, 45 mm. **Ruler:** Elizabeth II **Subject:** 1976 Montreal Olympics **Obv:** Young bust right, small maple leaf below, date at right **Rev:** Cycling, denomination below **Note:** Series III.

Date	Mintage	VF20	XF40	MS60	MS63	MS65
1974	—	—	—	—	40.00	—
1974	—	PF63 40.00				

KM# 96 10 DOLLARS
48.60 g., 0.925 Silver 1.4453 oz. ASW, 45 mm. **Ruler:** Elizabeth II **Subject:** 1976 Montreal Olympics **Obv:** Young bust right, small maple leaf below, date at right **Rev:** Lacrosse, denomination below **Note:** Series III.

Date	Mintage	VF20	XF40	MS60	MS63	MS65
1974	—	—	—	—	40.00	—
1974	—	PF63 40.00				

KM# 102 10 DOLLARS
48.60 g., 0.925 Silver 1.4453 oz. ASW, 45 mm. **Ruler:** Elizabeth II **Subject:** 1976 Montreal Olympics **Obv:** Young bust right, small maple leaf below, date at right **Rev:** Men's hurdles, denomination below **Note:** Series IV.

Date	Mintage	VF20	XF40	MS60	MS63	MS65
1975	—	—	—	—	40.00	—
1975	—	PF63 40.00				

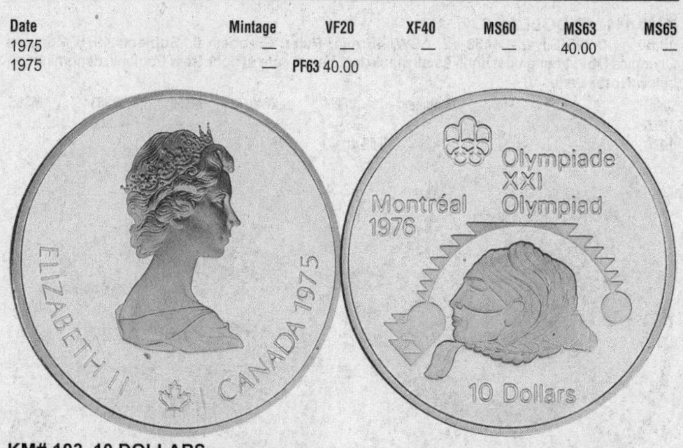

KM# 103 10 DOLLARS
48.60 g., 0.925 Silver 1.4453 oz. ASW, 45 mm. **Ruler:** Elizabeth II **Subject:** Montreal 1976 - 21st Summer Olympic Games **Obv:** Young bust right, small maple leaf below, date at right **Rev:** Women's shot put, denomination below **Note:** Series IV.

Date	Mintage	VF20	XF40	MS60	MS63	MS65
1975	—	—	—	—	40.00	—
1975	—	PF63 40.00				

KM# 104 10 DOLLARS
48.60 g., 0.925 Silver 1.4453 oz. ASW, 45 mm. **Ruler:** Elizabeth II **Subject:** 1976 Montreal Olympics **Obv:** Young bust right, small maple leaf below, date at right **Rev:** Sailing, denomination below **Note:** Series V.

Date	Mintage	VF20	XF40	MS60	MS63	MS65
1975	—	—	—	—	40.00	—
1975	—	PF63 40.00				

KM# 105 10 DOLLARS
48.60 g., 0.925 Silver 1.4453 oz. ASW, 45 mm. **Ruler:** Elizabeth II **Subject:** 1976 Montreal Olympics **Obv:** Young bust right, small maple leaf below, date at right **Rev:** Canoeing, denomination below **Note:** Series V.

Date	Mintage	VF20	XF40	MS60	MS63	MS65
1975	—	—	—	—	40.00	—
1975	—	PF63 40.00				

KM# 111 10 DOLLARS
48.60 g., 0.925 Silver 1.4453 oz. ASW, 45 mm. **Ruler:** Elizabeth II **Subject:** 1976 Montreal Olympics **Obv:** Young bust right, small maple leaf below, date at right **Rev:** Football, denomination below **Note:** Series VI.

Date	Mintage	VF20	XF40	MS60	MS63	MS65
1976	—	—	—	—	40.00	—
1976	—	PF63 40.00				

KM# 112 10 DOLLARS
48.60 g., 0.925 Silver 1.4453 oz. ASW, 45 mm. **Ruler:** Elizabeth II **Subject:** 1976 Montreal Olympics **Obv:** Young bust right, small maple leaf below, date at right **Rev:** Field hockey **Note:** Series VI.

Date	Mintage	VF20	XF40	MS60	MS63	MS65
1976	—	—	—	—	40.00	—
1976	—	PF63 40.00				

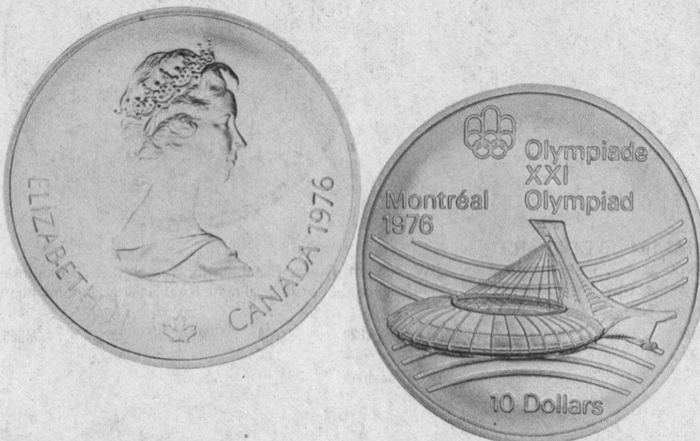

KM# 113 10 DOLLARS
48.60 g., 0.925 Silver 1.4453 oz. ASW, 45 mm. **Ruler:** Elizabeth II **Subject:** 1976 Montreal Olympics **Obv:** Young bust right, small maple leaf below, date at right **Rev:** Olympic Stadium, denomination below **Note:** Series VII.

Date	Mintage	VF20	XF40	MS60	MS63	MS65
1976	—	—	—	—	40.00	—
1976	—	PF63 40.00				

KM# 114 10 DOLLARS
48.60 g., 0.925 Silver 1.4453 oz. ASW, 45 mm. **Ruler:** Elizabeth II **Subject:** 1976 Montreal Olympics **Obv:** Young bust right, small maple leaf below, date at right **Rev:** Olympic Velodrome, denomination below **Note:** Series VII.

Date	Mintage	VF20	XF40	MS60	MS63	MS65
1976	—	—	—	—	40.00	—
1976	—	PF63 40.00				

KM# 215 15 DOLLARS
33.63 g., 0.925 Silver 1.0001 oz. ASW, 39 mm. **Ruler:** Elizabeth II **Subject:** 1992 Olympics **Obv:** Crowned head right, date at left, denomination below **Rev:** Coaching track

Date	Mintage	VF20	XF40	MS60	MS63	MS65
1992	—	PF60 32.00				

KM# 216 15 DOLLARS
33.63 g., 0.925 Silver 1.0001 oz. ASW **Ruler:** Elizabeth II **Subject:** 1992 Olympics **Obv:** Crowned head right, date at left, denomination below **Rev:** High jump, rings, speed skating

Date	Mintage	VF20	XF40	MS60	MS63	MS65
1992	—	PF60 32.00				

KM# 304 15 DOLLARS
33.63 g., 0.925 Silver 1.0001 oz. ASW with gold insert, 40 mm. **Ruler:** Elizabeth II **Subject:** Year of the Tiger **Obv:** Crowned head right **Rev:** Tiger within octagon at center, animal figures surround

Date	Mintage	VF20	XF40	MS60	MS63	MS65
1998	—	PF60 375				

KM# 331 15 DOLLARS
33.63 g., 0.925 Silver 1.0001 oz. ASW with gold insert **Ruler:** Elizabeth II **Subject:** Year of the Rabbitt **Obv:** Crowned head right **Rev:** Rabbit within octagon at center, animal figures surround

Date	Mintage	VF20	XF40	MS60	MS63	MS65
1999	77,791	PF60 100				

KM# 387 15 DOLLARS
33.63 g., 0.925 Silver 1.0001 oz. ASW with gold insert **Ruler:** Elizabeth II **Subject:** Year of the Dragon **Obv:** Crowned head right

Date	Mintage	VF20	XF40	MS60	MS63	MS65
2000	88,634	PF60 150				

KM# 71 20 DOLLARS
18.27 g., 0.900 Gold 0.5287 oz. AGW, 27.05 mm. **Ruler:** Elizabeth II **Subject:** Centennial **Obv:** Crowned head right **Rev:** Crowned and supported arms **Edge:** Reeded

Date	Mintage	VF20	XF40	MS60	MS63	MS65
1967 Specimen	334,288	—	—	—	900	—

KM# 145 20 DOLLARS
33.63 g., 0.925 Silver 1.0001 oz. ASW, 40 mm. **Ruler:** Elizabeth II **Subject:** 1988 Calgary Olympics **Obv:** Young bust right, maple leaf below, date at right **Rev:** Downhill skier, denomination below **Edge:** Lettered

Date	Mintage	VF20	XF40	MS60	MS63	MS65
1985	—	PF60 35.00				
1985	Inc. above	PF60 200				
Note: Plain edge						

KM# 146 20 DOLLARS
33.63 g., 0.925 Silver 1.0001 oz. ASW, 40 mm. **Ruler:** Elizabeth II **Subject:** 1988 Calgary Olympics **Obv:** Young bust right, small maple leaf below, date at right **Rev:** Speed skater, denomination below **Edge:** Lettered

Date	Mintage	VF20	XF40	MS60	MS63	MS65
1985	—	PF60 35.00				
1985	Inc. above	PF60 200				
Note: Plain edge						

KM# 147 20 DOLLARS
33.63 g., 0.925 Silver 1.0001 oz. ASW, 40 mm. **Ruler:** Elizabeth II **Subject:** 1988 Calgary Olympics **Obv:** Young bust right, small maple leaf below, date at right **Rev:** Biathlon, denomination below **Edge:** Lettered

Date	Mintage	VF20	XF40	MS60	MS63	MS65
1986	—	PF60 35.00				
1986	Inc. above	PF60 200				
Note: Plain edge						

KM# 148 20 DOLLARS
33.63 g., 0.925 Silver 1.0001 oz. ASW, 40 mm. **Ruler:** Elizabeth II **Subject:** 1988 Calgary Olympics **Obv:** Young bust right, small maple leaf below, date at right **Rev:** Hockey, denomination below **Edge:** Lettered

Date	Mintage	VF20	XF40	MS60	MS63	MS65
1986	—	PF60 35.00				
1986	Inc. above	PF60 200				
Note: Plain edge						

KM# 150 20 DOLLARS
33.63 g., 0.925 Silver 1.0001 oz. ASW, 40 mm. **Ruler:** Elizabeth II **Subject:** Calgary 1988 - 15th Winter Olympic Games **Obv:** Young bust right, small maple leaf below, date at right **Rev:** Cross-country skier, denomination below **Edge:** Lettered

Date	Mintage	VF20	XF40	MS60	MS63	MS65
1986	—	PF60 35.00				

KM# 151 20 DOLLARS
33.63 g., 0.925 Silver 1.0001 oz. ASW, 40 mm. **Ruler:** Elizabeth II **Subject:** 1988 Calgary Olympics **Obv:** Young bust right, small maple leaf below, date at right **Rev:** Free-style skier, denomination below **Edge:** Lettered

Date	Mintage	VF20	XF40	MS60	MS63	MS65
1986	—	PF60 35.00				
1986	Inc. above	PF60 200				
Note: Plain edge						

KM# 155 20 DOLLARS
34.11 g., 0.925 Silver 1.0143 oz. ASW, 40 mm. **Ruler:** Elizabeth II **Subject:** Calgary 1988 - 15th Winter Olympic Games **Obv:** Young bust right, small maple leaf below, date at right **Rev:** Figure skating pairs event, denomination below **Edge:** Lettered

Date	Mintage	VF20	XF40	MS60	MS63	MS65
1987	—	PF60 35.00				

KM# 156 20 DOLLARS
34.11 g., 0.925 Silver 1.0143 oz. ASW, 40 mm. **Ruler:** Elizabeth II **Subject:** 1988 Calgary Olympics **Obv:** Young bust right, small maple leaf below, date at right **Rev:** Curling, denomination below **Edge:** Lettered

Date	Mintage	VF20	XF40	MS60	MS63	MS65
1987	—	PF60 35.00				

KM# 159 20 DOLLARS
34.11 g., 0.925 Silver 1.0143 oz. ASW, 40 mm. **Ruler:** Elizabeth II **Subject:** 1988 Calgary Olympics **Obv:** Young bust right, small maple leaf below, date at right **Rev:** Ski jumper, denomination below **Edge:** Lettered

Date	Mintage	VF20	XF40	MS60	MS63	MS65
1987	—	PF60 35.00				

KM# 160 20 DOLLARS
34.11 g., 0.925 Silver 1.0143 oz. ASW, 40 mm. **Ruler:** Elizabeth II **Subject:** 1988 Calgary Olympics **Obv:** Young bust right, maple leaf below, date at right **Rev:** Bobsled, denomination below **Edge:** Lettered

Date	Mintage	VF20	XF40	MS60	MS63	MS65
1987	—	PF60 35.00				

KM# 172 20 DOLLARS
31.10 g., 0.925 Silver 0.925 oz. ASW gold cameo insert, 38 mm. **Ruler:** Elizabeth II **Subject:** Aviation **Obv:** Crowned head right, date below **Rev:** Lancaster, Fauquier in cameo, denomination below

Date	Mintage	VF20	XF40	MS60	MS63	MS65
1990	—	PF60 125				

KM# 173 20 DOLLARS
31.10 g., 0.925 Silver 0.925 oz. ASW with Gold cameo insert., 38 mm. **Ruler:** Elizabeth II **Subject:** Aviation **Obv:** Crowned head right, date below **Rev:** Anson and Harvard, Air Marshal Robert Leckie in cameo, denomination below

Date	Mintage	VF20	XF40	MS60	MS63	MS65
1990	—	PF60 42.00				

KM# 196 20 DOLLARS
31.10 g., 0.925 Silver 0.925 oz. ASW gold cameo insert, 38 mm. **Ruler:** Elizabeth II **Subject:** Aviation **Obv:** Crowned head right, date below **Rev:** Silver Dart, John A. D. McCurdy and F. W. "Casey" Baldwin in cameo, denomination below

Date	Mintage	VF20	XF40	MS60	MS63	MS65
1991	—	PF60 42.00				

KM# 197 20 DOLLARS
31.10 g., 0.925 Silver 0.925 oz. ASW gold cameo insert, 38 mm. **Ruler:** Elizabeth II **Subject:** Aviation **Obv:** Crowned head right, date below **Rev:** de Haviland Beaver, Philip C. Garratt in cameo, denomination below

Date	Mintage	VF20	XF40	MS60	MS63	MS65
1991	—	PF60 42.00				

KM# 224 20 DOLLARS
31.10 g., 0.925 Silver 0.925 oz. ASW gold cameo insert, 38 mm. **Ruler:** Elizabeth II **Subject:** Aviation **Obv:** Crowned head right, date below **Rev:** Curtiss JN-4 Canick ("Jenny"), Sir Frank W. Baillie in cameo, denomination below

Date	Mintage	VF20	XF40	MS60	MS63	MS65
1992	—	PF60 42.00				

KM# 225 20 DOLLARS
31.10 g., 0.925 Silver 0.925 oz. ASW with Gold cameo insert., 38 mm. **Ruler:** Elizabeth II **Subject:** Aviation **Obv:** Crowned head right, date below **Rev:** de Haviland Gypsy Moth, Murton A. Seymour in cameo, denomination below

Date	Mintage	VF20	XF40	MS60	MS63	MS65
1992	—	PF60 42.00				

KM# 236 20 DOLLARS
31.10 g., 0.925 Silver 0.925 oz. ASW with Gold cameo insert., 38 mm. **Ruler:** Elizabeth II **Subject:** Aviation **Obv:** Crowned head right, date below **Rev:** Fairchild 71C float plane, James A. Richardson, Sr. in cameo, denomination below

Date	Mintage	VF20	XF40	MS60	MS63	MS65
1993	—	PF60 42.00				

KM# 237 20 DOLLARS
31.10 g., 0.925 Silver 0.925 oz. ASW with Gold cameo insert., 38 mm. **Ruler:** Elizabeth II **Subject:** Aviation **Obv:** Crowned head right, date below **Rev:** Lockheed 14, Zebulon Lewis Leigh in cameo, denomination below

Date	Mintage	VF20	XF40	MS60	MS63	MS65
1993	—	PF60 42.00				

KM# 246 20 DOLLARS
31.10 g., 0.925 Silver 0.925 oz. ASW with Gold cameo insert., 38 mm. **Ruler:** Elizabeth II **Subject:** Aviation **Obv:** Crowned head right, date below **Rev:** Curtiss HS-2L seaplane, Stewart Graham in cameo, denomination below

Date	Mintage	VF20	XF40	MS60	MS63	MS65
1994	—	PF60 42.00				

KM# 247 20 DOLLARS
31.10 g., 0.925 Silver 0.925 oz. ASW with Gold cameo insert., 38 mm. **Ruler:** Elizabeth II **Subject:** Aviation **Obv:** Crowned head right, date below **Rev:** Vickers Vedette, Wilfred T. Reid in cameo, denomination below

Date	Mintage	VF20	XF40	MS60	MS63	MS65
1994	—	PF60 42.00				

KM# 271 20 DOLLARS
31.10 g., 0.925 Silver 0.925 oz. ASW gold cameo insert, 38 mm. **Ruler:** Elizabeth II **Subject:** Aviation **Obv:** Crowned head right, date below **Rev:** C-FEA1 Fleet Cannuck, denomination below

Date	Mintage	VF20	XF40	MS60	MS63	MS65
1995	17,438	PF60 42.00				

KM# 272 20 DOLLARS
31.10 g., 0.925 Silver 0.925 oz. ASW gold cameo insert, 38 mm. **Ruler:** Elizabeth II **Subject:** Aviation **Obv:** Crowned head right, date below **Rev:** DHC-1 Chipmunk, denomination below

Date	Mintage	VF20	XF40	MS60	MS63	MS65
1995	17,722	PF60 42.00				

KM# 276 20 DOLLARS
31.10 g., 0.925 Silver 0.925 oz. ASW gold cameo insert, 38 mm. **Ruler:** Elizabeth II **Subject:** Aviation **Obv:** Crowned head right, date below **Rev:** CF-100 Cannuck, denomination below

Date	Mintage	VF20	XF40	MS60	MS63	MS65
1996	18,508	PF60 42.00				

KM# 277 20 DOLLARS

31.10 g., 0.925 Silver 0.925 oz. ASW gold cameo insert, 38 mm. **Ruler:** Elizabeth II **Subject:** Aviation **Obv:** Crowned head right, date below **Obv. Legend:** CF-105 Arrow, denomination below

Date	Mintage	VF20	XF40	MS60	MS63	MS65
1996	—	PF60 100				

KM# 297 20 DOLLARS

31.10 g., 0.925 Silver 0.925 oz. ASW gold cameo insert, 38 mm. **Ruler:** Elizabeth II **Subject:** Aviation **Obv:** Crowned head right, date below **Rev:** Canadair F-86 Sabre, denomination below

Date	Mintage	VF20	XF40	MS60	MS63	MS65
1997	14,389	PF60 42.00				

KM# 298 20 DOLLARS

31.10 g., 0.925 Silver 0.925 oz. ASW with Gold cameo insert., 38 mm. **Ruler:** Elizabeth II **Subject:** Aviation **Obv:** Crowned head right, date below **Rev:** Canadair CT-114 Tutor, denomination below

Date	Mintage	VF20	XF40	MS60	MS63	MS65
1997	15,669	PF60 42.00				

KM# 329 20 DOLLARS

31.10 g., 0.925 Silver 0.925 oz. ASW gold cameo insert, 38 mm. **Ruler:** Elizabeth II **Subject:** Aviation **Obv:** Crowned *head*, right, date below **Rev:** CP-107 Argus, denomination below **Rev. Inscription:** Peter Mossman

Date	Mintage	VF20	XF40	MS60	MS63	MS65
1998	Est. 50000	PF60 50.00				

KM# 330 20 DOLLARS

31.10 g., 0.925 Silver 0.925 oz. ASW gold cameo insert, 38 mm. **Ruler:** Elizabeth II **Subject:** Aviation **Obv:** Crowned head right, date below **Rev:** CP-215 Waterbomber, denomination below

Date	Mintage	VF20	XF40	MS60	MS63	MS65
1998	Est. 50000	PF60 75.00				

KM# 339 20 DOLLARS

31.10 g., 0.925 Silver 0.925 oz. ASW gold cameo insert, 38 mm. **Ruler:** Elizabeth II **Subject:** Aviation **Obv:** Crowned head right, date below **Rev:** DHC-6 Twin Otter, denomination below

Date	Mintage	VF20	XF40	MS60	MS63	MS65
1999	Est. 50000	PF60 95.00				

KM# 340 20 DOLLARS

31.10 g., 0.925 Silver 0.925 oz. ASW gold cameo insert, 38 mm. **Ruler:** Elizabeth II **Subject:** Aviation **Obv:** Crowned head right, date below **Rev:** DHC-8 Dash 8, denomination below

Date	Mintage	VF20	XF40	MS60	MS63	MS65
1999	50,000	PF60 100				

KM# 395 20 DOLLARS

0.925 Silver, 38 mm. **Ruler:** Elizabeth II **Subject:** First Canadian locomotive **Obv:** Crowned head right, date below **Rev:** Locomotive below multicolored cameo, denomination below

Date	Mintage	VF20	XF40	MS60	MS63	MS65
2000	—	PF60 50.00				

KM# 396 20 DOLLARS

0.925 Silver, 38 mm. **Ruler:** Elizabeth II **Subject:** First Canadian self-propelled car **Obv:** Crowned head right, date below **Rev:** Car below multicolored cameo, denomination below

Date	Mintage	VF20	XF40	MS60	MS63	MS65
2000	—	PF60 50.00				

KM# 397 20 DOLLARS

0.925 Silver, 38 mm. **Ruler:** Elizabeth II **Subject:** Bluenose sailboat **Obv:** Crowned head right, date below **Rev:** Bluenose sailing left below multicolored cameo, denomination below

Date	Mintage	VF20	XF40	MS60	MS63	MS65
2000	—	PF60 150				

KM# 115 100 DOLLARS

13.34 g., 0.583 Gold 0.250 oz. AGW, 27 mm. **Ruler:** Elizabeth II **Subject:** 1976 Montreal Olympics **Obv:** Young bust right, maple leaf below, date at right, beaded borders **Rev:** Past and present Olympic figures, denomination at right

Date	Mintage	VF20	XF40	MS60	MS63	MS65
1976	650,000	—	—	—	375	—

KM# 116 100 DOLLARS

16.97 g., 0.917 Gold 0.5002 oz. AGW, 25 mm. **Ruler:** Elizabeth II **Subject:** 1976 Montreal Olympics **Obv:** Young bust right, maple leaf below, date at right, plain borders **Rev:** Past and present Olympic figures, denomination at right

Date	Mintage	VF20	XF40	MS60	MS63	MS65
1976	—	PF63 750				

KM# 119 100 DOLLARS

16.97 g., 0.917 Gold 0.5002 oz. AGW **Ruler:** Elizabeth II **Subject:** Queen's silver jubilee **Obv:** Young bust right **Rev:** Bouquet of provincial flowers, denomination below

Date	Mintage	VF20	XF40	MS60	MS63	MS65
1952-1977	180,396	PF63 750				

KM# 122 100 DOLLARS

16.97 g., 0.917 Gold 0.5002 oz. AGW **Ruler:** Elizabeth II **Subject:** Canadian unification **Obv:** Young bust right, denomination at left, date upper right **Rev:** Geese (representing the provinces) in flight formation

Date	Mintage	VF20	XF40	MS60	MS63	MS65
1978	—	PF63 750				

KM# 126 100 DOLLARS

16.97 g., 0.917 Gold 0.5002 oz. AGW **Ruler:** Elizabeth II **Subject:** International Year of the Child **Obv:** Young bust right **Rev:** Children with hands joined divide denomination and date

Date	Mintage	VF20	XF40	MS60	MS63	MS65
1979	—	PF63 750				

KM# 129 100 DOLLARS

16.97 g., 0.917 Gold 0.5002 oz. AGW **Ruler:** Elizabeth II **Subject:** Arctic Territories **Obv:** Young bust right, denomination at left, date above right **Rev:** Kayaker

Date	Mintage	VF20	XF40	MS60	MS63	MS65
1980	—	PF63 750				

KM# 131 100 DOLLARS

16.97 g., 0.917 Gold 0.5002 oz. AGW **Ruler:** Elizabeth II **Subject:** National anthem **Obv:** Young bust right, denomination at left, date above right **Rev:** Music score on map

Date	Mintage	VF20	XF40	MS60	MS63	MS65
1981	102,000	PF63 750				

KM# 137 100 DOLLARS

16.97 g., 0.917 Gold 0.5002 oz. AGW **Ruler:** Elizabeth II **Subject:** New Constitution **Obv:** Young bust right, denomination at left **Rev:** Open book, maple leaf on right page, date below

Date	Mintage	VF20	XF40	MS60	MS63	MS65
1982	121,708	PF63 750				

KM# 139 100 DOLLARS

16.97 g., 0.917 Gold 0.5002 oz. AGW **Ruler:** Elizabeth II **Subject:** 400th Anniversary of St. John's, Newfoundland **Obv:** Young bust right **Rev:** Anchor divides building and ship, denomination below, dates above

Date	Mintage	VF20	XF40	MS60	MS63	MS65
1583-1983	—	PF63 750				

KM# 142 100 DOLLARS

16.97 g., 0.917 Gold 0.5002 oz. AGW **Ruler:** Elizabeth II **Subject:** Jacques Cartier **Obv:** Young bust right **Rev:** Cartier head on right facing left, ship on left, date lower right, denomination above

Date	Mintage	VF20	XF40	MS60	MS63	MS65
1534-1984	—	PF63 750				

KM# 144 100 DOLLARS

16.97 g., 0.917 Gold 0.5002 oz. AGW **Ruler:** Elizabeth II **Subject:** National Parks **Obv:** Young bust right **Rev:** Bighorn sheep, denomination divides dates below

Date	Mintage	VF20	XF40	MS60	MS63	MS65
1885-1985	—	PF63 750				

KM# 152 100 DOLLARS

16.97 g., 0.917 Gold 0.5002 oz. AGW **Ruler:** Elizabeth II **Subject:** Peace **Obv:** Young bust right **Rev:** Maple leaves and letters intertwined, date at right, denomination below

Date	Mintage	VF20	XF40	MS60	MS63	MS65
1986	—	PF63 750				

KM# 158 100 DOLLARS

13.34 g., 0.583 Gold 0.250 oz. AGW **Ruler:** Elizabeth II **Subject:** 1988 Calgary Olympics **Obv:** Young bust right, maple leaf below, date at right **Rev:** Torch and logo, denomination below **Edge Lettering:** In English and French

Date	Mintage	VF20	XF40	MS60	MS63	MS65
1987 Proof, plain edge	Inc. above	PF65 375				
1987 Proof, letter edge	142,750	PF65 375				

KM# 162 100 DOLLARS

13.34 g., 0.583 Gold 0.250 oz. AGW **Ruler:** Elizabeth II **Subject:** Bowhead Whales, balaera mysticetus **Rev:** Whales left, date below, within circle, denomination below

Date	Mintage	VF20	XF40	MS60	MS63	MS65
1988	—	PF65 375				

KM# 169 100 DOLLARS

13.34 g., 0.583 Gold 0.250 oz. AGW **Ruler:** Elizabeth II **Subject:** Sainte-Marie **Obv:** Young bust right **Rev:** Huron Indian, Missionary and Mission building, denomination below, dates above

Date	Mintage	VF20	XF40	MS60	MS63	MS65
1639-1989	—	PF65 375				

KM# 171 100 DOLLARS

13.34 g., 0.583 Gold 0.250 oz. AGW **Ruler:** Elizabeth II **Subject:** International Literacy Year **Obv:** Crowned head right, date below **Rev:** Woman with children, denomination below

Date	Mintage	VF20	XF40	MS60	MS63	MS65
1990	—	PF65 375				

KM# 180 100 DOLLARS

13.34 g., 0.583 Gold 0.250 oz. AGW **Ruler:** Elizabeth II **Subject:** S.S. Empress of India **Obv:** Crowned head right, date below **Rev:** Ship,"SS Empress", denomination below

Date	Mintage	VF20	XF40	MS60	MS63	MS65
1991	—	PF65 375				

KM# 211 100 DOLLARS

13.34 g., 0.583 Gold 0.250 oz. AGW **Ruler:** Elizabeth II **Subject:** Montreal **Obv:** Crowned head right, date below **Rev:** Half figure in foreground with paper, buildings in back, denomination below

Date	Mintage	VF20	XF40	MS60	MS63	MS65
1992	—	PF65 375				

KM# 245 100 DOLLARS

13.34 g., 0.583 Gold 0.250 oz. AGW **Ruler:** Elizabeth II **Subject:** Antique Automobiles **Obv:** Crowned head right, date below **Rev:** German Bene Victoria; Simmonds Steam Carriage; French Panhard-Levassor's Daimler; American Duryea; Canadian Featherston Haugh in center, denomination below

Date	Mintage	VF20	XF40	MS60	MS63	MS65
1993	—	PF65 375				

KM# 249 100 DOLLARS

13.34 g., 0.583 Gold 0.250 oz. AGW **Ruler:** Elizabeth II **Subject:** World War II Home Front **Obv:** Crowned head right, date below **Rev:** Kneeling figure working on plane, denomination below

Date	Mintage	VF20	XF40	MS60	MS63	MS65
1994	16,201	PF65 375				

KM# 260 100 DOLLARS

13.34 g., 0.583 Gold 0.250 oz. AGW **Ruler:** Elizabeth II **Subject:** Louisbourg **Obv:** Crowned head right, date below **Rev:** Ship and buildings, dates and denomination above

Date	Mintage	VF20	XF40	MS60	MS63	MS65
1995	16,916	PF65 375				

KM# 273 100 DOLLARS

13.34 g., 0.583 Gold 0.250 oz. AGW **Ruler:** Elizabeth II **Subject:** Klondike Gold Rush Centennial **Obv:** Crowned head right, date below **Rev:** Scene of Kate Carmack panning for gold, dates above, denomination lower left

Date	Mintage	VF20	XF40	MS60	MS63	MS65
1896-1996	17,973	PF65 350				

KM# 287 100 DOLLARS

13.34 g., 0.583 Gold 0.250 oz. AGW **Ruler:** Elizabeth II **Subject:** Alexander Graham Bell **Obv:** Crowned head right, date below **Rev:** A. G. Bell head right, globe and telephone, denomination upper right

Date	Mintage	VF20	XF40	MS60	MS63	MS65
1997	14,775	PF65 375				

KM# 307 100 DOLLARS

13.34 g., 0.583 Gold 0.250 oz. AGW **Ruler:** Elizabeth II **Subject:** Discovery of Insulin **Obv:** Crowned head right, date below **Rev:** Nobel prize award figurine, dates at left, denomination at right

Date	Mintage	VF20	XF40	MS60	MS63	MS65
1998	11,220	PF65 375				

KM# 341 100 DOLLARS

13.34 g., 0.583 Gold 0.250 oz. AGW **Ruler:** Elizabeth II **Subject:** 50th Anniversary Newfoundland Unity With Canada **Obv:** Crowned head right, date below **Rev:** Two designs at front, mountains in back, denomination below

Date	Mintage	VF20	XF40	MS60	MS63	MS65
1999	10,242	PF65 375				

KM# 402 100 DOLLARS

13.34 g., 0.583 Gold 0.250 oz. AGW, 27 mm. **Ruler:** Elizabeth II **Subject:** McClure's Arctic expedition **Obv:** Crowned head right, date below **Rev:** Six men pulling supply sled to an icebound ship, denomination below **Edge:** Reeded

Date	Mintage	VF20	XF40	MS60	MS63	MS65
2000	—	PF65 375				

KM# 388 150 DOLLARS

13.61 g., 0.750 Gold 0.3282 oz. AGW **Ruler:** Elizabeth II **Subject:** Year of the Dragon **Obv:** Crowned head right

Date	Mintage	VF20	XF40	MS60	MS63	MS65
2000	—	PF63 625				

KM# 217 175 DOLLARS

16.97 g., 0.917 Gold 0.5003 oz. AGW **Ruler:** Elizabeth II **Subject:** 1992 Olympics **Obv:** Crowned head right, date at left, denomination below **Rev:** Passing the torch **Edge:** Lettered

Date	Mintage	VF20	XF40	MS60	MS63	MS65
1992	—	PF63 750				

KM# 178 200 DOLLARS

17.14 g., 0.9166 Gold 0.505 oz. AGW, 29 mm. **Ruler:** Elizabeth II **Subject:** Canadian flag silver jubilee **Obv:** Crowned head right, date below **Rev:** People with flag, denomination above

Date	Mintage	VF20	XF40	MS60	MS63	MS65
1990	—	PF63 775				

KM# 202 200 DOLLARS

17.14 g., 0.9166 Gold 0.505 oz. AGW, 29 mm. **Ruler:** Elizabeth II **Subject:** Hockey **Obv:** Crowned head right **Rev:** Hockey players, denomination above

Date	Mintage	VF20	XF40	MS60	MS63	MS65
1991	10,215	PF63 775				

KM# 230 200 DOLLARS

17.14 g., 0.9166 Gold 0.505 oz. AGW, 29 mm. **Ruler:** Elizabeth II **Subject:** Niagara Falls **Obv:** Crowned head right **Rev:** Niagara Falls, denomination above

Date	Mintage	VF20	XF40	MS60	MS63	MS65
1992	—	PF63 775				

KM# 244 200 DOLLARS

17.14 g., 0.9166 Gold 0.505 oz. AGW, 29 mm. **Ruler:** Elizabeth II **Subject:** Mounted police **Obv:** Crowned head right, date below **Rev:** Mountie with children, denomination above

Date	Mintage	VF20	XF40	MS60	MS63	MS65
1993	10,807	PF63 775				

KM# 250 200 DOLLARS

17.14 g., 0.9166 Gold 0.505 oz. AGW, 29 mm. **Ruler:** Elizabeth II **Subject:** Interpretation of 1908 novel by Lucy Maud Montgomery, 1874-1942, Anne of Green Gables **Obv:** Crowned head right **Rev:** Figure sitting in window, denomination above

Date	Mintage	VF20	XF40	MS60	MS63	MS65
1994	10,655	PF63 775				

KM# 265 200 DOLLARS

17.14 g., 0.9166 Gold 0.505 oz. AGW, 29 mm. **Ruler:** Elizabeth II **Subject:** Maple-syrup production **Obv:** Crowned head right, date below **Rev:** Maple syrup making, denomination at right

Date	Mintage	VF20	XF40	MS60	MS63	MS65
1995	—	PF63 775				

KM# 275 200 DOLLARS

17.14 g., 0.9166 Gold 0.505 oz. AGW, 29 mm. **Ruler:** Elizabeth II **Subject:** Transcontinental Canadian Railway **Obv:** Crowned head right, date below **Rev:** Train going through mountains, denomination below

Date	Mintage	VF20	XF40	MS60	MS63	MS65
1996	—	PF63 775				

KM# 288 200 DOLLARS
17.14 g., 0.9166 Gold 0.505 oz. AGW, 29 mm. **Ruler:** Elizabeth II **Subject:** Haida mask **Obv:** Crowned head right, date below **Rev:** Haida mask

Date	Mintage	VF20	XF40	MS60	MS63	MS65
1997	11,610	PF63 775				

KM# 317 200 DOLLARS
17.14 g., 0.9166 Gold 0.505 oz. AGW, 29 mm. **Ruler:** Elizabeth II **Subject:** Legendary white buffalo **Obv:** Crowned head right, date below **Rev:** Buffalo

Date	Mintage	VF20	XF40	MS60	MS63	MS65
1998	—	PF63 775				

KM# 358 200 DOLLARS
17.14 g., 0.9166 Gold 0.505 oz. AGW, 29 mm. **Ruler:** Elizabeth II **Subject:** Mikmaq butterfly **Obv:** Crowned head right **Rev:** Butterfly within design

Date	Mintage	VF20	XF40	MS60	MS63	MS65
1999	—	PF63 775				

KM# 403 200 DOLLARS
17.14 g., 0.9166 Gold 0.505 oz. AGW, 29 mm. **Ruler:** Elizabeth II **Subject:** Motherhood **Obv:** Crowned head right, date above, denomination at right **Rev:** Inuit mother with infant **Edge:** Reeded

Date	Mintage	VF20	XF40	MS60	MS63	MS65
2000	—	PF63 775				

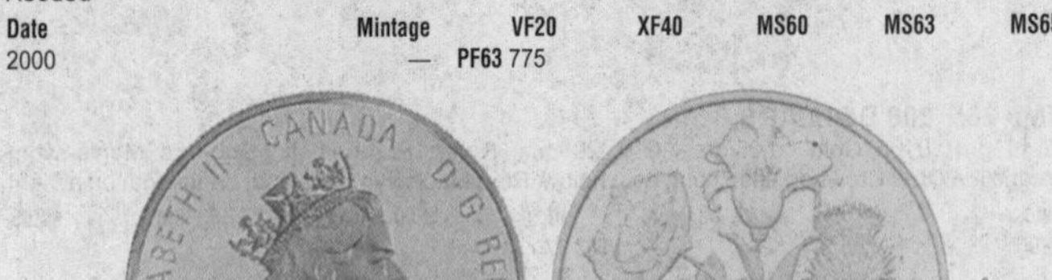

KM# 308 350 DOLLARS
38.05 g., 0.9999 Gold 1.2232 oz. AGW **Ruler:** Elizabeth II **Subject:** Flowers of Canada's Coat of Arms **Obv:** Crowned head right, date behind, denomination at bottom **Rev:** Flowers

Date	Mintage	VF20	XF40	MS60	MS63	MS65
1998	—	PF63 2,250				

KM# 370 350 DOLLARS
38.05 g., 0.9999 Gold 1.2232 oz. AGW **Ruler:** Elizabeth II **Rev:** Lady's slipper

Date	Mintage	VF20	XF40	MS60	MS63	MS65
1999	1,990	PF63 2,250				

KM# 404 350 DOLLARS
38.05 g., 0.9999 Gold 1.2232 oz. AGW, 34 mm. **Ruler:** Elizabeth II **Obv:** Crowned head right **Rev:** Three Pacific Dogwood flowers **Edge:** Reeded

Date	Mintage	VF20	XF40	MS60	MS63	MS65
2000	1,506	PF63 2,250				

SILVER BULLION COINAGE

KM# 163 5 DOLLARS
31.10 g., 0.9999 Silver 0.9998 oz. ASW **Ruler:** Elizabeth II **Obv:** Young bust right, denomination and date below **Rev:** Maple leaf flanked by 9999

Date	Mintage	VF20	XF40	MS60	MS63	MS65
1988	1,155,931	—	—	—	35.00	37.00
1989	—	PF63 40.00				
1989	3,332,200	—	—	—	35.00	37.00

KM# 187 5 DOLLARS
31.10 g., 0.9999 Silver 0.9998 oz. ASW **Ruler:** Elizabeth II **Obv:** Crowned head right, date and denomination below **Rev:** Maple leaf flanked by 9999

Date	Mintage	VF20	XF40	MS60	MS63	MS65
1990	1,708,800	—	—	—	35.00	37.00
1991	644,300	—	—	—	35.00	37.00
1992	343,800	—	—	—	35.00	37.00
1993	889,946	—	—	—	35.00	37.00
1994	1,133,900	—	—	—	35.00	37.00
1995	326,244	—	—	—	35.00	37.00
1996	250,445	—	—	—	42.50	45.00
1997	100,970	—	—	—	35.00	37.00
1998	591,359	—	—	—	35.00	37.00
1998 Tiger privy mark	25,000	—	—	—	35.00	37.00
1998 Titanic privy mark	26,000	—	—	—	85.00	90.00
1998 R.C.M.P. privy mark	25,000	—	—	—	35.00	37.00
1998 90th Anniversary R.C.M. privy mark	13,025	—	—	—	35.00	37.00
1999	1,229,442	—	—	—	35.00	37.00
1999 Rabbit privy mark	25,000	—	—	—	35.00	37.00
1999 Y2K privy mark	9,999	—	—	—	37.50	40.00
2000	403,652	—	—	—	35.00	37.00
2000 Dragon privy mark	25,000	—	—	—	35.00	37.00
2000 Expo Hanover privy mark	—	—	—	—	45.00	48.00

KM# 363 5 DOLLARS

31.10 g., 0.9999 Silver 0.9998 oz. ASW **Ruler:** Elizabeth II **Obv:** Crowned head right, date and denomination below **Rev:** Maple leaf flanked by 9999

Date		Mintage	VF20	XF40	MS60	MS63	MS65
1999/2000	Fireworks privy mark	298,775	—	—	—	35.00	37.00

KM# 326 50 DOLLARS

311.04 g., 0.9999 Silver 9.999 oz. ASW **Ruler:** Elizabeth II **Subject:** 10th Anniversary Silver Maple Leaf **Obv:** Crowned head right **Rev:** Maple leaf flanked by 9999 **Edge:** 10th ANNIVERSARY 10e ANNIVERSAIRE

Date	Mintage	VF20	XF40	MS60	MS63	MS65
1998	—	PF63 375				

GOLD BULLION COINAGE

KM# 238 DOLLAR

1.56 g., 0.9999 Gold 0.050 oz. AGW **Ruler:** Elizabeth II **Obv:** Crowned head right, denomination and date below **Rev:** Maple leaf flanked by 9999

Date	Mintage	VF20	XF40	MS60	MS63	MS65
1993	37,080	—	—	—	80.00	—
1994	78,860	—	—	—	80.00	—
1995	85,920	—	—	—	80.00	—
1996	56,520	—	—	—	80.00	—
1997	59,720	—	—	—	80.00	—
1998	44,260	—	—	—	80.00	—
1999 oval "20 YEARS ANS" privy mark	—	—	—	—	83.00	—
2000 oval "2000" privy mark	—	—	—	—	83.00	—

KM# 365 DOLLAR

1.56 g., 0.9999 Gold 0.050 oz. AGW **Ruler:** Elizabeth II **Obv:** Crowned head right **Rev:** Maple leaf hologram

Date	Mintage	VF20	XF40	MS60	MS63	MS65
1999	500	—	—	—	115	—

KM# 256 2 DOLLARS

2.07 g., 0.9999 Gold 0.0667 oz. AGW **Ruler:** Elizabeth II **Obv:** Crowned head right, denomination and date below **Rev:** Maple leaf flanked by 9999

Date	Mintage	VF20	XF40	MS60	MS63	MS65
1994	5,493	—	—	—	140	—

KM# 135 5 DOLLARS

3.12 g., 0.9999 Gold 0.1003 oz. AGW **Ruler:** Elizabeth II **Obv:** Young bust right, date and denomination below **Rev:** Maple leaf flanked by 9999

Date	Mintage	VF20	XF40	MS60	MS63	MS65
1982	246,000	—	—	—	145	—
1983	304,000	—	—	—	145	—
1984	262,000	—	—	—	145	—
1985	398,000	—	—	—	145	—
1986	529,516	—	—	—	145	—
1987	459,000	—	—	—	145	—
1988	506,500	—	—	—	145	—
1989	16,992	PF63 200				
1989	539,000	—	—	—	145	—

KM# 188 5 DOLLARS

3.12 g., 0.9999 Gold 0.1003 oz. AGW **Ruler:** Elizabeth II **Obv:** Elizabeth II effigy **Rev:** Maple leaf

Date	Mintage	VF20	XF40	MS60	MS63	MS65
1990	476,000	—	—	—	145	—
1991	322,000	—	—	—	145	—
1992	384,000	—	—	—	145	—
1993	248,630	—	—	—	145	—
1994	313,150	—	—	—	145	—
1995	294,890	—	—	—	145	—
1996	179,220	—	—	—	145	—
1997	188,540	—	—	—	145	—
1998	301,940	—	—	—	145	—
1999 oval "20 Years ANS" privy mark	—	—	—	—	152	—
2000 oval "2000" privy mark	—	—	—	—	152	—

KM# 366 5 DOLLARS

3.12 g., 0.9999 Gold 0.1003 oz. AGW **Ruler:** Elizabeth II **Rev:** Maple leaf hologram

Date	Mintage	VF20	XF40	MS60	MS63	MS65
1999	500	—	—	—	210	—

KM# 136 10 DOLLARS

7.79 g., 0.9999 Gold 0.2503 oz. AGW **Ruler:** Elizabeth II **Obv:** Young bust right, date and denomination below **Rev:** Maple leaf flanked by 9999

Date	Mintage	VF20	XF40	MS60	MS63	MS65
1982	184,000	—	—	—	350	—
1983	308,800	—	—	—	350	—
1984	242,400	—	—	—	350	—
1985	620,000	—	—	—	350	—
1986	915,200	—	—	—	350	—
1987	376,000	—	—	—	350	—
1988	436,000	—	—	—	350	—
1989	—	PF63 500				
1989	328,800	—	—	—	350	—

KM# 189 10 DOLLARS

7.79 g., 0.9999 Gold 0.2503 oz. AGW **Ruler:** Elizabeth II **Obv:** Crowned head right, date and denomination below **Rev:** Maple leaf flanked by 9999

Date	Mintage	VF20	XF40	MS60	MS63	MS65
1990	253,600	—	—	—	350	—
1991	166,400	—	—	—	350	—
1992	179,600	—	—	—	350	—
1993	158,452	—	—	—	350	—
1994	148,792	—	—	—	350	—
1995	127,596	—	—	—	350	—
1996	89,148	—	—	—	350	—
1997	98,104	—	—	—	350	—
1998	85,472	—	—	—	350	—
1999 oval "20 Years ANS" privy mark	—	—	—	—	365	—
2000 oval "2000" privy mark	—	—	—	—	365	—

KM# 367 10 DOLLARS

7.79 g., 0.9999 Gold 0.2503 oz. AGW **Ruler:** Elizabeth II **Rev:** Maple leaf hologram

Date	Mintage	VF20	XF40	MS60	MS63	MS65
1999	—	—	—	—	485	—

KM# 153 20 DOLLARS

15.55 g., 0.9999 Gold 0.4999 oz. AGW, 32 mm. **Ruler:** Elizabeth II **Obv:** Young bust right, date and denomination below **Rev;** Maple leaf flanked by 9999

Date	Mintage	VF20	XF40	MS60	MS63	MS65
1986	529,200	—	—	—	680	—
1987	332,800	—	—	—	680	—
1988	538,400	—	—	—	680	—
1989	259,200	—	—	—	680	—
1989	—	PF63 935				

KM# 190 20 DOLLARS

15.55 g., 0.9999 Gold 0.4999 oz. AGW **Ruler:** Elizabeth II **Obv:** Crowned head right, date and denomination below **Rev:** Maple leaf flanked by 9999

Date	Mintage	VF20	XF40	MS60	MS63	MS65
1990	174,400	—	—	—	680	—
1991	96,200	—	—	—	680	—
1992	108,000	—	—	—	680	—
1993	99,492	—	—	—	680	—
1994	104,766	—	—	—	680	—
1995	103,162	—	—	—	680	—
1996	66,246	—	—	—	680	—
1997	63,354	—	—	—	680	—
1998	65,366	—	—	—	680	—
1999 oval "20 Years ANS" privy mark	—	—	—	—	710	—
2000 oval "2000" privy mark	—	—	—	—	710	—

KM# 368 20 DOLLARS

15.55 g., 0.9999 Gold 0.4999 oz. AGW **Ruler:** Elizabeth II **Rev:** Maple leaf hologram

Date	Mintage	VF20	XF40	MS60	MS63	MS65
1999	500	—	—	—	935	—

KM# 125.1 50 DOLLARS
31.10 g., 0.999 Gold 0.999 oz. AGW **Ruler:** Elizabeth II **Obv:** Young bust right, denomination and date below **Rev:** Maple leaf flanked by .999

Date	Mintage	VF20	XF40	MS60	MS63	MS65
1979	1,000,000	—	—	—	1,325	—
1980	1,251,500	—	—	—	1,325	—
1981	863,000	—	—	—	1,325	—
1982	883,000	—	—	—	1,325	—

KM# 125.2 50 DOLLARS
31.10 g., 0.9999 Gold 0.9999 oz. AGW **Ruler:** Elizabeth II **Obv:** Young bust right, date and denomination below **Rev:** Maple leaf flanked by .9999

Date	Mintage	VF20	XF40	MS60	MS63	MS65
1983	843,000	—	—	—	1,325	—
1984	1,067,500	—	—	—	1,325	—
1985	1,908,000	—	—	—	1,325	—
1986	779,115	—	—	—	1,325	—
1987	978,000	—	—	—	1,325	—
1988	826,500	—	—	—	1,325	—
1989	17,781	PF63 1,900				
1989	856,000	—	—	—	1,325	—

KM# 191 50 DOLLARS
31.10 g., 0.9999 Gold 0.9999 oz. AGW **Ruler:** Elizabeth II **Obv:** Crowned head right, date and denomination below **Rev:** Maple leaf flanked by .9999

Date	Mintage	VF20	XF40	MS60	MS63	MS65
1990	815,000	—	—	—	1,325	—
1991	290,000	—	—	—	1,325	—
1992	368,900	—	—	—	1,325	—
1993	321,413	—	—	—	1,325	—
1994	180,357	—	—	—	1,325	—
1995	208,729	—	—	—	1,325	—
1996	143,682	—	—	—	1,325	—
1997	478,211	—	—	—	1,325	—
1998	593,704	—	—	—	1,325	—
1999 oval "20 Years ANS" privy mark	—	—	—	—	1,375	—
2000 oval "2000" privy mark	—	—	—	—	1,375	—
2000 oval fireworks privy mark	—	—	—	—	1,375	—

KM# 305 50 DOLLARS
31.10 g., 0.9999 Gold 0.9999 oz. AGW **Ruler:** Elizabeth II **Obv:** Crowned head denomination below, within circle, dates below **Rev:** Mountie at gallop right, within circle **Shape:** 10-sided

Date	Mintage	VF20	XF40	MS60	MS63	MS65
1997	12,913	—	—	—	1,850	—

KM# 369 50 DOLLARS
31.10 g., 0.9999 Gold 0.9999 oz. AGW **Ruler:** Elizabeth II **Obv:** Crowned head right, date and denomination below **Rev:** Maple leaf hologram flanked by 9999, with fireworks privy mark

Date	Mintage	VF20	XF40	MS60	MS63	MS65
2000	500	—	—	—	1,850	—

PLATINUM BULLION COINAGE

KM# 239 DOLLAR
1.56 g., 0.9995 Platinum 0.050 oz. APW **Ruler:** Elizabeth II **Obv:** Crowned head right, date and denomination below **Rev:** Maple leaf flanked by 9995

Date	Mintage	VF20	XF40	MS60	MS63	MS65
1993	2,120	—	—	—	68.00	—
1994	4,260	—	—	—	68.00	—
1995	460	—	—	—	150	—
1996	1,640	—	—	—	68.00	—
1997	1,340	—	—	—	68.00	—
1998	2,000	—	—	—	68.00	—
1999	2,000	—	—	—	68.00	—

KM# 257 2 DOLLARS
2.07 g., 0.9995 Platinum 0.0666 oz. APW **Ruler:** Elizabeth II **Obv:** Crowned head right, date and denomination below **Rev:** Maple leaf flanked by 9995

Date	Mintage	VF20	XF40	MS60	MS63	MS65
1994	1,470	—	—	—	240	—

KM# 164 5 DOLLARS
3.12 g., 0.9995 Platinum 0.1003 oz. APW **Ruler:** Elizabeth II **Obv:** Young bust right, date and denomination below **Rev:** Maple leaf flanked by 9995

Date	Mintage	VF20	XF40	MS60	MS63	MS65
1988	74,000	—	—	—	125	—
1989	18,000	—	—	—	125	—
1989	11,999	PF63 250				

KM# 192 5 DOLLARS
3.12 g., 0.9995 Platinum 0.1003 oz. APW **Ruler:** Elizabeth II **Rev:** Maple leaf

Date	Mintage	VF20	XF40	MS60	MS63	MS65
1990	9,000	—	—	—	125	—
1991	13,000	—	—	—	125	—
1992	16,000	—	—	—	125	—
1993	14,020	—	—	—	125	—
1994	19,190	—	—	—	125	—
1995	8,940	—	—	—	125	—
1996	8,820	—	—	—	125	—
1997	7,050	—	—	—	125	—
1998	5,710	—	—	—	125	—
1999	2,000	—	—	—	125	—

KM# 165 10 DOLLARS
7.79 g., 0.9995 Platinum 0.2502 oz. APW **Ruler:** Elizabeth II **Obv:** Young bust right, date and denomination below **Rev:** Maple leaf flanked by 9995

Date	Mintage	VF20	XF40	MS60	MS63	MS65
1988	93,600	—	—	—	295	—
1989	1,999	PF63 550				
1989	3,200	—	—	—	295	—

KM# 193 10 DOLLARS
7.79 g., 0.9995 Platinum 0.2502 oz. APW **Ruler:** Elizabeth II **Rev:** Maple leaf

Date	Mintage	VF20	XF40	MS60	MS63	MS65
1990	1,600	—	—	—	295	—
1991	7,200	—	—	—	295	—
1992	11,600	—	—	—	295	—
1993	8,048	—	—	—	295	—
1994	9,456	—	—	—	295	—
1995	6,524	—	—	—	295	—
1996	6,160	—	—	—	295	—
1997	4,552	—	—	—	295	—
1998	3,816	—	—	—	295	—
1999	2,000	—	—	—	295	—

KM# 166 20 DOLLARS

15.55 g., 0.9995 Platinum 0.4998 oz. APW **Ruler:** Elizabeth II **Obv:** Young bust right, denomination and date below **Rev:** Maple leaf flanked by 9995

Date	Mintage	VF20	XF40	MS60	MS63	MS65
1988	23,600	—	—	—	570	—
1989	4,800	—	—	—	570	—
1989	1,999	PF63 1,000				

KM# 194 20 DOLLARS

15.55 g., 0.9995 Platinum 0.4998 oz. APW **Ruler:** Elizabeth II **Rev:** Maple leaf

Date	Mintage	VF20	XF40	MS60	MS63	MS65
1990	2,600	—	—	—	570	—
1991	5,600	—	—	—	570	—
1992	12,800	—	—	—	570	—
1993	6,022	—	—	—	570	—
1994	6,710	—	—	—	570	—
1995	6,308	—	—	—	570	—
1996	5,490	—	—	—	570	—
1997	3,990	—	—	—	570	—
1998	5,486	—	—	—	570	—
1999	500	—	—	—	600	—

KM# 174 30 DOLLARS

3.11 g., 0.999 Platinum 0.0999 oz. APW **Ruler:** Elizabeth II **Obv:** Crowned head right **Rev:** Polar bear swimming, denomination below

Date	Mintage	VF20	XF40	MS60	MS63	MS65
1990	—	PF63 210				

KM# 198 30 DOLLARS

3.11 g., 0.999 Platinum 0.0999 oz. APW **Ruler:** Elizabeth II **Obv:** Crowned head right **Rev:** Snowy owl, denomination below

Date	Mintage	VF20	XF40	MS60	MS63	MS65
1991	—	PF63 210				

KM# 226 30 DOLLARS

3.11 g., 0.999 Platinum 0.0999 oz. APW **Ruler:** Elizabeth II **Obv:** Crowned head right **Rev:** Cougar head and shoulders, denomination below

Date	Mintage	VF20	XF40	MS60	MS63	MS65
1992	—	PF63 210				

KM# 240 30 DOLLARS

3.11 g., 0.999 Platinum 0.0999 oz. APW **Ruler:** Elizabeth II **Obv:** Crowned head right **Rev:** Arctic fox, denomination below

Date	Mintage	VF20	XF40	MS60	MS63	MS65
1993	—	PF63 210				

KM# 252 30 DOLLARS

3.11 g., 0.999 Platinum 0.0999 oz. APW **Ruler:** Elizabeth II **Obv:** Crowned head right, date below **Rev:** Sea otter, denomination below

Date	Mintage	VF20	XF40	MS60	MS63	MS65
1994	1,500	PF63 210				

KM# 266 30 DOLLARS

3.11 g., 0.999 Platinum 0.0999 oz. APW **Ruler:** Elizabeth II **Obv:** Crowned head right, date below **Rev:** Canadian lynx, denomination below

Date	Mintage	VF20	XF40	MS60	MS63	MS65
1995	—	PF63 210				

KM# 278 30 DOLLARS

3.11 g., 0.999 Platinum 0.0999 oz. APW **Ruler:** Elizabeth II **Obv:** Crowned head right, date below **Rev:** Falcon portrait, denomination below

Date	Mintage	VF20	XF40	MS60	MS63	MS65
1996	—	PF63 210				

KM# 300 30 DOLLARS

3.11 g., 0.9995 Platinum 0.0999 oz. APW **Ruler:** Elizabeth II **Obv:** Crowned head right, date below **Rev:** Bison head, denomination below

Date	Mintage	VF20	XF40	MS60	MS63	MS65
1997	—	PF63 210				

KM# 322 30 DOLLARS

3.11 g., 0.999 Platinum 0.0999 oz. APW **Ruler:** Elizabeth II **Obv:** Crowned head right, date below **Rev:** Grey wolf

Date	Mintage	VF20	XF40	MS60	MS63	MS65
1998	—	PF63 210				

KM# 359 30 DOLLARS

3.11 g., 0.9995 Platinum 0.0999 oz. APW **Ruler:** Elizabeth II **Obv:** Crowned head right, date below **Rev:** Musk ox

Date	Mintage	VF20	XF40	MS60	MS63	MS65
1999	1,500	PF63 210				

KM# 405 30 DOLLARS

3.11 g., 0.9995 Platinum 0.0999 oz. APW, 16 mm. **Ruler:** Elizabeth II **Obv:** Crowned head right, date below **Rev:** Pronghorn antelope head, denomination below **Edge:** Reeded

Date	Mintage	VF20	XF40	MS60	MS63	MS65
2000	—	PF63 210				

KM# 167 50 DOLLARS

31.10 g., 0.9995 Platinum 0.9995 oz. APW **Ruler:** Elizabeth II **Obv:** Young bust right, denomination and date below **Rev:** Maple leaf flanked by 9995

Date	Mintage	VF20	XF40	MS60	MS63	MS65
1988	37,500	—	—	—	1,100	—
1989	—	PF60 1,900				
1989	10,000	—	—	—	1,100	—

KM# 195 50 DOLLARS

31.10 g., 0.9995 Platinum 0.9995 oz. APW **Ruler:** Elizabeth II **Rev:** Maple leaf

Date	Mintage	VF20	XF40	MS60	MS63	MS65
1990	15,100	—	—	—	1,100	—
1991	31,900	—	—	—	1,100	—
1992	40,500	—	—	—	1,100	—
1993	17,666	—	—	—	1,100	—
1994	36,245	—	—	—	1,100	—
1995	25,829	—	—	—	1,100	—
1996	62,273	—	—	—	1,100	—
1997	25,480	—	—	—	1,100	—
1998	10,403	—	—	—	1,100	—
1999	1,300	—	—	—	1,150	—

KM# 175 75 DOLLARS

7.78 g., 0.999 Platinum 0.2498 oz. APW **Ruler:** Elizabeth II **Obv:** Crowned head right **Rev:** Polar bear resting, denomination below

Date	Mintage	VF20	XF40	MS60	MS63	MS65
1990	—	PF63 520				

KM# 199 75 DOLLARS
7.78 g., 0.999 Platinum 0.2498 oz. APW **Ruler:** Elizabeth II **Obv:** Crowned head right **Rev:** Snowy owls perched on branch, denomination below

Date	Mintage	VF20	XF40	MS60	MS63	MS65
1991	—	PF63 520				

KM# 227 75 DOLLARS
7.78 g., 0.999 Platinum 0.2498 oz. APW **Ruler:** Elizabeth II **Obv:** Crowned head right **Rev:** Cougar prowling, denomination below

Date	Mintage	VF20	XF40	MS60	MS63	MS65
1992	—	PF63 520				

KM# 241 75 DOLLARS
7.78 g., 0.999 Platinum 0.2498 oz. APW **Ruler:** Elizabeth II **Obv:** Crowned head right **Rev:** Two Arctic foxes, denomination below

Date	Mintage	VF20	XF40	MS60	MS63	MS65
1993	—	PF63 520				

KM# 253 75 DOLLARS
7.78 g., 0.999 Platinum 0.2498 oz. APW **Ruler:** Elizabeth II **Obv:** Crowned head right, date below **Rev:** Sea otter eating urchin, denomination below

Date	Mintage	VF20	XF40	MS60	MS63	MS65
1994	1,500	PF63 520				

KM# 267 75 DOLLARS
7.78 g., 0.999 Platinum 0.2498 oz. APW **Ruler:** Elizabeth II **Obv:** Crowned head right, date below **Rev:** Two lynx kittens, denomination below

Date	Mintage	VF20	XF40	MS60	MS63	MS65
1995	1,500	PF63 520				

KM# 279 75 DOLLARS
7.78 g., 0.999 Platinum 0.2498 oz. APW **Ruler:** Elizabeth II **Obv:** Crowned head right, date below **Rev:** Peregrine falcon, denomination below

Date	Mintage	VF20	XF40	MS60	MS63	MS65
1996	1,500	PF63 520				

KM# 301 75 DOLLARS
7.78 g., 0.999 Platinum 0.2498 oz. APW **Ruler:** Elizabeth II **Obv:** Crowned head right, date below **Rev:** Two bison calves, denomination below

Date	Mintage	VF20	XF40	MS60	MS63	MS65
1997	1,500	PF63 520				

KM# 323 75 DOLLARS
7.78 g., 0.999 Platinum 0.2498 oz. APW **Ruler:** Elizabeth II **Obv:** Crowned head right, date below **Rev:** Gray wolf

Date	Mintage	VF20	XF40	MS60	MS63	MS65
1998	1,000	PF63 520				

KM# 360 75 DOLLARS
7.78 g., 0.999 Platinum 0.2498 oz. APW **Ruler:** Elizabeth II **Obv:** Crowned head right, date below **Rev:** Musk ox

Date	Mintage	VF20	XF40	MS60	MS63	MS65
1999	—	PF63 520				

KM# 406 75 DOLLARS
7.78 g., 0.999 Platinum 0.2498 oz. APW, 20 mm. **Ruler:** Elizabeth II **Obv:** Crowned head right **Rev:** Standing pronghorn antelope, denomination below **Edge:** Reeded

Date	Mintage	VF20	XF40	MS60	MS63	MS65
2000	—	PF63 520				

KM# 176 150 DOLLARS
15.55 g., 0.999 Platinum 0.4995 oz. APW **Ruler:** Elizabeth II **Obv:** Crowned head right **Rev:** Polar bear walking, denomination below

Date	Mintage	VF20	XF40	MS60	MS63	MS65
1990	—	PF63 1,000				

KM# 200 150 DOLLARS
15.55 g., 0.999 Platinum 0.4995 oz. APW **Ruler:** Elizabeth II **Obv:** Crowned head right **Rev:** Snowy owl flying, denomination below

Date	Mintage	VF20	XF40	MS60	MS63	MS65
1991	—	PF63 1,000				

KM# 228 150 DOLLARS
15.55 g., 0.999 Platinum 0.4995 oz. APW **Ruler:** Elizabeth II **Obv:** Crowned head right **Rev:** Cougar mother and cub, denomination below

Date	Mintage	VF20	XF40	MS60	MS63	MS65
1992	—	PF63 1,000				

KM# 242 150 DOLLARS
15.55 g., 0.999 Platinum 0.4995 oz. APW **Ruler:** Elizabeth II **Obv:** Crowned head right **Rev:** Arctic fox by lake, denomination below

Date	Mintage	VF20	XF40	MS60	MS63	MS65
1993	—	PF63 1,000				

KM# 254 150 DOLLARS

15.55 g., 0.999 Platinum 0.4995 oz. APW **Ruler:** Elizabeth II **Obv:** Crowned head right, date below **Rev:** Sea otter mother carrying pup, denomination below

Date	Mintage	VF20	XF40	MS60	MS63	MS65
1994	—	PF63 1,000				

KM# 268 150 DOLLARS

15.55 g., 0.999 Platinum 0.4995 oz. APW **Ruler:** Elizabeth II **Obv:** Crowned head right, date below **Rev:** Prowling lynx, denomination below

Date	Mintage	VF20	XF40	MS60	MS63	MS65
1995	—	PF63 1,000				

KM# 280 150 DOLLARS

15.55 g., 0.999 Platinum 0.4995 oz. APW **Ruler:** Elizabeth II **Obv:** Crowned head right, date below **Rev:** Peregrine falcon on branch, denomination below

Date	Mintage	VF20	XF40	MS60	MS63	MS65
1996	100	PF63 1,000				

KM# 302 150 DOLLARS

15.55 g., 0.999 Platinum 0.4995 oz. APW **Ruler:** Elizabeth II **Obv:** Crowned head right, date below **Rev:** Bison bull, denomination below

Date	Mintage	VF20	XF40	MS60	MS63	MS65
1997	—	PF63 1,000				

KM# 324 150 DOLLARS

15.55 g., 0.999 Platinum 0.4995 oz. APW **Ruler:** Elizabeth II **Obv:** Crowned head right, date below **Rev:** Two gray wolf cubs, denomination below

Date	Mintage	VF20	XF40	MS60	MS63	MS65
1998	—	PF63 1,000				

KM# 361 150 DOLLARS

15.55 g., 0.999 Platinum 0.4995 oz. APW **Ruler:** Elizabeth II **Obv:** Crowned head right **Rev:** Musk ox, denomination below

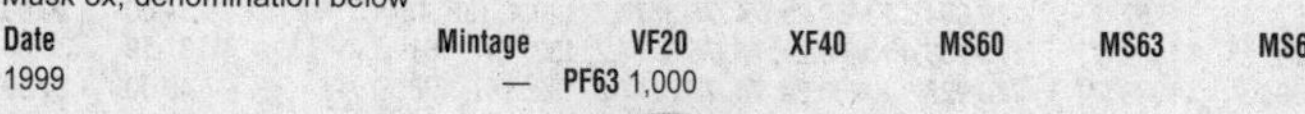

Date	Mintage	VF20	XF40	MS60	MS63	MS65
1999	—	PF63 1,000				

KM# 407 150 DOLLARS

15.55 g., 0.999 Platinum 0.4994 oz. APW, 25 mm. **Ruler:** Elizabeth II **Obv:** Crowned head right **Rev:** Two pronghorn antelope, denomination below **Edge:** Reeded

Date	Mintage	VF20	XF40	MS60	MS63	MS65
2000	—	PF63 1,000				

KM# 177 300 DOLLARS

31.10 g., 0.999 Platinum 0.999 oz. APW **Ruler:** Elizabeth II **Obv:** Crowned head right **Rev:** Polar bear mother and cub, denomination below

Date	Mintage	VF20	XF40	MS60	MS63	MS65
1990	—	PF63 1,950				

KM# 201 300 DOLLARS

31.10 g., 0.999 Platinum 0.999 oz. APW **Ruler:** Elizabeth II **Obv:** Crowned head right **Rev:** Snowy owl with chicks, denomination below

Date	Mintage	VF20	XF40	MS60	MS63	MS65
1991	—	PF63 1,950				

KM# 229 300 DOLLARS

31.10 g., 0.999 Platinum 0.999 oz. APW **Ruler:** Elizabeth II **Obv:** Crowned head right **Rev:** Cougar resting in tree, denomination below

Date	Mintage	VF20	XF40	MS60	MS63	MS65
1992	—	PF63 1,950				

KM# 243 300 DOLLARS

31.10 g., 0.999 Platinum 0.999 oz. APW **Ruler:** Elizabeth II **Obv:** Crowned head right **Rev:** Mother fox and three kits, denomination below

Date	Mintage	VF20	XF40	MS60	MS63	MS65
1993	—	PF63 1,950				

KM# 255 300 DOLLARS

31.10 g., 0.999 Platinum 0.999 oz. APW **Ruler:** Elizabeth II **Obv:** Crowned head right, date below **Rev:** Two otters swimming, denomination below

Date	Mintage	VF20	XF40	MS60	MS63	MS65
1994	—	PF63 1,950				

KM# 269 300 DOLLARS
31.10 g., 0.999 Platinum 0.999 oz. APW **Ruler:** Elizabeth II **Obv:** Crowned head right, date below **Rev:** Female lynx and three kittens, denomination below

Date	Mintage	VF20	XF40	MS60	MS63	MS65
1995	1,500	PF63 1,950				

KM# 281 300 DOLLARS
31.10 g., 0.999 Platinum 0.999 oz. APW **Ruler:** Elizabeth II **Obv:** Crowned head right, date below **Rev:** Peregrine falcon feeding nestlings, denomination below

Date	Mintage	VF20	XF40	MS60	MS63	MS65
1996	1,500	PF63 1,950				

KM# 303 300 DOLLARS
31.10 g., 0.999 Platinum 0.999 oz. APW **Ruler:** Elizabeth II **Obv:** Crowned head right, date below **Rev:** Bison family, denomination below

Date	Mintage	VF20	XF40	MS60	MS63	MS65
1997	1,500	PF63 1,950				

KM# 325 300 DOLLARS
31.10 g., 0.999 Platinum 0.999 oz. APW **Ruler:** Elizabeth II **Obv:** Crowned head right, date below **Rev:** Gray wolf and two cubs, denomination below

Date	Mintage	VF20	XF40	MS60	MS63	MS65
1998	—	PF63 1,950				

KM# 362 300 DOLLARS
31.10 g., 0.999 Platinum 0.999 oz. APW **Ruler:** Elizabeth II **Obv:** Crowned head right, date below **Rev:** Musk ox

Date	Mintage	VF20	XF40	MS60	MS63	MS65
1999	—	PF63 1,950				

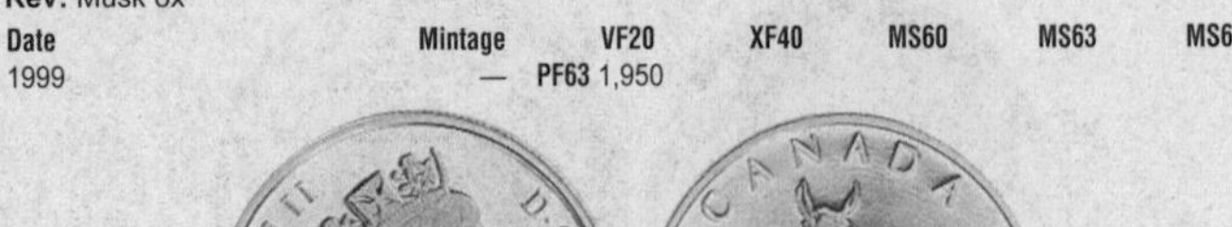

KM# 408 300 DOLLARS
31.10 g., 0.999 Platinum 0.999 oz. APW, 30 mm. **Ruler:** Elizabeth II **Obv:** Crowned head right, date below **Rev:** Four pronghorn antelope, denomination below **Edge:** Reeded

Date	Mintage	VF20	XF40	MS60	MS63	MS65
2000	—	PF63 1,950				

PATTERNS

Including off metal strikes

KM#	Date	Mintage	Identification	Mkt Val
Pn14	1911	—	Cent. Bronze. Similar to 1912-1920.	20,000
Pn15	1911	—	Dollar. Silver.	
Pn16	1911	—	Dollar. Lead.	250,000
Pn17	1911	—	5 Dollars. Gold.	70,000
Pn18	1911	—	10 Dollars. Gold.	70,000
Pn19	1928	—	5 Dollars. Bronze.	20,000
Pn20	1928	—	10 Dollars. Bronze.	22,000
Pn23	1964	—	Dollar. Tin. Piefort.	8,000
Pn24	1967	—	Dollar. Silver. Unique.	14,000

TRIAL STRIKES

KM#	Date	Mintage	Identification	Mkt Val
TS3	1928	—	5 Dollars. Bronze.	12,000
TS4	1928	—	10 Dollars. Bronze.	12,000
TS5	1937	—	Cent. Brass. Thick planchet.	5,500
TS6	1937	—	5 Cents. Brass. Thick planchet.	6,000
TS7	1937	—	10 Cents. Brass. Thick planchet.	6,000
TS8	1937	—	25 Cents. Brass. Thick planchet.	7,000
TS9	1937	—	25 Cents. Bronze.	3,500
TS10	1937	—	50 Cents. Brass. Thick planchet.	16,000
TS11	1942	—	5 Cents. Nickel. 12 sided.	6,000
TS12	1943	—	Cent. Copper Plated Steel.	—
TS13	1943	—	5 Cents. Steel.	—
TS14	1944	—	5 Cents. Tombac.	—
TS15	1951	—	5 Cents. Chrome Plated Steel.	4,000
TS16	1952	—	5 Cents.	2,000
TS17	1959	—	50 Cents. Tin.	6,000

CUSTOM PROOF-LIKE SETS (CPL)

KM#	Date	Mintage	Identification	Issue Price	Mkt Val
CPL1	1971 (7)	33,517	KM59.1 (2 pcs.), 60.1, 62b, 75.1, 77.1 ,79	6.50	5.00
CPL2	1971 (6)	38,198	KM59.1 (2 pcs.), 60.1, 62b, 75.1, 77.1	6.50	5.00
CPL3	1973 (6)	35,676	KM59.1 (2 pcs.), 60.1, 75.1, 77.1, 81.1 obv. 120 beads, 82	6.50	6.50
CPL4	1973 (7)	Inc. above	KM59.1 (2 pcs.), 60.1, 75.1, 77.1, 81.1 obv. 132 beads, 82	6.50	200
CPL5	1974 (5)	44,296	KM59.1 (2 pcs.), 60.1, 62b-75.1, 88	8.00	5.00
CPL6	1975 (6)	36,851	KM59.1 (2 pcs.), 60.1, 62b-75.1, 76.2, 77.1	8.00	5.00
CPL7	1976 (6)	28,162	KM59.1 (2 pcs.), 60.1, 62b-75.1, 76.2, 77.1	8.00	5.50
CPL8	1977 (6)	44,198	KM59.1 (2 pcs.), 60.1, 62b-75.2, 77.1, 117	8.15	7.50
CPL9	1978 (6)	41,000	KM59.1 (2 pcs.), 60.1, 62b-75.3, 77.1, 120.1	—	5.00
CPL10	1979 (6)	31,174	KM59.2 (2 pcs.), 60.2, 74, 75.3, 77.2, 120.1	10.75	5.00
CPL11	1980 (7)	41,447	KM60.2, 74, 75.3, 77.2, 120.1, 127 (2 pcs.)	10.75	6.00

MINT SETS

KM#	Date	Mintage	Identification	Issue Price	Mkt Val
MS1	1973 (4)	Inc. above	KM84, 85, 86.1, 87; Olympic Commemoratives, Series I	45.00	135
MS2	1974 (4)	Inc. above	KM89, 90, 93, 94; Olympic Commemoratives, Series II	48.00	135
MS3	1974 (4)	Inc. above	KM91-92, 95-96; Olympic Commemorative, Series III	48.00	135
MS4	1975 (4)	Inc. above	KM98, 99, 102, 103; Olympic Commemoratives, Series IV	48.00	135
MS5	1975 (4)	Inc. above	KM100, 101, 104, 105; Olympic Commemoratives, Series V	60.00	135
MS6	1976 (4)	Inc. above	KM107, 108, 111, 112; Olympic Commemoratives, Series VI	60.00	135
MS7	1976 (4)	Inc. above	KM109, 110, 113, 114; Olympic Commemoratives, Series VII	60.00	135

OLYMPIC COMMEMORATIVES (OCP)

KM#	Date	Mintage	Identification	Issue Price	Mkt Val
OCP1	1973 (4)	Inc. above	KM84-87, Series I	78.50	135
OCP2	1974 (4)	Inc. above	KM89-90, 93-94, Series II	88.50	135
OCP3	1974 (4)	Inc. above	KM91-92, 95-96, Series III	88.50	135
OCP4	1975 (4)	Inc. above	KM98-99, 102-103, Series IV	88.50	135
OCP5	1975 (4)	Inc. above	KM100-101, 104-105, Series V	88.50	135
OCP6	1976 (4)	Inc. above	KM107-108, 111-112, Series VI	88.50	135
OCP7	1976 (4)	Inc. above	KM109-110, 113-114, Series VII	88.50	135

PROOF SETS

KM#	Date	Mintage	Identification	Issue Price	Mkt Val
PS1	1981 (7)	199,000	KM60.2, 74, 75.3, 77.2, 120.1, 127, 130	36.00	30.00
PS2	1982 (7)	180,908	KM60.2a, 74, 75.3, 77.2, 120.1, 132, 133	36.00	37.50
PS3	1983 (7)	166,779	KM60.2a, 74, 75.3, 77.2, 120.1, 132, 138	36.00	27.50
PS4	1984 (7)	161,602	KM60.2a, 74, 75.3, 77.2, 120.1, 132, 140	30.00	27.50
PS5	1985 (7)	157,037	KM60.2a, 74, 75.3, 77.2, 120.1, 132, 143	30.00	30.00
PS6	1986 (7)	175,745	KM60.2a, 74, 75.3, 77.2, 120.1, 132, 149	30.00	29.00
PS7	1987 (7)	179,004	KM60.2a, 74, 75.3, 77.2, 120.1, 132, 154	34.00	30.00
PS8	1988 (7)	175,259	KM60.2a, 74, 75.3, 77.2, 132, 157, 161	37.50	34.00
PS9	1989 (7)	170,928	KM60.2a, 74, 75.3, 77.2, 132, 157, 168	40.00	34.00
PS10	1989 (4)	6,823	KM125.2, 135-136, 153	1,190	2,900
PS11	1989 (4)	1,995	KM164-167	1,700	3,750
PS12	1989 (3)	2,550	KM125.2, 163, 167	1,530	3,500
PS13	1989 (3)	9,979	KM135, 163, 164	165	475
PS14	1990 (7)	158,068	KM170, 181, 182, 183, 184, 185, 186	41.00	42.50
PS15	1990 (4)	2,629	KM174-177	1,720	3,700
PS16	1991 (7)	14,629	KM179, 181, 182, 183, 184, 185, 186	—	80.00
PS17	1991 (4)	873	KM198-201	1,760	3,700
PS18	1992 (11)	84,397	KM203a, 212a-214a, 218, 220a-223a, 231a-234a	—	92.50
PS19	1992 (7)	147,061	KM204-210	42.75	65.00
PS20	1992 (4)	3,500	KM226-229	1,680	3,700
PS22	1993 (4)	3,500	KM240-243	1,329	3,700
PS23	1994 (7)	47,303	KM181-186, 248	47.50	30.00
PS24	1994 (7)	99,121	KM181-186, 251	43.00	45.00
PS25	1994 (4)	1,500	KM252-255	915	3,700

KM#	Date	Mintage	Identification	Issue Price	Mkt Val
PS26	1995 (7)	Inc. above	KM181-186, 259	37.45	52.00
PS27	1995 (7)	50,000	KM181-185, 258, 259	49.45	52.00
PS28	1995 (4)	Inc. above	KM261-264	42.00	95.00
PS29	1995 (4)	682	KM266-269	1,555	3,700
PS30	1995 (2)	Inc. above	KM261-262	22.00	48.00
PS31	1995 (2)	Inc. above	KM263-264	22.00	46.00
PS32	1996 (4)	423	KM278-281	1,555	3,700
PS33	1996 (7)	Inc. above	KM181, 182a, 183a, 184a, 185a, 186, 274	49.00	60.00
PS34	1996 (4)	Inc. above	KM283-286	44.45	80.00
PS35	1997 (7)	Inc. above	KM182a, 183a, 184a, 270c, 282, 289, 290	60.00	75.00
PS36	1997 (4)	Inc. above	KM292-295	44.45	68.00
PS37	1997 (4)	Inc. above	KM300-303	1,530	3,700
PS38	1998 (8)	Inc. above	KM182a, 183a, 184a, 186, 270b, 289, 290a, 306	59.45	80.00
PS39	1998 (5)	25,000	KM309-313	73.50	55.00
PS40	1998 (2)	61,000	KM316 w/China Y-727	72.50	40.00
PS41	1998 (4)	Inc. above	KM318-321	44.45	68.00
PS42	1998 (4)	1,000	KM322-325	1,552	3,700
PS43	1998 (5)	25,000	KM310-313, 332	73.50	68.00
PS44	1999 (7)	Inc. above	KM182a-184a, 186, 270c, 289, 290a,	59.45	55.00
PS45	1999 (4)	Inc. above	KM335-338	39.95	140
PS46	1999 (12)	Inc. above	KM342a-353a	99.45	115
PS47	1999 (4)	Inc. above	KM359-362	1,425	3,700
PS48	2000 (12)	—	KM373a-383a, 384.2a	101	110
PS49	2000 (4)	—	KM389-392	44.00	80.00
PS50	2000 (4)	600	KM405-408	1,416	3,700

PROOF-LIKE DOLLARS

KM#	Date	Mintage	Identification	Issue Price	Mkt Val
D1.1	1951 (1)	—	KM46, Canoe	—	200
D1.2	1951 (1)	—	KM46, Arnprior	—	1,300
D2.1	1952 (1)	—	KM46, water lines	—	1,150
D2.2	1952 (1)	—	KM46, without water lines	—	200
D3	1953 (1)	1,200	KM54, Canoe w/shoulder fold	—	500
D4	1954 (1)	5,300	KM54, Canoe	1.25	175
D5	1955 (1)	7,950	KM54, Canoe	1.25	125
D5a	1955 (1)	Inc. above	KM54, Arnprior	1.25	225
D6	1956 (1)	10,212	KM54, Canoe	1.25	95.00
D7	1957 (1)	16,241	KM54, Canoe	1.25	50.00
D8	1958 (1)	33,237	KM55, British Columbia	1.25	30.00
D9	1959 (1)	45,160	KM54, Canoe	1.25	24.00
D10	1960 (1)	82,728	KM54, Canoe	1.25	22.00
D11	1961 (1)	120,928	KM54, Canoe	1.25	22.00
D12	1962 (1)	248,901	KM54, Canoe	1.25	22.00
D13	1963 (1)	963,525	KM54, Canoe	1.25	22.00
D14	1964 (1)	2,862,441	KM58, Charlottetown	1.25	22.00
D15	1965 (1)	2,904,352	KM64.1, Canoe	—	22.00
D16	1966 (1)	672,514	KM64.1, Canoe	—	22.00
D17	1967 (1)	1,036,176	KM70, Confederation	—	22.00

PROOF-LIKE SETS (PL)

KM#	Date	Mintage	Identification	Issue Price	Mkt Val
PL1	1953 (6)	1,200	KM49 w/o shoulder fold, 50-54	2.20	2,000
PL3	1954 (6)	3,000	KM49-54	2.50	650
PL4	1954 (6)	Inc. above	KM49 w/o shoulder fold, 50-54	2.50	1,600
PL5	1955 (6)	6,300	KM49, 50a, 51-54	2.50	400
PL6	1955 (6)	Inc. above	KM49, 50a, 51-54, Arnprior	2.50	500
PL7	1956 (5)	6,500	KM49, 50a, 51-54	2.50	200
PL8	1957 (6)	11,862	KM49, 50a, 51-54	2.50	150
PL9	1958 (6)	18,259	KM49, 50a, 51-53, 55	2.50	125
PL10	1959 (6)	31,577	KM49, 50a, 51, 52, 54, 56	2.50	60.00
PL11	1960 (6)	64,097	KM49, 50a, 51, 52, 54, 56	3.00	45.00
PL12	1961 (6)	98,373	KM49, 50a, 51, 52, 54, 56	3.00	45.00
PL13	1962 (6)	200,950	KM49, 50a, 51, 52, 54, 56	3.00	40.00
PL14	1963 (6)	673,006	KM49, 51, 52, 54, 56, 57	3.00	35.00
PL15	1964 (5)	1,653,162	KM49, 51, 52, 56-58	3.00	35.00
PL16	1965 (4)	2,904,352	KM59.1-60.1, 61-63, 64.1	4.00	35.00
PL17	1966 (5)	672,514	KM59.1-60.1, 61-63, 64.1	4.00	35.00
PL18	1967 (6)	961,887	KM65-70 (pliofilm flat pack)	4.00	35.00
PL18A	1967 (6)	70,583	KM65-70 Specimen Quality and Silver Medal (red box)	12.00	55.00
PL18B	1967 (7)	337,688	KM65-71 Specimen Quality (black box)	40.00	850
PL19	1968 (6)	521,641	KM59.1-60.1, 62b, 72a, 75.1-76.1	4.00	2.25
PL20	1969 (4)	326,203	KM59.1-60.1, 62b, 75.1-77.1	4.00	3.00
PL21	1970 (4)	349,120	KM59.1-60.1, 62b, 75.1, 77.1, 78	4.00	3.50
PL22	1971 (4)	253,311	KM59.1-60.1, 62b, 75.1, 77.1, 79	4.00	3.00
PL23	1972 (3)	224,275	KM59.1-60.1, 62b-77.1	4.00	3.00
PL24	1973 (6)	243,695	KM59.1-60.1, 62b-75.1 obv. 120 beads, 77.1, 81.1, 82	4.00	4.00
PL25	1973 (3)	Inc. above	KM59.1-60.1, 62b-75.1 obv. 132 beads, 77.1, 81.2, 82	4.00	250
PL26	1974 (6)	213,589	KM59.1-60.1, 62b-75.1, 77.1, 88	5.00	3.00
PL27.1	1975 (4)	197,372	KM59.1, 60.1, 62b-75.1, 76.2, 77.1	5.00	3.50
PL27.2	1975 (6)	Inc. above	KM59.1, 60.1, 62b-75.1, 76.3, 77.1	5.00	5.00
PL28	1976 (4)	171,737	KM59.1, 60.1, 62b-75.1, 76.2, 77.1	5.15	3.00
PL29	1977 (4)	225,307	KM59.1, 60.1, 62b, 75.2, 77.1, 117.1	5.15	3.00
PL30	1978 (6)	260,000	KM59.1-60.1, 62b, 75.3, 77.1, 120.1	5.25	4.25
PL31	1979 (6)	187,624	KM59.2-60.2, 74, 75.3, 77.2, 120.1	6.25	4.25
PL32	1980 (6)	410,842	KM60.2, 74, 75.3, 77.2, 120.1, 127	6.50	4.50
PL33	1981 (5)	186,250	KM60.2, 74, 75.3, 77.2, 120.1, 123	5.00	4.00
PL34	1982 (5)	203,287	KM60.2, 74, 75.3, 77.2, 120.1, 123	6.00	4.00
PL36	1983 (6)	190,838	KM60.2a, 74, 75.3, 77.2, 120.1, 132	5.00	5.00
PL36.1	1983 (6)	Inc. above	KM60.2a, 74, 75.3, 77.2, 120.1, 132; set in folder packaged by British Royal Mint Coin Club	—	10.00
PL37	1984 (6)	181,249	KM60.2a, 74, 75.3, 77.2, 120.1, 132	5.25	5.00
PL38	1985 (6)	173,924	KM60.2a, 74, 75.3, 77.2, 120.1, 132	5.25	24.00
PL39	1986 (6)	167,338	KM60.2a, 74, 75.3, 77.2, 120.1, 132	5.25	6.50
PL40	1987 (6)	212,136	KM60.2a, 74, 75.3, 77.2, 120.1, 132	5.25	7.00
PL41	1988 (6)	182,048	KM60.2a, 74, 75.3, 77.2, 132, 157	6.05	5.50
PL42	1989 (6)	173,622	KM60.2a, 74, 75.3, 77.2, 132, 157	6.60	8.00
PL43	1990 (6)	170,791	KM181-186	7.40	8.00
PL44	1991 (6)	147,814	KM181-186	7.40	25.00
PL45	1992 (6)	217,597	KM204-209	8.25	17.50
PL46	1993 (6)	171,680	KM181-186	8.25	5.00
PL47	1994 (6)	141,676	KM181-185, 258	8.50	5.50
PL48	1994 (6)	18,794	KM181-185, 258 (Oh Canada holder)	—	8.50
PL49	1995 (6)	143,892	KM181-186	6.95	5.50
PL50	1995 (6)	50,927	KM181-186 (Oh Canada holder)	14.65	8.50
PL51	1995 (6)	36,443	KM181-186 (Baby Gift holder)	—	9.00
PL52	1996 (4)	116,736	KM181-186	—	27.00
PL53	1996 (6)	29,747	KM181-186 (Baby Gift holder)	—	14.00
PL54	1996 (10)	Inc. above	KM181a-185a, 186	8.95	65.00
PL55	1996 (6)	Inc. above	KM181a-185a, 186 (Oh Canada holder)	14.65	12.00
PL56	1996 (6)	Inc. above	KM181a-185a, 186 (Baby Gift holder)	—	12.00
PL57	1997 (7)	Inc. above	KM182a-184a, 209, 270, 289-290	10.45	8.00
PL58	1997 (7)	Inc. above	KM182a-184a, 270, 289-291 (Oh Canada holder)	16.45	30.00
PL59	1997 (5)	Inc. above	KM182a-184a, 209, 270, 289-290 (Baby Gift holder)	18.50	25.00
PL60	1998 (7)	Inc. above	KM182-184, 186, 270, 289-290	10.45	25.00
PL61	1998 (7)	Inc. above	KM182-184, 186, 270, 289-290 (Oh Canada holder)	16.45	25.00
PL62	1998 (7)	Inc. above	KM182-184, 186, 270, 289-290 (Tiny Treasures holder)	16.45	25.00
PL63	1999 (12)	Inc. above	KM342-353	16.95	10.00
PL64	2000 (12)	—	KM373-384	16.95	10.00

SPECIMEN SETS (SS)

KM#	Date	Mintage	Identification	Issue Price	Mkt Val
SS12	1902 (5)	100	KM8-12	—	60,000
SS13	1902 (3)	Inc. above	KM9 (Large H), 10, 11	—	40,000
SS14	1903 (3)	Inc. above	KM10, 12, 13	—	7,000
SS15	1908 (5)	1,000	KM8, 10-13	—	3,500
SS16	1911 (5)	1,000	KM15-19	—	5,500
SS18	1921 (5)	Inc. above	KM22a-25a, 28	—	225,000
SS19	1922 (2)	Inc. above	KM28, 29	—	2,500
SS20	1923 (2)	Inc. above	KM28, 29	—	5,000
SS21	1924 (2)	Inc. above	KM28, 29	—	4,000
SS22	1925 (2)	Inc. above	KM28, 29	—	7,000
SS23	1926 (2)	Inc. above	KM28, 29 (Near 6)	—	5,000
SS24	1927 (3)	Inc. above	KM24a, 28, 29	—	8,000
SS25	1928 (4)	Inc. above	KM23a, 24a, 28, 29	—	12,000
SS26	1929 (5)	Inc. above	KM23a,-25a, 28, 29	—	35,000
SS27	1930 (4)	Inc. above	KM23a, 24a. 28, 29	—	35,000
SS28	1931 (5)	Inc. above	KM23a-25a, 28, 29	—	60,000
SS29	1932 (5)	Inc. above	KM23a-25a, 28, 29	—	20,000
SS30	1934 (2)	Inc. above	KM23-25, 28, 29	—	50,000
SS31	1936 (5)	Inc. above	KM23a-25a, 28, 29	—	12,000
SS32	1936 (5)	Inc. above	KM23a(dot), 24a(dot), 25a, 28(dot), 29, 30	—	550,000
SS33	1937 (6)	1,025	KM32-37, Matte Finish	—	1,600
SS34	1937 (4)	Inc. above	KM32-35, Mirror Fields	—	1,200
SS35	1937 (6)	75	KM32-37, Mirror Fields	—	3,000
SS-A36	1939 (5)	Inc. above	KM32-35, 38, Matte Finish	—	—
SS-B36	1939 (5)	Inc. above	KM32-35, 38, Mirror Fields	—	12,000
SS-C36	1942 (2)	Inc. above	KM32, 33	—	1,000
SS-D36	1943 (2)	Inc. above	KM32, 40	—	1,000
SS36	1938 (6)	Inc. above	KM32-37	—	40,000
SS-A37	1944 (2)	Inc. above	KM32, 40a	—	1,000
SS37	1944 (5)	3	KM32, 34-37, 40a	—	20,000
SS-A38	1945 (2)	Inc. above	KM32, 40a	—	1,000
SS38	1945 (5)	6	KM32, 34-37, 40a	—	12,500
SS39	1946 (5)	15	KM32, 34-37, 39a	—	9,000
SS40	1947 (6)	Inc. above	KM32, 34-36(7 curved), 37(7 pointed),	—	12,500
SS41	1947 (6)	Inc. above	KM32, 34-36(7 curved), 37(blunt 7), 39a	—	14,000
SS42	1947 (6)	Inc. above	KM32, 34-36(7 curved right), 37, 39a	—	10,000
SS44	1949 (4)	20	KM41-45, 47	—	8,000
SS44A	1949 (2)	Inc. above	KM47 (Proof)	—	2,600
SS45	1950 (4)	12	KM41-46	—	5,500
SS46	1950 (4)	Inc. above	KM41-45, 46 (Arnprior)	—	7,000
SS47	1951 (5)	12	KM41, 48, 42a, 43-46 (w/water lines)	—	6,500
SS48	1952 (5)	2,317	KM41, 42a, 43-46 (water lines)	—	6,500
SS48A	1952 (5)	Inc. above	KM41, 42a, 43-46 (w/o water lines)	—	6,500
SS49	1953 (6)	28	KM49 w/o straps, 50-54	—	6,500
SS50	1953 (6)	Inc. above	KM49 w/ straps, 50-54	—	6,500
SS51	1964 (5)	Inc. above	KM49, 51, 52, 56-58	—	2,400
SS52	1965 (4)	Inc. above	KM59.1-60.1, 61-63, 64.1	—	2,400
SS56	1971 (6)	66,860	KM59.1-60.1, 62b-75.1, 77.1, 79 (2 pcs.); Double Dollar Prestige Sets	12.00	14.50
SS57	1972 (5)	36,349	KM59.1,-60.1, 62b-75.1, 76.1 (2 pcs.)	12.00	18.00
SS58	1973 (6)	119,819	KM59.1-60.1, 75.1, 77.1, 81.1, 82, 83	12.00	16.00
SS59	1973 (6)	Inc. above	KM59.1-60.1, 75.1, 77.1, 81.2, 82, 83	—	1,600
SS60	1974 (5)	85,230	KM59.1-60.1, 62b-75.1, 77.1, 88, 88a	15.00	12.50
SS61	1975 (5)	97,263	KM59.1-60.1, 62b-75.1, 76.2, 77.1, 97	15.00	12.50
SS62	1976 (5)	87,744	KM59.1-60, 62b-75.1, 76.2, 77.1, 106	16.00	14.00
SS63	1977 (5)	142,577	KM59.1-60.1, 62b, 75.2, 77.1, 117.1, 118	16.50	14.50
SS64	1978 (6)	147,000	KM59.1-60.1, 62b, 75.3, 77.1, 120.1, 121	16.50	10.00
SS65	1979 (6)	155,698	KM59.2-60.2, 74, 75.3, 77.2, 120, 124	18.50	15.50
SS66	1980 (6)	162,875	KM60.2, 74-75.3, 77.2, 120, 127, 128	30.50	25.00
SS67	1981 (6)	71,300	KM60.2, 74, 75.3, 77.2, 120.1, 127; Regular Specimen Sets	10.00	5.50
SS68	1982 (10)	62,298	KM60.2a, 74, 75.3, 77.2, 120.1, 132	11.50	100
SS69	1983 (6)	60,329	KM60.2a, 74, 75.3, 77.2, 120.1, 132	12.75	9.00
SS70	1984 (2)	60,400	KM60.2a, 74, 75.3, 77.2, 120.1, 132	10.00	5.50
SS71	1985 (6)	61,553	KM60.2a, 74, 75.3, 77.2, 120.1, 132	10.00	23.50
SS72	1986 (6)	67,152	KM60.2a, 74, 75.3, 77.2, 120.1, 132	10.00	9.00
SS72A	1987 (6)	75,194	KM60.2a, 74, 75.3, 77.2, 120.1, 132	11.00	7.50
SS73	1988 (6)	70,205	KM60.2a, 74, 75.3, 77.2, 132, 157	12.30	7.50
SS74	1989 (6)	75,306	KM60.2a, 74, 75.3, 77.2, 132, 157	14.50	9.50
SS75	1990 (6)	76,611	KM181-186	15.50	8.50

KM#	Date	Mintage	Identification	Issue Price	Mkt Val
SS76	1991 (6)	68,552	KM181-186	15.50	17.50
SS77	1992 (6)	78,328	KM204-209	16.25	17.50
SS78	1993 (6)	77,351	KM181-186; Regular Specimen Sets Resumed	16.25	13.00
SS79	1994 (6)	77,349	KM181-186	16.50	9.50
SS80	1995 (6)	Inc. above	KM181-186	13.95	9.50
SS82	1996 (4)	Inc. above	KM181a-185a, 186	18.95	35.00
SS83	1997 (7)	Inc. above	KM182a-184a, 270, 289-291	19.95	47.50
SS84	1998 (7)	Inc. above	KM182-184, 186, 270, 289, 290	19.95	18.00
SS85	1999 (7)	Inc. above	KM182-184, 186, 270, 289a, 290	19.95	20.00

V.I.P. SPECIMEN SETS (VS)

KM#	Date	Mintage	Identification	Issue Price	Mkt Val
VS1	1969 (0)	4		—	2,000
VS2	1970 (0)	100	KM59.1-60.1, 74.1-75.1, 77.1, 78	—	525
VS3	1971 (0)	69	KM59.1-60.1, 74.1-75.1, 77.1, 79(2 pcs.)	—	525
VS4	1972 (0)	25	KM59.1-60.1, 74.1-75.1, 76.1, (2 pcs.), 77.1	—	650
VS5	1973 (0)	26	KM59.1-60.1, 75.1, 77.1, 81.1, 82, 83	—	650
VS6	1974 (0)	72	KM59.1-60.1, 74.1-75.1, 77.1, 88, 88a	—	525
VS7	1975 (0)	94	KM59.1-60.1, 74.1-75.1, 76.2, 77.1, 97	—	525
VS8	1976 (0)	Inc. above	KM59.1-60.1, 74.1-75.1, 76.2, 77.1, 106	—	525

NEWFOUNDLAND

PROVINCE

CIRCULATION COINAGE

KM# 9 LARGE CENT

Bronze **Obv:** Crowned bust right **Rev:** Crown and date within center circle, wreath surrounds, denomination above

Date	Mintage	VG8	F12	VF20	XF40	AU50	MS60	MS63	MS65
1904 H	100,000	10.00	18.00	30.00	75.00	175	400	1,300	—
1904 H	—	**PF60** 6,000							
1907	200,000	3.00	5.00	11.00	35.00	125	250	1,000	—
1909	200,000	3.00	5.00	9.00	27.50	65.00	125	250	—
1909	—	**PF60** 600							

KM# 16 LARGE CENT

Bronze **Obv:** Crowned bust left **Rev:** Crown and date within center circle, wreath surrounds, denomination above

Date	Mintage	VG8	F12	VF20	XF40	AU50	MS60	MS63	MS65
1913	400,000	1.50	2.50	3.50	9.00	30.00	60.00	125	—
1917 C	702,350	1.50	2.50	3.50	8.00	30.00	100	400	—
1917 C	—	**PF60** 950							
1919 C	300,000	1.50	2.50	4.00	14.00	50.00	225	750	—
1919 C	—	**PF60** 2,500							
1920 C	302,184	1.50	2.50	6.00	24.00	90.00	350	1,900	—
1929	300,000	1.50	2.50	3.50	7.00	30.00	85.00	175	—
1929 C	—	**PF60** 3,000							
1936	300,000	1.50	2.00	2.50	5.00	18.00	40.00	100	—

KM# 18 SMALL CENT

3.20 g., Bronze, 19 mm. **Obv:** Crowned head left **Rev:** Pitcher plant divides date, denomination below

Date	Mintage	VG8	F12	VF20	XF40	AU50	MS60	MS63	MS65
1938	500,000	0.45	0.95	1.25	3.50	9.00	24.00	70.00	—
1938	—	**PF60** 6,000							
1940	300,000	1.25	2.25	4.50	14.00	40.00	95.00	600	—
1940 Re-engraved date	Inc. above	45.00	60.00	85.00	150	300	650	2,400	—
1940	—	**PF60** 2,500							
1941 C	827,662	0.45	0.70	0.95	2.50	9.00	29.00	200	—
1941 C Re-engraved date	Inc. above	16.00	24.00	40.00	95.00	175	400	2,000	—
1942	1,996,889	0.45	0.70	0.95	2.50	13.50	40.00	250	—
1943 C	1,239,732	0.45	0.70	0.95	2.50	9.00	22.50	100	—
1944 C	1,328,776	1.50	2.50	9.00	35.00	100	300	2,000	—
1947 C	313,772	1.25	1.75	4.00	19.00	45.00	100	350	—
1947 C	—	**PF60** 3,000							

KM# 7 5 CENTS

1.18 g., 0.925 Silver 0.035 oz. ASW **Obv:** Crowned bust right **Rev:** Denomination and date within circle

Date	Mintage	VG8	F12	VF20	XF40	AU50	MS60	MS63	MS65
1903	100,000	5.00	11.00	29.00	70.00	175	450	1,700	—
1903	—	**PF60** 3,000							
1904 H	100,000	4.00	7.00	19.00	45.00	90.00	225	450	—
1904 H	—	**PF60** 1,800							
1908	400,000	4.00	7.00	18.00	45.00	100	250	1,100	—

KM# 13 5 CENTS

1.18 g., 0.925 Silver 0.035 oz. ASW **Obv:** Crowned bust left **Rev:** Denomination and date within circle

Date	Mintage	VG8	F12	VF20	XF40	AU50	MS60	MS63	MS65
1912	300,000	2.00	3.00	6.00	24.00	55.00	125	250	—
1912	—	**PF60** 2,400							
1917 C	300,319	2.00	5.00	8.00	27.00	100	350	1,200	—
1917 C	—	**PF60** 2,400							
1919 C	100,844	6.00	11.00	27.00	100	450	1,200	3,500	—
1919 C	—	**PF60** 2,400							
1929	300,000	2.00	3.00	4.00	14.00	65.00	175	400	—

KM# 19 5 CENTS

1.18 g., 0.925 Silver 0.035 oz. ASW **Obv:** Crowned head left **Rev:** Denomination and date within circle

Date	Mintage	VG8	F12	VF20	XF40	AU50	MS60	MS63	MS65
1938	100,000	1.50	2.50	3.00	11.00	30.00	100	300	—
1938	—	**PF60** 1,600							
1940 C	200,000	1.50	2.50	3.00	11.00	30.00	100	350	—
1940 C	—	**PF60** 3,200							
1941 C	621,641	0.60	1.75	2.50	4.00	9.00	22.00	35.00	—
1942 C	298,348	0.60	1.75	2.50	5.00	13.50	28.00	60.00	—
1943 C	351,666	0.60	1.50	2.50	5.00	10.50	22.00	45.00	—

KM# 19a 5 CENTS

1.17 g., 0.800 Silver 0.030 oz. ASW, 15.67 mm. **Obv:** Crowned head left **Rev:** Denomination and date within circle **Edge:** Reeded

Date	Mintage	VG8	F12	VF20	XF40	AU50	MS60	MS63	MS65
1944 C	286,504	1.50	1.75	2.50	9.00	22.00	70.00	150	—
1945 C	203,828	1.50	1.75	2.50	4.00	9.00	22.50	35.00	—
1946 C	2,041	**PF60** 3,000							
1946 C Prooflike	—	—	—	—	—	—	—	4,000	—
1946 C	—	**PF60** 3,500							
1947 C	38,400	3.00	5.00	8.00	30.00	45.00	100	250	—
1947 C Prooflike	—	—	—	—	—	—	—	2,100	—

KM# 8 10 CENTS

2.36 g., 0.925 Silver 0.0701 oz. ASW **Obv:** Crowned bust right **Rev:** Denomination and date within circle

Date	Mintage	VG8	F12	VF20	XF40	AU50	MS60	MS63	MS65
1903	100,000	11.00	30.00	90.00	250	650	2,400	5,500	—
1903	—	**PF60** 3,750							
1904 H	100,000	6.00	14.00	35.00	100	200	350	600	—
1904 H	—	**PF60** 2,250							

KM# 14 10 CENTS

2.36 g., 0.925 Silver 0.0701 oz. ASW **Obv:** Crowned bust left

Date	Mintage	VG8	F12	VF20	XF40	AU50	MS60	MS63	MS65
1912	150,000	4.00	5.50	14.00	45.00	100	225	350	—
1917 C	250,805	3.50	5.00	14.00	45.00	175	450	1,350	—
1919 C	54,342	4.00	11.00	22.00	70.00	125	250	350	—

KM# 20 10 CENTS

2.36 g., 0.925 Silver 0.0701 oz. ASW **Obv:** Crowned head left **Rev:** Denomination and date within circle

Date	Mintage	VG8	F12	VF20	XF40	AU50	MS60	MS63	MS65
1938	100,000	3.50	4.00	4.50	18.00	100	200	800	—
1938	—	**PF60** 3,200							
1940	100,000	3.00	3.50	4.50	14.00	45.00	100	400	—
1940	—	**PF60** 4,000							
1941 C	483,630	1.30	3.00	3.50	7.00	18.00	50.00	125	—
1942 C	293,736	1.30	3.00	3.50	7.00	22.00	70.00	200	—
1943 C	104,706	1.30	3.00	3.50	9.00	30.00	250	800	—
1944 C	151,471	1.30	3.50	11.00	27.00	65.00	350	1,300	—

KM# 20a 10 CENTS

2.33 g., 0.800 Silver 0.060 oz. ASW **Obv:** Crowned head left

Date	Mintage	VG8	F12	VF20	XF40	AU50	MS60	MS63	MS65
1945 C	175,833	1.10	2.50	3.00	7.00	22.00	100	400	—
1946 C	38,400	3.50	4.50	9.00	30.00	60.00	125	300	—
1946 C	—	**PF60** 1,200							
1947 C	61,988	3.00	3.50	7.00	20.00	45.00	100	350	—

KM# 10 20 CENTS

4.71 g., 0.925 Silver 0.1402 oz. ASW **Obv:** Crowned bust right **Rev:** Denomination and date within circle

Date	Mintage	VG8	F12	VF20	XF40	AU50	MS60	MS63	MS65
1904 H	75,000	13.00	35.00	65.00	300	900	2,700	7,000	—
1904 H	—	**PF60** 2,400							

KM# 15 20 CENTS

4.71 g., 0.925 Silver 0.1402 oz. ASW **Obv:** Crowned bust left **Rev:** Denomination and date within circle

Date	Mintage	VG8	F12	VF20	XF40	AU50	MS60	MS63	MS65
1912	350,000	5.50	8.00	18.00	65.00	175	300	750	—
1912	—	**PF60** 2,500							

KM# 17 25 CENTS

5.83 g., 0.925 Silver 0.1734 oz. ASW **Obv:** Crowned bust left **Rev:** Denomination and date within circle

Date	Mintage	VG8	F12	VF20	XF40	AU50	MS60	MS63	MS65
1917 C	464,779	7.00	8.00	10.00	18.00	50.00	200	400	—
1917 C	—	**PF60** 3,000							
1919 C	163,939	7.00	8.00	15.00	35.00	125	450	2,000	—
1919 C	—	**PF60** 3,000							

KM# 11 50 CENTS

11.78 g., 0.925 Silver 0.3503 oz. ASW, 30 mm. **Obv:** Crowned bust right

Date	Mintage	VG8	F12	VF20	XF40	AU50	MS60	MS63	MS65
1904 H	140,000	14.00	16.00	20.00	60.00	175	350	1,000	—
1904 H	—	**PF60** 2,900							
1907	100,000	14.00	16.00	25.00	75.00	225	400	1,200	—
1908	160,000	14.00	16.00	20.00	60.00	125	300	800	—
1909	200,000	14.00	16.00	22.00	60.00	150	350	1,000	—

KM# 12 50 CENTS

11.78 g., 0.925 Silver 0.3503 oz. ASW, 30 mm. **Obv:** Crowned bust left **Rev:** Denomination and date within circle

Date	Mintage	VG8	F12	VF20	XF40	AU50	MS60	MS63	MS65
1911	200,000	13.50	15.00	18.00	45.00	100	300	775	—
1917 C	375,560	13.00	14.00	16.00	40.00	80.00	175	500	—
1917 C	—	**PF60** 3,250							
1918 C	294,824	13.00	14.00	16.00	40.00	80.00	175	500	—
1919 C	306,267	13.00	14.00	16.00	42.00	100	300	1,200	—
1919 C	—	**PF60** 3,250							

TRIAL STRIKES

KM#	Date	Mintage	Identification	Mkt Val
TS3	1945H C	—	10 Cents. Nickel.	—

CAPE VERDE

The Republic of Cape Verde, Africa's smallest republic, is located in the Atlantic Ocean, about 370 miles (595 km.) west of Dakar, Senegal, off the coast of Africa. The 14-island republic has an area of 1,557 sq. mi. (4,033 sq. km.) and a population of 435,983. Capital: Praia. The refueling of ships and aircraft is the chief economic function of the country. Fishing is important and agriculture is widely practiced, but the Cape Verdes are not self-sufficient in food. Fish products, salt, bananas, and shellfish are exported.

The date of discovery of the islands is uncertain. Possibly they were visited by Venetian captain Alvise Cadamosto in 1456. Portuguese navigator Diogo Gomes claimed them for Portugal in May of 1460. Settlement began two years later. The early importance and wealth of the islands, which caused them to be attacked by Sir Francis Drake and the Dutch, resulted from the monopoly of the Guinea slave trade granted the inhabitants in 1466. Poverty and famine occasioned by frequent periods of severe drought have marked the history of the country since abolition of the slave trade in 1876.

After 500 years of Portuguese rule, the Cape Verdes became independent on July 5, 1975. At the first general election, all seats of the new national assembly were won by the Party for the Independence of Guinea-Bissau and Cape Verde (PAIGC). The PAIGC linked the two former colonies into one state. Antonio Mascarenhas Monteiro won the first free presidential election in 1991.

RULER

Portuguese, until 1975

MONETARY SYSTEM

100 Centavos = 1 Escudo

PORTUGUESE COLONY

COLONIAL COINAGE

KM# 1 5 CENTAVOS

Bronze **Obv:** Liberty head left **Rev:** Denomination at center, date below

Date	Mintage	VF20	XF40	MS60	MS63	MS65
1930	1,000,000	1.00	3.00	8.00	12.00	25.00

KM# 2 10 CENTAVOS

Bronze, 19 mm. **Obv:** Denomination at center, date below **Rev:** Liberty head left

Date	Mintage	VF20	XF40	MS60	MS63	MS65
1930	1,500,000	1.00	3.00	8.00	12.00	25.00

KM# 3 20 CENTAVOS

Bronze **Obv:** Denomination at center, date below **Rev:** Liberty head left

Date	Mintage	VF20	XF40	MS60	MS63	MS65
1930	1,500,000	1.00	3.00	10.00	14.00	28.00

KM# 4 50 CENTAVOS

4.32 g., Nickel-Bronze, 22.7 mm. **Obv:** Liberty head right, long loose hair **Rev:** Encircled arms within wreath, denomination below **Edge:** Reeded

Date	Mintage	VF20	XF40	MS60	MS63	MS65
1930	1,000,000	30.00	70.00	150	300	—

KM# 6 50 CENTAVOS

Nickel-Bronze **Obv:** Denomination **Rev:** Miniature crowns above encircled arms, date below

Date	Mintage	VF20	XF40	MS60	MS63	MS65
1949	1,000,000	0.50	1.00	3.50	7.00	10.00

KM# 11 50 CENTAVOS

3.40 g., Bronze, 20 mm. **Obv:** Denomination **Rev:** Miniature crowns above arms, date below

Date	Mintage	VF20	XF40	MS60	MS63	MS65
1968	1,000,000	0.50	0.75	1.50	3.00	5.00

KM# 5 ESCUDO

Nickel-Bronze, 26 mm. **Obv:** Liberty head right, long loose hair **Rev:** Encircled arms within wreath, denomination below

Date	Mintage	VF20	XF40	MS60	MS63	MS65
1930	50,000	35.00	80.00	250	500	—

KM# 7 ESCUDO

Nickel-Bronze, 26 mm. **Obv:** Denomination **Rev:** Miniature crowns above encircled arms, date below

Date	Mintage	VF20	XF40	MS60	MS63	MS65
1949	500,000	2.00	3.50	6.00	12.00	22.00

KM# 8 ESCUDO

8.00 g., Bronze, 26 mm. **Obv:** Denomination **Rev:** Miniature crowns above encircled arms, date below

Date	Mintage	VF20	XF40	MS60	MS63	MS65
1953	250,000	3.00	6.00	12.00	20.00	37.00
1968	500,000	1.00	2.00	3.50	6.00	10.00

KM# 9 2-1/2 ESCUDOS

3.50 g., Nickel-Bronze, 20 mm. **Obv:** Arms on cross, date below **Rev:** Miniature crowns above arms, denomination below

Date	Mintage	VF20	XF40	MS60	MS63	MS65
1953	500,000	7.00	25.00	50.00	75.00	100
1967	400,000	1.00	2.50	5.00	8.00	15.00

KM# 12 5 ESCUDOS

4.41 g., Nickel-Bronze, 21 mm. **Obv:** Miniature crowns above arms, denomination below **Rev:** Arms on cross, date below

Date	Mintage	VF20	XF40	MS60	MS63	MS65
1968	200,000	1.50	3.50	6.00	10.00	18.00

KM# 10 10 ESCUDOS

5.00 g., 0.720 Silver 0.1157 oz. ASW **Obv:** Arms on cross, date below **Rev:** Miniature crowns above arms, denomination below

Date	Mintage	VF20	XF40	MS60	MS63	MS65
1953	400,000	5.00	7.00	12.00	18.00	27.00

REPUBLIC

DECIMAL COINAGE

KM# 15 20 CENTAVOS

1.30 g., Aluminum, 21 mm. **Obv:** Emblem within wreath, date below **Rev:** Denomination above fish

Date	Mintage	VF20	XF40	MS60	MS63	MS65
1977	—	0.20	0.30	0.50	0.75	1.50
1980	—	0.20	0.30	0.50	0.75	1.50

KM# 16 50 CENTAVOS

2.10 g., Aluminum, 24.5 mm. **Obv:** Emblem within wreath, date below **Rev:** Denomination above fish

Date	Mintage	VF20	XF40	MS60	MS63	MS65
1977	—	0.25	0.40	0.65	0.85	1.75
1980	—	0.25	0.40	0.65	0.85	1.75

KM# 17 ESCUDO

4.10 g., Nickel-Bronze, 23.5 mm. **Series:** F.A.O. **Subject:** Education **Obv:** Emblem within wreath, denomination below, date at bottom **Rev:** Student at desk **Edge:** Reeded

Date	Mintage	VF20	XF40	MS60	MS63	MS65
1977	1,000,000	0.50	0.75	1.50	2.25	3.50
1980	—	0.50	0.75	1.50	2.25	3.50

KM# 23 ESCUDO

3.95 g., Brass Plated Steel, 23.5 mm. **Subject:** 10th Anniversary of Independence **Obv:** Emblem within wreath below denomination and date **Rev:** Inscription below building **Edge:** Reeded

Date	Mintage	VF20	XF40	MS60	MS63	MS65
1985	—	—	0.75	1.25	2.00	3.00
1985	—	PF65 150				

KM# 23a ESCUDO
4.00 g., 0.925 Silver 0.119 oz. ASW, 23.5 mm. **Subject:** 10th Anniversary of Independence **Obv:** Emblem within wreath below denomination and date **Rev:** Inscription below building

Date	Mintage	VF20	XF40	MS60	MS63	MS65
1985	—	PF65 250				

KM# 23b ESCUDO
6.00 g., 0.750 Gold 0.1447 oz. AGW **Subject:** 10th Anniversary of Independence **Obv:** Emblem within wreath below denomination and date **Rev:** Inscription below building

Date	Mintage	VF20	XF40	MS60	MS63	MS65
1985	50	PF65 400				

KM# 27 ESCUDO
2.50 g., Brass Plated Steel, 18 mm. **Obv:** Denomination on National emblem, date below **Rev:** Tartaruga Sea Turtle **Edge:** Plain

Date	Mintage	VF20	XF40	MS60	MS63	MS65
1994	—	—	—	1.00	1.25	1.50

KM# 18 2-1/2 ESCUDOS
7.00 g., Nickel-Bronze, 26 mm. **Series:** F.A.O. **Obv:** Emblem within wreath above denomination and date **Rev:** Coffee tree planting

Date	Mintage	VF20	XF40	MS60	MS63	MS65
1977	1,200,000	0.50	0.75	1.50	2.50	3.50
1980	—	0.50	0.75	1.50	2.50	3.50
1982	—	0.50	0.75	1.50	2.50	3.50

KM# 28 5 ESCUDOS
4.00 g., Copper Plated Steel, 21 mm. **Obv:** National emblem to right of denomination, date below **Rev:** Osprey

Date	Mintage	VF20	XF40	MS60	MS63	MS65
1994	—	—	—	1.50	2.00	3.00

KM# 31 5 ESCUDOS
4.00 g., Copper Plated Steel, 21 mm. **Obv:** National emblem to right of denomination, date below **Rev:** Flowers - Contra Bruxas

Date	Mintage	VF20	XF40	MS60	MS63	MS65
1994	—	—	—	1.00	1.25	2.00

KM# 36 5 ESCUDOS
4.00 g., Copper Plated Steel, 21 mm. **Obv:** National emblem to right of denomination, date below **Rev:** Sailboat - Belmira

Date	Mintage	VF20	XF40	MS60	MS63	MS65
1994	—	—	—	1.00	1.25	2.00

KM# 19 10 ESCUDOS
9.00 g., Copper-Nickel, 28.1 mm. **Obv:** Emblem within wreath above denomination and date **Rev:** Eduardo Mondlane

Date	Mintage	VF20	XF40	MS60	MS63	MS65
1977	—	0.50	1.00	2.00	3.00	5.00
1980	—	0.50	1.00	2.00	3.00	5.00
1982	—	0.40	0.75	2.00	3.00	5.00

KM# 24 10 ESCUDOS
Copper-Nickel **Subject:** 10th Anniversary of Independence **Obv:** Emblem within wreath below denomination and date **Rev:** Letter design at center, star above

Date	Mintage	VF20	XF40	MS60	MS63	MS65
1985	—	PF65 150				
1985	—	—	—	1.50	2.00	3.50

KM# 24a 10 ESCUDOS
9.00 g., 0.925 Silver 0.2677 oz. ASW **Subject:** 10th Anniversary of Independence **Obv:** Emblem within wreath below denomination and date **Rev:** Letter design at center, star above

Date	Mintage	VF20	XF40	MS60	MS63	MS65
1985	—	PF65 300				

KM# 24b 10 ESCUDOS
9.00 g., 0.750 Gold 0.217 oz. AGW **Subject:** 10th Anniversary of Independence **Obv:** Emblem within wreath below denomination and date **Rev:** Letter design at center, star above

Date	Mintage	VF20	XF40	MS60	MS63	MS65
1985	50	PF65 500				

KM# 29 10 ESCUDOS
4.57 g., Nickel Plated Steel, 22 mm. **Obv:** National emblem, date at left, denomination upper left **Rev:** Brown-headed Kingfisher

Date	Mintage	VF20	XF40	MS60	MS63	MS65
1994	—	—	—	1.50	2.25	4.00

KM# 32 10 ESCUDOS
4.57 g., Nickel Plated Steel, 22 mm. **Obv:** National emblem, date at left, denomination upper left **Rev:** Flowers - Lingua De Vaca

Date	Mintage	VF20	XF40	MS60	MS63	MS65
1994	—	—	—	1.25	2.00	3.00

KM# 41 10 ESCUDOS
4.57 g., Nickel Plated Steel, 22 mm. **Obv:** National emblem, date at left, denomination upper left **Rev:** Sailship "Carvalho"

Date	Mintage	VF20	XF40	MS60	MS63	MS65
1994	—	—	—	1.25	2.00	3.00

KM# 20 20 ESCUDOS
12.20 g., Copper-Nickel, 31 mm. **Obv:** Emblem within wreath above denomination and date **Rev:** Domingos Ramos

Date	Mintage	VF20	XF40	MS60	MS63	MS65
1977	—	0.80	1.50	2.25	4.00	7.50
1980	—	0.80	1.50	2.25	4.00	7.50
1982	—	0.60	1.25	2.00	3.50	7.50

KM# 30 20 ESCUDOS
5.90 g., Nickel Plated Steel, 25 mm. **Obv:** National emblem, date divided below, denomination at bottom **Rev:** Brown Booby

Date	Mintage	VF20	XF40	MS60	MS63	MS65
1994	—	—	—	1.25	2.50	4.00

KM# 33 20 ESCUDOS
5.90 g., Nickel Plated Steel, 25 mm. **Obv:** National emblem, date divided below, denomination at bottom **Rev:** Flowers - Carqueja **Edge:** Reeded

Date	Mintage	VF20	XF40	MS60	MS63	MS65
1994	—	—	—	1.00	1.75	3.00

KM# 42 20 ESCUDOS
5.90 g., Nickel Plated Steel, 25 mm. **Obv:** National emblem, date divided below, denomination at bottom **Rev:** Sailship "Novas de Alegria" **Edge:** Reeded

Date	Mintage	VF20	XF40	MS60	MS63	MS65
1994	—	—	—	1.00	1.75	3.00

KM# 21 50 ESCUDOS
16.20 g., Copper-Nickel, 34.1 mm. **Obv:** Emblem within wreath above denomination and date **Rev:** Head of Amilcar Lopes Cabral left, two dates on right

Date	Mintage	VF20	XF40	MS60	MS63	MS65
1977	—	1.50	2.50	4.00	7.00	10.00
1980	—	1.50	2.50	4.00	7.00	10.00

KM# 22 50 ESCUDOS
16.00 g., Copper-Nickel, 34 mm. **Series:** F.A.O. **Subject:** World Fisheries Conference **Rev:** White sea bream fish left, two dates below

Date	Mintage	VF20	XF40	MS60	MS63	MS65
1984	Est. 115000	—	—	—	18.00	25.00

KM# 22a 50 ESCUDOS
16.00 g., 0.925 Silver 0.4758 oz. ASW, 34 mm. **Series:** F.A.O. **Subject:** World Fisheries Conference **Rev:** White sea bream fish left, two dates below

Date	Mintage	VF20	XF40	MS60	MS63	MS65
1984	Est. 20000	PF65 55.00				

KM# 22b 50 ESCUDOS
27.00 g., 0.917 Gold 0.796 oz. AGW **Series:** F.A.O. **Subject:** World Fisheries Conference **Rev:** White sea bream fish left, two dates below

Date	Mintage	VF20	XF40	MS60	MS63	MS65
1984	Est. 100000	PF65 1,650				

KM# 37 50 ESCUDOS
7.40 g., Nickel Plated Steel, 28 mm. **Obv:** National emblem divides date, denomination above **Rev:** Cape Verde Sparrow left

Date	Mintage	VF20	XF40	MS60	MS63	MS65
1994	—	—	—	—	5.00	8.00

KM# 43 50 ESCUDOS
7.40 g., Nickel Plated Steel, 28 mm. **Obv:** National emblem divides date, denomination above **Rev:** Sailship "Senhor das Areias"

Date	Mintage	VF20	XF40	MS60	MS63	MS65
1994	—	—	—	—	3.00	5.00

KM# 44 50 ESCUDOS
7.40 g., Nickel Plated Steel, 28 mm. **Obv:** National emblem **Rev:** Macelina flowers

Date	Mintage	VF20	XF40	MS60	MS63	MS65
1994	—	—	—	—	3.00	5.00

KM# 25 100 ESCUDOS
Copper-Nickel **Subject:** Papal Visit **Obv:** Emblem within wreath above denomination and date **Rev:** Half figure of Pope

Date	Mintage	VF20	XF40	MS60	MS63	MS65
1990	—	—	—	—	4.00	7.00

KM# 25a 100 ESCUDOS
Silver **Subject:** Papal Visit **Obv:** Emblem within wreath above denomination and date **Rev:** Half figure of Pope

Date	Mintage	VF20	XF40	MS60	MS63	MS65
1990	—	PF65 30.00				

KM# 25b 100 ESCUDOS
33.40 g., 0.900 Gold 0.9665 oz. AGW **Subject:** Papal Visit **Obv:** Emblem within wreath above denomination and date **Rev:** Half figure of Pope

Date	Mintage	VF20	XF40	MS60	MS63	MS65
1990	—	PF65 1,700				

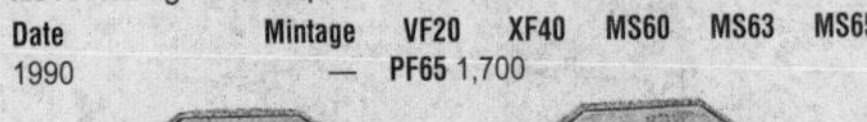

KM# 38 100 ESCUDOS
11.00 g., Bi-Metallic Copper-Nickel center in Bronze ring, 26 mm. **Obv:** National emblem divides date, denomination at top, value at bottom **Rev:** Saiao flowers **Shape:** 10-sided

Date	Mintage	VF20	XF40	MS60	MS63	MS65
1994	—	—	—	—	4.00	7.00

KM# 38a 100 ESCUDOS
11.00 g., Bi-Metallic Copper-Nickel center in Brass ring, 26 mm. **Obv:** National emblem divides date, denomination at top, value at bottom **Rev:** Saiao flowers **Edge:** Reeded

Date	Mintage	VF20	XF40	MS60	MS63	MS65
1994	—	—	—	—	5.00	8.00

KM# 39 100 ESCUDOS
11.00 g., Bi-Metallic Copper-Nickel center in Bronze ring, 26 mm. **Obv:** National emblem divides date, denomination at top, value at bottom **Rev:** Raza Lark left within circle **Shape:** 10-sided

Date	Mintage	VF20	XF40	MS60	MS63	MS65
1994	—	—	—	—	7.00	9.00

KM# 39a 100 ESCUDOS
11.00 g., Bi-Metallic Copper-Nickel center in Brass ring, 26 mm. **Obv:** National emblem divides date, denomination at top, value at bottom **Rev:** Calhandra do Ilheu Raso bird **Edge:** Reeded

Date	Mintage	VF20	XF40	MS60	MS63	MS65
1994	—	—	—	—	7.00	9.00

KM# 40 100 ESCUDOS
11.00 g., Bi-Metallic Copper-Nickel center in Bronze ring, 26 mm. **Obv:** National emblem divides date, denomination at top, value at bottom **Rev:** Sailship "Madalan" **Shape:** 10-sided

Date	Mintage	VF20	XF40	MS60	MS63	MS65
1994	—	—	—	—	5.00	8.00

KM# 40a 100 ESCUDOS
11.00 g., Bi-Metallic Copper-Nickel center in Brass ring, 26 mm. **Obv:** National emblem divides date, denomination at top, value at bottom **Rev:** Sailing ship "Madalan" **Edge:** Reeded

Date	Mintage	VF20	XF40	MS60	MS63	MS65
1994	—	—	—	—	5.00	8.00

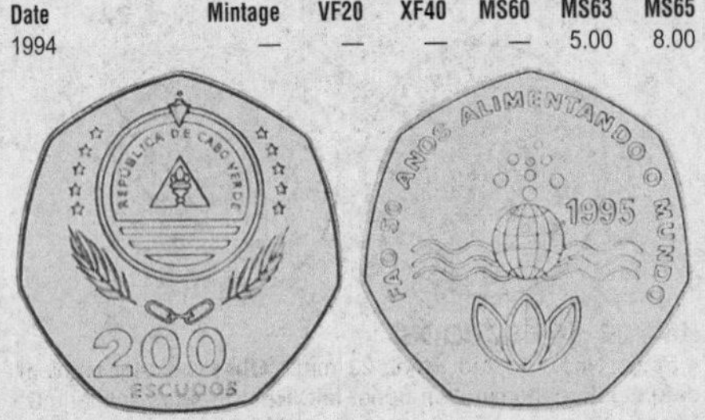

KM# 34 200 ESCUDOS
Copper-Nickel **Series:** F.A.O. **Obv:** National emblem above denomination **Rev:** Globe on water, date at right

Date	Mintage	VF20	XF40	MS60	MS63	MS65
1995	—	—	—	—	3.00	5.00

KM# 35 200 ESCUDOS
Copper-Nickel **Subject:** 20th Year of Independence **Obv:** National emblem above denomination **Rev:** Two figures back to back, two dates below

Date	Mintage	VF20	XF40	MS60	MS63	MS65
ND-1995	—	—	—	—	3.00	5.00

KM# 13 250 ESCUDOS
16.40 g., 0.900 Silver 0.4745 oz. ASW, 33.5 mm. **Subject:** 1st Anniversary of Independence **Obv:** Denomination at right above fish, date below **Rev:** Date in center, star divides chain at bottom

Date	Mintage	VF20	XF40	MS60	MS63	MS65
1976	3,525	PF65 37.00				
1976	13,000	—	—	—	15.00	20.00

KM# 26 1000 ESCUDOS
28.11 g., 0.925 Silver 0.836 oz. ASW **Subject:** Tordesilhas Treaty **Obv:** National emblem at center, denomination below **Rev:** Ship between maps, two dates above

Date	Mintage	VF20	XF40	MS60	MS63	MS65
ND-1994	Est. 10000	PF65 45.00				
ND-1994	—	—	—	—	25.00	30.00

KM# 14 2500 ESCUDOS
8.00 g., 0.900 Gold 0.2315 oz. AGW **Subject:** 1st Anniversary of Independence **Obv:** Emblem within wreath above denomination **Rev:** Head left, date below

Date	Mintage	VF20	XF40	MS60	MS63	MS65
1976	3,409	PF60 325	PF63 400	PF65 450		

PIEDFORT

KM#	Date	Mintage	Identification	Mkt Val
P1	1984	520	50 Escudos. 0.925. Silver. KM22a.	100

PROVAS

KM#	Date	Mintage	Identification	Mkt Val
Pr1	1930	—	5 Centavos. Bronze. Stamped "PROVA" in field. KM1.	55.00
Pr2	1930	—	10 Centavos. Bronze. Stamped "PROVA" in field. KM2.	55.00
Pr3	1930	—	20 Centavos. Bronze. Stamped "PROVA" in field. KM3.	55.00
Pr4	1930	—	50 Centavos. Nickel-Bronze. Stamped "PROVA" in field. KM4.	95.00
Pr5	1930	—	Escudo. Nickel-Bronze. Stamped "PROVA" in field. KM5.	120
Pr6	1949	—	50 Centavos. Nickel-Bronze. Stamped "PROVA" in field. KM6.	50.00
Pr7	1949	—	Escudo. Nickel-Bronze. Stamped "PROVA" in field. KM7.	55.00
Pr8	1953	—	Escudo. Bronze. Stamped "PROVA" in field. KM8.	55.00
Pr9	1953	—	2-1/2 Escudos. Nickel-Bronze. Stamped "PROVA" in field. KM9.	50.00
Pr10	1953	—	10 Escudos. Silver. Stamped "PROVA" in field. KM10.	55.00
Pr11	1954	—	Escudo. Stamped "PROVA" in field.	45.00
Pr12	1954	—	2-1/2 Escudos. Stamped "PROVA" in field.	50.00

Pr13	1955	—	Escudo. Stamped "PROVA" in field.	45.00
Pr14	1955	—	2-1/2 Escudos. Stamped "PROVA" in field.	50.00
Pr15	1956	—	Escudo. Stamped "PROVA" in field.	45.00
Pr16	1956	—	2-1/2 Escudos. Stamped "PROVA" in field.	50.00
Pr17	1957	—	Escudo. Stamped "PROVA" in field.	45.00
Pr18	1957	—	2-1/2 Escudos. Stamped "PROVA" in field.	50.00
Pr19	1958	—	Escudo. Stamped "PROVA" in field.	45.00
Pr20	1958	—	2-1/2 Escudos. Stamped "PROVA" in field.	50.00
Pr21	1959	—	Escudo. Stamped "PROVA" in field.	45.00
Pr22	1959	—	2-1/2 Escudos. Stamped "PROVA" in field.	50.00
Pr23	1960	—	Escudo. Stamped "PROVA" in field.	45.00
Pr24	1960	—	2-1/2 Escudos. Stamped "PROVA" in field.	50.00
Pr25	1961	—	Escudo. Stamped "PROVA" in field.	45.00
Pr26	1961	—	2-1/2 Escudos. Stamped "PROVA" in field.	50.00
Pr27	1962	—	Escudo. Stamped "PROVA" in field.	45.00
Pr28	1962	—	2-1/2 Escudos. Stamped "PROVA" in field.	50.00
Pr29	1963	—	Escudo. Stamped "PROVA" in field.	45.00
Pr30	1963	—	2-1/2 Escudos. Stamped "PROVA" in field.	50.00
Pr31	1964	—	Escudo. Stamped "PROVA" in field.	45.00
Pr32	1964	—	2-1/2 Escudos. Stamped "PROVA" in field.	50.00
Pr33	1965	—	Escudo. Stamped "PROVA" in field.	45.00
Pr34	1965	—	2-1/2 Escudos. Stamped "PROVA" in field.	50.00
Pr35	1966	—	Escudo. Stamped "PROVA" in field.	45.00
Pr36	1966	—	2-1/2 Escudos. Stamped "PROVA" in field.	50.00
Pr37	1967	—	Escudo. Stamped "PROVA" in field.	38.00
Pr38	1967	—	2-1/2 Escudos. Nickel-Bronze. Stamped "PROVA" in field. KM9.	45.00
Pr39	1968	—	50 Centavos. Bronze. Stamped "PROVA" in field. KM11.	38.00
Pr40	1968	—	Escudo. Bronze. Stamped "PROVA" in field. KM8.	45.00
Pr41	1968	—	5 Escudos. Nickel-Bronze. Stamped "PROVA" in field. KM12.	50.00

PROOF SETS

KM#	Date	Mintage	Identification	Issue Price	Mkt Val
PS1	1976-77 (4)	—	KM13-14 1976, KM17-18 1977	—	500
PSA2	1985 (2)	—	KM#23 & 24	—	300
PS2	1985 (2)	—	KM23a, 24a	—	550

CAYMAN ISLANDS

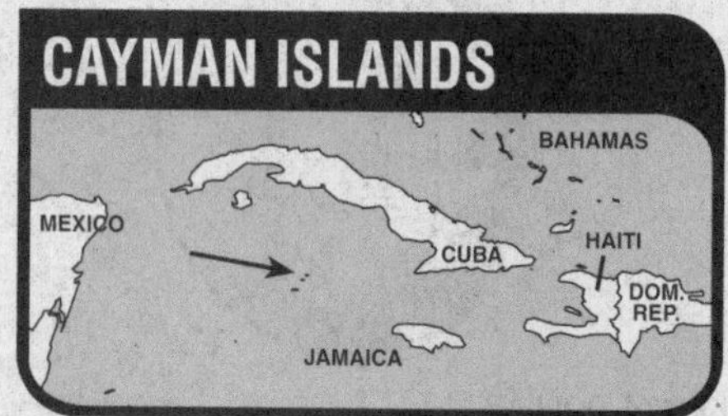

The Cayman Islands is a British Crown Colony situated about 180 miles (280 km) northwest of Jamaica. It consists of three islands: Grand Cayman, Little Cayman, and Cayman Brac. The islands have an area of 102 sq. mi. (259 sq. km.) and a population of 33,200. Capital: George Town. Seafaring, commerce, banking, and tourism are the principal industries. Rope, turtle shells, and sharkskins are exported.

The islands were discovered by Columbus in 1503, and named by him Tortugas (Spanish for turtles') because of the great number of turtles in the nearby waters. Ceded to Britain in 1670, they were colonized from Jamaica by the British and remained dependencies of Jamaica until 1959, when they became a unit territory within the Federation of the West Indies. They became a separate colony when the Federation was dissolved in 1962. Since 1972 a form of self-government has existed, with the Governor responsible for defense and certain other affairs.

While the islands used Jamaican currency for much of their history, the Caymans issued its first national coinage in 1972. The $25 gold and silver commemorative coins issued in 1972 to celebrate the silver wedding anniversary of Queen Elizabeth II and Prince Philip are the first coins in 300 years of Commonwealth coinage to portray a member of the British royal family other than the reigning monarch.

RULER
British

MINT MARKS
CHI - Valcambi
FM - Franklin Mint, U.S.A.*

MONETARY SYSTEM
100 Cents = 1 Dollar

BRITISH COLONY

DECIMAL COINAGE

KM# 1 CENT

2.85 g., Bronze, 17 mm. **Ruler:** Elizabeth II **Obv:** Young bust right **Rev:** Great Caiman Thrush

Date	Mintage	VF20	XF40	MS60	MS63	MS65
1972	2,155,000	—	0.15	0.25	0.75	1.00
1972	11,000	PF65 0.50				
1973	9,988	PF65 0.50				
1974	30,000	PF65 0.50				
1975	7,175	PF65 0.50				
1976	3,044	PF65 0.50				
1977	1,800,000	—	0.20	0.35	0.90	1.25
1977	1,970	PF65 1.00				
1979 FM	4,247	PF65 0.50				
1980 FM	—	—	0.15	0.25	0.75	1.00
1980 FM	1,215	PF65 1.25				
1981	865	PF65 1.50				
1982	—	—	0.15	0.25	0.75	1.00
1982	589	PF65 1.50				
1983	348	PF65 1.50				
1984	—	PF65 1.50				
1986	1,000	PF65 1.50				

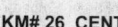

KM# 26 CENT

2.85 g., Bronze, 17 mm. **Ruler:** Elizabeth II **Subject:** 25th Anniversary of Coronation **Obv:** Young bust right **Rev:** Great Caiman Thrush

Date	Mintage	VF20	XF40	MS60	MS63	MS65
1978	1,303	PF65 2.00				

KM# 87 CENT

2.85 g., Bronze, 16 mm. **Ruler:** Elizabeth II **Obv:** Crowned bust right **Rev:** Great Caiman Thrush **Edge:** Plain

Date	Mintage	VF20	XF40	MS60	MS63	MS65
1987	—	—	0.15	0.30	0.75	1.00
1987	—	PF65 3.00				
1988	—	PF65 3.00				
1990	—	—	0.15	0.30	0.75	1.00

KM# 87a CENT

2.55 g., Copper Plated Steel, 17 mm. **Ruler:** Elizabeth II **Obv:** Crowned bust right **Rev:** Great Caiman Thrush **Edge:** Plain

Date	Mintage	VF20	XF40	MS60	MS63	MS65
1992	—	—	0.15	0.30	0.75	1.00
1996	8,000,000	—	0.15	0.30	0.75	1.00

KM# 131 CENT

2.55 g., Copper Plated Steel, 17 mm. **Ruler:** Elizabeth II **Obv:** Crowned head right **Rev:** Grand Caiman thrush **Edge:** Plain

Date	Mintage	VF20	XF40	MS60	MS63	MS65
1999	8,002,000	—	0.15	0.30	0.75	1.00

KM# 2 5 CENTS

2.20 g., Copper-Nickel, 18 mm. **Ruler:** Elizabeth II **Obv:** Young bust right **Rev:** Pink-spotted shrimp and value **Edge:** Plain

Date	Mintage	VF20	XF40	MS60	MS63	MS65
1972	300,000	—	0.15	0.50	1.00	1.50
1972	12,000	PF65 0.75				
1973	200,000	—	0.75	1.00	1.50	2.00

Note: 1973 Business strikes were not released to circulation

Date	Mintage	VF20	XF40	MS60	MS63	MS65
1973	9,988	PF65 0.75				
1974	30,000	PF65 0.75				
1975	7,175	PF65 0.75				
1976	3,044	PF65 0.75				
1977	600,000	—	0.15	0.50	1.00	1.50
1977	1,980	PF65 0.75				
1979	4,247	PF65 0.75				
1980	—	PF65 2.00				
1981	—	PF65 2.50				
1982	—	—	0.15	0.50	1.00	1.50
1982	348	PF65 2.50				
1983	—	PF65 2.50				
1984	—	PF65 2.50				
1986	1,000	PF65 2.50				

KM# 27 5 CENTS

2.20 g., Copper-Nickel, 18 mm. **Ruler:** Elizabeth II **Subject:** 25th Anniversary of Coronation **Obv:** Young bust right **Rev:** Pink-spotted shrimp

Date	Mintage	VF20	XF40	MS60	MS63	MS65
1978	1,303	PF65 3.00				

KM# 88 5 CENTS

2.20 g., Copper-Nickel, 18 mm. **Ruler:** Elizabeth II **Obv:** Crowned bust right **Rev:** Pink-spotted shrimp and value

Date	Mintage	VF20	XF40	MS60	MS63	MS65
1987	—	—	0.15	0.35	0.50	1.00
1987	—	PF65 5.00				
1988	—	PF65 5.00				
1990	—	—	0.15	0.35	0.50	1.00

KM# 88a 5 CENTS

2.00 g., Nickel Plated Steel, 18 mm. **Ruler:** Elizabeth II **Obv:** Crowned bust right **Rev:** Pink-spotted shrimp **Edge:** Plain

Date	Mintage	VF20	XF40	MS60	MS63	MS65
1992	—	—	0.20	0.50	0.75	1.25
1996	—	—	0.15	0.35	0.50	1.00

KM# 132 5 CENTS

2.00 g., Nickel Plated Steel, 18 mm. **Ruler:** Elizabeth II **Obv:** Crowned head right **Rev:** Pink-spotted shrimp **Edge:** Plain

Date	Mintage	VF20	XF40	MS60	MS63	MS65
1999	2,502,000	—	0.15	0.35	0.50	0.85

KM# 3 10 CENTS

3.90 g., Copper-Nickel, 21 mm. **Ruler:** Elizabeth II **Obv:** Young bust right **Rev:** Green Turtle surfacing **Edge:** Reeded

Date	Mintage	VF20	XF40	MS60	MS63	MS65
1972	550,000	0.25	0.40	0.75	1.00	1.25
1972	11,000	PF65 1.00				
1973	200,000	0.2.5	1.00	2.00	2.50	3.00

Note: 1973 Business strikes were not released to circulation

Date	Mintage	VF20	XF40	MS60	MS63	MS65
1973	9,988	PF65 1.00				
1974	30,000	PF65 1.00				
1975	7,175	PF65 1.00				
1976	3,044	PF65 1.00				
1977	960,000	—	0.40	0.75	1.00	1.25
1977	1,980	PF65 1.00				
1979 FM	4,247	PF65 1.00				
1980 FM	1,215	PF65 3.00				
1981 FM	865	PF65 3.00				
1982	—	—	0.40	0.60	0.75	1.00
1982 FM	589	PF65 3.00				
1983 FM	348	PF65 3.00				
1984 FM	—	PF65 3.00				
1986	1,000	PF65 3.00				

KM# 28 10 CENTS

3.90 g., Copper-Nickel, 21 mm. **Ruler:** Elizabeth II **Subject:** 25th Anniversary of Coronation **Obv:** Young bust right **Rev:** Green Turtle surfacing

Date	Mintage	VF20	XF40	MS60	MS63	MS65
1978	1,304	PF65 3.50				

KM# 89 10 CENTS

3.90 g., Copper-Nickel, 21 mm. **Ruler:** Elizabeth II **Obv:** Crowned bust right **Rev:** Green turtle surfacing **Edge:** Reeded

Date	Mintage	VF20	XF40	MS60	MS63	MS65
1987	—	—	0.40	0.60	0.75	1.00
1987	—	PF65 6.00				
1988	—	PF65 6.00				
1990	—	—	0.40	0.60	0.75	1.00

KM# 89a 10 CENTS

3.45 g., Nickel Plated Steel, 21 mm. **Ruler:** Elizabeth II **Obv:** Crowned bust right **Rev:** Green turtle surfacing **Edge:** Reeded

Date	Mintage	VF20	XF40	MS60	MS63	MS65
1992	—	—	0.40	0.60	0.75	1.00
1996	—	—	0.40	0.60	0.75	1.00

KM# 133 10 CENTS

3.45 g., Nickel Plated Steel, 21 mm. **Ruler:** Elizabeth II **Obv:** Head with tiara right **Rev:** Green turtle surfacing **Edge:** Reeded

Date	Mintage	VF20	XF40	MS60	MS63	MS65
1999	3,002,000	—	0.40	0.60	0.75	1.00

KM# 4 25 CENTS

5.67 g., Copper-Nickel, 24.26 mm. **Ruler:** Elizabeth II **Obv:** Young bust right **Rev:** Schooner sailing right **Edge:** Reeded

Date	Mintage	VF20	XF40	MS60	MS63	MS65
1972	350,000	0.40	0.60	1.00	1.25	1.50
1972	11,000	PF65 1.00				
1973	100,000	1.00	2.00	3.00	3.50	4.00

Note: 1973 Business strikes were not released to circulation

Date	Mintage	VF20	XF40	MS60	MS63	MS65
1973	9,988	PF65 1.00				
1974	30,000	PF65 1.00				
1975	7,175	PF65 1.00				
1976	3,044	PF65 1.00				
1977	520,000	0.40	0.60	1.00	1.25	1.50
1977	1,980	PF65 1.00				
1979	4,247	PF65 1.00				
1980	1,215	PF65 3.50				
1981	865	PF65 4.00				
1982	—	0.40	0.60	1.00	1.25	1.50
1982	589	PF65 4.00				
1983	348	PF65 4.00				
1984	—	PF65 4.00				
1986	1,000	PF65 4.00				

KM# 29 25 CENTS

5.67 g., Copper-Nickel, 24.26 mm. **Ruler:** Elizabeth II **Subject:** 25th Anniversary of Coronation **Obv:** Young bust right **Rev:** Schooner sailing right

Date	Mintage	VF20	XF40	MS60	MS63	MS65
1978	1,303	PF65 4.00				

KM# 90 25 CENTS

5.67 g., Copper-Nickel, 24.26 mm. **Ruler:** Elizabeth II **Obv:** Crowned head right **Rev:** Schooner sailing right **Edge:** Reeded

Date	Mintage	VF20	XF40	MS60	MS63	MS65
1987	—	0.40	0.60	1.00	1.25	1.50
1987	—	PF65 8.00				
1988	—	PF65 8.00				
1990	—	—	0.50	0.75	1.00	1.25

KM# 90a 25 CENTS

5.10 g., Nickel Plated Steel, 24.26 mm. **Ruler:** Elizabeth II **Obv:** Crowned head right **Rev:** Schooner sailing right **Edge:** Reeded

Date	Mintage	VF20	XF40	MS60	MS63	MS65
1992	—	—	0.50	0.75	1.00	1.25
1996	—	—	0.50	0.75	1.00	1.25

KM# 134 25 CENTS

5.10 g., Nickel Plated Steel, 24.26 mm. **Ruler:** Elizabeth II **Obv:** Head with tiara right **Rev:** Schooner sailing right **Edge:** Reeded

Date	Mintage	VF20	XF40	MS60	MS63	MS65
1999	2,500,000	—	0.50	0.75	1.00	1.25

KM# 5 50 CENTS

10.30 g., 0.925 Silver 0.3063 oz. ASW, 28.2 mm. **Ruler:** Elizabeth II **Obv:** Young bust right **Rev:** Caribbean Emperor Fish

Date	Mintage	VF20	XF40	MS60	MS63	MS65
1972	500	—	12.00	14.00	16.00	18.00
1972	11,000	PF65 9.00				
1973	9,988	PF65 9.00				
1974	30,000	PF65 9.00				
1975	7,175	PF65 9.00				
1976	3,044	PF65 9.00				
1977	1,980	PF65 9.00				
1979 FM	4,247	PF65 9.00				
1980 FM	1,215	PF65 12.00				
1981 FM	865	PF65 20.00				
1982 FM	589	PF65 20.00				

KM# 30 50 CENTS

10.30 g., 0.925 Silver 0.3063 oz. ASW, 28.2 mm. **Ruler:** Elizabeth II **Subject:** 25th Anniversary of Coronation **Obv:** Young bust right **Rev:** Caribbean Emperor Fish

Date	Mintage	VF20	XF40	MS60	MS63	MS65
1978	2,169	PF65 15.00				

KM# 73 50 CENTS

10.30 g., 0.925 Silver 0.3063 oz. ASW, 28.2 mm. **Ruler:** Elizabeth II **Obv:** Young bust right **Rev:** Morning Glory **Edge:** Reeded

Date	Mintage	VF20	XF40	MS60	MS63	MS65
1983 FM	348	PF65 18.00				
1984 FM	411	PF65 18.00				
1986	1,000	PF65 18.00				

KM# 91 50 CENTS

10.30 g., 0.925 Silver 0.3063 oz. ASW, 28.2 mm. **Ruler:** Elizabeth II **Obv:** Crowned head right **Rev:** Map of the Islands

Date	Mintage	VF20	XF40	MS60	MS63	MS65
1987	—	PF65 22.00				
1988	—	PF65 22.00				

KM# 6 DOLLAR

18.00 g., 0.925 Silver 0.5353 oz. ASW, 35 mm. **Ruler:** Elizabeth II **Obv:** Young bust right **Rev:** Poinciana flower

Date	Mintage	VF20	XF40	MS60	MS63	MS65
1972	500	—	—	20.00	25.00	28.00
1972	11,000	PF65 14.00				
1973	9,988	PF65 14.00				
1974	30,000	PF65 14.00				
1975	7,175	PF65 14.00				
1976	3,044	PF65 14.00				
1977	1,980	PF65 14.00				
1979 FM	4,247	PF65 14.00				
1980 FM	1,215	PF65 25.00				
1981 FM	865	PF65 35.00				
1982 FM	589	PF65 35.00				

KM# 31 DOLLAR

18.00 g., 0.925 Silver 0.5353 oz. ASW, 35 mm. **Ruler:** Elizabeth II **Subject:** 25th Anniversary of Coronation **Obv:** Young bust right **Rev:** Poinciana flower

Date	Mintage	VF20	XF40	MS60	MS63	MS65
1978	2,168	PF65 20.00				

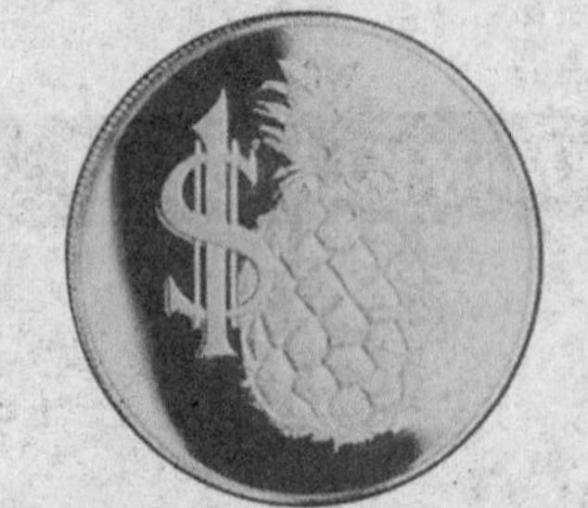

KM# 74 DOLLAR

18.00 g., 0.925 Silver 0.5353 oz. ASW, 35 mm. **Ruler:** Elizabeth II **Obv:** Young bust right **Rev:** Pineapple

Date	Mintage	VF20	XF40	MS60	MS63	MS65
1983 FM	1,686	PF65 22.50				
1984 FM	—	PF65 22.50				
1986	1,000	PF65 22.50				

KM# 92 DOLLAR

18.00 g., 0.925 Silver 0.5353 oz. ASW, 35 mm. **Ruler:** Elizabeth II **Obv:** Crowned bust right **Rev:** Map of the Islands

Date	Mintage	VF20	XF40	MS60	MS63	MS65
1987	—	PF65 30.00				
1988	—	PF65 30.00				

KM# 103 DOLLAR

18.14 g., 0.925 Silver 0.5395 oz. ASW **Ruler:** Elizabeth II **Obv:** Crowned bust right **Rev:** Green Turtle

Date	Mintage	VF20	XF40	MS60	MS63	MS65
1990	Est. 5000	PF65 55.00				

KM# 111 DOLLAR
18.14 g., 0.925 Silver 0.5395 oz. ASW **Ruler:** Elizabeth II **Obv:** Crowned bust right **Rev:** Lesser Caymans' Rock Iguana

Date	Mintage	VF20	XF40	MS60	MS63	MS65
1992	Est. 5000	PF65 35.00				

KM# 116 DOLLAR
18.14 g., 0.925 Silver 0.5395 oz. ASW, 35 mm. **Ruler:** Elizabeth II **Obv:** Crowned bust right **Rev:** Cayman Ironwood Tree

Date	Mintage	VF20	XF40	MS60	MS63	MS65
1994	10,000	PF65 30.00				

KM# 118 DOLLAR
28.28 g., 0.925 Silver 0.841 oz. ASW **Ruler:** Elizabeth II **Subject:** Royal Visit **Obv:** Crowned bust right **Rev:** Royal couple in cameo above yacht "Britannia

Date	Mintage	VF20	XF40	MS60	MS63	MS65
1994	Est. 10000	PF65 35.00				

KM# 120 DOLLAR
28.28 g., 0.925 Silver 0.841 oz. ASW **Ruler:** Elizabeth II **Obv:** Crowned bust right **Rev:** Queen Mother's arms

Date	Mintage	VF20	XF40	MS60	MS63	MS65
1994	Est. 20000	PF65 22.00				

KM# 121 DOLLAR
28.28 g., 0.925 Silver 0.841 oz. ASW, 38.6 mm. **Ruler:** Elizabeth II **Obv:** Crowned bust right **Rev:** Sir Francis Drake at left looking right, arms at right

Date	Mintage	VF20	XF40	MS60	MS63	MS65
1994	10,000	PF65 25.00				

KM# 125 DOLLAR
28.28 g., 0.925 Silver 0.841 oz. ASW, 38.6 mm. **Ruler:** Elizabeth II **Obv:** Crowned bust right **Rev:** Blue Rock Iguana left

Date	Mintage	VF20	XF40	MS60	MS63	MS65
1995	15,000	PF65 45.00				

KM# 122 DOLLAR
18.14 g., 0.925 Silver 0.5395 oz. ASW, 35 mm. **Ruler:** Elizabeth II **Obv:** Crowned bust right **Rev:** Amazona Leucocephala Caymanesis - Parrot right

Date	Mintage	VF20	XF40	MS60	MS63	MS65
1996	10,000	PF65 32.00				

KM# 124 DOLLAR
28.28 g., 0.925 Silver 0.841 oz. ASW, 38.6 mm. **Ruler:** Elizabeth II **Subject:** Olympics **Obv:** Crowned bust right **Rev:** Two sailboats

Date	Mintage	VF20	XF40	MS60	MS63	MS65
1996	30,000	PF65 22.50				

KM# 7 2 DOLLARS
29.45 g., 0.925 Silver 0.8758 oz. ASW, 40 mm. **Ruler:** Elizabeth II **Obv:** Young bust right **Rev:** Great Blue Heron

Date	Mintage	VF20	XF40	MS60	MS63	MS65
1972	500	—	—	—	32.00	37.00
1972	11,000	PF65 22.00				
1973	9,988	PF65 22.00				
1974	30,000	PF65 22.00				
1975	5,390	PF65 22.00				
1976	3,044	PF65 22.00				
1977	1,980	PF65 22.00				
1979 FM	4,247	PF65 22.00				
1980 FM	1,215	PF65 35.00				
1981 FM	865	PF65 40.00				
1982 FM	589	PF65 45.00				
1986	1,000	PF65 35.00				

KM# 32 2 DOLLARS
29.45 g., 0.925 Silver 0.8758 oz. ASW, 40 mm. **Ruler:** Elizabeth II **Subject:** 25th Anniversary of Coronation **Rev:** Great Blue Heron right

Date	Mintage	VF20	XF40	MS60	MS63	MS65
1978	2,169	PF65 35.00				

KM# 75 2 DOLLARS
29.45 g., 0.925 Silver 0.8758 oz. ASW, 40 mm. **Ruler:** Elizabeth II **Rev:** Parrot looking right

Date	Mintage	VF20	XF40	MS60	MS63	MS65
1983 FM	409	PF65 50.00				
1984 FM	—	PF65 60.00				

KM# 93 2 DOLLARS
29.45 g., 0.925 Silver 0.8758 oz. ASW, 40 mm. **Ruler:** Elizabeth II **Obv:** Crowned bust right **Rev:** Great Blue Heron

Date	Mintage	VF20	XF40	MS60	MS63	MS65
1987	—	PF65 45.00				
1988	—	PF65 45.00				

KM# 114 2 DOLLARS
28.28 g., 0.925 Silver 0.841 oz. ASW, 38.6 mm. **Ruler:** Elizabeth II **Obv:** Crowned bust right **Rev:** Wreck of the "Ten Sails"

Date	Mintage	VF20	XF40	MS60	MS63	MS65
1994	15,000	PF65 20.50				

KM# 127 2 DOLLARS
28.28 g., 0.925 Silver 0.841 oz. ASW, 38.6 mm. **Ruler:** Elizabeth II **Subject:** 25th Anniversary - Currency Board **Obv:** Crowned bust right **Rev:** Coins and arms within circle

Date	Mintage	VF20	XF40	MS60	MS63	MS65
ND-1996	2,000	PF65 50.00				

KM# 128 2 DOLLARS
28.28 g., 0.925 Silver 0.841 oz. ASW, 38.6 mm. **Ruler:** Elizabeth II **Subject:** Queen's Golden Wedding Anniversary **Obv:** Crowned bust right **Rev:** Royal couple in carriage above gold-plated shield

Date	Mintage	VF20	XF40	MS60	MS63	MS65
1997	30,000	PF65 35.00				

KM# 129 2 DOLLARS
28.28 g., 0.925 Silver 0.841 oz. ASW, 38.6 mm. **Ruler:** Elizabeth II **Subject:** Establishment of Cayman Islands Monetary Authority **Obv:** Crowned bust right **Rev:** Schooners Arbutus I and Goldfield under sail

Date	Mintage	VF20	XF40	MS60	MS63	MS65
1997	5,000	PF65 50.00				

KM# 130 2 DOLLARS
15.55 g., 0.999 Silver 0.4995 oz. ASW, 31.5 mm. **Ruler:** Elizabeth II **Subject:** Millennium **Obv:** Crowned bust right **Rev:** Ornate clock **Shape:** Scalloped

Date	Mintage	VF20	XF40	MS60	MS63	MS65
2000	30,000	PF65 38.00				

KM# 8 5 DOLLARS
35.50 g., 0.925 Silver 1.0557 oz. ASW, 42 mm. **Ruler:** Elizabeth II **Obv:** Young bust right **Rev:** Island arms

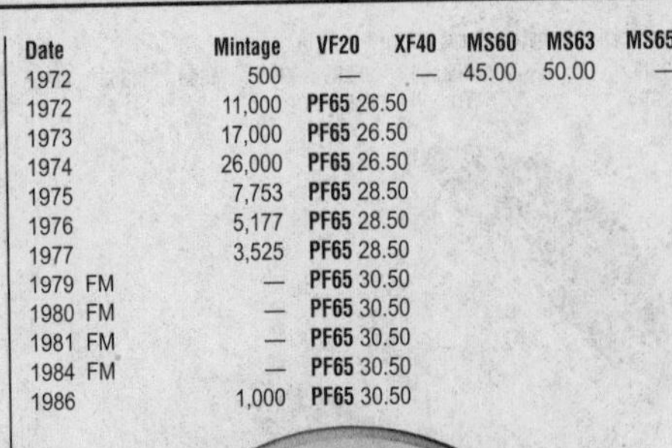

Date	Mintage	VF20	XF40	MS60	MS63	MS65
1972	500	—	—	45.00	50.00	—
1972	11,000	PF65 26.50				
1973	17,000	PF65 26.50				
1974	26,000	PF65 26.50				
1975	7,753	PF65 28.50				
1976	5,177	PF65 28.50				
1977	3,525	PF65 28.50				
1979 FM	—	PF65 30.50				
1980 FM	—	PF65 30.50				
1981 FM	—	PF65 30.50				
1984 FM	—	PF65 30.50				
1986	1,000	PF65 30.50				

KM# 33 5 DOLLARS
35.50 g., 0.925 Silver 1.0557 oz. ASW, 42 mm. **Ruler:** Elizabeth II **Subject:** 25th Anniversary of Coronation **Obv:** Young bust right

Date	Mintage	VF20	XF40	MS60	MS63	MS65
1978	2,168	PF65 40.00				

KM# 70 5 DOLLARS
35.50 g., 0.925 Silver 1.0557 oz. ASW, 42 mm. **Ruler:** Elizabeth II **Subject:** 150th Anniversary of Parliamentary Government **Obv:** Young bust right **Rev:** Island arms

Date	Mintage	VF20	XF40	MS60	MS63	MS65
1982 FM	1,105	PF65 45.00				

KM# 76 5 DOLLARS
35.50 g., 0.925 Silver 1.0557 oz. ASW, 42 mm. **Ruler:** Elizabeth II **Subject:** Royal Visit

Date	Mintage	VF20	XF40	MS60	MS63	MS65
1983 FM	419	PF65 75.00				

KM# 81 5 DOLLARS
28.28 g., 0.925 Silver 0.841 oz. ASW, 38.61 mm. **Ruler:** Elizabeth II **Subject:** 250th Anniversary of Royal Land Grant **Obv:** Crowned bust right **Rev:** Map of islands

Date	Mintage	VF20	XF40	MS60	MS63	MS65
1985	Est. 1000	PF65 50.00				

KM# 80 5 DOLLARS
28.28 g., 0.500 Silver 0.4546 oz. ASW **Ruler:** Elizabeth II **Subject:** Commonwealth Games **Obv:** Crowned bust right **Rev:** Long Jumper

Date	Mintage	VF20	XF40	MS60	MS63	MS65
1986	50,000	—	—	8.50	9.75	12.00

KM# 80a 5 DOLLARS
28.28 g., 0.925 Silver 0.841 oz. ASW **Ruler:** Elizabeth II **Subject:** Commonwealth Games **Obv:** Crowned bust right **Rev:** Long Jumper

Date	Mintage	VF20	XF40	MS60	MS63	MS65
1986	Est. 20000	PF65 21.50				

KM# 85 5 DOLLARS
28.28 g., 0.925 Silver 0.841 oz. ASW **Ruler:** Elizabeth II **Subject:** Queen Elizabeth II and Philip's 40th Wedding Anniversary **Obv:** Crowned bust right **Rev:** Monogram above dates within wreath

Date	Mintage	VF20	XF40	MS60	MS63	MS65
ND-1987	—	PF65 28.00				

KM# 85a 5 DOLLARS
35.64 g., 0.925 Silver 1.0599 oz. ASW **Ruler:** Elizabeth II **Subject:** Queen Elizabeth II and Philip's 40th Wedding Anniversary **Obv:** Crowned bust right **Rev:** Monogram above dates within wreath

Date	Mintage	VF20	XF40	MS60	MS63	MS65
ND-1987	—	PF65 65.00				

KM# 95 5 DOLLARS
28.28 g., 0.925 Silver 0.841 oz. ASW **Ruler:** Elizabeth II **Subject:** World Wildlife Fund **Obv:** Crowned bust right **Rev:** Cuban Amazon

Date	Mintage	VF20	XF40	MS60	MS63	MS65
1987	—	PF65 30.00				

KM# 94 5 DOLLARS
35.64 g., 0.925 Silver 1.0599 oz. ASW **Ruler:** Elizabeth II **Subject:** Seoul Olympics **Obv:** Crowned bust right **Rev:** Sailboats, denomination at left

Date	Mintage	VF20	XF40	MS60	MS63	MS65
1988	20,003	PF65 27.00				

KM# 96 5 DOLLARS
28.28 g., 0.925 Silver 0.841 oz. ASW **Ruler:** Elizabeth II **Subject:** 500th Anniversary of Columbus' Discovery of America **Obv:** Crowned bust right **Rev:** Columbus in cameo above ships

Date	Mintage	VF20	XF40	MS60	MS63	MS65
1988	10,000	PF65 28.00				

KM# 98 5 DOLLARS
28.28 g., 0.925 Silver 0.841 oz. ASW **Ruler:** Elizabeth II **Subject:** Visit of Princess Alexandra **Obv:** Crowned bust right **Rev:** Arms of Princess Alexandria

Date	Mintage	VF20	XF40	MS60	MS63	MS65
1988	Est. 5000	PF65 32.00				

KM# 143 5 DOLLARS
28.28 g., 0.925 Silver 0.841 oz. ASW **Ruler:** Elizabeth II **Subject:** Seoul Olympics **Obv:** Crowned bust right, value **Rev:** Sailboats

Date	Mintage	VF20	XF40	MS60	MS63	MS65
1988	318	PF65 750				

KM# 100 5 DOLLARS
28.28 g., 0.925 Silver 0.841 oz. ASW **Ruler:** Elizabeth II **Subject:** 100 Years of Postal Service **Rev:** Ship with small shield above

Date	Mintage	VF20	XF40	MS60	MS63	MS65
ND-1989	10,000	PF65 30.00				

KM# 102 5 DOLLARS
28.28 g., 0.925 Silver 0.841 oz. ASW **Ruler:** Elizabeth II **Subject:** Save the Children Fund **Obv:** Crowned bust right **Rev:** Two children sailing boats in water

Date	Mintage	VF20	XF40	MS60	MS63	MS65
1989	Est. 20000	PF65 22.00				

KM# 108 5 DOLLARS
28.28 g., 0.925 Silver 0.841 oz. ASW **Ruler:** Elizabeth II **Subject:** Queen Mother's Birth Centennial **Obv:** Crowned bust right **Rev:** Crowned monogram within flowers

Date	Mintage	VF20	XF40	MS60	MS63	MS65
ND-1990	Est. 10000	PF65 22.00				

KM# 109 5 DOLLARS
28.28 g., 0.925 Silver 0.841 oz. ASW, 38.6 mm. **Ruler:** Elizabeth II **Subject:** 20th Anniversary of the Currency Board **Obv:** Crowned bust right **Rev:** Islands and compass above ship within circle **Edge:** Reeded

Date	Mintage	VF20	XF40	MS60	MS63	MS65
ND-1991	2,500	PF65 35.00				

KM# 110 5 DOLLARS
28.28 g., 0.925 Silver 0.841 oz. ASW, 38.6 mm. **Ruler:** Elizabeth II **Subject:** 1992 Olympics - Barcelona **Obv:** Crowned bust right **Rev:** Cyclists

Date	Mintage	VF20	XF40	MS60	MS63	MS65
1992	200	PF65 125				

KM# 112 5 DOLLARS
28.28 g., 0.925 Silver 0.841 oz. ASW, 38.6 mm. **Ruler:** Elizabeth II **Subject:** 40th Anniversary - Coronation of Queen Elizabeth **Obv:** Crowned bust right **Rev:** Royal symbols

Date	Mintage	VF20	XF40	MS60	MS63	MS65
ND-1993	Est. 13000	PF65 32.00				

KM# 126 5 DOLLARS
28.28 g., 0.925 Silver 0.841 oz. ASW **Ruler:** Elizabeth II **Subject:** 70th Birthday of Queen Elizabeth II **Obv:** Crowned bust right **Rev:** The Queen on horseback divides monogram

Date	Mintage	VF20	XF40	MS60	MS63	MS65
ND-1996	12,500	PF65 37.00				

KM# 68 10 DOLLARS
Copper-Nickel **Ruler:** Elizabeth II **Subject:** Wedding of Prince Charles and Lady Diana **Obv:** Young bust right **Rev:** Facing busts, small island arms above

Date	Mintage	VF20	XF40	MS60	MS63	MS65
1981	—	—	—	12.00	13.50	15.00

KM# 68a 10 DOLLARS
28.28 g., 0.925 Silver 0.841 oz. ASW **Ruler:** Elizabeth II **Subject:** Wedding of Prince Charles and Lady Diana **Obv:** Young bust right **Rev:** Facing busts, small arms above

Date	Mintage	VF20	XF40	MS60	MS63	MS65
1981	40,000	PF65 22.00				

KM# 72 10 DOLLARS
27.89 g., 0.925 Silver 0.8294 oz. ASW **Ruler:** Elizabeth II **Subject:** International Year of the Child **Obv:** Young bust right **Rev:** Two children following sea turtle **Edge:** Reeded

Date	Mintage	VF20	XF40	MS60	MS63	MS65
1982	6,616	PF65 32.00				

KM# 77 10 DOLLARS
23.45 g., 0.925 Silver 0.6974 oz. ASW **Ruler:** Elizabeth II **Subject:** Royal Visit **Obv:** Young bust right **Rev:** Royal couple facing each other above small island arms

Date	Mintage	VF20	XF40	MS60	MS63	MS65
1983 FM	10,000	PF65 25.00				

KM# 9 25 DOLLARS
51.35 g., 0.925 Silver 1.5271 oz. ASW, 45 mm. **Ruler:** Elizabeth II **Subject:** Queen Elizabeth II and Philip's 25th Wedding Anniversary **Obv:** Young bust right **Rev:** Jugate heads right

Date	Mintage	VF20	XF40	MS60	MS63	MS65
1972	26,000	PF65 36.00				
1972	186,000	—	—	—	30.50	33.00

KM# 9a 25 DOLLARS
13.82 g., 0.500 Gold 0.2222 oz. AGW, 27 mm. **Ruler:** Elizabeth II **Subject:** Queen Elizabeth II and Philip's 25th Wedding Anniversary **Obv:** Young bust right **Rev:** Jugate heads right

Date	Mintage	VF20	XF40	MS60	MS63	MS65
1972	21,000	PF65 400				
1972	7,706	—	—	—	—	400

KM# 10 25 DOLLARS
51.35 g., 0.925 Silver 1,5271 oz. ASW, 45 mm. **Ruler:** Elizabeth II **Subject:** Churchill Centenary **Obv:** Island arms **Rev:** Bust facing

Date	Mintage	VF20	XF40	MS60	MS63	MS65
1974	1,200	—	—	40.00	45.00	—
1974	12,000	PF65 55.00				

Note: 4300 sets were issued in proof containing KM#10 and Turks & Caicos Islands 20 Crowns KM#2 with an issue price of $80.00

KM# 14 25 DOLLARS
51.35 g., 0.925 Silver 1.5271 oz. ASW, 45 mm. **Ruler:** Elizabeth II **Subject:** Queen's Silver Jubliee **Obv:** Young bust right **Rev:** Crowned arms with supporters

Date	Mintage	VF20	XF40	MS60	MS63	MS65
1977	7,854	PF65 60.00				
1977	3,600	—	—	45.00	50.00	—

KM# 16 25 DOLLARS
51.35 g., 0.925 Silver 1.5271 oz. ASW, 45 mm. **Ruler:** Elizabeth II **Subject:** Queen Mary I, 1553-1558 **Obv:** Young bust right **Rev:** Bust 3/4 facing

Date	Mintage	VF20	XF40	MS60	MS63	MS65
1977	2,720	PF63 37.00	PF65 50.00			

KM# 17 25 DOLLARS
51.35 g., 0.925 Silver 1.5271 oz. ASW, 45 mm. **Ruler:** Elizabeth II **Subject:** Elizabeth I, 1558-1603 **Obv:** Young bust right **Rev:** Bust with high ruffled collar 3/4 right

Date	Mintage	VF20	XF40	MS60	MS63	MS65
1977	2,677	PF63 37.00	PF65 50.00			

KM# 18 25 DOLLARS
51.35 g., 0.925 Silver 1.5271 oz. ASW, 45 mm. **Ruler:** Elizabeth II **Subject:** Queen Mary II, 1688-1694 **Obv:** Young bust right **Rev:** Bust 3/4 right

Date	Mintage	VF20	XF40	MS60	MS63	MS65
1977	2,653	PF63 37.00	PF65 50.00			

KM# 19 25 DOLLARS
51.35 g., 0.925 Silver 1.5271 oz. ASW, 45 mm. **Ruler:** Elizabeth II **Subject:** Queen Anne, 1702-1714 **Obv:** Young bust right **Rev:** Bust 3/4 facing

Date	Mintage	VF20	XF40	MS60	MS63	MS65
1977	2,630	PF63 37.00	PF65 50.00			

KM# 20 25 DOLLARS
51.35 g., 0.925 Silver 1.5271 oz. ASW, 45 mm. **Ruler:** Elizabeth II **Subject:** Queen Victoria, 1837-1901 **Obv:** Young bust right **Rev:** Crowned bust left

Date	Mintage	VF20	XF40	MS60	MS63	MS65
1977	2,623	PF63 37.00	PF65 50.00			

KM# 36 25 DOLLARS
51.35 g., 0.925 Silver 1.5271 oz. ASW, 45 mm. **Ruler:** Elizabeth II **Subject:** 25th Anniversary of Coronation **Obv:** Young bust right **Rev:** Ampulla

Date	Mintage	VF20	XF40	MS60	MS63	MS65
1978	5,000	PF65 45.00				

KM# 37 25 DOLLARS
51.35 g., 0.925 Silver 1.5271 oz. ASW, 45 mm. **Ruler:** Elizabeth

II **Subject:** 25th Anniversary of Coronation **Obv:** Young bust right **Rev:** Royal orb

Date	Mintage	VF20	XF40	MS60	MS63	MS65
1978	5,000	PF65 45.00				

KM# 38 25 DOLLARS

51.35 g., 0.925 Silver 1.5271 oz. ASW, 45 mm. **Ruler:** Elizabeth II **Subject:** 25th Anniversary of Coronation **Obv:** Young bust right **Rev:** St. Edward's crown

Date	Mintage	VF20	XF40	MS60	MS63	MS65
1978	5,000	PF65 45.00				

KM# 39 25 DOLLARS

51.35 g., 0.925 Silver 1.5271 oz. ASW, 45 mm. **Ruler:** Elizabeth II **Subject:** 25th Anniversary of Coronation **Obv:** Young bust right **Rev:** Coronation chair

Date	Mintage	VF20	XF40	MS60	MS63	MS65
1978	5,000	PF65 45.00				

KM# 40 25 DOLLARS

51.35 g., 0.925 Silver 1.5271 oz. ASW, 45 mm. **Ruler:** Elizabeth II **Subject:** 25th Anniversary of Coronation **Obv:** Young bust right **Rev:** Royal sceptre

Date	Mintage	VF20	XF40	MS60	MS63	MS65
1978	5,000	PF65 45.00				

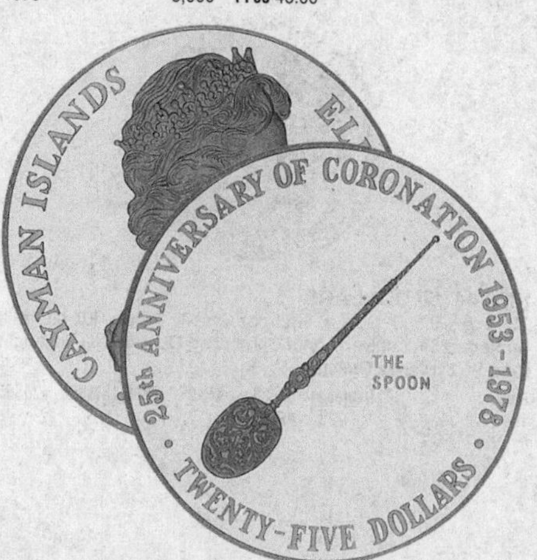

KM# 41 25 DOLLARS

51.35 g., 0.925 Silver 1.5271 oz. ASW, 45 mm. **Ruler:** Elizabeth II **Subject:** 25th Anniversary of Coronation **Obv:** Young bust right **Rev:** Spoon

Date	Mintage	VF20	XF40	MS60	MS63	MS65
1978	5,000	PF65 45.00				

KM# 48 25 DOLLARS

35.64 g., 0.500 Silver 0.5729 oz. ASW, 42 mm. **Ruler:** Elizabeth II **Obv:** Young bust right **Rev:** Saxon Kings

Date	Mintage	VF20	XF40	MS60	MS63	MS65
1980 CHI	12,000	PF63 18.00	PF65 28.00			

KM# 49 25 DOLLARS

35.64 g., 0.500 Silver 0.5729 oz. ASW, 42 mm. **Ruler:** Elizabeth II **Obv:** Young bust right **Rev:** Norman kings

Date	Mintage	VF20	XF40	MS60	MS63	MS65
1980 CHI	12,000	PF63 18.00	PF65 28.00			

KM# 50 25 DOLLARS

35.64 g., 0.500 Silver 0.5729 oz. ASW, 42 mm. **Ruler:** Elizabeth II **Obv:** Young bust right **Rev:** House of Plantagenet - I

Date	Mintage	VF20	XF40	MS60	MS63	MS65
1980 CHI	12,000	PF63 18.00	PF65 28.00			

KM# 51 25 DOLLARS

35.64 g., 0.500 Silver 0.5729 oz. ASW, 42 mm. **Ruler:** Elizabeth II **Obv:** Young bust right **Rev:** House of Plantagenet - II

Date	Mintage	VF20	XF40	MS60	MS63	MS65
1980 CHI	12,000	PF63 18.00	PF65 28.00			

KM# 52 25 DOLLARS

35.64 g., 0.500 Silver 0.5729 oz. ASW, 42 mm. **Ruler:** Elizabeth II **Obv:** Young bust right **Rev:** House of Lancaster

Date	Mintage	VF20	XF40	MS60	MS63	MS65
1980 CHI	12,000	PF63 18.00	PF65 28.00			

KM# 53 25 DOLLARS

35.64 g., 0.500 Silver 0.5729 oz. ASW, 42 mm. **Ruler:** Elizabeth II **Obv:** Young bust right **Rev:** House of York

Date	Mintage	VF20	XF40	MS60	MS63	MS65
1980 CHI	12,000	PF63 18.00	PF65 28.00			

KM# 54 25 DOLLARS

35.64 g., 0.500 Silver 0.5729 oz. ASW, 42 mm. **Ruler:** Elizabeth II **Obv:** Young bust right **Rev:** House of Tudor

Date	Mintage	VF20	XF40	MS60	MS63	MS65
1980 CHI	12,000	PF63 18.00	PF65 28.00			

KM# 55 25 DOLLARS

35.64 g., 0.500 Silver 0.5729 oz. ASW, 42 mm. **Ruler:** Elizabeth II **Obv:** Young bust right **Rev:** House of Stuart & Orange

Date	Mintage	VF20	XF40	MS60	MS63	MS65
1980 CHI	12,000	PF63 18.00	PF65 28.00			

KM# 56 25 DOLLARS
35.64 g., 0.500 Silver 0.5729 oz. ASW, 42 mm. **Ruler:** Elizabeth II **Obv:** Young bust right **Rev:** House of Hanover

Date	Mintage	VF20	XF40	MS60	MS63	MS65
1980 CHI	12,000	PF63 18.00	PF65 28.00			

KM# 57 25 DOLLARS
35.64 g., 0.500 Silver 0.5729 oz. ASW, 42 mm. **Ruler:** Elizabeth II **Obv:** Young bust right **Rev:** House of Saxe-Coburg and Windsor

Date	Mintage	VF20	XF40	MS60	MS63	MS65
1980 CHI	12,000	PF63 18.00	PF65 28.00			

KM# 78 25 DOLLARS
64.80 g., 0.925 Silver 1.9271 oz. ASW **Ruler:** Elizabeth II **Subject:** Royal Visit **Obv:** Young bust right **Rev:** Royal couple facing each other above small island arms

Date	Mintage	VF20	XF40	MS60	MS63	MS65
1983 FM	5,000	PF65 57.00				

KM# 104 25 DOLLARS
3.13 g., 0.999 Gold 0.1007 oz. AGW **Ruler:** Elizabeth II **Subject:** Winston Churchill **Obv:** Young bust right **Rev:** Evacuation of Dunkirk

Date	Mintage	VF20	XF40	MS60	MS63	MS65
1990	—	PF63 150	PF65 175			

KM# 12 50 DOLLARS
64.94 g., 0.925 Silver 1.9313 oz. ASW **Ruler:** Elizabeth II **Subject:** Sovereign Queens of England **Obv:** Young bust right **Rev:** Portraits of sovereign queens in circle with names and dates

Date	Mintage	VF20	XF40	MS60	MS63	MS65
1975	33,000	—	—	56.00	—	—
1975	7,800	PF65 56.00				
1976	1,292	—	—	61.00	—	—
1976	2,843	PF65 61.00				
1977	Inc. above	PF65 61.00				
1977	2,400	—	—	61.00	—	—

KM# 21 50 DOLLARS
11.34 g., 0.500 Gold 0.1823 oz. AGW **Ruler:** Elizabeth II **Subject:** Queen Mary I, 1553-1558 **Obv:** Young bust right **Rev:** Bust 3/4 facing

Date	Mintage	VF20	XF40	MS60	MS63	MS65
1977	1,999	PF65 300				

KM# 22 50 DOLLARS
11.34 g., 0.500 Gold 0.1823 oz. AGW **Ruler:** Elizabeth II **Subject:** Queen Elizabeth I, 1558-1603 **Obv:** Young bust right **Rev:** Bust with high ruffled collar 3/4 right

Date	Mintage	VF20	XF40	MS60	MS63	MS65
1977	1,969	PF65 300				

KM# 23 50 DOLLARS
11.34 g., 0.500 Gold 0.1823 oz. AGW **Ruler:** Elizabeth II **Subject:** Queen Mary II, 1688-1694 **Obv:** Young bust right **Rev:** Bust 3/4 right

Date	Mintage	VF20	XF40	MS60	MS63	MS65
1977	1,961	PF65 300				

KM# 24 50 DOLLARS
11.34 g., 0.500 Gold 0.1823 oz. AGW **Ruler:** Elizabeth II **Subject:** Queen Anne, 1702-1714 **Obv:** Young bust right **Rev:** Bust 3/4 left

Date	Mintage	VF20	XF40	MS60	MS63	MS65
1977	1,938	PF65 300				

KM# 25 50 DOLLARS
11.34 g., 0.500 Gold 0.1823 oz. AGW **Ruler:** Elizabeth II **Subject:** Queen Victoria, 1837-1901 **Obv:** Young bust right **Rev:** Crowned bust left

Date	Mintage	VF20	XF40	MS60	MS63	MS65
1977	1,932	PF65 300				

KM# 34 50 DOLLARS
64.94 g., 0.925 Silver 1.9313 oz. ASW **Ruler:** Elizabeth II **Obv:** Young bust right **Rev:** Coronation Anniversary legend added to KM#12

Date	Mintage	VF20	XF40	MS60	MS63	MS65
1978	5,775	PF65 61.00				

KM# 42 50 DOLLARS
11.34 g., 0.500 Gold 0.1823 oz. AGW **Ruler:** Elizabeth II **Subject:** 25th Anniversary of Coronation **Obv:** Young bust right **Rev:** The Ampulla

Date	Mintage	VF20	XF40	MS60	MS63	MS65
1978	771	PF65 350				

KM# 43 50 DOLLARS
11.34 g., 0.500 Gold 0.1823 oz. AGW **Ruler:** Elizabeth II **Subject:** 25th Anniversary of Coronation **Obv:** Young bust right **Rev:** Royal orb

Date	Mintage	VF20	XF40	MS60	MS63	MS65
1978	771	PF65 350				

KM# 44 50 DOLLARS
11.34 g., 0.500 Gold 0.1823 oz. AGW **Ruler:** Elizabeth II **Subject:** 25th Anniversary of Coronation **Obv:** Young bust right **Rev:** St. Edward's Crown

Date	Mintage	VF20	XF40	MS60	MS63	MS65
1978	771	PF65 350				

KM# 45 50 DOLLARS
11.34 g., 0.500 Gold 0.1823 oz. AGW **Ruler:** Elizabeth II **Subject:** 25th Anniversary of Coronation **Obv:** Young bust right **Rev:** Coronation chair

Date	Mintage	VF20	XF40	MS60	MS63	MS65
1978	771	PF65 350				

KM# 46 50 DOLLARS
11.34 g., 0.500 Gold 0.1823 oz. AGW **Ruler:** Elizabeth II **Subject:** 25th Anniversary of Coronation **Obv:** Young bust right **Rev:** Scepter

Date	Mintage	VF20	XF40	MS60	MS63	MS65
1978	771	PF65 350				

KM# 47 50 DOLLARS
11.34 g., 0.500 Gold 0.1823 oz. AGW **Ruler:** Elizabeth II **Subject:** 25th Anniversary of Coronation **Obv:** Young bust right **Rev:** Spoon

Date	Mintage	VF20	XF40	MS60	MS63	MS65
1978	771	PF65 350				

KM# 58 50 DOLLARS
11.34 g., 0.500 Gold 0.1823 oz. AGW, 27 mm. **Ruler:** Elizabeth II **Obv:** Young bust right **Rev:** Saxon Kings

Date	Mintage	VF20	XF40	MS60	MS63	MS65
1980	10,000	PF65 280				

KM# 59 50 DOLLARS
11.34 g., 0.500 Gold 0.1823 oz. AGW, 27 mm. **Ruler:** Elizabeth II **Obv:** Young bust right **Rev:** Norman Kings

Date	Mintage	VF20	XF40	MS60	MS63	MS65
1980	10,000	PF65 280				

KM# 60 50 DOLLARS
11.34 g., 0.500 Gold 0.1823 oz. AGW, 27 mm. **Ruler:** Elizabeth II **Obv:** Young bust right **Rev:** House of Plantagenet - I

Date	Mintage	VF20	XF40	MS60	MS63	MS65
1980	11,000	PF65 280				

KM# 61 50 DOLLARS
11.34 g., 0.500 Gold 0.1823 oz. AGW, 27 mm. **Ruler:** Elizabeth II **Obv:** Young bust right **Rev:** House of Plantagenet - II

Date	Mintage	VF20	XF40	MS60	MS63	MS65
1980	11,000	PF65 280				

KM# 62 50 DOLLARS
11.34 g., 0.500 Gold 0.1823 oz. AGW, 27 mm. **Ruler:** Elizabeth II **Obv:** Young bust right **Rev:** House of Lancaster

Date	Mintage	VF20	XF40	MS60	MS63	MS65
1980	11,000	PF65 280				

KM# 63 50 DOLLARS
11.34 g., 0.500 Gold 0.1823 oz. AGW, 27 mm. **Ruler:** Elizabeth II **Obv:** Young bust right **Rev:** House of York

Date	Mintage	VF20	XF40	MS60	MS63	MS65
1980	11,000	PF65 280				

KM# 64 50 DOLLARS
11.34 g., 0.500 Gold 0.1823 oz. AGW, 27 mm. **Ruler:** Elizabeth II **Obv:** Young bust right **Rev:** House of Tudor

Date	Mintage	VF20	XF40	MS60	MS63	MS65
1980	11,000	PF65 280				

KM# 65 50 DOLLARS
11.34 g., 0.500 Gold 0.1823 oz. AGW, 27 mm. **Ruler:** Elizabeth II **Obv:** Young bust right **Rev:** House of Stuart and Orange

Date	Mintage	VF20	XF40	MS60	MS63	MS65
1980	11,000	PF65 280				

KM# 66 50 DOLLARS
11.34 g., 0.500 Gold 0.1823 oz. AGW, 27 mm. **Ruler:** Elizabeth II **Obv:** Young bust right **Rev:** House of Hanover

Date	Mintage	VF20	XF40	MS60	MS63	MS65
1980	11,000	PF65 280				

KM# 67 50 DOLLARS
11.34 g., 0.500 Gold 0.1823 oz. AGW, 27 mm. **Ruler:** Elizabeth II **Obv:** Young bust right **Rev:** House of Saxe-Coburg and Windsor

Date	Mintage	VF20	XF40	MS60	MS63	MS65
1980	11,000	PF65 280				

KM# 71 50 DOLLARS
5.00 g., 0.900 Gold 0.1447 oz. AGW **Ruler:** Elizabeth II **Subject:** 150th Anniversary of Parliamentary Government **Obv:** Young bust right **Rev:** Island arms

Date	Mintage	VF20	XF40	MS60	MS63	MS65
1982	585	PF65 230				

KM# 79 50 DOLLARS
5.19 g., 0.917 Gold 0.153 oz. AGW **Ruler:** Elizabeth II **Subject:** Royal Visit **Obv:** Young bust right **Rev:** Royal couple facing each other above small arms

Date	Mintage	VF20	XF40	MS60	MS63	MS65
1983	5,000	—	—	—	235	250

KM# 83 50 DOLLARS
129.60 g., 0.925 Silver 3.8542 oz. ASW, 63 mm. **Ruler:** Elizabeth II **Subject:** Bird Conservation **Obv:** Crowned bust right **Rev:** Snowy Egret left

Date	Mintage	VF20	XF40	MS60	MS63	MS65
1985	10,000	PF63 85.00	PF65 100			

KM# 105 50 DOLLARS
7.81 g., 0.999 Gold 0.251 oz. AGW **Ruler:** Elizabeth II **Obv:** Crowned bust right **Rev:** Cameo Winston Churchill above Spitfires over Dover

Date	Mintage	VF20	XF40	MS60	MS63	MS65
1990	Est. 500	PF63 395	PF65 445			

KM# 115 50 DOLLARS
15.98 g., 0.917 Gold 0.4711 oz. AGW, 28.4 mm. **Ruler:** Elizabeth II **Obv:** Crowned bust right **Rev:** Wreck of the "Ten Sails"

Date	Mintage	VF20	XF40	MS60	MS63	MS65
1994	200	PF65 850				

KM# 11 100 DOLLARS
22.68 g., 0.500 Gold 0.3646 oz. AGW **Ruler:** Elizabeth II **Subject:** Winston Churchill Centenary **Obv:** Island arms **Rev:** Bust facing

Date	Mintage	VF20	XF40	MS60	MS63	MS65
1974	6,300	PF65 550				
1974	1,400	—	—	—	—	600

KM# 13 100 DOLLARS
22.68 g., 0.500 Gold 0.3646 oz. AGW **Ruler:** Elizabeth II **Obv:** Young bust right **Rev:** Sovereign Queens of England in circle

Date	Mintage	VF20	XF40	MS60	MS63	MS65
1975	4,950	PF65 575				
1975	8,053	—	—	—	—	550
1976	3,560	PF65 575				
1976	2,028	—	—	—	—	550
1977	2,845	PF65 575				
1977	—	—	—	—	—	550

KM# 15 100 DOLLARS
22.68 g., 0.500 Gold 0.3646 oz. AGW **Ruler:** Elizabeth II **Subject:** Queen's Silver Jubilee **Obv:** Young bust right **Rev:** Crowned arms with supporters

Date	Mintage	VF20	XF40	MS60	MS63	MS65
1977	562	—	—	—	—	600
1977	4,386	PF65 550				

KM# 35 100 DOLLARS
22.68 g., 0.500 Gold 0.3646 oz. AGW **Ruler:** Elizabeth II **Obv:** Young bust right **Rev:** Sovereign Queens of England in circle

Date	Mintage	VF20	XF40	MS60	MS63	MS65
1978	1,973	PF65 575				

KM# 69 100 DOLLARS
8.04 g., 0.917 Gold 0.2369 oz. AGW **Ruler:** Elizabeth II **Subject:** Wedding of Prince Charles and Lady Diana **Obv:** Young bust right **Rev:** Busts facing, small island arms above

Date	Mintage	VF20	XF40	MS60	MS63	MS65
1981	11,000	PF65 375				

KM# 97 100 DOLLARS
15.98 g., 0.917 Gold 0.4711 oz. AGW **Ruler:** Elizabeth II **Subject:** 500th Anniversary of Columbus' Discovery of America

Date	Mintage	VF20	XF40	MS60	MS63	MS65
1988	—	PF65 800				

KM# 101 100 DOLLARS
15.98 g., 0.917 Gold 0.4711 oz. AGW **Ruler:** Elizabeth II **Subject:** 100 Years of Postal Service **Obv:** Crowned bust right **Rev:** Ship with small shield above

Date	Mintage	VF20	XF40	MS60	MS63	MS65
1989	—	PF65 800				

KM# 106 100 DOLLARS
15.61 g., 0.999 Gold 0.5013 oz. AGW **Ruler:** Elizabeth II **Subject:** Winston Churchill **Obv:** Crowned bust right **Rev:** Evacuation of Dunkirk

Date	Mintage	VF20	XF40	MS60	MS63	MS65
1990	500	PF63 725	PF65 825			

KM# 117 100 DOLLARS
30.50 g., 0.917 Gold 0.8992 oz. AGW **Ruler:** Elizabeth II **Obv:** Crowned bust right **Rev:** Cayman Ironwood Tree

Date	Mintage	VF20	XF40	MS60	MS63	MS65
1994	Est. 15000	PF65 1,300				

KM# 123 100 DOLLARS
15.98 g., 0.917 Gold 0.4711 oz. AGW **Ruler:** Elizabeth II **Obv:** Crowned bust right **Rev:** Amazona Leucocephala Caymanesis - Parrot

Date	Mintage	VF20	XF40	MS60	MS63	MS65
1996	Est. 150	PF65 800				

KM# 82 250 DOLLARS
47.54 g., 0.917 Gold 1.4016 oz. AGW, 38.61 mm. **Ruler:** Elizabeth II **Subject:** 250th Anniversary of Royal Land Grant **Obv:** Crowned bust right **Rev:** Map of islands

Date	Mintage	VF20	XF40	MS60	MS63	MS65
1985	—	PF65 2,100				

KM# 84 250 DOLLARS
47.54 g., 0.917 Gold 1.4016 oz. AGW **Ruler:** Elizabeth II **Subject:** Commonwealth Games **Obv:** Crowned bust right **Rev:** Long jumper

Date	Mintage	VF20	XF40	MS60	MS63	MS65
1986	64	PF65 2,250				

KM# 86 250 DOLLARS
47.54 g., 0.917 Gold 1.4016 oz. AGW **Ruler:** Elizabeth II **Subject:** Queen Elizabeth II and Philip's 40th Wedding Anniversary **Obv:** Crowned bust right **Rev:** E & P monogram

Date	Mintage	VF20	XF40	MS60	MS63	MS65
ND (1987)	75	PF65 2,200				

KM# 99 250 DOLLARS
47.54 g., 0.917 Gold 1.4016 oz. AGW **Ruler:** Elizabeth II **Subject:** Visit of Princess Alexandra **Obv:** Crowned bust right **Rev:** Royal Arms of Princess Alexandra

Date	Mintage	VF20	XF40	MS60	MS63	MS65
1988	86	PF65 2,200				

KM# 107 250 DOLLARS
31.21 g., 0.999 Gold 1.0024 oz. AGW **Ruler:** Elizabeth II **Obv:** Crowned bust right **Rev:** Cameo Winston Churchill above Spitfires over Dover

Date	Mintage	VF20	XF40	MS60	MS63	MS65
1990	Est. 500	PF63 1,450	PF65 1,550			

KM# 144 250 DOLLARS
47.54 g., 0.916 Gold 1.4001 oz. AGW, 38.61 mm. **Ruler:** Elizabeth II **Subject:** Elizabeth, the Queen Mother, 90th Birthday **Rev:** Crowned monogram

Date	Mintage	VF20	XF40	MS60	MS63	MS65
1990	Est. 250	PF65 2,100				

KM# 113 250 DOLLARS
47.54 g., 0.917 Gold 1.4016 oz. AGW **Ruler:** Elizabeth II **Subject:** 40th Anniversary - Coronation of Queen Elizabeth II

Date	Mintage	VF20	XF40	MS60	MS63	MS65
1993	Est. 100	PF65 2,150				

KM# 119 250 DOLLARS
47.54 g., 0.917 Gold 1.4016 oz. AGW **Ruler:** Elizabeth II **Subject:** Royal Visit **Obv:** Crowned bust right **Rev:** Royal couple above yacht "Britannia"

Date	Mintage	VF20	XF40	MS60	MS63	MS65
1994	200	PF65 2,100				

PIEDFORT

KM#	Date	Mintage	Identification	Mkt Val
P1	1982	74	10 Dollars. Silver. KM72	150

MINT SETS

KM#	Date	Mintage	Identification	Issue Price	Mkt Val
MS1	1987 (4)	—	KM87-90	—	5.00
MS2	1992 (4)	—	KM87a-90a	8.00	8.00
MS3	1996 (4)	—	KM87a-90a	9.60	11.00
MS4	1999 (4)	—	KM#131-134	11.25	14.00

PROOF SETS

KM#	Date	Mintage	Identification	Issue Price	Mkt Val
PS1	1972 (8)	10,757	KM1-8	40.00	75.00
PS2	1973 (8)	9,988	KM1-8	40.00	75.00
PS3	1974 (8)	15,387	KM1-8	40.00	75.00
PS4	1974 (2)	2,400	KM10-11	245	700
PS5	1975 (8)	5,390	KM1-8	54.50	75.00
PS6	1975 (6)	1,785	KM1-6	31.50	30.00
PS7	1975 (2)	3,650	KM12-13	293	700
PS8	1976 (8)	3,044	KM1-8	54.50	85.00
PS9	1976 (2)	1,531	KM12-13	293	700
PS11	1977 (8)	1,970	KM1-8	52.50	95.00
PS12	1977 (6)	2,445	KM12, 16-20	315	400
PS13	1977 (6)	1,932	KM13, 21-25	651	2,250
PS14	1977 (2)	223	KM14-15	290	700
PS15	1978 (8)	1,303	KM26-33	79.50	125
PS16	1978 (6)	5,000	KM36-41	306	325
PS17	1978 (6)	771	KM42-47	600	2,100
PS18	1979 (8)	4,427	KM1-8	117	100
PS19	1980 (8)	1,215	KM1-8	147	110
PS20	1980 (10)	—	KM48-57	—	350
PS21	1981 (8)	865	KM1-8	147	120
PS22	1982 (8)	589	KM1-7, 70	147	125
PS23	1983 (8)	348	KM1-4, 73-76	157	145
PS24	1984 (8)	—	KM1-4, 8, 73-75	159	155
PS25	1986 (8)	330	KM1-4, 7-8, 73-74	150	125
PS26	1987 (8)	317	KM85a, 87-93	160	215
PS27	1988 (8)	318	KM87-94	170	310
PS28	1990 (4)	500	KM104-107	1,650	3,000

CENTRAL AFRICAN REPUBLIC

The Central African Republic, a landlocked country in Central Africa, bounded by Chad on the north, Cameroon on the west, Congo (Brazzaville) and Congo Democratic Republic, (formerly Zaire) on the south and the Sudan on the east, has an area of 240,324 sq. mi. (622,984 sq. km.) and a population of 3.2 million. Capital: Bangui. Deposits of uranium, iron ore, manganese and copper remain to be developed. Diamonds, cotton, timber and coffee are exported.

The area that is now the Central African Republic was constituted as the French territory of Ubangi-Shari in 1894. It was united with Chad in 1905 and joined with Middle Congo and Gabon in 1910, becoming one of the four territories of French Equatorial Africa. Upon dissolution of the federation on Dec. 1, 1958, the constituent territories became fully autonomous members of the French Community. Ubangi-Shari proclaimed its complete independence as the Central African Republic on Aug. 13, 1960.

On Jan. 1, 1966, Col. Jean-Bedel Bokassa, Chief of Staff of the Armed Forces, overthrew the government of President David Dacko and assumed power as president of the republic. President Bokassa abolished the constitution of 1959 and dissolved the National Assembly. In 1975 the Congress of the sole political party appointed Bokassa president for life. The republic became a constitutional monarchy on Dec. 4, 1976; President Bokassa was named Emperor Bokassa I. Bokassa was ousted as Central African emperor in a bloodless takeover of the government led by former president David Dacko on Sept. 20, 1979, and the African nation proclaimed once again a republic.

NOTE: For earlier coinage see French Equatorial Africa and Equatorial African States including later coinage as listed in Central African States.

RULERS
French, until 1960
Marshal Jean-Bedel Bokassa, 1976-1979

MINT MARKS
(a) - Paris, privy marks only

MONETARY SYSTEM
100 Centimes = 1 Franc

REPUBLIC

DECIMAL COINAGE

KM# 6 100 FRANCS
7.00 g., Nickel, 25.5 mm. **Obv:** Three giant eland left **Rev:** Denomination within circle

Date	Mintage	F12	VF20	XF40	MS60	MS63
1971 (a)	2,500,000	5.00	8.00	12.00	22.00	28.00
1972 (a)	3,500,000	5.00	8.00	12.00	22.00	28.00

KM# 7 100 FRANCS
7.00 g., Nickel, 25.5 mm. **Obv:** Three giant eland left **Rev:** Denomination, date below, within circle

Date	Mintage	F12	VF20	XF40	MS60	MS63
1975 (a)	—	4.00	7.00	10.00	18.00	22.50
1976 (a)	—	2.00	3.50	6.00	9.00	12.00
1979 (a)	—	6.00	12.50	18.00	28.00	35.00
1982 (a)	—	2.75	4.50	8.00	12.00	15.00
1983 (a)	—	2.75	4.50	9.00	14.00	20.00
1984 (a)	—	2.50	4.00	7.00	10.00	14.00
1985 (a)	—	2.50	4.00	7.00	10.00	14.00
1988 (a)	—	2.50	4.00	7.00	10.00	14.00
1990 (a)	—	2.00	3.50	6.00	9.00	12.00

KM# 8 100 FRANCS
7.00 g., Nickel, 25.5 mm. **Obv:** Three giant eland left **Rev:** Denomination and date within circle **Rev. Legend:** EMPIRE CENTRAFRICAIN

Date	Mintage	VF20	XF40	MS60	MS63	MS65
1978 (a)	—	45.00	95.00	225	450	750

Note: These were produced during the short-lived reign of dictator Jean-Bedel Bokassa as Emperor, but not released for circulation, though many are now available in the market

KM# 1 1000 FRANCS
3.50 g., 0.900 Gold 0.1013 oz. AGW **Subject:** 10th Anniversary of Independence **Obv:** Bust of President Jean Bedel Bokassa facing **Rev:** Three joined shields, radiant sun above center shield, denomination below

Date	Mintage	F12	VF20	XF40	MS60	MS63
1970	4,000	PF65 200				

KM# 2 3000 FRANCS
10.50 g., 0.900 Gold 0.3038 oz. AGW **Subject:** 10th Anniversary of Independence **Rev:** Bust with mortarboard facing, denomination below

Date	Mintage	F12	VF20	XF40	MS60	MS63
1970	4,000	PF65 600				

KM# 3 5000 FRANCS
17.50 g., 0.900 Gold 0.5064 oz. AGW **Subject:** 10th Anniversary of Independence; 1972 Munich Olympics **Obv:** Head left divides dates **Rev:** Wrestlers, date and denomination below

Date	Mintage	F12	VF20	XF40	MS60	MS63
1970	4,000	PF65 1,000				

KM# 4 10000 FRANCS
35.00 g., 0.900 Gold 1.0127 oz. AGW **Subject:** 10th Anniversary of Independence; ONU 24th Anniversary **Obv:** Head left divides dates **Rev:** Map at center, heads above, denomination below

Date	Mintage	F12	VF20	XF40	MS60	MS63
1970	4,000	PF65 2,000				

KM# 5 20000 FRANCS
70.00 g., 0.900 Gold 2.0255 oz. AGW **Subject:** 10th Anniversary of Independence; Operation Bokassa **Obv:** Head of Bokassa left, divides dates **Rev:** Symbols of independence, denomination below

Date	Mintage	F12	VF20	XF40	MS60	MS63
1970	4,000	PF65 4,000				

SECOND REPUBLIC

KM# 11 500 FRANCS
Copper-Nickel

Date	Mintage	VF20	XF40	MS60	MS63	MS65
1985	—	5.00	9.00	16.00	28.00	45.00
1986	—	5.00	9.00	16.00	28.00	45.00

ESSAIS

KM#	Date	Mintage	Identification	Mkt Val
E1	1970	—	1000 Francs. Bronze. KM1.	185
E1a	1970	—	1000 Francs. Nickel.	135
E2	1971	1,450	100 Francs. Nickel. KM6.	40.00
E3	1971	4	100 Francs. Gold. KM6.	3,250
E4	1975	1,700	100 Francs. Nickel. KM7.	35.00
E5	1978	1,900	100 Francs. Nickel. KM8.	450
E6	1985	1,700	500 Francs. Copper-Nickel. Plants divide date and denomination. Woman's head, 3/4 left. KM11.	50.00

PROOF SETS

KM#	Date	Mintage	Identification	Issue Price	Mkt Val
PS1	1970 (5)	4,000	KM1-5	375	7,800

CENTRAL AFRICAN STATES

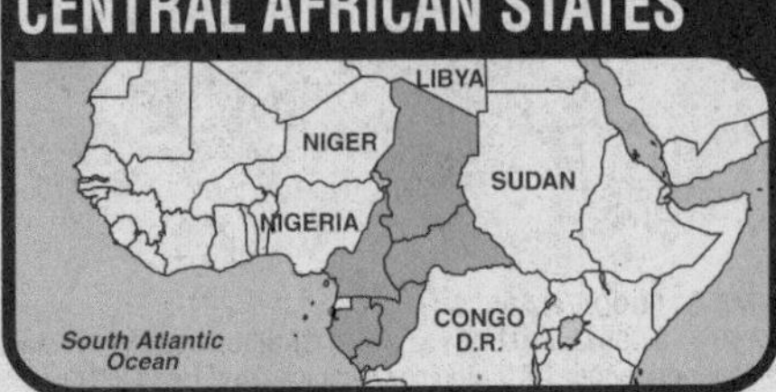

The Central African States, a monetary union comprised of Equatorial Guinea (a former Spanish possession), the former French possessions and now independent states of the Republic of Congo (Brazzaville), Gabon, Central African Republic, Chad and Cameroon, issues a common currency for the member states from a common central bank. The monetary unit, the African Financial Community franc, is tied to and supported by the French franc.

In 1960, an attempt was made to form a union of the newly independent republics of Chad, Congo, Central Africa and Gabon. The proposal was discarded when Chad refused to become a constituent member. The four countries then linked into an Equatorial Customs Unit, to which Cameroon became an associate member in 1961. A more extensive cooperation of the five republics, identified as the Central African Customs and Economic Union, was entered into force at the beginning of 1966.

In 1974 the Central Bank of the Equatorial African States, which had issued coins and paper currency in its own name and with the names of the constituent member nations, changed its name to the Bank of the Central African States. Equatorial Guinea converted to the CFA currency system issuing its first 100 Franc in 1985.

For earlier coinage see French Equatorial Africa.

Country Code Letters

To observe the movement of coinage throughout the states, the country of origin in which the coin is intended to circulate is designated by the following additional code letters:

A = Chad
B = Central African Republic
C = Congo
D = Gabon
E = Cameroon

By 1992 this practice was discontinued as the strategy had proved to be inconclusive.

MONETARY UNION

STANDARD COINAGE

KM# 8 FRANC

1.30 g., Aluminum, 23 mm. **Obv:** Three giant eland left, date below **Rev:** Denomination within wreath

Date	Mintage	VF20	XF40	MS60	MS63	MS65
1974	3,000,000	0.60	1.00	1.25	2.50	—
1976	4,000,000	0.60	1.00	1.25	2.50	—
1978	1,100,000	0.40	0.80	1.00	2.00	—
1979	250,000	0.40	0.80	1.00	2.00	—
1982	400,000	0.40	0.80	1.00	2.00	—
1985	300,000	0.40	0.80	1.00	2.00	—
1986	300,000	0.40	0.80	1.00	2.00	—
1988	100,000	0.40	0.80	1.00	2.00	—
1990	900,000	0.40	0.80	1.00	2.00	—
1992	300,000	0.40	0.80	1.00	2.00	—
1998 (a)	10,000,000	0.40	0.80	1.00	2.00	—

KM# 7 5 FRANCS

3.00 g., Aluminum-Bronze, 20 mm. **Obv:** Three giant eland left, date below **Rev:** Denomination within wreath

Date	Mintage	VF20	XF40	MS60	MS63	MS65
1973	26,000,000	0.30	0.60	0.85	1.65	2.50
1975	—	0.30	0.60	0.85	1.65	2.50
1976	—	0.30	0.60	0.85	1.65	2.50
1977	—	0.30	0.60	0.85	1.65	2.50
1978	—	0.30	0.60	0.85	1.65	2.50
1979	—	0.30	0.60	0.85	1.65	2.50
1980	—	0.30	0.60	0.75	1.35	2.50
1981	—	0.30	0.60	0.75	1.35	2.50
1982	—	0.30	0.60	0.75	1.35	2.50
1983	—	0.30	0.60	0.75	1.35	2.50
1984	—	0.30	0.60	0.75	1.35	2.50
1985	—	0.30	0.60	0.75	1.35	2.50
1992	—	0.30	0.60	0.75	1.35	2.50
1996 (a)	—	0.30	0.60	0.75	1.25	2.50
1998 (a)	—	0.30	0.60	0.75	1.25	2.50

KM# 9 10 FRANCS

4.00 g., Aluminum-Bronze, 23 mm. **Obv:** Three giant eland left, date below **Rev:** Denomination within wreath

Date	Mintage	VF20	XF40	MS60	MS63	MS65
1974	18,500,000	0.35	0.75	1.00	2.00	3.00
1975	—	0.35	0.75	1.00	2.00	3.00
1976	—	0.35	0.75	1.00	2.00	3.00
1977	—	0.35	0.75	1.00	2.00	3.00
1978	—	0.35	0.75	1.00	2.00	3.00
1979	—	0.35	0.75	1.00	2.00	3.00
1980	—	0.35	0.65	0.75	1.35	2.75
1981	—	0.35	0.65	0.75	1.35	2.75
1982	—	0.35	0.65	0.75	1.35	2.75
1983	—	0.35	0.65	0.75	1.35	2.75
1984	—	0.35	0.65	0.75	1.35	2.75
1985	—	0.35	0.65	0.75	1.35	2.75
1992	—	0.35	0.65	0.75	1.35	2.75
1996	—	0.35	0.65	0.85	1.65	3.00
1998 (a)	—	0.35	0.75	1.00	1.50	3.00

KM# 10 25 FRANCS

8.00 g., Aluminum-Bronze, 27.2 mm. **Obv:** Three giant eland left, date below **Rev:** Denomination within wreath

Date	Mintage	VF20	XF40	MS60	MS63	MS65
1975 (a)	—	1.00	1.75	2.25	3.00	5.00
1976 (a)	—	1.00	1.50	2.00	2.75	5.00
1978 (a)	—	1.00	1.50	2.00	2.75	5.00
1982 (a)	—	0.75	1.25	1.75	2.50	5.00
1983 (a)	—	0.75	1.25	1.75	2.50	5.00
1984 (a)	—	0.75	1.25	1.75	2.50	5.00
1985 (a)	—	0.75	1.25	1.75	2.50	5.00
1986 (a)	—	0.75	1.25	1.75	2.50	5.00
1988 (a)	—	0.75	1.25	1.75	2.50	5.00
1990 (a)	—	0.75	1.25	1.75	2.50	5.00
1991 (a)	—	0.75	1.25	1.75	2.50	5.00
1992 (a)	—	0.75	1.25	1.75	2.50	5.00
1996 (a)	—	0.75	1.25	1.75	2.50	5.00
1998 (a)	—	0.50	1.00	1.50	2.00	5.00

KM# 11 50 FRANCS

4.70 g., Nickel, 21.5 mm. **Obv:** Three giant eland left, date below **Rev:** Denomination within flower design **Edge:** Reeded **Note:** Starting in 1996 an extra flora item was added where the mintmark was formerly located.

Date	Mintage	VF20	XF40	MS60	MS63	MS65
1976 (a) A	10,000,000	2.00	3.00	5.00	7.00	13.50
1976 (a) B	Inc. above	2.00	3.00	5.00	7.00	13.50
1976 (a) C	Inc. above	2.00	3.00	5.00	7.00	13.50
1976 (a) D	Inc. above	2.00	3.00	5.00	7.00	13.50
1976 (a) E	Inc. above	2.00	3.00	5.00	7.00	13.50
1977 (a) A	—	1.25	2.50	4.00	6.00	10.50
1977 (a) B	—	1.25	2.50	4.00	6.00	10.50
1977 (a) C	—	1.00	2.00	3.00	5.00	8.50
1977 (a) D	—	1.00	2.00	3.00	5.00	8.50
1977 (a) E	—	1.00	2.00	3.00	5.00	8.50
1978 (a) A	—	1.25	2.50	4.00	6.00	10.50
1978 (a) B	—	1.25	2.50	4.00	6.00	10.50
1978 (a) C	—	1.00	2.00	3.00	5.00	8.50
1978 (a) D	—	1.00	2.00	3.00	5.00	8.50
1979 (a) E	—	1.00	2.00	3.00	5.00	8.50
1979 (a) B	—	1.00	2.00	3.00	5.00	8.50
1980 (a) A	—	1.25	2.50	4.00	6.00	10.00
1980 (a) C	—	1.00	2.00	3.00	5.00	7.50
1981 (a) C	—	1.00	2.00	3.00	5.00	7.50
1981 (a) D	—	1.00	2.00	3.00	5.00	7.50
1982 (a) A	—	1.25	2.50	4.00	6.00	10.00
1983 (a) B	—	1.00	2.00	3.00	5.00	7.50
1983 (a) D	—	1.00	2.00	3.00	5.00	7.50
1983 (a) E	—	1.00	2.00	3.00	5.00	7.50
1984 (a) A	—	1.25	2.50	4.00	6.00	10.00
1984 (a) B	—	1.25	2.50	4.00	6.00	10.00
1984 (a) C	—	1.00	2.00	3.00	5.00	7.50
1984 (a) D	—	1.00	2.00	3.00	5.00	7.50
1985 (a) A	—	1.25	2.50	4.00	6.00	10.00
1985 (a) B	—	1.25	2.50	4.00	6.00	10.00
1985 (a) D	—	1.00	2.00	3.00	5.00	7.50
1986 (a) B	—	1.25	2.50	4.00	6.00	10.00
1986 C	—	1.25	2.50	4.00	6.00	10.00
1986 (a) E	—	1.00	2.00	3.00	5.00	7.50
1988 (a) B	—	1.25	2.50	4.00	6.00	10.00
1989 (a) A	—	1.25	2.50	4.00	6.00	10.00
1990 A	—	1.25	2.50	4.00	6.00	10.00
1990 (a) B	—	1.25	2.50	4.00	6.00	10.00
1991 (a) A	—	1.25	2.50	4.00	6.00	10.00
1996 (a) Cocoa bean	—	1.00	2.00	3.00	5.00	7.50
1998 (a) Cocoa bean	—	1.00	2.00	3.00	5.00	7.50

KM# 13 100 FRANCS

7.05 g., Nickel, 25.5 mm. **Obv:** Three giant eland **Rev:** Denomination

Date	Mintage	VF20	XF40	MS60	MS63	MS65
1992 (a)	—	—	—	2.00	4.50	6.00
1996 (a)	—	—	—	2.00	4.50	6.00
1998 (a)	—	—	—	2.00	4.50	6.00

KM# 12 500 FRANCS

9.00 g., Nickel, 28 mm. **Obv:** Half figure of woman within circle, date lower right **Rev:** Eland head left divides denomination above

Date	Mintage	VF20	XF40	MS60	MS63	MS65
1976 A	4,000,000	3.00	5.00	7.00	12.00	18.00
1976 B	Inc. above	3.00	5.00	7.00	12.00	18.00
1976 C	Inc. above	2.50	4.00	6.00	10.00	18.00
1976 D	Inc. above	2.50	4.00	6.00	10.00	18.00
1976 E	Inc. above	2.50	4.00	6.00	10.00	18.00
1977 A	—	3.00	6.00	9.00	15.00	22.00
1977 B	—	3.00	6.00	9.00	15.00	22.00
1977 C	—	3.00	6.00	9.00	15.00	22.00
1977 D	—	2.50	4.00	6.00	10.00	18.00
1977 E	—	1.50	2.50	4.00	6.50	14.00
1979 D	—	2.00	3.00	4.50	7.50	15.00
1979 (a) B	—	2.00	3.00	4.50	7.50	15.00
1979 (a) E	—	2.00	3.00	4.50	7.50	15.00
1982 D	—	2.00	3.00	4.50	7.50	15.00
1984 A	—	2.00	3.00	4.50	7.50	15.00
1984 B	—	2.00	3.00	4.50	7.50	15.00
1984 C	—	2.00	3.00	4.50	7.50	15.00
1984 D	—	2.00	3.00	4.50	7.50	15.00
1984 E	—	2.00	3.00	4.50	7.50	15.00

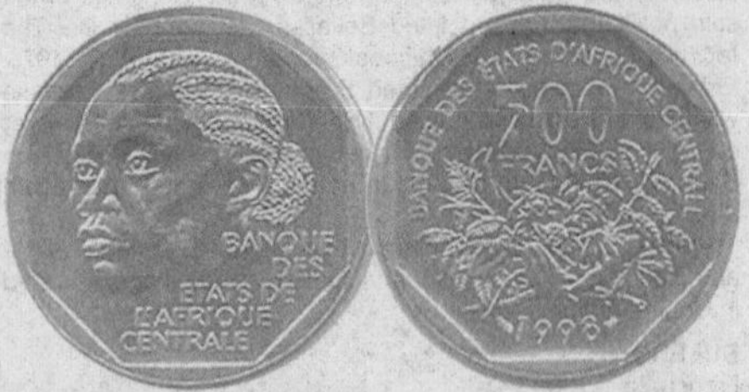

KM# 14 500 FRANCS

11.00 g., Copper-Nickel, 30 mm. **Obv:** Native woman's head half left **Rev:** Plant divides denomination and date **Edge:** Plain

Date	Mintage	VF20	XF40	MS60	MS63	MS65
1998 (a)	—	—	5.00	10.00	17.00	28.00

ESSAIS

Standard metals unless otherwise noted

KM#	Date	Mintage	Identification	Mkt Val
E1	1973	1,550	5 Francs. Aluminum-Bronze. KM7.	22.00
E2	1974	1,550	Franc. Aluminum. KM8.	20.00
E3	1974	1,550	10 Francs. Aluminum-Bronze. KM9.	20.00
EA4	1975	—	10 Francs. Aluminum-Bronze. KM9.	20.00
E4	1975	1,700	25 Francs. Aluminum-Bronze. KM10.	20.00
E5	1976	—	Franc. KM6.	20.00
E6	1976	—	5 Francs. Aluminum-Bronze. KM7.	20.00
E7	1976	—	10 Francs. Aluminum-Bronze. KM9.	22.00
E8	1976	—	50 Francs. Nickel. KM11.	45.00
Note: Essais exist with each letter - A, B, C, D and E				
E9	1976(a)	—	500 Francs. Nickel. KM12.	75.00
Note: Essais exist with each letter - A, B, C, D and E				
E10	1979	—	10 Francs. Aluminum-Bronze. KM9.	25.00
E11	1983	—	10 Francs. Aluminum-Bronze. KM9.	25.00
Note: Essais exist with each letter - A, B, C, D and E				

PATTERNS

Including off metal strikes

KM#	Date	Mintage	Identification	Mkt Val
Pn1	1956	33	40 Francs. Aluminum-Bronze.	1,000
Pn2	1956	33	40 Francs. Aluminum-Bronze.	1,000
Pn3	1956	33	40 Francs. Aluminum-Bronze.	1,000
Pn4	1956	33	40 Francs. Aluminum-Bronze.	1,000
Pn5	1956	33	40 Francs. Aluminum-Bronze.	1,000
Pn6	1956	33	40 Francs. Aluminum-Bronze.	1,000

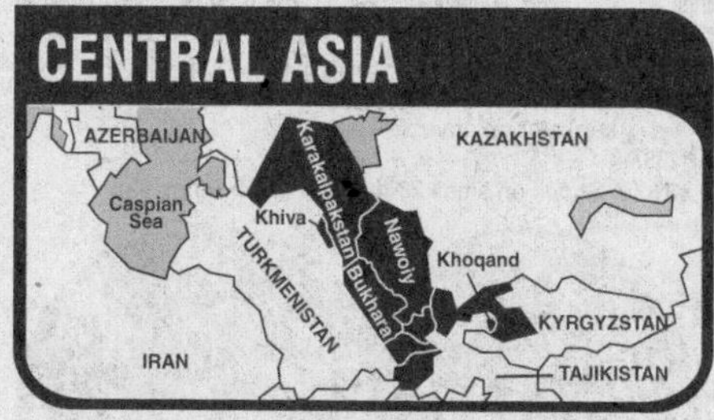

In the several centuries prior to 1500 which witnessed the breakup of the Mongol Empire and the subsequent rise of smaller successor states, no single power or dynasty was able to control the vast expanses of Western and Central Asia. The region known previously as Transoxiana, the land beyond the Oxus River (modern Amu Darya), became the domain of the Shaybanids, then the Janids. The territory ruled by these dynasties had no set borders, which rather expanded and contracted as the fortunes of the rulers ebbed and flowed. At their greatest extent, the khanate took in parts of what are now northern Iran and Afghanistan, as well as part or all of modern Turkmenistan, Uzbekistan, Kazakhstan, Tadzhikistan and Kyrgyzstan. Coins are known to have been struck by virtually every ruler, but some are quite scarce owing to short reigns or the ever-changing political and economic situation.

MINTS

Abivard

Akhshi/Akhshikath

اندجان اندگان

Andigan/Andijan

اسفراين

Asfarayin/Isfarayin

استراباد

Astarabad

اوبه

Awbah

بدخشان

Badakhshan

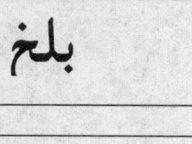

بلخ

Balkh

Bistam

بخارا

Bukhara

Damghan

هراة هرات

Herat

حصر

Hisar

Karmin

Kish

كوفن كوفين

Kufan/Kufin

Langar

ماروار

Marw

مشهد

Mashhad

Nasaf

نمرز نيمروز

Nimruz

نسا

Nisa

قرشى

Qarshi (copper only)

Qayin

قندوز

Qunduz

سبزوار

Sabzavar

سمرقند

Samarqand

تشكند

Tashkand (Tashkent)

ترمذ

Termez

Tun

Turbat

اردو

Urdu (camp mint)

Yazur

BUKHARA

Bukhara, a city and former emirate in southern Russian Turkestan, formed part (Sogdiana) of the Seleucid Empire after the conquest of Alexander the Great and incessantly remained an important region throughout the middle ages, often serving as the capital center for a succession of ruling dynasties of Iranian and Turkish origin until the 19th century. It became virtually a Russian vassal in1868 as a consequence of the Czarist invasion of 1866,following which it gradually became a part of Russian Turkestan and then part of Uzbekistan S.S.R., now Uzbekistan.

RULERS

Russian Vassal,
(since AH1284/1868AD)
Emir Abd al-Ahad,
AH1303-1328 / 1886-1910AD
Emir Sayyid Alim Khan,
AH1329-1339 / 1911-1920AD

MINT NAME

بخارا — Bukhara

بخاراي شريف — Bukhara-yi Sharif

MONETARY SYSTEM

Until AH1322/1905AD: 45 to 64 Pul (Fulus) = 4 Miri = 1 silver Tenga
19 to 21 Tenga = 1 Tilla (gold 4.55 g.)
Until AH1336-1338/1918-1920AD: copper Tenga or Tenga-fulus

Within the protectorate period, Russian currency of Roubles and Kopeks were officially in circulation: 1 silver Tenga = 20 Kopeks

Note: All copper, bronze and brass issues of Bukhara in the 20th century are anonymous. Some silver and gold issues traditionally bear the names of Emirs long since deceased.

Note: Denominations of 1/32 Tenga & Tilla are of very similar design under various rulers, but can be distinguished by date.

Note: Tilla coins are known with a date appearing as "134-", which is actually 1316 with the "1" and "6" stuck close together, appearing as a Persian "4".

Note: Most copper, bronze and brass AH1336-1338 dated coins of 2, 3, 10 and especially 20 Tenga exhibit considerable flat spots, die shifts and other defects. Well-struck specimens with fully struck design demand a considerable premium.

Note: The numerals "0" and "5" have variant forms in Bukhara, including an open 'J' – type symbol for "5" instead of a closed symbol:

0 ٥ and ٠

5 ل or ل instead of ٥ ٥

KHANATE

Muzaffar al-Din
AH1277-1303/1860-1886

HAMMERED COINAGE

KM# 70 TENGA

Silver, 11-18 mm. **Rev:** Mint and date **Note:** Varieties exist. Weight varies 3.06-3.25 grams; Size varies. Die varieties exist with and without date on reverse. Struck in the name of late Emir Haydar. Prev. KM#63.

Date	Mintage	G4	VG8	F12	VF20	XF40
AH1322	—	—	7.50	15.00	27.50	45.00

Note: Doubled flan errors dated AH1322/1322 consisting of two strikes forged together exist, weighing approximately 6.25 grams

Abd Al-Ahad
AH1303-1329/1886-1910AD

KM# 67.2 PUL (Fulus)

Copper **Obv:** Inscription and date **Obv. Inscription:** Bukhara **Rev:** Denomination and date

Date	Mintage	G4	VG8	F12	VF20	XF40
AH1319	—	—	—	—	—	—

KM# 86 1/32 TENGA (2 Fulus)

Copper **Obv:** Inscription and date **Obv. Inscription:** Fulus Bukhara **Rev:** "32" in 6-petal ornate cartouche **Note:** Varieties exist on round or irregular flans. Size varies 14-17 mm. Large "32" above Fulus indicates the denomination (1/32 Tenga). Prev. #Y4.1.

Date	Mintage	G4	VG8	F12	VF20	XF40
AH1322	—	—	5.00	8.50	16.50	25.00
AH1323	—	—	4.00	7.00	12.00	20.00
Note: Coins exist with denomination error "23"						
AH1324	—	—	4.00	7.00	12.00	20.00
AH1327	—	—	6.00	10.00	18.00	30.00
AH1328	—	—	6.00	10.00	18.00	30.00

KM# 87 1/32 TENGA (2 Fulus)

Copper **Obv:** Inscription and date **Obv. Inscription:** zarb Bukhara-yi sharif **Rev:** Inscription and date **Rev. Inscription:** Fulus 32 **Note:** Large "32" above Fulus indicates the denomination (1/32 Tenga). Varieties exist. Prev. Y#1.

Date	Mintage	G4	VG8	F12	VF20	XF40
AH1322	—	10.00	15.00	20.00	30.00	40.00
AH1324	—	10.00	15.00	20.00	30.00	40.00

KM# 75 TENGA

Silver **Rev:** Mint and date **Note:** Prev. KM#63.

Date	Mintage	G4	VG8	F12	VF20	XF40
AH1319//1308	—	—	30.00	50.00	75.00	100
AH1319//1311	—	—	30.00	50.00	75.00	100
AH1319 Recut 1311	—	—	12.00	20.00	35.00	60.00
AH1319	—	—	10.00	15.00	25.00	60.00
AH1320//1320	—	—	17.50	30.00	50.00	80.00
AH1320//1319	—	—	12.00	20.00	35.00	60.00
AH1321//1320	—	—	12.00	20.00	35.00	60.00
1321 recut from 1320						
AH1322	—	—	8.00	15.00	27.50	45.00
Note: Doubled flan errors dated AH1322/1322 consisting of two strikes forged together exist, weighing approximately 6.25 grams						

KM# 65 TILLA

4.55 g., Gold **Note:** Struck in the name of late Ma'sum Ghazi (Emir Shah Murad). Die varieties exist with and without date on reverse. Prev. #Y3.

Date	Mintage	G4	VG8	F12	VF20	XF40
AH1319	—	—	185	190	225	300
AH1321	—	—	200	260	385	575
AH1322//1322	—	—	185	190	225	300
AH1324/1324	—	—	185	190	225	300
AH1324//1316	—	—	200	260	385	575
AH1324//1321	—	—	200	260	385	575
AH1325//1325	—	—	185	190	225	300
AH1325//1325	—	—	190	240	360	525
Note: Reverse date recut from 1324						
AH1327	—	—	185	210	310	500
AH1328	—	—	185	210	310	500
AH1328//1292	—	—	275	385	535	825
AH1328//1304	—	—	200	260	385	575
AH1328//1321	—	—	275	385	535	825

Alim Khan
AH1329-1339/1910-1920AD

KM# A63 1/32 TENGA (2 Fulus)

Copper **Obv. Inscription:** Fulus Bukhara **Rev:** "32" in a 6-petal ornate cartouche **Note:** Size varies 12-14 mm. Similar to KM#86. "32" indicates denomination (1/32 Tenga). Numerous die varieties exist including placement of date for 1332 with date inside or below Fulus.

Date	Mintage	G4	VG8	F12	VF20	XF40
AH1329	—	—	6.00	12.00	20.00	35.00
AH1330	—	—	4.00	7.00	15.00	22.50
Note: Date appearing as "1335" is actually "1330" with small circle instead of dot for zero						
AH1331	—	—	5.00	8.50	16.50	25.00
AH1332	—	—	4.00	7.00	15.00	22.50
AH1333	—	—	6.00	12.00	20.00	35.00
Note: Exists with denomination errors 21, 201, 22, 31, etc.						
AH13-33	—	—	8.00	15.00	25.00	40.00
Divided date						
ND (1914)	—	—	12.50	25.00	40.00	75.00

KM# 42 2 FULUS

Copper **Obv:** Inscription and date **Obv. Inscription:** Fulus Bukhara **Rev:** "2" in 6-petal ornate cartouche **Note:** Many varieties exist, including placement of date for 1332 and 1333 with date inside or below Fulu. Size varies: 11-14mm. Prev. #Y4.

Date	Mintage	G4	VG8	F12	VF20	XF40
AH1330	—	—	15.00	27.50	45.00	70.00
AH1332	—	—	7.50	14.00	22.50	35.00
Note: This date exists with denomination error "6" and with "2" engraved above "32"						
AH1333	—	—	15.00	20.00	45.00	70.00
AH13-33	—	—	20.00	35.00	50.00	75.00
Divided date						
ND (1914)	—	—	20.00	35.00	50.00	75.00
Note: With 2 above crescent in circle resembling an Arabic "4"						

KM# 44 4 FULUS

Copper **Obv:** Sanah and date, inscription below **Obv. Inscription:** Bukhara **Rev. Inscription:** Chahar Fulus **Note:** Size varies: 14-16 mm. Die varieties exist. Prev. #Y5.

Date	Mintage	G4	VG8	F12	VF20	XF40
AH1334	—	—	5.00	8.50	16.50	25.00
AH1335	—	—	30.00	50.00	80.00	125

KM# 45 8 FULUS

Copper **Obv:** Inscription, date below double line **Obv. Inscription:** Bukhara **Rev. Inscription:** Hasht Fulus **Note:** Size varies: 15-18mm. Die varieties exist. Prev. #YA5.

Date	Mintage	G4	VG8	F12	VF20	XF40
AH1335	—	—	5.00	8.50	16.50	25.00

KM# A6 1/2 TENGA

Copper, 14 mm. **Obv. Inscription:** Inscription and date in hextagonal frame **Rev:** zarb Buhkhara **Rev. Inscription:** fulus nim tangah **Note:** Prev. #Y6.

Date	Mintage	G4	VG8	F12	VF20	XF40
AH1336	—	—	15.00	30.00	50.00	100

KM# 46.1 TENGA

Copper **Obv:** Inscription and date in dotted circle **Obv. Inscription:** zarb Bukhara **Rev. Inscription:** fulus yak tangah **Note:** Size varies 13-16mm. Small round or irregular flans, no border. Die varieties exist.

Date	Mintage	G4	VG8	F12	VF20	XF40
AH1336	—	—	20.00	35.00	55.00	80.00

KM# 46.2 TENGA

Copper **Obv:** Inscription and date in beaded circle **Obv. Inscription:** zarb Bukhara **Rev. Inscription:** fulus yak tangah **Note:** Size varies 17-20mm. Large round or irregular flans, irregular flans are scarcer than round flans. Many varieties exist. Prev. #Y6a.

Date	Mintage	G4	VG8	F12	VF20	XF40
AH1336	—	—	6.00	12.00	20.00	35.00
AH1337	—	—	6.00	12.00	20.00	35.00
Note: This date exists with 5-rayed (outlined and full), and 6-rayed (outlined) star on obverse						
(1918)	—	—	10.00	17.50	30.00	50.00
Note: Overstruck on 4 or 8 Fulus, KM#44 and 45						
AH1337	—	—	10.00	17.50	30.00	50.00
Note: Overstruck on 8 Fulus KM#45						
AH1338	—	—	75.00	100	135	185

KM# 47 2 TENGA

Bronze **Obv:** Inscription and date in dotted circle **Obv. Inscription:** zarb bukhara **Rev. Inscription:** fulus du tangah **Note:** Size varies 22-23mm. Varieties with upright and oblique milled edge exist, both years exist with 5-rayed (outlined and full), and 6-rayed (outlined) star on obverse. Prev. #Y7.

Date	Mintage	G4	VG8	F12	VF20	XF40
AH1336	—	—	6.00	12.00	25.00	55.00
AH1337	—	—	6.00	12.00	25.00	55.00
Note: Also exists without star (rare)						

KM# 48 3 TENGA

Bronze **Obv:** Inscription and date **Obv. Inscription:** zarb Bukhara **Rev. Inscription:** fulus se tangah **Note:** Greek meander circle both sides. Varieties with upright and oblique milled edge exist. Size varies 24-26mm. Prev. #Y8.

Date	Mintage	G4	VG8	F12	VF20	XF40
AH1336	—	—	6.00	12.00	25.00	50.00
AH1337	—	—	6.00	12.00	25.00	50.00
Note: Exists with 5-rayed outlined and full (whole or broken) star on obverse						
AH1337	—	—	—	—	—	—
Note: Struck on small 23 mm and thin 2 Tenga flan						

KM# 49 4 TENGA

Bronze, 30 mm. **Obv:** Inscription and date **Obv. Inscription:** zarb Bukhara **Rev. Inscription:** fulus chahar tangah **Note:** Floral design circle on both sides. Prev. #Y9.

Date	Mintage	G4	VG8	F12	VF20	XF40
AH1336 Rare	—	—	—	—	—	—
Note: This denomination was officially announced for circulation, but its production in quantity was reduced as it was considered excessive and economically senseless						

KM# 50 5 TENGA

Bronze **Obv:** Inscription and date in almond-shaped inner border **Obv. Inscription:** zarb Bukhara **Rev. Inscription:** fulus panj tangah **Note:** Greek meander circle on both sides. Varieties exist with upright and oblique milled edge. Size varies 28-30mm. Prev. #Y10.

Date	Mintage	G4	VG8	F12	VF20	XF40
AH1336	—	—	25.00	40.00	65.00	100
AH1337	—	—	25.00	40.00	65.00	100

KM# 53 10 TENGA
Brass, 29 mm. **Obv:** Inscription and date **Obv. Inscription:** zarb Bukhara **Rev:** Inscription and date **Rev. Inscription:** yakdah tangah **Note:** Square frames on both sides vary in size, varieties exist with upright and oblique milled edge. Reverse date varies in position and arrangement (full or divided dates with different combinations). Prev. #Y11.

Date	Mintage	G4	VG8	F12	VF20	XF40
AH1337//1337	—	—	8.00	15.00	25.00	40.00
Note: With chain border on both sides						
AH1337//1337	—	—	12.50	22.50	40.00	60.00
Note: With branch border (similar to 20 Tenga) on obverse						
AH1337//1338	—	—	10.00	17.50	32.50	50.00
AH1338//1338	—	—	30.00	45.00	80.00	125

KM# 51.1 20 TENGA
Brass or Bronze **Obv:** Inscription and date in crescent, 6-pointed circled star above **Obv. Inscription:** zarb Bukharayi sharif **Rev:** Inscription and date within 6-pointed star **Rev. Inscription:** bist tangah **Note:** Varieties exist with upright and oblique milled edge, obverse date varies in position and arrangement (full or divided dates with different combinations). Prev. KM#51 and #Y12.

Date	Mintage	G4	VG8	F12	VF20	XF40
AH1337	—	—	22.50	35.00	50.00	85.00
Note: Dated on both sides						
AH1337	—	—	27.50	45.00	75.00	110
Note: Dated reverse only						

KM# 51.2 20 TENGA
Brass, 33 mm. **Obv:** Inscription (mintname in error without second alif) and date in crescent, 6-pointed circled star above **Obv. Inscription:** zarb Bukhari sharif **Rev:** Inscription and date within 6-pointed star **Rev. Inscription:** bist tangah

Date	Mintage	G4	VG8	F12	VF20	XF40
AH1337	—	—	40.00	55.00	80.00	120
Note: Dated on both sides						

KM# A65 TILLA
4.55 g., Gold **Note:** Struck in the name of late Ma'sum Ghazi (Emir Shah Murad).

Date	Mintage	G4	VG8	F12	VF20	XF40
AH1329	—	—	155	175	215	325
AH1330	—	—	225	375	525	825
AH1331	—	—	190	275	375	575
AH1335	—	—	190	275	375	575

KHIVA

Khiva (Khwarezm), a present town, but once a great kingdom under the names of Chorasmia, Khwarezm and Urgenj, is located in Central Asia east of the Caspian Sea and south of the Aral Sea. It was the westernmost successor of the former Janid state, now divided between Uzbekistan and Turkmenistan.

Almost all coins bear the mint name Khwarizm (Khorezm), sometimes paired with the epithet dar al-islam. A few have the mint name Khivaq (for Khiva). The gold coins are rare, but generally well-struck, as are the early silver coins, until about AH1280/1863AD. The later silver is often weakly struck, and is usually found worn, as is the copper of all periods.

Russia established relations with Khwarezm (Khiva) in the 17th century, occupied it in AH1290/1873AD, and annexed it in 1875. Revolution concentrated Russia's preoccupation elsewhere during 1917 and Khwarezm (Khiva) seized this opportunity to declare its independence. It was able to sustain this status for a scant two years. By 1919 the Soviet regime had reestablished control over the region and extinguished the independent state. In AH1338/1920AD it became Khwarezm Soviet People's Republic and later became part of the Uzbekistan S.S.R., now Uzbekistan.

RULERS
Sayyid Abdullah Khan and Junaid Khan, AH1337-38/1918-20AD

MINT NAMES

خوارزم

Khwarezm

دار الاسلام خوارزم

Dar al-Islam

Note: All copper, bronze and brass issues of Khiva (Khorezm, Khwarezm) in the 20th century are anonymous, except the silver Tenga Y#8, which bears the name of a Khan, long since deceased.

KHANATE

Sayyid Muhammad Rahim
AH1282-1328 / 1865-1910 AD

HAMMERED COINAGE

Y# 3.1 PUL (Fulus)
Copper **Obv:** Inscription in circle **Obv. Inscription:** Khwarezm **Rev:** Inscription, date appears as "3" above "1" or "2" above "2" **Rev. Inscription:** fulus **Note:** Oblong or irregular flans.

Date	Mintage	G4	VG8	F12	VF20	XF40
AH1322	—	5.00	8.00	20.00	35.00	—
AH1323	—	5.00	8.00	20.00	35.00	—
AH1324	—	5.00	8.00	20.00	35.00	—
AH1325	—	5.00	8.00	20.00	35.00	—
AH1326	—	5.00	8.00	20.00	35.00	—

Isfandiyar
AH1328-1336 / 1910-1918 AD

Y# 3.2 PUL (Fulus)
Copper **Obv:** Inscription in circle **Obv. Inscription:** Khwarezm **Rev:** Inscription, date appears as "3" above "1" or "2" above "2" **Rev. Inscription:** fulus **Note:** Oblong or irregular flans, similar to Y#3.1.

Date	Mintage	G4	VG8	F12	VF20	XF40
AH1328	—	5.00	8.00	20.00	35.00	—
AH1329	—	5.00	8.00	20.00	35.00	—

Sayyid Abdullah and Junaid Khan
AH1337-1338 / 1919-1920 AD

Y# A9.1 TENGA
Copper **Obv:** Inscription and date in dotted or reeded circle **Obv. Inscription:** zarb Khwarezm **Rev:** Rising sun and crescent, inscription below **Rev. Inscription:** fulus bir tangah **Note:** Size varies: 17-19 mm.

Date	Mintage	G4	VG8	F12	VF20	XF40
AH1337	—	—	75.00	120	200	400

Y# A9.2 TENGA
Copper **Obv:** Inscription and date in dotted or reeded circle **Obv. Inscription:** zarb Khwarezm **Rev:** No crescent above rising sun **Rev. Inscription:** fulus bir tangah **Note:** Die varieties exist with different border patterns and date above or below mint name. Crudely struck specimens with Tajik inscription "fulus yak tangah" (instead of the Uzbek "bir tangah") are modern forgeries. Size varies: 17-19mm.

Date	Mintage	G4	VG8	F12	VF20	XF40
AH1337	—	—	60.00	100	150	250

Y# 8 TENGA
2.28 g., Silver **Note:** Struck in the name of Sayyid Muhammad Rahim; die varieties exist.

Date	Mintage	G4	VG8	F12	VF20	XF40
AH1337//1337	—	—	250	400	600	850
Note: The estimated number known to exist does not exceed 20 pieces						

Y# 9.1 2-1/2 TENGA
Copper or Bronze **Obv:** Inscription and date **Obv. Inscription:** zarb Dar al-Islam Khwarezm **Rev:** Rising sun and crescent, inscription below **Rev. Inscription:** fulus iki yarim tangah **Note:** Die varieties exist. Number of sun rays vary from 7 to 13. Date above mint name and strikes with additional date on reverse exist.

Date	Mintage	G4	VG8	F12	VF20	XF40
AH1337	—	—	30.00	45.00	75.00	120

Y# 9.2 2-1/2 TENGA
Brass or Bronze **Obv:** Inscription and date **Obv. Inscription:** zarb Dar al-Islam Khwarezm **Rev:** Full sun and crescent, inscription below **Rev. Inscription:** fulus iki yarim tangah **Note:** Many die varieties exist. Number of sun rays vary from 8 to 18, date above or below mintname. Strikes with additional date on reverse exist. Size varies 20-22mm.

Date	Mintage	G4	VG8	F12	VF20	XF40
AH1337	—	—	30.00	45.00	75.00	120
Note: Rare 1337 strikes over Russian Kopek Y#9.2 are known						

Y# 9.3 2-1/2 TENGA
Brass or Bronze **Obv:** Inscription and date **Obv. Inscription:** zarb Dar al-Islam Khwarezm **Rev:** Full sun and crescent, modified inscription below **Rev. Inscription:** iki yarim tangah fulus **Note:** Many die varieties exist. Number of sun rays vary from 10-13. Size varies 20-22mm.

Date	Mintage	G4	VG8	F12	VF20	XF40
AH1337	—	—	25.00	40.00	70.00	—
Note: Date above or below mint name						

Date	Mintage	G4	VG8	F12	VF20	XF40
AH1338	—	—	150	250	400	—

Note: Date below mint name

Y# 10.1 5 TENGA

Copper or Bronze, 30 mm. **Obv:** Inscription and date **Obv. Inscription:** zarb Dar al-Islam Khwarezm **Rev:** Rising sun and crescent, inscription below **Rev. Inscription:** fulus besh tangah

Date	Mintage	G4	VG8	F12	VF20	XF40
AH1337 Rare	—	—	—	—	—	—

Y# 10.2 5 TENGA

Copper or Bronze **Obv:** Inscription and date **Obv. Inscription:** zarb Dar al-Islam Khwarezm **Rev:** Full sun and crescent, inscription below **Rev. Inscription:** fulus besh tangah **Note:** Many die varieties exist. Number of sun rays vary from 9-20, date above or below mint name. Strikes with additional date on reverse exist. Size varies 29-32mm.

Date	Mintage	G4	VG8	F12	VF20	XF40
AH1337	—	—	25.00	40.00	70.00	125

Y# 10.3 5 TENGA

Brass or Bronze **Obv:** Inscription and date **Obv. Inscription:** zarb Dar al-Islam Khwarezm **Rev:** Full sun and crescent, modified inscription below **Rev. Inscription:** besh tangah fulus **Note:** Many die varieties exist. Number of sun rays vary from 9-18, date appears above or below mint name. Strikes with additional date on reverse exist. Size varies 29-32mm.

Date	Mintage	G4	VG8	F12	VF20	XF40
AH1337	—	—	20.00	35.00	60.00	90.00
Note: Rare 1337 strikes over Russian 3 Kopek Y#11.2 are known						
AH1338	—	—	35.00	55.00	80.00	120

Y# 11.1 15 TENGA

Bronze **Obv:** Inscription and date **Obv. Inscription:** zarb Dar al-Islam Khwarezm **Rev:** Inscription and date in crescent, 6-pointed circled star above **Rev. Inscription:** on besh tangah fulus **Note:** Size varies 28-31mm.

Date	Mintage	G4	VG8	F12	VF20	XF40
AH1338	—	—	120	200	350	600

Note: Struck on flans of 5 Tenga with obverse of 5 Tenga; In an attempt to replace 5 Tenga by 15 Tenga due to inflation, flans of 5 Tenga with obverse dies of 5 Tenga were used first; Confusion due to the similar size led to production and usage of special broader flans (see Y#11.2)

Y# 11.2 15 TENGA

Bronze **Obv. Inscription:** zarb Dar al-Islam Khwarezm **Rev:** Inscription and date in crescent, 6-pointed circled star above **Rev. Inscription:** on besh tangah fulus **Note:** Struck on broad flans. Strikes with or without date above mint name on obverse exist. Die varieties with different rim patterns on reverse exist. Size varies 32-34mm.

Date	Mintage	G4	VG8	F12	VF20	XF40
AH1338	—	—	100	175	250	400

KHOREZM PEOPLE'S SOVIET REPUBLIC

AH1338-1343 / 1920-1924 AD

Y# 15.1 20 ROUBLES

Copper or Bronze **Obv:** Inscription and date, star above, legend around **Obv. Legend:** zarb fulus Khwarezm shuralar qarari ilan **Obv. Inscription:** yigirma manat **Rev:** Divided arms above, inscription (in Russian) below **Note:** Die varieties exist. Both dates have 6 points in obverse star. Size varies 25-26mm.

Date	Mintage	G4	VG8	F12	VF20	XF40
AH1338	—	—	25.00	40.00	70.00	100
AH1339	—	—	40.00	70.00	100	150

Y# 15.2 20 ROUBLES

Copper or Bronze **Obv:** Inscription and date, star above, legend around **Obv. Legend:** zarb fulus Khwarezm shuralar qarari ilan **Obv. Inscription:** yigirma manat **Rev:** Crossed arms above, denomination "20 / RUB" (in Russian) below **Note:** Die varieties exist. Size varies 25-26mm.

Date	Mintage	G4	VG8	F12	VF20	XF40
AH1338	—	—	30.00	50.00	80.00	120
Note: 6 points in obverse star						
AH1339	—	—	20.00	35.00	50.00	80.00
Note: Varieties exist with 6 or 8 points in obverse star, with 8 stars much scarcer						

Y# 16.1 25 ROUBLES

Brass or Bronze **Obv:** Inscription and date above, legend below (starting on the right with "Khwarezm") **Obv. Legend:** zarb fulus Khwarezm shuralar qarari ilan **Obv. Inscription:** yigirma besh manat **Rev:** Arms in center, crescent and star above, denomination "25 RUBLES" (in Russian) around **Note:** Many die varieties exist with different arms design. Varieties exist with 8, 12, 16 or 18 points in reverse star. The strike with inverted "R" has 12 points in star. Size varies 24-26mm.

Date	Mintage	G4	VG8	F12	VF20	XF40
AH1339	—	—	17.50	30.00	40.00	75.00
AH1339	—	—	50.00	70.00	100	175
Note: With inverted Russian "R" in "Rubles"						

Y# 16.2 25 ROUBLES

Brass or Bronze **Obv:** Inscription and date above, legend below (starting on the right with "shuralar") **Obv. Legend:** zarb fulus Khwarezm shuralar qarari ilan **Obv. Inscription:** yigirma besh manat **Rev:** Arms in center, crescent and star above, denomination "25 Rubles" (in Russian) around **Note:** Many die varieties exist with different arms design. Varieties exist with 8, 12, 16 or 18 points in reverse star. The strike with inverted "R" has 12 points in star. Size varies 24-26mm.

Date	Mintage	G4	VG8	F12	VF20	XF40
AH1339	—	—	17.50	25.00	40.00	70.00
AH1339	—	—	50.00	70.00	100	175
Note: With inverted Russian "R" in "Rubles"						

Y# 17 100 ROUBLES

Bronze **Obv:** Crescent and star in center, inscription and date above, legend below **Obv. Legend:** zarb fulus Khwarezm shuralar qarari ilan **Obv. Inscription:** yuz manat **Rev:** Denomination "100 Rubles" (in Russian), arms below **Note:** Die varieties exist. Varieties exist with 6 or 8 points in obverse star. Size varies 20-22.

Date	Mintage	G4	VG8	F12	VF20	XF40
AH1339	—	—	22.50	40.00	60.00	90.00

Y# 18 500 ROUBLES

Bronze, 24 mm. **Obv:** Inscription in center, 12-pointed star and date above, legend around **Obv. Legend:** zarb fulus Khwarezmjumhuriyeti **Obv. Inscription:** 500 / besh yuz manat / 500 **Rev:** Arms with two stars above, "Rubles" (in Russian) / "500" below **Note:** Genuine specimens appear like the pictured coin, no die varieties exist.

Date	Mintage	G4	VG8	F12	VF20	XF40
AH1339	—	—	100	175	250	350

Y# 19.1 500 ROUBLES

Brass or Bronze **Obv:** Inscription (in one word) in center, star and divided date above, legend around **Obv. Legend:** zarb fulus jumhuriyeti Khwarezm **Obv. Inscription:** beshyuz manat **Rev:** Arms with two stars above, "Rubles" (in Russian) / "500" below **Note:** Die varieties exist. Varieties exist with 8 or 17 points in obverse star, the later is much scarcer. Size varies 18-20mm.

Date	Mintage	G4	VG8	F12	VF20	XF40
AH1339	—	—	20.00	35.00	50.00	80.00

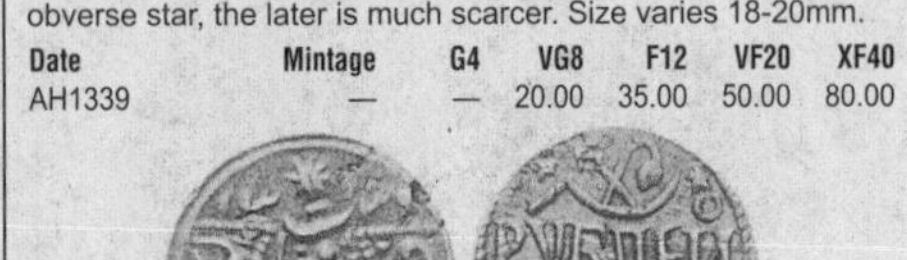

Y# 19.2 500 ROUBLES

Brass or Bronze **Obv:** Inscription (in 2 words) in center, star and divided date above, legend around **Obv. Legend:** zarb fulus jumhuriyeti Khwarezm **Obv. Inscription:** besh yuz manat **Rev:** Arms with two stars above, "Rubles" (in Russian) / "500" below **Note:** Die varieties exist. Two varieties of the arms design exist. Size varies 18-20mm.

Date	Mintage	G4	VG8	F12	VF20	XF40
AH1339	—	—	17.50	25.00	40.00	70.00

Note: Varieties exist with 5, 6, 8, 12 or 16 points in obverse star

Date	Mintage	G4	VG8	F12	VF20	XF40
AH1340	—	—	22.50	40.00	60.00	90.00

Note: Varieties exist with 5 or 6 points in obverse star

CEYLON

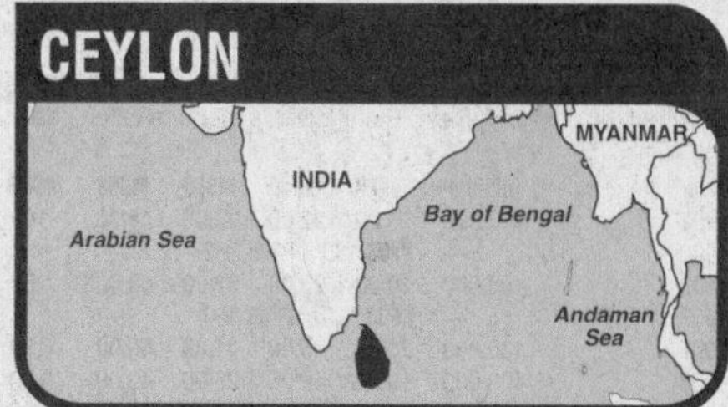

The earliest known inhabitants of Ceylon, the Veddahs, were subjugated by the Sinhalese from northern India in the 6th century B.C. Sinhalese rule was maintained until 1408, after which the island was controlled by China for 30 years. The Portuguese came to Ceylon in 1505 and maintained control of the coastal area for 150 years. The Dutch supplanted them in 1658, which were in turn supplanted by the British who seized the Dutch colonies in 1796, and made them a Crown Colony in 1802. In 1815, the British conquered the independent Kingdom of Kandy in the central part of the island. Constitutional changes in 1931 and 1946 granted the Ceylonese a measure of autonomy and a parliamentary form of government. Britain granted Ceylon independence as a self-governing state within the British Commonwealth on Feb. 4, 1948. On May 22, 1972, the Ceylonese adopted a new Constitution, which declared Ceylon to be the Republic of Sri Lanka –'Resplendent Island'

RULER

British, 1796-1948

BRITISH COLONY

DECIMAL COINAGE

100 Cents = 1 Rupee

KM# 90 1/4 CENT

1.18 g., Copper **Ruler:** Victoria **Obv:** Head left within circle **Obv. Legend:** QUEEN VICTORIA **Rev:** Tree within circle

Date	Mintage	F12	VF20	XF40	MS60	MS63
1901	216,000	1.75	4.00	10.00	14.00	22.00
1901	—	PF63 180	PF65 360			

KM# 100 1/4 CENT

1.18 g., Copper **Ruler:** Edward VII **Obv:** Crowned bust right **Rev:** Tree within circle, date below, denomination above

Date	Mintage	VF20	XF40	MS60	MS63	MS65
1904	103,000	5.00	12.00	20.00	35.00	—
1904	—	PF63 150	PF65 300			

KM# 100a 1/4 CENT

Gold **Ruler:** Edward VII **Obv:** Crowned bust right **Rev:** Tree within circle, date below, denomination above

Date	Mintage	VF20	XF40	MS60	MS63	MS65
1904	—	PF63 1,150	PF65 2,250			

KM# 91 1/2 CENT

2.35 g., Copper, 18.3 mm. **Ruler:** Victoria **Obv:** Head left within circle **Obv. Legend:** QUEEN VICTORIA **Rev:** Tree within circle

Date	Mintage	F12	VF20	XF40	MS60	MS63
1901	2,020,000	1.50	2.00	4.00	6.00	12.00

KM# 101 1/2 CENT

2.35 g., Copper **Ruler:** Edward VII **Obv:** Crowned bust right **Rev:** Tree within circle, date below, denomination above

Date	Mintage	VF20	XF40	MS60	MS63	MS65
1904	2,012,000	2.00	4.00	6.00	12.00	—
1904	—	PF63 120	PF65 240			
1905	1,000,000	3.00	5.00	7.00	15.00	—
1905	—	PF63 120	PF65 240			
1906	3,056,000	2.00	4.00	6.00	12.00	—
1906	—	PF63 120	PF65 240			
1908	1,000,000	3.00	5.00	7.00	15.00	—
1908	—	PF63 200	PF65 400			
1909	3,000,000	2.00	4.00	6.00	12.00	—
1909	—	PF63 120	PF65 240			

KM# 106 1/2 CENT

2.35 g., Copper, 18.2 mm. **Ruler:** George V **Obv:** Crowned bust left **Rev:** Tree within circle, date below, denomination above

Date	Mintage	VF20	XF40	MS60	MS63	MS65
1912	5,008,000	2.50	3.50	5.00	10.00	—
1912	—	PF63 120	PF65 240			
1914	2,000,000	2.75	5.00	7.00	12.00	—
1914	—	PF63 120	PF65 240			
1917	2,000,000	3.00	5.00	7.00	12.00	—
1917	—	PF63 120	PF65 240			
1926	5,000,000	1.00	2.00	3.00	5.00	10.00
1926	—	PF63 120	PF65 240			

KM# 110 1/2 CENT

2.35 g., Copper **Ruler:** George VI **Obv:** Crowned head left **Rev:** Tree within circle, date below, denomination above

Date	Mintage	VF20	XF40	MS60	MS63	MS65
1937	3,026,000	0.85	1.50	2.50	4.00	8.00
1937	—	PF63 175	PF65 350			
1940	5,080,000	0.65	1.25	2.00	3.50	7.50

KM# 92 CENT

4.72 g., Copper, 22.5 mm. **Ruler:** Victoria **Obv:** Head left within circle **Obv. Legend:** QUEEN VICTORIA **Rev:** Tree within circle

Date	Mintage	F12	VF20	XF40	MS60	MS63
1901	1,014,000	3.00	6.00	10.00	14.00	28.00

KM# 102 CENT

4.72 g., Copper **Ruler:** Edward VII **Obv:** Crowned bust right **Rev:** Tree within circle, date below, denomination above

Date	Mintage	VF20	XF40	MS60	MS63	MS65
1904	2,529,000	2.00	3.00	5.00	10.00	—
1904	—	PF63 125	PF65 250			
1905	1,509,000	2.00	3.00	5.00	15.00	—
1905	—	PF63 125	PF65 250			
1906	1,751,000	2.00	3.00	5.00	15.00	—
1906	—	PF63 125	PF65 250			
1908	—	1.50	2.50	4.00	10.00	—
1908	—	PF63 225	PF65 450			
1909	2,500,000	1.50	2.50	4.00	10.00	—
1909	—	PF63 125	PF65 250			
1910	8,236,000	1.00	2.00	3.00	10.00	—
1910	—	PF63 125	PF65 250			

KM# 107 CENT

4.72 g., Copper, 22.4 mm. **Ruler:** George V **Obv:** Crowned bust left **Rev:** Tree within circle, date below, denomination above

Date	Mintage	VF20	XF40	MS60	MS63	MS65
1912	5,855,000	0.75	1.25	3.00	9.00	25.00
1912	—	PF63 115	PF65 230			
1914	6,000,000	1.00	1.75	3.00	9.00	25.00
1914	—	PF63 115	PF65 230			
1917	1,000,000	1.75	2.25	7.00	15.00	25.00
1917	—	PF63 115	PF65 230			
1920	2,000,000	1.00	1.75	3.00	9.00	25.00
1920	—	PF63 115	PF65 230			
1922	2,930,000	1.00	1.75	3.00	9.00	25.00
1922	—	PF63 115	PF65 230			
1923	2,500,000	1.00	1.75	3.00	9.00	25.00
1923	—	PF63 115	PF65 230			
1925	7,490,000	0.75	1.00	1.50	5.00	20.00
1925	—	PF63 115	PF65 230			
1926	3,750,000	0.75	1.00	1.50	5.00	20.00
1926	—	PF63 115	PF65 230			
1928	2,500,000	0.75	1.00	1.50	5.00	20.00
1928	—	PF63 115	PF65 230			
1929	5,000,000	0.75	1.00	1.50	5.00	20.00
1929	—	PF63 115	PF65 230			

KM# 111 CENT

4.72 g., Copper, 22 mm. **Ruler:** George VI **Obv:** Crowned head left, PM below neck at right **Rev:** Tree within circle, date below, denomination above **Note:** High relief. Thickness: 1.73mm.

Date	Mintage	VF20	XF40	MS60	MS63	MS65
1937	4,538,000	0.50	0.75	1.25	3.00	10.00
1937	—	PF63 100	PF65 200			
1940	10,190,000	0.30	0.50	1.00	2.00	10.00
1940	—	PF63 75.00	PF65 150			
1942	20,780,000	0.30	0.50	1.00	2.00	10.00

KM# 111a CENT

2.35 g., Bronze, 22.35 mm. **Ruler:** George VI **Obv:** Crowned head left **Rev:** Tree within circle, date below, denomination above **Note:** Low relief. Thin planchet, .87mm.

Date	Mintage	VF20	XF40	MS60	MS63	MS65
1942	Inc. above	0.30	0.50	0.75	1.50	3.00
1942	—	PF63 75.00	PF65 150			
1943	43,705,000	0.30	0.50	0.75	1.25	3.00
1945	34,100,000	0.30	0.50	0.75	1.25	3.00
1945	—	PF60 20.00	PF63 50.00	PF65 100		

Note: Frozen year 1945, restruck until 1962

KM# 117 2 CENTS

2.59 g., Nickel-Brass, 18 mm. **Ruler:** George VI **Obv:** Crowned head left **Rev:** Denomination above date **Shape:** Scalloped

Date	Mintage	VF20	XF40	MS60	MS63	MS65
1944	30,165,000	0.25	0.35	0.60	1.25	3.00

KM# 119 2 CENTS

2.59 g., Nickel-Brass, 18 mm. **Ruler:** George VI **Obv:** Crowned head left, legend without EMPEROR OF INDIA **Rev:** Denomination above date **Shape:** Scalloped

Date	Mintage	VF20	XF40	MS60	MS63	MS65
1951	15,000,000	0.25	0.50	0.75	1.75	3.00
1951	150	PF63 50.00	PF65 100			

KM# 124 2 CENTS

2.59 g., Nickel-Brass, 18 mm. **Ruler:** Elizabeth II **Obv:** Laureate bust right **Rev:** Denomination above date **Shape:** Scalloped

Date	Mintage	VF20	XF40	MS60	MS63	MS65
1955	37,131,000	0.15	0.25	0.35	0.65	1.00
1957	38,200,000	0.15	0.25	0.35	0.65	1.00
1957	—	PF63 75.00	PF65 150			

KM# 103 5 CENTS
3.89 g., Copper-Nickel, 20 mm. **Ruler:** Edward VII **Obv:** Crowned bust right **Rev:** Denomination above date **Shape:** Square

Date	Mintage	VF20	XF40	MS60	MS63	MS65
1909	2,000,000	2.00	3.00	5.00	10.00	20.00
1910	4,000,000	2.00	3.00	4.00	9.00	20.00

KM# 108 5 CENTS
3.89 g., Copper-Nickel, 18 mm. **Ruler:** George V **Obv:** Crowned bust left **Rev:** Denomination above date **Shape:** 4-sided

Date	Mintage	VF20	XF40	MS60	MS63	MS65
1912 H	4,000,000	1.50	2.00	3.50	9.00	20.00
1920	6,000,000	1.00	1.25	2.50	7.00	20.00
1926	3,000,000	1.50	2.00	4.00	9.00	20.00

KM# 113.1 5 CENTS
3.89 g., Nickel-Brass, 18 mm. **Ruler:** George VI **Obv:** Crowned head left **Rev:** Denomination above date **Shape:** Square

Date	Mintage	VF20	XF40	MS60	MS63	MS65
1942	12,752,000	0.75	1.25	2.00	4.50	15.00
1942	—	PF63 50.00	PF65 100			
1943	Inc. above	0.75	1.25	2.00	4.50	15.00
1943	—	PF63 50.00	PF65 100			

KM# 113.2 5 CENTS
3.24 g., Nickel-Brass, 18 mm. **Ruler:** George VI **Obv:** Crowned head left **Rev:** Denomination above date **Note:** Thin planchet.

Date	Mintage	VF20	XF40	MS60	MS63	MS65
1944	18,064,000	0.35	0.50	1.00	2.00	5.00
1945	31,192,000	0.30	0.50	0.75	1.75	5.00
1945	—	PF60 60.00	PF63 120	PF65 300		

Note: Varieties exist in bust, denomination and legend placement for 1945; The date was frozen at 1945 and these coins were struck until 1962

KM# 120 5 CENTS
3.24 g., Nickel-Brass, 18 mm. **Ruler:** George VI **Obv:** Crowned head left, legend without EMPEROR OF INDIA **Rev:** Denomination above date **Shape:** Square

Date	Mintage	VF20	XF40	MS60	MS63	MS65
1951 Proof, restrike	—	PF60 15.00	PF63 35.00	PF65 75.00		
1951	150	PF60 50.00	PF63 100	PF65 200		

KM# 97 10 CENTS
1.17 g., 0.800 Silver 0.030 oz. ASW **Ruler:** Edward VII **Obv:** Crowned bust right **Rev:** Plant divides denomination above date

Date	Mintage	VF20	XF40	MS60	MS63	MS65
1902	1,000,000	2.00	3.50	7.00	25.00	75.00
1902	—	PF63 180	PF65 360			
1903	1,000,000	2.00	3.50	7.00	25.00	75.00
1903	—	PF63 180	PF65 360			
1907	500,000	6.00	9.00	18.00	30.00	50.00
1908	1,500,000	2.00	3.50	7.00	18.00	35.00
1909	1,000,000	2.00	3.50	7.00	18.00	35.00
1910	2,000,000	2.00	3.50	7.00	18.00	35.00

KM# 104 10 CENTS
1.17 g., 0.800 Silver 0.030 oz. ASW **Ruler:** George V **Obv:** Crowned bust left **Rev:** Plant divides denomination, date below

Date	Mintage	VF20	XF40	MS60	MS63	MS65
1911	1,000,000	2.00	3.00	6.00	14.00	35.00
1912	1,000,000	2.50	4.00	7.00	18.00	35.00
1913	2,000,000	1.75	2.50	5.00	12.00	35.00
1914	2,000,000	1.75	2.50	5.00	12.00	35.00
1914	—	PF63 180	PF65 360			
1917	879,000	3.00	5.00	9.00	20.00	50.00
1917	—	PF63 180	PF65 360			

KM# 104a 10 CENTS
1.17 g., 0.550 Silver 0.0206 oz. ASW, 15.5 mm. **Ruler:** George V **Obv:** Crowned bust left **Rev:** Plant divides denomination, date below

Date	Mintage	VF20	XF40	MS60	MS63	MS65
1919 B	750,000	4.00	6.00	12.00	25.00	75.00
1919 B	—	PF63 180	PF65 360			
1920 B	3,059,000	2.50	4.00	7.00	18.00	50.00
1920 B	—	PF63 180	PF65 360			
1921 B	1,583,000	1.75	3.00	6.00	12.00	35.00
1921	—	PF63 180	PF65 360			
1922	282,000	4.00	6.00	12.00	30.00	50.00
1922	—	PF63 180	PF65 360			
1924	1,508,000	1.75	3.00	5.00	12.00	35.00
1924	—	PF63 180	PF65 360			
1925	1,500,000	1.75	3.00	5.00	12.00	35.00
1925	—	PF63 180	PF65 360			
1926	1,500,000	1.75	3.00	5.00	12.00	35.00
1926	—	PF63 180	PF65 360			
1927	1,500,000	1.75	3.00	5.00	12.00	35.00
1927	—	PF63 180	PF65 360			
1928	1,500,000	1.75	3.00	5.00	12.00	35.00
1928	—	PF63 180	PF65 360			

KM# 112 10 CENTS
1.17 g., 0.800 Silver 0.030 oz. ASW, 15.5 mm. **Ruler:** George VI **Obv:** Crowned head left **Rev:** Plant divides denomination, date below **Edge:** Reeded

Date	Mintage	VF20	XF40	MS60	MS63	MS65
1941	16,271,000	1.50	2.00	3.00	7.00	10.00

KM# 118 10 CENTS
4.21 g., Nickel-Brass, 23 mm. **Ruler:** George VI **Obv:** Crowned head left **Rev:** Denomination above date **Shape:** Scalloped

Date	Mintage	VF20	XF40	MS60	MS63	MS65
1944	30,500,000	0.50	1.00	1.50	2.50	5.00
1944	—	PF60 100	PF63 200	PF65 500		

KM# 121 10 CENTS
4.21 g., Nickel-Brass, 23 mm. **Ruler:** George VI **Obv:** Crowned head left, legend without EMPEROR OF INDIA **Rev:** Denomination above date **Shape:** Scalloped

Date	Mintage	VF20	XF40	MS60	MS63	MS65
1951	34,760,000	0.20	0.40	0.60	1.25	3.00
1951	150	PF60 20.00	PF63 50.00	PF65 100		
1951 Proof, restrike	—	PF60 10.00	PF63 20.00	PF65 40.00		

Note: Frozen year 1951; restruck until 1962. Royal Mint strikes (1959-62) differ slightly in the formation of native inscriptions

KM# 98 25 CENTS
2.92 g., 0.800 Silver 0.075 oz. ASW **Ruler:** Edward VII **Obv:** Crowned bust right **Rev:** Plant divides denomination, date below

Date	Mintage	VF20	XF40	MS60	MS63	MS65
1902	400,000	10.00	22.00	32.00	48.00	100
1902	—	PF63 180	PF65 360			
1903	400,000	10.00	22.00	32.00	48.00	100
1903	—	PF63 180	PF65 360			
1907	120,000	25.00	35.00	45.00	60.00	150
1908	400,000	10.00	18.00	28.00	42.00	75.00
1909	400,000	10.00	18.00	28.00	42.00	75.00
1910	800,000	6.00	12.00	16.00	25.00	50.00

KM# 105 25 CENTS
2.92 g., 0.800 Silver 0.075 oz. ASW **Ruler:** George V **Obv:** Crowned bust left **Rev:** Plant divides denomination, date below

Date	Mintage	VF20	XF40	MS60	MS63	MS65
1911	400,000	7.00	14.00	18.00	36.00	100
1911	—	PF63 210	PF65 420			
1913	1,200,000	4.00	8.00	12.00	20.00	50.00
1913	—	PF63 210	PF65 420			
1914	400,000	7.00	14.00	20.00	30.00	75.00
1914	—	PF63 210	PF65 420			
1917	300,000	10.00	18.00	28.00	42.00	100
1917	—	PF63 210	PF65 420			

KM# 105a 25 CENTS
2.92 g., 0.550 Silver 0.0516 oz. ASW **Ruler:** George V **Obv:** Crowned bust left **Rev:** Plant divides denomination, date below

Date	Mintage	VF20	XF40	MS60	MS63	MS65
1919 B	1,400,000	3.50	7.00	15.00	25.00	85.00
1919 B	—	PF63 180	PF65 360			
1920 B	1,600,000	3.50	6.00	12.00	20.00	50.00
1920 B	—	PF63 180	PF65 360			
1921 B	600,000	7.00	12.00	25.00	45.00	100
1921 B	—	PF63 180	PF65 360			
1922	1,211,000	3.50	6.00	12.00	20.00	50.00
1922	—	PF63 180	PF65 360			
1925	1,004,000	3.50	6.00	12.00	20.00	50.00
1925	—	PF63 180	PF65 360			
1926	1,000,000	3.50	6.00	12.00	20.00	50.00
1926	—	PF63 180	PF65 360			

KM# 115 25 CENTS
2.75 g., Nickel-Brass, 19.3 mm. **Ruler:** George VI **Obv:** Crowned head left **Rev:** Crown at top divides date, denomination below **Note:** Frozen date 1943, restruck until 1951.

Date	Mintage	VF20	XF40	MS60	MS63	MS65
1943	13,920,000	0.50	1.00	1.50	2.50	5.00

KM# 122 25 CENTS
2.75 g., Nickel-Brass **Ruler:** George VI **Obv:** Legend without EMPEROR OF INDIA **Rev:** Crown divides date at top, denomination below

Date	Mintage	VF20	XF40	MS60	MS63	MS65
1951	25,940,000	0.30	0.60	1.00	1.75	5.00
1951	150	PF60 30.00	PF63 70.00	PF65 150		
1951 Proof, restrike	—	PF60 10.00	PF63 20.00	PF65 40.00		

Note: Frozen year 1951; restruck until 1962. Royal Mint strikes (1959-62) differ in numerals 9 and 5

KM# 99 50 CENTS
5.83 g., 0.800 Silver 0.150 oz. ASW **Ruler:** Edward VII **Obv:** Crowned bust right **Rev:** Plant divides denomination, date below

Date	Mintage	VF20	XF40	MS60	MS63	MS65
1902	200,000	12.00	30.00	50.00	85.00	150
1902	—	PF63 210	PF65 420			
1903	800,000	10.00	20.00	35.00	50.00	100
1903	—	PF63 210	PF65 420			
1910	200,000	16.00	32.00	50.00	95.00	150

KM# 109 50 CENTS
5.83 g., 0.800 Silver 0.150 oz. ASW **Ruler:** George V **Obv:** Crowned bust left **Rev:** Plant divides denomination, date below

Date	Mintage	VF20	XF40	MS60	MS63	MS65
1913	400,000	15.00	28.00	40.00	85.00	150
1913	—	PF63 210	PF65 420			
1914	200,000	15.00	28.00	40.00	85.00	150
1914	—	PF63 210	PF65 420			
1917	1,073,000	7.00	12.00	25.00	40.00	85.00
1917	—	PF63 210	PF65 420			

KM# 109a 50 CENTS
5.83 g., 0.550 Silver 0.1031 oz. ASW, 23.8 mm. **Ruler:** George V **Obv:** Crowned bust left **Rev:** Plant divides denomination, date below

Date	Mintage	VF20	XF40	MS60	MS63	MS65
1919 B	750,000	5.00	10.00	20.00	50.00	100
1919 B	—	PF63 145	PF65 290			
1920 B	800,000	5.00	10.00	20.00	50.00	100
1920 B	—	PF63 145	PF65 290			
1921 B	800,000	5.00	10.00	20.00	50.00	100
1921 B	—	PF63 145	PF65 290			
1922	1,040,000	5.00	10.00	20.00	50.00	100
1922	—	PF63 145	PF65 290			
1924	1,010,000	5.00	10.00	20.00	50.00	100
1924	—	PF63 145	PF65 290			
1925	500,000	7.00	12.00	20.00	35.00	75.00
1925	—	PF63 145	PF65 290			
1926	500,000	7.00	12.00	20.00	35.00	75.00
1926	—	PF63 145	PF65 290			
1927	500,000	7.00	12.00	20.00	35.00	75.00
1927	—	PF63 145	PF65 290			
1928	500,000	7.00	12.00	20.00	35.00	75.00
1928	—	PF63 145	PF65 290			
1929	500,000	7.00	12.00	20.00	35.00	75.00
1929	—	PF63 145	PF65 290			

KM# 114 50 CENTS
5.83 g., 0.800 Silver 0.150 oz. ASW **Ruler:** George VI **Obv:** Crowned head left **Rev:** Plant divides denomination, date below

Date	Mintage	VF20	XF40	MS60	MS63	MS65
1942	662,000	2.75	5.00	8.00	12.00	20.00

KM# 116 50 CENTS
5.51 g., Nickel-Brass **Ruler:** George VI **Obv:** Crowned head left **Rev:** Crown divides date above denomination **Note:** Frozen date 1943, restruck until 1951.

Date	Mintage	VF20	XF40	MS60	MS63	MS65
1943	8,600,000	0.75	1.50	3.00	5.00	35.00

KM# 123 50 CENTS
5.51 g., Nickel-Brass, 24 mm. **Ruler:** George VI **Obv:** Crowned head left, legend without EMPEROR OF INDIA **Rev:** Crown divides date above denomination

Date	Mintage	VF20	XF40	MS60	MS63	MS65
1951	19,980,000	0.35	0.75	1.25	1.75	5.00
1951	150	PF60 30.00	PF63 70.00	PF65 150		
1951 Proof, restrike	—	PF60 10.00	PF63 20.00	PF65 40.00		

Note: Frozen year 1951; restruck until 1962. Royal Mint strikes (1959-62) differ slightly in the formation of native inscriptions

BRITISH COMMONWEALTH

KM# 125 RUPEE
11.31 g., Copper-Nickel, 28 mm. **Ruler:** Elizabeth II **Subject:** 2,500 Years of Buddhism **Obv:** Date and design at center, denomination at left **Rev:** Temple above 2500, design in background

Date	Mintage	VF20	XF40	MS60	MS63	MS65
1957	2,000,000	—	—	1.00	3.00	5.00
1957	1,800	PF63 30.00	PF65 50.00			

KM# 126 5 RUPEES
28.26 g., 0.925 Silver 0.8404 oz. ASW, 39 mm. **Ruler:** Elizabeth II **Subject:** 2,500 Years of Buddhism **Obv:** Flowers and date at center, denomination at left **Rev:** 2500 within inner circle of flower, circle of animals surround, ducks encircle them

Date	Mintage	VF20	XF40	MS60	MS63	MS65
1957	500,000	15.50	28.00	35.00	45.00	60.00

Note: 258,000 returned in 1962 to be melted at The Royal Mint

Date	Mintage	VF20	XF40	MS60	MS63	MS65
1957	1,800	PF63 80.00	PF65 150			

DECIMAL COINAGE

KM# 127 CENT
0.70 g., Aluminum, 16.1 mm. **Ruler:** Elizabeth II **Obv:** Denomination at center, date below **Rev:** Crowned arms

Date	Mintage	VF20	XF40	MS60	MS63	MS65
1963	33,000,000	—	—	0.10	0.20	0.35
1965	12,000,000	—	—	0.10	0.20	0.35
1967	10,000,000	—	—	0.10	0.20	0.35
1968	22,505,000	—	—	0.10	0.20	0.35
1969	10,000,000	—	—	0.10	0.20	0.35
1970	15,000,000	—	—	0.10	0.20	0.35
1971	55,000,000	—	—	0.10	0.20	0.35
1971	—	PF65 0.50				

KM# 128 2 CENTS
0.78 g., Aluminum, 18.3 mm. **Ruler:** Elizabeth II **Obv:** Denomination at center, date below **Rev:** Crowned arms **Shape:** Scalloped

Date	Mintage	VF20	XF40	MS60	MS63	MS65
1963	26,000,000	—	0.10	0.15	0.25	0.40
1965	7,000,000	—	0.10	0.15	0.25	0.40
1967	15,000,000	—	0.10	0.15	0.25	0.40
1968	15,000,000	—	0.10	0.15	0.25	0.40
1970	13,000,000	—	0.10	0.15	0.25	0.40
1971	45,000,000	—	0.10	0.15	0.25	0.40
1971	—	PF65 1.00				

KM# 129 5 CENTS
3.24 g., Nickel-Brass, 18 mm. **Ruler:** Elizabeth II **Obv:** Denomination at center, date below **Rev:** Crowned arms **Shape:** 4-sided

Date	Mintage	VF20	XF40	MS60	MS63	MS65
1963	16,000,000	0.10	0.15	0.25	0.35	0.50
1965	9,000,000	0.10	0.15	0.25	0.35	0.50
1968	12,000,000	0.10	0.15	0.25	0.35	0.50
1969	2,500,000	0.10	0.15	0.25	0.40	0.75
1970	7,000,000	0.10	0.15	0.25	0.35	0.50
1971	32,000,000	0.10	0.15	0.25	0.35	0.50
1971	—	PF65 1.50				

KM# 130 10 CENTS
4.21 g., Nickel-Brass, 23 mm. **Ruler:** Elizabeth II **Obv:** Denomination at center, date below **Rev:** Crowned arms **Shape:** Scalloped

Date	Mintage	VF20	XF40	MS60	MS63	MS65
1963	14,000,000	0.10	0.15	0.25	0.35	0.50
1965	3,000,000	0.10	0.15	0.25	0.40	0.75
1969	6,000,000	0.10	0.15	0.25	0.35	0.50
1971	29,000,000	0.10	0.15	0.25	0.35	0.50
1971	—	PF65 1.25				

KM# 131 25 CENTS
3.24 g., Copper-Nickel, 18 mm. **Ruler:** Elizabeth II **Obv:** Denomination at center, date below **Rev:** Crowned arms

Date	Mintage	VF20	XF40	MS60	MS63	MS65
1963	30,000,000	0.10	0.20	0.40	0.55	0.80
1965	8,000,000	0.10	0.25	0.50	0.65	1.00
1971	24,000,000	0.10	0.15	0.30	0.45	0.75
1971	—	PF65 1.50				

KM# 132 50 CENTS
5.51 g., Copper-Nickel, 21.5 mm. **Ruler:** Elizabeth II **Obv:** Denomination at center, date below **Rev:** Crowned arms

Date	Mintage	VF20	XF40	MS60	MS63	MS65
1963	15,000,000	0.20	0.35	0.75	1.00	1.25
1965	7,000,000	0.20	0.35	0.75	1.00	1.25
1971	4,000,000	0.50	0.75	1.50	1.75	2.00
1971	—	PF65 2.50				
1972	—	0.50	0.75	1.50	1.75	2.00

KM# 133 RUPEE
7.13 g., Copper-Nickel, 25.3 mm. **Ruler:** Elizabeth II **Obv:** Denomination above date **Rev:** Crowned arms

Date	Mintage	VF20	XF40	MS60	MS63	MS65
1963	20,000,000	0.20	0.40	1.00	1.25	1.50
1965	5,000,000	0.25	0.50	1.25	1.50	1.75
1969	2,500,000	0.25	0.50	1.75	2.00	2.50
1971	5,000,000	0.25	0.50	1.50	1.75	2.00
1971	—	PF65 4.50				

KM# 134 2 RUPEES
12.52 g., Copper-Nickel, 32 mm. **Ruler:** Elizabeth II **Series:** F.A.O. **Obv:** Large denomination above date **Rev:** King Parakramabahu I (1153-1186) between wheat stalks **Edge:** Security

Date	Mintage	VF20	XF40	MS60	MS63	MS65
1968	500,000	1.50	2.25	4.50	7.00	10.00

PATTERNS

Including off metal strikes

KM#	Date	Mintage	Identification	Mkt Val
Pn8	1904	—	5 Cents. Copper.	15,000
Pn9	1942	—	Cent. Copper. plain. KM#111 struck in Black Bakelite.	600
Pn10	1943	—	50 Cents.	—
Pn11	1965	—	10 Cents. Nickel-Brass. Similar to KM#130, with "TRIAL" in raised letters on obverse and reverse, struck at Birmingham Mint.	—
Pn12	1968	—	5 Cents. Nickel-Brass. Similar to KM#129, with "TRIAL" in raised letters on obverse and reverse, struck at Birmingham Mint.	—

PROOF SETS

KM#	Date	Mintage	Identification	Issue Price	Mkt Val
PS1	1951 (6)	150	KM111a (1945), 119-123 (1951). Restrikes exist.	—	300
PS2	1957 (2)	400	KM125-126	—	200
PS3	1957 (2)	700	KM125-126, 2 each	—	400
PS4	1971 (7)	20,000	KM127-133	—	12.00

CHAD

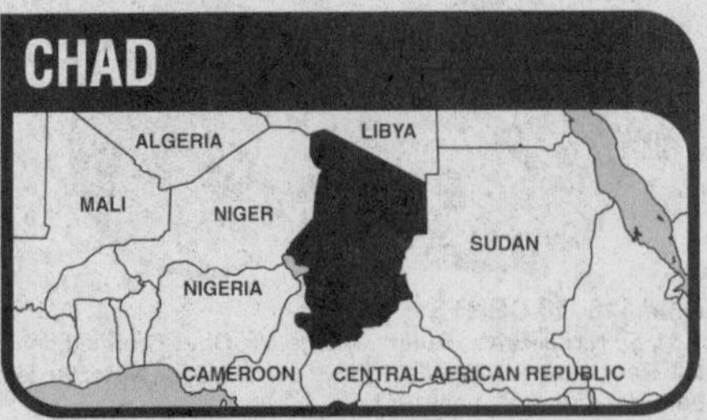

The Republic of Chad, a landlocked country of central Africa, is the largest country of former French Equatorial Africa. It has an area of 495,755 sq. mi. (1,284,000 sq. km.) and a population of *7.27 million. Capital: N'Djamena. An expanding livestock industry produces camels, cattle and sheep. Cotton (the chief product), ivory and palm oil are important exports.

Although supposedly known to Ptolemy, the Chad area was first visited by white men in 1823. Exaggerated estimates of its economic importance led to a race for its possession (1890-93), which resulted in the territory being divided by treaty between Great Britain, France and Germany. As a consequence of World War I, the German area was mandated to France in 1919. Chad was absorbed into the colony of French Equatorial Africa, as part of Ubangi-Shari, in 1910 and became a separate colony in 1920. Upon dissolution of French Equatorial Africa in 1959, the component states became autonomous members of the French Union. Chad became an independent republic on Aug. 11, 1960.

NOTE: For earlier and related coinage see French Equatorial Africa and the Equatorial African States. For later coinage see Central African States.

MINT MARKS
(a) - Paris, privy marks only
(b) = Brussels
NI - Numismatic Italiana, Arezzo, Italy

COMMEMORATIVE EDGE INSCRIPTIONS
1960 LIBERTE PROGRESS SOLIDARITE
1970/REPUBLIQUE DU TCHAD

REPUBLIC

DECIMAL COINAGE

KM# 1 100 FRANCS
5.00 g., 0.925 Silver 0.1487 oz. ASW **Subject:** 10th Anniversary of Independence **Obv:** Map of African continent **Rev:** Robert Francis Kennedy 3/4 right, denomination below

Date	Mintage	VF20	XF40	MS60	MS63	MS65
1970 (b)	975	PF60 100	PF63 120	PF65 150		

KM# 2 100 FRANCS
7.00 g., Nickel, 25.5 mm. **Obv:** Three Giant Eland left **Rev:** Denomination within circle, date below

Date	Mintage	VF20	XF40	MS60	MS63	MS65
1971 (a)	5,000,000	8.00	15.00	25.00	45.00	—
1972 (a)	5,000,000	8.00	15.00	25.00	45.00	—

KM# 3 100 FRANCS
7.00 g., Nickel, 25.5 mm. **Obv:** Three Giant Eland **Rev:** Denomination and date within circle

Date	Mintage	VF20	XF40	MS60	MS63	MS65
1975 (a)	—	7.00	12.00	20.00	35.00	—
1978 (a)	—	8.00	15.00	25.00	45.00	—
1980 (a)	—	7.00	13.00	22.00	40.00	—
1982 (a)	—	7.00	12.00	20.00	35.00	—
1984 (a)	—	7.00	12.00	20.00	35.00	—
1985 (a)	—	6.00	10.00	18.00	30.00	—
1988 (a)	—	6.00	10.00	18.00	30.00	—
1990 (a)	—	6.00	10.00	18.00	30.00	—
1991 (a)	—	6.00	10.00	18.00	30.00	—

KM# 4 200 FRANCS
15.00 g., 0.925 Silver 0.4461 oz. ASW **Subject:** 10th Anniversary of Independence **Obv:** Map of African continent **Rev:** Martin Luther King Jr. facing divides dates, denomination below

Date	Mintage	VF20	XF40	MS60	MS63	MS65
1970 (b)	952	PF60 125	PF63 145	PF65 225		

KM# 5 200 FRANCS
15.00 g., 0.800 Silver 0.3858 oz. ASW **Subject:** 10th Anniversary of Independence **Obv:** Map of African continent, denomination at left **Rev:** Charles de Gaulle 3/4 right divides dates

Date	Mintage	VF20	XF40	MS60	MS63	MS65
1970 (b)	442	PF60 135	PF63 175	PF65 275		

KM# 6 200 FRANCS
15.00 g., 0.800 Silver 0.3858 oz. ASW **Subject:** 10th Anniversary of Independence **Rev:** Egypt's President Nasser 3/4 facing

Date	Mintage	VF20	XF40	MS60	MS63	MS65
1970 (b)	435	PF60 135	PF63 175	PF65 275		

KM# 7 300 FRANCS
25.00 g., 0.925 Silver 0.7435 oz. ASW, 42 mm. **Subject:** 10th Anniversary of Independence **Obv:** Map of African continent **Rev:** John Fitzgerald Kennedy left, Space Shuttle at left, denomination below

Date	Mintage	VF20	XF40	MS60	MS63	MS65
1970 (b)	504	PF60 250	PF63 450	PF65 650		

KM# 13 500 FRANCS
Copper-Nickel **Obv:** Plants divide date and denomination **Rev:** Woman's head 3/4 left

Date	Mintage	VF20	XF40	MS60	MS63	MS65
1985 (a)	—	3.00	6.00	12.00	20.00	35.00

KM# 17 500 FRANCS
12.00 g., Silver, 30 mm. **Subject:** Millennium **Obv:** Native portrait right within circle, denomination below **Rev:** Date atop radiant map of Africa

Date	Mintage	VF20	XF40	MS60	MS63	MS65
2000	—	PF65 25.00				

KM# 8 1000 FRANCS
3.50 g., 0.900 Gold 0.1013 oz. AGW **Subject:** 10th Anniversary of Independence **Obv:** Nude half figure of woman right, shield of arms above, denomination at right **Rev:** Commandant Lamy 3/4 facing, date below

Date	Mintage	VF20	XF40	MS60	MS63	MS65
ND-1970 (a)NI	4,000	PF65 220				
ND-1970 NI	Inc. above	PF65 220				

KM# 16 1000 FRANCS
14.97 g., 0.985 Silver 0.4741 oz. ASW, 35 mm. **Obv:** Native portrait right within circle, denomination below **Rev:** Portrait of Galileo **Edge:** Plain

Date	Mintage	VF20	XF40	MS60	MS63	MS65
1999	—	PF65 25.00				

KM# 24 1000 FRANCS
15.00 g., 0.985 Silver 0.475 oz. ASW, 34 mm. **Rev:** Okapi Johnston

Date	Mintage	VF20	XF40	MS60	MS63	MS65
1999	—	PF65 30.00				

KM# 25 1000 FRANCS
15.00 g., 0.985 Silver 0.475 oz. ASW, 34 mm. **Rev:** Bird of Paradise

Date	Mintage	VF20	XF40	MS60	MS63	MS65
1999	—	PF65 35.00				

KM# 26 1000 FRANCS
15.00 g., 0.985 Silver 0.475 oz. ASW, 34 mm. **Rev:** Giraffe

Date	Mintage	VF20	XF40	MS60	MS63	MS65
1999	—	PF65 30.00				

KM# 27 1000 FRANCS
15.00 g., 0.985 Silver 0.475 oz. ASW, 34 mm. **Rev:** Hippopotamus

Date	Mintage	VF20	XF40	MS60	MS63	MS65
ND	—	PF65 45.00				

KM# 37 1000 FRANCS
Silver, 38 mm. **Subject:** FIFA World Cup, France **Obv:** Female bust right **Rev:** Soccer player and Eiffle tower

Date	Mintage	VF20	XF40	MS60	MS63	MS65
1999	—	PF65 40.00				

KM# 9 3000 FRANCS
10.50 g., 0.900 Gold 0.3038 oz. AGW **Subject:** 10th Anniversary of Independence **Obv:** Shield of arms above map, denomination below, right **Rev:** Governor Eboue 3/4 left, date below

Date	Mintage	VF20	XF40	MS60	MS63	MS65
ND-1970 (a)NI	4,000	PF65 475				
ND-1970 NI	Inc. above	PF65 475				

KM# 10 5000 FRANCS
17.50 g., 0.900 Gold 0.5064 oz. AGW **Subject:** 10th Anniversary of Independence **Obv:** Trees divide arch and arms, denomination below **Rev:** General Leclerc 3/4 facing, date below

Date	Mintage	VF20	XF40	MS60	MS63	MS65
ND-1970 (a)NI	4,000	PF65 850				
ND-1970 NI	Inc. above	PF65 850				

KM# 11 10000 FRANCS
36.00 g., 0.900 Gold 1.0417 oz. AGW **Subject:** 10th Anniversary of Independence **Obv:** Arms above double cross, denomination below **Rev:** General Charles de Gaulle right, date below

Date	Mintage	VF20	XF40	MS60	MS63	MS65
ND-1970 (a)NI	4,000	PF65 1,450				
ND (1970) NI	Inc. above	PF65 2,000				

KM# 14 10000 FRANCS
36.00 g., 0.900 Gold 1.0417 oz. AGW **Subject:** 10th Anniversary of Independence **Obv:** Map of African continent, denomination at left **Rev:** Egypt's President Nasser facing

Date	Mintage	VF20	XF40	MS60	MS63	MS65
1970 (b)	205	PF65 2,300				

KM# 15 10000 FRANCS
36.00 g., 0.900 Gold 1.0417 oz. AGW **Subject:** 10th Anniversary of Independence **Obv:** Map of Africa **Rev:** Charles de Gaulle facing

Date	Mintage	VF20	XF40	MS60	MS63	MS65
1970	90	PF65 2,450				

KM# 12 20000 FRANCS
70.00 g., 0.900 Gold 2.0255 oz. AGW **Subject:** 10th Anniversary of Independence **Obv:** Arms with supporters, denomination below

Date	Mintage	VF20	XF40	MS60	MS63	MS65
ND (1970) (a)NI	Est. 4000	PF65 4,000				
ND (1970) NI	Inc. above	PF65 4,000				

ESSAIS

Standard metals unless otherwise noted

KM#	Date	Mintage	Identification	Mkt Val
E1	1970(a)	—	10000 Francs. Copper-Nickel-Aluminum. Arms above double cross, denomination below. Head of de Gaulle right, date below. KM#11.	175
E3	1971(a)	1,400	100 Francs. Nickel. Three Giant Eland left. Denomination within circle, date below. KM#2.	60.00
E4	1971	4	100 Francs. Gold. KM#2.	2,750
E5	1975(a)	1,700	100 Francs. Nickel. KM#3.	35.00
E6	1985(a)	1,700	500 Francs. Copper-Nickel. Plants divide denomination and date. Woman's head 3/4 left. KM#13.	100

PROOF SETS

KM#	Date	Mintage	Identification	Issue Price	Mkt Val
PS1	1970 (5)	4,000	KM8-12	412	7,000
PS2	1970 (3)	—	KM1, 4, 7	33.00	1,000

CHEROKEE NATION

SOVEREIGN STATE

MEDALLIC COINAGE

KM# 1.1 50 EAGLES

32.71 g., 0.925 Silver 0.9728 oz. ASW, 41.7 mm. **Issuer:** Col. H. M. Williams **Obv:** Crossed tomahawk and peace pipe with feather behind **Rev:** Bust of Cherokee brave left **Edge:** Reeded **Note:** Without fineness stamping.

Date	Mintage	VF20	XF40	MS60	MS63	MS65
1980	800	PF63 75.00	PF65 90.00			

KM# 1.2 50 EAGLES

32.71 g., 0.925 Silver 0.9728 oz. ASW, 41.7 mm. **Issuer:** Col. H. M. Williams **Obv:** Crossed tomahawk and peace pipe with feather behind **Rev:** Bust of Cherokee brave left **Edge:** Reeded **Note:** With fineness stamping. Mintage Inc. X#1.1.

Date	Mintage	VF20	XF40	MS60	MS63	MS65
1980	Inc. above	PF63 120	PF65 135			

KM# 1a 50 EAGLES

Brass, 41.70 mm. **Issuer:** Col. H. M. Williams **Obv:** Crossed tomahawk and peace pipe with feather behind **Rev:** Bust of Cherokee brave left **Edge:** Reeded

Date	Mintage	VF20	XF40	MS60	MS63	MS65
1980	100	—	—	—	100	120

KM# 2 ADELA

31.05 g., 0.999 Silver 0.9973 oz. ASW, 38.8 mm. **Obv:** Seal (7-pointed star) in sprays, legend including native script **Obv. Legend:** SEAL OF THE CHEROKEE NATION - SEPT. 6. 1839 **Rev:** Bust of John Ross 3/4 left in outlined 7-pointed star, legend in native script **Edge:** Reeded

Date	Mintage	VF20	XF40	MS60	MS63	MS65
2000	4,000	PF63 65.00	PF65 80.00			

CHILE

The Republic of Chile, a ribbon-like country on the Pacific coast of southern South America, has an area of 292,135 sq. mi. (756,950 sq. km.) and a population of *15.21 million. Capital: Santiago. Historically, the economic base of Chile has been the rich mineral deposits of its northern provinces. Copper has accounted for more than 75 percent of Chile's export earnings in recent years. Other important mineral exports are iron ore, iodine and nitrate of soda. Fresh fruits and vegetables, as well as wine are increasingly significant in inter-hemispheric trade.

Chile had developed a strong democracy. This was displaced when rampant inflation characterized chaotic and subsequently repressive governments in the mid to late 20th century.

MINT MARK

So - Santiago

MONETARY SYSTEM

100 Centavos = 1 Peso

REPUBLIC

DECIMAL COINAGE

Often dual denominated in peso equivalent conodores

KM# 161.1 CENTAVO

3.50 g., Copper, 20 mm. **Obv:** Liberty head left **Rev:** Denomination within wreath, date below

Date	Mintage	F12	VF20	XF40	MS60	MS63
1904	—	0.75	1.50	3.00	8.00	12.00
1908	—	1.50	3.00	9.00	16.00	20.00

KM# 161.2 CENTAVO

2.50 g., Copper, 18 mm. **Obv:** Liberty head left **Rev:** Denomination within wreath, date below **Edge:** Plain

Date	Mintage	F12	VF20	XF40	MS60	MS63
1919	173,000	1.25	2.50	8.50	15.00	25.00
1991 Rare	Inc. above	—	—	—	—	—
Note: Error for 1919						

KM# 164 2 CENTAVOS

3.50 g., Copper, 21 mm. **Obv:** Liberty head left **Rev:** Denomination within wreath, date below

Date	Mintage	F12	VF20	XF40	MS60	MS63
1919	147,000	1.50	3.00	6.00	17.50	28.00

KM# 162 2-1/2 CENTAVOS

7.00 g., Copper, 25 mm. **Obv:** Liberty head left **Rev:** Denomination within wreath

Date	Mintage	F12	VF20	XF40	MS60	MS63
1904	277,000	3.50	7.50	20.00	50.00	75.00
1906	161,000	4.50	10.00	22.00	55.00	80.00
1907	262,000	3.50	7.50	20.00	45.00	70.00
Note: Varieties exist for 1907 dated coins						
1908	201,000	3.00	7.00	19.00	45.00	70.00

KM# 155.2 5 CENTAVOS

1.00 g., 0.500 Silver 0.0161 oz. ASW, 14 mm. **Obv:** Defiant Condor on rock left, 0.5 below condor **Rev:** Denomination above date within wreath **Note:** Varieties exist with 0.5, 0.5., 0/5.5., 0,5 or 05. below condor.

Date	Mintage	F12	VF20	XF40	MS60	MS63
1901/801	2,109,000	3.00	6.00	15.00	25.00	35.00
Note: With 05.						
1901/891	Inc. above	3.00	6.00	15.00	25.00	35.00
1901/896	Inc. above	3.00	6.00	15.00	25.00	35.00
1904/891/9	2,527,000	3.50	7.50	17.00	27.00	38.00
1904/894	Inc. above	3.50	7.50	17.00	27.00	38.00
1904/1	Inc. above	3.50	7.50	17.00	27.00	38.00
Note: With 0.5						
1904	Inc. above	2.00	5.00	10.00	20.00	32.00
Note: With 05 and 0.5						
1906/4	713,000	5.00	10.00	25.00	45.00	60.00
1906	Inc. above	2.00	5.00	10.00	20.00	32.00
1907	2,791,000	2.00	3.00	8.00	22.50	35.00
Note: Exists with both 0.5 and 0.5. obverse varieties						
1907	Inc. above	2.00	3.00	8.00	22.50	35.00

KM# 155.2a 5 CENTAVOS

1.00 g., 0.400 Silver 0.0129 oz. ASW, 14 mm. **Obv:** Defiant Condor on rock left **Rev:** Denomination above date within wreath **Edge:** Reeded **Note:** Without fineness below condor.

Date	Mintage	F12	VF20	XF40	MS60	MS63
1908/1	3,642,000	2.50	5.00	10.00	15.00	20.00
1908/2	Inc. above	2.50	5.00	10.00	15.00	20.00
1908	Inc. above	2.00	3.00	7.00	15.00	20.00
1909/1	1,177,000	2.00	4.00	9.00	15.00	20.00
1909/2	Inc. above	2.00	4.00	9.00	15.00	20.00
1909/8	Inc. above	2.00	4.00	9.00	15.00	20.00
1909	Inc. above	2.00	5.00	9.00	15.00	20.00
1909/899	Inc. above	2.50	6.00	12.00	22.00	35.00
1910/01	1,587,000	2.00	3.00	7.00	15.00	20.00
1910	Inc. above	2.00	3.00	7.00	15.00	20.00
1911	847,000	2.00	4.00	9.00	15.00	20.00
1913/1	2,573,000	2.50	5.00	10.00	15.00	20.00
1913/2	Inc. above	3.00	7.00	15.00	35.00	45.00
Note: Varieties exist with a dot below 1 in date for 1913						
1913	Inc. above	2.00	3.00	7.00	15.00	20.00
Note: Varieties exist with a dot below 1 in date for 1913						
1919	Inc. below	1.50	3.00	7.00	15.00	20.00
Note: With and without dash below second 9 in date						

KM# 155.3 5 CENTAVOS

1.00 g., 0.450 Silver 0.0145 oz. ASW, 14 mm. **Obv:** Defiant Condor on rock left, 0.45 below condor **Rev:** Denomination above date within wreath **Edge:** Reeded

Date	Mintage	F12	VF20	XF40	MS60	MS63
1915/1	2,250,000	1.50	3.50	6.00	12.00	25.00
1915	Inc. above	1.50	3.00	5.00	12.00	25.00
Note: 1915 exists with flat and curved top on 5						
1916/1	4,337,000	1.50	3.50	6.00	12.00	25.00
1916/5	Inc. above	1.50	3.50	6.00	12.00	25.00
1916	Inc. above	1.50	3.00	5.00	12.00	25.00
1919/1	1,494,000	3.00	7.00	15.00	35.00	50.00
Note: With dash below second 9 in date						
1919/2	Inc. above	2.00	4.00	8.00	15.00	35.00
1919/5	Inc. above	2.00	4.00	8.00	15.00	35.00
1919	Inc. above	3.00	5.00	9.00	15.00	35.00

KM# 165 5 CENTAVOS

2.00 g., Copper-Nickel, 16.5 mm. **Obv:** Defiant Condor on rock left, without designer's name O. ROTY at bottom **Rev:** Denomination above date within wreath **Edge:** Plain **Note:** Varieties exist.

Date	Mintage	F12	VF20	XF40	MS60	MS63
1920	718,000	1.00	1.50	3.00	10.00	15.00
1921	2,406,000	0.60	1.25	2.00	7.00	10.00
1922	3,872,000	0.60	1.25	2.00	7.00	10.00
1923	2,150,000	0.60	1.25	2.00	7.00	10.00
1925	994,000	0.60	1.25	2.00	7.00	10.00

Note: Obverse variety known with dot to left of right wing tip.

Date	Mintage	F12	VF20	XF40	MS60	MS63
1926	594,000	1.50	2.50	3.00	9.00	12.00
1927	1,276,000	0.50	1.00	2.00	6.00	10.00
1928	5,197,000	0.50	1.00	2.00	6.00	10.00
1933	3,000,000	5.00	10.00	25.00	55.00	75.00
1934	Inc. above	0.25	0.50	1.00	3.00	5.00
1936	2,000,000	0.25	0.50	1.00	3.00	5.00
1937	2,000,000	0.25	0.50	1.00	3.00	5.00
1938	2,000,000	0.25	0.50	1.00	3.00	5.00

KM# 156.2 10 CENTAVOS

2.00 g., 0.500 Silver 0.0322 oz. ASW, 17 mm. **Obv:** Defiant Condor on rock left, 0.5 below condor **Rev:** Denomination above date within wreath **Edge:** Reeded **Note:** Obverse varieties exist with 0.5, 0,5, 0.5. or 0.5/9 below condor. Struck by law of January 19, 1899.

Date	Mintage	F12	VF20	XF40	MS60	MS63
1901/891	Inc. above	20.00	36.00	65.00	120	175
1901/896	Inc. above	20.00	36.00	65.00	120	175
1904/896	779,000	2.50	4.00	8.00	15.00	25.00
1904/899	Inc. above	2.50	4.00	8.00	15.00	25.00
1906	139,000	3.00	5.00	10.00	17.00	28.00
1907/807	3,151,000	3.00	5.00	10.00	17.00	28.00
1907/2	Inc. above	3.00	5.00	10.00	17.00	28.00
1907	Inc. above	2.50	4.00	8.00	15.00	25.00

Note: Exists with both 0.5 and 0.5. obverse varieties.

KM# 156.2a 10 CENTAVOS

1.50 g., 0.400 Silver 0.0193 oz. ASW, 17 mm. **Obv:** Defiant Condor on rock left **Rev:** Denomination above date within wreath **Edge:** Reeded **Note:** Varieties exist.

Date	Mintage	F12	VF20	XF40	MS60	MS63
1908/1	4,149,000	1.50	3.00	6.00	12.00	17.00
1908	Inc. above	1.00	2.00	4.50	10.00	15.00
1908/inverted 6	Inc. above	1.50	3.00	6.00	12.00	17.00
1909/8	2,964,000	1.50	3.00	6.00	12.00	17.00
1909	Inc. above	1.00	2.00	4.50	10.00	15.00
1913	1,269,000	1.50	3.00	6.00	12.00	17.00
1919/8	883,000	3.00	6.00	12.00	25.00	35.00
1919	Inc. above	2.50	5.00	10.00	15.00	20.00
1920/5	2,109,000	1.50	3.00	6.00	12.00	17.00
1920	Inc. above	1.00	2.00	4.50	10.00	15.00

KM# 156.3 10 CENTAVOS

1.50 g., 0.450 Silver 0.0217 oz. ASW, 17 mm. **Obv:** Defiant Condor on rock left, 0.45 below condor **Rev:** Denomination above date within wreath **Edge:** Plain

Date	Mintage	F12	VF20	XF40	MS60	MS63
1915	1,620,000	1.00	1.50	3.00	5.00	7.50
1916	2,855,000	1.00	1.50	3.00	5.00	7.50
1917/1	736,000	2.00	3.50	7.00	12.00	18.00
1917	Inc. above	1.50	2.50	5.00	10.00	15.00
1918/5	—	2.00	3.50	7.00	12.00	18.00
1918	—	1.50	2.50	5.00	10.00	15.00
1919/3	—	2.00	3.50	7.00	12.00	18.00

KM# 166 10 CENTAVOS

3.00 g., Copper-Nickel, 19.5 mm. **Obv:** Defiant Condor on rock left, without designer's name O. ROTY at bottom **Rev:** Denomination above date within wreath **Edge:** Plain

Date	Mintage	F12	VF20	XF40	MS60	MS63
1920	451,000	1.50	3.50	7.00	15.00	25.00
1921	2,654,000	0.50	0.75	1.50	3.00	5.00
1922	4,017,000	0.50	0.75	1.50	3.00	5.00
1923	3,356,000	0.50	0.75	7.50	30.00	45.00
1924	1,445,000	0.50	0.75	1.50	3.00	5.00
1925	2,665,000	0.50	0.75	1.50	3.00	5.00
1927	523,000	1.00	2.00	3.50	7.00	10.00
1928	3,052,000	0.50	0.75	1.50	3.00	5.00
1932	1,500,000	1.00	2.00	3.50	7.00	10.00
1933/2	5,800,000	0.75	1.00	2.00	4.00	6.00
1933	Inc. above	0.25	0.50	1.00	2.00	5.00
1933 Over reversed 3	Inc. above	0.50	1.00	2.00	4.00	6.00
1934	900,000	0.50	0.75	1.50	3.00	5.00
1935	1,500,000	0.50	0.75	1.50	3.00	5.00
1936	3,300,000	0.25	0.50	1.00	2.00	5.00
1937	2,000,000	0.25	0.50	1.00	2.00	5.00
1937 Over reversed 3	Inc. above	0.50	1.00	2.00	3.00	5.00
1938	5,000,000	0.25	0.50	1.00	2.00	5.00
1938 Over reversed 3	Inc. above	0.50	1.00	2.00	3.00	5.00
1939	1,200,000	0.25	0.50	1.00	2.00	5.00
1939 Over reversed 3	Inc. above	0.50	1.00	2.00	3.00	5.00
1940	6,100,000	0.25	0.50	1.00	2.00	5.00
1941	900,000	1.00	2.00	3.00	4.00	6.00

KM# 151.2 20 CENTAVOS

4.00 g., 0.500 Silver 0.0643 oz. ASW, 21.5 mm. **Obv:** Defiant Condor on rock left, 0.5 below condor **Rev:** Denomination above date within wreath **Note:** Obverse varieties with 0.5 or 0.5. exist. Issued by law of January 19, 1899.

Date	Mintage	F12	VF20	XF40	MS60	MS63
1906/806	866,000	3.00	6.00	12.00	25.00	45.00
1906/896	Inc. above	3.00	6.00	12.00	25.00	45.00
1906	Inc. above	2.50	5.00	10.00	20.00	35.00
1907/807	7,625,000	2.50	5.00	10.00	20.00	35.00
1907/895	Inc. above	2.50	5.00	10.00	20.00	35.00
1907	Inc. above	2.25	4.50	10.00	20.00	35.00

KM# 151.3 20 CENTAVOS

3.00 g., 0.400 Silver 0.0386 oz. ASW, 21.5 mm. **Obv:** Defiant Condor on rock left, without 0.5 below condor **Rev:** Denomination above date within wreath **Edge:** Reeded

Date	Mintage	F12	VF20	XF40	MS60	MS63
1907/807	1,201,000	2.00	3.50	8.00	14.00	22.00
1907	Inc. above	1.50	3.00	7.00	13.00	22.00
1908/808	5,869,000	2.00	3.50	8.00	14.00	22.00
1908	Inc. above	1.35	3.00	6.00	12.00	20.00
1909	1,080,000	1.35	3.00	6.00	12.00	20.00
1913/1	3,507,000	1.50	4.00	8.00	14.00	22.00
1913/50	Inc. above	1.50	4.00	8.00	14.00	22.00
1913	Inc. above	2.00	4.00	8.00	14.00	22.00
1919	3,749,000	1.35	3.00	6.00	12.00	20.00
1920	4,189,000	1.35	3.00	6.00	12.00	20.00

KM# 151.4 20 CENTAVOS

3.00 g., 0.450 Silver 0.0434 oz. ASW, 21.5 mm. **Obv:** Defiant Condor on rock left, 0.45 below condor's wing, O'Roty at bottom **Rev:** Denomination above date within wreath **Edge:** Reeded

Date	Mintage	F12	VF20	XF40	MS60	MS63
1916	3,377,000	2.00	4.00	8.00	14.00	22.00

KM# 167.1 20 CENTAVOS

4.50 g., Copper-Nickel, 22.5 mm. **Obv:** Without designer's name O. ROTY at bottom **Rev:** Denomination and date within wreath, large numeral **Edge:** Plain

Date	Mintage	F12	VF20	XF40	MS60	MS63
1920	499,000	1.00	2.50	5.50	10.00	15.00
1921	6,547,000	0.35	1.00	3.00	7.00	10.00
1922	8,261,000	0.35	1.00	3.00	7.00	10.00
1923	5,439,000	0.35	1.00	3.00	7.00	10.00
1924	16,096,000	0.35	1.00	3.00	7.00	10.00
1925	9,830,000	0.35	1.00	3.00	7.00	10.00

Note: Varieties exist with dot under 5 in date for 1925

Date	Mintage	F12	VF20	XF40	MS60	MS63
1929	9,685,000	0.35	1.00	3.00	7.00	10.00

KM# 167.3 20 CENTAVOS

4.50 g., Copper-Nickel, 22.5 mm. **Obv:** Defiant Condor on rock left, with designer's name O. ROTY at bottom **Rev:** Denomination above date within wreath **Edge:** Plain

Date	Mintage	F12	VF20	XF40	MS60	MS63
1932	—	0.35	0.75	1.25	2.50	5.00
1932 Over reversed 3	—	0.50	1.00	2.00	3.50	6.00
1933	1,000,000	0.35	0.75	1.25	2.50	5.00
1933 Over reversed 3X	Inc. above	1.00	1.50	2.50	4.00	7.00
1933 Over reversed 33	Inc. above	1.00	1.50	2.50	4.00	7.00
1937	—	0.35	0.75	1.25	2.50	5.00
1937 Over reversed 3	—	1.00	1.50	2.50	4.00	7.00
1938	3,043,000	0.35	0.75	1.25	2.50	5.00
1938 3 over reversed 3	Inc. above	1.00	1.50	2.50	4.00	7.00
1939	5,283,000	0.35	0.75	1.25	2.00	3.50
1939 3 over reversed 3	Inc. above	1.00	1.50	2.50	4.00	7.00
1940	9,300,000	0.35	0.75	1.25	2.00	3.00
1941	3,000,000	0.35	0.75	1.25	2.00	3.50

KM# 167.4 20 CENTAVOS

Copper-Nickel **Obv:** With designer's name O. ROTY at bottom **Rev:** Denomination and date within wreath

Date	Mintage	F12	VF20	XF40	MS60	MS63
1929	Inc. above	1.00	2.50	5.00	7.00	9.00

KM# 167.2 20 CENTAVOS

4.50 g., Copper-Nickel, 22.65 mm. **Obv:** Without designer's name **Rev:** Denomination and date within wreath, small numeral

Date	Mintage	F12	VF20	XF40	MS60	MS63
1932	—	0.50	1.00	2.00	3.50	5.00
1932 Over reversed 3	—	0.75	1.50	3.00	5.00	8.00
1933 Over reversed 3X	—	0.50	1.00	2.00	3.50	5.00
1933/ Reversed 33	59,000,000	0.50	1.00	2.00	3.50	5.00
1933	Inc. above	0.35	0.75	1.25	3.50	5.00

KM# 177 20 CENTAVOS

3.00 g., Copper This coin is called: "Chaucha", 18 mm. **Obv:** Armored bust of General Bernardo O'Higgins right, Thenot on truncation, copihue flower left & right to denomination **Rev:** Denomination above date **Edge:** Plain

Date	Mintage	VF20	XF40	MS60	MS63	MS65
1942	30,000,000	0.25	1.00	2.00	4.00	7.50
1943	396,000,000	0.25	1.00	2.00	4.00	7.50
1944	29,100,000	0.25	1.00	2.00	4.00	7.50
1945	11,400,000	0.25	1.00	2.00	4.00	7.50
1946	13,800,000	0.25	1.00	2.00	4.00	7.50
1947	15,700,000	0.25	1.00	2.00	4.00	7.50
1948	15,200,000	0.25	1.00	2.00	4.00	7.50
1949	14,700,000	0.25	1.00	2.00	4.00	7.50
1950	15,200,000	0.25	1.00	2.00	4.00	7.50
1951	14,700,000	0.25	1.00	2.00	4.00	7.50
1952	15,500,000	0.25	1.00	2.00	4.00	7.50
1953	7,800,000	0.25	1.00	2.00	4.00	7.50

KM# 163 40 CENTAVOS
6.00 g., 0.400 Silver 0.0772 oz. ASW, 25 mm. **Obv:** Defiant Condor on rock, left **Rev:** Denomination above date within wreath **Edge:** Reeded

Date	Mintage	F12	VF20	XF40	MS60	MS63
1907	56,000	20.00	40.00	80.00	195	225
1908/6	1,452,000	7.00	14.00	28.00	55.00	75.00
1908	Inc. above	6.00	12.00	25.00	35.00	50.00

KM# 160 50 CENTAVOS
10.00 g., 0.700 Silver 0.2251 oz. ASW, 28 mm. **Obv:** Defiant Condor on rock left **Rev:** Denomination above date within wreath **Edge:** Reeded **Note:** Varieties with 0.7 or 0.7. exist.

Date	Mintage	F12	VF20	XF40	MS60	MS63
1902	2,022,000	8.00	12.00	22.50	30.00	50.00
1903	1,111,000	8.00	12.00	22.50	30.00	50.00
1905	1,075,000	8.00	12.00	22.50	30.00	50.00

KM# 178 50 CENTAVOS
4.00 g., Copper, 20.5 mm. **Obv:** Bust of General Bernardo O'Higgins right, Thenot on truncation **Rev:** Denomination above date **Edge:** Plain

Date	Mintage	VF20	XF40	MS60	MS63	MS65
1942	4,715,000	3.00	5.00	7.50	15.00	20.00

KM# 152.2 PESO
20.00 g., 0.700 Silver 0.4501 oz. ASW, 35 mm. **Obv:** Defiant Condor on rock, left, 0.7 below right wing **Rev:** Denomination above date within wreath

Date	Mintage	F12	VF20	XF40	MS60	MS63
1902	178,000	17.00	25.00	60.00	125	175
1903	372,000	15.00	19.00	38.00	80.00	125
1905	429,000	15.00	19.00	38.00	80.00	125

KM# 152.3 PESO
12.00 g., 0.900 Silver 0.3472 oz. ASW, 31.5 mm. **Obv:** Defiant Condor on rock, left, 0.9 below right wing **Rev:** Denomination above date within wreath **Edge:** Reeded

Date	Mintage	F12	VF20	XF40	MS60	MS63
1910	2,166,000	—	6.50	12.00	20.00	35.00

KM# 152.4 PESO
9.00 g., 0.720 Silver 0.2083 oz. ASW, 27.5 mm. **Obv:** Defiant Condor on rock, left, 0.72 below right wing **Rev:** Denomination above date within wreath **Edge:** Plain

Date	Mintage	F12	VF20	XF40	MS60	MS63
1915	6,032,000	—	3.75	10.00	12.00	15.00
1917	3,033,000	—	3.75	12.00	15.00	20.00

KM# 152.5 PESO
9.00 g., 0.500 Silver 0.1447 oz. ASW, 29 mm. **Obv:** Defiant Condor on rock, left, 0.5 below right wing **Rev:** Denomination above date within wreath **Edge:** Reeded

Date	Mintage	F12	VF20	XF40	MS60	MS63
1921	2,287,000	—	2.75	10.00	12.00	15.00
1922	2,718,000	—	2.75	10.00	12.00	15.00

KM# 152.6 PESO
9.00 g., 0.500 Silver 0.1447 oz. ASW, 29 mm. **Obv:** Defiant Condor on rock left, 0.5 below right wing **Rev:** Date and denomination within wreath **Edge:** Reeded **Note:** Struck with medal rotation.

Date	Mintage	F12	VF20	XF40	MS60	MS63
1924	1,748,000	—	2.75	10.00	12.00	15.00
1925	2,037,000	—	2.75	10.00	12.00	15.00

Note: Varieties of 1925 dated coins exist with flat and curved tops

KM# 142.2 PESO
25.00 g., 0.900 Silver 0.7234 oz. ASW, 37 mm. **Obv:** Plumed arms within wreath **Rev:** Defiant Condor above date, shield in right talon, flat top 3 **Edge:** Reeded **Note:** Medal alignment.

Date	Mintage	F12	VF20	XF40	MS60	MS63
1883(1925)	712,000	—	150	350	1,400	2,000

KM# 142.3 PESO
25.00 g., 0.900 Silver 0.7234 oz. ASW, 37 mm. **Obv:** Three plumes above shield within wreath, denomination below **Rev:** Defiant Condor above date, shield in right talon, flat-top 3 **Edge:** Reeded **Note:** Coin alignment. Minted in 1925-26 and most coins were melted down in 1927.

Date	Mintage	F12	VF20	XF40	MS60	MS63
1883(1926)	149,000	—	150	300	850	1,250

KM# A171.1 PESO
9.00 g., 0.500 Silver 0.1447 oz. ASW, 29 mm. **Obv:** Defiant Condor on rock left, 0.5 below right wing **Rev:** Date and denomination within wreath **Edge:** Reeded **Note:** A mule, with 0.5 and without mint mark on obverse.

Date	Mintage	VF20	XF40	MS60	MS63	MS65
1927	—	30.00	55.00	120	—	—

KM# 171.1 PESO
9.00 g., 0.500 Silver 0.1447 oz. ASW, 29 mm. **Obv:** Defiant Condor on rock left, 0.5 below right wing **Rev:** Denomination above date within wreath **Edge:** Reeded

Date	Mintage	F12	VF20	XF40	MS60	MS63
1927 So	3,890,000	—	2.75	6.00	10.00	15.00

KM# 171.2 PESO
9.00 g., 0.500 Silver 0.1447 oz. ASW, 29 mm. **Obv:** Defiant Condor on rock left, 0.5 below right wing **Rev:** Date and denomination within wreath, thick numeral **Edge:** Reeded **Note:** Varieties 0.5 and 0,5 exist. Total of 2,431,608 pieces dated 1921-1927 were melted down in 1932.

Date	Mintage	F12	VF20	XF40	MS60	MS63
1927 So	—	—	2.75	6.00	10.00	15.00

KM# 174 PESO
6.00 g., 0.400 Silver 0.0772 oz. ASW, 26 mm. **Obv:** Defiant Condor on rock left **Rev:** Denomination above date within wreath **Edge:** Reeded

Date	Mintage	F12	VF20	XF40	MS60	MS63
1932	4,000,000	—	2.50	4.00	7.00	12.00

KM# 176.1 PESO
10.00 g., Copper-Nickel, 29 mm. **Obv:** Defiant Condor on rock left **Rev:** Denomination above date within wreath **Edge:** Reeded

Date	Mintage	F12	VF20	XF40	MS60	MS63
1933	29,976,000	0.35	0.75	1.50	2.50	4.50

KM# 176.2 PESO
10.00 g., Copper-Nickel, 29 mm. **Obv:** Defiant Condor on rock left, O ROTY incuse on rock base **Rev:** Denomination above date within wreath **Edge:** Reeded

Date	Mintage	F12	VF20	XF40	MS60	MS63
1940	150,000	—	2.00	3.00	6.00	10.00

KM# 179 PESO
7.50 g., Copper, 25.2 mm. **Obv:** Armored bust of General Bernardo O'Higgins right **Rev:** Denomination above date **Edge:** Reeded

Date	Mintage	VF20	XF40	MS60	MS63	MS65
1942	15,150,000	0.35	2.00	4.00	9.00	15.00
1943	16,900,000	0.35	2.00	4.00	9.00	15.00
1944	12,050,000	0.35	2.00	4.00	9.00	15.00
1945	7,600,000	0.35	2.00	4.00	9.00	15.00
1946	2,050,000	0.35	5.00	7.00	15.00	25.00

Date	Mintage	VF20	XF40	MS60	MS63	MS65
1947	2,200,000	0.35	5.00	7.00	15.00	25.00
1948	5,900,000	0.25	2.00	3.00	5.00	7.50
1949	7,100,000	0.20	1.00	2.00	4.00	7.50
1950	7,250,000	0.20	1.00	2.00	4.00	7.50
1951	8,150,000	0.20	1.00	2.00	4.00	7.50
1952	10,400,000	0.20	1.00	2.00	4.00	7.50
1953 Short top 5	17,200,000	0.20	1.00	1.50	3.00	7.50
1953 Long top 5	Inc. above	0.20	1.00	1.50	3.00	7.50
1954	7,566,000	0.20	1.00	1.50	3.00	7.50

KM# 179a PESO
2.00 g., Aluminum, 25 mm. **Obv:** Armored bust, right **Rev:** Denomination above date **Edge:** Plain

Date	Mintage	VF20	XF40	MS60	MS63	MS65
1954	43,550,000	0.15	0.50	0.75	1.00	1.50
1954	—	PF63 25.00				
1955	69,050,000	0.15	0.50	0.75	1.00	1.50
1956	58,250,000	0.15	0.50	0.75	1.00	1.50
1956	—	PF63 25.00				
1957	49,250,000	0.15	0.50	0.75	1.00	1.50
1958	29,900	0.15	0.50	0.75	1.00	1.50

KM# 172 2 PESOS
18.00 g., 0.500 Silver 0.2894 oz. ASW, 33 mm. **Obv:** Defiant Condor on rock left **Rev:** Denomination above date within wreath **Edge:** Reeded **Note:** Obverse varieties 0.5 and 0,5 with curved top and flat top 5 exist. 459,510 pieces were melted down in 1932.

Date	Mintage	F12	VF20	XF40	MS60	MS63
1927	1,060,000	5.25	10.00	12.00	20.00	28.00

KM# 159 5 PESOS
3.00 g., 0.917 Gold 0.0883 oz. AGW, 16.5 mm. **Obv:** Head left **Rev:** Plumed arms with supporters **Edge:** Reeded

Date	Mintage	F12	VF20	XF40	MS60	MS63
1911	1,399	—	—	200	350	—

KM# 173.1 5 PESOS
25.00 g., 0.900 Silver 0.7234 oz. ASW, 37 mm. **Obv:** Defiant Condor on rock, left, 0.9 below right wing **Rev:** Denomination above date within wreath, wide 5, width = 3 mm **Edge:** Reeded

Date	Mintage	F12	VF20	XF40	MS60	MS63
1927	965,000	25.00	28.00	37.00	75.00	175

KM# 173.2 5 PESOS
25.00 g., 0.900 Silver 0.7234 oz. ASW **Obv:** Defiant Condor on rock left, 0.9 below right wing **Rev:** Denomination and date within wreath, narrow 5, width = 2.7 mm **Edge:** Reeded **Shape:** 37 **Note:** Varieties 0.9 and 0,9 exist. 436,510 pieces of KM#173.1 and #173.2 were melted down in 1932.

Date	Mintage	F12	VF20	XF40	MS60	MS63
1927	Inc. above	25.00	28.00	37.00	75.00	175

KM# 180 5 PESOS
2.40 g., Aluminum, 23.5 mm. **Obv:** Condor in flight **Rev:** Denomination above date flanked by grain sprigs **Edge:** Plain

Date	Mintage	VF20	XF40	MS60	MS63	MS65
1956	1,600,000	0.35	0.50	0.75	1.00	1.25

KM# 182 5 PESOS
22.50 g., 0.999 Silver 0.7227 oz. ASW, 35.5 mm. **Subject:** 150th Anniversary of Naval Academy **Obv:** Arms with supporters, date at left, denomination below **Rev:** Bust of Admiral Arturo Prat Chacon, 3/4 facing **Edge:** Reeded

Date	Mintage	VF20	XF40	MS60	MS63	MS65
1968	1,200	PF63 35.00	PF65 50.00			

KM# 157 10 PESOS
5.99 g., 0.917 Gold 0.1766 oz. AGW, 21 mm. **Obv:** Head left **Rev:** Plumed arms with supporters

Date	Mintage	F12	VF20	XF40	MS60	MS63
1901	1,651,000	—	—	225	300	335

KM# 181 10 PESOS
2.96 g., Aluminum, 29 mm. **Obv:** Condor in flight **Rev:** Denomination above date, grain sprigs flank **Edge:** Plain

Date	Mintage	VF20	XF40	MS60	MS63	MS65
1956	13,100,000	0.25	0.35	0.50	0.75	1.50
1957	28,800,000	0.25	0.35	0.50	0.75	1.50
1958	44,500,000	0.25	0.35	0.50	0.75	1.50
1959	10,220,000	0.50	0.75	1.00	1.50	2.50

KM# 183 10 PESOS
45.00 g., 0.999 Silver 1.4453 oz. ASW, 45 mm. **Subject:** Arrival of Liberation Fleet in 1820 under command of Lord Cochrane **Rev:** Liberation fleet, dates below **Edge:** Reeded

Date	Mintage	VF20	XF40	MS60	MS63	MS65
1968	1,215	PF63 95.00	PF65 125			

KM# 158 20 PESOS
11.98 g., 0.917 Gold 0.3533 oz. AGW, 27 mm. **Obv:** Head left **Rev:** Plumed arms with supporters

Date	Mintage	F12	VF20	XF40	MS60	MS63
1906	41,000	—	—	450	575	645
1907	12,000	—	—	450	575	645
1908	26,000	—	—	450	575	645
1910	28,000	—	—	450	575	625
1911	17,000	—	—	450	575	625
1913/11	18,000	—	—	450	575	625
1913	Inc. above	—	—	450	575	625
1914	22,000	—	—	450	575	625
1915	65,000	—	—	450	575	625
1916	36,000	—	—	450	575	625
1917	717,000	—	—	450	575	625

KM# 168 20 PESOS
4.07 g., 0.900 Gold 0.1177 oz. AGW, 18.5 mm. **Obv:** Head left, date below **Rev:** Arms with supporters, denomination above

Date	Mintage	F12	VF20	XF40	MS60	MS63
1926	85,000	—	—	150	185	215
1958	500	150	200	220	250	—
1959	25,000	—	—	150	185	215
1961	20,000	—	—	150	185	215
1964	—	—	—	150	185	215
1976	99,000	—	—	150	185	215
1977	38,000	—	—	150	185	215
1979	30,000	—	—	150	185	215
1980	30,000	—	—	150	185	215

KM# 188 20 PESOS
4.07 g., 0.900 Gold 0.1177 oz. AGW, 18.5 mm. **Obv:** Head left, date below **Rev:** Coat of arms on ornamental vines, denomination above

Date	Mintage	VF20	XF40	MS60	MS63	MS65
1976	Inc. above	—	150	185	215	—

KM# 169 50 PESOS
10.17 g., 0.900 Gold 0.2943 oz. AGW, 24.5 mm. **Obv:** Head left, date below **Rev:** Coat of arms, denomination above

Date	Mintage	F12	VF20	XF40	MS60	MS63
1926	126,000	—	—	375	475	525
1958	10,000	—	—	375	475	525
1961	20,000	—	—	375	475	525
1962	30,000	—	—	375	475	525
1965	—	—	—	375	475	525
1966	—	—	—	375	475	525
1967	—	—	—	375	475	525
1968	—	—	—	375	475	525
1969	—	—	—	375	475	525
1970	—	—	—	—	750	—
1974	—	—	—	375	475	525

KM# 184 50 PESOS
10.17 g., 0.900 Gold 0.2943 oz. AGW **Subject:** 150th

Anniversary of Military Academy **Obv:** Coat of arms above denomination **Rev:** Armored bust right of Bernardo O'Higgins, two dates below

Date	Mintage	VF20	XF40	MS60	MS63	MS65
1968	2,515	PF63 450	PF65 500			

KM# 170 100 PESOS

20.34 g., 0.900 Gold 0.5885 oz. AGW, 31 mm. **Obv:** Head left, date below **Rev:** Coat of arms, denomination above

Date	Mintage	F12	VF20	XF40	MS60	MS63
1926	678,000	—	—	750	925	975

KM# 175 100 PESOS

20.34 g., 0.900 Gold 0.5885 oz. AGW, 31 mm. **Obv:** Head left, date below, revised bust and legend style **Rev:** Coat of arms, denomination above, revised legend style

Date	Mintage	F12	VF20	XF40	MS60	MS63
1932	9,315	—	750	925	975	—
1946	260,000	—	—	750	925	975
1947	540,000	—	—	750	925	975
1948	420,000	—	—	750	925	975
1949	310,000	—	—	750	925	975
1950	20,000	—	—	750	925	975
1951	145,000	—	—	750	925	975
1952	245,000	—	—	750	925	975
1953	175,000	—	—	750	925	975
1954	190,000	—	—	750	925	975
1955	150,000	—	—	750	925	975
1956	60,000	—	—	750	925	975
1957	40,000	—	—	750	925	975
1958	157,000	—	—	750	925	975
1959	90,000	—	—	750	925	975
1960	200,000	—	—	750	925	975
1961	295,000	—	—	750	925	975
1962	260,000	—	—	750	925	975
1963	210,000	—	—	750	925	975
1964	—	—	—	750	925	975
1968	—	—	—	750	925	975
1969	—	—	—	750	925	975
1970	—	—	—	750	925	975
1971	—	—	—	750	925	975
1972	—	—	—	750	925	975
1973	—	—	—	750	925	975
1974	—	—	—	750	925	975
1976	172,000	—	—	750	925	975
1977	25,000	—	—	750	925	975
1979	100,000	—	—	750	925	975
1980	50,000	—	—	750	925	975

KM# 185 100 PESOS

20.34 g., 0.900 Gold 0.5885 oz. AGW, 31 mm. **Subject:** 150th Anniversary of National Coinage **Obv:** Coat of arms, date at left, denomination below **Rev:** Coinage press, liberty bust left

Date	Mintage	VF20	XF40	MS60	MS63	MS65
1968	1,815	PF63 950	PF65 1,000			

KM# 186 200 PESOS

40.68 g., 0.900 Gold 1.1771 oz. AGW **Subject:** 150th Anniversary of San Martin's passage through Andes Mountains, from a painting by Vila Prades **Obv:** Coat of arms, date at left, denomination below **Rev:** Riders passing through mountains, two dates below

Date	Mintage	VF20	XF40	MS60	MS63	MS65
1968	965	PF63 1,750	PF65 1,850			

KM# 187 500 PESOS

101.70 g., 0.900 Gold 2.9427 oz. AGW **Subject:** 150th Anniversary of National Flag **Rev:** Liberty bust left, waving flag in background, two dates below

Date	Mintage	VF20	XF40	MS60	MS63	MS65
1968	—	PF63 4,500	PF65 4,700			

REFORM COINAGE

10 Pesos = 1 Centesimo; 100 Centesimos = 1 Escudo

KM# 192 1/2 CENTESIMO

2.00 g., Aluminum, 25 mm. **Obv:** Condor in flight **Rev:** Denomination above date, grain sprigs flank **Edge:** Reeded

Date	Mintage	VF20	XF40	MS60	MS63	MS65
1962	3,750,000	0.10	0.30	0.50	1.00	1.50
1962	—	PF63 10.00				
1963	8,100,000	0.10	0.30	0.50	1.00	1.50

KM# 189 CENTESIMO

3.00 g., Aluminum, 28 mm. **Obv:** Condor in flight **Rev:** Denomination above date, grain sprigs flank **Edge:** Plain

Date	Mintage	VF20	XF40	MS60	MS63	MS65
1960	20,160,000	0.50	1.00	1.50	2.00	3.00
1960	—	PF63 45.00				
1961	Inc. above	0.50	1.00	1.50	2.00	3.00
1962	26,320,000	0.50	1.00	1.50	2.00	3.00
1963	27,100,000	0.50	1.00	1.50	2.00	3.00
1963	—	PF63 45.00				

KM# 193 2 CENTESIMOS

3.00 g., Aluminum-Bronze, 20 mm. **Obv:** Condor in flight **Rev:** Denomination above date, grain sprigs flank **Edge:** Plain

Date	Mintage	VF20	XF40	MS60	MS63	MS65
1960	2,050,000	—	—	—	50.00	—
Note: Not released for circulation						
1960	—	PF63 50.00				
1964	2,050,000	—	0.10	1.50	2.00	3.00
1965	32,550,000	—	0.10	1.50	2.00	3.00
1966	31,800,000	—	0.10	1.50	2.00	3.00
1967	34,750,000	—	0.10	1.50	2.00	3.00

Date	Mintage	VF20	XF40	MS60	MS63	MS65
1967	—	PF63 50.00				
1968	29,400,000	—	0.10	1.50	2.00	3.00
1969	—	—	—	—	3.00	5.00
1969	—	PF63 50.00				
1970	20,250,000	—	0.10	1.50	2.00	3.00

KM# 190 5 CENTESIMOS

4.12 g., Aluminum-Bronze, 23.3 mm. **Obv:** Condor in flight **Rev:** Denomination above date, grain sprigs flank **Edge:** Reeded

Date	Mintage	VF20	XF40	MS60	MS63	MS65
1960	—	—	—	—	75.00	—
Note: Not released for circulation						
1960	—	PF63 100				
1961	12,000	2.50	5.00	7.00	10.00	15.00
1962	—	2.00	4.00	6.00	10.00	15.00
1963	—	2.00	4.00	6.00	10.00	15.00
1964	16,628,000	0.10	0.15	1.00	2.00	3.00
1965	27,680,000	0.10	0.15	1.00	2.00	3.00
1966	32,360,000	0.10	0.15	1.00	2.00	3.00
1966	—	PF63 50.00				
1967	19,680,000	0.10	0.15	1.00	2.00	3.00
1968	4,400,000	0.10	0.15	1.00	2.00	3.00
1968	—	PF63 50.00				
1969	13,200,000	—	—	3.00	5.00	7.00
1969	—	PF63 50.00				
1970	30,680,000	0.10	0.15	1.00	2.00	3.00
1971	16,080,000	0.10	0.15	1.00	2.00	3.00

KM# 191 10 CENTESIMOS

8.10 g., Aluminum-Bronze, 27.17 mm. **Obv:** Condor in flight **Rev:** Denomination above date, grain sprigs flank **Edge:** Plain

Date	Mintage	VF20	XF40	MS60	MS63	MS65
1960	—	2.00	4.00	6.00	10.00	15.00
1960	—	PF63 70.00				
1961	1,915,000	0.10	1.00	2.00	4.00	6.00
1962	1,480,000	0.10	0.20	1.00	2.00	3.00
1963 Small date	10,980,000	0.10	0.20	1.00	2.00	3.00
1964	27,070,000	0.10	0.20	1.00	2.00	3.00
1965	49,480,000	0.10	0.20	1.00	2.00	3.00
1966	60,680,000	0.10	0.20	1.00	2.00	3.00
1967	27,520,000	0.10	0.25	1.00	2.00	3.00
1967	—	PF63 50.00				
1968	8,040,000	0.10	0.20	1.00	2.00	3.00
1969	15,660,000	—	—	3.00	5.00	7.00
1970 Large date	42,080,000	0.10	0.20	0.50	1.00	2.00

KM# 194 10 CENTESIMOS

2.50 g., Aluminum-Bronze, 18.10 mm. **Obv:** Armored bust of Bernardo O'Higgins, right **Rev:** Arms above denomination, date at left **Edge:** Plain

Date	Mintage	VF20	XF40	MS60	MS63	MS65
1971	99,700,000	—	—	0.10	0.15	0.25

KM# 195 20 CENTESIMOS

3.05 g., Aluminum-Bronze, 19.97 mm. **Obv:** Bust of Jose Manuel Balmaceda left **Rev:** Arms above denomination, date at left **Edge:** Plain

Date	Mintage	VF20	XF40	MS60	MS63	MS65
1971	89,200,000	—	—	0.10	0.20	0.35
1972	—	0.10	0.20	0.50	1.00	1.50

KM# 196 50 CENTESIMOS
4.15 g., Aluminum-Bronze, 21.9 mm. **Obv:** Bust of Manuel Rodriguez right **Rev:** Arms above denomination, date at left **Edge:** Plain

Date	Mintage	VF20	XF40	MS60	MS63	MS65
1971	58,300,000	0.10	0.15	0.20	0.25	0.45

KM# 197 ESCUDO
2.74 g., Copper-Nickel, 18.90 mm. **Obv:** Bust of Jose Miguel Carrera 3/4 facing **Rev:** Arms above denomination, date at left **Edge:** Reeded

Date	Mintage	VF20	XF40	MS60	MS63	MS65
1971	160,900,000	0.10	0.20	0.30	0.40	0.60
1972	Inc. above	0.10	0.20	0.30	0.40	0.60
1972	—	PF63 50.00				

KM# 198 2 ESCUDOS
Copper-Nickel **Obv:** Caupolican, Chief of Araucanian Indians **Rev:** Arms above denomination, date at left

Date	Mintage	VF20	XF40	MS60	MS63	MS65
1971	106	—	—	—	175	275
Note: Not released for circulation						
1971	—	PF63 150				

KM# 199 5 ESCUDOS
4.53 g., Copper-Nickel, 23.03 mm. **Obv:** Lautaro, Araucanian Indian, upriser against Spain **Rev:** Arms above denomination, date at left **Edge:** Reeded

Date	Mintage	VF20	XF40	MS60	MS63	MS65
1971	—	0.10	0.25	0.35	0.75	1.25
1972	—	0.10	0.25	0.35	0.75	1.25
1972	—	PF63 50.00				

KM# 199a 5 ESCUDOS
1.50 g., Aluminum, 22.8 mm. **Obv:** Lautaro, Araucanian Indian, upriser against Spain **Rev:** Arms above denomination, date at left **Edge:** Reeded

Date	Mintage	VF20	XF40	MS60	MS63	MS65
1972	—	—	0.10	0.15	0.20	0.50

KM# 200 10 ESCUDOS
2.00 g., Aluminum, 24.93 mm. **Obv:** Defiant Condor on rock left **Rev:** Denomination above date within wreath **Edge:** Plain

Date	Mintage	VF20	XF40	MS60	MS63	MS65
1974	33,750,000	—	0.10	0.15	0.35	0.50
1974	—	PF63 50.00				

Date	Mintage	VF20	XF40	MS60	MS63	MS65
1975	31,600,000	—	—	—	—	—

Note: Although recorded with mintage, no examples are known with this date

KM# 201 50 ESCUDOS
4.00 g., Nickel-Brass, 21.48 mm. **Obv:** Defiant Condor on rock left **Rev:** Denomination above date within wreath **Edge:** Plain **Shape:** 12-sided

Date	Mintage	VF20	XF40	MS60	MS63	MS65
1974	5,700,000	0.15	0.25	0.35	0.60	0.85
1975	20,300,000	0.15	0.20	0.25	0.50	0.75

KM# 202 100 ESCUDOS
5.01 g., Nickel-Brass, 23.5 mm. **Obv:** Defiant Condor on rock left **Rev:** Denomination above date within wreath **Edge:** Plain **Shape:** 12-sided

Date	Mintage	VF20	XF40	MS60	MS63	MS65
1974	32,100,000	0.20	0.35	0.50	0.75	1.00
1975	65,600,000	0.20	0.35	0.50	0.75	1.00

REFORM COINAGE

100 Centavos = 1 Peso; 1000 Old Escudos = 1 Peso

KM# 203 CENTAVO
2.00 g., Aluminum, 24.93 mm. **Obv:** Defiant Condor on rock left **Rev:** Denomination above date within wreath **Edge:** Plain

Date	Mintage	VF20	XF40	MS60	MS63	MS65
1975	2,000,000	0.10	0.15	0.25	0.50	0.75

KM# 204 5 CENTAVOS
3.95 g., Aluminum-Bronze, 21.6 mm. **Obv:** Defiant Condor on rock left **Rev:** Denomination above date within wreath **Edge:** Plain **Shape:** 12-sided

Date	Mintage	VF20	XF40	MS60	MS63	MS65
1975	5,400,000	—	0.10	0.15	0.25	0.75
1976	6,600,000	—	—	—	—	—

Note: Although recorded with mintage, no examples are known with this date

KM# 204a 5 CENTAVOS
1.50 g., Aluminum, 21.6 mm. **Obv:** Defiant Condor on rock left **Rev:** Date and denomination within wreath **Shape:** 12-sided

Date	Mintage	VF20	XF40	MS60	MS63	MS65
1976	5,000,000	—	0.10	0.15	0.25	0.75

KM# 205 10 CENTAVOS
5.01 g., Aluminum-Bronze, 23.75 mm. **Obv:** Defiant Condor on rock left **Rev:** Denomination above date within wreath **Edge:** Plain **Shape:** 12-sided

Date	Mintage	VF20	XF40	MS60	MS63	MS65
1975	8,600,000	—	0.10	0.15	0.25	0.75
1976	9,000,000	—	—	—	—	—

Note: Although recorded with mintage, no examples are known with this date

KM# 205a 10 CENTAVOS
2.05 g., Aluminum, 23.75 mm. **Obv:** Defiant Condor on rock left **Rev:** Denomination above date within wreath **Edge:** Plain **Shape:** 12-sided

Date	Mintage	VF20	XF40	MS60	MS63	MS65
1976	6,600,000	—	0.10	0.15	0.25	0.50
1977	57,800,000	—	0.10	0.15	0.25	0.50
1978	58,050,000	—	0.10	0.15	0.25	0.50
1979	101,950,000	—	0.10	0.15	0.25	0.50

KM# 206 50 CENTAVOS
4.13 g., Copper-Nickel, 22.17 mm. **Obv:** Defiant Condor on rock left **Rev:** Denomination above date within wreath **Edge:** Reeded

Date	Mintage	VF20	XF40	MS60	MS63	MS65
1975	38,000,000	—	0.10	0.15	0.25	0.50
1976	1,000,000	0.50	0.75	1.00	2.00	3.00
1977	10,000,000	—	0.10	0.15	0.25	0.50

KM# 206a 50 CENTAVOS
4.00 g., Aluminum-Bronze, 22.06 mm. **Obv:** Defiant Condor on rock left **Rev:** Denomination above date within wreath **Edge:** Reeded

Date	Mintage	VF20	XF40	MS60	MS63	MS65
1978	19,250,000	—	0.10	0.15	0.25	0.60
1979	28,000,000	—	0.10	0.15	0.25	0.60

KM# 207 PESO
5.00 g., Copper-Nickel, 24 mm. **Obv:** Armored bust of Bernardo O'Higgins right **Obv. Legend:** BERNARDO O'HIGGINS **Rev:** Denomination above date within wreath **Edge:** Reeded

Date	Mintage	VF20	XF40	MS60	MS63	MS65
1975	51,000,000	0.10	0.15	0.15	0.25	0.35

KM# 208 PESO
5.11 g., Copper-Nickel, 24 mm. **Obv:** Armored bust of Bernardo O'Higgins right **Obv. Legend:** LIBERTADOR. B. O'HIGGINS **Rev:** Denomination above date within wreath **Edge:** Reeded

Date	Mintage	VF20	XF40	MS60	MS63	MS65
1976	30,000,000	—	0.10	0.15	0.25	0.35
1977	20,000,000	—	0.10	0.15	0.25	0.35

KM# 208a PESO
5.00 g., Aluminum-Bronze, 24 mm. **Obv:** Armored bust of Bernardo O'Higgins right **Rev:** Denomination above date within wreath **Edge:** Reeded

Date	Mintage	VF20	XF40	MS60	MS63	MS65
1978	39,706,000	—	0.10	0.15	0.25	0.35
1979	63,000,000	—	0.10	0.15	0.25	0.35

KM# 216.1 PESO

2.00 g., Aluminum-Bronze, 17 mm. **Obv:** Armored bust right **Rev:** Denomination above date within wreath **Edge:** Plain **Note:** Reduced size. Wide date.

Date	Mintage	VF20	XF40	MS60	MS63	MS65
1981	40,000,000	—	—	0.10	0.20	0.30
1984	60,000,000	—	—	0.10	0.20	0.30
1985	20,000,000	—	—	0.10	0.20	0.30
1986	45,000,000	—	—	0.10	0.20	0.30
1987	80,000,000	—	—	0.10	0.20	0.30

KM# 216.2 PESO

2.00 g., Aluminum-Bronze, 17 mm. **Obv:** Armored bust, right **Rev:** Denomination above date within wreath **Edge:** Plain **Note:** Narrow date.

Date	Mintage	VF20	XF40	MS60	MS63	MS65
1988	105,000,000	—	—	0.10	0.20	0.30
1989	205,000,000	—	—	0.10	0.20	0.30
1990	140,000,000	—	—	0.10	0.20	0.30
1991	140,000,000	—	—	0.10	0.20	0.30

KM# 231 PESO

0.70 g., Aluminum, 15.5 mm. **Obv:** Gen. Bernardo O'Higgins bust right **Obv. Legend:** REPÚBLICA - DE CHILE **Rev:** Denomination above date within wreath **Edge:** Plain **Shape:** 8-sided **Note:** Varieties exist.

Date	Mintage	VF20	XF40	MS60	MS63	MS65
1992 So Wide date	—	—	—	—	0.10	0.20
1993 So Narrow date	—	—	—	—	0.10	0.20
1994 So Narrow date	—	—	—	—	0.10	0.20
1995 So Narrow date	—	—	—	—	0.10	0.20
1996 So Narrow date	—	—	—	—	0.10	0.20
1997 So Narrow date	—	—	—	—	0.10	0.20
1998 So Narrow date	—	—	—	—	0.10	0.20
1999 So Narrow date	—	—	—	—	0.10	0.20
2000 So Narrow date	—	—	—	—	0.10	0.20

KM# 209 5 PESOS

6.66 g., Copper-Nickel, 26 mm. **Subject:** 3rd Anniversary of New Government **Obv:** Winged figure with upraised arms, broken chain on wrists **Rev:** Denomination above date within wreath **Edge:** Reeded

Date	Mintage	VF20	XF40	MS60	MS63	MS65
1976	2,100,000	0.15	0.25	0.75	1.50	2.50
1977	28,300,000	0.15	0.25	0.75	1.50	2.50
1978	11,704,000	0.15	0.25	0.75	1.50	2.50
1980	8,200,000	0.15	0.25	0.75	1.50	2.50

KM# 217.1 5 PESOS

2.80 g., Aluminum-Bronze, 19 mm. **Obv:** Winged figure with arms upraised, broken chain on wrists **Rev:** Denomination above date within wreath **Edge:** Plain **Note:** Wide date.

Date	Mintage	VF20	XF40	MS60	MS63	MS65
1981	17,000,000	—	0.10	0.25	0.50	0.75
1982	20,000,000	—	0.10	0.25	0.50	0.75
1984	12,000,000	—	0.10	0.25	0.50	0.75
1985	16,000,000	—	0.10	0.25	0.50	0.75
1986	16,000,000	—	0.10	0.25	0.50	0.75
1987	8,000,000	—	0.10	0.25	0.50	0.75

KM# 217.2 5 PESOS

2.80 g., Aluminum-Bronze, 19 mm. **Obv:** Winged figure with arms upraised, broken chain on wrists **Rev:** Denomination above date within wreath **Edge:** Plain **Note:** Narrow date.

Date	Mintage	VF20	XF40	MS60	MS63	MS65
1988	27,000,000	—	0.10	0.25	0.50	0.75
1989	32,000,000	—	0.10	0.25	0.50	0.75
1990	23,000,000	—	0.10	0.25	0.50	0.75

KM# 229 5 PESOS

2.80 g., Aluminum-Bronze, 19 mm. **Obv:** Armored bust of Bernardo O'Higgins right **Rev:** Denomination above date within wreath **Edge:** Plain

Date	Mintage	VF20	XF40	MS60	MS63	MS65
1990	8,000,000	—	0.10	0.25	0.50	0.75
1991	2,000,000	—	0.10	0.25	0.50	0.75
1992	—	—	0.10	0.25	0.50	0.75

KM# 232 5 PESOS

2.20 g., Aluminum-Bronze, 15.5 mm. **Obv:** Gen. Bernardo O'Higgins bust right **Obv. Legend:** REPUBLICA - DE CHILE **Rev:** Denomination above date within wreath **Edge:** Plain **Shape:** 8-sided **Note:** Varieties exist.

Date	Mintage	VF20	XF40	MS60	MS63	MS65
1992 So	—	—	0.10	0.20	0.35	0.60
1993 So	—	—	0.10	0.20	0.35	0.60
1994 So	—	—	0.10	0.20	0.35	0.60
1995 So	—	—	0.10	0.20	0.35	0.60
1996 So	—	—	0.10	0.20	0.35	0.60
1997 So	—	—	0.10	0.20	0.35	0.60
1998 So	—	—	0.10	0.20	0.35	0.60
1999 So	—	—	0.10	0.20	0.35	0.60
2000 So	—	—	0.10	0.20	0.35	0.60

KM# 210 10 PESOS

8.90 g., Copper-Nickel, 28 mm. **Subject:** 3rd Anniversary of New Government **Obv:** Winged figure with arms upraised, broken chains on wrists **Rev:** Denomination above date within wreath **Edge:** Reeded

Date	Mintage	VF20	XF40	MS60	MS63	MS65
1976	2,100,000	0.10	0.20	0.75	1.25	1.50
1977	30,000,000	0.10	0.20	0.50	1.00	1.25
1978	20,004,000	0.10	0.20	0.50	1.00	1.25
1979	7,000,000	0.10	0.20	0.50	1.00	1.25
1980	20,000,000	0.10	0.20	0.50	1.00	1.25

KM# 211 10 PESOS

45.00 g., 0.999 Silver 1.4453 oz. ASW **Subject:** 3rd Anniversary of New Government **Obv:** Coat of arms above denomination **Rev:** Winged figure with arms upraised, two dates above **Edge:** Reeded

Date	Mintage	VF20	XF40	MS60	MS63	MS65
ND-1976	1,000	PF63 150		PF65 180		

KM# 218.1 10 PESOS

3.50 g., Aluminum-Bronze, 21 mm. **Obv:** Winged figure with arms upraised, broken chain on wrists **Rev:** Denomination above date within wreath **Edge:** Reeded **Note:** Wide date, narrow rim.

Date	Mintage	VF20	XF40	MS60	MS63	MS65
1981	55,000,000	0.10	0.20	0.30	0.50	0.75
1982	45,000,000	0.10	0.20	0.30	0.50	0.75
1984	30,000,000	0.10	0.20	0.30	0.50	0.75
1985	400,000	0.50	1.50	0.25	3.50	5.00
1986 Narrow date	25,000,000	0.10	0.20	0.30	0.50	0.75
1986 Wide date	Inc. above	0.10	0.20	0.30	0.50	0.75
1987	8,000,000	0.10	0.20	0.30	0.50	0.75

KM# 218.2 10 PESOS

3.50 g., Aluminum-Bronze, 21 mm. **Obv:** Winged figure with arms upraised, broken chain on wrists **Rev:** Denomination above date within wreath **Edge:** Reeded **Note:** Narrow date.

Date	Mintage	VF20	XF40	MS60	MS63	MS65
1988	45,000,000	0.10	0.20	0.30	0.50	0.75
1989	73,000,000	0.10	0.20	0.30	0.50	0.75

KM# 218.3 10 PESOS

3.50 g., Aluminum-Bronze, 21 mm. **Obv:** Winged figure with arms upraised, broken chain on wrists **Rev:** Denomination above date within wreath **Edge:** Reeded **Note:** Wide rim.

Date	Mintage	VF20	XF40	MS60	MS63	MS65
1990	10,000,000	0.10	0.20	0.30	0.50	0.75

KM# 228.1 10 PESOS

3.50 g., Aluminum-Bronze, 21 mm. **Obv:** Small bust of Bernardo

O'Higgins right, wide rim **Rev:** Denomination above date within wreath **Edge:** Reeded

Date	Mintage	VF20	XF40	MS60	MS63	MS65
1990	5,000,000	0.10	0.20	0.30	0.50	0.75

KM# 228.2 10 PESOS
3.50 g., Aluminum-Bronze, 21 mm. **Obv:** Bust of Gen. Bernardo O'Higgins right **Obv. Legend:** REPUBLICA - DE CHILE **Rev:** Denomination above date within sprays **Edge:** Reeded **Note:** All 9's are curl tail 9's except for the 1999 date, these are straight tail 9's. Normal rim.

Date	Mintage	VF20	XF40	MS60	MS63	MS65
1990 So	25,000,000	0.10	0.20	0.30	0.50	0.65
1991 So	—	0.10	0.20	0.30	0.50	0.65
1992 So	—	0.10	0.20	0.30	0.50	0.65
1993 So	—	0.10	0.20	0.30	0.50	0.65
1994 So	—	0.10	0.20	0.30	0.50	0.65
1995 So	—	0.10	0.20	0.30	0.50	0.65
1996 So	—	0.10	0.20	0.30	0.50	0.65
1997 So	—	0.10	0.20	0.30	0.50	0.65
1998 So	—	0.10	0.20	0.30	0.50	0.65
1999 So	—	0.10	0.20	0.30	0.50	0.65
2000 So	—	0.10	0.20	0.30	0.50	0.65

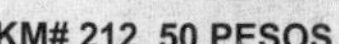

KM# 212 50 PESOS
10.15 g., 0.900 Gold 0.2937 oz. AGW **Subject:** 3rd Anniversary of New Government **Obv:** Coat of arms above denomination **Rev:** Winged figure with arms upraised, two dates above

Date	Mintage	VF20	XF40	MS60	MS63	MS65
ND-1976	1,900	—	—	—	550	600
ND-1976	Inc. above	PF65 700				

KM# 219.1 50 PESOS
7.00 g., Aluminum-Bronze, 25 mm. **Obv:** Armored bust right **Rev:** Denomination above date within wreath **Edge:** Ornamented **Shape:** 10-sided **Note:** Wide date.

Date	Mintage	VF20	XF40	MS60	MS63	MS65
1981	12,000,000	0.25	0.50	0.75	1.25	1.50
1982	14,000,000	0.25	0.50	0.75	1.25	1.50
1985	400,000	0.60	1.50	2.00	3.50	5.00
1986	1,000,000	0.25	0.50	0.75	1.25	1.50
1987	4,000,000	0.25	0.50	0.75	1.25	1.50

KM# 219.2 50 PESOS
7.00 g., Aluminum-Bronze, 25 mm. **Obv:** Bust of Gen. Bernardo O'Higgins right **Obv. Legend:** REPUBLICA - DE CHILE **Rev:** Denomination above date within sprays **Edge:** Ornamented **Shape:** 10-sided **Note:** Narrow date.

Date	Mintage	VF20	XF40	MS60	MS63	MS65
1988 So	4,800,000	0.25	0.50	0.75	1.25	1.50
1989 So	4,000,000	0.25	0.50	0.75	1.25	1.50
1991 So	10,845,000	0.25	0.50	0.75	1.25	1.50
1992 So	—	0.25	0.50	0.75	1.25	1.50
1993 So	—	0.25	0.50	0.75	1.25	1.50
1994 So	—	0.25	0.50	0.75	1.25	1.50
1995 So	—	0.25	0.50	0.75	1.25	1.50
1996 So	—	0.25	0.50	0.75	1.25	1.50
1997 So	—	0.25	0.50	0.75	1.25	1.50
1998 So	—	0.25	0.50	0.75	1.25	1.50
1999 So	—	0.25	0.50	0.75	1.25	1.50
2000 So	—	0.25	0.50	0.75	1.25	1.50

KM# 213 100 PESOS
20.30 g., 0.900 Gold 0.5874 oz. AGW **Subject:** 3rd Anniversary of New Government **Obv:** Coat of arms above date and denomination **Rev:** Winged figure with upraised arms, two dates above

Date	Mintage	VF20	XF40	MS60	MS63	MS65
1976	2,900	—	—	—	1,000	1,100
1976	100	PF65 1,250				

KM# 226.1 100 PESOS
9.00 g., Aluminum-Bronze, 27 mm. **Obv:** Coat of arms **Rev:** Denomination above date within wreath **Edge Lettering:** POR LA RAZON O LA FUERZA **Note:** Wide date with pointed 9.

Date	Mintage	VF20	XF40	MS60	MS63	MS65
1981	10,000,000	0.50	0.75	1.00	1.50	2.50
1984	8,000,000	0.50	0.75	1.00	1.50	2.50
1985	15,000,000	0.50	0.75	1.00	1.50	2.50
1986	11,000,000	0.50	0.75	1.00	1.50	2.50
1987	15,000,000	0.50	0.75	1.00	1.50	2.50

KM# 226.2 100 PESOS
9.00 g., Aluminum-Bronze, 27 mm. **Obv:** Coat of arms **Rev:** Denomination above date within wreath **Edge Lettering:** POR LA RAZON O LA FUERZA **Note:** Narrow date with curved 9.

Date	Mintage	VF20	XF40	MS60	MS63	MS65
1989 So	20,000,000	0.50	0.75	1.00	1.50	2.50
1991 So	4,320,000	0.50	0.75	1.00	1.50	2.50
1992 So	—	0.50	0.75	1.00	1.50	2.50
1993 So	—	0.50	0.75	1.00	1.50	2.50
1994 So	—	0.50	0.75	1.00	1.50	2.50
1995 So	—	0.50	0.75	1.00	1.50	2.50
1996 So	—	0.50	0.75	1.00	1.50	2.50
1997 So	—	0.50	0.75	1.00	1.50	2.50
1998 So	—	0.50	0.75	1.00	1.50	2.50
1999 So	—	0.50	0.75	1.00	1.50	2.50
2000 So	—	0.50	0.75	1.00	1.50	2.50

KM# 214 500 PESOS
102.27 g., 0.900 Gold 2.9592 oz. AGW **Subject:** 3rd Anniversary of New Government **Obv:** Coat of arms, denomination below **Rev:** Winged figure with upraised arms, two dates above **Note:** Similar to 100 Pesos, KM#213.

Date	Mintage	VF20	XF40	MS60	MS63	MS65
1976	500	—	—	—	5,250	5,500
1976	700	PF65 5,750				

KM# 235 500 PESOS
6.50 g., Bi-Metallic Aluminum-Bronze center in Copper-Nickel-Zinc ring, 26 mm. **Subject:** Cardinal Raul Silva Henriquez **Obv:** Bust of cardinal within inner ring facing left **Rev:** Denomination above date within wreath **Edge:** Reeded

Date	Mintage	VF20	XF40	MS60	MS63	MS65
2000 So	—	—	—	2.50	5.00	6.50
2000 So Proof	—	—	—	—	—	—

KM# 233 2000 PESOS
8.20 g., 0.500 Silver 0.1318 oz. ASW, 26.2 mm. **Subject:** 250th Anniversary of the Mint **Obv:** Building divides date and denomination **Rev:** Metal workers, two dates below **Edge:** Reeded

Date	Mintage	VF20	XF40	MS60	MS63	MS65
1993	50,000	—	—	8.00	12.00	15.00

KM# 230 10000 PESOS
27.00 g., 0.925 Silver 0.803 oz. ASW, 40 mm. **Series:** Ibero - American **Obv:** Inner circle holds Coat of Arms, denomination within outer circle, 13 shields surround **Rev:** Three dates below three ships, globe in background **Edge:** Reeded

Date	Mintage	VF20	XF40	MS60	MS63	MS65
1991	75,000	PF63 32.00	PF65 45.00			

PATTERNS

Including off metal strikes

KM#	Date	Mintage	Identification	Mkt Val
PnA26	1903	—	2-1/2 Centavos.	—
PnB26	1906	—	10 Centavos.	—
PnC26	1906	—	10 Centavos.	—
PnD26	1908	—	5 Centavos. Copper-Nickel.	400
PnE26	1908	—	10 Centavos. Brass.	—
PnF26	1914	—	50 Centavos. Silver.	—
Pn26	1914	—	Peso. Silver.	1,500
PnA27	1914	—	50 Centavos.	1,200
PnB27	1914	—	2 Pesos. Silver. Piefort, large flan.	850
Pn27	1914	—	2 Pesos. Silver. Piefort, small flan.	850
Pn28	1916	—	20 Centavos. Silver.	—
Pn29	1916	—	20 Centavos. Silver.	—
Pn30	1917	—	10 Centavos. Silver.	—
Pn31	1917	—	10 Centavos. Silver.	—
Pn32	1919	—	5 Centavos. Copper-Nickel.	—
Pn33	1919	—	5 Centavos. Silver.	—
Pn34	1919	—	5 Centavos. Silver.	—
Pn35	1919	—	10 Centavos. Copper-Nickel.	—
Pn36	1919	—	20 Centavos. Copper-Nickel.	—
Pn37	ND19xx (1919)	—	10 Centavos. Copper-Nickel. Center hole.	—
Pn38	1926	—	Peso. Silver. Indian, date below chin. Star within wreath divides denomination.	700
Pn39	1926	—	Peso. Silver. Fineness added.	700
Pn40	1926	—	Peso. Silver. Coat of arms. Without fineness.	750
Pn41	1926	—	2 Pesos. Silver. Condor. Coat of arms. Without fineness.	1,250
Pn42	1926	—	2 Pesos. Silver. Indian. Star in wreath. 5" fineness, Pn43.	750

KM#	Date	Mintage	Identification	Mkt Val
Pn43	1926	—	2 Pesos. Silver. Indian. Star in wreath. 72" fineness, Pn44.	750
Pn44	1926	—	5 Pesos.	1,900
Pn45	1926	—	5 Pesos. Silver. Weak or no fineness (effaced from die).	1,000
Pn46	1926	—	5 Pesos. Silver.	1,550
Pn47	1927	—	Peso. Copper-Nickel.	325
Pn48	1927	—	Peso. Silver.	625
Pn49	1927	—	5 Pesos. Silver.	375
PnA50	1928	—	5 Pesos. Indian head.	—
PnA51	1928	—	2 Pesos. Mine workers.	—
PnA54	1928	—	2 Pesos. Indian head.	—
Pn50	1929	—	20 Centavos. Copper-Nickel. Center hole.	450
Pn51	1929	—	20 Centavos. Copper-Nickel. Pn49 but "CHILE" on reverse instead of "20".	450
Pn52	1929	—	Peso. Silver.	650
Pn53	ND-1929	—	Peso. Silver. Without country, date or fineness.	650
Pn54	ND-1929	—	Peso. Silver. Similar to Pn52, without mountains on obverse.	650
Pn55	1930	—	20 Centavos. Copper-Nickel. Center hole.	1,000
Pn56	1930	—	20 Centavos. Copper-Nickel. Pn54 but "20" instead of "CHILE" on obverse, with center hole.	800
Pn57	1930	—	Peso. Silver. Worker and factory. Value.	1,200
Pn58	1930	—	2 Pesos. Copper-Nickel. Condor. Value and date in wreath.	1,000
PnA59	1933	—	Peso. Nickel. KM#176.1.	200
Pn59	1933	—	Peso. Copper-Nickel. Condor. Value and date in wreath.	350
PnA60	1933	—	Peso. Copper-Nickel. Condor. Value and date in wreath. Mint punched cancelled.	350
Pn60	1938	—	5 Pesos. Brass.	625
Pn61	1938	—	5 Pesos. Copper-Nickel.	—
PnA62	ND-1938	—	5 Pesos. Plain. Aluminum-Bronze or Silver.	500
Pn62	ND-1938	—	5 Pesos. Silver. Without date.	375
PnA63	1940	—	2 Pesos. Sitting condor, closed wings with and without date.	—
PnB63	1941	—	20 Centavos. Bronze.	125
Pn63	1942	—	Peso. Copper. Like KM#179, but smaller diameter.	125
Pn64	1947	—	100 Pesos. Copper.	—
Pn65	1948	—	Onza. Silver.	120
Pn65a	1948	—	Onza. Copper.	45.00
PnA66	1951	—	10 Pesos. Aluminum-Bronze. Thick flan.	120
Pn66	1953	—	20 Centavos. Aluminum.	155
Pn67	1956	—	5 Pesos. Brass. KM#180.	—
Pn68	1959	—	10 Pesos. Brass. KM#181.	—
Pn69	1960	—	2 Centesimos. Brass. Uniface.	130
PnA70	1960	—	2 Centesimos. Aluminum-Bronze.	95.00
Pn70	1960	—	2 Centesimos. Copper-Nickel.	80.00
Pn71	1960	—	5 Centesimos. Copper. KM#190.	130
Pn72	1960	—	5 Centesimos. Copper-Nickel. Plain. KM#190.	115
Pn73	1960	—	5 Centesimos. Copper-Nickel. Milled. KM#190.	95.00
Pn74	1960	—	10 Centesimos. Copper. KM#191.	130
Pn75	1960	—	10 Centesimos. Copper-Nickel. KM#191.	60.00
Pn76	1960	—	10 Centesimos. Brass. KM#191.	—
Pn77	1960	—	10 Centesimos. Brass.	—
Pn78	1960	—	10 Centesimos. Aluminum-Bronze. Legend. Arms flanked by C-M.	85.00
Pn79	1960	—	10 Centesimos. Copper-Nickel. Legend. Arms flanked by C-M.	85.00
Pn80	1964	—	2 Centesimos. Copper-Nickel. KM#193.	95.00
Pn81	1968	—	100 Pesos. Copper. Center hole.	150
Pn82	1969	—	Peso. Copper-Nickel. Ten sided. Ten sided, arms with "C.M." below.	125
Pn83	1971	—	Peso. Nickel.	—
Pn84	ND (1971)	—	50 Pesos. Aluminum-Bronze. Equestrian statue of Lautaro, left. Arms above denomiation within wreath.	—
Pn85	1971	—	2 Escudos. Silver. KM#198.	—
Pn86	1972	—	5 Escudos. Silver. KM#199.	—
Pn87	1972	—	Escudo. Silver. KM197.	—
Pn88	1974	—	10 Escudos. Aluminum.	—
Pn89	1979	5	100 Pesos. 0.500. Silver. Equestrian statue of O'Higgins.	—

PIEDFORT

KM#	Date	Mintage	Identification	Mkt Val
P4	1951	—	10 Pesos. Aluminum-Bronze. KM#181.	125

TRIAL STRIKES

KM#	Date	Mintage	Identification	Mkt Val
TS7	ND-1960	—	10 Centesimos. Copper-Nickel. Coat of arms flanked by C-M. Coat of arms flanked by C-M.	70.00
TS8	ND-1960	—	10 Centesimos. Aluminum-Bronze. Coat of arms flanked by C-M. Coat of arms flanked by C-M.	60.00

PROOF SETS

KM#	Date	Mintage	Identification	Issue Price	Mkt Val
PS1	1968 (6)	—	KM#182-187. Total of 12,000 coins struck for each denomination including those available singly.	560	8,500
PS2	1968 (4)	—	KM#184-187. Total of 12,000 coins struck for each denomination including those available singly.	528	8,000
PS3	1968 (2)	—	KM#182, 183. Total of 12,000 coins struck for each denomination including those available singly.	31.50	175
PS4	1971/2 (3)	—	KM#197 (1972), KM#198 (1971), KM#199 (1972). Total of 12,000 coins struck for each denomination including those available singly.	—	165

VALDIVIA

REPUBLIC

SILVER BULLION COINAGE

KM# 223 1/4 ONZA

7.78 g., 0.999 Silver 0.2498 oz. ASW **Subject:** 10th Anniversary of National Liberation

Date	Mintage	F12	VF20	XF40	MS60	MS63
ND-1983	1,000	PF65 20.00				

KM# 225 ONZA

31.11 g., 0.999 Silver 0.9991 oz. ASW **Subject:** 10th Anniversary of National Liberation

Date	Mintage	F12	VF20	XF40	MS60	MS63
ND-1983	1,000	PF65 50.00				

KM# 234 ONZA

31.10 g., 0.999 Silver 0.999 oz. ASW **Subject:** Numismatic Association of Chile **Obv:** Similar to 4 Escudos, KM#2 **Rev:** Similar to 1/2 Real, KM#90 obverse

Date	Mintage	F12	VF20	XF40	MS60	MS63
ND-1999	75	PF65 95.00				

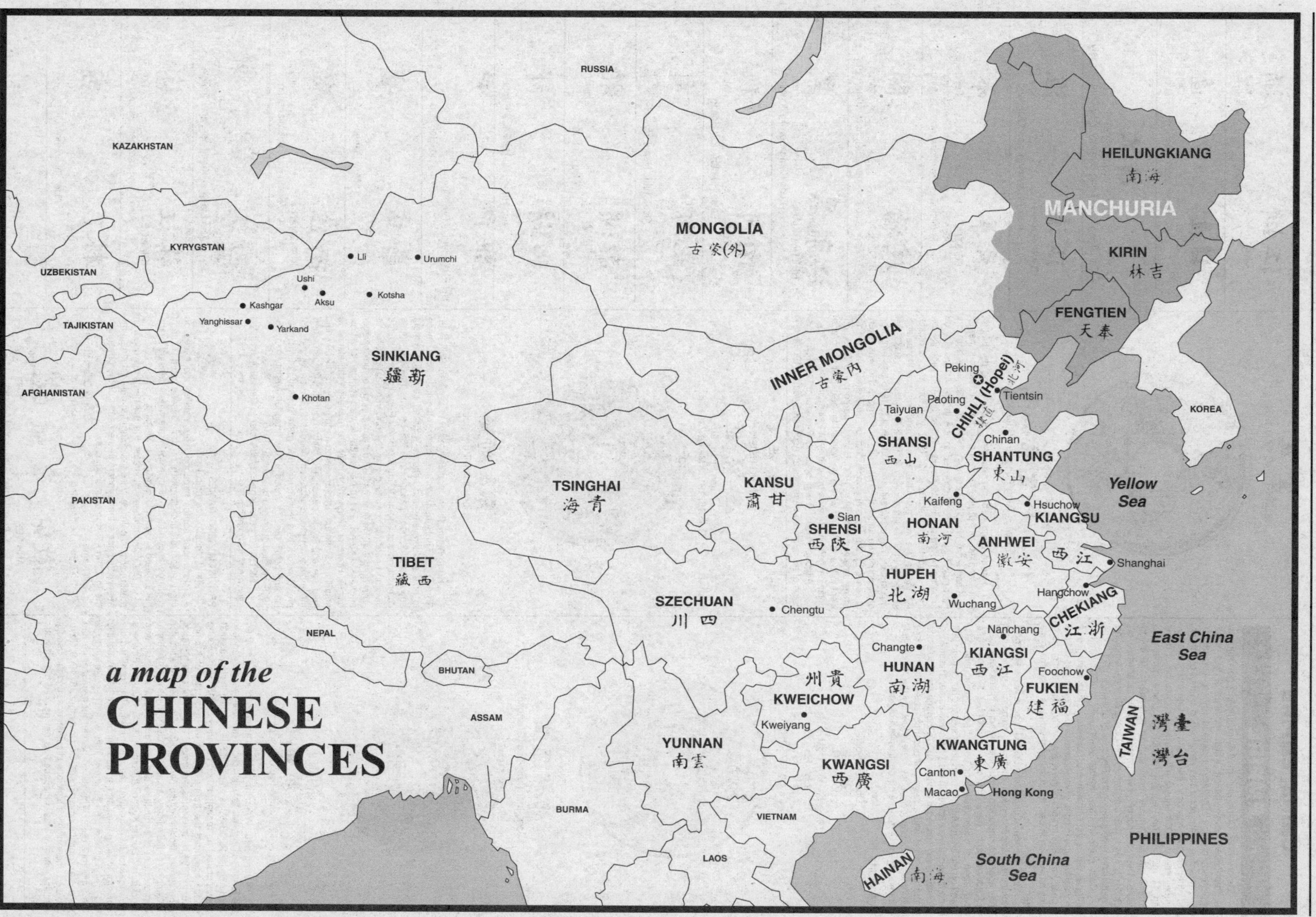
a map of the
CHINESE PROVINCES
RUSSIA
KAZAKHSTAN
KYRYGSTAN
UZBEKISTAN
TAJIKISTAN
AFGHANISTAN
PAKISTAN
MONGOLIA
古蒙(外)
SINKIANG
Lli
Urumchi
Ushi
Aksu
Kotsha
Kashgar
Yanghissar
Yarkand
Khotan
INNER MONGOLIA
古蒙内
MANCHURIA
HEILUNGKIANG
KIRIN
林吉
FENGTIEN
天奉
KOREA
Peking
CHIHLI (Hopei)
Tientsin
Paoting
Taiyuan
SHANSI
西山
Chinan
SHANTUNG
東山
Yellow Sea
TSINGHAI
海青
KANSU
肅甘
Sian
SHENSI
西陝
Kaifeng
HONAN
南河
Hsuchow
KIANGSU
ANHWEI
徽安
Shanghai
TIBET
藏西
HUPEH
北湖
Wuchang
Hangchow
CHEKIANG
江浙
SZECHUAN
川四
Chengtu
NEPAL
BHUTAN
ASSAM
Nanchang
KIANGSI
西江
Changte
HUNAN
南湖
East China Sea
州貴
KWEICHOW
Kweiyang
Foochow
FUKIEN
建福
TAIWAN
灣臺
灣台
YUNNAN
南雲
KWANGSI
西廣
KWANGTUNG
東廣
Canton
Macao
Hong Kong
BURMA
VIETNAM
LAOS
PHILIPPINES
HAINAN
South China Sea

CHINA, EMPIRE

EMPIRE

Before 1912, China was ruled by an imperial government. The republican administration which replaced it was itself supplanted on the Chinese mainland by a communist government in 1949, but it has remained in control of Taiwan and other offshore islands in the China Sea with a land area of approximately 14,000 square miles and a population of more than 14 million. The People's Republic of China administers some 3.7 million square miles and an estimated 1.19 billion people. This communist government, officially established on October 1, 1949, was admitted to the United Nations, replacing its nationalist predecessor, the Republic of China, in 1971.

Cast coins in base metals were used in China many centuries before the Christian era, but locally struck coinages of the western type in gold, silver, copper and other metals did not appear until 1888.In spite of the relatively short time that modern coins have been in use, the number of varieties is exceptionally large.

Both Nationalist and Communist China, as well as the pre-revolutionary Imperial government and numerous provincial or other agencies, including some foreign-administered agencies and governments, have issued coins in China. Most of these have been in dollar (yuan) or dollar-fraction denominations, based on the internationally used dollar system, but coins in tael denominations were issued in the 1920's and earlier. The striking of coins nearly ceased in the late 1930's through the 1940's due to the war effort and a period of uncontrollable inflation while vast amounts of paper currency were issued by the Nationalist, Communist and Japanese occupation institutions.

EMPERORS

Obverse Types

光緒
KUANG-HSÜ
德宗
Te Tsung 1875-1908

Type A
光緒通寶
Kuang-hsü T'ung-pao (Guangxu)

Type B
光緒重寶
Kuang-hsü Chung-pao

Kuang-hsü - When the previous emperor died, his mother, the Empress Dowager Tz'u-hsi, chose her four-year-old nephew, born August 14, 1871, as emperor. She adopted the boy so that she could act as regent and on February 25, 1875, the young prince ascended the throne, taking the reign title of Kuang-hsü. In 1898 he tried to assert himself and collected a group of progressive officials around him. He issued a series of edicts for revamping of the military, abolition of civil service examinations, improvement of agriculture and restructuring of administrative procedures. During Kuang-hsü's reign (1875-1908) the Empress Dowager totally dominated the government. She confined the emperor to his palace and spread rumors that he was deathly ill. Foreign powers let it be known they would not take kindly to the Emperor's death. This saved his life but thereafter he had no power over the government. On November 15, 1908, Tz'u-hsi died under highly suspicious circumstances and the usually healthy emperor was announced as having died the previous day.

宣統
HSÜAN-T'UNG 1908-1911

Type A
宣統
Hsüan-t'ung T'ung-pao (Xuantong)

Hsuan-t'ung - The last emperor of the Ch'ing dynasty in China and Japan's puppet emperor, under the assumed name of K'ang-te, in Manchoukuo from 1934 to 1945, was born on February 7, 1906. He succeeded to the throne at the age of three on November 14, 1908. He reigned under a regency for three years but on February 12, 1912, was forced to abdicate the throne. He was permitted to continue living in the palace in Peking until he left secretly in 1924. On March 9, 1932, he was installed as president, and from 1934 to 1945 was emperor of Manchoukuo under the reign title of K'ang-te. He was taken prisoner by the Russians in August of 1945 and returned to China as a war criminal in 1950. He was pardoned in 1959 and went to live in Peking where he worked in the repair shop of a botanical garden. He died peacefully in Peking in 1967.

Although Hsüan-t'ung became Emperor in 1908, all the coins of his reign are based on an Accession year of 1909.

憲洪
HUNG-HSIEN
宣統通
(Yuan Shih-k'ai)
Dec. 15, 1915 - March 21, 1916

憲洪 通寶
Hung-hsien T'ung-pao

Hung-hsien (more popularly known as Yuan Shih-K'ai). Born in 1859 in Honan Province, he was the first Han Chinese to hold a viceroyalty and become a grand councillor without any academic qualifications. In 1885 he was made Chinese commissioner at Seoul. During the Boxer Rebellion of 1900, the division under his command was the only remnant of China's army to survive. He enjoyed the trust and support of the dowager empress, Tz'u-hsi, and at her death he was stripped of all his offices. However, when the tide of the revolution threatened to engulf the Manchus Yuan appeared as the only man who could lead the country to peace and unity. Both the Emperor and the provisional president recommended that Yuan be the first president of China. He contrived to make himself president for life and boldly tried to create a new imperial dynasty in 1915-1916. He died of uremia on June 6, 1916.

NOTE: For other legend types refer to Rebel Issues listed after Yunnan-Szechuan.

PROVINCIAL MINT NAMES

(and other source indicators)

Provincial names throughout the catalog are based on the Wade-Giles transliteration of the Chinese word. Current spellings, known as the "Pinyin" form, are widely adopted by the printed media. Example: Sinkiang = Xinjiang.

The column at left illustrates the full name as used on most provincial coinage while the column at right illustrates the abbreviated name that appears in the center of the obverse of the Tai-Ch'ing-Ti-Kuo copper coinage.

Full Name — Single Character (1)
Right to Left reading

徽安 — 皖
ANHWEI — Huan
Also An-hwi, Anhui, now Anhui

江浙 — 浙
CHEKIANG — Che
Also Cheh-kiang, now Zhejiang

隸直 — 直
CHIHLI — Chih
Also Hopei (after 1928), now Hebei

CH'ING DYNASTY
Tai Ch'ing, also Tsing Dynasty, now Qing Dynasty

 — 
CHING-KIANG — Huai
Also Tsing-kiang, now Qingjiang

天奉 — 奉
FENGTIEN — Feng
Also Fung-tien, Fun-tien Shengching, Manchurian Provinces, now Liaoning

建福 — 閩
FUKIEN — Min
Also Foo-kien, F.K., now Fujian

江龍黑 — 
HEILUNGKIANG — Hei
Also Hei Lung Kiang, now Heilongjiang

南河 — 豫
HONAN — Yu
Also Ho-nan, now Henan

北河 — 冀
HOPEH — Chi
Also Chihli, Hopei, now Hebei

南湖 — 湘
HUNAN — Hsiang
Also Hu-nan

北湖 — 鄂
HUPEH — O
Also Hupei, Hu-peh, now Hubei

部戶 — 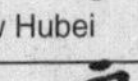
HU PU (Board of Revenue) — Hu
Also Hu Poo, Hoo Poo

肅甘 — 甘
KANSU — Kan
Now Gansu

南江 — 寗
KIANGNAN — Ning
Also Kiang Nan, now Jiangnan

西江 — 贛 — 贛
KIANGSI — Kan — or
Also Kiang-si, Kiang-see, now Jiangxi

蘇江 — 蘇
KIANGSU — Su
Also Kiang-soo, now Jiangsu

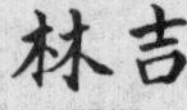 — 吉
KIRIN — Chi
Also Chi-lin, now Jilin

西廣 桂

KWANGSI, KWANGSEA Kuei

Also Kwang-si, now Guangxi

東廣 粵

KWANGTUNG Yüeh

Also Kwang-tung, now Guangdong

州貴 黔

KWEICHOW Ch'ien

Also Kweichou, now Guizhou

洋北

PEIYANG MINT (Tientsin)

Also Pei Yang

西山 山

SHANSI Shan

Now Shanxi (Chin)

西陝 陝

SHENSI Shan

Also Shen-si, now Shaanxi

東山 東

SHANTUNG TUNG

Also Shang-tung, Shan-tung, now Shandong (Lu)

魯

SIKANG

疆新 新

SINKIANG Hsin

(Chinese Turkestan)

Also Sin-kiang, Hsin-kiang Sungarei, now Xinjiang

川四 川 蜀

SZECHUAN Ch'uan

Also Szechwan Szechuen, now Sichuan (Shu)

灣臺 臺

TAIWAN T'ai

Also Tai-wan, now Taiwan

灣台 台

TAIWAN T'ai

(Alternate)

南雲 雲 滇

YÜNNAN Yün (Alternate) (Tien)

Also Yun-nan, now Yunnan

省三東

TUNG SAN SHENG

Manchuria

滇川

YUNNAN-SZECHUAN

GOVERNMENTAL NAMES

(and other source indicators)

Full Names (Right to left reading)

府政東冀

CHITUNG (Japanese puppet)

國和共埃維蘇華中

CHINESE SOVIET REPUBLIC

國洲滿大

MANCHOUKUO (Japanese puppet) (2)

行銀疆蒙

MENGCHIANG (Japanese puppet)

中華人民共和國

PEOPLES REPUBLIC OF CHINA (Communist) (3)

國民華中

REPUBLIC OF CHINA (Nationalist)

行銀備準合聯國中

NORTH CHINA (Japanese puppet)

(1) Single-character designators for provincial or regional mints are used primarily on copper coins of the Tai Ching Ti Kuo series.

(2) Vertical readings predominate.

(3) Reads left to right.

(4) For lists of mints in Sinkiang, see that section.]

ADDITIONAL CHARACTERS

The additional characters illustrated and defined below are found on the reverse of cast bronze cash coins, usually above the square center hole. In the period covered by this catalog the following mints produced cash coins with these additional marks: Board of Revenue and Board of Works in Peking, Kweichow, Aksu and Ili in Sinkiang, Shantung, Szechuan, and all three mints listed in Yunnan.

CHARACTERS

一	I, Yi	十一	Shih I	心	Hsin
二	Erh	合	Ho	宇	Yu
三	San	工	Kung	宙	Chou
四	Szu	主	Chu	來	Lai
五	Wu	川	Ch'uan	往	Wang
六	Liu	之	Chih	晋	Chin
七	Ch'i	正	Cheng	村	Ts'un
八	Pa	又	Yu	日	Jih
九	Chiu	山	Shan	列	Lieh
十	Shih	大	Ta	仁	Jen
主	Chung	中	Feng	手	Shang
順	Shun	云	Yun	手	Shou
天	T'ien	利	Li	穴	Kung
分	Fen				

MINT MARK IDENTIFIER

Boo-Clowan
(Peking)
Hu-Pu
Board of Revenue

Boo-Yuwan
(Peking)
Kung-Pu
Board of Public Works

Boo-an
An Mint
ANHWEI

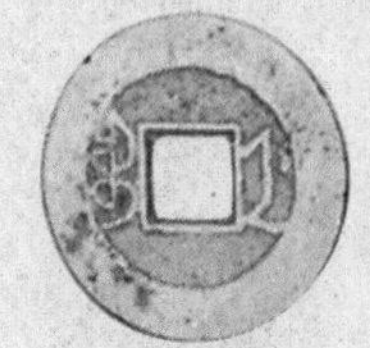

Boo-Je
Chê Mint
Hangchow
CHEKIANG

Boo-Ji
Chih Mint
Paoting
CHIHLI

Boo-GI
Chi Mint
Chichow
CHIHLI

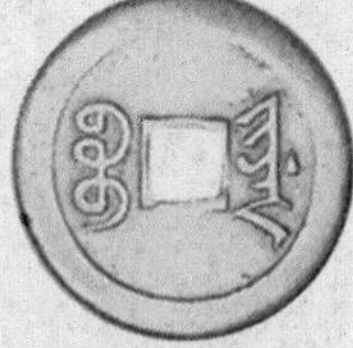

Boo-Jiyen
Ching Mint
Tientsin
CHIHLI

(Through Hsien-Feng era)

Boo-Fung
Fung Mint
FENGTIEN

Boo-Fu
Fu Mint
Fuchou
FUKIEN

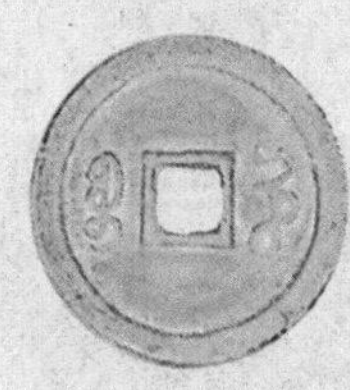

Boo-Ho
Ho Mint
K'aifeng
HONAN

Boo-Nan
Nan Mint
Ch'ang-sha
HUNAN

Boo-De
Teh Mint
Chengte
CHIHLI

Boo-U
Wu Mint
Wuch'ang
HUPEH

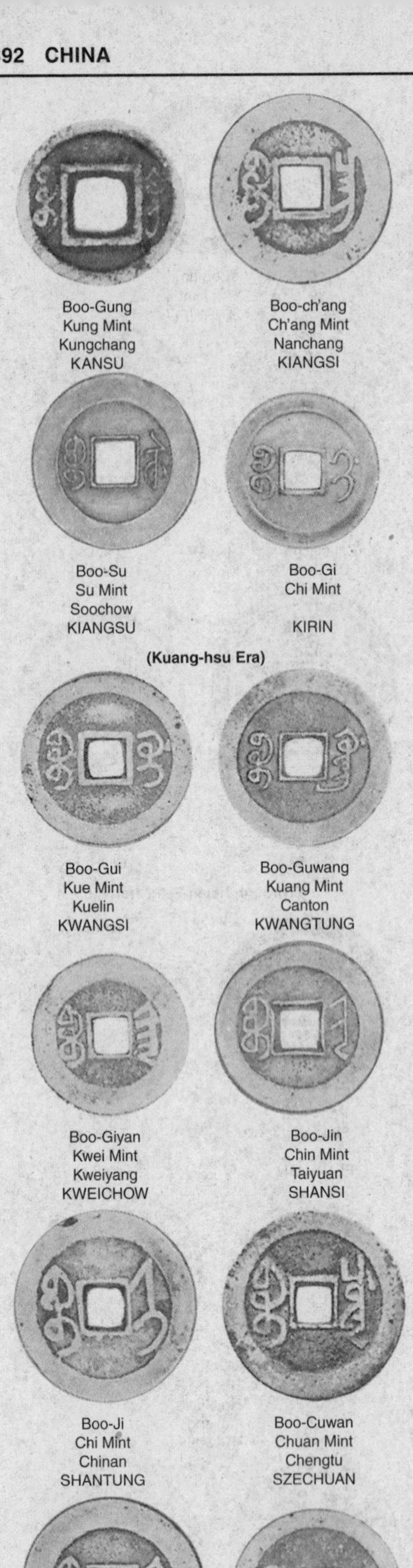

Boo-Gung
Kung Mint
Kungchang
KANSU

Boo-ch'ang
Ch'ang Mint
Nanchang
KIANGSI

Boo-Su
Su Mint
Soochow
KIANGSU

Boo-Gi
Chi Mint

KIRIN

(Kuang-hsu Era)

Boo-Gui
Kue Mint
Kuelin
KWANGSI

Boo-Guwang
Kuang Mint
Canton
KWANGTUNG

Boo-Giyan
Kwei Mint
Kweiyang
KWEICHOW

Boo-Jin
Chin Mint
Taiyuan
SHANSI

Boo-Ji
Chi Mint
Chinan
SHANTUNG

Boo-Cuwan
Chuan Mint
Chengtu
SZECHUAN

Boo-San
Shan Mint
Sian
SHENSI

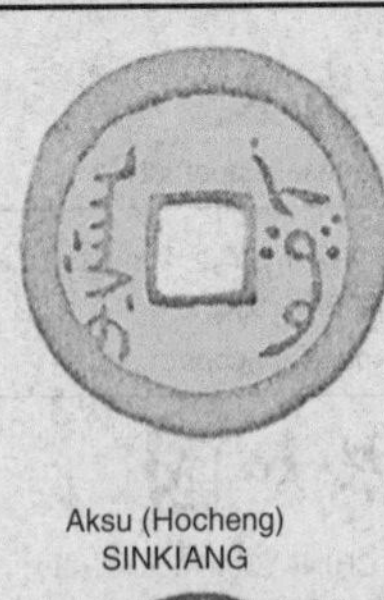

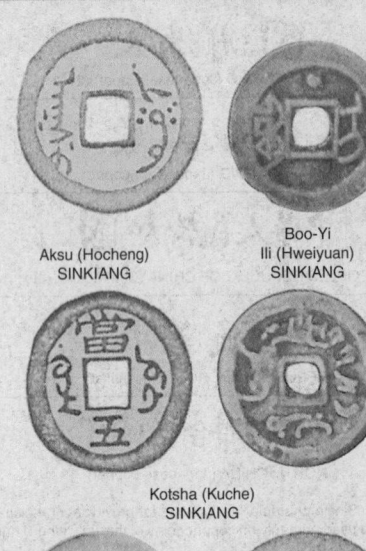

Aksu (Hocheng)
SINKIANG

Boo-Yi
Ili (Hweiyuan)
SINKIANG

Kotsha (Kuche)
SINKIANG

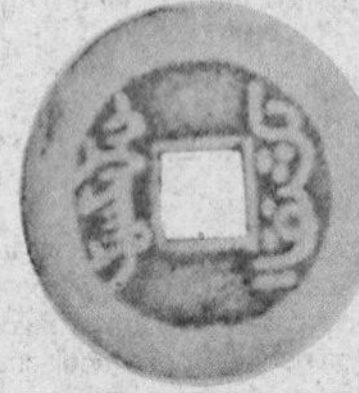

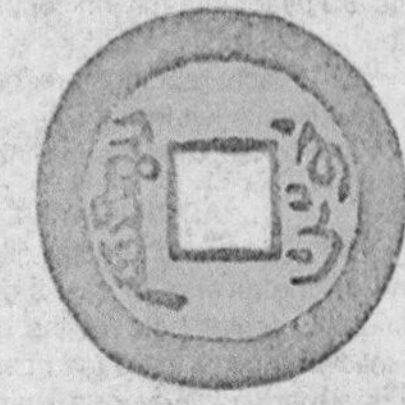

Kashgar (Shufu)
SINKIANG

Khotan (Hotien)
SINKIANG

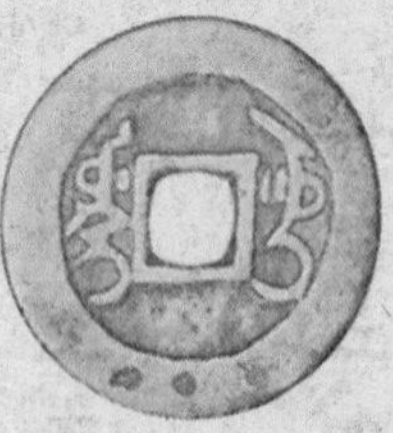

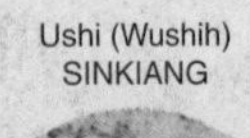

Boo-Di
Di Mint
Urumchi (Tihwa)
SINKIANG

Ushi (Wushih)
SINKIANG

Yarkand (Soche)
SINKIANG

Boo-Tai
Tai Mint
TAIWAN

Boo-Yôn
Yûn Mint
Yûnnan Fu
YUNNAN

Boo-Dong
Tung Mint
Tungch'uan
YUNNAN

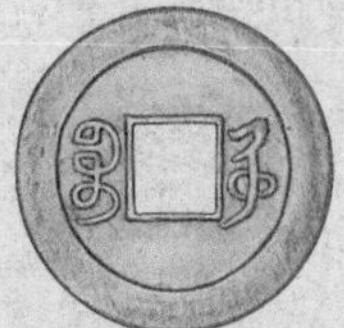

Boo-Gu
Ku Mint
Taku Arsenal
TIENTSIN, CHIHLI

Boo-Fu
Fu Mint
Fuchow
YUNNAN

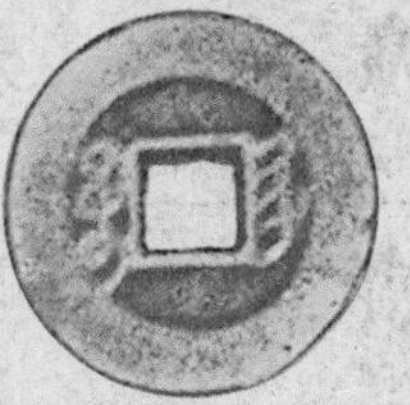

Boo-Jing
Ching Mint
Chingchow
HUPEH

NON-CIRCULATING ISSUES

Along with regular circulation coinage produced by the various mints certain cash types were cast in various sizes with the emperor's reign title on the obverse but with various characters and/or symbols not found in our mint identifiers. This listing is not complete but it will benefit the collector as an aid to proper identification.

PALACE ISSUES

(Palace Cash)

Usually 1-6 mace in weight, made of 60" copper and 40" zinc. Made for distribution in the palace during new year. Usually given to eunuchs and guards. Recipients hanged them under lamps - "lamp 'hanging' money."

Obv. inscription: Kuang-hsü T'ung-pao
Rev. inscription: T'ien-hsia T'ai-p'ing
"Peace under Heaven."

NOTE: The market value is about $60.00-100.00 in VF condition.

BIRTHDAY CASH

壽 福

These issues have the normal reign title on the obverse but the reverse has two Chinese characters *Fu* in normal or seal script (happiness), at right and *Shou* (birthday) at left. The market value is about $60.00-100.00 in F/VF condition. Some are palace issues, but most are made by private sources as good luck amulets.

Kuang-hsu

MONETARY UNITS

Dollar Amounts		
DOLLAR *(Yuan)*	元 or 員	圓 or 圜
HALF DOLLAR *(Pan Yuan)*	圓 半	元中
50¢ *(Chiao/Hao)*	角伍	毫伍
10¢ *(Chiao/Hao)*	角壹	毫壹
1¢ *(Fen/Hsien)*	分壹	仙壹

NUMERALS

NUMBER	CONVENTIONAL	FORMAL	COMMERCIAL
1	一 元	壹 弌	〡
2	二	弍 貳	〢
3	三	叁 弎	〣
4	四	肆	〤
5	五	伍	〥
6	六	陸	〦
7	七	柒	〧
8	八	捌	〨
9	九	玖	〩
10	十	拾 什	十
20	十 二 or 廿	拾貳	〢十
25	五 十 二 or 五廿	伍拾貳	〢十〥
30	十 三 or 卅	拾叁	〣十
100	百 一	佰壹	〡百
1,000	千 一	仟壹	〡千
10,000	萬 一	萬壹	〡万
100,000	萬十 億一	萬拾 億壹	十万
1,000,000	萬百一	萬佰壹	〡百万

NOTE: This table has been adapted from *Chinese Bank Notes* by Ward Smith and Brian Matravers.

COPPER AND CASH COIN AMOUNTS

COPPER (*Mei*)	枚	CASH (*Wen*)	文

Tael Amounts

1 TAEL (*Liang*)	兩
HALF TAEL (*Pan Liang*)	兩半
5 MACE (*Wu Ch'ien*)	钱伍
1 MACE (*I Ch'ien*)	钱壹
1 CANDEREEN (*I Fen*)	分壹

COMMON PREFIXES

COPPER (*T'ung*)	銅	GOLD (*Chin*)	金
SILVER (*Yin*)	銀	Ku Ping (*Tael*)*	平庫

NOTE: This table has been adapted from Chinese Bank Notes by Ward Smith and Brian Matravers.

MONETARY SYSTEM

Cash Coin System

800-1600 Cash = 1 Tael
400 Sinkiang 'red' cash = 1 Tael

In theory, 1000 cash were equal to a tael of silver, but in actuality the rate varied from time to time and place to place.

Dollar System

10 Cash (Wen, Ch'ien) = 1 Cent (Fen, Hsien)
10 Cents = 1 Chiao (Hao)
100 Cents = 1 Dollar (Yuan)
1 Dollar = 0.72 Kuping Tael

Imperial silver coins normally bore no denomination, but were inscribed with their weights as follows:

1 Dollar = 7 Mace and 2 Candareens, 26.86 g
50 Cents = 3 Mace and 6 Candareens, 13.43 g
20 Cents = 1 Mace and 4.4 Candareens, 5.37 g
10 Cents = 7.2 Candareens, 2.68 g
5 Cents = 3.6 Candareens, 1.34 g

NOTE: *Candareen* is spelled *Candarin* and misspelled as *Caindarin* on Kirin Province Imperial coinage.

Tael System

10 Li = 1 Fen (Candareen), .37 g
10 Fen (Candareen) = 1 Ch'ien (Mace), 3.73 g
10 Ch'ien (Mace) = 1 Kuping Liang (Tael), 37.31 g

DATING

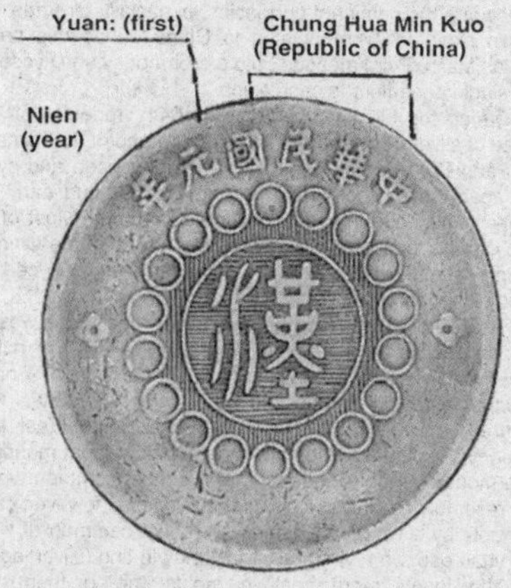

Most struck Chinese coins are dated by year within a given period, such as the regnal eras or the republican periods. A 1907 issue, for example, would be dated in the 33rd year of the Kuang Hsu era (1875 + 33 - 1 = 1907) or a 1926 issue is dated in the 15th year of the Republic (1912 + 15 - 1 = 1926). The mathematical discrepancy in both instances is accounted for by the fact that the first year is included in the elapsed time. Modern Chinese Communist coins are dated in western numerals using the western calendar, but earlier issues use conventional Chinese numerals. The coins of the Republic of China (Taiwan) are also dated in the year of the Republic, which is added to equal the calendar year. Still another method is a 60-year, repeating cycle, outlined in the table below. The date is shown by the combination of two characters, the first from the top row and the second from the column at left. In this catalog, when a cyclical date is used, the abbreviation CD appears before the AD date.

Dates not in parentheses are those which appear on the coins. For undated coins, dates appearing in parentheses are the years in which the coin was actually minted. Undated coins for which the year of minting is unknown are listed with ND (No Date) in the date or year column.

CYCLICAL DATES

	庚	辛	壬	癸	甲	乙	丙	丁	戊	己
戌	1850 1910		1862 1922		1874 1934		1886 1946		1838 1898	
亥		1851 1911		1863 1923		1875 1935		1887 1947		1839 1899
子	1840 1900		1852 1912		1864 1924		1876 1936		1888 1948	
丑		1841 1901		1853 1913		1865 1925		1877 1937		1889 1949
寅	1830 1890		1842 1902		1854 1914		1866 1926		1878 1938	
卯		1831 1891		1843 1903		1855 1915		1867 1927		1879 1939
辰	1880 1940		1832 1892		1844 1904		1856 1916		1868 1928	
巳		1881 1941		1833 1893		1845 1905		1857 1917		1869 1929
午	1870 1930		1882 1942		1834 1894		1846 1906		1858 1918	
未		1871 1931		1883 1943		1835 1895		1847 1907		1859 1919
申	1860 1920		1872 1932		1884 1944		1836 1896		1848 1908	
酉		1861 1921		1873 1933		1885 1945		1837 1897		1849 1909

NOTE: This table has been adapted from *Chinese Bank Notes* by Ward Smith and Brian Matravers.

GRADING

Chinese coins should not be graded entirely by western standards. In addition to Fine, Very Fine, Extremely Fine (XF), and Uncirculated, the type of strike should be considered weak, medium or sharp strike. China had no rigid minting rules as we know them. For instance, Kirin (Jilin) and Sinkiang (Xinjiang) Provinces used some dies made of iron - hence, they wore out rapidly. Some communist army issues were apparently struck by crude hand methods on soft dies (it is hard to find two coins of the same die!). In general, especially for some minor coins, dies were used until they were worn well beyond western standards. Subsequently, one could have an uncirculated coin struck from worn dies with little of the design or letters still visible, but still uncirculated! All prices quoted are for well-struck (sharp struck), well-centered specimens. Most silver coins can be found from very fine to uncirculated. Some copper coins are difficult to find except in poorer grades.

REFERENCES

The following references have been used for this section:

K - Edward Kann - Illustrated Catalog of Chinese Coins.

Hsu - T.K. Hsu - Illustrated Catalog of Chinese Coins, 1981 edition.

W - A.M. Tracey Woodward - The Minted Ten-Cash Coins of China.

NOTE: The die struck 10 and 20 Cash coins are often found silver plated. This was not done at the mint. They were apparently plated to be passed to the unwary as silver coins.

IDENTIFICATION

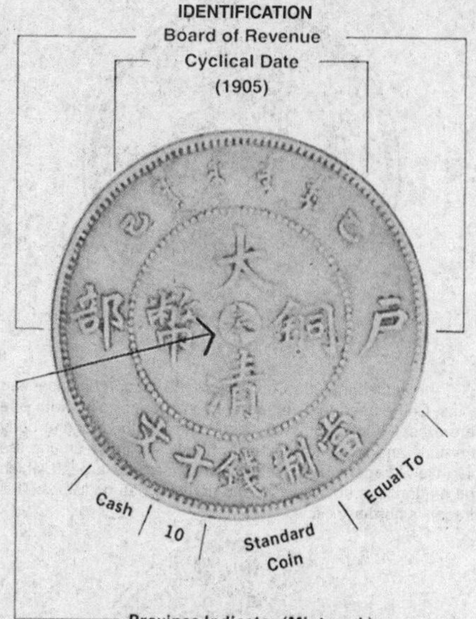

DRAGON TYPES

(Chinese Imperial Coins)

Side View Dragon-left (Silver Coins)

First used by the Kwangtung Mint in 1889. This was the standard (though not the only) dragon used on silver coins. Normally there is no circle around the dragon. Note the fireball beneath the dragon's chin. Normally there are seven flames on the fireball.

Side View Dragon-left (Copper Coins)

First used on copper coins in 1901 or 1902. The dragon may be circled or uncircled. Many varieties exist, with three to seven flames on the fireball.

Side View Dragon-right (Silver Coins)

First appears on the second series of Fukien. The dragon is redesigned with the dragon's body reversed.

Flying Dragon

Introduced in 1901. Copied from the dragon on Japanese coins. China used this dragon only on copper coins (with one rare exception). Note that the clouds around the dragon's body are curly and snake-like instead of puffy like those around the side view dragon. The fireball now appears as a pearl which the dragon is about to grasp, and normally has no flames. This dragon is normally circled.

Front View Dragon

Introduced about 1904, this type of dragon was not used by many mints. The dragon is usually uncircled and has few clouds around its body. Note the tiny mountain under the cloud beneath the fireball.

Tai Ch'ing Ti Kuo Dragon

In 1905 China carried out a coinage reform which standardized the designs of copper coins. All mints were ordered to use the same obverse and reverse designs, but to place a mint mark in the center of the obverse.

SYCEE (INGOTS)

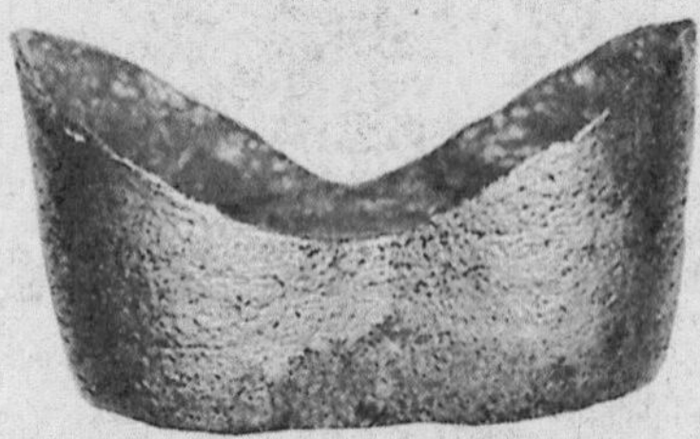

Prior to 1889 the general coinage issued by the Chinese government was the copper-alloy cash coin. Despite occasional shortlived experiments with silver and gold coinage, and disregarding paper money which tended to be unreliable, the government expected the people to get by solely with cash coins. This system worked well for individuals making purchases for themselves, but was unsatisfactory for trade and large business transactions, since a dollar's worth of cash coins weighed about four pounds. As a result, a private currency consisting of silver ingots, usually stamped by the firm which made them, came into use. These were the sycee ingots.

It is not known when these ingots first came into use. Some sources date them to the Yuan (Mongol) dynasty but they are certainly much older. Examples are known from as far back as the Han dynasty (206 BC - 220 AD) but prior to the Sung era (960 - 1280AD) they were used mainly for hoarding wealth. The development of commerce by the Sung dynasty, however, required the use of silver or gold to pay for large purchases. By the Mongol period (1280-1368) silver ingots and paper money had become the dominant currencies, especially for trade. The western explorers who traveled to China during this period (such as Marco Polo) mention both paper money and sycee but not a single one refers to cash coins.

During the Ming dynasty (1368-1644) trade fell off and the use of silver decreased. But toward the end of that dynasty, Dutch and British ships began a new China trade and sycee once again became common. During the 19th and early 20th centuries, the trade in sycee became enormous. Most of the sycee around today are from this period. In 1935 the Chinese government and in 1939 Sinkiang banned the use of sycee and it soon disappeared.

The word sycee (pronounced "sigh - see") is a western corruption of the Chinese word hsi-szu ("fine silk") or hsi yin ("fine silver") and is first known to have appeared in the English language in the late 1600's. By the early 1700's the word appeared regularly in the records of the British East India Company. Westerners also called these ingots "boat money" or "shoe money" owing to the fact that the most common type of ingot resembles a Chinese shoe. The Chinese, however, called the ingots by a variety of names, the most common of which were yuan pao, wen -yin (fine silver) and yin-ting (silver ingot).

The ingots were cast in molds (giving them their characteristic shapes) and while the metal was still semi-liquid, the inscription was impressed. It was due to this procedure that the sides of some sycee are higher than the center. The manufacturers were usually silver firms, often referred to as lu fang's, and after the sycee was finished it was occasionally tested and marked by the kung ku (public assayer).

Sycee were not circulated as we understand it. One didn't usually carry a sycee to market and spend it. Usually the ingots were used as a means of carrying a large amount of money on trips (as we would carry $100 bills instead of $5 bills) or for storing wealth. Large transactions between merchants or banks were paid by means of crates of sycee - each containing 60 fifty tael ingots.

Sycee are known in a variety of shapes the most common of which are the shoe or boat shaped, drum shaped, and loaf shaped (rectangular or hourglass-shaped, with a generally flat surface). Other shapes include one that resembles a double headed axe (this is the oldest type known), one that is square and flat, and others that are "fancy" (in the form of fish, butterflies, leaves, etc.).

Sycee have no denominations as they were simply ingots that passed by weight. Most are in more or less standard weights, however, the most common being 1, 5, 10 and 50 taels. Other weights known include 1/10, 1/5, 1/4, 1/3, 1/2, 2/3, 72/100 (this is the weight of a dollar), 3/4, 2, 3, 4, 6, 7, 8 and 25 taels. Most of the pieces weighing less than 5 taels were used as gifts or souvenirs.

The actual weight of any given value of sycee varied considerably due to the fact that the tael was not a single weight but a general term for a wide range of local weight standards. The weight of the tael varied depending upon location and type of tael in question. For example in one town, the weight of a tael of rice, of silver and of stones may each be different. In addition, the fineness of silver also varied depending upon location and type of tael in question. It was not true, as westerners often wrote, that sycee were made of pure silver. For most purposes, a weight of 37 grams may be used for the tael.

Weights and Current Market Value of Sycee
(Weights are approximate)

1/2 Tael	17-19 grams	$40.00
72/100 Tael	25-27 grams	
1 Tael	35-38 grams	$75.00
2 Taels	70-75 grams	$200
3 Taels	100-140 grams	$350
5 Taels	175-190 grams	$400
7 Taels	240-260 grams	$500
10 Taels	350-380 grams	$650
25 Taels	895-925 grams	$25,000
50 Taels	1790-1850 grams	$15,000
50 Taels, square	1790-1850 grams	$10,000

SZECHUAN WARLORD ISSUE

200 Cash

Obv: Mirror image of normal coin, Y#459.

NOTE: Certain coins found with degenerate or reversed English legends are usually considered to be local warlord issues while some authorities insist on referring to them as contemporary counterfeits.

CH'ING DYNASTY

Manchu, 1644 - 1911

Kuang-hsü

GENERAL CAST COINAGE

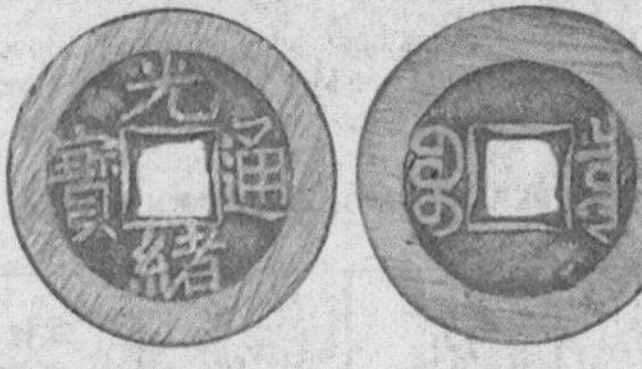

C# 1–16 CASH

Cast Brass **Obv. Inscription:** Kuang-hsü T'ung-pao **Rev. Inscription:** Boo-ciowan

Date	Mintage	G4	VG8	F12	VF20	XF40
ND(1875-1908)	—	2.00	2.50	3.00	5.00	—

Note: For crude cast, red copper issues, see Sinkiang General coinage

C# 1–16.1 CASH

Cast Brass **Series:** Thousand Character Classic **Obv. Inscription:** Kuang-hsü T'ung-pao **Rev:** Manchu inscription with "Chin" above **Rev. Inscription:** Boo-ciowan

Date	Mintage	G4	VG8	F12	VF20	XF40
ND(1875-1908)	—	8.00	11.00	17.00	25.00	—

C# 1–16.2 CASH

Cast Brass **Series:** Thousand Character Classic **Obv. Inscription:** Kuang-hsü T'ung-pao **Rev:** Manchu inscription with "Chou" above **Rev. Inscription:** Boo-ciowan

Date	Mintage	G4	VG8	F12	VF20	XF40
ND(1875-1908)	—	8.00	11.00	17.00	25.00	—

C# 1–16.3 CASH

Cast Brass **Series:** Thousand Character Classic **Obv. Inscription:** Kuang-hsü T'ung-pao **Rev:** Manchu inscription with "Jih" above **Rev. Inscription:** Boo-ciowan

Date	Mintage	G4	VG8	F12	VF20	XF40
ND(1875-1908)	—	8.00	11.00	17.00	25.00	—

C# 1–16.4 CASH

Cast Brass **Series:** Thousand Character Classic **Obv. Inscription:** Kuang-hsü T'ung-pao **Rev:** Manchu inscription with "Lai" above **Rev. Inscription:** Boo-ciowan

Date	Mintage	G4	VG8	F12	VF20	XF40
ND(1875-1908)	—	8.00	11.00	17.00	25.00	—

C# 1–16.5 CASH

Cast Brass **Series:** Thousand Character Classic **Obv. Inscription:** Kuang-hsü T'ung-pao **Rev:** Manchu inscription with "Lieh" above **Rev. Inscription:** Boo-ciowan

Date	Mintage	G4	VG8	F12	VF20	XF40
ND(1875-1908)	—	8.00	11.00	17.00	25.00	—

C# 1–16.6 CASH

Cast Brass **Series:** Thousand Character Classic **Obv. Inscription:** Kuang-hsü T'ung-pao **Rev:** Manchu inscription with "Wang" above **Rev. Inscription:** Boo-ciowan

Date	Mintage	G4	VG8	F12	VF20	XF40
ND(1875-1908)	—	8.00	11.00	17.00	25.00	—

C# 1–16.7 CASH

Cast Brass **Series:** Thousand Character Classic **Obv. Inscription:** Kuang-hsü T'ung-pao **Rev:** Manchu inscription with "Yu" above **Rev. Inscription:** Boo-ciowan

Date	Mintage	G4	VG8	F12	VF20	XF40
ND(1875-1908)	—	8.00	11.00	17.00	25.00	—

C# 1–16.10 CASH

Cast Brass **Series:** Thousand Character Classic **Obv. Inscription:** Kuang-hsü T'ung-pao **Rev:** Manchu inscription with "Shou" above **Rev. Inscription:** Boo-ciowan

Date	Mintage	G4	VG8	F12	VF20	XF40
ND(1875-1908)	—	8.00	11.00	17.00	25.00	—

C# 2–15 CASH

Cast Brass, 25-26 mm. **Obv. Inscription:** Kuang-hsü T'ung-pao **Rev:** Manchu inscription **Rev. Inscription:** Boo-yuwan **Note:** Size varies:.

Date	Mintage	G4	VG8	F12	VF20	XF40
ND(1875-1908)	—	2.00	4.00	8.00	9.00	—

Note: For crude cast copper strikes, see Sinkiang General Coinage

C# 1–16.8 CASH

Cast Brass **Obv. Inscription:** Kuang-hsü T'ung-pao **Rev:** Manchu inscription with dot below **Rev. Inscription:** Boo-ciowan

Date	Mintage	G4	VG8	F12	VF20	XF40
ND(1899-1901)	—	2.25	4.00	5.00	8.00	—

C# 1–16.9 CASH

Cast Brass **Obv. Inscription:** Kuang-hsü T'ung-pao **Rev:** Manchu inscription with dot above **Rev. Inscription:** Boo-ciowan

Date	Mintage	G4	VG8	F12	VF20	XF40
ND(1899-1901)	—	2.25	4.00	5.00	8.00	—

C# 2–15.1 CASH

Cast Brass, 19-20 mm. **Series:** Thousand Character Classic **Obv. Inscription:** Kuang-hsü T'ung-pao **Rev:** Manchu inscription with "Chou" above **Rev. Inscription:** Boo-yuwan **Note:** Size varies.

Date	Mintage	G4	VG8	F12	VF20	XF40
ND(1899-1901)	—	8.00	13.00	19.00	28.00	—

C# 2–15.2 CASH

Cast Brass **Series:** Thousand Character Classic **Obv. Inscription:** Kuang-hsü T'ung-pao **Rev:** Manchu inscription with "Lai" above **Rev. Inscription:** Boo-yuwan

Date	Mintage	G4	VG8	F12	VF20	XF40
ND(1899-1901)	—	8.00	13.00	19.00	28.00	—

C# 2–15.3 CASH

Cast Brass **Series:** Thousand Character Classic **Obv. Inscription:** Kuang-hsü T'ung-pao **Rev:** Manchu inscription with "Lieh" above **Rev. Inscription:** Boo-yuwan

Date	Mintage	G4	VG8	F12	VF20	XF40
ND(1899-1901)	—	8.00	13.00	19.00	28.00	—

C# 2–15.4 CASH

Cast Brass **Series:** Thousand Character Classic **Obv. Inscription:** Kuang-hsü T'ung-pao **Rev:** Manchu inscription with "Yu" above **Rev. Inscription:** Boo-yuwan

Date	Mintage	G4	VG8	F12	VF20	XF40
ND(1899-1901)	—	8.00	13.00	19.00	28.00	—

C# 2–15.5 CASH

Cast Brass, 20 mm. **Series:** Thousand Character Classic **Obv. Inscription:** Kuang-hsü T'ung-pao **Rev:** Manchu inscription with "Jih" above **Rev. Inscription:** Boo-yuwan

Date	Mintage	G4	VG8	F12	VF20	XF40
ND(1899-1901)	—	8.00	13.00	19.00	28.00	—

C# 2–15.6 CASH

Cast Brass **Series:** Thousand Character Classic **Obv. Inscription:** Kuang-hsü T'ung-pao **Rev:** Manchu inscription with "Wang" above **Rev. Inscription:** Boo-yuwan

Date	Mintage	G4	VG8	F12	VF20	XF40
ND(1899-1901)	—	8.00	13.00	19.00	28.00	—

C# 2–15.7 CASH

Cast Brass **Series:** Thousand Character Classic **Obv. Inscription:** Kuang-hsü T'ung-pao **Rev:** Manchu inscription with "Jih" above, dot below **Rev. Inscription:** Boo-yuwan

Date	Mintage	G4	VG8	F12	VF20	XF40
ND(1899-1901)	—	8.00	13.00	19.00	28.00	—

C# 2–16 5 CASH

Cast Brass **Obv. Inscription:** Kuang-hsü T'ung-pao **Rev:** Manchu inscription **Rev. Inscription:** Boo-yuwan

Date	Mintage	G4	VG8	F12	VF20	XF40
ND(1875-1908)	—	240	425	600	850	—

C# 1–17 10 CASH

Cast Brass, 30 mm. **Obv. Inscription:** Kuang-hsü Chung-pao **Rev:** Manchu inscription with normal "Shih" for 10 below **Rev. Inscription:** Boo-ciowan

Date	Mintage	G4	VG8	F12	VF20	XF40
ND(1875-1908)	—	3.00	5.00	8.00	10.00	—

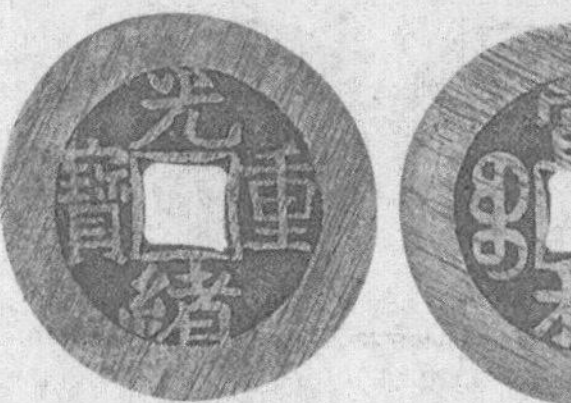

C# 1–18 10 CASH

Cast Brass, 28 mm. **Obv. Inscription:** Kuang-hsü Chung-pao **Rev:** Manchu inscription with official "Shih" for 10 below **Rev. Inscription:** Boo-ciowan

Date	Mintage	G4	VG8	F12	VF20	XF40
ND(1875-1908)	—	4.50	7.50	10.00	15.00	—

C# 1–18.1 10 CASH

Cast Brass, 22 mm. **Obv. Inscription:** Kuang-hsü Chung-pao **Rev:** Manchu inscription with official "Shih" for 10 below **Rev. Inscription:** Boo-ciowan

Date	Mintage	G4	VG8	F12	VF20	XF40
ND(1875-1908)	—	6.00	9.00	15.00	20.00	—

C# 2–17 10 CASH

Cast Brass, 31-32 mm. **Obv. Inscription:** Kuang-hsü Chung-pao **Rev:** Manchu inscription with normal Shih (10) below. **Rev. Inscription:** Boo-yuwan **Note:** Size varies.

Date	Mintage	G4	VG8	F12	VF20	XF40
ND(1875-1908)	—	4.50	7.50	10.00	25.00	—

C# 2–18 10 CASH

Cast Brass **Obv. Inscription:** Kuang-hsü T'ung-pao **Rev:** Manchu inscription with official Shih (10) below **Rev. Inscription:** Boo-yuwan

Date	Mintage	G4	VG8	F12	VF20	XF40
ND(1880-1908)	—	6.00	10.00	15.00	35.00	—

STANDARD UNIFIED GENERAL COINAGE

A Central mint opened at Tientsin in 1905, was made responsible for producing most of the dies for the Tai Ch'ing Hu Poo coinage and for the 1910 and 1911 unified coinage. The mint was burned down in 1912 but resumed operations in 1914 with Yuan Shih-k'ai dollar issues. It continued producing dies for selected branch mints until 1921. It was superseded as the Central mint of China by Nanking in 1927 and by the new Nationalist Government mint at Shanghai in 1933.

Y# 7 CASH

Brass **Obv. Legend:** Kuang-hsü **Rev:** Dragon **Note:** Struck.

Date	Mintage	VG8	F12	VF20	XF40	MS60
CD1908	—	1.50	5.00	9.00	25.00	—

Y# 8 2 CASH

Copper **Obv. Inscription:** Tai-ch'ing T'ung-pi **Rev:** Dragon

Date	Mintage	VG8	F12	VF20	XF40	MS60
CD1905 Hu-pu	—	4.00	7.00	15.00	35.00	—
CD1906 Hu-pu	—	5.00	9.00	20.00	50.00	—

Y# 8.1 2 CASH

Copper **Obv:** Four dots divide legend **Obv. Inscription:** Tai-ch'ing T'ung-pi **Rev:** Dragon

Date	Mintage	VG8	F12	VF20	XF40	MS60
CD1907	—	11.00	27.50	37.50	80.00	—

Y# 3 5 CASH

Copper **Obv. Inscription:** Kuang-hsü Yüan-pao **Rev:** Dragon **Rev. Legend:** HU POO

Date	Mintage	VG8	F12	VF20	XF40	MS60
ND(1903-05) Hu-pu	3,671,000	11.00	20.00	31.50	70.00	—

Y# 9 5 CASH

Copper **Obv. Inscription:** Tai-ch'ing T'ung-pi **Rev:** Dragon; smaller legend **Rev. Legend:** Kuang-hsü

Date	Mintage	VG8	F12	VF20	XF40	MS60
CD1905	—	8.00	15.00	30.00	70.00	—
CD1906 Rare	—	—	—	—	—	—

Y# 9.1 5 CASH

Copper **Obv:** Four dots divide legend **Obv. Legend:** Kuang-hsü **Obv. Inscription:** Tai-ch'ing T'ung-pi **Rev:** Dragon

Date	Mintage	VG8	F12	VF20	XF40	MS60
CD1907	—	25.00	60.00	115	250	—

Y# 4 10 CASH

Copper **Obv. Inscription:** Kuang-hsü Yüan-pao **Rev:** Side view dragon **Rev. Legend:** HU POO

Date	Mintage	VG8	F12	VF20	XF40	MS60
ND(1903-05)	281,171,000	1.00	3.00	5.00	9.00	50.00

Y# 4.1 10 CASH

Copper **Rev:** Side view dragon; different rosettes; smaller legend **Rev. Legend:** HU POO

Date	Mintage	VG8	F12	VF20	XF40	MS60
ND(1903-05)	Inc. above	0.50	1.50	3.00	8.00	40.00

Y# 10 10 CASH

Copper **Obv. Inscription:** Tai-ch'ing T'ung-pi **Rev:** Side view dragon **Rev. Legend:** Kuang-hsü Nien-tsao TAI-CHING-TI-KUO...

Date	Mintage	VG8	F12	VF20	XF40	MS60
CD1905	Inc. above	0.70	2.25	5.00	8.00	50.00

Y# 10.1 10 CASH

Copper **Obv. Inscription:** Tai-ch'ing T'ung-pi **Rev:** Different dragon; larger legend **Rev. Legend:** TAI-CHING-TI-KUO...

Date	Mintage	VG8	F12	VF20	XF40	MS60
CD1905	—	15.00	37.50	100	165	200

Y# 10.2 10 CASH

Copper **Obv. Inscription:** Tai-ch'ing T'ung-pi **Rev:** Dragon **Rev. Legend:** Kuang-hsü Nien-tsao TAI-CHING-TI-KUO

Date	Mintage	VG8	F12	VF20	XF40	MS60
CD1906	—	0.40	1.25	2.25	5.00	40.00

Y# 10.3 10 CASH

Copper **Obv:** Without dots **Obv. Inscription:** Tai-ch'ing T'ung-pi **Rev:** Dragon; legend without dot after "KUO" **Rev. Legend:** Kuang-hsü Nien-tsao TAI-CHING-TI-KUO

Date	Mintage	VG8	F12	VF20	XF40	MS60
CD1907	—	0.50	1.50	3.00	7.00	36.00

Y# 10.4 10 CASH

Copper **Obv. Inscription:** Tai-ch'ing T'ung-pi **Rev:** Dragon; legend with dot after "KUO" **Rev. Legend:** Kuang-hsü Nien-tsao TAI-CHING-TI-KUO.

Date	Mintage	VG8	F12	VF20	XF40	MS60
CD1907	—	0.50	1.50	3.00	7.00	36.00

Y# 10.4a 10 CASH

Brass **Obv:** Without dots **Obv. Inscription:** Tai-ch'ing T'ung-pi **Rev:** Dragon **Rev. Legend:** Kuang-hsü Nien-tsao TAI-CHING-TI-KUO.

Date	Mintage	VG8	F12	VF20	XF40	MS60
CD1907	—	2.75	8.00	30.00	55.00	160

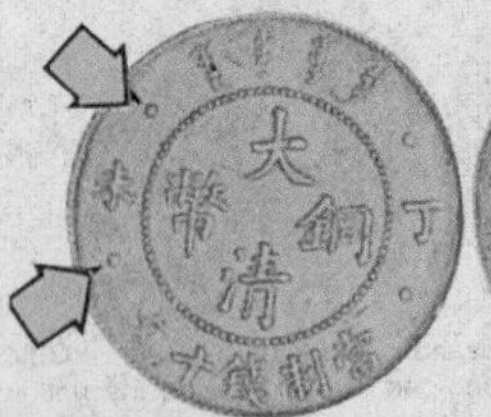

Y# 10.5 10 CASH

Copper **Obv:** Four dots divide legend **Obv. Inscription:** Tai-ch'ing T'ung-pi **Rev:** Dragon **Rev. Legend:** Kuang-hsü Nien-tsao TAI-CHING-TI-KUO.

Date	Mintage	VG8	F12	VF20	XF40	MS60
CD1907	—	0.50	1.50	3.00	7.00	36.00

Y# 10.5a 10 CASH

Brass **Obv. Inscription:** Tai-ch'ing T'ung-pi **Rev:** Dragon **Rev. Legend:** Kuang-hsü Nien-tsao TAI-CHING-TI-KUO.

Date	Mintage	VG8	F12	VF20	XF40	MS60
CD1907	—	2.75	8.00	22.50	60.00	170

Y# 5 20 CASH

Copper, 32 mm. **Obv. Inscription:** Kuang-hsü Yüan-pao **Rev:** Dragon **Rev. Legend:** HU POO

Date	Mintage	VG8	F12	VF20	XF40	MS60
ND(1903)	—	0.70	1.50	3.00	50.00	—

Y# 5.1 20 CASH

Copper, 32 mm. **Obv:** Four-point rosette in center **Obv. Inscription:** Kuang-hsü Yüan-pao **Rev:** Dragon **Rev. Legend:** HU POO

Date	Mintage	VG8	F12	VF20	XF40	MS60
ND(1903)	—	4.00	9.00	18.00	100	—

Y# 5.2 20 CASH

Copper, 32 mm. **Obv. Inscription:** Kuang-hsü Yüan-pao **Rev:** Head of dragon and clouds redesigned **Rev. Legend:** HU POO

Date	Mintage	VG8	F12	VF20	XF40	MS60
ND(1903) Restrike	—	4.00	9.00	18.00	100	—

Note: Y#5-5.2 were struck at the Wuchang Mint in 1917 from unused dies prepared in 1903

Y# 5aa 20 CASH

Copper, 32 mm. **Obv. Inscription:** Kuang-hsü Yüan-pao **Rev:** Dragon in circle of dots **Rev. Legend:** HU POO

Date	Mintage	VG8	F12	VF20	XF40	MS60
ND(1903-05)	—	45.00	75.00	130	250	—

Y# 11 20 CASH

Copper, 32 mm. **Obv. Inscription:** Tai-ch'ing T'ung-pi **Rev:** Dragon **Rev. Legend:** Kuang-hsü Nien-tsao, TAI-CHING-TI-KUO

Date	Mintage	VG8	F12	VF20	XF40	MS60
CD1905	—	19.00	45.00	75.00	150	—

Y# 11.1 20 CASH

Copper, 32 mm. **Obv. Inscription:** Tai-ch'ing T'ung-pi **Rev:** Dragon **Rev. Legend:** Kuang-hsü Nien-tsao, TAI-CHING-TI-KUO

Date	Mintage	VG8	F12	VF20	XF40	MS60
CD1906	—	19.00	45.00	75.00	150	—

Y# 11.2 20 CASH

Copper, 32 mm. **Obv:** Dots around date **Obv. Inscription:** Tai-ch'ing T'ung-pi **Rev:** Dragon **Rev. Legend:** Kuang-hsü Nien-tsao, TAI-CHING-TI-KUO **Note:** 1.2-1.7 mm. thick.

Date	Mintage	VG8	F12	VF20	XF40	MS60
CD1907	—	0.90	2.25	3.00	8.00	—

Y# 11.3 20 CASH

Copper, 32 mm. **Obv. Inscription:** Tai-ch'ing T'ung-pi **Rev:** Dragon **Rev. Legend:** Kuang-hsü Nien-tsao, TAI-CHING-TI-KUO **Note:** 2.0-2.3 mm. thick.

Date	Mintage	VG8	F12	VF20	XF40	MS60
CD1907	—	4.00	9.00	18.00	50.00	—

Y# 11.3a 20 CASH

Brass, 32 mm. **Obv. Inscription:** Tai-ch'ing T'ung-pi **Rev:** Dragon **Rev. Legend:** Kuang-hsü Nien-tsao, TAI-CHING-TI-KUO

Date	Mintage	VG8	F12	VF20	XF40	MS60
CD1907	—	5.00	12.00	22.50	60.00	—

K# 215 10 CENTS

2.70 g., 0.820 Silver 0.0712 oz. ASW **Obv. Inscription:** Tai-ch'ing T'ung-pi **Rev:** Dragon **Rev. Legend:** Kuang-hsü Nien-tsao, TAI-CHING-TI-KUO...

Date	Mintage	VG8	F12	VF20	XF40	MS60
CD1907	—	150	250	500	1,000	3,000

Y# 12 10 CENTS

2.70 g., 0.820 Silver 0.0712 oz. ASW **Obv. Inscription:** Kuang-hsü Yüan-pao **Rev:** Dragon **Rev. Legend:** Kuang-hsü Nien-tsao, TAI-CHING-TI-KUO...

Date	Mintage	VG8	F12	VF20	XF40	MS60
ND(1908)	—	18.00	45.00	75.00	350	950

K# 214 20 CENTS

5.50 g., 0.820 Silver 0.145 oz. ASW **Obv. Inscription:** Tai-ch'ing Yin-pi **Rev:** Dragon **Rev. Legend:** Kuang-hsü Nien-tsao, TAI-CHING-TI-KUO...

Date	Mintage	VG8	F12	VF20	XF40	MS60
CD1907	—	300	600	975	2,750	6,500

Y# 13 20 CENTS

5.30 g., 0.820 Silver 0.1397 oz. ASW **Obv. Inscription:** Kuang-hsü Yüan-pao **Rev:** Dragon **Rev. Legend:** Kuang-hsü Nien-tsao, TAI-CHING-TI-KUO...

Date	Mintage	VG8	F12	VF20	XF40	MS60
ND(1908)	—	30.00	90.00	175	450	1,650

K# 217w 20 CENTS

5.30 g., 0.820 Silver 0.1397 oz. ASW **Obv. Inscription:** Kuang-hsü Yüan-pao **Rev:** Dragon **Rev. Legend:** Kuang-hsü Nien-tsao, TAI-CHING-TI-KUO... with "COPPER COIN" (error)

Date	Mintage	VG8	F12	VF20	XF40	MS60
ND-1908 Rare	—	—	—	—	—	—

K# 213 50 CENTS

13.60 g., 0.860 Silver 0.376 oz. ASW **Obv. Inscription:** Tai-ch'ing Yin-pi **Rev:** Dragon **Rev. Legend:** Kuang-hsü Nien-tsao, TAI-CHING-TI-KUO...

Date	Mintage	VG8	F12	VF20	XF40	MS60
CD1907	—	750	1,200	1,800	5,000	11,500

K# 212 DOLLAR

26.90 g., 0.900 Silver 0.7784 oz. ASW **Obv. Inscription:** Tai-ch'ing Yin-pi **Rev:** Dragon **Rev. Legend:** Kuang-hsü Nien-tsao, TAI-CHING-TI-KOU...

Date	Mintage	VG8	F12	VF20	XF40	MS60
CD1907	—	1,500	2,250	3,750	12,500	25,000

Y# 14 DOLLAR

26.90 g., 0.900 Silver 0.7784 oz. ASW **Obv. Inscription:** Kuang-hsü Yüan-pao **Rev:** Dragon **Rev. Legend:** Kuang-hsü Nien-tsao, TAI-CHING-TI-KOU...

Date	Mintage	VG8	F12	VF20	XF40	MS60
ND(1908)	—	55.00	150	375	600	3,000

Hsüan-t'ung

GENERAL CAST COINAGE

C# 1-19.1 CASH

Cast Brass, 19 mm. **Obv. Inscription:** Hsüan-t'ung T'ung-pao **Rev:** Manchu inscription **Rev. Inscription:** Boo-ciowan

Date	Mintage	G4	VG8	F12	VF20	XF40
ND(1909-11)	—	8.00	11.00	15.00	30.00	—

C# 1-19.2 CASH

Cast Brass, 24 mm. **Obv. Inscription:** Hsüan-t'ung T'ung-pao **Rev:** Manchu inscription **Rev. Inscription:** Boo-ciowan

Date	Mintage	G4	VG8	F12	VF20	XF40
ND(1909-11)	—	15.00	22.50	37.50	70.00	—

C# 1-19a CASH

Iron, 23 mm. **Obv. Inscription:** Hsüan-t'ung T'ung-pao **Rev:** Manchu inscription **Rev. Inscription:** Boo-ciowan

Date	Mintage	G4	VG8	F12	VF20	XF40
ND(1909-11)	—	18.00	30.00	45.00	100	—

STANDARD UNIFIED GENERAL COINAGE

A Central mint opened at Tientsin in 1905, was made responsible for producing most of the dies for the Tai Ch'ing Hu Poo coinage and for the 1910 and 1911 unified coinage. The mint was burned down in 1912 but resumed operations in 1914 with Yuan Shih-k'ai dollar issues. It continued producing dies for selected branch mints until 1921. It was superseded as the Central mint of China by Nanking in 1927 and by the new Nationalist Government mint at Shanghai in 1933.

Y# 18 CASH

Brass **Obv. Legend:** Hsüan-t'ung **Rev:** Dragon **Note:** Struck.

Date	Mintage	VG8	F12	VF20	XF40	MS60
CD1909	—	37.50	75.00	130	270	—

Note: Inc. Y25

Y# 25 CASH

Brass **Obv. Inscription:** Tai-ch'ing T'ung-pi

Date	Mintage	VG8	F12	VF20	XF40	MS60
ND(1909)	92,126,000	1.50	2.25	3.00	6.00	—

Y# A18 2 CASH

Copper **Obv. Inscription:** Hsüan-t'ung

Date	Mintage	VG8	F12	VF20	XF40	MS60
CD1909 Rare	13,353,000	—	—	—	—	—

Y# 19 5 CASH

Copper **Obv. Legend:** Hsüan-t'ung

Date	Mintage	VG8	F12	VF20	XF40	MS60
CD1909	2,170,000	—	—	1,300	2,400	—

Y# 20 10 CASH

Copper **Obv. Inscription:** Tai-ch'ing T'ung-pi **Rev:** Waves below dragon **Rev. Legend:** Hsüan-t'ung Nien-tsao TAI-CHING-TI-KUO.

Date	Mintage	VG8	F12	VF20	XF40	MS60
CD1909	—	0.50	1.50	3.00	8.00	45.00

Y# 20.1 10 CASH
Copper **Obv. Inscription:** Tai-ch'ing T'ung-pi **Rev:** Rosette below dragon, "U" of "KUO" inverted "A" **Rev. Legend:** Hsüan-t'ung Nien-tsao TAI-CHING-TI-KUO.

Date	Mintage	VG8	F12	VF20	XF40	MS60
CD1909	—	2.75	8.00	18.00	50.00	120

Note: Although this coin bears no indication of its origin, it was minted in the Manchurian Provinces ca.1922

Y# 20x 10 CASH
Copper **Obv:** Rosette in center **Obv. Inscription:** Tai-ch'ing T'ung-pi **Rev:** Dragon **Rev. Legend:** Hsüan-t'ung Nien-tsao TAI-CHING-TI-KUO.

Date	Mintage	VG8	F12	VF20	XF40	MS60
CD1909	—	5.00	15.00	30.00	60.00	160

Note: Although this coin bears no indication of its origin, it was minted in Kirin Province

Y# 27 10 CASH
Bronze **Obv:** Dragon **Obv. Inscription:** Tai-ch'ing T'ung-pi **Rev. Legend:** Hsüan-t'ung...

Date	Mintage	VG8	F12	VF20	XF40	MS60
3(1911)	95,585,000	1.25	4.00	6.00	16.00	180
3(1911) Proof; Rare	—	—	—	—	—	—

Y# 27a 10 CASH
Brass **Obv:** Dragon **Obv. Inscription:** Tai-ch'ing T'ung-pi **Rev. Legend:** Hsüan-t'ung...

Date	Mintage	VG8	F12	VF20	XF40	MS60
3(1911)	—	18.00	45.00	70.00	190	300

Y# 21 20 CASH
Brass, 32 mm. **Obv. Inscription:** Tai-ch'ing T'ung-pi **Rev:** With dot between "KUO" and COPPER; six waves beneath dragon **Rev. Legend:** Hsüan-t'ung Nien-tsao, TAI-CHING-TI-KUO...

Date	Mintage	VG8	F12	VF20	XF40	MS60
CD1909	—	1.50	4.00	8.00	20.00	—

Y# 21.1 20 CASH
Copper, 32 mm. **Obv. Inscription:** Tai-ch'ing T'ung-pi **Rev:** With dot between "KUO" and "COPPER"; six waves beneath dragon **Rev. Legend:** Hsüan-t'ung Nien-tsao, TAI-CHING-TI-KUO... **Note:** 1.2-1.7 mm. thick.

Date	Mintage	VG8	F12	VF20	XF40	MS60
CD1909	—	3.00	8.00	14.00	40.00	100

Y# 21.2 20 CASH
Copper, 32 mm. **Obv. Inscription:** Tai-ch'ing T'ung-pi **Rev:** Without dot between "KUO" and "COPPER"; six waves beneath dragon **Rev. Legend:** Hsüan-t'ung Nien-tsao, TAI-CHING-TI-KUO... **Note:** 2.0-2.3 mm. thick.

Date	Mintage	VG8	F12	VF20	XF40	MS60
CD1909	—	3.00	9.00	16.00	45.00	150

Y# 21.3 20 CASH
Copper, 32 mm. **Obv. Inscription:** Tai-ch'ing T'ung-pi **Rev:** Without dot between "KUO" and "COPPER"; rosette beneath dragon **Rev. Legend:** Hsüan-t'ung Nien-tsao, TAI-CHING-TI-KUO...

Date	Mintage	VG8	F12	VF20	XF40	MS60
CD1909 Restrike	—	9.00	22.50	60.00	150	—

Note: Although this coin bears no indication of its origin, it was minted in the Manchurian Provinces ca.1922

Y# 21.4 20 CASH
Copper, 32 mm. **Obv. Inscription:** Tai-ch'ing T'ung-pi **Rev:** Without dot between "KUO" and "COPPER"; dot below dragon's chin **Rev. Legend:** Hsüan-t'ung Nien-tsao, TAI-CHING-TI-KUO...

Date	Mintage	VG8	F12	VF20	XF40	MS60
CD1909 Restrike	—	5.00	13.00	25.00	60.00	175

Note: Although this coin bears no indication of its origin, it was minted in the Manchurian Provinces ca.1922

Y# 21.5 20 CASH
Copper, 32 mm. **Obv:** Inner circle of large dots **Obv. Inscription:** Tai-ch'ing T'ung-pi **Rev:** Without dot between "KUO" and "COPPER"; five crude waves beneath dragon with redesigned forehead; inner circle of large dots **Rev. Legend:** Hsüan-t'ung Nien-tsao, TAI-CHING-TI-KUO...

Date	Mintage	VG8	F12	VF20	XF40	MS60
CD1909	—	2.00	5.00	9.00	60.00	200

K# 222 10 CENTS
3.20 g., 0.650 Silver 0.0669 oz. ASW **Obv. Inscription:** Tai-ch'ing Yin-pi **Rev:** Dragon **Rev. Legend:** Hsüan-t'ung Nien-tsao

Date	Mintage	VG8	F12	VF20	XF40	MS60
ND-1910	—	120	180	375	1,250	2,500
ND-1910	—	PF60 2,250				

Y# 28 10 CENTS
2.70 g., Silver **Obv. Legend:** Hsüan-t'ung **Obv. Inscription:** Tai-ch'ing Yin-pi **Rev:** Dragon **Rev. Legend:** Hsüan-t'ung Nien-tsao

Date	Mintage	VG8	F12	VF20	XF40	MS60
3(1911)	—	15.00	30.00	65.00	225	700

Note: Refer to Hunan Republic 10 Cents, K#762

Y# 29 20 CENTS
5.40 g., 0.820 Silver 0.1424 oz. ASW **Obv. Legend:** Hsüan-t'ung **Obv. Inscription:** Tai-ch'ing Yin-pi **Rev:** Dragon

Date	Mintage	VG8	F12	VF20	XF40	MS60
3(1911)	—	70.00	150	300	1,000	2,000

K# 221 25 CENTS
6.70 g., 0.800 Silver 0.1723 oz. ASW **Obv. Legend:** Hsüan-t'ung Nien-tsao **Obv. Inscription:** Tai-ch'ing Yin-pi **Rev:** Dragon

Date	Mintage	VG8	F12	VF20	XF40	MS60
ND-1910	1,410,000	100	300	600	1,500	3,000
ND-1910	—	PF60 5,000				

Y# 23 50 CENTS
13.40 g., 0.800 Silver 0.3447 oz. ASW **Obv. Inscription:** Tai-ch'ing Yin-pi **Rev:** Dragon **Rev. Legend:** Hsüan-t'ung Nien-tsao

Date	Mintage	VG8	F12	VF20	XF40	MS60
ND(1910)	1,571,000	100	200	400	1,500	3,500
ND (1910)	—	PF60 5,000				

Y# 30 50 CENTS
13.40 g., 0.800 Silver 0.3447 oz. ASW **Obv. Legend:** Hsüan-t'ung **Obv. Inscription:** Tai-ch'ing Yin-pi **Rev:** Dragon

Date	Mintage	VG8	F12	VF20	XF40	MS60
3(1911)	Inc. above	750	1,350	2,250	6,300	15,000
3(1911)	—	PF60 12,000				

K# 219 DOLLAR
26.90 g., 0.900 Silver 0.7784 oz. ASW **Obv. Inscription:** Tai-ch'ing Yin-pi **Rev:** Dragon **Rev. Legend:** Hsüan-t'ung Nien-tsao

Date	Mintage	VG8	F12	VF20	XF40	MS60
ND-1910	—	600	1,200	2,250	6,300	12,500
ND-1910	—	PF60 10,500				

Y# 31 DOLLAR

26.90 g., 0.900 Silver 0.7784 oz. ASW **Obv. Legend:** Hsüan-t'ung **Obv. Inscription:** Tai-ch'ing Yin-pi **Rev:** Dragon

Date	Mintage	F12	VF20	XF40	MS60	MS63
3(1911)	77,153,000	75.00	125	400	2,000	6,000

Note: Struck at the Tientsin, Nanking, and Wuchang Mints without distinctive marks

Y# 31.1 DOLLAR

26.90 g., 0.900 Silver 0.7784 oz. ASW **Obv. Legend:** Hsüan-t'ung **Obv. Inscription:** Tai-ch'ing Yin-pi **Rev:** Dragon; "dot" after "DOLLAR"

Date	Mintage	VG8	F12	VF20	XF40	MS60
3(1911)	Inc. above	60.00	100	200	550	2,800

PATTERNS

Peking Tael Series

KM#	Date	Mintage	Identification	Mkt Val
Pn290	29(1903)	—	5 Fen. Silver. K931.	5,000
Pn291	29(1903)	—	Ch'ien. Silver. K930.	2,800
Pn292	29(1903)	—	2 Ch'ien. Silver. K929.	7,600
Pn293	29(1903)	—	2 Ch'ien. Gold. K929v.	60,000
Pn294	29(1903)	—	5 Ch'ien. Silver. K928.	24,000
Pn295	29(1903)	—	Liang. Silver. K927.	96,000
Pn296	29(1903)	—	Liang. Gold. K927v.	160,000
Pn297	CD1906	—	Ch'ien. Silver. K937.	3,000
Pn298	CD1906	—	2 Ch'ien. Silver. K936.	3,600
Pn299	CD1906	—	5 Ch'ien. Silver. K935.	6,000
Pn300	CD1906	—	Liang. Silver. K934.	24,000
Pn301	CD1906	—	Liang. Gold. K1540. Tientsin Mint. 39.5mm, 37g. Large clouds, plain edge.	100,000
PnA302	CD1906	—	Liang. Gold. Tientsin Mint. 39.5mm, 37g. Small clouds, reeded edge. Rare.	—
Pn302	CD1907	—	Liang. Gold. K1541. Tientsin Mint. 39.5mm, 37g. Small clouds, reeded edge.	100,000
PnA303	CD1907	—	Liang. Gold. K1541a. Tientsin Mint. 39.5mm, 37g. Large clouds, plain edge. Rare.	—
Pn303	CD1907	—	Liang. Silver. K1541v.	26,000

PATTERNS

Standard Unified General

KM#	Date	Mintage	Identification	Mkt Val
Pn264	ND (1906)	—	Cash. Brass. Hsu4a, square hole.	800
Pn265	ND (1906)	—	Cash. Brass. Hsu4b, without hole.	800
Pn266	ND (1906)	—	Cash. Copper. Y#7.	800
Pn267	ND (1906)	—	Cash. Brass. Y#25; without hole.	800
Pn268	CD1907	—	Dollar. Copper. K212.	—
Pn269	ND-1908	—	20 Cents. Nickel. Milled. K217w.	—
Pn310	ND-1908	—	20 Cents. Nickel. K217y.	—
Pn250	ND-1910	—	10 Cents. Nickel. K222.	—
Pn251	ND-1910	—	1/4 Dollar. Silver. Plain. K221.	—
Pn272	ND-1910	—	Li. Copper. Hsu33.	800
Pn273	ND-1910	—	5 Li. Copper. Hsu34.	1,100
Pn274	ND-1910	—	5 Li. Bronze.	1,100
Pn275	ND-1910	—	2 Cash. Copper. Hsu13.	800
Pn276	ND-1910	—	2 Cash. Brass. With hole, Hsu13.	800
Pn277	ND-1910	—	Fen. Copper. Hsu35.	1,200
Pn278	ND-1910	—	Fen. Bronze.	1,200
Pn279	ND-1910	—	2 Fen. Copper. Hsu36.	2,000
Pn280	ND-1910	—	2 Fen. Bronze.	2,000
Pn281	3(1911)	—	5 Cash. Copper. Y26; Hsu30.	1,200
Pn282	3(1911)	—	5 Cash. Bronze. Y26a.	1,200
Pn283	3(1911)	—	20 Cash. Copper. Hsu32.	1,400
Pn284	3(1911)	—	20 Cash. Bronze.	1,400
Pn304	3(1911)	—	Dollar. Silver. K223.	50,000
Pn305	3(1911)	—	Dollar. Silver. K223a.	50,000
Pn306	3(1911)	—	Dollar. Silver. K223b.	—
Pn307	3(1911)	—	Dollar. Silver. K224.	70,000
Pn308	3(1911)	—	Dollar. Silver. K225.	50,000
Pn309	3(1911)	—	Dollar. Silver. K226.	40,000
Pn311	ND-1910	—	10 Cents. Nickel. K222y.	250

TRIAL STRIKES

KM#	Date	Mintage	Identification	Mkt Val
TS3	1(1910)	—	Fen. White Metal. Hsu35, KM#Pn275. Uniface obverse.	250

PROOF SETS

KM#	Date	Mintage	Identification	Issue Price	Mkt Val
PS1	ND(1910) (4)	—	Y#23, K#219, 221, 222	—	—

ANHWEI PROVINCE

Anhui

A province located in eastern China. Made a separate province during the Manchu dynasty in the 17th century. Principally agricultural with some mining of coal and iron ore. Spanish-American 8 Reales saw wide circulation in this province until the end of World War I. The provincial mint at Anking began operations in 1897, closed in 1899, and later reopened in 1902. The primary production of the mint was cash coins but included a series of silver coinage.

EMPIRE

Kuang-hsü

MILLED COINAGE

Y# 35 5 CASH

Copper **Obv. Legend:** An-hui Sheng Tsao **Obv. Inscription:** Kuang-hsü Yüan-pao **Rev:** Circled dragon **Rev. Legend:** AN-HWEI

Date	Mintage	VG8	F12	VF20	XF40	MS60
ND(1902)	—	150	200	300	680	—

Y# 35.1 5 CASH

Copper **Obv. Legend:** An-hui Sheng Tsao **Obv. Inscription:** Kuang-hsü Yüan-pao **Rev:** Uncircled dragon **Rev. Legend:** AN-HUI

Date	Mintage	VG8	F12	VF20	XF40	MS60
ND(ca. 1902) Rare	—	—	—	—	—	—

Y# 34 10 CASH

Copper **Obv. Legend:** An-hui Sheng Tsao **Obv. Inscription:** Kuang-hsü Yüan-pao **Rev:** Denomination: "ONE CEN" **Note:** May show various stages of recutting of "C" in "CEN".

Date	Mintage	VG8	F12	VF20	XF40	MS60
ND1902	—	35.00	50.00	85.00	150	—

Y# 34a 10 CASH

Copper **Obv. Legend:** An-hui Sheng Tsao **Obv. Inscription:** Kuang-hsü Yüan-pao **Rev:** Letter "A" inverted, denomination "ONE SEN"

Date	Mintage	VG8	F12	VF20	XF40	MS60
ND(1902)	—	50.00	80.00	125	350	—

Y# 34a.1 10 CASH

Copper **Obv. Legend:** An-hui Sheng Tsao **Rev:** Letter "A" corrected, denomination "ONE SEN"

Date	Mintage	VG8	F12	VF20	XF40	MS60
ND(1902)	—	40.00	65.00	100	250	—

Y# 36 10 CASH

Copper **Obv. Legend:** An-hui Sheng Tsao **Obv. Inscription:** Kuang-hsü Yüan-pao **Rev:** Letter "N" backwards in "AN-HWEI" and in "TEN"

Date	Mintage	VG8	F12	VF20	XF40	MS60
ND(1902-06)	—	6.00	12.00	20.00	65.00	—

Y# 36.1 10 CASH

Copper **Obv:** Small Manchu in center **Obv. Legend:** An-hui Sheng Tsao **Obv. Inscription:** Kuang-hsü Yüan-pao **Rev:** Rosettes close together, letter "N" corrected in "AN-HWEI" and in "TEN" **Edge:** Plain

Date	Mintage	VG8	F12	VF20	XF40	MS60
ND(1902-06)	—	1.25	3.00	6.00	25.00	—

Y# 36.1a 10 CASH

Copper **Obv:** Small Manchu in center **Obv. Legend:** An-hui Sheng Tsao **Obv. Inscription:** Kuang-hsü Yüan-pao **Rev:** Rosettes close together, letter "N" corrected in AN-HWEI and in TEN **Edge:** Milled

Date	Mintage	VG8	F12	VF20	XF40	MS60
ND(1902-06) Rare	—	—	—	—	—	—

Y# 36.2 10 CASH

Copper **Obv:** Smaller, redesigned rosettes, larger Manchu words in center **Obv. Legend:** An-hui Sheng Tsao **Obv. Inscription:** Kuang-hsü Yüan-pao **Rev:** Rosettes close together, larger clouds around redesigned dragon

Date	Mintage	VG8	F12	VF20	XF40	MS60
ND(1902-06)	—	1.75	5.00	7.00	50.00	225

Y# 36.3 10 CASH

Copper **Obv:** Rosettes crude and heavy **Obv. Legend:** An-hui Sheng Tsao **Obv. Inscription:** Kuang-hsü Yüan-pao **Rev:**

Rosettes close together, dragon's head redesigned

Date	Mintage	VG8	F12	VF20	XF40	MS60
ND(1902-08)	—	5.00	12.00	17.50	50.00	—

Y# 36.4 10 CASH

Copper **Obv. Legend:** An-hui Sheng Tsao **Obv. Inscription:** Kuang-hsü Yüan-pao **Rev:** Rosettes far apart

Date	Mintage	VG8	F12	VF20	XF40	MS60
ND(1902-06)	—	1.25	3.00	6.00	50.00	—

Y# 36a.1 10 CASH

Copper **Obv:** Small rosette **Obv. Legend:** An-hui Sheng Tsao **Obv. Inscription:** Kuang-hsu Yüan-pao **Rev:** Small English legend above dragon

Date	Mintage	F12	VF20	XF40	MS60	MS63
ND(1902-06)	—	4.00	7.00	20.00	250	450

Y# 36a.2 10 CASH

Copper **Obv. Legend:** An-hui Sheng Tsao **Obv. Inscription:** Kuang-hsü Yüan-pao **Rev:** Small English legend with larger clouds around dragon and only one cloud below dragon's tail

Date	Mintage	VG8	F12	VF20	XF40	MS60
ND(1902-06)	—	2.50	6.00	10.00	22.50	—

Y# 36a.3 10 CASH

Copper **Obv:** Large rosette at center, legend with 2 characters at bottom **Obv. Legend:** An-hui Sheng Tsao **Obv. Inscription:** Kuang-hsü Yüan-pao

Date	Mintage	VG8	F12	VF20	XF40	MS60
ND(1902-06)	—	1.25	3.00	6.00	18.00	—

Y# 36a.4 10 CASH

Copper **Obv:** Large rosette at center, legend with 5 characters at bottom **Obv. Legend:** An-hui Sheng Tsao **Obv. Inscription:** Kuang-hsü Yüan-pao

Date	Mintage	VG8	F12	VF20	XF40	MS60
ND(1902-06)	—	1.50	3.00	6.00	25.00	—

Y# 36a.5 10 CASH

Copper **Obv:** Legend with 2 characters at bottom **Obv. Legend:** An-hui Sheng Tsao **Obv. Inscription:** Kuang-hsü Yüan-pao **Rev:** Small English legend above dragon

Date	Mintage	VG8	F12	VF20	XF40	MS60
ND(1902-06)	—	4.00	9.00	18.00	36.00	—

Y# 36a.6 10 CASH

Copper **Obv:** Slightly smaller rosette at center with right Manchu word slightly higher than on Y#36a.5 **Obv. Legend:** An-hui Sheng Tsao **Obv. Inscription:** Kuang-hsü Yüan-pao **Rev:** Small English legend above dragon

Date	Mintage	VG8	F12	VF20	XF40	MS60
ND(1902-06)	—	1.25	3.00	6.00	25.00	—

Y# 36a 10 CASH

Copper **Obv:** Small rosette at center, legend with 5 characters at bottom **Obv. Legend:** An-hui Sheng Tsao **Obv. Inscription:** Kuang-hsü Yüan-pao **Rev:** Large English legend above dragon, without "TEN CASH"

Date	Mintage	VG8	F12	VF20	XF40	MS60
ND(1902-06)	—	1.25	3.00	6.00	22.50	—

Y# 38a.1 10 CASH

Copper **Obv:** Legend with 5 characters at bottom **Obv. Legend:** An-hui Sheng Tsao **Obv. Inscription:** Kuang-hsü Yüan-pao **Rev:** "Ten" spelled "TOEN"

Date	Mintage	VG8	F12	VF20	XF40	MS60
ND(1902-06)	—	35.00	70.00	150	250	—

Y# 38a 10 CASH

Copper **Obv:** Legend with 2 characters at bottom **Obv. Legend:** An-hui Sheng Tsao **Obv. Inscription:** Kuang-hsü Yüan-pao **Rev:** "Ten" spelled "TOEN"

Date	Mintage	VG8	F12	VF20	XF40	MS60
ND(1902-06)	—	8.00	15.00	30.00	75.00	450

Y# 38b.1 10 CASH

Copper **Obv:** Legend with 5 characters at bottom **Obv. Legend:** An-hui Sheng Tsao **Obv. Inscription:** Kuang-hsü Yüan-pao

Date	Mintage	VG8	F12	VF20	XF40	MS60
ND(1902-06)	—	15.00	35.00	50.00	140	—

Y# 38b 10 CASH

Copper **Obv:** Legend with 2 characters at bottom **Obv. Legend:** An-hui Sheng Tsao **Obv. Inscription:** Kuang-hsü Yüan-pao **Rev:** Without "TEN CASH"

Date	Mintage	VG8	F12	VF20	XF40	MS60
ND(1902-06)	—	5.00	12.00	25.00	65.00	—

Y# 39.1 10 CASH

Copper **Obv. Legend:** An-hui Sheng Tsao **Obv. Inscription:** Kuang-hsü Yüan-pao **Rev:** Stars at sides and "AN-HUI" above dragon

Date	Mintage	VG8	F12	VF20	XF40	MS60
ND(1902-06) Rare	—	—	—	—	—	—

Y# 39.2 10 CASH

Copper **Obv. Legend:** An-hui Sheng Tsao **Obv. Inscription:** Kuang-hsü Yüan-pao **Rev:** "AN-HUI", upright dragon **Note:** Square-holed center.

Date	Mintage	VG8	F12	VF20	XF40	MS60
ND(1902-06) Rare	—	—	—	—	—	—

Y# 39 10 CASH

Copper **Obv:** Legend with 7 characters at bottom **Obv. Legend:** An-hui Sheng Tsao **Obv. Inscription:** Kuang-hsü Yüan-pao **Rev:** Rosettes at side and "AN-HUI" above dragon

Date	Mintage	VG8	F12	VF20	XF40	MS60
ND(1902-06) Rare	—	—	—	—	—	—

Y# 10a 10 CASH

Copper **Obv:** Large mint mark at center **Obv. Inscription:** Tai-ch'ing T'ung-pi **Rev. Legend:** Kuang-hsü Nien-tsao, TAI-CHING-TI-KUO ...

Date	Mintage	VG8	F12	VF20	XF40	MS60
CD-1906	—	1.25	3.00	6.00	22.50	200

Y# 10a.1 10 CASH

Copper **Obv:** Small mint mark at center **Obv. Inscription:** Tai-ch'ing T'ung-pi **Rev. Legend:** Kuang-hsü Nien-tsao, TAI-CHING-TI-KUO ...

Date	Mintage	VG8	F12	VF20	XF40	MS60
CD-1906	—	1.75	4.00	7.00	22.50	200

Y# 10a.2 10 CASH
Copper **Obv:** More finely engraved, cloud near dragon's lower foot shaped like a 3 **Obv. Inscription:** Tai-ch'ing T'ung-pi **Rev:** More finely engraved **Rev. Legend:** Kuang-hsü Nien-tsao, TAI-CHING-TI-KUO ...

Date	Mintage	VG8	F12	VF20	XF40	MS60
CD1906	—	1.25	3.00	6.00	22.50	200

Y# 37 20 CASH
Copper **Obv. Legend:** An-hui Sheng Tsao **Obv. Inscription:** Kuang-hsü Yüan-pao

Date	Mintage	VG8	F12	VF20	XF40	MS60
ND(1902)	—	375	750	1,100	1,500	—

Y# 11a 20 CASH
Copper **Obv. Inscription:** Tai-ch'ing T'ung-pi **Rev:** TAI-CHING-TI-KUO ... **Rev. Inscription:** Kuang-hsü Nien-tsao

Date	Mintage	VG8	F12	VF20	XF40	MS60
CD1906	—	80.00	150	300	600	—

Y# 43.5 20 CENTS
5.30 g., 0.920 Silver 0.1568 oz. ASW **Obv. Inscription:** Kuang-hsü Yüan-pao **Rev:** Dragon

Date	Mintage	VG8	F12	VF20	XF40	MS60
27(1901) 1 known	—	—	—	—	—	—

Note: D.K.E. Ching Sale 6-91 VF++ realized $2,420

MILITARY TOKEN COINAGE

Given to An-hui Imperial troops by the Military Bureau for faithful and/or meritorious service.

KM# W45 10 CASH
Copper **Issuer:** Anhwei Military Bureau **Obv:** Large central Chinese character "Cheang" (reward) **Obv. Legend:** An-hui Wu Dih Buh Yuen **Rev:** Legend around dragon **Rev. Legend:** AN-HWEI***TEN CASH***

Date	Mintage	VG8	F12	VF20	XF40	MS60
ND(1902)	—	125	225	375	550	—

KM# W46 10 CASH
Copper **Issuer:** Anhwei Military Bureau **Obv. Legend:** An-hui Wu Dih Buh Yuen **Rev:** Legend around Dragon **Rev. Legend:** AN-HWEI***TEN CASH***

Date	Mintage	VG8	F12	VF20	XF40	MS60
ND(1902)	—	125	225	375	550	—

KM# W47 10 CASH
Copper **Issuer:** Anhwei Military Bureau **Obv. Legend:** An-hui Wu Dih Buh Yuen **Rev:** Legend without "TEN CASH"

Date	Mintage	VG8	F12	VF20	XF40	MS60
ND(1902)	—	200	350	600	900	—

Hsüan-t'ung

MILLED COINAGE

Y# 20a 10 CASH
Copper **Obv. Inscription:** Tai-ch'ing T'ung-pi **Rev. Legend:** Hsüan-t'ung Nien-tsao, TAI-CHING-TI-KUO ...

Date	Mintage	VG8	F12	VF20	XF40	MS60
CD1909	—	12.50	25.00	50.00	125	—

Y# 20a.1 10 CASH
Copper **Obv. Inscription:** Tai-ch'ing T'ung-pi **Rev:** Dot after "COIN" **Rev. Legend:** Hsüan-t'ung Nien-tsao, TAI-CHING-TI-KUO ...

Date	Mintage	VG8	F12	VF20	XF40	MS60
CD1909	—	35.00	65.00	130	225	—

CHEKIANG PROVINCE

A province located along the east coast of China. Although the smallest of the Chinese mainland provinces, it is one of the most densely populated. Economic interests are mostly agricultural with iron and coal mining and some fishing. A small mint opened in 1897. This was replaced by a larger mint which operated briefly 1898-99. Other mints opened in 1903 and 1905. These were merged with the Fukien Mint in 1906-07.

EMPIRE

Kuang-hsü

PROVINCIAL CAST COINAGE

C# 4–19 CASH
Cast Brass, 21-22 mm. **Obv:** Type A **Obv. Inscription:** Kuang-hsü T'ung-pao **Rev. Inscription:** Boo-je **Mint:** Chê **Note:** Size varies.

Date	Mintage	G4	VG8	F12	VF20	XF40
ND(1875-1908)	—	4.00	5.00	8.00	12.00	14.00

C# 4–19.1 CASH
Cast Brass **Obv. Inscription:** Kuang-hsü T'ung-pao **Rev:** More angular mint mark

Date	Mintage	G4	VG8	F12	VF20	XF40
ND(1875-1908)	—	2.50	4.00	5.00	7.00	10.00

MILLED COINAGE

Y# 8b 2 CASH
Copper **Obv. Inscription:** Tai-ch'ing T'ung-pi **Rev:** Dragon

Date	Mintage	VG8	F12	VF20	XF40	MS60
CD1906	—	5.00	10.00	16.00	30.00	—

Y# 9b 5 CASH
Copper **Obv. Inscription:** Tai-ch'ing T'ung-pi **Rev. Legend:** Kuang-hsü Nien-tsao, TAI-CHING-TI-KUO ...

Date	Mintage	F12	VF20	XF40	MS60	MS63
CD1906	—	10.00	16.00	30.00	225	375

Y# 49 10 CASH
Copper **Obv:** Ball in circle in center **Obv. Legend:** Che-kiang Sheng Tsao **Obv. Inscription:** Kuang-hsü Yüan-pao **Rev:** Dragon

Date	Mintage	VG8	F12	VF20	XF40	MS60
ND(1903-06)	—	0.60	1.75	3.00	5.00	—

Y# 49.1 10 CASH
Copper **Obv:** Rosette at center and large Manchu "Boo" at left **Obv. Legend:** Che-kiang Sheng Tsao **Obv. Inscription:** Kuang-hsü Yüan-pao **Rev:** Dragon

Date	Mintage	VF20	XF40	MS60	MS63	MS65
ND(1903-06)	—	2.50	4.50	150	275	450

Y# 49.1a 10 CASH
Brass **Obv:** Rosette at center and large Manchu "Boo" at left **Obv. Legend:** Che-kiang Sheng Tsao **Obv. Inscription:** Kuang-hsü Yüan-pao **Rev:** Dragon

Date	Mintage	F12	VF20	XF40	MS60	MS63
ND(1903-06)	—	5.00	10.00	18.00	200	350

Y# 49.2 10 CASH
Copper **Obv:** Small Manchu "Boo" at left **Obv. Legend:** Che-kiang Sheng Tsao **Obv. Inscription:** Kuang-hsü Yüan-pao **Rev:** Dragon **Note:** Similar to Y#49.1 but with coin die alignment

Date	Mintage	VG8	F12	VF20	XF40	MS60
ND(1903-06)	—	0.90	1.75	4.00	7.00	—

Y# 49.3 10 CASH
Copper **Obv:** Rosette at center and small Manchu word at left **Obv. Legend:** Che-kiang Sheng Tsao **Obv. Inscription:** Kuang-hsü Yüan-pao **Rev:** Small, cramped dragon with few clouds around body

Date	Mintage	VG8	F12	VF20	XF40	MS60
ND(1903-06)	—	0.90	1.75	4.00	7.00	—

Y# 49.4 10 CASH

Copper **Obv. Legend:** Che-kiang Sheng Tsao **Obv. Inscription:** Kuang-hsü Yüan-pao **Rev:** Dragon without ball in center circle

Date	Mintage	VG8	F12	VF20	XF40	MS60
ND(1903-06)	—	1.50	3.00	6.00	12.00	—

Y# 49a 10 CASH

Brass **Obv:** Legend has 4 characters at bottom **Obv. Legend:** Che-kiang Sheng Tsao **Obv. Inscription:** Kuang-hsü Yüan-pao **Rev:** Dragon

Date	Mintage	VG8	F12	VF20	XF40	MS60
ND(1903-06)	—	4.00	7.00	13.00	25.00	—

Y# 49b 10 CASH

Copper **Obv. Legend:** Che-kiang Sheng Tsao **Obv. Inscription:** Kuang-hsü Yüan-pao **Rev:** Dragon

Date	Mintage	VG8	F12	VF20	XF40	MS60
ND(1903-06)	—	7.00	14.00	30.00	55.00	—

Y# 10b 10 CASH

Copper **Obv. Inscription:** Tai-ch'ing T'ung-pi **Rev:** Dragon **Rev. Legend:** Kuang hsü Nien-tsao, TAI-CHING-TI-KUO with KUO spelled KIIO

Date	Mintage	F12	VF20	XF40	MS60	MS63
CD1906	—	2.50	5.00	10.00	375	550

Y# 10b.1 10 CASH

Copper **Obv. Inscription:** Tai-ch'ing T'ung-pi **Rev:** Dragon **Rev. Legend:** Kuang hsü Nien-tsao, TAI-CHING-TI-KUO with KUO spelled KUO

Date	Mintage	VG8	F12	VF20	XF40	MS60
CD1906	—	3.00	6.00	12.00	25.00	—

Note: Chekiang and other 10 Cash coin types found struck over Korean 5 Fun coins are known; Why they were overstruck in China is unknown

Y# 50 20 CASH

Copper **Obv. Legend:** Che-kiang Sheng Tsao **Obv. Inscription:** Kuang-hsü Yüan-pao **Rev:** Dragon **Note:** Two planchet sizes exist.

Date	Mintage	VG8	F12	VF20	XF40	MS60
ND(1903-04)	—	100	200	400	900	—

Y# 11b 20 CASH

Copper **Obv. Inscription:** Tai-ch'ing T'ung-Pi **Rev. Legend:** Kuang-hsü Nien-tsao, TAI-CHING-TI-KUO ...

Date	Mintage	VG8	F12	VF20	XF40	MS60
CD1906	—	60.00	100	200	350	—

REPUBLIC

Y# 371 10 CENTS

2.65 g., 0.650 Silver 0.0554 oz. ASW **Obv:** Crossed flags **Rev. Legend:** CHE-KIANG PROVINCE

Date	Mintage	F12	VF20	XF40	MS60	MS63
13(1924)	4,464,000	5.00	8.00	12.00	50.00	275

Y# 373 20 CENTS

5.30 g., Silver **Rev:** Large value "20" **Rev. Legend:** CHE-KIANG PROVINCE.

Date	Mintage	VG8	F12	VF20	XF40	MS60
13(1924)	—	120	350	600	1,000	1,800

PATTERNS

Including off metal strikes

KM#	Date	Mintage	Identification	Mkt Val
Pn4	ND-1902	—	5 Cents. Silver. CHE-KIANG. K123-I.	20,000
Pn5	ND-1902	—	10 Cents. Silver. CHE-KIANG. K122-I.	15,000
Pn6	ND-1902	—	20 Cents. Silver. CHE-KIANG. K121-I.	15,000
Pn7	ND-1902	—	Dollar. Silver. CHE-KIANG. K 119-I.	60,000
Pn8	ND-1902	—	Dollar. Copper. CHE-KIANG. K 119-I.	40,000
Pn9	ND-1903	—	10 Cash. Copper. Y49.3a.	1,000
Pn10	ND-1903	—	10 Cash. White Copper. Y49.3a. W132.	—
Pn11	13(1924)	—	20 Cents. Silver. Crossed flags. Y372.	2,000

CHIHLI PROVINCE

Hebei, Hopei

A province located in northeastern China which contains the eastern end of the Great Wall. An important producer of coal and some iron ore. In 1928 the provincial name was changed from Chihli to Hopei. The Paoting mint was established in 1745 and only produced cast cash coins.

A mint for struck cash was established in 1888 and the mint for the Peiyang silver coinage was added in 1896. This was destroyed during the Boxer Rebellion. A replacement mint was built in 1902 for the provincial coinage and merged with the Tientsin (Tianjin) Central mint in 1910.

EMPIRE

Kuang-hsü

PROVINCIAL CAST COINAGE

C# 3–1.1 CASH

Cast Brass, 23 mm. **Obv. Inscription:** Kuang-hsü T'ung-pao **Rev:** Type 1 mint mark, Manchu inscription **Rev. Inscription:** Boo-gu **Mint:** Ku

Date	Mintage	G4	VG8	F12	VF20	XF40
ND(1875-1908)	—	90.00	125	200	300	—

C# 3–1.2 CASH

Cast Brass, 22 mm. **Obv. Inscription:** Kuang-hsü T'ung-pao **Rev:** Type 2 mint mark, Manchu inscription **Rev. Inscription:** Boo-gu **Mint:** Ku

Date	Mintage	G4	VG8	F12	VF20	XF40
ND(1875-1908)	—	20.00	30.00	50.00	75.00	—

C# 8–1 CASH

Cast Brass, 23 mm. **Obv. Inscription:** Kuang-hsü T'ung-pao **Rev:** Manchu inscription **Mint:** Ching

Date	Mintage	G4	VG8	F12	VF20	XF40
ND(1875-1908)	—	2.50	4.50	7.50	12.00	—

C# 8–1.1 CASH

Cast Brass **Obv. Inscription:** Kuang-hsü T'ung-pao **Rev:** Dot above, Manchu inscription **Rev. Inscription:** Boo-jiyen **Mint:** Ching

Date	Mintage	G4	VG8	F12	VF20	XF40
ND(1875-1908)	—	2.75	4.50	7.50	15.00	—

C# 8–1.2 CASH

Cast Brass **Obv. Inscription:** Kuang-hsü T'ung-pao **Rev:** Dot below, Manchu inscription **Rev. Inscription:** Boo-jiyen **Mint:** Ching

Date	Mintage	G4	VG8	F12	VF20	XF40
ND(1875-1908)	—	2.00	3.50	6.00	10.00	—

C# 8–1.3 CASH

Cast Brass **Obv. Inscription:** Kuang-hsü T'ung-pao **Rev:** 2 dots below, Manchu inscription **Rev. Inscription:** Boo-jiyen **Mint:** Ching

Date	Mintage	G4	VG8	F12	VF20	XF40
ND(1875-1908)	—	3.50	5.50	9.00	15.00	—

C# 8–1.4 CASH

Cast Brass **Obv. Inscription:** Kuang-hsü T'ung-pao **Rev:** Circle above Manchu inscription **Rev. Inscription:** Boo-jiyen **Mint:** Ching

Date	Mintage	G4	VG8	F12	VF20	XF40
ND(1875-1908)	—	3.50	5.50	9.00	18.00	—

C# 8–1.5 CASH

Cast Brass **Obv. Inscription:** Kuang-hsü T'ung-pao **Rev:** Circle below Manchu inscription **Rev. Inscription:** Boo-jiyen **Mint:** Ching

Date	Mintage	G4	VG8	F12	VF20	XF40
ND(1875-1908)	—	3.50	5.50	9.00	18.00	—

C# 8–1.6 CASH

Cast Brass **Obv. Inscription:** Kuang-hsü T'ung-pao **Rev:** Crescent above Manchu inscription **Rev. Inscription:** Boo-jiyen **Mint:** Ching

Date	Mintage	G4	VG8	F12	VF20	XF40
ND(1875-1908)	—	3.50	5.50	9.00	18.00	—

C# 8–1.7 CASH

Cast Brass **Obv. Inscription:** Kuang-hsü T'ung-pao **Rev:** Crescent below Manchu inscription **Rev. Inscription:** Boo-jiyen **Mint:** Ching

Date	Mintage	G4	VG8	F12	VF20	XF40
ND(1875-1908)	—	2.00	3.75	7.50	17.00	—

C# 8–1.8 CASH

Cast Brass **Obv. Inscription:** Kuang-hsü T'ung-pao **Rev:** Dash below Manchu inscription **Rev. Inscription:** Boo-jiyen **Mint:** Ching

Date	Mintage	G4	VG8	F12	VF20	XF40
ND(1875-1908)	—	2.00	3.75	7.50	15.00	—

Note: Varieties exist with dots and crescents in different corners on reverse and also with incuse dots

C# 8–1.9 CASH
Brass, 22.3 mm. **Obv. Inscription:** Kuang-hsü T'ung-pao **Rev:** Dash above **Rev. Inscription:** Boo-jiyen **Mint:** Ching

Date	Mintage	G4	VG8	F12	VF20	XF40
ND(1875-1908)	—	2.00	3.75	7.50	15.00	—

C# 8–1.10 CASH
Brass, 22.1 mm. **Obv. Inscription:** Kuang-hsü T'ung-pao **Rev:** Dot at upper left **Rev. Inscription:** Boo-jiyen **Mint:** Ching

Date	Mintage	G4	VG8	F12	VF20	XF40
ND(1875-1908)	—	2.75	4.50	7.50	15.00	—

MILLED COINAGE

Y# 66 CASH
Brass **Obv. Inscription:** Kuang-hsü T'ung-pao **Mint:** Peiyang Arsenal **Note:** Struck at Chin Mint, Tientsin.

Date	Mintage	G4	VG8	F12	VF20	XF40
ND(1904-07)	—	1.50	4.00	6.00	12.00	28.00

Y# 7c CASH
Brass **Obv. Legend:** Kuang-hsü **Rev:** Dragon **Note:** Struck at Chin Mint(Peiyang Arsenal), Tientsin.

Date	Mintage	G4	VG8	F12	VF20	XF40
CD1908	—	1.00	2.50	4.50	7.50	13.50

Y# 8c 2 CASH
Copper **Note:** Struck at Chin Mint(Peiyang Arsenal), Tientsin.

Date	Mintage	VG8	F12	VF20	XF40	MS60
CD1906 Rare	—	—	—	—	—	—

Y# 9c 5 CASH
Copper **Obv. Inscription:** Tai-ch'ing T'ung-pi **Rev. Legend:** Kuang-hsü Nien-tsao, TAI-CHING-TI-KUO ... **Note:** Struck at Chin Mint (Peiyang Arsenal), Tientsin.

Date	Mintage	G4	VG8	F12	VF20	XF40
CD1906	—	4.00	10.00	20.00	35.00	50.00

Y# 10c 10 CASH
Copper **Obv. Inscription:** Tai-ch'ing T'ung-pi **Rev. Legend:** Kuang-hsü Nien-tsao, TAI-CHING-TI-KUO ... **Note:** Struck at Chin Mint (Peiyang Arsenal), Tientsin.

Date	Mintage	G4	VG8	F12	VF20	XF40
CD1906	—	0.50	1.25	2.50	4.00	6.00

Y# 67 10 CASH
Copper **Obv. Inscription:** Kuang-hsü Yüan-pao **Rev:** Side-view square-mouth dragon, hole in center of rosette **Rev. Legend:** PEI YANG **Note:** Struck at Chin Mint (Peiyang Arsenal), Tientsin.

Date	Mintage	G4	VG8	F12	VF20	XF40
ND (1906)	—	0.50	1.25	2.50	3.00	5.00

Note: Mulings exist with obverse of Kwangtung (Guangdong) Y#192 and reverse of Chihli Y#67; Refer to Kwangtung listings

Y# 67.1 10 CASH
Copper **Obv. Inscription:** Kuang-hsü Yüan-pao **Rev:** Dragon with round mouth **Note:** Struck at Chin Mint (Peiyang Arsenal), Tientsin.

Date	Mintage	G4	VG8	F12	VF20	XF40
ND (1906)	—	0.50	1.25	2.50	3.00	5.00

Y# 67.2 10 CASH
Copper **Obv. Inscription:** Kuang-hsü Yüan-pao **Rev:** Dot in center of rosettes, dragon with square mouth **Note:** Struck at Chin Mint (Peiyang Arsenal), Tientsin.

Date	Mintage	G4	VG8	F12	VF20	XF40
ND (1906)	—	0.50	1.25	2.50	3.00	5.00

Y# 67.3 10 CASH
Copper **Obv. Inscription:** Kuang-hsü Yüan-pao **Rev:** Dot in center of rosettes, dragon with round mouth **Note:** Struck at Chin Mint (Peiyang Arsenal), Tientsin.

Date	Mintage	G4	VG8	F12	VF20	XF40
ND (1906)	—	0.50	1.25	2.50	3.00	5.00

Y# 67.4 10 CASH
Copper **Obv. Inscription:** Kuang-hsü Yüan-pao **Rev:** Redesigned dragon with smaller body and smaller English legends **Note:** Struck at Chin Mint (Peiyang Arsenal), Tientsin.

Date	Mintage	G4	VG8	F12	VF20	XF40
ND (1906)	—	0.70	1.75	4.00	8.00	18.00

Y# 11c 20 CASH
Copper **Obv. Inscription:** Tai-ch'ing T'ung-pi **Rev. Legend:** Kuang-hsü Nien-tsao, TAI-CHING-TI-KUO ... **Note:** Struck at Chin Mint (Peiyang Arsenal), Tientsin.

Date	Mintage	VG8	F12	VF20	XF40	MS60
CD1906	—	15.00	30.00	60.00	135	—

Y# 68 20 CASH
Copper **Note:** Struck at Chin Mint (Peiyang Arsenal), Tientsin.

Date	Mintage	G4	VG8	F12	VF20	XF40
ND (1906)	—	10.00	20.00	30.00	40.00	100

Y# 68.1 20 CASH
Copper **Obv. Inscription:** Kuang-hsü Yüan-pao **Rev:** Smaller lettering **Note:** Struck at Chin Mint (Peiyang Arsenal), Tientsin.

Date	Mintage	VG8	F12	VF20	XF40	MS60
ND(1906)	—	25.00	35.00	50.00	120	—

Y# 68a 20 CASH
Brass **Obv. Inscription:** Kuang-hsü Yüan-pao **Rev:** Side view dragon **Rev. Legend:** PEI YANG **Note:** Struck at Chin Mint (Peiyang Arsenal), Tientsin.

Date	Mintage	VG8	F12	VF20	XF40	MS60
ND(1906) Rare	—	—	—	—	—	—

Y# 71a 20 CENTS
5.30 g., 0.820 Silver 0.1397 oz. ASW **Obv. Inscription:** Kuang-hsü Yüan-pao **Rev:** Side view dragon, legend at bottom **Rev. Legend:** PEI YANG **Note:** Struck at Chin Mint (Peiyang Arsenal), Tientsin.

Date	Mintage	VG8	F12	VF20	XF40	MS60
31(1905)	161,000	48.00	90.00	180	300	725

Y# 73 DOLLAR
26.70 g., 0.900 Silver 0.7726 oz. ASW **Obv. Inscription:** Kuang-hsü Yüan-pao **Rev:** Side view dragon, legend at bottom **Rev. Legend:** PEI YANG

Date	Mintage	VG8	F12	VF20	XF40	MS60
29(1903)	22,018,000	27.50	41.50	65.00	195	1,150

Y# 73.1 DOLLAR
26.70 g., 0.900 Silver 0.7726 oz. ASW **Obv. Inscription:** Kuang-hsü Yüan-pao **Rev:** Side view dragon, legend at bottom, period after legend **Rev. Legend:** PEI YANG **Note:** Struck at Chin Mint (Peiyang Arsenal), Tientsin.

Date	Mintage	VG8	F12	VF20	XF40	MS60
29(1903)	Inc. above	27.50	41.50	65.00	195	1,150

Y# 73.2 DOLLAR
26.70 g., 0.900 Silver 0.7726 oz. ASW **Obv. Inscription:** Kuang-hsü Yüan-pao **Rev:** Thinner side-view dragon, legend at bottom, year as "33rd" **Rev. Legend:** PEI YANG **Mint:** Peiyang Arsenal **Note:** Struck at Chin Mint (Peiyang Arsenal), Tientsin.

Date	Mintage	VG8	F12	VF20	XF40	MS60
33(1907)	2,341,000	27.50	45.50	80.00	230	1,450
34(1908)	—	22.50	32.50	45.50	130	650

Y# 73.3 DOLLAR
26.70 g., 0.900 Silver 0.7726 oz. ASW **Obv. Inscription:** Kuang-hsü Yüan-pao **Rev:** Side view dragon, legend at bottom, short center spine to tail **Rev. Legend:** PEI YANG **Note:** Struck at Chin Mint (Peiyang Arsenal), Tientsin. Restruck during Republican times.

Date	Mintage	VG8	F12	VF20	XF40	MS60
34(1908)	—	22.50	32.50	45.50	130	650

Y# 73.4 DOLLAR
26.70 g., 0.900 Silver 0.7726 oz. ASW **Obv. Inscription:** Kuang-hsü Yüan-pao **Rev:** Side view dragon, legend at bottom, crosslet 4 in date **Rev. Legend:** PEI YANG **Note:** Struck at Chin Mint (Peiyang Arsenal), Tientsin. Restruck during Republican times.

Date	Mintage	VG8	F12	VF20	XF40	MS60
34(1908)	—	39.00	65.00	165	350	1,950

Y# 74 TAEL
51.20 g., Silver **Obv. Inscription:** Kuang-hsü Yüan-pao **Rev:** Side view dragon, legend at bottom **Rev. Legend:** PEI YANG **Note:** Struck at Chin Mint (Peiyang Arsenal), Tientsin.

Date	Mintage	VG8	F12	VF20	XF40	MS60
33(1907)	—	—	—	15,000	25,000	50,000

Y# 74.1 TAEL
51.20 g., Silver **Obv. Inscription:** Kuang-hsü Yüan-pao **Rev:** Side view dragon, legend at bottom, 3 dots on pearl arranged horizontally **Rev. Legend:** PEI YANG **Note:** Struck at Chin Mint (Peiyang Arsenal), Tientsin.

Date	Mintage	VG8	F12	VF20	XF40	MS60
33(1907)	—	—	—	15,000	25,000	50,000

Y# 74.2 TAEL
51.20 g., Silver **Obv. Inscription:** Kuang-hsü Yüan-pao **Rev:** Side view dragon, legend at bottom, 3 dots on pearl arranged in arc **Rev. Legend:** PEI YANG **Note:** Struck at Chin Mint (Peiyang Arsenal), Tientsin.

Date	Mintage	VG8	F12	VF20	XF40	MS60
33(1907)	—	—	—	10,000	22,000	45,000

PATTERNS

Including off metal strikes

KM#	Date	Mintage	Identification	Mkt Val
Pn6	29(1903)	—	Dollar. Brass. Y73.	—
Pn7	33(1907)	—	Tael. Gold. Y74. Specialists suspect this is a counterfiet.	—

FENGTIEN PROVINCE

(Fungtien)
Liaoning

The southernmost province of the Three Eastern Provinces was known by a variety of names including Fengtien, Shengching, and Liaoning. The modern Mukden (Fengtien Province) Mint operated from 1897 to 1931.

EMPIRE

Kuang-hsü

PROVINCIAL CAST COINAGE

C# 9–1 CASH
Cast Brass **Obv:** Type A **Obv. Inscription:** Kuang-hsü T'ung-pao **Rev:** Manchu inscription **Rev. Inscription:** Boo-fung

Date	Mintage	G4	VG8	F12	VF20	XF40
ND(1875-1908)	—	20.00	30.00	45.00	70.00	120

MILLED COINAGE

Y# 88 10 CASH
Brass **Obv. Inscription:** Kuang-hsü Yüan-pao **Rev:** Province name spelled "FEN-TIEN"

Date	Mintage	VG8	F12	VF20	XF40	MS60
CD1903	—	50.00	140	275	550	—

Y# 89 10 CASH
Brass **Obv. Inscription:** Kuang-hsü Yüan-pao **Rev. Legend:** FUNG-TIEN PROVINCE

Date	Mintage	VG8	F12	VF20	XF40	MS60
CD1903	—	6.00	11.00	37.50	80.00	—
CD1904	—	2.00	5.00	8.00	20.00	—
CD1905	—	2.25	7.00	15.00	30.00	—
CD1906	35,036,000	5.00	9.00	37.50	70.00	—

Y# 89.1 10 CASH
Brass **Obv:** Manchu words in center reversed **Obv. Inscription:** Kuang-hsü Yüan-pao **Rev. Legend:** FUNG-TIEN PROVINCE

Date	Mintage	VG8	F12	VF20	XF40	MS60
CD1903	—	42.00	130	225	500	—

Y# 10e.1 10 CASH
Copper **Obv. Inscription:** Tai-ch'ing T'ung-pi **Rev:** Large pearl **Rev. Legend:** Kuang-hsü Nien-tsao, TAI-CHING-TI-KUO ...

Date	Mintage	VG8	F12	VF20	XF40	MS60
CD1905	—	4.00	12.00	25.00	80.00	—

Y# 10e 10 CASH
Copper **Obv. Inscription:** Tai-ch'ing T'ung-pi **Rev:** Dragon, small pearl **Rev. Legend:** Kuang-hsü Nien-tsao, TAI-CHING TI KUO ...

Date	Mintage	VG8	F12	VF20	XF40	MS60
CD1905	—	4.00	12.00	25.00	80.00	—

Y# 89.2 10 CASH
Brass **Obv. Inscription:** Kuang-hsü Yüan-pao **Rev:** Large pearl **Rev. Legend:** FUNG-TIEN PROVINCE

Date	Mintage	VG8	F12	VF20	XF40	MS60
CD1905	—	5.00	15.00	30.00	75.00	—

Y# 10e.2 10 CASH
Copper **Obv:** Mint mark on spherical disc in center **Obv. Inscription:** Tai-ch'ing T'ung-pi **Rev:** Large pearl **Rev. Legend:** Kuang-hsü Nien-tsao, TAI-CHING-TI KUO ...

Date	Mintage	VG8	F12	VF20	XF40	MS60
CD1907	130,000	3.00	9.00	18.00	120	275

Y# 10e.3 10 CASH
Copper **Obv:** Mint mark on flat disc in center **Obv. Inscription:** Tai-ch'ing T'ung-pi **Rev. Legend:** Kuang-hsü Nien-tsao, TAI CHING TI KUO ...

Date	Mintage	VG8	F12	VF20	XF40	MS60
CD1907	Inc. above	1.50	5.00	9.00	24.00	150

Y# 20e.1 10 CASH
Copper **Obv. Inscription:** Tai-ch'ing T'ung-pi **Rev. Legend:** Kuang-hsü Nien-tsao, TAI CHING TI KUO ... **Note:** Mule, obverse Y#20e, reverse Y#10e. Prev. #W286.

Date	Mintage	VG8	F12	VF20	XF40	MS60
CD1909 6 known	—	—	—	—	—	—

Y# 90 20 CASH
Brass **Obv. Legend:** Feng-tien Sheng Tsao **Obv. Inscription:** Kuang-hsü Yüan-pao **Rev. Legend:** FUNG TIEN PROVINCE

Date	Mintage	VG8	F12	VF20	XF40	MS60
CD1903	—	160	210	265	875	—
CD1904	—	12.00	22.50	47.25	275	725
CD1905	—	20.00	37.50	55.00	325	800

Y# 11e 20 CASH

Brass **Obv. Inscription:** Tai-ching T'ung-pi **Rev. Legend:** Kuang-hsü Nien-tsao, TAI-CHING-TI-KUO ...

Date	Mintage	VG8	F12	VF20	XF40	MS60
CD1905	—	8.00	15.00	37.50	180	475
CD1907	—	11.00	22.50	55.00	265	650

Y# 11g 20 CASH

Copper **Obv:** Inscription with Hu at right, Pu at left **Obv. Inscription:** Tai-ch'ing T'ung-pi **Rev:** Dragon **Rev. Legend:** Kuang-hsü Nien-tsao, TAI-CHING-TI-KUO...

Date	Mintage	VG8	F12	VF20	XF40	MS60
CD1905	—	—	—	—	—	—

Y# 11f 20 CASH

Copper **Obv:** Inscription with "CD" at left and right **Obv. Inscription:** Tai-ching T'ung-pi **Rev. Legend:** Kuang-hsü Nien-tsao, TAI-CHING-TI-KUO...

Date	Mintage	VG8	F12	VF20	XF40	MS60
CD1907	—	—	—	—	—	—

Y# 91 20 CENTS

Silver, 24 mm. **Obv. Legend:** Feng-tien Sheng Tsao **Obv. Inscription:** Kuang-hsü Yüan-pao **Rev:** Side view dragon, 8 rows of scales on dragon **Rev. Legend:** FUNG-TIEN PROVINCE

Date	Mintage	VG8	F12	VF20	XF40	MS60
CD1904	—	6.00	14.00	22.50	75.00	275

Y# 91.1 20 CENTS

Silver **Obv. Legend:** Feng-tien Sheng Tsao **Obv. Inscription:** Kuang-hsü Yüan-pao **Rev:** Side view dragon, 5 rows of scales on dragon **Rev. Legend:** FUNG-TIEN PROVINCE

Date	Mintage	VG8	F12	VF20	XF40	MS60
CD1904	—	8.00	15.00	27.50	90.00	300

Y# 92 DOLLAR

26.40 g., 0.850 Silver 0.7215 oz. ASW **Obv. Legend:** Feng-tien Sheng Tsao **Obv. Inscription:** Kuang-hsü Yüan-pao **Rev:** Side view dragon **Rev. Legend:** FUNG-TIEN PROVINCE

Date	Mintage	VG8	F12	VF20	XF40	MS60
CD1903	262,000	150	350	1,000	3,500	12,500

Y# 92.1 DOLLAR

26.40 g., 0.850 Silver 0.7215 oz. ASW **Obv:** Manchu "Boo-funs" in center are reversed **Obv. Legend:** Feng-tien Sheng Tsao **Obv. Inscription:** Kuang-hsü Yüan-pao **Rev:** Side view dragon **Rev. Legend:** FUNG-TIEN PROVINCE

Date	Mintage	VG8	F12	VF20	XF40	MS60
CD1903	Inc. above	150	375	1,200	4,000	13,500

TOKEN COINAGE

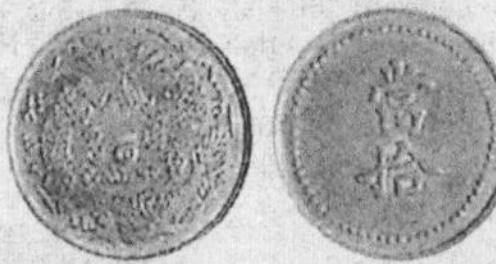

KM# TnA1 10 CENTS

Copper **Obv:** Dragon **Rev:** Tang-shih (10)

Date	Mintage	VG8	F12	VF20	XF40	MS60
ND(c.1904)	—	—	—	1,100	1,800	3,000

KM# Tn1 DOLLAR

Copper **Obv:** Reverse of 10 Cash, Y#10e, small spiral on pearl **Rev. Inscription:** Tang-yüan (1 Dollar) **Note:** Woodward #242.

Date	Mintage	VG8	F12	VF20	XF40	MS60
ND-1904	—	—	—	650	1,200	19,000

KM# Tn1a DOLLAR

Brass **Obv:** Reverse of 10 Cash, Y#10e, small spiral on pearl **Rev. Inscription:** Tang-yüan (1 Dollar)

Date	Mintage	VG8	F12	VF20	XF40	MS60
ND-1904	—	—	—	650	1,200	19,000

KM# Tn2 100 CENTS

Copper **Obv:** Dragon, large spiral on pearl **Obv. Legend:** FUNG TIEN PROVINCE **Rev. Inscription:** Tang Pai **Note:** Silver forgeries exist. Woodward #243.

Date	Mintage	VG8	F12	VF20	XF40	MS60
ND-1904	—	—	—	650	1,200	19,000

KM# Tn3 100 CENTS

Brass **Obv. Legend:** FUNG-TIEN PROVINCE **Rev. Inscription:** Tang Pai **Note:** Silver forgeries exist.

Date	Mintage	VG8	F12	VF20	XF40	MS60
ND-1904	—	—	—	—	—	—

Hsüan-t'ung

MILLED COINAGE

Y# 19e 5 CASH

Copper **Obv. Inscription:** Tai-ching T'ung-pi **Rev. Legend:** Hsüan-t'ung Nien-tsao, TAI-CHING-TI-KUO ...

Date	Mintage	VG8	F12	VF20	XF40	MS60
CD1909	—	55.00	115	190	400	—

Y# 20e 10 CASH

Copper **Obv:** Mint mark on flat disc in center **Obv. Inscription:** Tai-ch'ing T'ung-pi **Rev. Legend:** Hsüan-T'ung Nien-tsao, TAI-CHING-TI-KUO ...

Date	Mintage	VG8	F12	VF20	XF40	MS60
CD1909	—	4.00	12.00	27.50	90.00	200

Y# 21e 20 CASH

Brass **Obv. Inscription:** Tai-ching T'ung-pi **Rev. Legend:** Hsüan-t'ung Nien-tsao, TAI-CHING-TI-KUO ...

Date	Mintage	VG8	F12	VF20	XF40	MS60
CD1909	—	37.50	90.00	185	650	—

PATTERNS

Including off metal strikes

KM#	Date	Mintage	Identification	Mkt Val
PnA2	ND-1902	—	10 Cents. Brass. Regular provincial design.	—
Pn3	ND-1902	—	20 Cents. Brass. Regular provincial design.	—
Pn4	ND-1902	—	20 Cents. Brass. Error, TENG-TIEN.	—
Pn5	ND-1902	—	20 Cents. Silver.	—
Pn6	ND-1902	—	50 Cents. Brass.	—
Pn7	ND-1902	—	Dollar. Aluminum.	75,000
Pn8	ND-1902	—	Dollar. Silver. Error, TENG-TIEN.	—
Pn9	ND-1902	—	Dollar. Brass.	—
Pn10	ND-1902	—	10 Cash. Copper.	—
Pn11	CD1903	—	10 Cash. Copper. Y88.	—
Pn12	CD1903	—	10 Cash. Copper. Y89.	—
Pn13	CD1903	—	10 Cash. Copper. Y89.1.	—
Pn14	CD1903	—	20 Cash. Copper. Y90.	—
PnA15	CD1903	—	Tael. Silver. K931-I.	—
Note: Superior Goodman sale 6-91 about XF realized $187,000.				
Pn15	CD1904	—	10 Cash. Copper. Y89.	—
Pn16	CD1905	—	10 Cash. Copper. Y89.	—
Pn17	CD1905	—	20 Cash. Copper. Y90.	—

FUKIEN PROVINCE

Fujian

A province located on the southeastern coast of China, including the island of Taiwan until it became its own separate province in 1885. Although known mainly as an agricultural area, forestry and some mining, particularly iron ore and coal, are also important to the economy. The Foochow Mint operated throughout the Manchu dynasty. The Viceroy's or City mint was opened in 1896 for struck coinage. Two other mints were established in 1905, the Mamoi Arsenal Mint which struck the Custom-House issues until it closed in 1906, and the West Mint which later became the main Fukien (Fujian) Mint. It closed between 1914 and 1920. Various subsidiary mints were in operation from 1924 to 1925.

EMPIRE

MILLED COINAGE

Y# 8f 2 CASH

Brass **Obv: Inscription:** Tai-ching T'ung-pi **Rev:** Dragon **Mint:** Fu

Date	Mintage	VG8	F12	VF20	XF40	MS60
CD1906	—	5.00	12.00	20.00	80.00	—

Kuang-hsü

PROVINCIAL CAST COINAGE

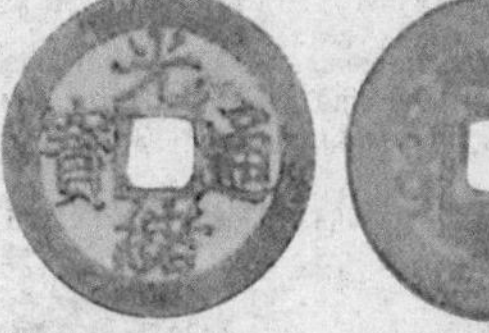

C# 10–25 CASH

Cast Brass **Obv. Inscription:** Kuang hsü T'ung-pao **Rev:** Manchu inscription **Rev. Inscription:** Boo-fu **Mint:** Fu **Note:** Schjöth #1581.

Date	Mintage	G4	VG8	F12	VF20	XF40
ND(1875-1908)	—	1.00	1.75	3.00	4.00	—

C# 10–25.1 CASH

Cast Brass **Obv. Inscription:** Kuang hsü T'ung-pao **Rev:** Dot at top of hole, Manchu inscription **Rev. Inscription:** Boo-fu **Mint:** Fu

Date	Mintage	G4	VG8	F12	VF20	XF40
ND(1875-1908)	—	3.00	5.00	8.00	12.00	—

C# 10–25.2 CASH

Cast Brass **Obv. Inscription:** Kuang-hsü T'ung-pao **Rev:** Inverted Manchu inscription **Rev. Inscription:** Boo-fu **Mint:** Fu

Date	Mintage	G4	VG8	F12	VF20	XF40
ND(1875-1908)	—	—	—	—	—	—

MILLED COINAGE

Y# 7f CASH

Brass **Obv. Inscription:** Kuang hsü **Rev:** Dragon **Mint:** Fu

Date	Mintage	VG8	F12	VF20	XF40	MS60
CD1908	—	55.00	115	165	350	—

Y# 95 CASH

Brass **Obv. Inscription:** Kuang hsü T'ung-pao **Rev. Inscription:** Manchu Boo-fu **Mint:** Fu

Date	Mintage	VG8	F12	VF20	XF40	MS60
ND(1908)	—	9.00	15.00	22.50	100	250

Y# 99 5 CASH

Copper **Obv. Legend:** Fu-kien Kuan Chü Tsao **Obv. Inscription:** Kuang-hsü Yüan-pao **Rev:** Dragon **Rev. Legend:** FOO-KIEN **Mint:** Fu

Date	Mintage	VG8	F12	VF20	XF40	MS60
ND(1901-03)	590,000	27.50	37.50	55.00	120	—

Y# 99a 5 CASH

Brass **Obv. Legend:** Fu-kien Kuan Chü Tsao **Obv. Inscription:** Kuang-hsü Yüan-pao **Rev:** Dragon **Rev. Legend:** FOO-KIEN **Mint:** Fu

Date	Mintage	VG8	F12	VF20	XF40	MS60
ND(1901-03)	—	18.00	37.50	75.00	150	—

Y# 97 10 CASH

Copper **Obv:** Large characters at left and right **Obv. Legend:** Fu-kien Kuan Chü Tsao **Obv. Inscription:** Kuang-hsü Yüan-pao **Rev:** Dragon **Rev. Legend:** F.K. CUSTOM-HOUSE **Mint:** Fu

Date	Mintage	VG8	F12	VF20	XF40	MS60
ND(1901-05)	417,031,000	0.90	4.00	8.00	25.00	130

Y# 97.1 10 CASH

Copper **Obv:** Small characters at left and right sides **Obv. Legend:** Fu-kien Kuan Chü Tsao **Obv. Inscription:** Kuang-hsü Yüan-pao **Rev:** Dragon **Rev. Legend:** F.K. CUSTOM-HOUSE **Mint:** Fu

Date	Mintage	VG8	F12	VF20	XF40	MS60
ND(1901-05)	Inc. above	1.25	4.00	8.00	25.00	130

Y# 98 10 CASH

Copper **Obv. Legend:** Fu-kien Kuan Chü Tsao **Obv. Inscription:** Kuang-hsü Yüan-pao **Rev:** Dragon **Rev. Legend:** FOO-KIEN CUSTOM **Mint:** Fu

Date	Mintage	VG8	F12	VF20	XF40	MS60
ND(1901-05)	Inc. above	55.00	150	225	500	—

Y# 100.1 10 CASH

Copper **Obv. Legend:** Fu-kien Kuan Chü Tsao **Obv. Inscription:** Kuang-hsü Yüan-pao **Rev:** 3 clouds left of pearl and without cl oud above tip of dragon's tail, dragon **Rev. Legend:** FOO-KIEN **Mint:** Fu

Date	Mintage	VG8	F12	VF20	XF40	MS60
ND(1901-05)	Inc. above	1.25	4.00	8.00	24.00	130

Y# 100.2 10 CASH

Copper **Obv. Legend:** Fu-kien Kuan Chü Tsao **Obv. Inscription:** Kuang-hsü Yüan-pao **Rev:** 3 clouds left of pearl and a cloud above tip of dragon's tail, dragon **Rev. Legend:** FOO-KIEN **Mint:** Fu

Date	Mintage	VG8	F12	VF20	XF40	MS60
ND(1901-05)	Inc. above	0.60	2.00	4.00	10.00	130

Y# 100.2a 10 CASH

Brass **Obv. Legend:** Fu-kien Kuan Chü Tsao **Obv. Inscription:** Kuang-hsü Yüan-pao **Rev:** Dragon **Rev. Legend:** FOO-KIEN **Mint:** Fu

Date	Mintage	VG8	F12	VF20	XF40	MS60
ND(1901-05)	Inc. above	—	—	—	—	—

Y# 100.3 10 CASH

Copper **Obv. Legend:** Fu-kien Kuan Chü Tsao **Obv. Inscription:** Kuang-hsü Yüan-pao **Rev:** Dragon, denomination: 10 CASHES **Rev. Legend:** FOO-KIEN **Mint:** Fu

Date	Mintage	VG8	F12	VF20	XF40	MS60
ND(1901-05)	Inc. above	6.00	18.00	30.00	90.00	—

Y# 100 10 CASH

Copper **Obv. Legend:** Fu-kien Kuan Chü Tsao **Obv. Inscription:** Kuang-hsü Yüan-pao **Rev:** 1 cloud left of pearl, dragon **Rev. Legend:** FOO-KIEN **Mint:** Fu

Date	Mintage	VG8	F12	VF20	XF40	MS60
ND(1901-05)	Inc. above	2.00	6.00	11.00	30.00	130

Y# 10f 10 CASH

Copper **Obv. Inscription:** Tai-ch'ing T'ung-pi **Rev:** Dragon, inscription, denomination 10 CASHES **Rev. Legend:** Kuang-hsü Nien-tsao, TAI-CHING-TI-KUO ... **Mint:** Fu

Date	Mintage	VG8	F12	VF20	XF40	MS60
CD1906	—	0.40	1.25	2.25	6.00	40.00

Y# 101 20 CASH

Copper **Obv. Legend:** Fu-kien Kuan Chü Tsao **Obv. Inscription:** Kuang-hsü Yüan-pao **Rev:** Dragon **Rev. Legend:** FOO-KIEN **Mint:** Fu

Date	Mintage	VG8	F12	VF20	XF40	MS60
ND(1901-02)	18,000	18.00	45.00	70.00	180	1,000

Y# 101.1 20 CASH

Copper **Obv. Legend:** Fu-kien Kuan Chü Tsao **Obv. Inscription:** Kuang-hsü Yüan-pao **Rev:** Dragon **Rev. Legend:** FOO-KIEN **Mint:** Fu

Date	Mintage	VG8	F12	VF20	XF40	MS60
ND(1901-02)	Inc. above	37.50	90.00	135	300	—

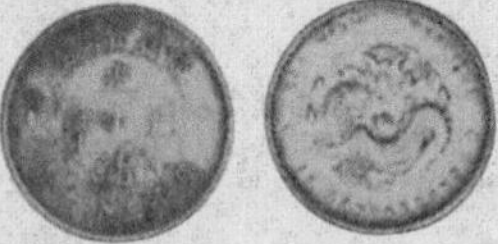

Y# 102 5 CENTS

1.35 g., 0.820 Silver 0.0356 oz. ASW **Obv:** Legend with 5 characters at top, inscription **Obv. Legend:** Fu-kien Kuan Chü Tsao **Obv. Inscription:** Kuang-hsü Yüan-pao **Rev:** Side view dragon left **Mint:** Fu

Date	Mintage	VG8	F12	VF20	XF40	MS60
ND(1896-1903)	—	6.00	16.00	27.50	50.00	190

Y# 102.1 5 CENTS

1.35 g., 0.820 Silver 0.0356 oz. ASW **Obv:** Legend with four characters at top **Obv. Legend:** Fu-kien Kuan Chü Tsao **Obv. Inscription:** Kuang-hsü Yüan-pao **Rev:** Rosette at either side of side view dragon right **Mint:** Fu

Date	Mintage	VG8	F12	VF20	XF40	MS60
ND(1903-08)	—	5.00	9.00	15.00	50.00	100

Y# 102.2 5 CENTS

1.35 g., 0.820 Silver 0.0356 oz. ASW **Obv. Legend:** Fu-kien Kuan Chü Tsao **Obv. Inscription:** Kuang-hsü Yüan-pao **Rev:** Rosette above dragon's head **Mint:** Fu

Date	Mintage	VG8	F12	VF20	XF40	MS60
ND(1903-08)	—	5.00	10.00	19.00	65.00	125

Y# 102.3 5 CENTS

1.35 g., 0.820 Silver 0.0356 oz. ASW **Obv. Legend:** Fu-kien Kuan Chü Tsao **Obv. Inscription:** Kuang-hsü Yüan-pao **Rev. Legend:** PROVINCE FOO-KIEN **Mint:** Fu

Date	Mintage	VG8	F12	VF20	XF40	MS60
ND(1903-08)	—	—	—	—	—	—

Y# 103 10 CENTS

2.70 g., 0.820 Silver 0.0712 oz. ASW **Obv:** Legend with 5 characters at top, inscription **Obv. Legend:** Fu-kien Kuan Chü Tsao **Obv. Inscription:** Kuang-hsü Yüan-pao **Rev:** Rosette at either side of side view dragon left **Mint:** Fu

Date	Mintage	VG8	F12	VF20	XF40	MS60
ND(1896-1903)	13,425,000	5.00	12.00	20.00	40.00	190

Y# 103.1 10 CENTS

2.70 g., 0.820 Silver 0.0712 oz. ASW **Obv. Legend:** Fu-kien Kuan Chü Tsao **Obv. Inscription:** Kuang-hsü Yüan-pao **Rev:** Dot at either side of side view dragon left **Mint:** Fu

Date	Mintage	VG8	F12	VF20	XF40	MS60
ND(1896-1903)	Inc. above	8.00	18.00	34.00	70.00	190

Y# 103.2 10 CENTS
2.70 g., 0.820 Silver 0.0712 oz. ASW **Obv:** Legend has 4 characters at top **Obv. Legend:** Fu-kien Kuan Chü Tsao **Obv. Inscription:** Kuang-hsü Yüan-pao **Rev:** Small side view dragon right **Mint:** Fu

Date	Mintage	VG8	F12	VF20	XF40	MS60
ND(1903-08)	Inc. above	2.75	5.00	10.00	31.25	80.00

Y# 103.3 10 CENTS
2.70 g., 0.820 Silver 0.0712 oz. ASW **Obv:** Legend has 4 characters at top **Obv. Legend:** Fu-kien Kuan Chü Tsao **Obv. Inscription:** Kuang-hsü Yüan-pao **Rev:** Large side view dragon right **Mint:** Fu

Date	Mintage	VG8	F12	VF20	XF40	MS60
ND(1903-08)	Inc. above	4.00	9.00	18.00	65.00	125

Y# 104 20 CENTS
5.40 g., 0.820 Silver 0.1424 oz. ASW **Obv:** Legend has 5 characters at top, inscription **Obv. Legend:** Fu-kien Kuan Chü Tsao **Obv. Inscription:** Kuang-hsü Yüan-pao **Rev:** Dot at either side of side view dragon left **Mint:** Fu

Date	Mintage	VG8	F12	VF20	XF40	MS60
ND(1896-1903)	31,772,000	5.00	10.00	16.00	30.00	165

Y# 104.1 20 CENTS
5.40 g., 0.820 Silver 0.1424 oz. ASW **Obv. Legend:** Fu-kien Kuan Chü Tsao **Obv. Inscription:** Kuang-hsü Yüan-pao **Rev:** Rosette at either side of side view dragon left **Mint:** Fu

Date	Mintage	VG8	F12	VF20	XF40	MS60
ND(1898-1903)	Inc. above	5.00	10.00	16.00	30.00	165

Y# 104.2 20 CENTS
5.40 g., 0.820 Silver 0.1424 oz. ASW **Obv:** Legend has 4 characters at top **Obv. Legend:** Fu-kien Kuan Chü Tsao **Obv. Inscription:** Kuang-hsü Yüan-pao **Rev:** Side view dragon right **Mint:** Fu **Note:** Variety with large side view dragon right on reverse exists.

Date	Mintage	VG8	F12	VF20	XF40	MS60
ND(1903-08)	Inc. above	5.00	8.00	11.00	33.75	90.00

Hsüan-T'ung

Y# 106 CASH
Brass **Obv. Inscription:** Hsüan-t'ung T'ung-pao **Rev:** Manchu inscription **Rev. Inscription:** Manchu Boo-fu **Mint:** Fu

Date	Mintage	VG8	F12	VF20	XF40	MS60
ND(1909)	—	22.50	37.50	75.00	200	600

Y# 20f 10 CASH
Copper **Obv. Inscription:** Tai-ch'ing T'ung-pi **Rev:** Dragon **Rev. Legend:** Hsüan-tung Nien-tsao, TAI-CHING-TI-KUO ... **Mint:** Fu

Date	Mintage	VG8	F12	VF20	XF40	MS60
CD1909	—	25.00	75.00	130	290	—

REPUBLIC

PROVINCIAL CAST COINAGE

Y# 374 CASH
Cast Brass **Obv. Inscription:** Fu-chien T'ung-pao **Rev:** 6 stripes on right flag

Date	Mintage	VG8	F12	VF20	XF40	MS60
ND(1912)	—	50.00	80.00	125	205	—

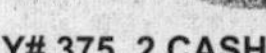

Y# 375 2 CASH
Cast Brass **Obv. Inscription:** Fu-chien T'ung-pao **Rev:** 5 stripes on right flag

Date	Mintage	VG8	F12	VF20	XF40	MS60
ND(1912)	—	12.50	17.50	22.50	37.50	—

Y# 375.1 2 CASH
Cast Brass **Obv. Inscription:** Fu-chien T'ung-pao **Rev:** 6 stripes on right flag

Date	Mintage	VG8	F12	VF20	XF40	MS60
ND(1912)	—	30.00	50.00	80.00	155	—

MILLED COINAGE

Y# 379 10 CASH
Copper **Obv. Legend:** Fu-Kien Tung Pien Tsang Tsao **Obv. Inscription:** Chung-hua Yüan-pao **Rev. Legend:** FOO-KIEN COPPER COIN

Date	Mintage	VG8	F12	VF20	XF40	MS60
ND(1912)	—	1.50	5.00	10.00	30.00	70.00

Y# 379a 10 CASH
Brass **Obv. Legend:** Fu-Kien Tung Pien Tsang Tsao **Obv. Inscription:** Chung-hua Yüan-pao **Rev. Legend:** FOO-KIEN COPPER COIN

Date	Mintage	VG8	F12	VF20	XF40	MS60
ND(1912)	—	22.50	45.00	60.00	175	250

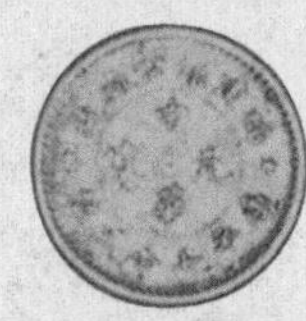

Y# 380 10 CENTS
2.60 g., Silver **Obv. Inscription:** Chung-hua Yüan-pao

Date	Mintage	VG8	F12	VF20	XF40	MS60
ND(1912)	—	30.00	48.00	120	400	700

Y# 382 10 CENTS
2.60 g., Silver **Obv. Inscription:** Chung-hua Yüan-pao

Date	Mintage	VG8	F12	VF20	XF40	MS60
ND(1913)	—	1.75	3.00	7.00	20.00	40.00

Y# 380a 10 CENTS
2.60 g., Silver **Obv:** Different legend in center **Obv. Inscription:** Chung-hua Yüan-pao **Note:** Similar to Y#380.

Date	Mintage	VG8	F12	VF20	XF40	MS60
CD1924	—	30.00	60.00	145	400	600

Y# 388 10 CENTS
2.60 g., Silver, 18 mm. **Subject:** Canton martyrs

Date	Mintage	VG8	F12	VF20	XF40	MS60
17(1928)	—	5.00	12.00	18.00	60.00	100
20(1931)	—	6.00	14.00	30.00	100	150

Y# 390 10 CENTS
2.60 g., Silver, 18 mm. **Subject:** Canton martyrs

Date	Mintage	VG8	F12	VF20	XF40	MS60
Yr. 21(1932)	—	48.00	120	180	400	800

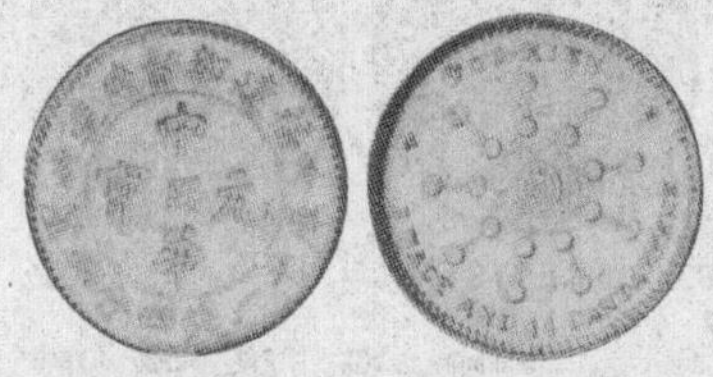

Y# 377 20 CENTS
5.00 g., Silver **Obv. Inscription:** Chung-hua Yüan-pao

Date	Mintage	VG8	F12	VF20	XF40	MS60
CD1911	—	5.00	12.00	25.00	70.00	200

Y# A381 20 CENTS
5.40 g., Silver **Obv. Inscription:** Chung-hua Yüan-pao

Date	Mintage	VG8	F12	VF20	XF40	MS60
ND(1912)	—	2.75	5.00	10.00	30.00	100

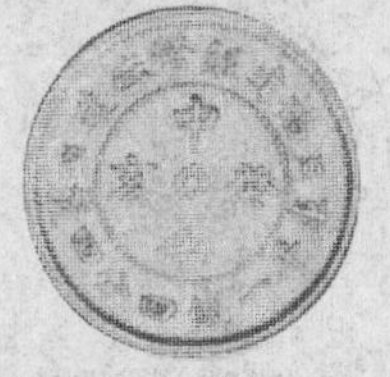

Y# 381 20 CENTS

5.30 g., Silver **Obv:** Rosettes at sides, dot in middle of rosette center **Rev:** Rosettes at sides

Date	Mintage	VG8	F12	VF20	XF40	MS60
CD1923	—	3.00	5.00	9.00	25.00	95.00

Y# 381.1 20 CENTS

5.30 g., Silver **Rev:** "MADE" spelled "MAIE" in legend

Date	Mintage	VG8	F12	VF20	XF40	MS60
CD1923	—	3.00	5.00	9.00	25.00	95.00

Y# 381.2 20 CENTS

5.30 g., Silver **Rev. Legend:** MADEIN FOO-KIENMINT

Date	Mintage	VG8	F12	VF20	XF40	MS60
CD1923	—	3.00	5.00	9.00	25.00	95.00

Y# 381.3 20 CENTS

5.30 g., Silver **Obv:** Without dot in middle of center rosette, 5-pointed star at sides in place of rosette

Date	Mintage	VG8	F12	VF20	XF40	MS60
CD1923	—	5.00	12.00	18.00	40.00	100

Y# 383 20 CENTS

5.20 g., Silver

Date	Mintage	VG8	F12	VF20	XF40	MS60
ND(1923)	—	2.50	4.00	7.00	20.00	80.00

Note: Kann dates this coin 1913, but evidence suggests that it was struck in 1923

Y# 381.4 20 CENTS

5.00 g., Silver **Obv:** Different legend in center

Date	Mintage	VG8	F12	VF20	XF40	MS60
CD1924	—	3.00	6.00	10.00	30.00	100

Y# 383a 20 CENTS

5.70 g., Silver

Date	Mintage	VG8	F12	VF20	XF40	MS60
13(1924)	—	14.00	42.00	60.00	140	180

Y# 384 20 CENTS

5.00 g., Silver **Subject:** Northern Expedition **Obv:** Crossed flags

Date	Mintage	VG8	F12	VF20	XF40	MS60
16(1927)	—	90.00	240	425	1,000	2,000

Y# 385 20 CENTS

5.30 g., Silver **Subject:** Northern Expedition **Obv:** Crossed flags

Date	Mintage	VG8	F12	VF20	XF40	MS60
16(1927)	—	240	775	1,200	2,700	4,000

Y# 389.1 20 CENTS

5.30 g., Silver, 23 mm. **Subject:** Canton martyrs **Obv:** Two rows of bricks at right of gate

Date	Mintage	VG8	F12	VF20	XF40	MS60
17(1928)	—	3.00	6.00	9.00	25.00	70.00
20(1931)	—	4.00	9.00	14.00	40.00	120

Y# 389.2 20 CENTS

5.50 g., Silver, 23 mm. **Subject:** Canton martyrs **Obv:** Half brick in 3rd row of bricks at right of gate

Date	Mintage	VG8	F12	VF20	XF40	MS60
17(1928)	—	3.00	5.00	8.00	20.00	60.00
20(1931)	—	4.00	7.00	12.00	35.00	110

Y# 389.3 20 CENTS

5.50 g., Silver, 23 mm. **Subject:** Canton martyrs **Rev:** 6-pointed star in legend

Date	Mintage	VG8	F12	VF20	XF40	MS60
20(1931)	—	—	—	—	—	—

Y# 391 20 CENTS

5.30 g., Silver, 23 mm. **Subject:** Canton martyrs **Rev:** Crossed flags

Date	Mintage	VG8	F12	VF20	XF40	MS60
21(1932)	—	25.00	55.00	90.00	250	500

PATTERNS

Including off metal strikes

KM#	Date	Mintage	Identification	Mkt Val
Pn3	ND-1912	—	2 Wen. Cast Brass. Obv. Ins: Fu-chien Sheng-tsao.	1,500
Pn4	ND-1912	—	2 Wen. Cast Brass. Obv. Ins: Fu-chien T'ung-pao.	1,500
Pn5	ND-1912	—	2 Wen. Cast Brass. Obv. Ins: Min-sheng T'ung-pao.	1,500
Pn6	16(1927)	—	20 Cents. Silver. Sun Yat-sen Memorial. K712.	3,750
Pn7	17(1928)	—	20 Cents. Brass. Y389.1.	—
Pn8	21(1932)	—	20 Cents. Brass. Y391.	—

HEILUNGKIANG PROVINCE

Heilongjiang

The northwesternmost of the former Three Eastern Provinces, bordering on Siberia. Though very large in extent, it is only sparsely populated, for wide areas are desert land. Economically the district was always backward. Heilungkiang (Heilongjiang) Province had no mint of its own, and seemingly no silver money bearing its name was ever placed in circulation although Imperial patterns in the standard dragon design exist for at least the dollar and 50 cent denominations. During the beginning of the 20th century it was suggested to contract for silver coins from the Berlin Mint.

PATTERNS

Including off metal strikes

KM#	Date	Mintage	Identification	Mkt Val
Pn1	ND(1903)	—	50 Cents. Brass. KM584x.	45,000
Pn2	ND-1903	—	Dollar. Silver. Rare.	—
Pn3	ND(1903)	—	Dollar. Brass.	75,000
Pn4	ND(1903)	—	Dollar. Silver Plated Brass.	—

HONAN PROVINCE

Henan

A province in east-central China. As well as being one of the most densely populated provinces it is also one of the most important agriculturally. It is the area of earliest settlement in China and has housed the capital during various dynasties. The Kaifeng Mint issued coins from its opening in 1647 through most of the rulers of the Manchu dynasty. In 1905 a modern mint opened at Kaifeng but closed in 1914. A mint in Loyang opened in 1924.

EMPIRE

Kuang-hsü

PROVINCIAL CAST COINAGE

C# 3–1.1a CASH

Zinc **Obv. Inscription:** Kuang-hsü T'ung-pao **Rev:** Dot at upper left, Manchu inscription **Rev. Inscription:** Boo-ho **Mint:** Ho

Date	Mintage	G4	VG8	F12	VF20	XF40
ND(1875-1908) Rare	—	—	—	—	—	—

C# 11–9 CASH

Cast Brass **Obv. Inscription:** Kuang-hsü T'ung-pao **Rev:** Manchu inscription **Rev. Inscription:** Boo-ho **Mint:** Ho

Date	Mintage	G4	VG8	F12	VF20	XF40
ND(1875-1908)	—	4.00	8.00	10.00	15.00	—

C# 11–9.1 CASH

Cast Brass **Obv. Inscription:** Kuang-hsü T'ung-pao **Rev:** Circle above, Manchu inscription **Rev. Inscription:** Boo-ho **Mint:** Ho

Date	Mintage	G4	VG8	F12	VF20	XF40
ND(1875-1908)	—	5.00	9.00	14.00	38.00	—

C# 11–9.2 CASH

Cast Brass **Obv. Inscription:** Kuang-hsü T'ung-pao **Rev:** Circle below, Manchu inscription **Rev. Inscription:** Boo-ho **Mint:** Ho

Date	Mintage	G4	VG8	F12	VF20	XF40
ND(1875-1908)	—	5.00	9.00	13.50	30.00	—

C# 11–9.3 CASH

Cast Brass **Obv. Inscription:** Kuang-hsü T'ung-pao **Rev:** Crescent above, Manchu inscription **Rev. Inscription:** Boo-ho **Mint:** Ho

Date	Mintage	G4	VG8	F12	VF20	XF40
ND(1875-1908)	—	5.00	9.00	13.50	30.00	—

C# 11–9.4 CASH

Cast Brass **Obv. Inscription:** Kuang-hsü T'ung-pao **Rev:** Crescent below, Manchu inscription **Rev. Inscription:** Boo-ho **Mint:** Ho

Date	Mintage	G4	VG8	F12	VF20	XF40
ND(1875-1908)	—	5.00	9.00	13.50	30.00	—

C# 11–9.5 CASH

Cast Brass **Obv. Inscription:** Kuang-hsü T'ung-pao **Rev:** Crescent above, dot below, Manchu inscription **Rev. Inscription:** Boo-ho **Mint:** Ho **Note:** Schjöth #1571.

Date	Mintage	G4	VG8	F12	VF20	XF40
ND(1875-1908)	—	5.00	9.00	13.50	30.00	—

C# 11-9.6 CASH

Cast Brass **Obv. Inscription:** Kuang-hsü T'ung-pao **Rev:** Dot above, Manchu inscription **Rev. Inscription:** Boo-ho **Mint:** Ho

Date	Mintage	G4	VG8	F12	VF20	XF40
ND(1875-1908)	—	5.00	9.00	13.50	27.00	—

C# 11-9.7 CASH

Cast Brass **Obv. Inscription:** Kuang-hsü T'ung-pao **Rev:** Dot below, Manchu inscription **Rev. Inscription:** Boo-ho **Mint:** Ho

Date	Mintage	G4	VG8	F12	VF20	XF40
ND(1875-1908)	—	5.00	9.00	13.50	27.00	—

C# 11-9.8 CASH

Cast Brass **Obv. Inscription:** Kuang-hsü T'ung-pao **Rev:** Dot at upper left, Manchu inscription **Rev. Inscription:** Boo-ho **Mint:** Ho **Note:** Crescent and dot varieties exist.

Date	Mintage	G4	VG8	F12	VF20	XF40
ND(1875-1908)	—	5.00	9.00	13.50	27.00	—

C# 11-9.9 CASH

Cast Brass **Obv. Inscription:** Kuang-hsü T'ung-pao **Rev:** Crescent above, circle below **Mint:** Ho

Date	Mintage	G4	VG8	F12	VF20	XF40
ND(1875-1908)	—	10.00	17.50	25.00	45.00	—

C# 11-9.10 CASH

Cast Brass **Obv. Inscription:** Kuang-hsü T'ung-pao **Rev:** Dot in circle below **Mint:** Ho

Date	Mintage	G4	VG8	F12	VF20	XF40
ND(1875-1908)	—	15.00	25.00	35.00	55.00	—

MILLED COINAGE

Y# 7g CASH

Brass **Obv. Legend:** Kuang-hsü **Rev:** Side view dragon

Date	Mintage	VG8	F12	VF20	XF40	MS60
CD1908	—	12.00	30.00	50.00	115	—

Y# 7ga CASH

Copper **Obv. Legend:** Kuang-hsü **Rev:** Side view dragon

Date	Mintage	VG8	F12	VF20	XF40	MS60
CD1908	—	25.00	60.00	100	225	—

Y# 108 10 CASH

Copper **Obv. Legend:** Ho-nan Sheng Tsao **Obv. Inscription:** Kuang-hsü Yüan-pao **Rev:** Circled dragon without mountain below pearl with 3 flames

Date	Mintage	VG8	F12	VF20	XF40	MS60
ND(1905)	—	5.00	12.00	25.00	90.00	—

Y# 108.1 10 CASH

Copper **Obv. Legend:** Ho-nan Sheng Tsao **Obv. Inscription:** Kuang-hsü Yüan-pao **Rev:** Circled dragon without mountain below pearl with 5 flames

Date	Mintage	VG8	F12	VF20	XF40	MS60
ND(1905)	—	1.25	4.00	6.00	22.50	75.00

Y# 108.2 10 CASH

Copper **Obv. Legend:** Ho-nan Sheng Tsao **Obv. Inscription:** Kuang-hsü Yüan-pao **Rev:** Circled dragon, mountain below pearl, very small English lettering

Date	Mintage	VG8	F12	VF20	XF40	MS60
ND(1905)	—	7.00	18.00	36.00	75.00	—

Y# 108.3 10 CASH

Copper **Obv. Legend:** Ho-nan Sheng Tsao **Obv. Inscription:** Kuang-hsü Yüan-pao **Rev:** Circled dragon, large English legend

Date	Mintage	VG8	F12	VF20	XF40	MS60
ND(1905)	—	6.00	12.00	18.00	45.00	—

Y# 108a.1 10 CASH

Copper **Obv:** Flat circled yin-yang **Obv. Legend:** Ho-nan Sheng Tsao **Obv. Inscription:** Kuang-hsü Yüan-pao **Rev:** Uncircled dragon

Date	Mintage	VG8	F12	VF20	XF40	MS60
ND(1905)	—	1.25	4.00	6.00	22.50	75.00

Y# 108a.2 10 CASH

Copper **Obv:** Curved line on raised yin-yang slanted more **Obv. Legend:** Ho-nan Sheng Tsao **Obv. Inscription:** Kuang-hsü Yüan-pao **Rev:** Uncircled dragon

Date	Mintage	VG8	F12	VF20	XF40	MS60
ND(1905)	—	1.25	4.00	6.00	20.00	50.00

Y# 108a.3 10 CASH

Copper **Obv:** Flat yin-yang slanted more **Obv. Legend:** Ho-nan Sheng Tsao **Obv. Inscription:** Kuang-hsü Yüan-pao **Rev:** Circled dragon, plain pearl

Date	Mintage	VG8	F12	VF20	XF40	MS60
ND(1905)	—	0.90	3.00	5.00	18.00	75.00

Note: Dies made in United States

Y# 108a.3a 10 CASH

Brass **Obv. Legend:** Ho-nan Sheng Tsao **Obv. Inscription:** Kuang-hsü Yüan-pao **Rev:** Dragon

Date	Mintage	VG8	F12	VF20	XF40	MS60
ND(1905)	—	3.00	6.00	12.00	30.00	—

Y# 108a.4 10 CASH

Copper **Obv. Legend:** Ho-nan Sheng Tsao **Obv. Inscription:** Kuang-hsü Yüan-pao **Rev:** Dragon, incuse swirl in pearl

Date	Mintage	VG8	F12	VF20	XF40	MS60
ND(1905)	—	1.25	4.00	6.00	18.00	—

Note: Dies made in United States

Y# 108a 10 CASH

Brass **Obv:** Raised circled yin-yang in center **Obv. Legend:** Ho-nan Sheng Tsao **Obv. Inscription:** Kuang-hsü Yüan-pao **Rev:** Uncircled dragon, Honan spelled HOU-NAN **Note:** Dies made in Japan.

Date	Mintage	VG8	F12	VF20	XF40	MS60
ND(1905) Rare	—	—	—	—	—	—

Y# 10g 10 CASH

Copper **Obv. Inscription:** Tai-ch'ing T'ung-pi **Rev:** Dragon, period after COIN in legend **Rev. Legend:** Kuang-hsü Nien-tsao, TAI-CHING-TI-KUO ...

Date	Mintage	VG8	F12	VF20	XF40	MS60
CD1906	132,000,000	1.00	2.50	6.00	15.00	—

Y# 10g.1 10 CASH

Copper **Obv. Inscription:** Tai-ch'ing T'ung-pi **Rev:** Dragon, period after COPPER in legend **Rev. Legend:** Kuang-hsü Nien-tsao, TAI-CHING-TI-KUO ...

Date	Mintage	VG8	F12	VF20	XF40	MS60
CD1906	—	1.50	4.00	7.00	18.00	—

Y# 10g.2 10 CASH

Copper **Obv. Inscription:** Tai-ch'ing T'ung-pi **Rev:** Dragon **Rev. Legend:** Kuang-hsü Nien-tsao, TAI-CHING-TI-KUO ... **Note:** Cyclical dates at sides.

Date	Mintage	VG8	F12	VF20	XF40	MS60
CD1907 Rare	—	—	—	—	—	—

Hsüan-t'ung

Y# 20g 10 CASH

Copper **Obv. Inscription:** Tai-ch'ing T'ung-pi **Rev:** Dragon **Rev. Legend:** Hsüan-t'ung Nien-tsao, TAI-CHING-TI-KUO ... **Note:** Normally encountered with weak legends.

Date	Mintage	VG8	F12	VF20	XF40	MS60
CD1909	—	25.00	48.00	70.00	190	—
CD1911	—	6.00	18.00	30.00	75.00	150

REPUBLIC

Y# A392.1 10 CASH

Copper **Obv:** Without lines above and below rosettes **Obv. Legend:** Chung Hua Min Kuo **Rev:** Crossed flags, florals at left and right **Rev. Legend:** HO-NAN

Date	Mintage	VG8	F12	VF20	XF40	MS60
ND(1913-14)	—	0.40	1.25	2.50	11.00	32.00

Y# A392a 10 CASH

Copper **Obv:** With lines above and below rosettes **Obv. Legend:** Chung Hua Min Kuo **Rev:** Crossed flags, florals at left and right **Rev. Legend:** HO-NAN

Date	Mintage	VG8	F12	VF20	XF40	MS60
ND(1913-14)	—	0.40	1.25	2.50	9.00	30.00

Y# A392.2 10 CASH

Copper **Obv. Legend:** Chung Hua Min Kuo **Rev:** Crossed flags, florals at left and right, letter "S" in "CASH" backwards **Rev. Legend:** HO-NAN

Date	Mintage	VG8	F12	VF20	XF40	MS60
ND(c.192)	—	7.00	20.00	36.00	90.00	—

Y# 392.1 10 CASH

Copper **Obv:** Rosette in center higher in relation to heart-shaped leaves below, Yuan at lower left with 2 horizontal strokes **Obv. Legend:** Chung Hua Min Kuo **Rev:** Crossed flags, florals at left and right **Rev. Legend:** HO-NAN

Date	Mintage	VG8	F12	VF20	XF40	MS60
ND(c.192)	—	0.80	2.50	4.00	11.00	32.00

Y# 392.2 10 CASH

Copper **Obv:** Yüan at lower left with 3 horizontal strokes. **Obv. Legend:** Chung Hua Min Kuo **Rev:** Crossed flags, florals at left and right **Rev. Legend:** HO-NAN

Date	Mintage	VG8	F12	VF20	XF40	MS60
ND(ca.192)	—	0.80	2.50	4.00	11.00	32.00

Y# 392 10 CASH

Copper **Obv:** Yüan at lower left with 2 horizontal strokes **Obv. Legend:** Chung Hua Min Kuo **Rev:** Value "TEN CASH" in larger letters at bottom **Rev. Legend:** HO-NAN

Date	Mintage	VG8	F12	VF20	XF40	MS60
ND(c.192)	—	0.30	0.90	1.75	6.00	27.50

Y# 393 20 CASH

Copper, 32 mm. **Obv:** Value in 6 characters at bottom **Obv. Legend:** Chung Hua Min Kuo **Rev:** Crossed flags, florals at left and right **Rev. Legend:** HO-NAN

Date	Mintage	G4	VG8	F12	VF20	XF40
ND(c.192)	—	1.50	3.00	6.00	15.00	45.00

Y# 393.1 20 CASH

Copper, 32 mm. **Obv:** Value in 5 characters at bottom **Obv. Legend:** Chung Hua Min Kuo **Rev:** Crossed flags, florals at left and right **Rev. Legend:** HO-NAN

Date	Mintage	G4	VG8	F12	VF20	XF40
ND(c.192)	—	1.25	2.50	5.00	12.00	30.00

Y# 393.2 20 CASH

Copper, 32 mm. **Obv:** Value in 6 characters below **Obv. Legend:** Chung Hua Min Kuo **Rev:** Crossed flags, florals at left and right **Rev. Legend:** CHINA

Date	Mintage	G4	VG8	F12	VF20	XF40
ND(c.1921)	—	15.00	30.00	55.00	265	—

Y# A397 20 CASH

Copper, 32 mm. **Obv:** Value in 6 characters below **Obv. Legend:** Chung Hua Min Kuo (year) Nien **Rev:** Star above crossed flags, florals at left and right

Date	Mintage	G4	VG8	F12	VF20	XF40
20(1931)	—	—	750	2,250	4,500	—

Y# 394 50 CASH

Copper, 38 mm. **Obv. Legend:** Chung Hua Min Kuo **Rev:** Crossed flags, florals at left and right, short flagpoles **Rev. Legend:** HO-NAN

Date	Mintage	G4	VG8	F12	VF20	XF40
ND(c.192)	—	3.00	8.00	15.00	40.00	140

Y# 394.1 50 CASH

Copper, 38 mm. **Obv. Legend:** Chung Hua Min Kuo **Rev:** Crossed flags, florals at left and right, long flagpoles **Rev. Legend:** HO-NAN

Date	Mintage	G4	VG8	F12	VF20	XF40
ND(c.192)	—	3.00	8.00	15.00	30.00	120

Y# 394b 50 CASH

Brass, 38 mm. **Obv. Legend:** Chung Hua Min Kuo **Rev:** Crossed flags, florals at left and right **Rev. Legend:** HO-NAN

Date	Mintage	G4	VG8	F12	VF20	XF40
ND(c.192)	—	15.00	30.00	60.00	170	450

Y# 394a 50 CASH

Copper, 38 mm. **Obv. Legend:** Chung Hua Min Kuo **Rev:** Crossed flags, florals at left and right **Rev. Legend:** CHINA

Date	Mintage	G4	VG8	F12	VF20	XF40
ND(c.1921)	—	10.00	19.00	37.50	120	350

Y# 397 50 CASH

Copper **Obv:** National star at center **Obv. Legend:** Chung Hua Min Kuo (year) Nien **Rev:** Star above value in grain sprays

Date	Mintage	VG8	F12	VF20	XF40	MS60
20(1931)	—	120	250	450	1,250	7,500

Y# 397a 50 CASH

Brass **Obv:** National star at center **Obv. Legend:** CHUNG HUA MIN KUO (year) NIEN **Rev:** Star above value in grain sprays

Date	Mintage	F12	VF20	XF40	MS60	MS63
20 (1931)	—	250	450	1,250	7,500	13,500

Y# 395 100 CASH

Copper, 40 mm. **Obv. Legend:** Chung Hua Min Kuo **Rev:** Crossed flags, florals at left and right, small star in right flag, tassels 4mm long **Rev. Legend:** HO-NAN

Date	Mintage	G4	VG8	F12	VF20	XF40
ND(ca. 1928)	—	6.00	9.00	18.00	60.00	220

Y# 395.1 100 CASH

Copper, 40 mm. **Rev:** Tassels 5mm long

Date	Mintage	G4	VG8	F12	VF20	XF40
ND(ca. 1928)	—	8.00	12.00	22.50	70.00	290

Y# 395.2 100 CASH

Copper, 40 mm. **Obv. Legend:** Chung Hua Min Kuo **Rev:** Crossed flags, florals at left and right, large star in right flag **Rev. Legend:** HO-NAN

Date	Mintage	G4	VG8	F12	VF20	XF40
ND(ca. 1928)	—	—	—	—	—	—

Y# 398 100 CASH
Copper, 40 mm. **Obv:** National star at center **Obv. Legend:** Chung Hua Min Kuo (year) Nien **Rev:** Star above value in grain sprays

Date	Mintage	VG8	F12	VF20	XF40	MS60
20(1931)	—	65.00	110	200	—	—

Y# 396 200 CASH
Copper, 42 mm. **Obv. Legend:** Chung Hua Min Kuo **Rev:** Crossed flags, florals at left and right, large square inside right flag **Rev. Legend:** HO-NAN

Date	Mintage	G4	VG8	F12	VF20	XF40
ND (1928)	—	6.00	9.00	18.00	60.00	260

Y# 396.1 200 CASH
Copper, 42 mm. **Obv. Legend:** Chung Hua Min Kuo **Rev:** Crossed flags, small panel with small star inside right flag, florals at left and right **Rev. Legend:** HO-NAN

Date	Mintage	G4	VG8	F12	VF20	XF40
ND (1928)	—	5.00	8.00	17.00	60.00	300

Y# 396.2 200 CASH
Copper, 42 mm. **Obv. Legend:** Chung Hua Min Kuo **Rev:** Crossed flags, small panel with large star inside right flag, florals at left and right **Rev. Legend:** HO-NAN

Date	Mintage	G4	VG8	F12	VF20	XF40
ND (1928)	—	5.00	8.00	17.00	60.00	300

Y# 396a 200 CASH
Brass, 42 mm. **Obv. Legend:** Chung Hua Min Kuo **Rev:** Crossed flags, small panel with large star inside right flag, florals at left and right **Rev. Legend:** HO-NAN

Date	Mintage	G4	VG8	F12	VF20	XF40
ND (1928)	—	7.00	18.00	27.50	55.00	180

PATTERNS

Including off metal strikes

KM#	Date	Mintage	Identification	Mkt Val
Pn1	CD1909	—	2 Cash. Brass.	—
Pn2	CD1909	—	5 Cash. Copper. Y19g.	—
Pn3	CD1909	—	20 Cash. Copper. Y21g.	—

HUNAN PROVINCE

A province in south-central China. Mining of coal, antimony, tungsten and tin is important as well as raising varied agricultural products. The Changsha Mint produced Cash coins from early in the Manchu dynasty. Its facility for struck coinage opened in 1897, and two further copper mints were added in 1905. All three mints were closed down in 1907, but one mint was reopened at a later date and produced vast quantities of republican copper coinage until 1926.

EMPIRE

BULLION COINAGE

Mace/Tael Series

K# 951 CH'IEN (MACE)
3.70 g., Silver **Issuer:** Fo-nau Official Bureau **Obv:** Two lines of two characters each **Rev:** Two lines of one character each

Date	Mintage	VG8	F12	VF20	XF40	MS60
ND-1906	—	115	225	300	600	1,200

K# 961 CH'IEN (MACE)
3.60 g., Silver **Obv:** Three lines of two characters each **Rev:** Two lines of two characters each

Date	Mintage	VG8	F12	VF20	XF40	MS60
ND-1906	—	—	—	—	—	—

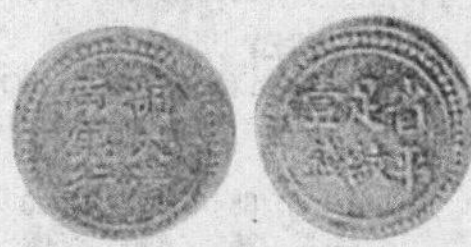

K# 971 CH'IEN (MACE)
3.70 g., Silver **Issuer:** Ta Ching Gov't. Bank **Obv:** Two lines of two characters each **Rev:** Two lines of two characters each

Date	Mintage	VG8	F12	VF20	XF40	MS60
ND-1908	—	75.00	750	1,050	1,800	2,500

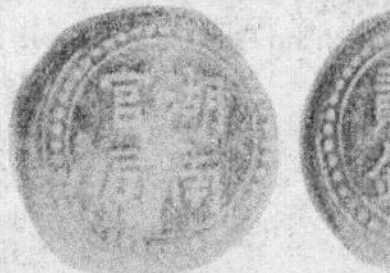

K# 984/5 CH'IEN (MACE)
3.70 g., Silver **Issuer:** Chien-I, Changsha **Obv:** Two lines of three characters each **Rev:** Two lines of one character each

Date	Mintage	VG8	F12	VF20	XF40	MS60
ND-1908	—	115	225	300	600	1,000

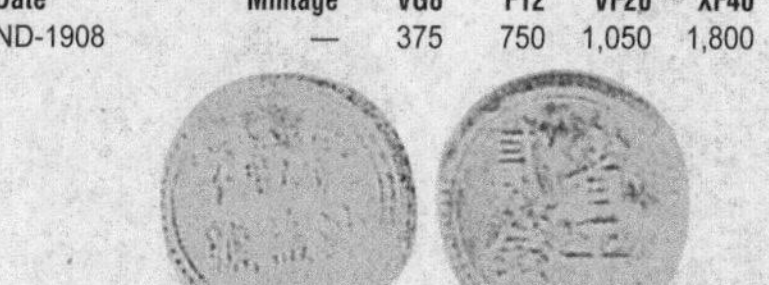

K# 950 2 CH'IEN (MACE)
7.30 g., Silver **Issuer:** Fo-nan Official Bureau **Obv:** Two lines of two characters each **Rev:** Two lines of two characters each

Date	Mintage	VG8	F12	VF20	XF40	MS60
ND-1906	—	115	225	300	600	1,200

K# 960 2 CH'IEN (MACE)
7.30 g., Silver **Obv:** Three lines of two characters each **Rev:** Two lines of two characters each **Mint:** Hunan

Date	Mintage	VG8	F12	VF20	XF40	MS60
ND-1906	—	—	—	—	—	—

K# 970 2 CH'IEN (MACE)
7.30 g., Silver **Issuer:** Ta Ch'ing Gov't. Bank **Obv:** Three lines of two characters each **Rev:** Two lines of three characters each

Date	Mintage	VG8	F12	VF20	XF40	MS60
ND-1908	—	375	750	1,050	1,800	2,500

K# 982/3 2 CH'IEN (MACE)
7.30 g., Silver **Issuer:** Chien-I, Changsha **Obv:** Two lines of three characters each **Rev:** Two lines of two characters each

Date	Mintage	VG8	F12	VF20	XF40	MS60
ND-1908	—	115	225	300	600	1,000

K# 949 3 CH'IEN (MACE)
10.70 g., Silver **Issuer:** Fo-nan Official Bureau **Obv:** Two lines of three characters each **Rev:** Two lines of three characters each

Date	Mintage	VG8	F12	VF20	XF40	MS60
ND-1906	—	130	265	375	700	1,500

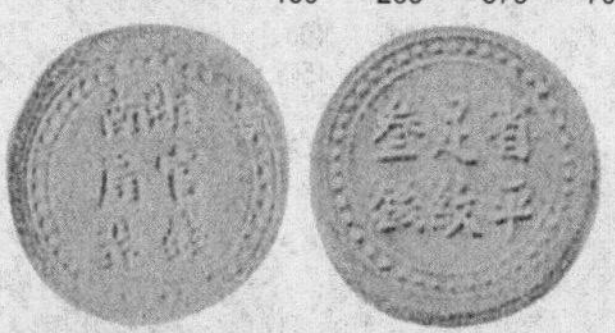

K# 959 3 CH'IEN (MACE)
10.70 g., Silver **Obv:** Three lines of two characters each **Rev:** Two lines of three characters each **Mint:** Hunan

Date	Mintage	VG8	F12	VF20	XF40	MS60
ND-1906	—	130	265	375	700	1,500

K# 969 3 CH'IEN (MACE)
10.70 g., Silver **Issuer:** Ta Ch'ing Gov't. Bank **Obv:** Three lines of two characters each **Rev:** Two lines of three characters each

Date	Mintage	VG8	F12	VF20	XF40	MS60
ND-1908	—	375	750	1,050	1,800	2,500

K# 981 3 CH'IEN (MACE)
10.70 g., Silver **Issuer:** Chien-I, Changsha **Obv:** Two lines of three characters each **Rev:** Two lines of three characters each

Date	Mintage	VG8	F12	VF20	XF40	MS60
ND-1908	—	130	265	375	700	1,350

K# 981a 3 CH'IEN (MACE)
10.70 g., Silver **Issuer:** Chien-I, Changsha **Obv:** Two lines of three characters each **Rev:** Two lines of three characters each **Note:** "official" character for three

Date	Mintage	VG8	F12	VF20	XF40	MS60
ND-1908	—	130	265	375	700	1,350

K# 948 4 CH'IEN (MACE)
14.30 g., Silver **Issuer:** Fo-nan Official Bureau **Obv:** Two lines of three characters each **Rev:** Two lines of three characters each

Date	Mintage	VG8	F12	VF20	XF40	MS60
ND-1906	—	130	265	375	700	1,500

K# 958 4 CH'IEN (MACE)
14.30 g., Silver **Obv:** Three lines of two characters each **Rev:** Two lines of three characters each **Mint:** Hunan

Date	Mintage	VG8	F12	VF20	XF40	MS60
ND-1906	—	—	—	—	—	—

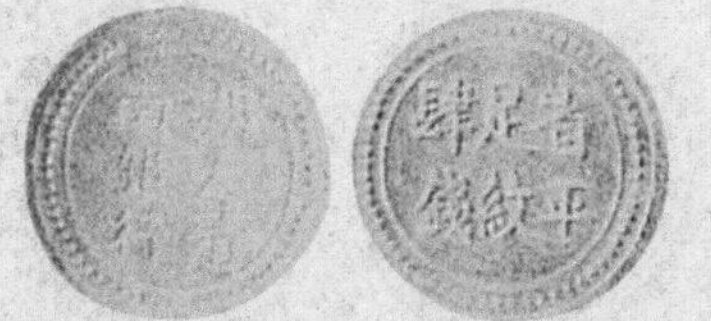

K# 968 4 CH'IEN (MACE)
14.30 g., Silver **Issuer:** Ta Ch'ing Gov't. Bank **Obv:** Three lines of two characters each **Rev:** Two lines of three characters each

Date	Mintage	VG8	F12	VF20	XF40	MS60
ND-1908	—	450	900	1,200	2,000	2,700

K# 980 4 CH'IEN (MACE)
14.30 g., Silver **Issuer:** Chien-I, Changsha **Obv:** Two lines of three characters each **Rev:** Two lines of three characters each

Date	Mintage	VG8	F12	VF20	XF40	MS60
ND-1908	—	130	265	375	700	1,350

K# 947 5 CH'IEN (MACE)
18.30 g., Silver **Issuer:** Fo-nan Official Bureau **Obv:** Two lines of three characters each **Rev:** Two lines of three characters each

Date	Mintage	VG8	F12	VF20	XF40	MS60
ND-1906	—	130	265	375	700	1,500

K# 957 5 CH'IEN (MACE)
18.30 g., Silver **Obv:** Three lines of two characters each **Rev:** Two lines of three characters each **Mint:** Hunan

Date	Mintage	VG8	F12	VF20	XF40	MS60
ND-1906	—	105	—	—	—	—

K# 967 5 CH'IEN (MACE)
18.30 g., Silver **Issuer:** Ta Ch'ing Gov't. Bank **Obv:** Three lines of two characters each **Rev:** Two lines of three characters each

Date	Mintage	VG8	F12	VF20	XF40	MS60
ND-1908	—	450	900	1,200	2,000	2,700

K# 979 5 CH'IEN (MACE)
18.30 g., Silver **Issuer:** Chien-I, Changsha **Obv:** Two lines of three characters each **Rev:** Two lines of three characters each

Date	Mintage	VG8	F12	VF20	XF40	MS60
ND-1908	—	130	265	375	700	1,350

K# 946 6 CH'IEN (MACE)
21.40 g., Silver **Issuer:** Fo-nan Official Bureau **Obv:** Two lines of three characters each **Rev:** Two lines of three characters each

Date	Mintage	VG8	F12	VF20	XF40	MS60
ND-1906	—	265	525	650	1,100	2,200

K# 956 6 CH'IEN (MACE)
21.40 g., Silver **Obv:** Three lines of two characters each **Rev:** Two lines of three characters each **Mint:** Hunan

Date	Mintage	VG8	F12	VF20	XF40	MS60
ND-1906	—	—	—	—	—	—

K# 966 6 CH'IEN (MACE)
21.40 g., Silver **Issuer:** Ta Ch'ing Gov't. Bank **Obv:** Three lines of two characters each **Rev:** Two lines of three characters each

Date	Mintage	VG8	F12	VF20	XF40	MS60
ND-1908	—	450	900	1,200	2,000	2,700

K# 978 6 CH'IEN (MACE)
21.40 g., Silver **Issuer:** Chien-I, Changsha **Obv:** Two lines of three characters each **Rev:** Two lines of three characters each

Date	Mintage	VG8	F12	VF20	XF40	MS60
ND-1908	—	165	350	450	800	1,650

K# 945 7 CH'IEN (MACE)
25.90 g., Silver **Issuer:** Fo-nan Official Bureau **Obv:** Two lines of three characters each **Rev:** Two lines of three characters each

Date	Mintage	VG8	F12	VF20	XF40	MS60
ND-1906	—	225	450	600	1,100	2,200

K# 955 7 CH'IEN (MACE)
25.90 g., Silver **Obv:** Three lines of two characters each **Rev:** Two lines of three characters each **Mint:** Hunan

Date	Mintage	VG8	F12	VF20	XF40	MS60
ND-1906	—	—	—	—	—	—

K# 965 7 CH'IEN (MACE)
25.90 g., Silver **Issuer:** Ta Ch'ing Gov't. Bank **Obv:** Three lines of two characters each **Rev:** Two lines of three characters each

Date	Mintage	VG8	F12	VF20	XF40	MS60
ND(ca.1908)	—	525	1,050	1,350	2,200	3,000

K# 977 7 CH'IEN (MACE)
25.90 g., Silver **Issuer:** Chien-I, Changsha **Obv:** Two lines of three characters each **Rev:** Two lines of three characters each

Date	Mintage	F12	VF20	XF40	MS60	MS63
ND-1908	—	265	375	700	1,750	4,250

K# 944 8 CH'IEN (MACE)
29.20 g., Silver **Issuer:** Fo-nan Official Bureau **Obv:** Two lines of three characters each **Rev:** Two lines of three characters each

Date	Mintage	VG8	F12	VF20	XF40	MS60
ND-1906	—	225	450	600	1,100	2,200

K# 954 8 CH'IEN (MACE)
29.20 g., Silver **Obv:** Three lines of two characters each **Rev:** Two lines of three characters each **Mint:** Hunan

Date	Mintage	VG8	F12	VF20	XF40	MS60
ND-1906	—	—	—	—	—	—

K# 964 8 CH'IEN (MACE)
29.20 g., Silver **Issuer:** Ta Ch'ing Gov't. Bank **Obv:** Three lines of two characters each **Rev:** Two lines of three characters each

Date	Mintage	VG8	F12	VF20	XF40	MS60
ND-1908	—	425	1,050	1,350	2,200	3,000

K# 976 8 CH'IEN (MACE)
29.20 g., Silver **Issuer:** Chien-I, Changsha **Obv:** Two lines of three characters each **Rev:** Two lines of three characters each

Date	Mintage	VG8	F12	VF20	XF40	MS60
ND-1908	—	265	525	650	1,100	2,200

K# 943 9 CH'IEN (MACE)
29.20 g., Silver **Issuer:** Fo-nan Official Bureau **Obv:** Two lines of three characters each **Rev:** Two lines of three characters each

Date	Mintage	VG8	F12	VF20	XF40	MS60
ND-1906	—	225	450	600	1,100	2,200

K# 953 9 CH'IEN (MACE)
29.20 g., Silver **Obv:** Three lines of two characters each **Rev:** Two lines of three characters each **Mint:** Hunan

Date	Mintage	VG8	F12	VF20	XF40	MS60
ND-1906	—	—	—	—	—	—

K# 963 9 CH'IEN (MACE)
29.20 g., Silver **Issuer:** Ta Ch'ing Gov't. Bank **Obv:** Three lines of two characters each **Rev:** Two lines of three characters each

Date	Mintage	VG8	F12	VF20	XF40	MS60
ND-1908	—	425	1,050	1,350	2,200	3,200

K# 975 9 CH'IEN (MACE)
29.20 g., Silver **Issuer:** Chien-I, Changsha **Obv:** Two lines of three characters each **Rev:** Two lines of three characters each

Date	Mintage	VG8	F12	VF20	XF40	MS60
ND-1908	—	265	525	650	1,100	2,250

K# 942 LIANG (Tael)
35.90 g., Silver **Issuer:** Fo-nan Official Bureau **Obv:** Two lines of three characters each **Rev:** Two lines of three characters each

Date	Mintage	VG8	F12	VF20	XF40	MS60
ND-1906	—	165	350	475	950	1,850

K# 952 LIANG (Tael)
35.90 g., Silver **Obv:** Three lines of two characters each **Rev:** Two lines of three characters each **Mint:** Hunan

Date	Mintage	VG8	F12	VF20	XF40	MS60
ND-1906	—	150	300	400	675	1,450

K# 942r LIANG (Tael)
35.90 g., Silver **Obv:** Three lines of four characters each **Mint:** Hunan

Date	Mintage	VG8	F12	VF20	XF40	MS60
ND-1908 Rare Uniface	—	300	600	750	1,200	2,350

K# 962 LIANG (Tael)
35.90 g., Silver **Issuer:** Ta Ch'ing Gov't. Bank **Obv:** Three lines of two characters each **Rev:** Two lines of three characters each

Date	Mintage	VG8	F12	VF20	XF40	MS60
ND-1908	—	375	900	1,200	2,000	3,000

K# 974 LIANG (Tael)
35.90 g., Silver **Issuer:** Chien-I, Changsha **Obv:** Two lines of

three characters each **Rev:** Two lines of three characters each

Date	Mintage	VG8	F12	VF20	XF40	MS60
ND-1908	—	190	375	500	900	1,750

Kuang-hsü

PROVINCIAL CAST COINAGE

C# 12–7 CASH

Cast Brass **Obv. Inscription:** Kuang-hsü T'ung-pao **Rev:** Manchu inscription **Rev. Inscription:** Boo-nan **Mint:** Nan

Date	Mintage	G4	VG8	F12	VF20	XF40
ND(1875-1908)	—	9.00	18.00	25.00	42.00	—

MILLED COINAGE

Y# 112 10 CASH

Copper **Obv:** Rosette in center with center of petals depressed; Manchu words at sides, "Tang Shih" at bottom **Obv. Legend:** Hu-nan Sheng Tsao **Obv. Inscription:** Kuang-hsü Yüan-pao **Rev:** Narrow spacing in HU-NAN above dragon **Rev. Legend:** HU-NAN

Date	Mintage	VG8	F12	VF20	XF40	MS60
ND(1902-06)	—	0.50	1.50	3.00	14.00	130

Y# 112.1 10 CASH

Copper **Obv. Legend:** Hu-nan Sheng Tsao **Obv. Inscription:** Kuang-hsü Yüan-pao **Rev:** Dragon; wide spacing in HU-NAN **Rev. Legend:** HU-NAN

Date	Mintage	F12	VF20	XF40	MS60	MS63
ND(1902-06)	—	3.00	6.00	20.00	135	—

Y# 112.2 10 CASH

Copper **Obv:** Petals of rosettes not depressed **Obv. Legend:** Hu-nan Sheng Tsao **Obv. Inscription:** Kuang-hsü Yüan-pao **Rev:** Dragon **Rev. Legend:** HU-NAN

Date	Mintage	VG8	F12	VF20	XF40	MS60
ND(1902-06)	—	0.70	2.25	4.00	15.00	130

Y# 112.3 10 CASH

Copper **Obv:** Two Manchu words in center, "T'ung Yüan" at bottom **Obv. Legend:** Hu-nan Sheng Tsao **Obv. Inscription:** Kuang-hsü Yüan-pao **Rev:** Dragon **Rev. Legend:** HU-NAN

Date	Mintage	VG8	F12	VF20	XF40	MS60
ND(1902-06)	—	1.50	5.00	9.00	25.00	150

Y# 112.4 10 CASH

Copper **Obv. Legend:** Hu-nan Sheng Tsao **Obv. Inscription:** Kuang-hsü Yüan-pao **Rev:** Dragon; narrow spacing in "HU-NAN" **Rev. Legend:** HU-NAN

Date	Mintage	VG8	F12	VF20	XF40	MS60
ND(1902-06)	—	0.70	2.25	4.00	15.00	130

Y# 112.5 10 CASH

Copper **Obv:** Rosette in center, "Tang Shih" at bottom **Obv. Legend:** Hu-nan Sheng Tsao **Obv. Inscription:** Kuang-hsü Yüan-pao **Rev:** Dragon; ring around pearl **Rev. Legend:** HU-NAN

Date	Mintage	VG8	F12	VF20	XF40	MS60
ND(1902-06)	—	0.60	2.00	3.00	14.00	130

Y# 112.6 10 CASH

Copper **Obv:** Centers of petals on rosette depressed **Obv. Legend:** Hu-nan Sheng Tsao **Obv. Inscription:** Kuang-hsü Yüan-pao **Rev:** Dragon **Rev. Legend:** HU-NAN

Date	Mintage	VG8	F12	VF20	XF40	MS60
ND(1902-06)	—	0.70	2.25	4.00	15.00	130

Y# 112.7 10 CASH

Copper **Obv:** two Manchu words in center, "T'ung Yüan" at bottom **Obv. Legend:** Hu-nan Sheng Tsao **Obv. Inscription:** Kuang-hsü Yüan-pao **Rev:** Dragon; ring around pearl **Rev. Legend:** HU-NAN

Date	Mintage	VG8	F12	VF20	XF40	MS60
ND(1902-06)	—	0.70	2.25	4.00	15.00	130

Y# 112.8 10 CASH

Copper **Obv:** Larger characters at left and right, and different characters below **Obv. Legend:** Hu-nan Sheng Tsao **Obv. Inscription:** Kuang-hsü Yüan-pao **Rev:** Dragon redesigned and small star at either side **Rev. Legend:** HU-NAN

Date	Mintage	VG8	F12	VF20	XF40	MS60
ND(1902-06)	—	2.75	8.00	15.00	40.00	165

Y# 112.9 10 CASH

Copper **Obv:** Rosette in center; legend: four characters at bottom **Obv. Legend:** Hu-nan Sheng Tsao **Obv. Inscription:** Kuang-hsü Yüan-pao **Rev:** Redesigned dragon without pearl; rosette at either side **Rev. Legend:** HU-NAN

Date	Mintage	VG8	F12	VF20	XF40	MS60
ND(1902-06)	—	4.00	11.00	22.50	60.00	200

Y# 112.10 10 CASH

Copper **Obv:** Two Manchu words in center with dot between; "T'ung Yüan" at bottom **Obv. Legend:** Hu-nan Sheng Tsao **Obv. Inscription:** Kuang-hsü Yüan-pao **Rev:** Dragon **Rev. Legend:** HU-NAN

Date	Mintage	VG8	F12	VF20	XF40	MS60
ND(1902-06)	—	0.50	1.50	3.00	14.00	130

Y# 112.11 10 CASH

Copper **Obv:** Without dot between Manchu words, "T'ung Yüan" at bottom **Obv. Legend:** Hu-nan Sheng Tsao **Obv. Inscription:** Kuang-hsü Yüan-pao **Rev:** Dragon **Rev. Legend:** HU-NAN

Date	Mintage	VG8	F12	VF20	XF40	MS60
ND(1902-06)	—	0.50	1.50	3.00	14.00	130

Y# 112.12 10 CASH

Copper **Obv:** Smaller 15.5 millimeter inner circle, with larger beads, "T'ung Yüan" at bottom **Obv. Legend:** Hu-nan Sheng Tsao **Obv. Inscription:** Kuang-hsü Yüan-pao **Rev:** Dragon **Rev. Legend:** HU-NAN

Date	Mintage	VG8	F12	VF20	XF40	MS60
ND(1902-06)	—	0.50	1.50	3.00	14.00	130

Y# 112.13 10 CASH

Copper **Obv:** Two Manchu words in center, 18.4mm inner circle; "Huang T'ung" at bottom **Obv. Legend:** Hu-nan Sheng Tsao **Obv. Inscription:** Kuang-hsü Yüan-pao **Rev:** Dragon **Rev. Legend:** HU-NAN

Date	Mintage	VG8	F12	VF20	XF40	MS60
ND(1902-06)	—	13.00	37.50	70.00	160	—

Y# 112.14 10 CASH

Copper **Obv:** Smaller 17.5mm inner circle; "Huang T'ung Yüan" at bottom **Obv. Legend:** Hu-nan Sheng Tsao **Obv. Inscription:** Kuang-hsü Yüan-pao **Rev:** Dragon **Rev. Legend:** HU-NAN

Date	Mintage	VG8	F12	VF20	XF40	MS60
ND(1902-06)	—	13.00	37.50	70.00	160	—

Y# 113 10 CASH

Copper **Obv. Legend:** Hu-nan Sheng Tsao, six characters at bottom **Obv. Inscription:** Kuang-hsü Yüan-pao **Rev:** Flying dragon **Rev. Legend:** HU-NAN **Edge:** Reeded

Date	Mintage	VG8	F12	VF20	XF40	MS60
ND(1902-06)	—	2.00	6.00	12.00	32.00	180

Y# 113.1 10 CASH

Copper **Obv. Legend:** Hu-nan Sheng Tsao **Obv. Inscription:** Kuang-hsü Yüan-pao **Rev:** Dragon **Rev. Legend:** Inverted U in HU-NAN **Edge:** Reeded

Date	Mintage	VG8	F12	VF20	XF40	MS60
ND(1902-06)	—	7.00	19.00	37.50	90.00	—

Y# 113a 10 CASH

Brass, 28 mm. **Obv. Legend:** Hu-nan Sheng Tsao, three characters at bottom **Obv. Inscription:** Kuang-hsü Yüan-pao **Rev:** Dragon **Rev. Legend:** HU-NAN

Date	Mintage	F12	VF20	XF40	MS60	MS63
ND(1902-06)	—	5.00	11.00	30.00	175	375

Y# 10h 10 CASH

Copper **Obv:** Upper and lower parts of character "Hu" connected **Obv. Inscription:** Tai-ch'ing T'ung-pi **Rev:** Dragon; dot between Chinese characters above dragon **Rev. Legend:** Kuang-hsü Nien-tsao, TAI-CHING-TI-KUO...

Date	Mintage	VG8	F12	VF20	XF40	MS60
CD1906	—	9.00	27.50	55.00	140	—

Y# 10h.1 10 CASH

Copper **Obv:** Upper and lower parts of character "Hu" not connected **Obv. Inscription:** Tai-ch'ing T'ung-pi **Rev:** Dragon; dot between Chinese characters at top **Rev. Legend:** Kuang-hsü Nien-tsao, TAI-CHING-TI-KUO...

Date	Mintage	VG8	F12	VF20	XF40	MS60
CD1906	—	9.00	27.50	55.00	140	—

Y# 10h.2 10 CASH

Copper **Obv. Inscription:** Tai-ch'ing T'ung-pi **Rev:** Dragon; seven flames on pearl **Rev. Legend:** Kuang-hsü Nien-tsao, TAI-CHING-TI-KUO...

Date	Mintage	VG8	F12	VF20	XF40	MS60
CD1906	—	1.00	3.00	6.00	20.00	135

Y# 10h.3 10 CASH

Copper **Obv. Inscription:** Tai-ch'ing T'ung-pi **Rev:** Dragon; seven-flame pearl ornamented with toothlike projections **Rev. Legend:** Kuang-hsü Nien-tsao, TAI-CHING-TI-KUO...

Date	Mintage	VG8	F12	VF20	XF40	MS60
CD1906	—	1.00	3.00	5.00	18.00	130

Y# 10h.4 10 CASH

Copper **Obv. Inscription:** Tai-ch'ing T'ung-pi **Rev:** Dragon; four flames on pearl **Rev. Legend:** Kuang-hsü Nien-tsao, TAI-CHING-TI-KUO...

Date	Mintage	VG8	F12	VF20	XF40	MS60
CD1906	—	1.50	5.00	9.00	25.00	150

Y# 10h.5 10 CASH

Copper **Obv. Inscription:** Tai-ch'ing T'ung-pi **Rev:** Redesigned dragon with high waves beneath **Rev. Legend:** Kuang-hsü Nien-tsao, TAI-CHING-TI-KUO...

Date	Mintage	VG8	F12	VF20	XF40	MS60
CD1906	—	20.00	60.00	120	300	—

Y# 10h.6 10 CASH

Copper **Obv:** Character "Hu" connected **Obv. Inscription:** Tai-ch'ing T'ung-pi **Rev:** Redesigned dragon, dot between COPPER COIN **Rev. Legend:** Kuang-hsü Nien-tsao, TAI-CHING-TI-KUO...

Date	Mintage	VG8	F12	VF20	XF40	MS60
CD1906	—	7.00	19.00	30.00	80.00	—

Y# 10h.7 10 CASH

Copper **Obv:** Character "Hu", connected **Obv. Inscription:** Tai-ch'ing T'ung-pi **Rev:** Redesigned dragon with five flames on pearl **Rev. Legend:** Kuang-hsü Nien-tsao, TAI-CHING-TI-KUO... **Note:** Woodward #342 and #343

Date	Mintage	VG8	F12	VF20	XF40	MS60
CD1906	—	15.00	45.00	70.00	160	—

Y# 114 5 CENTS

1.30 g., 0.820 Silver 0.0343 oz. ASW **Obv. Inscription:** Kuang-hsü Yüan-pao **Mint:** Nan **Note:** Kann #164.

Date	Mintage	F12	VF20	XF40	MS60	MS63
ND(c.1902) Rare	—	—	—	—	—	—

Y# 115 10 CENTS

2.50 g., 0.820 Silver 0.0659 oz. ASW **Obv:** Two rosettes at both sides **Obv. Inscription:** Kuang-hsü Yüan-pao **Mint:** Nan

Date	Mintage	F12	VF20	XF40	MS60	MS63
ND (1902)	—	11.00	22.50	45.00	200	—

Y# 116 20 CENTS

5.30 g., 0.820 Silver 0.1397 oz. ASW **Obv. Inscription:** Kuang-hsü Yüan-pao **Mint:** Nan

Date	Mintage	F12	VF20	XF40	MS60	MS63
ND (1902)	—	75.00	150	300	700	—

Hung-hsien

TRANSITIONAL COINAGE

Y# 401.1 10 CASH

Copper **Obv. Legend:** THE FIRST YEAR OF HUNG SHUAN **Rev. Legend:** Hung-hsien Yüan-nien

Date	Mintage	VG8	F12	VF20	XF40	MS60
1(1915)	—	55.00	90.00	200	300	450

Y# 401.2 10 CASH

Copper **Obv:** Wider space in legend

Date	Mintage	VG8	F12	VF20	XF40	MS60
1(1915)	—	15.00	30.00	45.00	100	—

REPUBLIC

MILLED COINAGE

Y# 339a 10 CASH

Brass **Obv. Legend:** Chung Hua Min Kuo **Obv. Inscription:** Hu-nan T'ung-Tüan

Date	Mintage	VG8	F12	VF20	XF40	MS60
ND(1912)	—	2.75	8.00	15.00	35.00	135

Y# 399 10 CASH

Copper **Obv:** Large rosette **Obv. Legend:** Chung Hua Min Kuo **Obv. Inscription:** Hu-nan Tung-Yuan **Rev:** Center of star convex

Date	Mintage	VG8	F12	VF20	XF40	MS60
ND(1912)	—	1.00	3.00	6.00	15.00	75.00

Y# 399.1 10 CASH

Copper **Obv:** Small rosette **Obv. Legend:** Chung Hua Min Kuo **Obv. Inscription:** Hu-nan Tung-Yuan **Rev:** Center of star convex

Date	Mintage	VG8	F12	VF20	XF40	MS60
ND(1912)	—	1.00	3.00	6.00	15.00	75.00

Y# 399.2 10 CASH

Copper **Obv. Legend:** Chung Hua Min Kuo **Obv. Inscription:** Hu-nan Tung-Yuan **Rev:** Center of star concave; star outlined

Date	Mintage	VG8	F12	VF20	XF40	MS60
ND(1912)	—	1.25	3.00	7.00	18.00	80.00

Y# 399.3 10 CASH

Copper **Obv. Legend:** Chung Hua Min Kuo **Obv. Inscription:** Hu-nan Tung-Yuan **Rev:** Star not outlined

Date	Mintage	VG8	F12	VF20	XF40	MS60
ND(1912)	—	1.25	3.00	7.00	18.00	80.00

Y# 399.4 10 CASH

Copper **Obv:** Large rosette **Obv. Legend:** Chung Hua Min Kuo **Obv. Inscription:** Hu-nan Tung-Yuan **Rev:** Center of star concave

Date	Mintage	VG8	F12	VF20	XF40	MS60
ND(1912)	—	1.25	3.00	7.00	18.00	80.00

Y# 399.5 10 CASH

Copper **Note:** Mule. General Issue, Y#306.

Date	Mintage	VG8	F12	VF20	XF40	MS60
ND(1912)	—	—	—	—	—	—

Y# 402 10 CASH

Copper **Subject:** Provincial Constitution **Obv:** Rosette above crossed flags **Obv. Legend:** THE REPUBLIC OF CHINA **Rev:** Trigram of the Pah Kwah in grain sprays

Date	Mintage	VG8	F12	VF20	XF40	MS60
11(1922)	—	22.50	37.50	55.00	120	225

Y# 402.1 10 CASH

Copper **Obv:** Star above crossed flags **Obv. Legend:** THE REPUBLIC OF CHINA **Rev:** Trigram of the Pah Kwah in grain sprays

Date	Mintage	VG8	F12	VF20	XF40	MS60
11(1922)	—	27.50	39.00	60.00	130	—

Y# 400.2 20 CASH

Copper **Rev. Legend:** Hu-Nan Shan Tsoh

Date	Mintage	VG8	F12	VF20	XF40	MS60
ND(1919)	—	2.00	3.00	9.00	24.00	—

Y# 400.3 20 CASH

Copper **Obv:** 25 small curls in ribbon at base of plant **Obv. Legend:** THE REPUBLIC OF CHINA **Rev. Legend:** Hu-Nan Shan Tsoh

Date	Mintage	VG8	F12	VF20	XF40	MS60
ND(1919)	—	2.00	3.00	9.00	24.00	—

Y# 400.4 20 CASH

Copper **Obv:** Smaller rice grains **Obv. Legend:** THE REPUBLIC OF CHINA **Rev:** Crossed flags, floral ornament at left smaller **Rev. Legend:** Hu-Nan Shan Tsoh

Date	Mintage	VG8	F12	VF20	XF40	MS60
ND(1919)	—	2.00	3.00	9.00	24.00	150

Y# 400.5 20 CASH

Copper **Obv:** Thin ribbon at base of plant **Obv. Legend:** THE REPUBLIC OF CHINA **Rev. Legend:** Hu-Nan Shan Tsoh

Date	Mintage	VG8	F12	VF20	XF40	MS60
ND(1919)	—	2.00	3.00	9.00	24.00	150

Y# 400.6 20 CASH

Copper **Obv. Legend:** THE REPUBLIC OF CHINA **Rev:** Small pentagonal rosette above crossed flags **Rev. Legend:** Hu-Nan Shan Tsoh

Date	Mintage	VG8	F12	VF20	XF40	MS60
ND(1919)	—	2.00	3.00	9.00	24.00	150

Y# 400.7 20 CASH

Copper **Obv. Legend:** THE REPUBLIC OF CHINA **Rev:** Larger star-shaped rosette above crossed flags **Rev. Legend:** Hu-Nan Shan Tsoh

Date	Mintage	VG8	F12	VF20	XF40	MS60
ND(1919)	—	3.00	8.00	12.00	28.00	160

Y# 400.7b 20 CASH

Brass **Obv. Legend:** THE REPUBLIC OF CHINA **Rev. Legend:** Hu-Nan Shan Tsoh

Date	Mintage	VG8	F12	VF20	XF40	MS60
ND(1919)	—	5.00	12.00	25.00	60.00	185

Y# 400.8 20 CASH

Copper **Obv:** Larger star-shaped rosette above flags **Obv. Legend:** THE REPUBLIC OF CHINA **Rev. Legend:** Hu-Nan Shan Tsoh

Date	Mintage	VG8	F12	VF20	XF40	MS60
ND(1919)	—	3.00	8.00	12.00	24.00	170

Y# 400.9 20 CASH

Copper **Obv. Legend:** THE REPUBLIC OF CHINA **Rev:** Sharp pointed star above crossed flags, long inner ribbons **Rev. Legend:** Hu-Nan Shan Tsoh

Date	Mintage	VG8	F12	VF20	XF40	MS60
ND(1919)	—	3.00	8.00	12.00	60.00	185

Y# 400.10 20 CASH

Copper **Obv. Legend:** THE REPUBLIC OF CHINA **Rev:** Sharp 5-pointed star over crossed flags, short inner ribbons **Rev. Legend:** Hu-nan Sheng Tsao

Date	Mintage	VG8	F12	VF20	XF40	MS60
ND(1919)	—	30.00	37.50	45.00	100	200

Y# 400 20 CASH

Copper **Obv. Legend:** THE REPUBLIC OF CHINA **Rev:** Rosette above crossed flags, florals at left and right, five characters at bottom in legend **Rev. Legend:** Hu Nan Shan Tsoh

Date	Mintage	VG8	F12	VF20	XF40	MS60
ND(1919)	—	2.00	5.00	11.00	40.00	—

Y# 400.11 20 CASH

Copper **Obv. Legend:** THE REPUBLIC OF CHINA **Rev:** Similar to Y#400.2; no dot in rosette above flags **Rev. Legend:** Hu-nan Sheng Tsao

Date	Mintage	VG8	F12	VF20	XF40	MS60
ND(1919)	—	—	—	—	—	—

Y# 400a 20 CASH

9.47 g., Copper **Obv:** Denomination: "20 CASH" **Obv. Legend:** THE REPUBLIC OF CHINA **Rev. Legend:** Hu-Nan Shan Tsoh

Date	Mintage	VG8	F12	VF20	XF40	MS60
ND(1919)	—	75.00	115	150	300	—

Y# 400b 20 CASH

Brass **Obv:** Denomination: "20 CASH" **Obv. Legend:** THE REPUBLIC OF CHINA **Rev. Legend:** Hu-Nan Shan Tsoh

Date	Mintage	VG8	F12	VF20	XF40	MS60
ND(1919)	—	5.00	12.00	30.00	80.00	—

Y# 403.1 20 CASH

Copper **Subject:** Provincial Constitution **Obv:** Rosette above crossed flags **Obv. Legend:** THE REPUBLIC OF CHINA **Rev:** Trigram of the Pah Kwah in large grain sprays

Date	Mintage	VG8	F12	VF20	XF40	MS60
11(1922)	—	33.75	55.00	100	180	350

Y# 403.2 20 CASH

Copper **Subject:** Provincial Constitution **Obv:** Rosette above crossed flags **Obv. Legend:** THE REPUBLIC OF CHINA **Rev:** Trigram of the Pah Kwah in smaller grain sprays

Date	Mintage	VG8	F12	VF20	XF40	MS60
11(1922)	—	55.00	115	150	300	500

Y# 404 DOLLAR
27.40 g., Silver **Subject:** Provincial Constitution **Obv. Legend:** THE REPUBLIC OF CHINA **Rev:** Trigram of the Pah Kwah in grain sprays

Date	Mintage	VG8	F12	VF20	XF40	MS60
11(1922)	—	350	675	1,350	3,750	9,500

Hung-hsien

TRANSITIONAL COINAGE

K# 762 10 CENTS
Silver **Obv. Legend:** Hung-hsien Yüan-nien **Obv. Inscription:** Chung-hua Yin-pi **Rev:** "Flying" dragon

Date	Mintage	VG8	F12	VF20	XF40	MS60
ND-1915	—	300	525	1,200	3,000	7,500

Note: Though Kann calls this coin as Essai, contemporary reports indicate that the coin actually circulated briefly in 1915. Not to be confused with Y#28, the obverse of which has a different legend in Chinese. (See General Issues - Empire.)

PATTERNS

Including off metal strikes

KM#	Date	Mintage	Identification	Mkt Val
Pn4	ND-1902	—	10 Cash. Copper. Three characters at bottom, Y#112.	22,000
Pn5	ND-1902	—	10 Cash. Copper. Three characters at bottom, Y#112.	17,500

Note: Two Heaton (Birmingham) proof patterns for a proposed brass coinage which wasn't adopted. Dies were recut with only 2 characters for issue.

KM#	Date	Mintage	Identification	Mkt Val
Pn6	ND-1915	—	10 Cents. Nickel. Plain. K#762x.	—
Pn7	ND-1915	—	10 Cents. Copper. Plain. K#762y.	18,000
Pn9	11(1922)	—	Dollar. Silver. General Chao Heng-ti.	—
Pn10	11(1922)	—	Dollar. Copper. General Chao Heng-ti.	—

HUPEH PROVINCE

Hubei

A province located in east-central China. Hilly, with some lakes and swamps, it has rich coal and iron deposits plus a varied agricultural program. The Wuchang Mint had been active from early in the Manchu dynasty and its modern equipment began operations in 1895. It probably closed in 1929.

EMPIRE

Kuang-hsü

PROVINCIAL CAST COINAGE

C# 13–11 CASH
Cast Brass **Obv. Inscription:** Kuang-hsü T'ung-pao **Rev. Inscription:** Manchu Boo-ching **Mint:** Ching

Date	Mintage	G4	VG8	F12	VF20	XF40
ND(1875-1908)	—	12.50	20.00	30.00	50.00	—

C# 13–11.1 CASH
Cast Brass **Obv. Inscription:** Kuang-hsü T'ung-pao **Rev. Inscription:** Manchu Boo-ching **Mint:** Ching **Note:** Attribution of this mint mark to Chingchow is uncertain. Some authorities claim the Taku (Dagu) Mint in Tientsin struck this coin.

Date	Mintage	G4	VG8	F12	VF20	XF40
ND(1875-1908)	—	12.00	15.00	22.50	35.00	—

MILLED COINAGE

Y# 121 CASH
Brass **Obv. Inscription:** Kuang-hsü Yüan-pao **Rev:** Dragon **Mint:** Ching

Date	Mintage	VG8	F12	VF20	XF40	MS60
ND(1906)	66,474,000	12.00	18.00	27.50	60.00	100

Y# 7j CASH
Brass **Obv:** Small mint mark on small disc in center **Obv. Legend:** Kuang-hsü **Rev:** Dragon

Date	Mintage	VG8	F12	VF20	XF40	MS60
CD1908	Inc. above	5.00	12.00	22.50	50.00	90.00

Y# 7j.1 CASH
Brass **Obv:** Large mint mark on small disc in center **Obv. Legend:** Kuang-hsü **Rev:** Dragon **Mint:** Ching

Date	Mintage	VG8	F12	VF20	XF40	MS60
CD1908	Inc. above	5.00	12.00	22.50	50.00	90.00

Y# 8j 2 CASH
Copper **Obv. Inscription:** Tai-ch'ing T'ung-pi **Rev:** Dragon **Mint:** Ching

Date	Mintage	VG8	F12	VF20	XF40	MS60
CD-1906	844,000	75.00	120	190	400	—

Y# 9j 5 CASH
Copper, 24 mm. **Obv. Inscription:** Tai-ch'ing T'ung-pi **Rev. Legend:** Kuang-hsü Nien-tsao, TAI-CHING-TI-KUO ... **Mint:** Ching

Date	Mintage	VG8	F12	VF20	XF40	MS60
CD1906	9,846,000	8.00	14.00	22.50	60.00	—

Y# 9j.1 5 CASH
Copper, 23 mm. **Obv. Inscription:** Tai-ch'ing T'ung-pi **Rev:** Dragon redesigned **Rev. Legend:** Kuang-hsü Nien-tsao, TAI-CHING-TI-KUO ... **Mint:** Ching

Date	Mintage	VG8	F12	VF20	XF40	MS60
CD1906	Inc. above	9.00	17.00	27.50	70.00	—

Y# 120.1 10 CASH
Copper **Obv. Legend:** Hu Peh Sheng Tsao **Obv. Inscription:** Kuang-hsü Yüan-pao **Rev:** Slightly larger English letters, wide face on dragon **Mint:** Ching

Date	Mintage	VG8	F12	VF20	XF40	MS60
ND(1902-05)	Inc. above	0.50	1.50	3.00	12.00	120

Y# 120.2 10 CASH
Copper **Obv. Legend:** Hu Peh Sheng Tsao **Obv. Inscription:** Kuang-hsü Yüan-pao **Rev:** Large pearl with many spines, narrower face on dragon **Mint:** Ching

Date	Mintage	VG8	F12	VF20	XF40	MS60
ND(1902-05)	Inc. above	0.40	1.25	2.25	8.00	120

Y# 120.3 10 CASH
Copper **Obv. Legend:** Hu Peh Sheng Tsao **Obv. Inscription:** Kuang-hsü Yüan-pao **Rev:** Smaller pearl with fewer spines on dragon **Mint:** Ching **Note:** Commonly found with medal alignment but also exists with coin alignment.

Date	Mintage	F12	VF20	XF40	MS60	MS63
ND(1902-05)	Inc. above	1.25	2.25	8.00	120	450

Y# 120.3a 10 CASH
Brass **Obv. Legend:** Hu Peh Sheng Tsao **Obv. Inscription:** Kuang-hsü Yüan-pao **Rev:** Dragon **Mint:** Ching

Date	Mintage	VG8	F12	VF20	XF40	MS60
ND(1902-05)	Inc. above	—	—	—	—	—

Y# 120.4 10 CASH
Copper **Obv:** 5-petaled rosette, small Manchu word at right **Obv. Legend:** Hu Peh Sheng Tsao **Obv. Inscription:** Kuang-hsü Yüan-pao **Rev:** 4 dots in shape of cross at either side of dragon, PROVINCE spelled PHOVINCE, with "V" an inverted "A" **Mint:** Ching

Date	Mintage	VG8	F12	VF20	XF40	MS60
ND(1902-05)	Inc. above	0.50	1.50	3.00	12.00	120

Y# 120.5 10 CASH
Copper **Obv:** Large Manchu at right **Obv. Legend:** Hu Peh Sheng Tsao **Obv. Inscription:** Kuang-hsü Yüan-pao **Rev:** "R" in PROVINCE inverted, "V" an inverted "A", dragon **Mint:** Ching

Date	Mintage	VG8	F12	VF20	XF40	MS60
ND(1902-05)	Inc. above	0.50	1.50	3.00	12.00	120

Y# 120.6 10 CASH
Copper **Obv. Legend:** Hu Peh Sheng Tsao **Obv. Inscription:**

Kuang-hsü Yüan-pao **Rev:** 6-pointed star at either side of dragon, hyphen in HU-PEH **Mint:** Ching

Date	Mintage	VG8	F12	VF20	XF40	MS60
ND(1902-05)	Inc. above	0.50	1.50	3.00	12.00	120

Y# 120.7 10 CASH

Copper **Obv. Legend:** Hu Peh Sheng Tsao **Obv. Inscription:** Kuang-hsü Yüan-pao **Rev:** 6-pointed star at either side of dragon, without hyphen in HU-PEH **Mint:** Ching

Date	Mintage	VG8	F12	VF20	XF40	MS60
ND(1902-05)	Inc. above	0.70	2.25	5.00	16.00	125

Y# 120.8 10 CASH

Copper **Obv:** 5-petaled rosette and small Manchu **Obv. Legend:** Hu Peh Sheng Tsao **Obv. Inscription:** Kuang-hsü Yüan-pao **Rev:** Dragon, very small pearl **Mint:** Ching

Date	Mintage	VG8	F12	VF20	XF40	MS60
ND(1902-05)	Inc. above	1.50	5.00	9.00	30.00	130

Y# 120.9 10 CASH

Copper **Obv:** Square in circle **Obv. Legend:** Hu Peh Sheng Tsao **Obv. Inscription:** Kuang-hsü Yüan-pao **Rev:** Dragon, hyphen in HU-PEH **Mint:** Ching

Date	Mintage	VG8	F12	VF20	XF40	MS60
ND(1902-05)	Inc. above	2.00	6.00	11.00	36.00	140

Y# 120.10 10 CASH

Copper **Obv:** Square in circle **Obv. Legend:** Hu Peh Sheng Tsao **Obv. Inscription:** Kuang-hsü Yüan-pao **Rev:** Dragon, without hyphen in HU-PEH **Mint:** Ching

Date	Mintage	VG8	F12	VF20	XF40	MS60
ND(1902-05)	Inc. above	0.70	2.25	4.00	14.00	120

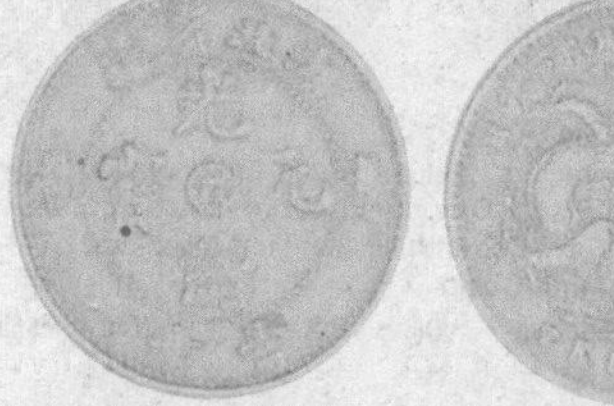

Y# 120 10 CASH

Copper **Obv:** 8-petaled rosette **Obv. Legend:** Hu Peh Sheng Tsao **Obv. Inscription:** Kuang-hsü Yüan-pao **Rev:** Dragon surrounded by clouds **Mint:** Ching

Date	Mintage	VG8	F12	VF20	XF40	MS60
ND(1902-05)	4,475,000	2.75	8.00	12.00	35.00	140

Y# 120a 10 CASH

Copper **Obv. Legend:** Hu Peh Sheng Tsao **Obv. Inscription:** Kuang-hsü Yüan-pao **Rev:** Uncircled large dragon **Mint:** Ching

Date	Mintage	VG8	F12	VF20	XF40	MS60
ND(1902-05)	Inc. above	1.50	5.00	11.00	30.00	135

Y# 122.1 10 CASH

Copper **Obv:** Second character from right "Pei" smaller **Obv. Legend:** Hu-peh Sheng Tsao **Obv. Inscription:** Kuang-hsü Yüan-pao **Rev:** Dragon **Mint:** Ching

Date	Mintage	VG8	F12	VF20	XF40	MS60
ND(1902-05)	Inc. above	0.30	0.70	2.25	8.00	120

Y# 122.3 10 CASH

Copper **Obv. Legend:** Hu-peh Sheng Tsao **Obv. Inscription:** Kuang-hsü Yüan-pao **Rev:** Clouds above dragon's head, 2 clouds below pearl instead of 1 **Mint:** Ching

Date	Mintage	VG8	F12	VF20	XF40	MS60
ND(1902-05)	Inc. above	1.00	3.00	8.00	24.00	140

Y# 122.4 10 CASH

Copper **Obv. Legend:** Hu-peh Sheng Tsao **Obv. Inscription:** Kuang-hsü Yüan-pao **Rev:** Dragon, small circle around lower part of pearl, without dots on either side of mountain **Mint:** Ching

Date	Mintage	VG8	F12	VF20	XF40	MS60
ND(1902-05)	Inc. above	1.00	3.00	8.00	24.00	140

Y# 122.5 10 CASH

Copper **Obv. Legend:** Hu-peh Sheng Tsao **Obv. Inscription:** Kuang-hsü Yüan-pao **Rev:** Dragon, larger circle around larger pearl, larger English letters **Mint:** Ching

Date	Mintage	VG8	F12	VF20	XF40	MS60
ND(1902-05)	Inc. above	1.00	3.00	8.00	24.00	135

Y# 122 10 CASH

7.18 g., Copper **Obv:** Second character from right at top is larger, 6-petalled rosette **Obv. Legend:** Hu-peh Sheng Tsao **Obv. Inscription:** Kuang-hsü Yüan-pao **Rev:** Front view dragon **Shape:** 28.04 **Mint:** Ching

Date	Mintage	F12	VF20	XF40	MS60	MS63
ND(1902-05)	Inc. above	0.90	2.25	8.00	120	300

Y# 122a 10 CASH

Copper **Obv. Legend:** Hu-peh Sheng Tsao **Obv. Inscription:** Kuang-hsü Yüan-pao **Rev:** Circled front view of dragon **Mint:** Ching

Date	Mintage	VG8	F12	VF20	XF40	MS60
ND(1902-05)	—	70.00	190	265	450	—

Y# 10j 10 CASH

Copper **Obv. Inscription:** Tai-ch'ing T'ung-pi **Rev:** Dragon, 7 flames on pearl **Rev. Legend:** Kuang hsü Nien-tsao, TAI-CHING-TI-KUO ... **Mint:** Ching

Date	Mintage	VG8	F12	VF20	XF40	MS60
CD1906	1,865,558,000	0.40	1.25	1.50	6.00	140

Y# 10j.1 10 CASH

Copper, 28-29 mm. **Obv. Inscription:** Tai-ch'ing T'ung-pi **Rev:** Redesigned dragon with wide lips, cloud-shaped bar below pearl with 5 flames **Rev. Legend:** Kuang hsü Nien-tsao, TAI-CHING-TI-KUO ... **Mint:** Ching

Date	Mintage	VG8	F12	VF20	XF40	MS60
CD1906	Inc. above	1.00	3.00	8.00	24.00	125

Y# 10j.2 10 CASH

Copper, 30 mm. **Obv. Inscription:** Tai-ch'ing T'ung-pi **Rev:** Dragon **Rev. Legend:** Kuang hsü Nien-tsao, TAI-CHING-TI-KUO ... **Mint:** Ching

Date	Mintage	VG8	F12	VF20	XF40	MS60
CD1906	Inc. above	1.00	3.00	8.00	24.00	125

Y# 10j.3 10 CASH

Copper **Obv. Inscription:** Tai-ch'ing T'ung-pi **Rev:** Different dragon with hook-shaped cloud beneath, pearl with 4 flames, large incuse swirl on pearl **Rev. Legend:** Kuang hsü Nien-tsao, TAI-CHING-TI-KUO ... **Mint:** Ching

Date	Mintage	VG8	F12	VF20	XF40	MS60
CD1906	Inc. above	0.50	1.50	3.00	8.00	120

Y# 10j.4 10 CASH

Copper **Obv. Inscription:** Tai-ch'ing T'ung-pi **Rev:** Dragon, small incuse swirl on pearl with 4 flames **Rev. Legend:** Kuang hsü Nien-tsao, TAI-CHING-TI-KUO ... **Mint:** Ching

Date	Mintage	VG8	F12	VF20	XF40	MS60
CD1906	Inc. above	0.30	0.70	1.50	6.00	120

Y# 10j.5 10 CASH
Copper **Obv. Inscription:** Tai-ch'ing T'ung-pi **Rev:** Dragon, swirl on pearl in relief with 4 flames **Rev. Legend:** Kuang hsü Nien-tsao, TAI-CHING-TI-KUO ... **Mint:** Ching

Date	Mintage	VG8	F12	VF20	XF40	MS60
CD1906	Inc. above	0.40	1.25	1.50	6.00	120

Y# 11j 20 CASH
Copper **Obv. Inscription:** Tai-ch'ing T'ung-pi **Rev:** Dragon **Rev. Legend:** Kuang-hsü Nien-tsao, TAI-CHING-TI-KUO ... **Mint:** Ching

Date	Mintage	VG8	F12	VF20	XF40	MS60
CD1906	3,710,000	225	375	725	1,900	—

Y# 123 5 CENTS
1.35 g., 0.820 Silver 0.0356 oz. ASW **Obv. Legend:** Hu-peh Sheng Tsao **Obv. Inscription:** Kuang-hsü Yüan-pao **Rev:** Dragon **Rev. Legend:** HU-PEH PROVINCE **Edge:** Reeded **Mint:** Ching

Date	Mintage	VG8	F12	VF20	XF40	MS60
ND(1895-1905)	4,278,000	17.50	50.00	100	200	500

Y# 124.1 10 CENTS
2.70 g., 0.820 Silver 0.0712 oz. ASW, 18.6 mm. **Obv. Legend:** Hu-peh Sheng Tsao **Obv. Inscription:** Kuang-hsü Yüan-pao **Rev:** Without characters beside dragon **Rev. Legend:** HU-PEH PROVINCE **Edge:** Reeded **Mint:** Ching

Date	Mintage	F12	VF20	XF40	MS60	MS63
ND(1895-1907)	—	4.00	8.00	30.00	130	425

Note: 2 varieties of edge milling exist

Y# 125.1 20 CENTS
5.30 g., 0.820 Silver 0.1397 oz. ASW **Obv. Legend:** Hu-peh Sheng Tsao **Obv. Inscription:** Kuang-hsü Yüan-pao **Rev:** Without characters beside dragon **Rev. Legend:** HU-PEH PROVINCE **Mint:** Ching

Date	Mintage	F12	VF20	XF40	MS60	MS63
ND(1895-1907)	—	9.00	17.00	35.00	140	500

Y# 126 50 CENTS
13.50 g., 0.860 Silver 0.3733 oz. ASW **Obv. Legend:** Hu-peh Sheng Tsao **Obv. Inscription:** Kuang-hsü Yüan-pao **Rev:** Dragon **Rev. Legend:** HU-PEH PROVINCE **Mint:** Ching

Date	Mintage	VG8	F12	VF20	XF40	MS60
ND(1895-1905)	—	38.00	75.00	150	600	1,750

Y# 127.1 DOLLAR
26.70 g., 0.900 Silver 0.7726 oz. ASW **Obv. Legend:** Hu-peh Sheng Tsao **Obv. Inscription:** Kuang-hsü Yüan-pao **Rev:** Without "Pen Sheng" at either side of dragon **Rev. Legend:** HU-PEH PROVINCE **Edge:** Reeded **Mint:** Ching

Date	Mintage	VG8	F12	VF20	XF40	MS60
ND(1895-1907)	19,935,000	30.00	50.00	100	400	1,300

BULLION TAEL COINAGE

Y# 128.1 TAEL
37.70 g., 0.877 Silver 1.063 oz. ASW **Obv:** Large inscription **Obv. Inscription:** Kuang-hsü Yin-pi **Rev:** Two dragons forming circle **Rev. Legend:** HU-PEH PROVINCE **Mint:** Ching

Date	Mintage	VG8	F12	VF20	XF40	MS60
30(1904)	648,000	525	900	1,800	7,500	11,500

Y# 128.2 TAEL
37.70 g., 0.877 Silver 1.063 oz. ASW **Obv:** Smaller inscription **Obv. Inscription:** Kuang-hsü Yin-pi **Rev:** Two dragons forming circle **Rev. Legend:** HU-PEH PROVINCE

Date	Mintage	F12	VF20	XF40	MS60	MS63
30(1904)	Inc. above	825	1,650	6,500	15,000	35,000

Hsüan-t'ung

MILLED COINAGE

Y# 20j 10 CASH
Copper **Obv. Inscription:** Tai-ch'ing T'ung-pi **Rev:** Dragon, large incuse swirl on pearl **Rev. Legend:** Hsüan-t'ung Nien-tsao, TAI-CHING-TI-KUO ... **Mint:** Ching

Date	Mintage	VG8	F12	VF20	XF40	MS60
CD1909	371,577,000	0.70	2.25	5.00	16.00	120

Y# 20j.1 10 CASH
Copper **Obv. Inscription:** Tai-ch'ing T'ung-pi **Rev:** Dragon, small swirl in relief on pearl **Rev. Legend:** Hsüan-t'ung Nien-tsao, TAI-CHING-TI-KUO ... **Mint:** Ching

Date	Mintage	VG8	F12	VF20	XF40	MS60
CD1909	Inc. above	0.70	2.25	5.00	16.00	120

Y# 20j.2 10 CASH
Copper **Obv:** CD1909 over CD1906 **Obv. Inscription:** Tai-ch'ing T'ung-pi **Rev:** Dragon **Rev. Legend:** Hsüan-t'ung Nien-tsao, TAI-CHING-TI-KUO ... **Mint:** Ching

Date	Mintage	VG8	F12	VF20	XF40	MS60
CD1909/1906	—	—	—	—	—	—

Y# 20j.3 10 CASH
Copper **Obv:** Characters "Hsuan T'ung" re-engraved over characters "Kuang Hsu" **Obv. Inscription:** Tai-ch'ing T'ung-pi **Rev:** Dragon **Rev. Legend:** Hsüan-t'ung Nien-tsao, TAI-CHING-TI-KUO ... **Mint:** Ching

Date	Mintage	VG8	F12	VF20	XF40	MS60
CD1909 Rare	—	—	—	—	—	—

Y# 129 10 CENTS
Silver **Obv. Legend:** Hu-peh Sheng Tsao **Obv. Inscription:** Hsüan-t'ung Yüan-pao **Rev:** Dragon **Rev. Legend:** HU-PEH PROVINCE **Mint:** Ching

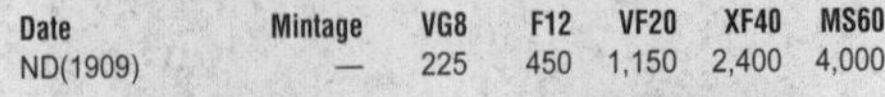

Date	Mintage	VG8	F12	VF20	XF40	MS60
ND(1909)	—	225	450	1,150	2,400	4,000

Y# 130 20 CENTS
Silver **Obv. Legend:** Hu-peh Sheng Tsao **Obv. Inscription:** Hsüan-t'ung Yüan-pao **Rev:** Dragon **Rev. Legend:** HU-PEH PROVINCE **Mint:** Ching

Date	Mintage	VG8	F12	VF20	XF40	MS60
ND(1909-11)	—	300	600	1,000	3,000	5,000

Y# 131 DOLLAR
27.00 g., 0.900 Silver 0.7813 oz. ASW **Obv. Legend:** Hu-peh Sheng Tsao **Obv. Inscription:** Hsüan-t'ung Yüan-pao **Rev:** Dragon **Mint:** Ching

Date	Mintage	VG8	F12	VF20	XF40	MS60
ND(1909-11)	2,703,000	33.00	55.00	100	270	1,200

REPUBLIC

Y# A405 20 CASH
Brass **Note:** Attribution is uncertain. Probably minted in Szechuan (Sichuan).

Date	Mintage	VG8	F12	VF20	XF40	MS60
ND(c.1914)	—	40.00	85.00	125	200	—

Y# 405 50 CASH
Copper or Brass **Obv. Legend:** Chung Hua Min Kuo (year) Nien **Note:** Crude strike. Similar coins dated Yr. 1 and Yr. 8 are known, but their status is uncertain.

Date	Mintage	G4	VG8	F12	VF20	XF40
3(1914)	—	375	575	850	1,100	—
7(1918)	—	250	400	600	850	—

Y# 405.1 50 CASH
Copper or Brass **Obv. Legend:** Chung Hua Min Kuo (year) Nien **Note:** Machine strike. Not to be confused with Szechuan (Sichuan) Y#449.

Date	Mintage	G4	VG8	F12	VF20	XF40
7(1918)	—	375	550	750	1,150	—

Y# 406 20 CENTS
5.20 g., Silver **Obv:** Characters "Tsao" at left and "Hu" at right of military bust of Yuan Shih-k'ai left **Note:** Do not confuse with Y#327 (see Republic-general issues).

Date	Mintage	VG8	F12	VF20	XF40	MS60
9(1920)	—	45.00	120	375	750	4,500

PATTERNS

Including off metal strikes

KM#	Date	Mintage	Identification	Mkt Val
PnA6	ND-1902	—	10 Cash. White Copper. Y122.5. W518.	—
Pn6	ND-1902	—	10 Cash. Brass. W480.	—
PnA7	3(1911)	—	10 Cents. Pewter. K48y.	—
Pn7	1(1916)	—	10 Cents. White Metal. K764x.	—

KANSU PROVINCE

Gansu

A province located in north-central China with a contrast of mountains and sandy plains. The west end of the Great Wall with its branches lies in Kansu (Gansu). Kansu (Gansu) was the eastern end of the "Silk Road" that led to central and western Asia. Two mints issued Cash coins. It has been reported, but not confirmed, that the Lanchow Mint operated as late as 1949.

REPUBLIC

CAST COINAGE

Y# C407 20 CASH
Brass **Obv:** Crossed flags, striped flag at right **Obv. Legend:** Chung Hua Min Kuo **Rev:** Value in grain sprays **Rev. Legend:** THE REPUBELIC OF CHINA **Edge:** Plain **Mint:** (no Mint Information)

Date	Mintage	G4	VG8	F12	VF20	XF40
ND (1920)	—	85.00	220	500	825	—

Y# E407 20 CASH
6.40 g., Brass, 31.85 mm. **Obv:** Crossed flags, striped flag at left **Obv. Legend:** Chung Hua Min Kuo **Rev:** Value in grain sprays **Rev. Legend:** TJ REPUBLIC OF CHINA + TEVC + **Edge:** Plain

Date	Mintage	G4	VG8	F12	VF20	XF40
ND (1920)	—	150	300	650	1,200	—

Y# D407 50 CASH
Brass **Obv:** Crossed flags in floral sprays, striped flag at right **Obv. Legend:** Chung Hua Min Kuo **Rev:** Value in grain sprays **Rev. Legend:** THE REPUBLIC OE CHINA **Edge:** Plain **Mint:** (no Mint Information)

Date	Mintage	G4	VG8	F12	VF20	XF40
ND (1920)	—	200	375	850	1,350	2,000

MILLED COINAGE

Y# 408 50 CASH
Copper **Obv. Legend:** Chung Hua Min Kuo (year) Nien **Mint:** (no Mint Information)

Date	Mintage	VG8	F12	VF20	XF40	MS60
15(1926)	2,564,000	100	220	350	650	—

Y# A408 50 CASH
Copper **Obv:** National star **Obv. Legend:** Chung Hua Min Kuo (year) Nien **Rev:** Crossed flags **Mint:** (no Mint Information)

Date	Mintage	VG8	F12	VF20	XF40	MS60
ND(1927)	—	625	1,150	2,000	—	—

Y# 409 100 CASH
Copper **Obv. Legend:** Chung Hua Min Kuo (year) Nien **Rev:** Crossed flags **Mint:** (no Mint Information)

Date	Mintage	VG8	F12	VF20	XF40	MS60
15(1926)	—	45.00	75.00	150	350	—

Y# 407 DOLLAR
26.60 g., Silver **Obv:** Military bust of Yüan Shih-kai left, "Su" at left, "Kan" at right **Obv. Legend:** Chung Hua Min Kuo (year) Nien **Rev:** Value in sprays **Mint:** (no Mint Information)

Date	Mintage	VG8	F12	VF20	XF40	MS60
3(1914)	—	350	750	5,000	15,000	35,000

Y# 410 DOLLAR
26.60 g., Silver **Obv:** Facing bust of Sun Yat-sen **Obv. Legend:** Chung Hua Min Kuo (year) Nien **Rev:** National star **Mint:** (no Mint Information)

Date	Mintage	VG8	F12	VF20	XF40	MS60
17(1928)	—	475	1,150	3,500	12,500	—

PATTERNS

Including off metal strikes

KM#	Date	Mintage	Identification	Mkt Val
Pn1	ND(ca.1928)	—	5 Cash. Copper. Hsu#385.	1,300
Pn2	ND(ca.1928)	—	10 Cash. Copper.	—
Pn3	ND(1928)	—	5 Fen. Copper. Hsu#383.	600
Pn4	17(1928)	—	50 Cash. Copper.	—
Pn5	ND(ca.1928)	—	10 Fen. Copper. Hsu#384.	800

KIANGNAN, PROVINCE

A district in eastern China made up of Anhwei (Anhui) and Kiangsu (Jiangsu) provinces. In 1667 the province of Kiangnan was divided into the present provinces of Anhwei (Anhui) and Kiangsu (Jiangsu). In 1723 Nanking, formerly the capital of Kiangnan, was made the capital of Liang-Chiang Chiang (an administrative area consisting of Anhwei (Anhui), Kiangsu (Jiangsu), and Kiangsi (Jiangxi) provinces).

Always highly regarded because of location, agriculture and manufacturing, Kiangnan has frequently been sought after by contending forces.

The Nanking Mint had been active during imperial times. Modern minting facilities began operations in 1897. A second mint was planned for the Kiangnan Arsenal in Shanghai in 1905. Mints for copper coins also operated in Chingkiang (Qingjiang) in central Kiangsu and at Soochow which is further south. A silver mint was planned for Shanghai in 1921. The Nanking Mint, the most important of the group, burned down in 1929. The Nationalist Government Central Mint was completed in Shanghai in 1930 and opened in 1933.

EMPIRE

Kuang-hsü

MILLED COINAGE

The initials HAH, SY, CH and TH are those of mint officials and were placed on the coins as a guarantee of the coin's fineness. The 5-, 10-, and 20-cent coins are often found without a decimal point between the numbers on the reverse. The 1904 dated dollar was restruck during Republican times.

Y# 7k CASH
Brass **Obv:** Bottom horizontal stroke in mint mark extends beyond outside vertical strokes **Obv. Legend:** Kuang-hsü **Rev:** Dragon

Date	Mintage	VG8	F12	VF20	XF40	MS60
CD-1908	25,450,000	4.00	7.00	13.00	32.00	—

Y# 7k.1 CASH
Brass **Obv:** Bottom horizontal stroke in mint mark does not extend beyond outside vertical strokes **Obv. Legend:** Kuang-hsü **Rev:** Dragon

Date	Mintage	VG8	F12	VF20	XF40	MS60
CD1908	Inc. above	5.00	10.00	19.00	43.00	—

Y# 9k.1 5 CASH
Copper **Obv:** Mint mark incused on raised disk **Obv. Inscription:** Tai-ch'ing T'ung-pi **Rev:** Dragon **Rev. Legend:** Kuang-hsü Nien-tsao, TAI-CHING-TI-KUO...

Date	Mintage	VG8	F12	VF20	XF40	MS60
CD1906	—	55.00	100	150	300	—

Y# 9k.1a 5 CASH
Brass **Obv. Inscription:** Tai-ch'ing T'ung-pi **Rev:** Dragon **Rev. Legend:** Kuang-hsü Nien-tsao, TAI-CHING-TI-KUO...

Date	Mintage	VG8	F12	VF20	XF40	MS60
CD1906	—	70.00	135	190	400	—

Y# 9k.2 5 CASH
Copper **Obv:** Mint mark in relief at center without disk **Obv. Inscription:** Tai-ch'ing T'ung-pi **Rev:** Dragon **Rev. Legend:** Kuang-hsü Nien-tsao, TAI-CHING-TI-KUO...

Date	Mintage	VG8	F12	VF20	XF40	MS60
CD1906	—	50.00	50.00	50.00	400	—

Y# 135 10 CASH
Copper **Obv. Legend:** Chiang-nan Sheng Tsao **Obv. Inscription:** Kuang-hsü Yüan-pao **Rev:** Dragon **Edge:** Reeded

Date	Mintage	VG8	F12	VF20	XF40	MS60
ND(1902)	—	15.00	45.00	90.00	200	—

Y# 135.1 10 CASH
Copper **Obv. Legend:** Chiang-nan Sheng Tsao **Obv. Inscription:** Kuang-hsü Yüan-pao **Rev:** Dragon **Edge:** Plain

Date	Mintage	VG8	F12	VF20	XF40	MS60
ND(1902)	—	15.00	45.00	90.00	200	—

Y# 135.2 10 CASH
Copper **Obv:** Small Manchu words in center **Obv. Legend:** Chiang-nan Sheng Tsao **Obv. Inscription:** Kuang-hsü Yüan-pao **Rev:** Dragon

Date	Mintage	F12	VF20	XF40	MS60	MS63
CD1902	—	2.25	5.00	8.00	80.00	—

Y# 135.3 10 CASH
Copper **Obv:** Large Manchu words in center **Obv. Legend:** Chiang-nan Sheng Tsao **Obv. Inscription:** Kuang-hsü Yüan-pao **Rev:** Dragon

Date	Mintage	VG8	F12	VF20	XF40	MS60
CD1902	—	3.00	10.00	19.00	50.00	200

Y# C140 10 CASH
Copper **Obv:** Kiang-nan **Obv. Legend:** Chiang-nan Sheng Tsao **Obv. Inscription:** Kuang-hsü Yüan-pao **Rev:** Dragon **Rev. Legend:** KIANG-SOO **Note:** Mule; often confused with Y#162.

Date	Mintage	VG8	F12	VF20	XF40	MS60
CD1902	—	—	—	—	—	—
ND(1902)	—	75.00	225	300	500	—

Y# 135.4 10 CASH
Copper **Obv. Legend:** Chiang-nan Sheng Tsao **Obv. Inscription:** Kuang-hsü Yüan-pao **Rev:** Dragon

Date	Mintage	VG8	F12	VF20	XF40	MS60
CD1903	—	2.00	6.00	8.00	14.00	130

Y# 135.5 10 CASH
Copper **Obv. Legend:** Chiang-nan Sheng Tsao **Obv. Inscription:** Kuang-hsü Yüan-pao **Rev:** Dragon; cloud above letter "T" looks like number "3"

Date	Mintage	VG8	F12	VF20	XF40	MS60
CD1904	351,974,000	0.50	1.50	3.00	10.00	130

Y# 135.6 10 CASH
Copper **Obv. Legend:** Chiang-nan Sheng Tsao **Obv. Inscription:** Kuang-hsü Yüan-pao **Rev:** Dragon; cloud above "T" redesigned; "CASH" spelled "GASH"

Date	Mintage	VG8	F12	VF20	XF40	MS60
CD1904	Inc. above	2.25	7.00	14.00	35.00	180

Y# 135.7 10 CASH
Copper **Obv. Legend:** Chiang-nan Sheng Tsao **Obv. Inscription:** Kuang-hsü Yüan-pao **Rev:** Thin-tailed dragon; third design of cloud above letter "T"

Date	Mintage	VG8	F12	VF20	XF40	MS60
CD1904	Inc. above	0.70	2.25	5.00	10.00	130

Y# 135.8 10 CASH
Copper **Obv. Legend:** Chiang-nan Sheng Tsao **Obv. Inscription:** Kuang-hsü Yüan-pao **Rev:** Fewer clouds around dragon; scales on dragon's body different, pearl smaller

Date	Mintage	VG8	F12	VF20	XF40	MS60
CD1904	Inc. above	2.25	7.00	14.00	35.00	180

Note: This coin is believed to be counterfeit

Y# 135.9 10 CASH
Copper **Obv. Legend:** Chiang-nan Sheng Tsao **Obv. Inscription:** Kuang-hsü Yüan-pao **Rev:** Small rosette at either side of dragon

Date	Mintage	VG8	F12	VF20	XF40	MS60
CD1905	496,020,000	0.50	1.50	3.00	10.00	120

Y# 135.10 10 CASH
Copper **Obv. Legend:** Chiang-nan Sheng Tsao **Obv. Inscription:** Kuang-hsü Yüan-pao **Rev:** Large oblong rosettes at either side of dragon

Date	Mintage	VG8	F12	VF20	XF40	MS60
CD1905	Inc. above	0.70	2.25	5.00	10.00	120

Y# 138 10 CASH

Copper **Obv. Legend:** Chiang-nan Sheng Tsao **Obv. Inscription:** Kuang-hsü Yüan-pao **Rev:** Dragon; denomination: "TEN-CASH"

Date	Mintage	VG8	F12	VF20	XF40	MS60
CD1905	Inc. above	2.00	5.00	9.00	24.00	130

Y# 138.1 10 CASH

Copper **Obv:** Rosette in center **Obv. Legend:** Chiang-nan Sheng Tsao **Obv. Inscription:** Kuang-hsü Yüan-pao **Rev:** Dragon; without hyphen in "TEN CASH"

Date	Mintage	VG8	F12	VF20	XF40	MS60
CD1905	Inc. above	0.40	1.25	2.25	10.00	120

Y# 10k 10 CASH

Copper **Obv:** Mint mark in relief on raised disc **Obv. Inscription:** Tai-ch'ing T'ung-pi **Rev:** Dragon with wide face and incuse eyes **Rev. Legend:** Kuang-hsü Nien-tsao, TAI-CHING-TI-KUO...

Date	Mintage	VG8	F12	VF20	XF40	MS60
CD1906	504,800,000	0.70	2.00	4.00	10.00	120

Y# 10k.1 10 CASH

Copper **Obv. Inscription:** Tai-ch'ing T'ung-pi **Rev:** Dragon with narrower face and raised dots for eyes **Rev. Legend:** Kuang-hsü Nien-tsao, TAI-CHING-TI-KUO...

Date	Mintage	VG8	F12	VF20	XF40	MS60
CD1906	Inc. above	0.70	2.00	4.00	10.00	120

Y# 10k.2 10 CASH

Copper **Obv:** Mint mark in relief without raised disc **Obv. Inscription:** Tai-ch'ing T'ung-pi **Rev:** Dragon with wide face and incuse eyes **Rev. Legend:** Kuang-hsü Nien-tsao, TAI-CHING-TI-KUO...

Date	Mintage	VG8	F12	VF20	XF40	MS60
CD1906	Inc. above	0.50	1.50	4.00	10.00	120

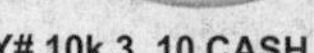

Y# 10k.3 10 CASH

Copper **Obv. Inscription:** Tai-ch'ing T'ung-pi **Rev:** Dragon with narrow face and raised dots for eyes **Rev. Legend:** Kuang-hsü Nien-tsao, TAI-CHING-TI-KUO...

Date	Mintage	VG8	F12	VF20	XF40	MS60
CD1906	Inc. above	0.50	1.50	4.00	10.00	120

Y# 10k.4 10 CASH

Copper **Obv:** Mint mark incuse on raised disc **Obv. Inscription:** Tai-ch'ing T'ung-pi **Rev:** Dragon **Rev. Legend:** Kuang-hsü Nien-tsao, TAI-CHING-TI-KUO...

Date	Mintage	VG8	F12	VF20	XF40	MS60
CD1906	Inc. above	7.00	19.00	37.50	90.00	—

Y# 10k.4a 10 CASH

Brass **Obv. Inscription:** Tai-ch'ing T'ung-pi **Rev:** Dragon **Rev. Legend:** Kuang-hsü Nien-tsao, TAI-CHING-TI-KUO...

Date	Mintage	VG8	F12	VF20	XF40	MS60
CD1906	—	—	—	—	—	—

Y# A140 10 CASH

Copper **Obv:** Y#10k.2 **Obv. Inscription:** Tai-ch'ing T'ung-Pi **Rev:** Dragon; Y#138 **Note:** Mule.

Date	Mintage	VG8	F12	VF20	XF40	MS60
CD1906	Inc. above	13.00	37.50	60.00	120	250

Y# B140 10 CASH

Copper **Obv:** Y#138 **Obv. Legend:** Chiang-nan Sheng Tsao **Obv. Inscription:** Kuang-hsü Yüan-pao **Rev:** Dragon; Y#10k **Note:** Mule.

Date	Mintage	VG8	F12	VF20	XF40	MS60
CD1906	Inc. above	15.00	45.00	75.00	140	—

Y# D140 10 CASH

Copper **Obv:** Y#138.1 **Obv. Legend:** Chiang-nan Sheng Tsao **Obv. Inscription:** Kuang-hsü Yüan-pao **Rev:** Dragon; Y#135 **Note:** Mule.

Date	Mintage	VG8	F12	VF20	XF40	MS60
CD1906	Inc. above	55.00	150	225	400	—

Note: Other Kiangnan mules exist, dated 1902 and 1903

Y# E140 10 CASH

Copper **Obv:** Y#10.5 **Obv. Inscription:** Tai-ch'ing T'ung-pi **Rev:** Dragon; Kiangnan Y#138.1 **Note:** Mule.

Date	Mintage	VG8	F12	VF20	XF40	MS60
CD1907	—	55.00	150	350	600	—

Y# 140.1 10 CASH

7.12 g., Copper, 28.6 mm. **Obv:** Y#10k **Obv. Inscription:** Tai-ch'ing T'ung-Pi **Rev:** Dragon; Y#138 **Note:** Mule; raised or incused mint mark.

Date	Mintage	VG8	F12	VF20	XF40	MS60
CD1906	Inc. above	1.50	5.00	8.00	24.00	140

Y# 140.2 10 CASH

Copper **Obv:** Y#10k **Obv. Inscription:** Tai-ch'ing T'ung-pi **Rev:** Dragon, Y#138 **Note:** Mule; mint mark incuse on raised disk.

Date	Mintage	VG8	F12	VF20	XF40	MS60
CD1906	Inc. above	1.50	5.00	8.00	24.00	140

Y# 10k.5 10 CASH

Copper **Obv:** Mint mark incuse on raised disc **Obv. Inscription:** Tai-ch'ing T'ung-pi **Rev:** Dragon with wide face; seven flames on pearl **Rev. Legend:** Kuang-hsü Nien-tsao, TAI-CHING-TI-KUO...

Date	Mintage	VG8	F12	VF20	XF40	MS60
CD1907	552,000,000	0.70	2.25	5.00	10.00	120

Y# 10k.6 10 CASH

Copper **Obv. Inscription:** Tai-ch'ing T'ung-pi **Rev:** Different dragon with narrow face and small mouth; five flames on pearl; dot after "COIN" **Rev. Legend:** Kuang-hsü Nien-tsao, TAI-CHING-TI-KUO...

Date	Mintage	VG8	F12	VF20	XF40	MS60
CD1907	Inc. above	0.50	1.50	3.00	9.00	120

Y# 10k.6a 10 CASH

Brass **Obv. Inscription:** Tai-ch'ing T'ung-pi **Rev:** Dragon **Rev. Legend:** Kuang-hsü Nien-tsao, TAI-CHING-TI-KUO...

Date	Mintage	VG8	F12	VF20	XF40	MS60
CD1907	Inc. above	5.00	14.00	27.50	60.00	—

Y# 10k.7 10 CASH

Copper **Obv. Inscription:** Tai-ch'ing T'ung-pi **Rev:** Dragon with large mouth and redesigned head; flame below pearl has long tail which touches dragon's body; "KUO" spelled "KIIO" **Rev. Legend:** Kuang-hsü Nien-tsao, TAI-CHING-TI-KUO...

Date	Mintage	VG8	F12	VF20	XF40	MS60
CD1907	Inc. above	0.50	1.50	4.00	10.00	120

Y# 10k.8 10 CASH

Copper **Obv. Inscription:** Tai-ch'ing T'ung-pi **Rev:** Tail of flame below pearl does not touch dragon's body; dash after word "COIN"; "KUO" spelled "KUO" **Rev. Legend:** Kuang-hsü Nien-tsao, TAI-CHING-TI-KUO...

Date	Mintage	VG8	F12	VF20	XF40	MS60
CD1907	Inc. above	0.50	1.50	4.00	10.00	120

Y# 10k.9 10 CASH

Copper **Obv. Inscription:** Tai-ch'ing T'ung-pi **Rev:** Dragon with square mouth; letter "K" in "KUO" larger than other letters; without dot or dash after "COIN" **Rev. Legend:** Kuang-hsü Nien-tsao, TAI-CHING-TI-KUO...

Date	Mintage	VG8	F12	VF20	XF40	MS60
CD1907	Inc. above	0.50	1.50	3.00	9.00	120

Y# 10k.9a 10 CASH

Copper **Obv. Inscription:** Tai-ch'ing T'ung-pi **Rev:** Large flat-faced dragon **Rev. Legend:** Kuang-hsü Nien-tsao, TAI-CHING-TI-KUO...

Date	Mintage	VG8	F12	VF20	XF40	MS60
CD1907	—	—	—	—	—	—

Y# 10k.10 10 CASH

Copper **Obv:** Mint mark incuse on raised disc **Obv. Inscription:** Tai-ch'ing T'ung-pi **Rev:** Dragon with small mouth; five-flame pearl; dot after "COIN"; "KUO" spelled "KUO" **Rev. Legend:** Kuang-hsü Nien-tsao, TAI-CHING-TI-KUO...

Date	Mintage	VG8	F12	VF20	XF40	MS60
CD1908	442,750,000	0.50	1.50	4.00	10.00	50.00

Y# 10k.12 10 CASH

Copper **Obv. Inscription:** Tai-ch'ing T'ung-pi **Rev:** Dragon; dash after "COIN"; "KUO" spelled "KUO" **Rev. Legend:** Kuang-hsü Nien-tsao, TAI-CHING-TI-KUO...

Date	Mintage	VG8	F12	VF20	XF40	MS60
CD1908	Inc. above	0.70	2.25	5.00	10.00	50.00

Y# 10k.13 10 CASH

Copper **Obv. Inscription:** Tai-ch'ing T'ung-pi **Rev:** Dragon's head redesigned; without dot or dash after "COIN"; "KUO" spelled "KIIO" **Rev. Legend:** Kuang-hsü Nien-tsao, TAI-CHING-TI-KUO...

Date	Mintage	VG8	F12	VF20	XF40	MS60
CD1908	Inc. above	0.50	1.50	3.00	8.00	40.00

Note: Most of the 1907 and 1908 ten cash above have copper spelled GOPPER

Y# 10k.14 10 CASH

Copper **Obv. Inscription:** Tai-ch'ing T'ung-pi **Rev:** Dragon's right mustache without hook **Rev. Legend:** TAI-GIIING-TI-KIIO GOPPER COIN

Date	Mintage	VG8	F12	VF20	XF40	MS60
CD1908	Inc. above	0.50	1.50	4.00	10.00	—

Y# 10k.15 10 CASH

Copper, 28.54 mm. **Obv. Inscription:** Tai-ch'ing T'ung-pi **Rev:** Dragon has large mouth and redesigned head; tail on cloud beneath pearl touches dragon's body. **Rev. Legend:** Kuang-hs? Nien-tsao, TAI-CHING-TI-KUO... **Edge:** Plain

Date	Mintage	VG8	F12	VF20	XF40	MS60
CD1908	Inc. above	0.50	1.50	3.00	8.00	40.00

Y# 141a 5 CENTS

13.00 g., 0.820 Silver 0.3427 oz. ASW **Obv. Legend:** Chiang-nan Sheng Tsao **Obv. Inscription:** Kuang-hsü Yüan-pao **Rev:** Without circle around dragon

Date	Mintage	VG8	F12	VF20	XF40	MS60
CD1901	—	75.00	175	375	1,100	1,800

Y# 142a.5 10 CENTS

2.60 g., 0.820 Silver 0.0685 oz. ASW **Obv:** Without initials **Obv. Legend:** Chiang-nan Sheng Tsao **Obv. Inscription:** Kuang-hsü Yüan-pao **Rev:** Large English letters

Date	Mintage	VG8	F12	VF20	XF40	MS60
CD1901	7,794,000	5.00	8.00	15.00	35.00	150

Y# 142a.6 10 CENTS

2.60 g., 0.820 Silver 0.0685 oz. ASW **Obv:** Without initials **Obv. Legend:** Chiang-nan Sheng Tsao **Obv. Inscription:** Kuang-hsü Yüan-pao **Rev:** Small English letters

Date	Mintage	VG8	F12	VF20	XF40	MS60
CD1901	Inc. above	5.00	8.00	15.00	35.00	150

Y# 142a.7 10 CENTS

2.60 g., 0.820 Silver 0.0685 oz. ASW **Obv:** Initials "HAH" **Obv. Legend:** Chiang-nan Sheng Tsao **Obv. Inscription:** Kuang-hsü Yüan-pao **Rev:** Large rosettes beside dragon

Date	Mintage	VG8	F12	VF20	XF40	MS60
CD1901	Inc. above	5.00	10.00	17.00	40.00	165

Y# 142a.8 10 CENTS

2.60 g., 0.820 Silver 0.0685 oz. ASW **Obv. Legend:** Chiang-nan Sheng Tsao **Obv. Inscription:** Kuang-hsü Yüan-pao **Rev:** Small rosettes beside dragon

Date	Mintage	VG8	F12	VF20	XF40	MS60
CD1901	Inc. above	5.00	10.00	17.00	40.00	165

Y# 142a.9 10 CENTS

2.60 g., 0.820 Silver 0.0685 oz. ASW **Obv. Legend:** Chiang-nan Sheng Tsao **Obv. Inscription:** Kuang-hsü Yüan-pao **Rev:** Large stars beside dragon

Date	Mintage	VG8	F12	VF20	XF40	MS60
CD1902	3,778,000	5.00	9.00	16.00	40.00	160

Y# 142a.10 10 CENTS

2.60 g., 0.820 Silver 0.0685 oz. ASW **Obv. Legend:** Chiang-nan Sheng Tsao **Obv. Inscription:** Kuang-hsü Yüan-pao **Rev:** Small stars beside dragon

Date	Mintage	VG8	F12	VF20	XF40	MS60
CD1902	Inc. above	6.00	12.00	20.00	45.00	215

Y# 142a.11 10 CENTS

2.60 g., 0.820 Silver 0.0685 oz. ASW **Obv:** Large rosette **Obv. Legend:** Chiang-nan Sheng Tsao **Obv. Inscription:** Kuang-hsü Yüan-pao

Date	Mintage	VG8	F12	VF20	XF40	MS60
CD1903	1,161,000	9.00	25.00	60.00	150	500

Y# 142a.12 10 CENTS

2.60 g., 0.820 Silver 0.0685 oz. ASW **Obv:** Small rosette **Obv. Legend:** Chiang-nan Sheng Tsao **Obv. Inscription:** Kuang-hsü Yüan-pao

Date	Mintage	VG8	F12	VF20	XF40	MS60
CD1903	Inc. above	9.00	25.00	60.00	150	500

Y# 142a.13 10 CENTS

2.60 g., 0.820 Silver 0.0685 oz. ASW **Obv:** Initials "HAH TH" **Obv. Legend:** Chiang-nan Sheng Tsao **Obv. Inscription:** Kuang-hsü Yüan-pao

Date	Mintage	VG8	F12	VF20	XF40	MS60
CD1904	897,000	7.00	12.00	25.00	75.00	625

Y# 142a.14 10 CENTS

2.60 g., 0.820 Silver 0.0685 oz. ASW **Obv:** Initials "SY" upside down **Obv. Legend:** Chiang-nan Sheng Tsao **Obv. Inscription:** Kuang-hsü Yüan-pao

Date	Mintage	VG8	F12	VF20	XF40	MS60
CD1905	681,000	8.00	14.00	40.00	95.00	500

Y# 142a.15 10 CENTS

2.60 g., 0.820 Silver 0.0685 oz. ASW **Obv:** Without SY initials

Date	Mintage	VG8	F12	VF20	XF40	MS60
CD-1905	Inc. above	5.00	10.00	20.00	65.00	500

Y# 143a.6 20 CENTS

5.30 g., 0.820 Silver 0.1397 oz. ASW **Obv:** Without initials **Obv. Legend:** Chiang-nan Sheng Tsao **Obv. Inscription:** Kuang-hsü Yüan-pao

Date	Mintage	VG8	F12	VF20	XF40	MS60
CD1901	47,114,000	8.00	13.00	20.00	50.00	250

Y# 143a.7 20 CENTS

5.30 g., 0.820 Silver 0.1397 oz. ASW **Obv:** Initials "HAH" **Obv. Legend:** Chiang-nan Sheng Tsao **Obv. Inscription:** Kuang-hsü Yüan-pao

Date	Mintage	VG8	F12	VF20	XF40	MS60
CD1901	Inc. above	6.00	10.00	15.00	45.00	375

Y# 143a.8 20 CENTS

5.30 g., 0.820 Silver 0.1397 oz. ASW **Obv. Legend:** Chiang-nan Sheng Tsao **Obv. Inscription:** Kuang-hsü Yüan-pao

Date	Mintage	VG8	F12	VF20	XF40	MS60
CD1902	15,754,000	6.00	10.00	15.00	45.00	375

Y# 143a.9 20 CENTS

5.30 g., 0.820 Silver 0.1397 oz. ASW **Obv:** Rosette in outer legend **Obv. Legend:** Chiang-nan Sheng Tsao **Obv. Inscription:** Kuang-hsü Yüan-pao

Date	Mintage	VG8	F12	VF20	XF40	MS60
CD1903	2,432,000	9.00	25.00	50.00	140	625

Y# 143a.10 20 CENTS

5.30 g., 0.820 Silver 0.1397 oz. ASW **Obv:** Without rosette **Obv. Legend:** Chiang-nan Sheng Tsao **Obv. Inscription:** Kuang-hsü Yüan-pao

Date	Mintage	VG8	F12	VF20	XF40	MS60
CD1903	Inc. above	20.00	40.00	100	250	1,000

Y# 143a.11 20 CENTS

5.30 g., 0.820 Silver 0.1397 oz. ASW **Obv:** Initials "HAH TH" **Obv. Legend:** Chiang-nan Sheng Tsao **Obv. Inscription:** Kuang-hsü Yüan-pao

Date	Mintage	VG8	F12	VF20	XF40	MS60
CD1904	1,172,000	10.00	30.00	70.00	150	750

Y# 143a.12 20 CENTS

5.30 g., 0.820 Silver 0.1397 oz. ASW **Obv:** Without initials **Obv. Legend:** Chiang-nan Sheng Tsao **Obv. Inscription:** Kuang-hsü Yüan-pao

Date	Mintage	VG8	F12	VF20	XF40	MS60
CD1905	828,000	8.00	25.00	60.00	125	200

Y# 143a.13 20 CENTS

5.30 g., 0.820 Silver 0.1397 oz. ASW **Obv:** Initials "SY" **Obv. Legend:** Chiang-nan Sheng Tsao **Obv. Inscription:** Kuang-hsü Yüan-pao

Date	Mintage	VG8	F12	VF20	XF40	MS60
CD1905	Inc. above	8.00	25.00	50.00	100	500

Y# 143a.14 20 CENTS

5.30 g., 0.820 Silver 0.1397 oz. ASW **Obv. Legend:** Chiang-nan Sheng Tsao **Obv. Inscription:** Kuang-hsü Yüan-pao **Rev. Legend:** ...MACI...

Date	Mintage	VG8	F12	VF20	XF40	MS60
CD1901	Inc. above	7.00	13.00	25.00	75.00	375

Y# 145a.5 DOLLAR

26.70 g., 0.900 Silver 0.7726 oz. ASW **Obv:** Without initials **Obv. Legend:** Chiang-nan Sheng Tsao **Obv. Inscription:** Kuang-hsü Yüan-pao **Note:** Kann#86.

Date	Mintage	VG8	F12	VF20	XF40	MS60
CD1901	2,377,000	150	450	600	1,250	6,300

Y# 145a.6 DOLLAR

26.70 g., 0.900 Silver 0.7726 oz. ASW **Obv:** Bold initials "HAH" without rosette **Obv. Legend:** Chiang-nan Sheng Tsao **Obv. Inscription:** Kuang-hsü Yüan-pao **Rev:** Petals of rosettes separated from each other

Date	Mintage	VG8	F12	VF20	XF40	MS60
CD1901	Inc. above	70.00	190	375	900	6,000

Y# 145a.7 DOLLAR

26.70 g., 0.900 Silver 0.7726 oz. ASW **Obv:** Initials "HAH" and rosette **Obv. Legend:** Chiang-nan Sheng Tsao **Obv. Inscription:** Kuang-hsü Yüan-pao **Rev:** Petals of rosettes run together

Date	Mintage	VG8	F12	VF20	XF40	MS60
CD1901	Inc. above	40.00	65.00	110	375	4,500

Y# 145a.21 DOLLAR

26.70 g., 0.900 Silver 0.7726 oz. ASW **Obv:** Fine initials "HAH" without rosette **Obv. Legend:** Chiang-nan Sheng Tsao **Obv. Inscription:** Kuang-hsü Yüan-pao **Rev:** Similar to Y#145a.6 **Note:** Kann#90.

Date	Mintage	VG8	F12	VF20	XF40	MS60
CD1901	Inc. above	65.00	190	375	750	3,750

Y# 145a.22 DOLLAR

26.70 g., 0.900 Silver 0.7726 oz. ASW **Obv:** Cross of six dots at upper right **Obv. Legend:** Chiang-nan Sheng Tsao **Obv. Inscription:** Kuang-hsü Yüan-pao **Rev:** Similar to Y#145a.6 **Note:** Kann#90b.

Date	Mintage	VG8	F12	VF20	XF40	MS60
CD1901	Inc. above	100	300	600	1,650	7,000

Y# 145a.8 DOLLAR

25.70 g., 0.900 Silver 0.7436 oz. ASW **Obv:** Small date, small "HAH" **Obv. Legend:** Chiang-nan Sheng Tsao **Obv. Inscription:** Kuang-hsü Yüan-pao **Rev:** Similar to Y#145a.4 **Note:** Kann#94.

Date	Mintage	VG8	F12	VF20	XF40	MS60
CD1902	3,562,000	44.00	70.00	150	450	3,000

Y# 145a.9 DOLLAR

27.00 g., 0.900 Silver 0.7813 oz. ASW **Obv:** Larger date, larger "HAH" **Obv. Legend:** Chiang-nan Sheng Tsao **Obv. Inscription:** Kuang-hsü Yüan-pao

Date	Mintage	VG8	F12	VF20	XF40	MS60
CD1902	Inc. above	44.00	70.00	150	450	3,000

Y# 145a.10 DOLLAR

26.90 g., 0.900 Silver 0.7784 oz. ASW **Obv:** "HAH" and rosettes in outer ring **Obv. Legend:** Chiang-nan Sheng Tsao **Obv. Inscription:** Kuang-hsü Yüan-pao **Note:** Kann#96.

Date	Mintage	VG8	F12	VF20	XF40	MS60
CD1903	1,489,000	50.00	120	250	825	6,000

Y# 145a.11 DOLLAR

27.00 g., 0.900 Silver 0.7813 oz. ASW **Obv:** Without rosette in outer ring **Obv. Legend:** Chiang-nan Sheng Tsao **Obv. Inscription:** Kuang-hsü Yüan-pao **Note:** Kann#96c.

Date	Mintage	VG8	F12	VF20	XF40	MS60
CD1903	Inc. above	500	1,400	2,000	4,500	18,000

Y# 145a.12 DOLLAR

26.70 g., 0.900 Silver 0.7726 oz. ASW **Obv:** Initials "HAH" and "CH" without dots or rosettes **Obv. Legend:** Chiang-nan Sheng Tsao **Obv. Inscription:** Kuang-hsü Yüan-pao **Rev:** Similar to Y#145a.4 **Note:** Kann#99.

Date	Mintage	VG8	F12	VF20	XF40	MS60
CD1904	44,725,000	50.00	80.00	130	300	2,000

Y# 145a.13 DOLLAR

27.00 g., 0.900 Silver 0.7813 oz. ASW **Obv:** Dot at either side **Obv. Legend:** Chiang-nan Sheng Tsao **Obv. Inscription:** Kuang-hsü Yüan-pao

Date	Mintage	VG8	F12	VF20	XF40	MS60
CD1904	Inc. above	50.00	80.00	130	350	2,150

Y# 145a.14 DOLLAR

27.00 g., 0.900 Silver 0.7813 oz. ASW **Obv. Inscription:** Kuang-hsü Yüan-pao **Rev:** Dot to left of numeral 7

Date	Mintage	VG8	F12	VF20	XF40	MS60
CD1904	Inc. above	50.00	80.00	130	350	2,250

Y# 145a.15 DOLLAR

27.00 g., 0.900 Silver 0.7813 oz. ASW **Obv:** Four-petalled rosette at either side "HAH" and "CH" **Obv. Legend:** Chiang-nan Sheng Tsao **Obv. Inscription:** Kuang-hsü Yüan-pao

Date	Mintage	VG8	F12	VF20	XF40	MS60
CD1904	Inc. above	80.00	150	400	975	2,700

Y# 145a.16 DOLLAR

27.00 g., 0.900 Silver 0.7813 oz. ASW **Obv:** Initials "HAH" and "TH" **Obv. Legend:** Chiang-nan Sheng Tsao **Obv. Inscription:** Kuang-hsü Yüan-pao

Date	Mintage	VG8	F12	VF20	XF40	MS60
CD1904	Inc. above	80.00	150	500	1,150	6,500

Y# 145a.19 DOLLAR

27.00 g., 0.900 Silver 0.7813 oz. ASW **Obv:** Dot at either side, without four central characters **Obv. Legend:** Chiang-nan Sheng Tsao **Obv. Inscription:** Kuang-hsü Yüan-pao

Date	Mintage	VG8	F12	VF20	XF40	MS60
CD1904	—	—	—	—	—	—

Y# 145a.17 DOLLAR

27.10 g., 0.900 Silver 0.7842 oz. ASW **Obv:** Initials "SY" **Obv. Legend:** Chiang-nan Sheng Tsao **Obv. Inscription:** Kuang-hsü Yüan-pao **Rev:** Similar to Y#145a.10

Date	Mintage	VG8	F12	VF20	XF40	MS60
CD1905	634,000	55.00	110	220	975	6,000

Hsüan-T'ung

Y# 146 10 CENTS

2.60 g., 0.820 Silver 0.0685 oz. ASW **Obv. Legend:** Chiang-nan Sheng Tsao **Obv. Inscription:** Hsüan-t'ung Yüan-pao **Rev:** Dragon

Date	Mintage	VG8	F12	VF20	XF40	MS60
ND(1911)	Est. 820000	9.00	30.00	60.00	165	750

Note: Includes 590,000 pieces struck in debased silver in 1916

Y# 147 20 CENTS

5.30 g., 0.820 Silver 0.1397 oz. ASW **Obv. Legend:** Chiang-nan Sheng Tsao **Obv. Inscription:** Hsüan-T'ung Yüan-pao **Rev:** Dragon

Date	Mintage	VG8	F12	VF20	XF40	MS60
ND(1911)	2,320,000	20.00	50.00	100	250	800

Note: Includes 2,005,000 pieces struck in debased silver in 1916

PATTERNS

Including off metal strikes

KM#	Date	Mintage	Identification	Mkt Val
Pn5	CD1906	—	2 Cash. Copper. Y#8k.	—
Pn6	CD1906	—	20 Cash. Copper. Y#11k.	—

KIANGSI PROVINCE

Jiangxi, Kiangsee

A province located in southeastern China. Mostly hilly with some mountains on the borders that produce coal and tungsten. Some of China's finest porcelain comes from this province. Kiangsi was visited by Marco Polo. A mint was opened in Nanchang in 1729, closed in 1733, reopened in 1736 and operated with reasonable continuity from that time. Modern machinery was introduced in 1901 although it only produced copper coins. The mint closed amidst internal problems in the 1920's.

EMPIRE

MILLED COINAGE

Horizontal rosette

Vertical rosette

Many Kiangsi (Jiangxi) coins have a six-petalled rosette in the center of the obverse, arranged so that two sides of the rosette are formed by two petals in line with each other. The remaining two sides have a single petal, standing out from the rest. The direction that these single petals point, determines whether the rosette is horizontal or vertical. A horizontal rosette has the single petals pointing left and right, while the single petals of the vertical rosette point up and down.

Y# 149 10 CASH
Copper **Obv:** Vertical rosette at center **Obv. Legend:** Chiang-hsi Sheng Tsao **Obv. Inscription:** Kuang-hsü Yüan-pao **Rev:** Province name spelled "KIANG-SEE"

Date	Mintage	VG8	F12	VF20	XF40	MS60
ND(1902)	—	8.00	15.00	22.50	60.00	150

Y# 149.1 10 CASH
Copper **Obv:** Horizontal rosette at center **Obv. Legend:** Chiang-hsi Sheng Tsao **Obv. Inscription:** Kuang-hsü Yüan-pao

Date	Mintage	VG8	F12	VF20	XF40	MS60
ND(1902)	—	8.00	15.00	22.50	60.00	—

Y# 149.2 10 CASH
Copper **Obv:** Different Manchu word at right **Obv. Legend:** Chiang-hsi Sheng Tsao **Obv. Inscription:** Kuang-hsü Yüan-pao **Rev:** Circled dragon **Note:** May be a pattern.

Date	Mintage	VG8	F12	VF20	XF40	MS60
ND(1902) Rare	—	—	—	—	—	—

Y# 150.1 10 CASH
Copper **Obv:** Manchu "Pao Ch'ang" at center and Chinese reading "Ku P'ing" at 3 and 9 o'clock **Obv. Legend:** Chiang-hsi Sheng Tsao **Obv. Inscription:** Kuang-hsü Yüan-pao

Date	Mintage	VG8	F12	VF20	XF40	MS60
ND(1902)	—	1.50	5.00	9.00	30.00	120

Y# 150.2 10 CASH
Copper **Obv:** Manchu "Pao Ch'ang" at 3 and 9 o'clock, horizontal rosette in center **Obv. Legend:** Chiang-hsi Sheng Tsao **Obv. Inscription:** Kuang-hsü Yüan-pao

Date	Mintage	VG8	F12	VF20	XF40	MS60
ND(1902)	—	0.50	1.50	3.00	12.00	120

Y# 150.2a 10 CASH
Brass **Obv. Legend:** Chiang-hsi Sheng Tsao **Obv. Inscription:** Kuang-hsü Yüan-pao

Date	Mintage	VG8	F12	VF20	XF40	MS60
ND(1902)	—	2.75	8.00	15.00	45.00	160

Y# 150.3 10 CASH
Copper **Obv:** Vertical rosette in center **Obv. Legend:** Chiang-hsi Sheng Tsao **Obv. Inscription:** Kuang-hsü Yüan-pao

Date	Mintage	VG8	F12	VF20	XF40	MS60
ND(1902)	—	0.50	1.50	3.00	12.00	120

Y# 150.4 10 CASH
Copper **Obv:** Horizontal rosette **Obv. Legend:** Chiang-hsi Sheng Tsao **Obv. Inscription:** Kuang-hsü Yüan-pao **Rev:** 1 star at either side of dragon, large English lettering

Date	Mintage	VG8	F12	VF20	XF40	MS60
ND(1902)	—	0.50	1.50	3.00	12.00	120

Y# 150.4a 10 CASH
Brass **Obv:** Horizontal rosette **Obv. Legend:** Chiang-hsi Sheng Tsao **Obv. Inscription:** Kuang-hsü Yüan-pao **Rev:** 1 star at either side of dragon, large English lettering

Date	Mintage	VG8	F12	VF20	XF40	MS60
ND(1902)	—	2.00	8.00	14.00	36.00	140

Y# 150.5 10 CASH
Copper **Obv:** Vertical rosette **Obv. Legend:** Chiang-hsi Sheng Tsao **Obv. Inscription:** Kuang-hsü Yüan-pao

Date	Mintage	VG8	F12	VF20	XF40	MS60
ND(1902)	—	0.50	1.50	3.00	12.00	120

Y# 150.6 10 CASH
Copper **Obv. Legend:** Chiang-hsi Sheng Tsao **Obv. Inscription:** Kuang-hsü Yüan-pao **Rev:** Smaller English lettering, 1 star at either side of dragon

Date	Mintage	VG8	F12	VF20	XF40	MS60
ND(1902)	—	0.50	1.50	3.00	12.00	120

Y# 150.7 10 CASH
Copper **Obv:** Small rosette center **Obv. Legend:** Chiang-hsi Sheng Tsao **Obv. Inscription:** Kuang-hsü Yüan-pao **Rev:** 1 star at either side of dragon

Date	Mintage	VG8	F12	VF20	XF40	MS60
ND(1902)	—	3.00	9.00	17.00	36.00	140

Y# 150.8 10 CASH
Copper **Obv. Legend:** Chiang-hsi Sheng Tsao **Obv. Inscription:** Kuang-hsü Yüan-pao **Rev:** 3 stars at either side of dragon

Date	Mintage	VG8	F12	VF20	XF40	MS60
ND(1902)	—	7.00	19.00	30.00	70.00	240

Y# 150 10 CASH
Copper **Obv:** Manchu "Pao Yuan" at 3 and 9 o'clock **Obv. Legend:** Chiang-hsi Sheng Tsao **Obv. Inscription:** Kuang-hsü Yüan-pao **Rev:** Province name spelled "KIANG-SI", 2 stars at either side of dragon

Date	Mintage	VG8	F12	VF20	XF40	MS60
ND(1902)	—	3.00	9.00	17.00	36.00	140

Y# 152.1 10 CASH
Copper **Obv:** Horizontal rosette in center, Manchu "Pao Ch'ang" at 3 and 9 o'clock **Obv. Legend:** Chiang-hsi Sheng Tsao **Obv. Inscription:** Kuang-hsü Yüan-pao

Date	Mintage	VG8	F12	VF20	XF40	MS60
ND(1902)	—	4.00	6.00	9.00	30.00	—

Y# 152.2 10 CASH
Copper **Obv:** Horizontal rosette in center, Manchu "Pao Ch'ang" at 3 and 9 o'clock, small character "10" **Obv. Legend:** Chiang-hsi Sheng Tsao **Obv. Inscription:** Kuang-hsü Yüan-pao

Date	Mintage	VG8	F12	VF20	XF40	MS60
ND(1902)	—	8.00	18.00	27.50	60.00	—

Y# 152.3 10 CASH
Copper **Obv:** Horizontal rosette in center, Manchu "Pao Ch'ang" at 3 and 9 o'clock, large character "10" **Obv. Legend:** Chiang-hsi Sheng Tsao **Obv. Inscription:** Kuang-hsü Yüan-pao **Rev:** Without mountain below dragon

Date	Mintage	VG8	F12	VF20	XF40	MS60
ND(1902)	—	5.00	12.00	18.00	40.00	—

Y# 152.4 10 CASH
Copper **Obv:** Horizontal rosette in center, small character "10" **Obv. Legend:** Chiang-hsi Sheng Tsao **Obv. Inscription:** Kuang-hsü Yüan-pao

Date	Mintage	VG8	F12	VF20	XF40	MS60
ND(1902)	—	5.00	12.00	18.00	40.00	—

Y# 152.5 10 CASH
Copper **Obv:** Manchu "Pao Ch'ang" in center, Chinese "K'u P'ing" at 3 and 9 o'clock **Obv. Legend:** Chiang-hsi Sheng Tsao **Obv. Inscription:** Kuang-hsü Yüan-pao **Rev:** Without mountain below pearl, dragon's body repositioned

Date	Mintage	VG8	F12	VF20	XF40	MS60
ND(1902)	—	5.00	13.00	19.00	40.00	—

Y# 152.6 10 CASH
Copper **Obv. Legend:** Chiang-hsi Sheng Tsao **Obv. Inscription:** Kuang-hsü Yüan-pao **Rev:** Mountain below dragon

Date	Mintage	VG8	F12	VF20	XF40	MS60
ND(1902)	—	5.00	11.00	17.00	36.00	—

Y# 152.7 10 CASH

Copper **Obv:** Vertical rosette in center **Obv. Legend:** Chiang-hsi Sheng Tsao **Obv. Inscription:** Kuang-hsü Yüan-pao

Date	Mintage	VG8	F12	VF20	XF40	MS60
ND(1902)	—	—	—	—	—	—

Y# 152 10 CASH

Copper **Obv:** Manchu "Pao Ch'ang" at 3 and 9 o'clock **Obv. Legend:** Chiang-hsi Sheng Tsao **Obv. Inscription:** Kuang-hsü Yüan-pao **Rev:** Province name spelled "KIANG-SI", front view dragon, mountain below pearl

Date	Mintage	VG8	F12	VF20	XF40	MS60
ND(1902)	—	4.00	4.00	9.00	30.00	—

Y# 153.1 10 CASH

Copper **Obv:** Manchu "Pao Ch'ang" at center and Chinese "K'u P'ing" at 3 and 9 o'clock **Obv. Legend:** Chiang-hsi Sheng Tsao **Obv. Inscription:** Kuang-hsü Yüan-pao **Note:** Found with and without a swirl on the pearl below dragon's mouth.

Date	Mintage	VG8	F12	VF20	XF40	MS60
ND(1902)	—	1.25	3.00	5.00	30.00	—

Y# 153.2 10 CASH

Copper **Obv:** Small Manchu "Pao Ch'ang" at 3 and 9 o'clock, small horizontal rosette in center **Obv. Legend:** Chiang-hsi Sheng Tsao **Obv. Inscription:** Kuang-hsü Yüan-pao **Note:** Found with and without a swirl on the pearl below dragon's mouth.

Date	Mintage	VG8	F12	VF20	XF40	MS60
ND(1902)	—	1.25	3.00	5.00	16.00	—

Y# 153.3 10 CASH

Copper **Obv:** Small vertical rosette in center **Obv. Legend:** Chiang-hsi Sheng Tsao **Obv. Inscription:** Kuang-hsü Yüan-pao **Note:** Found with and without a swirl on the pearl below dragon's mouth.

Date	Mintage	VG8	F12	VF20	XF40	MS60
ND(1902)	—	3.00	8.00	15.00	35.00	—

Y# 153 10 CASH

Copper **Obv. Legend:** Chiang-hsi Sheng Tsao **Obv. Inscription:** Kuang-hsü Yüan-pao **Rev:** Legend above front view dragon **Rev. Legend:** KIANG-SEE PROVINCE **Note:** Found with and without a swirl on the pearl below dragon's mouth.

Date	Mintage	VG8	F12	VF20	XF40	MS60
ND(1902)	—	3.00	7.00	11.00	30.00	—

Y# 154 10 CASH

Copper **Obv. Legend:** Chiang-hsi Sheng Tsao **Obv. Inscription:** Kuang-hsü Yüan-pao **Rev:** Legend above flying dragon **Rev. Legend:** KIANG SI

Date	Mintage	VG8	F12	VF20	XF40	MS60
ND(1902)	—	60.00	90.00	120	300	—

Y# 10m 10 CASH

Copper **Obv. Inscription:** Tai-ch'ing T'ung-pi **Rev:** Dragon's eyes in relief **Rev. Legend:** Kuang-hsü Nien-tsao, TAI-CHING-TI-KUO ...

Date	Mintage	VG8	F12	VF20	XF40	MS60
CD1906	—	2.00	5.00	9.00	30.00	—

Y# 10m.1 10 CASH

Copper **Obv. Inscription:** Tai-ch'ing T'ung-pi **Rev:** Dragon's eyes incuse **Rev. Legend:** Kuang-hsü Nien-tsao, TAI-CHING-TI-KUO ...

Date	Mintage	VG8	F12	VF20	XF40	MS60
CD1906	—	2.00	5.00	9.00	30.00	—

Y# 10m.2 10 CASH

Copper **Obv. Inscription:** Tai-ch'ing T'ung-pi **Rev:** Dragon redesigned, small faint cloud beneath pearl **Rev. Legend:** Kuang-hsü Nien-tsao, TAI-CHING-TI-KUO ...

Date	Mintage	VG8	F12	VF20	XF40	MS60
CD1906	—	8.00	18.00	27.50	70.00	—

REPUBLIC

Y# 412 10 CASH

5.90 g., Copper **Obv:** Date appears at 3 and 9 o'clock, value in 5 characters in legend **Obv. Legend:** Chiang-hsi Sheng-tsao **Rev:** 9-pointed star inside circle and 5-petalled rosette at 3 and 9 o'clock, value in 5 characters below

Date	Mintage	VG8	F12	VF20	XF40	MS60
CD1912	—	200	300	450	650	—

Y# 412a 10 CASH

6.70 g., Copper, 28.46 mm. **Obv:** Horizontal rosette in center with Chinese characters "Chiang Hsi" above and below; Value in 2 characters in legend **Obv. Legend:** Chung Hua Min Kuo **Rev:** 6-petalled rosette at either side, value in 2 characters below

Date	Mintage	VG8	F12	VF20	XF40	MS60
CD1912	—	2.00	5.00	9.00	20.00	—

Y# 412a.1 10 CASH

Copper **Obv:** Small, vertical rosette in center **Obv. Legend:** Chung Hua Min Kuo

Date	Mintage	VG8	F12	VF20	XF40	MS60
CD1912	—	2.00	5.00	9.00	20.00	—

Y# 412a.2 10 CASH

Copper **Obv:** Large, vertical rosette in center; thick, large-center characters **Obv. Legend:** Chung Hua Min Kuo **Rev:** Small, 5-petalled rosettes at either side

Date	Mintage	VG8	F12	VF20	XF40	MS60
CD1912	—	9.00	18.00	27.50	60.00	—

Y# 412a.3 10 CASH

Copper **Obv:** Large, vertical rosette in center; thin-center characters **Obv. Legend:** Chung Hua Min Kuo

Date	Mintage	VG8	F12	VF20	XF40	MS60
CD1912	—	2.00	5.00	9.00	24.00	—

REBEL COINAGE

Ta Han" was a rebel issue made before the revolution. Not only a symbol of defiance, this coin indicated secret membership. Ching law subjected those carrying these coins to execution.

Y# 411 10 CASH

Copper **Obv:** Mint mark incused on raised-disc center with Chinese characters on 4 sides, "Ta-Han T'ung-pi" character value in outer ring at bottom **Rev:** Ring of 9 balls without inscription

Date	Mintage	VG8	F12	VF20	XF40	MS60
CD1911 Rare	—	—	—	—	—	—

KIANGSU-CHINGKIANG, PROVINCE

PROVINCE

Kuang-hsü

MILLED COINAGE

Y# 77.1 10 CASH
Copper **Obv:** Large character at 3 o'clock **Obv. Inscription:** Kuang-hsü Yüan-pao **Rev. Legend:** * CHING * KIANG **Edge:** Plain **Mint:** Chingkiang

Date	Mintage	VG8	F12	VF20	XF40	MS60
ND(1905)	—	1.25	4.00	6.00	20.00	170

Y# 77.2 10 CASH
Copper **Obv:** Ring around center dot in rosette **Obv. Inscription:** Kuang-hsü Yüan-pao **Rev. Legend:** * CHING * KIANG **Edge:** Reeded **Mint:** Chingkiang

Date	Mintage	VG8	F12	VF20	XF40	MS60
ND(1905)	—	1.50	5.00	8.00	30.00	220

Y# 77.3 10 CASH
Copper **Obv:** Ring around center dot in rosette **Obv. Inscription:** Kuang-hsü Yüan-pao **Rev. Legend:** * CHING * KIANG **Edge:** Plain **Mint:** Chingkiang

Date	Mintage	VG8	F12	VF20	XF40	MS60
ND(1905)	—	5.00	14.00	18.00	40.00	250

Y# 77.4 10 CASH
Copper **Obv:** Smaller character at 3 o'clock **Obv. Inscription:** Kuang-hsü Yüan-pao **Rev. Legend:** * CHING * KIANG **Edge:** Reeded **Mint:** Chingkiang

Date	Mintage	VG8	F12	VF20	XF40	MS60
ND(1905)	—	2.00	5.00	9.00	32.00	225

Y# 77.5 10 CASH
Copper **Obv:** Smaller character at 3 o'clock **Obv. Inscription:** Kuang-hsü Yüan-pao **Rev. Legend:** * Ching * Kiang **Edge:** Plain **Mint:** Chingkiang

Date	Mintage	VG8	F12	VF20	XF40	MS60
ND(1905)	—	2.00	5.00	9.00	32.00	225

Y# 77.6 10 CASH
Copper **Obv:** Without rosette **Obv. Inscription:** Kuang-hsü Yüan-pao **Rev. Legend:** * CHING * KIANG **Edge:** Reeded **Mint:** Chingkiang

Date	Mintage	VG8	F12	VF20	XF40	MS60
ND(1905)	—	1.50	5.00	8.00	30.00	220

Y# 77.7 10 CASH
Copper **Obv:** Without rosette **Obv. Inscription:** Kuang-hsü Yüan-pao **Rev. Legend:** * CHING * KIANG **Edge:** Plain **Mint:** Chingkiang

Date	Mintage	VG8	F12	VF20	XF40	MS60
ND(1905)	—	2.75	8.00	10.00	32.00	225

Y# 77 10 CASH
Copper **Obv:** Large character at 3 o'clock **Obv. Inscription:** Kuang-hsü Yüan-pao **Rev. Legend:** * CHING * KIANG **Edge:** Reeded **Mint:** Chingkiang

Date	Mintage	VG8	F12	VF20	XF40	MS60
ND(1905)	—	1.25	4.00	6.00	20.00	180

Y# 78.1 10 CASH
Copper **Obv:** Large character at 3 o'clock **Obv. Inscription:** Kuang-hsü Yüan-pao **Rev. Legend:** TSING-KIANG **Edge:** Plain **Mint:** Chingkiang

Date	Mintage	VG8	F12	VF20	XF40	MS60
ND(1905)	—	1.50	5.00	8.00	30.00	220

Y# 78.2 10 CASH
Copper **Obv:** Small character at 3 o'clock **Obv. Inscription:** Kuang-hsü Yüan-pao **Rev. Legend:** TSING-KIANG **Edge:** Reeded **Mint:** Chingkiang

Date	Mintage	VG8	F12	VF20	XF40	MS60
ND(1905)	—	1.00	2.00	4.00	15.00	150

Y# 78.3 10 CASH
Copper **Obv:** Small character at 3 o'clock **Obv. Inscription:** Kuang-hsü Yüan-pao **Rev. Legend:** TSING-KIANG **Edge:** Plain **Mint:** Chingkiang

Date	Mintage	VG8	F12	VF20	XF40	MS60
ND(1905)	—	1.00	3.00	7.00	25.00	200

Y# 78.4 10 CASH
Copper **Obv:** Without rosette **Obv. Inscription:** Kuang-hsü Yüan-pao **Rev. Legend:** TSING-KIANG **Edge:** Reeded **Mint:** Chingkiang

Date	Mintage	VG8	F12	VF20	XF40	MS60
ND(1905)	—	2.00	5.00	9.00	35.00	235

Y# 78 10 CASH
Copper **Obv:** Large character at 3 o'clock **Obv. Inscription:** Kuang-hsü Yüan-pao **Rev. Legend:** TSING-KIANG **Edge:** Reeded **Mint:** Chingkiang

Date	Mintage	VG8	F12	VF20	XF40	MS60
ND(1905)	—	1.00	2.25	5.00	18.00	160

Y# 10d 10 CASH
Copper **Obv:** Small mint mark in center, without center raised disc **Obv. Inscription:** Tai-ch'ing T'ung-pi **Rev:** 5 flames on pearl **Rev. Legend:** Kuang-hsü Nien-tsao, TAI-CHING TI-KUO **Mint:** Chingkiang

Date	Mintage	VG8	F12	VF20	XF40	MS60
CD1906	—	13.00	37.50	75.00	250	—

Y# 10d.1 10 CASH
Copper **Obv:** Small mint mark **Obv. Inscription:** Tai-ch'ing T'ung-pi **Rev:** 7 flames on pearl **Rev. Legend:** Kuang-hsü Nien-tsao, TAI-CHING-TI-KUO **Mint:** Chingkiang

Date	Mintage	VG8	F12	VF20	XF40	MS60
CD1906	—	1.00	2.25	4.00	15.00	150

Y# 10d.2 10 CASH
Copper **Obv. Inscription:** Tai-ch'ing T'ung-pi **Rev:** 9 flames on pearl **Rev. Legend:** Kuang-hsü Nien-tsao, TAI-CHING - TI-KUO **Mint:** Chingkiang

Date	Mintage	VG8	F12	VF20	XF40	MS60
CD1906	—	1.00	2.00	3.00	15.00	150

Y# 10d.3 10 CASH
Copper **Obv:** Large mint mark **Obv. Inscription:** Tai-ch'ing T'ung-pi **Rev:** 5 flames on pearl **Rev. Legend:** Kuang-hsü Nien-tsao, TAI-CHING TI-KUO **Mint:** Chingkiang

Date	Mintage	VG8	F12	VF20	XF40	MS60
CD1906	—	1.00	2.25	4.00	15.00	150

Y# 10d.4 10 CASH
Copper **Obv. Inscription:** Tai-ch'ing T'ung-pi **Rev:** 7 flames on pearl **Rev. Legend:** Kuang-hsü Nien-tsao, TAI-CHING TI-KUO **Mint:** Chingkiang

Date	Mintage	VG8	F12	VF20	XF40	MS60
CD1906	—	1.00	2.25	4.00	15.00	150

Y# 10d.5 10 CASH
Copper **Obv. Inscription:** Tai-ch'ing T'ung-pi **Rev:** 9 flames on pearl **Rev. Legend:** Kuang-hsü Nien-tsao, TAI-CHING TI-KUO **Mint:** Chingkiang

Date	Mintage	VG8	F12	VF20	XF40	MS60
CD1906	—	1.00	2.25	4.00	15.00	150

Y# 10d.6 10 CASH
Copper **Obv:** Mint mark incused on raised disc **Obv. Inscription:** Tai-ch'ing T'ung-pi **Rev. Legend:** Kuang-hsü Nien-tsao, TAI-CHING TI-KUO... **Mint:** Chingkiang **Note:** Trial piece.

Date	Mintage	VG8	F12	VF20	XF40	MS60
CD1906	—	—	—	—	—	—

Note: 10 cash coins of Kiangsu (Jiangsu) and Chingkiang are often found plated with a silvery material. This was not done at the mint. Apparently they were plated so they could be passed to the unwary as silver coins.

KIANGSU-KIANGSOO PROVINCE

Jiangsu

A province located on the east coast of China. One of the smallest and most densely populated of all Chinese provinces. A mint opened in Soochow in 1667, but closed shortly after in 1670. A new mint opened in 1734 for producing cast coins and had continuous operation until about 1870. Modern equipment was introduced in 1898 and a second mint was opened in 1904. Both mints closed down production in 1906. Taels were produced in Shanghai by local silversmiths as early as 1856. These saw limited circulation in the immediate area.

EMPIRE

Kuang-hsü

PROVINCIAL CAST COINAGE

C# 16–12 CASH
Cast Brass **Obv. Inscription:** Kuang-hsü T'ung-pao **Rev:**

Manchu inscription **Rev. Inscription:** Boo-su **Mint:** Su

Date	Mintage	G4	VG8	F12	VF20	XF40
ND(1875-1908)	—	2.75	5.00	10.00	18.00	—

C# 16–12.1 CASH

Cast Brass **Obv. Inscription:** Kuang-hsü T'ung-pao **Rev:** Manchu inscription, circle above **Rev. Inscription:** Boo-su **Mint:** Su

Date	Mintage	G4	VG8	F12	VF20	XF40
ND(1875-1908)	—	4.00	7.00	13.00	22.50	—

C# 16–12.2 CASH

Cast Brass **Obv. Inscription:** Kuang-hsü T'ung-pao **Rev:** Manchu inscription, crescent above **Rev. Inscription:** Boo-su **Mint:** Su

Date	Mintage	G4	VG8	F12	VF20	XF40
ND(1875-1908)	—	4.00	7.00	13.00	22.50	—

MILLED COINAGE

Y# 158 5 CASH

Copper **Obv. Legend:** Chiang-hsü Sheng Tsao **Obv. Inscription:** Kuang-hsü Yüan-pao **Rev:** Side view dragon, "EIVE" for "FIVE"

Date	Mintage	VG8	F12	VF20	XF40	MS60
ND(1901)	—	18.00	48.75	85.00	200	—

Y# 9n 5 CASH

Brass **Obv. Inscription:** Tai-ching T'ung-pi **Rev. Legend:** Kuang-hsü Nien-tsao, TAI-CHING-TI-KUO ...

Date	Mintage	VG8	F12	VF20	XF40	MS60
CD-1906	—	37.50	115	190	400	—

Y# B162 10 CASH

Copper **Obv:** Kiangsu Y#162.8 **Obv. Legend:** Chiang-hsü Sheng Tsao **Obv. Inscription:** Kuang-hsü Yüan-pao **Rev:** Kiangnan Y#135 **Note:** Mule.

Date	Mintage	VG8	F12	VF20	XF40	MS60
CD-1902	—	90.00	270	450	3,000	—

Y# 162.1 10 CASH

Brass **Obv:** Manchu in center, rosettes at 2 and 10 o'clock **Obv. Legend:** Chiang-hsü Sheng Tsao **Obv. Inscription:** Kuang-hsü Yüan-pao

Date	Mintage	VG8	F12	VF20	XF40	MS60
ND(1902)	—	0.50	1.50	3.00	12.00	120

Y# 162.2 10 CASH

Brass **Obv. Legend:** Chiang-hsü Sheng Tsao **Obv. Inscription:** Kuang-hsü Yüan-pao **Edge:** Plain

Date	Mintage	VG8	F12	VF20	XF40	MS60
ND(1902)	—	0.50	1.50	3.00	14.00	130

Y# 162.3 10 CASH

Brass **Obv:** Tiny rosettes **Obv. Legend:** Chiang-hsü Sheng Tsao **Obv. Inscription:** Kuang-hsü Yüan-pao **Rev:** Tiny rosettes **Edge:** Reeded

Date	Mintage	VG8	F12	VF20	XF40	MS60
ND(1902)	—	0.70	2.00	4.00	14.00	130

Y# 162.4 10 CASH

Brass **Obv:** Rosette center, Manchu at 3 and 9 o'clock **Obv. Legend:** Chiang-hsü Sheng Tsao **Obv. Inscription:** Kuang-hsü Yüan-pao

Date	Mintage	VG8	F12	VF20	XF40	MS60
ND(1902)	—	0.50	1.50	3.00	14.00	130

Y# 162.5 10 CASH

Brass **Obv. Legend:** Chiang-hsü Sheng Tsao **Obv. Inscription:** Kuang-hsü Yüan-pao **Edge:** Plain

Date	Mintage	VG8	F12	VF20	XF40	MS60
ND(1902)	—	0.50	1.50	3.00	14.00	130

Y# 162 10 CASH

Brass **Obv:** Manchu words at center, without rosettes **Obv. Inscription:** Kuang-hsü Yüan-pao **Edge:** Reeded

Date	Mintage	VG8	F12	VF20	XF40	MS60
ND(1902)	—	2.00	6.00	9.00	30.00	140

Y# 162.6 10 CASH

Brass **Obv:** Rosette center, large Manchu at 3 and 9 o'clock, higher than on Y#162.4 **Obv. Legend:** Chiang-hsü Sheng Tsao **Obv. Inscription:** Kuang-hsü Yüan-pao **Edge:** Reeded

Date	Mintage	VG8	F12	VF20	XF40	MS60
ND(1902)	—	0.70	2.25	4.00	14.00	130

Y# 162.7 10 CASH

Copper **Obv. Legend:** Chiang-hsü Sheng Tsao **Obv. Inscription:** Kuang-hsü Yüan-pao **Edge:** Plain

Date	Mintage	VG8	F12	VF20	XF40	MS60
ND(1902)	—	0.70	2.25	4.00	14.00	130

Y# 162.7a 10 CASH

Brass **Obv. Legend:** Chiang-hsü Sheng Tsao **Obv. Inscription:** Kuang-hsü Yüan-pao

Date	Mintage	VG8	F12	VF20	XF40	MS60
ND(1902) Rare	—	—	—	—	—	—

Y# 162.8 10 CASH

Copper **Obv:** Manchu "Boo-su" at center **Obv. Legend:** Chiang-hsü Sheng Tsao **Obv. Inscription:** Kuang-hsü Yüan-pao **Edge:** Reeded

Date	Mintage	VG8	F12	VF20	XF40	MS60
CD-1902	—	1.00	3.00	6.00	16.00	135

Y# 162.13 10 CASH

Copper **Obv. Legend:** Chiang-hsü Sheng Tsao **Obv. Inscription:** Kuang-hsü Yüan-pao **Edge:** Plain

Date	Mintage	VG8	F12	VF20	XF40	MS60
CD-1902	—	—	—	—	—	—

Y# C162 10 CASH

Copper **Obv:** Kiangsu Y#162.9 **Obv. Legend:** Chiang-hsü Sheng Tsao **Obv. Inscription:** Kuang-hsü Yüan-pao **Rev:** Kiangnan Y#135 **Note:** Mule.

Date	Mintage	VG8	F12	VF20	XF40	MS60
CD-1903	—	90.00	270	450	3,000	—

Y# 162.9 10 CASH

Copper **Obv:** Manchu "Boo-su" at center **Obv. Legend:** Chiang-hsü Sheng Tsao **Obv. Inscription:** Kuang-hsü Yüan-pao **Edge:** Reeded

Date	Mintage	VG8	F12	VF20	XF40	MS60
CD-1903	—	2.75	8.00	11.00	30.00	180

Y# 160 10 CASH

Brass **Obv. Legend:** Chiang-hsü Sheng Tsao **Obv. Inscription:** Kuang-hsü Yüan-pao **Rev:** Cloud below all 3 letters of "SOO"

Date	Mintage	VG8	F12	VF20	XF40	MS60
ND(1904-05)	—	1.25	4.00	6.00	18.00	130

Y# 160.1 10 CASH

Brass **Obv. Legend:** Chiang-hsü Sheng Tsao **Obv. Inscription:** Kuang-hsü Yüan-pao **Rev:** Cloud below first 2 letters of "SOO", Manchu "Boo" at 9 o'clock higher, dragon's body thinner

Date	Mintage	VG8	F12	VF20	XF40	MS60
ND(1904-05)	—	1.25	4.00	6.00	18.00	130

Y# A162 10 CASH

Copper **Obv:** Kiangsu Y#162 **Obv. Legend:** Chiang-hsü Sheng Tsao **Obv. Inscription:** Kuang-hsü Yüan-pao **Rev:** Kiangnan Y#135 **Note:** Mule.

Date	Mintage	VG8	F12	VF20	XF40	MS60
ND(1905)	—	625	1,900	3,150	5,000	—

Y# 162.10 10 CASH

Copper **Obv:** Rosette center, small Manchu "Boo-su" at 3 and 9 o'clock **Obv. Legend:** Chiang-hsü Sheng Tsao **Obv. Inscription:** Kuang-hsü Yüan-pao **Edge:** Plain

Date	Mintage	VG8	F12	VF20	XF40	MS60
CD-1905	—	0.50	1.50	3.00	12.00	130

Y# 162.11 10 CASH

Copper **Obv:** Larger Manchu "Boo-su" **Obv. Legend:** Chiang-hsü Sheng Tsao **Obv. Inscription:** Kuang-hsü Yüan-pao

Date	Mintage	VG8	F12	VF20	XF40	MS60
CD1905	—	1.25	4.00	8.00	20.00	140

Y# 162.12 10 CASH
Copper **Obv. Legend:** Chiang-hsü Sheng Tsao **Obv. Inscription:** Kuang-hsü Yüan-pao **Rev:** Kiangsu spelled "KIANG-COO"

Date	Mintage	VG8	F12	VF20	XF40	MS60
CD1905	—	300	750	1,500	5,000	—

Note: Considered a contemporary counterfeit by some authorities

Y# 10n 10 CASH
Copper **Obv:** Mint mark incused on raised disc **Obv. Inscription:** Tai-ch'ing T'ung-pi **Rev. Legend:** Kuang-hsü Nien-tsao, TAI-CHING-TI-KUO ... **Edge:** Plain

Date	Mintage	VG8	F12	VF20	XF40	MS60
CD1906	—	0.85	2.50	5.00	15.00	90.00

Y# 10n.1 10 CASH
Copper **Obv:** Mint mark incused on raised disc **Obv. Inscription:** Tai-ch'ing T'ung-pi **Rev. Legend:** Kuang-hsü Nien-tsao, TAI-CHING-TI-KUO ... **Edge:** Reeded

Date	Mintage	VG8	F12	VF20	XF40	MS60
CD1906	—	3.00	9.00	17.00	40.00	200

Y# 10n.2 10 CASH
Copper **Obv:** Mint mark in relief in field at center without raised disc **Obv. Inscription:** Tai-ch'ing T'ung-pi **Rev. Legend:** Kuang-hsü Nien-tsao, TAI-CHING-TI-KUO ... **Edge:** Plain

Date	Mintage	VG8	F12	VF20	XF40	MS60
CD1906	—	3.00	9.00	17.00	40.00	200

Y# 163 20 CASH
Copper **Obv. Legend:** Chiang-hsü Sheng Tsao **Obv. Inscription:** Kuang-hsü Yüan-pao **Rev:** Dragon

Date	Mintage	F12	VF20	XF40	MS60	MS63
ND (1902)	—	60.00	90.00	200	750	2,000

Y# 163a 20 CASH
Brass **Obv. Legend:** Chiang-hsü Sheng Tsao **Obv. Inscription:** Kuang-hsü Yüan-pao **Rev:** Dragon

Date	Mintage	VG8	F12	VF20	XF40	MS60
ND(1902)	—	45.00	70.00	100	225	750

Y# 11n.1 20 CASH
Copper **Obv. Inscription:** Tai-ch'ing T'ung-pi **Rev. Legend:** Kuang-hsü Nien-tsao, TAI-CHING-TI-KUO ...

Date	Mintage	F12	VF20	XF40	MS60	MS63
CD1906	—	70.00	120	350	3,000	6,000

Y# 11n.1a 20 CASH
Brass **Obv. Inscription:** Tai-ch'ing T'ung-pi **Rev. Legend:** Kuang-hsü Nien-tsao, TAI-CHING-TI-KUO ...

Date	Mintage	VG8	F12	VF20	XF40	MS60
CD1906	—	75.00	150	350	2,000	—

PATTERNS

Including off metal strikes

KM#	Date	Mintage	Identification	Mkt Val
Pn2	ND-1901	—	2 Cash. Brass. Y159.	1,500
Pn3	CD1906	—	2 Cash. Brass. Y8n.	2,500
Pn4	ND-1906	—	5 Cash. Brass. EIVE for FIVE. Y161.1.	5,500
Pn5	ND-1906	—	5 Cash. Copper. EIVE for FIVE. Y161.1a.	6,500
Pn6	ND-1906	—	10 Cash. White Copper. Y162.5, W826.	65,000
Pn7	CD-1906	—	20 Cash. Copper. Character "Huai" in center. Y11d.	—

KIRIN PROVINCE

Jilin

A province of northeast China that was formed in 1945. Before that it was one of the three original provinces of Manchuria. Besides growing corn, wheat and tobacco, there is also coal mining. An arsenal in Kirin (Jilin) opened in 1881 and was chosen as a source for coinage attempts. In 1884 Tael trials were struck and regular coinage began in 1895. Modern equipment was installed in a new mint in Kirin (Jilin) in 1901. The issues of this mint were very prolific and many varieties exist due to the use of hand cut dies for the earlier issues. The mint burned down in 1911.

EMPIRE

Kuang-hsü

MILLED COINAGE

Errors in the English legends are very common in the Kirin coinage. It has been estimated there are over 2500 die varieties of Kirin (Jilin) silver coins and more than 1000 varieties of copper 10 Cash. Listed here are basic types and major varieties only.

Y# 175 2 CASH
Bronze **Obv. Inscription:** Kuang-hsü T'ung-pao **Mint:** Chi
Note: Mint mark: Manchu "Boo-gi".

Date	Mintage	VG8	F12	VF20	XF40	MS60
ND(1905)	—	120	180	240	500	—

Y# 174 10 CASH
Bronze **Obv. Inscription:** Kuang-hsü Yüan-pao **Mint:** Chi
Note: Mint mark: Manchu "Chi".

Date	Mintage	VG8	F12	VF20	XF40	MS60
ND(1901) Rare	—	—	—	—	—	—

Y# 176 10 CASH(ES)
Copper **Obv. Legend:** Chi-lin Sheng Tsao **Obv. Inscription:** Kuang-hsü Yüan-pao **Rev:** Dragon

Date	Mintage	VG8	F12	VF20	XF40	MS60
ND(1901)	—	55.00	90.00	135	290	—

Y# 176.1 10 CASH(ES)
Copper **Obv. Legend:** Chi-lin Sheng Tsao **Obv. Inscription:** Kuang-hsü Yüan-pao **Rev:** Thinner dragon

Date	Mintage	VG8	F12	VF20	XF40	MS60
ND(1901)	—	55.00	90.00	135	290	—

Y# 177 10 CASH(ES)
Copper **Obv:** Small rosettes **Obv. Legend:** Chi-lin Sheng Tsao **Obv. Inscription:** Kuang-hsü Yüan-pao **Rev:** Dragon; large rosettes

Date	Mintage	VG8	F12	VF20	XF40	MS60
ND(1903)	—	15.00	30.00	70.00	150	—

Y# 177.1 10 CASH(ES)
Copper **Obv. Legend:** Chi-lin Sheng Tsao **Obv. Inscription:** Kuang-hsü Yüan-pao **Rev:** Dragon; small stars

Date	Mintage	VG8	F12	VF20	XF40	MS60
ND(1903)	—	15.00	30.00	70.00	150	—

Y# 177.2 10 CASH(ES)
Copper **Obv:** Small stars **Obv. Legend:** Chi-lin Sheng Tsao **Obv. Inscription:** Kuang-hsü Yüan-pao **Rev:** Dragon; large rosettes

Date	Mintage	VG8	F12	VF20	XF40	MS60
ND(1903)	—	15.00	30.00	85.00	180	—

Y# 177.3 10 CASH(ES)
Copper **Obv:** Small stars **Obv. Legend:** Chi-lin Sheng Tsao **Obv. Inscription:** Kuang-hsü Yüan-pao **Rev:** Dragon; small stars

Date	Mintage	VG8	F12	VF20	XF40	MS60
ND(1903)	—	15.00	30.00	70.00	150	—

Y# 177.3a 10 CASH(ES)
Brass **Obv. Legend:** Chi-lin Sheng Tsao **Obv. Inscription:** Kuang-hsü Yüan-pao **Rev:** Dragon

Date	Mintage	VG8	F12	VF20	XF40	MS60
ND(1903)	—	15.00	30.00	85.00	180	—

Y# 177.4 10 CASH(ES)
Brass **Obv:** Large stars **Obv. Legend:** Chi-lin Sheng Tsao **Obv. Inscription:** Kuang-hsü Yüan-pao **Rev:** Dragon; large stars

Date	Mintage	VG8	F12	VF20	XF40	MS60
ND(1903)	—	12.00	20.00	55.00	110	—

Y# 177.5 10 CASH(ES)
Brass **Obv:** Large stars **Obv. Legend:** Chi-lin Sheng Tsao **Obv. Inscription:** Kuang-hsü Yüan-pao **Rev:** Dragon; large rosettes

Date	Mintage	VG8	F12	VF20	XF40	MS60
ND(1903)	—	12.00	20.00	55.00	110	—

Y# 177.6 10 CASH(ES)

Brass **Obv:** Medium rosettes **Obv. Legend:** Chi-lin Sheng Tsao **Obv. Inscription:** Kuang-hsü Yüan-pao **Rev:** Dragon

Date	Mintage	VG8	F12	VF20	XF40	MS60
ND(1903)	—	12.00	20.00	55.00	110	—

Y# 177.7 10 CASH(ES)

Brass **Obv. Legend:** Chi-lin Sheng Tsao **Obv. Inscription:** Kuang-hsü Yüan-pao **Rev:** Dragon; "CASHES" spelled "CASHIS"

Date	Mintage	VG8	F12	VF20	XF40	MS60
ND(1903)	—	90.00	150	240	500	—

Note: It is difficult to differentiate the stars and rosettes on worn coins; the rosettes have a raised dot in the center while the stars have a hole in the center; it has been estimated that 1000 varieties of Y#177 exist

Y# A176 20 CASH(ES)

Copper **Obv:** Manchu in center, eight characters below **Obv. Legend:** Chi-lin Sheng Tsao **Obv. Inscription:** Kuang-hsü Yüan-pao **Rev:** Dragon

Date	Mintage	VG8	F12	VF20	XF40	MS60
ND(1903)	—	120	300	600	1,400	—

Y# A176.1 20 CASH(ES)

Copper **Obv:** Rosette in center, three characters below **Obv. Legend:** Chi-lin Sheng Tsao **Obv. Inscription:** Kuang-hsü Yüan-pao **Rev:** Dragon

Date	Mintage	VG8	F12	VF20	XF40	MS60
ND(1903)	—	120	350	650	1,450	—

Y# 178 20 CASH(ES)

Copper **Obv. Legend:** Chi-lin Sheng Tsao **Obv. Inscription:** Kuang-hsü Yüan-pao **Rev:** Dragon

Date	Mintage	VG8	F12	VF20	XF40	MS60
ND(1903)	—	55.00	100	150	350	—

Y# 178.1 20 CASH(ES)

Copper **Obv. Inscription:** Kuang-hsü Yüan-pao **Rev:** Dragon, "CASHES" spelled "CASHIS"

Date	Mintage	VG8	F12	VF20	XF40	MS60
ND(1903)	—	55.00	100	150	350	—

Y# 21p 20 CASH(ES)

Copper **Obv. Inscription:** Tai-ch'ing T'ung-pi **Rev:** Dragon **Rev. Legend:** Hsüan-t'ung Nien-tsao, TAI-CHING-TI-KUO...

Date	Mintage	VG8	F12	VF20	XF40	MS60
CD1909	—	180	375	675	1,500	—

Y# E176 30 CASHES

Brass **Obv. Inscription:** Kuang-hsü Yüan-pao **Rev:** Side view dragon

Date	Mintage	VG8	F12	VF20	XF40	MS60
CD1901 Rare	—	—	—	—	—	—

Y# B176 50 CASHES

Brass **Obv:** Chi-lin Sheng Tsao **Obv. Inscription:** Kuang-hsü Yüan-pao **Rev:** Side view dragon

Date	Mintage	G4	VG8	F12	VF20	XF40
CD1901 3 known	—	—	—	—	—	—

Note: D.K.E. Ching Sale 6-91 VG-F realized $3,410; a similar 20 Cashes and silver 50 Cent have been reported and are believed to be fantasies by some authorities

Y# F176 100 CASHES

Brass **Obv. Inscription:** Kuang-hsü Yüan-pao **Rev:** Side view dragon

Date	Mintage	VG8	F12	VF20	XF40	MS60
CD1901	—	—	—	—	—	—

Y# C176 10 COPPERS

Brass **Obv. Inscription:** Kuang-hsü Yüan-pao **Rev:** Dragon **Note:** Similar to 50 Cashes, Y#B176

Date	Mintage	VG8	F12	VF20	XF40	MS60
CD1901	—	—	—	—	—	—

Y# 179.1 5 CENTS

1.27 g., Silver **Obv. Inscription:** Kuang-hsü Yüan-pao **Rev:** Side view dragon; without crosses flanking weight **Note:** Kann #394, 416, 549

Date	Mintage	VG8	F12	VF20	XF40	MS60
CD1906	—	7.00	17.00	47.00	110	650
CD1907	—	10.00	22.50	55.00	115	650
CD1908 Rare	—	—	—	—	—	—

Y# 179a 5 CENTS

1.27 g., Silver **Obv:** Yin-yang in center **Obv. Inscription:** Kuang-hsü Yüan-pao **Rev:** Side view dragon **Note:** Kann #444,465, 481, 510, 533.

Date	Mintage	VG8	F12	VF20	XF40	MS60
CD1901	—	7.00	14.00	43.00	110	600
CD1902	—	7.00	17.00	47.00	120	750
CD1903	—	14.00	33.00	95.00	215	1,300
CD1904	—	10.00	27.50	55.00	150	650
CD1905	—	10.00	19.00	55.00	130	600

Y# 180.1 10 CENTS

2.55 g., Silver **Obv:** Large flower vase center **Obv. Legend:** Chi-lin Sheng Tsao **Obv. Inscription:** Kuang-hsü Yüan-pao **Rev:** Side view dragon; without crosses flanking weight **Note:** Kann #393, 416, 546.

Date	Mintage	VG8	F12	VF20	XF40	MS60
CD1906	—	7.00	17.00	47.00	95.00	500
CD1907	—	55.00	130	350	750	2,350

Y# 180a 10 CENTS

2.55 g., Silver **Obv:** Yin-yang in center **Obv. Legend:** Chi-lin Sheng Tsao **Obv. Inscription:** Kuang-hsü Yüan-pao **Rev:** Side view dragon **Note:** Kann #440, 464, 484.

Date	Mintage	VG8	F12	VF20	XF40	MS60
CD1901	—	7.00	14.00	43.00	95.00	500
CD1902	—	7.00	19.00	55.00	130	600
CD1903	—	10.00	25.00	70.00	150	1,000
CD1904	—	40.75	90.00	215	550	2,550
CD1905	—	7.00	17.00	43.00	95.00	500

Y# 180c 10 CENTS

2.55 g., Silver **Obv:** Numeral 1 in center **Obv. Legend:** Chi-lin Tsao **Obv. Inscription:** Kuang-hsü Yüan-pao **Rev:** Side view dragon

Date	Mintage	VG8	F12	VF20	XF40	MS60
CD1908	—	65.00	180	425	650	1,800

Y# 181 20 CENTS

5.10 g., Silver **Obv:** Flower vase center **Obv. Legend:** Chi-lin Sheng Tsao **Obv. Inscription:** Kuang-hsü Yüan-pao **Rev:** Side view dragon

Date	Mintage	VG8	F12	VF20	XF40	MS60
CD1906	Inc. below	10.00	17.00	47.00	95.00	600
CD1907	Inc. below	10.00	17.00	47.00	95.00	600
CD1908	Inc. below	80.00	240	650	1,100	3,600

Y# 181a 20 CENTS

5.10 g., Silver **Obv:** Yin-yang in center **Obv. Legend:** Chi-lin Sheng Tsao **Obv. Inscription:** Kuang-hsü Yüan-pao **Rev:** Side view dragon

Date	Mintage	VG8	F12	VF20	XF40	MS60
CD1901	22,508,000	8.00	14.00	45.00	70.00	425
CD1902	Inc. above	8.00	14.00	45.00	70.00	425
CD1903	Inc. above	8.00	14.00	45.00	70.00	425
CD1904	Inc. above	8.00	14.00	45.00	70.00	425
CD1905	Inc. above	8.00	14.00	45.00	70.00	425

Y# 181b 20 CENTS

5.10 g., Silver **Obv:** Manchu words in center **Obv. Legend:** Chi-lin Tsao **Obv. Inscription:** Kuang-hsü Yüan-pao **Rev:** Side view dragon

Date	Mintage	VG8	F12	VF20	XF40	MS60
CD1908	Inc. above	38.00	110	290	425	1,450

Y# 181c 20 CENTS

5.10 g., Silver **Obv:** Numeral 2 center **Obv. Legend:** Chi-lin Tsao **Obv. Inscription:** Kuang-hsü Yüan-pao **Rev:** Side view dragon

Date	Mintage	VG8	F12	VF20	XF40	MS60
CD1908	Inc. above	18.00	55.00	145	240	1,050

Y# 182.3 50 CENTS

13.10 g., Silver **Obv. Legend:** Chi-lin Sheng Tsao **Obv. Inscription:** Kuang-hsü Yüan-pao **Rev:** Side view dragon

Date	Mintage	VG8	F12	VF20	XF40	MS60
CD1906	—	25.00	50.00	85.00	170	1,400
CD1907	—	25.00	50.00	85.00	170	1,400
CD1908	—	50.00	120	190	400	2,200

Y# 182a.1 50 CENTS

13.10 g., Silver **Obv:** Redesigned yin-yang in center **Obv. Legend:** Chi-lin Sheng Tsao **Obv. Inscription:** Kuang-hsü Yüan-pao **Rev:** Side view dragon

Date	Mintage	VG8	F12	VF20	XF40	MS60
CD1901	—	25.00	50.00	85.00	170	1,400
CD1902	—	25.00	50.00	85.00	170	1,400
CD1903	—	27.50	60.00	95.00	190	1,500
CD1904	—	25.00	50.00	85.00	170	1,400
CD1905	—	22.50	36.00	70.00	145	1,400

Y# 182b 50 CENTS

13.10 g., Silver **Obv:** Manchu words in center **Obv. Legend:** Chi-lin Tsao **Obv. Inscription:** Kuang-hsü Yüan-pao **Rev:** Side view dragon

Date	Mintage	VG8	F12	VF20	XF40	MS60
CD1908	—	600	1,200	4,500	12,500	27,500

Y# 183 DOLLAR

26.10 g., Silver **Obv:** Flower vase center **Obv. Legend:** Chi-lin Sheng Tsao **Obv. Inscription:** Kuang-hsü Yüan-pao **Rev:** Side view dragon; small rosettes before and after weight: "7 CANDARINS 2" or "7 CAINDARINS 2"

Date	Mintage	VG8	F12	VF20	XF40	MS60
CD1906	—	55.00	150	375	1,000	7,200
CD1907	—	180	500	800	2,100	13,000
CD1908	—	1,500	4,800	8,000	21,500	36,000

Y# 183a.1 DOLLAR

26.10 g., Silver **Obv:** Redesigned Yin-yang in center **Obv. Legend:** Chi-lin Sheng Tsao **Obv. Inscription:** Kuang-hsü Yüan-pao **Rev:** Coarse-scaled, beady-eyed dragon

Date	Mintage	VG8	F12	VF20	XF40	MS60
CD1901	—	65.00	200	425	1,000	7,000
CD1902	—	65.00	200	425	1,000	7,000

Y# 183a.2 DOLLAR

26.10 g., Silver **Obv. Legend:** Chi-lin Sheng Tsao **Obv. Inscription:** Kuang-hsü Yüan-pao **Rev:** Fine dot-scaled, beady-eyed dragon

Date	Mintage	VG8	F12	VF20	XF40	MS60
CD1902	—	55.00	150	425	1,000	7,000
CD1903	—	65.00	200	425	1,000	5,500
CD1904	—	65.00	200	425	950	5,200
CD1905	—	65.00	200	425	950	5,200

Y# 183.1 DOLLAR

26.10 g., Silver **Obv:** Large rosettes **Obv. Inscription:** Kuang-hsü Yüan-pao **Rev:** Side view dragon; without rosettes flanking weight

Date	Mintage	VG8	F12	VF20	XF40	MS60
ND(1905)	—	1,000	3,200	5,900	11,500	22,000

Y# 183a.3 DOLLAR

26.10 g., Silver **Obv. Legend:** Chi-lin Sheng Tsao **Obv. Inscription:** Kuang-hsü Yüan-pao **Rev:** Fine oval-scaled, round-eyed dragon

Date	Mintage	VG8	F12	VF20	XF40	MS60
CD1905	—	55.00	130	425	950	4,900

Y# 183.2 DOLLAR

26.10 g., Silver **Obv. Inscription:** Kuang-hsü Yüan-pao **Rev:** Side view dragon **Rev. Legend:** 3.2 CAINDARINS 2 (error)

Date	Mintage	VG8	F12	VF20	XF40	MS60
CD1906	—	400	950	1,300	2,750	6,000

Y# 183.3 DOLLAR

26.10 g., Silver **Obv:** Small rosettes **Obv. Inscription:** Kuang-hsü Yüan-pao **Rev:** Side view dragon; small rosettes before and after weight "7 CANDARINS 2"

Date	Mintage	VG8	F12	VF20	XF40	MS60
ND1906	—	200	425	650	1,400	5,500

Y# 183.4 DOLLAR

26.10 g., Silver **Obv:** Small leaves out of left basket **Obv. Legend:** Chi-lin Sheng Tsao **Obv. Inscription:** Kuang-hsü Yüan-pao **Rev:** Side view dragon; similar to Y#183.2

Date	Mintage	VG8	F12	VF20	XF40	MS60
ND1906	—	80.00	240	525	1,000	5,200

Y# 183b DOLLAR

26.10 g., Silver **Obv:** Manchu words in center **Obv. Legend:** Chi-lin Tsao **Obv. Inscription:** Kuang-hsü Yüan-pao **Rev:** Side view dragon

Date	Mintage	VG8	F12	VF20	XF40	MS60
CD1908	—	975	3,300	8,000	18,500	43,500

Y# 183c DOLLAR

26.10 g., Silver **Obv:** Numeral 11 in center **Obv. Legend:** Chi-lin Tsao **Obv. Inscription:** Kuang-hsü Yüan-pao **Rev:** Side view dragon

Date	Mintage	VG8	F12	VF20	XF40	MS60
CD1908	—	1,050	3,450	8,600	19,500	52,500

Note: The numeral 11 in center reflects the discount in subsidiary coinage; it took 11 dimes to equal the dollar

Hsüan-t'ung

Y# 20p 10 CASH(ES)

Copper **Obv:** Very small mint mark **Obv. Inscription:** Tai-ch'ing T'ung-pi **Rev. Legend:** Hsüan-t'ung Nien-tsao, TAI-CHING-TI-KUO...

Date	Mintage	VG8	F12	VF20	XF40	MS60
CD1909	—	25.00	45.00	75.00	180	—

Y# 20p.1 10 CASH(ES)

Copper **Obv:** Larger mint mark **Obv. Inscription:** Tai-ch'ing T'ung-pi **Rev:** Head of dragon, redesigned with more whiskers **Rev. Legend:** Hsüan-t'ung Nien-tsao, TAI-CHING-TI-KUO...

Date	Mintage	VG8	F12	VF20	XF40	MS60
CD1909	—	30.00	55.00	90.00	180	—

Y# 20p.2 10 CASH(ES)

Copper **Obv:** Larger mint mark **Obv. Inscription:** Tai-ch'ing

T'ung-pi **Rev:** Dragon similar to Y#20p **Rev. Legend:** Hsüan-t'ung Nien-tsao, TAI-CHING-TI-KUO...

Date	Mintage	VG8	F12	VF20	XF40	MS60
CD1909	—	30.00	55.00	90.00	180	—

Note: For Y#20x refer to General Issues-Empire

Y# 20p.3 10 CASH(ES)

Copper **Obv:** Y#20p **Obv. Inscription:** Tai-ch'ing T'ung-pi **Rev:** General Issue - Empire Y#20.1 **Rev. Legend:** Hsüan-t'ung Nien-tsao, TAI-CHING-TI-KUO... **Note:** Mule.

Date	Mintage	VG8	F12	VF20	XF40	MS60
CD1909 2 known	—	—	—	—	5,500	—

Note: Though dated 1909, minted at Mukden ca.1922

Y# 22 20 CENTS

5.10 g., Silver **Obv:** Mint mark in relief on raised disc at center **Obv. Legend:** Chi-lin Sheng Tsao **Obv. Inscription:** Hsüan-t'ung Yüan-pao **Rev:** Side view dragon

Date	Mintage	VG8	F12	VF20	XF40	MS60
ND(1909)	—	25.00	70.00	170	300	900

Y# 22.2 20 CENTS

5.10 g., Silver **Obv:** Mint mark in circle at center **Obv. Inscription:** Hsüan-t'ung Yüan-pao **Rev:** Side view dragon

Date	Mintage	VG8	F12	VF20	XF40	MS60
ND(1909)	—	25.00	70.00	170	300	900

PATTERNS

Including off metal strikes

KM#	Date	Mintage	Identification	Mkt Val
Pn10	CD1902	—	50 Cents. Brass. Y#182a.1.	—
Pn11	CD1908	—	20 Cents. Zinc. Y#181c.	—
Pn12	ND-1909	—	20 Cents. Silver. K#583, formerly Y#22.1.	—

KWANGSI-KWANGSEA, PROVINCE

Guangxi

A hilly region in southeast China with many forests. Large amounts of rice are grown adjacent to the many rivers. A mint opened in Kweilin in 1667, closed in 1670, reopened in 1679, closed again in 1681. It reopened in the mid-1700's and was a rather prolific issuer of Cash coins. In 1905 the government allowed modern mints to be established in Kwangsi (Guangxi) at Nanning (1905) and Kweilin (1905). The Nanning Mint began operation in 1919 and closed in 1923. In 1920 a new mint was opened at Wuchow and operated sporadically until 1929. In 1938 part of the Shanghai Central Mint was moved to Kweilin where it operated until at least 1945 and perhaps as late as 1949.

EMPIRE

Kuang-hsü

PROVINCIAL CAST COINAGE

C# 18–9 CASH

Cast Brass **Obv. Inscription:** Kuang-hsü T'ung-pao **Rev:** Manchu inscription **Rev. Inscription:** Boo-gui **Mint:** Kue

Date	Mintage	G4	VG8	F12	VF20	XF40
ND(1875-1908)	—	7.00	10.00	16.00	30.00	—

REPUBLIC

MILLED COINAGE

Y# 413 CENT

Brass **Obv. Legend:** KWANG-SEA PROVINCE

Date	Mintage	F12	VF20	XF40	MS60	MS63
8(1919)	—	225	375	800	2,750	5,000

Y# 413a CENT

Brass **Obv. Legend:** Chung Hua Min Kuo (year) Nien

Date	Mintage	VG8	F12	VF20	XF40	MS60
8(1919)	—	22.50	60.00	115	300	—

Y# A415 5 CENTS

Copper-Nickel **Obv. Legend:** Chung Hua Min Kuo (year) Nien **Rev:** Large "5" in sprays

Date	Mintage	VG8	F12	VF20	XF40	MS60
12(1923)	—	75.00	225	375	800	1,800

Y# 414 10 CENTS

2.70 g., Silver **Obv. Legend:** Chung Hua Min Kuo (year) Nien

Date	Mintage	VG8	F12	VF20	XF40	MS60
9(1920)	—	37.50	115	190	350	900

Y# 415 20 CENTS

5.30 g., Silver **Obv. Legend:** Chung Hua Min Kuo (year) Nien **Rev. Legend:** KWANG-SEA PROVINCE

Date	Mintage	F12	VF20	XF40	MS60	MS63
8(1919)	—	90.00	130	100	600	2,000
9(1920)	—	120	190	100	900	3,000

Y# 415a 20 CENTS

5.30 g., Silver **Obv. Legend:** Chung Hua Min Kuo (year) Nien **Rev. Legend:** KWANG-SI PROVINCE

Date	Mintage	F12	VF20	XF40	MS60	MS63
8(1919)	—	15.00	37.50	100	375	1,500
9(1920)	—	15.00	37.50	100	375	1,500
11(1922)	—	15.00	37.50	100	375	1,500
12(1923)	—	15.00	37.50	100	375	1,500
13(1924)	—	15.00	37.50	100	375	1,500
14(1925)	—	15.00	37.50	100	375	1,500

Y# 415a.1 20 CENTS

5.30 g., Silver **Obv:** Character "Kuei" in center instead of dot **Obv. Legend:** Chung Hua Min Kuo (year) Nien

Date	Mintage	VG8	F12	VF20	XF40	MS60
13(1924)	—	55.00	120	150	300	750

Y# 415b 20 CENTS

5.30 g., Silver **Obv:** Tiny character "Hsi" on dot center **Obv. Legend:** Chung Hua Min Kuo (year) Nien **Rev:** Wreath added around "20"

Date	Mintage	F12	VF20	XF40	MS60	MS63
15(1926)	—	8.00	11.00	25.00	50.00	175
15(1926)	—	8.00	11.00	25.00	50.00	175
Note: Without HSI						
16(1927)	—	8.00	11.00	25.00	50.00	175

Y# 416 20 CENTS

5.30 g., Silver **Obv. Legend:** Chung Hua Min Kuo (year) Nien **Rev:** Elephant nose rock at Kueilin

Date	Mintage	VG8	F12	VF20	XF40	MS60
38(1949)	—	60.00	150	265	500	1,150

PIEDFORT

KM#	Date	Mintage	Identification	Mkt Val
P1	10(1921)	—	10 Cents. Bronze. Y414c. KM#Pn5.	750
P2	10(1921)	—	10 Cents. Brass. Y414b. KM#Pn4.	450

PATTERNS

Including off metal strikes

KM#	Date	Mintage	Identification	Mkt Val
Pn1	ND-1905	—	10 Cash. Copper.	—
Pn2	CD1906	—	10 Cash. Copper.	—
Pn3	10(1921)	—	10 Cents. Copper. 2.11-2.22 grams. Y414a, K746-IIx.	2,500
Pn4	10(1921)	—	10 Cents. Brass. Y414b.	—
Pn5	10(1921)	—	10 Cents. Bronze. Y414c.	3,000
Pn6	10(1921)	—	10 Cents. Silver. Y414f.	—
Pn7	10(1921)	—	20 Cents. Copper. 4.68-4.97 grams. Y415c, K746-Ix.	2,500
Pn8	10(1921)	—	20 Cents. Bronze. Y415d.	—
Pn9	10(1921)	—	20 Cents. Brass. Y415e.	—
Pn10	10(1921)	—	20 Cents. Silver. Y415f.	15,000

KWANGTUNG PROVINCE

Guangdong

A province located on the southeast coast of China. Kwangtung (Guangdong) lies mostly in the tropics and has both mountains and plains. Its coastline is nearly 800 miles long and provides many good harbors. Because of the location of Guangzhou (Canton) in the province, Kwangtung (Guangdong) was the first to be visited by seaborne foreign traders. Hong Kong was ceded to Great Britain after the First Opium War in 1841. Kowloon was later ceded to Britain in 1860 and the New Territories (100 year lease) in 1898 and Macao to Portugal in 1887. Kwangchowwan was leased to France in 1898 (a property was restored in 1946). A modern mint opened in Guangzhou (Canton) in 1889 with Edward Wyon as superintendent. The mint was a large issuer of coins until it closed in 1931. The Nationalists reopened the mint briefly in 1949, striking a few silver dollars, before abandoning the mainland for their retreat to Taiwan.

The large island of Hainan was split off from Kwangtung (Guangdong) Province in 1988 and established as a separate province.

Hong Kong was returned to China by Britain on July 1, 1997 and established as a special administrative region, retaining its own coinage.

EMPIRE

MILLED COINAGE

Y# 204 CASH

Brass **Obv. Inscription:** Hsüan-t'ung T'uang pao **Rev:** Manchu inscription **Rev. Inscription:** Boo-guwang **Mint:** Kuang

Date	Mintage	VG8	F12	VF20	XF40	MS60
ND(1909-11)	—	0.40	1.00	2.00	4.00	65.00

Y# 206 DOLLAR
27.00 g., 0.900 Silver 0.7813 oz. ASW **Obv. Legend:** Kuang-tung Sheng Tsao **Obv. Inscription:** Hsüan-t'ung Yüan-pao **Rev:** Dragon

Date	Mintage	VG8	F12	VF20	XF40	MS60
ND(1909-11)	—	36.00	50.00	100	265	3,000

Kuang-hsü

PROVINCIAL CAST COINAGE

C# 19–7 CASH
Cast Brass **Obv. Inscription:** Kuang-hsü T'ung-pao **Rev:** Manchu inscription **Rev. Inscription:** Boo-guwang **Mint:** Kuang

Date	Mintage	G4	VG8	F12	VF20	XF40
ND(1875-1908)	—	14.00	28.00	40.00	60.00	—

MILLED COINAGE

Y# 190 CASH
2.70 g., Brass, 24 mm. **Obv:** "Kuang" in a different style **Obv. Inscription:** Kuang-hsü T'ung-pao **Rev:** Manchu inscription **Rev. Inscription:** Boo-guwang **Mint:** Kuang

Date	Mintage	VG8	F12	VF20	XF40	MS60
ND(1890-1908)	1,059,253,000	—	0.10	0.30	1.25	2.50

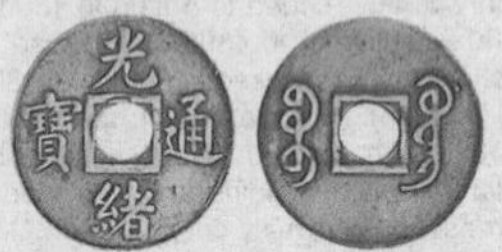

Y# 191 CASH
Brass **Obv. Inscription:** Kuang-hsü T'ung-pao **Rev:** Manchu inscription **Rev. Inscription:** Boo-guwang **Mint:** Kuang

Date	Mintage	VG8	F12	VF20	XF40	MS60
ND(1906-08)	—	—	0.20	0.50	2.00	40.00

Y# 192 CENT (10 Cash)
Copper **Obv. Legend:** Kuang-tung Sheng Tsao **Obv. Inscription:** Kuang-hsü Yüan-pao **Rev:** Dragon, ONE CENT

Date	Mintage	VG8	F12	VF20	XF40	MS60
ND(1900-06)	—	0.50	1.50	3.00	6.00	90.00

Y# 193 CENT (10 Cash)
7.52 g., Copper, 27.8 mm. **Obv. Legend:** Kuang-tung Sheng Tsao **Obv. Inscription:** Kuang-hsü Yüan-pao **Rev:** Dragon, TEN CASH

Date	Mintage	F12	VF20	XF40	MS60	MS63
ND(1900-06)	—	2.00	4.00	8.00	30.00	100

Note: Varieties in lettering exist, including spacing of characters.

Y# 10r CENT (10 Cash)
6.50 g., Copper, 28.1 mm. **Obv. Inscription:** Tai-ch'ing T'ung-pi **Rev:** Dragon **Rev. Legend:** Kuang-hsü Nien-tsao, TAI-CHING-TI KUO ...

Date	Mintage	VG8	F12	VF20	XF40	MS60
CD1906	79,000,000	0.70	2.00	4.00	12.00	175
CD1907	46,000,000	0.70	2.00	4.00	12.00	175
CD1908	62,736,000	0.70	2.00	4.00	12.00	175

Y# A193 CENT (10 Cash)
Copper **Obv:** Y#192 **Obv. Legend:** Kuang-tung Sheng Tsao **Obv. Inscription:** Kuang-hsü Yuan-pao **Rev:** Y#193, dragon, "TEN CASH" **Note:** Mule.

Date	Mintage	VG8	F12	VF20	XF40	MS60
ND(1906)	—	13.00	40.00	55.00	80.00	250

Y# B193 CENT (10 Cash)
Copper **Obv:** Y#193 **Obv. Legend:** Kuang-tung Sheng Tsao **Obv. Inscription:** Kuang-hsü Yuan-pao **Rev:** Y#192, dragon **Note:** Mule.

Date	Mintage	VG8	F12	VF20	XF40	MS60
ND(1906)	—	13.00	40.00	55.00	80.00	250

KM# B192 CENT
Copper **Obv. Legend:** Kuang-hsü Yüan-pao **Obv. Inscription:** Kuang-hsü Yüan-pao **Note:** Prev. W#896.

Date	Mintage	VG8	F12	VF20	XF40	MS60
ND-1906	—	45.00	130	200	300	575

Y# 199 5 CENTS
1.30 g., 0.820 Silver 0.0343 oz. ASW **Obv. Legend:** Kuang-tung Sheng Tsao **Obv. Inscription:** Kuang-hsü Yüan-pao **Rev:** English legend around dragon

Date	Mintage	F12	VF20	XF40	MS60	MS63
ND(1890-1905)	—	12.00	25.00	85.00	375	850

Y# 200 10 CENTS
2.70 g., 0.820 Silver 0.0712 oz. ASW **Obv. Legend:** Kuang-tung Sheng Tsao **Obv. Inscription:** Kuang-hsü Yüan-pao **Rev:** English legends around dragon **Mint:** Kuang

Date	Mintage	F12	VF20	XF40	MS60	MS63
ND(1890-1908)	—	10.00	20.00	50.00	275	375

Y# 201 20 CENTS
5.50 g., 0.800 Silver 0.1415 oz. ASW **Obv. Legend:** Kuang-tung Sheng Tsao **Obv. Inscription:** Kuang-hsü Yüan-pao **Rev:** Dragon

Date	Mintage	F12	VF20	XF40	MS60	MS63
ND(1890-1908)	—	10.00	15.00	35.00	100	250
ND(1890-1908) Proof, 10 known	—	PF60 3,000				

Y# 202 50 CENTS
13.50 g., 0.860 Silver 0.3733 oz. ASW **Obv. Legend:** Kuang-tung Sheng Tsao **Obv. Inscription:** Kuang-hsü Yüan-pao **Rev:** English legends around dragon

Date	Mintage	VG8	F12	VF20	XF40	MS60
ND(1890-1905)	—	37.50	55.00	105	375	1,250
ND(1890-1905)	—	PF60 2,000				

Y# 203 DOLLAR
27.00 g., 0.900 Silver 0.7813 oz. ASW **Obv. Legend:** Kuang-tung Sheng Tsao **Obv. Inscription:** Kuang-hsü Yüan-pao **Rev:** English legends around dragon

Date	Mintage	VG8	F12	VF20	XF40	MS60
ND(1890-1908)	—	37.50	70.00	125	285	1,450
ND(1890-1908)	—	PF60 5,000				

Hsuan-T'ung

Y# 20r 10 CASH
Copper **Obv. Inscription:** Tai-ch'ing T'ung-pi **Rev:** Dragon **Rev. Legend:** Hsüan-t'ung Nien-tsao, TAI-CHING-TI KUO ...

Date	Mintage	VG8	F12	VF20	XF40	MS60
CD1909	—	1.00	3.00	6.00	14.00	200

Y# 205 20 CENTS
5.50 g., 0.800 Silver 0.1415 oz. ASW **Obv. Inscription:** Hsüan-t'ung Yüan-pao **Rev:** Dragon **Note:** Two varieties of edge reeding known.

Date	Mintage	VG8	F12	VF20	XF40	MS60
ND(1909-11)	94,774,000	7.00	11.00	15.00	25.00	75.00

REPUBLIC

Y# 417 CENT
Bronze **Obv. Legend:** Chung Hua Min Kuo (year) Nien **Rev. Legend:** KWANG-TUNG PROVINCE

Date	Mintage	VG8	F12	VF20	XF40	MS60
1(1912)	18,836,000	1.00	3.00	5.00	16.00	65.00
3(1914)	14,750,000	1.00	3.00	5.00	16.00	65.00
4(1915)	6,350,000	3.00	9.00	14.00	45.00	110
5(1916)	18,388,000	1.50	5.00	8.00	22.50	90.00
7(1918)	—	6.00	17.00	27.50	60.00	140

Y# 417a CENT

Brass **Obv. Legend:** Chung Hua Min Kuo (year) Nien **Rev. Legend:** KWANG-TUNG PROVINCE

Date	Mintage	VG8	F12	VF20	XF40	MS60
1(1912)	Inc. above	—	—	—	—	—
3(1914)	Inc. above	1.50	5.00	12.00	30.00	75.00
4(1915)	Inc. above	2.25	8.00	17.00	45.00	95.00
5(1916)	Inc. above	1.00	3.00	8.00	18.00	60.00

Y# 418 2 CENTS

Brass **Obv. Legend:** Chung Hua Min Kuo (year) Nien **Rev. Legend:** KWANG-TUNG PROVINCE

Date	Mintage	VG8	F12	VF20	XF40	MS60
7(1918)	—	15.00	45.00	75.00	180	350

Y# 418a 2 CENTS

Copper **Obv. Legend:** Chung Hua Min Kuo (year) Nien **Rev. Legend:** KWANG-TUNG PROVINCE

Date	Mintage	VG8	F12	VF20	XF40	MS60
7(1918) Rare	—	—	—	—	—	—

Y# 420 5 CENTS

Copper-Nickel **Obv. Legend:** Chung Hua Min Kuo (year) Nien **Rev:** Large "5" in sprays **Rev. Legend:** KWANG-TUNG PROVINCE

Date	Mintage	VG8	F12	VF20	XF40	MS60
8(1919)	916,000	1.00	2.00	4.00	6.00	10.00

Y# 421 5 CENTS

Copper-Nickel **Obv. Legend:** Chung Hua Min Kuo (year) Nien **Rev:** Flag **Rev. Legend:** KWANG-TUNG PROVINCE

Date	Mintage	VG8	F12	VF20	XF40	MS60
10(1921)	666,000	0.70	2.00	5.00	13.00	25.00

Y# 420a 5 CENTS

Copper-Nickel **Obv. Legend:** Chung Hua Min Kuo (year) Nien **Rev:** Large "5" in sprays **Rev. Legend:** KWANG-TUNG PROVINCE

Date	Mintage	F12	VF20	XF40	MS60	MS63
12(1923)	480,000	1.50	3.00	5.00	12.00	—

Y# 422 10 CENTS

2.70 g., Silver **Obv. Legend:** Chung Hua Min Kuo (year) Nien **Rev:** Large "10" **Rev. Legend:** KWANG-TUNG PROVINCE

Date	Mintage	VG8	F12	VF20	XF40	MS60
2(1913)	8,798,000	6.00	8.00	12.00	16.00	30.00
3(1914)	Inc. above	6.00	10.00	14.00	18.00	36.00
11(1922)	—	6.00	12.00	22.50	30.00	75.00

Y# 425 10 CENTS

2.50 g., Silver **Obv. Legend:** Chung Hua Min Kuo (year) Nien **Rev:** Bust of Sun Yat-sen **Rev. Legend:** KWANG-TUNG PROVINCE

Date	Mintage	VG8	F12	VF20	XF40	MS60
18(1929)	48,960,000	5.00	8.00	12.00	16.00	28.00

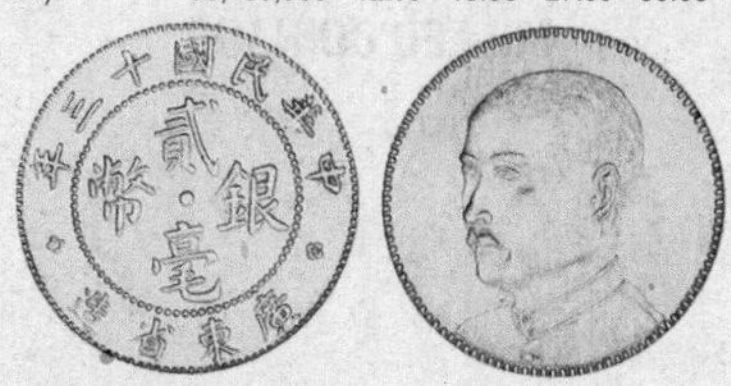

Y# 423 20 CENTS

5.40 g., Silver **Obv. Legend:** Chung Hua Min Kuo (year) Nien **Rev. Legend:** KWANG-TUNG PROVINCE **Note:** The fineness of many of these 20-cent pieces, especially those dated Yr. 13 (1924), is as low as .500. In 1924 the Anhwei (Anhui) Mint secretly produced quantities of Kwangtung (Guangdong) 20-cent pieces that were only .400 fine. Standard issues were struck with a small dot in the center, 2 small rosettes at 4 and 8 o'clock; varieties exist with a large dot and large rosettes.

Date	Mintage	VG8	F12	VF20	XF40	MS60
1(1912)	88,000,000	10.00	12.00	16.00	25.00	50.00
2(1913)	109,974,000	10.00	12.00	16.00	25.00	50.00
3(1914)	41,691,000	10.00	12.00	16.00	25.00	50.00
4(1915)	22,332,000	12.00	25.00	50.00	100	400
7(1918)	—	10.00	12.00	16.00	25.00	40.00
8(1919)	195,000,000	8.00	12.00	16.00	18.00	28.00
9(1920)	197,000,000	8.00	12.00	16.00	18.00	28.00
10(1921)	402,250,000	8.00	12.00	16.00	18.00	28.00
11(1922)	350,000,000	8.00	12.00	16.00	18.00	28.00
12(1923)	4,400,000	12.00	16.00	22.50	34.00	75.00
13(1924)	55,109,000	12.00	18.00	27.50	50.00	100

Y# 424 20 CENTS

5.30 g., Silver **Obv. Legend:** Chung Hua Min Kuo (year) Nien **Rev:** Bust of Sun Yat-sen **Rev. Legend:** KWANG-TUNG PROVINCE

Date	Mintage	VG8	F12	VF20	XF40	MS60
13(1924)	—	45.00	110	170	300	700

Y# 426 20 CENTS

5.30 g., Silver **Obv:** Value in sprays **Obv. Legend:** Chung Hua Min Kuo (year) Nien **Rev:** Bust of Sun Yat-sen **Rev. Legend:** KWANG-TUNG PROVINCE

Date	Mintage	VG8	F12	VF20	XF40	MS60
17(1928)	28,530,000	45.00	110	210	375	800
18(1929)	779,738,000	10.00	16.00	25.00	30.00	50.00
19(1930) 1 known	—	—	—	—	—	10,500

PATTERNS

Including off metal strikes

KM#	Date	Mintage	Identification	Mkt Val
Pn16	ND(ca. 1902)	—	1/2 Cent. Copper. Circled "flying" dragon.	—
Pn17	ND-1904	—	Tael. Silver. K932.	—
			Note: Superior Goodman sale 6-91 proof realized $41,800.	
Pn18	ND-1904	—	Tael. White Metal. K932y.	—
PnA18	ND-1904	—	Tael. Pewter. 6mm thick. K932x.	—
PnA19	ND-1906	—	20 Cash. Copper. TCTK.	—
Pn19	3(1914)	—	10 Cents. Copper. Y422.	—
PnA20	4(1915)	—	Cent. Red Copper. Y417.	—
PnB20	5(1916)	—	Cent. Red Copper. Y417.	—
PnC20	7(1918)	—	Cent. Red Copper. Y417.	—
Pn20	8(1919)	—	20 Cents. Copper. Y423.	300
Pn21	9(1920)	—	20 Cents. Copper. Y423.	300
Pn22	10(1921)	—	20 Cents. Copper. Y423.	300
PnA23	11(1922)	—	20 Cents. Copper. Y423.	300
Pn23	13(1924)	—	20 Cents. Gold. Y424.	5,000
Pn24	17(1928)	—	20 Cents. Copper. Y426.	—
Pn25	18(1929)	—	20 Cents. Copper. Y426.	—
Pn26	ND-1929	—	20 Cents. Gold. Y426.	5,000
Pn27	25(1936)	—	Cent. Bronze. Sun Yat Sen.	6,000
Pn28	25(1936)	—	Cent. Copper.	1,400

KWEICHOW PROVINCE

Guizhou

A province located in southern China. It is basically a plateau region that is somewhat remote from the general traffic of China. The Kweichow Mint opened in 1730 and produced Cash coins until the end of the reign of Kuang Hsu. The Republic issues for this province are enigmatic as to their origin, as a mint supposedly did not exist in Kweichow (Guizhou) at this time.

EMPIRE

Kuang-hsü

PROVINCIAL CAST COINAGE

C# 20–9 CASH

Cast Brass **Obv. Inscription:** Kuang-hsü T'ung-pao **Rev:** Manchu inscription **Rev. Inscription:** Boo-jiyan **Mint:** Kuei

Date	Mintage	G4	VG8	F12	VF20	XF40
ND(1875-1908)	—	5.00	9.00	13.00	20.00	—

C# 20–9.1 CASH

Cast Brass **Obv. Inscription:** Kuang-hsü T'ung-pao **Rev:** Manchu inscription **Rev. Inscription:** Boo-jiyan **Mint:** Kuei

Date	Mintage	G4	VG8	F12	VF20	XF40
ND(1875-1908)	—	6.00	11.00	15.00	22.50	—

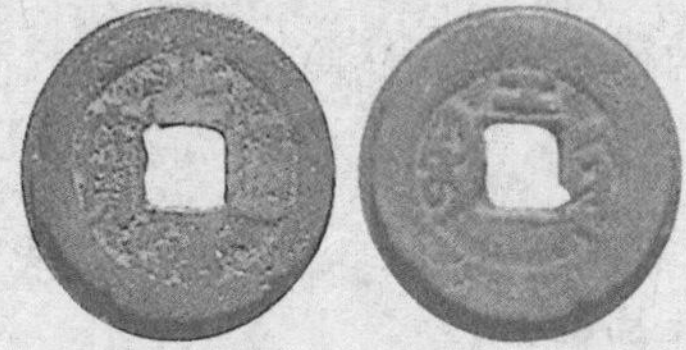

C# 20–9.2 CASH

Cast Brass **Obv. Inscription:** Kuang-hsü T'ung-pao **Rev:** Chinese "Kung" above **Rev. Inscription:** Boo-jiyan **Mint:** Kuei

Date	Mintage	G4	VG8	F12	VF20	XF40
ND(1875-1905)	—	10.00	14.00	20.00	35.00	—

REPUBLIC

MILLED COINAGE

Y# A429 1/2 CENT

Copper **Obv. Legend:** Chung Hua Min Kuo (year) Nien

Date	Mintage	VG8	F12	VF20	XF40	MS60
38(1949)	—	450	750	800	—	—

Y# A429a 1/2 CENT

Brass **Obv. Legend:** Chung Hua Min Kuo (year) Nien

Date	Mintage	VG8	F12	VF20	XF40	MS60
38(1949)	—	300	450	—	—	—

Y# A429a.2 1/2 CENT

Brass **Obv:** Narrow, thick characters **Obv. Legend:** Chung Hua Min Kuo (year) Nien

Date	Mintage	VG8	F12	VF20	XF40	MS60
38(1949)	—	450	650	—	—	—

Y# 429 10 CENTS

Antimony **Obv. Legend:** Chung Hua Min Kuo (year) Nien

Date	Mintage	VG8	F12	VF20	XF40	MS60
20(1931)	—	250	450	650	1,000	—

Y# 430 20 CENTS

Silver **Obv. Legend:** Chung Hua Min Kuo (year) Nien

Date	Mintage	VG8	F12	VF20	XF40	MS60
38(1949)	—	60.00	150	300	550	1,750

Y# 431 20 CENTS

Silver **Obv. Legend:** Chung Hua Min Kuo (year) Nien

Date	Mintage	VG8	F12	VF20	XF40	MS60
38(1949)	—	—	—	—	6,500	9,500

Y# 432 50 CENTS

Silver **Obv. Legend:** Chung Hua Min Kuo (year) Nien

Date	Mintage	VG8	F12	VF20	XF40	MS60
38(1949)	—	—	—	5,500	12,500	17,500

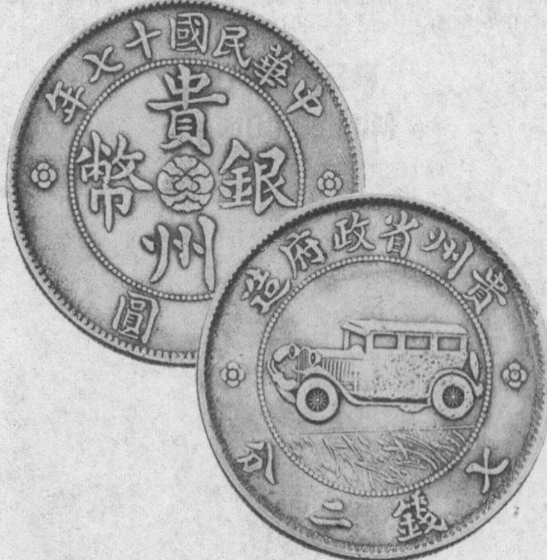

Y# 428 DOLLAR

25.80 g., Silver, 39 mm. **Subject:** First Road in Kweichow **Obv. Legend:** Chung Hua Min Kuo (year) Nien

Date	Mintage	VG8	F12	VF20	XF40	MS60
17(1928)	648,000	500	800	2,500	6,500	17,500

Note: This coin is known as the "Auto Dollar" as it purports to portray the governor's automobile; minor varieties exist in Chinese legends and various automobile designs

Y# 433 DOLLAR

26.40 g., Silver **Obv:** Round window in pavilion **Obv. Legend:** Chung Hua Min Kuo (year) Nien **Rev:** Bamboo

Date	Mintage	VG8	F12	VF20	XF40	MS60
38(1949)	—	600	1,250	3,000	8,500	28,000

Note: This coin is known as the "Bamboo Dollar".

Y# 433a DOLLAR

26.40 g., Silver **Obv:** Square window in pavilion **Obv. Legend:** Chung Hua Min Kuo (year) Nien **Note:** Many conterfeits exist.

Date	Mintage	VG8	F12	VF20	XF40	MS60
38(1949) Rare	—	650	1,300	3,250	9,500	30,000

Note: This coin is known as the "Bamboo Dollar".

MANCHURIAN PROVINCES

Since the 17th century, Manchuria has been divided into three provinces. The two northern provinces were called Heilungkiang and Kirin. Together the three provinces of Manchuria were known as the Manchurian Provinces in English or the Three Eastern Provinces in Chinese. Since the communist takeover in 1949, western Mongol-populated areas of Manchuria have been included in the Inner Mongolia Autonomous Region.

EMPIRE

Kuang-Hsü

MILLED COINAGE

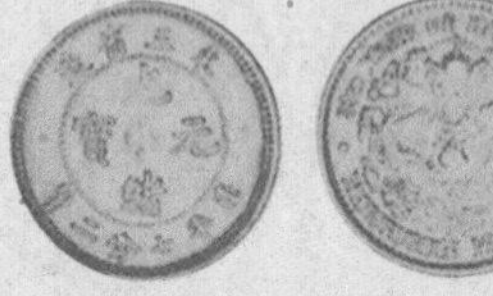

Y# 209 10 CENTS

2.60 g., 0.890 Silver 0.0744 oz. ASW **Obv. Legend:** Tung-san Sheng Tsao **Obv. Inscription:** Kuang-hsü Yüan-pao **Rev:** Legend at bottom **Rev. Legend:** MANCHURIAN PROVINCES

Date	Mintage	VG8	F12	VF20	XF40	MS60
33(1907)	1,079,000	5.00	15.00	37.50	60.00	240

Y# 210 20 CENTS

5.20 g., 0.890 Silver 0.1488 oz. ASW **Obv:** One dot at either side **Obv. Legend:** Tung-san Sheng Tsao **Obv. Inscription:** Kuang-hsü Yüan-pao **Rev:** Legend at bottom **Rev. Legend:** MANCHURIAN PROVINCES

Date	Mintage	VG8	F12	VF20	XF40	MS60
33(1907)	—	13.00	40.00	60.00	180	350

Y# 210a.1 20 CENTS

5.20 g., 0.890 Silver 0.1488 oz. ASW **Obv:** Three rosettes at either side **Obv. Legend:** Tung-san Sheng Tsao **Obv. Inscription:** Kuang-hsü Yüan-pao **Rev:** Legend at bottom **Rev. Legend:** MANCHURIAN PROVINCES

Date	Mintage	VG8	F12	VF20	XF40	MS60
33(1908)	249,219,000	10.00	18.00	35.00	110	210

Y# 210a.2 20 CENTS

5.20 g., 0.890 Silver 0.1488 oz. ASW **Obv:** One rosette at either side **Obv. Legend:** Tung-san Sheng Tsao **Obv. Inscription:** Kuang-hsü Yüan-pao **Rev:** Legend at bottom **Rev. Legend:** MANCHURIAN PROVINCES

Date	Mintage	VG8	F12	VF20	XF40	MS60
33(1908)	Inc. above	8.00	14.00	25.00	60.00	180

Y# 211 50 CENTS

13.10 g., 0.890 Silver 0.3748 oz. ASW **Obv. Legend:** Tung-san Sheng Tsao **Obv. Inscription:** Kuang-Hsü Yüan-pao **Rev:** Legend at bottom **Rev. Legend:** MANCHURIAN PROVINCES

Date	Mintage	VG8	F12	VF20	XF40	MS60
33(1907)	—	130	350	750	2,000	6,000

Y# 212 DOLLAR

26.40 g., 0.890 Silver 0.7554 oz. ASW **Obv. Legend:** Tung-san Sheng Tsao **Obv. Inscription:** Kuang-Hsü Yüan-pao **Rev:** Legend at bottom **Rev. Legend:** MANCHURIAN PROVINCES

Date	Mintage	F12	VF20	XF40	MS60	MS63
33(1907)	—	800	1,750	4,000	15,000	25,000

Hsüan-t'ung

Y# 213.2 20 CENTS

5.20 g., 0.890 Silver 0.1488 oz. ASW **Obv:** One large-petaled rosette at either side **Obv. Legend:** Tung-san Sheng Tsao **Obv. Inscription:** Hsüan-t'ung Yüan-pao **Rev:** Legend at bottom; date as 1ST YEAR **Rev. Legend:** MANCHURIAN PROVINCES

Date	Mintage	VG8	F12	VF20	XF40	MS60
1(1909)	Inc. above	6.00	10.00	20.00	60.00	140

Y# 213 20 CENTS

5.20 g., 0.890 Silver 0.1488 oz. ASW **Obv:** Two small stars flanking one large star at either side **Obv. Legend:** Tung-san Sheng Tsao **Obv. Inscription:** Hsüan-t'ung Yüan-pao **Rev:** Legend at bottom; date given as FIRST YEAR **Rev. Legend:** MANCHURIAN PROVINCES

Date	Mintage	VG8	F12	VF20	XF40	MS60
1(1910)	Inc. above	6.00	10.00	18.00	55.00	115

Y# 213.1 20 CENTS

5.20 g., 0.890 Silver 0.1488 oz. ASW **Obv:** One small star at either side **Obv. Legend:** Tung-san Sheng Tsao **Obv. Inscription:** Hsüan-t'ung Yüan-pao **Rev:** Legend at bottom **Rev. Legend:** MANCHURIAN PROVINCES

Date	Mintage	VG8	F12	VF20	XF40	MS60
1(1910)	Inc. above	6.00	10.00	20.00	60.00	130

Y# 213.3 20 CENTS
5.20 g., 0.890 Silver 0.1488 oz. ASW **Obv:** One large star between two dots **Obv. Legend:** Tung-san Sheng Tsao **Obv. Inscription:** Hsüan-t'ung Yüan-pao **Rev:** Legend at bottom **Rev. Legend:** MANCHURIAN PROVINCES

Date	Mintage	VG8	F12	VF20	XF40	MS60
1(1910)	Inc. above	6.00	10.00	20.00	60.00	130

Y# 213a 20 CENTS
5.20 g., 0.890 Silver 0.1488 oz. ASW **Obv:** Manchu "Boo-fu" at center **Obv. Legend:** Tung-san Sheng Tsao **Obv. Inscription:** Hsüan-t'ung Yüan-pao **Rev:** Error in legend **Rev. Legend:** MANCHURIAN PROVIENCES

Date	Mintage	VG8	F12	VF20	XF40	MS60
ND(1911)	Inc. above	6.00	10.00	18.00	55.00	120

Y# 213a.6 20 CENTS
5.20 g., 0.890 Silver 0.1488 oz. ASW **Obv:** Without Manchu "Boo-fu" at center **Obv. Legend:** Tung-san Sheng Tsao **Obv. Inscription:** Hsüan-t'ung Yüan-pao **Rev:** Error in legend **Rev. Legend:** MANCHURIAN PROVIENCES

Date	Mintage	VG8	F12	VF20	XF40	MS60
ND(1912)	Inc. above	7.00	12.00	20.00	60.00	140

Y# 213a.4 20 CENTS
5.20 g., 0.700 Silver 0.117 oz. ASW **Obv:** Without Manchu "Boo-fu" at center **Obv. Legend:** Tung-san Sheng Tsao **Obv. Inscription:** Hsüan-t'ung Yüan-pao **Rev:** Legend at top **Rev. Legend:** MANCHURIAN PROVINCES

Date	Mintage	VG8	F12	VF20	XF40	MS60
ND(1913)	Inc. above	6.00	10.00	20.00	60.00	140

Y# 213a.1 20 CENTS
5.20 g., 0.700 Silver 0.117 oz. ASW **Obv:** 5-petaled rosette in center with dot in center of rosette; dot below side rosettes **Obv. Legend:** Tung-san Sheng Tsao **Obv. Inscription:** Hsüan-t'ung Yüan-pao **Rev:** Legend at top **Rev. Legend:** MANCHURIAN PROVINCES

Date	Mintage	VG8	F12	VF20	XF40	MS60
ND(1914-15)	Inc. above	6.00	9.00	17.00	55.00	110

Y# 213a.2 20 CENTS
5.20 g., 0.700 Silver 0.117 oz. ASW **Obv:** With dot below side rosettes **Obv. Legend:** Tung-san Sheng Tsao **Obv. Inscription:** Hsüan-t'ung Yüan-pao **Rev:** Legend at top **Rev. Legend:** MANCHURIAN PROVINCES

Date	Mintage	VG8	F12	VF20	XF40	MS60
ND(1914-15)	Inc. above	6.00	9.00	17.00	55.00	110

Y# 213a.3 20 CENTS
5.20 g., 0.700 Silver 0.117 oz. ASW **Obv:** Without dot in center of 5-petaled rosette **Obv. Inscription:** Hsüan-t'ung Yüan-pao **Rev:** Legend at top **Rev. Legend:** MANCHURIAN PROVINCES

Date	Mintage	VG8	F12	VF20	XF40	MS60
ND(ca.1914-15)	Inc. above	6.00	9.00	17.00	55.00	110

REPUBLIC

Y# 434 CENT
Copper **Obv. Legend:** Chung Hua Min Kuo... **Rev:** Sunburst in floral sprays

Date	Mintage	F12	VF20	XF40	MS60	MS63
18(1929)	—	4.00	6.00	10.00	50.00	175

Y# 434a CENT
Brass **Obv. Legend:** Chung Hua Min Kuo... **Rev:** Sunburst in floral sprays

Date	Mintage	VG8	F12	VF20	XF40	MS60
18(1929)	—	—	—	—	—	—

PATTERNS

Including off metal strikes

KM#	Date	Mintage	Identification	Mkt Val
Pn1	18(1929)	—	Dollar. Silver.	—
Note: Superior Goodman sale 6-91 choice AU realized, $22,000.				
Pn2	18(1929)	—	Fen. Copper. Y#434 with formal Chinese "One Fen.	—

SHANSI PROVINCE

Shanxi

A province located in northeastern China that has some of the richest coal deposits in the world. Parts of the Great Wall cross the province. Extensive agriculture of early China started here. Cited as a "model province" in the new Chinese Republic. Intermittently active mints from 1645. The modern mint was established in 1919. It operated until the mid-1920's and closed because of the public's resistance against the coins that were being produced.

EMPIRE

Kuang-hsü

PROVINCIAL CAST COINAGE

C# 21–8 CASH
Cast Brass **Obv:** Manchu inscription **Obv. Inscription:** Kuang-hsü T'ung-pao **Rev. Inscription:** Boo-Jin **Mint:** Chin

Date	Mintage	G4	VG8	F12	VF20	XF40
ND(1875-1908)	—	7.00	13.00	19.00	38.00	—

REPUBLIC

MILLED COINAGE

Y# A435 10 CASH (1 Cent)
Copper **Obv:** Crossed flags **Obv. Legend:** Chung Hua Min Kuo **Rev:** Value in wheat sprays **Mint:** (no Mint Information)

Date	Mintage	VG8	F12	VF20	XF40	MS60
ND(1912)	—	350	950	1,750	3,000	—

Hsuan-Tung

Y# 217 20 CENTS
4.80 g., Silver **Obv. Legend:** Shan-hsi Sheng Tsao **Obv. Inscription:** Hsuan-t'ung Yuan-pao **Rev:** Side view dragon **Mint:** (no Mint Information)

Date	Mintage	VG8	F12	VF20	XF40	MS60
ND(1911)	—	1,000	2,000	3,500	5,000	—

Note: Several varieties exist similar to Y#217, but struck more crudely in base metal and with different Chinese legends at the top of the obverse. English legends are usually blundered. These were struck about 1913 and thought to be warlord issues. Do not confuse these with coins of Fengtien (Liaoning), from which this was copied.

PATTERNS

Including off metal strikes

KM#	Date	Mintage	Identification	Mkt Val
Pn2	14(1925)	—	5 Cents. Nickel. K823.	—

SHANTUNG PROVINCE

Shandong

A province located on the northeastern coast of China. Confucius was born in this province. Parts of the province were leased to Great Britain and to Germany. Farming, fishing and mining are the chief occupations. A mint was opened at Tsinan in 1647 and was an intermittent producer for the empire. A modern mint was opened at Tsinan in 1905, but closed in 1906. Patterns were prepared between 1926-1933 in anticipation of a new coinage, but none were struck for circulation.

EMPIRE

Kuang-hsü

PROVINCIAL CAST COINAGE

C# 22–6 CASH
Cast Brass **Obv. Inscription:** Kuang-hsü T'ung-pao **Rev:** Type 1 mint mark **Rev. Inscription:** Boo-ji **Mint:** Chi

Date	Mintage	G4	VG8	F12	VF20	XF40
ND(1875-1908)	—	15.00	28.00	42.00	60.00	—

Note: Refer to Tungch'uan, Yünnan Province, for 1 cash C#27 series coins previously listed here

MILLED COINAGE

Y# 8a 2 CASH
Copper **Obv. Inscription:** Kuang-hsü T'ung-pao **Rev:** Dragon

Date	Mintage	VG8	F12	VF20	XF40	MS60
CD1906	—	18.00	37.50	55.00	140	—

Y# 220 10 CASH
Copper **Obv. Inscription:** Kuang-hsü Yüan-pao **Rev:** Side view dragon

Date	Mintage	VG8	F12	VF20	XF40	MS60
ND(1904-05)	—	12.00	22.50	45.00	95.00	200

Y# 221.1 10 CASH
Copper **Obv:** Thick Manchu in center, flying dragon **Obv. Legend:** Shen-tung Sheng Tsao **Obv. Inscription:** Kuang-hsü Yüan-pao

Date	Mintage	VG8	F12	VF20	XF40	MS60
ND(1904-05)	—	2.25	5.00	15.00	80.00	160

Y# 221 10 CASH
Copper **Obv:** Thin Manchu words in center, flying dragon **Obv. Legend:** Shen-tung Sheng Tsao **Obv. Inscription:** Kuang-hsü Yüan-pao **Rev:** SHANTUNG

Date	Mintage	VG8	F12	VF20	XF40	MS60
ND(1904-05)	—	4.00	11.00	22.50	90.00	180

Y# 221.2 10 CASH
Copper **Obv:** Smaller stars, flying dragon **Obv. Legend:** Shen-tung Sheng Tsao **Obv. Inscription:** Kuang-hsü Yüan-pao

Date	Mintage	VG8	F12	VF20	XF40	MS60
ND(1904-05)	—	2.25	5.00	15.00	80.00	160

Y# 221.3 10 CASH
Copper **Obv:** Similar to Y#220, flying dragon **Obv. Legend:** Shen-tung Sheng Tsao **Obv. Inscription:** Kuang-hsü Yüan-pao **Rev:** Similar to Y#221

Date	Mintage	VG8	F12	VF20	XF40	MS60
ND(1904-05)	—	95.00	190	300	600	—

Y# 221a.1 10 CASH
Copper **Obv:** Thin Manchu in center, flying dragon **Obv. Legend:** Shen-tung Sheng Tsao **Obv. Inscription:** Kuang-hsü Yüan-pao

Date	Mintage	VG8	F12	VF20	XF40	MS60
ND(1904-05)	—	3.00	8.00	18.00	60.00	120

Y# 221a 10 CASH
Copper **Obv:** Thick Manchu in center, flying dragon **Obv. Legend:** Shen-tung Sheng Tsao **Obv. Inscription:** Kuang-hsü Yüan-pao **Rev:** SHANG-TUNG

Date	Mintage	VG8	F12	VF20	XF40	MS60
ND(1904-05)	—	1.50	4.00	9.00	60.00	120

Y# 10s 10 CASH
Brass **Obv. Inscription:** Tai-ch'ing T'ung-pi **Rev:** 6 large waves below dragon **Rev. Legend:** Kuang-hsü Nien-tsao, TAI-CHING-TI-KUO ...

Date	Mintage	VG8	F12	VF20	XF40	MS60
CD1906	—	3.00	9.00	18.00	60.00	120

Y# 10s.1 10 CASH
Copper **Obv. Inscription:** Tai-ch'ing T'ung-pi **Rev. Legend:** Kuang-hsü Nien-tsao, TAI-CHING-TI-KUO ...

Date	Mintage	VG8	F12	VF20	XF40	MS60
CD1906	—	4.00	11.00	25.00	70.00	140

Y# 10s.1a 10 CASH
Copper **Obv. Inscription:** Tai-ch'ing T'ung-pi **Rev:** 5 small waves below dragon **Rev. Legend:** Kuang-hsü Nien-tsao, TAI-CHING-TI-KUO ...

Date	Mintage	VG8	F12	VF20	XF40	MS60
CD1906	—	2.75	8.00	18.00	60.00	120

Y# 10s.2a 10 CASH
Copper **Obv. Inscription:** Tai-ch'ing T'ung-pi **Rev:** Dragon with larger forehead and narrower face, pearl redesigned **Rev. Legend:** Kuang-hsü Nien-tsao, TAI-CHING-TI-KUO ...

Date	Mintage	VG8	F12	VF20	XF40	MS60
CD1906	—	4.00	12.00	27.50	80.00	160

PATTERNS

Including off metal strikes

KM#	Date	Mintage	Identification	Mkt Val
Pn7	15(1926)	—	10 Dollars. Gold. K1536.	8,400
Pn8	15(1926)	—	10 Dollars. Pewter. K1536y.	—
Pn9	15(1926)	—	20 Dollars. Gold. K1535.	12,000
Pn10	15(1926)	—	20 Dollars. Pewter. K1535y.	—
Pn11	21(1932)	—	20 Cash. Copper. Wide flan.	—
Pn12	22(1933)	—	2 Cents. Nickel. K827.	—
Pn13	22(1933)	—	20 Cash. Copper.	—

SHENSI PROVINCE

Shaanxi

A province located in central China that is a rich agricultural area. A very important province in the early development of China. An active imperial mint was located at Sian (Xi'an).

EMPIRE

Kuang-hsü

PROVINCIAL CAST COINAGE

C# 23–13 CASH
Cast Brass **Obv:** Type A **Obv. Inscription:** Kuang-hsü T'ung-pao **Rev:** Manchu inscription **Rev. Inscription:** Boo-san

Date	Mintage	G4	VG8	F12	VF20	XF40
ND(1875-1908)	—	25.00	42.00	60.00	90.00	—

REPUBLIC

MILLED COINAGE

Y# 435 CENT
Copper **Obv:** Crossed flags **Obv. Legend:** IMTYPIF: "I Mei Ta Yuan Pi I (1) Fen" (One is 1/100 of Large Dollar Coin = 1 Cent) **Obv. Inscription:** Chung Hua Min Kuo **Rev:** Value above wheat sprays

Date	Mintage	VG8	F12	VF20	XF40	MS60
ND1928	—	37.50	60.00	140	300	—

Y# 436 2 CENTS
Copper **Obv:** Crossed flags, star between flags **Obv. Legend:** IMTYPEF: "I Mei Ta Yüan Pi Erh (2) Fen" **Obv. Inscription:** Chung Hua Min Kuo **Rev:** Value above wheat sprays **Note:** Dentilated borders.

Date	Mintage	VG8	F12	VF20	XF40	MS60
ND1928	—	55.00	90.00	180	320	—

Y# 436.1 2 CENTS
Copper **Obv:** Crossed flags, without star between flags **Obv. Legend:** IMTYPEF: "I Mei Ta Yüan Pi Erh (2) Fen" **Obv. Inscription:** Chung Hua Min Kuo **Rev:** Value above wheat sprays **Note:** Large Chinese legends.

Date	Mintage	VG8	F12	VF20	XF40	MS60
ND(c.1928)	—	22.50	37.50	90.00	170	650

Y# 436.2 2 CENTS
Copper **Obv:** Crossed flags, star in center **Obv. Legend:** IMTYPEF: "I Mei Ta Yüan Pi Erh (2) Fen" **Obv. Inscription:** Chung Hua Min Kuo **Rev:** Value above wheat sprays, star in center

Date	Mintage	VG8	F12	VF20	XF40	MS60
ND(c.1928)	—	60.00	115	240	500	—

Y# 436.3 2 CENTS
Copper **Obv:** Crossed flags, without star between flags **Obv. Legend:** IMTYPEF: "I Mei Ta Yüan Pi Erh (2) Fen" **Obv. Inscription:** Chung Hua Min Kuo **Rev:** Value above wheat sprays **Note:** Small Chinese legends.

Date	Mintage	VG8	F12	VF20	XF40	MS60
ND(c.1928)	—	37.50	75.00	160	280	—

Y# 436.5 2 CENTS
Copper **Obv:** Crossed flags, similar to Y#436.2 but with star between flags **Obv. Legend:** IMTYPEF: "I Mei Ta Yüan Pi Erh (2) Fen" **Obv. Inscription:** Chung Hua Min Kuo **Rev:** Value above wheat sprays **Note:** Large Chinese legends.

Date	Mintage	VG8	F12	VF20	XF40	MS60
ND(1928)	—	60.00	115	240	500	—

SINKIANG PROVINCE

Hsinkiang, Xinjiang
"New Dominion"

An autonomous region in western China, often referred to as Chinese Turkestan. High mountains surround 2000 ft. tableland on three sides with a large desert in center of this province. Many salt lakes, mining and some farming and oil. Inhabited by early man and was referred to as the "Silk Route" to the West. Sinkiang (Xinjiang) has been historically under the control of many factions, including Genghis Khan. It became a province in 1884. China has made claim to Sinkiang (Xinjiang) for many, many years. This rule has been more nominal than actual. Sinkiang (Xinjiang) had eight imperial mints, only three of which were in operation toward the end of the reign of Kuang Hsu. Only two mints operated during the early years of the republic. In 1949, due to a drastic coin shortage and lack of confidence in the inflated paper money, it was planned to mint some dollars in Sinkiang (Xinjiang). These did not see much circulation, however, due to the defeat of the nationalists, though they have recently appeared in considerable numbers in today's market.

PATTERNS

NOTE: A number of previously listed cast coins of Sinkiang Province are now known to be patterns - "mother" cash or "seed" cash for which no circulating issues are known. The following coins are, therefore, no longer listed. Most were probably manufactured in Beijing. They are generally made of brass rather than the purer copper usual to Sinkiang. The following coins are, therefore, no longer listed here: Craig #30-9, 30-11a, 30-12a, 30-14, 30-15a, 30-16, 30-17, 28-4.1, 28-8a,

28-9a,28-9c, 28-10, 31-1a, 31-1v, 31-2, 32-4, 32-5, 33-12, 33-21, 34-2, 34-3, 35-5a and 35-6.

MONETARY SYSTEM

2 Pul = 1 Cash
2 Cash = 5 Li
4 Cash = 10 Li = 1 Fen
25 Cash = 10 Fen = 1 Miscal = 1 Ch'ien, Mace, Tanga
10 Miscals (Mace) = 1 Liang (Tael or Sar)
20 Miscals (Tangas) = 1 Tilla

LOCAL MINT NAMES AND MARKS

Mint	Chinese	Uyghur	Manchu
Aksu	城阿	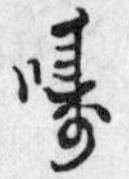	
Ili, now Yining	犁伊		
Kashgar, now Kashi	什喀	كشقر	
Khotan, now Hotan	闐和	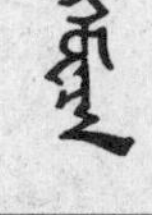	
Kuche, now Kuqa	車庫	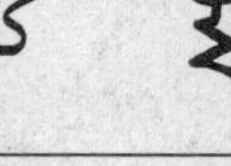	
Urumchi, now Urumqi	車庫	اوش	
Ushi, now Wushi (Uqturpan)	化廸	اوش	
Yangihissar, now Yengisar			
Yarkand, now Shache (Yarkant)	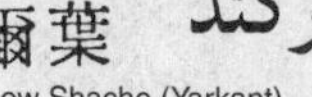	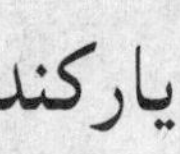	

EMPIRE

MILLED COINAGE

Y# B20.1 2 MISCALS (2 Mace)

7.32 g., Silver, 23 mm. **Obv. Legend:** Chinese and Turki around inscription Kuang-hsü Yüan-pao **Rev:** Dragon, lowest coil points right **Edge:** Reeded **Mint:** Kashgar

Date	Mintage	VG8	F12	VF20	XF40	MS60
AH1323	—	1,200	2,250	3,750	—	—

Y# B20.2 2 MISCALS (2 Mace)

7.32 g., Silver, 23 mm. **Obv. Legend:** Chinese and Turki around inscription Kuang-hsü Yüan-pao **Rev:** Dragon, lowest coil points left **Mint:** Kashgar

Date	Mintage	VG8	F12	VF20	XF40	MS60
AH1323	—	1,200	2,250	3,750	—	—

Y# 23 2 MISCALS (2 Mace)

7.20 g., Silver, 24 mm. **Obv:** Chinese and Turki legend around inscription **Obv. Inscription:** Ta-Ch'ing Yin-pi **Rev:** Dragon in circle surrounded by sprays

Date	Mintage	VG8	F12	VF20	XF40	MS60
AH1324 Rare	—	—	—	—	—	—
AH1325	—	30.00	60.00	100	220	—
AH1326	—	30.00	60.00	100	220	—
AH1327	—	37.50	75.00	120	300	—
AH1329	—	55.00	100	165	350	—

Y# 29 2 MISCALS (2 Mace)

7.20 g., Silver **Obv:** Turki legend around Yin-Yüan Êrh-ch'ien within a beaded circle **Rev:** Double ring around small dragon, floral pattern outside without legend **Mint:** Kashgar

Date	Mintage	VG8	F12	VF20	XF40	MS60
AH1329	—	85.00	135	225	500	—

Y# 29.1 2 MISCALS (2 Mace)

7.20 g., Silver **Obv:** Yin-yüan Êrh-ch'ien **Rev:** Turki legend below larger dragon within single circle **Mint:** Kashgar

Date	Mintage	VG8	F12	VF20	XF40	MS60
AH1329	—	115	190	300	650	—

Y# 30 3 MISCALS

10.50 g., Silver **Obv. Inscription:** Yin-yüan San-ch'ien **Rev:** Turki legend below small, side view dragon in circle **Mint:** Kashgar

Date	Mintage	VG8	F12	VF20	XF40	MS60
AH1329	—	300	525	900	2,000	—

Y# 21.1 5 MISCALS

17.20 g., Silver, 32 mm. **Obv:** Simple 5 in Chinese, date at lower right **Rev:** Dragon's tail points to right **Mint:** Kashgar

Date	Mintage	VG8	F12	VF20	XF40	MS60
AH1323	—	30.00	50.00	90.00	240	—

Y# 25.1 5 MISCALS

17.20 g., Silver **Obv:** Date at left or upper left **Rev:** Dragon **Mint:** Kashgar

Date	Mintage	VG8	F12	VF20	XF40	MS60
AH1325	—	33.75	60.00	130	300	—
AH1326	—	33.75	60.00	130	300	—
AH1327	—	33.75	60.00	130	300	—

Y# 25.2 5 MISCALS

17.20 g., Silver **Rev:** Dragon **Mint:** Kashgar **Note:** Similar to Y#25.1. Varieties exist in date placement.

Date	Mintage	VG8	F12	VF20	XF40	MS60
AH1325	—	33.75	60.00	130	300	—
AH1326	—	33.75	60.00	130	300	—
AH1327	—	33.75	60.00	130	300	—

Y# 25.3 5 MISCALS

17.20 g., Silver **Obv:** Inverted Turki legend, date at upper right, right, or lower right **Obv. Legend:** Dragon **Mint:** Kashgar

Date	Mintage	VG8	F12	VF20	XF40	MS60
AH1325	—	27.50	37.50	115	220	—
AH1326	—	27.50	37.50	115	220	—
AH1328	—	27.50	37.50	115	220	—

Note: Error for 1326

Y# 25.4 5 MISCALS

17.20 g., Silver **Obv:** "Kashgar" at top between standard Turki legend with date at upper right **Rev:** Dragon **Mint:** Kashgar

Date	Mintage	VG8	F12	VF20	XF40	MS60
AH1325	—	30.00	55.00	150	350	—

Y# 25.8 5 MISCALS

17.20 g., Silver **Obv:** Date at upper left or left **Rev:** Dragon **Mint:** Kashgar **Note:** Varieties exist.

Date	Mintage	VG8	F12	VF20	XF40	MS60
AH1325	—	27.50	37.50	115	220	—

Y# 25.9 5 MISCALS

17.20 g., Silver **Obv:** Similar to Y#25.4 **Rev:** Dragon, floral sprays reversed **Mint:** Kashgar

Date	Mintage	VG8	F12	VF20	XF40	MS60
AH1325	—	75.00	150	250	550	—

Y# 25.10 5 MISCALS
17.20 g., Silver **Obv:** Date at upper left **Rev:** Dragon, standard florals **Mint:** Kashgar

Date	Mintage	VG8	F12	VF20	XF40	MS60
AH1325	—	75.00	150	250	550	—

Y# 25.11 5 MISCALS
17.20 g., Silver **Obv:** Date at upper left **Rev:** Dragon, three rosettes at top **Mint:** Kashgar

Date	Mintage	VG8	F12	VF20	XF40	MS60
AH1325	—	900	1,200	1,500	2,400	—

Y# 26 SAR (Tael)
35.20 g., Silver, 40 mm. **Obv:** Chinese "Kashgar" at top wtih Turki "Kashgar" to left **Obv. Inscription:** Ta-ch'ing Yin-pi **Rev:** Side view dragon in sprays **Mint:** Kashgar

Date	Mintage	VG8	F12	VF20	XF40	MS60
AH1325	—	300	450	750	1,700	—

Y# 26.1 SAR (Tael)
35.20 g., Silver, 40 mm. **Obv:** "Kashgar Tao" at top **Mint:** Kashgar

Date	Mintage	VG8	F12	VF20	XF40	MS60
AH1325	—	1,800	4,150	7,500	14,000	—

Y# 26.2 SAR (Tael)
35.20 g., Silver, 40 mm. **Obv:** Chinese "Kashgar" at top wtih Turki "Kashgar" to right **Mint:** Kashgar

Date	Mintage	VG8	F12	VF20	XF40	MS60
AH1325	—	450	750	1,100	2,500	—

Hsüan-t'ung

PROVINCIAL CAST COINAGE

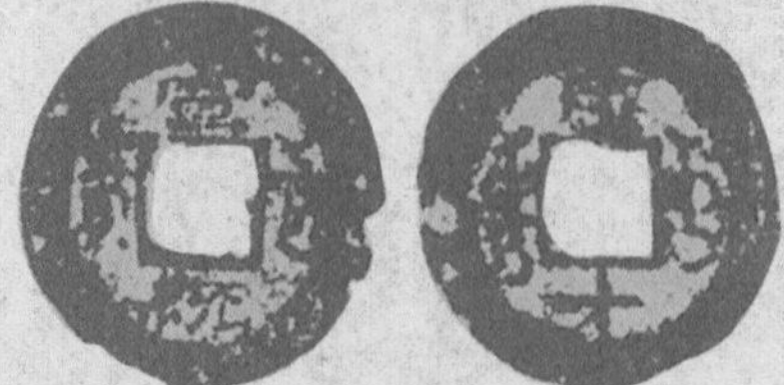

C# 34–4 10 CASH
Cast Copper **Rev:** "K'u" (Kuche) above, "Ushi" in Manchu and Turki right and left **Mint:** Ushi

Date	Mintage	G4	VG8	F12	VF20	XF40
ND(1909-1911)	—	75.00	120	225	—	—

Note: Cast in Ushi to the order of the Kuche Mint; it is the last of the "red" copper cash

MILLED COINAGE

Y# 2.1 10 CASH
Copper **Obv. Inscription:** Hsüan-t'ung Yüan-pao **Rev:** Without Chinese legend above side-view dragon

Date	Mintage	G4	VG8	F12	VF20	XF40
ND (1909)	—	31.25	55.00	95.00	265	—

Y# 2.2 10 CASH
Copper **Obv. Inscription:** Hsüan-t'ung Yüan-pao **Rev:** Chinese legend with "Nien" (year) added above dragon

Date	Mintage	G4	VG8	F12	VF20	XF40
CD1910	—	31.25	55.00	95.00	265	—
CD1911	—	37.50	65.00	125	300	—

Y# 2.3 10 CASH
Copper **Obv:** Double ring around star in center of inscription **Obv. Inscription:** Hsüan-t'ung Yüan-pao

Date	Mintage	G4	VG8	F12	VF20	XF40
CD1911	—	37.50	65.00	125	300	—

Y# 2a 10 CASH
Copper **Obv:** Large characters within center circle **Obv. Inscription:** Hsüan-t'ung Yüan-pao

Date	Mintage	VG8	F12	VF20	XF40	MS60
CD1910	—	—	—	—	37.50	100

Note: Modern copy

Y# 27 5 MISCALS
17.20 g., Silver **Obv:** "Kashgar" at top, Turki below; star in center **Obv. Inscription:** Hsüan-t'ung Yin-pi **Rev:** Dragon **Mint:** Kashgar

Date	Mintage	VG8	F12	VF20	XF40	MS60
AH1327	—	30.00	45.00	100	220	—
AH1328	—	37.50	75.00	135	300	—

Y# 27.1 5 MISCALS
17.20 g., Silver **Obv:** Official "Wu" (5) at right, dot in center **Rev:** Dragon **Mint:** Kashgar

Date	Mintage	VG8	F12	VF20	XF40	MS60
AH1328	—	55.00	100	225	450	—

Y# 27.2 5 MISCALS
17.20 g., Silver **Obv:** Rosette in center **Mint:** Kashgar

Date	Mintage	VG8	F12	VF20	XF40	MS60
AH1329	—	75.00	150	300	550	—

Y# A28.1 5 MISCALS
17.20 g., Silver **Obv:** Dot in center **Rev:** Side view dragon **Mint:** Kashgar **Note:** Prev. Y#27.4.

Date	Mintage	VG8	F12	VF20	XF40	MS60
AH1329	—	27.50	45.00	115	265	—

Y# A28.2 5 MISCALS
17.20 g., Silver **Obv:** Rosette in center **Rev:** Side view dragon **Mint:** Kashgar **Note:** Prev. Y#27.5.

Date	Mintage	VG8	F12	VF20	XF40	MS60
AH1329	—	27.50	45.00	115	265	—

Y# A28.3 5 MISCALS
17.20 g., Silver **Obv:** Official "Wu" (5) at right, star in center **Rev:** Side view dragon **Mint:** Kashgar **Note:** Prev. Y#27.6.

Date	Mintage	VG8	F12	VF20	XF40	MS60
AH1329	—	27.50	45.00	115	265	—

Y# A28 5 MISCALS
17.20 g., Silver **Obv:** "Kashgar" at top, normal "Wu" (5) at right, star in center **Obv. Inscription:** Hsüan-t'ung Yüan-pao **Rev:** Side view dragon **Mint:** Kashgar **Note:** Prev. Y#27.3.

Date	Mintage	VG8	F12	VF20	XF40	MS60
AH1329	—	27.50	45.00	115	265	—

Hung-hsien

Y# A38.1 10 CASH
Copper **Obv:** Chinese legend in inner dotted circle **Obv. Legend:** Hung-hsien T'ung-pi **Mint:** Kashgar

Date	Mintage	G4	VG8	F12	VF20	XF40
AH1334	—	155	235	325	—	—

Y# A38.2 10 CASH
Copper **Mint:** Kashgar

Date	Mintage	G4	VG8	F12	VF20	XF40
AH1334	—	155	235	325	—	—

Note: Y#A38.1 and A38.2 were issued for the brief reign of Yuan Shih-kai as Emperor Hung-hsien (1916)

Kuang-hsü

LOCAL CAST COINAGE

C# 30–18.1 10 CASH

Cast Copper **Rev:** "Asku" in Manchu at right, in Turki at left **Mint:** Aksu

Date	Mintage	G4	VG8	F12	VF20	XF40
ND(1875-1908)	—	11.00	18.00	28.00	50.00	—

C# 30–18 10 CASH

Cast Copper **Obv. Inscription:** Kuang-hsü Chung-pao **Rev:** Character "A" (for Aksu) above center hole, "Aksu" in Turki at right, in Manchu at left **Mint:** Aksu

Date	Mintage	G4	VG8	F12	VF20	XF40
ND(1875-1908)	—	4.00	6.00	10.00	20.00	—

C# 30–19 10 CASH

Cast Copper **Obv. Inscription:** Kuang-hsü T'ung-pao **Rev:** Character "K'a" (for Kashgar) above **Mint:** Aksu

Date	Mintage	G4	VG8	F12	VF20	XF40
ND(1886-1908)	—	6.00	12.00	16.00	33.00	—

Note: Cast in the Aksu Mint for the Kashgar Mint, beginning in 1886 during the reign of Kuang-Hsü

PROVINCIAL CAST COINAGE

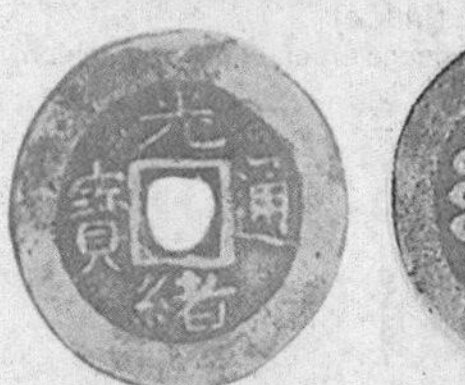

KM# 10 CASH

Cast Copper **Obv. Inscription:** Kuang-hsü T'ung-pao **Rev:** Manchu inscription for Hu-pu Board of Revenue **Rev. Inscription:** Boo Ciowan **Mint:** Kuche

Date	Mintage	G4	VG8	F12	VF20	XF40
ND(1875-1908)	—	3.00	7.00	13.00	20.00	—

KM# 11 CASH

Cast Copper **Rev:** Similar to KM#10 but entire reverse is in inverted mirror image **Mint:** Kuche

Date	Mintage	G4	VG8	F12	VF20	XF40
ND(1875-1908)	—	7.00	13.00	19.00	28.00	—

KM# 12 CASH

Cast Copper **Obv. Inscription:** Kuang-hsü T'ung-pao **Rev:** Similar to KM#11 **Mint:** Kuche

Date	Mintage	G4	VG8	F12	VF20	XF40
ND(1875-1908)	—	3.00	7.00	13.00	20.00	—

KM# 13 CASH

Cast Copper **Obv. Inscription:** Kuang-hsü T'ung-pao **Rev:** Illiterate Manchu inscription **Rev. Inscription:** Boo Chuan or Yuan **Mint:** Kuche

Date	Mintage	G4	VG8	F12	VF20	XF40
ND(1875-1908)	—	3.00	7.00	13.00	20.00	—

KM# 14 CASH

Cast Copper **Obv. Inscription:** Kuang-hsü T'ung-pao **Rev:** Illiterate Manchu inscription **Rev. Inscription:** Boo-Chuan **Mint:** Kuche

Date	Mintage	G4	VG8	F12	VF20	XF40
ND(1875-1908)	—	3.00	6.00	11.00	18.00	—

Note: The five one-cash varieties listed above could be confused with Beijing issues C1-16 or C2-15, but they are much more crudely cast, and are made of red copper rather than brass; see Landon Ross, 1986, Numismatics International Bulletin 20(3) for a more detailed review

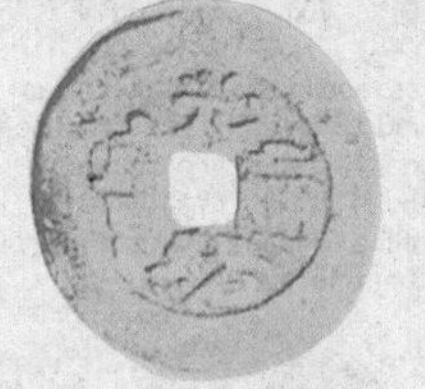
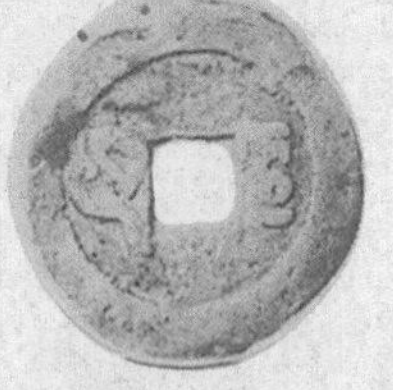

C# 33–23 CASH

Cast Copper **Obv. Inscription:** Kuang-hsü T'ung-pao **Mint:** Kuche

Date	Mintage	G4	VG8	F12	VF20	XF40
ND(1875-1908)	—	7.00	10.00	14.00	25.00	—

KM# 7.1 10 CASH

Cast Copper **Obv. Inscription:** Kuang-hsü T'ung-pao **Rev:** "Pao Ku" with "K'u" (for Kuche) above **Mint:** Kuche

Date	Mintage	G4	VG8	F12	VF20	XF40
ND(1875-1908)	—	4.00	7.00	13.00	28.00	—

KM# 7.2 10 CASH

Cast Copper **Obv. Inscription:** Kuang-hsü T'ung-pao **Rev:** "Pao" (for Kuche) at left reversed **Mint:** Kuche

Date	Mintage	G4	VG8	F12	VF20	XF40
ND(1875-1908)	—	13.00	25.00	40.00	65.00	—

KM# 8 10 CASH

Cast Copper **Obv. Inscription:** Kuang-hsü T'ung-pao **Rev:** "Manchu Boo Hsin" with "Hsin" (new, but here standing for the Tihwa (now Urumqi) Mint) above **Mint:** Urumqi

Date	Mintage	G4	VG8	F12	VF20	XF40
ND(1875-1908)	—	6.00	8.00	13.00	28.00	—

KM# 9 10 CASH

Cast Copper **Obv. Inscription:** Kuang-hsü T'ung-pao **Rev:** "Manchu Boo Hsin" (for Tihwa Mint) with "Hsin" (new) above **Mint:** Urumqi

Date	Mintage	G4	VG8	F12	VF20	XF40
ND(1875-1908)	—	6.00	8.00	13.00	28.00	—

C# 32–6.1 10 CASH

Cast Copper **Obv. Inscription:** Kuang-hsü T'ung-pao **Rev:** Turki-Manchu inscription (right-left) **Rev. Inscription:** Boo-Kashgar **Mint:** Kashgar

Date	Mintage	G4	VG8	F12	VF20	XF40
ND(1875-1908)	—	8.00	17.00	30.00	48.00	—

C# 32–6 10 CASH

Cast Copper **Obv. Inscription:** Kuang-hsü T'ung-pao **Rev:** "Kashgar" in Turki at left, in Manchu at right, "K'a" (Kashgar) above **Mint:** Kashgar

Date	Mintage	G4	VG8	F12	VF20	XF40
ND(1875-1908)	—	8.00	17.00	30.00	48.00	—

C# 33–16 10 CASH

Cast Copper **Obv. Inscription:** Kuang-hsü T'ung-pao **Mint:** Kuche

Date	Mintage	G4	VG8	F12	VF20	XF40
ND(1875-1908)	—	14.00	30.00	45.00	70.00	—

C# 33–18.1 10 CASH

Cast Copper **Rev:** Semi-circle at lower right **Mint:** Kuche

Date	Mintage	G4	VG8	F12	VF20	XF40
ND(1875-1908)	—	11.00	19.00	30.00	50.00	—

C# 33–18 10 CASH

Cast Copper **Obv. Inscription:** Kuang-hsü T'ung-pao **Rev:** Character "K'u" above **Mint:** Kuche

Date	Mintage	G4	VG8	F12	VF20	XF40
ND(1875-1908)	—	13.00	22.00	35.00	65.00	—

C# 33–19 10 CASH

Cast Copper **Obv. Inscription:** Kuang-hsü T'ung-pao **Rev:** Manchu inscription, "kuce" in simple style **Rev. Inscription:** Boo-kuce **Mint:** Kuche

Date	Mintage	G4	VG8	F12	VF20	XF40
ND(1875-1908)	—	6.00	7.00	27.50	47.00	—

GENERAL CAST COINAGE

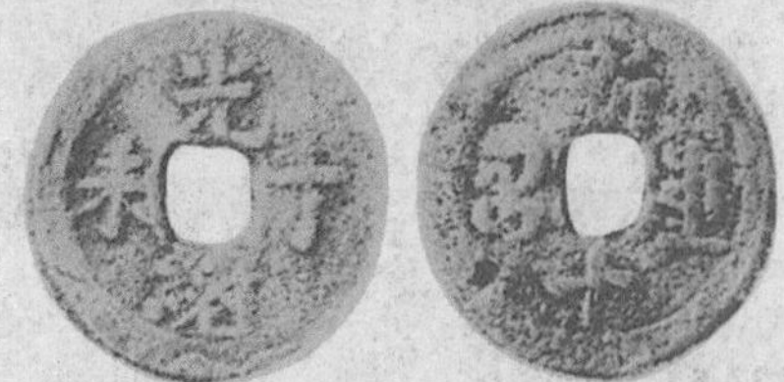

KM# 16 10 CASH
Cast Copper **Obv. Inscription:** Kuang-hsü Ting Wei **Rev:** "Boo-yuan?" with "Hsin" (new) above

Date	Mintage	G4	VG8	F12	VF20	XF40
CD1907	—	15.00	33.75	60.00	135	—

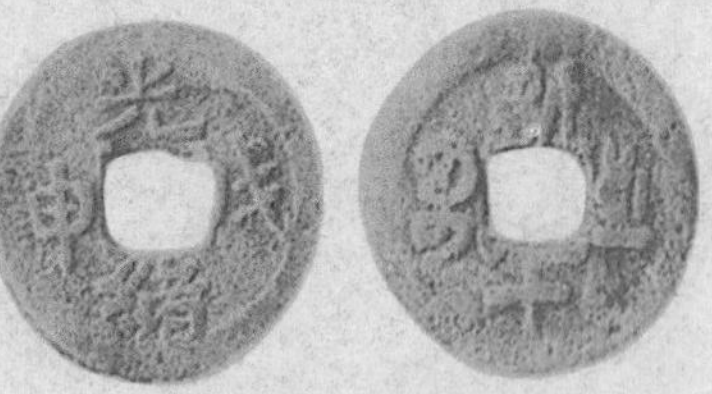

KM# 17 10 CASH
Cast Copper **Obv. Inscription:** Kuang-hsü Wu-shen

Date	Mintage	G4	VG8	F12	VF20	XF40
CD1908	—	22.50	48.75	90.00	165	—

MILLED COINAGE

Y# 1 FEN, 5 LI
Copper **Obv:** Large dots in circle, dentilated rims **Obv. Inscription:** Kuang-hsü Yüan-pao **Rev:** Front view dragon **Note:** Two varieties are reported.

Date	Mintage	G4	VG8	F12	VF20	XF40
ND (1906)	—	190	250	450	700	—

Y# 1a FEN, 5 LI
Copper **Obv:** Small dots in circle, dotted rims **Obv. Inscription:** Kuang-hsü Yüan-pao **Rev:** Front view dragon **Note:** Modern copy.

Date	Mintage	F12	VF20	XF40	MS60	MS63
ND (1906)	—	—	—	75.00	125	—

Note: The legend on this coin states that it is valued at 1 Fen 5 Li of silver (about 15 Cash); the coin is the size of a normal 10 Cash piece of Sinkiang (Xinjiang), but these pieces are usually larger than those of the other provinces; for this reason, it is assumed the coin was overvalued to benefit the government

Y# B1 2 FEN 5 LI
Copper **Obv. Inscription:** Kuang-hsü Yüan-pao **Rev:** Side view dragon

Date	Mintage	G4	VG8	F12	VF20	XF40
ND (1906) Rare	—	—	—	—	—	—

Note: Status unknown

Y# A2 2 FEN 5 LI
Copper **Obv. Inscription:** Kuang-hsü Yüan-pao **Rev:** Front view dragon

Date	Mintage	G4	VG8	F12	VF20	XF40
ND (1906) Rare	—	—	—	—	—	—

Note: This denomination was recalled shortly after issue and the dies re-engraved 1 Fen and 5 Li to produce Y#1; do not confuse poorly re-engraved Chinese numeral "172" examples of Y#1 for Y#A1; note the difference in spacing of the Chinese characters below the rosettes between Y#1 and Y#A1

Y# B16 MISCAL (Mace)
3.50 g., Silver **Obv:** "Kashgar" at right, value at left **Obv. Inscription:** Kuang-hsü Yin-yüan **Mint:** Kashgar

Date	Mintage	VG8	F12	VF20	XF40	MS60
AH1331 Error for 1321	—	75.00	130	265	525	—
AH1322	—	75.00	130	265	525	—

Y# C16 MISCAL (Mace)
3.50 g., Silver **Obv:** "Kashgar" in Chinese at right and left of value **Rev:** Turki inscription in sprays **Mint:** Kashgar

Date	Mintage	VG8	F12	VF20	XF40	MS60
AH1322	—	70.00	105	190	400	—

Y# 3 MISCAL (Mace)
3.50 g., Silver **Obv:** Outer legend: Turki without dot in center **Rev:** Without Turki legend

Date	Mintage	VG8	F12	VF20	XF40	MS60
ND(1905)	—	115	190	300	650	—

Y# 3.1 MISCAL (Mace)
3.50 g., Silver **Obv. Legend:** Turki with dot in center **Rev:** Without Turki legend

Date	Mintage	VG8	F12	VF20	XF40	MS60
ND(1905)	—	115	190	300	650	3,500

Y# 3.2 MISCAL (Mace)
3.50 g., Silver **Obv:** Without outer Turki legend **Rev:** Turki legend

Date	Mintage	VG8	F12	VF20	XF40	MS60
ND(1905)	—	500	825	1,350	3,000	—

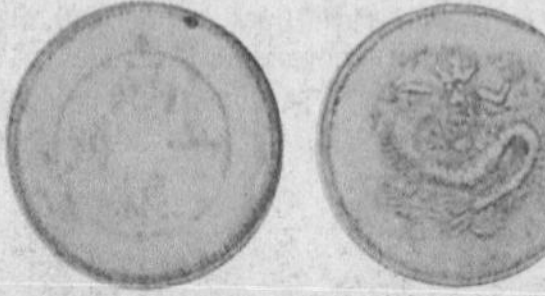

Y# 3.3 MISCAL (Mace)
3.50 g., Silver **Obv:** Without outer Turki legend **Rev:** Without outer Turki legend

Date	Mintage	VG8	F12	VF20	XF40	MS60
ND(1905)	—	135	225	375	800	—

Y# A20.1 MISCAL (Mace)
3.50 g., Silver **Obv:** Turki at right and left of value, date at lower left **Rev:** Side view dragon

Date	Mintage	VG8	F12	VF20	XF40	MS60
AH1323	—	300	525	900	2,000	—

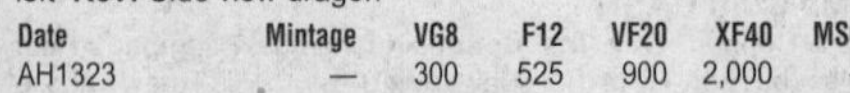

Y# A20.2 MISCAL (Mace)
3.50 g., Silver **Obv:** Turki at right and left of value, date at lower right **Rev:** Side view dragon **Mint:** Kashgar

Date	Mintage	VG8	F12	VF20	XF40	MS60
AH1323	—	300	525	900	2,000	—

Y# A20.3 MISCAL (Mace)
3.50 g., Silver **Obv:** Inverted Turki legends at right and left of value **Mint:** Kashgar

Date	Mintage	VG8	F12	VF20	XF40	MS60
AH1323	—	300	525	900	2,000	—

Y# 10 MISCAL (Mace)
3.50 g., Silver **Obv:** Without outer Turki legend **Rev:** Legend above dragon, 1 MACE below **Rev. Legend:** SUNGAREI

Date	Mintage	VG8	F12	VF20	XF40	MS60
ND(1906)	—	165	350	600	1,300	—

Y# A12 GOLD MISCAL (Mace)
7.80 g., Gold **Rev:** Legend above dragon, "2 MACE" below **Rev. Legend:** SUNGAREI **Note:** Similar to 2 Miscals (Silver) Y#11.

Date	Mintage	VG8	F12	VF20	XF40	MS60
ND(1906)	—	—	—	—	—	—

Note: Requires Confirmation

Y# 8 GOLD MISCAL (Mace)
3.90 g., Gold **Rev:** Turki legend around uncircled dragon

Date	Mintage	VG8	F12	VF20	XF40	MS60
ND(1907)	—	750	1,250	2,000	3,000	5,000

Y# 8.1 GOLD MISCAL (Mace)
3.90 g., Gold **Rev:** Without Turki legend around uncircled dragon

Date	Mintage	VG8	F12	VF20	XF40	MS60
ND(1907)	—	950	1,550	2,400	3,650	6,300

Y# 8.2 GOLD MISCAL (Mace)
3.90 g., Gold **Rev:** Turki legend at left differs

Date	Mintage	VG8	F12	VF20	XF40	MS60
ND(1907)	—	825	1,400	2,200	3,250	5,500

Y# 8.3 GOLD MISCAL (Mace)
3.90 g., Gold **Rev:** Turki legend in outer circle

Date	Mintage	VG8	F12	VF20	XF40	MS60
ND(1907)	—	1,150	1,900	3,750	5,000	7,000

Y# 9.1 GOLD 2 MISCALS
7.80 g., Gold **Obv:** Wide-spaced Chinese "2" **Rev:** Redesigned dragon

Date	Mintage	VG8	F12	VF20	XF40	MS60
ND(1906)	—	1,550	3,150	6,300	8,800	12,500

Y# 9 GOLD 2 MISCALS
7.80 g., Gold **Obv:** Narrow-spaced Chinese "2" **Rev:** Turki legend around uncircled dragon

Date	Mintage	VG8	F12	VF20	XF40	MS60
ND(1906)	—	1,150	1,900	3,750	6,300	9,500

Y# 17a 2 MISCALS (2 Mace)
7.20 g., Silver, 23 mm. **Obv:** Inscription between Kashgar and value **Obv. Inscription:** Kuang-hsü Yin-yüan **Mint:** Kashgar

Date	Mintage	VG8	F12	VF20	XF40	MS60
AH1319	—	20.00	35.00	60.00	175	350
AH1320	—	27.50	45.00	70.00	150	—

Y# 17a.1 2 MISCALS (2 Mace)
7.20 g., Silver, 23 mm. **Obv:** Inscription between "K'a Tsao" at right, value at left **Obv. Inscription:** Kuang-hsü Yin-yüan **Mint:** Kashgar

Date	Mintage	VG8	F12	VF20	XF40	MS60
AH1320 Rare	—	—	—	—	—	—
AH1321	—	27.50	45.00	70.00	150	—
AH1322	—	30.00	55.00	95.00	200	—

Y# 33 2 MISCALS (2 Mace)
Silver, 24 mm. **Obv:** Inscription between "Tihwa" and value with normal Êrh (2) at left **Obv. Inscription:** Kuang-hsü Yin-yüan **Rev:** Turki inscription in floral wreath **Rev. Inscription:** Urumchi **Mint:** Tihwa

Date	Mintage	VG8	F12	VF20	XF40	MS60
AH1321	—	22.50	33.00	85.00	180	—
AH1322	—	22.50	33.00	85.00	180	—
AH1323	—	27.50	45.00	85.00	180	—

Y# 4 2 MISCALS (2 Mace)
7.20 g., Silver **Obv:** Turki outer legend **Rev:** Without Turki legend

Date	Mintage	VG8	F12	VF20	XF40	MS60
ND(1905)	—	75.00	115	225	800	—

Y# 4.1 2 MISCALS (2 Mace)
7.20 g., Silver **Obv:** Continuous Turki outer legend **Rev:** Without Turki legend

Date	Mintage	VG8	F12	VF20	XF40	MS60
ND(1905)	—	150	225	375	650	—

Y# 4.2 2 MISCALS (2 Mace)
7.20 g., Silver **Obv:** Without outer Turki legend **Rev:** Turki legend

Date	Mintage	VG8	F12	VF20	XF40	MS60
ND(1905)	—	225	375	600	1,300	—

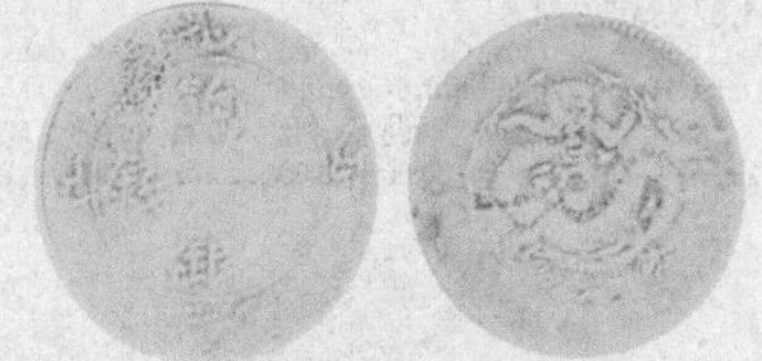

Y# 4.3 2 MISCALS (2 Mace)
7.20 g., Silver **Rev:** Redesigned dragon without Turki legends

Date	Mintage	VG8	F12	VF20	XF40	MS60
ND(1905)	—	225	375	600	1,300	—

Y# 4.4 2 MISCALS (2 Mace)
7.20 g., Silver **Obv:** Turki outer legend **Rev:** Circled dragon without Turki legend

Date	Mintage	VG8	F12	VF20	XF40	MS60
ND(1905) Rare	—	—	—	—	—	—

Y# 33.1 2 MISCALS (2 Mace)
Silver, 24 mm. **Obv:** Inscription between "Tihwa" and value with official Êrh (2) at left **Obv. Inscription:** Kuang-hsü Yin-yüan **Rev:** Turki inscription in floral wreath **Rev. Inscription:** Urumchi **Mint:** Tihwa

Date	Mintage	VG8	F12	VF20	XF40	MS60
AH1323	—	22.50	33.00	85.00	180	—
AH1324	—	22.50	33.00	85.00	180	—
AH1325	—	22.50	33.00	85.00	180	—

Y# 11 2 MISCALS (2 Mace)
7.20 g., Silver **Rev:** Legend above dragon, "2 MACE" below **Rev. Legend:** SUNGAREI

Date	Mintage	VG8	F12	VF20	XF40	MS60
ND(1906)	—	300	650	1,300	2,700	—

Y# 18a 3 MISCALS
10.50 g., Silver **Obv:** Inscription between Kashgar and value **Obv. Inscription:** Kuang-hsü Yin-yüan **Rev:** Turki in floral wreath **Mint:** Kashgar

Date	Mintage	VG8	F12	VF20	XF40	MS60
AH1319	—	20.00	30.00	50.00	130	—
AH1320	—	20.00	30.00	50.00	130	—

Y# 18a.1 3 MISCALS
10.50 g., Silver **Obv:** Inscription between "K'a Tsao" and value **Obv. Inscription:** Kuang-hsü Yin-yüan **Rev:** Turki in floral wreath **Mint:** Kashgar

Date	Mintage	VG8	F12	VF20	XF40	MS60
AH1320	—	15.00	30.00	50.00	130	—
AH1321	—	15.00	30.00	50.00	130	—
AH1322	—	15.00	30.00	50.00	130	—

Y# 34 3 MISCALS
10.30 g., Silver **Obv:** Inscription between "Tihwa" and value with normal "San" (3) at left **Obv. Inscription:** Kuang-hs? Yin-y?an **Rev:** Turki inscription in floral wreath **Rev. Inscription:** Urumchi **Edge:** Reeded **Mint:** Tihwa

Date	Mintage	VG8	F12	VF20	XF40	MS60
AH1321	—	27.50	45.00	115	220	—
AH1322	—	27.50	45.00	115	220	—
AH1323	—	27.50	45.00	115	220	—

Y# 34a 3 MISCALS
10.30 g., Silver **Obv:** Inscription between "Tihwa" and value with official "San" (3) at left **Obv. Inscription:** Kuang-hsü Yin-yüan **Rev:** Turki inscription in floral wreath **Rev. Inscription:** Urumchi **Mint:** Tihwa

Date	Mintage	VG8	F12	VF20	XF40	MS60
AH1322	—	15.00	30.00	50.00	130	—
AH1323	—	15.00	30.00	50.00	130	—
AH1324	—	15.00	30.00	50.00	130	—
AH1325	—	15.00	30.00	50.00	130	—

Y# 20 3 MISCALS
10.50 g., Silver, 27 mm. **Obv. Legend:** Turki and Chinese around inscription with normal "San"; (3) in Chinese at bottom **Obv. Inscription:** Ta-ch'ing Yüan-pao **Mint:** Kashgar

Date	Mintage	VG8	F12	VF20	XF40	MS60
AH1323	—	130	265	425	900	—

Y# 20.1 3 MISCALS
10.50 g., Silver, 27 mm. **Obv. Legend:** Turki and Chinese around inscription with official "San"; (3) in Chinese at bottom **Obv. Inscription:** Ta-ch'ing Yüan-pao **Mint:** Kashgar

Date	Mintage	VG8	F12	VF20	XF40	MS60
AH1323	—	150	300	500	1,100	—

Y# 20.2 3 MISCALS
10.50 g., Silver, 27 mm. **Obv. Legend:** Turki and Chinese around inscription with official "San", (3) in Chinese at bottom, date at lower right **Obv. Inscription:** Ta-ch'ing Yüan-pao **Mint:** Kashgar

Date	Mintage	VG8	F12	VF20	XF40	MS60
AH1323	—	150	300	550	1,200	—

Y# 5 4 MISCALS (4 Mace)
14.20 g., Silver

Date	Mintage	VG8	F12	VF20	XF40	MS60
ND(1905)	—	130	190	300	800	—

Y# 19a 5 MISCALS

17.20 g., Silver **Obv:** Inscription between "Kashgar" and value; Chinese characters "K'a Shih" at right **Obv. Inscription:** Kuang-hsü Yin-yüan **Rev:** Turki inscription within sprays **Mint:** Kashgar

Date	Mintage	VG8	F12	VF20	XF40	MS60
AH1319	—	27.50	37.50	75.00	220	450
AH1320	—	27.50	37.50	75.00	220	450

Y# 19a.1 5 MISCALS

17.20 g., Silver **Obv:** Inscription between "K'a Tsao" at right, value at left **Obv. Inscription:** Kuang-hsü Yin-yüan **Mint:** Kashgar

Date	Mintage	VG8	F12	VF20	XF40	MS60
AH1321	—	22.50	37.50	75.00	200	—
AH1322	—	22.50	37.50	75.00	200	—

Y# 35 5 MISCALS

17.90 g., Silver **Obv:** Inscription between "Tihwa" and value with normal "Wu" (5) at left **Obv. Inscription:** Kuang-hsü Yin-yüan **Rev:** Turki inscription in floral wreath **Rev. Inscription:** Urumchi **Mint:** Tihwa

Date	Mintage	VG8	F12	VF20	XF40	MS60
AH1321	—	30.00	60.00	120	300	—
AH1322	—	30.00	60.00	120	300	—
AH1323	—	30.00	60.00	120	300	—

Y# 21.2 5 MISCALS

17.20 g., Silver, 32 mm. **Obv:** Inverted Turki legend, date at lower right **Rev:** Dragon **Mint:** Kashgar

Date	Mintage	VG8	F12	VF20	XF40	MS60
AH1323	—	35.00	60.00	100	250	—

Y# 21.3 5 MISCALS

17.20 g., Silver, 32 mm. **Obv:** Normal "Wu" (5) at bottom, date at lower right **Rev:** Dragon **Mint:** Kashgar

Date	Mintage	VG8	F12	VF20	XF40	MS60
AH1323 Rare	—	—	—	—	—	—

Y# 21.4 5 MISCALS

17.20 g., Silver, 32 mm. **Obv:** Date at upper left **Rev:** Side view dragon's tail points to left **Mint:** Kashgar

Date	Mintage	VG8	F12	VF20	XF40	MS60
AH1323	—	22.50	37.50	75.00	200	—

Y# 21.5 5 MISCALS

17.20 g., Silver, 32 mm. **Obv:** Date at lower right **Rev:** Dragon **Mint:** Kashgar

Date	Mintage	VG8	F12	VF20	XF40	MS60
AH1323	—	22.50	37.50	75.00	200	—

Y# 21.6 5 MISCALS

17.20 g., Silver, 32 mm. **Obv:** Inverted Turki legend, date at lower right **Rev:** Dragon **Mint:** Kashgar

Date	Mintage	VG8	F12	VF20	XF40	MS60
AH1323	—	30.00	55.00	120	300	—

Y# 21.7 5 MISCALS

17.20 g., Silver, 32 mm. **Obv:** Date at upper right **Rev:** Dragon **Mint:** Kashgar

Date	Mintage	VG8	F12	VF20	XF40	MS60
AH1323	—	30.00	45.00	70.00	170	—

Y# 21 5 MISCALS

17.20 g., Silver, 32 mm. **Obv:** Chinese and Turki around inscription; date at upper left **Obv. Inscription:** Ta-ch'ing Yüan-pao **Rev:** Side view dragon's tail points to right **Mint:** Kashgar **Note:** Kann #1110.

Date	Mintage	VG8	F12	VF20	XF40	MS60
AH1323	—	30.00	45.00	70.00	150	350

Y# 35a 5 MISCALS

17.90 g., Silver **Obv:** Inscription between "Tihwa" and value with official "Wu" (5) at left **Obv. Inscription:** Kuang-hsü Yin-yüan **Rev:** Turki inscription in floral wreath **Rev. Inscription:** Urumchi **Mint:** Tihwa

Date	Mintage	VG8	F12	VF20	XF40	MS60
AH1323	—	30.00	60.00	120	300	—
AH1324	—	22.50	45.00	90.00	240	—
AH1325	—	22.50	45.00	90.00	240	—

Y# 25 5 MISCALS

17.20 g., Silver **Obv:** "Kashgar Tsao" at top between standard Turki legend; inscription: "Ta-ch'ing Yin-pi" **Rev:** Dragon **Mint:** Kashgar

Date	Mintage	VG8	F12	VF20	XF40	MS60
ND(1906)	—	33.75	60.00	130	325	—

Y# 31 5 MISCALS

17.20 g., Silver **Obv. Legend:** Legend "Kashgar" at top, Turki below around side view dragon, star at center and at right **Rev:** Inscription between value **Rev. Inscription:** "Hsiang-yin" (soldier's pay) **Mint:** Kashgar **Note:** Varieties with two and three tail spines on dragon exist.

Date	Mintage	VG8	F12	VF20	XF40	MS60
AH1329	—	30.00	60.00	150	375	—
AH1330	—	30.00	60.00	150	375	—
AH1321	—	30.00	60.00	150	375	—
Note: Error for 1331						
AH1331	—	30.00	60.00	150	375	—

Y# 31.2 5 MISCALS

17.20 g., Silver **Obv:** Rosettes in outer field **Mint:** Kashgar

Date	Mintage	VG8	F12	VF20	XF40	MS60
AH1329	—	75.00	150	250	550	—

Y# 31.3 5 MISCALS

17.20 g., Silver **Rev:** Rosettes in center **Mint:** Kashgar

Date	Mintage	VG8	F12	VF20	XF40	MS60
AH1329	—	33.75	115	150	375	—

Y# 6 5 MISCALS (5 Mace)

17.90 g., Silver **Obv:** Without dot or rosette in center **Rev:** Uncircled dragon

Date	Mintage	VG8	F12	VF20	XF40	MS60
ND(1905)	—	25.00	42.00	100	350	1,500

Y# 6.1 5 MISCALS (5 Mace)

17.90 g., Silver **Rev:** Circled dragon, without rosettes

Date	Mintage	VG8	F12	VF20	XF40	MS60
ND(1905)	—	25.00	42.00	100	350	—

Y# 6.2 5 MISCALS (5 Mace)

17.90 g., Silver **Rev:** Large rosettes at sides of dragon

Date	Mintage	VG8	F12	VF20	XF40	MS60
ND(1905)	—	25.00	42.00	100	350	—

Y# 6.3 5 MISCALS (5 Mace)

17.90 g., Silver **Obv:** Dot in center **Rev:** Without rosettes, circled dragon

Date	Mintage	VG8	F12	VF20	XF40	MS60
ND(1905)	—	25.00	42.00	100	350	—

Y# 6.4 5 MISCALS (5 Mace)
17.90 g., Silver **Obv:** Cross in center

Date	Mintage	VG8	F12	VF20	XF40	MS60
ND(1905)	—	25.00	42.00	100	350	—

Y# 6.5 5 MISCALS (5 Mace)
17.90 g., Silver **Obv:** Large rosette in center, middle of which is depressed

Date	Mintage	VG8	F12	VF20	XF40	MS60
ND(1905)	—	25.00	42.00	100	350	—

Y# 6.6 5 MISCALS (5 Mace)
17.90 g., Silver **Obv:** Eight-petalled rosette in center, middle of which is raised **Rev:** Small rosettes at sides of dragon

Date	Mintage	VG8	F12	VF20	XF40	MS60
ND(1905)	—	25.00	42.00	100	360	—

Y# 6.7 5 MISCALS (5 Mace)
17.90 g., Silver **Rev:** Bat above uncircled dragon's head

Date	Mintage	VG8	F12	VF20	XF40	MS60
ND(1905)	—	265	450	675	1,400	—

Y# 6.8 5 MISCALS (5 Mace)
17.90 g., Silver **Rev:** Turki legend around uncircled dragon

Date	Mintage	VG8	F12	VF20	XF40	MS60
ND(1905)	—	600	900	—	—	—

Y# 6.9 5 MISCALS (5 Mace)
17.90 g., Silver **Rev:** Legend above uncircled dragon, "5 MACE" below **Rev. Legend:** SUNGAREI

Date	Mintage	VG8	F12	VF20	XF40	MS60
ND(1906) Rare	—	—	—	—	—	—

Note: Some authorities consider this coin a fantasy

Y# 6.10 5 MISCALS (5 Mace)
17.90 g., Silver **Rev:** Without SUNGREI, with four bats and many clouds around dragon

Date	Mintage	VG8	F12	VF20	XF40	MS60
ND(1906) Rare	—	—	—	—	—	—

Y# 6.11 5 MISCALS (5 Mace)
17.90 g., Silver **Obv:** Turki legend rotated **Rev:** Bat above dragon's head

Date	Mintage	VG8	F12	VF20	XF40	MS60
ND(1906) Rare	—	—	—	—	—	—

Y# 7 SAR (Tael)
35.50 g., Silver **Obv:** Without Turki legend **Rev:** Without Turki legend, rosettes at sides of uncircled dragon

Date	Mintage	VG8	F12	VF20	XF40	MS60
ND(1905)	—	42.00	70.00	120	450	1,700

Y# 7.1 SAR (Tael)
35.50 g., Silver **Rev:** Turki legend around circled dragon, without rosettes

Date	Mintage	VG8	F12	VF20	XF40	MS60
ND(1905)	—	60.00	100	175	650	1,900

Y# 7.2 SAR (Tael)
35.50 g., Silver **Rev:** Turki legend around uncircled dragon

Date	Mintage	VG8	F12	VF20	XF40	MS60
ND(1905)	—	750	1,300	1,900	3,500	—

Y# 7.3 SAR (Tael)
35.50 g., Silver **Obv:** Outer Turki legend, rosette in center **Rev:** Without Turki legend, with rosettes at sides of uncircled dragon

Date	Mintage	VG8	F12	VF20	XF40	MS60
ND(1905)	—	150	450	825	3,200	—

REPUBLIC

PROVINCIAL CAST COINAGE

Y# 37.1 10 CASH
Cast Copper, 32 mm. **Obv. Inscription:** Chung Hua Min Kuo **Rev:** Crossed flags **Mint:** Aksu

Date	Mintage	G4	VG8	F12	VF20	XF40
ND (1912)	—	80.00	120	200	—	—

Y# 37.2 10 CASH
Cast Copper, 29 mm. **Obv. Inscription:** Chung Hua Min Kuo **Rev:** Crossed flags **Mint:** Aksu

Date	Mintage	G4	VG8	F12	VF20	XF40
ND (1912)	—	70.00	110	180	—	—

MILLED COINAGE

Y# A36.1 5 CASH
Copper **Obv:** Large Chinese inscription **Obv. Inscription:** "Chung-hua Min-kuo" between "T'ung-pi **Rev:** Flag **Rev. Legend:** Chinese outer, Turki inner, around flag **Mint:** Kashgar

Date	Mintage	G4	VG8	F12	VF20	XF40
ND (1912)	—	350	475	625	1,050	—

Y# A36.2 5 CASH
Copper **Obv:** Small Chinese inscription **Obv. Inscription:** "Chung-hua Min-kuo" between "T'ung-pi" **Rev:** Flag **Rev. Legend:** Chinese outer, Turki inner, around flag **Mint:** Kashgar

Date	Mintage	G4	VG8	F12	VF20	XF40
ND(ca.1912)	—	425	575	750	1,150	—

Y# 36 5 CASH
Copper **Obv. Legend:** Chinese around inscription "Chung-hua Min-kuo" **Rev:** Crossed flags **Rev. Inscription:** Turki above and below crossed flags **Mint:** Kashgar

Date	Mintage	G4	VG8	F12	VF20	XF40
AH1331	—	125	170	280	525	—

Y# B39.1 10 CASH
Copper **Obv:** Large character "Shih" (ten), normal "Pao" **Obv. Legend:** Chung Hua Min Kuo **Rev:** Crossed flags

Date	Mintage	G4	VG8	F12	VF20	XF40
ND (1910)	—	12.00	20.00	35.00	55.00	100

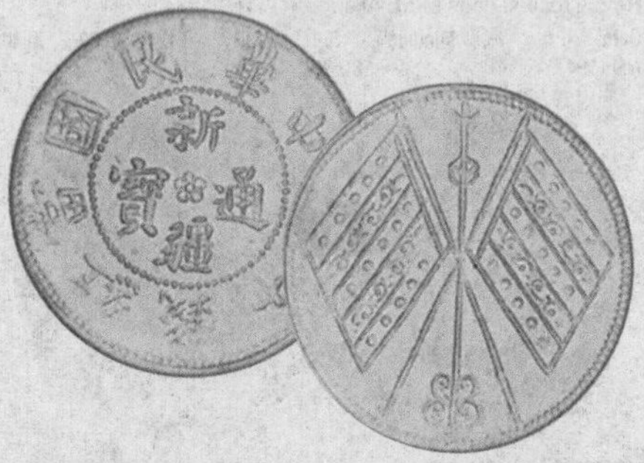

Y# B39.2 10 CASH
Copper **Obv:** Small character "Shih" (ten) **Obv. Legend:** Chung Hua Min Kuo **Rev:** Small crossed flags

Date	Mintage	G4	VG8	F12	VF20	XF40
ND (1910)	—	16.00	32.00	45.00	75.00	130

Y# B36.1 10 CASH
Copper **Obv:** Large Chinese inscription **Obv. Inscription:** "Chung-hua Min-kuo" between "T'ung-pi" **Rev:** Flag **Rev. Legend:** Chinese outer, Turki inner, around flag **Mint:** Kashgar

Date	Mintage	G4	VG8	F12	VF20	XF40
ND (1912)	—	31.25	47.00	65.00	135	—

Y# B36.2 10 CASH
Copper **Obv:** Small Chinese inscription **Obv. Inscription:** "Chung-hua Min-kuo" between "T'ung-pi" **Rev:** Flag **Rev. Legend:** Chinese outer, Turki inner, around flag **Mint:** Kashgar

Date	Mintage	G4	VG8	F12	VF20	XF40
ND (1912)	—	31.25	47.00	65.00	135	—

Y# 38.2 10 CASH
Copper **Rev:** Crossed flags, modified Turki legend with date at bottom **Mint:** Kashgar

Date	Mintage	G4	VG8	F12	VF20	XF40
AH1331	—	11.00	16.00	22.50	55.00	—
AH1332	—	11.00	16.00	22.50	55.00	—
AH1334	—	11.00	16.00	22.50	55.00	—
AH1335	—	11.00	16.00	22.50	55.00	—

Y# A39.1 10 CASH
Copper **Obv. Legend:** Chung Hua Min Kuo **Rev:** Large crossed flags with vertical stripes

Date	Mintage	G4	VG8	F12	VF20	XF40
CD1 (1912)	—	7.50	13.50	18.50	28.50	55.00

Y# A39.2 10 CASH
Copper **Rev:** Small crossed flags with vertical stripes

Date	Mintage	G4	VG8	F12	VF20	XF40
CD1	—	11.00	19.00	25.00	40.00	115
Note: This type exists with a great variety of the "Shih" (ten), and "Pao" characters						
CD1 (1912)	—	11.00	19.00	25.00	40.00	115

Y# 38.1 10 CASH
Copper **Obv:** Chinese legend: "Shih Wen" (10 Cash) at upper left **Rev:** Crossed flags, date at upper center **Mint:** Kashgar

Date	Mintage	G4	VG8	F12	VF20	XF40
ND (1913)	—	9.00	19.00	25.00	60.00	—
AH1332	—	9.00	19.00	25.00	60.00	—
AH1333	—	9.00	19.00	25.00	60.00	—
AH1334	—	9.00	19.00	25.00	60.00	—

Y# 38.3 10 CASH
Copper **Obv:** Two lower right Chinese characters different **Obv. Inscription:** Chung Hua Min Kuo **Rev:** Crossed flags, AH date at top **Mint:** Kashgar

Date	Mintage	G4	VG8	F12	VF20	XF40
AH133-4	—	65.00	95.00	155	300	—

Y# 38.5 10 CASH
Copper **Obv:** Outer Chinese legend wtihout "Shih" of "Kashgar" at lower left **Obv. Inscription:** Chung Hua Min Kuo **Rev:** Crossed flags, Turki legend in florals with "Zarb Kashgar" at top **Mint:** Kashgar **Note:** Rev: similar to Y#A38.2

Date	Mintage	G4	VG8	F12	VF20	XF40
AH1334	—	47.00	75.00	125	265	—

Y# 38.6 10 CASH
Copper **Obv. Inscription:** Chung Hua Min Kuo **Rev:** Single flower in lower Turki legend **Mint:** Kashgar

Date	Mintage	G4	VG8	F12	VF20	XF40
AH1334	—	—	—	—	—	—

Y# 38.7 10 CASH
Copper **Obv. Inscription:** Chung Hua Min Kuo **Rev:** Without flowers or florals in Turki legends **Mint:** Kashgar

Date	Mintage	G4	VG8	F12	VF20	XF40
AH1334	—	—	—	—	—	—

Y# 38a.1 10 CASH
Copper **Obv:** Chinese date at upper right with rosette **Obv. Inscription:** Chung Hua Min Kuo **Mint:** Kashgar

Date	Mintage	G4	VG8	F12	VF20	XF40
AH1340	—	8.00	13.00	19.00	42.00	—
AH1339	—	8.00	13.00	19.00	42.00	—

Y# 38a.2 10 CASH
Copper **Obv:** Outer Chinese legend without "Shih" of "Kashgar" at upper left **Obv. Inscription:** Chung Hua Min Kuo **Rev:** Crossed flags **Mint:** Kashgar

Date	Mintage	G4	VG8	F12	VF20	XF40
AH134x	—	8.00	13.00	19.00	42.00	—

Y# 38a.3 10 CASH
Copper **Obv. Inscription:** Chung Hua Min Kuo **Rev:** Crossed flags, Turki legend rearranged **Mint:** Kashgar

Date	Mintage	G4	VG8	F12	VF20	XF40
AH1340	—	8.00	13.00	19.00	42.00	—
AH1339	—	8.00	13.00	19.00	42.00	—

Y# 38a.5 10 CASH

Copper **Obv:** Crowded Chinese year "11" **Obv. Inscription:** Chung Hua Min Kuo **Rev:** Crossed flags **Mint:** Kashgar

Date	Mintage	G4	VG8	F12	VF20	XF40
AH1340	—	32.00	50.00	80.00	150	—

Y# 38b.1 10 CASH

Copper **Obv:** Chinese legend "Min-kuo T'ung-yüan" in inner circle with "Kashgar" at right **Obv. Inscription:** Min Kuo T'ung Yüan **Rev:** Crossed flags **Mint:** Kashgar

Date	Mintage	G4	VG8	F12	VF20	XF40
AH1340	—	19.00	37.50	50.00	110	—

Y# 38b.2 10 CASH

Copper **Obv:** Outer Chinese legend rotated **Obv. Inscription:** Min Kuo T'ung Yüan **Rev:** Crossed flags **Mint:** Kashgar

Date	Mintage	G4	VG8	F12	VF20	XF40
AH134x	—	19.00	37.50	50.00	110	—

Y# C39 10 CASH

Copper **Obv. Inscription:** Chung Hua Min Kuo **Rev:** Turki legend around crossed flags

Date	Mintage	G4	VG8	F12	VF20	XF40
CD1921 Rare	—	—	—	—	—	—

Note: Status unknown

Y# A44.1 10 CASH

Copper **Obv. Inscription:** Chung Hua Min Kuo **Rev:** Crossed flags **Mint:** Kashgar

Date	Mintage	G4	VG8	F12	VF20	XF40
11(1922)	—	65.00	95.00	125	225	—

Y# A44.2 10 CASH

Copper **Obv. Inscription:** Chung Hua Min Kuo **Rev:** Crossed flags reversed **Mint:** Kashgar

Date	Mintage	G4	VG8	F12	VF20	XF40
11(1922)	—	65.00	95.00	125	225	—

Y# B38.1 10 CASH

Copper **Obv:** Chinese legend in inner circle; Chinese date at left and right of upper legend **Obv. Inscription:** Min Kuo T'ung Yüan **Rev:** Chinese characters "T'ung Yüan" in solid sunburst

Date	Mintage	G4	VG8	F12	VF20	XF40
CD1928	—	50.00	100	150	300	—

Y# B38.2 10 CASH

Copper **Obv:** Upper legend **Obv. Legend:** Hsinchiang Kashgar Tsao **Obv. Inscription:** Min Kuo T'ung Yüan **Rev:** Outlined sunburst **Rev. Inscription:** Small T'ung Yüan **Mint:** Kashgar

Date	Mintage	G4	VG8	F12	VF20	XF40
CD1928	—	37.50	90.00	125	270	—

Note: A similar coin with same upper legend and cyclical date 1929 at sides is reported

Y# B38.3 10 CASH

Copper **Obv:** Upper legend **Obv. Legend:** Hsinchiang K'a Tsao **Obv. Inscription:** Min Kuo T'ung Yüan **Rev:** Outlined sunburst **Rev. Inscription:** Large T'ung Yüan **Mint:** Kashgar

Date	Mintage	G4	VG8	F12	VF20	XF40
CD1928	—	19.00	30.00	37.50	85.00	—

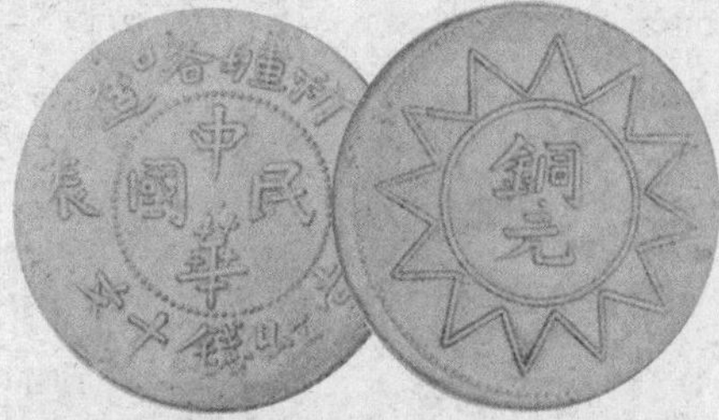

Y# B38.4 10 CASH

Copper **Obv:** Chinese date at left and right **Obv. Inscription:** Chung Hua Min Kuo **Rev:** Outlined sunburst **Rev. Inscription:** T'ung Yüan **Mint:** Kashgar

Date	Mintage	G4	VG8	F12	VF20	XF40
CD1928	—	6.00	10.00	15.00	37.50	—
CD1929	—	10.00	14.00	27.50	55.00	—

Y# B38.5 10 CASH

Copper **Obv. Inscription:** Chung Hua Min Kuo **Rev:** Outlined finely rayed sunburst **Rev. Inscription:** T'ung Yüan **Mint:** Kashgar

Date	Mintage	G4	VG8	F12	VF20	XF40
CD1928	—	75.00	115	175	300	—

Y# B38.7 10 CASH

Copper **Obv. Legend:** HSINCHIANG KASHGAR TSAO **Obv. Inscription:** Chung Hua Min Kuo **Rev:** Outlined sunburst (as Y#B38.3) **Rev. Inscription:** Large T'ung Yüan **Mint:** Kashgar

Date	Mintage	G4	VG8	F12	VF20	XF40
CD1928	—	19.00	30.00	65.00	—	—

Y# B38b.1 10 CASH

Copper **Obv. Inscription:** Chung Hua Min Kuo **Rev:** Turki legend in solid sunburst **Mint:** Kashgar

Date	Mintage	G4	VG8	F12	VF20	XF40
AH1346	—	155	220	375	675	—

Y# B38b.2 10 CASH

Copper **Obv:** Similar to Y#B838d **Obv. Inscription:** Chung Hua Min Kuo **Rev:** Turki legend in solid sunburst **Mint:** Kashgar

Date	Mintage	G4	VG8	F12	VF20	XF40
AH1346	—	190	250	450	750	—

Y# B38c.1 10 CASH

Copper **Obv. Inscription:** Min Kuo T'ung Yüan **Rev:** Chinese character "Jih" in solid sunburst

Date	Mintage	G4	VG8	F12	VF20	XF40
CD1928	—	220	350	525	900	—

Y# B38c.2 10 CASH

Copper **Obv:** Like B38c.1 **Obv. Inscription:** Min Kuo T'ung Yüan **Rev:** Chinese character "Jih" in rayed sunburst **Mint:** Kashgar

Date	Mintage	G4	VG8	F12	VF20	XF40
CD1928	—	220	350	525	900	—

Y# B38c.3 10 CASH

Copper **Obv:** Like Y#B38b.1 **Obv. Inscription:** Min Kuo T'ung Yüan **Rev:** Like Y#B38c.1 **Mint:** Kashgar

Date	Mintage	G4	VG8	F12	VF20	XF40
CD1928	—	220	350	525	900	—

Y# B38c.4 10 CASH

Copper **Obv. Legend:** Cyclic date at left and right like Y#B38.4 **Obv. Inscription:** Min Kuo T'ung Yüan

Date	Mintage	G4	VG8	F12	VF20	XF40
CD1928	—	220	350	525	900	—

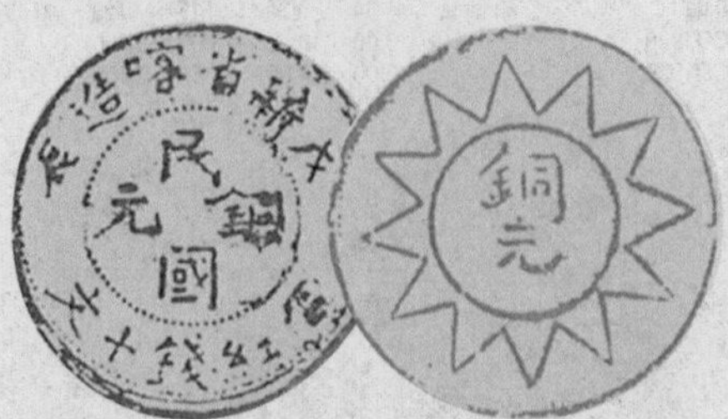

Y# B38d 10 CASH
Copper **Obv:** Chinese legend in inner circle **Obv. Inscription:** Min Kuo T'ung Yüan **Rev:** Chinese characters "T'ung Yüan" in solid sunburst **Mint:** Kashgar

Date	Mintage	G4	VG8	F12	VF20	XF40
CD1928	—	155	220	375	675	—

Y# B38.6 10 CASH
Copper **Obv. Inscription:** Chung Hua Min Kuo **Rev:** Sunburst **Rev. Inscription:** T'ung Yüan **Mint:** Kashgar

Date	Mintage	G4	VG8	F12	VF20	XF40
CD1929	—	50.00	75.00	125	255	—

Y# B38a.1 10 CASH
Copper **Obv:** Chinese characters for date to left and right of "Chung Hua Min Kuo" in inner circle **Obv. Inscription:** Chung Hua Min Kuo **Rev:** Turki legend in oulined sunburst **Mint:** Kashgar

Date	Mintage	G4	VG8	F12	VF20	XF40
CD1929	—	125	205	325	525	—

Y# B38a.2 10 CASH
Copper **Obv. Legend:** Hsinchiang K'ashih Tsao **Obv. Inscription:** Chung Hua Min Kuo **Rev:** Sunburst **Mint:** Kashgar

Date	Mintage	G4	VG8	F12	VF20	XF40
CD1929	—	95.00	125	175	270	—

Y# 40.2 10 CASH
Copper **Obv:** Large starburst in center **Obv. Inscription:** Chung Hua Min Kuo **Rev:** Long streamers

Date	Mintage	G4	VG8	F12	VF20	XF40
CD1929 Rare	—	9.00	15.00	20.00	37.50	70.00

Note: Y#40 inscribed "Sheng Ch'eng" (provincial capital) in upper legend refers to Tihwa (Urumchi, now Ürümqi)

Y# 40.3 10 CASH
Copper **Obv:** Cyclical date at upper right in legend **Obv. Inscription:** Chung Hua Min Kuo **Mint:** Kashgar

Date	Mintage	G4	VG8	F12	VF20	XF40
CD1930 Rare	—	—	—	—	—	—

Y# 40.41 10 CASH
Copper **Obv:** Chinese legend in inner circle with "Hsin Chiang" at upper right **Obv. Inscription:** Chung Hua Min Kuo **Rev:** Flags with solid sunbursts with inner circles

Date	Mintage	G4	VG8	F12	VF20	XF40
CD1929	—	9.00	15.00	20.00	37.50	70.00
CD1930 Rare	—	—	—	—	—	—

Note: The cyclical date character at left exists closed, which is rare, and open for CD1929

Y# 44.1 10 CASH
Copper **Obv. Legend:** Hsinchiang K'ashih Tsao **Obv. Inscription:** Chung Hua Min Kuo **Rev:** Crossed flags with wide outlined sunbursts; flags at right with inner circle **Mint:** Kashgar

Date	Mintage	G4	VG8	F12	VF20	XF40
CD1929	—	6.00	12.00	22.50	50.00	—

Y# 44.2 10 CASH
Copper **Obv:** Small eight-petaled rosette in center **Obv. Inscription:** Chung Hua Min Kuo **Rev:** Flag at right without inner circle **Mint:** Kashgar

Date	Mintage	G4	VG8	F12	VF20	XF40
CD1929	—	9.00	14.00	22.50	42.00	—
CD1930	—	9.00	14.00	22.50	42.00	—

Y# 44.3 10 CASH
Copper **Obv:** Star with rays in center **Obv. Inscription:** Chung Hua Min Kuo **Rev:** Crossed flags **Mint:** Kashgar

Date	Mintage	G4	VG8	F12	VF20	XF40
CD1930	—	11.00	22.50	27.50	55.00	—

Y# 44.4 10 CASH
Copper **Obv:** Eight-petaled rosette in center **Obv. Inscription:** Chung Hua Min Kuo **Rev:** Crossed flags with narrow outlined sunbursts **Mint:** Kashgar

Date	Mintage	G4	VG8	F12	VF20	XF40
CD1930	—	13.00	25.00	45.00	95.00	—

Y# 44.5 10 CASH
Copper **Obv. Inscription:** Chung Hua Min Kuo **Rev:** Crossed flags with solid sunbursts **Mint:** Kashgar

Date	Mintage	G4	VG8	F12	VF20	XF40
CD1933	—	8.00	15.00	27.50	55.00	—

Y# 44.6 10 CASH
Copper **Obv. Inscription:** Chung Hua Min Kuo **Rev:** Reversed flags with large solid sunbursts **Mint:** Kashgar

Date	Mintage	G4	VG8	F12	VF20	XF40
CD1929	—	6.00	14.00	25.00	45.00	—
CD1930	—	8.00	15.00	27.50	55.00	—

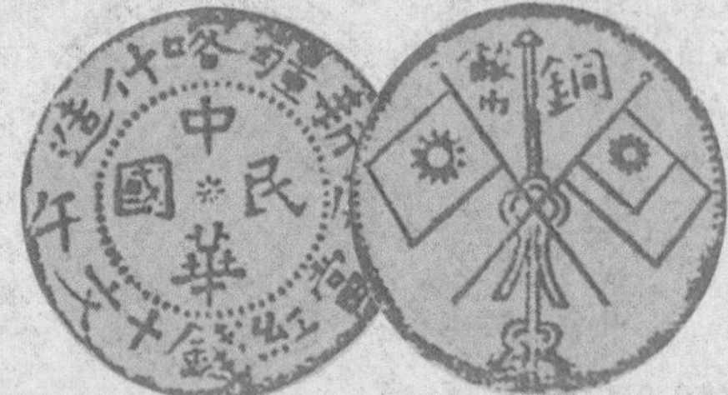

Y# 44.7 10 CASH
Copper **Obv. Inscription:** Chung Hua Min Kuo **Rev:** Reversed crossed flags with small solid sunbursts **Mint:** Kashgar

Date	Mintage	G4	VG8	F12	VF20	XF40
CD1930	—	31.25	65.00	125	265	—

Y# 44.8 10 CASH
Copper **Obv:** Upper legend **Obv. Legend:** Hsinchiang K'ashih Tsao **Obv. Inscription:** Chung Hua Min Kuo **Rev:** Crossed flags **Mint:** Kashgar

Date	Mintage	G4	VG8	F12	VF20	XF40
CD1929	—	95.00	125	175	270	—

Y# 44.9 10 CASH
Copper **Obv. Inscription:** Chung Hua Min Kuo **Rev:** Reversed crossed flags with large "flower petal" outlined sunbursts **Mint:** Kashgar

Date	Mintage	G4	VG8	F12	VF20	XF40
CD1930	—	8.00	15.00	27.50	55.00	—

Y# 44.10 10 CASH
Copper **Obv. Inscription:** Chung Hua Min Kuo **Rev:** Crossed flags reversed **Mint:** Kashgar

Date	Mintage	G4	VG8	F12	VF20	XF40
CD1930	—	—	—	—	—	—

Y# 48 20 CASH
Copper **Obv. Inscription:** Chung Hua Min Kuo **Rev:** Crossed flags **Mint:** Kashgar

Date	Mintage	G4	VG8	F12	VF20	XF40
AH133x Rare	—	—	—	—	—	—

Y# A41.1 20 CASH
Copper **Obv:** Chinese legend in inner circle with "Hsin Chiang" at upper right **Obv. Inscription:** Chung Hua Min Kuo **Rev:** Crossed flags

Date	Mintage	G4	VG8	F12	VF20	XF40
CD1929	—	95.00	155	250	450	—
CD1930	—	105	175	280	500	—

Note: Y#A41.1 inscribed "Sheng Ch'eng" (provincial capital) in upper legend refers to Tihwa (Urumchi now Urumqi)

Y# A41.2 20 CASH
Copper **Obv:** Cyclical date at upper right **Obv. Inscription:** Chung Hua Min Kuo **Rev:** Crossed flags

Date	Mintage	G4	VG8	F12	VF20	XF40
CD1930 Rare	—	—	—	—	—	—

Y# 39.1 20 CASH
Copper **Obv:** 8-petaled rosette in center **Obv. Inscription:** Hsin Chiang T'ung Pao **Rev:** Two stripes in crossed flags have arabesques

Date	Mintage	VG8	F12	VF20	XF40	MS60
ND(1931)	—	13.00	22.50	32.50	55.00	300

Y# 39.2 20 CASH
Copper **Obv:** 5-petaled rosette in center **Obv. Inscription:** Hsin Chiang T'ung Pao **Rev:** Crossed flags

Date	Mintage	VG8	F12	VF20	XF40	MS60
ND(1931)	—	65.00	125	190	350	550

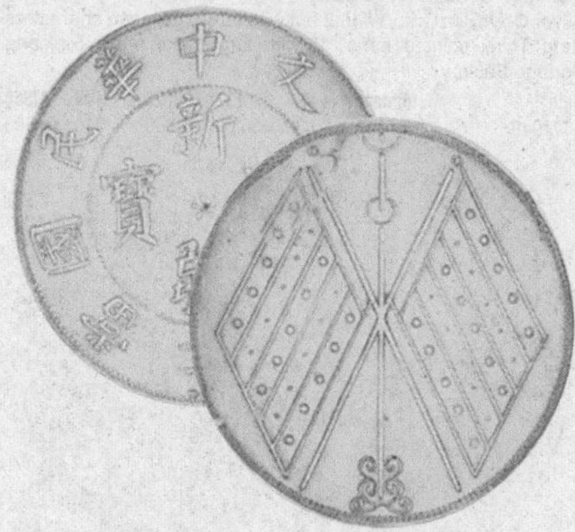

Y# 39.3 20 CASH
Copper **Obv. Inscription:** Hsin Chiang T'ung Pao **Rev:** Crossed flags without arabesques

Date	Mintage	VG8	F12	VF20	XF40	MS60
ND(1931) Restrike	—	—	—	—	75.00	300

Y# 43 5 MISCALS
17.30 g., Silver **Obv:** Stars dividing Chinese legends **Obv. Inscription:** Chung Hua Min Kuo **Rev:** Crossed flags dividing Turki legend **Mint:** Kashgar

Date	Mintage	VG8	F12	VF20	XF40	MS60
AH1331	—	50.00	95.00	200	425	—
AH1332	—	50.00	95.00	200	425	—

Y# 43.1 5 MISCALS
17.30 g., Silver **Obv:** Rosettes dividing Chinese legend **Obv. Inscription:** Chung Hua Min Kuo **Rev:** Crossed flags **Mint:** Kashgar **Note:** Varieties exist.

Date	Mintage	VG8	F12	VF20	XF40	MS60
AH1330	—	55.00	100	210	450	—
AH1331	—	55.00	100	210	450	—
AH1332	—	55.00	100	210	450	—
AH13-32	—	55.00	100	210	450	—

Y# 43.2 5 MISCALS
17.30 g., Silver **Obv:** Rosettes dividing Chinese legend **Obv. Inscription:** Chung Hua Min Kuo **Rev:** Crossed flags **Mint:** Kashgar

Date	Mintage	VG8	F12	VF20	XF40	MS60
AH1334	—	70.00	135	300	650	—
AH133-4	—	70.00	135	300	650	—

Note: Varieties exist

Y# 43.3 5 MISCALS
17.30 g., Silver **Obv:** Rosette in center, floral arrangements dividing Chinese legend **Obv. Inscription:** Chung Hua Min Kuo **Rev:** Crossed flags **Mint:** Kashgar **Note:** Varieties exist.

Date	Mintage	VG8	F12	VF20	XF40	MS60
AH13-32	—	60.00	115	240	550	—
AH133-2	—	60.00	115	240	550	—
AH133-4	—	70.00	135	300	650	—

Y# 43.4 5 MISCALS
17.30 g., Silver **Obv:** Stars divide rotated outer Chinese legend **Obv. Inscription:** Chung Hua Min Kuo **Rev:** Crossed flags **Mint:** Kashgar

Date	Mintage	VG8	F12	VF20	XF40	MS60
AHx13x	—	—	—	—	—	—

Note: Considered contemporary forgeries by some experts

Y# 41 5 MISCALS (5 Mace)
17.90 g., Silver **Obv. Legend:** Chung Hua Min Kuo (year) Nien **Rev:** Two stripes in crossed flags have arabesques

Date	Mintage	VG8	F12	VF20	XF40	MS60
1(1912)	—	60.00	100	225	450	—

Y# 41a 5 MISCALS (5 Mace)
17.90 g., Silver **Obv. Legend:** Chung Hua Min Kuo (year) Nien **Rev:** Four stripes in crossed flags have arabesques

Date	Mintage	VG8	F12	VF20	XF40	MS60
1(1912)	—	60.00	100	225	450	—

Y# 42 SAR (Tael)
35.90 g., Silver **Obv. Legend:** Chung Hua Min Kuo (year) Nien **Rev:** Two stripes in crossed flags have arabesques

Date	Mintage	VG8	F12	VF20	XF40	MS60
1(1912)	—	70.00	120	240	425	1,750

Y# 42a SAR (Tael)
35.90 g., Silver **Obv:** Similar to Y#42 **Obv. Legend:** Chung Hua Min Kuo (year) Nien **Rev:** Four stripes in crossed flags have arabesques

Date	Mintage	VG8	F12	VF20	XF40	MS60
1(1912)	—	70.00	120	240	425	2,250

Y# 45 SAR (Tael)
35.00 g., Silver **Obv:** Large characters **Rev:** Rosette at top between wheat ears **Mint:** Ti-hua

Date	Mintage	VG8	F12	VF20	XF40	MS60
6(1917)	—	32.50	48.00	85.00	240	—

Y# 45.1 SAR (Tael)
35.00 g., Silver **Obv:** Similar to Y#45 but with small characters **Rev:** Without rosette at top **Mint:** Ti-hua

Date	Mintage	VG8	F12	VF20	XF40	MS60
6(1917)	—	32.50	48.00	70.00	120	—

Y# 45.2 SAR (Tael)
35.00 g., Silver **Rev:** Rosette at top between more ornate branches **Mint:** Ti-hua

Date	Mintage	VG8	F12	VF20	XF40	MS60
7(1918)	—	35.00	50.00	90.00	240	600

Y# 46.1 DOLLAR (Yuan)
Silver **Obv:** Similar to Y#46.2 but with larger Chinese characters **Rev:** Think pointed base "1" with large serif **Mint:** Sinkiang Pouring Factory

Date	Mintage	VG8	F12	VF20	XF40	MS60
38//1949	—	30.00	36.00	60.00	210	550

Y# 46.2 DOLLAR (Yuan)
Silver **Obv:** Smaller Chinese characters **Rev:** Thin pointed base "1" **Mint:** Sinkiang Pouring Factory

Date	Mintage	VG8	F12	VF20	XF40	MS60
38//1949	—	30.00	40.00	70.00	220	575

Y# 46.3 DOLLAR (Yuan)
Silver **Rev:** Square-based "1" **Mint:** Sinkiang Pouring Factory

Date	Mintage	VG8	F12	VF20	XF40	MS60
38//1949	—	32.50	50.00	90.00	240	—

Y# 46.4 DOLLAR (Yuan)
Silver **Obv:** Outlined Chinese characters "Yüan" in center **Mint:** Sinkiang Pouring Factory

Date	Mintage	VG8	F12	VF20	XF40	MS60
38//1949	—	70.00	120	180	350	—

Y# 46.5 DOLLAR (Yuan)
Silver **Mint:** Sinkiang Pouring Factory **Note:** 9-4-9-1 (1949) at bottom.

Date	Mintage	VG8	F12	VF20	XF40	MS60
38//1949	—	180	350	600	1,200	—

Y# 46 DOLLAR (Yuan)
Silver **Obv:** Similar to Y#46.2 but with larger Chinese characters **Rev:** Think pointed base "1" **Mint:** Sinkiang Pouring Factory **Note:** Kann #1267a reports a variety in the character "Kuo".

Date	Mintage	VG8	F12	VF20	XF40	MS60
38//1949	—	30.00	36.00	60.00	210	550

Kuang-hsü

Y# F38 10 CASH
Copper **Obv:** Chinese characters "Shih Wen" (10 Wen) at lower left **Rev:** Crossed flags, upper Turki legend inverted

Date	Mintage	G4	VG8	F12	VF20	XF40
AH1332	—	45.00	80.00	120	265	—

ISLAMIC REPUBLIC OF EASTERN TURKESTAN

Y# E38.1 20 CASH
Copper, 32-34 mm. **Rev:** Crossed flags

Date	Mintage	G4	VG8	F12	VF20	XF40
AH1352	—	100	200	475	900	—

Y# E38.2 20 CASH
Copper **Rev:** Crossed flags reversed

Date	Mintage	G4	VG8	F12	VF20	XF40
AH1352	—	100	200	475	900	—

Y# E38.3 20 CASH
Copper, 32-34 mm. **Rev:** Crossed flags, sun in partial frame in left flag, denomination given as two wen (sic)

Date	Mintage	G4	VG8	F12	VF20	XF40
AH1352	—	125	250	550	1,000	—

Y# E38.4 20 CASH
Copper, **Rev:** Crossed flags, large sun in national flag at left **Note:** Varieties exist.

Date	Mintage	G4	VG8	F12	VF20	XF40
AH1352	—	125	250	550	1,000	—

Note: Crudely cut Chinese denomination appears as 2 instead of 20; also encountered overstruck on 10 Cash, Y#44 varieties

Y# G38 20 CASH
Copper **Obv:** Similar to 20 Cash, Y#E38.3 **Rev:** Crossed flags, small flag at left

Date	Mintage	G4	VG8	F12	VF20	XF40
AH1352	—	125	250	550	1,000	—

Y# E39 MISCAL
Silver **Obv:** Turki legend around central Turki legend **Obv. Legend:** "Sharket Turkhestan Cumhuriyet Islamiyesi" around "Muskuk, sanah 1252" **Rev:** Turki legend **Rev. Legend:** Zarb Kashgar

Date	Mintage	G4	VG8	F12	VF20	XF40
AH1352 Rare	—	—	—	—	—	—

Note: Varieties of sun with eight and nine rays exist

UIGHURISTAN REPUBLIC

Y# D38.1 10 CASH
Copper **Rev:** Crossed flags, flag at right without fringe

Date	Mintage	G4	VG8	F12	VF20	XF40
AH1352	—	60.00	120	225	375	—

Y# D38.2 10 CASH
Copper **Rev:** Crossed flags, flag at right with partial fringe

Date	Mintage	G4	VG8	F12	VF20	XF40
AH1352	—	60.00	120	225	375	—

Y# D38.3 10 CASH
Copper **Rev:** Crossed flags, flag at right with full fringe

Date	Mintage	G4	VG8	F12	VF20	XF40
AH1352	—	60.00	120	225	375	—

Note: Encountered overstruck on various earlier Republican Series 10 Cash

PATTERNS

Including off metal strikes

KM#	Date	Mintage	Identification	Mkt Val
Pn40	AH1324 (1906)	—	Tael. Silver.	—
Pn41	ND-1906	—	Mace. Copper. Y#10; Kann#1034.	3,500
Pn42	ND-1906	—	2 Mace. Silver. Y#11; Kann #1033.	7,000
Pn43	ND-1906	—	2 Mace. Copper. Kann #1033x.	2,700
Pn44	ND-1906	—	4 Mace. Silver.	17,000
Pn45	ND-1906	—	4 Mace. Brass.	2,900
Pn46	ND-1906	—	5 Mace. Silver. Kann #1032.	—
Pn47	ND-1906	—	7 Mace. Silver. 2 Candareens, Y#12. Kann #1031.	—

SUIYUAN PROVINCE

In November 1913, the central government grouped together 19 Mongolian and 12 Shansi districts to form the Suiyuan Special Administrative Zone. In 1928, the name was changed to Suiyuan Province. The province was joined with other Mongolian provinces to form Inner Mongolia after the communist takeover in 1949.

REPUBLIC

MILLED COINAGE

KM# 3 FEN
Shell Casing Brass **Ruler:** (no ruler information) **Obv:** White Tower **Rev:** Ancient spade coin between Yi and Fen

Date	Mintage	VG8	F12	VF20	XF40	MS60
38(1949)	—	275	500	950	2,250	4,000

KM# 5 5 FEN
Shell Casing Brass **Ruler:** (no ruler information) **Obv:** White Tower **Rev:** Ancient spade coin between Wu(5) and Fen

Date	Mintage	VG8	F12	VF20	XF40	MS60
38(1949)	—	600	800	1,500	2,500	—

SZECHUAN PROVINCE

Sichuan

A province located in south-central China. The largest of the traditional Chinese provinces, Szechuan (Sichuan) is a plateau region watered by many rivers. These rivers carry much trading traffic. Agriculture or mining are the occupational choices of most of the populace. In World War II the national capital was moved to Chungking in Szechuan (Sichuan). Chengtu was an active imperial mint that opened in 1732 and was in practically continuous operation until the advent of modern equipment. Modern minting was introduced in the province when Chengtu began milled coinage in 1898. A mint was authorized for Chungking in 1905 but it did not begin operations until 1913. The Chengtu Mint was looted by soldiers in 1925. The last republic issues from Szechuan (Sichuan) were dated 1932.

The machinery for the first Szechuan (Sichuan) Mint was produced in New Jersey and the dies were engraved in Philadelphia. The mint was opened in 1898, but closed within a few months and did not reopen until 1901. There is no doubt now that Y#234-238 (K#145-149) were the first issues of this mint, contrary to the Kann listings.

EMPIRE

MILLED COINAGE

Y# 11t 20 CASH
Copper **Obv. Inscription:** Ta-ch'ing T'ung-pi

Date	Mintage	VG8	F12	VF20	XF40	MS60
CD1906	51,028,000	13.00	27.50	60.00	120	—

Y# 21t.1 20 CASH
Copper **Obv:** Bottom of Manchu word at 11 o'clock curls right **Obv. Inscription:** Ta-ch'ing T'ung-pi

Date	Mintage	VG8	F12	VF20	XF40	MS60
CD1909	33,414,000	20.00	35.00	70.00	140	—

Y# 21t.1a 20 CASH
Brass **Obv. Inscription:** Ta-ch'ing T'ung-pi

Date	Mintage	VG8	F12	VF20	XF40	MS60
CD1909	Inc. above	32.00	45.00	120	200	—

Y# 21t.2 20 CASH
Copper **Obv:** Bottom of Manchu word at 11 o'clock curls left **Obv. Inscription:** Ta-ch'ing T'ung-pi

Date	Mintage	VG8	F12	VF20	XF40	MS60
CD1909	—	20.00	35.00	70.00	140	—

Kuang-hsü

PROVINCIAL CAST COINAGE

C# 24–9 CASH
Cast Brass **Obv. Inscription:** Kuang-hsü T'ung-pao **Rev:** Manchu inscription **Rev. Inscription:** Boo-Cuwan **Mint:** Chuan

Date	Mintage	G4	VG8	F12	VF20	XF40
ND(1875-1908)	—	6.00	9.00	14.00	28.00	—

MILLED COINAGE

Y# 225 5 CASH
Copper **Obv:** Manchu at center **Obv. Legend:** Szu-ch'uan Kuan Chü Tsao **Obv. Inscription:** Kuang-hsü Yüan-pao **Rev:** Side view dragon

Date	Mintage	VG8	F12	VF20	XF40	MS60
ND(1903-04)	85,000	65.00	90.00	150	235	—

Y# 225a 5 CASH
Brass **Obv. Legend:** Szu-ch'uan Kuan Chü Tsao **Obv. Inscription:** Kuang-hsü Yüan-pao

Date	Mintage	VG8	F12	VF20	XF40	MS60
ND(1903-04) Rare	Inc. above	—	—	—	—	—

Y# 228 5 CASH

Brass **Obv:** Flower at center **Obv. Legend:** Szu-ch'uan Sheng Tsao **Obv. Inscription:** Kuang-hsü Yüan-pao **Rev:** Flying dragon

Date	Mintage	VG8	F12	VF20	XF40	MS60
ND(1903-04)	Inc. above	450	625	1,150	—	—

Y# A229 5 CASH

Brass **Obv:** Flower at center **Obv. Legend:** Szu-ch-uan Sheng Tsao **Obv. Inscription:** Kuang-hsü Yüan-pao **Rev:** Side view dragon **Note:** Prev. Y#A228.

Date	Mintage	VG8	F12	VF20	XF40	MS60
ND(1903-04)	Inc. above	125	175	300	500	—

Y# 226 10 CASH

Copper **Obv:** Thick Manchu in center, large rosettes **Obv. Legend:** Szu-ch'uan Kuan Chü Tsao **Obv. Inscription:** Kuang-hsü Yüan-pao

Date	Mintage	VG8	F12	VF20	XF40	MS60
ND(1903-05)	95,960,000	19.00	37.50	65.00	120	—

Y# 226.1 10 CASH

Copper **Obv:** Thin Manchu in center, small rosettes **Obv. Legend:** Szu-ch'uan Kuan Chü Tsao **Obv. Inscription:** Kuang-hsü Yüan-pao

Date	Mintage	VG8	F12	VF20	XF40	MS60
ND(1903-05)	Inc. above	34.50	70.00	130	225	—

Y# 226.2 10 CASH

Copper **Obv:** Large rosettes **Obv. Legend:** Szu-ch'uan Kuan Chü Tsao **Obv. Inscription:** Kuang-hsü Yüan-pao

Date	Mintage	VG8	F12	VF20	XF40	MS60
ND(1903-05)	Inc. above	32.00	60.00	110	200	—

Y# 229 10 CASH

Copper **Obv:** Legend with two characters at bottom, 6-9mm apart **Obv. Legend:** Szu-ch'uan Sheng Tsao **Obv. Inscription:** Kuang-hsü Yüan-pao **Rev:** Trident-shaped flame on dragon's body below letters CHU

Date	Mintage	VG8	F12	VF20	XF40	MS60
ND(1903-05)	Inc. above	6.00	11.00	22.50	50.00	—

Y# 229.1 10 CASH

Copper **Obv:** Legend with characters at bottom, 4-5mm apart **Obv. Legend:** Szu-ch'uan Sheng Tsao **Obv. Inscription:** Kuang-hsü Yüan-pao

Date	Mintage	VG8	F12	VF20	XF40	MS60
ND(1903-05)	Inc. above	6.00	11.00	22.50	50.00	—

Y# 229.2 10 CASH

Copper **Obv:** Manchu at 3 o'clock is lower in relation to center characters **Obv. Legend:** Szu-ch'uan Sheng Tsao **Obv. Inscription:** Kuang-hsü Yüan-pao

Date	Mintage	VG8	F12	VF20	XF40	MS60
ND(1903-05)	Inc. above	6.00	11.00	22.50	50.00	—

Y# 229.3 10 CASH

Copper **Obv:** Characters 6-9mm apart **Obv. Legend:** Szu-ch'uan Sheng Tsao **Obv. Inscription:** Kuang-hsü Yüan-pao **Rev:** Trident-shaped flame below letters HUE

Date	Mintage	VG8	F12	VF20	XF40	MS60
ND(1903-05)	Inc. above	6.00	11.00	22.50	50.00	—

Y# 229.3a 10 CASH

Brass **Obv. Legend:** Szu-ch'uan Sheng Tsao **Obv. Inscription:** Kuang-hsü Yüan-pao

Date	Mintage	VG8	F12	VF20	XF40	MS60
ND(1903-05)	Inc. above	6.00	11.00	22.50	50.00	—

Y# 229.4 10 CASH

Brass **Obv:** Characters 4-5mm apart **Obv. Legend:** Szu-ch'uan Sheng Tsao **Obv. Inscription:** Kuang-hsü Yüan-pao

Date	Mintage	VG8	F12	VF20	XF40	MS60
ND(1903-05)	Inc. above	6.00	11.00	22.50	50.00	—

Y# 229.5 10 CASH

Brass **Obv:** Bottom characters 6-9mm apart **Obv. Legend:** Szu-ch'uan Sheng Tsao **Obv. Inscription:** Kuang-hsü Yüan-pao **Rev:** Without trident-shaped flame, instead a cloud pointing to the letter U

Date	Mintage	VG8	F12	VF20	XF40	MS60
ND(1903-05)	Inc. above	5.00	8.00	17.00	35.00	—

Y# 229.5a 10 CASH

Copper **Obv. Legend:** Szu-ch'uan Sheng Tsao **Obv. Inscription:** Kuang-hsü Yüan-pao

Date	Mintage	VG8	F12	VF20	XF40	MS60
ND(1903-05)	Inc. above	6.00	10.00	22.50	45.00	—

Y# 229.6 10 CASH

Brass **Obv:** Characters 4-5mm apart **Obv. Legend:** Szu-ch'uan Sheng Tsao **Obv. Inscription:** Kuang-hsü Yüan-pao

Date	Mintage	VG8	F12	VF20	XF40	MS60
ND(1903-05)	Inc. above	6.00	11.00	22.50	50.00	—

Y# 229.6a 10 CASH

Copper **Obv. Legend:** Szu-ch'uan Sheng Tsao **Obv. Inscription:** Kuang-hsü Yüan-pao

Date	Mintage	VG8	F12	VF20	XF40	MS60
ND(1903-05)	Inc. above	4.00	6.00	12.00	25.00	—

Y# 229.7 10 CASH

Brass **Obv:** Manchu at 3 o'clock is lower **Obv. Legend:** Szu-ch'uan Sheng Tsao **Obv. Inscription:** Kuang-hsü Yüan-pao

Date	Mintage	VG8	F12	VF20	XF40	MS60
ND(1903-05)	Inc. above	6.00	11.00	22.50	50.00	—

Y# 229.7a 10 CASH

Copper **Obv. Legend:** Szu-ch'uan Sheng Tsao **Obv. Inscription:** Kuang-hsü Yüan-pao

Date	Mintage	VG8	F12	VF20	XF40	MS60
ND(1903-05)	Inc. above	4.00	6.00	14.00	30.00	—

Y# 229.8 10 CASH

Brass **Obv:** Characters 4-5mm apart **Obv. Legend:** Szu-ch'uan Sheng Tsao **Obv. Inscription:** Kuang-hsü Yüan-pao **Rev:** Without cloud below CHU, high point of dragon's body below letter "C", tail joins body above "S" in "CASH"

Date	Mintage	VG8	F12	VF20	XF40	MS60
ND(1903-05)	Inc. above	8.00	15.00	35.00	75.00	—

Y# 229.8a 10 CASH

Copper **Obv. Legend:** Szu-ch'uan Sheng Tsao **Obv. Inscription:** Kuang-hsü Yüan-pao

Date	Mintage	VG8	F12	VF20	XF40	MS60
ND(1903-05)	Inc. above	3.00	5.00	9.00	18.00	—

Y# 229.9 10 CASH

Copper **Obv. Legend:** Szu-ch'uan Sheng Tsao **Obv. Inscription:** Kuang-hsü Yüan-pao **Rev:** High point of dragon's body below letter H, tail joins body above letter "C" in "CASH"

Date	Mintage	VG8	F12	VF20	XF40	MS60
ND(1903-05)	Inc. above	3.00	5.00	9.00	18.00	—

Y# 231 10 CASH

Copper **Obv. Legend:** Szu-ch'uan Sheng Tsao **Obv. Inscription:** Kuang-hsü Yüan-pao

Date	Mintage	VG8	F12	VF20	XF40	MS60
ND(1903-05)	Inc. above	225	300	400	550	—

Y# 10t 10 CASH

Copper **Obv. Inscription:** Ta-ch'ing T'ung-pi **Rev. Legend:** Kuang-hsü Nien-tsao, TAI-CHING-TI-KUO...

Date	Mintage	VG8	F12	VF20	XF40	MS60
CD-1906	337,748,000	4.00	9.00	22.50	45.00	—

Y# 227 20 CASH

Copper **Obv. Inscription:** Kuang-hsü Yüan-pao

Date	Mintage	VG8	F12	VF20	XF40	MS60
ND(1903-05)	25,319,000	150	190	325	525	—

Y# 230 20 CASH

Copper **Obv:** Small Manchu at 3 and 9 o'clock **Obv. Legend:** Szu-ch'uan Sheng Tsao **Obv. Inscription:** Kuang-hsü Yüan-pao **Rev:** Trident flame points to "E" of "SZE"

Date	Mintage	VG8	F12	VF20	XF40	MS60
ND(1903-05)	Inc. above	15.00	22.50	55.00	100	—

Y# 230.1 20 CASH

Copper **Obv:** Large Manchu at 3 and 9 o'clock **Obv. Legend:** Szu-ch'uan Sheng Tsao **Obv. Inscription:** Kuang-hsü Yüan-pao **Rev:** Large trident flame points to "C" of "CHUEN" **Note:** Varieties exist.

Date	Mintage	VG8	F12	VF20	XF40	MS60
ND(1903-05)	Inc. above	45.00	75.00	145	270	—

Y# 230.3 20 CASH

Copper **Obv:** Large Manchu **Obv. Legend:** Szu-ch'uan Sheng Tsao **Obv. Inscription:** Kuang-hsü Yüan-pao **Rev:** Trident flame below "ZE"

Date	Mintage	VG8	F12	VF20	XF40	MS60
ND(1903-05)	Inc. above	22.50	45.00	90.00	145	—

Y# 230.4 20 CASH

Copper **Obv. Legend:** Szu-ch'uan Sheng Tsao **Obv. Inscription:** Kuang-hsü Yüan-pao **Rev:** Trident flame below "CHU" of "CHUEN", large letters

Date	Mintage	VG8	F12	VF20	XF40	MS60
ND(1903-05)	—	45.00	90.00	180	285	—

Y# 230.5 20 CASH

Copper **Obv. Legend:** Szu-ch'uan Sheng Tsao **Obv. Inscription:** Kuang-hsü Yüan-pao **Rev:** Trident flame points to "E" of "CHUEN", small letters

Date	Mintage	VG8	F12	VF20	XF40	MS60
ND(1903-05)	Inc. above	—	—	—	—	—

Y# 230.6 20 CASH

Copper **Obv:** Different small Manchu **Obv. Legend:** Szu-ch'uan Sheng Tsao **Obv. Inscription:** Kuang-hsü Yüan-pao **Rev:** Large 5-petaled rosettes, dragon differs

Date	Mintage	VG8	F12	VF20	XF40	MS60
ND(1903-05)	Inc. above	20.00	32.00	65.00	130	—

Y# 230.7a 20 CASH

Brass **Obv:** Small Manchu **Obv. Legend:** Szu-ch'uan Sheng Tsao **Obv. Inscription:** Kuang-hsü Yüan-pao **Rev:** Larger cloud below "CHUEN"

Date	Mintage	VG8	F12	VF20	XF40	MS60
ND(1903-05)	Inc. above	22.50	37.50	70.00	140	—

Y# 234 5 CENTS

1.30 g., 0.820 Silver 0.0343 oz. ASW, 15.82 mm. **Obv. Legend:** Szu-ch'uan Sheng Tsao **Obv. Inscription:** Kuang-hsü Yüan-pao **Edge:** Reeded

Date	Mintage	VG8	F12	VF20	XF40	MS60
ND(1898; 1901-08)	671,000	25.00	60.00	120	250	500

Y# 234.1 5 CENTS

1.30 g., 0.820 Silver 0.0343 oz. ASW, 15.82 mm. **Obv. Legend:** Szu-ch'uan Sheng Tsao **Obv. Inscription:** Kuang-hsü Yüan-pao **Rev:** With errors in the English legend **Rev. Legend:** 8ZECHUEN PROVIN(D inverted) EI? (errors) **Edge:** Reeded

Date	Mintage	VG8	F12	VF20	XF40	MS60
ND(1901-08)	Inc. above	8.00	22.50	37.50	100	600

Y# 235 10 CENTS

2.60 g., 0.820 Silver 0.0685 oz. ASW **Obv. Legend:** Szu-ch'uan Sheng Tsao **Obv. Inscription:** Kuang-hsü Yüan-pao

Date	Mintage	VG8	F12	VF20	XF40	MS60
ND(1898; 1901-08)	1,274,000	16.00	45.00	110	225	550

Y# 236 20 CENTS

5.30 g., 0.820 Silver 0.1397 oz. ASW **Obv. Legend:** Szu-ch'uan Sheng Tsao **Obv. Inscription:** Kuang-hsü Yüan-pao **Rev:** Five flames on pearl

Date	Mintage	VG8	F12	VF20	XF40	MS60
ND(1898; 1901-08)	897,000	25.00	50.00	115	240	600

Y# 236.1 20 CENTS

5.30 g., 0.820 Silver 0.1397 oz. ASW **Obv. Legend:** Szu-ch'uan Sheng Tsao **Obv. Inscription:** Kuang-hsü Yüan-pao **Rev:** Six flames on pearl

Date	Mintage	VG8	F12	VF20	XF40	MS60
ND(1898; 1901-08)	Inc. above	25.00	50.00	115	240	600

Y# 236.2 20 CENTS

5.30 g., 0.820 Silver 0.1397 oz. ASW **Obv. Legend:** Szu-ch'uan Sheng Tsao **Obv. Inscription:** Kuang-hsü Yüan-pao **Rev:** Seven flames on pearl

Date	Mintage	VG8	F12	VF20	XF40	MS60
ND(1898; 1901-08)	Inc. above	25.00	50.00	115	240	600

Y# 236.3 20 CENTS

5.30 g., 0.820 Silver 0.1397 oz. ASW **Obv. Legend:** Szu-ch'uan Sheng Tsao **Obv. Inscription:** Kuang-hsü Yüan-pao **Rev:** Various errors in English legend

Date	Mintage	VG8	F12	VF20	XF40	MS60
ND(1901-08)	Inc. above	8.00	22.50	37.50	100	400

Y# 237 50 CENTS

13.20 g., 0.860 Silver 0.365 oz. ASW **Obv. Legend:** Szu-ch'uan Sheng Tsao **Obv. Inscription:** Kuang-hsü Yüan-pao **Rev:** Dragon with narrow face, small cross at either side, large fireball

Date	Mintage	VG8	F12	VF20	XF40	MS60
ND(1898; 1901-08)	474,000	60.00	140	300	1,000	5,500

Y# 237.1 50 CENTS

13.20 g., 0.860 Silver 0.365 oz. ASW **Obv. Legend:** Szu-ch'uan Sheng Tsao **Obv. Inscription:** Kuang-hsü Yüan-pao **Rev:** Various errors in English legend

Date	Mintage	VG8	F12	VF20	XF40	MS60
ND(1901-08)	Inc. above	27.50	55.00	115	425	3,750

Y# 237.2 50 CENTS

13.20 g., 0.860 Silver 0.365 oz. ASW **Obv. Legend:** Szu-ch'uan Sheng Tsao **Obv. Inscription:** Kuang-hsü Yüan-pao **Rev:** Dragon with tapering face and small chin, small fireball, small cross at either side of dragon

Date	Mintage	VG8	F12	VF20	XF40	MS60
ND(1901-08)	Inc. above	22.50	45.00	90.00	375	2,500

Y# 237.3 50 CENTS

13.20 g., 0.860 Silver 0.365 oz. ASW **Obv. Legend:** Szu-ch'uan Sheng Tsao **Obv. Inscription:** Kuang-hsü Yüan-pao **Rev:** Dragon with wide face and smaller fireball, thicker spines on top of dragon's head, small cross at either side of dragon

Date	Mintage	VG8	F12	VF20	XF40	MS60
ND(1901-08)	Inc. above	22.50	45.00	90.00	375	2,500

Y# 238 DOLLAR

26.80 g., 0.900 Silver 0.7755 oz. ASW **Obv. Legend:** Szu-ch'uan Sheng Tsao **Obv. Inscription:** Kuang-hsü Yüan-pao **Rev:** Dragon with narrow face and large fireball, small cross at either side of dragon

Date	Mintage	VG8	F12	VF20	XF40	MS60
ND(1901-08)	6,487,000	35.00	55.00	95.00	300	5,000

Y# 238.1 DOLLAR
26.80 g., 0.900 Silver 0.7755 oz. ASW **Obv. Legend:** Szu-ch'uan Sheng Tsao **Obv. Inscription:** Kuang-hsü Yüan-pao **Rev:** Inverted "A" instead of "V" in "PROVINCE" in legend

Date	Mintage	VG8	F12	VF20	XF40	MS60
ND(1901-08)	Inc. above	35.00	55.00	90.00	275	5,000

Y# 238.2 DOLLAR
26.80 g., 0.900 Silver 0.7755 oz. ASW **Obv. Inscription:** Kuang-hsü Yüan-pao **Rev:** Dragon with wider face and flatter pearl, small cross at either side of dragon

Date	Mintage	VG8	F12	VF20	XF40	MS60
ND(1901-08)	Inc. above	35.00	55.00	85.00	250	5,000

Y# 238.3 DOLLAR
26.80 g., 0.900 Silver 0.7755 oz. ASW **Obv. Legend:** Szu-ch'uan Sheng Tsao **Obv. Inscription:** Kuang-hsü Yüan-pao **Rev:** "7 MACE" and "3 CANDAREENS" instead of "2 CANDAREENS"

Date	Mintage	VG8	F12	VF20	XF40	MS60
ND(1901-08)	Inc. above	42.00	85.00	150	500	7,000

Hsüan-t'ung

Y# 20t.1 10 CASH
Copper **Obv:** Bottom of Manchu word at 11 o'clock curls to left **Obv. Inscription:** Ta-ch'ing T'ung-pi **Rev. Legend:** Hsüan-t'ung Nien-tsao, TAI-CHING-TI-KUO...

Date	Mintage	VG8	F12	VF20	XF40	MS60
CD-1909	231,930,000	1.25	2.50	6.00	15.00	—

Y# 20t.1a 10 CASH
Brass **Obv. Inscription:** Ta-ch'ing T'ung-pi **Rev. Legend:** Hsüan-t'ung Nien-tsao, TAI-CHING-TI-KUO...

Date	Mintage	VG8	F12	VF20	XF40	MS60
CD-1909	Inc. above	4.00	6.00	22.50	40.00	—

Y# 20t.2 10 CASH
Copper **Obv:** Bottom of Manchu word at 11 o'clock curls to right **Obv. Inscription:** Ta-ch'ing T'ung-pi **Rev. Legend:** Hsüan-t'ung Nien-tsao, TAI-CHING-TI-KUO...

Date	Mintage	VG8	F12	VF20	XF40	MS60
CD1909	Inc. above	6.00	11.00	22.50	40.00	—

Y# 239 5 CENTS
1.30 g., 0.820 Silver 0.0343 oz. ASW **Obv. Legend:** Szu-ch'uan Sheng Tsao **Obv. Inscription:** Hsüan-t'ung Yüan-pao

Date	Mintage	VG8	F12	VF20	XF40	MS60
ND(1910)	566,000	15.00	37.50	60.00	200	800

Y# 240 10 CENTS
2.60 g., 0.820 Silver 0.0685 oz. ASW **Obv. Legend:** Szu-ch'uan Sheng Tsao **Obv. Inscription:** Hsüan-t'ung Yüan-pao

Date	Mintage	VG8	F12	VF20	XF40	MS60
ND(1909-11)	278,000	13.00	37.50	45.00	140	500

Y# 241 20 CENTS
5.30 g., 0.820 Silver 0.1397 oz. ASW **Obv. Legend:** Szu-ch'uan Sheng Tsao **Obv. Inscription:** Hsüan-t'ung Yüan-pao

Date	Mintage	VG8	F12	VF20	XF40	MS60
ND(1909-11) Rare	41,000	—	—	—	—	—

Y# 242 50 CENTS
13.20 g., 0.860 Silver 0.365 oz. ASW **Obv. Legend:** Szu-ch'uan Sheng Tsao **Obv. Inscription:** Hsüan-t'ung Yüan-pao

Date	Mintage	VG8	F12	VF20	XF40	MS60
ND(1909-11)	38,000	45.00	130	225	750	4,000

Y# 242.1 50 CENTS
13.20 g., 0.860 Silver 0.365 oz. ASW **Obv. Legend:** Szu-ch'uan Sheng Tsao **Obv. Inscription:** Hsüan-t'ung Yüan-pao **Rev:** Inverted "A" in place of "V" in "PROVINCE" in legend

Date	Mintage	VG8	F12	VF20	XF40	MS60
ND(1901-11)	Inc. above	45.00	130	225	750	4,000

Y# 243 DOLLAR
26.80 g., 0.900 Silver 0.7755 oz. ASW **Obv. Legend:** Szu-ch'uan Sheng Tsao **Obv. Inscription:** Hsüan-t'ung Yüan-pao **Rev:** Large spines on dragon's body

Date	Mintage	VG8	F12	VF20	XF40	MS60
ND(1909-11)	2,846,000	35.00	55.00	100	325	6,000

Y# 243.1 DOLLAR
26.80 g., 0.900 Silver 0.7755 oz. ASW **Obv. Legend:** Szu-ch'uan Sheng Tsao **Obv. Inscription:** Hsüan-t'ung Yüan-pao **Rev:** Inverted "A" instead of "V" in "PROVINCE"

Date	Mintage	VG8	F12	VF20	XF40	MS60
ND(1909-11)	Inc. above	35.00	55.00	110	350	5,500

Y# 243.2 DOLLAR
26.80 g., 0.900 Silver 0.7755 oz. ASW **Obv. Legend:** Szu-ch'uan Sheng Tsao **Obv. Inscription:** Hsüan-t'ung Yüan-pao **Rev:** Small spines on dragon's body

Date	Mintage	VG8	F12	VF20	XF40	MS60
ND(1909-11)	Inc. above	45.00	100	150	500	6,000

REPUBLIC

CUT MILLED COINAGE

Y# 459y 50 CASH
Brass **Note:** 200 Cash, Y#459 cut into quarters.

Date	Mintage	VG8	F12	VF20	XF40	MS60
2(1913)	—	45.00	55.00	60.00	75.00	—

Y# 459x 100 CASH
Copper or Brass **Note:** 200 Cash, Y#459 cut in half.

Date	Mintage	VG8	F12	VF20	XF40	MS60
2(1913)	—	6.00	15.00	30.00	70.00	—

MILLED COINAGE

Y# 466 100 CASH
Copper **Obv. Legend:** "Chung Hua Min Kuo Nien" - (Years) **Obv. Inscription:** Ch'uan **Note:** Beware of modern forgeries

Date	Mintage	VG8	F12	VF20	XF40	MS60
15 (1926)	—	190	280	375	700	—
19 (1930)	—	155	190	250	825	—

Y# 466a 100 CASH
Brass **Obv. Legend:** CHUNG HUA MIN KUO NIEN (Years) **Obv. Inscription:** Ch'uan **Rev:** Manchu "Boo-yuan" with Chinese "K'u" (for Kuche) above **Note:** Beware of modern forgeries

Date	Mintage	VG8	F12	VF20	XF40	MS60
19 (1930)	—	155	190	280	625	—

DECIMAL COINAGE

Y# 441 5 CASH
Copper **Obv:** Crossed flags **Obv. Legend:** Chung Hua Min Kuo (year) Nien **Rev:** Lion standing left **Note:** Varieties exist.

Date	Mintage	VG8	F12	VF20	XF40	MS60
1(1912)	471,000	75.00	150	375	850	—

Y# 441a 5 CASH
Brass **Obv:** Crossed flags **Obv. Legend:** Chung Hua Min Kuo (year) Nien **Rev:** Lion standing left

Date	Mintage	VG8	F12	VF20	XF40	MS60
1(1912)	Inc. above	—	—	—	—	—

Y# 441b 5 CASH
Silver **Obv:** Crossed flags **Obv. Legend:** Chung Hua Min Kuo (year) Nien **Rev:** Lion standing left

Date	Mintage	VG8	F12	VF20	XF40	MS60
1(1912)	—	—	—	1,500	2,500	—

Note: Modern forgeries of Y#441 in copper and of Y#441b in silver exist

Y# 443 5 CASH
Copper **Obv. Legend:** Chung Hua Min Kuo (year) Nien

Date	Mintage	VG8	F12	VF20	XF40	MS60
1(1912)	Inc. above	43.75	90.00	165	225	—

Y# 443a 5 CASH
Brass **Obv. Legend:** Chung Hua Min Kuo (year) Nien

Date	Mintage	VG8	F12	VF20	XF40	MS60
1(1912) Rare	—	—	—	—	—	—

Y# 446 5 CASH
Copper **Obv. Legend:** Chung Hua Min Kuo (year) Nien

Date	Mintage	VG8	F12	VF20	XF40	MS60
1(1912) Rare	Inc. above	—	—	—	—	—

Y# 446a 5 CASH
Brass **Obv:** Chung Hua Min Kuo (year) Nien

Date	Mintage	VG8	F12	VF20	XF40	MS60
1(1912) Rare	Inc. above	—	—	—	—	—

Y# 447 10 CASH

Copper **Obv:** Two rosettes **Obv. Legend:** Chung Hua Min Kuo (year) Nien

Date	Mintage	VG8	F12	VF20	XF40	MS60
1(1912)	108,618,000	2.75	5.00	20.00	45.00	—
2(1913)	Inc. above	9.00	22.50	50.00	110	—

Y# 447a 10 CASH

Brass **Obv. Legend:** Chung Hua Min Kuo (year) Nien

Date	Mintage	VG8	F12	VF20	XF40	MS60
1(1912)	Inc. above	1.50	3.00	8.00	20.00	—
2(1913)	Inc. above	2.50	6.00	16.00	40.00	—

Y# 447.1a 10 CASH

Brass **Obv:** Three rosettes **Obv. Legend:** Chung Hua Min Kuo (year) Nien

Date	Mintage	VG8	F12	VF20	XF40	MS60
2(1913) Rare	Inc. above	—	—	—	—	—

Y# 475 10 CASH

Red Copper **Obv:** Characters in five-petaled flower **Obv. Legend:** Chung Hua Min Kuo (year) Nien **Rev:** Denomination above sun

Date	Mintage	VG8	F12	VF20	XF40	MS60
19(1930) Rare	—	—	—	—	—	—

Y# 448 20 CASH

Copper, 32 mm. **Obv:** Two rosettes **Obv. Legend:** Chung Hua Min Kuo (year) Nien

Date	Mintage	VG8	F12	VF20	XF40	MS60
1(1912)	115,061,000	2.25	5.00	12.00	30.00	—

Note: Character for "first" instead of number one in date

Y# 448a 20 CASH

Brass, 32 mm. **Obv. Legend:** Chung Hua Min Kuo (year) Nien

Date	Mintage	VG8	F12	VF20	XF40	MS60
1(1912)	Inc. above	1.50	3.00	8.00	20.00	—
2(1913)	Inc. above	2.00	4.00	10.00	25.00	—

Note: Character for "first" instead of number one in date

Y# 448.1 20 CASH

Copper, 32 mm. **Obv:** Three rosettes

Date	Mintage	VG8	F12	VF20	XF40	MS60
2(1913)	Inc. above	375	525	900	1,600	—
3(1914)	Inc. above	375	525	900	1,600	—

Y# 448.1a 20 CASH

Brass, 32 mm. **Obv. Legend:** Chung Hua Min Kuo (year) Nien

Date	Mintage	VG8	F12	VF20	XF40	MS60
2(1913)	Inc. above	4.00	9.00	25.00	50.00	—
3(1914)	Inc. above	4.00	9.00	25.00	50.00	—

Note: There are many varieties of this 20 Cash; small and large rosettes; open and closed size characters and exaggerated size character with horns

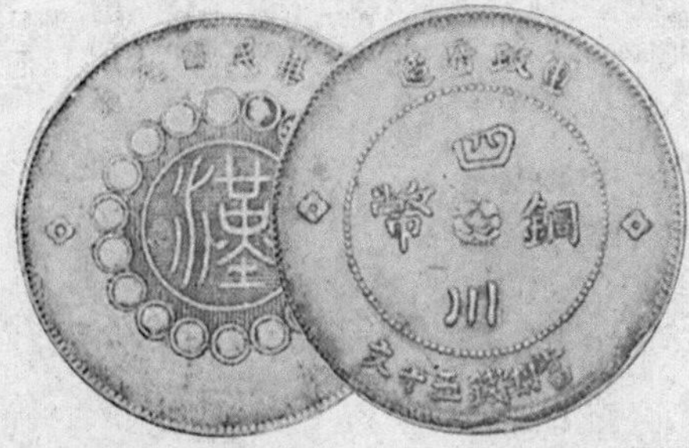

Y# 449 50 CASH

Copper, 36 mm. **Obv. Legend:** Chung Hua Min Kuo (year) Nien **Rev:** Small flower in center

Date	Mintage	VG8	F12	VF20	XF40	MS60
1(1912)	489,382,000	3.00	6.00	16.00	36.00	—

Y# 449.1 50 CASH

Copper, 36 mm. **Obv. Legend:** Chung Hua Min Kuo (year) Nien **Rev:** Larger flower in center

Date	Mintage	VG8	F12	VF20	XF40	MS60
1(1912)	Inc. above	3.00	8.00	20.00	45.00	—

Y# 449.1a 50 CASH

Brass, 36 mm. **Obv. Legend:** Chung Hua Min Kuo (year) Nien

Date	Mintage	VG8	F12	VF20	XF40	MS60
1(1912)	Inc. above	4.00	9.00	25.00	55.00	—

Note: A Yr. 7 is reported, but its authenticity is not verified

Y# 449a 50 CASH

Brass, 36 mm. **Obv. Legend:** Chung Hua Min Kuo (year) Nien

Date	Mintage	VG8	F12	VF20	XF40	MS60
1(1912)	Inc. above	2.25	5.00	14.00	30.00	—

Y# 449.2 50 CASH

Copper, 36 mm. **Obv:** Three rosettes **Obv. Legend:** Chung Hua Min Kuo (year) Nien **Rev:** Small flower in center

Date	Mintage	VG8	F12	VF20	XF40	MS60
2(1913)	Inc. above	3.00	8.00	22.50	50.00	—

Y# 449.2a 50 CASH

Brass, 36 mm. **Obv. Legend:** Chung Hua Min Kuo (year) Nien

Date	Mintage	VG8	F12	VF20	XF40	MS60
2(1913)	Inc. above	3.00	8.00	22.50	50.00	—
3(1914)	Inc. above	3.00	8.00	22.50	50.00	—

Y# 462 50 CASH

Copper **Obv. Legend:** Chung Hua Min Kuo (year) Nien

Date	Mintage	VG8	F12	VF20	XF40	MS60
15(1926)	90,000	27.50	55.00	130	240	—

Y# 462a 50 CASH

Brass **Obv. Legend:** Chung Hua Min Kuo (year) Nien

Date	Mintage	VG8	F12	VF20	XF40	MS60
15(1926)	Inc. above	25.00	48.75	110	200	—

Y# 450 100 CASH

Copper, 39 mm. **Obv:** Two rosettes **Obv. Legend:** Chung Hua Min Kuo (year) Nien **Rev:** Large flower in center

Date	Mintage	VG8	F12	VF20	XF40	MS60
2(1913)	399,212,000	5.00	11.00	18.00	40.00	—
3(1914)	—	45.00	60.00	95.00	125	—

Y# 450.1 100 CASH

Copper, 39 mm. **Obv:** Three rosettes **Obv. Legend:** Chung Hua Min Kuo (year) Nien **Rev:** Small flower in center

Date	Mintage	VG8	F12	VF20	XF40	MS60
2(1913)	Inc. above	5.00	14.00	30.00	60.00	—
3(1914)	—	—	—	—	—	—

Y# 450a 100 CASH

Brass, 39 mm. **Obv. Legend:** Chung Hua Min Kuo (year) Nien

Date	Mintage	VG8	F12	VF20	XF40	MS60
2(1913)	Inc. above	3.00	5.00	14.00	30.00	—

Y# 463.1 100 CASH

Copper **Obv. Legend:** Chung Hua Min Kuo (year) Nien **Rev:** Large value "100", large leaves

Date	Mintage	VG8	F12	VF20	XF40	MS60
15(1926)	7,055,000	5.00	14.00	30.00	60.00	—

Y# 463.2 100 CASH

Copper **Obv. Legend:** Chung Hua Min Kuo (year) Nien **Rev:** Small value "100", small leaves

Date	Mintage	VG8	F12	VF20	XF40	MS60
15(1926)	Inc. above	5.00	14.00	30.00	60.00	—

Y# 463a.1 100 CASH

Brass **Obv. Legend:** Chung Hua Min Kuo (year) Nien **Rev:** Large value "100", large leaves

Date	Mintage	VG8	F12	VF20	XF40	MS60
15(1926)	Inc. above	5.00	12.00	25.00	55.00	—

Y# 463a.2 100 CASH

Brass **Obv. Legend:** Chung Hua Min Kuo (year) Nien **Rev:** Small value "100", small leaves

Date	Mintage	VG8	F12	VF20	XF40	MS60
15(1926)	Inc. above	5.00	12.00	25.00	55.00	—

Y# 464.1 200 CASH

Copper **Obv. Legend:** Chung Hua Min Kuo (year) Nien **Obv. Inscription:** Ch'uan **Edge:** Reeded

Date	Mintage	VG8	F12	VF20	XF40	MS60
15(1926)	Inc. above	9.00	22.00	55.00	100	—

Y# 459 200 CASH

Copper **Obv:** Flowers **Obv. Legend:** Chung Hua Min Kuo (year) Nien **Rev:** Crossed flags, short tassels **Rev. Legend:** THE REPUBLIC OF CHINA

Date	Mintage	VG8	F12	VF20	XF40	MS60
2(1913) Rare	—	—	—	—	—	—

Y# 459.1 200 CASH

Copper **Obv:** Flowers **Obv. Legend:** Chung Hua Min Kuo (year) Nien **Rev:** Crossed flags, long tassels **Rev. Legend:** THE REPUBLIC OF CHINA

Date	Mintage	VG8	F12	VF20	XF40	MS60
2(1913)	Inc. above	9.00	15.00	50.00	95.00	—

Y# 459.1a 200 CASH

Brass **Obv:** Flowers **Obv. Legend:** Chung Hua Min Kuo (year) Nien **Rev:** Crossed flags, long tassels **Rev. Legend:** THE REPUBLIC OF CHINA

Date	Mintage	VG8	F12	VF20	XF40	MS60
2(1913)	—	7.00	12.00	40.00	75.00	—

Y# 459.2 200 CASH

Copper **Obv:** Flowers **Obv. Legend:** Chung Hua Min Kuo (year) Nien **Rev:** Crossed flags **Rev. Legend:** THE REPUBLIC OF CHINA

Date	Mintage	VG8	F12	VF20	XF40	MS60
2(1913)	Inc. above	5.00	9.00	45.00	85.00	—

Note: For cut segments refer to 50 Cash, Y#459y and 100 Cash, Y#459x

Y# 459a 200 CASH

Brass **Obv:** Flowers **Obv. Legend:** Chung Hua Min Kuo (year) Nien **Rev:** Crossed flags, short tassels **Rev. Legend:** THE REPUBLIC OF CHINA

Date	Mintage	VG8	F12	VF20	XF40	MS60
2(1913)	—	30.00	60.00	160	270	—

Y# 464 200 CASH

Copper **Obv. Legend:** Chung Hua Min Kuo (year) Nien **Obv. Inscription:** Ch'uan **Edge:** Plain

Date	Mintage	VG8	F12	VF20	XF40	MS60
15(1926)	—	8.00	18.00	36.00	75.00	—

Y# 464.1a 200 CASH

Brass **Obv. Legend:** Chung Hua Min Kuo (year) Nien **Obv. Inscription:** Ch'uan **Edge:** Reeded

Date	Mintage	VG8	F12	VF20	XF40	MS60
15(1926)	Inc. above	—	—	—	—	—

Y# 464.2 200 CASH

Brass **Obv:** Similar to Y#464 **Obv. Legend:** Chung Hua Min Kuo (year) Nien **Obv. Inscription:** Ch'uan **Rev:** Dot within first 0 of 200

Date	Mintage	VG8	F12	VF20	XF40	MS60
15(1926)	Inc. above	—	—	—	—	—

Note: Many varieties: open and closed buds; overstruck on earlier pieces and on virgin flans; different sizes and thicknesses

Y# 464a 200 CASH

Brass **Obv. Legend:** Chung Hua Min Kuo (year) Nien **Obv. Inscription:** Ch'uan **Edge:** Plain

Date	Mintage	VG8	F12	VF20	XF40	MS60
15(1926)	Inc. above	8.00	18.00	36.00	75.00	—

Y# 476 2 CENTS

Copper **Obv. Legend:** Chung Hua Min Kuo (year) Nien

Date	Mintage	VG8	F12	VF20	XF40	MS60
19(1930) Rare	—	—	—	—	—	—

Y# 476a 2 CENTS

Brass **Obv. Legend:** Chung Hua Min Kuo (year) Nien

Date	Mintage	VG8	F12	VF20	XF40	MS60
19(1930)	—	—	—	—	—	—

Y# 453 10 CENTS

2.60 g., Silver **Obv. Legend:** Chung Hua Min Kuo (year) Nien

Date	Mintage	VG8	F12	VF20	XF40	MS60
1(1912)	370,000	13.00	37.50	80.00	200	400

Y# 468 10 CENTS

Copper-Nickel **Obv. Legend:** Chung Hua Min Kuo (year) Nien

Date	Mintage	VG8	F12	VF20	XF40	MS60
ND(1926)	—	7.00	19.00	40.00	100	250

Y# 468a 10 CENTS

Silver **Obv. Legend:** Chung Hua Min Kuo (year) Nien

Date	Mintage	VG8	F12	VF20	XF40	MS60
ND(1926)	—	18.00	55.00	150	250	500

Y# 468b 10 CENTS

Iron **Obv. Legend:** Chung Hua Min Kuo (year) Nien

Date	Mintage	VG8	F12	VF20	XF40	MS60
ND(1926)	—	10.00	30.00	100	140	300

Y# 454 20 CENTS

5.20 g., Silver **Obv. Legend:** Chung Hua Min Kuo (year) Nien

Date	Mintage	VG8	F12	VF20	XF40	MS60
1(1912)	95,000	25.00	75.00	200	500	1,000

K# 795 20 CENTS

5.20 g., Silver, 25 mm. **Subject:** Sikang Szechuan Army in the Tibetan War **Obv:** Bust of governor Liu Wen-hwei of Szechuan facing **Obv. Legend:** Chung Hua Min Kuo (year) Nien **Rev:** Crossed flags

Date	Mintage	VG8	F12	VF20	XF40	MS60
1932	—	4,500	7,500	9,000	11,500	27,000

Y# 455 50 CENTS

12.90 g., Silver **Obv. Legend:** Chung Hua Min Kuo (year) Nien

Date	Mintage	VG8	F12	VF20	XF40	MS60
1(1912)	37,942,000	15.00	25.00	42.00	110	250
2(1913) Rare	Inc. above	—	—	—	—	—

Y# 473 50 CENTS

10.50 g., Silver **Subject:** Sun Yat-sen **Obv. Legend:** Chung Hua Min Kuo (year) Nien

Date	Mintage	VG8	F12	VF20	XF40	MS60
17(1928)	Inc. above	—	—	—	—	—

Y# 456 DOLLAR

25.60 g., Silver **Obv. Legend:** Chung Hua Min Kuo (year) Nien

Date	Mintage	VG8	F12	VF20	XF40	MS60
1(1912)	55,670,000	30.00	40.00	60.00	150	700
2 Rare	Inc. above	—	—	—	—	—

Y# 456.1 DOLLAR

25.60 g., Silver **Obv. Legend:** Chung Hua Min Kuo (year) Nien **Rev:** Righthand character with two dots instead of horizontal stroke

Date	Mintage	VG8	F12	VF20	XF40	MS60
1(1912)	Inc. above	32.00	42.00	85.00	250	1,100

Note: Silver content ranged from 0.880 to 0.500 fine

Y# 474 DOLLAR
25.50 g., Silver **Subject:** Sun Yat-sen **Obv. Legend:** Chung Hua Min Kuo (year) Nien

Date	Mintage	VG8	F12	VF20	XF40	MS60
17(1928)	Inc. above	—	—	—	—	—

PATTERNS

Including off metal strikes

KM#	Date	Mintage	Identification	Mkt Val
Pn16	ND-1901	—	20 Cents. Aluminum. Dragon type.	—
Pn17	ND-1902	—	5 Cents. Brass. K#149y.	550
Pn18	ND-1902	—	10 Cents. Brass. K#148y.	650
Pn19	ND-1902	—	20 Cents. Brass. K#147y.	750
Pn20	ND-1902	—	50 Cents. Brass. K#146y.	950
Pn21	ND-1902	—	Dollar. Brass. K#145y.	1,850
Pn22	CD1906	—	2 Cash. Copper. Y#8t.	—
Pn23	CD1906	—	5 Cash. Copper. Y#9t.	—
Pn24	CD1908	—	Cash. Brass. Y#7t.	550
Pn25	CD1908	—	5 Cash. Brass.	—
Pn26	ND-1912	—	10 Cents. Copper.	—
Pn27	1(1912)	—	50 Cents. Copper. Y#455.	—
Pn28	ND-1926	—	10 Cents. Brass. Y#468.	—
Pn29	17(1928)	—	Dollar. Copper. Y#474.	—
Pn30	ND-1941	—	50 Cents. Temple. Spade. World War II.	—

YUNNAN PROVINCE

A province located in south China bordering Burma, Laos and Vietnam. It is very mountainous with many lakes. Yunnan was the home of various active imperial mints. A modern mint was established at Kunming in 1905 and the first struck copper coins were issued in 1906 and the first struck silver coins in 1908. General Tang Chi-yao issued coins in gold, silver and copper with his portrait in 1919. The last Republican coins were struck here in 1949.

EMPIRE

MILLED COINAGE

Y# 10u 10 CASH
Copper **Obv:** Inscription: Tai-ching T'ung-pi with large mint mark "Yun" in center **Rev:** Side view dragon

Date	Mintage	VG8	F12	VF20	XF40	MS60
CD1906	36,701,000	15.00	33.00	60.00	130	—

Y# 10u.1 10 CASH
Copper **Obv:** Inscription with small mint mark "Yun" in center **Obv. Inscription:** Tai-ching T'ung-pi **Rev:** Side view dragon

Date	Mintage	VG8	F12	VF20	XF40	MS60
CD1906	Inc. above	37.50	85.00	135	280	—

Y# 10v 10 CASH
Copper **Obv:** Inscription with mint mark "Tien" in center **Obv. Inscription:** Tai-ching T'ung-pi **Rev:** Side view dragon

Date	Mintage	VG8	F12	VF20	XF40	MS60
CD1906	Inc. above	19.00	45.00	70.00	150	—

Y# 11u.1 20 CASH
Copper **Obv:** Inscription with small mint mark "Yun" in center **Obv. Inscription:** Tai-ching T'ung-pi **Rev:** Side view dragon

Date	Mintage	VG8	F12	VF20	XF40	MS60
CD1906	—	50.00	50.00	50.00	1,100	—

Y# 11u 20 CASH
Copper **Obv:** Inscription with large mint mark "Yun" in center **Obv. Inscription:** Tai-ching T'ung-pi **Rev:** Side view dragon

Date	Mintage	VG8	F12	VF20	XF40	MS60
CD1906	645,000	190	265	350	600	—

Y# 11v.1 20 CASH
Copper **Obv:** Inscription with mint mark "Tien" in center **Obv. Inscription:** Tai-ching T'ung-pi **Rev:** Side view dragon

Date	Mintage	VG8	F12	VF20	XF40	MS60
CD1906	Inc. above	225	425	600	1,100	—

Y# 11v.1a 20 CASH
Brass **Obv. Inscription:** Tai-ching T'ung-pi **Rev:** Side view dragon

Date	Mintage	VG8	F12	VF20	XF40	MS60
CD1906	Inc. above	265	525	675	1,200	—

Kuang-hsü

PROVINCIAL CAST COINAGE

C# 26–9.1 CASH
Cast Brass **Obv. Inscription:** Kuang-hsü T'ung-pao **Rev:** Manchu inscription, "Kung" above **Rev. Inscription:** Boo-yôn **Mint:** Yûn

Date	Mintage	G4	VG8	F12	VF20	XF40
ND(1875-1908)	—	2.50	6.00	9.00	13.00	—

C# 26–9.2 CASH
Cast Brass **Obv. Inscription:** Kuang-hsü T'ung-pao **Rev:** Manchu inscription, "Szu" (four) above **Rev. Inscription:** Boo-yôn **Mint:** Yûn

Date	Mintage	G4	VG8	F12	VF20	XF40
ND(1875-1908)	—	3.00	6.00	9.00	13.00	—

C# 26–9.3 CASH
Cast Brass **Obv. Inscription:** Kuang-hsü T'ung-pao **Rev:** Manchu inscription, "Chin" above **Rev. Inscription:** Boo-yôn **Mint:** Yûn

Date	Mintage	G4	VG8	F12	VF20	XF40
ND(1875-1908)	—	3.00	6.00	9.00	13.00	—

C# 26–9.4 CASH
Cast Brass **Obv. Inscription:** Kuang-hsü T'ung-pao **Rev:** Manchu inscription, crescent above, dot below **Rev. Inscription:** Boo-yôn **Mint:** Yûn

Date	Mintage	G4	VG8	F12	VF20	XF40
ND(1875-1908)	—	3.00	6.00	9.00	14.00	—

C# 26–9.5 CASH
Cast Brass **Obv. Inscription:** Kuang-hsü T'ung-pao **Rev:** Manchu inscription, dot above hole **Rev. Inscription:** Boo-yôn **Mint:** Yûn

Date	Mintage	G4	VG8	F12	VF20	XF40
ND(1875-1908)	—	3.00	6.00	9.00	14.00	—

C# 26–9 CASH
Cast Brass **Obv. Inscription:** Kuang-hsü T'ung-pao **Rev:** Manchu inscription **Rev. Inscription:** Boo-yôn **Mint:** Yûn

Date	Mintage	G4	VG8	F12	VF20	XF40
ND(1875-1908)	—	2.50	5.00	8.00	12.00	—

C# 27–6 CASH
Cast Brass **Obv. Inscription:** Kuang-hsü T'ung-pao **Rev:** Manchu inscription **Rev. Inscription:** Boo-dong **Mint:** Tung

Date	Mintage	G4	VG8	F12	VF20	XF40
ND(1875-1908)	—	5.00	8.00	11.00	18.00	—

C# 27–6.1 CASH
Cast Brass **Obv. Inscription:** Kuang-hsü T'ung-pao **Rev:** Manchu inscription, "Chin" above **Rev. Inscription:** Boo-dong **Mint:** Tung

Date	Mintage	G4	VG8	F12	VF20	XF40
ND(1875-1908)	—	6.00	9.00	12.00	18.00	—

C# 27–6.2 CASH
Cast Brass **Obv. Inscription:** Kuang-hsü T'ung-pao **Rev:** Manchu inscription, "Ts'un" below **Rev. Inscription:** Boo-dong **Mint:** Tung

Date	Mintage	G4	VG8	F12	VF20	XF40
ND(1875-1908)	—	6.00	9.00	12.00	18.00	—

MILLED COINAGE

Y# 252 20 CENTS
Brass **Obv. Legend:** Yün-nan Sheng Tsao **Obv. Inscription:** Kuang-hsü Yuan-pao **Rev:** Side view dragon **Note:** Many minor varieties.

Date	Mintage	F12	VF20	XF40	MS60	MS63
ND (1908)	532,000	27.50	55.00	120	350	1,000

Y# 253 50 CENTS
13.20 g., 0.800 Silver 0.3395 oz. ASW **Obv. Legend:** Yün-nan Sheng Tsao **Obv. Inscription:** Kuang-hsü Yuan-pao **Rev:** Side view dragon

Date	Mintage	VG8	F12	VF20	XF40	MS60
ND(1908)	—	15.00	20.00	30.00	75.00	600

Y# 254 DOLLAR
26.80 g., 0.900 Silver 0.7755 oz. ASW **Obv. Legend:** Yün-nan Sheng Tsao **Obv. Inscription:** Kuang-hsü Yüan-pao **Rev:** Side view dragon

Date	Mintage	VG8	F12	VF20	XF40	MS60
ND(1908)	—	40.00	70.00	150	550	3,200

Hsüan-t'ung

PROVINCIAL CAST COINAGE

C# 27–7 CASH
Cast Brass **Obv. Inscription:** Hsuan-t'ung T'ung-pao **Rev:** "Ts'un" below inscription **Rev. Inscription:** Manchu Boo-dong **Mint:** Tung

Date	Mintage	G4	VG8	F12	VF20	XF40
ND(1909-11) Rare	—	—	—	—	—	—

C# 26–11 CASH
Cast Brass **Obv. Inscription:** Hsuan-t'ung T'ung-pao **Rev:** "Kung" above hole **Rev. Inscription:** Manchu Boo-yôn **Mint:** Yûn **Note:** Struck at Yûn Mint (Yünnanfu).

Date	Mintage	G4	VG8	F12	VF20	XF40
ND(1909-11)	—	115	150	225	325	—

C# 26–12 CASH
Cast Brass **Obv. Inscription:** Hsuan-t'ung T'ung-pao **Rev:** "Shan" above hole **Rev. Inscription:** Manchu Boo-yôn

Date	Mintage	G4	VG8	F12	VF20	XF40
ND(1909-11)	—	45.00	60.00	75.00	150	—

C# 26–13 CASH
Cast Brass **Obv. Inscription:** Hsuan-t'ung T'ung-pao **Rev:** Without character above hole **Rev. Inscription:** Manchu Boo-yôn **Mint:** Yûn

Date	Mintage	G4	VG8	F12	VF20	XF40
ND(1909-11)	—	55.00	70.00	85.00	150	—

MILLED COINAGE

Y# 259 50 CENTS
13.20 g., 0.800 Silver 0.3395 oz. ASW **Obv. Legend:** Yün-nan Sheng Tsao **Obv. Inscription:** Hsüan-t'ung-pao **Rev:** Side view dragon; seven flames on pearl

Date	Mintage	VG8	F12	VF20	XF40	MS60
ND(1909-11)	—	15.00	22.50	35.00	100	600

Y# 259.1 50 CENTS
13.20 g., 0.800 Silver 0.3395 oz. ASW **Obv. Legend:** Yün-nan Sheng Tsao **Obv. Inscription:** Hsüan-t'ung-pao **Rev:** Side view dragon; nine flames on pearl

Date	Mintage	VG8	F12	VF20	XF40	MS60
ND(1909-11)	—	18.00	25.00	40.00	110	500

Y# 260 DOLLAR
26.80 g., 0.900 Silver 0.7755 oz. ASW **Obv. Legend:** Yün-nan Sheng Tsao **Obv. Inscription:** Hsüan-t'ung T'ung-pao **Rev:** Side view dragon

Date	Mintage	VG8	F12	VF20	XF40	MS60
ND(1909-11)	—	45.00	85.00	150	550	2,750

Y# 260.1 DOLLAR
26.80 g., 0.900 Silver 0.7755 oz. ASW **Obv. Legend:** Yün-nan Sheng Tsao **Obv. Inscription:** Hsüan-t'ung T'ung-pao **Rev:** Side view dragon

Date	Mintage	VG8	F12	VF20	XF40	MS60
CD1910 Rare	—	—	—	—	—	—

REPUBLIC

TRANSITIONAL COINAGE

In the name of the Republic

KM# 5 CASH
Cast Copper or Brass **Obv. Inscription:** Min-kuo T'ung-pao **Rev:** Inscription **Rev. Inscription:** Tung-ch'uan **Mint:** Tung

Date	Mintage	G4	VG8	F12	VF20	XF40
ND-1912	—	15.00	30.00	75.00	165	—

KM# 5a CASH
Cast Copper or Brass **Obv. Inscription:** Min-kuo T'ung-pao **Rev:** Inscription **Rev. Inscription:** Boo-yôn **Mint:** Yûn

Date	Mintage	G4	VG8	F12	VF20	XF40
ND-1912	—	100	125	225	—	—

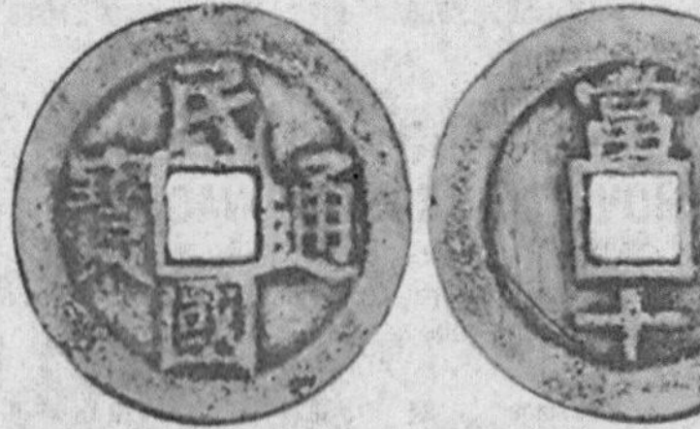

KM# 4 10 CASH
Brass **Obv. Inscription:** Min-kuo T'ung-pao

Date	Mintage	G4	VG8	F12	VF20	XF40
ND-1912	—	22.50	37.50	85.00	175	—

RESTRUCK IMPERIAL COINAGE

The following imperial coins are reign-dated 1875-1908. These coins were apparently restruck from previously unused dies at intervals from 1911 through to 1949, and with a progressively reduced silver content. The dates and silver content shown are approximate.

Y# 255 10 CENTS
2.65 g., 0.650 Silver 0.0554 oz. ASW **Obv. Legend:** Yün-nan Sheng Tsao **Obv. Inscription:** Kuang-hsü Yüan-pao **Rev:** Side view dragon with two circles beneath pearl

Date	Mintage	VG8	F12	VF20	XF40	MS60
ND(1911-15)	902,000	8.00	22.50	45.00	100	240

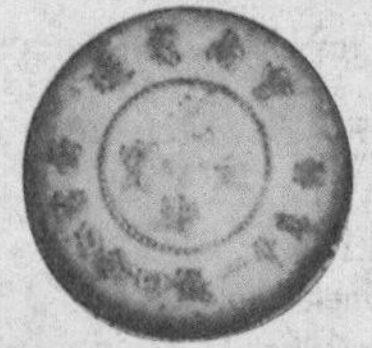 

Y# 256 20 CENTS
5.30 g., 0.800 Silver 0.1363 oz. ASW **Obv. Legend:** Yün-nan Sheng Tsao **Obv. Inscription:** Kuang-hsü Yüan-pao **Rev:** Side view dragon with two circles beneath pearl

Date	Mintage	VG8	F12	VF20	XF40	MS60
ND(1911-15)	—	7.00	19.00	27.50	65.00	150

Y# 256a 20 CENTS
5.30 g., 0.650 Silver 0.1108 oz. ASW **Obv. Legend:** Yün-nan Sheng Tsao **Obv. Inscription:** Kuang-hsü Yüan-pao **Rev:** Side view dragon with three circles beneath pearl

Date	Mintage	VG8	F12	VF20	XF40	MS60
ND(1911-15)	—	7.00	20.00	35.00	85.00	250

Y# 256b 20 CENTS
5.30 g., 0.400 Silver 0.0682 oz. ASW **Obv. Legend:** Yün-nan Sheng Tsao **Obv. Inscription:** Kuang-hsü Yüan-pao **Rev:** Side view dragon with two or three circles beneath pearl

Date	Mintage	VG8	F12	VF20	XF40	MS60
ND(1920-31)	—	—	—	—	—	—

Y# 257 50 CENTS
13.20 g., 0.800 Silver 0.3395 oz. ASW **Obv. Legend:** Yün-nan Sheng Tsao **Obv. Inscription:** Kuang-hsü Yüan-pao **Rev:** Side view dragon with two circles below pearl

Date	Mintage	VG8	F12	VF20	XF40	MS60
ND(1911-15)	—	15.00	18.00	22.50	55.00	120

Note: There are more than 30 minor varieties of Y#257.

Y# 257.1 50 CENTS
13.20 g., 0.800 Silver 0.3395 oz. ASW **Obv. Legend:** Yün-nan Sheng Tsao **Obv. Inscription:** Kuang-hsü Yüan-pao **Rev:** Side view dragon with three circles below pearl

Date	Mintage	VG8	F12	VF20	XF40	MS60
ND(1911-15)	—	14.00	17.00	20.00	50.00	110

Y# 257.2 50 CENTS
13.20 g., 0.500 Silver 0.2122 oz. ASW **Obv. Legend:** Yün-nan Sheng Tsao **Obv. Inscription:** Kuang-hsü Yüan-pao **Rev:** Side view dragon with four circles below pearl

Date	Mintage	VG8	F12	VF20	XF40	MS60
ND(1920-31)	—	14.00	17.00	20.00	50.00	110

Y# 257.3 50 CENTS
13.20 g., 0.500 Billon 0.2122 oz. **Obv. Legend:** Yün-nan Sheng Tsao **Obv. Inscription:** Kuang-hsü Yuan-pao **Rev:** Side view dragon with two circles beneath pearl, large circle around center circle of rosettes

Date	Mintage	VG8	F12	VF20	XF40	MS60
ND(1949)	—	—	—	10.00	20.00	35.00

Y# 258 DOLLAR
26.80 g., 0.900 Silver 0.7755 oz. ASW **Obv. Legend:** Yün-nan Sheng Tsao **Obv. Inscription:** Kuang-hsü Yüan-pao **Rev:** Side view dragon with one circle below pearl

Date	Mintage	VG8	F12	VF20	XF40	MS60
ND(1911-15)	—	45.00	65.00	95.00	350	1,100

Y# 258.1 DOLLAR
26.80 g., 0.900 Silver 0.7755 oz. ASW **Obv. Legend:** Yün-nan Sheng Tsao **Obv. Inscription:** Kuang-hsü Yüan-pao **Rev:** Side view dragon with four circles below pearl

Date	Mintage	VG8	F12	VF20	XF40	MS60
ND(1920-22)	—	40.00	60.00	80.00	300	1,000

STANDARD COINAGE

Y# 488 CENT

Brass **Obv:** Crossed flags **Obv. Legend:** Chung Hua Min Kuo

Date	Mintage	VG8	F12	VF20	XF40	MS60
21 Rare	—	—	—	—	—	—

Y# 489 2 CENTS

Brass **Obv:** Crossed flags **Obv. Legend:** Chung Hua Min Kuo

Date	Mintage	VG8	F12	VF20	XF40	MS60
21	—	350	650	1,000	2,250	—

Y# 478 50 CASH

Brass **Obv:** Crossed flags **Obv. Legend:** Yün-nan Sheng Tsao **Rev:** Bust of General T'ang Chi-yao facing

Date	Mintage	VG8	F12	VF20	XF40	MS60
ND(1919)	—	20.00	40.00	90.00	300	—

Y# 478a 50 CASH

Copper **Obv:** Crossed flags **Obv. Legend:** Yün-nan Sheng Tsao **Rev:** Bust of General T'ang Chi-yao facing

Date	Mintage	VG8	F12	VF20	XF40	MS60
ND(1919)	—	40.00	80.00	170	450	—

Y# 485 5 CENTS

Copper-Nickel **Obv. Legend:** Chung Hua Min Kuo (year) Nien **Rev:** Flag

Date	Mintage	VG8	F12	VF20	XF40	MS60
12(1923)	—	45.00	65.00	95.00	225	—

Y# 490 5 CENTS

Copper **Obv:** Crossed flags **Obv. Legend:** Chung Hua Min Kuo

Date	Mintage	VG8	F12	VF20	XF40	MS60
21(1932)	—	250	350	500	700	—

Y# 486 10 CENTS

Copper-Nickel **Obv. Legend:** Chung Hua Min Kuo (year) Nien **Rev:** Flag **Edge:** Reeded

Date	Mintage	VG8	F12	VF20	XF40	MS60
12(1923)	—	4.00	5.00	8.00	22.50	—

Y# 486.1 10 CENTS

Copper-Nickel **Obv. Legend:** Chung Hua Min Kuo (year) Nien **Rev:** Flag **Edge:** Plain

Date	Mintage	VG8	F12	VF20	XF40	MS60
12(1923)	—	5.00	8.00	13.00	37.50	—

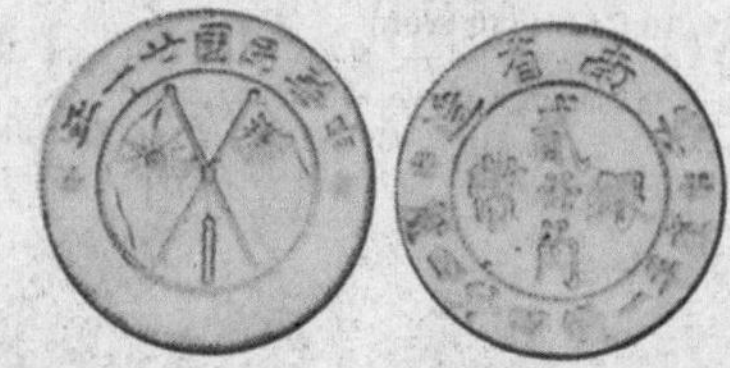

Y# 491 20 CENTS

5.60 g., Silver **Obv:** Crossed flags **Obv. Legend:** Chung Hua Min Kuo (year) Nien

Date	Mintage	VG8	F12	VF20	XF40	MS60
21(1932)	—	9.00	12.00	16.00	36.00	75.00

Y# 493 20 CENTS

5.60 g., Silver **Rev:** Provincial capitol

Date	Mintage	VG8	F12	VF20	XF40	MS60
38(1949)	—	10.00	13.00	18.00	200	500

Y# 480 50 CENTS

13.10 g., 0.850 Silver 0.358 oz. ASW **Obv:** Bust of General T'ang Chi-yao right **Rev:** Crossed flags

Date	Mintage	VG8	F12	VF20	XF40	MS60
ND(1916)	—	25.00	45.00	85.00	375	1,850

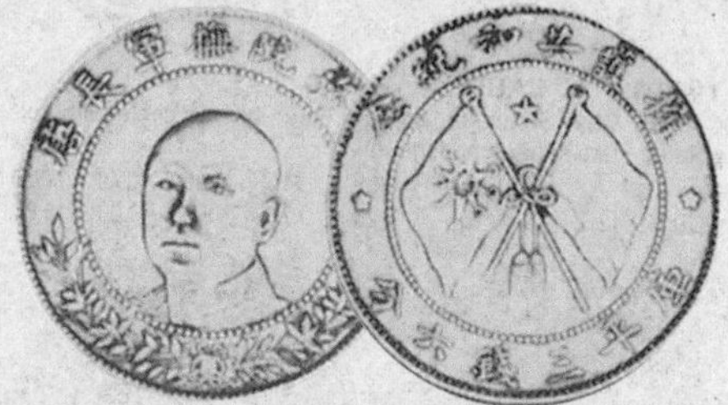

Y# 479 50 CENTS

13.10 g., 0.850 Silver 0.358 oz. ASW, 33 mm. **Obv:** Bust of General T'ang Chi-yao facing **Rev:** Crossed flags

Date	Mintage	VG8	F12	VF20	XF40	MS60
ND(1917)	—	20.00	30.00	50.00	120	350

Y# 479.1 50 CENTS

13.10 g., 0.850 Silver 0.358 oz. ASW, 33 mm. **Obv:** Bust of General T'ang Chi-yao facing **Rev:** Crossed flags with circle in center of flag at left

Date	Mintage	VG8	F12	VF20	XF40	MS60
ND(1917)	—	20.00	30.00	50.00	120	350

Y# 492 50 CENTS

13.10 g., 0.500 Silver 0.2106 oz. ASW **Obv:** Crossed flags **Obv. Legend:** Chung Hua Min Kuo (year) Nien

Date	Mintage	VG8	F12	VF20	XF40	MS60
21	—	12.00	18.00	24.00	60.00	150

K# 1521 5 DOLLARS

Gold **Obv. Inscription:** Equal to 5 (silver) Dollars **Note:** Uniface; Similar to 10 Dollars, K#1520.

Date	Mintage	VG8	F12	VF20	XF40	MS60
ND-1917 Rare	—	—	—	—	—	—

Y# 481 5 DOLLARS

4.50 g., 0.750 Gold 0.1085 oz. AGW, 18 mm. **Obv:** Bust of General T'ang Chi-yao facing **Rev:** With numeral 2 below flag tassels

Date	Mintage	F12	VF20	XF40	MS60	MS63
ND (1919)	Est. 60000	800	1,150	1,950	2,650	4,000

Y# 481.1 5 DOLLARS

4.50 g., 0.750 Gold 0.1085 oz. AGW, 18 mm. **Obv:** Bust of General T'ang Chi-yao facing **Rev:** Without numeral 2 below flag tassels

Date	Mintage	F12	VF20	XF40	MS60	MS63
ND (1919)	Inc. above	—	—	—	—	—

Note: Requires Confirmation

K# 1529 5 DOLLARS

4.50 g., 0.750 Gold 0.1085 oz. AGW **Obv. Inscription:** Wu(5)-Yüan Chin-pi **Rev:** Tien in wheat sprays **Edge:** Plain

Date	Mintage	F12	VF20	XF40	MS60	MS63
ND-1925	—	—	1,750	2,550	3,800	5,000

K# 1520 10 DOLLARS

Gold **Obv. Inscription:** Equal to 10 Silver Dollars **Note:** Uniface.

Date	Mintage	VG8	F12	VF20	XF40	MS60
ND(1917) Rare	—	—	—	—	—	—

Y# 482 10 DOLLARS

8.50 g., 0.750 Gold 0.205 oz. AGW, 23 mm. **Obv:** Bust of General T'ang Chi-yao facing **Rev:** With numeral 1 below flag tassels

Date	Mintage	F12	VF20	XF40	MS60	MS63
ND (1919)	900,000	1,100	1,850	2,550	3,450	6,200

Y# 482.1 10 DOLLARS

8.50 g., 0.750 Gold 0.205 oz. AGW, 23 mm. **Obv:** Bust of General T'ang Chi-yao facing **Rev:** Without numeral 1 below flag tassels

Date	Mintage	F12	VF20	XF40	MS60	MS63
ND (1919)	Inc. above	1,100	1,900	2,600	3,600	6,500

K# 1528 10 DOLLARS

8.50 g., 0.750 Gold 0.205 oz. AGW **Obv. Inscription:** Shih(10)-yüan Chin-pi **Rev:** Tien in wheat sprays **Edge:** Plain

Date	Mintage	VG8	F12	VF20	XF40	MS60
ND-1925	—	—	—	3,450	6,900	10,500

PATTERNS

Including off metal strikes

KM#	Date	Mintage	Identification	Mkt Val
Pn1	ND(ca.1902) (1902)	—	Cash. Brass. Tungch'uwan.	—
Pn2	ND-1908	—	10 Cash. Copper.	900
Pn3	ND-1908	—	50 Cents. Copper. Y#253.	750
Pn4	ND-1908	—	50 Cents. Brass. Y#253.	900
Pn5	ND-1908	—	50 Cents. Copper. Y#257.	750
Pn6	ND-1908	—	Dollar. Copper. Y#254.	1,200
Pn7	ND-1925	—	5 Dollars. Silver.	750
Pn8	ND-1925	—	10 Dollars. Silver.	1,050
Pn9	ND-1925	—	10 Dollars. Pewter. K#1528y.	—

YUNNAN-SZECHUAN PROVINCE

Yunnan-Sichuan

These two coins have a 2-character mint mark in the center of the obverse, indicating the provinces of Yunnan and Szechuan (Sichuan).

EMPIRE

Kuang-hsü

PROVINCIAL CAST COINAGE

Y# 10w 10 CASH
Copper **Obv. Inscription:** Ta-ching T'ung-pi **Rev. Legend:** Kuang-hsu Nien Tsao, TAI-CHING-TI-KUO... **Mint:** (no Mint Information)

Date	Mintage	F12	VF20	XF40	MS60	MS63
CD 1906	—	40.00	80.00	275	1,350	4,750

Y# 11w 20 CASH
Copper **Obv. Inscription:** Ta-ch'ing T'ung-pi **Rev. Legend:** Kuang-hsü Nien Tsao, TAI-CHING-TI-KUO... **Mint:** (no Mint Information)

Date	Mintage	VG8	F12	VF20	XF40	MS60
CD 1906	—	100	150	200	400	1,500

CHINA, REPUBLIC OF

EMPIRE

On December 15, 1915 Yuan Shih-K'ai had himself formally chosen and proclaimed emperor. Opposition developed within China and among various foreign powers. A rebellion broke out in Yünnan and spread to other southern provinces. Opposition was so great that Yuan rescinded the monarchy on March 21, 1916. On June 6th he died.

TRANSITIONAL COINAGE

KM# 1 5 CASH (5 Wen)
Copper **Ruler:** Hung-hsien **Obv:** Inscription: Hung-hsien T'ung-pao

Date	Mintage	VG8	F12	VF20	XF40	MS60
ND(1916) Rare	—	—	—	—	—	—

Note: Questionable, believed to be a fantasy by some authorities

REPUBLIC

STANDARD COINAGE

Y# 301 10 CASH (10 Wen)
Copper **Obv:** Crossed flags, florals at left and right **Rev:** Double circle with small rosettes separating legend

Date	Mintage	VG8	F12	VF20	XF40	MS60
ND(ca.1912)	—	0.20	0.50	0.75	1.50	15.00

Y# 301.1 10 CASH (10 Wen)
Copper **Obv:** Second character from right in bottom legend is rounded **Rev:** Double circle with three dots separating legend

Date	Mintage	VG8	F12	VF20	XF40	MS60
ND(ca.1912)	—	0.35	1.00	2.00	5.00	22.00

Y# 301.2 10 CASH (10 Wen)
Copper **Obv:** Second character from right in bottom legend is rounded **Rev:** Double circle with two dots separating legend

Date	Mintage	VG8	F12	VF20	XF40	MS60
ND(ca.1912)	—	0.20	0.50	1.00	2.50	16.00

Y# 301.3 10 CASH (10 Wen)
Copper **Obv:** Small star on flag **Rev:** Double circle with six-pointed stars separating legend

Date	Mintage	VG8	F12	VF20	XF40	MS60
ND(ca.1912)	—	0.25	0.75	1.50	3.00	18.00

Y# 301.4 10 CASH (10 Wen)
Copper **Obv:** Large star on flag extending to edges of flag **Rev:** Double circle with six-pointed stars separating legend

Date	Mintage	VG8	F12	VF20	XF40	MS60
ND(ca.1912)	—	3.50	10.00	15.00	25.00	65.00

Y# 301.4a 10 CASH (10 Wen)
Brass **Obv:** Large star on flag extending to edges of flag **Rev:** Double circle with six-pointed stars separating legend

Date	Mintage	VG8	F12	VF20	XF40	MS60
ND(ca.1912)	—	—	—	—	—	—

Y# 301.5 10 CASH (10 Wen)
Copper **Obv:** Flower wtih many stems **Rev:** Single circle

Date	Mintage	VG8	F12	VF20	XF40	MS60
ND(ca.1912)	—	0.25	0.75	1.50	3.00	20.00

Y# 301.6 10 CASH (10 Wen)
Copper **Obv:** Flower wtih fewer stems **Rev:** Single circle

Date	Mintage	VG8	F12	VF20	XF40	MS60
ND(ca.1912)	—	0.25	0.75	1.50	3.00	20.00

Y# 301a 10 CASH (10 Wen)
Brass **Obv:** Crossed flags, florals at left and right **Rev:** Double circle with small rosettes separating legend

Date	Mintage	VG8	F12	VF20	XF40	MS60
ND(ca.1912)	—	—	—	—	—	—

Y# 309 10 CASH (10 Wen)
Copper

Date	Mintage	VG8	F12	VF20	XF40	MS60
ND(1914-17)	—	3.50	10.00	20.00	40.00	120

Note: Pieces with L. GIORGI near rim are patterns

Y# 307 10 CASH (10 Wen)
Copper **Obv:** One large rosette on either side **Rev:** Slender leaves and short ribbon

Date	Mintage	VG8	F12	VF20	XF40	MS60
ND(1919)	421,138,000	0.20	0.50	1.00	3.00	14.00

Y# 307.1 10 CASH (10 Wen)
Copper **Rev:** Larger leaves and longer ribbon

Date	Mintage	VG8	F12	VF20	XF40	MS60
ND(1919)	Inc. above	3.50	10.00	20.00	40.00	100

Y# 307a.1 10 CASH (10 Wen)
6.64 g., Copper, 28.05 mm. **Obv:** Crossed flags, three rosettes on either side, ornate right flag **Rev:** Short ribbon and smaller wheat ears

Date	Mintage	VG8	F12	VF20	XF40	MS60
ND(1919)	Inc. above	3.50	10.00	20.00	40.00	100

Y# 307a 10 CASH (10 Wen)
Copper **Obv:** Crossed flags, three rosettes on either side, ornate right flag **Rev:** Long ribbon

Date	Mintage	VG8	F12	VF20	XF40	MS60
ND(1919)	Inc. above	0.40	1.00	2.00	4.00	12.50

Y# 307b 10 CASH (10 Wen)
Brass **Obv:** Crossed flags, three rosettes at either side, ornate right flag **Rev:** Long ribbon

Date	Mintage	VG8	F12	VF20	XF40	MS60
ND(1919)	—	—	—	—	—	—

Y# 302.1 10 CASH (10 Wen)

Copper **Obv:** Crossed flags, florals at left and right **Rev:** Vine above leaf at 12-o'clock, wreath tied at bottom; M-shaped leaves at base of larger wheat ears

Date	Mintage	VG8	F12	VF20	XF40	MS60
ND(ca.192)	—	0.35	1.00	3.50	6.50	20.00

Y# 302.2 10 CASH (10 Wen)

Copper **Rev:** Vine beneath leaf at 12-o'clock; wreath not tied at bottom; without M-shaped leaves at base of wheat ears

Date	Mintage	VG8	F12	VF20	XF40	MS60
ND(ca.192)	—	0.50	1.50	4.00	8.00	22.00

Y# 302.3 10 CASH (10 Wen)

Copper **Rev:** Leaves pointing clockwise

Date	Mintage	VG8	F12	VF20	XF40	MS60
ND(ca.192)	—	10.00	30.00	40.00	60.00	115

Y# 302 10 CASH (10 Wen)

Copper **Rev:** Vine above leaf at 12-o'clock; wreath tied at bottom; M-shaped leaves at base of wheat ears

Date	Mintage	VG8	F12	VF20	XF40	MS60
ND(ca.192)	—	0.20	0.60	1.50	3.00	18.00

Y# 302a 10 CASH (10 Wen)

Brass **Obv:** Crossed flags, florals at left and right **Rev:** Vine above leaf at 12-o'clock; wreath tied at bottom; M-shaped leaves at base of wheat ears

Date	Mintage	VG8	F12	VF20	XF40	MS60
ND(ca.192)	—	—	—	—	—	—

Y# 303.1 10 CASH (10 Wen)

Copper **Obv:** Crossed flags, left flag's star in relief, small star-shaped rosettes at left and right **Rev:** Small 4-petaled rosettes separating legend

Date	Mintage	VG8	F12	VF20	XF40	MS60
ND(ca.192)	—	0.20	0.50	1.00	2.00	15.00

Y# 303.3 10 CASH (10 Wen)

Copper **Obv:** Large rosettes replace stars **Rev:** Stars separating legend

Date	Mintage	VG8	F12	VF20	XF40	MS60
ND(ca.192)	—	1.00	3.00	6.25	12.50	25.00

Y# 303.4 10 CASH (10 Wen)

Copper **Obv:** Crossed flags, very small pentagonal rosettes at left and right

Date	Mintage	VG8	F12	VF20	XF40	MS60
ND(ca.192)	—	0.25	0.75	1.50	3.00	15.00

Y# 303.4a 10 CASH (10 Wen)

Brass **Obv:** Crossed flags, very small pentagonal rosettes at left and right **Rev:** Stars separating legend

Date	Mintage	VG8	F12	VF20	XF40	MS60
ND(ca.192)	—	1.00	3.00	6.25	12.50	25.00

Y# 303.5 10 CASH (10 Wen)

Brass **Obv:** Crossed flags, three large rosettes at left and right **Rev:** Stars separate legend

Date	Mintage	VG8	F12	VF20	XF40	MS60
ND(ca.192)	—	—	—	—	—	—

Y# 303 10 CASH (10 Wen)

Copper **Obv:** Crossed flags, small star-shaped rosettes at left and right **Rev:** Small 4-petaled rosettes separating legend

Date	Mintage	VG8	F12	VF20	XF40	MS60
ND(ca.192)	—	0.20	0.50	1.00	2.00	15.00

Y# 303a 10 CASH (10 Wen)

Brass **Obv:** Crossed flags, stars replace rosettes at left and right **Rev:** Small 4-petaled rosettes separating legend

Date	Mintage	VG8	F12	VF20	XF40	MS60
ND(ca.192)	—	0.50	1.50	4.00	10.00	22.50

Y# 304 10 CASH (10 Wen)

Copper **Obv:** Circled flags flanked by pentagonal rosettes

Date	Mintage	VG8	F12	VF20	XF40	MS60
ND(ca.192)	—	3.75	11.50	21.50	42.50	85.00

Y# 305 10 CASH (10 Wen)

Copper **Rev:** Chrysanthemum

Date	Mintage	VG8	F12	VF20	XF40	MS60
ND(ca.192)	—	5.00	15.00	25.00	50.00	115

Y# 306.1 10 CASH (10 Wen)

Copper **Obv:** Crossed flags, florals at left and right **Rev:** Wheat ear design within circle

Date	Mintage	VG8	F12	VF20	XF40	MS60
ND(ca.192)	—	0.20	0.50	1.25	3.00	14.00

Y# 306.1b 10 CASH (10 Wen)

Copper **Obv:** Crossed flags, florals at left and right **Rev:** Thin leaf blade between lower wheat ears

Date	Mintage	VG8	F12	VF20	XF40	MS60
ND(ca.192)	—	1.75	5.00	7.50	14.00	30.00

Y# 306.2 10 CASH (10 Wen)

Copper **Obv:** Crossed flags, florals at left and right, dot on either side of upper legend **Rev:** Wheat ear design within circle

Date	Mintage	VG8	F12	VF20	XF40	MS60
ND(ca.192)	—	0.35	1.00	2.00	3.50	15.00

Y# 306.2b 10 CASH (10 Wen)

Brass **Obv:** Crossed flags, florals at left and right, dot on either side of upper legend **Rev:** Thin leaf blade between lower wheat ears

Date	Mintage	VG8	F12	VF20	XF40	MS60
ND(ca.192)	—	0.45	1.25	3.00	5.00	15.00

Y# 306.3 10 CASH (10 Wen)

Copper **Obv:** Star between flags **Rev:** Wheat ear design within circle

Date	Mintage	VG8	F12	VF20	XF40	MS60
ND(ca.192)	—	6.50	20.00	40.00	75.00	—

Y# 306.4 10 CASH (10 Wen)

Copper **Obv:** Elongated rosettes, different characters in bottom legend **Rev:** Thin leaf blade between lower wheat ears

Date	Mintage	VG8	F12	VF20	XF40	MS60
ND(ca.192)	—	9.00	27.50	55.00	85.00	215

Y# 306a 10 CASH (10 Wen)

Copper **Obv:** Crossed flags, five characters in lower legend

Date	Mintage	VG8	F12	VF20	XF40	MS60
ND(ca.192)	—	1.75	5.00	12.00	25.00	65.00

Y# 306b 10 CASH (10 Wen)

Brass **Obv:** Crossed flags, five characters in lower legend

Date	Mintage	VG8	F12	VF20	XF40	MS60
ND(ca.192)	—	0.35	1.00	2.50	5.00	18.00

Y# 311 10 CASH (10 Wen)

Copper

Date	Mintage	VG8	F12	VF20	XF40	MS60
13	—	65.00	175	350	500	850

Y# 308 20 CASH (20 Wen)

Copper, 32.3 mm. **Obv:** Crossed flags **Rev:** Value in sprays

Date	Mintage	VG8	F12	VF20	XF40	MS60
8	200,861,000	0.50	1.50	3.00	7.50	30.00

Y# 308b 20 CASH (20 Wen)

Cast Brass **Obv:** Crossed flags **Rev:** Value in sprays

Date	Mintage	G4	VG8	F12	VF20	XF40
8(1919)	—	10.00	15.00	18.50	27.50	—

Note: A "warlord" issue; refer to note under Szechuan - Republic

Y# 308a 20 CASH (20 Wen)

Copper **Obv:** Crossed flags **Rev:** Value in sprays

Date	Mintage	VG8	F12	VF20	XF40	MS60
10	Inc. above	0.35	1.00	2.50	6.00	30.00

Y# 310 20 CASH (20 Wen)

Copper **Obv:** Crossed flags **Rev:** Value in sprays

Date	Mintage	VG8	F12	VF20	XF40	MS60
ND(ca.1921)	—	5.00	15.00	30.00	70.00	135

Note: Some sources date these 20 Cash pieces bearing crossed flags ca.1912, but many were not struck until the 1920s; this coin is usually found weakly struck and lightweight

Y# 312 20 CASH (20 Wen)

Copper **Obv. Legend:** REPUBLIC OF CHINA **Obv. Inscription:** Chung-hua T'ung-pien **Rev:** Value in sprays, date above

Date	Mintage	VG8	F12	VF20	XF40	MS60
13 (1924)	—	3.50	10.00	30.00	70.00	135

Note: This coin is usually found weakly struck

HSU# 9 20 CASH (20 Wen)

Copper **Obv:** Crossed flags **Rev:** Value in sprays **Note:** Nationalist commemorative.

Date	Mintage	VG8	F12	VF20	XF40	MS60
ND(1927-28)	—	75.00	225	400	650	900

HSU# 445a 500 CASH (500 Wen)

Copper **Subject:** Nationalist Commemorative **Obv:** Crossed flags **Rev:** Value in sprays

Date	Mintage	VG8	F12	VF20	XF40	MS60
ND(1927/8) Rare	12	—	—	—	—	—

Y# 323 1/2 CENT (1/2 Fen)

Bronze

Date	Mintage	VG8	F12	VF20	XF40	MS60
5	1,789,000	1.75	5.00	10.00	20.00	45.00

Y# 346 1/2 CENT (1/2 Fen)

Bronze

Date	Mintage	VG8	F12	VF20	XF40	MS60
25	64,720,000	0.25	0.75	1.50	3.00	7.50
28 Rare	—	—	—	—	—	—

Y# 324 CENT (1 Fen)

Bronze

Date	Mintage	VG8	F12	VF20	XF40	MS60
5	—	1.75	5.00	10.00	20.00	50.00

Note: Pieces with "L. GIORGI" near rim are patterns

Y# 324a CENT (1 Fen)

Bronze

Date	Mintage	VG8	F12	VF20	XF40	MS60
22	—	2.75	8.00	15.00	30.00	100

Y# 347 CENT (1 Fen)

Copper **Obv. Legend:** Chung Hua Min Kuo (year) Nien **Rev:** Large "Kuel" mint mark below Pu

Date	Mintage	VG8	F12	VF20	XF40	MS60
25	311,780,000	0.15	0.40	0.75	1.75	2.50
26	307,198,000	0.15	0.45	1.00	1.50	3.00
27	12,000,000	1.00	3.00	5.00	8.00	16.00
28	75,000,000	0.65	2.00	4.00	7.00	15.00

KM# 347.1 CENT (1 Fen)

Copper **Obv. Legend:** Chung Hua Min Kuo (year) Nien **Rev:** Small "Kuel" mint mark below Pu

Date	Mintage	VG8	F12	VF20	XF40	MS60
28 (1939) Rare	—	—	—	—	—	—

Y# 353 CENT (1 Fen)

Brass **Note:** Shi Kwan Cent.

Date	Mintage	VG8	F12	VF20	XF40	MS60
28(1939)	—	13.50	40.00	60.00	120	200

Y# 355 CENT (1 Fen)

Aluminum

Date	Mintage	VG8	F12	VF20	XF40	MS60
29	150,000,000	—	0.10	0.25	0.50	1.50

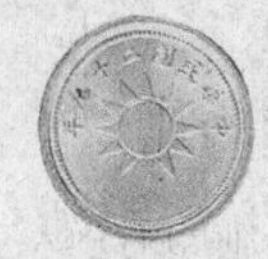

Y# 357 CENT (1 Fen)

Brass

Date	Mintage	VG8	F12	VF20	XF40	MS60
29	50,000,000	0.25	0.75	1.00	2.00	4.00

Y# 363 CENT (1 Fen)

Bronze

Date	Mintage	VG8	F12	VF20	XF40	MS60
37	—	1.50	4.00	10.00	15.00	20.00

Y# 325a 2 CENTS (2 Fen)

Bronze

Date	Mintage	VG8	F12	VF20	XF40	MS60
22(1933)	—	13.50	40.00	60.00	95.00	150

Y# 354 2 CENTS (2 Fen)

Brass

Date	Mintage	VG8	F12	VF20	XF40	MS60
28(1939)	300,000,000	3.50	10.00	15.00	25.00	50.00

Y# 358 2 CENTS (2 Fen)

Brass

Date	Mintage	VG8	F12	VF20	XF40	MS60
29(1940)	—	0.20	0.50	1.00	1.50	2.00
30(1941) Rare	—	—	—	—	—	—

Y# 348 5 CENTS (5 Fen)

3.07 g., Nickel, 18.5 mm.

Date	Mintage	VG8	F12	VF20	XF40	MS60
25(1936)	72,844,000	0.35	1.00	1.50	3.00	6.00
27(1938)	34,325,000	0.75	2.50	4.50	8.00	15.00
28(1939)	6,000,000	3.50	10.00	15.00	25.00	50.00

Y# 348.1 5 CENTS (5 Fen)

Nickel **Rev:** A mint mark below spade (Vienna)

Date	Mintage	VG8	F12	VF20	XF40	MS60
25(1936)	20,000,000	0.35	1.00	2.00	3.50	15.00

Y# 348.2 5 CENTS (5 Fen)

Nickel **Obv:** Character "P'ing" on both sides of portrait

Date	Mintage	VG8	F12	VF20	XF40	MS60
25	—	17.50	50.00	80.00	125	175

Y# 348.3 5 CENTS (5 Fen)

Nickel **Obv:** Character "Ch'ing" on both sides of portrait

Date	Mintage	VG8	F12	VF20	XF40	MS60
25	—	17.50	50.00	80.00	125	175

Y# 356 5 CENTS (5 Fen)

1.10 g., Aluminum, 20 mm.

Date	Mintage	VG8	F12	VF20	XF40	MS60
29(1940)	350,000,000	0.20	0.50	1.00	2.50	4.00

Y# 359 5 CENTS (5 Fen)

Copper-Nickel

Date	Mintage	VG8	F12	VF20	XF40	MS60
29(1940)	57,000,000	0.10	0.25	1.50	2.50	5.00
30(1941)	96,000,000	0.10	0.25	1.50	2.50	6.00

K# 602 10 CENTS (1 Chiao)

2.30 g., Silver, 18 mm. **Subject:** Sun Yat-sen Founding of the Republic **Obv:** Bust left within circle **Rev:** Two 5-pointed stars dividing legend at top **Note:** vertical reeding

Date	Mintage	VG8	F12	VF20	XF40	MS60
ND(1912)	—	65.00	200	500	700	1,250

K# 602b 10 CENTS (1 Chiao)

2.30 g., Silver, 18 mm. **Subject:** Sun Yat-sen Founding of the Republic **Obv:** Bust left within circle **Rev:** Two 5-pointed stars dividing legend at top **Edge:** Engrailed with circles

Date	Mintage	VG8	F12	VF20	XF40	MS60
ND(1912)	—	—	—	700	850	1,500

Y# 326 10 CENTS (1 Chiao)

2.70 g., 0.700 Silver 0.0608 oz. ASW

Date	Mintage	VG8	F12	VF20	XF40	MS60
3	—	2.50	6.00	12.00	25.00	85.00
3 Specimen	—	PF60 600				
5	—	8.00	25.00	42.00	70.00	180
5 Specimen	—	PF60 900				

Y# 334 10 CENTS (1 Chiao)

Silver **Subject:** Unadopted design of national emblem

Date	Mintage	VG8	F12	VF20	XF40	MS60
15	—	10.00	20.00	30.00	110	650

Y# 339 10 CENTS (1 Chiao)

2.50 g., Silver, 18 mm. **Subject:** Death of Sun Yat-sen

Date	Mintage	VG8	F12	VF20	XF40	MS60
16	—	12.00	30.00	120	250	500

Y# 349 10 CENTS (1 Chiao)

Nickel, 21 mm.

Date	Mintage	VG8	F12	VF20	XF40	MS60
25(1936)	73,866,000	0.20	0.60	1.00	3.00	7.50
27(1938)	110,203,000	0.65	2.00	4.25	8.00	20.00
28(1939)	68,000,000	0.50	1.50	3.50	10.00	27.50

Y# 349.1 10 CENTS (1 Chiao)

Nickel **Rev:** Mint mark A below spade (Vienna Mint)

Date	Mintage	VG8	F12	VF20	XF40	MS60
25(1936)A	60,000,000	0.35	1.00	2.00	8.00	25.00

Y# 349a 10 CENTS (1 Chiao)

Non-Magnetic Nickel Alloy

Date	Mintage	VG8	F12	VF20	XF40	MS60
25(1936)	1,000,000	6.00	18.00	30.00	40.00	65.00

Note: All of the Y#349 coins were supposed to have been minted in pure nickel at the Shanghai Mint; However, in 1936 a warlord had the Tientsin Mint produce about one million 10 Cent pieces of heavily alloyed nickel; The result is that the Shanghai pieces are attracted to a magnet while the Tientsin pieces are not

Y# 360 10 CENTS (1 Chiao)

Copper-Nickel, 21 mm. **Edge:** Reeded

Date	Mintage	VG8	F12	VF20	XF40	MS60
29(1940)	68,000,000	0.20	0.50	2.50	8.00	15.00
30(1941)	254,000,000	0.20	0.50	1.50	2.50	5.00
31(1942)	10,000,000	8.50	25.00	60.00	80.00	120

Y# 360.1 10 CENTS (1 Chiao)

Copper-Nickel **Edge:** Plain

Date	Mintage	VG8	F12	VF20	XF40	MS60
29(1940) Rare	Inc. above	—	—	—	—	—
30(1941)	Inc. above	0.65	2.00	7.50	10.00	15.00

Y# 317 20 CENTS (2 Chiao)

5.20 g., Silver, 23 mm. **Subject:** Founding of the Republic

Date	Mintage	VG8	F12	VF20	XF40	MS60
ND(1912)	155,000	18.00	30.00	48.00	90.00	180

Y# 327 20 CENTS (2 Chiao)

5.40 g., 0.700 Silver 0.1215 oz. ASW, 22.88 mm.

Date	Mintage	VG8	F12	VF20	XF40	MS60
3	—	3.00	4.00	7.00	14.00	85.00
3 Specimen	—	PF60 300				
5	—	3.00	4.00	7.00	18.00	110
5 Specimen	—	PF60 600				
9	—	55.00	120	325	600	1,800

Y# 335 20 CENTS (2 Chiao)

5.20 g., Silver **Subject:** Unadopted design of national emblem

Date	Mintage	VG8	F12	VF20	XF40	MS60
15	—	12.00	25.00	45.00	125	750

Y# 340 20 CENTS (2 Chiao)
5.30 g., Silver, 23 mm. **Subject:** Death of Sun Yat-sen

Date	Mintage	VG8	F12	VF20	XF40	MS60
16(1927)	—	27.50	40.00	100	200	400

Y# 350 20 CENTS (20 Fen)
6.05 g., Nickel, 24.06 mm.

Date	Mintage	VG8	F12	VF20	XF40	MS60
25(1936)	49,620,000	0.20	0.50	2.50	6.00	10.00
27(1938)	61,248,000	0.35	1.00	2.00	7.00	12.00
28(1939)	38,000,000	0.65	2.00	5.00	10.00	15.00

Y# 350.1 20 CENTS (20 Fen)
Nickel **Rev:** Mint mark A below spade (Vienna Mint)

Date	Mintage	VG8	F12	VF20	XF40	MS60
25(1936) A	40,000,000	0.35	1.00	2.00	3.50	6.00

Y# 361 20 CENTS (20 Fen)
Copper-Nickel

Date	Mintage	VG8	F12	VF20	XF40	MS60
31(1942)	32,300,000	0.15	0.40	1.00	2.25	4.00

Y# 328 50 CENTS (1/2 Yuan)
13.60 g., 0.700 Silver 0.3061 oz. ASW

Date	Mintage	VG8	F12	VF20	XF40	MS60
3	—	10.00	30.00	55.00	90.00	300
3 Specimen	—	PF60 1,200				

Y# 362 50 CENTS (1/2 Yuan)
9.06 g., Copper-Nickel, 28 mm. **Edge:** Reeded

Date	Mintage	VG8	F12	VF20	XF40	MS60
31(1942)	57,000,000	0.50	1.50	3.00	7.50	15.00
32(1943)	4,000,000	2.00	4.00	10.00	20.00	40.00

Y# 318 DOLLAR (Yuan)
26.90 g., 0.900 Silver 0.7784 oz. ASW, 39 mm. **Subject:** Sun Yat-sen Founding of the Republic **Obv:** Sun Yat-sen facing left **Rev:** Two five-pointed stars dividing legend at top

Date	Mintage	VG8	F12	VF20	XF40	MS60
ND(1912)	—	75.00	225	450	675	1,700

Y# 318.1 DOLLAR (Yuan)
26.90 g., 0.900 Silver 0.7784 oz. ASW, 39 mm. **Obv:** Dot below ear

Date	Mintage	VG8	F12	VF20	XF40	MS60
ND(1912)	—	—	—	—	—	—

Note: For similar issue with rosettes see Y#318a.1 (1927)

Y# 319 DOLLAR (Yuan)
27.30 g., 0.900 Silver 0.7899 oz. ASW, 39 mm. **Obv:** Sun Yat-sen facing left

Date	Mintage	VG8	F12	VF20	XF40	MS60
ND(1912)	—	55.00	150	425	700	2,500

Y# 320 DOLLAR (Yuan)
26.50 g., Silver, 39 mm. **Subject:** Li Yüan-hung Founding of Republic

Date	Mintage	VG8	F12	VF20	XF40	MS60
ND(1912)	—	225	675	1,350	2,750	4,750

Y# 320.1 DOLLAR (Yuan)
26.50 g., Silver, 39 mm. **Rev. Legend:** OE for OF

Date	Mintage	VG8	F12	VF20	XF40	MS60
ND(1912)	—	265	825	1,650	3,000	—

Y# 320.2 DOLLAR (Yuan)
26.50 g., Silver **Rev. Legend:** CIIINA for CHINA

Date	Mintage	VG8	F12	VF20	XF40	MS60
ND(1912)	—	265	825	1,650	3,000	—

Y# 321 DOLLAR (Yuan)
26.50 g., Silver, 39 mm. **Subject:** Li Yüan-hung Founding of Republic

Date	Mintage	VG8	F12	VF20	XF40	MS60
ND(1912)	—	75.00	150	275	750	1,650

Y# 321.1 DOLLAR (Yuan)
26.50 g., Silver, 39 mm. **Rev:** H of "THE" in legend engraved as I I

Date	Mintage	VG8	F12	VF20	XF40	MS60
ND(1912)	—	75.00	150	285	775	1,750

Y# 322 DOLLAR (Yuan)
26.70 g., 0.900 Silver 0.7726 oz. ASW, 39 mm. **Subject:** Yüan Shih-kai Founding of Republic **Note:** 2.8mm thickness.

Date	Mintage	VG8	F12	VF20	XF40	MS60
ND(1914)	20,000	150	265	450	850	4,500

Y# 322.1 DOLLAR (Yuan)
26.70 g., 0.900 Silver 0.7726 oz. ASW, 39 mm. **Subject:** Yüan Shih-kai Founding of Republic **Note:** 3.25mm thickness.

Date	Mintage	VG8	F12	VF20	XF40	MS60
ND(ca.1918)	—	150	265	450	850	4,500

Note: A restrike made about 1918 for collectors

Y# 329.1 DOLLAR (Yuan)
26.40 g., 0.890 Silver 0.7554 oz. ASW, 39 mm. **Note:** Edge engrailed with circles.

Date	Mintage	VG8	F12	VF20	XF40	MS60
3	—	40.00	120	300	2,000	4,400

Y# 329.2 DOLLAR (Yuan)
26.40 g., 0.890 Silver 0.7554 oz. ASW, 39 mm. **Edge:** Ornamented with alternating T's

Date	Mintage	VG8	F12	VF20	XF40	MS60
3	—	40.00	120	300	2,000	4,400

Y# 329.3 DOLLAR (Yuan)
26.40 g., 0.890 Silver 0.7554 oz. ASW, 39 mm. **Edge:** Plain

Date	Mintage	VG8	F12	VF20	XF40	MS60
3	—	18.00	40.00	75.00	500	800

Y# 329.4 DOLLAR (Yuan)
26.40 g., 0.890 Silver 0.7554 oz. ASW, 39 mm. **Note:** Tiny circle in ribbon bow. This is a mint mark, but it is not clear what mint is indicated.

Date	Mintage	VG8	F12	VF20	XF40	MS60
3	—	32.00	40.00	80.00	170	400

Y# 329 DOLLAR (Yuan)
26.40 g., 0.890 Silver 0.7554 oz. ASW, 39 mm. **Subject:** Yüan Shih-kai **Obv:** Six characters above head **Note:** Vertical reeding.

Date	Mintage	VG8	F12	VF20	XF40	MS60
3	—	30.00	34.00	40.00	60.00	120

Y# 332 DOLLAR (Yuan)
26.80 g., Silver, 39 mm. **Ruler:** Hung-hsien **Subject:** Inauguration of Hung-hsien Regime **Obv:** Bust of Hung-hsien in military uniform with plumed hat facing **Rev:** Winged dragon left **Note:** K#663.

Date	Mintage	VG8	F12	VF20	XF40	MS60
ND(1916)	—	150	600	1,000	1,600	4,500

Y# 329.6 DOLLAR (Yuan)
26.40 g., 0.890 Silver 0.7554 oz. ASW **Obv:** Seven characters above head

Date	Mintage	VG8	F12	VF20	XF40	MS60
8	—	30.00	34.00	40.00	90.00	300
9	—	30.00	34.00	40.00	60.00	120

Date	Mintage	VG8	F12	VF20	XF40	MS60
10	—	30.00	34.00	40.00	60.00	120

Y# 329.5 DOLLAR (Yuan)
26.40 g., 0.890 Silver 0.7554 oz. ASW **Edge:** Oblique reeding

Date	Mintage	VG8	F12	VF20	XF40	MS60
10	—	16.00	20.00	32.50	45.00	75.00

K# 676 DOLLAR (Yuan)
26.50 g., Silver, 39 mm. **Subject:** President Hsu Shih-chang **Edge:** Reeded

Date	Mintage	VG8	F12	VF20	XF40	MS60
10	—	190	375	750	2,750	5,000

K# 676.1 DOLLAR (Yuan)
26.50 g., Silver, 39 mm. **Edge:** Plain

Date	Mintage	VG8	F12	VF20	XF40	MS60
10	—	300	750	1,200	3,000	6,500

Y# 336 DOLLAR (Yuan)
26.80 g., Silver **Subject:** Unadopted design of national emblem **Rev:** Value in small characters

Date	Mintage	VG8	F12	VF20	XF40	MS60
12	—	300	750	1,350	2,500	11,000

Y# 336.1 DOLLAR (Yuan)
26.73 g., 0.900 Silver 0.7734 oz. ASW **Subject:** Unadopted design of national emblem **Rev:** Value in large characters

Date	Mintage	VG8	F12	VF20	XF40	MS60
12	—	375	750	1,500	4,500	17,500

K# 677 DOLLAR (Yuan)
26.73 g., 0.900 Silver 0.7734 oz. ASW, 39 mm. **Obv:** Bust of President Tsao Kun facing

Date	Mintage	VG8	F12	VF20	XF40	MS60
ND(1923)	50,000	190	375	800	3,500	8,000

K# 678 DOLLAR (Yuan)
26.93 g., 0.900 Silver 0.7792 oz. ASW, 39 mm. **Obv:** Bust of President Tsao Kun in military uniform facing

Date	Mintage	VG8	F12	VF20	XF40	MS60
ND(1923)	—	—	—	750	2,750	6,500

K# 683 DOLLAR (Yuan)
26.73 g., 0.900 Silver 0.7734 oz. ASW, 39 mm. **Obv:** Bust of President Tuan Chi-jui facing

Date	Mintage	VG8	F12	VF20	XF40	MS60
ND(1924)	20,000	190	300	750	2,500	6,500

Y# 318a.1 DOLLAR (Yuan)
26.73 g., 0.900 Silver 0.7734 oz. ASW **Obv:** Bust of Sun Yat-sen left **Rev:** Two rosettes dividing legend at top **Edge:** Incuse reeding

Date	Mintage	VG8	F12	VF20	XF40	MS60
ND(1927)	—	32.00	36.00	40.00	60.00	100

Y# 318a.2 DOLLAR (Yuan)
26.73 g., 0.900 Silver 0.7734 oz. ASW **Edge:** Reeding in relief

Date	Mintage	VG8	F12	VF20	XF40	MS60
ND(1927)	—	32.00	36.00	40.00	60.00	100

Note: Varieties exist with errors in the English legend. For similar coins with 5-pointed stars dividing legends, see Y#318 (1912). In 1949 the Canton Mint restruck Memento dollars. There are modern restrikes in red copper and brass.

K# 609 DOLLAR (Yuan)
26.73 g., 0.900 Silver 0.7734 oz. ASW **Obv:** Bust of Sun Yat-sen **Rev:** Sun Yat-sen Memorial

Date	Mintage	VG8	F12	VF20	XF40	MS60
16(1927)	480	1,150	2,250	4,500	7,500	19,000

K# 690 DOLLAR (Yuan)
26.73 g., 0.900 Silver 0.7734 oz. ASW, 39 mm. **Obv:** Bust of General Chu Yu-pu facing

Date	Mintage	VG8	F12	VF20	XF40	MS60
ND(1927)	—	—	—	7,500	18,000	50,000

Y# 344 DOLLAR (Yuan)
26.73 g., 0.900 Silver 0.7734 oz. ASW **Obv:** Bust of Sun Yat-sen left **Rev:** 3 wild geese flying above junk, rising sun

Date	Mintage	VG8	F12	VF20	XF40	MS60
21(1932)	2,260,000	150	265	450	600	1,200

Y# 345 DOLLAR (Yuan)
26.73 g., 0.900 Silver 0.7734 oz. ASW **Obv:** Bust of Sun-Yat Sen left **Rev:** Without birds above junk or rising sun

Date	Mintage	VG8	F12	VF20	XF40	MS60
22(1933)	46,400,000	30.00	34.00	40.00	65.00	110
23(1934)	128,740,000	30.00	34.00	40.00	55.00	80.00

Note: In 1949, three U.S. mints restruck a total of 30 million "Junk Dollars" dated Year 23. Several varieties are known. Most carry the same value, with the exception of the six ropes variety listed below.

Date	Mintage	VG8	F12	VF20	XF40	MS60
23 (1934) six ropes	Inc. above	60.00	80.00	165	285	500

Note: six rope lines between sails at center

Y# 333 10 DOLLARS
7.05 g., Red Gold **Ruler:** Hung-hsien **Obv:** Bust of Hung-hsien left **Rev:** Winged dragon left **Note:** K#1515.

Date	Mintage	VG8	F12	VF20	XF40	MS60
1	—	—	—	5,400	8,400	11,500

Y# 333a 10 DOLLARS
7.05 g., Yellow Gold **Ruler:** Hung-hsien

Date	Mintage	VG8	F12	VF20	XF40	MS60
1	—	—	—	5,400	8,400	11,500

Y# 330 10 DOLLARS
8.15 g., 0.850 Gold 0.2227 oz. AGW **Ruler:** Hung-hsien **Note:** K#1531.

Date	Mintage	VG8	F12	VF20	XF40	MS60
8	—	—	—	4,200	5,700	7,800

Y# 331 20 DOLLARS
16.30 g., 0.850 Gold 0.4454 oz. AGW **Ruler:** Hung-hsien **Note:** K#1530.

Date	Mintage	VG8	F12	VF20	XF40	MS60
8	—	—	—	—	8,400	13,000

TOKEN COINAGE

KM# Tn1 FEN
Brass

Date	Mintage	F12	VF20	XF40	MS60	MS63
17	—	75.00	125	175	300	—

Note: This token is usually found with small punch marks near center on obverse and reverse

KM# Tn2 2 FEN
Brass

Date	Mintage	F12	VF20	XF40	MS60	MS63
17	—	150	250	400	650	—

Note: This token has always been found with small punch marks near center on obverse and reverse

KM# Tn3 5 FEN
Brass **Note:** Similar to 2 Fen, KM#Tn2.

Date	Mintage	F12	VF20	XF40	MS60	MS63
17	—	450	750	1,250	—	—

Note: This token has always been found with small punch marks near center on obverse and reverse

KM# Tn4 10 FEN
Brass **Note:** Similar to 2 Fen, KM#Tn2.

Date	Mintage	F12	VF20	XF40	MS60	MS63
17	—	450	750	1,250	—	—

Note: This token has always been found with small punch marks near center on obverse and reverse

PATTERNS

Including off metal strikes

KM#	Date	Mintage	Identification	Mkt Val
Pn2	ND(1912)	—	Cash. Copper or Brass.	—
Pn3	ND(1912)	—	Cash. Zinc.	—
Pn4	ND(1912)	—	Cash. Iron.	—
Pn5	ND(1912)	—	10 Cash. Copper. Hsu13.	1,000
PnA6	ND(1912)	—	10 Cash. Copper. Similar to Pn5 but larger bust; W972.	—
Pn6	ND(1912)	—	10 Cash. Gold.	—
PnA7	ND(1912)	—	5 Cash. Copper. Crossed flags.	—
PnB7	ND(1912)	—	20 Cash. Copper. Crossed flags.	3,000
PnC7	ND(1912)	—	50 Cash. Copper. Crossed flags.	8,000
Pn7	ND(1912)	—	20 Cents. Gold. Y#317.	4,500
Pn8	ND(1912)	—	Dollar. Gold. Y#318.	25,000
Pn9	ND(1912)	—	Dollar. Gold. Y#318 - K#1550.	20,000
PnA10	ND(1912)	—	Dollar. Silver. Li Yuan-hung.	—
Pn10	ND(1912)	—	Dollar. Silver. Chin Teh-chuen, K#672. Many counterfeits exist.	50,000
Pn11	ND(1912)	—	Dollar. Eyes in relief. Chin Teh-chuen, K#672a.	—
Note: All known examples are counterfeit.				
Pn12	ND(1912)	—	Dollar. Bronze. K#672x.	—
Note: All known examples are counterfeit.				
PnA13	ND(1914)	—	10 Cash. Copper. With L. GEORGI; Y#309.	35,000
Pn13	3(1914)	—	5 Cents. Nickel. K#815.	—
Pn14	3(1914)	—	5 Cents. Nickel. Plain. Essay, K#815a.	20,000
Pn15	3(1914)	—	5 Cents. Nickel. Milled. Essay, K#815b; with G. L.	—
Pn16	3(1914)	—	5 Cents. Silver. Milled. Essay, K#815c; with G. L.	350
Pn17	3(1914)	—	5 Cents. Copper. Essay, K#815x.	225
Pn18	3(1914)	—	5 Cents. Pewter. Plain. Essay, K#815y.	—
Pn19	3(1914)	—	5 Cents. Copper. With G. L., essay, K#815z.	—
Pn20	3(1914)	—	10 Cents. Silver. With G. L., K#659a.	700
Pn21	3(1914)	—	10 Cents. Copper. Y#326.	45.00
Pn22	3(1914)	—	10 Cents. Nickel. Y#326.	350
Pn23	3(1914)	—	20 Cents. Silver. With G. L.; K#657a.	900
Pn24	3(1914)	—	20 Cents. Copper. Y#327.	65.00
Pn25	3(1914)	—	20 Cents. Nickel. Y#327.	375
Pn26	3(1914)	—	20 Cents. Pewter. Y#327.	300
Pn27	3(1914)	—	50 Cents. Silver. With L. GIORGI; Yuan Shih-kai, K#655a.	8,500
Pn28	ND(1914)	—	Dollar. Silver. With L. GIORGI; Yuan Shih-kai, K#642a.	18,000
Pn29	ND(1914)	—	Dollar. Gold. With L. GIORGI, Yuan Shih-kai; K#1558.	25,000
Pn30	ND(1914)	—	Dollar. Silver. Yuan Shih-kai, plumes of hat touch rim; K#644.	10,500
Pn31	ND(1914)	—	Dollar. Silver. With L. GIORGI; Yuan Shih-kai, K#645.	15,000
Pn32	3(1914)	—	Dollar. Silver. K#643.	70,000
Pn33	3(1914)	—	Dollar. Silver. With L. GIORGI; K#643a.	35,000
Pn34	ND(1914)	—	Dollar. Copper. Y#322.	500
Pn35	ND(1914)	—	Dollar. Brass. Y#322.	600
Pn36	ND(1914)	—	Dollar. Gold. Y#329.	25,000
Pn37	ND(1914)	—	Dollar. Copper. Y#329.	450
Pn38	ND(1914)	—	Dollar. Brass. Y#329.	400
PnA39	ND(1914)	—	5 Dollars. Gold. K#1517.	6,000
Pn39	5(1916)	—	1/2 Cent. Copper. Without center hole; Y#323.	375
Pn40	5(1916)	—	10 Cash. Copper. Without center hole; Y#324.	400
Pn41	5(1916)	—	10 Cash. Copper. With L. GIORGI; Y#324.3.	65,000
Pn42	5(1916)	—	20 Cash. Copper. Hsu44.	650
Pn43	5(1916)	—	20 Cents. Copper. Y#327.	—
Pn44	ND(1916)	—	Dollar. Gold. Y#332. It has been verified that the San Francisco Mint actually struck 2 pieces in gold in 1928.	15,000
Pn45	ND(1916)	—	Dollar. White Metal. Y#332.	—
Pn47	ND(1916)	—	Dollar. Silver. With L. GIORGI; plumes don't touch rim; K#663a.	25,000
Pn48	ND(1916)	—	Dollar. Silver. With L. GIORGI; K#663d.	15,000
Pn50	1(1916)	—	10 Dollars. Gold. with L. G. Hung-hsien, near shoulder; K#1515a.	—
Pn51	1(1916)	—	10 Dollars. Copper. with L. G. Hung-hsien, near shoulder; K#1515y.	—

Pn52	ND(1916)	—	Dollar. Silver. Plumes of hat touch rim; K#664.	10,500
Pn53	ND(1916)	—	Dollar. Gold. With L. GIORGI; K#1560.	50,000
Pn54	1(1916)	—	10 Dollars. Silver. Y#333.	—
Pn55	1(1916)	—	10 Dollars. Copper. Y#333.	375
Pn56	8(1919)	—	10 Cash. Copper. Hsu29.	1,000
Pn57	8(1919)	—	10 Cash. Copper. Hsu30.	1,000
Pn59	8(1919)	—	10 Dollars. Copper. Y#330.	350
Pn60	8(1919)	—	10 Dollars. Brass. Y#330.	350
Pn61	8(1919)	—	20 Dollars. Copper. Y#331.	500
Pn62	10(1921)	—	Dollar. Gold. K#1570.	25,000
Pn63	10(1921)	—	Dollar. Silver. Reeded. K#676a.1.	2,500
Pn64	10(1921)	—	Dollar. Silver. Plain. K#676a.2.	2,500
Pn65	10(1921)	—	Dollar. Gold. Reeded. K#1570.	30,000
Pn66	10(1921)	—	Dollar. Gold. Plain. K#1570a.	35,000
Pn67	ND(1923)	—	Dollar. Gold. K#1572.	20,000
Pn68	ND(1923)	—	Dollar. Copper. K#677x.	450
Pn69	ND(1923)	—	Dollar. Brass. K#677y.	450
Pn70	12(1923)	—	Dollar. Gold. Y#336.	25,000
Pn71	12(1923)	—	Dollar. Copper. Y#336.	—
Pn72	12(1923)	—	Dollar. Gold. Y#336.1.	—
Pn73	ND(1924)	—	Dollar. Gold. K#1577.	25,000
Pn74	ND(1924)	—	Dollar. Copper. K#683x.	700
Pn75	ND(1924)	—	Dollar. Pewter. K#683y.	700
Pn76	15(1926)	—	10 Cents. Copper. Y#334.	125
Pn77	15(1926)	—	10 Cents. Lead. Y#334.	90.00
Pn78	15(1926)	—	20 Cents. Copper. Y#335.	65.00
PnA79	15(1926)	—	Dollar. Silver. K#604.	150,000
Pn79	15(1926)	—	Dollar. Silver. K#685.	48,450
Pn80	16(1927)	—	10 Cents. Copper. Y#339.	—
Pn81	16(1927)	—	10 Cents. Gold. Y#339.	—
Pn82	ND(1927)	—	Dollar. Gold. Y#318.	—
Pn83	ND(1927)	—	Dollar. Copper. Y#318.	225
Pn84	ND(1927)	—	Dollar. Silver. K#687.	60,000
Pn85	16(1927)	—	Dollar. Silver. K#686.	65,000
Pn86	ND(1928)	—	20 Cash. Copper. Y#337.	—
Pn87	ND(1928)	—	20 Cash. Copper. Similar to 1 Chiao.	—
Pn90	17(1928)	—	Dollar. Silver. K#688.	50,000
Pn91	17(1928)	—	Dollar. Copper. K#688x.	3,500
PnA92	17(1928)	—	Dollar. Gold. K#688z.	45,000
Pn92	17(1928)	—	Dollar. Pewter. K#688y.	6,500
Pn93	18(1929)	—	20 Cents. Silver. K#611.	—
Pn94	18(1929)	—	10 Cents. Copper-Nickel. Vienna; K#617yVI.	850
Pn95	18(1929)	—	20 Cents. Copper-Nickel. Vienna; K#617yV.	—
Pn96	18(1929)	—	50 Cents. Copper-Nickel. Vienna; K#617yIV.	—
Pn97	18(1929)	—	Dollar. Silver. Italian; K#614.	13,000
Pn98	18(1929)	—	Dollar. Silver. With designer's name. K#614a.	45,000
Pn99	18(1929)	—	Dollar. Silver. English; K#615.	11,000
Pn100	18(1929)	—	Dollar. Silver. American; K#616.	13,000
Pn101	18(1929)	—	Dollar. Silver. Austrian; K#61.	12,000
Pn102	18(1929)	—	Dollar. Silver. Japanese; K#618.	17,000

Note: In 1929 China invited several mints to submit designs for a new Sun Yat-sen Dollar, with his bust on one side and a junk on the other. All designs were very much alike, differing mainly in details of the portrait, the waves, and the junk.

Pn103	18(1929)	—	10 Cents. Silver. K#617yIII.	850
Pn104	18(1929)	—	20 Cents. Silver. K#617yII.	850
Pn105	18(1929)	—	50 Cents. Silver. K#617yI.	850
Pn106	18(1929)	—	Dollar. Silver. K#610.	50,000
Pn107	18(1929)	—	20 Cents. Silver. K#611.	5,000
Pn108	18(1929)	—	Dollar. Silver. Wreath. K#612.	—
Pn109	ND(1929)	—	Dollar. Silver. Memento. K#620.	—
Pn110	ND(1929)	—	Dollar. Copper. K#620x.	—
Pn111	ND(1929)	—	Dollar. White Metal. K#620y.	—
Pn112	ND(1929)	—	Dollar. Silver. Wreath. K#620k.	—
Pn113	ND(1929)	—	Dollar. White Metal. K#620m.	—
Pn114	21(1932)	—	Cent. Bronze.	—
Pn115	21(1932)	—	Cent. Bronze. Without center hole.	—
Pn118	21(1932)	—	2 Cents. Nickel. Milled. K#830.	1,200
Pn119	21(1932)	—	2 Cents. Nickel. Plain. K#830a.	1,200
Pn120	21(1932)	—	2 Cents. Nickel. Without center hole; K#830b.	2,000
Pn121	21(1932)	—	5 Cents. Nickel. Milled. K#829.	600
Pn122	21(1932)	—	5 Cents. Nickel. Plain. K#829a.	600
Pn123	21(1932)	—	5 Cents. Nickel. Without center; K#829b.	600
Pn124	21(1932)	—	10 Cents. Silver. K#631.	—
Pn125	21(1932)	—	10 Cents. Silver. Plain. K#631a.	—
Pn126	21(1932)	—	10 Cents. Copper. K#631.	—
Pn127	21(1932)	—	20 Cents. Silver. Milled. K#630.	—
Pn128	21(1932)	—	20 Cents. Silver. Plain. K#630a.	—
Pn129	21(1932)	—	20 Cents. Copper. K#630x.	—
Pn130	21(1932)	—	1/2 Dollar. Silver. Milled. K#629.	4,500
Pn131	21(1932)	—	1/2 Dollar. Silver. Plain. K#629a.	4,500
Pn132	21(1932)	—	1/2 Dollar. Copper. K#629x.	—
Pn133	21(1932)	—	Dollar. Silver. Milled. K#628.	—
Pn134	21(1932)	—	Dollar. Silver. Plain. K#628a.	10,000
Pn135	21(1932)	—	Dollar. Silver. Cherry blossom edge.	10,000
Pn136	21(1932)	—	Dollar. Copper. K#628x.	95,000
Pn137	21(1932)	—	Dollar. Copper. Y#344, K#622x.	275
Pn138	22(1933)	—	Dollar. Copper. Y#345.	8,500
Pn139	23(1934)	—	Dollar. Copper. Y#345.	—
Pn140	24(1935)	—	5 Cents. Nickel. K#833.	450
Pn141	24(1935)	—	5 Cents. Copper. K#833x.	—
Pn142	24(1935)	—	10 Cents. Nickel. K#832.	450
Pn143	24(1935)	—	10 Cents. Copper. K#832x.	—
Pn144	24(1935)	—	20 Cents. Nickel. K#831.	450
Pn145	24(1935)	—	20 Cents. Copper. K#831x.	—
PnA146	24(1935)	—	1/2 Dollar. Silver. K#625k.	—
PnB146	24(1935)	—	1/2 Dollar. Copper. K#625x.	—
Pn146	24(1935)	—	Dollar. Silver. K#625.	—
Pn146a	24(1935)	—	Dollar. Copper or Brass. Reduced size Pn146.	1,550
Pn147	24(1935)	—	Dollar. Copper. Y#345.	—
Pn148	25//1936	—	Mei. Copper. Character "Chin".	—
Pn149	25//1936	—	Mei. Copper.	—
Pn150	25//1936	—	2 Mei. Copper.	—
Pn151	25//1936	—	5 Mei. Copper.	—
Pn152	25//1936	—	10 Mei. Copper.	—
Pn153	25//1936	—	50 Mei. Copper.	—
Pn154	25//1936	—	20 Wen. Copper.	—
PnA155	25//1936	—	1/2 Fen. Copper. Character "P'ing" lower.	—

Note: This may also exist with character under spade on reverse

Pn155	25(1936)	—	Fen. Copper.	—
PnA156	25//1936	—	Fen. Copper. Character "P'ing" lower.	—
PnB156	25//1936	—	Fen. Copper. Character "P'ing" under spade.	—
PnC156	25//1936	—	Fen. Copper. Character "Ch'ing" lower.	—
PnD156	25//1936	—	Fen. Copper. Character "Ch'ing" under spade.	—
Pn156	25(1936)	—	5 Cents. Copper. Y#348.	—
Pn157	25(1936)	—	10 Cents. Nickel. Character "Ch'ing" in field or on portrait.	500
Pn158	25(1936)	—	10 Cents. Nickel. Character "P'ing" in field or on portrait.	500
Pn159	25(1936)	—	10 Cents. Nickel. Character "Ch'ing" on side of portrait.	500
Pn160	25(1936)	—	10 Cents. Nickel. Character "P'ing" on side of portrait.	500
Pn161	25(1936)	—	10 Cents. Copper. Y#349.	—
Pn162	25(1936)	—	10 Cents. Aluminum. Y#349.	—
Pn163	25(1936)	—	10 Cents. Aluminum-Bronze. Y#349.	—
Pn164	25(1936)	—	10 Cents. Lead. Y#349.	—
Pn165	25(1936)	—	20 Cents. Copper. Y#350.	—
Pn166	25(1936)	—	20 Cents. Aluminum. Y#350.	—
Pn167	25(1936)	—	20 Cents. Aluminum-Bronze. Y#350.	—
Pn168	25(1936)	—	20 Cents. Pewter. Y#350.	100
Pn169	25(1936)	—	50 Cents. Silver. K#635.	37,500
Pn170	25(1936)	—	50 Cents. Silver. K#633.	—
Pn171	25(1936)	—	50 Cents. Silver. Similar to K#633 without Greek border.	—
Pn172	25(1936)	—	Dollar. Silver. K#634.	80,000
Pn173	25(1936)	—	Dollar. Silver. Similar to K#632 without Greek border.	—
Pn174	25(1936)	—	Dollar. Silver. K#632.	9,000
Pn175	25(1936)	—	Dollar. Copper. K#632x.	2,500
Pn176	25(1936)	—	Dollar. Nickel. K#632y.	2,500
Pn177	25(1936)	—	Dollar. Brass. K#632z.	2,500
Pn178	25(1936)	—	Dollar. Silver. Chiang Kai-shek.	40,000
Pn179	25(1936)	—	Dollar. Copper. Chiang Kai-shek.	7,500
Pn180	26(1937)	—	5 Cents. Nickel. Y#348.2.	—
Pn181	26(1937)	—	10 Cents. Nickel. "P'ing" on side of portrait; Y#349.7.	—
Pn183	26(1937)	—	20 Cents. Nickel. Y#350.1.	—
Pn184	26(1937)S (1937)	—	50 Cents. Silver. K#637.	—
Pn185	26(1937)S (1937)	—	Dollar. Silver. K#636.	—
Pn186	27(1938)	—	5 Cents. Copper. Y#348.	—
Pn187	27(1938)	—	10 Cents. Copper. Y#349.	—
Pn188	27(1938)	—	20 Cents. Copper. Y#350.	—
Pn189	27(1938)	—	20 Cents. Pewter. Y#350.	150
Pn190	28(1939)	—	5 Cents. Copper. Y#348.	—
Pn191	28(1939)	—	5 Cents. Brass. Y#348.	—
PnA192	28(1939)	—	20 Cents. Copper. K#857x.	175
PnB192	29(1940)	—	1/2 Dollar. Copper.	250
Pn192	30(1941)	—	10 Cents. Copper. Y#360.	250
Pn193	30(1941)	—	10 Cents. Brass. Y#360.	—
PnA194	30(1941)	—	20 Cents. Nickel. K#863 IV.	250
PnB194	30(1941)	—	1/2 Dollar. Silver. K#696x.	—
PnC194	30(1941)	—	1/2 Dollar. Nickel. K#863 III.	2,000
Pn194	31(1942)	—	10 Cents. Copper-Nickel. Character "Kuei" below the spade.	—
Pn195	31(1942)	—	10 Cents. Copper. Y#360.	—
Pn196	31(1942)	—	10 Cents. Brass. Y#360.	—
Pn197	31(1942)	—	20 Cents. Copper-Nickel. Character "Kuei" below spade.	—
Pn198	31(1942)	—	20 Cents. Copper. Y#361.	—
Pn199	31(1942)	—	50 Cents. Copper-Nickel. Character "Kuei" between legs of space. K#866m.	—
Pn200	31(1942)	—	50 Cents. Copper. Y#362.	200
Pn201	31(1942)	—	50 Cents. Bronze. Y#362.	200
Pn202	31(1942)	—	50 Cents. Silver. Y#362.	1,500
PnA203	32(1943)	—	50 Cents. Copper-Nickel. Character "Kuei" between legs of spade.	—
Pn203	32(1943)	—	50 Cents. Copper. Y#362.	200
Pn204	32(1943)	—	50 Cents. Bronze. Y#362.	200
PnA205	37(1948)	—	50 Cents. Silver. Ch'ing right; K#698.	—
Pn205	37(1948)	—	Dollar. Silver. K#637yII.	—
Pn206	37(1948)	—	2 Dollars. Silver. K#637yI; denomination.	200

TRIAL STRIKES

KM#	Date	Mintage	Identification	Mkt Val
TS1	ND(1912)	—	Dollar. Silver. Uniface. Chin Te-chuan; K#672b.	8,000
TS2	37(1948)	—	50 Cents. Silver. K#698w.	750

CHINESE SOVIET REPUBLIC

CONSOLIDATED SOVIET REPUBLIC

(Kiangsi)

STANDARD COINAGE

Y# 506 CENT

Copper **Ruler:** Mao Tse-tung **Obv:** Large "1" on hammer and sickle **Rev:** Star above value in wheat stalks

Date	Mintage	F12	VF20	XF40	MS60	MS63
ND(ca.1932)	—	45.00	85.00	175	450	600

Y# 506a CENT

Copper **Ruler:** Mao Tse-tung **Obv:** Large "1" on hammer and sickle **Rev:** Star above value in wheat stalks

Date	Mintage	F12	VF20	XF40	MS60	MS63
ND(ca.196) Restrike	—	—	—	18.00	45.00	70.00

Y# 507 5 CENTS

Copper **Ruler:** Mao Tse-tung **Obv:** Hammer and sickle on map outline **Rev:** Star over value in wheat stalks **Edge:** Plain **Note:** Varieties exist.

Date	Mintage	F12	VF20	XF40	MS60	MS63
ND(ca.1932)	—	70.00	120	350	700	1,300

Y# 507.1 5 CENTS

Copper **Ruler:** Mao Tse-tung **Obv:** Hammer and sickle on map outline **Rev:** Star over value in wheat stalks **Edge:** Reeded **Note:** Varieties exist.

Date	Mintage	VG8	F12	VF20	XF40	MS60
ND(ca.1932)	—	45.00	70.00	120	350	—

Y# 507a 5 CENTS
Copper **Ruler:** Mao Tse-tung **Obv:** Hammer and sickle on map outline **Rev:** Star over value in wheat stalks

Date	Mintage	F12	VF20	XF40	MS60	MS63
ND(ca.196) Restrike	—	—	—	37.50	70.00	145

Y# 508 20 CENTS
5.50 g., Silver **Ruler:** Mao Tse-tung **Obv:** Star over hammer and sickle on globe in wheat stalks **Rev:** Denomination **Note:** Many minor varieties exist.

Date	Mintage	VG8	F12	VF20	XF40	MS60
1932	—	70.00	135	300	650	—
1933	—	45.00	75.00	100	225	450

KM# 5 DOLLAR
Silver **Ruler:** Mao Tse-tung **Obv:** Crude facing portrait of Lenin **Rev:** Hammer, sickle, and value within ornamental wreath

Date	Mintage	VG8	F12	VF20	XF40	MS60
1931 Rare	—	—	—	—	—	—

PATTERNS

Including off metal strikes

KM#	Date	Mintage	Identification	Mkt Val
Pn1	1932	—	20 Cents. Copper. Y#508.	2,250

HSIANG-O-HSI SOVIET

(Kiangsi-West Hupeh)

SOVIET CONTROLLED PROVINCE

STANDARD COINAGE

KM# 1 FEN
Copper **Obv:** Legend around large star **Rev:** Denomination within wreath, legend around

Date	Mintage	VG8	F12	VF20	XF40	MS60
ND(1931) Rare	—	—	—	—	—	—

HUNAN SOVIET

SOVIET CONTROLLED PROVINCE

STANDARD COINAGE

KM# 1.1 DOLLAR
Silver **Obv:** Large star **Obv. Legend:** Hu-nan Sheng Su-wei-ai Cheng-fu **Rev:** Denomination within sprays

Date	Mintage	VG8	F12	VF20	XF40	MS60
1931	—	2,000	3,000	5,500	9,500	—

KM# 1.2 DOLLAR
Silver **Obv:** Hammer and sickle within small star **Rev:** Denomination within sprays

Date	Mintage	VG8	F12	VF20	XF40	MS60
1931	—	650	1,250	2,500	—	—

HUPEH-HONAN-ANWHEI SOVIET

The Hupeh-Honan-Anwhei Soviet District was a large revolutionary base. It was formerly made up of three separate special districts: East Hupeh, South Honan and West Anwhei which united until after 1930. Between 1931 and 1932 this Bank has issued a quantity of copper and silver coins as well as banknotes.

SOVIET CONTROLLED PROVINCE

STANDARD COINAGE

Y# 503 DOLLAR
26.80 g., Silver **Obv:** Hammer and sickle on globe at center **Rev:** Lower legend appears in crude Russian, denomination within circle at center **Rev. Legend:** SOVETS....

Date	Mintage	VG8	F12	VF20	XF40	MS60
1932	—	1,500	3,200	6,500	12,000	—

Note: Attribution of Y#503 to the Hupeh-Honan-Anwhei Soviet is not definite.

Y# 504 DOLLAR
27.20 g., Silver **Obv:** Hammer and sickle on globe at center **Rev:** Denomination within center circle

Date	Mintage	VG8	F12	VF20	XF40	MS60
1932	—	1,200	2,500	4,250	7,500	—

P'ING CHIANG COUNTY SOVIET

SOVIET CONTROLLED PROVINCE

STANDARD COINAGE

KM# 1 DOLLAR
Silver **Obv:** Star in center circle holds sickle and hammer, legend in 8 Chinese characters **Obv. Legend:** P'ing Chiang... **Rev:** Denomination within wreath

Date	Mintage	VG8	F12	VF20	XF40	MS60
1931 Rare	—	—	—	—	—	—

SHENSI-NORTH SOVIET

SOVIET CONTROLLED PROVINCE

STANDARD COINAGE

Date is given in the 5th year of the Chinese Soviet Republic. They were issued after the Long March.

KM# 1.1 DOLLAR
Silver **Obv:** Large hammer and sickle **Rev:** Value in plain field, yr.5 at bottom

Date	Mintage	VG8	F12	VF20	XF40	MS60
5 (1936)	—	8,500	12,500	20,000	—	—

KM# 1.2 DOLLAR
Silver **Obv:** Star at left, slightly lower **Rev:** Denomination within center circle, legend rotated with yr.5 at top

Date	Mintage	VG8	F12	VF20	XF40	MS60
5 (1936)	—	8,500	12,500	20,000	—	—

KM# 2 DOLLAR
Silver **Obv:** Large hammer and sickle **Rev:** Value within wheat stalks

Date	Mintage	VG8	F12	VF20	XF40	MS60
5 (1936)	—	12,500	20,000	40,000	—	—

SZECHUAN-SHENSI SOVIET

SOVIET CONTROLLED PROVINCES

STANDARD COINAGE

Y# 510 200 CASH
Copper **Obv:** Three stars around hammer and sickle **Rev:** Denomination at center

Date	Mintage	G4	VG8	F12	VF20	XF40
1933	—	100	200	400	1,000	—

Y# 510.1 200 CASH
Copper **Obv:** Three stars around hammer and sickle **Rev:** Small "200" at center

Date	Mintage	G4	VG8	F12	VF20	XF40
1933	—	70.00	140	275	750	—

Y# 510.2 200 CASH
Copper **Obv:** Three stars around hammer and sickle **Rev:** Large "200" at center

Date	Mintage	G4	VG8	F12	VF20	XF40
1933	—	70.00	140	275	750	—

Y# 510.3 200 CASH
Copper **Obv:** Three stars around hammer and sickle **Rev:** Square 0's in "200" at center

Date	Mintage	G4	VG8	F12	VF20	XF40
1933	—	85.00	170	325	900	—

Y# 510.4 200 CASH
Copper **Obv:** Solid hammer and sickle reversed **Rev:** 200 retrograde at center

Date	Mintage	G4	VG8	F12	VF20	XF40
1933	—	110	240	450	1,250	—

Y# 510.5 200 CASH
Copper **Obv:** Shaded hammer and sickle reversed, three stars above **Rev:** Denomination within wreath at center **Note:** Varieties exist.

Date	Mintage	G4	VG8	F12	VF20	XF40
1933	—	95.00	190	375	1,000	—

Y# 511 200 CASH
Copper **Obv:** Hammer and sickle at center of large star, date with closed 3 and backwards 4 **Rev:** Denomination within circle **Note:** Modern forgeries of this variety exist.

Date	Mintage	VG8	F12	VF20	XF40	MS60
1934	—	65.00	130	220	425	2,000

Y# 511.1 200 CASH
Copper **Obv:** Hammer and sickle within large star, date with open 3 and backwards 4 **Rev:** Denomination within circle

Date	Mintage	VG8	F12	VF20	XF40	MS60
1934	—	65.00	130	220	425	—

Y# 511.2 200 CASH
Copper **Obv:** Hammer and sickle within large star, date with 4 corrected **Rev:** Denomination within circle

Date	Mintage	VG8	F12	VF20	XF40	MS60
1934	—	130	260	450	950	5,000

Y# 511a 200 CASH
Copper **Obv:** Hammer and sickle within large star, date with 4 corrected **Rev:** Denomination within circle

Date	Mintage	F12	VF20	XF40	MS60	MS63
1934 Restrike	—	—	—	35.00	95.00	175

Note: Many varieties of 200 Cash pieces exist; well struck, usually found in choice condition; unlisted varieties do not carry a premium

Y# 512 500 CASH
Copper **Obv:** Hammer and sickle within small star, small stars flanking date **Rev:** Denomination within circle

Date	Mintage	VG8	F12	VF20	XF40	MS60
1934	—	240	325	550	1,000	—

Y# 512.1 500 CASH
Copper **Obv:** Large stars flanking date; hammer handle across lower leg of star **Rev:** Denomination within circle

Date	Mintage	VG8	F12	VF20	XF40	MS60
1934	—	160	300	550	1,000	—

Y# 512.2 500 CASH
Copper, 33-34 mm. **Obv:** Hammer handle extends between right leg of star **Rev:** Denomination within circle

Date	Mintage	VG8	F12	VF20	XF40	MS60
1934	—	80.00	160	350	650	—

Note: Many varieties of 500 Cash pieces exist; unlisted varieties do not carry a premium

Y# 513 DOLLAR
26.30 g., Silver **Obv:** Globe with hammer and sickle **Rev:** Denomination within circle, large, decorative, solid stars

Date	Mintage	VG8	F12	VF20	XF40	MS60
1934	—	500	950	1,850	6,500	—

Y# 513.1 DOLLAR
26.30 g., Silver **Obv:** Globe with outlined hammer and sickle, hammer handle over sickle blade **Rev:** Denomination within circle, medium solid stars

Date	Mintage	VG8	F12	VF20	XF40	MS60
1934	—	450	900	1,750	6,000	—

Y# 513.2 DOLLAR
26.30 g., Silver **Obv:** Globe with outlined hammer and sickle **Rev:** Denomination within circle, small solid stars

Date	Mintage	VG8	F12	VF20	XF40	MS60
1933 Rare	—	—	—	—	—	—
1934	—	450	900	1,750	6,000	—

Y# 513.3 DOLLAR
26.30 g., Silver **Obv:** Globe with hammer and sickle **Rev:** Denomination within circle, outlined stars

Date	Mintage	VG8	F12	VF20	XF40	MS60
1934	—	700	1,600	3,750	7,000	—

Y# 513.4 DOLLAR
26.30 g., Silver **Obv:** Globe with hammer and sickle **Rev:** Denomination within circle, pentagram stars **Note:** Many minor varieties exist.

Date	Mintage	VG8	F12	VF20	XF40	MS60
1934	—	450	900	1,850	6,250	—

Y# 513.5 DOLLAR
26.30 g., Silver **Obv:** Globe with outlined hammer and sickle **Rev:** Denomination within circle, large solid stars

Date	Mintage	VG8	F12	VF20	XF40	MS60
1934	—	450	1,000	2,000	6,750	—

Y# 513.6 DOLLAR
26.30 g., Silver **Obv:** Globe with outlined hammer and sickle, sickle blade over hammer handle **Rev:** Denomination within circle, small solid stars

Date	Mintage	VG8	F12	VF20	XF40	MS60
1934	—	450	900	1,750	6,000	—

COUNTERMARKED COINAGE

K# 650k DOLLAR
26.40 g., Silver **Obv:** Bust, left, countermark of uncertain origin meaning "SOVIET" **Rev:** Denomination within wreath **Countermark:** Three Chinese characters in rectangular box **Note:** Countermark on Y#329.

CM Date	Host Date	VG8	F12	VF20	XF40	MS60
ND(1934)		500	900	1,500	2,800	—

WAN-HSI-PEI-SOVIET

(Northwest Anhwei)

SOVIET CONTROLLED PROVINCE

STANDARD COINAGE

KM# 1 50 CASH
Brass **Obv:** Legend around globe with hammer and sickle **Rev:** Value in star within wreath, all within legend

Date	Mintage	G4	VG8	F12	VF20	XF40
1931	—	1,200	2,500	3,500	5,500	—

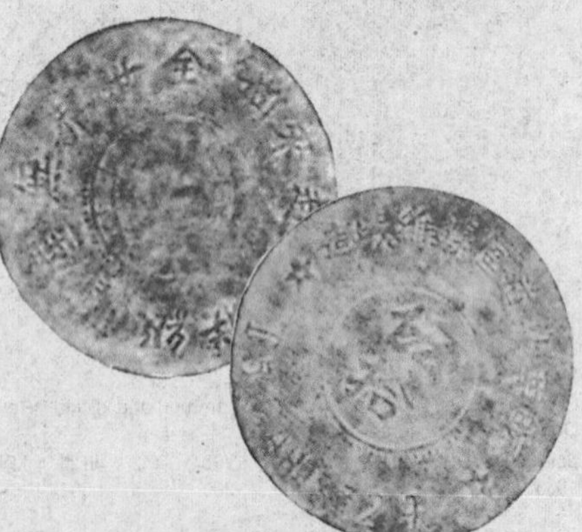

KM# 2 50 CASH
Copper **Obv:** Legend around globe with hammer and sickle **Rev:** Value in circle, Chinese legend above, Western legend below

Date	Mintage	VG8	F12	VF20	XF40	MS60
ND(1931-32) Rare	—	—	—	—	—	—

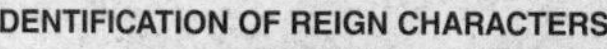

CHINA-JAPANESE PUPPET STATES

Shortly after World War I the greatest external threat to the territorial integrity of China was posed by Japan. The Japanese had large investments in Manchuria (a name given by non-Chinese to the three northeastern provinces of China), which allowed them privileges that compromised Chinese sovereignty. On the night of Sept. 18-19, 1931, with a contrived incident for an excuse, Japanese forces seized the city of Mukden (Shenyang), and within a few weeks completely demolished Chinese power north of the Great Wall.

In Feb. 1932, after the Japanese occupation of Manchuria, they set up Manchoukuo as an independent republic. Jehol (Rehe) was occupied by the Japanese in 1933 and added to Manchoukuo. Manchoukuo was established as an empire in 1934 with the deposed Manchu emperor Hsuan T'ung (the late Henry Pu Yi) as the puppet emperor K'ang Te. Lacking the means to face the Japanese armies in the field, the Chinese could only trade space for time.

Not content with confining its control of China to the areas north of the Great Wall, the Japanese launched a major campaign in 1937, and by the fall of 1938 had occupied in addition to Manchuria the provinces of Hopei (Hebei) and Chahar, most of the port cities, and the major cities as far west as Hankow (Hankou), now part of Wuhan. In addition, they dominated or threatened the provinces of Suiyuan, Shansi (Shanxi) and Shantung (Shandong).

Still the Chinese did not yield. The struggle was prolonged until the advent of World War II, which brought about the defeat of Japan and the return of the puppet states to Chinese control.

As the victorious Japanese armies swept deeper into China, Japan established central banks under control of the Bank of Japan in the conquered provinces for the purpose of establishing control over banking and finance in the puppet states. These included the Chi Tung Bank,which had its main office in Tientsin (Tianjin) with branches in Peking (Beijing), Chinan (Jinan) and Tangshan, the Federal Reserve Bank of China with its main office in Peking (Beijing) and branches in 37 other cities; and the Hua Hsing Bank with its main office in Shanghai and two branches. The puppet states of Manchukuo, previously detailed in this introduction, and Mengchiang, which comprised a greater part of Inner Mongolia, were also major coin-issuing entities.

EAST HOPEI

The Chi Tung Bank was the banking institution of the "East Hopei Anti-Comintern Autonomous Government" established by the Japanese in 1936 to undermine the political position of China in the northwest provinces. It issued both coins and notes between 1937 and 1939 with a restraint uncharacteristic of the puppet banks of the China-Japanese puppet states.

ANTI-COMINTERN AUTONOMOUS GOVERNMENT

STANDARD COINAGE

Y# 516 5 LI

Copper **Ruler:** (no ruler information) **Issuer:** Chi Tung Bank **Obv:** Japanese character "first" **Rev:** Value in grain stalks

Date	Mintage	VG8	F12	VF20	XF40	MS60
26(1937)	—	13.00	32.50	60.00	115	350

Y# 517 FEN

Copper **Ruler:** (no ruler information) **Issuer:** Chi Tung Bank **Obv:** Japanese character "first" **Rev:** Value in grain stalks

Date	Mintage	VG8	F12	VF20	XF40	MS60
26(1937)	—	4.00	9.00	18.00	28.00	115

Y# 518 5 FEN

Copper-Nickel **Ruler:** (no ruler information) **Issuer:** Chi Tung Bank **Obv:** Japanese character "first" **Rev:** Value in grain stalks

Date	Mintage	VG8	F12	VF20	XF40	MS60
26(1937)	—	3.00	8.00	14.00	22.00	90.00

Y# 519 CHIAO

Copper-Nickel **Ruler:** (no ruler information) **Issuer:** Chi Tung Bank **Obv:** T'ien-ning Pagoda in Peking **Rev:** Value in grain stalks

Date	Mintage	VG8	F12	VF20	XF40	MS60
26(1937)	—	3.00	8.00	14.00	20.00	85.00

Y# 520 2 CHIAO

Copper-Nickel **Ruler:** (no ruler information) **Issuer:** Chi Tung Bank **Obv:** T'ien-ning Pagoda in Peking **Rev:** Value in grain stalks

Date	Mintage	VG8	F12	VF20	XF40	MS60
26(1937)	—	4.00	9.00	18.00	40.00	130

MANCHUKUO

The former Japanese puppet state of Manchoukuo (largely Manchuria), comprising the northeastern Chinese provinces of Fengtien (Liaoning), Kirin (Jilin), Heilungkiang (Heilongjiang) and Jehol (Rehe), had an area of 503,143 sq. mi. (1,303,134 sq. km.) and a population of 43.3 million. Capital: Changchun, renamed Hsinking. The area is rich in fertile soil, timber and mineral resources, including coal, iron and gold.

Until the closing years of the 19th century when Chinese influence became predominant, Manchuria was chiefly a domain of the tribal Manchus and their Mongol allies. Coincident with the rise of Chinese influence, foreign imperialistic powers began to appreciate the value of the area to their expansionist philosophy. Japan, overpopulated and poor in resources, desired it as a source of raw materials and for increased living area. Russia wanted it as the eastern terminus of the Trans-Siberian railway that was to unite its Asian empire. The inevitable conflict of Japanese, Chinese and Russian interests required that one or more of the powers be eliminated. After eliminating Russia in their war of 1904-05, Japan eliminated China on the night of Sept. 18, 1931, when, on the pretext of a contrived incident, it moved militarily to seize control of the Three Eastern Provinces. Early in 1932 Japan declared Manchuria independent by virtue of a voluntary separatist movement and established the state of Manchoukuo. To give the puppet state an aura of legitimacy, the deposed emperor of the former Manchu dynasty was recalled from retirement and designated "chief executive". The area was restored to China at the end of World War II.

RULERS

Ta T'ung, 1932-1934

K'ang Te, 1934-1945

The puppet emperor under the assumed name of K'ang Te was previously the last emperor of China (P'u-yi, or Hsuan T'ung, 1909-11).

MONETARY SYSTEM

10 Li = 1 Fen

10 Fen = 1 Chiao

IDENTIFICATION OF REIGN CHARACTERS

'Nien' Year 1932-1934 Ta T'ung

'Nien' Year 1934-1945 K'ang Te

DATE ABBREVIATIONS

TT - Ta T'ung

KT - K'ang Te

GREEK RIM BORDER VARIETIES

Narrow Design

Wide Design

MARKET VALUATIONS

Uncirculated aluminum coins without any planchet defects are worth up to twice the market valuations given.

JAPANESE OCCUPATION

STANDARD COINAGE

Y# 1 5 LI

Bronze **Ruler:** Ta-t'ung **Obv:** Flag **Rev:** Value in floral sprays

Date	Mintage	VG8	F12	VF20	XF40	MS60
TT 2(1933)	—	25.00	60.00	100	150	350
TT 3(1934)	—	5.00	13.00	27.50	45.00	110

Y# 5 5 LI

Bronze **Ruler:** K'ang-te **Obv:** Character Yuan for "first", flag **Rev:** Value in floral sprays

Date	Mintage	VG8	F12	VF20	XF40	MS60
KT 1(1934)	—	4.00	9.00	22.50	35.00	90.00
KT 2(1935)	—	4.00	9.00	22.50	35.00	90.00
KT 3(1936)	—	18.00	42.00	65.00	90.00	195
KT 4(1937)	—	5.00	13.00	32.00	42.00	100
KT 6(1939)	—	115	225	300	400	675

Y# 2 FEN

5.01 g., Bronze, 23.97 mm. **Ruler:** Ta-t'ung **Obv:** Flag **Rev:** Value in floral sprays

Date	Mintage	VG8	F12	VF20	XF40	MS60
TT 2(1933)	—	2.25	6.00	13.00	25.00	90.00
TT 3(1934)	—	2.00	5.00	9.00	15.00	70.00

Y# 6 FEN

Bronze **Ruler:** K'ang-te **Obv:** Character Yuan for "first", flag **Rev:** Value in floral sprays

Date	Mintage	VG8	F12	VF20	XF40	MS60
KT 1(1934)	—	1.25	3.00	9.00	18.00	55.00
KT 2(1935)	—	1.25	3.00	9.00	15.00	37.50
KT 3(1936)	—	1.25	3.00	9.00	15.00	37.50
KT 4(1937)	—	1.25	3.00	9.00	15.00	37.50
KT 5(1938)	—	1.25	3.00	9.00	15.00	37.50
KT 6(1939)	—	1.25	3.00	9.00	18.00	55.00

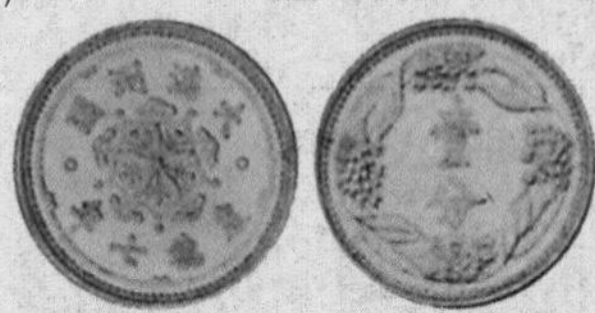

Y# 9 FEN

Aluminum, 19 mm. **Ruler:** K'ang-te **Obv:** National symbol **Rev:** Value in floral wreath

Date	Mintage	VG8	F12	VF20	XF40	MS60
KT 6(1939)	—	0.50	1.25	2.25	6.00	18.00
KT 7(1940)	—	0.50	1.25	2.25	6.00	18.00
KT 8(1941)	—	0.50	1.25	2.25	6.00	18.00
KT 9(1942)	—	0.50	1.25	2.25	6.00	18.00
KT 10(1943)	—	0.50	1.25	2.25	6.00	18.00

Y# 13 FEN

Aluminum **Ruler:** K'ang-te **Obv:** Legend around large "1" **Rev:** Floral wreath

Date	Mintage	VG8	F12	VF20	XF40	MS60
KT 10(1943)	—	1.00	2.25	6.00	15.00	37.50
KT 11(1944)	—	1.00	2.25	6.00	15.00	37.50

Y# 13a FEN

Fiber red **Ruler:** K'ang-te **Obv:** Legend around large "1" **Rev:** Floral wreath

Date	Mintage	G4	VG8	F12	VF20	XF40
KT 12(1945)	—	6.00	9.00	14.00	28.00	55.00

Y# 13a.1 FEN

Fiber Brown in color **Ruler:** K'ang-te **Obv:** Legend around large "1" **Rev:** Floral wreath

Date	Mintage	G4	VG8	F12	VF20	XF40
KT 12(1945)	—	6.00	9.00	22.50	45.00	70.00

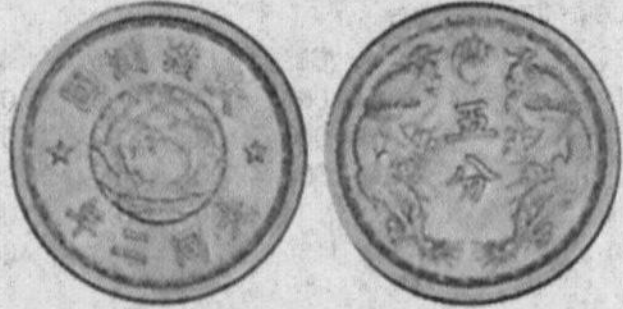

Y# 3 5 FEN

3.50 g., Copper-Nickel **Ruler:** Ta-t'ung **Obv:** Lotus flower **Rev:** Pearl above value between facing dragons

Date	Mintage	VG8	F12	VF20	XF40	MS60
TT 2(1933)	—	1.00	2.25	6.00	15.00	55.00
TT 3(1934)	—	0.50	1.25	3.00	6.00	37.50

Y# 7 5 FEN

Copper-Nickel **Ruler:** K'ang-te **Rev:** Pearl above value between facing dragons

Date	Mintage	VG8	F12	VF20	XF40	MS60
KT 1(1934)	—	0.70	2.00	5.00	9.00	20.00
Note: Character Yuan for "first".						
KT 2(1935)	—	0.70	2.00	5.00	9.00	20.00
KT 3(1936)	—	0.70	2.00	5.00	9.00	20.00
Note: Narrow border design						
KT 3(1936)	—	1.50	4.00	9.00	18.00	45.00
Note: Wide border design						
KT 4(1937)	—	1.25	3.00	6.00	13.00	28.00
KT 6(1939)	—	1.25	3.00	6.00	13.00	28.00

Y# 11 5 FEN

Aluminum **Ruler:** K'ang-te **Obv:** Legend around large "5" **Rev:** National symbol above value in floral sprays

Date	Mintage	VG8	F12	VF20	XF40	MS60
KT 7	—	0.70	2.00	5.00	9.00	20.00
KT 8	—	0.50	1.25	2.25	6.00	15.00
KT 9	—	0.50	1.25	2.25	6.00	15.00
KT 10	—	0.50	1.25	2.25	6.00	15.00

Y# A13 5 FEN

Aluminum **Ruler:** K'ang-te **Obv:** Legend around small "5" **Rev:** Wreath

Date	Mintage	VG8	F12	VF20	XF40	MS60
KT 10	—	1.25	3.00	8.00	15.00	45.00
KT 11	—	1.25	3.00	8.00	15.00	45.00

Y# A13a 5 FEN

Fiber red **Ruler:** K'ang-te **Obv:** Legend around small "5" **Rev:** Wreath

Date	Mintage	VG8	F12	VF20	XF40	MS60
KT 11	—	8.00	14.00	27.50	45.00	—
KT 12	—	125	175	225	—	—

Y# A13a.1 5 FEN

Fiber Brown in color **Ruler:** K'ang-te **Obv:** Legend around small "5" **Rev:** Floral wreath

Date	Mintage	VG8	F12	VF20	XF40	MS60
KT 11	—	15.00	31.25	45.00	75.00	—

Y# 4 CHIAO (10 Fen)

Copper-Nickel **Ruler:** Ta-t'ung **Obv:** Lotus flower **Rev:** Pearl above value between facing dragons

Date	Mintage	VG8	F12	VF20	XF40	MS60
TT 2	—	2.00	5.00	9.00	22.50	55.00
TT 3	—	0.90	2.25	6.00	13.00	45.00

Y# 8 CHIAO (10 Fen)

Copper-Nickel **Ruler:** K'ang-te **Rev:** Pearl above value between facing dragons

Date	Mintage	VG8	F12	VF20	XF40	MS60
KT 1	—	1.25	2.25	6.00	9.00	27.50
Note: Character Yuan for "first".						
KT 2	—	1.25	2.25	6.00	9.00	27.50
KT 5	—	1.25	2.25	6.00	9.00	27.50
KT 6	—	1.25	2.25	6.00	9.00	27.50
KT 6 Proof	—	—	—	—	—	—

Y# 10 CHIAO (10 Fen)

Copper-Nickel **Ruler:** K'ang-te **Obv:** Two winged horses **Rev:** National symbol above value with stylized sunrise

Date	Mintage	VG8	F12	VF20	XF40	MS60
KT 7	—	6.00	9.00	15.00	32.50	90.00

Y# 12 CHIAO (10 Fen)

Aluminum **Ruler:** K'ang-te **Obv:** Legend around "10" on "Fundo" weight outline **Rev:** National symbol above value in floral sprays

Date	Mintage	VG8	F12	VF20	XF40	MS60
KT 7	—	1.25	2.25	6.00	9.00	27.50
KT 8	—	1.25	2.25	6.00	9.00	27.50
KT 9	—	1.25	2.25	6.00	9.00	27.50
KT 10	—	175	400	600	750	1,150

Y# 14 CHIAO (10 Fen)

Aluminum **Ruler:** K'ang-te **Rev:** Legend around large "10"

Date	Mintage	VG8	F12	VF20	XF40	MS60
KT 10	—	2.00	5.00	9.00	15.00	45.00

PATTERNS

Including off metal strikes

KM#	Date	Mintage	Identification	Mkt Val
Pn1	KT5(1938)	—	5 Chiao. Copper-Nickel. Medieval emperor's bust. Portrait.	—
Pn2	KT5(1938)	—	5 Chiao. Copper-Nickel. Two facing phoenix. Chinese characters.	—
Pn3	KT9(1942)	—	Chiao. Silver. Specimen.	1,450
Pn4	KT9(1942)	—	Chiao. Copper-Nickel. Specimen.	900
Pn5	KT9(1942)	—	Chiao. Brass. Specimen.	700
Pn6	KT9(1942)	—	Chiao. Nickel-Bronze. Specimen.	700
Pn7	KT12(1945)	—	Fen. Copper Plated Steel. Y#13a.	—

MENG CHIANG

As Japanese troops moved into North China in 1937, the political situation became fluid in several provinces bordering on Manchoukuo, which were sometimes referred to as Inner Mongolia. On September 27, 1937, the Chanan Bank was established. As the situation became more settled the Japanese effected the merger of two local banks with the Bank of Chanan under a new title, Meng Chiang (Mongolian Borderlands or Mongol Territory) Bank. The Meng Chiang Bank was organized on November 27 and opened on December 1, 1937, with headquarters in Kalgan (Zhangjiakou) and branch offices in about a dozen locations throughout the region. Its notes were declared the exclusive currency for the area. The bank closed at the end of the war.

JAPANESE OCCUPATION

STANDARD COINAGE

Y# 521 5 CHIAO

Copper-Nickel **Obv:** Legend in floral design **Rev:** Value in facing dragons

Date	Mintage	VG8	F12	VF20	XF40	MS60
27(1938)	—	3.00	6.00	11.00	22.50	55.00

PATTERNS

Including off metal strikes

KM#	Date	Mintage	Identification	Mkt Val
Pn1	738(1943)	—	Fen. Aluminum. Ram's head. Value above phoenix. This coin uses the Kublai Khan (KK) dating system.	—
Pn2	738(1943)	—	5 Fen. Aluminum. Ram's head. Value above phoenix. This coin uses the Kublai Khan (KK) dating system.	3,750
Pn3	738(1943)	—	Chiao. Aluminum. Ram's head. Value above phoenix. This coin uses the Kublai Khan (KK) dating system.	5,200

PROVISIONAL GOVT. OF CHINA

In late 1937 the Japanese North China Expeditionary Army established the "Provisional Government of China" at Peking (Beijing).

FEDERAL RESERVE BANK

The Federal Reserve Bank of China was opened in 1938 by Japanese military authorities in Peking (Beijing). It was the puppet financial agency of the Japanese in northeast China. The puppet bank issued both coins and currency, but in modest amounts.

JAPANESE OCCUPATION

STANDARD COINAGE

Y# 523 FEN

Aluminum **Issuer:** Federal Reserve Bank **Obv:** Legend around FR Bank symbol **Rev:** Temple of Heaven

Date	Mintage	VG8	F12	VF20	XF40	MS60
30	—	1.50	3.00	6.00	8.00	27.50
31	—	0.70	1.50	3.00	6.00	20.00
32	—	3.00	8.00	15.00	32.00	70.00

Y# 524 5 FEN

Aluminum **Issuer:** Federal Reserve Bank **Obv:** Legend around FR Bank symbol **Rev:** Temple of Heaven **Note:** The 5 Fen pieces were struck on thick (1 gram) and thin (.8 gram) planchets.

Date	Mintage	VG8	F12	VF20	XF40	MS60
30	—	1.50	3.00	6.00	8.00	27.50
31	—	0.70	1.50	3.00	6.00	20.00
32	—	3.00	8.00	15.00	32.00	70.00

Y# 525 CHIAO

Aluminum, 22 mm. **Issuer:** Federal Reserve Bank **Obv:** Legend around FR Bank symbol **Rev:** Temple of Heaven **Note:** The 1 Chiao pieces were struck on thick (1.5 gram), thin (1.2 gram), and very thin (1.0 gram) planchets.

Date	Mintage	VG8	F12	VF20	XF40	MS60
30	—	1.50	3.00	6.00	8.00	27.50
31	—	0.70	1.50	3.00	6.00	20.00
32	—	2.25	5.00	8.00	14.00	65.00

PATTERNS

Including off metal strikes

KM#	Date	Mintage	Identification	Mkt Val
Pn1	30(1941)	—	Fen. Silver. KM#523, R.Y.30.	1,500
Pn2	30(1941)	—	5 Fen. Silver. KM#524, R.Y.30.	1,500

REFORMED GOVT. OF CHINA

On March 28, 1938 the Japanese Central China Expeditionary Army established the Reformed Government of the Republic of China at Nanking (Nanjing).

HUA HSING COMMERCIAL BANK

The Hua Hsing Commerce Bank was a financial agency created and established by the government of Japan and its puppet authorities in Shanghai in May 1939. Notes and coins were issued until sometime in 1941, with the quantities restricted by Chinese aversion to accepting them.

JAPANESE OCCUPATION

STANDARD COINAGE

Y# A522 FEN

Bronze **Obv:** Legend around character "Hua" above pair of wings **Rev:** Stylized character divides value

Date	Mintage	VG8	F12	VF20	XF40	MS60
29(1940)	—	75.00	150	300	450	750

Y# 522 10 FEN

Copper-Nickel **Obv:** Legend around character "Hua" above pair of wings **Rev:** Floral bouquet divides value

Date	Mintage	VG8	F12	VF20	XF40	MS60
29(1940)	—	0.70	1.50	3.00	5.00	14.00

Note: Metal alloys vary

PATTERNS

Including off metal strikes

KM#	Date	Mintage	Identification	Mkt Val
Pn1	29(1940)	—	Fen. Copper-Nickel.	1,200
Pn2	29(1940)	—	Fen. Silver.	1,450
Pn3	29(1940)	—	5 Fen. Copper-Nickel. Liu-ho Pagoda.	1,200
Pn4	29(1940)	—	20 Fen. Copper-Nickel. Junk.	4,200

CHINA / Peoples Republic

The Peoples Republic of China, located in eastern Asia, has an area of 3,696,100 sq. mi. (9,596,960 sq. km.) (including Manchuria and Tibet) and a population of *1.20 billion. Capital: Peking (Beijing). The economy is based on agriculture, mining, and manufacturing. Textiles, clothing, metal ores, tea and rice are exported.

China's ancient civilization began in east-central Henan's Huayang county, 2800-2300 B.C. The warring feudal states comprising early China were first united under Emperor Ch'in Shih (246-210 B.C.) who gave China its name and first central government. Subsequent dynasties alternated brilliant cultural achievements with internal disorder until the Empire was brought down by the revolution of 1911, and the Republic of China installed in its place. Chinese culture attained a pre-eminence in art, literature and philosophy, but a traditional backwardness in industry and administration ill prepared China for the demands of 19th century Western expansionism which exposed it to military and political humiliations, and mandated a drastic revision of political practice in order to secure an accommodation with the modern world.

The Republic of 1911 barely survived the stress of World War I, and was subsequently all but shattered by the rise of nationalism and the emergence of the Chinese Communist movement. Moscow, which practiced a policy of cooperation between Communists and other parties in movements for national liberation, sought to establish an entente between the Chinese Communist Party and the Kuomintang ('National Peoples Party') of Sun Yat-sen. The ensuing cooperation was based on little more than the hope each had of using the other.

An increasingly uneasy association between the Kuomintang and the Chinese Communist Party developed and continued until April 12, 1927, when Chiang Kai-shek, Sun Yat-sen's political heir, instituted a bloody purge to stamp out the Communists within the Kuomintang and the government and virtually paralyzed their ranks throughout China. Some time after the mid-1927 purges, the Chinese Communist Party turned to armed force to resist Chiang Kai-shek and during the period of 1930-34 acquired control over large parts of Kiangsi (Jiangxi), Fukien (Fujian), Hunan and Hupeh (Hubei). The Nationalist Nanking government responded with a series of campaigns against the soviet power bases and, by October of 1934, succeeded in driving the remnants of the Communist army to a refuge in Shensi (Shaanxi) Province. There the Communists reorganized under the leadership of Mao Tse-tung, defeated the Nationalist forces, and on Sept. 21, 1949, established the Peoples Republic of China. Thereafter relations between Russia and Communist China steadily deteriorated until 1958, when China emerged as an independent center of Communist power.

MONETARY SYSTEM

After 1949

10 Fen (Cents) = 1 Jiao

10 Jiao = 1 Renminbi Yuan

MINT MARKS

(b) - Beijing (Peking)

(s) - Shanghai

(y) - Shenyang (Mukden)

OBVERSE LEGENDS

中华人民共和国

ZHONGHUA RENMIN GONGHEGUO

(Peoples Republic of China)

中国人民银行

ZHONGGUO RENMIN YINHANG

(Peoples Bank of China)

PEOPLES REPUBLIC

STANDARD COINAGE

KM# 1 FEN

0.70 g., Aluminum, 18 mm. **Obv:** National emblem **Rev:** Value in wreath, date below **Edge:** Reeded **Note:** Prev. Y#1.

Date	Mintage	XF40	MS60	MS63	MS65	MS66
1955	—	1.50	10.00	36.00	45.00	78.00
1956	—	2.50	15.00	54.00	75.00	400
1957	—	3.50	20.00	72.00	90.00	270
1958	—	0.75	5.00	18.00	22.50	220
1959	—	0.75	5.00	18.00	22.50	170
1961	—	0.75	5.00	18.00	25.00	320
1963	—	0.50	3.00	11.00	15.00	90.00
1964	—	0.50	2.00	7.00	10.00	25.00
1971	—	0.50	2.00	7.00	10.00	20.00
1972	—	0.50	2.00	7.00	12.00	50.00
1973	—	0.50	3.00	11.00	15.00	40.00
1974	—	0.50	2.00	7.00	12.00	30.00
1975	500,000	0.50	2.00	7.00	10.00	20.00
1976	—	0.25	1.00	4.00	9.00	30.00
1977	—	0.25	1.00	4.00	7.00	22.00
1978	—	0.25	1.00	4.00	6.00	17.00
1979	—	1.00	9.00	12.00	15.00	22.00
1980	—	0.25	1.00	3.00	7.00	20.00
1980 Proof	—	—	—	—	—	—
1981	—	0.25	1.00	3.00	7.00	20.00
1981	—	**PF65** 270	**PF67** 328	**PF69** 428		
1982	—	0.25	1.00	3.00	7.00	20.00
1982	—	**PF65** 50.00				
1983	2,412,000	0.10	0.50	1.50	15.00	35.00
1983	—	**PF65** 30.00				
1984	3,283,000	0.10	0.50	1.50	15.00	35.00
1984	—	**PF65** 85.00				
1985	—	0.10	0.50	1.50	15.00	35.00
1985	—	**PF65** 110				
1986	—	0.10	0.50	3.00	7.00	20.00
1986	—	**PF65** 1,200				
1987	—	0.10	0.50	3.00	7.00	20.00
1991	—	0.10	0.50	3.00	7.00	20.00
1991	—	**PF65** 35.00				
1992	—	0.10	0.50	1.50	15.00	35.00

Date	Mintage	XF40	MS60	MS63	MS65	MS66
1992	—	PF65 85.00				
1993 Sets only	—	—	—	—	4.50	—
1993	—	PF65 12.00				
1994 Sets only	—	—	—	—	4.50	—
1994	—	PF65 12.00				
1995 Sets only	—	—	—	—	4.50	—
1995	—	PF65 12.00				
1996 Sets only	—	—	—	—	4.50	—
1996	—	PF65 12.00				
1997	—	—	0.35	1.00	6.00	—
1998	—	—	0.35	1.00	6.00	—
1999	—	—	0.35	1.00	6.00	—
2000	—	—	0.35	1.00	6.00	—

KM# 2 2 FEN

1.05 g., Aluminum, 21 mm. **Obv:** National emblem **Rev:** Value in wreath, date below **Edge:** Reeded **Note:** Prev. Y#2.

Date	Mintage	XF40	MS60	MS63	MS65	MS66
1956	—	0.75	3.00	14.00	20.00	56.00
1959	—	1.00	8.00	30.00	70.00	800
1960	—	1.00	8.00	30.00	50.00	600
1961	—	0.75	3.00	14.00	25.00	180
1962	—	0.75	3.00	14.00	40.00	250
1963	—	0.75	3.00	14.00	60.00	900
1964	—	0.50	2.50	12.00	15.00	20.00
1974	—	0.50	3.00	14.00	20.00	45.00
1975	—	0.50	2.00	10.00	20.00	75.00
1976	—	0.50	2.00	10.00	12.50	20.00
1977	360,000	0.50	1.50	6.00	10.00	28.00
1978	—	0.40	1.25	5.50	7.50	20.00
1979	—	0.40	1.25	5.50	7.50	20.00
1980	—	0.40	1.25	5.50	7.50	20.00
1980	—	PF65 80.00				
1981	—	0.40	1.25	4.50	7.00	20.00
1981	—	PF65 60.00				
1982	—	0.40	1.25	4.50	7.00	20.00
1982	—	PF65 75.00				
1983	1,790,000	0.20	0.75	2.50	4.00	10.00
1983	—	PF65 40.00				
1984	1,963,000	0.20	0.75	2.50	4.00	10.00
1984	—	PF65 70.00				
1985	—	0.20	0.75	2.50	4.00	10.00
1985	—	PF65 50.00				
1986	—	0.35	1.50	10.00	85.00	110
1986	—	PF65 120				
1987	—	0.20	0.75	5.00	8.00	22.00
1988	—	0.20	0.75	5.00	8.00	22.00
1989	—	0.20	0.75	5.00	8.00	22.00
1990	—	0.20	0.75	5.00	8.00	22.00
1991	—	0.20	0.75	5.00	8.00	22.00
1991	—	PF65 15.00				
1992	—	0.20	0.75	2.50	4.00	10.00
1992	—	PF65 15.00				
1993 Sets only	—	—	—	—	5.00	9.00
1993	—	PF65 15.00				
1994 Sets only	—	—	—	—	5.00	9.00
1994	—	PF65 15.00				
1995 Sets only	—	—	—	—	5.00	9.00
1995	—	PF65 15.00				
1996 Sets only	—	—	—	—	5.00	9.00
1996	—	PF65 15.00				
1997	—	—	1.50	5.00	8.00	22.00
1998	—	—	1.50	5.00	8.00	22.00
1999	—	—	1.50	5.00	8.00	22.00
2000	—	—	1.50	5.00	8.00	22.00

KM# 3 5 FEN

1.60 g., Aluminum, 24 mm. **Obv:** National emblem **Rev:** Value in wreath, date below **Edge:** Reeded **Note:** Prev. Y#3.

Date	Mintage	XF40	MS60	MS63	MS65	MS66
1955	—	2.00	20.00	40.00	50.00	60.00
1956	—	0.75	4.00	18.00	22.00	25.00
1957	—	0.75	5.00	21.00	32.00	50.00
1974	—	0.50	3.00	12.00	16.00	28.00
1975	—	0.50	3.00	12.00	16.00	28.00
1976	350,000	0.50	1.50	7.50	12.50	21.00
1979	—	1.25	20.00	65.00	—	—
1980	—	0.50	1.50	7.50	12.50	21.00
1980	—	PF67 110				
1981	—	0.50	1.50	7.50	12.50	21.00
1981	—	PF67 110				
1982	—	0.50	1.50	7.50	12.50	21.00
1982	—	PF67 110				
1983	484,000	0.25	1.25	5.00	8.00	17.00
1983	—	PF67 110				
1984	600,000	0.25	1.25	5.00	8.00	17.00
1984	—	PF67 110				
1985	—	0.25	1.25	5.00	8.00	17.00
1985	—	PF67 110				
1986	—	0.25	1.30	7.00	12.00	30.00
1986	—	PF67 110				
1987	—	0.25	1.30	7.00	12.00	30.00
1988	—	0.25	1.30	7.00	12.00	30.00
1989	—	0.25	1.30	7.00	12.00	30.00
1990	—	0.25	1.30	7.00	12.00	30.00
1991	—	0.25	1.30	7.00	12.00	30.00
1991	—	PF67 110				
1992	—	0.25	1.25	5.00	8.00	17.00
1992	—	PF67 100				
1993 Sets only	—	—	—	—	4.50	—
1993	—	PF65 15.00				
1994 Sets only	—	—	—	—	4.50	—
1994	—	PF65 15.00				
1995 Sets only	—	—	—	—	4.50	—
1995	—	PF65 15.00				
1996 Sets only	—	—	—	—	4.50	—
1996	—	PF65 15.00				
1997	—	—	1.50	4.50	7.50	15.00
1998	—	—	1.50	4.50	7.50	15.00
1999	—	—	1.50	4.50	7.50	15.00
2000	—	—	1.50	4.50	7.50	15.00

KM# 15 JIAO

2.60 g., Brass, 20 mm. **Obv:** National emblem **Rev:** Denomination above wreath, date below **Note:** Prev. Y#24.

Date	Mintage	XF40	MS60	MS63	MS65	MS66
1980	—	—	2.50	10.00	15.00	35.00
1980	—	PF67 60.00				
1981	—	—	2.50	10.00	15.00	25.00
1981	—	PF67 60.00				
1982	—	PF67 60.00				
1983	3,100,000	—	2.50	10.00	15.00	140
1983	—	PF67 75.00				
1984	3,500,000	—	2.50	10.00	15.00	40.00
1984	—	PF67 65.00				
1985	—	PF67 160 PF69 600				
1985	—	—	2.50	10.00	15.00	70.00
1986	—	PF67 40.00				

KM# 155 JIAO

Brass **Series:** 6th National Games **Subject:** Gymnast **Obv:** Stylized torch divides date below **Rev:** Gymnast above date, denomination at left **Note:** Prev. Y#148.

Date	Mintage	XF40	MS60	MS63	MS65	MS66
1987	10,570,000	1.00	2.00	3.00	5.00	12.00

KM# 156 JIAO

Brass **Series:** 6th National Games **Subject:** Soccer **Obv:** Stylized torch divides date below **Rev:** Soccer player divides date and denomination **Note:** Prev. Y#149.

Date	Mintage	XF40	MS60	MS63	MS65	MS66
1987	Inc. above	1.00	2.00	3.00	5.00	12.00

KM# 157 JIAO

Brass **Series:** 6th National Games **Subject:** Volleyball **Obv:** Stylized torch divides date below **Rev:** Volleyball player, date below, denomination at right **Note:** Prev. Y#150.

Date	Mintage	XF40	MS60	MS63	MS65	MS66
1987	Inc. above	1.00	2.00	3.00	5.00	12.00

KM# 335 JIAO

2.30 g., Aluminum, 22.5 mm. **Obv:** National emblem, date below **Rev:** Peony blossom, denomination at right **Edge:** Plain **Note:** Prev. Y#328.

Date	Mintage	XF40	MS60	MS63	MS65	MS66
1991	—	—	0.50	1.50	4.50	10.00
1991	—	PF65 20.00				
1992	—	—	0.50	1.50	4.50	10.00
1992	—	PF65 20.00				
1993	—	—	0.50	1.50	4.50	10.00
1993	—	PF65 20.00				
1994	—	—	0.50	1.50	4.50	10.00
1994	—	PF65 20.00				
1995	—	—	0.50	1.50	4.50	10.00
1995	—	PF65 20.00				
1996	—	—	0.50	1.50	4.50	10.00
1996	—	PF65 20.00				
1997	—	—	0.50	1.50	4.50	10.00
1998	—	—	0.50	1.50	4.50	10.00
1999	—	—	0.50	1.50	4.50	10.00
1999	—	PF65 20.00				

KM# 1210 JIAO

1.12 g., Aluminum, 19 mm. **Obv:** Denomination, date below **Rev:** Orchid **Rev. Legend:** ZHONGGUA RENMIN YINHANG **Edge:** Plain **Note:** Prev. Y#1068.

Date	Mintage	XF40	MS60	MS63	MS65	MS66
1999	—	—	0.50	1.00	2.00	3.50
2000	—	—	0.50	1.00	2.00	3.50

KM# 16 2 JIAO

4.15 g., Brass, 23 mm. **Obv:** National emblem **Rev:** Denomination above wreath, date below **Note:** Prev. Y#25.

Date	Mintage	XF40	MS60	MS63	MS65	MS66
1980	—	—	0.75	2.50	6.00	15.00
1980	—	PF65 45.00 PF67 100				
1981	—	—	0.75	2.50	6.00	15.00
1981	—	PF65 45.00 PF67 100 PF69 120				
1982	—	PF65 60.00 PF67 130				
1983	4,200,000	—	0.75	2.50	6.00	15.00
1983	—	PF65 45.00 PF67 100				
1984	2,500,000	—	0.75	2.00	6.00	15.00
1984	—	PF65 45.00 PF67 100				
1985	—	PF65 45.00 PF67 100				
1986	—	PF65 45.00 PF67 100				

KM# 17 5 JIAO

6.00 g., Brass, 26 mm. **Obv:** National emblem **Rev:** Denomination above wreath, date below **Note:** Prev. Y#26.

Date	Mintage	XF40	MS60	MS63	MS65	MS66
1980	—	0.75	2.50	9.00	25.00	45.00
1980	—	PF65 60.00 PF67 120				
1981	—	0.75	2.50	9.00	25.00	45.00
1981	—	PF65 60.00 PF67 120				
1982	—	PF65 60.00 PF67 120				
1983	3,000,000	0.75	2.50	9.00	25.00	45.00
1983	—	PF65 45.00 PF67 100 PF69 110				
1984	3,500,000	0.75	2.50	9.00	25.00	45.00
1984	—	PF65 45.00 PF67 100				
1985	—	0.75	2.50	9.00	25.00	45.00
1985	—	PF65 45.00 PF67 100				
1986	—	PF65 45.00 PF67 100				

KM# 65 5 JIAO
2.20 g., 0.900 Silver 0.0637 oz. ASW, 14 mm. **Obv:** Building divides date and denomination **Rev:** Marco Polo looking left, two dates below **Note:** Prev. Y#53.

Date	Mintage	XF40	MS60	MS63	MS65	MS66
1983	7,050	PF65 165	PF67 200			

KM# 265 5 JIAO
2.00 g., 0.999 Silver 0.0642 oz. ASW, 14 mm. **Obv:** Great wall, date below **Rev:** Denomination divides phoenix and dragon representing good luck **Note:** Prev. Y#205.

Date	Mintage	XF40	MS60	MS63	MS65	MS66
1990	55,000	PF65 30.00	PF67 50.00			

KM# 336 5 JIAO
3.80 g., Brass, 20.5 mm. **Obv:** National emblem, date below **Rev:** Denomination above flowers **Edge:** Segmented reeding **Note:** Prev. Y#329.

Date	Mintage	XF40	MS60	MS63	MS65	MS66
1991	—	—	1.00	2.50	7.50	20.00
1991	—	PF65 10.00	PF67 30.00			
1992	—	—	1.00	2.50	7.50	20.00
1992	—	PF65 10.00	PF67 30.00			
1993	—	—	1.00	2.50	7.50	20.00
1993	—	PF65 10.00	PF67 30.00			
1994	—	—	1.00	2.50	7.50	20.00
1994	—	PF65 10.00	PF67 30.00			
1995	—	—	1.00	2.50	7.50	20.00
1995	—	PF65 10.00	PF67 30.00			
1996	—	—	1.00	2.50	7.50	20.00
1996	—	PF65 10.00	PF67 30.00			
1997	—	—	1.00	2.50	7.50	20.00
1998	—	—	1.00	2.50	7.50	20.00
1999	—	—	1.00	2.50	7.50	20.00
2000	—	—	1.00	2.50	7.50	20.00

KM# 18 YUAN
9.30 g., Copper-Nickel, 30 mm. **Obv:** National emblem, date below **Rev:** Great wall **Note:** Prev. Y#27.

Date	Mintage	XF40	MS60	MS63	MS65	MS66
1980	—	—	3.50	7.00	18.00	150
1980	—	PF65 35.00	PF67 55.00			
1981	—	—	3.50	7.00	18.00	30.00
1981	—	PF65 35.00	PF67 55.00			
1982	—	PF65 35.00	PF67 55.00			
1983	3,100,000	—	3.50	7.00	18.00	60.00
1983	—	PF65 35.00	PF67 55.00			
1984	4,100,000	—	3.50	7.00	18.00	50.00
1984	—	PF65 35.00	PF67 55.00			
1985	—	—	3.50	7.00	18.00	50.00
1985	—	PF65 35.00	PF67 55.00			
1986	—	PF65 35.00	PF67 55.00			

KM# 19 YUAN
Brass **Series:** Lake Placid - 13th Winter Olympic Games **Subject:** Figure skating **Obv:** National emblem, Olympic logo at left, denomination below **Rev:** Woman figure skater within snowflake design **Note:** Prev. Y#16.

Date	Mintage	XF40	MS60	MS63	MS65	MS66
1980	29,000	PF65 42.00	PF67 60.00			

KM# 20 YUAN
Brass **Series:** Lake Placid - 13th Winter Olympic Games **Subject:** Biathlon **Obv:** National emblem, Olympic logo at left, denomination below **Rev:** Biathlete within snowflake **Note:** Prev. Y#17.

Date	Mintage	XF40	MS60	MS63	MS65	MS66
1980	29,000	PF65 42.00	PF67 60.00			

KM# 21 YUAN
Brass, 30 mm. **Series:** Lake Placid - 13th Winter Olympic Games **Subject:** Alpine Skiing **Obv:** National emblem , Olympic logo at left, denomination below **Rev:** Skier within snowflake design **Note:** Prev. Y#14.

Date	Mintage	XF40	MS60	MS63	MS65	MS66
1980	29,000	PF65 42.00	PF67 60.00			

KM# 22 YUAN
Brass **Series:** Lake Placid - 13th Winter Olympic Games **Subject:** Women's speed Skating **Obv:** National emblem, Olympic logo at left, denomination below **Rev:** Speed skater within snowflake design **Note:** Prev. Y#15.

Date	Mintage	XF40	MS60	MS63	MS65	MS66
1980	29,000	PF65 42.00	PF67 60.00			

KM# 29 YUAN
Brass, 30 mm. **Series:** 1980 Olympics **Subject:** Archery **Obv:** National emblem above denomination **Rev:** Archers, date below, Olympic logo upper left **Note:** Prev. Y#10.

Date	Mintage	XF40	MS60	MS63	MS65	MS66
1980	40,000	PF65 45.00	PF67 65.00			

KM# 30 YUAN
Brass, 30 mm. **Series:** 1980 Olympics **Subject:** Wrestling **Obv:** National emblem, denomination below **Rev:** Wrestlers, date below, Olympic logo upper left **Note:** Prev. Y#11.

Date	Mintage	XF40	MS60	MS63	MS65	MS66
1980	40,000	PF65 45.00	PF67 65.00			

KM# 31 YUAN
Brass, 30 mm. **Series:** 1980 Olympics **Subject:** Equestrian **Obv:** National emblem, denomination below **Rev:** Equestrians, date below, Olympic logo, upper left **Note:** Prev. Y#12.

Date	Mintage	XF40	MS60	MS63	MS65	MS66
1980	40,000	PF65 45.00	PF67 65.00			

KM# 32 YUAN
Brass, 30 mm. **Series:** 1980 Olympics **Subject:** Soccer **Obv:** National emblem, denomination below **Rev:** Two soccer players in ancient garb **Note:** Prev. Y#13.

Date	Mintage	XF40	MS60	MS63	MS65	MS66
1980	40,000	PF65 45.00	PF67 65.00			

KM# 58 YUAN
Brass **Subject:** World Cup Soccer **Obv:** National emblem, date below **Rev:** Soccer player, within ring, kicking the ball, denomination bottom right **Note:** Prev. Y#34.

Date	Mintage	XF40	MS60	MS63	MS65	MS66
1982	20,000	PF65 25.00	PF67 35.00			

KM# 66 YUAN
12.70 g., Brass, 32 mm. **Rev:** Panda seated with bamboo branch, within octagon line border

Date	Mintage	XF40	MS60	MS63	MS65	MS66
1983	30,000	PF65 30.00	PF67 40.00			

KM# 85 YUAN
Brass **Obv:** National emblem, date below **Rev:** Panda within octagon **Note:** Prev. Y#58.

Date	Mintage	XF40	MS60	MS63	MS65	MS66
1983	30,000	PF65 325	PF67 375			
1984	30,000	PF65 325	PF67 375			

KM# 104 YUAN
Copper-Nickel **Subject:** 35th Anniversary - Peoples Republic **Obv:** National emblem above buildings, dates below **Rev:** Republic figures **Note:** Prev. Y#85.

Date	Mintage	XF40	MS60	MS63	MS65	MS66
ND-1984	—	PF65 65.00	PF67 75.00			
ND-1984	20,410,000	—	55.00	—	—	—

KM# 105 YUAN
Copper-Nickel **Subject:** 35th Anniversary - Peoples Republic **Obv:** National emblem **Rev:** Dancers **Note:** Prev. Y#86.

Date	Mintage	XF40	MS60	MS63	MS65	MS66
ND-1984	Inc. above	—	7.00	9.00	15.00	25.00
ND-1984	—	PF65 18.00	PF67 22.00			

KM# 106 YUAN
Copper-Nickel **Subject:** 35th Anniversary - Peoples Republic **Obv:** National emblem above buildings, dates below **Rev:** Monument amid cranes in flight **Note:** Prev. Y#87.

Date	Mintage	XF40	MS60	MS63	MS65	MS66
ND-1984	Inc. above	—	7.00	9.00	15.00	25.00
ND-1984	—	PF65 18.00	PF67 22.00			

KM# 112 YUAN
12.70 g., Brass, 32 mm. **Rev:** Panda seated with bamboo in octagon linear border

Date	Mintage	XF40	MS60	MS63	MS65	MS66
1984	30,000	PF65 45.00	PF67 65.00			

KM# 110 YUAN
Copper-Nickel **Subject:** 20th Anniversary - Tibet Autonomous Region **Obv:** National emblem, date below **Rev:** Potala Palace **Note:** Prev. Y#96.

Date	Mintage	XF40	MS60	MS63	MS65	MS66
1985	2,612,000	15.00	25.00	40.00	60.00	—
1985	10,000	PF65 55.00	PF67 75.00			

KM# 111 YUAN
Copper-Nickel **Subject:** 30th Anniversary - Xinjiang Autonomous Region **Note:** Prev. Y#109.

Date	Mintage	XF40	MS60	MS63	MS65	MS66
1985	10,000	PF65 65.00	PF67 85.00			
1985	4,500,000	50.00	55.00	—	—	—

KM# 130 YUAN
Copper-Nickel **Subject:** Year of Peace **Obv:** National emblem, date below **Rev:** Seated woman with doves **Note:** Prev. Y#151.

Date	Mintage	XF40	MS60	MS63	MS65	MS66
1986	27,048,000	—	6.00	8.00	12.00	20.00

KM# 158 YUAN
Copper-Nickel **Subject:** 40th Anniversary - Mongolian Autonomous Region **Obv:** Building, date below **Rev:** Riders, sheep below, denomination at left **Note:** Prev. Y#140.

Date	Mintage	XF40	MS60	MS63	MS65	MS66
1987	9,054,000	3.00	7.00	9.00	15.00	25.00

KM# 180 YUAN
Copper-Nickel **Subject:** 30th Anniversary - Kwangsi Autonomous Region **Obv:** Mountains and water, inscription and date below **Rev:** Native dancers, denomination at right, two dates upper left **Note:** Prev. Y#198.

Date	Mintage	XF40	MS60	MS63	MS65	MS66
1988	4,072,000	—	10.00	13.00	18.00	30.00

KM# 181 YUAN
Copper-Nickel **Subject:** 30th Anniversary - Ningxia Autonomous Region **Rev:** Women with plants, denomination at right, within circle, dates below **Note:** Prev. Y#211.

Date	Mintage	XF40	MS60	MS63	MS65	MS66
1988	1,560,000	—	18.00	25.00	45.00	75.00

KM# 182 YUAN
Copper-Nickel **Subject:** 40th Anniversary - Peoples Bank **Obv:** National emblem, date below **Rev:** Building divides dates **Note:** Prev. Y#212.

Date	Mintage	XF40	MS60	MS63	MS65	MS66
1988	2,068,000	45.00	65.00	125	200	300

KM# 220 YUAN
Copper-Nickel **Subject:** 40th Anniversary - Peoples Republic **Obv:** National emblem above buildings, date below **Rev:** Music score divides artistic year and dates **Note:** Prev. Y#204.

Date	Mintage	XF40	MS60	MS63	MS65	MS66
1989	2,000,000	—	7.00	15.00	25.00	45.00

KM# 264 YUAN
Nickel Clad Steel **Series:** 11th Asian Games - Beijing 1990 **Obv:** Building, Roman numeral above, inscription and date below **Rev:** Female archer, denomination above, panda archer below **Note:** Prev. Y#256.

Date	Mintage	XF40	MS60	MS63	MS65	MS66
1990	Inc. above	—	7.00	15.00	25.00	45.00

KM# 266 YUAN
Nickel Clad Steel **Series:** XI Asian Games **Obv:** Building, Roman numerals above, inscription and date below **Rev:** Sword Dancer, panda dancer at left, denomination at right **Note:** Prev. Y#264.

Date	Mintage	XF40	MS60	MS63	MS65	MS66
1990	25,608,000	—	7.00	15.00	25.00	45.00

KM# 337 YUAN
6.10 g., Nickel Plated Steel, 25 mm. **Obv:** National emblem, date below **Rev:** Denomination above flowers **Edge:** Plain **Note:** Prev. Y#330.

Date	Mintage	XF40	MS60	MS63	MS65	MS66
1991	—	—	1.50	3.50	9.00	15.00
1991	—	PF65 12.00	PF67 20.00			
1992	—	—	1.50	3.50	9.00	15.00
1992	—	PF65 12.00	PF67 20.00			
1993	—	—	1.50	3.50	9.00	15.00
1993	—	PF65 12.00	PF67 20.00			
1994	—	—	1.50	3.50	9.00	15.00
1994	—	PF65 12.00	PF67 20.00			
1995	—	—	1.50	3.50	9.00	15.00
1995	—	PF65 12.00	PF67 20.00			
1996	—	—	1.50	3.50	9.00	15.00
1996	—	PF65 12.00	PF67 20.00			
1997	—	—	1.50	3.50	9.00	15.00
1997	—	PF65 12.00	PF67 20.00			
1998	—	—	1.50	3.50	9.00	15.00
1998	—	PF65 12.00	PF67 20.00			
1999	—	—	1.50	3.50	9.00	15.00
1999	—	PF65 12.00	PF67 20.00			

KM# 338 YUAN
Nickel Clad Steel, 25 mm. **Subject:** Planting Trees Festival **Rev:** Head of young woman **Note:** Prev. Y#279.

Date	Mintage	XF40	MS60	MS63	MS65	MS66
1991	10,000,000	—	3.25	6.00	10.00	18.00

KM# 339 YUAN

Nickel Clad Steel, 25 mm. **Subject:** Planting Trees Festival **Obv:** Trees, inscription, and numbers within circle **Rev:** Monument on globe divides birds in flight, date below **Note:** Prev. Y#280.

Date	Mintage	XF40	MS60	MS63	MS65	MS66
1991	10,000,000	—	3.25	6.00	10.00	18.00

KM# 340 YUAN

Nickel Clad Steel, 25 mm. **Subject:** Planting Trees Festival **Obv:** Trees, inscription, and numbers within circle **Rev:** Seedling, date below **Note:** Prev. Y#281.

Date	Mintage	XF40	MS60	MS63	MS65	MS66
1991	10,000,000	—	3.25	6.00	10.00	18.00

KM# 341 YUAN

5.91 g., Nickel Plated Steel, 25 mm. **Subject:** 70th Anniversary of the Founding of the Chinese Communist Party **Obv:** National emblem, date below **Rev:** House of Shanghai **Note:** Prev. Y#284.

Date	Mintage	XF40	MS60	MS63	MS65	MS66
1991	30,000,000	—	3.25	6.00	10.00	18.00

KM# 342 YUAN

5.81 g., Nickel Plated Steel, 25 mm. **Subject:** 70th Anniversary of the Founding of the Chinese Communist Party **Rev:** House in Tsun-i (Zunyi), Kweichow Province **Note:** Prev. Y#285.

Date	Mintage	XF40	MS60	MS63	MS65	MS66
1991	30,000,000	—	3.25	6.00	10.00	18.00

KM# 343 YUAN

5.84 g., Nickel Plated Steel, 25 mm. **Subject:** 70th Anniversary of the Founding of the Chinese Communist Party - Meeting in Tiananmen Square, 1978 **Obv:** National emblem, date below **Rev:** Flags, monument, and building **Note:** Prev. Y#286.

Date	Mintage	XF40	MS60	MS63	MS65	MS66
1991	30,000,000	—	3.25	6.00	10.00	18.00

KM# 344 YUAN

Nickel Plated Steel, 25 mm. **Subject:** 1st Women's World Football Cup **Obv:** Conjoined soccer balls, artistic woman design on top **Rev:** Goalie, date at right **Note:** Prev. Y#316.

Date	Mintage	XF40	MS60	MS63	MS65	MS66
1991	10,000,000	—	4.00	7.00	12.00	20.00

KM# 345 YUAN

Nickel Plated Steel, 25 mm. **Subject:** 1st Women's World Football Cup **Obv:** Conjoined soccer balls, artistic woman design on top **Rev:** Player, soccer ball background, date at lower right **Note:** Prev. Y#317.

Date	Mintage	XF40	MS60	MS63	MS65	MS66
1991	10,000,000	—	4.00	7.00	12.00	20.00

KM# 390 YUAN

Nickel Clad Steel, 25 mm. **Subject:** 10th Anniversary - Constitution **Obv:** National emblem, date below **Rev:** Constitution, denomination at right, dates and flower below **Note:** Prev. Y#364.

Date	Mintage	XF40	MS60	MS63	MS65	MS66
1992	10,000,000	—	3.25	6.00	10.00	18.00

KM# 470 YUAN

Nickel Clad Steel, 25 mm. **Subject:** 100th Birthday of Soong Ching Ling - Second Wife of Sun Yat-sen **Obv:** Building, date below **Rev:** Bust of Ching-ling, 1892-1981, half left, revolutionary stateswoman **Note:** Prev. Y#365.

Date	Mintage	XF40	MS60	MS63	MS65	MS66
1993	10,448,000	—	5.50	7.50	12.50	20.00
1993	—	PF65 20.00	PF67 35.00			

KM# 471 YUAN

Nickel Clad Steel, 25 mm. **Subject:** 100th Anniversary - Birth of Chairman Mao **Obv:** Buildings and mountains, date below **Rev:** Mao's head, left **Note:** Prev. Y#399.

Date	Mintage	XF40	MS60	MS63	MS65	MS66
1993	20,000,000	—	5.00	7.00	12.00	20.00
1993 Prooflike	—	—	8.00	10.00	17.00	28.00

KM# 610 YUAN

Nickel Clad Steel, 25 mm. **Series:** Children's Year **Subject:** Project Hope **Obv:** National emblem, date below **Rev:** Two children, denomination lower left **Note:** Prev. Y#455.

Date	Mintage	XF40	MS60	MS63	MS65	MS66
1994	—	—	4.00	6.00	10.00	18.00

KM# 710 YUAN

Nickel Plated Steel, 25 mm. **Subject:** Table Tennis **Obv:** Building divides design and date **Rev:** Table tennis player, denomination lower left **Note:** Prev. Y#487.

Date	Mintage	XF40	MS60	MS63	MS65	MS66
1995	10,000,000	—	5.00	7.00	12.00	20.00
1995	20,000	PF65 20.00	PF67 35.00			

KM# 711 YUAN

5.94 g., Nickel Plated Steel, 25 mm. **Subject:** 50th Anniversary - Defeat of Fascism and Japan **Obv:** Great Wall and mountains, date below **Rev:** Statue of rock and soldiers, dates and denomination below **Note:** Prev. Y#528.

Date	Mintage	XF40	MS60	MS63	MS65	MS66
1995	10,000,000	—	5.00	7.00	12.00	20.00

KM# 712 YUAN

6.03 g., Nickel Plated Steel, 25 mm. **Subject:** 50th Anniversary - United Nations **Obv:** National emblem above wall, denomination below **Rev:** United Nations logo and anniversary numbers, date lower right **Note:** Prev. Y#529.

Date	Mintage	XF40	MS60	MS63	MS65	MS66
1995	10,000,000	—	5.00	7.00	12.00	20.00

KM# 713 YUAN

Nickel Plated Steel, 25 mm. **Subject:** 4th UN Women's Conference **Obv:** Small building within design **Rev:** Half moon and dove above inscription, denomination and dates below **Note:** Prev. Y#530.

Date	Mintage	XF40	MS60	MS63	MS65	MS66
1995	10,000,000	—	5.00	7.00	12.00	20.00

KM# 880 YUAN

6.05 g., Nickel Plated Steel, 25 mm. **Obv:** Zhu De's home in Sichuan, date below **Rev:** Marshal Zhu De, 3/4 left **Edge:** Lettered **Edge Lettering:** "ZHONGGUO" twice **Note:** Prev. Y#1124.

Date	Mintage	XF40	MS60	MS63	MS65	MS66
1996	580,000	—	5.00	7.00	12.00	20.00

KM# 1120 YUAN

Nickel Clad Steel, 25 mm. **Subject:** 100th Birthday - Chou (Zhou) Enlai **Obv:** Chou (Zhou) birth place, date below **Rev:** Chou (Zhou) bust left **Note:** Prev. Y#721.

Date	Mintage	XF40	MS60	MS63	MS65	MS66
1998	—	—	5.00	7.00	12.00	20.00

KM# 1121 YUAN

6.10 g., Nickel Clad Steel, 24.9 mm. **Subject:** Liu Shao-chi **Obv:** Building, denomination and date **Rev:** Bust of Liu left **Edge Lettering:** ZHONGGUO twice **Note:** Prev. Y#1057.

Date	Mintage	XF40	MS60	MS63	MS65	MS66
1998	—	—	6.00	8.00	14.00	25.00

KM# 1211 YUAN

6.10 g., Nickel Clad Steel, 24.9 mm. **Subject:** 50th Anniversary - People's Political Consultative Conference **Obv:** Emblem, date within, above inscription and dates **Rev:** Building, date below **Note:** Prev. Y#1058.

Date	Mintage	XF40	MS60	MS63	MS65	MS66
1999	—	—	6.00	8.00	14.00	25.00

KM# 1212 YUAN

6.10 g., Nickel Plated Steel, 24.9 mm. **Obv:** Denomination, date below **Rev:** Chrysanthemum **Rev. Legend:** ZHONGGUA RENMIN YINHANG **Edge:** "RMB" three times, separated by diamonds **Note:** Prev. Y#1069.

Date	Mintage	XF40	MS60	MS63	MS65	MS66
1999	—	—	—	1.00	2.50	4.50
2000	—	—	—	1.50	3.50	6.00

KM# 1301 YUAN

6.10 g., Nickel Clad Steel, 25 mm. **Subject:** Dunhuang Cave **Obv:** Pagoda, date below **Rev:** Standing and floating figures **Edge:** "RMB" 3 times **Note:** Prev. Y#1037.

Date	Mintage	XF40	MS60	MS63	MS65	MS66
2000	—	—	6.00	8.00	14.00	25.00

KM# 402 3 YUAN

15.00 g., 0.900 Silver 0.434 oz. ASW **Subject:** Ancient Chinese Paper **Note:** Prev. Y#363.

Date	Mintage	XF40	MS60	MS63	MS65	MS66
1992	Est. 20000	PF65 42.00	PF67 60.00			

KM# 403 3 YUAN

15.00 g., 0.900 Silver 0.434 oz. ASW **Subject:** Ancient Chinese Coins **Note:** Prev. Y#362.

Date	Mintage	XF40	MS60	MS63	MS65	MS66
1992	23,000	PF65 42.00	PF67 60.00			

KM# 472 3 YUAN

15.00 g., 0.900 Silver 0.434 oz. ASW **Rev:** Chinese Gods Fu, Lu and Shu **Note:** Prev. Y#403.

Date	Mintage	XF40	MS60	MS63	MS65	MS66
1993	20,000	PF65 50.00	PF67 70.00			

KM# 734 3 YUAN

15.00 g., 0.900 Silver 0.434 oz. ASW **Subject:** Yin and Yang Concept **Obv:** Great Wall tower, date below **Rev:** Chinese gods Fu, Lu and Shu with Yin Yang symbol, denomination below **Note:** Prev. Y#733.

Date	Mintage	XF40	MS60	MS63	MS65	MS66
1995	—	PF65 45.00	PF67 65.00			

KM# 824 3 YUAN

15.00 g., 0.900 Silver 0.434 oz. ASW **Subject:** Great Wall of China **Obv:** Great Wall view, date below **Rev:** Great Wall construction scene, denomination above **Note:** Prev. Y#734.

Date	Mintage	XF40	MS60	MS63	MS65	MS66
1995	—	PF65 45.00	PF67 65.00			

KM# 1035 3 YUAN

15.00 g., 0.900 Silver 0.434 oz. ASW, 30 mm. **Subject:** World Wildlife Federation **Obv:** State emblem, date below **Rev:** Panda seated right eating leaves, denomination at right **Edge:** Reeded **Note:** Prev. Y#1081.

Date	Mintage	XF40	MS60	MS63	MS65	MS66
1997	50,000	PF65 40.00	PF67 80.00	PF69 170		

KM# 77 5 YUAN

22.22 g., 0.900 Silver 0.643 oz. ASW **Obv:** Building **Rev:** Marco Polo bust, right, facing left, above ships, denomination below, dates at left of bust **Note:** Prev. Y#54.

Date	Mintage	XF40	MS60	MS63	MS65	MS66
1983	15,000	PF65 175	PF67 190	PF69 200		

KM# 76 5 YUAN

22.00 g., 0.900 Silver 0.6366 oz. ASW, 22 mm. **Subject:** Marco Polo

Date	Mintage	XF40	MS60	MS63	MS65	MS66
1984	15,000	PF65 90.00	PF67 100	PF69 120		

KM# 97 5 YUAN

8.45 g., 0.800 Silver 0.2173 oz. ASW **Series:** 1984 Summer and Winter Olympics **Obv:** Mural of athletes divides emblem and date **Rev:** High jumper, Olympic torch below, denomination at left **Note:** Prev. Y#61.

Date	Mintage	XF40	MS60	MS63	MS65	MS66
1984	10,000	PF65 75.00	PF67 185	PF69 260		

KM# 98 5 YUAN

22.22 g., 0.900 Silver 0.643 oz. ASW **Rev:** Soldier statue from archaeological discovery, kneeling, right, denomination lower right **Note:** Prev. Y#70.

Date	Mintage	XF40	MS60	MS63	MS65	MS66
1984	14,000	PF65 40.00	PF67 50.00	PF69 65.00		

KM# 99 5 YUAN

22.22 g., 0.900 Silver 0.643 oz. ASW **Rev:** Soldier statue, 3/4 left, from archaeological discovery, denomination lower left **Note:** Prev. Y#68.

Date	Mintage	XF40	MS60	MS63	MS65	MS66
1984	14,000	PF65 40.00	PF67 50.00	PF69 65.00		

KM# 100 5 YUAN

22.22 g., 0.900 Silver 0.643 oz. ASW **Rev:** Soldier statue with horse, right, from archaeological discovery, denomination below **Note:** Prev. Y#71.

Date	Mintage	XF40	MS60	MS63	MS65	MS66
1984	14,000	PF65 40.00	PF67 50.00	PF69 65.00		

KM# 101 5 YUAN

22.22 g., 0.900 Silver 0.643 oz. ASW **Rev:** Soldier statue, right, from archaeological discovery, denomination lower right **Note:** Prev. Y#69.

Date	Mintage	XF40	MS60	MS63	MS65	MS66
1984	14,000	PF65 40.00	PF67 50.00	PF69 65.00		

KM# 121 5 YUAN

22.22 g., 0.900 Silver 0.643 oz. ASW **Subject:** Founders of Chinese Culture **Obv:** State seal **Rev:** Lao-Tse riding water buffalo **Note:** Prev. Y#90.

Date	Mintage	XF40	MS60	MS63	MS65	MS66
1985	8,175	PF65 65.00	PF67 85.00	PF69 110		

KM# 122 5 YUAN
22.22 g., 0.900 Silver 0.643 oz. ASW **Subject:** Founders of Chinese Culture **Rev:** Sun Wu, right, denomination at left **Note:** Prev. Y#92.

Date	Mintage	XF40	MS60	MS63	MS65	MS66
1985	8,175	PF65 65.00	PF67 85.00	PF69 110		

KM# 123 5 YUAN
22.22 g., 0.900 Silver 0.643 oz. ASW **Subject:** Founders of Chinese Culture **Rev:** Qu Yuan, left, facing , denomination at right **Note:** Prev. Y#91.

Date	Mintage	XF40	MS60	MS63	MS65	MS66
1985	8,175	PF65 65.00	PF67 85.00	PF69 110		

KM# 124 5 YUAN
22.22 g., 0.900 Silver 0.643 oz. ASW **Subject:** Founders of Chinese Culture **Rev:** Chen Sheng and Wu Guang, denomination at left **Note:** Prev. Y#93.

Date	Mintage	XF40	MS60	MS63	MS65	MS66
1985	8,175	PF65 65.00	PF67 85.00	PF69 110		

KM# 139 5 YUAN
18.61 g., 0.925 Silver 0.5535 oz. ASW **Subject:** Soccer **Obv:** National emblem, inscription and date below **Rev:** Soccer player, denomination lower right **Note:** Prev. Y#112.

Date	Mintage	XF40	MS60	MS63	MS65	MS66
1986	8,500	PF65 90.00	PF67 185	PF69 300		

KM# 139a 5 YUAN
17.06 g., 0.800 Silver 0.4388 oz. ASW **Note:** Prev. Y#112a.

Date	Mintage	XF40	MS60	MS63	MS65	MS66
1986	1,000	—	—	325	—	—

Note: Satin finish

KM# 140 5 YUAN
18.61 g., 0.925 Silver 0.5535 oz. ASW **Subject:** Soccer **Obv:** National emblem above inscription and date **Rev:** Two players, denomination above right **Note:** Prev. Y#197.

Date	Mintage	XF40	MS60	MS63	MS65	MS66
1986	10,000	PF65 90.00	PF67 185	PF69 300		

KM# 140a 5 YUAN
16.83 g., 0.800 Silver 0.4329 oz. ASW **Note:** Prev. Y#197a.

Date	Mintage	XF40	MS60	MS63	MS65	MS66
1986 Satin finish	1,000	—	—	375	—	—

KM# 141 5 YUAN
22.22 g., 0.900 Silver 0.643 oz. ASW **Subject:** Chinese Culture **Rev:** Sima Qian, Historian, denomination below **Note:** Prev. Y#116.

Date	Mintage	XF40	MS60	MS63	MS65	MS66
1986	9,675	PF65 55.00	PF67 75.00	PF69 120		

KM# 142 5 YUAN
22.22 g., 0.900 Silver 0.643 oz. ASW **Subject:** Chinese Culture **Rev:** Zhang Heng, Astronomer, left, denomination lower right **Note:** Prev. Y#114.

Date	Mintage	XF40	MS60	MS63	MS65	MS66
1986	9,675	PF65 55.00	PF67 75.00	PF69 120		

KM# 143 5 YUAN
22.22 g., 0.900 Silver 0.643 oz. ASW **Subject:** Chinese Culture **Rev:** Cai Lun - papermaking, denomination upper right **Note:** Prev. Y#113.

Date	Mintage	XF40	MS60	MS63	MS65	MS66
1986	9,675	PF65 55.00	PF67 75.00	PF69 120		

KM# 144 5 YUAN
22.22 g., 0.900 Silver 0.643 oz. ASW **Subject:** Chinese Culture **Rev:** Zu Chong Zhi, Mathematician, denomination at right **Note:** Prev. Y#115.

Date	Mintage	XF40	MS60	MS63	MS65	MS66
1986	9,675	PF65 55.00	PF67 75.00	PF69 120		

KM# 148 5 YUAN
18.61 g., 0.925 Silver 0.5535 oz. ASW **Subject:** Year of Peace **Obv:** National emblem, date below **Rev:** Seated woman, doves in flight, denomination at left **Note:** Prev. Y#119.

Date	Mintage	XF40	MS60	MS63	MS65	MS66
1986	1,350	PF65 1,000	PF67 1,400	PF69 2,600		

KM# 150 5 YUAN
22.22 g., 0.900 Silver 0.643 oz. ASW. **Subject:** 25th Anniversary, World Wildlife Fund **Obv:** National emblem, date below **Rev:** Giant panda divides mountains and denomination **Note:** Prev. Y#106.

Date	Mintage	XF40	MS60	MS63	MS65	MS66
1986	20,000	PF67 125	PF69 135			
1986	20,000	—	—	90.00	100	110

KM# 152 5 YUAN
26.70 g., 0.900 Silver 0.7726 oz. ASW **Obv:** Great Wall, date below **Rev:** The Empress of China, first American ship to make a trade voyage to China. Denomination below **Note:** Prev. Y#132.

Date	Mintage	XF40	MS60	MS63	MS65	MS66
1986	75,000	PF67 80.00	PF69 110			

KM# 172 5 YUAN
31.47 g., 0.900 Silver 0.9106 oz. ASW **Rev:** Princess Chen Wen and Song Zan Gan Bu strolling to left, denomination at left **Note:** Prev. Y#138.

Date	Mintage	XF40	MS60	MS63	MS65	MS66
1987	4,000	PF67 60.00	PF69 70.00			

KM# 173 5 YUAN
31.47 g., 0.900 Silver 0.9106 oz. ASW **Subject:** Bridge Builder - Li Chun **Rev:** Li Chun, left, denomination lower left **Note:** Prev. Y#137.

Date	Mintage	XF40	MS60	MS63	MS65	MS66
1987	4,000	PF67 60.00	PF69 70.00			

KM# 174 5 YUAN
31.47 g., 0.900 Silver 0.9106 oz. ASW **Rev:** Poet Li Bai, left, denomination at right **Note:** Prev. Y#135.

Date	Mintage	XF40	MS60	MS63	MS65	MS66
1987	4,000	PF67 60.00	PF69 70.00			

KM# 175 5 YUAN
31.47 g., 0.900 Silver 0.9106 oz. ASW **Rev:** Poet Du Fu walking right, denomination at left **Note:** Prev. Y#136.

Date	Mintage	XF40	MS60	MS63	MS65	MS66
1987	4,000	PF67 60.00	PF69 70.00			

KM# 201 5 YUAN
30.25 g., 0.875 Silver 0.851 oz. ASW **Series:** Winter Olympics **Obv:** National emblem, date below **Rev:** Downhill skier with snowflakes, denomination at left **Note:** Prev. Y#129.

Date	Mintage	XF40	MS60	MS63	MS65	MS66
1988	10,000	PF65 125	PF67 250	PF69 400		

KM# 202 5 YUAN
30.25 g., 0.875 Silver 0.851 oz. ASW **Series:** Seoul 1988 - 24th Summer Olympic Games **Obv:** National emblem, date below **Rev:** Woman hurdler, denomination below **Note:** Prev. Y#130.

Date	Mintage	XF40	MS60	MS63	MS65	MS66
1988	20,000	PF67 60.00	PF69 70.00			

KM# 203 5 YUAN
30.25 g., 0.875 Silver 0.851 oz. ASW **Series:** Olympics **Obv:** National emblem, date below **Rev:** Sailboat racing, denomination at left **Note:** Prev. Y#171.

Date	Mintage	XF40	MS60	MS63	MS65	MS66
1988	20,000	PF65 65.00	PF67 80.00	PF69 100		

KM# 204 5 YUAN
30.25 g., 0.875 Silver 0.851 oz. ASW **Series:** Seoul 1988 - 24th Summer Olympic Games **Obv:** National emblem, date below **Rev:** Woman fencer, date at left, denomination below **Note:** Prev. Y#172.

Date	Mintage	XF40	MS60	MS63	MS65	MS66
1988	20,000	PF65 65.00	PF67 85.00	PF69 110		

KM# 207 5 YUAN
22.22 g., 0.900 Silver 0.643 oz. ASW **Subject:** Song Dynasty Poet **Rev:** Su Shi, standing left, holding document, waves in background **Note:** Prev. Y#162.

Date	Mintage	XF40	MS60	MS63	MS65	MS66
1988	9,500	PF65 50.00	PF67 60.00	PF69 70.00		

KM# 208 5 YUAN
22.22 g., 0.900 Silver 0.643 oz. ASW **Subject:** Poetess of Song Dynasty **Rev:** Li Qingzhao, facing, looking left, denomination at left **Note:** Prev. Y#163.

Date	Mintage	XF40	MS60	MS63	MS65	MS66
1988	13,000	PF65 50.00	PF67 60.00	PF69 70.00		

KM# 209 5 YUAN
22.22 g., 0.900 Silver 0.643 oz. ASW **Subject:** Inventor of Movable-type Printing **Rev:** Bi Sheng, 3/4 facing, denomination at right **Note:** Prev. Y#161.

Date	Mintage	XF40	MS60	MS63	MS65	MS66
1988	14,000	PF65 50.00	PF67 60.00	PF69 70.00		

KM# 210 5 YUAN
22.22 g., 0.900 Silver 0.643 oz. ASW **Subject:** Military Hero of Song Dynasty - Yue Fei **Rev:** Yue Fei, left, denomination at lower left **Note:** Prev. Y#160.

Date	Mintage	XF40	MS60	MS63	MS65	MS66
1988	13,000	PF65 50.00	PF67 60.00	PF69 70.00		

KM# 245 5 YUAN
27.00 g., 0.925 Silver 0.803 oz. ASW **Subject:** Soccer **Rev:** 2 soccer players, date upper left, denomination below **Note:** Prev. Y#243.

Date	Mintage	XF40	MS60	MS63	MS65	MS66
1989	30,000	PF65 85.00	PF67 100	PF69 120		

KM# 246 5 YUAN
27.00 g., 0.925 Silver 0.803 oz. ASW **Subject:** Soccer **Obv:** National emblem, date below **Rev:** 2 soccer players, denomination below **Note:** Prev. Y#297.

Date	Mintage	XF40	MS60	MS63	MS65	MS66
1989	30,000	PF65 70.00	PF67 80.00	PF69 90.00		

KM# 247 5 YUAN
27.00 g., 0.925 Silver 0.803 oz. ASW **Subject:** Soccer **Rev:** Goalie, denomination at left **Note:** Prev. Y#298.

Date	Mintage	XF40	MS60	MS63	MS65	MS66
1989	30,000	PF65 70.00	PF67 80.00	PF69 90.00		

KM# 248 5 YUAN
22.22 g., 0.900 Silver 0.643 oz. ASW **Obv:** National emblem, date below **Rev:** Kublai Khan, Emperor **Note:** Prev. Y#213.

Date	Mintage	XF40	MS60	MS63	MS65	MS66
1989	10,000	PF65 70.00	PF67 80.00	PF69 90.00		

KM# 249 5 YUAN
22.22 g., 0.900 Silver 0.643 oz. ASW **Rev:** Guan Hanqing, Playwright, denomination at left **Note:** Prev. Y#214.

Date	Mintage	XF40	MS60	MS63	MS65	MS66
1989	8,000	PF65 70.00	PF67 80.00	PF69 90.00		

KM# 250 5 YUAN
22.22 g., 0.900 Silver 0.643 oz. ASW **Rev:** Guo Shoujing, Scientist, right, denomination at left **Note:** Prev. Y#215.

Date	Mintage	XF40	MS60	MS63	MS65	MS66
1989	8,500	PF65 70.00	PF67 80.00	PF69 90.00		

KM# 251 5 YUAN
22.22 g., 0.900 Silver 0.643 oz. ASW **Obv:** National emblem, date below **Rev:** Huang Dao-po, facing, looking left, 13th century inventor of hydraulic spinning, denomination at right **Note:** Prev. Y#216.

Date	Mintage	XF40	MS60	MS63	MS65	MS66
1989	8,000	PF65 70.00	PF67 80.00	PF69 90.00		

KM# 260 5 YUAN
22.22 g., 0.900 Silver 0.643 oz. ASW **Series:** Save The Children Fund **Obv:** National emblem, date below **Rev:** Children and panda, denomination at right **Note:** Prev. Y#230.

Date	Mintage	XF40	MS60	MS63	MS65	MS66
1989	25,000	PF65 70.00	PF67 120	PF69 160		

KM# 42 5 YUAN
15.00 g., 0.900 Silver 0.434 oz. ASW, 33 mm. **Series:** Artifacts **Rev:** Elephant statue

Date	Mintage	XF40	MS60	MS63	MS65	MS66
1990	5,000	PF65 120	PF67 180	PF69 200		

KM# 43 5 YUAN
15.00 g., 0.999 Silver 0.4818 oz. ASW, 33 mm. **Series:** Artifacts **Rev:** Rhino statue

Date	Mintage	XF40	MS60	MS63	MS65	MS66
1990	5,000	PF65 120	PF67 180	PF69 200		

KM# 44 5 YUAN
15.00 g., 0.900 Silver 0.434 oz. ASW, 33 mm. **Series:** Artifacts **Rev:** Dragon statue

Date	Mintage	XF40	MS60	MS63	MS65	MS66
1990	5,000	PF65 120	PF67 180	PF69 200		

KM# 45 5 YUAN
15.00 g., 0.900 Silver 0.434 oz. ASW, 33 mm. **Series:** Artifacts **Rev:** Lizard statue

Date	Mintage	XF40	MS60	MS63	MS65	MS66
1990	5,000	PF65 120	PF67 180	PF69 200		

KM# 310 5 YUAN
22.22 g., 0.900 Silver 0.643 oz. ASW **Rev:** Li Zicheng, Revolutionary, right, denomination upper right **Note:** Prev. Y#303.

Date	Mintage	XF40	MS60	MS63	MS65	MS66
1990	Est. 30500	PF65 50.00	PF67 60.00	PF69 70.00		

KM# 311 5 YUAN
22.22 g., 0.900 Silver 0.643 oz. ASW **Rev:** Li Shi Zhen, Herbalist, seated left, denomination upper left **Note:** Prev. Y#304.

Date	Mintage	XF40	MS60	MS63	MS65	MS66
1990	Est. 30500	PF65 50.00	PF67 60.00	PF69 70.00		

KM# 312 5 YUAN
22.22 g., 0.900 Silver 0.643 oz. ASW **Rev:** Zheng He, Seafarer, looking left, denomination at left **Note:** Prev. Y#305.

Date	Mintage	XF40	MS60	MS63	MS65	MS66
1990	Est. 30500	PF65 50.00	PF67 60.00	PF69 70.00		

KM# 313 5 YUAN
22.22 g., 0.900 Silver 0.643 oz. ASW **Rev:** Luo Guanzhong, Historian, seated left, denomination at right **Note:** Prev. Y#302.

Date	Mintage	XF40	MS60	MS63	MS65	MS66
1990	Est. 30000	PF65 50.00	PF67 60.00	PF69 70.00		

KM# 315 5 YUAN
2.00 g., 0.999 Silver 0.0642 oz. ASW, 15 mm. **Rev:** Dragon and Phoenix

Date	Mintage	XF40	MS60	MS63	MS65	MS66
1990	50,000	PF65 55.00	PF67 65.00	PF69 80.00		

KM# 322 5 YUAN
15.00 g., 0.900 Silver 0.434 oz. ASW **Rev:** 3 buildings joined by bridges, denomination below **Note:** Prev. Y#679.

Date	Mintage	XF40	MS60	MS63	MS65	MS66
1990	2,000	PF65 95.00	PF67 110	PF69 120		

KM# 323 5 YUAN
15.00 g., 0.900 Silver 0.434 oz. ASW **Rev:** Pondside building, denomination below **Note:** Prev. Y#677.

Date	Mintage	XF40	MS60	MS63	MS65	MS66
1990	2,000	PF65 95.00	PF67 110	PF69 120		

KM# 324 5 YUAN
15.00 g., 0.900 Silver 0.434 oz. ASW **Subject:** Taiwan Scenery Series **Obv:** Great Wall **Rev:** Tall, narrow building, denomination below **Note:** Prev. Y#676.

Date	Mintage	XF40	MS60	MS63	MS65	MS66
1990	2,000	PF65 95.00	PF67 110	PF69 120		

KM# 325 5 YUAN
15.00 g., 0.900 Silver 0.434 oz. ASW **Rev:** Hillside building, denomination below **Note:** Prev. Y#678.

Date	Mintage	XF40	MS60	MS63	MS65	MS66
1990	2,000	PF65 95.00	PF67 110	PF69 120		

KM# 377 5 YUAN
22.22 g., 0.900 Silver 0.643 oz. ASW **Rev:** Song Yingxing, Scientist **Note:** Prev. Y#322.

Date	Mintage	XF40	MS60	MS63	MS65	MS66
1991	Est. 25000	PF65 60.00	PF67 75.00	PF69 90.00		

KM# 378 5 YUAN
22.22 g., 0.900 Silver 0.643 oz. ASW **Rev:** Cao Xueqin, Writer **Note:** Prev. Y#323.

Date	Mintage	XF40	MS60	MS63	MS65	MS66
1991	Est. 25000	PF65 60.00	PF67 75.00	PF69 90.00		

KM# 379 5 YUAN
22.22 g., 0.900 Silver 0.643 oz. ASW **Rev:** Lin Zexu, high ranking official **Note:** Prev. Y#324.

Date	Mintage	XF40	MS60	MS63	MS65	MS66
1991	Est. 25000	PF65 60.00	PF67 75.00	PF69 90.00		

KM# 380 5 YUAN
22.22 g., 0.900 Silver 0.643 oz. ASW **Rev:** Hong Xuquan, Revolutionary **Note:** Prev. Y#325.

Date	Mintage	XF40	MS60	MS63	MS65	MS66
1991	Est. 25000	PF65 60.00	PF67 75.00	PF69 90.00		

KM# 75 5 YUAN
15.00 g., 0.900 Silver 0.434 oz. ASW, 33 mm. **Subject:** Marco Polo **Rev:** Bust and two temples

Date	Mintage	XF40	MS60	MS63	MS65	MS66
1992	30,000	PF65 65.00	PF67 110	PF69 140		

KM# 404 5 YUAN
22.22 g., 0.900 Silver 0.643 oz. ASW **Subject:** Archaeological Finds **Obv:** Great Wall, date below **Rev:** Ancient ships and shipbuilding, denomination at left **Note:** Prev. Y#331.

Date	Mintage	XF40	MS60	MS63	MS65	MS66
1992	15,000	PF65 75.00	PF67 120	PF69 150		

KM# 405 5 YUAN
22.22 g., 0.900 Silver 0.643 oz. ASW **Subject:** First Seismograph **Obv:** Great wall, date below **Rev:** First seismograph **Note:** Prev. Y#333.

Date	Mintage	XF40	MS60	MS63	MS65	MS66
1992	15,000	PF65 75.00	PF67 120	PF69 150		

KM# 406 5 YUAN
22.22 g., 0.900 Silver 0.643 oz. ASW **Subject:** Ancient Kite Flying **Obv:** Great Wall, date below **Rev:** Butterfly, kites in background, denomination below **Note:** Prev. Y#334.

Date	Mintage	XF40	MS60	MS63	MS65	MS66
1992	15,000	PF65 75.00	PF67 120	PF69 150		

KM# 407 5 YUAN
22.22 g., 0.900 Silver 0.643 oz. ASW **Subject:** First Compass **Obv:** Great Wall, date below **Rev:** Ancient compass, men on horseback, empty biga, denomination below **Note:** Prev. Y#332.

Date	Mintage	XF40	MS60	MS63	MS65	MS66
1992	15,000	PF65 75.00	PF67 120	PF69 150		

KM# 408 5 YUAN
22.22 g., 0.900 Silver 0.643 oz. ASW **Obv:** Great Wall, date below **Rev:** Bronze Age metal working scene, denomination below **Edge:** Fine or coarse reeding

Date	Mintage	XF40	MS60	MS63	MS65	MS66
1992	15,000	PF65 75.00	PF67 120	PF69 150		

KM# 446 5 YUAN
22.22 g., 0.900 Silver 0.643 oz. ASW **Obv:** National emblem **Rev:** Wang Zhaojun, Princess, Peacemaker, Sponsor of the Arts, denomination at right **Note:** Prev. Y#552.

Date	Mintage	XF40	MS60	MS63	MS65	MS66
1992	Est. 7000	PF65 85.00	PF67 130	PF69 160		

KM# 447 5 YUAN
22.22 g., 0.900 Silver 0.643 oz. ASW **Obv:** National emblem **Rev:** Hua Mulan, soldier, 2nd Century Heroine on horseback, denomination upper right **Note:** Prev. Y#551.

Date	Mintage	XF40	MS60	MS63	MS65	MS66
1992	—	PF65 85.00	PF67 130	PF69 160		

KM# 448 5 YUAN
22.22 g., 0.900 Silver 0.643 oz. ASW **Obv:** National emblem **Rev:** Cai Wenji, 177-254AD, Poet, kneeling left, denomination at right **Note:** Prev. Y#550.

Date	Mintage	XF40	MS60	MS63	MS65	MS66
1992	Est. 7000	PF65 85.00	PF67 130	PF69 160		

KM# 449 5 YUAN
22.22 g., 0.900 Silver 0.643 oz. ASW **Obv:** National emblem **Rev:** Xiao Zhuo, 953-1009AD, Strategist, left, denomination below **Note:** Prev. Y#553.

Date	Mintage	XF40	MS60	MS63	MS65	MS66
1992	Est. 7000	PF65 85.00	PF67 130	PF69 160		

KM# 450 5 YUAN
22.22 g., 0.900 Silver 0.643 oz. ASW **Obv:** National emblem, date below **Rev:** Zheng Chenggong portrait, pointing right, denomination upper left **Note:** Prev. Y#549.

Date	Mintage	XF40	MS60	MS63	MS65	MS66
1992	—	PF65 85.00	PF67 130	PF69 160		

KM# 457 5 YUAN
15.00 g., 0.900 Silver 0.434 oz. ASW **Subject:** Archaeological Finds **Obv:** National emblem **Rev:** Bighorn sheep **Note:** Prev. Y#752.

Date	Mintage	XF40	MS60	MS63	MS65	MS66
1992	3,000	PF65 150	PF67 225	PF69 300		

KM# 458 5 YUAN
15.00 g., 0.900 Silver 0.434 oz. ASW **Subject:** Archeological Finds **Obv:** National emblem **Rev:** Panther sculpture **Note:** Prev. Y#751.

Date	Mintage	XF40	MS60	MS63	MS65	MS66
1992	3,000	PF65 150	PF67 225	PF69 300		

KM# 459 5 YUAN
15.00 g., 0.900 Silver 0.434 oz. ASW **Subject:** Archaeological Finds **Obv:** National emblem **Rev:** Resting deer with long antlers **Note:** Prev. Y#750.

Date	Mintage	XF40	MS60	MS63	MS65	MS66
1992	3,000	PF65 150	PF67 225	PF69 300		

KM# 460 5 YUAN
15.00 g., 0.900 Silver 0.434 oz. ASW **Subject:** Archaeological Finds **Obv:** National emblem **Rev:** Changzin court lantern **Note:** Prev. Y#753.

Date	Mintage	XF40	MS60	MS63	MS65	MS66
1992	3,000	PF65 150	PF67 225	PF69 300		

KM# 465 5 YUAN
22.22 g., 0.900 Silver 0.643 oz. ASW **Subject:** United Nations Environmental Protection **Obv:** National emblem, date below **Rev:** Woman drawing water from stream, denomination below **Note:** Prev. Y#548.

Date	Mintage	XF40	MS60	MS63	MS65	MS66
1992	20,000	PF65 100	PF67 125	PF69 150		

KM# 467 5 YUAN
15.00 g., 0.900 Silver 0.434 oz. ASW **Obv:** National emblem, date below **Rev:** Marco Polo bust, looking right, buildings and dates at right, denomination below

Date	Mintage	XF40	MS60	MS63	MS65	MS66
1992	12,000	PF65 65.00	PF67 75.00	PF69 90.00		

KM# 469 5 YUAN
Copper **Obv:** National emblem, date below **Obv. Legend:** ZHONGCHUA RENMIN GONGHEFUO **Rev:** 2 Pandas eating bamboo, denomination below **Note:** Prev. Y#359.

Date	Mintage	XF40	MS60	MS63	MS65	MS66
1993	2,000,000	—	22.00	30.00	35.00	40.00

KM# 488 5 YUAN
22.22 g., 0.900 Silver 0.643 oz. ASW **Subject:** Mathematical Definition of Zero **Obv:** Great Wall, date below **Rev:** Mathematicians, abacus, denomination lower right **Note:** Prev. Y#558.

Date	Mintage	XF40	MS60	MS63	MS65	MS66
1993	15,000	PF65 85.00	PF67 125	PF69 140		

KM# 489 5 YUAN
22.22 g., 0.900 Silver 0.643 oz. ASW **Subject:** Chin-Yin Yang **Rev:** Two figures, one standing and one kneeling, denomination below **Note:** Prev. Y#377.

Date	Mintage	XF40	MS60	MS63	MS65	MS66
1993	15,000	PF65 85.00	PF67 125	PF69 140		

KM# 490 5 YUAN
22.22 g., 0.900 Silver 0.643 oz. ASW **Subject:** Invention of the Stirrup **Obv:** Great Wall **Rev:** Early polo game, denomination below **Note:** Prev. Y#559.

Date	Mintage	XF40	MS60	MS63	MS65	MS66
1993	15,000	PF65 85.00	PF67 125	PF69 140		

KM# 491 5 YUAN
22.22 g., 0.900 Silver 0.643 oz. ASW **Subject:** Invention of the Umbrella **Obv:** Great Wall, date below **Rev:** Figures with umbrellas above umbrella makers, denomination at right **Note:** Prev. Y#400.

Date	Mintage	XF40	MS60	MS63	MS65	MS66
1993	15,000	PF65 85.00	PF67 125	PF69 140		

KM# 492 5 YUAN
22.22 g., 0.900 Silver 0.643 oz. ASW **Subject:** The Terracotta Army **Obv:** Great Wall, date below **Rev:** The unearthing of the terracotta figurines, denomination at right **Note:** Prev. Y#560.

Date	Mintage	XF40	MS60	MS63	MS65	MS66
1993	15,000	PF65 85.00	PF67 125	PF69 140		

KM# 530 5 YUAN
22.22 g., 0.900 Silver 0.643 oz. ASW **Obv:** National emblem **Rev:** Chou En-Lai, facing, denomination upper left **Note:** Prev. Y#534.

Date	Mintage	XF40	MS60	MS63	MS65	MS66
1993	Est. 25000	PF65 65.00	PF67 95.00	PF69 110		

KM# 531 5 YUAN
22.22 g., 0.900 Silver 0.643 oz. ASW **Obv:** National emblem **Rev:** Chu Teh, 3/4 facing, arm raised, denomination upper right **Note:** Prev. Y#536.

Date	Mintage	XF40	MS60	MS63	MS65	MS66
1993	—	PF65 65.00	PF67 95.00	PF69 110		

KM# 532 5 YUAN
22.22 g., 0.900 Silver 0.643 oz. ASW **Obv:** National emblem **Rev:** Liu Shaoqi, 3/4 left, denomination at left **Note:** Prev. Y#535.

Date	Mintage	XF40	MS60	MS63	MS65	MS66
1993	Est. 25000	PF65 65.00	PF67 95.00	PF69 110		

KM# 533 5 YUAN
22.22 g., 0.900 Silver 0.643 oz. ASW **Obv:** National emblem **Rev:** Li Da-Chao, facing, denomination at right **Note:** Prev. Y#537.

Date	Mintage	XF40	MS60	MS63	MS65	MS66
1993	Est. 25000	PF65 65.00	PF67 95.00	PF69 110		

KM# 545 5 YUAN
1.56 g., 0.999 Gold 0.050 oz. AGW **Subject:** Goddess of Mercy **Obv:** Great Wall, date below **Rev:** Goddess left, denomination at right **Note:** Prev. Y#498.

Date	Mintage	XF40	MS60	MS63	MS65	MS66
1993 Prooflike	40,000	—	—	80.00	160	250

KM# 546 5 YUAN
1.56 g., 0.999 Gold 0.050 oz. AGW **Rev:** Goddess Kuan Yin - Seated in Flowers **Note:** Prev. Y#500.

Date	Mintage	XF40	MS60	MS63	MS65	MS66
1993	1,000	PF65 120	PF67 180	PF69 220		

KM# 567 5 YUAN
15.00 g., 0.900 Silver 0.434 oz. ASW **Subject:** Archeological Finds **Obv:** National emblem **Rev:** Ox lantern **Note:** Prev. Y#768.

Date	Mintage	XF40	MS60	MS63	MS65	MS66
1993	2,000	PF65 200	PF67 270	PF69 310		

KM# 568 5 YUAN
15.00 g., 0.900 Silver 0.434 oz. ASW **Subject:** Archeological Finds **Obv:** National emblem **Rev:** Human figure lantern **Note:** Prev. Y#769.

Date	Mintage	XF40	MS60	MS63	MS65	MS66
1993	2,000	PF65 200	PF67 270	PF69 310		

KM# 569 5 YUAN
15.00 g., 0.900 Silver 0.434 oz. ASW **Subject:** Archeological Finds **Obv:** National emblem **Rev:** Pig statue **Note:** Prev. Y#771.

Date	Mintage	XF40	MS60	MS63	MS65	MS66
1993	2,000	PF65 200	PF67 270	PF69 310		

KM# 570 5 YUAN
15.00 g., 0.900 Silver 0.434 oz. ASW **Subject:** Archeological Finds **Obv:** National emblem **Rev:** Horse statue **Note:** Prev. Y#770.

Date	Mintage	XF40	MS60	MS63	MS65	MS66
1993	2,000	PF65 200	PF67 270	PF69 310		

KM# 575 5 YUAN
15.00 g., 0.900 Silver 0.434 oz. ASW **Subject:** Taiwan Temple **Obv:** Great Wall **Rev:** Tower temple **Note:** Prev. Y#444.

Date	Mintage	XF40	MS60	MS63	MS65	MS66
1993	2,000	PF65 70.00	PF67 90.00	PF69 110		

KM# 576 5 YUAN
15.00 g., 0.900 Silver 0.434 oz. ASW **Subject:** Taiwan Temple **Obv:** Great Wall **Rev:** Large temple **Note:** Prev. Y#442.

Date	Mintage	XF40	MS60	MS63	MS65	MS66
1993	2,000	PF65 70.00	PF67 90.00	PF69 110		

KM# 577 5 YUAN
15.00 g., 0.900 Silver 0.434 oz. ASW **Subject:** Taiwan Temple **Obv:** Great Wall **Rev:** Small temple **Note:** Prev. Y#443.

Date	Mintage	XF40	MS60	MS63	MS65	MS66
1993	2,000	PF65 70.00	PF67 90.00	PF69 110		

KM# 578 5 YUAN
15.00 g., 0.900 Silver 0.434 oz. ASW **Obv:** Great Wall **Rev:** Taiwan Temple Buddha Statue **Note:** Prev. Y#441.

Date	Mintage	XF40	MS60	MS63	MS65	MS66
1993	2,000	PF65 70.00	PF67 90.00	PF69 110		

KM# 583 5 YUAN
1.56 g., 0.999 Gold 0.050 oz. AGW **Subject:** Homeland Scenery **Obv:** Great Wall **Rev:** Temple at Mount Song **Note:** Prev. Y#773.

Date	Mintage	XF40	MS60	MS63	MS65	MS66
1993	8,888	PF65 80.00	PF67 120	PF69 140		

KM# 627 5 YUAN
22.22 g., 0.900 Silver 0.643 oz. ASW **Subject:** Oriental Invention **Obv:** Great Wall, date below **Rev:** First records of comets, denomination at right **Note:** Prev. Y#618.

Date	Mintage	XF40	MS60	MS63	MS65	MS66
1994	15,000	PF65 75.00	PF67 90.00	PF69 110		

KM# 628 5 YUAN
22.22 g., 0.900 Silver 0.643 oz. ASW **Subject:** Oriental Inventions **Obv:** Great Wall, date below **Rev:** First tuned bells, denomination at left **Note:** Prev. Y#616.

Date	Mintage	XF40	MS60	MS63	MS65	MS66
1994	15,000	PF65 75.00	PF67 90.00	PF69 110		

KM# 629 5 YUAN
22.22 g., 0.900 Silver 0.643 oz. ASW **Subject:** Oriental Inventions **Obv:** Great Wall, date below **Rev:** First silken fabric, denomination lower right **Note:** Prev. Y#617.

Date	Mintage	XF40	MS60	MS63	MS65	MS66
1994	15,000	PF65 75.00	PF67 90.00	PF69 110		

KM# 630 5 YUAN
22.22 g., 0.900 Silver 0.643 oz. ASW **Subject:** Oriental Inventions **Obv:** Great Wall, date below **Rev:** First chain pumps used to draw water, denomination below **Note:** Prev. Y#620.

Date	Mintage	XF40	MS60	MS63	MS65	MS66
1994	15,000	PF65 75.00	PF67 90.00	PF69 110		

KM# 631 5 YUAN
22.22 g., 0.900 Silver 0.643 oz. ASW **Subject:** Oriental Inventions **Obv:** Great Wall, date below **Rev:** First masts for sailing, denomination lower right **Note:** Prev. Y#619.

Date	Mintage	XF40	MS60	MS63	MS65	MS66
1994	15,000	PF65 75.00	PF67 90.00	PF69 110		

KM# 659 5 YUAN
15.55 g., 0.999 Silver 0.4995 oz. ASW **Rev:** Goddess Kuan Yin - with bottle **Note:** Prev. Y#507.

Date	Mintage	XF40	MS60	MS63	MS65	MS66
1994	3,000	PF65 100	PF67 130	PF69 160		

KM# 660 5 YUAN
15.55 g., 0.999 Silver 0.4995 oz. ASW **Rev:** Goddess Kuan Yin - standing, denomination at right **Note:** Prev. Y#508.

Date	Mintage	XF40	MS60	MS63	MS65	MS66
1994	3,000	PF65 100	PF67 130	PF69 160		

KM# 661 5 YUAN
15.55 g., 0.999 Silver 0.4995 oz. ASW **Rev:** Goddess Kuan Yin - with child, denomination at left **Note:** Prev. Y#506.

Date	Mintage	XF40	MS60	MS63	MS65	MS66
1994	3,000	PF65 100	PF67 130	PF69 160		

KM# 674 5 YUAN
1.56 g., 0.999 Gold 0.050 oz. AGW **Obv:** Crowned figure on horseback, date lower right **Rev:** Unicorn, denomination at left **Note:** Prev. Y#419.

Date	Mintage	XF40	MS60	MS63	MS65	MS66
1994	31,100	PF65 95.00	PF67 110	PF69 130		

KM# 714 5 YUAN
Bronze **Obv:** National emblem, date below **Obv. Legend:** ZHONGHUA RENMIN GONGHEGUO **Rev:** Golden monkey, denomination at right **Note:** Prev. Y#547.

Date	Mintage	XF40	MS60	MS63	MS65	MS66
1995	—	—	10.00	15.00	22.00	50.00

KM# 735 5 YUAN
22.22 g., 0.900 Silver 0.643 oz. ASW **Subject:** Oriental Inventions **Obv:** Great Wall, date below **Rev:** Soldiers with cannon and gunpowder, denomination lower left **Note:** Prev. Y#627.

Date	Mintage	XF40	MS60	MS63	MS65	MS66
1995	15,000	PF65 75.00	PF67 95.00	PF69 120		

KM# 736 5 YUAN
22.22 g., 0.900 Silver 0.643 oz. ASW **Subject:** Oriental Inventions **Obv:** Great Wall, date below **Rev:** Potter, denomination lower left **Note:** Prev. Y#630.

Date	Mintage	XF40	MS60	MS63	MS65	MS66
1995	15,000	PF65 75.00	PF67 95.00	PF69 120		

KM# 737 5 YUAN
22.22 g., 0.900 Silver 0.643 oz. ASW **Subject:** Oriental Inventions **Obv:** Great Wall, date below **Rev:** Individual block printing, denomination at right **Note:** Prev. Y#628.

Date	Mintage	XF40	MS60	MS63	MS65	MS66
1995	15,000	PF65 75.00	PF67 95.00	PF69 120		

KM# 738 5 YUAN
22.22 g., 0.900 Silver 0.643 oz. ASW **Subject:** Oriental Inventions **Obv:** Great Wall **Rev:** Teacher with chart of human body **Note:** Prev. Y#631.

Date	Mintage	XF40	MS60	MS63	MS65	MS66
1995	15,000	PF65 75.00	PF67 95.00	PF69 120		

KM# 739 5 YUAN
20.00 g., 0.900 Silver 0.5787 oz. ASW, 36 mm. **Subject:** Oriental Inventions - Chess **Obv:** The Great Wall, date below **Rev:** Chess players, denomination upper right **Note:** Prev. Y#629.

Date	Mintage	XF40	MS60	MS63	MS65	MS66
1995	15,000	PF65 75.00	PF67 95.00	PF69 120		

KM# 774 5 YUAN
22.22 g., 0.900 Silver 0.643 oz. ASW **Obv:** Temple, date below **Rev:** Sea goddess bust, 3/4 left, denomination at right **Note:** Prev. Y#481.

Date	Mintage	XF40	MS60	MS63	MS65	MS66
1995	8,000,000	PF65 90.00	PF67 170	PF69 300		

KM# 778 5 YUAN
22.22 g., 0.900 Silver 0.643 oz. ASW **Obv:** Temple, date below **Rev:** Goddess Kuan Yin, facing, - with Lotus flower, denomination at left **Note:** Prev. Y#516.

Date	Mintage	XF40	MS60	MS63	MS65	MS66
1995	3,000	PF65 90.00	PF67 150	PF69 200		

KM# 779 5 YUAN
22.22 g., 0.900 Silver 0.643 oz. ASW **Obv:** Temple, date below **Rev:** Goddess Kuan Yin, 3/4 left, - with sceptre, denomination at left **Note:** Prev. Y#518.

Date	Mintage	XF40	MS60	MS63	MS65	MS66
1995	3,000	PF65 90.00	PF67 150	PF69 200		

KM# A781 5 YUAN
22.22 g., 0.900 Silver 0.643 oz. ASW **Obv:** Temple, date below **Rev:** Goddess Kuan Yin - with wheel, 3/4 left, denomination at right **Note:** Prev. Y#517.

Date	Mintage	XF40	MS60	MS63	MS65	MS66
1995	3,000	PF65 90.00	PF67 150	PF69 200		

KM# 781 5 YUAN
22.22 g., 0.900 Silver 0.643 oz. ASW **Obv:** Temple, date below **Rev:** Goddess Kuan Yin - with bowl, 3/4 left, denomination at right **Note:** Prev. Y#519.

Date	Mintage	XF40	MS60	MS63	MS65	MS66
1995	3,000	PF65 90.00	PF67 150	PF69 200		

KM# 794 5 YUAN
1.56 g., 0.999 Gold 0.050 oz. AGW **Obv:** Eastern unicorn rearing, left, date below **Rev:** Western unicorn with offspring, denomination at left **Note:** Prev. Y#736.

Date	Mintage	XF40	MS60	MS63	MS65	MS66
1995	20,000	PF65 135	PF67 185	PF69 230		

KM# 823 5 YUAN
22.22 g., 0.900 Silver 0.643 oz. ASW **Subject:** Chinese Culture Series **Obv:** Great Wall seen through arch, date below **Rev:** Female opera role, denomination upper right **Note:** Prev. Y#798.

Date	Mintage	XF40	MS60	MS63	MS65	MS66
1995	20,000	PF65 65.00	PF67 85.00	PF69 100		

KM# 825 5 YUAN
22.22 g., 0.900 Silver 0.643 oz. ASW **Subject:** Chinese Culture Series **Obv:** Great Wall seen through arch, date below **Rev:** Tang Taizong seated, denomination at left **Note:** Prev. Y#796.

Date	Mintage	XF40	MS60	MS63	MS65	MS66
1995	20,000	PF65 65.00	PF67 85.00	PF69 100		

KM# 826 5 YUAN
22.22 g., 0.900 Silver 0.643 oz. ASW **Subject:** Chinese Culture Series **Obv:** Great Wall seen through arch **Rev:** Lion dance **Note:** Prev. Y#797.

Date	Mintage	XF40	MS60	MS63	MS65	MS66
1995	20,000	PF65 65.00	PF67 85.00	PF69 100		

KM# 827 5 YUAN
22.22 g., 0.900 Silver 0.643 oz. ASW **Subject:** Chinese Culture Series **Obv:** Great Wall seen through arch, date below **Rev:** Mencius seated at table, denomination below **Note:** Prev. Y#795.

Date	Mintage	XF40	MS60	MS63	MS65	MS66
1995	20,000	PF65 65.00	PF67 85.00	PF69 100		

KM# 828 5 YUAN
22.22 g., 0.900 Silver 0.643 oz. ASW **Subject:** Chinese Culture Series **Obv:** Great Wall seen through arch, date below **Rev:** Pagoda of Six Harmonies, denomination at left **Note:** Prev. Y#794.

Date	Mintage	XF40	MS60	MS63	MS65	MS66
1995	20,000	PF65 65.00	PF67 85.00	PF69 100		

KM# 866 5 YUAN
22.22 g., 0.900 Silver 0.643 oz. ASW **Rev:** Silk spinner, denomination at right **Note:** Prev. Y#603.

Date	Mintage	XF40	MS60	MS63	MS65	MS66
1995	Est. 15000	PF65 55.00	PF67 70.00	PF69 80.00		

KM# 867 5 YUAN
22.22 g., 0.900 Silver 0.643 oz. ASW **Rev:** Silk merchant and customer, denomination at right **Note:** Prev. Y#602.

Date	Mintage	XF40	MS60	MS63	MS65	MS66
1995	15,000	PF65 55.00	PF67 70.00	PF69 80.00		

KM# 868 5 YUAN
22.22 g., 0.900 Silver 0.643 oz. ASW **Rev:** 2 men leading camel, denomination below **Note:** Prev. Y#600.

Date	Mintage	XF40	MS60	MS63	MS65	MS66
1995	15,000	PF65 75.00	PF67 95.00	PF69 110		

KM# 869 5 YUAN
22.22 g., 0.900 Silver 0.643 oz. ASW **Rev:** Dancer, denomination lower right **Note:** Prev. Y#601.

Date	Mintage	XF40	MS60	MS63	MS65	MS66
1995	15,000	PF65 60.00	PF67 80.00	PF69 100		

KM# 881 5 YUAN
Bronze **Obv:** National emblem, date below **Obv. Legend:** ZONGHUA RENMIN GONGHEGUO **Rev:** Tiger, denomination at left **Note:** Prev. Y#729.

Date	Mintage	XF40	MS60	MS63	MS65	MS66
1996	—	—	7.00	12.00	20.00	25.00

KM# 882 5 YUAN
Bronze **Obv:** National emblem, date below **Rev:** Pair of baiji dolphins, denomination above **Note:** Prev. Y#730.

Date	Mintage	XF40	MS60	MS63	MS65	MS66
1996	—	—	7.00	12.00	20.00	25.00

KM# 909 5 YUAN
22.22 g., 0.900 Silver 0.643 oz. ASW **Subject:** Chinese Inventions and Discoveries Series **Obv:** Great Wall **Rev:** Horse cart, denomination below **Note:** Prev. Y#875.

Date	Mintage	XF40	MS60	MS63	MS65	MS66
1996	15,000	PF65 150	PF67 180	PF69 200		

KM# 910 5 YUAN
22.22 g., 0.900 Silver 0.643 oz. ASW **Subject:** Chinese Inventions and Discoveries Series **Obv:** Great Wall, date below **Rev:** Three musicians, denomination at left **Note:** Prev. Y#871.

Date	Mintage	XF40	MS60	MS63	MS65	MS66
1996	15,000	PF65 150	PF67 180	PF69 200		

KM# 911 5 YUAN
22.22 g., 0.900 Silver 0.643 oz. ASW **Subject:** Chinese Inventions and Discoveries Series **Obv:** Great Wall **Rev:** Sailing ship, denomination at right **Note:** Prev. Y#874.

Date	Mintage	XF40	MS60	MS63	MS65	MS66
1996	15,000	PF65 150	PF67 180	PF69 200		

KM# 912 5 YUAN
22.22 g., 0.900 Silver 0.643 oz. ASW **Subject:** Chinese Inventions and Discoveries Series **Obv:** Great Wall, date below **Rev:** Suspension bridge, denomination at right **Note:** Prev. Y#872.

Date	Mintage	XF40	MS60	MS63	MS65	MS66
1996	15,000	PF65 150	PF67 180	PF69 200		

KM# 913 5 YUAN
22.22 g., 0.900 Silver 0.643 oz. ASW **Subject:** Chinese Inventions and Discoveries Series **Obv:** Great Wall **Rev:** Astronomical clock, denomination at right **Note:** Prev. Y#873.

Date	Mintage	XF40	MS60	MS63	MS65	MS66
1996	15,000	PF65 150	PF67 180	PF69 200		

KM# 933 5 YUAN
1.56 g., 0.999 Gold 0.050 oz. AGW **Subject:** Goddess Guanyin **Obv:** Temple, date below **Rev:** Goddess holding flower, denomination at left **Note:** Prev. Y#885.

Date	Mintage	XF40	MS60	MS63	MS65	MS66
1996	—	PF65 75.00	PF67 225	PF69 300		

KM# 934 5 YUAN
15.55 g., 0.999 Silver 0.4994 oz. ASW, 33 mm. **Obv:** Temple, date below **Rev:** Goddess holding vase and twig, denomination at right **Edge:** Reeded **Note:** Prev. Y#1196.

Date	Mintage	XF40	MS60	MS63	MS65	MS66
1996	5,000	PF65 90.00	PF67 285	PF69 350		

KM# 935 5 YUAN
1.56 g., 0.999 Gold 0.0499 oz. AGW, 14 mm. **Subject:** Goddess Guanyin **Obv:** Temple **Rev:** Goddess holding vase and twig **Edge:** Reeded **Note:** Prev. Y#1197.

Date	Mintage	XF40	MS60	MS63	MS65	MS66
1996	35,000	PF65 75.00	PF67 275	PF69 350		

KM# 938 5 YUAN
15.55 g., 0.999 Silver 0.4995 oz. ASW **Obv:** Eastern unicorn, date below **Rev:** Western unicorn rearing, left, denomination lower left **Note:** Prev. Y#883.

Date	Mintage	XF40	MS60	MS63	MS65	MS66
1996	—	—	—	55.00	—	—

KM# 939 5 YUAN
1.56 g., 0.999 Gold 0.050 oz. AGW **Obv:** Eastern unicorn, date below **Rev:** Head of western unicorn, right, denomination at right **Note:** Prev. Y#740.

Date	Mintage	XF40	MS60	MS63	MS65	MS66
1996	—	—	—	85.00	110	120
1996	5,000	PF65 165	PF67 200	PF69 280		

KM# 940 5 YUAN
1.56 g., 0.999 Platinum 0.050 oz. APW **Obv:** Eastern unicorn, date below **Rev:** Head of western unicorn, right, denomination at right **Note:** Prev. Y#740a.

Date	Mintage	XF40	MS60	MS63	MS65	MS66
1996	8,000	—	—	150	250	320

KM# 971 5 YUAN
22.22 g., 0.900 Silver 0.643 oz. ASW **Rev:** Musicians on camel, denomination at left **Note:** Prev. Y#607.

Date	Mintage	XF40	MS60	MS63	MS65	MS66
1996	15,000	PF65 75.00	PF67 100	PF69 130		

KM# 972 5 YUAN
22.22 g., 0.900 Silver 0.643 oz. ASW **Rev:** Fairy above Magao Sanctuary, denomination upper right **Note:** Prev. Y#605.

Date	Mintage	XF40	MS60	MS63	MS65	MS66
1996	15,000	PF65 75.00	PF67 100	PF69 130		

KM# 973 5 YUAN
22.22 g., 0.900 Silver 0.643 oz. ASW **Rev:** Various historic

sculptures, denomination lower left **Note:** Prev. Y#606.

Date	Mintage	XF40	MS60	MS63	MS65	MS66
1996	15,000	PF65 75.00		PF67 100	PF69 130	

KM# 974 5 YUAN

22.22 g., 0.900 Silver 0.643 oz. ASW **Rev:** Caravan route market scene, denomination below **Note:** Prev. Y#604.

Date	Mintage	XF40	MS60	MS63	MS65	MS66
1996	15,000	PF65 75.00		PF67 100	PF69 130	

KM# 980 5 YUAN

Bronze **Obv:** National emblem, date below **Obv. Legend:** ZHONGHUA RENMIN GONGHEGUO **Rev:** Crested Ibis, left, denomination at left **Note:** Prev. Y#731.

Date	Mintage	XF40	MS60	MS63	MS65	MS66
1997	—	—	7.00	12.00	20.00	30.00

KM# 981 5 YUAN

Bronze **Obv:** National emblem, date below **Obv. Legend:** ZHONGHUA RENMIN GONGHEGUO **Rev:** Red-crowned Crane, right, denomination at right **Note:** Prev. Y#732.

Date	Mintage	XF40	MS60	MS63	MS65	MS66
1997	—	—	7.00	12.00	20.00	30.00

KM# 1025 5 YUAN

15.51 g., 0.999 Silver 0.4982 oz. ASW, 33 mm. **Series:** Kuan Yin **Rev:** Female holding plant and jug, inscription at right

Date	Mintage	XF40	MS60	MS63	MS65	MS66
1997	10,000	PF65 75.00		PF67 95.00	PF69 120	

KM# 1026 5 YUAN

15.51 g., 0.999 Silver 0.4982 oz. ASW, 33 mm. **Series:** Kuan Yin **Rev:** Female holding jug and plant, inscription at left

Date	Mintage	XF40	MS60	MS63	MS65	MS66
1997	10,000	PF65 75.00		PF67 95.00	PF69 120	

KM# 1027 5 YUAN

1.55 g., 0.999 Gold 0.0498 oz. AGW, 14 mm. **Series:** Kuan Yin **Rev:** Female holding jug and plant

Date	Mintage	XF40	MS60	MS63	MS65	MS66
1997	35,000	PF65 200		PF67 285	PF69 350	

KM# 1030 5 YUAN

20.00 g., 0.999 Silver 0.6424 oz. ASW **Obv:** 2 Eastern unicorns, date below **Rev:** 1 Western unicorn, denomination below **Note:** Prev. Y#911.

Date	Mintage	XF40	MS60	MS63	MS65	MS66
1997	5,000	PF65 50.00		PF67 70.00	PF69 90.00	

KM# 1057 5 YUAN

1.56 g., 0.999 Gold 0.0499 oz. AGW, 14 mm. **Obv:** Ornamental column **Rev:** Child holding a carp **Edge:** Reeded **Note:** Prev. Y#1198.

Date	Mintage	XF40	MS60	MS63	MS65	MS66
1997	100,000	—	—	—	90.00	120

KM# 1058 5 YUAN

15.55 g., 0.999 Silver 0.4995 oz. ASW **Subject:** Traditional Chinese Mascot **Obv:** Ornamental column **Rev:** Child holding carp **Note:** Prev. Y#916.1

Date	Mintage	XF40	MS60	MS63	MS65	MS66
1997	80,000	—	—	—	55.00	70.00

KM# 1058a 5 YUAN

15.55 g., 0.999 Silver 0.4994 oz. ASW, 36 mm. **Obv:** Ornamental column **Rev:** Multicolor child holding carp **Edge:** Reeded **Note:** Prev. Y#916.2.

Date	Mintage	XF40	MS60	MS63	MS65	MS66
1997	100,000	PF65 60.00		PF67 80.00	PF69 100	

KM# 1067 5 YUAN

22.00 g., 0.900 Silver 0.6366 oz. ASW, 36 mm. **Obv:** Great Wall **Rev:** Building, denomination below **Edge:** Reeded **Note:** Prev. Y#1190.

Date	Mintage	XF40	MS60	MS63	MS65	MS66
1997 (y)	35,000	—	—	—	55.00	70.00

KM# 1068 5 YUAN

22.00 g., 0.900 Silver 0.6366 oz. ASW, 36 mm. **Obv:** Great Wall **Rev:** Gymnast, denomination at right **Edge:** Reeded **Note:** Prev. Y#1189.

Date	Mintage	XF40	MS60	MS63	MS65	MS66
1997 (y)	35,000	—	—	75.00	85.00	110

KM# 1069 5 YUAN

22.00 g., 0.900 Silver 0.6366 oz. ASW, 36 mm. **Obv:** Great Wall **Rev:** Man with extended open hand, denomination at right **Edge:** Reeded **Note:** Prev. Y#1187.

Date	Mintage	XF40	MS60	MS63	MS65	MS66
1997 (y)	35,000	—	—	—	55.00	70.00

KM# 1070 5 YUAN

22.00 g., 0.900 Silver 0.6366 oz. ASW, 36 mm. **Obv:** Great Wall **Rev:** Astronomer, denomination at left **Edge:** Reeded **Note:** Prev. Y#1188.

Date	Mintage	XF40	MS60	MS63	MS65	MS66
1997 (y)	35,000	—	—	—	55.00	70.00

KM# 1071 5 YUAN

22.00 g., 0.900 Silver 0.6366 oz. ASW, 36 mm. **Obv:** Great Wall view, date below **Rev:** Man with flag, denomination lower left **Edge:** Reeded **Note:** Prev. Y#1186.

Date	Mintage	XF40	MS60	MS63	MS65	MS66
1997 (y)	35,000	—	—	—	55.00	70.00

KM# 1103 5 YUAN

22.00 g., 0.900 Silver 0.6366 oz. ASW, 36 mm. **Series:** Silk Road **Rev:** Camels entering gate

Date	Mintage	XF40	MS60	MS63	MS65	MS66
1997	15,000	PF65 200		PF67 280	PF69 320	

KM# 1104 5 YUAN

22.00 g., 0.900 Silver 0.6366 oz. ASW, 36 mm. **Series:** Silk Road **Rev:** Statue within nitch

Date	Mintage	XF40	MS60	MS63	MS65	MS66
1997	15,000	PF65 200		PF67 280	PF69 320	

KM# 1105 5 YUAN

22.00 g., 0.900 Silver 0.6366 oz. ASW, 36 mm. **Series:** Silk Road **Rev:** People inspecting cloth

Date	Mintage	XF40	MS60	MS63	MS65	MS66
1997	—	PF65 200		PF67 280	PF69 320	

KM# 1106 5 YUAN

22.00 g., 0.900 Silver 0.6366 oz. ASW, 36 mm. **Series:** Silk Road **Rev:** Musicians and dancer

Date	Mintage	XF40	MS60	MS63	MS65	MS66
1997	15,000	PF65 200		PF67 280	PF69 320	

KM# 1122 5 YUAN

Bronze **Subject:** Chinese Alligator **Obv:** National emblem, date below **Obv. Legend:** ZHONGHUA RENMIN GONGHEGUO **Rev:** Alligator, right, denomination above **Note:** Prev. Y#941.

Date	Mintage	XF40	MS60	MS63	MS65	MS66
1998	—	—	7.00	12.00	20.00	30.00

KM# 1123 5 YUAN

Bronze **Subject:** Brown-eared Pheasant **Obv:** National emblem, date below **Rev:** Pheasant, left, denomination above **Note:** Prev. Y#940.

Date	Mintage	XF40	MS60	MS63	MS65	MS66
1998	—	—	7.00	12.00	20.00	30.00

KM# A1134 5 YUAN

51.50 g., 0.999 Silver 1.6541 oz. ASW, 33 mm. **Subject:** Honk Kong International Coin Convention **Rev:** Panda seated eating bamboo leaves

Date	Mintage	XF40	MS60	MS63	MS65	MS66
1998	30,000	PF65 65.00		PF67 85.00	PF69 100	

KM# 1158 5 YUAN

51.50 g., 0.999 Silver 1.6541 oz. ASW, 33 mm. **Series:** Kuan Yin **Rev:** Female standing holding branch

Date	Mintage	XF40	MS60	MS63	MS65	MS66
1998	10,000	PF65 65.00		PF67 85.00	PF69 100	

KM# 1159 5 YUAN

51.51 g., 0.999 Silver 1.6544 oz. ASW, 33 mm. **Series:** Kuan Yin **Rev:** Female with hands in prayer

Date	Mintage	XF40	MS60	MS63	MS65	MS66
1998	10,000	PF65 65.00	PF67 85.00	PF69 100		

KM# 1172 5 YUAN

15.60 g., 0.999 Silver 0.501 oz. ASW, 36 mm. **Obv:** Radiant winged pillar monument above flowers **Rev:** Multicolor child holding vase, elephant at left **Edge:** Reeded **Note:** Prev. Y#1130.

Date	Mintage	XF40	MS60	MS63	MS65	MS66
1998	100,000	PF65 85.00	PF67 100	PF69 120		

KM# 1173 5 YUAN

15.60 g., 0.999 Silver 0.501 oz. ASW, 33 mm. **Obv:** Radiant winged pillar monument above flowers **Rev:** Child holding vase, elephant at left **Edge:** Reeded **Note:** Prev. Y#1129.

Date	Mintage	XF40	MS60	MS63	MS65	MS66
1998	80,000	—	—	65.00	80.00	110

KM# 1213 5 YUAN

13.30 g., Bronze, 31.9 mm. **Obv:** State emblem **Rev:** Butterfly **Edge:** Reeded and plain sections **Note:** Prev. Y#1053.

Date	Mintage	XF40	MS60	MS63	MS65	MS66
1999	—	—	7.00	12.00	20.00	30.00

KM# 1214 5 YUAN

13.30 g., Bronze, 31.9 mm. **Obv:** State emblem **Rev:** Sturgeon **Edge:** Plain and reeded sections **Note:** Prev. Y#1054.

Date	Mintage	XF40	MS60	MS63	MS65	MS66
1999	—	—	7.00	12.00	20.00	30.00

KM# 78 10 YUAN

1.20 g., 0.900 Gold 0.0347 oz. AGW, 14 mm. **Obv:** Building, denomination at right **Rev:** Marco Polo bust, left, dates below **Note:** Prev. Y#55.

Date	Mintage	XF40	MS60	MS63	MS65	MS66
1983	50,000	PF65 65.00	PF67 85.00	PF69 100		

KM# 95 10 YUAN

17.06 g., 0.800 Silver 0.4388 oz. ASW **Series:** Olympics **Obv:** National emblem, date below **Rev:** Speed skater, denomination lower right **Note:** Prev. Y#64.

Date	Mintage	XF40	MS60	MS63	MS65	MS66
1984	6,000	PF65 120	PF67 200	PF69 260		

KM# 96 10 YUAN

16.81 g., 0.925 Silver 0.4999 oz. ASW **Series:** Los Angeles 1984 - 23rd Summer Olympic Games **Obv:** National emblem, date below **Rev:** Volleyball player serving, denomination at left **Note:** Prev. Y#63.

Date	Mintage	XF40	MS60	MS63	MS65	MS66
1984 Matte	1,000	—	250	1,000	—	—

KM# 96a 10 YUAN

17.06 g., 0.800 Silver 0.4388 oz. ASW **Note:** Prev. Y#63a.

Date	Mintage	XF40	MS60	MS63	MS65	MS66
1984	4,500	PF65 145	PF67 285			

KM# 103 10 YUAN

27.00 g., 0.900 Silver 0.7813 oz. ASW **Subject:** 110th Anniversary - Birth of Dr. Cheng Jiageng **Obv:** Jie Mei School **Rev:** Bust, facing, divides dates **Note:** Prev. Y#88.

Date	Mintage	XF40	MS60	MS63	MS65	MS66
1984	6,000	PF65 200	PF67 400	PF69 600		

KM# 126 10 YUAN

16.81 g., 0.925 Silver 0.4999 oz. ASW **Subject:** Women's Decade **Obv:** National emblem, denomination below **Rev:** Heads of three women, dates upper right **Note:** Prev. Y#62.

Date	Mintage	XF40	MS60	MS63	MS65	MS66
ND-1984	4,000	PF65 250	PF67 500			

KM# 127 10 YUAN

34.56 g., 0.900 Silver 1.000 oz. ASW **Subject:** 20th Anniversary - Tibet Autonomous Region **Obv:** National emblem, date below **Rev:** Potala Palace, denomination upper right **Note:** Prev. Y#97.

Date	Mintage	XF40	MS60	MS63	MS65	MS66
1985	3,000	PF65 1,500	PF67 1,800	PF69 2,000		

KM# 128 10 YUAN

34.56 g., 0.900 Silver 1.000 oz. ASW **Subject:** 30th Anniversary - Xinjiang Autonomous Region **Obv:** Building, date below **Rev:** Woman carrying tray, animals below, denomination at right, circle surrounds **Note:** Prev. Y#110.

Date	Mintage	XF40	MS60	MS63	MS65	MS66
1985	1,400	PF65 500	PF67 750	PF69 1,000		

KM# 146 10 YUAN

29.19 g., 0.925 Silver 0.8681 oz. ASW **Subject:** 120th Anniversary - Birth of Sun Yat-sen **Obv:** Bust, facing, divides dates, date below **Rev:** Sun Yat-sen's residence, denomination below **Note:** Prev. Y#111.

Date	Mintage	XF40	MS60	MS63	MS65	MS66
1986	8,450	PF65 200	PF67 300	PF69 400		

KM# 212 10 YUAN

27.00 g., 0.925 Silver 0.803 oz. ASW **Subject:** Rare Animal Protection **Rev:** Baiji dolphins, denomination above **Note:** Prev. Y#166.

Date	Mintage	XF40	MS60	MS63	MS65	MS66
1988	35,000	PF65 95.00	PF67 110	PF69 120		

KM# 213 10 YUAN

27.00 g., 0.925 Silver 0.803 oz. ASW **Subject:** Rare Animal Protection **Rev:** Crested Ibis, right, denomination at right **Note:** Prev. Y#165.

Date	Mintage	XF40	MS60	MS63	MS65	MS66
1988	35,000	PF65 95.00	PF67 110	PF69 120		

KM# 231 10 YUAN

15.00 g., 0.850 Silver 0.4099 oz. ASW **Subject:** Year of the Snake **Obv:** Shanhaiguan City Gate, date below **Rev:** Snake left, denomination below **Note:** Prev. Y#177.

Date	Mintage	XF40	MS60	MS63	MS65	MS66
1989	15,000	PF65 110	PF67 220	PF69 250		

KM# 240 10 YUAN

27.00 g., 0.925 Silver 0.803 oz. ASW **Subject:** 1990 Asian Games **Obv:** Monument, stadium, Great Wall segment and sun **Rev:** Tennis player, denomination above **Note:** Prev. Y#201.

Date	Mintage	XF40	MS60	MS63	MS65	MS66
1989	20,000	PF65 75.00	PF67 80.00	PF69 90.00		

KM# 241 10 YUAN

27.00 g., 0.925 Silver 0.803 oz. ASW **Subject:** 1990 Asian Games **Obv:** Monument, stadium, Great Wall segment and sun **Rev:** Bicyclist, denomination lower right **Note:** Prev. Y#202.

Date	Mintage	XF40	MS60	MS63	MS65	MS66
1989	20,000	PF65 75.00	PF67 80.00	PF69 90.00		

KM# 242 10 YUAN

27.00 g., 0.925 Silver 0.803 oz. ASW **Subject:** 1990 Asian Games **Obv:** Monument, stadium, Great Wall segment and sun **Rev:** Weight lifter, left, denomination at left **Note:** Prev. Y#199.

Date	Mintage	XF40	MS60	MS63	MS65	MS66
1989	20,000	PF65 75.00	PF67 80.00	PF69 90.00		

KM# 243 10 YUAN

27.00 g., 0.925 Silver 0.803 oz. ASW **Subject:** 11th Asian Games - Beijing 1990 **Obv:** Monument, stadium, Great Wall segment and sun **Rev:** Platform diver, denomination at left **Note:** Prev. Y#200.

Date	Mintage	XF40	MS60	MS63	MS65	MS66
1989	20,000	PF65 75.00	PF67 80.00	PF69 90.00		

KM# 253 10 YUAN

27.00 g., 0.925 Silver 0.803 oz. ASW **Subject:** Endangered Animals **Obv:** National emblem, date below **Rev:** Red-crowned crane, right, wings spread, denomination at left **Note:** Prev. Y#249.

Date	Mintage	XF40	MS60	MS63	MS65	MS66
1989	10,000	PF65 95.00	PF67 115			

KM# 254 10 YUAN

27.00 g., 0.925 Silver 0.803 oz. ASW **Subject:** Endangered Animals **Obv:** National emblem, date below **Rev:** Skia deer, denomination at left **Note:** Prev. Y#248.

Date	Mintage	XF40	MS60	MS63	MS65	MS66
1989	10,000	PF65 90.00	PF67 110			

KM# 256 10 YUAN

27.00 g., 0.925 Silver 0.803 oz. ASW **Subject:** 40th Anniversary of Peoples Republic **Obv:** National emblem divides dates **Rev:** Great Wall with eagles in flight above, denomination at left **Note:** Prev. Y#236.

Date	Mintage	XF40	MS60	MS63	MS65	MS66
ND-1989	5,000	PF65 120	PF67 225			

KM# 257 10 YUAN

27.00 g., 0.925 Silver 0.803 oz. ASW **Subject:** 40th Anniversary of Peoples Republic **Rev:** Tiananmen Square, birds flying above, denomination at right **Note:** Prev. Y#235.

Date	Mintage	XF40	MS60	MS63	MS65	MS66
ND-1989	5,000	PF65 120	PF67 225			

KM# 291 10 YUAN

27.00 g., 0.925 Silver 0.803 oz. ASW **Subject:** XI Asian Games **Obv:** Roman numerals above building, date below **Rev:** Gymnast on rings, denomination lower right **Note:** Prev. Y#253.

Date	Mintage	XF40	MS60	MS63	MS65	MS66
1990	20,000	PF65 70.00	PF67 75.00	PF69 80.00		

KM# 292 10 YUAN

27.00 g., 0.925 Silver 0.803 oz. ASW **Subject:** XI Asian Games **Rev:** Javelin thrower, denomination below **Note:** Prev. Y#251.

Date	Mintage	XF40	MS60	MS63	MS65	MS66
1990	20,000	PF65 70.00	PF67 75.00	PF69 80.00		

KM# 293 10 YUAN

27.00 g., 0.925 Silver 0.803 oz. ASW **Subject:** XI Asian Games **Obv:** Roman numeral above building, date below **Rev:** Soccer player, denomination lower right **Note:** Prev. Y#254.

Date	Mintage	XF40	MS60	MS63	MS65	MS66
1990	20,000	PF65 70.00	PF67 75.00	PF69 80.00		

KM# 294 10 YUAN

27.00 g., 0.925 Silver 0.803 oz. ASW **Subject:** XI Asian Games **Rev:** Baseball player, denomination at left **Note:** Prev. Y#252.

Date	Mintage	XF40	MS60	MS63	MS65	MS66
1990	20,000	PF65 70.00	PF67 75.00	PF69 80.00		

KM# 300 10 YUAN
27.00 g., 0.900 Silver 0.7813 oz. ASW **Series:** Summer Olympics **Obv:** National emblem, date below **Rev:** Bicycle racers, denomination below **Note:** Prev. Y#283.

Date	Mintage	XF40	MS60	MS63	MS65	MS66
1990	30,000	PF65 65.00	PF67 70.00	PF69 80.00		

KM# 301 10 YUAN
30.00 g., 0.900 Silver 0.8681 oz. ASW **Series:** Barcelona 1992 - 25th Summer Olympic Games **Obv:** National emblem, date below **Rev:** Platform diver, denomination lower left **Note:** Prev. Y#366.

Date	Mintage	XF40	MS60	MS63	MS65	MS66
1990	30,000	PF65 70.00	PF67 80.00	PF69 95.00		

KM# 302 10 YUAN
27.00 g., 0.900 Silver 0.7813 oz. ASW **Series:** Barcelona 1992 - 25th Summer Olympic Games **Obv:** National emblem, date below **Rev:** Woman high jumper, denomination at right **Note:** Prev. Y#300.

Date	Mintage	XF40	MS60	MS63	MS65	MS66
1990	30,000	PF65 70.00	PF67 80.00	PF69 95.00		

KM# 305 10 YUAN
27.00 g., 0.925 Silver 0.803 oz. ASW **Obv:** National emblem, date below **Rev:** Thomas Alva Edison holding lightbulb, facing, denomination at right **Note:** Prev. Y#247.

Date	Mintage	XF40	MS60	MS63	MS65	MS66
1990	30,000	PF65 65.00	PF67 100	PF69 120		

KM# 306 10 YUAN
27.00 g., 0.925 Silver 0.803 oz. ASW **Obv:** National emblem, date below **Rev:** William Shakespeare, seated, denomination upper left **Note:** Prev. Y#245.

Date	Mintage	XF40	MS60	MS63	MS65	MS66
1990	30,000	PF65 65.00	PF67 100	PF69 120		

KM# 307 10 YUAN
27.00 g., 0.925 Silver 0.803 oz. ASW **Obv:** National emblem, date below **Rev:** Ludwig van Beethoven, seated at piano, denomination above **Note:** Prev. Y#246.

Date	Mintage	XF40	MS60	MS63	MS65	MS66
1990	30,000	PF65 65.00	PF67 100	PF69 120		

KM# 308 10 YUAN
27.00 g., 0.925 Silver 0.803 oz. ASW **Obv:** National emblem, date below **Rev:** Half figure of Homer, Poet, denomination at right **Note:** Prev. Y#244.

Date	Mintage	XF40	MS60	MS63	MS65	MS66
1990	30,000	PF65 65.00	PF67 100	PF69 120		

KM# 316 10 YUAN
31.10 g., 0.999 Silver 0.9989 oz. ASW **Obv:** Great Wall, date below **Rev:** Phoenix and dragon, denomination at right **Note:** Prev. Y#261.

Date	Mintage	XF40	MS60	MS63	MS65	MS66
1990	12,000	PF65 90.00	PF67 115	PF69 130		

KM# 317 10 YUAN
1.00 g., 0.999 Gold 0.0321 oz. AGW, 14 mm. **Obv:** Great Wall, date below **Rev:** Phoenix and dragon, denomination at left **Note:** Prev. Y#206.

Date	Mintage	XF40	MS60	MS63	MS65	MS66
1990	34,000	PF65 85.00	PF67 100	PF69 110		

KM# 296 10 YUAN
30.00 g., 0.900 Silver 0.8681 oz. ASW **Series:** Olympics **Obv:** National emblem, date below **Rev:** Downhill skier, denomination lower left **Note:** Prev. Y#367.

Date	Mintage	XF40	MS60	MS63	MS65	MS66
1991	30,000	PF65 65.00	PF67 70.00	PF69 80.00		

KM# 299 10 YUAN
30.00 g., 0.900 Silver 0.8681 oz. ASW **Series:** Barcelona 1992 - 25th Summer Olympic Games **Obv:** National emblem, date below **Rev:** Woman playing table tennis, denomination at right **Note:** Prev. Y#456.

Date	Mintage	XF40	MS60	MS63	MS65	MS66
1991	30,000	PF65 95.00	PF67 115			

KM# 369 10 YUAN
27.08 g., 0.925 Silver 0.8053 oz. ASW **Subject:** Women's 1st World Football Championships **Obv:** 5 story building, date below **Rev:** Women's soccer, 3 players, denomination below **Note:** Prev. Y#319.

Date	Mintage	XF40	MS60	MS63	MS65	MS66
1991	2,800	PF65 150	PF67 275			

KM# 370 10 YUAN
27.08 g., 0.925 Silver 0.8053 oz. ASW **Subject:** 1st Women's World Football Championship **Obv:** 5 story building, date below **Rev:** Women's soccer, 2 players, denomination at right **Note:** Prev. Y#318.

Date	Mintage	XF40	MS60	MS63	MS65	MS66
1991	2,800	PF65 150	PF67 275			

KM# 372 10 YUAN

27.08 g., 0.925 Silver 0.8053 oz. ASW **Rev:** Columbus **Note:** Prev. Y#348.

Date	Mintage	XF40	MS60	MS63	MS65	MS66
1991	—	PF65 65.00	PF67 70.00	PF69 85.00		

KM# 373 10 YUAN

27.08 g., 0.925 Silver 0.8053 oz. ASW **Obv:** National emblem, date below **Rev:** Mark Twain seated with book, denomination at left **Note:** Prev. Y#350.

Date	Mintage	XF40	MS60	MS63	MS65	MS66
1991	—	PF65 65.00	PF67 70.00	PF69 85.00		

KM# 374 10 YUAN

27.08 g., 0.925 Silver 0.8053 oz. ASW **Rev:** Mozart seated at piano, two dates upper right, denomination at left **Note:** Prev. Y#347.

Date	Mintage	XF40	MS60	MS63	MS65	MS66
1991	—	PF65 65.00	PF67 70.00	PF69 85.00		

KM# 375 10 YUAN

27.08 g., 0.925 Silver 0.8053 oz. ASW **Rev:** Einstein **Note:** Prev. Y#349.

Date	Mintage	XF40	MS60	MS63	MS65	MS66
1991	—	PF65 50.00	PF67 65.00	PF69 80.00		

KM# 383 10 YUAN

31.10 g., 0.999 Silver 0.999 oz. ASW **Subject:** 80th Anniversary - 1911 Revolution **Obv:** Building, two dates below **Rev:** Sun Yat Sen in civilian clothes, denomination at right **Note:** Prev. Y#476.

Date	Mintage	XF40	MS60	MS63	MS65	MS66
ND-1991	2,500	PF65 145	PF67 285	PF69 310		

KM# 438 10 YUAN

26.95 g., 0.900 Silver 0.7798 oz. ASW **Series:** Lillehammer 1994 - 17th Winter Olympic Games **Obv:** National emblem, date below **Rev:** Ski jumper, denomination at right **Note:** Prev. Y#490.

Date	Mintage	XF40	MS60	MS63	MS65	MS66
1992	30,000	PF65 75.00	PF67 110	PF69 140		

KM# 439 10 YUAN

26.83 g., 0.900 Silver 0.7763 oz. ASW **Series:** 1994 Winter Olympics **Obv:** National emblem, date below **Rev:** Cross country skier, denomination at right **Note:** Prev. Y#368.

Date	Mintage	XF40	MS60	MS63	MS65	MS66
1992	7,500	PF65 125	PF67 135	PF69 150		

KM# 441 10 YUAN

27.00 g., 0.925 Silver 0.803 oz. ASW **Subject:** International Celebrities **Obv:** National emblem, date below **Rev:** Leonardo Da Vinci with painting of Mona Lisa, denomination below **Note:** Prev. Y#755.

Date	Mintage	XF40	MS60	MS63	MS65	MS66
1992	30,000	PF65 70.00	PF67 75.00	PF69 80.00		

KM# 442 10 YUAN

27.00 g., 0.925 Silver 0.803 oz. ASW **Subject:** International Celebrities **Obv:** National emblem, date below **Rev:** Wolfgang Von Goethe, denomination at right **Note:** Prev. Y#756.

Date	Mintage	XF40	MS60	MS63	MS65	MS66
1992	30,000	PF65 70.00	PF67 75.00	PF69 80.00		

KM# 443 10 YUAN

27.11 g., 0.900 Silver 0.7844 oz. ASW **Obv:** National emblem, date below **Rev:** Tschaikovsky leaning against piano, denomination lower left **Note:** Prev. Y#709.

Date	Mintage	XF40	MS60	MS63	MS65	MS66
1992	30,000	PF65 70.00	PF67 75.00	PF69 80.00		

KM# 444 10 YUAN

27.00 g., 0.925 Silver 0.803 oz. ASW **Subject:** International Celebrities **Obv:** National emblem, date below **Rev:** Alfred Nobel, denomination at left **Note:** Prev. Y#757.

Date	Mintage	XF40	MS60	MS63	MS65	MS66
1992	30,000	PF65 70.00	PF67 75.00	PF69 80.00		

KM# 454 10 YUAN

27.00 g., 0.925 Silver 0.803 oz. ASW **Subject:** Wildlife **Obv:** National emblem **Rev:** White storks, denomination at right **Note:** Prev. Y#486.

Date	Mintage	XF40	MS60	MS63	MS65	MS66
1992	7,260	PF65 120	PF67 150	PF69 180		

KM# 455 10 YUAN

26.95 g., 0.900 Silver 0.7798 oz. ASW **Obv:** National emblem, date below **Rev:** Snow leopard, denomination above **Note:** Prev. Y#584.

Date	Mintage	XF40	MS60	MS63	MS65	MS66
1992	7,260	PF65 120	PF67 150	PF69 180		

KM# 466 10 YUAN

31.10 g., 0.999 Silver 0.999 oz. ASW **Subject:** Environmental Protection **Obv:** National emblem, date below **Rev:** Kneeling woman fetching water at stream, denomination below **Note:** Prev. Y#942.

Date	Mintage	XF40	MS60	MS63	MS65	MS66
1992	60,000	—	75.00	80.00	100	120

KM# 493 10 YUAN
30.00 g., 0.900 Silver 0.8681 oz. ASW, 40 mm. **Subject:** Yin and Yang Concept **Obv:** Great Wall blockhouse, date below **Rev:** Four men studying the symbol,denomination below **Edge:** Reeded **Note:** Prev. Y#1077.

Date	Mintage	XF40	MS60	MS63	MS65	MS66
1993	—	—	70.00	75.00	120	140

Note: Probably minted at a much later date.

KM# 494 10 YUAN
31.10 g., 0.999 Silver 0.999 oz. ASW, 40 mm. **Series:** Scientific and technical inventions **Rev:** Four men standing around scroll

Date	Mintage	XF40	MS60	MS63	MS65	MS66
1993	11,800	PF65 125	PF67 135	PF69 145		

KM# 520 10 YUAN
24.26 g., 0.900 Silver 0.7018 oz. ASW **Subject:** World Cup Soccer - 1994 **Obv:** National emblem, date below **Rev:** Soccer players, denomination lower left **Note:** Prev. Y#418.

Date	Mintage	XF40	MS60	MS63	MS65	MS66
1993	30,000	PF65 90.00	PF67 130	PF69 165		

KM# 521 10 YUAN
27.00 g., 0.925 Silver 0.803 oz. ASW **Subject:** World Cup Soccer **Obv:** National emblem, date below **Rev:** 3 soccer players, denomination below **Note:** Prev. Y#779.

Date	Mintage	XF40	MS60	MS63	MS65	MS66
1993	30,000	PF65 80.00	PF67 120	PF69 160		

KM# 524 10 YUAN
30.00 g., 0.900 Silver 0.8681 oz. ASW **Subject:** Olympics Centennial **Obv:** National emblem, date below **Rev:** Fencing, denomination below **Note:** Prev. Y#493.

Date	Mintage	XF40	MS60	MS63	MS65	MS66
1993	30,000	PF65 75.00	PF67 85.00	PF69 95.00		

KM# 525 10 YUAN
30.00 g., 0.900 Silver 0.8681 oz. ASW **Series:** Olympics **Obv:** National emblem, date below **Rev:** Runners, denomination below **Note:** Prev. Y#492.

Date	Mintage	XF40	MS60	MS63	MS65	MS66
1993	30,000	PF65 75.00	PF67 85.00	PF69 95.00		

KM# 537 10 YUAN
30.00 g., 0.900 Silver 0.8681 oz. ASW **Obv:** National emblem **Rev:** 3/4-length figure of Soong Ching-ling, 1892-1981, half left, birds in background, denomination at right **Note:** Prev. Y#759.

Date	Mintage	XF40	MS60	MS63	MS65	MS66
1993	20,000	PF65 90.00	PF67 100	PF69 110		

KM# 538 10 YUAN
30.00 g., 0.900 Silver 0.8681 oz. ASW **Obv:** National emblem **Rev:** Song Qingling, seated, denomination st right **Note:** Prev. Y#758.

Date	Mintage	XF40	MS60	MS63	MS65	MS66
1993	20,000	PF65 90.00	PF67 100	PF69 110		

KM# 540.1 10 YUAN
27.00 g., 0.925 Silver 0.803 oz. ASW **Subject:** Mao Tse Tung **Obv:** Building on cliff **Rev:** Bust facing, denomination at right **Note:** Prev. Y#412.1.

Date	Mintage	XF40	MS60	MS63	MS65	MS66
1993	30,000	—	—	115	120	130

KM# 540.2 10 YUAN
27.00 g., 0.925 Silver 0.803 oz. ASW **Obv:** Building on cliff, date at right **Rev:** Revised bust facing, denomination at right **Note:** Prev. Y#412.2.

Date	Mintage	XF40	MS60	MS63	MS65	MS66
1993	—	—	—	115	120	130

KM# 547 10 YUAN
3.11 g., 0.999 Gold 0.0999 oz. AGW **Rev:** Goddess Guanyin seated in flowers, denomination at left **Note:** Prev. Y#501.

Date	Mintage	XF40	MS60	MS63	MS65	MS66
1993	1,000	PF65 225	PF67 285	PF69 320		

KM# 548 10 YUAN
3.11 g., 0.999 Gold 0.0999 oz. AGW **Obv:** Building above date **Rev:** Goddess of Mercy holding flower, denomination at left **Note:** Prev. Y#499.

Date	Mintage	XF40	MS60	MS63	MS65	MS66
1993 Prooflike	20,000	—	—	185	200	210

KM# 563 10 YUAN
27.00 g., 0.925 Silver 0.803 oz. ASW **Rev:** 2 Bactrian camels, denomination below **Note:** Prev. Y#579.

Date	Mintage	XF40	MS60	MS63	MS65	MS66
1993	4,825	PF65 120	PF67 135	PF69 150		

KM# 564 10 YUAN
27.00 g., 0.925 Silver 0.803 oz. ASW **Rev:** Pere David deer, denomination above **Note:** Prev. Y#580.

Date	Mintage	XF40	MS60	MS63	MS65	MS66
1993	4,825	PF65 120	PF67 135	PF69 150		

KM# 584 10 YUAN
31.11 g., 0.999 Silver 0.999 oz. ASW, 39.9 mm. **Subject:** Mt. Heng **Obv:** Great Wall, date below **Rev:** Cliffside building, denomination below **Edge:** Reeded **Note:** Prev. Y#1229.

Date	Mintage	XF40	MS60	MS63	MS65	MS66
1993	60,000	PF65 90.00	PF67 100	PF69 120		

KM# 585 10 YUAN

31.11 g., 0.999 Silver 0.999 oz. ASW **Subject:** Mt. Tai **Obv:** Great Wall, date below **Rev:** Small building with long staircase, denomination upper left **Note:** Prev. Y#933.

Date	Mintage	XF40	MS60	MS63	MS65	MS66
1993	60,000	PF65 90.00	PF67 100	PF69 120		

KM# 586 10 YUAN

31.11 g., 0.999 Silver 0.999 oz. ASW **Subject:** Mt. Hua **Obv:** Great Wall, date below **Rev:** Bird's eye view of mountain tops, shelter, denomination at left **Note:** Prev. Y#934.

Date	Mintage	XF40	MS60	MS63	MS65	MS66
1993	60,000	PF65 90.00	PF67 100	PF69 120		

KM# 587 10 YUAN

31.11 g., 0.999 Silver 0.999 oz. ASW **Subject:** Homeland scenery **Obv:** Great Wall, date below **Rev:** Large building, islands in background, denomination upper right **Note:** Prev. Y#932.

Date	Mintage	XF40	MS60	MS63	MS65	MS66
1993	60,000	PF65 90.00	PF67 100	PF69 120		

KM# 588 10 YUAN

3.10 g., 0.999 Gold 0.0997 oz. AGW, 18 mm. **Subject:** Homeland Scenery **Obv:** Great Wall **Rev:** Cliffside building **Note:** Prev. Y#774.

Date	Mintage	XF40	MS60	MS63	MS65	MS66
1993	8,888	PF65 200	PF67 300			

KM# 589 10 YUAN

31.11 g., 0.999 Silver 0.999 oz. ASW **Subject:** Mt. Song **Obv:** Great Wall, date below **Rev:** Tall domed building, denomination at right **Note:** Prev. Y#935.

Date	Mintage	XF40	MS60	MS63	MS65	MS66
1993	60,000	PF65 90.00	PF67 100	PF69 120		

KM# 594 10 YUAN

3.11 g., 0.999 Gold 0.0999 oz. AGW **Obv:** Temple of Harmony **Rev:** 2 peacocks, denomination above **Note:** Prev. Y#474.

Date	Mintage	XF40	MS60	MS63	MS65	MS66
1993 Prooflike	—	—	—	350	—	—

KM# 595 10 YUAN

31.10 g., 0.999 Silver 0.9989 oz. ASW **Obv:** Temple of Harmony, date below **Rev:** Peacocks, denomination above **Note:** Prev. Y#352.

Date	Mintage	XF40	MS60	MS63	MS65	MS66
1993	7,000	PF65 200	PF67 350	PF69 500		
1997 Matte	50,000	—	—	100	115	130

KM# 522 10 YUAN

27.20 g., 0.925 Silver 0.8089 oz. ASW **Obv:** National emblem, date below **Rev:** Soccer player, denomination at left

Date	Mintage	XF40	MS60	MS63	MS65	MS66
1994	30,000	PF65 60.00	PF67 80.00	PF69 100		

KM# 526 10 YUAN

31.10 g., 0.999 Silver 0.999 oz. ASW **Series:** Olympics Centennial **Obv:** National emblem, date below **Rev:** Female archer shooting, denomination lower left **Note:** Prev. Y#495.

Date	Mintage	XF40	MS60	MS63	MS65	MS66
1994	30,000	PF65 90.00	PF67 100	PF69 110		

KM# 527 10 YUAN

31.10 g., 0.999 Silver 0.999 oz. ASW **Series:** Olympics **Obv:** National emblem, date below **Rev:** Basketball player, denomination at left **Note:** Prev. Y#494.

Date	Mintage	XF40	MS60	MS63	MS65	MS66
1994	30,000	PF65 90.00	PF67 100	PF69 110		

KM# 528 10 YUAN

31.10 g., 0.999 Silver 0.999 oz. ASW **Series:** Olympics **Obv:** National emblem, date below **Rev:** Boxing match, denomination at right **Note:** Prev. Y#496.

Date	Mintage	XF40	MS60	MS63	MS65	MS66
1994	30,000	PF65 90.00	PF67 100	PF69 110		

KM# 651 10 YUAN

27.00 g., 0.925 Silver 0.803 oz. ASW **Subject:** Hiroshima 1994 - 12th Asian Games **Rev:** Runners, denomination lower right **Note:** Prev. Y#439.

Date	Mintage	XF40	MS60	MS63	MS65	MS66
1994	5,000	PF65 95.00	PF67 125	PF69 160		

KM# 652 10 YUAN

27.00 g., 0.925 Silver 0.803 oz. ASW **Subject:** Hiroshima 1994 - 12th Asian Games **Obv:** National emblem, athletic figures above date **Rev:** Swimming, denomination at left **Note:** Prev. Y#438.

Date	Mintage	XF40	MS60	MS63	MS65	MS66
1994	5,000	PF65 95.00	PF67 125	PF69 160		

KM# 654 10 YUAN

27.00 g., 0.925 Silver 0.803 oz. ASW **Obv:** National emblem **Rev:** Confucius, denomination at right **Note:** Prev. Y#539.

Date	Mintage	XF40	MS60	MS63	MS65	MS66
1994	—	PF65 85.00	PF67 100	PF69 120		

KM# 655 10 YUAN
27.00 g., 0.925 Silver 0.803 oz. ASW **Rev:** Socrates, denomination lower left **Note:** Prev. Y#540.

Date	Mintage	XF40	MS60	MS63	MS65	MS66
1994	—	PF65 85.00	PF67 100	PF69 120		

KM# 656 10 YUAN
27.00 g., 0.925 Silver 0.803 oz. ASW **Rev:** Rembrandt, denomination at left **Note:** Prev. Y#541.

Date	Mintage	XF40	MS60	MS63	MS65	MS66
1994	—	PF65 85.00	PF67 100	PF69 120		

KM# 657 10 YUAN
27.00 g., 0.925 Silver 0.803 oz. ASW **Rev:** Verdi, denomination at right **Note:** Prev. Y#542.

Date	Mintage	XF40	MS60	MS63	MS65	MS66
1994	—	PF65 85.00	PF67 100	PF69 120		

KM# 662 10 YUAN
3.11 g., 0.999 Gold 0.0999 oz. AGW **Obv:** Great Wall above date **Rev:** Guanyin-Goddess of Mercy, holding child, facing, denomination at left **Note:** Prev. Y#510.

Date	Mintage	XF40	MS60	MS63	MS65	MS66
1994 Prooflike	8,000	—	—	185	275	350

KM# 663 10 YUAN
31.10 g., 0.999 Silver 0.999 oz. ASW **Obv:** Great Wall, date below **Rev:** Guanyin - Goddess of Mercy, holding child, facing, denomination at left **Note:** Prev. Y#482.

Date	Mintage	XF40	MS60	MS63	MS65	MS66
1994	30,000	PF65 75.00	PF67 95.00	PF69 110		

KM# 671 10 YUAN
20.74 g., 0.900 Silver 0.600 oz. ASW **Obv:** Building, date below **Rev:** Black-billed Magpies on branch, denomination below **Shape:** 12-sided **Note:** Prev. Y#681.

Date	Mintage	XF40	MS60	MS63	MS65	MS66
1994	3,900	PF65 115	PF67 235	PF69 280		

KM# 673 10 YUAN
4.00 g., 0.999 Bi-Metallic 0.1285 oz. Gold center in silver ring, 23 mm. **Rev:** Dragon and Phoenix

Date	Mintage	XF40	MS60	MS63	MS65	MS66
1994	2,500	PF65 700	PF67 1,600	PF69 3,000		

KM# 675 10 YUAN
31.10 g., 0.999 Silver 0.9989 oz. ASW **Obv:** Figure on Eastern unicorn, date below **Rev:** Unicorn, sprays of roses below, denomination at left **Note:** Prev. Y#420.

Date	Mintage	XF40	MS60	MS63	MS65	MS66
1994	50,000	—	—	70.00	85.00	100
1994	4,000	PF65 200	PF67 300			

KM# 676 10 YUAN
3.11 g., 0.999 Gold 0.0999 oz. AGW **Rev:** Unicorn looking back towards right **Note:** Prev. Y#421.

Date	Mintage	XF40	MS60	MS63	MS65	MS66
1994	5,100	PF65 300	PF67 500			

KM# 686 10 YUAN
31.10 g., 0.999 Silver 0.999 oz. ASW **Subject:** Sino - Singapore Friendship **Obv:** Great Wall, date below **Rev:** City view of Singapore, denomination below **Note:** Prev. Y#710.

Date	Mintage	XF40	MS60	MS63	MS65	MS66
1994	30,000	PF65 75.00	PF67 90.00	PF69 100		

KM# 690 10 YUAN
31.10 g., 0.999 Silver 0.999 oz. ASW **Subject:** Children at Play **Obv:** Imperial Palace, corner building **Rev:** Three children carrying tray, denomination below **Note:** Prev. Y#783.

Date	Mintage	XF40	MS60	MS63	MS65	MS66
1994	2,500	PF65 300	PF67 500			

KM# 691 10 YUAN
31.10 g., 0.999 Silver 0.999 oz. ASW **Subject:** Children at Play **Obv:** Imperial Palace, corner building **Rev:** Three children playing on ground, denomination above **Note:** Prev. Y#784.

Date	Mintage	XF40	MS60	MS63	MS65	MS66
1994	2,500	PF65 125	PF67 250			

KM# 692 10 YUAN
31.10 g., 0.999 Silver 0.999 oz. ASW **Subject:** Children at Play **Rev:** 2 children and cat, denomination below **Note:** Prev. Y#457.

Date	Mintage	XF40	MS60	MS63	MS65	MS66
1994	8,500	PF65 150	PF67 225	PF69 300		

KM# 693 10 YUAN
31.10 g., 0.999 Silver 0.999 oz. ASW **Subject:** Children at Play **Obv:** Building, date below **Rev:** 3 children and toy boat, denomination below **Note:** Prev. Y#458.

Date	Mintage	XF40	MS60	MS63	MS65	MS66
1994	8,500	PF65 150	PF67 225	PF69 300		

KM# 755 10 YUAN
31.10 g., 0.999 Silver 0.999 oz. ASW **Subject:** Table Tennis **Obv:** Tianjing Stadium **Rev:** Two table tennis players, denomination at left **Note:** Prev. Y#837.

Date	Mintage	XF40	MS60	MS63	MS65	MS66
1995	3,000	PF65 190	PF67 240			

KM# 756 10 YUAN
31.10 g., 0.999 Silver 0.999 oz. ASW **Subject:** Table Tennis **Obv:** Tianjing Stadium **Rev:** Table tennis player, denomination at left **Note:** Prev. Y#836.

Date	Mintage	XF40	MS60	MS63	MS65	MS66
1995	3,000	PF65 190	PF67 240			

KM# 758 10 YUAN
27.00 g., 0.925 Silver 0.803 oz. ASW **Series:** 1996 Olympics **Obv:** National emblem, date below **Rev:** Kick boxer, denomination at right **Note:** Prev. Y#714.

Date	Mintage	XF40	MS60	MS63	MS65	MS66
1995	—	PF65 75.00	PF67 95.00	PF69 110		

KM# 759 10 YUAN
27.00 g., 0.925 Silver 0.803 oz. ASW **Series:** 1996 Olympics **Obv:** National emblem, date below **Rev:** Handball player, denomination lower right **Note:** Prev. Y#713.

Date	Mintage	XF40	MS60	MS63	MS65	MS66
1995	—	PF65 75.00	PF67 95.00	PF69 110		

KM# 760 10 YUAN
31.10 g., 0.999 Silver 0.999 oz. ASW **Series:** 1996 Olympics **Obv:** National emblem, date below **Rev:** Female shooter, denomination below **Note:** Prev. Y#842.

Date	Mintage	XF40	MS60	MS63	MS65	MS66
1995	30,000	PF65 75.00	PF67 95.00	PF69 110		

KM# 761 10 YUAN
31.10 g., 0.999 Silver 0.999 oz. ASW **Series:** Olympics **Obv:** National emblem, date below **Rev:** Gymnast, denomination at right **Note:** Prev. Y#841.

Date	Mintage	XF40	MS60	MS63	MS65	MS66
1995	30,000	PF65 75.00	PF67 95.00	PF69 110		

KM# 766 10 YUAN
27.00 g., 0.925 Silver 0.803 oz. ASW **Subject:** Painter Zu Beihong **Obv:** Portrait **Rev:** Horse running left, denomination at left **Note:** Prev. Y#820.

Date	Mintage	XF40	MS60	MS63	MS65	MS66
1995	8,000	PF65 100	PF67 110	PF69 130		

KM# 767 10 YUAN
27.00 g., 0.925 Silver 0.803 oz. ASW **Subject:** Painter Zu Beihong **Obv:** Portrait, facing, divides dates **Rev:** Cat stalking, denomination at left **Note:** Prev. Y#819.

Date	Mintage	XF40	MS60	MS63	MS65	MS66
1995	8,000	PF65 100	PF67 110	PF69 130		

KM# 775 10 YUAN
31.10 g., 0.999 Silver 0.999 oz. ASW, 40 mm. **Subject:** Goddess of Mazu **Rev:** Female bust right with flat topped hat

Date	Mintage	XF40	MS60	MS63	MS65	MS66
1995	50,000	PF65 150	PF67 275	PF69 400		

KM# 776 10 YUAN
31.10 g., 0.999 Silver 0.999 oz. ASW, 40 mm. **Subject:** Goddess of Mazu **Rev:** Female bust facing

Date	Mintage	XF40	MS60	MS63	MS65	MS66
1995	50,000	PF65 150	PF67 275	PF69 400		

KM# 782 10 YUAN
3.11 g., 0.999 Gold 0.0999 oz. AGW **Obv:** Building, date below **Rev:** Guanyin - Goddess of Mercy with lotus flower, facing, denomination at left **Note:** Prev. Y#520.

Date	Mintage	XF40	MS60	MS63	MS65	MS66
1995	3,000	PF65 180	PF67 210	PF69 240		

KM# 783 10 YUAN
3.11 g., 0.999 Gold 0.0999 oz. AGW **Obv:** Building, date below **Rev:** Guanyin - Goddess of Mercy with sceptre, denomination at left **Note:** Prev. Y#522.

Date	Mintage	XF40	MS60	MS63	MS65	MS66
1995	3,000	PF65 180	PF67 210	PF69 240		

KM# 784 10 YUAN
3.11 g., 0.999 Gold 0.0999 oz. AGW **Obv:** Building, date below **Rev:** Guanyin, Goddess of Mercy with bowl, denomination at left **Note:** Prev. Y#523.

Date	Mintage	XF40	MS60	MS63	MS65	MS66
1995	3,000	PF65 180	PF67 210	PF69 240		

KM# 785 10 YUAN
3.11 g., 0.999 Gold 0.0999 oz. AGW **Obv:** Building, date below **Rev:** Guanyin, Goddess of Mercy with wheel, denomination at left **Note:** Prev. Y#521.

Date	Mintage	XF40	MS60	MS63	MS65	MS66
1995	3,000	PF65 180	PF67 210	PF69 240		

KM# 786 10 YUAN
31.10 g., 0.999 Silver 0.999 oz. ASW **Obv:** Building, date below **Rev:** Guanyin, Goddess of Mercy with sceptre, denomination at left **Note:** Prev. Y#489.

Date	Mintage	XF40	MS60	MS63	MS65	MS66
1995 Prooflike	30,000	—	—	90.00	110	120

KM# 791 10 YUAN
27.00 g., 0.925 Silver 0.803 oz. ASW **Subject:** Dinosaurs **Rev:** Pterodactylus, denomination at right **Note:** Prev. Y#469.

Date	Mintage	XF40	MS60	MS63	MS65	MS66
1995	Est. 5000	PF65 250	PF67 325	PF69 400		

KM# 792 10 YUAN
27.00 g., 0.925 Silver 0.803 oz. ASW **Subject:** Dinosaurs **Rev:** Stegosaurus, denomination below **Note:** Prev. Y#470.

Date	Mintage	XF40	MS60	MS63	MS65	MS66
1995	—	PF65 250	PF67 325	PF69 400		

KM# 795 10 YUAN
31.11 g., 0.999 Silver 0.999 oz. ASW **Obv:** Eastern Unicorn, date below **Rev:** Unicorn with offspring, denomination at left **Note:** Prev. Y#683.

Date	Mintage	XF40	MS60	MS63	MS65	MS66
1995	—	PF65 250	PF67 325	PF69 400		

KM# 796 10 YUAN
3.11 g., 0.999 Gold 0.0999 oz. AGW **Obv:** Eastern unicorn, date below **Rev:** Western unicorn with offspring, denomination at left **Note:** Prev. Y#737.

Date	Mintage	XF40	MS60	MS63	MS65	MS66
1995	5,000	PF65 300	PF67 375	PF69 450		

KM# 806 10 YUAN
31.11 g., 0.999 Silver 0.999 oz. ASW **Subject:** 50th Anniversary of Anti-Japanese War **Obv:** National emblem, date below **Rev:** Chou and Mao above soldiers, denomination below **Note:** Prev. Y#684.

Date	Mintage	XF40	MS60	MS63	MS65	MS66
1995	3,750	PF65 125	PF67 140	PF69 160		

KM# 807 10 YUAN
31.11 g., 0.999 Silver 0.999 oz. ASW **Obv:** National emblem, date below **Rev:** Attacking soldiers above bridge guarded by lion, denomination at right **Note:** Prev. Y#685.

Date	Mintage	XF40	MS60	MS63	MS65	MS66
1995	3,750	PF65 125	PF67 140	PF69 160		

KM# 811 10 YUAN
31.11 g., 0.999 Silver 0.999 oz. ASW **Subject:** 4th UN World Women's Congress **Obv:** Logo above building **Rev:** Three women with flowers and birds **Note:** Prev. Y#686.

Date	Mintage	XF40	MS60	MS63	MS65	MS66
1995	30,500	PF65 90.00	PF67 100	PF69 120		

KM# 813 10 YUAN
27.00 g., 0.925 Silver 0.803 oz. ASW **Series:** 50th Anniversary - United Nations **Obv:** UN logo **Rev:** UN building **Note:** Prev. Y#682.

Date	Mintage	XF40	MS60	MS63	MS65	MS66
1995	115,000	PF65 75.00	PF67 95.00	PF69 110		

KM# 815 10 YUAN
31.10 g., 0.999 Silver 0.999 oz. ASW **Subject:** Return of Hong Kong to China **Obv:** Tiananmen Square, date below **Rev:** Deng Xiao Ping bust, left, buildings below, denomination at bottom **Note:** Prev. Y#531.

Date	Mintage	XF40	MS60	MS63	MS65	MS66
1995	88,000	PF65 100	PF67 110	PF69 120		

KM# 818 10 YUAN
27.00 g., 0.925 Silver 0.803 oz. ASW **Rev:** Sailing ship, denomination above **Note:** Prev. Y#647.

Date	Mintage	XF40	MS60	MS63	MS65	MS66
1995	10,000	PF65 500	PF67 650	PF69 800		

KM# 819 10 YUAN
27.00 g., 0.925 Silver 0.803 oz. ASW **Rev:** Junk, denomination below **Note:** Prev. Y#650.

Date	Mintage	XF40	MS60	MS63	MS65	MS66
1995	10,000	PF65 500	PF67 650	PF69 800		

KM# 830 10 YUAN
3.11 g., 0.999 Gold 0.0999 oz. AGW **Subject:** Chinese Culture Series **Obv:** Great Wall seen through arch **Rev:** Mencius seated at table, denomination below **Note:** Prev. Y#800.

Date	Mintage	XF40	MS60	MS63	MS65	MS66
1995	25,000	PF65 185	PF67 300	PF69 400		

KM# 831 10 YUAN
3.11 g., 0.999 Gold 0.0999 oz. AGW **Subject:** Chinese Culture Series **Obv:** Great Wall seen through arch **Rev:** Female opera role **Note:** Prev. Y#803.

Date	Mintage	XF40	MS60	MS63	MS65	MS66
1995	25,000	PF65 185	PF67 300	PF69 400		

KM# 832 10 YUAN
3.11 g., 0.999 Gold 0.0999 oz. AGW **Subject:** Chinese Culture Series **Obv:** Great Wall seen through arch **Rev:** Tang Taizong seated, denomination at left **Note:** Prev. Y#801.

Date	Mintage	XF40	MS60	MS63	MS65	MS66
1995	25,000	PF65 185	PF67 300	PF69 400		

KM# 833 10 YUAN
3.11 g., 0.999 Gold 0.0999 oz. AGW **Subject:** Chinese Culture Series **Obv:** Great Wall seen through arch, date below **Rev:** Pagoda of six harmonies, denomination at left **Note:** Prev. Y#799.

Date	Mintage	XF40	MS60	MS63	MS65	MS66
1995	25,000	PF65 185	PF67 300	PF69 400		

KM# 834 10 YUAN
3.11 g., 0.999 Gold 0.0999 oz. AGW **Subject:** Chinese Culture Series **Obv:** Great Wall seen through arch **Rev:** Lion dance, denomination lower left **Note:** Prev. Y#802.

Date	Mintage	XF40	MS60	MS63	MS65	MS66
1995	25,000	PF65 185	PF67 300	PF69 400		

KM# 840 10 YUAN
27.00 g., 0.925 Silver 0.803 oz. ASW **Obv:** Dragon in inner circle, date below **Rev:** Huang Di in chariot, denomination at lower right **Note:** Prev. Y#588.

Date	Mintage	XF40	MS60	MS63	MS65	MS66
1995	5,000	PF65 100	PF67 140	PF69 180		

KM# 841 10 YUAN
27.00 g., 0.925 Silver 0.803 oz. ASW **Obv:** Dragon in inner circle **Rev:** Half figure of Yan Di, wearing skins, facing, denomination lower right **Note:** Prev. Y#589.

Date	Mintage	XF40	MS60	MS63	MS65	MS66
1995	5,000	PF65 100	PF67 140	PF69 180		

KM# 842 10 YUAN
27.00 g., 0.925 Silver 0.803 oz. ASW **Obv:** Dragon in inner circle **Rev:** Half figure of Yao holding feathers, facing, denomination lower right **Note:** Prev. Y#590.

Date	Mintage	XF40	MS60	MS63	MS65	MS66
1995	5,000	PF65 100	PF67 140	PF69 180		

KM# 843 10 YUAN
27.00 g., 0.925 Silver 0.803 oz. ASW **Obv:** Dragon in inner circle **Rev:** Half figure of Shun with urn, facing, denomination lower left **Note:** Prev. Y#591.

Date	Mintage	XF40	MS60	MS63	MS65	MS66
1995	5,000	PF65 100	PF67 140	PF69 180		

KM# 847 10 YUAN
27.00 g., 0.925 Silver 0.803 oz. ASW **Subject:** Romance of the Three Kingdoms Series **Obv:** Luo Guanzhong bust, facing, date below **Rev:** Liu Bei standing holding rod, denomination at right **Note:** Prev. Y#825.

Date	Mintage	XF40	MS60	MS63	MS65	MS66
1995	7,000	PF65 300	PF67 350	PF69 400		

KM# 848 10 YUAN
27.00 g., 0.925 Silver 0.803 oz. ASW **Subject:** Romance of the Three Kingdoms Series **Obv:** Luo Guanzhong bust **Rev:** Zhuge Liang on throne, denomination at right **Note:** Prev. Y#828.

Date	Mintage	XF40	MS60	MS63	MS65	MS66
1995	7,000	PF65 300	PF67 350	PF69 400		

KM# 849 10 YUAN
27.00 g., 0.925 Silver 0.803 oz. ASW **Subject:** Romance of the Three Kingdoms Series **Obv:** Luo Guanzhong bust **Rev:** Guan Yo reading, denomination above **Note:** Prev. Y#826.

Date	Mintage	XF40	MS60	MS63	MS65	MS66
1995	7,000	PF65 300	PF67 350	PF69 400		

KM# 850 10 YUAN
27.00 g., 0.925 Silver 0.803 oz. ASW **Subject:** Romance of the Three Kingdoms Series **Obv:** Luo Guanzhong bust **Rev:** Zhang Fei on horse, denomination at left **Note:** Prev. Y#827.

Date	Mintage	XF40	MS60	MS63	MS65	MS66
1995	7,000	PF65 300	PF67 350	PF69 400		

KM# 858 10 YUAN
31.10 g., 0.999 Silver 0.999 oz. ASW **Subject:** 50th Anniversary - Return of Taiwan to China **Obv:** Great Wall **Rev:** Zhongshan Hall **Note:** Prev. Y#812.

Date	Mintage	XF40	MS60	MS63	MS65	MS66
1995	5,000	PF65 215	PF67 325	PF69 450		

KM# 859 10 YUAN
31.10 g., 0.999 Silver 0.999 oz. ASW **Subject:** 50th Anniversary - Return of Taiwan to China **Obv:** Great Wall **Rev:** Taiwan and China maps **Note:** Prev. Y#811.

Date	Mintage	XF40	MS60	MS63	MS65	MS66
1995	5,000	PF65 215	PF67 325	PF69 450		

KM# 871 10 YUAN
20.73 g., 0.900 Silver 0.5999 oz. ASW **Obv:** Great Wall, date below **Rev:** Eagle in flight, denomination at left **Shape:** 12-sided **Note:** Prev. Y#809.

Date	Mintage	XF40	MS60	MS63	MS65	MS66
1995	3,900	PF65 190	PF67 375	PF69 700		

KM# 762 10 YUAN
27.00 g., 0.925 Silver 0.803 oz. ASW **Series:** Olympics **Obv:** National emblem, date below **Rev:** Sailboarder, denomination at left **Note:** Prev. Y#890.

Date	Mintage	XF40	MS60	MS63	MS65	MS66
1996	30,000	PF65 75.00	PF67 95.00	PF69 110		

KM# 902 10 YUAN
27.00 g., 0.925 Silver 0.803 oz. ASW **Subject:** Beijing Coin Fair **Obv:** Temple of Heaven within inner circle with additional legend **Rev:** Seated panda eating with cub, gold insert **Note:** Prev. Y#846.

Date	Mintage	XF40	MS60	MS63	MS65	MS66
1996	2,000	PF65 125	PF67 250			

KM# 903 10 YUAN
27.00 g., 0.925 Silver 0.803 oz. ASW **Subject:** Ninth Asian Stamp Exhibition **Obv:** Temple of Heaven, date below, within circle, with additional legend **Rev:** Seated panda eating with cub **Note:** Prev. Y#845.

Date	Mintage	XF40	MS60	MS63	MS65	MS66
1996	2,000	PF65 125	PF67 250			

KM# 904 10 YUAN
31.10 g., 0.999 Silver 0.999 oz. ASW **Subject:** 9th Asian Stamp Exhibition **Obv:** Stamp, date below **Rev:** Radiant Imperial Stamp, with additional legend above and to right **Note:** Prev. Y#866.

Date	Mintage	XF40	MS60	MS63	MS65	MS66
1996	20,000	PF65 140	PF67 160	PF69 180		

KM# 905 10 YUAN
31.10 g., 0.999 Silver 0.999 oz. ASW **Subject:** 45th Anniversary - Chinese Aviation Industry **Obv:** National emblem **Rev:** Jet airplane, denomination at right **Note:** Prev. Y#862.

Date	Mintage	XF40	MS60	MS63	MS65	MS66
1996	20,000	PF65 75.00	PF67 95.00	PF69 110		

KM# 906 10 YUAN
31.10 g., 0.999 Silver 0.999 oz. ASW **Subject:** 45th Anniversary - Chinese Aviation Industry **Obv:** National emblem, date below **Rev:** Propeller airplane, denomination below **Note:** Prev. Y#861.

Date	Mintage	XF40	MS60	MS63	MS65	MS66
1996	20,000	PF65 75.00	PF67 95.00	PF69 110		

KM# 907 10 YUAN
31.10 g., 0.999 Silver 0.999 oz. ASW **Subject:** 40th Anniversary - Chinese Aviation Industry **Obv:** National emblem above Great Wall **Rev:** Rocket and satellites, denomination at right **Note:** Prev. Y#864.

Date	Mintage	XF40	MS60	MS63	MS65	MS66
1996	20,000	PF65 75.00	PF67 95.00	PF69 110		

KM# 908 10 YUAN
31.10 g., 0.999 Silver 0.999 oz. ASW **Subject:** 40th Anniversary - Chinese Aviation Industry **Obv:** National emblem above Great Wall **Rev:** Satellites, denomination at left **Note:** Prev. Y#863.

Date	Mintage	XF40	MS60	MS63	MS65	MS66
1996	20,000	PF65 75.00	PF67 95.00	PF69 110		

KM# 931 10 YUAN
31.10 g., 0.999 Silver 0.999 oz. ASW **Obv:** Building **Rev:** Sun Yat-Sen bust, facing, denomination below, 3/4 wreath of fans surrounds **Note:** Prev. Y#858.

Date	Mintage	XF40	MS60	MS63	MS65	MS66
1996	20,000	PF65 75.00	PF67 95.00	PF69 110		

KM# 936 10 YUAN
31.10 g., 0.999 Silver 0.999 oz. ASW **Subject:** Goddess of Mercy - Guanyin **Obv:** Temple, date below **Rev:** Goddess holding flower, denomination at left **Note:** Prev. Y#886.

Date	Mintage	XF40	MS60	MS63	MS65	MS66
1996	30,000	PF65 70.00	PF67 120	PF69 200		

KM# 937 10 YUAN
3.11 g., 0.999 Gold 0.0999 oz. AGW **Subject:** Goddess Guanyin **Obv:** Temple **Rev:** Goddess holding flower **Note:** Prev. Y#887.

Date	Mintage	XF40	MS60	MS63	MS65	MS66
1996	10,000	PF65 185	PF67 300	PF69 400		

KM# 941 10 YUAN
31.11 g., 0.999 Silver 0.999 oz. ASW **Obv:** Eastern unicorn, date below **Rev:** Western unicorn in wreath, denomination lower left **Note:** Prev. Y#741.

Date	Mintage	XF40	MS60	MS63	MS65	MS66
1996	8,000	PF65 200	PF67 240	PF69 280		

KM# 942 10 YUAN
3.11 g., 0.999 Gold 0.0999 oz. AGW **Obv:** Eastern unicorn, date below **Rev:** Western unicorn in wreath, denomination lower left **Note:** Prev. Y#742.

Date	Mintage	XF40	MS60	MS63	MS65	MS66
1996	5,000	PF65 300	PF67 350	PF69 400		

KM# 951 10 YUAN
31.10 g., 0.999 Silver 0.999 oz. ASW **Subject:** 60th Anniversary - Long March **Obv:** Flag above building, date below **Rev:** Chairman Mao on horse, denomination above horse head **Note:** Prev. Y#868.

Date	Mintage	XF40	MS60	MS63	MS65	MS66
1996	20,000	PF65 100	PF67 110	PF69 120		

KM# 952 10 YUAN
31.10 g., 0.999 Silver 0.999 oz. ASW **Subject:** 60th Anniversary - Long March **Obv:** Flag above Baota Mountain, date below **Rev:** Two armies enjoined in battle, denomination below **Note:** Prev. Y#869.

Date	Mintage	XF40	MS60	MS63	MS65	MS66
1996	20,000	PF65 100	PF67 110	PF69 120		

KM# 954 10 YUAN
31.10 g., 0.999 Silver 0.999 oz. ASW **Subject:** Centennial of Chinese Post Office **Obv:** Modern stamp **Rev:** Radiant Imperial stamp, no legend above **Note:** Prev. Y#865.

Date	Mintage	XF40	MS60	MS63	MS65	MS66
1996	20,000	PF65 40.00	PF67 50.00	PF69 65.00		

KM# 956 10 YUAN
31.10 g., 0.999 Silver 0.999 oz. ASW **Subject:** Return of Hong Kong to China **Obv:** Tiananmen Square, date below **Rev:** Law book above Hong Kong harbor view, denomination below **Note:** Prev. Y#860.

Date	Mintage	XF40	MS60	MS63	MS65	MS66
1996	88,000	PF65 50.00	PF67 60.00	PF69 70.00		

KM# 959 10 YUAN
27.00 g., 0.925 Silver 0.803 oz. ASW **Subject:** Romance of the Three Kingdoms Series **Obv:** Luo Guanzhong portrait **Rev:** Cao Cao standing with spear, denomination at right **Note:** Prev. Y#876.

Date	Mintage	XF40	MS60	MS63	MS65	MS66
1996	7,000	PF65 100	PF67 110	PF69 130		

KM# 960 10 YUAN
27.00 g., 0.925 Silver 0.803 oz. ASW **Subject:** Romance of the Three Kingdoms Series **Obv:** Luo Guanzhong portrait **Rev:** Cao Pi seated at desk, denomination at right **Note:** Prev. Y#877.

Date	Mintage	XF40	MS60	MS63	MS65	MS66
1996	7,000	PF65 100	PF67 110	PF69 130		

KM# 961 10 YUAN
27.00 g., 0.925 Silver 0.803 oz. ASW **Subject:** Romance of the Three Kingdoms Series **Obv:** Luo Guanzhong portrait **Rev:** Cao Zhi standing with scroll and flags, denomination lower left **Note:** Prev. Y#878.

Date	Mintage	XF40	MS60	MS63	MS65	MS66
1996	7,000	PF65 100	PF67 110	PF69 130		

KM# 962 10 YUAN
27.00 g., 0.925 Silver 0.803 oz. ASW **Subject:** Romance of the Three Kingdoms Series **Obv:** Luo Guanzhong portrait **Rev:** Sima Yi on horse with spear, denomination at left **Note:** Prev. Y#879.

Date	Mintage	XF40	MS60	MS63	MS65	MS66
1996	7,000	PF65 100	PF67 110	PF69 130		

KM# 982 10 YUAN
Bi-Metallic Copper-Nickel center in Brass ring **Subject:** Return of Hong Kong **Obv:** Stylized flower within circle, date below **Rev:** City view, denomination above, circle surrounds **Note:** Prev. Y#722.

Date	Mintage	XF40	MS60	MS63	MS65	MS66
1997	—	—	6.00	—	—	—

Note: 5,000 pieces were struck and issued in boxes with certificates and are valued at $350

KM# 983 10 YUAN
Bi-Metallic Brass center in Copper-Nickel ring **Subject:** Hong Kong - Constitution **Obv:** Stylized flower within circle, date below **Rev:** Document with state emblem within circle, denomination below **Note:** Prev. Y#723.

Date	Mintage	XF40	MS60	MS63	MS65	MS66
1997	—	—	6.00	—	—	—

KM# 1004 10 YUAN
31.10 g., 0.999 Silver 0.999 oz. ASW **Subject:** Shanghai International Stamp & Coin Expo **Obv:** Building within circle, legend outside **Rev:** Panda, left, denomination below, gold insert **Note:** Prev. Y#895.

Date	Mintage	XF40	MS60	MS63	MS65	MS66
1997	30,000	PF65 125	PF67 150	PF69 200		

KM# 1017 10 YUAN
31.10 g., 0.999 Silver 0.999 oz. ASW, 27.2 x 42 mm. **Subject:** Painting Master Qi Baishi **Rev:** Shrimps **Shape:** Rectangular

Date	Mintage	XF40	MS60	MS63	MS65	MS66
1997	11,800	PF65 125	PF67 150	PF69 200		

KM# 1018 10 YUAN
31.10 g., 0.999 Silver 0.999 oz. ASW, 27.5 x 42 mm. **Subject:** Painting Master Qi Baishi **Rev:** Two squirrels **Shape:** Rectangular

Date	Mintage	XF40	MS60	MS63	MS65	MS66
1997	11,800	PF65 150	PF67 170	PF69 220		

KM# 1028 10 YUAN
31.10 g., 0.999 Silver 0.999 oz. ASW, 40 mm. **Series:** Kuan Yin **Rev:** Female holding jug

Date	Mintage	XF40	MS60	MS63	MS65	MS66
1997	30,000	PF65 125	PF67 150	PF69 180		

KM# 1029 10 YUAN
3.11 g., 0.999 Gold 0.0999 oz. AGW **Subject:** Goddess Guanyin **Obv:** Putuo Hill Temple **Rev:** Goddess holding jug of dew **Note:** Prev. Y#913, 985.

Date	Mintage	XF40	MS60	MS63	MS65	MS66
1997	10,000	PF65 180	PF67 200	PF69 220		

KM# 1031 10 YUAN
31.10 g., 0.999 Silver 0.999 oz. ASW **Obv:** Eastern unicorn, date below **Rev:** Western unicorn, denomination below **Note:** Prev. Y#912.

Date	Mintage	XF40	MS60	MS63	MS65	MS66
1997 Prooflike	—	—	—	75.00	—	—
1997	8,000	PF65 150	PF67 180	PF69 220		

KM# 1032 10 YUAN
3.11 g., 0.999 Gold 0.0999 oz. AGW **Obv:** Eastern unicorn **Rev:** Western unicorn **Note:** Prev. Y#912a.

Date	Mintage	XF40	MS60	MS63	MS65	MS66
1997	5,000	PF65 400	PF67 475	PF69 550		

KM# 1037 10 YUAN
31.10 g., 0.999 Silver 0.999 oz. ASW **Subject:** Wildlife of China **Obv:** National emblem, date below **Rev:** Swan with young, denomination lower left **Note:** Prev. Y#920.

Date	Mintage	XF40	MS60	MS63	MS65	MS66
1997	68,000	PF65 100	PF67 115	PF69 130		

KM# 1038 10 YUAN
31.10 g., 0.999 Silver 0.999 oz. ASW **Subject:** Wildlife of China **Obv:** National emblem, date below **Rev:** Chinese white dolphins, denomination lower right **Note:** Prev. Y#919.

Date	Mintage	XF40	MS60	MS63	MS65	MS66
1997	68,000	PF65 100	PF67 115	PF69 130		

KM# 1039 10 YUAN
31.10 g., 0.999 Silver 0.999 oz. ASW, 40 mm. **Series:** Endangered wildlife **Rev:** Swan

Date	Mintage	XF40	MS60	MS63	MS65	MS66
1997	68,000	PF65 150	PF67 170	PF69 200		

KM# 1041 10 YUAN
31.10 g., 0.999 Silver 0.999 oz. ASW **Subject:** Peoples Liberation Army **Obv:** Radiant star above Great Wall, date below **Rev:** Founding of PLA scene, denomination below **Note:** Prev. Y#908.

Date	Mintage	XF40	MS60	MS63	MS65	MS66
1997	30,000	PF65 75.00	PF67 90.00	PF69 100		

KM# 1042 10 YUAN

31.10 g., 0.999 Silver 0.999 oz. ASW **Obv:** Radiant star above Great Wall, date below **Rev:** Three members of the PRC Army, Air Force and Navy Airplanes, boats and missile in background, denomination at left **Note:** Prev. Y#909.

Date	Mintage	XF40	MS60	MS63	MS65	MS66
1997	30,000	PF65 75.00	PF67 90.00	PF69 100		

KM# 1045 10 YUAN

31.10 g., 0.999 Silver 0.999 oz. ASW **Subject:** Return of Hong Kong to China **Obv:** Tiananmen Square, date below **Rev:** Flag and fireworks over city, denomination below **Note:** Prev. Y#902.

Date	Mintage	XF40	MS60	MS63	MS65	MS66
1997	800,000	—	—	90.00	—	—
1997	88,000	PF65 140	PF67 180	PF69 210		

KM# 1047 10 YUAN

31.10 g., 0.999 Silver 0.999 oz. ASW **Subject:** Return of Macao to China **Obv:** Tiananmen Square **Rev:** Deng Xiaoping viewing Macao, denomination at right **Note:** Prev. Y#905.

Date	Mintage	XF40	MS60	MS63	MS65	MS66
1997	88,000	PF65 125	PF67 140	PF69 160		

KM# 1051 10 YUAN

31.10 g., 0.999 Silver 0.999 oz. ASW **Subject:** Sino - Thailand Friendship **Obv:** Forbidden City and Thai Royal Palace, date below **Rev:** Two Buddha statues, one in cameo, denomination lower left **Note:** Prev. Y#711.

Date	Mintage	XF40	MS60	MS63	MS65	MS66
1997	45,000	PF65 70.00	PF67 90.00	PF69 100		

KM# 1053 10 YUAN

31.20 g., 0.999 Silver 1.0021 oz. ASW **Subject:** Yi Nationality **Obv:** Towered building, date below **Rev:** Madame She Ziang with sword, soldiers at right above denomination **Note:** Prev. Y#938.

Date	Mintage	XF40	MS60	MS63	MS65	MS66
1997	28,000	PF65 70.00	PF67 90.00	PF69 100		

KM# 1054 10 YUAN

31.20 g., 0.999 Silver 1.0021 oz. ASW **Subject:** Gesal, King of Tibet **Obv:** Towered building, date below **Rev:** King on horseback, denomination at right, figures in a row below **Note:** Prev. Y#936.

Date	Mintage	XF40	MS60	MS63	MS65	MS66
1997	28,000	PF65 70.00	PF67 90.00	PF69 100		

KM# 1055 10 YUAN

31.20 g., 0.999 Silver 1.0021 oz. ASW **Subject:** Li Nationality **Obv:** Towered building, date below **Rev:** Madame Zian reading scroll, denomination at right **Note:** Prev. Y#939.

Date	Mintage	XF40	MS60	MS63	MS65	MS66
1997	28,000	PF65 70.00	PF67 90.00	PF69 100		

KM# 1056 10 YUAN

31.20 g., 0.999 Silver 1.0021 oz. ASW **Subject:** Gadamellin of Mongolia **Obv:** Towered building, date below **Rev:** Cavalry attack with swords, denomination at right **Note:** Prev. Y#937.

Date	Mintage	XF40	MS60	MS63	MS65	MS66
1997	28,000	PF65 70.00	PF67 90.00	PF69 100		

KM# 1059 10 YUAN

31.10 g., 0.999 Silver 0.999 oz. ASW **Subject:** Traditional Chinese Mascot **Obv:** Monument in Tiananmen Square, sprays below **Rev:** Child holding carp, denomination below **Note:** Prev. Y#917.1.

Date	Mintage	XF40	MS60	MS63	MS65	MS66
1997	80,000	PF65 75.00	PF67 95.00	PF69 110		

KM# 1059a 10 YUAN

31.10 g., 0.999 Silver 0.999 oz. ASW **Subject:** Traditional Chinese Mascot **Obv:** Monument in Tiananmen Square, sprays below, circle surrounds, date below **Rev:** Multicolor version of child holding carp, denomination below **Note:** Prev. Y#917.2.

Date	Mintage	XF40	MS60	MS63	MS65	MS66
1997	100,000	PF65 90.00	PF67 110	PF69 130		

KM# 1060 10 YUAN

3.11 g., 0.999 Gold 0.0999 oz. AGW, 18 mm. **Obv:** Ornamental column **Rev:** Child holding a carp **Edge:** Reeded **Note:** Prev. Y#1199.1

Date	Mintage	XF40	MS60	MS63	MS65	MS66
1997	100,000	—	—	175	—	—

KM# 1060a 10 YUAN

3.11 g., 0.999 Gold 0.0999 oz. AGW, 18 mm. **Obv:** Ornamental column **Rev:** Multicolor child holding a carp **Edge:** Reeded **Note:** Prev. Y#1199.2

Date	Mintage	XF40	MS60	MS63	MS65	MS66
1997	20,000	PF65 180	PF67 220	PF69 245		

KM# 1062 10 YUAN
31.10 g., 0.999 Silver 0.999 oz. ASW **Subject:** Celebrating Spring **Obv:** Radiant lantern, date below **Rev:** Children setting off firecrackers, denomination above **Note:** Prev. Y#914.1.

Date	Mintage	XF40	MS60	MS63	MS65	MS66
1997	60,000	—	—	75.00	—	—
1997	60,000	PF65 75.00	PF67 85.00	PF69 95.00		

KM# 1063 10 YUAN
3.11 g., 0.999 Gold 0.0999 oz. AGW **Subject:** Celebrating Spring **Obv:** Lantern **Rev:** Children setting off firecrackers **Note:** Prev. Y#983.

Date	Mintage	XF40	MS60	MS63	MS65	MS66
1997	60,000	—	—	165	170	180

KM# 1072 10 YUAN
3.11 g., 0.999 Gold 0.0999 oz. AGW, 18 mm. **Obv:** Great Wall, date below **Rev:** Astronomer, denomination upper left **Edge:** Reeded **Note:** Prev. Y#1193.

Date	Mintage	XF40	MS60	MS63	MS65	MS66
1997 (y)	16,000	—	—	180	185	195

KM# 1073 10 YUAN
3.11 g., 0.999 Gold 0.0999 oz. AGW, 18 mm. **Obv:** Great Wall, date below **Rev:** Gymnast, denomination at right **Edge:** Reeded **Note:** Prev. Y#1194.

Date	Mintage	XF40	MS60	MS63	MS65	MS66
1997 (y)	16,000	—	—	180	185	195

KM# 1074 10 YUAN
3.11 g., 0.999 Gold 0.0999 oz. AGW, 18 mm. **Obv:** Great Wall, date below **Rev:** Man with extended open hand, denomination at right **Edge:** Reeded **Note:** Prev. Y#1192.

Date	Mintage	XF40	MS60	MS63	MS65	MS66
1997 (y)	16,000	—	—	180	185	195

KM# 1075 10 YUAN
3.11 g., 0.999 Gold 0.0999 oz. AGW, 18 mm. **Obv:** Great Wall, date below **Rev:** Building, denomination below **Edge:** Reeded **Note:** Prev. Y#1195.

Date	Mintage	XF40	MS60	MS63	MS65	MS66
1997 (y)	16,000	—	—	180	185	195

KM# 1076 10 YUAN
3.11 g., 0.999 Gold 0.0999 oz. AGW, 18 mm. **Obv:** Great Wall, date below **Rev:** Man with flag, denomination at left **Edge:** Reeded **Note:** Prev. Y#1191.

Date	Mintage	XF40	MS60	MS63	MS65	MS66
1997 (y)	16,000	—	—	180	185	195

KM# 1077 10 YUAN
27.00 g., 0.925 Silver 0.803 oz. ASW, 38 mm. **Subject:** Ancient Chinese Culture Series **Obv:** Dragon seal **Rev:** Bronze wares **Edge:** Reeded **Note:** Prev. Y#1099.

Date	Mintage	XF40	MS60	MS63	MS65	MS66
1997	10,000	PF65 115	PF67 155	PF69 180		

KM# 1078 10 YUAN
27.00 g., 0.925 Silver 0.803 oz. ASW, 38 mm. **Subject:** Ancient Chinese Culture Series **Obv:** Dragon seal **Rev:** Coinage **Edge:** Reeded **Note:** Prev. Y#1102.

Date	Mintage	XF40	MS60	MS63	MS65	MS66
1997	10,000	PF65 115	PF67 155	PF69 180		

KM# 1079 10 YUAN
27.00 g., 0.925 Silver 0.803 oz. ASW, 38 mm. **Subject:** Ancient Chinese Culture Series **Obv:** Dragon seal **Rev:** Calligraphy **Edge:** Reeded **Note:** Prev. Y#1101.

Date	Mintage	XF40	MS60	MS63	MS65	MS66
1997	10,000	PF65 115	PF67 155	PF69 180		

KM# 1080 10 YUAN
27.00 g., 0.925 Silver 0.803 oz. ASW, 38 mm. **Subject:** Ancient Chinese Culture Series **Obv:** Dragon seal **Rev:** Pottery **Edge:** Reeded **Note:** Prev. Y#1100.

Date	Mintage	XF40	MS60	MS63	MS65	MS66
1997	10,000	PF65 115	PF67 155	PF69 180		

KM# 1084 10 YUAN
27.00 g., 0.925 Silver 0.803 oz. ASW, 38.6 mm. **Series:** Classic literature

Date	Mintage	XF40	MS60	MS63	MS65	MS66
1997	10,000	PF65 120	PF67 125	PF69 130		

KM# 1085 10 YUAN
27.00 g., 0.925 Silver 0.803 oz. ASW, 38.6 mm. **Series:** Classic literature **Rev:** Man seated, incense burning at right

Date	Mintage	XF40	MS60	MS63	MS65	MS66
1997	—	PF65 120	PF67 125	PF69 130		

KM# 1086 10 YUAN
27.00 g., 0.925 Silver 0.803 oz. ASW, 38.6 mm. **Rev:** Warrior standing, four horsemen in background

Date	Mintage	XF40	MS60	MS63	MS65	MS66
1997	—	PF65 120	PF67 125	PF69 130		

KM# 1087 10 YUAN
27.00 g., 0.925 Silver 0.803 oz. ASW, 38.6 mm. **Series:** Classical literature **Rev:** Bearded man standing, dragon in background

Date	Mintage	XF40	MS60	MS63	MS65	MS66
1997	10,000	PF65 120	PF67 125	PF69 130		

KM# 1091 10 YUAN
20.73 g., 0.900 Silver 0.5999 oz. ASW, 35 mm. **Subject:** Wildlife of China **Obv:** The Great Wall, date below **Rev:** Two penguins, denomination upper left **Edge:** Plain **Shape:** 12-sided **Note:** Prev. Y#1079.

Date	Mintage	XF40	MS60	MS63	MS65	MS66
1997	8,800	PF65 150	PF67 275	PF69 400		

KM# 1093 10 YUAN
31.44 g., 0.999 Silver 1.0098 oz. ASW, 39.8 mm. **Subject:** Forbidden City **Obv:** Exterior view of the Forbidden City **Rev:** Main interior approach and gatehouse to the palaces **Edge:** Reeded **Note:** Prev. Y#1092.

Date	Mintage	XF40	MS60	MS63	MS65	MS66
1997	—	PF65 100	PF67 110	PF69 120		

KM# 1094 10 YUAN
31.14 g., 0.999 Silver 1.000 oz. ASW, 39.8 mm. **Subject:** Forbidden City **Obv:** Exterior view of the Forbidden City **Rev:** Causeway to palace **Edge:** Reeded **Note:** Prev. Y#1093.

Date	Mintage	XF40	MS60	MS63	MS65	MS66
1997	—	PF65 100	PF67 110	PF69 120		

KM# 1095 10 YUAN
31.14 g., 0.999 Silver 1.000 oz. ASW, 39.8 mm. **Subject:** Forbidden City **Obv:** Exterior view of the Forbidden City **Rev:** Interior view **Edge:** Reeded **Note:** Prev. Y#1095.

Date	Mintage	XF40	MS60	MS63	MS65	MS66
1997	—	PF65 100	PF67 110	PF69 120		

KM# 1096 10 YUAN
31.10 g., 0.999 Silver 0.999 oz. ASW, 40 mm. **Series:** Forbidden City **Rev:** Garden pagoda

Date	Mintage	XF40	MS60	MS63	MS65	MS66
1997	80,000	PF65 125	PF67 135	PF69 145		

KM# 1097 10 YUAN
3.11 g., 0.999 Gold 0.0999 oz. AGW **Obv:** Forbidden city, date below **Rev:** Bronze chinze, denomination upper right **Note:** Prev. Y#984; 1094.

Date	Mintage	XF40	MS60	MS63	MS65	MS66
1997	11,000	PF65 180	PF67 250	PF69 300		

KM# 1036 10 YUAN
27.00 g., 0.925 Silver 0.803 oz. ASW, 38 mm. **Subject:** World Wildlife Fund **Obv:** National emblem, date below **Rev:** Clouded leopard on branch, denomination below **Edge:** Reeded **Note:** Prev. Y#1063.

Date	Mintage	XF40	MS60	MS63	MS65	MS66
1998	40,000	PF65 90.00	PF67 100	PF69 120		

KM# A1135 10 YUAN
31.10 g., 0.999 Silver 0.999 oz. ASW, 40 mm. **Subject:** Bejing International Coin Exposition **Rev:** Gilt panda seated

Date	Mintage	XF40	MS60	MS63	MS65	MS66
1998	30,000	PF65 125	PF67 140	PF69 160		

KM# 1136 10 YUAN
31.10 g., 0.999 Silver 0.999 oz. ASW, 40 mm. **Subject:** China International Aviation & Aerospace Exposition **Rev:** Panda seated on rock, gift insert at left

Date	Mintage	XF40	MS60	MS63	MS65	MS66
1998	50,000	PF65 125	PF67 140	PF69 160		

KM# 1151 10 YUAN
31.02 g., 0.999 Silver 0.9964 oz. ASW **Subject:** 100th Birthday - Zhou Enlai **Obv:** Zhou Enlai Memorial Hall, date below **Rev:** Zhou on horseback, denomination at right, two dates at left **Note:** Prev. Y#724.

Date	Mintage	XF40	MS60	MS63	MS65	MS66
1998	38,000	PF65 75.00	PF67 90.00	PF69 100		

KM# 1152 10 YUAN
31.02 g., 0.999 Silver 0.9964 oz. ASW **Subject:** 100th Birthday - Zhou Enlai **Obv:** Zhou Enlai Memorial Hall, date below **Rev:** Zhou standing facing 3/4 right, denomination at right **Note:** Prev. Y#725.

Date	Mintage	XF40	MS60	MS63	MS65	MS66
1998	38,000	PF65 90.00	PF67 100	PF69 110		

KM# 1154 10 YUAN
31.10 g., 0.999 Silver 0.999 oz. ASW, 40 mm. **Series:** 100th Anniversary Birth of Liu Shaoqi **Rev:** Bust facing wearing neckerchief

Date	Mintage	XF40	MS60	MS63	MS65	MS66
1998	30,000	PF65 125	PF67 135	PF69 145		

KM# 1155 10 YUAN
31.10 g., 0.999 Silver 0.999 oz. ASW, 40 mm. **Subject:** 100th Anniversary Birth of Liu Shaoqui **Rev:** Liu Shaoqui standing at microphone

Date	Mintage	XF40	MS60	MS63	MS65	MS66
1998	30,000	PF65 125	PF67 135	PF69 145		

KM# 1157 10 YUAN
31.39 g., 0.999 Silver 1.0082 oz. ASW **Obv:** National emblem, date below **Rev:** Portrait of Dr. Norman Bethune with surgery scene, denomination at left **Note:** Prev. Y#727.

Date	Mintage	XF40	MS60	MS63	MS65	MS66
1998	61,000	PF65 60.00	PF67 65.00	PF69 70.00		

KM# 1161 10 YUAN
31.10 g., 0.999 Silver 0.999 oz. ASW, 40 mm. **Series:** Kuan Yin **Rev:** Seated figure on lotis

Date	Mintage	XF40	MS60	MS63	MS65	MS66
1998	88,000	PF65 125	PF67 175	PF69 400		

KM# 1162 10 YUAN
3.11 g., 0.999 Gold 0.0999 oz. AGW, 18 mm. **Subject:** Dragon culture **Rev:** Dragon circle

Date	Mintage	XF40	MS60	MS63	MS65	MS66
1998	6,000	PF65 400	PF67 600	PF69 800		

KM# 1168 10 YUAN
31.10 g., 0.999 Silver 0.999 oz. ASW, 40 mm. **Subject:** Macao's return to China **Rev:** Birds flying over lablet, lighthouse at left, gate at right

Date	Mintage	XF40	MS60	MS63	MS65	MS66
1998	88,000	PF65 120	PF67 125	PF69 135		

KM# 1174.1 10 YUAN
31.10 g., 0.999 Silver 0.9989 oz. ASW, 40 mm. **Obv:** Radiant winged pillar monument above flowers **Rev:** Child holding vase, elephant at left **Edge:** Reeded **Note:** Prev. Y#1131.1.

Date	Mintage	XF40	MS60	MS63	MS65	MS66
1998	80,000	—	—	70.00	75.00	80.00

KM# 1174.2 10 YUAN
31.10 g., 0.999 Silver 0.9989 oz. ASW, 40 mm. **Obv:** Radiant winged pillar monument above flowers **Rev:** Multicolor child holding vase, elephant at left **Edge:** Reeded **Note:** Prev. Y#1131.2.

Date	Mintage	XF40	MS60	MS63	MS65	MS66
1998	100,000	PF65 100	PF67 125			

KM# 1175 10 YUAN
3.11 g., 0.999 Gold 0.0999 oz. AGW Colorized, 18 mm. **Series:** Traditional Chinese auspicious matter **Rev:** White elephant and man in red outfit

Date	Mintage	XF40	MS60	MS63	MS65	MS66
1998	20,000	PF65 170	PF67 200			

KM# 1176 10 YUAN
31.47 g., 0.999 Silver 1.0108 oz. ASW **Subject:** Celebrating Spring **Obv:** Radiant lantern, date below **Rev:** Three children about to fly kites, denomination below **Note:** Prev. Y#744.

Date	Mintage	XF40	MS60	MS63	MS65	MS66
1998	80,000	—	—	60.00	65.00	70.00
1998	60,000	PF65 70.00	PF67 80.00	PF69 90.00		

KM# A1179 10 YUAN
31.10 g., 0.999 Silver 0.999 oz. ASW, 40 mm. **Subject:** Spring greetings **Obv:** Lantern and rays **Rev:** Three figures

Date	Mintage	XF40	MS60	MS63	MS65	MS66
1998	60,000	PF65 125	PF67 135	PF69 145		

KM# 1196 10 YUAN
31.10 g., 0.999 Silver 0.999 oz. ASW, 40 mm. **Subject:** Vault Protector **Obv:** Denomination, inscription and ornamental design,square cutout at center **Rev:** Old cash coin characters, square cutout at center **Edge:** Reeded **Note:** Square holed cash coin design. Prev. Y#1064.

Date	Mintage	XF40	MS60	MS63	MS65	MS66
1998	100,000	PF65 65.00	PF67 70.00	PF69 75.00		

KM# 1197 10 YUAN
3.11 g., 0.999 Gold 0.0999 oz. AGW, 18 mm. **Subject:** Vault Protector **Obv:** Denomination, inscription and ornamental design **Rev:** Old cash coin characters **Edge:** Reeded **Note:** Square holed cash coin design. Prev. Y#1065.

Date	Mintage	XF40	MS60	MS63	MS65	MS66
1998	—	PF65 200	PF67 250	PF69 280		

KM# 1224 10 YUAN
31.10 g., 0.999 Silver 0.999 oz. ASW, 40 mm. **Subject:** Bejing Coin and Stamp Fair **Rev:** Gilt panda seated on rock

Date	Mintage	XF40	MS60	MS63	MS65	MS66
1999	40,000	PF65 150	PF67 170	PF69 190		

KM# 1240 10 YUAN
31.10 g., 0.999 Silver 0.999 oz. ASW, 27.5 x 42 mm. **Subject:** Master Painter Zhang Daqian **Obv:** Bust facing **Rev:** Large flower **Shape:** Rectangle

Date	Mintage	XF40	MS60	MS63	MS65	MS66
1999	10,000	PF65 150	PF67 170	PF69 190		

KM# 1241 10 YUAN
31.10 g., 0.999 Silver 0.999 oz. ASW, 27.5 x 42 mm. **Subject:** Master Painter Zhang Daiqian **Obv:** Portrait facing **Rev:** Bud on flora bench **Shape:** Rectangle

Date	Mintage	XF40	MS60	MS63	MS65	MS66
1999	10,000	PF65 150	PF67 170	PF69 190		

KM# 1242 10 YUAN
30.92 g., 0.999 Silver 0.9931 oz. ASW, 40 mm. **Subject:** Yin and Yang Concept **Obv:** Gate, date below **Rev:** Gold-plated standing goddess, denomination at right **Edge:** Reeded **Note:** Prev. Y#1078.

Date	Mintage	XF40	MS60	MS63	MS65	MS66
1999	—	PF65 120	PF67 130	PF69 140		

KM# 1243 10 YUAN
31.10 g., 0.999 Silver 0.999 oz. ASW, 40 mm. **Obv:** Building on top of E Mei Mountain, date below **Rev:** The Kuan Yin Buddha, denomination at left **Edge:** Reeded **Note:** Prev. Y#1207.

Date	Mintage	XF40	MS60	MS63	MS65	MS66
1999	60,000	—	—	90.00	100	110

KM# 1244 10 YUAN
31.10 g., 0.999 Silver 0.999 oz. ASW, 40 mm. **Subject:** Kuan Yin **Obv:** Temple **Rev:** Female holding mirror

Date	Mintage	XF40	MS60	MS63	MS65	MS66
1999	60,000	PF65 60.00	PF67 65.00	PF69 70.00		

KM# 1246 10 YUAN
31.10 g., 0.999 Silver 0.999 oz. ASW, 40 mm. **Subject:** 50th Anniversary - PRC **Rev:** Three soldiers

Date	Mintage	XF40	MS60	MS63	MS65	MS66
1999	84,900	PF65 125	PF67 135	PF69 150		

KM# 1247 10 YUAN
7.80 g., Bi-Metallic Brass center in Copper-Nickel ring, 25.5 mm. **Subject:** 50th Anniversary - People's Republic **Obv:** Fireworks above building **Rev:** Birds above "50" **Edge:** Reeded and plain sections **Note:** Prev. Y#1059.

Date	Mintage	XF40	MS60	MS63	MS65	MS66
1999	—	—	9.00	12.00	—	—

KM# 1248 10 YUAN
31.10 g., 0.999 Silver 0.999 oz. ASW **Subject:** 50th Anniversary PRC **Rev:** Arrow, progress scenes

Date	Mintage	XF40	MS60	MS63	MS65	MS66
1999	84,900	PF65 120	PF67 130	PF69 140		

KM# 1252 10 YUAN
31.10 g., 0.999 Silver 0.999 oz. ASW **Obv:** Wan Chun Pavilion, date below **Rev:** Gold-plated Chinese roses, denomination at lower left **Note:** Prev. Y#943.

Date	Mintage	XF40	MS60	MS63	MS65	MS66
1999	100,000	—	—	125	—	—

KM# 1253 10 YUAN
31.10 g., 0.999 Silver 0.999 oz. ASW **Obv:** Da Guan Tower in Kunming, date below **Rev:** Multicolor camellias, denomination upper right **Note:** Prev. Y#944.

Date	Mintage	XF40	MS60	MS63	MS65	MS66
1999	100,000	PF65 120	PF67 130	PF69 140		

KM# 1254 10 YUAN
31.10 g., 0.999 Silver 0.999 oz. ASW, 40 mm. **Subject:** 22nd World Philatelic Congress **Rev:** UPO logo

Date	Mintage	XF40	MS60	MS63	MS65	MS66
1999	50,000	PF65 110	PF67 120	PF69 130		

KM# 1255 10 YUAN
31.10 g., 0.999 Silver 0.999 oz. ASW, 40 mm. **Subject:** 22nd World Philatelic Congress **Obv:** Logo **Rev:** Congress arch, stamps

Date	Mintage	XF40	MS60	MS63	MS65	MS66
1999	50,000	PF65 90.00	PF67 100	PF69 110		

KM# 1257 10 YUAN
31.10 g., 0.999 Silver 0.999 oz. ASW, 40 mm. **Series:** Traditional Chinese suspicious matters **Rev:** Boy holding up large carp

Date	Mintage	XF40	MS60	MS63	MS65	MS66
1999	100,000	PF65 120	PF67 130	PF69 140		

KM# 1258 10 YUAN
31.10 g., 0.999 Silver 0.999 oz. ASW, 40 mm. **Obv:** Radiant winged pillar above flowers **Rev:** Multicolor child holding a red carp above his head **Edge:** Reeded **Note:** Prev. Y#1228.

Date	Mintage	XF40	MS60	MS63	MS65	MS66
1999	—	PF65 100	PF67 110	PF69 120		

KM# 1259 10 YUAN
31.26 g., 0.999 Silver 1.004 oz. ASW **Subject:** Celebrating Spring **Obv:** Radiant lantern, date below **Rev:** Multicolor, children lighting firecrackers, denomination above **Note:** Prev. Y#914.2.

Date	Mintage	XF40	MS60	MS63	MS65	MS66
1999	—	PF65 110	PF67 120	PF69 135		

KM# 1260 10 YUAN
31.10 g., 0.999 Silver 0.999 oz. ASW Colorized, 40 mm. **Series:** Rare bird **Rev:** Bird amongst flora **Note:** Colorized

Date	Mintage	XF40	MS60	MS63	MS65	MS66
1999	100,000	PF65 120	PF67 130	PF69 140		

KM# 1262 10 YUAN
31.10 g., 0.999 Silver 0.999 oz. ASW, 42 x 27.5 mm. **Series:** Ancient Chinese famous paintings **Obv:** Two horse carts one right other left **Rev:** Warrior chariot left **Shape:** Rectangle

Date	Mintage	XF40	MS60	MS63	MS65	MS66
1999	13,800	PF65 120	PF67 130	PF69 140		

KM# 1263 10 YUAN
31.10 g., 0.999 Silver 0.999 oz. ASW, 42 x 27.5 mm. **Series:** Ancient Chinese famous paintings **Obv:** Two horse carts one right other left **Rev:** Royal boat left **Shape:** Rectangle

Date	Mintage	XF40	MS60	MS63	MS65	MS66
1999	13,800	PF65 120	PF67 130	PF69 140		

KM# 1264 10 YUAN
31.10 g., 0.999 Silver 0.999 oz. ASW, 42 x 27.5 mm. **Series:** Ancient Chinese famous paintings **Rev:** Horseman left **Shape:** Rectangle

Date	Mintage	XF40	MS60	MS63	MS65	MS66
1999	13,800	PF65 120	PF67 130	PF69 140		

KM# 1265 10 YUAN
31.10 g., 0.999 Silver 0.999 oz. ASW, 42 x 27.5 mm. **Series:** Ancient Chinese famous paintings **Obv:** Two horse carts one right other left **Rev:** Trees **Shape:** Rectangle

Date	Mintage	XF40	MS60	MS63	MS65	MS66
1999	13,800	PF65 120	PF67 130	PF69 140		

KM# 1266 10 YUAN
31.10 g., 0.999 Silver 0.999 oz. ASW, 42 x 27.5 mm. **Series:** Ancient Chinese famous paintings **Obv:** Two horse carts one right other left **Rev:** Trees and groups of people **Shape:** Rectangle

Date	Mintage	XF40	MS60	MS63	MS65	MS66
1999	13,800	PF65 120	PF67 130	PF69 140		

KM# 1267 10 YUAN
31.10 g., 0.999 Silver 0.999 oz. ASW, 42 x 27.5 mm. **Series:** Ancient Chinese famous paintings **Obv:** Two horse carts one right other left **Rev:** Trees and river **Shape:** Rectangle

Date	Mintage	XF40	MS60	MS63	MS65	MS66
1999	13,800	PF65 120	PF67 130	PF69 140		

KM# 1268 10 YUAN
31.10 g., 0.999 Silver 0.999 oz. ASW, 42 x 27.5 mm. **Series:** Ancient Chinese famous paintings **Obv:** Two horse carts one right other left **Rev:** Rocks in river **Shape:** Rectangle

Date	Mintage	XF40	MS60	MS63	MS65	MS66
1999	13,800	PF65 120	PF67 130	PF69 140		

KM# 1269 10 YUAN
31.10 g., 0.999 Silver 0.999 oz. ASW, 42 x 27.5 mm. **Series:** Ancient Chinese famous paintings **Obv:** Two horse carts one right other left **Rev:** People and horses **Shape:** Rectangle

Date	Mintage	XF40	MS60	MS63	MS65	MS66
1999	13,800	PF65 120	PF67 130	PF69 140		

KM# 1270 10 YUAN
31.10 g., 0.999 Silver 0.999 oz. ASW, 42 x 27.5 mm. **Series:** Tall tower in arc **Subject:** Suzhou Gardens **Obv:** Bridge and river, temple **Shape:** Rectangle

Date	Mintage	XF40	MS60	MS63	MS65	MS66
1999	11,800	PF65 120	PF67 130	PF69 140		

KM# 1271 10 YUAN
31.10 g., 0.999 Silver 0.999 oz. ASW, 42 x 27.5 mm. **Subject:** Suzhou Gardens **Obv:** Two tall towered temple **Rev:** Water side temple **Shape:** Rectangle

Date	Mintage	XF40	MS60	MS63	MS65	MS66
1999	11,800	PF65 120	PF67 130	PF69 140		

KM# 1272 10 YUAN
31.10 g., 0.999 Silver 0.999 oz. ASW, 42 x 27.5 mm. **Series:** Temple at right in arc **Subject:** Suzhou Gardens **Obv:** Lakeside temple with reflection **Shape:** Rectangle

Date	Mintage	XF40	MS60	MS63	MS65	MS66
1999	11,800	PF65 120	PF67 130	PF69 140		

KM# 1273 10 YUAN
31.10 g., 0.999 Silver 0.999 oz. ASW, 42 x 27.5 mm. **Subject:** Suzhou Garden **Obv:** Temple in arc **Rev:** Temple by bridge and rock formation **Shape:** Rectangle

Date	Mintage	XF40	MS60	MS63	MS65	MS66
1999	11,800	PF65 120	PF67 130	PF69 140		

KM# 1274 10 YUAN
31.10 g., 0.999 Silver 0.999 oz. ASW, 40 mm. **Subject:** 10th Anniversary of Hope Project **Obv:** Logo and flora below **Rev:** Two children holding plaque

Date	Mintage	XF40	MS60	MS63	MS65	MS66
1999	60,000	PF65 120	PF67 130	PF69 140		

KM# 1275 10 YUAN
31.10 g., 0.999 Silver 0.999 oz. ASW, 14 x 120 mm. **Subject:** Fan paintings **Obv:** Rice plant design in arc **Rev:** Flora plants **Shape:** Arc

Date	Mintage	XF40	MS60	MS63	MS65	MS66
1999	11,800	PF65 100	PF67 110	PF69 120		

KM# 1276 10 YUAN
31.10 g., 0.999 Silver 0.999 oz. ASW, 14 x 120 mm. **Subject:** Fan paintings **Obv:** Rice plant desing in arc **Rev:** Boat, trees and mountain scene **Shape:** Arc

Date	Mintage	XF40	MS60	MS63	MS65	MS66
1999	11,800	PF65 100	PF67 110	PF69 120		

KM# 1277 10 YUAN
31.10 g., 0.999 Silver 0.999 oz. ASW, 14 x 120 mm. **Subject:** Fan paintings **Obv:** Rice plant desing in arc **Rev:** One tree **Shape:** Arc

Date	Mintage	XF40	MS60	MS63	MS65	MS66
1999	11,800	PF65 100	PF67 110	PF69 120		

KM# 1278 10 YUAN
31.10 g., 0.999 Silver 0.999 oz. ASW, 31.1035 mm. **Subject:** Fan paintings **Obv:** Rice plant in arc **Rev:** Fisherman and fish **Shape:** Arc

Date	Mintage	XF40	MS60	MS63	MS65	MS66
1999	11,800	PF65 100	PF67 110	PF69 120		

KM# A1279 10 YUAN
31.10 g., 0.999 Silver 0.999 oz. ASW, 40 mm. **Subject:** Return of Macao **Rev:** Large 99 above buildings

Date	Mintage	XF40	MS60	MS63	MS65	MS66
1999	88,000	PF65 120	PF67 130	PF69 140		

KM# 1279 10 YUAN
7.78 g., Bi-Metallic Brass center in Copper-Nickel ring, 25.48 mm. **Subject:** Return of Macau **Obv:** Stylized water lily **Rev:** Modern harbor and city view, birds and banner above **Edge:** Segmented reeding **Note:** Prev. Y#1056.

Date	Mintage	XF40	MS60	MS63	MS65	MS66
1999	—	—	7.00	9.00	—	—

KM# 1283 10 YUAN
31.10 g., 0.999 Silver 0.999 oz. ASW, 40 mm. **Subject:** Bejing opera **Rev:** Actress with long red ribbon **Note:** Colorized

Date	Mintage	XF40	MS60	MS63	MS65	MS66
1999	38,000	PF65 120	PF67 130	PF69 140		

KM# 1284 10 YUAN
31.10 g., 0.999 Silver 0.999 oz. ASW, 40 mm. **Subject:** Bejing opera **Rev:** Female standing holding round fan **Note:** Colorized

Date	Mintage	XF40	MS60	MS63	MS65	MS66
1999	38,000	PF65 120	PF67 130	PF69 140		

KM# 1285 10 YUAN
31.10 g., 0.999 Silver 0.999 oz. ASW, 40 mm. **Subject:** Bejing opera **Rev:** Figure standing holding whip **Note:** Colorized

Date	Mintage	XF40	MS60	MS63	MS65	MS66
1999	38,000	PF65 120	PF67 130	PF69 140		

KM# 1286 10 YUAN
31.10 g., 0.999 Silver 0.999 oz. ASW, 40 mm. **Subject:** Bejing opera **Rev:** Actor standing holding sword

Date	Mintage	XF40	MS60	MS63	MS65	MS66
1999	38,000	PF65 120	PF67 130	PF69 140		

KM# 1300 10 YUAN
7.80 g., Bi-Metallic Copper-Nickel center in Brass ring, 25.5 mm. **Obv:** Rocket and city view above wheel **Rev:** Number two and eye above map of China **Edge:** Segmented reeding **Note:** Prev. Y#1123.

Date	Mintage	XF40	MS60	MS63	MS65	MS66
2000	—	—	9.00	—	—	—

KM# 1311 10 YUAN
31.10 g., 0.999 Silver 0.999 oz. ASW, 40 mm. **Series:** Classic literature **Subject:** Dream of red mansion **Rev:** Female seated, child standing, three herons **Shape:** Octagon **Note:** Colorized

Date	Mintage	XF40	MS60	MS63	MS65	MS66
2000	38,000	PF65 125	PF67 135	PF69 150		

KM# 1312 10 YUAN
31.10 g., 0.999 Silver 0.999 oz. ASW, 40 mm. **Series:** Classical literature **Subject:** Dream of red mansion **Rev:** Female standing by red fence **Shape:** Octagon **Note:** Colorized

Date	Mintage	XF40	MS60	MS63	MS65	MS66
2000	38,000	PF65 125	PF67 135	PF69 150		

KM# 1313 10 YUAN
31.10 g., 0.999 Silver 0.999 oz. ASW, 40 mm. **Series:** Classical literature **Subject:** Dream of red mansion **Rev:** Female in yellow kimono in room with red curtains **Shape:** Octagon **Note:** Colorized

Date	Mintage	XF40	MS60	MS63	MS65	MS66
2000	38,000	PF65 125	PF67 135	PF69 150		

KM# 1314 10 YUAN
31.10 g., 0.999 Silver 0.999 oz. ASW, 40 mm. **Series:** Classical literature **Subject:** Dream of red mansion **Rev:** Female in blue kimono, cherry blossom **Shape:** Octagon **Note:** Colorized

Date	Mintage	XF40	MS60	MS63	MS65	MS66
2000	38,000	PF65 125	PF67 135	PF69 150		

KM# 1317 10 YUAN
31.10 g., 0.999 Silver 0.999 oz. ASW, 40 mm. **Subject:** Dragons **Shape:** Round **Note:** Prev. Y#1048.

Date	Mintage	XF40	MS60	MS63	MS65	MS66
2000	50,000	—	—	—	200	220

KM# 1318 10 YUAN
23.04 g., 0.900 Silver 0.6666 oz. ASW, 40 mm. **Obv:** Building within circle, date below **Rev:** Multicolor dragon, denomination at right **Note:** Prev. Y#993.

Date	Mintage	XF40	MS60	MS63	MS65	MS66
2000	100,000	—	—	—	125	130

KM# 1328 10 YUAN
31.10 g., 0.999 Silver 0.999 oz. ASW, 40 mm. **Series:** Rare bird **Rev:** Bird on pink blossom **Note:** Colorized

Date	Mintage	XF40	MS60	MS63	MS65	MS66
2000	100,000	PF65 50.00	PF67 60.00	PF69 70.00		

KM# 1330 10 YUAN
3.11 g., 0.999 Gold 0.0999 oz. AGW, 18 mm. **Subject:** Goddess Kuan Yin **Obv:** Putuo Mountain Gate **Rev:** Standing Kuan Yin with holographic background **Edge:** Reeded **Note:** Prev. Y#996.

Date	Mintage	XF40	MS60	MS63	MS65	MS66
2000	33,000	—	—	—	180	210

KM# 1331 10 YUAN
31.10 g., 0.999 Silver 0.999 oz. ASW, 40 mm. **Subject:** Y2K **Obv:** Monument **Rev:** World Globe as an eye above value **Edge:** Reeded **Note:** Prev. Y#1235.

Date	Mintage	XF40	MS60	MS63	MS65	MS66
2000	88,000	PF65 100	PF67 110	PF69 125		

KM# 1332 10 YUAN
3.11 g., 0.999 Gold 0.0999 oz. AGW **Subject:** Y2K **Note:** Prev. Y#994.

Date	Mintage	XF40	MS60	MS63	MS65	MS66
2000	50,000	—	—	—	175	185

KM# 1338 10 YUAN
31.10 g., 0.999 Silver 0.999 oz. ASW, 40 mm. **Subject:** Beijing opera **Rev:** 2 figures with chairs **Note:** Colorized

Date	Mintage	XF40	MS60	MS63	MS65	MS66
2000	38,000	PF65 125	PF67 135	PF69 150		

KM# 1339 10 YUAN
31.10 g., 0.999 Silver 0.999 oz. ASW, 40 mm. **Subject:** Beijing opera **Rev:** 2 figures one with sword **Note:** Colorized

Date	Mintage	XF40	MS60	MS63	MS65	MS66
2000	38,000	PF65 125	PF67 135	PF69 150		

KM# 1340 10 YUAN
31.10 g., 0.999 Silver 0.999 oz. ASW, 40 mm. **Subject:** Beijing opera **Rev:** Two figures both in yellow kimonos **Note:** Colorized

Date	Mintage	XF40	MS60	MS63	MS65	MS66
2000	38,000	PF65 125	PF67 135	PF69 150		

KM# 1341 10 YUAN
31.10 g., 0.999 Silver 0.999 oz. ASW, 40 mm. **Subject:** Beijing opera **Rev:** Two figures one with blue and white diamond kimono **Note:** Colorized

Date	Mintage	XF40	MS60	MS63	MS65	MS66
2000	38,000	PF65 125	PF67 135	PF69 150		

KM# 33 15 YUAN
10.00 g., 0.800 Silver 0.2572 oz. ASW **Series:** Olympics **Obv:** National emblem, denomination below **Rev:** Ancient archers, date below **Note:** Piedfort-type planchet. Prev. Y#745.

Date	Mintage	XF40	MS60	MS63	MS65	MS66
1980	15,000	—	—	100	110	120

KM# 34 20 YUAN
10.35 g., 0.850 Silver 0.2828 oz. ASW, 28 mm. **Series:** 1980 Olympics **Subject:** Wrestling **Obv:** National emblem, denomination below **Rev:** Wrestlers, date below **Note:** Prev. Y#18.

Date	Mintage	XF40	MS60	MS63	MS65	MS66
1980	29,000	PF65 50.00	PF67 60.00	PF69 70.00		

KM# 318 20 YUAN
62.21 g., 0.999 Silver 1.998 oz. ASW **Rev:** Phoenix and dragon **Note:** Prev. Y#207.

Date	Mintage	XF40	MS60	MS63	MS65	MS66
1990	5,000	PF65 700	PF67 950	PF69 1,200		

KM# 452 20 YUAN
62.21 g., 0.999 Silver 1.998 oz. ASW **Obv:** Great Wall, date below **Rev:** Horse and dragon, denomination at right **Note:** Prev. Y#888.

Date	Mintage	XF40	MS60	MS63	MS65	MS66
1992	6,000	PF65 700	PF67 800	PF69 1,000		

Note: Issued in 1996

KM# 966 20 YUAN
62.21 g., 0.999 Silver 1.998 oz. ASW **Obv:** Bai Di city gate, date at bottom **Rev:** Yangtze River scene, denomination at bottom **Shape:** Rectangular **Note:** Prev. Y#595.

Date	Mintage	XF40	MS60	MS63	MS65	MS66
1996	8,000	PF65 225	PF67 325	PF69 400		

KM# 967 20 YUAN
62.21 g., 0.999 Silver 1.998 oz. ASW **Obv:** Qu Yuan Temple, date at bottom **Rev:** River scene, denomination below **Shape:** Rectangular **Note:** Prev. Y#596.

Date	Mintage	XF40	MS60	MS63	MS65	MS66
1996	8,000	PF65 225	PF67 325	PF69 400		

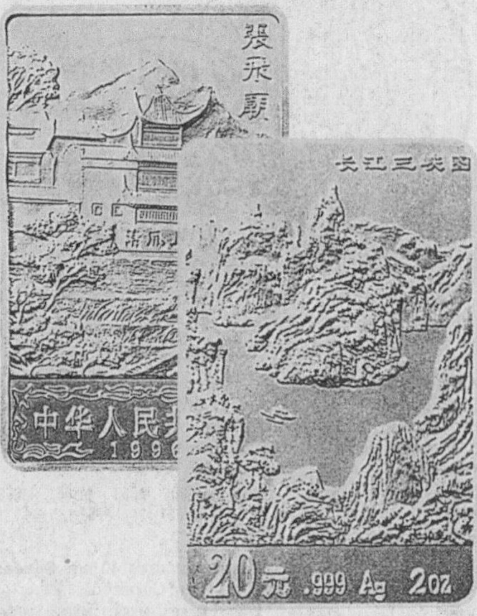

KM# 968 20 YUAN
62.21 g., 0.999 Silver 1.998 oz. ASW **Obv:** Zhang Fei Temple, date at bottom **Rev:** River scene, denomination below **Shape:** Rectangular **Note:** Prev. Y#597.

Date	Mintage	XF40	MS60	MS63	MS65	MS66
1996	8,000	PF65 225	PF67 325	PF69 400		

KM# 969 20 YUAN
62.21 g., 0.999 Silver 1.998 oz. ASW **Obv:** Zhao Jun Temple, date at bottom **Rev:** River scene, denomination below **Shape:** Rectangular **Note:** Prev. Y#598.

Date	Mintage	XF40	MS60	MS63	MS65	MS66
1996	8,000	PF65 225	PF67 325	PF69 400		

KM# 1164 20 YUAN

62.21 g., 0.999 Silver 1.998 oz. ASW, 55 x 36 mm. **Subject:** New look of Hong Kong **Obv:** Two flags, sprigs below **Rev:** Suspension bridge **Shape:** Rectangle

Date	Mintage	XF40	MS60	MS63	MS65	MS66
1998	11,800	PF65 250	PF67 350			

KM# 1165 20 YUAN

62.25 g., 0.999 Silver 1.9994 oz. ASW, 55 x 36 mm. **Subject:** New look of Hong Kong **Obv:** Two flags, sprigs below **Rev:** Modern tower and buildings **Shape:** Rectangle

Date	Mintage	XF40	MS60	MS63	MS65	MS66
1998	11,800	PF65 250	PF67 350			

KM# 1166 20 YUAN

62.21 g., 0.999 Silver 1.998 oz. ASW, 55 x 36 mm. **Subject:** New look of Hong Kong **Obv:** Two flags, sprigs below **Rev:** Modern domed building, skyline **Shape:** Rectangle

Date	Mintage	XF40	MS60	MS63	MS65	MS66
1998	11,800	PF65 250	PF67 350			

KM# 1167 20 YUAN

62.21 g., 0.999 Silver 1.998 oz. ASW, 55 x 36 mm. **Subject:** New look of Hong Kong **Obv:** Two flags, sprigs below **Rev:** Large buda statue **Shape:** Rectangle

Date	Mintage	XF40	MS60	MS63	MS65	MS66
1998	11,800	PF65 250	PF67 350			

KM# 1181 20 YUAN

62.21 g., 0.999 Silver 1.998 oz. ASW, 55 x 36 mm. **Series:** Ancient paintings **Obv:** Tall temple and buildings **Rev:** Large black horse in rural scene **Shape:** Rectangle

Date	Mintage	XF40	MS60	MS63	MS65	MS66
1998	18,800	PF65 300	PF67 320	PF69 330		

KM# 1182 20 YUAN

62.21 g., 0.999 Silver 1.998 oz. ASW, 55 x 36 mm. **Series:** Ancient paintings **Obv:** Tall temple and buildings **Rev:** Buildings in rural scene **Shape:** Rectangle

Date	Mintage	XF40	MS60	MS63	MS65	MS66
1998	18,800	PF65 300	PF67 320	PF69 330		

KM# 1183 20 YUAN

62.21 g., 0.999 Silver 1.998 oz. ASW, 55 x 36 mm. **Series:** Ancient paintings **Obv:** Tall temple and buildings **Rev:** More buildings in rural scene **Shape:** Rectangle

Date	Mintage	XF40	MS60	MS63	MS65	MS66
1998	18,800	PF65 300	PF67 320	PF69 330		

KM# 1184 20 YUAN

62.21 g., 0.999 Silver 1.998 oz. ASW, 55 x 36 mm. **Series:** Ancient paintings **Obv:** Tall temple and buildings **Rev:** Buildings and ships in scene **Shape:** Rectangle

Date	Mintage	XF40	MS60	MS63	MS65	MS66
1998	18,800	PF65 300	PF67 320	PF69 330		

KM# 1185 20 YUAN

62.21 g., 0.999 Silver 1.998 oz. ASW, 55 x 36 mm. **Series:** Ancient paintings **Obv:** Tall temple and buildings **Rev:** Arch and buildings **Shape:** Rectangle

Date	Mintage	XF40	MS60	MS63	MS65	MS66
1998	18,800	PF65 250	PF67 270	PF69 280		

KM# 1186 20 YUAN

62.21 g., 0.999 Silver 1.998 oz. ASW, 55 x 36 mm. **Series:** Ancient paintings **Obv:** Tall temple and buildings **Rev:** Ships and rural scene **Shape:** Rectangle

Date	Mintage	XF40	MS60	MS63	MS65	MS66
1998	18,800	PF65 300	PF67 320	PF69 330		

KM# 1189 20 YUAN

62.21 g., 0.999 Silver 1.998 oz. ASW, 19 x 29 mm. **Series:** Guilien scenery **Obv:** Natural bridge archway at sea shore **Rev:** Tall coastal islands **Shape:** Rectangle

Date	Mintage	XF40	MS60	MS63	MS65	MS66
1998	18,800	PF65 300	PF67 320	PF69 330		

KM# 1190 20 YUAN

62.21 g., 0.999 Silver 1.998 oz. ASW, 19 x 29 mm. **Series:** Guilien scenery **Obv:** 4 arched bridge **Rev:** Tall coastal islands **Shape:** Rectangle

Date	Mintage	XF40	MS60	MS63	MS65	MS66
1998	18,800	PF65 250	PF67 270	PF69 280		

KM# A1191 20 YUAN

62.21 g., 0.999 Silver 1.998 oz. ASW, 19 x 29 mm. **Series:** Guilien scenery **Obv:** Tall out crop with pagoda at top **Rev:** Tall coastal islands **Shape:** Rectangle

Date	Mintage	XF40	MS60	MS63	MS65	MS66
1998	18,800	PF65 250	PF67 275	PF69 300		

KM# 1191 20 YUAN

62.21 g., 0.999 Silver 1.998 oz. ASW, 19 x 29 mm. **Series:** Guilien scenery **Obv:** Long arched bridge **Rev:** Tall coastal islands **Shape:** Rectangle

Date	Mintage	XF40	MS60	MS63	MS65	MS66
1998	18,800	PF65 300	PF67 330	PF69 350		

KM# 1344 20 YUAN

62.21 g., 0.999 Silver 1.998 oz. ASW, 55 x 36 mm. **Subject:** 100th Anniversary of finding Dun Huang Grottoes scripture cave **Obv:** Temple **Rev:** Figure in flight left **Shape:** Rectangle

Date	Mintage	XF40	MS60	MS63	MS65	MS66
2000	11,800	PF65 255	PF67 375	PF69 500		

KM# 1345 20 YUAN

62.21 g., 0.999 Silver 1.998 oz. ASW, 55 x 36 mm. **Subject:** 100th Anniversary of finding Dun Huang Grottoes Scripture Cave **Rev:** Figure in flight right, circled around **Shape:** Rectangle

Date	Mintage	XF40	MS60	MS63	MS65	MS66
2000	11,800	PF65 255	PF67 375	PF69 500		

KM# 1346 20 YUAN

62.21 g., 0.999 Silver 1.998 oz. ASW, 55 x 36 mm. **Subject:** 100th Anniversary of finding Duan Huang Grottoes Scripture Cave **Obv:** Temple **Rev:** Figure in flight right holding lyre **Shape:** Rectangle

Date	Mintage	XF40	MS60	MS63	MS65	MS66
2000	11,800	PF65 255	PF67 375	PF69 500		

KM# 1347 20 YUAN

62.21 g., 0.999 Silver 1.998 oz. ASW, 55 x 36 mm. **Subject:** 100th Anniversary of finding Dun Huang Grottoes Scripture Cave **Obv:** Temple **Rev:** Figure in flight left, hand outstretched right **Shape:** Rectangle

Date	Mintage	XF40	MS60	MS63	MS65	MS66
2000	11,800	PF65 255	PF67 375	PF69 500		

KM# 1348 20 YUAN

62.21 g., 0.999 Silver 1.998 oz. ASW, 55 x 36 mm. **Subject:** 100th Anniversary of finding Dun Huang Grottoes Scripture Cave **Rev:** Figure in flight left, playing lyre **Shape:** Rectangle

Date	Mintage	XF40	MS60	MS63	MS65	MS66
2000	11,800	PF65 255	PF67 375	PF69 500		

KM# 1349 20 YUAN

62.21 g., 0.999 Silver 1.998 oz. ASW, 55 x 36 mm. **Subject:** 100th Anniversary of finding Dun Huang Grottoes Scripture Cave **Rev:** Figure in flight right, with tray service **Shape:** Rectangle

Date	Mintage	XF40	MS60	MS63	MS65	MS66
2000	11,800	PF65 255	PF67 375	PF69 500		

KM# 59 25 YUAN

19.44 g., 0.800 Silver 0.500 oz. ASW **Subject:** World Soccer Cup **Obv:** National emblem, date below **Rev:** Soccer players, denomination below **Note:** Prev. Y#36.

Date	Mintage	XF40	MS60	MS63	MS65	MS66
1982	40,000	PF65 75.00	PF67 85.00	PF69 95.00		

KM# 60 25 YUAN

19.44 g., 0.800 Silver 0.500 oz. ASW **Subject:** World Soccer Cup **Obv:** National emblem, date below **Rev:** Soccer players, denomination upper right **Note:** Prev. Y#35.

Date	Mintage	XF40	MS60	MS63	MS65	MS66
1982	40,000	PF65 75.00	PF67 85.00	PF69 95.00		

KM# 453 25 YUAN

7.78 g., 0.999 Gold 0.2498 oz. AGW **Obv:** Great Wall **Rev:** Horse and dragon **Note:** Prev. Y#889.

Date	Mintage	XF40	MS60	MS63	MS65	MS66
1992	5,000	PF65 1,000	PF67 1,400	PF69 1,600		

Note: Issued in 1996

KM# 461 25 YUAN

8.48 g., 0.917 Gold 0.250 oz. AGW **Subject:** Bronze Age Sculptures **Obv:** National emblem **Rev:** Ram **Note:** Prev. Y#555.

Date	Mintage	XF40	MS60	MS63	MS65	MS66
1992	—	PF65 1,200				

KM# 462 25 YUAN

8.48 g., 0.917 Gold 0.250 oz. AGW **Subject:** Bronze Age Sculptures **Rev:** Panther **Note:** Prev. Y#556.

Date	Mintage	XF40	MS60	MS63	MS65	MS66
1992	—	PF65 1,200				

KM# 495 25 YUAN

7.78 g., 0.999 Gold 0.2498 oz. AGW **Rev:** Chinese Gods: Fu, Lu, and Shu **Note:** Prev. Y#404.

Date	Mintage	XF40	MS60	MS63	MS65	MS66
1993	Est. 3000	—	—	—	550	—

KM# 496 25 YUAN

7.78 g., 0.9995 Platinum 0.2499 oz. APW **Series:** Chinese Inventions and Discoveries **Obv:** Great Wall **Rev:** Mathematicians using an abacus **Note:** Prev. Y#1074.

Date	Mintage	XF40	MS60	MS63	MS65	MS66
1993	100	PF65 4,000	PF67 7,500	PF69 10,000		

KM# 497 25 YUAN

7.78 g., 0.9995 Platinum 0.2499 oz. APW **Series:** Chinese Inventions and Discoveries **Obv:** Great Wall **Rev:** Two men and Yin and Yang symbol **Note:** Prev. Y#1075.

Date	Mintage	XF40	MS60	MS63	MS65	MS66
1993	100	PF65 4,000	PF67 7,500	PF69 10,000		

KM# 498 25 YUAN

7.78 g., 0.9995 Platinum 0.2499 oz. APW, 21.95 mm. **Series:** Chinese Inventions and Discoveries **Obv:** Great Wall **Rev:** Stirrup and equestrians **Edge:** Reeded **Note:** Prev. Y#1072.

Date	Mintage	XF40	MS60	MS63	MS65	MS66
1993	100	PF65 4,000	PF67 7,500	PF69 10,000		

KM# 499 25 YUAN

7.78 g., 0.9995 Platinum 0.2499 oz. APW **Series:** Chinese Inventions and Discoveries **Obv:** Great Wall **Rev:** Umbrella use and repair scene **Note:** Prev. Y#1073.

Date	Mintage	XF40	MS60	MS63	MS65	MS66
1993	100	PF65 4,000	PF67 7,500	PF69 10,000		

KM# 500 25 YUAN

7.78 g., 0.9995 Platinum 0.2499 oz. APW **Series:** Chinese Inventions and Discoveries **Obv:** Great Wall **Rev:** Excavating the Terra-cotta army **Note:** Prev. Y#1076.

Date	Mintage	XF40	MS60	MS63	MS65	MS66
1993	100	PF65 4,000	PF67 7,500	PF69 10,000		

KM# 549 25 YUAN

7.78 g., 0.999 Gold 0.2497 oz. AGW **Rev:** Goddess Kuan Yin seated in flower, denomination at left **Note:** Prev. Y#502.

Date	Mintage	XF40	MS60	MS63	MS65	MS66
1993	1,000	PF65 550	PF67 575	PF69 600		

KM# 571 25 YUAN

8.49 g., 0.917 Gold 0.2503 oz. AGW **Subject:** Bronze Age Sculptures **Obv:** National emblem, date below **Rev:** Pig, left, denomination below **Note:** Prev. Y#409.

Date	Mintage	XF40	MS60	MS63	MS65	MS66
1993	—	PF65 1,000	PF67 1,200			

KM# 572 25 YUAN

8.49 g., 0.917 Gold 0.2503 oz. AGW **Subject:** Bronze Age Sculptures **Obv:** National emblem, date below **Rev:** Unicorn, right, denomination lower right **Note:** Prev. Y#408.

Date	Mintage	XF40	MS60	MS63	MS65	MS66
1993	—	PF65 1,000	PF67 1,200			

KM# 590 25 YUAN

7.78 g., 0.999 Gold 0.2497 oz. AGW **Subject:** Homeland Scenery **Obv:** Great Wall **Rev:** Large temple at Mount Heng **Note:** Prev. Y#775.

Date	Mintage	XF40	MS60	MS63	MS65	MS66
1993	8,888	PF65 475	PF67 550			

KM# 596 25 YUAN
7.78 g., 0.999 Gold 0.2497 oz. AGW **Obv:** Temple of Heaven **Rev:** Two peacocks, denomination above **Note:** Prev. Y#475.

Date	Mintage	XF40	MS60	MS63	MS65	MS66
1993 Prooflike	—	—	—	—	550	—

KM# 632 25 YUAN
7.78 g., 0.9995 Platinum 0.2499 oz. APW, 21.95 mm. **Subject:** Oriental Inventions **Obv:** Great Wall **Rev:** First records of comets **Note:** Prev. Y#1120; 1183.

Date	Mintage	XF40	MS60	MS63	MS65	MS66
1994	100	PF65 4,000	PF67 7,500	PF69 10,000		

KM# 633 25 YUAN
7.78 g., 0.9995 Platinum 0.2499 oz. APW, 21.95 mm. **Subject:** Oriental Inventions **Obv:** Great Wall **Rev:** First tuned bells **Note:** Prev. Y#1118; 1181.

Date	Mintage	XF40	MS60	MS63	MS65	MS66
1994	100	PF65 4,000	PF67 7,500	PF69 10,000		

KM# 634 25 YUAN
7.78 g., 0.9995 Platinum 0.2499 oz. APW, 21.95 mm. **Subject:** Oriental Inventions **Obv:** Great Wall **Rev:** First silken fabric **Note:** Prev. Y#1119; 1182.

Date	Mintage	XF40	MS60	MS63	MS65	MS66
1994	100	PF65 4,000	PF67 7,500	PF69 10,000		

KM# 635 25 YUAN
7.78 g., 0.9995 Platinum 0.2499 oz. APW, 21.95 mm. **Subject:** Oriental Inventions **Obv:** Great Wall **Rev:** First chain pumps used to draw water **Note:** Prev. Y#1122; 1185.

Date	Mintage	XF40	MS60	MS63	MS65	MS66
1994	100	PF65 4,000	PF67 7,500	PF69 10,000		

KM# 636 25 YUAN
7.78 g., 0.9995 Platinum 0.2499 oz. APW, 21.95 mm. **Subject:** Oriental Inventions **Obv:** Great Wall **Rev:** First masts for sailing **Note:** Prev. Y#1121.

Date	Mintage	XF40	MS60	MS63	MS65	MS66
1994	100	PF65 4,000	PF67 7,500	PF69 10,000		

KM# 664 25 YUAN
3.11 g., 0.999 Gold 0.0999 oz. AGW **Obv:** Great Wall, date below **Rev:** Goddess Kuan Yin holding child, facing, denomination at left **Note:** Prev. Y#511.

Date	Mintage	XF40	MS60	MS63	MS65	MS66
1994	1,000	PF65 500	PF67 1,000	PF69 1,500		

KM# 665 25 YUAN
3.11 g., 0.999 Gold 0.0999 oz. AGW **Obv:** Great Wall, date below **Rev:** Goddess Kuan Yin standing, denomination at right **Note:** Prev. Y#513.

Date	Mintage	XF40	MS60	MS63	MS65	MS66
1994	1,000	PF65 500	PF67 1,000	PF69 1,500		

KM# 666 25 YUAN
3.11 g., 0.999 Gold 0.0999 oz. AGW **Obv:** Great Wall, date below **Rev:** Goddess Kuan Yin with bottle, 3/4 left, denomination at right **Note:** Prev. Y#512.

Date	Mintage	XF40	MS60	MS63	MS65	MS66
1994	1,000	PF65 500	PF67 1,000	PF69 1,500		

KM# 667 25 YUAN
3.11 g., 0.999 Gold 0.0999 oz. AGW **Obv:** Great Wall, date below **Rev:** Goddess Kuan Yin seated, denomination at right **Note:** Prev. Y#514.

Date	Mintage	XF40	MS60	MS63	MS65	MS66
1994	1,000	PF65 500	PF67 1,000	PF69 1,500		

KM# 678 25 YUAN
7.78 g., 0.999 Gold 0.2497 oz. AGW **Obv:** Figure on Eastern unicorn, date below **Rev:** Unicorn, denomination at left, rose sprays below **Note:** Prev. Y#423.

Date	Mintage	XF40	MS60	MS63	MS65	MS66
1994	5,100	PF65 600	PF67 650	PF69 700		

KM# 694 25 YUAN
7.78 g., 0.999 Gold 0.2499 oz. AGW, 22 mm. **Series:** Famous paintings **Rev:** Three children playing with model ship

Date	Mintage	XF40	MS60	MS63	MS65	MS66
1994	1,000	PF65 600	PF67 1,250	PF69 2,000		

KM# 695 25 YUAN
7.78 g., 0.999 Gold 0.2499 oz. AGW, 22 mm. **Series:** Famous paintings **Rev:** Two children with dog

Date	Mintage	XF40	MS60	MS63	MS65	MS66
1994	1,000	PF65 475	PF67 650	PF69 800		

KM# 777 25 YUAN
7.83 g., 0.999 Gold 0.2515 oz. AGW **Subject:** Sea Goddess Mazhu **Obv:** Mazhu Temple **Rev:** Mazhu's portrayal **Note:** Prev. Y#835.

Date	Mintage	XF40	MS60	MS63	MS65	MS66
1995	3,000	PF65 475	PF67 650	PF69 800		

KM# 787 25 YUAN
7.78 g., 0.999 Gold 0.2497 oz. AGW, 22 mm. **Obv:** Pu-Tow temple **Rev:** Goddess of Mercy - with Lotus flower **Note:** Prev. Y#524.

Date	Mintage	XF40	MS60	MS63	MS65	MS66
1995	1,000	PF65 525	PF67 850	PF69 1,200		

KM# 788 25 YUAN
7.78 g., 0.999 Gold 0.2497 oz. AGW **Rev:** Goddess of Mercy with sceptre **Note:** Prev. Y#526.

Date	Mintage	XF40	MS60	MS63	MS65	MS66
1995	1,000	PF65 525	PF67 850	PF69 1,200		

KM# 789 25 YUAN
7.78 g., 0.999 Gold 0.2497 oz. AGW **Rev:** Goddess of Mercy with bowl **Note:** Prev. Y#527.

Date	Mintage	XF40	MS60	MS63	MS65	MS66
1995	1,000	PF65 525	PF67 850	PF69 1,200		

KM# 790 25 YUAN
7.78 g., 0.999 Gold 0.2497 oz. AGW **Rev:** Goddess of Mercy with wheel **Note:** Prev. Y#525.

Date	Mintage	XF40	MS60	MS63	MS65	MS66
1995	1,000	PF65 525	PF67 850	PF69 1,200		

KM# 797 25 YUAN
7.78 g., Bi-Metallic Gold center in Silver ring **Obv:** Building within circle, date below **Rev:** Unicorn with offspring, denomination at left, circle surrounds **Note:** Prev. Y#687; 1061.

Date	Mintage	XF40	MS60	MS63	MS65	MS66
1995	—	PF65 300	PF67 400	PF69 500		

KM# 798 25 YUAN
7.83 g., 0.999 Gold 0.2515 oz. AGW **Obv:** Eastern unicorn rearing, date below **Rev:** Western unicorn with offspring, denomination at left **Note:** Prev. Y#738.

Date	Mintage	XF40	MS60	MS63	MS65	MS66
1995	5,000	PF65 700	PF67 800	PF69 900		

KM# 943 25 YUAN
7.78 g., 0.999 Gold 0.2498 oz. AGW **Obv:** Eastern unicorn, date below **Rev:** Western unicorn and maiden, denomination at left **Note:** Prev. Y#743.

Date	Mintage	XF40	MS60	MS63	MS65	MS66
1996	3,000	PF65 700	PF67 800	PF69 900		

KM# 944 25 YUAN
7.78 g., 0.9995 Platinum 0.2499 oz. APW, 21.9 mm. **Subject:** Unicorn **Obv:** Eastern unicorn, full body, date below **Rev:** Western unicorn head, right, denomination at right **Edge:** Reeded **Note:** Prev. Y#955.

Date	Mintage	XF40	MS60	MS63	MS65	MS66
1996	—	PF65 800	PF67 1,000	PF69 1,200		

KM# 955 25 YUAN
7.78 g., 0.999 Gold 0.2498 oz. AGW **Subject:** Centennial of Chinese Post Office **Obv:** Modern postal stamp, date below **Rev:** Imperial postal stamp, denomination at right **Note:** Prev. Y#867.

Date	Mintage	XF40	MS60	MS63	MS65	MS66
1996	3,000	PF65 450	PF67 700	PF69 900		

KM# 1064 25 YUAN
7.78 g., 0.999 Gold 0.2498 oz. AGW **Subject:** Celebrating Spring **Obv:** Radiant lantern, date below **Rev:** Children setting off firecrackers, denomination above **Note:** Prev. Y#915.

Date	Mintage	XF40	MS60	MS63	MS65	MS66
1997	10,000	PF65 450	PF67 550	PF69 650		

KM# 1098 25 YUAN
7.78 g., 0.999 Gold 0.2498 oz. AGW **Subject:** China Palace Museum **Obv:** Forbidden City **Rev:** Inner view of palace **Note:** Prev. Y#1000.

Date	Mintage	XF40	MS60	MS63	MS65	MS66
1997	4,000	PF65 475	PF67 650	PF69 800		

KM# 1099 25 YUAN
7.78 g., 0.999 Gold 0.2498 oz. AGW **Subject:** China Palace Museum **Obv:** Forbidden City **Rev:** Imperial Gardens **Note:** Prev. Y#997.

Date	Mintage	XF40	MS60	MS63	MS65	MS66
1997	4,000	PF65 475	PF67 650	PF69 800		

KM# 1100 25 YUAN
7.78 g., 0.999 Gold 0.2498 oz. AGW **Subject:** China Palace Museum **Obv:** Forbidden City **Rev:** Jin Shui **Note:** Prev. Y#998.

Date	Mintage	XF40	MS60	MS63	MS65	MS66
1997	4,000	PF65 475	PF67 650	PF69 800		

KM# 1102 25 YUAN
7.78 g., 0.999 Gold 0.2498 oz. AGW **Subject:** China Palace Museum **Obv:** Forbidden City **Rev:** Quan Quin Palace **Note:** Prev. Y#999.

Date	Mintage	XF40	MS60	MS63	MS65	MS66
1997	4,000	PF65 475	PF67 650	PF69 800		

KM# A1180 25 YUAN
7.65 g., 0.999 Gold 0.2457 oz. AGW, 22 mm. **Subject:** Spring greeting **Obv:** Lantern in rays **Rev:** Three figures dancing

Date	Mintage	XF40	MS60	MS63	MS65	MS66
1998	10,000	PF65 450	PF67 625	PF69 750		

KM# 1329 25 YUAN
7.78 g., 0.9999 Gold 0.250 oz. AGW **Subject:** Bird **Rev:** Multicolored. **Note:** Prev. Y#1136.

Date	Mintage	XF40	MS60	MS63	MS65	MS66
2000	8,800	—	—	475	—	—

KM# 23 30 YUAN
16.00 g., Silver **Series:** Lake Placid 1980 - 13th Winter Olympic Games **Obv:** National emblem, denomination below **Rev:** Woman figure skater, within snowflake **Note:** Prev. Y#747.

Date	Mintage	XF40	MS60	MS63	MS65	MS66
1980	20,000	PF65 90.00	PF67 110	PF69 120		

KM# 24 30 YUAN
16.00 g., Silver **Series:** 1980 Olympics **Obv:** National emblem, denomination below **Rev:** Biathalon skier, within snowflake **Note:** Prev. Y#748.

Date	Mintage	XF40	MS60	MS63	MS65	MS66
1980	20,000	PF65 90.00	PF67 110	PF69 120		

KM# 25 30 YUAN
16.00 g., Silver **Series:** 1980 Olympics **Obv:** National emblem, denomination below **Rev:** Downhill skier, within snowflake **Note:** Prev. Y#746.

Date	Mintage	XF40	MS60	MS63	MS65	MS66
1980	20,000	PF65 90.00	PF67 110	PF69 120		

KM# 26 30 YUAN
15.00 g., 0.850 Silver 0.4099 oz. ASW **Series:** Lake Placid 1980 - 13th Winter Olympic Games **Obv:** National emblem, denomination below **Rev:** Woman speed skater, within snowflake **Note:** Prev. Y#21.

Date	Mintage	XF40	MS60	MS63	MS65	MS66
1980	20,000	PF65 90.00	PF67 110	PF69 120		

KM# 35 30 YUAN
15.00 g., 0.850 Silver 0.4099 oz. ASW **Series:** 1980 Olympics **Subject:** Equestrian **Obv:** National emblem, denomination below **Rev:** Horse racing, date below **Note:** Prev. Y#19.

Date	Mintage	XF40	MS60	MS63	MS65	MS66
1980	29,000	PF65 90.00	PF67 110	PF69 120		

KM# 36 30 YUAN
15.00 g., 0.850 Silver 0.4099 oz. ASW **Series:** 1980 Olympics **Obv:** National emblem, denomination below **Rev:** Soccer, date below **Note:** Prev. Y#20.

Date	Mintage	XF40	MS60	MS63	MS65	MS66
1980	29,000	PF65 90.00	PF67 110	PF69 120		

KM# 8 35 YUAN
19.44 g., 0.800 Silver 0.500 oz. ASW **Subject:** UNICEF and IYC **Obv:** National emblem and date above sprays **Rev:** Children planting a flower, denomination below **Note:** Prev. Y#8.

Date	Mintage	XF40	MS60	MS63	MS65	MS66
1979 Matte	1,000	—	5,500	—	—	—
1979	14,000	PF65 550	PF67 650	PF69 700		

KM# 50 35 YUAN
33.58 g., 0.800 Silver 0.8637 oz. ASW **Subject:** 70th Anniversary - 1911 Revolution **Obv:** Statue of Sun Yat-sen divides dates **Rev:** Mausoleum, denomination below **Note:** Prev. Y#46.

Date	Mintage	XF40	MS60	MS63	MS65	MS66
1981	3,885	PF65 1,350	PF67 1,450	PF69 1,550		

KM# 147 50 YUAN
155.50 g., 0.999 Silver 4.9944 oz. ASW, 70 mm. **Subject:** 120th Anniversary - Birth of Sun Yat-sen **Rev:** Sun Yat-sen standing, facing, denomination at left, circle surrounds **Note:** Illustration reduced. Prev. Y#108.

Date	Mintage	XF40	MS60	MS63	MS65	MS66
1986	3,000	PF65 850	PF67 1,000	PF69 1,200		

KM# 205 50 YUAN
155.50 g., 0.999 Silver 4.9944 oz. ASW, 70 mm. **Series:** Seoul 1988 - 24th Summer Olympic Games **Rev:** Volleyball game, denomination below **Note:** Illustration reduced. Prev. Y#170.

Date	Mintage	XF40	MS60	MS63	MS65	MS66
1988	3,898	PF65 1,200	PF67 1,400	PF69 1,600		

KM# 297 50 YUAN
155.68 g., 0.999 Silver 5.0002 oz. ASW **Series:** Albertville 1992 - 16th Winter Olympic Games **Obv:** National emblem, date below **Rev:** 3 speed skaters, denomination above **Note:** Illustration reduced. Prev. Y#321.

Date	Mintage	XF40	MS60	MS63	MS65	MS66
1990	10,000	PF65 550	PF67 650	PF69 750		

KM# 326 50 YUAN
15.55 g., 0.999 Gold 0.4995 oz. AGW **Subject:** Taiwan Scenery Series **Obv:** Great Wall **Rev:** Three buildings joined by docks and bridge **Note:** Prev. Y#707.

Date	Mintage	XF40	MS60	MS63	MS65	MS66
1990	—	PF65 1,200	PF67 1,400	PF69 1,600		

KM# 327 50 YUAN
15.55 g., 0.999 Gold 0.4995 oz. AGW **Subject:** Taiwan Scenery Series **Obv:** Great Wall **Rev:** Pondside building **Note:** Prev. Y#705.

Date	Mintage	XF40	MS60	MS63	MS65	MS66
1990	—	PF65 1,200	PF67 1,400	PF69 1,600		

KM# 328 50 YUAN
15.55 g., 0.999 Gold 0.4995 oz. AGW **Subject:** Taiwan Scenery Series **Obv:** Great Wall **Rev:** Pagoda **Note:** Prev. Y#704.

Date	Mintage	XF40	MS60	MS63	MS65	MS66
1990	—	PF65 1,200	PF67 1,400	PF69 1,600		

KM# 329 50 YUAN
15.55 g., 0.999 Gold 0.4995 oz. AGW **Subject:** Taiwan Scenery Series **Obv:** Great Wall **Rev:**. Hillside building **Note:** Prev. Y#706.

Date	Mintage	XF40	MS60	MS63	MS65	MS66
1990	—	PF65 1,200	PF67 1,400	PF69 1,600		

KM# 303 50 YUAN
155.50 g., 0.999 Silver 4.9944 oz. ASW **Series:** Barcelona 1992 - 25th Summer Olympic Games **Obv:** National emblem, date below **Rev:** Female runners, denomination above **Note:** Prev. Y#472.

Date	Mintage	XF40	MS60	MS63	MS65	MS66
1991	10,000	PF65 650	PF67 725	PF69 800		

KM# 382 50 YUAN
155.50 g., 0.999 Silver 4.9944 oz. ASW **Subject:** 80th Anniversary - 1911 Revolution **Obv:** Similar to 10 Yuan, Y#476,(building with two dates below) **Rev:** Sun Yat-Sen in uniform, facing, denomination at left **Note:** Prev. Y#477.

Date	Mintage	XF40	MS60	MS63	MS65	MS66
1991	1,000	PF65 3,500	PF67 4,500	PF69 6,000		

KM# 409 50 YUAN
155.50 g., 0.999 Silver 4.9944 oz. ASW, 70 mm. **Series:** Scientific and technical inventions **Rev:** Compass

Date	Mintage	XF40	MS60	MS63	MS65	MS66
1992	3,000	PF65 800	PF67 900	PF69 1,000		

KM# 463 50 YUAN
16.96 g., 0.917 Gold 0.500 oz. AGW **Subject:** Bronze Age Sculptures **Obv:** National emblem, date below **Rev:** Kneeling figure, denomination below **Note:** Prev. Y#557.

Date	Mintage	XF40	MS60	MS63	MS65	MS66
1992	—	PF65 2,500				

KM# 501 50 YUAN
15.55 g., 0.999 Gold 0.4995 oz. AGW **Subject:** Chinese Inventions and Discoveries **Obv:** Great Wall, denomination below **Rev:** Chin with Yin Yang, denomination below **Note:** Prev. Y#378.

Date	Mintage	XF40	MS60	MS63	MS65	MS66
1993	1,200	PF65 2,850	PF67 4,000	PF69 5,000		

KM# 502 50 YUAN
15.56 g., 0.999 Gold 0.4998 oz. AGW, 40 mm. **Series:** Scientific and technical inventions **Rev:** Three men standing over printing form

Date	Mintage	XF40	MS60	MS63	MS65	MS66
1993	1,200	PF65 2,850	PF67 4,000	PF69 5,000		

KM# 503 50 YUAN
15.55 g., 0.999 Gold 0.4995 oz. AGW **Subject:** Chinese Inventions and Discoveries **Obv:** Great Wall **Rev:** Stirrup **Note:** Prev. Y#765.

Date	Mintage	XF40	MS60	MS63	MS65	MS66
1993	1,200	PF65 2,850	PF67 4,000	PF69 5,000		

KM# 504 50 YUAN
15.55 g., 0.999 Gold 0.4995 oz. AGW **Subject:** Chinese Inventions and Discoveries **Obv:** Great Wall, date below **Rev:** Invention of the Umbrella, denomination at right **Note:** Prev. Y#401.

Date	Mintage	XF40	MS60	MS63	MS65	MS66
1993	1,200	PF65 2,850	PF67 4,000	PF69 5,000		

KM# 505 50 YUAN
15.55 g., 0.999 Gold 0.4995 oz. AGW **Subject:** Chinese Inventions and Discoveries **Obv:** Great Wall **Rev:** Excavation of the Terra-cotta Army **Note:** Prev. Y#766.

Date	Mintage	XF40	MS60	MS63	MS65	MS66
1993	1,200	PF65 2,850	PF67 4,000	PF69 5,000		

KM# 506 50 YUAN
15.55 g., 0.999 Gold 0.4995 oz. AGW **Subject:** Chinese Inventions and Discoveries **Obv:** Great Wall **Rev:** Discovery of mathematical zero **Note:** Prev. Y#767.

Date	Mintage	XF40	MS60	MS63	MS65	MS66
1993	1,200	PF65 2,850	PF67 4,000	PF69 4,000		

KM# 507 50 YUAN
155.52 g., 0.999 Silver 4.995 oz. ASW **Subject:** Chinese Gods: Fu, Lu and Shu **Obv:** Building and Great Wall, date below **Rev:** Three gods with symbol on panel and child **Note:** Prev. Y#405.

Date	Mintage	XF40	MS60	MS63	MS65	MS66
1993	1,000	PF65 1,700	PF67 2,400	PF69 3,000		

KM# 542 50 YUAN
15.55 g., 0.999 Gold 0.4995 oz. AGW **Subject:** Chairman Mao **Rev:** Bust, 3/4 left, denomination at left **Note:** Prev. Y#414.

Date	Mintage	XF40	MS60	MS63	MS65	MS66
1993	—	PF65 1,600	PF67 2,000	PF69 2,500		
1993 (s)	—	PF65 2,800	PF67 3,200	PF69 3,500		

KM# 543 50 YUAN
155.52 g., 0.999 Silver 4.995 oz. ASW, 70 mm. **Rev:** Chairman Mao writing, denomination at right **Note:** Illustration reduced. Prev. Y#413.

Date	Mintage	XF40	MS60	MS63	MS65	MS66
1993	1,500	PF65 1,500	PF67 1,650	PF69 1,800		

KM# 550 50 YUAN
15.55 g., 0.999 Gold 0.4995 oz. AGW **Obv:** Great Wall, date below **Rev:** Goddess Kuan Yin - seated in flower, denomination at left **Note:** Prev. Y#503.

Date	Mintage	XF40	MS60	MS63	MS65	MS66
1993	1,000	PF65 1,800				

KM# 565 50 YUAN

155.55 g., 0.999 Silver 4.9961 oz. ASW **Subject:** Chinese Wildlife **Obv:** National emblem, date below **Rev:** Brown bear and cub, denomination at right **Note:** Illustration reduced. Prev. Y#772.

Date	Mintage	XF40	MS60	MS63	MS65	MS66
1993	4,500	PF65 2,500		PF67 3,500	PF69 4,500	

KM# 573 50 YUAN

16.98 g., 0.917 Gold 0.5006 oz. AGW **Subject:** Bronze Age Sculptures **Obv:** National emblem, date below **Rev:** Kneeling man lantern, denomination at right **Note:** Prev. Y#410.

Date	Mintage	XF40	MS60	MS63	MS65	MS66
1993	500	PF65 2,250		PF67 3,200	PF69 4,000	

KM# 579 50 YUAN

15.55 g., 0.999 Gold 0.4995 oz. AGW **Subject:** Taiwan Temples **Obv:** Great Wall, date below **Rev:** Large temple, denomination below **Note:** Prev. Y#446.

Date	Mintage	XF40	MS60	MS63	MS65	MS66
1993	1,000	PF65 1,650		PF67 2,350	PF69 3,000	

KM# 580 50 YUAN

15.55 g., 0.999 Gold 0.4995 oz. AGW **Subject:** Taiwan Temples **Obv:** Great Wall, date below **Rev:** Small temple, denomination below **Note:** Prev. Y#447.

Date	Mintage	XF40	MS60	MS63	MS65	MS66
1993	1,000	PF65 1,650		PF67 2,350	PF69 3,000	

KM# 581 50 YUAN

15.55 g., 0.999 Gold 0.4995 oz. AGW **Subject:** Taiwan Temples **Obv:** Great Wall, date below **Rev:** Tower temple, denomination below **Note:** Prev. Y#448.

Date	Mintage	XF40	MS60	MS63	MS65	MS66
1993	—	PF65 1,650		PF67 2,350	PF69 3,000	

KM# 582 50 YUAN

15.55 g., 0.999 Gold 0.4995 oz. AGW **Subject:** Taiwan Temples **Obv:** Great Wall, date below **Rev:** Buddha statue, denomination below **Note:** Prev. Y#445.

Date	Mintage	XF40	MS60	MS63	MS65	MS66
1993	1,000	PF65 1,650		PF67 2,350	PF69 3,000	

KM# 591 50 YUAN

155.55 g., 0.999 Silver 4.9961 oz. ASW **Obv:** Great Wall **Rev:** Mount Hau and river **Note:** Prev. Y#776.

Date	Mintage	XF40	MS60	MS63	MS65	MS66
1993	8,888	PF65 600				

KM# 597 50 YUAN

155.50 g., 0.999 Silver 4.9944 oz. ASW **Obv:** Temple of Harmony **Rev:** Two peacocks **Note:** Prev. Y#353.

Date	Mintage	XF40	MS60	MS63	MS65	MS66
1993	888	PF65 4,500		PF67 6,500	PF69 8,000	

KM# 79 50 YUAN

155.50 g., 0.999 Silver 4.9944 oz. ASW, 70 mm. **Subject:** Marco Polo **Rev:** Bust and two temples

Date	Mintage	XF40	MS60	MS63	MS65	MS66
1994	1,500	PF65 1,500		PF67 1,850	PF69 2,200	

KM# 637 50 YUAN

15.55 g., 0.999 Gold 0.4995 oz. AGW **Subject:** Oriental Inventions - Astronomy **Obv:** Great Wall **Rev:** First records of comets **Note:** Prev. Y#623.

Date	Mintage	XF40	MS60	MS63	MS65	MS66
1994	1,200	PF65 3,500		PF67 4,250	PF69 5,000	

KM# 638 50 YUAN

15.55 g., 0.999 Gold 0.4995 oz. AGW **Subject:** Oriental Inventions **Obv:** Great Wall **Rev:** First tuned bells **Note:** Prev. Y#621.

Date	Mintage	XF40	MS60	MS63	MS65	MS66
1994	1,200	PF65 3,500		PF67 4,250	PF69 5,000	

KM# 639 50 YUAN

15.55 g., 0.999 Gold 0.4995 oz. AGW **Subject:** Oriental Inventions **Obv:** Great Wall **Rev:** First silken fabric **Note:** Prev. Y#622.

Date	Mintage	XF40	MS60	MS63	MS65	MS66
1994	1,200	PF65 3,500		PF67 4,250	PF69 5,000	

KM# 640 50 YUAN

15.55 g., 0.999 Gold 0.4995 oz. AGW **Subject:** Oriental Inventions **Obv:** Great Wall **Rev:** First chain pumps used to draw water **Note:** Prev. Y#625.

Date	Mintage	XF40	MS60	MS63	MS65	MS66
1994	1,200	PF65 3,500		PF67 4,250	PF69 5,000	

KM# 641 50 YUAN

15.55 g., 0.999 Gold 0.4995 oz. AGW **Subject:** Oriental Inventions **Obv:** Great Wall **Rev:** First masts for sailing **Note:** Prev. Y#624.

Date	Mintage	XF40	MS60	MS63	MS65	MS66
1994	1,200	PF65 3,500		PF67 4,250	PF69 5,000	

KM# 669 50 YUAN

155.52 g., 0.999 Silver 4.995 oz. ASW **Rev:** Taiwan temple **Note:** Prev. Y#708.

Date	Mintage	XF40	MS60	MS63	MS65	MS66
1994	500	PF65 1,250				

KM# 679 50 YUAN

155.50 g., 0.999 Silver 4.9944 oz. ASW **Obv:** Figure on Eastern unicorn, date below **Rev:** Unicorn looking right, denomination at left, rose sprays below **Note:** Prev. Y#424.

Date	Mintage	XF40	MS60	MS63	MS65	MS66
1994	1,100	PF65 1,650		PF67 1,850	PF69 2,100	

KM# 680 50 YUAN

15.55 g., 0.999 Gold 0.4995 oz. AGW **Obv:** Figure on Eastern unicorn, date below **Rev:** Unicorn looking right, rose sprays below, denomination at left **Note:** Prev. Y#425.

Date	Mintage	XF40	MS60	MS63	MS65	MS66
1994	1,100	PF65 3,500		PF67 4,000	PF69 4,500	

KM# 687 50 YUAN

155.52 g., 0.999 Silver 4.995 oz. ASW **Subject:** Sino-Singapore Friendship **Obv:** Great Wall **Rev:** Singapore harbor view **Note:** Prev. Y#785.

Date	Mintage	XF40	MS60	MS63	MS65	MS66
1994	300	PF65 6,000				

KM# 696 50 YUAN

155.50 g., 0.999 Silver 4.9944 oz. ASW **Subject:** Children At Play **Obv:** Temple of Heaven **Rev:** Two children with cat **Note:** Prev. Y#461.

Date	Mintage	XF40	MS60	MS63	MS65	MS66
1994	500	PF65 5,000		PF67 8,500	PF69 12,000	

KM# 697 50 YUAN

15.55 g., 0.999 Gold 0.4995 oz. AGW **Subject:** Children At Play **Obv:** Temple of Heaven **Rev:** Three children with toy boat, denomination below **Note:** Prev. Y#460.

Date	Mintage	XF40	MS60	MS63	MS65	MS66
1994	1,888	PF65 3,500		PF67 4,250	PF69 5,000	

KM# 698 50 YUAN

15.55 g., 0.999 Gold 0.4995 oz. AGW **Subject:** Children At Play **Rev:** Two children with cat, denomination below **Note:** Prev. Y#459.

Date	Mintage	XF40	MS60	MS63	MS65	MS66
1994	1,888	PF65 3,500		PF67 4,250	PF69 5,000	

KM# 740 50 YUAN

15.55 g., 0.999 Gold 0.4995 oz. AGW **Subject:** Oriental Inventions **Obv:** Great Wall, date below **Rev:** Soldiers with cannon and gunpowder, denomination lower left **Note:** Prev. Y#632.

Date	Mintage	XF40	MS60	MS63	MS65	MS66
1995	1,200	PF65 2,200		PF67 3,000	PF69 4,000	

KM# 741 50 YUAN

15.55 g., 0.999 Gold 0.4995 oz. AGW **Subject:** Oriental Inventions **Obv:** Great Wall **Rev:** Potter **Note:** Prev. Y#634.

Date	Mintage	XF40	MS60	MS63	MS65	MS66
1995	1,200	PF65 2,200		PF67 3,000	PF69 4,000	

KM# 742 50 YUAN

15.55 g., 0.999 Gold 0.4995 oz. AGW **Subject:** Oriental Inventions **Obv:** Great Wall, date below **Rev:** Individual block printing, denomination at right **Note:** Prev. Y#633.

Date	Mintage	XF40	MS60	MS63	MS65	MS66
1995	1,200	PF65 2,200		PF67 3,000	PF69 4,000	

KM# 743 50 YUAN

15.55 g., 0.999 Gold 0.4995 oz. AGW **Subject:** Oriental Inventions **Obv:** Great Wall, date below **Rev:** Teacher with anatomy chart of human body, denomination at left **Note:** Prev. Y#636.

Date	Mintage	XF40	MS60	MS63	MS65	MS66
1995	1,200	PF65 2,200		PF67 3,000	PF69 4,000	

KM# 744 50 YUAN

15.55 g., 0.999 Gold 0.4995 oz. AGW **Subject:** Oriental Inventions **Obv:** Great Wall **Rev:** Chess players **Note:** Prev. Y#635.

Date	Mintage	XF40	MS60	MS63	MS65	MS66
1995	1,200	PF65 2,200		PF67 3,000	PF69 4,000	

KM# 757 50 YUAN
155.52 g., 0.999 Silver 4.995 oz. ASW **Series:** 1996 Summer Olympics **Obv:** National emblem, date below **Rev:** Table tennis player, date at right, denomination at left **Note:** Illustration reduced. Prev. Y#891.

Date	Mintage	XF40	MS60	MS63	MS65	MS66
1995	—	PF65 500	PF67 650	PF69 800		
1996	3,000	PF65 550	PF67 700	PF69 850		

KM# 763 50 YUAN
10.37 g., 0.999 Gold 0.333 oz. AGW **Subject:** Table Tennis **Obv:** Tianjing Stadium **Rev:** Table tennis player **Note:** Prev. Y#838.

Date	Mintage	XF40	MS60	MS63	MS65	MS66
1995	2,000	PF65 700	PF67 850	PF69 950		

KM# 768 50 YUAN
7.90 g., 0.916 Gold 0.2327 oz. AGW **Obv:** Bust of painter Xu Beihong, facing, date below **Rev:** Lion, denomination lower right **Note:** Prev. Y#821.

Date	Mintage	XF40	MS60	MS63	MS65	MS66
1995	3,000	PF65 1,200	PF67 1,350	PF69 1,500		

KM# 769 50 YUAN
151.00 g., 0.999 Silver 4.8499 oz. ASW, 70 mm. **Subject:** 100th Anniversary Birth of Xu Beihong **Rev:** Figure riding oxen

Date	Mintage	XF40	MS60	MS63	MS65	MS66
1995	300	PF65 850	PF67 950	PF69 1,100		

KM# 771 50 YUAN
155.52 g., 0.999 Silver 4.995 oz. ASW **Obv:** Chiqian building **Rev:** Zheng Chenggong standing with flag and ships **Note:** Prev. Y#822.

Date	Mintage	XF40	MS60	MS63	MS65	MS66
1995	250	PF65 1,550	PF67 1,650	PF69 1,800		

KM# 793 50 YUAN
15.55 g., 0.999 Gold 0.4995 oz. AGW **Subject:** Dinosaur **Obv:** Tall building, date below **Rev:** Brontosaurus, denomination at left **Note:** Prev. Y#471.

Date	Mintage	XF40	MS60	MS63	MS65	MS66
1995	—	PF65 1,100	PF67 1,150	PF69 1,200		

KM# 799 50 YUAN
15.55 g., 0.9995 Platinum 0.4997 oz. APW, 26.8 mm. **Subject:** Unicorn **Obv:** Eastern unicorn, rearing, date below **Rev:** Western unicorn with offspring, denomination at left **Edge:** Reeded **Note:** Prev. Y#739a.

Date	Mintage	XF40	MS60	MS63	MS65	MS66
1995	1,015	PF65 1,700	PF67 1,850	PF69 2,000		

KM# 800 50 YUAN
155.50 g., 0.999 Silver 4.9944 oz. ASW, 69 mm. **Rev:** Unicorn with offspring, denomination at left **Note:** Illustration reduced. Prev. Y#688.

Date	Mintage	XF40	MS60	MS63	MS65	MS66
1995	1,500	PF65 1,200	PF67 1,300	PF69 1,400		

KM# 801 50 YUAN
15.55 g., 0.999 Gold 0.4995 oz. AGW **Obv:** Eastern unicorn, rearing, date below **Rev:** Western unicorn with offspring, denomination at left **Note:** Prev. Y#739.

Date	Mintage	XF40	MS60	MS63	MS65	MS66
1995	1,250	PF65 1,650	PF67 1,800	PF69 2,100		

KM# 808 50 YUAN
15.55 g., 0.999 Gold 0.4995 oz. AGW **Subject:** 50th Anniversary - Anti-Japanese War **Obv:** National emblem, date below **Rev:** Zhou and Mao above soldiers, denomination below **Note:** Prev. Y#690.

Date	Mintage	XF40	MS60	MS63	MS65	MS66
1995	2,500	PF65 1,150	PF67 1,300	PF69 1,400		

KM# 812 50 YUAN
10.36 g., Bi-Metallic Gold center in Silver ring **Subject:** World Women's Conference **Obv:** Logo above building **Rev:** Three women, denomination above within circle **Note:** Prev. Y#691.

Date	Mintage	XF40	MS60	MS63	MS65	MS66
1995	3,000	PF65 600	PF67 700	PF69 800		

KM# 814 50 YUAN
15.55 g., 0.999 Gold 0.4995 oz. AGW **Series:** 50th Anniversary - United Nations **Obv:** United Nations logo, date below **Rev:** United Nations building, denomination upper left, dates at right **Note:** Prev. Y#488.

Date	Mintage	XF40	MS60	MS63	MS65	MS66
1995	17,500	PF65 950	PF67 1,100	PF69 1,200		

KM# 816 50 YUAN
15.55 g., 0.999 Gold 0.4995 oz. AGW **Subject:** Return of Hong Kong to China - Series I **Obv:** Tiananmen building and monument **Rev:** Deng Xiaoping's portrait above Hong Kong skyline **Note:** Prev. Y#532.

Date	Mintage	XF40	MS60	MS63	MS65	MS66
1995	11,800	PF65 1,000	PF67 1,250	PF69 1,400		

KM# 820 50 YUAN
15.55 g., 0.999 Gold 0.4995 oz. AGW **Rev:** Sailing ship **Note:** Prev. Y#648.

Date	Mintage	XF40	MS60	MS63	MS65	MS66
1995	1,000	PF65 2,200	PF67 2,350	PF69 2,500		

KM# 821 50 YUAN
15.55 g., 0.999 Gold 0.4995 oz. AGW **Rev:** Junk **Note:** Prev. Y#651.

Date	Mintage	XF40	MS60	MS63	MS65	MS66
1995	1,000	PF65 2,200	PF67 2,350	PF69 2,500		

KM# 822 50 YUAN
155.50 g., 0.999 Silver 4.9944 oz. ASW, 70 mm. **Rev:** Junk, denomination below **Note:** Illustration reduced. Prev. Y#689.

Date	Mintage	XF40	MS60	MS63	MS65	MS66
1995	1,000	PF65 1,000	PF67 1,200	PF69 1,400		

KM# 844 50 YUAN
15.55 g., 0.999 Gold 0.4995 oz. AGW **Subject:** Yellow River culture **Rev:** Nu Wa Rising, denomination below **Note:** Prev. Y#593.

Date	Mintage	XF40	MS60	MS63	MS65	MS66
1995	2,500	PF65 2,500	PF67 2,850	PF69 3,200		

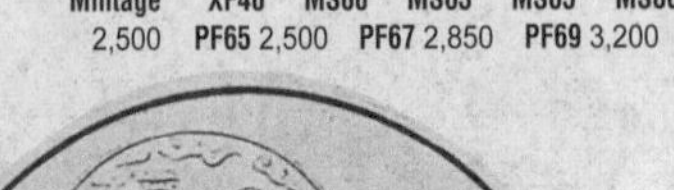

KM# 845 50 YUAN
155.50 g., 0.999 Silver 4.9944 oz. ASW, 70 mm. **Rev:** Da Yu walking through water, denomination at left **Note:** Illustration reduced. Prev. Y#592.

Date	Mintage	XF40	MS60	MS63	MS65	MS66
1995	500	PF65 2,300	PF67 2,500	PF69 2,800		

KM# 851 50 YUAN
15.55 g., 0.4995 Gold 0.2497 oz. AGW **Subject:** Romance of Three Kingdoms **Obv:** Luo Guanzhong **Rev:** Three figures **Note:** Prev. Y#829a.

Date	Mintage	XF40	MS60	MS63	MS65	MS66
1995	2,000	PF65 1,500	PF67 1,700	PF69 2,000		

KM# 852 50 YUAN
155.52 g., 0.999 Silver 4.995 oz. ASW **Subject:** Romance of Three Kingdoms **Obv:** Luo Guanzhong **Rev:** Three figures **Note:** Prev. Y#829.

Date	Mintage	XF40	MS60	MS63	MS65	MS66
1995	7,000	PF65 2,400	PF67 2,750	PF69 3,000		

KM# 860 50 YUAN
15.55 g., 0.999 Gold 0.4995 oz. AGW **Subject:** 50th Anniversary - For the return of Taiwan to China **Obv:** Great Wall **Rev:** Zhongshan Hall **Note:** Prev. Y#815.

Date	Mintage	XF40	MS60	MS63	MS65	MS66
1995	3,000	PF65 1,150	PF67 1,350	PF69 1,500		

KM# 861 50 YUAN
15.55 g., 0.999 Gold 0.4995 oz. AGW **Subject:** 50th Anniversary - For the return of Taiwan to China **Obv:** Great Wall **Rev:** Taiwan and China maps **Note:** Prev. Y#814.

Date	Mintage	XF40	MS60	MS63	MS65	MS66
1995	3,000	PF65 1,150	PF67 1,350	PF69 1,500		

KM# 862 50 YUAN
155.52 g., 0.999 Silver 4.995 oz. ASW **Subject:** 50th Anniversary - For the return of Taiwan to China **Obv:** Great Wall **Rev:** Taiwan and China maps **Note:** Prev. Y#813.

Date	Mintage	XF40	MS60	MS63	MS65	MS66
1995	999	PF65 2,000	PF67 2,250	PF69 2,500		

KM# 870 50 YUAN
11.32 g., 0.916 Gold 0.3333 oz. AGW **Subject:** Silk Road **Obv:** National emblem, date below **Rev:** Man riding camel, denomination at right **Note:** Prev. Y#608.

Date	Mintage	XF40	MS60	MS63	MS65	MS66
1995	10,000	PF65 750	PF67 1,000	PF69 1,300		

KM# 914 50 YUAN
15.50 g., 0.999 Gold 0.4978 oz. AGW, 27 mm. **Series:** Scientific and technical inventions **Obv:** Tower on Great Wall **Rev:** Man in two horse cart

Date	Mintage	XF40	MS60	MS63	MS65	MS66
1996	1,200	PF65 2,750	PF67 3,750	PF69 5,000		

KM# 915 50 YUAN
15.50 g., 0.999 Gold 0.4978 oz. AGW, 27 mm. **Series:** Scientific and technical inventions **Obv:** Tower on Great Wall **Rev:** Three men seated playing musical instruments

Date	Mintage	XF40	MS60	MS63	MS65	MS66
1996	1,200	PF65 2,750	PF67 3,750	PF69 5,000		

KM# 916 50 YUAN
15.50 g., 0.999 Gold 0.4978 oz. AGW, 27 mm. **Subject:** Scientific and technical inventions **Obv:** Tower on Great Wall **Rev:** Boat in river

Date	Mintage	XF40	MS60	MS63	MS65	MS66
1996	1,200	PF65 2,750	PF67 3,750	PF69 5,000		

KM# 917 50 YUAN
15.50 g., 0.999 Gold 0.4978 oz. AGW, 27 mm. **Series:** Scientific and techinical inventions **Obv:** Tower on Great Wall **Rev:** Bridge

Date	Mintage	XF40	MS60	MS63	MS65	MS66
1996	1,200	PF65 2,750	PF67 3,750	PF69 5,000		

KM# 918 50 YUAN
15.50 g., 0.999 Gold 0.4978 oz. AGW, 27 mm. **Series:** Scientific and techinical inventions **Obv:** Tower on Great Wall **Rev:** Tower

Date	Mintage	XF40	MS60	MS63	MS65	MS66
1996	1,200	PF65 2,750	PF67 3,750	PF69 5,000		

KM# 932 50 YUAN
15.55 g., 0.999 Gold 0.4995 oz. AGW **Obv:** Building, date below **Rev:** Sun Yat-sen bust facing, denomination below, fan sprays 3/4 around **Note:** Prev. Y#859.

Date	Mintage	XF40	MS60	MS63	MS65	MS66
1996	3,000	PF65 2,000				

KM# 945 50 YUAN
155.52 g., 0.999 Silver 4.995 oz. ASW, 70.2 mm. **Subject:** Unicorn **Obv:** Eastern unicorn, full body, date below **Rev:** Western unicorn with maiden, denomination at left **Edge:** Reeded **Note:** Illustration reduced. Prev. Y#1038.

Date	Mintage	XF40	MS60	MS63	MS65	MS66
1996	—	PF65 2,500				

KM# 946 50 YUAN
15.55 g., 0.999 Gold 0.4995 oz. AGW, 27 mm. **Subject:** Unicorn **Obv:** Eastern unicorn, full body **Rev:** Western unicorn in wreath **Edge:** Reeded **Note:** Prev. Y#1039; 1091.

Date	Mintage	XF40	MS60	MS63	MS65	MS66
1996	1,000	PF65 2,750	PF67 3,250	PF69 4,000		

KM# 953 50 YUAN
15.55 g., 0.999 Gold 0.4995 oz. AGW **Subject:** 60th Anniversary - Long March **Obv:** Flag above building, date below **Rev:** Chairman Mao portrait, denomination at right **Note:** Prev. Y#870.

Date	Mintage	XF40	MS60	MS63	MS65	MS66
1996	6,000	PF65 1,150				

KM# 957 50 YUAN
15.55 g., 0.999 Gold 0.4995 oz. AGW **Subject:** Return of Hong Kong to China Series II **Obv:** Hong Kong Harbor **Note:** Prev. Y#658.

Date	Mintage	XF40	MS60	MS63	MS65	MS66
1996	11,800	PF65 1,000	PF67 1,650	PF69 2,100		

KM# 963 50 YUAN
15.55 g., 0.999 Gold 0.4995 oz. AGW **Subject:** Romance of the Three Kingdoms Series **Obv:** Luo Guanzhong portrait **Rev:** Guand Du on horseback, leading his troops **Note:** Prev. Y#881.

Date	Mintage	XF40	MS60	MS63	MS65	MS66
1996	2,000	PF65 1,500	PF67 1,650	PF69 1,800		

KM# 964 50 YUAN
155.52 g., 0.999 Silver 4.995 oz. ASW, 80 mm. **Subject:** Romance of the Three Kingdoms Series **Obv:** Bust of Luo Guanzhong, 3/4 right, date below **Rev:** Battle scene, denomination below **Note:** Illustration reduced. Prev. Y#880.

Date	Mintage	XF40	MS60	MS63	MS65	MS66
1996	500	PF65 1,700	PF67 2,000	PF69 2,200		

KM# 970 50 YUAN
15.55 g., 0.999 Gold 0.4995 oz. AGW **Obv:** Yangtze River scene, denomination lower left corner **Rev:** Large dam **Shape:** Rectangular **Note:** Prev. Y#599.

Date	Mintage	XF40	MS60	MS63	MS65	MS66
1996	6,000	PF65 1,350	PF67 1,750	PF69 2,150		

KM# 975 50 YUAN
11.32 g., 0.916 Gold 0.3333 oz. AGW **Subject:** Silk Road **Obv:** National emblem, date below **Rev:** Water vendor, denomination lower right **Note:** Prev. Y#609.

Date	Mintage	XF40	MS60	MS63	MS65	MS66
1996	10,000	PF65 1,000	PF67 1,350	PF69 2,000		

KM# 1019 50 YUAN
151.26 g., 0.999 Silver 4.8583 oz. ASW, 70 mm. **Subject:** Painting Master Qi Baishi **Rev:** Basket

Date	Mintage	XF40	MS60	MS63	MS65	MS66
1997	999	PF65 475	PF67 500	PF69 600		

KM# 1020 50 YUAN
15.55 g., 0.999 Gold 0.4995 oz. AGW **Obv:** Portrait of Qi Bashi **Rev:** Squirrels eating grapes **Shape:** Rectangular **Note:** Prev. Y#1005, 1029.

Date	Mintage	XF40	MS60	MS63	MS65	MS66
1997	5,000	PF65 1,500	PF67 1,800	PF69 2,000		

KM# 1040 50 YUAN
15.55 g., 0.999 Gold 0.4995 oz. AGW **Subject:** Chinese Wildlife **Obv:** National emblem, date below **Rev:** Two white dolphins, denomination at right **Note:** Prev. Y#921.

Date	Mintage	XF40	MS60	MS63	MS65	MS66
1997	30,000	PF65 975	PF67 1,250	PF69 1,400		

KM# 1043 50 YUAN
15.56 g., 0.999 Gold 0.4996 oz. AGW **Subject:** People's Liberation Army **Obv:** Radiant star above Great Wall **Rev:** Youthful Chairman Mao standing **Note:** Prev. Y#910.

Date	Mintage	XF40	MS60	MS63	MS65	MS66
1997	12,000	PF65 975	PF67 1,250	PF69 1,400		

KM# 1044 50 YUAN
15.55 g., 0.999 Gold 0.4995 oz. AGW **Subject:** Return of Hong Kong to China - Series III **Obv:** Tiananmen Square - Forbidden City **Rev:** Flag and fireworks above Hong Kong, denomination below **Note:** Prev. Y#903.

Date	Mintage	XF40	MS60	MS63	MS65	MS66
1997	11,800	PF65 1,000		PF67 1,450	PF69 1,800	

KM# 1048 50 YUAN
155.52 g., 0.999 Silver 4.995 oz. ASW, 80 mm. **Subject:** Return of Macao to China **Obv:** Tiananmen Square - Forbidden City, date above leaf sprays below **Rev:** Deng Xiaoping viewing Macao, denomination at right **Note:** Illustration reduced. Prev. Y#906.

Date	Mintage	XF40	MS60	MS63	MS65	MS66
1997	—	PF65 775		PF67 975	PF69 1,100	

KM# 1049 50 YUAN
15.56 g., 0.999 Gold 0.4996 oz. AGW **Subject:** Return of Macao to China **Obv:** Tiananmen Square - Forbidden City **Rev:** Deng Xiaoping viewing Macao **Note:** Prev. Y#906a.

Date	Mintage	XF40	MS60	MS63	MS65	MS66
1997	11,800	PF65 1,000		PF67 1,250	PF69 1,400	

KM# 1061 50 YUAN
155.52 g., 0.999 Silver 4.995 oz. ASW **Subject:** Traditional Chinese Mascot **Obv:** Ornamental column **Rev:** Child holding carp **Note:** Prev. Y#918.

Date	Mintage	XF40	MS60	MS63	MS65	MS66
1997	3,800	PF65 500		PF67 650	PF69 800	

KM# 1081 50 YUAN
15.55 g., 0.999 Gold 0.4995 oz. AGW **Subject:** Huang (Yellow) River Culture **Obv:** Archer **Rev:** Dragon **Note:** Prev. Y#1004.

Date	Mintage	XF40	MS60	MS63	MS65	MS66
1997	3,000	PF65 1,400		PF67 1,500	PF69 1,600	

KM# 1082 50 YUAN
155.50 g., 0.999 Silver 4.9944 oz. ASW, 70 mm. **Series:** Yellow river culture **Rev:** Female in flight

Date	Mintage	XF40	MS60	MS63	MS65	MS66
1997	1,000	PF65 1,500		PF67 1,650	PF69 1,800	

KM# 1088 50 YUAN
15.55 g., 0.9999 Gold 0.4999 oz. AGW **Subject:** Romance of the Three Kingdoms **Rev:** Soldiers on a boat **Note:** Prev. Y#1179.

Date	Mintage	XF40	MS60	MS63	MS65	MS66
1997	3,000	PF65 1,300		PF67 1,450	PF69 1,600	

KM# 1089 50 YUAN
151.50 g., 0.999 Silver 4.866 oz. ASW, 70 mm. **Series:** Classic literature **Rev:** Man and woman and 4 others standing by banners

Date	Mintage	XF40	MS60	MS63	MS65	MS66
1997	1,500	PF65 875		PF67 975	PF69 1,100	

KM# 1107 50 YUAN
10.10 g., 0.916 Gold 0.2974 oz. AGW, 23 mm. **Series:** Silk Road **Rev:** Man with horse

Date	Mintage	XF40	MS60	MS63	MS65	MS66
1997	10,000	PF65 650		PF67 750	PF69 900	

KM# 1153 50 YUAN
15.55 g., 0.999 Gold 0.4995 oz. AGW **Subject:** Zhou Enlai **Note:** Prev. Y#1007.

Date	Mintage	XF40	MS60	MS63	MS65	MS66
1998	8,000	PF65 1,100		PF67 1,300	PF69 1,500	

KM# 1156 50 YUAN
15.55 g., 0.9999 Gold 0.4999 oz. AGW **Subject:** Liu Shao Qi **Obv:** Portrait **Rev:** Temple **Note:** Prev. Y#1180.

Date	Mintage	XF40	MS60	MS63	MS65	MS66
1998	8,000	PF65 1,100		PF67 1,300	PF69 1,500	

KM# 1160 50 YUAN
100.00 g., 0.999 Silver 3.2119 oz. ASW, 60 mm. **Series:** Kuan Yin **Rev:** Multi armed seated statue

Date	Mintage	XF40	MS60	MS63	MS65	MS66
1998	—	PF65 500		PF67 650	PF69 800	

KM# 1169 50 YUAN
15.56 g., 0.999 Gold 0.4998 oz. AGW, 27 mm. **Subject:** Macao's return to China **Rev:** Birds flying over lablet, lighthouse at left, gate at right

Date	Mintage	XF40	MS60	MS63	MS65	MS66
1998	11,800	PF65 1,000		PF67 1,100	PF69 1,200	

KM# 1170 50 YUAN
151.50 g., 0.999 Silver 4.866 oz. ASW, 70 mm. **Subject:** Macao's return to China **Rev:** Birds flying over lablet, lighthouse at left, gate at right

Date	Mintage	XF40	MS60	MS63	MS65	MS66
1998	5,000	PF65 850		PF67 950	PF69 1,100	

KM# 1179 50 YUAN
155.50 g., 0.999 Silver 4.9944 oz. ASW, 70 mm. **Subject:** Spring greeting **Obv:** Lantern and rays **Rev:** Three figures

Date	Mintage	XF40	MS60	MS63	MS65	MS66
1998	1,500	PF65 850		PF67 950	PF69 1,100	

KM# 1187 50 YUAN
155.50 g., 0.999 Silver 4.9944 oz. ASW Colorized, 90 x 40 mm. **Obv:** Long budding **Rev:** Six females **Shape:** Rectangle

Date	Mintage	XF40	MS60	MS63	MS65	MS66
1998	18,800	PF65 850		PF67 950	PF69 1,100	

KM# 1192 50 YUAN
15.50 g., 0.999 Gold 0.4978 oz. AGW, 19 x 29 mm. **Series:** Guilien scenery **Obv:** Pastural bridge archway at sea shore **Rev:** Tall coastal islands **Shape:** Rectangle

Date	Mintage	XF40	MS60	MS63	MS65	MS66
1998	1,600	PF65 1,650		PF67 2,750	PF69 4,000	

KM# 1193 50 YUAN
15.50 g., 0.999 Gold 0.4978 oz. AGW, 19 x 29 mm. **Series:** Guilien scenery **Obv:** 4 arched bridge **Rev:** Tall coastal islands **Shape:** Rectangle

Date	Mintage	XF40	MS60	MS63	MS65	MS66
1998	1,600	PF65 1,650		PF67 2,750	PF69 4,000	

KM# 1194 50 YUAN
15.50 g., 0.999 Gold 0.4978 oz. AGW, 19 x 29 mm. **Series:** Guilien scenery **Obv:** Long arched bridge **Rev:** Tall coastal islands **Shape:** Rectangle

Date	Mintage	XF40	MS60	MS63	MS65	MS66
1998	1,600	PF65 1,650		PF67 2,750	PF69 4,000	

KM# 1195 50 YUAN
15.50 g., 0.999 Gold 0.4978 oz. AGW, 19 x 29 mm. **Series:** Guilien scenery **Obv:** Tall out crop with pagoda at top **Rev:** Tall coastal islands **Shape:** Rectangle

Date	Mintage	XF40	MS60	MS63	MS65	MS66
1998	1,600	PF65 1,650		PF67 2,750	PF69 4,000	

KM# 1245 50 YUAN
15.56 g., 0.999 Gold 0.4998 oz. AGW, 19 x 29 mm. **Subject:** Master Painter Zhang Daqian **Obv:** Bust facing **Rev:** Two riders on oxen **Shape:** Rectangle

Date	Mintage	XF40	MS60	MS63	MS65	MS66
1999	6,000	PF65 1,150		PF67 1,350	PF69 1,500	

KM# 1250 50 YUAN
15.55 g., 0.999 Gold 0.4995 oz. AGW **Subject:** 50th Anniversary of People's Republic **Note:** Prev. Y#1008.

Date	Mintage	XF40	MS60	MS63	MS65	MS66
1999	15,700	PF65 1,100		PF67 1,250	PF69 1,400	

KM# A1259 50 YUAN
151.50 g., 0.999 Silver 4.866 oz. ASW, 70 mm. **Series:** Traditional Chinese suspicious matters **Obv:** Winged column and rays

Date	Mintage	XF40	MS60	MS63	MS65	MS66
1999	5,000	PF65 850		PF67 1,100	PF69 1,300	

KM# 1261 50 YUAN
151.50 g., 0.999 Silver 4.866 oz. ASW, 90 x 40 mm. **Series:** Ancient Chinese painting **Rev:** Men on horseback right **Shape:** Rectangle **Note:** Colorized

Date	Mintage	XF40	MS60	MS63	MS65	MS66
1999	18,800	PF65 850		PF67 1,100	PF69 1,300	

KM# 1280 50 YUAN
15.50 g., 0.999 Gold 0.4978 oz. AGW, 27 mm. **Subject:** Return of Macao **Rev:** 99 above buildings

Date	Mintage	XF40	MS60	MS63	MS65	MS66
1999	11,800	PF65 1,000		PF67 1,250	PF69 1,400	

KM# 1281 50 YUAN
155.50 g., 0.999 Silver 4.9944 oz. ASW, 70 mm. **Subject:** Return of Macao **Rev:** Views of Macao

Date	Mintage	XF40	MS60	MS63	MS65	MS66
1999	5,000	PF65 850		PF67 1,100	PF69 1,300	

KM# 1287 50 YUAN
15.50 g., 0.999 Gold 0.4978 oz. AGW, 27 mm. **Subject:** Beijing opera **Rev:** Actor bowing

Date	Mintage	XF40	MS60	MS63	MS65	MS66
1999	8,000	PF65 1,450		PF67 1,650	PF69 2,000	

KM# 1288 50 YUAN
155.00 g., 0.999 Silver 4.9784 oz. ASW, 90 x 40 mm. **Rev:** 5 actors, one with banner **Shape:** Rectangle **Note:** Colorized

Date	Mintage	XF40	MS60	MS63	MS65	MS66
1999	11,800	PF65 850		PF67 1,200	PF69 1,500	

KM# 1315 50 YUAN
15.50 g., 0.999 Gold 0.4978 oz. AGW, 27 mm. **Series:** Classic literature **Subject:** Dream of red mansion **Rev:** Female standing looking at flora, parrots **Shape:** Octagonal **Note:** Colorized

Date	Mintage	XF40	MS60	MS63	MS65	MS66
2000	8,800	PF65 1,200		PF67 1,400	PF69 1,600	

KM# 1316 50 YUAN
155.50 g., 0.999 Silver 4.9944 oz. ASW, 28.5 x 120 mm. **Series:** Classic literature **Subject:** Dream of red mansion **Rev:** Two figures standing around basin **Shape:** Arc **Note:** Colorized

Date	Mintage	XF40	MS60	MS63	MS65	MS66
2000	11,800	PF65 850		PF67 1,100	PF69 1,250	

KM# 1323 50 YUAN
155.52 g., 0.999 Silver 4.995 oz. ASW **Rev:** Dragons **Shape:** Rectangle **Note:** Prev. Y#1049.

Date	Mintage	XF40	MS60	MS63	MS65	MS66
2000	1,888	PF65 1,250		PF67 1,350	PF69 1,450	

KM# 1333 50 YUAN
17.00 g., 0.999 Gold 0.546 oz. AGW, 27 mm. **Subject:** Y2K **Obv:** Monument **Rev:** World Globe as an eye above value within silver plated outer ring **Edge:** Reeded **Note:** Prev. Y#1236.

Date	Mintage	XF40	MS60	MS63	MS65	MS66
2000	20,000	PF65 3,000		PF67 3,500	PF69 4,000	

KM# 1334 50 YUAN
Bi-Metallic Gold center in Silver ring **Subject:** Y-2-K **Note:** Prev. Y#1137.

Date	Mintage	XF40	MS60	MS63	MS65	MS66
2000	20,000	PF65 1,500		PF67 1,750	PF69 2,100	

KM# 1342 50 YUAN
15.50 g., 0.999 Gold 0.4978 oz. AGW, 27 mm. **Subject:** Beijing opera **Rev:** Performer and kettle drum **Note:** Colorized

Date	Mintage	XF40	MS60	MS63	MS65	MS66
2000	8,000	PF65 1,200		PF67 1,400	PF69 1,600	

KM# 1343 50 YUAN
155.50 g., 0.999 Silver 4.9944 oz. ASW, 90 x 40 mm. **Subject:** Bejing opera **Rev:** Five performers **Shape:** Rectangle **Note:** Colorized

Date	Mintage	XF40	MS60	MS63	MS65	MS66
2000	11,800	PF65 850		PF67 1,100	PF69 1,250	

KM# 80 100 YUAN
11.00 g., 0.900 Gold 0.3183 oz. AGW **Obv:** Building, date at right **Rev:** Marco Polo bust, top right, ship below, denomination at bottom **Note:** Prev. Y#56.

Date	Mintage	XF40	MS60	MS63	MS65	MS66
1983	1,030	PF65 1,750		PF67 1,850	PF69 2,200	

KM# 102 100 YUAN
11.32 g., 0.917 Gold 0.3337 oz. AGW **Obv:** National emblem,

date below **Rev:** Emperor Huang Di, denomination below **Note:** Prev. Y#72.

Date	Mintage	XF40	MS60	MS63	MS65	MS66
1984	10,000	PF65 775	PF67 875	PF69 1,100		

KM# 125 100 YUAN
11.32 g., 0.917 Gold 0.3337 oz. AGW, 23 mm. **Subject:** Founders of Chinese Culture **Rev:** Confucius, denomination at right **Note:** Prev. Y#94.

Date	Mintage	XF40	MS60	MS63	MS65	MS66
1985	7,000	PF65 775	PF67 875	PF69 1,100		

KM# 145 100 YUAN
11.32 g., 0.917 Gold 0.3337 oz. AGW, 23 mm. **Subject:** Chinese Culture **Obv:** National emblem, date below **Rev:** Revolutionary Soldier, Liu Bang on horseback, denomination at left **Note:** Prev. Y#117.

Date	Mintage	XF40	MS60	MS63	MS65	MS66
1986	7,000	PF65 775	PF67 875	PF69 1,100		

KM# 149 100 YUAN
11.32 g., 0.917 Gold 0.3337 oz. AGW **Subject:** Year of Peace **Rev:** Statue of seated female **Note:** Prev. Y#120.

Date	Mintage	XF40	MS60	MS63	MS65	MS66
1986	1,000	PF65 2,850	PF67 3,500	PF69 4,200		

KM# 151 100 YUAN
11.32 g., 0.917 Gold 0.3337 oz. AGW **Subject:** Wildlife **Obv:** National emblem, date below **Rev:** Wild Yak, left, denomination at left **Note:** Prev. Y#107.

Date	Mintage	XF40	MS60	MS63	MS65	MS66
1986	3,000	PF65 850	PF67 1,150	PF69 1,400		

KM# 176 100 YUAN
11.32 g., 0.917 Gold 0.3337 oz. AGW **Obv:** National emblem, date below **Rev:** Emperor Li Shih on horseback, denomination at right **Note:** Prev. Y#139.

Date	Mintage	XF40	MS60	MS63	MS65	MS66
1987	7,000	PF65 750	PF67 850	PF69 900		

KM# 177 100 YUAN
373.24 g., 0.999 Silver 11.9878 oz. ASW, 80 mm. **Subject:** 125th Anniversary - Birth of Zhan Tianyou **Obv:** National emblem, date below **Rev:** Bust of Zhan Tianyou facing above steam locomotive on bridge, denomination below, dates above **Note:** Illustration reduced. Prev. Y#131.

Date	Mintage	XF40	MS60	MS63	MS65	MS66
1987	2,911	PF65 900	PF67 1000	PF69 1,200		

KM# 206 100 YUAN
15.55 g., 0.999 Gold 0.4994 oz. AGW **Series:** Seoul 1988 - 24th Summer Olympic Games **Obv:** National emblem, date below **Rev:** Rhythmic gymnast, denomination at right **Note:** Prev. Y#173.

Date	Mintage	XF40	MS60	MS63	MS65	MS66
1988	5,500	PF65 1,450	PF67 2,000	PF69 2,400		

KM# 211 100 YUAN
11.32 g., 0.917 Gold 0.3337 oz. AGW **Rev:** Emperor Zhao Kuangyin, denomination at right **Note:** Prev. Y#164.

Date	Mintage	XF40	MS60	MS63	MS65	MS66
1988	Est. 7000	PF65 775	PF67 875	PF69 1,100		

KM# 214 100 YUAN
8.00 g., 0.917 Gold 0.2359 oz. AGW **Subject:** Rare Animal Protection **Obv:** National emblem, date below **Rev:** Golden monkey, denomination at left **Note:** Prev. Y#167.

Date	Mintage	XF40	MS60	MS63	MS65	MS66
1988	29,000	PF65 625	PF67 725	PF69 800		

KM# 244 100 YUAN
8.00 g., 0.917 Gold 0.2359 oz. AGW **Subject:** 11th Asian Games - Beijing 1990 **Obv:** Stadium **Rev:** Ribbon dancer, denomination below **Note:** Prev. Y#203.

Date	Mintage	XF40	MS60	MS63	MS65	MS66
1989	Est. 7000	PF65 525	PF67 600	PF69 700		

KM# 252 100 YUAN
11.32 g., 0.917 Gold 0.3337 oz. AGW **Obv:** National emblem, date below **Rev:** Genghis Khan on horseback, denomination at left **Note:** Prev. Y#217.

Date	Mintage	XF40	MS60	MS63	MS65	MS66
1989	—	PF65 800	PF67 950	PF69 1,100		

KM# 255 100 YUAN
8.00 g., 0.917 Gold 0.2359 oz. AGW **Series:** Endangered Animals **Obv:** National emblem, date below **Rev:** Chinese tiger, denomination at left **Note:** Prev. Y#250.

Date	Mintage	XF40	MS60	MS63	MS65	MS66
1989	14,000	PF65 700	PF67 800	PF69 900		

KM# 258 100 YUAN
7.78 g., 0.999 Gold 0.2497 oz. AGW **Subject:** 40th Anniversary of People's Republic **Obv:** National emblem, date at right **Rev:** Pair of flying cranes, denomination at left **Note:** Prev. Y#299.

Date	Mintage	XF40	MS60	MS63	MS65	MS66
1989	1,000	PF65 750	PF67 850	PF69 1,000		

KM# 261 100 YUAN
11.32 g., 0.917 Gold 0.3337 oz. AGW **Series:** Save the Children Fund **Obv:** National emblem, date below **Rev:** Child running flying kites, denomination lower right **Note:** Prev. Y#231.

Date	Mintage	XF40	MS60	MS63	MS65	MS66
1989	5,000	PF65 750	PF67 850	PF69 1,000		

KM# 267 100 YUAN
8.00 g., 0.917 Gold 0.2359 oz. AGW **Subject:** XI Asian Games - Beijing 1990 **Obv:** Roman numeral above stadium, date below **Rev:** Swimmer, denomination lower left **Note:** Prev. Y#256.

Date	Mintage	XF40	MS60	MS63	MS65	MS66
1990	10,000	PF65 600	PF67 700	PF69 800		

KM# 304 100 YUAN
10.37 g., 0.999 Gold 0.3331 oz. AGW **Series:** Barcelona 1992 - 25th Summer Olympic Games **Obv:** National emblem, date below **Rev:** 2 women playing basketball, denomination at right **Note:** Prev. Y#327.

Date	Mintage	XF40	MS60	MS63	MS65	MS66
1990	10,000	—	—	650	725	800

KM# 309 100 YUAN
11.32 g., 0.917 Gold 0.3337 oz. AGW **Obv:** National emblem, date below **Rev:** First emperor, Huang Di standing, denomination at right **Note:** Prev. Y#287.

Date	Mintage	XF40	MS60	MS63	MS65	MS66
1990	10,000	PF65 1,250	PF67 1,450	PF69 1,600		

KM# 314 100 YUAN
11.32 g., 0.917 Gold 0.3337 oz. AGW **Obv:** National emblem, date below **Rev:** Emperor Zhu Yuanzhang seated, denomination upper left **Note:** Prev. Y#306.

Date	Mintage	XF40	MS60	MS63	MS65	MS66
1990	—	—	—	675	750	800

KM# 298 100 YUAN
10.37 g., 0.999 Gold 0.3331 oz. AGW **Series:** Albertville 1992 - 16th Winter Olympic Games **Obv:** National emblem, date below **Rev:** Pairs figure skating, denomination lower right **Note:** Prev. Y#473.

Date	Mintage	XF40	MS60	MS63	MS65	MS66
1991	10,000	PF65 1,000	PF67 1,150	PF69 1,300		

KM# 371 100 YUAN
8.00 g., 0.916 Gold 0.2356 oz. AGW **Subject:** Women's 1st World Football Cup **Obv:** Stadium, date below **Rev:** Woman kicking ball, denomination at right **Note:** Prev. Y#320.

Date	Mintage	XF40	MS60	MS63	MS65	MS66
1991	1,400	PF65 950	PF67 1,100	PF69 1,200		

KM# 376 100 YUAN
11.32 g., 0.917 Gold 0.3337 oz. AGW **Rev:** Emperor Yan Di, denomination upper right **Note:** Prev. Y#545.

Date	Mintage	XF40	MS60	MS63	MS65	MS66
1991	10,000	PF65 1,250	PF67 1,750	PF69 2,200		

KM# 381 100 YUAN
11.32 g., 0.333 Gold 0.1212 oz. AGW **Subject:** Emperor Kang Xi, denomination at left **Obv:** National emblem, date below **Note:** Prev. Y#326.

Date	Mintage	XF40	MS60	MS63	MS65	MS66
1991	Est. 7000	PF65 1,250	PF67 1,750	PF69 2,200		

KM# 384 100 YUAN
31.10 g., 0.999 Gold 0.999 oz. AGW **Obv:** Building, two dates below **Rev:** Sun Yat-sen in uniform, facing, denomination at left **Note:** Illustration reduced. Prev. Y#479.

Date	Mintage	XF40	MS60	MS63	MS65	MS66
ND-1991	1,000	PF65 6,500	PF67 7,500	PF69 9,000		

KM# 385 100 YUAN
8.60 g., 0.917 Gold 0.2535 oz. AGW **Subject:** 80th Anniversary - 1911 Revolution **Obv:** Building **Rev:** Sun Yat-sen writing, denomination at right **Note:** Prev. Y#478.

Date	Mintage	XF40	MS60	MS63	MS65	MS66
1991	2,500	PF65 2,250	PF67 2,500	PF69 3,000		

KM# 410 100 YUAN
31.10 g., 0.9995 Platinum 0.9995 oz. APW, 32 mm. **Series:** Scientific and technical inventions **Rev:** Ship

Date	Mintage	XF40	MS60	MS63	MS65	MS66
1992	100	PF67 14,000	PF69 16,000			

KM# 411 100 YUAN
31.10 g., 0.9995 Platinum 0.9995 oz. APW, 32 mm. **Series:** Scientific and technical inventions **Rev:** Large urn

Date	Mintage	XF40	MS60	MS63	MS65	MS66
1992	100	PF67 14,000	PF69 16,000			

KM# 412 100 YUAN
31.10 g., 0.9995 Platinum 0.9995 oz. APW, 32 mm. **Series:** Scientific and technical inventions **Rev:** Kite flying

Date	Mintage	XF40	MS60	MS63	MS65	MS66
1992	100	PF67 14,000	PF69 16,000			

KM# 413 100 YUAN
31.10 g., 0.9995 Platinum 0.9995 oz. APW, 32 mm. **Series:** Scientific and technical inventions

Date	Mintage	XF40	MS60	MS63	MS65	MS66
1992	100	PF67 14,000	PF69 16,000			

KM# 414 100 YUAN
31.10 g., 0.9995 Platinum 0.9995 oz. APW, 32 mm. **Series:** Scientific and technical inventions **Rev:** Large urn with flange

Date	Mintage	XF40	MS60	MS63	MS65	MS66
1992	100	PF67 14,000	PF69 16,000			

KM# 415 100 YUAN
31.10 g., 0.999 Gold 0.999 oz. AGW **Subject:** Chinese Inventions **Obv:** Great Wall, date below **Rev:** Ancient ships and shipbuilding, denomination lower left **Note:** Prev. Y#336.

Date	Mintage	XF40	MS60	MS63	MS65	MS66
1992	1,000	PF65 5,000	PF67 6,000	PF69 7,500		

KM# 416 100 YUAN
31.10 g., 0.999 Gold 0.999 oz. AGW **Subject:** Chinese Inventions **Rev:** First seismograph, denomination below **Note:** Prev. Y#338.

Date	Mintage	XF40	MS60	MS63	MS65	MS66
1992	1,000	PF65 5,000	PF67 6,000	PF69 7,500		

KM# 417 100 YUAN
31.10 g., 0.999 Gold 0.999 oz. AGW **Subject:** Chinese Inventions **Obv:** Great Wall **Rev:** First kite, denomination below **Note:** Prev. Y#339.

Date	Mintage	XF40	MS60	MS63	MS65	MS66
1992	1,000	PF65 5,000	PF67 6,000	PF69 7,500		

KM# 418 100 YUAN
31.10 g., 0.999 Gold 0.999 oz. AGW **Subject:** Chinese Inventions **Rev:** First compass, denomination below **Note:** Prev. Y#337.

Date	Mintage	XF40	MS60	MS63	MS65	MS66
1992	1,000	PF65 5,000	PF67 6,000	PF69 7,500		

KM# 419 100 YUAN
31.10 g., 0.999 Gold 0.999 oz. AGW **Obv:** Great Wall, date below **Rev:** Bronze Age Metal Working, large urn, denomination below **Note:** Prev. Y#340.

Date	Mintage	XF40	MS60	MS63	MS65	MS66
1992	1,000	PF65 5,000	PF67 6,000	PF69 7,500		

KM# 440 100 YUAN
11.32 g., 0.917 Gold 0.3337 oz. AGW **Series:** 1994 Olympics **Obv:** Temple of Heaven **Rev:** Male figure skater, denomination below **Note:** Prev. Y#692.

Date	Mintage	XF40	MS60	MS63	MS65	MS66
1992	1,500	PF65 1,750	PF67 2,000	PF69 2,300		

KM# 445 100 YUAN
11.32 g., 0.333 Gold 0.1212 oz. AGW **Obv:** National emblem, date below **Rev:** Emperor Da Yu, denomination at right **Note:** Prev. Y#546.

Date	Mintage	XF40	MS60	MS63	MS65	MS66
1992	Est. 10000	PF65 1,250	PF67 1,450	PF69 1,600		

KM# 451 100 YUAN
11.32 g., 0.917 Gold 0.3337 oz. AGW **Obv:** National emblem, date below **Rev:** Wu Zetian "The Iron Lady" 603-705AD, Stateswoman, denomination at right **Note:** Prev. Y#554.

Date	Mintage	XF40	MS60	MS63	MS65	MS66
1992	2,500	PF65 1,250	PF67 1,450	PF69 1,600		

KM# 456 100 YUAN
8.00 g., 0.917 Gold 0.2359 oz. AGW **Series:** Endangered Wildlife **Rev:** Mountain sheep, denomination below **Note:** Prev. Y#693.

Date	Mintage	XF40	MS60	MS63	MS65	MS66
1992	1,500	PF65 775	PF67 1,000	PF69 1,300		

KM# 464 100 YUAN
33.96 g., 0.916 Gold 1.0001 oz. AGW **Subject:** Archeological Finds **Obv:** National emblem **Rev:** Resting deer with long antlers **Note:** Prev. Y#754.

Date	Mintage	XF40	MS60	MS63	MS65	MS66
1992	500	PF65 3,500	PF67 4,000	PF69 4,500		

KM# 508 100 YUAN
31.10 g., 0.999 Gold 0.999 oz. AGW **Obv:** Building and Great Wall **Rev:** Chinese Gods: Fu, Lu, and Shu **Note:** Prev. Y#406.

Date	Mintage	XF40	MS60	MS63	MS65	MS66
1993	888	PF65 5,000	PF67 6,000	PF69 7,000		

KM# 523 100 YUAN
10.36 g., 0.917 Gold 0.3054 oz. AGW **Subject:** World Cup Soccer **Obv:** National emblem, date below **Rev:** Player kicking ball, denomination at left **Note:** Prev. Y#491.

Date	Mintage	XF40	MS60	MS63	MS65	MS66
1993	5,000	PF65 750	PF67 1,000	PF69 1,200		

KM# 534 100 YUAN
11.32 g., 0.917 Gold 0.3337 oz. AGW **Obv:** National emblem, date below **Rev:** Bust of Chairman Mao Zedong, right, denomination at left **Note:** Prev. Y#538.

Date	Mintage	XF40	MS60	MS63	MS65	MS66
1993	4,500	PF65 1,850	PF67 2,350	PF69 2,600		

KM# 535 100 YUAN
31.10 g., 0.999 Gold 0.999 oz. AGW **Obv:** Home of Sun Yat-sen **Rev:** Bust of Sun Yat-sen, facing, denomination at right **Note:** Prev. Y#763.

Date	Mintage	XF40	MS60	MS63	MS65	MS66
1993	8,888	PF65 2,000	PF67 2,400	PF69 2,700		

KM# 539 100 YUAN
8.00 g., 0.916 Gold 0.2356 oz. AGW **Obv:** National emblem, date below **Rev:** Bust of Soong Ching-ling half left, 1892-1981, Revolutionary Stateswoman, denomination at right **Note:** Prev. Y#760.

Date	Mintage	XF40	MS60	MS63	MS65	MS66
1993	2,000	PF65 700	PF67 900	PF69 1,200		

KM# 551 100 YUAN
31.10 g., 0.999 Gold 0.999 oz. AGW **Obv:** Great Wall, date below **Rev:** Guanyin, Goddess of Mercy, seated in flower, denomination at left **Note:** Prev. Y#504.

Date	Mintage	XF40	MS60	MS63	MS65	MS66
1993	1,000	PF65 2,200	PF67 2,600	PF69 3,000		

KM# 574 100 YUAN
33.95 g., 0.917 Gold 1.0009 oz. AGW **Subject:** Bronze Age Sculptures **Obv:** National emblem, date below **Rev:** Bull lantern, denomination at left **Note:** Prev. Y#411.

Date	Mintage	XF40	MS60	MS63	MS65	MS66
1993	500	PF65 4,000	PF67 5,500	PF69 7,000		

KM# 592 100 YUAN
31.10 g., 0.999 Gold 0.999 oz. AGW **Subject:** Mount Tai **Obv:** Great Wall **Rev:** Temple **Note:** Prev. Y#777.

Date	Mintage	XF40	MS60	MS63	MS65	MS66
1993	8,888	PF65 1,900	PF67 2,100	PF69 2,300		

KM# 598 100 YUAN
31.13 g., 0.999 Gold 0.9999 oz. AGW **Obv:** Temple, date below **Rev:** Two peacocks, denomination above **Note:** Prev. Y#354.

Date	Mintage	XF40	MS60	MS63	MS65	MS66
1993	1,200	PF65 7,000	PF67 9,500	PF69 11,000		

KM# 529 100 YUAN
10.37 g., 0.333 Gold 0.111 oz. AGW **Series:** Centennial Olympics, Atlanta 1994 - 26th Summer Olympic Games **Rev:** Female torch runner, denomination lower left **Note:** Prev. Y#497.

Date	Mintage	XF40	MS60	MS63	MS65	MS66
1994	5,000	PF65 1,300	PF67 1,500	PF69 1,800		

KM# 566 100 YUAN
8.00 g., 0.916 Gold 0.2356 oz. AGW, 23 mm. **Series:** Endangered wildlife **Rev:** Panda climbing tree

Date	Mintage	XF40	MS60	MS63	MS65	MS66
1994	5,000	PF65 900	PF67 1,100	PF69 1,400		

KM# 653 100 YUAN
8.00 g., 0.917 Gold 0.2359 oz. AGW **Subject:** 12th Asian Games **Obv:** National emblem, row of athletic figures below, date at bottom **Rev:** Gymnast on bars, denomination at right **Note:** Prev. Y#440.

Date	Mintage	XF40	MS60	MS63	MS65	MS66
1994	3,000	PF65 625	PF67 725	PF69 850		

KM# 658 100 YUAN
10.36 g., 0.917 Gold 0.3054 oz. AGW **Obv:** National emblem **Rev:** Emperor Zhou Wenwang, denomination at left **Note:** Prev. Y#543.

Date	Mintage	XF40	MS60	MS63	MS65	MS66
1994	Est. 10000	PF65 1,600	PF67 2,000	PF69 2,300		

KM# 672 100 YUAN
15.55 g., 0.916 Gold 0.4579 oz. AGW **Obv:** Building, date below **Rev:** Black-billed magpie on branch, denomination below **Shape:** 12-sided **Note:** Prev. Y#695.

Date	Mintage	XF40	MS60	MS63	MS65	MS66
1994	1,300	PF65 1,500	PF67 1,700	PF69 1,900		

KM# 681 100 YUAN
373.24 g., 0.999 Silver 11.9878 oz. ASW, 85 mm. **Rev:** Unicorn with offspring, denomination at left **Note:** Illustration reduced. Prev. Y#426.

Date	Mintage	XF40	MS60	MS63	MS65	MS66
1994	2,000	PF65 2,500	PF67 2,800	PF69 3,200		

KM# 682 100 YUAN
31.10 g., 0.999 Gold 0.999 oz. AGW **Obv:** Child riding Eastern Unicorn, date below **Rev:** Unicorn, denomination at left, rose sprays below **Note:** Prev. Y#427.

Date	Mintage	XF40	MS60	MS63	MS65	MS66
1994	1,100	PF65 3,000	PF67 4,000	PF69 5,000		

KM# 699 100 YUAN
373.24 g., 0.999 Silver 11.9879 oz. ASW, 80 mm. **Rev:** Two children with dog

Date	Mintage	XF40	MS60	MS63	MS65	MS66
1994	400	PF65 3,500	PF67 4,500	PF69 5,500		

KM# 764 100 YUAN
10.37 g., 0.999 Gold 0.333 oz. AGW **Series:** Olympics **Obv:** National emblem, date below **Rev:** Ribbon dancer, denomination at right **Note:** Prev. Y#844.

Date	Mintage	XF40	MS60	MS63	MS65	MS66
1995	10,000	PF65 775	PF67 950	PF69 1,100		

KM# 765 100 YUAN
10.37 g., 0.999 Gold 0.333 oz. AGW **Series:** 1996 Olympics **Obv:** National emblem, date below **Rev:** High diver, denomination below **Note:** Prev. Y#843.

Date	Mintage	XF40	MS60	MS63	MS65	MS66
1995	10,000	PF65 775	PF67 950	PF69 1,100		

KM# 772 100 YUAN
373.24 g., 0.999 Silver 11.988 oz. ASW **Subject:** Zheng Chenggong **Obv:** Chiqian building **Rev:** Standing figure with flag and ships **Note:** Prev. Y#823.

Date	Mintage	XF40	MS60	MS63	MS65	MS66
1995	150	PF65 1,350	PF67 1,750	PF69 2,150		

KM# 802 100 YUAN
373.24 g., 0.999 Silver 11.9878 oz. ASW, 98 mm. **Rev:** Unicorn with offspring, denomination at left **Note:** Illustration reduced. Prev. Y#698.

Date	Mintage	XF40	MS60	MS63	MS65	MS66
1995	—	PF65 4,000	PF67 6,000	PF69 8,000		

KM# 803 100 YUAN
31.10 g., 0.999 Gold 0.999 oz. AGW, 32 mm. **Subject:** Unicorn **Obv:** Eastern unicorn **Rev:** Western unicorn with offspring **Edge:** Reeded **Note:** Prev. Y#1012; 1062.

Date	Mintage	XF40	MS60	MS63	MS65	MS66
1995	504	PF65 4,000	PF67 5,500	PF69 7,000		

KM# 809 100 YUAN
31.10 g., 0.999 Gold 0.999 oz. AGW **Rev:** Soldiers above bridge guarded by chinze, denomination at right **Note:** Prev. Y#697.

Date	Mintage	XF40	MS60	MS63	MS65	MS66
1995	1,400	PF65 2,000	PF67 2,500	PF69 3,000		

KM# 810 100 YUAN
31.10 g., 0.999 Gold 0.999 oz. AGW **Subject:** 50th Anniversary - Anti-Japanese War **Rev:** People at wall, denomination below **Note:** Prev. Y#696.

Date	Mintage	XF40	MS60	MS63	MS65	MS66
1995	1,400	PF65 2,000	PF67 2,500	PF69 3,000		

KM# 835 100 YUAN
31.01 g., 0.999 Gold 0.996 oz. AGW **Subject:** Chinese Culture Series **Obv:** Great Wall seen through arch **Rev:** Mencius seated at table **Note:** Prev. Y#805.

Date	Mintage	XF40	MS60	MS63	MS65	MS66
1995	1,000	PF65 7,000	PF67 10,000	PF69 12,000		

KM# 836 100 YUAN
31.01 g., 0.999 Gold 0.996 oz. AGW **Subject:** Chinese Culture Series **Obv:** Great Wall seen through arch **Rev:** Lion dance **Note:** Prev. Y#807.

Date	Mintage	XF40	MS60	MS63	MS65	MS66
1995	1,000	PF65 7,000	PF67 10,000	PF69 12,000		

KM# 837 100 YUAN
31.01 g., 0.999 Gold 0.996 oz. AGW **Subject:** Chinese Culture Series **Obv:** Great Wall seen through arch **Rev:** Tang Taizong seated **Note:** Prev. Y#806.

Date	Mintage	XF40	MS60	MS63	MS65	MS66
1995	1,000	PF65 7,000	PF67 10,000	PF69 12,000		

KM# 838 100 YUAN
31.10 g., 0.999 Gold 0.999 oz. AGW **Subject:** Chinese Culture Series **Obv:** Great Wall seen through arch **Rev:** Pagoda of Six Harmonies **Note:** Prev. Y#804.

Date	Mintage	XF40	MS60	MS63	MS65	MS66
1995	1,000	PF65 7,000	PF67 10,000	PF69 12,000		

KM# 839 100 YUAN
31.10 g., 0.999 Gold 0.999 oz. AGW **Subject:** Chinese Culture Series **Obv:** Great Wall seen through arch **Rev:** Female opera role **Note:** Prev. Y#808.

Date	Mintage	XF40	MS60	MS63	MS65	MS66
1995	1,000	PF65 7,000	PF67 10,000	PF69 12,000		

KM# 853 100 YUAN
31.10 g., 0.999 Gold 0.999 oz. AGW **Subject:** Romance of the Three Kingdoms **Obv:** Luo Guanzhong **Rev:** Standing Liu Bei with flags **Note:** Prev. Y#830.

Date	Mintage	XF40	MS60	MS63	MS65	MS66
1995	1,500	PF65 3,000	PF67 5,000	PF69 6,500		

KM# 854 100 YUAN
31.10 g., 0.999 Gold 0.999 oz. AGW **Subject:** Romance of the Three Kingdoms **Obv:** Luo Guanzhong **Rev:** Seated Guan Yu reading **Note:** Prev. Y#831.

Date	Mintage	XF40	MS60	MS63	MS65	MS66
1995	1,500	PF65 3,000	PF67 5,000	PF69 6,500		

KM# 855 100 YUAN
31.10 g., 0.999 Gold 0.999 oz. AGW **Subject:** Romance of the Three Kingdoms **Obv:** Luo Guanzhong **Rev:** Zhuge Liang seated on throne **Note:** Prev. Y#833.

Date	Mintage	XF40	MS60	MS63	MS65	MS66
1995	1,500	PF65 3,000	PF67 5,000	PF69 6,500		

KM# 856 100 YUAN
31.10 g., 0.999 Gold 0.999 oz. AGW **Subject:** Romance of the Three Kingdoms **Obv:** Luo Guanzhong **Rev:** Zhang Fei on horseback **Note:** Prev. Y#832.

Date	Mintage	XF40	MS60	MS63	MS65	MS66
1995	1,500	PF65 3,000	PF67 5,000	PF69 6,500		

KM# 872 100 YUAN
16.98 g., 0.916 Gold 0.500 oz. AGW **Obv:** Great Wall, date below **Rev:** Perched eagle, denomination lower right **Shape:** 12-sided **Note:** Prev. Y#810.

Date	Mintage	XF40	MS60	MS63	MS65	MS66
1995	1,300	PF65 3,000	PF67 5,000	PF69 6,500		

KM# 948 100 YUAN
31.10 g., 0.999 Platinum 0.999 oz. APW, 32 mm. **Subject:** Unicorn **Obv:** Eastern unicorn, full body **Rev:** Western unicorn and maiden **Edge:** Reeded **Note:** Prev. Y#956a.

Date	Mintage	XF40	MS60	MS63	MS65	MS66
1996	500	PF65 7,000	PF67 8,500	PF69 10,000		

KM# 1021 100 YUAN
373.24 g., 0.999 Silver 11.9879 oz. ASW, 80 mm. **Subject:** Painting Master Qi Baishi **Rev:** Leaves & praying mantis

Date	Mintage	XF40	MS60	MS63	MS65	MS66
1997	80	PF65 6,000	PF67 7,000	PF69 8,000		

KM# 1034 100 YUAN
31.10 g., 0.9995 Platinum 0.9995 oz. APW **Obv:** Eastern unicorn **Rev:** Western unicorn **Note:** Prev. Y#966.

Date	Mintage	XF40	MS60	MS63	MS65	MS66
1997	500	PF65 8,000	PF67 9,500	PF69 12,000		

KM# 1092 100 YUAN
16.98 g., 0.916 Gold 0.500 oz. AGW, 26.5 mm. **Subject:** Wildlife of China **Obv:** The Great Wall **Rev:** Penguin **Edge:** Plain **Note:** Prev. Y#1080.

Date	Mintage	XF40	MS60	MS63	MS65	MS66
1997	2,800	PF65 1,500	PF67 2,200	PF69 3,200		

KM# 319 150 YUAN
622.04 g., 0.999 Silver 19.979 oz. ASW **Rev:** Phoenix and dragon **Note:** Prev. Y#208.

Date	Mintage	XF40	MS60	MS63	MS65	MS66
1990	1,500	PF65 5,000	PF67 6,500	PF69 8,000		

KM# 599 150 YUAN
622.04 g., 0.999 Silver 19.979 oz. ASW **Obv:** Temple of Harmony **Rev:** Two peacocks, denomination below **Note:** Prev. Y#355.

Date	Mintage	XF40	MS60	MS63	MS65	MS66
1993	500	PF65 9,500	PF67 11,000	PF69 13,000		

KM# 683 150 YUAN
622.04 g., 0.999 Silver 19.979 oz. ASW **Obv:** Figure on Eastern unicorn, date below **Rev:** Unicorn, denomination at left, rose sprays below **Note:** Prev. Y#428.

Date	Mintage	XF40	MS60	MS63	MS65	MS66
1994	500	PF65 5,000	PF67 6,000	PF69 7,000		

KM# 804 150 YUAN
622.04 g., 0.999 Silver 19.979 oz. ASW, 98 mm. **Obv:** Eastern unicorn, rearing, date below **Rev:** Unicorn with offspring **Note:** Illustration reduced. Prev. Y#699.

Date	Mintage	XF40	MS60	MS63	MS65	MS66
1995	500	PF65 6,000	PF67 7,000	PF69 8,000		

KM# 976 150 YUAN
622.04 g., 0.999 Silver 19.979 oz. ASW **Obv:** Eastern unicorn, date below **Rev:** Western unicorn, rearing, denomination below **Note:** Prev. Y#884.

Date	Mintage	XF40	MS60	MS63	MS65	MS66
1996	500	PF65 5,500	PF67 6,500	PF69 7,500		

KM# 46 200 YUAN
8.47 g., 0.917 Gold 0.2497 oz. AGW **Subject:** Chinese Bronze Age Finds **Obv:** National emblem **Rev:** Leopard, denomination below **Note:** Prev. Y#28.

Date	Mintage	XF40	MS60	MS63	MS65	MS66
1981	1,000	PF65 4,500	PF67 5,500	PF69 6,500		

KM# 47 200 YUAN
8.47 g., 0.917 Gold 0.2497 oz. AGW **Subject:** Chinese Bronze Age Finds **Obv:** National emblem **Rev:** Winged creature, denomination below **Note:** Prev. Y#29.

Date	Mintage	XF40	MS60	MS63	MS65	MS66
1981	1,000	PF65 4,500	PF67 5,500	PF69 6,500		

KM# 61 200 YUAN
8.47 g., 0.917 Gold 0.2497 oz. AGW **Subject:** World Cup Soccer **Obv:** National emblem, date below **Rev:** Player kicking, denomination below **Note:** Prev. Y#37.

Date	Mintage	XF40	MS60	MS63	MS65	MS66
1982	1,261	PF65 1,400	PF67 1,700	PF69 2,100		

KM# 320 200 YUAN
62.21 g., 0.999 Gold 1.998 oz. AGW **Obv:** Great Wall, date below **Rev:** Denomination between Phoenix and dragon **Note:** Prev. Y#209.

Date	Mintage	XF40	MS60	MS63	MS65	MS66
1990	2,538	PF65 7,000	PF67 8,000	PF69 9,000		

KM# 420 200 YUAN
1000.00 g., 0.999 Silver 32.1186 oz. ASW, 100 mm. **Series:** Scientific and technical inventions **Rev:** Ship

Date	Mintage	XF40	MS60	MS63	MS65	MS66
1992	250	PF65 30,000	PF67 40,000	PF69 50,000		

KM# 421 200 YUAN
1000.00 g., 0.999 Silver 32.1186 oz. ASW, 100 mm. **Series:** Scientific and technical inventions **Rev:** Large urn

Date	Mintage	XF40	MS60	MS63	MS65	MS66
1992	250	PF65 30,000	PF67 40,000	PF69 50,000		

KM# 422 200 YUAN
1000.00 g., 0.999 Silver 32.1186 oz. ASW, 100 mm. **Series:** Scientific and technical inventions **Rev:** Kite flying

Date	Mintage	XF40	MS60	MS63	MS65	MS66
1992	250	PF65 30,000	PF67 40,000	PF69 50,000		

KM# 423 200 YUAN
1000.00 g., 0.999 Silver 32.1186 oz. ASW, 100 mm. **Series:** Scientific and technical inventions **Rev:** Spoon on table

Date	Mintage	XF40	MS60	MS63	MS65	MS66
1992	250	PF65 30,000	PF67 40,000	PF69 50,000		

KM# 424 200 YUAN
1000.00 g., 0.999 Silver 32.1186 oz. ASW, 100 mm. **Series:** Scientific and technical inventions **Rev:** Large urn with flags

Date	Mintage	XF40	MS60	MS63	MS65	MS66
1992	250	PF65 30,000	PF67 40,000	PF69 50,000		

KM# 863 200 YUAN
1000.00 g., 0.999 Silver 32.1186 oz. ASW, 100 mm. **Subject:** 50th Anniversary - Return of Taiwan to China **Obv:** Great Wall **Rev:** Taiwan and China maps **Note:** Prev. Y#816.

Date	Mintage	XF40	MS60	MS63	MS65	MS66
1995	100	PF65 12,000	PF67 17,000	PF69 21,000		

KM# 1022 200 YUAN
1000.00 g., 0.999 Silver 32.1186 oz. ASW, 100 mm. **Subject:** Painting Master Qui Baishi **Rev:** Two baskets

Date	Mintage	XF40	MS60	MS63	MS65	MS66
1997	188	PF65 6,500	PF67 9,500	PF69 11,000		

KM# 1052 200 YUAN
1000.00 g., 0.999 Silver 32.1186 oz. ASW **Subject:** Sino - Thailand Friendship **Obv:** Forbidden City and Thai Royal Palace **Rev:** 2 Buddha statues, one in cameo **Note:** Prev. Y#712.

Date	Mintage	XF40	MS60	MS63	MS65	MS66
1997	880	PF65 3,500	PF67 4,250	PF69 5,000		

KM# 1198 200 YUAN
1000.00 g., 0.999 Silver 32.1186 oz. ASW **Subject:** Vault protector of the Tang Dynasty **Obv:** Cash coin **Rev:** Value and flora **Shape:** 120

Date	Mintage	XF40	MS60	MS63	MS65	MS66
1998	2,800	PF65 5,500	PF67 6,500	PF69 8,000		

KM# 28 250 YUAN
8.00 g., 0.917 Gold 0.2359 oz. AGW **Subject:** 1980 Winter Olympics **Obv:** State seal **Rev:** Down hill skier **Note:** Prev. Y#22.

Date	Mintage	XF40	MS60	MS63	MS65	MS66
1980	20,000	PF65 700	PF67 850	PF69 1,100		

KM# 37 300 YUAN
10.00 g., 0.917 Gold 0.2948 oz. AGW **Series:** 1980 Olympics **Subject:** Archery **Obv:** National emblem, denomination below **Rev:** Two archers, date below **Note:** Prev. Y#23.

Date	Mintage	XF40	MS60	MS63	MS65	MS66
1980	15,000	PF65 1,350	PF67 1,450	PF69 1,600		

KM# 668 300 YUAN
103.13 g., 0.999 Gold 3.3122 oz. AGW **Obv:** Great Wall, date below **Rev:** Guanyin, Goddess of Mercy, holding child, facing, denomination at left **Note:** Prev. Y#515.

Date	Mintage	XF40	MS60	MS63	MS65	MS66
1994	128	PF65 7,500	PF67 9,500	PF69 11,000		

KM# 1335 300 YUAN
1000.00 g., 0.999 Silver 32.1186 oz. ASW, 100 mm. **Subject:** The millennium **Rev:** Globe within eye design

Date	Mintage	XF40	MS60	MS63	MS65	MS66
2000	3,000	PF65 2,000	PF67 2,500	PF69 2,900		

KM# 4 400 YUAN
16.95 g., 0.917 Gold 0.4997 oz. AGW **Obv:** National emblem, two dates below **Rev:** 30th Anniversary of People's Republic - Tiananmen, denomination below **Note:** Prev. Y#4.

Date	Mintage	XF40	MS60	MS63	MS65	MS66
ND-1979	Est. 23000	PF65 1,100	PF67 1,400	PF69 1,800		

KM# 5 400 YUAN
16.95 g., 0.917 Gold 0.4997 oz. AGW **Subject:** 30th Anniversary of People's Republic **Obv:** National emblem, two dates below **Rev:** People's Heroes Monument, denomination below **Note:** Prev. Y#5.

Date	Mintage	XF40	MS60	MS63	MS65	MS66
ND-1979	Est. 23000	PF65 1,100	PF67 1,400	PF69 1,800		

KM# 6 400 YUAN
16.95 g., 0.917 Gold 0.4997 oz. AGW **Subject:** 30th Anniversary of People's Republic **Obv:** National emblem, two dates below **Rev:** Chairman Mao Memorial Hall, denomination below **Note:** Prev. Y#6.

Date	Mintage	XF40	MS60	MS63	MS65	MS66
ND-1979	Est. 23000	PF65 1,100	PF67 1,400	PF69 1,800		

KM# 7 400 YUAN
16.95 g., 0.917 Gold 0.4997 oz. AGW **Subject:** 30th Anniversary of People's Republic **Obv:** National emblem **Rev:** Great Hall of the People **Note:** Prev. Y#7.

Date	Mintage	XF40	MS60	MS63	MS65	MS66
ND-1979	—	PF65 1,100	PF67 1,400	PF69 1,800		

KM# 48 400 YUAN
16.95 g., 0.917 Gold 0.4997 oz. AGW **Subject:** Chinese Bronze Age Finds **Obv:** State seal **Rev:** Rhinoceros, left, denomination below **Note:** Prev. Y#30.

Date	Mintage	XF40	MS60	MS63	MS65	MS66
1981	1,000	PF65 4,500	PF67 5,500	PF69 6,500		

KM# 51 400 YUAN
13.36 g., 0.917 Gold 0.3939 oz. AGW **Subject:** 70th Anniversary of 1911 Revolution **Obv:** Bust of Sun-Yat-sen, facing, two dates below **Rev:** Nationalist troops attacking, denomination and date below **Note:** Prev. Y#47.

Date	Mintage	XF40	MS60	MS63	MS65	MS66
1981	1,338	PF65 3,500	PF67 4,000	PF69 5,000		

KM# 9 450 YUAN
17.17 g., 0.900 Gold 0.4968 oz. AGW **Series:** International Year of the Child **Obv:** State seal above floral sprays **Rev:** Two children planting flower **Note:** Prev. Y#9.

Date	Mintage	XF40	MS60	MS63	MS65	MS66
1979	Est. 12000	PF65 2,000	PF67 2,500	PF69 3,000		

KM# 81 500 YUAN
155.52 g., 0.999 Gold 4.9949 oz. AGW, 60 mm. **Subject:** Marco Polo bust on left, looking right, buildings at right, denomination below **Note:** Illustration reduced. Prev. Y#395.

Date	Mintage	XF40	MS60	MS63	MS65	MS66
1993	100	PF65 35,000	PF67 55,000			

KM# 509 500 YUAN
155.52 g., 0.999 Gold 4.9949 oz. AGW, 60 mm. **Subject:** Chinese Gods: Fu, Lu and Shu, denomination below **Obv:** Building and Great Wall, date below **Rev:** Three gods with symbol on panel and child **Note:** Illustration reduced. Prev. Y#407.

Date	Mintage	XF40	MS60	MS63	MS65	MS66
1993	99	PF65 65,000	PF67 85,000			

KM# 519 500 YUAN
155.52 g., 0.999 Gold 4.9949 oz. AGW, 60 mm. **Subject:** Yandi, Semi-mythical First Emperor **Obv:** National emblem **Rev:** 3/4 figure looking left, denomination over right shoulder **Note:** Illustration reduced. Prev. Y#417.

Date	Mintage	XF40	MS60	MS63	MS65	MS66
1993	99	PF65 125,000	PF67 145,000			

KM# 536 500 YUAN
155.52 g., 0.999 Gold 4.9949 oz. AGW **Subject:** Sun Yat-sen **Obv:** Home of Sun Yat-sen, date below **Rev:** Bust of Sun Yat-sen, facing, denomination at right **Note:** Prev. Y#764.

Date	Mintage	XF40	MS60	MS63	MS65	MS66
1993	99	PF65 65,000	PF67 85,000			

KM# 544 500 YUAN
155.52 g., 0.999 Gold 4.9949 oz. AGW, 60 mm. **Subject:** Chairman Mao **Obv:** Tall building, date at right **Rev:** 3/4 figure of Mao looking left, denomination at right **Note:** Illustration reduced. Prev. Y#415.

Date	Mintage	XF40	MS60	MS63	MS65	MS66
1993	100	PF65 50,000	PF67 70,000			

KM# 593 500 YUAN
155.52 g., 0.999 Gold 4.9949 oz. AGW **Subject:** Tomb of Emperor Huang **Obv:** Great Wall, date below **Rev:** Tomb, denomination below **Note:** Prev. Y#778.

Date	Mintage	XF40	MS60	MS63	MS65	MS66
1993	99	PF65 45,000	PF67 65,000			

KM# 600 500 YUAN
155.52 g., 0.999 Gold 4.9949 oz. AGW **Obv:** Temple of Harmony **Rev:** Two peacocks **Note:** Prev. Y#356.

Date	Mintage	XF40	MS60	MS63	MS65	MS66
1993	99	PF65 45,000	PF67 65,000			

KM# 670 500 YUAN
155.52 g., 0.999 Gold 4.9949 oz. AGW, 60 mm. **Obv:** Taiwan Temple, date below **Rev:** Buddha statue, denomination below **Note:** Illustration reduced. Prev. Y#449.

Date	Mintage	XF40	MS60	MS63	MS65	MS66
1994	76	PF65 55,000	PF67 75,000			

KM# 684 500 YUAN
155.52 g., 0.999 Gold 4.9949 oz. AGW **Obv:** Eastern unicorn with rider, date below **Rev:** Unicorn above sprays of roses, denomination at left **Note:** Prev. Y#429.

Date	Mintage	XF40	MS60	MS63	MS65	MS66
1994	99	PF65 35,000	PF67 55,000			

KM# 688 500 YUAN
155.52 g., 0.999 Gold 4.9949 oz. AGW **Subject:** Sino-Singapore Friendship **Obv:** Great Wall, date below **Rev:** Singapore Harbor, denomination below **Note:** Illustration reduced. Prev. Y#701.

Date	Mintage	XF40	MS60	MS63	MS65	MS66
1994	91	PF65 55,000	PF67 75,000			

KM# 700 500 YUAN
155.52 g., 0.999 Gold 4.9949 oz. AGW, 60 mm. **Subject:** Children At Play **Rev:** Two children with cat, denomination below **Note:** Illustration reduced. Prev. Y#462.

Date	Mintage	XF40	MS60	MS63	MS65	MS66
1994	99	PF65 45,000	PF67 65,000			

KM# 770 500 YUAN
151.00 g., 0.999 Gold 4.8499 oz. AGW, 60 mm. **Subject:** 100th Anniversary Birth of Xu Beihong **Rev:** Figure riding oxen

Date	Mintage	XF40	MS60	MS63	MS65	MS66
1995	100	PF65 45,000	PF67 65,000			

KM# 773 500 YUAN
155.52 g., 0.9999 Gold 4.9995 oz. AGW **Subject:** Zheng Chenggong **Obv:** Chiqian Building **Rev:** Standing figure with flag, war ships in background, two dates upper right, denomination lower right **Note:** Prev. Y#824.

Date	Mintage	XF40	MS60	MS63	MS65	MS66
1995	99	PF65 45,000	PF67 65,000			

KM# 805 500 YUAN
155.52 g., 0.999 Gold 4.9949 oz. AGW, 60 mm. **Subject:** Unicorn **Obv:** Eastern unicorn **Rev:** Unicorn mother and baby **Edge:** Reeded **Note:** Prev. Y#656.

Date	Mintage	XF40	MS60	MS63	MS65	MS66
1995	99	PF65 45,000	PF67 65,000			

KM# 817 500 YUAN
155.52 g., 0.999 Gold 4.9949 oz. AGW **Subject:** Return of Hong Kong to China - Series I **Obv:** Tiananmen Square, date below **Rev:** Bust of Deng Xiaoping over Hong Kong city view **Note:** Prev. Y#533.

Date	Mintage	XF40	MS60	MS63	MS65	MS66
1995	228	PF65 30,000	PF67 50,000			

KM# A823 500 YUAN
155.52 g., 0.999 Gold 4.9949 oz. AGW, 60 mm. **Rev:** Dragon boat, denomination below **Note:** Illustration reduced. Prev. Y#649.

Date	Mintage	XF40	MS60	MS63	MS65	MS66
1995	99	PF65 50,000	PF67 70,000			

KM# 846 500 YUAN
155.52 g., 0.999 Gold 4.9949 oz. AGW, 60 mm. **Subject:** Yellow River culture **Rev:** Nu Wa Rising, denomination below **Note:** Illustration reduced. Prev. Y#594.

Date	Mintage	XF40	MS60	MS63	MS65	MS66
1995	99	PF65 40,000	PF67 60,000			

KM# 857 500 YUAN
155.52 g., 0.9999 Gold 4.9995 oz. AGW **Subject:** Romance of the Three Kingdoms Series **Obv:** Bust of Luo Guanzhong, looking right **Rev:** Three heroes of Shu Han, denomination above **Note:** Prev. Y#834.

Date	Mintage	XF40	MS60	MS63	MS65	MS66
1995	99	PF65 35,000	PF67 55,000			

KM# 864 500 YUAN
155.52 g., 0.9999 Gold 4.9995 oz. AGW **Subject:** 50th Anniversary - Taiwan's Return to China **Obv:** Great Wall, date below **Rev:** Taiwan and China maps, date at right, denomination lower left **Note:** Illustration reduced. Prev. Y#817.

Date	Mintage	XF40	MS60	MS63	MS65	MS66
1995	99	PF65 45,000	PF67 65,000			

KM# 949 500 YUAN
155.52 g., 0.9999 Gold 4.9995 oz. AGW **Obv:** Western unicorn on hind legs, surrounded by roses **Rev:** Eastern unicorn standing **Note:** Prev. Y#657.

Date	Mintage	XF40	MS60	MS63	MS65	MS66
1996	108	PF65 45,000	PF67 65,000			

KM# 958 500 YUAN
155.52 g., 0.9999 Gold 4.9995 oz. AGW **Subject:** Return of Hong Kong to China - Series II **Note:** Prev. Y#659.

Date	Mintage	XF40	MS60	MS63	MS65	MS66
1996	228	PF65 16,000	PF67 36,000			

KM# 965 500 YUAN
155.52 g., 0.999 Gold 4.995 oz. AGW **Subject:** Romance of the Three Kingdoms Series **Obv:** Bust of Luo Guanzhong **Rev:** Guan Du on horseback leading troops, denomination at left **Note:** Illustration reduced. Prev. Y#882.

Date	Mintage	XF40	MS60	MS63	MS65	MS66
1996	99	PF65 45,000	PF67 65,000			

KM# 1023 500 YUAN
155.51 g., 0.999 Gold 4.9948 oz. AGW, 60 mm. **Subject:** Painting Master Qi Baishi

Date	Mintage	XF40	MS60	MS63	MS65	MS66
1997	99	PF65 65,000	PF67 85,000			

KM# 1046 500 YUAN
155.52 g., 0.999 Gold 4.995 oz. AGW **Subject:** Return of Hong Kong to China - Series III **Obv:** Tiananmen Square **Rev:** Bust of Deng Xiaoping above city, denomination at left **Note:** Prev. Y#904.

Date	Mintage	XF40	MS60	MS63	MS65	MS66
1997	228	PF65 16,000	PF67 36,000			

KM# 1050 500 YUAN
155.52 g., 0.999 Gold 4.995 oz. AGW **Subject:** Return of Macao to China **Obv:** Tiananmen Square **Rev:** Deng Xiaoping standing viewing Macao, denomination at right **Note:** Prev. Y#907.

Date	Mintage	XF40	MS60	MS63	MS65	MS66
1997	228	PF65 15,000	PF67 35,000			

KM# 1066 500 YUAN
155.52 g., 0.999 Gold 4.995 oz. AGW **Subject:** Greeting Spring **Obv:** Lantern **Rev:** Children lighting firecrackers **Note:** Prev. Y#1022.

Date	Mintage	XF40	MS60	MS63	MS65	MS66
1997	108	PF65 30,000	PF67 50,000			

KM# 1083 500 YUAN
151.50 g., 0.999 Gold 4.866 oz. AGW, 60 mm. **Series:** Yellow river culture **Rev:** Kneeling archer shooting skyward right

Date	Mintage	XF40	MS60	MS63	MS65	MS66
1997	128	PF65 45,000	PF67 65,000			

KM# 1090 500 YUAN
151.50 g., 0.999 Gold 4.866 oz. AGW, 60 mm. **Series:** Classic literature **Rev:** Warrior standing on prow

Date	Mintage	XF40	MS60	MS63	MS65	MS66
1997	168	PF65 45,000	PF67 65,000			

KM# 1171 500 YUAN
151.50 g., 0.999 Gold 4.866 oz. AGW, 60 mm. **Subject:** Macao's return to China **Rev:** Birds flying over tablet, lighthouse at left, gate at right

Date	Mintage	XF40	MS60	MS63	MS65	MS66
1998	228	PF65 27,000	PF67 47,000			

KM# 1180 500 YUAN
155.52 g., 0.999 Gold 4.995 oz. AGW **Subject:** Greeting Spring **Obv:** Lantern **Rev:** Children making kites **Note:** Prev. Y#1023.

Date	Mintage	XF40	MS60	MS63	MS65	MS66
1998	128	PF65 35,000	PF67 55,000			

KM# 1251 500 YUAN
155.52 g., 0.999 Gold 4.995 oz. AGW **Subject:** 50th Anniversary of People's Republic Founding Ceremony **Shape:** Rectangular **Note:** Prev. Y#1026.

Date	Mintage	XF40	MS60	MS63	MS65	MS66
1999	990	PF65 22,500	PF67 32,500			

KM# 1282 500 YUAN
155.50 g., 0.999 Gold 4.9944 oz. AGW, 60 mm. **Subject:** Return of Macao **Rev:** Views of Macao

Date	Mintage	XF40	MS60	MS63	MS65	MS66
1999	228	PF65 15,000	PF67 30,000			

KM# 1336 500 YUAN
155.52 g., 0.999 Gold 4.995 oz. AGW **Subject:** Y2K **Note:** Prev. Y#1028.

Date	Mintage	XF40	MS60	MS63	MS65	MS66
2000	1,000	PF65 13,000	PF67 24,000			

KM# 49 800 YUAN
33.20 g., 0.917 Gold 0.9788 oz. AGW **Subject:** Chinese Bronze Age Finds **Obv:** National emblem, date below **Rev:** Elephant statue, left, denomination below **Note:** Prev. #Y31.

Date	Mintage	XF40	MS60	MS63	MS65	MS66
1981	1,000	PF65 7,500	PF67 9,500			

KM# 259 1500 YUAN
622.60 g., 0.999 Gold 19.997 oz. AGW, 90 mm. **Subject:** Anniversary of People's Republic **Obv:** National emblem above city view with fireworks in sky **Rev:** Man giving speech, people in background, denomination below **Note:** Illustration reduced. Prev. #Y232.

Date	Mintage	XF40	MS60	MS63	MS65	MS66
1989	100	PF65 90,000	PF67 110,000			

KM# 321 1500 YUAN
622.60 g., 0.999 Gold 19.997 oz. AGW **Obv:** Great Wall **Rev:** Denomination divides Phoenix and dragon **Note:** Prev. #Y210.

Date	Mintage	XF40	MS60	MS63	MS65	MS66
1990	250	PF65 55,000	PF67 75,000			

KM# 552 1500 YUAN
562.51 g., 0.999 Gold 18.0669 oz. AGW, 85 mm. **Rev:** Guanyin, Goddess of Mercy, seated in flower, denomination at left **Note:** Illustration reduced. Prev. #Y505.

Date	Mintage	XF40	MS60	MS63	MS65	MS66
1993	88	PF65 80,000	PF67 100,000			

KM# 601 1500 YUAN
622.60 g., 0.999 Gold 19.997 oz. AGW **Obv:** Temple of Harmony **Rev:** Two peacocks **Note:** Prev. #Y357.

Date	Mintage	XF40	MS60	MS63	MS65	MS66
1993	66	PF65 65,000	PF67 85,000			

KM# 425 2000 YUAN
1000.00 g., 0.999 Gold 32.1186 oz. AGW **Subject:** Chinese Inventions and Discoveries **Obv:** Great Wall **Rev:** Seismograph **Note:** Prev. #Y749.

Date	Mintage	XF40	MS60	MS63	MS65	MS66
1992	Est. 4	PF65 300,000	PF67 350,000			

KM# 426 2000 YUAN
1000.00 g., 0.999 Gold 32.1186 oz. AGW, 100 mm. **Subject:** Chinese inventions **Rev:** First compass, denomination below **Note:** Illustration reduced. Prev. #Y402.

Date	Mintage	XF40	MS60	MS63	MS65	MS66
1992	10	PF65 250,000	PF67 280,000			

KM# 685 2000 YUAN
1000.00 g., 0.999 Gold 32.1186 oz. AGW **Obv:** Figure on Eastern unicorn, date below **Rev:** Unicorn, denomination below, rose sprays below **Note:** Prev. #Y430.

Date	Mintage	XF40	MS60	MS63	MS65	MS66
1994	20	PF65 200,000	PF67 220,000			

KM# 689 2000 YUAN
1000.00 g., 0.999 Gold 32.1186 oz. AGW, 112 mm. **Subject:** Sino-Singapore Friendship **Obv:** Great Wall, date below **Rev:** Singapore Harbor, denomination below **Note:** Illustration reduced. Prev. #Y703.

Date	Mintage	XF40	MS60	MS63	MS65	MS66
1994	15	PF65 95,000	PF67 115,000			

KM# 865 2000 YUAN
1000.00 g., 0.999 Gold 32.1186 oz. AGW **Subject:** 50th Anniversary - Taiwan's Return to China **Obv:** Great Wall **Rev:** Taiwan and China maps **Note:** Prev. #Y818.

Date	Mintage	XF40	MS60	MS63	MS65	MS66
1995	25	PF65 200,000	PF67 220,000			

KM# 950 2000 YUAN
1000.00 g., 0.999 Gold 32.1186 oz. AGW **Obv:** Eastern unicorn **Rev:** Western unicorn with maiden **Note:** Prev. #Y957.

Date	Mintage	XF40	MS60	MS63	MS65	MS66
1996	18	PF65 150,000	PF67 170,000			

KM# 1024 2000 YUAN
1000.00 g., 0.999 Gold 32.1186 oz. AGW, 100 mm. **Subject:** Painting Master Qi Baishi **Rev:** Two fruit baskets

Date	Mintage	XF40	MS60	MS63	MS65	MS66
1997	25	PF65 150,000	PF67 170,000			

KM# 1199 2000 YUAN
1000.00 g., 0.999 Gold 32.1186 oz. AGW, 100 mm. **Subject:** Vault protector of the Tang Dynasty **Obv:** Cash coin **Rev:** Value and flora

Date	Mintage	XF40	MS60	MS63	MS65	MS66
1998	68	PF65 100,000	PF67 120,000			

KM# 1337 30000 YUAN
10000.00 g., 0.9999 Gold 321.4751 oz. AGW, 180 mm. **Subject:** Third Millennium **Obv:** China Centenary Altar **Rev:** Denominations **Edge:** Plain **Note:** Previous Y # 1070.

Date	Mintage	XF40	MS60	MS63	MS65	MS66
2000	20	PF65 575,000	PF67 600,000			

SILVER BULLION COINAGE

Lunar Series

KM# 73 10 YUAN
15.00 g., 0.850 Silver 0.4099 oz. ASW **Subject:** Year of the Pig **Rev:** Pigs, denomination below **Note:** Prev. Y#44.

Date	Mintage	XF40	MS60	MS63	MS65	MS66
1983	6,790	PF65 1,400	PF67 1,700	PF69 2,100		

KM# 93 10 YUAN
15.00 g., 0.850 Silver 0,4099 oz. ASW **Subject:** Year of the Rat **Obv:** Building, date below **Rev:** Rat eating squash, denomination below **Note:** Prev. Y#59.

Date	Mintage	XF40	MS60	MS63	MS65	MS66
1984	11,000	PF65 400	PF67 550	PF69 700		

KM# 119 10 YUAN
15.00 g., 0.900 Silver 0.434 oz. ASW **Subject:** Year of the Ox **Rev:** Ox above denomination **Note:** Prev. Y#78.

Date	Mintage	XF40	MS60	MS63	MS65	MS66
1985	22,000	PF65 300	PF67 400	PF69 450		

KM# 137 10 YUAN
15.00 g., 0.900 Silver 0.434 oz. ASW **Subject:** Year of the Tiger **Obv:** Qing Dynasty Palace, date below **Rev:** Tiger, after a painting by He Ziang Ning, denomination upper left **Note:** Prev. Y#98.

Date	Mintage	XF40	MS60	MS63	MS65	MS66
1986	15,000	PF65 300	PF67 350	PF69 400		

KM# 169 10 YUAN
15.00 g., 0.900 Silver 0.434 oz. ASW **Subject:** Year of the Rabbit **Obv:** Yellow Crane Pavilion above legend **Rev:** 2 rabbits above denomination **Note:** Prev. Y#121.

Date	Mintage	XF40	MS60	MS63	MS65	MS66
1987	14,000	PF65 400	PF67 500	PF69 650		

KM# A193 10 YUAN
31.10 g., 0.999 Silver 0.9989 oz. ASW **Subject:** Year of the Dragon **Obv:** Temple of Heaven, date below **Rev:** Dragons, denomination below center

Date	Mintage	XF40	MS60	MS63	MS65	MS66
1988	20,000	PF65 300	PF67 350	PF69 400		

KM# 193 10 YUAN
15.00 g., 0.900 Silver 0.434 oz. ASW **Subject:** Year of the Dragon **Obv:** Great Wall, date below **Rev:** Dragon above denomination **Note:** Prev. Y#141.

Date	Mintage	XF40	MS60	MS63	MS65	MS66
1988	15,000	PF65 300	PF67 350	PF69 400		

KM# 232 10 YUAN
31.10 g., 0.999 Silver 0.9989 oz. ASW **Subject:** Year of the Snake **Obv:** National emblem **Rev:** Snake above denomination **Note:** Prev. Y#183.

Date	Mintage	XF40	MS60	MS63	MS65	MS66
1989	6,000	PF65 500	PF67 550	PF69 650		

KM# 282 10 YUAN

15.00 g., 0.850 Silver 0.4099 oz. ASW **Subject:** Year of the Horse **Obv:** Temple of Confucius, date below **Rev:** Horse galloping left, denomination below **Note:** Prev. Y#221.

Date	Mintage	XF40	MS60	MS63	MS65	MS66
1990	15,000	PF65 250	PF67 300	PF69 350		

KM# 283 10 YUAN

31.10 g., 0.999 Silver 0.9989 oz. ASW **Subject:** Year of the Horse **Rev:** Saddled horse, left, denomination lower right **Note:** Prev. Y#222.

Date	Mintage	XF40	MS60	MS63	MS65	MS66
1990	12,000	PF65 250	PF67 300	PF69 350		

KM# 360 10 YUAN

15.00 g., 0.900 Silver 0.434 oz. ASW **Subject:** Year of the Goat **Obv:** Chinese building and legend **Rev:** Goat, denomination upper left **Note:** Prev. Y#270.

Date	Mintage	XF40	MS60	MS63	MS65	MS66
1991	15,000	PF65 240	PF67 320	PF69 390		

KM# 361 10 YUAN

31.10 g., 0.999 Silver 0.9989 oz. ASW **Subject:** Year of the Goat **Obv:** National emblem, date below **Rev:** Three goats, denomination below **Note:** Prev. Y#271.

Date	Mintage	XF40	MS60	MS63	MS65	MS66
1991	8,000	PF65 300	PF67 375	PF69 460		

KM# 427 10 YUAN

15.00 g., 0.900 Silver 0.434 oz. ASW **Subject:** Year of the Monkey **Obv:** Building, date below **Rev:** Seated monkey, denomination at right **Note:** Prev. Y#288.

Date	Mintage	XF40	MS60	MS63	MS65	MS66
1992	—	PF65 240	PF67 320	PF69 400		

KM# 428 10 YUAN

31.10 g., 0.999 Silver 0.9989 oz. ASW **Subject:** Year of the Monkey **Rev:** Monkey, denomination at left **Note:** Prev. Y#294.

Date	Mintage	XF40	MS60	MS63	MS65	MS66
1992	8,000	PF65 300	PF67 350	PF69 430		

KM# 510 10 YUAN

31.10 g., 0.999 Silver 0.9989 oz. ASW **Subject:** Year of the Rooster **Obv:** National emblem, date below **Rev:** Rooster and hen, denomination at left **Note:** Prev. Y#567.

Date	Mintage	XF40	MS60	MS63	MS65	MS66
1993	—	PF65 325	PF67 425	PF69 500		

KM# 511 10 YUAN

20.75 g., 0.999 Silver 0.6665 oz. ASW **Subject:** Year of the Rooster **Obv:** Building, date below **Rev:** Rooster and sunflowers, denomination at left **Shape:** Scalloped **Note:** Prev. Y#480.

Date	Mintage	XF40	MS60	MS63	MS65	MS66
1993	6,800	PF65 425	PF67 500	PF69 550		

KM# 642 10 YUAN

20.75 g., 0.999 Silver 0.6665 oz. ASW, 36 mm. **Subject:** Year of the Dog **Obv:** Traditional style building **Rev:** Value and dog **Edge:** Plain **Shape:** Scalloped **Note:** Prev. Y#1246.

Date	Mintage	XF40	MS60	MS63	MS65	MS66
1994	—	PF65 350	PF67 400	PF69 450		

KM# 643 10 YUAN

31.10 g., 0.999 Silver 0.9989 oz. ASW **Subject:** Year of the Dog **Note:** Prev. Y#396.

Date	Mintage	XF40	MS60	MS63	MS65	MS66
1994	8,000	PF65 300	PF67 350	PF69 400		

KM# 745 10 YUAN

31.11 g., 0.999 Silver 0.999 oz. ASW **Subject:** Year of the Pig **Obv:** National emblem, date below **Rev:** Pig, denomination at right **Note:** Prev. Y#450.

Date	Mintage	XF40	MS60	MS63	MS65	MS66
1995	8,000	PF65 400	PF67 475	PF69 560		

KM# 752 10 YUAN

20.75 g., 0.999 Silver 0.6665 oz. ASW **Subject:** Year of the Pig **Obv:** Building, date below **Rev:** Two pigs, denomination lower left **Shape:** Scalloped **Note:** Prev. Y#452.

Date	Mintage	XF40	MS60	MS63	MS65	MS66
1995	6,800	PF65 400	PF67 475	PF69 560		

KM# 927 10 YUAN

31.10 g., 0.999 Silver 0.999 oz. ASW **Subject:** Year of the Rat **Rev:** Rat by oil lamp, denomination below **Note:** Prev. Y#585.

Date	Mintage	XF40	MS60	MS63	MS65	MS66
1996	8,000	PF65 400	PF67 475	PF69 560		

KM# 928 10 YUAN

23.04 g., 0.900 Silver 0.6666 oz. ASW **Subject:** Year of the Rat **Obv:** Dengdu Pavilion **Rev:** Rat eating corn cob **Shape:** Scalloped **Note:** Prev. Y#854.

Date	Mintage	XF40	MS60	MS63	MS65	MS66
1996	6,800	PF65 300	PF67 350	PF69 410		

KM# 1013.1 10 YUAN

31.10 g., 0.999 Silver 0.999 oz. ASW **Subject:** Year of the Ox **Obv:** State seal **Rev:** Water buffalo **Note:** Prev. Y#899.1.

Date	Mintage	XF40	MS60	MS63	MS65	MS66
1997	8,000	PF65 300	PF67 350	PF69 410		

KM# 1013.2 10 YUAN

31.10 g., 0.999 Silver 0.999 oz. ASW, 40 mm. **Subject:** Year of the Ox **Obv:** National emblem, date below **Rev:** Bull, drinking, denomination below **Note:** Increased size. Prev. Y#899.2.

Date	Mintage	XF40	MS60	MS63	MS65	MS66
1997	50,000	—	—	90.00	100	110

KM# 1014 10 YUAN
23.04 g., 0.900 Silver 0.6666 oz. ASW **Subject:** Year of the Ox **Obv:** Mingyuan Pavilion **Rev:** Bull, denomination below **Shape:** Scalloped **Note:** Prev. Y#896.

Date	Mintage	XF40	MS60	MS63	MS65	MS66
1997	6,800	PF65 300	PF67 370	PF69 440		

KM# 1137 10 YUAN
31.10 g., 0.999 Silver 0.999 oz. ASW, 32 mm. **Rev:** Tiger on rock outcrop

Date	Mintage	XF40	MS60	MS63	MS65	MS66
1998	8,000	PF65 300	PF67 370	PF69 440		

KM# 1138 10 YUAN
31.10 g., 0.999 Silver 0.999 oz. ASW, 40 mm. **Subject:** Year of the Tiger **Obv:** National emblem **Rev:** Tiger on rock, denomination at right **Note:** Prev. Y#922.

Date	Mintage	XF40	MS60	MS63	MS65	MS66
1998	50,000	—	—	100	120	140

KM# 1138a 10 YUAN
31.10 g., 0.999 Silver 0.999 oz. ASW **Subject:** Year of the Tiger **Obv:** Badaling building **Rev:** Multicolor tiger cub, denomination at right **Note:** Prev. Y#923.

Date	Mintage	XF40	MS60	MS63	MS65	MS66
1998	100,000	—	—	100	120	140

KM# 1148 10 YUAN
23.04 g., 0.900 Silver 0.6666 oz. ASW **Subject:** Year of the Tiger **Obv:** Badaling building, date below **Rev:** Tiger **Shape:** Scalloped **Note:** Prev. Y#926.

Date	Mintage	XF40	MS60	MS63	MS65	MS66
1998	6,800	PF65 300	PF67 330	PF69 360		

KM# 1225 10 YUAN
31.10 g., 0.999 Silver 0.999 oz. ASW, 32 mm. **Subject:** Year of the rabbit

Date	Mintage	XF40	MS60	MS63	MS65	MS66
1999	8,000	PF65 300	PF67 330	PF69 360		

KM# 1226 10 YUAN
31.10 g., 0.999 Silver 0.999 oz. ASW, 40 mm. **Subject:** Year of the rabbit

Date	Mintage	XF40	MS60	MS63	MS65	MS66
1999	100,000	PF65 300	PF67 330	PF69 360		

KM# A1227 10 YUAN
31.10 g., 0.999 Silver 0.999 oz. ASW, 40 mm. **Subject:** Year of the rabbit **Note:** Colorized

Date	Mintage	XF40	MS60	MS63	MS65	MS66
1999	50,000	PF65 290	PF67 330	PF69 360		

KM# 1236 10 YUAN
20.53 g., 0.900 Silver 0.594 oz. ASW, 36 mm. **Subject:** Year of the rabbit **Shape:** Scalloped

Date	Mintage	XF40	MS60	MS63	MS65	MS66
1999	6,800	PF65 250	PF67 350	PF69 410		

KM# 1321 10 YUAN
31.10 g., 0.999 Silver 0.999 oz. ASW, 43.2 x 26.5 mm. **Subject:** Year of the Dragon **Obv:** Shanhaiguan gate tower of the Great, date above **Rev:** Dragon, denomination lower right **Edge:** Plain **Shape:** Fan **Note:** Prev. Y#1110.

Date	Mintage	XF40	MS60	MS63	MS65	MS66
2000	66,000	PF65 325	PF67 360	PF69 420		

KM# 1325 10 YUAN
23.04 g., 0.900 Silver 0.6666 oz. ASW **Subject:** Year of the Dragon **Obv:** Building **Rev:** Dragon **Shape:** Scalloped **Note:** Prev. Y#978.

Date	Mintage	XF40	MS60	MS63	MS65	MS66
2000	6,800	PF65 500	PF67 600	PF69 760		

KM# 56 20 YUAN
15.00 g., 0.850 Silver 0.4099 oz. ASW **Subject:** Year of the Dog **Obv:** Temple of Heaven, date lower right **Rev:** Dog above denomination **Note:** Prev. Y#38.

Date	Mintage	XF40	MS60	MS63	MS65	MS66
1982	8,825	PF65 650	PF67 750	PF69 880		

KM# 40 30 YUAN
15.00 g., 0.850 Silver 0.4099 oz. ASW **Subject:** Year of the Rooster **Obv:** Shoreline temple, date lower left **Rev:** Rooster, denomination at left **Note:** Prev. Y#32.

Date	Mintage	XF40	MS60	MS63	MS65	MS66
1981	10,000	PF65 750	PF67 800	PF69 900		

KM# 170 50 YUAN
155.50 g., 0.999 Silver 4.9944 oz. ASW **Subject:** Year of the Rabbit **Obv:** Pagoda, date below **Rev:** Two rabbits, denomination below **Note:** Prev. Y#122.

Date	Mintage	XF40	MS60	MS63	MS65	MS66
1987	4,000	PF65 1,200	PF67 1,250	PF69 1,300		

KM# 194 50 YUAN
155.50 g., 0.999 Silver 4.9944 oz. ASW, 70 mm. **Subject:** Year of the Dragon **Obv:** Great Wall, date below **Rev:** Inner circle holds three dragons, four dragons surround, denomination below **Note:** Illustration reduced. Prev. Y#142.

Date	Mintage	XF40	MS60	MS63	MS65	MS66
1988	5,000	PF65 1,150	PF67 1,200	PF69 1,250		

KM# 233 50 YUAN
155.50 g., 0.999 Silver 4.9944 oz. ASW, 70 mm. **Subject:** Year of the Snake **Obv:** Shanhaiguan Pass Gate **Rev:** Snake left, denomination below **Note:** Illustration reduced. Prev. Y#178.

Date	Mintage	XF40	MS60	MS63	MS65	MS66
1989	1,000	PF65 2,150	PF67 2,200	PF69 2,300		

KM# 284 50 YUAN

155.50 g., 0.999 Silver 4.9944 oz. ASW, 70 mm. **Subject:** Year of the Horse **Obv:** Temple of Confucius **Rev:** Two horses drinking at stream, denomination below **Note:** Illustration reduced. Prev. Y#223.

Date	Mintage	XF40	MS60	MS63	MS65	MS66
1990	2,000	PF65 1,300		PF67 1,450		PF69 1,600

KM# 362 50 YUAN

155.50 g., 0.999 Silver 4.9944 oz. ASW, 60 mm. **Subject:** Year of the Goat **Obv:** Chinese building and legend **Rev:** Goats, denomination above **Note:** Illustration reduced. Prev. Y#272.

Date	Mintage	XF40	MS60	MS63	MS65	MS66
1991	2,000	PF65 1,300		PF67 1,450		PF69 1,600

KM# 429 50 YUAN

155.50 g., 0.999 Silver 4.9944 oz. ASW **Subject:** Year of the Monkey **Obv:** Building **Rev:** Monkey **Note:** Prev. Y#289.

Date	Mintage	XF40	MS60	MS63	MS65	MS66
1992	1,000	PF65 1,500		PF67 1,600		PF69 1,700

KM# 512 50 YUAN

155.50 g., 0.999 Silver 4.9944 oz. ASW **Subject:** Year of the Rooster **Note:** Prev. Y#381.

Date	Mintage	XF40	MS60	MS63	MS65	MS66
1993	1,000	PF65 1,500		PF67 1,600		PF69 1,700

KM# 644 50 YUAN

155.50 g., 0.999 Silver 4.9944 oz. ASW **Subject:** Year of the Dog **Note:** Prev. Y#386.

Date	Mintage	XF40	MS60	MS63	MS65	MS66
1994	1,000	PF65 1,500		PF67 1,600		PF69 1,700

KM# 746 50 YUAN

155.52 g., 0.999 Silver 4.995 oz. ASW **Subject:** Year of the Pig **Obv:** Traditional building **Rev:** Sow and 4 piglets **Note:** Prev. Y#464.

Date	Mintage	XF40	MS60	MS63	MS65	MS66
1995	1,000	PF65 1,800		PF67 1,900		PF69 2,100

KM# 926 50 YUAN

155.52 g., 0.999 Silver 4.995 oz. ASW **Subject:** Year of the Rat **Obv:** Dengdu Pavilion **Rev:** Rat and grapes, denomination above **Note:** Prev. Y#855.

Date	Mintage	XF40	MS60	MS63	MS65	MS66
1996	1,000	PF65 1,500		PF67 1,600		PF69 1,700

KM# 1011 50 YUAN

155.52 g., 0.999 Silver 4.995 oz. ASW, 80 mm. **Subject:** Year of the Ox **Obv:** Mingyuan Pavilion, date below **Rev:** Bull ox, left, denomination above **Note:** Illustration reduced. Prev. Y#897.

Date	Mintage	XF40	MS60	MS63	MS65	MS66
1997	1,000	PF65 1,500		PF67 1,600		PF69 1,700

KM# 1140 50 YUAN

155.52 g., 0.999 Silver 4.995 oz. ASW **Subject:** Year of the Tiger **Obv:** Badaling building **Rev:** Tiger on rock, denomination at right **Note:** Prev. Y#927.

Date	Mintage	XF40	MS60	MS63	MS65	MS66
1998	1,000	PF65 1,500		PF67 1,600		PF69 1,700

KM# 1230 50 YUAN

151.50 g., 0.999 Silver 4.866 oz. ASW, 70 mm. **Subject:** Year of the rabbit

Date	Mintage	XF40	MS60	MS63	MS65	MS66
1999	1,000	PF65 1,500		PF67 1,600		PF69 1,700

KM# 195 100 YUAN

373.24 g., 0.999 Silver 11.9878 oz. ASW, 80 mm. **Subject:** Year of the Dragon **Obv:** Great Wall, date below **Rev:** Two dragons facing, denomination below **Note:** Illustration reduced. Prev. Y#143.

Date	Mintage	XF40	MS60	MS63	MS65	MS66
1988	3,000	PF65 2,500		PF67 2,600		PF69 2,700

KM# 234 100 YUAN

373.24 g., 0.999 Silver 11.9878 oz. ASW **Subject:** Year of the Snake **Obv:** Shanhaiguan Pass Gate **Rev:** Snake left within beaded circle, denomination below **Note:** Illustration reduced. Prev. Y#179.

Date	Mintage	XF40	MS60	MS63	MS65	MS66
1989	400	PF65 3,000		PF67 3,200		PF69 3,500

KM# 285 100 YUAN

373.24 g., 0.999 Silver 11.9878 oz. ASW, 80 mm. **Subject:** Year of the Horse **Obv:** Temple of Confucius **Rev:** Two horses galloping left, denomination below **Note:** Illustration reduced. Prev. Y#285.

Date	Mintage	XF40	MS60	MS63	MS65	MS66
1990	1,000	PF65 1,450		PF67 1,650		PF69 1,800

KM# 363 100 YUAN

373.24 g., 0.999 Silver 11.9878 oz. ASW, 80 mm. **Subject:** Year of the Goat **Rev:** Two goats, denomination at left **Note:** Illustration reduced. Prev. Y#273.

Date	Mintage	XF40	MS60	MS63	MS65	MS66
1991	1,000	PF65 1,450		PF67 1,650		PF69 1,800

KM# 431 100 YUAN

373.24 g., 0.999 Silver 11.9878 oz. ASW **Subject:** Year of the Monkey **Obv:** Building **Rev:** Family of monkeys **Note:** Prev. Y#290.

Date	Mintage	XF40	MS60	MS63	MS65	MS66
1992	500	PF65 2,400		PF67 2,600		PF69 2,800

KM# 514 100 YUAN

373.24 g., 0.999 Silver 11.9878 oz. ASW **Subject:** Year of the Rooster **Note:** Prev. Y#383.

Date	Mintage	XF40	MS60	MS63	MS65	MS66
1993	500	PF65 2,400		PF67 2,600		PF69 2,800

KM# 646 100 YUAN

373.24 g., 0.999 Silver 11.9878 oz. ASW **Subject:** Year of the Dog **Note:** Prev. Y#388.

Date	Mintage	XF40	MS60	MS63	MS65	MS66
1994	500	PF65 2,400		PF67 2,600		PF69 2,800

KM# 747 100 YUAN

373.24 g., 0.999 Silver 11.988 oz. ASW, 80 mm. **Subject:** Year of the Pig **Rev:** Sow and five piglets **Note:** Prev. Y#466.

Date	Mintage	XF40	MS60	MS63	MS65	MS66
1995	—	PF65 3,500		PF67 3,600		PF69 3,720

KM# 925 100 YUAN

373.24 g., 0.999 Silver 11.9879 oz. ASW, 80 mm. **Subject:** Year of the rat **Rev:** Rat on balance scale

Date	Mintage	XF40	MS60	MS63	MS65	MS66
1996	500	PF65 2,500		PF67 2,600		PF69 2,750

KM# 1010 100 YUAN

373.24 g., 0.999 Silver 11.9878 oz. ASW **Subject:** Year of the Ox **Note:** Prev. Y#669.

Date	Mintage	XF40	MS60	MS63	MS65	MS66
1997	500	—	—	2,400	2,600	2,750

KM# 1141 100 YUAN
373.24 g., 0.999 Silver 11.988 oz. ASW **Subject:** Year of the Tiger **Obv:** Badaling building **Rev:** Tiger on rock, denomination at right **Note:** Prev. Y#928.

Date	Mintage	XF40	MS60	MS63	MS65	MS66
1998	500	PF65 2,600		PF67 2,700	PF69 2,850	

KM# 1231 100 YUAN
373.00 g., 0.999 Silver 11.9802 oz. ASW, 80 mm. **Subject:** Year of the rabbit

Date	Mintage	XF40	MS60	MS63	MS65	MS66
1999	500	PF65 2,600		PF67 2,700	PF69 2,850	

KM# 436 200 YUAN
1000.00 g., 0.999 Silver 32.1186 oz. ASW, 120 mm. **Subject:** Completion of 150 Yuan Lunar - Animal Coin Series **Obv:** Monument divides date and denomination within circle **Rev:** Ying/Yang symbols within octagon surrounded by twelve animal coins **Note:** Illustration reduced. Prev. Y#700.

Date	Mintage	XF40	MS60	MS63	MS65	MS66
1992	185	PF65 17,500		PF67 25,000	PF69 40,000	

KM# 1239 200 YUAN
1000.00 g., 0.999 Silver 32.1186 oz. ASW **Subject:** Completion of 12-Year Lunar Cycle **Note:** Prev. Y#976.

Date	Mintage	XF40	MS60	MS63	MS65	MS66
1999	1,000	PF65 7,000		PF67 7,100	PF69 7,300	

SILVER BULLION COINAGE

Panda Series

KM# 483 5 YUAN
15.55 g., 0.999 Silver 0.4995 oz. ASW **Obv:** Temple of Heaven within circle, date below **Rev:** Panda facing forward, denomination below **Note:** Prev. Y#392.

Date	Mintage	XF40	MS60	MS63	MS65	MS66
1993	—	—	—	27.50	40.00	50.00

KM# 621 5 YUAN
15.55 g., 0.999 Silver 0.4995 oz. ASW **Rev:** Panda approaching water, denomination above **Note:** Prev. Y#436.

Date	Mintage	XF40	MS60	MS63	MS65	MS66
1994	—	—	—	30.00	45.00	60.00

KM# 731 5 YUAN
15.77 g., 0.999 Silver 0.5066 oz. ASW **Obv:** Temple of Heaven **Rev:** Panda climbing tree branch **Note:** Prev. Y#791.

Date	Mintage	XF40	MS60	MS63	MS65	MS66
1995	—	PF65 45.00		PF67 55.00	PF69 65.00	

KM# 898 5 YUAN
15.55 g., 0.999 Silver 0.4995 oz. ASW **Obv:** Temple of Heaven **Rev:** Panda seated on shore **Note:** Large and small date varieties exist. Prev. Y#847.

Date	Mintage	XF40	MS60	MS63	MS65	MS66
1996	—	—	18.00	25.00	28.00	30.00

KM# 993 5 YUAN
15.63 g., 0.999 Silver 0.502 oz. ASW **Obv:** Temple of Heaven within circle, date below **Rev:** Panda crossing stream, denomination at lower left **Note:** Large and small date varieties exist. Prev. Y#728; 892.

Date	Mintage	XF40	MS60	MS63	MS65	MS66
1997	—	PF67 27.50		PF69 30.00		

KM# 995 5 YUAN
15.60 g., 0.999 Silver 0.501 oz. ASW, 36 mm. **Obv:** Temple of Heaven **Rev:** Multicolor panda and flora **Edge:** Reeded **Note:** Large and small date varieties exist. Prev. Y#962.

Date	Mintage	XF40	MS60	MS63	MS65	MS66
1997	100,000	—	—	30.00	35.00	40.00

KM# 1005 5 YUAN
15.55 g., 0.999 Silver 0.4995 oz. ASW **Obv:** Temple of Heaven with additional legend on Hong Kong's return **Rev:** Panda crossing stream, denomination lower left **Note:** Large and small date varieties exist. Prev. Y#893.

Date	Mintage	XF40	MS60	MS63	MS65	MS66
1997	30,000	PF65 60.00		PF67 65.00	PF69 75.00	

KM# 1124 5 YUAN
15.56 g., 0.999 Silver 0.4998 oz. ASW, 33 mm. **Rev:** Panda seated eating bamboo leaf

Date	Mintage	XF40	MS60	MS63	MS65	MS66
1998	200,000	PF65 30.00		PF67 35.00	PF69 40.00	

KM# 1131 5 YUAN
15.55 g., 0.999 Silver 0.4995 oz. ASW **Rev:** Multicolor panda **Note:** Large and small date varieties exist. Prev. Y#964.

Date	Mintage	XF40	MS60	MS63	MS65	MS66
1998	100,000	—	—	30.00	35.00	40.00

KM# 67 10 YUAN
27.00 g., 0.900 Silver 0.7813 oz. ASW **Obv:** Temple of Heaven, date below **Rev:** Two pandas, denomination below **Note:** Prev. Y#57.

Date	Mintage	XF40	MS60	MS63	MS65	MS66
1983	10,000	PF65 550		PF67 600	PF69 630	
1983 Frosted Proof	Inc. above	PF65 570		PF67 620	PF69 680	

KM# 87 10 YUAN
27.00 g., 0.925 Silver 0.803 oz. ASW **Obv:** Temple of Heaven, date below **Rev:** Panda and cub, denomination at right **Note:** Prev. Y#67.

Date	Mintage	XF40	MS60	MS63	MS65	MS66
1984	10,000	PF65 450		PF67 500	PF69 530	

KM# 114 10 YUAN
27.00 g., 0.900 Silver 0.7813 oz. ASW **Obv:** Temple of Heaven, date below **Rev:** Panda with cub on back, denomination below **Note:** Prev. Y#95.

Date	Mintage	XF40	MS60	MS63	MS65	MS66
1985	10,000	PF65 500		PF67 550	PF69 620	

KM# 167 10 YUAN
31.10 g., 0.999 Silver 0.9989 oz. ASW **Obv:** Temple of Heaven, date below **Rev:** Panda climbing tree, denomination at right **Note:** Prev. Y#133.

Date	Mintage	XF40	MS60	MS63	MS65	MS66
1987	31,000	PF65 325		PF67 375	PF69 410	

KM# A221 10 YUAN
31.10 g., 0.999 Silver 0.9989 oz. ASW **Obv:** Temple of Heaven, date below **Rev:** Baby panda on grid background, date at bottom

Date	Mintage	XF40	MS60	MS63	MS65	MS66
1989	250,000	—	—	70.00	75.00	80.00
1989	25,000	PF65 145		PF67 150	PF69 160	

KM# 276 10 YUAN
31.10 g., 0.999 Silver 0.9989 oz. ASW **Obv:** Temple of Heaven, date below **Rev:** Panda, denomination below **Note:** Prev. Y#237.

Date	Mintage	XF40	MS60	MS63	MS65	MS66
1990	200,000	—	—	70.00	75.00	80.00
1990 P in circle	20,000	PF65 145	PF67 150	PF69 160		

KM# 356 10 YUAN
62.20 g., 0.999 Silver 1.9978 oz. ASW **Obv:** Temple of Heaven, date below **Rev:** Panda climbing bamboo branch, denomination upper right **Note:** Prev. Y#314.

Date	Mintage	XF40	MS60	MS63	MS65	MS66
1991	10,000	PF65 250	PF67 270	PF69 290		

KM# 386.1 10 YUAN
31.10 g., 0.999 Silver 0.9989 oz. ASW **Obv:** Temple of Heaven, date below with bottom serifs **Rev:** Panda sitting with hind feet in water, denomination at left **Note:** Prev. Y#308.1.

Date	Mintage	XF40	MS60	MS63	MS65	MS66
1991	100,000	—	—	215	235	250

KM# 386.2 10 YUAN
31.10 g., 0.999 Silver 0.9989 oz. ASW **Obv:** Temple of Heaven, date below **Rev:** P behind panda **Note:** Prev. Y#308.2.

Date	Mintage	XF40	MS60	MS63	MS65	MS66
1991	20,000	PF65 250	PF67 260	PF69 280		

KM# 386.3 10 YUAN
31.10 g., 0.999 Silver 0.9989 oz. ASW **Obv:** Building, date below without bottom serifs **Note:** Prev. Y#308.3.

Date	Mintage	XF40	MS60	MS63	MS65	MS66
1991	Inc. above	—	—	100	110	120

KM# A397 10 YUAN
31.10 g., 0.999 Silver 0.999 oz. ASW, 40 mm. **Rev:** Panda climbing right on eucalyptus branch, denomination above.

Date	Mintage	XF40	MS60	MS63	MS65	MS66
1992 P	20,000	PF67 45.00	PF69 50.00			
1992 P	—	PF67 100	PF69 120			

KM# 397 10 YUAN
31.10 g., 0.999 Silver 0.9989 oz. ASW **Obv:** Temple of Heaven within circle, date below **Rev:** Panda climbing right on eucalyptus branch, denomination above **Note:** Prev. Y#346.

Date	Mintage	XF40	MS60	MS63	MS65	MS66
1992	100,000	—	—	200	215	230
1992	5,202	PF65 450	PF67 500	PF69 550		

KM# 478 10 YUAN
31.10 g., 0.999 Silver 0.9989 oz. ASW **Obv:** Temple of Heaven, date below **Rev:** Mother panda nurturing cub **Note:** Prev. Y#360.

Date	Mintage	XF40	MS60	MS63	MS65	MS66
1993	20,000	PF67 100	PF69 120			

KM# 485 10 YUAN
31.10 g., 0.999 Silver 0.9989 oz. ASW **Obv:** Temple of Heaven, date below **Rev:** Panda on flat rock **Note:** Prev. Y#361.

Date	Mintage	XF40	MS60	MS63	MS65	MS66
1993	120,000	—	—	80.00	85.00	90.00

KM# 616 10 YUAN
31.10 g., 0.999 Silver 0.9989 oz. ASW **Obv:** Temple of Heaven, date below **Rev:** Panda sitting on branch of tree **Note:** Prev. Y#437.

Date	Mintage	XF40	MS60	MS63	MS65	MS66
1994	20,000	PF65 200	PF67 215	PF69 230		

KM# A623 10 YUAN
31.10 g., 0.999 Silver 0.9989 oz. ASW **Obv:** Temple of Heaven within circle, date below **Rev:** Seated panda eating, denomination below

Date	Mintage	XF40	MS60	MS63	MS65	MS66
1994	120,000	—	—	75.00	80.00	85.00

KM# 723 10 YUAN
31.10 g., 0.999 Silver 0.999 oz. ASW **Obv:** Temple of Heaven **Rev:** Panda approaching water from right **Note:** Prev. Y#787.

Date	Mintage	XF40	MS60	MS63	MS65	MS66
1995	10,000	PF65 150	PF67 165	PF69 180		

KM# 732.1 10 YUAN
31.10 g., 0.999 Silver 0.999 oz. ASW **Obv:** Temple of Heaven **Rev:** Panda sitting on branch eating large twig (nine leaf) **Note:** Prev. Y#485.1.

Date	Mintage	XF40	MS60	MS63	MS65	MS66
1995	—	—	—	60.00	70.00	75.00

KM# 732.2 10 YUAN
31.10 g., 0.999 Silver 0.999 oz. ASW **Obv:** Temple of Heaven, date below **Rev:** Panda eating small twig (three leaf) **Note:** Prev. Y#485.2.

Date	Mintage	XF40	MS60	MS63	MS65	MS66
1995	—	—	—	50.00	55.00	60.00

KM# 733 10 YUAN
31.10 g., 0.999 Silver 0.999 oz. ASW **Subject:** Beijing Stamp Fair **Obv:** Temple of Heaven with additional legend below **Rev:** Panda approaching water from right **Note:** Prev. Y#792.

Date	Mintage	XF40	MS60	MS63	MS65	MS66
1995	18,000	PF65 60.00	PF67 70.00	PF69 80.00		

KM# 892 10 YUAN
31.10 g., 0.999 Silver 0.999 oz. ASW **Obv:** Temple of Heaven within circle, date below **Rev:** Seated panda mother and cub, denomination upper left **Note:** Large and small date varieties exist. Prev. Y#583.

Date	Mintage	XF40	MS60	MS63	MS65	MS66
1996 Prooflike	—	—	—	50.00	55.00	60.00

KM# 900 10 YUAN
31.23 g., 0.999 Silver 1.0031 oz. ASW, 39.8 mm. **Obv:** Temple of Heaven **Rev:** Seated panda facing left **Edge:** Reeded **Note:** Large and small date varieties exist. Prev. Y#1096.

Date	Mintage	XF40	MS60	MS63	MS65	MS66
1996	8,000	PF65 125				

KM# 986 10 YUAN
31.10 g., 0.999 Silver 0.999 oz. ASW **Obv:** Temple of Heaven within circle, date below **Rev:** Panda on thick branch, left, denomination below **Note:** Large and small date varieties exist. Prev. Y#715.

Date	Mintage	XF40	MS60	MS63	MS65	MS66
1997	50,000	—	—	40.00	45.00	50.00

KM# 996 10 YUAN
31.10 g., 0.999 Silver 0.999 oz. ASW, 40 mm. **Obv:** Temple of Heaven within circle, date below **Rev:** Multicolor panda and flora, denomination at right **Edge:** Reeded **Note:** Large and small date varieties exist. Prev. #Y1060.

Date	Mintage	XF40	MS60	MS63	MS65	MS66
1997	—	—	70.00	85.00	90.00	95.00

KM# 1002 10 YUAN
31.22 g., 0.999 Silver 1.0027 oz. ASW **Obv:** Temple of Heaven and date within circle, - "Visit China '97" around outside **Rev:** Panda on large tree branch, denomination below **Note:** Large and small date varieties exist. Prev. Y#726.

Date	Mintage	XF40	MS60	MS63	MS65	MS66
1997	50,000	—	—	40.00	45.00	50.00

KM# 1003 10 YUAN
31.10 g., 0.999 Silver 0.999 oz. ASW **Obv:** Temple of Heaven - "Founding of Chongqing Municipality" **Rev:** Panda on branch **Note:** Large and small date varieties exist. Prev. Y#894.

Date	Mintage	XF40	MS60	MS63	MS65	MS66
1997	50,000	PF65 65.00				

KM# 1126 10 YUAN
31.10 g., 0.999 Silver 0.999 oz. ASW **Obv:** Temple of Heaven, date below **Rev:** Panda **Note:** Large and small date varieties exist. Prev. Y#969.

Date	Mintage	XF40	MS60	MS63	MS65	MS66
1998	250,000	—	—	65.00	70.00	75.00

KM# 1132 10 YUAN
31.10 g., 0.999 Silver 0.999 oz. ASW **Obv:** Temple of Heaven, date below **Rev:** Multicolor panda **Note:** Large and small date varieties exist. Prev. Y#970.

Date	Mintage	XF40	MS60	MS63	MS65	MS66
1998	100,000	—	—	65.00	70.00	75.00

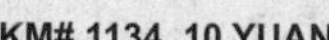

KM# 1134 10 YUAN
31.06 g., 0.999 Silver 0.9976 oz. ASW, 39.9 mm. **Subject:** 1998 Beijing Internatipnal Coin Exposition **Obv:** Temple of Heaven **Rev:** Gilt Panda reclining on rock **Edge:** Reeded

Date	Mintage	XF40	MS60	MS63	MS65	MS66
1998	30,000	—	—	90.00	95.00	105

KM# 1135 10 YUAN
31.05 g., 0.999 Silver 0.9973 oz. ASW, 39.91 mm. **Subject:** 1999 Beijing International Coin Exposition **Obv:** Temple of Heaven **Rev:** Gilt Panda laying on rock **Edge:** Reeded

Date	Mintage	XF40	MS60	MS63	MS65	MS66
1999	40,000	—	—	70.00	75.00	80.00

KM# 1216 10 YUAN
31.10 g., 0.999 Silver 0.999 oz. ASW **Obv:** Temple of Heaven within circle, date below **Rev:** Panda on rock, denomination at left **Note:** Large and small date varieties exist. Prev. Y#931.

Date	Mintage	XF40	MS60	MS63	MS65	MS66
1999	—	—	—	70.00	75.00	80.00
1999	—	PF65 100				

KM# 1217 10 YUAN
31.10 g., 0.999 Silver 0.999 oz. ASW **Obv:** Temple of Heaven, date below **Rev:** Multicolor panda **Note:** Large and small date varieties exist. Prev. Y#974.

Date	Mintage	XF40	MS60	MS63	MS65	MS66
1999	100,000	—	—	60.00	65.00	70.00

KM# 1310 10 YUAN
31.10 g., 0.999 Silver 0.999 oz. ASW **Obv:** Temple of Heaven within circle, date below **Rev:** Panda seated, holding bamboo branch, denomination below **Note:** Large and small date varieties exist. Prev. Y#979.

Date	Mintage	XF40	MS60	MS63	MS65	MS66
2000	—	—	—	60.00	65.00	70.00

Note: Domestic Chinese examples struck with mirror fields, overseas examples struck with frosted fields

KM# 168 50 YUAN
155.50 g., 0.999 Silver 4.9944 oz. ASW, 70 mm. **Obv:** Temple of Heaven **Rev:** Panda clinging to tree trunk **Note:** Prev. Y#134.

Date	Mintage	XF40	MS60	MS63	MS65	MS66
1987	8,540	PF65 350	PF67 370	PF69 410		

KM# 188 50 YUAN
155.50 g., 0.999 Silver 4.9944 oz. ASW **Obv:** Temple of Heaven **Rev:** Two pandas in tree **Note:** Prev. Y#168.

Date	Mintage	XF40	MS60	MS63	MS65	MS66
1988	11,000	PF65 400	PF67 430	PF69 460		

KM# 222 50 YUAN
155.50 g., 0.999 Silver 4.9944 oz. ASW **Obv:** Temple of Heaven **Rev:** Mother panda with cub **Note:** Prev. Y#218.

Date	Mintage	XF40	MS60	MS63	MS65	MS66
1989	9,599	PF65 425	PF67 475	PF69 520		

KM# 273 50 YUAN
155.50 g., 0.999 Silver 4.9944 oz. ASW **Obv:** Temple of Heaven **Rev:** Two pandas, one in tree **Note:** Prev. Y#262.

Date	Mintage	XF40	MS60	MS63	MS65	MS66
1990	4,000	PF65 550	PF67 600	PF69 650		

KM# 353 50 YUAN
155.50 g., 0.999 Silver 4.9944 oz. ASW **Obv:** Temple of Heaven, date below **Rev:** Pandas at water's edge, denomination above **Note:** Prev. Y#373.

Date	Mintage	XF40	MS60	MS63	MS65	MS66
1991	5,000	PF65 525	PF67 575	PF69 650		

KM# 398 50 YUAN
155.50 g., 0.999 Silver 4.9944 oz. ASW **Obv:** Temple of Heaven, date below **Rev:** Pandas **Note:** Prev. Y#374.

Date	Mintage	XF40	MS60	MS63	MS65	MS66
1992	4,000	PF65 600	PF67 700	PF69 750		

KM# 475 50 YUAN
155.50 g., 0.999 Silver 4.9944 oz. ASW, 70 mm. **Obv:** Temple of Heaven **Rev:** Pandas playing on stump, denomination at left **Note:** Prev. Y#379.

Date	Mintage	XF40	MS60	MS63	MS65	MS66
1993	3,000	PF65 850	PF67 950	PF69 1,200		

KM# 479 50 YUAN
155.50 g., 0.999 Silver 4.9944 oz. ASW, 70 mm. **Rev:** Two panda playing on stump

Date	Mintage	XF40	MS60	MS63	MS65	MS66
1993	3,000	PF65 500	PF67 650	PF69 800		

KM# 617 50 YUAN
155.50 g., 0.999 Silver 4.9944 oz. ASW **Obv:** Temple of Heaven **Rev:** Two pandas, one in tree **Note:** Prev. Y#638.

Date	Mintage	XF40	MS60	MS63	MS65	MS66
1994	3,000	PF65 2,000	PF67 3,500	PF69 5,000		

KM# 727 50 YUAN
155.50 g., 0.999 Silver 4.9944 oz. ASW **Obv:** Temple of Heaven **Rev:** Two pandas on river bank, denomination above **Note:** Prev. Y#645.

Date	Mintage	XF40	MS60	MS63	MS65	MS66
1995	1,500	PF65 2,250	PF67 3,250	PF69 3,500		

KM# 189 100 YUAN
373.24 g., 0.999 Silver 11.9878 oz. ASW, 70 mm. **Obv:** Temple of Heaven **Rev:** Two pandas in tree **Note:** Prev. Y#169.

Date	Mintage	XF40	MS60	MS63	MS65	MS66
1988	5,000	PF65 800	PF67 1,200	PF69 1,500		

KM# 225 100 YUAN
373.24 g., 0.999 Silver 11.9878 oz. ASW, 80 mm. **Obv:** Temple of Heaven **Rev:** Panda with two cubs **Note:** Prev. Y#219, Y#228

Date	Mintage	XF40	MS60	MS63	MS65	MS66
1989	6,000	PF65 1,000	PF67 1,400	PF69 1,700		

KM# 274 100 YUAN
373.24 g., 0.999 Silver 11.9878 oz. ASW, 80 mm. **Obv:** Temple of Heaven **Rev:** Three curious pandas **Note:** Prev. Y#263.

Date	Mintage	XF40	MS60	MS63	MS65	MS66
1990	2,500	PF65 1,000	PF67 1,200	PF69 1,500		

KM# 352 100 YUAN
373.24 g., 0.999 Silver 11.9878 oz. ASW, 80 mm. **Obv:** Temple of Heaven **Rev:** Pandas with two cubs, one in tree **Note:** Prev. Y#375, KM#354

Date	Mintage	XF40	MS60	MS63	MS65	MS66
1991	2,500	PF65 1,150	PF67 1,250	PF69 1,400		

KM# 399 100 YUAN
373.24 g., 0.999 Silver 11.9878 oz. ASW, 80 mm. **Obv:** Temple of Heaven, date below **Rev:** Pandas **Note:** Prev. Y#376.

Date	Mintage	XF40	MS60	MS63	MS65	MS66
1992	2,500	PF65 1,150	PF67 1,250	PF69 1,400		

KM# 480 100 YUAN
373.24 g., 0.999 Silver 11.9878 oz. ASW, 80 mm. **Obv:** Temple of Heaven **Rev:** Pandas **Note:** Prev. Y#380.

Date	Mintage	XF40	MS60	MS63	MS65	MS66
1993	2,000	PF65 1,800	PF67 2,500	PF69 3,100		

KM# 618 100 YUAN
373.24 g., 0.999 Silver 11.9878 oz. ASW **Obv:** Temple of Heaven **Rev:** Panda with two cubs at water's edge, denomination lower right, circle surrounds **Note:** Prev. Y#652.

Date	Mintage	XF40	MS60	MS63	MS65	MS66
1994	2,000	PF65 3,500	PF67 4,000	PF69 4,500		

KM# 720 100 YUAN
373.24 g., 0.999 Silver 11.9878 oz. ASW, 80 mm. **Obv:** Temple of Heaven **Rev:** Panda family **Note:** Prev. Y#646.

Date	Mintage	XF40	MS60	MS63	MS65	MS66
1995	1,000	PF65 6,000	PF67 7,000	PF69 8,000		

KM# 899 100 YUAN
373.24 g., 0.999 Silver 11.9879 oz. ASW, 80 mm. **Rev:** Three pandas playing

Date	Mintage	XF40	MS60	MS63	MS65	MS66
1996	800	PF65 4,500	PF67 5,250	PF69 6,000		

KM# 994 100 YUAN
373.24 g., 0.999 Silver 11.9879 oz. ASW, 80 mm. **Rev:** Three pandas playing

Date	Mintage	XF40	MS60	MS63	MS65	MS66
1997	2,500	PF65 1,800	PF67 2,600	PF69 3,200		

KM# 1133 200 YUAN
1000.00 g., 0.999 Silver 32.1186 oz. ASW **Obv:** Temple of Heaven **Rev:** Panda **Note:** Large and small date varieties exist. Prev. Y#968.

Date	Mintage	XF40	MS60	MS63	MS65	MS66
1998	1,998	PF65 3,350	PF67 3,850	PF69 4,400		

KM# 1222 200 YUAN
1000.21 g., 0.999 Silver 32.1253 oz. ASW, 100 mm. **Obv:** Temple of Heaven within circle **Rev:** Panda on rock left, denomination at left **Note:** Illustration reduced. Large and small date varieties exist. Prev. Y#971.

Date	Mintage	XF40	MS60	MS63	MS65	MS66
1999	—	PF65 4,000	PF67 4,850	PF69 5,600		

KM# 1303 300 YUAN
1000.00 g., 0.999 Silver 32.1186 oz. ASW, 100 mm. **Obv:** Temple of Heaven **Rev:** Panda seated on leaves **Edge:** Plain **Note:** Large and small date varieties exist. Prev. Y#1071.

Date	Mintage	XF40	MS60	MS63	MS65	MS66
2000	2,000	PF65 2,800	PF67 3,000	PF69 3,300		

KM# 1308 300 YUAN
1000.00 g., 0.999 Silver 32.1186 oz. ASW, 100 mm. **Rev:** Panda seated eating bamboo

Date	Mintage	XF40	MS60	MS63	MS65	MS66
2000	2,000	PF65 2,800	PF67 3,000	PF69 3,300		

GOLD BULLION COINAGE

Panda Series

KM# 351 3 YUAN
1.00 g., 0.999 Gold 0.0321 oz. AGW **Obv:** Temple of Heaven **Rev:** Seated panda left, denomination at left **Note:** Prev. Y#307.

Date	Mintage	XF40	MS60	MS63	MS65	MS66
1991	110,000	PF65 100	PF67 110	PF69 120		

KM# 68 5 YUAN
1.56 g., 0.999 Gold 0.050 oz. AGW **Obv:** Temple of Heaven, date below **Rev:** Panda on all fours right, within circle **Note:** Prev. Y#48.

Date	Mintage	XF40	MS60	MS63	MS65	MS66
1983	75,454	PF65 110	PF67 120	PF69 130		

KM# 86 5 YUAN
1.56 g., 0.999 Gold 0.050 oz. AGW **Obv:** Temple of Heaven, date below **Rev:** Panda holding bamboo branch, reclined, denomination at right **Note:** Prev. Y#73.

Date	Mintage	XF40	MS60	MS63	MS65	MS66
1984	77,869	PF65 80.00	PF67 85.00	PF69 95.00		

KM# 113 5 YUAN
1.56 g., 0.999 Gold 0.050 oz. AGW **Obv:** Temple of Heaven, date below **Rev:** Panda hanging from branch, denomination upper left **Note:** Prev. Y#80.

Date	Mintage	XF40	MS60	MS63	MS65	MS66
1985	21,075	PF65 80.00	PF67 85.00	PF69 95.00		

KM# 131 5 YUAN
1.56 g., 0.999 Gold 0.050 oz. AGW **Obv:** Temple of Heaven, date below **Rev:** Panda, denomination below **Note:** Prev. Y#101.

Date	Mintage	XF40	MS60	MS63	MS65	MS66
1986 P	10,000	PF65 120	PF67 130	PF69 150		
1986	79,194	—	—	75.00	80.00	85.00

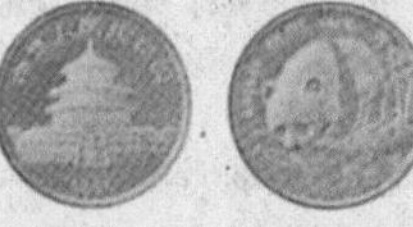

KM# 159 5 YUAN
1.56 g., 0.999 Gold 0.050 oz. AGW **Obv:** Temple of Heaven, date below **Rev:** Panda left, denomination below **Note:** Prev. Y#124.

Date	Mintage	XF40	MS60	MS63	MS65	MS66
1987 (y)	Inc. above	—	—	75.00	80.00	85.00
1987 (s)	133,080	—	—	75.00	80.00	85.00
1987 P	10,000	PF65 120	PF67 130	PF69 150		

KM# 221 5 YUAN
1.56 g., 0.999 Gold 0.050 oz. AGW **Obv:** Temple of Heaven, date below **Rev:** Panda pawing bamboo **Note:** Prev. Y#152.

Date	Mintage	XF40	MS60	MS63	MS65	MS66
1988	10,000	PF65 120	PF67 130	PF69 150		
1988	468,683	—	—	75.00	80.00	85.00

KM# 183 5 YUAN
1.55 g., 0.999 Gold 0.0498 oz. AGW, 14 mm. **Rev:** Panda seated with bamboo

Date	Mintage	XF40	MS60	MS63	MS65	MS66
1989	—	PF65 120	PF67 130	PF69 150		
1989	268,738	—	—	75.00	80.00	85.00

KM# 268 5 YUAN
1.56 g., 0.999 Gold 0.050 oz. AGW **Obv:** Temple of Heaven, date below **Rev:** Panda climbing rock, denomination below **Note:** Prev. Y#238.

Date	Mintage	XF40	MS60	MS63	MS65	MS66
1990	348,246	—	—	75.00	80.00	85.00
1990	5,000	PF65 125	PF67 1,350	PF69 160		

KM# 346 5 YUAN
1.56 g., 0.999 Gold 0.050 oz. AGW **Obv:** Temple of Heaven **Rev:** Panda with hind feet in water eating bamboo **Note:** Prev. Y#309.

Date	Mintage	XF40	MS60	MS63	MS65	MS66
1991	206,254	—	—	85.00	90.00	95.00
1991	3,500	PF65 135	PF67 150	PF69 165		

KM# 391 5 YUAN
1.56 g., 0.999 Gold 0.050 oz. AGW **Obv:** Temple of Heaven **Rev:** Panda on branch **Note:** Prev. Y#341.

Date	Mintage	XF40	MS60	MS63	MS65	MS66
1992	216,305	—	—	85.00	90.00	95.00
1992	—	PF65 250	PF67 275	PF69 300		

KM# 473 5 YUAN
1.56 g., 0.999 Gold 0.050 oz. AGW **Obv:** Temple of Heaven, date below **Rev:** Panda pawing bamboo **Note:** Prev. Y#610.

Date	Mintage	XF40	MS60	MS63	MS65	MS66
1993	158,364	—	—	85.00	90.00	95.00
1993	—	PF65 145	PF67 165	PF69 180		

KM# 611 5 YUAN
1.56 g., 0.999 Gold 0.050 oz. AGW **Obv:** Temple of Heaven, date below **Rev:** Panda sitting, denomination below **Note:** Prev. Y#431.

Date	Mintage	XF40	MS60	MS63	MS65	MS66
1994	133,226	—	—	85.00	90.00	95.00
1994	2,500	PF65 200	PF67 225	PF69 250		

KM# 715 5 YUAN
1.56 g., 0.999 Gold 0.050 oz. AGW **Obv:** Temple of Heaven, date below **Rev:** Panda holding bamboo stick, denomination at left **Note:** Prev. Y#640.

Date	Mintage	XF40	MS60	MS63	MS65	MS66
1995	97,910	—	—	150	155	160

KM# 883 5 YUAN

1.56 g., 0.999 Gold 0.050 oz. AGW **Obv:** Temple of Heaven, date below **Rev:** Panda in tree looking down, denomination lower left **Note:** Large and small date varieties exist. Prev. Y#581.

Date	Mintage	XF40	MS60	MS63	MS65	MS66
1996	145,347	—	—	120	125	130

KM# 984 5 YUAN

1.56 g., 0.999 Gold 0.050 oz. AGW **Obv:** Temple of Heaven **Rev:** Panda on branch **Note:** Large and small date varieties exist. Prev. Y#716.

Date	Mintage	XF40	MS60	MS63	MS65	MS66
1997	54,853	—	—	120	125	130

Note: Exists in large and small date varieties

KM# 1125 5 YUAN

1.56 g., 0.999 Gold 0.0501 oz. AGW **Obv:** Temple of Heaven **Rev:** Panda seated on rock **Note:** Prev. Y#990.

Date	Mintage	XF40	MS60	MS63	MS65	MS66
1998	27,483	—	—	350	370	380

Note: Exists in Large and Small date varieties.

KM# 1215 5 YUAN

1.56 g., 0.999 Gold 0.0501 oz. AGW **Obv:** Temple of Heaven **Rev:** Panda on ledge **Note:** Prev. Y#981.

Date	Mintage	XF40	MS60	MS63	MS65	MS66
1999	37,171	—	—	150	155	160

Note: Exists in Large and Small date varieties.

KM# 1302 5 YUAN

1.56 g., 0.999 Gold 0.0501 oz. AGW **Obv:** Temple of Heaven **Rev:** Panda seated on leaves **Note:** Large and small date varieties exist. Prev. Y#945.

Date	Mintage	XF40	MS60	MS63	MS65	MS66
2000 Frosted fields	Inc. above	—	—	150	165	180
2000 Mirror fields	41,837	—	—	500	525	550

Note: Domestic Chinese examples struck with mirror fields, overseas examples struck with frosted fields

KM# 69 10 YUAN

3.11 g., 0.999 Gold 0.0999 oz. AGW **Obv:** Temple of Heaven, date below **Rev:** Panda right **Note:** Prev. Y#49.

Date	Mintage	XF40	MS60	MS63	MS65	MS66
1983	82,013	—	—	210	220	230

KM# 88 10 YUAN

3.11 g., 0.999 Gold 0.0999 oz. AGW **Obv:** Temple of Heaven **Rev:** Panda holding bamboo branch, reclined, denomination at right **Note:** Prev. Y#74.

Date	Mintage	XF40	MS60	MS63	MS65	MS66
1984	86,404	—	—	190	200	220

KM# 115 10 YUAN

3.11 g., 0.999 Gold 0.0999 oz. AGW **Obv:** Temple of Heaven, date below **Rev:** Panda hanging from branch, denomination upper left **Note:** Prev. Y#81.

Date	Mintage	XF40	MS60	MS63	MS65	MS66
1985	143,062	—	—	165	170	180

KM# 132 10 YUAN

3.11 g., 0.999 Gold 0.0999 oz. AGW **Obv:** Temple of Heaven **Rev:** Panda, denomination below **Note:** Prev. Y#102.

Date	Mintage	XF40	MS60	MS63	MS65	MS66
1986	65,596	—	—	165	170	180
1986 P	10,000	PF65 215	PF67 225	PF69 235		

KM# 163 10 YUAN

3.11 g., 0.999 Gold 0.0999 oz. AGW **Obv:** Temple of Heaven, date below **Rev:** Panda, denomination below **Note:** Prev. Y#125.

Date	Mintage	XF40	MS60	MS63	MS65	MS66
1987 (s)	134,598	—	—	165	170	175
1987 (y)	Inc. above	—	—	165	170	175
1987 P	10,000	PF65 215	PF67 225	PF69 235		

KM# 184 10 YUAN

3.11 g., 0.999 Gold 0.0999 oz. AGW **Obv:** Temple of Heaven, date below **Rev:** Panda pawing bamboo, denomination below **Note:** Prev. Y#153.

Date	Mintage	XF40	MS60	MS63	MS65	MS66
1988	213,653	—	—	165	170	175
1988	10,000	PF65 215	PF67 225	PF69 235		

KM# 223 10 YUAN

3.11 g., 0.999 Gold 0.0999 oz. AGW, 14 mm. **Rev:** Panda seated with bamboo, linear grid background

Date	Mintage	XF40	MS60	MS63	MS65	MS66
1989	8,000	PF65 215	PF67 225	PF69 235		
1989	89,058	—	—	165	170	175

KM# 269 10 YUAN

3.11 g., 0.999 Gold 0.0999 oz. AGW **Obv:** Temple of Heaven, date below **Rev:** Panda, denomination below **Note:** Prev. Y#239.

Date	Mintage	XF40	MS60	MS63	MS65	MS66
1990	21,654	—	—	165	170	175
1990	5,000	PF65 250	PF67 260	PF69 275		

KM# 347 10 YUAN

3.11 g., 0.999 Gold 0.0999 oz. AGW **Obv:** Temple of Heaven **Rev:** Panda with hind feet in water eating bamboo **Note:** Similar to 100 Yuan, KM# 350. Prev. Y#310.

Date	Mintage	XF40	MS60	MS63	MS65	MS66
1991	81,792	—	—	165	170	175
1991	—	PF65 300	PF67 330	PF69 360		

KM# 392 10 YUAN

3.11 g., 0.999 Gold 0.0999 oz. AGW **Obv:** Temple of Heaven, date below **Rev:** Panda climbing right on eucalyptus branch **Note:** Prev. Y#342.

Date	Mintage	XF40	MS60	MS63	MS65	MS66
1992	116,999	—	—	165	170	175
1992	—	PF65 500	PF67 550	PF69 610		

KM# 474 10 YUAN

3.11 g., 0.999 Gold 0.0999 oz. AGW **Obv:** Temple of Heaven **Rev:** Panda on flat rock **Note:** Prev. Y#484; 611; 1203.

Date	Mintage	XF40	MS60	MS63	MS65	MS66
1993	86,318	—	—	165	170	175
1993	—	PF65 300	PF67 325	PF69 350		

KM# 612 10 YUAN

3.11 g., 0.999 Gold 0.0999 oz. AGW **Obv:** Temple of Heaven, date below **Rev:** Seated panda eating, denomination below **Note:** Prev. Y#432.

Date	Mintage	XF40	MS60	MS63	MS65	MS66
1994	55,182	—	—	240	250	255
1994	—	PF65 400	PF67 420	PF69 440		

KM# 716 10 YUAN

3.11 g., 0.999 Gold 0.0999 oz. AGW **Obv:** Temple of Heaven **Rev:** Panda eating bamboo, denomination at left **Note:** Prev. Y#641.

Date	Mintage	XF40	MS60	MS63	MS65	MS66
1995	45,007	—	—	300	310	320

KM# 884 10 YUAN

3.11 g., 0.999 Gold 0.0999 oz. AGW **Obv:** Temple of Heaven, date below **Rev:** Panda in tree **Note:** Large and small date varieties exist. Prev. Y#575.

Date	Mintage	XF40	MS60	MS63	MS65	MS66
1996	57,203	—	—	225	235	250

KM# 889 10 YUAN

3.11 g., 0.999 Gold 0.0999 oz. AGW **Subject:** 15th Anniversary - Gold Panda Coins **Obv:** Temple of Heaven with additional legend **Rev:** Panda in tree **Note:** Large and small date varieties exist. Prev. Y#848.

Date	Mintage	XF40	MS60	MS63	MS65	MS66
1996	20,000	PF65 235	PF67 275	PF69 310		

KM# 987 10 YUAN

3.11 g., 0.999 Gold 0.0999 oz. AGW **Obv:** Temple of Heaven **Rev:** Panda on branch **Note:** Large and small date varieties exist. Prev. Y#717.

Date	Mintage	XF40	MS60	MS63	MS65	MS66
1997	46,628	—	—	190	200	210

KM# 1127 10 YUAN

3.11 g., 0.999 Gold 0.0999 oz. AGW **Obv:** Temple of Heaven **Rev:** Panda seated on rock **Note:** Large and small date varieties exist. Prev. Y#988.

Date	Mintage	XF40	MS60	MS63	MS65	MS66
1998	8,502	—	—	500	550	600

KM# 1218 10 YUAN

3.11 g., 0.999 Gold 0.0999 oz. AGW **Obv:** Temple of Heaven **Rev:** Panda on ledge **Note:** Prev. Y#989. Large and small date varieties exist.

Date	Mintage	XF40	MS60	MS63	MS65	MS66
1999	25,501	—	—	270	275	280

KM# 1304 10 YUAN

3.11 g., 0.999 Gold 0.0999 oz. AGW **Obv:** Temple of Heaven **Rev:** Panda seated on leaves **Note:** Mirror and frosed exist. Prev. Y#946.

Date	Mintage	XF40	MS60	MS63	MS65	MS66
2000	44,511	PF65 260	PF67 320	PF69 380		

KM# 70 25 YUAN

7.78 g., 0.999 Gold 0.2497 oz. AGW **Obv:** Temple of Heaven, date below **Rev:** Panda walking right, in inner circle, denomination below **Note:** Prev. Y#50.

Date	Mintage	XF40	MS60	MS63	MS65	MS66
1983	43,827	—	—	500	525	560

KM# 89 25 YUAN

7.78 g., 0.999 Gold 0.2497 oz. AGW **Obv:** Temple of Heaven, date below **Rev:** Lounging Panda with bamboo **Note:** Prev. Y#75.

Date	Mintage	XF40	MS60	MS63	MS65	MS66
1984	35,970	—	—	500	550	600

KM# 116 25 YUAN

7.78 g., 0.999 Gold 0.2497 oz. AGW **Obv:** Temple of Heaven, date below **Rev:** Panda hanging on bamboo branch, denomination upper left **Note:** Prev. Y#82.

Date	Mintage	XF40	MS60	MS63	MS65	MS66
1985	89,044	—	—	500	560	620

KM# 133 25 YUAN

7.78 g., 0.999 Gold 0.2497 oz. AGW **Obv:** Temple of Heaven **Rev:** Facing panda standing, denomination below **Note:** Prev. Y#103.

Date	Mintage	XF40	MS60	MS63	MS65	MS66
1986 P	10,000	PF65 550	PF67 575	PF69 630		
1986	42,229	—	—	425	475	510

KM# 161 25 YUAN
7.78 g., 0.999 Gold 0.2497 oz. AGW **Obv:** Temple of Heaven, date below **Rev:** Panda drinking, denomination below **Note:** Prev. Y#126.

Date	Mintage	XF40	MS60	MS63	MS65	MS66
1987 (y)	Inc. above	—	—	425	475	510
1987 (s)	97,358	—	—	425	475	510
1987 P	10,000	PF65 550	PF67 575	PF69 630		

KM# 185 25 YUAN
7.78 g., 0.999 Gold 0.2497 oz. AGW **Obv:** Temple of Heaven **Rev:** Panda pawing bamboo **Note:** Prev. Y#154.

Date	Mintage	XF40	MS60	MS63	MS65	MS66
1988	10,000	PF65 550	PF67 575	PF69 630		
1988	142,634	—	—	425	475	510

KM# 224 25 YUAN
7.78 g., 0.999 Gold 0.2497 oz. AGW **Obv:** Temple of Heaven, date below **Rev:** Panda reclining, grid behind, denomination below **Note:** Prev. Y#189.

Date	Mintage	XF40	MS60	MS63	MS65	MS66
1989	221,688	—	—	425	475	510
1989	—	PF65 550	PF67 575	PF69 630		

KM# 270 25 YUAN
7.78 g., 0.999 Gold 0.2497 oz. AGW **Obv:** Temple of Heaven, date below **Rev:** Panda, denomination lower right **Note:** Prev. Y#240.

Date	Mintage	XF40	MS60	MS63	MS65	MS66
1990	31,148	—	—	425	475	510
1990	5,000	PF65 650	PF67 750	PF69 810		

KM# 359 25 YUAN
7.78 g., 0.999 Gold 0.2497 oz. AGW, 22 mm. **Obv:** Temple of Heaven, date below **Edge:** Reeded **Note:** Prev. Y#311.

Date	Mintage	XF40	MS60	MS63	MS65	MS66
1991	54,548	—	—	425	475	510
1991	—	PF65 700	PF67 800	PF69 860		

KM# 393 25 YUAN
7.78 g., 0.999 Gold 0.2497 oz. AGW **Obv:** Temple of Heaven, date below **Rev:** Panda on limb **Note:** Prev. Y#343.

Date	Mintage	XF40	MS60	MS63	MS65	MS66
1992	72,537	—	—	425	475	510
1992	—	PF65 1,100	PF67 1,200	PF69 1,300		

KM# A613 25 YUAN
7.78 g., 0.999 Gold 0.2497 oz. AGW, 22 mm. **Obv:** Temple of Heaven **Rev:** Panda seated on flat rock **Edge:** Reeded

Date	Mintage	XF40	MS60	MS63	MS65	MS66
1993	80,006	—	—	425	475	510
1993P	2,500	PF65 650	PF67 700	PF69 730		

KM# 613 25 YUAN
7.78 g., 0.999 Gold 0.2497 oz. AGW **Obv:** Temple of Heaven, date below **Rev:** Panda tugging on bamboo sprig **Note:** Prev. Y#433.

Date	Mintage	XF40	MS60	MS63	MS65	MS66
1994	20,386	—	—	425	475	510
1994	2,500	PF65 750	PF67 800	PF69 860		

KM# 717 25 YUAN
7.76 g., 0.999 Gold 0.2492 oz. AGW **Obv:** Temple of Heaven, date below **Rev:** Panda **Note:** Prev. Y#642.

Date	Mintage	XF40	MS60	MS63	MS65	MS66
1995	13,710	—	—	750	800	850

KM# 885 25 YUAN
7.83 g., 0.999 Gold 0.2515 oz. AGW **Obv:** Temple of Heaven, date below **Rev:** Panda **Note:** Large and small date varieties exist. Prev. Y#576.

Date	Mintage	XF40	MS60	MS63	MS65	MS66
1996	17,589	—	—	600	650	680

KM# 891 25 YUAN
7.78 g., 0.999 Gold 0.2498 oz. AGW **Subject:** 15th Anniversary - Gold Panda Coinage **Obv:** Temple of Heaven with additional legend **Rev:** Panda in tree **Note:** Large and small date varieties exist. Prev. Y#849.

Date	Mintage	XF40	MS60	MS63	MS65	MS66
1996	8,000	PF65 750	PF67 775	PF69 820		

KM# 989 25 YUAN
7.78 g., 0.999 Gold 0.2498 oz. AGW **Obv:** Temple of Heaven **Rev:** Panda on branch **Note:** Prev. Y#718.

Date	Mintage	XF40	MS60	MS63	MS65	MS66
1997	21,909	—	—	550	575	600

Note: Exists in Large and Small date varieties.

KM# 1128 25 YUAN
7.78 g., 0.999 Gold 0.2497 oz. AGW **Obv:** Temple of Heaven **Rev:** Panda seated on rock **Note:** Large and small date varieties exist. Prev. Y#1002.

Date	Mintage	XF40	MS60	MS63	MS65	MS66
1998	13,009	—	—	800	825	850

Note: Exists in both large and small date varieties

KM# 1219 25 YUAN
7.78 g., 0.999 Gold 0.2497 oz. AGW **Obv:** Temple of Heaven **Rev:** Panda on ledge **Note:** Large and small date varieties exist. Prev. Y#1003.

Date	Mintage	XF40	MS60	MS63	MS65	MS66
1999	18,013	—	—	600	650	680

KM# 1305 25 YUAN
7.78 g., 0.999 Gold 0.2497 oz. AGW **Obv:** Temple of Heaven **Rev:** Panda seated on leaves **Note:** Large and small date varieties exist. Prev. Y#947.

Date	Mintage	XF40	MS60	MS63	MS65	MS66
2000	24,811	—	—	500	525	550

Note: Domestic Chinese examples struck with mirror fields, overseas examples struck with frosted fields

KM# 71 50 YUAN
15.55 g., 0.999 Gold 0.4995 oz. AGW **Obv:** Temple of Heaven, date below **Rev:** Panda walking right, in inner circle, date below **Note:** Prev. Y#51.

Date	Mintage	XF40	MS60	MS63	MS65	MS66
1983	28,596	PF65 850	PF67 950	PF69 1,000		

KM# 90 50 YUAN
15.55 g., 0.999 Gold 0.4995 oz. AGW **Obv:** Temple of Heaven, date below **Rev:** Lounging panda with bamboo sprig, denomination at right **Note:** Prev. Y#76.

Date	Mintage	XF40	MS60	MS63	MS65	MS66
1984	20,057	PF65 850	PF67 950	PF69 1,000		

KM# 117 50 YUAN
15.55 g., 0.999 Gold 0.4995 oz. AGW **Obv:** Temple of Heaven, date below **Rev:** Panda hanging from bamboo branch, denomination upper left **Note:** Prev. Y#83.

Date	Mintage	XF40	MS60	MS63	MS65	MS66
1985	62,675	—	—	800	850	900

KM# 134 50 YUAN
15.55 g., 0.999 Gold 0.4995 oz. AGW **Obv:** Temple of Heaven, date below **Rev:** Facing panda standing, denomination below **Note:** Prev. Y#104.

Date	Mintage	XF40	MS60	MS63	MS65	MS66
1986	48,618	—	—	775	800	830
1986 P	10,000	PF65 850	PF67 950	PF69 1,000		

KM# 162 50 YUAN
15.55 g., 0.999 Gold 0.4995 oz. AGW **Obv:** Temple of Heaven, date below **Rev:** Panda drinking water, denomination below **Note:** Prev. Y#127.

Date	Mintage	XF40	MS60	MS63	MS65	MS66
1987 (s)	97,076	—	—	775	800	830
1987 (y)	Inc. above	—	—	775	800	830
1987 P	10,000	PF65 850	PF67 950	PF69 1,000		

KM# 186 50 YUAN
15.55 g., 0.999 Gold 0.4995 oz. AGW **Obv:** Temple of Heaven, date below **Rev:** Panda pawing bamboo within circle, denomination below **Note:** Prev. Y#155.

Date	Mintage	XF40	MS60	MS63	MS65	MS66
1988	220,430	—	—	775	800	830
1988	10,000	PF65 850	PF67 950	PF69 1,000		

KM# 226 50 YUAN
15.55 g., 0.999 Gold 0.4995 oz. AGW **Obv:** Temple of Heaven **Rev:** Grid behind panda **Note:** Prev. Y#190.

Date	Mintage	XF40	MS60	MS63	MS65	MS66
1989	120,588	—	—	775	800	830
1989	—	PF65 850	PF67 950	PF69 1,000		

KM# 271 50 YUAN
15.55 g., 0.999 Gold 0.4995 oz. AGW **Obv:** Temple of Heaven, date below **Rev:** Panda **Note:** Prev. Y#241.

Date	Mintage	XF40	MS60	MS63	MS65	MS66
1990	35,091	—	—	800	850	880
1990	5,000	PF65 900	PF67 1,000			

KM# 349 50 YUAN
15.55 g., 0.999 Gold 0.4995 oz. AGW **Obv:** Temple of Heaven, date below **Rev:** Panda tugging on bamboo sprig, denomination below, within circle, date below **Note:** Prev. Y#312.

Date	Mintage	XF40	MS60	MS63	MS65	MS66
1991	32,717	—	—	800	850	880
1991	—	PF65 850	PF67 900	PF69 920		

KM# 357 50 YUAN
31.10 g., 0.999 Gold 0.999 oz. AGW **Subject:** 10th Anniversary of Panda Coinage **Obv:** Temple of Heaven, date below **Rev:** Panda climbing bamboo branch **Note:** Double thickness. Prev. Y#315.

Date	Mintage	XF40	MS60	MS63	MS65	MS66
1991	2,500	PF65 3,000	PF67 3,500	PF69 4,000		

KM# 476 50 YUAN
15.55 g., 0.999 Gold 0.4995 oz. AGW **Obv:** Temple of Heaven **Rev:** Pandas **Note:** Prev. Y#613.

Date	Mintage	XF40	MS60	MS63	MS65	MS66
1992	26,495	—	—	900	—	—
1992	—	PF65 2,000	PF67 2,500	PF69 2,800		

KM# A614 50 YUAN
15.55 g., 0.999 Gold 0.4994 oz. AGW, 27 mm. **Obv:** Temple of Heaven **Rev:** Panda seated on flat rock **Edge:** Reeded

Date	Mintage	XF40	MS60	MS63	MS65	MS66
1993P	2,500	PF65 1,500	PF67 2,000	PF69 2,800		
1993	31,254	—	—	800	875	960

KM# 614 50 YUAN
15.55 g., 0.999 Gold 0.4995 oz. AGW **Obv:** Temple of Heaven **Rev:** Panda seated, eating bamboo shoots, denomination below **Note:** Prev. Y#434.

Date	Mintage	XF40	MS60	MS63	MS65	MS66
1994	16,788	—	—	850	—	—
1994	—	PF65 2,200	PF67 3,200	PF69 4,000		

KM# 718 50 YUAN
15.55 g., 0.999 Gold 0.4995 oz. AGW **Obv:** Temple of Heaven **Rev:** Panda eating bamboo, denomination at left **Note:** Large and small date varieties exist. Prev. Y#643.

Date	Mintage	XF40	MS60	MS63	MS65	MS66
1995	11,749	—	—	1,200	1,275	1,320

KM# 886 50 YUAN
15.55 g., 0.999 Gold 0.4995 oz. AGW **Obv:** Temple of Heaven, date below **Rev:** Panda in tree **Note:** Large and small date varieties exist. Prev. Y#577.

Date	Mintage	XF40	MS60	MS63	MS65	MS66
1996	13,849	—	—	900	1,000	1,100

KM# 990 50 YUAN
15.55 g., 0.999 Gold 0.4995 oz. AGW **Obv:** Temple of Heaven within circle, date below **Rev:** Panda on large tree branch, denomination below **Note:** Prev. Y#719. Large and small date varieties exist.

Date	Mintage	XF40	MS60	MS63	MS65	MS66
1997	15,483	—	—	850	950	1,000

KM# 1129 50 YUAN
15.55 g., 0.999 Gold 0.4995 oz. AGW **Obv:** Temple of Heaven **Rev:** Panda seated on rock **Note:** Prev. Y#1010. Large and small date varieties exist.

Date	Mintage	XF40	MS60	MS63	MS65	MS66
1998	4,168	—	—	1,500	2,000	2,600

KM# 1220 50 YUAN
15.55 g., 0.999 Gold 0.4995 oz. AGW **Obv:** Temple of Heaven **Rev:** Panda on ledge **Note:** Prev. Y#1011.

Date	Mintage	XF40	MS60	MS63	MS65	MS66
1999	12,482	—	—	900	1,100	1,200

Note: Exists in Large and Small date varieties

KM# 1306 50 YUAN
15.55 g., 0.999 Gold 0.4995 oz. AGW **Obv:** Temple of Heaven **Rev:** Panda seated on leaves **Note:** Large and small date varieties exist. Prev. Y#948.

Date	Mintage	XF40	MS60	MS63	MS65	MS66
2000	20,811	PF65 950	PF67 1,150	PF69 1,350		

Note: Domestic Chinese examples struck with mirror fields, overseas examples struck with frosted fields.

KM# 72 100 YUAN
31.13 g., 0.999 Gold 0.9999 oz. AGW **Obv:** Temple of Heaven, date below **Rev:** Panda right within circle, date below **Note:** Prev. Y#52.

Date	Mintage	XF40	MS60	MS63	MS65	MS66
1983	25,363	—	—	1,800	1,900	2,000

KM# 91 100 YUAN
31.13 g., 0.999 Gold 0.9999 oz. AGW **Obv:** Temple of Heaven, date below **Rev:** Lounging panda with bamboo sprigs, denomination at right **Note:** Prev. Y#77.

Date	Mintage	XF40	MS60	MS63	MS65	MS66
1984	25,193	—	—	1,800	1,900	2,000

KM# 118 100 YUAN
31.13 g., 0.999 Gold 0.9999 oz. AGW **Obv:** Temple of Heaven, date below **Rev:** Panda hanging from branch, denomination upper left **Note:** Prev. Y#84.

Date	Mintage	XF40	MS60	MS63	MS65	MS66
1985	55,539	—	—	—	1,600	1,800

KM# 135 100 YUAN
31.13 g., 0.999 Gold 0.9999 oz. AGW **Obv:** Temple of Heaven, date below **Rev:** Panda amongst bamboo plants **Note:** Prev. Y#105.

Date	Mintage	XF40	MS60	MS63	MS65	MS66
1986	107,124	—	—	—	1,400	1,500
1986 P	10,000	PF69 2,200				

KM# 166 100 YUAN
31.13 g., 0.999 Gold 0.9999 oz. AGW **Obv:** Temple of Heaven, date below **Rev:** Panda drinking at stream, denomination below **Note:** Prev. Y#128.

Date	Mintage	XF40	MS60	MS63	MS65	MS66
1987 (s)	156,178	—	—	—	1,400	1,600
1987 (y)	Inc. above	—	—	—	1,400	1,600
1987 P	10,000	PF69 2,000				

KM# 187 100 YUAN
31.13 g., 0.999 Gold 0.9999 oz. AGW **Obv:** Temple of Heaven, date below **Rev:** Panda pawing bamboo within circle, denomination below **Note:** Prev. Y#156.

Date	Mintage	XF40	MS60	MS63	MS65	MS66
1988	289,055	—	—	—	1,300	1,400
1988	10,000	PF69 2,500				

KM# 229 100 YUAN
31.13 g., 0.999 Gold 0.9999 oz. AGW **Obv:** Temple of Heaven, date below **Rev:** Panda reclining, grid behind, denomination below **Note:** Prev. Y#191.

Date	Mintage	XF40	MS60	MS63	MS65	MS66
1989	115,187	—	—	—	1,300	1,400
1989	8,000	PF69 2,600				

KM# 272 100 YUAN
31.13 g., 0.999 Gold 0.9999 oz. AGW **Obv:** Temple of Heaven, date below **Rev:** Panda climbing rock, denomination below **Note:** Prev. Y#242.

Date	Mintage	XF40	MS60	MS63	MS65	MS66
1990	53,898	—	—	—	1,400	1,500
1990	5,000	PF69 4,000				

KM# 350 100 YUAN
31.13 g., 0.999 Gold 0.9999 oz. AGW **Obv:** Temple of Heaven, date below **Rev:** Seated panda with hind feet in water, eating bamboo, denomination at left **Note:** Prev. Y#313.

Date	Mintage	XF40	MS60	MS63	MS65	MS66
1991	36,367	—	—	—	1,650	1,700
1991	—	PF67 2,500	PF69 4,000			

KM# 395 100 YUAN
31.10 g., 0.999 Gold 0.999 oz. AGW **Obv:** Temple of Heaven within circle, date below **Rev:** Panda on branch, denomination above **Note:** Prev. Y#345.

Date	Mintage	XF40	MS60	MS63	MS65	MS66
1992	41,120	—	—	—	1,650	1,700
1992	—	PF67 3,200	PF69 4,500			

KM# 477 100 YUAN
31.10 g., 0.999 Gold 0.999 oz. AGW **Obv:** Temple of Heaven **Rev:** Panda seated on rock **Note:** Prev. Y#614.

Date	Mintage	XF40	MS60	MS63	MS65	MS66
1993	40,449	—	—	—	1,650	1,700

KM# A615 100 YUAN
8.00 g., 0.916 Gold 0.2356 oz. AGW **Obv:** National emblem, date below **Rev:** Panda climbing tree, denomination at right

Date	Mintage	XF40	MS60	MS63	MS65	MS66
1994	—	PF67 600	PF69 700			

KM# 615 100 YUAN
31.10 g., 0.999 Gold 0.999 oz. AGW **Obv:** Temple of Heaven,

date below **Rev:** Panda seated, eating bamboo shoots, denomination below **Note:** Prev. Y#435.

Date	Mintage	XF40	MS60	MS63	MS65	MS66
1994	24,438	—	—	—	1,650	1,700

KM# 719 100 YUAN
31.10 g., 0.999 Gold 0.999 oz. AGW **Obv:** Temple of Heaven **Rev:** Panda eating bamboo **Note:** Prev. Y#644.

Date	Mintage	XF40	MS60	MS63	MS65	MS66
1995	17,412	—	—	—	2,450	2,600

KM# 726 100 YUAN
31.01 g., 0.999 Gold 0.996 oz. AGW **Obv:** Temple of Heaven within circle, date below **Rev:** Panda approaching water from right, denomination below **Note:** Prev. Y#790.

Date	Mintage	XF40	MS60	MS63	MS65	MS66
1995	2,000	PF65 7,000	PF67 10,000	PF69 12,000		

KM# 887 100 YUAN
31.10 g., 0.999 Gold 0.999 oz. AGW **Obv:** Temple of Heaven within circle, date below **Rev:** Panda in tree, denomination at left **Note:** Large and small date varieties exist. Prev. Y#578.

Date	Mintage	XF40	MS60	MS63	MS65	MS66
1996	22,009	—	—	—	1,650	1,800

KM# 896 100 YUAN
31.10 g., 0.999 Gold 0.999 oz. AGW **Subject:** 15th Anniversary - Gold Panda Coins **Obv:** Temple of Heaven with additional legend **Rev:** Panda in tree **Note:** Large and small date varieties exist. Previous Y # 850.

Date	Mintage	XF40	MS60	MS63	MS65	MS66
1996	1,500	PF67 3,500	PF69 4,500			

KM# 901 100 YUAN
31.10 g., 0.999 Gold 0.999 oz. AGW **Obv:** Temple of Heaven **Rev:** Panda sitting on rock **Note:** Large and small date varieties exist. Prev. Y#1013.

Date	Mintage	XF40	MS60	MS63	MS65	MS66
1996	1,500	PF67 7,000	PF69 9,000			

KM# 991 100 YUAN
31.10 g., 0.999 Gold 0.999 oz. AGW **Obv:** Temple of Heaven **Rev:** Panda on large branch, denomination below **Note:** Large and small date varieties exist. Prev. Y#720.

Date	Mintage	XF40	MS60	MS63	MS65	MS66
1997	30,457	—	—	—	1,650	1,800

Note: Exists in large and small date varieties

KM# 1130 100 YUAN
31.13 g., 0.999 Gold 0.9999 oz. AGW **Obv:** Temple of Heaven **Rev:** Panda seated on rock **Note:** Large and small date varieties exist. Prev. Y#1016.

Date	Mintage	XF40	MS60	MS63	MS65	MS66
1998	20,507	—	—	—	2,250	2,450

KM# 1221 100 YUAN
31.13 g., 0.999 Gold 0.9999 oz. AGW **Obv:** Temple of Heaven **Rev:** Panda on ledge **Note:** Large and small date varieties exist. Prev. Y#1017.

Date	Mintage	XF40	MS60	MS63	MS65	MS66
1999	32,439	—	—	—	1,650	1,800

KM# 1307 100 YUAN
31.10 g., 0.999 Gold 0.999 oz. AGW **Obv:** Temple of Heaven **Rev:** Panda seated on leaves **Note:** Large and small date varieties exist. Prev. Y#949.

Date	Mintage	XF40	MS60	MS63	MS65	MS66
2000	29,011	—	—	—	1,650	1,800

Note: Domestic Chinese examples struck with mirror fields, overseas examples struck with frosted fields

KM# 164 500 YUAN
155.52 g., 0.999 Gold 4.9949 oz. AGW, 60 mm. **Obv:** Temple of Heaven **Rev:** Panda with cub, denomination below **Note:** Illustration reduced. Prev. Y#147.

Date	Mintage	XF40	MS60	MS63	MS65	MS66
1987	3,000	PF69 14,000				

KM# 190 500 YUAN
155.52 g., 0.999 Gold 4.9949 oz. AGW **Obv:** Temple of Heaven **Rev:** Two pandas in tree, denomination upper left **Note:** Prev. Y#233.

Date	Mintage	XF40	MS60	MS63	MS65	MS66
1988	3,000	PF69 14,000				

KM# 400 500 YUAN
155.52 g., 0.999 Gold 4.9949 oz. AGW **Obv:** Temple of Heaven, date below **Rev:** Pandas **Note:** Prev. Y#369.

Date	Mintage	XF40	MS60	MS63	MS65	MS66
1992	99	PF69 35,000				

KM# 481 500 YUAN
155.52 g., 0.999 Gold 4.9949 oz. AGW **Obv:** Temple of Heaven **Rev:** Two pandas climbing tree stumps **Note:** Prev. Y#761.

Date	Mintage	XF40	MS60	MS63	MS65	MS66
1993	99	PF69 40,000				

KM# 619 500 YUAN
155.52 g., 0.999 Gold 4.9949 oz. AGW **Obv:** Temple of Heaven **Rev:** Two pandas, one in tree, denomination above **Note:** Prev. Y#639.

Date	Mintage	XF40	MS60	MS63	MS65	MS66
1994	99	PF69 45,000				

KM# 92 1000 YUAN
373.24 g., 0.999 Gold 11.9878 oz. AGW, 70 mm. **Obv:** Temple of Heaven **Rev:** Panda seated left, denomination beloOw **Note:** Illustration reduced. Prev. #Y66.

Date	Mintage	XF40	MS60	MS63	MS65	MS66
1984	250	PF69 40,000				

Note: A typical sealed proof exhibits some scuffing and is valued as above, while perfect examples can bring up to a 100% premium

KM# 136.1 1000 YUAN
373.24 g., 0.999 Gold 11.9878 oz. AGW, 70 mm. **Obv:** Temple of Heaven **Rev:** Panda eating bamboo shoot with cub, denomination at right **Note:** Illustration reduced. Prev. #Y118.1.

Date	Mintage	XF40	MS60	MS63	MS65	MS66
1986	2,550	PF69 30,000				

KM# 136.2 1000 YUAN
373.24 g., 0.999 Gold 11.9878 oz. AGW **Obv:** Temple of Heaven **Rev:** Panda eating bamboo shoot with cub **Edge:** Plain **Note:** Prev. #Y118.2.

Date	Mintage	XF40	MS60	MS63	MS65	MS66
1986 Proof	—	—	—	—	—	—

Note: 2 known; Last traded privately at $45,000

KM# 165 1000 YUAN
373.24 g., 0.999 Gold 11.9878 oz. AGW **Obv:** Temple of Heaven **Rev:** Panda with cub, denomination below **Shape:** 70 **Note:** Illustration reduced. Prev. #Y157.

Date	Mintage	XF40	MS60	MS63	MS65	MS66
1987	2,445	PF69 28,000				

KM# 191 1000 YUAN
373.24 g., 0.999 Gold 11.9878 oz. AGW **Obv:** Temple of Heaven **Rev:** Pandas in tree **Note:** Similar to 500 Yuan, KM # 190. Prev. #Y234.

Date	Mintage	XF40	MS60	MS63	MS65	MS66
1988	1,650	PF69 22,000				

KM# 275 1000 YUAN
373.24 g., 0.999 Gold 11.9878 oz. AGW, 70 mm. **Obv:** Temple of Heaven **Rev:** Three pandas, denomination upper right **Note:** Prev. #Y282. Illustration reduced.

Date	Mintage	XF40	MS60	MS63	MS65	MS66
1990	500	PF69 40,000				

KM# 355 1000 YUAN
373.24 g., 0.999 Gold 11.9878 oz. AGW **Obv:** Temple of Heaven, date below **Rev:** Pandas **Note:** Prev. #Y371.

Date	Mintage	XF40	MS60	MS63	MS65	MS66
1991	400	PF69 45,000				

KM# 401 1000 YUAN
373.24 g., 0.999 Gold 11.9878 oz. AGW **Obv:** Temple of Heaven **Rev:** Pandas **Note:** Prev. #Y372.

Date	Mintage	XF40	MS60	MS63	MS65	MS66
1992	99	PF69 45,000				

KM# 482 1000 YUAN
373.24 g., 0.999 Gold 11.9878 oz. AGW **Obv:** Temple of Heaven **Rev:** Panda family of three **Note:** Prev. #Y762.

Date	Mintage	XF40	MS60	MS63	MS65	MS66
1993	99	PF69 60,000				

KM# 620 1000 YUAN
373.24 g., 0.999 Gold 11.988 oz. AGW, 70 mm. **Obv:** Temple of Heaven **Rev:** Panda and two cubs at water's edge **Edge:** Reeded **Note:** Prev. #Y1089.

Date	Mintage	XF40	MS60	MS63	MS65	MS66
1994	99	PF69 80,000				

KM# 721 1000 YUAN
373.24 g., 0.999 Gold 11.988 oz. AGW, 70 mm. **Obv:** Temple of Heaven **Rev:** Two adult pandas with cub **Edge:** Reeded **Note:** Illustration reduced. Prev. #Y1090.

Date	Mintage	XF40	MS60	MS63	MS65	MS66
1995	99	PF69 80,000				

KM# 992 2000 YUAN
1000.00 g., 0.999 Gold 32.1186 oz. AGW **Obv:** Temple of Heaven **Rev:** Panda **Note:** Large and small date varieties exist. Prev. #Y961.

Date	Mintage	XF40	MS60	MS63	MS65	MS66
1997	58	PF69 260,000				

KM# A1130 2000 YUAN
1000.00 g., 0.999 Gold 32.1186 oz. AGW **Obv:** Temple of Heaven **Rev:** Panda **Note:** Large and small date varieties exist.

Date	Mintage	XF40	MS60	MS63	MS65	MS66
1998	58	PF69 260,000				

KM# 1223 2000 YUAN
1000.21 g., 0.999 Gold 32.1253 oz. AGW **Obv:** Temple of Heaven **Rev:** Panda on rock **Note:** Large and small date varieties exist. Prev. #Y972.

Date	Mintage	XF40	MS60	MS63	MS65	MS66
1999	68	PF69 230,000				

KM# 1309 3000 YUAN
1000.00 g., 0.999 Gold 32.1186 oz. AGW, 90 mm. **Rev:** Panda seated eating bamboo

Date	Mintage	XF40	MS60	MS63	MS65	MS66
2000	68	PF69 230,000				

KM# 358 10000 YUAN
4851.60 g., 0.999 Gold 155.8265 oz. AGW **Subject:** 10th Anniversary of Gold Panda Issue **Obv:** Temple of Heaven **Rev:** Panda on branch, denomination at right, in center of 10 panda coin designs **Note:** Prev. #Y358.

Date	Mintage	XF40	MS60	MS63	MS65	MS66
1991 Proof, Rare	10	—	—	—	—	—

GOLD BULLION COINAGE

Lunar Series

KM# 1012 10 YUAN
3.11 g., 0.999 Gold 0.0999 oz. AGW **Subject:** Year of the Ox **Obv:** Mingyuan Pavilion **Rev:** Calf **Note:** Prev. Y#901.

Date	Mintage	XF40	MS60	MS63	MS65	MS66
1997	48,000	PF65 265	PF67 325	PF69 400		

KM# 1139 10 YUAN
3.11 g., 0.999 Gold 0.0999 oz. AGW **Subject:** Year of the Tiger **Obv:** Badaling building, date below **Rev:** Tiger cub, denomination at right **Note:** Prev. Y#924.

Date	Mintage	XF40	MS60	MS63	MS65	MS66
1998	48,000	PF65 265	PF67 325	PF69 400		

KM# 1139a 10 YUAN
3.11 g., 0.999 Gold 0.0999 oz. AGW **Subject:** Year of the Tiger **Obv:** Badaling building, date below **Rev:** Multicolor tiger head, facing, denomination at right **Note:** Prev. Y#925.

Date	Mintage	XF40	MS60	MS63	MS65	MS66
1998	30,000	PF65 400	PF67 550	PF69 650		

KM# 1228 10 YUAN
3.11 g., 0.999 Gold 0.0999 oz. AGW **Subject:** Year of the Rabbit **Note:** Prev. Y#980.

Date	Mintage	XF40	MS60	MS63	MS65	MS66
1999	—	PF65 220	PF67 300	PF69 380		

KM# A1229 10 YUAN
3.11 g., 0.999 Gold 0.0999 oz. AGW **Rev:** Multicolor rabbit **Note:** Prev. Y#991.

Date	Mintage	XF40	MS60	MS63	MS65	MS66
1999	30,000	PF65 350	PF67 425	PF69 500		

KM# 1319 10 YUAN
3.11 g., 0.999 Gold 0.0999 oz. AGW **Subject:** Year of the Dragon **Note:** Prev. Y#992.

Date	Mintage	XF40	MS60	MS63	MS65	MS66
2000	48,000	PF65 300	PF67 400	PF69 450		

KM# 1320 10 YUAN
3.11 g., 0.999 Gold 0.0999 oz. AGW, 18 mm. **Subject:** Year of the dragon **Note:** Colorized

Date	Mintage	XF40	MS60	MS63	MS65	MS66
2000	30,000	PF65 450	PF67 525	PF69 600		

KM# 1322 50 YUAN
15.55 g., 0.999 Gold 0.4995 oz. AGW **Subject:** Year of the Dragon **Shape:** Fan

Date	Mintage	XF40	MS60	MS63	MS65	MS66
2000	6,600	—	—	—	1,300	1,400

KM# 196 100 YUAN
31.13 g., 0.999 Gold 0.9999 oz. AGW **Subject:** Year of the Dragon **Obv:** Temple of Heaven **Rev:** 2 floating dragons **Note:** Prev. Y#175.

Date	Mintage	XF40	MS60	MS63	MS65	MS66
1988	10,000	PF65 2,200	PF67 3,200	PF69 4,000		

KM# 235 100 YUAN
31.13 g., 0.999 Gold 0.9999 oz. AGW **Subject:** Year of the Snake **Obv:** National emblem **Rev:** Snake left, denomination below **Note:** Prev. Y#184.

Date	Mintage	XF40	MS60	MS63	MS65	MS66
1989	3,000	PF65 2,300	PF67 2,800	PF69 3,600		

KM# 286 100 YUAN
31.13 g., 0.999 Gold 0.9999 oz. AGW **Subject:** Year of the Horse **Obv:** National emblem, date below **Rev:** Prancing horse left, denomination lower right **Note:** Prev. Y#225.

Date	Mintage	XF40	MS60	MS63	MS65	MS66
1990	6,000	PF65 2,300	PF67 3,000	PF69 4,000		

KM# 364 100 YUAN
31.13 g., 0.999 Gold 0.9999 oz. AGW **Subject:** Year of the Goat **Obv:** National emblem **Rev:** Two goats butting heads, denomination below **Note:** Prev. Y#274.

Date	Mintage	XF40	MS60	MS63	MS65	MS66
1991	1,800	PF65 2,600	PF67 3,500	PF69 5,000		

KM# 432 100 YUAN
31.10 g., 0.999 Gold 0.999 oz. AGW **Subject:** Year of the Monkey **Rev:** Monkey seated on branch, denomination at left **Note:** Prev. Y#295.

Date	Mintage	XF40	MS60	MS63	MS65	MS66
1992	1,800	PF65 2,800	PF67 3,700	PF69 5,000		

KM# 515 100 YUAN
15.55 g., 0.917 Gold 0.4585 oz. AGW **Subject:** Year of the Rooster **Obv:** City gate, date below **Rev:** Rooster with sunflowers, denomination at left **Shape:** Scalloped **Note:** Prev. Y#568.

Date	Mintage	XF40	MS60	MS63	MS65	MS66
1993	—	PF65 1,300	PF67 2,000	PF69 2,500		

KM# 516 100 YUAN
31.10 g., 0.999 Gold 0.999 oz. AGW **Subject:** Year of the Rooster **Obv:** National emblem **Rev:** Rooster and hen, denomination at left **Note:** Prev. Y#570.

Date	Mintage	XF40	MS60	MS63	MS65	MS66
1993	1,900	PF65 2,800	PF67 3,700	PF69 5,000		

KM# 647 100 YUAN
16.40 g., 0.916 Gold 0.4829 oz. AGW **Subject:** Year of the Dog **Obv:** Phoenix Pavilion, date below **Rev:** Lap dog, denomination at left **Shape:** Scalloped **Note:** Prev. Y#780.

Date	Mintage	XF40	MS60	MS63	MS65	MS66
1994	2,300	PF65 1,300	PF67 2,000	PF69 2,500		

KM# 648 100 YUAN
31.13 g., 0.999 Gold 0.9999 oz: AGW **Subject:** Year of the Dog **Rev:** Two dogs, denomination lower left **Note:** Prev. Y#397.

Date	Mintage	XF40	MS60	MS63	MS65	MS66
1994	1,800	PF65 2,800	PF67 3,700	PF69 5,000		

KM# 748 100 YUAN
31.10 g., 0.999 Gold 0.999 oz. AGW **Subject:** Year of the Pig **Obv:** National emblem, date below **Rev:** Pig, denomination at right **Note:** Prev. Y#451.

Date	Mintage	XF40	MS60	MS63	MS65	MS66
1995	1,800	PF65 3,200	PF67 4,700	PF69 6,000		

KM# 753 100 YUAN
15.56 g., 0.999 Gold 0.4996 oz. AGW **Subject:** Year of the Pig **Obv:** Building, date below **Rev:** Two pigs, denomination at lower left **Shape:** Scalloped **Note:** Prev. Y#453.

Date	Mintage	XF40	MS60	MS63	MS65	MS66
1995	2,300	PF65 1,300	PF67 2,200	PF69 3,000		

KM# 924 100 YUAN
31.10 g., 0.999 Gold 0.999 oz. AGW **Subject:** Year of the Rat **Rev:** Rat by oil lamp, denomination below **Note:** Prev. Y#586.

Date	Mintage	XF40	MS60	MS63	MS65	MS66
1996	1,800	PF65 8,000	PF67 12,000	PF69 16,000		

KM# 929 100 YUAN
16.98 g., 0.916 Gold 0.500 oz. AGW **Subject:** Year of the Rat **Obv:** Dengdu Pavilion, date below **Rev:** Rat on corn cob, denomination upper left **Shape:** Scalloped **Note:** Prev. Y#856.

Date	Mintage	XF40	MS60	MS63	MS65	MS66
1996	2,300	PF65 1,300	PF67 2,200	PF69 3,000		

KM# 1009 100 YUAN
31.10 g., 0.999 Gold 0.999 oz. AGW **Subject:** Year of the Ox **Obv:** National emblem, date below **Rev:** Ox, denomination below **Note:** Prev. Y#900.

Date	Mintage	XF40	MS60	MS63	MS65	MS66
1997	1,600	PF65 2,700	PF67 3,500	PF69 4,500		

KM# 1015 100 YUAN
15.56 g., 0.999 Gold 0.4996 oz. AGW **Subject:** Year of the Ox **Shape:** Scalloped **Note:** Prev. Y#670.

Date	Mintage	XF40	MS60	MS63	MS65	MS66
1997	2,300	PF65 1,200	PF67 2,000	PF69 2,600		

KM# 1142 100 YUAN
31.10 g., 0.999 Gold 0.999 oz. AGW **Subject:** Year of the Tiger **Obv:** State seal **Rev:** Tiger **Note:** Prev. Y#929.

Date	Mintage	XF40	MS60	MS63	MS65	MS66
1998	1,600	PF65 3,000	PF67 4,000	PF69 5,000		

KM# 1149 100 YUAN
15.56 g., 0.999 Gold 0.4996 oz. AGW **Subject:** Year of the Tiger **Shape:** Scalloped **Note:** Prev. Y#1015.

Date	Mintage	XF40	MS60	MS63	MS65	MS66
1998	2,300	PF65 1,300	PF67 2,000	PF69 2,600		

KM# 1229 100 YUAN
15.56 g., 0.999 Gold 0.4996 oz. AGW **Subject:** Year of the Rabbit **Shape:** Scalloped **Note:** Prev. Y#1019.

Date	Mintage	XF40	MS60	MS63	MS65	MS66
1999 Prof	—	PF67 2,500	PF69 3,000			

KM# 1232 100 YUAN
31.10 g., 0.999 Gold 0.999 oz. AGW **Subject:** Year of the Rabbit **Note:** Prev. Y#1018.

Date	Mintage	XF40	MS60	MS63	MS65	MS66
1999	—	PF65 3,000	PF67 4,000	PF69 5,000		

KM# 1326 100 YUAN
15.55 g., 0.916 Gold 0.458 oz. AGW **Rev:** Dragons **Shape:** Scalloped **Note:** Prev. Y#1051.

Date	Mintage	XF40	MS60	MS63	MS65	MS66
2000	2,300	PF67 3,500	PF69 4,500			

KM# 74 150 YUAN
8.00 g., 0.917 Gold 0.2359 oz. AGW **Subject:** Year of the Pig **Obv:** Hillside pagoda, waterfront, date lower right **Rev:** Two pigs, denomination below **Note:** Prev. Y#45.

Date	Mintage	XF40	MS60	MS63	MS65	MS66
1983	2,035	PF65 3,500	PF67 4,500	PF69 5,500		

KM# 94 150 YUAN
8.00 g., 0.917 Gold 0.2359 oz. AGW **Subject:** Year of the Rat **Obv:** Fortress, date lower right **Rev:** Rat with squash, denomination below **Note:** Prev. Y#60.

Date	Mintage	XF40	MS60	MS63	MS65	MS66
1984	2,248	PF65 5,000	PF67 6,000	PF69 7,000		

KM# 120 150 YUAN
8.00 g., 0.917 Gold 0.2359 oz. AGW **Subject:** Year of the Ox **Obv:** Houseboat in harbor **Rev:** Ox left, denomination below **Note:** Prev. Y#79.

Date	Mintage	XF40	MS60	MS63	MS65	MS66
1985	Est. 16000	PF65 700	PF67 1,250	PF69 1,450		

KM# 138 150 YUAN
8.00 g., 0.917 Gold 0.2359 oz. AGW **Subject:** Year of the Tiger **Obv:** Qing Dynasty Palace, date below **Rev:** Tiger advancing left, after a painting by He Ziang Ning, denomination above **Note:** Prev. Y#99.

Date	Mintage	XF40	MS60	MS63	MS65	MS66
1986	5,480	PF65 900	PF67 1,300	PF69 1,500		

KM# 171 150 YUAN
8.00 g., 0.917 Gold 0.2359 oz. AGW **Subject:** Year of the Rabbit **Obv:** Pagoda, date below **Rev:** Two rabbits, denomination below **Note:** Prev. Y#123.

Date	Mintage	XF40	MS60	MS63	MS65	MS66
1987	4,780	PF65 900	PF67 1,300	PF69 1,500		

KM# 198 150 YUAN
8.00 g., 0.917 Gold 0.2359 oz. AGW **Subject:** Year of the Dragon **Obv:** Great Wall of China, date below **Rev:** Dragon attacking, denomination below **Note:** Prev. Y#144.

Date	Mintage	XF40	MS60	MS63	MS65	MS66
1988	7,600	PF65 750	PF67 1,000	PF69 1,200		

KM# 237 150 YUAN
8.00 g., 0.917 Gold 0.2359 oz. AGW **Subject:** Year of the Snake **Obv:** Shanhaiguan Pass Gate, date below **Rev:** Snake left, denomination below **Note:** Prev. Y#180.

Date	Mintage	XF40	MS60	MS63	MS65	MS66
1989	7,500	PF65 600	PF67 800	PF69 1,000		

KM# 288 150 YUAN
8.00 g., 0.917 Gold 0.2359 oz. AGW **Subject:** Year of the Horse **Obv:** Temple of Confucius, date below **Rev:** Horse galloping, denomination at left **Note:** Prev. Y#227.

Date	Mintage	XF40	MS60	MS63	MS65	MS66
1990	7,500	PF65 600	PF67 800	PF69 1,000		

KM# 366 150 YUAN
8.00 g., 0.917 Gold 0.2359 oz. AGW **Subject:** Year of the Goat **Obv:** Chinese building and legend **Rev:** Goat reclining, denomination below **Note:** Prev. Y#276.

Date	Mintage	XF40	MS60	MS63	MS65	MS66
1991	7,500	PF65 600	PF67 800	PF69 1,000		

KM# 433 150 YUAN
8.00 g., 0.917 Gold 0.2359 oz. AGW **Subject:** Year of the Monkey **Obv:** Pavilion of Emperor Teng **Rev:** Monkey sitting, denomination at right **Note:** Prev. Y#291.

Date	Mintage	XF40	MS60	MS63	MS65	MS66
1992	5,000	PF65 600	PF67 800	PF69 1,000		

KM# 57 200 YUAN
8.47 g., 0.917 Gold 0.2497 oz. AGW **Subject:** Year of the Dog **Obv:** Temple of Heaven, date below **Rev:** Dog, denomination below **Note:** Prev. Y#39.

Date	Mintage	XF40	MS60	MS63	MS65	MS66
1982	2,500	PF65 2,000	PF67 3,000	PF69 4,000		

KM# 41 250 YUAN
8.00 g., 0.917 Gold 0.2359 oz. AGW **Subject:** Year of the Rooster **Obv:** Monument, date lower left **Rev:** Rooster left, denomination at left **Note:** Prev. Y#33.

Date	Mintage	XF40	MS60	MS63	MS65	MS66
1981	5,015	PF65 1,200	PF67 1,800	PF69 2,200		

KM# 199 500 YUAN
155.52 g., 0.999 Gold 4.9949 oz. AGW, 60 mm. **Subject:** Year of the Dragon **Obv:** Great Wall **Rev:** Inner circle holds three dragons, four dragons surround, denomination below **Note:** Illustration reduced. Prev. Y#145.

Date	Mintage	XF40	MS60	MS63	MS65	MS66
1988	3,000	PF65 12,000	PF67 15,000	PF69 18,000		

KM# 238 500 YUAN
155.52 g., 0.999 Gold 4.9949 oz. AGW, 60 mm. **Subject:** Year of the Snake **Obv:** National emblem **Rev:** Snake left, denomination below, within beaded circle **Note:** Illustration reduced. Prev. Y#181.

Date	Mintage	XF40	MS60	MS63	MS65	MS66
1989	500	PF65 14,000	PF67 24,000	PF69 30,000		

KM# 289 500 YUAN
155.52 g., 0.999 Gold 4.9949 oz. AGW, 60 mm. **Obv:** Temple of Confucius **Rev:** Two horses drinking water, denomination below **Note:** Illustration reduced. Prev. Y#228.

Date	Mintage	XF40	MS60	MS63	MS65	MS66
1990	500	PF65 15,000	PF67 25,000	PF69 30,000		

KM# 367 500 YUAN
155.52 g., 0.999 Gold 4.9949 oz. AGW, 60 mm. **Subject:** Year of the Goat **Obv:** Two goats, one nursing offspring, denomination above **Note:** Illustration reduced. Prev. Y#277.

Date	Mintage	XF40	MS60	MS63	MS65	MS66
1991	250	PF65 17,000	PF67 27,000	PF69 32,000		

KM# 434 500 YUAN
155.52 g., 0.999 Gold 4.9949 oz. AGW, 60 mm. **Subject:** Year of the Monkey **Obv:** Chinese building **Rev:** Monkey seated, denomination at right **Note:** Illustration reduced. Prev. Y#292.

Date	Mintage	XF40	MS60	MS63	MS65	MS66
1992	99	PF65 30,000	PF67 40,000	PF69 55,000		

KM# 517 500 YUAN
155.52 g., 0.999 Gold 4.9949 oz. AGW **Subject:** Year of the Rooster **Note:** Prev. Y#384.

Date	Mintage	XF40	MS60	MS63	MS65	MS66
1993	99	PF65 30,000	PF67 40,000	PF69 55,000		

KM# 649 500 YUAN
155.52 g., 0.999 Gold 4.9949 oz. AGW **Subject:** Year of the Dog **Note:** Prev. Y#389.

Date	Mintage	XF40	MS60	MS63	MS65	MS66
1994	99	PF65 32,000	PF67 45,000	PF69 60,000		

KM# 750 500 YUAN
155.52 g., 0.999 Gold 4.9949 oz. AGW **Subject:** Year of the Pig **Note:** Prev. Y#467.

Date	Mintage	XF40	MS60	MS63	MS65	MS66
1995	99	PF65 32,000	PF67 45,000	PF69 60,000		

KM# 922 500 YUAN
155.52 g., 0.9999 Gold 4.9995 oz. AGW **Subject:** Year of the Rat **Rev:** Rat eating grapes, denomination above **Note:** Prev. Y#663.

Date	Mintage	XF40	MS60	MS63	MS65	MS66
1996	99	PF65 32,000	PF67 45,000		PF69 60,000	

KM# 1007 500 YUAN
155.52 g., 0.999 Gold 4.995 oz. AGW **Subject:** Year of the Ox **Note:** Prev. Y#672.

Date	Mintage	XF40	MS60	MS63	MS65	MS66
1997	99	PF65 32,000	PF67 45,000		PF69 60,000	

KM# 1144 500 YUAN
155.52 g., 0.999 Gold 4.995 oz. AGW **Subject:** Year of the Tiger **Note:** Prev. Y#1024.

Date	Mintage	XF40	MS60	MS63	MS65	MS66
1998	99	PF65 32,000	PF67 45,000		PF69 60,000	

KM# 1227 500 YUAN
155.52 g., 0.999 Gold 4.995 oz. AGW **Subject:** Year of the Rabbit **Note:** Prev. Y#1025.

Date	Mintage	XF40	MS60	MS63	MS65	MS66
1999	99	PF65 30,000	PF67 40,000		PF69 50,000	

KM# 1324 500 YUAN
155.52 g., 0.999 Gold 4.995 oz. AGW **Subject:** Year of the Dragon **Shape:** Rectangular **Note:** Prev. Y#1027.

Date	Mintage	XF40	MS60	MS63	MS65	MS66
2000	118	PF65 35,000	PF67 45,000		PF69 60,000	

KM# 200 1000 YUAN
373.24 g., 0.999 Gold 11.9878 oz. AGW, 70 mm. **Subject:** Year of the Dragon **Obv:** Great Wall **Rev:** Two facing dragons, denomination below **Note:** Illustration reduced. Prev. #Y146.

Date	Mintage	XF40	MS60	MS63	MS65	MS66
1988	518	PF65 32,000	PF67 42,000		PF69 55,000	

KM# 239 1000 YUAN
373.24 g., 0.999 Gold 11.9878 oz. AGW, 70 mm. **Subject:** Year of the Snake **Obv:** National emblem **Rev:** Snake left within beaded circle, denomination below **Note:** Prev. #Y182.

Date	Mintage	XF40	MS60	MS63	MS65	MS66
1989	200	PF65 35,000	PF67 45,000		PF69 60,000	

KM# 290 1000 YUAN
373.24 g., 0.999 Gold 11.9878 oz. AGW, 70 mm. **Subject:** Year of the Horse **Obv:** Temple of Confucius **Rev:** Two horses running, denomination below **Note:** Illustration reduced. Prev. #Y229.

Date	Mintage	XF40	MS60	MS63	MS65	MS66
1990	500	PF65 35,000	PF67 45,000		PF69 60,000	

KM# 368 1000 YUAN
373.24 g., 0.999 Gold 11.9878 oz. AGW **Subject:** Year of the Goat **Obv:** Chinese building and legend **Rev:** Three goats, denomination at left **Note:** Illustration reduced. Prev. #Y278.

Date	Mintage	XF40	MS60	MS63	MS65	MS66
1991	200	PF65 35,000	PF67 45,000		PF69 60,000	

KM# 435 1000 YUAN
373.24 g., 0.999 Gold 11.9878 oz. AGW **Subject:** Year of the Monkey **Obv:** Chinese building **Rev:** Five monkeys, denomination at left **Note:** Illustration reduced. Prev. #Y293.

Date	Mintage	XF40	MS60	MS63	MS65	MS66
1992	99	PF69 80,000				

KM# 518 1000 YUAN
373.24 g., 0.999 Gold 11.9878 oz. AGW **Subject:** Year of the Rooster **Note:** Prev. #Y385.

Date	Mintage	XF40	MS60	MS63	MS65	MS66
1993	99	PF69 80,000				

KM# 650 1000 YUAN
373.24 g., 0.999 Gold 11.9878 oz. AGW **Subject:** Year of the Dog **Note:** Prev. #Y390.

Date	Mintage	XF40	MS60	MS63	MS65	MS66
1994	99	PF69 80,000				

KM# 751 1000 YUAN
373.24 g., 0.999 Gold 11.9878 oz. AGW **Subject:** Year of the Pig **Note:** Prev. #Y468.

Date	Mintage	XF40	MS60	MS63	MS65	MS66
1995	99	PF69 80,000				

KM# 921 1000 YUAN
373.24 g., 0.999 Gold 11.9878 oz. AGW **Subject:** Year of the Rat **Note:** Prev. #Y664.

Date	Mintage	XF40	MS60	MS63	MS65	MS66
1996	99	PF69 80,000				

KM# 1006 1000 YUAN
373.24 g., 0.999 Gold 11.9878 oz. AGW **Subject:** Year of the Ox **Note:** Prev. #Y673.

Date	Mintage	XF40	MS60	MS63	MS65	MS66
1997	99	PF69 80,000				

KM# 1145 1000 YUAN
373.24 g., 0.999 Gold 11.9878 oz. AGW **Subject:** Year of the Tiger **Note:** Prev. #Y1030.

Date	Mintage	XF40	MS60	MS63	MS65	MS66
1998	99	PF69 80,000				

KM# 1235 1000 YUAN
373.24 g., 0.999 Gold 11.9878 oz. AGW **Subject:** Year of the Rabbit **Note:** Prev. #Y1031.

Date	Mintage	XF40	MS60	MS63	MS65	MS66
1999	99	PF69 80,000				

KM# 437 2000 YUAN
1000.00 g., 0.999 Gold 32.1186 oz. AGW, 100 mm. **Subject:** Completion of 150 Yuan Lunar Animal Coin Series **Obv:** Monument divides date and denomination within circle **Rev:** Ying/Yang symbol within octagon, twelve animal coins surround **Note:** Illustration reduced. Prev. #Y702.

Date	Mintage	XF40	MS60	MS63	MS65	MS66
1992	21	PF69 230,000				

KM# 754 2000 YUAN
1000.00 g., 0.999 Gold 32.1186 oz. AGW **Subject:** Year of the Pig **Edge:** Scalloped **Note:** Prev. #Y660.

Date	Mintage	XF40	MS60	MS63	MS65	MS66
1995	15	PF69 235,000				

KM# 930 2000 YUAN
1000.00 g., 0.999 Gold 32.1186 oz. AGW **Subject:** Year of the Rat **Shape:** Scalloped **Note:** Prev. #Y665.

Date	Mintage	XF40	MS60	MS63	MS65	MS66
1996	15	PF69 235,000				

KM# 1016 2000 YUAN
1000.00 g., 0.999 Gold 32.1186 oz. AGW **Subject:** Year of the Ox **Note:** Prev. #Y674.

Date	Mintage	XF40	MS60	MS63	MS65	MS66
1997	15	PF69 235,000				

KM# 1150 2000 YUAN
1000.00 g., 0.999 Gold 32.1186 oz. AGW **Subject:** Year of the Tiger **Shape:** Scalloped **Note:** Prev. #Y967.

Date	Mintage	XF40	MS60	MS63	MS65	MS66
1998	15	PF69 235,000				

KM# 1238 2000 YUAN
1000.00 g., 0.999 Gold 32.1186 oz. AGW **Subject:** Year of the Rabbit **Shape:** Scalloped **Note:** Prev. #Y975.

Date	Mintage	XF40	MS60	MS63	MS65	MS66
1999	15	PF69 235,000				

KM# 1327 2000 YUAN
1000.21 g., 0.999 Gold 32.1253 oz. AGW, Scalloped mm. **Subject:** Year of the Dragon **Note:** Prev. #Y977.

Date	Mintage	XF40	MS60	MS63	MS65	MS66
2000	15	PF69 235,000				

PALLADIUM BULLION COINAGE

Panda Series

KM# 227 50 YUAN
31.10 g., 0.999 Palladium 0.999 oz. APW **Obv:** Building, date below **Rev:** Panda on grid background, denomination lower right **Note:** Prev. Y#220.

Date	Mintage	XF40	MS60	MS63	MS65	MS66
1989	3,000	PF67 16,000				

PLATINUM BULLION COINAGE

Panda Series

KM# 484 5 YUAN
1.56 g., 0.9995 Platinum 0.050 oz. APW **Obv:** Temple of Heaven within circle, date below **Rev:** Panda seated on rock, denomination upper left **Note:** Prev. Y#483.

Date	Mintage	XF40	MS60	MS63	MS65	MS66
1993	—	—	—	—	450	500

KM# 729 5 YUAN
1.55 g., 0.9995 Platinum 0.0498 oz. APW, 14 mm. **Rev:** Panda with bamboo staff

Date	Mintage	XF40	MS60	MS63	MS65	MS66
1995	10,000	—	—	450	480	520

KM# 888 5 YUAN
1.56 g., 0.999 Platinum 0.050 oz. APW **Obv:** Temple of Heaven, date below **Rev:** Panda in tree looking down, denomination lower left **Note:** Prev. Y#581a.

Date	Mintage	XF40	MS60	MS63	MS65	MS66
1996	5,000	—	—	—	175	230

KM# 985 5 YUAN
1.56 g., 0.999 Platinum 0.050 oz. APW **Obv:** Temple of Heaven **Rev:** Panda on branch **Note:** Prev. Y#716a.

Date	Mintage	XF40	MS60	MS63	MS65	MS66
1997	5,000	—	—	—	1,700	1,850

KM# 277 10 YUAN
3.11 g., 0.9995 Platinum 0.0999 oz. APW **Obv:** Temple of Heaven, date below **Rev:** Panda with branch, denomination below **Note:** Prev. Y#267.

Date	Mintage	XF40	MS60	MS63	MS65	MS66
1990	4,500	PF65 350	PF67 550	PF69 750		

KM# 486 10 YUAN
3.11 g., 0.9995 Platinum 0.0999 oz. APW **Obv:** Temple of Heaven within circle, date below **Rev:** Panda seated on rock, denomination upper left **Note:** Prev. Y#484a.

Date	Mintage	XF40	MS60	MS63	MS65	MS66
1993	2,500	PF65 450	PF67 650	PF69 800		

KM# 623 10 YUAN
3.11 g., 0.999 Platinum 0.0999 oz. APW **Obv:** Temple of Heaven, date below **Rev:** Seated panda eating, denomination below **Note:** Prev. Y#432a.

Date	Mintage	XF40	MS60	MS63	MS65	MS66
1994	2,500	—	—	—	550	650

KM# 730 10 YUAN
3.11 g., 0.999 Platinum 0.0999 oz. APW **Obv:** Temple of Heaven, date below **Rev:** Panda eating bamboo, denomination at left **Note:** Prev. Y#641a.

Date	Mintage	XF40	MS60	MS63	MS65	MS66
1995	5,000	—	—	—	450	650

KM# 890 10 YUAN
3.11 g., 0.999 Platinum 0.0999 oz. APW **Obv:** Temple of Heaven, date below **Rev:** Panda in tree **Note:** Prev. Y#575a.

Date	Mintage	XF40	MS60	MS63	MS65	MS66
1996	2,500	—	—	—	550	750

KM# 988 10 YUAN
3.11 g., 0.999 Platinum 0.0999 oz. APW **Obv:** Temple of Heaven **Rev:** Panda on branch **Note:** Prev. Y#717a.

Date	Mintage	XF40	MS60	MS63	MS65	MS66
1997	2,500	—	—	—	1,350	1,600

KM# 278 25 YUAN
7.78 g., 0.9995 Platinum 0.2499 oz. APW **Obv:** Temple of Heaven, date below **Rev:** Panda climbing tree, denomination at right **Note:** Prev. Y#268.

Date	Mintage	XF40	MS60	MS63	MS65	MS66
1990	—	PF65 575	PF67 750	PF69 950		

KM# 279 50 YUAN
15.55 g., 0.9995 Platinum 0.4997 oz. APW **Obv:** Temple of Heaven, date below **Rev:** Panda eating bamboo on rock, denomination below **Note:** Prev. Y#269.

Date	Mintage	XF40	MS60	MS63	MS65	MS66
1990	2,500	PF65 1,250	PF67 1,450	PF69 1,600		

KM# A163 100 YUAN
31.10 g., 0.9995 Platinum 0.9995 oz. APW **Obv:** Temple of Heaven, date below **Rev:** Panda drinking at stream, denomination below **Note:** Prev. Y#158.

Date	Mintage	XF40	MS60	MS63	MS65	MS66
1987	2,000	PF65 2,000	PF67 2,500	PF69 3,000		

KM# 192 100 YUAN
31.10 g., 0.9995 Platinum 0.9995 oz. APW **Obv:** Temple of Heaven, date below **Rev:** Panda grasping bamboo shoot, within circle, denomination below **Note:** Prev. Y#159.

Date	Mintage	XF40	MS60	MS63	MS65	MS66
1988	2,000	PF65 2,000	PF67 2,700	PF69 3,500		

KM# 230 100 YUAN
31.10 g., 0.9995 Platinum 0.9995 oz. APW **Obv:** Temple of Heaven, date below **Rev:** Panda reclining, grid behind, denomination lower right **Note:** Prev. Y#191a.

Date	Mintage	XF40	MS60	MS63	MS65	MS66
1989	3,000	PF65 2,250	PF67 3,000	PF69 4,000		

KM# 280 100 YUAN
31.14 g., 0.9995 Platinum 1.0007 oz. APW **Obv:** Temple of Heaven, date below **Rev:** Panda on rock, denomination below **Note:** Prev. Y#735.

Date	Mintage	XF40	MS60	MS63	MS65	MS66
1990	1,300	PF65 3,500	PF67 5,000	PF69 6,000		

PLATINUM BULLION COINAGE

Lunar Series

KM# 197 100 YUAN
31.10 g., 0.9995 Platinum 0.9995 oz. APW **Subject:** Year of the Dragon **Obv:** Temple of Heaven **Rev:** 2 floating dragons **Note:** Prev. Y#176.

Date	Mintage	XF40	MS60	MS63	MS65	MS66
1988	2,000	PF67 3,750	PF69 4,000			

KM# 236 100 YUAN
31.10 g., 0.9995 Platinum 0.9995 oz. APW **Subject:** Year of the Snake **Obv:** National emblem **Rev:** Snake, left, denomination below **Note:** Prev. Y#185.

Date	Mintage	XF40	MS60	MS63	MS65	MS66
1989	1,000	PF67 3,250	PF69 3,500			

KM# 287 100 YUAN
31.10 g., 0.9995 Platinum 0.9995 oz. APW **Subject:** Year of the Horse **Obv:** National emblem **Rev:** Prancing horse **Note:** Prev. Y#225a.

Date	Mintage	XF40	MS60	MS63	MS65	MS66
1990	2,000	PF67 2,850	PF69 3,200			

KM# 365 100 YUAN
31.10 g., 0.9995 Platinum 0.9995 oz. APW **Subject:** Year of the Goat **Obv:** National emblem **Rev:** Two goats butting heads, denomination below **Note:** Prev. Y#274a.

Date	Mintage	XF40	MS60	MS63	MS65	MS66
1991	500	PF69 9,500				

KM# 430 100 YUAN

31.10 g., 0.9995 Platinum 0.9995 oz. APW **Subject:** Year of the Monkey **Rev:** Monkey seated on branch, denomination at left **Note:** Prev. Y#295a.

Date	Mintage	XF40	MS60	MS63	MS65	MS66
1992	300	PF69 13,000				

KM# 513 100 YUAN

31.10 g., 0.9995 Platinum 0.9995 oz. APW **Subject:** Year of the Rooster **Note:** Prev. Y#382.

Date	Mintage	XF40	MS60	MS63	MS65	MS66
1993	300	PF69 10,000				

KM# 645 100 YUAN

31.10 g., 0.9995 Platinum 0.9995 oz. APW **Subject:** Year of the Dog **Note:** Prev. Y#397a.

Date	Mintage	XF40	MS60	MS63	MS65	MS66
1994	300	PF69 10,000				

KM# 749 100 YUAN

31.10 g., 0.9995 Platinum 0.9995 oz. APW **Subject:** Year of the Pig **Note:** Prev. Y#465.

Date	Mintage	XF40	MS60	MS63	MS65	MS66
1995	300	PF69 10,000				

KM# 923 100 YUAN

31.10 g., 0.9995 Platinum 0.9995 oz. APW **Subject:** Year of the Rat **Rev:** Rat by oil lamp, denomination below **Note:** Prev. Y#586a.

Date	Mintage	XF40	MS60	MS63	MS65	MS66
1996	300	PF69 15,000				

KM# 1008 100 YUAN

31.10 g., 0.9995 Platinum 0.9995 oz. APW **Subject:** Year of the Ox **Obv:** National emblem **Rev:** Ox, denomination below **Note:** Prev. Y#900a.

Date	Mintage	XF40	MS60	MS63	MS65	MS66
1997	300	PF69 10,000				

KM# 1143 100 YUAN

31.10 g., 0.999 Platinum 0.999 oz. APW **Subject:** Year of the Tiger **Obv:** National emblem **Rev:** Tiger **Note:** Prev. Y#929a.

Date	Mintage	XF40	MS60	MS63	MS65	MS66
1998	300	PF69 10,000				

KM# 1233 100 YUAN

31.10 g., 0.999 Platinum 0.999 oz. APW **Subject:** Year of the Rabbit **Note:** Prev. Y#1018a.

Date	Mintage	XF40	MS60	MS63	MS65	MS66
1999	—	PF69 10,000				

BI-METALLIC BULLION COINAGE

KM# 677 25 YUAN

7.78 g., Bi-Metallic Gold center in Silver ring **Obv:** Building within circle, date below **Rev:** Unicorn, denomination at left, within circle **Note:** Prev. Y#422.

Date	Mintage	XF40	MS60	MS63	MS65	MS66
1994	1,100	PF67 2,750	PF69 3,000			

BI-METALLIC MEDALLIC BULLION COINAGE

Silver / Gold

KM# 396 10 YUAN

3.11 g., Bi-Metallic Gold center in Silver ring **Obv:** Temple of Heaven within circle, date below **Rev:** Panda on branch, denomination above, within circle **Note:** Prev. Y#391.

Date	Mintage	XF40	MS60	MS63	MS65	MS66
1992	—	PF67 1,000	PF69 1,200			

KM# 468 10 YUAN

3.15 g., 0.999 Gold and Silver 0.1012 oz. **Obv:** Temple of Heaven **Rev:** Panda

Date	Mintage	XF40	MS60	MS63	MS65	MS66
1992	—	—	—	—	275	350

KM# A625 10 YUAN

3.11 g., Bi-Metallic Gold center in Silver ring **Obv:** Temple of Heaven within circle, date below **Rev:** Panda tugging bamboo sprig, denomination below, within circle **Note:** Prev. Y#680.

Date	Mintage	XF40	MS60	MS63	MS65	MS66
1994	—	PF65 500	PF67 650	PF69 750		

KM# 625 10 YUAN

3.11 g., Bi-Metallic Gold center in Silver ring **Rev:** Phoenix and dragon **Note:** Prev. Y#463.

Date	Mintage	XF40	MS60	MS63	MS65	MS66
1994	2,500	—	—	—	800	950

KM# 701 10 YUAN

Obv: Temple of Heaven **Rev:** Panda

Date	Mintage	XF40	MS60	MS63	MS65	MS66
1994	—	—	—	—	225	280

KM# 722 10 YUAN

3.11 g., Bi-Metallic Gold center in Silver ring **Obv:** Temple of Heaven, date below **Rev:** Panda at stream, denomination below **Note:** Prev. Y#571.

Date	Mintage	XF40	MS60	MS63	MS65	MS66
1995	2,000	PF65 500	PF67 650	PF69 750		

KM# 873 10 YUAN

3.15 g., 0.999 Gold and Silver 0.1012 oz. **Obv:** Temple of Heaven **Rev:** Panda

Date	Mintage	XF40	MS60	MS63	MS65	MS66
1995	—	—	—	—	250	280

KM# 893 10 YUAN

3.11 g., Bi-Metallic Gold center in Silver ring **Obv:** Temple of Heaven **Rev:** Panda seated in rock **Note:** Prev. Y#851.

Date	Mintage	XF40	MS60	MS63	MS65	MS66
1996	2,500	PF65 400	PF67 500	PF69 550		

KM# 977 10 YUAN

3.15 g., 0.999 Gold and Silver 0.1012 oz. **Obv:** Temple of Heaven **Rev:** Panda

Date	Mintage	XF40	MS60	MS63	MS65	MS66
1996	—	—	—	—	225	310

KM# 998 10 YUAN

3.11 g., Bi-Metallic Gold center in Silver ring **Obv:** Temple of Heaven, date below **Rev:** Panda climbing tree **Note:** Prev. Y#986.

Date	Mintage	XF40	MS60	MS63	MS65	MS66
1997	2,800	PF65 700	PF67 800	PF69 900		

KM# 1108 10 YUAN

3.15 g., Gold and Silver **Obv:** Temple of Heaven **Rev:** Panda

Date	Mintage	XF40	MS60	MS63	MS65	MS66
1997	—	—	—	—	350	450

KM# 348 25 YUAN

7.78 g., Bi-Metallic Gold center in Silver ring **Obv:** Temple of Heaven, date below **Rev:** Seated panda, denomination at left, date below **Note:** Prev. Y#301.

Date	Mintage	XF40	MS60	MS63	MS65	MS66
1991	2,000	PF65 1,000	PF67 1,300	PF69 1,500		

KM# 386 25 YUAN

8.50 g., Gold and Silver **Obv:** Temple of Heaven **Rev:** Panda

Date	Mintage	XF40	MS60	MS63	MS65	MS66
1991	—	—	—	—	1,000	1,100

KM# 487 25 YUAN

7.78 g., Bi-Metallic Gold center in Silver ring **Obv:** Temple of Heaven, date below **Rev:** Panda on rock **Note:** Prev. Y#930.

Date	Mintage	XF40	MS60	MS63	MS65	MS66
1993	2,500	PF65 1,000	PF67 1,300	PF69 1,500		

KM# 602 25 YUAN

8.50 g., 0.999 Gold and Silver 0.273 oz. **Obv:** Temple of Heaven **Rev:** Panda

Date	Mintage	XF40	MS60	MS63	MS65	MS66
1993	—	—	—	—	400	500

KM# 626 25 YUAN

7.78 g., Bi-Metallic Gold center in Silver ring **Obv:** Temple of Heaven within circle, date below **Rev:** Panda tugging on bamboo sprig, denomination below, within circle, date below **Note:** Prev. Y#544.

Date	Mintage	XF40	MS60	MS63	MS65	MS66
1994	—	PF65 1,000	PF67 1,300	PF69 1,500		

KM# 702 25 YUAN

8.50 g., 0.999 Gold and Silver 0.273 oz. **Obv:** Temple of Heaven **Rev:** Panda

Date	Mintage	XF40	MS60	MS63	MS65	MS66
1994	—	—	—	—	300	400

KM# 724 25 YUAN

7.78 g., Bi-Metallic Gold center in Silver ring **Obv:** Temple of Heaven, date below **Rev:** Panda at stream, denomination below, within circle **Note:** Prev. Y#572.

Date	Mintage	XF40	MS60	MS63	MS65	MS66
1995	—	PF65 1,000	PF67 1,300	PF69 1,500		

KM# 874 25 YUAN

8.50 g., 0.999 Gold and Silver 0.273 oz. **Obv:** Temple of Heaven **Rev:** Panda

Date	Mintage	XF40	MS60	MS63	MS65	MS66
1995	—	—	—	—	475	550

KM# 894 25 YUAN

7.78 g., Bi-Metallic Gold center in Silver ring **Obv:** Temple of Heaven **Rev:** Panda seated on rock **Note:** Prev. Y#852.

Date	Mintage	XF40	MS60	MS63	MS65	MS66
1996	2,500	PF67 1,750	PF69 2,000			

KM# 978 25 YUAN

8.50 g., 0.999 Gold and Silver 0.273 oz. **Obv:** Temple of Heaven **Rev:** Panda

Date	Mintage	XF40	MS60	MS63	MS65	MS66
1996	—	—	—	—	475	550

KM# 999 25 YUAN
7.78 g., 0.999 Bi-Metallic 0.2497 oz. Gold center in Silver ring **Obv:** Temple of Heaven, date below **Rev:** Panda climbing tree **Note:** Prev. Y#1001.

Date	Mintage	XF40	MS60	MS63	MS65	MS66
1997	2,800	PF67 2,250	PF69 2,500			

KM# 1109 25 YUAN
8.50 g., 0.999 Gold and Silver 0.273 oz. **Obv:** Temple of Heaven **Rev:** Panda

Date	Mintage	XF40	MS60	MS63	MS65	MS66
1997	—	—	—	—	750	820

KM# 281 50 YUAN
15.55 g., 0.999 Bi-Metallic 0.4995 oz. Gold center in Silver ring **Obv:** Temple of Heaven, date below, within circle **Rev:** Panda walking, denomination below, within circle, date below **Note:** Prev. Y#266.

Date	Mintage	XF40	MS60	MS63	MS65	MS66
1990	2,000	PF65 1,600	PF67 1,800	PF69 2,000		

KM# 330 50 YUAN
15.55 g., 0.999 Gold and Silver 0.4994 oz. **Obv:** Temple of Heaven **Rev:** Panda

Date	Mintage	XF40	MS60	MS63	MS65	MS66
1990	—	—	—	—	1,600	1,700

KM# 725 50 YUAN
21.77 g., 0.999 Bi-Metallic 0.6993 oz. Gold center in Silver ring **Obv:** Temple of Heaven within circle, date below **Rev:** Panda at stream, denomination below, within circle **Note:** Prev. Y#573.

Date	Mintage	XF40	MS60	MS63	MS65	MS66
1995	—	PF65 1,600	PF67 1,800	PF69 2,100		

KM# 875 50 YUAN
15.55 g., 0.999 Gold and Silver 0.4994 oz. **Obv:** Temple of Heaven **Rev:** Panda

Date	Mintage	XF40	MS60	MS63	MS65	MS66
1995	—	—	—	—	850	920

KM# 876 50 YUAN
10.50 g., 0.999 Gold and Silver 0.3372 oz. **Rev:** United Nations

Date	Mintage	XF40	MS60	MS63	MS65	MS66
1995	—	—	—	—	1,600	1,750

KM# 895 50 YUAN
15.55 g., 0.999 Bi-Metallic 0.4995 oz. Gold center in Silver ring **Obv:** Temple of Heaven **Rev:** Panda seated on rock **Note:** Prev. Y#853.

Date	Mintage	XF40	MS60	MS63	MS65	MS66
1996	2,500	PF65 2,000	PF67 2,250	PF69 2,500		

KM# 979 50 YUAN
15.55 g., Gold and Silver **Obv:** Temple of Heaven **Rev:** Panda

Date	Mintage	XF40	MS60	MS63	MS65	MS66
1996	—	—	—	—	850	920

KM# 1000 50 YUAN
15.55 g., 0.999 Bi-Metallic 0.4995 oz. Gold center in Silver ring **Obv:** Temple of Heaven, date below **Rev:** Panda climbing tree **Note:** Prev. Y#1009.

Date	Mintage	XF40	MS60	MS63	MS65	MS66
1997	2,800	PF65 2,300	PF67 3,000	PF69 3,500		

KM# 1110 50 YUAN
15.55 g., 0.999 Gold and Silver 0.4994 oz. **Obv:** Temple of Heaven **Rev:** Panda

Date	Mintage	XF40	MS60	MS63	MS65	MS66
1997	—	—	—	—	1,000	1,200

KM# 728 500 YUAN
155.52 g., 0.9999 Bi-Metallic 4.9995 oz. Gold center in Silver ring **Obv:** Temple of Heaven **Rev:** Two pandas sitting on rock, denomination above, within circle **Note:** Prev. Y#793.

Date	Mintage	XF40	MS60	MS63	MS65	MS66
1995	199	PF65 25,000	PF67 35,000	PF69 40,000		

KM# 897 500 YUAN
155.52 g., 0.999 Bi-Metallic 4.995 oz. Gold center in Silver ring **Obv:** Temple of Heaven, date below **Rev:** Panda **Note:** Prev. Y#1020.

Date	Mintage	XF40	MS60	MS63	MS65	MS66
1996	199	PF65 30,000	PF67 40,000	PF69 50,000		

KM# 997 500 YUAN
155.52 g., 0.999 Bi-Metallic 4.995 oz. Gold center in Silver ring **Obv:** Temple of Heaven **Rev:** Two pandas resting near stream **Note:** Prev. Y#1021.

Date	Mintage	XF40	MS60	MS63	MS65	MS66
1997	199	PF65 60,000	PF67 70,000	PF69 75,000		

PATTERNS

Including off metal strikes

KM#	Date	Mintage	Identification	Mkt Val
Pn1	1983	—	5 Yuan. Denomination between sprays. Marco Polo bust at upper right, ships below, dates at left, denomination below. Silvered base metal, Marco Polo.	2,600
Pn2	1983	—	100 Yuan. Bronze Gilt.	2,250
Pn3	1985	—	200 Yuan. Gold. Decade for Women.	—
Pn4	1991	—	Yuan. Nickel Plated Steel. Raised character "pattern". KM#341.	550
Pn5	1991	—	Yuan. Nickel Plated Steel. Raised character "pattern". KM#342.	550
Pn6	1991	—	Yuan. Nickel Plated Steel. Raised character "pattern".	550
Pn7	1991	—	Yuan. Nickel Plated Steel. Raised character "pattern". KM#357.	725
Pn8	1991	—	Yuan. Nickel Plated Steel. Raised character "pattern". KM#345.	550
Pn9	1991	—	10000 Yuan. Gold.	—

PIEDFORT

KM#	Date	Mintage	Identification	Mkt Val
P1	1979	2,000	35 Yuan. 0.800. Silver. KM#8.	15,000
P2	1979	500	450 Yuan. 0.900. Gold. KM#9.	35,000
P3	1980	2,500	Yuan. Copper. KM#29.	600
P4	1980	2,500	Yuan. Copper. KM#30.	600
P5	1980	2,500	Yuan. Copper. KM#31.	600
P6	1980	2,500	Yuan. Copper. KM#32.	600
P7	1980	1,000	Yuan. Copper. KM#21.	600
P8	1980	1,000	Yuan. Copper. KM#22.	600
P9	1980	1,000	Yuan. Copper. KM#19.	600
P10	1980	1,000	Yuan. Copper. KM#20.	600
P11	1980	2,000	15 Yuan. 0.800. Silver. KM#33. Archery.	1,000
P12	1980	2,000	20 Yuan. 0.800. Silver. KM#34, Wrestling.	1,000
P13	1980	1,000	30 Yuan. 0.800. Silver. KM#35. Equestrian.	1,000
P14	1980	1,000	30 Yuan. 0.800. Silver. KM#36. Soccer.	1,000
P15	1980	2,000	30 Yuan. 0.800. Silver. KM#26. Speed skating.	1,000
P16	1980	2,000	30 Yuan. 0.800. Silver. KM#25. Alpine skiing.	1,000
P17	1980	2,000	30 Yuan. 0.800. Silver. KM#24. Biathalon.	1,000
P18	1980	2,000	30 Yuan. 0.800. Silver. KM#23. Figure skating.	1,000
P19	1980	360	250 Yuan. 0.917. Gold. KM#28. Alpine skiing.	15,000
P20	1980	500	300 Yuan. 0.917. Gold. KM#37. Archery.	15,000
PA21	1991	—	10 Yuan. 0.999. Silver. Panda - Hind feet in water. KM#347.	900
P21	1992	Est. 2500	5 Yuan. 0.900. Silver. KM#404. Ancient ship building.	2,200
P22	1992	Est. 2500	5 Yuan. 0.900. Silver. KM#407. First compass.	2,200
P23	1992	Est. 2500	5 Yuan. 0.900. Silver. KM#405. First seismograph.	2,200
P24	1992	Est. 2500	5 Yuan. 0.900. Silver. KM#406. Ancient kite flying.	2,200
P25	1992	Est. 2500	5 Yuan. 0.900. Silver. KM#408. Bronze metal working.	2,200
P26	1996	5,000	5 Yuan. 0.999. Silver. KM#933. Goddess holding flower.	—
P27	1996	5,000	5 Yuan. 0.999. Silver. KM#934. Goddess holding vase and twig.	—
P28	1997	80,000	5 Yuan. 0.999. Silver. KM#1058.	850
P29	1997	80,000	5 Yuan. 0.999. Silver. KM#1058. Child w/carp.	—
P30	1997	80,000	10 Yuan. 0.999. Silver. KM#1059. Child w/carp.	—
P31	1998	—	10 Yuan. 0.999. Silver. KM#1138.	700
P32	1998	100,000	10 Yuan. 0.999. Silver. KM#1059.	475

MINT SETS

KM#	Date	Mintage	Identification	Issue Price	Mkt Val
MS1	1979 (s) (3)	—	KM#1-3, Medal	—	150
MS2	1980 (b) (6)	—	KM#1-3, 15-17	—	400
MS4	1986 (2)	—	KM#130 (2)	—	25.00
MS5	1990 (2)	—	KM#266-267	—	20.00
MS6	1991 (6)	—	KM#1-3, 335-337	—	20.00
MS7	1991 (2)	—	KM344-345	—	10.00
MS8	1992 (6)	—	KM1-3, 335-337	—	20.00
MS9	1993 (6)	—	KM#1-3, 335-337	—	20.00
MS10	1994 (6)	—	KM#1-3, 335-337	—	20.00
MS11	1995 (6)	—	KM#1-3, 335-337	—	20.00
MS12	1996 (6)	—	KM#1-3, 335-337	—	20.00
MS13	1997 (6)	—	KM#1-3, 335-337	—	11.00
MS14	1998 (6)	—	KM#1-3, 335-337	—	11.00
MS15	1999 (6)	—	KM#1-3, 335-337	—	11.00
MS16	2000 (6)	—	KM#1-3, 336, 1210, 1212	—	11.00

PROOF SETS

KM#	Date	Mintage	Identification	Issue Price	Mkt Val
PS1	1979 (4)	70,000	KM#4-7	1,695	3,800
PS2	1980 (14)	1,000	KM#19-22, 26, 28, 29-32, 34-37	1,750	2,100
PS3	1980 (7)	—	KM#1-3, 15-18	—	100
PS4	1980 (4)	—	KM#29-32	—	70.00
PS5	1980 (4)	—	KM#19-22	—	80.00
PS6	1980 (3)	1,000	KM#34-36	—	150
PS7	1981(s) (7)	10,000	KM#1-3, 15-18, Medal	2.00	1,500
PS8	1981 (4)	1,000	KM#46-49	2,950	16,000
PS9	1982(s) (7)	—	KM#1-3, 15-18, Medal	2.00	500
PS10	1983(s) (7)	—	KM#1-3, 15-18, Book	2.00	300
PS11	1983(s) (7)	—	KM#1-3, 15-18, Medal (paper cover)	2.00	300
PS12	1984(y) (7)	—	KM#1-3, 15-18, Medal	—	650
PS13	1984 (4)	—	KM#98-101	—	200
PS14	1984 (3)	—	KM#104-106	—	85.00
PS15	1985 (2)	—	KM#110, 127	45.00	2,750
PS16	1985(y) (7)	—	KM#1-3, 15-18, Medal	—	750
PS17	1985 (2)	—	KM#111, 128	45.00	320
PS18	1985 (4)	—	KM#121-124	—	300
PS19	1986(y) (7)	—	KM#1-3, 15-18, Medal	10.00	500
PS20	1986 (5)	10,000	KM#131-135	—	2,700
PS21	1986 (4)	—	KM#141-144	—	260
PS22	1987 (4)	10,000	KM#159, 161, 162, 166	—	2,700
PS23	1987 (2)	—	KM#167-168	278	575
PS24	1987 (4)	—	KM#172-175	—	240
PS25	1988 (4)	—	KM#207-210	200	260
PS26	1988 (5)	10,000	KM#184-187, 221	—	2,700
PS27	1989 (6)	8,000	KM224-229	—	4,000
PS28	1989 (4)	—	KM#248-251	—	320
PS29	1990 (5)	5,000	KM#268-272	—	2,700
PS30	1990 (3)	2,500	KM#277-279	1,095	2,150
PS31	1990 (1)	2,000	KM#281 and medal	995	500
PSA32	1990 (5)	10,000	KM#267, 291-294	—	800
PS32	1991 (6)	—	KM#1-3, 335-337	—	35.00
PS33	1991 (1)	2,000	KM#348 and medal	575	350
PS34	1991 (5)	350	KM#346, 347, 349, 350, 359	—	3,700
PS35	1992 (6)	—	KM#1-3, 335-337	—	35.00
PS36	1992 (5)	2,500	KMP#21-25 Piefort	—	9,000
PS37	1992 (5)	1,000	KM#415-419	—	10,000
PS38	1992 (5)	—	KM#391-395	—	3,525
PS39	1993 (4)	2,000	KM#575-578	200	280
PS40	1993 (4)	1,000	KM#579-582	1,600	3,900
PS41	1993 (3)	—	KM#595, 597-598	—	3,050
PS42	1993 (3)	—	KM#473, 476, 477	—	2,850
PS43	1993 (6)	—	KM#1-3, 335-337	—	35.00
PSA44	1993 (2)	2,500	KM#486-487	—	850
PS44	1993 (5)	100	KM#496-500	1,875	5,750
PS45	1994 (11)	50	KM#674-684	—	24,100
PS46	1994 (10)	50	KM#674-683	—	6,550
PS47	1994 (5)	1,000	KM#674, 676-678, 680	—	2,400
PS48	1994 (4)	2,500	KM#674-676, 678	645	900

PS49	1994 (6)	1,000	KM#675-679, 681	—	1,950
PS50	1994 (2)	400	KM#675, 683	—	1,500
PS51	1994 (5)	—	KM#611-614, 626	—	2,100
PS52	1994 (6)	—	KM#1-3, 335-337	—	35.00
PS53	1995 (3)	2,000	KM#791-793	485	1,225
PS54	1995 (3)	2,000	KM#772, 724, 725	—	925
PS55	1995 (2)	3,000	KM#791-792	89.00	250
PS56	1995 (4)	15,000	KM#866-869	—	300
PS57	1995 (4)	9,000	KM#840-843	—	400
PS58	1995 (6)	—	KM#1-3, 335-337	—	35.00
PS59	1995 (5)	1,000	KM#794, 796-798, 801	—	2,300
PS60	1996 (4)	15,000	KM#971-974	—	260
PS61	1996 (4)	8,000	KM#966-969	—	900
PS62	1996 (6)	—	KM#1-3, 335-337	—	35.00
PS63	1996 (4)	750	KM#939, 941-943, plus bottle	—	1,150
PS64	1997 (4)	28,000	KM#1053-1056	—	300
PS65	1997 (4)	10,000	KM#1077-1080	—	460
PS66	1998 (2)	61,000	China KM#1157 and Canada KM#316	72.50	80.00

REPUBLIC OF CHINA

East China Sea
JAPAN
CHINA
Philippine Sea

The Republic of China, comprising Taiwan (an island located 90 miles (145 km.) off the southeastern coast of mainland China), the offshore islands of Quemoy and Matsu and nearby islets of the Pescadores chain, has an area of 14,000 sq. mi. (35,980 sq. km.) and a population of 20.2 million. Capital: Taipei. During the past decade, manufacturing has replaced agriculture in importance. Fruits, vegetables, plywood, textile yarns and fabrics and clothing are exported.

Chinese migration to Taiwan began as early as the 6th century. The Dutch established a base on the island in 1624 and held it until 1661, when they were driven out by supporters of the Ming dynasty who used it as a base for their unsuccessful attempt to displace the ruling Manchu dynasty of mainland China. After being occupied by Manchu forces in 1683, Taiwan remained under the suzerainty of China until its cession to Japan in 1895. It was returned to China following World War II. On Dec. 8, 1949, Taiwan became the last remnant of Sun Yat-sen's vast Republic of China. Chiang Kai-Shek had quickly moved his government and nearly exhausted army from the mainland leaving the Communist forces under Mao Tse-tung victorious.

The coins of Nationalist China do not carry A.D. dating, but are dated according to the year of the republic, which was established in 1911. However, republican years are added to 1911 to find the western year. Thus republican year 38 plus 1911 equals Gregorian calendar year 1949AD.

MONETARY SYSTEM

10 Cents = 1 Chiao

10 Chiao = 1 Yuan (Dollar)

REPUBLIC

STANDARD COINAGE

Y# 531 CHIAO

4.50 g., Brass, 21 mm. **Obv:** Bust of Sun Yat-sen left **Rev:** Map, symbols on sides

Date	Mintage	F12	VF20	XF40	MS60	MS63
38(1949)	157,600,000	0.15	0.30	1.00	4.00	5.00

Y# 533 CHIAO

1.15 g., Aluminum, 19 mm. **Obv:** Bust of Sun Yat-sen left **Rev:** Map, symbols on sides **Edge:** Reeded

Date	Mintage	F12	VF20	XF40	MS60	MS63
44(1955)	583,980,000	—	0.10	0.15	1.00	1.50

Y# 545 CHIAO

1.15 g., Aluminum, 19 mm. **Obv:** Single-heart orchid **Rev:** Two Chinese symbols

Date	Mintage	F12	VF20	XF40	MS60	MS63
56(1967)	89,999,000	—	0.10	0.15	0.75	1.00
59(1970)	30,000,000	—	0.10	0.25	1.00	1.25
60(1971)	19,925,000	—	0.20	0.40	1.50	2.00
61(1972)	11,141,000	0.10	0.40	0.60	2.00	2.50
62(1973)	111,400,000	—	—	0.10	0.75	1.00
63(1974)	71,930,000	—	0.10	0.25	1.00	1.25

Y# 534 2 CHIAO

1.80 g., Aluminum, 23 mm. **Obv:** Bust of Sun Yat-sen left **Rev:** Map, symbols at sides **Edge:** Plain

Date	Mintage	F12	VF20	XF40	MS60	MS63
39(1950)	327,495,000	—	0.10	0.50	3.00	3.50

Y# 532 5 CHIAO

5.00 g., 0.720 Silver 0.1157 oz. ASW, 24 mm. **Obv:** Bust of Sun Yat-sen left **Rev:** Map, symbols at sides

Date	Mintage	F12	VF20	XF40	MS60	MS63
38(1949)	—	2.50	3.00	5.00	7.50	10.00

Y# 535 5 CHIAO

7.00 g., Aluminum-Bronze, 27 mm. **Obv:** Bust of Sun Yat-sen left **Rev:** Map, symbols at sides **Edge:** Reeded

Date	Mintage	F12	VF20	XF40	MS60	MS63
43(1954)	279,624,000	—	0.10	0.25	1.00	1.50

Y# 546 5 CHIAO

3.70 g., Nickel-Brass, 23 mm. **Obv:** Mayling orchid **Rev:** Two Chinese characters **Edge:** Reeded

Date	Mintage	F12	VF20	XF40	MS60	MS63
56(1967)	109,999,000	—	0.10	0.15	0.50	0.75
59(1970)	6,010,000	0.15	0.30	0.60	1.25	1.50
60(1971)	4,434,000	0.20	0.40	0.80	1.50	1.75
61(1972)	21,171,000	—	0.10	0.20	1.00	1.25
62(1973)	88,840,000	—	0.10	0.20	1.00	1.25
69(1980)	3,972,000	—	0.10	0.20	1.00	1.25
70(1981)	100,000,000	—	0.10	0.20	1.00	1.25

Y# 550 1/2 YUAN

3.00 g., Bronze, 18 mm. **Obv:** Orchid **Rev:** Value and Chinese symbols **Edge:** Plain

Date	Mintage	F12	VF20	XF40	MS60	MS63
70(1981)	103,800,000	—	0.10	0.20	1.00	1.25
70(1981)	—	PF63 10.00		PF65 12.00		
75(1986)	22,000,000	—	0.10	0.20	1.00	1.25
77(1988)	10,000,000	—	0.15	0.30	1.25	1.50
84(1995)	—	—	0.15	0.30	1.00	1.25
84(1995)	—	PF63 10.00		PF65 12.00		
85(1996)	—	—	0.15	0.30	1.00	1.25
85(1996)	—	PF63 10.00		PF65 12.00		
86(1997)	—	—	0.15	0.30	1.00	1.25
86(1997)	—	PF63 10.00		PF65 12.00		
87(1998)	—	—	0.15	0.30	1.00	1.25
87(1998)	—	PF63 10.00		PF65 12.00		
88(1999)	—	—	0.15	0.30	1.00	1.25
88(1999)	—	PF63 10.00		PF65 12.00		
89(2000)	—	—	0.15	0.30	1.00	1.25
89(2000)	—	PF63 10.00		PF65 12.00		

Y# 536 YUAN

6.00 g., Copper-Nickel-Zinc, 25 mm. **Obv:** Plum blossom **Rev:** Orchid **Edge:** Reeded

Date	Mintage	F12	VF20	XF40	MS60	MS63
49(1960)	321,717,000	—	0.10	0.20	0.50	0.65
59(1970)	48,800,000	0.10	0.20	0.50	1.00	1.25
60(1971)	41,532,000	0.10	0.20	0.50	1.00	1.25
61(1972)	105,309,000	—	0.10	0.20	0.50	0.65
62(1973)	353,924,000	—	0.10	0.20	0.50	0.65
63(1974)	535,605,000	—	0.10	0.20	0.50	0.65
64(1975)	456,874,000	—	0.10	0.20	0.50	0.65
65(1976)	634,497,000	—	0.10	0.20	0.50	0.65
66(1977)	116,900,000	—	0.10	0.20	0.50	0.65
67(1978)	104,245,000	—	0.10	0.20	0.50	0.65
68(1979)	—	0.10	0.20	0.50	0.80	1.00
69(1980)	113,900,000	—	0.10	0.20	0.50	0.65

Y# A537 YUAN

Silver **Subject:** 50th Anniversary of the Republic **Obv:** Chiang Kai-shek left **Rev:** Value at center within flower wreath

Date	Mintage	F12	VF20	XF40	MS60	MS63
50(1961)	—	—	—	—	350	400

Note: This coin was released accidentally or was released and quickly withdrawn and is very scarce today

Y# 543 YUAN

Copper-Nickel **Subject:** 80th Birthday of Chiang Kai-shek **Obv:** Bust of Chiang Kai-shek **Rev:** Chinese value in center

Date	Mintage	F12	VF20	XF40	MS60	MS63
55(1966)	—	0.25	0.35	0.50	1.00	1.50

Y# 547 YUAN

Copper-Nickel-Zinc, 25 mm. **Series:** F.A.O. **Obv:** Orchid **Rev:** Farmer in field, value below **Edge:** Reeded

Date	Mintage	F12	VF20	XF40	MS60	MS63
58(1969)	10,000,000	0.25	0.35	0.50	1.00	1.50

Y# 551 YUAN
3.80 g., Aluminum-Bronze, 20 mm. **Obv:** Bust of Chiang Kai-shek left **Rev:** Chinese value in center, 1 below **Edge:** Reeded

Date	Mintage	F12	VF20	XF40	MS60	MS63
70(1981)	1,080,000,000	—	—	0.10	0.15	0.25
70(1981)	—	PF63 12.50	PF65 15.00			
71(1982)	780,000,000	—	—	0.10	0.15	0.25
72(1983)	420,000,000	—	—	0.10	0.15	0.25
73(1984)	110,000,000	—	—	0.10	0.15	0.25
74(1985)	200,000,000	—	—	0.10	0.15	0.25
75(1986)	200,000,000	—	—	0.10	0.15	0.25
76(1987)	110,000,000	—	—	0.10	0.15	0.25
77(1988)	40,000,000	—	—	0.20	0.50	0.65
81(1992)	—	—	—	0.15	0.25	0.35
82(1993)	—	—	—	0.15	0.25	0.35
83(1994)	—	—	—	0.15	0.25	0.35
84(1995)	—	—	—	0.15	0.25	0.35
84(1995)	—	PF63 12.50	PF65 15.00			
85(1996)	—	—	—	0.15	0.25	0.35
85(1996)	—	PF63 12.50	PF65 15.00			
86(1997)	—	—	—	0.15	0.25	0.35
86(1997)	—	PF63 12.50	PF65 15.00			
87(1998)	—	—	—	0.15	0.30	0.35
87(1998)	—	PF63 12.50	PF65 15.00			
88(1999)	—	—	—	0.15	0.30	0.35
88(1999)	—	PF63 12.50	PF65 15.00			
89(2000)	—	—	—	0.15	0.30	0.35
89(2000)	—	PF63 12.50	PF65 15.00			

Y# 537 5 YUAN
Copper-Nickel **Obv:** Bust of Sun Yat-sen left **Rev:** Mausoleum in Nanking **Edge:** Reeded

Date	Mintage	F12	VF20	XF40	MS60	MS63
54(1965)	—	0.35	0.75	1.50	5.00	6.50

Y# 548 5 YUAN
9.50 g., Copper-Nickel, 29 mm. **Obv:** Bust of Chiang Kai-shek left **Rev:** Chinese symbols in center **Edge:** Reeded

Date	Mintage	F12	VF20	XF40	MS60	MS63
59(1970)	12,360,000	0.20	0.40	0.80	1.50	2.00
60(1971)	20,575,000	0.20	0.35	0.50	1.00	1.50
61(1972)	27,998,000	0.20	0.35	0.50	1.00	1.50
62(1973)	50,122,000	0.20	0.35	0.50	0.80	1.25
63(1974)	418,068,000	0.20	0.35	0.50	0.80	1.25
64(1975)	39,520,000	0.20	0.35	0.50	0.80	1.25
65(1976)	140,000,000	0.20	0.35	0.50	0.80	1.25
66(1977)	50,260,000	0.20	0.35	0.50	0.80	1.25
67(1978)	78,082,000	0.20	0.35	0.50	0.80	1.25
68(1979)	—	0.20	0.35	0.50	0.80	1.25
69(1980)	273,000,000	0.20	0.35	0.50	0.80	1.25
70(1981)	162,000,000	0.20	0.35	0.50	0.80	1.25

Y# 552 5 YUAN
4.40 g., Copper-Nickel, 22 mm. **Obv:** Bust of Chiang Kai-shek left **Rev:** Chinese value in center, 5 below **Edge:** Reeded

Date	Mintage	F12	VF20	XF40	MS60	MS63
70(1981)	522,432,000	—	0.15	0.20	0.50	0.75
70(1981)	—	PF63 12.50	PF65 15.00			
71(1982)	6,600,000	—	0.15	0.20	0.50	0.75
72(1983)	34,000,000	—	0.15	0.20	0.50	0.75
73(1984)	280,000,000	—	0.15	0.20	0.50	0.75
77(1988)	200,000,000	—	0.15	0.20	0.50	0.75
78(1989)	—	—	0.15	0.20	0.50	0.75
84(1995)	—	—	0.15	0.25	0.50	0.75
84(1995)	—	PF63 12.50	PF65 15.00			
85(1996)	—	—	0.15	0.25	0.50	0.75
85(1996)	—	PF63 12.50	PF65 15.00			
86(1997)	—	—	0.15	0.25	0.50	0.75
86(1997)	—	PF63 12.50	PF65 15.00			
87(1998)	—	—	0.15	0.25	0.50	0.75
87(1998)	—	PF63 12.50	PF65 15.00			
88(1999)	—	—	0.15	0.25	0.50	0.75
88(1999)	—	PF63 12.50	PF65 15.00			
89(2000)	—	—	0.15	0.25	0.50	0.75
89(2000)	—	PF63 12.50	PF65 15.00			

Y# 538 10 YUAN
Copper-Nickel, 26 mm. **Obv:** Bust of Sun Yat-sen left **Rev:** Mausoleum in Nanking

Date	Mintage	F12	VF20	XF40	MS60	MS63
54(1965)	—	0.50	1.00	2.00	6.00	7.50

Y# 553 10 YUAN
7.50 g., Copper-Nickel, 26 mm. **Obv:** Bust of Chiang Kai-shek left **Rev:** Chinese value in center, 10 below **Edge:** Reeded

Date	Mintage	F12	VF20	XF40	MS60	MS63
70(1981)	123,000,000	—	0.30	0.45	0.75	1.00
70(1981)	—	PF63 15.00	PF65 18.00			
71(1982)	361,000,000	—	0.30	0.45	0.75	1.00
72(1983)	196,000,000	—	0.30	0.45	0.75	1.00
73(1984)	220,000,000	—	0.30	0.45	0.75	1.00
74(1985)	200,000,000	—	0.30	0.45	0.75	1.00
75(1986)	100,000,000	—	0.30	0.45	0.75	1.00
76(1987)	90,000,000	—	0.30	0.45	0.75	1.00
77(1988)	100,000,000	—	0.30	0.45	0.75	1.00
78(1989)	—	—	0.30	0.45	0.75	1.00
79(1990)	—	—	0.30	0.45	0.75	1.00
80(1991)	—	—	0.30	0.45	0.75	1.00
81(1992)	—	—	0.30	0.45	0.75	1.00
82(1993)	—	—	0.30	0.45	0.75	1.00
83(1994)	—	—	0.30	0.45	0.75	1.00
84(1995)	—	—	0.25	0.45	0.75	1.00
84(1995)	—	PF63 15.00	PF65 18.00			
85(1996)	—	—	0.25	0.45	0.75	1.00
85(1996)	—	PF63 15.00	PF65 18.00			
86(1997)	—	—	0.25	0.45	0.75	1.00
86(1997)	—	PF63 15.00	PF65 18.00			
87(1998)	—	—	0.25	0.45	0.75	1.00
87(1998)	—	PF63 15.00	PF65 18.00			
88(1999)	—	—	0.25	0.45	0.75	1.00
88(1999)	—	PF63 15.00	PF65 18.00			
89(2000)	—	—	0.25	0.45	0.75	1.00
89(2000)	—	PF63 15.00	PF65 18.00			

Y# 555 10 YUAN
7.50 g., Copper-Nickel, 26 mm. **Subject:** 50th Anniversary - Taiwan's Liberation from Japan **Obv:** Map with dates flanking **Rev:** Chinese symbols in center, 10 below **Edge:** Reeded

Date	Mintage	F12	VF20	XF40	MS60	MS63
84(1995)	—	—	—	—	2.50	3.00

Y# 558 10 YUAN
7.50 g., Copper-Nickel, 26 mm. **Subject:** 50th Anniversary - Taiwan Yuan (Dollar) **Obv:** Coins **Rev:** Anniversary dates above denomination **Edge:** Reeded

Date	Mintage	F12	VF20	XF40	MS60	MS63
88(1999)	30,000,000	—	—	—	2.75	3.50

Y# 560 10 YUAN
7.50 g., Copper-Nickel, 26 mm. **Subject:** Year of the Dragon **Obv:** Stylized dragon above denomination **Rev:** Dragon **Edge:** Reeded

Date	Mintage	F12	VF20	XF40	MS60	MS63
89(2000)	—	—	—	—	3.00	3.50

Y# 539 50 YUAN
17.10 g., 0.750 Silver 0.4123 oz. ASW **Obv:** Bust of Sun Yat-sen left **Rev:** Chinese symbols in center, bird above, deer below

Date	Mintage	F12	VF20	XF40	MS60	MS63
54(1965)	—	—	—	16.50	32.00	40.00

Y# 554 50 YUAN
8.25 g., Nickel-Brass, 24 mm. **Obv:** Orchid burst **Rev:** Chinese symbols center, 50 below, flower wreath circle

Date	Mintage	F12	VF20	XF40	MS60	MS63
81-1992	—	—	0.50	1.00	3.50	4.00
82-1993	—	—	0.50	1.00	3.50	4.00
84-1995	—	—	0.50	1.00	3.50	4.00
84-1995	—	PF63 17.00	PF65 20.00			
85-1996	—	—	0.50	1.00	3.50	4.00
85-1996	—	PF63 17.00	PF65 20.00			
86-1997	—	—	0.50	1.00	3.50	4.00
86-1997	—	PF63 17.00	PF65 20.00			
87-1998	—	—	0.50	1.00	3.50	4.00
87-1998	—	PF63 17.00	PF65 20.00			
88-1999	—	—	0.50	1.00	3.50	4.00
88-1999	—	PF63 17.00	PF65 20.00			
89-2000	—	—	0.50	1.00	3.50	4.00
89-2000	—	PF63 17.00	PF65 20.00			

Y# 556 50 YUAN
10.00 g., Bi-Metallic Aluminum-Bronze center in Copper-Nickel ring, 28 mm. **Obv:** Parliament building **Rev:** Value left, Chinese symbols at bottom

Date	Mintage	F12	VF20	XF40	MS60	MS63
84-1995	—	—	—	—	5.75	6.50
84-1995	—	PF63 19.00	PF65 22.00			
85-1996	—	—	—	—	5.75	6.50

Date	Mintage	F12	VF20	XF40	MS60	MS63
85-1996	—	PF63 19.00	PF65 22.00			
86-1997	—	—	—	—	5.75	6.50
86-1997	—	PF63 19.00	PF65 22.00			
87-1998	—	—	—	—	5.75	6.50
87-1998	—	PF63 19.00	PF65 22.00			
88-1999	—	—	—	—	5.75	6.50
88-1999	—	PF63 19.00	PF65 22.00			
89-2000	—	—	—	—	5.75	6.50
89-2000	—	PF63 19.00	PF65 22.00			

Y# 562 50 YUAN

15.57 g., 0.999 Silver 0.500 oz. ASW, 33 mm. **Subject:** Late President - Chiang Ching-Kuo **Obv:** Bust of Ching-kuo facing **Rev:** Mausoleum above denomination **Edge:** Reeded

Date	Mintage	VF20	XF40	MS60	MS63	MS65
87 (1998)	70,000	—	—	30.00	32.50	35.00

Y# 559 50 YUAN

15.55 g., 0.925 Silver 0.4624 oz. ASW **Subject:** 50 Years - Taiwan Yuan (Dollar) **Obv:** Coins **Rev:** Denomination including coin design and date

Date	Mintage	VF20	XF40	MS60	MS63	MS65
88(1999)	390,000	—	—	25.00	27.50	30.00

Y# 564 50 YUAN

15.57 g., 0.999 Silver 0.500 oz. ASW, 33 mm. **Subject:** Year 2000 **Obv:** Celestial globe **Rev:** Dragon **Edge:** Reeded

Date	Mintage	VF20	XF40	MS60	MS63	MS65
89 (2000)	120,000	—	—	30.00	32.50	35.00

Y# 540 100 YUAN

22.21 g., 0.750 Silver 0.5356 oz. ASW **Obv:** Bust of Sun Yat-sen left

Date	Mintage	F12	VF20	XF40	MS60	MS63
54(1965)	—	—	—	18.50	32.50	42.00

Y# 561 100 YUAN

15.57 g., 0.999 Silver 0.500 oz. ASW, 33 mm. **Subject:** 50th Anniversary - 2-28 Incident **Obv:** Monument **Rev:** Geometrical design **Edge:** Reeded

Date	Mintage	VF20	XF40	MS60	MS63	MS65
86(1997)	55,000	—	—	30.00	35.00	40.00

Y# 557 200 YUAN

31.14 g., 0.999 Silver 1.000 oz. ASW **Subject:** First Popular Election Vote **Obv:** Bust of President Lee Teng-hui and Vice President Lien Chan **Rev:** National emblem above text

Date	Mintage	VF20	XF40	MS60	MS63	MS65
85(1996)	—	PF63 80.00	PF65 85.00			

Y# 566 200 YUAN

31.35 g., 0.999 Silver 1.0069 oz. ASW, 38 mm. **Subject:** Second Popular Vote Presidential Election **Obv:** Bust of the President and Vice-president **Rev:** National emblem above inscription **Edge:** Reeded

Date	Mintage	VF20	XF40	MS60	MS63	MS65
89 (2000)	—	—	—	—	85.00	95.00

Y# 541 1000 YUAN

15.00 g., 0.900 Gold 0.434 oz. AGW **Obv:** Bust of Sun Yat-sen left

Date	Mintage	F12	VF20	XF40	MS60	MS63
54(1965)	—	—	—	—	650	725

Y# 563 1000 YUAN

15.55 g., 0.999 Gold 0.4996 oz. AGW, 25 mm. **Obv:** Bust of Chiang Ching-kuo facing **Rev:** Mausoleum **Edge:** Reeded

Date	Mintage	F12	VF20	XF40	MS60	MS63
87(1998)	30,000	—	—	—	775	850

Y# 542 2000 YUAN

30.00 g., 0.900 Gold 0.8681 oz. AGW **Obv:** Bust of Sun Yat-sen left **Rev:** Chinese symbols at center, budding branch wrapped around

Date	Mintage	F12	VF20	XF40	MS60	MS63
54(1965)	—	—	—	—	1,350	1,500

Y# 544 2000 YUAN

31.06 g., 0.900 Gold 0.8987 oz. AGW **Subject:** 80th Birthday of Chiang Kai-shek **Rev:** Two cranes standing on rock

Date	Mintage	F12	VF20	XF40	MS60	MS63
55(1966)	—	—	—	—	1,450	1,600

Y# 575 2000 YUAN

31.11 g., 0.9999 Gold 1.000 oz. AGW, 33 mm. **Subject:** Inauguration of the President of the People's Republic of China

Date	Mintage	VF20	XF40	MS60	MS63	MS65
2000	125,000	PF63 1,750	PF65 1,950			

PATTERNS

Yuan System; Including off metal strikes

KM#	Date	Mintage	Identification	Mkt Val
Pn1	ND38(1949)	—	Chiao. Bronze. KG#12a.	180
Pn2	38(1949)	—	Chiao. Aluminum. KG#12b.	180
Pn3	38(1949)	—	Chiao. Copper. KG#12c.	180
Pn4	38(1949)	—	Chiao. Copper. KG#12d.	180
Pn5	38(1949)	—	Chiao. Aluminum. K#12e; without reeded edge.	180
Pn6	38(1949)	—	Chiao. Copper. k#13.	180
Pn7	38(1949)	—	Chiao. Copper. KG#14.	180
Pn8	38(1949)	—	5 Chiao. Aluminum-Bronze. KG#15a.	425
Pn9	38(1949)	—	5 Chiao. Aluminum. KG#15b.	300
Pn10	38(1949)	—	5 Chiao. Silver. KG#16.	475
Pn11	38(1949)	—	5 Chiao. Copper. KG#16a.	350
Pn12	38(1949)	—	5 Chiao. Silver. KG#17.	450
Pn13	38(1949)	—	5 Chiao. Silver. KG#18.	725
Pn14	38(1949)	—	5 Chiao. Silver. KG#19.	875
Pn15	38(1949)	—	5 Chiao. Silver. KG#20.	475
Pn16	38(1949)	—	Yuan. Silver. KG#21i.	475
PnA17	38(1949)	—	Yuan. Nickel. Plain.	—
PnB17	38(1949)	—	20 Yuan. Bronze.	1,450
Pn17	39(1950)	—	2 Chiao. Aluminum. Reeded. KG#21a.	150
Pn18	39(1950)	—	2 Chiao. Aluminum-Bronze. KG#21b.	180
Pn19	39(1950)	—	2 Chiao. Aluminum-Bronze. KG#21c; without reeded edge.	180
Pn20	39(1950)	—	2 Chiao. Copper. KG#21d.	180
Pn21	39(1950)	—	Yuan. Silver.	850
Pn22	39(1950)	—	Yuan. Copper-Nickel.	350
Pn23	39(1950)	—	Yuan. Copper-Nickel.	350
Pn24	39(1950)	—	Yuan. Aluminum-Bronze. KG#22a.	240
Pn25	39(1950)	—	Yuan. Aluminum. KG#22b.	425
Pn26	43(1954)	—	5 Chiao. Aluminum-Bronze. KG#23.	500
Pn27	43(1954)	—	5 Chiao. Aluminum-Bronze. Reeded. KG#23a.	500
Pn28	43(1954)	—	5 Chiao. Copper. KG#23b.	500
Pn29	43(1954)	—	5 Chiao. Aluminum-Bronze. KG#23c.	500
Pn30	43(1954)	—	5 Chiao. Aluminum-Bronze. KG#24.	500
Pn31	43(1954)	—	5 Chiao. Aluminum-Bronze. KG#25.	500
Pn32	43(1954)	—	5 Chiao. Aluminum-Bronze. KG#25a.	500
Pn33	43(1954)	—	5 Chiao. Bronze. KG#26a.	500
Pn34	44(1955)	—	Chiao. Aluminum. Simplified "TAI", KG#27a.	500
Pn35	44(1955)	—	Chiao. Bronze. KG#27b.	210
PnA36	45(1956)	—	2 Chiao. Aluminum-Bronze.	—
Pn36	45(1956)	—	2 Chiao. Copper-Nickel. Y#534.	210
PnA37	45(1956)	—	Yuan. Copper-Nickel. Ocean unlined.	—
PnB37	45(1956)	—	Yuan. Aluminum-Bronze. Pn37 with simplified "TAI" character.	—
Pn37	45(1956)	—	Yuan. Copper-Nickel.	350
Pn38	48(1959)	—	Yuan. Nickel.	400
Pn39	48(1959)	—	Yuan. Nickel-Silver.	300
Pn40	49(1960)	—	Yuan. Nickel-Silver. Y#536.	300
Pn41	49(1960)	—	Yuan. Nickel-Silver. Large flan.	375
Pn42	49(1960)	—	Yuan. Nickel-Silver. With Taiwan-sheng.	375
Pn43	49(1960)	—	Yuan. Nickel-Silver. With 1 Yuan.	325
Pn44	49(1960)	—	Yuan. Nickel-Silver. With 1 Kinmen.	325
Pn45	49(1960)	—	5 Yuan. Nickel.	—
Pn46	49(1960)	—	5 Yuan. Nickel. Ancient Chinese symbols.	—
PnA47	50(1961)	—	Yuan. Copper-Nickel. Reeded. Y#536.	775
Pn47	50(1961)	—	Yuan. Nickel-Silver. Sun Yat-sen.	270
Pn48	50(1961)	—	Yuan. Nickel-Aluminum. Chiang Kai-shek.	270
PnA49	50(1961)	—	Yuan. Nickel. Chiang Kai-shek.	2,250
PnB49	50(1961)	—	Yuan. Nickel-Aluminum. Chiang Kai-shek.	2,250
Pn49	50(1961)	—	Yuan. Nickel-Silver. Similar to Pn48 but eleven characters above bust.	270
Pn50	51(1962)	—	5 Yuan. Nickel.	350
Pn51	53(1964)	—	5 Yuan. Copper-Nickel.	350
Pn52	54(1965)	—	10 Yuan. Copper-Nickel. Clouds replace mountains. Y#538.	475
Pn53	54(1965)	—	10 Yuan. Copper-Nickel. Without clouds. Y#538.	475
Pn54	55(1966)	—	2000 Yuan. Silver Gilt. Madam and President Chiang. Y#544.	775
Pn55	38(1949)	—	Chien. Aluminum-Bronze. KG#7b.	425
Pn56	38(1949)	—	Chien. Silver. KG#6a.	600
Pn57	38(1949)	—	Chien. Aluminum-Bronze. KG#6b.	425
Pn58	38(1949)	—	2 Chien. Aluminum-Bronze. KG#4b.	425
Pn59	38(1949)	—	2 Chien. Aluminum-Bronze. KG#3b.	425
Pn60	38(1949)	—	5 Chien. Aluminum-Bronze. KG#2b.	425
Pn62	45(1956)	—	2 Chien. Copper-Nickel.	300
Pn63	45(1956)	—	2 Chien. Aluminum-Bronze.	300
Pn64	45(1956)	—	2 Chien. Aluminum.	300
Pn65	62(1973)	—	5 Yuan. Gold. Y#548.	2,000
Pn66	64(1975)	—	Yuan. Gold. Y#536.	1,500
Pn67	64(1975)	—	Yuan. Aluminum. Y#536.	240

MINT SETS

KM#	Date	Mintage	Identification	Issue Price	Mkt Val
MS1	54(1965) (4)	—	Y#537-540	—	85.00
MS2	70(1981) (4)	—	Y#550-553	—	50.00
MS3	84(1995) (5)	—	Y#550-554	—	15.00
MS4	85(1996) (5)	—	Y#550-554	—	15.00
MS5	86(1997) (5)	—	Y#550-554	—	15.00
MS6	87(1998) (5)	—	Y#550-554	—	15.00
MSA7	88(1999) (2)	260,000	Y#558-559	—	27.50
MS7	88(1999) (5)	—	Y#550-554	—	15.00
MS8	89(2000) (5)	—	Y#550-554	—	15.00

PROOF SETS

KM#	Date	Mintage	Identification	Issue Price	Mkt Val
PS1	70(1981) (4)	—	Y#550-553	—	50.00
PS2	82(1993) (5)	50,000	Y#550-554	14.75	300
PS3	83(1994) (5)	70,000	Y#550-554	14.75	80.00
PS4	84(1995) (5)	70,000	Y#550-554	17.65	70.00
PS5	85(1996) (5)	70,000	Y#550-553 & 556	17.65	70.00
PS6	86(1997) (5)	70,000	Y#550-553 & 556	17.65	70.00
PS7	87(1998) (5)	100,000	Y#550-553 & 556	20.60	70.00
PS8	88(1999) (5)	100,000	Y#550-554	20.60	70.00
PS9	89(2000) (5)	100,000	Y#550-553 & 556	22.05	70.00

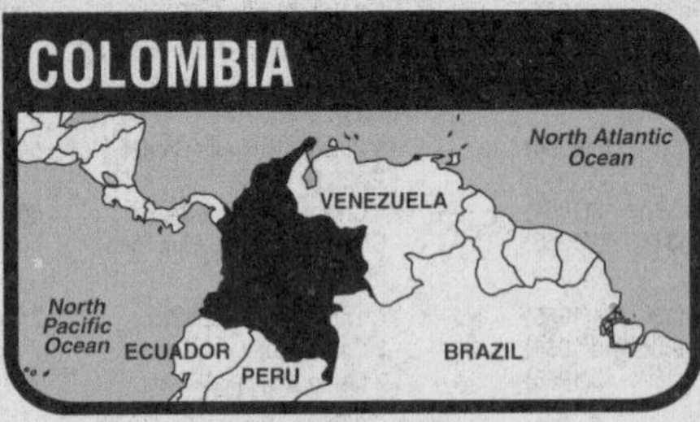

The Republic of Colombia, in the northwestern corner of South America, has an area of 440,831 sq. mi. (1,138,910 sq. km.) and a population of*42.3 million. Capital: Bogota. The economy is primarily agricultural with a mild, rich coffee being the chief crop. Colombia has the world's largest platinum deposits and important reserves of coal, iron ore, petroleum and limestone; other precious metals and emeralds are also mined. Coffee, crude oil, bananas, sugar and emeralds are exported.

The northern coast of present Colombia was one of the first parts of the American continent to be visited by Spanish navigators. At Darien in Panama is the site of the first permanent European settlement on the American mainland in 1510. New Granada, as Colombia was known until 1861, stemmed from the settlement of Santa Marta in 1525. New Granada was established as a Spanish colony in 1549. Independence was declared in 1810, and secured in 1819 when Simon Bolivar united Colombia, Venezuela, Panama and Ecuador as the Republic of Gran Colombia. Venezuela withdrew from the Republic in 1829; Ecuador in 1830; and Panama in 1903.

MINT MARKS

A, M – Medellin (capital), Antioquia (state)
B - BOGOTA
(D) Denver, USA
H – Birmingham (Heaton & Sons)
(m) - Medellin, w/o mint mark
(Mo) - Mexico City
NI - Numismatica Italiana, Arezzo, Italy
mint marks stylized in wreath
(P) - Philadelphia
(S) - San Francisco, USA.
(W) - Waterbury, CT (USA, Scoville mint)

REPUBLIC

DECIMAL COINAGE

100 Centavos = 1 Peso

KM# 275 CENTAVO

2.00 g., Copper-Nickel, 17 mm. **Obv:** Liberty head right **Rev:** Denomination within wreath **Note:** Erratically punched final two digits of date are common on these issues, especially 1935-1948. A very faint "17" is often observable beneath the final two digits on many dates of this type.

Date	Mintage	VF20	XF40	MS60	MS63	MS65
1918	430,000	6.00	15.00	35.00	125	—
1919	Inc. above	8.00	25.00	60.00	140	—
1920 (D)	7,540,000	6.50	13.50	32.00	120	—
1921 (D)	12,460,000	6.50	12.50	30.00	60.00	—
1933 (P)	3,000,000	0.50	3.00	5.00	10.00	—
1935 (P)	5,000,000	0.50	3.00	7.00	15.00	—
1936	1,540,000	2.00	5.00	15.00	45.00	—
1938 (P)	7,920,000	0.25	0.50	2.00	6.00	—
1941 B	1,000,000	0.50	1.00	3.00	10.00	—
1946 B	2,096,000	0.35	0.75	2.50	6.50	—
1947/17 B	1,835,000	1.00	3.50	6.00	12.00	—
1947/37 B	Inc. above	1.00	3.50	6.00	12.00	—
1947/6 B	Inc. above	1.00	3.50	6.00	12.00	—
1947 B	Inc. above	0.50	1.00	2.00	5.00	—
1948/38 B	1,139,000	1.00	3.50	6.00	12.00	—
1948 B	Inc. above	0.50	1.00	2.00	5.00	—

KM# 205 CENTAVO

2.00 g., Bronze, 17.2 mm. **Obv:** Liberty cap within wreath **Rev:** Coffee bean sprigs flank denomination, cornucopia above **Note:** Several date varieties exist.

Date	Mintage	VF20	XF40	MS60	MS63	MS65
1942	1,000,000	1.00	2.00	4.50	12.50	—
1942 B	Inc. above	1.00	3.50	9.00	28.00	—
1943	—	0.50	1.00	2.50	7.00	—
1943 B	4,515,000	0.50	1.00	2.50	7.00	—
1944 B	4,515,000	0.35	0.65	1.50	5.00	—
1945 B	3,769,000	0.50	1.00	2.50	7.00	—
1945 B over reversed B	—	0.35	0.65	1.50	5.00	—
1948 B	585,000	0.50	1.00	3.00	10.00	—
1949 B	4,255,000	0.35	0.65	1.50	5.00	—
1950 B	5,827,000	0.45	0.75	2.50	8.00	—
1951 B	Inc. above	0.35	0.65	1.75	5.50	—
1957	2,500,000	0.25	0.45	0.75	2.00	3.00
1958	590,000	0.25	0.45	1.00	2.25	3.50
1959	2,677,000	0.15	0.25	0.50	1.25	2.50
1960	2,500,000	0.15	0.25	0.50	1.25	2.50
1961 Widely spaced date	3,673,000	0.15	0.25	0.50	1.25	2.50
1961 Narrowly spaced date	Inc. above	0.15	0.25	0.45	1.00	2.50
1962	4,065,000	0.15	0.25	0.50	1.25	2.50
1963	1,845,000	0.15	0.25	0.75	2.00	3.00
1964/44	3,165,000	0.50	1.50	2.50	5.00	7.50
1964	Inc. above	0.15	0.25	0.50	1.25	2.50
1965 Large date	5,510,000	0.15	0.25	0.45	1.00	2.50
1965 Small date	Inc. above	0.15	0.25	0.45	1.00	2.50
1966	3,910,000	0.15	0.25	0.50	1.25	2.50

KM# 275a CENTAVO

2.00 g., Nickel Clad Steel, 17 mm. **Obv:** Liberty head right **Rev:** Denomination within wreath **Note:** Erratically punched final two digits of date are common on these issues.

Date	Mintage	VF20	XF40	MS60	MS63	MS65
1952/12 B	—	0.20	0.50	1.50	4.00	8.00
1952 B	Inc. above	0.10	0.15	0.75	3.00	7.50
1954 B	5,080,000	0.10	0.15	0.50	2.00	7.00
1956	1,315,000	0.20	0.50	1.00	5.00	9.00
1957	900,000	0.35	0.75	2.50	7.50	12.00
1958/48	—	0.35	0.75	2.00	6.00	10.00
1958	1,596,000	0.20	0.45	1.00	3.00	7.50

KM# 218 CENTAVO

Bronze, 17 mm. **Subject:** Uprising Sesquicentennial **Obv:** Liberty cap within wreath **Rev:** Coffee bean sprigs flank denomination, cornucopia above **Note:** This and the other issues in the uprising commemorative series offer the usual design of the period with the dates 1810-1960 added at the bottom of the obverse.

Date	Mintage	VF20	XF40	MS60	MS63	MS65
ND-1960	500,000	1.50	3.00	8.00	12.00	18.00

KM# 205a CENTAVO

2.00 g., Copper Clad Steel, 17.2 mm. **Obv:** Liberty cap within wreath **Rev:** Coffee bean sprigs flank denomination, cornucopia above **Note:** Several date varieties exist.

Date	Mintage	VF20	XF40	MS60	MS63	MS65
1967	5,730,000	—	0.10	0.15	0.45	1.00
1968	7,390,000	—	0.10	0.15	0.45	1.00
1969	6,870,000	—	0.10	0.15	0.45	1.00
1970	3,839,000	—	0.10	0.20	0.60	1.00
1971	3,020,000	—	0.10	0.20	0.60	1.00
1972	3,100,000	—	0.10	0.20	0.60	1.00
1973	—	—	—	0.15	0.40	1.00
1974	2,000,000	—	—	0.15	0.40	1.00
1975	1,000,000	—	—	0.15	0.40	1.00
1976	1,000,000	—	—	0.15	0.40	1.00
1977	900,000	—	0.15	0.40	0.75	1.00
1978	224,000	—	0.25	0.50	1.00	2.00

KM# 198 2 CENTAVOS

3.00 g., Copper-Nickel **Obv:** Liberty head right, date below **Rev:** Denomination within wreath **Note:** Erratically punched final two digits exist for 1946-1947. A very faint "17" is often observable beneath the final two digits on many dates of this type.

Date	Mintage	VF20	XF40	MS60	MS63	MS65
1918	930,000	7.00	15.00	30.00	80.00	—
1919	Inc. above	16.50	30.00	60.00	135	—
1920	3,855,000	3.00	6.50	18.50	50.00	—
1921 (D)	11,145,000	2.50	5.00	15.00	40.00	—
1922 10 pieces known	—	1,350	2,800	—	—	—
1933 (P)	3,500,000	0.50	1.50	4.00	10.00	—
1935 (P)	2,500,000	0.35	1.00	3.50	8.00	—
1938 (P)	3,872,000	0.35	1.00	3.25	7.00	—
1941 B	500,000	1.00	2.00	7.00	20.00	—
1942 B	500,000	1.50	2.50	8.00	16.50	—
1946/36 B	2,593,000	1.00	2.50	6.00	12.50	—
1946 B	Inc. above	0.75	1.50	4.75	11.00	—
1947/3 B	1,337,000	0.75	1.50	4.00	10.00	—
1947/36 B	Inc. above	0.75	1.50	4.00	10.00	—
1947 B	Inc. above	0.35	1.00	3.00	8.00	—

KM# 210 2 CENTAVOS

3.03 g., Bronze, 19.04 mm. **Obv:** Liberty cap within wreath, date below **Rev:** Coffee bean sprigs flank denomination, cornucopia above **Mint:** Bogota

Date	Mintage	VF20	XF40	MS60	MS63	MS65
1948 B	2,648,000	0.35	1.00	4.00	10.00	15.00
1949 B	1,278,000	0.75	2.00	7.00	15.00	20.00
1950 B	2,285,000	0.75	1.50	7.00	18.00	25.00

KM# 211 2 CENTAVOS

3.10 g., Aluminum-Bronze, 19 mm. **Obv:** Head left, date below, divided legend **Rev:** Denomination within wreath

Date	Mintage	VF20	XF40	MS60	MS63	MS65
1952 B Small date	5,038,000	0.15	0.25	0.50	2.00	5.00
1965/3	1,830,000	0.10	0.20	0.40	1.00	3.00
1965 Large date	Inc. above	0.15	0.25	0.50	2.00	5.00

KM# 214 2 CENTAVOS

2.93 g., Aluminum-Bronze, 19 mm. **Obv:** Head left, date below, continuous legend **Rev:** Denomination within wreath **Mint:** Bogota

Date	Mintage	VF20	XF40	MS60	MS63	MS65
1955 Large date	2,513,000	0.15	0.30	1.00	3.00	5.00
1955 B Large date	Inc. above	0.15	0.30	0.75	2.00	3.50
1959 Small date	4,609,000	0.10	0.20	0.50	1.50	2.50

KM# 219 2 CENTAVOS

Aluminum-Bronze, 19 mm. **Subject:** Uprising Sesquicentennial **Obv:** Head left, date below **Rev:** Denomination within wreath **Mint:** Bogota

Date	Mintage	VF20	XF40	MS60	MS63	MS65
ND-1960	250,000	1.00	2.00	3.00	8.00	15.00

KM# 190 2-1/2 CENTAVOS

Copper-Nickel, 14.3 mm. **Obv:** Liberty cap within circle **Rev:** Denomination within circle **Mint:** Scoville Mfg. Co. **Note:** It is probable that te scarcity of this coin, and KM#184, result from the fact of being placed in circulation within the then-Columbian state of Panama. After a brief US-aided rebellion gained independence for Panama and the US gained canal rights, US-made silver coinage replaced the short-lived copper-nickel Columbian coinage.

Date	Mintage	F12	VF20	XF40	MS60	MS63
1902	Est. 400000	—	—	—	500	900

KM# 184 5 CENTAVOS

Copper-Nickel, 20 mm. **Obv:** Head left **Rev:** Large denomination, sprays flank **Mint:** Scoville Mfg. Co. **Note:** It is probable that the scarcity of this coin and KM#190, result from the fact that they were placed in circulation within the then-Columbian state of Panama. After a brief US-aided rebellion gained independence from Panama and the US gained canal rights, US-made silver coinage replaced the short-lived copper-nickel Columbian coinage.

Date	Mintage	F12	VF20	XF40	MS60	MS63
1902	Est. 400000	—	200	400	650	850

KM# 191 5 CENTAVOS

1.25 g., 0.666 Silver 0.0268 oz. ASW, 14 mm. **Obv:** Head left, date below **Rev:** Small denomination within two cornucopias **Edge:** Plain **Mint:** Philadelphia

Date	Mintage	F12	VF20	XF40	MS60	MS63
1902 (P)	400,000	—	1.25	2.50	5.00	12.00

KM# 199 5 CENTAVOS

4.00 g., Copper-Nickel, 21 mm. **Obv:** Head right, date below **Rev:** Denomination within wreath **Note:** Varieties exist. Erratically punched final two digits of date are common on these issues, especially 1935-1950. A very faint "17" is often observable beneath the final two digits on many dates of this type. A cursive numeral form is found on some 1941 strikes or is obvious for the one's in the date. May only occur on some with "B" mm on reverse.

Date	Mintage	VF20	XF40	MS60	MS63	MS65
1918	767,000	11.00	25.00	50.00	100	—
1919	1,926,000	16.50	30.00	65.00	125	—
1920	2,062,000	11.00	25.00	50.00	100	—
1920 H	—	10.00	27.50	45.00	100	—
1921	1,574,000	16.50	30.00	65.00	125	—
1921 H	—	16.50	30.00	65.00	125	—
1922	2,623,000	16.50	30.00	65.00	125	—
1922 H	—	16.50	30.00	65.00	125	—
1924	120,000	18.50	35.00	70.00	125	—
1933 (P)	2,000,000	1.00	2.00	6.00	15.00	—
1935/24	1,616,000	5.00	12.00	30.00	60.00	—
1935 (P)	10,000,000	0.75	1.75	3.50	10.00	—
1936	—	45.00	75.00	150	350	—
1938 B	2,000,000	1.00	2.50	5.50	13.00	—
1938	3,867,000	2.00	3.75	8.00	15.00	—
1938 Large 38 in date	Inc. above	2.00	4.50	10.00	20.00	—
1939/5	2,000,000	1.75	3.00	6.00	13.00	—
1939	Inc. above	0.75	1.50	3.50	8.00	—
1941	—	2.50	5.50	9.00	23.00	—
1941 B	500,000	3.00	6.00	10.00	25.00	—
1946 (P) (S) Small date	40,000,000	0.25	0.50	1.00	3.00	—
1946 (m) Large date	3,330,000	2.00	4.00	8.50	23.00	—
1949 B	2,750,000	0.45	1.00	2.50	6.00	—
1950 B Large 50 in date	3,611,000	6.00	12.00	25.00	45.00	—
1950 B Small 50 in date	Inc. above	0.45	1.00	3.00	6.00	—

KM# 206 5 CENTAVOS

4.12 g., Bronze, 21 mm. **Obv:** Liberty cap within wreath, date below **Rev:** Coffee bean sprigs flank denomination, cornucopia above **Note:** Some coins of 1942-1956 have weak "B" mint mark.

Date	Mintage	VF20	XF40	MS60	MS63	MS65
1942	—	2.00	4.00	12.00	30.00	—
1942 B	800,000	1.00	2.50	4.50	12.00	—
1943	—	5.00	9.00	18.00	35.00	—
1943 B	6,053,000	0.75	1.50	3.00	10.00	—
1944	—	0.75	1.50	3.00	10.00	—
1944 B	9,013,000	0.75	1.50	3.00	10.00	—
1945/4	—	0.75	1.50	3.00	10.00	—
1945	—	0.75	1.50	3.00	10.00	—
1945 B	11,101,000	0.25	0.75	1.25	4.00	—
1946/5	—	1.25	3.50	4.50	12.50	—
1946	—	0.50	1.25	2.00	7.00	—
1952	—	1.25	2.50	3.50	10.00	—
1952 B	3,985,000	0.15	0.40	1.00	2.50	5.00
1953 B	5,180,000	0.10	0.25	0.75	2.00	5.00
1954 B	1,159,000	0.25	0.50	0.75	2.00	5.00
1955 B	6,819,000	0.10	0.25	0.75	2.00	5.00
1956	8,772,000	0.10	0.25	0.50	1.00	3.00
1956 B	—	0.75	1.50	4.50	12.50	20.00
1957	8,912,000	0.10	0.25	0.75	2.00	4.00
1958	15,016,000	0.10	0.25	0.50	1.50	3.00
1959	14,271,000	0.10	0.25	0.50	1.50	3.00
1960/660	11,716,000	0.25	0.75	1.00	2.25	4.00
1960/70	Inc. above	0.25	0.75	1.00	2.25	4.00
1960	Inc. above	0.10	0.25	0.50	1.25	3.00
1961	11,200,000	0.10	0.25	0.50	1.25	3.00
CD1962	10,928,000	—	0.10	0.35	1.00	3.00
1963/53	15,113,000	—	—	—	—	—
1963	Inc. above	—	0.10	0.35	1.00	3.00
1964	9,336,000	—	0.10	0.35	1.00	3.00
1965	6,460,000	—	0.10	0.35	1.00	3.00
1966	7,170,000	—	0.10	0.35	1.00	3.00

KM# 206a 5 CENTAVOS

3.23 g., Copper Clad Steel, 21.29 mm. **Obv:** Liberty cap within wreath, date below **Rev:** Coffee bean sprigs flank denomination, cornucopia above **Note:** Varieties exist for 1967, 1970, and 1973.

Date	Mintage	VF20	XF40	MS60	MS63	MS65
1967	10,280,000	—	0.10	0.25	0.50	1.00
1968	8,900,000	—	0.10	0.25	0.50	1.00
1969	17,800,000	—	0.10	0.25	0.50	1.00
1970	14,842,000	—	0.10	0.15	0.25	0.50
1971	10,730,000	—	0.10	0.15	0.25	0.50
1972	10,170,000	—	0.10	0.15	0.25	0.50
1973	10,525,000	—	0.10	0.15	0.25	0.50
1974	5,310,000	—	0.10	0.15	0.25	0.50
1975	5,631,000	—	0.10	0.15	0.25	0.50
1976	3,009,000	—	0.10	0.15	0.25	0.50
1977	2,000,000	0.15	0.25	0.35	0.45	0.75
1978	468,000	0.15	0.25	0.50	0.75	1.50
1979	8,087,000	—	—	—	—	—

KM# 220 5 CENTAVOS

Bronze, 21 mm. **Subject:** Uprising Sesquicentennial **Obv:** Liberty cap within wreath **Rev:** Coffee bean sprigs flank denomination, cornucopia above

Date	Mintage	VF20	XF40	MS60	MS63	MS65
ND-1960	400,000	1.75	3.50	7.50	28.00	65.00

KM# 196.1 10 CENTAVOS

2.50 g., 0.900 Silver 0.0723 oz. ASW, 18 mm. **Obv:** Simon Bolivar head right, date below **Rev:** Arms and value **Note:** Varieties exist.

Date	Mintage	F12	VF20	XF40	MS60	MS63
1911	5,065,000	—	2.75	3.00	11.00	30.00
1913	8,305,000	—	2.75	3.00	10.00	25.00
1914	3,840,000	—	2.75	3.00	11.00	30.00
1920	2,149,000	—	2.75	3.00	11.00	30.00
1934/24	Inc. above	—	7.00	15.00	30.00	65.00
1934 B B on obverse	140,000	—	3.00	8.00	20.00	45.00
1934	Inc. above	—	7.00	14.00	30.00	65.00
1937 B	—	—	6.00	13.00	25.00	50.00
1938/7 B	2,055,000	—	2.75	4.00	7.00	22.50
1938 B Wide date	Inc. above	—	2.75	3.00	4.00	12.00
1938 Narrow date	Inc. above	—	2.75	3.00	4.00	12.00
1940	450,000	—	2.75	3.00	5.00	18.00
1941	4,415,000	—	2.75	3.00	4.00	10.00
1942	3,140,000	—	6.00	11.00	18.00	42.00
1942 B B on reverse	Inc. above	—	2.75	3.00	4.00	8.00

KM# 196.2 10 CENTAVOS

2.50 g., 0.900 Silver 0.0723 oz. ASW, 18 mm. **Obv:** Simon Bolivar head right **Rev:** National arms recut

Date	Mintage	F12	VF20	XF40	MS60	MS63
1920	Inc. above	—	3.00	7.00	13.00	35.00

KM# 207.1 10 CENTAVOS

2.50 g., 0.500 Silver 0.0402 oz. ASW, 18 mm. **Obv:** Francisco de Paula Santander head right **Rev:** Denomination within wreath, mint mark at bottom

Date	Mintage	VF20	XF40	MS60	MS63	MS65
1945 B	4,830,000	1.50	1.75	3.00	6.00	12.00
1945 B-B	—	—	—	—	—	—
1945 Backwards B	—	1.50	1.75	3.00	6.00	12.00
1946/5 B	—	1.50	2.00	4.00	7.50	15.00
1946 B	—	1.50	2.00	4.00	7.50	15.00
1947/5 B	7,366,000	1.75	3.00	5.00	9.00	18.00
1947/6 B	Inc. above	1.75	3.00	5.00	9.00	18.00
1947 B	Inc. above	1.75	3.00	5.00	9.00	18.00

KM# 207.2 10 CENTAVOS

2.50 g., 0.500 Silver 0.0402 oz. ASW, 18 mm. **Obv:** Head of Santander right, date below **Rev:** Denomination within wreath, mint mark at top **Note:** Varieties exist. Almost all dies for 1946-1951 show at least faint traces of overdating from 1945. Coins with absolutely no underdate, and those with very bold underdate, are generally worth more to advanced specialists.

Date	Mintage	VF20	XF40	MS60	MS63	MS65
1947/5 B	Inc. above	2.25	4.00	7.00	12.50	25.00
1947 B	Inc. above	2.25	4.00	7.00	12.50	25.00
1948/5 B	3,629,000	1.50	2.00	5.00	9.00	18.00
1948 B	Inc. above	1.50	1.75	3.00	5.50	11.00
1949/5 B	5,923,000	3.00	6.00	10.00	15.00	30.00
1949 B	Inc. above	1.50	1.75	2.50	4.50	9.00
1950 B	6,783,000	1.50	1.75	3.00	5.00	10.00
1951/5 B	5,185,000	1.50	1.75	3.00	5.00	10.00
1951 B	Inc. above	1.50	1.75	2.50	4.50	9.00
1952 B	1,060,000	1.75	2.50	4.50	7.50	15.00

KM# 212.1 10 CENTAVOS

Copper-Nickel, 18 mm. **Obv:** Arms above date **Rev:** Head of Chief Calarca right divides denomination **Mint:** Bogota

Date	Mintage	VF20	XF40	MS60	MS63	MS65
1952 B	6,035,000	0.35	1.00	3.50	5.00	15.00
1953 B	6,985,000	0.25	0.50	1.50	3.00	6.00

KM# 212.2 10 CENTAVOS

2.33 g., Copper-Nickel, 18.5 mm. **Obv:** Arms above date **Rev:** Head of Chief Calarca right divides denomination **Mint:** Bogota **Note:** Varieties exist.

Date	Mintage	VF20	XF40	MS60	MS63	MS65
1954 B	13,006,000	0.20	0.50	1.25	1.75	3.00
1955 B	9,968,000	0.20	0.50	1.25	1.75	3.00
1956	36,010,000	0.10	0.20	0.50	0.75	1.50
1956 B	—	0.10	0.20	0.50	0.75	1.50
1958	41,695,000	—	—	—	—	—
1959	36,653,000	0.10	0.20	0.50	0.75	1.50

Date	Mintage	VF20	XF40	MS60	MS63	MS65
1960	32,290,000	0.10	0.20	0.50	1.00	2.00
1961	17,780,000	0.10	0.20	0.50	1.00	2.00
1962	8,930,000	0.10	0.20	0.50	1.00	2.00
1963	37,540,000	0.10	0.20	0.50	1.00	1.50
1964	61,672,000	0.10	0.20	0.50	1.00	1.50
1965	12,804,000	0.10	0.25	0.75	1.50	3.00
1966 Large date	23,544,000	0.10	0.20	0.50	0.75	1.50

KM# 221 10 CENTAVOS

Copper-Nickel, 18.5 mm. **Subject:** Uprising Sesquicentennial **Obv:** Arms above two dates **Rev:** Head of Chief Calarca right divides denomination

Date	Mintage	VF20	XF40	MS60	MS63	MS65
ND-1960	1,000,000	1.00	2.00	3.50	4.00	8.00

KM# 226 10 CENTAVOS

2.51 g., Nickel Clad Steel, 18.3 mm. **Obv:** Head of Santander right, date below **Rev:** Denomination within circular wreath

Date	Mintage	VF20	XF40	MS60	MS63	MS65
1967	26,980,000	—	0.10	0.20	0.50	1.00
1968	23,670,000	—	0.10	0.20	0.50	1.00
1969	29,450,000	—	0.10	0.20	0.50	1.00

KM# 236 10 CENTAVOS

2.52 g., Nickel Clad Steel, 18.3 mm. **Obv:** Head of Santander right, date below **Rev:** Denomination within wreath

Date	Mintage	VF20	XF40	MS60	MS63	MS65
1969	Inc. above	—	0.10	0.20	0.50	1.00
1970	38,935,000	—	0.10	0.20	0.50	1.00
1971	53,314,000	—	0.10	0.20	0.50	1.00

KM# 243 10 CENTAVOS

Nickel Clad Steel, 18.3 mm. **Obv:** Legend divided after REPUBLICA

Date	Mintage	VF20	XF40	MS60	MS63	MS65
1970	—	—	—	—	—	—
1971	—	—	—	—	—	—

KM# 253 10 CENTAVOS

2.52 g., Nickel Clad Steel, 18.4 mm. **Obv:** Head right, date below, continuous legend **Rev:** Denomination within wreath **Edge:** Reeded **Note:** Varieties exist.

Date	Mintage	VF20	XF40	MS60	MS63	MS65
1972	58,000,000	—	0.10	0.15	0.25	0.50
1973	46,549,000	—	0.10	0.15	0.25	0.50
1974	49,740,000	—	0.10	0.15	0.25	0.50
1975	46,037,000	—	0.10	0.15	0.25	0.50
1976	46,084,000	—	0.10	0.15	0.25	0.50
1977	8,127,000	—	0.10	0.15	0.25	0.50
1978	97,081,000	—	0.10	0.15	0.25	0.50
1980	18,929,000	—	0.10	0.15	0.25	0.50
1989	—	—	0.10	0.15	0.25	0.50

KM# 197 20 CENTAVOS

5.00 g., 0.900 Silver 0.1447 oz. ASW **Obv:** Head of Simon Bolivar right, date below **Rev:** Arms, denomination above

Date	Mintage	F12	VF20	XF40	MS60	MS63
1911	1,206,000	—	5.25	6.00	10.00	20.00
1913	1,630,000	—	5.25	6.00	10.00	25.00
1914	2,560,000	—	5.25	6.00	11.00	27.50
1920 Wide date	1,242,000	—	5.25	7.00	14.00	35.00
1920 Narrow date	Inc. above	—	5.25	7.00	14.00	35.00
1921	372,000	—	8.00	17.00	40.00	95.00
1922	45,000	—	33.00	60.00	95.00	250
1933 B	330,000	—	5.25	8.00	17.00	38.00
Note: Mint mark on obverse						
1933 B	Inc. above	—	14.00	27.50	50.00	145
Note: Mint mark on reverse						
1933 B	Inc. above	—	6.00	11.00	22.50	55.00
Note: Mint mark on both sides						
1938/1	1,410,000	—	5.25	9.00	19.00	38.00
1938	Inc. above	—	5.25	6.00	11.00	25.00
1941	—	—	5.25	7.00	13.00	30.00
1942	155,000	—	10.00	22.50	37.50	75.00
1942 B	Inc. above	—	5.25	6.00	10.00	22.50
Note: Mint mark on reverse						

KM# 208.1 20 CENTAVOS

5.00 g., 0.500 Silver 0.0804 oz. ASW **Obv:** Francisco de Paula Santander **Rev:** Mint mark in field below CENTAVOS

Date	Mintage	VF20	XF40	MS60	MS63	MS65
1945 B	1,675,000	3.00	3.50	8.00	12.00	18.00
1945 BB	Inc. above	7.00	13.00	28.00	35.00	55.00
Note: 1945BB has extra B on wreath at bottom						
1946/5 B	6,599,000	3.00	3.50	7.00	11.00	17.00
1946 B	Inc. above	3.00	3.50	10.00	15.00	22.50
1947/5 B	9,708,000	3.00	7.00	13.00	18.00	30.00
1947 B	—	3.00	7.00	13.00	18.00	30.00

KM# 208.2 20 CENTAVOS

5.00 g., 0.500 Silver 0.0804 oz. ASW **Obv:** Francisco de Paula Santander **Rev:** Mint mark on wreath at top **Note:** Almost all dies for 1946-1951 show at least faint traces of overdating from 1945. Coins with absolutely no underdate, and those with very bold underdate, are generally worth more to advanced specialists. Varieties exist.

Date	Mintage	VF20	XF40	MS60	MS63	MS65
1947/5 B	Inc. above	6.00	11.00	22.50	55.00	75.00
1948/5 B	Inc. above	3.00	3.50	6.00	13.00	22.00
1948 B	Inc. above	3.00	3.50	6.00	15.00	25.00
1949/5 B	403,000	4.00	9.00	20.00	50.00	70.00
1949 B	Inc. above	3.00	6.00	11.00	35.00	55.00
1950/45 B	1,899,000	3.00	7.00	17.00	55.00	75.00
1950 B	Inc. above	3.00	7.00	15.00	42.00	65.00
1951/45 B	7,498,000	3.00	3.50	7.00	16.00	28.00
1951 B	Inc. above	3.00	3.50	7.00	16.00	28.00

KM# 208.3 20 CENTAVOS

5.00 g., 0.500 Silver 0.0804 oz. ASW **Obv:** Francisco de Paula Santander **Rev:** Without mint mark

Date	Mintage	VF20	XF40	MS60	MS63	MS65
1946 (m)	—	3.00	8.00	17.00	35.00	55.00
1946/5 (m)	—	4.00	10.00	18.00	45.00	70.00
1947 (m)	1,748,000	6.00	9.00	17.00	38.00	60.00

KM# 213 20 CENTAVOS

5.00 g., 0.300 Silver 0.0482 oz. ASW **Obv:** Arms, date below **Rev:** Bust of Simon Bolivar left, divides denomination

Date	Mintage	VF20	XF40	MS60	MS63	MS65
1952 B Rare	3,887	—	—	—	—	—
1953 B	17,819,000	1.00	1.75	2.00	4.00	8.00

KM# 215.1 20 CENTAVOS

5.00 g., Copper-Nickel, 23.2 mm. **Obv:** Head of Simon Bolivar right, small date below **Rev:** Denomination above arms, half circle of stars below

Date	Mintage	VF20	XF40	MS60	MS63	MS65
1956	39,778,000	—	0.10	0.15	0.50	1.50
1959	55,519,000	—	0.10	0.15	0.50	1.50

KM# 215.2 20 CENTAVOS

4.93 g., Copper-Nickel, 23.4 mm. **Obv:** Head of Simon Bolivar right, large date below **Rev:** Denomination above arms, half circle of stars below

Date	Mintage	VF20	XF40	MS60	MS63	MS65
1963	12,035,000	—	—	0.10	0.50	1.50
1964	29,075,000	—	—	0.10	0.50	1.50
1965	19,180,000	—	0.10	0.25	0.75	2.50

KM# 215.3 20 CENTAVOS

4.80 g., Copper-Nickel, 23.4 mm. **Obv:** Head of Simon Bolivar right, medium date **Rev:** Denomination above arms, half circle of stars below

Date	Mintage	VF20	XF40	MS60	MS63	MS65
1966	23,060,000	—	0.10	0.15	0.50	1.50

KM# 222 20 CENTAVOS

Copper-Nickel **Subject:** Uprising Sesquicentennial **Obv:** Head right divides dates below **Rev:** Denomination above arms, half circle of stars below

Date	Mintage	VF20	XF40	MS60	MS63	MS65
ND-1960	500,000	1.50	2.00	3.00	5.00	9.00

KM# 224 20 CENTAVOS

Copper-Nickel **Obv:** Arms above denomination **Rev:** Bust of Jorge Eliecer Gaitan left, date below

Date	Mintage	VF20	XF40	MS60	MS63	MS65
1965	1,000,000	—	0.20	0.50	0.75	2.00

KM# 227 20 CENTAVOS

4.50 g., Nickel Clad Steel, 23.6 mm. **Obv:** Head of Santander right, large date and continuous legend **Rev:** Denomination within wreath

Date	Mintage	VF20	XF40	MS60	MS63	MS65
1967	15,720,000	—	0.10	0.20	0.50	1.00
1968	26,680,000	—	0.10	0.20	0.50	1.00
1969	22,470,000	—	0.10	0.20	0.50	1.00

KM# 237 20 CENTAVOS

4.50 g., Nickel Clad Steel, 23.6 mm. **Obv:** Refined detailed portrait of Santander right, with smaller date and legend **Rev:** Denomination within wreath

Date	Mintage	VF20	XF40	MS60	MS63	MS65
1969	Inc. above	—	—	—	—	—
1970	44,358,000	—	0.10	0.20	0.60	1.00

KM# 245 20 CENTAVOS

4.55 g., Nickel Clad Steel, 23.4 mm. **Obv:** Head right, legend divided after REPUBLICA DE **Rev:** Denomination within wreath

Date	Mintage	VF20	XF40	MS60	MS63	MS65
1971	77,526,000	—	0.10	0.35	0.50	0.75

KM# 246.1 20 CENTAVOS

4.50 g., Nickel Clad Steel, 23.6 mm. **Obv:** Head right, date below, legend continuous **Rev:** Denomination within wreath

Note: Varieties exist with and without dots.

Date	Mintage	VF20	XF40	MS60	MS63	MS65
1971	Inc. above	—	0.10	0.35	0.50	0.75
1972	41,891,000	—	0.10	0.35	0.50	0.75
1973/1	41,440,000	—	0.10	0.35	0.50	0.75
1973	Inc. above	—	0.15	0.25	0.50	0.75
1974/1	45,941,000	—	0.25	0.35	0.60	1.00
1974	Inc. above	—	0.10	0.35	0.50	0.75
1975	28,635,000	—	0.10	0.35	0.50	0.75
1976	29,590,000	—	0.10	0.35	0.50	0.75
1977	2,054,000	—	0.20	0.40	0.60	1.00
1978	10,630,000	—	0.10	0.35	0.50	0.75

KM# 246.2 20 CENTAVOS

Nickel Clad Steel **Obv:** Head right, date below, smaller letters in legend **Rev:** Wreath with larger 20 and smaller CENTAVOS

Date	Mintage	VF20	XF40	MS60	MS63	MS65
1979	16,655,000	—	0.10	0.20	0.50	1.00

KM# 267 25 CENTAVOS

Aluminum-Bronze **Obv:** Head of Simon Bolivar right, date below **Rev:** Denomination within lines

Date	Mintage	VF20	XF40	MS60	MS63	MS65
1979	88,874,000	0.10	0.15	0.20	0.35	0.50
1980	46,168,000	0.10	0.15	0.20	0.35	0.50

KM# 186.2 50 CENTAVOS

12.50 g., 0.835 Silver 0.3356 oz. ASW, 30 mm. **Obv:** Liberty head left, incuse lettering on headband, date below **Rev:** Denomination above arms **Edge Lettering:** DIOS LEI LIBERTAD **Mint:** Bogota **Note:** Similar to KM#186.1a.

Date	Mintage	VG8	F12	VF20	XF40	MS60
1906	446,000	13.00	17.00	30.00	55.00	115
1907	1,126,000	12.00	13.00	20.00	42.50	90.00
1908/7	871,000	25.00	36.00	55.00	90.00	200
1908	Inc. above	13.00	15.00	25.00	50.00	110

KM# 192 50 CENTAVOS

12.50 g., 0.835 Silver 0.3356 oz. ASW, 30 mm. **Obv:** Liberty head left, date below **Rev:** Denomination above arms **Mint:** Philadelphia

Date	Mintage	F12	VF20	XF40	MS60	MS63
1902 (P)	960,000	12.00	20.00	40.00	80.00	150

KM# 193.1 50 CENTAVOS

12.50 g., 0.900 Silver 0.3617 oz. ASW, 30 mm. **Obv:** Simon Bolivar, sharper featured head right, date below **Rev:** Denomination above arms, left wing and flags far from legend **Note:** Struck at Birmingham and Bogota mints. Date varieties exist.

Date	Mintage	F12	VF20	XF40	MS60	MS63
1912	1,207,000	14.00	16.00	40.00	55.00	90.00
1912 Proof; rare	—	—	—	—	—	—
1913	417,000	14.00	16.00	40.00	55.00	90.00
1914 Closed 4	769,000	14.00	18.00	45.00	65.00	100
1915 Small date	946,000	14.00	16.00	32.00	50.00	85.00
1915 Small date; Proof; rare	—	—	—	—	—	—
1915 Large date	Inc. above	—	—	—	—	—
1915 Proof; rare	—	—	—	—	—	—
1916 Small date	1,060,000	14.00	15.00	25.00	36.00	60.00
1917 Normal 7	99,000	14.00	25.00	50.00	70.00	110
1917 Foot on 7	Inc. above	14.00	25.00	50.00	70.00	110
1917 Curved top	Inc. above	14.00	25.00	55.00	75.00	120
1918	400,000	14.00	15.00	30.00	55.00	90.00
1919	Inc. above	18.00	28.00	45.00	65.00	100
1922	150,000	14.00	17.00	32.00	55.00	90.00
1923	150,000	14.00	17.00	32.00	55.00	90.00
1931/21 B	—	14.00	15.00	25.00	36.00	60.00
1931 B	700,000	14.00	15.00	25.00	36.00	60.00
1931	Inc. above	80.00	145	200	265	425
1932/12 B	300,000	14.00	17.00	32.00	55.00	90.00
1932/22 B	Inc. above	14.00	18.00	40.00	60.00	95.00
1932 B	Inc. above	14.00	15.00	25.00	36.00	60.00
1932 Flat top 3, no B	Inc. above	25.00	35.00	50.00	70.00	110
1933/13 B	1,000,000	14.00	15.00	22.00	32.00	55.00
1933/23 B	Inc. above	14.00	15.00	28.00	36.00	60.00
1933 B	Inc. above	—	14.00	15.00	20.00	35.00

KM# 193.2 50 CENTAVOS

12.50 g., 0.900 Silver 0.3617 oz. ASW, 30 mm. **Obv:** Simon Bolivar, sharper featured head right, date below **Rev:** Denomination above arms, larger letters, left wing and flags close to legend **Mint:** Medellin **Note:** Date varieties exist.

Date	Mintage	F12	VF20	XF40	MS60	MS63
1914 Open 4	—	14.00	16.00	35.00	60.00	95.00
1915/4 Large date	—	55.00	75.00	125	160	240
1915 Large date	—	65.00	110	150	200	300
1918/4	—	14.00	25.00	40.00	55.00	90.00
1918	—	14.00	15.00	30.00	50.00	80.00
1919/8	—	14.00	18.00	32.00	52.00	85.00
1919	—	14.00	18.00	32.00	52.00	85.00
1921	300,000	14.00	18.00	32.00	52.00	85.00
1922	—	14.00	15.00	30.00	50.00	80.00
1932/22 M	1,200,000	25.00	45.00	75.00	120	175
1932 M	Inc. above	—	14.00	17.00	22.00	38.00
1932 Round top 3, no M	Inc. above	22.50	40.00	65.00	100	150
1933 M	800,000	—	14.00	25.00	36.00	60.00
1933/23 Round top 3s, no M	Inc. above	18.00	30.00	40.00	55.00	90.00

KM# 274 50 CENTAVOS

12.50 g., 0.900 Silver 0.3617 oz. ASW, 30 mm. **Obv:** Simon Bolivar, rounder featured head right, date below **Rev:** Denomination above arms **Note:** Struck at the Philadelphia and San Francisco mints. Sculptor of this Bolivar bust was Roulin.

Date	Mintage	VF20	XF40	MS60	MS63	MS65
1916 (P)	1,300,000	—	14.00	30.00	60.00	—
1917 (P)	142,000	13.00	22.50	45.00	90.00	—
1921 (P)	1,000,000	—	14.00	25.00	55.00	—
1922 (P)	3,000,000	—	14.00	20.00	50.00	85.00
1934 (S)	10,000,000	—	14.00	20.00	50.00	85.00

KM# 209 50 CENTAVOS

12.50 g., 0.500 Silver 0.2009 oz. ASW, 30 mm. **Obv:** Simon Bolivar (in military uniform) bust left, date below **Rev:** Denomination within circular wreath **Mint:** Bogota

Date	Mintage	VF20	XF40	MS60	MS63	MS65
1947/6	1,240,000	8.00	12.00	22.50	35.00	55.00
1947	Inc. above	15.00	20.00	32.00	50.00	85.00
1948/6	707,000	8.00	12.00	22.50	35.00	55.00
1948 inverted B	Inc. above	32.00	45.00	65.00	95.00	140
1948	Inc. above	12.00	15.00	28.00	45.00	95.00

KM# 217 50 CENTAVOS

12.56 g., Copper-Nickel, 30.5 mm. **Obv:** Denomination below arms **Rev:** Head of Simon Bolivar by Tererani, right, date below **Note:** Various sizes of date exist.

Date	Mintage	VF20	XF40	MS60	MS63	MS65
1958	3,596,000	0.50	1.25	3.50	7.50	10.00
1958 Medal Rotation	Inc. above	12.00	22.00	40.00	—	—
1959	13,466,000	0.30	1.00	3.00	5.00	7.00
1959 Medal Rotation	Inc. above	3.50	6.00	10.00	—	—
1960	4,360,000	0.50	1.50	3.50	5.00	7.00
1961	3,260,000	0.50	1.50	3.50	5.00	7.00
1962	2,336,000	0.50	1.50	3.50	5.00	7.00
1963	4,098,000	0.50	1.00	3.00	5.00	7.00
1964	9,274,000	0.30	1.00	3.00	5.00	7.00
1965	5,800,000	0.30	1.00	3.00	5.00	7.00
1966	2,820,000	0.50	1.00	3.00	5.00	7.00

KM# 223 50 CENTAVOS

Copper-Nickel, 30.5 mm. **Subject:** Uprising Sesquicentennial **Obv:** Denomination below arms **Rev:** Head right, two dates below

Date	Mintage	VF20	XF40	MS60	MS63	MS65
ND-1960	200,000	4.00	8.00	12.00	14.00	18.00

KM# 225 50 CENTAVOS

Copper-Nickel, 30.5 mm. **Obv:** Arms and denomination **Rev:** Jorge Eliecer Gaitan bust left, date below

Date	Mintage	VF20	XF40	MS60	MS63	MS65
1965	600,000	0.25	0.50	0.80	2.00	5.00

KM# 228 50 CENTAVOS
Nickel Clad Steel, 30 mm. **Obv:** Head of Francisco de Paula Santander (from bust by Pierre-Jean David d'Angers), right, date below **Rev:** Denomination within circular wreath

Date	Mintage	VF20	XF40	MS60	MS63	MS65
1967	3,460,000	0.25	0.50	0.75	1.25	1.75
1968	5,460,000	0.20	0.40	0.75	1.25	1.75
1969	1,590,000	0.25	0.50	0.75	1.50	2.00

KM# 244.1 50 CENTAVOS
4.40 g., Nickel Clad Steel, 23.3 mm. **Obv:** Head right, flat truncation, date below **Rev:** Denomination within wreath, 5 far from wreath **Edge:** Reeded **Shape:** 12-sided **Note:** Date varieties exist.

Date	Mintage	VF20	XF40	MS60	MS63	MS65
1970	30,906,000	—	0.10	0.15	0.50	0.75
1971	32,650,000	—	0.10	0.15	0.50	0.75
1972	25,290,000	—	0.10	0.15	0.50	0.75
1973	8,060,000	—	0.10	0.15	0.50	0.75
1974	19,541,000	—	0.10	0.15	0.50	0.75
1975	4,325,000	—	0.20	0.30	0.75	1.00
1976	13,181,000	—	0.10	0.15	0.45	0.75
1977	10,413,000	—	0.10	0.15	0.45	0.75
1978	10,736,000	—	0.10	0.15	0.45	0.75

KM# 244.2 50 CENTAVOS
4.40 g., Nickel Clad Steel, 23.3 mm. **Obv:** Head right, angled truncation, date below **Rev:** Denomination within wreath, 5 close to wreath **Edge:** Reeded **Shape:** 12-sided **Note:** Various sizes of dates exist.

Date	Mintage	VF20	XF40	MS60	MS63	MS65
1979	22,584,000	—	0.10	0.15	0.45	0.75
1980	16,433,000	—	0.10	0.15	0.45	0.75
1982	10,107,000	—	0.10	0.15	0.45	0.75

KM# 244.3 50 CENTAVOS
4.40 g., Nickel Clad Steel, 23.3 mm. **Obv:** Head right, angled truncation, date below **Rev:** Denomination within wreath, 5 far from wreath **Edge:** Reeded **Shape:** 12-sided **Note:** Mule.

Date	Mintage	VF20	XF40	MS60	MS63	MS65
1979	—	10.00	20.00	30.00	50.00	75.00

KM# 216 PESO
25.00 g., 0.900 Silver 0.7234 oz. ASW, 37 mm. **Subject:** 200th Anniversary of Popayan Mint **Obv:** Arms above denomination **Rev:** Monument, sprays flank, date above **Mint:** Mexico City

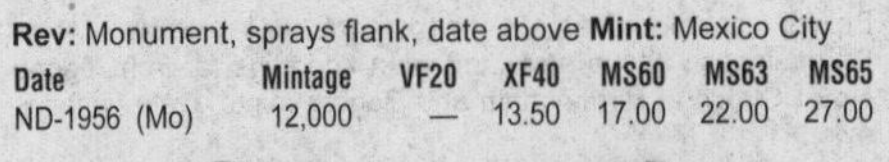

Date	Mintage	VF20	XF40	MS60	MS63	MS65
ND-1956 (Mo)	12,000	—	13.50	17.00	22.00	27.00

KM# 229 PESO
Copper-Nickel, 30 mm. **Obv:** Head of Simon Bolivar right, date below **Rev:** Denomination within circular wreath **Shape:** 10-sided

Date	Mintage	VF20	XF40	MS60	MS63	MS65
1967	4,000,000	0.25	0.50	0.75	1.50	2.00

KM# 258.1 PESO
Copper-Nickel, 25.3 mm. **Obv:** Bust of Simon Bolivar 3/4 facing, small date below **Rev:** Denomination, ears of corn flank

Date	Mintage	VF20	XF40	MS60	MS63	MS65
1974	56,020,000	—	0.10	0.15	0.50	0.75
1975 medium date	117,714,000	—	0.10	0.15	0.40	0.60
1976	98,728,000	—	0.10	0.15	0.40	0.60

KM# 258.2 PESO
Copper-Nickel, 25.3 mm. **Obv:** Bust of Simon Bolivar 3/4 facing, large date below **Rev:** Denomination, ears of corn flank

Date	Mintage	VF20	XF40	MS60	MS63	MS65
1976	Inc. above	—	0.10	0.15	0.40	0.60
1977	62,083,000	—	0.10	0.15	0.40	0.60
1978	48,624,000	—	0.10	0.15	0.40	0.60
1979	83,908,000	—	0.10	0.15	0.40	0.60
1980	93,406,000	—	0.10	0.15	0.40	0.60
1981	65,219,000	—	0.10	0.15	0.40	0.60
1989 Requires confirmation	138	—	—	—	—	—

KM# 263 2 PESOS
7.80 g., Bronze, 23.8 mm. **Obv:** Bust of Simon Bolivar 3/4 facing, date below **Rev:** Denomination within wreath **Note:** Varieties exist.

Date	Mintage	VF20	XF40	MS60	MS63	MS65
1977	76,661,000	0.10	0.15	0.25	0.50	0.75
1978	69,575,000	0.10	0.15	0.25	0.50	0.75
1979	56,537,000	0.10	0.15	0.25	0.50	0.75
1980	108,521,000	0.10	0.15	0.25	0.50	0.75
1981	40,368,000	0.10	0.15	0.25	0.50	0.75
1983	8,358,000	0.20	0.30	0.50	0.75	1.00
1987	13,832,500	0.10	0.15	0.25	0.50	0.75
1988	16,218,225	0.10	0.15	0.25	0.50	0.75

KM# 194 2-1/2 PESOS
3.99 g., 0.917 Gold 0.1178 oz. AGW **Obv:** Native, date below **Rev:** Arms and denomination

Date	Mintage	F12	VF20	XF40	MS60	MS63
1913	18,000	—	150	215	225	250

KM# 200 2-1/2 PESOS
3.99 g., 0.917 Gold 0.1178 oz. AGW **Obv:** Simon Bolivar large head right, date below **Rev:** Arms and denomination

Date	Mintage	VF20	XF40	MS60	MS63	MS65
1919 A	—	150	200	250	—	—
Note: Two varieties, with large or small first 1 in date						
1919 B	—	—	—	—	—	—
1919	34,000	150	200	250	—	—
1920/19 A	—	150	200	250	—	—
1920 A	—	150	200	250	—	—
1920	34,000	150	200	250	—	—

KM# 203 2-1/2 PESOS
3.99 g., 0.917 Gold 0.1178 oz. AGW **Obv:** Simon Bolivar small head, MEDELLIN below, date at bottom **Rev:** Arms and denomination

Date	Mintage	VF20	XF40	MS60	MS63	MS65
1924	—	150	200	225	250	—
1925 Rare	—	—	—	—	—	—
1927	—	150	200	225	250	—
1928	14,000	150	200	225	250	—
1929 Rare	—	—	—	—	—	—

KM# 195.1 5 PESOS
7.99 g., 0.917 Gold 0.2355 oz. AGW **Obv:** Native, date below **Rev:** Arms and denomination **Note:** Various rotations of dies exist.

Date	Mintage	F12	VF20	XF40	MS60	MS63
1913	17,000	—	300	425	450	475
1918/3	423,000	—	300	375	425	450
1918	Inc. above	—	300	375	425	450
1919	2,181,000	—	300	375	425	450
1919 Long-tail 9	Inc. above	—	300	375	425	450
1919 Dot over 9	Inc. above	—	300	375	425	450

KM# 195.2 5 PESOS
7.99 g., 0.917 Gold 0.2355 oz. AGW **Obv:** Native, date below **Rev:** Arms and denomination **Note:** Medallic die rotation. Unless otherwise noted mintage is included in KM#195.1.

Date	Mintage	F12	VF20	XF40	MS60	MS63
1913	Inc. above	—	300	375	425	450
1917	43,000	—	300	375	425	450
1918	Inc. above	—	300	375	425	450
1919	Inc. above	—	300	375	425	450

KM# 201.1 5 PESOS
7.99 g., 0.917 Gold 0.2355 oz. AGW **Obv:** Simon Bolivar, large head right **Rev:** Arms and denomination **Note:** 1920A dated coins come with mint mark centered or on right side of coat of arms; 1923B dated coins come with B on the left or right of coat of arms. The 1923B mint mark to right carries a 25% premium in value. Various rotations of dies exist.

Date	Mintage	VF20	XF40	MS60	MS63	MS65
1919	Inc. above	—	300	425	450	—
Note: Narrow or wide dates, with multiple varieties of numeral alignment						
1919 A	Inc. above	300	375	425	450	—
Note: Narrow or wide date						
1919 B	—	300	375	425	450	—
1920	870,000	300	375	425	450	—
1920 A	Inc. above	300	375	425	450	—
Note: Placement of A below coat of arms varies						

Date	Mintage	VF20	XF40	MS60	MS63	MS65
1920 B	108,000	300	375	425	450	—
Note: Placement of B varies						
1921 A	—	—	—	—	—	—
1922 B	29,000	300	375	425	450	—
Note: Two varieties known, with B touching or separated from coat of arms						
1923 B	74,000	300	375	425	450	—
1924 B	705,000	300	375	425	450	—
Note: Placement of B varies						

KM# 201.2 5 PESOS

7.99 g., 0.917 Gold 0.2355 oz. AGW **Obv:** Simon Bolivar, large head **Rev:** Arms and denomination **Note:** Medallic die rotation.

Date	Mintage	VF20	XF40	MS60	MS63	MS65
1920	Inc. above	300	375	425	450	—

KM# 204 5 PESOS

7.99 g., 0.917 Gold 0.2355 oz. AGW **Obv:** Simon Bolivar, small head, MEDELLIN below, date at bottom **Rev:** Arms and denomination **Note:** 1924 dated coins have several varieties in size of 2 and 4. 1925 dated coins exist with an Arabic and a Spanish style 5. 1930 dated coins have three varieties in size and placement of 3.

Date	Mintage	VF20	XF40	MS60	MS63	MS65
1924 Large 2	120,000	—	300	425	450	—
1924 Large 4	Inc. above	300	375	425	450	—
1924 Small 4	Inc. above	300	375	425	450	—
1924 MFDELLIN	Inc. above	300	375	425	450	—
1925/4	668,000	300	375	425	450	—
1925 MFDELLIN	Inc. above	300	375	425	450	—
Note: Wide or narrow date						
1925 MFDFLLIN	Inc. above	300	375	425	450	—
Note: Wide or narrow date						
1926	383,000	300	375	425	450	—
1926 MFDFLLIN	Inc. above	300	375	425	450	—
1926 MFDFLLIN	Inc. above	300	375	425	450	—
Note: With large 6 in date						
1927 MFDFLLIN	365,000	300	375	425	450	—
Note: Wide or narrow date						
1928 MFDFLLIN	314,000	300	375	425	450	—
Note: Narrow or wide date with large or normal 2						
1929 MFDFLLIN	321,000	300	375	425	450	—
Note: Narrow or wide date						
1930 MFDFLLIN	502,000	300	375	425	450	—
Note: Varieties known with aligned date or dropped 3 in date						

KM# 230 5 PESOS

Copper-Nickel, 34 mm. **Subject:** International Eucharistic Congress **Obv:** Denomination within wheat stalks, date below **Rev:** Design within circle, within square, at center

Date	Mintage	VF20	XF40	MS60	MS63	MS65
1968 B	660,000	0.25	0.50	0.80	2.00	3.00

KM# 247 5 PESOS

Nickel Clad Steel, 30 mm. **Subject:** 6th Pan-American Games in Cali **Obv:** Torches flank denomination at center, date below **Rev:** Games logo

Date	Mintage	VF20	XF40	MS60	MS63	MS65
1971	2,000,000	0.25	0.50	0.75	1.75	2.50

KM# 268 5 PESOS

Bronze, 26.3 mm. **Obv:** Seated figure right **Rev:** Denomination and buildings

Date	Mintage	VF20	XF40	MS60	MS63	MS65
1980	146,268,000	0.25	0.50	0.75	1.50	2.00
1.981	9,148,000	0.25	0.50	0.75	1.50	2.00
1.982	—	0.25	0.50	1.00	2.00	3.00
1983	84,107,000	0.25	0.50	0.75	1.50	2.00
1985	—	0.25	0.50	0.75	1.50	2.00
1986	14,700,000	0.25	0.50	0.75	1.50	2.00
1987	20,214,040	0.25	0.50	0.75	1.50	2.00
1988 Small date	45,003,894	0.25	0.50	0.75	1.50	2.00
1988 Large inverted date	Inc. above	0.25	0.50	0.75	1.50	2.00
1989	106,825,973	0.25	0.50	0.75	1.50	2.00

KM# 280 5 PESOS

2.60 g., Aluminum-Bronze, 17.3 mm. **Obv:** Arms above date **Rev:** Denomination within wreath **Edge:** Reeded **Note:** Varieties exist, such as 1989 where some have 72 beads on the obverse and reverse and some have 66 beads.

Date	Mintage	VF20	XF40	MS60	MS63	MS65
1989	—	—	—	0.25	0.50	0.75
Note: Included with KM#268, 1989.						
1990	100,700,000	—	—	0.25	0.50	0.75
1991	60,000,000	—	—	0.25	0.50	0.75
1992	20,000,000	—	—	0.20	0.35	0.65
1993	40,000,000	—	—	0.20	0.35	0.65

KM# 202 10 PESOS

15.98 g., 0.917 Gold 0.471 oz. AGW **Obv:** Head of Simon Bolivar right, date below **Rev:** Arms and denomination

Date	Mintage	VF20	XF40	MS60	MS63	MS65
1919	101,000	600	700	850	950	—
1924 B	55,000	600	700	850	950	—
Note: Varieties with aligned date and dropped 4 in date						

KM# 270 10 PESOS

10.00 g., Copper-Nickel-Zinc, 28.1 mm. **Obv:** Figure on horseback and standing, date at left **Rev:** Map showing San Andreas Island and Providencia, denomination below **Note:** Date varieties exist.

Date	Mintage	VF20	XF40	MS60	MS63	MS65
1.981	104,554,000	—	0.15	0.25	0.50	1.25
1.982	83,605,000	—	0.15	0.25	0.50	1.25
1983	104,051,000	—	0.15	0.25	0.50	1.25
1985	80,000,000	—	0.15	0.25	0.50	1.25
1988	50,704,091	—	0.15	0.25	0.50	1.25
1989	184,206,150	—	0.15	0.25	0.50	1.25

KM# 281.1 10 PESOS

3.30 g., Copper-Nickel-Zinc, 18.75 mm. **Obv:** Flagged arms, date below **Rev:** Denomination within wreath, wide 10 (5mm) - wreath nearly touches beads in rim **Edge:** Reeded **Note:** Varieties exist.

Date	Mintage	VF20	XF40	MS60	MS63	MS65
1989	—	—	—	0.25	0.50	0.75
Note: Included with KM#270, 1989						
1990	91,300,000	—	—	0.25	0.50	0.75
1991	60,000,000	—	—	0.25	0.50	0.75
1992	47,256,100	—	—	0.25	0.50	0.75
1993	15,000,000	—	—	0.25	0.50	0.75
1994	20,000,000	—	—	0.25	0.50	0.75

KM# 281.2 10 PESOS

3.30 g., Copper-Nickel-Zinc, 18.75 mm. **Obv:** Flagged arms, date below **Rev:** Narrow 10 (4.5mm) - wreath is 1 mm away from beads in rim

Date	Mintage	VF20	XF40	MS60	MS63	MS65
1993	—	—	—	1.50	3.00	5.00
Note: Included with KM#281.1, 1993.						
1994	—	—	—	1.50	3.00	5.00
Note: Included with KM#281.1, 1994.						

KM# 271 20 PESOS

6.10 g., Aluminum-Bronze, 25 mm. **Obv:** Vase, date below **Rev:** Denomination within wreath **Note:** 1985 and 1988 coins exist with large and small dates.

Date	Mintage	VF20	XF40	MS60	MS63	MS65
1982	—	—	0.15	0.20	0.30	0.50
1984	64,066,000	—	0.15	0.20	0.30	0.50
1985	100,690,000	—	0.15	0.20	0.30	0.50
1986	18,300,000	—	0.15	0.20	0.30	0.50
1987	70,000,000	—	0.15	0.20	0.30	0.50
1988	72,002,490	—	0.15	0.20	0.30	0.50
1989	—	—	0.15	0.20	0.30	0.50
Note: Included with KM#282.1, 1989.						

KM# 282.1 20 PESOS

3.60 g., Aluminum-Bronze, 20.25 mm. **Obv:** Flagged arms above date, 72 beads circle around the rim **Rev:** Denomination within wreath **Edge:** Reeded **Note:** Varieties exist.

Date	Mintage	VF20	XF40	MS60	MS63	MS65
1989	90,062,949	—	—	0.25	0.50	0.75
1990	130,000,000	—	—	0.25	0.50	0.75
1991	167,432,500	—	—	0.25	0.50	0.75
1992	132,600,000	—	—	0.25	0.50	0.75
1993	19,312,500	—	—	0.25	0.50	0.75
1994	95,000,000	—	—	0.25	0.50	0.75

KM# 282.2 20 PESOS

3.60 g., Aluminum-Bronze, 20.25 mm. **Obv:** Flagged arms, 68 beads circle around the rim **Rev:** Denomination within wreath

Date	Mintage	VF20	XF40	MS60	MS63	MS65
1994	—	—	—	0.25	0.50	0.75
Note: Included with KM#282.1, 1994.						

KM# 272 50 PESOS

8.40 g., Copper-Nickel, 26.8 mm. **Subject:** National Constitution **Obv:** Arms above denomination, sprigs flank date below **Rev:** Building, stars below, within circle

Date	Mintage	VF20	XF40	MS60	MS63	MS65
1986	14,900,000	—	—	0.75	1.25	1.50
1987 Large date	40,042,000	—	—	0.75	1.25	1.50
1988 Small date	100,002,000	—	—	0.75	1.25	1.50
1989	80,696,450	—	—	0.75	1.25	1.50

KM# 283.1 50 PESOS
4.50 g., Copper-Nickel-Zinc, 21.8 mm. **Obv:** Flagged arms above date **Rev:** Denomination within wreath, 66 beads circle around rim **Edge:** Reeded **Note:** Varieties exist.

Date	Mintage	VF20	XF40	MS60	MS63	MS65
1989	—	—	0.30	0.50	0.75	1.00
Note: Included with KM#272, 1989.						
1990	120,000,000	—	0.30	0.50	0.75	1.00
1991	150,000,000	—	0.30	0.50	0.75	1.00
1992	50,000,000	—	0.30	0.50	0.75	1.00
1993	35,000,000	—	0.30	0.50	0.75	1.00

KM# 283.2 50 PESOS
4.60 g., Copper-Nickel-Zinc, 21.8 mm. **Obv:** National arms, date below **Rev:** Denomination within wreath, 72 beads circle around rim **Edge:** Reeded

Date	Mintage	VF20	XF40	MS60	MS63	MS65
1989	—	—	0.30	0.50	0.75	1.00
Note: Included with KM#272, 1989						
1990	—	—	0.30	0.50	0.75	1.00
Note: Included with KM#283.1, 1990.						
1994	155,000,000	—	0.30	0.50	0.75	1.00

KM# 231 100 PESOS
4.30 g., 0.900 Gold 0.1244 oz. AGW **Subject:** International Eucharistic Congress **Obv:** Arms divide denomination **Rev:** Bust of Pope Paul VI left and Bogota's Cathedral at left, date below

Date	Mintage	VF20	XF40	MS60	MS63	MS65
1968	8,000	PF65 250	PF67 275			
1968	108,000	—	—	225	245	—

KM# 238 100 PESOS
4.30 g., 0.900 Gold 0.1244 oz. AGW **Subject:** Battle of Boyaca - Joachim Paris **Obv:** Bust of Bolivar 3/4 facing **Rev:** Bust of Paris 3/4 facing, dates above, denomination below

Date	Mintage	VF20	XF40	MS60	MS63	MS65
ND-1969 B	6,000	PF65 250	PF67 275			
ND-1969 NI	—	PF65 250	PF67 275			

KM# 248 100 PESOS
4.30 g., 0.900 Gold 0.1244 oz. AGW **Subject:** 6th Pan-American Games **Obv:** Games logo, date below **Rev:** Javelin thrower within circle, denomination below, 3/4 circle of athletes surround

Date	Mintage	VF20	XF40	MS60	MS63	MS65
1971	6,000	PF65 250	PF67 275			

KM# 285.1 100 PESOS
5.31 g., Aluminum-Bronze, 23 mm. **Obv:** Flagged arms above date **Rev:** Denomination within wreath, numerals 4.5mm tall **Edge:** Segmented reeded and lettered **Edge Lettering:** CIEN PESOS (twice)

Date	Mintage	VF20	XF40	MS60	MS63	MS65
1992	50,000,000	—	—	0.45	0.65	1.25
1993	180,500,000	—	—	0.45	0.65	1.25
1994	255,000,000	—	—	0.45	0.65	1.25

KM# 285.2 100 PESOS
5.31 g., Aluminum-Bronze, 23 mm. **Obv:** Flagged arms above date **Rev:** Denomination within wreath, numerals 6mm tall **Edge:** Segmented reeding and lettered **Edge Lettering:** CIEN PESOS (twice) **Note:** Edge varieties exist.

Date	Mintage	VF20	XF40	MS60	MS63	MS65
1994	—	—	0.50	0.75	1.00	1.50
Note: Included with KM#285.1, 1994.						
1995	180,000,000	—	0.50	0.75	1.00	1.50

KM# 232 200 PESOS
8.60 g., 0.900 Gold 0.2488 oz. AGW **Subject:** International Eucharistic Congress **Obv:** Bust of Pope Paul VI left and Bogota's Cathedral at left, date below **Rev:** Arms divide denomination

Date	Mintage	VF20	XF40	MS60	MS63	MS65
1968	108,000	—	—	—	—	450
1968	8,000	PF65 460	PF67 485			

KM# 239 200 PESOS
8.60 g., 0.900 Gold 0.2488 oz. AGW **Subject:** Battle of Boyaca - Carlos Soublette **Obv:** Bust of Bolivar 3/4 facing **Rev:** Bust of Soublette 3/4 facing, dates above, denomination below

Date	Mintage	VF20	XF40	MS60	MS63	MS65
1969 B	6,000	PF65 460	PF67 485			
1969 NI	Inc. above	PF65 460	PF67 485			

KM# 249 200 PESOS
8.60 g., 0.900 Gold 0.2488 oz. AGW **Subject:** 6th Pan-American Games in Cali **Obv:** Games logo, date below **Rev:** Runner within circle, denomination below, 3/4 circle of athletes surround

Date	Mintage	VF20	XF40	MS60	MS63	MS65
1971	6,000	PF65 460	PF67 485			

KM# 287 200 PESOS
7.08 g., Copper-Nickel-Zinc, 24.4 mm. **Obv:** Denomination within lined circle, date below **Rev:** Quimbaya artwork **Edge Lettering:** MOTIVO QUIMBAYA - 200 PESOS

Date	Mintage	VF20	XF40	MS60	MS63	MS65
1994	115,000,000	—	0.50	0.75	1.00	1.50
1995	150,000,000	—	0.50	0.75	1.00	1.50
1996	80,000,000	—	0.50	0.75	1.00	1.50
1997	37,000,000	—	0.50	0.75	1.00	1.50

KM# 233 300 PESOS
12.90 g., 0.900 Gold 0.3733 oz. AGW **Subject:** International Eucharistic Congress **Obv:** Bust of Pope Paul VI 3/4 left and Bogota's Cathedral at left, date below **Rev:** Arms above denomination

Date	Mintage	VF20	XF40	MS60	MS63	MS65
1968	62,000	—	—	—	650	—
1968	8,000	PF65 675	PF67 700			

KM# 240 300 PESOS
12.90 g., 0.900 Gold 0.3733 oz. AGW **Subject:** Battle of Boyaca - Jose Anzoategui **Obv:** Bust of Bolivar 3/4 facing **Rev:** Bust of Anzoategui 3/4 facing, dates above, denomination below

Date	Mintage	VF20	XF40	MS60	MS63	MS65
1969 B	Inc. above	PF65 700	PF67 750			
1969 NI	6,000	PF65 700	PF67 750			

KM# 250 300 PESOS
12.90 g., 0.900 Gold 0.3733 oz. AGW **Subject:** 6th Pan-American Games **Obv:** Games logo, date below **Rev:** Two figures within circle, denomination below, 3/4 circle of athletes surround

Date	Mintage	VF20	XF40	MS60	MS63	MS65
1971	6,000	PF65 700	PF67 750			

KM# 234 500 PESOS
21.50 g., 0.900 Gold 0.6221 oz. AGW **Subject:** International Eucharistic Congress **Obv:** Bust of Pope Paul VI 3/4 left and Bogota's Cathedral left, date below **Rev:** Arms above denomination

Date	Mintage	VF20	XF40	MS60	MS63	MS65
1968	8,000	PF65 1,200	PF67 1,250			
1968	14,000	—	—	—	1,150	—

KM# 241 500 PESOS
21.50 g., 0.900 Gold 0.6221 oz. AGW **Subject:** Battle of Boyaca **Obv:** Bust of Simon Bolivar 3/4 facing **Rev:** Bust of Juan Jose Rondon 3/4 facing, dates above, denomination below

Date	Mintage	VF20	XF40	MS60	MS63	MS65
ND-1969 B	6,000	PF65 1,200	PF67 1,250			
ND-1969 NI	Inc. above	PF65 1,200	PF67 1,250			

KM# 251 500 PESOS

21.50 g., 0.900 Gold 0.6221 oz. AGW **Subject:** 6th Pan-American Games in Cali **Obv:** Games logo, date below **Rev:** Two figures within circle, denomination below, 3/4 circle of athletes surround

Date	Mintage	VF20	XF40	MS60	MS63	MS65
1971	6,000	PF65 1,200	PF67 1,250			

KM# 264 500 PESOS

28.28 g., 0.925 Silver 0.841 oz. ASW **Subject:** Conservation **Obv:** Tomas Cipriano de Mosquera bust left, dates below **Rev:** Orinoco Crocodile, denomination below

Date	Mintage	VF20	XF40	MS60	MS63	MS65
1978	2,678	—	—	—	35.00	42.00
1978	3,233	PF65 40.00	PF67 45.00			
1979	—	PF65 40.00	PF67 45.00			

KM# 286 500 PESOS

7.14 g., Bi-Metallic Aluminum-Bronze center in Copper-Zinc-Nickel ring, 23.7 mm. **Obv:** Guacari tree within circle **Rev:** Denomination within circle, date below **Edge:** Segmented reeding

Date	Mintage	VF20	XF40	MS60	MS63	MS65
1993	15,642,000	—	0.75	1.25	2.00	3.00
1994	90,000,000	—	0.75	1.25	2.00	3.00
1995	90,000,000	—	0.75	1.25	2.00	3.00
1996	55,000,000	—	0.75	1.25	2.00	3.00
1997	50,000,000	—	0.75	1.25	2.00	3.00

KM# 265 750 PESOS

35.00 g., 0.925 Silver 1.0409 oz. ASW **Subject:** Conservation **Obv:** Tomas Cipriano de Mosquera bust left **Rev:** Chestnut-bellied hummingbird, denomination below

Date	Mintage	VF20	XF40	MS60	MS63	MS65
1978	2,656	—	—	—	42.00	45.00
1978	3,100	PF65 40.00	PF67 45.00			
1979	—	PF65 42.00	PF67 50.00			

KM# 254 1000 PESOS

4.30 g., 0.900 Gold 0.1244 oz. AGW **Subject:** 100th Anniversary - Birth of Guillermo Valencia **Obv:** Shield above denomination **Rev:** Head right

Date	Mintage	VF20	XF40	MS60	MS63	MS65
1973	10,003	PF65 225	PF67 245			

KM# 259 1000 PESOS

4.30 g., 0.900 Gold 0.1244 oz. AGW **Subject:** 450th Anniversary - City of Santa Marta **Obv:** Bust 3/4 right, denomination below **Rev:** Symbol at center, dates below

Date	Mintage	VF20	XF40	MS60	MS63	MS65
ND-1975	2,500	PF65 245	PF67 275			

KM# 260 1000 PESOS

4.30 g., 0.900 Gold 0.1244 oz. AGW **Subject:** Tricentennial - City of Medellin **Obv:** City gate on shield, sprays flank, dates below **Rev:** Symbol at center, denomination below **Shape:** Square

Date	Mintage	VF20	XF40	MS60	MS63	MS65
ND-1975	4,000	PF65 240	PF67 265			

KM# 288 1000 PESOS

7.30 g., Aluminum-Bronze, 21.67 mm. **Obv:** Value and date **Rev:** Filagreed design **Edge:** Reeded and lettered **Edge Lettering:** CULTURA SINU MIL PESOS

Date	Mintage	VF20	XF40	MS60	MS63	MS65
1996	60,000,000	—	—	1.25	2.25	3.00
1997	35,000,000	—	—	1.25	2.25	3.00
1998	85,300,000	—	—	1.25	2.25	3.00

KM# 235 1500 PESOS

64.50 g., 0.900 Gold 1.8663 oz. AGW **Subject:** International Eucharistic Congress **Obv:** Pope's bust 3/4 left, cathedral at left **Rev:** Arms above denomination

Date	Mintage	VF20	XF40	MS60	MS63	MS65
1968	5,722	—	—	—	—	3,200
1968	8,000	PF65 3,000	PF67 3,250			

KM# 242 1500 PESOS

64.50 g., 0.900 Gold 1.8663 oz. AGW **Subject:** Battle of Boyaca **Obv:** Armored bust of Bolivar 3/4 facing **Rev:** Head of Santander right, arms divide dates above, denomination below

Date	Mintage	VF20	XF40	MS60	MS63	MS65
ND-1969 B	6,000	PF65 3,000	PF67 3,250			
ND-1969 NI	Inc. above	PF65 3,000	PF67 3,250			

KM# 252 1500 PESOS

64.50 g., 0.900 Gold 1.8663 oz. AGW **Subject:** 6th Pan-American Games **Obv:** Games logo, date below **Rev:** Symbols on raft within circle, denomination below, 3/4 circle of athletes surrounds

Date	Mintage	VF20	XF40	MS60	MS63	MS65
1971	6,000	PF65 3,000	PF67 3,250			

KM# 255 1500 PESOS

19.10 g., 0.900 Gold 0.5527 oz. AGW **Subject:** 50th Anniversary - Gold Museum of Central Bank of Bogota **Rev:** Pre-Columbian urn made by Chibcha Indians

Date	Mintage	VF20	XF40	MS60	MS63	MS65
ND-1973	50,000	PF65 950	PF67 1,000			

KM# 256 1500 PESOS
8.60 g., 0.900 Gold 0.2488 oz. AGW **Subject:** Guillermo Valencia, 100th Anniversary of Birth **Obv:** Shield **Rev:** Bust right

Date	Mintage	VF20	XF40	MS60	MS63	MS65
1973	5,000	PF65 425	PF67 450			

KM# 257 2000 PESOS
12.90 g., 0.900 Gold 0.3733 oz. AGW **Subject:** 100th Anniversary - Birth of Guillermo Valencia **Obv:** Shield above denomination, date below **Rev:** Bust right, two dates below

Date	Mintage	VF20	XF40	MS60	MS63	MS65
1973	5,003	PF65 650	PF67 700			

KM# 261 2000 PESOS
8.60 g., 0.900 Gold 0.2488 oz. AGW **Subject:** 450th Anniversary - City of Santa Marta **Obv:** Bust 3/4 right, denomination below **Rev:** Symbol, dates below

Date	Mintage	VF20	XF40	MS60	MS63	MS65
ND-1975	2,500	PF65 450	PF67 475			

KM# 262 2000 PESOS
8.60 g., 0.900 Gold 0.2488 oz. AGW **Subject:** Tricentennial - City of Medellin **Obv:** City gate on shield, sprays flank, two dates below **Rev:** Symbol at center, denomination below **Shape:** Square

Date	Mintage	VF20	XF40	MS60	MS63	MS65
ND-1975	4,000	PF65 425	PF67 450			

KM# 293 5000 PESOS
15.30 g., Nickel **Subject:** 50th Anniversary - Organization of American States **Obv:** Denomination, date below **Rev:** Circle of flags

Date	Mintage	VF20	XF40	MS60	MS63	MS65
1998	50,000	—	—	1.50	4.00	7.50

Note: Minted in 1999

KM# 284 10000 PESOS
27.00 g., 0.925 Silver 0.803 oz. ASW, 40 mm. **Series:** Ibero - American **Subject:** Bogota Mint **Obv:** Arms at center, denomination below, shields surround **Obv. Legend:** ENCUENTRO DE DOS MONDOS 1992 **Rev:** Old Bogota Mint building **Edge:** Reeded

Date	Mintage	VF20	XF40	MS60	MS63	MS65
1991	20,000	PF65 50.00	PF67 55.00			

KM# 266 15000 PESOS
33.44 g., 0.900 Gold 0.9675 oz. AGW **Subject:** Conservation **Obv:** Armored bust left **Rev:** Ocelot left, denomination below

Date	Mintage	VF20	XF40	MS60	MS63	MS65
1978	490	—	—	—	1,650	1,700
1978	148	PF65 2,550	PF67 2,750			

KM# 276 15000 PESOS
17.29 g., 0.900 Gold 0.5003 oz. AGW **Subject:** 150th Anniversary - Death of Antonio Jose De Sucre **Obv:** Armored bust 3/4 left divides dates **Rev:** Cornucopias enclose symbol at center, denomination below

Date	Mintage	VF20	XF40	MS60	MS63	MS65
1980	250	PF65 875	PF67 925			

KM# 278 15000 PESOS
17.29 g., 0.900 Gold 0.5003 oz. AGW **Subject:** 150th Anniversary - Death of Jose Maria Cordova **Obv:** Bust 3/4 facing, divides dates **Rev:** Cornucopias enclose symbol at center, denomination below

Date	Mintage	VF20	XF40	MS60	MS63	MS65
1980	250	PF65 875	PF67 925			

KM# 289 20000 PESOS
8.64 g., 0.900 Gold 0.250 oz. AGW **Subject:** Birth Centennial **Obv:** Bust of Alfonso Lopez-Pumarejo facing divides dates **Rev:** Building, denomination below

Date	Mintage	VF20	XF40	MS60	MS63	MS65
ND-1986	1,351	PF65 425	PF67 450			

KM# 269 30000 PESOS
34.58 g., 0.900 Gold 1.0006 oz. AGW **Subject:** Death of Bolivar **Obv:** Funeral scene, dates below **Rev:** Cornucopias flank symbol at center, denomination below

Date	Mintage	VF20	XF40	MS60	MS63	MS65
1980	500	PF65 1,600	PF67 1,700			

KM# 273 35000 PESOS
8.64 g., 0.900 Gold 0.250 oz. AGW **Subject:** 100th Anniversary - Birth of President Santos **Obv:** Bust facing divides dates **Rev:** Inscription within wreath

Date	Mintage	VF20	XF40	MS60	MS63	MS65
ND-1988	900	PF65 425	PF67 450			

KM# 292 40000 PESOS
17.28 g., 0.900 Gold 0.500 oz. AGW **Subject:** Centennial - Birthday of Alfonso Lopez-Pumarejo **Obv:** Bust facing divides dates **Rev:** Building, denomination below

Date	Mintage	VF20	XF40	MS60	MS63	MS65
ND-1986	1,351	PF65 875	PF67 900			

KM# 290 50000 PESOS
8.64 g., 0.900 Gold 0.250 oz. AGW **Subject:** Centennial - Birthday of Mariano Ospina P **Obv:** Portrait facing divides dates **Rev:** Inscription within wreath

Date	Mintage	VF20	XF40	MS60	MS63	MS65
ND-1991	900	PF65 400	PF67 425			

KM# 277 70000 PESOS
17.28 g., 0.900 Gold 0.500 oz. AGW **Subject:** 100th Anniversary - Birth of President Santos **Obv:** Bust 3/4 facing divides dates **Rev:** Inscription within wreath

Date	Mintage	VF20	XF40	MS60	MS63	MS65
ND-1988	600	PF65 875	PF67 925			

KM# 291 100000 PESOS
17.28 g., 0.900 Gold 0.500 oz. AGW **Subject:** Centennial - Birthday of Mariano Ospina P **Obv:** Head facing divides dates **Rev:** Inscription within wreath

Date	Mintage	VF20	XF40	MS60	MS63	MS65
ND-1991	600	PF65 825	PF67 875			

INFLATIONARY COINAGE

Beginning about 1886, Colombia fell victim to rampant printing press inflation and a debased, vanishing coinage. Left without solid backing, the peso gradually fell until it was worth 1 centavo of the old silver-based currency. The copper-nickel 1, 2, and 5 peso p/m coins reflected this inflation, and later circulated at par with the newer 1, 2, and 5 centavo coins.

P/M - Papel Moneda

KM# A279 PESO (Papel Moneda)
2.00 g., Copper-Nickel, 17 mm. **Obv:** Liberty head right **Rev:** Denomination, p/m below, within wreath

Date	Mintage	F12	VF20	XF40	MS60	MS63
1907 AM	2,860,000	1.25	3.50	7.00	14.00	22.50
1907 AM	—	PF63 100	PF65 150			
1910 AM	1,205,000	3.50	7.00	10.00	17.50	25.00
1911 AM	2,816,000	2.75	6.00	9.00	12.00	20.00
1912 AM	6,094,000	2.00	5.00	7.00	12.00	18.50
1912 H Without crossbar	2,000,000	1.50	3.00	5.00	12.50	22.00
1912 H With crossbar	Inc. above	1.50	3.00	5.00	12.50	22.00
1913 AM	306,000	5.00	8.00	12.00	22.50	50.00
1914 AM	552,000	6.00	9.00	13.00	18.50	42.50
1916/4 AM	234,000	11.00	15.00	20.00	35.00	65.00
1916 AM	Inc. above	11.00	15.00	20.00	35.00	65.00

KM# B279 2 PESOS (Papel Moneda)
3.00 g., Copper-Nickel, 19 mm. **Obv:** Liberty head right, date below **Rev:** Denomination, p/m below, within wreath **Note:** Date varieties exist.

Date	Mintage	F12	VF20	XF40	MS60	MS63
1907 AM	4,161,000	1.75	3.75	8.00	16.00	27.00
1907 AM	—	PF63 100	PF65 150			
1910/07 AM	1,189,000	7.50	13.50	16.50	25.00	42.50
1910 AM	Inc. above	6.75	12.50	18.00	30.00	50.00
1914 AM	1,000,000	4.50	12.00	15.00	22.50	40.00

KM# 279 5 PESOS (Papel Moneda)
4.00 g., Copper-Nickel, 21 mm. **Obv:** Liberty head right, date below **Rev:** Denomination, p/m below, within wreath

Date	Mintage	VF20	XF40	MS60	MS63	MS65
1907 AM	6,143,000	7.50	12.50	22.50	40.00	60.00
1907 AM	—	PF63 100	PF65 150			
1909 AM	4,000,000	8.50	16.00	25.00	45.00	65.00
1912 H	2,000,000	10.00	20.00	30.00	60.00	75.00
1912 AM	1,897,000	10.00	20.00	30.00	60.00	75.00
1913 AM	Inc. above	10.00	22.00	35.00	65.00	80.00
1914 AM	Inc. above	20.00	35.00	50.00	75.00	90.00

LEPROSARIUM COINAGE

Special coinage for use in the three government leper colonies of Agua de Dios, Cano de Lord, and Contratacion. The hospitals were closed in the late 1950s and patients were allowed to exchange these special coins for regular currency at any bank.

Bogota Mint

KM# L9 CENTAVO
2.00 g., Copper-Nickel, 17 mm. **Obv:** LAZARETO on cross with circles at quarters, date below **Rev:** Denomination within wreath

Date	Mintage	G4	VG8	F12	VF20	XF40
1921 RH	300,000	0.75	1.50	3.50	7.00	10.00

KM# L10 2 CENTAVOS
3.00 g., Copper-Nickel, 18.89 mm. **Obv:** LAZARETO on cross with circles at quarters, date below **Rev:** Denomination within wreath

Date	Mintage	G4	VG8	F12	VF20	XF40
1921 RH	350,000	0.50	0.65	2.00	6.75	10.00

KM# L1 2-1/2 CENTAVOS
1.30 g., Brass **Obv:** Denomination within circle, date below **Rev:** LAZARETO on cross with circles at quarters

Date	Mintage	G4	VG8	F12	VF20	XF40
1901 Rare	20,000	—	—	—	—	3,500

Note: Only a few examples of this type are currently known to have survived.

KM# L2 5 CENTAVOS
Brass **Obv:** Denomination within circle **Rev:** LAZARETO on cross with circles at quarters, date below **Note:** Weight varies: 2.3-2.55 g.

Date	Mintage	G4	VG8	F12	VF20	XF40
1901 B	15,000	6.00	12.50	22.00	45.00	60.00

KM# L11 5 CENTAVOS
4.00 g., Copper-Nickel, 22.88 mm. **Obv:** LAZARETO on cross with circles at quarters, date below **Rev:** Denomination within wreath, large 5

Date	Mintage	G4	VG8	F12	VF20	XF40
1921 H	200,000	1.00	2.00	4.50	9.00	15.00

KM# L3 10 CENTAVOS
Brass **Obv:** Denomination above date **Rev:** LAZARETO on cross with circles at quarters **Note:** Weight varies: 3.3-3.69 g.

Date	Mintage	G4	VG8	F12	VF20	XF40
1901 B	10,000	10.00	15.00	28.00	50.00	75.00

KM# L12 10 CENTAVOS
5.10 g., Copper-Nickel, 22.89 mm. **Obv:** LAZARETO on cross with circles at quarters, date below **Rev:** Denomination within wreath

Date	Mintage	G4	VG8	F12	VF20	XF40
1921 RH	200,000	1.00	2.00	4.50	9.00	15.00

KM# L4 20 CENTAVOS
Brass **Obv:** LAZARETO on cross with circles at quarters, date below **Rev:** Denomination above arms **Note:** Weight varies: 4.85-5.1 g.

Date	Mintage	G4	VG8	F12	VF20	XF40
1901 B	30,000	10.00	15.00	28.00	50.00	75.00

KM# L5 50 CENTAVOS
Brass **Obv:** LAZARETO on cross with circles at quarters, date below **Rev:** Denomination above arms **Note:** Weight varies: 12-12.4 g.

Date	Mintage	G4	VG8	F12	VF20	XF40
1901 B	26,000	13.50	20.00	35.00	75.00	100

KM# L5a 50 CENTAVOS
Copper **Obv:** LAZARETO on cross with circles at quarters, date below **Rev:** Denomination above arms **Note:** Weight varies: 12-12.4 g.

Date	Mintage	G4	VG8	F12	VF20	XF40
1901 2 known	—	—	—	—	—	—

KM# L13 50 CENTAVOS
9.80 g., Copper-Nickel, 30 mm.

Date	Mintage	G4	VG8	F12	VF20	XF40
1921 RH	120,000	2.00	4.00	7.50	16.00	25.00

KM# L14 50 CENTAVOS
9.80 g., Brass

Date	Mintage	G4	VG8	F12	VF20	XF40
1928 RH	50,000	2.00	4.50	9.00	18.00	30.00

KM# L14a 50 CENTAVOS
9.80 g., Copper

Date	Mintage	G4	VG8	F12	VF20	XF40
1928 Proof; Rare	Inc. above	—	—	—	—	—

INFLATIONARY LEPROSARIUM COINAGE

1 Peso was equal in value to 1 Centavo of the old silver currency. It later circulated at par with the newer 1 Centavo coins.

P/M - Papel Moneda

KM# L6 PESO (Papel Moneda)
Copper-Nickel, 18 mm. **Obv:** Denomination, P.M., below, within wreath **Rev:** LAZARETO within circle **Note:** Weight varies: 2.45-2.65 g.

Date	Mintage	G4	VG8	F12	VF20	XF40
1907/0	792,000	—	—	—	—	—
1907	Inc. above	5.00	10.00	20.00	45.00	—

KM# L7 5 PESOS (Papel Moneda)
4.75 g., Copper-Nickel, 23 mm.

Date	Mintage	G4	VG8	F12	VF20	XF40
1907	159,000	30.00	60.00	100	200	—

KM# L8 10 PESOS (Papal Moneda)
9.50 g., Copper-Nickel, 28 mm.

Date	Mintage	G4	VG8	F12	VF20	XF40
1907	129,000	40.00	75.00	125	250	—

PROVINCE OF SANTANDER

CIVIL WAR COINAGE

KM# A1 10 CENTAVOS
0.50 g., Brass **Obv:** Numeric denomination above 'C' **Note:** Uniface.

Date	Mintage	VG8	F12	VF20	XF40	MS60
ND-1902	—	10.00	18.50	28.50	60.00	100

KM# A2 20 CENTAVOS
0.70 g., Brass **Obv:** Numeric denomination within "C" **Note:** Uniface.

Date	Mintage	VG8	F12	VF20	XF40	MS60
1902	—	18.00	35.00	55.00	80.00	125

KM# A3 50 CENTAVOS
1.45 g., Brass **Obv:** Numeric denomination within "C" **Note:** Uniface. Varieties exist in shape of "0" in denomination: a fully rounded zero commands double the listed values. Later 20th Century counterfeits are known.

Date	Mintage	VG8	F12	VF20	XF40	MS60
1902	—	2.00	4.00	7.50	16.50	30.00

PATTERNS

Including off metal strikes

KM#	Date	Mintage	Identification	Mkt Val
Pn84	1909	—	5 Centavos. Copper-Nickel.	—
Pn85	1913	—	5 Decimos. Thin Bolivar head.	—
Pn86	1913	—	5 Decimos. Thin Bolivar head, canceled obverse die.	—
Pn87	1913	—	2-1/2 Pesos. Gold. ENSAYO; KM#194.	—
Pn88	1913	—	5 Pesos. Gold. ENSAYO; KM#195.	—
Pn89	1915	—	2-1/2 Pesos. Gold. ENSAYO; KM#194.	—
Pn90	1917	—	5 Centavos. Copper-Nickel. PAZ on cap band; otherwise as KM#199.	—
Pn91	1917	—	5 Centavos. Copper-Nickel. KM#199.	—
Pn92	1923	—	2-1/2 Pesos. Gold. ENSAYO; KM#203.	6,000
Pn93	1923	—	2-1/2 Pesos. Silver. ESSAI; KM#203.	—
Pn94	1923	—	5 Pesos. Gold. ENSAYO, KM#204.	—
Pn95	1923	—	5 Pesos. Silver. ESSAI; KM#204.	—
Pn96	1941	—	5 Centavos. Copper-Nickel.	—
Pn97	1946	—	50 Centavos. Copper-Nickel. 10-sided planchet.	—
Pn98	1946	—	50 Centavos. 0.500. Silver. Reeded.	—
Pn99	1950	—	20 Centavos. 0.500. Silver.	200
Pn100	1950	—	50 Centavos. 0.900. Silver. Bolivar military bust, condor over large shield.	200
Pn101	1950	—	50 Centavos. 0.900. Silver. Condor over small shield.	200
Pn102	1950	—	50 Centavos. 0.900. Silver.	—
Pn103	1951	—	50 Centavos. Silver.	200
Pn104	1952	—	50 Centavos. Silver.	200
PnA105	1956	—	20 Centavos. Copper-Nickel. Reeded edge.	—
Pn105	1956	—	50 Centavos. Copper-Nickel.	225
Pn106	1956	—	Peso. Gold.	—
Pn107	1957	—	50 Centavos. Copper-Nickel.	225
Pn108	1963	—	Peso. Copper-Nickel. Prev. KM#Pn57.	225
Pn109	1968	—	Peso. Copper-Nickel. Prev. KM#Pn58.	225
Pn110	1969	—	50 Centavos. Copper-Nickel. Prev. KM#Pn59.	145
Pn111	1969	—	50 Centavos. Copper-Nickel. Prev. KM#Pn60.	145
Pn112	1969	—	Peso. Copper-Nickel. Prev. KM#Pn61.	225
Pn113	1969	—	Peso. Copper-Nickel. Prev. KM#Pn62.	225
Pn114	1969	—	Peso. Copper-Nickel. Prev. KM#Pn63.	225
Pn115	1970	—	Centavo. Aluminum. Prev. KM#Pn64.	75.00
Pn116	1970	—	5 Centavos. Aluminum. Prev. KM#Pn65.	80.00
Pn117	1971	—	10 Centavos. Aluminum. Prev. KM#Pn66.	85.00
Pn118	1971	—	50 Centavos. Copper-Nickel. Prev. KM#Pn67.	125
Pn119	1974	—	Peso. Silver. Prev. KM#Pn68.	275
Pn120	1979	—	5 Pesos. Copper-Nickel. Inverted date. Prev. KM#Pn69.	—

PIEDFORT

KM#	Date	Mintage	Identification	Mkt Val
P3	1913	—	50 Centavos. 0.900. Silver. Ensayo.	2,500
P4	1915	—	10 Centavos. 0.900. Silver. Ensayo.	—
P5	1915	—	20 Centavos. 0.900. Silver. Ensayo.	—

TRIAL STRIKES

KM#	Date	Mintage	Identification	Mkt Val
TS15	1911	—	10 Centavos. Lead. Uniface.	—
TS16	1911	—	20 Centavos. Lead. Uniface.	—
TS14	ND (1914)	—	50 Centavos. Lead.	—
TS17	1946	—	20 Centavos. Nickel.	—
TS18	1946	—	20 Centavos. Nickel.	—

PROOF SETS

KM#	Date	Mintage	Identification	Issue Price	Mkt Val
PS1	1968 (5)	8,000	KM#231-235	340	5,650
PS2	1969 (5)	6,000	KM#238-242	—	5,800
PS3	1971 (5)	6,000	KM#248-252	—	5,800
PS4	1973 (3)	—	KM#254, 256, 257	—	1,075
PS5	1975 (2)	2,500	KM#260, 262	195	720
PS6	1975 (2)	4,000	KM#259, 261	195	690
PS7	1979 (2)	—	KM#264-265	—	90.00

COMOROS

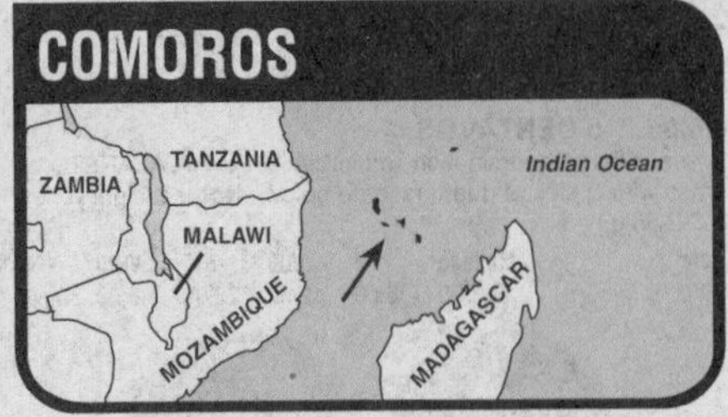

The Union of the Comoros, a volcanic archipelago located in the Mozambique Channel of the Indian Ocean 300 miles (483 km.) northwest of Madagascar, has an area of 719 sq. mi. (2,171 sq. km.) and a population of *714,000. Capital: Moroni. The economy of the islands is based on agriculture. There are practically no mineral resources. Vanilla, essence for perfumes, copra, and sisal are exported.

Ancient Phoenician traders were probably the first visitors to the Comoro Islands, but the first detailed knowledge of the area was gathered by Arab sailors. Arab dominion and culture were firmly established when the Portuguese, Dutch, and French arrived in the 16th century. In 1843 a Malagasy ruler ceded the island of Mayotte to France; the other three principal islands of the archipelago-Anjouan, Moheli, and Grand Comore came under French protection in 1886. The islands were joined administratively with Madagascar in 1912. The Comoros became partially autonomous, with the status of a French overseas territory, in 1946, and achieved complete internal autonomy in 1961. On Dec. 31, 1975, after 133 years of French association, the Comoro Islands became the independent Republic of the Comoros.

Mayotte retained the option of determining its future ties and in 1976 voted to remain French. Its present status is that of a French Territorial Collectivity. French currency now circulates there.

TITLES

دولة انجزنجية

Daulat Anjazanchiyah

RULER
French, 1886-1975

MINT MARKS
(a) Paris, privy marks only
A - Paris

MONETARY SYSTEM
100 Centimes = 1 Franc

FRENCH COLONIAL

TOKEN COINAGE

KM# Tn1 25 CENTIMES
1.20 g., Aluminum **Issuer:** Societe Anonyme **Obv:** Legend at center and surrounding **Rev:** Denomination

Date	Mintage	F12	VF20	XF40	MS60	MS63
ND-1915	—	30.00	60.00	100	150	250

KM# Tn1a 25 CENTIMES
4.60 g., Brass **Issuer:** Societe Anonyme **Obv:** Legend at center and surrounding **Rev:** Denomination

Date	Mintage	F12	VF20	XF40	MS60	MS63
ND-1922	—	45.00	90.00	125	225	300

KM# Tn2 50 CENTIMES
Aluminum **Obv:** Legend at center and surrounding **Rev:** Denomination

Date	Mintage	F12	VF20	XF40	MS60	MS63
ND-1915	—	35.00	70.00	125	250	450

KM# Tn2a 50 CENTIMES
Brass **Obv:** Legend at center and surrounding **Rev:** Denomination

Date	Mintage	F12	VF20	XF40	MS60	MS63
ND-1915	—	—	—	450	600	800

KM# Tn3 FRANC
1.30 g., Aluminum **Obv:** Legend at center and surrounding **Rev:** Denomination

Date	Mintage	F12	VF20	XF40	MS60	MS63
ND-1915	—	40.00	80.00	135	260	425

KM# Tn3a FRANC
Brass **Obv:** Legend at center and surrounding **Rev:** Denomination

Date	Mintage	F12	VF20	XF40	MS60	MS63
ND-1922	—	—	—	300	500	700

KM# Tn4 2 FRANCS
Aluminum **Obv:** Legend at center and surrounding **Rev:** Denomination

Date	Mintage	F12	VF20	XF40	MS60	MS63
ND-1915	—	50.00	100	185	350	450

KM# Tn5 2 FRANCS
Aluminum **Note:** Uniface.

Date	Mintage	F12	VF20	XF40	MS60	MS63
1915	—	50.00	100	185	350	450

DECIMAL COINAGE

KM# 4 FRANC
Aluminum **Obv:** Winged Liberty bust left, cargo ships in background, date below **Rev:** Trees surrounding denomination

Date	Mintage	VF20	XF40	MS60	MS63	MS65
1964 (a)	500,000	0.25	0.40	1.25	3.00	6.00

KM# 5 2 FRANCS
2.21 g., Aluminum, 27.1 mm. **Obv:** Winged Liberty bust left, date below, cargo ships in background **Rev:** Trees surround denomination

Date	Mintage	VF20	XF40	MS60	MS63	MS65
1964 (a)	600,000	0.25	0.50	1.50	3.50	7.00

KM# 6 5 FRANCS
3.73 g., Aluminum, 31.1 mm. **Obv:** Winged Liberty bust left, date below, cargo ships in background **Rev:** Trees surround denomination

Date	Mintage	VF20	XF40	MS60	MS63	MS65
1964 (a)	1,000,000	0.40	0.65	2.00	4.00	8.00

KM# 7 10 FRANCS
3.01 g., Aluminum-Bronze **Obv:** Winged Liberty bust left, date below, cargo ships in background **Rev:** Plants on mantle with shells flanking, denomination at center, fish below

Date	Mintage	VF20	XF40	MS60	MS63	MS65
1964 (a)	600,000	0.50	1.00	2.50	5.00	7.50

KM# 8 20 FRANCS
3.89 g., Aluminum-Bronze, 23.8 mm. **Obv:** Winged Liberty bust left, date below, cargo ships in background **Rev:** Plants on mantle, shells flank, denomination at center, fish below

Date	Mintage	VF20	XF40	MS60	MS63	MS65
1964 (a)	500,000	0.65	1.25	3.00	5.50	8.00

FEDERAL ISLAMIC REPUBLIC

STANDARD COINAGE

KM# 10 5000 FRANCS
44.83 g., 0.925 Silver 1.3332 oz. ASW **Issuer:** Etat Comorien **Obv:** Flowers, date at left, denomination below **Rev:** Bust of Said Mohamed Cheikh facing divides dates

Date	Mintage	XF40	MS60	MS63	MS65	MS66
1976	700	—	145	185	225	250
1976	1,000	PF65 220	PF67 250	PF69 275		

KM# 11 10000 FRANCS
3.07 g., 0.900 Gold 0.0888 oz. AGW **Issuer:** Etat Comorien **Obv:** Anjouan sunbird, denomination below **Rev:** Bust of Said Mohamed Cheikh facing divides dates

Date	Mintage	XF40	MS60	MS63	MS65	MS66
1976	500	—	—	175	300	350
1976	500	PF65 275	PF67 325	PF69 375		

KM# 12 20000 FRANCS
6.14 g., 0.900 Gold 0.1777 oz. AGW **Issuer:** Etat Comorien **Obv:** Coelacanth fish right, denomination below **Rev:** Bust of Said Mohamed Cheikh facing divides dates

Date	Mintage	XF40	MS60	MS63	MS65	MS66
1976	500	—	—	325	400	450
1976	500	PF65 375	PF67 450	PF69 500		

INSTITUT D'EMISSION COINAGE

KM# 9 50 FRANCS
6.09 g., Nickel, 24.1 mm. **Subject:** Independence of Republic **Obv:** Building with tall tower **Rev:** Half moon on cross above denomination, date below

Date	Mintage	VF20	XF40	MS60	MS63	MS65
1975 (a)	1,200,000	0.40	0.75	1.25	2.25	3.50

KM# 13 100 FRANCS
10.00 g., Nickel, 28.5 mm. **Series:** F.A.O. **Obv:** Half moon and stars above denomination, date below **Rev:** Boat and fish

Date	Mintage	VF20	XF40	MS60	MS63	MS65
1977 (a)	1,500,000	0.60	1.00	2.00	3.50	5.00

BANQUE CENTRAL COINAGE

KM# 15 5 FRANCS
3.85 g., Aluminum, 31 mm. **Subject:** World Fisheries Conference **Obv:** Trees surround denomination, date upper right **Rev:** Coelacanth fish left

Date	Mintage	VF20	XF40	MS60	MS63	MS65
1984 (a)	1,010,000	0.25	0.50	1.50	4.00	7.50
1992 (a)	—	0.25	0.50	1.50	4.00	7.50

KM# 17 10 FRANCS
3.91 g., Aluminum-Bronze, 22.4 mm. **Obv:** Half moon with four stars vertical from point to point **Rev:** Denomination above date

Date	Mintage	VF20	XF40	MS60	MS63	MS65
1992 (a)	—	—	—	1.25	2.00	3.00

KM# 14 25 FRANCS
3.97 g., Nickel, 20 mm. **Series:** F.A.O. **Obv:** Chickens **Rev:** Denomination above date

Date	Mintage	VF20	XF40	MS60	MS63	MS65
1981 (a)	1,000,000	1.50	2.50	6.00	10.00	16.00
1982 (a)	2,007,000	0.20	0.40	1.00	2.50	5.00

KM# 16 50 FRANCS
5.60 g., Nickel, 23.93 mm. **Obv:** Crescent and stars above denomination, date below **Rev:** Building with tall tower **Edge:** Reeded

Date	Mintage	VF20	XF40	MS60	MS63	MS65
1990 (a)	—	—	—	1.00	2.50	3.50
1994 (a) bee	—	—	—	1.00	2.50	3.50

KM# 18 100 FRANCS
10.00 g., Nickel, 28 mm. **Subject:** Circulation Type **Obv:** Denomination, crescent and stars above, date below **Rev:** Boat and fish **Edge:** Plain

Date	Mintage	VF20	XF40	MS60	MS63	MS65
1999 (a) bee	—	—	—	—	3.00	4.50

ESSAIS

Standard metals unless otherwise noted

KM#	Date	Mintage	Identification	Mkt Val
E1	1964(a)	1,700	Franc. KM4.	55.00
E2	1964(a)	1,700	2 Francs. KM5.	55.00
E3	1964(a)	1,700	5 Francs. KM6.	55.00
E4	1964(a)	1,700	10 Francs. KM7.	55.00
E5	1964(a)	1,700	20 Francs. KM8.	55.00
E6	1975(a)	1,800	50 Francs. KM9.	55.00
E7	1977(a)	1,900	100 Francs. KM13.	65.00
E8	1982(a)	1,900	25 Francs.	45.00
E9	1984(a)	1,700	5 Francs. KM15.	50.00

FDC SETS

KM#	Date	Mintage	Identification	Issue Price	Mkt Val
SS1	1964 (5)	—	KM4-8. Issued with Reunion set.	—	35.00

MINT SETS

KM#	Date	Mintage	Identification	Issue Price	Mkt Val
MS1	1976 (3)	500	KM10-12	—	950

PROOF SETS

KM#	Date	Mintage	Identification	Issue Price	Mkt Val
PS1	1976 (3)	500	KM10-12	229	1,050

CONGO FREE STATE

In ancient times the territory comprising former Zaire was occupied by Negrito peoples (Pygmies) pushed into the mountains by Bantu and Nilotic invaders. The interior was first explored by the American correspondent Henry Stanley, who was subsequently commissioned by King Leopold II of Belgium to conclude development treaties with the local chiefs. The Berlin conference of 1885 awarded the area to Leopold, who administered and exploited it as his private property until it was annexed to Belgium in 1908.

For later issues, see Belgian Congo.

RULER
Leopold II

ROYAL DOMAIN

1865-1908

STANDARD COINAGE

KM# 9 5 CENTIMES
Copper-Nickel, 19 mm. **Ruler:** Leopold II **Obv:** Crowned monograms surround center hole, within circle **Rev:** Hole at center of radiant star, denomination above, date below

Date	Mintage	F12	VF20	XF40	MS60	MS63
1906	100,000	5.00	10.00	25.00	50.00	100
1908	180,000	4.00	8.00	20.00	35.00	75.00
1908/6	—	—	—	—	—	225

KM# 10 10 CENTIMES
Copper-Nickel, 22 mm. **Ruler:** Leopold II **Obv:** Hole at center of crowned monograms within circle **Rev:** Hole at center of radiant star, denomination above, date below

Date	Mintage	F12	VF20	XF40	MS60	MS63
1906	100,000	5.00	12.00	28.00	50.00	100
1908	800,000	3.00	8.00	20.00	35.00	85.00

KM# 11 20 CENTIMES
Copper-Nickel, 25 mm. **Ruler:** Leopold II **Obv:** Hole at center of crowned monograms within circle **Rev:** Hole at center of radiant star, denomination above, date below

Date	Mintage	F12	VF20	XF40	MS60	MS63
1906	100,000	5.00	12.00	32.00	120	150
1908	400,000	4.00	8.00	20.00	85.00	135

PATTERNS

Including off metal strikes

KM#	Date	Mintage	Identification	Mkt Val
Pn21	1906	—	20 Centimes. Aluminum-Bronze.	750
Note: Unpunched center-hole				
Pn22	1911	—	5 Centimes. Copper-Nickel. Unpunched center-hole.	500
Note: Unpunched center-hole				

CONGO REPUBLIC

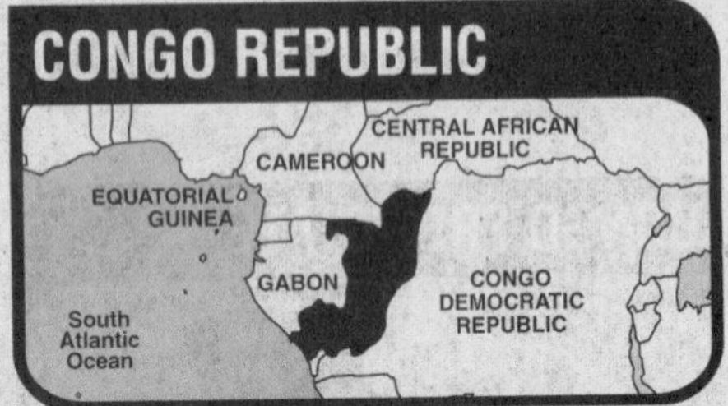

The Republic of the Congo (formerly the Peoples Republic of the Congo), located on the equator in west-central Africa, has an area of 132,047 sq. mi. (342,000 sq. km.) and a population of *2.98 million. Capital: Brazzaville. Agriculture forestry, mining, and food processing are the principal industries. Timber, industrial diamonds, potash, peanuts, and cocoa beans are exported.

The Portuguese were the first Europeans to explore the Congo (Brazzaville) area, 14th century. They conducted a slave trade with the tribal kingdoms of Teke, Loango, and Kongo without attempting developmental colonization. French influence was established in 1883 when the king of Teke signed a treaty with Savorgnan de Brazza, thereby placing his kingdom under the protection of France. While a French protectorate, the area was known as Middle Congo. In 1910 Middle Congo became a part of French Equatorial Africa, which also included Gabon, Ubangi-Shari (now the Central African Republic), and Chad. Following World War II, during which it was an important center of Free French activities, the Middle Congo was given a large measure of internal autonomy, and its inhabitants were made French citizens. Upon approval of the constitution of the Fifth French Republic, 1958, it became a member of the new French Community. On Aug. 15, 1960, Middle Congo became the independent Republic of the Congo-Brazzaville. In Jan. 1970 the country's name was changed to Peoples Republic of the Congo. A new constitution which asserts the government's advocacy of socialism was adopted in 1973.

In June and July of 1992, a new 125-member National Assembly was elected. Later that year a new president, Pascal Lissouba was elected. In November, President Lissouba dismissed the previous government and dissolved the National Assembly. A new 23-member government, including members of the opposition, was formed in December, 1992, and the name was changed to Republique du Congo.

NOTE: For earlier and related coinage see French Equatorial Africa and the Equatorial African States. For later coinage see Central African States.

RULER
French until 1960

MINT MARK
(a) - Paris, privy marks only

MONETARY SYSTEM
100 Centimes = 1 Franc

PEOPLE'S REPUBLIC

Republique Populaire du Congo

DECIMAL COINAGE

KM# 1 100 FRANCS
7.00 g., Nickel, 25.5 mm. **Obv:** Three Giant Eland left **Rev:** Denomination within circle, date below

Date	Mintage	VF20	XF40	MS60	MS63	MS65
1971 (a)	2,700,000	3.50	7.50	15.00	25.00	45.00
1972 (a)	2,500,000	3.50	7.50	15.00	25.00	45.00

KM# 2 100 FRANCS
7.00 g., Nickel, 25.5 mm. **Obv:** Three Giant Eland left **Rev:** Denomination within circle, date below

Date	Mintage	VF20	XF40	MS60	MS63	MS65
1975 (a)	—	2.50	5.00	8.00	12.00	25.00
1982 (a)	—	2.50	5.00	8.00	10.00	15.00
1983 (a)	—	2.50	5.00	8.00	10.00	15.00
1985 (a)	—	2.00	4.00	7.00	10.00	15.00
1990 (a)	—	2.00	4.00	7.00	10.00	15.00

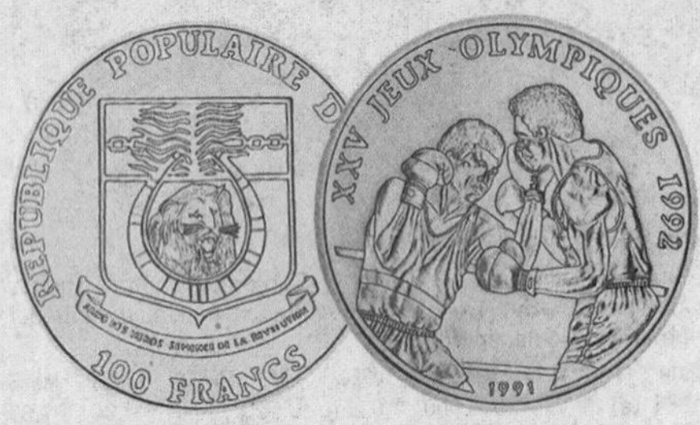

KM# 7 100 FRANCS
Nickel Plated Steel **Subject:** Olympics **Obv:** National arms, denomination below **Rev:** Boxers, date below

Date	Mintage	VF20	XF40	MS60	MS63	MS65
1991	5,000	—	—	—	12.00	15.00

KM# 8 100 FRANCS
Nickel Plated Steel **Subject:** Olympics **Obv:** National arms, denomination below **Rev:** Hurdler, date lower right

Date	Mintage	VF20	XF40	MS60	MS63	MS65
1991	5,000	—	—	—	12.00	15.00

KM# 10 100 FRANCS
Nickel Plated Steel **Series:** Old Ships **Obv:** National arms, denomination below **Rev:** Spanish galleon, date below

Date	Mintage	VF20	XF40	MS60	MS63	MS65
1991	—	—	—	—	10.00	12.00

KM# 30 100 FRANCS
Copper **Series:** Old ships **Obv:** National arms, denomination below **Obv. Legend:** Republique Populaire du Congo **Rev:** Spanish galleon, date below

Date	Mintage	VF20	XF40	MS60	MS63	MS65
1991	Est. 100	PF65 55.00	PF67 60.00			

KM# 22 100 FRANCS
Copper **Series:** Protection of Nature **Obv:** National arms, denomination below **Rev:** Congolese peacock

Date	Mintage	VF20	XF40	MS60	MS63	MS65
1992	—	—	—	—	18.00	20.00

KM# 22a 100 FRANCS
Copper-Nickel **Series:** Protection of Nature **Obv:** National arms, denomination below **Obv. Legend:** Republique Populaire du Congo **Rev:** Congolese peacock **Note:** Prev. KM#31.

Date	Mintage	VF20	XF40	MS60	MS63	MS65
1992	Est. 333	—	—	—	45.00	50.00

KM# 4 500 FRANCS
Copper-Nickel **Obv:** Plants divide date and denomination, within octagon **Rev:** Inscription lower right of woman's head 3/4 left, within octagon

Date	Mintage	VF20	XF40	MS60	MS63	MS65
1985 (a)	—	3.50	6.50	10.00	18.50	—
1986 (a)	—	3.50	6.50	10.00	18.50	—

KM# 5 500 FRANCS
16.00 g., 0.999 Silver 0.5139 oz. ASW **Series:** Old Ships **Obv:** National arms, denomination below **Rev:** Spanish galleon, date below

Date	Mintage	VF20	XF40	MS60	MS63	MS65
1991	—	PF65 30.00	PF67 35.00			

KM# 6 500 FRANCS
12.00 g., 0.999 Silver 0.3854 oz. ASW **Subject:** World Cup Soccer **Obv:** National arms, denomination below **Rev:** Soccer players, date at left

Date	Mintage	VF20	XF40	MS60	MS63	MS65
1991	—	—	—	—	25.00	30.00

KM# 9 500 FRANCS
16.07 g., 0.999 Silver 0.5161 oz. ASW **Subject:** Olympics **Obv:** National arms, denomination below **Rev:** Hurdler

Date	Mintage	VF20	XF40	MS60	MS63	MS65
1991	—	PF65 25.00	PF67 28.00			

KM# 9a 500 FRANCS
20.00 g., 0.999 Silver 0.6424 oz. ASW **Subject:** Olympics **Obv:** National arms, denomination below **Rev:** Hurdler

Date	Mintage	VF20	XF40	MS60	MS63	MS65
1991	5,000	—	—	—	25.00	30.00

KM# 11 500 FRANCS
20.00 g., 0.999 Silver 0.6424 oz. ASW **Subject:** World Cup Soccer **Obv:** National arms, denomination below **Rev:** Player and date left of Statue of Liberty

Date	Mintage	VF20	XF40	MS60	MS63	MS65
1992	—	PF65 32.00	PF67 35.00			

KM# 12 500 FRANCS
19.95 g., 0.999 Silver 0.6408 oz. ASW **Subject:** Protection of Nature **Obv:** National arms, denomination below **Rev:** Congolese peacock

Date	Mintage	VF20	XF40	MS60	MS63	MS65
1992	—	PF65 35.00	PF67 40.00			

REPUBLIC

Republique du Congo

KM# 18 100 FRANCS
Copper-Nickel **Obv:** Woman seated with tablet, denomination below **Rev:** Four-masted sailing ship - "Herzogin Cecilie", date below

Date	Mintage	VF20	XF40	MS60	MS63	MS65
1993	—	—	—	—	10.00	12.00

KM# 20 100 FRANCS
Copper **Subject:** Preservation of Nature **Obv:** Woman seated with tablet, denomination below **Rev:** Four elephants, tusks below, date at lower left

Date	Mintage	VF20	XF40	MS60	MS63	MS65
1993	—	—	—	—	22.00	25.00

KM# 32 100 FRANCS
Copper **Obv:** Woman seated with tablet, denomination below **Rev:** Four-masted sailing ship - "Herzogin Cecilie", date below

Date	Mintage	VF20	XF40	MS60	MS63	MS65
1993	Est. 100	PF65 50.00	PF67 55.00			

KM# 33 100 FRANCS
Copper **Subject:** Prehistoric Animals **Obv:** Woman seated with tablet, denomination below **Rev:** Brachiosaurus in water, date below

Date	Mintage	VF20	XF40	MS60	MS63	MS65
1993	Est. 100	PF65 50.00	PF67 55.00			

KM# 16 100 FRANCS
Copper-Nickel **Subject:** Prehistoric Animals **Obv:** Woman seated with tablet, denomination below **Rev:** Polacanthus left, date below

Date	Mintage	VF20	XF40	MS60	MS63	MS65
1994	—	—	—	—	20.00	22.00

KM# 19 100 FRANCS
Copper-Nickel **Subject:** Prehistoric Animals **Obv:** Woman seated with tablet, denomination below **Rev:** Spinosaurus left, date lower left

Date	Mintage	VF20	XF40	MS60	MS63	MS65
1994	—	—	—	—	20.00	22.00

KM# 34 100 FRANCS
Copper-Nickel **Subject:** Prehistoric Animals **Obv:** Woman seated with tablet, denomination below **Rev:** Mammuthus 3/4 facing

Date	Mintage	VF20	XF40	MS60	MS63	MS65
1994	Est. 100	PF65 50.00	PF67 55.00			

KM# 21 100 FRANCS
Copper-Nickel **Obv:** Woman seated with tablet, denomination below **Rev:** Junkers JU52 trimotor airplane left, date at right **Note:** Multicolored.

Date	Mintage	VF20	XF40	MS60	MS63	MS65
1995	25,000	—	—	—	22.00	27.00

KM# 35 100 FRANCS
Copper-Nickel **Subject:** XXVII Olympiade **Obv:** Woman seated with tablet, denomination below **Rev:** Shot putter, date at left **Note:** Prev. KM#45.

Date	Mintage	VF20	XF40	MS60	MS63	MS65
1999	10,000	—	—	—	7.00	9.00

KM# 42 500 FRANCS
13.81 g., 0.999 Silver 0.4436 oz. ASW, 30 mm. **Obv:** Woman seated with tablet, denomination below **Rev:** Multicolor lion head, date at right **Edge:** Plain

Date	Mintage	VF20	XF40	MS60	MS63	MS65
1996	—	PF65 38.00	PF67 42.00			

KM# 38 500 FRANCS
9.96 g., Silver, 29.9 mm. **Series:** 2000 Olympics **Subject:** Basketball **Obv:** Seated woman with tablet **Rev:** Basketball player and map of Australia

Date	Mintage	VF20	XF40	MS60	MS63	MS65
1998	—	PF65 22.00	PF67 27.00			

KM# 13 1000 FRANCS
20.00 g., 0.999 Silver 0.6424 oz. ASW **Subject:** Preservation of Nature **Obv:** Woman seated with tablet, denomination below **Rev:** Elephants, tusks below, date lower left

Date	Mintage	VF20	XF40	MS60	MS63	MS65
1993	—	PF65 40.00	PF67 45.00			

KM# 14 1000 FRANCS
15.90 g., 0.999 Silver 0.5107 oz. ASW **Subject:** Prehistoric Animals **Obv:** Woman seated with tablet, denomination below **Rev:** Brachiosaurus, date below

Date	Mintage	VF20	XF40	MS60	MS63	MS65
1993	—	PF65 30.00	PF67 35.00			

KM# 15 1000 FRANCS
20.10 g., 0.999 Silver 0.6456 oz. ASW **Obv:** Woman seated with tablet, denomination below **Rev:** 4-masted sailing ship - "Herzogin Cecilie", date below

Date	Mintage	VF20	XF40	MS60	MS63	MS65
1993	Est. 100	—	—	—	100	120
1993	—	PF65 30.00	PF67 35.00			

KM# 17 1000 FRANCS
15.88 g., 0.999 Silver 0.510 oz. ASW **Subject:** Prehistoric Animals **Obv:** Woman seated with tablet, denomination below **Rev:** Mammoth, date lower left

Date	Mintage	VF20	XF40	MS60	MS63	MS65
1994	—	PF65 30.00	PF67 35.00			

KM# 23 1000 FRANCS
20.00 g., 0.999 Silver 0.6424 oz. ASW **Subject:** 1996 Olympics **Obv:** Woman seated with tablet **Rev:** Discus throwing, date at left

Date	Mintage	VF20	XF40	MS60	MS63	MS65
1995	15,000	PF65 25.00	PF67 28.00			

KM# 24 1000 FRANCS
20.00 g., 0.999 Silver 0.6424 oz. ASW **Obv:** Woman seated with tablet **Rev:** Multicolor Swiss airliner - Junkers JU 52, left, date at right

Date	Mintage	VF20	XF40	MS60	MS63	MS65
1995	15,000	PF65 45.00	PF67 50.00			

KM# 25 1000 FRANCS
20.00 g., 0.999 Silver 0.6424 oz. ASW **Obv:** Woman seated with tablet, denomination below **Rev:** Multicolor Panther head facing, date upper right

Date	Mintage	VF20	XF40	MS60	MS63	MS65
1996	—	PF65 45.00	PF67 50.00			

KM# 26.1 1000 FRANCS
20.00 g., 0.999 Silver 0.6424 oz. ASW **Subject:** World Cup Soccer **Obv:** Woman seated with tablet, denomination below **Rev:** Two soccer players, date at right

Date	Mintage	VF20	XF40	MS60	MS63	MS65
1996	—	PF65 35.00	PF67 40.00			

KM# 26.2 1000 FRANCS
31.10 g., 0.999 Silver 0.9989 oz. ASW

Date	Mintage	VF20	XF40	MS60	MS63	MS65
1996	Est. 100	—	—	—	75.00	90.00

KM# 27 1000 FRANCS
20.00 g., 0.999 Silver 0.6424 oz. ASW **Subject:** World Cup Soccer **Obv:** Woman seated with tablet, denomination below **Rev:** Multicolor Eiffel Tower, soccer ball and French flag,

Date	Mintage	VF20	XF40	MS60	MS63	MS65
1996	—	PF65 32.00	PF67 37.00			

KM# 40 1000 FRANCS
20.00 g., 0.999 Silver 0.6424 oz. ASW, 38.1 mm. **Obv:** Woman seated with tablet, denomination below **Rev:** Multicolor elephant **Edge:** Reeded

Date	Mintage	VF20	XF40	MS60	MS63	MS65
1996	—	PF65 45.00	PF67 50.00			

KM# 52 1000 FRANCS
Silver, 38 mm. **Rev:** Giraffe in color

Date	Mintage	VF20	XF40	MS60	MS63	MS65
1996	—	PF65 50.00	PF67 55.00			

KM# 53 1000 FRANCS
31.11 g., 0.999 Silver 0.999 oz. ASW **Rev:** Sir Henry Morgan in color

Date	Mintage	VF20	XF40	MS60	MS63	MS65
1996	Est. 10000	PF65 65.00	PF67 70.00			

KM# 54 1000 FRANCS
31.11 g., 0.999 Silver 0.999 oz. ASW **Rev:** David Livingstone in color

Date	Mintage	VF20	XF40	MS60	MS63	MS65
1996	Est. 10000	PF65 65.00	PF67 70.00			

KM# 28.1 1000 FRANCS
20.00 g., 0.999 Silver 0.6424 oz. ASW **Subject:** XXVII Olympiade **Obv:** Woman seated with tablet, denomination below **Rev:** Multicolored boxers

Date	Mintage	VF20	XF40	MS60	MS63	MS65
1997	Est. 100	—	—	—	100	120
1997	Est. 500	PF65 55.00	PF67 60.00			

KM# 28.2 1000 FRANCS
15.88 g., 0.999 Silver 0.510 oz. ASW **Subject:** XXVII Olympiade **Obv:** Woman seated with tablet, denomination below **Rev:** Multicolored boxers

Date	Mintage	VF20	XF40	MS60	MS63	MS65
1998	Est. 100	—	—	—	100	120
1998	5,000	PF65 35.00	PF67 40.00			

KM# 29 1000 FRANCS
15.00 g., 0.999 Silver 0.4818 oz. ASW **Obv:** Woman seated with tablet, denomination below **Rev:** Ancient Roman ship, date below

Date	Mintage	VF20	XF40	MS60	MS63	MS65
1997	5,000	PF65 28.00	PF67 32.00			

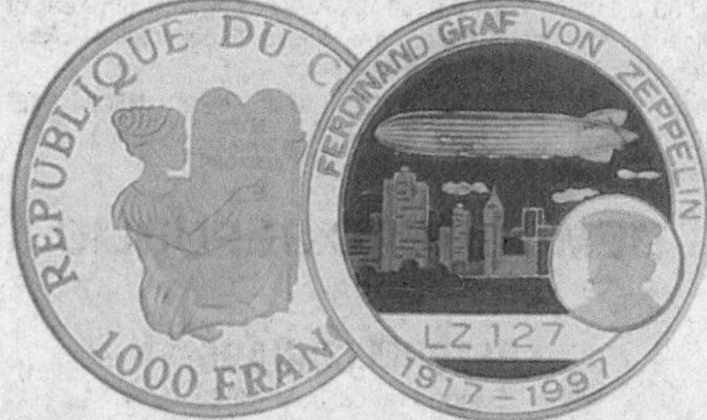

KM# 37 1000 FRANCS
15.00 g., 0.999 Silver 0.4818 oz. ASW, 34.9 mm. **Subject:** Graf Zeppelin **Obv:** Woman with tablet **Rev:** Multicolor New York City view with Zeppelin in flight and a cameo insert at lower right of Count Zeppelin **Edge:** Plain **Note:** Prev. KM#107.

Date	Mintage	VF20	XF40	MS60	MS63	MS65
ND-1997	—	PF65 35.00	PF67 40.00			

KM# 39 1000 FRANCS
15.00 g., 0.999 Silver 0.4818 oz. ASW, 35 mm. **Obv:** Woman seated with tablet, denomination below **Rev:** Soccer player, date lower right **Edge:** Plain

Date	Mintage	VF20	XF40	MS60	MS63	MS65
1997	—	PF65 40.00	PF67 45.00			

KM# 41 1000 FRANCS
31.10 g., 0.999 Silver 0.9989 oz. ASW, 45 mm. **Obv:** Woman seated with tablet, denomination below **Rev:** Map of East Central African countries with two elephants and a crocodile **Edge:** Plain

Date	Mintage	VF20	XF40	MS60	MS63	MS65
1997	—	PF67 125				

KM# 55 1000 FRANCS
15.00 g., 0.999 Silver 0.4818 oz. ASW, 35 mm. **Rev:** Two soccer players in color with Eifle tower

Date	Mintage	VF20	XF40	MS60	MS63	MS65
1997	—	PF65 50.00	PF67 55.00			

KM# 56 1000 FRANCS
20.00 g., 0.999 Silver 0.6424 oz. ASW **Subject:** 16th World Cup, France **Rev:** Eifle tower and soccer player

Date	Mintage	VF20	XF40	MS60	MS63	MS65
1997	Est. 2950	PF65 40.00	PF67 45.00			

KM# 57 1000 FRANCS
20.00 g., 0.999 Silver 0.6424 oz. ASW **Subject:** 16th World Cup, France **Rev:** Golie with ball

Date	Mintage	VF20	XF40	MS60	MS63	MS65
1997	2,950	PF65 40.00	PF67 45.00			

KM# 58 1000 FRANCS
31.11 g., 0.999 Silver 0.999 oz. ASW **Rev:** Horsemen of the Tuareg **Shape:** Rectangular

Date	Mintage	VF20	XF40	MS60	MS63	MS65
1997	—	PF65 50.00	PF67 55.00			

KM# 59 1000 FRANCS
31.11 g., 0.999 Silver 0.999 oz. ASW **Rev:** Sphinx and pyramids

Date	Mintage	VF20	XF40	MS60	MS63	MS65
1997	Est. 5000	PF65 50.00	PF67 55.00			

KM# 60 1000 FRANCS
31.11 g., 0.999 Silver 0.999 oz. ASW **Rev:** Palm fan **Shape:** Rectangular

Date	Mintage	VF20	XF40	MS60	MS63	MS65
1997	Est. 5000	PF65 50.00	PF67 55.00			

KM# 61 1000 FRANCS
31.11 g., 0.999 Silver 0.999 oz. ASW **Rev:** Caravelle ship **Shape:** Rectangle

Date	Mintage	VF20	XF40	MS60	MS63	MS65
1997	Est. 5000	PF65 50.00	PF67 55.00			

KM# 62 1000 FRANCS
31.11 g., 0.999 Silver 0.999 oz. ASW **Rev:** Cape fur seal **Shape:** Rectangle

Date	Mintage	VF20	XF40	MS60	MS63	MS65
1997	—	PF65 50.00	PF67 55.00			

KM# 63 1000 FRANCS
15.00 g., 0.999 Silver 0.4818 oz. ASW, 35 mm. **Rev:** South African crowned cranes in color

Date	Mintage	VF20	XF40	MS60	MS63	MS65
1997	Est. 2500	PF65 40.00	PF67 45.00			

KM# 64 1000 FRANCS
15.00 g., 0.999 Silver 0.4818 oz. ASW **Subject:** Summer Olympics, Sidney, 2000 **Rev:** Boxing

Date	Mintage	VF20	XF40	MS60	MS63	MS65
1998	Est. 5000	PF65 32.00	PF67 37.00			

KM# 36 1000 FRANCS
20.10 g., 0.999 Silver 0.6456 oz. ASW **Subject:** XXVII Olympiade **Obv:** Woman seated with tablet, denomination below **Rev:** Shot putter, date at left

Date	Mintage	VF20	XF40	MS60	MS63	MS65
1999	5,000	PF65 25.00	PF67 28.00			

KM# 43 1000 FRANCS
15.00 g., 0.999 Silver 0.4818 oz. ASW, 35 mm. **Obv:** Woman seated with tablet, denomination below **Rev:** Charles Darwin **Edge:** Plain

Date	Mintage	VF20	XF40	MS60	MS63	MS65
1999	—	PF65 45.00	PF67 50.00			

KM# 65 1000 FRANCS
Silver **Rev:** S.S. Europa

Date	Mintage	VF20	XF40	MS60	MS63	MS65
1999 Proof	—	—	—	—	—	—

KM# 66 1000 FRANCS
0.999 Silver, 42x24 mm. **Subject:** African Wildlife **Shape:** Rectangle

Date	Mintage	VF20	XF40	MS60	MS63	MS65
1999	—	PF65 60.00	PF67 65.00			

KM# 44 1000 FRANCS
15.00 g., 0.999 Silver 0.4818 oz. ASW, 35 mm. **Obv:** Woman seated with tablet, denomination below **Rev:** Graf Ferdinand von Zeppelin **Edge:** Plain

Date	Mintage	VF20	XF40	MS60	MS63	MS65
ND(2000)	—	PF65 30.00	PF67 35.00			

KM# 45 1000 FRANCS
15.00 g., 0.999 Silver 0.4818 oz. ASW, 35 mm. **Obv:** Woman seated with tablet, denomination below **Rev:** White stork, date at right **Edge:** Plain

Date	Mintage	VF20	XF40	MS60	MS63	MS65
2000	—	—	—	—	25.00	30.00

ESSAIS

Standard metals unless otherwise noted

KM#	Date	Mintage	Identification	Mkt Val
E1	1971(a)	1,450	100 Francs.	35.00
E2	1971(a)	4	100 Francs. Gold.	1,700
E3	1975(a)	1,700	100 Francs.	30.00
E5	1985(a)	1,700	500 Francs. Plants between denomination and date within octagon. Inscription at lower right of womans head.	50.00

PIEDFORT

KM#	Date	Mintage	Identification	Mkt Val
P1	1991	110	500 Francs. 0.999. Silver. National arms, denomination below. Spanish galleon, date below. KM5.	125

TRIAL STRIKES

KM#	Date	Mintage	Identification	Mkt Val
TS1	1984	3	10 Francs. Silver. Fencing. Uniface.	600
TS2	1984	3	50 Francs. Silver. Shot put. Uniface.	600

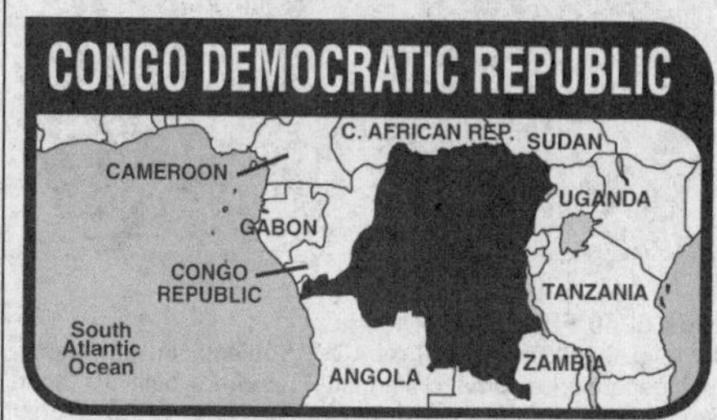

The Democratic Republic of the Congo (formerly the Republic of Zaire, and earlier the Belgian Congo), located in the south-central part of Africa, has an area of 905,568 sq. mi. (2,345,410 sq. km.) and a population of *47.4 million. Capital: Kinshasa. The mineral-rich country produces copper, tin, diamonds, gold, zinc, cobalt and uranium.

In ancient times the territory comprising former Zaire was occupied by Negrito peoples (Pygmies) pushed into the mountains by Bantu and Nilotic invaders. The interior was first explored by the American correspondent Henry Stanley, who was subsequently commissioned by King Leopold II of Belgium to conclude development treaties with the local chiefs. The Berlin conference of 1885 awarded the area to Leopold, who administered and exploited it as his private property until it was annexed to Belgium in 1908. Belgium received the mandate for the German territory of Ruanda-Urundi as a result of the international treaties after WWI. During World War II, Belgian Congolese troops fought on the side of the Allies, notably in Ethiopia. Following the eruption of bloody independence riots in 1959, Belgium granted the Belgian Congo independence as the Republic of the Congo on June 30, 1960. The nation officially changed its name to Zaire on Oct. 27, 1971, and following a Civil War in 1997 changed its name to the "Democratic Republic of the Congo."

MINT MARKS

(b) – Brussels, privy marks only

REPUBLIC

1960 - 1971

DECIMAL COINAGE

KM# 1 10 FRANCS

3.27 g., Aluminum, 29.8 mm. **Obv:** Denomination above date **Rev:** Lion face **Note:** Many recalled and melted, but large numbers still remain available to collectors, mostly in Brilliant Uncirculated grades.

Date	Mintage	VF20	XF40	MS60	MS63	MS65
1965 (b)	Est. 100000000	—	—	5.00	10.00	20.00

KM# 2 10 FRANCS

3.23 g., 0.900 Gold 0.0933 oz. AGW **Subject:** 5th Anniversary of Independence **Obv:** President Joseph Kasa-Vubu **Rev:** Crossed palm trees, denomination below **Note:** Approximately 70 percent melted.

Date	Mintage	VF20	XF40	MS60	MS63	MS65
1965	Est. 3000	PF65 175				

KM# 3 20 FRANCS

6.45 g., 0.900 Gold 0.1867 oz. AGW **Subject:** 5th Anniversary of Independence **Obv:** Uniformed bust of President Joseph Kasa-Vubu 3/4 right **Rev:** Crossed palm trees, denomination below **Note:** Approximately 70 percent melted.

Date	Mintage	VF20	XF40	MS60	MS63	MS65
1965	—	PF65 325				

KM# 4 25 FRANCS

8.06 g., 0.900 Gold 0.2333 oz. AGW **Subject:** 5th Anniversary of Independence **Rev:** Elephant left **Note:** Approximately 70 percent melted.

Date	Mintage	VF20	XF40	MS60	MS63	MS65
1965	Est. 3000	PF65 400				

KM# 4a 25 FRANCS

Silver **Subject:** 5th Anniversary of Independence **Rev:** Elephant left

Date	Mintage	VF20	XF40	MS60	MS63	MS65
1965	—	PF65 75.00				

KM# 5 50 FRANCS

16.13 g., 0.900 Gold 0.4667 oz. AGW **Subject:** 5th Anniversary of Independence **Obv:** Uniformed President's bust 3/4 right **Rev:** Elephant left, denomination and date below **Note:** Approximately 70 percent melted.

Date	Mintage	VF20	XF40	MS60	MS63	MS65
1965	Est. 3000	PF65 825				

KM# 6 100 FRANCS

32.26 g., 0.900 Gold 0.9334 oz. AGW **Subject:** 5th Anniversary of Independence **Obv:** Uniformed bust of President Joseph Kasa-Vubu 3/4 right **Rev:** Elephant left **Note:** Approximately 70 percent melted.

Date	Mintage	VF20	XF40	MS60	MS63	MS65
1965	Est. 3000	PF65 1,650				

KM# 6a 100 FRANCS

Silver **Subject:** 5th Anniversary of Independence **Obv:** President Joseph Kasa-Vubu **Rev:** Elephant left

Date	Mintage	VF20	XF40	MS60	MS63	MS65
1965	—	PF65 110				

REFORM COINAGE

100 Sengis = 1 Likuta;
100 Makuta (plural of Likuta) = 1 Zaire

KM# 7 10 SENGIS

0.70 g., Aluminum, 17 mm. **Obv:** Denomination within circle **Rev:** Leopard crouching on branch, date below **Edge:** Reeded

Date	Mintage	VF20	XF40	MS60	MS63	MS65
1967	90,996,000	0.15	0.25	0.50	1.00	3.00
1967	—	PF65 235				

KM# 10 10 SENGIS

3.20 g., 0.900 Gold 0.0926 oz. AGW **Subject:** 5th Year of Mobutu Presidency **Obv:** Arms above denomination **Rev:** Military bust of President Joseph Desire Mobutu 3/4 facing, date below

Date	Mintage	VF20	XF40	MS60	MS63	MS65
1970	1,000	—	—	—	160	170
1970	1,000	PF65 180				

KM# 10a 10 SENGIS

Brass Gilt **Subject:** 5th Year of Mobutu Presidency **Obv:** Arms **Rev:** Bust of President Joseph Desire Mobutu

Date	Mintage	VF20	XF40	MS60	MS63	MS65
1970	—	PF65 70.00				

KM# 8 LIKUTA

1.27 g., Aluminum, 20.9 mm. **Obv:** Denomination within circle **Rev:** Arms above date

Date	Mintage	VF20	XF40	MS60	MS63	MS65
1967	49,180,000	0.15	0.50	1.25	2.00	5.00
1967	—	PF65 225				

KM# 9 5 MAKUTA

6.41 g., Copper-Nickel, 25 mm. **Obv:** Denomination within circle **Rev:** Bust of President Mobutu 3/4 left, date below

Date	Mintage	VF20	XF40	MS60	MS63	MS65
1967	2,470,000	0.50	1.00	2.00	4.00	9.00
1967	—	PF65 225				

KM# 11 25 MAKUTAS

Brass Gilt **Subject:** 5th Year of Mobutu Presidency **Obv:** Arms above denomination **Rev:** President's bust 3/4 facing, date below

Date	Mintage	VF20	XF40	MS60	MS63	MS65
1970	—	PF65 100				

KM# 11a 25 MAKUTAS

8.00 g., 0.900 Gold 0.2315 oz. AGW **Subject:** 5th Year of Mobutu Presidency **Obv:** Arms above denomination **Rev:** President's bust facing

Date	Mintage	VF20	XF40	MS60	MS63	MS65
1970	1,000	—	—	—	400	420
1970	1,000	PF65 435				

KM# 12 50 MAKUTAS

Brass Gilt **Subject:** 5th Year of Mobutu Presidency **Obv:** Arms above denomination **Rev:** President's bust 3/4 facing

Date	Mintage	VF20	XF40	MS60	MS63	MS65
1970	—	PF65 125				

KM# 12a 50 MAKUTAS

16.00 g., 0.900 Gold 0.463 oz. AGW **Subject:** 5th Year of Mobutu Presidency **Obv:** Arms above denomination **Rev:** President's bust 3/4 facing, date below

Date	Mintage	VF20	XF40	MS60	MS63	MS65
1970	1,000	—	—	—	800	820
1970	1,000	PF65 835				

KM# 13 ZAIRE

Brass Gilt **Subject:** 5th Year of Mobutu Presidency **Obv:** Arms above denomination **Rev:** President's bust 3/4 facing

Date	Mintage	VF20	XF40	MS60	MS63	MS65
1970	—	PF65 200				

KM# 13a ZAIRE

32.00 g., 0.900 Gold 0.9259 oz. AGW **Subject:** 5th Year of Mobutu Presidency **Obv:** Arms above denomination **Rev:** President's bust, 3/4 facing, date below

Date	Mintage	VF20	XF40	MS60	MS63	MS65
1970	1,000	—	—	—	1,600	1,625
1970	1,000	PF65 1,650				

DEMOCRATIC REPUBLIC

1998 -

REFORM COINAGE

Congo Francs; July 1998

KM# 73 5 FRANCS

24.30 g., Copper-Nickel, 38.5 mm. **Subject:** Royals of Europe **Obv:** Lion **Rev:** Multicolor portrait of Queen Juliana (1948-80) and crowned arms **Edge:** Reeded

Date	Mintage	VF20	XF40	MS60	MS63	MS65
1999	—	PF65 15.00	PF67 18.00			

KM# 84 5 FRANCS

24.30 g., Copper-Nickel, 38.5 mm. **Subject:** Anna Paulowna **Obv:** Lion within inner circle, denomination below in outer circle **Rev:** Multicolor portrait applique within inner circle **Edge:** Reeded

Date	Mintage	VF20	XF40	MS60	MS63	MS65
1999	—	PF65 15.00	PF67 18.00			

KM# 85 5 FRANCS

24.30 g., Copper-Nickel, 38.5 mm. **Subject:** Willem I **Obv:** Lion within inner circle, denomination below in outer circle **Rev:** Multicolor portrait applique within inner circle **Edge:** Reeded

Date	Mintage	VF20	XF40	MS60	MS63	MS65
1999	—	PF65 15.00	PF67 18.00			

KM# 86 5 FRANCS

24.30 g., Copper-Nickel, 38.5 mm. **Subject:** Willem III **Obv:** Lion within inner circle, denomination below in outer circle **Rev:** Multicolor portrait applique within inner circle **Edge:** Reeded

Date	Mintage	VF20	XF40	MS60	MS63	MS65
1999	—	PF65 15.00	PF67 18.00			

KM# 87 5 FRANCS

24.30 g., Copper-Nickel, 38.5 mm. **Subject:** Wilhelmina **Obv:** Lion within inner circle, denomination below in outer circle **Rev:** Multicolor portrait applique within inner circle **Edge:** Reeded

Date	Mintage	VF20	XF40	MS60	MS63	MS65
1999	—	PF65 15.00	PF67 18.00			

KM# 88 5 FRANCS

24.30 g., Copper-Nickel, 38.5 mm. **Subject:** Bernhard **Obv:** Lion within inner circle, denomination in outer circle **Rev:** Multicolor portrait applique within inner circle **Edge:** Reeded

Date	Mintage	VF20	XF40	MS60	MS63	MS65
1999	—	PF65 15.00	PF67 18.00			

KM# 89 5 FRANCS

24.30 g., Copper-Nickel, 38.5 mm. **Subject:** Claus **Obv:** Lion within inner circle, denomination below in outer circle **Rev:** Multicolor portrait applique within inner circle **Edge:** Reeded

Date	Mintage	VF20	XF40	MS60	MS63	MS65
1999	—	PF65 15.00	PF67 18.00			

KM# 90 5 FRANCS

24.30 g., Copper-Nickel, 38.5 mm. **Subject:** Willem-Alexander **Obv:** Lion within inner circle, denomination below in outer circle **Rev:** Multicolor portrait applique within inner circle **Edge:** Reeded

Date	Mintage	VF20	XF40	MS60	MS63	MS65
1999	—	PF65 15.00	PF67 18.00			

KM# 24 5 FRANCS

Copper-Nickel **Subject:** Panama Canal **Obv:** Standing lion facing, denomination below **Rev:** Sailing ship above inscription and map **Note:** Prev. KM#47.

Date	Mintage	VF20	XF40	MS60	MS63	MS65
2000	—	—	—	—	—	15.00

KM# 39 5 FRANCS

27.16 g., Copper-Nickel, 37.3 mm. **Series:** Wild Life Protection **Obv:** Standing lion facing, denomination below **Rev:** Multicolor holographic parrot with folded wings right **Edge:** Reeded **Note:** Prev. KM#62.

Date	Mintage	VF20	XF40	MS60	MS63	MS65
2000	—	PF65 25.00				

KM# 40 5 FRANCS

Copper-Nickel 27.16, 37.3 mm. **Series:** Wild Life Protection **Obv:** Standing lion facing, denomination below **Rev:** Multicolor holographic parrot with open wings left **Edge:** Reeded **Note:** Prev. KM#63.

Date	Mintage	VF20	XF40	MS60	MS63	MS65
2000	—	PF65 25.00				

KM# 41 5 FRANCS

27.16 g., Copper-Nickel, 37.3 mm. **Series:** Wild Life Protection **Obv:** Standing lion facing, denomination below **Rev:** Multicolor holographic toucan left **Note:** Prev. KM#64.

Date	Mintage	VF20	XF40	MS60	MS63	MS65
2000	—	PF65 25.00				

KM# 63 5 FRANCS

28.75 g., Copper-Nickel, 38 mm. **Subject:** Lady Diana - Visit to India **Obv:** Standing lion facing, denomination below **Rev:** Lady Diana at left, Taj Mahal at right, cameo of Queen Mother top center **Edge:** Reeded **Note:** Prev. KM#86.

Date	Mintage	VF20	XF40	MS60	MS63	MS65
ND-2000	—	PF65 12.00				

KM# 64 5 FRANCS

28.75 g., Copper-Nickel, 38 mm. **Subject:** Lady Diana - Meeting with Pope John Paul II **Obv:** Standing lion facing, denomination below **Rev:** Lady Diana front left, Pope John Paul II facing left, cameo of Queen Mother top center **Edge:** Reeded **Note:** Prev. KM#87.

Date	Mintage	VF20	XF40	MS60	MS63	MS65
ND-2000	—	PF65 12.00				

KM# 121 5 FRANCS

Copper-Nickel, 40 mm. **Obv:** Lion standing looking forward, denomination below **Rev:** Multicolor applique King Baudouin I (1930-1993) facing, dates at right **Edge:** Reeded

Date	Mintage	VF20	XF40	MS60	MS63	MS65
2000	—	—	—	—	10.00	12.00

KM# 160 5 FRANCS
26.53 g., Copper-Nickel, 37.3 mm. **Subject:** Marine-Life Protection **Obv:** Standing lion facing, denomination below **Rev:** Multicolor fish scene, date below **Edge:** Reeded

Date	Mintage	VF20	XF40	MS60	MS63	MS65
2000	—	PF65 20.00	PF67 25.00			

KM# 14 10 FRANCS
20.00 g., 0.925 Silver 0.5948 oz. ASW **Series:** Endangered Wildlife **Obv:** Lion within inner circle, date below in outer circle **Rev:** Bonobos female chimpanzee with young, denomination below **Note:** Prev. KM#35.

Date	Mintage	VF20	XF40	MS60	MS63	MS65
1999	10,000	PF65 32.00	PF67 35.00			

KM# 15 10 FRANCS
20.00 g., 0.925 Silver 0.5948 oz. ASW **Series:** Endangered Wildlife **Obv:** Lion within inner circle, date below in outer circle **Rev:** Pygmy hippopotamus right, denomination below **Note:** Prev. KM#36.

Date	Mintage	VF20	XF40	MS60	MS63	MS65
1999	10,000	PF65 32.00	PF67 35.00			

KM# 16 10 FRANCS
20.00 g., 0.925 Silver 0.5948 oz. ASW **Series:** Endangered Wildlife **Obv:** Lion within inner circle, date below in outer circle **Rev:** Crocodile left, denomination below **Note:** Prev. KM#37.

Date	Mintage	VF20	XF40	MS60	MS63	MS65
1999	10,000	PF65 32.00	PF67 35.00			

KM# 17 10 FRANCS
20.00 g., 0.925 Silver 0.5948 oz. ASW **Series:** Endangered Wildlife **Obv:** Lion within inner circle, date below in outer circle **Rev:** Water chevrotain left, denomination below **Note:** Prev. KM#38.

Date	Mintage	VF20	XF40	MS60	MS63	MS65
1999	10,000	PF65 32.00	PF67 35.00			

KM# 18 10 FRANCS
20.00 g., 0.925 Silver 0.5948 oz. ASW **Series:** Endangered Wildlife **Obv:** Lion within inner circle, date below in outer circle **Rev:** Tree pangolin on branch right, denomination below **Note:** Prev. KM#39.

Date	Mintage	VF20	XF40	MS60	MS63	MS65
1999	10,000	PF65 32.00	PF67 35.00			

KM# 19 10 FRANCS
20.00 g., 0.925 Silver 0.5948 oz. ASW **Series:** Endangered Wildlife **Obv:** Lion within inner circle, date below in outer circle **Rev:** Poto hanging on branches, denomination below **Note:** Prev. KM#40.

Date	Mintage	VF20	XF40	MS60	MS63	MS65
1999	10,000	PF65 32.00	PF67 35.00			

KM# 20 10 FRANCS
25.31 g., 0.925 Silver 0.7527 oz. ASW **Subject:** Explorers of Africa-Dr. David Livingstone **Obv:** Lion within inner circle, date below in outer circle **Rev:** Head facing, land and ship in background, denomination at left **Note:** Prev. KM#41.

Date	Mintage	VF20	XF40	MS60	MS63	MS65
1999	10,000	PF65 20.00	PF67 22.00			

KM# 21 10 FRANCS
25.31 g., 0.925 Silver 0.7527 oz. ASW **Subject:** Explorers of Africa-Sir Henry Morton Stanley **Obv:** Lion within inner circle, date below in outer circle **Rev:** Bust facing, denomination at right **Note:** Prev. KM#42.

Date	Mintage	VF20	XF40	MS60	MS63	MS65
1999	10,000	PF65 20.00	PF67 22.00			

KM# 22 10 FRANCS
25.31 g., 0.925 Silver 0.7527 oz. ASW **Subject:** 30th Anniversary of the Lunar Landing **Obv:** Lion within inner circle, date below in outer circle **Rev:** First lunar landing scene, denomination at left, two dates above **Note:** Prev. KM#43.

Date	Mintage	VF20	XF40	MS60	MS63	MS65
1999	10,000	PF65 20.00	PF67 22.00			

KM# 23 10 FRANCS
25.31 g., 0.925 Silver 0.7527 oz. ASW **Subject:** Sydney 2000 **Obv:** Roaring lion bust left within inner circle, date below in outer circle **Rev:** Diver and opera house, denomination at left **Note:** Prev. KM#44.

Date	Mintage	VF20	XF40	MS60	MS63	MS65
1999	10,000	PF65 20.00	PF67 22.00			

KM# 25 10 FRANCS
25.13 g., 0.925 Silver 0.7474 oz. ASW **Subject:** Panama Canal **Obv:** Standing lion facing, denomination below **Rev:** Sailing ship above inscription and map **Note:** Prev. KM#48.

Date	Mintage	VF20	XF40	MS60	MS63	MS65
2000	—	PF65 45.00	PF67 50.00			

KM# 26 10 FRANCS
25.13 g., 0.925 Silver 0.7474 oz. ASW **Subject:** Panama Cañal **Obv:** Standing lion facing, denomination below **Rev:** Cargo ship over map of Panama, date at left **Note:** Prev. KM#49.

Date	Mintage	VF20	XF40	MS60	MS63	MS65
2000	—	PF65 45.00	PF67 50.00			

KM# 27 10 FRANCS
25.13 g., 0.925 Silver 0.7474 oz. ASW **Subject:** 25th Anniversary - Visit of Pope John Paul II **Obv:** Standing lion facing, denomination below **Rev:** Bust 3/4 right of Pope John Paul II, date below **Note:** Prev. KM#50.

Date	Mintage	VF20	XF40	MS60	MS63	MS65
2000	—	PF65 35.00	PF67 40.00			

KM# 28 10 FRANCS
25.13 g., 0.925 Silver 0.7474 oz. ASW **Subject:** 25th Anniversary - Visit of Pope John Paul II **Obv:** Standing lion facing, denomination below **Rev:** Half-length bust of Pope John Paul II facing, date below **Note:** Prev. KM#51.

Date	Mintage	VF20	XF40	MS60	MS63	MS65
2000	—	PF65 25.00	PF67 30.00			

KM# 30 10 FRANCS
25.45 g., 0.925 Silver 0.7569 oz. ASW, 37.3 mm. **Subject:** Wild Life Protection **Obv:** Standing lion facing, denomination below **Rev:** Multicolor parrot with open wings left **Edge:** Reeded **Note:** Prev. KM#53.

Date	Mintage	VF20	XF40	MS60	MS63	MS65
2000	—	PF65 65.00	PF67 70.00			

KM# 31 10 FRANCS
25.45 g., 0.925 Silver 0.7569 oz. ASW, 37.3 mm. **Subject:** Wild Life Protection **Obv:** Standing lion facing, denomination below **Rev:** Toucan with folded wings right **Edge:** Reeded **Note:** Prev. KM#54.

Date	Mintage	VF20	XF40	MS60	MS63	MS65
2000	—	PF65 65.00	PF67 70.00			

KM# 32 10 FRANCS
31.26 g., 0.999 Silver 1.004 oz. ASW, 47.7 x 27.1 mm. **Subject:** Millennium - space travel **Obv:** Standing lion facing, denomination below **Rev:** Footprint on the moon **Edge:** Plain **Shape:** Rectangle **Note:** Prev. KM#55.

Date	Mintage	VF20	XF40	MS60	MS63	MS65
2000	—	PF65 32.00	PF67 37.00			

KM# 33 10 FRANCS
31.26 g., 0.999 Silver 1.004 oz. ASW, 45.1 x 23.4 mm. **Subject:** Animal Protection **Obv:** Standing lion facing within triangle, denomination below **Rev:** Chimpanzee hanging from branches **Edge:** Plain **Shape:** Triangle **Note:** Prev. KM#56.

Date	Mintage	VF20	XF40	MS60	MS63	MS65
2000	—	PF65 32.00	PF67 37.00			

KM# 34 10 FRANCS
31.26 g., 0.999 Silver 1.004 oz. ASW, 45.1 x 23.4 mm. **Subject:** Animal Protection **Obv:** Standing lion facing within triangle, denomination below **Rev:** 2 chimpanzees in trees **Edge:** Plain **Shape:** Triangle **Note:** Prev. KM#57.

Date	Mintage	VF20	XF40	MS60	MS63	MS65
2000	—	PF65 32.00	PF67 37.00			

KM# 35 10 FRANCS
31.26 g., 0.999 Silver 1.004 oz. ASW, 45.1 x 23.4 mm. **Subject:** Animal Protection **Obv:** Standing lion facing within triangle, denomination below **Rev:** Female chimpanzee with young one **Edge:** Plain **Shape:** Triangle **Note:** Prev. KM#58.

Date	Mintage	VF20	XF40	MS60	MS63	MS65
2000	—	PF65 32.00	PF67 37.00			

KM# 36 10 FRANCS
31.26 g., 0.999 Silver 1.004 oz. ASW, 45.1 x 23.4 mm. **Subject:** Animal Protection **Obv:** Standing lion facing within triangle, denomination below **Rev:** 2 chimpanzees on the ground **Edge:** Plain **Shape:** Triangle **Note:** Prev. KM#59.

Date	Mintage	VF20	XF40	MS60	MS63	MS65
2000	—	PF65 32.00	PF67 37.00			

KM# 37 10 FRANCS
20.00 g., 0.925 Silver 0.5948 oz. ASW, 38 mm. **Subject:** Millennium - Jesus **Obv:** Standing lion facing, denomination below **Rev:** Portrait of Jesus facing within beaded circles, date below **Edge:** Plain **Note:** Prev. KM#60.

Date	Mintage	VF20	XF40	MS60	MS63	MS65
2000	—	PF65 32.00	PF67 37.00			

KM# 44 10 FRANCS
19.92 g., 0.925 Silver 0.5924 oz. ASW, 41.1 mm. **Series:** Olympics **Obv:** Standing lion facing, date below **Rev:** Long jumper, denomination at right **Edge:** Reeded **Note:** Prev. KM#67.

Date	Mintage	VF20	XF40	MS60	MS63	MS65
2000	—	PF65 30.00	PF67 32.00			

KM# 45 10 FRANCS
19.92 g., 0.925 Silver 0.5924 oz. ASW, 41.1 mm. **Series:** Olympics **Obv:** Standing lion facing, date below **Rev:** Two divers, denomination at left **Edge:** Reeded **Note:** Prev. KM#68.

Date	Mintage	VF20	XF40	MS60	MS63	MS65
2000	—	PF65 30.00	PF67 32.00			

KM# 46 10 FRANCS
19.92 g., 0.925 Silver 0.5924 oz. ASW, 41.1 mm. **Series:** Olympics **Obv:** Standing lion facing, date below **Rev:** Tennis player, denomination at right **Edge:** Reeded **Note:** Prev. KM#69.

Date	Mintage	VF20	XF40	MS60	MS63	MS65
2000	—	PF65 30.00	PF67 32.00			

KM# 47 10 FRANCS
19.92 g., 0.925 Silver 0.5924 oz. ASW, 41.1 mm. **Series:** Olympics **Obv:** Standing lion facing, date below **Rev:** Weight lifter, denomination at left **Edge:** Reeded **Note:** Prev. KM#70.

Date	Mintage	VF20	XF40	MS60	MS63	MS65
2000	—	PF65 30.00	PF67 32.00			

KM# 48 10 FRANCS
19.92 g., 0.925 Silver 0.5924 oz. ASW, 41.1 mm. **Series:** Olympics **Obv:** Standing lion facing, date below **Rev:** Two fencers, denomination below **Edge:** Plain **Note:** Prev. KM#71.

Date	Mintage	VF20	XF40	MS60	MS63	MS65
2000	—	PF65 30.00	PF67 32.00			

KM# 49 10 FRANCS
19.92 g., 0.925 Silver 0.5924 oz. ASW, 41.1 mm. **Series:** Olympics **Obv:** Standing lion facing, date below **Rev:** Two boxers, denomination below **Edge:** Reeded **Note:** Prev. KM#72.

Date	Mintage	VF20	XF40	MS60	MS63	MS65
2000	—	PF65 30.00	PF67 32.00			

KM# 50 10 FRANCS
19.92 g., 0.925 Silver 0.5924 oz. ASW, 41.1 mm. **Series:** Olympics **Obv:** Standing lion facing, date below **Rev:** Rowing, denomination below **Edge:** Reeded **Note:** Prev. KM#73.

Date	Mintage	VF20	XF40	MS60	MS63	MS65
2000	—	PF65 30.00	PF67 32.00			

KM# 51 10 FRANCS
19.92 g., 0.925 Silver 0.5924 oz. ASW, 41.1 mm. **Series:** Olympics **Obv:** Standing lion facing, date below **Rev:** Archer, denomination at lower left **Edge:** Reeded **Note:** Prev. KM#74.

Date	Mintage	VF20	XF40	MS60	MS63	MS65
2000	—	PF65 30.00	PF67 32.00			

KM# 52 10 FRANCS
19.92 g., 0.925 Silver 0.5924 oz. ASW, 41.1 mm. **Series:** Olympics **Obv:** Standing lion facing, date below **Rev:** Judo match, denomination below **Edge:** Reeded **Note:** Prev. KM#75.

Date	Mintage	VF20	XF40	MS60	MS63	MS65
2000	—	PF65 30.00	PF67 32.00			

KM# 53 10 FRANCS
19.92 g., 0.925 Silver 0.5924 oz. ASW, 41.1 mm. **Series:** Olympics **Obv:** Standing lion facing, date below **Rev:** Ribbon dancer, denomination at right **Edge:** Reeded **Note:** Prev. KM#76.

Date	Mintage	VF20	XF40	MS60	MS63	MS65
2000	—	PF65 30.00	PF67 32.00			

KM# 54 10 FRANCS
19.92 g., 0.925 Silver 0.5924 oz. ASW, 41.1 mm. **Series:** Olympics **Obv:** Standing lion facing, date below **Rev:** Badminton player, denomination below **Edge:** Reeded **Note:** Prev. KM#77.

Date	Mintage	VF20	XF40	MS60	MS63	MS65
2000	—	PF65 30.00	PF67 32.00			

KM# 55 10 FRANCS
25.45 g., 0.925 Silver 0.7569 oz. ASW, 37.2 mm. **Series:** Wild Life Protection **Obv:** Standing lion facing, denomination below **Rev:** Multicolored toucan hologram left **Edge:** Reeded **Note:** Prev. KM#78.

Date	Mintage	VF20	XF40	MS60	MS63	MS65
2000	—	PF65 65.00	PF67 70.00			

KM# 92 10 FRANCS
30.87 g., 0.999 Silver 0.9915 oz. ASW, 38.7 mm. **Obv:** Standing lion facing, date below **Rev:** African crocodile left, denomination below **Edge:** Reeded

Date	Mintage	VF20	XF40	MS60	MS63	MS65
2000	—	PF65 35.00	PF67 38.00			

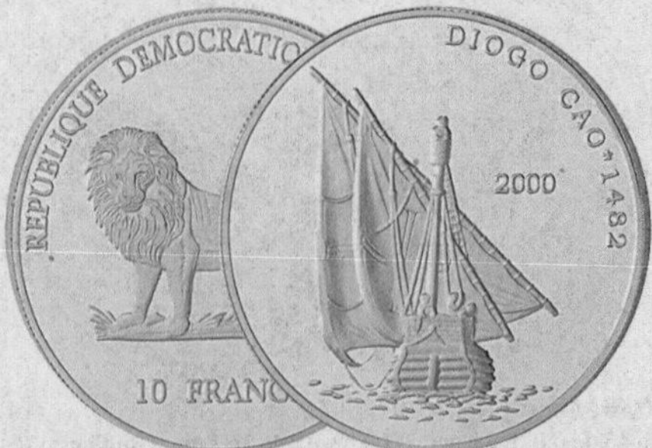

KM# 98 10 FRANCS
31.55 g., 0.925 Silver 0.9383 oz. ASW, 38.7 mm. **Subject:** Diogo Cao 1482 **Obv:** Standing lion facing, denomination below **Rev:** Portuguese sailing ship, date at right **Edge:** Reeded

Date	Mintage	VF20	XF40	MS60	MS63	MS65
2000	—	PF65 25.00	PF67 28.00			

KM# 161 10 FRANCS

19.76 g., 0.925 Silver 0.5877 oz. ASW, 38.6 mm. **Obv:** Standing lion facing, denomination below **Rev:** Gorilla on all fours facing, date below **Edge:** Reeded

Date	Mintage	VF20	XF40	MS60	MS63	MS65
2000	—	PF65 45.00	PF67 50.00			

KM# 29 20 FRANCS

1.53 g., 0.999 Gold 0.0491 oz. AGW **Subject:** 25th Anniversary - Visit of Pope John Paul II **Obv:** Standing lion facing, denomination below **Rev:** Bust right of Pope John Paul II **Note:** Prev. KM#52.

Date	Mintage	VF20	XF40	MS60	MS63	MS65
2000	—	PF65 70.00	PF67 80.00			

KM# 62 20 FRANCS

62.20 g., 0.9999 Silver 1.9996 oz. ASW, 40 mm. **Subject:** Japanese New 500 Yen Coin **Obv:** Standing lion facing, denomination below **Rev:** Japanese 500 yen coin Y-125, embedded over the obverse and reverse design of the Y-99 500 yen coin **Edge:** Reeded **Note:** Prev. KM#85.

Date	Mintage	VF20	XF40	MS60	MS63	MS65
2000	1,500	—	—	—	70.00	80.00

KM# 183 20 FRANCS

1.22 g., Gold, 13.85 mm. **Subject:** Arican art **Obv:** Lion standing right **Rev:** statue at right **Edge:** Reeded

Date	Mintage	VF20	XF40	MS60	MS63	MS65
2000	—	PF65 70.00	PF67 80.00			

KM# 177 100 FRANCS

39.20 g., Gold **Obv:** Roaring lion **Rev:** Dr. Livingstone and river boat **Edge:** Reeded

Date	Mintage	VF20	XF40	MS60	MS63	MS65
1999	—	PF67 1,750				

KM# 42 100 FRANCS

31.54 g., 0.9999 Gold 1.0139 oz. AGW, 37.3 mm. **Subject:** Wild Life Protection **Obv:** Standing lion facing, denomination below **Rev:** Multicolor holographic parrot with folded wings right **Edge:** Reeded **Note:** Prev. KM#65.

Date	Mintage	VF20	XF40	MS60	MS63	MS65
2000	25	PF67 1,850				

KM# 43 100 FRANCS

31.54 g., 0.9999 Gold 1.0139 oz. AGW, 37.3 mm. **Subject:** Wild Life Protection **Obv:** Standing lion facing, denomination below **Rev:** Multicolor holographic parrot with open wings left **Edge:** Reeded **Note:** Prev. KM#66.

Date	Mintage	VF20	XF40	MS60	MS63	MS65
2000	25	PF67 1,850				

ESSAIS

KM#	Date	Mintage	Identification	Mkt Val
E1	1965	—	10 Francs. Silver.	—
E2	1965(b)	—	10 Francs. Gold.	—

Note: Aluminum and copper-nickel essais of the 10 Francs are valued at $500 and $650 respectively. These are considered off-metal pieces created as die trials or set-up strikes in the process of producing the official silver and gold coins.

KM#	Date	Mintage	Identification	Mkt Val
E3	1970	—	50 Makutas. Pewter. KM12.	275
E4	1970	—	Zaire. Pewter. KM13.	350
E5	1970	—	Zaire. Silver. KM13.	175
E6	1970	10	Zaire. Gold. ESSAI.	1,750

PATTERNS

Including off metal strikes

KM#	Date	Mintage	Identification	Mkt Val
Pn1	1965	—	10 Francs. Copper. 3.2 mm thick.	1,000
Pn3	1965	—	100 Francs. KM#6, Type II variety.	1,000
Pn5	1999	—	100 Francs. Gilt. Stanley.	450
Pn6	1999	—	100 Francs. Gilt. Livingston.	450

PIEDFORT WITH ESSAI

KM#	Date	Mintage	Identification	Mkt Val
PE1	1970	10	Zaire. Silver. 2.4 mm thick.	700
PE2	1970	10	Zaire. Silver. 4.7 mm thick.	1,500

TRIAL STRIKES

KM#	Date	Mintage	Identification	Mkt Val
TS1	1965	—	10 Francs. Bronze. Uniface reverse, KM1, piefort thickness.	900

MINT SETS

KM#	Date	Mintage	Identification	Issue Price	Mkt Val
MS1	1970 (4)	1,000	KM10, 11a-13a	1,300	3,000

PROOF SETS

KM#	Date	Mintage	Identification	Issue Price	Mkt Val
PS1	1965 (5)	3,000	KM2-6. Approximately 70 percent melted.	490	3,400
PS2	1970 (4)	1,000	KM10, 11a-13a	—	3,150
PS3	2000 (4)	—	KM#33-36	—	170

COOK ISLANDS

Cook Islands, a self-governing dependency of New Zealand consisting of 15 islands, is located in the South Pacific Ocean about 2,000 miles (3,218 km.) northeast of New Zealand. It has an area of 93 sq. mi. (234 sq. km.) and a population of 17,185. Capital: Avarua. The United States claims the islands of Danger, Manahiki, Penrhyn, and Rakahanga atolls. Citrus and canned fruits and juices, copra, clothing, jewelry, and mother-of-pearl shell are exported.

Spanish navigator Alvaro de Mendada first sighted the islands in 1595. Portuguese navigator Pedro Fernandes de Quieros landed on Rakahanga in 1606. English navigator Capt. James Cook sailed to the islands on three occasions: 1773, 1774 and 1777. He named them Hervey Islands, in honor of Augustus John Hervey, a lord of the Admiralty. The islands were declared a British protectorate in 1888, and were annexed to New Zealand in 1901. They were granted internal self-government in 1965. New Zealand provides an annual subsidy and retains responsibility for defense and foreign affairs.

RULER

British

MINT MARKS

(b) - British Royal Mint

FM - Franklin Mint, U.S.A. *

PM - Pobjoy Mint

***NOTE**: From 1975-1985 the Franklin Mint produced coinage in up to three different qualities. Qualities of issue are designated in () after each date and are defined as follows:

(M) MATTE - Normal circulation strike or a dull finish produced by sandblasting special uncirculated (polish finish) or proof quality dies.

(U) SPECIAL UNCIRCULATED - Polished or proof-like in appearance without any frosted features.

(P) PROOF - The highest quality obtainable having mirror-like fields and frosted features.

MONETARY SYSTEM

(Until 1967)

12 Pence = 1 Shilling
20 Shillings = 1 Pound
(Commencing 1967)
100 Cents = 1 Dollar

DEPENDENCY OF NEW ZEALAND

DECIMAL COINAGE

KM# 1 CENT

2.07 g., Bronze, 17.53 mm. **Ruler:** Elizabeth II **Obv:** Young bust right, date below **Rev:** Taro leaf, denomination at right

Date	Mintage	F12	VF20	XF40	MS60	MS63
1972	17,000	PF63 0.50	PF65 0.75			
1972	117,000	—	—	0.10	0.20	0.35
1973	13,000	PF63 0.50	PF65 0.75			
1973	8,500	—	—	0.10	0.20	0.35
1974	300,000	—	—	0.10	0.20	0.35
1974	7,300	PF63 0.50	PF65 0.75			
1975	429,000	—	—	0.10	0.20	0.35
1975 FM (P)	21,000	PF63 0.50	PF65 0.75			
1975 FM (M)	1,000	—	—	—	0.50	0.65
1975 FM (U)	2,251	—	—	—	0.20	0.35
1976 FM (M)	1,001	—	—	—	0.50	0.65
1976 FM (P)	18,000	PF63 0.50	PF65 0.75			
1976 FM (U)	1,066	—	—	—	0.20	0.35
1977 FM (M)	1,171	—	—	—	0.50	0.65
1977 FM (U)	1,002	—	—	—	0.20	0.35
1977 FM (P)	5,986	PF63 0.50	PF65 0.75			
1979 FM (M)	1,000	—	—	—	0.50	0.65
1979 FM (U)	500	—	—	—	1.00	1.25
1979 FM (P)	4,058	PF63 0.50	PF65 0.75			
1983	10,000	PF63 0.50	PF65 0.75			
1983	—	—	—	0.10	0.20	0.35

KM# 1a CENT

2.07 g., Bronze, 17.53 mm. **Ruler:** Elizabeth II **Obv:** Young bust right, date below **Rev:** Taro leaf, denomination **Edge Lettering:** 1728 • CAPT. JAMES COOK • 1978

Date	Mintage	VF20	XF40	MS60	MS63	MS65
1978 FM (U)	767	—	—	0.75	1.00	—
1978 FM (M)	1,000	—	—	0.85	1.15	—
1978 FM (P)	6,287	PF63 0.50	PF65 0.75			

KM# 1b CENT

2.07 g., Bronze, 17.53 mm. **Ruler:** Elizabeth II **Subject:** Wedding of Prince Charles and Lady Diana **Obv:** Young bust right **Edge Lettering:** THE ROYAL WEDDING 29 JULY 1981

Date	Mintage	VF20	XF40	MS60	MS63	MS65
1981 FM (U)	1,100	—	—	0.50	0.65	—
1981 FM (M)	1,000	—	—	0.50	0.65	—
1981 FM (P)	9,205	PF63 0.40	PF65 0.65			

KM# 2 2 CENTS

4.14 g., Bronze, 21.08 mm. **Ruler:** Elizabeth II **Obv:** Young bust right, date below **Rev:** Pineapple, denomination at right

Date	Mintage	F12	VF20	XF40	MS60	MS63
1972	63,000	—	0.10	0.15	0.30	0.50
1972	17,000	PF63 0.75	PF65 1.00			
1973	8,500	—	0.15	0.20	0.40	0.60
1973	13,000	PF63 0.75	PF65 1.00			
1974	120,000	—	0.10	0.15	0.30	0.50
1974	7,300	PF63 0.75	PF65 1.00			
1975	129,000	—	0.10	0.15	0.25	0.45
1975 FM (U)	2,251	—	—	—	0.30	0.50
1975 FM (M)	1,000	—	—	—	0.50	0.75
1975 FM (P)	21,000	PF63 0.75	PF65 1.00			
1976 FM (U)	1,066	—	—	—	0.30	0.50
1976 FM (M)	1,001	—	—	—	0.75	1.00
1976 FM (P)	18,000	PF63 0.75	PF65 1.00			
1977 FM (U)	1,002	—	—	—	0.30	0.50
1977 FM (M)	1,171	—	—	—	0.75	1.00
1977 FM (P)	5,986	PF63 0.75	PF65 1.00			
1979 FM (U)	500	—	—	—	0.30	0.50
1979 FM (M)	1,000	—	—	—	0.75	1.00
1979 FM (P)	4,058	PF63 0.75	PF65 1.00			
1983	—	—	0.10	0.15	0.25	0.45
1983	10,000	PF63 0.75	PF65 1.00			

KM# 2a 2 CENTS

4.14 g., Bronze, 21.08 mm. **Ruler:** Elizabeth II **Obv:** Young bust right **Rev:** Pineapple, denomination at right **Edge Lettering:** 1728 • CAPT. JAMES COOK • 1978

Date	Mintage	VF20	XF40	MS60	MS63	MS65
1978 FM (U)	767	—	—	0.85	1.15	—
1978 FM (M)	1,000	—	—	0.75	1.00	—
1978 FM (P)	6,287	PF63	0.50	PF65	0.75	

KM# 2b 2 CENTS

4.14 g., Bronze, 21.08 mm. **Ruler:** Elizabeth II **Subject:** Wedding of Prince Charles and Lady Diana **Obv:** Young bust right, date below **Edge Lettering:** THE ROYAL WEDDING 29 JULY 1981

Date	Mintage	VF20	XF40	MS60	MS63	MS65
1981 FM (U)	1,100	—	—	0.75	1.00	—
1981 FM (M)	1,000	—	—	0.75	1.00	—
1981 FM (P)	9,205	PF63	0.50	PF65	0.75	

KM# 3 5 CENTS

2.83 g., Copper-Nickel, 19.41 mm. **Ruler:** Elizabeth II **Obv:** Young bust right, date below **Rev:** Hibiscus, denomination below **Edge:** Reeded

Date	Mintage	F12	VF20	XF40	MS60	MS63
1972	32,000	—	0.10	0.20	0.40	0.60
1972	17,000	PF63	1.00	PF65	1.25	
1973	8,500	—	0.15	0.25	0.50	0.75
1973	13,000	PF63	1.00	PF65	1.25	
1974	80,000	—	0.10	0.20	0.40	0.60
1974	7,300	PF63	1.00	PF65	1.25	
1975	89,000	—	0.10	0.20	0.40	0.60
1975 FM (U)	2,251	—	—	—	0.40	0.60
1975 FM (M)	1,000	—	—	—	1.00	1.25
1975 FM (P)	21,000	PF63	0.85	PF65	1.25	
1976 FM (U)	1,066	—	—	—	0.40	0.60
1976 FM (M)	1,001	—	—	—	1.00	1.25
1976 FM (P)	18,000	PF63	0.85	PF65	1.25	
1977 FM (U)	1,002	—	—	—	0.40	0.60
1977 FM (M)	1,171	—	—	—	1.00	1.25
1977 FM (P)	5,986	PF63	1.00	PF65	1.25	
1979 FM (U)	500	—	—	—	0.40	0.60
1979 FM (M)	1,000	—	—	—	1.00	1.25
1979 FM (P)	4,058	PF63	1.00	PF65	1.25	
1983	—	—	0.10	0.20	0.40	0.60
1983	10,000	PF63	1.00	PF65	1.25	

KM# 3a 5 CENTS

2.83 g., Copper-Nickel, 19.41 mm. **Ruler:** Elizabeth II **Subject:** 250th Anniversary of the Birth of Captain James Cook **Obv:** Young bust right, date below **Rev:** Hibiscus, denomination below **Edge:** Reeded, with plain lettered segment **Edge Lettering:** 1728 • CAPT. JAMES COOK • 1978

Date	Mintage	VF20	XF40	MS60	MS63	MS65
1978 FM (U)	767	—	—	0.75	1.00	—
1978 FM (M)	1,000	—	—	1.00	1.25	—
1978 FM (P)	6,287	PF63	0.50	PF65	0.75	

KM# 3b 5 CENTS

2.83 g., Copper-Nickel, 19.41 mm. **Ruler:** Elizabeth II **Subject:** Wedding of Prince Charles and Lady Diana **Obv:** Young bust right, date below **Edge Lettering:** THE ROYAL WEDDING 29 JULY 1981

Date	Mintage	VF20	XF40	MS60	MS63	MS65
1981 FM (U)	1,100	—	—	1.00	1.25	—
1981 FM (M)	1,000	—	—	1.00	1.25	—
1981 FM (P)	9,205	PF63	0.50	PF65	0.75	

KM# 33 5 CENTS

2.83 g., Copper-Nickel, 19.41 mm. **Ruler:** Elizabeth II **Obv:** Crowned head right, date below **Rev:** Hibiscus, value below **Edge:** Reeded

Date	Mintage	VF20	XF40	MS60	MS63	MS65
1987	—	—	0.15	0.35	0.50	—
1987	—	PF63	1.00	PF65	1.25	
1988	—	—	0.15	0.35	0.50	—
1988	—	PF63	1.00	PF65	1.25	
1992	—	—	0.15	0.35	0.50	—
1992	—	PF63	1.00	PF65	1.25	
1994	20,000	—	0.15	0.35	0.50	—
1994	200	PF63	1.50	PF65	1.75	

KM# 369 5 CENTS

4.43 g., Nickel Clad Steel, 24.05 mm. **Ruler:** Elizabeth II **Subject:** F.A.O. **Obv:** Head with tiara right, date below **Rev:** Statue of Tangaroa divides denomination **Edge:** Plain

Date	Mintage	VF20	XF40	MS60	MS63	MS65
2000	—	—	—	1.00	1.50	—
2000	—	PF63	3.50	PF65	5.00	

KM# 4 10 CENTS

5.65 g., Copper-Nickel, 23.6 mm. **Ruler:** Elizabeth II **Obv:** Young bust right, date below **Rev:** Orange, denomination above **Edge:** Reeded

Date	Mintage	F12	VF20	XF40	MS60	MS63
1972	35,000	—	0.10	0.20	0.65	0.85
1972	17,000	PF63	1.25	PF65	1.50	
1973	59,000	—	0.10	0.20	0.65	0.85
1973	13,000	PF63	1.25	PF65	1.50	
1974	50,000	—	0.10	0.20	0.50	0.85
1974	7,300	PF63	1.25	PF65	1.50	
1975	59,000	—	0.10	0.20	0.50	0.85
1975 FM (U)	2,251	—	—	—	0.50	0.85
1975 FM (M)	1,000	—	—	—	1.25	1.50
1975 FM (P)	21,000	PF63	1.25	PF65	1.50	
1976 FM (U)	1,066	—	—	—	0.50	0.65
1976 FM (M)	1,001	—	—	—	1.25	1.50
1976 FM (P)	18,000	PF63	1.25	PF65	1.50	
1977 FM (M)	1,171	—	—	—	1.25	1.50
1977 FM (U)	1,002	—	—	—	0.50	0.65
1977 FM (P)	5,986	PF63	1.25	PF65	1.50	
1983	—	—	0.10	0.20	0.50	0.65
1983	10,000	PF63	1.25	PF65	1.50	

KM# 4a 10 CENTS

5.65 g., Copper-Nickel, 23.6 mm. **Ruler:** Elizabeth II **Obv:** Young bust right, date below **Rev:** Orange, denomination above **Edge Lettering:** 1728 • CAPT. JAMES COOK • 1978

Date	Mintage	VF20	XF40	MS60	MS63	MS65
1978 FM (U)	767	—	—	1.25	1.50	—
1978 FM (M)	1,000	—	—	1.25	1.50	—
1978 FM (P)	6,287	PF63	1.00	PF65	1.25	

KM# 4b 10 CENTS

5.65 g., Copper-Nickel, 23.6 mm. **Ruler:** Elizabeth II **Series:** F.A.O. **Obv:** Young bust right, date below **Rev:** Orange, denomination above

Date	Mintage	VF20	XF40	MS60	MS63	MS65
1979 FM (U)	500	—	—	1.50	1.75	—
1979 FM (M)	9,000	—	—	1.00	1.25	—
1979 FM (P)	4,058	PF63	1.25	PF65	1.50	

KM# 4c 10 CENTS

5.65 g., Copper-Nickel, 23.6 mm. **Ruler:** Elizabeth II **Subject:** Wedding of Prince Charles and Lady Diana **Obv:** Young bust right, date below **Edge Lettering:** THE ROYAL WEDDING 29 JULY 1981

Date	Mintage	VF20	XF40	MS60	MS63	MS65
1981 FM (U)	1,100	—	—	1.25	1.50	—
1981 FM (M)	1,000	—	—	1.25	1.50	—
1981 FM (P)	9,205	PF63	0.75	PF65	1.00	

KM# 34 10 CENTS

5.65 g., Copper-Nickel, 23.6 mm. **Ruler:** Elizabeth II **Obv:** Crowned head right, date below **Rev:** Orange, denomination above **Edge:** Reeded

Date	Mintage	VF20	XF40	MS60	MS63	MS65
1987	—	—	0.20	0.50	0.75	—
1987	—	PF63	1.25	PF65	1.50	
1988	—	—	0.20	0.50	0.75	—
1988	—	PF63	1.25	PF65	1.50	
1992	—	—	0.20	0.50	0.75	—
1992	—	PF63	1.25	PF65	1.50	
1994	20,000	—	0.20	0.50	0.75	—
1994	200	PF63	1.75	PF65	2.00	

KM# 5 20 CENTS

11.31 g., Copper-Nickel, 28.52 mm. **Ruler:** Elizabeth II **Obv:** Young bust right, date below **Rev:** Fairy Tern right, denomination below **Edge:** Reeded

Date	Mintage	VF20	XF40	MS60	MS63	MS65
1972	31,000	0.20	0.40	0.75	1.00	—
1972	17,000	PF63	1.50	PF65	1.75	
1973	49,000	0.20	0.40	0.75	1.00	—
1973	13,000	PF63	1.50	PF65	1.75	
1974	5,500	0.20	0.45	0.85	1.25	—
1974	7,300	PF63	1.50	PF65	1.75	
1975	60,000	0.20	0.40	0.75	1.00	—
1975 FM (U)	2,251	—	—	0.85	1.25	—
1975 FM (M)	1,000	—	—	1.50	1.75	—
1975 FM (P)	21,000	PF63	1.50	PF65	1.75	
1983	—	0.20	0.40	0.85	1.25	—
1983	10,000	PF63	1.50	PF65	1.75	

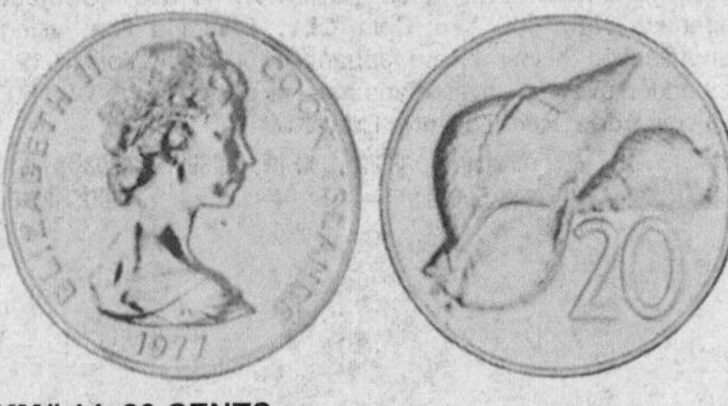

KM# 14 20 CENTS

11.31 g., Copper-Nickel, 28.52 mm. **Ruler:** Elizabeth II **Obv:** Young bust right, date below **Rev:** Two Pacific Triton shells, denomination lower right **Edge:** Reeded

Date	Mintage	VF20	XF40	MS60	MS63	MS65
1976 FM (U)	1,066	—	—	1.00	1.25	—
1976 FM (M)	1,001	—	—	1.50	1.75	—
1976 FM (P)	18,000	PF63	1.50	PF65	1.75	
1977 FM (U)	1,002	—	—	1.00	1.25	—
1977 FM (M)	1,171	—	—	1.50	1.75	—
1977 FM (P)	5,986	PF63	1.50	PF65	1.75	
1979 FM (U)	500	—	—	2.00	2.50	—
1979 FM (M)	1,000	—	—	1.50	1.75	—
1979 FM (P)	4,058	PF63	1.50	PF65	1.75	

KM# 14a 20 CENTS

11.31 g., Copper-Nickel, 28.52 mm. **Ruler:** Elizabeth II **Obv:** Young bust right, date below **Rev:** Shells, denomination at right **Edge Lettering:** 1728 • CAPT. JAMES COOK • 1978

Date	Mintage	VF20	XF40	MS60	MS63	MS65
1978 FM (U)	767	—	—	2.00	2.50	—
1978 FM (M)	1,000	—	—	1.50	1.75	—
1978 FM (P)	6,287	PF63	1.50	PF65	1.75	

KM# 14b 20 CENTS

11.31 g., Copper-Nickel, 28.52 mm. **Ruler:** Elizabeth II **Subject:** Wedding of Prince Charles and Lady Diana **Obv:** Young bust right, date below **Rev:** Shells, denomination at right **Edge Lettering:** THE ROYAL WEDDING 29 JULY 1981

Date	Mintage	VF20	XF40	MS60	MS63	MS65
1981 FM (U)	1,100	—	—	1.50	1.75	—
1981 FM (M)	1,000	—	—	1.50	1.75	—
1981 FM (P)	9,205	PF63	1.00	PF65	1.25	

KM# 35 20 CENTS

11.31 g., Copper-Nickel, 28.52 mm. **Ruler:** Elizabeth II **Obv:** Crowned head right, date below **Rev:** Fairy Tern, denomination below **Edge:** Reeded

Date	Mintage	VF20	XF40	MS60	MS63	MS65
1987	—	—	0.25	0.75	1.00	—
1987	—	PF63 1.50	PF65 1.75			
1988	—	—	0.25	0.75	1.00	—
1988	—	PF63 1.50	PF65 1.75			
1992	—	—	0.25	0.75	1.00	—
1992	—	PF63 1.50	PF65 1.75			
1994	20,000	—	0.25	0.75	1.00	—
1994	200	PF63 2.00	PF65 2.50			

KM# 6.1 50 CENTS

13.60 g., Copper-Nickel, 31.75 mm. **Ruler:** Elizabeth II **Obv:** Young bust right, date below **Rev:** Bonito fish, denomination upper left **Edge:** Segmented reeding

Date	Mintage	VF20	XF40	MS60	MS63	MS65
1972	31,000	—	0.65	1.25	2.00	—
1972	17,000	PF63 3.00	PF65 4.00			
1973	19,000	—	0.65	1.25	2.00	—
1973	13,000	PF63 3.00	PF65 4.00			
1974	10,000	—	0.65	1.25	2.00	—
1974	7,300	PF63 3.00	PF65 4.00			
1975	19,000	—	0.65	1.25	2.00	—
1975 FM (U)	2,251	—	—	1.50	2.00	—
1975 FM (M)	1,000	—	—	2.00	3.00	—
1975 FM (P)	21,000	PF63 2.50	PF65 3.00			
1976 FM (U)	1,066	—	—	1.50	2.00	—
1976 FM (M)	1,001	—	—	2.00	3.00	—
1976 FM (P)	18,000	PF63 2.50	PF65 3.00			
1977 FM (U)	1,002	—	—	1.50	2.00	—
1977 FM (M)	1,171	—	—	2.00	3.00	—
1977 FM (P)	5,986	PF63 3.00	PF65 4.00			
1983	—	—	0.65	1.25	2.00	—
1983	10,000	PF63 3.50	PF65 5.00			

KM# 6.2 50 CENTS

13.60 g., Copper-Nickel, 31.75 mm. **Ruler:** Elizabeth II **Obv:** Young bust right, date below **Edge Lettering:** 1728 • CAPT. JAMES COOK • 1978

Date	Mintage	VF20	XF40	MS60	MS63	MS65
1978 FM (U)	767	—	—	2.00	3.00	—
1978 FM (M)	1,000	—	—	2.00	3.00	—
1978 FM (P)	6,287	PF63 2.00	PF65 2.50			

KM# 6.3 50 CENTS

13.60 g., Copper-Nickel, 31.75 mm. **Ruler:** Elizabeth II **Series:** F.A.O. **Obv:** Young bust right, date below **Rev:** F.A.O. logo, Bonito fish, denomination upper left **Edge:** Segmented reeding

Date	Mintage	VF20	XF40	MS60	MS63	MS65
1979 FM (U)	500	—	—	2.50	3.50	—
1979 FM (M)	9,000	—	0.75	1.25	2.00	—
1979 FM (P)	4,058	PF63 2.25	PF65 2.75			

KM# 6.4 50 CENTS

13.60 g., Copper-Nickel, 31.75 mm. **Ruler:** Elizabeth II **Subject:** Wedding of Prince Charles and Lady Diana **Obv:** Young bust right, date below **Edge Lettering:** THE ROYAL WEDDING 29 JULY 1981

Date	Mintage	VF20	XF40	MS60	MS63	MS65
1981 FM (U)	1,100	—	—	2.00	3.00	—
1981 FM (M)	1,000	—	—	2.00	3.00	—
1981 FM (P)	9,205	PF63 1.50	PF65 1.75			

KM# 36 50 CENTS

13.60 g., Copper-Nickel, 31.75 mm. **Ruler:** Elizabeth II **Obv:** Crowned head right, date below **Rev:** Bonito fish, denomination upper left **Edge:** Segmented reeding

Date	Mintage	VF20	XF40	MS60	MS63	MS65
1987	—	—	0.65	1.50	2.00	—
1987	—	PF63 2.00	PF65 2.50			
1992	—	—	0.65	1.50	2.00	—

KM# 307 50 CENTS

Copper-Nickel **Ruler:** Elizabeth II **Obv:** Crowned head right, date below **Rev:** Head 3/4 facing, dates and denomination below

Date	Mintage	VF20	XF40	MS60	MS63	MS65
1997	—	PF63 8.50	PF65 10.00			
1997	—	—	—	—	6.00	—

KM# 338 50 CENTS

26.90 g., Copper-Nickel **Ruler:** Elizabeth II **Obv:** Crowned head right, date below **Rev:** Multicolor cartoon cat "Garfield", denomination below **Edge:** Reeded

Date	Mintage	VF20	XF40	MS60	MS63	MS65
1999	—	PF63 7.50	PF65 9.50			

KM# 41 50 TENE

13.60 g., Copper-Nickel, 31.75 mm. **Ruler:** Elizabeth II **Obv:** Crowned head right, date below **Rev:** Hawksbill turtle right, denomination above

Date	Mintage	VF20	XF40	MS60	MS63	MS65
1988	60,000	—	0.50	2.00	3.50	—
1988	1,000	PF63 5.00	PF65 6.00			
1992	—	—	—	2.00	3.50	—
1992	—	PF63 5.00	PF65 6.00			
1994	20,000	—	—	2.00	3.50	—
1994	200	PF63 6.00	PF65 7.00			

KM# 7 DOLLAR

27.20 g., Copper-Nickel, 38.5 mm. **Ruler:** Elizabeth II **Obv:** Young bust right, date below **Rev:** Tangaroa, Polynesian God of Creation, divides denominations

Date	Mintage	VF20	XF40	MS60	MS63	MS65
1972	31,000	1.00	1.50	2.50	4.00	—
1972	27,000	PF63 4.00	PF65 5.00			
1973	49,000	1.00	1.50	2.50	4.00	—
1973	13,000	PF63 6.00	PF65 7.00			
1974	20,000	1.00	1.50	2.50	4.00	—
1974	7,300	PF63 6.00	PF65 7.00			
1975	29,000	1.00	1.50	2.50	4.00	—
1975 FM (U)	2,251	—	—	3.50	5.00	—
1975 FM (M)	1,000	—	—	4.50	6.00	—
1975 FM (P)	21,000	PF63 6.00	PF65 7.00			
1976 FM (U)	1,066	—	—	4.50	6.00	—
1976 FM (M)	1,001	—	—	4.50	6.00	—
1976 FM (P)	18,000	PF63 5.00	PF65 6.00			
1977 FM (U)	1,002	—	—	4.50	6.00	—
1977 FM (M)	1,171	—	—	4.50	6.00	—
1977 FM (P)	5,986	PF63 6.50	PF65 7.50			
1979 FM (U)	500	—	—	5.50	7.00	—
1979 FM (M)	1,000	—	—	4.50	6.00	—
1979 FM (P)	4,058	PF63 6.50	PF65 7.50			
1983	—	1.00	1.50	3.50	5.00	—
1983	10,000	PF63 5.00	PF65 6.00			

KM# 7a DOLLAR

27.20 g., Copper-Nickel, 38.5 mm. **Ruler:** Elizabeth II **Obv:** Young bust right, date below **Rev:** Tangaroa, Polynesian God of Creation, divides denominations **Edge Lettering:** 1728 • CAPT. JAMES COOK • 1978

Date	Mintage	VF20	XF40	MS60	MS63	MS65
1978 FM (U)	767	—	—	6.00	7.50	—
1978 FM (M)	1,000	—	—	6.00	7.50	—
1978 FM (P)	6,287	PF63 5.50	PF65 6.50			

KM# 7b DOLLAR

27.20 g., Copper-Nickel, 38.5 mm. **Ruler:** Elizabeth II **Subject:** Wedding of Prince Charles and Lady Diana **Obv:** Young bust right, date below **Rev:** Tangaroa, Polynesian God of Creation, divides denominations **Edge Lettering:** THE ROYAL WEDDING 29 JULY 1981

Date	Mintage	VF20	XF40	MS60	MS63	MS65
1981 FM (U)	1,100	—	—	5.00	6.50	—
1981 FM (M)	1,000	—	—	5.00	6.50	—
1981 FM (P)	9,205	PF63 5.00	PF65 6.00			

KM# 30 DOLLAR

27.20 g., Copper-Nickel, 38.5 mm. **Ruler:** Elizabeth II **Subject:** 16th Forum, 2nd P.I.C. and Mini Games **Obv:** Young bust right, date below **Rev:** Tangaroa, Polynesian God of Creation

Date	Mintage	VF20	XF40	MS60	MS63	MS65
1985	—	—	—	3.50	5.00	—

KM# 30a DOLLAR

27.22 g., 0.925 Silver 0.8095 oz. ASW, 38.5 mm. **Ruler:** Elizabeth II **Subject:** 16th Forum, 2nd P.I.C. and Mini Games **Obv:** Young bust right, date below **Rev:** Tangaroa, Polynesian God of Creation

Date	Mintage	VF20	XF40	MS60	MS63	MS65
1985	Est. 2500	PF65 32.00				

KM# 30b DOLLAR

39.80 g., 0.917 Gold 1.1734 oz. AGW, 38.5 mm. **Ruler:** Elizabeth II **Subject:** 16th Forum, 2nd P.I.C. and Mini Games **Obv:** Young bust right, date below **Rev:** Tangaroa, Polynesian God of Creation

Date	Mintage	VF20	XF40	MS60	MS63	MS65
1985	Est. 25	PF65 2,250				

KM# 31 DOLLAR
27.20 g., Copper-Nickel, 38.5 mm. **Ruler:** Elizabeth II **Subject:** 60th Birthday of Queen Elizabeth II **Obv:** Crowned bust right, date below **Rev:** Cameos of family members in circle

Date	Mintage	VF20	XF40	MS60	MS63	MS65
1986	20,000	—	—	2.75	3.50	—

KM# 31a DOLLAR
27.22 g., 0.925 Silver 0.8095 oz. ASW, 38.5 mm. **Ruler:** Elizabeth II **Subject:** 60th Birthday of Queen Elizabeth II **Obv:** Crowned bust right, date below **Rev:** Cameos of family members in circle

Date	Mintage	VF20	XF40	MS60	MS63	MS65
1986	Est. 2500	PF65 32.00				

KM# 31b DOLLAR
44.00 g., 0.917 Gold 1.2972 oz. AGW, 38.5 mm. **Ruler:** Elizabeth II **Subject:** 60th Birthday of Queen Elizabeth II **Obv:** Crowned bust right, date below **Rev:** Cameos of family members in circle

Date	Mintage	VF20	XF40	MS60	MS63	MS65
1986	Est. 60	PF65 2,400				

KM# 32 DOLLAR
27.20 g., Copper-Nickel, 38.5 mm. **Ruler:** Elizabeth II **Subject:** Prince Andrew's Wedding **Obv:** Crowned head right, date below **Rev:** Busts of Andrew and Sarah facing each other within wreath

Date	Mintage	VF20	XF40	MS60	MS63	MS65
1986	Est. 20000	—	—	2.75	3.50	—

KM# 32a DOLLAR
27.22 g., 0.925 Silver 0.8095 oz. ASW, 38.5 mm. **Ruler:** Elizabeth II **Subject:** Prince Andrews Wedding **Obv:** Crowned bust right, date below **Rev:** Busts of Andrew and Sarah facing each other within wreath

Date	Mintage	VF20	XF40	MS60	MS63	MS65
1986	Est. 2500	PF65 32.00				

KM# 32b DOLLAR
44.00 g., 0.917 Gold 1.2972 oz. AGW, 38.5 mm. **Ruler:** Elizabeth II **Subject:** Prince Andrews Wedding **Obv:** Crowned bust right, date below **Rev:** Busts of Andrew and Sarah facing each other within wreath

Date	Mintage	VF20	XF40	MS60	MS63	MS65
1986	—	PF65 2,400				

KM# 37 DOLLAR
Copper-Nickel, 28.52 mm. **Ruler:** Elizabeth II **Obv:** Crowned head right, date below **Rev:** Tangaroa statue divides denominations **Shape:** Scalloped

Date	Mintage	VF20	XF40	MS60	MS63	MS65
1987	—	—	1.00	2.50	3.50	—
1987	—	PF63 4.50	PF65 5.50			
1988	—	—	1.00	2.50	3.50	—
1988	—	PF63 4.50	PF65 5.50			
1992	—	—	1.00	2.50	3.50	—
1992	—	PF63 4.50	PF65 5.50			
1994	20,000	—	1.00	2.50	3.50	—
1994	200	PF63 5.50	PF65 6.50			

KM# 147 DOLLAR
27.20 g., Copper-Nickel, 38.5 mm. **Ruler:** Elizabeth II **Obv:** Crowned head right, date below **Rev:** Tangaroa, Polynesian God of Fertility

Date	Mintage	VF20	XF40	MS60	MS63	MS65
1992	—	—	—	2.75	4.00	—

KM# 266 DOLLAR
27.20 g., Copper-Nickel, 38.5 mm. **Ruler:** Elizabeth II **Obv:** Crowned head right, date below **Rev:** Queen Mother and daughters within circle, denomination below

Date	Mintage	VF20	XF40	MS60	MS63	MS65
1995	Est. 30000	PF65 3.00				

KM# 267 DOLLAR
10.00 g., 0.500 Silver 0.1608 oz. ASW **Ruler:** Elizabeth II **Subject:** 1996 Summer Olympics **Obv:** Crowned head right, date below **Rev:** Horse jumping left within circle, denomination below

Date	Mintage	VF20	XF40	MS60	MS63	MS65
1996	Est. 10000	PF65 7.50				

KM# 268 DOLLAR
Copper-Nickel **Ruler:** Elizabeth II **Obv:** Crowned head right, date below **Rev:** Sir Francis Drake left and sailing ship right, denomination below

Date	Mintage	VF20	XF40	MS60	MS63	MS65
1996	—	PF65 3.00				

KM# 277 DOLLAR
Copper-Nickel **Ruler:** Elizabeth II **Subject:** Yellowstone National Park **Obv:** Crowned head right, date below **Rev:** Multi-colored Grizzly Bear and cub

Date	Mintage	VF20	XF40	MS60	MS63	MS65
1996	—	—	—	—	5.50	7.00

KM# 278 DOLLAR
Copper-Nickel **Ruler:** Elizabeth II **Subject:** Olympic National Park **Obv:** Crowned head right, date below **Rev:** Multicolor Bald Eagle in flight

Date	Mintage	VF20	XF40	MS60	MS63	MS65
1996	—	—	—	—	5.50	7.00

KM# 311 DOLLAR
9.97 g., 0.500 Silver 0.1603 oz. ASW **Ruler:** Elizabeth II **Subject:** Endangered Wildlife **Obv:** Crowned head right, date below **Rev:** Mother elephant with calf, denomination below

Date	Mintage	VF20	XF40	MS60	MS63	MS65
1996	—	PF65 12.00				

KM# 326 DOLLAR
31.10 g., 0.999 Silver 0.999 oz. ASW **Ruler:** Elizabeth II **Subject:** Lunar Year of the Mouse **Obv:** Crowned head right, date below **Rev:** Mouse in basket

Date	Mintage	VF20	XF40	MS60	MS63	MS65
1996	—	PF65 35.00				

KM# 327 DOLLAR
31.10 g., 0.999 Silver 0.999 oz. ASW **Ruler:** Elizabeth II **Obv:** Crowned head right, date below **Rev:** Multicolor carnation

Date	Mintage	VF20	XF40	MS60	MS63	MS65
1996	—	PF65 37.50				

KM# 341 DOLLAR
Copper-Nickel **Ruler:** Elizabeth II **Subject:** Endangered Wildlife **Obv:** Crowned head right, date below **Rev:** Senegalese lion, denomination below

Date	Mintage	VF20	XF40	MS60	MS63	MS65
1996	—	—	—	—	9.00	12.00

KM# 342 DOLLAR
28.43 g., Copper-Nickel, 38.68 mm. **Ruler:** Elizabeth II **Subject:** Endangered Wildlife **Obv:** Crowned head right **Rev:** European otters **Edge:** Reeded

Date	Mintage	VF20	XF40	MS60	MS63	MS65
1996	—	—	—	—	9.00	12.00

KM# 343 DOLLAR
28.43 g., Copper-Nickel, 38.68 mm. **Ruler:** Elizabeth II **Subject:** Endangered Wildlife **Obv:** Crowned head right **Rev:** Jackass penguins **Edge:** Reeded

Date	Mintage	VF20	XF40	MS60	MS63	MS65
1996	—	—	—	—	9.00	12.00

KM# 344 DOLLAR
28.43 g., Copper-Nickel, 38.68 mm. **Ruler:** Elizabeth II **Subject:** Endangered Wildlife **Obv:** Crowned head right **Rev:** Fallow deer **Edge:** Reeded

Date	Mintage	VF20	XF40	MS60	MS63	MS65
1996	—	—	—	—	9.00	12.00

KM# 345 DOLLAR
28.43 g., Copper-Nickel, 38.68 mm. **Ruler:** Elizabeth II **Subject:** Endangered Wildlife **Obv:** Crowned head right **Rev:** Heaviside's dolphins **Edge:** Reeded

Date	Mintage	VF20	XF40	MS60	MS63	MS65
1996	—	—	—	—	9.00	12.00

KM# 346 DOLLAR
28.43 g., Copper-Nickel, 38.68 mm. **Ruler:** Elizabeth II **Subject:** Endangered Wildlife **Obv:** Crowned head right **Rev:** Cougar and cub **Edge:** Reeded

Date	Mintage	VF20	XF40	MS60	MS63	MS65
1996	—	—	—	—	9.00	12.00

KM# 347 DOLLAR
28.43 g., Copper-Nickel, 38.68 mm. **Ruler:** Elizabeth II **Subject:** Endangered Wildlife **Obv:** Crowned head right **Rev:** Lowland gorilla **Edge:** Reeded

Date	Mintage	VF20	XF40	MS60	MS63	MS65
1996	—	—	—	—	9.00	12.00

KM# 348 DOLLAR
28.43 g., Copper-Nickel, 38.68 mm. **Ruler:** Elizabeth II **Subject:** Endangered Wildlife **Obv:** Crowned head right **Rev:** Peregrine falcon **Edge:** Reeded

Date	Mintage	VF20	XF40	MS60	MS63	MS65
1996	—	—	—	—	9.00	12.00

KM# 349 DOLLAR
28.43 g., Copper-Nickel, 38.68 mm. **Ruler:** Elizabeth II **Subject:** Endangered Wildlife **Obv:** Crowned head right **Rev:** Kangaroo **Edge:** Reeded

Date	Mintage	VF20	XF40	MS60	MS63	MS65
1996	—	—	—	—	9.00	12.00

KM# 350 DOLLAR
28.43 g., Copper-Nickel, 38.68 mm. **Ruler:** Elizabeth II **Subject:** Endangered Wildlife **Obv:** Crowned head right **Rev:** Bee hummingbird **Edge:** Reeded

Date	Mintage	VF20	XF40	MS60	MS63	MS65
1996	—	—	—	—	9.00	12.00

KM# 351 DOLLAR
28.43 g., Copper-Nickel, 38.68 mm. **Ruler:** Elizabeth II **Subject:** Endangered Wildlife **Obv:** Crowned head right **Rev:** Butterfly and thistle **Edge:** Reeded

Date	Mintage	VF20	XF40	MS60	MS63	MS65
1996	—	—	—	—	9.00	12.00

KM# 352 DOLLAR
28.43 g., Copper-Nickel, 38.68 mm. **Ruler:** Elizabeth II **Subject:** Endangered Wildlife **Obv:** Crowned head right **Rev:** Ring-tailed lemurs **Edge:** Reeded

Date	Mintage	VF20	XF40	MS60	MS63	MS65
1996	—	—	—	—	9.00	12.00

KM# 353 DOLLAR
28.43 g., Copper-Nickel, 38.68 mm. **Ruler:** Elizabeth II **Subject:** Endangered Wildlife **Obv:** Crowned head right **Rev:** Szechuan takins **Edge:** Reeded

Date	Mintage	VF20	XF40	MS60	MS63	MS65
1996	—	—	—	—	9.00	12.00

KM# 354 DOLLAR
28.43 g., Copper-Nickel, 38.68 mm. **Ruler:** Elizabeth II **Subject:** Endangered Wildlife **Obv:** Crowned head right **Rev:** Eagle owl **Edge:** Reeded

Date	Mintage	VF20	XF40	MS60	MS63	MS65
1996	—	—	—	—	9.00	12.00

KM# 355 DOLLAR
28.43 g., Copper-Nickel, 38.68 mm. **Ruler:** Elizabeth II **Subject:** Endangered Wildlife **Obv:** Crowned head right **Rev:** White-tailed deer **Edge:** Reeded

Date	Mintage	VF20	XF40	MS60	MS63	MS65
1996	—	—	—	—	9.00	12.00

KM# 356 DOLLAR
28.43 g., Copper-Nickel, 38.68 mm. **Ruler:** Elizabeth II **Subject:** Endangered Wildlife **Obv:** Crowned head right **Rev:** Drill monkey **Edge:** Reeded

Date	Mintage	VF20	XF40	MS60	MS63	MS65
1996	—	—	—	—	9.00	12.00

KM# 387 DOLLAR
28.43 g., Copper-Nickel, 38.68 mm. **Ruler:** Elizabeth II **Subject:** Endangered Wildlife **Obv:** Crowned head right **Rev:** Alpine Ibex on mountain **Edge:** Reeded

Date	Mintage	VF20	XF40	MS60	MS63	MS65
1996	—	—	—	—	9.00	12.00

KM# 308.1 DOLLAR
31.46 g., 0.999 Silver 1.0105 oz. ASW **Ruler:** Elizabeth II **Obv:** Crowned head right, date below **Rev:** Princess Diana's portrait, dates **Note:** Polished fields with matte portraits.

Date	Mintage	VF20	XF40	MS60	MS63	MS65
1997	—	PF65 37.50				

KM# 308.2 DOLLAR
34.46 g., 0.999 Silver 1.1068 oz. ASW **Ruler:** Elizabeth II **Obv:** Crowned head right, date below **Rev:** Princess Diana's bust facing, dates **Note:** Matte fields with polished portraits.

Date	Mintage	VF20	XF40	MS60	MS63	MS65
1997 Matte Proof	—	PF65 40.00				

KM# 848 DOLLAR
Copper-Nickel **Ruler:** Elizabeth II **Subject:** Theodore Roosevelt National Park **Note:** S#381.

Date	Mintage	VF20	XF40	MS60	MS63	MS65
1997	—	—	—	—	—	15.00

KM# 856 DOLLAR
Copper-Nickel **Ruler:** Elizabeth II **Subject:** Great Smoky Mountains National Park

Date	Mintage	VF20	XF40	MS60	MS63	MS65
1997	—	—	—	—	—	15.00

KM# 863 DOLLAR
28.00 g., Copper-Nickel **Ruler:** Elizabeth II **Subject:** Hawaii Volcano National Park

Date	Mintage	VF20	XF40	MS60	MS63	MS65
1997	—	—	—	—	—	15.00

KM# 873 DOLLAR
Copper-Nickel **Ruler:** Elizabeth II **Subject:** Crater Lake National Park **Note:** S#411.

Date	Mintage	VF20	XF40	MS60	MS63	MS65
1997	—	—	—	—	—	15.00

KM# 900 DOLLAR
Copper-Nickel **Ruler:** Elizabeth II **Subject:** Grand Portage National Monument

Date	Mintage	VF20	XF40	MS60	MS63	MS65
1997	—	—	—	—	—	15.00

KM# 910 DOLLAR
Copper-Nickel **Ruler:** Elizabeth II **Subject:** Yosemite National Park

Date	Mintage	VF20	XF40	MS60	MS63	MS65
1997	—	—	—	—	—	15.00

KM# 314 DOLLAR
31.64 g., 0.999 Silver 1.0161 oz. ASW **Ruler:** Elizabeth II **Subject:** Australian Fauna **Obv:** Crowned head right, date below **Rev:** Multicolor ring-tailed gecko, in beaded circle, denomination lower right

Date	Mintage	VF20	XF40	MS60	MS63	MS65
1998	Est. 4000	PF65 45.00				

KM# 315 DOLLAR
31.64 g., 0.999 Silver 1.0161 oz. ASW **Ruler:** Elizabeth II **Subject:** Australian Fauna **Obv:** Crowned head right, date below **Rev:** Multicolor bilby (mouse)

Date	Mintage	VF20	XF40	MS60	MS63	MS65
1998	Est. 4000	PF65 37.50				

KM# 316 DOLLAR
31.64 g., 0.999 Silver 1.0161 oz. ASW **Ruler:** Elizabeth II **Subject:** Australian Fauna **Obv:** Crowned head right, date below **Rev:** Multicolor platypus

Date	Mintage	VF20	XF40	MS60	MS63	MS65
1998	Est. 4000	PF65 40.00				

KM# 317 DOLLAR
31.64 g., 0.999 Silver 1.0161 oz. ASW **Ruler:** Elizabeth II **Subject:** Australian Fauna **Obv:** Crowned head right, date below **Rev:** Multicolor ghost bat

Date	Mintage	VF20	XF40	MS60	MS63	MS65
1998	Est. 4000	PF65 45.00				

KM# 318 DOLLAR
31.64 g., 0.999 Silver 1.0161 oz. ASW **Ruler:** Elizabeth II **Subject:** Australian Fauna **Obv:** Crowned head right, date below **Rev:** Multicolor hatback turtle

Date	Mintage	VF20	XF40	MS60	MS63	MS65
1998	Est. 4000	PF65 45.00				

KM# 931 DOLLAR
10.00 g., 0.500 Silver 0.1608 oz. ASW **Ruler:** Elizabeth II **Subject:** World Cup Soccer, Paris

Date	Mintage	VF20	XF40	MS60	MS63	MS65
1998	10,000	PF65 9.50				

KM# 933 DOLLAR
Copper-Nickel **Ruler:** Elizabeth II **Subject:** Petrified Forest National Park

Date	Mintage	VF20	XF40	MS60	MS63	MS65
1998	—	—	—	—	—	15.00

KM# 942 DOLLAR
Copper-Nickel **Ruler:** Elizabeth II **Subject:** Glacier Bay National Park and Preserve

Date	Mintage	VF20	XF40	MS60	MS63	MS65
1998	—	—	—	—	—	15.00

KM# 951 DOLLAR
Copper-Nickel **Ruler:** Elizabeth II **Series:** North Cascades National Park

Date	Mintage	VF20	XF40	MS60	MS63	MS65
1998	—	—	—	—	—	15.00

KM# 960 DOLLAR
Copper-Nickel **Ruler:** Elizabeth II **Subject:** Grand Canyon National Park

Date	Mintage	VF20	XF40	MS60	MS63	MS65
1998	—	—	—	—	—	15.00

KM# 969 DOLLAR
Copper-Nickel **Ruler:** Elizabeth II **Subject:** Gulf Islands National Seashore

Date	Mintage	VF20	XF40	MS60	MS63	MS65
1998	—	—	—	—	—	15.00

KM# 979 DOLLAR
Copper-Nickel **Ruler:** Elizabeth II **Subject:** Big Cypress National Preserve

Date	Mintage	VF20	XF40	MS60	MS63	MS65
1998	—	—	—	—	—	15.00

KM# 989 DOLLAR
Copper-Nickel **Ruler:** Elizabeth II **Subject:** Everglades National Park

Date	Mintage	VF20	XF40	MS60	MS63	MS65
1998	—	—	—	—	—	15.00

KM# 999 DOLLAR
Copper-Nickel **Ruler:** Elizabeth II **Subject:** Wind Cave National Park

Date	Mintage	VF20	XF40	MS60	MS63	MS65
1998	—	—	—	—	—	15.00

KM# 1009 DOLLAR
Copper-Nickel **Ruler:** Elizabeth II **Subject:** Bryce Canyon National Park

Date	Mintage	VF20	XF40	MS60	MS63	MS65
1998	—	—	—	—	—	15.00

KM# 1019 DOLLAR
Copper-Nickel **Ruler:** Elizabeth II **Subject:** Gates of the Arctic National Park and Preserve

Date	Mintage	VF20	XF40	MS60	MS63	MS65
1998 Proof	—	—	—	—	—	15.00

KM# 1029 DOLLAR
Copper-Nickel **Ruler:** Elizabeth II **Subject:** Badlands National Park

Date	Mintage	VF20	XF40	MS60	MS63	MS65
1998	—	—	—	—	—	15.00

KM# 1039 DOLLAR
Copper-Nickel **Ruler:** Elizabeth II **Subject:** Grand Teton National Park

Date	Mintage	VF20	XF40	MS60	MS63	MS65
1998	—	—	—	—	—	15.00

KM# 1048 DOLLAR
Copper-Nickel **Ruler:** Elizabeth II **Subject:** Kajoko Honokhau National Historic Park

Date	Mintage	VF20	XF40	MS60	MS63	MS65
1998	—	—	—	—	—	15.00

KM# 1058 DOLLAR
Copper-Nickel **Ruler:** Elizabeth II **Subject:** Virgin Islands National Park

Date	Mintage	VF20	XF40	MS60	MS63	MS65
1998	—	—	—	—	—	15.00

KM# 1068 DOLLAR
Copper-Nickel **Ruler:** Elizabeth II **Subject:** Mammoth Cave National Park

Date	Mintage	VF20	XF40	MS60	MS63	MS65
1998	—	—	—	—	—	15.00

KM# 1078 DOLLAR
Copper-Nickel **Ruler:** Elizabeth II **Subject:** Rocky Mountain National Park

Date	Mintage	VF20	XF40	MS60	MS63	MS65
1998	—	—	—	—	—	15.00

KM# 361 DOLLAR
31.68 g., 0.999 Silver 1.0175 oz. ASW **Ruler:** Elizabeth II **Subject:** Tropical Fish **Obv:** Crowned head right, date below **Rev:** Multicolored lemonpeel angelfish **Edge:** Reeded

Date	Mintage	VF20	XF40	MS60	MS63	MS65
1999	—	PF65 37.00				

KM# 362 DOLLAR
31.68 g., 0.999 Silver 1.0175 oz. ASW **Ruler:** Elizabeth II **Subject:** Tropical Fish **Obv:** Crowned head right, date below **Rev:** Multicolor clown triggerfish **Edge:** Reeded

Date	Mintage	VF20	XF40	MS60	MS63	MS65
1999	—	PF65 37.00				

KM# 363 DOLLAR
31.68 g., 0.999 Silver 1.0175 oz. ASW **Ruler:** Elizabeth II **Subject:** Tropical Fish **Obv:** Crowned head right, date below **Rev:** Multicolor regal angelfish **Edge:** Reeded

Date	Mintage	VF20	XF40	MS60	MS63	MS65
1999	—	PF65 37.00				

KM# 364 DOLLAR
31.68 g., 0.999 Silver 1.0175 oz. ASW **Ruler:** Elizabeth II **Subject:** Tropical Fish **Obv:** Crowned head right, date below **Rev:** Multicolor serpent starfish **Edge:** Reeded

Date	Mintage	VF20	XF40	MS60	MS63	MS65
1999	—	PF65 42.00				

KM# 365 DOLLAR
31.68 g., 0.999 Silver 1.0175 oz. ASW **Ruler:** Elizabeth II **Subject:** Tropical Fish **Obv:** Crowned head right, date below **Rev:** Multicolor clown fish on anemone **Edge:** Reeded

Date	Mintage	VF20	XF40	MS60	MS63	MS65
1999	—	PF65 37.00				

KM# 380 DOLLAR
28.28 g., 0.925 Silver 0.841 oz. ASW, 38.6 mm. **Ruler:** Elizabeth II **Subject:** Queen's Golden Jubilee **Obv:** Crowned head right, date below **Rev:** Flags over roof tops, denomination below **Edge:** Reeded

Date	Mintage	VF20	XF40	MS60	MS63	MS65
2000	15,000	PF65 28.00				

KM# 437 DOLLAR
31.80 g., 0.999 Silver 1.0214 oz. ASW, 40.5 mm. **Ruler:** Elizabeth II **Obv:** Crowned head right, date below **Rev:** Queen Mother multicolor portrait **Edge:** Reeded

Date	Mintage	VF20	XF40	MS60	MS63	MS65
2000	19,500	PF65 37.50				

KM# 1096 DOLLAR
Copper-Nickel **Ruler:** Elizabeth II **Rev:** Sagebrush in color

Date	Mintage	VF20	XF40	MS60	MS63	MS65
2000	Est. 5000	—	—	—	—	50.00

KM# 1101 DOLLAR
31.64 g., 0.999 Silver 1.0161 oz. ASW **Ruler:** Elizabeth II **Subject:** Australian Wildlife **Rev:** Cucko Wasp in color

Date	Mintage	VF20	XF40	MS60	MS63	MS65
2000	Est. 5000	PF65 50.00				

KM# 1102 DOLLAR
31.64 g., 0.999 Silver 1.0161 oz. ASW **Ruler:** Elizabeth II **Subject:** Australian Wildlife **Rev:** Jewel Beetle in color

Date	Mintage	VF20	XF40	MS60	MS63	MS65
2000	Est. 5000	PF65 50.00				

KM# 1103 DOLLAR
31.64 g., 0.999 Silver 1.0161 oz. ASW **Ruler:** Elizabeth II **Subject:** Australian Wildlife **Rev:** Ulysses Butterfly (blue/black) in color

Date	Mintage	VF20	XF40	MS60	MS63	MS65
2000	Est. 5000	PF65 50.00				

KM# 1104 DOLLAR
31.64 g., 0.999 Silver 1.0161 oz. ASW **Ruler:** Elizabeth II **Subject:** Australian Wildlife **Rev:** Goliath stick insect

Date	Mintage	VF20	XF40	MS60	MS63	MS65
2000	Est. 5000	PF65 50.00				

KM# 1105 DOLLAR
31.64 g., 0.999 Silver 1.0161 oz. ASW **Ruler:** Elizabeth II **Subject:** Australian Wildlife **Rev:** Sapphire Rockmaster Damselfly in color

Date	Mintage	VF20	XF40	MS60	MS63	MS65
2000	Est. 5000	PF65 50.00				

KM# 8 2 DOLLARS

25.70 g., 0.925 Silver 0.7643 oz. ASW, 39 mm. **Ruler:** Elizabeth II **Subject:** 20th Anniversary of Coronation **Obv:** Young bust right, date below

Date	Mintage	VF20	XF40	MS60	MS63	MS65
1973	46,000	PF65 30.00				
1973	16,000	—	—	25.00	28.00	—

KM# 38 2 DOLLARS

Copper-Nickel, 28.52 mm. **Ruler:** Elizabeth II **Obv:** Crowned head right, date below **Rev:** Kumete table, morter and pestle from Atiu Island, denomination above **Shape:** 3-sided

Date	Mintage	VF20	XF40	MS60	MS63	MS65
1987	—	PF63 6.00	PF65 7.00			
1987	—	—	2.25	3.50	5.00	—
1988	—	—	2.25	3.50	5.00	—
1988	—	PF63 6.00	PF65 7.00			
1992	—	—	2.25	3.25	4.50	—
1992	—	PF63 6.00	PF65 7.00			
1994	20,000	—	2.25	3.25	4.50	—
1994	200	PF63 6.50	PF65 7.50			

KM# 279 2 DOLLARS

10.00 g., 0.500 Silver 0.1608 oz. ASW **Ruler:** Elizabeth II **Subject:** Yellowstone National Park **Obv:** Crowned head right, date below **Rev:** Grizzly bears, denomination below

Date	Mintage	VF20	XF40	MS60	MS63	MS65
1996	—	PF65 12.00				

KM# 280 2 DOLLARS

10.00 g., 0.500 Silver 0.1608 oz. ASW **Ruler:** Elizabeth II **Subject:** Olympic National Park **Obv:** Crowned head right, date below **Rev:** Eagle flying in the mountain tops

Date	Mintage	VF20	XF40	MS60	MS63	MS65
1996	—	PF65 12.00				

KM# 328 2 DOLLARS

10.00 g., 0.500 Silver 0.1608 oz. ASW **Ruler:** Elizabeth II **Subject:** Petrified Forest National Park **Obv:** Crowned head right, date below **Rev:** Pronghorn antelope

Date	Mintage	VF20	XF40	MS60	MS63	MS65
1997 Proof	—	—	—	—	—	—
1998	—	PF65 12.00				

KM# 329 2 DOLLARS

10.00 g., 0.500 Silver 0.1608 oz. ASW **Ruler:** Elizabeth II **Subject:** Crater Lake National Park **Obv:** Crowned head right, date below **Rev:** White-tailed deer

Date	Mintage	VF20	XF40	MS60	MS63	MS65
1997 Proof	—	—	—	—	—	—
1998	—	PF65 12.00				

KM# 371 2 DOLLARS

10.00 g., 0.500 Silver 0.1608 oz. ASW, 30 mm. **Ruler:** Elizabeth II **Subject:** Great Smoky Mountains National Park **Obv:** Crowned head right, date below **Rev:** Red wolf and two cubs **Edge:** Reeded

Date	Mintage	VF20	XF40	MS60	MS63	MS65
1997	—	PF65 12.00				

KM# 372 2 DOLLARS

10.00 g., 0.500 Silver 0.1608 oz. ASW, 30 mm. **Ruler:** Elizabeth II **Subject:** Theodore Roosevelt National Park **Obv:** Crowned head right, date below **Rev:** Bison, denomination below **Edge:** Reeded

Date	Mintage	VF20	XF40	MS60	MS63	MS65
1997	—	PF65 12.00				

KM# 373 2 DOLLARS

10.00 g., 0.500 Silver 0.1608 oz. ASW, 30 mm. **Ruler:** Elizabeth II **Subject:** Yosemite National Park **Obv:** Crowned head right, date below **Rev:** Peregrine falcon **Edge:** Reeded

Date	Mintage	VF20	XF40	MS60	MS63	MS65
1997	—	PF65 12.00				

KM# 376 2 DOLLARS

15.84 g., 0.999 Silver 0.5088 oz. ASW, 28.3 mm. **Ruler:** Elizabeth II **Subject:** British Queen Mother **Obv:** Crowned head right, date below **Rev:** Queen Mother and daughters, circa 1936 within circle, denomination below **Edge:** Reeded

Date	Mintage	VF20	XF40	MS60	MS63	MS65
1997	—	PF65 12.00				

KM# 436 2 DOLLARS

20.40 g., 0.500 Silver 0.3279 oz. ASW, 33.9 mm. **Ruler:** Elizabeth II **Obv:** Crowned head right, date below **Rev:** Queen Mother and daughters circa 1980 **Edge:** Reeded

Date	Mintage	VF20	XF40	MS60	MS63	MS65
1997	—	PF65 15.00				

KM# 864 2 DOLLARS

10.00 g., 0.500 Silver 0.1608 oz. ASW **Ruler:** Elizabeth II **Subject:** Hawaii Volcano National Park

Date	Mintage	VF20	XF40	MS60	MS63	MS65
1997	—	—	—	—	—	15.00

KM# 901 2 DOLLARS

10.00 g., 0.500 Silver 0.1608 oz. ASW **Ruler:** Elizabeth II **Subject:** Grand Portage National Monument

Date	Mintage	VF20	XF40	MS60	MS63	MS65
1997	—	PF65 12.50				

KM# 321 2 DOLLARS

42.41 g., 0.925 Silver 1.2614 oz. ASW **Ruler:** Elizabeth II **Obv:** Crowned head right, date below **Rev:** Cook Islands attractions and features, denomination at right **Shape:** 1/3 circular segment

Date	Mintage	VF20	XF40	MS60	MS63	MS65
1998	Est. 20000	PF65 50.00				

Note: This coin is part of a tri-national, three coin matching set with Fiji and Samoa

KM# 374 2 DOLLARS

10.00 g., 0.500 Silver 0.1608 oz. ASW, 30 mm. **Ruler:** Elizabeth II **Subject:** North Cascades National Park **Obv:** Crowned head right, date below **Rev:** Spotted owl, denomination below **Edge:** Reeded

Date	Mintage	VF20	XF40	MS60	MS63	MS65
1998	—	PF65 12.00				

KM# 943 2 DOLLARS

10.00 g., 0.500 Silver 0.1608 oz. ASW **Ruler:** Elizabeth II **Subject:** Glacier Bay National Park and Preserve **Rev:** Humpback whale

Date	Mintage	VF20	XF40	MS60	MS63	MS65
1998	—	PF65 15.00				

KM# 961 2 DOLLARS

10.00 g., 0.500 Silver 0.1608 oz. ASW **Ruler:** Elizabeth II **Subject:** Grand Canyon National Park **Rev:** California Condor

Date	Mintage	VF20	XF40	MS60	MS63	MS65
1998	—	PF65 15.00				

KM# 970 2 DOLLARS

10.00 g., 0.500 Silver 0.1608 oz. ASW **Ruler:** Elizabeth II **Subject:** Gulf Islands National Seashore

Date	Mintage	VF20	XF40	MS60	MS63	MS65
1998	—	PF65 15.00				

KM# 980 2 DOLLARS
10.00 g., 0.500 Silver 0.1608 oz. ASW **Ruler:** Elizabeth II **Subject:** Big Cypress National Preserve **Rev:** Puma

Date	Mintage	VF20	XF40	MS60	MS63	MS65
1998	—	PF65 15.00				

KM# 990 2 DOLLARS
10.00 g., 0.500 Silver 0.1608 oz. ASW **Ruler:** Elizabeth II **Subject:** Everglades National Park **Rev:** Crocodile

Date	Mintage	VF20	XF40	MS60	MS63	MS65
1998	—	PF65 15.00				

KM# 1000 2 DOLLARS
10.00 g., 0.500 Silver 0.1608 oz. ASW **Ruler:** Elizabeth II **Subject:** Wind Cave National Park **Rev:** Swift fox

Date	Mintage	VF20	XF40	MS60	MS63	MS65
1998	—	PF65 15.00				

KM# 1010 2 DOLLARS
10.00 g., 0.500 Silver 0.1608 oz. ASW **Ruler:** Elizabeth II **Subject:** Bryce Canyon National Park **Rev:** Prairie dog

Date	Mintage	VF20	XF40	MS60	MS63	MS65
1998	—	PF65 15.00				

KM# 1020 2 DOLLARS
10.00 g., 0.500 Silver 0.1608 oz. ASW **Ruler:** Elizabeth II **Subject:** Gates of the Arctic National Park and Preserve **Rev:** Falcon

Date	Mintage	VF20	XF40	MS60	MS63	MS65
1998	—	PF65 15.00				

KM# 1030 2 DOLLARS
10.00 g., 0.500 Silver 0.1608 oz. ASW **Ruler:** Elizabeth II **Subject:** Badlands National Park **Rev:** Black-footed ferret

Date	Mintage	VF20	XF40	MS60	MS63	MS65
1998	—	PF65 15.00				

KM# 1040 2 DOLLARS
10.00 g., 0.500 Silver 0.1608 oz. ASW **Ruler:** Elizabeth II **Subject:** Grand Teton National Park **Rev:** Whooping Crane

Date	Mintage	VF20	XF40	MS60	MS63	MS65
1998	—	PF65 15.00				

KM# 1049 2 DOLLARS
10.00 g., 0.500 Silver 0.1608 oz. ASW **Ruler:** Elizabeth II **Subject:** Kajoko Honokhau National Historic Park **Rev:** Hawaiian Duck

Date	Mintage	VF20	XF40	MS60	MS63	MS65
1998	—	PF65 15.00				

KM# 1059 2 DOLLARS
10.00 g., 0.500 Silver 0.1608 oz. ASW **Ruler:** Elizabeth II **Subject:** Virgin Islands National Park **Rev:** Brown Pelican

Date	Mintage	VF20	XF40	MS60	MS63	MS65
1998	—	PF65 15.00				

KM# 1069 2 DOLLARS
10.00 g., 0.500 Silver 0.1608 oz. ASW **Ruler:** Elizabeth II **Subject:** Mammoth Cave National Park **Rev:** Grey Bat

Date	Mintage	VF20	XF40	MS60	MS63	MS65
1998	—	PF65 15.00				

KM# 1079 2 DOLLARS
10.00 g., 0.500 Silver 0.1608 oz. ASW **Ruler:** Elizabeth II **Subject:** Rocky Mountain National Park **Rev:** Purple trout

Date	Mintage	VF20	XF40	MS60	MS63	MS65
1998	—	PF65 15.00				

KM# 339 2 DOLLARS
31.10 g., 0.999 Silver 0.999 oz. ASW **Ruler:** Elizabeth II **Obv:** Crowned head right, date below **Rev:** Multicolor cartoon cat, Garfield, flipping coin **Edge:** Reeded

Date	Mintage	VF20	XF40	MS60	MS63	MS65
1999	—	PF65 37.50				

KM# 340 2 DOLLARS
31.10 g., 0.999 Silver 0.999 oz. ASW **Ruler:** Elizabeth II **Obv:** Crowned head right, date below **Rev:** Multicolor cartoon cat, Garfield, tricking Odie **Edge:** Reeded

Date	Mintage	VF20	XF40	MS60	MS63	MS65
1999	—	PF65 37.50				

KM# 9 2-1/2 DOLLARS
27.35 g., 0.925 Silver 0.8134 oz. ASW, 38 mm. **Ruler:** Elizabeth II **Subject:** Captain James Cook's 2nd Pacific Voyage **Obv:** Young bust right, date below **Rev:** H.M.S. Resolution and H.M.S. Adventure above world globe

Date	Mintage	VF20	XF40	MS60	MS63	MS65
1973	12,000	PF65 30.00				
1973	6,000	—	—	—	—	32.00
1974	2,000	—	—	—	—	35.00
1974	12,000	PF65 30.00				

KM# 1088 4 DOLLARS
1.04 g., 0.999 Silver 0.0334 oz. ASW **Ruler:** Elizabeth II **Rev:** Two dolphins

Date	Mintage	VF20	XF40	MS60	MS63	MS65
1998	—	PF65 25.00				

KM# 15 5 DOLLARS
27.30 g., 0.500 Silver 0.4389 oz. ASW **Ruler:** Elizabeth II **Subject:** Wildlife Conservation **Obv:** Young bust right, date below **Rev:** Mangara kingfisher, denomination below

Date	Mintage	VF20	XF40	MS60	MS63	MS65
1976 FM (U)	2,192	—	—	—	—	20.00
1976 FM (M)	251	—	—	—	—	32.50
1976 FM (P)	28,000	PF65 17.00				

KM# 17 5 DOLLARS
27.30 g., 0.500 Silver 0.4389 oz. ASW **Ruler:** Elizabeth II **Obv:** Young bust right, date below **Rev:** Atiu swiftlet, denomination below **Edge Lettering:** Wildlife Conservation

Date	Mintage	VF20	XF40	MS60	MS63	MS65
1977 FM (U)	4,032	—	—	—	—	20.00
1977 FM (M)	252	—	—	—	—	40.00
1977 FM (P)	11,000	PF65 17.00				

KM# 20 5 DOLLARS
27.30 g., 0.500 Silver 0.4389 oz. ASW **Ruler:** Elizabeth II **Subject:** Wildlife Conservation **Obv:** Young bust right, date below **Rev:** Polynesian warblers by nest in branches, denomination below **Edge Lettering:** 1728 • CAPT. JAMES COOK • 1978

Date	Mintage	VF20	XF40	MS60	MS63	MS65
1978 FM (U)	3,659	—	—	—	—	18.00
1978 FM (M)	250	—	—	—	—	30.00
1978 FM (P)	11,000	PF65 17.00				

KM# 24 5 DOLLARS
27.30 g., 0.500 Silver 0.4389 oz. ASW **Ruler:** Elizabeth II **Subject:** Wildlife Conservation **Obv:** Young bust right, date below **Rev:** Rarotongan fruit doves on branch, denomination below

Date	Mintage	VF20	XF40	MS60	MS63	MS65
1979 FM (U)	2,500	—	—	—	—	27.00
1979 FM (P)	8,612	PF65 17.00				

KM# 39 5 DOLLARS
Aluminum-Bronze, 31.51 mm. **Ruler:** Elizabeth II **Obv:** Crowned head right, date below **Rev:** Conch shell, denomination above **Shape:** 12-sided

Date	Mintage	VF20	XF40	MS60	MS63	MS65
1987	—	—	3.50	5.50	7.50	—
1987	—	PF65 9.00				
1988	—	—	3.50	5.50	7.50	—
1988	—	PF65 9.00				
1992	—	—	3.50	5.50	7.50	—
1992	—	PF65 9.00				
1994	20,000	—	3.50	5.50	7.50	—
1994	200	PF63 12.00	PF65 15.00			

KM# 39a 5 DOLLARS
Copper-Nickel, 31.51 mm. **Ruler:** Elizabeth II **Obv:** Crowned head right, date below **Rev:** Conch shell **Shape:** 12-sided **Note:** Mint error, struck on Australian 50 cents planchet.

Date	Mintage	VF20	XF40	MS60	MS63	MS65
1988	—	—	—	—	—	—

KM# 181 5 DOLLARS

Copper-Nickel **Ruler:** Elizabeth II **Subject:** Endangered World Wildlife **Obv:** Crowned head right, date below **Rev:** Tiger

Date	Mintage	VF20	XF40	MS60	MS63	MS65
1990	—	—	—	—	7.50	12.50

KM# 808 5 DOLLARS

Copper-Nickel **Ruler:** Elizabeth II **Subject:** Endangered World Wildlife **Rev:** Ursus arctos horribilis

Date	Mintage	VF20	XF40	MS60	MS63	MS65
1990 PM	100,000	—	—	—	—	12.00

KM# 809 5 DOLLARS

Copper-Nickel **Ruler:** Elizabeth II **Subject:** Endangered World Wildlife **Rev:** Black rhino (Diceros Bicornis)

Date	Mintage	VF20	XF40	MS60	MS63	MS65
1990 PM	100,000	—	—	—	—	12.00

KM# 810 5 DOLLARS

Copper-Nickel **Ruler:** Elizabeth II **Subject:** Endangered World Wildlife **Rev:** Chimpanzie (Pan troglogytes)

Date	Mintage	VF20	XF40	MS60	MS63	MS65
1990 PM	100,000	—	—	—	—	12.00

KM# 811 5 DOLLARS

Copper-Nickel **Ruler:** Elizabeth II **Subject:** Endangered World Wildlife **Rev:** Ovis orientalis musimon

Date	Mintage	VF20	XF40	MS60	MS63	MS65
1990 PM	100,000	—	—	—	—	12.00

KM# 149 5 DOLLARS

9.95 g., 0.500 Silver 0.1599 oz. ASW **Ruler:** Elizabeth II **Subject:** World Cup Soccer **Obv:** Crowned head right, date below **Rev:** Three soccer players

Date	Mintage	VF20	XF40	MS60	MS63	MS65
1991	150,000	PF65 7.50				

KM# 217 5 DOLLARS

9.85 g., 0.500 Silver 0.1583 oz. ASW **Ruler:** Elizabeth II **Obv:** Crowned head right, date below **Rev:** Christopher Columbus 3/4 facing, ship at left, denomination below

Date	Mintage	VF20	XF40	MS60	MS63	MS65
1991	Est. 50000	—	—	—	7.00	9.00

KM# 218 5 DOLLARS

9.95 g., 0.500 Silver 0.1599 oz. ASW **Ruler:** Elizabeth II **Subject:** Endangered Wildlife **Obv:** Crowned head right, date below **Rev:** European otters

Date	Mintage	VF20	XF40	MS60	MS63	MS65
1991	Est. 100000	—	—	—	9.00	12.00

KM# 219 5 DOLLARS

9.95 g., 0.500 Silver 0.1599 oz. ASW **Ruler:** Elizabeth II **Subject:** Endangered Wildlife **Obv:** Crowned head right, date below **Rev:** Penguins

Date	Mintage	VF20	XF40	MS60	MS63	MS65
1991	Est. 100000	—	—	—	9.00	12.00

KM# 220 5 DOLLARS

9.95 g., 0.500 Silver 0.1599 oz. ASW **Ruler:** Elizabeth II **Subject:** Endangered Wildlife **Obv:** Crowned head right, date below **Rev:** Deer

Date	Mintage	VF20	XF40	MS60	MS63	MS65
1991	Est. 100000	—	—	—	9.00	12.00

KM# 221 5 DOLLARS

9.95 g., 0.500 Silver 0.1599 oz. ASW **Ruler:** Elizabeth II **Subject:** Endangered Wildlife **Obv:** Crowned head right, date below **Rev:** Cape dolphins

Date	Mintage	VF20	XF40	MS60	MS63	MS65
1991	Est. 100000	—	—	—	9.00	12.00

KM# 222 5 DOLLARS

9.95 g., 0.500 Silver 0.1599 oz. ASW **Ruler:** Elizabeth II **Subject:** Endangered Wildlife **Obv:** Crowned head right, date below **Rev:** Cougar

Date	Mintage	VF20	XF40	MS60	MS63	MS65
1991	Est. 100000	—	—	—	9.00	12.00

KM# 223 5 DOLLARS

9.95 g., 0.500 Silver 0.1599 oz. ASW **Ruler:** Elizabeth II **Subject:** Endangered Wildlife **Obv:** Crowned head right, date below **Rev:** Ibex

Date	Mintage	VF20	XF40	MS60	MS63	MS65
1991	Est. 100000	—	—	—	9.00	12.00

KM# 224 5 DOLLARS

9.95 g., 0.500 Silver 0.1599 oz. ASW **Ruler:** Elizabeth II **Subject:** Endangered Wildlife **Obv:** Crowned head right, date below **Rev:** Eagle owl

Date	Mintage	VF20	XF40	MS60	MS63	MS65
1991	Est. 100000	—	—	—	9.00	12.00

KM# 225 5 DOLLARS

9.95 g., 0.500 Silver 0.1599 oz. ASW **Ruler:** Elizabeth II **Subject:** Endangered Wildlife **Obv:** Crowned head right, date below **Rev:** Peregrine falcon

Date	Mintage	VF20	XF40	MS60	MS63	MS65
1991	Est. 100000	—	—	—	9.00	12.00

KM# 226 5 DOLLARS

9.95 g., 0.500 Silver 0.1599 oz. ASW **Ruler:** Elizabeth II **Subject:** Endangered Wildlife **Obv:** Crowned head right, date below **Rev:** African lion

Date	Mintage	VF20	XF40	MS60	MS63	MS65
1991	Est. 100000	—	—	—	9.00	12.00

KM# 227 5 DOLLARS

9.95 g., 0.500 Silver 0.1599 oz. ASW **Ruler:** Elizabeth II **Subject:** Endangered Wildlife **Obv:** Crowned head right, date below **Rev:** Bee hummingbird

Date	Mintage	VF20	XF40	MS60	MS63	MS65
1991	Est. 100000	—	—	—	9.00	12.00

KM# 228 5 DOLLARS

9.95 g., 0.500 Silver 0.1599 oz. ASW **Ruler:** Elizabeth II **Subject:** Endangered Wildlife **Obv:** Crowned head right, date below **Rev:** Kangaroo

Date	Mintage	VF20	XF40	MS60	MS63	MS65
1991	Est. 100000	—	—	—	9.00	12.00

KM# 229 5 DOLLARS

9.95 g., 0.500 Silver 0.1599 oz. ASW **Ruler:** Elizabeth II **Subject:** Endangered Wildlife **Obv:** Crowned head right, date below **Rev:** Persian fallow deer

Date	Mintage	VF20	XF40	MS60	MS63	MS65
1991	Est. 100000	—	—	—	9.00	12.00

KM# 230 5 DOLLARS

9.95 g., 0.500 Silver 0.1599 oz. ASW **Ruler:** Elizabeth II **Subject:** Endangered Wildlife **Obv:** Crowned head right, date below **Rev:** Lowland gorilla

Date	Mintage	VF20	XF40	MS60	MS63	MS65
1991	Est. 100000	—	—	—	9.00	12.00

KM# 253 5 DOLLARS

10.13 g., 0.500 Silver 0.1628 oz. ASW **Ruler:** Elizabeth II **Obv:** Crowned head right, date below **Rev:** First man on the moon, denomination below

Date	Mintage	VF20	XF40	MS60	MS63	MS65
1991	—	PF65 8.00				

KM# 137 5 DOLLARS

10.00 g., 0.500 Silver 0.1608 oz. ASW **Ruler:** Elizabeth II **Subject:** Environmental Protection **Obv:** Crowned head right, date below **Rev:** Child watching butterfly

Date	Mintage	VF20	XF40	MS60	MS63	MS65
1992	Est. 25000	PF65 7.50				

KM# 150 5 DOLLARS

10.00 g., 0.500 Silver 0.1608 oz. ASW **Ruler:** Elizabeth II **Obv:** Crowned head right, date below **Rev:** Johann Sebastian Bach

Date	Mintage	VF20	XF40	MS60	MS63	MS65
1992	—	PF65 7.50				

KM# 160 5 DOLLARS

10.00 g., 0.500 Silver 0.1608 oz. ASW **Ruler:** Elizabeth II **Obv:** Crowned head right, date below **Rev:** Sailing ship Astrolabe

Date	Mintage	VF20	XF40	MS60	MS63	MS65
1992	—	PF65 7.50				

KM# 231 5 DOLLARS

10.00 g., 0.500 Silver 0.1608 oz. ASW **Ruler:** Elizabeth II **Subject:** Endangered Wildlife **Obv:** Crowned head right, date below **Rev:** Mandrill right, denomination below

Date	Mintage	VF20	XF40	MS60	MS63	MS65
1992	Est. 100000	—	—	—	9.00	12.00

KM# 232 5 DOLLARS

10.00 g., 0.500 Silver 0.1608 oz. ASW **Ruler:** Elizabeth II **Subject:** Endangered Wildlife **Obv:** Crowned head right, date below **Rev:** Butterfly

Date	Mintage	VF20	XF40	MS60	MS63	MS65
1992	Est. 100000	—	—	—	7.00	9.00

KM# 233 5 DOLLARS

10.00 g., 0.500 Silver 0.1608 oz. ASW **Ruler:** Elizabeth II **Subject:** Endangered Wildlife **Obv:** Crowned head right, date below **Rev:** Takin

Date	Mintage	VF20	XF40	MS60	MS63	MS65
1992	Est. 100000	—	—	—	7.00	9.00

KM# 252 5 DOLLARS
9.95 g., 0.500 Silver 0.1599 oz. ASW **Ruler:** Elizabeth II **Subject:** 1992 Olympics **Obv:** Crowned head right, date below **Rev:** High jump, denomination below

Date	Mintage	VF20	XF40	MS60	MS63	MS65
1992	150,000	PF65 7.50				

KM# 816 5 DOLLARS
1.24 g., 0.9999 Gold 0.0399 oz. AGW, 13.92 mm. **Ruler:** Elizabeth II **Rev:** Papillon dog

Date	Mintage	VF20	XF40	MS60	MS63	MS65
1992	7,089	PF65 85.00				
1994	4,012	PF65 95.00				

KM# 821 5 DOLLARS
Copper-Nickel **Ruler:** Elizabeth II **Rev:** Lemur

Date	Mintage	VF20	XF40	MS60	MS63	MS65
1992	Est. 100000	—	—	—	—	12.00

KM# 234 5 DOLLARS
10.00 g., 0.500 Silver 0.1608 oz. ASW **Ruler:** Elizabeth II **Subject:** Endangered Wildlife **Obv:** Crowned head right, date below **Rev:** African elephant

Date	Mintage	VF20	XF40	MS60	MS63	MS65
1995	Est. 25000	PF65 12.00				

KM# 255 5 DOLLARS
31.47 g., 0.925 Silver 0.9359 oz. ASW **Ruler:** Elizabeth II **Subject:** Queen Elizabeth II's 25th Wedding Anniversary **Obv:** Crowned head right, date below **Rev:** St. Paul's Cathedral

Date	Mintage	VF20	XF40	MS60	MS63	MS65
1995	Est. 30000	PF65 27.50				

KM# 269 5 DOLLARS
31.47 g., 0.925 Silver 0.9359 oz. ASW **Ruler:** Elizabeth II **Subject:** Endangered Wildlife **Obv:** Crowned head right, date below **Rev:** Cheetah

Date	Mintage	VF20	XF40	MS60	MS63	MS65
1996	Est. 15000	PF65 30.00				

KM# 281 5 DOLLARS
28.00 g., 0.925 Silver 0.8327 oz. ASW **Ruler:** Elizabeth II **Subject:** Yellowstone National Park **Obv:** Crowned head right, date below **Rev:** Multicolor grizzly bear and cub

Date	Mintage	VF20	XF40	MS60	MS63	MS65
1996	25,000	PF65 28.00				

KM# 282 5 DOLLARS
28.00 g., 0.925 Silver 0.8327 oz. ASW **Ruler:** Elizabeth II **Subject:** Olympic National Park **Obv:** Crowned head right, date below **Rev:** Multicolor bald eagle in flight

Date	Mintage	VF20	XF40	MS60	MS63	MS65
1996	25,000	PF65 28.00				

KM# 301 5 DOLLARS
28.00 g., 0.925 Silver 0.8327 oz. ASW **Ruler:** Elizabeth II **Subject:** Endangered Wildlife **Obv:** Crowned head right, date below **Rev:** Crocodile on river bank

Date	Mintage	VF20	XF40	MS60	MS63	MS65
1996	—	PF65 30.00				

KM# 302 5 DOLLARS
28.00 g., 0.925 Silver 0.8327 oz. ASW **Ruler:** Elizabeth II **Subject:** Endangered Wildlife **Obv:** Crowned head right, date below **Rev:** Lion, lioness and cubs

Date	Mintage	VF20	XF40	MS60	MS63	MS65
1996	—	PF65 25.00				

KM# 303 5 DOLLARS
28.00 g., 0.925 Silver 0.8327 oz. ASW **Ruler:** Elizabeth II **Subject:** Endangered Wildlife **Obv:** Crowned head right, date below **Rev:** Female gorilla and offspring

Date	Mintage	VF20	XF40	MS60	MS63	MS65
1996	—	PF65 25.00				

KM# 304 5 DOLLARS
28.00 g., 0.925 Silver 0.8327 oz. ASW **Ruler:** Elizabeth II **Subject:** Endangered Wildlife **Obv:** Crowned head right, date below **Rev:** Penguin family

Date	Mintage	VF20	XF40	MS60	MS63	MS65
1996	—	PF65 25.00				

KM# 366 5 DOLLARS
31.47 g., 0.925 Silver 0.9359 oz. ASW **Ruler:** Elizabeth II **Subject:** Protect Our World **Obv:** Crowned head right, date below **Rev:** Charles Darwin bust at right, map and tortoise, denomination below **Edge:** Reeded

Date	Mintage	VF20	XF40	MS60	MS63	MS65
1996	—	PF65 27.50				

KM# 368 5 DOLLARS
28.00 g., 0.925 Silver 0.8327 oz. ASW **Ruler:** Elizabeth II **Subject:** Great Smoky Mountains National Park **Obv:** Crowned head right, date below **Rev:** Red wolf and two cubs **Edge:** Reeded

Date	Mintage	VF20	XF40	MS60	MS63	MS65
1996	—	PF65 28.00				

KM# 370 5 DOLLARS
31.50 g., 0.925 Silver 0.9368 oz. ASW, 38.6 mm. **Ruler:** Elizabeth II **Subject:** Olympics **Obv:** Crowned head right, date below **Rev:** Pole vaulter and runner **Edge:** Reeded

Date	Mintage	VF20	XF40	MS60	MS63	MS65
1996	—	PF65 25.00				

KM# 377 5 DOLLARS
31.50 g., 0.925 Silver 0.9368 oz. ASW, 38.6 mm. **Ruler:** Elizabeth II **Subject:** Endangered Wildlife **Obv:** Crowned head right, date below **Rev:** Two adult polar bears with cub **Edge:** Reeded

Date	Mintage	VF20	XF40	MS60	MS63	MS65
1996	—	PF65 30.00				

KM# 379 5 DOLLARS
31.47 g., 0.925 Silver 0.9359 oz. ASW, 38.6 mm. **Ruler:** Elizabeth II **Subject:** Queen Mother **Obv:** Crowned head right, date below **Rev:** Queen Mother and daughters, circa 1936, within circle, denomination below **Edge:** Reeded

Date	Mintage	VF20	XF40	MS60	MS63	MS65
1996	—	PF65 25.00				

KM# 846 5 DOLLARS
31.47 g., 0.925 Silver 0.9359 oz. ASW **Ruler:** Elizabeth II **Rev:** Catamarian **Note:** S#359.

Date	Mintage	VF20	XF40	MS60	MS63	MS65
1996	—	PF65 40.00				

KM# 312 5 DOLLARS
1.24 g., 0.9999 Gold 0.040 oz. AGW **Ruler:** Elizabeth II **Obv:** Crowned head right, date below **Rev:** Portrait of Princess Diana, dates, denomination below

Date	Mintage	VF20	XF40	MS60	MS63	MS65
1997	—	PF65 75.00				

KM# 335 5 DOLLARS
15.52 g., 0.999 Silver 0.4985 oz. ASW **Ruler:** Elizabeth II **Subject:** Japanese Samurai **Obv:** Crowned head right, date below **Rev:** 3/4 bust Yoshinobu Tokugawa facing, denomination at right, 3/4 braided circle surrounds **Edge:** Reeded

Date	Mintage	VF20	XF40	MS60	MS63	MS65
1997 FM	—	PF65 20.00				

KM# 457 5 DOLLARS
1.20 g., 0.9995 Platinum 0.0386 oz. APW **Ruler:** Elizabeth II **Subject:** Love Angels

Date	Mintage	VF20	XF40	MS60	MS63	MS65
1997	250	PF65 90.00				

KM# 849 5 DOLLARS
28.00 g., 0.925 Silver 0.8327 oz. ASW **Ruler:** Elizabeth II **Subject:** Theodore Roosevelt National Park **Rev:** Bison

Date	Mintage	VF20	XF40	MS60	MS63	MS65
1997	—	PF65 35.00				

KM# 865 5 DOLLARS
28.00 g., 0.925 Silver 0.8327 oz. ASW **Ruler:** Elizabeth II **Series:** Hawaii Volcano National Park

Date	Mintage	VF20	XF40	MS60	MS63	MS65
1997	—	PF65 35.00				

KM# 874 5 DOLLARS
10.00 g., 0.500 Silver 0.1608 oz. ASW **Ruler:** Elizabeth II **Subject:** Crater Lake National Park **Note:** S#413.

Date	Mintage	VF20	XF40	MS60	MS63	MS65
1997	—	PF65 15.00				

KM# 882 5 DOLLARS
15.55 g., 0.925 Silver 0.4624 oz. ASW **Ruler:** Elizabeth II **Rev:** Jean d'Arc, Christopher Columbus, John F. Kennedy

Date	Mintage	VF20	XF40	MS60	MS63	MS65
1997	—	—	—	—	30.00	—

KM# 902 5 DOLLARS
28.00 g., 0.925 Silver 0.8327 oz. ASW **Ruler:** Elizabeth II **Subject:** Grand Portage National Monument

Date	Mintage	VF20	XF40	MS60	MS63	MS65
1997	—	PF65 27.00				

KM# 911 5 DOLLARS
28.00 g., 0.925 Silver 0.8327 oz. ASW **Ruler:** Elizabeth II **Subject:** Yosemite National Park

Date	Mintage	VF20	XF40	MS60	MS63	MS65
1997	—	PF65 30.00				

KM# 918 5 DOLLARS
1.20 g., 0.999 Gold 0.0385 oz. AGW, 13.92 mm. **Ruler:** Elizabeth II **Subject:** Christmas

Date	Mintage	VF20	XF40	MS60	MS63	MS65
1997	100	PF65 95.00				

KM# 918a 5 DOLLARS
1.20 g., 0.9999 Platinum 0.0386 oz. APW, 13.92 mm. **Ruler:** Elizabeth II **Subject:** Christmas

Date	Mintage	VF20	XF40	MS60	MS63	MS65
1997	100	PF65 100				

KM# 923 5 DOLLARS
1.20 g., 0.999 Gold 0.0385 oz. AGW **Ruler:** Elizabeth II **Subject:** Christmas **Rev:** Angel with book and vine

Date	Mintage	VF20	XF40	MS60	MS63	MS65
1997	500	PF65 85.00				

KM# 923a 5 DOLLARS
1.20 g., 0.999 Platinum 0.0385 oz. APW **Ruler:** Elizabeth II **Subject:** Christmas **Rev:** Angel with book and vine

Date	Mintage	VF20	XF40	MS60	MS63	MS65
1997	500	PF65 100				

KM# 934 5 DOLLARS
28.00 g., 0.925 Silver 0.8327 oz. ASW **Ruler:** Elizabeth II **Subject:** Petrified Forest National Park **Rev:** Pronghorn

Date	Mintage	VF20	XF40	MS60	MS63	MS65
1998	—	PF65 35.00				

KM# 944 5 DOLLARS
28.00 g., 0.925 Silver 0.8327 oz. ASW **Ruler:** Elizabeth II **Subject:** Glacier Bay National Park and Preserve **Rev:** Humpback whale

Date	Mintage	VF20	XF40	MS60	MS63	MS65
1998	—	PF65 27.50				

KM# 952 5 DOLLARS
28.00 g., 0.925 Silver 0.8327 oz. ASW **Ruler:** Elizabeth II **Subject:** North Cascades National Park **Rev:** Northern Lights

Date	Mintage	VF20	XF40	MS60	MS63	MS65
1998	—	PF65 27.50				

KM# 962 5 DOLLARS
28.00 g., 0.925 Silver 0.8327 oz. ASW **Ruler:** Elizabeth II **Subject:** Grand Canyon National Park **Rev:** California Condor

Date	Mintage	VF20	XF40	MS60	MS63	MS65
1998	—	PF65 27.50				

KM# 971 5 DOLLARS
28.00 g., 0.925 Silver 0.8327 oz. ASW **Ruler:** Elizabeth II **Subject:** Gulf Islands National Seashore

Date	Mintage	VF20	XF40	MS60	MS63	MS65
1998	—	PF65 27.50				

KM# 981 5 DOLLARS
28.00 g., 0.925 Silver 0.8327 oz. ASW **Ruler:** Elizabeth II **Subject:** Big Cypress National Preserve **Rev:** Puma

Date	Mintage	VF20	XF40	MS60	MS63	MS65
1998	—	PF65 27.50				

KM# 991 5 DOLLARS
28.00 g., 0.925 Silver 0.8327 oz. ASW **Ruler:** Elizabeth II **Subject:** Everglades National Park **Rev:** Corcodile

Date	Mintage	VF20	XF40	MS60	MS63	MS65
1998	—	PF65 27.50				

KM# 1001 5 DOLLARS
28.00 g., 0.925 Silver 0.8327 oz. ASW **Ruler:** Elizabeth II **Subject:** Wind Cave National Park **Rev:** Swift Fox

Date	Mintage	VF20	XF40	MS60	MS63	MS65
1998	—	PF65 27.50				

KM# 1011 5 DOLLARS
28.00 g., 0.925 Silver 0.8327 oz. ASW **Ruler:** Elizabeth II **Subject:** Bryce Canyon National Park **Rev:** Prairie Dog

Date	Mintage	VF20	XF40	MS60	MS63	MS65
1998	—	PF65 27.50				

KM# 1021 5 DOLLARS
28.00 g., 0.925 Silver 0.8327 oz. ASW **Ruler:** Elizabeth II **Subject:** Gates of the Arctic National Park and Preserve **Rev:** Falcon

Date	Mintage	VF20	XF40	MS60	MS63	MS65
1998	—	PF65 27.50				

KM# 1031 5 DOLLARS
28.00 g., 0.925 Silver 0.8327 oz. ASW **Ruler:** Elizabeth II **Subject:** Badlands National Park **Rev:** Black-footed Ferret

Date	Mintage	VF20	XF40	MS60	MS63	MS65
1998	—	PF65 27.50				

KM# 1041 5 DOLLARS
28.00 g., 0.925 Silver 0.8327 oz. ASW **Ruler:** Elizabeth II **Subject:** Grand Teton National Park **Rev:** Whooping Crane

Date	Mintage	VF20	XF40	MS60	MS63	MS65
1998	—	PF65 27.50				

KM# 1050 5 DOLLARS
28.00 g., 0.925 Silver 0.8327 oz. ASW **Ruler:** Elizabeth II **Subject:** Kajoko Honokhau National Historic Park **Rev:** Hawaiian Duck

Date	Mintage	VF20	XF40	MS60	MS63	MS65
1998	—	PF65 27.50				

KM# 1060 5 DOLLARS
28.00 g., 0.925 Silver 0.8327 oz. ASW **Ruler:** Elizabeth II **Subject:** Virgin Islands National Park **Rev:** Brown Pelican

Date	Mintage	VF20	XF40	MS60	MS63	MS65
1998	—	PF65 27.50				

KM# 1070 5 DOLLARS
28.00 g., 0.925 Silver 0.8327 oz. ASW **Ruler:** Elizabeth II **Subject:** Mammoth Cave National Park **Rev:** Grey Bat

Date	Mintage	VF20	XF40	MS60	MS63	MS65
1998	—	PF65 27.50				

KM# 1080 5 DOLLARS
28.00 g., 0.925 Silver 0.8327 oz. ASW **Ruler:** Elizabeth II **Subject:** Rocky Mountain National Park **Rev:** Purple trout

Date	Mintage	VF20	XF40	MS60	MS63	MS65
1998	—	PF65 27.50				

KM# 1089 5 DOLLARS
1.24 g., 0.999 Gold 0.0398 oz. AGW **Ruler:** Elizabeth II **Rev:** Two dolphins

Date	Mintage	VF20	XF40	MS60	MS63	MS65
1998	—	PF65 90.00				

KM# 367 5 DOLLARS
31.45 g., 0.925 Silver 0.9353 oz. ASW **Ruler:** Elizabeth II **Subject:** Millennium - 2000 A.D. **Obv:** Crowned head right, date below **Rev:** Christian symbol above Tangaroa, Pagan God of Creation, denomination below **Edge:** Plain **Shape:** 7-sided

Date	Mintage	VF20	XF40	MS60	MS63	MS65
1999	—	PF65 37.50				

KM# 378 5 DOLLARS
31.50 g., 0.925 Silver 0.9368 oz. ASW, 38.6 mm. **Ruler:** Elizabeth II **Subject:** Takitumu Conservation Area **Obv:**

Crowned head right, date below **Rev:** Rarotongan Monarch Flycatcher, denomination at left **Edge:** Reeded

Date	Mintage	VF20	XF40	MS60	MS63	MS65
1999	—	PF65 30.00				

KM# 444 5 DOLLARS

62.21 g., 0.999 Silver 1.998 oz. ASW, 50 mm. **Ruler:** Elizabeth II **Obv:** Crowned head right, date below **Rev:** SS Sofia Jane, steam and sail ship **Edge:** Reeded

Date	Mintage	VF20	XF40	MS60	MS63	MS65
1999 Antiqued finish	5,000	—	—	90.00	—	—

KM# 445 5 DOLLARS

62.21 g., 0.999 Silver 1.998 oz. ASW, 50 mm. **Ruler:** Elizabeth II **Obv:** Crowned head right, date below **Rev:** Scottish Bard, barque type ship **Edge:** Reeded

Date	Mintage	VF20	XF40	MS60	MS63	MS65
1999 Antiqued finish	5,000	—	—	90.00	—	—

KM# 446 5 DOLLARS

62.21 g., 0.999 Silver 1.998 oz. ASW, 50 mm. **Ruler:** Elizabeth II **Obv:** Crowned head right, date below **Rev:** Cutty Sark, clipper ship **Edge:** Reeded

Date	Mintage	VF20	XF40	MS60	MS63	MS65
1999 Antiqued finish	5,000	—	—	90.00	—	—

KM# 447 5 DOLLARS

62.21 g., 0.999 Silver 1.998 oz. ASW, 50 mm. **Ruler:** Elizabeth II **Obv:** Crowned head right, date below **Rev:** HMS Sirius, 20 gun naval ship circa 1788 **Edge:** Reeded

Date	Mintage	VF20	XF40	MS60	MS63	MS65
1999 Antiqued finish	5,000	—	—	90.00	—	—

KM# 448 5 DOLLARS

62.21 g., 0.999 Silver 1.998 oz. ASW, 50 mm. **Ruler:** Elizabeth II **Obv:** Crowned head right, date below **Rev:** 18 ft. Skiff **Edge:** Reeded

Date	Mintage	VF20	XF40	MS60	MS63	MS65
1999 Antiqued finish	5,000	—	—	90.00	—	—

KM# 456 5 DOLLARS

31.50 g., 0.925 Silver 0.9368 oz. ASW, 38.6 mm. **Ruler:** Elizabeth II **Obv:** Crowned head right, date below **Rev:** Sail Ship Archimedes **Edge:** Reeded

Date	Mintage	VF20	XF40	MS60	MS63	MS65
1999	—	PF65 37.50				

KM# 1315 5 DOLLARS

Silver **Ruler:** Elizabeth II **Subject:** Moon landing

Date	Mintage	VF20	XF40	MS60	MS63	MS65
1999	—	PF65 50.00				

KM# 375 5 DOLLARS

28.10 g., 0.925 Silver 0.8357 oz. ASW with gold plated outer circle, 38.6 mm. **Ruler:** Elizabeth II **Subject:** Queen Mother's 100th Birthday **Obv:** Crowned head right, date below **Rev:** Queen Mother and daughters, circa 1980 **Edge:** Reeded

Date	Mintage	VF20	XF40	MS60	MS63	MS65
2000	1,000	PF65 30.00				

KM# 1097 5 DOLLARS

25.00 g., 0.925 Silver 0.7435 oz. ASW **Ruler:** Elizabeth II **Rev:** Sagebrush in color

Date	Mintage	VF20	XF40	MS60	MS63	MS65
2000	—	PF65 65.00				

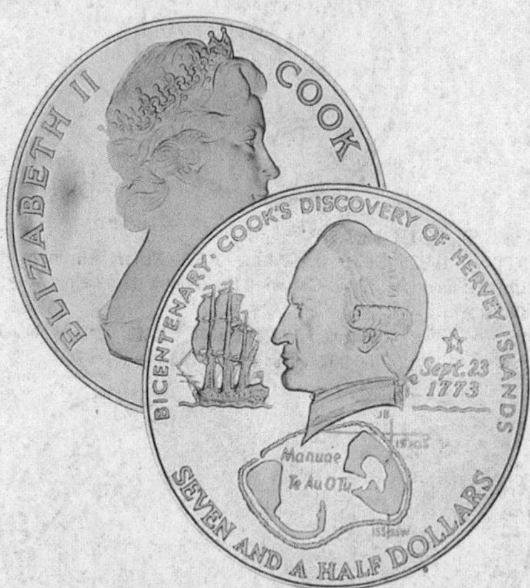

KM# 10 7-1/2 DOLLARS

33.80 g., 0.925 Silver 1.0052 oz. ASW, 42 mm. **Ruler:** Elizabeth II **Subject:** Capt. James Cook's 2nd Pacific Voyage **Obv:** Young bust right, date below **Rev:** H.M.S. Resolution and Cook's profile above map of Hervey Islands

Date	Mintage	VF20	XF40	MS60	MS63	MS65
1973	6,000	—	—	—	—	37.00
1973	12,000	PF65 35.00				
1974	2,000	—	—	—	—	40.00
1974	13,000	PF65 35.00				

KM# 21 10 DOLLARS

27.90 g., 0.925 Silver 0.8297 oz. ASW **Ruler:** Elizabeth II **Subject:** 25th Anniversary of Coronation **Obv:** Young bust right, date below **Rev:** Crown with supporters, dates below, denomination at bottom

Date	Mintage	VF20	XF40	MS60	MS63	MS65
1978 FM	11,000	PF65 30.00				
1978 FM (U)	5,350	—	—	—	—	32.00

KM# 72 10 DOLLARS

10.00 g., 0.925 Silver 0.2974 oz. ASW **Ruler:** Elizabeth II **Subject:** Endangered World Wildlife **Obv:** Crowned head right, date below **Rev:** Elephants head left

Date	Mintage	VF20	XF40	MS60	MS63	MS65
1990	25,000	PF63 9.00	PF65 12.50			

KM# 73 10 DOLLARS

10.00 g., 0.925 Silver 0.2974 oz. ASW **Ruler:** Elizabeth II **Subject:** Endangered World Wildlife **Obv:** Crowned head right, date below **Rev:** Tiger

Date	Mintage	VF20	XF40	MS60	MS63	MS65
1990	—	PF63 9.00	PF65 12.50			

KM# 79 10 DOLLARS

10.00 g., 0.925 Silver 0.2974 oz. ASW **Ruler:** Elizabeth II **Subject:** Olympics **Obv:** Crowned head right, date below **Rev:** Runner

Date	Mintage	VF20	XF40	MS60	MS63	MS65
1990	150,000	PF63 8.00	PF65 11.50			

KM# 80 10 DOLLARS

10.00 g., 0.925 Silver 0.2974 oz. ASW, 30 mm. **Ruler:** Elizabeth II **Subject:** Endangered World Wildlife **Obv:** Crowned head right, date below **Rev:** African elephants **Edge:** Reeded

Date	Mintage	VF20	XF40	MS60	MS63	MS65
1990	Est. 25000	PF63 9.00	PF65 12.50			

KM# 81 10 DOLLARS

28.00 g., 0.925 Silver 0.8327 oz. ASW **Ruler:** Elizabeth II **Subject:** Save the Children **Obv:** Crowned head right, date below **Rev:** Grass-skirted dancers

Date	Mintage	VF20	XF40	MS60	MS63	MS65
1990	20,000	PF65 30.00				

KM# 90 10 DOLLARS

10.00 g., 0.925 Silver 0.2974 oz. ASW **Ruler:** Elizabeth II **Subject:** 500 Years of America **Obv:** Crowned head right, date below **Rev:** Bust at left looking right, ship at right, denomination below

Date	Mintage	VF20	XF40	MS60	MS63	MS65
1990	Est. 150000	PF63 8.00	PF65 11.50			

KM# 91 10 DOLLARS

10.00 g., 0.925 Silver 0.2974 oz. ASW **Ruler:** Elizabeth II **Subject:** 1991 Winter Olympics **Obv:** Crowned head right, date below **Rev:** Cross-country skier, denomination below

Date	Mintage	VF20	XF40	MS60	MS63	MS65
1990	150,000	PF63 7.50	PF65 11.00			

KM# 121 10 DOLLARS

10.00 g., 0.925 Silver 0.2974 oz. ASW **Ruler:** Elizabeth II **Subject:** 500 Years of America **Obv:** Crowned head right, date below **Rev:** Columbus and ship

Date	Mintage	VF20	XF40	MS60	MS63	MS65
1990	Est. 150000	PF63 8.00	PF65 11.50			

KM# 136 10 DOLLARS

31.47 g., 0.925 Silver 0.9359 oz. ASW **Ruler:** Elizabeth II **Obv:** Crowned head right, date below **Rev:** Bust with planet earth revolving around radiant sun in background

Date	Mintage	VF20	XF40	MS60	MS63	MS65
1992	—	PF65 30.00				

KM# 254 10 DOLLARS

31.47 g., 0.925 Silver 0.9359 oz. ASW **Ruler:** Elizabeth II **Subject:** World Cup '94 **Obv:** Crowned head right, date below **Rev:** Goalie catching ball

Date	Mintage	VF20	XF40	MS60	MS63	MS65
1992	Est. 20000	PF65 35.00				

KM# 817 10 DOLLARS

3.11 g., 0.9999 Gold 0.100 oz. AGW **Ruler:** Elizabeth II **Rev:** Papillon dog

Date	Mintage	VF20	XF40	MS60	MS63	MS65
1992	4,506	PF65 180				
1994	2,016	PF65 195				

KM# 358 10 DOLLARS

14.80 g., 0.925 Silver 0.4401 oz. ASW **Ruler:** Elizabeth II **Subject:** Captain Cook **Obv:** Crowned head right, date below **Rev:** Captain Cook wading ashore, denomination at right **Edge:** Reeded

Date	Mintage	VF20	XF40	MS60	MS63	MS65
1994 FM	—	PF63 12.00	PF65 17.00			

KM# 832 10 DOLLARS

31.11 g., 0.999 Silver 0.999 oz. ASW **Ruler:** Elizabeth II **Subject:** World War II - Japan invades China

Date	Mintage	VF20	XF40	MS60	MS63	MS65
1995	—	PF65 45.00				

KM# 833 10 DOLLARS

31.11 g., 0.999 Silver 0.999 oz. ASW **Ruler:** Elizabeth II **Subject:** WWII, Attack of Pearl Harbor **Note:** S#833.

Date	Mintage	VF20	XF40	MS60	MS63	MS65
1995	—	PF65 45.00				

KM# 834 10 DOLLARS

31.11 g., 0.999 Silver 0.999 oz. ASW **Ruler:** Elizabeth II **Subject:** WWII, Landing of the Allies at Normandy

Date	Mintage	VF20	XF40	MS60	MS63	MS65
1995	—	PF65 45.00				

KM# 835 10 DOLLARS

31.11 g., 0.999 Silver 0.999 oz. ASW **Ruler:** Elizabeth II **Subject:** WWII, Atom Bomb drop at Heroshima

Date	Mintage	VF20	XF40	MS60	MS63	MS65
1995	—	PF65 45.00				

KM# 283 10 DOLLARS

28.00 g., 0.925 Silver 0.8327 oz. ASW **Ruler:** Elizabeth II **Subject:** Olympic National Park **Obv:** Crowned head right, date below **Rev:** Multicolor Bald eagle in flight over mountain tops, denomination below

Date	Mintage	VF20	XF40	MS60	MS63	MS65
1996	10,000	PF65 32.50				

KM# 284 10 DOLLARS

28.00 g., 0.925 Silver 0.8327 oz. ASW **Ruler:** Elizabeth II **Subject:** Yellowstone National Park **Obv:** Crowned head right, date below **Rev:** Multicolor Grizzly bear and cub

Date	Mintage	VF20	XF40	MS60	MS63	MS65
1996	10,000	PF65 35.00				

KM# 285 10 DOLLARS

1.24 g., 0.999 Gold 0.040 oz. AGW **Ruler:** Elizabeth II **Subject:** Olympic National Park **Obv:** Crowned head right, date below **Rev:** Eagle's head right, denomination below

Date	Mintage	VF20	XF40	MS60	MS63	MS65
1996	—	PF65 75.00				

KM# 286 10 DOLLARS

1.24 g., 0.999 Gold 0.040 oz. AGW **Ruler:** Elizabeth II **Subject:** Yellowstone National Park **Obv:** Crowned head right, date below

Date	Mintage	VF20	XF40	MS60	MS63	MS65
1996	—	PF65 85.00				

KM# 359 10 DOLLARS
28.00 g., 0.925 Silver 0.8327 oz. ASW **Ruler:** Elizabeth II **Subject:** Theodore Roosevelt National Park **Obv:** Crowned head right, date below **Rev:** Multicolor bison **Edge:** Reeded

Date	Mintage	VF20	XF40	MS60	MS63	MS65
1996	—	PF65 35.00				
1997	—	PF65 35.00				

KM# 330 10 DOLLARS
28.00 g., 0.925 Silver 0.8327 oz. ASW **Ruler:** Elizabeth II **Subject:** Great Smoky Mountains National Park **Obv:** Crowned head right, date below **Rev:** Multicolor red wolf with two cubs

Date	Mintage	VF20	XF40	MS60	MS63	MS65
1997	—	PF65 37.50				

KM# 331 10 DOLLARS
28.00 g., 0.925 Silver 0.8327 oz. ASW **Ruler:** Elizabeth II **Subject:** Yosemite National Park **Obv:** Crowned head right, date below **Rev:** Multicolor Peregrine falcon

Date	Mintage	VF20	XF40	MS60	MS63	MS65
1997	—	PF65 37.50				

KM# 360 10 DOLLARS
28.00 g., 0.925 Silver 0.8327 oz. ASW **Ruler:** Elizabeth II **Subject:** Glacier Bay National Park **Obv:** Crowned head right, date below **Rev:** Multicolor Humpback whale breaking the water

Date	Mintage	VF20	XF40	MS60	MS63	MS65
1997	—	PF65 35.00				

KM# 458 10 DOLLARS
2.50 g., 0.9995 Platinum 0.0803 oz. APW **Ruler:** Elizabeth II **Subject:** Love Angels

Date	Mintage	VF20	XF40	MS60	MS63	MS65
1997	250	PF65 185				

KM# 555 10 DOLLARS
Silver **Ruler:** Elizabeth II **Subject:** Hawaii Volcanos National Park **Obv:** Bust right **Rev:** Hawaii Volcanos, multicolor tourtise

Date	Mintage	VF20	XF40	MS60	MS63	MS65
1997	—	PF65 37.50				

KM# 852 10 DOLLARS
1.24 g., 0.999 Gold 0.0398 oz. AGW **Ruler:** Elizabeth II **Subject:** Theodore Roosevelt National Park **Rev:** Bison

Date	Mintage	VF20	XF40	MS60	MS63	MS65
1997	—	PF65 75.00				

KM# 859 10 DOLLARS
1.24 g., 0.999 Gold 0.0398 oz. AGW **Ruler:** Elizabeth II **Subject:** Great Smoky Mountains National Park **Rev:** Red wolf **Note:** S#397.

Date	Mintage	VF20	XF40	MS60	MS63	MS65
1997	—	PF65 75.00				

KM# 866 10 DOLLARS
28.00 g., 0.925 Silver 0.8327 oz. ASW **Ruler:** Elizabeth II **Subject:** Hawaii Volcano National Park

Date	Mintage	VF20	XF40	MS60	MS63	MS65
1997	—	PF65 30.00				

KM# 869 10 DOLLARS
1.24 g., 0.999 Gold 0.0398 oz. AGW **Ruler:** Elizabeth II **Subject:** Hawaii Volcano National Park

Date	Mintage	VF20	XF40	MS60	MS63	MS65
1997	—	PF65 75.00				

KM# 875 10 DOLLARS
28.00 g., 0.925 Silver 0.8327 oz. ASW **Ruler:** Elizabeth II **Subject:** Crater Lake National Park **Note:** S#415.

Date	Mintage	VF20	XF40	MS60	MS63	MS65
1997	—	PF65 45.00				

KM# 878 10 DOLLARS
1.24 g., 0.999 Gold 0.0398 oz. AGW **Ruler:** Elizabeth II **Subject:** Crater Lake National Park

Date	Mintage	VF20	XF40	MS60	MS63	MS65
1997	—	PF65 75.00				

KM# 903 10 DOLLARS
28.00 g., 0.925 Silver 0.8327 oz. ASW **Ruler:** Elizabeth II **Subject:** Grand Portage National Monument **Rev:** Landscape in color

Date	Mintage	VF20	XF40	MS60	MS63	MS65
1997	—	PF65 28.00				

KM# 906 10 DOLLARS
1.24 g., 0.999 Gold 0.0398 oz. AGW **Ruler:** Elizabeth II **Subject:** Grand Portage National Monument **Rev:** North American Reindeer

Date	Mintage	VF20	XF40	MS60	MS63	MS65
1997	—	PF65 75.00				

KM# 914 10 DOLLARS
1.24 g., 0.999 Gold 0.0398 oz. AGW **Ruler:** Elizabeth II **Subject:** Yosemite National Park **Rev:** Waterfall

Date	Mintage	VF20	XF40	MS60	MS63	MS65
1997	—	PF65 75.00				

KM# 919 10 DOLLARS
2.50 g., 0.999 Gold 0.0803 oz. AGW, 17.95 mm. **Ruler:** Elizabeth II **Subject:** Christmas

Date	Mintage	VF20	XF40	MS60	MS63	MS65
1997	100	PF65 150				

KM# 919a 10 DOLLARS
2.50 g., 0.9999 Platinum 0.0804 oz. APW, 17.95 mm. **Ruler:** Elizabeth II **Subject:** Christmas

Date	Mintage	VF20	XF40	MS60	MS63	MS65
1997	100	PF65 175				

KM# 924 10 DOLLARS
2.50 g., 0.999 Gold 0.0803 oz. AGW **Ruler:** Elizabeth II **Subject:** Christmas **Rev:** Angel with book and vine

Date	Mintage	VF20	XF40	MS60	MS63	MS65
1997	500	PF65 140				

KM# 924a 10 DOLLARS
2.50 g., 0.999 Platinum 0.0803 oz. APW **Ruler:** Elizabeth II **Subject:** Christmas **Rev:** Angel with book and vine

Date	Mintage	VF20	XF40	MS60	MS63	MS65
1997	500	PF65 190				

KM# 332 10 DOLLARS
28.00 g., 0.925 Silver 0.8327 oz. ASW **Ruler:** Elizabeth II **Subject:** Grand Teton National park **Obv:** Crowned head right, date below **Rev:** Multicolor Whooping crane

Date	Mintage	VF20	XF40	MS60	MS63	MS65
1998	—	PF65 37.50				

KM# 333 10 DOLLARS
28.00 g., 0.925 Silver 0.8327 oz. ASW **Ruler:** Elizabeth II **Subject:** Grand Canyon National Park **Obv:** Crowned head right, date below **Rev:** Multicolor California condor in flight over canyon

Date	Mintage	VF20	XF40	MS60	MS63	MS65
1998	—	PF65 37.50				

KM# 935 10 DOLLARS
28.00 g., 0.925 Silver 0.8327 oz. ASW **Ruler:** Elizabeth II **Subject:** Petrified Forest National Park **Rev:** Landscape in color

Date	Mintage	VF20	XF40	MS60	MS63	MS65
1998	—	PF65 37.50				

KM# 938 10 DOLLARS
1.24 g., 0.999 Gold 0.0398 oz. AGW **Ruler:** Elizabeth II **Subject:** Petrified Forest National Park **Rev:** Pronghorn

Date	Mintage	VF20	XF40	MS60	MS63	MS65
1998	—	PF65 75.00				

KM# 947 10 DOLLARS
1.24 g., 0.999 Gold 0.0398 oz. AGW **Ruler:** Elizabeth II **Rev:** Humpback whale

Date	Mintage	VF20	XF40	MS60	MS63	MS65
1998	—	PF65 75.00				

KM# 953 10 DOLLARS
28.00 g., 0.925 Silver 0.8327 oz. ASW **Ruler:** Elizabeth II **Subject:** North Cascades National Park **Rev:** Landscape in color

Date	Mintage	VF20	XF40	MS60	MS63	MS65
1998	—	PF65 37.50				

KM# 956 10 DOLLARS
1.24 g., 0.999 Gold 0.0398 oz. AGW **Ruler:** Elizabeth II **Subject:** North Cascades National Park **Rev:** Northern Lights

Date	Mintage	VF20	XF40	MS60	MS63	MS65
1998	—	PF65 75.00				

KM# 972 10 DOLLARS
28.00 g., 0.925 Silver 0.8327 oz. ASW **Ruler:** Elizabeth II **Subject:** Gulf Islands National Seashore **Rev:** Landscape in color

Date	Mintage	VF20	XF40	MS60	MS63	MS65
1998	—	PF65 37.50				

KM# 975 10 DOLLARS
1.24 g., 0.999 Gold 0.0398 oz. AGW **Ruler:** Elizabeth II **Subject:** Gulf Islands National Seashore

Date	Mintage	VF20	XF40	MS60	MS63	MS65
1998	—	PF65 75.00				

KM# 982 10 DOLLARS
28.00 g., 0.925 Silver 0.8327 oz. ASW **Ruler:** Elizabeth II **Subject:** Big Cypress National Preserve **Rev:** Landscape in color

Date	Mintage	VF20	XF40	MS60	MS63	MS65
1998	—	PF65 37.50				

KM# 985 10 DOLLARS
1.24 g., 0.999 Gold 0.0398 oz. AGW **Ruler:** Elizabeth II **Subject:** Big Cypress National Preserve **Rev:** Puma

Date	Mintage	VF20	XF40	MS60	MS63	MS65
1998	—	PF65 75.00				

KM# 992 10 DOLLARS
28.00 g., 0.925 Silver 0.8327 oz. ASW **Ruler:** Elizabeth II **Subject:** Everglades National Park **Rev:** Landscape in color

Date	Mintage	VF20	XF40	MS60	MS63	MS65
1998	—	PF65 37.50				

KM# 995 10 DOLLARS
1.24 g., 0.999 Gold 0.0398 oz. AGW **Ruler:** Elizabeth II **Subject:** Everglades National Park **Rev:** Crocodile

Date	Mintage	VF20	XF40	MS60	MS63	MS65
1998	—	PF65 75.00				

KM# 1002 10 DOLLARS
28.00 g., 0.999 Silver 0.8993 oz. ASW **Ruler:** Elizabeth II **Subject:** Wind Cave National Park **Rev:** Landscape in color

Date	Mintage	VF20	XF40	MS60	MS63	MS65
1998	—	PF65 37.50				

KM# 1005 10 DOLLARS
1.24 g., 0.999 Gold 0.0398 oz. AGW **Ruler:** Elizabeth II **Subject:** Wind Cave National Park **Rev:** Swift Fox

Date	Mintage	VF20	XF40	MS60	MS63	MS65
1998	—	PF65 75.00				

KM# 1012 10 DOLLARS
28.00 g., 0.925 Silver 0.8327 oz. ASW **Ruler:** Elizabeth II **Subject:** Bryce Canyon National Park **Rev:** Landscape in color

Date	Mintage	VF20	XF40	MS60	MS63	MS65
1998	—	PF65 37.50				

KM# 1015 10 DOLLARS
1.24 g., 0.999 Gold 0.0398 oz. AGW **Ruler:** Elizabeth II **Subject:** Bryce Canyon National Park **Rev:** Prairie Dog

Date	Mintage	VF20	XF40	MS60	MS63	MS65
1998	—	PF65 75.00				

KM# 1022 10 DOLLARS
28.00 g., 0.925 Silver 0.8327 oz. ASW **Ruler:** Elizabeth II **Subject:** Gates of the Arctic National Park and Preserve **Rev:** Landscape in color

Date	Mintage	VF20	XF40	MS60	MS63	MS65
1998 proof	—	PF65 50.00				

KM# 1025 10 DOLLARS
1.24 g., 0.999 Gold 0.0398 oz. AGW **Ruler:** Elizabeth II **Subject:** Gates of the Arctic National Park and Preserve **Rev:** Falcon

Date	Mintage	VF20	XF40	MS60	MS63	MS65
1998	—	PF65 75.00				

KM# 1032 10 DOLLARS
28.00 g., 0.925 Silver 0.8327 oz. ASW **Ruler:** Elizabeth II **Subject:** Badlands National Park **Rev:** Landscape in color

Date	Mintage	VF20	XF40	MS60	MS63	MS65
1998	—	PF65 37.50				

KM# 1035 10 DOLLARS
1.24 g., 0.999 Gold 0.0398 oz. AGW **Ruler:** Elizabeth II **Subject:** Badlands National Park **Rev:** Black-footed Ferret

Date	Mintage	VF20	XF40	MS60	MS63	MS65
1998	—	PF65 75.00				

KM# 1044 10 DOLLARS
1.24 g., 0.999 Gold 0.0398 oz. AGW **Ruler:** Elizabeth II **Subject:** Grand Teton National Park **Rev:** Whooping Crane

Date	Mintage	VF20	XF40	MS60	MS63	MS65
1998	—	PF65 75.00				

KM# 1051 10 DOLLARS
28.00 g., 0.925 Silver 0.8327 oz. ASW **Ruler:** Elizabeth II **Subject:** Kajoko Honokhau National Historic Park **Rev:** Landscape in color

Date	Mintage	VF20	XF40	MS60	MS63	MS65
1998	—	PF65 37.50				

KM# 1054 10 DOLLARS
1.24 g., 0.999 Gold 0.0398 oz. AGW **Ruler:** Elizabeth II **Subject:** Kajoko Honokhau National Historic Park **Rev:** Hawaiian Duck

Date	Mintage	VF20	XF40	MS60	MS63	MS65
1998	—	PF65 75.00				

KM# 1061 10 DOLLARS
28.00 g., 0.925 Silver 0.8327 oz. ASW **Ruler:** Elizabeth II **Subject:** Virgin Islands National Park **Rev:** Landscape in color

Date	Mintage	VF20	XF40	MS60	MS63	MS65
1998	—	PF65 37.50				

KM# 1064 10 DOLLARS
1.24 g., 0.999 Gold 0.0398 oz. AGW **Ruler:** Elizabeth II **Subject:** Virgin Islands National Park **Rev:** Brown Pelican

Date	Mintage	VF20	XF40	MS60	MS63	MS65
1998	—	PF65 75.00				

KM# 1071 10 DOLLARS
28.00 g., 0.925 Silver 0.8327 oz. ASW **Ruler:** Elizabeth II **Subject:** Mammoth Cave National Park **Rev:** Landscape in color

Date	Mintage	VF20	XF40	MS60	MS63	MS65
1998	—	PF65 37.50				

KM# 1074 10 DOLLARS
1.24 g., 0.999 Gold 0.0398 oz. AGW **Ruler:** Elizabeth II **Subject:** Mammoth Cave National Park **Rev:** Grey Bat

Date	Mintage	VF20	XF40	MS60	MS63	MS65
1998	—	PF65 75.00				

KM# 1081 10 DOLLARS
28.00 g., 0.925 Silver 0.8327 oz. ASW **Ruler:** Elizabeth II **Subject:** Rocky Mountain National Park **Rev:** Landscape in color

Date	Mintage	VF20	XF40	MS60	MS63	MS65
1998	—	PF65 37.50				

KM# 1084 10 DOLLARS
1.24 g., 0.999 Gold 0.0398 oz. AGW **Ruler:** Elizabeth II **Subject:** Rocky Mountain National Park **Rev:** Purple trout

Date	Mintage	VF20	XF40	MS60	MS63	MS65
1998	—	PF65 75.00				

KM# 1090 10 DOLLARS
3.11 g., 0.999 Gold 0.0999 oz. AGW **Ruler:** Elizabeth II **Rev:** Two dolphins

Date	Mintage	VF20	XF40	MS60	MS63	MS65
1998	—	PF65 185				

KM# 476 10 DOLLARS
1.22 g., Gold, 13.88 mm. **Ruler:** Elizabeth II **Subject:** 1996 Solar Eclipse **Obv:** Crowned bust right **Rev:** Outlined earth latitudes in rays **Edge:** Reeded

Date	Mintage	VF20	XF40	MS60	MS63	MS65
1999	—	PF65 75.00				

KM# 477 10 DOLLARS
1.22 g., Gold, 1.22 mm. **Ruler:** Elizabeth II **Obv:** Crowned bust right **Rev:** Bottle-nosed Dolphin **Edge:** Reeded

Date	Mintage	VF20	XF40	MS60	MS63	MS65
2000	—	PF65 75.00				

KM# 1098 10 DOLLARS
1.24 g., 0.999 Gold 0.0398 oz. AGW **Ruler:** Elizabeth II **Rev:** Sagebrush

Date	Mintage	VF20	XF40	MS60	MS63	MS65
2000	—	PF65 75.00				

KM# 1100 10 DOLLARS
1.24 g., 0.999 Gold 0.0398 oz. AGW **Ruler:** Elizabeth II **Subject:** Wildlife **Rev:** Bottlenose dolphin

Date	Mintage	VF20	XF40	MS60	MS63	MS65
2000	—	PF65 75.00				

KM# 1106 10 DOLLARS
312.35 g., 0.999 Silver 10.0321 oz. ASW **Ruler:** Elizabeth II **Rev:** Planets lined up in a row

Date	Mintage	VF20	XF40	MS60	MS63	MS65
2000	Est. 5000	PF65 375				

KM# 28 20 DOLLARS
28.28 g., 0.925 Silver 0.841 oz. ASW **Ruler:** Elizabeth II **Subject:** International Year of the Scout **Obv:** Young bust right, date below **Rev:** Boy Scouts, dates at left, denomination at right

Date	Mintage	VF20	XF40	MS60	MS63	MS65
1983	10,000	—	—	—	—	32.50
1983	10,000	PF65 35.00				

KM# 818 20 DOLLARS
6.22 g., 0.999 Gold 0.1998 oz. AGW **Ruler:** Elizabeth II **Rev:** Papillon dog

Date	Mintage	VF20	XF40	MS60	MS63	MS65
1992	3,580	PF65 350				
1994	1,511	PF65 375				

KM# 151 20 DOLLARS
31.47 g., 0.925 Silver 0.9359 oz. ASW **Ruler:** Elizabeth II **Obv:** Crowned head right, date below **Rev:** Friedrich von Schiller

Date	Mintage	VF20	XF40	MS60	MS63	MS65
1993	—	PF65 35.00				

KM# 152 20 DOLLARS
31.47 g., 0.925 Silver 0.9359 oz. ASW **Ruler:** Elizabeth II **Obv:** Crowned head right, date below **Rev:** Bust of Charles Darwin facing left, tortoise and map, denomination below

Date	Mintage	VF20	XF40	MS60	MS63	MS65
1993	10,000	PF65 35.00				

KM# 161 20 DOLLARS
31.47 g., 0.925 Silver 0.9359 oz. ASW **Ruler:** Elizabeth II **Subject:** 1996 Olympics **Obv:** Crowned head right, date below **Rev:** Pole vaulter and sprinter

Date	Mintage	VF20	XF40	MS60	MS63	MS65
1993	50,000	PF65 35.00				

KM# 235 20 DOLLARS
31.47 g., 0.925 Silver 0.9359 oz. ASW **Ruler:** Elizabeth II **Obv:** Crowned head right, date below **Rev:** Tainui Catamaran

Date	Mintage	VF20	XF40	MS60	MS63	MS65
1995	Est. 15000	PF65 35.00				

KM# 236 20 DOLLARS
1.24 g., 0.999 Gold 0.040 oz. AGW **Ruler:** Elizabeth II **Subject:** 500 Years of America **Obv:** Crowned head right, date below **Rev:** Columbus claims the New World, denomination below

Date	Mintage	VF20	XF40	MS60	MS63	MS65
1995	Est. 25000	—	—	—	65.00	70.00

KM# 237 20 DOLLARS
1.24 g., 0.999 Silver Gilt 0.040 oz. **Ruler:** Elizabeth II **Subject:** 500 Years of America **Obv:** Crowned head right, date below **Rev:** Washington crossing the Delaware, denomination below

Date	Mintage	VF20	XF40	MS60	MS63	MS65
1995	Est. 25000	—	—	—	65.00	70.00

KM# 256 20 DOLLARS
31.47 g., 0.925 Silver 0.9359 oz. ASW **Ruler:** Elizabeth II **Obv:** Crowned head right, date below **Rev:** Queen Mother and daughters within circle, denomination below

Date	Mintage	VF20	XF40	MS60	MS63	MS65
1995	Est. 30000	PF65 37.50				

KM# 257 20 DOLLARS
1.24 g., 0.9999 Gold 0.040 oz. AGW **Ruler:** Elizabeth II **Subject:** 500 Years of America **Obv:** Crowned head right, date below **Rev:** Statue of Liberty, denomination below

Date	Mintage	VF20	XF40	MS60	MS63	MS65
1995	—	—	—	—	65.00	70.00

KM# 258 20 DOLLARS
1.24 g., 0.9999 Gold 0.040 oz. AGW **Ruler:** Elizabeth II **Subject:** 500 Years of America **Obv:** Crowned head right, date below **Rev:** Capt. James Cook bust right, denomination below

Date	Mintage	VF20	XF40	MS60	MS63	MS65
1995	Est. 25000	PF65 70.00				

KM# 270 20 DOLLARS
1.24 g., 0.9999 Gold 0.040 oz. AGW **Ruler:** Elizabeth II **Subject:** 500 Years of America **Obv:** Crowned head right, date below **Rev:** Astronaut on moon, denomination below

Date	Mintage	VF20	XF40	MS60	MS63	MS65
1995	Est. 25000	PF65 70.00				

KM# 287 20 DOLLARS
155.52 g., 0.999 Silver 4.995 oz. ASW, 82 mm. **Ruler:** Elizabeth II **Subject:** Olympic National Park **Obv:** Crowned head right, date below **Rev:** Bald eagle **Note:** Illustration reduced.

Date	Mintage	VF20	XF40	MS60	MS63	MS65
1996	1,000	PF65 145				

KM# 288 20 DOLLARS
155.52 g., 0.999 Silver 4.995 oz. ASW **Ruler:** Elizabeth II **Subject:** Yellowstone National Park **Obv:** Crowned head right, date below **Rev:** Grizzly bear

Date	Mintage	VF20	XF40	MS60	MS63	MS65
1996	1,000	PF65 145				

KM# 298 20 DOLLARS
3.00 g., 0.9999 Gold 0.0964 oz. AGW **Ruler:** Elizabeth II **Subject:** Year of the Mouse **Obv:** Crowned head right, date below **Rev:** Multicolor Mickey Mouse portrait facing, denomination below

Date	Mintage	VF20	XF40	MS60	MS63	MS65
1996	—	PF65 175				

KM# 475 20 DOLLARS
1.22 g., Gold, 13.89 mm. **Ruler:** Elizabeth II **Obv:** Crowned bust right **Rev:** 1/2 length figure of Friedrich von Schiller at right seated at table, bell at left **Edge:** Reeded

Date	Mintage	VF20	XF40	MS60	MS63	MS65
1996	—	PF65 65.00				

KM# 843 20 DOLLARS
3.13 g., 0.999 Gold 0.1006 oz. AGW **Ruler:** Elizabeth II **Subject:** Mother's day

Date	Mintage	VF20	XF40	MS60	MS63	MS65
1996	—	PF65 200				

KM# 847 20 DOLLARS
1.24 g., 0.999 Gold 0.0398 oz. AGW **Ruler:** Elizabeth II **Subject:** Friedrich von Schiller **Note:** S#360.

Date	Mintage	VF20	XF40	MS60	MS63	MS65
1996 Proof	—	—	—	—	—	70.00

KM# 334 20 DOLLARS
32.02 g., 0.925 Silver 0.9523 oz. ASW **Ruler:** Elizabeth II **Subject:** 12th Century **Obv:** Crowned head right, date below **Rev:** Genghis Khan on horse left, soldier on camel at right, denominaition at left

Date	Mintage	VF20	XF40	MS60	MS63	MS65
1997	—	PF65 32.00				

KM# 336 20 DOLLARS
31.88 g., 0.925 Silver 0.9481 oz. ASW **Ruler:** Elizabeth II **Subject:** 18th Century **Obv:** Crowned head right, date below **Rev:** Signing of the Declaration of Independence, denomination lower right **Edge:** Reeded

Date	Mintage	VF20	XF40	MS60	MS63	MS65
1997 FM	—	PF65 32.00				

KM# 337 20 DOLLARS
31.88 g., 0.925 Silver 0.9481 oz. ASW **Ruler:** Elizabeth II **Subject:** 19th Century **Obv:** Crowned head right, date below **Rev:** Waving driver with two passengers in horseless carriage, bicycle at right in back, denomination at left **Edge:** Reeded

Date	Mintage	VF20	XF40	MS60	MS63	MS65
1997 FM	—	PF65 32.00				

KM# 459 20 DOLLARS
5.00 g., 0.9995 Platinum 0.1607 oz. APW **Ruler:** Elizabeth II **Subject:** Love Angels

Date	Mintage	VF20	XF40	MS60	MS63	MS65
1997	250	PF65 350				

KM# 850 20 DOLLARS
155.50 g., 0.999 Silver 4.9944 oz. ASW **Ruler:** Elizabeth II **Subject:** Theodore Roosevelt National Park **Rev:** Bison **Note:** S#385.

Date	Mintage	VF20	XF40	MS60	MS63	MS65
1997	—	PF65 175				

KM# 857 20 DOLLARS
155.50 g., 0.999 Silver 4.9944 oz. ASW **Ruler:** Elizabeth II **Subject:** Great Smoky Mountains National Park **Rev:** Red wolf

Date	Mintage	VF20	XF40	MS60	MS63	MS65
1997	—	PF65 175				

KM# 867 20 DOLLARS
155.50 g., 0.999 Silver 4.9944 oz. ASW **Ruler:** Elizabeth II **Subject:** Hawaii Volcano National Park

Date	Mintage	VF20	XF40	MS60	MS63	MS65
1997	—	PF65 185				

KM# 876 20 DOLLARS
155.50 g., 0.999 Silver 4.9944 oz. ASW **Ruler:** Elizabeth II **Subject:** Crater Lake National Park

Date	Mintage	VF20	XF40	MS60	MS63	MS65
1997	—	PF65 185				

KM# 883 20 DOLLARS
31.11 g., 0.925 Silver 0.925 oz. ASW **Ruler:** Elizabeth II **Rev:** Birth of Jesus

Date	Mintage	VF20	XF40	MS60	MS63	MS65
1997		—	—	—	—	30.00

KM# 884 20 DOLLARS
31.11 g., 0.925 Silver 0.925 oz. ASW **Ruler:** Elizabeth II **Rev:** Paper Making in China

Date	Mintage	VF20	XF40	MS60	MS63	MS65
1997	—	PF65 30.00				

KM# 885 20 DOLLARS
31.11 g., 0.925 Silver 0.925 oz. ASW **Ruler:** Elizabeth II **Rev:** Roman Empire

Date	Mintage	VF20	XF40	MS60	MS63	MS65
1997	—	PF65 30.00				

KM# 886 20 DOLLARS
31.11 g., 0.925 Silver 0.925 oz. ASW **Ruler:** Elizabeth II **Rev:** Constantin the Great

Date	Mintage	VF20	XF40	MS60	MS63	MS65
1997	—	PF65 30.00				

KM# 887 20 DOLLARS
31.11 g., 0.925 Silver 0.925 oz. ASW **Ruler:** Elizabeth II **Rev:** Demise of the Western Empire

Date	Mintage	VF20	XF40	MS60	MS63	MS65
1997	—	PF65 30.00				

KM# 888 20 DOLLARS
31.11 g., 0.925 Silver 0.925 oz. ASW **Ruler:** Elizabeth II **Rev:** Emperior Justinian

Date	Mintage	VF20	XF40	MS60	MS63	MS65
1997	—	PF65 30.00				

KM# 889 20 DOLLARS
31.11 g., 0.925 Silver 0.925 oz. ASW **Ruler:** Elizabeth II **Rev:** Founding of Islam

Date	Mintage	VF20	XF40	MS60	MS63	MS65
1997	—	PF65 30.00				

KM# 890 20 DOLLARS
31.11 g., 0.925 Silver 0.925 oz. ASW **Ruler:** Elizabeth II **Rev:** Charles I

Date	Mintage	VF20	XF40	MS60	MS63	MS65
1997	—	PF65 30.00				

KM# 891 20 DOLLARS
31.11 g., 0.925 Silver 0.925 oz. ASW **Ruler:** Elizabeth II **Rev:** Calif of Bagdad

Date	Mintage	VF20	XF40	MS60	MS63	MS65
1997	—	PF65 30.00				

KM# 892 20 DOLLARS
31.11 g., 0.925 Silver 0.925 oz. ASW **Ruler:** Elizabeth II **Rev:** 10th Century

Date	Mintage	VF20	XF40	MS60	MS63	MS65
1997	—	PF65 30.00				

KM# 893 20 DOLLARS
31.11 g., 0.925 Silver 0.925 oz. ASW **Ruler:** Elizabeth II **Rev:** Norman invasion of England

Date	Mintage	VF20	XF40	MS60	MS63	MS65
1997	—	PF65 45.00				

KM# 895 20 DOLLARS
31.11 g., 0.925 Silver 0.925 oz. ASW **Ruler:** Elizabeth II **Rev:** Artistic Renaissance

Date	Mintage	VF20	XF40	MS60	MS63	MS65
1997	—	PF65 45.00				

KM# 896 20 DOLLARS
31.11 g., 0.925 Silver 0.925 oz. ASW **Ruler:** Elizabeth II **Rev:** Christopher Columbus

Date	Mintage	VF20	XF40	MS60	MS63	MS65
1997	—	PF65 45.00				

KM# 897 20 DOLLARS
31.11 g., 0.925 Silver 0.925 oz. ASW **Ruler:** Elizabeth II **Rev:** William Shakespeare

Date	Mintage	VF20	XF40	MS60	MS63	MS65
1997	—	PF65 45.00				

KM# 898 20 DOLLARS
31.11 g., 0.925 Silver 0.925 oz. ASW **Ruler:** Elizabeth II **Rev:** Sir Isaac Newton

Date	Mintage	VF20	XF40	MS60	MS63	MS65
1997	—	PF65 45.00				

KM# 899 20 DOLLARS
31.11 g., 0.925 Silver 0.925 oz. ASW **Ruler:** Elizabeth II **Rev:** Neil Armstrong and the Moon landing

Date	Mintage	VF20	XF40	MS60	MS63	MS65
1997	—	PF65 45.00				

KM# 904 20 DOLLARS
155.50 g., 0.999 Silver 4.9944 oz. ASW **Ruler:** Elizabeth II **Rev:** North American Reindeer

Date	Mintage	VF20	XF40	MS60	MS63	MS65
1997	—	PF65 185				

KM# 912 20 DOLLARS
155.50 g., 0.999 Silver 4.9944 oz. ASW **Ruler:** Elizabeth II **Subject:** Yosemite National Park **Rev:** Waterfall

Date	Mintage	VF20	XF40	MS60	MS63	MS65
1997	—	PF65 185				

KM# 920 20 DOLLARS
5.00 g., 0.999 Gold 0.1606 oz. AGW **Ruler:** Elizabeth II **Subject:** Christmas

Date	Mintage	VF20	XF40	MS60	MS63	MS65
1997	100	PF65 325				

KM# 920a 20 DOLLARS
5.00 g., 0.9999 Platinum 0.1607 oz. APW **Ruler:** Elizabeth II **Subject:** Christmas

Date	Mintage	VF20	XF40	MS60	MS63	MS65
1997	100	PF65 375				

KM# 925 20 DOLLARS
5.00 g., 0.999 Gold 0.1606 oz. AGW **Ruler:** Elizabeth II **Subject:** Christmas **Rev:** Angel with book and vine

Date	Mintage	VF20	XF40	MS60	MS63	MS65
1997	500	PF65 285				

KM# 925a 20 DOLLARS
5.00 g., 0.999 Platinum 0.1606 oz. APW **Ruler:** Elizabeth II **Subject:** Christmas **Rev:** Angel with book and vine

Date	Mintage	VF20	XF40	MS60	MS63	MS65
1997	500	PF65 350				

KM# 936 20 DOLLARS
155.50 g., 0.999 Silver 4.9944 oz. ASW **Ruler:** Elizabeth II **Subject:** Petrified Forest National Park

Date	Mintage	VF20	XF40	MS60	MS63	MS65
1998	—	PF65 185				

KM# 945 20 DOLLARS
155.50 g., 0.999 Silver 4.9944 oz. ASW **Ruler:** Elizabeth II **Subject:** Glacier Bay National Park and Preserve **Rev:** Humpback whale

Date	Mintage	VF20	XF40	MS60	MS63	MS65
1998	—	PF65 185				

KM# 954 20 DOLLARS
155.50 g., 0.999 Silver 4.9944 oz. ASW **Ruler:** Elizabeth II **Subject:** North Cascades National Park **Rev:** Northern Lights

Date	Mintage	VF20	XF40	MS60	MS63	MS65
1998	—	PF65 185				

KM# 963 20 DOLLARS
155.50 g., 0.999 Silver 4.9944 oz. ASW **Ruler:** Elizabeth II **Subject:** Grand Canyon National Park **Rev:** California Condor

Date	Mintage	VF20	XF40	MS60	MS63	MS65
1998	—	PF65 185				

KM# 973 20 DOLLARS
155.50 g., 0.999 Silver 4.9944 oz. ASW **Ruler:** Elizabeth II **Subject:** Gulf Islands National Seashore

Date	Mintage	VF20	XF40	MS60	MS63	MS65
1998	—	PF65 185				

KM# 983 20 DOLLARS
155.50 g., 0.999 Silver 4.9944 oz. ASW **Ruler:** Elizabeth II **Subject:** Big Cypress National Preserve **Rev:** Puma

Date	Mintage	VF20	XF40	MS60	MS63	MS65
1998	—	PF65 185				

KM# 993 20 DOLLARS
155.50 g., 0.999 Silver 4.9944 oz. ASW **Ruler:** Elizabeth II **Subject:** Everglades National Park **Rev:** Crocodile

Date	Mintage	VF20	XF40	MS60	MS63	MS65
1998	—	PF65 185				

KM# 1003 20 DOLLARS
155.50 g., 0.925 Silver 4.6245 oz. ASW **Ruler:** Elizabeth II **Subject:** Wind Cave National Park **Rev:** Swift Fox

Date	Mintage	VF20	XF40	MS60	MS63	MS65
1998	—	PF65 185				

KM# 1013 20 DOLLARS
155.50 g., 0.999 Silver 4.9944 oz. ASW **Ruler:** Elizabeth II **Subject:** Bryce Canyon National Park **Rev:** Prairie Dog

Date	Mintage	VF20	XF40	MS60	MS63	MS65
1998	—	PF65 185				

KM# 1023 20 DOLLARS
155.50 g., 0.999 Silver 4.9944 oz. ASW **Ruler:** Elizabeth II **Subject:** Gates of the Arctic National Park and Preserve **Rev:** Falcon

Date	Mintage	VF20	XF40	MS60	MS63	MS65
1998	—	PF65 185				

KM# 1033 20 DOLLARS
155.50 g., 0.999 Silver 4.9944 oz. ASW **Ruler:** Elizabeth II **Subject:** Badlands National Park **Rev:** Black-footed Ferret

Date	Mintage	VF20	XF40	MS60	MS63	MS65
1998	—	PF65 185				

KM# 1042 20 DOLLARS
155.50 g., 0.999 Silver 4.9944 oz. ASW **Ruler:** Elizabeth II **Subject:** Grand Teton National Park **Rev:** Whooping Crane

Date	Mintage	VF20	XF40	MS60	MS63	MS65
1998	—	PF65 185				

KM# 1052 20 DOLLARS
155.50 g., 0.999 Silver 4.9944 oz. ASW **Ruler:** Elizabeth II **Subject:** Kajoko Honokhau National Historic Park **Rev:** Hawaiian Duck

Date	Mintage	VF20	XF40	MS60	MS63	MS65
1998	—	PF65 185				

KM# 1062 20 DOLLARS
155.50 g., 0.999 Silver 4.9944 oz. ASW **Ruler:** Elizabeth II **Subject:** Virgin Islands National Park **Rev:** Brown Pelican

Date	Mintage	VF20	XF40	MS60	MS63	MS65
1998	—	PF65 185				

KM# 1072 20 DOLLARS
155.50 g., 0.999 Silver 4.9944 oz. ASW **Ruler:** Elizabeth II **Subject:** Mammoth Cave National Park **Rev:** Grey Bat

Date	Mintage	VF20	XF40	MS60	MS63	MS65
1998	—	PF65 185				

KM# 1082 20 DOLLARS
155.50 g., 0.999 Silver 4.9944 oz. ASW **Ruler:** Elizabeth II **Subject:** Rocky Mountain National Park **Rev:** Purple trout

Date	Mintage	VF20	XF40	MS60	MS63	MS65
1998	—	PF65 185				

KM# 1091 20 DOLLARS
6.22 g., 0.999 Gold 0.1998 oz. AGW **Ruler:** Elizabeth II **Rev:** Two dolphins

Date	Mintage	VF20	XF40	MS60	MS63	MS65
1998	—	PF65 375				

KM# 18 25 DOLLARS
48.85 g., 0.925 Silver 1.4528 oz. ASW **Ruler:** Elizabeth II **Subject:** Queen's Silver Jubilee **Obv:** Crowned head right, date below **Rev:** Crowned EIIR monogram between flowers

Date	Mintage	VF20	XF40	MS60	MS63	MS65
1977 FM	17,000	PF65 55.00				
1977 FM (M)	100	—	—	—	—	70.00
1977 FM (U)	4,068	—	—	—	—	60.00

KM# 42 25 DOLLARS
37.00 g., 0.925 Silver 1.1004 oz. ASW **Ruler:** Elizabeth II **Subject:** 100th Anniversary of British Rule **Obv:** Crowned head right, date below **Rev:** Sailing ship at bottom right, bust of Makea Takau Ariki, island chief at left, mountains behind, denomination below

Date	Mintage	VF20	XF40	MS60	MS63	MS65
1988	3,000	PF65 42.00				

KM# 83 25 DOLLARS
1.21 g., 0.999 Gold 0.039 oz. AGW **Ruler:** Elizabeth II **Subject:** Endangered Wildlife **Obv:** Crowned head right, date below **Rev:** Bison head left, denomination below

Date	Mintage	VF20	XF40	MS60	MS63	MS65
1990	100,000	PF65 65.00				

KM# 84 25 DOLLARS
1.21 g., 0.999 Gold 0.039 oz. AGW **Ruler:** Elizabeth II **Subject:** Endangered Wildlife **Obv:** Crowned head right, date below **Rev:** Longhorn sheep head facing, denomination below

Date	Mintage	VF20	XF40	MS60	MS63	MS65
1990	Est. 100000	PF65 65.00				

KM# 85 25 DOLLARS
1.21 g., 0.999 Gold 0.039 oz. AGW **Ruler:** Elizabeth II **Subject:** Endangered Wildlife **Obv:** Crowned head right, date below **Rev:** Tiger head, denomination below

Date	Mintage	VF20	XF40	MS60	MS63	MS65
1990	—	PF65 65.00				

KM# 86 25 DOLLARS
1.21 g., 0.999 Gold 0.039 oz. AGW **Ruler:** Elizabeth II **Subject:** Endangered Wildlife **Obv:** Crowned head right, date below **Rev:** Eagle

Date	Mintage	VF20	XF40	MS60	MS63	MS65
1990	Est. 100000	PF65 65.00				

KM# 87 25 DOLLARS
1.21 g., 0.999 Gold 0.039 oz. AGW **Ruler:** Elizabeth II **Subject:** Endangered Wildlife **Obv:** Crowned head right, date below **Rev:** Elephant head left, denomination below

Date	Mintage	VF20	XF40	MS60	MS63	MS65
1990	Est. 100000	PF65 65.00				

KM# 88 25 DOLLARS
1.21 g., 0.999 Gold 0.039 oz. AGW **Ruler:** Elizabeth II **Subject:** Endangered Wildlife **Obv:** Crowned head right, date below **Rev:** Lynx head left, denomination below

Date	Mintage	VF20	XF40	MS60	MS63	MS65
1990	Est. 100000	PF65 65.00				

KM# 239 25 DOLLARS
1.21 g., 0.999 Gold 0.039 oz. AGW **Ruler:** Elizabeth II **Subject:** Endangered Wildlife **Obv:** Crowned head right, date below **Rev:** Bee hummingbird right, denomination below

Date	Mintage	VF20	XF40	MS60	MS63	MS65
1990	Est. 100000	PF65 65.00				

KM# 240 25 DOLLARS
1.21 g., 0.999 Gold 0.039 oz. AGW **Ruler:** Elizabeth II **Subject:** Endangered Wildlife **Obv:** Crowned head right, date below **Rev:** Koala bear, denomination below

Date	Mintage	VF20	XF40	MS60	MS63	MS65
1991	Est. 100000	PF65 65.00				

KM# 241 25 DOLLARS
1.21 g., 0.999 Gold 0.039 oz. AGW **Ruler:** Elizabeth II **Subject:** Endangered Wildlife **Obv:** Crowned head right, date below **Rev:** Panda bear, denomination below

Date	Mintage	VF20	XF40	MS60	MS63	MS65
1991	Est. 100000	PF65 65.00				
1997 PM	—	PF65 65.00				

KM# 138 25 DOLLARS
1.21 g., 0.999 Gold 0.039 oz. AGW **Ruler:** Elizabeth II **Subject:** Endangered Wildlife **Obv:** Crowned head right, date below **Rev:** Przewalski's horse galloping right, denomination below

Date	Mintage	VF20	XF40	MS60	MS63	MS65
1992	—	PF65 65.00				

KM# 242 25 DOLLARS
1.21 g., 0.999 Gold 0.039 oz. AGW **Ruler:** Elizabeth II **Subject:** Endangered Wildlife **Obv:** Crowned head right, date below **Rev:** African lion, denomination below

Date	Mintage	VF20	XF40	MS60	MS63	MS65
1992	Est. 100000	PF65 65.00				

KM# 243 25 DOLLARS
1.21 g., 0.999 Gold 0.039 oz. AGW **Ruler:** Elizabeth II **Subject:** Endangered Wildlife **Obv:** Crowned head right, date below **Rev:** Butterfly, denomination below

Date	Mintage	VF20	XF40	MS60	MS63	MS65
1992	Est. 100000	PF65 65.00				

KM# 238 25 DOLLARS
6.22 g., 0.583 Gold 0.1166 oz. AGW **Ruler:** Elizabeth II **Subject:** 1996 Olympics **Obv:** Crowned head right, date below **Rev:** Ancient archer within circle, denomination below

Date	Mintage	VF20	XF40	MS60	MS63	MS65
1995	Est. 5000	PF65 220				

KM# 271 25 DOLLARS
155.52 g., 0.999 Silver 4.995 oz. ASW **Ruler:** Elizabeth II **Subject:** Endangered Wildlife **Obv:** Crowned head right, date below **Rev:** Koala bear and baby, denomination below

Date	Mintage	VF20	XF40	MS60	MS63	MS65
1996	Est. 10000	PF65 175				

KM# 272 25 DOLLARS
155.52 g., 0.999 Silver 4.995 oz. ASW **Ruler:** Elizabeth II **Subject:** Endangered Wildlife **Obv:** Crowned head right, date below **Rev:** Family of chimpanzees

Date	Mintage	VF20	XF40	MS60	MS63	MS65
1996	Est. 10000	PF65 175				

KM# 273 25 DOLLARS
155.52 g., 0.999 Silver 4.995 oz. ASW **Ruler:** Elizabeth II **Subject:** Endangered Wildlife **Obv:** Crowned head right, date below **Rev:** Family of elephants

Date	Mintage	VF20	XF40	MS60	MS63	MS65
1996	Est. 10000	PF65 175				

KM# 274 25 DOLLARS
155.52 g., 0.999 Silver 4.995 oz. ASW **Ruler:** Elizabeth II **Subject:** Endangered Wildlife **Obv:** Crowned head right, date below **Rev:** Family of whooping cranes

Date	Mintage	VF20	XF40	MS60	MS63	MS65
1996	Est. 10000	PF65 175				

KM# 289 25 DOLLARS
155.52 g., 0.999 Silver 4.995 oz. ASW **Ruler:** Elizabeth II **Subject:** Olympic National Park **Obv:** Crowned head right, date below **Rev:** Multicolor Bald eagle in flight

Date	Mintage	VF20	XF40	MS60	MS63	MS65
1996	1,000	PF65 175				

KM# 290 25 DOLLARS
155.52 g., 0.999 Silver 4.995 oz. ASW **Ruler:** Elizabeth II **Subject:** Yellowstone Natonal Park **Obv:** Crowned head right, date below **Rev:** Multicolor Grizzly bear and cub

Date	Mintage	VF20	XF40	MS60	MS63	MS65
1996	1,000	PF65 175				

KM# 291 25 DOLLARS
3.11 g., 0.999 Gold 0.0999 oz. AGW **Ruler:** Elizabeth II **Subject:** Olympic National Park **Obv:** Crowned head right, date below **Rev:** Bald eagle head right, denomination below

Date	Mintage	VF20	XF40	MS60	MS63	MS65
1996	—	PF65 170				

KM# 292 25 DOLLARS
3.11 g., 0.999 Gold 0.0999 oz. AGW **Ruler:** Elizabeth II **Subject:** Yellowstone National Park **Obv:** Crowned head right, date below **Rev:** Grizzly bear

Date	Mintage	VF20	XF40	MS60	MS63	MS65
1996	—	PF65 170				

KM# 474 25 DOLLARS
7.82 g., 0.9999 Gold 0.2514 oz. AGW, 19.97 mm. **Ruler:** Elizabeth II **Subject:** Death of Princess Diana **Obv:** Crowned bust right **Rev:** Head of Diana 3/4 right **Edge:** Reeded

Date	Mintage	VF20	XF40	MS60	MS63	MS65
1997	—	PF65 450				

KM# 851 25 DOLLARS
155.50 g., 0.999 Silver 4.9944 oz. ASW **Ruler:** Elizabeth II **Subject:** Theodore Roosevelt National Park **Rev:** Mountian landscape, multicolor **Note:** S#386.

Date	Mintage	VF20	XF40	MS60	MS63	MS65
1997	—	PF65 190				

KM# 853 25 DOLLARS
3.11 g., 0.999 Gold 0.0999 oz. AGW **Ruler:** Elizabeth II **Subject:** Theodore Roosevelt National Park **Rev:** Bison **Note:** S#388.

Date	Mintage	VF20	XF40	MS60	MS63	MS65
1997	—	PF65 165				

KM# 858 25 DOLLARS
155.50 g., 0.999 Silver 4.9944 oz. ASW **Ruler:** Elizabeth II **Subject:** Great Smoky Mountains National Park **Rev:** Mountain skyline in color **Note:** S#396.

Date	Mintage	VF20	XF40	MS60	MS63	MS65
1997	—	PF65 190				

KM# 860 25 DOLLARS
3.11 g., 0.999 Gold 0.0999 oz. AGW **Ruler:** Elizabeth II **Subject:** Great Smoky Mountains National Park **Rev:** Red wolf

Date	Mintage	VF20	XF40	MS60	MS63	MS65
1997	—	PF65 170				

KM# 868 25 DOLLARS
155.50 g., 0.999 Silver 4.9944 oz. ASW **Ruler:** Elizabeth II **Subject:** Hawaii Volcano National Park

Date	Mintage	VF20	XF40	MS60	MS63	MS65
1997	—	PF65 215				

KM# 870 25 DOLLARS
3.11 g., 0.999 Gold 0.0999 oz. AGW **Ruler:** Elizabeth II **Subject:** Hawaii Volcano National Park **Note:** S#408.

Date	Mintage	VF20	XF40	MS60	MS63	MS65
1997	—	PF65 175				

KM# 877 25 DOLLARS
155.50 g., 0.999 Silver 4.9944 oz. ASW **Ruler:** Elizabeth II **Subject:** Crater Lake National Park **Rev:** Mountian view in multicolor

Date	Mintage	VF20	XF40	MS60	MS63	MS65
1997	—	PF65 215				

KM# 879 25 DOLLARS
3.11 g., 0.999 Gold 0.0999 oz. AGW **Ruler:** Elizabeth II **Subject:** Crater Lake National Park

Date	Mintage	VF20	XF40	MS60	MS63	MS65
1997	—	PF65 175				

KM# 905 25 DOLLARS
155.50 g., 0.999 Silver 4.9944 oz. ASW **Ruler:** Elizabeth II **Subject:** Grand Portage National Monument **Rev:** Landscape in color

Date	Mintage	VF20	XF40	MS60	MS63	MS65
1997	—	PF65 215				

KM# 907 25 DOLLARS
3.11 g., 0.999 Gold 0.0999 oz. AGW **Ruler:** Elizabeth II **Subject:** Grand Portage National Monument **Rev:** North American Reindeer

Date	Mintage	VF20	XF40	MS60	MS63	MS65
1997	—	PF65 175				

KM# 913 25 DOLLARS
155.50 g., 0.999 Silver 4.9944 oz. ASW **Ruler:** Elizabeth II **Subject:** Yosemite National Park **Rev:** Landscape in color

Date	Mintage	VF20	XF40	MS60	MS63	MS65
1997	—	PF65 215				

KM# 915 25 DOLLARS
3.11 g., 0.999 Gold 0.0999 oz. AGW **Ruler:** Elizabeth II **Subject:** Yosemite National Park **Rev:** Waterfall

Date	Mintage	VF20	XF40	MS60	MS63	MS65
1997	—	PF65 175				

KM# 932 25 DOLLARS
155.50 g., 0.999 Silver 4.9944 oz. ASW **Ruler:** Elizabeth II **Subject:** 2000 Summer Olympics - Sydney **Rev:** Triathlon

Date	Mintage	VF20	XF40	MS60	MS63	MS65
1998	Est. 3000	PF65 190				

KM# 937 25 DOLLARS
155.50 g., 0.999 Silver 4.9944 oz. ASW **Ruler:** Elizabeth II **Subject:** Petrified Forest National Park **Rev:** Landscape in color

Date	Mintage	VF20	XF40	MS60	MS63	MS65
1998	—	PF65 215				

KM# 939 25 DOLLARS
3.11 g., 0.999 Gold 0.0999 oz. AGW **Ruler:** Elizabeth II **Subject:** Petrified Forest National Park **Rev:** Pronghorn

Date	Mintage	VF20	XF40	MS60	MS63	MS65
1998	—	PF65 175				

KM# 946 25 DOLLARS
155.50 g., 0.999 Silver 4.9944 oz. ASW **Ruler:** Elizabeth II **Rev:** Landscape in color

Date	Mintage	VF20	XF40	MS60	MS63	MS65
1998	—	PF65 215				

KM# 948 25 DOLLARS
3.11 g., 0.999 Gold 0.0999 oz. AGW **Ruler:** Elizabeth II **Subject:** Glacier Bay National Park and Preserve **Rev:** Humpback whale

Date	Mintage	VF20	XF40	MS60	MS63	MS65
1998	—	PF65 175				

KM# 955 25 DOLLARS
155.50 g., 0.999 Silver 4.9944 oz. ASW **Ruler:** Elizabeth II **Subject:** North Cascades National Park **Rev:** Northern Lights in color

Date	Mintage	VF20	XF40	MS60	MS63	MS65
1998	—	PF65 215				

KM# 957 25 DOLLARS
3.11 g., 0.925 Gold 0.0925 oz. AGW **Ruler:** Elizabeth II **Subject:** North Cascades National Park **Rev:** Northern Lights

Date	Mintage	VF20	XF40	MS60	MS63	MS65
1998	—	PF65 175				

KM# 964 25 DOLLARS
155.50 g., 0.999 Silver 4.9944 oz. ASW **Ruler:** Elizabeth II **Subject:** Grand Canyon National Park **Rev:** Landscape in color

Date	Mintage	VF20	XF40	MS60	MS63	MS65
1998	—	PF65 215				

KM# 965 25 DOLLARS
1.24 g., 0.999 Gold 0.0398 oz. AGW **Ruler:** Elizabeth II **Subject:** Grand Canyon National Park **Rev:** California Condor

Date	Mintage	VF20	XF40	MS60	MS63	MS65
1998	—	PF65 75.00				

KM# 966 25 DOLLARS
3.11 g., 0.999 Gold 0.0999 oz. AGW **Ruler:** Elizabeth II **Subject:** Grand Canyon National Park **Rev:** California Condor

Date	Mintage	VF20	XF40	MS60	MS63	MS65
1998	—	PF65 175				

KM# 974 25 DOLLARS
155.50 g., 0.999 Silver 4.9944 oz. ASW **Ruler:** Elizabeth II **Subject:** Gulf Islands National Seashore **Rev:** Landscape in color

Date	Mintage	VF20	XF40	MS60	MS63	MS65
1998	—	PF65 215				

KM# 976 25 DOLLARS
3.11 g., 0.999 Gold 0.0999 oz. AGW **Ruler:** Elizabeth II **Subject:** Gulf Islands National Seashore

Date	Mintage	VF20	XF40	MS60	MS63	MS65
1998	—	PF65 175				

KM# 984 25 DOLLARS
155.50 g., 0.999 Silver 4.9944 oz. ASW **Ruler:** Elizabeth II **Subject:** Big Cypress National Preserve **Rev:** Landscape in color

Date	Mintage	VF20	XF40	MS60	MS63	MS65
1998	—	PF65 215				

KM# 986 25 DOLLARS
3.11 g., 0.999 Gold 0.0999 oz. AGW **Ruler:** Elizabeth II **Subject:** Big Cypress National Preserve **Rev:** Puma

Date	Mintage	VF20	XF40	MS60	MS63	MS65
1998	—	PF65 175				

KM# 994 25 DOLLARS
155.50 g., 0.999 Silver 4.9944 oz. ASW **Ruler:** Elizabeth II **Subject:** Everglades National Park **Rev:** Landscape in color

Date	Mintage	VF20	XF40	MS60	MS63	MS65
1998	—	PF65 215				

KM# 996 25 DOLLARS
3.11 g., 0.999 Gold 0.0999 oz. AGW **Ruler:** Elizabeth II **Subject:** Everglades National Park **Rev:** Crocodile

Date	Mintage	VF20	XF40	MS60	MS63	MS65
1998	—	PF65 175				

KM# 1004 25 DOLLARS
155.50 g., 0.999 Silver 4.9944 oz. ASW **Ruler:** Elizabeth II **Subject:** Wind Cave National Park **Rev:** Landscape in color

Date	Mintage	VF20	XF40	MS60	MS63	MS65
1998	—	PF65 215				

KM# 1006 25 DOLLARS
3.11 g., 0.999 Gold 0.0999 oz. AGW **Ruler:** Elizabeth II **Subject:** Wind Cave National Park **Rev:** Swift Fox

Date	Mintage	VF20	XF40	MS60	MS63	MS65
1998	—	PF65 175				

KM# 1014 25 DOLLARS
155.50 g., 0.999 Silver 4.9944 oz. ASW **Ruler:** Elizabeth II **Subject:** Bryce Canyon National Park **Rev:** Landscape in color

Date	Mintage	VF20	XF40	MS60	MS63	MS65
1998	—	PF65 215				

KM# 1016 25 DOLLARS
3.11 g., 0.999 Gold 0.0999 oz. AGW **Ruler:** Elizabeth II **Subject:** Bryce Canyon National Park **Rev:** Prairie Dog

Date	Mintage	VF20	XF40	MS60	MS63	MS65
1998	—	PF65 175				

KM# 1024 25 DOLLARS
155.50 g., 0.999 Silver 4.9944 oz. ASW **Ruler:** Elizabeth II **Subject:** Gates of the Arctic National Park and Preserve **Rev:** Landscape in color

Date	Mintage	VF20	XF40	MS60	MS63	MS65
1998	—	PF65 215				

KM# 1026 25 DOLLARS
3.11 g., 0.999 Gold 0.0999 oz. AGW **Ruler:** Elizabeth II **Subject:** Gates of the Arctic National Park and Preserve **Rev:** Falcon

Date	Mintage	VF20	XF40	MS60	MS63	MS65
1998	—	PF65 175				

KM# 1034 25 DOLLARS
155.50 g., 0.999 Silver 4.9944 oz. ASW **Ruler:** Elizabeth II **Subject:** Badlands National Park **Rev:** Landscape in color

Date	Mintage	VF20	XF40	MS60	MS63	MS65
1998	—	PF65 215				

KM# 1036 25 DOLLARS
3.11 g., 0.999 Gold 0.0999 oz. AGW **Ruler:** Elizabeth II **Subject:** Badlands National Park **Rev:** Black-footed Ferret

Date	Mintage	VF20	XF40	MS60	MS63	MS65
1998	—	PF65 175				

KM# 1043 25 DOLLARS
155.50 g., 0.999 Silver 4.9944 oz. ASW **Ruler:** Elizabeth II **Subject:** Grand Teton National Park **Rev:** Landscape in color

Date	Mintage	VF20	XF40	MS60	MS63	MS65
1998	—	PF65 215				

KM# 1045 25 DOLLARS
3.11 g., 0.999 Gold 0.0999 oz. AGW **Ruler:** Elizabeth II **Subject:** Grand Teton National Park **Rev:** Whopping Crane

Date	Mintage	VF20	XF40	MS60	MS63	MS65
1998	—	PF65 175				

KM# 1053 25 DOLLARS
155.50 g., 0.999 Silver 4.9944 oz. ASW **Ruler:** Elizabeth II **Subject:** Kajoko Honokhau National Historic Park **Rev:** Landscape in color

Date	Mintage	VF20	XF40	MS60	MS63	MS65
1998	—	PF65 215				

KM# 1055 25 DOLLARS
3.11 g., 0.999 Gold 0.0999 oz. AGW **Ruler:** Elizabeth II **Subject:** Kajoko Honokhau National Historic Park **Rev:** Hawaiian Duck

Date	Mintage	VF20	XF40	MS60	MS63	MS65
1998	—	PF65 175				

KM# 1063 25 DOLLARS
155.50 g., 0.999 Silver 4.9944 oz. ASW **Ruler:** Elizabeth II **Subject:** Virgin Islands National Park **Rev:** Landscape in color

Date	Mintage	VF20	XF40	MS60	MS63	MS65
1998	—	PF65 215				

KM# 1065 25 DOLLARS
3.11 g., 0.999 Gold 0.0999 oz. AGW **Ruler:** Elizabeth II **Subject:** Virgin Islands National Park **Rev:** Brown Pelican

Date	Mintage	VF20	XF40	MS60	MS63	MS65
1998	—	PF65 175				

KM# 1073 25 DOLLARS
155.50 g., 0.999 Silver 4.9944 oz. ASW **Ruler:** Elizabeth II **Subject:** Mammoth Cave National Park **Rev:** Landscape in color

Date	Mintage	VF20	XF40	MS60	MS63	MS65
1998	—	PF65 215				

KM# 1075 25 DOLLARS
3.11 g., 0.999 Gold 0.0999 oz. AGW **Ruler:** Elizabeth II **Subject:** Mammoth Cave National Park **Rev:** Grey Bat

Date	Mintage	VF20	XF40	MS60	MS63	MS65
1998	—	PF65 175				

KM# 1083 25 DOLLARS
155.50 g., 0.999 Silver 4.9944 oz. ASW **Ruler:** Elizabeth II **Subject:** Rocky Mountain National Park **Rev:** Landscape in color

Date	Mintage	VF20	XF40	MS60	MS63	MS65
1998	—	PF65 215				

KM# 1085 25 DOLLARS
3.11 g., 0.999 Gold 0.0999 oz. AGW **Ruler:** Elizabeth II **Subject:** Rocky Mountain National Park **Rev:** Purple trout

Date	Mintage	VF20	XF40	MS60	MS63	MS65
1998	—	PF65 175				

KM# 1092 25 DOLLARS
7.81 g., 0.999 Gold 0.2507 oz. AGW **Ruler:** Elizabeth II **Rev:** Garfield standing with arms crossed in color

Date	Mintage	VF20	XF40	MS60	MS63	MS65
1999	—	PF65 450				

KM# 1099 25 DOLLARS
15.55 g., 0.999 Gold 0.4994 oz. AGW **Ruler:** Elizabeth II **Rev:** Sagebrush

Date	Mintage	VF20	XF40	MS60	MS63	MS65
2000	Est. 250	PF65 875				

KM# 309 30 DOLLARS

1000.10 g., 0.999 Silver 32.1218 oz. ASW **Ruler:** Elizabeth II **Obv:** Crowned head right, date below **Rev:** Princess Diana's portrait, dates

Date	Mintage	VF20	XF40	MS60	MS63	MS65
1997 Matte Proof	—	PF63 1,150				

KM# 928 30 DOLLARS

5.00 g., 0.999 Gold 0.1606 oz. AGW **Ruler:** Elizabeth II **Subject:** Year of the tiger **Rev:** Garfield in color

Date	Mintage	VF20	XF40	MS60	MS63	MS65
1998	—	PF65 285				

KM# 1093 30 DOLLARS

7.81 g., 0.999 Gold 0.2507 oz. AGW **Ruler:** Elizabeth II **Rev:** Garfield head and arms crossed in color

Date	Mintage	VF20	XF40	MS60	MS63	MS65
1999	—	PF65 450				

KM# 1094 30 DOLLARS

5.00 g., 0.999 Gold 0.1606 oz. AGW **Ruler:** Elizabeth II **Subject:** Year of the Rabbit **Rev:** Buggs Bunny in color

Date	Mintage	VF20	XF40	MS60	MS63	MS65
1999	—	PF65 285				

KM# 1095 30 DOLLARS

5.00 g., 0.999 Gold 0.1606 oz. AGW **Ruler:** Elizabeth II **Subject:** Year of the Rabbit **Rev:** Bugs Bunny windsurfing in color

Date	Mintage	VF20	XF40	MS60	MS63	MS65
1999	—	PF65 285				

KM# 11 50 DOLLARS

97.20 g., 0.925 Silver 2.8907 oz. ASW, 58 mm. **Ruler:** Elizabeth II **Subject:** Winston Churchill Centenary **Obv:** Young bust right, date below **Rev:** Churchill head at right looking left, castle, Big Ben clock, flag, denomination below

Date	Mintage	VF20	XF40	MS60	MS63	MS65
1974	1,202	—	—	—	110	120
1974	2,502	PF65 115				

KM# 11a 50 DOLLARS

97.20 g., 0.925 Silver Gilt 2.8907 oz., 58 mm. **Ruler:** Elizabeth II **Subject:** Winston Churchill Centenary **Obv:** Young bust right, date below **Rev:** Churchill head at right looking left, flag above castle and clock tower

Date	Mintage	VF20	XF40	MS60	MS63	MS65
1974	2,002	PF65 110				

KM# 203 50 DOLLARS

3.95 g., 0.500 Gold 0.0634 oz. AGW **Ruler:** Elizabeth II **Obv:** Young bust right, date below **Rev:** Denomination above plant

Date	Mintage	VF20	XF40	MS60	MS63	MS65
1980	—	PF65 115				

KM# 27 50 DOLLARS

3.95 g., 0.500 Gold 0.0634 oz. AGW **Ruler:** Elizabeth II **Subject:** Wedding of Prince Charles and Lady Diana **Obv:** Young bust right, date below **Rev:** Denomination below symbol

Date	Mintage	VF20	XF40	MS60	MS63	MS65
1981	220	—	—	—	—	115
1981	1,309	PF65 120				

KM# 40 50 DOLLARS

28.28 g., 0.925 Silver 0.841 oz. ASW **Ruler:** Elizabeth II **Subject:** 1988 Olympics **Obv:** Crowned bust right, date below **Rev:** Torch bearer, globe in background

Date	Mintage	VF20	XF40	MS60	MS63	MS65
1987 PM	20,000	PF65 30.00				

KM# 61 50 DOLLARS

20.94 g., 0.925 Silver 0.6227 oz. ASW **Ruler:** Elizabeth II **Subject:** Great Explorers **Obv:** Crowned head right, date below **Rev:** Stanley and Livingstone, denomination lower right

Date	Mintage	VF20	XF40	MS60	MS63	MS65
1988 (P)	—	PF65 20.00				

KM# 62 50 DOLLARS

20.94 g., 0.925 Silver 0.6227 oz. ASW **Ruler:** Elizabeth II **Subject:** Great Explorers **Obv:** Crowned head right, date below **Rev:** Capt. James Cook

Date	Mintage	VF20	XF40	MS60	MS63	MS65
1988 FM (P)	—	PF65 20.00				

KM# 63 50 DOLLARS

20.94 g., 0.925 Silver 0.6227 oz. ASW **Ruler:** Elizabeth II **Subject:** Great Explorers **Obv:** Crowned head right, date below **Rev:** Vasco Nuñez de Balboa

Date	Mintage	VF20	XF40	MS60	MS63	MS65
1988 FM (P)	—	PF65 20.00				

KM# 64 50 DOLLARS

20.94 g., 0.925 Silver 0.6227 oz. ASW **Ruler:** Elizabeth II **Subject:** Great Explorers **Obv:** Crowned head right, date below **Rev:** Ferdinand Magellan's ships: Vittoria and Trinidad

Date	Mintage	VF20	XF40	MS60	MS63	MS65
1988 FM (P)	—	PF65 20.00				

KM# 65 50 DOLLARS

20.94 g., 0.925 Silver 0.6227 oz. ASW **Ruler:** Elizabeth II **Subject:** Great Explorers **Obv:** Crowned head right, date below **Rev:** Marco Polo on camel, denomination at right

Date	Mintage	VF20	XF40	MS60	MS63	MS65
1988 FM (P)	—	PF65 20.00				

KM# 66 50 DOLLARS

20.94 g., 0.925 Silver 0.6227 oz. ASW **Ruler:** Elizabeth II **Subject:** Great Explorers **Obv:** Crowned head right, date below **Rev:** Vasco da Gama

Date	Mintage	VF20	XF40	MS60	MS63	MS65
1988 FM (P)	—	PF65 20.00				

KM# 67 50 DOLLARS

20.94 g., 0.925 Silver 0.6227 oz. ASW **Ruler:** Elizabeth II **Subject:** Great Explorers **Obv:** Crowned head right, date below **Rev:** Christopher Columbus

Date	Mintage	VF20	XF40	MS60	MS63	MS65
1988 FM (P)	—	PF65 20.00				

KM# 68 50 DOLLARS
20.94 g., 0.925 Silver 0.6227 oz. ASW **Ruler:** Elizabeth II
Subject: Great Explorers **Obv:** Crowned head right, date below
Rev: Sir Francis Drake

Date	Mintage	VF20	XF40	MS60	MS63	MS65
1988 FM (P)	—	PF65 20.00				

KM# 69 50 DOLLARS
20.94 g., 0.925 Silver 0.6227 oz. ASW **Ruler:** Elizabeth II
Subject: Great Explorers **Obv:** Crowned head right, date below
Rev: Sieur de la Salle

Date	Mintage	VF20	XF40	MS60	MS63	MS65
1988 FM (P)	—	PF65 20.00				

KM# 96 50 DOLLARS
20.94 g., 0.925 Silver 0.6227 oz. ASW **Ruler:** Elizabeth II
Subject: Great Explorers **Obv:** Crowned head right, date below
Rev: Alexander the Great

Date	Mintage	VF20	XF40	MS60	MS63	MS65
1988 FM (P)	—	PF65 20.00				

KM# 97 50 DOLLARS
20.94 g., 0.925 Silver 0.6227 oz. ASW **Ruler:** Elizabeth II
Subject: Great Explorers **Obv:** Crowned head right, date below
Rev: Leif Ericson, denomination at right

Date	Mintage	VF20	XF40	MS60	MS63	MS65
1988 FM (P)	—	PF65 20.00				

KM# 98 50 DOLLARS
20.94 g., 0.925 Silver 0.6227 oz. ASW **Ruler:** Elizabeth II
Subject: Great Explorers **Obv:** Crowned head right, date below
Rev: Amerigo Vespucci

Date	Mintage	VF20	XF40	MS60	MS63	MS65
1988 FM (P)	—	PF65 20.00				

KM# 99 50 DOLLARS
20.94 g., 0.925 Silver 0.6227 oz. ASW **Ruler:** Elizabeth II
Subject: Great Explorers **Obv:** Crowned head right, date below
Rev: Bartolomeu Diaz

Date	Mintage	VF20	XF40	MS60	MS63	MS65
1988 FM (P)	—	PF65 20.00				

KM# 100 50 DOLLARS
20.94 g., 0.925 Silver 0.6227 oz. ASW **Ruler:** Elizabeth II
Subject: Great Explorers **Obv:** Crowned head right, date below
Rev: Juan Ponce de Léon

Date	Mintage	VF20	XF40	MS60	MS63	MS65
1988 FM (P)	—	PF65 20.00				

KM# 101 50 DOLLARS
20.94 g., 0.925 Silver 0.6227 oz. ASW **Ruler:** Elizabeth II
Subject: Great Explorers **Obv:** Crowned head right, date below
Rev: Hernando Cortés

Date	Mintage	VF20	XF40	MS60	MS63	MS65
1988 FM (P)	—	PF65 20.00				

KM# 102 50 DOLLARS
20.94 g., 0.925 Silver 0.6227 oz. ASW **Ruler:** Elizabeth II
Subject: Great Explorers **Obv:** Crowned head right, date below
Rev: Francisco Coronado

Date	Mintage	VF20	XF40	MS60	MS63	MS65
1988 FM (P)	—	PF65 20.00				

KM# 103 50 DOLLARS
20.94 g., 0.925 Silver 0.6227 oz. ASW **Ruler:** Elizabeth II
Subject: Great Explorers **Obv:** Crowned head right, date below
Rev: Francisco Pizarro and map, denomination at left

Date	Mintage	VF20	XF40	MS60	MS63	MS65
1988 FM (P)	—	PF65 20.00				

KM# 104 50 DOLLARS
20.94 g., 0.925 Silver 0.6227 oz. ASW **Ruler:** Elizabeth II
Subject: Great Explorers **Obv:** Crowned head right, date below
Rev: Samuel de Champlain

Date	Mintage	VF20	XF40	MS60	MS63	MS65
1988 FM (P)	—	PF65 20.00				

KM# 105 50 DOLLARS
20.94 g., 0.925 Silver 0.6227 oz. ASW **Ruler:** Elizabeth II
Subject: Great Explorers **Obv:** Crowned head right, date below
Rev: John Cabot

Date	Mintage	VF20	XF40	MS60	MS63	MS65
1988 FM (P)	—	PF65 20.00				

KM# 106 50 DOLLARS
20.94 g., 0.925 Silver 0.6227 oz. ASW **Ruler:** Elizabeth II
Subject: Great Explorers **Obv:** Crowned head right, date below
Rev: Abel Janszoon Tasman

Date	Mintage	VF20	XF40	MS60	MS63	MS65
1988 FM (P)	—	PF65 20.00				

KM# 107 50 DOLLARS
20.94 g., 0.925 Silver 0.6227 oz. ASW **Ruler:** Elizabeth II
Subject: Great Explorers **Obv:** Crowned head right, date below
Rev: Lewis and Clark, denomination at left

Date	Mintage	VF20	XF40	MS60	MS63	MS65
1988 FM (P)	—	PF65 20.00				

KM# 108 50 DOLLARS

20.94 g., 0.925 Silver 0.6227 oz. ASW **Ruler:** Elizabeth II **Subject:** Great Explorers **Obv:** Crowned head right, date below **Rev:** Fridtjof Nansen

Date	Mintage	VF20	XF40	MS60	MS63	MS65
1988 FM (P)	—	PF65 20.00				

KM# 109 50 DOLLARS

20.94 g., 0.925 Silver 0.6227 oz. ASW **Ruler:** Elizabeth II **Subject:** Great Explorers **Obv:** Crowned head right, date below **Rev:** Robert Peary

Date	Mintage	VF20	XF40	MS60	MS63	MS65
1988 FM (P)	—	PF65 20.00				

KM# 110 50 DOLLARS

20.94 g., 0.925 Silver 0.6227 oz. ASW **Ruler:** Elizabeth II **Subject:** Great Explorers **Obv:** Crowned head right, date below **Rev:** Roald Amundsen

Date	Mintage	VF20	XF40	MS60	MS63	MS65
1988 FM (P); Proof	—	PF65 20.00				

KM# 111 50 DOLLARS

20.94 g., 0.925 Silver 0.6227 oz. ASW **Ruler:** Elizabeth II **Subject:** Great Explorers **Obv:** Crowned head right, date below **Rev:** Richard Byrd, map at left, denomination above

Date	Mintage	VF20	XF40	MS60	MS63	MS65
1988 FM (P)	—	PF65 20.00				

KM# 45 50 DOLLARS

19.40 g., 0.925 Silver 0.5769 oz. ASW **Ruler:** Elizabeth II **Subject:** 500 Years of America **Obv:** Crowned head right, date below **Rev:** Sir Francis Drake

Date	Mintage	VF20	XF40	MS60	MS63	MS65
1989	15,000	PF65 20.00				
1990	—	PF65 20.00				

KM# 46 50 DOLLARS

31.10 g., 0.999 Silver 0.9989 oz. ASW **Ruler:** Elizabeth II **Subject:** 500 Years of America **Obv:** Crowned head right, date below **Rev:** Capt. James Cook

Date	Mintage	VF20	XF40	MS60	MS63	MS65
1989	15,000	PF65 35.00				

KM# 47 50 DOLLARS

29.90 g., 0.925 Silver 0.8892 oz. ASW **Ruler:** Elizabeth II **Subject:** 500 Years of America **Obv:** Crowned head right, date below **Rev:** Christopher Columbus **Edge Lettering:** CHRISTOPHER COLUMBUS WITH THE SANTA MARIA

Date	Mintage	VF20	XF40	MS60	MS63	MS65
1989	Est. 15000	PF65 35.00				

Note: Prior to the 27th edition, the illustration for KM#47 was incorrect. Please see KM#182 for correct listing.

KM# 49 50 DOLLARS

31.10 g., 0.925 Silver 0.9249 oz. ASW **Ruler:** Elizabeth II **Subject:** 500 Years of America **Obv:** Crowned head right, date below **Rev:** Ferdinand Magellan at right, map at left, denomination below

Date	Mintage	VF20	XF40	MS60	MS63	MS65
1989	15,000	PF65 35.00				
1991	Est. 60000	PF65 30.00				

KM# 60 50 DOLLARS

28.28 g., 0.925 Silver 0.841 oz. ASW **Ruler:** Elizabeth II **Subject:** 1990 Olympics **Obv:** Crowned bust right, date below **Rev:** Runners and biathalon

Date	Mintage	VF20	XF40	MS60	MS63	MS65
1989	40,000	PF65 30.00				

KM# 70 50 DOLLARS

28.28 g., 0.925 Silver 0.841 oz. ASW **Ruler:** Elizabeth II **Subject:** Soccer World Championship **Obv:** Crowned bust right, date below **Rev:** Two soccer players and ball

Date	Mintage	VF20	XF40	MS60	MS63	MS65
1989	—	PF65 30.00				

KM# 806 50 DOLLARS

28.28 g., 0.925 Silver 0.841 oz. ASW **Ruler:** Elizabeth II **Subject:** XXV Summer Olympics, Barcelonia **Rev:** Swimmer, Breast stroke

Date	Mintage	VF20	XF40	MS60	MS63	MS65
1989 PM	5	PF65 3,000				

KM# 43 50 DOLLARS

31.10 g., 0.925 Silver 0.9249 oz. ASW **Ruler:** Elizabeth II **Subject:** 500 Years of America **Obv:** Crowned head right, date below **Rev:** Jacques Cartier

Date	Mintage	VF20	XF40	MS60	MS63	MS65
1990	60,000	PF65 34.00				
1991	—	PF65 32.00				

KM# 44 50 DOLLARS

31.10 g., 0.999 Silver 0.9989 oz. ASW **Ruler:** Elizabeth II **Subject:** 500 Years of America **Obv:** Crowned head right, date below **Rev:** Vasco Nunez de Balboa, left, denomination below

Date	Mintage	VF20	XF40	MS60	MS63	MS65
1990	15,000	PF65 36.00				
1991	—	PF65 34.00				

KM# 48 50 DOLLARS
31.10 g., 0.999 Silver 0.9989 oz. ASW **Ruler:** Elizabeth II **Subject:** 500 Years of America **Obv:** Crowned head right, date below **Rev:** President Abraham Lincoln in foreground of capitol

Date	Mintage	VF20	XF40	MS60	MS63	MS65
1990	15,000	PF65 36.00				
1991	—	PF65 34.00				

KM# 52 50 DOLLARS
19.40 g., 0.925 Silver 0.5769 oz. ASW **Ruler:** Elizabeth II **Subject:** Endangered World Wildlife **Obv:** Crowned head right, date below **Rev:** Grizzly bear

Date	Mintage	VF20	XF40	MS60	MS63	MS65
1990 PM	2,500	PF65 25.00				
1990 PM Matte Proof	550	PF65 45.00				

KM# 53 50 DOLLARS
19.40 g., 0.925 Silver 0.5769 oz. ASW **Ruler:** Elizabeth II **Subject:** Endangered World Wildlife **Obv:** Crowned head right, date below **Rev:** African elephant

Date	Mintage	VF20	XF40	MS60	MS63	MS65
1990 Matte Proof	1,000	PF65 35.00				
1990	25,000	PF65 22.50				

KM# 54 50 DOLLARS
19.40 g., 0.925 Silver 0.5769 oz. ASW **Ruler:** Elizabeth II **Subject:** Endangered World Wildlife **Obv:** Crowned head right, date below **Rev:** Lynx

Date	Mintage	VF20	XF40	MS60	MS63	MS65
1990	25,000	PF65 22.50				

KM# 55 50 DOLLARS
19.40 g., 0.925 Silver 0.5769 oz. ASW **Ruler:** Elizabeth II **Subject:** Endangered World Wildlife **Obv:** Crowned head right, date below **Rev:** Black rhinoceros

Date	Mintage	VF20	XF40	MS60	MS63	MS65
1990	Est. 25000	PF65 22.50				

KM# 56 50 DOLLARS
19.40 g., 0.925 Silver 0.5769 oz. ASW **Ruler:** Elizabeth II **Subject:** Endangered World Wildlife **Obv:** Crowned head right, date below **Rev:** Bighorn sheep, denomination below

Date	Mintage	VF20	XF40	MS60	MS63	MS65
1990	Est. 25000	PF65 22.50				

KM# 57 50 DOLLARS
19.40 g., 0.925 Silver 0.5769 oz. ASW **Ruler:** Elizabeth II **Subject:** Endangered World Wildlife **Obv:** Crowned head right, date below **Rev:** Koala bear

Date	Mintage	VF20	XF40	MS60	MS63	MS65
1990	Est. 25000	PF65 22.50				

KM# 58 50 DOLLARS
19.40 g., 0.925 Silver 0.5769 oz. ASW **Ruler:** Elizabeth II **Subject:** Endangered World Wildlife **Obv:** Crowned head right, date below **Rev:** Buffalo, denomination below

Date	Mintage	VF20	XF40	MS60	MS63	MS65
1990	25,000	PF65 22.50				
1990	600	—	—	—	40.00	45.00

KM# 59 50 DOLLARS
19.40 g., 0.925 Silver 0.5769 oz. ASW **Ruler:** Elizabeth II **Subject:** Endangered World Wildlife **Obv:** Crowned head right, date below **Rev:** Chimpanzee, denomination below

Date	Mintage	VF20	XF40	MS60	MS63	MS65
1990	Est. 25000	PF65 22.50				

KM# 89 50 DOLLARS
31.10 g., 0.925 Silver 0.9249 oz. ASW **Ruler:** Elizabeth II **Subject:** 500 Years of America **Obv:** Crowned head right, date below **Rev:** 3/4 figure of Henry Hudson at right looking left, ship at left, denomination below

Date	Mintage	VF20	XF40	MS60	MS63	MS65
1990	60,000	PF65 30.00				

KM# 112 50 DOLLARS
19.20 g., 0.925 Silver 0.571 oz. ASW **Ruler:** Elizabeth II **Subject:** 1992 Olympics **Obv:** Crowned head right, date below **Rev:** Runner

Date	Mintage	VF20	XF40	MS60	MS63	MS65
1990	40,000	PF65 20.00				

KM# 115 50 DOLLARS
19.80 g., 0.925 Silver 0.5888 oz. ASW **Ruler:** Elizabeth II **Subject:** Endangered World Wildlife **Obv:** Crowned head right, date below **Rev:** Blackbuck left, denomination below

Date	Mintage	VF20	XF40	MS60	MS63	MS65
1990	—	PF65 30.00				

KM# 117 50 DOLLARS
19.80 g., 0.925 Silver 0.5888 oz. ASW **Ruler:** Elizabeth II **Subject:** Endangered World Wildlife **Obv:** Crowned head right, date below **Rev:** Whooping crane, denomination below

Date	Mintage	VF20	XF40	MS60	MS63	MS65
1990	—	PF65 30.00				

KM# 134 50 DOLLARS
31.10 g., 0.925 Silver 0.9249 oz. ASW **Ruler:** Elizabeth II **Subject:** 500 Years of America **Obv:** Crowned head right, date below **Rev:** Cabral bust at right, two figures with cross at left, denomination below

Date	Mintage	VF20	XF40	MS60	MS63	MS65
1990	Est. 60000	PF65 30.00				

KM# 135 50 DOLLARS
31.10 g., 0.925 Silver 0.9249 oz. ASW **Ruler:** Elizabeth II **Subject:** 500 Years of America **Obv:** Crowned head right, date below **Rev:** Half figure of Bolivar at left facing right, denomination below

Date	Mintage	VF20	XF40	MS60	MS63	MS65
1990	—	PF65 30.00				

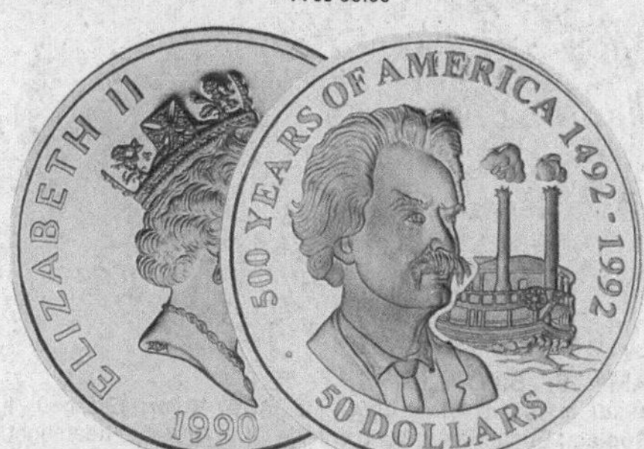

KM# 139 50 DOLLARS
31.26 g., 0.925 Silver 0.9297 oz. ASW **Ruler:** Elizabeth II **Subject:** 500 Years of America **Obv:** Crowned head right, date below **Rev:** Samuel Clemens at left looking right, steamboat in background, denomination below

Date	Mintage	VF20	XF40	MS60	MS63	MS65
1990	Est. 60000	PF65 30.00				

KM# 144 50 DOLLARS
19.40 g., 0.925 Silver 0.5769 oz. ASW **Ruler:** Elizabeth II **Subject:** Endangered World Wildlife **Obv:** Crowned head right, date below **Rev:** European hedgehog left, denomination below

Date	Mintage	VF20	XF40	MS60	MS63	MS65
1990	Est. 25000	PF65 27.50				

KM# 182 50 DOLLARS
31.35 g., 0.925 Silver 0.9323 oz. ASW **Ruler:** Elizabeth II **Subject:** 500 Years of America **Obv:** Crowned head right, date below **Rev:** Columbus' portrait with Santa Maria in background

Date	Mintage	VF20	XF40	MS60	MS63	MS65
1990	—	PF65 30.00				

KM# 184 50 DOLLARS
31.35 g., 0.925 Silver 0.9323 oz. ASW **Ruler:** Elizabeth II **Subject:** 500 Years of America **Obv:** Crowned head right, date below **Rev:** Inca Prince

Date	Mintage	VF20	XF40	MS60	MS63	MS65
1990	Est. 60000	PF65 30.00				

KM# 185 50 DOLLARS
31.35 g., 0.925 Silver 0.9323 oz. ASW **Ruler:** Elizabeth II **Subject:** 500 Years of America **Obv:** Crowned head right, date below **Rev:** Cortez and Montezuma, denomination below

Date	Mintage	VF20	XF40	MS60	MS63	MS65
1990	Est. 60000	PF65 30.00				

KM# 186 50 DOLLARS
31.35 g., 0.925 Silver 0.9323 oz. ASW **Ruler:** Elizabeth II **Subject:** 500 Years of America **Obv:** Crowned head right, date below **Rev:** Samuel de Champlain bust looking right, denomination below

Date	Mintage	VF20	XF40	MS60	MS63	MS65
1990	Est. 60000	PF65 30.00				

KM# 188 50 DOLLARS
31.35 g., 0.925 Silver 0.9323 oz. ASW **Ruler:** Elizabeth II **Subject:** 500 Years of America **Obv:** Crowned head right, date below **Rev:** Sir Walter Raleigh at right facing left, ship at left, denomination below

Date	Mintage	VF20	XF40	MS60	MS63	MS65
1990	Est. 60000	PF65 30.00				

KM# 205 50 DOLLARS
19.20 g., 0.925 Silver 0.571 oz. ASW **Ruler:** Elizabeth II **Subject:** Endangered World Wildlife **Obv:** PM mint mark below truncation **Rev:** European bison and calf

Date	Mintage	VF20	XF40	MS60	MS63	MS65
1990 PM	—	PF65 27.50				

KM# 206 50 DOLLARS
19.20 g., 0.925 Silver 0.571 oz. ASW **Ruler:** Elizabeth II **Subject:** Endangered World Wildlife **Obv:** Crowned head right, date below **Rev:** Tiger

Date	Mintage	VF20	XF40	MS60	MS63	MS65
1990	Est. 25000	PF65 27.50				

KM# 207 50 DOLLARS
19.20 g., 0.925 Silver 0.571 oz. ASW **Ruler:** Elizabeth II **Subject:** Endangered World Wildlife **Obv:** Crowned head right, date below **Rev:** Dama gazelles, denomination below

Date	Mintage	VF20	XF40	MS60	MS63	MS65
1990	Est. 25000	PF65 27.50				

KM# 208 50 DOLLARS
19.20 g., 0.925 Silver 0.571 oz. ASW **Ruler:** Elizabeth II **Subject:** Endangered World Wildlife **Obv:** Crowned head right, date below **Rev:** Cougars

Date	Mintage	VF20	XF40	MS60	MS63	MS65
1990 PM	—	PF65 27.50				

KM# 209 50 DOLLARS
19.20 g., 0.925 Silver 0.571 oz. ASW **Ruler:** Elizabeth II **Subject:** Endangered World Wildlife **Obv:** Crowned head right, date below **Rev:** Eagle Owl, denomination below

Date	Mintage	VF20	XF40	MS60	MS63	MS65
1990 (b)	—	PF65 27.50				

KM# 210 50 DOLLARS
19.20 g., 0.925 Silver 0.571 oz. ASW **Ruler:** Elizabeth II **Subject:** Endangered World Wildlife **Obv:** Crowned head right, date below **Rev:** Heaviside's dolphins

Date	Mintage	VF20	XF40	MS60	MS63	MS65
1990 (b)	—	PF65 27.50				

KM# 211 50 DOLLARS
19.20 g., 0.925 Silver 0.571 oz. ASW **Ruler:** Elizabeth II **Subject:** Endangered World Wildlife **Obv:** Crowned head right, date below **Rev:** European otters

Date	Mintage	VF20	XF40	MS60	MS63	MS65
1990	—	PF65 27.50				

KM# 212 50 DOLLARS
19.20 g., 0.925 Silver 0.571 oz. ASW **Ruler:** Elizabeth II **Subject:** Endangered World Wildlife **Obv:** Crowned head right, date below **Rev:** Alpine ibex

Date	Mintage	VF20	XF40	MS60	MS63	MS65
1990	—	PF65 27.50				

KM# 213 50 DOLLARS
19.20 g., 0.925 Silver 0.571 oz. ASW **Ruler:** Elizabeth II **Subject:** Endangered World Wildlife **Obv:** Crowned head right, date below **Rev:** Senegalese lion, denomination below

Date	Mintage	VF20	XF40	MS60	MS63	MS65
1990	—	PF65 27.50				
1991	—	PF65 27.50				

KM# 214 50 DOLLARS
19.20 g., 0.925 Silver 0.571 oz. ASW **Ruler:** Elizabeth II **Subject:** Endangered World Wildlife **Obv:** Crowned head right, date below **Rev:** Fallow deer, denomination below

Date	Mintage	VF20	XF40	MS60	MS63	MS65
1990	—	PF65 27.50				

KM# 215 50 DOLLARS
19.20 g., 0.925 Silver 0.571 oz. ASW **Ruler:** Elizabeth II **Subject:** Endangered World Wildlife **Obv:** Crowned head right, date below **Rev:** Bee hummingbird

Date	Mintage	VF20	XF40	MS60	MS63	MS65
1990	—	PF65 27.50				

KM# 216 50 DOLLARS
19.20 g., 0.925 Silver 0.571 oz. ASW **Ruler:** Elizabeth II **Subject:** Endangered World Wildlife **Obv:** Crowned head right, date below **Rev:** Jackass penguins

Date	Mintage	VF20	XF40	MS60	MS63	MS65
1990	—	PF65 27.50				

KM# 265 50 DOLLARS
28.30 g., 0.925 Silver 0.8416 oz. ASW **Ruler:** Elizabeth II **Subject:** World Cup Soccer **Obv:** Crowned head right, date below **Rev:** Soccer players, denomination below

Date	Mintage	VF20	XF40	MS60	MS63	MS65
1990	—	PF65 27.50				

KM# 357 50 DOLLARS
19.20 g., 0.925 Silver 0.571 oz. ASW **Ruler:** Elizabeth II **Subject:** Endangered World Wildlife **Obv:** Crowned head right, date below **Rev:** Peregrine falcon

Date	Mintage	VF20	XF40	MS60	MS63	MS65
1990 (b)	—	PF65 27.50				

KM# 812 50 DOLLARS
10.00 g., 0.925 Silver 0.2974 oz. ASW **Ruler:** Elizabeth II **Subject:** Endangered World Wildlife **Rev:** Macropus rufus

Date	Mintage	VF20	XF40	MS60	MS63	MS65
1990	25,000	PF65 25.00				

KM# 813 50 DOLLARS
10.00 g., 0.925 Silver 0.2974 oz. ASW **Ruler:** Elizabeth II **Subject:** Endangered World Wildlife **Rev:** White-tailed deer, doe and fawn

Date	Mintage	VF20	XF40	MS60	MS63	MS65
1990	25,000	PF65 25.00				

KM# 44a 50 DOLLARS
31.10 g., 0.925 Silver 0.9249 oz. ASW **Ruler:** Elizabeth II **Subject:** 500 Years of America **Obv:** Crowned head right, date below **Rev:** Vasco Nuñez de Balboa

Date	Mintage	VF20	XF40	MS60	MS63	MS65
1991	60,000	PF65 32.00				

KM# 46a 50 DOLLARS
31.10 g., 0.925 Silver 0.9249 oz. ASW **Ruler:** Elizabeth II **Subject:** 500 Years of America **Obv:** Crowned head right, date below **Rev:** Capt. James Cook

Date	Mintage	VF20	XF40	MS60	MS63	MS65
1991	Est. 60000	PF65 32.00				

KM# 93 50 DOLLARS
19.80 g., 0.925 Silver 0.5888 oz. ASW **Ruler:** Elizabeth II **Subject:** Endangered Wildlife **Obv:** Crowned head right, date below **Rev:** Eagle owl

Date	Mintage	VF20	XF40	MS60	MS63	MS65
1991	Est. 25000	PF65 22.50				

KM# 94 50 DOLLARS
31.10 g., 0.925 Silver 0.9249 oz. ASW **Ruler:** Elizabeth II **Subject:** 500 Years of America **Obv:** Crowned head right, date below **Rev:** Sitting Bull, denomination below

Date	Mintage	VF20	XF40	MS60	MS63	MS65
1991	Est. 15000	PF65 35.00				

KM# 95 50 DOLLARS
19.20 g., 0.925 Silver 0.571 oz. ASW **Ruler:** Elizabeth II **Subject:** Endangered Wildlife **Obv:** Crowned head right, date below **Rev:** Heaviside's dolphins

Date	Mintage	VF20	XF40	MS60	MS63	MS65
1991	—	PF65 22.50				

KM# 118 50 DOLLARS
19.20 g., 0.925 Silver 0.571 oz. ASW **Ruler:** Elizabeth II **Subject:** Endangered Wildlife **Obv:** Crowned head right, date below **Rev:** European otters

Date	Mintage	VF20	XF40	MS60	MS63	MS65
1991	—	PF65 22.50				

KM# 119 50 DOLLARS
19.20 g., 0.925 Silver 0.571 oz. ASW **Ruler:** Elizabeth II **Subject:** Endangered Wildlife **Obv:** Crowned head right, date below **Rev:** Peregrine falcon

Date	Mintage	VF20	XF40	MS60	MS63	MS65
1991	—	PF65 22.50				

KM# 120 50 DOLLARS
19.20 g., 0.925 Silver 0.571 oz. ASW **Ruler:** Elizabeth II **Subject:** Endangered Wildlife **Obv:** Crowned head right, date below **Rev:** Alpine ibex

Date	Mintage	VF20	XF40	MS60	MS63	MS65
1991	Est. 25000	PF65 22.50				

KM# 122 50 DOLLARS
19.20 g., 0.925 Silver 0.571 oz. ASW **Ruler:** Elizabeth II **Subject:** Endangered Wildlife **Obv:** Crowned head right, date below **Rev:** Senegalese lion

Date	Mintage	VF20	XF40	MS60	MS63	MS65
1991	—	PF65 22.50				

KM# 123 50 DOLLARS
19.20 g., 0.925 Silver 0.571 oz. ASW **Ruler:** Elizabeth II **Subject:** Endangered Wildlife **Obv:** Crowned head right, date below **Rev:** Deer

Date	Mintage	VF20	XF40	MS60	MS63	MS65
1991	Est. 25000	PF65 22.50				

KM# 124 50 DOLLARS
19.20 g., 0.925 Silver 0.571 oz. ASW **Ruler:** Elizabeth II **Subject:** Endangered Wildlife **Obv:** Crowned head right, date below **Rev:** Kangaroo

Date	Mintage	VF20	XF40	MS60	MS63	MS65
1991	Est. 25000	PF65 22.50				

KM# 125 50 DOLLARS
19.20 g., 0.925 Silver 0.571 oz. ASW **Ruler:** Elizabeth II **Subject:** Endangered Wildlife **Obv:** Crowned head right, date below **Rev:** Cougar and cub

Date	Mintage	VF20	XF40	MS60	MS63	MS65
1991	Est. 25000	PF65 22.50				

KM# 126 50 DOLLARS
19.20 g., 0.925 Silver 0.571 oz. ASW **Ruler:** Elizabeth II **Subject:** Endangered Wildlife **Obv:** Crowned head right, date below **Rev:** Fallow deer

Date	Mintage	VF20	XF40	MS60	MS63	MS65
1991	Est. 25000	PF65 22.50				

KM# 127 50 DOLLARS
19.20 g., 0.925 Silver 0.571 oz. ASW **Ruler:** Elizabeth II **Subject:** Endangered Wildlife **Obv:** Crowned head right, date below **Rev:** Bee hummingbird

Date	Mintage	VF20	XF40	MS60	MS63	MS65
1991	Est. 25000	PF65 22,50				

KM# 128 50 DOLLARS
19.20 g., 0.925 Silver 0.571 oz. ASW **Ruler:** Elizabeth II **Subject:** Endangered Wildlife **Obv:** Crowned head right, date below **Rev:** Jackass penguins

Date	Mintage	VF20	XF40	MS60	MS63	MS65
1991	—	PF65 22.50				

KM# 140 50 DOLLARS
31.26 g., 0.925 Silver 0.9297 oz. ASW **Ruler:** Elizabeth II **Subject:** 500 Years of America **Obv:** Crowned head right, date below **Rev:** Mayflower and pilgrims, denomination below

Date	Mintage	VF20	XF40	MS60	MS63	MS65
1991	—	PF65 30.00				
1992	60,000	PF65 30.00				

KM# 141 50 DOLLARS
31.26 g., 0.925 Silver 0.9297 oz. ASW **Ruler:** Elizabeth II **Subject:** 500 Years of America **Obv:** Crowned head right, date below **Rev:** Alexander Mackenzie bust looking right, figure in canoe at right, denomination below

Date	Mintage	VF20	XF40	MS60	MS63	MS65
1991	60,000	PF65 30.00				

KM# 145 50 DOLLARS
7.78 g., 0.5833 Gold 0.1458 oz. AGW **Ruler:** Elizabeth II **Subject:** 500 Years of America **Obv:** Crowned head right, date below **Rev:** Columbus kneeling with flag, denomination below

Date	Mintage	VF20	XF40	MS60	MS63	MS65
1991	Est. 60000	PF65 265				

KM# 148 50 DOLLARS
31.10 g., 0.925 Silver 0.9249 oz. ASW **Ruler:** Elizabeth II **Subject:** 500 Years of America **Obv:** Crowned head right, date below **Rev:** Aztec Priest, denomination below

Date	Mintage	VF20	XF40	MS60	MS63	MS65
1991	Est. 15000	PF65 35.00				

KM# 189 50 DOLLARS
31.10 g., 0.925 Silver 0.9249 oz. ASW **Ruler:** Elizabeth II **Subject:** 500 Years of America **Obv:** Crowned head right, date below **Rev:** Francisco Pizarro bust at left looking right, arms at right, denomination below

Date	Mintage	VF20	XF40	MS60	MS63	MS65
1991	Est. 60000	PF65 30.00				

KM# 190 50 DOLLARS
31.10 g., 0.925 Silver 0.9249 oz. ASW **Ruler:** Elizabeth II **Subject:** 500 Years of America **Obv:** Crowned head right, date below **Rev:** Jesuit Church in Cuzco, denomination below

Date	Mintage	VF20	XF40	MS60	MS63	MS65
1991	—	PF65 30.00				

KM# 191 50 DOLLARS
31.10 g., 0.925 Silver 0.9249 oz. ASW **Ruler:** Elizabeth II **Subject:** 500 Years of America **Obv:** Crowned head right, date below **Rev:** Peter Minuit's purchase of Manhattan Island, denomination below

Date	Mintage	VF20	XF40	MS60	MS63	MS65
1991	Est. 60000	PF65 30.00				

KM# 192 50 DOLLARS
31.10 g., 0.925 Silver 0.9249 oz. ASW **Ruler:** Elizabeth II **Subject:** 500 Years of America **Obv:** Crowned head right, date below **Rev:** Boston Tea Party, denomination below

Date	Mintage	VF20	XF40	MS60	MS63	MS65
1991	Est. 60000	PF65 30.00				

KM# 193 50 DOLLARS
31.10 g., 0.925 Silver 0.9249 oz. ASW **Ruler:** Elizabeth II **Subject:** 500 Years of America **Obv:** Crowned head right, date below **Rev:** Marquis de Lafayette bust at right looking left, figures at left, denomination below

Date	Mintage	VF20	XF40	MS60	MS63	MS65
1991	—	PF65 30.00				

KM# 194 50 DOLLARS
31.10 g., 0.925 Silver 0.9249 oz. ASW **Ruler:** Elizabeth II **Subject:** 500 Years of America **Obv:** Crowned head right, date below **Rev:** Robert Fulton, denomination below

Date	Mintage	VF20	XF40	MS60	MS63	MS65
1991	—	PF65 30.00				

KM# 195 50 DOLLARS
31.10 g., 0.925 Silver 0.9249 oz. ASW **Ruler:** Elizabeth II **Subject:** 500 Years of America **Obv:** Crowned head right, date below **Rev:** First U.S. transcontinental railroad, two busts above at left, denomination below

Date	Mintage	VF20	XF40	MS60	MS63	MS65
1991	—	PF65 30.00				

KM# 196 50 DOLLARS
31.10 g., 0.925 Silver 0.9249 oz. ASW **Ruler:** Elizabeth II **Subject:** 500 Years of America **Obv:** Crowned head right, date below **Rev:** Emperor Maximilian of Mexico on horseback, denomination below

Date	Mintage	VF20	XF40	MS60	MS63	MS65
1991	—	PF65 30.00				

KM# 305 50 DOLLARS
31.10 g., 0.925 Silver 0.9249 oz. ASW **Ruler:** Elizabeth II **Subject:** 500 Years of America **Obv:** Crowned head right, date below **Rev:** Capt. James Cook

Date	Mintage	VF20	XF40	MS60	MS63	MS65
1991	Est. 60000	PF65 30.00				

KM# 807 50 DOLLARS
31.11 g., 0.925 Silver 0.925 oz. ASW **Ruler:** Elizabeth II **Subject:** Ferdinand Magellan

Date	Mintage	VF20	XF40	MS60	MS63	MS65
1991	—	PF65 35.00				

KM# 815 50 DOLLARS
7.78 g., 0.583 Gold 0.1458 oz. AGW **Ruler:** Elizabeth II **Rev:** Koalas

Date	Mintage	VF20	XF40	MS60	MS63	MS65
1991	Est. 100000	PF65 275				

KM# 114 50 DOLLARS
31.10 g., 0.925 Silver 0.9249 oz. ASW **Ruler:** Elizabeth II **Subject:** 500 Years of America **Obv:** Crowned head right, date below **Rev:** Coronado's discovery of the Grand Canyon, denomination below

Date	Mintage	VF20	XF40	MS60	MS63	MS65
1992	Est. 15000	PF65 35.00				

KM# 129 50 DOLLARS
7.78 g., 0.583 Gold 0.1458 oz. AGW **Ruler:** Elizabeth II **Subject:** Endangered Wildlife **Obv:** Crowned head right, date below **Rev:** Eagles head

Date	Mintage	VF20	XF40	MS60	MS63	MS65
1992	—	PF65 265				

KM# 131 50 DOLLARS
7.78 g., 0.583 Gold 0.1458 oz. AGW **Ruler:** Elizabeth II **Subject:** Endangered Wildlife **Obv:** Crowned head right, date below **Rev:** Elephant head

Date	Mintage	VF20	XF40	MS60	MS63	MS65
1992	—	PF65 265				

KM# 132 50 DOLLARS
7.78 g., 0.583 Gold 0.1458 oz. AGW **Ruler:** Elizabeth II **Subject:** Endangered Wildlife **Obv:** Crowned head right, date below **Rev:** Tiger head

Date	Mintage	VF20	XF40	MS60	MS63	MS65
1992	—	PF65 265				

KM# 142 50 DOLLARS
31.26 g., 0.925 Silver 0.9297 oz. ASW **Ruler:** Elizabeth II **Subject:** 500 Years of America **Obv:** Crowned head right, date below **Rev:** John Davis' strait marked on map, ship at right, denomination below

Date	Mintage	VF20	XF40	MS60	MS63	MS65
1992	Est. 60000	PF65 30.00				

KM# 143 50 DOLLARS
31.26 g., 0.925 Silver 0.9297 oz. ASW **Ruler:** Elizabeth II **Subject:** 500 Years of America **Obv:** Crowned head right, date below **Rev:** Vitus Bering, denomination below

Date	Mintage	VF20	XF40	MS60	MS63	MS65
1992	Est. 60000	PF65 30.00				

KM# 156 50 DOLLARS
31.10 g., 0.925 Silver 0.925 oz. ASW **Ruler:** Elizabeth II **Subject:** 500 Years of America **Obv:** Crowned head right, date below **Rev:** Pedro de Valdivia bust at left looking right, denomination below

Date	Mintage	VF20	XF40	MS60	MS63	MS65
1992	—	PF65 30.00				

KM# 157 50 DOLLARS
31.10 g., 0.925 Silver 0.925 oz. ASW **Ruler:** Elizabeth II **Subject:** 500 Years of America **Obv:** Crowned head right, date below **Rev:** Diego de Almagro, denomination below

Date	Mintage	VF20	XF40	MS60	MS63	MS65
1992	—	PF65 30.00				

KM# 162 50 DOLLARS
31.10 g., 0.925 Silver 0.925 oz. ASW **Ruler:** Elizabeth II **Subject:** 500 Years of America **Obv:** Crowned head right, date below **Rev:** Francisco de Coronado

Date	Mintage	VF20	XF40	MS60	MS63	MS65
1992	—	PF65 30.00				

KM# 176 50 DOLLARS
7.78 g., 0.5833 Gold 0.1458 oz. AGW **Ruler:** Elizabeth II **Subject:** 500 Years of America **Obv:** Crowned head right, date below **Rev:** Robert de La Salle

Date	Mintage	VF20	XF40	MS60	MS63	MS65
1992	—	PF65 265				

KM# 183 50 DOLLARS
31.10 g., 0.925 Silver 0.925 oz. ASW **Ruler:** Elizabeth II **Subject:** 500 Years of America **Obv:** Crowned head right, date below **Rev:** Giovanni da Verrazano, denomination below

Date	Mintage	VF20	XF40	MS60	MS63	MS65
1992	—	PF65 30.00				

KM# 197 50 DOLLARS
31.10 g., 0.925 Silver 0.925 oz. ASW **Ruler:** Elizabeth II **Subject:** 500 Years of America **Obv:** Crowned head right, date below **Rev:** Juan Ponce de Leon, denomination below

Date	Mintage	VF20	XF40	MS60	MS63	MS65
1992	—	PF65 30.00				

KM# 198 50 DOLLARS
31.10 g., 0.925 Silver 0.925 oz. ASW **Ruler:** Elizabeth II **Subject:** 500 Years of America **Obv:** Crowned head right,

date below **Rev:** 3/4 bust of Pedro de Mendoza at left, historic monuments at right, denomination below

Date	Mintage	VF20	XF40	MS60	MS63	MS65
1992	Est. 60000	PF65 30.00				

KM# 199 50 DOLLARS
31.10 g., 0.925 Silver 0.925 oz. ASW **Ruler:** Elizabeth II **Subject:** 500 Years of America **Obv:** Crowned head right, date below **Rev:** Pedro Menendez de Aviles on horseback at lower right, monument at left, denomination below

Date	Mintage	VF20	XF40	MS60	MS63	MS65
1992	—	PF65 30.00				

KM# 200 50 DOLLARS
31.10 g., 0.925 Silver 0.925 oz. ASW **Ruler:** Elizabeth II **Subject:** 500 Years of America **Obv:** Crowned head right, date below **Rev:** Independence Hall, figures above denomination

Date	Mintage	VF20	XF40	MS60	MS63	MS65
1992	—	PF65 32.50				

KM# 201 50 DOLLARS
31.10 g., 0.925 Silver 0.925 oz. ASW **Ruler:** Elizabeth II **Subject:** 500 Years of America **Obv:** Crowned head right, date below **Rev:** Sacagawea guiding Lewis and Clark, denomination below

Date	Mintage	VF20	XF40	MS60	MS63	MS65
1992	Est. 60000	PF65 30.00				

KM# 202 50 DOLLARS
31.10 g., 0.925 Silver 0.925 oz. ASW **Ruler:** Elizabeth II **Subject:** 500 Years of America **Obv:** Crowned head right, date below **Rev:** Oregon Trail, conestoga wagon in front of U.S. map outline, denomination below

Date	Mintage	VF20	XF40	MS60	MS63	MS65
1992	—	PF65 30.00				

KM# 204 50 DOLLARS
7.78 g., 0.5833 Gold 0.1458 oz. AGW **Ruler:** Elizabeth II **Subject:** 500 Years of America **Obv:** Crowned head right, date below **Rev:** Bust of John Cabot at left, ship at right, denomination below

Date	Mintage	VF20	XF40	MS60	MS63	MS65
1992	5,000	PF65 265				

KM# 244 50 DOLLARS
19.20 g., 0.925 Silver 0.571 oz. ASW **Ruler:** Elizabeth II **Obv:** Crowned head right, date below **Rev:** Poplar Admiral Butterfly and thistle, denomination below

Date	Mintage	VF20	XF40	MS60	MS63	MS65
1992	—	PF65 22.50				

KM# 249 50 DOLLARS
7.78 g., 0.583 Gold 0.1458 oz. AGW **Ruler:** Elizabeth II **Subject:** 500 Years of America **Obv:** Crowned head right, date below **Rev:** Busts of Ferdinand and Isabella half right, denomination below

Date	Mintage	VF20	XF40	MS60	MS63	MS65
1992	Est. 5000	PF65 265				

KM# 259 50 DOLLARS
7.78 g., 0.583 Gold 0.1458 oz. AGW **Ruler:** Elizabeth II **Subject:** 500 Years of America **Obv:** Crowned head right, date below **Rev:** Paul de Maisonneuve, map and city view, denomination below

Date	Mintage	VF20	XF40	MS60	MS63	MS65
1992	Est. 5000	PF65 265				

KM# 260 50 DOLLARS
7.78 g., 0.583 Gold 0.1458 oz. AGW **Ruler:** Elizabeth II **Subject:** 500 Years of America **Obv:** Crowned head right, date below **Rev:** Jakob le Maire, ship and map, denomination below

Date	Mintage	VF20	XF40	MS60	MS63	MS65
1992	Est. 5000	PF65 265				

KM# 261 50 DOLLARS
19.20 g., 0.925 Silver 0.571 oz. ASW **Ruler:** Elizabeth II **Subject:** Endangered Wildlife **Obv:** Crowned head right, date below **Rev:** Szechuan Takins, denomination below

Date	Mintage	VF20	XF40	MS60	MS63	MS65
1992	25,000	PF65 22.50				

KM# 262 50 DOLLARS
19.20 g., 0.925 Silver 0.571 oz. ASW **Ruler:** Elizabeth II **Subject:** Endangered Wildlife **Obv:** Crowned head right, date below **Rev:** Ring-tailed lemurs

Date	Mintage	VF20	XF40	MS60	MS63	MS65
1992	25,000	PF65 22.50				

KM# 263 50 DOLLARS
19.20 g., 0.925 Silver 0.571 oz. ASW **Ruler:** Elizabeth II **Subject:** Endangered Wildlife **Obv:** Crowned head right, date below **Rev:** Mandrill, denomination below

Date	Mintage	VF20	XF40	MS60	MS63	MS65
1992	25,000	PF65 22.50				

KM# 264 50 DOLLARS
19.20 g., 0.925 Silver 0.571 oz. ASW **Ruler:** Elizabeth II **Subject:** Endangered Wildlife **Obv:** Crowned head right, date below **Rev:** Lowland gorilla

Date	Mintage	VF20	XF40	MS60	MS63	MS65
1992	25,000	PF65 22.50				

KM# 310 50 DOLLARS
31.00 g., 0.925 Silver 0.9219 oz. ASW **Ruler:** Elizabeth II **Obv:** Crowned head right, date below **Rev:** Aztec kneels before Alvarado, denomination below **Edge Lettering:** PEDRO DE ALVARADO CONQUEROR of the AZTEC EMPIRE

Date	Mintage	VF20	XF40	MS60	MS63	MS65
1992	—	PF65 30.00				

KM# 822 50 DOLLARS
7.78 g., 0.583 Gold 0.1458 oz. AGW **Ruler:** Elizabeth II **Rev:** Soccerfield

Date	Mintage	VF20	XF40	MS60	MS63	MS65
1992	2,500	PF65 275				

KM# 153 50 DOLLARS
7.78 g., 0.5833 Gold 0.1458 oz. AGW **Ruler:** Elizabeth II **Subject:** Endangered Wildlife **Obv:** Crowned head right, date below **Rev:** Ibex

Date	Mintage	VF20	XF40	MS60	MS63	MS65
1993	—	PF65 260				

KM# 154 50 DOLLARS
7.78 g., 0.5833 Gold 0.1458 oz. AGW **Ruler:** Elizabeth II **Subject:** Endangered Wildlife **Obv:** Crowned head right, date below **Rev:** Owl and parrot

Date	Mintage	VF20	XF40	MS60	MS63	MS65
1993	—	PF65 260				

KM# 155 50 DOLLARS
31.10 g., 0.925 Silver 0.925 oz. ASW **Ruler:** Elizabeth II **Subject:** 500 Years of America **Obv:** Crowned head right, date below **Rev:** Father Jacques Marquette, denomination below

Date	Mintage	VF20	XF40	MS60	MS63	MS65
1993	—	PF65 30.00				

KM# 163 50 DOLLARS
31.10 g., 0.925 Silver 0.925 oz. ASW **Ruler:** Elizabeth II **Subject:** 500 Years of America **Obv:** Crowned head right, date below **Rev:** Francisco de Orellana bust at right looking left, ship at left, denomination below

Date	Mintage	VF20	XF40	MS60	MS63	MS65
1993	—	PF65 30.00				

KM# 164 50 DOLLARS
31.10 g., 0.925 Silver 0.925 oz. ASW **Ruler:** Elizabeth II **Subject:** 500 Years of America **Obv:** Crowned head right, date below **Rev:** Pinzon brothers, denomination below

Date	Mintage	VF20	XF40	MS60	MS63	MS65
1993	—	PF65 30.00				

KM# 165 50 DOLLARS
31.10 g., 0.925 Silver 0.925 oz. ASW **Ruler:** Elizabeth II **Subject:** 500 Years of America **Obv:** Crowned head right, date below **Rev:** Juan de la Cosa

Date	Mintage	VF20	XF40	MS60	MS63	MS65
1993	—	PF65 30.00				

KM# 166 50 DOLLARS
31.10 g., 0.925 Silver 0.925 oz. ASW **Ruler:** Elizabeth II **Subject:** 500 Years of America **Obv:** Crowned head right, date below **Rev:** William Penn

Date	Mintage	VF20	XF40	MS60	MS63	MS65
1993	—	PF65 30.00				

KM# 167 50 DOLLARS
31.10 g., 0.925 Silver 0.925 oz. ASW **Ruler:** Elizabeth II **Subject:** 500 Years of America **Obv:** Crowned head right, date below **Rev:** Diego de Velasquez

Date	Mintage	VF20	XF40	MS60	MS63	MS65
1993	—	PF65 30.00				

KM# 168 50 DOLLARS
31.10 g., 0.925 Silver 0.925 oz. ASW **Ruler:** Elizabeth II **Subject:** 500 Years of America **Obv:** Crowned head right, date below **Rev:** Miner panning for gold

Date	Mintage	VF20	XF40	MS60	MS63	MS65
1993	—	PF65 30.00				

KM# 169 50 DOLLARS
31.10 g., 0.925 Silver 0.925 oz. ASW **Ruler:** Elizabeth II **Subject:** 500 Years of America **Obv:** Crowned head right, date below **Rev:** Sir Martin Frobisher bust at left facing right, rocks at right, denomination below

Date	Mintage	VF20	XF40	MS60	MS63	MS65
1993	—	PF65 30.00				

KM# 170 50 DOLLARS
31.10 g., 0.925 Silver 0.925 oz. ASW **Ruler:** Elizabeth II **Subject:** 500 Years of America **Obv:** Crowned head right, date below **Rev:** George Vancouver

Date	Mintage	VF20	XF40	MS60	MS63	MS65
1993	—	PF65 30.00				

KM# 171 50 DOLLARS
31.10 g., 0.925 Silver 0.925 oz. ASW **Ruler:** Elizabeth II **Subject:** 500 Years of America **Obv:** Crowned head right, date below **Rev:** John Hawkins at right, ship at left, denomination below

Date	Mintage	VF20	XF40	MS60	MS63	MS65
1993	—	PF65 30.00				

KM# 172 50 DOLLARS
31.10 g., 0.925 Silver 0.925 oz. ASW **Ruler:** Elizabeth II **Subject:** 500 Years of America **Obv:** Crowned head right, date below **Rev:** Amerigo Vespucci head within map outline, ship at right, denomination below

Date	Mintage	VF20	XF40	MS60	MS63	MS65
1993	—	PF65 30.00				

KM# 173 50 DOLLARS
7.78 g., 0.5833 Gold 0.1458 oz. AGW **Ruler:** Elizabeth II **Subject:** 500 Years of America **Obv:** Crowned head right, date below **Rev:** George Washington

Date	Mintage	VF20	XF40	MS60	MS63	MS65
1993	—	PF65 260				

KM# 174 50 DOLLARS
7.78 g., 0.5833 Gold 0.1458 oz. AGW **Ruler:** Elizabeth II **Subject:** 500 Years of America **Obv:** Crowned head right, date below **Rev:** Alonso de Hojeda

Date	Mintage	VF20	XF40	MS60	MS63	MS65
1993	—	PF65 260				

KM# 175 50 DOLLARS
7.78 g., 0.5833 Gold 0.1458 oz. AGW **Ruler:** Elizabeth II **Subject:** 500 Years of America **Obv:** Crowned head right, date below **Rev:** Thomas Jefferson

Date	Mintage	VF20	XF40	MS60	MS63	MS65
1993	—	PF65 260				

KM# 177 50 DOLLARS
7.78 g., 0.5833 Gold 0.1458 oz. AGW **Ruler:** Elizabeth II **Subject:** 500 Years of America **Obv:** Crowned head right, date below **Rev:** Captain James Cook

Date	Mintage	VF20	XF40	MS60	MS63	MS65
1993	—	PF65 260				

KM# 178 50 DOLLARS
7.78 g., 0.5833 Gold 0.1458 oz. AGW **Ruler:** Elizabeth II **Subject:** 500 Years of America **Obv:** Crowned head right, date below **Rev:** Christopher Columbus

Date	Mintage	VF20	XF40	MS60	MS63	MS65
1993	—	PF65 260				

KM# 179 50 DOLLARS
7.78 g., 0.5833 Gold 0.1458 oz. AGW **Ruler:** Elizabeth II **Subject:** 500 Years of America **Obv:** Crowned head right, date below **Rev:** Statue of Liberty

Date	Mintage	VF20	XF40	MS60	MS63	MS65
1993	—	PF65 250				

KM# 180 50 DOLLARS
7.78 g., 0.5833 Gold 0.1458 oz. AGW **Ruler:** Elizabeth II **Subject:** 1996 Olympics **Obv:** Crowned head right, date below **Rev:** Ribbon dancer, denomination below

Date	Mintage	VF20	XF40	MS60	MS63	MS65
1993	Est. 5000	PF65 260				

KM# 245 50 DOLLARS
7.78 g., 0.5833 Gold 0.1458 oz. AGW **Ruler:** Elizabeth II **Subject:** Endangered Wildlife **Obv:** Crowned head right, date below **Rev:** African lion, denomination below

Date	Mintage	VF20	XF40	MS60	MS63	MS65
1993	Est. 10000	PF65 265				

KM# 248 50 DOLLARS
31.10 g., 0.925 Silver 0.925 oz. ASW **Ruler:** Elizabeth II **Subject:** 500 Years of America **Obv:** Crowned head right, date below **Rev:** Jose de San Martin at right, figures on horseback at left, denomination below

Date	Mintage	VF20	XF40	MS60	MS63	MS65
1993	Est. 60000	PF65 30.00				

KM# 472 50 DOLLARS
7.65 g., 0.583 Gold 0.1434 oz. AGW, 24.96 mm. **Ruler:** Elizabeth II **Obv:** Crowned bust right **Rev:** Parrot's head **Edge:** Reeded

Date	Mintage	VF20	XF40	MS60	MS63	MS65
1993	—	PF65 265				

KM# 246 50 DOLLARS
7.78 g., 0.583 Gold 0.1458 oz. AGW **Ruler:** Elizabeth II **Subject:** Endangered Wildlife **Obv:** Crowned head right, date below **Rev:** Sea otter head, denomination below

Date	Mintage	VF20	XF40	MS60	MS63	MS65
1994	Est. 10000	PF65 265				

KM# 247 50 DOLLARS
7.78 g., 0.583 Gold 0.1458 oz. AGW **Ruler:** Elizabeth II **Subject:** Endangered Wildlife **Obv:** Crowned head right, date below **Rev:** Przewalski's horse

Date	Mintage	VF20	XF40	MS60	MS63	MS65
1994	Est. 10000	PF65 265				

KM# 275 50 DOLLARS
7.78 g., 0.583 Gold 0.1458 oz. AGW **Ruler:** Elizabeth II **Subject:** Endangered Wildlife **Obv:** Crowned head right, date below **Rev:** Poplar Admiral butterflies

Date	Mintage	VF20	XF40	MS60	MS63	MS65
1994	Est. 10000	PF65 265				

KM# 276 50 DOLLARS
7.78 g., 0.583 Gold 0.1458 oz. AGW **Ruler:** Elizabeth II **Obv:** Crowned head right, date below **Rev:** Queen Mother and daughters

Date	Mintage	VF20	XF40	MS60	MS63	MS65
1995	Est. 5000	PF65 260				

KM# 823 50 DOLLARS
3.00 g., 0.999 Gold 0.0964 oz. AGW **Ruler:** Elizabeth II **Subject:** Year of the Pig **Note:** S#288.

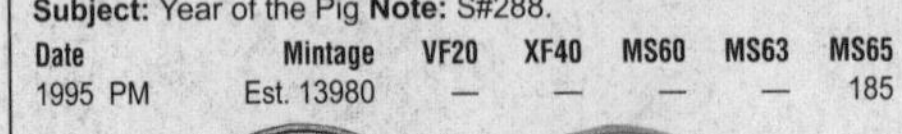

Date	Mintage	VF20	XF40	MS60	MS63	MS65
1995 PM	Est. 13980	—	—	—	—	185

KM# 299 50 DOLLARS
8.00 g., 0.9999 Gold 0.2572 oz. AGW **Ruler:** Elizabeth II **Subject:** Year of the Mouse **Obv:** Crowned head right, date below **Rev:** Mickey and Minnie Mouse portrait, denomination below

Date	Mintage	VF20	XF40	MS60	MS63	MS65
1996	—	PF65 450				

KM# 841 50 DOLLARS
8.00 g., 0.999 Gold 0.2569 oz. AGW **Ruler:** Elizabeth II **Subject:** Year of the Rat

Date	Mintage	VF20	XF40	MS60	MS63	MS65
1996 Proof	—	—	—	—	—	450

KM# 844 50 DOLLARS
7.81 g., 0.999 Gold 0.2507 oz. AGW **Ruler:** Elizabeth II **Subject:** Mother's day

Date	Mintage	VF20	XF40	MS60	MS63	MS65
1996	—	PF65 475				

KM# 306 50 DOLLARS
Bi-Metallic Platinum center in Gold ring **Ruler:** Elizabeth II **Obv:** Crowned head right within circle, date below **Rev:** Mother seal with pup within circle, date below

Date	Mintage	VF20	XF40	MS60	MS63	MS65
1997	—	PF65 425				

KM# 322 50 DOLLARS
32.22 g., 0.925 Silver 0.9583 oz. ASW **Ruler:** Elizabeth II **Subject:** 2nd Century **Obv:** Crowned head right, date below **Rev:** Chinese papermaker, denomination at left

Date	Mintage	VF20	XF40	MS60	MS63	MS65
1997	—	PF65 35.50				

KM# 323 50 DOLLARS
32.22 g., 0.925 Silver 0.9583 oz. ASW **Ruler:** Elizabeth II **Subject:** 8th Century **Obv:** Crowned head right, date below **Rev:** Coronation of Charlemagne

Date	Mintage	VF20	XF40	MS60	MS63	MS65
1997	—	PF65 32.50				

KM# 324 50 DOLLARS
32.22 g., 0.925 Silver 0.9583 oz. ASW **Ruler:** Elizabeth II **Subject:** 12th Century **Obv:** Crowned head right, date below **Rev:** Genghis Khan **Rev. Inscription:** GENGHIS KHAN BEGINS ASIAN CONQUEST

Date	Mintage	VF20	XF40	MS60	MS63	MS65
1997	—	PF65 32.50				

KM# 325.1 50 DOLLARS
32.22 g., 0.925 Silver 0.9583 oz. ASW **Ruler:** Elizabeth II **Subject:** 13th Century **Obv:** Crowned head right, date below **Rev:** Marco Polo and Kublai Khan **Note:** Prev. KM#325.

Date	Mintage	VF20	XF40	MS60	MS63	MS65
1997	—	PF65 32.50				

KM# 325.2 50 DOLLARS
32.34 g., 0.925 Silver 0.9618 oz. ASW, 38.7 mm. **Ruler:** Elizabeth II **Subject:** 13th Century **Obv:** Crowned head right, date below **Rev:** Inscription in polished rectangle **Rev. Inscription:** MARCO POLO AT KUBLAI KHAN'S COURT **Edge:** Reeded

Date	Mintage	VF20	XF40	MS60	MS63	MS65
1997 FM	—	PF65 32.50				

KM# 381 50 DOLLARS
4.12 g., 0.5833 Gold 0.0773 oz. AGW, 20.9 mm. **Ruler:** Elizabeth II **Subject:** Explorers **Obv:** Crowned head right, date below **Rev:** Leif Ericson with battle axe facing, denomination at right **Edge:** Reeded

Date	Mintage	VF20	XF40	MS60	MS63	MS65
1997	—	PF65 130				
1997 FM	—	PF65 140				

KM# 382 50 DOLLARS
4.60 g., 0.5833 Gold 0.0863 oz. AGW, 20.9 mm. **Ruler:** Elizabeth II **Subject:** Explorers **Obv:** Crowned head right, date below **Rev:** Marco Polo on camel **Edge:** Reeded

Date	Mintage	VF20	XF40	MS60	MS63	MS65
1997 FM	—	PF65 150				

KM# 383 50 DOLLARS
4.60 g., 0.5833 Gold 0.0863 oz. AGW, 20.9 mm. **Ruler:** Elizabeth II **Subject:** Explorers **Obv:** Crowned head right, date below **Rev:** Vasco da Gama **Edge:** Reeded

Date	Mintage	VF20	XF40	MS60	MS63	MS65
1997 FM	—	PF65 150				

KM# 384 50 DOLLARS
4.60 g., 0.5833 Gold 0.0863 oz. AGW **Ruler:** Elizabeth II **Subject:** Explorers **Obv:** Crowned head right, date below **Rev:** Vasco de Nuñez Balboa **Edge:** Reeded

Date	Mintage	VF20	XF40	MS60	MS63	MS65
1997 FM	—	PF65 150				

KM# 385 50 DOLLARS
4.60 g., 0.5833 Gold 0.0863 oz. AGW, 20.9 mm. **Ruler:** Elizabeth II **Subject:** Explorers **Obv:** Crowned head right, date below **Rev:** Hernando Cortes **Edge:** Reeded

Date	Mintage	VF20	XF40	MS60	MS63	MS65
1997 FM	—	PF65 150				

KM# 386 50 DOLLARS
4.60 g., 0.5833 Gold 0.0863 oz. AGW, 20.9 mm. **Ruler:** Elizabeth II **Subject:** Explorers **Obv:** Crowned head right, date below **Rev:** Magellan's ships: Vittoria and Trinidad **Edge:** Reeded

Date	Mintage	VF20	XF40	MS60	MS63	MS65
1997 FM	—	PF65 150				

KM# 390 50 DOLLARS
4.60 g., 0.5833 Gold 0.0863 oz. AGW, 20.9 mm. **Ruler:** Elizabeth II **Subject:** Explorers **Obv:** Crowned head right, date below **Rev:** Alexander the Great with sword on horseback, denomination above **Edge:** Reeded

Date	Mintage	VF20	XF40	MS60	MS63	MS65
1997 FM	—	PF65 150				

KM# 391 50 DOLLARS
4.60 g., 0.5833 Gold 0.0863 oz. AGW, 20.9 mm. **Ruler:** Elizabeth II **Subject:** Explorers **Obv:** Crowned head right, date below **Rev:** Christopher Columbus **Edge:** Reeded

Date	Mintage	VF20	XF40	MS60	MS63	MS65
1997 FM	—	PF65 150				

KM# 392 50 DOLLARS
4.60 g., 0.5833 Gold 0.0863 oz. AGW, 20.9 mm. **Ruler:** Elizabeth II **Subject:** Explorers **Obv:** Crowned head right, date below **Rev:** Sir Francis Drake **Edge:** Reeded

Date	Mintage	VF20	XF40	MS60	MS63	MS65
1997 FM	—	PF65 150				

KM# 393 50 DOLLARS
4.60 g., 0.5833 Gold 0.0863 oz. AGW, 20.9 mm. **Ruler:** Elizabeth II **Subject:** Explorers **Obv:** Crowned head right, date below **Rev:** Abel Janszoon Tasman **Edge:** Reeded

Date	Mintage	VF20	XF40	MS60	MS63	MS65
1997 FM	—	PF65 150				

KM# 394 50 DOLLARS
4.60 g., 0.5833 Gold 0.0863 oz. AGW, 20.9 mm. **Ruler:** Elizabeth II **Subject:** Explorers **Obv:** Crowned head right, date below **Rev:** Capt. James Cook **Edge:** Reeded

Date	Mintage	VF20	XF40	MS60	MS63	MS65
1997 FM	—	PF65 150				

KM# 395 50 DOLLARS
4.60 g., 0.5833 Gold 0.0863 oz. AGW, 20.9 mm. **Ruler:** Elizabeth II **Subject:** Explorers **Obv:** Crowned head right, date below **Rev:** Richard E. Byrd **Edge:** Reeded

Date	Mintage	VF20	XF40	MS60	MS63	MS65
1997 FM	—	PF65 150				

KM# 395.1 50 DOLLARS
6.37 g., 0.5833 Gold 0.1195 oz. AGW, 21 mm. **Ruler:** Elizabeth II **Obv:** Crowned head right, date below **Rev:** Admiral Richard C. Byrd **Edge:** Reeded

Date	Mintage	VF20	XF40	MS60	MS63	MS65
1997 FM	8	PF65 400				

Note: Struck on thicker than normal planchet resulting in a 38.5% heavier weight. 8 Pieces known.

KM# 399 50 DOLLARS
31.90 g., 0.925 Silver 0.9487 oz. ASW, 38.7 mm. **Ruler:** Elizabeth II **Subject:** 1st Century **Obv:** Crowned head right, date below **Rev:** Nativity scene **Edge:** Reeded

Date	Mintage	VF20	XF40	MS60	MS63	MS65
1997 FM	—	PF65 32.50				

KM# 400 50 DOLLARS
32.10 g., 0.925 Silver 0.9546 oz. ASW, 38.7 mm. **Ruler:** Elizabeth II **Subject:** 3rd Century **Obv:** Crowned head right, date below **Rev:** Roman citizens **Edge:** Reeded

Date	Mintage	VF20	XF40	MS60	MS63	MS65
1997 FM	—	PF65 32.50				

KM# 401 50 DOLLARS
30.91 g., 0.925 Silver 0.9192 oz. ASW, 38.7 mm. **Ruler:** Elizabeth II **Subject:** 4th Century **Obv:** Crowned head right, date below **Rev:** Constantine the Great **Edge:** Reeded

Date	Mintage	VF20	XF40	MS60	MS63	MS65
1997 FM	—	PF65 32.50				

KM# 402 50 DOLLARS
32.32 g., 0.925 Silver 0.9612 oz. ASW, 38.7 mm. **Ruler:** Elizabeth II **Subject:** 5th Century **Obv:** Crowned head right, date below **Rev:** The sacking of Rome **Edge:** Reeded

Date	Mintage	VF20	XF40	MS60	MS63	MS65
1997 FM	—	PF65 32.50				

KM# 403 50 DOLLARS
30.82 g., 0.925 Silver 0.9166 oz. ASW, 38.7 mm. **Ruler:** Elizabeth II **Subject:** 6th Century **Obv:** Crowned head right, date below **Rev:** Emperor Justinian **Edge:** Reeded

Date	Mintage	VF20	XF40	MS60	MS63	MS65
1997 FM	—	PF65 32.50				

KM# 404 50 DOLLARS
31.10 g., 0.925 Silver 0.9249 oz. ASW, 38.7 mm.

Ruler: Elizabeth II **Subject:** 7th Century **Obv:** Crowned head right, date below **Rev:** Establishment of Islam, domed building, denomination at left **Edge:** Reeded

Date	Mintage	VF20	XF40	MS60	MS63	MS65
1997 FM	—	PF65 32.50				

KM# 405 50 DOLLARS
29.53 g., 0.925 Silver 0.8782 oz. ASW, 38.7 mm. **Ruler:** Elizabeth II **Subject:** 9th Century **Obv:** Crowned head right, date below **Rev:** Caliph of Baghdad **Edge:** Reeded

Date	Mintage	VF20	XF40	MS60	MS63	MS65
1997 FM	—	PF65 32.50				

KM# 406 50 DOLLARS
32.13 g., 0.925 Silver 0.9555 oz. ASW, 38.7 mm. **Ruler:** Elizabeth II **Subject:** 10th Century **Obv:** Crowned head right, date below **Rev:** Monk writing **Rev. Inscription:** THE DARK AGES OF EUROPE **Edge:** Reeded

Date	Mintage	VF20	XF40	MS60	MS63	MS65
1997 FM	—	PF65 35.50				

KM# 407 50 DOLLARS
31.76 g., 0.925 Silver 0.9445 oz. ASW, 38.7 mm. **Ruler:** Elizabeth II **Subject:** 11th Century **Obv:** Crowned head right, date below **Rev:** Norman landing scene **Rev. Inscription:** THE NORMAN CONQUEST **Edge:** Reeded

Date	Mintage	VF20	XF40	MS60	MS63	MS65
1997 FM	—	PF65 32.50				

KM# 408 50 DOLLARS
31.75 g., 0.925 Silver 0.9442 oz. ASW, 38.7 mm. **Ruler:** Elizabeth II **Subject:** 14th Century **Obv:** Crowned head right, date below **Rev:** Renaissance buildings **Rev. Inscription:** BIRTH OF THE RENAISSANCE **Edge:** Reeded

Date	Mintage	VF20	XF40	MS60	MS63	MS65
1997 FM	—	PF65 32.50				

KM# 409 50 DOLLARS
31.44 g., 0.925 Silver 0.935 oz. ASW, 38.7 mm. **Ruler:** Elizabeth II **Subject:** 15th Century **Obv:** Crowned head right, date below **Rev:** Columbus and ship **Rev. Inscription:** AGE OF EXPLORATION: CHRISTOPHER COLUMBUS **Edge:** Reeded

Date	Mintage	VF20	XF40	MS60	MS63	MS65
1997 FM	—	PF65 32.50				

KM# 410 50 DOLLARS
32.61 g., 0.925 Silver 0.9698 oz. ASW, 38.7 mm. **Ruler:** Elizabeth II **Subject:** 16th Century **Obv:** Crowned head right, date below **Rev:** William Shakespeare **Edge:** Reeded

Date	Mintage	VF20	XF40	MS60	MS63	MS65
1997 FM	—	PF65 32.50				

KM# 411 50 DOLLARS
32.05 g., 0.925 Silver 0.9531 oz. ASW, 38.7 mm. **Ruler:** Elizabeth II **Subject:** 17th Century **Obv:** Crowned head right, date below **Rev:** Isaac Newton **Edge:** Reeded

Date	Mintage	VF20	XF40	MS60	MS63	MS65
1997 FM	—	PF65 32.50				

KM# 412 50 DOLLARS
32.34 g., 0.925 Silver 0.9618 oz. ASW, 38.7 mm. **Ruler:** Elizabeth II **Subject:** 18th Century **Obv:** Crowned head right, date below **Rev:** Declaration of Independence signing scene **Edge:** Reeded

Date	Mintage	VF20	XF40	MS60	MS63	MS65
1997 FM	—	PF65 32.50				

KM# 413 50 DOLLARS
31.63 g., 0.925 Silver 0.9407 oz. ASW, 38.7 mm. **Ruler:** Elizabeth II **Subject:** 19th Century **Obv:** Crowned head right, date below **Rev:** Early automobile **Edge:** Reeded

Date	Mintage	VF20	XF40	MS60	MS63	MS65
1997 FM	—	PF65 32.50				

KM# 414 50 DOLLARS
31.24 g., 0.925 Silver 0.9291 oz. ASW, 38.7 mm. **Ruler:** Elizabeth II **Subject:** 20th Century **Obv:** Crowned head right, date below **Rev:** Moon landing scene, denomination at left **Edge:** Reeded

Date	Mintage	VF20	XF40	MS60	MS63	MS65
1997 FM	—	PF65 32.50				

KM# 460 50 DOLLARS
10.00 g., 0.9995 Platinum 0.3213 oz. APW **Ruler:** Elizabeth II **Subject:** Love Angels

Date	Mintage	VF20	XF40	MS60	MS63	MS65
1997	250	PF65 625				

KM# 921 50 DOLLARS
10.00 g., 0.999 Gold 0.3212 oz. AGW **Ruler:** Elizabeth II **Subject:** Christmas

Date	Mintage	VF20	XF40	MS60	MS63	MS65
1997	100	PF65 575				

KM# 921a 50 DOLLARS
10.00 g., 0.9999 Platinum 0.3215 oz. APW, 27 mm. **Ruler:** Elizabeth II **Subject:** Christmas

Date	Mintage	VF20	XF40	MS60	MS63	MS65
1997	100	PF65 675				

KM# 926 50 DOLLARS
10.00 g., 0.999 Gold 0.3212 oz. AGW **Ruler:** Elizabeth II **Subject:** Christmas **Rev:** Angel with book and vine

Date	Mintage	VF20	XF40	MS60	MS63	MS65
1997	500	PF65 575				

KM# 926a 50 DOLLARS
10.00 g., 0.999 Platinum 0.3212 oz. APW **Ruler:** Elizabeth II **Subject:** Christmas **Rev:** Angel with book and vine

Date	Mintage	VF20	XF40	MS60	MS63	MS65
1997 Proof	500	—	—	—	—	650

KM# 929 50 DOLLARS
10.00 g., 0.999 Gold 0.3212 oz. AGW **Ruler:** Elizabeth II **Rev:** Betty Boop in color

Date	Mintage	VF20	XF40	MS60	MS63	MS65
1998	—	PF65 575				

KM# 461 75 DOLLARS
15.00 g., 0.9995 Platinum 0.482 oz. APW **Ruler:** Elizabeth II **Subject:** Love Angels

Date	Mintage	VF20	XF40	MS60	MS63	MS65
1997	250	PF65 950				

KM# 922 75 DOLLARS
15.00 g., 0.999 Gold 0.4818 oz. AGW, 30 mm. **Ruler:** Elizabeth II **Subject:** Christmas

Date	Mintage	VF20	XF40	MS60	MS63	MS65
1997	100	PF65 875				

KM# 922a 75 DOLLARS
15.00 g., 0.9999 Platinum 0.4822 oz. APW, 30 mm. **Ruler:** Elizabeth II **Subject:** Christmas

Date	Mintage	VF20	XF40	MS60	MS63	MS65
1997	100	PF65 1,000				

KM# 927 75 DOLLARS
15.00 g., 0.999 Gold 0.4818 oz. AGW **Ruler:** Elizabeth II **Subject:** Christmas **Rev:** Angel with book and vine

Date	Mintage	VF20	XF40	MS60	MS63	MS65
1997	500	PF65 850				

KM# 927a 75 DOLLARS
15.00 g., 0.999 Platinum 0.4818 oz. APW **Ruler:** Elizabeth II **Subject:** Christmas **Rev:** Angel with book and vine

Date	Mintage	VF20	XF40	MS60	MS63	MS65
1997	500	PF65 950				

KM# 930 75 DOLLARS
15.00 g., 0.999 Gold 0.4818 oz. AGW **Ruler:** Elizabeth II **Rev:** Popeye in color

Date	Mintage	VF20	XF40	MS60	MS63	MS65
1998	—	PF65 900				

KM# 12 100 DOLLARS
16.72 g., 0.917 Gold 0.4929 oz. AGW, 27 mm. **Ruler:** Elizabeth II **Subject:** Winston Churchill Centenary **Obv:** Young bust right, date below **Rev:** Churchill head at right looking left, Big Ben and flag at left, denomination below

Date	Mintage	VF20	XF40	MS60	MS63	MS65
1974	368	—	—	—	—	860
1974	1,453	PF65 870				

KM# 13 100 DOLLARS
9.60 g., 0.900 Gold 0.2778 oz. AGW, 26 mm. **Ruler:** Elizabeth II **Subject:** Bicentennial - Return of Captain James Cook from Second Pacific Voyage **Obv:** Young bust right, date below **Rev:** Ship divides portraits in cameos, denomination below

Date	Mintage	VF20	XF40	MS60	MS63	MS65
1975 FM (M)	100	—	—	—	—	525
1975 FM (U)	7,447	—	—	—	—	495
1975 FM	17,000	PF65 480				

KM# 16 100 DOLLARS
9.60 g., 0.900 Gold 0.2778 oz. AGW, 26 mm. **Ruler:** Elizabeth II **Subject:** U.S. Bicentennial **Obv:** Young bust right, date below **Rev:** Conjoined heads of Benjamin Franklin and James Cook left, denomination below

Date	Mintage	VF20	XF40	MS60	MS63	MS65
1976 FM (M)	50	—	—	—	—	540
1976 FM	9,373	PF65 480				
1976 FM (U)	852	—	—	—	—	495

KM# 19 100 DOLLARS
9.60 g., 0.900 Gold 0.2778 oz. AGW, 26 mm. **Ruler:** Elizabeth II **Subject:** Queen's Silver Jubilee **Obv:** Young bust right, date below **Rev:** Crowned EIIR monogram

Date	Mintage	VF20	XF40	MS60	MS63	MS65
1977 FM (M)	50	—	—	—	—	540
1977 FM	9,364	PF65 480				
1977 FM (P)	562	—	—	—	—	495

KM# 25 100 DOLLARS
9.60 g., 0.900 Gold 0.2778 oz. AGW, 26 mm. **Ruler:** Elizabeth II **Subject:** Membership in Commonwealth of Nations **Obv:** Young bust right, date below **Rev:** Tangaroa head left, divides denomination, circle surrounds

Date	Mintage	VF20	XF40	MS60	MS63	MS65
1979 FM	3,367	PF65 495				
1979 FM (U)	400	—	—	—	—	525

KM# 74 100 DOLLARS
1.24 g., 0.999 Gold 0.040 oz. AGW **Ruler:** Elizabeth II **Subject:** Endangered World Wildlife **Obv:** Crowned head right, date below **Rev:** American bald eagle head left, beak open, denomination below

Date	Mintage	VF20	XF40	MS60	MS63	MS65
1990 Prooflike	1,320	—	—	—	65.00	70.00

KM# 75 100 DOLLARS
1.24 g., 0.999 Gold 0.040 oz. AGW, 14 mm. **Ruler:** Elizabeth II **Subject:** Endangered World Wildlife **Obv:** Crowned head right, date below **Rev:** Bison

Date	Mintage	VF20	XF40	MS60	MS63	MS65
1990 Prooflike	320	—	—	—	70.00	75.00

KM# 76 100 DOLLARS
1.24 g., 0.999 Gold 0.040 oz. AGW, 14 mm. **Ruler:** Elizabeth II **Subject:** Endangered World Wildlife **Obv:** Crowned head right, date below **Rev:** Elephant

Date	Mintage	VF20	XF40	MS60	MS63	MS65
1990 Prooflike	720	—	—	—	67.00	73.00

KM# 77 100 DOLLARS
1.24 g., 0.999 Gold 0.040 oz. AGW, 14 mm. **Ruler:** Elizabeth II **Subject:** Endangered World Wildlife **Obv:** Crowned head right, date below **Rev:** Tiger

Date	Mintage	VF20	XF40	MS60	MS63	MS65
1990 Prooflike	420	—	—	—	80.00	90.00

KM# 78 100 DOLLARS
1.24 g., 0.999 Gold 0.040 oz. AGW, 14 mm. **Ruler:** Elizabeth II **Subject:** Endangered World Wildlife **Obv:** Crowned head right, date below **Rev:** European Mouflon

Date	Mintage	VF20	XF40	MS60	MS63	MS65
1990 Prooflike	320	—	—	—	70.00	75.00

KM# 92 100 DOLLARS
3.46 g., 0.900 Gold 0.100 oz. AGW, 18 mm. **Ruler:** Elizabeth II **Subject:** 1992 Summer Olympics **Obv:** Crowned head right, date below **Rev:** Bicyclists, denomination below

Date	Mintage	VF20	XF40	MS60	MS63	MS65
1990	—	PF65 175				

KM# 113 100 DOLLARS
172.11 g., 0.925 Silver 5.1185 oz. ASW, 65 mm. **Ruler:** Elizabeth II **Subject:** 500 Years of America **Obv:** Crowned head right, date below **Rev:** Ferdinand Magellan **Note:** Illustration reduced.

Date	Mintage	VF20	XF40	MS60	MS63	MS65
1990	Est. 3000	PF65 185				

KM# 297 100 DOLLARS
155.65 g., 0.999 Silver 4.9993 oz. ASW **Ruler:** Elizabeth II **Subject:** Endangered Wildlife **Obv:** Crowned head right, date below **Rev:** Three elephants **Note:** Illustration reduced.

Date	Mintage	VF20	XF40	MS60	MS63	MS65
1991	—	PF65 200				

KM# 319 100 DOLLARS
170.60 g., 0.925 Silver 5.0735 oz. ASW, 65 mm. **Ruler:** Elizabeth II **Subject:** 500 Years of America **Obv:** Crowned head right, date below **Rev:** Mt. Rushmore, eagle with wings spread below, denomination at bottom **Note:** Illustration reduced.

Date	Mintage	VF20	XF40	MS60	MS63	MS65
1991	—	PF65 175				

KM# 320 100 DOLLARS
170.60 g., 0.925 Silver 5.0735 oz. ASW **Ruler:** Elizabeth II **Subject:** 500 Years of America **Obv:** Crowned head right, date below **Rev:** Bust of Columbus at left facing right, three ships at right, denomination below **Note:** Illustration reduced.

Date	Mintage	VF20	XF40	MS60	MS63	MS65
1992	—	PF65 175				

KM# 819 100 DOLLARS
15.55 g., 0.9999 Gold 0.4999 oz. AGW **Ruler:** Elizabeth II **Rev:** Papillon dog

Date	Mintage	VF20	XF40	MS60	MS63	MS65
1992	322	PF65 875				

KM# 158 100 DOLLARS
155.52 g., 0.999 Silver 4.995 oz. ASW **Ruler:** Elizabeth II **Subject:** Endangered Wildlife **Obv:** Crowned head right, date below **Rev:** Manchurian cranes **Note:** Illustration reduced.

Date	Mintage	VF20	XF40	MS60	MS63	MS65
1993	—	PF65 185				

KM# 159 100 DOLLARS
155.52 g., 0.999 Silver 4.995 oz. ASW **Ruler:** Elizabeth II **Subject:** 500 Years of America **Obv:** Crowned head right, date below **Rev:** Hudson's "Half Moon" and New York City skyline, denomination below **Note:** Illustration reduced.

Date	Mintage	VF20	XF40	MS60	MS63	MS65
1993	—	PF65 175				

KM# 250 100 DOLLARS
7.78 g., 0.999 Platinum 0.2498 oz. APW **Ruler:** Elizabeth II **Obv:** Crowned head right, date below **Rev:** Javelin throwing

Date	Mintage	VF20	XF40	MS60	MS63	MS65
1995	Est. 1000	PF65 550				

KM# 824 100 DOLLARS
8.00 g., 0.999 Gold 0.2569 oz. AGW **Ruler:** Elizabeth II **Subject:** Year of the Pig **Note:** S#824.

Date	Mintage	VF20	XF40	MS60	MS63	MS65
1995 PM	Est. 8980	—	—	—	—	475

KM# 293 100 DOLLARS
7.78 g., 0.999 Gold 0.2499 oz. AGW **Ruler:** Elizabeth II **Subject:** Olympic National Park **Obv:** Crowned head right, date below **Rev:** Eagles head right, denomination below

Date	Mintage	VF20	XF40	MS60	MS63	MS65
1996	—	PF65 450				

KM# 294 100 DOLLARS
7.78 g., 0.999 Gold 0.2499 oz. AGW **Ruler:** Elizabeth II **Subject:** Yellowstone National Park **Obv:** Crowned head right, date below **Rev:** Grizzly Bear, denomination below

Date	Mintage	VF20	XF40	MS60	MS63	MS65
1996	—	PF65 450				

KM# 300 100 DOLLARS
15.00 g., 0.9999 Gold 0.4822 oz. AGW **Ruler:** Elizabeth II **Subject:** Year of the Mouse **Obv:** Crowned head right, date below **Rev:** Mickey Mouse sailboarding, denomination below

Date	Mintage	VF20	XF40	MS60	MS63	MS65
1996	—	PF65 850				

KM# 388 100 DOLLARS
7.78 g., 0.999 Gold 0.2499 oz. AGW, 22 mm. **Ruler:** Elizabeth II **Subject:** Yellowstone National Park **Obv:** Crowned head right, date below **Rev:** Bear on tree branch **Edge:** Reeded

Date	Mintage	VF20	XF40	MS60	MS63	MS65
1996	—	PF65 450				

KM# 842 100 DOLLARS
15.00 g., 0.999 Gold 0.4818 oz. AGW **Ruler:** Elizabeth II **Subject:** Year of the mouse **Note:** S#322.

Date	Mintage	VF20	XF40	MS60	MS63	MS65
1996	—	PF65 850				

KM# 854 100 DOLLARS
7.78 g., 0.999 Gold 0.2499 oz. AGW **Ruler:** Elizabeth II **Subject:** Theodore Roosevelt National Park **Rev:** Bison

Date	Mintage	VF20	XF40	MS60	MS63	MS65
1997	—	PF65 425				

KM# 861 100 DOLLARS
7.78 g., 0.999 Gold 0.2499 oz. AGW **Ruler:** Elizabeth II **Subject:** Great Smoky Mountains National Park **Rev:** Red wolf **Note:** S#399.

Date	Mintage	VF20	XF40	MS60	MS63	MS65
1997	—	PF65 425				

KM# 871 100 DOLLARS
7.78 g., 0.999 Gold 0.2499 oz. AGW **Ruler:** Elizabeth II **Subject:** Hawaii Volcano National Park

Date	Mintage	VF20	XF40	MS60	MS63	MS65
1997	—	PF65 425				

KM# 880 100 DOLLARS
7.78 g., 0.999 Gold 0.2499 oz. AGW **Ruler:** Elizabeth II **Subject:** Crater Lake National Park

Date	Mintage	VF20	XF40	MS60	MS63	MS65
1997	—	PF65 425				

KM# 908 100 DOLLARS
7.78 g., 0.999 Gold 0.2499 oz. AGW **Ruler:** Elizabeth II **Subject:** Grand Portage National Monument **Rev:** North American Reindeer

Date	Mintage	VF20	XF40	MS60	MS63	MS65
1997	—	PF65 425				

KM# 916 100 DOLLARS
7.78 g., 0.999 Gold 0.2499 oz. AGW **Ruler:** Elizabeth II **Subject:** Yosemite National Park **Rev:** Waterfall

Date	Mintage	VF20	XF40	MS60	MS63	MS65
1997	—	PF65 425				

KM# 940 100 DOLLARS
7.78 g., 0.999 Gold 0.2499 oz. AGW **Ruler:** Elizabeth II **Subject:** Petrified Forest National Park **Rev:** Pronghorn

Date	Mintage	VF20	XF40	MS60	MS63	MS65
1998	—	PF65 425				

KM# 949 100 DOLLARS
7.78 g., 0.999 Gold 0.2499 oz. AGW **Ruler:** Elizabeth II **Subject:** Glacier Bay National Park and Preserve **Rev:** Humpback whale

Date	Mintage	VF20	XF40	MS60	MS63	MS65
1998	—	PF65 425				

KM# 958 100 DOLLARS
7.78 g., 0.999 Gold 0.2499 oz. AGW **Ruler:** Elizabeth II **Subject:** North Cascades National Park **Rev:** Northern Lights

Date	Mintage	VF20	XF40	MS60	MS63	MS65
1998	—	PF65 425				

KM# 967 100 DOLLARS
7.78 g., 0.999 Gold 0.2499 oz. AGW **Ruler:** Elizabeth II **Subject:** Grand Canyon National Park **Rev:** California Condor

Date	Mintage	VF20	XF40	MS60	MS63	MS65
1998	—	PF65 425				

KM# 977 100 DOLLARS
7.78 g., 0.999 Gold 0.2499 oz. AGW **Ruler:** Elizabeth II **Subject:** Gulf Islands National Seashore

Date	Mintage	VF20	XF40	MS60	MS63	MS65
1998	—	PF65 425				

KM# 987 100 DOLLARS
7.78 g., 0.999 Gold 0.2499 oz. AGW **Ruler:** Elizabeth II **Subject:** Big Cypress National Preserve **Rev:** Puma

Date	Mintage	VF20	XF40	MS60	MS63	MS65
1998	—	PF65 425				

KM# 997 100 DOLLARS
7.78 g., 0.999 Gold 0.2499 oz. AGW **Ruler:** Elizabeth II **Subject:** Everglades National Park **Rev:** Crocodile

Date	Mintage	VF20	XF40	MS60	MS63	MS65
1998	—	PF65 425				

KM# 1007 100 DOLLARS
7.78 g., 0.999 Gold 0.2499 oz. AGW **Ruler:** Elizabeth II **Subject:** Wind Cave National Park **Rev:** Swift Fox

Date	Mintage	VF20	XF40	MS60	MS63	MS65
1998	—	PF65 425				

KM# 1017 100 DOLLARS
7.78 g., 0.999 Gold 0.2499 oz. AGW **Ruler:** Elizabeth II **Subject:** Bryce Canyon National Park **Rev:** Prairie Dog

Date	Mintage	VF20	XF40	MS60	MS63	MS65
1998	—	PF65 425				

KM# 1027 100 DOLLARS
7.78 g., 0.999 Gold 0.2499 oz. AGW **Ruler:** Elizabeth II **Subject:** Gates of the Arctic National Park and Preserve **Rev:** Falcon

Date	Mintage	VF20	XF40	MS60	MS63	MS65
1998	—	PF65 425				

KM# 1037 100 DOLLARS
7.78 g., 0.999 Gold 0.2499 oz. AGW **Ruler:** Elizabeth II **Subject:** Badlands National Park **Rev:** Black-footed Ferret

Date	Mintage	VF20	XF40	MS60	MS63	MS65
1998	—	PF65 425				

KM# 1046 100 DOLLARS
7.78 g., 0.999 Gold 0.2499 oz. AGW **Ruler:** Elizabeth II **Subject:** Grand Teton National Park **Rev:** Whooping Crane

Date	Mintage	VF20	XF40	MS60	MS63	MS65
1998	—	PF65 425				

KM# 1056 100 DOLLARS
7.75 g., 0.999 Gold 0.2489 oz. AGW **Ruler:** Elizabeth II **Subject:** Kajoko Honokhau National Historic Park **Rev:** Hawaiian Duck

Date	Mintage	VF20	XF40	MS60	MS63	MS65
1998	—	PF65 425				

KM# 1066 100 DOLLARS
7.78 g., 0.999 Gold 0.2499 oz. AGW **Ruler:** Elizabeth II **Subject:** Virgin Islands National Park **Rev:** Brown Pelican

Date	Mintage	VF20	XF40	MS60	MS63	MS65
1998	—	PF65 425				

KM# 1076 100 DOLLARS
7.78 g., 0.999 Gold 0.2499 oz. AGW **Ruler:** Elizabeth II **Subject:** Mammoth Cave National Park **Rev:** Grey Bat

Date	Mintage	VF20	XF40	MS60	MS63	MS65
1998	—	PF65 425				

KM# 1086 100 DOLLARS
7.78 g., 0.999 Gold 0.2499 oz. AGW **Ruler:** Elizabeth II **Subject:** Rocky Mountain National Park **Rev:** Purple trout

Date	Mintage	VF20	XF40	MS60	MS63	MS65
1998	—	PF65 425				

KM# 826 150 DOLLARS
10.00 g., 0.999 Gold 0.3212 oz. AGW **Ruler:** Elizabeth II **Subject:** Year of the Pig **Note:** S#291.

Date	Mintage	VF20	XF40	MS60	MS63	MS65
1995	—	PF65 525				

KM# 827 150 DOLLARS
10.00 g., 0.999 Gold 0.3212 oz. AGW **Ruler:** Elizabeth II **Subject:** Year of the Pig **Note:** S#292.

Date	Mintage	VF20	XF40	MS60	MS63	MS65
1995	—	PF65 525				

KM# 828 150 DOLLARS
10.00 g., 0.999 Gold 0.3212 oz. AGW **Ruler:** Elizabeth II **Subject:** Year of the Pig. **Note:** S#293.

Date	Mintage	VF20	XF40	MS60	MS63	MS65
1995	—	PF65 525				

KM# 836 150 DOLLARS
10.00 g., 0.999 Gold 0.3212 oz. AGW **Ruler:** Elizabeth II **Subject:** World War II, Japan invades China **Note:** S#301.

Date	Mintage	VF20	XF40	MS60	MS63	MS65
1995	—	PF65 525				

KM# 837 150 DOLLARS
10.00 g., 0.999 Gold 0.3212 oz. AGW **Ruler:** Elizabeth II **Subject:** WWII, Attack on Pearl Harbor **Note:** S#302.

Date	Mintage	VF20	XF40	MS60	MS63	MS65
1995	—	PF65 525				

KM# 838 150 DOLLARS
10.00 g., 0.999 Gold 0.3212 oz. AGW **Ruler:** Elizabeth II **Subject:** WWII, Allied landing at Normandy **Note:** S#303.

Date	Mintage	VF20	XF40	MS60	MS63	MS65
1995	—	PF65 525				

KM# 839 150 DOLLARS
10.00 g., 0.999 Gold 0.3212 oz. AGW **Ruler:** Elizabeth II **Subject:** WWII, Atom Bomb at Hiroshima

Date	Mintage	VF20	XF40	MS60	MS63	MS65
1995	—	PF65 525				

KM# 840 150 DOLLARS
10.00 g., 0.999 Gold 0.3212 oz. AGW **Ruler:** Elizabeth II **Subject:** WWII, Flag raising at Iwo Jima **Note:** S#305.

Date	Mintage	VF20	XF40	MS60	MS63	MS65
1995	—	PF65 525				

KM# 22 200 DOLLARS
16.60 g., 0.900 Gold 0.4803 oz. AGW **Ruler:** Elizabeth II **Subject:** Bicentennial - Discovery of Hawaii by Capt. James Cook **Obv:** Young bust right, date below **Rev:** Capt. James Cook with crew, denomination below

Date	Mintage	VF20	XF40	MS60	MS63	MS65
1978 FM	3,216	PF65 830				
1978 FM (M)	26	—	—	—	—	900
1978 FM (U)	621	—	—	—	—	850

KM# 26 200 DOLLARS
16.60 g., 0.900 Gold 0.4803 oz. AGW **Ruler:** Elizabeth II **Subject:** Legacy of Capt. James Cook **Obv:** Young bust right, date below **Rev:** Bird flying right above banner, denomination below

Date	Mintage	VF20	XF40	MS60	MS63	MS65
1979 FM	1,939	PF65 850				
1979 FM (U)	271	—	—	—	—	875

KM# 29 200 DOLLARS
15.98 g., 0.917 Gold 0.4711 oz. AGW **Ruler:** Elizabeth II **Subject:** International Year of the Scout **Obv:** Young bust right, date below **Rev:** Circle of stars around symbol at center, dates at lower left, denomination at lower right

Date	Mintage	VF20	XF40	MS60	MS63	MS65
1983	—	PF65 850				

KM# 820 200 DOLLARS
31.11 g., 0.9999 Gold 0.9999 oz. AGW **Ruler:** Elizabeth II **Rev:** Papillon dog

Date	Mintage	VF20	XF40	MS60	MS63	MS65
1992	Est. 59	PF65 1,800				

KM# 251 200 DOLLARS
15.55 g., 0.999 Platinum 0.4995 oz. APW **Ruler:** Elizabeth II **Obv:** Crowned head right, date below **Rev:** Wrestling

Date	Mintage	VF20	XF40	MS60	MS63	MS65
1995	1,000	PF65 950				

KM# 845 200 DOLLARS
31.16 g., 0.999 Gold 1.0009 oz. AGW **Ruler:** Elizabeth II **Subject:** Mother's Day **Rev:** Flower

Date	Mintage	VF20	XF40	MS60	MS63	MS65
1996	—	PF65 1,775				

KM# 23 250 DOLLARS
17.90 g., 0.900 Gold 0.5179 oz. AGW **Ruler:** Elizabeth II **Subject:** 250th Anniversary - Birth of James Cook **Obv:** Young bust right, date below **Rev:** Head left, denomination below

Date	Mintage	VF20	XF40	MS60	MS63	MS65
1978 FM (M)	25	—	—	—	1,000	—
1978 FM (U)	200	—	—	—	950	—
1978 FM	1,757	PF63 900				

KM# 50 250 DOLLARS
7.78 g., 0.999 Gold 0.2497 oz. AGW **Ruler:** Elizabeth II **Subject:** 500 Years of America **Obv:** Crowned head right, date below **Rev:** Cameos of Cook and Franklin flank sailing ship, denomination below

Date	Mintage	VF20	XF40	MS60	MS63	MS65
1989	3,000	PF65 425				
1990	3,000	PF65 425				

KM# 51 250 DOLLARS
7.78 g., 0.999 Gold 0.2497 oz. AGW **Ruler:** Elizabeth II **Subject:** 500 Years of America **Obv:** Crowned head right, date below **Rev:** Amerigo Vespucci bust at right looking left, ship at left

Date	Mintage	VF20	XF40	MS60	MS63	MS65
1990	Est. 3000	PF65 425				

KM# 82 250 DOLLARS
9.60 g., 0.900 Gold 0.2778 oz. AGW **Ruler:** Elizabeth II **Subject:** Save the Children **Obv:** Crowned head right, date below **Rev:** Child behind large shell, denomination below

Date	Mintage	VF20	XF40	MS60	MS63	MS65
1990	3,000	PF65 475				

KM# 814 250 DOLLARS
7.75 g., 0.999 Gold 0.2489 oz. AGW, 30 mm. **Ruler:** Elizabeth II **Rev:** Hernando de Soto and ship

Date	Mintage	VF20	XF40	MS60	MS63	MS65
1990	Est. 3000	PF65 475				

KM# 71 250 DOLLARS
7.78 g., 0.999 Gold 0.2497 oz. AGW **Ruler:** Elizabeth II **Subject:** 1992 Olympics **Obv:** Crowned head right, date below **Rev:** Torch, denomination below

Date	Mintage	VF20	XF40	MS60	MS63	MS65
1991	Est. 5000	PF65 450				

KM# 825 250 DOLLARS
18.00 g., 0.999 Gold 0.5781 oz. AGW **Ruler:** Elizabeth II **Subject:** Year of the Pig **Note:** S#290.

Date	Mintage	VF20	XF40	MS60	MS63	MS65
1995 PM	3,980	—	—	—	1,000	1,100

KM# 295 250 DOLLARS
31.10 g., 0.999 Gold 0.999 oz. AGW **Ruler:** Elizabeth II **Subject:** Olympic National Park **Obv:** Crowned head right, date below **Rev:** Multicolor bald eagle in flight

Date	Mintage	VF20	XF40	MS60	MS63	MS65
1996	1,000	PF65 1,750				

KM# 296 250 DOLLARS
31.10 g., 0.999 Gold 0.999 oz. AGW **Ruler:** Elizabeth II **Subject:** Yellowstone National Park **Obv:** Crowned head right, date below **Rev:** Multicolored grizzly bear and cub

Date	Mintage	VF20	XF40	MS60	MS63	MS65
1996	1,000	PF65 1,750				

KM# 855 250 DOLLARS
31.11 g., 0.999 Gold 0.999 oz. AGW **Ruler:** Elizabeth II **Subject:** Theodore Roosevelt National Park **Rev:** Bison **Note:** S#390.

Date	Mintage	VF20	XF40	MS60	MS63	MS65
1997	—	PF65 1,725				

KM# 862 250 DOLLARS
31.11 g., 0.999 Gold 0.999 oz. AGW **Ruler:** Elizabeth II **Subject:** Great Smoky Mountains National Park **Rev:** Red wolf

Date	Mintage	VF20	XF40	MS60	MS63	MS65
1997	—	PF65 1,750				

KM# 872 250 DOLLARS
31.11 g., 0.999 Gold 0.999 oz. AGW **Ruler:** Elizabeth II **Subject:** Hawaii Volcano National Park **Note:** S#410.

Date	Mintage	VF20	XF40	MS60	MS63	MS65
1997	—	PF65 1,800				

KM# 881 250 DOLLARS
31.11 g., 0.999 Gold 0.999 oz. AGW **Ruler:** Elizabeth II **Subject:** Crater Lake National Park

Date	Mintage	VF20	XF40	MS60	MS63	MS65
1997	—	PF65 1,800				

KM# 909 250 DOLLARS
31.11 g., 0.999 Gold 0.999 oz. AGW **Ruler:** Elizabeth II **Subject:** Grand Portage National Monument **Rev:** North American Reindeer

Date	Mintage	VF20	XF40	MS60	MS63	MS65
1997	—	PF65 1,800				

KM# 917 250 DOLLARS
31.11 g., 0.999 Silver 0.999 oz. ASW **Ruler:** Elizabeth II **Subject:** Yosemite National Park **Rev:** Waterfall

Date	Mintage	VF20	XF40	MS60	MS63	MS65
1997	—	PF65 1,800				

KM# 941 250 DOLLARS
31.11 g., 0.999 Gold 0.999 oz. AGW **Ruler:** Elizabeth II **Subject:** Petrified Forest National Park **Rev:** Pronghorn

Date	Mintage	VF20	XF40	MS60	MS63	MS65
1998	—	PF65 1,800				

KM# 950 250 DOLLARS
31.11 g., 0.999 Gold 0.999 oz. AGW **Ruler:** Elizabeth II **Subject:** Glacier Bay National Park and Preserve **Rev:** Humpback whale

Date	Mintage	VF20	XF40	MS60	MS63	MS65
1998	—	PF65 1,800				

KM# 959 250 DOLLARS
31.11 g., 0.999 Gold 0.999 oz. AGW **Ruler:** Elizabeth II **Subject:** North Cascades National Park **Rev:** Northern Lights

Date	Mintage	VF20	XF40	MS60	MS63	MS65
1998	—	PF65 1,800				

KM# 968 250 DOLLARS
31.11 g., 0.999 Gold 0.999 oz. AGW **Ruler:** Elizabeth II **Subject:** Grand Canyon National Park **Rev:** California Condor

Date	Mintage	VF20	XF40	MS60	MS63	MS65
1998	—	PF65 1,800				

KM# 978 250 DOLLARS
31.11 g., 0.999 Gold 0.999 oz. AGW **Ruler:** Elizabeth II **Subject:** Gulf Islands National Seashore

Date	Mintage	VF20	XF40	MS60	MS63	MS65
1998	—	PF65 1,800				

KM# 988 250 DOLLARS
31.11 g., 0.999 Gold 0.999 oz. AGW **Ruler:** Elizabeth II **Subject:** Big Cypress National Preserve **Rev:** Puma

Date	Mintage	VF20	XF40	MS60	MS63	MS65
1998	—	PF65 1,800				

KM# 998 250 DOLLARS
31.11 g., 0.999 Gold 0.999 oz. AGW **Ruler:** Elizabeth II **Subject:** Everglades National Park **Rev:** Crocodile

Date	Mintage	VF20	XF40	MS60	MS63	MS65
1998	—	PF65 1,800				

KM# 1008 250 DOLLARS
31.11 g., 0.999 Gold 0.999 oz. AGW **Ruler:** Elizabeth II **Subject:** Wind Cave National Park **Rev:** Swift Fox

Date	Mintage	VF20	XF40	MS60	MS63	MS65
1998	—	PF65 1,800				

KM# 1018 250 DOLLARS
31.11 g., 0.999 Gold 0.999 oz. AGW **Ruler:** Elizabeth II **Subject:** Bryce Canyon National Park **Rev:** Prairie Dog

Date	Mintage	VF20	XF40	MS60	MS63	MS65
1998	—	PF65 1,800				

KM# 1028 250 DOLLARS
31.11 g., 0.999 Gold 0.999 oz. AGW **Ruler:** Elizabeth II **Subject:** Gates of the Arctic National Park and Preserve **Rev:** Falcon

Date	Mintage	VF20	XF40	MS60	MS63	MS65
1998	—	PF65 1,800				

KM# 1038 250 DOLLARS
31.11 g., 0.999 Gold 0.999 oz. AGW **Ruler:** Elizabeth II **Subject:** Badlands National Park **Rev:** Black-footed Ferret

Date	Mintage	VF20	XF40	MS60	MS63	MS65
1998	—	PF65 1,800				

KM# 1047 250 DOLLARS
31.11 ,g., 0.999 Gold 0.999 oz. AGW **Ruler:** Elizabeth II **Subject:** Grand Teton National Park **Rev:** Whooping Crane

Date	Mintage	VF20	XF40	MS60	MS63	MS65
1998	—	PF65 1,800				

KM# 1057 250 DOLLARS
31.11 g., 0.999 Gold 0.999 oz. AGW **Ruler:** Elizabeth II **Subject:** Kajoko Honokhau National Historic Park **Rev:** Hawaiian Duck

Date	Mintage	VF20	XF40	MS60	MS63	MS65
1998	—	PF65 1,800				

KM# 1067 250 DOLLARS
31.11 g., 0.999 Gold 0.999 oz. AGW **Ruler:** Elizabeth II **Subject:** Virgin Islands National Park **Rev:** Brown Pelican

Date	Mintage	VF20	XF40	MS60	MS63	MS65
1998	—	PF65 1,800				

KM# 1077 250 DOLLARS
31.11 g., 0.999 Gold 0.999 oz. AGW **Ruler:** Elizabeth II **Subject:** Mammoth Cave National Park **Rev:** Grey Bat

Date	Mintage	VF20	XF40	MS60	MS63	MS65
1998	—	PF65 1,800				

KM# 1087 250 DOLLARS
31.11 g., 0.999 Gold 0.999 oz. AGW **Ruler:** Elizabeth II **Subject:** Rocky Mountain National Park **Rev:** Purple trout

Date	Mintage	VF20	XF40	MS60	MS63	MS65
1998	—	PF65 1,800				

KM# 313 500 DOLLARS
14.74 g., 0.999 Platinum 0.4734 oz. APW **Ruler:** Elizabeth II **Obv:** Crowned head right, date below **Rev:** Marco Polo, oriental building in background, denomination below

Date	Mintage	VF20	XF40	MS60	MS63	MS65
1995	Est. 1000	PF65 875				

KM# 415 500 DOLLARS
14.74 g., 0.999 Platinum 0.4734 oz. APW, 25.8 mm. **Ruler:** Elizabeth II **Obv:** Crowned head right, date below **Rev:** Two of Ferdinand Magellan's ships **Edge:** Reeded

Date	Mintage	VF20	XF40	MS60	MS63	MS65
1995 FM	1,000	PF65 875				

KM# 829 500 DOLLARS
30.00 g., 0.999 Gold 0.9636 oz. AGW **Ruler:** Elizabeth II **Subject:** Year of the Pig **Note:** S#294.

Date	Mintage	VF20	XF40	MS60	MS63	MS65
1995	—	PF65 1,700				

KM# 830 500 DOLLARS
30.00 g., 0.999 Gold 0.9636 oz. AGW **Ruler:** Elizabeth II **Subject:** Year of the Pig

Date	Mintage	VF20	XF40	MS60	MS63	MS65
1995	—	PF65 1,700				

KM# 831 500 DOLLARS
30.00 g., 0.999 Gold 0.9636 oz. AGW **Ruler:** Elizabeth II **Subject:** Year of the Pig **Note:** S#296.

Date	Mintage	VF20	XF40	MS60	MS63	MS65
1995	—	PF65 1,700				

PIEDFORT

KM#	Date	Mintage	Identification	Mkt Val
P1	1985	250	Dollar. 0.925. Silver.	250
P2	1986	500	Dollar. 0.925. Silver.	95.00
P3	1986	500	Dollar. 0.925. Silver. Reeded.	95.00

TRIAL STRIKES

KM#	Date	Mintage	Identification	Mkt Val
TS1	ND (1976)	—	20 Cents. Copper-Nickel. KM#14. Reverse of KM#14.	—

MINT SETS

KM#	Date	Mintage	Identification	Issue Price	Mkt Val
MS1	1972 (7)	11,045	KM1-5, 6.1, 7	7.50	9.50
MS2	1973 (9)	3,652	KM1-5, 6.1, 7, 9, 10	52.50	75.00
MS3	1973 (7)	3,023	KM1-5, 6.1, 7	10.00	15.00
MS4	1973 (2)	2,348	KM9, 10	45.00	65.00
MS5	1974 (9)	913	KM1-5, 6.1, 7. 9. 10	58.50	80.00
MS6	1974 (7)	2,087	KM1-5, 6.1, 7	10.00	15.00
MS7	1974 (2)	587	KM9, 10	45.00	65.00
MS8	1975 (7)	2,251	KM1-5, 6.1, 7	10.00	9.50
MS9	1976 (8)	1,066	KM1-4, 6.1,7, 14, 15	20.00	30.00
MS10	1977 (8)	1,171	KM1-4, 6.1, 7, 14, 17	20.00	32.50
MS11	1978 (8)	767	KM1a-4a, 6.2, 7a, 14a, 20	20.00	30.00
MS12	1979 (8)	500	KM1-3, 4b, 6.3 7, 14, 24	—	30.00
MS13	1981 (7)	1,100	KM1b-3b, 4c, 6.4, 7b, 14b	—	16.00
MS14	1983 (7)	—	KM1-5, 6.1, 7	—	13.50
MS15	1987 (7)	—	KM33-39	—	22.50
MS16	1988 (7)	—	KM33-35, 37-39, 41	—	22.50
MS17	1992 (7)	—	KM33-35, 37-39, 41	—	22.50
MS18	1999 (5)	5,000	KM#444-448	417	450

PROOF SETS

KM#	Date	Mintage	Identification	Issue Price	Mkt Val
PS1	1972 (7)	17,101	KM1-5, 6.1, 7	20.00	12.00
PS2	1973 (9)	7,395	KM1-5, 6.1, 7, 9-10	89.50	80.00
PS3	1973 (7)	5,136	KM1-5, 6.1, 7	29.50	14.00
PS4	1973 (2)	4,754	KM9-10	60.00	65.00
PS5	1974 (9)	4,444	KM1-5, 6.1, 7, 9-10	95.00	80.00
PS6	1974 (7)	5,300	KM1-5, 6.1, 7	32.50	14.00
PS7	1974 (2)	2,856	KM9-10	65.00	65.00
PS8	1975 (7)	21,290	KM1-5, 6.1, 7	31.50	13.50
PS9	1976 (8)	17,658	KM1-4, 6.1, 7, 14-15	40.00	30.00
PS10	1977 (8)	5,986	KM1-4, 6.1, 7, 14, 17	42.00	31.50
PS11	1978 (8)	6,287	KM1a-4a, 6.2, 7a, 14a, 20	42.00	28.50
PS12	1979 (8)	4,058	KM1-3, 4b, 6.3, 7, 14, 24	44.00	30.00
PS13	1981 (7)	9,205	KM1b-3b, 4c, 6.4, 7b, 14b	39.50	12.50
PS14	1983 (7)	10,000	KM1-5, 6.1, 7	29.95	13.50
PS15	1987 (7)	—	KM33-39	—	32.50
PSA16	1988 (25)	—	KM#61-69, 96-111	—	575
PS16	1988 (7)	—	KM33-35, 37-39, 41	—	32.50
PS17	1991 (12)	1,000	KM93, 95, 118-120, 122-128	—	300
PS18	1992 (7)	—	KM33-35, 37-39, 41	—	32.50
PS19	1994 (7)	200	KM33-35, 37-39, 41	—	37.50
PS20	1996 (3)	—	KM298-300	—	1,475
PS21	1996 (6)	—	KM284, 286, 288, 292, 294, 296	—	2,685
PS22	1998 (5)	4,000	KM314-318	185	225
PS23	1999 (3)	—	KM338-340	98.00	110
PS24	1999 (5)	4,000	KM361-365	122	225

PROOF-LIKE SETS (PL)

KM#	Date	Mintage	Identification	Issue Price	Mkt Val
PLS1	1990 (5)	—	KM74-78	325	400
PLS2	1997 (5)	250	KM#457-461	—	2,250

COSTA RICA

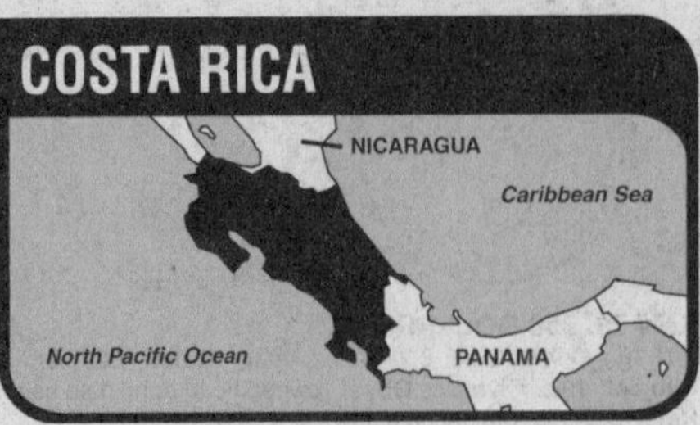

The Republic of Costa Rica, located in southern Central America between Nicaragua and Panama, has an area of 19,730 sq. mi. (51,100 sq. km.) and a population of 3.4 million. Capital: San Jose. Agriculture predominates; tourism and coffee, bananas, beef and sugar contribute heavily to the country's export earnings.

Costa Rica was discovered by Christopher Columbus in 1502, during his last voyage to the New World, and was a colony of Spain from 1522 until independence in 1821. Established as a republic in 1848, Costa Rica adopted democratic reforms in the 1870's and 80's. Today, Costa Rica remains a model of orderly democracy in Latin America, although, like most of the hemisphere - its economy is in stress.

MINT MARKS
CR - San Jose 1825-1947
(P) – Philadelphia, 1905-1961
(L) – London, 1937, 1948

ISSUING BANK INITIALS - MINTS
BCCR - Philadelphia 1951-1958,1961
BICR - Philadelphia 1935
BNCR - London 1937,1948
BNCR - San Jose 1942-1947
GCR - Philadelphia 1905-1908,1929
GCR - San Jose 1917-1941

KEY TO MINT IDENTIFICATION

Key Letter	Mint
(a)	Armant Metalurgica, Santiago, Chile
(c)	Casa de Moneda, Mexico City Mint
(cc)	Casa de Moneda, Brazil
(co)	Colombia Republican Banko
(g)	Guatemala Mint
(i)	Italcambio Mint
(p) or (P)	Philadelphia Mint, USA
(r) RCM	Royal Canadian Mint
(rm)	Royal Mint, London
(s)	San Francisco
(sj)	San Jose
(sm)	Sherrit Mint, Toronto
(v)	Vereingte Deutsche Metallwerke, Karlsruhe
(w)	Westain, Toronto

ASSAYERS' INITIALS
CY – Carlos Ygle sias, 1902
JCV – Jesus Cubrero Vargas, 1903
GCR – Gobierno de Costa Rica

MONETARY SYSTEM
8 Reales = 1 Peso
16 Pesos = 8 Escudos = 1 Onza

REPUBLIC

REFORM COINAGE

1897, 100 Centimos = 1 Colon

KM# 144 2 CENTIMOS
1.00 g., Copper-Nickel **Obv:** Large numeral above date **Rev:** Denomination above sprays **Edge:** Plain

Date	Mintage	F12	VF20	XF40	MS60	MS63
1903 (P)	630,000	0.50	1.00	3.00	10.00	15.00

Note: 274,342 of this type were used as planchets for KM178 in 1942.

KM# 145 5 CENTIMOS
1.00 g., 0.900 Silver 0.0289 oz. ASW **Obv:** National arms, date below **Rev:** Denomination within wreath **Edge:** Reeded

Date	Mintage	F12	VF20	XF40	MS60	MS63
1905 (P)	500,000	0.50	1.25	3.00	9.00	13.00
1910 (P)	400,000	0.50	1.25	3.00	9.00	15.00
1912 (P)	540,000	0.50	1.25	3.00	9.00	12.00
1914 (P)	510,000	0.50	1.25	3.00	9.00	11.00

KM# 146 10 CENTIMOS
2.00 g., 0.900 Silver 0.0579 oz. ASW, 18 mm. **Obv:** National arms, date below **Rev:** Denomination within wreath

Date	Mintage	F12	VF20	XF40	MS60	MS63
1905 (P)	400,000	1.10	1.50	5.00	15.00	25.00
1910 (P)	400,000	1.10	1.50	5.00	15.00	25.00
1912 (P)	270,000	1.10	1.50	5.00	17.00	28.00
1914 (P)	150,000	1.10	1.50	5.00	20.00	35.00

KM# 143 50 CENTIMOS
10.00 g., 0.900 Silver 0.2894 oz. ASW, 29 mm. **Obv:** National arms, date below **Rev:** Denomination within wreath

Date	Mintage	F12	VF20	XF40	MS60	MS63
1902 CY	120,000	25.00	60.00	100	300	500
1903 JCV	382,000	15.00	45.00	75.00	225	350

Note: Of the total mintage for this date, San Jose Mint struck 132,140 in 1903 and Philadelphia Mint struck an additional 250,000 in 1904 with the 1903 date; the two strikings are indistinguishable, because all the dies were reportedly made in Philadelphia.

Date	Mintage	F12	VF20	XF40	MS60	MS63
1914 (P) GCR	202,213	—	1,000	2,000	2,500	3,000

Note: Most coins dated 1914 were later counterstamped UN COLON/ 1923; See KM#164.

KM# 139 2 COLONES
1.56 g., 0.900 Gold 0.045 oz. AGW **Obv:** National arms **Rev:** Bust of Colombus right

Date	Mintage	F12	VF20	XF40	MS60	MS63
1915 (P)	5,000	57.00	90.00	110	175	215
1916 (P)	5,000	57.00	90.00	110	175	215
1921 (P)	3,000	57.00	100	130	240	325
1922 (P)	13,000	57.00	90.00	90.00	140	190
1926 (P)	15,000	57.00	90.00	85.00	125	165
1928 (P)	25,000	57.00	90.00	80.00	115	140

REFORM COINAGE

1917, 100 Centavos = 1 Colon

KM# 147 5 CENTAVOS
1.00 g., Brass **Obv:** National arms, date below **Rev:** Denomination within wreath **Edge:** Plain

Date	Mintage	F12	VF20	XF40	MS60	MS63
1917 (sj) Rare	400,000	10.00	50.00	175	500	750
1918 (sj)	1,000,000	1.00	5.00	20.00	65.00	100
1919 (sj)	500,000	1.00	5.00	20.00	65.00	100

KM# 148 10 CENTAVOS
2.00 g., 0.500 Silver 0.0322 oz. ASW, 18 mm. **Obv:** National arms, date below **Rev:** Denomination within wreath **Edge:** Reeded

Date	Mintage	F12	VF20	XF40	MS60	MS63
1917 (sj)	100,000	0.60	2.00	5.00	10.00	12.00

KM# 149.1 10 CENTAVOS
2.00 g., Brass, 18 mm. **Obv:** National arms, date below **Rev:** Denomination within wreath, GCR at lower right

Date	Mintage	F12	VF20	XF40	MS60	MS63
1917 GCR	500,000	2.00	10.00	25.00	100	175

KM# 149.2 10 CENTAVOS
2.00 g., Brass, 18 mm. **Obv:** National arms, date below **Rev:** Denomination within wreath, GCR at bottom center

Date	Mintage	F12	VF20	XF40	MS60	MS63
1917 GCR	Inc. above	1.50	6.00	25.00	75.00	200
1918 GCR	900,000	1.00	5.00	15.00	50.00	125
1919 GCR	250,000	1.00	5.00	15.00	45.00	100

KM# 150 50 CENTAVOS
10.00 g., 0.500 Silver 0.1608 oz. ASW, 29 mm. **Obv:** National arms **Note:** All but 10 examples of the 1917 issue and the complete 1918 mintage were counterstamped UN COLON/1923. See KM#165.

Date	Mintage	F12	VF20	XF40	MS60	MS63
1917 GCR	9,400	—	—	2,000	3,000	4,000
1918 GCR	30,000	—	—	—	—	—

COUNTERSTAMPED COINAGE

In the financially stressful years between 1914 and 1925 many Latin American countries saw their currencies lose much of its former purchasing power. Governments reacted in several ways: In Peru, Chile, Brazil and most of Central America, this took the form of devaluing their monetary unit relative to such standards as the U.S. dollar and Swiss franc. Costa Rica began issuing coins of .500 fine silver and brass to replace the .900 fine silver issues of the past. A decree of 1923 also made provisions for the old .900 fine silver coins to be revalued, doubling their previous face values, by dated counterstamping conducted at the San Jose Mint through 1923 and into 1924.

Obverse counterstamp: 1923 in 11mm circle.

Reverse counterstamp: 50/CENTIMOS in 11mm circle.

NOTE: The total mintage for KM#154-159 was 1,866,000 pieces.

Type VIII ï 1923

KM# 154 50 CENTIMOS
6.40 g., 0.903 Silver 0.1858 oz. ASW **Obv:** '1923' an old shield **Rev:** '50 centimos' within circle **Note:** Counterstamped on 1/4 Peso, KM#103

Date	Mintage	VG8	F12	VF20	XF40	MS60
1850 JB	—	400	700	—	—	—

KM# 155 50 CENTIMOS
6.25 g., 0.750 Silver 0.1507 oz. ASW, 25 mm. **Obv:** '1923' an old shield **Rev:** '50 centimos' in circle **Note:** Counterstamped on 25 Centavos, KM#105

Date	Mintage	G4	VG8	F12	VF20	XF40
1864 GW	—	125	225	350	—	—

KM# 156 50 CENTIMOS
6.25 g., 0.750 Silver 0.1507 oz. ASW, 25 mm. **Obv:** '1923' an old shield **Rev:** '50 centimos' in circle **Note:** Counterstamped on 25 Centavos KM#106

Date	Mintage	G4	VG8	F12	VF20	XF40
1865 GW	—	50.00	100	150	—	—
1864 GW	—	150	300	—	—	—
1875 GW	—	40.00	100	150	—	—

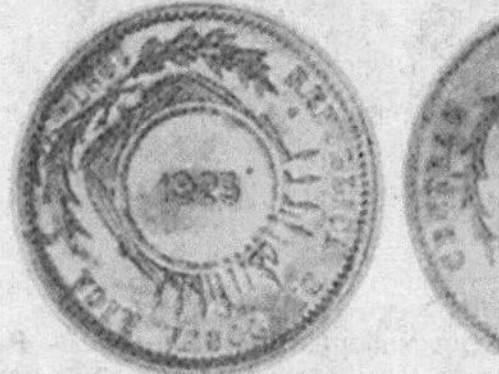

KM# 157 50 CENTIMOS
6.25 g., 0.750 Silver 0.1507 oz. ASW, 25 mm. **Obv:** '1923' an old shield **Rev:** '50 centimos' in circle **Note:** Counterstamped on 25 Centavos, KM#127.1

Date	Mintage	VG8	F12	VF20	XF40	MS60
1887 GW	—	6.00	8.00	13.00	19.00	—
1886 GW	—	8.00	10.00	15.00	25.00	—

KM# 158 50 CENTIMOS
6.25 g., 0.750 Silver 0.1507 oz. ASW, 25 mm. **Obv:** '1923' an old shield **Rev:** '50 centimos' in circle **Note:** Counterstamped on 25 Centavos, KM#127.2

Date	Mintage	VG8	F12	VF20	XF40	MS60
1887 GW	—	6.00	8.00	13.00	19.00	—
1886 GW	—	10.00	13.00	19.00	37.50	—

KM# 159 50 CENTIMOS
6.30 g., 0.750 Silver 0.1519 oz. ASW, 25 mm. **Obv:** '1923' an old shield **Rev:** '50 centimos' within circle **Note:** Counterstamped on 25 Centavos, KM#130.

Date	Mintage	F12	VF20	XF40	MS60	MS63
1890/80 HEATON	—	7.00	8.00	12.00	30.00	—
1889 HEATON	—	7.00	8.00	12.00	30.00	—
1890 HEATON	—	7.00	8.00	12.00	30.00	—
1892 HEATON	—	7.00	8.00	12.00	30.00	—
1893 HEATON	—	7.00	8.00	12.00	30.00	—

COUNTERSTAMPED COINAGE

Obverse counterstamp: 1923 in 14mm circle.

Reverse counterstamp: UN/COLON in 14mm circle.

NOTE: The total mintage for KM#162-164 was 421,810 pieces. Host dates of 1867 GW, 1870 GW and 1872 GW are listed, but no examples are currently known to exist.

Type IX ï 1923

KM# 162 COLON
12.50 g., 0.750 Silver 0.3014 oz. ASW **Note:** Counterstamped on 50 Centavos, KM#112.

Date	Mintage	VG8	F12	VF20	XF40	MS60
1866/5 GW	—	100	200	—	—	—
1865 GW	—	100	200	—	—	—
1867 GW	—	200	400	—	—	—
1870 GW	—	400	—	—	—	—
1872 GW	—	800	—	—	—	—
1875 GW	—	100	200	350	—	—

KM# 165 COLON
10.00 g., 0.500 Silver 0.1608 oz. ASW, 29 mm. **Obv:** Denomination on shield, date below **Rev:** Date within circle, wreath surrounds **Note:** Counterstamped on 50 Centavos, KM#150.

Date	Mintage	F12	VF20	XF40	MS60	MS63
1918 GCR	28,800	20.00	40.00	80.00	140	—
1917 GCR	9,390	11.00	20.00	42.00	105	—

KM# 163 COLON (Un)
12.50 g., 0.750 Silver 0.3014 oz. ASW **Obv:** Date within circle, wreath surrounds **Rev:** Liberty cap and flags above shield, turned 3/4 right, denomination within circle on shield **Note:** Counterstamped on 50 Centavos, KM#124.

Date	Mintage	F12	VF20	XF40	MS60	MS63
1885 GW	—	13.00	17.00	35.00	75.00	—
1880 GW	—	13.00	17.00	35.00	75.00	—
1886 GW	—	17.00	25.00	42.00	100	—
1887 GW	—	13.00	17.00	35.00	75.00	—
1890 GW	—	13.00	17.00	27.50	65.00	—

KM# 164 COLON (Un)
10.00 g., 0.900 Silver 0.2894 oz. ASW, 29 mm. **Obv:** Date within circle, wreath surrounds **Rev:** Denomination within circle on shield **Note:** Counterstamped on 50 Centavos, KM#143.

Date	Mintage	F12	VF20	XF40	MS60	MS63
1903 JCV	—	12.00	15.00	25.00	42.00	—
1902 CY	—	14.00	20.00	31.50	49.00	—
1914 GCR	—	12.00	17.00	27.50	42.00	—

REFORM COINAGE

1920, 100 Centimos = 1 Colon

KM# 151 5 CENTIMOS
1.00 g., Brass **Obv:** National arms, date below **Rev:** Denomination within wreath, G.C.R. lower right **Edge:** Plain

Date	Mintage	F12	VF20	XF40	MS60	MS63
1920	500,000	1.50	5.00	20.00	50.00	100
1921	500,000	1.50	5.00	25.00	60.00	125
1922	500,000	1.50	5.00	15.00	35.00	75.00
1936	1,500,000	1.00	2.00	5.00	15.00	35.00
1938	1,000,000	1.00	2.00	7.00	25.00	40.00
1940	1,300,000	1.00	2.00	4.00	15.00	35.00
1941	1,000,000	1.00	2.00	4.00	15.00	35.00

KM# 169 5 CENTIMOS
1.00 g., Bronze **Obv:** National arms, date below **Rev:** Denomination within wreath, G.C.R. lower right

Date	Mintage	VF20	XF40	MS60	MS63	MS65
1929 (P)	1,500,000	2.00	4.00	12.00	30.00	45.00

KM# 178 5 CENTIMOS
1.00 g., Copper-Nickel **Obv:** National arms, date below **Rev:** Denomination within wreath, star below divides B.N. at left from C.R. at right

Date	Mintage	F12	VF20	XF40	MS60	MS63
1942	274,000	0.65	1.00	4.00	10.00	15.00

Note: Struck over 2 Centimos, KM#144. Overstrikes with clear evidence of the undertype command a 10-15% premium.

KM# 179 5 CENTIMOS
1.00 g., Brass **Obv:** National arms, date below **Rev:** Denomination within wreath, star below divides B.N. at left from C.R. at right

Date	Mintage	F12	VF20	XF40	MS60	MS63
1942	1,730,000	0.50	1.50	3.00	12.00	35.00
1943	1,000,000	0.50	1.50	3.00	12.00	35.00
1946	1,000,000	0.50	1.50	4.00	15.00	40.00
1947	3,000,000	0.50	1.00	3.00	10.00	15.00

KM# A184 5 CENTIMOS
1.00 g., Copper-Nickel **Obv:** National arms, date below **Rev:** Denomination within wreath, star below divides B.C. at left from C.R. at right **Note:** Struck in Philadelphia 1951-52.

Date	Mintage	VF20	XF40	MS60	MS63	MS65
1951 (P)	3,000,000	0.50	1.00	2.00	3.50	5.00

KM# 184.1 5 CENTIMOS

1.00 g., Copper-Nickel **Obv:** National arms, ribbon above, date below **Rev:** Denomination within wreath, B.C.C.R. below **Note:** Struck in Philadelphia, 1952.

Date	Mintage	VF20	XF40	MS60	MS63	MS65
1951 (P)	7,000,000	0.15	0.35	0.75	1.50	2.00

KM# 184.1a 5 CENTIMOS

0.88 g., Stainless Steel, 14.92 mm. **Obv:** National arms, ribbon above, date below **Rev:** Denomination within wreath, B.C.C.R. below **Note:** 1967 date struck in San Francisco.

Date	Mintage	VF20	XF40	MS60	MS63	MS65
1953 (P)	9,040,000	—	0.10	0.25	0.40	0.75
1958 (P)	19,940,000	—	0.10	0.15	0.25	0.50
Note: Struck in 1959						
1967 (s)	10,900,000	—	0.10	0.20	0.35	0.65

KM# 184.2 5 CENTIMOS

1.00 g., Copper-Nickel, 15 mm. **Obv:** Small ships, 7 stars on arms, no flag on near ship, date below **Rev:** Denomination within wreath, B.C.C.R. below **Edge:** Reeded **Note:** Varieties exist for shields of each date.

Date	Mintage	VF20	XF40	MS60	MS63	MS65
1969	20,000,000	—	0.10	0.15	0.25	0.50
1976	—	—	0.10	0.15	0.25	0.50
1976	5,000	PF65 2.50				
1978	7,520,000	—	0.10	0.15	0.25	0.50

KM# 184.3 5 CENTIMOS

1.02 g., Copper-Nickel, 14.98 mm. **Obv:** Large ships, 7 stars on arms, flag on near ship, date below arms **Rev:** Denomination within wreath, B.C.C.R. below, '5' varieties **Note:** Dies vary for each date.

Date	Mintage	VF20	XF40	MS60	MS63	MS65
1972 (g)	12,550,000	—	0.10	0.15	0.25	0.50
1973 (g)	20,000,000	—	0.10	0.15	0.25	0.50
1976 (g) thick '5'	15,000,000	—	0.10	0.15	0.25	0.50
1976 (g) thin '5'	—	—	0.10	0.15	0.25	0.50

KM# 184.3a 5 CENTIMOS

0.98 g., Brass, 15 mm. **Obv:** National arms, ribbon above, large date below **Rev:** Denomination within wreath, B.C.C.R. below

Date	Mintage	VF20	XF40	MS60	MS63	MS65
1979 (g)	60,000,000	—	0.10	0.15	0.25	0.50

KM# 152 10 CENTIMOS

2.00 g., Brass, 18 mm. **Obv:** National arms, date below **Rev:** Denomination within wreath, G.C.R. at lower right

Date	Mintage	F12	VF20	XF40	MS60	MS63
1920 GCR	850,000	1.00	5.00	15.00	35.00	90.00
1921 GCR	750,000	1.00	5.00	20.00	50.00	125
1922 GCR	750,000	1.00	5.00	10.00	25.00	50.00

KM# 170 10 CENTIMOS

2.00 g., Bronze, 18 mm. **Obv:** National arms, date below **Rev:** Denomination within wreath, G.C.R. at bottom

Date	Mintage	F12	VF20	XF40	MS60	MS63
1929 (P) GCR	500,000	1.50	3.50	10.00	25.00	50.00

KM# 174 10 CENTIMOS

Brass, 18 mm. **Obv:** National arms, date below **Rev:** Denomination within wreath, G.C.R. below

Date	Mintage	F12	VF20	XF40	MS60	MS63
1936 (sj)	750,000	1.00	2.00	5.00	15.00	25.00
1941 (sj)	500,000	1.00	2.00	5.00	20.00	45.00

KM# 180 10 CENTIMOS

2.00 g., Brass, 18 mm. **Obv:** National arms, date below **Rev:** Denomination within wreath, B.N. - C.R. divided below

Date	Mintage	F12	VF20	XF40	MS60	MS63
1942 (sj)	1,000,000	1.00	3.00	8.00	15.00	35.00
1943 (sj)	500,000	1.00	3.00	8.00	15.00	35.00
1946 (sj)	500,000	1.00	3.00	8.00	15.00	35.00
1947 (sj)	1,500,000	0.50	1.00	3.00	8.00	15.00
Note: Edge varieties exist on 1947 strikes						

KM# 185.1 10 CENTIMOS

2.00 g., Copper-Nickel, 18 mm. **Obv:** Small ships, 5 stars in shield, date below arms **Rev:** Denomination within wreath, B.C.C.R. below **Edge:** Reeded

Date	Mintage	VF20	XF40	MS60	MS63	MS65
1951 (P)	2,500,000	0.20	0.70	1.25	2.00	3.00
Note: Struck in 1952						

KM# 185.1a 10 CENTIMOS

1.75 g., Stainless Steel, 18 mm. **Obv:** National arms, date below **Rev:** Denomination within wreath, B.C.C.R. below **Edge:** Reeded

Date	Mintage	VF20	XF40	MS60	MS63	MS65
1953 (P)	5,290,000	—	0.10	0.75	0.75	1.25
1958 (P)	10,470,000	—	0.10	0.25	0.50	1.00
Note: Struck in 1959						
1967 (s)	5,500,000	—	0.10	0.25	0.50	1.00

KM# 185.2 10 CENTIMOS

2.00 g., Copper-Nickel, 18 mm. **Obv:** Small ships, 7 stars in field, date below arms **Rev:** Denomination within wreath, B.C.C.R. below **Edge:** Reeded **Note:** Dies vary for each date

Date	Mintage	VF20	XF40	MS60	MS63	MS65
1969 (d)	10,000,000	—	0.10	0.15	0.25	0.50
1976 (sm)	40,000,000	—	0.10	0.15	0.25	0.50
1976	5,000	PF65 2.50				

KM# 185.2b 10 CENTIMOS

2.00 g., Nickel Clad Steel, 18 mm. **Obv:** National arms **Rev:** Denomination within wreath, B.C.C.R. below **Edge:** Reeded

Date	Mintage	VF20	XF40	MS60	MS63	MS65
1979 (sm)	10,000,000	—	0.10	0.15	0.25	0.50

KM# 185.2a 10 CENTIMOS

Aluminum, 18 mm. **Obv:** National arms, small ships, 7 stars in field **Rev:** Denomination within wreath, B.C.C.R. below

Date	Mintage	VF20	XF40	MS60	MS63	MS65
1982 (v)	40,000,000	—	0.10	0.15	0.25	0.50

KM# 185.3 10 CENTIMOS

2.00 g., Copper-Nickel, 18 mm. **Obv:** Large ships, 7 stars in field, date below arms **Rev:** Denomination within wreath B.C.C.R. below, large 10 **Edge:** Reeded

Date	Mintage	VF20	XF40	MS60	MS63	MS65
1972 (g)	20,000,000	—	0.10	0.15	0.25	0.50
1975 (g)	5,000,000	—	0.10	0.15	0.25	0.50

KM# 168 25 CENTIMOS

3.45 g., 0.650 Silver 0.0721 oz. ASW **Obv:** National arms, date below **Rev:** Denomination within wreath, G.C.R. below at right **Edge:** Reeded

Date	Mintage	F12	VF20	XF40	MS60	MS63
1924	1,340,000	3.00	5.00	9.00	18.00	30.00

Note: Typical examples of KM#168 are weak at centers, fully struck up XF and Unc pieces command a 50% premium.

KM# 171 25 CENTIMOS

3.45 g., Copper-Nickel **Obv:** National arms, date below **Rev:** Denomination within wreath, B.I.C.R. below **Edge:** Incuse lettered

Date	Mintage	F12	VF20	XF40	MS60	MS63
1935 (P)	1,200,000	0.25	0.75	2.50	15.00	25.00

KM# 175 25 CENTIMOS

3.33 g., Copper-Nickel **Obv:** National arms, date below **Rev:** Denomination within wreath, B.N.C.R. below

Date	Mintage	F12	VF20	XF40	MS60	MS63
1937 (L)	1,600,000	0.25	0.75	2.00	8.00	15.00
1937 (L)	—	PF65 250				
Note: In proof sets only.						
1948 (L)	9,200,000	0.10	0.20	0.40	2.00	4.00
1948 (L) Specimen	—	—	—	—	—	250

KM# 181 25 CENTIMOS

3.50 g., Yellow Brass **Obv:** National arms, date below **Rev:** Denomination within wreath, star divides B.N. from C.R. below **Edge:** Reeded

Date	Mintage	F12	VF20	XF40	MS60	MS63
1944 (sj)	800,000	0.50	1.00	3.00	12.00	25.00
1945 (sj)	1,200,000	0.50	1.00	3.00	12.00	25.00
1946 (sj)	1,200,000	0.50	1.00	3.00	12.00	25.00

KM# 181a 25 CENTIMOS

3.50 g., Red Brass or bronze **Obv:** National arms, date below **Rev:** Denomination within wreath, star below divides B.N. and C.R. **Edge:** Reeded

Date	Mintage	F12	VF20	XF40	MS60	MS63
1945 (sj)	Inc. above	3.00	10.00	20.00	50.00	90.00

KM# 188.1 25 CENTIMOS

3.46 g., Copper-Nickel, 23.03 mm. **Obv:** Small ships, 7 stars on arms, date below **Rev:** Denomination within wreath, B.C.C.R. below **Note:** Dies vary for each date.

Date	Mintage	VF20	XF40	MS60	MS63	MS65
1967 (L)	4,000,000	—	0.10	0.50	1.00	1.50
1969 (d)	4,000,000	—	0.10	0.50	1.00	1.50
1974 (v)	—	—	0.10	0.30	0.75	1.25
1976 (sm)	12,000,000	—	0.10	0.30	0.75	1.25
1976	5,000	PF65 2.50				
1978 (a)	10,000,000	—	0.10	0.30	0.75	1.25

KM# 188.1a 25 CENTIMOS

Nickel Clad Steel **Obv:** National arms, date below **Rev:** Denomination within wreath, B.C.C.R. below **Note:** Beaded rims.

Date	Mintage	VF20	XF40	MS60	MS63	MS65
1980 (sm)	30,000,000	—	0.10	0.25	0.75	1.25

KM# 188.1b 25 CENTIMOS

Aluminum **Obv:** National arms, date below **Rev:** Denomination within wreath, B.C.C.R. below **Edge:** Plain

Date	Mintage	VF20	XF40	MS60	MS63	MS65
1982 (r)	30,000,000	—	0.10	0.25	0.75	1.25

KM# 188.2 25 CENTIMOS

3.38 g., Copper-Nickel, 23 mm. **Obv:** Large ships, 7 stars in field

Date	Mintage	VF20	XF40	MS60	MS63	MS65
1972 (g)	8,000,000	—	0.10	0.25	0.75	1.25

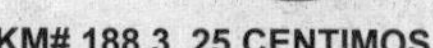

KM# 188.3 25 CENTIMOS

1.05 g., Aluminum, 17 mm. **Obv:** National arms, date below **Rev:** Denomination within wreath, B.C.C.R. below **Edge:** Reeded **Note:** Reduced size. Dies vary for each date.

Date	Mintage	VF20	XF40	MS60	MS63	MS65
1983 (r)	60,000,000	—	0.10	0.20	0.75	1.25
1986 (c)	60,000,000	—	0.10	0.20	0.75	1.25
1989 (c)	60,000,000	—	0.10	0.20	0.75	1.25

KM# 172 50 CENTIMOS

6.25 g., Copper-Nickel, 25.02 mm. **Obv:** National arms, date below **Rev:** Denomination within wreath, B.I.C.R. below

Date	Mintage	F12	VF20	XF40	MS60	MS63
1935 (P)	700,000	0.50	1.00	8.00	20.00	50.00

KM# 176 50 CENTIMOS

7.00 g., Copper-Nickel, 25 mm. **Obv:** National arms, date below **Rev:** Denomination within wreath, B.N.C.R. below

Date	Mintage	F12	VF20	XF40	MS60	MS63
1937 (L)	600,000	0.50	1.50	3.00	15.00	35.00
1937 (L)	—	PF65 250				
Note: In proof sets only.						
1948 (L)	4,000,000	—	0.25	0.50	3.00	5.00
1948 (L) Specimen	—	—	—	—	—	250

KM# 189.1 50 CENTIMOS

Copper-Nickel, 26 mm. **Obv:** Small ships, 7 stars on shield, date below arms **Rev:** Small value '50' within wreath, B.C.C.R. below **Note:** Medal rotation.

Date	Mintage	VF20	XF40	MS60	MS63	MS65
1965 (L)	1,000,000	0.10	0.25	0.75	1.25	1.50

KM# 189.3 50 CENTIMOS

7.29 g., Copper-Nickel, 26 mm. **Obv:** National arms, date below **Rev:** Denomination within wreath, B.C.C.R. below, large 50 **Edge Lettering:** -BCCR- (repeated) **Note:** Dies vary for each date - the main varieties are an open or closed "5" in "50", or large and small dates.

Date	Mintage	VF20	XF40	MS60	MS63	MS65
1968 (P)	2,000,000	0.10	0.15	0.50	1.00	1.50
1970 (P)	4,000,000	0.10	0.15	0.35	1.00	1.50
1976 (sm)	6,000,000	0.10	0.15	0.35	1.00	1.50
1976	5,000	PF65 2.50				
1978 (v)	10,000,000	0.10	0.15	0.35	1.00	1.50

KM# 189.2 50 CENTIMOS

7.01 g., Copper-Nickel, 26 mm. **Obv:** Large ships, 7 stars in shield, date below arms **Rev:** Denomination within wreath, B.C.C.R. below, large 50

Date	Mintage	VF20	XF40	MS60	MS63	MS65
1972 (g)	4,000,000	0.10	0.15	0.35	1.00	1.50
1975 (g) Large date	524,000	0.10	0.15	0.35	1.00	1.50
1975 (g) Small date	Inc. above	0.10	0.15	0.35	1.00	1.50

KM# 209.1 50 CENTIMOS

2.18 g., Stainless Steel, 19.11 mm. **Obv:** Large ships, letters incuse on ribbon, date below arms **Rev:** Denomination within wreath, B.C.C.R. below, thick 50 **Edge:** Plain

Date	Mintage	VF20	XF40	MS60	MS63	MS65
1982 (c)	12,000,000	—	0.15	0.35	1.00	1.50
1983 (c)	24,000,000	—	0.15	0.35	1.00	1.50
1990 (c)	24,000,000	—	0.15	0.35	1.00	1.50

KM# 209.2 50 CENTIMOS

2.20 g., Stainless Steel, 18.95 mm. **Obv:** Small ships, letters in relief on ribbon **Rev:** Denomination within wreath

Date	Mintage	VF20	XF40	MS60	MS63	MS65
1984 (L)	42,000,000	—	0.15	0.35	1.00	1.50
1990 (c)	24,000,000	—	0.15	0.35	1.00	1.50

KM# 173 COLON

10.00 g., Copper-Nickel, 29 mm. **Obv:** National arms, date below **Rev:** Denomination within wreath, B.I.C.R below **Edge:** Incuse BICR; plain **Note:** Beaded rims.

Date	Mintage	F12	VF20	XF40	MS60	MS63
1935 (P)	350,000	1.00	4.00	12.00	35.00	90.00
Note: Struck in 1936.						

KM# 177 COLON

Copper-Nickel, 29 mm. **Obv:** National arms, date below **Rev:** Denomination within wreath, B.N.C.R. below **Edge Lettering:** -BNCR- (repeated)

Date	Mintage	F12	VF20	XF40	MS60	MS63
1937 (L)	300,000	0.75	2.00	6.00	25.00	50.00
1937 (L)	—	PF65 350				
1948 (L)	1,350,000	0.20	0.40	1.00	3.00	5.00
1948 (L) Specimen	—	—	—	—	—	300

KM# 186.1 COLON

8.67 g., Stainless Steel, 29 mm. **Obv:** Small ships, 5 stars in shield, date below **Rev:** Denomination within wreath, B.C.C.R. below **Edge Lettering:** -BCCR- (repeated)

Date	Mintage	VF20	XF40	MS60	MS63	MS65
1954 (P)	987,000	0.35	1.00	5.00	7.50	12.00

KM# 186.1a COLON

10.00 g., Copper-Nickel, 29 mm. **Obv:** National arms, date below **Rev:** Denomination within wreath, B.C.C.R. below

Date	Mintage	VF20	XF40	MS60	MS63	MS65
1961 (P)	1,000,000	0.20	0.50	2.00	3.00	5.00

KM# 186.2 COLON

10.00 g., Copper-Nickel, 29 mm. **Obv:** Small ships, 7 stars in shield, date below **Rev:** Denomination within wreath, B.C.C.R. below, small 1 **Edge Lettering:** -BCCR- (repeated) **Note:** Dies vary for each date

Date	Mintage	VF20	XF40	MS60	MS63	MS65
1965 (v)	1,000,000	0.20	0.30	0.75	1.50	3.00
1968 (P)	2,000,000	0.20	0.30	0.75	1.50	3.00
1970 (P)	2,000,000	0.20	0.30	0.75	1.50	3.00
1974 (v)	2,000,000	0.20	0.30	0.75	1.50	3.00
1978 (v)	10,000,000	0.20	0.30	0.75	1.50	3.00

KM# 186.3 COLON

10.00 g., Copper-Nickel, 29 mm. **Obv:** Large ships, 7 stars in shield, date below **Rev:** Denomination within wreath, B.C.C.R. below

Date	Mintage	VF20	XF40	MS60	MS63	MS65
1972 (g)	2,000,000	0.20	0.30	0.75	1.50	3.00
1975 (g)	1,028,000	0.20	0.30	0.75	1.50	3.00

KM# 186.4 COLON

10.00 g., Copper-Nickel, 29 mm. **Obv:** Small ships, 7 stars in shield **Rev:** Denomination within wreath, large "1" **Edge Lettering:** -BCCR- (repeated) **Note:** Dies vary for each date.

Date	Mintage	VF20	XF40	MS60	MS63	MS65
1976 (sm)	12,000,000	0.20	0.30	0.75	1.50	3.00
1976 (sm)	5,000					
1977 (sm)	22,000,000	0.20	0.30	0.75	1.50	3.00

KM# 210.1 COLON

3.20 g., Stainless Steel, 21 mm. **Obv:** Letters incuse on ribbon, date below arms **Rev:** Denomination within wreath, B.C.C.R. below

Date	Mintage	VF20	XF40	MS60	MS63	MS65
1982 (cc)	12,000,000	—	0.15	0.35	0.50	1.00
1983 (cc)	24,000,000	—	0.15	0.35	0.50	1.00
1984 (L)	60,000,000	—	0.15	0.35	0.50	1.00
1991 (cc)	30,000,000	—	0.15	0.35	0.50	1.00

KM# 210.2 COLON

3.20 g., Stainless Steel, 21 mm. **Obv:** Letters in relief on ribbon, date below arms **Rev:** Denomination within wreath, B.C.C.R. below **Note:** Varieties exist with a "slim 1" in the value for 1984 & 1989, and a "fat 1" in the value for 1993 & 1994.

Date	Mintage	VF20	XF40	MS60	MS63	MS65
1984 (L)	Inc. above	—	0.15	0.35	0.50	0.80
1989 (c)	50,000,000	—	0.15	0.35	0.50	0.80
1993 (sm)	50,000,000	—	0.15	0.35	0.50	0.80
1994 (v)	15,000,000	—	0.15	0.35	0.50	0.80

KM# 233 COLON

2.78 g., Brass, 15.04 mm. **Obv:** National arms, date below **Rev:** Denomination above spray, B.C.C.R. below

Date	Mintage	VF20	XF40	MS60	MS63	MS65
1998 (a)	15,000,000	—	0.25	0.75	0.10	1.50

KM# 183 2 COLONES

Copper-Nickel, 32 mm. **Obv:** National arms, date below **Rev:** Denomination within wreath, B.N.C.R. below **Edge Lettering:** -BNCR- (repeated)

Date	Mintage	F12	VF20	XF40	MS60	MS63
1948 (L)	1,380,000	0.50	1.00	3.00	8.00	12.00
1948 (L)	—	PF65 350				

KM# 187.1 2 COLONES

12.00 g., Stainless Steel, 32 mm. **Obv:** National arms with small ships, 5 stars in shield, date below arms **Rev:** Denomination within wreath, B.C.C.R. below **Edge Lettering:** -BCCR- (repeated)

Date	Mintage	VF20	XF40	MS60	MS63	MS65
1954 (P)	1,028,000	1.00	3.00	6.00	10.00	25.00

KM# 187.1a 2 COLONES

14.00 g., Copper-Nickel, 32 mm. **Obv:** National arms, date below **Rev:** Denomination within wreath, B.C.C.R. below **Edge Lettering:** -BCCR- (repeated)

Date	Mintage	VF20	XF40	MS60	MS63	MS65
1961 (P)	1,000,000	0.30	0.50	1.00	1.50	3.00

KM# 187.2 2 COLONES

14.00 g., Copper-Nickel, 32 mm. **Obv:** Small ships, 7 stars in shield, date below arms **Rev:** Denomination within wreath, B.C.C.R. below **Edge Lettering:** -BCCR- (repeated) **Note:** Dies vary for each date.

Date	Mintage	VF20	XF40	MS60	MS63	MS65
1968 (L)	2,000,000	0.30	0.45	1.00	1.50	3.00
1970 (P)	1,000,000	0.30	0.45	1.00	1.50	3.00
1972 (v)	2,000,000	0.30	0.45	1.00	1.50	3.00
1978 (v)	10,000,000	0.30	0.45	1.00	1.50	3.00

KM# 190 2 COLONES

4.30 g., 0.999 Silver 0.1381 oz. ASW **Subject:** 20th Anniversary of the Central Bank **Rev:** Bank above denomination

Date	Mintage	VF20	XF40	MS60	MS63	MS65
1970	5,157	PF65 12.00				

Note: Also exists with a small oval with 1000 inside above the S in COLONES.

KM# 211.1 2 COLONES

4.25 g., Stainless Steel, 23.1 mm. **Obv:** Letters incuse on ribbon, date below arms **Rev:** Denomination within wreath, B.C.C.R. below

Date	Mintage	VF20	XF40	MS60	MS63	MS65
1982 (cc)	12,000,000	—	0.20	0.60	1.00	1.50
1983 (cc)	24,000,000	—	0.20	0.60	1.00	1.50

KM# 211.2 2 COLONES

4.25 g., Stainless Steel, 23.1 mm. **Obv:** Letters in relief on ribbon, date below arms **Rev:** Denomination within wreath, B.C.C.R. below

Date	Mintage	VF20	XF40	MS60	MS63	MS65
1984 (L)	72,000,000	—	0.20	0.50	0.75	1.25

KM# 191 5 COLONES

10.78 g., 0.999 Silver 0.3462 oz. ASW **Subject:** 400th Year - The Founding of New Carthage Juan Vazquez de Coronado **Obv:** National arms, date below **Rev:** Bust with ruffled collar facing, raised 1000 hallmark in oval below "o" of "Cartago" **Edge:** Reeded

Date	Mintage	VF20	XF40	MS60	MS63	MS65
1970	5,157	PF65 15.00				

KM# 203 5 COLONES

Nickel, 29.5 mm. **Subject:** 25th Anniversary of the Central Bank **Obv:** National arms, denomination below **Rev:** Plants with two dates at right

Date	Mintage	VF20	XF40	MS60	MS63	MS65
ND-1975	2,000,000	0.15	0.25	0.45	0.65	1.00
ND-1975	5,000	PF65 2.00				

KM# 214.1 5 COLONES

7.25 g., Stainless Steel, 25.9 mm. **Obv:** Small ship, letters in relief on ribbon, date below arms **Rev:** Denomination above spray, B.C.C.R. below **Edge:** Reeded

Date	Mintage	VF20	XF40	MS60	MS63	MS65
1983 (cc)	24,000,000	0.10	0.25	0.75	1.00	1.50
1989 (v)	20,000,000	0.10	0.25	0.75	1.00	1.50
1993	—	0.10	0.25	0.75	1.00	1.50

KM# 214.2 5 COLONES

7.25 g., Stainless Steel, 25.9 mm. **Obv:** Large ship, letters incuse on ribbon **Rev:** B.C.C.R. below sprays **Edge:** Reeded

Date	Mintage	VF20	XF40	MS60	MS63	MS65
1985 (cc)	25,000,000	0.10	0.25	0.50	0.75	1.00

KM# 214.3 5 COLONES

7.25 g., Nickel Plated Stainless Steel, 25.9 mm. **Obv:** Small ship, letters in relief on ribbon, date below arms **Rev:** Denomination above spray, B.C.C.R. below

Date	Mintage	VF20	XF40	MS60	MS63	MS65
1993	2,000,000	0.10	0.25	0.50	0.75	1.00

KM# 227 5 COLONES

4.03 g., Bronze, 21.5 mm. **Obv:** National arms, date below **Obv. Legend:** REPUBLICA DE COSTA RICA **Rev:** Denomination above sprays, B.C.C.R. below, thick '5' **Edge:** Segmented reeding

Date	Mintage	VF20	XF40	MS60	MS63	MS65
1995 (w)	15,500,000	—	0.25	0.50	0.75	1.00

KM# 227a 5 COLONES

4.00 g., Copper-Aluminum-Nickel, 21.6 mm. **Obv:** National arms, large date below, large letters in legend **Rev:** Denomination above spray, B.C.C.R. below, thick '5' **Edge:** Segmented reeding

Date	Mintage	VF20	XF40	MS60	MS63	MS65
1997 (a)	15,000,000	—	0.15	0.50	0.75	1.00

KM# 227a.1 5 COLONES

4.00 g., Copper-Aluminum-Nickel, 21.6 mm. **Obv:** National arms, date below, smaller letters in legend and smaller date, shield is outlined **Obv. Legend:** REPUBLICA DE COSTA RICA **Rev:** Denomination above sprays, B.C.C.R. below, thick '5' **Edge:** Segmented reeding

Date	Mintage	VF20	XF40	MS60	MS63	MS65
1999 (co)	15,000,000	—	0.15	0.50	1.00	1.50

KM# 192 10 COLONES

21.70 g., 0.999 Silver 0.697 oz. ASW, 40 mm. **Subject:** Attempt of Unification of Middle America **Obv:** National arms, date below **Rev:** Kapok tree (ceiba petandra), five mountains in background, denomination below

Date	Mintage	VF20	XF40	MS60	MS63	MS65
1970	5,157	PF63 20.00	PF65 35.00			

KM# 204 10 COLONES

Nickel, 32 mm. **Subject:** 25th Anniversary of the Central Bank **Obv:** National arms, denomination below **Rev:** Two dates above tree at center

Date	Mintage	VF20	XF40	MS60	MS63	MS65
ND-1975 (v)	495,115	2.00	3.00	7.00	9.00	12.00
ND-1975 (v)	5,000	PF65 16.00				

KM# 215.1 10 COLONES

8.45 g., Stainless Steel, 28.3 mm. **Obv:** Letters in relief on ribbon, date below arms **Rev:** Denomination above spray, B.C.C.R. below **Edge:** Reeded

Date	Mintage	VF20	XF40	MS60	MS63	MS65
1983 (v)	12,000,000	0.20	0.35	0.75	1.50	2.00
1992 (v)	25,000,000	0.20	0.35	0.75	1.50	2.00

KM# 215.2 10 COLONES

8.45 g., Stainless Steel, 28.3 mm. **Obv:** Letters incuse on ribbon, date below arms **Rev:** Denomination above spray, B.C.C.R. below

Date	Mintage	VF20	XF40	MS60	MS63	MS65
1985 (cc)	20,000,000	0.20	0.35	0.75	1.50	2.00

KM# 228 10 COLONES

5.00 g., Bronze Plated Steel, 23.5 mm. **Obv:** National arms, date below **Rev:** Denomination above spray, B.C.C.R. below, thick 1 in numeral **Edge:** Segmented reeding

Date	Mintage	VF20	XF40	MS60	MS63	MS65
1995 (w)	15,500,000	—	0.35	0.75	1.00	1.25

KM# 228a 10 COLONES

5.05 g., Copper-Aluminum-Nickel, 23.5 mm. **Obv:** National arms, date below, large letters in legend and date, shield outlined **Obv. Legend:** REPUBLICA DE COSTA RICA **Rev:** Denomination above sprays, B.C.C.R. below, thick 1 in numeral **Edge:** Segmented reeding

Date	Mintage	VF20	XF40	MS60	MS63	MS65
1997 (a)	15,000,000	—	—	0.75	1.00	1.25

KM# 228a.1 10 COLONES

5.00 g., Copper-Aluminum-Nickel, 23.5 mm. **Obv:** National arms and date below, small letters in legend **Rev:** Thin "1" in value above spray, B.C.C.R. below. Legends smaller than on KM#228a. **Edge:** Segmented reeding

Date	Mintage	VF20	XF40	MS60	MS63	MS65
1999 (co)	30,000,000	—	—	0.75	1.00	1.25

KM# 193 20 COLONES

43.70 g., 0.999 Silver 1.4036 oz. ASW, 50.8 mm. **Rev:** "Venus de Milo" statue, raised 1000 hallmark in oval below "O" in "MILO"

Date	Mintage	VF20	XF40	MS60	MS63	MS65
1970	7,500	PF63 35.00	PF65 45.00			

KM# 205 20 COLONES

Nickel, 36 mm. **Subject:** 25th Anniversary of the Central Bank **Obv:** National arms above denomination **Rev:** Flowers divide dates **Edge:** Reeded

Date	Mintage	VF20	XF40	MS60	MS63	MS65
ND-1975 (v)	1,995,111	1.00	1.50	3.50	3.00	5.00
ND-1975 (v)	5,000	PF65 15.00				

KM# 216.1 20 COLONES

9.80 g., Stainless Steel, 31.25 mm. **Obv:** Letters in relief on ribbon, date below arms **Rev:** Denomination above spray, B.C.C.R. below **Edge:** Reeded

Date	Mintage	VF20	XF40	MS60	MS63	MS65
1983 (v)	16,000,000	0.35	0.55	1.00	1.50	2.00
1994	—	0.35	0.65	1.75	2.00	—

KM# 216.2 20 COLONES

9.70 g., Stainless Steel, 31.25 mm. **Obv:** Letters incuse on ribbon, date below arms **Rev:** Denomination above spray, B.C.C.R. below **Edge:** Reeded

Date	Mintage	VF20	XF40	MS60	MS63	MS65
1985 (cc)	25,000,000	0.35	0.55	1.00	1.50	2.00

KM# 216.3 20 COLONES

9.70 g., Nickel Plated Stainless Steel, 31.25 mm. **Obv:** Letters incuse on ribbon, date below arms **Rev:** Denomination above spray, B.C.C.R. below **Edge:** Reeded

Date	Mintage	VF20	XF40	MS60	MS63	MS65
1994 (sm)	10,000,000	0.35	0.65	1.00	1.25	1.75

KM# 194 25 COLONES

53.90 g., 0.999 Silver 1.7312 oz. ASW, 60 mm. **Subject:** 25 Years of Social Legislation **Obv:** National arms, date below **Rev:** "Materniad" sculpture by F. Zuniga, denomination below

Date	Mintage	VF20	XF40	MS60	MS63	MS65
1970	6,800	PF63 50.00	PF65 70.00			

KM# 229 25 COLONES

7.00 g., Brass Plated Steel, 25.5 mm. **Obv:** National arms, date below **Rev:** Denomination above spray, B.C.C.R. below **Edge:** Segmented reeding

Date	Mintage	VF20	XF40	MS60	MS63	MS65
1995	15,000,000	—	—	0.75	1.00	1.50

KM# 195.1 50 COLONES
7.45 g., 0.900 Gold 0.2156 oz. AGW **Subject:** Inter-American Human Rights Convention **Obv:** National arms, date below **Rev:** Nude on globe background, denomination below

Date	Mintage	VF20	XF40	MS60	MS63	MS65
1970	3,507	PF63 400				

KM# 195.2 50 COLONES
7.45 g., 0.900 Gold 0.2156 oz. AGW **Obv:** National arms, date below **Rev:** 1 "AR" countermark above fineness statement

Date	Mintage	VF20	XF40	MS60	MS63	MS65
1970	Inc. above	PF63 420				

KM# 200 50 COLONES
25.55 g., 0.500 Silver 0.4107 oz. ASW, 38.6 mm. **Subject:** Conservation **Obv:** National arms, date below **Rev:** Green turtles, denomination below

Date	Mintage	VF20	XF40	MS60	MS63	MS65
1974	7,599	—	—	10.00	15.00	22.00

KM# 200a 50 COLONES
28.28 g., 0.925 Silver 0.841 oz. ASW, 38.6 mm. **Subject:** Conservation **Obv:** National arms, date below **Rev:** Green Turtle, denomination below

Date	Mintage	VF20	XF40	MS60	MS63	MS65
1974	11,000	PF63 22.00	PF65 30.00			

KM# 231 50 COLONES
7.80 g., Copper-Aluminum-Nickel, 27.5 mm. **Obv:** National arms, large letters, large date below **Obv. Legend:** REPUBLICA DE COSTA RICA **Rev:** Value above spray **Rev. Legend:** B. C. C. R. **Edge:** Segmented reeding

Date	Mintage	VF20	XF40	MS60	MS63	MS65
1997 (a)	15,000,000	—	—	1.00	1.50	2.00

KM# 231.1 50 COLONES
7.80 g., Copper-Aluminum-Nickel, 27.5 mm. **Obv:** National arms, date below, small letters and date **Obv. Legend:** REPUBLICA DE COSTA RICA **Rev:** Value above spray, smaller letters in legend **Rev. Legend:** B. C. C. R. **Edge:** Segmented reeding

Date	Mintage	VF20	XF40	MS60	MS63	MS65
1999	25,000,000	—	—	1.00	1.50	2.00

KM# 196 100 COLONES
14.90 g., 0.900 Gold 0.4311 oz. AGW **Obv:** National arms **Rev:** Gold Vulture pendant in the style of the Chibcha Indians, denomination below

Date	Mintage	VF20	XF40	MS60	MS63	MS65
1970	3,507	PF63 700	PF65 750			

KM# 201 100 COLONES
32.10 g., 0.500 Silver 0.516 oz. ASW, 42 mm. **Subject:** Conservation **Obv:** National arms, date below divides BC from CR **Rev:** Manatee, denomination below

Date	Mintage	VF20	XF40	MS60	MS63	MS65
1974	7,599	—	9.50	14.00	18.00	25.00

KM# 201a 100 COLONES
35.00 g., 0.925 Silver 1.0409 oz. ASW, 42 mm. **Subject:** Conservation **Obv:** National arms **Rev:** Manatee

Date	Mintage	VF20	XF40	MS60	MS63	MS65
1974	11,000	PF63 25.00	PF65 30.00			

KM# 206 100 COLONES
35.00 g., 0.925 Silver 1.0409 oz. ASW **Subject:** International Year of the Child **Rev:** Three birds in nest, date below

Date	Mintage	VF20	XF40	MS60	MS63	MS65
1979	9,500	—	—	20.00	25.00	30.00
1979	5,000	PF63 27.00	PF65 35.00			

KM# 224 100 COLONES
Nickel **Obv:** National arms, denomination below **Rev:** Bust of President Dr. Oscar Arias S. divides dates

Date	Mintage	VF20	XF40	MS60	MS63	MS65
1987 (sm)	25,000	—	—	5.00	7.00	9.00

KM# 230 100 COLONES
9.10 g., Brass Plated Steel, 29.5 mm. **Obv:** National arms above date **Rev:** Denomination above spray, B.C.C.R. below **Edge:** Segmented reeding

Date	Mintage	VF20	XF40	MS60	MS63	MS65
1995 (w)	15,000,000	—	—	1.00	1.50	2.50

KM# 230a 100 COLONES
9.00 g., Copper-Aluminum-Nickel, 29.5 mm. **Obv:** National arms, date below, large letters in legend and date, shield outlined **Rev:** Value above spray, B.C.C.R. below **Edge:** Segmented reeding

Date	Mintage	VF20	XF40	MS60	MS63	MS65
1997 (a)	15,000,000	—	—	1.00	1.50	2.50
1998 (a)	15,000,000	—	—	1.00	1.50	2.50

KM# 230a.1 100 COLONES
9.00 g., Copper-Aluminum-Nickel, 29.5 mm. **Obv:** National arms, date below, small letters in legend **Rev:** Denomination above spray, B.C.C.R. below, small letters in legend **Edge:** Segmented reeding

Date	Mintage	VF20	XF40	MS60	MS63	MS65
1999 (co)	30,000,000	—	—	1.00	1.50	2.50

KM# 240 100 COLONES
9.10 g., Copper-Aluminum-Nickel, 29.5 mm. **Obv:** New design with much smaller legend and date **Rev:** Value **Edge:** Segmented reeding

Date	Mintage	VF20	XF40	MS60	MS63	MS65
2000 (a)	35,000,000	—	—	1.00	1.50	2.50

KM# 197 200 COLONES
29.80 g., 0.900 Gold 0.8623 oz. AGW **Obv:** National arms **Rev:** Juan Santamaria and cannon

Date	Mintage	VF20	XF40	MS60	MS63	MS65
1970 (i)	3,507	PF63 1,500	PF65 1,600			

KM# 212 250 COLONES
30.33 g., 0.925 Silver 0.902 oz. ASW **Subject:** Conservation **Obv:** National arms **Rev:** Jaguar head facing

Date	Mintage	VF20	XF40	MS60	MS63	MS65
1982 FM	1,109	PF63 145	PF65 165	PF67 185		

KM# 217 250 COLONES
30.33 g., 0.925 Silver 0.902 oz. ASW **Obv:** National arms **Rev:** National flower, denomination below

Date	Mintage	VF20	XF40	MS60	MS63	MS65
1983 FM	393	PF63 150	PF65 175	PF67 195		

KM# 207 300 COLONES
10.97 g., 0.925 Silver 0.3262 oz. ASW **Subject:** 125th Anniversary - Death of Juan Santamaria **Obv:** National arms, denomination below **Rev:** Juan Santamaria standing with torch and rifle divides dates

Date	Mintage	VF20	XF40	MS60	MS63	MS65
1981 (sm)	10,000	PF63 12.00	PF65 15.00			

KM# 223 300 COLONES
10.97 g., 0.925 Silver 0.3262 oz. ASW **Subject:** 200th Anniversary - Founding of Alajuela **Obv:** National arms, denomination below **Rev:** Head facing, divides dates

Date	Mintage	VF20	XF40	MS60	MS63	MS65
1981 (sm)	—	PF63 12.00	PF65 15.00			

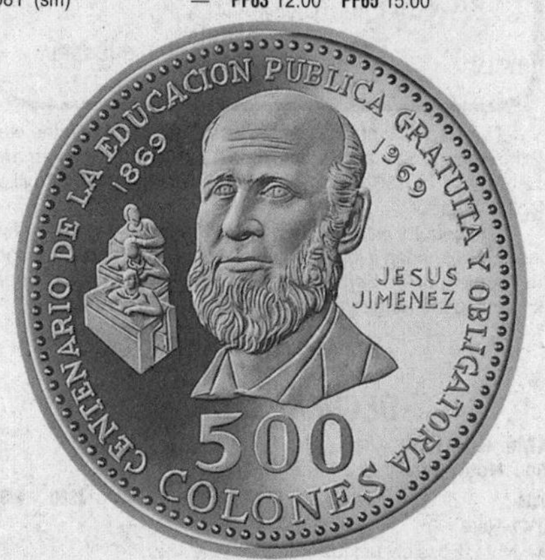

KM# 198 500 COLONES
74.52 g., 0.900 Gold 2.1563 oz. AGW **Subject:** 100th Anniversary of Public Education **Obv:** National arms **Rev:** Jesus Jimenez and students at desks

Date	Mintage	VF20	XF40	MS60	MS63	MS65
1970 (i)	3,507	PF63 3,400	PF65 3,600			

KM# 236 500 COLONES
9.80 g., Brass **Subject:** 50 Years - Central Bank **Obv:** National arms, date below **Rev:** Bank building, value below

Date	Mintage	VF20	XF40	MS60	MS63	MS65
2000 (a)	5,000,000	—	—	1.00	1.50	2.00
2000 (a)	500	PF65 15.00				

KM# 199 1000 COLONES
149.04 g., 0.900 Gold 4.3126 oz. AGW **Subject:** 150th Anniversary of Central American Independence **Obv:** National arms **Rev:** Face on radiant sun above mountains, water and map, denomination below **Note:** Illustration reduced.

Date	Mintage	VF20	XF40	MS60	MS63	MS65
1970 (i)	3,507	PF63 7,250	PF65 7,500			

KM# 225 1000 COLONES
10.97 g., 0.925 Silver 0.3262 oz. ASW **Obv:** National arms, denomination below **Rev:** Head of President Dr. Oscar Arias S. divides dates

Date	Mintage	VF20	XF40	MS60	MS63	MS65
1987 (sm)	10,000	—	—	10.00	12.00	15.00

KM# 202 1500 COLONES
33.44 g., 0.900 Gold 0.9675 oz. AGW **Subject:** Conservation **Obv:** National arms, date below divides B.C. from C.R. **Rev:** Giant anteater, denomination below

Date	Mintage	VF20	XF40	MS60	MS63	MS65
1974	2,418	—	—	1,350	1,550	1,750
1974	726	PF63 1,750	PF65 1,850			

KM# 213 1500 COLONES
6.98 g., 0.500 Gold 0.1122 oz. AGW **Rev:** Busts of Francisco Coronado and Christopher Columbus, denomination above **Note:** Although considered legal tender, these coins were never officially authorized for circulation.

Date	Mintage	VF20	XF40	MS60	MS63	MS65
1982 FM (P)	724	PF63 235	PF65 250	PF67 275		

KM# 218 1500 COLONES
6.98 g., 0.500 Gold 0.1122 oz. AGW **Obv:** National arms, date below **Rev:** Native figurine, denomination above, spray below

Date	Mintage	VF20	XF40	MS60	MS63	MS65
1983 FM (P)	272	PF63 245	PF65 285	PF67 350		

KM# 234 3000 COLONES
25.36 g., 0.925 Silver 0.7542 oz. ASW **Subject:** 150th Anniversary San Juan de Dios Hospital **Obv:** National arms, denomination below **Rev:** Hospital building divides dates

Date	Mintage	VF20	XF40	MS60	MS63	MS65
1994 (rm)	—	PF63 22.00	PF65 30.00			

KM# 208 5000 COLONES
15.00 g., 0.900 Gold 0.434 oz. AGW **Subject:** 125th Anniversary - Death of Juan Santamaria **Obv:** National arms, denomination below **Rev:** Figure standing with torch and rifle divides dates

Date	Mintage	VF20	XF40	MS60	MS63	MS65
1981 (sm)	—	—	—	650	700	800
1981 (sm)	2,000	PF63 800	PF65 900			

KM# 232 5000 COLONES
15.00 g., 0.900 Gold 0.434 oz. AGW **Subject:** Founding of Alajuela **Obv:** National arms **Rev:** Portrait of Ramirez

Date	Mintage	VF20	XF40	MS60	MS63	MS65
1981 (sm)	2,000	PF63 800	PF65 900			

KM# 235 5000 COLONES
25.06 g., 0.925 Silver 0.7453 oz. ASW **Subject:** Centennial of the Colon **Obv:** National arms, denomination below **Rev:** Bust of Columbus right, two dates below denomination

Date	Mintage	VF20	XF40	MS60	MS63	MS65
1997 (a)	—	PF63 30.00	PF65 40.00			

KM# 237 5000 COLONES
31.10 g., 0.925 Silver 0.9249 oz. ASW **Subject:** 50 Years

- Central Bank **Obv:** National arms, date below **Rev:** Man working screw press, denomination at right

Date	Mintage	VF20	XF40	MS60	MS63	MS65
2000 (a)	7,500	PF63 28.00	PF65 40.00			

KM# 226 25000 COLONES

15.00 g., 0.900 Gold 0.434 oz. AGW **Obv:** National arms, denomination below **Rev:** Bust of President Dr. Oscar Arias S., divides dates

Date	Mintage	VF20	XF40	MS60	MS63	MS65
1987 (sm)	5,000	PF63 700	PF65 750			

KM# 238 100000 COLONES

15.55 g., 0.900 Gold 0.4499 oz. AGW **Subject:** 50 Years - Central Bank **Obv:** National arms **Rev:** Three standing citizens, denomination at right

Date	Mintage	VF20	XF40	MS60	MS63	MS65
2000 (a)	2,500	PF63 750	PF65 800			

LEPROSARIUM COINAGE

KM# L1 5 CENTIMOS

Copper-Nickel, 15 mm. **Note:** 4mm hole punched through 5 Centimos, KM#178.

Date	Mintage	VG8	F12	VF20	XF40	MS60
1942	2,000	—	—	—	—	—

Note: Prospective buyers should proceed with caution, as many examples were produced in the early 1970's and no definitive proof of original examples currently exists.

KM# L2 25 CENTIMOS

Copper-Nickel **Note:** 6mm hole punched through 25 Centimos, KM#171. Prospective buyers should proceed with caution, as modern fabrications are prevalent.

Date	Mintage	VG8	F12	VF20	XF40	MS60
1935 Rare	2,000	—	—	—	—	—

KM# L3 25 CENTIMOS

Copper-Nickel **Note:** 6mm hole punched through 25 Centimos, KM#175. Prospective buyers should proceed with caution, as modern fabrications are prevalent.

Date	Mintage	VG8	F12	VF20	XF40	MS60
1937 Rare	Inc. above	—	—	—	—	—

KM# L4 50 CENTIMOS

Copper-Nickel, 25 mm. **Note:** 8mm hole punched through 50 Centimos, KM#172. Prospective buyers should proceed with caution, as modern fabrications are prevalent.

Date	Mintage	VG8	F12	VF20	XF40	MS60
1935 Rare	800	—	—	—	—	—

KM# L5 50 CENTIMOS

Copper-Nickel, 25 mm. **Note:** 8mm hole punched through 50 Centimos, KM#176. Prospective buyers should proceed with caution, as modern fabrications are prevalent.

Date	Mintage	VG8	F12	VF20	XF40	MS60
1937 Rare	Inc. above	—	—	—	—	—

KM# L6 COLON

Copper-Nickel, 29 mm. **Note:** 9mm hole punched through 1 Colon, KM#173. Prospective buyers should proceed with caution, as modern fabrications are prevalent.

Date	Mintage	VG8	F12	VF20	XF40	MS60
1935 Rare	1,000	—	—	—	—	—

KM# L7 COLON

Copper-Nickel, 29 mm. **Note:** 9mm hole punched through 1 Colon, KM#177. Prospective buyers should proceed with caution, as modern fabrications are prevalent.

Date	Mintage	VG8	F12	VF20	XF40	MS60
1937 Rare	Inc. above	—	—	—	—	—

PATTERNS

Including off metal strikes

KM#	Date	Mintage	Identification	Mkt Val
Pn11	1923	—	25 Centimos. Brass. Obverse of gold 5 pesos type KM#117 or 118, reverse as KM#168.	—
Pn12	1924	—	25 Centimos. Brass. KM#168. Considered false.	—
Pn13	19xx (1928)	—	5 Centimos. Copper-Nickel. Similar to 1929 issue.	65.00
Pn14	19xx (1928)	—	5 Centimos. Brass. Similar to KM#151 type, 1936-1941 issues.	120
Pn15	19xx (1928)	—	10 Centimos. Copper-Nickel. Similar to 1929 issue. Prev.# KMPn10.	85.00
Pn16	1944	—	25 Centimos. Silver.	—
Pn17	1944	—	25 Centimos. Brass. Polished dies.	150

PIEDFORT

KM#	Date	Mintage	Identification	Mkt Val
P6	1946	—	25 Centimos. Brass.	250
P7	1946	—	25 Centimos. Copper-Nickel. 50 pieces.	350

MINT SETS

KM#	Date	Mintage	Identification	Issue Price	Mkt Val
MS1	1972 (6)	—	KM#184.4, 185.3-186.3, 187.2, 188.2-189.2	—	7.00
MS2	1975 (3)	—	KM#203-205	—	15.00

PROOF SETS

KM#	Date	Mintage	Identification	Issue Price	Mkt Val
PS2	1937 (3)	—	KM#175-177	—	850
PS3	1970 (10)	570	KM#190-199	—	13,500
PS4	1970 (5)	4,650	KM#190-194	52.00	150
PS5	1970 (5)	3,000	KM#195-199	832	13,000
PS6	1974 (2)	30,000	KM#200a-201a	50.00	55.00
PS7	1975 (3)	—	KM#203-205	—	20.00
PS8	1976 (5)	5,000	KM#184.3, 185.2, 186.4, 188.1, 189.1	10.00	7.00
PS9	2000 (3)	500	KM#236-238	—	850

CRETE

The island of Crete (Kriti), located 60 miles southeast of the Peloponnesus, was the center of a brilliant civilization that flourished before the advent of Greek culture. After being conquered by the Romans, Byzantines, Moslems and Venetians, Crete became part of the Turkish Empire in 1669. As a consequence of the Greek Revolution of the1820s, it was ceded to Egypt. Egypt returned the island to the Turks in 1840, and they ceded it to Greece in 1913, after the Second Balkan War.

RULER

Prince George, 1898-1906

MINT MARKS

A - Paris

(a) - Paris (privy marks only)

GREEK ADMINISTRATION

STANDARD COINAGE

KM# 1 LEPTON

Bronze, 15 mm. **Ruler:** Prince George **Obv:** Crown **Rev:** Denomination within wreath

Date	Mintage	F12	VF20	XF40	MS60	MS63
1900 A	289,283	12.00	20.00	50.00	150	300
1901 A	1,710,717	8.00	12.00	27.50	75.00	125

KM# 2 2 LEPTA

Bronze, 20 mm. **Ruler:** Prince George **Obv:** Crown **Rev:** Denomination within wreath

Date	Mintage	F12	VF20	XF40	MS60	MS63
1900 A	793,079	8.00	12.50	37.00	125	245
1901 A	707,000	7.00	12.00	35.00	85.00	145

KM# 6 50 LEPTA

2.50 g., 0.835 Silver 0.0671 oz. ASW, 18 mm. **Ruler:** Prince George **Obv:** Head right **Rev:** Crowned arms, denomination below

Date	Mintage	F12	VF20	XF40	MS60	MS63
1901 (a)	600,000	25.00	55.00	150	750	1,500

KM# 7 DRACHMA

5.00 g., 0.835 Silver 0.1342 oz. ASW, 23 mm. **Ruler:** Prince George **Obv:** Head right **Rev:** Crowned, mantled and supported arms, denomination below

Date	Mintage	F12	VF20	XF40	MS60	MS63
1901 (a)	500,000	35.00	100	750	1,750	3,500

KM# 8 2 DRACHMAI

10.00 g., 0.835 Silver 0.2685 oz. ASW, 27 mm. **Ruler:** Prince George **Obv:** Head right **Rev:** Crowned, mantled and supported arms, denomination below

Date	Mintage	F12	VF20	XF40	MS60	MS63
1901 (a)	175,000	75.00	200	1,000	5,500	10,000

KM# 9 5 DRACHMAI

25.00 g., 0.900 Silver 0.7234 oz. ASW, 37 mm. **Ruler:** Prince George **Obv:** Head right **Rev:** Crowned, mantled and supported arms, denomination below

Date	Mintage	F12	VF20	XF40	MS60	MS63
1901 (a)	150,000	100	250	1,200	10,000	20,000

CROATIA

The Republic of Croatia, (Hrvatska) bordered on the west by the Adriatic Sea and the northeast by Hungary, has an area of 21,829 sq. mi. (56,538 sq. km.) and a population of 4.7 million. Capital: Zagreb.

The country was attached to the Kingdom of Hungary until Dec. 1, 1918, when it joined with the Serbs and Slovenes to form the Kingdom of the Serbs, Croats and Slovenes, which changed its name to the Kingdom of Yugoslavia on Oct. 3, 1929.

KINGDOM

DECIMAL COINAGE

KM# 1 KUNA

Zinc **Note:** Similar to 2 Kune, KM#2.

Date	Mintage	F12	VF20	XF40	MS60	MS63
1941 Rare	—	—	—	—	—	—

Note: Possibly unique

KM# 2 2 KUNE
2.26 g., Zinc, 19.1 mm. **Edge:** Plain **Note:** Medal rotation

Date	Mintage	F12	VF20	XF40	MS60	MS63
1941	—	5.00	10.00	20.00	35.00	—
1941	—	PF63 80.00				

KM# A3 500 KUNA
9.95 g., 0.900 Gold 0.2879 oz. AGW **Obv:** Ante Pavelió, date below **Rev:** Denomination above arms within braided circle

Date	Mintage	F12	VF20	XF40	MS60	MS63
1941	170	—	1,750	2,250	3,000	—

KM# B3 500 KUNA
9.95 g., 0.900 Gold 0.2879 oz. AGW **Obv:** Kneeling figure with sheaf of grain, date below **Rev:** Denomination above arms within braided circle

Date	Mintage	F12	VF20	XF40	MS60	MS63
1941	—	—	—	—	3,400	—

REPUBLIC

REFORM COINAGE

For the circulating minor coins, the reverse legend (name of item) is in Croatian for odd dated years and Latin for even dated years.

May 30, 1994 - 1000 Dinara = 1 Kuna; 100 Lipa = 1 Kuna

KM# 3 LIPA
0.70 g., Aluminum, 17 mm. **Obv:** Denomination above crowned arms **Obv. Legend:** REPUBLIKA HRVATSKA **Rev:** Ears of corn, date below **Rev. Legend:** KUKURUZ **Edge:** Plain

Date	Mintage	VF20	XF40	MS60	MS63	MS65
1993	57,834,100	—	0.20	0.35	0.50	—
1993	17,000	PF65 1.00				
1995 With dot	—	—	0.20	0.35	0.50	—
1995	7,101,000	—	0.20	0.35	0.50	—
1995 With dot, Proof	4,000	PF65 2.00				
1997	5,019,000	—	0.20	0.35	0.50	—
1997	2,000	PF65 1.00				
1999	8,000,000	—	0.20	0.35	0.50	—
1999	2,000	PF65 1.50				

KM# 3a LIPA
Silver, 17 mm. **Obv:** Denomination above arms **Rev:** Ears of corn

Date	Mintage	VF20	XF40	MS60	MS63	MS65
1993 Proof, rare	5	—	—	—	—	—

KM# 3b LIPA
Gold, 17 mm. **Obv:** Denomination above arms **Rev:** Ears of corn

Date	Mintage	VF20	XF40	MS60	MS63	MS65
1993 Proof, rare	5	—	—	—	—	—

KM# 12 LIPA
0.70 g., Aluminum, 17 mm. **Obv:** Denomination above crowned arms **Obv. Legend:** REPUBLIKA HRVATSKA **Rev:** Ears of corn, date below **Rev. Legend:** ZEA MAYS **Edge:** Plain

Date	Mintage	VF20	XF40	MS60	MS63	MS65
1994	2,003,097	—	0.40	0.75	1.00	1.25
1994	4,000	PF65 2.00				
1996	2,000,000	—	0.40	0.75	1.00	1.25
1996	5,000	PF65 1.00				
1998	2,000,000	—	0.40	0.75	1.00	1.25
1998	2,000	PF65 2.50				
2000	2,000,000	—	0.40	0.75	1.00	1.25
2000	1,000	PF65 2.50				

KM# 13 LIPA
0.70 g., Aluminum, 17 mm. **Obv:** Denomination above crowned arms **Rev:** Ears of corn, date below **Rev. Legend:** FAO

Date	Mintage	VF20	XF40	MS60	MS63	MS65
ND-1995	1,000,000	—	0.35	0.75	1.00	—
ND-1995	5,000	PF65 1.50				

KM# 4 2 LIPE
0.92 g., Aluminum, 19 mm. **Obv:** Denomination above crowned arms on half braid **Obv. Legend:** REPUBLIKA HRVATSKA **Rev:** Grapevine, date below **Rev. Legend:** VINOVA LOZA **Edge:** Plain

Date	Mintage	VF20	XF40	MS60	MS63	MS65
1993	17,958,962	—	0.40	0.75	1.00	1.25
1993	17,000	PF65 2.00				
1995	7,498,000	—	0.40	0.75	1.00	1.25
1995	4,000	PF65 2.00				
1997	4,996,000	—	0.40	0.75	1.00	1.25
1997	2,000	PF65 2.50				
1999	8,000,000	—	0.40	0.75	1.00	1.25
1999	2,000	PF65 2.50				

KM# 4a 2 LIPE
Silver, 19 mm. **Obv:** Denomination above crowned arms on half braid **Rev:** Grapevine above date

Date	Mintage	VF20	XF40	MS60	MS63	MS65
1993 Proof, rare	5	—	—	—	—	—

KM# 4b 2 LIPE
Gold, 19 mm. **Obv:** Denomination above crowned arms on half braid **Rev:** Grapevine

Date	Mintage	VF20	XF40	MS60	MS63	MS65
1993 Proof, rare	5	—	—	—	—	—

KM# 14 2 LIPE
0.92 g., Aluminum, 19 mm. **Obv:** Denomination above crowned arms on half braid **Obv. Legend:** REPUBLIKA HRVATSKA **Rev:** Grapevine, date below **Rev. Legend:** VITIS VINIFERA **Edge:** Plain

Date	Mintage	VF20	XF40	MS60	MS63	MS65
1994	2,001,063	—	0.80	1.25	1.50	2.00
1994	4,000	PF65 2.25				
1996	2,006,000	—	0.80	1.25	1.50	2.00
1996	5,000	PF65 2.25				
1998	2,000,000	—	0.80	1.25	1.50	2.00
1998	2,000	PF65 2.50				
2000	2,000,000	—	0.80	1.25	1.50	2.00
2000	1,000	PF65 3.00				

KM# 36 2 LIPE
0.92 g., Aluminum, 19 mm. **Subject:** Olympics **Obv:** Denomination above crowned arms on half braid **Rev:** Olympic logo, torch above date below **Edge:** Plain

Date	Mintage	VF20	XF40	MS60	MS63	MS65
1996	1,000,000	—	0.75	1.00	1.50	2.00
1996	5,000	PF65 2.50				

KM# 5 5 LIPA
2.50 g., Brass Plated Steel, 18 mm. **Obv:** Denomination above crowned arms **Obv. Legend:** REPUBLIKA HRVATSKA **Rev:** Oak leaves, date below **Rev. Legend:** HRAST LUZNJAK **Edge:** Plain

Date	Mintage	VF20	XF40	MS60	MS63	MS65
1993	42,686,969	—	0.40	1.00	1.50	2.00
1993	17,000	PF65 2.25				
1995	17,308,000	—	0.40	0.60	1.00	1.50
1995	4,000	PF65 3.00				
1997	29,964,000	—	0.40	0.60	1.00	1.50
1997	2,000	PF65 3.50				
1999	25,402,000	—	0.40	0.60	1.00	1.50
1999	2,000	PF65 3.50				

KM# 5a 5 LIPA
Silver, 18 mm. **Obv:** Denomination above crowned arms **Rev:** Oak leaves, date below

Date	Mintage	VF20	XF40	MS60	MS63	MS65
1993 Proof, rare	5	—	—	—	—	—

KM# 5b 5 LIPA
Gold, 18 mm. **Obv:** Denomination above crowned arms **Rev:** Oak leaves, date below

Date	Mintage	VF20	XF40	MS60	MS63	MS65
1993 Proof, rare	5	—	—	—	—	—

KM# 15 5 LIPA
2.50 g., Brass Plated Steel, 18 mm. **Obv:** Denomination above crowned arms **Obv. Legend:** REPUBLIKA HRVATSKA **Rev:** Oak leaves, date below **Rev. Legend:** QUERCUS ROBUR **Edge:** Plain

Date	Mintage	VF20	XF40	MS60	MS63	MS65
1994	2,009,346	—	0.80	1.25	1.50	2.00
1994	4,000	PF65 2.25				
1996	2,004,000	—	0.80	1.25	1.50	2.00
1996	5,000	PF65 2.50				
1998	2,000,000	—	0.80	1.25	1.50	2.00
1998	2,000	PF65 3.00				
2000	4,500,000	—	0.80	1.25	1.50	2.00
2000	1,000	PF65 4.00				

KM# 37 5 LIPA
2.50 g., Brass Plated Steel, 18 mm. **Subject:** Olympics **Obv:** Denomination above crowned arms **Rev:** Olympic logo, torch above, date below

Date	Mintage	VF20	XF40	MS60	MS63	MS65
1996	900,000	—	1.00	1.50	2.00	2.50
1996	5,000	PF65 3.50				

KM# 6 10 LIPA
3.25 g., Brass Plated Steel, 20 mm. **Obv:** Denomination above crowned arms **Obv. Legend:** REPUBLIKA HRVATSKA **Rev:** Tobacco plant, date below **Rev. Legend:** DUHAN **Edge:** Plain

Date	Mintage	VF20	XF40	MS60	MS63	MS65
1993	63,689,778	—	0.40	0.75	1.50	2.00
1993	17,000	PF65 3.00				
1995	26,335,500	—	0.40	0.75	1.50	2.00
1995	4,000	PF65 4.00				
1997	39,995,500	—	0.40	0.75	1.50	2.00
1997	2,000	PF65 4.50				
1999	51,500,000	—	0.40	0.75	1.50	2.00
1999	2,000	PF65 4.50				

KM# 6a 10 LIPA
Silver, 20 mm. **Obv:** Denomination above crowned arms on half braid **Rev:** Tobacco plant, date below

Date	Mintage	VF20	XF40	MS60	MS63	MS65
1993 Proof, rare	5	—	—	—	—	—

KM# 6b 10 LIPA

Gold, 20 mm. **Obv:** Denomination above crowned arms on half braid **Rev:** Oak leaves, date below

Date	Mintage	VF20	XF40	MS60	MS63	MS65
1993 Proof, rare	5	—	—	—	—	—

KM# 16 10 LIPA

3.25 g., Brass Plated Steel, 20 mm. **Obv:** Denomination above crowned arms on half braid **Obv. Legend:** REPUBLIKA HRVATSKA **Rev:** Tobacco plant, date below **Rev. Legend:** NICOTIANA TABACUM **Edge:** Plain

Date	Mintage	VF20	XF40	MS60	MS63	MS65
1994	2,000,127	—	0.80	1.25	2.00	2.50
1994	4,000	PF65 4.00				
1996	2,000,000	—	0.80	1.25	2.00	2.50
1996	5,000	PF65 3.50				
1998	2,000,000	—	0.80	1.25	2.00	2.50
1998	2,000	PF65 4.50				
2000	3,000,000	—	0.80	1.25	2.00	2.50
2000	1,000	PF65 5.00				

KM# 38 10 LIPA

3.25 g., Brass Plated Steel, 20 mm. **Subject:** 50th Anniversary - UN **Obv:** Denomination above crowned arms above half braid **Rev:** UN logo, dates below

Date	Mintage	VF20	XF40	MS60	MS63	MS65
ND-1995	900,000	—	1.00	1.50	2.00	2.50
ND-1995	5,000	PF65 4.00				

KM# 7 20 LIPA

2.90 g., Nickel Plated Steel, 18.5 mm. **Obv:** Denomination above crowned arms on half braid **Obv. Legend:** REPUBLIKA HRVATSKA **Rev:** Olive branch, date below **Rev. Legend:** MASLINA **Edge:** Plain

Date	Mintage	VF20	XF40	MS60	MS63	MS65
1993	25,206,442	—	0.50	0.75	1.50	2.00
1993	17,000	PF65 3.00				
1995	39,718,500	—	0.50	0.75	1.50	2.00
1995	4,000	PF65 4.00				
1997	9,999,000	—	0.45	0.75	1.50	2.00
1997	2,000	PF65 4.50				
1999	33,500,000	—	0.45	0.75	1.50	2.00
1999	2,000	PF65 4.50				

KM# 7a 20 LIPA

Silver, 18.5 mm. **Obv:** Denomination above crowned arms on half braid **Rev:** Olive branch, date below

Date	Mintage	VF20	XF40	MS60	MS63	MS65
1993 Proof, rare	5	—	—	—	—	—

KM# 7b 20 LIPA

Gold, 18.5 mm. **Obv:** Denomination above crowned arms on half braid **Rev:** Olive branch, date below

Date	Mintage	VF20	XF40	MS60	MS63	MS65
1993 Proof, rare	5	—	—	—	—	—

KM# 17 20 LIPA

2.90 g., Nickel Plated Steel, 18.5 mm. **Obv:** Denomination above crowned arms on half braid **Obv. Legend:** REPUBLIKA HRVATSKA **Rev:** Olive branch, date below **Rev. Legend:** OLEA EUROPAEA **Edge:** Plain

Date	Mintage	VF20	XF40	MS60	MS63	MS65
1994	2,072,862	—	0.80	1.25	2.00	2.50
1994	4,000	PF65 3.00				
1996	2,000,000	—	0.80	1.25	2.00	2.50
1996	5,000	PF65 4.00				
1998	2,000,000	—	0.80	1.25	2.00	2.50
1998	2,000	PF65 4.50				
2000	2,000,000	—	0.80	1.25	2.00	2.50
2000	1,000	PF65 5.00				

KM# 18 20 LIPA

2.90 g., Nickel Plated Steel, 18.5 mm. **Subject:** F.A.O. **Obv:** Denomination above crowned arms on half braid **Rev:** Olive branch, date below

Date	Mintage	VF20	XF40	MS60	MS63	MS65
ND-1995	1,000,000	—	0.65	0.85	1.75	2.50
ND-1995	5,000	PF65 4.50				

KM# 8 50 LIPA

3.65 g., Nickel Plated Steel, 20.5 mm. **Obv:** Denomination above crowned arms on half braid **Obv. Legend:** REPUBLIKA HRVATSKA **Rev:** Flowers, date below **Rev. Legend:** VELEBITSKA DEGENIJA **Edge:** Plain

Date	Mintage	VF20	XF40	MS60	MS63	MS65
1993	51,456,267	—	0.60	0.80	1.50	2.00
1993	17,000	PF65 4.00				
1995	22,077,000	—	0.60	0.80	1.50	2.00
1995	4,000	PF65 4.50				
1997	1,473,000	—	0.60	0.80	1.50	2.00
1997	2,000	PF65 5.00				
1999	1,000,000	—	0.60	0.80	1.50	2.00
1999	2,000	PF65 5.00				

KM# 8a 50 LIPA

Silver, 20.5 mm. **Obv:** Denomination above crowned arms on half braid **Rev:** Flowers, date below

Date	Mintage	VF20	XF40	MS60	MS63	MS65
1993 Proof, rare	5	—	—	—	—	—

KM# 8b 50 LIPA

Gold, 20.5 mm. **Obv:** Denomination above crowned arms on half braid **Rev:** Flowers, date below

Date	Mintage	VF20	XF40	MS60	MS63	MS65
1993 Proof, rare	5	—	—	—	—	—

KM# 19 50 LIPA

3.65 g., Nickel Plated Steel, 20.5 mm. **Obv:** Denomination above crowned arms on half braid **Obv. Legend:** REPUBLIKA HRVATSKA **Rev:** Flowers, date below **Rev. Legend:** DEGENIA VELEBITICA **Edge:** Plain

Date	Mintage	VF20	XF40	MS60	MS63	MS65
1994	2,001,131	—	0.80	1.25	2.00	2.50
1994	4,000	PF65 4.00				
1996	2,000,000	—	0.80	1.25	2.00	2.50
1996	5,000	PF65 4.00				
1998	2,000,000	—	0.80	1.25	2.00	2.50
1998	2,000	PF65 4.50				
2000	3,500,000	—	0.80	1.25	2.00	2.50
2000	1,000	PF65 5.00				

KM# 39 50 LIPA

3.65 g., Nickel Plated Steel, 20.5 mm. **Subject:** European soccer **Obv:** Denomination above crowned arms on half braid **Rev:** Checkered shield, soccer ball at bottom, date above

Date	Mintage	VF20	XF40	MS60	MS63	MS65
1996	900,000	—	—	1.25	2.00	2.50
1996	5,000	PF65 5.00				

KM# 9.1 KUNA

5.00 g., Copper-Nickel-Zinc, 22.5 mm. **Obv:** Marten back of numeral, arms divide branches below **Obv. Legend:** REPUBLIKA HRVATSKA **Rev:** Nightingale left, two dates **Rev. Legend:** SLAVUJ **Edge:** Reeded

Date	Mintage	VF20	XF40	MS60	MS63	MS65
1993	49,913,770	—	0.50	1.00	1.75	2.25
1993	17,000	PF65 3.00				
1995	33,707,000	—	0.50	1.00	1.75	2.25
1995	4,000	PF65 3.50				
1997	6,205,000	—	0.50	1.00	1.75	2.25
1997	2,000	PF65 4.00				

KM# 9.1a KUNA

Silver, 22.5 mm. **Obv:** Marten back of numeral, arms divide branches below **Rev:** Nightingale left

Date	Mintage	VF20	XF40	MS60	MS63	MS65
1993 Proof, rare	—	—	—	—	—	—

KM# 9.1b KUNA

Gold, 22.5 mm. **Obv:** Marten back of numeral, arms divide branches below **Rev:** Nightingale left

Date	Mintage	VF20	XF40	MS60	MS63	MS65
1993 Proof, rare	—	—	—	—	—	—

KM# 9.2 KUNA

5.00 g., Copper-Nickel-Zinc, 22.5 mm. **Obv:** Crowned arms flanked by sprays, denomination above on marten **Rev:** Nightingale, left, '1994' above, date below **Edge:** Reeded

Date	Mintage	VF20	XF40	MS60	MS63	MS65
1999	27,000,000	—	0.50	1.00	1.50	2.50
1999	2,000	PF65 4.00				

KM# 20.1 KUNA

5.00 g., Copper-Nickel-Zinc, 22.5 mm. **Obv:** Marten back of numeral, arms divide branches below **Rev:** Nightingale left, date below **Rev. Legend:** Error spelling "LUSCINNIA MEGARHYNCHOS" **Edge:** Reeded **Note:** Formerly KM-20

Date	Mintage	VF20	XF40	MS60	MS63	MS65
1994	2,000,133	—	0.50	1.00	2.00	2.50
1994	4,000	PF65 4.00				

KM# 20.2 KUNA

5.00 g., Copper-Nickel-Zinc, 22.5 mm. **Obv:** Marten back of numeral, arms divide branches below **Obv. Legend:** REPUBLIKA HRVATSKA **Rev:** Nightingale left, date below **Rev. Legend:** Correct spelling "LUSCINIA MEGARHYNCHOS" **Edge:** Reeded

Date	Mintage	VF20	XF40	MS60	MS63	MS65
1996	2,000,000	—	1.00	2.00	3.00	4.00
1996	5,000	PF65 5.00				
1998	1,000,000	—	1.00	2.00	3.00	4.00
1998	2,000	PF65 5.00				
2000	2,000,000	—	1.00	2.00	3.00	4.00
2000	1,000	PF65 5.00				

KM# 40 KUNA

5.00 g., Copper-Nickel-Zinc, 22.5 mm. **Subject:** Olympics **Obv:** Marten back of numeral, arms divide branches below **Rev:** Olympic logo, torch above, date below **Edge:** Reeded

Date	Mintage	VF20	XF40	MS60	MS63	MS65
1996	1,000,000	—	1.50	2.50	3.00	4.00
1996	5,000	PF65 4.00				

KM# 10 2 KUNE

6.20 g., Copper-Nickel-Zinc, 24.5 mm. **Obv:** Marten back of numeral, arms divide branches below **Obv. Legend:** REPUBLIKA HRVATSKA **Rev:** Bluefin tuna right, date below **Rev. Legend:** TUNJ **Edge:** Reeded

Date	Mintage	VF20	XF40	MS60	MS63	MS65
1993	19,774,119	—	1.00	1.50	2.00	3.00
1993	17,000	PF65 4.50				
1995	9,304,000	—	1.00	1.50	2.00	3.00
1995	4,000	PF65 5.50				
1997	1,305,000	—	1.00	1.75	2.25	3.50
1997	2,000	PF65 6.00				
1999	2,500,000	—	1.00	1.75	2.25	3.50
1999	2,000	PF65 6.00				

KM# 10a 2 KUNE

Silver, 24.5 mm. **Obv:** Marten back of numeral, arms divide branches below **Rev:** Tuna right, date below

Date	Mintage	VF20	XF40	MS60	MS63	MS65
1993 Proof, rare	5	—	—	—	—	—

KM# 10b 2 KUNE

Gold, 24.5 mm. **Obv:** Marten back of numeral, arms divide branches below **Rev:** Tuna right, date below

Date	Mintage	VF20	XF40	MS60	MS63	MS65
1993 Proof, rare	5	—	—	—	—	—

KM# 21 2 KUNE

6.20 g., Copper-Nickel-Zinc, 24.5 mm. **Obv:** Marten back of numeral, arms divide branches below **Obv. Legend:** REPUBLIKA HRVATSKA **Rev:** Bluefin tuna right, date below **Rev. Legend:** THUNNUS - THYNNUS **Edge:** Reeded

Date	Mintage	VF20	XF40	MS60	MS63	MS65
1994	2,000,758	—	1.50	2.00	3.00	4.00
1994	4,000	PF65 5.00				
1996	2,000,000	—	1.50	2.00	3.00	4.00
1996	5,000	PF65 4.50				
1998	2,000,000	—	1.50	2.00	3.00	4.00
1998	2,000	PF65 5.50				
2000	2,000,000	—	1.50	2.00	3.00	4.00
2000	1,000	PF65 6.00				

KM# 22 2 KUNE

6.20 g., Copper-Nickel-Zinc, 24.5 mm. **Obv:** Marten back of numeral, arms divide branches below **Rev:** Bluefin tuna right, date below **Rev. Legend:** FAO **Edge:** Reeded

Date	Mintage	VF20	XF40	MS60	MS63	MS65
ND-1995	500,000	—	0.75	2.00	3.00	4.00
ND-1995	5,000	PF65 5.50				

KM# 11 5 KUNA

7.45 g., Copper-Nickel-Zinc, 26.7 mm. **Obv:** Marten back of numeral, arms divide branches below **Obv. Legend:** REPUBLIKA HRVATSKA **Rev:** Brown bear left, date below **Rev. Legend:** MRKI MEDVJED **Edge:** Reeded

Date	Mintage	VF20	XF40	MS60	MS63	MS65
1993	4,989,330	—	1.50	2.50	3.50	5.00
1993	17,000	PF65 7.50				
1995	3,724,000	—	1.50	2.50	3.50	5.00
1995	4,000	PF65 7.50				
1997	1,165,000	—	1.50	3.00	5.00	7.00
1997	2,000	PF65 7.50				
1999	4,000,000	—	1.50	2.50	3.50	5.00
1999	2,000	PF65 7.50				

KM# 11a 5 KUNA

Silver, 26.7 mm. **Obv:** Marten back of numeral, arms divide branches below **Rev:** Brown bear left, date below

Date	Mintage	VF20	XF40	MS60	MS63	MS65
1993 Proof, rare	5	—	—	—	—	—

KM# 11b 5 KUNA

Gold, 26.7 mm. **Obv:** Marten back of numeral, arms divide branches below **Rev:** Brown bear left, date below

Date	Mintage	VF20	XF40	MS60	MS63	MS65
1993 Proof, rare	5	—	—	—	—	—

KM# 23 5 KUNA

7.45 g., Copper-Nickel-Zinc, 26.5 mm. **Obv:** Marten back of numeral, arms divide branches below **Obv. Legend:** REPUBLIKA HRVATSKA **Rev:** Brown bear left, date below **Rev. Legend:** URSUS ARCTOS **Edge:** Reeded

Date	Mintage	VF20	XF40	MS60	MS63	MS65
1994	2,001,422	—	2.00	3.50	5.00	7.00
1994	4,000	PF65 8.00				
1996	2,000,000	—	2.00	3.50	5.00	7.00
1996	5,000	PF65 8.00				
1998	2,000,000	—	2.00	3.50	5.00	7.00
1998	2,000	PF65 8.00				
2000	7,700,000	—	1.50	3.00	5.00	7.00
2000	1,000	PF65 9.00				

KM# 24 5 KUNA

7.45 g., Copper-Nickel, 26.5 mm. **Subject:** 500th Anniversary - Senj **Obv:** Denomination on square divides arms above from shield below, circle surrounds **Rev:** Anniversary dates on symbol within circle

Date	Mintage	VF20	XF40	MS60	MS63	MS65
1994	1,000,000	—	—	3.50	5.00	6.00
1994	5,000	PF65 8.00				

KM# 24a 5 KUNA

Silver, 26.7 mm. **Subject:** 500th Anniversary - Senj **Obv:** Denomination on square divides arms above from shield below, circle surrounds **Rev:** Anniversary dates on symbols within circle

Date	Mintage	VF20	XF40	MS60	MS63	MS65
1994	—	PF65 275				

KM# 24b 5 KUNA

12.00 g., 0.900 Gold 0.3472 oz. AGW, 26.2 mm. **Subject:** 500th Anniversary - Senj **Obv:** Denomination on square divides arms above from shield below, circle surrounds **Rev:** Anniversary dates on symbols within circle

Date	Mintage	VF20	XF40	MS60	MS63	MS65
1994	200	—	—	—	—	650

KM# 47 25 KUNA

12.75 g., Bi-Metallic Brass center in Copper-Nickel ring, 32 mm. **Subject:** Danube Border Region **Obv:** 3D denomination on marten within circle, crowned arms below divide branches **Rev:** Regional map, date below **Shape:** 12-sided

Date	Mintage	VF20	XF40	MS60	MS63	MS65
1997	300,000	—	—	7.00	8.00	9.00
1997	2,000	PF65 22.50				

KM# 48 25 KUNA

12.75 g., Bi-Metallic Brass center in Copper-Nickel ring, 32 mm. **Subject:** 5th Anniversary - UN Membership **Obv:** 3D denomination on marten within circle, crowned arms divide branches below **Rev:** UN emblem within wreath, date below **Shape:** 12-sided

Date	Mintage	VF20	XF40	MS60	MS63	MS65
1997	2,000	PF65 22.50				
1997	300,000	—	—	7.00	8.00	9.00

KM# 49 25 KUNA

12.75 g., Bi-Metallic Brass center in Copper-Nickel ring, 32 mm. **Subject:** First Croatian Esperanto Congress **Obv:** 3D denomination on marten within circle, crowned arms below divide branches **Rev:** Logo, date below **Shape:** 12-sided

Date	Mintage	VF20	XF40	MS60	MS63	MS65
1997	2,000	PF65 22.50				
1997	300,000	—	—	7.00	8.00	9.00

KM# 63 25 KUNA

12.75 g., Bi-Metallic Brass center in Copper-Nickel ring, 32 mm. **Subject:** Lisbon Expo **Obv:** 3D denomination on marten within circle, crowned arms below divide branches **Rev:** Sailboat, date upper right **Shape:** 12-sided

Date	Mintage	VF20	XF40	MS60	MS63	MS65
1998	300,000	—	—	7.00	7.00	9.00
1998	1,000	PF65 25.00				

KM# 64 25 KUNA

12.75 g., Bi-Metallic Brass center in Copper-Nickel ring, 31 mm. **Subject:** European Union **Obv:** 3D denomination on marten within circle, crowned arms below divide branches **Rev:** 12 stars on a large "E", date below **Edge:** Plain **Shape:** 12-sided

Date	Mintage	VF20	XF40	MS60	MS63	MS65
1999	300,000	—	—	7.00	8.00	9.00
1999	1,000	PF65 25.00				

KM# 65 25 KUNA
12.75 g., Bi-Metallic Brass center in Copper-Nickel ring, 32 mm. **Obv:** 3D denomination on marten within circle, crowned arms below divide branches **Rev:** Human fetus within radiant circle, date below **Edge:** Plain **Shape:** 12-sided

Date	Mintage	VF20	XF40	MS60	MS63	MS65
2000	300,000	—	—	7.00	8.00	9.00
2000	1,000	PF65 25.00				

KM# 25.1 100 KUNA
15.00 g., 0.999 Silver 0.4818 oz. ASW, 32 mm. **Subject:** 900th Anniversary - St. Blaza Church **Obv:** Buildings divide arms and denomination **Rev:** Altar at St. Blaza divides dates

Date	Mintage	VF20	XF40	MS60	MS63	MS65
ND-1994	3,000	PF63 50.00	PF65 60.00			

KM# 25.2 100 KUNA
15.00 g., 0.999 Silver 0.4818 oz. ASW, 32 mm. **Subject:** 900th Anniversary - St. Blaza Church **Obv:** Buildings divide denomination and arms, series II mark added **Rev:** Altar at St. Blaza divides dates

Date	Mintage	VF20	XF40	MS60	MS63	MS65
ND-1994	1,000	PF63 75.00	PF65 90.00			

KM# 26 100 KUNA
33.63 g., 0.925 Silver 1.0001 oz. ASW, 40 mm. **Rev:** Half-length bust of Pope John Paul II

Date	Mintage	VF20	XF40	MS60	MS63	MS65
1994	10,000	PF63 70.00	PF65 80.00			

KM# 27 100 KUNA
20.00 g., 0.925 Silver 0.5948 oz. ASW, 34 mm. **Subject:** 5th Anniversary of Independence

Date	Mintage	VF20	XF40	MS60	MS63	MS65
ND-1995	6,000	PF63 38.00	PF65 45.00			

KM# 50 100 KUNA
20.00 g., 0.925 Silver 0.5948 oz. ASW, 34 mm. **Subject:** City of Split **Obv:** Towered building, denomination at left **Rev:** Ancient depiction of king on throne, dates at left

Date	Mintage	VF20	XF40	MS60	MS63	MS65
ND-1995	5,000	PF63 35.00	PF65 40.00			

KM# 41 100 KUNA
20.00 g., 0.925 Silver 0.5948 oz. ASW, 34 mm. **Subject:** Olympics **Obv:** Sailboat racing, denomination above **Rev:** Wheelchair-bound javelin thrower, crowned arms above

Date	Mintage	VF20	XF40	MS60	MS63	MS65
1996	2,000	PF63 40.00	PF65 50.00			

KM# 42 100 KUNA
20.00 g., 0.925 Silver 0.5948 oz. ASW, 34 mm. **Subject:** Olympics **Obv:** Rowing, denomination above **Rev:** Water polo player, crowned arms above

Date	Mintage	VF20	XF40	MS60	MS63	MS65
1996	2,000	PF63 40.00	PF65 50.00			

KM# 28 150 KUNA
24.00 g., 0.925 Silver 0.7137 oz. ASW, 37 mm. **Subject:** 5th Anniversary of Independence **Obv:** Denomination below crowned arms **Rev:** Assorted symbols on portioned background

Date	Mintage	VF20	XF40	MS60	MS63	MS65
1995	5,000	PF63 45.00	PF65 55.00			

KM# 43 150 KUNA
24.00 g., 0.925 Silver 0.7137 oz. ASW, 37 mm. **Subject:** Olympics **Obv:** Gymnast, denomination at right **Rev:** Basketball players, crowned arms above

Date	Mintage	VF20	XF40	MS60	MS63	MS65
1996	2,000	PF63 45.00	PF65 55.00			

KM# 44 150 KUNA
24.00 g., 0.925 Silver 0.7137 oz. ASW, 37 mm. **Subject:** Olympics **Obv:** Table tennis and paddle, denomination at top **Rev:** Marksmanship eye design, crowned arms divide date above, circle surrounds

Date	Mintage	VF20	XF40	MS60	MS63	MS65
1996	2,000	PF63 45.00	PF65 55.00			

KM# 56 150 KUNA
24.00 g., 0.925 Silver 0.7137 oz. ASW, 37 mm. **Subject:** 800th Anniversary - City of Osijek **Obv:** Crowned arms above denomination **Rev:** City view

Date	Mintage	VF20	XF40	MS60	MS63	MS65
ND-1996	1,000	PF63 60.00	PF65 70.00			

KM# 59 150 KUNA
24.00 g., 0.925 Silver 0.7137 oz. ASW, 37 mm. **Obv:** Denomination above arms, date divided below **Rev:** Bust left

Date	Mintage	VF20	XF40	MS60	MS63	MS65
1997	10,000	PF63 40.00	PF65 50.00			

KM# 67 150 KUNA
24.00 g., 0.925 Silver 0.7137 oz. ASW, 37 mm. **Subject:** Vukovar **Obv:** Ceramic container, arms below **Rev:** Courtyard, date at right **Edge:** Plain

Date	Mintage	VF20	XF40	MS60	MS63	MS65
1997	2,000	PF63 55.00	PF65 65.00			

KM# 69 150 KUNA
24.00 g., 0.925 Silver 0.7137 oz. ASW, 37 mm. **Obv:** Wild flowers, denomination at right, arms at top **Rev:** White-tailed eagle on branch **Edge:** Plain

Date	Mintage	VF20	XF40	MS60	MS63	MS65
1997	1,000	PF63 55.00	PF65 65.00			

KM# 75 150 KUNA
24.00 g., 0.925 Silver 0.7137 oz. ASW, 37 mm. **Subject:** 150 Years of Croatian as an Official Language **Obv:** Two hands writing **Rev:** Old document **Edge:** Plain

Date	Mintage	VF20	XF40	MS60	MS63	MS65
1997	1,000	PF63 50.00	PF65 60.00			

KM# 73 150 KUNA
24.00 g., 0.925 Silver 0.7137 oz. ASW, 37 mm. **Obv:** Small national arms above religious arms and value **Rev:** Cardinal Stepinac (1898-1960) right **Edge:** Plain

Date	Mintage	VF20	XF40	MS60	MS63	MS65
1998	3,000	PF63 38.00	PF65 45.00			

KM# 29.1 200 KUNA
20.00 g., 0.999 Silver 0.6424 oz. ASW, 38 mm. **Obv:** St. Marka Church **Rev:** Portal of St. Marka Church

Date	Mintage	VF20	XF40	MS60	MS63	MS65
ND-1994	3,000	PF63 70.00	PF65 85.00			

KM# 29.2 200 KUNA
20.00 g., 0.999 Silver 0.6424 oz. ASW, 38 mm. **Obv:** St. Marka Church, Series II mark added **Rev:** Portal of St. Marka Church

Date	Mintage	VF20	XF40	MS60	MS63	MS65
ND-1994	1,000	PF63 85.00	PF65 100			

KM# 30 200 KUNA
33.63 g., 0.925 Silver 1.0001 oz. ASW, 40 mm. **Subject:** 5th Anniversary of Independence

Date	Mintage	VF20	XF40	MS60	MS63	MS65
ND-1995	4,000	PF63 65.00	PF65 80.00			

KM# 51 200 KUNA
33.63 g., 0.925 Silver 1.0001 oz. ASW, 40 mm. **Subject:** Spalatum **Obv:** Diocletian's palace, denomination and arms above **Rev:** Sarcophagus, two dates above

Date	Mintage	VF20	XF40	MS60	MS63	MS65
ND-1995	5,000	PF63 45.00	PF65 55.00			

KM# 45 200 KUNA
33.63 g., 0.925 Silver 1.0001 oz. ASW, 40 mm. **Subject:** Olympics **Obv:** High jumper **Rev:** Tennis player

Date	Mintage	VF20	XF40	MS60	MS63	MS65
ND (1996)	2,000	PF63 50.00	PF65 60.00			

KM# 46 200 KUNA
33.63 g., 0.925 Silver 1.0001 oz. ASW, 40 mm. **Subject:** Olympics **Obv:** Diving swimmers, denomination above **Rev:** Basketball game, crowned arms above

Date	Mintage	VF20	XF40	MS60	MS63	MS65
1996	2,000	PF63 50.00	PF65 60.00			

KM# 54 200 KUNA
33.63 g., 0.925 Silver 1.0001 oz. ASW, 40 mm. **Subject:** University in Zadar **Obv:** Circle of arches, denomination at top, arms below **Rev:** Saint reading within circle, dates below

Date	Mintage	VF20	XF40	MS60	MS63	MS65
ND-1996	1,000	PF63 55.00	PF65 65.00			

KM# 57 200 KUNA
33.63 g., 0.925 Silver 1.0001 oz. ASW, 40 mm. **Subject:** 500th Anniversary - City of Osijek **Obv:** National arms above denomination **Rev:** City view

Date	Mintage	VF20	XF40	MS60	MS63	MS65
ND-1996	1,000	PF63 55.00	PF65 65.00			

KM# 60 200 KUNA
33.63 g., 0.925 Silver 1.0001 oz. ASW, 40 mm. **Obv:** Denomination above national arms **Rev:** Bust left

Date	Mintage	VF20	XF40	MS60	MS63	MS65
1997	5,000	PF63 45.00	PF65 55.00			

KM# 71 200 KUNA
33.63 g., 0.925 Silver 1.0001 oz. ASW, 40 mm. **Obv:** Wild flowers **Obv. Legend:** REPUBLIKA HRVATSKA **Rev:** Three black storks **Rev. Legend:** CRNA RODA **Edge:** Plain

Date	Mintage	VF20	XF40	MS60	MS63	MS65
1997	1,000	PF63 60.00	PF65 70.00			

KM# 76 200 KUNA
33.63 g., 0.925 Silver 1.0001 oz. ASW, 40 mm. **Obv:** National arms above a page of illuminated text, denomination below **Rev:** Juraj Julija Klovic, 1498-1578, looking right **Edge:** Plain

Date	Mintage	VF20	XF40	MS60	MS63	MS65
1998	2,000	PF63 45.00	PF65 55.00			

KM# 77 200 KUNA

33.63 g., 0.925 Silver 1.0001 oz. ASW, 40 mm. **Obv:** National arms and value above book, quill and oil lamp **Rev:** Ivana Brlic Mazuranic, seated looking right **Edge:** Plain

Date	Mintage	VF20	XF40	MS60	MS63	MS65
1998	2,000	PF63 45.00	PF65 55.00			

KM# 80 200 KUNA

33.63 g., 0.925 Silver 1.0001 oz. ASW, 40 mm. **Obv:** Cakovec old town view **Rev:** Katarina Zrinska **Edge:** Plain

Date	Mintage	VF20	XF40	MS60	MS63	MS65
1999	2,000	PF63 45.00	PF65 55.00			

KM# 81 200 KUNA

33.63 g., 0.925 Silver 1.0001 oz. ASW, 40 mm. **Obv:** Aquarelle painting **Rev:** Zlava Raskaj

Date	Mintage	VF20	XF40	MS60	MS63	MS65
2000	2,000	PF63 45.00	PF65 55.00			

KM# 31.1 500 KUNA

3.50 g., 0.999 Gold 0.1124 oz. AGW, 20 mm. **Obv:** Izborna Cathedral, denomination below **Rev:** Arms at top and bottom, cherubs flank

Date	Mintage	VF20	XF40	MS60	MS63	MS65
1994	1,000	PF63 300	PF65 350			

KM# 31.2 500 KUNA

3.50 g., 0.999 Gold 0.1124 oz. AGW, 20 mm. **Obv:** Izborna Cathedral, Series II added **Rev:** Arms at top and bottom, cherubs flank

Date	Mintage	VF20	XF40	MS60	MS63	MS65
1994	1,000	PF63 300	PF65 350			

KM# 32 500 KUNA

3.50 g., 0.986 Gold 0.111 oz. AGW, 18 mm. **Subject:** 5th Anniversary of Independence

Date	Mintage	VF20	XF40	MS60	MS63	MS65
1995	4,000	PF63 250	PF65 300			

KM# 52 500 KUNA

3.50 g., 0.986 Gold 0.111 oz. AGW, 18 mm. **Subject:** City of Split **Obv:** Towered building, denomination at left **Rev:** Ancient depiction of king on throne, dates at left

Date	Mintage	VF20	XF40	MS60	MS63	MS65
ND-1995	6,000	PF63 250	PF65 300			

KM# 55 500 KUNA

3.50 g., 0.986 Gold 0.111 oz. AGW, 18 mm. **Subject:** University of Zadar **Obv:** Circle of arches, denomination at top, arms below **Rev:** Saint reading within circle, dates below

Date	Mintage	VF20	XF40	MS60	MS63	MS65
ND-1996	1,000	PF63 250	PF65 300			

KM# 58 500 KUNA

3.50 g., 0.986 Gold 0.111 oz. AGW, 18 mm. **Subject:** 800th Anniversary - City of Osijek **Obv:** Crowned arms, denomination below **Rev:** City view

Date	Mintage	VF20	XF40	MS60	MS63	MS65
ND-1996	1,000	PF63 250	PF65 300			

KM# 68 500 KUNA

3.50 g., 0.986 Gold 0.111 oz. AGW, 18 mm. **Subject:** Vukovar **Obv:** Ceramic container, denomination at upper right **Rev:** Courtyard, date at right **Edge:** Plain

Date	Mintage	VF20	XF40	MS60	MS63	MS65
1997	2,000	PF63 210	PF65 245			

KM# 70 500 KUNA

3.50 g., 0.986 Gold 0.111 oz. AGW, 18 mm. **Obv:** Wild flowers, denomination at right, arms above **Rev:** White-tailed eagle on branch **Edge:** Plain

Date	Mintage	VF20	XF40	MS60	MS63	MS65
1997	1,000	PF63 210	PF65 250			

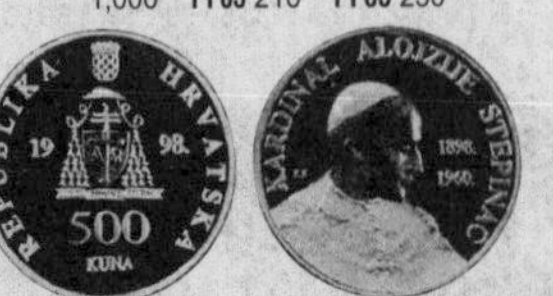

KM# 74 500 KUNA

3.50 g., 0.986 Gold 0.111 oz. AGW, 18 mm. **Obv:** Small national arms above religious arms and value, date divided **Rev:** Bust of Cardinal Stepinac (1898-1960) right **Edge:** Plain

Date	Mintage	VF20	XF40	MS60	MS63	MS65
1998	3,000	PF63 210	PF65 250			

KM# 82 500 KUNA

3.50 g., 0.986 Gold 0.111 oz. AGW, 18 mm. **Subject:** 10th Anniversary of Parliament **Obv:** View of session **Rev:** Parliament building

Date	Mintage	VF20	XF40	MS60	MS63	MS65
ND (2000)	500	PF63 210	PF65 265			

KM# 33 1000 KUNA

7.00 g., 0.986 Gold 0.2219 oz. AGW, 25 mm. **Obv:** Crowned arms divides date above denomination **Rev:** Half-length portrait of Pope John Paul II, looking left

Date	Mintage	VF20	XF40	MS60	MS63	MS65
1994	4,000	PF63 450	PF65 500			

KM# 34 1000 KUNA

7.00 g., 0.986 Gold 0.2219 oz. AGW, 22 mm. **Subject:** 5th Anniversary of Independence **Obv:** Arms divide sprays below denomination, dotted background **Rev:** Map, inscription, and dates, dotted background

Date	Mintage	VF20	XF40	MS60	MS63	MS65
ND-1995	3,000	PF63 450	PF65 500			

KM# 53 1000 KUNA

7.00 g., 0.986 Gold 0.2219 oz. AGW, 22 mm. **Subject:** Spalatum **Obv:** Diocletian's palace, denomination and arms above **Rev:** Sarcophagus, dates above

Date	Mintage	VF20	XF40	MS60	MS63	MS65
ND-1995	3,000	PF63 450	PF65 500			

KM# 61 1000 KUNA

7.00 g., 0.986 Gold 0.2219 oz. AGW, 22 mm. **Subject:** Death of Dr. Tudman **Obv:** National arms **Rev:** Dr. Tudman **Edge:** Plain

Date	Mintage	VF20	XF40	MS60	MS63	MS65
1997	3,000	PF63 450	PF65 500			

KM# 72 1000 KUNA

7.00 g., 0.986 Gold 0.2219 oz. AGW, 22 mm. **Obv:** Wild flowers, arms above, denomination at right **Obv. Legend:** REPUBLIKA HRVATSKA **Rev:** Three Black Storks **Rev. Legend:** CRNA RODA **Edge:** Plain

Date	Mintage	VF20	XF40	MS60	MS63	MS65
1997	1,000	PF63 450	PF65 500			

TRADE COINAGE

KM# 35 DUCAT

3.50 g., 0.986 Gold 0.111 oz. AGW, 20 mm. **Obv:** Crowned arms with supporters, denomination below **Rev:** Ruder Boskovic bust at left facing, dates at left

Date	Mintage	VF20	XF40	MS60	MS63	MS65
1994 Proof	5,000	—	—	—	—	265

KM# 62 DUCAT

3.50 g., 0.986 Gold 0.111 oz. AGW, 20 mm. **Subject:** Liberation of Knin **Obv:** Crowned arms, denomination below **Rev:** Regional view within circle

Date	Mintage	VF20	XF40	MS60	MS63	MS65
ND-1995	3,000	—	—	—	—	265

PATTERNS

Including off metal strikes

KM#	Date	Mintage	Identification	Mkt Val
Pn5	1934	—	5 Kuna. Bronze.	350
Pn6	1934	—	5 Kuna. Copper-Nickel.	400
Pn7	1934	—	5 Kuna. 0.900. Silver.	450
Pn8	1934	—	5 Kuna. Zinc.	—
Pn9	1941	—	25 Banica. Zinc. With initials. 16 or 17 mm.	—
Pn10	1941	—	25 Banica. Zinc. Without initials. 16 or 17 mm.	—
Pn11	1941	—	25 Banica. Nickel. 16 or 17 mm.	—
Pn12	1941	—	25 Banica. Gold. 16 or 17 mm.	3,500
Pn13	1941	—	50 Banica. Nickel.	—
Pn14	1941	—	50 Banica. Zinc.	—
Pn15	1941	—	50 Banica. Silver.	—
Pn16	1941	—	50 Banica. Gold.	4,500
Pn17	1941	—	Kuna. Zinc.	—
Pn18	1941	—	Kuna. Copper.	—
Pn19	1941	—	Kuna. Aluminum.	200
Pn20	1941	—	Kuna. Nickel.	—
Pn21	1941	—	Kuna. Silver.	450
Pn22	1941	—	Kuna. Gold.	3,500
Pn23	1941	—	Kuna. Silver. Without undulating background.	—
Pn24	1941	—	2 Kune. Aluminum.	—
Pn25	1941	—	2 Kune. Nickel.	—
Pn26	1941	—	2 Kune. Silver.	—
Pn27	1941	—	2 Kune. Gold.	4,500
Pn28	1941	—	10 Kuna. Similar to Pn 19. 10 Kuna above shield within wheat border. Requires Confirmation.	—
Pn29	1941	—	500 Kuna. Aluminum. Pn 26. Similar to B3.	—
Pn30	1941	—	500 Kuna. Copper-Nickel. Pn 26. Similar to B3.	—
Pn31	1941	—	500 Kuna. Aluminum. Chain.	—
Pn32	1941	—	500 Kuna. Aluminum-Bronze.	—
Pn33	1941	—	500 Kuna. Copper.	—
Pn34	1941	—	500 Kuna. Copper-Nickel.	—
Pn35	1941	—	500 Kuna. Silver.	—
Pn36	1941	—	500 Kuna. Aluminum. Head left, date below. Denomination above arms, wheat chain surrounds.	650
Pn37	1941	—	500 Kuna. Gold. Chain. KMA3.	—
Pn38	1941	—	500 Kuna. Nickel. KMA3.	—
Pn39	1941	—	500 Kuna. Aluminum. KMA3.	—
Pn40	1941	—	500 Kuna. Brass. KMA3.	400
Pn41	1943	—	5 Kuna.	—
Pn42	1943	—	10 Kuna.	—

MINT SETS

KM#	Date	Mintage	Identification	Issue Price	Mkt Val
MS1	1993 (9)	50,000	KM3-11	8.00	16.50

PROOF SETS

KM#	Date	Mintage	Identification	Issue Price	Mkt Val
PS1	1993 (9)	17,000	KM3-11	15.20	30.00
PS2	1993 (9)	10	KM3a-11a, rare	—	—
PS3	1993 (9)	5	KM3b-11b, rare	—	—
PS4	1994 (9)	4,000	KM12, 14-17, 19-21, 23	15.20	35.00
PS5	1994 (3)	500	KM21, 23, 24a	—	285
PS6	1994 (3)	250	KM21, 23, 24b	—	650
PS7	1994 (2)	1,000	KM26, 33	240	510
PS8	ND (1994) (3)	250	KM25.1, 29.1, 31.1	154	450
PS9	ND (1994) (3)	500	KM25.2, 29.2, 31.2	154	475
PS13	1995 (9)	4,000	KM3-11	15.20	36.00
PS14	1995 (5)	—	KM27, 28, 30, 32, 34	—	880
PS15	ND (1995) (4)	1,000	KM50-53	375	790
PS16	ND (1995) (2)	1,000	KM50, 51	62.50	95.00
PS17	ND (1995) (2)	1,000	KM50, 52	125	300
PS18	ND (1995) (2)	1,000	KM51, 53	250	490
PS19	ND (1995) (2)	1,000	KM52, 53	312	695
PS20	ND (1995) (5)	1,000	KM 27, 28, 30, 32, 34	406	880
PS21	ND (1995) (3)	2,000	KM 27, 30, 34	270	550
PS22	1995 (2)	2,000	KM28, 32	135	350
PS23	1996 (6)	1,000	KM41-46	187	350
PS24	1996 (9)	5,000	KM12, 14-17, 19-21, 23	8.00	32.50
PS25	ND (1996) (2)	500	KM54-55	146	350
PS26	ND (1996) (3)	300	KM56-58	177	425
PS27	1997 (3)	300	KM59-61	281	530
PS28	1997 (2)	300	KM#69, 70	141	325
PS29	1997 (2)	300	KM#71, 72	260	525
PS30	1997 (4)	300	KM#69, 70, 71, 72	401	835
PS31	1997 (9)	—	KM#3-8, 9.1, 10-11	—	40.00
PS32	1998 (2)	500	KM#73, 74	141	300
PS33	1998 (9)	—	KM#12, 14-17, 19, 20.2, 21, 23	—	40.00
PS34	1999 (9)	—	KM#3-8, 9.2, 10-11	—	40.00
PS35	2000 (9)	—	KM#12, 14-17, 19, 20.2, 21, 23	—	45.00

CUBA

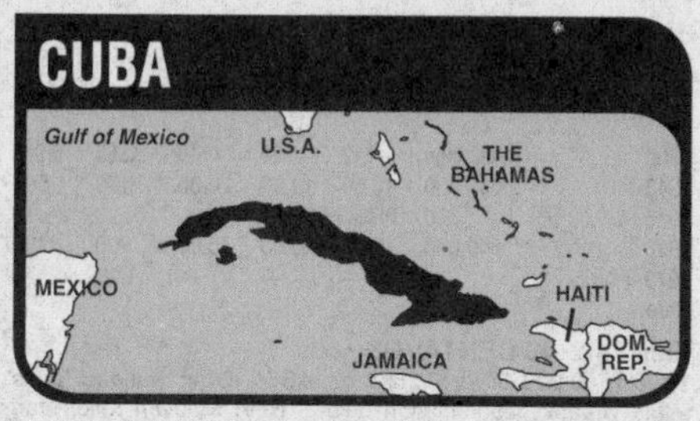

The Republic of Cuba, situated at the northern edge of the Caribbean Sea about 90 miles (145 km.) south of Florida, has an area of 42,804 sq. mi. (110,860 sq. km.) and a population of *11.2 million. Capital: Havana. The Cuban economy is based on the cultivation and refining of sugar, which provides 80 percent of export earnings.

Discovered by Columbus in 1492 and settled by Diego Velasquez in the early 1500s, Cuba remained a Spanish possession until 1898, except for a brief British occupancy of Havana in 1762-63. Cuban attempts to gain freedom were crushed, even while Spain was granting independence to its other American possessions. Ten years of warfare, 1868-78, between Spanish troops and Cuban rebels exacted guarantees of rights which were never implemented. The final revolt, begun in 1895, evoked American sympathy, and with the aid of U.S. troops independence was proclaimed on May 20, 1902. Fulgencio Batista seized the government in 1952 and established a dictatorship. Opposition to Batista, led by Fidel Castro, drove him into exile on Jan. 1, 1959. A communist-type, 25-member collective leadership headed by Castro was inaugurated in March, 1962.

RULER

Spanish, until 1898

MINT MARK

Key - Havana, 1977-

MONETARY SYSTEM

100 Centavos = 1 Peso

FIRST REPUBLIC

1902 - 1962

DECIMAL COINAGE

KM# 9.1 CENTAVO

2.50 g., Copper-Nickel, 17 mm. **Obv:** National arms within wreath, denomination below **Rev:** Roman denomination within circle of star, date below, 2.5 G. 250M

Date	Mintage	F12	VF20	XF40	MS60	MS63
1915	9,396,000	—	1.00	2.00	10.00	50.00
1915	200	PF60 750				
1916	9,318,000	—	1.00	2.00	10.00	50.00
1916	104	PF60 750				
1920	19,378,000	—	1.00	2.00	10.00	40.00
1938	2,000,000	—	1.50	3.00	15.00	50.00

KM# 9.2a CENTAVO

2.30 g., Brass, 17 mm. **Obv:** National arms within wreath, denomination below **Rev:** Roman denomination within circle of star, 2.3 GR. 300M

Date	Mintage	VF20	XF40	MS60	MS63	MS65
1943	20,000,000	0.40	1.25	5.00	20.00	—

KM# 9.2 CENTAVO

2.50 g., Copper-Nickel, 17 mm. **Obv:** National arms within wreath, denomination below **Rev:** Roman denomination within circle of star, 2.5 GR. 250M

Date	Mintage	F12	VF20	XF40	MS60	MS63
1946	50,000,000	—	0.20	1.00	5.00	15.00
1961	100,000,000	—	0.25	0.60	1.50	5.00

KM# 26 CENTAVO

2.30 g., Brass, 17 mm. **Subject:** Birth of Jose Marti Centennial **Obv:** Star on triangular shield divides denomination **Rev:** Bust left

Date	Mintage	F12	VF20	XF40	MS60	MS63
1953	50,000,000	—	0.15	0.75	5.00	20.00
1953 Proof; Rare	100	—	—	—	—	—

KM# 30 CENTAVO

Copper-Nickel, 17 mm. **Obv:** Star on triangular shield divides denomination **Rev:** Bust of Jose Marti left, date at left

Date	Mintage	F12	VF20	XF40	MS60	MS63
1958	50,000,000	—	0.15	0.75	5.00	35.00

KM# A10 2 CENTAVOS

3.50 g., Copper-Nickel, 19 mm. **Obv:** National arms within wreath, denomination below **Rev:** Roman denomination within circle of star, date below

Date	Mintage	VF20	XF40	MS60	MS63	MS65
1915	6,090,000	1.25	3.00	15.00	75.00	—
1915	150	PF60 800				
1916	5,322,000	1.25	3.50	15.00	80.00	—
1916	100	PF60 800				

KM# 11.1 5 CENTAVOS

5.00 g., Copper-Nickel, 21 mm. **Obv:** National arms within wreath above denomination **Rev:** Roman denomination within circle of star, date below, 5.0 G. 250M

Date	Mintage	F12	VF20	XF40	MS60	MS63
1915	5,096,000	—	1.00	4.00	15.00	75.00
1915	150	PF60 1,000				
1916	1,714,000	—	1.50	5.00	20.00	100
1916	100	PF60 800				
1920	10,000,000	—	1.00	3.00	20.00	75.00

KM# 11.2 5 CENTAVOS

5.00 g., Copper-Nickel, 21 mm. **Obv:** National arms within wreath, denomination below **Rev:** Roman denomination within circle of star, 5.0 G 250M **Note:** No period after G

Date	Mintage	F12	VF20	XF40	MS60	MS63
1920	—	—	1.75	20.00	150	750

KM# 11.3a 5 CENTAVOS

4.60 g., Brass, 21 mm. **Obv:** National arms within wreath **Rev:** Roman denominations within star, 4.6 GR. 300M **Note:** Prev. KM#11.2a.

Date	Mintage	VF20	XF40	MS60	MS63	MS65
1943	6,000,000	1.00	2.00	5.00	25.00	—

KM# 11.3 5 CENTAVOS

5.00 g., Copper-Nickel, 21 mm. **Obv:** National arms within wreath, denomination below **Rev:** Roman denomination within circle of star, date below, 5 GR. 250M **Note:** Prev. KM #11.2.

Date	Mintage	F12	VF20	XF40	MS60	MS63
1946	40,000,000	—	0.50	0.75	4.00	20.00
1960	20,000,000	—	0.75	1.25	5.00	15.00
1961	70,000,000	—	0.15	0.40	1.00	2.00

KM# A12 10 CENTAVOS
2.50 g., 0.900 Silver 0.0723 oz. ASW, 17.8 mm. **Obv:** National arms within wreath, denomination below **Rev:** Star **Edge:** Reeded

Date	Mintage	VF20	XF40	MS60	MS63	MS65
1915	5,690,000	4.00	5.00	25.00	150	—
1915	125	PF60 2,000				
1916	560,000	5.00	15.00	100	300	—
1916	50	PF60 2,000				
1920	3,090,000	4.00	10.00	50.00	200	—
1948	5,120,000	3.00	4.00	6.00	15.00	—
1949	9,880,000	3.00	4.00	6.00	15.00	—

KM# 23 10 CENTAVOS
2.50 g., 0.900 Silver 0.0723 oz. ASW, 18 mm. **Subject:** 50th Year of Republic **Obv:** Two dates left of flag, tower at right, denomination below **Rev:** Star above tree, spoked wheel below

Date	Mintage	F12	VF20	XF40	MS60	MS63
1952	10,000,000	—	3.00	4.00	15.00	25.00

KM# 13.1 20 CENTAVOS
5.00 g., 0.900 Silver 0.1447 oz. ASW, 23 mm. **Obv:** National arms within wreath **Rev:** High relief star

Date	Mintage	F12	VF20	XF40	MS60	MS63
1915 Fine reeding	7,915,000	5.00	9.00	25.00	175	500
1915 Coarse reeding	Inc. above	50.00	150	300	900	2,000
1915	125	PF60 2,000				

KM# 13.2 20 CENTAVOS
5.00 g., 0.900 Silver 0.1447 oz. ASW, 23 mm. **Obv:** National arms within wreath, denomination below **Rev:** Low relief star, date below **Note:** Coins with high relief stars normally exhibit a weak key and palm tree on the reverse. Coins with low relief stars tend to exhibit much more distinct lines in the valleys running towards the center of the star.

Date	Mintage	F12	VF20	XF40	MS60	MS63
1915 Coarse reeding	7,915,150	5.00	6.00	10.00	25.00	150
Note: Mintage included in KM#13.1						
1915 Fine reeding	—	15.00	50.00	175	750	1,500
Note: Mintage included in KM#13.1						
1916	2,535,000	5.00	7.50	15.00	50.00	350
1916	50	PF60 3,500				
1920	6,130,000	—	5.00	8.00	30.00	125
1932	184,000	22.00	55.00	200	800	1,750
1948	6,830,000	—	5.00	6.00	8.00	15.00
1949	13,170,000	—	5.00	6.00	8.00	15.00

KM# 24 20 CENTAVOS
5.00 g., 0.900 Silver 0.1447 oz. ASW, 23 mm. **Subject:** 50th Year of Republic **Obv:** Two dates left of flag, tower at right, denomination below **Rev:** Star above tree, spoked wheel below

Date	Mintage	F12	VF20	XF40	MS60	MS63
1952	8,700,000	—	5.00	6.00	10.00	20.00

KM# 27 25 CENTAVOS
6.25 g., 0.900 Silver 0.1808 oz. ASW, 24 mm. **Subject:** Centennial - Birth of Jose Marti **Obv:** Liberty cap on post, denomination at right **Rev:** Bust, left

Date	Mintage	F12	VF20	XF40	MS60	MS63
1953	19,000,000	4.00	6.00	8.00	10.00	30.00
1953 Proof; Rare	—	—	—	—	—	—

KM# 14 40 CENTAVOS
10.00 g., 0.900 Silver 0.2894 oz. ASW **Obv:** National arms within wreath, denomination below **Rev:** High relief star, date below

Date	Mintage	F12	VF20	XF40	MS60	MS63
1915	2,633,000	10.00	12.00	20.00	100	500
1915	100	PF60 1,500				
1920	540,000	15.00	40.00	75.00	200	700
1920 Proof; Rare	—	—	—	—	—	—

KM# 14.2 40 CENTAVOS
10.00 g., 0.900 Silver 0.2894 oz. ASW **Obv:** National arms within wreath, denomination below **Rev:** Medium relief star, date below

Date	Mintage	F12	VF20	XF40	MS60	MS63
1915	Inc. above	30.00	100	275	750	1,200

KM# 14.3 40 CENTAVOS
10.00 g., 0.900 Silver 0.2894 oz. ASW **Obv:** National arms within wreath, denomination below **Rev:** Low relief star, date below **Note:** Coins with high relief stars normally exhibit a weak key and palm tree on the reverse. Coins with low relief stars tend to exhibit much more distinct lines in the valleys running towards the center of the star.

Date	Mintage	F12	VF20	XF40	MS60	MS63
1915	Inc. above	10.00	15.00	30.00	250	600
1916	188,000	15.00	60.00	150	750	1,500
1916	50	PF60 2,500				
1920	Inc. above	15.00	40.00	75.00	250	600

KM# 25 40 CENTAVOS
10.00 g., 0.900 Silver 0.2894 oz. ASW, 28 mm. **Subject:** 50th Year of Republic **Obv:** Two dates left of flag, tower at right, denomination below **Rev:** Star above tree, spoked wheel below

Date	Mintage	F12	VF20	XF40	MS60	MS63
1952	1,250,000	10.00	11.00	12.00	25.00	50.00

KM# 28 50 CENTAVOS
12.50 g., 0.900 Silver 0.3617 oz. ASW, 31 mm. **Subject:** Centennial - Birth of Jose Marti **Obv:** Inscription on scroll, denomination at right **Rev:** Bust, left

Date	Mintage	F12	VF20	XF40	MS60	MS63
ND-1953	2,000,000	10.00	12.00	14.00	16.00	35.00
ND-1953 Proof; Rare	—	—	—	—	—	—

KM# 15.1 PESO
26.73 g., 0.900 Silver 0.7734 oz. ASW, 38 mm. **Obv:** National arms within wreath, denomination below **Rev:** High relief star, date below

Date	Mintage	F12	VF20	XF40	MS60	MS63
1915	1,976,000	20.00	24.00	30.00	250	1,000
1915	100	PF60 3,000				

KM# 15.2 PESO
26.73 g., 0.900 Silver 0.7734 oz. ASW, 38 mm. **Obv:** National arms within wreath, denomination below **Rev:** Low relief star, date below **Note:** Coins with high relief stars normally exhibit a weak key and palm tree on the obverse. Coins with low relief stars tend to exhibit much more distinct lines in the valleys running towards the center of the star.

Date	Mintage	F12	VF20	XF40	MS60	MS63
1915	Inc. above	20.00	40.00	100	1,500	8,500
1916	843,000	25.00	40.00	70.00	500	3,200
1916	50	PF60 5,000				
1932	3,550,000	—	20.00	30.00	110	350
1933	6,000,000	—	20.00	30.00	100	200
1934	3,000,000	—	20.00	30.00	100	200

KM# 16 PESO
1.67 g., 0.900 Gold 0.0484 oz. AGW **Obv:** National arms within wreath, denomination below **Rev:** Head of Jose Marti right, date below

Date	Mintage	F12	VF20	XF40	MS60	MS63
1915	6,850	85.00	100	150	225	400
1915	140	PF60 3,000				
1916	11,000	85.00	100	150	250	400
1916	100	PF60 3,000				

KM# 22 PESO
26.73 g., 0.900 Silver 0.7734 oz. ASW, 38 mm. **Obv:** National arms within wreath at right, denomination at left **Rev:** Laureate bust right, date lower right **Note:** Known as the "ABC" Peso.

Date	Mintage	F12	VF20	XF40	MS60	MS63
1934	7,000,000	33.00	40.00	45.00	150	350
1934 Matte proof	—	PF60 5,250				
1935	12,500,000	33.00	40.00	45.00	140	300
1936	16,000,000	33.00	40.00	45.00	140	400
1937	11,500,000	85.00	250	400	1,100	5,000
1938	10,800,000	33.00	40.00	45.00	140	400
1939	9,200,000	33.00	40.00	45.00	140	400

KM# 29 PESO
26.73 g., 0.900 Silver 0.7734 oz. ASW, 38 mm. **Subject:** Centennial of Jose Marti **Obv:** Radiant sun rising above water, denomination below **Rev:** Bust left, two dates

Date	Mintage	F12	VF20	XF40	MS60	MS63
ND-1953	1,000,000	33.00	40.00	45.00	50.00	125
ND-1953 Proof; Rare	—	—	—	—	—	—

KM# 17 2 PESOS
3.34 g., 0.900 Gold 0.0967 oz. AGW **Obv:** National arms within wreath, denomination below **Rev:** Head right, date below

Date	Mintage	F12	VF20	XF40	MS60	MS63
1915	10,000	170	180	200	300	500
1915	100	PF60 5,000				
1916	150,000	170	180	190	230	400
1916 Proof; Rare	8	—	—	—	—	—

KM# 18 4 PESOS
6.69 g., 0.900 Gold 0.1935 oz. AGW **Obv:** National arms within wreath, denomination below **Rev:** Head right, date below

Date	Mintage	F12	VF20	XF40	MS60	MS63
1915	6,300	340	350	375	1,200	3,000
1915	100	PF60 6,000				
1916	129,000	340	350	360	375	700
1916	90	PF60 4,500				

KM# 19 5 PESOS
8.36 g., 0.900 Gold 0.2419 oz. AGW **Obv:** National arms within wreath, denomination below **Rev:** Head right, date below

Date	Mintage	F12	VF20	XF40	MS60	MS63
1915	696,000	415	425	435	475	850
1915	—	PF60 5,000				
1916	1,132,000	415	425	435	450	600
1916	—	PF60 6,500				

Note: American Numismatic Rarities Eliasberg sale 4-05, Proof 65 realized $13,800.

KM# 20 10 PESOS
16.72 g., 0.900 Gold 0.4838 oz. AGW **Obv:** National arms within wreath, denomination below **Rev:** Head right, date below

Date	Mintage	F12	VF20	XF40	MS60	MS63
1915	95,000	825	835	845	875	1,200
1915	—	PF60 7,500				
1916	1,169,000	825	835	845	875	1,200
1916 Proof, Rare	—	—	—	—	—	—

Note: David Akers John Jay Pittman sale 8-99 very choice Proof realized $19,550, choice Proof realized $14,950. American Numismatic Rarities Eliasberg sale 4-05, Proof 62 realized $29,900.

KM# 21 20 PESOS
33.44 g., 0.900 Gold 0.9675 oz. AGW **Subject:** Jose Marti **Obv:** National arms within wreath, denomination below **Rev:** Head right, date below

Date	Mintage	F12	VF20	XF40	MS60	MS63
1915	57,000	1,500	1,600	1,700	1,850	3,500
1915 Proof; Rare	—	—	—	—	—	—

Note: David Akers John Jay Pittman sale 8-99 very choice proof 1915 realized $11,500.

Date	Mintage	F12	VF20	XF40	MS60	MS63
1916 Proof; Rare	10	—	—	—	—	—

Note: David Akers John Jay Pittman sale 8-99 nearly choice Proof 1916 realized $43,125.

SECOND REPUBLIC

1962 - Present

KM# 33.1 CENTAVO
0.75 g., Aluminum, 16.76 mm. **Obv:** National arms within wreath, denomination below **Rev:** Roman denomination within circle of star, date below **Rev. Legend:** PATRIA Y LIBERTAD **Note:** Shield varieties exist.

Date	Mintage	VF20	XF40	MS60	MS63	MS65
1963	200,020,000	0.10	0.30	0.60	1.25	1.50
1966	50,000,000	0.10	0.40	0.80	1.75	2.00
1969	50,000,000	0.10	0.40	0.80	1.75	2.00
1970	50,000,000	0.10	0.40	0.80	1.75	2.00
1971	49,960,000	0.40	0.80	1.50	3.00	3.50
1972	100,000,000	0.10	0.40	0.80	1.75	2.00
1978	50,000,000	0.10	0.40	0.80	1.75	2.00
1979	100,000,000	0.10	0.40	0.80	1.75	2.00
1981	100,000,000	0.10	0.40	0.80	1.75	2.00
1982	50,000,000	0.10	0.40	0.80	1.75	2.00

KM# 33.2 CENTAVO
0.75 g., Aluminum, 16.76 mm. **Obv:** National arms within wreath, denomination below **Rev:** Roman denomination within circle of star, date below **Rev. Legend:** PATRIA O MUERTE **Note:** Shield varieties exist.

Date	Mintage	VF20	XF40	MS60	MS63	MS65
1983	—	0.10	0.40	0.80	1.75	2.00
1984	—	0.10	0.40	0.80	1.75	2.00
1985	—	0.10	0.40	0.80	1.75	2.00
1986	—	0.10	0.40	0.80	1.75	2.00
1987	—	0.10	0.40	0.80	1.75	2.00
1988	—	0.10	0.40	0.80	1.75	2.00

KM# 33.3 CENTAVO
0.75 g., Aluminum, 16.76 mm. **Obv:** Cuban arms within wreath, denomination below **Rev:** Roman denomination within circle of star, date below **Edge:** Plain **Note:** Shield varieties exist.

Date	Mintage	VF20	XF40	MS60	MS63	MS65
1998	—	—	0.40	0.80	1.75	2.00

KM# 104.1 2 CENTAVOS
1.00 g., Aluminum, 19.31 mm. **Obv:** National arms within wreath, denomination below **Rev:** Roman denomination within circle of star, date below **Note:** Small lettered legends, long edge denticles on both sides of coin

Date	Mintage	VF20	XF40	MS60	MS63	MS65
1983	3,996,000	0.10	0.25	1.00	2.00	2.50

KM# 104.2 2 CENTAVOS
1.00 g., Aluminum, 19.31 mm. **Obv:** National arms within wreath, denomination below **Rev:** Roman denomination within circle of star, date below **Note:** Large lettered legends, short edge denticles on both sides of coin

Date	Mintage	VF20	XF40	MS60	MS63	MS65
1983	50,010,000	0.10	0.20	0.50	1.00	1.25
1984	62,500,000	0.10	0.25	1.00	2.00	2.50
1985	70,000,000	0.10	0.20	0.50	1.00	1.25
1986	15,000,000	0.10	0.20	0.50	1.00	1.25

KM# 34 5 CENTAVOS
1.50 g., Aluminum, 21.21 mm. **Obv:** National arms within wreath, denomination below **Rev:** Roman denomination within circle of star, date below **Note:** Shield varieties exist.

Date	Mintage	VF20	XF40	MS60	MS63	MS65
1963	80,000,000	0.10	0.25	0.75	1.50	1.75
1966	50,000,000	0.15	0.35	1.50	2.50	3.00
1968 Kremnica	100,000,000	0.15	0.35	1.50	2.50	3.00
1968 Leningrad	103,000,000	0.25	0.50	2.50	3.00	3.50
1971	100,020,000	0.10	0.25	0.75	1.50	1.75
1972	100,000,000	0.10	0.25	0.75	1.50	1.75

KM# 31 20 CENTAVOS
6.40 g., Copper-Nickel, 24 mm. **Subject:** Jose Marti **Obv:** National arms within wreath, denomination below **Rev:** Bust left, date lower left **Edge:** Reeded

Date	Mintage	VF20	XF40	MS60	MS63	MS65
1962	83,860,000	1.00	1.50	3.00	5.00	7.00
1968	25,750,000	1.25	2.00	4.00	6.00	8.00

KM# 35.1 20 CENTAVOS
2.00 g., Aluminum, 24 mm. **Obv:** Cuban arms within wreath, denomination below **Rev:** Roman denomination within circle of star, date below **Note:** Shield varieties exist.

Date	Mintage	VF20	XF40	MS60	MS63	MS65
1969	25,000,000	1.00	1.50	2.50	4.50	6.00
1971	29,560,000	1.00	1.50	2.50	4.50	6.00
1972	25,000,000	1.00	1.50	2.50	4.50	6.00

KM# 35.2 20 CENTAVOS
2.00 g., Aluminum, 24 mm. **Obv:** National arms, revised shield **Rev:** Roman denomination within circle of star

Date	Mintage	VF20	XF40	MS60	MS63	MS65
ND (1980)	—	7.00	10.00	15.00	—	—

KM# 360 25 CENTAVOS
Copper-Nickel **Subject:** Carlos J. Finlay **Obv:** National arms within wreath, denomination below **Rev:** Bust at right looking left, dates below

Date	Mintage	VF20	XF40	MS60	MS63	MS65
ND (1988)	—	—	10.00	25.00	45.00	60.00

KM# 361 25 CENTAVOS
Copper-Nickel **Subject:** Alexander von Humboldt **Obv:** National arms within wreath, denomination below **Rev:** Bust in cameo at left and bird at right divide dates

Date	Mintage	VF20	XF40	MS60	MS63	MS65
1989	—	—	8.00	20.00	35.00	50.00

KM# 32 40 CENTAVOS
9.60 g., Copper-Nickel **Subject:** Camilo Cienfuegos Gornaran **Obv:** National arms within wreath, denomination below **Rev:** Uniformed bust right, date at left

Date	Mintage	VF20	XF40	MS60	MS63	MS65
1962	15,250,000	3.00	5.00	7.00	12.00	14.00

KM# 186 PESO
11.40 g., Copper-Nickel, 29.98 mm. **Subject:** Carlos Manuel de Cespedes **Obv:** National arms **Rev:** Bust facing **Edge:** Plain

Date	Mintage	VF20	XF40	MS60	MS63	MS65
ND-1977	3,000	—	—	—	7.00	11.00

KM# 187 PESO
Copper-Nickel, 30 mm. **Subject:** Ignacio Agramonte **Obv:** National arms within wreath, denomination below **Rev:** Bust facing, date at left

Date	Mintage	VF20	XF40	MS60	MS63	MS65
1977	3,000	—	—	—	7.00	11.00

KM# 188 PESO
Copper-Nickel, 30 mm. **Subject:** Maximo Gomez

Date	Mintage	VF20	XF40	MS60	MS63	MS65
1977	3,000	—	—	—	7.00	11.00

KM# 189 PESO
Copper-Nickel, 30 mm. **Subject:** Antonio Maceo

Date	Mintage	VF20	XF40	MS60	MS63	MS65
1977	3,000	—	—	—	7.00	11.00

KM# 190 PESO
Copper-Nickel, 30 mm. **Subject:** 60th Anniversary of Socialist Revolution - Lenin **Obv:** National arms within wreath, denomination below **Rev:** Bust left divides dates

Date	Mintage	VF20	XF40	MS60	MS63	MS65
ND(1977)	6,000	—	—	—	20.00	45.00

KM# 191 PESO
Copper-Nickel, 30 mm. **Subject:** Nonaligned Nations Conference **Obv:** National arms within wreath, denomination below **Rev:** Design left of date

Date	Mintage	VF20	XF40	MS60	MS63	MS65
1979	3,000	—	—	—	5.00	7.00

KM# 46 PESO
Copper-Nickel, 30 mm. **Subject:** Cuban Flower - Mariposa

Date	Mintage	VF20	XF40	MS60	MS63	MS65
1980	3,000	—	—	—	5.00	8.00

KM# 192 PESO
Copper-Nickel, 30 mm. **Series:** Olympics **Obv:** National arms within wreath, denomination below **Rev:** Athletes in frames

Date	Mintage	VF20	XF40	MS60	MS63	MS65
1980	3,000	—	—	—	5.00	8.00

KM# 193 PESO
Copper-Nickel, 30 mm. **Series:** Olympics **Rev:** Three athletic figures

Date	Mintage	VF20	XF40	MS60	MS63	MS65
1980	3,000	—	—	—	5.00	8.00

KM# 194 PESO
Copper-Nickel, 30 mm. **Subject:** Soviet - Cuban Space Flight **Obv:** National arms within wreath, denomination below **Rev:** Shuttle orbiting planet, date below

Date	Mintage	VF20	XF40	MS60	MS63	MS65
1980	3,000	—	—	—	5.00	8.00

KM# 53 PESO
Copper-Nickel, 30 mm. **Subject:** Cuban Flowers **Rev:** Azahar flower

Date	Mintage	VF20	XF40	MS60	MS63	MS65
1981	3,000	—	—	—	5.00	8.00

KM# 54 PESO
Copper-Nickel, 30 mm. **Subject:** Cuban Flowers **Rev:** Orquidea flower

Date	Mintage	VF20	XF40	MS60	MS63	MS65
1981	3,000	—	—	—	6.00	8.00

KM# 55 PESO
Copper-Nickel, 30 mm. **Subject:** Cuban Fauna **Obv:** National arms within wreath, denomination below **Rev:** Cuban Crocodiles, date above

Date	Mintage	VF20	XF40	MS60	MS63	MS65
1981	5,000	—	—	—	7.00	10.00

KM# 56 PESO
Copper-Nickel, 30 mm. **Subject:** Cuban Fauna **Rev:** Emerald Hummingbird

Date	Mintage	VF20	XF40	MS60	MS63	MS65
1981	5,000	—	—	—	7.00	8.00

KM# 57 PESO
Copper-Nickel, 30 mm. **Subject:** Cuban Fauna **Rev:** Bee Hummingbird

Date	Mintage	VF20	XF40	MS60	MS63	MS65
1981	5,000	—	—	—	7.00	8.00

KM# 58 PESO
Copper-Nickel, 30 mm. **Subject:** Soccer World Championship - Spain 1982 **Obv:** National arms within wreath, denomination below **Rev:** Soccer player kicking ball, soccer ball background, date at right

Date	Mintage	VF20	XF40	MS60	MS63	MS65
1981	10,000	—	—	—	5.00	8.00

KM# 59 PESO
Copper-Nickel, 30 mm. **Subject:** World Food Day - Sugar Production **Obv:** National arms within wreath, denomination below **Rev:** Sugarcane plants, date lower right

Date	Mintage	VF20	XF40	MS60	MS63	MS65
1981	10,000	—	—	—	5.00	8.00

KM# 60 PESO
Copper-Nickel, 30 mm. **Subject:** XIV Central American and Caribbean Games **Obv:** National arms within wreath, denomination below **Rev:** Cartoon crocodile, date at left

Date	Mintage	VF20	XF40	MS60	MS63	MS65
1981	5,000	—	—	—	7.00	8.00

KM# 61 PESO
Copper-Nickel, 30 mm. **Subject:** XIV Central American and Caribbean Games **Obv:** National arms within wreath, denomination below **Rev:** Three athletes

Date	Mintage	VF20	XF40	MS60	MS63	MS65
1981	5,000	—	—	—	5.00	8.00

KM# 62 PESO
Copper-Nickel, 30 mm. **Subject:** XIV Central American and Caribbean Games **Obv:** National arms within wreath, denomination below **Rev:** Boxers

Date	Mintage	VF20	XF40	MS60	MS63	MS65
1981	5,000	—	—	—	5.00	8.00

KM# 63 PESO
Copper-Nickel, 30 mm. **Subject:** Cuban Fauna **Obv:** National arms within wreath, denomination below **Rev:** Cuban Trogon

Date	Mintage	VF20	XF40	MS60	MS63	MS65
1981	5,000	—	—	—	7.00	10.00

KM# 64 PESO
Copper-Nickel, 30 mm. **Subject:** Cuban Fauna **Obv:** National arms within wreath, denomination below **Rev:** Cuban Solendodon

Date	Mintage	VF20	XF40	MS60	MS63	MS65
1981	5,000	—	—	—	7.00	10.00

KM# 65 PESO
Copper-Nickel, 30 mm. **Subject:** Cuban Fauna **Obv:** National arms within wreath, denomination below **Rev:** Giant Gar Fish

Date	Mintage	VF20	XF40	MS60	MS63	MS65
1981	5,000	—	—	—	7.00	10.00

KM# 66 PESO
Copper-Nickel, 30 mm. **Obv:** National arms within wreath, denomination below **Rev:** Columbus' ship - Nina, date at right

Date	Mintage	VF20	XF40	MS60	MS63	MS65
1981	10,000	—	—	—	9.00	12.00

KM# 67 PESO
Copper-Nickel, 30 mm. **Obv:** National arms within wreath, denomination below **Rev:** Columbus' ship - Pinta

Date	Mintage	VF20	XF40	MS60	MS63	MS65
1981	10,000	—	—	—	9.00	12.00

KM# 68 PESO
Copper-Nickel, 30 mm. **Obv:** National arms within wreath, denomination below **Rev:** Columbus' ship - Santa Maria

Date	Mintage	VF20	XF40	MS60	MS63	MS65
1981	10,000	—	—	—	9.00	12.00

KM# 88 PESO
Copper-Nickel, 30 mm. **Subject:** Ernest Hemingway **Obv:** National arms within wreath, denomination below **Rev:** Bust facing, three dates

Date	Mintage	VF20	XF40	MS60	MS63	MS65
1982	7,000	—	—	—	10.00	13.00

KM# 89 PESO

Copper-Nickel, 30 mm. **Subject:** Ernest Hemingway **Obv:** National arms within wreath, denomination below **Rev:** Fishing yacht

Date	Mintage	VF20	XF40	MS60	MS63	MS65
1982	7,000	—	—	—	10.00	13.00

KM# 90 PESO

Copper-Nickel, 30 mm. **Subject:** Ernest Hemingway **Obv:** National arms within wreath, denomination below **Rev:** Small boat

Date	Mintage	VF20	XF40	MS60	MS63	MS65
ND-1982	7,000	—	—	—	10.00	13.00

KM# 91 PESO

Copper-Nickel, 30 mm. **Subject:** Miquel De Cervantes **Obv:** National arms within wreath, denomination below **Rev:** Bust with ruffled collar 3/4 right, three dates

Date	Mintage	VF20	XF40	MS60	MS63	MS65
1982	7,000	—	—	—	6.00	9.00

KM# 92 PESO

Copper-Nickel, 30 mm. **Subject:** Hidalgo Don Quijote **Obv:** National arms within wreath, denomination below **Rev:** Figure on horseback with lance divides dates

Date	Mintage	VF20	XF40	MS60	MS63	MS65
1982	7,000	—	—	—	6.00	9.00

KM# 93 PESO

Copper-Nickel, 30 mm. **Subject:** Hidalgo Don Quijote and Sancho Panza **Obv:** National arms within wreath **Rev:** Small figure on mule, larger figure with lance on horse

Date	Mintage	VF20	XF40	MS60	MS63	MS65
1982	7,000	—	—	—	6.00	9.00

KM# 94 PESO

Copper-Nickel, 30 mm. **Series:** F.A.O. **Rev:** Citrus fruit

Date	Mintage	VF20	XF40	MS60	MS63	MS65
1982	6,609	—	—	—	5.00	8.00

KM# 95 PESO

Copper-Nickel, 30 mm. **Series:** F.A.O. **Obv:** National arms within wreath **Rev:** Cow on grass left

Date	Mintage	VF20	XF40	MS60	MS63	MS65
1982	5,684	—	—	—	7.00	10.00

KM# 105 PESO

6.00 g., Nickel-Brass, 24.5 mm. **Obv:** National arms within wreath, denomination below **Rev:** Star, date below

Date	Mintage	VF20	XF40	MS60	MS63	MS65
1983	10,000,000	0.50	1.00	1.50	2.00	3.00
1984	10,000,000	0.50	1.00	1.50	2.00	3.00
1985	10,300,000	0.50	1.00	1.50	2.00	3.00
1986	20,000,000	0.50	1.00	1.50	2.00	3.00
1987	10,000,000	0.50	1.00	1.50	2.00	3.00
1988	15,000,000	0.50	1.00	1.50	2.00	3.00
1989	15,000,000	0.50	1.00	1.50	2.00	3.00

KM# 106 PESO

Copper-Nickel, 30 mm. **Subject:** Railroad **Obv:** National arms within wreath, denomination below **Rev:** Train engine, date below

Date	Mintage	VF20	XF40	MS60	MS63	MS65
1983	7,000	—	—	—	6.00	10.00

KM# 107 PESO

Copper-Nickel, 30 mm. **Subject:** World Fisheries Conference **Obv:** National arms within wreath, denomination below **Rev:** Spiny lobster

Date	Mintage	VF20	XF40	MS60	MS63	MS65
1983	5,000	—	—	—	6.00	10.00

KM# 173 PESO

Copper-Nickel, 30 mm. **Series:** 1984 Olympics **Obv:** National arms within wreath, denomination **Rev:** Runner

Date	Mintage	VF20	XF40	MS60	MS63	MS65
1983	3,000	—	—	—	5.00	8.00

KM# 174 PESO

Copper-Nickel, 30 mm. **Series:** 1984 Olympics **Obv:** National arms within wreath, denomination **Rev:** Discus thrower

Date	Mintage	VF20	XF40	MS60	MS63	MS65
1983	3,000	—	—	—	5.00	8.00

KM# 175 PESO

Copper-Nickel, 30 mm. **Series:** 1984 Olympics **Obv:** National arms within wreath, denomination below **Rev:** Judo, date upper right

Date	Mintage	VF20	XF40	MS60	MS63	MS65
1983	3,000	—	—	—	5.00	8.00

KM# 195 PESO

Copper-Nickel, 30 mm. **Series:** Olympics **Obv:** National arms within wreath, denomination **Rev:** Woman holding torch

Date	Mintage	VF20	XF40	MS60	MS63	MS65
1983	3,000	—	—	—	5.00	8.00

KM# 196 PESO

Copper-Nickel, 30 mm. **Series:** Olympics **Rev:** Two hockey players

Date	Mintage	VF20	XF40	MS60	MS63	MS65
1983	3,000	—	—	—	5.00	8.00

KM# 197 PESO
Copper-Nickel, 30 mm. **Series:** Olympics **Obv:** National arms within wreath, denomination **Rev:** Downhill skier

Date	Mintage	VF20	XF40	MS60	MS63	MS65
1983	3,000	—	—	—	4.00	6.00

KM# 116 PESO
Copper-Nickel, 30 mm. **Subject:** Transportation **Obv:** National arms within wreath, denomination **Rev:** Freighter

Date	Mintage	VF20	XF40	MS60	MS63	MS65
1984	5,000	—	—	—	5.00	8.00

KM# 118 PESO
Copper-Nickel, 30 mm. **Subject:** Santisima Trinidad **Obv:** National arms within wreath, denomination below **Rev:** Ship with full sails, date at left

Date	Mintage	VF20	XF40	MS60	MS63	MS65
1984	3,000	—	—	—	9.00	13.00

KM# 130 PESO
Copper-Nickel, 30 mm. **Subject:** Transportation **Obv:** National arms within wreath, denomination **Rev:** Volanta coach

Date	Mintage	VF20	XF40	MS60	MS63	MS65
1984	5,000	—	—	—	5.00	8.00

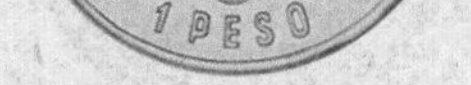

KM# 140 PESO
Copper-Nickel, 30 mm. **Subject:** Castillos **Obv:** National arms within wreath, denomination below **Rev:** El Morro La Habana

Date	Mintage	VF20	XF40	MS60	MS63	MS65
1984	5,000	—	—	—	5.00	10.00

KM# 142 PESO
Copper-Nickel, 30 mm. **Subject:** Castillos **Obv:** National arms within wreath, denomination below **Rev:** La Fuerza La Habana

Date	Mintage	VF20	XF40	MS60	MS63	MS65
1984	5,000	—	—	—	7.00	11.00

KM# 144 PESO
Copper-Nickel, 30 mm. **Subject:** Castillos **Obv:** National arms within wreath, denomination below **Rev:** El Morro Santiago De Cuba

Date	Mintage	VF20	XF40	MS60	MS63	MS65
1984	5,000	—	—	—	5.00	10.00

KM# 172 PESO
Copper-Nickel, 30 mm. **Subject:** Transportation **Obv:** National arms within wreath, denomination below **Rev:** Hot air balloon, date at left

Date	Mintage	VF20	XF40	MS60	MS63	MS65
1984	23	—	—	—	1,800	—

KM# 120 PESO
Copper-Nickel, 30 mm. **Subject:** International Year of Music **Obv:** National arms within wreath, denomination **Rev:** Bust of Bach at left, musical score at right

Date	Mintage	VF20	XF40	MS60	MS63	MS65
1985	2,000	—	—	—	7.00	12.00

KM# 124 PESO
Copper-Nickel, 30 mm. **Subject:** Wildlife Preservation **Obv:** National arms within wreath, denomination below **Rev:** Cuban crocodile (head only)

Date	Mintage	VF20	XF40	MS60	MS63	MS65
1985	5,000	—	—	—	12.00	17.00

KM# 126 PESO
Copper-Nickel, 30 mm. **Subject:** Wildlife Preservation **Obv:** National arms within wreath, denomination below **Rev:** Cuban rock iguana (half body)

Date	Mintage	VF20	XF40	MS60	MS63	MS65
1985	5,000	—	—	—	12.00	17.00

KM# 128 PESO
Copper-Nickel, 30 mm. **Subject:** Wildlife Preservation **Obv:** National arms within wreath, denomination below **Rev:** Cuban amazon parrot (head)

Date	Mintage	VF20	XF40	MS60	MS63	MS65
1985	5,000	—	—	—	12.00	17.00

KM# 132 PESO
Copper-Nickel, 30 mm. **Subject:** 40th Anniversary of F.A.O. **Obv:** National arms within wreath, denomination below **Rev:** Sugar cane, lobster, palm tree, and F.A.O. logo

Date	Mintage	VF20	XF40	MS60	MS63	MS65
ND-1985	5,000	—	—	—	4.00	6.00

KM# 133 PESO
Copper-Nickel, 30 mm. **Series:** F.A.O. **Obv:** National arms within wreath, denomination below **Rev:** Two people amid forest

Date	Mintage	VF20	XF40	MS60	MS63	MS65
1985	5,000	—	—	—	4.00	6.00

KM# 181 PESO
11.26 g., Copper-Nickel, 30 mm. **Series:** Wildlife Preservation **Obv:** National arms **Rev:** Crocodile **Edge:** Plain

Date	Mintage	VF20	XF40	MS60	MS63	MS65
1985	Est. 3000	—	—	—	17.00	27.00

KM# 182 PESO

11.26 g., Copper-Nickel, 30 mm. **Series:** Wildlife Preservation **Obv:** National arms **Rev:** Cuban rock iguana **Edge:** Plain

Date	Mintage	VF20	XF40	MS60	MS63	MS65
1985	Est. 3000	—	—	—	17.00	27.00

KM# 183 PESO

11.26 g., Copper-Nickel, 30 mm. **Series:** Wildlife Preservation **Obv:** National arms **Rev:** Parrot perched on branch right **Edge:** Plain

Date	Mintage	VF20	XF40	MS60	MS63	MS65
1985	Est. 3000	—	—	—	17.00	27.00

KM# 122 PESO

Copper-Nickel, 30 mm. **Subject:** Soccer World Championship - Mexico '85 **Obv:** National arms within wreath, denomination **Rev:** Two soccer players

Date	Mintage	VF20	XF40	MS60	MS63	MS65
ND-1986	5,000	—	—	—	5.00	8.00

KM# 134 PESO

Copper-Nickel, 30 mm. **Subject:** 100th Anniversary of Automobile **Obv:** National arms within wreath, denomination below **Rev:** Daimler-Benz, two dates below

Date	Mintage	VF20	XF40	MS60	MS63	MS65
ND-1986	3,000	—	—	—	9.00	16.00

KM# 136 PESO

Copper-Nickel, 30 mm. **Subject:** 30th Anniversary - Voyage of the Granma **Obv:** National arms within wreath, denomination **Rev:** Large ship at sea, dates above

Date	Mintage	VF20	XF40	MS60	MS63	MS65
ND-1986	3,000	—	—	—	7.00	12.00

KM# 138 PESO

Copper-Nickel, 30 mm. **Series:** Olympic Rings **Obv:** National arms within wreath, denomination **Rev:** Speed skater

Date	Mintage	VF20	XF40	MS60	MS63	MS65
1986	1,000	—	—	—	18.00	25.00

KM# 156 PESO

Copper-Nickel, 30 mm. **Subject:** International Year of Peace **Obv:** National arms within wreath, denomination below **Rev:** Dove with olive branch in flight, date at right

Date	Mintage	VF20	XF40	MS60	MS63	MS65
1986	5,000	—	—	—	6.00	10.00
1986	5,000	PF65 20.00				

KM# 198 PESO

Copper-Nickel, 30 mm. **Obv:** National arms within wreath, denomination below **Rev:** Speed skater, without rings above skater, date lower left

Date	Mintage	VF20	XF40	MS60	MS63	MS65
1986	3,000	—	—	—	5.00	11.00

KM# 148 PESO

Copper-Nickel, 30 mm. **Obv:** National arms within wreath, denomination below **Rev:** Cathedral in Santiago

Date	Mintage	VF20	XF40	MS60	MS63	MS65
1987	3,000	—	—	—	9.00	14.00

KM# 150 PESO

Copper-Nickel, 30 mm. **Obv:** National arms within wreath, denomination below **Rev:** Cathedral in Caridad del Cobre

Date	Mintage	VF20	XF40	MS60	MS63	MS65
1987	3,000	—	—	—	9.00	14.00

KM# 152 PESO

Copper-Nickel, 30 mm. **Obv:** National arms within wreath, denomination below **Rev:** Cathedral in Trinidad, date below

Date	Mintage	VF20	XF40	MS60	MS63	MS65
1987	3,000	—	—	—	9.00	14.00

KM# 154 PESO

Copper-Nickel, 30 mm. **Subject:** 40th Anniversary - Expedition of Kon-Tiki **Obv:** National arms within wreath, denomination **Rev:** Full masted ships, dates

Date	Mintage	VF20	XF40	MS60	MS63	MS65
ND-1987	3,000	—	—	—	9.00	14.00

KM# 158 PESO

Copper-Nickel, 30 mm. **Subject:** 20th Anniversary - Demise of Ernesto Che Guevara **Obv:** National arms within wreath, denomination **Rev:** Facing bust divides dates

Date	Mintage	VF20	XF40	MS60	MS63	MS65
ND-1987	6,000	—	—	—	35.00	45.00
ND-1987	200	PF65 100				

KM# 160 PESO

Copper-Nickel, 30 mm. **Subject:** 70th Anniversary of Bolshevik Revolution **Obv:** National arms within wreath, denomination below **Rev:** Russian cruiser Aurora, date at right

Date	Mintage	VF20	XF40	MS60	MS63	MS65
1987	5,000	—	—	—	9.00	14.00

KM# 165 PESO

Copper-Nickel, 30 mm. **Subject:** 100th Anniversary of the Souvenir Peso **Obv:** National arms within wreath, denomination below **Rev:** Womans head right

Date	Mintage	VF20	XF40	MS60	MS63	MS65
1987	3,000	—	—	—	9.00	14.00
1987	3,000	PF65 25.00				

KM# 167 PESO

Copper-Nickel, 30 mm. **Subject:** 100th Anniversary - Abolition of Slavery **Obv:** National arms within wreath, denomination below **Rev:** Half figure of slave breaking chains, three dates

Date	Mintage	VF20	XF40	MS60	MS63	MS65
1987	2,000	—	—	—	15.00	25.00

KM# 179 PESO

Copper-Nickel, 30 mm. **Subject:** Chess Centennial **Obv:** National arms within wreath, denomination **Rev:** Jose Capablanca at match

Date	Mintage	VF20	XF40	MS60	MS63	MS65
ND-1988	1,000	—	—	—	17.00	27.00

KM# 184 PESO

Copper-Nickel, 30 mm. **Subject:** Soccer - 1986 Mexico **Obv:** National arms within wreath, denomination below **Rev:** Soccer players, date at left

Date	Mintage	VF20	XF40	MS60	MS63	MS65
1988	1,000	—	—	—	15.00	22.00

KM# 200 PESO

Copper-Nickel, 30 mm. **Subject:** Chess Centennial **Rev:** Chess pieces

Date	Mintage	VF20	XF40	MS60	MS63	MS65
ND-1988	6,000	—	—	—	9.00	14.00

KM# 244 PESO

Copper-Nickel, 30 mm. **Subject:** Soccer World Championship - Italy 1990 **Obv:** Three towers above key on crowned shield within wreath **Rev:** Soccer players, date above

Date	Mintage	VF20	XF40	MS60	MS63	MS65
1988	2,000	—	—	—	12.00	16.00

KM# 245 PESO

Copper-Nickel, 30 mm. **Subject:** European World Soccer Championship - Federal Republic of Germany **Obv:** National arms within wreath, denomination below **Rev:** Three players

Date	Mintage	VF20	XF40	MS60	MS63	MS65
1988	2,000	—	—	—	12.00	16.00

KM# 246 PESO

Copper-Nickel, 30 mm. **Subject:** European World Soccer Championship - Federal Republic of Germany **Obv:** National arms within wreath, denomination below **Rev:** Four players

Date	Mintage	VF20	XF40	MS60	MS63	MS65
1988	2,000	—	—	—	12.00	16.00

KM# 258 PESO

Copper-Nickel, 30 mm. **Subject:** World Health Organization **Obv:** National arms within wreath, denomination below **Rev:** Nurse with baby, building in background

Date	Mintage	VF20	XF40	MS60	MS63	MS65
1988	2,000	—	—	—	8.00	13.00

KM# 269 PESO

Copper-Nickel, 30 mm. **Subject:** Transportation **Obv:** National arms within wreath, denomination **Rev:** Zeppelin

Date	Mintage	VF20	XF40	MS60	MS63	MS65
1988	1,000	—	—	—	45.00	60.00

KM# 276 PESO

Copper-Nickel, 30 mm. **Subject:** 40th Anniversary of Cuban National Ballet **Obv:** National arms within wreath, denomination below **Rev:** Womans head right, looking up

Date	Mintage	VF20	XF40	MS60	MS63	MS65
ND-1988	2,000	—	—	—	10.00	13.00

KM# 277 PESO

Copper-Nickel, 30 mm. **Subject:** 150th Anniversary of Havana Grand Theater **Obv:** National arms within wreath, denomination below **Rev:** Theater building, dates at left

Date	Mintage	VF20	XF40	MS60	MS63	MS65
ND-1977	2,000	—	—	—	10.00	13.00

KM# 282 PESO

Copper-Nickel, 30 mm. **Obv:** National arms within wreath, denomination **Rev:** Carlos J. Finlay

Date	Mintage	VF20	XF40	MS60	MS63	MS65
ND-1988	2,000	—	—	—	9.00	12.00

KM# 324 PESO

Copper-Nickel, 30 mm. **Subject:** Assault of the Moncada Garrison **Obv:** National arms within wreath, denomination **Rev:** Battle scene

Date	Mintage	VF20	XF40	MS60	MS63	MS65
1988	2,000	—	—	—	9.00	14.00

KM# 363 PESO

Brass, 30 mm. **Obv:** National arms within wreath, denomination below **Rev:** Head of Jose Marti right, date below

Date	Mintage	VF20	XF40	MS60	MS63	MS65
1988	—	—	—	—	12.00	16.00

KM# 512 PESO

Copper **Obv:** National arms within wreath, denomination below **Rev:** Bust at lower right looking left, dates below

Date	Mintage	VF20	XF40	MS60	MS63	MS65
ND-1988	2,500	—	—	—	12.00	17.00

KM# 513 PESO
Copper **Subject:** Transportation **Obv:** National arms within wreath, denomination **Rev:** Zeppelin, date lower left

Date	Mintage	VF20	XF40	MS60	MS63	MS65
1988	2,500	—	—	—	28.00	38.00

KM# 247 PESO
Copper-Nickel, 30 mm. **Subject:** World Soccer Championship - Italy 1990 **Obv:** National arms within wreath, denomination below **Rev:** Three players

Date	Mintage	VF20	XF40	MS60	MS63	MS65
1989	4,000	—	—	—	7.00	11.00

KM# 248 PESO
Copper-Nickel, 30 mm. **Subject:** World Soccer Championship - Italy 1990 **Obv:** National arms within wreath, denomination below **Rev:** Colosseum

Date	Mintage	VF20	XF40	MS60	MS63	MS65
1989	2,000	—	—	—	20.00	30.00

KM# 253 PESO
Copper-Nickel, 30 mm. **Subject:** 30th Anniversary of Revolution **Obv:** National arms within wreath, denomination below **Rev:** Castro with gun standing before radiant sun, dates at left

Date	Mintage	VF20	XF40	MS60	MS63	MS65
ND-1989	5,000	—	—	—	11.00	16.00

KM# 254 PESO
Copper-Nickel, 30 mm. **Subject:** 30th Anniversary of Revolution **Obv:** National arms within wreath, denomination below **Rev:** Facing busts of Jose Marti and Castro

Date	Mintage	VF20	XF40	MS60	MS63	MS65
1989	5,000	—	—	—	11.00	16.00

KM# 255 PESO
Copper-Nickel, 30 mm. **Subject:** 30th Anniversary of Revolution **Obv:** National arms within wreath, denomination below **Rev:** Cienfuegos and Castro, dates at right

Date	Mintage	VF20	XF40	MS60	MS63	MS65
ND-1989	5,000	—	—	—	11.00	16.00

KM# 257 PESO
Copper-Nickel, 30 mm. **Subject:** Triumph of the Revolution **Obv:** National arms within wreath, denomination below **Rev:** Castro with revolutionaries, dates below

Date	Mintage	VF20	XF40	MS60	MS63	MS65
1989	2,000	—	—	—	11.00	16.00

KM# 259 PESO
Copper-Nickel, 30 mm. **Subject:** Cuban Tobacco **Obv:** National arms within wreath, denomination below **Rev:** Native smoking above tobacco plant, parrot at right, date below

Date	Mintage	VF20	XF40	MS60	MS63	MS65
1989	1,000	—	—	—	20.00	30.00

KM# 260 PESO
Copper-Nickel, 30 mm. **Subject:** 160th Anniversary of First Railroad in England **Obv:** National arms within wreath, denomination below **Rev:** Railroad carts, dates below and above

Date	Mintage	VF20	XF40	MS60	MS63	MS65
1989	2,000	—	—	—	10.00	20.00

KM# 261 PESO
Copper-Nickel, 30 mm. **Subject:** 500th Anniversary - Discovery of America **Obv:** National arms within wreath, denomination below **Rev:** Three ships, date at left

Date	Mintage	VF20	XF40	MS60	MS63	MS65
1989	3,145	—	—	—	10.00	20.00

KM# 270 PESO
Copper-Nickel, 30 mm. **Subject:** 30th Anniversary - The March to Victory **Obv:** National arms within wreath, denomination **Rev:** Uniformed figures marching, dates

Date	Mintage	VF20	XF40	MS60	MS63	MS65
1989	2,000	—	—	—	8.00	13.00

KM# 271 PESO
Copper-Nickel, 30 mm. **Subject:** 200th Anniversary of French Revolution **Obv:** National arms within wreath, denomination below **Rev:** Female Allegory of Revolution

Date	Mintage	VF20	XF40	MS60	MS63	MS65
ND-1989	2,000	—	—	—	8.00	13.00

KM# 272 PESO
Copper-Nickel, 30 mm. **Subject:** 200th Anniversary of French Revolution - Bastille **Obv:** National arms within wreath, denomination below **Rev:** Castle scene, dates below

Date	Mintage	VF20	XF40	MS60	MS63	MS65
ND-1989	2,000	—	—	—	8.00	13.00

KM# 274 PESO
Copper-Nickel, 30 mm. **Subject:** First Spanish Railroad **Obv:** National arms within wreath, denomination below **Rev:** Train on track, three dates

Date	Mintage	VF20	XF40	MS60	MS63	MS65
1989	2,000	—	—	—	10.00	20.00

KM# 275 PESO
Copper-Nickel, 30 mm. **Subject:** First Cuban Railroad **Obv:** National arms within wreath, denomination below **Rev:** Train engine divides dates

Date	Mintage	VF20	XF40	MS60	MS63	MS65
1989	2,000	—	—	—	10.00	20.00

KM# 278 PESO
Copper-Nickel, 30 mm. **Subject:** 5th Centennial - Discovery of America **Obv:** National arms within wreath, denomination below **Rev:** Three ships at sea, date at left

Date	Mintage	VF20	XF40	MS60	MS63	MS65
1989	2,000	—	—	—	8.00	13.00

KM# 283 PESO
Copper-Nickel, 30 mm. **Subject:** Alexander von Humboldt **Obv:** National arms within wreath, denomination below **Rev:** Cameo of Alexander von Humboldt, birds on branch

Date	Mintage	VF20	XF40	MS60	MS63	MS65
1989	2,000	—	—	—	10.00	15.00

KM# 284 PESO
Copper-Nickel, 30 mm. **Series:** 1992 Olympics **Obv:** National arms within wreath, denomination below **Rev:** Two boxers

Date	Mintage	VF20	XF40	MS60	MS63	MS65
1989	1,000	—	—	—	20.00	30.00

KM# 285 PESO
Copper-Nickel, 30 mm. **Obv:** National arms within wreath, denomination below **Rev:** Bust of Camillo Cienfuegos, date at left

Date	Mintage	VF20	XF40	MS60	MS63	MS65
1989	2,000	—	—	—	10.00	20.00

KM# 286 PESO
Copper-Nickel, 30 mm. **Obv:** National arms within wreath, denomination below **Rev:** Profile of Ernesto Che Guevara

Date	Mintage	VF20	XF40	MS60	MS63	MS65
1989	2,000	—	—	—	25.00	35.00

KM# 287 PESO
Copper-Nickel, 30 mm. **Obv:** National arms within wreath, denomination below **Rev:** Bust of Tania La Guerrillera, Argentinian revolutionary

Date	Mintage	VF20	XF40	MS60	MS63	MS65
1989	2,000	—	—	—	15.00	25.00

KM# 436 PESO
Copper **Obv:** National arms within wreath, denomination below **Rev:** Cameo of Alexander von Humboldt, Condors

Date	Mintage	VF20	XF40	MS60	MS63	MS65
1989	—	—	—	—	13.00	17.00

KM# 250 PESO
Copper, 30 mm. **Obv:** National arms within wreath, denomination below **Rev:** Esperanto at right, world globe at left

Date	Mintage	VF20	XF40	MS60	MS63	MS65
1990	6,000	—	—	—	8.00	10.00

KM# 273 PESO
Copper, 30 mm. **Subject:** Discovery of America **Obv:** National arms within wreath, denomination below **Rev:** Scene depicting Columbus departing from Spain

Date	Mintage	VF20	XF40	MS60	MS63	MS65
1990	12,000	—	—	—	8.00	13.00

KM# 279 PESO
Copper-Nickel, 30 mm. **Subject:** 5th Centennial of Columbus' Arrival in Cuba **Obv:** National arms within wreath, denomination below **Rev:** Ship at sea, map in background, date at right

Date	Mintage	VF20	XF40	MS60	MS63	MS65
1990	2,000	—	—	—	8.00	13.00

KM# 288 PESO
Copper-Nickel, 30 mm. **Obv:** National arms within wreath, denomination below **Rev:** Columbus meeting natives

Date	Mintage	VF20	XF40	MS60	MS63	MS65
1990	2,000	—	—	—	8.00	13.00

KM# 289 PESO
Copper-Nickel, 30 mm. **Obv:** National arms within wreath, denomination below **Rev:** Three soccer balls at left, map of Italy at right

Date	Mintage	VF20	XF40	MS60	MS63	MS65
1990	—	—	—	—	6.00	9.00

KM# 306 PESO
Copper-Nickel, 30 mm. **Subject:** 500th Anniversary - Discovery of America **Obv:** National arms within wreath, denomination below **Rev:** King Ferdinand of Spain

Date	Mintage	VF20	XF40	MS60	MS63	MS65
1990	3,000	—	—	—	7.00	11.00

KM# 307 PESO
Copper-Nickel, 30 mm. **Subject:** 500th Anniversary - Discovery of America **Obv:** National arms within wreath, denomination below **Rev:** Queen Isabella of Spain

Date	Mintage	VF20	XF40	MS60	MS63	MS65
1990	3,000	—	—	—	7.00	11.00

KM# 308 PESO
Copper-Nickel, 30 mm. **Subject:** 500th Anniversary - Discovery of America **Obv:** National arms within wreath, denomination below **Rev:** Christopher Columbus 3/4 left

Date	Mintage	VF20	XF40	MS60	MS63	MS65
1990	3,000	—	—	—	7.00	11.00

KM# 309 PESO

Copper-Nickel, 30 mm. **Subject:** 500th Anniversary - Discovery of America **Obv:** National arms within wreath, denomination below **Rev:** Juan de la Cosa

Date	Mintage	VF20	XF40	MS60	MS63	MS65
1990	3,000	—	—	—	5.00	8.00

KM# 310 PESO

Copper-Nickel, 30 mm. **Subject:** Pan American Games **Obv:** National arms within wreath, denomination below **Rev:** High jumper

Date	Mintage	VF20	XF40	MS60	MS63	MS65
1990	5,000	—	—	—	5.00	8.00

KM# 311 PESO

Copper-Nickel, 30 mm. **Subject:** Pan American Games **Obv:** National arms within wreath, denomination below **Rev:** Volleyball

Date	Mintage	VF20	XF40	MS60	MS63	MS65
1990	5,000	—	—	—	5.00	8.00

KM# 312 PESO

Copper-Nickel, 30 mm. **Subject:** Pan American Games **Obv:** National arms within wreath, denomination below **Rev:** Baseball game on baseball background

Date	Mintage	VF20	XF40	MS60	MS63	MS65
1990	5,000	—	—	—	7.00	11.00

KM# 325 PESO

Copper-Nickel, 30 mm. **Obv:** National arms within wreath, denomination below **Rev:** Columbus' ships sailing west

Date	Mintage	VF20	XF40	MS60	MS63	MS65
1990	12,000	—	—	—	6.00	8.00

KM# 340 PESO

Copper-Nickel, 30 mm. **Subject:** Celia Sanchez Manduley 1920-80, revolutionary **Obv:** National arms within wreath, denomination below **Rev:** Head looking left, dates below

Date	Mintage	VF20	XF40	MS60	MS63	MS65
1990	—	—	—	—	5.00	8.00

KM# 387 PESO

Copper-Nickel, 30 mm. **Obv:** National arms within wreath, denomination below **Rev:** Route of first voyage by Columbus

Date	Mintage	VF20	XF40	MS60	MS63	MS65
1990	2,000	—	—	—	9.00	11.00

KM# 471 PESO

Copper, 40 mm. **Obv:** National arms within wreath, denomination below **Rev:** Columbus meeting natives

Date	Mintage	VF20	XF40	MS60	MS63	MS65
1990	—	—	—	—	10.00	15.00

KM# 514 PESO

Copper-Nickel, 30 mm. **Subject:** Simon Bolivar - Libertador **Obv:** National arms within wreath, denomination **Rev:** Uniformed bust facing, dates

Date	Mintage	VF20	XF40	MS60	MS63	MS65
1990	2,000	—	—	—	13.00	19.00

KM# 347 PESO

5.52 g., Brass Plated Steel, 24.5 mm. **Subject:** Jose Marti **Obv:** National arms within wreath, denomination below **Rev:** Smaller Bust facing, denomination at left **Rev. Legend:** PATRIA O MUERTE **Note:** Rim varieties exist.

Date	Mintage	VF20	XF40	MS60	MS63	MS65
1991	—	—	1.00	2.50	3.50	5.00
1992	—	—	1.00	2.00	3.00	4.00
1992 Proof	—	—	—	—	—	—
1994	—	—	1.00	2.00	3.00	4.00

KM# 364 PESO

Nickel Bonded Steel, 30 mm. **Obv:** National arms within wreath, denomination below **Rev:** Hatuey tribesman head left, date at right

Date	Mintage	VF20	XF40	MS60	MS63	MS65
1991	3,000	—	—	—	9.00	11.00

KM# 365 PESO

Nickel Bonded Steel, 30 mm. **Obv:** National arms within wreath, denomination below **Rev:** Pinzon brothers

Date	Mintage	VF20	XF40	MS60	MS63	MS65
1991	3,000	—	—	—	6.00	8.00

KM# 366 PESO

Nickel Bonded Steel, 30 mm. **Subject:** 500th Anniversary of New World **Obv:** National arms within wreath, denomination below **Rev:** Bust of Queen Joanna, 1479-1555, daughter of Isabella I

Date	Mintage	VF20	XF40	MS60	MS63	MS65
1991	3,000	—	—	—	6.00	8.00

KM# 367 PESO

Nickel Bonded Steel, 30 mm. **Obv:** National arms within wreath, denomination below **Rev:** Diego Velazquez

Date	Mintage	VF20	XF40	MS60	MS63	MS65
1991	3,000	—	—	—	6.00	8.00

KM# 388 PESO

Nickel Bonded Steel, 30 mm. **Subject:** Madrid **Obv:** National arms within wreath, denomination below **Rev:** Alcala Gate

Date	Mintage	VF20	XF40	MS60	MS63	MS65
1991	10,000	—	—	—	6.00	8.00

KM# 389 PESO

Nickel Bonded Steel, 30 mm. **Subject:** Barcelona **Obv:** National arms within wreath, denomination below **Rev:** Olympic stadium

Date	Mintage	VF20	XF40	MS60	MS63	MS65
1991	—	—	—	—	6.00	8.00

KM# 390 PESO

Nickel Bonded Steel, 30 mm. **Subject:** Seville **Obv:** National arms within wreath, denomination below **Rev:** La Giralda Tower

Date	Mintage	VF20	XF40	MS60	MS63	MS65
1991	—	—	—	—	6.00	8.00

KM# 368 PESO

Copper-Nickel, 30 mm. **Subject:** Postal Ship **Obv:** National arms within wreath, denomination below **Rev:** Ship at sea, date at left

Date	Mintage	VF20	XF40	MS60	MS63	MS65
1992	—	—	—	—	9.00	11.00

KM# 391 PESO

Nickel Bonded Steel, 30 mm. **Subject:** 25th Anniversary - Death of Ernesto Che Guevara **Obv:** National arms within wreath, denomination below **Rev:** Ernesto Che Guevara

Date	Mintage	VF20	XF40	MS60	MS63	MS65
1992	—	—	—	—	12.00	18.00

KM# 392 PESO

Nickel Bonded Steel, 30 mm. **Obv:** National arms within wreath, denomination below **Rev:** Bartolome de Las Casas

Date	Mintage	VF20	XF40	MS60	MS63	MS65
1992	3,000	—	—	—	6.00	8.00

KM# 393 PESO

Nickel Bonded Steel, 30 mm. **Obv:** National arms within wreath, denomination below **Rev:** Half figure of Chief Guama blowing shell, date at left

Date	Mintage	VF20	XF40	MS60	MS63	MS65
1992	3,000	—	—	—	9.00	11.00

KM# 394 PESO

Nickel Bonded Steel, 30 mm. **Obv:** National arms within wreath, denomination below **Rev:** King Philipp of Spain

Date	Mintage	VF20	XF40	MS60	MS63	MS65
1992	3,000	—	—	—	6.00	8.00

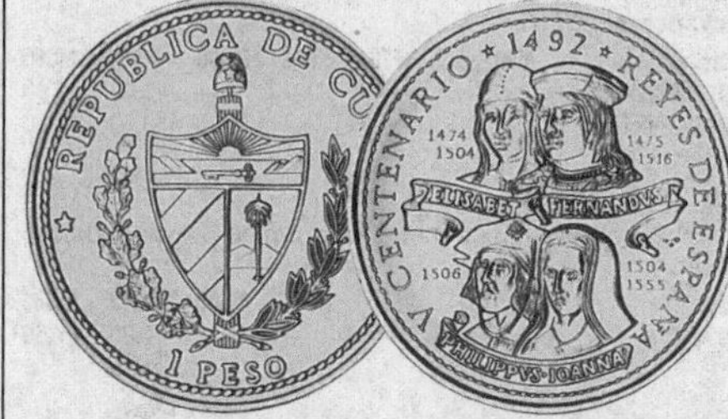

KM# 395 PESO

Nickel Bonded Steel, 30 mm. **Subject:** Spanish Royalty **Obv:** National arms within wreath, denomination below **Rev:** Banners below royal busts at top and bottom, dates flanking

Date	Mintage	VF20	XF40	MS60	MS63	MS65
ND-1992	3,000	—	—	—	6.00	8.00

KM# 401 PESO

Copper-Nickel, 30 mm. **Obv:** National arms within wreath, denomination below **Rev:** Seville Tower of Gold

Date	Mintage	VF20	XF40	MS60	MS63	MS65
1992	—	—	—	—	6.00	8.00

KM# 402 PESO

Copper-Nickel, 30 mm. **Subject:** El Escorial **Obv:** National arms within wreath, denomination below **Rev:** City view, date below

Date	Mintage	VF20	XF40	MS60	MS63	MS65
1992	—	—	—	—	6.00	8.00

KM# 403 PESO

Copper-Nickel, 30 mm. **Obv:** National arms within wreath, denomination below **Rev:** St. Jorge Palace, date below

Date	Mintage	VF20	XF40	MS60	MS63	MS65
1992	10,000	—	—	—	6.00	8.00

KM# 437 PESO

Copper **Subject:** 25th Anniversary - Death of Ernesto Che Guevara **Obv:** National arms within wreath, denomination **Rev:** Uniformed bust facing, dates

Date	Mintage	VF20	XF40	MS60	MS63	MS65
ND-1992	—	—	—	—	17.00	27.00

KM# 462 PESO

Nickel Bonded Steel, 30 mm. **Subject:** Introduction of Africans to America **Obv:** National arms within wreath, denomination below **Rev:** Figure with back facing at left, ship at sea at right, inscription below

Date	Mintage	VF20	XF40	MS60	MS63	MS65
1992	—	—	—	—	11.00	15.00

KM# 396 PESO

Copper **Subject:** Millennium of St. Jacobi **Obv:** National arms within wreath, denomination **Rev:** Armored figure on rearing horse right

Date	Mintage	VF20	XF40	MS60	MS63	MS65
1993	—	—	—	—	12.00	17.00

KM# 397.1 PESO

29.43 g., Copper Plated Bronze, 37.9 mm. **Subject:** 40th Anniversary of the attack on Moncada Barracks by revolutionaries led by Fidel Castro on July 26, 1953. **Obv:** National arms, denomination below **Obv. Legend:** REPUBLICA DE CUBA **Rev:** Uniformed bust of Castro left **Rev. Legend:** 40 ANIVERSARIO DEL MONCADA **Edge:** Plain, beveled rim

Date	Mintage	VF20	XF40	MS60	MS63	MS65
1993	—	—	—	—	18.00	28.00

KM# 397.2 PESO

30.02 g., Copper Plated Bronze, 37.9 mm. **Subject:** 40th Anniversary of the attack on Moncada Barracks by revolutionaries led by Fidel Castro on July 26, 1953 **Obv:** National arms, denomination below **Obv. Legend:** REPUBLICA DE CUBA **Rev:** Uniformed bust of Castro left **Rev. Legend:** 40 ANIVERSARIO DEL MONCADA **Edge:** Plain, flat rim

Date	Mintage	VF20	XF40	MS60	MS63	MS65
1993	—	—	—	—	18.00	28.00

KM# 404 PESO

Copper-Nickel, 30 mm. **Series:** Prehistoric Animals **Obv:** National arms within wreath, denomination below **Rev:** Chalicotherium standing with tree, date below

Date	Mintage	VF20	XF40	MS60	MS63	MS65
1993	—	—	—	—	20.00	30.00

KM# 429 PESO

Copper-Nickel, 30 mm. **Subject:** Federico Garcia Lorca **Obv:** National arms within wreath, denomination **Rev:** Bust facing, dates at left

Date	Mintage	VF20	XF40	MS60	MS63	MS65
1993	—	—	—	—	8.00	10.00

KM# 509 PESO

Copper, 38 mm. **Obv:** National arms within wreath, denomination below **Rev:** President Abraham Lincoln, map of United States behind

Date	Mintage	VF20	XF40	MS60	MS63	MS65
1993	—	—	—	—	13.00	17.00

KM# 515 PESO

Copper **Obv:** National arms within wreath, denomination below **Rev:** Bolivar and Marti

Date	Mintage	VF20	XF40	MS60	MS63	MS65
1993 Plain finish	—	—	—	—	13.00	17.00
1993 Antiqued finish	—	—	—	—	13.00	17.00

KM# 915 PESO

Nickel Plated Steel, 32.5 mm. **Rev:** Simon Bolivar and Jose Marti

Date	Mintage	VF20	XF40	MS60	MS63	MS65
1993	Est. 3000	—	—	—	6.00	7.50

KM# 438 PESO

Copper-Nickel Plated Steel, 30 mm. **Series:** Prehistoric Animals **Obv:** National arms within wreath, denomination below **Rev:** Stegosaurus

Date	Mintage	VF20	XF40	MS60	MS63	MS65
1994	—	—	—	—	20.00	30.00

KM# 439 PESO

Nickel Plated Steel, 30 mm. **Series:** Caribbean Fauna **Obv:** National arms within wreath, denomination below **Rev:** Multicolored Bottle-nosed Dolphins

Date	Mintage	VF20	XF40	MS60	MS63	MS65
1994	25,000	—	—	—	12.00	—

KM# 460 PESO

Nickel Plated Steel, 30 mm. **Series:** Caribbean Fauna **Obv:** National arms within wreath, denomination below **Rev:** Multicolored Spotted Eagle Ray left, date below

Date	Mintage	VF20	XF40	MS60	MS63	MS65
1994	25,000	—	—	—	12.00	—

KM# 463 PESO

Nickel Bonded Steel, 30 mm. **Subject:** Isla del Evangelista **Obv:** National arms within wreath, denomination below **Rev:** Parrot, ship, and sea chest

Date	Mintage	VF20	XF40	MS60	MS63	MS65
1994	—	—	—	—	8.00	10.00

KM# 464 PESO

Nickel Bonded Steel, 30 mm. **Subject:** Sailing Ships **Obv:** National arms within wreath, denomination below **Rev:** NAO VICTORIA

Date	Mintage	VF20	XF40	MS60	MS63	MS65
1994	—	—	—	—	8.00	10.00

KM# 465 PESO

Nickel Bonded Steel, 30 mm. **Subject:** Sailing Ships **Obv:** National arms within wreath, denomination below **Rev:** LA INDIA

Date	Mintage	VF20	XF40	MS60	MS63	MS65
1994	—	—	—	—	8.00	10.00

KM# 466.1 PESO

Nickel Plated Steel, 30 mm. **Series:** Caribbean Fauna **Obv:** National arms within wreath, denomination below **Rev:** Multicolored Yellow Sea Bass (Coney), 7 lines in the tail, slimmer fish

Date	Mintage	VF20	XF40	MS60	MS63	MS65
1994	25,000	—	—	—	22.00	—

KM# 466.2 PESO

Nickel Plated Steel, 30 mm. **Subject:** Caribbean Fauna **Obv:** National arms within wreath, denomination below **Rev:** Multicolored Yellow Sea Bass (Coney), 5 lines in the tail

Date	Mintage	VF20	XF40	MS60	MS63	MS65
1994	Inc. above	—	—	—	12.00	—

KM# 467.1 PESO
Nickel Plated Steel, 30 mm. **Series:** Caribbean Fauna **Obv:** National arms within wreath, denomination below **Rev:** Multicolored sailfish, small water splashes, thin nose

Date	Mintage	VF20	XF40	MS60	MS63	MS65
1994	25,000	—	—	—	22.00	—

KM# 467.2 PESO
Nickel Plated Steel, 30 mm. **Subject:** Caribbean Fauna **Obv:** National arms within wreath, denomination below **Rev:** Multicolored sailfish, large water splashes, wider nose

Date	Mintage	VF20	XF40	MS60	MS63	MS65
1994	Inc. above	—	—	—	12.00	—

KM# 497 PESO
Nickel Plated Steel, 30 mm. **Series:** Caribbean Fauna **Obv:** National arms within wreath, denomination below **Rev:** Multicolor pelican

Date	Mintage	VF20	XF40	MS60	MS63	MS65
1994	25,000	—	—	—	13.00	—

KM# 498.1 PESO
Nickel Plated Steel, 30 mm. **Series:** Caribbean Fauna **Obv:** National arms within wreath, denomination below **Rev:** Multicolored flamingos, thin water splashes

Date	Mintage	VF20	XF40	MS60	MS63	MS65
1994	25,000	—	—	—	23.00	—

KM# 498.2 PESO
Nickel Plated Steel, 30 mm. **Subject:** Caribbean Fauna **Obv:** National arms within wreath, denomination below **Rev:** Multicolored flamingos, wide water splashes

Date	Mintage	VF20	XF40	MS60	MS63	MS65
1994	Inc. above	—	—	—	13.00	—

KM# 516 PESO
Copper **Subject:** Montecristi Manifesto **Obv:** National arms within wreath, denomination below **Rev:** Two seated figures facing each other, date lower left

Date	Mintage	VF20	XF40	MS60	MS63	MS65
1994 Plain finish	—	—	—	—	13.00	17.00
1994 Antiqued finish	—	—	—	—	13.00	17.00

KM# 517 PESO
Copper **Obv:** National arms within wreath, denomination below **Rev:** Nao Victoria

Date	Mintage	VF20	XF40	MS60	MS63	MS65
1994	2,500	—	—	—	13.00	17.00

KM# 518 PESO
12.70 g., Nickel Bonded Steel, 32.68 mm. **Series:** World War I fighter airplanes **Obv:** National arms **Rev:** German Fokker Dr.I multicolor **Edge:** Plain

Date	Mintage	VF20	XF40	MS60	MS63	MS65
1994	—	—	—	—	18.00	22.00

KM# 547 PESO
12.70 g., Nickel Bonded Steel, 32.68 mm. **Series:** World War I fighter airplanes **Obv:** National arms **Rev:** English Albatross II multicolor **Edge:** Plain

Date	Mintage	VF20	XF40	MS60	MS63	MS65
1994	25,000	—	—	—	18.00	22.00

KM# 606 PESO
Copper **Subject:** 500th Anniversary - Discovery of Evangelista Island **Obv:** National arms within wreath, denomination below **Rev:** Parrot, chest, and ship

Date	Mintage	VF20	XF40	MS60	MS63	MS65
1994	—	—	—	—	13.00	17.00

KM# 918 PESO
Nickel Plated Steel, 32.5 mm. **Obv:** National Arms **Rev:** Jose Marti and Maximo Gomez

Date	Mintage	VF20	XF40	MS60	MS63	MS65
1994	Est. 5000	—	—	—	5.00	7.00

KM# 472.1 PESO
Copper-Nickel, 30 mm. **Subject:** Pirates of the Caribbean **Obv:** Roman I in denomination, lower relief, more refined shield **Rev:** Blackbeard

Date	Mintage	VF20	XF40	MS60	MS63	MS65
1995	Est. 25000	—	—	12.00	—	—

KM# 472.2 PESO
Copper-Nickel, 30 mm. **Subject:** Pirates of the Caribbean **Obv:** Arabic 1 in denomination, higher relief shield **Rev:** Blackbeard

Date	Mintage	VF20	XF40	MS60	MS63	MS65
1995	Inc. above	—	—	12.00	—	—

KM# 472.3 PESO
Copper-Nickel, 30 mm. **Subject:** Pirates of the Caribbean **Obv:** National arms within wreath, denomination below **Rev:** Blackbeard **Rev. Legend:** Mariposas del Caribe **Note:** Struck on trial planchet

Date	Mintage	VF20	XF40	MS60	MS63	MS65
1995 Rare	—	—	—	—	—	—

KM# 473.1 PESO
Copper-Nickel, 30 mm. **Subject:** Pirates of the Caribbean **Obv:** Roman I in denomination, lower relief, more refined shield **Rev:** Sir Henry Morgan

Date	Mintage	VF20	XF40	MS60	MS63	MS65
1995	25,000	—	—	12.00	—	—

KM# 473.2 PESO
Copper-Nickel, 30 mm. **Subject:** Pirates of the Caribbean **Obv:** Arabic 1 in denomination, higher relief shield **Rev:** Sir Henry Morgan

Date	Mintage	VF20	XF40	MS60	MS63	MS65
1995	Inc. above	—	—	12.00	—	—

KM# 473.3 PESO
Copper-Nickel, 30 mm. **Subject:** Pirates of the Caribbean **Obv:** National arms within wreath, denomination below **Rev:** Sir Henry Morgan **Rev. Legend:** Mariposas del Caribe **Note:** Struck on trial planchet.

Date	Mintage	VF20	XF40	MS60	MS63	MS65
1995 Rare	—	—	—	—	—	—

KM# 474.1 PESO
Copper-Nickel, 30 mm. **Subject:** Pirates of the Caribbean **Obv:** Roman I in denomination, lower relief, more refined shield **Rev:** Anne Bonny

Date	Mintage	VF20	XF40	MS60	MS63	MS65
1995	—	—	—	12.00	—	—

KM# 474.2 PESO
Copper-Nickel, 30 mm. **Subject:** Pirates of the Caribbean **Obv:** Arabic 1 in denomination, higher relief shield **Rev:** Anne Bonny

Date	Mintage	VF20	XF40	MS60	MS63	MS65
1995	Inc. above	—	—	12.00	—	—

KM# 474.3 PESO
Copper-Nickel, 30 mm. **Subject:** Pirates of the Caribbean **Obv:** National arms within wreath, denomination **Rev:** Anne Bonny **Rev. Legend:** Mariposas del Caribe **Note:** Struck on trial planchet.

Date	Mintage	VF20	XF40	MS60	MS63	MS65
1995 Rare	—	—	—	—	—	—

KM# 475.1 PESO
Copper-Nickel, 30 mm. **Subject:** Pirates of the Caribbean **Obv:** Roman I in denomination, lower relief, more refined shield **Rev:** Mary Read

Date	Mintage	VF20	XF40	MS60	MS63	MS65
1995	—	—	—	12.00	—	—

KM# 475.2 PESO
Copper-Nickel, 30 mm. **Subject:** Pirates of the Caribbean **Obv:** Arabic 1 in denomination, higher relief shield **Rev:** Mary Read

Date	Mintage	VF20	XF40	MS60	MS63	MS65
1995	Inc. above	—	—	12.00	—	—

KM# 475.3 PESO

Copper-Nickel, 30 mm. **Subject:** Pirates of the Caribbean **Obv:** National arms within wreath, denomination below **Rev:** Mary Read **Rev. Legend:** Mariposas del caribe **Note:** Struck on trial planchet.

Date	Mintage	VF20	XF40	MS60	MS63	MS65
1995 Rare	—	—	—	—	—	—

KM# 476.1 PESO

Copper-Nickel, 30 mm. **Subject:** Pirates of the Caribbean **Obv:** Roman I in denomination, lower relief, more refined shield **Rev:** Captain Kidd

Date	Mintage	VF20	XF40	MS60	MS63	MS65
1995	Est. 25000	—	—	12.00	—	—

KM# 476.2 PESO

Copper-Nickel, 30 mm. **Subject:** Pirates of the Caribbean **Obv:** Arabic 1 in denomination, higher relief shield **Rev:** Captain Kidd

Date	Mintage	VF20	XF40	MS60	MS63	MS65
1995	Inc. above	—	—	12.00	—	—

KM# 476.3 PESO

Copper-Nickel, 30 mm. **Subject:** Pirates of the Caribbean **Obv:** National arms within wreath, denomination below **Rev:** Captain Kidd **Rev. Legend:** Mariposas del Caribe **Note:** Struck on trial planchet.

Date	Mintage	VF20	XF40	MS60	MS63	MS65
1995 Rare	—	—	—	—	—	—

KM# 477.1 PESO

Copper-Nickel, 30 mm. **Subject:** Pirates of the Caribbean **Obv:** Roman I in denomination, lower relief, more refined shield **Rev:** Piet Heyn

Date	Mintage	VF20	XF40	MS60	MS63	MS65
1995	Est. 25000	—	—	12.00	—	—

KM# 477.2 PESO

Copper-Nickel, 30 mm. **Subject:** Pirates of the Caribbean **Obv:** Arabic 1 in denomination, higher relief shield **Rev:** Piet Heyn

Date	Mintage	VF20	XF40	MS60	MS63	MS65
1995	Inc. above	—	—	12.00	—	—

KM# 477.3 PESO

Copper-Nickel, 30 mm. **Subject:** Pirates of the Caribbean **Obv:** National arms within wreath, denomination below **Rev:** Piet Heyn **Rev. Legend:** Mariposas del Caribe **Note:** Struck on trial planchet

Date	Mintage	VF20	XF40	MS60	MS63	MS65
1995 Rare	—	—	—	—	—	—

KM# 519 PESO

Copper **Subject:** Centennial - Death of Jose Marti in combat **Obv:** National arms within wreath, denomination below **Rev:** Bust of Marti facing, date at right

Date	Mintage	VF20	XF40	MS60	MS63	MS65
1995 Plain finish	—	—	—	15.00	20.00	—
1995 Antiqued finish	3,000	—	—	15.00	20.00	—

KM# 520 PESO

Copper **Subject:** Centennial 1895-1995 **Obv:** National arms within wreath, denomination below **Rev:** Three conjoined busts, right of sword, facing right, dates below

Date	Mintage	VF20	XF40	MS60	MS63	MS65
ND-1995 Plain finish	Inc. below	—	—	15.00	20.00	—
ND-1995 Antiqued finish	2,000	—	—	15.00	20.00	—

KM# 521 PESO

Nickel Bonded Steel, 30 mm. **Subject:** Centennial - Jose Marti in combat **Obv:** National arms within wreath, denomination below **Rev:** Bust of Marti looking left, date at right

Date	Mintage	VF20	XF40	MS60	MS63	MS65
1995	—	—	—	—	8.00	12.00

KM# 522 PESO

12.70 g., Nickel Bonded Steel, 32.5 mm. **Obv:** National arms within wreath, denomination below **Rev:** Multicolored SIAI Marchetti Seaplane, date at left

Date	Mintage	VF20	XF40	MS60	MS63	MS65
1995	—	—	—	—	18.00	22.00

KM# 523 PESO

Copper-Nickel **Subject:** 50th Anniversary - United Nations **Obv:** National arms within wreath, denomination below **Rev:** Five people, assorted ages and race, UN logo in front, dove outline behind, dates below

Date	Mintage	VF20	XF40	MS60	MS63	MS65
ND-1995	—	—	—	—	13.00	17.00

KM# 607 PESO

Nickel Bonded Steel, 30 mm. **Subject:** 50th Anniversary - F.A.O. **Obv:** National arms within wreath, denomination below **Rev:** Farmer plowing behind two oxen

Date	Mintage	VF20	XF40	MS60	MS63	MS65
ND-1995	—	—	—	—	12.00	16.00

KM# 549 PESO

Nickel Bonded Steel, 30 mm. **Series:** Caribbean Fauna **Obv:** National arms within wreath, denomination below **Rev:** Multicolored Purple-throated Carib Hummingbird

Date	Mintage	VF20	XF40	MS60	MS63	MS65
1996	10,000	—	—	—	—	17.00

KM# 550 PESO

Nickel Bonded Steel, 30 mm. **Series:** Caribbean Fauna **Obv:** National arms within wreath, denomination below **Rev:** Multicolored Yellow Perch

Date	Mintage	VF20	XF40	MS60	MS63	MS65
1996	10,000	—	—	—	—	17.00

KM# 551 PESO

Nickel Bonded Steel, 30 mm. **Series:** Caribbean Fauna **Obv:** National arms within wreath, denomination below **Rev:** Multicolored Cuban Tody Bird

Date	Mintage	VF20	XF40	MS60	MS63	MS65
1996	10,000	—	—	—	—	17.00

KM# 552 PESO

Nickel Bonded Steel, 30 mm. **Series:** Caribbean Fauna **Obv:** National arms within wreath, denomination below **Rev:** Multicolored Wood Duck

Date	Mintage	VF20	XF40	MS60	MS63	MS65
1996	10,000	—	—	—	—	17.00

KM# 562 PESO
13.04 g., Nickel Bonded Steel, 32.78 mm. **Series:** Caribbean Fauna **Obv:** National arms **Rev:** Multicolored Vaca Anil Fish **Edge:** Plain

Date	Mintage	VF20	XF40	MS60	MS63	MS65
1996	10,000	—	—	—	—	17.00

KM# 565 PESO
Nickel Bonded Steel, 30 mm. **Series:** Caribbean Fauna **Obv:** National arms within wreath, denomination below **Rev:** Multicolored Papilio butterfly

Date	Mintage	VF20	XF40	MS60	MS63	MS65
1996	10,000	—	—	—	—	17.00

KM# 614 PESO
25.91 g., Copper-Nickel, 37.9 mm. **Subject:** 40th Anniversary of the "Granma" Landing **Obv:** National arms within wreath, denomination below **Rev:** Portrait above ship **Edge:** Plain

Date	Mintage	VF20	XF40	MS60	MS63	MS65
ND-1996	—	PF65 15.00				

KM# 731 PESO
25.83 g., Copper-Nickel, 37.9 mm. **Series:** F.A.O. **Obv:** National arms within wreath, denomination below **Rev:** Woman picking fruit **Edge:** Plain

Date	Mintage	VF20	XF40	MS60	MS63	MS65
1996	—	—	—	—	18.50	—

KM# 835 PESO
Copper-Nickel, 38 mm. **Subject:** Swiss Railway's 150th Anniversary

Date	Mintage	VF20	XF40	MS60	MS63	MS65
1996	—	—	—	—	—	40.00

KM# 612 PESO
Copper-Nickel, 37.9 mm. **Subject:** Fidel Castro's visit to the Vatican **Obv:** National arms within wreath, denomination below **Rev:** Pope and Castro meeting

Date	Mintage	VF20	XF40	MS60	MS63	MS65
1997	—	—	—	—	15.00	—

KM# 617 PESO
Copper-Nickel, 37 mm. **Subject:** 30th Anniversary - Death of Ernesto Che Guevara **Obv:** National arms within wreath, denomination below **Rev:** Full figure of Guevara with rifle walking down road between anniversary dates, mountains behind

Date	Mintage	VF20	XF40	MS60	MS63	MS65
1997	—	—	—	—	15.00	—

KM# 618 PESO
25.86 g., Copper-Nickel, 37.92 mm. **Subject:** Che Guevara's Death **Obv:** National arms, inscription **Rev:** Bearded portrait **Edge:** Plain

Date	Mintage	VF20	XF40	MS60	MS63	MS65
ND(1997)	—	—	—	—	15.00	—

KM# 619 PESO
12.92 g., Copper-Nickel, 32.61 mm. **Subject:** Ruellia Tuberosa **Obv:** National arms **Rev:** Multicolor flower **Edge:** Plain

Date	Mintage	VF20	XF40	MS60	MS63	MS65
1997	5,000	—	—	—	12.00	—

KM# 620 PESO
12.92 g., Nickel Bonded Steel, 32.61 mm. **Subject:** Turnera Ulmifola **Obv:** National arms **Rev:** Multicolor flower **Edge:** Plain

Date	Mintage	VF20	XF40	MS60	MS63	MS65
1997	5,000	—	—	—	12.00	—

KM# 621 PESO
12.92 g., Nickel Bonded Steel, 32.61 mm. **Subject:** Cordia Sebestena **Obv:** National arms **Rev:** Multicolor flower **Edge:** Plain

Date	Mintage	VF20	XF40	MS60	MS63	MS65
1997	5,000	—	—	—	12.00	—

KM# 722 PESO
12.92 g., Nickel Bonded Steel, 32.61 mm. **Subject:** Hibiscus Elatus **Obv:** National arms **Rev:** Multicolored flower **Edge:** Plain

Date	Mintage	VF20	XF40	MS60	MS63	MS65
1997	5,000	—	—	—	12.00	—

KM# 737 PESO
12.92 g., Nickel Bonded Steel, 32.61 mm. **Subject:** Lochnera Rosea **Obv:** National arms **Rev:** Multicolor flower **Edge:** Plain

Date	Mintage	VF20	XF40	MS60	MS63	MS65
1997	5,000	—	—	—	12.00	—

KM# 738 PESO
12.92 g., Nickel Bonded Steel, 32.61 mm. **Subject:** Bidens Pilosa **Obv:** National arms **Rev:** Multicolor flower **Edge:** Plain

Date	Mintage	VF20	XF40	MS60	MS63	MS65
1997	5,000	—	—	—	12.00	—

KM# 935 PESO
Nickel Plated Steel **Rev:** Ruellia in color

Date	Mintage	VF20	XF40	MS60	MS63	MS65
1997	—	—	—	—	—	30.00

KM# 936 PESO
Nickel Plated Steel **Rev:** Damiana in color

Date	Mintage	VF20	XF40	MS60	MS63	MS65
1997	—	—	—	—	—	30.00

KM# 937 PESO
Nickel Plated Steel **Rev:** Riger lilac in color

Date	Mintage	VF20	XF40	MS60	MS63	MS65
1997	—	—	—	—	—	30.00

KM# 938 PESO
Nickel Plated Steel **Rev:** Scarlet Cordia in color

Date	Mintage	VF20	XF40	MS60	MS63	MS65
1997	—	—	—	—	—	30.00

KM# 939 PESO
Nickel Plated Steel **Rev:** Madagascar evergreen in color

Date	Mintage	VF20	XF40	MS60	MS63	MS65
1997	—	—	—	—	—	30.00

KM# 940 PESO
155.50 g., 0.999 Silver 4.9944 oz. ASW **Rev:** Hibiscus elatus in color

Date	Mintage	VF20	XF40	MS60	MS63	MS65
1997	—	PF65 200				

KM# 622 PESO
11.30 g., Copper-Nickel, 30 mm. **Subject:** AIDS **Obv:** National arms within wreath, denomination below **Rev:** AIDS ribbon on silhouette before world map

Date	Mintage	VF20	XF40	MS60	MS63	MS65
1998	50,000	—	—	—	15.00	—

KM# 732 PESO
25.83 g., Copper-Nickel, 37.9 mm. **Subject:** Papal Visit **Obv:** National arms within wreath, denomination below **Rev:** Half figure of Pope John Paul II facing left, cathedral at left **Edge:** Plain

Date	Mintage	VF20	XF40	MS60	MS63	MS65
1998	20,000	—	—	—	16.50	—
1998	—	PF65 30.00				

KM# 662 PESO
26.00 g., Copper-Nickel, 37.9 mm. **Subject:** 40th Anniversary - The Triumph of the Revolution

Date	Mintage	VF20	XF40	MS60	MS63	MS65
1999	10,000	—	—	—	15.00	—

KM# 842 PESO
26.00 g., Copper-Nickel, 40 mm. **Subject:** International Global Conference

Date	Mintage	VF20	XF40	MS60	MS63	MS65
1999	200	—	—	—	—	60.00

KM# 663 PESO
Copper-Nickel **Subject:** Hacia un Nuevo Milenio - Towards a New Millennium

Date	Mintage	VF20	XF40	MS60	MS63	MS65
2000	5,000	—	—	—	15.00	—

KM# 664 PESO
26.00 g., Copper-Nickel, 38 mm. **Subject:** Welcome the Third Millennium

Date	Mintage	VF20	XF40	MS60	MS63	MS65
2000	5,000	—	—	—	15.00	—

KM# 665 PESO
26.00 g., Copper-Nickel, 38 mm. **Subject:** Welcome to the New Millennium

Date	Mintage	VF20	XF40	MS60	MS63	MS65
2000	5,000	—	—	—	15.00	—

KM# 823 PESO
Copper-Nickel, 37.9 mm. **Series:** Shipbuilding Relics **Obv:** National arms **Rev:** Submarine "Peral" **Rev. Legend:** RELIQUIAS DE LA NAVEGÀCIÓN

Date	Mintage	VF20	XF40	MS60	MS63	MS65
2000	—	—	—	—	10.00	12.00

KM# 824 PESO
Copper-Nickel, 37.9 mm. **Series:** Shipbuilding Relics **Obv:** National arms **Rev:** Sailing ship "Juan Sebastion Elcano" **Rev. Legend:** RELIQUIAS DE LA NAVEGÀCIÓN

Date	Mintage	VF20	XF40	MS60	MS63	MS65
2000	—	—	—	—	10.00	12.00

KM# 825 PESO
Copper-Nickel, 37.9 mm. **Series:** Shipbuilding Relics **Obv:** National arms **Rev:** Ship "Galatea" **Rev. Legend:** RELIQUIAS DE LA NAVEGÀCIÓN

Date	Mintage	VF20	XF40	MS60	MS63	MS65
2000	—	—	—	—	10.00	12.00

KM# 826 PESO
Copper-Nickel, 37.9 mm. **Series:** Shipbuilding Relics **Obv:** National arms **Rev:** Steam paddleboat "BUENAVENTURA" **Rev. Legend:** RELIQUIAS DE LA NAVEGÀCIÓN

Date	Mintage	VF20	XF40	MS60	MS63	MS65
2000	—	—	—	—	10.00	12.00

KM# 827 PESO
Copper-Nickel, 37.9 mm. **Series:** Shipbuilding Relics **Obv:** National arms **Rev:** Nativity scene in center of ship's compass **Rev. Legend:** RELIQUIAS DE LA NAVEGÀCIÓN

Date	Mintage	VF20	XF40	MS60	MS63	MS65
2000	—	—	—	—	10.00	12.00

KM# 843 PESO
26.00 g., Copper-Nickel, 38 mm. **Subject:** International Globalization Conference

Date	Mintage	VF20	XF40	MS60	MS63	MS65
2000	200	—	—	—	—	40.00

KM# 946 PESO
Copper-Nickel **Subject:** Shipbuilding **Rev:** Von Isaac Peral Caballero, Submarine building

Date	Mintage	VF20	XF40	MS60	MS63	MS65
2000	—	—	—	—	—	18.00

KM# 947 PESO
Copper-Nickel **Subject:** Shipbuilding **Rev:** Juan Sebastian de Elcano, sail training vessel

Date	Mintage	VF20	XF40	MS60	MS63	MS65
2000	—	—	—	—	—	18.00

KM# 948 PESO

Copper-Nickel **Subject:** Shipbuilding **Rev:** Galatea

Date	Mintage	VF20	XF40	MS60	MS63	MS65
2000	—	—	—	—	—	18.00

KM# 949 PESO

Copper-Nickel **Subject:** Shipbuilding **Rev:** Buenaventura

Date	Mintage	VF20	XF40	MS60	MS63	MS65
2000	—	—	—	—	—	18.00

KM# 346 3 PESOS

9.00 g., Copper-Nickel, 26.5 mm. **Subject:** Ernesto Che Guevara **Obv:** National arms within wreath, denomination below **Rev:** Head facing, date below **Note:** Shield varieties exist.

Date	Mintage	VF20	XF40	MS60	MS63	MS65
1990	4,050,000	—	2.50	5.00	7.00	9.00
1992	500	PF65 15.00				

KM# 346a 3 PESOS

8.00 g., Nickel Plated Steel, 26.5 mm. **Obv:** National arms within wreath, denomination below **Rev:** Head facing, date below **Note:** Shield varieties exist.

Date	Mintage	VF20	XF40	MS60	MS63	MS65
1992	—	—	2.50	5.00	7.00	9.00
1995	—	—	2.50	5.00	7.00	9.00

KM# 36 5 PESOS

13.33 g., 0.900 Silver 0.3857 oz. ASW **Subject:** 25th Anniversary - National Bank of Cuba **Obv:** Star behind arms above 1/2 wreath, denomination below **Rev:** Multi-storied building

Date	Mintage	VF20	XF40	MS60	MS63	MS65
ND-1975	50,000	PF65 18.00				

KM# 47 5 PESOS

12.00 g., 0.999 Silver 0.3854 oz. ASW **Subject:** First Soviet-Cuban Space Flight **Obv:** National arms within wreath, denomination below **Rev:** Shuttle orbiting planet, date below

Date	Mintage	VF20	XF40	MS60	MS63	MS65
1980	10,000	—	—	—	—	15.00
1980	5,000	PF65 60.00				

KM# 48 5 PESOS

12.00 g., 0.999 Silver 0.3854 oz. ASW **Subject:** Moscow Olympics **Obv:** National arms within wreath, denomination **Rev:** Three small squares depict athletes

Date	Mintage	VF20	XF40	MS60	MS63	MS65
1980	10,000	—	—	—	—	15.00

KM# 49 5 PESOS

12.00 g., 0.999 Silver 0.3854 oz. ASW **Obv:** National arms within wreath, denomination below **Rev:** Cuban flower - Mariposa

Date	Mintage	VF20	XF40	MS60	MS63	MS65
1980	10,000	—	—	—	—	15.00
1980	2,000	PF65 25.00				

KM# 69 5 PESOS

12.00 g., 0.999 Silver 0.3854 oz. ASW **Obv:** National arms within wreath, denomination below **Rev:** Cuban flower - Azahar

Date	Mintage	VF20	XF40	MS60	MS63	MS65
1981	10,000	—	—	—	—	16.50
1981	2,000	PF65 25.00				

KM# 70 5 PESOS

12.00 g., 0.999 Silver 0.3854 oz. ASW **Obv:** National arms within wreath, denomination below **Rev:** Cuban flower - Orquidea

Date	Mintage	VF20	XF40	MS60	MS63	MS65
1981	10,000	—	—	—	—	15.00
1981	2,000	PF65 25.00				

KM# 71 5 PESOS

12.00 g., 0.999 Silver 0.3854 oz. ASW **Obv:** National arms within wreath, denomination below **Rev:** Columbus' ship - Nina

Date	Mintage	VF20	XF40	MS60	MS63	MS65
1981	10,000	—	—	—	—	25.00
1981	1,000	PF65 60.00				

KM# 72 5 PESOS

12.00 g., 0.999 Silver 0.3854 oz. ASW **Obv:** National arms within wreath, denomination below **Rev:** Columbus' ship - Pinta

Date	Mintage	VF20	XF40	MS60	MS63	MS65
1981	10,000	—	—	—	—	25.00
1981	1,000	PF65 60.00				

KM# 73 5 PESOS

12.00 g., 0.999 Silver 0.3854 oz. ASW **Obv:** National arms within wreath, denomination below **Rev:** Columbus' ship - Santa Maria

Date	Mintage	VF20	XF40	MS60	MS63	MS65
1981	10,000	—	—	—	—	25.00
1981	1,000	PF65 60.00				

KM# 74 5 PESOS

12.00 g., 0.999 Silver 0.3854 oz. ASW **Series:** Cuban Fauna **Obv:** National arms within wreath, denomination below **Rev:** Crocodiles, date above

Date	Mintage	VF20	XF40	MS60	MS63	MS65
1981	5,000	—	—	—	—	25.00
1981	1,000	PF65 42.00				

KM# 75 5 PESOS

12.00 g., 0.999 Silver 0.3854 oz. ASW **Series:** Cuban Fauna **Obv:** National arms within wreath, denomination below **Rev:** Emerald Hummingbird

Date	Mintage	VF20	XF40	MS60	MS63	MS65
1981	5,000	—	—	—	—	25.00
1981	1,000	PF65 42.00				

KM# 76 5 PESOS

12.00 g., 0.999 Silver 0.3854 oz. ASW **Series:** Cuban Fauna **Obv:** National arms within wreath, denomination below **Rev:** Bee Hummingbird

Date	Mintage	VF20	XF40	MS60	MS63	MS65
1981	5,000	—	—	—	—	25.00
1981	1,000	PF65 42.00				

KM# 77 5 PESOS

12.00 g., 0.999 Silver 0.3854 oz. ASW **Subject:** Soccer Games - Spain 1982 **Obv:** National arms within wreath, denomination below **Rev:** Soccer player

Date	Mintage	VF20	XF40	MS60	MS63	MS65
1981	4,000	PF65 27.50				

KM# 78 5 PESOS

12.00 g., 0.999 Silver 0.3854 oz. ASW **Subject:** World Food Day - Sugar Production **Obv:** National arms within wreath, denomination below **Rev:** Sugarcane plant, date at right

Date	Mintage	VF20	XF40	MS60	MS63	MS65
1981	7,000	—	—	—	—	22.50
1981	1,560	PF65 40.00				

KM# 79 5 PESOS

12.00 g., 0.999 Silver 0.3854 oz. ASW **Subject:** XIV Central American and Caribbean Games **Obv:** National arms within wreath, denomination below **Rev:** Animated Mascot

Date	Mintage	VF20	XF40	MS60	MS63	MS65
1981	5,000	—	—	—	—	16.50
1981	2,000	PF65 35.00				

KM# 80 5 PESOS

12.00 g., 0.999 Silver 0.3854 oz. ASW **Subject:** XIV Central American and Caribbean Games **Obv:** National arms within wreath, denomination below **Rev:** Three athletes

Date	Mintage	VF20	XF40	MS60	MS63	MS65
1981	5,000	—	—	—	—	16.50
1981	2,000	PF65 35.00				

KM# 81 5 PESOS

12.00 g., 0.999 Silver 0.3854 oz. ASW **Subject:** XIV Central American and Caribbean Games **Obv:** National arms within wreath, denomination below **Rev:** Boxers

Date	Mintage	VF20	XF40	MS60	MS63	MS65
1981	5,000	—	—	—	—	16.50
1981	2,000	PF65 35.00				

KM# 82 5 PESOS

12.00 g., 0.999 Silver 0.3854 oz. ASW **Series:** Cuban Fauna **Obv:** National arms within wreath, denomination below **Rev:** Cuban Tocororo

Date	Mintage	VF20	XF40	MS60	MS63	MS65
1981	5,000	—	—	—	—	22.50
1981	1,000	PF65 42.00				

KM# 83 5 PESOS

12.00 g., 0.999 Silver 0.3854 oz. ASW **Series:** Cuban Fauna **Obv:** National arms within wreath, denomination below **Rev:** Cuban Solenodon left, date below

Date	Mintage	VF20	XF40	MS60	MS63	MS65
1981	5,000	—	—	—	—	22.50
1981	1,000	PF65 42.00				

KM# 84 5 PESOS

12.00 g., 0.999 Silver 0.3854 oz. ASW **Series:** Cuban Fauna **Obv:** National arms within wreath, denomination below **Rev:** Giant Garfish left, date above

Date	Mintage	VF20	XF40	MS60	MS63	MS65
1981	5,000	—	—	—	—	22.50
1981	1,000	PF65 42.00				

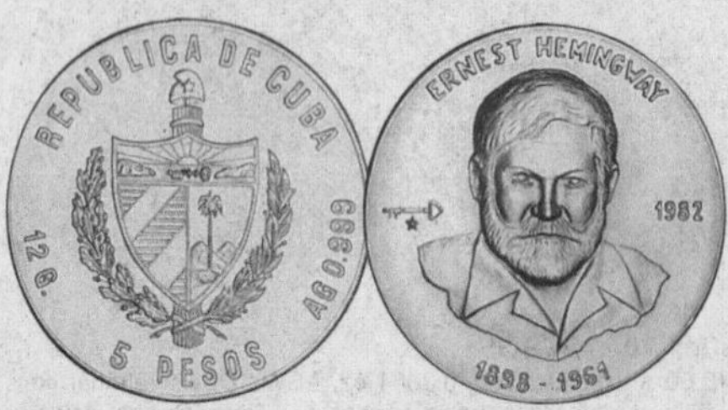

KM# 96 5 PESOS

12.00 g., 0.999 Silver 0.3854 oz. ASW **Obv:** National arms within wreath, denomination below **Rev:** Bust facing, three dates

Date	Mintage	VF20	XF40	MS60	MS63	MS65
1982	1,000	PF65 55.00				
1982	5,000	—	—	—	—	25.00

KM# 97 5 PESOS

12.00 g., 0.999 Silver 0.3854 oz. ASW **Obv:** National arms within wreath, denomination below **Rev:** Ernest Hemingway's fishing yacht

Date	Mintage	VF20	XF40	MS60	MS63	MS65
1982	5,000	—	—	—	—	25.00
1982	1,000	PF65 55.00				

KM# 98 5 PESOS

12.00 g., 0.999 Silver 0.3854 oz. ASW **Obv:** National arms within wreath, denomination below **Rev:** Ernest Hemingway - small boat

Date	Mintage	VF20	XF40	MS60	MS63	MS65
1982	5,000	—	—	—	—	25.00
1982	1,000	PF65 55.00				

KM# 99 5 PESOS

12.00 g., 0.999 Silver 0.3854 oz. ASW, 29.8 mm. **Obv:** National arms **Rev:** Bust of Miguel De Cervantes Saavedra 3/4 right **Edge:** Reeded

Date	Mintage	VF20	XF40	MS60	MS63	MS65
1982	7,000	—	—	—	—	18.00
1982	2,000	PF65 45.00				

KM# 100 5 PESOS

12.00 g., 0.999 Silver 0.3854 oz. ASW **Obv:** National arms within wreath, denomination below **Rev:** Hidalgo Don Quijote on horse

Date	Mintage	VF20	XF40	MS60	MS63	MS65
1982	7,000	—	—	—	—	18.00
1982	2,000	PF65 45.00				

KM# 101 5 PESOS

12.00 g., 0.999 Silver 0.3854 oz. ASW **Subject:** Hidalgo Don Quijote and Sancho Panza **Obv:** National arms within wreath, denomination below **Rev:** Small figure on mule, larger figure with lance on horse

Date	Mintage	VF20	XF40	MS60	MS63	MS65
1982	7,000	—	—	—	—	18.00
1982	2,000	PF65 45.00				

KM# 102 5 PESOS

12.00 g., 0.999 Silver 0.3854 oz. ASW **Series:** F.A.O. **Obv:** National arms within wreath, denomination below **Rev:** Citrus fruit

Date	Mintage	VF20	XF40	MS60	MS63	MS65
1982	3,125	—	—	—	—	25.00
1982	1,040	PF65 42.00				

KM# 103 5 PESOS

12.00 g., 0.999 Silver 0.3854 oz. ASW **Series:** F.A.O. **Obv:** National arms within wreath, denomination below **Rev:** Cow on grass left

Date	Mintage	VF20	XF40	MS60	MS63	MS65
1982	4,177	—	—	—	—	25.00
1982	1,000	PF65 42.00				

KM# 108 5 PESOS

12.00 g., 0.999 Silver 0.3854 oz. ASW **Series:** 1984 Winter Olympics - Hockey **Obv:** National arms within wreath, denomination below

Date	Mintage	VF20	XF40	MS60	MS63	MS65
1983	5,000	PF65 20.00				

KM# 109 5 PESOS
12.00 g., 0.999 Silver 0.3854 oz. ASW **Series:** 1984 Summer Olympics **Obv:** National arms within wreath, denomination below **Rev:** Runner

Date	Mintage	VF20	XF40	MS60	MS63	MS65
1983	5,000	PF65 20.00				

KM# 110 5 PESOS
12.00 g., 0.999 Silver 0.3854 oz. ASW **Obv:** National arms within wreath, denomination below **Rev:** Train on track, date below

Date	Mintage	VF20	XF40	MS60	MS63	MS65
1983	5,000	—	—	—	—	18.00
1983	2,000	PF65 35.00				

KM# 111 5 PESOS
12.00 g., 0.999 Silver 0.3854 oz. ASW **Subject:** World Fisheries **Obv:** National arms within wreath, denomination below **Rev:** Spiny lobster

Date	Mintage	VF20	XF40	MS60	MS63	MS65
1983	5,000	—	—	—	—	25.00
1983	1,000	PF65 45.00				

KM# 112 5 PESOS
12.00 g., 0.999 Silver 0.3854 oz. ASW **Subject:** Winter Olympics **Obv:** National arms within wreath, denomination below **Rev:** Woman holding torch

Date	Mintage	VF20	XF40	MS60	MS63	MS65
1983	5,000	PF65 20.00				

KM# 113 5 PESOS
12.00 g., 0.999 Silver 0.3854 oz. ASW **Series:** Winter Olympics **Obv:** National arms within wreath, denomination below **Rev:** Downhill skier

Date	Mintage	VF20	XF40	MS60	MS63	MS65
1983	5,000	PF65 20.00				

KM# 114 5 PESOS
12.00 g., 0.999 Silver 0.3854 oz. ASW **Series:** Summer Olympics **Obv:** National arms within wreath, denomination below **Rev:** Discus thrower

Date	Mintage	VF20	XF40	MS60	MS63	MS65
1983	5,000	PF65 20.00				

KM# 115 5 PESOS
12.00 g., 0.999 Silver 0.3854 oz. ASW **Series:** Summer Olympics **Obv:** National arms within wreath, denomination below **Rev:** Judo match, date at right

Date	Mintage	VF20	XF40	MS60	MS63	MS65
1983	5,000	PF65 20.00				

KM# 117 5 PESOS
12.00 g., 0.999 Silver 0.3854 oz. ASW **Subject:** Transportation **Obv:** National arms within wreath, denomination below **Rev:** Freighter, date below

Date	Mintage	VF20	XF40	MS60	MS63	MS65
1984	5,000	—	—	—	—	22.50
1984	1,000	PF65 45.00				

KM# 119 5 PESOS
12.00 g., 0.999 Silver 0.3854 oz. ASW **Obv:** National arms within wreath, denomination below **Rev:** Santisimo Trinidad, date at left

Date	Mintage	VF20	XF40	MS60	MS63	MS65
1984	5,000	—	—	—	—	22.50

KM# 131 5 PESOS
12.00 g., 0.999 Silver 0.3854 oz. ASW **Subject:** Transportation **Obv:** National arms within wreath, denomination below **Rev:** Volanta coach

Date	Mintage	VF20	XF40	MS60	MS63	MS65
1984	5,000	—	—	—	—	18.00
1984	1,000	PF65 45.00				

KM# 141 5 PESOS
12.00 g., 0.999 Silver 0.3854 oz. ASW **Subject:** Fortress - El Morro La Habana **Obv:** National arms within wreath, denomination below **Rev:** Fortress, date at left

Date	Mintage	VF20	XF40	MS60	MS63	MS65
1984	5,000	—	—	—	—	20.00
1984	1,000	PF65 55.00				

KM# 143 5 PESOS
12.00 g., 0.999 Silver 0.3854 oz. ASW **Subject:** La Fuerza La Habana **Obv:** National arms within wreath, denomination below **Rev:** Fortress

Date	Mintage	VF20	XF40	MS60	MS63	MS65
1984	5,000	—	—	—	—	20.00
1984	1,000	PF65 55.00				

KM# 145 5 PESOS
12.00 g., 0.999 Silver 0.3854 oz. ASW **Subject:** El Morro Santiago De Cuba **Obv:** National arms within wreath, denomination below **Rev:** Fortress

Date	Mintage	VF20	XF40	MS60	MS63	MS65
1984	5,000	—	—	—	—	20.00
1984	1,000	PF65 55.00				

KM# 666 5 PESOS
12.00 g., 0.999 Silver 0.3854 oz. ASW **Subject:** Transportation **Obv:** National arms within wreath, denomination below **Rev:** Hot air balloon

Date	Mintage	VF20	XF40	MS60	MS63	MS65
1984	2	—	—	—	—	4,000

KM# 121 5 PESOS
12.00 g., 0.999 Silver 0.3854 oz. ASW **Subject:** International Year of Music - Bach

Date	Mintage	VF20	XF40	MS60	MS63	MS65
1985	2,000	—	—	—	—	30.00
1985	—	PF65 50.00				

KM# 123 5 PESOS
12.00 g., 0.999 Silver 0.3854 oz. ASW, 29.83 mm. **Subject:** XIII World Football Championship - Mexico 1986 **Obv:** National arms **Rev:** Two soccer players **Edge:** Reeded

Date	Mintage	VF20	XF40	MS60	MS63	MS65
1985	5,000	—	—	—	—	22.50
1985	—	PF65 42.00				

KM# 125 5 PESOS
12.00 g., 0.999 Silver 0.3854 oz. ASW **Subject:** Wildlife Preservation **Obv:** National arms within wreath, denomination below **Rev:** Cuban crocodile

Date	Mintage	VF20	XF40	MS60	MS63	MS65
1985	5,000	—	—	—	—	42.00

KM# 127 5 PESOS
12.00 g., 0.999 Silver 0.3854 oz. ASW **Subject:** Wildlife Preservation **Obv:** National arms within wreath, denomination below **Rev:** Cuban Rock Iquana

Date	Mintage	VF20	XF40	MS60	MS63	MS65
1985	5,000	—	—	—	—	42.00

KM# 129 5 PESOS
12.00 g., 0.999 Silver 0.3854 oz. ASW **Subject:** Wildlife Preservation **Obv:** National arms within wreath, denomination below **Rev:** Cuban Amazon Parrot

Date	Mintage	VF20	XF40	MS60	MS63	MS65
1985	5,000	—	—	—	—	42.00

KM# 146 5 PESOS
12.00 g., 0.999 Silver 0.3854 oz. ASW **Subject:** 40th Anniversary of F.A.O. **Obv:** National arms within wreath, denomination below **Rev:** Lobster, palm tree, and sugar cane

Date	Mintage	VF20	XF40	MS60	MS63	MS65
ND-1985	4,500	—	—	—	—	20.00
ND-1985	500	PF65 55.00				

KM# 147 5 PESOS
12.00 g., 0.999 Silver 0.3854 oz. ASW **Series:** F.A.O. **Subject:** Forestry **Obv:** National arms within wreath, denomination below **Rev:** Stylized forest

Date	Mintage	VF20	XF40	MS60	MS63	MS65
ND-1985	4,500	—	—	—	—	18.00
ND-1985	500	PF65 50.00				

KM# 135 5 PESOS
12.00 g., 0.999 Silver 0.3854 oz. ASW **Subject:** 100th Anniversary of the Automobile **Obv:** National arms within wreath, denomination below **Rev:** Daimler-Benz

Date	Mintage	VF20	XF40	MS60	MS63	MS65
ND-1986	2,500	—	—	—	—	30.00

KM# 137 5 PESOS
12.00 g., 0.999 Silver 0.3854 oz. ASW **Subject:** 30th Anniversary - Voyage of the Granma **Obv:** National arms within wreath, denomination below **Rev:** Large ship at sea, dates

Date	Mintage	VF20	XF40	MS60	MS63	MS65
ND-1986	2,500	—	—	—	—	27.50

KM# 139.1 5 PESOS
12.00 g., 0.999 Silver 0.3854 oz. ASW **Series:** Olympics **Obv:** National arms within wreath, denomination below **Rev:** Skater

Date	Mintage	VF20	XF40	MS60	MS63	MS65
1986	2,500	—	—	—	—	45.00

KM# 139.2 5 PESOS
12.00 g., 0.999 Silver 0.3854 oz. ASW **Series:** Olympics **Obv:** National arms within wreath, denomination below **Rev:** Without rings above skater

Date	Mintage	VF20	XF40	MS60	MS63	MS65
1986	10,000	—	—	—	—	16.50

KM# 157 5 PESOS
12.00 g., 0.999 Silver 0.3854 oz. ASW **Series:** F.A.O. **Subject:** International Year of Peace **Obv:** National arms within wreath, denomination below

Date	Mintage	VF20	XF40	MS60	MS63	MS65
1986	10,000	—	—	—	—	27.50
1986	2,000	PF65 35.00				

KM# 149 5 PESOS
12.00 g., 0.999 Silver 0.3854 oz. ASW **Subject:** Cathedral in Santiago **Obv:** National arms within wreath, denomination below **Rev:** Cathedral, date above

Date	Mintage	VF20	XF40	MS60	MS63	MS65
1987	2,500	—	—	—	—	30.00

KM# 151 5 PESOS
12.00 g., 0.999 Silver 0.3854 oz. ASW **Subject:** Cathedral in Caridad del Cobre **Obv:** National arms within wreath, denomination below **Rev:** Cathedral

Date	Mintage	VF20	XF40	MS60	MS63	MS65
1987	2,500	—	—	—	—	30.00

KM# 153 5 PESOS
12.00 g., 0.999 Silver 0.3854 oz. ASW **Subject:** Cathedral in Trinidad **Obv:** National arms within wreath, denomination below **Rev:** Cathedral

Date	Mintage	VF20	XF40	MS60	MS63	MS65
1987	2,500	—	—	—	—	30.00

KM# 155 5 PESOS
12.00 g., 0.999 Silver 0.3854 oz. ASW **Subject:** 40th Anniversary - Expedition of Kon-Tiki **Obv:** National arms within wreath, denomination below **Rev:** Full masted ships, dates

Date	Mintage	VF20	XF40	MS60	MS63	MS65
ND-1987	5,000	—	—	—	—	25.00

KM# 159 5 PESOS
12.00 g., 0.999 Silver 0.3854 oz. ASW **Subject:** 20th Anniversary - Demise of Ernesto Che Guevara **Obv:** National arms within wreath, denomination below **Rev:** Bust facing divides dates

Date	Mintage	VF20	XF40	MS60	MS63	MS65
ND-1987	5,000	—	—	—	—	42.00
ND-1987	200	PF65 150				

KM# 161 5 PESOS
12.00 g., 0.999 Silver 0.3854 oz. ASW **Subject:** 70th Anniversary - Bolshevik Revolution **Obv:** National arms within wreath, denomination below **Rev:** Ship at sea, date at right

Date	Mintage	VF20	XF40	MS60	MS63	MS65
1987	3,000	—	—	—	—	30.00
1987	1,000	PF65 55.00				

KM# 166 5 PESOS
12.00 g., 0.999 Silver 0.3854 oz. ASW **Subject:** 100th Anniversary - Souvenir Peso **Obv:** National arms within wreath, denomination **Rev:** Head right

Date	Mintage	VF20	XF40	MS60	MS63	MS65
1987	3,000	—	—	—	—	30.00

KM# 326 5 PESOS
12.00 g., 0.999 Silver 0.3854 oz. ASW **Subject:** Abolition of Slavery **Obv:** National arms within wreath, denomination **Rev:** Slave breaking chains, dates

Date	Mintage	VF20	XF40	MS60	MS63	MS65
1987	2,000	—	—	—	—	35.00

KM# 180 5 PESOS
12.00 g., 0.999 Silver 0.3854 oz. ASW **Subject:** Jose Capablanca Chess Championship - Player **Obv:** National arms within wreath, denomination below **Rev:** Man with chessboard, dates at right

Date	Mintage	VF20	XF40	MS60	MS63	MS65
ND (1988)	5,000	—	—	—	—	30.00

KM# 185 5 PESOS
12.00 g., 0.999 Silver 0.3854 oz. ASW **Subject:** Soccer - Mexico 1986 **Obv:** National arms within wreath, denomination below **Rev:** Soccer players, date at left

Date	Mintage	VF20	XF40	MS60	MS63	MS65
1988	5,000	—	—	—	—	25.00
1988	—	PF65 35.00				

KM# 216 5 PESOS
6.00 g., 0.999 Silver 0.1927 oz. ASW **Subject:** Soccer - Italy 1990 **Obv:** Three towers above key on crowned shield within wreath **Rev:** Soccer players, date above

Date	Mintage	VF20	XF40	MS60	MS63	MS65
1988	—	—	—	—	—	15.00

KM# 216a 5 PESOS
12.00 g., 0.999 Silver 0.3854 oz. ASW **Subject:** Soccer - Italy 1990 **Obv:** Three towers above key on crowned shield within wreath **Rev:** Soccer players, two dates

Date	Mintage	VF20	XF40	MS60	MS63	MS65
1988	5,000	—	—	—	—	—

Note: Existence in doubt.

KM# 217 5 PESOS
12.00 g., 0.999 Silver 0.3854 oz. ASW **Subject:** Soccer - West Germany **Obv:** Three towers above key on crowned shield within wreath, denomination below **Rev:** Three players

Date	Mintage	VF20	XF40	MS60	MS63	MS65
1988	5,000	—	—	—	—	25.00

KM# 218 5 PESOS
12.00 g., 0.999 Silver 0.3854 oz. ASW **Subject:** Soccer - West Germany **Obv:** Three towers above key on crowned shield within wreath, denomination below **Rev:** Four players

Date	Mintage	VF20	XF40	MS60	MS63	MS65
1988	5,000	—	—	—	—	25.00

KM# 219 5 PESOS
16.00 g., 0.999 Silver 0.5139 oz. ASW **Subject:** 40th Anniversary - Cuban National Ballet **Obv:** National arms within wreath, denomination **Rev:** Head of Alicia Alonso right, ballet dancer, dates below

Date	Mintage	VF20	XF40	MS60	MS63	MS65
ND-1988	2,000	PF65 50.00				

KM# 220.1 5 PESOS
16.00 g., 0.999 Silver 0.5139 oz. ASW **Obv:** National arms within wreath, denomination **Rev:** Graf Zeppelin

Date	Mintage	VF20	XF40	MS60	MS63	MS65
1988	3,000	PF65 200				

KM# 220.2 5 PESOS
15.94 g., 0.999 Silver 0.512 oz. ASW **Obv:** National arms within wreath, thicker wreath **Rev:** Graf Zeppelin

Date	Mintage	VF20	XF40	MS60	MS63	MS65
1988	—	PF65 120				

KM# 221 5 PESOS
16.00 g., 0.999 Silver 0.5139 oz. ASW **Obv:** National arms within wreath, denomination below **Rev:** Carlos J. Finlay

Date	Mintage	VF20	XF40	MS60	MS63	MS65
ND-1988	2,000	PF65 50.00				

KM# 222 5 PESOS
16.00 g., 0.999 Silver 0.5139 oz. ASW **Subject:** World Health Organization **Obv:** National arms within wreath, denomination **Rev:** Nurse with baby, building in background

Date	Mintage	VF20	XF40	MS60	MS63	MS65
ND-1988	2,000	PF65 50.00				

KM# 223 5 PESOS
16.00 g., 0.999 Silver 0.5139 oz. ASW **Subject:** 150th Anniversary - Grand National Theater in Havana **Obv:** National arms within wreath, denomination below **Rev:** Theater building, dates and inscription at left

Date	Mintage	VF20	XF40	MS60	MS63	MS65
ND-1988	2,000	PF65 60.00				

KM# 224.1 5 PESOS
16.00 g., 0.999 Silver 0.5139 oz. ASW **Series:** Olympics - Barcelona **Obv:** National arms within wreath, plain bars **Rev:** Boxing

Date	Mintage	VF20	XF40	MS60	MS63	MS65
1989	10,000	PF65 37.50				

KM# 224.2 5 PESOS
16.00 g., 0.999 Silver 0.5139 oz. ASW **Subject:** Olympics - Barcelona **Obv:** National arms within wreath, striped bars **Rev:** Boxing

Date	Mintage	VF20	XF40	MS60	MS63	MS65
1989	Inc. above	PF65 37.50				

KM# 225.1 5 PESOS
16.00 g., 0.999 Silver 0.5139 oz. ASW **Series:** Olympics - Italy **Obv:** Small thin towers, lower relief, larger rectangular indentations in the tower and the crown **Rev:** Three soccer players

Date	Mintage	VF20	XF40	MS60	MS63	MS65
1989	10,000	PF65 37.50				

KM# 225.2 5 PESOS
16.00 g., 0.999 Silver 0.5139 oz. ASW **Subject:** Olympics - Italy **Obv:** Large, thick towers, higher relief, smaller oval indentations in the tower and the crown **Rev:** Three players

Date	Mintage	VF20	XF40	MS60	MS63	MS65
1989	Inc. above	PF65 37.50				

KM# 226.1 5 PESOS
16.00 g., 0.999 Silver 0.5139 oz. ASW **Series:** Olympics - Italy **Obv:** Small, thin towers, lower relief, larger rectangular indentations in the towers and crown **Rev:** Colosseum

Date	Mintage	VF20	XF40	MS60	MS63	MS65
1989	10,000	PF65 40.00				

KM# 226.2 5 PESOS
16.00 g., 0.999 Silver 0.5139 oz. ASW **Subject:** Olympics - Italy **Obv:** Large, thick towers, lower relief, smaller oval indentations in the towers and crown **Rev:** Colosseum

Date	Mintage	VF20	XF40	MS60	MS63	MS65
1989	Inc. above	PF65 40.00				

KM# 226.3 5 PESOS
16.00 g., 0.999 Silver 0.5139 oz. ASW **Subject:** Olympics - Italy **Obv:** High relief **Rev:** Colosseum

Date	Mintage	VF20	XF40	MS60	MS63	MS65
1989	Inc. above	PF65 65.00				

KM# 227.1 5 PESOS
16.00 g., 0.999 Silver 0.5139 oz. ASW **Subject:** Cuban tobacco **Obv:** Arms with plain field at lower right, thin wreath surrounds, denomination below **Rev:** Native smoking above tobacco plant, parrot at right, date below

Date	Mintage	VF20	XF40	MS60	MS63	MS65
1989	2,000	PF65 65.00				

KM# 227.2 5 PESOS
16.00 g., 0.999 Silver 0.5139 oz. ASW **Subject:** Cuban tobacco **Obv:** Arms with striped field at lower right, thick wreath **Rev:** Native smoking above tobacco plant, parrot at right, date below

Date	Mintage	VF20	XF40	MS60	MS63	MS65
1989	Inc. above	PF65 65.00				

KM# 231 5 PESOS
16.00 g., 0.999 Silver 0.5139 oz. ASW **Subject:** Alexander von Humboldt **Obv:** National arms within wreath, denomination **Rev:** Bust in cameo left of birds, dates

Date	Mintage	VF20	XF40	MS60	MS63	MS65
1989	3,000	PF65 60.00				

KM# 251.1 5 PESOS
16.00 g., 0.999 Silver 0.5139 oz. ASW **Subject:** Universal Congress of Esperanto **Obv:** Arms with plain field at lower right, thin wreath surrounds, denomination below **Rev:** Bust to right of globe looking left, date below

Date	Mintage	VF20	XF40	MS60	MS63	MS65
1990	6,000	PF65 50.00				

KM# 251.2 5 PESOS
16.00 g., 0.999 Silver 0.5139 oz. ASW **Subject:** Universal Congress of Esperanto **Obv:** Arms with striped field at lower right, thick wreath **Rev:** Bust to right of globe looking left

Date	Mintage	VF20	XF40	MS60	MS63	MS65
1990	Inc. above	PF65 50.00				

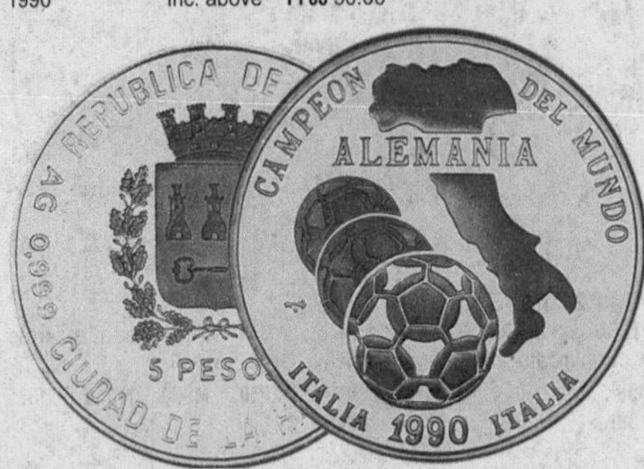

KM# 290.1 5 PESOS
16.00 g., 0.999 Silver 0.5139 oz. ASW **Subject:** Soccer **Obv:** Small, thin towers, lower relief, larger rectangular indentations in the towers and crown **Rev:** Map of Italy and soccer balls

Date	Mintage	VF20	XF40	MS60	MS63	MS65
1990	10,000	PF65 35.00				

KM# 290.2 5 PESOS
16.00 g., 0.999 Silver 0.5139 oz. ASW **Subject:** Soccer **Obv:** Large, thick towers, higher relief, smaller oval indentations in the towers and the crown **Rev:** Map of Italy and soccer balls

Date	Mintage	VF20	XF40	MS60	MS63	MS65
1990	Inc. above	PF65 35.00				

KM# 290.3 5 PESOS
16.00 g., 0.999 Silver 0.5139 oz. ASW **Subject:** Soccer **Obv:** National arms within wreath, denomination **Rev:** Map of Italy and soccer balls **Note:** Mule

Date	Mintage	VF20	XF40	MS60	MS63	MS65
1990	—	PF65 100				

KM# 338 5 PESOS
12.00 g., 0.999 Silver 0.3854 oz. ASW **Subject:** Soccer Championship **Obv:** National arms within wreath, denomination **Rev:** Two players

Date	Mintage	VF20	XF40	MS60	MS63	MS65
1991 Proof	10,000	—	—	—	—	36.00

KM# 405 5 PESOS
6.00 g., 0.999 Silver 0.1927 oz. ASW **Series:** Prehistoric Animals **Obv:** National arms within wreath, denomination below **Rev:** Apatosaurus

Date	Mintage	VF20	XF40	MS60	MS63	MS65
1993	30,000	PF65 33.00				

KM# 524.1 5 PESOS
15.00 g., 0.999 Silver 0.4818 oz. ASW **Subject:** Historia Postal de Cuba Steamship **Obv:** National arms within wreath, denomination below, thin letters **Rev:** Side-wheel steamship, date below, straight end 9 s

Date	Mintage	VF20	XF40	MS60	MS63	MS65
1993	25,000	PF65 30.00				

KM# 524.2 5 PESOS
15.00 g., 0.999 Silver 0.4818 oz. ASW **Subject:** Historia Postal de Cuba Steamship **Obv:** National arms, thin letters and wreath **Rev:** Side-wheel steamship, curved end 9s in date

Date	Mintage	VF20	XF40	MS60	MS63	MS65
1993	Inc. above	PF65 30.00				

KM# 524.3 5 PESOS
15.00 g., 0.999 Silver 0.4818 oz. ASW, 33 mm. **Subject:** Historia Postal de Cuba Steamship **Obv:** National arms, thick letters and wreath **Rev:** Side-wheel steamship, curved end 9s in date **Edge:** Reeded

Date	Mintage	VF20	XF40	MS60	MS63	MS65
1993	—	PF65 55.00				

KM# 524.4 5 PESOS
15.00 g., 0.999 Silver 0.4818 oz. ASW **Subject:** Historia Postal de Cuba Steamship **Obv:** National arms, thin letters and wreath, large (5mm) gap between 15 and G **Rev:** Side-Wheel steamship, curved end 9s in date

Date	Mintage	VF20	XF40	MS60	MS63	MS65
1993	—	PF65 55.00				

KM# 440 5 PESOS
16.00 g., 0.999 Silver 0.5139 oz. ASW **Series:** Prehistoric Animals **Obv:** National arms within wreath, denomination below **Rev:** Triceratops

Date	Mintage	VF20	XF40	MS60	MS63	MS65
1994	10,000	PF65 60.00				

KM# 573 5 PESOS
16.00 g., 0.999 Silver 0.5139 oz. ASW **Series:** Prehistoric Animals **Obv:** National arms within wreath, denomination below **Rev:** Maiasaura

Date	Mintage	VF20	XF40	MS60	MS63	MS65
1994	—	PF65 60.00				

KM# 581 5 PESOS
7.00 g., 0.999 Silver 0.2248 oz. ASW **Obv:** National arms within wreath, denomination below **Rev:** Multicolored hibiscus

Date	Mintage	VF20	XF40	MS60	MS63	MS65
1997	—	PF65 18.00				

KM# 623 5 PESOS
7.00 g., 0.999 Silver 0.2248 oz. ASW, 30 mm. **Subject:** AIDS **Obv:** National arms within wreath, denomination below **Rev:** AIDS ribbon on silhouette before world map

Date	Mintage	VF20	XF40	MS60	MS63	MS65
1998	50,000	PF65 16.00				

KM# 655 5 PESOS
7.00 g., 0.999 Silver 0.2248 oz. ASW **Subject:** Expo 2000 - Philadelphia **Obv:** National arms within wreath, denomination below **Rev:** Cartoon above building

Date	Mintage	VF20	XF40	MS60	MS63	MS65
1999	31,250	PF65 14.00				

KM# 656 5 PESOS
7.00 g., 0.999 Silver 0.2248 oz. ASW **Subject:** Expo 2000 - Hannover **Obv:** National arms within wreath, denomination below **Rev:** Cartoon above city hall

Date	Mintage	VF20	XF40	MS60	MS63	MS65
1999	31,250	PF65 14.00				

KM# 657 5 PESOS
7.00 g., 0.999 Silver 0.2248 oz. ASW **Subject:** Expo 2000 - Osaka **Obv:** National arms within wreath, denomination below **Rev:** Cartoon above city view

Date	Mintage	VF20	XF40	MS60	MS63	MS65
1999	31,250	PF65 14.00				

KM# 658 5 PESOS
7.00 g., 0.999 Silver 0.2248 oz. ASW **Subject:** Expo 2000 - Montreal **Obv:** National arms within wreath, denomination below **Rev:** Cartoon above sports buildings

Date	Mintage	VF20	XF40	MS60	MS63	MS65
1999	31,250	PF65 14.00				

KM# 659 5 PESOS
7.00 g., 0.999 Silver 0.2248 oz. ASW **Subject:** Expo 2000 - Twipsy **Obv:** National arms within wreath, denomination below **Rev:** "Twipsy" in square

Date	Mintage	VF20	XF40	MS60	MS63	MS65
1999	31,250	PF65 14.00				

KM# 660 5 PESOS
7.00 g., 0.999 Silver 0.2248 oz. ASW **Subject:** Expo 2000 **Obv:** National arms within wreath, denomination below **Rev:** World map with logo center square

Date	Mintage	VF20	XF40	MS60	MS63	MS65
1999	31,250	PF65 14.00				

KM# 673 5 PESOS
1.55 g., 0.999 Gold 0.0498 oz. AGW, 14 mm. **Subject:** Zunzuncita **Obv:** National arms within wreath, denomination below **Rev:** Hummingbird

Date	Mintage	VF20	XF40	MS60	MS63	MS65
1999	—	PF65 95.00				
(1999) Proof	—	—	—	—	—	—

KM# 37 10 PESOS
26.66 g., 0.900 Silver 0.7714 oz. ASW **Subject:** 25th Anniversary - National Bank of Cuba **Obv:** Star behind national arms above half wreath, denomination below **Rev:** Multi-storied building

Date	Mintage	VF20	XF40	MS60	MS63	MS65
1975	55,000	PF65 37.50				

KM# 50 10 PESOS
18.00 g., 0.999 Silver 0.5781 oz. ASW **Subject:** First Soviet-Cuban Space Flight **Obv:** National arms within wreath, denomination below **Rev:** Shuttle orbiting planet, date below

Date	Mintage	VF20	XF40	MS60	MS63	MS65
1980	10,000	—	—	—	27.00	—
1980	5,000	PF65 45.00				
1980 Matte proof	—	—	—	—	50.00	—

KM# 51 10 PESOS
18.00 g., 0.999 Silver 0.5781 oz. ASW **Subject:** Moscow Olympics **Obv:** National arms within wreath, denomination **Rev:** Three athletic symbols in relief, date below

Date	Mintage	VF20	XF40	MS60	MS63	MS65
1980	10,000	—	—	—	27.00	—
1980 Matte proof	—	PF65 65.00				

KM# 162 10 PESOS
31.10 g., 0.999 Silver 0.9989 oz. ASW **Subject:** Triumph of the Revolution **Obv:** National arms on star background above half wreath, denomination below **Rev:** Castro with revolutionaries divide dates

Date	Mintage	VF20	XF40	MS60	MS63	MS65
1987	2,000	PF65 50.00				
1988	4,000	PF65 40.00				
1989	2,000	PF65 50.00				

KM# 163 10 PESOS
31.10 g., 0.999 Silver 0.9989 oz. ASW **Subject:** 60th Anniversary - Birth of Ernesto Che Guevara **Obv:** National arms on star background above half wreath, denomination below **Rev:** Bust right, date at left

Date	Mintage	VF20	XF40	MS60	MS63	MS65
1987	2,000	PF65 55.00				
1988	4,000	PF65 45.00				
1989	2,000	PF65 55.00				

KM# 164 10 PESOS
31.10 g., 0.999 Silver 0.9989 oz. ASW **Subject:** 30th Anniversary - The March to Victory **Obv:** National arms on star background above half wreath, denomination below **Rev:** Uniformed figures on march

Date	Mintage	VF20	XF40	MS60	MS63	MS65
1987	2,000	PF65 50.00				
1988	4,000	PF65 40.00				
1989	2,000	PF65 50.00				

KM# 205 10 PESOS
31.10 g., 0.999 Silver 0.9989 oz. ASW **Subject:** 150th Anniversary - First Railroad in Spanish America **Obv:** National arms on star background above half wreath, denomination below **Rev:** Train engine on track divides dates

Date	Mintage	VF20	XF40	MS60	MS63	MS65
1988	5,000	PF65 45.00				

KM# 206 10 PESOS
31.10 g., 0.999 Silver 0.9989 oz. ASW **Subject:** 140th Anniversary - First Railroad in Spain **Obv:** National arms on star background above half wreath, denomination below **Rev:** Train on track, dates below

Date	Mintage	VF20	XF40	MS60	MS63	MS65
1988	5,000	PF65 45.00				

KM# 207 10 PESOS
31.10 g., 0.999 Silver 0.9989 oz. ASW **Subject:** 160th Anniversary - World's First Railroad **Obv:** National arms on star background above half wreath, denomination below **Rev:** Railroad carts divide dates

Date	Mintage	VF20	XF40	MS60	MS63	MS65
1988	5,000	PF65 45.00				

KM# 211 10 PESOS
3.11 g., 0.999 Gold 0.0999 oz. AGW **Obv:** National arms within wreath, denomination below **Rev:** Jose Marti

Date	Mintage	VF20	XF40	MS60	MS63	MS65
1988	50	—	—	—	185	275
1988	10	PF65 285				
1989	50	—	—	—	185	275
1989	15	PF65 285				
1990	15	—	—	—	185	275
1990	12	PF65 285				

KM# 228 10 PESOS
31.10 g., 0.999 Silver 0.9989 oz. ASW **Subject:** Tania La Guerrillera, Argentinian revolutionary **Obv:** National arms on star background above half wreath, denomination below **Rev:** Bust facing

Date	Mintage	VF20	XF40	MS60	MS63	MS65
1988	5,000	PF65 45.00				

KM# 229 10 PESOS
31.10 g., 0.999 Silver 0.9989 oz. ASW **Subject:** Camilo Cienfuegos **Obv:** National arms on star background above half wreath, denomination below **Rev:** Bust facing

Date	Mintage	VF20	XF40	MS60	MS63	MS65
1988	5,000	PF65 45.00				

KM# 230 10 PESOS
31.10 g., 0.999 Silver 0.9989 oz. ASW **Subject:** 35th Anniversary - Assault of the Moncada Garrison **Obv:** National arms on star background above half wreat, denomination below **Rev:** Armed figures, dates below

Date	Mintage	VF20	XF40	MS60	MS63	MS65
ND-1988	5,000	PF65 40.00				

KM# 24.2 10 PESOS
31.10 g., 0.999 Silver 0.9989 oz. ASW **Subject:** 30th Anniversary of Revolution **Obv:** Arms with striped field at lower right, thick wreath **Rev:** Jose Marti and Castro

Date	Mintage	VF20	XF40	MS60	MS63	MS65
1989	Inc. above	PF65 65.00				
1989	Inc. above	—	—	—	40.00	—

KM# 238 10 PESOS
20.00 g., 0.999 Silver 0.6424 oz. ASW **Subject:** 5th Centennial - Discovery of America **Obv:** National arms within wreath, denomination below **Rev:** Three ships at sea, date below and at left

Date	Mintage	VF20	XF40	MS60	MS63	MS65
1989	3,145	—	—	—	42.00	—

KM# 239 10 PESOS
26.72 g., 0.999 Silver 0.8582 oz. ASW **Subject:** 200th Anniversary of French Revolution - Lady Justice **Obv:** National arms within wreath, denomination below **Rev:** 3/4 Figure of Lady Justice, dates above

Date	Mintage	VF20	XF40	MS60	MS63	MS65
ND-1989	500	—	—	—	75.00	—
ND-1989	2,000	PF65 50.00				

KM# 240 10 PESOS
26.72 g., 0.999 Silver 0.8582 oz. ASW **Subject:** 200th Anniversary of French Revolution **Obv:** Small national arms within wreath, denomination below **Rev:** Bastille

Date	Mintage	VF20	XF40	MS60	MS63	MS65
ND-1989	500	—	—	—	75.00	—
ND-1989	2,000	PF65 50.00				

KM# 241.1 10 PESOS
31.10 g., 0.999 Silver 0.9989 oz. ASW **Subject:** 30th Anniversary of Revolution **Obv:** Arms with plain field at lower right, thin wreath **Rev:** Castro

Date	Mintage	VF20	XF40	MS60	MS63	MS65
ND-1989	5,000	—	—	—	40.00	—
ND-1989	5,000	PF65 50.00				

KM# 241.2 10 PESOS
31.10 g., 0.999 Silver 0.9989 oz. ASW **Subject:** 30th Anniversary of Revolution **Obv:** Arms with striped field at lower right, thick wreath **Rev:** Castro

Date	Mintage	VF20	XF40	MS60	MS63	MS65
ND-1989	Inc. above	—	—	—	40.00	—
ND-1989	Inc. above	PF65 50.00				

KM# 242.1 10 PESOS
31.10 g., 0.999 Silver 0.9989 oz. ASW **Subject:** 30th Anniversary of Revolution **Obv:** Arms with plain field at lower right, thin wreath **Rev:** Jose Marti and Castro

Date	Mintage	VF20	XF40	MS60	MS63	MS65
1989	5,000	—	—	—	40.00	—
1989	5,000	PF65 50.00				

KM# 243.1 10 PESOS
31.10 g., 0.999 Silver 0.9989 oz. ASW **Subject:** 30th Anniversary of Revolution **Obv:** Arms with plain field at lower right, thin wreath **Rev:** Camilo Cienfuegos and Fidel Castro, inscription above, dates at right

Date	Mintage	VF20	XF40	MS60	MS63	MS65
ND-1989	5,000	—	—	—	40.00	—
ND-1989	5,000	PF65 65.00				

KM# 243.2 10 PESOS
31.10 g., 0.999 Silver 0.9989 oz. ASW **Subject:** 30th Anniversary of Revolution **Obv:** Arms with striped field at lower right, thick wreath **Rev:** Camilo Cienfuegos and Fidel Castro

Date	Mintage	VF20	XF40	MS60	MS63	MS65
ND-1989	Inc. above	—	—	—	40.00	—
ND-1989	Inc. above	PF65 50.00				

KM# 249.1 10 PESOS
20.00 g., 0.999 Silver 0.6424 oz. ASW **Subject:** Discovery of America **Obv:** Arms with plain field at lower right, thin wreath, denomination below **Rev:** Three sailing ships, date below and at left

Date	Mintage	VF20	XF40	MS60	MS63	MS65
1989	8,855	PF65 38.00				

KM# 249.2 10 PESOS
20.00 g., 0.999 Silver 0.6424 oz. ASW **Subject:** Discovery of America **Obv:** Arms with striped field at lower right, thick wreath **Rev:** Three sailing ships

Date	Mintage	VF20	XF40	MS60	MS63	MS65
1989	Inc. above	PF65 40.00				

KM# 383 10 PESOS
3.11 g., 0.999 Gold 0.0999 oz. AGW **Obv:** National arms within wreath, denomination below **Rev:** Alexander von Humboldt

Date	Mintage	VF20	XF40	MS60	MS63	MS65
1989	500	—	—	—	—	190
1989	—	PF65 185				

KM# 252.1 10 PESOS
20.00 g., 0.999 Silver 0.6424 oz. ASW **Subject:** Discovery of America **Obv:** Arms with plain field at lower right, thin wreath **Rev:** Ship and map of Cuba, date at right

Date	Mintage	VF20	XF40	MS60	MS63	MS65
1990	10,000	PF65 38.00				

KM# 252.2 10 PESOS
20.00 g., 0.999 Silver 0.6424 oz. ASW **Subject:** Discovery of America **Obv:** Arms with striped field at lower right, thick wreath **Rev:** Ship and map of Cuba

Date	Mintage	VF20	XF40	MS60	MS63	MS65
1990	Inc. above	PF65 40.00				

KM# 256.1 10 PESOS
20.00 g., 0.999 Silver 0.6424 oz. ASW **Subject:** 500th Anniversary of Columbus Meeting Native Americans **Obv:** Arms with plain field at lower right, thin wreath **Rev:** Columbus meeting natives, date below

Date	Mintage	VF20	XF40	MS60	MS63	MS65
1990	10,000	PF65 40.00				

KM# 256.2 10 PESOS
20.00 g., 0.999 Silver 0.6424 oz. ASW **Subject:** 500th Anniversary of Columbus Meeting Native Americans **Obv:** Arms with striped field at lower right, thick wreath

Date	Mintage	VF20	XF40	MS60	MS63	MS65
1990	Inc. above	PF65 40.00				

KM# 262.1 10 PESOS
31.10 g., 0.999 Silver 0.999 oz. ASW **Obv:** Arms with plain field at lower right, thin wreath **Rev:** Celia Sanchez Manduley

Date	Mintage	VF20	XF40	MS60	MS63	MS65
1990	2,000	PF65 55.00				

KM# 262.2 10 PESOS
31.10 g., 0.999 Silver 0.999 oz. ASW **Obv:** Arms with striped bars at lower right, thick wreath **Rev:** Celia Sanchez Manduley

Date	Mintage	VF20	XF40	MS60	MS63	MS65
1990	Inc. above	PF65 55.00				

KM# 263 10 PESOS
31.10 g., 0.999 Silver 0.999 oz. ASW **Subject:** Discovery of America **Obv:** National arms within wreath, denomination **Rev:** King Ferdinand bust 3/4 right within wreath, two dates

Date	Mintage	VF20	XF40	MS60	MS63	MS65
1990	5,000	PF65 45.00				

KM# 264 10 PESOS
31.10 g., 0.999 Silver 0.999 oz. ASW **Subject:** Discovery of America **Obv:** National arms within wreath, denomination **Rev:** Queen Isabella

Date	Mintage	VF20	XF40	MS60	MS63	MS65
1990	5,000	PF65 45.00				

KM# 265 10 PESOS
31.10 g., 0.999 Silver 0.999 oz. ASW **Subject:** Discovery of America **Obv:** National arms within wreath, denomination below **Rev:** Christopher Columbus

Date	Mintage	VF20	XF40	MS60	MS63	MS65
1990	5,000	PF65 45.00				

KM# 266 10 PESOS
31.10 g., 0.999 Silver 0.999 oz. ASW **Subject:** Discovery of America **Obv:** National arms within wreath, denomination below **Rev:** Juan de la Cosa

Date	Mintage	VF20	XF40	MS60	MS63	MS65
1990	5,000	PF65 45.00				

KM# 267.1 10 PESOS
20.00 g., 0.999 Silver 0.6424 oz. ASW **Subject:** Discovery of America **Obv:** Arms with plain field at lower right, thin wreath **Rev:** Map of Columbus' route

Date	Mintage	VF20	XF40	MS60	MS63	MS65
1990	10,000	PF65 35.00				

KM# 267.2 10 PESOS
20.00 g., 0.999 Silver 0.6424 oz. ASW **Subject:** Discovery of America **Obv:** Arms with striped field at lower right, thick wreath **Rev:** Map of Columbus' route

Date	Mintage	VF20	XF40	MS60	MS63	MS65
1990	Inc. above	PF65 37.50				

KM# 280 10 PESOS
25.00 g., 0.999 Silver 0.803 oz. ASW **Subject:** Simon Bolivar **Obv:** National arms within wreath, denomination **Rev:** Uniformed bust right

Date	Mintage	VF20	XF40	MS60	MS63	MS65
1990	3,300	PF65 45.00				

KM# 291 10 PESOS
31.10 g., 0.999 Silver 0.9989 oz. ASW **Subject:** Pan American Games **Obv:** National arms within wreath, denomination **Rev:** High jumper

Date	Mintage	VF20	XF40	MS60	MS63	MS65
1990	3,000	PF65 55.00				

KM# 292 10 PESOS
31.10 g., 0.999 Silver 0.9989 oz. ASW **Subject:** Pan American Games **Obv:** National arms within wreath, denomination **Rev:** Volleyball

Date	Mintage	VF20	XF40	MS60	MS63	MS65
1990	3,000	PF65 55.00				

KM# 293 10 PESOS
31.10 g., 0.999 Silver 0.9989 oz. ASW **Subject:** Pan American Games **Obv:** National arms within wreath, denomination **Rev:** Baseball game scene

Date	Mintage	VF20	XF40	MS60	MS63	MS65
1990	3,000	PF65 60.00				

KM# 336.1 10 PESOS
28.00 g., 0.925 Silver 0.8327 oz. ASW **Series:** Summer Olympics **Obv:** Small characters **Rev:** Hurdler, tiny date at left

Date	Mintage	VF20	XF40	MS60	MS63	MS65
1990	25,000	PF65 32.00				

KM# 336.2 10 PESOS
28.00 g., 0.925 Silver 0.8327 oz. ASW **Subject:** Summer Olympics **Obv:** Tall (4mm) characters **Rev:** Hurdler

Date	Mintage	VF20	XF40	MS60	MS63	MS65
1990	Inc. above	PF65 50.00				

KM# 342 10 PESOS
3.11 g., 0.999 Gold 0.0999 oz. AGW **Series:** Olympics **Obv:** National arms within wreath, denomination below **Rev:** Basketball hoop, ball and hands, small date between arms below

Date	Mintage	VF20	XF40	MS60	MS63	MS65
1990	Est. 5000	PF65 185				

KM# 344.1 10 PESOS
28.00 g., 0.925 Silver 0.8327 oz. ASW **Series:** Summer Olympics **Obv:** Small characters **Rev:** Volleyball

Date	Mintage	VF20	XF40	MS60	MS63	MS65
1990	25,000	PF65 32.00				

KM# 344.2 10 PESOS
28.00 g., 0.925 Silver 0.8327 oz. ASW **Subject:** Summer Olympics **Obv:** Tall (4mm) characters **Rev:** Volleyball

Date	Mintage	VF20	XF40	MS60	MS63	MS65
1990	Inc. above	PF65 100				

KM# 345 10 PESOS
28.00 g., 0.925 Silver 0.8327 oz. ASW **Series:** Summer Olympics **Obv:** Small characters **Rev:** High jumper

Date	Mintage	VF20	XF40	MS60	MS63	MS65
1990	25,000	PF65 32.00				

KM# 362.1 10 PESOS
28.00 g., 0.925 Silver 0.8327 oz. ASW **Series:** Olympics **Obv:** Small characters **Rev:** Basketball players

Date	Mintage	VF20	XF40	MS60	MS63	MS65
1990	25,000	PF65 32.00				

KM# 362.2 10 PESOS
28.00 g., 0.925 Silver 0.8327 oz. ASW **Subject:** Olympics **Obv:** Tall (4mm) characters **Rev:** Basketball

Date	Mintage	VF20	XF40	MS60	MS63	MS65
1990	Inc. above	PF65 50.00				

KM# 369 10 PESOS
28.00 g., 0.999 Silver 0.8993 oz. ASW **Series:** Olympics **Rev:** Figure on pommel horse, date below

Date	Mintage	VF20	XF40	MS60	MS63	MS65
1990	—	PF65 32.00				

KM# 327 10 PESOS
31.10 g., 0.999 Silver 0.9989 oz. ASW **Obv:** National arms within wreath, denomination **Rev:** Vicente and Martin Pinzon in cameos

Date	Mintage	VF20	XF40	MS60	MS63	MS65
1991	3,000	PF65 50.00				

KM# 328 10 PESOS
31.10 g., 0.999 Silver 0.9989 oz. ASW **Obv:** National arms within wreath, denomination **Rev:** Hatuey tribesman

Date	Mintage	VF20	XF40	MS60	MS63	MS65
1991	3,000	PF65 50.00				

KM# 329 10 PESOS
25.00 g., 0.999 Silver 0.803 oz. ASW **Subject:** American International Monetary Conference **Obv:** National arms within wreath, denomination divided above **Rev:** Bust facing, dates below

Date	Mintage	VF20	XF40	MS60	MS63	MS65
ND-1991	3,300	PF65 40.00				

KM# 337 10 PESOS
27.00 g., 0.999 Silver 0.8672 oz. ASW **Subject:** Ibero - American **Obv:** National arms within wreath, denomination below within inner circle, circle of arms surround **Rev:** Statue of Columbus at Cardenas, dates at right

Date	Mintage	VF20	XF40	MS60	MS63	MS65
1991	51,000	PF65 42.50				

KM# 348 10 PESOS
31.10 g., 0.999 Silver 0.9989 oz. ASW **Subject:** Madrid **Obv:** National arms within wreath, denomination **Rev:** Alcala Gate

Date	Mintage	VF20	XF40	MS60	MS63	MS65
1991	—	PF65 50.00				

KM# 349 10 PESOS
31.10 g., 0.999 Silver 0.9989 oz. ASW **Subject:** Seville **Obv:** National arms within wreath, denomination **Rev:** La Giralda Tower

Date	Mintage	VF20	XF40	MS60	MS63	MS65
1991	—	PF65 50.00				

KM# 350 10 PESOS
31.10 g., 0.999 Silver 0.9989 oz. ASW **Subject:** Barcelona **Obv:** National arms within wreath, denomination **Rev:** Olympic Stadium

Date	Mintage	VF20	XF40	MS60	MS63	MS65
1991	3,250	PF65 50.00				

KM# 525 10 PESOS
31.10 g., 0.999 Silver 0.9989 oz. ASW **Obv:** National arms within wreath, denomination **Rev:** Diego Velazquez

Date	Mintage	VF20	XF40	MS60	MS63	MS65
1991	3,000	PF65 50.00				

KM# 526 10 PESOS
31.10 g., 0.999 Silver 0.9989 oz. ASW, 37.9 mm. **Subject:** 500th Anniversary of New World **Obv:** National arms within wreath, denomination **Rev:** Head of Queen Joanna, right, (1479-1555), daughter of Isabella I

Date	Mintage	VF20	XF40	MS60	MS63	MS65
1991	3,000	PF65 50.00				

KM# 341.1 10 PESOS
20.00 g., 0.999 Silver 0.6424 oz. ASW **Subject:** Postal History of Cuba **Obv:** 1992 style national arms **Rev:** Spanish galleon sailship, 1765 date

Date	Mintage	VF20	XF40	MS60	MS63	MS65
1992	10,000	PF65 32.00				

KM# 341.2 10 PESOS
20.00 g., 0.999 Silver 0.6424 oz. ASW **Subject:** Postal History **Obv:** Pre-1990 detailed, styled arms **Rev:** Sailing ship

Date	Mintage	VF20	XF40	MS60	MS63	MS65
1992	—	PF65 32.00				

KM# 351 10 PESOS
31.10 g., 0.999 Silver 0.9989 oz. ASW **Subject:** Seville **Obv:** National arms within wreath, denomination **Rev:** Tower of Gold

Date	Mintage	VF20	XF40	MS60	MS63	MS65
1992	2,050	PF65 55.00				

KM# 352 10 PESOS
31.10 g., 0.999 Silver 0.9989 oz. ASW **Obv:** National arms within wreath, denomination **Rev:** El Escorial

Date	Mintage	VF20	XF40	MS60	MS63	MS65
1992	2,050	PF65 55.00				

KM# 353 10 PESOS
31.10 g., 0.999 Silver 0.9989 oz. ASW **Subject:** 500th Anniversary of Philipp's rule **Obv:** National arms within wreath, denomination **Rev:** Bust of Philip I 3/4 right, date at right, within wreath

Date	Mintage	VF20	XF40	MS60	MS63	MS65
1992	3,000	PF65 50.00				

KM# 354.1 10 PESOS
20.00 g., 0.999 Silver 0.6424 oz. ASW **Subject:** Ptolomeo and Toscanelli **Obv:** National arms within wreath, denomination **Rev:** Medieval symbolic table, figure at top with globe, bust lower right

Date	Mintage	VF20	XF40	MS60	MS63	MS65
1992	—	PF65 35.00				

KM# 354.2 10 PESOS
20.00 g., 0.999 Silver 0.6424 oz. ASW **Obv:** Arms with thick wreath of the pre-1990 style **Rev:** Medieval symbolic table, figure at top with globe, bust lower right

Date	Mintage	VF20	XF40	MS60	MS63	MS65
1992	—	PF65 35.00				

KM# 355 10 PESOS
31.10 g., 0.999 Silver 0.9989 oz. ASW **Obv:** National arms within wreath, denomination **Rev:** Guama tribesman

Date	Mintage	VF20	XF40	MS60	MS63	MS65
1992	2,050	PF65 55.00				

KM# 370 10 PESOS
20.00 g., 0.999 Silver 0.6424 oz. ASW **Subject:** Postal History **Obv:** National arms within wreath, denomination **Rev:** Steam powered sailing ship, date below

Date	Mintage	VF20	XF40	MS60	MS63	MS65
1992	10,000	PF65 35.00				

KM# 371.1 10 PESOS
20.00 g., 0.999 Silver 0.6424 oz. ASW **Subject:** Introduction of Africans into America **Obv:** National arms within thin wreath **Rev:** Native at left, ship at sea on right

Date	Mintage	VF20	XF40	MS60	MS63	MS65
1992	10,000	PF65 40.00				

KM# 371.2 10 PESOS
20.00 g., 0.999 Silver 0.6424 oz. ASW **Obv:** National arms within thick wreath **Rev:** Native at left, ship at sea at right

Date	Mintage	VF20	XF40	MS60	MS63	MS65
1992	—	PF65 40.00				

KM# 372 10 PESOS
31.00 g., 0.999 Silver 0.9957 oz. ASW **Obv:** National arms within wreath, denomination below **Rev:** Seated figure left, writing, date at left

Date	Mintage	VF20	XF40	MS60	MS63	MS65
1992	2,050	PF65 55.00				

KM# 373 10 PESOS
31.00 g., 0.999 Silver 0.9957 oz. ASW **Subject:** Spanish Kings and Queens **Obv:** National arms within wreath **Rev:** Two heads left above and below banners

Date	Mintage	VF20	XF40	MS60	MS63	MS65
ND-1992	2,050	PF65 55.00				

KM# 374 10 PESOS
31.00 g., 0.999 Silver 0.9957 oz. ASW **Subject:** San Jorge Palace **Obv:** National arms within wreath, denomination **Rev:** Palace view

Date	Mintage	VF20	XF40	MS60	MS63	MS65
1992	2,050	PF65 55.00				

KM# 458.1 10 PESOS
20.00 g., 0.999 Silver 0.6424 oz. ASW **Subject:** World Cup Soccer **Obv:** Arms with plain field at lower right, thin wreath, thick characters **Rev:** Native in headdress on left, soccer player and date at right

Date	Mintage	VF20	XF40	MS60	MS63	MS65
1992	—	PF65 35.00				

KM# 458.2 10 PESOS
20.00 g., 0.999 Silver 0.6424 oz. ASW **Subject:** World Cup Soccer **Obv:** Arms with plain field at lower right, thin wreath, thin characters **Rev:** Native in headdress on left, soccer player and date at right

Date	Mintage	VF20	XF40	MS60	MS63	MS65
1992	—	PF65 35.00				

KM# 458.3 10 PESOS
20.00 g., 0.999 Silver 0.6424 oz. ASW **Subject:** World Cup Soccer **Obv:** Arms with striped field at lower right, thick wreath **Rev:** Native in headdress at left, soccer player and date at right

Date	Mintage	VF20	XF40	MS60	MS63	MS65
1992	—	PF65 35.00				

KM# 527.1 10 PESOS
20.00 g., 0.999 Silver 0.6424 oz. ASW **Subject:** 25th Anniversary - Death of Ernesto Che Guevara **Obv:** Arms with plain field at lower right, thin wreath **Rev:** Bust facing, dates

Date	Mintage	VF20	XF40	MS60	MS63	MS65
ND-1992	10,000	PF65 60.00				

KM# 527.2 10 PESOS
20.00 g., 0.999 Silver 0.6424 oz. ASW **Subject:** 25th Anniversary - Death of Ernesto Che Guevara **Obv:** Arms with striped field at lower right, thick wreath **Rev:** Bust facing, dates

Date	Mintage	VF20	XF40	MS60	MS63	MS65
ND-1992	Inc. above	PF65 40.00				

KM# 561 10 PESOS

20.00 g., 0.999 Silver 0.6424 oz. ASW **Subject:** Postal History **Obv:** National arms within wreath, denomination **Rev:** Old steam and sailship, date at right

Date	Mintage	VF20	XF40	MS60	MS63	MS65
1992	—	PF65 40.00				

KM# 375.1 10 PESOS

20.00 g., 0.999 Silver 0.6424 oz. ASW **Obv:** Arms with plain field at lower right, thin wreath **Rev:** President Abraham Lincoln

Date	Mintage	VF20	XF40	MS60	MS63	MS65
1993	—	PF65 55.00				

KM# 375.2 10 PESOS

20.00 g., 0.999 Silver 0.6424 oz. ASW **Obv:** Arms with striped field at lower right, thick wreath **Rev:** President Abraham Lincoln

Date	Mintage	VF20	XF40	MS60	MS63	MS65
1993	—	PF65 40.00				

KM# 398 10 PESOS

31.10 g., 0.999 Silver 0.9989 oz. ASW **Obv:** National arms within wreath, denomination **Rev:** Frosted bust of Fidel Castro left

Date	Mintage	VF20	XF40	MS60	MS63	MS65
1993	5,000	PF65 60.00				

KM# 399 10 PESOS

31.10 g., 0.999 Silver 0.9989 oz. ASW **Subject:** St. Jacobi **Obv:** Two sets of shielded arms, denomination **Rev:** Armored figure on rearing horse right

Date	Mintage	VF20	XF40	MS60	MS63	MS65
1993	5,000	PF65 45.00				

KM# 406.1 10 PESOS

31.10 g., 0.999 Silver 0.999 oz. ASW **Obv:** Arms with plain field at lower right, thin wreath **Rev:** Bolivar and Marti

Date	Mintage	VF20	XF40	MS60	MS63	MS65
1993	3,000	PF65 55.00				

KM# 406.2 10 PESOS

31.10 g., 0.999 Silver 0.999 oz. ASW **Obv:** Arms with striped field at lower right, thick wreath **Rev:** Bolivar and Marti

Date	Mintage	VF20	XF40	MS60	MS63	MS65
1993	Inc. above	PF65 45.00				

KM# 407.1 10 PESOS

31.10 g., 0.999 Silver 0.9989 oz. ASW **Subject:** Federico Garcia Lorca **Obv:** Arms with plain field at lower right, thin wreath **Rev:** Bust facing, dates at left

Date	Mintage	VF20	XF40	MS60	MS63	MS65
1993	3,300	PF65 55.00				

KM# 407.2 10 PESOS

31.10 g., 0.999 Silver 0.9989 oz. ASW **Obv:** Arms with striped field at lower right, thick wreath **Rev:** Frederico Garcia Lorca

Date	Mintage	VF20	XF40	MS60	MS63	MS65
1993	Inc. above	PF65 45.00				

KM# 496 10 PESOS

19.96 g., 0.999 Silver 0.6411 oz. ASW **Subject:** Postal History **Rev:** Steamship Almendares

Date	Mintage	VF20	XF40	MS60	MS63	MS65
1993	—	PF65 37.00				

KM# 408 10 PESOS

19.96 g., 0.999 Silver 0.6411 oz. ASW **Subject:** Montecristi Manifesto **Obv:** National arms within wreath, denomination below **Rev:** Two seated figures facing each other, date lower left

Date	Mintage	VF20	XF40	MS60	MS63	MS65
1994	3,300	PF65 45.00				

KM# 427 10 PESOS

20.00 g., 0.999 Silver 0.6424 oz. ASW **Obv:** National arms within wreath, denomination below **Rev:** Sailing ship - LA INDIA

Date	Mintage	VF20	XF40	MS60	MS63	MS65
1994	10,000	PF65 38.00				

KM# 428 10 PESOS

20.00 g., 0.999 Silver 0.6424 oz. ASW **Obv:** National arms within wreath, denomination below **Rev:** Sailing ship - NAO VICTORIA

Date	Mintage	VF20	XF40	MS60	MS63	MS65
1994	10,000	PF65 38.00				

KM# 441 10 PESOS

20.00 g., 0.999 Silver 0.6424 oz. ASW **Subject:** Evangelista Island **Obv:** Map of island, small arms lower right **Rev:** Ship at sea, treasure chest, parrot

Date	Mintage	VF20	XF40	MS60	MS63	MS65
1994	—	PF65 38.00				

KM# 442.1 10 PESOS

20.00 g., 0.999 Silver 0.6424 oz. ASW **Series:** Caribbean Fauna **Obv:** Thin characters **Rev:** Multicolored flamingos, thin water splashes

Date	Mintage	VF20	XF40	MS60	MS63	MS65
1994	10,000	PF65 45.00				

KM# 442.2 10 PESOS

20.00 g., 0.999 Silver 0.6424 oz. ASW **Subject:** Caribbean Fauna **Obv:** Thick characters **Rev:** Multicolored flamingos, wide water splashes

Date	Mintage	VF20	XF40	MS60	MS63	MS65
1994	Inc. above	PF65 38.00				

KM# 443.1 10 PESOS
20.00 g., 0.999 Silver 0.6424 oz. ASW **Series:** Caribbean Fauna **Obv:** Thin characters **Rev:** Multicolored Yellow Sea Bass (Coney), 7 lines in tail, slimmer fish

Date	Mintage	VF20	XF40	MS60	MS63	MS65
1994	10,000	PF65 45.00				

KM# 443.2 10 PESOS
20.00 g., 0.999 Silver 0.6424 oz. ASW **Subject:** Caribbean Fauna **Obv:** Thin characters **Rev:** Multicolored Yellow Sea Bass (Coney), 5 lines in tail

Date	Mintage	VF20	XF40	MS60	MS63	MS65
1994	Inc. above	PF65 38.00				

KM# 468 10 PESOS
20.00 g., 0.999 Silver 0.6424 oz. ASW **Subject:** Environmental Protection **Obv:** National arms within wreath, denomination **Rev:** Scale on left joined with tree on right, date lower right

Date	Mintage	VF20	XF40	MS60	MS63	MS65
1994	Est. 5000	PF65 42.00				

KM# 469 10 PESOS
20.00 g., 0.999 Silver 0.6424 oz. ASW **Series:** 1996 Olympics **Obv:** National arms within wreath, denomination **Rev:** Boxers

Date	Mintage	VF20	XF40	MS60	MS63	MS65
1994	Est. 30000	PF65 28.00				

KM# 470 10 PESOS
20.00 g., 0.999 Silver 0.6424 oz. ASW **Rev:** Red Baron Plane - multicolored Fokker Dr. I

Date	Mintage	VF20	XF40	MS60	MS63	MS65
1994	—	PF65 50.00				

KM# 499.1 10 PESOS
20.00 g., 0.999 Silver 0.6424 oz. ASW **Series:** Caribbean Fauna **Obv:** Thin characters **Rev:** Multicolored bottle-nosed dolphins

Date	Mintage	VF20	XF40	MS60	MS63	MS65
1994	Est. 10000	PF65 37.00				

KM# 499.2 10 PESOS
20.00 g., 0.999 Silver 0.6424 oz. ASW **Subject:** Caribbean Fauna **Obv:** Thick characters **Rev:** Multicolored bottle-nosed dolphins

Date	Mintage	VF20	XF40	MS60	MS63	MS65
1994	Inc. above	PF65 35.00				

KM# 500.1 10 PESOS
20.00 g., 0.999 Silver 0.6424 oz. ASW **Series:** Caribbean Fauna **Obv:** Thin characters **Rev:** Multicolored sailfish, smaller water splashes

Date	Mintage	VF20	XF40	MS60	MS63	MS65
1994	10,000	PF65 42.00				

KM# 500.2 10 PESOS
20.00 g., 0.999 Silver 0.6424 oz. ASW **Subject:** Caribbean Fauna **Obv:** Thick characters **Rev:** Multicolored sailfish, larger water splashes

Date	Mintage	VF20	XF40	MS60	MS63	MS65
1994	Inc. above	PF65 37.00				

KM# 501.1 10 PESOS
20.00 g., 0.999 Silver 0.6424 oz. ASW **Series:** Caribbean Fauna **Obv:** Thin characters **Rev:** Multicolored Brown Pelican

Date	Mintage	VF20	XF40	MS60	MS63	MS65
1994	10,000	PF65 42.00				

KM# 501.2 10 PESOS
20.00 g., 0.999 Silver 0.6424 oz. ASW **Subject:** Caribbean Fauna **Obv:** Thick characters **Rev:** Multicolored Brown Pelican

Date	Mintage	VF20	XF40	MS60	MS63	MS65
1994	Inc. above	PF65 37.00				

KM# 502.1 10 PESOS
20.00 g., 0.999 Silver 0.6424 oz. ASW **Series:** Caribbean Fauna **Obv:** Thin characters **Rev:** Multicolored Spotted Eagle Ray

Date	Mintage	VF20	XF40	MS60	MS63	MS65
1994	10,000	PF65 40.00				

KM# 502.2 10 PESOS
20.00 g., 0.999 Silver 0.6424 oz. ASW **Subject:** Caribbean Fauna **Obv:** Thick characters **Rev:** Multicolored Spotter Eagle Ray

Date	Mintage	VF20	XF40	MS60	MS63	MS65
1994	Inc. above	PF65 35.00				

KM# 510.1 10 PESOS
20.00 g., 0.999 Silver 0.6424 oz. ASW **Subject:** World Cup Soccer **Obv:** Thin characters **Rev:** Two players with bridge in background, date above

Date	Mintage	VF20	XF40	MS60	MS63	MS65
1994	Est. 10000	PF65 37.00				

KM# 510.2 10 PESOS
20.00 g., 0.999 Silver 0.6424 oz. ASW **Subject:** World Cup Soccer **Obv:** Thick characters **Rev:** Two players with bridge in background, date above

Date	Mintage	VF20	XF40	MS60	MS63	MS65
1994	Inc. above	PF65 37.00				

KM# 528 10 PESOS
20.00 g., 0.999 Silver 0.6424 oz. ASW **Obv:** National arms within wreath, denomination **Rev:** Multicolored Albatross DII fighter plane

Date	Mintage	VF20	XF40	MS60	MS63	MS65
1994	—	PF65 45.00				

KM# 541 10 PESOS
27.00 g., 0.925 Silver 0.803 oz. ASW **Subject:** Environmental Protection **Obv:** National arms within wreath, denomination **Rev:** Ivory-billed Woodpecker

Date	Mintage	VF20	XF40	MS60	MS63	MS65
1994	20,000	PF65 38.00				

KM# 478 10 PESOS

20.00 g., 0.999 Silver 0.6424 oz. ASW **Subject:** Pirates of the Caribbean **Obv:** National arms within wreath, denomination below **Rev:** Blackbeard within circle, date below

Date	Mintage	VF20	XF40	MS60	MS63	MS65
1995	Est. 10000	PF65 60.00				

KM# 479 10 PESOS

20.00 g., 0.999 Silver 0.6424 oz. ASW **Subject:** Pirates of the Caribbean **Obv:** National arms within wreath, denomination below **Rev:** Sir Henry Morgan

Date	Mintage	VF20	XF40	MS60	MS63	MS65
1995	Est. 10000	PF65 60.00				

KM# 480 10 PESOS

20.00 g., 0.999 Silver 0.6424 oz. ASW **Subject:** Pirates of the Caribbean **Obv:** National arms within wreath, denomination below **Rev:** Anne Bonny

Date	Mintage	VF20	XF40	MS60	MS63	MS65
1995	Est. 10000	PF65 60.00				

KM# 481 10 PESOS

20.00 g., 0.999 Silver 0.6424 oz. ASW **Subject:** Pirates of the Caribbean **Obv:** National arms within wreath, denomination below **Rev:** Mary Read

Date	Mintage	VF20	XF40	MS60	MS63	MS65
1995	Est. 10000	PF65 60.00				

KM# 482 10 PESOS

20.00 g., 0.999 Silver 0.6424 oz. ASW **Subject:** Pirates of the Caribbean **Obv:** National arms within wreath, denomination below **Rev:** Captain Kidd

Date	Mintage	VF20	XF40	MS60	MS63	MS65
1995	Est. 10000	PF65 60.00				

KM# 483 10 PESOS

20.00 g., 0.999 Silver 0.6424 oz. ASW **Subject:** Pirates of the Caribbean **Obv:** National arms within wreath, denomination below **Rev:** Piet Heyn

Date	Mintage	VF20	XF40	MS60	MS63	MS65
1995	Est. 10000	PF65 60.00				

KM# 511 10 PESOS

20.00 g., 0.999 Silver 0.6424 oz. ASW **Obv:** National arms within wreath, denomination **Rev:** Arnaldo Tamayo Mendez

Date	Mintage	VF20	XF40	MS60	MS63	MS65
1995	—	PF65 40.00				

KM# 529 10 PESOS

20.00 g., 0.999 Silver 0.6424 oz. ASW **Subject:** F.A.O. 50th Anniversary **Obv:** National arms within wreath, denomination below **Rev:** Farmer plowing with two oxen, logo and dates above

Date	Mintage	VF20	XF40	MS60	MS63	MS65
ND-1995	3,000	PF65 40.00				

KM# 530 10 PESOS

31.10 g., 0.999 Silver 0.9989 oz. ASW **Subject:** Centennial 1895-1995 **Obv:** National arms within wreath, denomination **Rev:** Sword to right of three conjoined busts right, dates below

Date	Mintage	VF20	XF40	MS60	MS63	MS65
ND-1995	500	PF65 70.00				

KM# 540 10 PESOS

28.28 g., 0.925 Silver 0.841 oz. ASW **Subject:** 50th Anniversary - United Nations **Obv:** National arms within wreath, denomination below **Rev:** Five persons of assorted ages and race, UN logo in front, outline of dove in back

Date	Mintage	VF20	XF40	MS60	MS63	MS65
ND-1995	Est. 105000	PF65 37.00				

KM# 548 10 PESOS

Silver **Subject:** Seaplane **Obv:** National arms within wreath, denomination **Rev:** Multicolored SIAI Marchetti S55

Date	Mintage	VF20	XF40	MS60	MS63	MS65
1995	15,000	PF65 42.00				

KM# 574 10 PESOS

20.00 g., 0.999 Silver 0.6424 oz. ASW, 37.9 mm. **Subject:** Death of Jose Marti **Obv:** National arms within wreath, denomination below

Date	Mintage	VF20	XF40	MS60	MS63	MS65
1995	—	—	—	—	—	40.00

KM# 553 10 PESOS
20.00 g., 0.999 Silver 0.6424 oz. ASW **Series:** Caribbean Fauna **Obv:** National arms within wreath, denomination below **Rev:** Multicolored Purple Throated Carib Hummingbird, right, date at right

Date	Mintage	VF20	XF40	MS60	MS63	MS65
1996	5,000	PF65 45.00				

KM# 554 10 PESOS
20.00 g., 0.999 Silver 0.6424 oz. ASW **Series:** Caribbean Fauna **Obv:** National arms within wreath, denomination below **Rev:** Multicolored Yellow Perch

Date	Mintage	VF20	XF40	MS60	MS63	MS65
1996	5,000	PF65 40.00				

KM# 555 10 PESOS
20.00 g., 0.999 Silver 0.6424 oz. ASW **Series:** Caribbean Fauna **Obv:** National arms within wreath, denomination below **Rev:** Multicolored Cuban Tody Bird

Date	Mintage	VF20	XF40	MS60	MS63	MS65
1996	5,000	PF65 40.00				

KM# 556 10 PESOS
20.00 g., 0.999 Silver 0.6424 oz. ASW **Series:** Caribbean Fauna **Obv:** National arms within wreath, denomination below **Rev:** Multicolored Wood Duck

Date	Mintage	VF20	XF40	MS60	MS63	MS65
1996	5,000	PF65 40.00				

KM# 563 10 PESOS
20.00 g., 0.999 Silver 0.6424 oz. ASW, 38 mm. **Series:** Caribbean Fauna **Obv:** National arms within wreath, denomination below **Rev:** Multicolored Vaca Anil (Blue Cow) Fish

Date	Mintage	VF20	XF40	MS60	MS63	MS65
1996	—	PF65 40.00				

KM# 566 10 PESOS
20.00 g., 0.999 Silver 0.6424 oz. ASW **Series:** Caribbean Fauna **Obv:** National arms within wreath, denomination below **Rev:** Multicolored Papilio Butterfly

Date	Mintage	VF20	XF40	MS60	MS63	MS65
1996	5,000	PF65 50.00				

KM# 582 10 PESOS
15.00 g., 0.999 Silver 0.4818 oz. ASW **Subject:** First Railroads - Germany **Obv:** National arms within wreath, denomination below **Rev:** First German locomotive, date 1835-1996

Date	Mintage	VF20	XF40	MS60	MS63	MS65
1996	—	PF65 30.00				

KM# 583 10 PESOS
15.00 g., 0.999 Silver 0.4818 oz. ASW **Subject:** First Railroads - Austria **Obv:** National arms within wreath, denomination below **Rev:** First Austrian locomotive, date 1848-1996

Date	Mintage	VF20	XF40	MS60	MS63	MS65
1996	—	PF65 30.00				

KM# 584 10 PESOS
15.00 g., 0.999 Silver 0.4818 oz. ASW **Subject:** First Railroads - Switzerland **Obv:** National arms within wreath, denomination below **Rev:** First Swiss locomotive, date 1847-1997

Date	Mintage	VF20	XF40	MS60	MS63	MS65
1996	—	PF65 30.00				

KM# 585 10 PESOS
15.00 g., 0.999 Silver 0.4818 oz. ASW **Subject:** El Mundo de la Aventura **Obv:** National arms within wreath, denomination below **Rev:** Multicolor submarine and cameo portrait of Capt. Nemo

Date	Mintage	VF20	XF40	MS60	MS63	MS65
1996	—	PF65 55.00				

KM# 586 10 PESOS
20.00 g., 0.999 Silver 0.6424 oz. ASW **Subject:** Campeonato Mundial de Futbol - Francia **Obv:** National arms within wreath, denomination below **Rev:** Joan of Arc with France's flag before soccer ball

Date	Mintage	VF20	XF40	MS60	MS63	MS65
1996	—	PF65 35.00				

KM# 587 10 PESOS
20.00 g., 0.999 Silver 0.6424 oz. ASW **Subject:** America - El Nuevo Mundo **Obv:** National arms within wreath, denomination below **Rev:** Ship and cameo portrait of Amerigo Vespucci

Date	Mintage	VF20	XF40	MS60	MS63	MS65
1996	—	PF65 35.00				

KM# 588 10 PESOS
20.00 g., 0.999 Silver 0.6424 oz. ASW **Subject:** World Food Summit **Obv:** National arms within wreath, denomination below **Rev:** Woman picking fruit, F.A.O. logo, dates

Date	Mintage	VF20	XF40	MS60	MS63	MS65
1996	—	PF65 35.00				

KM# 589 10 PESOS
31.10 g., 0.999 Silver 0.999 oz. ASW **Subject:** 40th Anniversary of the Granma's Landing **Obv:** National arms within wreath, denomination below **Rev:** Castro's portrait above the Granma

Date	Mintage	VF20	XF40	MS60	MS63	MS65
1996	—	PF65 50.00				

KM# 590 10 PESOS
20.00 g., 0.999 Silver 0.6424 oz. ASW **Subject:** Circumnavigation of Cuba - Pinzon **Obv:** National arms within wreath, denomination below **Rev:** Sailship and cameo portrait of Vincente Pinzon

Date	Mintage	VF20	XF40	MS60	MS63	MS65
1997	—	PF65 37.50				

KM# 591 10 PESOS
15.00 g., 0.999 Silver 0.4818 oz. ASW **Subject:** XXVII Olympics **Obv:** National arms within wreath, denomination below **Rev:** Two fencers

Date	Mintage	VF20	XF40	MS60	MS63	MS65
1997	—	PF65 35.00				

KM# 592 10 PESOS
15.00 g., 0.999 Silver 0.4818 oz. ASW **Subject:** XXVII Olympics **Obv:** National arms within wreath, denomination below **Rev:** Multicolored baseball player at bat, baseball background, small date below

Date	Mintage	VF20	XF40	MS60	MS63	MS65
1997	—	PF65 35.00				

KM# 593 10 PESOS
15.00 g., 0.999 Silver 0.4818 oz. ASW **Subject:** Wonders of the Ancient World **Obv:** National arms within wreath, denomination below **Rev:** Hanging Gardens of Babylon

Date	Mintage	VF20	XF40	MS60	MS63	MS65
1997	—	PF65 30.00				

KM# 594 10 PESOS
15.00 g., 0.999 Silver 0.4818 oz. ASW **Subject:** Wonders of the Ancient World **Obv:** National arms within wreath, denomination below **Rev:** Temple of Artemis

Date	Mintage	VF20	XF40	MS60	MS63	MS65
1997	—	PF65 30.00				

KM# 595 10 PESOS
15.00 g., 0.999 Silver 0.4818 oz. ASW **Subject:** Wonders of the Ancient World **Obv:** National arms within wreath, denomination below **Rev:** Lighthouse of Alexandria

Date	Mintage	VF20	XF40	MS60	MS63	MS65
1997	—	PF65 30.00				

KM# 596 10 PESOS
15.00 g., 0.999 Silver 0.4818 oz. ASW **Subject:** Wonders of the Ancient World **Obv:** National arms within wreath, denomination below **Rev:** Statue of Colossus of Rhodes over breakwater

Date	Mintage	VF20	XF40	MS60	MS63	MS65
1997	—	PF65 30.00				

KM# 597 10 PESOS
15.00 g., 0.999 Silver 0.4818 oz. ASW **Subject:** Wonders of the Ancient World **Obv:** National arms within wreath, denomination below **Rev:** Painting above Egyptian pyramids and excavation

Date	Mintage	VF20	XF40	MS60	MS63	MS65
1997	—	PF65 30.00				

KM# 598 10 PESOS
15.00 g., 0.999 Silver 0.4818 oz. ASW **Subject:** Wonders of the Ancient World - Temple of Jupiter **Obv:** National arms within wreath, denomination below **Rev:** Statue of Jupiter inside temple

Date	Mintage	VF20	XF40	MS60	MS63	MS65
1997	—	PF65 30.00				

KM# 599 10 PESOS
15.00 g., 0.999 Silver 0.4818 oz. ASW **Subject:** Wonders of the Ancient World **Obv:** National arms within wreath, denomination below **Rev:** Mausoleum of Halicarnas

Date	Mintage	VF20	XF40	MS60	MS63	MS65
1997	—	PF65 35.00				

KM# 600 10 PESOS
15.00 g., 0.999 Silver 0.4818 oz. ASW **Subject:**. Caribbean Flora **Obv:** National arms within wreath, denomination below **Rev:** Multicolor flower, Ruelia tuberosa

Date	Mintage	VF20	XF40	MS60	MS63	MS65
1997	3,000	PF65 35.00				

KM# 601 10 PESOS
15.00 g., 0.999 Silver 0.4818 oz. ASW **Subject:** Caribbean Flora **Obv:** National arms within wreath, denomination below **Rev:** Multicolored flower, "Cordia sebestena"

Date	Mintage	VF20	XF40	MS60	MS63	MS65
1997	—	PF65 30.00				

KM# 602 10 PESOS
15.00 g., 0.999 Silver 0.4818 oz. ASW **Subject:** Caribbean Flora **Obv:** National arms within wreath, denomination below **Rev:** Multicolor flower, "Lochnera rosea"

Date	Mintage	VF20	XF40	MS60	MS63	MS65
1997	—	PF65 30.00				

KM# 603 10 PESOS
15.00 g., 0.999 Silver 0.4818 oz. ASW **Subject:** Caribbena Flora **Obv:** National arms within wreath, denomination below **Rev:** Multicolored flower, "Turnera ulmifolia"

Date	Mintage	VF20	XF40	MS60	MS63	MS65
1997	—	PF65 30.00				

KM# 604 10 PESOS
15.00 g., 0.999 Silver 0.4818 oz. ASW **Subject:** Caribbean Flora **Obv:** National arms within wreath, denomination below **Rev:** Multicolored flower, "Bidens pilosa"

Date	Mintage	VF20	XF40	MS60	MS63	MS65
1997	—	PF65 30.00				

KM# 609 10 PESOS
15.00 g., 0.999 Silver 0.4818 oz. ASW **Subject:** Sesquicentennial of First Stearn/Sail Powered Ship **Obv:** National arms within wreath, denomination below **Rev:** Ship, date

Date	Mintage	VF20	XF40	MS60	MS63	MS65
1997	5,000	PF65 35.00				

KM# 613 10 PESOS
31.10 g., 0.999 Silver 0.999 oz. ASW, 37.9 mm. **Subject:** Castro Visit to Vatican **Obv:** National arms within wreath, denomination below **Rev:** Pope and Castro meeting

Date	Mintage	VF20	XF40	MS60	MS63	MS65
1997	—	—	—	—	50.00	—

KM# 624 10 PESOS
31.10 g., 0.999 Silver 0.9989 oz. ASW, 38 mm. **Obv:** National arms within wreath, denomination **Rev:** Deng Xiaoping bust facing

Date	Mintage	VF20	XF40	MS60	MS63	MS65
1997	10,000	PF65 40.00				

KM# 625 10 PESOS
27.00 g., 0.925 Silver 0.803 oz. ASW **Subject:** Ibero - American **Obv:** National arms and denomination within circle of arms **Rev:** Two rumba dancers, bongo drummer at left

Date	Mintage	VF20	XF40	MS60	MS63	MS65
1997	—	—	—	—	50.00	—

KM# 635 10 PESOS
31.10 g., 0.999 Silver 0.9989 oz. ASW, 38 mm. **Obv:** National arms within wreath, denomination **Rev:** Pope John Paul II, cathedral

Date	Mintage	VF20	XF40	MS60	MS63	MS65
1997	10,000	PF65 50.00				

KM# 650a 10 PESOS
15.00 g., 0.999 Silver 0.4818 oz. ASW, 38 mm. **Subject:** Expo 2000 - London **Rev:** Cartoon and Exhibition hall in color

Date	Mintage	VF20	XF40	MS60	MS63	MS65
1997	—	PF65 35.00				

KM# 667 10 PESOS
31.10 g., 0.999 Silver 0.9989 oz. ASW, 42 mm. **Subject:** 450th Anniversary - Birth of Cervantes **Obv:** National arms within wreath, denomination below **Rev:** Don Quixote tilting windmill

Date	Mintage	VF20	XF40	MS60	MS63	MS65
1997	—	PF65 55.00				

KM# 723 10 PESOS
31.10 g., 0.999 Silver 0.999 oz. ASW, 42 mm. **Subject:** 25th Anniversary - Ernesto Che Guevara's Death **Obv:** National arms and inscription **Rev:** Ernesto Che Guevara walking

Date	Mintage	VF20	XF40	MS60	MS63	MS65
ND-1997	10,000	PF65 47.00				

KM# 724 10 PESOS
31.10 g., 0.999 Silver 0.999 oz. ASW, 42 mm. **Subject:** 30th Anniversary - Ernesto Che Guevara's Death **Obv:** National arms within wreath, denomination **Rev:** Bust left **Edge:** Reeded

Date	Mintage	VF20	XF40	MS60	MS63	MS65
ND-1997	10,000	PF65 47.00				

KM# 747 10 PESOS
3.11 g., Gold, 16 mm. **Obv:** National arms and inscription **Rev:** Che Guevara standing

Date	Mintage	VF20	XF40	MS60	MS63	MS65
1997	500	PF65 195				

KM# 748 10 PESOS
3.11 g., Gold, 16 mm. **Obv:** National arms within wreath, denomination **Rev:** Bust of Che Guevara

Date	Mintage	VF20	XF40	MS60	MS63	MS65
1997	500	PF65 195				

KM# 750 10 PESOS
31.10 g., 0.999 Silver 0.9989 oz. ASW, 38 mm. **Obv:** National arms within wreath, denomination **Rev:** Deng Xiaoping viewing Hong Kong

Date	Mintage	VF20	XF40	MS60	MS63	MS65
1997	10,000	PF65 37.00				

KM# 927 10 PESOS
3.11 g., 0.999 Gold 0.0999 oz. AGW **Rev:** Ernesto "Che" Guevara

Date	Mintage	VF20	XF40	MS60	MS63	MS65
1997	—	—	—	—	—	200

KM# 928 10 PESOS
3.11 g., 0.999 Gold 0.0999 oz. AGW **Rev:** Ernesto "Che" Guevara in the Sierra Maestra

Date	Mintage	VF20	XF40	MS60	MS63	MS65
1997	—	—	—	—	—	200

KM# 931 10 PESOS
31.11 g., 0.999 Silver 0.999 oz. ASW **Subject:** Deng Xiaoping **Rev:** Deng as a Party official at a young age

Date	Mintage	VF20	XF40	MS60	MS63	MS65
1997	—	PF65 70.00				

KM# 932 10 PESOS
31.11 g., 0.999 Silver 0.999 oz. ASW **Subject:** Deng Ziaoping **Rev:** Hong Kong and Great Wall

Date	Mintage	VF20	XF40	MS60	MS63	MS65
1997	—	PF65 70.00				

KM# 944 10 PESOS
31.11 g., 0.999 Silver 0.999 oz. ASW **Rev:** Pope John Paul II and Cathedral of Saint Christopher in Havana

Date	Mintage	VF20	XF40	MS60	MS63	MS65
1997	Est. 2000	PF65 70.00				

KM# 610 10 PESOS
15.00 g., 0.999 Silver 0.4818 oz. ASW **Subject:** Mississippi **Obv:** National arms within wreath, denomination below **Rev:** Riverboat

Date	Mintage	VF20	XF40	MS60	MS63	MS65
1998	5,000	PF65 35.00				

KM# 611 10 PESOS
15.00 g., 0.999 Silver 0.4818 oz. ASW **Obv:** National arms within wreath, denomination below **Rev:** The ship Rio Bravo

Date	Mintage	VF20	XF40	MS60	MS63	MS65
1998	—	PF65 35.00				

KM# 644 10 PESOS
31.10 g., 0.999 Silver 0.999 oz. ASW **Subject:** Centenary - Explosion del Maine **Obv:** National arms within wreath, denomination below **Rev:** Explosion scene

Date	Mintage	VF20	XF40	MS60	MS63	MS65
1998	5,000	PF65 65.00				

KM# 645 10 PESOS
31.10 g., 0.999 Silver 0.999 oz. ASW **Subject:** Centenary - Naval battle of Santiago **Obv:** National arms within wreath, denomination below **Rev:** Cameo of Admiral Cervera and burning ship

Date	Mintage	VF20	XF40	MS60	MS63	MS65
1998	5,000	PF65 65.00				

KM# 646 10 PESOS
31.10 g., 0.999 Silver 0.999 oz. ASW **Subject:** Centenary - Calixto Garcia - Combate en Oriente **Obv:** National arms within wreath, denomination below **Rev:** Portrait above three Cuban cavalry troopers

Date	Mintage	VF20	XF40	MS60	MS63	MS65
1998	5,000	PF65 65.00				

KM# 647 10 PESOS
31.10 g., 0.999 Silver 0.999 oz. ASW **Obv:** National arms within wreath, denomination **Rev:** Souvenir peso design, bust of Leonor Molina right

Date	Mintage	VF20	XF40	MS60	MS63	MS65
1998	5,000	PF65 60.00				

KM# 648 10 PESOS
15.00 g., 0.999 Silver 0.4818 oz. ASW **Subject:** Expo 2000 - Twipsy **Obv:** National arms within wreath, denomination below **Rev:** "Twipsy" cartoon logo

Date	Mintage	VF20	XF40	MS60	MS63	MS65
1998	18,750	PF65 30.00				

KM# 648a 10 PESOS
15.00 g., 0.999 Silver 0.4818 oz. ASW, 38 mm. **Subject:** Expo 2000 - "Twipsy" **Rev:** Character in color

Date	Mintage	VF20	XF40	MS60	MS63	MS65
1998	—	PF65 30.00				

KM# 649 10 PESOS
15.00 g., 0.999 Silver 0.4818 oz. ASW **Subject:** Expo 2000 - Germany **Obv:** National arms within wreath, denomination below **Rev:** Map of Germany, flag colored background

Date	Mintage	VF20	XF40	MS60	MS63	MS65
1998	18,750	PF65 30.00				

KM# 649a 10 PESOS
15.00 g., 0.999 Silver 0.4818 oz. ASW, 38 mm. **Subject:** Expo 2000 - Germany **Rev:** Map of Germany, color flag background

Date	Mintage	VF20	XF40	MS60	MS63	MS65
1998	—	PF65 30.00				

KM# 650 10 PESOS
15.00 g., 0.999 Silver 0.4818 oz. ASW **Subject:** Expo 2000 - London **Obv:** National arms within wreath, denomination below **Rev:** Cartoon over exhibit hall

Date	Mintage	VF20	XF40	MS60	MS63	MS65
1998	18,750	PF65 30.00				

KM# 651 10 PESOS
15.00 g., 0.999 Silver 0.4818 oz. ASW **Subject:** Expo 2000 - Paris **Obv:** National arms within wreath, denomination below **Rev:** Cartoon and Eiffel Tower

Date	Mintage	VF20	XF40	MS60	MS63	MS65
1998	18,750	PF65 30.00				

KM# 651a 10 PESOS
15.00 g., 0.999 Silver 0.4818 oz. ASW, 38 mm. **Subject:** Expo 2000 - France **Rev:** Cartoon and Eiffel Tower in color

Date	Mintage	VF20	XF40	MS60	MS63	MS65
1998	—	PF65 30.00				

KM# 652 10 PESOS
15.00 g., 0.999 Silver 0.4818 oz. ASW **Subject:** Expo 2000 - Brussels **Obv:** National arms within wreath, denomination below **Rev:** Cartoon and Atomium structure

Date	Mintage	VF20	XF40	MS60	MS63	MS65
1998	18,750	PF65 30.00				

KM# 652a 10 PESOS
15.00 g., 0.999 Silver 0.4818 oz. ASW, 38 mm. **Subject:** Expo 2000 - Brussels **Rev:** Cartoon and Atomium structure in color

Date	Mintage	VF20	XF40	MS60	MS63	MS65
1998	—	PF65 30.00				

KM# 653 10 PESOS
15.00 g., 0.999 Silver 0.4818 oz. ASW **Subject:** Expo 2000 - Postrimerias **Obv:** National arms within wreath, denomination below **Rev:** Cartoon on tree bearing world globe

Date	Mintage	VF20	XF40	MS60	MS63	MS65
1998	18,750	PF65 30.00				

KM# 653a 10 PESOS
15.00 g., 0.999 Silver 0.4818 oz. ASW, 38 mm. **Subject:** Expo 2000 - Postrimerias **Rev:** Cartoon and tree in color on globe

Date	Mintage	VF20	XF40	MS60	MS63	MS65
1998	—	PF65 30.00				

KM# 668 10 PESOS
31.10 g., 0.999 Silver 0.999 oz. ASW, 45.2 x 35.1 mm. **Subject:** Havana Puzzle - Frigate Oquendo **Obv:** National arms within wreath, denomination below **Rev:** Two sailing ships **Edge:** Plain **Shape:** Rectangular

Date	Mintage	VF20	XF40	MS60	MS63	MS65
1998	—	PF65 60.00				

KM# 669 10 PESOS
31.10 g., 0.999 Silver 0.999 oz. ASW, 45.2 x 35.1 mm. **Subject:** Havana Puzzle - City of Havana **Obv:** National arms within wreath, denomination below **Rev:** Havana city view **Edge:** Plain **Shape:** Rectangular

Date	Mintage	VF20	XF40	MS60	MS63	MS65
1998	3,000	PF65 60.00				

KM# 670 10 PESOS
31.18 g., 0.999 Silver 1.0015 oz. ASW, 45.2 x 35.1 mm. **Subject:** Havana Puzzle - Sailing Ship San Genaro **Obv:** National arms within wreath, denomination below **Rev:** Three sailing ships **Edge:** Plain **Shape:** Rectangular

Date	Mintage	VF20	XF40	MS60	MS63	MS65
1998	3,000	PF65 60.00				

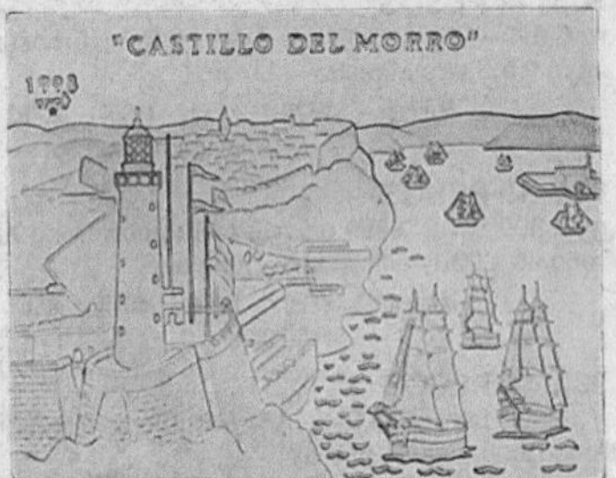

KM# 671 10 PESOS
31.18 g., 0.999 Silver 1.0015 oz. ASW, 45.2 x 35.1 mm. **Subject:** Havana Puzzle - El Morro **Obv:** National arms within wreath, denomination below **Rev:** Light house and sailing ships **Edge:** Plain **Shape:** Rectangular

Date	Mintage	VF20	XF40	MS60	MS63	MS65
1998	3,000	PF65 60.00				

KM# 751 10 PESOS
20.00 g., 0.999 Silver 0.6424 oz. ASW, 24x42 mm. **Obv:** National arms within wreath, denomination **Rev:** Cruise ship Hanseatic

Date	Mintage	VF20	XF40	MS60	MS63	MS65
1998	2,500	PF65 50.00				

KM# 945 10 PESOS
31.11 g., 0.999 Silver 0.999 oz. ASW **Rev:** Passenger luxury liner Hanseatic **Shape:** Rectangle

Date	Mintage	VF20	XF40	MS60	MS63	MS65
1998 Proof	Est. 2500	—	—	—	—	—

KM# 661 10 PESOS
31.10 g., 0.999 Silver 0.999 oz. ASW **Subject:** Zunzuncito **Obv:** National arms **Rev:** Hummingbird **Edge:** Plain

Date	Mintage	VF20	XF40	MS60	MS63	MS65
1999	—	PF65 50.00				

KM# 672 10 PESOS
31.10 g., 0.999 Silver 0.999 oz. ASW **Subject:** 40th Anniversary - Triumph of the Revolution

Date	Mintage	VF20	XF40	MS60	MS63	MS65
1999	—	PF65 45.00				

KM# 674 10 PESOS
31.10 g., 0.999 Silver 0.999 oz. ASW, 37.9 mm. **Subject:** Spanish Royal Visit - Fidel Castro receives King Juan Carlos I **Rev:** Castro and Juan Carlos I

Date	Mintage	VF20	XF40	MS60	MS63	MS65
1999	—	PF65 55.00				

KM# 675 10 PESOS
31.10 g., 0.999 Silver 0.999 oz. ASW, 37.9 mm. **Subject:** Spanish Royal Visit - King Juan Carlos and Queen Sofia **Rev:** Juan Carlos and Sofia with fort in distance

Date	Mintage	VF20	XF40	MS60	MS63	MS65
1999	—	PF65 55.00				

KM# 676 10 PESOS
31.10 g., 0.999 Silver 0.999 oz. ASW, 37.9 mm. **Subject:** Spanish Royal Visit - 2 Peoples United **Rev:** Map of Spain and Cuba

Date	Mintage	VF20	XF40	MS60	MS63	MS65
1999	—	PF65 55.00				

KM# 677 10 PESOS
31.10 g., 0.999 Silver 0.999 oz. ASW, 37.9 mm. **Subject:** Spanish Royal Visit - Homage to the Spanish Soldier **Rev:** Shields of Cuba and Spain above inscription

Date	Mintage	VF20	XF40	MS60	MS63	MS65
1999	—	PF65 55.00				

KM# 725 10 PESOS
3.11 g., 0.999 Gold 0.0999 oz. AGW, 18 mm. **Subject:** Zunzuncito **Obv:** National arms **Rev:** Hummingbird **Edge:** Reeded

Date	Mintage	VF20	XF40	MS60	MS63	MS65
1999	1,000	PF65 185				

KM# 736 10 PESOS
14.93 g., 0.999 Silver 0.4795 oz. ASW, 35.1 mm. **Subject:** Johann Wolfgang von Goethe **Obv:** National arms **Rev:** Seated figure outdoors **Edge:** Plain

Date	Mintage	VF20	XF40	MS60	MS63	MS65
1999	1,749	PF65 50.00				

KM# 749 10 PESOS
3.11 g., Gold, 18 mm. **Obv:** National arms within wreath, denomination **Rev:** Hummingbird in flight

Date	Mintage	VF20	XF40	MS60	MS63	MS65
1999	1,000	PF65 185				

KM# 752 10 PESOS
20.00 g., 0.999 Silver 0.6424 oz. ASW, 38 mm. **Subject:** First International Globalization Conference **Obv:** National arms within wreath, denomination **Rev:** World map

Date	Mintage	VF20	XF40	MS60	MS63	MS65
1999	200	PF65 145				

KM# 753 10 PESOS
15.00 g., 0.999 Silver 0.4818 oz. ASW, 35 mm. **Subject:** Goethe's birthplace **Obv:** National arms within wreath, denomination **Rev:** Building at left, bust at right looking left

Date	Mintage	VF20	XF40	MS60	MS63	MS65
1999	1,749	PF65 45.00				

KM# 754 10 PESOS
15.00 g., 0.999 Silver 0.4818 oz. ASW, 35 mm. **Subject:** Goeth's Weimar home **Obv:** National arms within wreath, denomination **Rev:** Building at right, bust at left looking right

Date	Mintage	VF20	XF40	MS60	MS63	MS65
1999	1,749	PF65 45.00				

KM# 755 10 PESOS
15.00 g., 0.999 Silver 0.4818 oz. ASW, 35 mm. **Obv:** National arms within wreath, denomination **Rev:** Christopher Columbus, ship, and arms

Date	Mintage	VF20	XF40	MS60	MS63	MS65
1999	1,950	PF65 45.00				

KM# 678 10 PESOS
31.10 g., 0.999 Silver 0.999 oz. ASW **Subject:** Maritime Relics - Peral Submarine **Obv:** National arms within wreath, denomination **Rev:** Submarine under water, small ship above

Date	Mintage	VF20	XF40	MS60	MS63	MS65
2000	1,500	PF65 38.00				

KM# 679 10 PESOS
31.10 g., 0.999 Silver 0.999 oz. ASW **Subject:** Maritime Relics - School Ship Galatea **Obv:** National arms within wreath, denomination **Rev:** Ship with full sails at sea

Date	Mintage	VF20	XF40	MS60	MS63	MS65
2000	1,500	PF65 38.00				

KM# 680 10 PESOS
31.10 g., 0.999 Silver 0.999 oz. ASW **Subject:** Maritime Relics - School Ship JS Elcano **Obv:** National arms within wreath, denomination **Rev:** Ship with many full sails at sea

Date	Mintage	VF20	XF40	MS60	MS63	MS65
2000	1,500	PF65 38.00				

KM# 681 10 PESOS
31.10 g., 0.999 Silver 0.999 oz. ASW **Subject:** Maritime Relics - Maritime Ambulance Buena Ventura **Obv:** National arms within wreath, denomination **Rev:** Two ships at sea

Date	Mintage	VF20	XF40	MS60	MS63	MS65
2000	1,500	PF65 38.00				

KM# 682 10 PESOS
20.00 g., 0.999 Silver 0.6424 oz. ASW **Subject:** Maritime Relics - Nautical Rose of Juan de la Cosa **Obv:** National arms within wreath, denomination **Rev:** Madonna and child with angels at center of radiant sun design

Date	Mintage	VF20	XF40	MS60	MS63	MS65
2000	1,500	PF65 38.00				

KM# 683 10 PESOS
20.00 g., 0.999 Silver 0.6424 oz. ASW **Subject:** Hacia un Nuevo Milenio (Towards a New Millennium) **Obv:** National arms within wreath, denomination below **Rev:** Dove of Peace covering world map

Date	Mintage	VF20	XF40	MS60	MS63	MS65
2000	—	PF65 50.00				

KM# 684 10 PESOS
20.00 g., 0.999 Silver 0.6424 oz. ASW **Subject:** Welcome to the New Millennium **Obv:** National arms within wreath, denomination below **Rev:** Hot air balloons above earth

Date	Mintage	VF20	XF40	MS60	MS63	MS65
2000	—	PF65 50.00				

KM# 685 10 PESOS
20.00 g., 0.999 Silver 0.6424 oz. ASW **Subject:** Welcome to the New Millennium **Obv:** National arms within wreath, denomination below **Rev:** Stars and Solar System

Date	Mintage	VF20	XF40	MS60	MS63	MS65
2000	—	PF65 50.00				

KM# 686 10 PESOS
15.00 g., 0.999 Silver 0.4818 oz. ASW **Subject:** Palaces of the World **Obv:** National arms within wreath, denomination **Rev:** Versailles Palace

Date	Mintage	VF20	XF40	MS60	MS63	MS65
2000	—	PF65 30.00				

KM# 687 10 PESOS
15.00 g., 0.999 Silver 0.4818 oz. ASW **Subject:** Palaces of the World **Obv:** National arms within wreath, denomination **Rev:** Windsor Palace

Date	Mintage	VF20	XF40	MS60	MS63	MS65
2000	—	PF65 30.00				

KM# 688 10 PESOS
15.00 g., 0.999 Silver 0.4818 oz. ASW **Subject:** Palaces of the World **Obv:** National arms within wreath, denomination **Rev:** San Soucci Palace

Date	Mintage	VF20	XF40	MS60	MS63	MS65
2000	—	PF65 30.00				

KM# 689 10 PESOS
15.00 g., 0.999 Silver 0.4818 oz. ASW **Subject:** Palaces of the World **Obv:** National arms within wreath, denomination **Rev:** Schonbrunn Palace

Date	Mintage	VF20	XF40	MS60	MS63	MS65
2000	—	PF65 30.00				

KM# 690 10 PESOS
15.00 g., 0.999 Silver 0.4818 oz. ASW **Subject:** Palaces of the World - Neuschwanstein Castles

Date	Mintage	VF20	XF40	MS60	MS63	MS65
2000	—	PF65 30.00				

KM# 691 10 PESOS
15.00 g., 0.999 Silver 0.4818 oz. ASW, 35 mm. **Subject:** Palaces of the World - Hradschinn Castle

Date	Mintage	VF20	XF40	MS60	MS63	MS65
2000	—	PF65 30.00				

KM# 735 10 PESOS
27.00 g., 0.925 Silver 0.803 oz. ASW, 40.1 mm. **Subject:** Ibero-America - Man and Horse **Obv:** National arms and denomination within circle of arms **Rev:** Horse in center within pictures of horses being ridden **Edge:** Reeded

Date	Mintage	VF20	XF40	MS60	MS63	MS65
2000	—	PF65 60.00				

KM# 756 10 PESOS
31.10 g., 0.999 Silver 0.999 oz. ASW, 38 mm. **Obv:** National arms within wreath, denomination **Rev:** Hummingbird feeding nestlings

Date	Mintage	VF20	XF40	MS60	MS63	MS65
2000	20,000	PF65 35.00				

KM# 757 10 PESOS
20.00 g., 0.999 Silver 0.6424 oz. ASW, 38 mm. **Subject:** Second International Globalization Conference **Obv:** National arms within wreath, denomination **Rev:** World map

Date	Mintage	VF20	XF40	MS60	MS63	MS65
2000	100	PF65 150				

KM# 758 10 PESOS
15.00 g., 0.999 Silver 0.4818 oz. ASW, 35 mm. **Obv:** National arms within wreath, denomination **Rev:** Sailing ship Santisima Trinidad

Date	Mintage	VF20	XF40	MS60	MS63	MS65
2000	2,500	PF65 40.00				

KM# 759 10 PESOS
15.00 g., 0.999 Silver 0.4818 oz. ASW, 35 mm. **Obv:** National arms within wreath, denomination **Rev:** Ship Vecero Rayo

Date	Mintage	VF20	XF40	MS60	MS63	MS65
2000	2,500	PF65 40.00				

KM# 760 10 PESOS
15.00 g., 0.999 Silver 0.4818 oz. ASW, 35 mm. **Obv:** National arms within wreath, denomination **Rev:** Sailing ship, San Pedro De Alcantara

Date	Mintage	VF20	XF40	MS60	MS63	MS65
2000	2,500	PF65 40.00				

KM# 761 10 PESOS
20.00 g., 0.999 Silver 0.6424 oz. ASW, 38 mm. **Obv:** National arms within wreath, denomination **Rev:** 50" in design

Date	Mintage	VF20	XF40	MS60	MS63	MS65
2000	1,250	PF65 50.00				

KM# 212 15 PESOS
3.88 g., 0.999 Gold 0.1246 oz. AGW **Obv:** National arms within wreath, denomination below **Rev:** Jose Marti head right, date below

Date	Mintage	VF20	XF40	MS60	MS63	MS65
1988	50	—	—	—	275	325
1988	15	PF65 300				
1989	50	—	—	—	275	325
1989	15	PF65 300				
1990	15	—	—	—	300	350
1990	12	PF65 325				

KM# 38 20 PESOS
26.00 g., 0.925 Silver 0.7732 oz. ASW **Subject:** Ignacio Agramonte **Obv:** Flagged arms, liberty cap above **Rev:** Bust 3/4 facing, date at left

Date	Mintage	VF20	XF40	MS60	MS63	MS65
1977	25,000	PF65 37.00				

KM# 39 20 PESOS
26.00 g., 0.925 Silver 0.7732 oz. ASW **Subject:** Maximo Gomez **Obv:** Liberty cap above flagged arms **Rev:** Bust facing

Date	Mintage	VF20	XF40	MS60	MS63	MS65
1977	75,000	PF65 32.00				

KM# 40 20 PESOS
26.00 g., 0.925 Silver 0.7732 oz. ASW **Subject:** Antonio Maceo **Obv:** Liberty cap above flagged arms **Rev:** Bust facing looking right

Date	Mintage	VF20	XF40	MS60	MS63	MS65
1977	75,000	PF65 32.00				

KM# 41 20 PESOS
26.00 g., 0.925 Silver 0.7732 oz. ASW **Subject:** 60th Anniversary Socialist Revolution - Lenin **Obv:** National arms within wreath, denomination **Rev:** Bust left

Date	Mintage	VF20	XF40	MS60	MS63	MS65
1977	100	PF65 1,400				

KM# 44 20 PESOS
26.00 g., 0.925 Silver 0.7732 oz. ASW **Subject:** Nonaligned Nations Conference **Obv:** National arms within wreath, denomination below **Rev:** Design left of date

Date	Mintage	VF20	XF40	MS60	MS63	MS65
1979	20,000	—	—	—	32.00	35.00
1979	—	PF65 60.00				
1979 Matte Proof	—	PF65 100				

KM# 169 20 PESOS
62.20 g., 0.999 Silver 1.9978 oz. ASW **Subject:** Triumph of the Revolution **Obv:** Arms on star background above half wreath **Rev:** Rejoicing scene

Date	Mintage	VF20	XF40	MS60	MS63	MS65
1987	500	PF65 95.00				
1988	1,000	PF65 85.00				
1989	500	PF65 95.00				

KM# 170 20 PESOS
62.20 g., 0.999 Silver 1.9978 oz. ASW **Subject:** 60th Anniversary - Birth of Ernesto Che Guevara **Obv:** Arms on star background above half wreath **Rev:** Bust right

Date	Mintage	VF20	XF40	MS60	MS63	MS65
1987	500	PF65 110				
1988	1,000	PF65 95.00				
1989	500	PF65 110				

KM# 171 20 PESOS
62.20 g., 0.999 Silver 1.9978 oz. ASW **Subject:** 30th Anniversary - The March to Victory **Obv:** Arms on star background above half wreath **Rev:** Soldiers on the march

Date	Mintage	VF20	XF40	MS60	MS63	MS65
1987	333	PF65 95.00				
1988	1,000	PF65 85.00				
1989	500	PF65 95.00				

KM# 232 20 PESOS
62.20 g., 0.999 Silver 1.9978 oz. ASW **Subject:** 150th Anniversary - First Railroad in Cuba **Obv:** Arms on star background above half wreath **Rev:** Train engine right

Date	Mintage	VF20	XF40	MS60	MS63	MS65
1988	Est. 1000	PF65 85.00				

KM# 233 20 PESOS
62.20 g., 0.999 Silver 1.9978 oz. ASW **Subject:** 140th Anniversary - First Railroad in Spain **Obv:** Arms on star background above half wreath **Rev:** Train left, dates

Date	Mintage	VF20	XF40	MS60	MS63	MS65
ND-1988	Est. 1000	PF65 85.00				

KM# 234 20 PESOS
62.20 g., 0.999 Silver 1.9978 oz. ASW **Subject:** 160th Anniversary - First Railroad in England **Obv:** Arms on star background above half wreath **Rev:** Ancient train with boxcar, dates

Date	Mintage	VF20	XF40	MS60	MS63	MS65
1988	Est. 1000	PF65 85.00				

KM# 235 20 PESOS
62.20 g., 0.999 Silver 1.9978 oz. ASW **Subject:** Tania La Guerrillera, Argentinian revolutionary **Obv:** Arms on star background above half wreath **Rev:** Bust facing

Date	Mintage	VF20	XF40	MS60	MS63	MS65
1988	1,000	PF65 85.00				

KM# 236 20 PESOS
62.20 g., 0.999 Silver 1.9978 oz. ASW **Subject:** Camilo Cienfuegos **Obv:** Arms on star background above half wreath **Rev:** Bust facing, dates

Date	Mintage	VF20	XF40	MS60	MS63	MS65
1988	1,000	PF65 85.00				

KM# 237 20 PESOS
62.20 g., 0.999 Silver 1.9978 oz. ASW **Subject:** 35th Anniversary - Assault of the Moncada Garrison **Obv:** Arms on star background above half wreath **Rev:** Armed figures, dates below

Date	Mintage	VF20	XF40	MS60	MS63	MS65
ND-1988	1,000	PF65 85.00				

KM# 531 20 PESOS
62.20 g., 0.999 Silver 1.9978 oz. ASW **Obv:** National arms within wreath, denomination **Rev:** Jose Raul playing chess

Date	Mintage	VF20	XF40	MS60	MS63	MS65
ND-1988	1,000	PF65 95.00				

KM# 532 20 PESOS

62.20 g., 0.999 Silver 1.9978 oz. ASW **Subject:** 25th Anniversary - Death of Ernesto Che Guevara **Obv:** National arms **Rev:** Head facing, dates

Date	Mintage	VF20	XF40	MS60	MS63	MS65
ND-1992	1,000	PF65 100				

KM# 471.1 20 PESOS

62.20 g., 0.999 Silver 1.9978 oz. ASW **Subject:** Fidel Castro - 40th Anniversary of Moncada **Obv:** National arms within wreath, denomination **Rev:** Uniformed bust left

Date	Mintage	VF20	XF40	MS60	MS63	MS65
1993	—	PF65 100				

KM# 459 20 PESOS

62.20 g., 0.999 Silver 1.9978 oz. ASW **Subject:** Cuban Railroad **Obv:** National arms **Rev:** Train engine, date below

Date	Mintage	VF20	XF40	MS60	MS63	MS65
1994	—	PF65 95.00				

KM# 533 20 PESOS

62.20 g., 0.999 Silver 1.9978 oz. ASW **Subject:** Transportation **Obv:** National arms **Rev:** Zeppelin, date below

Date	Mintage	VF20	XF40	MS60	MS63	MS65
1995	1,000	PF65 110				

KM# 836 20 PESOS

40.00 g., 0.999 Silver 1.2847 oz. ASW, 38 mm. **Subject:** Fauna **Obv:** National arms within wreath, denomination below **Rev:** Multicolored Papilio Butterfly, individually numbered

Date	Mintage	VF20	XF40	MS60	MS63	MS65
1996	500	PF65 95.00				

KM# 837 20 PESOS

40.00 g., 0.999 Silver 1.2847 oz. ASW, 38 mm. **Subject:** Fauna **Obv:** National arms within wreath, denomination below **Rev:** Multicolored (Blue Cow) fish, individually numbered

Date	Mintage	VF20	XF40	MS60	MS63	MS65
1996	500	PF65 95.00				

KM# 838 20 PESOS

40.00 g., 0.999 Silver 1.2847 oz. ASW, 38 mm. **Subject:** Fauna **Obv:** National arms within wreath, denomination below **Rev:** Multicolored Purple Throated Carib Hummingbird, individually numbered

Date	Mintage	VF20	XF40	MS60	MS63	MS65
1996	500	PF65 95.00				

KM# 839 20 PESOS

40.00 g., 0.999 Silver 1.2847 oz. ASW, 38 mm. **Subject:** Fauna **Obv:** National arms within wreath, denomination below **Rev:** Multicolored Yellow Perch, individually numbered

Date	Mintage	VF20	XF40	MS60	MS63	MS65
1996	500	PF65 95.00				

KM# 840 20 PESOS

40.00 g., 0.999 Silver 1.2847 oz. ASW, 38 mm. **Subject:** Fauna **Obv:** National arms within wreath, denomination below **Rev:** Multicolored Cuban Tody Bird, individually numbered

Date	Mintage	VF20	XF40	MS60	MS63	MS65
1996	500	PF65 95.00				

KM# 841 20 PESOS

40.00 g., 0.999 Silver 1.2847 oz. ASW, 38 mm. **Subject:** Fauna **Obv:** National arms within wreath, denomination below **Rev:** Multicolored Wood Duck, individually numbered

Date	Mintage	VF20	XF40	MS60	MS63	MS65
1996	500	PF65 95.00				

KM# 213 25 PESOS

7.77 g., 0.999 Gold 0.2496 oz. AGW **Subject:** Jose Marti **Obv:** National arms within wreath, denomination below **Rev:** Head right

Date	Mintage	VF20	XF40	MS60	MS63	MS65
1988	50	—	—	—	450	500
1988	15	PF65 550				
1989	50	—	—	—	450	500
1989	15	PF65 550				
1990	12	—	—	—	475	525
1990	12	PF65 575				

KM# 692 25 PESOS

7.78 g., 0.999 Gold 0.2498 oz. AGW, 20 mm. **Subject:** Zunzuncito **Obv:** National arms **Rev:** Hummingbird **Edge:** Reeded

Date	Mintage	VF20	XF40	MS60	MS63	MS65
1999	1,000	PF65 450				

KM# 422 30 PESOS

93.25 g., 0.999 Silver 2.9951 oz. ASW **Rev:** Vincente and Martin Pinzon

Date	Mintage	VF20	XF40	MS60	MS63	MS65
1991	1,000	PF65 145				

KM# 423 30 PESOS

93.25 g., 0.999 Silver 2.9951 oz. ASW **Rev:** Hatuey People

Date	Mintage	VF20	XF40	MS60	MS63	MS65
1991	1,000	PF65 125				

KM# 430 30 PESOS

93.30 g., 0.999 Silver 2.9967 oz. ASW **Series:** 500th Anniversary of the New World **Subject:** Queen Joanna 1479-1555, daughter of Isabella I **Obv:** National arms within wreath **Rev:** Bust 3/4 right above half wreath

Date	Mintage	VF20	XF40	MS60	MS63	MS65
1991	1,000	PF65 160				

KM# 431 30 PESOS

93.30 g., 0.999 Silver 2.9967 oz. ASW **Series:** 500th Anniversary of the New World **Subject:** Diego Velazquez **Obv:** National arms within wreath **Rev:** Bust 3/4 left above wreath

Date	Mintage	VF20	XF40	MS60	MS63	MS65
1991	1,000	PF65 160				

KM# 376 30 PESOS

93.25 g., 0.999 Silver 2.9951 oz. ASW **Series:** 500th Anniversary of the New World **Subject:** Guama native **Obv:** National arms within wreath **Rev:** Native figure drinking from large shell

Date	Mintage	VF20	XF40	MS60	MS63	MS65
1992	550	PF65 125				

KM# 377 30 PESOS

93.25 g., 0.999 Silver 2.9951 oz. ASW **Series:** 500th Anniversary of the New World **Subject:** Bartolome de Las Casas **Obv:** National arms within wreath **Rev:** Figure at desk writing a letter with a quill pen

Date	Mintage	VF20	XF40	MS60	MS63	MS65
1992	550	PF65 125				

KM# 378 30 PESOS
93.25 g., 0.999 Silver 2.9951 oz. ASW **Series:** 500th Anniversary of the New World **Subject:** King Philipp **Obv:** National arms within wreath **Rev:** Bust 3/4 right above half wreath

Date	Mintage	VF20	XF40	MS60	MS63	MS65
1992	550	PF65 125				

KM# 379 30 PESOS
93.25 g., 0.999 Silver 2.9951 oz. ASW **Series:** 500th Anniversary of the New World **Subject:** Fernando and Elisabeth, Philipp and Johanna **Obv:** National arms within wreath **Rev:** Spanish kings and queens

Date	Mintage	VF20	XF40	MS60	MS63	MS65
ND-1992	550	PF65 125				

KM# 208 50 PESOS
15.55 g., 0.999 Gold 0.4994 oz. AGW **Subject:** 30th Anniversary - The March to Victory **Obv:** Arms on star background above half wreath **Rev:** Soldiers on the march, date above

Date	Mintage	VF20	XF40	MS60	MS63	MS65
1988	150	PF65 900				

KM# 209 50 PESOS
15.55 g., 0.999 Gold 0.4994 oz. AGW **Subject:** 60th Anniversary - Birth of Ernesto Che Guevara **Obv:** Arms on star background above half wreath **Rev:** Bust right, date at left

Date	Mintage	VF20	XF40	MS60	MS63	MS65
1988	150	PF65 900				

KM# 210 50 PESOS
15.55 g., 0.999 Gold 0.4994 oz. AGW **Subject:** Triumph of the Revolutionary **Obv:** Arms on star background above half wreath **Rev:** Castro with revolutionaries, divide dates

Date	Mintage	VF20	XF40	MS60	MS63	MS65
1988	150	PF65 900				

KM# 214 50 PESOS
15.55 g., 0.999 Gold 0.4994 oz. AGW **Subject:** Jose Marti **Obv:** National arms within wreath, denomination **Rev:** Head right

Date	Mintage	VF20	XF40	MS60	MS63	MS65
1988	12	—	—	—	900	925
1988	15	PF65 900				
1989	150	—	—	—	875	900
1989	15	PF65 900				
1990	15	—	—	—	900	925
1990	12	PF65 925				

KM# 313 50 PESOS
15.55 g., 0.999 Gold 0.4994 oz. AGW **Subject:** 160th Anniversary - First Train in England **Rev:** Train, Liverpool - Manchester

Date	Mintage	VF20	XF40	MS60	MS63	MS65
1989	150	PF65 900				

KM# 314 50 PESOS
15.55 g., 0.999 Gold 0.4994 oz. AGW **Subject:** 150th Anniversary - First Train in Spanish America **Rev:** Train **Rev. Legend:** HABANA-BEJUCAL

Date	Mintage	VF20	XF40	MS60	MS63	MS65
1989	150	PF65 900				

KM# 315 50 PESOS
15.55 g., 0.999 Gold 0.4994 oz. AGW **Subject:** 140th Anniversary - First Train in Spain **Rev:** Train **Rev. Legend:** BARCELONA-MATARD

Date	Mintage	VF20	XF40	MS60	MS63	MS65
1989	150	PF65 900				

KM# 330 50 PESOS
15.55 g., 0.999 Gold 0.4994 oz. AGW **Subject:** Tania La Guerrillera **Rev:** Portrait of female guerilla fighter

Date	Mintage	VF20	XF40	MS60	MS63	MS65
1989	150	PF65 900				

KM# 331 50 PESOS
15.55 g., 0.999 Gold 0.4994 oz. AGW **Subject:** Camilo Cienfuegos Gornaran **Rev:** Portrait of Camilo Cienfuegos

Date	Mintage	VF20	XF40	MS60	MS63	MS65
1989	150	PF65 900				

KM# 332 50 PESOS
15.55 g., 0.999 Gold 0.4994 oz. AGW **Subject:** Assault of the Moncada Garrison **Rev:** Battle scene

Date	Mintage	VF20	XF40	MS60	MS63	MS65
1989	150	PF65 900				

KM# 281 50 PESOS
15.55 g., 0.999 Gold 0.4994 oz. AGW **Subject:** Simon Bolivar **Rev:** Portrait of Simon Bolivar

Date	Mintage	VF20	XF40	MS60	MS63	MS65
1990	50	PF65 900				

KM# 294 50 PESOS
155.52 g., 0.999 Silver 4.9949 oz. ASW, 65 mm. **Subject:** 500th Anniversary - Discovery of America **Obv:** National arms within wreath **Rev:** Christopher Columbus

Date	Mintage	VF20	XF40	MS60	MS63	MS65
1990	2,000	PF65 185				

KM# 295 50 PESOS
155.52 g., 0.999 Silver 4.9949 oz. ASW **Subject:** 500th Anniversary - Discovery of America **Obv:** National arms within wreath **Rev:** King Ferdinand of Spain

Date	Mintage	VF20	XF40	MS60	MS63	MS65
1990	2,000	PF65 185				

KM# 296 50 PESOS
155.52 g., 0.999 Silver 4.9949 oz. ASW **Subject:** 500th Anniversary - Discovery of America **Obv:** National arms within wreath **Rev:** Queen Isabella of Spain

Date	Mintage	VF20	XF40	MS60	MS63	MS65
1990	2,000	PF65 185				

KM# 297 50 PESOS
155.52 g., 0.999 Silver 4.9949 oz. ASW **Subject:** 500th Anniversary - Discovery of America **Obv:** National arms within wreath **Rev:** Juan de la Cosa

Date	Mintage	VF20	XF40	MS60	MS63	MS65
1990	2,000	PF65 185				

KM# 298 50 PESOS
15.55 g., 0.999 Gold 0.4994 oz. AGW **Subject:** 500th Anniversary - Discovery of America **Obv:** National arms within wreath **Rev:** Portrait of Christopher Columbus

Date	Mintage	VF20	XF40	MS60	MS63	MS65
1990	250	PF65 875				

KM# 299 50 PESOS
15.55 g., 0.999 Gold 0.4994 oz. AGW **Subject:** 500th Anniversary - Discovery of America **Obv:** National arms within wreath **Rev:** Portrait of King Ferdinand V

Date	Mintage	VF20	XF40	MS60	MS63	MS65
1990	250	PF65 875				

KM# 300 50 PESOS
15.55 g., 0.999 Gold 0.4994 oz. AGW **Subject:** 500th Anniversary - Discovery of America **Obv:** National arms within wreath **Rev:** Portrait of Queen Isabella of Spain

Date	Mintage	VF20	XF40	MS60	MS63	MS65
1990	250	PF65 875				

KM# 301 50 PESOS
15.55 g., 0.999 Gold 0.4994 oz. AGW **Subject:** 500th Anniversary - Discovery of America **Obv:** National arms within wreath **Rev:** Portrait of Juan de la Cosa

Date	Mintage	VF20	XF40	MS60	MS63	MS65
1990	250	PF65 875				

KM# 321 50 PESOS
15.55 g., 0.999 Gold 0.4994 oz. AGW **Subject:** Pan American Games - Baseball **Obv:** National arms within wreath, denomination **Rev:** Baseball players

Date	Mintage	VF20	XF40	MS60	MS63	MS65
1990	15	PF65 950				

KM# 322 50 PESOS
15.55 g., 0.999 Gold 0.4994 oz. AGW **Subject:** Pan American Games - High Jump **Obv:** National arms within wreath, denomination **Rev:** High jumper clearing pole

Date	Mintage	VF20	XF40	MS60	MS63	MS65
1990	15	PF65 950				

KM# 323 50 PESOS
15.55 g., 0.999 Gold 0.4994 oz. AGW **Subject:** Pan American Games - Volleyball **Obv:** National arms within wreath, denomination **Rev:** Volleyball players

Date	Mintage	VF20	XF40	MS60	MS63	MS65
1990	15	PF65 950				

KM# 339 50 PESOS
15.55 g., 0.999 Gold 0.4994 oz. AGW **Rev:** Hatuey tribesman

Date	Mintage	VF20	XF40	MS60	MS63	MS65
1991	200	PF65 875				

KM# 343 50 PESOS
155.50 g., 0.999 Silver 4.9944 oz. ASW **Series:** Olympics **Obv:** National arms within wreath **Rev:** Stadium

Date	Mintage	VF20	XF40	MS60	MS63	MS65
1991	1,050	PF65 225				

KM# 356 50 PESOS
155.50 g., 0.999 Silver 4.9944 oz. ASW **Subject:** Madrid - Alcala Gate **Obv:** National arms within wreath **Rev:** Building with arches

Date	Mintage	VF20	XF40	MS60	MS63	MS65
1991	550	PF65 275				

KM# 357 50 PESOS
155.50 g., 0.999 Silver 4.9944 oz. ASW **Subject:** Seville - La Giralda Tower **Obv:** National arms within wreath **Rev:** Tower, date at right

Date	Mintage	VF20	XF40	MS60	MS63	MS65
1991	550	PF65 275				

KM# 432 50 PESOS
155.50 g., 0.999 Silver 4.9944 oz. ASW **Series:** 500th Anniversary of the New World **Subject:** Queen Joanna 1479-1555, daughter of Isabella I **Obv:** National arms within wreath **Rev:** Head 3/4 right above half wreath

Date	Mintage	VF20	XF40	MS60	MS63	MS65
1991	1,000	PF65 225				

KM# 433 50 PESOS
155.50 g., 0.999 Silver 4.9944 oz. ASW **Series:** 500th Anniversary of the New World **Subject:** Diego Valezquez **Obv:** National arms within wreath **Rev:** Bust 3/4 left above half wreath

Date	Mintage	VF20	XF40	MS60	MS63	MS65
1991	1,000	PF65 225				

KM# 434 50 PESOS
155.50 g., 0.999 Silver 4.9944 oz. ASW **Series:** 500th Anniversary of the New World **Subject:** Pinzon Brothers **Obv:** National arms within wreath, denomination below **Rev:** Portraits in cameos, small ship above

Date	Mintage	VF20	XF40	MS60	MS63	MS65
1991	1,000	PF65 225				

KM# 435 50 PESOS
155.50 g., 0.999 Silver 4.9944 oz. ASW **Series:** 500th Anniversary of the New World **Subject:** Hatuey Tribesman **Obv:** National arms within wreath, denomination **Rev:** Head stretching left

Date	Mintage	VF20	XF40	MS60	MS63	MS65
1991	1,000	PF65 225				

KM# 444 50 PESOS
15.55 g., 0.999 Gold 0.4994 oz. AGW **Subject:** Queen Joanna

Date	Mintage	VF20	XF40	MS60	MS63	MS65
1991	200	PF65 875				

KM# 445 50 PESOS
15.55 g., 0.999 Gold 0.4994 oz. AGW **Subject:** Diego Valezquez

Date	Mintage	VF20	XF40	MS60	MS63	MS65
1991	200	PF65 875				

KM# 446 50 PESOS
15.55 g., 0.999 Gold 0.4994 oz. AGW **Subject:** Pinzon Brothers

Date	Mintage	VF20	XF40	MS60	MS63	MS65
1991	200	PF65 875				

KM# 358 50 PESOS
155.50 g., 0.999 Silver 4.9944 oz. ASW **Series:** 500th Anniversary of the New World **Subject:** Philipp I **Obv:** National arms within wreath **Rev:** Bust right above half wreath

Date	Mintage	VF20	XF40	MS60	MS63	MS65
1992	550	PF65 250				

KM# 359 50 PESOS

155.50 g., 0.999 Silver 4.9944 oz. ASW **Series:** 500th Anniversary of the New World **Subject:** Chief Guama **Obv:** National arms within wreath **Rev:** Native drinking from large shell

Date	Mintage	VF20	XF40	MS60	MS63	MS65
1992	550	PF65 250				

KM# 380 50 PESOS

155.73 g., 0.999 Silver 5.0018 oz. ASW **Series:** 500th Anniversary of the New World **Subject:** Bartolome de Las Casas **Obv:** National arms within wreath, denomination below **Rev:** Seated figure writing with quill

Date	Mintage	VF20	XF40	MS60	MS63	MS65
1992	550	PF65 250				

KM# 381 50 PESOS

155.73 g., 0.999 Silver 5.0018 oz. ASW **Series:** 500th Anniversary of the New World **Subject:** Ferdinand and Elisabeth, Philipp and Joanna **Obv:** National arms within wreath, denomination below **Rev:** Busts of Spanish Kings and Queens left

Date	Mintage	VF20	XF40	MS60	MS63	MS65
ND-1992	550	PF65 250				

KM# 382 50 PESOS

155.73 g., 0.999 Silver 5.0018 oz. ASW **Obv:** National arms within wreath, denomination below **Rev:** San Jorge Palace

Date	Mintage	VF20	XF40	MS60	MS63	MS65
1992	550	PF65 250				

KM# 568 50 PESOS

155.73 g., 0.999 Silver 5.0018 oz. ASW **Subject:** Cuban Fauna **Obv:** National arms within wreath, denomination below **Rev:** Multicolored Papilio butterfly

Date	Mintage	VF20	XF40	MS60	MS63	MS65
1992	—	PF65 250				

KM# 641 50 PESOS

155.73 g., 0.999 Silver 5.0018 oz. ASW **Subject:** 1982 - Ano de Espana **Obv:** National arms within wreath, denomination below **Rev:** Seville's Tower of Gold

Date	Mintage	VF20	XF40	MS60	MS63	MS65
1992	—	PF65 250				

KM# 914 50 PESOS

155.50 g., 0.999 Silver 4.9944 oz. ASW **Subject:** European Culture Capital - Madrid 1992

Date	Mintage	VF20	XF40	MS60	MS63	MS65
1992	Est. 550	PF65 225				

KM# 400 50 PESOS

155.52 g., 0.999 Silver 4.9949 oz. ASW **Obv:** National arms, denomination below on left, crowned arms on right **Rev:** St. Jacobi on rearing horse

Date	Mintage	VF20	XF40	MS60	MS63	MS65
1993	1,000	PF65 250				

KM# 693 50 PESOS

15.55 g., 0.999 Gold 0.4995 oz. AGW **Subject:** 40th Anniversary - Assault on Moncada Garrison

Date	Mintage	VF20	XF40	MS60	MS63	MS65
1993	—	PF65 900				

KM# 503 50 PESOS

155.52 g., 0.999 Silver 4.9949 oz. ASW **Subject:** Caribbean Fauna **Obv:** National arms within wreath, denomination below **Rev:** Multicolor bottle-nosed dophins **Edge:** Reeded

Date	Mintage	VF20	XF40	MS60	MS63	MS65
1994	2,500	PF65 250				

KM# 504 50 PESOS

155.52 g., 0.999 Silver 4.9949 oz. ASW **Subject:** Caribbean Fauna **Obv:** National arms within wreath, denomination below **Rev:** Multicolor sailfish

Date	Mintage	VF20	XF40	MS60	MS63	MS65
1994	2,500	PF65 225				

KM# 505 50 PESOS

155.52 g., 0.999 Silver 4.9949 oz. ASW **Subject:** Caribbean Fauna **Obv:** National arms within wreath, denomination below **Rev:** Multicolored brown pelican

Date	Mintage	VF20	XF40	MS60	MS63	MS65
1994	2,500	PF65 225				

KM# 506 50 PESOS

155.52 g., 0.999 Silver 4.9949 oz. ASW **Subject:** Caribbean Fauna **Obv:** National arms within wreath, denomination below **Rev:** Multicolored flamingos

Date	Mintage	VF20	XF40	MS60	MS63	MS65
1994	2,500	PF65 225				

KM# 507 50 PESOS

155.52 g., 0.999 Silver 4.9949 oz. ASW **Subject:** Caribbean Fauna **Obv:** National arms within wreath, denomination below **Rev:** Multicolored Yellow Grouper

Date	Mintage	VF20	XF40	MS60	MS63	MS65
1994	2,500	PF65 225				

KM# 508 50 PESOS

155.52 g., 0.999 Silver 4.9949 oz. ASW **Subject:** Caribbean Fauna **Obv:** National arms within wreath, denomination below **Rev:** Multicolored spotted eagle ray

Date	Mintage	VF20	XF40	MS60	MS63	MS65
1994	2,500	PF65 225				

KM# 484 50 PESOS

155.52 g., 0.999 Silver 4.9949 oz. ASW **Subject:** Pirates of the Caribbean **Obv:** National arms within wreath, denomination below **Rev:** Blackbeard within circle, date below

Date	Mintage	VF20	XF40	MS60	MS63	MS65
1995	—	PF65 250				

KM# 485 50 PESOS

155.52 g., 0.999 Silver 4.9949 oz. ASW **Series:** Pirates of the Caribbean **Subject:** Sir Henry Morgan **Obv:** National arms within wreath, denomination below **Rev:** Pirate with rifle over right shoulder left

Date	Mintage	VF20	XF40	MS60	MS63	MS65
1995	Est. 3000	PF65 250				

KM# 486 50 PESOS

155.52 g., 0.999 Silver 4.9949 oz. ASW **Series:** Pirates of the Caribbean **Subject:** Anne Bonny **Obv:** National arms within wreath, denomination below **Rev:** Bare-breasted woman and pirates drinking within circle, date below

Date	Mintage	VF20	XF40	MS60	MS63	MS65
1995	Est. 3000	PF65 250				

KM# 487 50 PESOS

155.52 g., 0.999 Silver 4.9949 oz. ASW **Series:** Pirates of the Caribbean **Subject:** Mary Read **Obv:** National arms within wreath, denomination below **Rev:** Pirates fighting on the beach

Date	Mintage	VF20	XF40	MS60	MS63	MS65
1995	Est. 3000	PF65 250				

KM# 488 50 PESOS

155.52 g., 0.999 Silver 4.9949 oz. ASW **Series:** Pirates of the Caribbean **Subject:** Captain Kidd **Obv:** National arms within wreath, denomination below **Rev:** Pirates aboard ship

Date	Mintage	VF20	XF40	MS60	MS63	MS65
1995	Est. 3000	PF65 250				

KM# 489 50 PESOS

155.52 g., 0.999 Silver 4.9949 oz. ASW **Subject:** Piet Heyn **Obv:** National arms within wreath, denomination below **Rev:** Pirates having sword fight

Date	Mintage	VF20	XF40	MS60	MS63	MS65
1995	—	PF65 250				

KM# 490 50 PESOS

13.00 g., 0.917 Gold 0.3833 oz. AGW **Series:** Pirates of the Caribbean **Subject:** Blackbeard **Obv:** National arms within wreath, denomination below **Rev:** Bust 3/4 facing within circle, date below

Date	Mintage	VF20	XF40	MS60	MS63	MS65
1995	Est. 1000	PF65 750				

KM# 491 50 PESOS
13.00 g., 0.917 Gold 0.3833 oz. AGW **Series:** Pirates of the Caribbean **Subject:** Sir Henry Morgan **Obv:** National arms within wreath, denomination below **Rev:** Bust 3/4 right

Date	Mintage	VF20	XF40	MS60	MS63	MS65
1995	Est. 1000	PF65 750				

KM# 492 50 PESOS
13.00 g., 0.917 Gold 0.3833 oz. AGW **Series:** Pirates of the Caribbean **Subject:** Anne Bonny **Obv:** National arms within wreath, denomination below **Rev:** Half-length female figure facing, ship in distance

Date	Mintage	VF20	XF40	MS60	MS63	MS65
1995	Est. 1000	PF65 750				

KM# 493 50 PESOS
13.00 g., 0.917 Gold 0.3833 oz. AGW **Series:** Pirates of the Caribbean **Subject:** Mary Read **Obv:** National arms within wreath, denomination below **Rev:** Half-length female figure facing, ship in distance

Date	Mintage	VF20	XF40	MS60	MS63	MS65
1995	Est. 1000	PF65 750				

KM# 494 50 PESOS
13.00 g., 0.917 Gold 0.3833 oz. AGW **Series:** Pirates of the Caribbean **Subject:** Captain Kidd **Obv:** National arms within wreath, denomination below **Rev:** Half-length figure looking right, ships in distance

Date	Mintage	VF20	XF40	MS60	MS63	MS65
1995	Est. 1000	PF65 750				

KM# 495 50 PESOS
13.00 g., 0.917 Gold 0.3833 oz. AGW **Series:** Pirates of the Caribbean **Subject:** Piet Heyn **Obv:** National arms within wreath, denomination below **Rev:** Half-length bust facing, ships in distance

Date	Mintage	VF20	XF40	MS60	MS63	MS65
1995	Est. 1000	PF65 750				

KM# 557 50 PESOS
155.00 g., 0.999 Silver 4.9784 oz. ASW **Series:** Caribbean Fauna **Obv:** National arms within wreath, denomination below **Rev:** Purple-throated Carib Hummingbird

Date	Mintage	VF20	XF40	MS60	MS63	MS65
1996	950	PF65 285				

KM# 558 50 PESOS
155.00 g., 0.999 Silver 4.9784 oz. ASW **Series:** Caribbean Fauna **Obv:** National arms within wreath, denomination below **Rev:** Yellow perch

Date	Mintage	VF20	XF40	MS60	MS63	MS65
1996	950	PF65 285				

KM# 559 50 PESOS
155.00 g., 0.999 Silver 4.9784 oz. ASW **Series:** Caribbean Fauna **Obv:** National arms within wreath, denomination below **Rev:** Cuban Tody bird

Date	Mintage	VF20	XF40	MS60	MS63	MS65
1996	950	PF65 285				

KM# 560 50 PESOS
155.00 g., 0.999 Silver 4.9784 oz. ASW **Series:** Caribbean Fauna **Obv:** National arms within wreath, denomination below **Rev:** Wood duck

Date	Mintage	VF20	XF40	MS60	MS63	MS65
1996	950	PF65 285				

KM# 564 50 PESOS
155.00 g., 0.999 Silver 4.9784 oz. ASW **Series:** Caribbean Fauna **Obv:** National arms within wreath, denomination below **Rev:** Vaca anil fish

Date	Mintage	VF20	XF40	MS60	MS63	MS65
1996	950	PF65 285				

KM# 567 50 PESOS
155.00 g., 0.999 Silver 4.9784 oz. ASW **Series:** Caribbean Fauna **Obv:** National arms within wreath, denomination below **Rev:** Papilio butterfly

Date	Mintage	VF20	XF40	MS60	MS63	MS65
1996	950	PF65 285				

KM# 694 50 PESOS
155.00 g., 0.999 Silver 4.9784 oz. ASW **Subject:** Caribbean Flora **Obv:** National arms within wreath, denomination below **Rev:** Multicolor flower, "Bidens Romerillo"

Date	Mintage	VF20	XF40	MS60	MS63	MS65
1997	—	PF65 285				

KM# 695 50 PESOS
155.00 g., 0.999 Silver 4.9784 oz. ASW **Subject:** Caribbean Flora **Obv:** National arms within wreath, denomination below **Rev:** Multicolor flower, "Cordia Vomitel"

Date	Mintage	VF20	XF40	MS60	MS63	MS65
1997	—	PF65 285				

KM# 697 50 PESOS
155.00 g., 0.999 Silver 4.9784 oz. ASW **Subject:** Wonders of the Ancient World **Rev:** Temple of Artemis

Date	Mintage	VF20	XF40	MS60	MS63	MS65
1997	—	PF65 260				

KM# 698 50 PESOS
155.00 g., 0.999 Silver 4.9784 oz. ASW **Subject:** Wonders of the Ancient World **Rev:** Pyramids

Date	Mintage	VF20	XF40	MS60	MS63	MS65
1997	—	PF65 260				

KM# 699 50 PESOS
155.00 g., 0.999 Silver 4.9784 oz. ASW **Subject:** Wonders of the Ancient World **Rev:** Hanging Gardens of Babylon

Date	Mintage	VF20	XF40	MS60	MS63	MS65
1997	—	PF65 260				

KM# 700 50 PESOS
155.00 g., 0.999 Silver 4.9784 oz. ASW **Subject:** Wonders of the Ancient World **Rev:** Statue of Jupiter at Olympus

Date	Mintage	VF20	XF40	MS60	MS63	MS65
1997	—	PF65 260				

KM# 701 50 PESOS
155.00 g., 0.999 Silver 4.9784 oz. ASW **Subject:** Wonders of the Ancient World **Rev:** Colossus of Rhodes

Date	Mintage	VF20	XF40	MS60	MS63	MS65
1997	—	PF65 260				

KM# 702 50 PESOS
155.00 g., 0.999 Silver 4.9784 oz. ASW **Subject:** Wonders of the Ancient World **Rev:** Mausoleum at Halicarnasos

Date	Mintage	VF20	XF40	MS60	MS63	MS65
1997	—	PF65 260				

KM# 941 50 PESOS
155.50 g., 0.999 Silver 4.9944 oz. ASW **Rev:** Ruellie in color

Date	Mintage	VF20	XF40	MS60	MS63	MS65
1997	—	PF65 220				

KM# 942 50 PESOS
155.50 g., 0.999 Silver 4.9944 oz. ASW **Rev:** Damiana in color

Date	Mintage	VF20	XF40	MS60	MS63	MS65
1997	—	PF65 220				

KM# 943 50 PESOS
155.50 g., 0.999 Silver 4.9944 oz. ASW **Rev:** Madagascar evergreen in color

Date	Mintage	VF20	XF40	MS60	MS63	MS65
1997	—	PF65 220				

KM# 638 50 PESOS
15.55 g., 0.999 Gold 0.4994 oz. AGW, 30 mm. **Subject:** AIDS **Obv:** National arms within wreath **Rev:** AIDS ribbon on silhouette before world map

Date	Mintage	VF20	XF40	MS60	MS63	MS65
1998	2,000	PF65 875				

KM# 654 50 PESOS
15.55 g., 0.999 Gold 0.4994 oz. AGW **Subject:** Expo 2000 **Obv:** National arms within wreath **Rev:** Twipsy cartoon logo

Date	Mintage	VF20	XF40	MS60	MS63	MS65
1998	3,125	PF65 875				

KM# 703 50 PESOS
15.55 g., 0.999 Gold 0.4994 oz. AGW **Subject:** 40th Anniversary - Triumph of the Revolution

Date	Mintage	VF20	XF40	MS60	MS63	MS65
1999	—	PF65 875				

KM# 704 50 PESOS
15.55 g., 0.999 Gold 0.4995 oz. AGW, 32.5 mm. **Obv:** National arms **Rev:** Hummingbird **Edge:** Reeded

Date	Mintage	VF20	XF40	MS60	MS63	MS65
1999	1,000	PF65 875				

KM# 705 50 PESOS
15.55 g., 0.999 Gold 0.4994 oz. AGW **Subject:** Welcome the New Millennium

Date	Mintage	VF20	XF40	MS60	MS63	MS65
2000	—	PF65 875				

KM# 706 50 PESOS
15.55 g., 0.999 Gold 0.4994 oz. AGW **Subject:** Welcome the Third Millennium

Date	Mintage	VF20	XF40	MS60	MS63	MS65
2000	—	PF65 875				

KM# 707 50 PESOS
15.55 g., 0.999 Gold 0.4994 oz. AGW **Subject:** Hacia un Nuevo Milenio (Towards a new Millennium)

Date	Mintage	VF20	XF40	MS60	MS63	MS65
2000	—	PF65 875				

KM# 42 100 PESOS
12.00 g., 0.917 Gold 0.3538 oz. AGW **Subject:** 60th Anniversary of Socialist Revolution - Lenin **Obv:** National arms within wreath, denomination below **Rev:** Bust left divides dates

Date	Mintage	VF20	XF40	MS60	MS63	MS65
ND-1977	10	PF65 10,000				

KM# 43 100 PESOS
12.00 g., 0.917 Gold 0.3538 oz. AGW **Obv:** Liberty cap above flagged arms, denomination **Rev:** Carlos Manuel de Cespedes

Date	Mintage	VF20	XF40	MS60	MS63	MS65
ND-1977	25,000	PF65 725				

KM# 45 100 PESOS
12.00 g., 0.917 Gold 0.3538 oz. AGW **Subject:** Nonaligned Nations Conference **Obv:** National arms within wreath **Rev:** Number six within design

Date	Mintage	VF20	XF40	MS60	MS63	MS65
1979	2,000	—	—	—	735	750
1979	20,000	PF65 725				

KM# 52 100 PESOS
12.00 g., 0.917 Gold 0.3538 oz. AGW **Subject:** First Soviet-Cuban space flight **Obv:** Arms **Rev:** Shuttle orbiting planet, date below

Date	Mintage	VF20	XF40	MS60	MS63	MS65
1980	1,000	—	—	—	600	625

KM# 85 100 PESOS
12.00 g., 0.917 Gold 0.3538 oz. AGW **Obv:** National arms within wreath, denomination below **Rev:** Columbus' ship - Niña

Date	Mintage	VF20	XF40	MS60	MS63	MS65
1981	2,000	—	—	—	600	625

KM# 86 100 PESOS
12.00 g., 0.917 Gold 0.3538 oz. AGW **Obv:** National arms within wreath, denomination below **Rev:** Columbus' ship - Pinta

Date	Mintage	VF20	XF40	MS60	MS63	MS65
1981	2,000	—	—	—	600	625

KM# 87 100 PESOS
12.00 g., 0.917 Gold 0.3538 oz. AGW **Obv:** National arms within wreath, denomination below **Rev:** Columbus' ship - Santa Maria

Date	Mintage	VF20	XF40	MS60	MS63	MS65
1981	2,000	—	—	—	600	625

KM# 202 100 PESOS
31.10 g., 0.999 Gold 0.999 oz. AGW **Subject:** 30th Anniversary of March to Victory **Obv:** Arms on star background above half wreath **Rev:** Soldiers on the march

Date	Mintage	VF20	XF40	MS60	MS63	MS65
1988	100	PF65 1,750				

KM# 203 100 PESOS
31.10 g., 0.999 Gold 0.999 oz. AGW **Subject:** 60th Anniversary - Birth of Ernesto Che Guevara **Obv:** Arms on star background above half wreath **Rev:** Bust right, dates at left

Date	Mintage	VF20	XF40	MS60	MS63	MS65
1988	100	PF65 1,750				

KM# 204 100 PESOS
31.10 g., 0.999 Gold 0.999 oz. AGW **Subject:** 30th Anniversary - Triumph of the Revolution **Obv:** Arms on star background above half wreath **Rev:** Scene of triumph, dates

Date	Mintage	VF20	XF40	MS60	MS63	MS65
1988	100	PF65 1,750				

KM# 215 100 PESOS
31.10 g., 0.999 Gold 0.999 oz. AGW **Subject:** Jose Marti **Obv:** National arms within wreath, denomination below **Rev:** Head right, date below

Date	Mintage	VF20	XF40	MS60	MS63	MS65
1988	50	—	—	—	1,700	1,725
1988	15	PF65 1,750				
1989	150	—	—	—	1,700	1,725
1989	15	PF65 1,750				

Date	Mintage	VF20	XF40	MS60	MS63	MS65
1990	15	—	—	—	1,700	1,725
1990	12	PF65 1,775				

KM# 316 100 PESOS
31.10 g., 0.999 Gold 0.999 oz. AGW **Subject:** 160th Anniversary - First train in England **Rev:** Train **Rev. Legend:** LIVERPOOL-MANCHESTER

Date	Mintage	VF20	XF40	MS60	MS63	MS65
1989	150	PF65 1,650				

KM# 317 100 PESOS
31.10 g., 0.999 Gold 0.999 oz. AGW **Subject:** 150th Anniversary - First train in Spanish America **Rev:** Train **Rev. Legend:** HABANA-BEJUCAL

Date	Mintage	VF20	XF40	MS60	MS63	MS65
1989	150	PF65 1,650				

KM# 318 100 PESOS
31.10 g., 0.999 Gold 0.999 oz. AGW **Subject:** 140th Anniversary - First train in Spain **Rev:** Train **Rev. Legend:** BARCELONA-MATARO

Date	Mintage	VF20	XF40	MS60	MS63	MS65
1989	150	PF65 1,650				

KM# 319 100 PESOS
31.10 g., 0.999 Gold 0.999 oz. AGW **Subject:** 200th Anniversary of French Revolution - Lady Justice **Rev:** Female revolutionary raising flag

Date	Mintage	VF20	XF40	MS60	MS63	MS65
1989	150	PF65 1,650				

KM# 320 100 PESOS
31.10 g., 0.999 Gold 0.999 oz. AGW **Subject:** 200th Anniversary of French Revolution - Bastille **Rev:** Bastille, soldiers in foreground

Date	Mintage	VF20	XF40	MS60	MS63	MS65
1989	150	PF65 1,650				

KM# 333 100 PESOS
31.10 g., 0.999 Gold 0.999 oz. AGW **Subject:** Tania La Guerrillera **Rev:** Portrait of female guerilla fighter

Date	Mintage	VF20	XF40	MS60	MS63	MS65
1989	150	PF65 1,650				

KM# 334 100 PESOS
31.10 g., 0.999 Gold 0.999 oz. AGW **Subject:** Camilo Cienfuegos Gornaran **Rev:** Portrait of Camilo Cienfuegos

Date	Mintage	VF20	XF40	MS60	MS63	MS65
1989	150	PF65 1,650				

KM# 335 100 PESOS
31.10 g., 0.999 Gold 0.999 oz. AGW **Subject:** 35th Anniversary - Assault of the Moncada Garrison **Rev:** Battle scene

Date	Mintage	VF20	XF40	MS60	MS63	MS65
1989	150	PF65 1,650				

KM# 447 100 PESOS
31.10 g., 0.999 Gold 0.999 oz. AGW **Subject:** 30th Anniversary of Revolution **Obv:** National arms within wreath, denomination **Rev:** Armed, uniformed figure standing right

Date	Mintage	VF20	XF40	MS60	MS63	MS65
1989	250	PF65 1,550				

KM# 448 100 PESOS
31.10 g., 0.999 Gold 0.999 oz. AGW **Subject:** 30th Anniversary of Revolution **Obv:** National arms within wreath, denomination **Rev:** Armed, uniformed figure standing right

Date	Mintage	VF20	XF40	MS60	MS63	MS65
1989	250	PF65 1,550				

KM# 449 100 PESOS
31.10 g., 0.999 Gold 0.999 oz. AGW **Subject:** 30th Anniversary of Revolution **Obv:** National arms within wreath, denomination **Rev:** Armed, uniformed figure standing right

Date	Mintage	VF20	XF40	MS60	MS63	MS65
1989	250	PF65 1,550				

KM# 302 100 PESOS
31.10 g., 0.999 Gold 0.999 oz. AGW **Subject:** 500th Anniversary - Discovery of America **Rev:** Portrait of Columbus

Date	Mintage	VF20	XF40	MS60	MS63	MS65
1990	250	PF65 1,550				

KM# 303 100 PESOS
31.10 g., 0.999 Gold 0.999 oz. AGW **Subject:** 500th Anniversary - Discovery of America **Rev:** Portrait of King Ferdinand V

Date	Mintage	VF20	XF40	MS60	MS63	MS65
1990	250	PF65 1,550				

KM# 304 100 PESOS
31.10 g., 0.999 Gold 0.999 oz. AGW **Subject:** 500th Anniversary - Discovery of America **Rev:** Portrait of Queen Isabella

Date	Mintage	VF20	XF40	MS60	MS63	MS65
1990	250	PF65 1,550				

KM# 305 100 PESOS
31.10 g., 0.999 Gold 0.999 oz. AGW **Subject:** 500th Anniversary - Discovery of America **Rev:** Portrait of Juan de la Cosa

Date	Mintage	VF20	XF40	MS60	MS63	MS65
1990	250	PF65 1,550				

KM# 450 100 PESOS
31.10 g., 0.999 Gold 0.999 oz. AGW **Subject:** Pinzon brothers **Obv:** National arms within wreath

Date	Mintage	VF20	XF40	MS60	MS63	MS65
1991	200	PF65 1,550				

KM# 451 100 PESOS
31.10 g., 0.999 Gold 0.999 oz. AGW **Subject:** 500th Anniversary of the New World **Rev:** Head of Queen Joanna half right, 1479-1555, daughter of Queen Isabella I

Date	Mintage	VF20	XF40	MS60	MS63	MS65
1991	200	PF65 1,550				

KM# 452 100 PESOS
31.10 g., 0.999 Gold 0.999 oz. AGW **Subject:** 500th Anniversary **Obv:** National arms within wreath **Rev:** Diego Velazquez

Date	Mintage	VF20	XF40	MS60	MS63	MS65
1991	200	PF65 1,550				

KM# 534 100 PESOS
31.10 g., 0.999 Gold 0.999 oz. AGW **Series:** Olympics **Rev:** Stadium

Date	Mintage	VF20	XF40	MS60	MS63	MS65
1991	225	PF65 1,550				

KM# 535 100 PESOS
31.10 g., 0.999 Gold 0.999 oz. AGW **Subject:** Madrid - Alcala Gate **Rev:** Building with arches

Date	Mintage	VF20	XF40	MS60	MS63	MS65
1991	225	PF65 1,550				

KM# 569 100 PESOS
31.10 g., 0.999 Gold 0.999 oz. AGW **Subject:** Hatuey People

Date	Mintage	VF20	XF40	MS60	MS63	MS65
1991	—	PF65 1,550				

KM# 384 100 PESOS
31.10 g., 0.999 Gold 0.999 oz. AGW **Subject:** Seville - Tower of Gold **Rev:** Tower of Gold in Seville

Date	Mintage	VF20	XF40	MS60	MS63	MS65
1992	225	PF65 1,550				

KM# 385 100 PESOS
31.10 g., 0.999 Gold 0.999 oz. AGW **Subject:** El Escorial **Rev:** El Escorial palace

Date	Mintage	VF20	XF40	MS60	MS63	MS65
1992	225	PF65 1,550				

KM# 453 100 PESOS
31.10 g., 0.999 Gold 0.999 oz. AGW **Subject:** 500th Anniversary **Obv:** National arms within wreath **Rev:** Bartolome de las Casas

Date	Mintage	VF20	XF40	MS60	MS63	MS65
1992	100	PF65 1,650				

KM# 454 100 PESOS
31.10 g., 0.999 Gold 0.999 oz. AGW **Subject:** 500th Anniversary **Obv:** National arms within wreath **Rev:** Guama Tribesman

Date	Mintage	VF20	XF40	MS60	MS63	MS65
1992	100	PF65 1,650				

KM# 455 100 PESOS
31.10 g., 0.999 Gold 0.999 oz. AGW **Subject:** 500th Anniversary **Obv:** National arms within wreath **Rev:** King Philipp

Date	Mintage	VF20	XF40	MS60	MS63	MS65
1992	100	PF65 1,650				

KM# 456 100 PESOS
31.10 g., 0.999 Gold 0.999 oz. AGW **Subject:** 500th Anniversary **Obv:** National arms within wreath **Rev:** Spanish kings and queens

Date	Mintage	VF20	XF40	MS60	MS63	MS65
1992	100	PF65 1,650				

KM# 536 100 PESOS
31.10 g., 0.999 Gold 0.999 oz. AGW **Subject:** San Jorge Palace

Date	Mintage	VF20	XF40	MS60	MS63	MS65
1992	225	PF65 1,550				

KM# 570 100 PESOS
31.10 g., 0.999 Gold 0.999 oz. AGW **Subject:** Ernesto Che Guevara **Obv:** National arms within wreath

Date	Mintage	VF20	XF40	MS60	MS63	MS65
1992	—	PF65 1,650				

KM# 537 100 PESOS
31.10 g., 0.999 Gold 0.999 oz. AGW **Subject:** 40th Anniversary of Moncada **Rev:** Fidel Castro

Date	Mintage	VF20	XF40	MS60	MS63	MS65
1993	100	PF65 1,650				

KM# 538 100 PESOS
31.10 g., 0.999 Gold 0.999 oz. AGW **Obv:** Two sets of arms and denomination **Rev:** St. Jacobi

Date	Mintage	VF20	XF40	MS60	MS63	MS65
1993	100	PF65 1,650				

KM# 539 100 PESOS
31.10 g., 0.999 Gold 0.999 oz. AGW **Rev:** Federico Garcia Lorca

Date	Mintage	VF20	XF40	MS60	MS63	MS65
1993	100	PF65 1,650				

KM# 916 100 PESOS
31.11 g., 0.999 Gold 0.999 oz. AGW **Obv:** National Arms **Rev:** Bolivar on horseback, Marti profile at right

Date	Mintage	VF20	XF40	MS60	MS63	MS65
1993	12	—	—	—	—	2,150
1993 Proof, polished	12	PF65 2,200				
1993 Proof, matte	12	PF65 2,200				

KM# 571 100 PESOS
31.10 g., 0.999 Gold 0.999 oz. AGW **Obv:** National arms within wreath **Rev:** Jose Marti

Date	Mintage	VF20	XF40	MS60	MS63	MS65
1994	—	PF65 1,650				

KM# 572 100 PESOS
31.10 g., 0.999 Gold 0.999 oz. AGW **Subject:** Centennial of the Necessary War

Date	Mintage	VF20	XF40	MS60	MS63	MS65
1995	—	PF65 1,650				

KM# 920 100 PESOS
31.11 g., 0.999 Gold 0.999 oz. AGW, 38 mm. **Subject:** Landing of the Granma, 40th Anniversary **Rev:** The Granma, and Bust of Fidel Castro

Date	Mintage	VF20	XF40	MS60	MS63	MS65
1996	—	PF65 1,650				

KM# 708 100 PESOS
31.10 g., 0.999 Gold 0.999 oz. AGW **Subject:** Meeting of Fidel Castro and Pope John Paul II in the Vatican

Date	Mintage	VF20	XF40	MS60	MS63	MS65
1997	—	PF65 1,650				

KM# 709 100 PESOS
31.10 g., 0.999 Gold 0.999 oz. AGW **Subject:** Papal visit to Cuba

Date	Mintage	VF20	XF40	MS60	MS63	MS65
1997	—	PF65 1,650				

KM# 929 100 PESOS
31.11 g., 0.999 Gold 0.999 oz. AGW **Rev:** Ernesto "Che" Guevara

Date	Mintage	VF20	XF40	MS60	MS63	MS65
1997	—	PF65 1,650				

KM# 930 100 PESOS
31.11 g., 0.999 Gold 0.999 oz. AGW **Rev:** Ernesto "Che" Guevara in the Sierra Maestra

Date	Mintage	VF20	XF40	MS60	MS63	MS65
1997	—	PF65 1,650				

KM# 933 100 PESOS
31.11 g., 0.999 Gold 0.999 oz. AGW **Subject:** Deng Ziaping **Rev:** Ziaoping as a Party Official at a young age

Date	Mintage	VF20	XF40	MS60	MS63	MS65
1997	—	PF65 1,650				

KM# 934 100 PESOS
31.11 g., 0.999 Gold 0.999 oz. AGW **Subject:** Deng Xiaoping **Rev:** Hong Kong and Great Wall

Date	Mintage	VF20	XF40	MS60	MS63	MS65
1997	—	PF65 1,650				

KM# 710 100 PESOS
31.10 g., 0.999 Gold 0.999 oz. AGW **Subject:** 90th Anniversary - Triumph of the Revolution

Date	Mintage	VF20	XF40	MS60	MS63	MS65
1999	—	PF65 1,650				

KM# 719 100 PESOS
31.10 g., 0.999 Gold 0.999 oz. AGW, 38 mm. **Obv:** National arms **Rev:** Hummingbird **Edge:** Reeded **Note:** Prev. KM#728.

Date	Mintage	VF20	XF40	MS60	MS63	MS65
1999	1,000	PF65 1,650				

KM# 711 100 PESOS
31.10 g., 0.999 Gold 0.999 oz. AGW **Subject:** Macia un Nuevo Milenio (Towards a new millennium)

Date	Mintage	VF20	XF40	MS60	MS63	MS65
2000	—	PF65 1,650				

KM# 712 100 PESOS
31.10 g., 0.999 Gold 0.999 oz. AGW **Subject:** Welcome to the third millennium

Date	Mintage	VF20	XF40	MS60	MS63	MS65
2000	—	PF65 1,650				

KM# 713 100 PESOS
31.10 g., 0.999 Gold 0.999 oz. AGW **Subject:** Welcome to the new millennium

Date	Mintage	VF20	XF40	MS60	MS63	MS65
2000	—	PF65 1,650				

KM# 714 100 PESOS
31.10 g., 0.999 Gold 0.999 oz. AGW **Subject:** Maritime relics - school ship Galatea

Date	Mintage	VF20	XF40	MS60	MS63	MS65
2000	—	PF65 1,650				

KM# 715 100 PESOS
31.10 g., 0.999 Gold 0.999 oz. AGW **Subject:** Maritime relics - maritime ambulance Buena Ventura

Date	Mintage	VF20	XF40	MS60	MS63	MS65
2000	—	PF65 1,650				

KM# 716 100 PESOS
31.10 g., 0.999 Gold 0.999 oz. AGW **Subject:** Maritime relics - nautical rise of Juan de la Cosa

Date	Mintage	VF20	XF40	MS60	MS63	MS65
2000	—	PF65 1,650				

KM# 717 100 PESOS
31.10 g., 0.999 Gold 0.999 oz. AGW **Subject:** Maritime relics - school ship JS Elcana

Date	Mintage	VF20	XF40	MS60	MS63	MS65
2000	—	PF65 1,650				

KM# 718 100 PESOS
31.10 g., 0.999 Gold 0.999 oz. AGW **Subject:** Maritime relics - Peral submarine

Date	Mintage	VF20	XF40	MS60	MS63	MS65
2000	—	PF65 1,650				

KM# 642 150 PESOS
411.42 g., 0.999 Silver 13.2143 oz. ASW **Series:** Cuban Fauna **Obv:** National arms within wreath **Rev:** Multicolored Cuban Trogon **Note:** The Cuban Trogon is the Cuban National Bird.

Date	Mintage	VF20	XF40	MS60	MS63	MS65
1996	Est. 420	PF65 450				

KM# 542 200 PESOS
31.10 g., Gold **Obv:** National arms within wreath **Rev:** Bolivar and Marti

Date	Mintage	VF20	XF40	MS60	MS63	MS65
1993	100	PF65 1,650				
1993	100	—	—	—	—	1,600

KM# 543 200 PESOS
31.10 g., Gold **Series:** Prehistoric Animals **Obv:** National arms within wreath **Rev:** Apatosaurus

Date	Mintage	VF20	XF40	MS60	MS63	MS65
1993	100	PF65 1,650				

KM# 544 200 PESOS
31.10 g., Gold **Series:** Prehistoric Animals **Rev:** Chalicotherium

Date	Mintage	VF20	XF40	MS60	MS63	MS65
1993	100	PF65 1,650				

KM# 545 200 PESOS
31.10 g., Gold **Subject:** Montecristi Manifesto **Rev:** Two seated figures facing each other, date lower left

Date	Mintage	VF20	XF40	MS60	MS63	MS65
1994	100	PF65 1,650				

KM# 643 300 PESOS
822.84 g., 0.999 Silver 26.4286 oz. ASW **Series:** Cuban Fauna **Obv:** National arms within wreath **Rev:** Multicolor Mariposa butterfly

Date	Mintage	VF20	XF40	MS60	MS63	MS65
1996	Est. 800	PF65 850				

KM# 457 500 PESOS
155.55 g., 0.999 Gold 4.996 oz. AGW **Rev:** Christopher Columbus

Date	Mintage	VF20	XF40	MS60	MS63	MS65
1990	15	PF65 8,750				

KM# 386 500 PESOS
155.55 g., 0.999 Gold 4.996 oz. AGW **Subject:** 500th Anniversary **Obv:** National arms within wreath **Rev:** Spanish Kings and Queens

Date	Mintage	VF20	XF40	MS60	MS63	MS65
ND-1992	15	PF65 8,750				

KM# 605 500 PESOS
155.55 g., 0.999 Platinum 4.996 oz. APW **Subject:** Castro **Rev:** Fidel Castro

Date	Mintage	VF20	XF40	MS60	MS63	MS65
1993	—	PF65 9,250				

KM# 917 500 PESOS
155.52 g., 0.999 Gold 4.9951 oz. AGW **Obv:** National Arms **Rev:** Castro bust left in military uniform

Date	Mintage	VF20	XF40	MS60	MS63	MS65
1993	Est. 20	PF65 9,000				

KM# 720 500 PESOS
49.00 g., 0.999 Gold with Silver 1.5738 oz. **Subject:** Che Guevara

Date	Mintage	VF20	XF40	MS60	MS63	MS65
2000	101	PF65 2,500				

KM# 950 500 PESOS
Gold and Silver 49g .999 Gold and 25g .999 Silver, 50 mm. **Rev:** Ernesto "Che" Guevara de la Serna

Date	Mintage	VF20	XF40	MS60	MS63	MS65
2000	Est. 101	PF65 3,000				

PESO CONVERTIBLE SERIES

KM# 729 CENTAVO
1.70 g., Copper Plated Steel, 15 mm. **Obv:** National arms within wreath, denomination below **Rev:** Tower and denomination **Edge:** Reeded

Date	Mintage	VF20	XF40	MS60	MS63	MS65
2000	—	—	—	1.25	2.50	4.00

KM# 733 CENTAVO
0.75 g., Aluminum, 16.75 mm. **Obv:** Cuban arms **Rev:** Tower and denomination **Edge:** Plain

Date	Mintage	VF20	XF40	MS60	MS63	MS65
2000	—	—	—	1.00	2.00	3.50

KM# 575.1 5 CENTAVOS
2.65 g., Nickel Plated Steel, 18 mm. **Obv:** National arms within wreath, denomination and date below **Rev:** Casa Colonial, denomination above **Note:** Medal alignment

Date	Mintage	VF20	XF40	MS60	MS63	MS65
1994	—	—	—	0.50	1.00	1.50

KM# 575.2 5 CENTAVOS
2.65 g., Nickel Plated Steel, 18 mm. **Obv:** National arms **Rev:** Casa Colonial **Note:** Coin alignment, recut designs.

Date	Mintage	VF20	XF40	MS60	MS63	MS65
1996	—	—	—	0.50	1.00	1.50
1998	—	—	—	0.50	1.00	1.50
1999	—	—	—	0.50	1.00	1.50
2000	—	—	—	0.50	1.00	1.50

KM# 576.1 10 CENTAVOS
4.00 g., Nickel Bonded Steel, 20 mm. **Obv:** National arms within wreath, denomination and date below **Rev:** Castillo de la Fuerza, denomination above **Note:** Medal alignment.

Date	Mintage	VF20	XF40	MS60	MS63	MS65
1994	—	—	—	1.00	2.00	3.50

KM# 576.2 10 CENTAVOS

4.00 g., Nickel Plated Steel, 20 mm. **Obv:** National arms **Rev:** Castillo de la Fuerza **Note:** Coin alignment, recut designs.

Date	Mintage	VF20	XF40	MS60	MS63	MS65
1996	—	—	—	1.00	2.00	3.50
1999	—	—	—	1.00	2.00	3.50
2000	—	—	—	1.00	2.00	3.50

KM# 577.1 25 CENTAVOS

5.65 g., Nickel Bonded Steel, 23 mm. **Obv:** National arms within wreath, denomination and date below **Rev:** Trinidad, denomination upper right **Note:** Medal alignment. Prev. KM#577.

Date	Mintage	VF20	XF40	MS60	MS63	MS65
1994	—	—	—	1.25	2.50	4.00

KM# 577.2 25 CENTAVOS

5.65 g., Nickel Plated Steel, 23 mm. **Obv:** National arms **Rev:** Trinidad **Note:** Coin alignment.

Date	Mintage	VF20	XF40	MS60	MS63	MS65
1998	—	—	—	1.25	2.50	4.00
2000	—	—	—	1.25	2.50	4.00

KM# 578.1 50 CENTAVOS

7.53 g., Nickel Plated Steel, 25 mm. **Obv:** National arms within wreath, denomination and date below **Rev:** Cathedral of Havana, denomination above **Note:** Medal alignment.

Date	Mintage	VF20	XF40	MS60	MS63	MS65
1994	—	—	—	2.25	4.50	6.00

KM# 579.1 PESO

8.50 g., Nickel Plated Steel, 27 mm. **Obv:** National arms within wreath, denomination and date below **Rev:** Guama, denomination upper left **Note:** Medal alignment.

Date	Mintage	VF20	XF40	MS60	MS63	MS65
1994	—	—	—	2.25	4.50	6.00

KM# 579.2 PESO

8.50 g., Nickel Plated Steel, 27 mm. **Obv:** National arms **Rev:** Guama **Edge:** Reeded **Note:** Coin alignment.

Date	Mintage	VF20	XF40	MS60	MS63	MS65
1998	—	—	—	1.75	3.50	5.00
2000	—	—	—	1.75	3.50	5.00

KM# 730 5 PESOS

4.50 g., Bi-Metallic Nickel Plated Steel center in Brass Plated Steel ring, 23 mm. **Obv:** National arms within wreath, denomination below **Rev:** Bust right, denomination at right, within circle **Edge:** Reeded **Note:** Medal alignment.

Date	Mintage	VF20	XF40	MS60	MS63	MS65
1999	—	—	—	7.50	12.00	15.00

VISITOR'S COINAGE

KM# 409 CENTAVO

Copper-Nickel **Obv:** Stag, date below **Rev:** Palm tree within logo and denomination

Date	Mintage	VF20	XF40	MS60	MS63	MS65
1988	—	0.35	0.75	1.50	3.00	—

KM# 410 CENTAVO

Aluminum **Obv:** Palm tree within logo **Rev:** Denomination

Date	Mintage	VF20	XF40	MS60	MS63	MS65
1988	—	0.35	0.75	1.50	5.00	—

KM# 411 5 CENTAVOS

3.50 g., Copper-Nickel, 19.9 mm. **Obv:** Mollusk and date **Rev:** Palm tree within logo, denomination

Date	Mintage	VF20	XF40	MS60	MS63	MS65
1981	—	0.50	1.00	2.00	4.00	—

KM# 412.1 5 CENTAVOS

Copper-Nickel **Obv:** Mollusk and date **Rev:** Palm tree within logo, denomination

Date	Mintage	VF20	XF40	MS60	MS63	MS65
1981	—	0.50	1.00	2.00	4.00	—

KM# 412.2 5 CENTAVOS

3.40 g., Copper-Nickel, 20 mm. **Obv:** Mollusk and date **Rev:** Palm tree within logo, denomination

Date	Mintage	VF20	XF40	MS60	MS63	MS65
1981	—	0.50	1.00	2.00	4.00	—

KM# 412.3 5 CENTAVOS

3.50 g., Copper-Nickel, 20 mm. **Obv:** Mollusk and date **Rev:** Palm tree within logo, small 5

Date	Mintage	VF20	XF40	MS60	MS63	MS65
1989	—	0.35	0.75	1.50	3.00	—

KM# 413 5 CENTAVOS

1.00 g., Aluminum, 20 mm. **Obv:** Palm tree within logo, date below **Rev:** Denomination

Date	Mintage	VF20	XF40	MS60	MS63	MS65
1988	—	0.75	1.50	3.00	5.00	—

KM# 412.3a 5 CENTAVOS

Stainless Steel **Obv:** Palm tree within logo, denomination **Rev:** Mollusk and date

Date	Mintage	VF20	XF40	MS60	MS63	MS65
1989	—	0.75	1.50	3.00	6.00	—

KM# 414 10 CENTAVOS

Copper-Nickel **Obv:** Hummingbird in flight right, date below **Rev:** Palm tree within logo, denomination

Date	Mintage	VF20	XF40	MS60	MS63	MS65
1981	—	0.50	1.00	2.00	4.00	5.00

KM# 415.1 10 CENTAVOS

Copper-Nickel **Obv:** Hummingbird in flight right, date below **Rev:** Palm tree within logo, large "10"

Date	Mintage	VF20	XF40	MS60	MS63	MS65
1981	—	0.75	1.50	3.00	5.00	7.00

KM# 415.2 10 CENTAVOS

Copper-Nickel **Obv:** Hummingbird in flight right, date below **Rev:** Palm tree within logo, small "10"

Date	Mintage	VF20	XF40	MS60	MS63	MS65
1981	—	0.50	1.00	2.00	4.00	15.00

KM# 416 10 CENTAVOS

Aluminum **Obv:** Palm tree within logo, date below **Rev:** Denomination

Date	Mintage	VF20	XF40	MS60	MS63	MS65
1988	—	0.50	1.00	2.00	4.00	—

KM# 415.2a 10 CENTAVOS

3.95 g., Stainless Steel, 21.4 mm. **Obv:** Hummingbird in flight right **Rev:** Palm tree within logo, small "10"

Date	Mintage	VF20	XF40	MS60	MS63	MS65
1989	—	1.00	2.00	4.00	9.00	18.00

KM# 415.3 10 CENTAVOS

Copper-Nickel **Obv:** Hummingbird in flight right **Rev:** Palm tree within logo, denomination **Note:** Reduced size.

Date	Mintage	VF20	XF40	MS60	MS63	MS65
1989	—	1.25	2.50	5.00	10.00	—

KM# 417 25 CENTAVOS

6.32 g., Copper-Nickel **Obv:** Flower, date below **Rev:** Palm tree within logo, denomination

Date	Mintage	VF20	XF40	MS60	MS63	MS65
1981	—	0.65	1.25	2.50	6.00	—

KM# 418.1 25 CENTAVOS

6.44 g., Copper-Nickel, 24.4 mm. **Obv:** Flower, date below **Rev:** Palm tree within logo, large 25

Date	Mintage	VF20	XF40	MS60	MS63	MS65
1981	—	0.75	1.50	3.00	7.00	—

KM# 418.2 25 CENTAVOS

Copper-Nickel **Obv:** Flower, date below **Rev:** Palm tree within logo, small 25

Date	Mintage	VF20	XF40	MS60	MS63	MS65
1989	—	0.75	1.50	3.00	7.00	—

KM# 418.2a 25 CENTAVOS

6.20 g., Stainless Steel, 23.8 mm. **Obv:** Flower and date **Rev:** Palm tree within logo, denomination

Date	Mintage	VF20	XF40	MS60	MS63	MS65
1989	—	1.50	3.00	6.00	12.00	—

KM# 419 25 CENTAVOS

Aluminum **Obv:** Palm tree within logo, date below **Rev:** Denomination

Date	Mintage	VF20	XF40	MS60	MS63	MS65
1988	—	0.65	1.25	2.50	5.00	—

KM# 420 50 CENTAVOS

Copper-Nickel **Obv:** Palm tree within logo, date below **Rev:** Denomination and logo

Date	Mintage	VF20	XF40	MS60	MS63	MS65
1981	—	2.00	4.00	7.50	15.00	—

Note: Varieties exist in the number of lines below the palm tree.

KM# 461 50 CENTAVOS

Copper-Nickel **Obv:** Palm tree within logo, denomination **Rev:** Denomination and logo

Date	Mintage	VF20	XF40	MS60	MS63	MS65
1989	—	2.50	5.00	10.00	18.00	—

KM# 421 PESO

Copper-Nickel **Obv:** Lighthouse **Rev:** Palm tree within logo, denomination

Date	Mintage	VF20	XF40	MS60	MS63	MS65
1981	—	3.50	7.00	12.50	22.00	—

KM# 580 PESO

Copper-Nickel **Obv:** Lighthouse **Rev:** Palm tree within logo, denomination

Date	Mintage	VF20	XF40	MS60	MS63	MS65
1989	—	3.50	7.00	12.50	22.00	—

TRIAL STRIKES

KM#	Date	Mintage	Identification	Mkt Val
TS1	1977	—	20 Pesos. Brass. Antonio Maceo, KM40. Prev. KM#TS5.	300
TS2	1977	—	20 Pesos. Brass. Maximo Gomez, KM39. Prev. KM#TS6.	300
TS3	1977	—	20 Pesos. Brass. Ignacio Aramonte, KM38. Prev. KM#TS7.	300
TS4	1977	—	20 Pesos. Copper-Nickel. Antonio Maceo, KM40. Prev. KM#TS8.	500
TS5	1977	—	100 Pesos. Brass. de Cespedes, KM43. Prev. KM#TS9.	300
TS6	1994	10	100 Pesos. Gold. Reverse of KM467, uniface. Prev. KM#TS2.	2,200
TS7	1994	1	50 Pesos. Silver. KM503; dolphins green and red. Prev. KM#TS3.	—
TS8	1994	1	50 Pesos. Silver. KM503, dolphins green and red.	—

PATTERNS

Including off metal strikes

KM#	Date	Mintage	Identification	Mkt Val
PnA10	1915	—	Centavo. Bronze.	—
PnC10	1915	—	2 Centavos. Bronze.	2,000
PnA11	1970	—	Peso. 0.999. Silver. KM158.	500
PnB11	1970	—	Peso. 0.999. Silver. KM158.	500
PnC11	1986	—	5 Pesos. 0.900. Copper. KM326.	—
PnD11	1986	—	5 Pesos. 0.050. Silver. KM326.	—
PnE11	1986	—	5 Pesos. 0.050. Gold. KM326.	—
PnF11	1987	—	5 Pesos. Copper. KM166.	—
PnG11	1987	—	5 Pesos. Copper. .900 Copper, .050 Silver, .050 Gold, KM#26.	—
Pn11	1987	3	5 Pesos. 0.999. Gold. KM159.	6,500
PnA12	1988	6	5 Pesos. 0.999. Silver.	1,150
Pn12	1988	6	5 Pesos. Silver.	1,150
PnA13	1988	6	100 Pesos. 0.999. Gold.	5,500
PnB13	1988	—	100 Pesos. 0.999. Gold.	5,500
Pn13	1988	6	100 Pesos. Gold.	—
Pn14	1993	34	10 Pesos. Silver. Mirror bust with frosted field. KM398.	600
Pn15	1994	25	10 Pesos. Silver. KM510, player's #9 on the back is matte.	600
Pn16	1995	22	10 Pesos. Silver. Key mint mark in proof.	800
Pn17	1995	100	Peso. Copper-Nickel. Pirates del Carib, Sir Francis Drake, proof.	120
Pn106	1999	—	Peso. Copper-Nickel. KM662.	100
Pn107	1999	—	10 Pesos. Silver. KM672.	200
Pn108	1999	—	100 Pesos. Gold. KM710.	1,500
Pn109	2000	—	Peso. Copper-Nickel. KM665.	—
Pn110	2000	—	Peso. Copper-Nickel. KM664.	100
Pn111	2000	—	Peso. Copper-Nickel. KM663.	100
Pn112	2000	—	10 Pesos. Silver. KM685.	200
Pn113	2000	—	10 Pesos. Silver. KM681.	200
Pn114	2000	—	10 Pesos. Silver. KM678.	200
Pn115	2000	—	10 Pesos. Silver. KM678.	200
Pn116	2000	—	10 Pesos. Silver. KM680.	200
Pn118	2000	—	10 Pesos. Silver. KM691.	200
Pn119	2000	—	10 Pesos. Silver. KM689.	200
Pn120	2000	—	10 Pesos. Silver. KM688.	200
Pn121	2000	—	10 Pesos. Silver. KM687.	200
Pn122	2000	—	10 Pesos. Silver. KM686.	200
Pn123	2000	—	10 Pesos. Silver. KM690.	200
Pn124	2000	—	10 Pesos. Silver. Ship Rays 1749-1805.	200
Pn125	2000	—	10 Pesos. Silver. Ship: Sand Pedro de Alcantara.	200
Pn126	2000	—	10 Pesos. Silver. Ship: Santisma Trinidad.	200
Pn127	2000	—	10 Pesos. Silver. KM684.	200
Pn128	2000	—	10 Pesos. Silver. KM683.	200
Pn129	2000	—	100 Pesos. Gold. KM712.	1,500
Pn130	2000	—	100 Pesos. Gold. KM711.	1,500
Pn131	2000	—	100 Pesos. Gold. KM713.	1,500
Pn132	2000	—	100 Pesos. Gold. KM718.	1,500
Pn133	2000	—	100 Pesos. Gold. KM717.	1,250
Pn134	2000	—	100 Pesos. Gold. KM714.	1,500
Pn135	2000	—	100 Pesos. Gold. KM715.	1,500
Pn136	2000	—	100 Pesos. Gold. KM716.	1,500

PIEDFORT

KM#	Date	Mintage	Identification	Mkt Val
P3	1983	100	5 Pesos. Silver. KM10.	200
P4	1988	30	10 Pesos. Gold. KM211.	1,200
P5	1988	30	10 Pesos. Gold. KM211.	1,200
P6	1988	15	15 Pesos. Gold. KM212.	1,200
P7	1988	15	15 Pesos. Gold. KM212.	1,200
P8	1988	10	25 Pesos. Gold. KM213.	1,600
P9	1988	10	25 Pesos. Gold. KM213.	1,600
P10	1988	10	50 Pesos. Gold. KM214.	1,600
P11	1988	10	50 Pesos. Gold. KM214.	1,600
P12	1988	10	100 Pesos. Gold. KM215.	2,200
P13	1988	10	100 Pesos. Gold. KM215.	2,200
P14	1989	30	10 Pesos. Gold. KM211.	1,200
P15	1989	30	10 Pesos. Gold. KM211.	1,200
P16	1989	150	10 Pesos. Silver. KM239.	200
P17	1989	150	10 Pesos. Silver. KM240.	200
P18	1989	15	15 Pesos. Gold. KM212.	1,200
P19	1989	15	15 Pesos. Gold. KM212.	1,200
P20	1989	10	25 Pesos. Gold. KM213.	1,600
P21	1989	15	25 Pesos. Gold. KM213.	1,600
P22	1989	10	50 Pesos. Gold. KM214.	2,200
P23	1989	15	50 Pesos. Gold. KM214.	2,200
P24	1989	12	50 Pesos. Gold. KM313.	1,800
P25	1989	12	50 Pesos. Gold. KM314.	1,800
P26	1989	12	50 Pesos. Gold. KM315.	1,800
P27	1989	15	100 Pesos. Silver. KM215.	—
P28	1989	10	100 Pesos. Gold. KM215.	2,200
P29	1989	15	100 Pesos. Gold. KM215.	2,200
P30	1989	12	100 Pesos. Gold. KM316.	1,800
P31	1989	12	100 Pesos. Gold. KM317.	1,800
P32	1989	12	100 Pesos. Gold. KM318.	1,800
P33	1989	12	100 Pesos. Gold. KM319.	2,200
P34	1989	12	100 Pesos. Gold. KM320.	2,200
P35	1990	50	10 Pesos. Silver. Ship and Cub; KM252.	400
P36	1990	15	10 Pesos. Silver. KM280.	900
P37	1990	100	10 Pesos. Silver. KM291.	250
P38	1990	100	10 Pesos. Silver. KM292.	160
P39	1990	100	10 Pesos. Silver. KM293.	160
P40	1990	12	10 Pesos. Gold. KM211.	1,200
P41	1990	12	10 Pesos. Gold. KM211.	1,200
P42	1990	12	15 Pesos. Gold. KM212.	1,200
P43	1990	12	15 Pesos. Gold. KM212.	1,200
P44	1990	12	25 Pesos. Gold. KM213.	—
P45	1990	12	25 Pesos. Gold. KM213.	—
P46	1990	12	50 Pesos. Gold. KM214.	2,200
P47	1990	12	50 Pesos. Gold. KM214.	2,200
P48	1990	12	50 Pesos. Gold. KM321.	2,200
P49	1990	12	50 Pesos. Gold. KM322.	2,200
P50	1990	12	50 Pesos. Gold. KM323.	2,200
P51	1990	12	100 Pesos. Gold. KM215.	2,200
P52	1990	15	100 Pesos. Gold. KM215.	2,200
P53	1992	50	10 Pesos. Silver. KM341.	150
P54	1993	150	5 Pesos. Silver. KM405.	200
P55	1993	—	10 Pesos. Silver. KM406.	250
P56	1993	15	200 Pesos. Gold. KM542.	2,200
P58	1993	—	100 Pesos. Gold. Similar to 200 Pesos; KM542.	—
P57	1994	10	100 Pesos. Gold. KM545.	1,850

P65	1999 (1995)	—	10 Pesos. Silver. KM672.	200
P66	2000	—	10 Pesos. Silver. KM684.	200
P67	2000	—	10 Pesos. Silver. KM685.	200
P68	2000	—	10 Pesos. Silver. KM683.	200

MINT SETS

KM#	Date	Mintage	Identification	Issue Price	Mkt Val
MS1	1953 (4)	—	KM#26-29	—	250
MS2	1994 (5)	—	KM#575.1-576.1, 577-579	—	35.00

PROOF SETS

KM#	Date	Mintage	Identification	Issue Price	Mkt Val
PS1	1915 (7)	20	KM#9-15	—	10,800
PS2	1915 (6)	24	KM#16-21; Rare	—	—
PS3	1916 (7)	20	KM#9-15	—	17,000
PS4	1916 (6)	—	KM#16-21; Rare	—	—
PS5	1953 (4)	—	KM#26-29; Rare	—	—
PS6	1975 (2)	—	KM#36, 37	—	60.00
PSA7	1977 (3)	—	KM#38-40	—	110
PS7	1977 (4)	—	KM#38-40, 43	290	850
PS8	1979 (2)	—	KM#44, 45	240	810
PS9	1988 (5)	15	KM#211-215	—	3,800
PS10	1998 (4)	—	KM#668-671	—	260
PS11	1999 (4)	—	KM#671, 673, 692, 704, 719	—	1,500

CURAÇAO

The island of Curacao, the largest of the six islands that comprise the Netherlands Antilles, which is an autonomous part of the Kingdom of the Netherlands located in the Caribbean Sea 40 miles off the coast of Venezuela, has an area of 173 sq. mi. (472 sq. km.) and a population of 145,000. Capital: Willemstad. The chief industries are banking and tourism. Salt, phosphates and cattle are exported. Formerly a part of the Netherlands Antilles, achieved on Oct. 10, 2011 a special status, as the fourth state under the Dutch crown.

Curacao was discovered by Spanish navigator Alonsode Ojeda in 1499 and was settled by Spain in 1527. The Dutch West India Company took the island from Spain in 1634 and administered it until 1787, when it was surrendered to the United Netherlands. The Dutch held it thereafter except for two periods during the Napoleonic Wars, 1800-1803 and 1807-16, when it was occupied by the British. During World War II, Curacao refined 60 percent of the oil used by the Allies; the refineries were protected by U.S. troops after Germany invaded the Netherlands in1940.

During the second occupation of the Napoleonic period, the British created an emergency coinage for Curacao by cutting the Spanish dollar into 5 equal segments and countermarking each piece with a rosette indent.

DUTCH ADMINISTRATION

1941-1945

MINT MARKS

D - Denver
P - Philadelphia
(u) - Utrecht

KINGDOM OF NETHERLANDS

MODERN COINAGE

100 Cents = 1 Gulden

KM# 39b CENT

Brass, 19 mm. **Obv:** Rampant lion left within circle, date below **Rev:** Denomination within wreath **Edge:** Reeded

Date	Mintage	F12	VF20	XF40	MS60	MS63
1942 P	—	40.00	75.00	150	300	500

KM# 39a CENT

2.50 g., Bronze, 19 mm. **Obv:** Rampant lion left within circle, date below **Rev:** Denomination within wreath **Edge:** Reeded

Date	Mintage	F12	VF20	XF40	MS60	MS63
1942 P	2,500,000	1.25	2.50	5.00	10.00	25.00

Note: This coin was also circulated in Suriname. For similar coins dated 1943P & 1957-1960, see Suriname.

KM# 41 CENT

2.50 g., Bronze, 19 mm. **Obv:** Rampant lion left within circle, date below **Rev:** Denomination within wreath **Edge:** Reeded

Date	Mintage	F12	VF20	XF40	MS60	MS63
1944 D D between 4 and O	3,000,000	—	0.50	1.50	5.00	10.00
1944 D D nearer to O	Inc. above	—	1.00	3.00	8.00	15.00
1947 (u)	1,500,000	2.00	3.25	7.00	15.00	30.00
1947 (u)	80	PF63 80.00				

KM# 42 2-1/2 CENTS

4.00 g., Bronze, 23.4 mm. **Obv:** Rampant lion left within circle, date below **Rev:** Denomination within wreath **Edge:** Reeded

Date	Mintage	F12	VF20	XF40	MS60	MS63
1944 D	1,000,000	1.00	2.00	5.00	42.00	20.00
1947 (u)	500,000	1.25	3.00	6.50	15.00	25.00
1947 (u)	80	PF63 80.00				
1948 (u)	1,000,000	1.00	2.00	5.00	12.00	20.00
1948 (u)	75	PF63 80.00				

KM# 40 5 CENTS

4.50 g., Copper-Nickel, 18 mm.

Date	Mintage	F12	VF20	XF40	MS60	MS63
1943	8,595,000	1.25	2.50	6.00	12.00	20.00

Note: The above piece does not bear either a palm tree privy mark or a mint mark, but it was struck expressly for use in Curacao and Surinam. This homeland type of KM#153 was last issued in the Netherlands in 1940. A slightly lighter weight version, at 4.35g, with 65% Copper, 12% Nickel and 23% Zinc was struck with a mintage of 585,000, likely a portion of the mintage total shown above.

KM# 47 5 CENTS

4.48 g., Copper-Nickel, 18 mm. **Obv:** Flower within inner circle **Rev:** Denomination within circle divides date at sides, shells at corners **Shape:** 4-sided

Date	Mintage	F12	VF20	XF40	MS60	MS63
1948 (u)	1,000,000	1.25	2.50	6.00	12.00	20.00
1948 (u)	75	PF63 80.00				

KM# 37 10 CENTS

1.40 g., 0.640 Silver 0.0288 oz. ASW, 15 mm. **Obv:** Head left **Rev:** Denomination and date within wreath **Edge:** Reeded

Date	Mintage	F12	VF20	XF40	MS60	MS63
1941 P	800,000	4.00	9.00	18.00	36.00	50.00
1942 P	1,500,100	3.00	7.00	16.00	32.00	45.00

Note: Both these coins were also circulated in Surinam. For coins dated 1942P, see also Surinam.

Date	Mintage	F12	VF20	XF40	MS60	MS63
1943 P	4,500,000	2.50	6.00	15.00	30.00	40.00

Note: 500,000 struck for circulation in Curacao, bulk of mintage for circulation in Surinam

KM# 38 25 CENTS

3.58 g., 0.640 Silver 0.0737 oz. ASW, 18.5 mm. **Obv:** Head left **Rev:** Denomination above date within wreath **Edge:** Reeded

Date	Mintage	F12	VF20	XF40	MS60	MS63
1941 P	1,100,000	3.50	6.50	12.50	25.00	35.00
1943/1 P	2,500,000	25.00	40.00	100	200	300

Note: Determined to be a die crack, not an overdate

Date	Mintage	F12	VF20	XF40	MS60	MS63
1943 P	Inc. above	2.50	4.50	7.50	15.00	25.00

Note: Both coins were also circulated in Surinam. For similar coins dated 1943, 1944 & 1945-P with acorn mint mark, see Netherlands.

KM# 36 1/10 GULDEN

1.40 g., 0.640 Silver 0.0288 oz. ASW **Obv:** Head left **Rev:** Crowned arms divide denomination, date below **Edge:** Reeded

Date	Mintage	F12	VF20	XF40	MS60	MS63
1901	300,000	10.00	20.00	45.00	100	180
1901	40	PF65 1,000				

KM# 43 1/10 GULDEN

1.30 g., 0.640 Silver 0.0267 oz. ASW, 15 mm. **Obv:** Head left **Rev:** Denomination, date below **Edge:** Reeded

Date	Mintage	F12	VF20	XF40	MS60	MS63
1944 D	1,500,000	0.85	1.75	3.50	10.00	16.00
1947 (u)	1,000,000	1.50	3.50	7.50	12.50	25.00
1947 (u)	80	PF63 90.00				

KM# 48 1/10 GULDEN

1.40 g., 0.640 Silver 0.0288 oz. ASW, 15 mm. **Obv:** Head left **Rev:** Denomination, date below **Edge:** Reeded

Date	Mintage	F12	VF20	XF40	MS60	MS63
1948 (u)	1,000,000	1.25	3.50	7.50	12.50	20.00
1948 (u)	75	PF63 100				

KM# 44 1/4 GULDEN

3.58 g., 0.640 Silver 0.0737 oz. ASW, 18.8 mm. **Obv:** Head left **Rev:** Denomination, date below **Edge:** Reeded

Date	Mintage	F12	VF20	XF40	MS60	MS63
1944 D D further from edge	1,500,000	2.50	3.75	7.50	12.50	20.00
1944 D D nearer to edge	Inc. above	2.50	3.75	7.50	12.50	20.00
1947 (u)	1,000,000	2.50	3.50	7.50	12.00	18.00
1947 (u)	80	PF63 80.00				

KM# 45 GULDEN

10.00 g., 0.720 Silver 0.2315 oz. ASW, 28 mm. **Obv:** Head left **Rev:** Crowned shield **Edge Lettering:** GOD * ZIJ * MET * ONS *

Date	Mintage	F12	VF20	XF40	MS60	MS63
1944 D	500,000	8.00	15.00	45.00	65.00	100

Note: Four variations in position of palmtree and D mint-mark are known

KM# 46 2-1/2 GULDEN
25.00 g., 0.720 Silver 0.5787 oz. ASW, 38 mm. **Obv:** Head left **Rev:** Crowned arms divide denomination, date below **Edge Lettering:** GOD * ZIJ * MET * ONS *

Date	Mintage	F12	VF20	XF40	MS60	MS63
1944 D	200,000	—	10.50	20.00	25.00	30.00

Note: 60,000 coins melted down after minting.

PATTERNS

Including off metal strikes

KM#	Date	Mintage	Identification	Mkt Val
Pn3	1944	—	1/4 Gulden. Nickel. Head left. Denomination, date below. Reeded.	3,300
Pn4	1944	—	1/10 Gulden. Nickel. Head left. Denomination, date below. Reeded. Mint sign: Palm Tree No "D".	3,300
Pn5	1947	—	1/4 Gulden. Nickel. Head left. Denomination, date below. Reeded.	2,000

PROOF SETS

KM#	Date	Mintage	Identification	Issue Price	Mkt Val
PS1	1901 (2)	40	KM36(1901), KM35(1900)	—	2,000
PS2	1947 (4)	80	KM41-44	—	400
PS3	1948 (3)	75	KM42, 47-48	—	250

The island of Cyprus lies in the eastern Mediterranean Sea 44 miles (71 km.) south of Turkey and 60 miles (97 km.) off the Syrian coast. It is the third largest island in the Mediterranean Sea, having an area of 3,572 sq. mi. (9,251 sq. km.) and a population of 736,636. Capital: Nicosia. Agriculture, light manufacturing and tourism are the chief industries. Citrus fruit, potatoes, footwear and clothing are exported

The importance of Cyprus dates from the Bronze Age when it was desired as a principal source of copper (from which the island derived its name) and as a strategic trading center. It was during this period that large numbers of Greeks settled on the island and gave it the predominantly Greek character. Its role as an international marketplace made it a prime disseminator of the then prevalent cultures, a role that still influences the civilization of Western man. Because of its fortuitous position and influential role, Cyprus was conquered by a succession of empires: the Assyrian, Egyptian, Persian, Macedonian, Ptolemaic, Roman and Byzantine. It was taken from Isaac Comnenus by Richard the Lion-Heart in 1191, sold to the Templar Knights and for the following 7 centuries was ruled by the Franks, the Venetians and the Ottomans. During the Ottoman period Cyprus acquired its Turkish community (18 percent of its population). In 1878 the island fell into British hands and was made a crown colony of Britain in 1925. Finally, on Aug. 16, 1960, it became an independent republic.

In 1964, the ethnic Turks withdrew from active participation in the government. Turkish forces invaded Cyprus in 1974, gained control of 40 percent of the island and forcibly separated the Greek and Turkish communities. In 1983, Turkish Cypriots proclaimed their own state in northern Cyprus, which remains without international recognition.

Cyprus is a member of the Commonwealth of Nations. The president is Chief of State and Head of Government. Cyprus is also a member of the European Union.

RULER
British, until 1960

MINT MARKS
no mint mark - Royal Mint, London, England
H - Birmingham, England

MONETARY SYSTEM
9 Piastres = 1 Shilling
20 Shillings = 1 Pound

BRITISH COLONY

PIASTRE COINAGE

KM# 1.2 1/4 PIASTRE
Bronze, 21 mm. **Obv:** Crowned head left **Rev:** Denomination within circle

Date	Mintage	F12	VF20	XF40	MS60	MS63
1901	72,000	20.00	50.00	150	400	—

KM# 8 1/4 PIASTRE
Bronze **Obv:** Crowned bust right **Rev:** Denomination within circle, date below **Shape:** 12-sided

Date	Mintage	F12	VF20	XF40	MS60	MS63
1902	72,000	40.00	50.00	120	350	850
1905	422,000	10.00	30.00	85.00	250	500
1908	36,000	50.00	150	275	600	—

KM# 16 1/4 PIASTRE
Bronze **Obv:** Crowned bust left **Rev:** Denomination within circle, date below

Date	Mintage	F12	VF20	XF40	MS60	MS63
1922	72,000	40.00	75.00	150	300	—
1926	360,000	8.00	16.00	35.00	125	375
1926	—	PF60 850	PF63 2,250	PF65 4,750		

KM# 11 1/2 PIASTRE
Bronze **Obv:** Crowned bust right **Rev:** Denomination within circle, date at right

Date	Mintage	F12	VF20	XF40	MS60	MS63
1908	36,000	80.00	200	500	900	—

KM# 17 1/2 PIASTRE
Bronze **Obv:** Crowned bust left **Rev:** Denomination within circle, date at right

Date	Mintage	F12	VF20	XF40	MS60	MS63
1922	36,000	60.00	100	250	500	—
1927	108,000	10.00	30.00	60.00	150	—
1927	—	PF60 600	PF63 700	PF65 950		
1930	180,000	10.00	30.00	60.00	200	—
1930	—	PF60 600	PF63 700	PF65 950		
1931	90,000	25.00	40.00	100	200	—
1931	—	PF60 600	PF63 700	PF65 950		

KM# 20 1/2 PIASTRE
2.50 g., Copper-Nickel, 19.4 mm. **Obv:** Crowned bust left **Rev:** Denomination, date at right **Shape:** Scalloped

Date	Mintage	F12	VF20	XF40	MS60	MS63
1934	1,440,000	1.00	3.00	7.50	25.00	80.00
1934	—	PF60 550	PF63 600			

KM# 22 1/2 PIASTRE
2.50 g., Copper-Nickel, 19.4 mm. **Obv:** Crowned head left **Rev:** Denomination, date at right **Shape:** Scalloped

Date	Mintage	F12	VF20	XF40	MS60	MS63
1938	1,080,000	0.35	2.00	5.00	20.00	35.00
1938	—	PF60 500	PF63 550			

KM# 22a 1/2 PIASTRE
2.50 g., Bronze, 19.4 mm. **Obv:** Crowned head left **Rev:** Denomination, date at right **Shape:** Scalloped

Date	Mintage	F12	VF20	XF40	MS60	MS63
1942	1,080,000	2.00	4.00	10.00	50.00	—

Note: A large portion of the mintage was destroyed during WWII

Date	Mintage	F12	VF20	XF40	MS60	MS63
1942	—	PF60 600	PF63 650			
1943	1,620,000	0.25	1.00	2.50	25.00	35.00
1944	2,160,000	0.25	1.00	2.50	12.50	20.00
1945	1,080,000	0.25	1.00	2.50	25.00	35.00
1945	—	PF60 400	PF63 450			

KM# 29 1/2 PIASTRE
2.50 g., Bronze, 19.4 mm. **Obv:** Crowned head left **Rev:** Denomination, date at right **Shape:** Scalloped

Date	Mintage	F12	VF20	XF40	MS60	MS63
1949	1,080,000	0.25	0.50	1.50	7.50	45.00
1949	—	PF60 350	PF63 400			

KM# 12 PIASTRE
Bronze **Obv:** Crowned bust right **Rev:** Denomination within circle, date at right

Date	Mintage	F12	VF20	XF40	MS60	MS63
1908	27,000	100	250	550	1,650	3,500

KM# 18 PIASTRE
Bronze **Obv:** Crowned bust left **Rev:** Denomination within circle, date at right

Date	Mintage	F12	VF20	XF40	MS60	MS63
1922	54,000	30.00	100	250	500	—
1927	127,000	10.00	30.00	100	200	450
1927	—	PF60 700	PF63 2,500			
1930	96,000	10.00	25.00	100	200	450
1930	—	PF60 700	PF63 2,500	PF65 14,000		
1931	45,000	50.00	150	300	600	—
1931	—	PF60 850	PF63 3,500			

KM# 21 PIASTRE
Copper-Nickel **Obv:** Crowned bust left **Rev:** Denomination, date at right **Shape:** Scalloped

Date	Mintage	F12	VF20	XF40	MS60	MS63
1934	1,440,000	1.50	3.50	10.00	45.00	150
1934	—	PF60 550	PF63 600			

KM# 23 PIASTRE
Copper-Nickel **Obv:** Crowned head left **Rev:** Denomination, date at right **Shape:** Scalloped

Date	Mintage	F12	VF20	XF40	MS60	MS63
1938	2,700,000	0.60	1.50	3.00	12.50	35.00
1938	—	PF60 400	PF63 450			

KM# 23a PIASTRE
5.22 g., Bronze **Obv:** Crowned head left **Rev:** Denomination, date at right

Date	Mintage	F12	VF20	XF40	MS60	MS63
1942	1,260,000	1.00	2.00	5.00	20.00	35.00
1942	—	PF60 250	PF63 300			
1943	2,520,000	0.50	1.00	2.50	15.00	25.00
1944	3,240,000	0.50	1.00	2.50	10.00	25.00
1945	1,080,000	0.60	1.50	3.00	20.00	35.00
1945	—	PF60 250	PF63 300			
1946	1,080,000	0.60	1.50	3.00	20.00	35.00
1946	—	PF60 275	PF63 350			

KM# 30 PIASTRE
Bronze **Obv:** Crowned head left **Obv. Legend:** ... DEI GRATIA REX **Rev:** Denomination, date at right **Shape:** Scalloped

Date	Mintage	F12	VF20	XF40	MS60	MS63
1949	1,080,000	0.25	0.75	1.50	4.50	12.00
1949	—	PF60 225	PF63 275			

KM# 4 3 PIASTRES
1.89 g., 0.925 Silver 0.0561 oz. ASW **Obv:** Crowned and veiled bust left **Rev:** Crown over denomination divides date, circle surrounds

Date	Mintage	F12	VF20	XF40	MS60	MS63
1901	300,000	30.00	70.00	180	500	900
1901	—	PF60 850	PF63 1,750			

KM# 5 4-1/2 PIASTRES
2.83 g., 0.925 Silver 0.0841 oz. ASW, 19 mm. **Obv:** Crowned and veiled bust left **Rev:** Crowned arms divide date, denomination below

Date	Mintage	F12	VF20	XF40	MS60	MS63
1901	400,000	12.00	25.00	70.00	180	—
1901	—	PF60 950				

KM# 15 4-1/2 PIASTRES
2.83 g., 0.925 Silver 0.0841 oz. ASW, 19 mm. **Obv:** Crowned bust left **Rev:** Crowned arms divide date, denomination below

Date	Mintage	F12	VF20	XF40	MS60	MS63
1921	600,000	6.00	12.00	60.00	120	—

KM# 24 4-1/2 PIASTRES
2.83 g., 0.925 Silver 0.0841 oz. ASW, 19 mm. **Obv:** Crowned head left **Rev:** Two stylized rampant lions left, denomination and date 3/4 surround

Date	Mintage	F12	VF20	XF40	MS60	MS63
1938	192,000	4.00	7.00	25.00	45.00	75.00
1938	—	PF60 400	PF63 450			

KM# 6 9 PIASTRES
5.66 g., 0.925 Silver 0.1682 oz. ASW **Obv:** Crowned and veiled bust left **Rev:** Crowned arms divide date, denomination below

Date	Mintage	F12	VF20	XF40	MS60	MS63
1901	600,000	18.00	48.00	120	240	—
1901	—	PF60 1,250				

KM# 9 9 PIASTRES
5.66 g., 0.925 Silver 0.1682 oz. ASW **Obv:** Crowned bust right **Rev:** Crowned arms divide date, denomination below

Date	Mintage	F12	VF20	XF40	MS60	MS63
1907	60,000	45.00	125	375	850	—

KM# 13 9 PIASTRES
5.66 g., 0.925 Silver 0.1682 oz. ASW **Obv:** Crowned bust left **Rev:** Crowned arms divide date, denomination below

Date	Mintage	F12	VF20	XF40	MS60	MS63
1913	50,000	48.00	150	350	775	—
1919	400,000	7.00	14.00	90.00	180	300
1921	490,000	7.00	14.00	90.00	180	300

KM# 25 9 PIASTRES
5.66 g., 0.925 Silver 0.1682 oz. ASW **Obv:** Crowned head left **Rev:** Two stylized rampant lions left, date at right, denomination below

Date	Mintage	F12	VF20	XF40	MS60	MS63
1938	504,000	7.00	11.00	18.00	35.00	60.00
1938	—	PF60 400	PF63 450			
1940	800,000	6.00	10.00	14.00	20.00	40.00
1940	—	PF60 400	PF63 450			

KM# 27 SHILLING
5.63 g., Copper-Nickel **Obv:** Crowned head left **Rev:** Two stylized rampant lions left, date below, denomination above

Date	Mintage	F12	VF20	XF40	MS60	MS63
1947	1,440,000	2.50	5.00	12.00	25.00	50.00
1947	—	PF60 300	PF63 350			

KM# 31 SHILLING
Copper-Nickel **Obv:** Crowned head left **Obv. Legend:** ... DEI GRATIA REX **Rev:** Two stylized rampant lions left, date below, denomination above

Date	Mintage	F12	VF20	XF40	MS60	MS63
1949	1,440,000	2.50	5.00	12.00	25.00	50.00
1949	—	PF60 300	PF63 350			

KM# 7 18 PIASTRES
11.31 g., 0.925 Silver 0.3364 oz. ASW **Obv:** Crowned and veiled bust left **Rev:** Crowned arms divide date and denomination below

Date	Mintage	F12	VF20	XF40	MS60	MS63
1901	200,000	50.00	185	475	1,200	—
1901	—	PF60 3,500				

KM# 10 18 PIASTRES
11.31 g., 0.925 Silver 0.3364 oz. ASW **Obv:** Crowned bust right **Rev:** Crowned arms divide date and denomination below

Date	Mintage	F12	VF20	XF40	MS60	MS63
1907	20,000	180	425	900	2,000	—

KM# 14 18 PIASTRES
11.31 g., 0.925 Silver 0.3364 oz. ASW **Obv:** Crowned bust left **Rev:** Crowned arms divide date and denomination below

Date	Mintage	F12	VF20	XF40	MS60	MS63
1913	25,000	150	300	650	1,350	—
1921	155,000	48.00	120	300	550	950

KM# 26 18 PIASTRES
11.31 g., 0.925 Silver 0.3364 oz. ASW **Obv:** Crowned head left **Rev:** Two stylized rampant lions left, date and denomination 3/4 surround

Date	Mintage	F12	VF20	XF40	MS60	MS63
1938	200,000	12.00	15.00	30.00	50.00	100
1938	—	PF60 425	PF63 500			
1940	100,000	20.00	30.00	60.00	90.00	150
1940	—	PF60 425	PF63 500			

KM# 28 2 SHILLING
4.00 g., Copper-Nickel, 28.3 mm. **Obv:** Crowned head left **Rev:** Two stylized rampant lions left, date below, denomination above

Date	Mintage	F12	VF20	XF40	MS60	MS63
1947	720,000	2.50	5.00	12.00	30.00	75.00
1947	—	PF60 375	PF63 450			

KM# 32 2 SHILLING
Copper-Nickel, 28.3 mm. **Obv:** Crowned head left **Rev:** Two stylized rampant lions left, date below, denomination above

Date	Mintage	F12	VF20	XF40	MS60	MS63
1949	720,000	2.50	5.00	15.00	35.00	80.00
1949	—	PF60 375	PF63 450			

KM# 19 45 PIASTRES
28.28 g., 0.925 Silver 0.8409 oz. ASW, 38 mm. **Subject:** 50th Anniversary of British Rule **Obv:** Crowned bust left **Rev:** Two stylized rampant lions left, date at right, denomination below

Date	Mintage	F12	VF20	XF40	MS60	MS63
ND-1928	80,000	25.00	35.00	75.00	125	275
ND(1928)	—	PF60 750	PF63 850			

DECIMAL COINAGE

50 Mils = 1 Shilling; 20 Shillings = 1 Pound; 1000 Mils = 1 Pound

KM# 33 3 MILS
2.80 g., Bronze, 20 mm. **Obv:** Crowned bust right **Rev:** Flying fish divides date and denomination

Date	Mintage	F12	VF20	XF40	MS60	MS63
1955	6,250,000	—	—	0.10	1.00	1.50
1955	2,000	PF65 2.50				

KM# 34 5 MILS
5.50 g., Bronze **Obv:** Crowned bust right **Rev:** Standing figure of Bronze Age man holding copper bar on shoulders, date and denomination below

Date	Mintage	F12	VF20	XF40	MS60	MS63
1955	10,000,000	—	0.15	0.25	1.00	1.50
1955	2,000	PF65 3.00				
1956	2,950,000	—	0.15	0.30	1.00	1.50
1956	—	PF65 3.00				

KM# 35 25 MILS
Copper-Nickel **Obv:** Crowned bust right **Rev:** Bulls head above denomination, date below

Date	Mintage	F12	VF20	XF40	MS60	MS63
1955	2,500,000	—	0.25	1.00	3.00	5.00
1955	2,000	PF65 3.00				

KM# 36 50 MILS
5.65 g., Copper-Nickel, 23.6 mm. **Obv:** Crowned bust right **Rev:** Fern leaves divide denomination, date below **Edge:** Reeded

Date	Mintage	F12	VF20	XF40	MS60	MS63
1955	4,000,000	—	0.35	0.50	1.00	1.50
1955	2,000	PF65 3.00				

KM# 37 100 MILS
Copper-Nickel, 28 mm. **Obv:** Crowned bust right **Rev:** Stylized ancient merchant ship, denomination upper left, date below

Date	Mintage	F12	VF20	XF40	MS60	MS63
1955	2,500,000	—	0.50	0.75	3.00	5.00
1955	2,000	PF65 4.50				
1957	Est. 500000	—	—	20.00	40.00	75.00

Note: 490,000 were melted down by the Central Bank of Cyprus in 1968.

Date	Mintage	F12	VF20	XF40	MS60	MS63
1957	—	PF65 4.50				

REPUBLIC

KM# 38 MIL
0.75 g., Aluminum, 18.5 mm. **Obv:** Shielded arms within wreath, date above **Rev:** Denomination within wreath **Shape:** 12-sided

Date	Mintage	F12	VF20	XF40	MS60	MS63
1963	5,000,000	—	—	—	1.00	1.50
1963	25,000	PF65 1.00				
1971	500,000	—	—	—	1.00	1.50
1972	500,000	—	—	—	1.00	1.50
1972	—	PF65 2.00				

KM# 39 5 MILS
5.74 g., Bronze **Obv:** Shielded arms within wreath, date above **Rev:** Stylized ancient merchant ship, denomination upper left

Date	Mintage	F12	VF20	XF40	MS60	MS63
1963	12,000,000	—	—	—	1.00	1.50
1963	25,000	PF65 1.25				
1970	2,500,000	—	—	—	3.00	5.00
1971	2,500,000	—	—	—	1.00	1.50
1972	2,500,000	—	—	—	1.00	1.50
1973	5,000,000	—	—	—	1.00	1.50
1974	2,500,000	—	—	—	1.00	1.50
1976	2,000,000	—	—	—	1.00	1.50
1977	2,000,000	—	—	—	1.00	1.50
1978	2,000,000	—	—	—	1.00	1.50
1979	2,000,000	—	—	—	1.00	1.50
1980	4,000,000	—	—	—	1.00	1.50
1980	—	PF65 2.50				

KM# 50.1 5 MILS
1.20 g., Aluminum, 20 mm. **Obv:** Shielded arms within wreath, date above **Rev:** Stylized ancient merchant ship, denomination upper left **Shape:** 12-sided

Date	Mintage	F12	VF20	XF40	MS60	MS63
1981	12,500,000	—	—	—	1.00	1.50

KM# 50.2 5 MILS
1.20 g., Aluminum, 20 mm. **Obv:** Shielded arms within wreath, date above **Rev:** Stylized ancient merchant ship, denomination upper left **Shape:** 12-sided

Date	Mintage	F12	VF20	XF40	MS60	MS63
1982	15,000,000	—	—	—	1.00	1.50
1982	—	PF65 2.00				

KM# 40 25 MILS
2.83 g., Copper-Nickel, 19.41 mm. **Obv:** Shielded arms within wreath, date above **Rev:** Cedar of Lebanon, denomination at left **Edge:** Reeded

Date	Mintage	F12	VF20	XF40	MS60	MS63
1963	2,500,000	—	—	—	1.00	1.50
1963	25,000	PF65 1.50				
1968	1,500,000	—	—	—	5.00	10.00
1971	1,000,000	—	—	—	1.00	1.50
1972	500,000	—	—	—	1.00	1.50
1973	1,000,000	—	—	—	1.00	1.50
1974	1,000,000	—	—	—	1.00	1.50
1976	2,000,000	—	—	—	1.00	1.50
1977	500,000	—	—	—	1.00	1.50
1978	500,000	—	—	—	1.00	1.50
1979	1,000,000	—	—	—	1.00	1.50
1980	2,000,000	—	—	—	1.00	1.50
1981	3,000,000	—	—	—	1.00	1.50
1982	1,000,000	—	—	—	1.00	1.50
1982	—	PF65 3.00				

KM# 41 50 MILS
5.65 g., Copper-Nickel, 23.6 mm. **Obv:** Shielded arms within wreath, date above **Rev:** Grape cluster above denomination **Edge:** Reeded

Date	Mintage	F12	VF20	XF40	MS60	MS63
1963	2,800,000	—	—	—	1.00	1.50
1963	25,000	PF65 1.75				
1970	500,000	—	—	—	2.00	5.00
1971	500,000	—	—	—	1.25	1.75
1972	750,000	—	—	—	1.00	1.50
1973	750,000	—	—	—	1.00	1.50
1974	1,500,000	—	—	—	1.00	1.50
1976	1,500,000	—	—	—	1.00	1.50
1977	500,000	—	—	—	1.00	1.50
1978	500,000	—	—	—	1.00	1.50
1979	1,000,000	—	—	—	1.00	1.50
1980	3,000,000	—	—	—	1.00	1.50
1981	4,000,000	—	—	—	1.00	1.50
1982	2,000,000	—	—	—	1.00	1.50
1982	—	PF65 3.50				

KM# 42 100 MILS
11.31 g., Copper-Nickel, 28.5 mm. **Obv:** Shielded arms within wreath, date above **Rev:** Cyprus Mouflon left, denomination below **Edge:** Reeded

Date	Mintage	F12	VF20	XF40	MS60	MS63
1963	1,750,000	—	—	0.70	2.00	3.00
1963	25,000	PF65 2.50				
1971	500,000	—	—	0.75	2.00	3.00
1973	750,000	—	—	0.70	2.00	3.00
1974	1,000,000	—	—	0.75	2.00	3.00
1976	1,500,000	—	—	0.70	2.00	3.00
1977	500,000	—	—	0.75	2.00	3.00
1978	1,000,000	—	—	0.75	2.00	3.00
1979	1,000,000	—	—	0.70	2.00	3.00
1980	1,000,000	—	—	0.70	2.00	3.00
1981	2,000,000	—	—	0.70	2.00	3.00
1982	2,000,000	—	—	0.70	2.00	3.00
1982	—	PF65 5.00				

KM# 43 500 MILS
Copper-Nickel, 36 mm. **Series:** F.A.O. **Obv:** Double cornucopia, as on the ancient coins of Ptolemy II **Rev:** Figure holding tray of fruit, denomination at right

Date	Mintage	F12	VF20	XF40	MS60	MS63
1970	80,000	—	—	5.00	9.00	12.00

KM# 43a 500 MILS
22.62 g., 0.800 Silver 0.5818 oz. ASW, 36 mm. **Series:** F.A.O **Obv:** Double cornucopia, as on the ancient coins of Ptolemy **Rev:** Figure holding tray of fruit, denomination

Date	Mintage	F12	VF20	XF40	MS60	MS63
1970	5,000	PF63 25.00	PF65 40.00			

KM# 44 500 MILS
Copper-Nickel, 32 mm. **Obv:** Shielded arms within wreath, date above **Rev:** Hercules and the Nemean lion, denomination at right **Edge:** Reeded

Date	Mintage	F12	VF20	XF40	MS60	MS63
1975	500,000	—	—	1.75	3.00	7.50
1977	300,000	—	—	2.00	5.00	10.00
1977	—	PF65 15.00				

KM# 44a 500 MILS
14.14 g., 0.800 Silver 0.3637 oz. ASW **Obv:** Shielded arms within wreath **Rev:** Hercules and denomination

Date	Mintage	F12	VF20	XF40	MS60	MS63
1975	10,000	PF63 20.00	PF65 30.00			

KM# 45 500 MILS
Copper-Nickel, 32 mm. **Subject:** Refugees, denomination and date at right **Obv:** Shielded arms within wreath, date above **Edge:** Reeded

Date	Mintage	F12	VF20	XF40	MS60	MS63
1976	25,000	—	1.25	2.00	4.00	7.50

KM# 45a 500 MILS
14.14 g., 0.925 Silver 0.4205 oz. ASW **Obv:** Shielded arms within wreath **Rev:** Refugees, denomination at right

Date	Mintage	F12	VF20	XF40	MS60	MS63
1976	25,000	PF63 17.00	PF65 22.00			

KM# 48 500 MILS
Copper-Nickel, 32 mm. **Subject:** Human Rights **Obv:** Flame within wreath divides dates **Rev:** Stylized crying dove above denomination

Date	Mintage	F12	VF20	XF40	MS60	MS63
ND(1978)	50,000	—	1.25	2.00	3.50	7.50

KM# 48a 500 MILS
14.14 g., 0.925 Silver 0.4205 oz. ASW **Subject:** Human Rights **Obv:** Flame within wreath divides denomination **Rev:** Crying dove above denomination

Date	Mintage	F12	VF20	XF40	MS60	MS63
ND-1978	5,000	PF65 65.00				

KM# 49 500 MILS
Copper-Nickel **Series:** Summer Olympic Games **Obv:** Shielded arms within wreath, date above **Rev:** Olympic logo divides date and denomination, sprays surround

Date	Mintage	F12	VF20	XF40	MS60	MS63
1980	50,000	—	1.25	2.50	5.00	9.00

KM# 49a 500 MILS
14.14 g., 0.925 Silver 0.4205 oz. ASW **Obv:** Shielded arms within wreath **Rev:** Olympic logo divides date and denomination, sprays surround

Date	Mintage	F12	VF20	XF40	MS60	MS63
1980	7,500	PF65 60.00				

KM# 51 500 MILS
Copper-Nickel, 32 mm. **Subject:** World Food Day **Obv:** Shielded arms within wreath, date above **Rev:** Denomination divides swordfish and grain sprig, date above **Edge:** Reeded

Date	Mintage	F12	VF20	XF40	MS60	MS63
ND(1981)	50,000	—	1.25	2.00	5.00	10.00

KM# 51a 500 MILS
14.14 g., 0.925 Silver 0.4205 oz. ASW **Obv:** Shielded arms within wreath **Rev:** Denomination divides swordfish and grain sprig

Date	Mintage	F12	VF20	XF40	MS60	MS63
ND(1978)	7,500	PF65 70.00				

KM# 46 POUND
Copper-Nickel, 38.5 mm. **Subject:** Refugee Commemorative **Obv:** Shielded arms within wreath, date above **Rev:** Refugees, date and denomination at right **Note:** Also known with a doubled die reverse, especially noticeable with the date.

Date	Mintage	F12	VF20	XF40	MS60	MS63
1976	25,000	—	—	2.50	5.00	10.00

KM# 46a POUND
28.28 g., 0.925 Silver 0.841 oz. ASW **Obv:** Shielded arms within wreath **Rev:** Refugees, denomination at right **Note:** Refugee Commemorative.

Date	Mintage	F12	VF20	XF40	MS60	MS63
1976	25,000	PF63 20.00	PF65 30.00			

KM# 47 50 POUNDS
15.98 g., 0.917 Gold 0.4711 oz. AGW **Obv:** Archbishop Makarios right, two dates **Rev:** Ship above map, dolphins, date and denomination below

Date	Mintage	F12	VF20	XF40	MS60	MS63
1977	39,000	—	—	—	—	750
1977	51,000	PF65 800				

REFORM COINAGE

100 Cents = 1 Pound

KM# 52 HALF CENT
1.20 g., Aluminum, 20 mm. **Obv:** Shield within wreath, date below **Rev:** Cyclamen, denomination at right **Shape:** 12-sided

Date	Mintage	VF20	XF40	MS60	MS63	MS65
1983	10,000,000	—	0.10	0.15	0.25	0.35
1983	6,250	PF65 1.50				

KM# 53.1 CENT
2.00 g., Nickel-Brass, 16.5 mm. **Obv:** Shielded arms within wreath, date below **Rev:** Stylized bird on a branch, value number surrounded by single line

Date	Mintage	VF20	XF40	MS60	MS63	MS65
1983	15,000,000	—	0.10	0.20	0.30	0.45
1983	6,250	PF65 1.50				

KM# 53.2 CENT
2.00 g., Nickel-Brass, 16.5 mm. **Obv:** Shielded arms within wreath, date below **Rev:** Stylized bird on a branch, value number surrounded by double line

Date	Mintage	VF20	XF40	MS60	MS63	MS65
1985	5,000,000	—	0.10	0.20	0.30	0.45
1987	5,000,000	—	0.10	0.20	0.30	0.45
1988	5,000,000	—	0.10	0.20	0.30	0.45
1990	4,000,000	—	0.10	0.20	0.30	0.45

KM# 53.3 CENT
2.00 g., Nickel-Brass, 16.5 mm. **Obv:** Shielded arms within altered wreath, date below **Rev:** Stylized bird on a branch, denomination at left **Edge:** Plain

Date	Mintage	VF20	XF40	MS60	MS63	MS65
1991	4,000,000	—	0.10	0.20	0.30	0.45
1992	4,000,000	—	0.10	0.20	0.30	0.45
1993	7,000,000	—	0.10	0.20	0.30	0.45
1994	10,000,000	—	0.10	0.20	0.30	0.45
1996	12,000,000	—	0.10	0.20	0.30	0.45
1998	15,000,000	—	0.10	0.20	0.30	0.45

KM# 54.1 2 CENTS
2.50 g., Nickel-Brass, 19 mm. **Obv:** Shielded arms within wreath, date below **Rev:** Stylized goats, value number surrounded by single line

Date	Mintage	VF20	XF40	MS60	MS63	MS65
1983	12,000,000	—	0.15	0.25	0.35	0.50
1983	6,250	PF65 1.50				

KM# 54.2 2 CENTS
2.50 g., Nickel-Brass, 19 mm. **Obv:** Shielded arms within wreath, date below **Rev:** Stylized goats, value number surrounded by double line

Date	Mintage	VF20	XF40	MS60	MS63	MS65
1985	8,000,000	—	0.15	0.25	0.35	0.50
1988	5,150,000	—	0.15	0.25	0.35	0.50
1990	4,000,000	—	0.15	0.25	0.35	0.50

KM# 54.3 2 CENTS
2.50 g., Nickel-Brass, 19 mm. **Obv:** Shielded arms within altered wreath, date below **Rev:** Stylized goats, denomination upper right **Edge:** Plain

Date	Mintage	VF20	XF40	MS60	MS63	MS65
1991	4,000,000	—	0.15	0.25	0.35	0.50
1992	4,000,000	—	0.15	0.25	0.35	0.50
1993	4,000,000	—	0.15	0.25	0.35	0.50
1994	10,000,000	—	0.15	0.25	0.35	0.50
1996	12,000,000	—	0.15	0.25	0.35	0.50
1998	10,000,000	—	0.15	0.25	0.35	0.50

KM# 55.1 5 CENTS
3.75 g., Nickel-Brass, 22 mm. **Obv:** Shielded arms within wreath, date below **Rev:** Stylized bull's head, value number surrounded by single line **Note:** REV: Value number surrounded by single line

Date	Mintage	VF20	XF40	MS60	MS63	MS65
1983	15,000,000	—	0.20	0.50	0.75	1.00
1983	6,250	PF65 2.00				

KM# 55.2 5 CENTS
3.75 g., Nickel-Brass, 22 mm. **Obv:** Shielded arms within wreath, date below **Rev:** Value number surrounded by double line

Date	Mintage	VF20	XF40	MS60	MS63	MS65
1985	5,000,000	—	0.20	0.50	0.75	1.00
1987	5,000,000	—	0.20	0.50	0.75	1.00
1988	5,060,000	—	0.20	0.50	0.75	1.00
1990	—	—	0.20	0.50	0.75	1.00

KM# 55.3 5 CENTS
3.75 g., Nickel-Brass, 22 mm. **Obv:** Altered wreath around arms **Rev:** Stylized bull's head above denomination **Edge:** Plain

Date	Mintage	VF20	XF40	MS60	MS63	MS65
1991	4,000,000	—	0.20	0.50	0.75	1.00
1992	4,000,000	—	0.20	0.50	0.75	1.00
1993	5,000,000	—	0.20	0.50	0.75	1.00
1994	8,000,000	—	0.20	0.50	0.75	1.00
1998	1,000,000	—	0.20	0.50	0.75	1.00

KM# 56.1 10 CENTS
5.50 g., Nickel-Brass, 24.5 mm. **Obv:** Shielded arms within wreath, date below **Rev:** Decorative vase, value number surrounded by single line **Edge:** Reeded

Date	Mintage	VF20	XF40	MS60	MS63	MS65
1983	10,000,000	—	0.35	0.75	1.00	1.25
1983	6,250	PF65 3.00				

KM# 56.2 10 CENTS
5.50 g., Nickel-Brass, 24.5 mm. **Obv:** Shielded arms within wreath, date below **Rev:** Value number framed by double line **Edge:** Reeded

Date	Mintage	VF20	XF40	MS60	MS63	MS65
1985	5,000,000	—	0.35	0.75	1.00	1.25
1988	5,035,000	—	0.35	0.75	1.00	1.25
1990	4,000,000	—	0.35	0.75	1.00	1.25

KM# 56.3 10 CENTS
5.50 g., Nickel-Brass, 24.5 mm. **Obv:** Altered wreath around arms **Rev:** Decorative vase, denomination above **Edge:** Reeded

Date	Mintage	VF20	XF40	MS60	MS63	MS65
1991	4,000,000	—	0.35	0.75	1.00	1.25
1992	3,000,000	—	0.35	0.75	1.00	1.25
1993	3,000,000	—	0.35	0.75	1.00	1.25
1994	8,000,000	—	0.35	0.75	1.00	1.25
1998	5,000,000	—	0.35	0.75	1.00	1.25

KM# 57.1 20 CENTS
7.75 g., Nickel-Brass, 27.25 mm. **Obv:** Shielded arms within wreath, date below **Rev:** Value number framed by single line **Edge:** Reeded

Date	Mintage	VF20	XF40	MS60	MS63	MS65
1983	10,000,000	—	0.50	2.00	3.00	3.50
1983	6,200	PF65 5.00				

KM# 57.2 20 CENTS
7.75 g., Nickel-Brass, 27.25 mm. **Obv:** Shielded arms within wreath, date below **Rev:** Value number framed by double line **Edge:** Reeded

Date	Mintage	VF20	XF40	MS60	MS63	MS65
1985	5,040,000	—	0.50	2.00	3.00	3.50
1988	1,000,000	—	0.50	2.00	4.00	5.00

KM# 62.1 20 CENTS
7.75 g., Nickel-Brass, 27.25 mm. **Obv:** Shielded arms within wreath, date below **Rev:** Head left, denomination at right **Edge:** Reeded

Date	Mintage	VF20	XF40	MS60	MS63	MS65
1989	2,000,000	—	—	1.00	1.25	1.50
1989	—	PF65 50.00				
1990	3,000,000	—	—	1.00	1.25	1.50

KM# 62.2 20 CENTS
7.75 g., Nickel-Brass, 27.25 mm. **Obv:** Altered wreath around arms **Rev:** Head left, denomination at right **Edge:** Reeded

Date	Mintage	VF20	XF40	MS60	MS63	MS65
1991	4,000,000	—	—	1.00	1.25	1.50
1992	3,000,000	—	—	1.00	1.25	1.50
1993	4,000,000	—	—	1.00	1.25	1.50
1994	8,000,000	—	—	1.00	1.25	1.50
1998	5,000,000	—	—	1.00	1.25	1.50

KM# 58 50 CENTS
Copper-Nickel, 32 mm. **Series:** F.A.O. **Subject:** Forestry **Obv:** Shielded arms within wreath, date above **Rev:** Goddess Diana in the shape of a stylized tree, denomination at right

Date	Mintage	VF20	XF40	MS60	MS63	MS65
1985	33,000	—	3.00	7.00	10.00	16.00

KM# 58a 50 CENTS
14.14 g., 0.925 Silver 0.4205 oz. ASW, 32 mm. **Series:** F.A.O. **Obv:** Shielded arms within wreath, date below **Rev:** Goddess Diana in the shape of a stylized tree

Date	Mintage	VF20	XF40	MS60	MS63	MS65
1985	4,000	PF65 50.00				

KM# 60 50 CENTS
Copper-Nickel **Subject:** Olympics **Obv:** Shielded arms within wreath, date below **Rev:** Symbols divide denomination, Olympic logo at right

Date	Mintage	VF20	XF40	MS60	MS63	MS65
1988	14,000	—	—	3.00	5.00	9.00

KM# 60a 50 CENTS
14.14 g., 0.925 Silver 0.4205 oz. ASW **Obv:** Shielded arms within wreath, date below **Rev:** Symbols divide denomination, logo at right

Date	Mintage	VF20	XF40	MS60	MS63	MS65
1988	4,000	PF65 75.00				

KM# 66 50 CENTS
7.00 g., Copper-Nickel, 26 mm. **Subject:** Abduction of Europa **Obv:** National arms, date below **Rev:** Female figure riding bull right within square, denomination below **Edge:** Plain **Shape:** 7-sided

Date	Mintage	VF20	XF40	MS60	MS63	MS65
1991 narrow date	3,005,000	—	—	1.75	2.50	3.25
1993 wide date	300,000	—	—	2.00	3.00	5.00
1994 wide date	500,000	—	—	2.00	3.00	5.00
1996	5,000,000	—	—	1.75	2.50	3.25
1998	5,000,000	—	—	1.75	2.50	3.25

KM# 66a 50 CENTS

7.00 g., 0.925 Silver 0.2082 oz. ASW, 26 mm. **Obv:** Shielded arms within wreath, date below **Rev:** Figure riding bull within square, denomination below

Date	Mintage	VF20	XF40	MS60	MS63	MS65
1991	5,000	PF65 70.00				

KM# 59 POUND

Copper-Nickel **Subject:** World Wildlife Fund **Obv:** Shielded arms within wreath, date below **Rev:** Cyprian wild sheep (Moufflon), denomination below

Date	Mintage	VF20	XF40	MS60	MS63	MS65
1986	39,000	—	—	7.00	10.00	15.00

KM# 59a POUND

0.925 Silver **Obv:** Shielded arms within wreath, date below **Rev:** Wild sheep, denomination below

Date	Mintage	VF20	XF40	MS60	MS63	MS65
1986	13,000	PF65 60.00				

KM# 61 POUND

Copper-Nickel **Series:** Olympics **Obv:** Shielded arms within wreath, date below **Rev:** Symbols, denomination below

Date	Mintage	VF20	XF40	MS60	MS63	MS65
1988	14,000	—	—	5.00	8.00	12.00

KM# 61a POUND

28.28 g., 0.925 Silver 0.841 oz. ASW **Obv:** Shielded arms within wreath, date below **Rev:** Symbols and denomination

Date	Mintage	VF20	XF40	MS60	MS63	MS65
1988	4,000	PF65 85.00				

KM# 63 POUND

Copper-Nickel **Subject:** Small European States Games **Rev:** Winged figure divides Olympic logos, denomination below

Date	Mintage	VF20	XF40	MS60	MS63	MS65
1989	19,000	—	—	4.00	7.00	12.00

Note: 4,000 issued in plastic case, 15,000 issued uncased

KM# 63a POUND

28.28 g., 0.925 Silver 0.841 oz. ASW **Subject:** Small European States Games **Rev:** Winged figure divides logos, denomination below

Date	Mintage	VF20	XF40	MS60	MS63	MS65
1989	4,000	PF65 65.00				

KM# 64 POUND

Copper-Nickel **Series:** Save the Children Fund **Obv:** Shielded arms within wreath **Rev:** Two boys at play

Date	Mintage	VF20	XF40	MS60	MS63	MS65
1989	19,000	—	—	4.00	7.00	12.00

Note: 4,000 issued in plastic case, 15,000 issued uncased

KM# 64a POUND

28.28 g., 0.925 Silver 0.841 oz. ASW **Series:** Save the Children Fund **Obv:** Shielded arms within wreath **Rev:** Two boys at play

Date	Mintage	VF20	XF40	MS60	MS63	MS65
1989	4,000	PF65 65.00				

KM# 67 POUND

Copper-Nickel **Series:** Olympics **Obv:** Small arms **Rev:** Relay Racing, denomination above Olympic logo

Date	Mintage	VF20	XF40	MS60	MS63	MS65
1992	8,000	—	—	6.00	10.00	18.00

KM# 67a POUND

28.28 g., 0.925 Silver 0.841 oz. ASW **Series:** Olympics **Obv:** Small arms **Rev:** Relay racing, denomination above logo

Date	Mintage	VF20	XF40	MS60	MS63	MS65
1992	4,000	PF65 75.00				

KM# 69 POUND

Copper-Nickel **Subject:** 50th Anniversary - United Nations **Obv:** Shielded arms within wreath, date below **Rev:** Tree of flag shields divides denomination and logo

Date	Mintage	VF20	XF40	MS60	MS63	MS65
1995	—	—	—	6.00	12.00	20.00

KM# 69a POUND

28.28 g., 0.925 Silver 0.841 oz. ASW **Series:** 50th Anniversary - United Nations **Obv:** Shielded arms within wreath, date below **Rev:** Tree of flag shields, denomination and logo

Date	Mintage	VF20	XF40	MS60	MS63	MS65
1995	—	PF65 60.00				

KM# 70 POUND

Copper-Nickel **Subject:** 50th Anniversary - F.A.O. **Obv:** Shielded arms within wreath, date below **Rev:** Bovine portrait, wheat and denominaton

Date	Mintage	VF20	XF40	MS60	MS63	MS65
1995	—	—	—	7.00	15.00	22.00

KM# 70a POUND

28.28 g., 0.925 Silver 0.841 oz. ASW **Series:** 50th Anniversary - F.A.O. **Obv:** Shielded arms within wreath, date below **Rev:** Bovine Portrait, wheat and denomination

Date	Mintage	VF20	XF40	MS60	MS63	MS65
1995	—	PF65 75.00				

KM# 71 POUND

Copper-Nickel **Series:** 1996 Olympics **Obv:** Shielded arms within wreath, date below **Rev:** Olympic rings, stylized flames, olive branch, denomination above

Date	Mintage	VF20	XF40	MS60	MS63	MS65
1996	3,000	—	—	—	25.00	45.00

KM# 71a POUND

28.28 g., 0.925 Silver 0.841 oz. ASW **Series:** 1996 Olympics **Obv:** Shielded arms within wreath, date below **Rev:** Olympic rings, stylized flames, olive branch

Date	Mintage	VF20	XF40	MS60	MS63	MS65
1996	—	PF65 65.00				

KM# 72 POUND

Copper-Nickel **Subject:** World Wildlife Fund - Conserving Nature **Obv:** Shielded arms within wreath, date below **Rev:** Green turtle, denomination above

Date	Mintage	VF20	XF40	MS60	MS63	MS65
1997	3,000	—	—	—	15.00	25.00

KM# 72a POUND

28.28 g., 0.925 Silver 0.841 oz. ASW **Obv:** Shielded arms within wreath, date below **Rev:** Green turtle

Date	Mintage	VF20	XF40	MS60	MS63	MS65
1997	Est. 15000	PF65 45.00				

KM# 90 POUND

Copper-Nickel **Subject:** Cyprus Orchid

Date	Mintage	VF20	XF40	MS60	MS63	MS65
1999	2,000	—	—	—	55.00	—

KM# 91 POUND

Copper-Nickel **Subject:** Cyprus Bird

Date	Mintage	VF20	XF40	MS60	MS63	MS65
2000	2,000	—	—	—	55.00	—

KM# 92 POUND

Copper-Nickel **Subject:** Sydney Olympic Games

Date	Mintage	VF20	XF40	MS60	MS63	MS65
2000	2,000	—	—	—	55.00	—

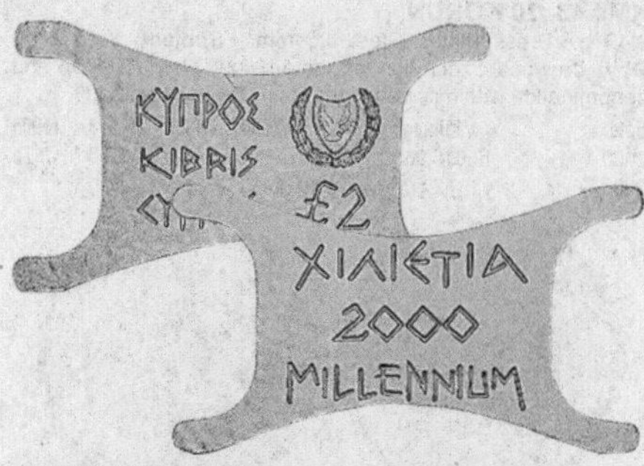

KM# 73 2 POUNDS

Bronze, 44.5 x 25 mm. **Subject:** Millennium **Obv:** National arms and denomination at right **Rev:** Three line inscription **Shape:** Ox-hide shape of ancient ingot

Date	Mintage	VF20	XF40	MS60	MS63	MS65
2000	1,000	—	—	—	100	150

KM# 73a 2 POUNDS

15.00 g., 0.925 Silver 0.4461 oz. ASW, 44.5 x 25 mm. **Subject:** Millennium **Obv:** National arms and denomination **Rev:** Three line inscription **Edge:** Plain **Shape:** 4-sided

Date	Mintage	VF20	XF40	MS60	MS63	MS65
2000	32,000	PF65 50.00				

KM# 65 20 POUNDS

7.99 g., 0.917 Gold 0.2355 oz. AGW, 22 mm. **Subject:** 30th Anniversary of the Republic **Obv:** Shielded arms within wreath, date below **Rev:** Denomination within circle on stylized bird

Date	Mintage	VF20	XF40	MS60	MS63	MS65
1990	5,000	PF65 500				

KM# 68 20 POUNDS

7.99 g., 0.917 Gold 0.2355 oz. AGW **Subject:** Museum Building Fund **Obv:** Shielded arms within wreath, date below **Rev:** Winged statue, left, denomination below

Date	Mintage	VF20	XF40	MS60	MS63	MS65
1992	5,000	PF65 500				

KM# 93 20 POUNDS

7.99 g., 0.9155 Gold 0.2351 oz. AGW **Subject:** Fund

Date	Mintage	VF20	XF40	MS60	MS63	MS65
1994	4,000	PF65 550				

KM# 74 100 POUNDS

30.00 g., 0.9167 Gold 0.8842 oz. AGW **Subject:** Millennium **Obv:** National arms and denomination at right **Rev:** Three line inscription **Shape:** Ox-hide shape of ancient ingot

Date	Mintage	VF20	XF40	MS60	MS63	MS65
2000	750	—	—	—	—	3,250

TRIAL STRIKES

KM#	Date	Mintage	Identification	Mkt Val
TS2	ND (1928)	—	45 Piastres. 0.917. Gold. Uniface.	—

Note: 1 known

MINT SETS

KM#	Date	Mintage	Identification	Issue Price	Mkt Val
MS1	1955 (5)	2,550	KM33-37	2.20	25.00
MS2	1963 (5)	8,050	KM38-42	1.95	15.00
MS3	1971 (5)	3,000	KM38-42	1.65	25.00
MS4	1972 (4)	30,000	KM38-41	2.35	20.00
MS5	1973 (4)	5,000	KM39-42	2.75	15.00
MS6	1974 (4)	5,000	KM39-42	3.25	5.00
MS7	1976 (3)	5,000	KM40-42	1.25	4.50
MS8	1976 (2)	25,000	KM45-46	6.50	14.00
MS9	1977 (5)	10,000	KM39-42, 44	—	14.00
MS10	1978 (5)	—	KM39-42, 48	5.50	12.50
MS11	1979 (4)	—	KM39-42	—	6.50
MS12	1980 (4)	—	KM39-42	—	6.50
MS13	1981 (5)	—	KM40-42, 50.1, 51	5.00	18.00
MS14	1981 (4)	—	KM40-42, 50.1	5.00	6.50
MS15	1982 (4)	5,000	KM40-42, 50.2	5.00	13.50
MS16	1983 (6)	11,400	KM52,53.1-57.1	15.00	15.00
MS17	1988 (5)	—	KM53.2-57.2	—	10.00
MS18	1989 (5)	—	KM53.2-56.2, 62.1	—	10.00
MS19	1990 (5)	—	KM53.2-56.2, 62.1	10.00	10.00

PROOF SETS

KM#	Date	Mintage	Identification	Issue Price	Mkt Val
PS4	1901 (4)	—	KM4-7	—	5,550
PS5	1931 (2)	—	KM17-18	—	2,000
PS6	1934 (2)	—	KM20-21	—	1,000
PS7	1938 (5)	—	KM-22-26	—	2,300
PS8	1947 (2)	—	KM27-28	—	800
PS9	1949 (2)	—	KM31-32	—	800
PS10	1949 (4)	—	KM29-32	—	1,300
PS11	1955 (5)	2,000	KM33-37	5.50	40.00
PS12	1963 (5)	24,501	KM38-42	9.00	20.00
PS13	1963 (5)	500	KM38-42	8.70	50.00
PS15	1976 (2)	25,000	KM45a-46a	50.00	85.00
PS16	1983 (6)	6,250	KM52, 53.1-57.1	20.00	75.00

CZECH REPUBLIC

The Czech Republic was formerly united with Slovakia as Czechoslovakia. It is bordered in the west by Germany, to the north by Poland, to the east by Slovakia and to the south by Austria. It consists of 3 major regions: Bohemia, Moravia and Silesia and has an area of 30,450 sq. mi. (78,864 sq. km.) and a population of 10.4 million. Capital: Prague (Praha). Agriculture and livestock are chief occupations while coal deposits are the main mineral resources.

The Czech lands were united with the Slovaks to form the Czechoslovak State, which came into existence on Oct. 28, 1918 upon the dissolution of the Austrian-Hungarian Empire. In 1938, this territory was broken up for the benefit of Germany, Poland, and Hungary by the Munich (Munchen) Agreement. In March 1939 the German influenced Slovak government proclaimed Slovakia independent. Germany incorporated the Czech lands into the Third Reich as the "Protectorate of Bohemia and Moravia." A Czech government-in-exile was set up in London in July 1940. The Soviets and USA forces liberated the area by May 1945. Communist influence increased steadily while pressure for liberalization culminated in the overthrow of the Stalinist leader Antonin Novotny and his associates in 1968. The Communist Party then introduced far reaching reforms which resulted in warnings from Moscow (Moskva), followed by occupation and stationing of Soviet forces. Mass demonstrations for reform began again in Nov. 1989 and the Federal Assembly abolished the Communist Party's sole right to govern. The new government formed was the Czech and Slovak Federal Republic. A movement for Democratic Slovakia was apparent in the June 1992 elections and on December 31, 1992, the CSFR was dissolved and the two new republics came into being on Jan. 1, 1993.

NOTE: For earlier issues see Czechoslovakia, Bohemia and Moravia or Slovakia listings.

MINT MARKS

(c) - castle = Hamburg
(cr) - cross = British Royal Mint
(l) - leaf = Royal Canadian
(m) - crowned *b* or *CM* = Jablonec nad Nisou
(mk) - *MK* in circle = Kremnica
(o) - broken circle = Vienna (Wien)

MONETARY SYSTEM

1 Czechoslovak Koruna (Kcs) = 1 Czech Koruna (Kc)
1 Koruna = 100 Haleru

REPUBLIC

STANDARD COINAGE

KM# 6 10 HALERU

0.60 g., Aluminum, 15.5 mm. **Obv:** Crowned Czech lion left, date below **Rev:** Denomination and stylized river **Edge:** Plain **Note:** Two varieties of mint marks exist for 1994.

Date	Mintage	VF20	XF40	MS60	MS63	MS65
1993 (c)	100,000,000	—	—	—	0.20	0.25
Note: 200 pieces destroyed						
1993 (m)	94,902,000	—	—	—	0.20	0.25
1994 (c)	2,500	—	—	—	2.50	3.00
Sets only						
1994 (m)	53,127,024	—	—	—	0.20	0.25
1994 (m)	2,000	PF65 6.00				
Proof, dull						
1994 (c)	27,500	PF65 3.00				
Proof, bright						
1995 (m)	106,918,596	—	—	—	0.20	0.25
1996 (m)	61,498,678	—	—	—	0.20	0.25
1997 (m)	40,968,395	—	—	—	0.20	0.25
Note: 85,778 pieces destroyed						
1997 (m)	1,500	PF65 30.00				
1998 (m)	41,027,073	—	—	—	0.20	0.25
1998 (m)	—	PF65 15.00				
1999 (m)	54,428,800	—	—	—	0.20	0.25
1999 (m)	2,000	PF65 12.50				
2000 (m)	52,497,440	—	—	—	0.20	0.25
2000 (m)	—	PF65 10.00				

KM# 2.1 20 HALERU

0.74 g., Aluminum, 17 mm. **Obv:** Crowned Czech lion left, date above **Rev:** Linden leaf within denomination; closed 2, "h" above flat line **Edge:** Reeded **Note:** Medallic coin alignment.

Date	Mintage	VF20	XF40	MS60	MS63	MS65
1993 (c)	80,000,000	—	—	—	0.30	0.40
1993 (m)	30,558,000	—	—	—	0.30	0.40
1994 (c)	9,310,000	—	—	—	0.30	0.40
1994 (m)	81,291,201	—	—	—	0.30	0.40
1994 (m)	2,500	PF65 3.00				
Proof, dull						
1994 (m)	17,500	PF65 1.00				
Proof, bright						
1995 (c)	450,000	—	—	—	1.75	2.00
1995 (m)	80,960,374	—	—	—	0.30	0.40
1996 (m)	61,086,142	—	—	—	0.30	0.40
1997 (m)	51,013,450	—	—	—	0.30	0.40
Note: 78,835 pieces destroyed						
1997 (m)	1,500	PF65 50.00				

KM# 2.2 20 HALERU

0.74 g., Aluminum, 17 mm. **Obv:** Crowned Czech lion left, date above **Rev:** Linden leaf and value, "h" above flat line, closed 2 in denomination **Edge:** Reeded **Note:** Coin alignment.

Date	Mintage	VF20	XF40	MS60	MS63	MS65
1993	Inc. above	—	—	—	4.00	5.00

KM# 2.3 20 HALERU

0.74 g., Aluminum, 17 mm. **Obv:** Crowned Czech lion left, date above **Rev:** Open 2 in denomination, "h" above angle line **Edge:** Reeded **Note:** Medal alignment.

Date	Mintage	VF20	XF40	MS60	MS63	MS65
1998 (m)	51,135,904	—	—	—	0.30	0.40
1998 (m)	—	PF65 10.00				
1999 (m)	20,820,612	—	—	—	0.30	0.40
1999 (m)	—	PF65 17.50				
2000 (m)	31,466,085	—	—	—	0.30	0.40
2000 (m)	—	PF65 12.50				

KM# 3.1 50 HALERU

0.90 g., Aluminum, 19 mm. **Obv:** Crowned Czech lion left, date below **Rev:** Large denomination **Edge:** Segmented reeding **Note:** Prev. KM#3.

Date	Mintage	VF20	XF40	MS60	MS63	MS65
1993 (c)	70,003,000	—	—	—	0.50	0.60
Note: 201 pieces destroyed						
1993 (m)	30,474,000	—	—	—	0.50	0.60
1994 (m)	21,109,425	—	—	—	0.50	0.60
Note: Closed 9 in date or a broken line in O						
1994 (m)	2,500	PF65 3.00				
Proof, dull						
Note: Open 9 in date						
1994 (m)	27,500	PF65 1.00				
Proof, bright						
Note: Open 9 in date						
1995 (m)	30,940,000	—	—	—	0.50	0.60
1996 (m)	35,904,000	—	—	—	0.50	0.60
1997 (m)	25,713,443	—	—	—	0.50	0.60

Date	Mintage	VF20	XF40	MS60	MS63	MS65
Note: 35,610 pieces destroyed						
1997 (m)	1,500	PF65 50.00				
1998 (m)	25,000	—	—	—	0.50	0.60
1998 (m)	2,600	PF65 15.00				
1999 (m)	21,024,800	—	—	—	0.50	0.60
Note: 8,687 pieces destroyed						
1999 (m)	2,000	PF65 17.50				
2000 (m)	15,753,440	—	—	—	0.50	0.60
2000 (m)	—	PF65 12.50				

KM# 7 KORUNA

3.60 g., Nickel Plated Steel, 20 mm. **Obv:** Crowned Czech lion left, date below **Rev:** Denomination above crown **Edge:** Reeded **Note:** Two varieties of mint marks exist for 1996. 2000-03 have two varieties in the artist monogram.

Date	Mintage	VF20	XF40	MS60	MS63	MS65
1993 (l)	102,431,000	—	—	—	0.60	0.75
1994 (m)	52,162,620	—	—	—	0.60	0.75
1995 (m)	40,668,280	—	—	—	0.60	0.75
1996 (m)	35,344,913	—	—	—	0.60	0.75
Note: Figure 1 with and without serif, three varieties of designer's signature.						
1997 (m)	15,055,501	—	—	—	0.60	0.75
1997 (m)	1,500	PF65 60.00				
1998 (m)	25,000	—	—	—	0.60	0.75
1998 (m)	—	PF65 15.00				
Note: 90 pieces destroyed.						
1999 (m)	24,904	—	—	—	0.60	0.75
1999 (m)	2,000	PF65 22.50				
2000 (m)	15,568,697	—	—	—	0.60	0.75
2000 (m)	2,500	PF65 20.00				

KM# 9 2 KORUNY

3.70 g., Nickel Plated Steel, 21.5 mm. **Obv:** Crowned Czech lion left, date below **Rev:** Large denomination, pendant design at left **Edge:** Plain **Shape:** 11-sided **Note:** Two varieties of designer monograms exist for 2001-04.

Date	Mintage	VF20	XF40	MS60	MS63	MS65
1993 (l)	80,001,000	—	—	—	0.65	0.80
1994 (l)	18,360,000	—	—	—	0.65	0.80
1994 (m)	30,310,327	—	—	—	0.65	0.80
1995 (m)	30,520,405	—	—	—	0.65	0.80
1996 (m)	15,201,750	—	—	—	0.65	0.80
1997 (m)	15,040,245	—	—	—	0.65	0.80
1997 (m)	1,500	PF65 80.00				
1998 (m)	10,455,480	—	—	—	0.65	0.80
1998 (m)	2,600	PF65 20.00				
Note: 90 pieces destroyed						
1999 (m)	28,768	—	—	—	0.65	0.80
Note: 1098 pieces destroyed.						
1999 (m)	2,000	PF65 30.00				
2000 (m)	25,000	—	—	—	0.65	0.80
2000 (m)	—	PF65 25.00				

KM# 8 5 KORUN

4.80 g., Nickel Plated Steel, 23 mm. **Obv:** Crowned Czech lion left, date below **Rev:** Large denomination, Charles bridge and linden leaf **Edge:** Plain

Date	Mintage	VF20	XF40	MS60	MS63	MS65
1993 (l)	70,001,000	—	—	—	1.00	1.25
1994 (l)	14,400,000	—	—	—	1.00	1.25
1994 (m)	30,475,491	—	—	—	1.00	1.25
1995 (m)	20,155,218	—	—	—	1.00	1.25
Note: Two varieties of figure 5 and designer's signature.						
1996 (m)	5,053,730	—	—	—	1.00	1.25
1997 (m)	40,000	—	—	—	1.00	1.25
1997 (m)	1,500	PF65 100				
1998 (m)	25,000	—	—	—	1.00	1.25
Note: 10,207 pieces destroyed						
1998 (m)	—	PF65 25.00				
Note: 90 Pieces destroyed.						
1999 (m)	29,490	—	—	—	1.00	1.25
1999 (m)	2,000	PF65 35.00				
2000 (m)	26,431	—	—	—	1.00	1.25

Date	Mintage	VF20	XF40	MS60	MS63	MS65
2000 (m)	—	PF65 27.50				

KM# 4 10 KORUN

7.62 g., Copper Plated Steel, 24.5 mm. **Obv:** Crowned Czech lion left, date below **Rev:** Brno Cathedral, denomination below **Edge:** Reeded **Note:** Position of designer's initials on reverse change during the 1995 strike.

Date	Mintage	VF20	XF40	MS60	MS63	MS65
1993 (c)	70,000,000	—	—	—	2.00	2.50
1993 (c)	1,000	75.00	125	175	250	—
Small Kc						
1994 (m)	2,064,220	—	—	—	1.50	1.75
1994 (m)	30,000	—	—	—	2.00	2.25
bright						
1995 (m)	152,388	—	—	—	1.50	1.75
1995 (m) LK	20,530,459	—	—	—	1.50	1.75
below						
1996 (m)	20,644,143	—	—	—	1.50	1.75
1997 (m)	48,215	—	—	—	1.50	1.75
1997 (m)	1,500	PF65 120				
1998 (m)	25,000	—	—	—	1.50	1.75
1998 (m)	—	PF65 30.00				
Note: 90 pieces melted.						
1999 (m)	29,490	—	—	—	1.50	1.75
Note: 2,036 pieces melted.						
1999 (m)	2,000	PF65 40.00				
2000 (m)	25,000	—	—	—	1.50	1.75
2000 (m)	—	PF65 30.00				

KM# 42 10 KORUN

7.62 g., Copper Plated Steel, 24.5 mm. **Subject:** Year 2000 **Obv:** Crowned Czech lion left, date below **Rev:** Clock works above denomination, within circle **Edge:** Reeded

Date	Mintage	VF20	XF40	MS60	MS63	MS65
2000	10,032,799	—	—	—	1.50	1.75
2000	2,500	PF65 37.50				

KM# 5 20 KORUN

8.43 g., Brass Plated Steel, 26 mm. **Obv:** Crowned Czech lion left, date below **Rev:** St. Wenceslas (Duke Vaclav) on horse **Edge:** Plain **Shape:** 13-sided **Note:** Two varieties of mint marks and style of 9's exist for 1997.

Date	Mintage	VF20	XF40	MS60	MS63	MS65
1993 (c)	55,001,000	—	1.00	—	3.00	3.25
1994 (c)	100,000	—	—	—	3.50	3.75
1995 (m)	101,837	—	—	—	2.50	2.75
1996 (m)	101,150	—	—	—	2.50	2.75
1997 (m)	8,091,219	—	—	—	2.50	2.75
1997 (m)	1,500	PF65 160				
1998 (m)	15,725,000	—	—	—	2.50	2.75
Note: 41,786 pieces destroyed.						
1998 (m)	—	PF65 35.00				
Note: 90 pieces destroyed						
1999 (m)	26,274,900	—	—	—	2.50	2.75
Note: 1,422 pieces destroyed.						
1999 (m)	2,000	PF65 60.00				
2000 (m)	5,694,581	—	—	—	2.50	2.75
2000 (m)	—	PF65 45.00				

KM# 43 20 KORUN

8.43 g., Brass Plated Steel, 26 mm. **Subject:** Year 2000 **Obv:** Crowned Czech lion left, date below **Rev:** Astrolab and denomination within circle **Edge:** Plain **Shape:** 13-sided

Date	Mintage	VF20	XF40	MS60	MS63	MS65
2000	10,015,065	—	—	—	2.50	2.75
2000	2,500	PF65 40.00				

KM# 1 50 KORUN

9.70 g., Bi-Metallic Brass Plated Steel center in Copper Plated Steel ring, 27.5 mm. **Obv:** Crowned Czech lion left **Rev:** Prague city view **Edge:** Plain

Date	Mintage	VF20	XF40	MS60	MS63	MS65
1993 (c)	35,001,000	—	2.50	3.50	7.50	8.00
1994 (c)	100,000	—	—	—	9.00	9.50
1995 (m)	102,977	—	—	—	9.00	9.50
1996 (m)	103,073	—	—	—	9.00	9.50
1997 (m)	40,000	—	—	—	9.00	9.50
1997 (m)	1,500	PF65 350				
1998 (m)	25,000	—	—	—	9.00	9.50
Note: 2,600 pieces destroyed.						
1998 (m)	—	PF65 85.00				
Note: 90 pieces destroyed						
1999 (m)	29,490	—	—	—	9.00	9.50
1999 (m)	2,000	PF65 115				
2000 (m)	26,436	—	—	—	9.00	9.50
2000 (m)	—	PF65 90.00				

KM# 10 200 KORUN

13.00 g., 0.900 Silver 0.3762 oz. ASW, 31 mm. **Subject:** 1st Anniversary of Constitution **Obv:** Quartered stylized arms above denomination and date **Rev:** Inscription above vertical dates **Note:** 7,420 pieces, uncirculated and 1,433 proof, were melted by the Czech National Bank in 1997.

Date	Mintage	VF20	XF40	MS60	MS63	MS65
1993	22,529	—	—	—	11.50	13.50
Note: Milled edge						
1993	3,563	PF65 200				
Note: Plain edge						

KM# 11 200 KORUN

13.00 g., 0.900 Silver 0.3762 oz. ASW, 31 mm. **Subject:** 650th Anniversary **Obv:** Quartered arms above denomination **Rev:** St. Vitus Cathedral and Archbishop's arms **Note:** 6,940 pieces uncircualted melted.

Date	Mintage	VF20	XF40	MS60	MS63	MS65
ND-1994	23,515	—	—	—	11.50	13.50
Note: Milled edge.						
ND-1994	2,497	PF65 150				
Note: Plain edge.						

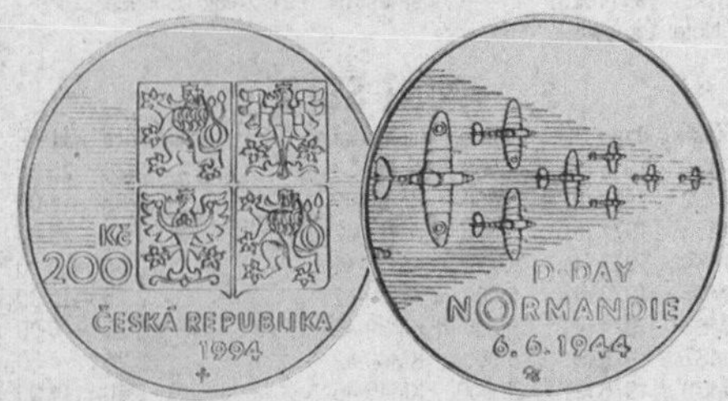

KM# 12 200 KORUN

13.00 g., 0.900 Silver 0.3762 oz. ASW, 31 mm. **Subject:**

50th Anniversary - Normandy Invasion **Obv:** Quartered arms, denomination at left, date below **Rev:** Spitfires in formation **Note:** 6,940 pieces, Unc and Proof, were melted by the Czech National Bank in 1997.

Date	Mintage	VF20	XF40	MS60	MS63	MS65
1994	20,929	—	—	—	15.50	17.50
Note: Milled edge						
1994	4,082	PF65 325				
Note: Plain edge						

KM# 13 200 KORUN

13.00 g., 0.900 Silver 0.3762 oz. ASW, 31 mm. **Subject:** 125th Anniversary of Brno Tramway **Obv:** Elongated, stylized, unbordered, quartered arms above date and denomination **Rev:** Tramway **Note:** 5,420 pieces uncirculated and 40 proof were remelted.

Date	Mintage	VF20	XF40	MS60	MS63	MS65
1994	19,525	—	—	—	13.00	15.00
Note: Milled edge						
1994	1,957	PF65 145				
Note: Plain edge						

KM# 14 200 KORUN

13.00 g., 0.900 Silver 0.3762 oz. ASW, 31 mm. **Subject:** Environmental Protection **Obv:** Stylized quartered arms divide date, denomination below **Rev:** Nude on globe, animals and plants in background **Note:** 4400 pieces uncirculated, were melted by the Czech National Bank in 1997.

Date	Mintage	VF20	XF40	MS60	MS63	MS65
1994	20,541	—	—	—	13.00	15.00
Note: Milled edge						
1994	1,997	PF65 300				
Note: Plain edge						

KM# 15 200 KORUN

13.00 g., 0.900 Silver 0.3762 oz. ASW, 31 mm. **Subject:** 50th Anniversary - Victory Over Fascism **Note:** 5,830 pieces, uncirculated, were melted by the Czech National Bank in 1997.

Date	Mintage	VF20	XF40	MS60	MS63	MS65
ND-1995	19,115	—	—	—	13.00	15.00
Note: Milled edge						
ND-1995	1,997	PF65 220				
Note: Plain edge						

KM# 16 200 KORUN

13.00 g., 0.900 Silver 0.3762 oz. ASW, 31 mm. **Subject:** 200th Anniversary - Birth of Pavel Josef Safarik **Note:** 6,450 pieces, uncirculated and 7 proof, were melted by the Czech National Bank in 1997.

Date	Mintage	VF20	XF40	MS60	MS63	MS65
1995	18,492	—	—	—	13.00	15.00
Note: Milled edge						
1995	1,998	PF65 260				
Note: Plain edge						

KM# 17 200 KORUN

13.00 g., 0.900 Silver 0.3762 oz. ASW, 31 mm. **Subject:** 50th Anniversary - United Nations **Obv:** Quartered arms above denomination **Rev:** UN logo, dates within wreath at left **Note:** 5,130 pieces, uncirculated and 53 proof, were melted by the Czech National Bank in 1997.

Date	Mintage	VF20	XF40	MS60	MS63	MS65
ND-1995	19,293	—	—	—	13.00	15.00
Note: Milled edge						
ND-1995	2,443	PF65 45.00				
Note: Plain edge						

KM# 22 200 KORUN

13.00 g., 0.900 Silver 0.3762 oz. ASW, 31 mm. **Subject:** Czech Philharmonic **Obv:** Quartered arms above denomination **Rev:** Building and musical instruments, dates above **Note:** Three varieties in the artisit's monogram exist. 5,820 pieces, uncirculated and 1 proof, were melted by the Czech National Bank in 1997.

Date	Mintage	VF20	XF40	MS60	MS63	MS65
1996	18,632	—	—	—	13.00	15.00
Note: Milled edge						
1996	2,496	PF65 70.00				
Note: Plain edge						

KM# 23 200 KORUN

13.00 g., 0.900 Silver 0.3762 oz. ASW, 31 mm. **Subject:** Karel Svolinsky **Obv:** Stylized quartered arms above denomination **Rev:** Bird on vase holding bouquet **Note:** 6,120 pieces, uncirculated and 1 proof, were melted by the Czech National Bank in 1997.

Date	Mintage	VF20	XF40	MS60	MS63	MS65
ND-1996	18,330	—	—	—	13.00	15.00
Note: Milled edge						
ND-1996	1,996	PF65 70.00				
Note: Plain edge						

KM# 24 200 KORUN

13.00 g., 0.900 Silver 0.3762 oz. ASW, 31 mm. **Subject:** Jean-Baptiste Gaspard Deburau **Obv:** Elongated, stylized, unbordered, quartered arms, denomination and date below **Rev:** Seated artistic portrait of Deburau **Note:** 7,380 pieces uncirculated and 1 proof were remelted.

Date	Mintage	VF20	XF40	MS60	MS63	MS65
1996	17,070	—	—	—	14.00	16.00
Note: Milled edge						
1996	1,996	PF65 45.00				
Note: Plain edge						

KM# 25 200 KORUN

13.00 g., 0.900 Silver 0.3762 oz. ASW, 31 mm. **Subject:** 200th Anniversary - Czech Christmas Mass by Jakub J. Ryba **Obv:** Quartered arms within circle, denomination below **Rev:** Angel with horn, stars above, church lower left, circle surrounds, dates at right **Note:** 6,170 pieces uncirculated and 1 proof were remelted.

Date	Mintage	VF20	XF40	MS60	MS63	MS65
ND-1996	18,781	—	—	—	13.00	15.00
Note: Milled edge						
ND-1996	2,496	PF65 225				
Note: Plain edge						

KM# 26 200 KORUN

13.00 g., 0.900 Silver 0.3762 oz. ASW, 31 mm. **Subject:** Centennial - First Automobile in Bohemia **Obv:** National arms **Rev:** Side view of antique automobile - President **Note:** 4,380 uncirculated and 1 proof were remelted.

Date	Mintage	VF20	XF40	MS60	MS63	MS65
ND-1997	18,075	—	—	—	13.00	15.00
Note: Milled edge						
ND-1997	2,996	PF65 285				
Note: Plain edge						

KM# 27 200 KORUN

13.00 g., 0.900 Silver 0.3762 oz. ASW, 31 mm. **Subject:** Millennium - St. Adalbert's Death **Obv:** Unbordered quartered arms, denomination below **Rev:** Bishop's portrait right, dates at right **Note:** 2,370 pieces uncirculated were remelted.

Date	Mintage	VF20	XF40	MS60	MS63	MS65
ND-1997	20,076	—	—	—	13.00	15.00
Note: Milled edge						
ND-1997	2,997	PF65 30.00				
Note: Plain edge						

KM# 28 200 KORUN

13.00 g., 0.900 Silver 0.3762 oz. ASW, 31 mm. **Subject:** Czech Amateur Athletic Union **Obv:** Unbordered arms **Rev:** Runners **Note:** 5,930 pieces uncirculated and 617 proof were remelted.

Date	Mintage	VF20	XF40	MS60	MS63	MS65
ND-1997	16,514	—	—	—	160	175
ND-1997	2,380	PF65 150				

KM# 29 200 KORUN

13.00 g., 0.900 Silver 0.3762 oz. ASW, 31 mm. **Subject:** 650th Anniversary - Na Slovanech-Emauzy Monastery **Obv:** Unbordered, quartered arms above denomination **Rev:** Seated saintly figure, date above **Note:** 5,060 pieces uncirculated and 49 proof were remelted.

Date	Mintage	VF20	XF40	MS60	MS63	MS65
ND-1997	17,391	—	—	—	13.00	15.00
Note: Milled edge						
ND-1997	2,945	PF65 165				
Note: Plain edge						

KM# 30 200 KORUN

13.00 g., 0.900 Silver 0.3762 oz. ASW, 31 mm. **Subject:** 650th Anniversary - Charles University in Prague **Obv:** Quartered arms within circle, patterned circle surrounds **Rev:** Charles IV portrait and document seal **Note:** 96 pieces uncirculated were remelted.

Date	Mintage	VF20	XF40	MS60	MS63	MS65
ND-1998	26,472	—	—	—	13.00	15.00
Note: Milled edge						
ND-1998	2,997	PF65 80.00				
Note: Plain edge with CESKA NARODNI BANKA *0.900* 13g						

KM# 31 200 KORUN

13.00 g., 0.900 Silver 0.3762 oz. ASW, 31 mm. **Subject:** 200th Aniversary - Birth of Frantisek Palacky **Obv:** National arms **Rev:** Head of Palacky left **Note:** 3,700 pieces uncirculated and 359 proof were remelted.

Date	Mintage	VF20	XF40	MS60	MS63	MS65
ND-1998	16,242	—	—	—	18.00	23.00
Note: Milled edge						
ND-1998	2,638	PF65 195				
Note: Plain edge with CESKA NARODNI BANKA *0.900* 13g						

KM# 32 200 KORUN

13.00 g., 0.900 Silver 0.3762 oz. ASW, 31 mm. **Subject:** 800th Anniversary - Coronation of King Premysl I Otakar **Obv:** Quartered arms above denomination **Rev:** Half facing head at right, coin design at left **Note:** 3,110 pieces uncirculated and 6 proof were remelted.

Date	Mintage	VF20	XF40	MS60	MS63	MS65
ND-1998	16,842	—	—	—	13.00	15.00
Note: Milled edge						
ND-1998	2,991	PF65 165				
Note: Plain edge with CESKA NARODNI BANKA *0.900* 13g						

KM# 33 200 KORUN

13.00 g., 0.900 Silver 0.3762 oz. ASW, 31 mm. **Subject:** 150th Anniversary - Birth of Frantisek Kmoch **Obv:** National arms **Rev:** Head of Kmoch facing left, dates **Note:** 4,120 pieces uncirculated and 580 proof were remelted.

Date	Mintage	VF20	XF40	MS60	MS63	MS65
ND-1998	15,830	—	—	—	11.50	14.00
Note: Milled edge						
ND-1998	2,416	PF65 170				
Note: Plain edge with CESKA NARODNI BANKA *0.900* 13g						

KM# 34 200 KORUN

13.00 g., 0.900 Silver 0.3762 oz. ASW, 31 mm. **Subject:** 50th Anniversary - NATO **Obv:** Unbordered, quartered arms, denomination below **Rev:** NATO style cross with dates on horizontals **Note:** 245 pieces uncirculated and 1 proof were remelted.

Date	Mintage	VF20	XF40	MS60	MS63	MS65
ND-1999	17,887	—	—	—	13.00	15.00
Note: Edge: CESKA REPUBLIKA CLENSKA ZEME NATO 1999						
ND-1999	2,996	PF65 30.00				
Note: Plain edge with CESKA NARODNI BANKA *0.900* 13g						

KM# 35 200 KORUN

13.00 g., 0.900 Silver 0.3762 oz. ASW, 31 mm. **Subject:** 200 Years - Prague Fine Arts Academy **Obv:** Stylized and quartered national arms within 1/2 circle, denomination at left **Rev:** Stylized design, dates at left **Edge:** Reeded **Note:** 2,740 pieces uncirculated and 198 proof were remelted.

Date	Mintage	VF20	XF40	MS60	MS63	MS65
ND-1999	14,137	—	—	—	13.00	15.00
Note: Milled edge						
ND-1999	2,699	PF65 145				
Note: Plain edge with CESKA NARODNI BANKA *0.900* 13g						

KM# 36 200 KORUN

13.00 g., 0.900 Silver 0.3762 oz. ASW, 31 mm. **Subject:** 100 Years - Brno University of Technology **Obv:** Unbordered, quartered arms, denomination below **Rev:** Stylized design, dates below **Note:** 1,790 pieces uncirculated were remelted.

Date	Mintage	VF20	XF40	MS60	MS63	MS65
ND-1999	16,579	—	—	—	13.00	15.00
Note: Milled edge						
ND-1999	3,072	PF65 28.00				
Note: Plain edge with CESKA NARODNI BANKA *0.900* 13g						

KM# 37 200 KORUN

13.00 g., 0.900 Silver 0.3762 oz. ASW, 31 mm. **Subject:** 100th Birthday - Ondrej Sekora **Obv:** National arms **Rev:** Ant holding flowers **Note:** 1,150 pieces uncirculated and 15 proof were remelted.

Date	Mintage	VF20	XF40	MS60	MS63	MS65
ND-1999	14,739	—	—	—	13.00	15.00
Note: Milled edge						
ND-1999	2,682	PF65 28.00				
Note: Plain edge with CESKA NARODNI BANKA *0.900* 13g						

KM# 46 200 KORUN

13.00 g., 0.900 Silver 0.3762 oz. ASW **Subject:** 700th Anniversary - Currency Reform **Obv:** Quartered arms above coin design which divides denomination **Rev:** Seated figure divides coin designs **Note:** 1,750 pieces uncirculated were remelted.

Date	Mintage	VF20	XF40	MS60	MS63	MS65
2000	3,397	PF65 28.00				
Note: Plain edge with CESKA NARODNI BANKA *0.900* 13g						
2000	14,203	—	—	—	14.00	16.00
Note: Milled edge						

KM# 47 200 KORUN

13.00 g., 0.900 Silver 0.3762 oz. ASW **Subject:** 100th Anniversary - Birth of Poet Vitezslav Nezval **Obv:** Quartered arms above denomination **Rev:** Stylized head left, dates at right **Note:** 3,180 pieces uncirculated were remelted.

Date	Mintage	VF20	XF40	MS60	MS63	MS65
2000	12,765	—	—	—	14.00	15.50
Note: Milled edge						
2000	2,885	PF65 28.00				
Note: Plain edge with CESKA NARODNI BANKA *0.900* 13g						

KM# 48 200 KORUN

13.00 g., 0.900 Silver 0.3762 oz. ASW, 31 mm. **Subject:** 150th Anniversary - Birth of Zdenek Fibich, Musical Composer **Obv:** National arms **Rev:** Portrait **Note:** 1,900 pieces uncirculated and 1 proof were remelted.

Date	Mintage	VF20	XF40	MS60	MS63	MS65
2000	13,028	—	—	—	13.00	15.00
Note: Milled edge						
2000	2,896	PF65 120				
Note: Plain edge with CESKA NARODNI BANKA *0.900* 13g						

KM# 49 200 KORUN

13.00 g., 0.900 Silver 0.3762 oz. ASW, 31 mm. **Subject:** International Monetary Fund and Prague World Bank Group **Obv:** Crowned lion in swirling dots **Rev:** Circle of swirling dots **Note:** 519 pieces uncirculated and 3 proof were remelted.

Date	Mintage	VF20	XF40	MS60	MS63	MS65
2000	14,914	—	—	—	13.00	15.00
Note: Milled edge						
2000	4,294	PF65 100				
Note: Plain edge with CESKA NARODNI BANKA *0.900* 13g						

KM# 50 200 KORUN

13.00 g., 0.900 Silver 0.3762 oz. ASW, 31 mm. **Subject:** New Millennium **Obv:** Elongated, stylized, unbordered arms, denomination below **Rev:** Stylized phoenix design, date below **Note:** 99 pieces uncirculated and 1 proof remelted.

Date	Mintage	VF20	XF40	MS60	MS63	MS65
2000	16,775	—	—	—	13.00	15.00
Note: Milled edge						

Date	Mintage	VF20	XF40	MS60	MS63	MS65
2000	3,500	PF65 28.00				

Note: Plain edge with CESKA NARODNI BANKA *0.900* 13g

KM# 18 1000 KORUN

3.11 g., 0.9999 Gold 0.100 oz. AGW, 16 mm. **Subject:** Historic Coins - Tolar of Silesian Estates 12-1/2 tolar 1620. **Obv:** Imperial eagle, denomination below **Rev:** Tablet with four line inscription within circle

Date	Mintage	VF20	XF40	MS60	MS63	MS65
1995	1,997	—	—	—	—	165
1996	3,252	—	—	—	—	165
1996	—	PF65 200				
1997	2,245	PF65 175				

KM# 38 1000 KORUN

3.11 g., 0.9999 Gold 0.100 oz. AGW, 16 mm. **Subject:** Karlstejn Castle **Obv:** Czech lion in gothic shield, 1348-1998 below **Rev:** Old coin design at right, quartered design in center

Date	Mintage	VF20	XF40	MS60	MS63	MS65
1998 Milled edge	2,097	—	—	—	—	165
1998 Proof, Plain edge	—	PF65 175				
1999	1,997	PF65 175				

KM# 44 2000 KORUN

34.21 g., 0.999 Bi-Metallic 1.0989 oz. Gold plated insert on silver planchet., 40 mm. **Subject:** Millennium **Obv:** National arms hologram on gold inlay **Rev:** Stylized 2000 **Edge Lettering:** *CNB* Ag 0.999* 31.103 g *CNB* AU 999.9 *3. 111 g* **Note:** With a 3.111 gram, .999 gold, .0999 ounce actual gold weight gold inlay.

Date	Mintage	VF20	XF40	MS60	MS63	MS65
ND-1999 (m)	10,157	—	—	—	165	170
ND-1999 (m)	2,993	PF65 220				

KM# 19 2500 KORUN

7.78 g., 0.9999 Gold 0.250 oz. AGW, 22 mm. **Subject:** Historic Coins - 1620 Tolar of Moravian Estates **Obv:** Imperial eagle within circle, denomination below **Rev:** Vine climbing tower within circle

Date	Mintage	VF20	XF40	MS60	MS63	MS65
1995	1,995	—	—	—	—	425
1996	1,253	—	—	—	—	425
1996	—	PF65 450				
1997	1,685	PF65 425				

KM# 39 2500 KORUN

7.78 g., 0.9999 Gold 0.250 oz. AGW, 22 mm. **Obv:** Three gothic shield with Czech Lion, Moravian and Silesian Eagle, 1348-1998 **Rev:** Seal of Karel IV with legal document

Date	Mintage	VF20	XF40	MS60	MS63	MS65
1998	1,078	—	—	—	—	425
Note: Milled edge						
1998	1,845	PF65 450				
Note: Plain edge						
1999	1,396	PF65 425				

KM# 20 5000 KORUN

15.55 g., 0.9999 Gold 0.4999 oz. AGW, 28 mm. **Subject:** Historic Coins **Obv:** Czech lion left within circle, denomination below **Rev:** Bohemian Maley Gros of 1587

Date	Mintage	VF20	XF40	MS60	MS63	MS65
1995	996	—	—	—	—	850
1996	1,251	—	—	—	—	850
1996	—	PF65 875				
1997	1,495	PF65 875				

KM# 40 5000 KORUN

15.55 g., 0.9999 Gold 0.500 oz. AGW, 28 mm. **Obv:** Three shielded arms, 1348-1998 above, denomination below **Rev:** Karel IV, Charles University founder

Date	Mintage	VF20	XF40	MS60	MS63	MS65
1998	1,041	—	—	—	—	850
Note: Milled edge						
1998	1,854	PF65 875				
Note: Plain edge with CESKA NARODNI BANKA 15.553g.						
1999	1,497	PF65 875				
Note: Plain edge with CESKA NARODNI BANKA 15.553g.						

KM# 21 10000 KORUN

31.10 g., 0.9999 Gold 0.9999 oz. AGW, 34 mm. **Subject:** Historic Coins **Obv:** Elongated, stylized, unbordered arms, date and denomination below **Rev:** Lion holding Prague Groschen

Date	Mintage	VF20	XF40	MS60	MS63	MS65
1995	996	—	—	—	—	1,650
1996	1,251	—	—	—	—	1,650
1996	—	PF65 1,750				
1997	1,494	PF65 1,700				

KM# 41 10000 KORUN

31.11 g., 0.9999 Gold 1.000 oz. AGW, 34 mm. **Obv:** Three gothic shield and St. Wencelas crown **Rev:** Karel IV and seals of Nove Mesto

Date	Mintage	VF20	XF40	MS60	MS63	MS65
1998	1,111	—	—	—	—	1,650
Note: Milled edge						
1998 Proof	1,996	—	—	—	—	—
Note: Plain edge with CESKA NARODNI BANKA 31.107g.						
1999 Proof	1,297	—	—	—	—	—
Note: Plain edge with CESKA NARODNI BANKA 31.107g.						

KM# 45 10000 KORUN

31.11 g., 0.9999 Gold 1.000 oz. AGW **Subject:** Karl IV **Obv:** Three gothic shields and St. Wenceslas crown **Rev:** Karl IV with 3 coin designs **Edge Lettering:** *CESKA NARODNI BANKA 31.107g*

Date	Mintage	VF20	XF40	MS60	MS63	MS65
1999 (m) Proof	1,297	—	—	—	—	—

MINT SETS

KM#	Date	Mintage	Identification	Issue Price	Mkt Val
MS1	1993 (9)	20,000	KM#1, 2.1, 3-9	—	14.00
MS2	1994 (9)	13,400	KM#1, 2.1, 3-9	—	18.00
MS3	1995 (9)	19,400	KM#1, 2.1, 3-9	—	14.50
MS4	1996 (9)	14,188	KM#1, 2.1, 3-9	—	14.50
MS5	1996 (9)	11,052	KM#1, 2.1, 3-9 w/ EURO 96 medal	—	14.50
MS6	1997 (9)	15,000	KM#1, 2.1, 3-9	—	14.50
MS7	1998 (9)	5,000	KM#1, 2.3, 3-9, Olympic Hockey Folder	—	14.50
MS8	1998 (9)	10,000	KM#1, 2.3, 3-9, Winter Scene Folder	—	14.50
MS9	1999 (9)	8,000	KM#1, 2.3, 3-9, Parler Folder	—	14.50
MS10	1999 (9)	5,000	KM#1, 2.3, 3-9, NATO Folder	—	14.50
MS11	1999 (9)	4,000	KM#1, 2.3, 3-9, Childrens Motif Folder	—	14.50
MS12	2000 (9)	10,000	KM#1, 2.3, 3.1, 6-9, 42-43 International Monetary Fund Folder	—	14.50
MS13	2000 (11)	13,000	KM#1, 2.3, 3.1, 4-9, 42-43, Space	—	90.00

PROOF SETS

KM#	Date	Mintage	Identification	Issue Price	Mkt Val
PS1	1994 (3)	2,000	KM2.1, 3, 6	—	12.50
PS2	1997 (9)	1,500	KM1, 2.1, 3-9, plus silver medal	35.00	900
PS3	1998 (9)	2,500	KM1, 2.3, 3.1, 4-9, plus silver medal	35.00	230
PS4	1999 (9)	2,000	KM1, 2.3, 3.1 4-9, plus silver medal	35.00	330
PS5	2000 (11)	2,500	KM#1, 2.3, 3.1, 4-9, 42-43	35.00	325

CZECHOSLOVAKIA

The Republic of Czechoslovakia, founded at the end of World War I, was part of the old Austrian-Hungarian Empire. It had an area of 49,371 sq. mi. (127,870 sq. km.) and a population of 15.6 million. Capital: Prague (Praha).

Czechoslovakia proclaimed itself a republic on Oct. 28, 1918, with Tomas G. Masaryk as President. Hitler's rise to power in Germany provoked Czechoslovakia's German minority in the Sudetenland to agitate for autonomy. At Munich (Munchen) in Sept. of 1938, France and Britain, seeking to avoid World War II, forced the cession of the Sudetenland to Germany. In March, 1939, Germany invaded Czechoslovakia and established the "protectorate of Bohemia and Moravia". Bohemia is a historic province in northwest Czechoslovakia that includes the city of Prague, one of the oldest continually occupied sites in Europe. Moravia is an area of considerable mineral wealth in central Czechoslovakia. Slovakia, a province in southeastern Czechoslovakia under Nazi influence was constituted as a republic. The end of World War II saw the re-established independence of Czechoslovakia, while bringing it within the Russian sphere of influence. On Feb. 23-25, 1948, the Communists seized control of the government in a coup d'etat, and adopted a constitution making the country a 'people's republic'. A new constitution adopted June 11, 1960, converted the country into a 'socialist republic', which lasted until 1989. On Nov. 11, 1989, demonstrations against the communist government began and in Dec. of that same year, communism was overthrown, and the Czech and Slovak Federal Republic was formed. In 1993 the CSFR split into the Czech Republic and The Republic of Slovakia.

NOTE: For additional listings see Bohemia and Moravia, Czech Republic and Slovakia.

MINT MARKS
(k) - Kremnica
(l) - Leningrad

MONETARY SYSTEM
100 Haleru = 1 Koruna

REPUBLIC

DECIMAL COINAGE

KM# 5 2 HALERE

2.00 g., Zinc, 17 mm. **Obv:** Czech lion with Slovak shield **Rev:** Charles Bridge in Praha, denomination below **Edge:** Plain

Date	Mintage	VF20	XF40	MS60	MS63	MS65
1923	2,700,000	5.00	10.00	16.00	—	—
1924	17,300,000	3.50	5.00	9.00	—	—
1925	2,000,000	5.00	7.50	17.00	—	—

KM# 6 5 HALERU

1.70 g., Bronze, 16.2 mm. **Obv:** Czech lion with Slovak shield, date below **Rev:** Charles Bridge in Praha, denomination below **Edge:** Plain

Date	Mintage	VF20	XF40	MS60	MS63	MS65
1923	37,800,000	0.30	0.50	2.00	3.50	—
1924	10	—	2,500	5,000	—	—
Note: There are two varieties of the number 4 in 1924 dated coins: with and without seraphs						
1925	12,000,000	0.30	0.50	2.50	3.75	—
1926	1,084,000	4.00	20.00	60.00	75.00	—
1927	8,916,000	0.35	0.75	2.50	3.75	—
1928	5,320,000	0.45	0.75	2.50	3.75	—
1929	12,680,000	0.35	0.75	2.50	3.75	—
1930	5,000,000	3.50	15.00	50.00	70.00	—
1931	7,448,000	0.35	0.75	2.50	3.75	—
1932	3,556,000	3.50	12.00	35.00	50.00	—
1938	14,244,000	0.35	0.75	2.00	3.50	—

KM# 3 10 HALERU

1.96 g., Bronze, 18 mm. **Obv:** Czech lion with Slovak shield, date below **Rev:** Charles Bridge of Praha, denomination below **Edge:** Plain

Date	Mintage	VF20	XF40	MS60	MS63	MS65
1922	6,000,000	0.45	1.00	2.75	4.00	—
1923	24,000,000	0.35	0.75	2.00	3.50	—
1924	5,320,000	0.45	1.00	3.00	4.50	—
1925	24,680,000	0.35	0.60	2.25	3.75	—
1926	10,000,000	0.35	0.75	2.25	3.75	—
1927	10,000,000	0.35	0.75	2.25	3.75	—
1928	14,290,000	0.35	0.75	2.25	3.75	—
1929	5,710,000	2.50	10.00	25.00	35.00	—
1930	6,980,000	0.45	1.00	2.50	3.75	—
1931	6,740,000	0.45	1.00	2.50	3.75	—
1932	11,280,000	0.35	0.75	2.00	3.50	—
1933	4,190,000	3.50	12.00	25.00	35.00	—
1934	13,200,000	0.35	0.75	2.00	3.50	—
1935	3,420,000	3.50	12.00	25.00	35.00	—
1936	8,560,000	0.35	0.75	2.00	3.50	—
1937	20,200,000	0.35	0.75	1.50	3.00	—
1938	21,400,000	0.35	0.75	1.50	3.00	—

KM# 1 20 HALERU

3.33 g., Copper-Nickel, 20 mm. **Obv:** Czech lion with Slovak shield, date below **Rev:** Sheaf with sickle, linden branch, denomination at left **Edge:** Plain

Date	Mintage	VF20	XF40	MS60	MS63	MS65
1921	40,000,000	0.35	0.60	2.50	3.75	—
1922	9,100,000	0.35	0.60	2.50	3.75	—
1924	20,931,000	0.35	0.60	2.50	3.75	—
1925	4,244,000	3.40	12.00	25.00	35.00	—
1926	14,825,000	0.35	0.60	2.50	3.75	—
1927	11,757,000	0.35	0.60	2.50	3.75	—
1928	14,018,000	0.35	0.60	2.50	3.75	—
1929	4,225,000	0.50	1.25	3.50	4.50	—
1930	—	2.00	5.00	14.00	20.00	—
1931	5,000,000	0.40	0.75	3.00	4.00	—
1933	Inc. above	25.00	80.00	160	200	—
1937	8,208,000	0.35	0.60	2.50	3.75	—
1938	18,787,000	0.35	0.60	2.50	3.75	—

KM# 16 25 HALERU

4.00 g., Copper-Nickel, 21 mm. **Obv:** Czech lion with Slovak shield, date below **Rev:** Large denomination **Edge:** Milled

Date	Mintage	VF20	XF40	MS60	MS63	MS65
1932	—	1,000	1,500	2,200	3,000	—
1933	22,711,000	1.00	2.00	4.00	5.00	—

KM# 2 50 HALERU

5.00 g., Copper-Nickel, 22 mm. **Obv:** Czech lion with Slovak shield, date below **Rev:** Linden branches and wheat sprigs bound with ribbon **Edge:** Milled

Date	Mintage	VF20	XF40	MS60	MS63	MS65
1921	3,000,000	0.50	1.00	3.00	4.00	—
1922	37,000,000	0.40	0.60	2.50	3.75	—
1924	10,000,000	0.40	0.60	3.00	4.00	—
1925	1,415,000	1.00	2.50	5.00	10.00	—
1926	1,585,000	9.00	15.00	25.00	45.00	—
1927	2,000,000	1.00	2.00	5.00	10.00	—
1931	6,000,000	0.50	1.00	2.50	5.00	—

KM# 4 KORUNA

6.66 g., Copper-Nickel, 25 mm. **Obv:** Czech lion with Slovak shield, date below **Rev:** Woman with sheaf and sickle, denomination at left **Edge:** Milled

Date	Mintage	VF20	XF40	MS60	MS63	MS65
1922	50,000,000	0.50	0.75	2.00	3.50	—
1923	15,385,000	0.50	0.75	2.00	3.50	—
1924	21,041,000	0.50	0.75	2.00	3.50	—
1925	8,574,000	0.60	1.25	4.00	7.50	—
1929	5,000,000	0.75	1.25	3.50	5.00	—
1930	5,000,000	0.60	1.25	5.00	7.50	—
1937	3,806,000	0.60	1.00	3.00	5.00	—
1938	8,582,000	0.60	1.00	3.00	5.00	—

KM# 10 5 KORUN

10.00 g., Copper-Nickel, 30 mm. **Obv:** Czech lion with Slovak shield, date below **Rev:** Industrial factory and large value

Date	Mintage	VF20	XF40	MS60	MS63	MS65
1925	16,474,500	2.50	3.50	6.00	12.00	—
1926	8,912,000	2.75	4.00	7.00	15.00	—
1927	4,613,500	20.00	80.00	140	175	—

KM# 11 5 KORUN

7.00 g., 0.500 Silver 0.1125 oz. ASW, 27 mm. **Obv:** Czech lion with Slovak shield, date below **Rev:** Industrial factory and large value **Edge:** Plain with crosses and waves

Date	Mintage	VF20	XF40	MS60	MS63	MS65
1928	1,710,000	5.00	8.00	14.00	20.00	—
Note: Edge varieties exist for 1928						
1929	12,861,000	3.00	6.00	12.00	15.00	—
1930	10,429,000	3.00	6.00	12.00	15.00	—
1931	2,000,000	5.00	18.00	35.00	50.00	—
1932	1,000,000	9.00	22.00	50.00	75.00	—

KM# 11a 5 KORUN

7.00 g., Nickel, 27 mm. **Obv:** Czech lion with Slovak shield, date below **Rev:** Industrial factory and large value

Date	Mintage	F12	VF20	XF40	MS60	MS63
1937	36,000	400	900	1,400	2,500	3,500
1938	17,200,000	1.25	2.50	4.00	6.50	10.00

KM# 12 10 KORUN

10.00 g., 0.700 Silver 0.2251 oz. ASW, 30 mm. **Subject:** 10th Anniversary of Independence **Obv:** Denomination above state shield within circle, dates below **Rev:** Bust right **Edge:** Milled

Date	Mintage	VF20	XF40	MS60	MS63	MS65
1918-1928	1,000,000	7.00	9.00	14.00	18.00	—

KM# 15 10 KORUN

10.00 g., 0.700 Silver 0.2251 oz. ASW, 30 mm. **Obv:** State emblem, date below **Rev:** Republic holding linden tree, denomination above **Edge:** Milled

Date	Mintage	VF20	XF40	MS60	MS63	MS65
1930	4,949,000	7.00	10.00	17.00	22.00	—
1931	6,689,000	6.00	9.00	15.00	20.00	—
1932	11,447,500	6.00	9.00	15.00	20.00	—
1933	915,000	600	1,200	2,000	3,200	—

KM# 17 20 KORUN

12.00 g., 0.700 Silver 0.2701 oz. ASW, 34 mm. **Obv:** State emblem, date above **Rev:** Three figures: Industry, Agriculture, and Business, divide denomination **Edge:** Plain with crosses and waves

Date	Mintage	VF20	XF40	MS60	MS63	MS65
1933	2,280,000	6.00	9.00	12.00	16.00	—
1934	3,280,000	6.00	9.00	12.00	16.00	—

KM# 18 20 KORUN

12.00 g., 0.700 Silver 0.2701 oz. ASW, 34 mm. **Subject:** Death of President Masaryk **Obv:** Denomination above state emblem **Rev:** Bust right, dates at left **Edge:** Plain with crosses and waves

Date	Mintage	VF20	XF40	MS60	MS63	MS65
1850-1937	1,000,000	7.00	10.00	22.00	35.00	—

TRADE COINAGE

KM# 7 DUKAT

3.49 g., 0.986 Gold 0.1106 oz. AGW **Subject:** 5th Anniversary of the Republic **Obv:** Shield with Czech lion and Slovak shield **Rev:** Duke Wenceslas (Vaclav) half-length figure facing **Edge:** Milled **Note:** Serially numbered below the duke. The number is in the die.

Date	Mintage	VF20	XF40	MS60	MS63	MS65
1923	1,000	1,000	2,500	5,000	—	—

KM# 8 DUKAT

3.49 g., 0.986 Gold 0.1106 oz. AGW **Obv:** Czech lion with Slovak shield, date below **Rev:** Duke Wenceslas (Vaclav) half-length figure facing **Edge:** Milled **Note:** Similar to KM#7 but without serial numbers.

Date	Mintage	VF20	XF40	MS60	MS63	MS65
1923	61,861	140	185	230	—	—
1924	32,814	140	185	230	—	—
1925	66,279	140	185	230	—	—
1926	58,669	140	185	230	—	—
1927	25,774	140	185	230	—	—
1928	18,983	140	190	255	—	—
1929	10,253	140	200	280	—	—
1930	11,338	140	200	280	—	—
1931	43,482	140	185	230	—	—
1932	26,617	140	185	230	—	—
1933	57,597	140	185	230	—	—
1934	9,729	185	200	280	—	—
1935	13,178	140	190	255	—	—

Date	Mintage	VF20	XF40	MS60	MS63	MS65
1936	14,566	140	190	255	—	—
1937	324	—	2,400	3,000	—	—
1938	56	—	1,750	16,500	—	—
1939	276	—	—	8,000	—	—

Note: Czech reports show mintage of 20 for Czechoslovakia and 256 for state of Slovakia

Date	Mintage	VF20	XF40	MS60	MS63	MS65
1951	500	—	2,400	3,000	—	—

KM# 9 2 DUKATY

6.98 g., 0.986 Gold 0.2213 oz. AGW, 25 mm. **Obv:** Czech lion with Slovak shield, denomination divides date below **Rev:** Duke Wenceslas (Vaclav) half-length figure facing **Edge:** Milled

Date	Mintage	VF20	XF40	MS60	MS63	MS65
1923	4,000	365	580	950	—	—
1929	3,262	365	580	950	—	—
1930	Inc. above	365	680	1,150	—	—
1931	2,994	365	580	950	—	—
1932	5,496	365	580	950	—	—
1933	4,671	365	580	950	—	—
1934	2,403	365	680	1,150	—	—
1935	2,577	365	680	1,150	—	—
1936	819	450	950	1,750	—	—
1937	8	—	—	60,000	—	—
1938	186	—	—	8,000	—	—

Note: Czech reports show mintage of 14 for Czechoslovakia and 172 for state of Slovakia

Date	Mintage	VF20	XF40	MS60	MS63	MS65
1951	200	—	—	5,000	—	—

KM# 13 5 DUKATU

17.45 g., 0.986 Gold 0.5532 oz. AGW, 34 mm. **Obv:** Czech lion with Slovak shield, denomination and date below **Rev:** Duke Wenceslas (Vaclav) on horseback right **Edge:** Milled

Date	Mintage	VF20	XF40	MS60	MS63	MS65
1929	1,827	900	1,450	2,200	—	—
1930	543	950	1,950	2,950	—	—
1931	1,528	900	1,450	2,200	—	—
1932	1,827	900	1,450	2,200	—	—
1933	1,752	900	1,450	2,200	—	—
1934	1,101	900	1,450	2,200	—	—
1935	1,037	900	1,450	2,200	—	—
1936	728	1,100	3,850	5,000	—	—
1937 Rare	4	—	—	—	—	—
1938	56	—	—	20,000	—	—

Note: Czech reports show mintage of 12 for Czechoslovakia and 44 for state of Slovakia

Date	Mintage	VF20	XF40	MS60	MS63	MS65
1951	100	—	—	10,000	—	—

KM# 14 10 DUKATU

34.90 g., 0.986 Gold 1.1064 oz. AGW, 42 mm. **Obv:** Czech lion with Slovak shield, denomination and date below **Rev:** Duke Wenceslas (Vaclav) on horseback right

Date	Mintage	VF20	XF40	MS60	MS63	MS65
1929	1,564	1,900	3,400	5,000	6,000	—
1930	394	2,400	5,900	8,000	9,000	—
1931	1,239	1,900	3,400	5,000	6,000	—
1932	1,035	1,900	3,400	5,000	6,000	—
1933	1,780	1,900	3,400	5,000	6,000	—
1934	1,298	1,900	3,400	5,000	6,000	—
1935	600	2,400	3,900	6,000	7,000	—
1936	633	2,400	4,900	7,500	8,500	—
1937 Rare	34	—	—	—	—	—
1938	192	—	—	45,000	—	—
1951	100	—	—	17,500	—	—

Note: Czech reports show mintage of 20 for Czechoslovakia and 172 for state of Slovakia.

POST WAR COINAGE

KM# 20 20 HALERU

2.00 g., Bronze, 18 mm. **Obv:** Czech lion with Slovak shield, date below **Rev:** Sheaf with sickle, linden branch, denomination at left **Edge:** Plain

Date	Mintage	VF20	XF40	MS60	MS63	MS65
1947	—	125	175	225	350	—
1948	24,340,000	0.15	0.40	1.25	1.75	—
1949	25,660,000	0.15	0.40	1.25	1.75	—
1950	11,132,000	0.15	0.40	1.25	2.00	—

KM# 31 20 HALERU

0.53 g., Aluminum, 16 mm. **Obv:** Czech lion with Slovak shield, date below **Rev:** Wheat sheaf, sickle, linden branch, denomination at left **Edge:** Plain

Date	Mintage	VF20	XF40	MS60	MS63	MS65
1951	46,800,000	0.15	0.25	1.00	1.50	—
1952	80,340,000	0.15	0.25	1.00	1.50	—

KM# 21 50 HALERU

Bronze, 20 mm. **Obv:** Czech lion with Slovak shield, date below **Rev:** Linden branches and wheat sprigs bound with ribbon **Edge:** Plain

Date	Mintage	VF20	XF40	MS60	MS63	MS65
1947	50,000,000	0.25	0.40	1.00	1.50	—
1948	20,000,000	0.25	0.40	1.00	1.50	—
1949	12,715,000	0.25	0.40	1.00	1.50	—
1950	17,415,000	0.25	0.40	1.00	1.50	—

KM# 32 50 HALERU

Aluminum, 18 mm. **Obv:** Czech lion with Slovak shield, date below **Rev:** Linden branches and wheat sprigs bound with ribbon **Edge:** Plain

Date	Mintage	VF20	XF40	MS60	MS63	MS65
1951	60,000,000	0.35	0.50	1.00	1.50	—
1952	60,000,000	0.45	0.60	1.00	1.50	—
1953	34,920,000	2.50	6.00	8.00	12.00	—

KM# 19 KORUNA

Copper-Nickel, 21 mm. **Obv:** Czech lion with Slovak shield, date below **Rev:** Woman with sheaf and sickle, denomination at left **Edge:** Milled

Date	Mintage	VF20	XF40	MS60	MS63	MS65
1946	88,000,000	0.25	0.50	1.00	1.50	—
1947	12,550,000	2.50	3.75	5.50	7.50	—

Note: Varieties exist for "4" in 1946 strikes

KM# 22 KORUNA

1.34 g., Aluminum, 21 mm. **Obv:** Czech lion with Slovak shield, date below **Rev:** Woman with sheaf and sickle, denomination at left **Edge:** Milled

Date	Mintage	VF20	XF40	MS60	MS63	MS65
1947	—	450	700	1,200	2,000	—

Note: Counterfeits, with prooflike fields, are known.

Date	Mintage	VF20	XF40	MS60	MS63	MS65
1950	62,190,000	0.35	0.45	1.00	1.25	—
1951	61,395,000	0.35	0.45	1.25	1.50	—
1952	101,105,000	0.30	0.40	0.80	1.00	—
1953	73,905,000	0.75	1.75	3.50	5.00	—

KM# 23 2 KORUNY

Copper-Nickel, 23.5 mm. **Obv:** Czech lion with Slovak shield, date below **Rev:** Juraj Janosik bust right, wearing hat, denomination at right **Edge:** Milled

Date	Mintage	VF20	XF40	MS60	MS63	MS65
1947	20,000,000	0.40	0.60	1.25	2.00	—
1948	20,476,000	0.40	0.60	1.50	2.50	—

KM# 23a 2 KORUNY

Aluminum-Bronze, 23 mm. **Obv:** Czech lion with Slovak shield, date below **Rev:** Juraj Janosik bust right, wearing hat, denomination at right **Edge:** Milled

Date	Mintage	VF20	XF40	MS60	MS63	MS65
1948	Est. 10000000	—	—	—	—	—

Note: Nearly entire mintage remelted, less than 20 known

KM# 34 5 KORUN

Aluminum, 23 mm. **Obv:** Czech lion with Slovak shield, date below **Rev:** Industrial factory and large value

Date	Mintage	VF20	XF40	MS60	MS63	MS65
1951	—	300	700	1,200	1,600	—

Note: Not released for circulation. Almost the entire mintage was melted

Date	Mintage	VF20	XF40	MS60	MS63	MS65
1952	40,715,000	50.00	75.00	120	160	—

Note: Weakly struck counterfeits are known

KM# 24 50 KORUN

10.00 g., 0.500 Silver 0.1608 oz. ASW, 28 mm. **Subject:** 1944 Slovak Uprising **Obv:** Czech lion with Slovak shield **Rev:** Veiled female standing, holding linden branch, denomination at left **Edge:** Plain with stars and waves

Date	Mintage	VF20	XF40	MS60	MS63	MS65
ND-1947	1,000,000	5.00	6.50	9.00	12.50	—

KM# 25 50 KORUN

10.00 g., 0.500 Silver 0.1608 oz. ASW, 28 mm. **Subject:** 3rd Anniversary - Prague Uprising **Obv:** Czech lion with Slovak shield **Rev:** Liberator divides denomination, date at right **Edge:** Plain with stars and waves

Date	Mintage	VF20	XF40	MS60	MS63	MS65
ND-1948	1,000,000	5.00	6.50	9.00	12.50	—

KM# 28 50 KORUN
10.00 g., 0.500 Silver 0.1608 oz. ASW, 28 mm. **Subject:** 70th Birthday - Josef Stalin **Obv:** Czech lion with Slovak shield within lined frame, denomination above **Rev:** Uniformed bust left **Edge:** Plain with stars and waves

Date	Mintage	VF20	XF40	MS60	MS63	MS65
ND-1949	1,000,000	5.00	6.50	9.00	12.50	—

KM# 26 100 KORUN
14.00 g., 0.500 Silver 0.2251 oz. ASW, 31 mm. **Subject:** 600th Anniversary - Charles University **Obv:** Czech lion with Slovak shield, date below **Rev:** King Charles kneeling before Duke Wenceslas, two shields at left, denomination below

Date	Mintage	VF20	XF40	MS60	MS63	MS65
1948	1,000,000	6.00	7.50	11.50	15.00	—

KM# 27 100 KORUN
14.00 g., 0.500 Silver 0.2251 oz. ASW, 31 mm. **Subject:** 30th Anniversary of Independence **Obv:** Czech lion with Slovak shield within lined frame **Rev:** Man with flag and laurel branch divides dates, denomination below **Edge:** Plain with stars and waves

Date	Mintage	VF20	XF40	MS60	MS63	MS65
ND-1948	1,000,000	6.00	7.50	11.50	15.00	—

KM# 29 100 KORUN
14.00 g., 0.500 Silver 0.2251 oz. ASW, 31 mm. **Subject:** 700th Anniversary - Jihlava Mining Privileges **Obv:** Czech lion with Slovak shield above inscription and date **Rev:** Seated figure, denomination below **Edge:** Plain with stars and waves

Date	Mintage	VF20	XF40	MS60	MS63	MS65
1949	1,000,000	6.00	7.50	11.50	15.00	—

KM# 30 100 KORUN
14.00 g., 0.500 Silver 0.2251 oz. ASW, 31 mm. **Subject:** 70th Birthday - Josef V. Stalin **Obv:** Czech lion with Slovak shield, denomination above **Rev:** Uniformed bust left, date at right **Edge:** Plain with stars and waves

Date	Mintage	VF20	XF40	MS60	MS63	MS65
ND-1949	1,000,000	6.00	8.00	14.00	22.00	—

KM# 33 100 KORUN
14.00 g., 0.500 Silver 0.2251 oz. ASW, 31 mm. **Subject:** 30th Anniversary - Communist party **Obv:** Czech lion with Slovak shield, denomination above **Rev:** Party Chairman bust right divides dates **Edge:** Plain with stars and waves

Date	Mintage	VF20	XF40	MS60	MS63	MS65
ND-1951	1,000,000	6.00	7.50	11.50	15.00	—

PEOPLES REPUBLIC

DECIMAL COINAGE

KM# 35 HALER
0.50 g., Aluminum, 16 mm. **Obv:** Czech lion with Slovak shield, date below **Rev:** Large denomination within linden wreath, star above **Edge:** Plain

Date	Mintage	VF20	XF40	MS60	MS63	MS65
1953	188,885,000	—	0.10	0.25	0.50	0.75
1954	—	—	0.10	0.25	0.50	0.75
1955	—	—	0.15	0.35	0.60	0.85
1956	—	—	0.10	0.25	0.50	0.75
1957	—	—	0.10	0.25	0.50	0.75
1958	—	0.25	0.35	0.50	0.70	1.00
1959	—	—	0.15	0.50	0.70	1.00
1960	—	—	0.10	0.25	0.50	0.75

KM# 36 3 HALERE
0.66 g., Aluminum, 18 mm. **Obv:** Czech lion with Slovak shield, date below **Rev:** Large denomination within linden wreath, star above **Edge:** Plain

Date	Mintage	VF20	XF40	MS60	MS63	MS65
1953	90,001,000	0.10	0.15	0.30	0.50	0.75
1954	Inc. above	0.10	0.15	0.30	0.50	0.75

KM# 37 5 HALERU
0.80 g., Aluminum, 20 mm. **Obv:** Czech lion with Slovak shield, date below **Rev:** Large denomination within linden wreath, star above **Edge:** Plain

Date	Mintage	VF20	XF40	MS60	MS63	MS65
1953	160,233,000	0.15	0.25	0.50	0.70	1.00
1954	Inc. above	0.15	0.25	0.50	0.70	1.00
1955	Inc. above	3.50	30.00	60.00	120	—

KM# 38 10 HALERU
1.16 g., Aluminum, 22 mm. **Obv:** Czech lion with Slovak shield, date below **Rev:** Large denomination within linden wreath, star above **Edge:** Reeded

Date	Mintage	VF20	XF40	MS60	MS63	MS65
1953	160,000	0.15	1.00	5.00	7.00	10.00
Note: Leningrad Mint-133 notches in milled edge						
1953	—	0.15	1.00	5.00	7.00	10.00
Note: Unknown Mint-125 notches in milled edge						
1954	—	0.50	2.00	7.00	9.00	12.00
1955	—	2.50	12.00	25.00	45.00	75.00
1956	—	0.15	1.00	5.00	7.00	10.00
1958	—	5.00	25.00	45.00	65.00	90.00

KM# 39 25 HALERU
1.43 g., Aluminum, 24 mm. **Obv:** Czech lion with Slovak shield, date below **Rev:** Large denomination within linden wreath, star above **Edge:** Reeded

Date	Mintage	VF20	XF40	MS60	MS63	MS65
1953	215,002,000	0.20	0.30	3.00	4.00	6.00
Note: Kremnica Mint - 134 notches in milled edge						
1953	Inc. above	0.50	0.60	3.50	5.00	7.00
Note: Leningrad Mint - 145 notches in milled edge						
1954	Inc. above	18.00	35.00	65.00	85.00	150

KM# 46 KORUNA
4.00 g., Aluminum-Bronze, 23 mm. **Obv:** Czech lion with Slovak shield, date below **Rev:** Woman kneeling planting linden tree, denomination at left **Edge:** Reeded

Date	Mintage	VF20	XF40	MS60	MS63	MS65
1957	137,000,000	0.30	0.45	2.50	5.00	7.00
1958	Inc. above	0.30	0.45	3.00	7.00	9.00
1959	Inc. above	0.25	0.35	2.00	4.50	6.00
1960	Inc. above	0.25	0.35	2.00	4.50	6.00

KM# 40 10 KORUN
12.00 g., 0.500 Silver 0.1929 oz. ASW, 30 mm. **Subject:** 10th Anniversary - Slovak Uprising **Obv:** Czech lion with Slovak shield **Rev:** Soldier standing right, train and construction site in background, denomination at left, dates below **Edge:** Milled **Note:** 65,810 pieces, Unc and Proof, were melted by the Czech National Bank in 1999.

Date	Mintage	VF20	XF40	MS60	MS63	MS65
ND-1954	250,000	—	5.00	7.00	9.00	12.00
ND-1954	5,000	PF65 45.00				

KM# 42 10 KORUN
12.00 g., 0.500 Silver 0.1929 oz. ASW, 30 mm. **Subject:** 10th Anniversary - Liberation from Germany **Obv:** Czech lion with Slovak shield **Rev:** Soldier kneeling left holding child, denomination at left, dates at right **Edge:** Milled **Note:** 95,552 pieces Unc and Proof, were melted by the Czech National Bank in 1999.

Date	Mintage	VF20	XF40	MS60	MS63	MS65
ND-1955	300,000	—	6.00	8.00	14.00	17.00
ND-1955	5,000	PF65 35.00				

KM# 47.1 10 KORUN
12.00 g., 0.500 Silver 0.1929 oz. ASW, 30 mm. **Subject:** 250th Anniversary - Technical College **Obv:** Czech lion with Slovak shield, denomination below **Rev:** Bust left, hand on chin **Edge:** Plain with stars and waves **Note:** Raised designer initials.

Date	Mintage	VF20	XF40	MS60	MS63	MS65
1957	75,000	—	5.00	7.00	9.00	12.00

Note: See note below KM#47.2

KM# 47.2 10 KORUN
12.00 g., 0.500 Silver 0.1929 oz. ASW, 30 mm. **Obv:** Czech lion with Slovak shield **Rev:** Bust left, hand on chin **Note:** Incuse designer initials.

Date	Mintage	VF20	XF40	MS60	MS63	MS65
1957	Est. 5000	PF65 16.00				

Note: 238 pieces, Unc and Proof, were melted by the Czech National Bank in 1999

KM# 48 10 KORUN
12.00 g., 0.500 Silver 0.1929 oz. ASW, 30 mm. **Obv:** Czech lion with Slovak shield, date above **Rev:** Bust right of the Bishop of the Moravian Brotherhood, denomination below **Edge:** Milled **Note:** 7,854 pieces Unc and Proof, were melted by the Czech National Bank in 1999.

Date	Mintage	VF20	XF40	MS60	MS63	MS65
1957	150,000	—	5.00	7.00	9.00	12.00
1957	5,000	PF65 16.00				

KM# 41 25 KORUN
16.00 g., 0.500 Silver 0.2572 oz. ASW, 34 mm. **Subject:** 10th Anniversary - Slovak Unprising **Obv:** State emblem: Czech lion with Slovak shield **Rev:** Soldier standing right, train and construction site in background, denomination at left, dates below **Edge:** Milled **Note:** 110,933 Pieces, Unc and Proof, were melted by the Czech National Bank in 1999.

Date	Mintage	VF20	XF40	MS60	MS63	MS65
ND-1954	250,000	—	—	8.00	10.00	15.00
ND-1954	—	PF65 60.00				

KM# 43 25 KORUN
16.00 g., 0.500 Silver 0.2572 oz. ASW, 34 mm. **Subject:** 10th Anniversary - Liberation from Germany **Obv:** Czech lion with Slovak shield **Rev:** Mother and child greeting soldier divides dates and denomination **Edge:** Milled **Note:** 78,643 pieces, Unc and Proof, were melted by the Czech National Bank in 1999.

Date	Mintage	VF20	XF40	MS60	MS63	MS65
ND-1955	200,000	—	—	8.00	10.00	15.00
ND-1955	5,000	PF65 32.00				

KM# 44 50 KORUN
20.00 g., 0.900 Silver 0.5787 oz. ASW, 37 mm. **Subject:** 10th Anniversary - Liberation from Germany **Obv:** Czech lion with Slovak shield **Rev:** Soldier with rifle raised divides dates, denomination lower right **Edge:** Milled **Note:** 36,650 pieces were melted by the Czech National Bank in 1999.

Date	Mintage	VF20	XF40	MS60	MS63	MS65
1955	120,000	—	12.00	18.00	22.00	28.00

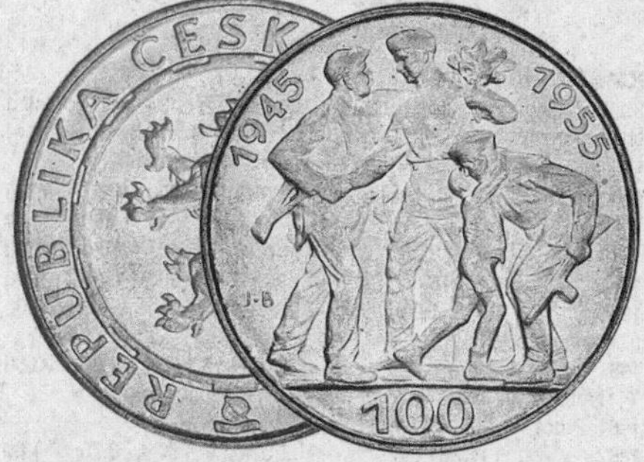

KM# 45 100 KORUN
24.00 g., 0.900 Silver 0.6945 oz. ASW, 40 mm. **Subject:** 10th Anniversary - Liberation from Germany **Obv:** Czech lion with Slovak shield within circle **Rev:** Father and young boy greeting two returning soldiers, dates divided at top, denomination below **Note:** 22,244 pieces were melted by the Czech National Bank in 1999.

Date	Mintage	VF20	XF40	MS60	MS63	MS65
ND-1955	Est. 75000	—	15.00	22.00	35.00	48.00

SOCIALIST REPUBLIC

KM# 51 HALER
0.50 g., Aluminum, 16 mm. **Obv:** Czech lion with socialist shield within shield, date below **Rev:** Denomination within linden wreath, star above **Edge:** Plain

Date	Mintage	VF20	XF40	MS60	MS63	MS65
1962	20,056,000	—	0.10	0.15	0.25	0.50
1963	Inc. above	—	0.10	0.15	0.25	0.50
1986	3,360,000	—	—	1.00	2.00	3.00

KM# 52 3 HALERE
0.66 g., Aluminum, 18 mm. **Obv:** Czech lion with socialist shield within shield, date below **Rev:** Denomination within linden wreath, star above **Edge:** Plain

Date	Mintage	VF20	XF40	MS60	MS63	MS65
1962	Inc. below	150	200	250	300	—
Note: Counterfeits, with prooflike fields, are known.						
1963	5,130,000	—	0.10	0.15	0.25	0.50

KM# 53 5 HALERU
0.80 g., Aluminum, 20 mm. **Obv:** Czech lion with socialist shield within shield, date below **Rev:** Denomination within linden wreath, star above **Edge:** Plain

Date	Mintage	VF20	XF40	MS60	MS63	MS65
1962	55,150,000	0.10	0.15	0.25	0.35	0.60
1963	Inc. above	0.10	0.15	0.25	0.35	0.60
1966	Inc. above	0.10	0.15	0.25	0.35	0.60
1966 Proof	—	—	—	—	—	—
1967	20,770,000	0.10	0.15	0.25	0.35	0.60
1970	5,090,000	0.10	0.15	0.20	0.30	0.50
1972	10,090,000	0.10	0.15	0.20	0.30	0.50
1973	10,140,000	0.10	0.15	0.20	0.30	0.50
1974	15,510,000	0.10	0.15	0.20	0.30	0.50
1975	15,510,000	0.10	0.15	0.20	0.30	0.50
1976	15,550,000	0.10	0.15	0.20	0.30	0.50

KM# 53a 5 HALERU
2.00 g., Brass **Obv:** Czech lion with socialist shield within shield **Rev:** Value within linden wreath, star above

Date	Mintage	VF20	XF40	MS60	MS63	MS65
1967	—	—	300	400	500	—

KM# 86 5 HALERU
0.70 g., Aluminum, 16.2 mm. **Obv:** Czech lion with socialist shield within shield, date below **Rev:** Large denomination, star above **Edge:** Plain

Date	Mintage	VF20	XF40	MS60	MS63	MS65
1977	26,710,000	—	0.10	0.25	0.35	0.60
1978	51,110,000	—	0.10	0.25	0.35	0.60
1979	72,380,000	—	0.10	0.25	0.35	0.60
1980	50,600	—	—	0.25	0.35	0.60
Note: Sets only						
1981	66,160	—	—	0.50	0.75	1.25
Note: Sets only						
1981 Proof	—	—	—	—	—	—
1982	53,847	—	—	1.00	2.00	3.00
Note: Sets only						
1983	60,000	—	—	0.50	0.75	1.25
Note: Sets only						
1984	39,957	—	—	0.75	1.00	1.50
Note: Sets only						
1985	39,791	—	—	0.75	1.00	1.50
Note: Sets only						
1986	20,020,000	—	0.10	0.25	0.35	0.50
1987	520,000	—	0.10	0.35	0.50	0.75
1988	8,029,999	—	0.10	0.25	0.35	0.50
1989	110,000	—	0.10	0.50	0.75	1.25
1990	13,950,000	—	0.10	0.25	0.35	0.50

KM# 49.1 10 HALERU
1.18 g., Aluminum, 22 mm. **Obv:** Star above Czech lion with socialist shield within shield **Rev:** Large denomination within linden wreath, star above **Edge:** Reeded

Date	Mintage	VF20	XF40	MS60	MS63	MS65
1961	314,480,000	0.10	0.20	0.35	0.50	0.75
1962	Inc. above	0.10	0.20	0.35	0.50	0.75
1963	Inc. above	0.10	0.20	0.35	0.50	0.75
1964	Inc. above	0.10	0.20	0.35	0.50	0.75
1965	Inc. above	0.10	0.20	0.35	0.50	0.75
1966	Inc. above	0.10	0.20	0.35	0.50	0.75
1966 Proof	—	—	—	—	—	—
1967	46,990,000	0.10	0.20	0.35	0.50	0.75
1968	37,275,000	0.10	0.20	0.35	0.50	0.75
1969	80,000,000	0.10	0.15	0.35	0.50	0.75
1970	50,005,000	0.10	0.20	0.35	0.50	0.75
1971	30,450,000	0.10	0.20	0.35	0.50	0.75

KM# 49.2 10 HALERU
1.18 g., Aluminum, 22 mm. **Obv:** Star above Czech lion with socialist shield within shield, flat-top 3 in date below **Rev:** Denomination within linden wreath, star above **Edge:** Reeded **Note:** Obverse muled from 50 Haleru, KM 55.1.

Date	Mintage	VF20	XF40	MS60	MS63	MS65
1963	Est. 3600	25.00	60.00	120	175	—

Note: Weakly struck counterfeits are known.

KM# 49.1a 10 HALERU

2.40 g., Brass, 22 mm. **Obv:** Star above Czech lion with socialist shield within shield **Rev:** Large denomination within linden wreath, star above

Date	Mintage	VF20	XF40	MS60	MS63	MS65
1968	Est. 20	—	300	400	500	—

KM# 80 10 HALERU

0.90 g., Aluminum, 18.2 mm. **Obv:** Czech lion with socialist shield within shield, fat date below **Rev:** Large thick denomination, star above **Note:** Varieties exist.

Date	Mintage	VF20	XF40	MS60	MS63	MS65
1974	11,470,000	—	0.10	0.25	0.35	0.50
1975	41,002,000	—	0.10	0.25	0.35	0.50
1976	182,000,000	—	0.10	0.25	0.35	0.50
1977	151,760,000	—	0.10	0.25	0.35	0.50
1978	62,620,000	—	0.10	0.25	0.35	0.50
1979	30,240,000	—	0.10	0.25	0.35	0.50
1980	31,280,000	—	0.10	0.25	0.35	0.50
1981	43,616,160	—	0.10	0.25	0.35	0.50
1981 Proof	—	—	—	—	—	—
1982	74,568,847	—	0.10	0.25	0.35	0.50
1983	50,560,000	—	0.10	0.25	0.35	0.50
1984	40,369,957	—	0.10	0.25	0.35	0.50
1985	92,929,791	—	0.10	0.25	0.35	0.50
1986	87,260,000	—	0.10	0.25	0.35	0.50
1987	30,030,000	—	0.10	0.25	0.35	0.50
1988	47,479,999	—	0.10	0.25	0.35	0.50
1989	50,300,000	—	0.10	0.25	0.35	0.50
1990	25,220,000	—	0.10	0.25	0.35	0.50

KM# 74 20 HALERU

2.60 g., Nickel-Brass, 19.5 mm. **Obv:** Czech lion with socialist shield within shield, thick date below **Rev:** Large thick denomination, star above **Edge:** Reeded **Note:** Varieties exist.

Date	Mintage	VF20	XF40	MS60	MS63	MS65
1972	25,820,000	0.10	0.20	0.40	0.60	1.00
1973	39,095,000	0.10	0.20	0.40	0.60	1.00
1974	24,795,000	0.10	0.20	0.40	0.60	1.00
1975	30,025,000	0.10	0.20	0.40	0.60	1.00
1976	30,540,000	0.10	0.20	0.40	0.60	1.00
1977	30,655,000	0.10	0.20	0.40	0.60	1.00
1978	30,095,000	0.10	0.20	0.40	0.60	1.00
1979	12,120,000	0.10	0.20	0.40	0.60	1.00
1980	52,301,000	0.10	0.15	0.30	0.50	0.75
1981	35,126,160	0.10	0.15	0.30	0.50	0.75
1981 Proof	—	—	—	—	—	—
1982	41,238,847	0.10	0.15	0.30	0.50	0.75
1983	50,160,000	0.10	0.15	0.30	0.50	0.75
1984	33,684,957	0.10	0.15	0.30	0.50	0.75
1985	40,454,791	0.10	0.15	0.30	0.50	0.75
1986	37,055,000	0.10	0.15	0.30	0.50	0.75
1987	26,975,000	0.10	0.15	0.30	0.50	0.75
1988	18,259,999	0.10	0.15	0.30	0.50	0.75
1989	29,980,000	0.10	0.15	0.30	0.50	0.75
1990	15,030,000	0.10	0.15	0.30	0.50	0.75

KM# 54 25 HALERU

1.43 g., Aluminum, 24 mm. **Obv:** Czech lion with socialist shield within shield, date below **Rev:** Large denomination within linden wreath, star above **Edge:** Reeded **Note:** This denomination ceased to be legal tender in 1972.

Date	Mintage	VF20	XF40	MS60	MS63	MS65
1962	69,880,000	0.15	0.20	0.35	0.60	1.00
1963	Inc. above	0.15	0.20	0.35	0.60	1.00
1964	Inc. above	0.15	0.20	0.35	0.60	1.00

KM# 55.1 50 HALERU

3.00 g., Bronze, 21.5 mm. **Obv:** Czech lion with socialist shield within shield, date below **Rev:** Large denomination within linden wreath, star above **Edge:** Reeded

Date	Mintage	VF20	XF40	MS60	MS63	MS65
1963	80,560,000	0.20	0.30	0.45	0.75	1.00
1964	Inc. above	0.20	0.30	0.45	0.75	1.00
1965	Inc. above	0.20	0.30	0.45	0.75	1.00
1969	9,876,000	0.20	0.30	0.45	0.75	1.00
1970	31,536,000	0.20	0.30	0.40	0.70	1.00
1971	20,800,000	0.20	0.30	0.40	0.70	1.00

KM# 55.2 50 HALERU

3.00 g., Bronze, 21.5 mm. **Obv:** Czech lion with socialist shield within shield, small date, without dots **Rev:** Value within linden wreath, star above **Edge:** Reeded **Note:** Obverse muled with 10 Haleru, KM 49.1.

Date	Mintage	VF20	XF40	MS60	MS63	MS65
1969	—	22.50	40.00	60.00	75.00	—

KM# 89 50 HALERU

3.20 g., Copper-Nickel, 20.8 mm. **Obv:** Czech lion with socialist shield within shield, thick date below **Rev:** Thick denomination, star above **Edge:** Reeded **Note:** Date varieties exist.

Date	Mintage	VF20	XF40	MS60	MS63	MS65
1977	—	—	500	750	1,000	—
1978	40,480,000	—	0.10	0.50	0.75	1.00
1979	76,116,000	—	0.10	0.50	0.75	1.00
1980	51,000	—	—	1.50	2.00	3.00
Note: Sets only						
1981	66,000	—	—	1.50	2.00	3.00
Note: Sets only						
1981 Proof	—	—	—	—	—	—
1982	14,261,847	—	0.10	0.50	0.75	1.00
1983	16,168,000	—	0.10	0.50	0.75	1.00
1984	16,207,957	—	0.10	0.50	0.75	1.00
1985	10,467,791	—	0.10	0.50	0.75	1.00
1986	10,020,000	—	0.10	0.50	0.75	1.00
1987	5,138,000	—	0.10	0.50	0.75	1.00
1988	5,089,999	—	0.10	0.50	0.75	1.00
1989	13,030,000	—	0.10	0.50	0.75	1.00
1990	7,742,000	—	0.10	0.50	0.75	1.00

KM# 50 KORUNA

4.00 g., Aluminum-Bronze, 23 mm. **Obv:** Czech lion with socialist shield within shield, date below **Rev:** Woman planting linden tree, denomination at left **Edge:** Reeded **Note:** Date varieties exist.

Date	Mintage	VF20	XF40	MS60	MS63	MS65
1961	146,964,000	0.15	0.30	0.60	0.85	1.25
1962	Inc. above	0.15	0.30	0.60	0.85	1.25
1963	Inc. above	0.15	0.30	0.60	0.85	1.25
1964	Inc. above	0.15	0.30	0.60	0.85	1.25
1965	Inc. above	0.15	0.30	0.60	0.85	1.25
1966	Inc. above	0.65	0.90	1.25	1.50	2.00
1967	7,924,000	0.15	0.30	0.60	0.85	1.25
1968	10,696,000	0.15	0.30	0.60	0.85	1.25
1969	21,820,000	0.15	0.30	0.60	0.85	1.25
1970	31,036,000	0.15	0.30	0.60	0.85	1.25
1971	10,152,000	0.15	0.30	0.60	0.85	1.25
1975	6,657,000	0.15	0.30	0.60	0.85	1.25
1976	14,211,000	0.15	0.30	0.60	0.85	1.25
1977	10,434,000	0.15	0.30	0.75	1.00	1.50
1979	Inc. below	0.15	0.30	0.75	1.00	1.50
1980	24,513,000	0.15	0.30	0.75	1.00	1.50
1981 Proof	—	—	—	—	—	—
1981	7,179,000	0.15	0.30	0.75	1.00	1.50
1982	17,162,847	0.15	0.30	0.75	1.00	1.50
1983	4,758,000	0.15	0.30	0.75	1.00	1.50
1984	9,732,957	0.15	0.30	0.75	1.00	1.50
1985	10,545,751	0.15	0.30	0.75	1.00	1.50
1986	2,789,000	0.15	0.30	0.75	1.00	1.50
1987	30,000	—	—	—	2.50	—
Note: Sets only						
1988	29,999	—	—	—	2.50	—
Note: Sets only						
1989	1,038,000	0.15	0.30	0.50	0.75	1.25
1990	19,368,000	0.15	0.30	0.50	0.75	1.25

KM# 75 2 KORUNY

6.00 g., Copper-Nickel, 24 mm. **Obv:** Czech lion with socialist shield within shield, date below **Rev:** Star above hammer and sickle, large value at right **Edge:** Ornamented

Date	Mintage	VF20	XF40	MS60	MS63	MS65
1972	20,344,000	0.25	0.45	0.75	1.00	1.50
1973	21,087,000	0.25	0.45	0.75	1.00	1.50
Note: 1973 date exists with edge of 5 Korun KM#60, value: $15.00						
1974	27,957,000	0.25	0.45	0.75	1.00	1.50
1975	35,094,000	0.25	0.45	0.75	1.00	1.50
1976	1,100,000	0.25	0.45	0.75	1.00	1.50
1977	4,201,000	0.25	0.65	1.00	1.50	2.00
1980	14,943,000	0.25	0.35	0.50	0.75	1.25
1981	17,264,000	0.25	0.35	0.50	0.75	1.25
1981 Proof	—	—	—	—	—	—
1982	8,108,000	0.25	0.35	0.50	0.75	1.25
1983	10,190,000	0.25	0.35	0.50	0.75	1.25
1984	8,634,000	0.25	0.35	0.50	0.75	1.25
1985	6,772,000	0.25	0.35	0.50	0.75	1.25
1986	10,262,000	0.25	0.35	0.50	0.75	1.25
1987	30,000	—	—	—	2.50	—
Note: Sets only						
1988	30,000	—	—	—	2.50	—
Note: Sets only						
1989	9,092,000	0.25	0.35	0.50	0.75	1.25
1990	10,672,000	0.25	0.35	0.50	0.75	1.25

KM# 57 3 KORUNY

5.50 g., Copper-Nickel, 23.5 mm. **Obv:** Czech lion with socialist shield within shield, date below **Rev:** Branch of five linden leaves within banner, large value at right **Edge:** Linden leaves and waves

Date	Mintage	VF20	XF40	MS60	MS63	MS65
1965	15,000,000	0.50	1.00	1.50	2.50	3.00
1966	Inc. above	0.50	1.00	1.50	2.50	3.00
1966 Proof	—	—	—	—	—	—
1968	7,000,000	0.45	0.85	1.25	2.00	3.00
1969	10,080,000	0.40	0.75	1.00	1.50	2.00

KM# 60 5 KORUN

7.00 g., Copper-Nickel, 26 mm. **Obv:** Czech lion with socialist shield within shield, date below **Rev:** Geometric design and large denomination **Edge:** Ornamented

Date	Mintage	VF20	XF40	MS60	MS63	MS65
1966	6,383,000	0.75	1.00	1.50	2.00	3.00
Note: 1966 varieties on obverse of coin: large date: no space between letter B in REPUBLIC and coat of arms; small date: space between letter B in REPUBLIC and coat of arms; plain edge: no ornamental inscription on edge (error coin). So far there has been no indication of any of the varieties as being scarce						
1966 Proof	—	—	—	—	—	—
1967	4,544,000	—	0.75	1.00	1.50	2.00
1968	14,120,000	—	0.75	1.00	1.50	2.00
1969	5,486,000	—	0.75	1.00	1.50	2.00
Note: Straight date						
1969	Inc. above	1.50	5.00	7.00	9.00	12.00
Note: Date in semi-circle						
1970	10,073,000	—	0.75	1.00	1.50	2.00
1973	15,620,000	—	0.75	1.00	1.25	1.50
Note: Two variations in 3 of date						
1974	20,053,000	—	0.75	1.00	1.25	1.50
Note: Three variations in 4 of date						
1975	17,158,000	—	0.75	1.00	1.25	1.50
1978	5,317,000	—	0.75	1.00	1.25	1.50
1979	9,219,000	—	0.75	1.00	1.25	1.50
1980	12,559,000	—	0.75	1.00	1.25	1.50
1981	8,620,160	—	0.75	1.00	1.25	1.50

Date	Mintage	VF20	XF40	MS60	MS63	MS65
1981 Proof	—	—	—	—	—	—
1982	6,903,847	—	0.75	1.00	1.25	1.50
1983	6,704,000	—	0.75	1.00	1.25	1.50
1984	6,856,957	—	0.75	1.00	1.25	1.50
1985	6,763,791	—	0.75	1.00	1.25	1.50
1986	20,000	—	—	—	35.00	—
Note: Sets only						
1987	30,000	—	—	—	7.00	—
Note: Sets only						
1988	29,999	—	—	—	5.00	—
1989	5,039,000	—	0.75	1.00	1.25	1.50
1990	2,783,000	—	0.75	1.00	1.25	1.50

KM# 56 10 KORUN

12.00 g., 0.500 Silver 0.1929 oz. ASW, 30 mm. **Subject:** 20th Anniversary - 1944 Slovak Uprising **Obv:** Star above Czech lion with socialist shield within shield **Rev:** Three hands and linden sprig divide dates and denomination **Edge Lettering:** SLOVENSKE NARODNE POVSTANIE **Note:** 11,476 pieces were melted by the Czech National Bank in 1999.

Date	Mintage	VF20	XF40	MS60	MS63	MS65
ND-1964	120,000	—	—	5.00	7.00	10.00

KM# 58 10 KORUN

12.00 g., 0.500 Silver 0.1929 oz. ASW, 30 mm. **Subject:** 550th Anniversary - Death of Jan Hus **Obv:** Star above Czech lion with socialist shield within shield **Rev:** Bust right, denomination below **Edge Lettering:** 550 LET UPALENI M, JANA HUSA **Note:** 380 pieces, Unc and Proof, were melted by the Czech National Bank in 1999.

Date	Mintage	VF20	XF40	MS60	MS63	MS65
ND-1965	55,000	—	—	7.00	13.00	15.00
ND-1965	5,000	PF65 20.00				

KM# 61 10 KORUN

12.00 g., 0.500 Silver 0.1929 oz. ASW, 30 mm. **Subject:** 1100th Anniversary of Great Moravia **Obv:** Star above Czech lion with socialist shield within shield **Rev:** Medal with horseman with falcon and plot of church, denomination upper right **Edge:** Plain with ellipse and rings **Note:** 9,446 pieces, Unc and Proof, were melted by the Czech National Bank in 1999.

Date	Mintage	VF20	XF40	MS60	MS63	MS65
1966	115,000	—	—	5.00	7.00	10.00
1966	5,000	PF65 16.00				

KM# 62 10 KORUN

12.00 g., 0.500 Silver 0.1929 oz. ASW, 30 mm. **Subject:** 500th Anniversary - Bratislava University **Obv:** Czech lion with socialist shield above stylized three mountains and river, denomination below **Rev:** University seal and building, date lower right **Edge:** Plain with Rhombs and waves **Note:** 103 pieces, Unc and Proof, were melted by the Czech National Bank in 1999.

Date	Mintage	VF20	XF40	MS60	MS63	MS65
ND-1967	45,000	—	—	10.00	18.00	20.00
ND-1967	5,000	PF65 30.00				

KM# 63 10 KORUN

12.00 g., 0.500 Silver 0.1929 oz. ASW, 30 mm. **Subject:** Centennial - Prague (Praha) National Theater **Obv:** Czech lion with socialist shield within shield, denomination below **Rev:** Female goddess in three-horse chariot, dates below **Edge:** Plain with crosses and waves **Note:** 50 pieces, Unc and Proof, were melted by the Czech National Bank in 1999.

Date	Mintage	VF20	XF40	MS60	MS63	MS65
ND-1968	55,000	—	—	12.00	25.00	32.00
ND-1968	5,000	PF65 125				

KM# 76 20 KORUN

9.00 g., 0.500 Silver 0.1447 oz. ASW, 29 mm. **Subject:** Centennial - Death of Andrej Sladkovic **Obv:** Czech lion with socialist shield within shield, denomination below **Rev:** Head left, dates below **Note:** 3,842 pieces, Unc and Proof, were melted by the Czech National Bank in 1999.

Date	Mintage	VF20	XF40	MS60	MS63	MS65
ND-1972	55,000	—	—	3.00	5.50	8.00
ND-1972	5,000	PF65 13.50				

KM# 59 25 KORUN

16.00 g., 0.500 Silver 0.2572 oz. ASW, 34 mm. **Subject:** 20th Anniversary - Czechoslovakian Liberation **Obv:** Czech lion with socialist shield within shield **Rev:** Female head left, dove with linden branch, denomination below, dates above and left **Edge Lettering:** 20 LET OSVOBOZENI CSSR **Note:** 18,114 pieces, Unc and Proof, were melted by the Czech National Bank in 1999.

Date	Mintage	VF20	XF40	MS60	MS63	MS65
ND-1965	150,000	—	—	8.00	10.00	13.00
ND-1965	5,000	PF65 17.00				

KM# 64 25 KORUN

16.00 g., 0.500 Silver 0.2572 oz. ASW, 34 mm. **Subject:** 150th Anniversary - Prague (Praha) National Museum **Obv:** Czech lion with socialist shield within shield, three line inscription below **Rev:** National Museum building, denomination below **Edge:** Plain with crosses and waves **Note:** 151 pieces, Unc and Proof, were melted by the Czech National Bank in 1999.

Date	Mintage	VF20	XF40	MS60	MS63	MS65
ND-1968	51,000	—	—	13.00	27.00	32.00
ND-1968	5,000	PF65 125				

KM# 66 25 KORUN

16.00 g., 0.500 Silver 0.2572 oz. ASW, 34 mm. **Subject:** 100th Anniversary - Death of J. E. Purkyne **Obv:** Czech lion with socialist shield within shield, denomination below **Rev:** Head right, dates at right **Edge Lettering:** FYSIOLOG, FILOSOF, BUDITEL, BASNIK **Note:** Edge varieties exist; 140 pieces, Unc and Proof, were melted by the Czech National Bank in 1999.

Date	Mintage	VF20	XF40	MS60	MS63	MS65
ND-1969	45,000	—	—	9.00	12.00	16.00
ND-1969	5,000	PF65 32.00				

KM# 67 25 KORUN

16.00 g., 0.500 Silver 0.2572 oz. ASW, 34 mm. **Subject:** 25th Anniversary - 1944 Slovak Uprising **Obv:** Czech lion with socialist shield within shield, three line inscription and denomination below **Rev:** Three mountains and plant, date at top **Edge Lettering:** 25. VYROCIE SLOVENSKEHO NARODNEHO POVSTANIA **Note:** Edge varieties exist; 40 pieces, Unc and Proof, were melted by the Czech National Bank in 1999.

Date	Mintage	VF20	XF40	MS60	MS63	MS65
ND-1969	25,000	—	—	40.00	55.00	70.00
ND-1969	5,000	PF65 90.00				

KM# 68 25 KORUN

10.00 g., 0.500 Silver 0.1608 oz. ASW, 30 mm. **Subject:** 50th Anniversary - Slovak National Theater **Obv:** Czech lion with socialist shield within square, denomination below **Rev:** Stylized head of muse within square divides dates **Note:** 4,923 pieces, Unc and Proof, were melted by the Czech National Bank in 1999.

Date	Mintage	VF20	XF40	MS60	MS63	MS65
ND-1970	45,000	—	—	5.00	8.00	10.00
ND-1970	5,000	PF65 50.00				

KM# 69 25 KORUN

10.00 g., 0.500 Silver 0.1608 oz. ASW, 30 mm. **Subject:** 25th Anniversary of Liberation **Obv:** Czech lion with socialist shield within shield, three line inscription below **Rev:** Sun of Liberation, landscape, denomination below **Edge:** - x - **Note:** 23,777 pieces, Unc and Proof, were melted by the Czech National Bank in 1999.

Date	Mintage	VF20	XF40	MS60	MS63	MS65
ND-1970	95,000	—	—	4.00	6.00	8.00
ND-1970	5,000	PF65 15.00				

KM# 65 50 KORUN

20.00 g., 0.900 Silver 0.5787 oz. ASW, 37 mm. **Subject:** 50th Anniversary of Czechoslovakia 20th Anniversary - People's Republic **Obv:** Czech lion with socialist shield divides dates, inscription and denomination below **Rev:** Woman's head left, wearing linden and floral wreath, date at left **Note:** 650 pieces, Unc and Proof, were melted by the Czech National Bank in 1999.

Date	Mintage	VF20	XF40	MS60	MS63	MS65
ND-1968	58,000	—	—	17.00	30.00	40.00
ND-1968	2,000	PF65 225				

KM# 70 50 KORUN

13.00 g., 0.700 Silver 0.2926 oz. ASW, 31 mm. **Subject:** Centennial - Birth of Lenin **Obv:** Czech lion with socialist shield within shield, denomination below **Rev:** Head right, date at left **Note:** 451 pieces, Unc and Proof, were melted by the Czech National Bank in 1999.

Date	Mintage	VF20	XF40	MS60	MS63	MS65
ND-1970	44,000	—	—	8.00	11.00	13.00
ND-1970	6,200	PF65 30.00				

KM# 71 50 KORUN

13.00 g., 0.700 Silver 0.2926 oz. ASW, 31 mm. **Subject:** 50th Anniversary - Czechoslovak Communist Party **Obv:** Czech lion with socialist shield within shield, denomination below **Rev:** Five figures standing within hammer and sickle, star above, dates below **Edge:** Wave, star, wave **Note:** 4,850 pieces, Unc and Proof, were melted by the Czech National Bank in 1999.

Date	Mintage	VF20	XF40	MS60	MS63	MS65
ND-1971	45,000	—	—	8.00	11.00	13.00
ND-1971	5,000	PF65 28.00				

KM# 72 50 KORUN

13.00 g., 0.700 Silver 0.2926 oz. ASW, 31 mm. **Subject:** 50th Anniversary - Death of Pavol Orsagh-Hviezdoslav **Obv:** Czech lion with socialist shield within shield, denomination below **Rev:** Head left, dates at right **Note:** 4,300 pieces, Unc and Proof, were melted by the Czech National Bank in 1999.

Date	Mintage	VF20	XF40	MS60	MS63	MS65
ND-1971	45,000	—	—	9.00	12.00	16.00
ND-1971	5,000	PF65 45.00				

KM# 77 50 KORUN

13.00 g., 0.700 Silver 0.2926 oz. ASW, 31 mm. **Subject:** 50th Anniversary - Death of J. V. Myslbek **Obv:** Czech lion with socialist shield within shield, denomination below **Rev:** Head left, dates at right **Edge Lettering:** J. V. MYSLBEK *1922-1972* **Note:** 6,439 pieces, Unc and Proof, were melted by the Czech National Bank in 1999.

Date	Mintage	VF20	XF40	MS60	MS63	MS65
ND-1972	45,000	—	—	8.00	11.00	13.00
ND-1972	5,000	PF65 22.00				

KM# 78 50 KORUN

13.00 g., 0.700 Silver 0.2926 oz. ASW, 31 mm. **Subject:** 25th Anniversary - Victory of Communist Party **Obv:** Czech lion with socialist shield within shield **Rev:** Soldier standing before large star, hammer and sickle at right **Edge Lettering:** 25. VYROCI VITEZNEHO UNORA* **Note:** 5,340 pieces, Unc and Proof, were melted by the Czech National Bank in 1999.

Date	Mintage	VF20	XF40	MS60	MS63	MS65
ND-1973	55,000	—	—	8.00	11.00	13.00
ND-1973	5,000	PF65 22.00				

KM# 79 50 KORUN

13.00 g., 0.700 Silver 0.2926 oz. ASW, 31 mm. **Subject:** 200th Anniversary - Birth of Josef Jungmann **Obv:** Czech lion with socialist shield within shield, denomination below **Rev:** Head right, dates below **Note:** 2,084 pieces, Unc and Proof, were melted by the Czech National Bank in 1999.

Date	Mintage	VF20	XF40	MS60	MS63	MS65
ND-1973	45,000	—	—	7.00	10.00	12.00
ND-1973	5,000	PF65 20.00				

KM# 81 50 KORUN

13.00 g., 0.700 Silver 0.2926 oz. ASW, 31 mm. **Subject:** Centennial - Birth of Janko Jesensky **Obv:** Czech lion with socialist shield within shield, denomination below **Rev:** Head 3/4 right, date at right **Edge:** Plain with wave star wave **Note:** 112,038 pieces, Unc and Proof, were melted by the Czech National Bank in 1999.

Date	Mintage	VF20	XF40	MS60	MS63	MS65
ND-1974	55,000	—	—	7.00	10.00	12.00
ND-1974	5,000	PF65 20.00				

KM# 83 50 KORUN

13.00 g., 0.700 Silver 0.2926 oz. ASW, 31 mm. **Subject:** Centennial - Birth of S. K. Neumann **Obv:** Czech lion with socialist shield within shield, denomination below **Rev:** Head right, dates at right **Edge:** Milled **Note:** 11,537 pieces, Unc and Proof, were melted by the Czech National Bank in 1999.

Date	Mintage	VF20	XF40	MS60	MS63	MS65
ND-1975	55,000	—	—	7.00	10.00	12.00
ND-1975	5,000	PF65 20.00				

KM# 87 50 KORUN

13.00 g., 0.700 Silver 0.2926 oz. ASW, 31 mm. **Subject:** 125th Anniversary - Death of Jan Kollar **Obv:** Czech lion with socialist shield within shield, denomination below **Rev:** Head facing, dates below **Edge:** Milled **Note:** 19,743 pieces, Unc and Proof, were melted by the Czech National Bank in 1999.

Date	Mintage	VF20	XF40	MS60	MS63	MS65
ND-1977	75,000	—	—	7.00	10.00	12.00
ND-1977	5,000	PF65 20.00				

KM# 90 50 KORUN

13.00 g., 0.700 Silver 0.2926 oz. ASW, 31 mm. **Subject:** Centennial - Birth of Zdenek Nejedly **Obv:** Czech lion with socialist shield within shield, denomination below **Rev:** Bust right, dates at left **Edge:** Milled **Note:** 20,538 pieces, Unc and Proof, were melted by the Czech National Bank in 1999.

Date	Mintage	VF20	XF40	MS60	MS63	MS65
ND-1978	75,000	—	—	7.00	10.00	12.00
ND-1978	5,000	PF65 20.00				

KM# 91 50 KORUN

13.00 g., 0.700 Silver 0.2926 oz. ASW, 31 mm. **Subject:** 650th Anniversary of Kremnica Mint **Obv:** Czech lion with socialist shield within shield, denomination below **Rev:** Montage of five coin designs, dates below **Note:** 22,037 pieces, Unc and Proof, were melted by the Czech National Bank in 1999.

Date	Mintage	VF20	XF40	MS60	MS63	MS65
ND-1978	93,000	—	—	7.00	10.00	12.00
ND-1978	7,000	PF65 20.00				

KM# 98 50 KORUN

13.00 g., 0.700 Silver 0.2926 oz. ASW, 31 mm. **Subject:** 30th Anniversary of 9th Congress **Obv:** Czech lion with socialist shield within shield, linden leaves flanking, three line inscription above denomination below **Rev:** Hammer and sickle in gear at center, linden leaves at left, dates below **Edge:** Milled **Note:** 30,089 pieces, Unc and Proof, were melted by the Czech National Bank in 1999.

Date	Mintage	VF20	XF40	MS60	MS63	MS65
ND-1979	94,000	—	—	7.00	10.00	12.00
ND-1979	6,000	PF65 20.00				

KM# 121 50 KORUN
7.00 g., 0.500 Silver 0.1125 oz. ASW, 27 mm. **Obv:** Czech lion with socialist shield within shield, denomination and dates below **Rev:** Prague (Praha) city view **Note:** 6,838 pieces, Unc and Proof, were melted by the Czech National Bank in 1999.

Date	Mintage	VF20	XF40	MS60	MS63	MS65
1986	90,000	—	—	—	5.00	8.00
1986	10,000	PF65 10.00				

KM# 122 50 KORUN
7.00 g., 0.500 Silver 0.1125 oz. ASW, 27 mm. **Obv:** Czech lion with socialist shield divides denomination, three line inscription and date below **Rev:** Levoca city view above three statues **Note:** 9,438 pieces Unc and Proof, were melted by the Czech National Bank in 1999.

Date	Mintage	VF20	XF40	MS60	MS63	MS65
1986	69,000	—	—	—	5.00	8.00
1986	10,000	PF65 10.00				

KM# 124 50 KORUN
7.00 g., 0.500 Silver 0.1125 oz. ASW, 27 mm. **Obv:** Czech lion with socialist shield divides denomination, three line inscription and date below **Rev:** Three building facades in Telc **Note:** 13,438 pieces Unc and Proof, were melted by the Czech National Bank in 1999.

Date	Mintage	VF20	XF40	MS60	MS63	MS65
1986	69,000	—	—	—	5.00	8.00
1986	10,000	PF65 10.00				

KM# 125 50 KORUN
7.00 g., 0.500 Silver 0.1125 oz. ASW, 27 mm. **Obv:** Czech lion with socialist shield divides denomination, three line inscription and date below **Rev:** Bratislava city view **Note:** 12,188 pieces, Unc and Proof, were melted by the Czech National Bank in 1999.

Date	Mintage	VF20	XF40	MS60	MS63	MS65
1986	69,000	—	—	—	5.00	8.00
1986	10,000	PF65 10.00				

KM# 126 50 KORUN
7.00 g., 0.500 Silver 0.1125 oz. ASW, 27 mm. **Obv:** Czech lion with socialist shield within shield, date and denomination below **Rev:** Cesky Krumlov city view **Note:** 11,338 pieces Unc and Proof, were melted by the Czech National Bank in 1999.

Date	Mintage	VF20	XF40	MS60	MS63	MS65
1986	69,000	—	—	—	5.00	8.00
1986	10,000	PF65 10.00				

KM# 127 50 KORUN
7.00 g., 0.500 Silver 0.1125 oz. ASW, 27 mm. **Subject:** Environmental Protection **Obv:** Czech lion with socialist shield within shield, date and denomination below **Rev:** Two Przewalski's horses **Note:** 338 pieces Unc and Proof, were melted by the Czech National Bank in 1999.

Date	Mintage	VF20	XF40	MS60	MS63	MS65
1987	55,000	—	—	—	22.50	25.00
1987	5,000	PF65 30.00				

KM# 129 50 KORUN
7.00 g., 0.500 Silver 0.1125 oz. ASW, 27 mm. **Subject:** 300th Anniversary - Birth of Juraj Janosik **Obv:** Czech lion with socialist shield divides denomination, three line inscription below **Rev:** Standing, caped man divides dates, bird at left **Note:** 735 pieces Unc and Proof, were melted by the Czech National Bank in 1999.

Date	Mintage	VF20	XF40	MS60	MS63	MS65
ND-1988	53,000	—	—	—	6.00	10.00
ND-1988	5,000	PF65 12.00				

KM# 133 50 KORUN
7.00 g., 0.500 Silver 0.1125 oz. ASW, 27 mm. **Subject:** 150th Anniversary - Breclav to Brno Railroad **Obv:** Czech lion with socialist shield within shield, denomination below **Rev:** Early steam locomotive, dates below **Note:** 1,835 pieces Unc and Proof, were melted by the Czech National Bank in 1999.

Date	Mintage	VF20	XF40	MS60	MS63	MS65
ND-1989	67,000	—	—	—	6.00	10.00
ND-1989	3,000	PF65 12.00				

KM# 73 100 KORUN
15.00 g., 0.700 Silver 0.3376 oz. ASW, 33 mm. **Subject:** Centennial - Death of Josef Manes **Obv:** Czech lion with socialist shield within shield, three line inscription and denomination below **Rev:** Bust right divides dates **Note:** 6,803 pieces, Unc and Proof, were melted by the Czech National Bank in 1999.

Date	Mintage	VF20	XF40	MS60	MS63	MS65
ND-1971	45,000	—	—	10.00	12.50	15.00
ND-1971	5,000	PF65 20.00				

KM# 82 100 KORUN
15.00 g., 0.700 Silver 0.3376 oz. ASW, 33 mm. **Subject:** Sesquicentennial - Birth of Bedrich Smetana **Obv:** Czech lion with socialist shield within shield, denomination below **Rev:** Head right, dates at left **Edge:** Plain with 150 LET OD NAROZENI **Note:** 6,201 pieces, Unc and Proof, were melted by the Czech National Bank in 1999.

Date	Mintage	VF20	XF40	MS60	MS63	MS65
ND-1974	75,000	—	—	10.00	12.50	15.00
ND-1974	5,000	PF65 20.00				

KM# 84 100 KORUN
15.00 g., 0.700 Silver 0.3376 oz. ASW, 33 mm. **Subject:** Centennial - Death of Janko Kral **Obv:** Czech lion with socialist shield within shield, denomination below **Rev:** Head right, dates lower right **Edge Lettering:** BASNIK * REVOLUCIONAR **Note:** 19,839 pieces, Unc and Proof, were melted by the Czech National Bank in 1999.

Date	Mintage	VF20	XF40	MS60	MS63	MS65
ND-1976	75,000	—	—	10.00	12.50	15.00
ND-1976	5,000	PF65 20.00				

KM# 85 100 KORUN
15.00 g., 0.700 Silver 0.3376 oz. ASW, 33 mm. **Subject:** Centennial - Birth of Viktor Kaplan **Obv:** Czech lion with socialist shield within shield, denomination below **Rev:** Bust right, dates at left **Edge:** - * - **Note:** 22,339 pieces, Unc and Proof, were melted by the Czech National Bank in 1999.

Date	Mintage	VF20	XF40	MS60	MS63	MS65
ND-1976	75,000	—	—	10.00	12.00	14.00
ND-1976	5,000	PF65 20.00				

KM# 88 100 KORUN
15.00 g., 0.700 Silver 0.3376 oz. ASW, 33 mm. **Subject:** 300th Anniversary - Death of Vaclav Hollar **Obv:** Czech lion with socialist shield within shield, denomination below **Rev:** Head left, dates lower left **Edge:** Plain with waves and dots **Note:** 32,789 pieces, Unc and Proof, were melted by the Czech National Bank in 1999.

Date	Mintage	VF20	XF40	MS60	MS63	MS65
ND-1977	95,000	—	—	10.00	12.00	14.00
ND-1977	5,000	PF65 20.00				

KM# 92 100 KORUN

15.00 g., 0.700 Silver 0.3376 oz. ASW, 33 mm. **Subject:** 75th Anniversary - Birth of Julius Fucik **Obv:** Czech lion with socialist shield within shield, denomination below **Rev:** Head left, dates at right **Edge Lettering:** LIDE, MEL JSEM VAS RAD, BDETE! **Note:** 24,840 pieces, Unc and Proof, were melted by the Czech National Bank in 1999.

Date	Mintage	VF20	XF40	MS60	MS63	MS65
ND-1978	75,000	—	—	10.00	12.00	14.00
ND-1978	5,000	PF65 20.00				

KM# 93 100 KORUN

15.00 g., 0.700 Silver 0.3376 oz. ASW, 33 mm. **Subject:** 600th Anniversary - Death of Charles IV **Obv:** Czech lion with socialist shield within shield, three line inscription, denomination and date below **Rev:** Crowned bust right, dates below **Note:** 32,638 pieces, Unc and Proof, were melted by the Czech National Bank in 1999.

Date	Mintage	VF20	XF40	MS60	MS63	MS65
1978	90,000	—	—	10.00	12.00	14.00
1978	10,000	PF65 20.00				

KM# 99 100 KORUN

15.00 g., 0.700 Silver 0.3376 oz. ASW, 33 mm. **Subject:** 150th Anniversary - Birth of Jan Botto **Obv:** Czech lion with socialist shield within shield, three line inscription above denomination below **Rev:** Head 3/4 left, date below **Edge:** ooo star ooo **Note:** 26,740 pieces, Unc and Proof, were melted by the Czech National Bank in 1999.

Date	Mintage	VF20	XF40	MS60	MS63	MS65
ND-1979	75,000	—	—	10.00	12.00	14.00
ND-1979	5,000	PF65 20.00				

KM# 100 100 KORUN

15.00 g., 0.700 Silver 0.3376 oz. ASW, 33 mm. **Subject:** 150th Anniversary - Birth of Peter Parler **Obv:** Czech lion with socialist shield within shield, medieval arches in background, three line inscription above denomination below **Rev:** Bust facing, medieval arches in background, date at left and below **Edge:** Plain with waves and dots **Note:** 54,738 pieces, Unc and Proof, were melted by the Czech National Bank in 1999.

Date	Mintage	VF20	XF40	MS60	MS63	MS65
ND-1980	91,000	—	—	10.00	12.00	14.00
ND-1980	9,000	PF65 20.00				

KM# 101 100 KORUN

9.00 g., 0.500 Silver 0.1447 oz. ASW, 29 mm. **Subject:** Fifth Spartakiade Games **Obv:** Czech lion with socialist shield within shield divides denomination, inscription below **Rev:** Seven female gymnastic figures, shadowing, date at left **Note:** 50,391 pieces, Unc and Proof, were melted by the Czech National Bank in 1999.

Date	Mintage	VF20	XF40	MS60	MS63	MS65
1980	110,000	—	—	—	12.00	14.00
1980	10,000	PF65 18.00				

KM# 102 100 KORUN

9.00 g., 0.500 Silver 0.1447 oz. ASW, 29 mm. **Subject:** Centennial - Birth of Bohumir Smeral **Obv:** Czech lion with socialist shield within shield, denomination below **Rev:** Bust 3/4 facing, dates lower right **Edge:** Milled **Note:** 29,943 pieces, Unc and Proof, were melted by the Czech National Bank in 1999.

Date	Mintage	VF20	XF40	MS60	MS63	MS65
ND-1980	74,000	—	—	—	10.00	12.00
ND-1980	6,000	PF65 16.00				

KM# 103 100 KORUN

9.00 g., 0.500 Silver 0.1447 oz. ASW, 29 mm. **Subject:** 20th Anniversary - Manned Space Flight **Obv:** Czech lion with socialist shield within shield, denomination below **Rev:** Cosmonaut Gagarin left, dates at right **Edge:** Milled **Note:** 31,639 pieces, Unc and Proof, were melted by the Czech National Bank in 1999.

Date	Mintage	VF20	XF40	MS60	MS63	MS65
ND-1981	95,000	—	—	—	10.00	12.00
ND-1981	5,000	PF65 16.00				

KM# 104 100 KORUN

9.00 g., 0.500 Silver 0.1447 oz. ASW, 29 mm. **Subject:** Centennial - Birth of Prof. Otakar Spaniel **Obv:** Czech lion with socialist shield within shield, denomination below **Rev:** Head left, dates below **Edge:** Milled **Note:** 56,189 pieces, Unc and Proof, were melted by the Czech National Bank in 1999.

Date	Mintage	VF20	XF40	MS60	MS63	MS65
ND-1981	115,000	—	—	—	10.00	12.00
ND-1981	5,000	PF65 16.00				

KM# 106 100 KORUN

9.00 g., 0.500 Silver 0.1447 oz. ASW, 29 mm. **Subject:** Centennial - Birth of Ivan Olbracht **Obv:** Czech lion with socialist shield within shield divides denomination **Rev:** Head with hat left, dates at right **Edge:** Milled **Note:** 24,140 pieces, Unc and Proof, were melted by the Czech National Bank in 1999.

Date	Mintage	VF20	XF40	MS60	MS63	MS65
ND-1982	76,000	—	—	—	10.00	12.00
ND-1982	4,000	PF65 18.00				

KM# 107 100 KORUN

9.00 g., 0.500 Silver 0.1447 oz. ASW, 29 mm. **Subject:** 150th Anniversary - Ceske Budejovice Horse Drawn Railway **Obv:** Czech lion with socialist shield within shield, denomination and inscription below **Rev:** Horse-drawn train carriage, dates below **Note:** 14,939 pieces, Unc and Proof, were melted by the Czech National Bank in 1999.

Date	Mintage	VF20	XF40	MS60	MS63	MS65
ND-1982	76,000	—	—	—	10.00	12.00
ND-1982	7,000	PF65 16.00				

KM# 108 100 KORUN

9.00 g., 0.500 Silver 0.1447 oz. ASW, 29 mm. **Subject:** 100th Anniversary - Death of Karl Marx **Obv:** Czech lion with socialist shield within shield divides denomination, inscription below **Rev:** Head facing, dates at left **Edge:** Milled **Note:** 23,793 pieces, Unc and Proof, were melted by the Czech National Bank in 1999.

Date	Mintage	VF20	XF40	MS60	MS63	MS65
ND-1983	76,000	—	—	—	10.00	12.00
ND-1983	4,000	PF65 18.00				

KM# 109 100 KORUN

9.00 g., 0.500 Silver 0.1447 oz. ASW, 29 mm. **Subject:** Centennial - Birth of Jaroslav Hasek **Obv:** Czech lion with socialist shield within shield, denomination below **Rev:** Bust facing, date below **Edge:** Milled **Note:** 21,538 pieces, Unc and Proof, were melted by the Czech National Bank in 1999.

Date	Mintage	VF20	XF40	MS60	MS63	MS65
ND-1983	76,000	—	—	—	12.00	12.00
ND-1983	4,000	PF65 18.00				

KM# 110 100 KORUN

9.00 g., 0.500 Silver 0.1447 oz. ASW, 29 mm. **Subject:** Centennial - Death of Samo Chalupka **Obv:** Czech lion with socialist shield within shield, inscription and denomination below **Rev:** Bust 3/4 facing, dates at left **Edge:** Milled **Note:** 27,938 pieces, Unc and Proof, were melted by the Czech National Bank in 1999.

Date	Mintage	VF20	XF40	MS60	MS63	MS65
ND-1983	76,000	—	—	—	10.00	12.00
ND-1983	4,000	PF65 18.00				

KM# 111 100 KORUN

9.00 g., 0.500 Silver 0.1447 oz. ASW, 29 mm. **Subject:** 100th Anniversary of National Theater of Prague **Obv:** Czech lion with socialist shield within shield, denomination below **Rev:** View of the National Theater in Prague, dates below **Edge:** Milled **Note:** 23,538 pieces, Unc and Proof, were melted by the Czech National Bank in 1999.

Date	Mintage	VF20	XF40	MS60	MS63	MS65
ND-1983	140,000	—	—	—	10.00	12.00
ND-1983	10,000	PF65 16.00				

KM# 113 100 KORUN

9.00 g., 0.500 Silver 0.1447 oz. ASW, 29 mm. **Subject:** 300th Anniversary - Birth of Matej Bel **Obv:** Czech lion with socialist shield within shield, denomination below **Rev:** Seated figure, dates at right **Edge:** Milled **Note:** 5288 pieces, Unc and Proof, were melted by the Czech National Bank in 1999.

Date	Mintage	VF20	XF40	MS60	MS63	MS65
ND-1984	57,000	—	—	—	10.00	12.00
ND-1984	3,000	PF65 18.00				

KM# 114 100 KORUN

9.00 g., 0.500 Silver 0.1447 oz. ASW, 29 mm. **Subject:** 150th Anniversary - Birth of Jan Neruda **Obv:** Czech lion with socialist shield within shield, denomination below **Rev:** Head 3/4 left, house and dates at left **Edge:** Milled **Note:** 12,539 pieces, Unc and Proof, were melted by the Czech National Bank in 1999.

Date	Mintage	VF20	XF40	MS60	MS63	MS65
ND-1984	76,000	—	—	—	10.00	12.00
ND-1984	4,000	PF65 18.00				

KM# 115 100 KORUN

9.00 g., 0.500 Silver 0.1447 oz. ASW, 29 mm. **Subject:** Centennial - Birth of Antonin Zapotocky **Obv:** Czech lion with socialist shield within shield divides denomination, inscription below **Rev:** Head 3/4 right, dates at left **Edge:** Milled **Note:** 19,938 pieces, Unc and Proof, were melted by the Czech National Bank in 1999.

Date	Mintage	VF20	XF40	MS60	MS63	MS65
ND-1984	76,000	—	—	—	10.00	12.00
ND-1984	4,000	PF65 18.00				

KM# 116 100 KORUN

9.00 g., 0.500 Silver 0.1447 oz. ASW, 29 mm. **Subject:** 200th Anniversary - Birth of Jan Holly **Obv:** Czech lion with socialist shield within shield divides denomination, inscription below **Rev:** Head 3/4 facing, dates at left **Edge:** Milled **Note:** 9,338 pieces, Unc and Proof, were melted by the Czech National Bank in 1999.

Date	Mintage	VF20	XF40	MS60	MS63	MS65
ND-1985	62,000	—	—	—	10.00	12.00
ND-1985	3,000	PF65 18.00				

KM# 117 100 KORUN

9.00 g., 0.500 Silver 0.1447 oz. ASW, 29 mm. **Subject:** 1985 Ice Hockey Championships **Obv:** Czech lion with socialist shield within shield, denomination below **Rev:** Hockey player skating left, dates at left **Edge:** Milled **Note:** 2,788 pieces, Unc and Proof, were melted by the Czech National Bank in 1999.

Date	Mintage	VF20	XF40	MS60	MS63	MS65
1985	66,000	—	—	—	10.00	12.00
1985	4,000	PF65 18.00				

KM# 118 100 KORUN

9.00 g., 0.500 Silver 0.1447 oz. ASW, 29 mm. **Subject:** 125th Anniversary - Birth of Martin Kukucin **Obv:** Czech lion with socialist shield within shield, denomination below **Rev:** Bust facing, dates at left **Edge:** Milled **Note:** 11,838 pieces, Unc and Proof, were melted by the Czech National Bank in 1999.

Date	Mintage	VF20	XF40	MS60	MS63	MS65
ND-1985	62,000	—	—	—	10.00	12.00
ND-1985	3,000	PF65 18.00				

KM# 119 100 KORUN

9.00 g., 0.500 Silver 0.1447 oz. ASW, 29 mm. **Subject:** 10th Anniversary of Helsinki Conference **Obv:** Czech lion with socialist shield within shield divides denomination, inscription below **Rev:** Stylized dove embracing European map, dates at lower left **Edge:** Milled **Note:** 18,838 pieces, Unc and Proof, were melted by the Czech National Bank in 1999.

Date	Mintage	VF20	XF40	MS60	MS63	MS65
ND-1985	75,000	—	—	—	10.00	12.00
ND-1985	5,000	PF65 18.00				

KM# 120 100 KORUN

9.00 g., 0.500 Silver 0.1447 oz. ASW, 29 mm. **Subject:** 250th Anniversary - Death of Petr Brandl **Obv:** Czech lion with socialist shield within shield, denomination below **Rev:** Bust facing, large rock in background, dates at right **Edge:** Milled **Note:** 16,038 pieces, Unc and Proof, were melted by the Czech National Bank in 1999.

Date	Mintage	VF20	XF40	MS60	MS63	MS65
ND-1985	71,000	—	—	—	10.00	12.00
ND-1985	4,000	PF65 18.00				

KM# 123 100 KORUN

13.00 g., 0.500 Silver 0.209 oz. ASW, 31 mm. **Subject:** 150th Anniversary - Death of Karel Hynek Macha **Obv:** Czech lion with socialist shield within shield divides denomination, inscription below **Rev:** Head 3/4 left, dates at right **Edge:** Milled **Note:** 10,288 pieces, Unc and Proof, were melted by the Czech National Bank in 1999.

Date	Mintage	VF20	XF40	MS60	MS63	MS65
ND-1986	63,000	—	—	—	10.00	12.00
ND-1986	5,000	PF65 18.00				

KM# 128 100 KORUN

13.00 g., 0.500 Silver 0.209 oz. ASW, 31 mm. **Subject:** 225th Anniversary of Mining Academy **Obv:** Czech lion with socialist shield within shield, denomination below **Rev:** Mining equipment, dates above small shield at right **Edge:** Milled **Note:** 6,438 pieces, Unc and Proof, were melted by the Czech National Bank in 1999.

Date	Mintage	VF20	XF40	MS60	MS63	MS65
ND-1987	55,000	—	—	—	12.00	14.00
ND-1987	5,000	PF65 20.00				

KM# 130 100 KORUN

13.00 g., 0.500 Silver 0.209 oz. ASW, 31 mm. **Subject:** Prague Philatelic Exposition **Obv:** Czech lion with socialist shield within shield, denomination and date below **Rev:** City views of Prague presented as four stamps **Edge:** Milled **Note:** 4,235 pieces, Unc and Proof, were melted by the Czech National Bank in 1999.

Date	Mintage	VF20	XF40	MS60	MS63	MS65
1988	66,000	—	—	—	12.50	15.00
1988	5,000	PF65 22.00				

KM# 132 100 KORUN

13.00 g., 0.500 Silver 0.209 oz. ASW, 31 mm. **Subject:** Centennial - Birth of Martin Benka **Obv:** Czech lion with socialist shield within shield, denomination below **Rev:** Young Slovak woman in national costume with dove, dates at right, based on painting by Martin Benko **Edge:** Milled **Note:** 8,635 pieces, Unc and Proof, were melted by the Czech National Bank in 1999.

Date	Mintage	VF20	XF40	MS60	MS63	MS65
ND-1988	55,000	—	—	—	12.50	15.00
ND-1988	5,000	PF65 25.00				

KM# 135 100 KORUN
13.00 g., 0.500 Silver 0.209 oz. ASW, 31 mm. **Subject:** 50th Anniversary of Student Organization Against Occupation and Fascism **Obv:** Czech lion with socialist shield within shield, denomination below **Rev:** Barbed wire and medieval document seal, dates above **Edge:** Milled **Note:** 4,335 pieces, Unc and Proof, were melted by the Czech National Bank in 1999.

Date	Mintage	VF20	XF40	MS60	MS63	MS65
ND-1989	67,000	—	—	—	12.00	14.00
ND-1989	—	PF65 32.00				

KM# 137 100 KORUN
13.00 g., 0.500 Silver 0.209 oz. ASW, 31 mm. **Subject:** 100th Anniversary - Birth of Karel Capek **Obv:** Czech lion with socialist shield within shield, inscription and denomination below **Rev:** Head left, dates at right **Edge:** Milled **Note:** 7,920 pieces, Unc and Proof, were melted by the Czech National Bank in 1999.

Date	Mintage	VF20	XF40	MS60	MS63	MS65
ND-1990	67,000	—	—	—	12.00	14.00
ND-1990	3,500	PF65 45.00				

KM# 138 100 KORUN
13.00 g., 0.500 Silver 0.209 oz. ASW, 31 mm. **Subject:** 250th Anniversary - Death of Jan Kupecky **Obv:** Czech lion with socialist shield within shield, denomination below **Rev:** Half-length figure holding paintbrush and palette right, dates at left **Edge:** Milled **Note:** 7,570 pieces, Unc and Proof, were melted by the Czech National Bank in 1999.

Date	Mintage	VF20	XF40	MS60	MS63	MS65
ND-1990	58,000	—	—	—	12.00	14.00
ND-1990	2,500	PF65 50.00				

KM# 105 500 KORUN
24.00 g., 0.900 Silver 0.6945 oz. ASW, 40 mm. **Subject:** 125th Anniversary - Death of Ludovit Stur **Obv:** Czech lion with socialist shield within shield, inscription and denomination below **Rev:** Head facing, dates below **Edge Lettering:** 125 ROKOV OD SMRTI L' STURA **Note:** 7,057 pieces, Unc and Proof, were melted by the Czech National Bank in 1999.

Date	Mintage	VF20	XF40	MS60	MS63	MS65
ND-1981	51,000	—	—	—	40.00	50.00
ND-1981	1,586	PF65 115				

KM# 112 500 KORUN
24.00 g., 0.900 Silver 0.6945 oz. ASW, 40 mm. **Subject:** 100th Anniversary of National Theater in Prague **Obv:** Czech lion with socialist shield within shield, denomination below **Rev:** Woman with lyre, theater facade at right, dates below **Edge Lettering:** NAROD SOBE **Note:** 4,740 pieces, Unc and Proof, were melted by the Czech National Bank in 1999.

Date	Mintage	VF20	XF40	MS60	MS63	MS65
ND-1983	55,000	—	—	—	45.00	55.00
ND-1983	5,000	PF65 85.00				

KM# 136 500 KORUN
24.00 g., 0.900 Silver 0.6945 oz. ASW, 40 mm. **Subject:** 100th Anniversary - Birth of Josef Lada **Obv:** Czech lion with socialist shield within shield divides denomination, inscription below **Rev:** Town view, children building snowmen divide dates **Edge Lettering:** CESKY MALIR NARODNI UMELEC **Note:** 2,238 pieces, Unc and Proof, were melted by the Czech National Bank in 1999.

Date	Mintage	VF20	XF40	MS60	MS63	MS65
ND-1987	48,000	—	—	—	50.00	60.00
ND-1987	5,000	PF65 90.00				

KM# 131 500 KORUN
24.00 g., 0.900 Silver 0.6945 oz. ASW, 40 mm. **Subject:** 20th Anniversary of National Federation **Obv:** Czech lion with socialist shield within shield, inscription and denomination below **Rev:** Stylized linden tree encircled by ribbon in shape of country, dates below **Edge Lettering:** 20. VYROCIE CESKOSLOVENSKEJ FEDERACIE oM **Note:** 6,435 pieces, Unc and Proof, were melted by the Czech National Bank in 1999.

Date	Mintage	VF20	XF40	MS60	MS63	MS65
ND-1988	46,000	—	—	—	45.00	55.00
ND-1988	3,000	PF65 85.00				

KM# 134 500 KORUN
24.00 g., 0.900 Silver 0.6945 oz. ASW, 40 mm. **Subject:** 125th Anniversary of Matica Slovenska Institute **Obv:** Czech lion with socialist shield within shield, denomination below **Rev:** Woman standing in national costume holding book and linden sprigs, dates at right **Edge Lettering:** HOJ VLAST MOJA TY ZEM DRAHA **Note:** 6,338 pieces, Unc and Proof, were melted by the Czech National Bank in 1999.

Date	Mintage	VF20	XF40	MS60	MS63	MS65
ND-1988	44,000	—	—	—	45.00	55.00
ND-1988	5,000	PF65 80.00				

CZECH SLOVAK FEDERAL REPUBLIC

KM# 149 HALER
0.79 g., Aluminum, 16 mm. **Obv:** CSFR above quartered shield, linden leaves flanking, date below **Rev:** Denomination within linden wreath **Edge:** Plain

Date	Mintage	VF20	XF40	MS60	MS63	MS65
1991	55,000	—	—	—	1.00	2.50
1992	50,000	—	—	—	1.00	2.50

KM# 150 5 HALERU
0.75 g., Aluminum, 16.2 mm. **Obv:** CSFR above quartered shield, linden leaves flanking, date below **Rev:** Large, thick, denomination **Edge:** Plain

Date	Mintage	VF20	XF40	MS60	MS63	MS65
1991	10,055,000	—	—	—	0.10	0.25
1992	50,000	—	—	—	—	2.00

Note: Sets only

KM# 146 10 HALERU
Aluminum, 18.2 mm. **Obv:** CSFR above quartered shield, linden leaves flanking, date below **Rev:** Large, thick denomination

Date	Mintage	VF20	XF40	MS60	MS63	MS65
1991	40,055,000	—	—	—	0.25	0.50
1992	45,050,000	—	—	—	0.25	0.50

KM# 143 20 HALERU
Aluminum-Bronze, 19.5 mm. **Obv:** CSFR above quartered shield, linden leaves flanking, date below **Rev:** Large, thick denomination **Edge:** Milled

Date	Mintage	VF20	XF40	MS60	MS63	MS65
1991	41,105,000	—	—	—	0.25	0.50
1992	35,050,000	—	—	—	0.25	0.50

KM# 144 50 HALERU
3.00 g., Copper-Nickel, 20.8 mm. **Obv:** CSFR above quartered shield, linden leaves flanking, date below **Rev:** Large, thick denomination **Edge:** Reeded

Date	Mintage	VF20	XF40	MS60	MS63	MS65
1991	24,463,000	—	—	—	0.35	0.75
1992	15,062,000	—	—	—	0.35	0.75

KM# 151 KORUNA
4.08 g., Copper-Aluminum, 23 mm. **Obv:** CSFR above quartered shield, linden leaves flanking, date below **Rev:** Female planting linden tree, denomination at left **Edge:** Reeded

Date	Mintage	VF20	XF40	MS60	MS63	MS65
1991	20,056,000	—	—	—	0.50	1.00
1992	20,387,000	—	—	—	0.50	1.00

KM# 148 2 KORUNY
5.90 g., Copper-Nickel, 24 mm. **Obv:** CSFR above quartered shield, linden leaves flanking, date below **Rev:** Linden leaf, large value at right **Edge:** Ornamented

Date	Mintage	VF20	XF40	MS60	MS63	MS65
1991 (k)	25,201,000	—	—	—	0.60	1.25
1991 (l)	20,000,000	—	—	—	0.60	1.25
1992	1,051,000	—	—	—	0.65	1.35

KM# 152 5 KORUN
Copper-Nickel, 26 mm. **Obv:** CSFR above quartered shield, linden leaves flanking, date below **Rev:** Geometric design, large value **Edge:** Eight plain and eight milled areas

Date	Mintage	VF20	XF40	MS60	MS63	MS65
1991 (k)	18,564,000	—	—	—	0.75	2.00
1991 (l)	10,000,750	—	—	—	0.75	2.00
1992	50,000	—	—	—	2.50	6.00

Note: Sets only

KM# 139.1 10 KORUN
Nickel-Bronze, 24.5 mm. **Obv:** CSFR above quartered shield, date below, denomination at left **Rev:** Bust right, dates at left **Edge:** Segmented reeding **Note:** Designer initials (MR) below bust, four varieties exist.

Date	Mintage	VF20	XF40	MS60	MS63	MS65
1990	9,990,000	—	—	—	2.00	4.50
1993	2,500,000	—	—	—	2.00	5.00

KM# 139.2 10 KORUN
Nickel-Bronze, 24.5 mm. **Obv:** CSFR above shield, date below, denomination at left **Rev:** Tomas G. Masaryk bust, right, dates at left **Edge:** Segmented reeding **Note:** Designer name below bust: RONAI.

Date	Mintage	VF20	XF40	MS60	MS63	MS65
1990	Inc. above	—	—	2.00	5.00	10.00

KM# 153 10 KORUN
Nickel-Bronze, 24.5 mm. **Obv:** CSFR above quartered shield, date below, denomination at left **Rev:** Uniformed bust left, dates at right

Date	Mintage	VF20	XF40	MS60	MS63	MS65
1991	10,036,000	—	—	—	2.00	4.00
1993	2,500,000	—	—	—	2.50	5.00

KM# 159 10 KORUN
Nickel-Bronze, 24.5 mm. **Obv:** CSFR above quartered shield, date below, denomination at left **Rev:** Bust right, dates at left **Edge:** Eight plain and eight milled areas

Date	Mintage	VF20	XF40	MS60	MS63	MS65
1992	5,050,000	—	—	—	2.00	4.00

KM# 140.1 50 KORUN
7.00 g., 0.500 Silver 0.1125 oz. ASW, 27 mm. **Obv:** CSFR quartered shield with designer's initials (LK) below denomination **Rev:** Veiled head left, date upper left **Edge:** Milled **Note:** See note with KM#140.2. Designer emblem exists with and without initials.

Date	Mintage	VF20	XF40	MS60	MS63	MS65
1990	147,000	—	—	—	6.00	10.00
1990	3,000	PF65 18.00				

KM# 140.2 50 KORUN
7.00 g., 0.500 Silver 0.1125 oz. ASW, 27 mm. **Obv:** CSFR quartered shield, without designer's initials (LK) **Rev:** Veiled head left **Note:** 12,070 pieces, Unc and Proof of either KM#140.1 or 140.2, were melted by the Czech National Bank in 1999.

Date	Mintage	VF20	XF40	MS60	MS63	MS65
1990	Inc. above	—	—	—	12.00	25.00

KM# 145 50 KORUN
7.00 g., 0.500 Silver 0.1125 oz. ASW, 27 mm. **Obv:** CSFR quartered shield, denomination below **Rev:** Steamship Bohemia, dates below **Edge:** Milled **Note:** 4,470 pieces, Unc and Proof, were melted by the Czech National Bank in 1999.

Date	Mintage	VF20	XF40	MS60	MS63	MS65
ND-1991	77,000	—	—	—	8.00	12.00
ND-1991	3,000	PF65 20.00				

KM# 155 50 KORUN
7.00 g., 0.700 Silver 0.1575 oz. ASW, 27 mm. **Obv:** CSFR quartered shield, denomination below **Rev:** Piestany Spa building, shield below **Edge:** Milled **Note:** 17,920 pieces, Unc and Proof, were melted by the Czech National Bank in 1999.

Date	Mintage	VF20	XF40	MS60	MS63	MS65
1991	75,000	—	—	—	5.50	9.00
1991	Est. 5000	PF65 16.50				

KM# 156 50 KORUN
7.00 g., 0.700 Silver 0.1575 oz. ASW, 27 mm. **Obv:** CSFR quartered shield, denomination below, date above **Rev:** Marianske Lazne Spa buildings **Edge:** Milled **Note:** 16,520 pieces, Unc and Proof, were melted by the Czech National Bank in 1999.

Date	Mintage	VF20	XF40	MS60	MS63	MS65
1991	75,000	—	—	—	6.00	10.00
1991	5,000	PF65 35.00				

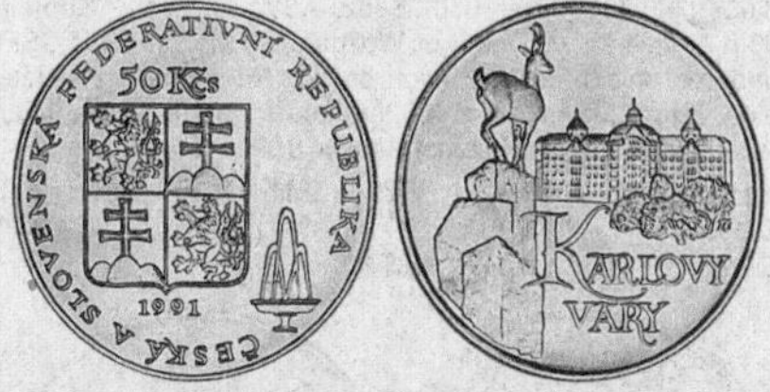

KM# 157 50 KORUN
7.00 g., 0.700 Silver 0.1575 oz. ASW, 27 mm. **Obv:** CSFR quartered shield, denomination above, date below **Rev:** Chamois on rock, Karlovy Vary Spa buildings **Edge:** Milled **Note:** 15,920, pieces, Unc and Proof, were melted by the Czech National Bank in 1999.

Date	Mintage	VF20	XF40	MS60	MS63	MS65
1991	75,000	—	—	—	12.00	15.00
1991	5,000	PF65 20.00				

KM# 141 100 KORUN
13.00 g., 0.500 Silver 0.209 oz. ASW, 31 mm. **Obv:** CSFR quartered shield, denomination at right **Rev:** Two horsemen right, date below **Edge:** Milled **Note:** 3,170 pieces, Unc and Proof, were melted by the Czech National Bank in 1999.

Date	Mintage	VF20	XF40	MS60	MS63	MS65
1990	67,000	—	—	—	16.00	22.00
1990	3,000	PF65 125				

KM# 142 100 KORUN
13.00 g., 0.500 Silver 0.209 oz. ASW, 31 mm. **Subject:** 100th

Anniversary - Birth of Bohuslav Martinu **Obv:** CSFR quartered shield, denomination below **Rev:** Head facing, dates at right **Edge:** Milled **Note:** 8,170 pieces, Unc and Proof, were melted by the Czech National Bank in 1999.

Date	Mintage	VF20	XF40	MS60	MS63	MS65
ND-1990	53,000	—	—	—	16.00	22.00
ND-1990	2,000	PF65 125				

KM# 147 100 KORUN

13.00 g., 0.500 Silver 0.209 oz. ASW, 31 mm. **Subject:** 150th Anniversary - Birth of A. Dvorak **Obv:** CSFR quartered shield, inscription and denomination below **Rev:** Stylized head right, dates below **Edge:** Milled **Note:** 16,220 pieces, Unc and Proof, were melted by the Czech National Bank in 1999.

Date	Mintage	VF20	XF40	MS60	MS63	MS65
1991	75,000	—	—	—	12.00	18.00
1991	5,000	PF65 100				

KM# 154 100 KORUN

13.00 g., 0.700 Silver 0.2926 oz. ASW, 31 mm. **Subject:** 200th Anniversary - Death of Wolfgang A. Mozart **Obv:** CSFR quartered shield, denomination below **Rev:** Bust right, dates below **Edge:** Milled **Note:** 2,620 pieces, Unc and Proof, were melted by the Czech National Bank in 1999.

Date	Mintage	VF20	XF40	MS60	MS63	MS65
ND-1991	75,000	—	—	—	14.00	20.00
ND-1991	5,000	PF65 100				

KM# 160 100 KORUN

13.00 g., 0.500 Silver 0.209 oz. ASW, 31 mm. **Subject:** 175th Anniversary - Moravian Museum **Obv:** CSFR quartered shield, denomination above, date below **Rev:** Moravian Museum, Moravian eagle **Edge:** Milled **Note:** 226,977 pieces, Unc and Proof, were melted by the Czech National Bank in 1999.

Date	Mintage	VF20	XF40	MS60	MS63	MS65
1992	73,000	—	—	—	12.00	18.00
1992	5,000	PF65 100				

KM# 161 100 KORUN

13.00 g., 0.500 Silver 0.209 oz. ASW, 31 mm. **Subject:** Nazi Massacres at Lidice and Lezaky **Obv:** CSFR quartered shield, denomination below, date above **Rev:** Cross with barbed wire loop **Edge:** Milled **Note:** 24,620 pieces, Unc and Proof, were melted by the Czech National Bank in 1999.

Date	Mintage	VF20	XF40	MS60	MS63	MS65
1992	70,000	—	—	—	12.00	18.00
1992	3,000	PF65 120				

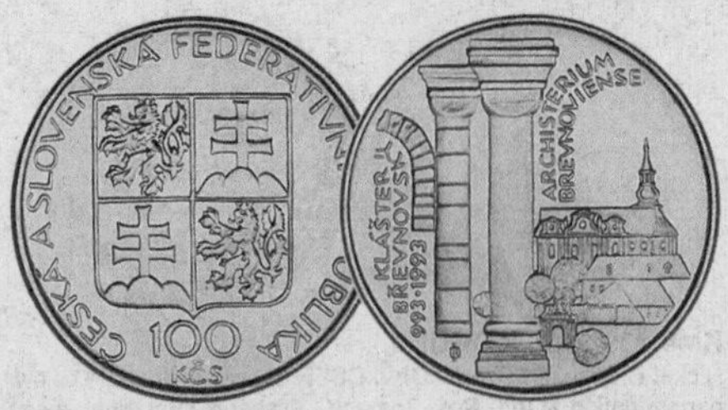

KM# 162 100 KORUN

13.00 g., 0.500 Silver 0.209 oz. ASW, 31 mm. **Subject:** 1000 Years of Brevnov Monastery **Obv:** CSFR quartered shield, denomination below **Rev:** Church and cloister columns, dates at left **Edge:** Milled **Note:** 25,932 pieces, Unc and Proof, were melted by the Czech National Bank in 1999.

Date	Mintage	VF20	XF40	MS60	MS63	MS65
ND-1993	70,000	—	—	—	12.00	18.00
ND-1993	3,000	PF65 120				

KM# 163 100 KORUN

13.00 g., 0.500 Silver 0.209 oz. ASW, 31 mm. **Subject:** Slovak Museum Centennial **Obv:** CSFR quartered shield, inscription and denomination below **Rev:** Historic folk art designs, dates lower left **Edge:** Milled **Note:** 31,932 pieces, Unc and Proof, were melted by the Czech National Bank in 1999.

Date	Mintage	VF20	XF40	MS60	MS63	MS65
ND-1993	70,000	—	—	—	12.00	18.00
ND-1993	3,000	PF65 120				

KM# 158 500 KORUN

24.00 g., 0.900 Silver 0.6945 oz. ASW, 40 mm. **Subject:** 400th Anniversary - Birth of J. A. Komensky **Obv:** CSFR quartered shield, date above, denomination below **Rev:** J. A. Komensky standing, dates at left **Edge:** Milled **Note:** 14,820 pieces, Unc and Proof, were melted by the Czech National Bank in 1999.

Date	Mintage	VF20	XF40	MS60	MS63	MS65
1992	60,000	—	—	—	35.00	45.00
1992	5,000	PF65 70.00				

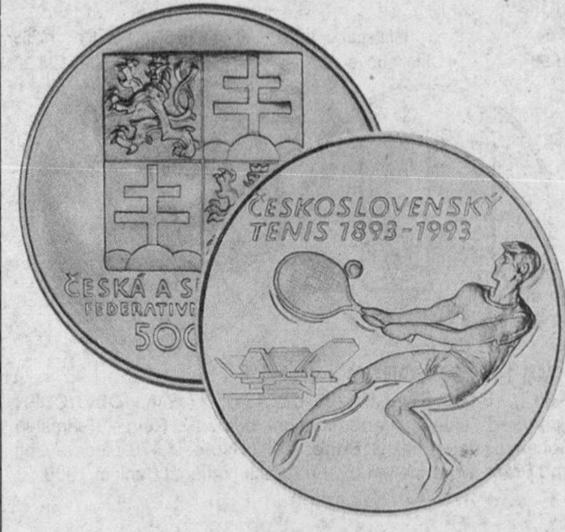

KM# 164 500 KORUN

24.00 g., 0.900 Silver 0.6945 oz. ASW, 40 mm. **Subject:** 100th Year of Czech Tennis **Obv:** CSFR quartered shield, inscription and denomination below **Rev:** Male tennis player, stadium at left, dates above **Edge:** Milled **Note:** 27,074 pieces, Unc and Proof, were melted by the Czech National Bank in 1999.

Date	Mintage	VF20	XF40	MS60	MS63	MS65
ND-1993	62,000	—	—	—	40.00	50.00
ND-1993	1,157	PF65 185				

PATTERNS

Including off-metal strikes

KM#	Date	Mintage	Identification	Mkt Val
Pn5	1920	—	20 Haleru. Copper-Nickel. Obv. KM# 2, Rev. KM#1.	1,850
Pn8	1932	—	25 Haleru. Copper-Nickel.	35,000

PROBA

KM#	Date	Mintage	Identification	Mkt Val
PrA1	1921	—	5 Korun. Silver. KM#10. "ZKOUSKA" on rim on both sides.	—
Pr1	1922	—	Koruna. Aluminum.	—
Pr2	1922	—	Koruna. Copper-Nickel.	—
Pr4	1932	2	25 Haleru. Copper-Nickel. W/ dense notches.	—
Pr5	1932	2	25 Haleru. Copper-Nickel. Thin notches.	—
Pr6	1932	10	25 Haleru. Copper-Nickel.	—
Pr3	1951	—	5 Koruna. Aluminum-Copper Magnesium.	—
Pr7	1976	—	3 Koruny.	—
Pr8	ND-1990	2,500	100 Korun.	225

MINT SETS

KM#	Date	Mintage	Identification	Issue Price	Mkt Val
MS1	1980 (7)	50,000	KM50, 60, 74-75, 80, 86, 89	5.00	5.25
MS2	1981 (7)	66,000	KM50, 60, 74-75, 80, 86, 89	—	5.50
MS3	1982 (7)	53,000	KM50, 60, 74-75, 80, 86, 89	—	5.50
MS4	1983 (7)	50,000	KM50, 60, 74-75, 80, 86, 89	—	4.50
MS5	1984 (7)	39,000	KM50, 60, 74-75, 80, 86, 89	—	6.50
MS6	1985 (7)	39,000	KM50, 60, 74-75, 80, 86, 89	—	6.50
MS7	1986 (7)	20,000	KM50, 60, 74-75, 80, 86, 89	—	50.00
MS8	1987 (7)	30,000	km50, 60, 74-75, 80, 86, 89	—	15.00
MS9	1988 (7)	29,000	KM50, 60, 74-75, 80, 86, 89	—	11.50
MS10	1989 (7)	30,000	KM50, 60, 74-75, 80, 86, 89	—	10.00
MS11	1990 (7)	30,000	KM50, 60, 74-75, 80, 86, 89	—	10.00
MS12	1991 (9)	25,000	KM143-144, 146, 148-153	—	14.00
MS13	1991 (8)	30,000	KM143-144, 146, 148-152	—	12.50
MS14	1992 (9)	49,000	KM143-144, 146, 148-152, 159	—	20.00
MS15	1992 (8)	49,000	KM143-144,146, 148-152	—	15.00

PROOF SETS

KM#	Date	Mintage	Identification	Issue Price	Mkt Val
PS1	1966 (4)	—	KM49.1, 53, 57, 60	—	—
PS2	1981 (7)	—	KM50, 60, 74-75, 80, 86, 89	—	—

DAHOMEY

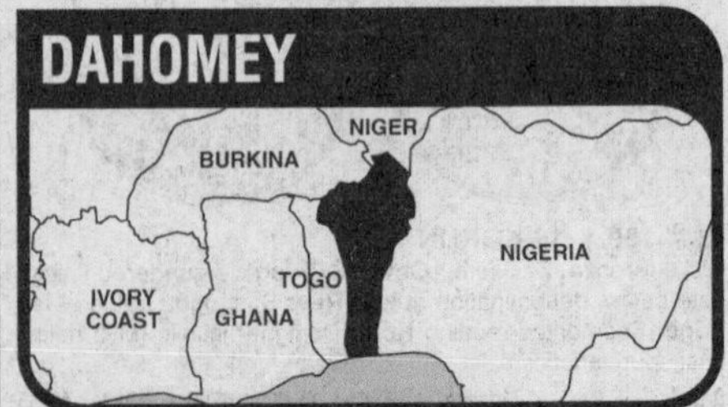

Porto-Novo, on the Bight of Benin, was founded as a trading post by the Portuguese in the 17th century. At that time, Dahomey (Benin) was composed of an aggregation of mutually suspicious tribes, the majority of which were tributary to the powerful northern Kingdom of Abomey. In 1863, the King of Porto-Novo petitioned France for protection from Abomey. The French subjugated other militant tribes as well, and in 1892 organized the area as a protectorate of France; in 1904 it was incorporated into French West Africa as the Territory of Dahomey. After the establishment of the Fifth French Republic, the Territory at Dahomey became an autonomous state within the French community. On Aug. 1, 1960, it became the fully independent Republic of Dahomey. In 1974, the republic began a transition to a socialist society with Marxism-Leninism as its revolutionary philosophy under Col. Ahmed Kerekow. On Nov. 30, 1975, the name of the Republic of Dahomey was changed to the Peoples Republic of Benin. As a result of Benin's first free presidential election in 30 years, Nicephore Soglo defeated Colonel Kerekou.

MINT MARK

1 AR - Uno-A-Erre, Arezzo, Italy

REPUBLIC

STANDARD COINAGE

KM# 1.1 100 FRANCS

5.10 g., 0.999 Silver 0.1638 oz. ASW **Subject:** 10th Anniversary of Independence **Obv:** Facing cornucopias top supported arms, date above, denomination below **Rev:** Buildings on Lake Ganvié **Note:** Hallmark "999.9" above denomination.

Date	Mintage	VF20	XF40	MS60	MS63	MS65
1971	4,650	PF63 38.00	PF65 45.00	PF67 65.00		

KM# 1.2 100 FRANCS

5.10 g., 0.999 Silver 0.1638 oz. ASW **Obv:** Facing cornucopias top supported arms, date above, denomination below **Rev:** Buildings on Lake Ganvié **Note:** Hallmark "999.9" right of denomination.

Date	Mintage	VF20	XF40	MS60	MS63	MS65
1971	Inc. above	PF63 38.00	PF65 45.00	PF67 65.00		

KM# 1.3 100 FRANCS

5.10 g., 0.999 Silver 0.1638 oz. ASW **Obv:** Facing cornucopias top supported arms, date above, denomination below **Rev:** Buildings on Lake Ganvié **Note:** Hallmark "1000" lower right "S" in "FRANCS".

Date	Mintage	VF20	XF40	MS60	MS63	MS65
1971	Inc. above	PF63 38.00	PF65 45.00	PF67 65.00		

KM# 2.1 200 FRANCS

10.25 g., 0.999 Silver 0.3292 oz. ASW **Subject:** 10th Anniversary of Independence **Obv:** Facing cornucopias top supported arms, date above, denomination below **Rev:** Abomey woman 3/4 left **Note:** Hallmark "999.9" between "200" and "FRANCS".

Date	Mintage	VF20	XF40	MS60	MS63	MS65
1971	5,150	PF63 48.00	PF65 55.00	PF67 75.00		

KM# 2.2 200 FRANCS

10.25 g., 0.999 Silver 0.3292 oz. ASW **Obv:** Facing cornucopias top supported arms, date above, denomination below **Rev:** Abomey woman 3/4 left **Note:** Hallmark "1000" lower right of "S" in "FRANCS".

Date	Mintage	VF20	XF40	MS60	MS63	MS65
1971	Inc. above	PF63 48.00	PF65 55.00	PF67 75.00		

KM# 2.3 200 FRANCS

10.25 g., 0.999 Silver 0.3292 oz. ASW **Obv:** Facing cornucopias top supported arms, date above, denomination below **Rev:** Abomey woman 3/4 left **Note:** Hallmark "999.9" lower right of "S" in "FRANCS".

Date	Mintage	VF20	XF40	MS60	MS63	MS65
1971	Inc. above	PF63 48.00	PF65 55.00	PF67 75.00		

KM# 2.4 200 FRANCS

10.25 g., 0.999 Silver 0.3292 oz. ASW **Obv:** Facing cornucopias top supported arms, date above, denomination below **Rev:** Abomey woman 3/4 left **Note:** Hallmark "999.9" in oval below "F" in "CFA".

Date	Mintage	VF20	XF40	MS60	MS63	MS65
1971	Inc. above	PF63 58.00	PF65 65.00	PF67 85.00		

KM# 3.1 500 FRANCS

25.20 g., 0.999 Silver 0.8094 oz. ASW, 40 mm. **Subject:** 10th Anniversary of Independence **Obv:** Facing cornucopias top supported arms, date above, denomination below **Rev:** Ouémé woman right **Note:** 1000" in oval below "S" in "FRANCS".

Date	Mintage	VF20	XF40	MS60	MS63	MS65
1971	5,550	PF63 100	PF65 115	PF67 140		

KM# 3.2 500 FRANCS

25.20 g., 0.999 Silver 0.8094 oz. ASW, 40 mm. **Obv:** Facing cornucopias top supported arms, date above, denomination below **Rev:** Ouémé woman right **Note:** 1 AR" and "1000" to right of "CFA".

Date	Mintage	VF20	XF40	MS60	MS63	MS65
1971	Inc. above	PF63 110	PF65 125	PF67 150		

KM# 4.1 1000 FRANCS

51.50 g., 0.999 Silver 1.6541 oz. ASW, 55 mm. **Subject:** 10th Anniversary of Independence **Obv:** Facing cornucopias top supported arms, date above, denomination below **Rev:** Somba woman facing **Note:** 1000" in oval below "S" in "FRANCS".

Date	Mintage	VF20	XF40	MS60	MS63	MS65
1971	6,500	PF63 180	PF65 200	PF67 225		

KM# 4.2 1000 FRANCS

51.50 g., 0.999 Silver 1.6541 oz. ASW, 55 mm. **Obv:** Facing cornucopias top supported arms, date above, denomination below **Rev:** Somba woman facing **Note:** "1 AR" and "1000" to right of "CFA".

Date	Mintage	VF20	XF40	MS60	MS63	MS65
1971	Inc. above	PF63 225	PF65 275	PF67 300		

KM# 6 2500 FRANCS

8.88 g., 0.900 Gold 0.2569 oz. AGW **Subject:** 10th Anniversary of Independence **Rev:** Dancers

Date	Mintage	VF20	XF40	MS60	MS63	MS65
1971	960	PF63 450	PF65 475	PF67 500		

KM# 7 5000 FRANCS

17.77 g., 0.900 Gold 0.5142 oz. AGW **Subject:** 10th Anniversary of Independence **Obv:** Similar to 2500 Francs, KM#6 **Rev:** Water buffalos (suncerus caffer-bovidae)

Date	Mintage	VF20	XF40	MS60	MS63	MS65
1971	610	PF63 875	PF65 900	PF67 950		

KM# 8 10000 FRANCS
35.55 g., 0.900 Gold 1.0287 oz. AGW **Subject:** 10th Anniversary of Independence **Obv:** Facing cornucopias top supported arms, date above, denomination below **Rev:** Acanthopholis

Date	Mintage	VF20	XF40	MS60	MS63	MS65
1971	470	PF63 1,750		PF65 1,800		PF67 1,900

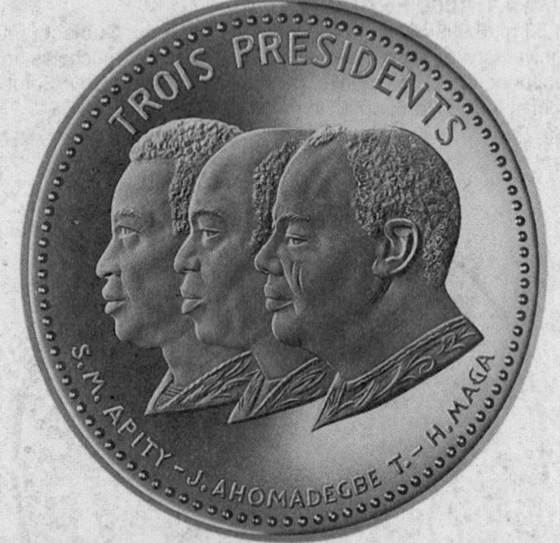

KM# 9 25000 FRANCS
88.88 g., 0.900 Gold 2.5718 oz. AGW **Subject:** 10th Anniversary of Independence **Obv:** Facing cornucopias top supported arms, date above, denomination below **Rev:** Aligned Presidents busts, left **Rev. Legend:** TROIS PRESIDENTS above, S.M. APITY - J. AHOMADEGBE T. - H. MAGA below

Date	Mintage	VF20	XF40	MS60	MS63	MS65
1971	380	PF63 4,450		PF65 4,500		PF67 4,650

PROOF SETS

KM#	Date	Mintage	Identification	Issue Price	Mkt Val
PS1	1971 (8)	380	KM#1.1-4.1, 6-9	—	8,100
PS2	1971 (4)	4,270	KM#1.1-4.1	36.00	400

DANISH WEST INDIES

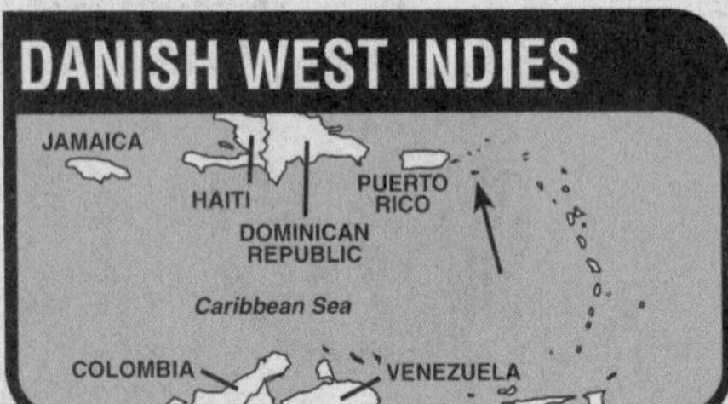

The Danish West Indies (now the U.S. organized unincorporated territory of the Virgin Islands of the United States) consisted of the islands of St. Thomas, St. John, St. Croix, and 62 islets in the Caribbean Sea roughly 40 miles (64 km.) east of Puerto Rico. The islands have a combined area of 133 sq. mi. (352 sq. km.) and a population of *106,000. Capital: Charlotte Amalie. Tourism is the principal industry. Watch movements, costume jewelry, pharmaceuticals, and rum are exported.

The Virgin Islands were discovered by Columbus, in 1493, during his second voyage to America. During the 17th century, individual islands, actually the peaks of a submerged mountain range, were held by Spain, Holland, England, France and Denmark. These islands were also the favorite resorts of the buccaneers operating in the Caribbean and the coastal waters of eastern North America. Control of most of the 100-island group finally passed to Denmark, with England securing the easterly remainder. The Danish islands had their own coinage from the early 18th century, based on but unequal to, Denmark's homeland system. In the late 18th and early 19th centuries, Danish minor copper and silver coinage augmented the islands currency. The Danish islands were purchased by the United States in 1917 for $25 million, mainly to forestall their acquisition by Germany and because they command the Anegada Passage into the Caribbean Sea, a strategic point on the defense perimeter of the Panama Canal.

RULER
Danish, until 1917

MINTMASTERS' INITIALS

Letter	Date	Name
P, VBP	1893-1918	Vilhelm Burchard Poulsen

MONEYERS' INITIALS

Letter	Date	Name
GI, J	1901-1933	(Knub) Gunnar Jensen
AH	1908-1924	Andreas Frederik Vilhelm Hansen

MONETARY SYSTEM
(1904-1934)
5 Bit = 1 Cent
100 Bit = 1 Franc
5 Francs = 1 Daler

DANISH COLONY

DECIMAL COINAGE

20 Cents = 1 Franc

KM# 74 1/2 CENT (2-1/2 Bit)
Bronze **Ruler:** Christian IX **Obv:** Crowned monogram above date **Rev:** Denominations divided by trident, caduceus and sickle **Note:** Mintmaster's initial: P. Moneyer's initials: GJ.

Date	Mintage	F12	VF20	XF40	MS60	MS63
1905 (h)	190,000	2.85	6.25	14.00	25.00	45.00
1905 (h) Prooflike	—	—	—	—	—	—

Note: Specimen strike

KM# 75 CENT (5 Bit)
Bronze, 23 mm. **Ruler:** Christian IX **Rev:** Denominations divided by trident, caduceus and sickle **Note:** Mintmaster's initial: P. Moneyer's initials: GJ.

Date	Mintage	F12	VF20	XF40	MS60	MS63
1905 (h)	500,000	4.50	8.75	22.00	45.00	75.00

KM# 83 CENT (5 Bit)
Bronze **Obv:** Crowned monogram above date **Rev:** Denominations divided by trident, caduceus and sickle **Note:** Mintmaster's initials: VBP. Moneyer's initials: AH-GJ.

Date	Mintage	F12	VF20	XF40	MS60	MS63
1913 (h)	200,000	7.50	15.00	35.00	75.00	115

KM# 76 2 CENTS (10 Bit)
Bronze **Ruler:** Christian IX **Obv:** Crowned monogram above date **Rev:** Denominations divided by trident, caduceus and sickle **Note:** Mintmaster's initial: P. Moneyer's initials: GJ.

Date	Mintage	F12	VF20	XF40	MS60	MS63
1905 (h)	150,000	6.00	12.00	28.00	65.00	100
1905 (h) Prooflike	20	—	—	—	—	—

Note: Specimen strike

KM# 77 5 CENTS (25 Bit)
4.00 g., Nickel, 21 mm. **Ruler:** Christian IX **Obv:** Crowned monogram above date **Rev:** Denominations divided by trident, caduceus and sickle **Note:** Mintmaster's initial: P. Moneyer's initials: GJ.

Date	Mintage	F12	VF20	XF40	MS60	MS63
1905 (h)	199,000	3.75	9.50	18.50	40.00	80.00
1905 (h) Prooflike	20	—	—	—	—	—

Note: Specimen strike

KM# 78 10 CENTS (50 Bit)
2.50 g., 0.800 Silver 0.0643 oz. ASW **Ruler:** Christian IX **Obv:** Head left **Rev:** Plant divides denominations **Note:** Mintmaster's initial: P. Moneyer's initials: GJ.

Date	Mintage	F12	VF20	XF40	MS60	MS63
1905 (h)	175,000	5.00	12.00	25.00	45.00	85.00
1905 (h) Prooflike	20	—	—	—	—	—

Note: Specimen strike

KM# 79 20 CENTS (1 Franc)
5.00 g., 0.800 Silver 0.1286 oz. ASW **Ruler:** Christian IX **Obv:** Uniformed bust left **Rev:** Three liberty figures divide denominations, date below **Note:** Mintmaster's initial: P. Moneyer's initials: GJ.

Date	Mintage	F12	VF20	XF40	MS60	MS63
1905 (h)	150,000	14.00	35.00	75.00	125	200
1905 (h) Prooflike	20	—	—	—	—	—

Note: Specimen strike

KM# 81 20 CENTS (1 Franc)
5.00 g., 0.800 Silver 0.1286 oz. ASW, 23 mm. **Obv:** Head left **Rev:** Three liberty figures divide denominations, date below **Edge:** Reeded **Note:** Mintmaster's initial: P. Moneyer's initials: GJ.

Date	Mintage	F12	VF20	XF40	MS60	MS63
1907 (h)	101,000	17.50	40.00	95.00	175	275
1907 (h) Prooflike	10	—	—	—	—	—

Note: Specimen strike

KM# 80 40 CENTS (2 Francs)
10.00 g., 0.800 Silver 0.2572 oz. ASW **Ruler:** Christian IX **Note:** Mintmaster's initial: P. Moneyer's initials: GJ.

Date	Mintage	F12	VF20	XF40	MS60	MS63
1905 (h)	38,000	25.00	55.00	115	265	375
1905 (h) Prooflike	20	—	—	—	—	—

Note: Specimen strike

KM# 82 40 CENTS (2 Francs)
10.00 g., 0.800 Silver 0.2572 oz. ASW **Obv:** Head left **Rev:** Three liberty figures divide denominations, date below **Note:** Mintmaster's initial: P. Moneyer's initials: GJ.

Date	Mintage	F12	VF20	XF40	MS60	MS63
1907 (h)	25,000	35.00	75.00	150	325	475
1907 (h) Prooflike	10	—	—	—	—	1,200

Note: Specimen strike

KM# 72 4 DALER (20 Francs)
6.45 g., 0.900 Gold 0.1867 oz. AGW **Ruler:** Christian IX **Obv:** Head left **Rev:** Seated liberty figure divides denominations **Note:** Mintmaster's initial: P. Moneyer's initials: GJ.

Date	Mintage	F12	VF20	XF40	MS60	MS63
1904 (h)	121,000	325	350	550	850	1,500
1905 (h)	Inc. above	350	375	600	1,000	1,750

KM# 73 10 DALER (50 Francs)
16.13 g., 0.900 Gold 0.4667 oz. AGW **Ruler:** Christian IX **Obv:** Head left **Rev:** Seated liberty figure divides denominations, date below **Note:** Mintmaster's initial: P. Moneyer's initials: GJ.

Date	Mintage	F12	VF20	XF40	MS60	MS63
1904 (h)	2,005	1,250	2,250	4,500	7,500	—

TRIAL STRIKES

KM#	Date	Mintage	Identification	Mkt Val
TS1	1904	—	20 Francs. Copper. KM#72.	—
TS2	1904	—	20 Francs. Copper. KM#72.	—

PROOF-LIKE SETS (PL)

KM#	Date	Mintage	Identification	Issue Price	Mkt Val
PL4	1905 (5)	20	KM#76-80	—	—
PL5	1907 (2)	10	KM#81-82	—	—

Danzig is an important seaport on the northern coast of Poland with access to the Baltic Sea. It has at different times belonged to the Teutonic Knights, Pomerania, Russia, and Prussia. It was part of the Polish Kingdom from 1587-1772.

Danzig (Gdansk) was a free city from 1919 to 1939 during which most of its modern coinage was made.

MONETARY SYSTEM

Until 1923
100 Pfennig = 1 Mark

Commencing 1923
100 Pfennig = 1 Gulden

FREE CITY
STANDARD COINAGE

KM# 140 PFENNIG
1.63 g., Bronze, 17.03 mm. **Obv:** Denomination **Rev:** Arms divide date

Date	Mintage	VF20	XF40	MS60	MS63	MS65
1923	4,000,000	3.00	6.00	12.00	35.00	75.00
1923	—	PF63 350				
1926	1,500,000	4.50	8.00	18.00	50.00	110
1929	1,000,000	7.00	12.00	25.00	55.00	115
1930	2,000,000	4.00	7.00	14.00	40.00	90.00
1937	3,000,000	4.00	7.00	14.00	40.00	90.00

KM# 141 2 PFENNIG
Bronze **Obv:** Denomination **Rev:** Arms divide date

Date	Mintage	VF20	XF40	MS60	MS63	MS65
1923	1,000,000	5.00	9.00	20.00	50.00	110
1923	—	PF63 400				
1926	1,750,000	5.00	9.00	20.00	50.00	110
1937	500,000	7.00	12.00	25.00	55.00	115

KM# 142 5 PFENNIG
Copper-Nickel **Obv:** Denomination **Rev:** Arms divide date within snowflake design

Date	Mintage	VF20	XF40	MS60	MS63	MS65
1923	3,000,000	4.00	7.00	15.00	40.00	90.00
1923	—	PF63 975				
1928	1,000,000	7.00	15.00	35.00	75.00	150
1928	—	PF63 1,150				

KM# 151 5 PFENNIG
Aluminum-Bronze **Obv:** Denomination **Rev:** Turbot left, date below

Date	Mintage	VF20	XF40	MS60	MS63	MS65
1932	4,000,000	5.00	8.00	25.00	60.00	125

KM# 143 10 PFENNIG
Copper-Nickel **Obv:** Denomination **Rev:** Arms divide date within snowflake design

Date	Mintage	VF20	XF40	MS60	MS63	MS65
1923	5,000,000	7.00	12.00	25.00	55.00	115
1923	—	PF63 600				

KM# 152 10 PFENNIG
Aluminum-Bronze **Obv:** Denomination **Rev:** Codfish (godus morrhua) left, date below

Date	Mintage	VF20	XF40	MS60	MS63	MS65
1932	5,000,000	7.00	12.00	35.00	75.00	150

KM# 144 1/2 GULDEN
2.50 g., 0.750 Silver 0.0603 oz. ASW, 20 mm. **Obv:** Date divided by shielded arms, denomination above **Rev:** Ship at sea **Edge:** Reeded

Date	Mintage	VF20	XF40	MS60	MS63	MS65
1923	1,000,000	15.00	35.00	75.00	125	285
1923	—	PF63 1,250				
1927	400,000	25.00	50.00	100	350	1,500
1927	—	PF63 1,600				

KM# 153 1/2 GULDEN
3.00 g., Nickel, 19.5 mm. **Obv:** Crowned vertical crosses **Rev:** Denomination above date

Date	Mintage	VF20	XF40	MS60	MS63	MS65
1932	1,400,000	15.00	35.00	75.00	125	275

KM# 145 GULDEN
5.00 g., 0.750 Silver 0.1206 oz. ASW **Obv:** Ship and star divide denomination **Rev:** Shielded arms with supporters, star above, date below

Date	Mintage	VF20	XF40	MS60	MS63	MS65
1923	2,500,000	20.00	45.00	100	250	375
1923	—	PF63 1,150				

KM# 154 GULDEN
5.00 g., Nickel, 23.5 mm. **Obv:** Large numeric denomination within circle **Rev:** Arms divide date

Date	Mintage	VF20	XF40	MS60	MS63	MS65
1932	2,500,000	15.00	25.00	90.00	175	350

KM# 146 2 GULDEN
10.00 g., 0.750 Silver 0.2411 oz. ASW **Obv:** Ship and star divide denomination **Rev:** Shielded arms with supporters, star above, date below

Date	Mintage	VF20	XF40	MS60	MS63	MS65
1923	1,250,000	75.00	150	275	450	950
1923	—	PF63 1,850				

KM# 155 2 GULDEN
10.00 g., 0.500 Silver 0.1608 oz. ASW **Obv:** Ship afloat within circle, denomination below **Rev:** Shielded arms with supporters, date above

Date	Mintage	VF20	XF40	MS60	MS63	MS65
1932	1,250,000	125	250	600	1,000	2,000

KM# 147 5 GULDEN
25.00 g., 0.750 Silver 0.6028 oz. ASW **Obv:** Marienkirche within circle **Rev:** Shielded arms with supporters, denomination below, star above

Date	Mintage	VF20	XF40	MS60	MS63	MS65
1923	700,000	125	25.00	550	900	1,750
1923	—	PF63 2,250				
1927	160,000	250	450	750	1,500	2,500
1927	—	PF63 4,500				

KM# 156 5 GULDEN
14.82 g., 0.500 Silver 0.2382 oz. ASW **Obv:** Marienkirche within circle, denomination below **Rev:** Shielded arms with supporters, date above

Date	Mintage	VF20	XF40	MS60	MS63	MS65
1932	430,000	300	750	1,500	2,500	—

KM# 157 5 GULDEN
14.82 g., 0.500 Silver 0.2382 oz. ASW **Obv:** Grain elevator by harbor within circle, denomination below **Rev:** Shielded arms with supporters, date above

Date	Mintage	VF20	XF40	MS60	MS63	MS65
1932	430,000	300	750	1,600	2,750	—

KM# 158 5 GULDEN
11.00 g., Nickel, 29 mm. **Obv:** Ship with three crowns asea, numeric denomination at left, circle surrounds, denomination below circle, date at right **Rev:** Arms with supporters on oval shield

Date	Mintage	VF20	XF40	MS60	MS63	MS65
1935	800,000	175	300	600	1,000	2,000

KM# 159 10 GULDEN
17.00 g., Nickel, 34 mm. **Obv:** Town hall tower, numeric denomination at right, circle surrounds, denomination below, date at right **Rev:** Arms with supporters on oval shield

Date	Mintage	VF20	XF40	MS60	MS63	MS65
1935	380,000	500	900	1,750	3,000	5,000

KM# 148 25 GULDEN
7.99 g., 0.917 Gold 0.2355 oz. AGW, 22 mm. **Obv:** Arms between columns with supporters, date below **Rev:** Statue from the Neptune fountain, denomination at left and divided below **Note:** Presented to senate members.

Date	Mintage	VF20	XF40	MS60	MS63	MS65
1923	800	2,000	3,500	6,500	9,000	—
1923	200	PF63 10,000				

KM# 150 25 GULDEN
7.99 g., 0.917 Gold 0.2355 oz. AGW, 22 mm. **Obv:** Arms with supporters, date below **Rev:** Statue from the Neptune fountain, denomination at left and divided below **Note:** Never offcially released for circulation. A few were distributed on Sept. 1, 1939, in VIP presentation cases. A small hoard was discovered in the early 21st century making hundreds of the coins available to the numismatic market and driving prices down to current levels.

Date	Mintage	VF20	XF40	MS60	MS63	MS65
1930	Est. 4000	—	—	1,200	1,500	2,200

TOKEN COINAGE

KM# Tn1 10 PFENNIG
Zinc **Obv:** Angel head above oval arms within circle, date below **Rev:** Denomination within cartouche **Note:** Small "10" in cartouche.

Date	Mintage	F12	VF20	XF40	MS60	MS63
1920	876,000	18.00	30.00	50.00	75.00	150

KM# Tn2 10 PFENNIG
Zinc **Note:** Large "10", no cartouche

Date	Mintage	F12	VF20	XF40	MS60	MS63
1920	124,000	75.00	120	185	325	—

PATTERNS

Including off metal strikes

KM#	Date	Mintage	Identification	Mkt Val
Pn43	1920	30	10 Pfennig. Silver.	3,250
Pn44	1920	30	10 Pfennig. Silver. Large 10.	3,250
Pn45	1923	—	5 Pfennig. Brass.	175
Pn46	1923	—	10 Pfennig. Brass.	185
Pn47	1923	10	Gulden. Gold. KM145.	7,500
Pn48	1927	—	2 Pfennig. Brass.	—
Pn49	1935	—	5 Gulden. Nickel. PROBE.	—
Pn50	1935	—	10 Gulden. Nickel. PROBE.	—
Pn51	1935	—	10 Gulden. Tin.	120

PROOF SETS

KM#	Date	Mintage	Identification	Issue Price	Mkt Val
PS1	1923 (8)	—	KM140-147	—	9,000

The Kingdom of Denmark (Danmark), a constitutional monarchy located at the mouth of the Baltic Sea, has an area of 16,639 sq. mi. (43,070 sq. km.) and a population of 5.2 million. Capital: Copenhagen. Most of the country is arable. Agriculture is conducted by large farms served by cooperatives. The largest industries are food processing, iron and metal, and shipping. Machinery, meats (chiefly bacon), dairy products and chemicals are exported.

The present decimal system of currency was introduced in 1874. As a result of a referendum held September 28, 2000, the currency of the European Monetary Union, the Euro, will not be introduced in Denmark in the foreseeable future.

RULERS
Christian IX, 1863-1906
Frederik VIII, 1906-1912
Christian X, 1912-1947
Frederik IX, 1947-1972
Margrethe II, 1972—

MINT MARKS
(h) - Copenhagen, heart

MINT OFFICIALS' INITIALS

Copenhagen Mint

Letter	Date	Name
*P, VBP	1893-1918	Vilhelm Buchard Poulsen
HCN	1919-1927	Hans Christian Nielsen
N	1927-1955	Niels Peter Nielsen
C	1956-1971	Alfred Frederik Christiansen
S	1971-1978	Vagn Sorensen
B	1978-1981	Peter M Biarno
R, NR	1982-1989	N. Norregaard Rasmussen
LG - JP	1990-2001	Laust Grove / J Petersen

NOTE: The letter P was only used on Danish West Indies coins and on Denmark, KM#802.

MONEYERS' INITIALS

Copenhagen Mint

Letter	Date	Name
GI, GJ	1901-1933	Knud Gunnar Jensen
AH	1908-1924	Andreas Frederik Vilhelm Hansen
HS, S	1933-1968	Harald Salomon
B	1968-1983	Frode Bahnsen
A	1986-	Johan Alkjaer (designer)
HV	1986-	Hanne Varming (sculptor)
JP	1989-	Jan Petersen

MONETARY SYSTEM
100 Øre = 1 Krone

KINGDOM

DECIMAL COINAGE

100 Øre = 1 Krone; 1874-present

KM# 792.2 ØRE
2.00 g., Bronze **Ruler:** Christian IX **Obv:** Crowned CIX monogram, date at lower lerft, mint mark and initials VBP at lower right **Rev:** Denomination above porpoise and barley ear

Date	Mintage	F12	VF20	XF40	MS60	MS63
1902/802 (h) VBP	2,977,000	0.80	2.25	5.50	15.00	22.50
1902 (h) VBP	Inc. above	0.60	2.00	5.00	13.50	17.50
1904/804 (h) VBP	4,962,000	0.80	2.25	4.50	11.00	15.00
1904 (h) VBP	Inc. above	0.60	2.00	4.00	10.00	12.50

KM# 804 ØRE
2.00 g., Bronze **Ruler:** Frederik VIII **Obv:** Crowned F8F monogram, initials GJ at lower right **Rev:** Denomination within circle, date and initials VBP below **Rev. Legend:** THE KINGDOM OF DENMARK

Date	Mintage	F12	VF20	XF40	MS60	MS63
1907 (h) VBP GJ	5,975,000	0.50	1.75	3.50	8.50	12.50
1909 (h) VBP GJ	2,985,000	0.50	1.75	3.50	10.00	17.50
1910 (h) VBP; GJ	2,994,000	0.50	1.75	4.50	15.00	22.50
1912 (h) VBP; GJ	3,006,000	0.50	1.75	3.50	10.00	17.50

KM# 812.1 ØRE
2.00 g., Bronze **Ruler:** Christian X **Obv:** Crowned CX monogram, initials VBP and mint mark at lower left, date and initials GJ at lower right **Rev:** Thick denomination, ornaments flanking

Date	Mintage	F12	VF20	XF40	MS60	MS63
1913 (h) VBP; GJ	5,011,000	0.25	1.00	1.75	4.50	6.00
1915 (h) VBP; GJ	4,940,000	0.50	1.75	3.50	10.00	12.50
1916 (h) VBP; GJ	2,439,000	0.50	1.75	3.50	10.00	12.50
1917 (h) VBP; GJ	4,564,000	8.00	12.50	20.00	50.00	75.00

KM# 812.1a ØRE
1.74 g., Iron **Ruler:** Christian X **Obv:** Crowned CX monogram, initials VBP and mint mark at lower left, date and initials GJ at lower right **Rev:** Thick denomination, ornaments flanking

Date	Mintage	F12	VF20	XF40	MS60	MS63
1918 (h) VBP; GJ	6,776,000	0.60	2.00	6.00	32.50	50.00
(1919) HCN; GJ	931,000	—	—	—	—	—

KM# 812.2 ØRE
2.00 g., Bronze **Ruler:** Christian X **Obv:** Crowned CX monogram, initials HCN and mint mark at lower left, date and initials GJ at lower right **Rev:** Value, ornaments flanking

Date	Mintage	F12	VF20	XF40	MS60	MS63
1919 (h) HCN; GJ	4,586,000	0.40	1.25	2.75	7.00	10.00
1920 (h) HCN; GJ	2,367,000	1.00	3.50	8.00	40.00	60.00
1921 (h) HCN; GJ	3,121,000	0.40	1.25	2.75	7.00	10.00
1922 (h) HCN; GJ	3,267,000	0.40	1.25	2.75	7.00	10.00
1923 (h) HCN; GJ	2,938,000	0.40	1.25	2.75	7.00	10.00

KM# 812.2a ØRE
1.74 g., Iron **Ruler:** Christian X **Obv:** Crowned CX monogram, initials HCN and mint mark at lower left, date and initials GJ at lower right **Rev:** Value, ornaments flanking

Date	Mintage	F12	VF20	XF40	MS60	MS63
1919 (h) HCN; GJ	931,000	3.00	8.00	15.00	65.00	100

KM# 826.1 ØRE

1.90 g., Bronze **Ruler:** Christian X **Obv:** Crowned CXC monogram within title "KING OF DENMARK", initials GJ below **Rev:** Country name and date above center hole, denomination, mint mark, and initials HCN below

Date	Mintage	F12	VF20	XF40	MS60	MS63
1926 (h) HCN; GJ	12,691,428	1.25	2.25	8.00	40.00	65.00
1927 (h) HCN; GJ	Inc. above	0.10	0.20	2.00	15.00	25.00

KM# 826.2 ØRE

1.90 g., Bronze **Ruler:** Christian X **Obv:** Crowned CXC monogram within title "KING OF DENMARK", initials GJ below **Rev:** Country name and date above center hole, denomination, mint mark, and initial N below **Note:** For coins dated 1941 refer to Faeroe Islands listings.

Date	Mintage	VF20	XF40	MS60	MS63	MS65
1927 (h) N; GJ	i.a.	3.00	10.00	50.00	85.00	140
1928 (h) N; GJ	16,999,905	0.25	3.00	10.00	15.00	22.50
1929 (h) N; GJ	5,172,000	0.25	3.00	14.00	20.00	30.00
1930 (h) N; GJ	5,306,000	0.25	3.00	14.00	20.00	30.00
1932 (h) N; GJ	5,089,000	0.25	3.00	14.00	20.00	30.00
1933 (h) N; GJ	2,095,000	0.35	5.00	17.50	40.00	60.00
1934 (h) N; GJ	3,665,000	0.10	0.75	7.50	12.50	18.00
1935 (h) N; GJ	5,668,000	0.10	0.75	7.50	12.50	18.00
1936 (h) N; GJ	5,584,000	0.10	0.50	5.00	8.00	12.00
1937 (h) N; GJ	6,877,000	0.10	0.50	5.00	8.00	12.00
1938 (h) N; GJ	3,850,000	0.10	0.50	3.00	5.00	8.00
1939 (h) N; GJ	5,662,000	0.10	0.50	3.00	5.00	8.00
1940 (h) N; GJ	1,965,000	0.10	0.50	3.00	5.00	8.00

KM# 832 ØRE

1.60 g., Zinc **Ruler:** Christian X **Obv:** Crowned CX monogram divides date, mint mark and initials N-S below **Rev:** Oak and beech leaves divide value

Date	Mintage	F12	VF20	XF40	MS60	MS63
1941 (h) N; S	21,570,000	0.10	0.20	1.50	20.00	35.00
1942 (h) N; S	6,997,000	0.10	0.20	1.50	20.00	35.00
1943 (h) N; S	15,082,000	0.10	0.20	1.50	20.00	35.00
1944 (h) N; S	11,981,000	0.10	0.50	1.50	20.00	35.00
1945 (h) N; S	916,000	1.00	2.00	6.00	22.50	40.00
1946 (h) N; S	712,000	1.50	3.00	8.00	37.50	60.00

KM# 839.1 ØRE

1.60 g., Zinc, 16 mm. **Ruler:** Frederik IX **Obv:** Crowned F IX R monogram divides date **Rev:** Mint mark, initials N-S below value

Date	Mintage	F12	VF20	XF40	MS60	MS63
1948 (h) N; S	460,000	1.00	2.50	5.00	30.00	50.00
1949 (h) N; S	2,513,000	0.75	2.00	5.00	40.00	65.00
1950 (h) N; S	9,453,000	0.50	1.50	3.00	20.00	35.00
1951 (h) N; S	2,931,000	0.75	2.00	3.00	25.00	45.00
1952 (h) N; S	7,626,000	—	0.10	0.75	10.00	20.00
1953 (h) N; S	11,994,000	—	0.10	0.25	8.50	17.50
1954 (h) N; S	12,642,000	—	0.10	0.20	8.00	15.00
1955 (h) N; S	14,177,000	—	—	0.10	2.50	5.00

KM# 839.2 ØRE

1.60 g., Zinc, 16 mm. **Ruler:** Frederik IX **Obv:** Crowned F IX R monogram divides date **Rev:** Mint mark, initials C-S below value

Date	Mintage	VF20	XF40	MS60	MS63	MS65
1956 (h) C; S	20,211,000	—	—	2.00	4.00	10.00
1957 (h) C; S	20,900,000	—	—	1.35	3.75	9.00
1958 (h) C; S	16,021,000	—	—	0.90	3.50	8.00
1959 (h) C; S	15,929,000	—	—	0.50	2.50	6.00
1960 (h) C; S	23,982,000	—	—	0.30	2.00	5.00
1961 (h) C; S	18,986,000	—	—	0.10	1.50	3.00
1962 (h) C; S	16,992,000	—	—	0.10	1.50	3.00
1963 (h) C; S	28,986,000	—	—	—	1.00	2.50
1964 (h) C; S	21,971,000	—	—	—	1.00	2.50
1965 (h) C; S	29,943,000	—	—	—	0.15	1.25
1966 (h) C; S	35,907,000	—	—	—	0.15	1.00
1967 (h) C; S	32,959,000	—	—	—	0.10	0.75
1968 (h) C; S	21,889,000	—	—	—	0.10	0.75
1969 (h) C; S	29,243,000	—	—	—	0.10	0.40
1970 (h) C; S	22,970,000	—	—	—	0.10	0.40
1971 (h) C; S	21,983,000	—	—	—	0.10	0.40

KM# 839.3 ØRE

1.60 g., Zinc, 16 mm. **Ruler:** Frederik IX **Obv:** Crowned F IX R monogram divides date **Rev:** Mint mark, initials S-S below value

Date	Mintage	VF20	XF40	MS60	MS63	MS65
1972 (h) S; S	13,000,000	—	—	—	0.15	0.50

KM# 846 ØRE

1.80 g., Zinc, 16 mm. **Ruler:** Frederik IX **Obv:** Crowned F IX R monogram divides date **Rev:** Two barley stalks around value, initials below **Note:** Never released for circulation, see note at 2 Ore, KM#847.

Date	Mintage	VF20	XF40	MS60	MS63	MS65
1960 (h) C; S	8,990,000	—	—	—	0.90	2.00
1962 (h) C; S	Inc. above	—	—	—	0.90	2.00
1963 (h) C; S	9,980,000	—	—	—	0.90	2.00
1964 (h) C; S	2,990,000	—	—	—	0.90	2.00

KM# 793.2 2 ØRE

4.00 g., Bronze **Ruler:** Christian IX **Obv:** Crowned CIX monogram, date at lower lerft, mint mark and initials VBP at lower right **Rev:** Denomination above porpoise and barley ear

Date	Mintage	F12	VF20	XF40	MS60	MS63
1902/802 (h) VBP	3,502,000	1.25	4.00	8.50	25.00	37.50
1902 (h) VBP	Inc. above	1.00	3.50	7.50	22.50	30.00
1906 (h) VBP	2,498,000	1.25	4.00	8.50	25.00	37.50

KM# 805 2 ØRE

4.00 g., Bronze **Ruler:** Frederik VIII **Obv:** Crowned F8F monogram, initials GJ at lower right **Rev:** Denomination within circle, date and initials VBP below

Date	Mintage	F12	VF20	XF40	MS60	MS63
1907 (h) VBP; GJ	2,502,000	0.40	2.75	5.00	22.50	30.00
1909 (h) VBP; GJ	2,485,000	0.40	2.75	5.00	30.00	45.00
1912 (h) VBP; GJ	2,480,000	0.40	2.75	5.00	22.50	30.00

KM# 813.1 2 ØRE

4.00 g., Bronze **Ruler:** Christian X **Obv:** Crowned CX monogram, initials VBP and mint mark at lower left, date and initials GJ at lower right **Rev:** Value, ornament flanking

Date	Mintage	F12	VF20	XF40	MS60	MS63
1913 (h) VBP; GJ	373,000	12.50	25.00	50.00	160	225
1914 (h) VBP; GJ	2,126,000	0.75	3.00	6.00	14.00	20.00
1915 (h) VBP; GJ	2,485,000	0.75	3.00	6.00	14.00	20.00
1916 (h) VBP; GJ	1,383,000	0.75	3.00	6.00	14.00	20.00
1917 (h) VBP; GJ	1,837,000	6.00	12.00	20.00	60.00	90.00

KM# 813.1a 2 ØRE

3.47 g., Iron **Ruler:** Christian X **Obv:** Crowned CX monogram, initials VBP and mint mark at lower left, date and initials GJ at lower right **Rev:** Value, ornament flanking

Date	Mintage	F12	VF20	XF40	MS60	MS63
1918 (h) VBP; GJ	4,160,999	2.00	4.50	10.00	55.00	95.00

KM# 813.2 2 ØRE

4.00 g., Bronze **Ruler:** Christian X **Obv:** Crowned CX monogram, initials HCN and mint mark at lower left, date and initials GJ at lower right **Rev:** Thick denomination, ornaments flanking

Date	Mintage	F12	VF20	XF40	MS60	MS63
1919 (h) HCN; GJ	5,503,000	2.50	5.00	10.00	27.50	40.00
1920 (h) HCN; GJ	2,528,000	0.50	1.50	3.00	8.00	15.00
1921 (h) HCN; GJ	2,158,000	0.75	3.00	6.00	14.00	20.00
1923 (h) HCN; GJ	2,625,000	0.75	3.00	6.00	14.00	20.00

KM# 813.2a 2 ØRE

3.47 g., Iron **Ruler:** Christian X **Obv:** Crowned CX monogram, initials HCN and mint mark at lower left, date and initials GJ at lower right **Rev:** Value, ornament flanking

Date	Mintage	F12	VF20	XF40	MS60	MS63
1919 (h) HCN; GJ	1,944,000	10.00	20.00	40.00	160	225

KM# 827.1 2 ØRE

3.80 g., Bronze **Ruler:** Christian X **Obv:** Crowned CXC monogram within title "KING OF DENMARK", initials GJ below **Rev:** Country name and date above center hole, denomination, mint mark, and initials HCN below

Date	Mintage	F12	VF20	XF40	MS60	MS63
1926 (h) HCN; GJ	301,000	35.00	65.00	130	375	525
1927 (h) HCN; GJ	15,359,000	0.10	0.25	4.00	17.50	32.50

KM# 827.2 2 ØRE

3.80 g., Bronze **Ruler:** Christian X **Obv:** Crowned CXC monogram within title "KING OF DENMARK", initials GJ below **Rev:** Country name and date above center hole, denomination, mint mark, and initial N below **Note:** For coins dated 1941 refer to Faeroe Islands listings.

Date	Mintage	F12	VF20	XF40	MS60	MS63
1927 (h) N; GJ	Inc. above	1.00	2.50	10.00	50.00	120
1928 (h) N; GJ	5,758,000	0.10	0.25	4.00	15.00	25.00
1929 (h) N; GJ	6,817,000	0.10	0.25	4.00	17.50	30.00
1930 (h) N; GJ	2,327,000	0.20	0.75	5.00	20.00	35.00
1931 (h) N; GJ	5,135,000	0.10	0.25	4.00	17.50	27.50
1932 (h) N; GJ	Inc. above	0.35	1.00	6.00	22.50	37.50
1934 (h) N; GJ	756,000	0.15	0.50	3.00	13.50	20.00
1935 (h) N; GJ	1,391,000	0.15	0.50	3.00	13.50	20.00
1936 (h) N; GJ	2,973,000	0.15	0.50	3.00	13.50	20.00
1937 (h) N; GJ	3,437,000	0.15	0.50	3.00	13.50	20.00
1938 (h) N; GJ	2,177,000	0.10	0.20	1.00	6.50	9.00
1939 (h) N; GJ	3,165,000	0.10	0.20	0.85	6.50	9.00
1940 (h) N; GJ	1,582,000	0.10	0.25	0.50	3.00	5.00

KM# 833 2 ØRE

1.20 g., Aluminum **Ruler:** Christian X **Obv:** Crowned CX monogram divides date within title: "KING OF DENMARK"; mint mark and initials N-S below **Rev:** Oak and beach leaves divide value

Date	Mintage	F12	VF20	XF40	MS60	MS63
1941 (h) N; S	26,205,000	0.10	0.20	1.50	8.50	12.50
1941 (h) N; S	—	PF63 350				

KM# 833a 2 ØRE

3.20 g., Zinc **Ruler:** Christian X **Obv:** Crowned CX monogram divides date, mint mark and initials N-S below **Rev:** Oak and beach leaves divide value

Date	Mintage	F12	VF20	XF40	MS60	MS63
1942 (h) N; S	12,934,000	0.10	0.20	1.50	17.50	27.50
1943 (h) N; S	9,603,000	0.10	0.20	1.50	17.50	27.50
1944 (h) N; S	6,069,000	0.10	0.20	1.50	17.50	27.50
1945 (h) N; S	329,000	2.50	5.00	10.00	55.00	100
1947 (h) N; S	589,000	1.25	2.50	6.00	47.50	90.00

KM# 840.1 2 ØRE

3.20 g., Zinc, 20.8 mm. **Ruler:** Frederik IX **Obv:** Crowned F IX R monogram and date **Rev:** Mint mark, initials N-S below value

Date	Mintage	VF20	XF40	MS60	MS63	MS65
1948 (h) N; S	1,927,000	1.50	3.00	20.00	40.00	90.00
1949 (h) N; S	1,603,000	5.00	10.00	55.00	120	200
1950 (h) N; S	4,544,000	1.25	3.00	17.50	30.00	85.00
1951 (h) N; S	3,766,000	3.00	6.00	40.00	75.00	140
1952 (h) N; S	4,874,000	0.20	2.00	15.00	35.00	80.00
1953 (h) N; S	8,112,000	0.10	0.25	5.00	15.00	40.00

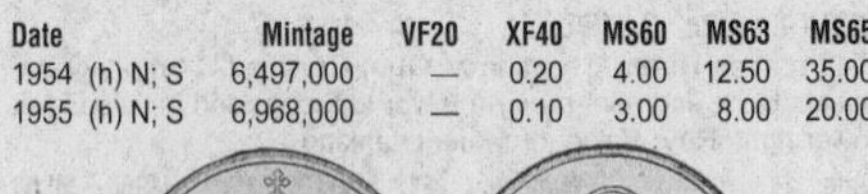

Date	Mintage	VF20	XF40	MS60	MS63	MS65
1954 (h) N; S	6,497,000	—	0.20	4.00	12.50	35.00
1955 (h) N; S	6,968,000	—	0.10	3.00	8.00	20.00

KM# 840.2 2 ØRE

3.20 g., Zinc, 20.8 mm. **Ruler:** Frederik IX **Obv:** Crowned F IX R monogram divides date **Rev:** Mint mark, initials C-S below value

Date	Mintage	VF20	XF40	MS60	MS63	MS65
1956 (h) C; S	10,004,000	—	—	1.50	5.00	15.00
1957 (h) C; S	15,329,000	—	—	1.00	3.00	10.00
1958 (h) C; S	8,119,999	—	—	0.50	2.00	8.00
1959 (h) C; S	10,462,000	—	—	0.40	1.20	5.00
1960 (h) C; S	16,504,000	—	—	0.35	1.00	3.50
1961 (h) C; S	15,504,000	—	—	—	0.80	2.50
1962 (h) C; S	10,980,000	—	—	—	0.80	2.50
1963 (h) C; S	19,470,000	—	—	—	0.60	2.00
1964 (h) C; S	15,411,000	—	—	—	0.60	2.00
1965 (h) C; S	20,173,000	—	—	—	0.40	1.50
1966 (h) C; S	21,949,000	—	—	—	0.40	1.50
1967 (h) C; S	22,439,000	—	—	—	0.25	1.50
1968 (h) C; S	17,632,000	—	—	—	0.25	1.50
1969 (h) C; S	29,276,000	—	—	—	0.20	1.00
1970 (h) C; S	23,864,000	—	—	—	0.20	1.00
1971 (h) C; S	35,811,000	—	—	—	0.15	1.00

KM# 847 2 ØRE

3.60 g., Bronze **Ruler:** Frederik IX **Obv:** Crowned F IX R monogram, date **Rev:** Two barley stalks around value, mint mark and initials C-S below **Note:** KM#847 was never released for circulation. Together with the 4 dates of 1 Øre, KM#846, they were sold as a 10 coin set to collectors by the mint. Approximately 100,000 sets were sold, remaining coins were melted. The date 1963 was produced exclusively for the set in 1973

Date	Mintage	VF20	XF40	MS60	MS63	MS65
1960 (h) C; S	Inc. above	—	—	—	0.90	2.00
1962 (h) C; S	Inc. above	—	—	—	0.90	2.00
1963 (h) C; S	100,000	—	—	—	0.90	2.00
1964 (h) C; S	3,990,000	—	—	—	0.90	2.00
1965 (h) C; S	11,980,000	—	—	—	0.90	2.00
1966 (h) C; S	12,000,000	—	—	—	0.90	2.00

KM# 840.3 2 ØRE

3.20 g., Zinc **Ruler:** Frederik IX **Obv:** Crowned F IX R monogram and date **Rev:** Mint mark, initials S-S below value

Date	Mintage	F12	VF20	XF40	MS60	MS63
1972 (h) S; S	6,496,000	—	—	—	—	0.30

KM# 794.2 5 ØRE

8.00 g., Bronze, 27 mm. **Ruler:** Christian IX **Obv:** Crowned CIX monogram, date at lower left, mint mark and initials VBP at lower right **Rev:** Value above porpoise and barley ear

Date	Mintage	F12	VF20	XF40	MS60	MS63
1902 (h) VBP	601,000	4.50	7.00	27.50	120	175
1904 (h) VBP	397,000	6.00	12.00	40.00	160	250
1906 (h) VBP	1,000,000	5.00	8.00	32.50	130	210

KM# 806 5 ØRE

8.00 g., Bronze **Ruler:** Frederik VIII **Obv:** Crowned F VIII R monogram, initials VBP at lower right **Rev:** Value within circle, date and initials VP below

Date	Mintage	F12	VF20	XF40	MS60	MS63
1907 (h) VBP; GJ	1,000,000	5.00	12.50	20.00	50.00	80.00
1908 (h) VBP; GJ	1,198,000	6.00	15.00	25.00	60.00	95.00
1912 (h) VBP; GJ	999,000	6.00	15.00	25.00	60.00	95.00

KM# 814.1 5 ØRE

8.00 g., Bronze, 27 mm. **Ruler:** Christian X **Obv:** Crowned CX monogram, initials VBP and mint mark lower at left, date and initials GJ at lower right **Rev:** Thick value, ornaments flanking

Date	Mintage	F12	VF20	XF40	MS60	MS63
1913 (h) VBP; GJ	216,000	40.00	90.00	150	350	500
1914 (h) VBP; GJ	785,000	4.00	7.00	15.00	35.00	47.50
1916 (h) VBP; GJ	887,000	5.00	10.00	20.00	47.50	65.00
1917 (h) VBP; GJ	494,000	8.00	17.50	30.00	70.00	100

KM# 814.1a 5 ØRE

6.94 g., Iron **Ruler:** Christian X **Obv:** Crowned CX monogram, initials VBP and mint mark at lower left, date and initials GJ at lower right **Rev:** Value, ornament flanking

Date	Mintage	F12	VF20	XF40	MS60	MS63
1918 (h) VBP; GJ	1,918,000	6.00	12.00	35.00	100	150

KM# 814.2 5 ØRE

8.00 g., Bronze **Ruler:** Christian X **Obv:** Crowned CX monogram, initials HCN and mint mark at lower left, date and initials GJ at lower right **Rev:** Thick value, ornaments flanking

Date	Mintage	F12	VF20	XF40	MS60	MS63
1919 (h) HCN; GJ	994,000	3.00	5.00	10.00	22.50	30.00
1920 (h) HCN; GJ	2,618,000	4.50	7.00	12.50	27.50	40.00
1921 (h) HCN; GJ	3,248,000	3.00	5.00	10.00	22.50	30.00
1923 (h) HCN; GJ	369,000	75.00	150	250	500	675

KM# 814.2a 5 ØRE

6.94 g., Iron **Ruler:** Christian X **Obv:** Crowned CX monogram, initials HCN and mint mark at lower left, date and initials GJ at lower right **Rev:** Value, ornament flanking

Date	Mintage	F12	VF20	XF40	MS60	MS63
1919 (h) HCN; GJ	1,034,999	8.00	20.00	50.00	150	275

KM# 828.1 5 ØRE

7.60 g., Bronze, 27.4 mm. **Ruler:** Christian X **Obv:** Crowned CXC monogram within title "KING OF DENMARK", initials GJ below **Rev:** Country name and date above center hole, denomination, mint mark, and initials HCN below

Date	Mintage	F12	VF20	XF40	MS60	MS63
1927 (h) HCN; GJ	7,129,000	0.10	0.20	0.50	6.00	15.00

KM# 828.2 5 ØRE

7.60 g., Bronze **Ruler:** Christian X **Obv:** Crowned CXC monogram within title "KING OF DENMARK", initials GJ below **Rev:** Country name and date above center hole, denomination, mint mark, and initial N below **Note:** For coins dated 1941 refer to Faeroe Islands.

Date	Mintage	F12	VF20	XF40	MS60	MS63
1927 (h) N; GJ	Inc. above	2.00	8.00	20.00	90.00	200
1928 (h) N; GJ	4,685,000	0.10	0.20	0.50	6.00	15.00
1929 (h) N; GJ	1,387,000	0.15	0.40	2.50	20.00	37.50
1930 (h) N; GJ	1,339,000	0.15	0.40	2.00	17.50	30.00
1932 (h) N; GJ	1,010,999	0.15	0.40	2.00	17.50	30.00
1932 (h) N; GJ	—					PF63 200
1934 (h) N; GJ	524,000	0.15	0.30	0.75	12.50	22.50
1935 (h) N; GJ	1,124,000	1.00	4.00	10.00	70.00	125
1936 (h) N; GJ	1,091,000	0.15	0.30	0.75	12.50	22.50
1937 (h) N; GJ	1,209,000	0.15	0.30	0.75	9.00	17.50
1938 (h) N; GJ	1,093,000	0.15	0.30	0.75	9.00	17.50
1939 (h) N; GJ	1,402,000	0.10	0.25	0.50	4.50	6.50
1940 (h) N; GJ	2,735,000	0.10	0.20	0.50	4.50	5.50

KM# 834 5 ØRE

2.40 g., Aluminum **Ruler:** Christian X **Obv:** Crowned CX monogram divides date, mint mark and initials N-S below **Rev:** Oak and beech leaves divide value

Date	Mintage	F12	VF20	XF40	MS60	MS63
1941 (h) N; S	16,984,000	—	0.15	1.25	10.00	20.00
1941 (h) N; S	—	PF63 350				

KM# 834a 5 ØRE

6.40 g., Zinc **Ruler:** Christian X **Obv:** Crowned CX monogram and date within title: "KING OF DENMARK"; mint mark and initials N-S below **Rev:** Value between oak and beech leaves

Date	Mintage	VF20	XF40	MS60	MS63	MS65
1942 (h) N; S	2,963,000	0.50	5.00	30.00	70.00	150
1943 (h) N; S	4,522,000	0.50	3.00	20.00	40.00	80.00
1944 (h) N; S	3,744,000	0.50	3.00	20.00	40.00	80.00
1945 (h) N; S	864,000	6.00	20.00	50.00	80.00	150

KM# 843.1 5 ØRE

6.40 g., Zinc **Ruler:** Frederik IX **Obv:** Crowned F IX R monogram, divides date **Rev:** Mint mark, initials N-S below value

Date	Mintage	XF40	AU50	MS60	MS63	MS65
1950 (h) N; S	657,000	20.00	40.00	60.00	85.00	160
1951 (h) N; S Straight 5	1,858,000	6.00	15.00	25.00	40.00	90.00
1951 (h) N; S Slant 5	Inc. above	6.00	15.00	25.00	40.00	90.00
1952 (h) N; S	3,562,000	3.00	10.00	15.00	25.00	60.00
1953 (h) N; S	5,944,000	2.00	8.00	13.50	17.50	40.00
1954 (h) N; S	3,060,000	2.25	9.00	14.00	20.00	45.00
1955 (h) N; S	2,314,000	5.50	12.50	17.50	30.00	70.00

KM# 843.2 5 ØRE

6.40 g., Zinc **Ruler:** Frederik IX **Obv:** Crowned F IX R monogram, divides date **Rev:** Mint mark, initials C-S below value

Date	Mintage	VF20	XF40	MS60	MS63	MS65
1956 (h) C; S	5,888,000	0.10	0.75	3.00	5.00	10.00
1957 (h) C; S	8,606,000	0.10	0.75	3.00	5.00	10.00
1958 (h) C; S	9,598,000	0.10	0.75	2.75	4.50	8.00
1959 (h) C; S	6,110,000	0.10	0.75	2.75	4.50	8.00
1960 (h) C; S	11,800,000	—	0.10	2.00	3.50	6.00
1961 (h) C; S	8,995,000	—	—	0.60	1.00	3.00
1962 (h) C; S	9,729,000	—	—	0.60	1.00	3.00
1963 (h) C; S	8,980,000	—	—	0.60	1.00	3.00
1964 (h) C; S	6,738,000	0.10	0.75	3.00	5.00	10.00

KM# 848.1 5 ØRE

6.00 g., Bronze, 24 mm. **Ruler:** Frederik IX **Obv:** Crowned F IX R monogram, divides date **Rev:** Two barley stalks around denomination, initials C-S below

Date	Mintage	VF20	XF40	MS60	MS63	MS65
1960 (h) C; S	3,760,000	0.20	0.60	1.75	5.00	12.50
1962 (h) C; S	5,873,000	0.40	0.90	2.50	7.50	20.00
1963 (h) C; S	23,287,000	—	—	—	0.40	2.00
1964 (h) C; S	41,521,000	—	—	—	0.40	2.00
1965 (h) C; S	14,229,000	—	—	—	0.50	2.50
1966 (h) C; S	23,410,000	—	—	—	0.40	2.00
1967 (h) C; S	15,094,000	—	—	—	0.50	2.50
1968 (h) C; S	16,105,000	—	—	—	0.40	2.00
1969 (h) C; S	23,594,000	—	—	—	0.25	1.50
1970 (h) C; S	26,176,000	—	—	—	0.10	1.00
1971 (h) C; S	10,076,000	—	—	—	0.10	0.65

KM# 848.2 5 ØRE

6.00 g., Bronze, 24 mm. **Ruler:** Frederik IX **Obv:** Crowned F IX R monogram, date **Rev:** Two barley stalks around value, initials S-S below

Date	Mintage	VF20	XF40	MS60	MS63	MS65
1972 (h) S; S	27,938,000	—	—	—	0.10	0.50

KM# 859.1 5 ØRE

1.60 g., Copper Clad Iron, 15.5 mm. **Ruler:** Margrethe II **Obv:** Crowned MIIR monogram divides date; mint mark, initials S-B **Rev:** DANMARK above denomination

Date	Mintage	VF20	XF40	MS60	MS63	MS65
1973 (h) S; B	75,138,000	—	—	—	—	0.15
1974 (h) S; B	71,796,000	—	—	—	—	0.15
1975 (h) S; B	45,004,000	—	—	—	—	0.15
1976 (h) S; B	73,296,000	—	—	—	—	0.15
1977 (h) S; B	74,066,000	—	—	—	—	0.15
1978 (h) S; B	52,425,000	—	—	—	—	0.15

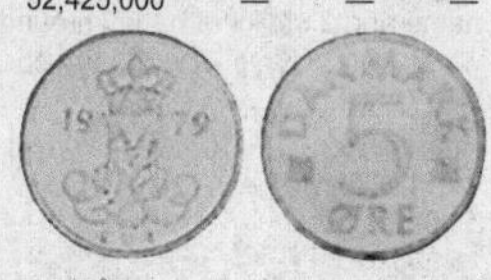

KM# 859.2 5 ØRE

1.60 g., Copper Clad Iron, 15.5 mm. **Ruler:** Margrethe II **Obv:** Crowned MIIR monogram divides date; mint mark, initials B-B **Rev:** DANMARK above denomination

Date	Mintage	VF20	XF40	MS60	MS63	MS65
1979 (h) B; B	58,953,000	—	—	—	—	0.15
1980 (h) B; B	54,362,000	—	—	—	—	0.15
1981 (h) B; B	52,201,000	—	—	—	—	0.15

KM# 859.3 5 ØRE

1.60 g., Copper Clad Iron, 15.5 mm. **Ruler:** Margrethe II **Obv:** Crowned MIIR monogram divides date; mint mark, initials R-B **Rev:** DANMARK above value

Date	Mintage	VF20	XF40	MS60	MS63	MS65
1982 (h) R; B	74,296,000	—	—	—	—	0.15
1983 (h) R; B	70,655,000	—	—	—	—	0.15
1984 (h) R; B	27,599,000	—	—	—	—	0.15
1985 (h) R; B	56,676,000	—	—	—	—	0.15
1986 (h) R; B	62,496,000	—	—	—	—	0.15
1987 (h) R; B	71,798,000	—	—	—	—	0.15
1988 (h) R; B	48,925,000	—	—	—	—	0.15

KM# 795.2 10 ØRE

1.45 g., 0.400 Silver 0.0186 oz. ASW **Ruler:** Christian IX **Obv:** Head right, date mint mark and initials below **Rev:** Denomination above porpoise and barley stalk, star at top

Date	Mintage	F12	VF20	XF40	MS60	MS63
1903/803 (h) VBP	3,007,000	0.50	5.50	9.50	24.00	37.50
1903 (h) VBP	Inc. above	0.50	5.00	8.50	20.00	32.50
1904 (h) VBP	2,449,000	5.50	12.50	22.50	70.00	100
1905 (h) VBP	1,571,000	0.50	4.00	7.00	17.50	27.50

KM# 807 10 ØRE

1.45 g., 0.400 Silver 0.0186 oz. ASW **Ruler:** Frederik VIII **Obv:** Head left, initials GJ below **Rev:** Value, date, mint mark, initials VBP within circle, lily ornamentation surrounds

Date	Mintage	F12	VF20	XF40	MS60	MS63
1907 (h) VBP; GJ	3,068,000	3.50	5.50	9.00	22.50	30.00
1910 (h) VBP; GJ	2,530,000	3.50	5.50	9.00	22.50	30.00
1911 (h) VBP; GJ	579,000	17.50	25.00	37.50	90.00	140
1912 (h) VBP; GJ	1,951,000	4.50	7.00	12.50	22.50	30.00

KM# 818.1 10 ØRE

1.45 g., 0.400 Silver 0.0186 oz. ASW **Ruler:** Christian X **Obv:** Crowned CX monogram, initials VBP and mint mark at lower left, date and initials GJ at lower right **Rev:** Value, ornaments flanking

Date	Mintage	F12	VF20	XF40	MS60	MS63
1914 (h) VBP; GJ	2,128,000	2.75	3.75	6.50	14.00	18.00
1915 (h) VBP; GJ	915,000	3.50	5.00	9.00	20.00	27.50
1916 (h) VBP; GJ	2,699,000	2.75	3.75	6.50	14.00	18.00
1917 (h) VBP; GJ	6,003,000	2.00	3.00	5.50	11.50	16.00
1918 (h) VBP; GJ	5,042,000	0.50	2.50	4.50	11.00	14.00

KM# 818.2 10 ØRE

1.45 g., 0.400 Silver 0.0186 oz. ASW **Ruler:** Christian X **Obv:** Crowned CX monogram, initials HCN and mint mark at lower left, date and initials GJ at lower right **Rev:** Value, ornament flanking

Date	Mintage	F12	VF20	XF40	MS60	MS63
1919 (h) HCN; GJ	10,184,000	—	0.50	2.50	4.75	7.00

KM# 818.2a 10 ØRE

1.50 g., Copper-Nickel, 15 mm. **Ruler:** Christian X **Obv:** Crowned CX monogram, initials HCN and mint mark at lower left, date and initials GJ at lower right **Rev:** Value, ornaments flanking

Date	Mintage	F12	VF20	XF40	MS60	MS63
1920 (h) HCN; GJ	10,234,000	3.00	5.50	12.50	25.00	35.00
1921 (h) HCN; GJ	8,064,000	3.00	5.50	12.50	25.00	35.00
1922 (h) HCN; GJ	3,065,000	10.00	22.50	37.50	80.00	120
1923 (h) HCN; GJ	1,790,000	275	425	600	1,100	1,400

KM# 822.1 10 ØRE

3.00 g., Copper-Nickel **Ruler:** Christian X **Obv:** Crowned CXR monogram around center hole, date, mint mark and initials HCN-GJ below hole **Rev:** Center hole flanked by spiral ornamentation dividing value **Edge:** Reeded

Date	Mintage	XF40	AU50	MS60	MS63	MS65
1924 (h) HCN; GJ	14,661,000	3.00	8.50	11.00	17.50	27.50
1925 (h) HCN; GJ	Inc. above	4.00	11.00	15.50	22.50	32.50
1926 (h) HCN; GJ	4,107,000	5.00	12.50	17.50	27.50	37.50

KM# 822.2 10 ØRE

3.00 g., Copper-Nickel **Ruler:** Christian X **Obv:** Crowned CXR monogram around center hole, date, mint mark and initial N-GJ below hole **Rev:** Center hole flanked by spiral ornamentation dividing value **Edge:** Reeded **Note:** For coins dated 1941 without mint mark or initials refer to Faeroe Islands listings.

Date	Mintage	F12	VF20	XF40	MS60	MS63
1929 (h) N; GJ	5,037,000	0.20	0.35	5.00	17.50	27.50
1931 (h) N; GJ	3,054,000	0.20	0.35	5.00	17.50	27.50
Small N						
1931 (h) N; GJ	Inc. above	0.20	0.35	5.00	17.50	27.50
Large N						
1933 (h) N; GJ	1,274,000	2.00	5.00	14.00	60.00	95.00
1934 (h) N; GJ	2,013,000	0.15	0.30	3.50	14.00	18.00
1935 (h) N; GJ	2,848,000	0.15	0.30	3.50	14.00	18.00
1936 (h) N; GJ	3,320,000	0.15	0.30	3.50	14.00	18.00
1937 (h) N; GJ	2,234,000	0.15	0.30	3.50	14.00	18.00
1938 (h) N; GJ	2,991,000	0.20	0.35	5.00	16.00	25.00
1939 (h) N; GJ	2,973,000	0.15	0.30	3.00	12.00	17.50
1940 (h) N; GJ	2,998,000	0.10	0.25	2.50	11.00	15.00
1941 (h) N; GJ	748,000	0.20	0.35	5.00	17.50	25.00
1946 (h) N; GJ	460,000	0.15	0.25	2.50	9.50	14.00
1947 (h) N; GJ	1,292,000	30.00	55.00	95.00	200	250

KM# 822.2a 10 ØRE

2.40 g., Zinc **Ruler:** Christian X **Obv:** Crowned CXR monogram around center hole, date, mint mark and initials N-GJ below hole **Rev:** Center hole flanked by spiral ornamentation dividing value

Date	Mintage	F12	VF20	XF40	MS60	MS63
1941 (h) N; GJ	7,706,000	0.10	0.25	2.75	12.00	17.50
1942 (h) N; GJ	8,676,000	0.10	0.25	2.75	12.00	17.50
1943 (h) N; GJ	2,181,000	0.20	0.35	3.50	14.00	20.00
1944 (h) N; GJ	7,994,000	0.10	0.25	2.75	12.00	17.50
1945 (h) N; GJ	1,280,000	25.00	50.00	85.00	190	260

KM# 841.1 10 ØRE

3.00 g., Copper-Nickel, 18 mm. **Ruler:** Frederik IX **Obv:** Crowned FIXR monogram divides date, oak and beech branches below **Rev:** Denomination, country name, mint mark, initials N-S

Date	Mintage	VF20	XF40	MS60	MS63	MS65
1948 (h) N; S	5,317,000	0.10	0.20	3.50	8.00	20.00
1949 (h) N; S	7,595,000	0.10	0.20	2.00	4.00	12.00
1950 (h) N; S	6,886,000	0.10	0.20	2.00	4.00	12.00
1951 (h) N; S	8,763,000	0.10	0.20	2.00	4.00	12.00
1952 (h) N; S	6,810,000	0.10	0.20	2.25	4.50	14.00
1953 (h) N; S	11,946,000	0.10	0.20	1.25	2.50	8.00
1954 (h) N; S	19,739,000	0.10	0.20	1.25	2.50	8.00
1955 (h) N; S	17,623,000	0.10	0.20	1.25	2.50	8.00

KM# 841.2 10 ØRE

3.00 g., Copper-Nickel, 18 mm. **Ruler:** Frederik IX **Obv:** Crowned FIXR monogram divides date, oak and beech branches below **Rev:** Denomination, country name, mint mark, initials C-S

Date	Mintage	VF20	XF40	MS60	MS63	MS65
1956 (h) C; S	12,323,000	0.10	0.20	1.25	2.50	8.00
1957 (h) C; S	13,227,000	0.10	0.20	1.00	2.00	5.00
1958 (h) C; S	10,870,000	0.10	0.20	1.00	2.00	5.00
1959 (h) C; S	1,255,000	20.00	35.00	85.00	120	200
1960 (h) C; S	5,107,000	0.10	0.20	1.50	4.00	8.00

KM# 849.1 10 ØRE

3.00 g., Copper-Nickel, 18 mm. **Ruler:** Frederik IX **Obv:** Crowned FIXR monogram divides date, mint mark and initials C-S below **Rev:** Denomination, country name above oak branches

Date	Mintage	VF20	XF40	MS60	MS63	MS65
1960 (h) C; S	Inc. above	—	—	0.20	1.00	4.00
1961 (h) C; S	20,258,000	—	—	—	—	2.00
1962 (h) C; S	12,785,000	—	—	—	—	1.50
1963 (h) C; S	17,171,000	—	—	—	—	1.00
1964 (h) C; S	14,282,000	—	—	—	—	0.75
1965 (h) C; S	21,857,000	—	—	—	—	0.50
1966 (h) C; S	24,160,000	—	—	—	—	0.50
1967 (h) C; S	21,544,000	—	—	—	—	0.40
1968 (h) C; S	7,586,000	—	—	—	—	0.40
1969 (h) C; S	31,534,000	—	—	—	—	0.40
1970 (h) C; S	37,813,000	—	—	—	—	0.30
1971 (h) C; S	17,719,000	—	—	—	—	0.30

KM# 849.2 10 ØRE

3.00 g., Copper-Nickel, 18 mm. **Ruler:** Frederik IX **Obv:** Crowned FIXR above mint mark and initials S-S **Rev:** Value, country name above oak branches

Date	Mintage	VF20	XF40	MS60	MS63	MS65
1972 (h) S; S	46,959,000	—	—	—	—	0.30

KM# 860.1 10 ØRE

3.00 g., Copper-Nickel, 18 mm. **Ruler:** Margrethe II **Obv:** Crowned MIIR monogram divides date, mint mark and initials S-B below **Rev:** Value flanked by oak leaves

Date	Mintage	VF20	XF40	MS60	MS63	MS65
1973 (h) S; B	37,538,000	—	—	—	—	0.30
1974 (h) S; B	38,570,000	—	—	—	—	0.30
1975 (h) S; B	62,633,000	—	—	—	—	0.30
1976 (h) S; B	64,358,999	—	—	—	—	0.30
1977 (h) S; B	61,994,000	—	—	—	—	0.30
1978 (h) S; B	30,302,000	—	—	—	—	0.30

KM# 860.2 10 ØRE

3.00 g., Copper-Nickel, 18 mm. **Ruler:** Margrethe II **Obv:** Crowned MIIR monogram divides date, mint mark and initials B-B below **Rev:** Value flanked by oak leaves

Date	Mintage	VF20	XF40	MS60	MS63	MS65
1979 (h) B; B	10,224,000	—	—	—	—	0.30
1980 (h) B; B	37,233,000	—	—	—	—	0.30
1981 (h) B; B	51,565,000	—	—	—	—	0.30

KM# 860.3 10 ØRE

3.00 g., Copper-Nickel, 18 mm. **Ruler:** Margrethe II **Obv:** Crowned MIIR monogram divides date, mint mark and initials R-B below **Rev:** Value flanked by oak leaves

Date	Mintage	VF20	XF40	MS60	MS63	MS65
1982 (h) R; B	40,195,000	—	—	—	—	0.30
1983 (h) R; B	35,634,000	—	—	—	—	0.30
1984 (h) R; B	17,828,000	—	—	—	—	0.30

Date	Mintage	VF20	XF40	MS60	MS63	MS65
1985 (h) R; B	29,317,000	—	—	—	—	0.30
1986 (h) R; B	46,254,000	—	—	—	—	0.30
1987 (h) R; B	27,898,000	—	—	—	—	0.30
1988 (h) R; B	29,400,000	—	—	—	—	0.30

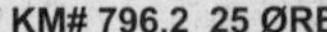

KM# 796.2 25 ØRE

2.42 g., 0.600 Silver 0.0467 oz. ASW **Ruler:** Christian IX **Obv:** Head right, date mint mark and initials below **Rev:** Value above porpoise and barley stalk, star at top

Date	Mintage	F12	VF20	XF40	MS60	MS63
1904 (h) VBP	1,922,000	10.00	25.00	45.00	120	150
1905/805 (h) VBP	1,722,000	10.00	25.00	45.00	120	150
1905 (h) VBP	Inc. above	8.00	20.00	35.00	80.00	120

KM# 808 25 ØRE

2.42 g., 0.600 Silver 0.0467 oz. ASW **Ruler:** Frederik VIII **Obv:** Head left, initials GJ below **Rev:** Value, date, mint mark, initials VBP within circle, lily ornamentation surrounds

Date	Mintage	F12	VF20	XF40	MS60	MS63
1907 (h) VBP; GJ	2,009,000	6.00	11.00	18.00	40.00	50.00
1911 (h) VBP; GJ	2,015,000	6.00	11.00	18.00	40.00	50.00

KM# 815.1 25 ØRE

2.42 g., 0.600 Silver 0.0467 oz. ASW **Ruler:** Christian X **Obv:** Crowned CX monogram, initials VBP and mint mark lower left, date and initials GJ lower right **Rev:** Value, ornaments flanking

Date	Mintage	F12	VF20	XF40	MS60	MS63
1913 (h) VBP; GJ	2,016,000	4.00	7.00	11.00	22.50	32.50
1914 (h) VBP; GJ	347,000	55.00	85.00	110	225	300
1915 (h) VBP; GJ	2,862,000	4.00	7.00	11.00	22.50	32.50
1916 (h) VBP; GJ	938,000	6.00	10.00	17.50	32.50	40.00
1917 (h) VBP; GJ	1,354,000	25.00	40.00	60.00	115	150
1918 (h) VBP; GJ	2,089,999	4.00	7.00	11.00	22.50	32.50

KM# 815.2 25 ØRE

2.42 g., 0.600 Silver 0.0467 oz. ASW **Ruler:** Christian X **Obv:** Crowned CX monogram, initials HCN and mint mark lower left, date and initials GJ lower right **Rev:** Value, ornament flanking

Date	Mintage	F12	VF20	XF40	MS60	MS63
1919 (h) HCN; GJ	9,295,000	2.50	4.00	7.50	15.00	20.00

KM# 815.2a 25 ØRE

2.40 g., Copper-Nickel **Ruler:** Christian X **Obv:** Crowned CX monogram, initials HCN and mint mark lower left, date and initials GJ lower right **Rev:** Value, ornament flanking

Date	Mintage	F12	VF20	XF40	MS60	MS63
1920 (h) HCN; GJ	12,288,000	2.50	4.00	7.50	20.00	35.00
1921 (h) HCN; GJ	9,444,000	2.50	4.00	7.50	20.00	35.00
1922 (h) HCN; GJ	5,701,000	12.50	22.50	32.50	60.00	90.00

KM# 823.1 25 ØRE

4.50 g., Copper-Nickel **Ruler:** Christian X **Obv:** Crowned CXR monogram around center hole, date, mint mark and initials HCN-GJ below hole **Rev:** Center hole flanked by designs divide value **Edge:** Reeded

Date	Mintage	F12	VF20	XF40	MS60	MS63
1924 (h) HCN; GJ	8,035,000	0.20	1.00	3.50	20.00	35.00
1925 (h) HCN; GJ	1,906,000	3,00	9.00	18.00	60.00	85.00
1926 (h) HCN; GJ	2,659,000	0.75	3.50	8.00	40.00	60.00

KM# 823.2 25 ØRE

4.50 g., Copper-Nickel **Ruler:** Christian X **Obv:** Crowned CXR monogram around center hole, date, mint mark and initials N-GJ below hole **Rev:** Center hole flanked by spiral ornamentations dividing value **Edge:** Reeded **Note:** For coins dated 1941 refer to Faeroe Islands listings.

Date	Mintage	F12	VF20	XF40	MS60	MS63
1929 (h) N; GJ	886,000	0.75	3.50	8.00	40.00	60.00
1930 (h) N; GJ	3,423,000	0.75	3.50	8.00	40.00	60.00
1932 (h) N; GJ	846,000	4.00	10.00	22.50	70.00	90.00
1933 (h) N; GJ	479,000	15.00	25.00	40.00	85.00	130
1934 (h) N; GJ	1,660,000	0.75	3.50	8.00	40.00	60.00
1935 (h) N; GJ	1,032,000	10.00	20.00	32.50	70.00	100
1936 (h) N; GJ	1,453,000	0.75	3.50	8.00	40.00	60.00
1937 (h) N; GJ	1,612,000	0.75	3.50	8.00	40.00	60.00
1938 (h) N; GJ	1,794,000	0.75	3.50	8.00	40.00	60.00
1939 (h) N; GJ	1,972,000	8.00	13.50	22.50	60.00	85.00
1940 (h) N; GJ	1,356,000	0.75	3.50	8.00	40.00	60.00
1946 (h) N; GJ	2,323,000	0.50	2.50	4.50	14.00	20.00
1947 (h) N; GJ	1,751,000	0.75	3.50	5.50	15.00	25.00

KM# 823.2a 25 ØRE

3.60 g., Zinc **Ruler:** Christian X **Obv:** Crowned CXR monogram around center hole, date, mint mark and initials N-GJ below hole **Rev:** Center hole flanked by spiral ornamentations dividing value

Date	Mintage	F12	VF20	XF40	MS60	MS63
1941 (h) N; GJ	15,332,000	0.75	6.00	17.50	32.50	45.00
1942 (h) N; GJ	997,000	0.75	6.00	17.50	32.50	45.00
1943 (h) N; GJ	5,784,000	0.75	6.00	17.50	42.50	65.00
1944 (h) N; GJ	10,665,000	0.75	6.00	17.50	37.50	52.50
1945 (h) N; GJ	4,543,000	0.75	6.00	17.50	40.00	60.00

KM# 842.1 25 ØRE

4.50 g., Copper-Nickel, 23 mm. **Ruler:** Frederik IX **Obv:** Crowned F IX R monogram divides value, oak and beech branches below **Rev:** Value, country name, mint mark, initials N-S

Date	Mintage	VF20	XF40	MS60	MS63	MS65
1948 (h) N; S	1,853,000	3.00	6.00	17.50	25.00	40.00
1949 (h) N; S	15,000,000	0.10	0.50	5.00	8.00	17.50
1950 (h) N; S	13,771,000	0.10	0.50	5.00	8.00	17.50
1951 (h) N; S	5,045,000	0.15	0.65	7.50	12.50	30.00
1952 (h) N; S	2,017,999	0.30	1.00	8.50	15.00	35.00
1953 (h) N; S	9,553,000	0.10	0.50	5.50	10.00	20.00
1954 (h) N; S	11,337,000	—	0.40	4.75	7.50	12.50
1955 (h) N; S	6,385,000	—	0.40	4.75	7.50	12.50

KM# 842.2 25 ØRE

4.50 g., Copper-Nickel, 23 mm. **Ruler:** Frederik IX **Obv:** Crowned F IX R monogram divides date, oak and beech branches below **Rev:** Value, country name, mint mark, initials C-S

Date	Mintage	VF20	XF40	MS60	MS63	MS65
1956 (h) C; S	10,228,000	—	0.20	2.50	4.00	7.00
1957 (h) C; S	7,421,000	—	0.20	2.50	4.00	7.00
1958 (h) C; S	3,600,000	—	0.25	2.75	5.00	8.00
1959 (h) C; S	2,211,000	1.00	2.50	7.00	10.00	20.00
1960 (h) C; S	3,453,000	—	0.30	1.35	2.00	4.00

KM# 850 25 ØRE

4.50 g., Copper-Nickel, 23 mm. **Ruler:** Frederik IX **Obv:** Crowned F IX R monogram divides date, oak and beech branches below **Rev:** Value, country name, mint mark, initials C-S

Date	Mintage	VF20	XF40	MS60	MS63	MS65
1960 (h) C; S	Inc. above	5.00	8.00	15.00	20.00	35.00
1961 (h) C; S	20,860,000	—	—	—	—	1.25
1962 (h) C; S	12,563,000	—	—	—	—	1.25
1964 (h) C; S	6,175,000	—	—	—	—	1.25
1965 (h) C; S	13,492,000	—	—	—	—	1.25
1966 (h) C; S	50,220,000	—	—	—	—	1.25
1967 (h) C; S	87,468,000	5.00	8.00	15.00	20.00	35.00

KM# 855.1 25 ØRE

4.30 g., Copper-Nickel, 23 mm. **Ruler:** Frederik IX **Obv:** Crowned F IX R monogram, date below, to left of center hole, beech branch to right, initials C-S and mint mark at bottom **Rev:** Value, country name and 2 stalks of barley around center hole

Date	Mintage	VF20	XF40	MS60	MS63	MS65
1966 (h) C; S	Inc. above	—	—	—	0.20	0.70
1967 (h) C; S	Inc. above	—	—	—	—	0.70
1968 (h) C; S	39,142,000	—	—	—	—	0.70
1969 (h) C; S	16,974,000	—	—	—	—	0.70
1970 (h) C; S	5,393,000	—	—	—	—	0.70
1971 (h) C; S	12,725,000	—	—	—	—	0.70

KM# 855.2 25 ØRE

4.30 g., Copper-Nickel, 23 mm. **Ruler:** Frederik IX **Obv:** Crowned F IX R monogram and date to left of center hole, beech branch to right, initial S-S and mint mark at bottom **Rev:** Value, country name and 2 stalks of barley around center hole

Date	Mintage	VF20	XF40	MS60	MS63	MS65
1972 (h) S; S	31,422,000	—	—	—	—	0.50

KM# 861.1 25 ØRE

4.30 g., Copper-Nickel, 23 mm. **Ruler:** Margrethe II **Obv:** Crowned MIIR monogram to left, oak branch to right of center hole, date above, mint mark and initials S-B below **Rev:** Denomination divided by center hole, stylized stalks flank

Date	Mintage	VF20	XF40	MS60	MS63	MS65
1973 (h) S; B	30,834,000	—	—	—	—	0.40
1974 (h) S; B	22,178,000	—	—	—	—	0.40
1975 (h) S; B	28,798,000	—	—	—	—	0.40
1976 (h) S; B	48,388,000	—	—	—	—	0.40
1977 (h) S; B	32,238,999	—	—	—	—	0.40
1978 (h) S; B	17,444,000	—	—	—	—	0.40

KM# 861.2 25 ØRE

4.30 g., Copper-Nickel, 23 mm. **Ruler:** Margrethe II **Obv:** Crowned MIIR monogram to left, oak branch to right of center hole, date above, mint mark and initials B-B below **Rev:** Value divided by center hole, stylized stalks flank

Date	Mintage	VF20	XF40	MS60	MS63	MS65
1979 (h) B; B	24,261,000	—	—	—	—	0.40
1980 (h) B; B	30,448,000	—	—	—	—	0.40
1981 (h) B; B	1,427,000	—	—	—	—	0.40

KM# 861.3 25 ØRE

4.30 g., Copper-Nickel, 23 mm. **Ruler:** Margrethe II **Obv:** Crowned MIIR monogram to left, oak branch to right of center hole, date above, mint mark and initials B-B below **Rev:** Value divided by center hole, stylized stalks flank

Date	Mintage	VF20	XF40	MS60	MS63	MS65
1982 (h) R; B	24,671,000	—	—	—	—	0.40

Date	Mintage	VF20	XF40	MS60	MS63	MS65
1983 (h) R; B	32,706,000	—	—	—	—	0.40
1984 (h) R; B	22,882,000	—	—	—	—	0.40
1985 (h) R; B	29,048,000	—	—	—	—	0.40
1986 (h) R; B	53,496,000	—	—	—	—	0.40
1987 (h) R; B	30,575,000	—	—	—	—	0.40
1988 (h) R; B	23,370,000	—	—	—	—	0.40

KM# 868.1 25 ØRE

2.80 g., Bronze, 17.5 mm. **Ruler:** Margrethe II **Obv:** Large crown divides date above, initial to right of country **Rev:** Denomination, small heart above, mint mark and initials LG-JP below **Note:** Beginning in 1996 and ending with 1998, the words "DANMARK" and "ØRE" have raised edges. Heart mint mark under "ØRE"; Prev. KM#868.

Date	Mintage	VF20	XF40	MS60	MS63	MS65
1990 LG; JP; A	109,084,000	—	—	—	—	0.15
1991 LG; JP; A	102,162,000	—	—	—	—	0.15
1992 LG; JP; A	6,293,000	—	—	—	—	0.50
1993 LG; JP; A	14,756,000	—	—	—	—	0.40
1994 LG; JP; A	35,750,000	—	—	—	—	0.15
1995 LG; JP; A	40,000,000	—	—	—	—	0.15
1996 LG; JP; A	46,760,000	—	—	—	—	0.15
1997 LG; JP; A	30,306,000	—	—	—	—	0.15
1998 LG; JP; A	17,200,000	—	—	—	—	0.15
1999 LG; JP; A	18,748,000	—	—	—	—	0.15
2000 LG; JP; A	14,500,000	—	—	—	—	0.15

KM# 866.1 50 ØRE

4.30 g., Bronze, 21.5 mm. **Ruler:** Margrethe II **Obv:** Date above large crown, country name below, initial A to right **Rev:** Large heart above value, mint mark and initials NR-JP below **Note:** Heart mint mark under the word "Øre".

Date	Mintage	VF20	XF40	MS60	MS63	MS65
1989 NR; JP; A	92,236,000	—	—	—	—	0.30

KM# 866.2 50 ØRE

4.30 g., Bronze, 21.5 mm. **Ruler:** Margrethe II **Obv:** Large crown divides date above, initial to right of country name **Rev:** Large heart above value, mint mark and initials LG-JP below **Note:** Beginning in 1996 and ending with 1998, the words "DANMARK" and "ØRE" have raised edges. Heart mint mark under the word "ØRE".

Date	Mintage	VF20	XF40	MS60	MS63	MS65
1990 LG; JP; A	63,518,000	—	—	—	—	0.30
1991 LG; JP; A	11,115,000	—	—	—	—	0.50
1992 LG; JP; A	14,397,000	—	—	—	—	0.50
1993 LG; JP; A	14,328,000	—	—	—	—	0.50
1994 LG; JP; A	25,055,000	—	—	—	—	0.30
1995 LG; JP; A	15,988,000	—	—	—	—	0.30
1996 LG; JP; A	11,536,000	—	—	—	—	0.30
1997 LG; JP; A	15,574,000	—	—	—	—	0.30
1998 LG; JP; A	13,120,000	—	—	—	—	0.30
1999 LG; JP; A	14,186,000	—	—	—	—	0.30
2000 LG; JP; A	15,500,000	—	—	—	—	0.30

KM# 831.1 1/2 KRONE

3.00 g., Aluminum-Bronze, 20 mm. **Ruler:** Christian X **Obv:** Crowned CXC monogram, date, mint mark, and initials HCN-GJ **Rev:** Value above, country name below large crown

Date	Mintage	F12	VF20	XF40	MS60	MS63
1924 (h) HCN; GJ	2,150,000	2.00	5.00	10.00	45.00	70.00
1925 (h) HCN; GJ	3,432,000	2.00	5.00	10.00	45.00	80.00
1926 (h) HCN; GJ	716,000	4.00	7.00	12.50	50.00	85.00

KM# 831.2 1/2 KRONE

3.00 g., Aluminum-Bronze **Ruler:** Christian X **Obv:** Crowned CXC monogram, date, mint mark, and initial N-GJ **Rev:** Value above, country name below large crown

Date	Mintage	F12	VF20	XF40	MS60	MS63
1939 (h) N; GJ	226,000	35.00	50.00	75.00	150	200
1940 (h) N; GJ	1,871,000	2.00	4.50	8.00	25.00	35.00

KM# 819 KRONE

7.50 g., 0.800 Silver 0.1929 oz. ASW **Ruler:** Christian X **Obv:** Head of Christian X, right, with titles, date, mint mark and initials AH at neck, and VBP at date **Rev:** Crowned royal arms with porpoise to left, barley stalk to right, value below

Date	Mintage	F12	VF20	XF40	MS60	MS63
1915 (h) VBP; AH	1,410,000	5.00	7.50	11.00	22.50	30.00
1916 (h) VBP; AH	992,000	6.00	8.00	12.50	25.00	35.00

KM# 824.1 KRONE

6.50 g., Aluminum-Bronze, 25.5 mm. **Ruler:** Christian X **Obv:** Crowned CXC monogram, date, mint mark, and initials HCN-GJ **Rev:** Denomination above large crown, country name below

Date	Mintage	F12	VF20	XF40	MS60	MS63
1924 (h) HCN; GJ	999,000	100	350	1,000	3,000	4,250
1925 (h) HCN; GJ	6,314,000	1.00	10.00	40.00	120	200
1926 (h) HCN; GJ	2,706,000	1.00	10.00	40.00	120	200

KM# 824.2 KRONE

6.50 g., Aluminum-Bronze, 25.5 mm. **Ruler:** Christian X **Obv:** Crowned CXC monogram, date, mint mark, and initials N-GJ **Rev:** Denomination above large crown, country name below

Date	Mintage	F12	VF20	XF40	MS60	MS63
1929 (h) N; GJ	501,000	4.00	15.00	55.00	200	325
1930 (h) N; GJ	540,000	10.00	20.00	60.00	275	450
1931 (h) N; GJ	540,000	3.50	12.50	45.00	140	200
1934 (h) N; GJ	529,000	3.50	12.50	45.00	140	200
1935 (h) N; GJ	505,000	15.00	25.00	70.00	250	375
1936 (h) N; GJ	558,000	3.50	12.50	45.00	140	200
1938 (h) N; GJ	407,000	8.50	15.00	40.00	175	250
1939 (h) N; GJ	1,517,000	1.00	4.00	12.50	35.00	60.00
1940 (h) N; GJ	1,496,000	1.00	4.00	12.50	35.00	60.00
1941 (h) N; GJ	661,000	10.00	17.50	50.00	200	275

KM# 835 KRONE

6.50 g., Aluminum-Bronze, 25.5 mm. **Ruler:** Christian X **Obv:** Head right, with titles, mint mark, initials N-S **Rev:** Value divided by stalk of wheat and oats crossed, date

Date	Mintage	F12	VF20	XF40	MS60	MS63
1942 (h) N; S	3,952,000	1.00	2.25	7.50	27.50	40.00
1943 (h) N; S	798,000	3.00	9.00	30.00	130	225
1944 (h) N; S	1,760,000	1.00	2.25	7.50	27.50	40.00
1945 (h) N; S	2,581,000	1.25	2.75	10.00	35.00	65.00
1946 (h) N; S	4,321,000	0.75	2.00	4.00	14.00	22.50
1947 (h) N; S	5,060,000	0.60	1.50	3.75	12.00	15.00

KM# 837.1 KRONE

6.50 g., Aluminum-Bronze, 25.5 mm. **Ruler:** Frederik IX **Obv:** Head right, titles, mint mark, initials N-S **Rev:** Crowned royal arms divide date, value above

Date	Mintage	F12	VF20	XF40	MS60	MS63
1947 (h) N; S	Inc. above	1.00	2.25	7.50	20.00	30.00
1948 (h) N; S	4,248,000	0.60	1.00	3.00	10.00	15.00
1949 (h) N; S	1,300,000	2.00	3.25	12.00	35.00	50.00
1952 (h) N; S	2,124,000	1.00	2.25	7.50	20.00	30.00
1953 (h) N; S	573,000	1.25	2.75	10.00	32.50	42.50
1954 (h) N; S	584,000	5.00	12.50	25.00	70.00	100
1955 (h) N; S	1,359,000	1.75	2.50	9.00	27.50	40.00

KM# 837.2 KRONE

6.50 g., Aluminum-Bronze, 25.5 mm. **Ruler:** Frederik IX **Obv:** Head right, titles, mint mark, initials C-S **Rev:** Crowned royal arms divide date, value above

Date	Mintage	F12	VF20	XF40	MS60	MS63
1956 (h) C; S	2,858,000	0.75	2.00	5.00	15.50	20.00
1957 (h) C; S	10,896,000	0.50	1.00	2.00	3.75	4.50
1958 (h) C; S	1,507,000	0.50	1.00	2.00	3.75	4.50
1959 (h) C; S	243,000	5.00	9.00	17.50	37.50	50.00
1960 (h) C; S	100	—	—	—	7,000	8,500

Note: 1960 dated coins were not released into circulation, however, approximately 50 pieces did eventually make their way into the collector's market in 1969.

KM# 851.1 KRONE

6.80 g., Copper-Nickel, 25.5 mm. **Ruler:** Frederik IX **Obv:** Older head right, titles, mint mark, initials C-S **Rev:** Crowned and quartered royal arms divide date, value above **Edge:** Reeded

Date	Mintage	VF20	XF40	MS60	MS63	MS65
1960 (h) C; S	1,000,000	—	—	1.75	3.00	8.00
1961 (h) C; S	10,348,000	—	—	—	3.00	11.00
1962 (h) C; S	27,068,000	—	—	—	2.00	12.50
1963 (h) C; S	32,083,000	—	—	—	—	3.00
1964 (h) C; S	5,984,000	—	—	—	—	4.00
1965 (h) C; S	13,799,000	—	—	—	—	3.00
1966 (h) C; S	10,890,000	—	—	—	—	2.50
1967 (h) C; S	18,304,000	—	—	—	—	2.50
1968 (h) C; S	8,212,999	—	—	—	—	2.00
1969 (h) C; S	9,597,000	—	—	—	—	2.00
1970 (h) C; S	9,460,000	—	—	—	—	1.50
1971 (h) C; S	13,985,000	—	—	—	—	1.00

KM# 851.2 KRONE

6.80 g., Copper-Nickel, 25.5 mm. **Ruler:** Frederik IX **Obv:** Older head right, titles, mint mark, initials S-S **Rev:** Crowned and quartered royal arms divide date, value above **Edge:** Reeded

Date	Mintage	VF20	XF40	MS60	MS63	MS65
1972 (h) S; S	21,019,000	—	—	—	—	0.75

KM# 862.1 KRONE

6.80 g., Copper-Nickel, 25.5 mm. **Ruler:** Margrethe II **Obv:** Head right, with titles, mint mark, initials S-B below **Rev:** Crowned and quartered royal arms divide date, value below **Edge:** Reeded

Date	Mintage	VF20	XF40	MS60	MS63	MS65
1973 (h) S; B	18,268,000	—	—	—	—	1.00
Note: Narrow rim (0.7mm)						
1973 (h) S; B	Inc. above	—	—	—	—	1.00
Note: Wide rim (1.1mm)						
1974 (h) S; B	17,742,000	—	—	—	—	1.00
1975 (h) S; B	20,136,000	—	—	—	—	0.75
1976 (h) S; B	28,049,000	—	—	—	—	0.75
1977 (h) S; B	25,685,000	—	—	—	—	0.75
1978 (h) S; B	11,286,000	—	—	—	—	0.75

KM# 862.2 KRONE
6.80 g., Copper-Nickel, 25.5 mm. **Ruler:** Margrethe II **Obv:** Head right, mint mark and initials B-B below **Rev:** Crowned and quartered royal arms divide date, value below **Edge:** Reeded

Date	Mintage	VF20	XF40	MS60	MS63	MS65
1979 (h) B; B	25,216,000	—	—	—	—	0.75
1980 (h) B; B	25,825,000	—	—	—	—	0.75
1981 (h) B; B	8,889,000	—	—	—	—	1.00

KM# 862.3 KRONE
6.80 g., Copper-Nickel, 25.5 mm. **Ruler:** Margrethe II **Obv:** Head right with titles, mint mark, initials R-B below **Rev:** Crowned and quartered royal arms divide date, value below **Edge:** Reeded

Date	Mintage	VF20	XF40	MS60	MS63	MS65
1982 (h) R; B	5,011,000	—	—	—	—	1.00
1983 (h) R; B	13,946,000	—	—	—	—	0.75
1984 (h) R; B	36,439,000	—	—	—	—	0.75
1985 (h) R; B	10,843,000	—	—	—	—	0.75
1986 (h) R; B	12,556,000	—	—	—	—	0.75
1987 (h) R; B	20,120,000	—	—	—	—	0.75
1988 (h) R; B	32,073,999	—	—	—	—	0.50
1989 (h) R; B	15,704,000	—	—	—	—	0.75

KM# 873.1 KRONE
3.60 g., Copper-Nickel, 20.25 mm. **Ruler:** Margrethe II **Obv:** 3 crowned MII monograms around center hole, date, mint mark, and initials LG-JP-A below **Rev:** Wave design surrounds center hole, value above, hearts flank **Edge:** Reeded **Note:** Prev. KM#873.

Date	Mintage	VF20	XF40	MS60	MS63	MS65
1992 LG; JP; A	81,621,000	—	—	—	—	0.40
1993 LG; JP; A	15,844,000	—	—	—	—	0.40
1994 LG; JP; A	23,658,000	—	—	—	—	0.40
1995 LG; JP; A	34,966,000	—	—	—	—	0.40
1996 LG; JP; A	10,081,000	—	—	—	—	0.40
1997 LG; JP; A	10,121,807	—	—	—	—	0.40
1998 LG; JP; A	13,100,000	—	—	—	—	0.40
1999 LG; JP; A	6,479,000	—	—	—	—	0.40
2000 LG; JP; A	21,500,000	—	—	—	—	0.40

KM# 802 2 KRONER
15.00 g., 0.800 Silver 0.3858 oz. ASW, 31 mm. **Ruler:** Christian IX **Subject:** 40th Anniversary of Reign **Obv:** Armored bust right, with titles and anniversary dates, date and "P" below bust **Rev:** Seated woman holding royal shield; flying dove to the left; Motto: "With God for honor and justice"; value in exergue

Date	Mintage	F12	VF20	XF40	MS60	MS63
1903 (h) P; GJ	103,392	12.50	17.50	22.50	35.00	47.50

KM# 803 2 KRONER
15.00 g., 0.800 Silver 0.3858 oz. ASW, 31 mm. **Ruler:** Frederik VIII **Subject:** Death of Christian IX and Accession of Frederik VIII **Obv:** Armored bust left with titles, motto, date, initials VBP **Rev:** Bust left with titles, date of death, value, initials GJ

Date	Mintage	F12	VF20	XF40	MS60	MS63
1906 (h) VBP GJ	151,000	12.50	17.50	22.50	35.00	45.00

KM# 811 2 KRONER
15.00 g., 0.800 Silver 0.3858 oz. ASW, 31 mm. **Ruler:** Christian X **Subject:** Death of Frederik VIII and Accession of Christian X **Obv:** Head right with initials AH at neck, date, mint mark and initials VBP below **Rev:** Head right with initials AH, value below, date of death **Note:** Coin rotation.

Date	Mintage	F12	VF20	XF40	MS60	MS63
1912 (h) VBP; AH	101,917	12.50	17.50	22.50	35.00	45.00

KM# 820 2 KRONER
15.00 g., 0.800 Silver 0.3858 oz. ASW, 31 mm. **Ruler:** Christian X **Obv:** Head right with initials AH at neck, date, mint mark and initial VBP below **Rev:** Crowned royal arms, porpoise and barley stalk flanking, value below

Date	Mintage	F12	VF20	XF40	MS60	MS63
1915 (h) VBP; AH	657,000	12.50	15.00	18.00	30.00	40.00
1916 (h) VBP; AH	402,000	14.00	17.50	22.50	37.50	50.00

KM# 821 2 KRONER
15.00 g., 0.800 Silver 0.3858 oz. ASW, 31 mm. **Ruler:** Christian X **Subject:** Silver Wedding Anniversary **Obv:** Heads of Christian X and Queen Alexandrine right, initials GJ **Rev:** Crowned arms within anniversary dates, initials HCN, denomination below

Date	Mintage	F12	VF20	XF40	MS60	MS63
1923 (h) HCN; GJ	203,357	7.25	12.50	16.00	27.50	37.50

KM# 825.1 2 KRONER
13.00 g., Aluminum-Bronze, 31 mm. **Ruler:** Christian X **Obv:** Crowned CXC monogram, date, mint mark, and initials HCN-GJ **Rev:** Denomination above large crown, country name below

Date	Mintage	F12	VF20	XF40	MS60	MS63
1924 (h) HCN; GJ	1,138,000	20.00	50.00	400	1,400	1,800
1925 (h) HCN; GJ	3,248,000	1.50	12.50	35.00	140	200
1926 (h) HCN; GJ	1,126,000	2.00	10.00	35.00	180	260

KM# 825.2 2 KRONER
13.00 g., Aluminum-Bronze, 31 mm. **Ruler:** Christian X **Obv:** Crowned CXC monogram, date, mint mark, and initials N-GJ **Rev:** Denomination above large crown, country name below

Date	Mintage	F12	VF20	XF40	MS60	MS63
1936 (h) N; GJ	400,000	3.00	15.00	50.00	200	375
1938 (h) N; GJ	191,000	7.00	20.00	60.00	220	375
1939 (h) N; GJ	723,000	2.50	9.00	20.00	40.00	60.00
1940 (h) N; GJ	743,000	3.00	11.00	25.00	55.00	75.00
1941 (h) N; GJ	129,000	35.00	65.00	200	450	600

KM# 829 2 KRONER
15.00 g., 0.800 Silver 0.3858 oz. ASW, 31 mm. **Ruler:** Christian X **Subject:** King's 60th Birthday **Obv:** Head right, date, mint mark, initials AH at neck, N below **Rev:** Draped and supported national arms, value below, initials HS, two dates at top

Date	Mintage	VF20	XF40	MS60	MS63	MS65
1930 (h) N; AH/HS	302,640	—	—	7.25	12.50	25.00

KM# 830 2 KRONER
15.00 g., 0.800 Silver 0.3858 oz. ASW, 31 mm. **Ruler:** Christian X **Subject:** 25th Anniversary of Reign **Obv:** Head right, mint mark and initials N-S below **Rev:** Crowned royal arms, value below

Date	Mintage	VF20	XF40	MS60	MS63	MS65
ND-1937 (h) N; S	208,699	—	—	7.25	14.00	30.00

KM# 836 2 KRONER
15.00 g., 0.800 Silver 0.3858 oz. ASW, 31 mm. **Ruler:** Christian X **Subject:** King's 75th Birthday **Obv:** Head right, mint mark and initials N-S below **Rev:** Dates of birth and 75th birthday year within wreath, legend around, denomination below **Rev. Legend:** (Translated) "IN ONE WITH HIS PEOPLE IN SORROW AND VICTORY"

Date	Mintage	VF20	XF40	MS60	MS63	MS65
ND-1945 (h) N; S	156,642	—	—	12.50	18.00	40.00

KM# 838.1 2 KRONER
13.00 g., Aluminum-Bronze, 31 mm. **Ruler:** Frederik IX **Obv:** Head right, mint mark and initials N-S below **Rev:** Crowned royal arms divide date, value above

Date	Mintage	F12	VF20	XF40	MS60	MS63
1947 (h) N; S	1,151,000	1.00	4.00	10.00	30.00	40.00
1948 (h) N; S	857,000	0.75	3.00	7.50	22.50	32.50
1949 (h) N; S	272,000	4.00	12.00	25.00	50.00	70.00
1951 (h) N; S	1,576,000	0.75	3.00	6.00	20.00	30.00
1952 (h) N; S	1,958,000	0.75	2.75	5.50	17.50	27.50
1953 (h) N; S	432,000	1.00	4.50	12.00	30.00	42.50
1954 (h) N; S	716,000	1.00	4.50	12.00	30.00	42.50
1955 (h) N; S	457,000	1.00	4.50	12.00	30.00	42.50

KM# 838.2 2 KRONER
13.00 g., Aluminum-Bronze, 31 mm. **Ruler:** Frederik IX **Obv:** Head right, mint mark and initials C-S below **Rev:** Crowned royal arms divide date, value above

Date	Mintage	F12	VF20	XF40	MS60	MS63
1956 (h) C; S	1,444,000	0.75	2.75	4.00	10.00	15.00
1957 (h) C; S	2,610,000	0.65	2.50	3.75	9.00	13.50
1958 (h) C; S	2,605,000	0.65	2.50	3,075	9.00	17.50
1959 (h) C; S	192,000	10.00	18.00	25.00	47.50	60.00

KM# 844 2 KRONER

15.00 g., 0.800 Silver 0.3858 oz. ASW, 31 mm. **Ruler:** Frederik IX **Subject:** Foundation for the Campaign against Tuberculosis in Greenland **Obv:** Conjoined heads right, date, mint mark and initials N-S below **Rev:** Map of Greenland, country name in Greenlandic language, denomination below **Note:** Greenland Commemorative.

Date	Mintage	VF20	XF40	MS60	MS63	MS65
1953 (h) N; S	151,710	7.25	17.50	30.00	37.50	60.00

KM# 845 2 KRONER

15.00 g., 0.800 Silver 0.3858 oz. ASW, 31 mm. **Ruler:** Frederik IX **Subject:** Princess Margrethe's 18th Birthday **Obv:** Head right with titles, mint mark and initials C-S below **Rev:** Head left, date of 18th birthday, value below

Date	Mintage	VF20	XF40	MS60	MS63	MS65
ND-1958 (h) C; S	301,426	—	7.50	20.00	30.00	50.00

KM# 874.1 2 KRONER

5.90 g., Copper-Nickel, 24.5 mm. **Ruler:** Margrethe II **Obv:** 3 crowned MII monograms around center hole, date and initials LG-JP-A below **Rev:** Design surrounds center hole, denomination above, hearts flank **Edge:** Segmented reeding **Note:** Prev. KM#874.

Date	Mintage	VF20	XF40	MS60	MS63	MS65
1992 LG; JP; A	41,648,000	—	—	—	—	0.80
1993 LG; JP; A	43,864,000	—	—	—	—	0.80
1994 LG; JP; A	27,629,000	—	—	—	—	0.80
1995 LG; JP; A	19,850,000	—	—	—	—	0.80
1996 LG; JP; A	2,884,000	—	—	—	—	1.00
1997 LG; JP; A	25,874,000	—	—	—	—	0.80
1998 LG; JP; A	4,360,000	—	—	—	—	0.80
1999 LG; JP; A	20,608,000	—	—	—	—	0.80
2000 LG; JP; A	10,400,000	—	—	—	—	0.80

KM# 852 5 KRONER

17.00 g., 0.800 Silver 0.4372 oz. ASW, 33 mm. **Ruler:** Frederik IX **Subject:** Silver Wedding Anniversary **Obv:** Conjoined heads right, within titles **Rev:** Crowned double FI monogram, silver anniversary dates above, 2 barley stalks, value, mint mark and initials C-S below

Date	Mintage	VF20	XF40	MS60	MS63	MS65
ND-1960 (h) C; S	409,858	—	8.50	15.00	20.00	50.00

KM# 853.1 5 KRONER

15.00 g., Copper-Nickel, 33 mm. **Ruler:** Frederik IX **Obv:** Head right, titles, mint mark and initials C-S below **Rev:** Crowned and quartered arms divide date within two oak branches, value above

Date	Mintage	VF20	XF40	MS60	MS63	MS65
1960 (h) C; S	6,418,000	—	1.50	4.00	6.00	25.00
1961 (h) C; S	9,744,000	—	1.75	5.00	7.00	17.50
1962 (h) C; S	2,073,999	1.50	2.50	7.00	10.00	25.00
1963 (h) C; S	709,000	1.50	2.50	7.00	10.00	25.00
1964 (h) C; S	1,443,000	—	1.75	5.00	7.00	17.50
1965 (h) C; S	2,574,000	—	—	3.00	6.00	15.00
1966 (h) C; S	4,370,000	—	—	3.00	6.00	15.00
1967 (h) C; S	1,864,000	—	—	3.00	6.00	15.00
1968 (h) C; S	4,131,999	—	—	3.00	6.00	15.00
1969 (h) C; S	72,000	—	—	4.00	8.00	19.00
1970 (h) C; S	2,246,000	—	—	—	—	3.50
1971 (h) C; S	4,767,000	—	—	—	—	3.00

KM# 853.2 5 KRONER

15.00 g., Copper-Nickel, 33 mm. **Ruler:** Frederik IX **Obv:** Head right, titles, mint mark and initials S-S below **Rev:** Crowned and quartered arms divide date within two oak branches, value above

Date	Mintage	VF20	XF40	MS60	MS63	MS65
1972 (h) S; S	2,599,000	—	—	—	—	2.50

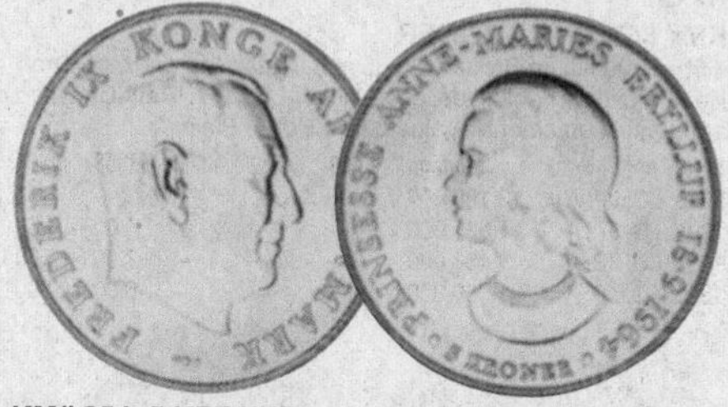

KM# 854 5 KRONER

17.00 g., 0.800 Silver 0.4372 oz. ASW, 33 mm. **Ruler:** Frederik IX **Subject:** Wedding of Princess Anne Marie **Obv:** Head right, mint mark and initials C-S **Rev:** Head left within title and wedding date

Date	Mintage	VF20	XF40	MS60	MS63	MS65
1964 (h) C; S	359,473	—	8.50	15.00	20.00	50.00

KM# 863.1 5 KRONER

15.00 g., Copper-Nickel, 33 mm. **Ruler:** Margrethe II **Obv:** Head right, mint mark and initials S-B below **Rev:** Crowned and quartered royal arms divide date and oak leaves, value below **Edge:** Reeded

Date	Mintage	VF20	XF40	MS60	MS63	MS65
1973 (h) S; B	3,774,000	—	—	—	2.00	4.00
Note: Narrow rim (1.0mm)						
1973 (h) S; B	Inc. above	—	—	—	2.00	4.00
Note: Wide rim (1.5mm)						
1974 (h) S; B	5,239,000	—	—	—	2.00	4.00
1975 (h) S; B	5,810,000	—	—	—	3.00	6.00
1976 (h) S; B	7,651,000	—	—	—	2.00	4.00
1977 (h) S; B	6,885,000	—	—	—	2.00	4.00
1978 (h) S; B	2,984,000	—	—	—	2.00	4.00

KM# 863.2 5 KRONER

15.00 g., Copper-Nickel, 33 mm. **Ruler:** Margrethe II **Obv:** Head right, mint mark and initials B-B below **Rev:** Crowned and quartered royal arms divide date and oak leaves, value below **Edge:** Reeded

Date	Mintage	VF20	XF40	MS60	MS63	MS65
1979 (h) B; B	2,861,000	—	—	—	2.00	4.00
1980 (h) B; B	3,622,000	—	—	—	2.50	4.00
1981 (h) B; B	1,057,000	—	—	—	2.50	5.00

KM# 863.3 5 KRONER

15.00 g., Copper-Nickel, 33 mm. **Ruler:** Margrethe II **Obv:** Head right, mint mark and initials R-B below **Rev:** Crowned and quartered royal arms divide date and oak leaves, value below **Edge:** Reeded

Date	Mintage	VF20	XF40	MS60	MS63	MS65
1982 (h) R; B	1,002,000	—	—	—	2.50	5.00
1983 (h) R; B	1,044,000	—	—	—	2.50	5.00
1984 (h) R; B	713,000	—	—	—	3.25	7.50
1985 (h) R; B	621,000	—	—	—	3.25	7.50
1986 (h) R; B	1,042,000	—	—	—	2.00	4.00
1987 (h) R; B	611,000	—	—	—	2.00	4.00
1988 (h) R; B	648,000	—	—	—	1.75	3.50

KM# 869.1 5 KRONER

9.20 g., Copper-Nickel, 28.5 mm. **Ruler:** Margrethe II **Obv:** 3 crowned MII monograms around center hole, date and initials LG-JP-A below **Rev:** Wave design surrounds center hole, denomination above, hearts flank **Edge:** Reeded **Note:** Large and small date varieties exist.

Date	Mintage	VF20	XF40	MS60	MS63	MS65
1990 LG; JP; A	46,745,000	—	—	—	—	2.50
1991 LG; JP; A	3,752,000	—	—	—	—	3.00
1992 LG; JP; A	2,426,000	—	—	—	—	3.00
1993 LG; JP; A	1,538,000	—	—	—	—	3.50
1994 LG; JP; A	7,920,000	—	—	—	—	2.00
1995 LG; JP; A	5,850,000	—	—	—	—	2.00
1997 LG; JP; A	5,258,000	—	—	—	—	2.00
1998 LG; JP; A	6,450,000	—	—	—	—	1.75
1999 LG; JP; A	4,786,000	—	—	—	—	1.75
2000 LG; JP; A	2,800,000	—	—	—	—	1.75

KM# 809 10 KRONER

4.48 g., 0.900 Gold 0.1296 oz. AGW **Ruler:** Frederik VIII **Obv:** Head left with titles **Rev:** Draped crowned national arms above date, value, mint mark and initials VBP

Date	Mintage	F12	VF20	XF40	MS60	MS63
1908 (h) VBP; GJ	308,000	—	—	165	235	275
1909 (h) VBP; GJ	153,000	—	—	165	235	275

KM# 816 10 KRONER

4.48 g., 0.900 Gold 0.1296 oz. AGW **Ruler:** Christian X **Obv:** Head right with title, date, mint mark, initials VBP. Initials AH at neck **Rev:** Draped crowned national arms above date, value, mint mark and initials VBP **Edge:** Reeded

Date	Mintage	F12	VF20	XF40	MS60	MS63
1913 (h) VBP;AH	312,000	—	165	175	230	265
1917 (h) VBP;AH	132,000	—	165	175	230	265

Note: These coins are still being sold in UNC condition by the Danish National Bank at bullion-related prices.

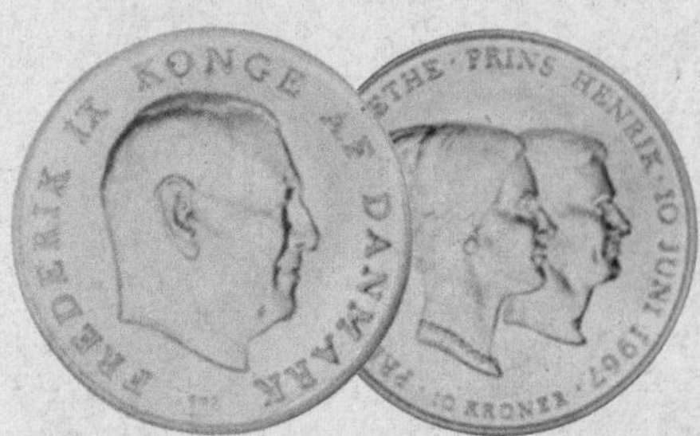

KM# 856 10 KRONER

20.40 g., 0.800 Silver 0.5247 oz. ASW, 36 mm. **Ruler:** Frederik IX **Subject:** Wedding of Princess Margrethe **Obv:** Head right with titles, mint mark, initials C-S **Rev:** Heads of Prince and Princess right, value below

Date	Mintage	VF20	XF40	MS60	MS63	MS65
ND-1967 (h) C; S	419,542	—	—	10.00	20.00	35.00

Note: 78,383 pieces were melted.

KM# 857 10 KRONER

20.40 g., 0.800 Silver 0.5247 oz. ASW, 36 mm. **Ruler:** Frederik IX **Subject:** Wedding of Princess Benedikte **Obv:** Head right, mint mark and initials C-S below **Rev:** Head left, value below

Date	Mintage	VF20	XF40	MS60	MS63	MS65
ND-1968 (h) C; S	253,837	—	—	10.00	20.00	40.00

Note: 42,923 were melted.

KM# 858 10 KRONER

20.40 g., 0.800 Silver 0.5247 oz. ASW, 36 mm. **Ruler:** Margrethe II **Subject:** Death of Frederik IX and Accession of Margrethe II **Obv:** Head right, motto, titles, mint mark and initials S-B **Rev:** Head right with titles, date of death, value below

Date	Mintage	VF20	XF40	MS60	MS63	MS65
1972 (h) S; S	402,000	—	—	10.00	16.00	27.50

KM# 864.1 10 KRONER

12.50 g., Copper-Nickel, 28 mm. **Ruler:** Margrethe II **Obv:** Head right with tiara, mint mark and initials B-B below **Rev:** Large 10 on horizontal grid, two rye stalks flanking, date above

Date	Mintage	VF20	XF40	MS60	MS63	MS65
1979 (h) B; B	76,801,000	—	—	—	—	4.50
1981 (h) B; B	10,520,000	—	—	—	3.00	7.00

KM# 864.2 10 KRONER

12.50 g., Copper-Nickel, 28 mm. **Ruler:** Margrethe II **Obv:** Head right with tiara, mint mark and initials R-B below **Rev:** Large 10 on horizontal grid, two rye stalks flanking, date above

Date	Mintage	VF20	XF40	MS60	MS63	MS65
1982 (h) R; B	1,065,000	—	—	—	4.00	10.00
1983 (h) R; B	1,123,000	—	—	—	4.00	10.00
1984 (h) R; B	748,000	—	—	—	5.50	12.50
1985 (h) R; B	720,000	—	—	—	5.50	12.50
1987 (h) R; B	719,000	—	—	—	4.00	10.00
1988 (h) R; B	718,000	—	—	—	3.50	9.00

KM# 865 10 KRONER

12.50 g., Copper-Nickel, 28 mm. **Ruler:** Margrethe II **Subject:** Crown Prince's 18th Birthday **Obv:** Head of Margrethe II with tiara right, mint mark and initials R-A below **Rev:** Head of crown prince Frederik left, date of 18th birthday, value below **Edge:** Plain

Date	Mintage	VF20	XF40	MS60	MS63	MS65
ND-1986 (h) R; A	1,090,351	—	—	—	3.00	6.00
ND-1986 (h) R; A	2,000	PF65 225				

Note: In folder

KM# 865a 10 KRONER

14.30 g., 0.800 Silver 0.3678 oz. ASW, 28 mm. **Ruler:** Margrethe II **Obv:** Head with tiara right, mint mark and initials R-A below **Rev:** Head of Crown Prince Frederik left, date of 18th birthday, value below

Date	Mintage	F12	VF20	XF40	MS60	MS63
1986 (h) R; A	24,000	PF65 100				

KM# 867.1 10 KRONER

7.00 g., Aluminum-Bronze, 23.35 mm. **Ruler:** Margrethe II **Obv:** Head with tiara right, titles, date, initials NR-JP-A **Rev:** Crowned arms within ornaments, value below **Edge:** Plain

Date	Mintage	VF20	XF40	MS60	MS63	MS65
1989 NR; JP; A	38,346,000	—	—	—	—	3.50

KM# 867.2 10 KRONER

7.00 g., Aluminum-Bronze, 23.35 mm. **Ruler:** Margrethe II **Obv:** Head with tiara right, titles, date, initials LG-JP-A **Rev:** Crowned arms within ornaments, value below **Edge:** Plain

Date	Mintage	VF20	XF40	MS60	MS63	MS65
1990 LG; JP; A	12,193,000	—	—	—	—	4.50
1991 LG; JP; A	1,065,000	—	—	—	4.00	7.50
1992 LG; JP; A	484,000	—	—	—	7.00	12.50
1993 LG; JP; A	1,069,000	—	—	—	6.00	10.00

KM# 877 10 KRONER

7.00 g., Aluminum-Bronze, 23.35 mm. **Ruler:** Margrethe II **Obv:** New portrait right, date below **Rev:** Crowned arms within ornaments, value below **Edge:** Plain **Note:** Beginning with strikes in 1995 and ending in 1998, letters and numbers on reverse have raised edges.

Date	Mintage	VF20	XF40	MS60	MS63	MS65
1994 LG; JP; A	4,058,000	—	—	—	—	4.00
1995 LG; JP; A	9,461,000	—	—	—	—	4.00
1997 LG; JP; A	3,725,000	—	—	—	—	4.00
1998 LG; JP; A	6,000,000	—	—	—	—	4.00
1999 LG; JP; A	4,034,749	—	—	—	—	4.00

KM# 810 20 KRONER

8.96 g., 0.900 Gold 0.2593 oz. AGW **Ruler:** Frederik VIII **Obv:** Head left, with titles **Rev:** Crowned and mantled arms above date, value, mint mark and initials VBP

Date	Mintage	F12	VF20	XF40	MS60	MS63
1908 (h) VBP;GJ	243,000	—	—	330	450	500
1909 (h) VBP;GJ	365,000	—	—	330	450	500
1910 (h) VBP;GJ	200,000	—	—	330	450	500
1911 (h) VBP;GJ	183,000	—	—	330	450	500
1912 (h) VBP;GJ	184,000	—	—	330	450	500

KM# 817.1 20 KRONER

8.96 g., 0.900 Gold 0.2593 oz. AGW **Ruler:** Christian X **Obv:** Head right with title, date, mint mark, initials VBP, initials AH at neck **Rev:** Crowned and mantled arms above date, value, mint mark and initials VBP

Date	Mintage	F12	VF20	XF40	MS60	MS63
1913 (h) VBP;AH	815,000	—	—	330	450	500
1914 (h) VBP;AH	920,000	—	—	330	450	500
1915 (h) VBP;AH	532,000	—	—	330	450	500
1916 (h) VBP;AH	1,401,000	—	—	330	450	500
1917 (h) VBP;AH	Inc. above	—	—	330	450	500

Note: The 1915 and 1916 coins are still being sold in UNC condition by the Danish National Bank at bullion-related prices.

KM# 817.2 20 KRONER

8.96 g., 0.900 Gold 0.2593 oz. AGW **Ruler:** Christian X **Obv:** Head right with title, date, mint mark, and initials HCN, initials AH at neck **Rev:** Crowned and mantled arms above date, value, mint mark, and initials HCN **Note:** 1926-1927 dated 20 Kroners were not released for circulation.

Date	Mintage	VF20	XF40	MS60	MS63	MS65
1926 (h) HCN;GJ	358,000	—	—	—	8,500	15,000
1927 (h) HCN;GJ	Inc. above	—	—	—	8,500	15,000

KM# 817.3 20 KRONER

8.96 g., 0.900 Gold 0.2593 oz. AGW **Ruler:** Christian X **Obv:** Head right with title, date, mint mark, and initials HCN. Initials AH at neck **Rev:** Crowned and mantled arms above date, value, mint mark and initials HCN **Note:** The 1930-1931 dated 20 Kroners were not released for circulation.

Date	Mintage	VF20	XF40	MS60	MS63	MS65
1930 (h) N;GJ	1,285,000	—	—	—	8,500	15,000
1931 (h) N;GJ	Inc. above	—	—	—	8,500	15,000

KM# 870 20 KRONER

9.30 g., Aluminum-Bronze, 27 mm. **Ruler:** Margrethe II **Subject:** 50th Birthday of Queen Margrethe **Obv:** Head with hat right, mint mark after 2 in legend, initials LG left of shoulder **Rev:** Large crown above daisy flower divides dates, value below **Edge:** Alternate reeded and plain sections

Date	Mintage	VF20	XF40	MS60	MS63	MS65
ND-1990 (h) LG	1,000,988	—	—	—	—	5.00

KM# 871 20 KRONER

9.30 g., Aluminum-Bronze, 27 mm. **Ruler:** Margrethe II **Obv:** Head with tiara right, titles, date, initials LG-JP-A, mint mark after II in legend **Rev:** Crowned arms within ornaments and value **Edge:** Alternate reeded and plain sections **Note:** Large and small date varieties exist.

Date	Mintage	VF20	XF40	MS60	MS63	MS65
1990 (h) LG; JP ; A	34,368,000	—	—	—	—	7.00
1991 (h) LG; JP; A	11,563,000	—	—	—	—	9.00
1993 (h) LG; JP; A	674,000	—	—	—	—	11.00

KM# 875 20 KRONER

9.30 g., Aluminum-Bronze, 27 mm. **Ruler:** Margrethe II **Subject:** Silver Wedding Anniversary **Obv:** Heads of Prince

Henrik and Margrethe II facing each other, anniversary dates below **Rev:** Fairy tale house, mint mark and initials LG at lower left, denomination at left **Edge:** Alternate reeded and plain sections

Date	Mintage	VF20	XF40	MS60	MS63	MS65
ND-1992 (h) LG	994,000	—	—	—	—	5.50

KM# 878 20 KRONER
9.30 g., Aluminum-Bronze, 27 mm. **Ruler:** Margrethe II **Obv:** New portrait right, date, mint mark and initials LG-JP-A below **Rev:** Crowned arms within ornament and value **Edge:** Alternating reeded and plain sections **Note:** Strikes dated 1996 and 1998 have letters and numbers on reverse with raised edges.

Date	Mintage	VF20	XF40	MS60	MS63	MS65
1994 (h) LG JP; A	2,565,000	—	—	—	—	6.00
1996 (h) LG JP; A	8,651,000	—	—	—	—	6.00
1998 (h) LG JP; A	4,000,000	—	—	—	—	6.00
1999 (h) LG JP; A	4,133,363	—	—	—	—	6.00

KM# 879 20 KRONER
9.30 g., Aluminum-Bronze, 27 mm. **Ruler:** Margrethe II **Subject:** 1000 Years of Danish Coinage **Obv:** Head with cloche left, inner legend in runic letters **Rev:** Large crown on cross, mint mark and initials LG **Edge:** Alternate reeded and plain sections

Date	Mintage	VF20	XF40	MS60	MS63	MS65
ND-1995 (h) LG; JP; A	1,000,000	—	—	—	—	7.00

KM# 881 20 KRONER
9.30 g., Aluminum-Bronze, 27 mm. **Ruler:** Margrethe II **Subject:** Wedding of Prince Joachim **Obv:** New portrait right, mint mark after II in legend, initials LG below at date **Rev:** Schackenborg castle at center, value below **Edge:** Alternate reeded and plain sections

Date	Mintage	VF20	XF40	MS60	MS63	MS65
1995 (h) LG JP	1,000,000	—	—	—	—	5.00

Note: Although dated 1995, this coin was minted at the end of the year and included in a 1996 mint set.

KM# 883 20 KRONER
9.30 g., Aluminum-Bronze, 27 mm. **Ruler:** Margrethe II **Subject:** 25th Anniversary - Queen's Reign **Obv:** Full-length portrait, mint mark and initials LG **Rev:** Crowned arms within anniversary date and value **Edge:** Alternate reeded and plain sections

Date	Mintage	VF20	XF40	MS60	MS63	MS65
ND-1997 (h) LG; JP	1,000,000	—	—	—	—	7.00

KM# 885 20 KRONER
9.30 g., Aluminum-Bronze, 27 mm. **Ruler:** Margrethe II **Subject:** 60th Birthday of Queen Margrethe II **Obv:** Bust right **Rev:** Crown divides dates above daisy flowers, denomination below **Edge:** Alternating reeded and plain sections

Date	Mintage	VF20	XF40	MS60	MS63	MS65
ND-2000 (h) LG	1,000,000	—	—	—	—	5.00

KM# 872 200 KRONER
31.10 g., 0.800 Silver 0.7999 oz. ASW, 38 mm. **Ruler:** Margrethe II **Subject:** 50th Birthday of Queen Margrethe **Obv:** Bust with hat right, mint mark after 2 in legend, initials LG and Fox mark above shoulder **Rev:** Large crown above daisy flower divides dates, value below **Edge:** Plain

Date	Mintage	VF20	XF40	MS60	MS63	MS65
ND-1990 (h) LG	100,855	—	—	—	—	35.00

KM# 876 200 KRONER
31.10 g., 0.999 Silver 0.9989 oz. ASW, 38 mm. **Ruler:** Margrethe II **Subject:** Silver Wedding Anniversary **Obv:** Heads of Prince Henrik and Queen Margrethe II facing each other, anniversary dates below **Rev:** Fairy tale house, mint mark and initials LG at lower left, denomination **Edge:** Plain

Date	Mintage	VF20	XF40	MS60	MS63	MS65
ND-1992 (h) LG	83,576	—	—	—	—	40.00

KM# 880 200 KRONER
31.10 g., 0.999 Silver 0.9989 oz. ASW, 38 mm. **Ruler:** Margrethe II **Subject:** 1000 Year of Danish Coinage **Obv:** Head with cloche left, runic lettering within legend **Rev:** Large crown on cross, mint mark at left, initials LG at bottom, denomination at left **Edge:** Plain

Date	Mintage	VF20	XF40	MS60	MS63	MS65
ND-1995 (h) LG	27,727	—	—	—	—	50.00

KM# 882 200 KRONER
31.10 g., 0.999 Silver 0.9989 oz. ASW, 38 mm. **Ruler:** Margrethe II **Subject:** Wedding of Prince Joachim **Obv:** New portrait right, date below **Rev:** Schackenburg Castle, denomination below **Edge:** Plain

Date	Mintage	VF20	XF40	MS60	MS63	MS65
1995 (h) LG	52,600	—	—	—	—	35.00

KM# 884 200 KRONER
31.10 g., 0.999 Silver 0.9989 oz. ASW, 38 mm. **Ruler:** Margrethe II **Subject:** 25th Anniversary - Queen's Reign **Obv:** Full-length portrait **Rev:** Quartered arms, denomination below, anniversary date at right **Edge:** Plain

Date	Mintage	VF20	XF40	MS60	MS63	MS65
ND-1997 (h) LG	60,022	—	—	—	—	45.00

KM# 886 200 KRONER
31.10 g., 0.999 Silver 0.9989 oz. ASW, 38 mm. **Ruler:** Margrethe II **Subject:** 60th Birthday of Queen Margrethe II **Obv:** Bust with tiara right **Rev:** Crown above flowers divides dates, denomination below **Edge:** Plain

Date	Mintage	VF20	XF40	MS60	MS63	MS65
ND-2000 (h) LG	59,900	—	—	—	—	42.00

PATTERNS

Including off metal strikes

KM#	Date	Mintage	Identification	Mkt Val
Pn67	1926(h) HCN; GJ	—	5 Øre. Bronze. KM#828.1. Thomas Holland Sale 11-00 $8600. Beware of counterfeits. Another example of the 1926 5 Øre was auctioned at Thomas Høiland Auction 20, lot 1574. The coin was defaced on the obv. which the catalogers see as a proof that the coin is a pattern.	—
PnB63	1940	—	25 Øre. Zinc. KM#823.	—
Pn63	1941	—	Øre. Aluminum. KM#832.	3,300
PnA64	1941	—	2 Øre. Zinc. KM#833.	—

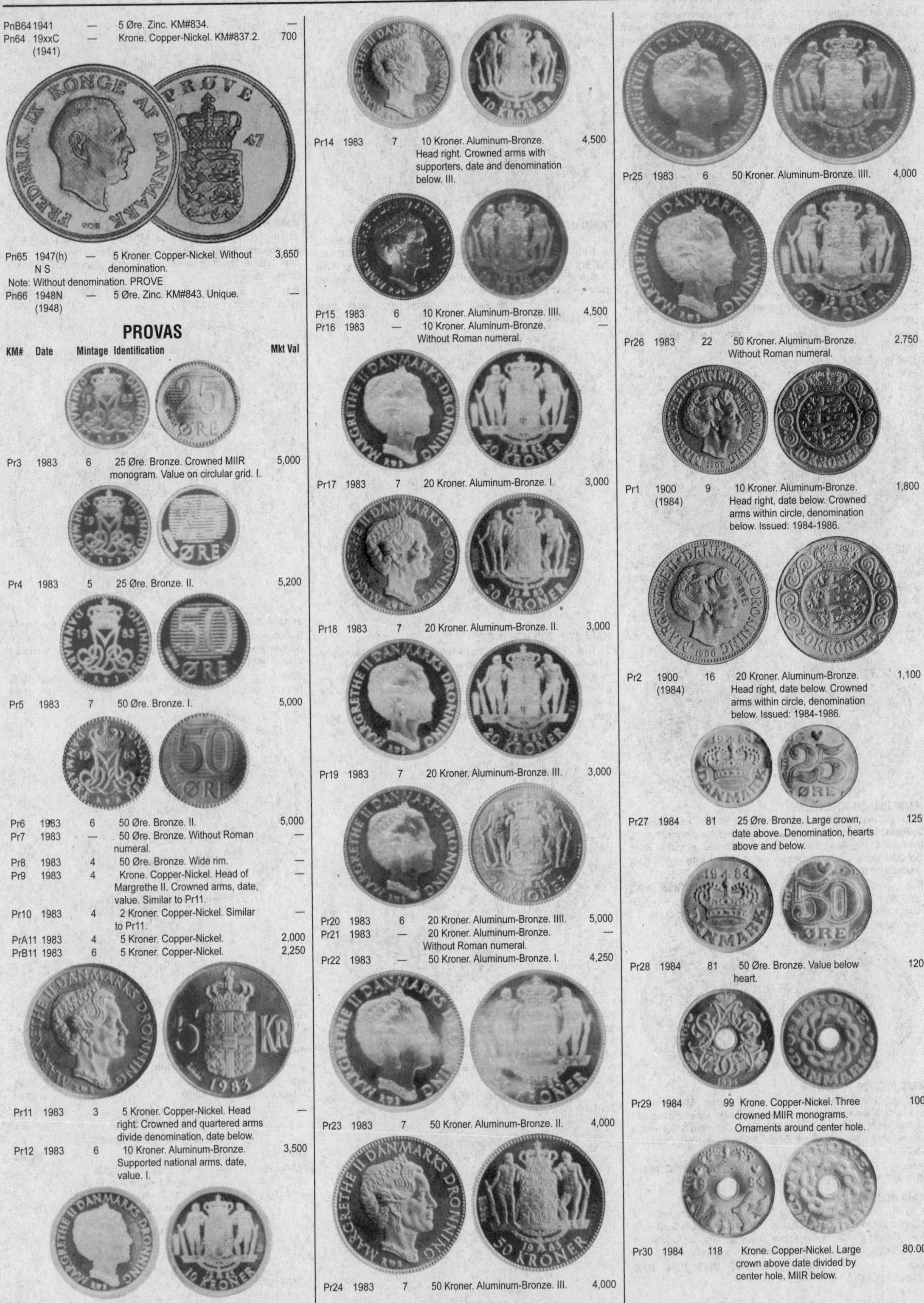

KM#	Date	Mintage	Identification	Mkt Val
PnB64	1941	—	5 Øre. Zinc. KM#834.	—
Pn64	19xxC (1941)	—	Krone. Copper-Nickel. KM#837.2.	700
Pn65	1947(h) N S	—	5 Kroner. Copper-Nickel. Without denomination.	3,650

Note: Without denomination. PROVE

KM#	Date	Mintage	Identification	Mkt Val
Pn66	1948N (1948)	—	5 Øre. Zinc. KM#843. Unique.	—

PROVAS

KM#	Date	Mintage	Identification	Mkt Val
Pr3	1983	6	25 Øre. Bronze. Crowned MIIR monogram. Value on circular grid. I.	5,000
Pr4	1983	5	25 Øre. Bronze. II.	5,200
Pr5	1983	7	50 Øre. Bronze. I.	5,000
Pr6	1983	6	50 Øre. Bronze. II.	5,000
Pr7	1983	—	50 Øre. Bronze. Without Roman numeral.	—
Pr8	1983	4	50 Øre. Bronze. Wide rim.	—
Pr9	1983	4	Krone. Copper-Nickel. Head of Margrethe II. Crowned arms, date, value. Similar to Pr11.	—
Pr10	1983	4	2 Kroner. Copper-Nickel. Similar to Pr11.	—
PrA11	1983	4	5 Kroner. Copper-Nickel.	2,000
PrB11	1983	6	5 Kroner. Copper-Nickel.	2,250
Pr11	1983	3	5 Kroner. Copper-Nickel. Head right. Crowned and quartered arms divide denomination, date below.	—
Pr12	1983	6	10 Kroner. Aluminum-Bronze. Supported national arms, date, value. I.	3,500
Pr13	1983	7	10 Kroner. Aluminum-Bronze. II.	2,900
Pr14	1983	7	10 Kroner. Aluminum-Bronze. Head right. Crowned arms with supporters, date and denomination below. III.	4,500
Pr15	1983	6	10 Kroner. Aluminum-Bronze. IIII.	4,500
Pr16	1983	—	10 Kroner. Aluminum-Bronze. Without Roman numeral.	—
Pr17	1983	7	20 Kroner. Aluminum-Bronze. I.	3,000
Pr18	1983	7	20 Kroner. Aluminum-Bronze. II.	3,000
Pr19	1983	7	20 Kroner. Aluminum-Bronze. III.	3,000
Pr20	1983	6	20 Kroner. Aluminum-Bronze. IIII.	5,000
Pr21	1983	—	20 Kroner. Aluminum-Bronze. Without Roman numeral.	—
Pr22	1983	—	50 Kroner. Aluminum-Bronze. I.	4,250
Pr23	1983	7	50 Kroner. Aluminum-Bronze. II.	4,000
Pr24	1983	7	50 Kroner. Aluminum-Bronze. III.	4,000
Pr25	1983	6	50 Kroner. Aluminum-Bronze. IIII.	4,000
Pr26	1983	22	50 Kroner. Aluminum-Bronze. Without Roman numeral.	2,750
Pr1	1900 (1984)	9	10 Kroner. Aluminum-Bronze. Head right, date below. Crowned arms within circle, denomination below. Issued: 1984-1986.	1,800
Pr2	1900 (1984)	16	20 Kroner. Aluminum-Bronze. Head right, date below. Crowned arms within circle, denomination below. Issued: 1984-1986.	1,100
Pr27	1984	81	25 Øre. Bronze. Large crown, date above. Denomination, hearts above and below.	125
Pr28	1984	81	50 Øre. Bronze. Value below heart.	120
Pr29	1984	99	Krone. Copper-Nickel. Three crowned MIIR monograms. Ornaments around center hole.	100
Pr30	1984	118	Krone. Copper-Nickel. Large crown above date divided by center hole, MIIR below.	80.00

Pr31 1984 203 Krone. Copper-Nickel. Ornaments surround center hole, hearts flank, denomination above country name below. Center hole divides date, crown above, MIIR below. Reverse of 1986. 60.00

Pr32 1984 — Krone. Copper-Nickel. Similar to Pr30 but without hole. 900

Pr33 1984 191 2 Kroner. Copper-Nickel. Triple monogram. Ornaments around center hole, value above. 70.00

Pr34 1984 103 2 Kroner. Copper-Nickel. Milled. 115

Pr35 1984 201 2 Kroner. Copper-Nickel. Interrupted milling 6 or 7 notches. Reverse of 1986. 70.00

Pr36 1984 85 5 Kroner. Copper-Nickel. Triple monogram. Ornament around center hole, value. 125

Pr37 1984 108 5 Kroner. Copper-Nickel. Milled. 125

Pr38 1984 202 5 Kroner. Copper-Nickel. Milled. Reverse of 1986. 70.00

Pr39 1984 6 5 Kroner. Copper-Nickel. As Pr36 except for added date at top and country name at bottom. Large 5 above ornament and denomination. 3,500

Pr40 1984 85 10 Kroner. Aluminum-Bronze. Crowned arms, ornament, value. 175

PrA41 1984 4 10 Kroner. Aluminum-Bronze. Without "Prove". —

PrB41 1984 3 10 Kroner. Aluminum-Bronze. Different ornaments and value style. Without "Prove". —

Pr41 1984 112 20 Kroner. Aluminum-Bronze. Head right, date below. Crowned arms within circle, denomination below. 140

Pr42 1984 4 20 Kroner. Aluminum-Bronze. Without "PROVE". —

PrA43 1984 51 20 Kroner. Aluminum-Bronze. Without "Prove". 250

Pr45 19(84) (1984) 23 50 Øre. Bronze. 500

Pr43 1986 183 25 Øre. Bronze. 80.00

Pr44 1986 210 25 Øre. Bronze. 75.00

Pr46 1986 181 50 Øre. Bronze. 85.00

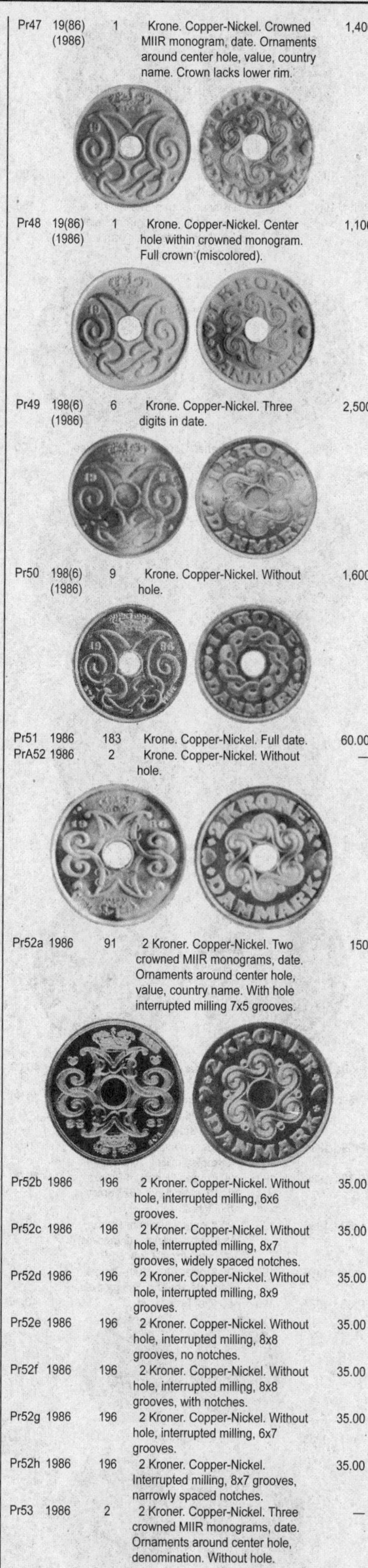

Pr47 19(86) (1986) 1 Krone. Copper-Nickel. Crowned MIIR monogram, date. Ornaments around center hole, value, country name. Crown lacks lower rim. 1,400

Pr48 19(86) (1986) 1 Krone. Copper-Nickel. Center hole within crowned monogram. Full crown (miscolored). 1,100

Pr49 198(6) (1986) 6 Krone. Copper-Nickel. Three digits in date. 2,500

Pr50 198(6) (1986) 9 Krone. Copper-Nickel. Without hole. 1,600

Pr51 1986 183 Krone. Copper-Nickel. Full date. 60.00

PrA52 1986 2 Krone. Copper-Nickel. Without hole. —

Pr52a 1986 91 2 Kroner. Copper-Nickel. Two crowned MIIR monograms, date. Ornaments around center hole, value, country name. With hole interrupted milling 7x5 grooves. 150

Pr52b 1986 196 2 Kroner. Copper-Nickel. Without hole, interrupted milling, 6x6 grooves. 35.00

Pr52c 1986 196 2 Kroner. Copper-Nickel. Without hole, interrupted milling, 8x7 grooves, widely spaced notches. 35.00

Pr52d 1986 196 2 Kroner. Copper-Nickel. Without hole, interrupted milling, 8x9 grooves. 35.00

Pr52e 1986 196 2 Kroner. Copper-Nickel. Without hole, interrupted milling, 8x8 grooves, no notches. 35.00

Pr52f 1986 196 2 Kroner. Copper-Nickel. Without hole, interrupted milling, 8x8 grooves, with notches. 35.00

Pr52g 1986 196 2 Kroner. Copper-Nickel. Without hole, interrupted milling, 6x7 grooves. 35.00

Pr52h 1986 196 2 Kroner. Copper-Nickel. Interrupted milling, 8x7 grooves, narrowly spaced notches. 35.00

Pr53 1986 2 2 Kroner. Copper-Nickel. Three crowned MIIR monograms, date. Ornaments around center hole, denomination. Without hole. —

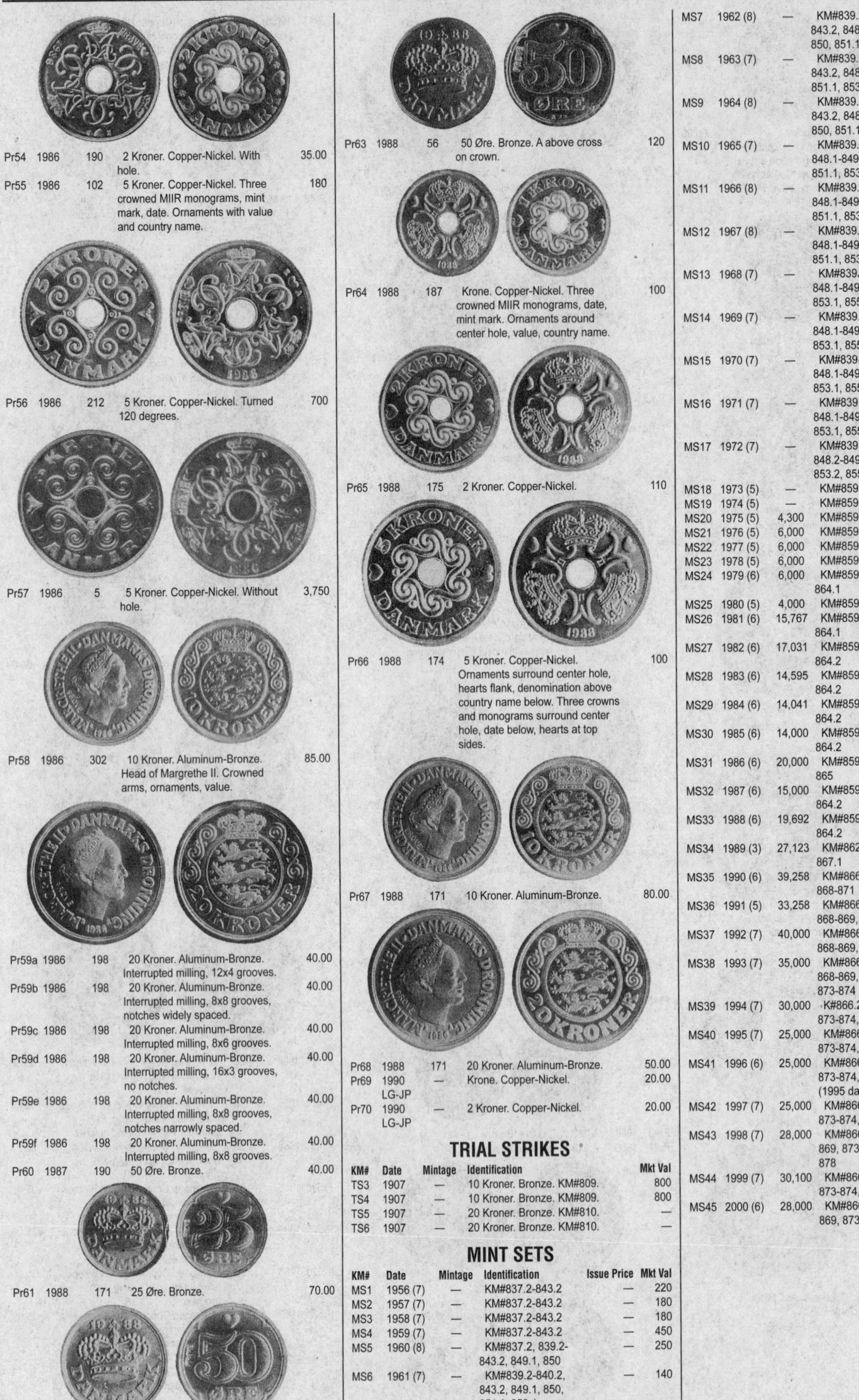

KM#	Date	Mintage	Identification	Mkt Val
Pr54	1986	190	2 Kroner. Copper-Nickel. With hole.	35.00
Pr55	1986	102	5 Kroner. Copper-Nickel. Three crowned MIIR monograms, mint mark, date. Ornaments with value and country name.	180
Pr56	1986	212	5 Kroner. Copper-Nickel. Turned 120 degrees.	700
Pr57	1986	5	5 Kroner. Copper-Nickel. Without hole.	3,750
Pr58	1986	302	10 Kroner. Aluminum-Bronze. Head of Margrethe II. Crowned arms, ornaments, value.	85.00
Pr59a	1986	198	20 Kroner. Aluminum-Bronze. Interrupted milling, 12x4 grooves.	40.00
Pr59b	1986	198	20 Kroner. Aluminum-Bronze. Interrupted milling, 8x8 grooves, notches widely spaced.	40.00
Pr59c	1986	198	20 Kroner. Aluminum-Bronze. Interrupted milling, 8x6 grooves.	40.00
Pr59d	1986	198	20 Kroner. Aluminum-Bronze. Interrupted milling, 16x3 grooves, no notches.	40.00
Pr59e	1986	198	20 Kroner. Aluminum-Bronze. Interrupted milling, 8x8 grooves, notches narrowly spaced.	40.00
Pr59f	1986	198	20 Kroner. Aluminum-Bronze. Interrupted milling, 8x8 grooves.	40.00
Pr60	1987	190	50 Øre. Bronze.	40.00
Pr61	1988	171	25 Øre. Bronze.	70.00
Pr62	1988	178	50 Øre. Bronze.	100
Pr63	1988	56	50 Øre. Bronze. A above cross on crown.	120
Pr64	1988	187	Krone. Copper-Nickel. Three crowned MIIR monograms, date, mint mark. Ornaments around center hole, value, country name.	100
Pr65	1988	175	2 Kroner. Copper-Nickel.	110
Pr66	1988	174	5 Kroner. Copper-Nickel. Ornaments surround center hole, hearts flank, denomination above country name below. Three crowns and monograms surround center hole, date below, hearts at top sides.	100
Pr67	1988	171	10 Kroner. Aluminum-Bronze.	80.00
Pr68	1988	171	20 Kroner. Aluminum-Bronze.	50.00
Pr69	1990 LG-JP	—	Krone. Copper-Nickel.	20.00
Pr70	1990 LG-JP	—	2 Kroner. Copper-Nickel.	20.00

TRIAL STRIKES

KM#	Date	Mintage	Identification	Mkt Val
TS3	1907	—	10 Kroner. Bronze. KM#809.	800
TS4	1907	—	10 Kroner. Bronze. KM#809.	800
TS5	1907	—	20 Kroner. Bronze. KM#810.	—
TS6	1907	—	20 Kroner. Bronze. KM#810.	—

MINT SETS

KM#	Date	Mintage	Identification	Issue Price	Mkt Val
MS1	1956 (7)	—	KM#837.2-843.2	—	220
MS2	1957 (7)	—	KM#837.2-843.2	—	180
MS3	1958 (7)	—	KM#837.2-843.2	—	180
MS4	1959 (7)	—	KM#837.2-843.2	—	450
MS5	1960 (8)	—	KM#837.2, 839.2-843.2, 849.1, 850	—	250
MS6	1961 (7)	—	KM#839.2-840.2, 843.2, 849.1, 850, 851.1, 853.1	—	140
MS7	1962 (8)	—	KM#839.2-840.2, 843.2, 848.1-849.1, 850, 851.1, 853.1	—	140
MS8	1963 (7)	—	KM#839.2-840.2, 843.2, 848.1-849.1, 851.1, 853.1	—	95.00
MS9	1964 (8)	—	KM#839.2-840.2, 843.2, 848.1-849.1, 850, 851.1, 853.1	—	70.00
MS10	1965 (7)	—	KM#839.2-840.2, 848.1-849.1, 850, 851.1, 853.1	—	75.00
MS11	1966 (8)	—	KM#839.2-840.2, 848.1-849.1, 850, 851.1, 853.1, 855.1	—	70.00
MS12	1967 (8)	—	KM#839.2-840.2, 848.1-849.1, 850, 851.1, 853.1, 855.1	—	85.00
MS13	1968 (7)	—	KM#839.2-840.2, 848.1-849.1, 851.1, 853.1, 855.1	—	50.00
MS14	1969 (7)	—	KM#839.2-840.2, 848.1-849.1, 851.1, 853.1, 855.1	—	50.00
MS15	1970 (7)	—	KM#839.2-840.2, 848.1-849.1, 851.1, 853.1, 855.1	—	22.00
MS16	1971 (7)	—	KM#839.2-840.2, 848.1-849.1, 851.1, 853.1, 855.1	—	22.00
MS17	1972 (7)	—	KM#839.3-840.3, 848.2-849.2, 851.2, 853.2, 855.2	—	9.00
MS18	1973 (5)	—	KM#859.1-863.1	—	13.00
MS19	1974 (5)	—	KM#859.1-863.1	6.00	9.00
MS20	1975 (5)	4,300	KM#859.1-863.1	6.00	175
MS21	1976 (5)	6,000	KM#859.1-863.1	3.55	75.00
MS22	1977 (5)	6,000	KM#859.1-863.1	—	75.00
MS23	1978 (5)	6,000	KM#859.1-863.1	—	30.00
MS24	1979 (6)	6,000	KM#859.2-863.2, 864.1	—	27.50
MS25	1980 (5)	4,000	KM#859.2-863.2	—	275
MS26	1981 (6)	15,767	KM#859.2-863.2, 864.1	—	30.00
MS27	1982 (6)	17,031	KM#859.3-863.3, 864.2	—	42.50
MS28	1983 (6)	14,595	KM#859.3-863.3, 864.2	—	40.00
MS29	1984 (6)	14,041	KM#859.3-863.3, 864.2	—	47.50
MS30	1985 (6)	14,000	KM#859.3-863.3, 864.2	—	47.50
MS31	1986 (6)	20,000	KM#859.3-863.3, 865	—	40.00
MS32	1987 (6)	15,000	KM#859.3-863.3, 864.2	—	50.00
MS33	1988 (6)	19,692	KM#859.3-863.3, 864.2	—	27.00
MS34	1989 (3)	27,123	KM#862.3, 866.1, 867.1	12.00	20.00
MS35	1990 (6)	39,258	KM#866.2, 867.2, 868-871	15.00	27.50
MS36	1991 (5)	33,258	KM#866.2, 867.2, 868-869, 871	15.00	35.00
MS37	1992 (7)	40,000	KM#866.2, 867.2, 868-869, 873-875	15.00	50.00
MS38	1993 (7)	35,000	KM#866.2, 867.2, 868-869, 871, 873-874	15.00	50.00
MS39	1994 (7)	30,000	K#866.2, 868-869, 873-874, 877-878	15.00	27.50
MS40	1995 (7)	25,000	KM#866.2, 868-869, 873-874, 877, 879	15.00	27.50
MS41	1996 (6)	25,000	KM#866.2, 868, 873-874, 878, 881 (1995 date)	15.00	25.00
MS42	1997 (7)	25,000	KM#866.2, 868-869, 873-874, 877, 883	15.00	35.00
MS43	1998 (7)	28,000	KM#866.2, 868, 869, 873-874, 877, 878	15.00	30.00
MS44	1999 (7)	30,100	KM#866.2, 868-869, 873-874, 877, 878	15.00	30.00
MS45	2000 (6)	28,000	KM#866.2, 868, 869, 873, 874, 885	15.00	75.00

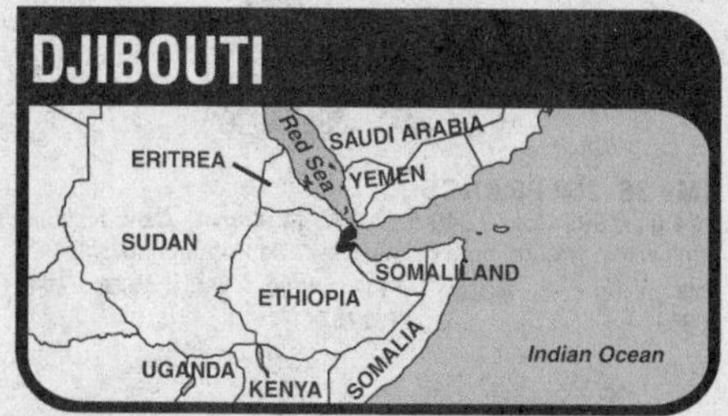

The Republic of Djibouti (formerly French Somaliland and the French Overseas Territory of Afars and Issas), located in northeast Africa at the Bab el Mandeb Strait connecting the Suez Canal and the Red Sea with the Gulf of Aden and the Indian Ocean, has an area of 8,950 sq. mi. (22,000 sq. km.) and a population of 421,320. Capital: Djibouti. The tiny nation has less than one sq. mi. of arable land, and no natural resources except salt, sand, and camels. The commercial activities of the transshipment port of Djibouti and the Addis Abada-Djibouti railroad are the basis of the economy. Salt, fish and hides are exported.

French interest in former French Somaliland began in 1839 with concessions obtained by a French naval lieutenant from the provincial sultans. French Somaliland was made a protectorate in 1884 and its boundaries were delimited by the Franco-British and Ethiopian accords of 1887 and 1897. It became a colony in 1896 and a territory within the French Union in 1946. In 1958 it voted to join the new French Community as an overseas territory, and reaffirmed that choice by a referendum in March, 1967. Its name was changed from French Somaliland to the French Territory of Afars and Issas on July 5, 1967.

The French Tricolor, which had flown over the strategically important territory for 115 years, was lowered for the last time on June 27, 1977, when French Afars and Issas became Africa's 49th independent state, under the name of the Republic of Djibouti.

Djibouti, a seaport and capital city of the Republic of Djibouti (and formerly of French Somaliland and French Afars and Issas) is located on the east coast of Africa at the southernmost entrance to the Red Sea. The capital was moved from Obok to Djibouti in 1892 and established as the transshipment point for Ethiopia's foreign trade via the Franco-Ethiopian railway linking Djibouti and Addis Ababa.

RULER

French, until 1977

COLONY

TOKEN COINAGE

KM# Tn1 5 CENTIMES

Zinc **Issuer:** Chamber of Commerce

Date	Mintage	F12	VF20	XF40	MS60	MS63
1920	—	25.00	60.00	120	180	300

KM# Tn5 5 CENTIMES

Aluminum **Issuer:** Chamber of Commerce **Obv:** Horned deer left of tree, date below **Rev:** Denomination within wreath

Date	Mintage	F12	VF20	XF40	MS60	MS63
1921	—	20.00	40.00	80.00	135	225

KM# Tn2 10 CENTIMES

Zinc **Issuer:** Chamber of Commerce

Date	Mintage	F12	VF20	XF40	MS60	MS63
1920	—	30.00	70.00	125	195	325

KM# Tn6 10 CENTIMES

Aluminum **Issuer:** Chamber of Commerce

Date	Mintage	F12	VF20	XF40	MS60	MS63
1921	—	25.00	55.00	100	150	250

KM# Tn7 25 CENTIMES

Aluminum, 22.5 mm. **Issuer:** Chamber of Commerce **Obv:** Horned deer left of tree, date below **Rev:** Denomination within wreath

Date	Mintage	F12	VF20	XF40	MS60	MS63
1921	—	30.00	70.00	125	195	325

KM# Tn3 50 CENTIMES

Zinc **Issuer:** Chamber of Commerce

Date	Mintage	F12	VF20	XF40	MS60	MS63
1920	—	40.00	90.00	175	270	450

KM# Tn8 50 CENTIMES

Bronze-Aluminum **Issuer:** Chamber of Commerce **Obv:** Country name between hearts at center, date below, beaded outline surrounds **Rev:** Large denomination **Shape:** Six sided coin

Date	Mintage	F12	VF20	XF40	MS60	MS63
1921	—	30.00	70.00	125	195	325

KM# Tn9 50 CENTIMES

Bronze **Issuer:** Chamber of Commerce

Date	Mintage	F12	VF20	XF40	MS60	MS63
1921	—	40.00	90.00	175	270	450

KM# Tn10 50 CENTIMES

Aluminum **Issuer:** Chamber of Commerce

Date	Mintage	F12	VF20	XF40	MS60	MS63
1922	—	45.00	100	200	300	500

KM# Tn4 FRANC

Aluminum **Issuer:** Chamber of Commerce

Date	Mintage	F12	VF20	XF40	MS60	MS63
1920	—	50.00	120	240	360	600

REPUBLIC

STANDARD COINAGE

KM# 20 FRANC

1.30 g., Aluminum, 23 mm. **Obv:** National arms within wreath, date below **Rev:** Giant eland head with headdress facing, divides denomination, shell on fish flank below

Date	Mintage	F12	VF20	XF40	MS60	MS63
1977 (a)	300,000	0.50	0.75	1.50	5.00	7.00
1996 (a)	—	0.50	0.75	1.50	4.00	6.00
1997 (a)	350	—	—	—	30.00	45.00
Note: Sets only						
1999 (a)	1,800	—	—	—	12.00	15.00
Note: Sets only						

KM# 37 FRANC

33.00 g., Aluminum-Bronze, 40.9 mm. **Subject:** 50th Anniversary French Djibouti **Obv:** National arms **Obv. Legend:** REPUBLIQUE DE DJIBOUTI **Rev:** Large value above 50e ANNIVERSAIRE **Rev. Legend:** UNITÉ - ÉGALITÉ - PAIX **Edge:** Plain

Date	Mintage	F12	VF20	XF40	MS60	MS63
1999 (a)	—	—	—	—	—	250
1999 (a)	500	PF65 300				

KM# 21 2 FRANCS

2.20 g., Aluminum, 27.1 mm. **Obv:** National arms within wreath, date below **Rev:** Giant eland head with headdress facing, divides denomination, shell on fish flank below

Date	Mintage	F12	VF20	XF40	MS60	MS63
1977 (a)	200,000	0.75	1.00	1.75	5.00	7.00
1991 (a)	—	0.75	1.00	1.75	4.00	6.00
1996 (a)	—	0.75	1.00	1.75	4.00	6.00
1997 (a)	350	—	—	—	30.00	40.00
Note: Sets only						
1999 (a)	1,800	—	—	—	12.00	15.00
Note: Sets only						

KM# 22 5 FRANCS

3.75 g., Aluminum, 31.1 mm. **Obv:** National arms within wreath, date below **Rev:** Giant eland head with headdress facing, divides denomination, shell on fish flank below

Date	Mintage	F12	VF20	XF40	MS60	MS63
1977 (a)	400,000	0.75	1.25	2.00	4.00	6.00
1986 (a)	—	0.75	1.00	1.75	3.50	5.50
1989 (a)	—	0.75	1.00	1.75	3.50	5.50
1991 (a)	—	0.75	1.00	1.75	3.50	5.50
1996 (a)	—	0.75	1.00	1.75	3.50	5.50
1997 (a)	350	—	—	—	30.00	45.00
Note: Sets only						
1999 (a)	1,800	—	—	—	12.00	15.00
Note: Sets only						

KM# 23 10 FRANCS

3.00 g., Aluminum-Bronze, 20 mm. **Obv:** National arms within wreath, date below **Rev:** Boats on water, denomination above **Note:** Varieties exist.

Date	Mintage	F12	VF20	XF40	MS60	MS63
1977 (a)	600,000	0.45	0.85	1.50	3.00	5.00
1983 (a)	—	0.50	1.00	1.75	3.50	5.50
1989 (a)	—	0.45	0.75	1.25	2.50	4.50
1991 (a)	—	0.45	0.75	1.25	2.50	4.50
1996 (a)	—	0.45	0.75	1.25	2.50	4.50
1997 (a)	350	—	—	—	20.00	28.00
Note: Sets only						
1999 (a)	1,800	—	—	—	10.00	12.00
Note: Sets only						

KM# 24 20 FRANCS

4.00 g., Aluminum-Bronze, 23.5 mm. **Obv:** National arms within wreath, date below **Rev:** Boats on water, denomination above **Note:** Varieties exist.

Date	Mintage	F12	VF20	XF40	MS60	MS63
1977 (a)	700,000	0.50	1.00	1.50	3.00	5.00
1982 (a)	—	0.50	1.00	1.75	3.50	5.50
1983 (a)	—	0.50	1.00	1.50	3.00	5.00
1986 (a)	—	0.45	0.75	1.25	2.50	4.50
1991 (a)	—	0.45	0.75	1.25	2.50	4.50
1996 (a)	—	0.45	0.75	1.25	2.50	4.50
1997 (a)	350	—	—	—	25.00	40.00
Note: Sets only						
1999 (a)	1,800	—	—	—	12.00	15.00
Note: Sets only						

KM# 25 50 FRANCS
7.05 g., Copper-Nickel, 25.7 mm. **Obv:** National arms within wreath, date below **Rev:** Pair of dromedary camels right, denomination above

Date	Mintage	F12	VF20	XF40	MS60	MS63
1977 (a)	1,500,000	0.75	1.50	3.00	7.00	10.00
1982 (a)	—	0.75	1.50	3.00	6.00	9.00
1983 (a)	—	0.50	1.00	2.25	6.00	9.00
1986 (a)	—	0.50	1.00	2.25	6.00	9.00
1989 (a)	—	0.50	1.00	2.25	6.00	9.00
1991 (a)	—	0.50	1.00	2.25	6.00	9.00
1997 (a)	350	—	—	—	25.00	35.00
Note: Sets only						
1999 (a)	1,800	—	—	—	15.00	20.00
Note: Sets only						

KM# 35 50 FRANCS
0.925 Silver **Subject:** Wildlife of Africa **Rev:** One lion in a tree, two lions under a tree

Date	Mintage	F12	VF20	XF40	MS60	MS63
1997	—	PF65 70.00				

KM# 26 100 FRANCS
12.00 g., Copper-Nickel, 30 mm. **Obv:** National arms within wreath, date below **Rev:** Pair of dromedary camels right, denomination above

Date	Mintage	F12	VF20	XF40	MS60	MS63
1977 (a)	1,500,000	1.00	2.00	3.00	9.00	12.00
1983 (a)	—	1.00	2.50	3.50	8.00	10.00
1991 (a)	—	1.00	1.75	2.75	7.50	8.00
1996 (a)	—	1.00	1.75	2.25	7.00	8.00
1997 (a)	350	—	—	—	25.00	35.00
Note: Sets only						
1999 (a)	1,800	—	—	—	15.00	20.00
Note: Sets only						

KM# 29 100 FRANCS
31.47 g., 0.925 Silver 0.9359 oz. ASW **Subject:** World Cup Soccer **Obv:** National arms within wreath, date below **Rev:** Soccer player divides maps, denomination below

Date	Mintage	F12	VF20	XF40	MS60	MS63
1994	Est. 15000	PF63 40.00	PF65 45.00			

KM# 30 100 FRANCS
31.47 g., 0.925 Silver 0.9359 oz. ASW **Series:** 1996 Olympic Games **Obv:** National arms within wreath, date below **Rev:** Runner, denomination at right

Date	Mintage	F12	VF20	XF40	MS60	MS63
1994	Est. 30000	PF63 35.00	PF65 40.00			

KM# 31 100 FRANCS
31.47 g., 0.925 Silver 0.9359 oz. ASW **Obv:** National arms within wreath, date below **Rev:** Frigate "Bateau" flag and denomination below

Date	Mintage	F12	VF20	XF40	MS60	MS63
1994	Est. 15000	PF63 45.00	PF65 50.00			

KM# 32 100 FRANCS
31.47 g., 0.925 Silver 0.9359 oz. ASW **Subject:** Endangered Wildlife **Obv:** National arms within wreath, date below **Rev:** Grevy zebras running right, denomination below

Date	Mintage	F12	VF20	XF40	MS60	MS63
1994	Est. 15000	PF63 40.00	PF65 45.00			

KM# 33 100 FRANCS
31.47 g., 0.925 Silver 0.9359 oz. ASW **Obv:** National arms within wreath, date below **Rev:** Portuguese "Nao" ship within circle, denomination below

Date	Mintage	F12	VF20	XF40	MS60	MS63
1996	Est. 15000	PF63 40.00	PF65 45.00			

KM# 36 250 FRANCS
1.24 g., 0.999 Gold 0.040 oz. AGW, 13.95 mm. **Obv:** National arms within wreath, date below **Rev:** Old Portuguese Ship

Date	Mintage	F12	VF20	XF40	MS60	MS63
1996	—	PF65 75.00				

KM# 27 500 FRANCS
Aluminum-Bronze **Obv:** National arms within wreath, date below **Rev:** Denomination within sprays

Date	Mintage	VF20	XF40	MS60	MS63	MS65
1989 (a)	—	4.00	6.00	12.00	15.00	20.00
1991 (a)	—	3.00	5.00	8.00	12.00	14.00
1997 (a)	350	—	10.00	15.00	25.00	35.00
Note: Sets only						
1999 (a)	1,800	—	—	12.00	20.00	25.00
Note: Sets only						

KM# 28 15000 FRANCS
0.999 Gold **Obv:** National arms within wreath, date below **Rev:** Map at center, denomination below

Date	Mintage	VF20	XF40	MS60	MS63	MS65
1991	Est. 10000	—	—	100	125	200

ESSAIS

Standard metals unless otherwise noted

KM#	Date	Mintage	Identification	Mkt Val
E1	1977	1,700	Franc. KM20.	20.00
E2	1977	1,700	2 Francs. KM21.	20.00
E3	1977	1,700	5 Francs. KM22.	22.00
E4	1977	1,700	10 Francs. KM23.	25.00
E5	1977	1,700	20 Francs. KM24.	25.00
E6	1977	1,700	50 Francs. KM25.	28.00
E7	1977	1,700	100 Francs. KM26.	30.00

MINT SETS

KM#	Date	Mintage	Identification	Issue Price	Mkt Val
MS1	1997 (8)	350	KM#20-27	—	300
MS2	1999 (8)	1,800	KM#20-27	—	125

DOMINICA

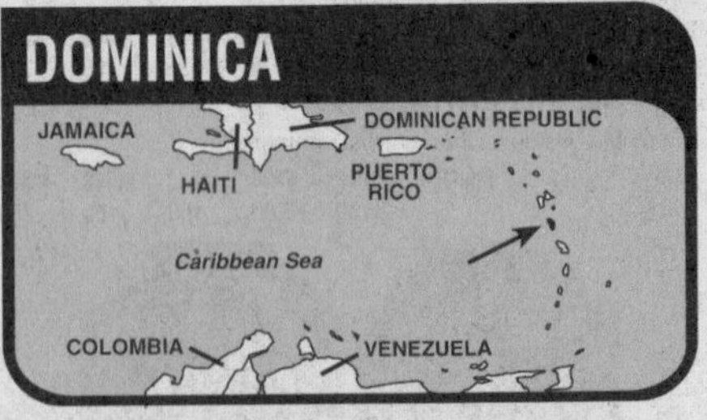

The Commonwealth of Dominica, situated in the Lesser Antilles midway between Guadeloupe to the north and Martinique to the south, has an area of 290 sq. mi. (750 sq. km.) and a population of 82,608, Capital: Roseau. Agriculture is the chief economic activity of the mountainous island. Bananas are the chief export.

Columbus discovered and named the island on Nov. 3, 1493. Spain neglected it and it was finally colonized by the French in 1632. The British drove the French from the island in 1756. Thereafter it changed hands between the French and British a dozen or more times before becoming permanently British in 1805. Around 1761, pierced or mutilated silver from Martinique was used on the island. A council in 1798 acknowledged and established value for these mutilated coins and ordered other cut and countermarked to be made in

Dominica. These remained in use until 1862, when they were demonetized and sterling became the standard. Throughout the greater part of its British history, Dominica was a presidency of the Leeward Islands. In 1940 its administration was transferred to the Windward Islands and it was established as a separate colony with considerable local autonomy. From 1955, Dominica was a member of the currency board of the British Caribbean Territories (Eastern Group), which issued its own coins until 1965. Dominica became a West Indies associated state with a built in option for independence in 1967. Full independence was attained on Nov. 3, 1978. Dominica, which has a republican form of government, is a member of the Commonwealth of Nations.

RULER

British, until 1978

MINT MARKS

CHI in circle - Valcambi, Chiasso, Italy
(ml) - maple leaf - Canadian Royal Mint

MONETARY SYSTEM

(Commencing 1813)
16 Bits = 12 Shillings = 1 Dollar (Spanish)
100 Cents = 1 Dollar (Dominican)

BRITISH COLONY

MODERN COINAGE

KM# 11 4 DOLLARS

Copper-Nickel, 38.5 mm. **Series:** F.A.O. **Rev:** Sugar cane and banana tree branch, denomination below **Note:** This 4-dollar F.A.O. commemorative coin is part of a group. The others are listed individually under their respective country names: Antigua, Barbados, Dominica, Grenada, Montserrat, St. Kitts, St. Lucia, and St. Vincent.

Date	Mintage	VF20	XF40	MS60	MS63	MS65
1970	13,000	6.00	10.00	22.00	35.00	—
1970	2,000	PF63 50.00				

COMMONWEALTH

KM# 12.1 10 DOLLARS

20.50 g., 0.925 Silver 0.6097 oz. ASW **Subject:** Independence - History of Carnival **Obv:** Young bust right **Rev:** Six dancing women, denomination below, with mint mark

Date	Mintage	VF20	XF40	MS60	MS63	MS65
ND-1978 CHI	1,500	—	—	20.00	25.00	32.50
ND-1978 CHI	2,000	PF65 37.50				

KM# 12.2 10 DOLLARS

20.50 g., 0.925 Silver 0.6097 oz. ASW **Subject:** Independence - History of Carnival **Obv:** Young bust right **Rev:** Six dancing women, denomination below, without mint mark

Date	Mintage	VF20	XF40	MS60	MS63	MS65
ND-1978	—	—	—	18.00	22.50	27.50

KM# 12.3 10 DOLLARS

20.50 g., 0.925 Silver 0.6097 oz. ASW **Subject:** Independence - History of Carnival **Obv:** Young bust right **Rev:** Six dancing women, denomination below, Canadian mint mark and fineness

Date	Mintage	VF20	XF40	MS60	MS63	MS65
ND-1978 (ml)	Est. 18	—	—	—	—	—
ND-1978 (ml)	Est. 233	PF65 125				

KM# 16 10 DOLLARS

20.50 g., 0.925 Silver 0.6097 oz. ASW **Subject:** Visit of Pope John Paul II **Obv:** Young bust right **Rev:** Head with beanie left, denomination below

Date	Mintage	VF20	XF40	MS60	MS63	MS65
ND-1979 CHI	1,150	—	—	22.50	30.00	37.00
ND-1979 CHI	3,450	PF65 42.00				

KM# 20 10 DOLLARS

Copper-Nickel **Subject:** Royal Visit **Obv:** Crowned bust right **Rev:** Lion tops arms with parrots, circle surrounds

Date	Mintage	VF20	XF40	MS60	MS63	MS65
1985	Est. 100000	—	—	4.00	8.00	16.00

KM# 20a 10 DOLLARS

28.28 g., 0.925 Silver 0.841 oz. ASW **Subject:** Royal Visit **Obv:** Crowned bust right **Rev:** Lion tops arms with parrots, circle surrounds

Date	Mintage	VF20	XF40	MS60	MS63	MS65
1985	Est. 5000	PF65 35.00				

KM# 13.1 20 DOLLARS

40.91 g., 0.925 Silver 1.2166 oz. ASW **Subject:** Independence and 50th Anniversary of Graf Zeppelin **Obv:** Young bust right divides dates **Rev:** Blimp above denomination

Date	Mintage	VF20	XF40	MS60	MS63	MS65
ND-1978 CHI	500	—	—	50.00	90.00	125
ND-1978 CHI	1,000	PF65 135				

KM# 13.2 20 DOLLARS

40.91 g., 0.925 Silver 1.2166 oz. ASW **Subject:** Independence and 50th Anniversary of Graf Zeppelin **Obv:** Young bust right divides dates **Rev:** Blimp above denomination, Canadian mint mark and .925 fineness stamp added

Date	Mintage	VF20	XF40	MS60	MS63	MS65
ND-1978 (ml)	—	—	—	—	—	—
ND-1978 (ml)	Est. 233	PF65 195				

KM# 13.3 20 DOLLARS

Silver, 45.2 mm. **Obv:** Young bust right **Rev:** Blimp above denomination **Edge:** Reeded **Note:** No mint marks or fineness.

Date	Mintage	VF20	XF40	MS60	MS63	MS65
ND-1978	—	PF65 225				

KM# 17 20 DOLLARS

40.91 g., 0.925 Silver 1.2166 oz. ASW **Subject:** Israel and Egypt Peace Treaty **Obv:** Young bust right **Rev:** Portrait of Sadat, Begin, and Carter, with small flags, denomination below

Date	Mintage	VF20	XF40	MS60	MS63	MS65
ND-1979 CHI	Est. 200	—	—	65.00	110	145
ND-1979 CHI	Est. 200	PF65 175				

KM# 21 100 DOLLARS

129.59 g., 0.925 Silver 3.8539 oz. ASW, 63 mm. **Subject:** Tropical Birds - Imperial Parrots **Obv:** Lion tops arms with parrots, circle surrounds, date below **Rev:** Parrots in trees, denomination above **Note:** Illustration reduced.

Date	Mintage	VF20	XF40	MS60	MS63	MS65
1988	Est. 10000	PF63 100	PF65 125			

KM# 14.1 150 DOLLARS

9.60 g., 0.900 Gold 0.2778 oz. AGW **Subject:** Independence - Imperial Parrot **Obv:** Young bust right **Rev:** Map of Dominica and parrot, without fineness, denomination at left

Date	Mintage	VF20	XF40	MS60	MS63	MS65
ND-1978	300	—	—	—	—	500
ND-1978	400	PF65 525				

KM# 14.2 150 DOLLARS

9.60 g., 0.900 Gold 0.2778 oz. AGW **Subject:** Independence - Imperial Parrot **Obv:** Young bust right **Rev:** Parrot and map, denomination at left, Canadian mint mark and .900 fineness added

Date	Mintage	VF20	XF40	MS60	MS63	MS65
ND-1978 (ml)	18	—	—	—	—	—
ND-1978 (ml)	116	PF65 575				

KM# 18 150 DOLLARS

9.60 g., 0.900 Gold 0.2778 oz. AGW **Subject:** Israel and Egypt Peace Treaty **Obv:** Young bust right **Rev:** Heads of Carter, Sadat, and Begin with flags, denomination below

Date	Mintage	VF20	XF40	MS60	MS63	MS65
ND-1979 CHI	100	—	—	—	—	750
ND-1979 CHI	100	PF65 800				

KM# 15.1 300 DOLLARS

19.20 g., 0.900 Gold 0.5556 oz. AGW **Subject:** Independence - Arms **Obv:** Young bust right **Rev:** Lion tops arms with parrots, denomination below, without fineness

Date	Mintage	VF20	XF40	MS60	MS63	MS65
ND-1978	500	—	—	—	—	950
ND-1978	800	PF65 975				

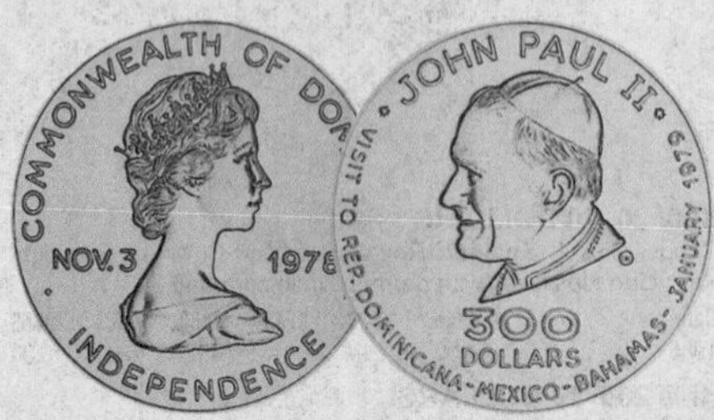

KM# 15.2 300 DOLLARS

19.20 g., 0.900 Gold 0.5556 oz. AGW **Subject:** Independence - Arms **Obv:** Young bust right **Rev:** National arms, Canadian mint mark and .900 fineness added

Date	Mintage	VF20	XF40	MS60	MS63	MS65
ND-1978 (ml)	18	—	—	—	—	—
ND-1978 (ml)	82	PF65 1,000				

KM# 19 300 DOLLARS

19.20 g., 0.900 Gold 0.5556 oz. AGW **Subject:** Visit of Pope John Paul II **Obv:** Young bust right **Rev:** Head with beanie left, denomination below

Date	Mintage	VF20	XF40	MS60	MS63	MS65
ND-1979 CHI	5,000	—	—	—	—	950
ND-1979 CHI	300	—	—	—	—	980

KM# 22 500 DOLLARS

47.54 g., 0.917 Gold 1.4016 oz. AGW **Subject:** Royal Visit **Obv:** Crowned bust right **Rev:** Lion tops arms with parrots, circle surrounds

Date	Mintage	VF20	XF40	MS60	MS63	MS65
1985	—	PF65 2,500				

PROOF SETS

KM#	Date	Mintage	Identification	Issue Price	Mkt Val
PS1	1978 (2)	—	KM#12.3, 13.2	—	325
PS2	1978 (4)	—	KM#12.3, 13.2, 14.2, 15.2	—	1,950

DOMINICAN REPUBLIC

The Dominican Republic, which occupies the eastern two-thirds of the island of Hispaniola, has an area of 18,704 sq. mi. (48,734 sq. km.) and a population of 7.9 million. Capital: Santo Domingo. The largely agricultural economy produces sugar, coffee, tobacco and cocoa. Tourism and casino gaming are also a rising source of revenue.

Columbus discovered Hispaniola in 1492, and named it La Isla Espanola - 'the Spanish Island'. Santo Domingo, the oldest white settlement in the Western Hemisphere, was the base from which Spain conducted its exploration of the New World. Later, French buccaneers settled the western third of Hispaniola, naming the colony St. Dominique, which in 1697, was ceded to France by Spain. In 1804, following a bloody revolt by former slaves, the French colony became the Republic of Haiti - mountainous country'. The Spanish called their part of Hispaniola Santo Domingo. In 1822, the Haitians conquered the entire island and held it until 1844, when Juan Pablo Duarte, the national hero of the Dominican Republic, drove them out of Santo Domingo and established an independent Dominican Republic. The republic returned voluntarily to Spanish dominion from 1861 to 1865, after being rejected by France, Britain and the United States. Independence was reclaimed in 1866.

MINT MARKS

(c) - Stylized maple leaf, Royal Canadian Mint
Mo – Mexico City
(o) - CHI in oval - Valcambi, Chiasso, Italy
(t) - Tower, Tower Mint, London

MONETARY SYSTEM

100 Centavos = 1 Peso Oro

REPUBLIC

REFORM COINAGE

1937: 100 Centavos = 1 Peso Oro

KM# 17 CENTAVO

3.11 g., Bronze, 19 mm. **Obv:** National arms **Rev:** Palm tree divides denomination and weight, date below

Date	Mintage	VF20	XF40	MS60	MS63	MS65
1937	1,000,000	1.50	7.50	30.00	75.00	150
1937	—	PF63 1,000				
1939	2,000,000	1.25	5.00	60.00	125	275
1941	2,000,000	0.50	3.00	7.50	12.00	40.00
1942	2,000,000	0.50	3.00	9.00	15.00	50.00
1944	5,000,000	0.50	1.50	5.00	10.00	30.00
1947	3,000,000	0.50	1.00	4.00	8.00	25.00
1949	3,000,000	0.40	1.00	4.00	8.00	25.00
1951	3,000,000	0.35	0.75	4.00	8.00	20.00
1952	3,000,000	0.35	0.75	4.00	8.00	20.00
1955	3,000,000	0.35	0.75	3.00	6.00	20.00
1956	3,000,000	0.35	0.75	3.00	6.00	20.00
1957	5,000,000	0.25	0.75	2.50	5.00	15.00
1959	5,000,000	0.25	0.75	2.50	5.00	50.00
1961	5,000,000	0.20	0.50	1.00	2.00	15.00
1961 10 known; Proof	—	PF63 800				

KM# 25 CENTAVO

Bronze, 19 mm. **Subject:** 100th Anniversary - Restoration of the Republic **Obv:** National arms, date below **Rev:** Taino Indian divides denomination and weight, date below

Date	Mintage	VF20	XF40	MS60	MS63	MS65
1963	13,000,000	—	0.10	0.40	0.75	1.25

KM# 31 CENTAVO

3.02 g., Bronze **Obv:** National arms **Rev:** Profile of native princess left divides denomination and weight, date below

Date	Mintage	VF20	XF40	MS60	MS63	MS65
1968	5,000,000	—	0.10	0.20	0.50	0.85
1971	6,000,000	—	0.10	0.20	0.50	0.85
1972	3,000,000	—	0.10	0.20	0.50	0.85
1972	500	PF65 20.00				
1975	500,000	0.10	0.20	0.30	0.60	1.00

KM# 32 CENTAVO

3.02 g., Bronze **Series:** F.A.O. **Obv:** National arms, date below **Rev:** Profile of native princess left divides denomination and weight, date below

Date	Mintage	VF20	XF40	MS60	MS63	MS65
1969	5,000,000	—	0.10	0.30	0.60	1.00

KM# 40 CENTAVO

Bronze **Subject:** Centennial - Death of Juan Pablo Duarte **Obv:** National arms, two dates below **Rev:** Bust facing divides denomination and weight, date below

Date	Mintage	VF20	XF40	MS60	MS63	MS65
1976	3,995,000	—	0.10	0.20	0.50	0.85
1976	5,000	PF65 1.00				

KM# 48 CENTAVO

Bronze **Subject:** Death of Juan Pablo Duarte **Obv:** National arms without memorial legend **Rev:** Bust facing divides denomination and weight, date below

Date	Mintage	VF20	XF40	MS60	MS63	MS65
1978	2,995,000	—	0.10	0.15	0.30	0.50
1978	5,000	PF65 2.00				
1979	2,985,000	—	0.10	0.15	0.30	0.50
1979	500	PF65 15.00				
1980	200,000	—	0.10	1.00	3.00	5.00
1980	3,000	PF65 1.00				
1981	3,000	PF65 1.00				

Note: KM#48a previously listed here has been moved to the Pattern section

KM# 64 CENTAVO

2.00 g., Copper Plated Zinc, 19 mm. **Subject:** Human Rights **Obv:** National arms **Rev:** Bust of Caonabo right **Edge:** Plain

Date	Mintage	VF20	XF40	MS60	MS63	MS65
1984 Mo	10,000,000	—	0.10	0.25	0.50	0.75
1984 Mo	1,600	PF65 1.50				
1986	18,067,000	—	0.10	0.25	0.50	0.75
1986	1,600	PF65 1.50				
1987	15,000,000	—	0.10	0.25	0.50	0.75
1987 (t)	1,600	PF65 1.50				

KM# 64a CENTAVO

2.00 g., 0.900 Silver 0.0579 oz. ASW, 19.03 mm. **Subject:** Human Rights **Obv:** National arms **Rev:** Bust of Caonabo right **Edge:** Plain

Date	Mintage	VF20	XF40	MS60	MS63	MS65
1984 Mo	100	PF65 20.00				
1986	100	PF65 20.00				

KM# 72 CENTAVO

Copper Plated Zinc, 19.1 mm. **Obv:** National arms, date below **Rev:** Triangular artifact, denomination below

Date	Mintage	VF20	XF40	MS60	MS63	MS65
1989	1,115	—	0.65	1.25	1.50	2.00

KM# 72a CENTAVO

3.70 g., 0.925 Silver 0.110 oz. ASW, 19.1 mm. **Obv:** National arms, date below **Rev:** Triangular artifact

Date	Mintage	VF20	XF40	MS60	MS63	MS65
1989 Proof	2,600	—	—	—	—	—

KM# 18 5 CENTAVOS

5.00 g., Copper-Nickel, 21 mm. **Obv:** National arms **Rev:** Profile of native princess left divides denomination and weight, date below

Date	Mintage	VF20	XF40	MS60	MS63	MS65
1937	2,000,000	1.75	5.00	15.00	35.00	100
1937	—	PF63 750				
1939	200,000	15.00	35.00	100	175	350
1951	2,000,000	1.25	2.00	10.00	20.00	35.00
1956	1,000,000	0.50	0.80	5.00	15.00	30.00
1959	1,000,000	0.50	0.80	3.50	10.00	15.00
1961	4,000,000	0.20	0.35	0.75	2.00	3.50
1961 10 known; Proof	—	PF63 1,000				
1971	440,000	0.40	0.60	1.50	2.50	4.00
1972	2,000,000	0.15	0.20	0.50	1.00	1.50
1972	500	PF63 15.00				
1974	5,000,000	—	0.15	0.45	1.00	1.50
1974	500	PF63 15.00				

KM# 18a 5 CENTAVOS

5.00 g., 0.350 Silver 0.0563 oz. ASW, 21 mm. **Obv:** National arms **Rev:** Profile of native princess left divides denomination and weight, date below

Date	Mintage	VF20	XF40	MS60	MS63	MS65
1944	2,000,000	4.00	8.00	60.00	120	225

KM# 26 5 CENTAVOS

5.00 g., Copper-Nickel, 21 mm. **Subject:** 100th Anniversary - Restoration of the Republic **Obv:** National arms, two dates below **Rev:** Profile of native princess left divides denomination and weight, date below

Date	Mintage	VF20	XF40	MS60	MS63	MS65
1963	4,000,000	0.10	0.15	0.60	1.25	1.50

KM# 41 5 CENTAVOS

Copper-Nickel, 41 mm. **Subject:** Centennial - Death of Juan Pablo Duarte **Obv:** National arms, two dates below **Rev:** Bust facing divides denomination and weight, date below

Date	Mintage	VF20	XF40	MS60	MS63	MS65
1976	5,595,000	—	0.10	0.50	0.75	1.00
1976	5,000	PF65 2.00				

KM# 49 5 CENTAVOS

5.00 g., Copper-Nickel, 21 mm. **Obv:** National arms without memorial legend **Rev:** Bust facing divides denomination and weight, date below

Date	Mintage	VF20	XF40	MS60	MS63	MS65
1978	1,996,000	—	0.10	0.35	0.65	1.00
1978	5,000	PF65 1.50				
1979	2,988,000	—	0.10	0.35	0.65	1.00
1979	500	PF65 15.00				
1980	5,300,000	—	0.10	0.35	0.65	1.00
1980	3,000	PF65 2.00				
1981	4,500,000	—	0.10	0.35	0.65	1.00
1981	3,000	PF65 2.00				

Note: KM#49a previously listed here has been moved to the Pattern section

KM# 59 5 CENTAVOS

5.00 g., Copper-Nickel, 21.19 mm. **Subject:** Human Rights **Obv:** National arms **Rev:** Conjoined busts right, denomination above **Edge:** Plain

Date	Mintage	VF20	XF40	MS60	MS63	MS65
1983	3,998,000	—	0.10	0.30	0.60	1.00
1983 (t)	1,600	PF65 2.00				
1984 Mo	10,000,000	—	0.10	0.30	0.60	1.00
1984 Mo	1,600	PF65 2.00				
1986	12,898,000	—	0.10	0.30	0.60	1.00
1986	1,600	PF65 2.00				
1987	10,000,000	—	0.10	0.30	0.60	1.00
1987 (t)	1,700	PF65 2.00				

KM# 59a 5 CENTAVOS

5.00 g., 0.900 Silver 0.1447 oz. ASW, 21.19 mm. **Subject:** Human Rights **Obv:** National arms **Rev:** Conjoined busts right, denomination above **Edge:** Plain

Date	Mintage	VF20	XF40	MS60	MS63	MS65
1983 (t)	100	PF65 30.00				
1984 Mo	100	PF65 30.00				
1986	100	PF65 30.00				

KM# 69 5 CENTAVOS

Nickel Clad Steel, 21 mm. **Subject:** Native Culture **Obv:** National arms, date below **Rev:** Native drummer, denomination at left

Date	Mintage	VF20	XF40	MS60	MS63	MS65
1989	50,000,000	—	—	0.35	0.65	1.00

KM# 69a 5 CENTAVOS

5.83 g., 0.925 Silver 0.1734 oz. ASW, 21 mm. **Subject:** Native Culture **Obv:** National arms, date below **Rev:** Native drummer, denomination at left

Date	Mintage	VF20	XF40	MS60	MS63	MS65
1989 Proof	2,600	—	—	—	—	—

KM# 19 10 CENTAVOS

2.50 g., 0.900 Silver 0.0723 oz. ASW, 17.9 mm. **Obv:** National arms **Rev:** Profile of native princess left divides denomination and weight

Date	Mintage	VF20	XF40	MS60	MS63	MS65
1937	1,000,000	3.00	20.00	40.00	70.00	100
1937	—	PF63 1,200				
1939	150,000	25.00	100	200	350	500
1942	2,000,000	4.00	15.00	35.00	60.00	90.00
1944	1,000,000	4.00	25.00	60.00	135	185
1951	500,000	4.00	5.00	10.00	25.00	40.00
1952	500,000	4.00	5.00	10.00	20.00	35.00
1953	750,000	4.00	5.00	8.00	16.00	25.00
1956	1,000,000	3.00	5.00	8.00	16.00	25.00
1959	2,000,000	2.75	4.00	7.00	15.00	30.00
1961	2,000,000	2.75	4.00	6.00	12.00	18.00

KM# 19a 10 CENTAVOS

2.50 g., Copper-Nickel, 17.9 mm. **Obv:** National arms **Rev:** Profile of native princess left divides denomination and weight, date below **Edge:** Plain

Date	Mintage	VF20	XF40	MS60	MS63	MS65
1967	10,000,000	—	0.15	0.50	0.75	1.00
1973	8,000,000	—	0.15	0.50	0.75	1.00
1973	500	PF65 20.00				
1975	8,000,000	—	0.15	0.50	0.75	1.00

KM# 27 10 CENTAVOS

2.50 g., 0.650 Silver 0.0522 oz. ASW, 17.9 mm. **Subject:** 100th Anniversary - Restoration of the Republic **Obv:** National arms **Rev:** Profile of native princess left divides denomination and weight

Date	Mintage	VF20	XF40	MS60	MS63	MS65
1963	4,000,000	1.00	1.75	2.75	3.50	5.00

KM# 42 10 CENTAVOS

Copper-Nickel, 17.9 mm. **Subject:** Centennial - Death of Juan Pablo Duarte **Obv:** National arms **Rev:** Bust facing, date below

Date	Mintage	VF20	XF40	MS60	MS63	MS65
1976	5,595,000	—	0.10	0.75	1.00	1.50
1976	5,000	PF65 2.00				

KM# 50 10 CENTAVOS

2.56 g., Copper-Nickel, 17.9 mm. **Obv:** National arms **Rev:** Bust facing divides denomination and weight, date below

Date	Mintage	VF20	XF40	MS60	MS63	MS65
1978	3,000,000	—	0.10	0.50	0.75	1.00
1978	5,000	PF65 2.00				
1979	4,020,000	—	0.10	0.50	0.75	1.00
1979	500	PF65 20.00				
1980	4,400,000	—	0.10	0.35	0.65	1.00
1980	3,000	PF65 3.00				
1981	6,000,000	—	0.10	0.35	0.65	1.00
1981	3,000	PF65 3.00				

Note: KM#50a previously listed here has been moved to the Pattern section

KM# 60 10 CENTAVOS

2.50 g., Copper-Nickel, 17.88 mm. **Subject:** Human Rights **Obv:** National arms, date below **Rev:** Head left, denomination above **Edge:** Reeded

Date	Mintage	VF20	XF40	MS60	MS63	MS65
1983	4,998,000	—	0.10	0.35	0.65	1.00
1983 (t)	4,000,000	—	0.10	0.35	0.65	1.00
1983 (t)	1,600	PF65 2.50				
1984 Mo	15,000,000	—	0.10	0.25	0.50	0.75
Note: Coarse reeding						
1984 Mo	1,600	PF65 2.50				
Note: Coarse reeding						
1986	15,515,000	—	0.10	0.25	0.50	0.75
1986	1,600	PF65 2.50				
1987	20,000,000	—	0.10	0.25	0.50	0.75
1987 (t)	1,700	PF65 2.50				

KM# 60a 10 CENTAVOS

2.50 g., 0.900 Silver 0.0723 oz. ASW, 17.88 mm. **Subject:** Human Rights **Obv:** National arms **Rev:** Head left, denomination above **Edge:** Reeded

Date	Mintage	VF20	XF40	MS60	MS63	MS65
1983 (t)	100	PF65 30.00				
1984 Mo	100	PF65 30.00				
1986	100	PF65 30.00				

KM# 70 10 CENTAVOS

2.27 g., Nickel Clad Steel, 17.9 mm. **Obv:** National arms, date below **Rev:** Indigenous fruits and vegetables divide denomination **Edge:** Reeded

Date	Mintage	VF20	XF40	MS60	MS63	MS65
1989	40,000,000	—	—	0.40	0.70	1.25
1991	3,500,000	—	—	0.40	0.70	1.25

KM# 70a 10 CENTAVOS

2.90 g., 0.925 Silver 0.0862 oz. ASW, 17.9 mm. **Obv:** National arms **Rev:** Indigenous fruits and vegetables divide denomination

Date	Mintage	VF20	XF40	MS60	MS63	MS65
1989 Proof	2,600	—	—	—	—	—

KM# 20 25 CENTAVOS

6.25 g., 0.900 Silver 0.1808 oz. ASW, 24 mm. **Obv:** National arms **Rev:** Profile of native princess left divides denomination and weight, date below

Date	Mintage	VF20	XF40	MS60	MS63	MS65
1937	560,000	10.00	25.00	60.00	120	180
1937	—	PF63 1,200				
1939 (p)	160,000	20.00	125	325	750	1,250
1942 (p)	560,000	9.50	35.00	100	150	225
1944	400,000	9.50	35.00	100	150	225
1947 (p)	400,000	9.50	25.00	85.00	175	250
1951 (p)	400,000	9.50	25.00	85.00	175	250
1952	400,000	7.50	9.50	16.50	75.00	150
1956	400,000	6.50	8.50	14.50	30.00	60.00
1960 (p)	600,000	6.50	8.50	14.50	30.00	70.00
1961	800,000	6.50	8.50	14.50	30.00	50.00

KM# 20a.1 25 CENTAVOS

6.25 g., Copper-Nickel, 24 mm. **Obv:** National arms **Rev:** Profile of native princess left divides denomination and weight, date below **Edge:** Plain

Date	Mintage	VF20	XF40	MS60	MS63	MS65
1967	5,000,000	0.10	0.20	0.75	1.00	1.50
1972	800,000	0.10	0.40	1.00	1.50	2.00
1972	500	PF65 20.00				

KM# 20a.2 25 CENTAVOS

6.25 g., Copper-Nickel, 24 mm. **Obv:** National arms **Rev:** Profile of native princess left divides denomination and weight, date below **Edge:** Reeded

Date	Mintage	VF20	XF40	MS60	MS63	MS65
1974	500	PF65 20.00				
1974	2,000,000	0.10	0.40	1.00	1.50	2.00

KM# 28 25 CENTAVOS

6.25 g., 0.650 Silver 0.1306 oz. ASW, 24 mm. **Subject:** 100th Anniversary - Restoration of the Republic **Obv:** National arms, two dates below **Rev:** Profile of native princess left divides denomination and weight, date below

Date	Mintage	VF20	XF40	MS60	MS63	MS65
1963	2,400,000	2.50	4.00	5.00	7.00	9.00

KM# 43 25 CENTAVOS

6.25 g., Copper-Nickel, 24 mm. **Subject:** Centennial - Death of Juan Pablo Duarte **Obv:** National arms, two dates below **Rev:** Bust facing divides denomination and weight, date below

Date	Mintage	VF20	XF40	MS60	MS63	MS65
1976	3,195,000	0.10	0.40	1.00	1.50	2.00
1976	5,000	PF65 2.50				

KM# 51 25 CENTAVOS

6.27 g., Copper-Nickel, 24 mm. **Obv:** National arms without memorial legend **Rev:** Bust facing divides denomination and weight, date below

Date	Mintage	VF20	XF40	MS60	MS63	MS65
1978	996,000	—	0.35	0.75	1.00	1.50
1978	5,000	PF65 3.00				
1979	2,089,000	—	0.15	0.50	0.75	1.00
1979	500	PF65 25.00				
1980	2,600,000	—	0.15	0.50	0.75	1.00
1980	3,000	PF65 3.00				
1981	3,200,000	—	0.15	0.50	0.75	1.00
1981	3,000	PF65 3.00				

Date	Mintage	VF20	XF40	MS60	MS63	MS65

Note: KM#51a previously listed here has been moved to the Pattern section

KM# 61.1 25 CENTAVOS

6.25 g., Copper-Nickel, 24.45 mm. **Subject:** Human Rights **Obv:** National arms, date below, denomination at left **Rev:** Profiles of the Mirabel sisters left, Patria, Minerva & Maria Teresa, human rights martyrs murdered 25.11.1960 by Trujillo **Edge:** Fine reeding **Note:** Medal rotation.

Date	Mintage	VF20	XF40	MS60	MS63	MS65
1983	793,000	—	0.15	0.50	0.75	1.00
1983 (t)	5,000	—	—	2.50	3.50	5.00
1983 (t)	1,600	PF65 8.00				
1984 Mo Coarse reeding	6,400,000	—	0.15	0.40	0.75	1.00
1984 Mo Proof; coarse reeding	1,600	PF65 8.00				
1986	—	—	—	2.50	3.50	5.00

KM# 61.1a 25 CENTAVOS

6.25 g., 0.900 Silver 0.1808 oz. ASW, 24 mm. **Subject:** Human Rights **Obv:** National arms **Rev:** Profile of the Mirabel sisters left

Date	Mintage	VF20	XF40	MS60	MS63	MS65
1983 (t)	100	PF65 40.00				
1984 Mo	100	PF65 40.00				

KM# 61.2 25 CENTAVOS

6.25 g., Copper-Nickel, 24 mm. **Subject:** Human Rights **Obv:** National arms, date below, denomination at left **Rev:** Profiles of the Mirabel sisters left, Patria, Minerva and Maria Teresa, human rights martyrs murdered 25.11.1960 by Trujillo **Edge:** Fine reeding **Note:** Coin rotation.

Date	Mintage	VF20	XF40	MS60	MS63	MS65
1986 Coarse reeding	10,132,000	—	0.15	0.40	0.75	1.00
1986	1,600	PF65 8.00				
1987	6,000,000	—	0.15	0.40	0.75	1.00
1987 (t)	1,700	PF65 8.00				

KM# 61.2a 25 CENTAVOS

Silver **Subject:** Human Rights **Obv:** National arms **Rev:** Profile of the Mirabel sisters left

Date	Mintage	VF20	XF40	MS60	MS63	MS65
1986	—	PF65 40.00				

KM# 71.1 25 CENTAVOS

5.70 g., Nickel Clad Steel, 24.2 mm. **Subject:** Native Culture **Obv:** National arms, date below **Rev:** Two oxen pulling cart, denomination above

Date	Mintage	VF20	XF40	MS60	MS63	MS65
1989 Coarse reeding	16,000,000	—	—	0.60	1.25	1.50
1991 Fine reeding	38,000,000	—	—	0.60	1.25	1.50

KM# 71.1a 25 CENTAVOS

6.74 g., 0.925 Silver 0.2004 oz. ASW, 24 mm. **Subject:** Native Culture **Obv:** National arms **Rev:** Two oxen pulling cart

Date	Mintage	VF20	XF40	MS60	MS63	MS65
1989 Proof	2,600	—	—	—	—	—

KM# 71.2 25 CENTAVOS

5.70 g., Nickel Clad Steel, 24.2 mm. **Subject:** Native Culture **Obv:** National arms, date below **Rev:** Two oxen pulling cart, denomination above **Edge:** Coarse reeding **Note:** Obverse and reverse legends and designs in beaded circle. Varieties exist.

Date	Mintage	VF20	XF40	MS60	MS63	MS65
1990	20,000,000	—	—	0.60	1.25	1.50

KM# 21 1/2 PESO
12.50 g., 0.900 Silver 0.3617 oz. ASW, 30.5 mm. **Obv:** National arms **Rev:** Profile of native princess left divides denomination and weight

Date	Mintage	VF20	XF40	MS60	MS63	MS65
1937	500,000	16.00	30.00	70.00	120	250
1937	—	PF63 1,800				
1944	100,000	20.00	100	200	375	550
1947	200,000	16.00	75.00	175	275	400
1951	200,000	16.00	50.00	100	200	350
1952	140,000	16.00	18.00	35.00	70.00	125
1959	100,000	15.00	17.00	30.00	60.00	100
1960	100,000	15.00	17.00	30.00	50.00	80.00
1961	400,000	14.00	16.00	25.00	35.00	60.00

KM# 21a.1 1/2 PESO
Copper-Nickel, 30.5 mm. **Obv:** National arms **Rev:** Profile of native princess left divides denomination and weight **Edge:** Plain

Date	Mintage	VF20	XF40	MS60	MS63	MS65
1967	1,500,000	0.20	0.40	1.50	2.50	4.00
1968	600,000	0.30	0.50	2.50	3.50	5.00

KM# 29 1/2 PESO
12.50 g., 0.650 Silver 0.2612 oz. ASW, 30.5 mm. **Subject:** 100th Anniversary - Restoration of the Republic **Obv:** National arms **Rev:** Profile of native princess left divides denomination and weight

Date	Mintage	VF20	XF40	MS60	MS63	MS65
1963	300,000	4.75	9.50	12.00	14.00	16.00

KM# 21a.2 1/2 PESO
12.50 g., Copper-Nickel, 30.5 mm. **Obv:** National arms **Rev:** Profile of native princess left divides denomination and weight **Edge:** Reeded

Date	Mintage	VF20	XF40	MS60	MS63	MS65
1973	600,000	0.20	0.40	1.25	1.75	2.50
1973	500	PF65 30.00				
1975	600,000	0.20	0.40	1.25	1.75	2.50

KM# 44 1/2 PESO
Copper-Nickel, 30.5 mm. **Subject:** Centennial - Death of Juan Pablo Duarte **Obv:** National arms, two dates below **Rev:** Bust facing divides denomination and weight, date below

Date	Mintage	VF20	XF40	MS60	MS63	MS65
1976	195,000	0.20	0.40	1.25	1.75	2.50
1976	5,000	PF65 3.00				

KM# 52 1/2 PESO
12.38 g., Copper-Nickel, 30.5 mm. **Obv:** National arms without memorial legend **Rev:** Bust facing divides denomination and weight, date below

Date	Mintage	VF20	XF40	MS60	MS63	MS65
1978	296,000	0.20	0.40	1.25	1.75	2.50
1978	5,000	PF65 4.00				
1979	967,000	0.20	0.40	1.25	1.75	2.50
1979	500	PF65 30.00				
1980	1,000,000	0.20	0.40	1.25	1.75	2.50
1980	3,000	PF65 5.00				
1981	1,300,000	0.20	0.40	1.25	1.75	2.50
1981	3,000	PF65 5.00				

Note: KM#52a previously listed here has been moved to the Pattern section

KM# 62.1 1/2 PESO
12.50 g., Copper-Nickel, 30.87 mm. **Subject:** Human Rights **Obv:** National arms, date below, denomination at left **Rev:** Three profiles right **Edge:** Fine reeding **Note:** Medal rotation.

Date	Mintage	VF20	XF40	MS60	MS63	MS65
1983	393,000	0.20	0.40	1.25	1.75	2.50
1983 (t)	5,000	—	—	3.50	4.50	6.00
1983 (t)	1,600	PF65 15.00				
1984 Mo Coarse reeding	3,200,000	0.20	0.40	1.25	1.75	2.50
1984 Mo Proof; coarse reeding	1,600	PF65 15.00				

KM# 62.1a 1/2 PESO
12.50 g., 0.900 Silver 0.3617 oz. ASW, 30.5 mm. **Subject:** Human Rights **Obv:** National arms, date below **Rev:** Three profiles right

Date	Mintage	VF20	XF40	MS60	MS63	MS65
1983 (t)	100	PF65 50.00				
1984 Mo	100	PF65 50.00				

KM# 62.2 1/2 PESO
12.50 g., Copper-Nickel, 30.5 mm. **Subject:** Human Rights **Obv:** National arms, date below, denomination at left **Rev:** Three profiles right **Edge:** Fine reeding **Note:** Coin rotation.

Date	Mintage	VF20	XF40	MS60	MS63	MS65
1986	5,225,000	0.20	0.40	1.25	1.75	2.50
1986	1,600	PF65 15.00				
1987	3,000,000	0.20	0.40	1.25	1.75	2.50
1987 (t)	1,700	PF65 15.00				

KM# 62.2a 1/2 PESO
12.50 g., 0.900 Silver 0.3617 oz. ASW **Subject:** Human rights **Obv:** National arms, date below **Rev:** 3 profiles right

Date	Mintage	VF20	XF40	MS60	MS63	MS65
1986	100	PF65 50.00				

KM# 73.1 1/2 PESO
11.32 g., Nickel Clad Steel, 30.5 mm. **Subject:** National Culture **Obv:** National arms **Rev:** Beacon at Colon

Date	Mintage	VF20	XF40	MS60	MS63	MS65
1989	8,000,000	—	—	1.25	2.00	3.00

KM# 73.1a 1/2 PESO
14.65 g., 0.925 Silver 0.4357 oz. ASW, 30.5 mm. **Subject:** National Culture **Obv:** National arms **Rev:** Beacon at Colon

Date	Mintage	VF20	XF40	MS60	MS63	MS65
1989 Proof	2,600	—	—	—	—	—

KM# 73.2 1/2 PESO
Nickel Clad Steel, 30.5 mm. **Subject:** National Culture **Obv:** National arms, date below **Rev:** Beacon at Colon, denomination at left

Date	Mintage	VF20	XF40	MS60	MS63	MS65
1990	1,500,000	—	—	1.25	2.00	3.00

KM# 22 PESO
26.70 g., 0.900 Silver 0.7726 oz. ASW, 38 mm. **Obv:** National arms **Rev:** HP below head of native princess left

Date	Mintage	VF20	XF40	MS60	MS63	MS65
1939 (p)	15,000	35.00	100	300	550	1,250
1939 (p) Proof, unique	—	PF63 15,000				
1952	20,000	—	14.50	25.00	35.00	65.00

KM# 23 PESO
26.70 g., 0.900 Silver 0.7726 oz. ASW, 38 mm. **Subject:** 25th Anniversary of Trujillo Regime **Obv:** National arms **Rev:** Bust right divides date and denomination **Note:** 30,550 officially melted following Trujillo's assassination in 1961.

Date	Mintage	VF20	XF40	MS60	MS63	MS65
1955 (p)	50,000	—	18.00	30.00	45.00	80.00

KM# 30 PESO
26.70 g., 0.650 Silver 0.558 oz. ASW, 38 mm. **Subject:** 100th Anniversary - Restoration of the Republic **Obv:** Memorial legend around national arms, two dates below **Rev:** Profile of native princess left divides denomination and weight, date below

Date	Mintage	VF20	XF40	MS60	MS63	MS65
1963	20,000	—	—	20.00	25.00	32.00
1963	—	PF63 1,200				

KM# 33 PESO
Copper-Nickel, 38 mm. **Subject:** 125th Anniversary of the Republic **Obv:** Memorial legend around national arms, two dates below **Rev:** Pueblo entrance within circle holding legend divides denomination and weight, date below

Date	Mintage	VF20	XF40	MS60	MS63	MS65
1969	30,000	—	—	2.50	4.50	7.00

KM# 34 PESO

26.70 g., 0.900 Silver 0.7726 oz. ASW, 38 mm. **Subject:** 25th Anniversary - Central Bank **Obv:** Memorial legend around national arms **Rev:** Bank door in inner circle divides denomination and weight, date below

Date	Mintage	VF20	XF40	MS60	MS63	MS65
1972	27,000	—	—	—	18.00	25.00
1972	3,000	PF65 35.00				

KM# 35 PESO

26.70 g., 0.900 Silver 0.7726 oz. ASW, 38 mm. **Subject:** 12th Central American and Caribbean Games **Obv:** National arms without memorial legend **Rev:** Coat of arms within circle, on map, denomination and date below

Date	Mintage	VF20	XF40	MS60	MS63	MS65
1974	50,000	—	—	—	18.00	25.00
1974	5,000	PF65 32.00				

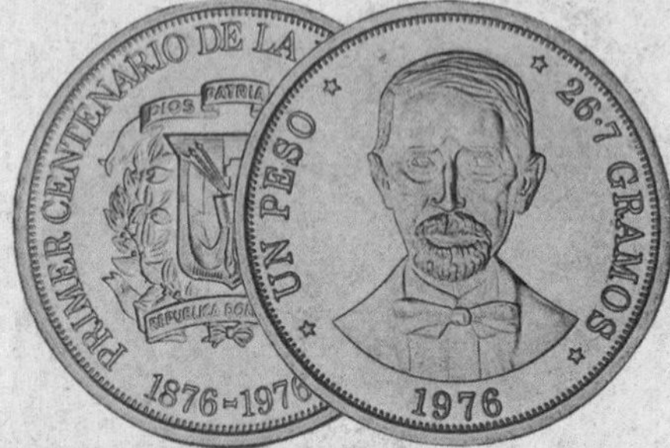

KM# 45 PESO

Copper-Nickel **Subject:** Centennial - Death of Juan Pablo Duarte **Obv:** National arms, two dates below **Rev:** Bust facing divides denomination and weight, date below

Date	Mintage	VF20	XF40	MS60	MS63	MS65
1976	25,000	—	1.00	2.00	3.50	5.00
1976	5,000	PF65 7.50				

KM# 53 PESO

26.60 g., Copper-Nickel, 38 mm. **Obv:** National arms without memorial legend **Rev:** Bust facing divides denomination and weight, date below

Date	Mintage	VF20	XF40	MS60	MS63	MS65
1978	35,000	—	1.00	2.00	3.50	5.00
1978	5,000	PF65 7.50				
1979	45,000	—	1.00	2.00	3.50	5.00
1979	500	PF65 35.00				
1980	20,000	—	1.00	2.00	3.50	5.00
1980	3,000	PF65 6.50				
1981	3,000	PF65 6.50				

Note: KM#53a previously listed here has been moved to the Pattern section

KM# 63.1 PESO

16.90 g., Copper-Nickel, 33.54 mm. **Subject:** Human Rights **Obv:** National arms, date below, denomination at left **Rev:** Three profiles right **Edge:** Fine reeding **Shape:** 10-sided **Note:** Medal rotation.

Date	Mintage	VF20	XF40	MS60	MS63	MS65
1983	5,000	—	—	5.00	7.50	12.50
1983 (t)	93,000	—	1.00	2.50	4.00	5.50
1983 (t)	1,600	PF65 15.00	PF67 18.00			
1984 Mo Coarse reeding	120,000	—	1.00	2.50	4.00	5.50
1984 Mo Proof; coarse reeding	1,600	PF65 15.00	PF67 18.00			

KM# 63.1a PESO

17.00 g., 0.900 Silver 0.4919 oz. ASW **Subject:** Human Rights **Obv:** National arms, denomination **Rev:** Three profiles right **Shape:** 10-sided

Date	Mintage	VF20	XF40	MS60	MS63	MS65
1983 (t)	100	PF65 125	PF67 150			
1984	100	PF65 100	PF67 125			

KM# 63.2 PESO

16.90 g., Copper-Nickel, 33.2 mm. **Subject:** Human Rights **Obv:** National arms, date below, denomination at left **Rev:** Three profiles right **Edge:** Fine reeding **Shape:** 10-sided **Note:** Coin rotation.

Date	Mintage	VF20	XF40	MS60	MS63	MS65
1986	—	—	1.00	2.50	4.00	5.50

KM# 65 PESO

Nickel Bonded Steel **Subject:** 15th Central American and Caribbean Games **Obv:** National arms, date below, denomination at left **Rev:** St. George and coat of arms **Shape:** Round

Date	Mintage	VF20	XF40	MS60	MS63	MS65
1986	100,000	—	1.00	3.00	5.00	7.00
1986	2,000	PF65 15.00	PF67 18.00			

KM# 65a PESO

6.50 g., Copper-Nickel **Subject:** 15th Central American and Caribbean Games **Obv:** National arms, denomination **Rev:** St. George and coat of arms **Shape:** Round

Date	Mintage	VF20	XF40	MS60	MS63	MS65
1986	548	—	—	—	40.00	60.00
1986 Proof	48	—	—	—	—	—

KM# 65b PESO

10.00 g., Copper-Nickel **Subject:** 15th Central American and Caribbean Games **Obv:** National arms and denomination **Rev:** St. George and coat of arms **Shape:** Round

Date	Mintage	VF20	XF40	MS60	MS63	MS65
1986	550	—	—	—	40.00	60.00
1986 Proof	50	—	—	—	—	—

KM# 66 PESO

19.84 g., Copper-Nickel **Subject:** 500th Anniversary - Discovery and Evangelization **Obv:** National arms, date below, denomination at left **Rev:** 3 ships at sea, date below

Date	Mintage	VF20	XF40	MS60	MS63	MS65
1988 (c)	150,000	—	—	2.50	3.50	5.00
1988 (c)	1,500	PF65 10.00	PF67 12.50			

KM# 66a PESO

21.10 g., 0.999 Silver 0.6778 oz. ASW **Subject:** 500th Anniversary - Discovery and Evangelization **Obv:** Denomination, national arms **Rev:** 3 ships at sea

Date	Mintage	VF20	XF40	MS60	MS63	MS65
1988	10,000	PF65 22.50	PF67 25.00			

KM# 66b PESO

31.10 g., 0.999 Gold 0.999 oz. AGW **Subject:** 500th Anniversary - Discovery and Evangelization **Obv:** Denomination, national arms **Rev:** 3 ships at sea

Date	Mintage	VF20	XF40	MS60	MS63	MS65
1988	—	PF67 1,700				

KM# 74 PESO

Copper-Nickel **Subject:** 500th Anniversary - Discovery and Evangelization **Obv:** Denomination, national arms **Rev:** Sailship landing

Date	Mintage	VF20	XF40	MS60	MS63	MS65
1989 (c)	—	—	—	2.50	3.50	5.00

KM# 74a PESO

31.10 g., 0.999 Silver 0.999 oz. ASW **Subject:** 500th Anniversary - Discovery and Evangelization **Obv:** Denomination, national arms **Rev:** Sailship landing

Date	Mintage	VF20	XF40	MS60	MS63	MS65
1989	10,000	PF65 30.00	PF67 32.00			

KM# 74b PESO

31.10 g., 0.999 Gold 0.999 oz. AGW **Subject:** 500th Anniversary - Discovery and Evangelization **Obv:** Denomination, national arms **Rev:** Sailship landing

Date	Mintage	VF20	XF40	MS60	MS63	MS65
1989 (c)	30	PF67 2,300				

KM# 77 PESO

Copper-Nickel **Subject:** 500th Anniversary - Discovery and Evangelization **Obv:** National arms, date below, denomination at left **Rev:** Two standing figures, date below

Date	Mintage	VF20	XF40	MS60	MS63	MS65
1990 (c)	30,000	—	—	2.50	3.50	5.00

KM# 77a PESO

31.10 g., 0.999 Silver 0.999 oz. ASW **Subject:** 500th Anniversary - Discovery and Evangelization **Obv:** National arms and denomination **Rev:** Two standing figures

Date	Mintage	VF20	XF40	MS60	MS63	MS65
1990	10,000	PF65 30.00	PF67 32.00			

KM# 77b PESO

31.10 g., 0.999 Gold 0.999 oz. AGW **Subject:** 500th Anniversary - Discovery and Evangelization **Obv:** National arms **Rev:** Two standing figures

Date	Mintage	VF20	XF40	MS60	MS63	MS65
1990	50	PF67 1,850				

KM# 80.1 PESO

6.50 g., Brass, 25 mm. **Subject:** Juan Pablo Duarte **Obv:** National arms and denomination **Rev:** DUARTE on bust 3/4 left, date below **Shape:** 11-sided **Note:** Coin die alignment.

Date	Mintage	VF20	XF40	MS60	MS63	MS65
1991	40,000,000	—	—	2.00	2.50	3.50
1992	35,000,000	—	—	2.00	2.50	3.50

KM# 81 PESO

Copper-Nickel **Subject:** Pinzon brothers on ship at sea **Obv:** National arms, date below, denomination at left **Rev:** Conjoined busts 3/4 left, on ship at sea, date below

Date	Mintage	VF20	XF40	MS60	MS63	MS65
1991 (c)	50,000	—	—	2.50	3.50	5.00

KM# 81a PESO

31.10 g., 0.999 Silver 0.999 oz. ASW **Subject:** Pinzon brothers on ship at sea **Obv:** Denomination, national arms **Rev:** Conjoined busts left on ship at sea

Date	Mintage	VF20	XF40	MS60	MS63	MS65
1991	10,000	PF65 32.00	PF67 35.00			

KM# 81b PESO

31.10 g., 0.999 Gold 0.999 oz. AGW **Subject:** Pinzon brothers on ship at sea **Obv:** Denomination, national arms **Rev:** Conjoined busts left on ship at sea

Date	Mintage	VF20	XF40	MS60	MS63	MS65
1991	35	PF67 2,000				

KM# 80.2 PESO

6.49 g., Brass, 25 mm. **Subject:** Juan Pablo Duarte **Obv:** National arms and denomination **Rev:** DUARTE below bust, date below **Note:** Coin die alignment.

Date	Mintage	VF20	XF40	MS60	MS63	MS65
1992	35,000,000	—	—	2.00	2.50	3.50
1993	40,000,000	—	—	2.00	2.50	3.50
1997	20,000,000	—	—	2.00	2.50	3.50
2000	30,000,000	—	—	2.00	2.50	3.50

KM# 82 PESO

Copper-Nickel, 34 mm. **Subject:** Christopher Columbus **Obv:** National arms, date below, denomination at left **Rev:** Bust 3/4 left, date below

Date	Mintage	VF20	XF40	MS60	MS63	MS65
1992 (c)	50,000	—	—	2.50	3.50	5.00

KM# 82a PESO

31.10 g., 0.999 Silver 0.999 oz. ASW **Subject:** Christopher Columbus **Obv:** Denomination, national arms **Rev:** Bust 3/4 left

Date	Mintage	VF20	XF40	MS60	MS63	MS65
1992	10,000	PF65 32.00	PF67 35.00			

KM# 82b PESO

31.10 g., 0.999 Gold 0.999 oz. AGW **Subject:** Christopher Columbus **Obv:** Denomination, national arms **Rev:** Bust 3/4 left

Date	Mintage	VF20	XF40	MS60	MS63	MS65
1992 (c)	35	PF67 2,300				

KM# 87 PESO

Copper-Nickel **Subject:** UN - Peace **Obv:** National arms, stars flank date below, denomination at left, **Rev:** UN logo, two doves, two dates above

Date	Mintage	VF20	XF40	MS60	MS63	MS65
1995	—	—	—	7.00	9.00	10.00

KM# 87a PESO

28.44 g., 0.925 Silver 0.8458 oz. ASW **Subject:** UN - Peace **Obv:** Denomination, arms, stars **Rev:** UN logo, two doves

Date	Mintage	VF20	XF40	MS60	MS63	MS65
1995	—	PF65 32.00	PF67 35.00			

KM# 80.3 PESO

Brass, 25 mm. **Subject:** Juan Pablo Duarte **Obv:** National arms and denomination **Rev:** DUARTE below bust **Note:** Medal die alignment

Date	Mintage	VF20	XF40	MS60	MS63	MS65
1997	—	—	—	2.00	2.50	3.50

KM# 88 5 PESOS

Bi-Metallic Stainless Steel center in Brass ring, 23 mm. **Subject:** 50th Anniversary - Central Bank **Obv:** Denomination and national arms within circle, date below **Rev:** Head facing within circle, two dates below

Date	Mintage	VF20	XF40	MS60	MS63	MS65
1997	—	—	—	2.50	3.00	4.50

KM# 37 10 PESOS

28.00 g., 0.900 Silver 0.8102 oz. ASW, 40 mm. **Subject:** International Bankers' Conference - First Hispaniola Coinage of Carlos and Johanna **Obv:** National arms, denomination and date below **Rev:** Arms of Castille in inner ring

Date	Mintage	VF20	XF40	MS60	MS63	MS65
1975	26,000	—	—	—	28.00	35.00
1975	—	PF65 50.00	PF67 60.00			

KM# 38 10 PESOS

30.00 g., 0.900 Silver 0.8681 oz. ASW **Subject:** Taino Art **Obv:** National arms **Rev:** Ancient figurine "Pueblo Viejo Mine" divides dates, date below

Date	Mintage	VF20	XF40	MS60	MS63	MS65
1975	45,000	—	—	—	—	—
1975	5,000	PF65 32.00	PF67 37.00			

KM# 57 10 PESOS

23.33 g., 0.925 Silver 0.6938 oz. ASW, 38.61 mm. **Subject:** International Year of the Child **Obv:** National arms **Rev:** 1/2 length figure of child drawing a house, small logos at left and right **Rev. Legend:** AÑO INTERNACIONAL DEL NIÑO **Edge:** Reeded

Date	Mintage	VF20	XF40	MS60	MS63	MS65
1982 (o)	8,482	PF65 25.00	PF67 30.00			

KM# 91 10 PESOS

2.45 g., 0.999 Silver 0.0787 oz. ASW, 18 mm. **Obv:** National arms **Rev:** St. Andrews Chapel

Date	Mintage	VF20	XF40	MS60	MS63	MS65
2000	3,000	—	—	—	—	17.50

KM# 92 10 PESOS

2.45 g., 0.999 Silver 0.0787 oz. ASW, 18 mm. **Obv:** National arms **Rev:** Our Lady of Carmen Church

Date	Mintage	VF20	XF40	MS60	MS63	MS65
2000	3,000	—	—	—	—	17.50

KM# 93 10 PESOS

2.45 g., 0.999 Silver 0.0787 oz. ASW, 18 mm. **Obv:** National arms **Rev:** Regina Angelorum Church

Date	Mintage	VF20	XF40	MS60	MS63	MS65
2000	3,000	—	—	—	—	17.50

KM# 94 10 PESOS

2.45 g., 0.999 Silver 0.0787 oz. ASW, 18 mm. **Obv:** National arms **Rev:** Chapel of the Remedies

Date	Mintage	VF20	XF40	MS60	MS63	MS65
2000	3,000	—	—	—	—	17.50

KM# 95 10 PESOS

2.45 g., 0.999 Silver 0.0787 oz. ASW, 18 mm. **Obv:** National arms **Rev:** St. Lazarus Church

Date	Mintage	VF20	XF40	MS60	MS63	MS65
2000	3,000	—	—	—	—	17.50

KM# 96 10 PESOS

2.45 g., 0.999 Silver 0.0787 oz. ASW, 18 mm. **Obv:** National arms **Rev:** St. Michael's Church

Date	Mintage	VF20	XF40	MS60	MS63	MS65
2000	3,000	—	—	—	—	17.50

KM# 97 10 PESOS

2.45 g., 0.999 Silver 0.0787 oz. ASW, 18 mm. **Obv:** National arms **Rev:** Church of Santa Barbara

Date	Mintage	VF20	XF40	MS60	MS63	MS65
2000	3,000	—	—	—	—	17.50

KM# 98 10 PESOS

2.45 g., 0.999 Silver 0.0787 oz. ASW, 18 mm. **Obv:** National arms **Rev:** Our Lady of the Rosary Church

Date	Mintage	VF20	XF40	MS60	MS63	MS65
2000	3,000	—	—	—	—	17.50

KM# 99 10 PESOS

2.45 g., 0.999 Silver 0.0787 oz. ASW, 18 mm. **Obv:** National arms **Rev:** Church of Banica

Date	Mintage	VF20	XF40	MS60	MS63	MS65
2000	3,000	—	—	—	—	17.50

KM# 100 10 PESOS

2.45 g., 0.999 Silver 0.0787 oz. ASW, 18 mm. **Obv:** National arms **Rev:** Church of Boya

Date	Mintage	VF20	XF40	MS60	MS63	MS65
2000	3,000	—	—	—	—	17.50

KM# 101 10 PESOS

2.45 g., 0.999 Silver 0.0787 oz. ASW, 18 mm. **Obv:** National arms **Rev:** Santo Domingo Cathedral

Date	Mintage	VF20	XF40	MS60	MS63	MS65
2000	3,000	—	—	—	—	17.50

KM# 102 10 PESOS

2.45 g., 0.999 Silver 0.0787 oz. ASW, 18 mm. **Obv:** National arms **Rev:** Holy Cross Cathedral of El Seibo

Date	Mintage	VF20	XF40	MS60	MS63	MS65
2000	3,000	—	—	—	—	17.50

KM# 103 10 PESOS

2.45 g., 0.999 Silver 0.0787 oz. ASW, 18 mm. **Obv:** National arms **Rev:** Higney Sanctuary

Date	Mintage	VF20	XF40	MS60	MS63	MS65
2000	3,000	—	—	—	—	17.50

KM# 110 10 PESOS

3.14 g., 0.9999 Gold 0.1008 oz. AGW, 16 mm. **Obv:** National arms **Rev:** Santa María de la Encarnación cathedral

Date	Mintage	VF20	XF40	MS60	MS63	MS65
2000	2,000	—	—	—	—	175

KM# 111 10 PESOS

3.14 g., 0.9999 Gold 0.1008 oz. AGW, 16 mm. **Obv:** National arms **Rev:** Banica church

Date	Mintage	VF20	XF40	MS60	MS63	MS65
2000	2,000	—	—	—	—	175

KM# 112 10 PESOS

3.14 g., 0.9999 Gold 0.1008 oz. AGW, 16 mm. **Obv:** National arms **Rev:** Boya church

Date	Mintage	VF20	XF40	MS60	MS63	MS65
2000	2,000	—	—	—	—	175

KM# 113 10 PESOS

3.14 g., 0.9999 Gold 0.1008 oz. AGW, 16 mm. **Obv:** National arms **Rev:** Nuestra Señora del Carmen church

Date	Mintage	VF20	XF40	MS60	MS63	MS65
2000	2,000	—	—	—	—	175

KM# 114 10 PESOS
3.14 g., 0.9999 Gold 0.1008 oz. AGW, 16 mm. **Obv:** National arms **Rev:** Nuestra Señora del Rosario church

Date	Mintage	VF20	XF40	MS60	MS63	MS65
2000	2,000	—	—	—	—	175

KM# 115 10 PESOS
3.14 g., 0.9999 Gold 0.1008 oz. AGW, 16 mm. **Obv:** National arms **Rev:** Santa Barbara church

Date	Mintage	VF20	XF40	MS60	MS63	MS65
2000	2,000	—	—	—	—	175

KM# 116 10 PESOS
3.14 g., 0.9999 Gold 0.1008 oz. AGW, 16 mm. **Obv:** National arms **Rev:** Santa Cruz de El Seibo church

Date	Mintage	VF20	XF40	MS60	MS63	MS65
2000	2,000	—	—	—	—	175

KM# 117 10 PESOS
3.14 g., 0.9999 Gold 0.1008 oz. AGW, 16 mm. **Obv:** National arms **Rev:** San Lázaro church

Date	Mintage	VF20	XF40	MS60	MS63	MS65
2000	2,000	—	—	—	—	175

KM# 118 10 PESOS
3.14 g., 0.9999 Gold 0.1008 oz. AGW, 16 mm. **Obv:** National arms **Rev:** San Miguel church

Date	Mintage	VF20	XF40	MS60	MS63	MS65
2000	2,000	—	—	—	—	175

KM# 119 10 PESOS
3.14 g., 0.9999 Gold 0.1008 oz. AGW, 16 mm. **Obv:** National arms **Rev:** Regina Angelorum chuch

Date	Mintage	VF20	XF40	MS60	MS63	MS65
2000	2,000	—	—	—	—	175

KM# 120 10 PESOS
3.14 g., 0.9999 Gold 0.1008 oz. AGW, 16 mm. **Obv:** National arms **Rev:** Sanctuary at Higuey

Date	Mintage	VF20	XF40	MS60	MS63	MS65
2000	2,000	—	—	—	—	175

KM# 121 10 PESOS
3.14 g., 0.9999 Gold 0.1008 oz. AGW, 16 mm. **Obv:** National arms **Rev:** Chapel of the Remedios

Date	Mintage	VF20	XF40	MS60	MS63	MS65
2000	2,000	—	—	—	—	175

KM# 122 10 PESOS
3.14 g., 0.9999 Gold 0.1008 oz. AGW, 16 mm. **Obv:** National arms **Rev:** Chapel of San Andrés

Date	Mintage	VF20	XF40	MS60	MS63	MS65
2000	2,000	—	—	—	—	175

KM# 54 25 PESOS
65.00 g., 0.925 Silver 1.9331 oz. ASW **Subject:** Pope John Paul II's Visit **Obv:** National arms, denomination below **Rev:** Bust left, Vatican City and date at left **Edge:** Reeded

Date	Mintage	VF20	XF40	MS60	MS63	MS65
ND-1979	3,000	—	—	—	55.00	65.00
ND-1979	6,000	PF65 75.00	PF67 85.00			

KM# 24 30 PESOS
29.62 g., 0.900 Gold 0.8571 oz. AGW, 32 mm. **Subject:** 25th Anniversary of Trujillo regime **Obv:** National arms, denomination below **Rev:** Head left, date below

Date	Mintage	VF20	XF40	MS60	MS63	MS65
1955	33,000	—	—	1,150	1,500	1,700

KM# 36 30 PESOS
11.70 g., 0.900 Gold 0.3385 oz. AGW **Subject:** 12th Central American and Caribbean Games **Obv:** National arms **Rev:** Games symbol, denomination and date below

Date	Mintage	VF20	XF40	MS60	MS63	MS65
1974	25,000	—	—	—	600	625
1974	5,000	PF65 650	PF67 675			

KM# 46 30 PESOS
78.00 g., 0.925 Silver 2.3197 oz. ASW **Subject:** 30th Anniversary of Central Bank **Obv:** National arms, denomination at left, date below **Rev:** Bank building, two dates below

Date	Mintage	VF20	XF40	MS60	MS63	MS65
1977	5,000	—	—	—	65.00	80.00
1977	2,000	PF65 100	PF67 110			

KM# 104 50 PESOS
28.35 g., 0.925 Silver 0.8431 oz. ASW, 38 mm. **Subject:** 50th Anniversary - Central Bank **Obv:** National arms **Rev:** Seated woman holding up coin **Edge:** Reeded

Date	Mintage	VF20	XF40	MS60	MS63	MS65
ND (1997)	3,000	—	—	—	—	32.00
ND (1997)	2,000	PF65 50.00	PF67 55.00			

KM# 39 100 PESOS
10.00 g., 0.900 Gold 0.2894 oz. AGW **Subject:** Taino Art **Obv:** National arms, date below **Rev:** Native art divides denomination, date below

Date	Mintage	VF20	XF40	MS60	MS63	MS65
1975	18,000	—	—	—	550	600
1975	2,000	PF65 850	PF67 950			

KM# 55 100 PESOS
12.00 g., 0.900 Gold 0.3472 oz. AGW **Subject:** Pope John Paul II's Visit **Obv:** National arms, denomination below **Rev:** Bust left, Vatican City and date at left

Date	Mintage	VF20	XF40	MS60	MS63	MS65
ND (1979)	1,000	—	—	—	600	675
ND (1979)	3,000	PF65 650	PF67 675			

KM# 67 100 PESOS
155.50 g., 0.999 Silver 4.9944 oz. ASW, 65 mm. **Subject:** Discovery of America - Native Americans

Date	Mintage	VF20	XF40	MS60	MS63	MS65
1988	5,300	PF65 125	PF67 145			

KM# 75 100 PESOS
155.50 g., 0.999 Silver 4.9944 oz. ASW **Subject:** 500th Anniversary of Discovery and Evangelization of America **Obv:** Arms **Rev:** Columbus and crew, date below

Date	Mintage	VF20	XF40	MS60	MS63	MS65
1989 (c)	1,500	PF65 150	PF67 170			

KM# 75a 100 PESOS
155.50 g., 0.999 Gold 4.9944 oz. AGW **Subject:** 500th Anniversary of Discovery and Evangelization of America **Obv:** Arms **Rev:** Columbus and crew

Date	Mintage	VF20	XF40	MS60	MS63	MS65
1989	30	PF67 8,500				

KM# 78 100 PESOS
155.50 g., 0.999 Silver 4.9944 oz. ASW, 65 mm. **Subject:** 500th Anniversary of Discovery and Evangelization of America **Obv:**

National arms **Rev:** Building a stockade, date below **Note:** Illustration reduced.

Date	Mintage	VF20	XF40	MS60	MS63	MS65
1990	1,000	PF65 165	PF67 185			

KM# 78a 100 PESOS
155.53 g., 0.999 Gold 4.9954 oz. AGW, 65 mm. **Subject:** 500th Anniversary of Discovery and Evangelization of America **Obv:** National arms **Rev:** Building a stockade **Note:** Illustration reduced.

Date	Mintage	VF20	XF40	MS60	MS63	MS65
1990	50	PF67 8,500				

KM# 83 100 PESOS
155.53 g., 0.999 Silver 4.9954 oz. ASW, 65 mm. **Subject:** 500th Anniversary of Discovery and Evangelization of America **Obv:** National arms **Rev:** Columbus Presenting Native American to Court **Note:** Illustration reduced.

Date	Mintage	VF20	XF40	MS60	MS63	MS65
1991	1,500	PF65 150	PF67 170			

KM# 83a 100 PESOS
155.53 g., 0.999 Gold 4.9954 oz. AGW, 65 mm. **Subject:** 500th Anniversary of Discovery and Evangelization of America **Obv:** National arms **Rev:** Columbus Presenting Native American to Court **Note:** Illustration reduced.

Date	Mintage	VF20	XF40	MS60	MS63	MS65
1991	35	PF67 8,500				

KM# 84 100 PESOS
155.53 g., 0.999 Silver 4.9954 oz. ASW, 65 mm. **Subject:** 500th Anniversary - Discovery and Evangelization of America **Obv:** National arms **Rev:** Columbus bust left, and anchored ship, date below **Note:** Illustration reduced.

Date	Mintage	VF20	XF40	MS60	MS63	MS65
1992	1,500	PF65 165	PF67 185			

KM# 84a 100 PESOS
155.53 g., 0.999 Gold 4.9954 oz. AGW, 65 mm. **Subject:** 500th Anniversary - Discovery and Evangelization of America **Obv:** National arms **Rev:** Bust left and anchored ship

Date	Mintage	VF20	XF40	MS60	MS63	MS65
1992	35	PF67 8,500				

KM# 47 200 PESOS
31.00 g., 0.800 Gold 0.7973 oz. AGW **Subject:** Centennial - Death of Juan Pablo Duarte **Obv:** National arms, date below **Rev:** Head facing divides denomination, two dates below **Note:** Large quantities of both varieties were melted for bullion.

Date	Mintage	VF20	XF40	MS60	MS63	MS65
1977	1,000	—	—	—	1,400	1,650
1977	2,000	PF65 1,650	PF67 1,750			

KM# 58 200 PESOS
17.17 g., 0.900 Gold 0.4968 oz. AGW **Subject:** International Year of the Child **Obv:** National arms, date below **Rev:** Children dancing, denomination below

Date	Mintage	VF20	XF40	MS60	MS63	MS65
1982	4,290	PF65 850	PF67 900			

KM# 105 200 PESOS
12.00 g., 0.900 Gold 0.3472 oz. AGW, 25 mm. **Subject:** 50th Anniversary - Central Bank **Obv:** National arms **Rev:** Seated woman holding up coin **Edge:** Reeded

Date	Mintage	VF20	XF40	MS60	MS63	MS65
ND (1997)	500	—	—	—	—	600
ND (1997)	2,000	PF65 600	PF67 625			

KM# 56 250 PESOS
31.10 g., 0.900 Gold 0.8999 oz. AGW **Subject:** Visit of Pope John Paul II

Date	Mintage	VF20	XF40	MS60	MS63	MS65
1979	1,000	—	—	—	1,500	1,550
1979	3,000	PF65 1,550	PF67 1,600			

KM# 68 500 PESOS
31.10 g., 0.999 Gold 0.9989 oz. AGW **Subject:** Discovery of America - Columbus

Date	Mintage	VF20	XF40	MS60	MS63	MS65
1988	2,600	PF65 1,700	PF67 1,750			

KM# 76 500 PESOS
31.10 g., 0.999 Gold 0.9989 oz. AGW **Subject:** 500th Anniversary - Discovery and Evangelization of America **Obv:** National arms, denomination below **Rev:** Portraits of Ferdinand and Isabella, date below

Date	Mintage	VF20	XF40	MS60	MS63	MS65
1989	600	PF65 1,750	PF67 1,800			

KM# 76a 500 PESOS
31.10 g., 0.999 Platinum 0.9989 oz. APW **Subject:** 500th Anniversary - Discovery and Evangelization of America **Obv:** National arms **Rev:** Portraits of Ferdinand and Isabella

Date	Mintage	VF20	XF40	MS60	MS63	MS65
1989	30	PF67 2,800				

KM# 79 500 PESOS
16.96 g., 0.917 Gold 0.500 oz. AGW **Subject:** 500th Anniversary - Discovery and Evangelization of America **Obv:** National arms, denomination below **Rev:** Santa Maria and landing crew, date below

Date	Mintage	VF20	XF40	MS60	MS63	MS65
1990	1,500	PF65 850	PF67 900			

KM# 79a 500 PESOS
15.55 g., 0.999 Platinum 0.4994 oz. APW **Subject:** 500th Anniversary - Discovery and Evangelization of America **Obv:** National arms **Rev:** Santa Maria and landing crew

Date	Mintage	VF20	XF40	MS60	MS63	MS65
1990	50	PF67 1,300				

KM# 85 500 PESOS
16.96 g., 0.917 Gold 0.500 oz. AGW **Subject:** 500th Anniversary - Discovery and Evangelization of America **Obv:** National arms, denomination below **Rev:** American fruits, date below

Date	Mintage	VF20	XF40	MS60	MS63	MS65
1991	1,500	PF65 850	PF67 900			

KM# 85a 500 PESOS
15.55 g., 0.999 Platinum 0.4994 oz. APW **Subject:** 500th Anniversary - Discovery and Evangelization of America **Obv:** National arms **Rev:** American fruits

Date	Mintage	VF20	XF40	MS60	MS63	MS65
1991	35	PF67 1,300				

KM# 86 500 PESOS
16.96 g., 0.917 Gold 0.500 oz. AGW **Subject:** 500th Anniversary - Discovery and Evangelization of America **Obv:** National arms, denomination below **Rev:** Enshrined tomb of Christopher Columbus, date below

Date	Mintage	VF20	XF40	MS60	MS63	MS65
1992	2,000	PF65 850	PF67 900			

KM# 86a 500 PESOS
15.50 g., 0.999 Platinum 0.4978 oz. APW **Subject:** 500th Anniversary - Discovery and Evangelization of America **Obv:** National arms **Rev:** Enshrined tomb of Christopher Columbus

Date	Mintage	VF20	XF40	MS60	MS63	MS65
1992	35	PF67 1,300				

KM# 108 2000 PESOS
62.77 g., 0.9167 Gold 1.8499 oz. AGW, 38 mm. **Subject:** Third Millennium of Christianity **Obv:** National arms **Rev:** Doves, globe **Rev. Legend:** TERCER MILENO - DEL CRISTIANISMO

Date	Mintage	VF20	XF40	MS60	MS63	MS65
2000	2,000	PF65 3,000	PF67 3,250			

KM# 109 2000 PESOS
31.16 g., 0.9995 Platinum 1.0013 oz. APW, 30 mm. **Subject:** Third Millenium of Christianity **Obv:** National arms **Rev:** Doves, globe **Rev. Legend:** TERCER MILENO - DEL CRISTIANISMO

Date	Mintage	VF20	XF40	MS60	MS63	MS65
2000	200	PF67 2,000				

PATTERNS

Including off metal strikes

KM#	Date	Mintage	Identification	Mkt Val
Pn6	1937	—	50 Centavos. Silver. Obverse only.	—
Pn7	1937	—	50 Centavos. Copper. Obverse only.	—
Pn8	1937	—	50 Centavos. Silver. Reverse only.	—
Pn9	1961	—	5 Centavos. Copper Bonded Steel.	—
Pn10	1961	—	5 Centavos. Copper Bonded Steel.	—
Pn11	1961	—	5 Centavos. Copper Bonded Steel. Same design both sides.	—
Pn12	1961	—	10 Centavos. Copper Bonded Steel.	—
Pn13	1961	—	25 Centavos. Chrome Plated Steel.	—
Pn14	1968	3	50 Centavos. Reeded edge.	—
Pn15	1972	1	25 Centavos. Reeded edge.	—
Pn16	1975	1	10 Pesos. Silver.	—
Pn17	1975	11	10 Pesos. 0.500. Gold.	1,000
Pn18	1975	1	10 Pesos. 0.294. Gold.	2,000
Pn19	1975	1	10 Pesos. 0.400. Gold.	2,000
Pn20	1975	1	10 Pesos. 0.800. Gold.	2,500
Pn21	1975	1	100 Pesos. 0.900. Gold. without matte details.	2,000
Pn22	1975	1	100 Pesos. 0.800. Gold. alloyed with .050 Silver and .150 Copper.	1,500
Pn23	1975	5	100 Pesos. 0.800. Gold. alloyed with .150 Silver.	1,000
Pn24	1975	5	100 Pesos. 0.800. Gold. alloyed with .150 Silver and .050 Copper, Proof.	1,000
Pn25	1976	3	10 Centavos. Plain rim.	600
Pn26	1977	5	30 Pesos. Gold. Proof.	—
Pn27	1978	3	Centavo. Aluminum.	—
Pn28	1978	3	Centavo. Copper and Zinc.	500
Pn29	1978	—	Centavo. 0.900. Silver.	500
Pn30	1978	—	5 Centavos. 0.900. Silver. Without memorial legend.	500
Pn31	1978	—	10 Centavos. 0.900. Silver. Without memorial legend.	500
Pn32	1978	3	25 Centavos. 6-1/2 Gramos.	600
Pn33	1978	—	25 Centavos. 0.900. Silver. Without memorial legend.	600
Pn34	1978	—	1/2 Peso. 0.900. Silver. Without memorial legend.	400
Pn35	1978	—	Peso. 0.900. Silver. Without memorial legend. Portrait of Duarte.	500
Pn36	1979	15	Centavo. 0.900. Silver.	400
Pn37	1979	—	5 Centavos. 0.900. Silver. Without memorial legend.	500
Pn38	1979	—	10 Centavos. 0.900. Silver. Without memorial legend.	500
Pn39	1979	3	25 Centavos. 6-1/2 Gramos.	300
Pn40	1979	—	25 Centavos. 0.900. Silver. Without memorial legend.	500
Pn41	1979	—	1/2 Peso. 0.900. Silver. Without memorial legend.	300
Pn42	1979	—	Peso. 0.900. Silver. Without memorial legend. Portrait of Duarte.	300
Pn43	1980	—	Centavo. 0.900. Silver.	250

KM#	Date	Mintage	Identification	Mkt Val
Pn44	1980	—	5 Centavos. 0.900. Silver. Without memorial legend.	400
Pn45	1980	—	10 Centavos. 0.900. Silver. Without memorial legend.	400
Pn46	1980	—	25 Centavos. 0.900. Silver. Without memorial legend.	400
Pn47	1980	—	1/2 Peso. 0.900. Silver. Without memorial legend.	400
Pn48	1980	—	Peso. 0.900. Silver. Without memorial legend. Portrait of Duarte.	400
Pn49	1981	—	Centavo. 0.900. Silver.	400
Pn50	1981	—	5 Centavos. 0.900. Silver. Without memorial legend.	400
Pn51	1981	—	10 Centavos. 0.900. Silver. Without memorial legend.	400
Pn52	1981	—	25 Centavos. 0.900. Silver. Without memorial legend.	400
Pn53	1981	—	1/2 Peso. 0.900. Silver. Without memorial legend.	400
Pn54	1981	—	Peso. 0.900. Silver. Without memorial legend. Portrait of Duarte.	500
Pn55	1982	80	10 Pesos. Silver. KM#57.	250
Pn56	1983	15	25 Centavos. Nickel Bonded Steel.	300
Pn57	1984	3	25 Centavos. Nickel Bonded Steel.	300
Pn58	1984	5	Peso. Nickel Bonded Steel.	300
Pn59	1986	500	Peso. Copper-Nickel.	300

Note: Several issues previously listed under Patterns have now been correctly identified as commercially inspired, privately contracted Medallic Issues and have been moved to that section. The remaining patterns have been renumbered

PIEDFORT

KM#	Date	Mintage	Identification	Mkt Val
P1	1977	5	30 Pesos. Gold. Piefort.	10,000
P2	1982	262	10 Pesos.	200
P3	1982	42	200 Pesos.	2,700
P4	1983 H	300	5 Centavos.	25.00
P5	1983 H	300	10 Centavos. Nickel Bonded Steel.	35.00
P6	1983	300	25 Centavos. Copper-Nickel. KM#61.	40.00
P7	1983 H	300	25 Centavos. Copper-Nickel.	40.00
P8	1983	300	1/2 Peso. Copper-Nickel. KM#62.	45.00
P9	1983	300	Peso. Copper-Nickel. KM#63.	55.00
P10	1984Mo	300	Centavo. KM64.	15.00
P11	1984Mo	300	5 Centavos. KM59.	15.00
P12	1984Mo	300	10 Centavos. KM60.	15.00
P13	1984Mo	300	25 Centavos. KM61.1.	25.00
P14	1984Mo	300	1/2 Peso. KM62.1.	15.00
P15	1984Mo	300	Peso. KM63.1.	27.00
P16	1986	300	Peso. Nickel Bonded Steel.	30.00
P17	1986	50	Peso. Copper-Nickel.	30.00
P18	1986	300	Centavo. Copper Plated Zinc.	15.00
P19	1986	300	5 Centavos. Copper-Nickel.	15.00
P20	1986	300	10 Centavos. Copper-Nickel.	20.00
P21	1986	300	25 Centavos. Copper-Nickel.	25.00
P22	1986	300	1/2 Peso. Copper-Nickel.	27.00
P23	1987	300	Centavo. 0.925. Silver.	30.00
P24	1987	300	5 Centavos. 0.925. Silver.	32.00
P25	1987	300	10 Centavos. 0.925. Silver.	35.00
P26	1987	300	25 Centavos. 0.925. Silver.	40.00
P27	1987	300	1/2 Peso. 0.925. Silver.	50.00
P28	1988	100	Peso. 0.999. Silver. KM#67.	70.00
P29	1988	100	100 Pesos. 0.999. Silver. KM#67.	350
P30	1989	300	Centavo. 0.925. Silver. KM#72a.	—
P31	1989	300	5 Centavos. 0.925. Silver. KM#69a.	—
P32	1989	300	10 Centavos. 0.925. Silver. KM#70a.	—
P33	1989	300	25 Centavos. 0.925. Silver. KM#71a.	—
P34	1989	300	1/2 Peso. 0.925. Silver. KM#73a.	—
P35	1989	10,000	Peso. 0.999. Silver. KM#74.	45.00
P36	1989	200	100 Pesos. 0.999. Silver. KM#75.	375
P37	1990	10,000	Peso. 0.999. Silver. KM#77.	45.00
P38	1990	200	100 Pesos. 0.999. Silver. KM#78.	325
P39	1991	10,000	Peso. 0.999. Silver. KM#81.	45.00
P40	1992	10,000	Peso. 0.999. Silver. KM#82.	45.00

MINT SETS

KM#	Date	Mintage	Identification	Issue Price	Mkt Val
MS1	1983 (5)	2,000	KM#59-63	10.00	45.00
MS2	1984 (6)	2,000	KM#59-64	—	10.00
MS3	1986 (5)	2,000	KM#59-62, 64	10.00	10.00
MS4	1987 (5)	1,000	KM#59-62, 64	10.00	30.00
MS5	1989 (5)	1,000	KM#69,70,71.1,72,73.1	—	14.00

PROOF SETS

KM#	Date	Mintage	Identification	Issue Price	Mkt Val
PS1	1937 (5)	—	KM#17-21	—	6,000
PS2	1972 (4)	500	KM#18, 20a.1, 31, 34	20.00	90.00
PS3	1973 (2)	500	KM#19a, 21a.2	5.00	50.00
PS4	1974 (2)	500	KM#18, 20a.2	5.00	35.00
PS5	1974 (2)	500	KM#35-36	120	710
PS6	1975 (2)	500	KM#38-39	200	745
PS7	1976 (6)	5,000	KM#40-45	10.00	20.00
PS8	1978 (6)	5,000	KM#48-53	10.00	20.00
PS9	1978 (6)	15	KM#Pn29-31, Pn33-35	175	2,200
PS10	1979 (6)	500	KM#48-53	15.00	140
PS11	1979 (6)	15	KM#Pn36-38, Pn40-42	255	2,200
PS12	1980 (6)	3,000	KM#48-53	15.00	22.50
PS13	1980 (6)	15	KM#Pn43-48	255	1,500
PS14	1981 (6)	3,000	KM#48-53	15.00	22.50
PS15	1981 (6)	15	KM#Pn49-54	300	1,500
PS16	1983 (2)	1,600	KM#59-60	10.00	10.00
PS17	1983 (2)	300	KM-P4, P5	25.00	50.00
PS18	1983 (2)	100	KM#59a, 60a	45.00	60.00
PS19	1983 (3)	1,570	KM#61-63	20.00	38.00
PS20	1983 (3)	270	KM-P7, 8, 9	45.00	125
PS21	1983 (3)	70	KM#61.1a-63.1a	125	190
PS22	1984 (6)	1,570	KM#59-64	20.00	45.00
PS23	1984 (6)	270	KM-P10, 11, 12, 13, 14, 15	30.00	85.00
PS24	1984 (6)	70	KM#59a-60a, 61.1a, 62.1a, 63.1a, 64a	250	270
PS25	1986 (5)	1,570	KM#59-62, 64	30.00	30.00
PS26	1986 (4)	270	KM-P17, 19, 20, 21, 22	40.00	75.00
PS28	1987 (6)	1,600	KM#59-62, 64	—	32.50
PS29	1987 (5)	300	KM-P23, 24, 25, 26, 27	—	165
PS30	1989 (5)	2,500	KM#69a-70a, 71.1a, 72a, 73.1a	—	—
PS31	1989 (5)	300	KM-P30, 31, 32, 33, 34	—	—
PS32	2000 (13)	—	KM#91-103	—	225

SPECIAL SETS

KM#	Date	Mintage	Identification	Issue Price	Mkt Val
SS1	1983 (15)	30	KM#61-63, 61a-63a, all mint marks, including Piefort	200	300
SS2	1984 (24)	30	KM#59-64, including Piefort	400	400
SS3	1986 (20)	30	KM#59-64	300	300
SS4	1986 (2)	1,700	KM65, Proof & Unc.	35.00	25.00
SS5	1986 (3)	300	KM#65, Proof & Unc., KM-P16	75.00	45.00
SS6	1986 (2)	23	KM#65a, Proof & Unc.	—	—
SS7	1986 (3)	25	KM#65a, Proof & Unc., KM-P17	—	—
SS8	1986 (3)	25	KM#65b, Proof & Unc., P#17	—	—
SS9	1986 (3)	25	KM#65b, Proof & Unc., P#17	—	—
SS10	1987 (15)	100	KM#59-62, 64, KM-P23, 24, 25, 26, 27	—	200
SS11	1989 (9)	100	KM#69-73, KM-P31, 32, 33, 34, 35	—	200

EAST AFRICA

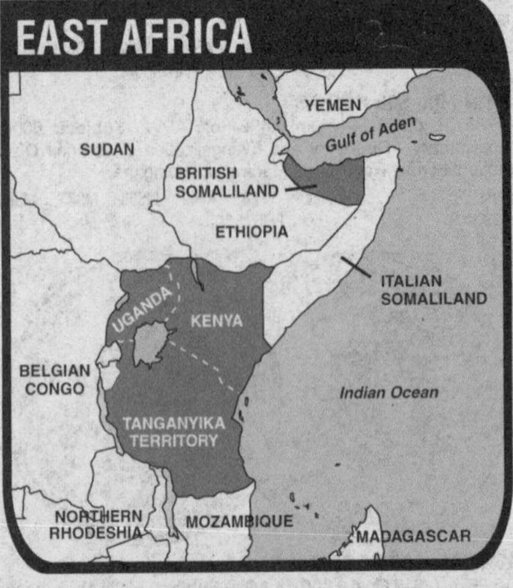

East Africa was an administrative grouping of five separate British territories: Kenya, Uganda, the Sultanate of Zanzibar and British Somaliland.

The common interest of Kenya, Tanganyika and Uganda invited cooperation in economic matters and consideration of political union. The territorial governors, organized as the East Africa High Commission, met periodically to administer such common activities as taxation, industrial development and education. The authority of the Commission did not infringe upon the constitution and internal autonomy of the individual colonies. A common coinage and banknotes, which were also legal tender in Aden, were provided for use of the member colonies by the East Africa Currency Board. The coinage through 1919 had the legend "East Africa and Uganda Protectorate".

NOTE: For later coinage see Kenya, Tanzania and Uganda.

RULER

British

MINT MARKS

A - Ackroyd & Best, Morley
I - Bombay Mint
H - Heaton Mint, Birmingham, England
K, KN - King's Norton Mint, Birmingham, England
SA - Pretoria Mint, South Africa
No mint mark – British Royal Mint, London

EAST AFRICA AND UGANDA PROTECTORATES

DECIMAL COINAGE

50 Cents = 1 Shilling; 100 Cents = 1 Florin

KM# 6 1/2 CENT

Aluminum **Ruler:** Edward VII **Edge:** Plain

Date	Mintage	F12	VF20	XF40	MS60	MS63
1908	900,000	15.00	25.00	75.00	200	300

KM# 6a 1/2 CENT

Copper-Nickel **Ruler:** Edward VII **Obv:** Center hole divides crown and denomination, fleurs flank **Rev:** Tusks flank center hole, denomination above, circle surrounds **Edge:** Plain

Date	Mintage	VF20	XF40	MS60	MS63	MS65
1909	900,000	12.00	35.00	75.00	135	200

KM# 5 CENT

Aluminum **Ruler:** Edward VII **Obv:** Center hole divides crown and denomination, fleurs flank **Rev:** Tusks flank center hole, denomination above, circle surrounds **Edge:** Plain

Date	Mintage	F12	VF20	XF40	MS60	MS63
1907	6,948,000	5.00	10.00	30.00	80.00	150
1907	—	PF63 1,250	PF65 3,250			
1908	2,871,000	8.00	16.00	35.00	100	175

KM# 5a CENT

2.88 g., Copper-Nickel, 22.35 mm. **Ruler:** Edward VII **Obv:** Center hole divides crown and denomination, fleurs flank **Rev:** Tusks flank center hole, denomination above, circle surrounds **Edge:** Plain

Date	Mintage	VF20	XF40	MS60	MS63	MS65
1909	25,000,000	1.25	3.00	7.00	12.00	20.00
1910	6,000,000	1.25	4.00	12.00	15.00	25.00

KM# 7 CENT

Copper-Nickel **Ruler:** George V **Obv:** Center hole divides crown and denomination, fleurs flank **Rev:** Tusks flank center hole, denomination above, circle surrounds **Edge:** Plain

Date	Mintage	F12	VF20	XF40	MS60	MS63
1911 H	25,000,000	0.25	1.00	5.00	15.00	35.00
1912 H	20,000,000	0.25	1.00	3.00	8.00	20.00
1913	4,529,000	0.75	1.50	8.00	20.00	40.00
1914 S	6,000,000	0.75	1.75	5.00	15.00	35.00
1914 H	2,500,000	1.00	3.00	8.00	20.00	40.00
1916 H	1,824,000	1.25	4.00	10.00	25.00	50.00
1917 H	3,176,000	0.75	2.00	5.00	15.00	35.00
1918 H	10,000,000	0.50	1.00	3.25	12.00	30.00

KM# A11 5 CENTS
Copper-Nickel **Ruler:** Edward VII

Date	Mintage	VF20	XF40	MS60	MS63	MS65
1907 Rare	—	—	—	—	—	—

KM# 11 5 CENTS
Copper-Nickel **Ruler:** George V **Obv:** Center hole divides crown and denomination, fleurs flank **Rev:** Tusks flank center hole, denomination above, circle surrounds **Edge:** Plain

Date	Mintage	F12	VF20	XF40	MS60	MS63
1913 H	300,000	1.50	4.00	20.00	35.00	90.00
1914 K	1,240,000	0.75	3.25	12.00	22.50	35.00
1914 K	—	PF63 200				
Note: The 1914K was issued with British West Africa KM#8 in a double (4 pieces) Specimen Set						
1919 H	200,000	10.00	15.00	40.00	120	220

KM# 2 10 CENTS
Copper-Nickel **Ruler:** Edward VII **Obv:** Center hole divides crown and denomination, fleurs flank **Rev:** Tusks flank center hole, denomination above, circle surrounds **Edge:** Plain

Date	Mintage	F12	VF20	XF40	MS60	MS63
1906	—	1,200	1,700	2,500	4,000	—
1907	1,000,000	1.50	4.00	16.00	30.00	50.00
1907	—	PF63 850				
1910	500,000	6.00	12.00	75.00	200	350

KM# 8 10 CENTS
Copper-Nickel **Ruler:** George V **Obv:** Center hole divides crown and denomination, fleurs flank **Rev:** Tusks flank center hole, denomination above, circle surrounds **Edge:** Plain

Date	Mintage	F12	VF20	XF40	MS60	MS63
1911 H	1,250,000	2.00	5.00	25.00	40.00	90.00
1912 H	1,050,000	2.00	5.00	30.00	55.00	120
1913	50,000	75.00	150	300	700	—
1918 H	400,000	10.00	20.00	80.00	150	285

KM# 3 25 CENTS
2.92 g., 0.800 Silver 0.075 oz. ASW **Ruler:** Edward VII **Obv:** Bust of King Edward VII right **Rev:** Lion and mountains within 3/4 circle with fleur ends, denomination and date below **Edge:** Reeded

Date	Mintage	F12	VF20	XF40	MS60	MS63
1906	400,000	3.00	7.00	35.00	60.00	100
1906 Proof	—	—	—	—	—	—
1910 H	200,000	4.00	8.00	50.00	90.00	150

KM# 10 25 CENTS
2.92 g., 0.800 Silver 0.075 oz. ASW **Ruler:** George V **Obv:** Bust of King George V left **Rev:** Lion and mountains within 3/4 circle with fleur ends, date and denomination below **Edge:** Reeded

Date	Mintage	F12	VF20	XF40	MS60	MS63
1912	180,000	4.00	15.00	45.00	80.00	120
1913	300,000	3.50	10.00	35.00	60.00	90.00
1914 H	80,000	20.00	35.00	60.00	100	170
1914 H	—	PF63 400				
1918 H	40,000	150	300	500	900	—

KM# 4 50 CENTS
5.83 g., 0.800 Silver 0.150 oz. ASW **Ruler:** Edward VII **Obv:** Bust of King Edward VII right **Rev:** Lion and mountains within circle with fleur ends, denomination and date below **Edge:** Reeded

Date	Mintage	F12	VF20	XF40	MS60	MS63
1906	200,000	6.00	30.00	80.00	120	200
1906	—	PF63 400				
1909	100,000	15.00	50.00	155	300	—
1910	100,000	10.00	45.00	100	175	250

KM# 9 50 CENTS
5.83 g., 0.800 Silver 0.150 oz. ASW **Ruler:** George V **Obv:** Bust of King George V left **Rev:** Lion and mountains within circle with fleur ends, denomination and date below **Edge:** Reeded

Date	Mintage	F12	VF20	XF40	MS60	MS63
1911	150,000	7.50	35.00	85.00	140	225
1911	—	PF63 250				
1912	100,000	8.00	45.00	75.00	125	200
1913	200,000	6.00	30.00	65.00	100	175
1914 H	180,000	6.00	30.00	65.00	100	175
1918 H	60,000	60.00	200	350	500	—
1919	100,000	250	350	900	1,500	—

BRITISH COLONIES

KM# 12 CENT
Copper-Nickel **Ruler:** George V **Obv:** Center hole divides crown and denomination, fleurs flank **Rev:** Tusks flank center hole, denomination above, circle surrounds **Edge:** Plain

Date	Mintage	F12	VF20	XF40	MS60	MS63
1920 H	Est. 2908000	30.00	60.00	110	275	450
Note: Only about 30% of the total mintage was released into circulation						
1920 H	—	PF63 575				
Note: 20-30 pcs						
1920	—	—	—	—	750	—
1921	920,000	—	—	—	4,500	—
Note: Not released for circulation						

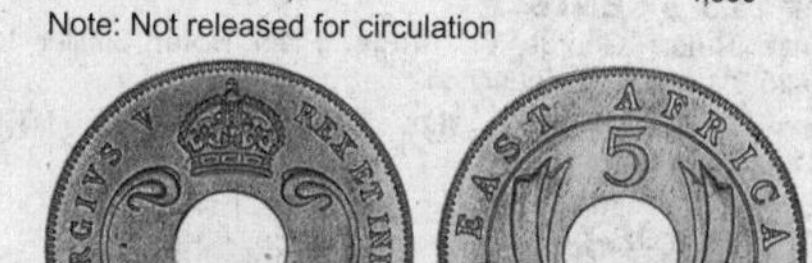

KM# 13 5 CENTS
Copper-Nickel **Ruler:** George V **Obv:** Center hole divides crown and denomination, fleurs flank **Rev:** Tusks flank center hole, denomination above, circle surrounds **Edge:** Plain

Date	Mintage	F12	VF20	XF40	MS60	MS63
1920 H	Est. 550000	75.00	150	225	325	450
Note: Only about 30% of the total mintage was released into circulation						
1920 H	—	PF63 575				
Note: 20-30 pcs						

KM# 14 10 CENTS
Copper-Nickel **Ruler:** George V **Obv:** Center hole divides crown and denomination, fleurs flank **Rev:** Tusks flank center hole, denomination above, circle surrounds **Edge:** Plain

Date	Mintage	F12	VF20	XF40	MS60	MS63
1920 H	Est. 700000	120	150	225	400	800
1920 H	—	PF63 700				
Note: 20-30 pcs						

KM# 15 25 CENTS
2.92 g., 0.500 Silver 0.0469 oz. ASW **Ruler:** George V **Obv:** Bust of King George V left **Rev:** Lion and mountains within circle with fleur ends, date and denomination below **Edge:** Reeded

Date	Mintage	F12	VF20	XF40	MS60	MS63
1920 H	748,000	25.00	35.00	75.00	150	225
1920 H	—	PF63 275				
Note: 20-30 pieces						

KM# 16 50 CENTS
5.83 g., 0.500 Silver 0.0937 oz. ASW **Ruler:** George V **Obv:** Bust of King George V left **Rev:** Lion and mountains within circle with fleur ends, date and denomination below **Edge:** Reeded **Note:** Not released for circulation.

Date	Mintage	F12	VF20	XF40	MS60	MS63
1920 A	12,000	1,500	2,000	3,000	4,000	—
1920 H	62,000	500	1,000	1,500	2,500	3,500
1920 H	—	PF63 4,000				
Note: 20-30 pieces						

KM# 17 FLORIN
11.66 g., 0.500 Silver 0.1875 oz. ASW **Ruler:** George V **Obv:** Bust of King George V left **Rev:** Lion and mountains within circle with fleur ends, denomination and date below **Edge:** Reeded

Date	Mintage	F12	VF20	XF40	MS60	MS63
1920	1,479,000	15.00	75.00	200	325	450
1920 A	542,000	200	500	1,100	2,000	—
1920 H	9,689,000	12.50	60.00	125	225	325
1920 H	—	PF63 800				
Note: 20-30 pieces						
1921	2	—	—	—	4,500	—

REFORM COINAGE

Commencing May 1921; 100 Cents = 1 Shilling

KM# 22 CENT
1.91 g., Bronze **Ruler:** George V **Obv:** Center hole divides crown and denomination, fleurs flank **Rev:** Tusks flank center hole, denomination above, circle surrounds **Edge:** Plain

Date	Mintage	F12	VF20	XF40	MS60	MS63
1922	8,250,000	0.25	1.00	8.00	15.00	22.00
1922 H	43,750,000	0.25	0.50	3.50	6.50	9.00

Date	Mintage	F12	VF20	XF40	MS60	MS63
1923	50,000,000	0.25	0.50	3.50	6.50	9.00
1924	Inc. above	0.25	0.75	5.00	10.00	15.00
1924 H	17,500,000	0.25	0.75	4.00	8.00	11.00
1924 KN	10,720,000	0.25	0.75	4.00	8.00	11.00
1924 KN	—	PF60 125	PF63 225	PF65 350		
1925	6,000,000	40.00	90.00	175	250	375
1925 KN	6,780,000	2.00	4.00	18.00	35.00	52.00
1927	10,000,000	0.25	0.75	5.00	10.00	15.00
1927	—	PF60 125	PF63 225			
1928 H	12,000,000	0.25	0.75	4.00	8.00	11.00
1928 KN	11,764,000	0.50	2.00	8.00	18.00	27.00
1928 KN	—	PF60 125	PF63 225			
1930	15,000,000	0.25	0.75	2.50	5.00	8.00
1930	—	PF60 150	PF63 300			
1935	10,000,000	0.25	0.50	1.75	3.50	6.00

KM# 29 CENT

1.95 g., Bronze **Ruler:** George VI **Obv:** Center hole divides crown and denomination, fleurs flank **Rev:** Tusks flank center hole, denomination above, circle surrounds **Edge:** Plain

Date	Mintage	VF20	XF40	MS60	MS63	MS65
1942	25,000,000	0.25	1.25	2.50	4.00	6.00
1942 I	15,000,000	0.30	1.50	3.00	5.00	7.00

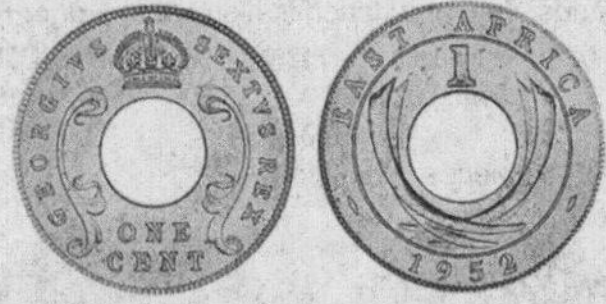

KM# 32 CENT

1.70 g., Bronze **Ruler:** George VI **Obv:** Center hole divides crown and denomination, fleurs flank **Obv. Legend:** ET IND. IMP. dropped from legend **Rev:** Tusks flank center hole, denomination above, circle surrounds **Edge:** Plain

Date	Mintage	VF20	XF40	MS60	MS63	MS65
1949	4,000,000	0.75	2.00	4.00	8.00	10.00
1949	—	PF63 225				
1950	16,000,000	0.25	1.25	2.50	3.50	5.00
1950	—	PF63 300				
1951 H	9,000,000	0.25	1.25	2.50	3.50	5.00
1951 H	—	PF63 225				
1951 KN	11,140,000	0.25	1.25	2.50	3.50	5.00
1951 KN	—	PF63 225				
1952	7,000,000	0.25	1.25	2.50	3.50	5.00
1952	—	PF63 300				
1952 H	13,000,000	0.25	1.25	2.50	3.50	5.00
1952 H	—	PF63 225				
1952 KN	5,230,000	0.35	1.50	4.00	8.00	10.00

KM# 35 CENT

2.00 g., Bronze, 20 mm. **Ruler:** Elizabeth II **Obv:** Center hole divides crown and denomination, fleurs flank **Rev:** Tusks flank center hole, denomination above, circle surrounds **Edge:** Plain

Date	Mintage	VF20	XF40	MS60	MS63	MS65
1954	8,000,000	0.25	0.85	2.50	3.50	5.00
1954	—	PF63 275				
1955	5,000,000	0.25	0.50	1.75	2.25	3.00
1955	—	PF63 300				
1955 H	6,384,000	0.20	0.65	1.75	2.25	3.00
1955 KN	4,000,000	0.20	0.65	1.75	2.25	3.00
1956 H	15,616,000	0.15	0.30	1.25	2.00	3.00
1956 KN	9,680,000	0.20	0.40	1.25	2.00	3.00
1957	15,000,000	0.20	0.65	1.75	2.25	3.00
1957 H	5,000,000	3.00	6.00	12.00	15.00	22.00
1957 KN	Inc. above	0.20	0.65	1.75	2.25	3.00
1959 H	10,000,000	0.20	0.40	1.25	2.00	3.00
1959 KN	10,000,000	0.20	0.40	1.25	2.00	3.00
1961	1,800,000	0.40	2.00	3.50	5.00	7.00
1961	—	PF63 250	PF65 500			
1961 H	1,800,000	0.40	2.00	3.50	5.00	7.00
1962 H	10,320,000	0.20	0.40	1.25	2.00	3.00

KM# 18 5 CENTS

6.50 g., Bronze, 25.3 mm. **Ruler:** George V **Edge:** Plain

Date	Mintage	F12	VF20	XF40	MS60	MS63
1921	1,000,000	2.00	4.00	15.00	32.00	50.00
1922	2,500,000	0.50	1.25	4.50	12.50	15.00
1923	2,400,000	0.50	1.25	6.00	15.00	18.00
1923	—	PF60 150	PF63 300			
1924	4,800,000	0.50	1.00	5.00	15.00	21.00
1925	6,600,000	0.50	1.00	4.00	10.00	15.00
1925	—	PF60 125	PF63 250			
1928	1,200,000	1.50	3.00	10.00	25.00	35.00
1928	—	PF60 150	PF63 300			
1933	5,000,000	0.50	1.00	5.00	10.00	15.00
1934	3,910,000	0.50	1.00	7.50	15.00	21.00
1934	—	PF60 165	PF63 350			
1935	5,800,000	0.50	1.00	5.00	10.00	15.00
1935	—	PF60 185	PF63 375			
1936	1,000,000	2.00	5.00	20.00	35.00	65.00

KM# 23 5 CENTS

6.70 g., Bronze, 26 mm. **Ruler:** Edward VIII **Obv:** Center hole divides crown and denomination, fleurs flank **Rev:** Tusks flank center hole, denomination above, circle surrounds **Edge:** Plain

Date	Mintage	VF20	XF40	MS60	MS63	MS65
1936 H	3,500,000	0.50	2.00	5.50	7.50	10.00
1936 H	—	PF63 175				
1936 KN	2,150,000	0.50	2.00	5.50	7.50	10.00
1936 KN	—	PF63 175				

KM# 25.1 5 CENTS

6.32 g., Bronze **Ruler:** George VI **Obv:** Center hole divides crown and denomination, fleurs flank **Rev:** Tusks flank center hole, denomination above, circle surrounds **Edge:** Plain **Note:** Thick flan.

Date	Mintage	VF20	XF40	MS60	MS63	MS65
1937 H	3,000,000	1.00	2.00	4.00	7.00	9.00
1937 KN	3,000,000	1.00	2.00	5.00	8.00	10.00
1939 H	2,000,000	1.00	5.00	12.50	17.50	20.00
1939 KN	2,000,000	1.00	5.00	12.50	17.50	20.00
1941	—	10.00	20.00	35.00	55.00	75.00
1941 I	20,000,000	1.00	2.00	4.00	7.00	9.00

KM# 25.2 5 CENTS

5.67 g., Bronze **Ruler:** George VI **Obv:** Center hole divides crown and denomination, fleurs flank **Rev:** Tusks flank center hole, denomination above, circle surrounds **Edge:** Plain **Note:** Thin flan, reduced weight.

Date	Mintage	VF20	XF40	MS60	MS63	MS65
1941 I	Inc. above	1.00	2.00	4.00	7.00	9.00
1942	16,000,000	1.00	2.00	4.00	7.00	9.00
1942 SA	4,120,000	6.00	12.00	25.00	40.00	55.00
1943 SA	17,880,000	0.25	0.50	1.00	2.00	4.00

KM# 25.3 5 CENTS

Bronze **Ruler:** George VI **Edge:** Plain **Note:** Similar to KM#25.2, but hole not punched.

Date	Mintage	VF20	XF40	MS60	MS63	MS65
1942	—	—	—	100	—	—

KM# 33 5 CENTS

5.55 g., Bronze, 25.5 mm. **Ruler:** George VI **Obv:** Center hole divides crown and denomination, fleurs flank **Obv. Legend:** ET IND. IMP. dropped from legend **Rev:** Tusks flank center hole, denomination above, circle surrounds **Edge:** Plain

Date	Mintage	VF20	XF40	MS60	MS63	MS65
1949	4,000,000	0.50	3.00	5.00	7.00	10.00
1949	—	PF63 200				
1951 H	6,000,000	0.50	2.00	4.00	6.00	8.00
1951 H	—	PF63 200				
1952	11,200,000	0.40	1.00	2.00	3.00	6.00
1952	—	PF63 300				

KM# 37 5 CENTS

5.77 g., Bronze **Ruler:** Elizabeth II **Obv:** Center hole divides crown and denomination, fleurs flank **Rev:** Tusks flank center hole, denomination above, circle surrounds **Edge:** Plain

Date	Mintage	VF20	XF40	MS60	MS63	MS65
1955	2,000,000	0.25	0.75	1.25	2.00	3.50
1955	—	PF63 200				
1955 H	4,000,000	0.50	1.25	1.75	3.50	5.00
1955 H	—	PF63 200				
1955 KN	2,000,000	0.80	2.50	3.00	5.00	8.00
1956 H	3,000,000	0.35	1.00	2.00	3.00	5.00
1956 KN	3,000,000	3.00	5.00	7.00	10.00	15.00
1956 KN	—	PF63 175				
1957 H	5,000,000	0.25	0.75	1.25	2.00	3.50
1957 KN	5,000,000	0.25	0.75	1.25	2.00	3.50
1961 H	4,000,000	0.35	1.00	2.00	3.00	5.50
1963	12,600,000	0.10	0.30	0.50	0.75	1.50
1963	—	PF63 200				

KM# 39 5 CENTS

5.69 g., Bronze **Obv:** Fleurs flank center hole, country name below, denomination above and right **Rev:** Tusks flank center hole, denomination above, circle surrounds **Edge:** Plain **Note:** Post-independence issue.

Date	Mintage	VF20	XF40	MS60	MS63	MS65
1964	7,600,000	0.10	0.20	0.50	0.75	1.00

KM# 19 10 CENTS

11.14 g., Bronze **Ruler:** George V **Obv:** Center hole divides crown and denomination, fleurs flank **Rev:** Tusks flank center hole, denomination above, circle surrounds **Edge:** Plain

Date	Mintage	F12	VF20	XF40	MS60	MS63
1921	130,000	5.00	20.00	45.00	75.00	135
1922	7,120,000	1.00	3.00	8.00	20.00	35.00
1923	1,200,000	1.25	4.00	20.00	40.00	55.00
1924	4,900,000	0.65	2.25	14.00	25.00	40.00
1925	4,800,000	0.65	2.25	14.00	25.00	40.00
1927	2,000,000	0.75	2.50	12.50	20.00	35.00
1928	3,800,000	0.75	2.50	15.00	30.00	45.00
1928	—	PF60 135	PF63 175			
1933	6,260,000	0.75	2.50	6.50	17.50	25.00
1934	3,649,000	0.75	2.50	15.00	30.00	45.00
1935	7,300,000	0.65	2.00	8.00	18.00	25.00
1936	500,000	1.50	15.00	30.00	50.00	—

KM# 24 10 CENTS

10.74 g., Bronze, 30.5 mm. **Ruler:** Edward VIII **Obv:** Center hole divides crown and denomination, fleurs flank **Rev:** Tusks flank center hole, denomination above, circle surrounds **Edge:** Plain **Note:** For listing of mule dated 1936H with obverse of KM#24 and reverse of British West Africa KM#16 refer to British West Africa listings.

Date	Mintage	VF20	XF40	MS60	MS63	MS65
1936	2,000,000	3.50	8.00	25.00	30.00	45.00
1936	—	PF63 200				

Date	Mintage	VF20	XF40	MS60	MS63	MS65
1936 H	4,330,000	0.50	1.50	6.50	8.50	12.00
1936 H	—	PF63 325				
1936 KN	4,142,000	0.50	1.50	6.50	8.50	12.00
1936 KN	—	PF63 145				

KM# 24a 10 CENTS

Copper-Nickel **Ruler:** Edward VIII **Obv:** Center hole divides crown and denomination, fleurs flank **Rev:** Tusks flank center hole, denomination above, circle surrounds **Edge:** Plain

Date	Mintage	VF20	XF40	MS60	MS63	MS65
1936 KN	—	—	—	—	—	—

KM# 26.1 10 CENTS

11.34 g., Bronze **Ruler:** George VI **Obv:** Center hole divides crown and denomination, fleurs flank **Rev:** Tusks flank center hole, denomination above, circle surrounds **Edge:** Plain **Note:** Thick flan.

Date	Mintage	VF20	XF40	MS60	MS63	MS65
1937	2,000,000	0.75	2.50	5.00	7.00	9.00
1937	—	PF63 175				
1937 H	2,500,000	0.75	2.50	7.00	10.00	13.00
1937 H	—	PF63 175				
1937 KN	2,500,000	0.75	2.50	7.00	10.00	13.00
1937 KN	—	PF63 175				
1939 H	2,000,000	0.70	5.50	12.00	15.00	20.00
1939 KN	2,029,999	0.70	5.50	12.00	15.00	20.00
1939 KN	—	PF63 175				
1941 I	15,682,000	1.00	6.00	13.00	16.00	23.00
1941 I	—	PF63 175				
1941	—	1.50	7.50	15.00	20.00	25.00
1941	—	PF63 175				

KM# 26.2 10 CENTS

Bronze **Ruler:** George VI **Obv:** Center hole divides crown and denomination, fleurs flank **Rev:** Tusks flank center hole, denomination above, circle surrounds **Edge:** Plain **Note:** Thin flan, reduced weight.

Date	Mintage	VF20	XF40	MS60	MS63	MS65
1942	12,000,000	0.50	1.75	4.00	7.00	10.00
1942	—	PF63 175				
1942 I	4,317,000	5.00	10.00	20.00	28.00	45.00
1943 SA	14,093,000	0.50	4.50	10.00	15.00	25.00
1945 SA	5,000,000	0.50	5.00	12.50	16.00	27.00

KM# 34 10 CENTS

9.50 g., Bronze **Ruler:** George VI **Obv:** Center hole divides crown and denomination, fleurs flank **Obv. Legend:** ET IND. IMP. dropped from legend **Rev:** Tusks flank center hole, denomination above, circle surrounds **Edge:** Plain

Date	Mintage	VF20	XF40	MS60	MS63	MS65
1949	4,000,000	2.50	5.00	12.00	15.00	22.00
1949	—	PF63 175				
1950	8,000,000	0.40	1.75	4.00	7.00	10.00
1950	—	PF63 200				
1951	14,500,000	0.40	1.25	3.00	6.00	9.00
1951	—	PF63 175				
1952	15,800,000	0.40	1.25	3.00	6.00	9.00
1952	—	PF63 250				
1952 H	2,000,000	5.00	10.00	20.00	25.00	30.00

KM# 38 10 CENTS

9.36 g., Bronze **Ruler:** Elizabeth II **Obv:** Center hole divides crown and denomination, fleurs flank **Rev:** Tusks flank center hole, denomination above, circle surrounds **Edge:** Plain

Date	Mintage	VF20	XF40	MS60	MS63	MS65
1956	6,001,000	1.00	2.50	8.00	10.00	15.00
1956	—	PF63 175				
1964 H Rare	—	—	—	—	—	—

KM# 40 10 CENTS

9.40 g., Bronze **Obv:** Fleurs flank center hole, country name below, denomination above and right **Rev:** Tusks flank center hole, denomination above, circle surrounds **Edge:** Plain **Note:** Post-independence issue.

Date	Mintage	VF20	XF40	MS60	MS63	MS65
1964 H	10,002,000	0.15	0.30	1.00	1.50	2.00

KM# 20 50 CENTS

3.89 g., 0.250 Silver 0.0312 oz. ASW **Ruler:** George V **Obv:** Crowned bust of King George V left **Rev:** Lion and mountains within 3/4 circle with fleur ends, date below divides denominations **Edge:** Reeded

Date	Mintage	F12	VF20	XF40	MS60	MS63
1921	6,200,000	1.25	5.00	17.50	30.00	45.00
1922	Inc. above	1.25	4.00	16.00	27.50	40.00
1923	396,000	5.00	18.00	45.00	80.00	150
1924	1,000,000	2.00	14.00	25.00	40.00	60.00

KM# 27 50 CENTS

3.89 g., 0.250 Silver 0.0312 oz. ASW **Ruler:** George VI **Obv:** Crowned head of King George VI left **Rev:** Lion and mountains within 3/4 circle with fleur ends, date and denomination below and right **Edge:** Reeded

Date	Mintage	VF20	XF40	MS60	MS63	MS65
1937 H	4,000,000	1.75	5.50	12.50	25.00	50.00
1937 H	—	PF63 275				
1942 H	5,000,000	1.75	9.00	20.00	30.00	60.00
1943 I	2,000,000	5.00	17.50	30.00	45.00	85.00
1944 SA	1,000,000	6.00	18.00	32.50	50.00	95.00

KM# 30 50 CENTS

3.89 g., Copper-Nickel **Ruler:** George VI **Obv:** Crowned head of King George VI left **Obv. Legend:** ET INDIA IMPERATOR dropped from legend **Rev:** Lion and mountains within 3/4 circle with fleur ends, date divides denominations below **Edge:** Reeded

Date	Mintage	VF20	XF40	MS60	MS63	MS65
1948	7,290,000	0.40	2.00	5.00	7.00	10.00
1948	—	PF63 250				
1949	12,960,000	0.30	1.50	4.00	8.00	10.00
1949	—	PF63 325				
1952 KN	2,000,000	0.40	2.00	5.00	8.00	10.00

KM# 36 50 CENTS

4.00 g., Copper-Nickel, 21 mm. **Ruler:** Elizabeth II **Obv:** Crowned bust right **Rev:** Lion and mountains within 3/4 circle with fleur ends, date divides denominations below **Edge:** Reeded **Note:** The KHN mint marks exist because the master dies were produced with both the KN and H mint marks for use at either mint. Each mint was required to remove the other's mint mark before striking, but this was not always meticulously done. When one or the other mint mark was not fully removed a weak trace would remain creating the appearance of a wide space K N with a weak H in the middle or an H flanked by a weak K and N, in the field below the lion.

Date	Mintage	VF20	XF40	MS60	MS63	MS65
1954	3,720,000	0.35	1.00	3.00	5.00	8.00
1954	—	PF63 225				
1955 H	1,600,000	3.00	5.00	7.00	12.00	15.00
1955 H	—	PF63 225				
1955 KHN	—	20.00	55.00	75.00	95.00	—
1955 KN	—	0.35	1.75	3.00	5.00	8.00
1956 H	2,000,000	0.25	1.25	2.50	4.00	8.00
1956 H	—	PF63 225				
1956 KHN	—	20.00	35.00	55.00	75.00	—
1956 KN	2,000,000	0.35	1.75	3.00	5.00	8.00
1958 H	2,600,000	0.40	2.00	4.00	6.00	9.00
1958 KHN	—	20.00	55.00	75.00	95.00	—
1960	4,000,000	0.25	1.25	2.50	4.00	8.00
1962 KN	4,000,000	0.35	1.75	3.00	5.00	8.00
1963	6,000,000	0.25	1.25	2.50	4.00	8.00

KM# 21 SHILLING

7.78 g., 0.250 Silver 0.0625 oz. ASW, 27.8 mm. **Ruler:** George V **Obv:** Bust of King George V left **Edge:** Reeded

Date	Mintage	F12	VF20	XF40	MS60	MS63
1921	6,141,000	3.50	6.75	18.00	30.00	45.00
1921 H	4,240,000	3.00	4.00	25.00	40.00	60.00
1922	18,858,000	3.50	3.25	14.00	28.00	40.00
1922 H	20,052,000	3.50	3.25	14.00	28.00	40.00
1923	4,000,000	5.00	10.00	30.00	45.00	60.00
1924	44,604,000	2.25	3.00	8.00	18.00	25.00
1925	28,405,000	2.25	3.00	8.00	20.00	30.00
1925	—	PF60 225	PF63 250			

KM# 28.1 SHILLING

7.60 g., 0.250 Silver 0.0611 oz. ASW, 27.7 mm. **Ruler:** George VI **Obv:** Crowned head of King George VI left **Rev:** Lion and mountains within 3/4 circle with fleur ends, date divides denominations below **Edge:** Reeded **Note:** REV; Type I, thin rim and short milling, EAST AFRICA further from edge than Type II, larger loop on right side of coin below diamond in legend. Edge reeding spaced out

Date	Mintage	VF20	XF40	MS60	MS63	MS65
1937 H	7,672,000	3.00	7.00	15.00	25.00	40.00
1937 H	—	PF63 300				
1941 I	7,000,000	3.00	7.00	20.00	30.00	50.00
1942 H	4,430,000	3.00	7.00	20.00	30.00	50.00
1942 H	—	PF63 300				
1944 H	10,000,000	3.00	7.00	25.00	40.00	65.00

KM# 28.2 SHILLING

7.78 g., 0.250 Silver 0.0625 oz. ASW **Ruler:** George VI **Obv:** Crowned head left **Rev:** Type II, thicker rim and larger milling, EAST AFRICA and leaves very near the edge, small leaf (loop) under diamond on right side **Edge:** Reeded

Date	Mintage	VF20	XF40	MS60	MS63	MS65
1941 I Rare	—	—	—	—	—	—

KM# 28.3 SHILLING

7.78 g., 0.250 Silver 0.0625 oz. ASW **Ruler:** George VI **Obv:** Crowned head left **Rev:** Type III, retouched central image, especially tuft of grass in front of lion **Edge:** Reeded

Date	Mintage	VF20	XF40	MS60	MS63	MS65
1942 I	3,900,000	3.25	14.00	22.00	32.00	55.00
1943 I	—	600	900	1,200	—	—

Note: 25-50 pieces

KM# 28.4 SHILLING

7.78 g., 0.250 Silver 0.0625 oz. ASW **Ruler:** George VI **Obv:** Crowned head left **Rev:** Lion and mountains within 3/4 circle with fleur ends, date divides denominations below **Edge:** Reeded **Note:** Obverse and reverse as KM#28.1, edge reeding close. For more in-depth comparison of these reverse variety types, see The Guidebook and Catalogue of British Commonwealth Coins, 1649-1971, 3rd Edition, Remick, J. Winnipeg, Regency Coin and Stamp, 1971.

Date	Mintage	VF20	XF40	MS60	MS63	MS65
1944 SA	5,820,000	4.00	17.00	30.00	45.00	75.00
1945 SA	10,080,000	3.50	13.00	27.50	40.00	65.00
1946 SA	18,260,000	3.00	12.00	20.00	30.00	50.00

KM# 31 SHILLING

7.81 g., Copper-Nickel, 27.8 mm. **Ruler:** George VI **Obv:** Crowned head of King George VI left **Obv. Legend:** ET INDIA IMPERATOR dropped from legend **Rev:** Lion and mountains within 3/4 circle with fleur ends, date and denomination below **Edge:** Reeded

Date	Mintage	VF20	XF40	MS60	MS63	MS65
1948	19,704,000	0.90	2.00	3.00	5.00	12.00
1949	38,318,000	0.90	2.00	3.00	5.00	12.00
1949	—	PF63 250				
1949 H	12,584,000	0.90	2.25	4.00	7.00	14.00
1949 KN	15,060,000	0.90	3.00	5.00	7.50	12.50
1950	56,362,000	0.60	1.50	3.00	5.00	12.00
1950	—	PF63 250				
1950 H	12,416,000	0.90	3.00	5.00	7.00	15.00
1950 KN	10,040,000	0.70	2.00	3.50	6.00	13.50
1952	55,605,000	0.60	1.50	3.00	5.00	12.00
1952	—	PF63 175				
1952 H	8,023,999	0.60	1.75	3.00	5.00	12.00
1952 KN	9,360,000	0.60	1.75	3.00	5.00	12.00

PATTERNS

Including off metal strikes

KM#	Date	Mintage	Identification	Mkt Val
Pn6	1906	—	Cent. Aluminum. KM#5.	2,500
Pn7	1907	5	1/2 Cent. Aluminum. KM#6.	3,500
Pn8	1907	—	5 Cents. Copper-Nickel. KM#11.	4,000
Pn9	1908	—	Cent. Copper-Nickel. KM#5a.	2,250
Pn10	1920 (a)	—	50 Cents. Aluminum. KM#16.	3,000
Pn11	1920 (a)	—	Florin. Aluminum. KM#17.	2,000
Pn12	1924	—	Cent. Nickel.	
Pn13	1925KN	—	Cent. Bronze. Uniface obverse.	250
Pn14	1925KN	—	Cent. Bronze.	
Pn15	1929KN	—	Cent. Bronze. Uniface obverse.	250
Pn16	1929KN	—	Cent. Bronze.	

MINT SETS

KM#	Date	Mintage	Identification	Issue Price	Mkt Val
MS1	1921-1922 (5)	—	KM#18-22. The 5 cent coin is dated 1921, all others are 1922.	—	2,000

PROOF SETS

KM#	Date	Mintage	Identification	Issue Price	Mkt Val
PSA1	1920H (6)	—	KM#12-17; 20-30 pieces	—	6,000
PS1	1906-1907 (6)	—	KM#2-5, Pn7-8; Rare	—	—
PS2	1949 (5)	—	KM#30-34	—	1,100
PS3	1950 (3)	—	KM#31, 32, 34	—	600
PS4	1952 (3)	—	KM#32, 33, 34	—	600

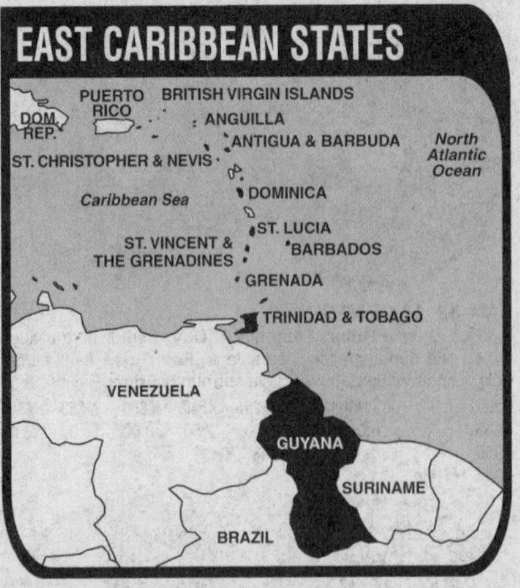

The East Caribbean States, formerly the British Caribbean Territories (Eastern Group), formed a currency board in 1950 to provide the constituent territories of Trinidad & Tobago, Barbados, British Guiana (now Guyana), British Virgin Islands, Anguilla, St. Kitts, Nevis, Antigua, Dominica, St. Lucia, St. Vincent and Grenada with a common currency, thereby permitting withdrawal of the regular British Pound currency. This was dissolved in 1965 and after the breakup, the East Caribbean Territories, a grouping including Barbados, the Leeward and Windward Islands, came into being. Coinage of the dissolved 'Eastern Group' continues to circulate. Paper currency of the East Caribbean Authority was first issued in 1965 and although Barbados withdrew from the group they continued using them prior to 1973 when Barbados issued a decimal coinage.

A series of 4-dollar coins tied to the FAO coinage program were released in 1970 under the name of the Caribbean Development Bank by eight loosely federated island groupings in the eastern Caribbean. These issues are listed individually in this volume under Antigua, Barbados, Dominica, Grenada, Montserrat, St. Kitts, St. Lucia and St. Vincent.

BRITISH CARIBBEAN TERRITORIES

STANDARD COINAGE

100 Cents = 1 British West Indies Dollar

KM# 1 1/2 CENT

5.63 g., Bronze, 20.4 mm. **Ruler:** Elizabeth II **Subject:** Humphrey Paget **Obv:** Crowned bust right **Rev:** Denomination above date

Date	Mintage	VF20	XF40	MS60	MS63	MS65
1955	500,000	0.50	0.75	1.00	1.75	2.50
1955	2,000	PF63 3.00				
1958	200,000	0.75	1.00	1.50	2.25	3.00
1958	20	PF63 145				

KM# 2 CENT

5.64 g., Bronze **Ruler:** Elizabeth II **Obv:** Crowned bust right **Rev:** Denomination within wreath, date below

Date	Mintage	VF20	XF40	MS60	MS63	MS65
1955	8,000,000	0.25	0.35	0.60	1.00	1.25
1955	2,000	PF63 3.00				
1957	3,000,000	0.25	1.00	1.75	2.25	3.00
1957	—	PF63 100				
1958	1,500,000	0.50	1.50	4.50	5.50	7.50
1958	20	PF63 165				
1959	500,000	0.60	2.50	6.00	12.00	20.00
1959	—	PF63 100				
1960	2,500,000	0.25	0.35	0.60	1.00	1.25
1960	—	PF63 100				
1961	2,280,000	0.35	0.50	0.75	1.25	1.50
1961	—	PF63 100				
1962	2,000,000	0.25	0.35	0.60	1.00	1.25
1962	—	PF63 100				
1963	750,000	0.70	1.00	1.25	2.00	2.50
1963	—	PF63 100				
1964	2,500,000	—	—	0.20	0.30	0.45
1964	—	PF63 100				
1965	4,800,000	—	—	0.20	0.30	0.45
1965 Prooflike	—	—	—	—	—	0.75
1965	—	PF63 5.00				

KM# 3 2 CENTS

9.55 g., Bronze, 30.5 mm. **Ruler:** Elizabeth II **Obv:** Crowned bust right **Rev:** Denomination within wreath, date below

Date	Mintage	VF20	XF40	MS60	MS63	MS65
1955	5,500,000	0.25	0.35	0.50	0.75	1.00
1955	2,000	PF63 3.00				
1957	1,250,000	0.25	0.75	1.25	2.00	2.50
1957	—	PF63 110				
1958	1,250,000	0.25	1.25	2.50	3.75	5.00
1958	20	PF63 185				
1960	750,000	0.25	1.00	1.75	2.75	3.50
1960	—	PF63 110				
1961	788,000	0.25	1.00	1.75	2.75	3.50
1961	—	PF63 110				
1962	1,060,000	0.20	0.30	0.50	0.65	0.85
1962	—	PF63 110				
1963	250,000	0.75	1.00	1.50	3.75	5.00
1963	—	PF63 110				
1964	1,188,000	0.20	0.30	0.45	0.55	0.75
1964	—	PF63 110				
1965	2,001,000	0.10	0.15	0.25	0.30	0.45
1965 Prooflike	—	—	—	—	—	0.75
1965	—	PF63 5.00				

KM# 4 5 CENTS

5.00 g., Nickel-Brass, 21 mm. **Ruler:** Elizabeth II **Obv:** Crowned head right **Rev:** Sir Francis Drake's Golden Hind divides denomination, date below **Edge:** Reeded

Date	Mintage	VF20	XF40	MS60	MS63	MS65
1955	8,600,000	0.25	0.35	0.60	1.00	1.25
1955	2,000	PF63 4.50				
1956	2,000,000	0.25	0.35	0.60	0.75	1.00
1956	—	PF63 300				
1960	1,000,000	0.30	0.45	0.90	1.25	1.50
1960	—	PF63 150				
1962	1,300,000	0.25	0.35	0.60	0.75	1.00
1962	—	PF63 150				
1963	200,000	0.35	0.75	1.20	1.50	2.00
1963	—	PF63 150				
1964	1,350,000	0.10	0.20	0.35	0.55	0.75
1964	—	PF63 150				
1965	2,400,000	0.10	0.15	0.25	0.40	0.50
1965 Prooflike	—	—	—	—	—	0.75
1965	—	PF63 5.00				

KM# 5 10 CENTS

2.60 g., Copper-Nickel, 18 mm. **Ruler:** Elizabeth II **Obv:** Crowned head right **Rev:** Sir Francis Drake's Golden Hind divides denomination, date below **Edge:** Reeded

Date	Mintage	VF20	XF40	MS60	MS63	MS65
1955	5,000,000	0.25	0.35	0.45	0.55	0.75
1955	2,000	PF63 4.50				
1956	4,000,000	0.25	0.35	0.45	0.55	0.75
1956	—	PF63 175				
1959	2,000,000	0.25	0.35	0.60	0.75	1.00
1959	—	PF63 175				
1961	1,260,000	0.30	0.40	0.75	1.00	1.25
1961	—	PF63 175				
1962	1,200,000	0.25	0.35	0.60	0.75	1.00
1962	—	PF63 175				
1964	1,400,000	0.20	0.25	0.35	0.50	0.65
1965	3,200,000	0.20	0.25	0.35	0.50	0.65
1965 Prooflike	—	—	—	—	—	0.75
1965	—	PF63 5.00				

KM# 6 25 CENTS
6.51 g., Copper-Nickel, 24 mm. **Ruler:** Elizabeth II **Obv:** Crowned bust right **Rev:** Sir Francis Drake's Golden Hind divides denomination, date below **Edge:** Reeded

Date	Mintage	VF20	XF40	MS60	MS63	MS65
1955	7,000,000	0.50	0.60	0.75	1.00	1.25
1955	2,000	PF63 6.50				
1957	800,000	1.00	1.25	2.25	3.25	4.50
1957	—	PF63 225				
1959	1,000,000	0.50	0.75	1.25	1.75	2.25
1959	—	PF63 225				
1961	744,000	0.75	1.25	2.50	3.75	5.00
1961	—	PF63 225				
1962	480,000	0.50	0.75	1.25	2.00	2.50
1962	—	PF63 225				
1963	480,000	0.50	1.75	1.25	2.00	2.50
1963	—	PF63 225				
1964	480,000	0.50	0.75	1.25	1.50	2.00
1964	—	PF63 225				
1965	1,280,000	0.50	0.75	1.25	1.50	2.00
1965 Prooflike	—	—	—	—	—	1.50
1965	—	PF63 7.50				

KM# 7 50 CENTS
13.00 g., Copper-Nickel, 30 mm. **Ruler:** Elizabeth II **Obv:** Crowned bust right **Rev:** Figure and horseheads above shielded arms and circular pictures, denomination and date divided below

Date	Mintage	VF20	XF40	MS60	MS63	MS65
1955	1,500,000	1.25	1.50	2.25	2.75	3.75
1955	2,000	PF63 12.50				
1965	100,000	4.00	5.50	7.50	11.50	15.00
1965 Prooflike	—	—	—	—	—	7.50
1965	—	PF63 10.00				

EAST CARIBBEAN TERRITORIES

STANDARD COINAGE

100 Cents = 1 Dollar

KM# 8 10 DOLLARS
28.28 g., Copper-Nickel, 38.61 mm. **Ruler:** Elizabeth II **Subject:** 10th Anniversary of Caribbean Development Bank **Obv:** Sir Francis Drake's Golden Hind divides denomination, date below **Rev:** Map on grid within circle, dates below **Note:** Prev. KM#1.

Date	Mintage	VF20	XF40	MS60	MS63	MS65
1980	—	—	—	2.50	4.50	7.00

KM# 8a 10 DOLLARS
28.28 g., 0.925 Silver 0.841 oz. ASW, 38.8 mm. **Ruler:** Elizabeth II **Obv:** Sir Francis Drake's Golden Hind divides denomination, date below **Rev:** Map on grid within circle, two dates below **Note:** Prev. KM#1a.

Date	Mintage	VF20	XF40	MS60	MS63	MS65
1980	10,000	PF63 21.50	PF65 30.00			

KM# 9 10 DOLLARS
28.28 g., Copper-Nickel, 38.61 mm. **Ruler:** Elizabeth II **Subject:** Wedding of Prince Charles and Lady Diana **Obv:** Young bust right **Rev:** Sir Francis Drake's Golden Hind and map of island chain, denomination below **Note:** Prev. KM#2.

Date	Mintage	VF20	XF40	MS60	MS63	MS65
1981	50,000	—	—	2.50	4.50	7.00

KM# 9a 10 DOLLARS
28.28 g., 0.925 Silver 0.841 oz. ASW, 38.8 mm. **Ruler:** Elizabeth II **Obv:** Young bust right **Rev:** Sir Francis Drake's Golden Hind and map of island chain, denomination below **Note:** Prev. KM#2a.

Date	Mintage	VF20	XF40	MS60	MS63	MS65
1981	30,000	PF63 18.50	PF65 25.00			

EAST CARIBBEAN STATES

KM# 10 CENT
0.90 g., Aluminum, 18.4 mm. **Ruler:** Elizabeth II **Obv:** Young bust right **Rev:** Wreath divides denomination, date upper right **Shape:** Scalloped **Note:** Prev. KM#1.

Date	Mintage	VF20	XF40	MS60	MS63	MS65
1981	—	—	—	0.20	0.30	0.40
1981	5,000	PF65 1.25				
1983	—	—	—	0.20	0.30	0.40
1984	—	—	—	0.20	0.30	0.40
1986	—	—	—	0.20	0.30	0.40
1986	2,500	PF65 1.25				
1987	—	—	—	0.20	0.30	0.40
1989	—	—	—	0.20	0.30	0.40
1991	—	—	—	0.20	0.30	0.40
1992	—	—	—	0.20	0.30	0.40
1993	—	—	—	0.20	0.30	0.40
1994	—	—	—	0.20	0.30	0.40
1995	—	—	—	0.20	0.30	0.40
1996	—	—	—	0.20	0.30	0.40
1997	—	—	—	0.20	0.30	0.40
1998	—	—	—	0.20	0.30	0.40
1999	—	—	—	0.20	0.30	0.40
2000	—	—	—	0.20	0.30	0.40

KM# 11 2 CENTS
1.00 g., Aluminum, 18.3 mm. **Ruler:** Elizabeth II **Obv:** Young bust right **Rev:** Wreath divides denomination, date upper right **Shape:** Square **Note:** Prev. KM#2.

Date	Mintage	VF20	XF40	MS60	MS63	MS65
1981	—	—	0.10	0.25	0.35	0.50
1981	5,000	PF65 1.50				
1984	—	—	0.10	0.25	0.35	0.50
1986	—	—	0.10	0.25	0.35	0.50
1986	2,500	PF65 1.50				
1987	—	—	0.10	0.25	0.35	0.50
1989	—	—	0.10	0.25	0.35	0.50
1991	—	—	0.10	0.25	0.35	0.50
1992	—	—	0.10	0.25	0.35	0.50
1993	—	—	0.10	0.25	0.35	0.50
1994	—	—	0.10	0.25	0.35	0.50
1995	—	—	0.10	0.25	0.35	0.50
1996	—	—	0.10	0.25	0.35	0.50
1997	—	—	0.10	0.25	0.35	0.50
1998	—	—	0.10	0.25	0.35	0.50
1999	—	—	0.10	0.25	0.35	0.50
2000	—	—	0.10	0.25	0.35	0.50

KM# 12 5 CENTS
1.31 g., Aluminum, 23.1 mm. **Ruler:** Elizabeth II **Obv:** Young bust right **Rev:** Wreath divides denomination, date upper right **Shape:** Scalloped **Note:** Prev. KM#3.

Date	Mintage	VF20	XF40	MS60	MS63	MS65
1981	—	—	0.10	0.30	0.45	0.65
1981	5,000	PF65 2.25				
1984	—	—	0.10	0.30	0.45	0.65
1986	—	—	0.10	0.30	0.45	0.65
1986	2,500	PF65 2.25				
1987	—	—	0.10	0.30	0.45	0.65
1989	—	—	0.10	0.30	0.45	0.65
1991	—	—	0.10	0.30	0.45	0.65
1992	—	—	0.10	0.30	0.45	0.65
1993	—	—	0.10	0.30	0.45	0.65
1994	—	—	0.10	0.30	0.45	0.65
1995	—	—	0.10	0.30	0.45	0.65
1996	—	—	0.10	0.30	0.45	0.65
1997	—	—	0.10	0.30	0.45	0.65
1998	—	—	0.10	0.30	0.45	0.65
1999	—	—	0.10	0.30	0.45	0.65
2000	—	—	0.10	0.30	0.45	0.65

KM# 13 10 CENTS
2.59 g., Copper-Nickel, 18.06 mm. **Ruler:** Elizabeth II **Obv:** Young bust right **Rev:** Sir Francis Drake's Golden Hind, denomination below and left, date at right **Edge:** Reeded **Note:** Prev. KM#4.

Date	Mintage	VF20	XF40	MS60	MS63	MS65
1981	—	0.10	0.15	0.40	0.60	0.75
1981	5,000	PF65 3.00				
1986	—	0.10	0.15	0.40	0.60	0.75
1986	2,500	PF65 3.00				
1987	—	0.10	0.15	0.40	0.60	0.75
1989	—	0.10	0.15	0.40	0.60	0.75
1991	—	0.10	0.15	0.40	0.60	0.75
1992	—	0.10	0.15	0.40	0.60	0.75
1993	—	0.10	0.15	0.40	0.60	0.75
1994	—	0.10	0.15	0.40	0.60	0.75
1995	—	0.10	0.15	0.40	0.60	0.75
1996	—	0.10	0.15	0.40	0.60	0.75
1997	—	0.10	0.15	0.40	0.60	0.75
1998	—	0.10	0.15	0.40	0.60	0.75
1999	—	0.10	0.15	0.40	0.60	0.75
2000	—	0.10	0.15	0.40	0.60	0.75

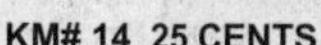

KM# 14 25 CENTS
6.48 g., Copper-Nickel, 23.98 mm. **Ruler:** Elizabeth II **Obv:** Young bust right **Rev:** Sir Francis Drake's Golden Hind, divides denomination, date at right **Edge:** Reeded **Note:** Prev. KM#5.

Date	Mintage	VF20	XF40	MS60	MS63	MS65
1981	—	0.15	0.20	0.50	0.75	1.00
1981	5,000	PF65 4.00				
1986	—	0.15	0.20	0.50	0.75	1.00
1986	2,500	PF65 4.00				
1987	—	0.15	0.20	0.50	0.75	1.00
1989	—	0.15	0.20	0.50	0.75	1.00
1991	—	0.15	0.20	0.50	0.75	1.00
1992	—	0.15	0.20	0.50	0.75	1.00
1993	—	0.15	0.20	0.50	0.75	1.00
1994	—	0.15	0.20	0.50	0.75	1.00
1995	—	0.15	0.20	0.50	0.75	1.00
1996	—	0.15	0.20	0.50	0.75	1.00
1997	—	0.15	0.20	0.50	0.75	1.00
1998	—	0.15	0.20	0.50	0.75	1.00
1999	—	0.15	0.20	0.50	0.75	1.00
2000	—	0.15	0.20	0.50	0.75	1.00

KM# 15 DOLLAR
8.20 g., Aluminum-Bronze, 26.9 mm. **Ruler:** Elizabeth II **Obv:** Young bust right **Rev:** Sir Francis Drake's Golden Hind divides denomination, date at right **Note:** Prev. KM#6.

Date	Mintage	VF20	XF40	MS60	MS63	MS65
1981	—	0.50	0.75	1.50	2.00	2.50
1981	5,000	PF65 8.00				
1986	—	0.50	0.75	1.50	2.00	2.50
1986	2,500	PF65 8.00				

KM# 20 DOLLAR
8.00 g., Copper-Nickel, 27.5 mm. **Ruler:** Elizabeth II **Obv:** Young bust right **Rev:** Sir Francis Drake's Golden Hind divides denomination, date at right **Shape:** 10-sided **Note:** Prev. KM#11.

Date	Mintage	VF20	XF40	MS60	MS63	MS65
1989	—	—	—	2.25	2.75	3.25
1991	—	—	—	2.25	2.75	3.25
1992	—	—	—	2.25	2.75	3.25
1993	—	—	—	2.25	2.75	3.25
1994	—	—	—	2.25	2.75	3.25
1995	—	—	—	2.25	2.75	3.25
1996	—	—	—	2.25	2.75	3.25
1997	—	—	—	2.00	2.50	3.00
1998	—	—	—	2.00	2.50	3.00
1999	—	—	—	2.00	2.50	3.00
2000	—	—	—	2.00	2.50	3.00

KM# 24 2 DOLLARS
Copper-Nickel **Ruler:** Elizabeth II **Subject:** 10th Anniversary of Central Bank **Obv:** Bank building, dates below **Rev:** Bust facing, denomination below **Note:** Prev. KM#15.

Date	Mintage	VF20	XF40	MS60	MS63	MS65
ND-1993	—	—	—	5.00	7.00	9.00

KM# 16 10 DOLLARS
Copper-Nickel **Ruler:** Elizabeth II **Series:** F.A.O. **Subject:** World Food Day **Obv:** Denomination within wreath, date below **Rev:** Grain sprig within circle divides date and FAO logo **Note:** Prev. KM#7.

Date	Mintage	VF20	XF40	MS60	MS63	MS65
1981	—	—	—	8.00	10.00	12.00

KM# 16a 10 DOLLARS
28.28 g., 0.500 Silver 0.4546 oz. ASW **Ruler:** Elizabeth II **Obv:** Denomination within wreath, date below **Rev:** Grain sprig within circle divides date and FAO logo **Note:** Prev. KM#7a.

Date	Mintage	VF20	XF40	MS60	MS63	MS65
1981	10,000	—	—	12.00	17.00	22.00
1981	5,000	PF63 45.00	PF65 55.00			

KM# 22 10 DOLLARS
28.28 g., 0.925 Silver 0.841 oz. ASW **Ruler:** Elizabeth II **Subject:** Queen Mother's 90th Birthday **Obv:** Crowned bust right, denomination below **Rev:** Crowned monogram with flowers flanking, dates below **Note:** Prev. KM#13.

Date	Mintage	VF20	XF40	MS60	MS63	MS65
ND-1990	—	PF63 25.00	PF65 35.00	PF67 40.00		

KM# 23 10 DOLLARS
28.28 g., 0.925 Silver 0.841 oz. ASW **Ruler:** Elizabeth II **Subject:** 40th Anniversary - Coronation of Queen Elizabeth **Obv:** Crowned bust right, denomination below **Rev:** Crowned and seated 1/2 figure holding scepter and royal orb, dates below **Note:** Prev. KM#14.

Date	Mintage	VF20	XF40	MS60	MS63	MS65
ND-1993	10,000	PF63 25.00	PF65 35.00	PF67 40.00		

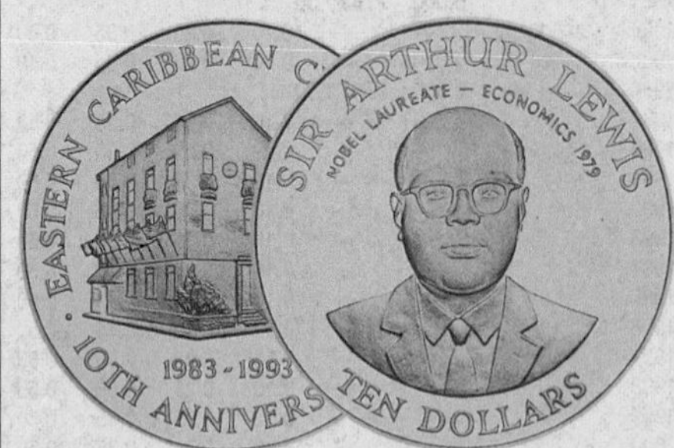

KM# 25 10 DOLLARS
28.28 g., 0.925 Silver 0.841 oz. ASW **Ruler:** Elizabeth II **Subject:** 10th Anniversary of Central Bank **Obv:** Bank building, dates below **Rev:** Bust facing, denomination below **Note:** Prev. KM#16.

Date	Mintage	VF20	XF40	MS60	MS63	MS65
ND-1993	2,500	PF63 35.00	PF65 55.00	PF67 65.00		

KM# 27 10 DOLLARS
31.47 g., 0.925 Silver 0.9359 oz. ASW **Ruler:** Elizabeth II **Subject:** World Cup Soccer **Rev:** Buildings, soccer ball at right, denomination below **Note:** Prev. KM#18.

Date	Mintage	VF20	XF40	MS60	MS63	MS65
1994	10,000	PF63 30.00	PF65 40.00	PF67 45.00		

KM# 33 10 DOLLARS
28.50 g., 0.925 Silver 0.8476 oz. ASW, 38.5 mm. **Ruler:** Elizabeth II **Subject:** Reeded **Obv:** Queens portrait **Rev:** The Royal Launch, denomination divides dates below **Edge:** Reeded

Date	Mintage	VF20	XF40	MS60	MS63	MS65
1996	—	PF63 25.00	PF65 35.00	PF67 40.00		

KM# 32 10 DOLLARS
28.50 g., 0.925 Silver 0.8476 oz. ASW, 38.5 mm. **Ruler:** Elizabeth II **Subject:** Queen Elizabeth and Philip's Golden Wedding Anniversary **Obv:** Crowned bust right, date below **Rev:** The royal couple waving behind gold inset shield, within circle, denomination below **Edge:** Reeded

Date	Mintage	VF20	XF40	MS60	MS63	MS65
1997	—	PF63 25.00	PF65 35.00	PF67 40.00		

KM# 30 10 DOLLARS
28.28 g., 0.925 Silver 0.841 oz. ASW **Ruler:** Elizabeth II **Subject:** Montserrat Volcano Appeal Fund **Obv:** Queens portrait **Rev:** Multicolor rainbow and volcano, date below **Note:** Prev. KM#30.

Date	Mintage	VF20	XF40	MS60	MS63	MS65
1998	10,000	PF63 30.00	PF65 45.00	PF67 50.00		

KM# 28 10 DOLLARS
28.28 g., 0.925 Silver 0.841 oz. ASW **Ruler:** Elizabeth II **Subject:** 50th Anniversary - University of the West Indies **Obv:** Bust facing, denomination below **Rev:** University arms, dates below, Pelican above **Note:** Prev. KM#19.

Date	Mintage	VF20	XF40	MS60	MS63	MS65
ND-1999	1,000	PF63 50.00	PF65 65.00	PF67 75.00		

KM# 31 2000 CENTS (20 Dollars)
7.98 g., 0.917 Gold 0.2353 oz. AGW **Ruler:** Elizabeth II **Series:** Millennium **Subject:** British Royal Mint **Obv:** Young bust right **Rev:** Ship, palm trees and radiant sun within circle divided by words "millennium", denomination below **Edge:** Reeded **Note:** Prev. KM#22.

Date	Mintage	VF20	XF40	MS60	MS63	MS65
2000	—	—	—	—	400	425

KM# 19 50 DOLLARS
28.28 g., 0.925 Silver 0.841 oz. ASW **Ruler:** Elizabeth II **Series:** International Year of Disabled Persons **Obv:** Young bust right **Rev:** Two winged figures divide date and denomination **Note:** Prev. KM#10.

Date	Mintage	VF20	XF40	MS60	MS63	MS65
1981	10,000	—	—	—	25.00	30.00
1981	10,000	PF65 40.00	PF67 45.00			

KM# 17 50 DOLLARS
28.28 g., 0.925 Silver 0.841 oz. ASW **Ruler:** Elizabeth II **Series:** International Year of the Scout **Rev:** Boy scouts, denomination below, date at left **Note:** Prev. KM#8.

Date	Mintage	VF20	XF40	MS60	MS63	MS65
ND-1983	10,000	—	—	—	27.00	32.00
ND-1983	10,000	PF65 42.00	PF67 48.00			

KM# 26 100 DOLLARS
15.98 g., 0.917 Gold 0.471 oz. AGW **Ruler:** Elizabeth II **Subject:** 10th Anniversary of Central Bank **Obv:** Bank building, dates below **Rev:** Bust facing, denomination below **Note:** Prev. KM#17.

Date	Mintage	VF20	XF40	MS60	MS63	MS65
1993	150	PF67 850				

KM# 29 100 DOLLARS
15.98 g., 0.917 Gold 0.471 oz. AGW **Ruler:** Elizabeth II **Subject:** 50th Anniversary - University of West Indies **Obv:** Bust facing, denomination below **Rev:** University arms, pelican above, dates below **Note:** Prev. KM#20.

Date	Mintage	VF20	XF40	MS60	MS63	MS65
ND-1999	300	PF65 800	PF67 825			

KM# 21 500 DOLLARS
15.98 g., 0.917 Gold 0.4711 oz. AGW **Ruler:** Elizabeth II **Series:** International Year of Disabled Persons **Obv:** Young bust right **Rev:** Two figures raising center figure, denomination above, date at right **Note:** Prev. KM#12.

Date	Mintage	VF20	XF40	MS60	MS63	MS65
1981	—	—	—	—	750	800
1981	—	PF65 850	PF67 875			

KM# 18 500 DOLLARS
15.98 g., 0.917 Gold 0.4711 oz. AGW **Ruler:** Elizabeth II **Series:** International Year of the Scout **Obv:** Queens portrait **Rev:** One scout standing, pointing; one scout kneeling with map, denomination below, date at right **Note:** Prev. KM#9.

Date	Mintage	VF20	XF40	MS60	MS63	MS65
ND-1983	2,000	—	—	—	750	800
ND-1983	2,000	PF65 825	PF67 850			

PIEDFORT

KM#	Date	Mintage	Identification	Mkt Val
P1	1981	1,000	50 Dollars. Silver. KM#19.	80.00
P2	1981	—	500 Dollars. Gold. KM#21.	1,750

MINT SETS

KM#	Date	Mintage	Identification	Issue Price	Mkt Val
MS1	1986 (6)	—	KM#10-15	—	18.00
MS2	1991 (6)	—	KM#10-14, 20	19.95	14.00
MS3	1992 (6)	—	KM#10-14, 20	—	12.00
MS4	1993 (6)	—	KM#10-14, 20	30.00	12.00
MS5	1994 (6)	—	KM#10-14,20	30.00	12.00
MS6	1995 (6)	—	KM#10-14, 20	30.00	12.00
MS8	1996 (6)	—	KM#10-14, 20	30.00	12.00
MS9	1997 (6)	—	KM#10-14, 20	30.00	12.00
MS10	1998 (6)	—	KM#10-14, 20	30.00	12.00
MS11	1999 (6)	—	KM#10-14, 20	25.00	15.00
MS12	2000 (7)	—	KM#10-14, 20, 31	139	450

PROOF SETS

KM#	Date	Mintage	Identification	Issue Price	Mkt Val
PS1	1955 (7)	2,000	KM#1-7	—	37.00
PS2	1958 (3)	20	KM#1-3	—	500
PS3	1965 (6)	—	KM#2-7	—	37.50
PS5	1981 (6)	5,000	KM#10-15	29.00	20.00
PS6	1986 (6)	2,500	KM#10-15	30.75	20.00

ECUADOR

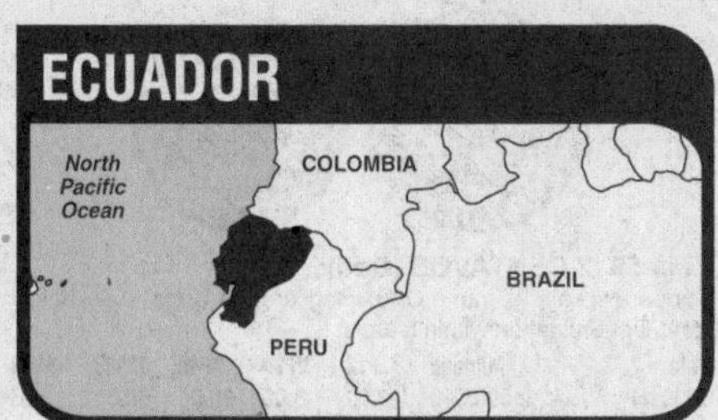

The Republic of Ecuador, located astride the equator on the Pacific Coast of South America, has an area of 105,037 sq. mi. (283,560 sq. km.) and a population of 10.9 million. Capital: Quito. Agriculture is the mainstay of the economy but there are appreciable deposits of minerals and petroleum. It is one of the world's largest exporters of bananas and balsa wood. Coffee, cacao, sugar and petroleum are also valuable exports.

Ecuador was first sighted in 1526 by Francisco Pizarro. Conquest was undertaken by Sebastian de Benalcazar, who founded Quito in 1534. Ecuador was part of the Viceroyalty of New Granada through the 16th and 17th centuries. After previous attempts to attain independence were crushed, Antonio Sucre, the able lieutenant of Bolivar, secured Ecuador's freedom in the Battle of Pinchincha, May 24, 1822. It then joined Venezuela and Colombia in a confederation known as Gran Colombia, and became an independent republic when it left the confederacy in 1830.

MINT MARKS
BIRMm - Birmingham, Heaton
Birmingham - Birmingham
D - Denver
H - Heaton, Birmingham
HF - LeLocle (Swiss)
LIMA - Lima
Mo - Mexico
PHILA.U.S.A. - Philadelphia
PHILADELPHIA - Philadelphia
PHILA - Philadelphia

MONETARY SYSTEM
10 Centavos = 1 Decimo
10 Decimos = 1 Sucre
25 Sucres = 1 Condor

REPUBLIC

DECIMAL COINAGE

10 Centavos = 1 Decimo; 10 Decimos = 1 Sucre;
25 Sucres = 1 Condor

KM# 57 1/2 CENTAVO (Medio)
Copper-Nickel, 15 mm. **Obv:** Flag draped arms, date below **Rev:** Denomination within laurels

Date	Mintage	F12	VF20	XF40	MS60	MS63
1909 H	4,000,000	2.00	8.00	15.00	45.00	100
1909 H	—	PF63 250				

KM# 58 CENTAVO (Un)
Copper-Nickel, 17 mm. **Obv:** Flag draped arms, date below **Rev:** Denomination within laurels

Date	Mintage	F12	VF20	XF40	MS60	MS63
1909 H	3,000,000	2.00	8.00	15.00	45.00	100
1909 H	—	PF63 250				

KM# 67 CENTAVO (Un)
6.25 g., Bronze, 20 mm. **Obv:** Flag draped arms, date below **Rev:** Denomination within laurels

Date	Mintage	F12	VF20	XF40	MS60	MS63
1928	2,016,000	0.50	0.75	2.00	15.00	35.00

KM# 59 2 CENTAVOS (Dos)
Copper-Nickel, 19 mm. **Obv:** Flag draped arms, date below **Rev:** Denomination within laurels

Date	Mintage	F12	VF20	XF40	MS60	MS63
1909 H	2,500,000	2.00	8.00	20.00	60.00	125
1909 H	—	PF63 250				

KM# 61 2-1/2 CENTAVOS
Copper-Nickel, 19 mm. **Obv:** Flag draped arms, date below **Rev:** Denomination within laurels

Date	Mintage	F12	VF20	XF40	MS60	MS63
1917	1,600,000	6.00	15.00	55.00	175	250

KM# 68 2-1/2 CENTAVOS
Nickel, 18.5 mm. **Obv:** Flag draped arms, date below **Rev:** Denomination within laurels

Date	Mintage	F12	VF20	XF40	MS60	MS63
1928	4,000,000	1.00	2.00	10.00	25.00	75.00

KM# 55.1 1/2 DECIMO (Medio)
1.25 g., 0.900 Silver 0.0362 oz. ASW, 15 mm. **Obv:** Head of Sucre left **Rev:** Flag-draped arms, denomination upper left

Date	Mintage	F12	VF20	XF40	MS60	MS63
1902/892 LIMA JF	1,000,000	1.00	2.00	6.00	25.00	45.00
1902/802 LIMA JF	Inc. above	1.00	2.00	6.00	25.00	45.00
1902 LIMA JF	Inc. above	1.00	2.00	6.00	25.00	45.00
1905/805 LIMA JF	500,000	1.00	2.00	9.00	30.00	50.00
1905/2 LIMA JF	Inc. above	1.00	2.00	9.00	30.00	50.00
1905 LIMA JF	Inc. above	1.00	2.00	9.00	30.00	50.00
1912/05 LIMA FG	20,000	2.00	3.00	12.00	35.00	60.00
1912 LIMA FG	Inc. above	2.00	3.00	12.00	35.00	60.00
1912 LIMA FG	Inc. above	2.00	3.00	15.00	45.00	75.00

Note: FCUADOR (obverse error)

KM# 55.2 1/2 DECIMO (Medio)
1.25 g., 0.900 Silver 0.0362 oz. ASW, 15 mm. **Obv:** Head of Sucre left, date below **Rev:** Modified flag draped arms, denomination upper left

Date	Mintage	F12	VF20	XF40	MS60	MS63
1915 BIRMm	2,000,000	1.25	1.75	3.00	8.00	15.00
1915 BIRMm	—	PF63 200				

KM# 60.1 5 CENTAVOS (Cinco)
Copper-Nickel, 21 mm. **Obv:** Flag draped arms with tails on flagpoles pointing outward, date below **Rev:** Denomination within laurels

Date	Mintage	F12	VF20	XF40	MS60	MS63
1909 H	2,000,000	4.50	10.00	30.00	150	250
1909 H	—	PF63 300				

KM# 60.2 5 CENTAVOS (Cinco)
Copper-Nickel, 21 mm. **Obv:** Flag draped arms with tails on flagpoles pointing downward, date below **Rev:** Denomination within laurels **Note:** Thin planchet.

Date	Mintage	F12	VF20	XF40	MS60	MS63
1917	1,200,000	8.00	15.00	50.00	125	200
1918	7,980,000	3.00	8.00	15.00	40.00	75.00

KM# 63 5 CENTAVOS (Cinco)
Copper-Nickel, 20 mm. **Obv:** Flag draped arms, date below **Rev:** Denomination within laurels

Date	Mintage	F12	VF20	XF40	MS60	MS63
1919	12,000,000	1.00	2.00	5.00	12.00	35.00
Note: 3 berries to left of "C" on reverse						
1919	—	PF63 200				
Note: 3 berries to left of "C" on reverse						
1919	Inc. above	1.00	2.00	15.00	30.00	50.00
Note: 4 berries to left of "C" on reverse. Varieties exist with loose or tight groupings of these berries						

KM# 65 5 CENTAVOS (Cinco)
Copper-Nickel, 16.5 mm. **Obv:** Flag draped arms, date below **Rev:** Head right within wreath, denomination below

Date	Mintage	F12	VF20	XF40	MS60	MS63
1924 H	10,000,000	1.00	2.00	8.00	25.00	45.00
1924 H	—	PF63 125				

KM# 69 5 CENTAVOS (Cinco)
3.00 g., Nickel, 19.5 mm. **Obv:** Flag draped arms, date below **Rev:** Head right within wreath, denomination below

Date	Mintage	F12	VF20	XF40	MS60	MS63
1928	16,000,000	1.00	2.00	3.00	6.50	15.00

KM# 75 5 CENTAVOS (Cinco)
2.00 g., Nickel, 17.1 mm. **Obv:** Flag draped arms, date below **Rev:** Denomination within wreath

Date	Mintage	F12	VF20	XF40	MS60	MS63
1937 HF	15,000,000	0.10	0.20	0.75	2.00	3.50

KM# 75a 5 CENTAVOS (Cinco)
Brass, 17.1 mm. **Obv:** Flag draped arms, date below **Rev:** Denomination within wreath

Date	Mintage	VF20	XF40	MS60	MS63	MS65
1942	2,000,000	2.00	5.00	10.00	17.00	35.00
1944	3,000,000	2.00	5.00	10.00	17.00	35.00

KM# 75b 5 CENTAVOS (Cinco)
2.00 g., Copper-Nickel, 17 mm. **Obv:** Flag draped arms, date below **Rev:** Denomination within wreath

Date	Mintage	VF20	XF40	MS60	MS63	MS65
1946	40,000,000	—	0.40	1.00	1.50	3.00

KM# 75c 5 CENTAVOS (Cinco)
Nickel Clad Steel **Obv:** Flag draped arms, date below **Rev:** Denomination within wreath

Date	Mintage	VF20	XF40	MS60	MS63	MS65
1970	—	—	0.15	0.25	0.50	1.00
1970	—	—	1.00	2.50	5.00	7.50
Note: ECADOR (obverse legend error, from weak struck U)						

KM# 50.3 DECIMO (Un)
2.50 g., 0.900 Silver 0.0723 oz. ASW, 18 mm. **Obv:** Head left, legend without "LEY" **Rev. Legend:** Flag-draped arms

Date	Mintage	F12	VF20	XF40	MS60	MS63
1902 LIMA JF	519,000	2.00	3.00	8.00	15.00	25.00
Note: With JR below fasces on reverse						
1902 LIMA JF	Inc. above	2.00	3.00	8.00	15.00	25.00
Note: Without JR below fasces on reverse						
1902 LIMA JF/TF	—	2.00	3.00	8.00	15.00	25.00
1905 LIMA JF	250,000	2.00	3.00	8.00	15.00	25.00
1912 LIMA FG	30,000	3.00	5.00	12.00	25.00	60.00

KM# 50.4 DECIMO (Un)
2.50 g., 0.900 Silver 0.0723 oz. ASW, 18 mm. **Obv:** Head of Sucre left, date below **Rev:** Flag draped arms, denomination upper left

Date	Mintage	F12	VF20	XF40	MS60	MS63
1915 BIRMm	1,000,000	—	1.50	3.00	8.00	15.00
1915 BIRMm	—	PF63 300				

KM# 50.5 DECIMO (Un)
2.50 g., 0.900 Silver 0.0723 oz. ASW, 18 mm. **Obv:** Head of Sucre left **Rev:** Flag draped arms

Date	Mintage	F12	VF20	XF40	MS60	MS63
1916 PHILA	2,000,000	—	1.50	3.00	8.00	15.00

KM# 62 10 CENTAVOS (Diez)
Copper-Nickel, 22 mm. **Obv:** Flag draped arms, date below **Rev:** Denomination within wreath

Date	Mintage	F12	VF20	XF40	MS60	MS63
1918	1,000,000	5.00	10.00	35.00	100	200

KM# 64 10 CENTAVOS (Diez)
Copper-Nickel, 25 mm. **Obv:** Flag draped arms, date below **Rev:** Denomination within wreath

Date	Mintage	F12	VF20	XF40	MS60	MS63
1919	2,000,000	1.00	2.00	8.00	20.00	45.00
1919	—	PF63 200				

KM# 66 10 CENTAVOS (Diez)
3.00 g., Copper-Nickel, 19.5 mm. **Obv:** Flag draped arms, date below **Rev:** Head of Bolivar left within wreath, denomination below **Note:** The H mint mark is very small and is located above the date.

Date	Mintage	F12	VF20	XF40	MS60	MS63
1924 H	5,000,000	1.00	2.00	5.00	15.00	35.00
1924 H	—	PF63 250				

KM# 70 10 CENTAVOS (Diez)

Nickel, 21.5 mm. **Obv:** Flag draped arms, date below **Rev:** Head of Bolivar right within wreath, denomination below

Date	Mintage	F12	VF20	XF40	MS60	MS63
1928	16,000,000	1.00	2.00	5.00	15.00	35.00

KM# 76 10 CENTAVOS (Diez)

3.00 g., Nickel, 19 mm. **Obv:** Flag draped arms, date below **Rev:** Denomination in wreath

Date	Mintage	F12	VF20	XF40	MS60	MS63
1937 HF	7,500,000	0.25	0.50	1.00	3.50	5.00

KM# 76a 10 CENTAVOS (Diez)

Brass, 19 mm. **Obv:** Flag-draped arms, date below **Rev:** Denomination within wreath

Date	Mintage	VF20	XF40	MS60	MS63	MS65
1942	5,000,000	1.00	5.00	10.00	25.00	45.00

KM# 76b 10 CENTAVOS (Diez)

3.00 g., Copper-Nickel, 19 mm. **Obv:** Flag draped arms, date below **Rev:** Denomination within wreath

Date	Mintage	VF20	XF40	MS60	MS63	MS65
1946	40,000,000	0.15	0.25	1.00	1.50	3.00

KM# 76c 10 CENTAVOS (Diez)

2.80 g., Nickel Clad Steel, 19 mm. **Obv:** Flag draped arms, date below **Rev:** Denomination within wreath **Note:** Varieties exist.

Date	Mintage	VF20	XF40	MS60	MS63	MS65
1964	20,000,000	—	0.20	0.75	1.00	1.50
1968	15,000,000	—	0.20	0.75	1.00	1.50
1972	20,000,000	—	0.15	0.65	1.00	1.50

KM# 76d 10 CENTAVOS (Diez)

Copper-Nickel Clad Steel, 19 mm. **Obv:** Flag draped arms, date below **Rev:** Denomination within wreath

Date	Mintage	VF20	XF40	MS60	MS63	MS65
1976	10,000,000	—	0.15	0.65	1.00	1.50

KM# 51.3 2 DECIMOS (Dos)

5.00 g., 0.900 Silver 0.1447 oz. ASW, 23 mm. **Obv:** Head of Sucre left **Rev:** Flag-draped arms, legend without "LEI" **Note:** Santiago and Lima Mints

Date	Mintage	F12	VF20	XF40	MS60	MS63
1912/18 FG	50,000	5.00	10.00	30.00	90.00	150
1912 FG	Inc. above	5.00	10.00	30.00	90.00	150
1914 FG LIMA.	110,000	5.00	10.00	17.00	75.00	125
1914 FG LIMA	Inc. above	5.00	10.00	15.00	60.00	125
1915 FG	157,000	5.00	10.00	40.00	125	225

Note: Small "R" below fasces on reverse

KM# 51.4 2 DECIMOS (Dos)

5.00 g., 0.900 Silver 0.1447 oz. ASW, 23 mm. **Obv:** Head of Sucre left **Rev:** Flag-draped arms, mint name in legend below **Rev. Legend:** PHILADELPHIA at bottom

Date	Mintage	F12	VF20	XF40	MS60	MS63
1914 TF	2,500,000	3.00	5.00	10.00	30.00	50.00
1916 TF	1,000,000	3.00	5.00	10.00	25.00	45.00

KM# 77.1 20 CENTAVOS

4.00 g., Nickel, 21 mm. **Obv:** Flag draped arms, date below **Rev:** Denomination within wreath

Date	Mintage	F12	VF20	XF40	MS60	MS63
1937 HF	7,500,000	0.25	0.50	1.00	2.00	3.50

KM# 77.1a 20 CENTAVOS

3.72 g., Brass, 21 mm. **Obv:** Flag draped arms, date below **Rev:** Denomination within wreath

Date	Mintage	VF20	XF40	MS60	MS63	MS65
1942	5,000,000	0.75	3.00	10.00	20.00	40.00
1944 D	15,000,000	0.75	3.00	8.00	15.00	30.00

KM# 77.1b 20 CENTAVOS

4.00 g., Copper-Nickel, 21 mm. **Obv:** Flag draped arms, date below **Rev:** Denomination within wreath

Date	Mintage	VF20	XF40	MS60	MS63	MS65
1946	30,000,000	0.75	1.00	2.00	3.50	5.00

KM# 77.1c 20 CENTAVOS

3.60 g., Nickel Clad Steel, 21 mm. **Obv:** Flag draped arms, date below **Rev:** Denomination within wreath

Date	Mintage	VF20	XF40	MS60	MS63	MS65
1959	14,400,000	—	0.20	0.45	0.65	1.00
1962	14,400,000	—	0.20	0.45	0.65	1.00
1966	24,000,000	—	0.20	0.45	0.65	1.00
1969	24,000,000	—	0.20	0.45	0.65	1.00
1971	12,000,000	—	0.20	0.45	0.65	1.00
1972	48,432,000	—	0.20	0.45	0.65	1.00

KM# 77.2 20 CENTAVOS

Copper-Nickel, 21 mm. **Obv:** Modified flag draped arms, date below **Rev:** Denomination within wreath

Date	Mintage	F12	VF20	XF40	MS60	MS63
1974	19,562,000	—	—	0.15	0.45	0.65

KM# 77.2a 20 CENTAVOS

Nickel Plated Steel, 21 mm. **Obv:** Flag draped arms, date below **Rev:** Denomination within wreath

Date	Mintage	VF20	XF40	MS60	MS63	MS65
1975	52,437,000	—	0.15	0.35	0.50	1.00

Date	Mintage	VF20	XF40	MS60	MS63	MS65
1978	37,500,000	—	0.15	0.35	0.50	1.00
1980	18,000,000	—	0.15	0.35	0.50	1.00
1981	21,000,000	—	0.15	0.35	0.50	1.00

KM# 71 50 CENTAVOS (Cincuenta)

2.50 g., 0.720 Silver 0.0579 oz. ASW, 18 mm. **Obv:** Head of Sucre left, date below **Rev:** Flag draped arms, denomination above, mint name below **Rev. Legend:** PHILA • U • S • A at bottom

Date	Mintage	F12	VF20	XF40	MS60	MS63
1928	1,000,000	2.00	3.00	10.00	25.00	60.00
1930	155,000	2.00	3.00	15.00	40.00	75.00

KM# 81 50 CENTAVOS (Cincuenta)

5.00 g., Nickel Clad Steel, 23 mm. **Obv:** Flag draped arms, date below **Rev:** Denomination within wreath **Edge:** Reeded

Date	Mintage	VF20	XF40	MS60	MS63	MS65
1963	20,000,000	0.15	0.25	0.50	0.85	1.00
1971	5,000,000	0.15	0.25	0.50	0.85	1.00
1974	—	0.15	0.25	0.50	0.85	1.00
1975	—	0.15	0.25	0.50	0.85	1.00
1977	40,000,000	0.10	0.20	0.35	0.75	1.00
1979	25,000,000	0.10	0.20	0.35	0.75	1.00
1982	20,000,000	0.10	0.20	0.35	0.75	1.00

KM# 87 50 CENTAVOS (Cincuenta)

Nickel Clad Steel **Obv:** Modified flag draped arms, date below **Rev:** Denomination within wreath

Date	Mintage	VF20	XF40	MS60	MS63	MS65
1985	30,000,000	0.10	0.20	0.30	0.50	0.75

KM# 90 50 CENTAVOS (Cincuenta)

Nickel Clad Steel **Obv:** Flag draped arms, date below **Rev:** Denomination within square **Note:** The circulation strikes were withdrawn from circulation and remelted. Approximately 100,000 pieces were released.

Date	Mintage	VF20	XF40	MS60	MS63	MS65
1988	—	—	—	0.20	0.30	0.50
1988 Proof	—	—	—	—	—	—

KM# 72 SUCRE (Un)

5.00 g., 0.720 Silver 0.1157 oz. ASW, 23.5 mm. **Obv:** Head of Sucre left, date below **Rev:** Flag draped arms, denomination above, mint name in legend below **Rev. Legend:** PHILA • U • S • A at bottom

Date	Mintage	F12	VF20	XF40	MS60	MS63
1928	3,000,000	2.25	3.00	8.00	15.00	30.00
1930	400,000	2.25	3.00	8.00	35.00	60.00
1934	2,000,000	2.25	3.00	8.00	15.00	30.00

KM# 78.1 SUCRE (Un)
6.75 g., Nickel, 26.5 mm. **Obv:** Flag draped arms, date below **Rev:** Head of Sucre left within wreath, denomination below **Edge:** Reeded

Date	Mintage	F12	VF20	XF40	MS60	MS63
1937 HF	9,000,000	0.50	1.00	2.00	3.00	5.00

KM# 78.2 SUCRE (Un)
6.75 g., Nickel, 26 mm. **Obv:** Flag-draped arms, date below **Rev:** Head of Sucre left **Edge:** Reeded

Date	Mintage	F12	VF20	XF40	MS60	MS63
1946	18,000,000	0.10	0.25	0.50	1.00	2.00

KM# 78a SUCRE (Un)
7.00 g., Copper-Nickel, 26 mm. **Obv:** Different ship in flag draped arms, date below **Rev:** Head of Sucre left within wreath, denomination below

Date	Mintage	VF20	XF40	MS60	MS63	MS65
1959	8,400,000	0.25	0.50	0.75	1.00	1.25
1959	—	PF63 250				

KM# 78b SUCRE (Un)
6.50 g., Nickel Clad Steel, 26 mm. **Obv:** Flag draped arms, date below **Rev:** Head left within wreath, denomination below **Edge:** Reeded **Note:** Ship in arms similar to KM#78

Date	Mintage	VF20	XF40	MS60	MS63	MS65
1964	20,000,000	0.10	0.25	0.75	1.00	1.25
1970	24,000,000	0.10	0.25	0.75	1.00	1.25
1971	8,092,000	0.10	0.25	0.75	1.00	1.25
1974	40,308,000	0.10	0.25	0.50	1.00	1.25
1978	32,000,000	0.10	0.25	0.50	1.00	1.25
1979	32,000,000	0.10	0.25	0.50	1.00	1.25
1980	110,000,000	0.10	0.25	0.50	1.00	1.25
1981	70,000,000	0.10	0.25	0.50	1.00	1.25

KM# 83 SUCRE (Un)
6.50 g., Nickel Clad Steel, 26 mm. **Obv:** Modified flag draped arms, date below **Rev:** Head left within wreath, denomination below **Edge:** Reeded **Note:** Ship in arms similar to KM #78

Date	Mintage	VF20	XF40	MS60	MS63	MS65
1974	32,000,000	0.10	0.20	0.40	0.75	1.00
1975	32,000,000	0.10	0.20	0.40	0.75	1.00
1975	—	PF65 150				
1977	32,000,000	0.10	0.20	0.35	0.75	1.00

KM# 85.1 SUCRE (Un)
6.50 g., Nickel Clad Steel, 26 mm. **Obv:** Modified coat of arms **Rev:** Large head right within wreath **Edge:** Reeded

Date	Mintage	VF20	XF40	MS60	MS63	MS65
1985	—	—	—	0.50	0.75	1.00

KM# 85.2 SUCRE (Un)
6.50 g., Nickel Clad Steel, 26 mm. **Obv:** Flag draped arms, date below **Rev:** Small head left within wreath, denomination below **Edge:** Reeded

Date	Mintage	VF20	XF40	MS60	MS63	MS65
1986	—	—	—	0.50	0.75	1.00

KM# 89 SUCRE (Un)
Nickel Clad Steel **Obv:** Flag draped arms, date below **Rev:** Head left within wreath, denomination below **Note:** The 1988 circulation strikes were reportedly withdrawn from circulation and remelted. Approximately 100,000 pieces were released.

Date	Mintage	VF20	XF40	MS60	MS63	MS65
1988	—	—	—	0.40	0.50	0.75
1988 Proof	—	—	—	—	—	—
1990	—	—	—	0.40	0.50	0.75

KM# 111 SUCRE (Un)
31.10 g., 0.900 Gold 0.8999 oz. AGW, 40 mm. **Subject:** Central Bank's 70th Anniversary **Obv:** Partial view of bank building **Rev:** Coin designs of 1 escudo KM-15 **Edge:** Reeded

Date	Mintage	VF20	XF40	MS60	MS63	MS65
ND (1997)	2,000	PF65 1,600				

KM# 73 2 SUCRES (Dos)
10.00 g., 0.720 Silver 0.2315 oz. ASW, 28.8 mm. **Obv:** Head of Sucre left, date below **Rev:** Flag draped arms, denomination above, mint name below **Rev. Legend:** PHILA • U • S • A at bottom

Date	Mintage	F12	VF20	XF40	MS60	MS63
1928	500,000	7.00	9.00	20.00	65.00	125
1930	100,000	8.00	12.00	30.00	75.00	175

KM# 80 2 SUCRES (Dos)
10.00 g., 0.720 Silver 0.2315 oz. ASW, 28.8 mm. **Obv:** Head of Sucre left, date below **Rev:** Flag draped arms, denomination above **Rev. Legend:** MEXICO at bottom

Date	Mintage	F12	VF20	XF40	MS60	MS63
1944 Mo	1,000,000	7.00	8.00	10.00	20.00	35.00

KM# 82 2 SUCRES (Dos)
Copper-Nickel **Obv:** Flag draped arms, date below **Rev:** Head 3/4 facing, divides denomination **Note:** Not released to circulation. Hundreds available in the numismatic market.

Date	Mintage	VF20	XF40	MS60	MS63	MS65
1973	2,000,000	—	—	75.00	125	225

KM# 79 5 SUCRES (Cinco)
25.00 g., 0.720 Silver 0.5787 oz. ASW **Obv:** Head of Sucre left, date below **Rev:** Flag draped arms, denomination above **Rev. Legend:** MEXICO at bottom **Edge:** Reeded

Date	Mintage	F12	VF20	XF40	MS60	MS63
1943 Mo	1,000,000	—	—	11.00	16.00	30.00
1944 Mo	2,600,000	—	—	11.00	16.00	30.00

KM# 84 5 SUCRES (Cinco)
Copper-Nickel **Obv:** Flag draped arms, date below **Rev:** Head of Sucre left within wreath, denomination below

Date	Mintage	VF20	XF40	MS60	MS63	MS65
1973	500	—	—	275	450	650

Note: While much of the original mintage was reported to have been melted, at least 100 or more pieces have made their way into the numismatic market.

KM# 91 5 SUCRES (Cinco)
5.29 g., Nickel Clad Steel, 22 mm. **Obv:** Flag draped arms, date below **Rev:** Denomination within lines, design in background **Note:** The 1988 circulation strikes were reportedly withdrawn from circulation and remelted. Approximately 100,000 pieces released.

Date	Mintage	VF20	XF40	MS60	MS63	MS65
1988	—	—	—	0.45	0.65	0.85
1988 Proof	—	—	—	—	—	—
1991	—	—	—	0.45	0.65	0.85

KM# 92.1 10 SUCRES (Diez)
Nickel Clad Steel, 24 mm. **Obv:** Flag draped arms, date below **Rev:** Denomination to right of statuette **Note:** Similar to KM#92.2 but small arms and letters. The circulation strikes were withdrawn from circulation and remelted. Approximately 100,000 pieces were released.

Date	Mintage	VF20	XF40	MS60	MS63	MS65
1988	—	—	—	0.50	0.75	1.00
1988 Proof	—	—	—	—	—	—

KM# 92.2 10 SUCRES (Diez)

6.17 g., Nickel Clad Steel, 24 mm. **Obv:** Flag draped arms, date below, large arms and letters **Rev:** Denomination to right of statuette

Date	Mintage	VF20	XF40	MS60	MS63	MS65
1991	—	—	—	0.50	0.75	1.00

KM# 94.1 20 SUCRES

Nickel Clad Steel, 26 mm. **Obv:** Flag draped arms, date below **Rev:** Denomination to right of small monument **Note:** The circulation strikes were withdrawn from circulation and remelted. Approximately 100,000 pieces released.

Date	Mintage	VF20	XF40	MS60	MS63	MS65
1988	—	—	—	0.65	1.00	1.50
1988 Proof	25	—	—	—	—	—

KM# 94.2 20 SUCRES

Nickel Clad Steel, 26 mm. **Obv:** Modified coat of arms **Rev:** Denomination to right of small monument

Date	Mintage	VF20	XF40	MS60	MS63	MS65
1991	—	—	—	0.65	1.00	1.50

KM# 93 50 SUCRES

Nickel Clad Steel, 29 mm. **Obv:** Flag draped arms, date below **Rev:** Denomination to left of native mask **Note:** The 1988 circulation strikes were withdrawn from circulation and remelted. Approximately 100,000 pieces released.

Date	Mintage	VF20	XF40	MS60	MS63	MS65
1988 Narrow date	—	—	—	1.00	1.50	2.50
Note: 141 denticles in obverse border						
1988 Proof	25	—	—	—	—	—
1991 Wide date	—	—	—	1.00	1.50	2.50
Note: 141 denticles in obverse border						
1991 Narrow date	—	—	—	1.00	1.50	2.50
Note: 161 denticles in obverse border						

KM# 96 100 SUCRES

Bi-Metallic Bronze plated Steel center in Nickel plated Steel ring, 19 mm. **Subject:** National Bicentennial **Obv:** Flag draped arms within circle, date below **Rev:** Bust left within circle, denomination below

Date	Mintage	VF20	XF40	MS60	MS63	MS65
1995	—	0.35	0.55	0.80	1.00	2.00

KM# 101 100 SUCRES

3.60 g., Bi-Metallic Brass clad steel center in Stainless Steel ring, 19.9 mm. **Subject:** 70th Anniversary - Central Bank **Obv:** Bust of Antonio Jose de Sucre left within circle, dates below **Rev:** Denomination within circle, grain sprigs flank

Date	Mintage	VF20	XF40	MS60	MS63	MS65
ND-1997	—	0.25	0.50	0.75	1.00	2.00

KM# 97 500 SUCRES

Bi-Metallic Bronze plated Steel center in Nickel plated Steel ring, 21.5 mm. **Subject:** State Reform **Obv:** Flag draped arms within circle, date below **Rev:** Isidro Ayora facing within circle, denomination below

Date	Mintage	VF20	XF40	MS60	MS63	MS65
1995	—	—	—	1.00	1.25	2.50

KM# 102 500 SUCRES

5.75 g., Bi-Metallic Aluminumn-Bronze center in Copper-Nickel ring, 21.5 mm. **Subject:** 70th Anniversary - Central Bank **Obv:** Isidro Ayora head facing within circle, dates below **Rev:** Denomination within circle, grain sprigs flank

Date	Mintage	VF20	XF40	MS60	MS63	MS65
ND-1997	—	—	—	1.00	1.25	2.50

KM# 86 1000 SUCRES

23.33 g., 0.925 Silver 0.6938 oz. ASW **Subject:** Championship Soccer **Obv:** Flag draped arms, date below **Rev:** Soccer player, globe in background, denomination below

Date	Mintage	VF20	XF40	MS60	MS63	MS65
1986	8,125	PF60 20.00	PF63 30.00	PF65 45.00		

KM# 88 1000 SUCRES

23.33 g., 0.925 Silver 0.6938 oz. ASW **Subject:** Championship Soccer **Obv:** Flag draped arms, date below **Rev:** Soccer players, globe in background, denomination below

Date	Mintage	VF20	XF40	MS60	MS63	MS65
1986	Est. 10000	PF60 20.00	PF63 30.00	PF65 45.00		

KM# 99 1000 SUCRES

Bi-Metallic Brass center in Stainless Steel ring, 23.5 mm. **Obv:** Flag draped arms within circle, date below **Rev:** Eugenio Espejo head right within circle, denomination below

Date	Mintage	VF20	XF40	MS60	MS63	MS65
1996	—	—	—	1.25	2.25	3.50

KM# 103 1000 SUCRES

7.19 g., Bi-Metallic Aluminumn-Bronze center in Copper-Nickel ring, 23.9 mm. **Subject:** 70th Anniversary - Central Bank **Obv:** Eugenio Espejo head right within circle, dates below **Rev:** Denomination within circle, grain sprigs flank **Edge:** Reeded

Date	Mintage	VF20	XF40	MS60	MS63	MS65
ND-1997	—	—	—	1.25	2.25	3.50

KM# 95 5000 SUCRES

27.00 g., 0.925 Silver 0.803 oz. ASW **Subject:** Ibero - American Series **Obv:** Flag draped arms and date within inner circle, circle of shields surround **Rev:** Native mask and dates above three ships, denomination below

Date	Mintage	VF20	XF40	MS60	MS63	MS65
1991	50,000	PF60 20.00	PF63 30.00	PF65 50.00		

KM# 98 5000 SUCRES

27.00 g., 0.925 Silver 0.803 oz. ASW **Subject:** Environmental Protection - Galapagos Penguins **Rev:** Two penguins, date at right, denomination below

Date	Mintage	VF20	XF40	MS60	MS63	MS65
1994	20,000	PF60 30.00	PF63 50.00	PF65 70.00		

KM# 100 5000 SUCRES

27.00 g., 0.925 Silver 0.803 oz. ASW **Subject:** Ibero-American Series - Native Costumes

Date	Mintage	VF20	XF40	MS60	MS63	MS65
1997	20,000	PF60 25.00	PF63 40.00	PF65 55.00		

KM# 109 5000 SUCRES

27.10 g., 0.925 Silver 0.8059 oz. ASW, 40 mm. **Subject:** Ibero-America Series **Obv:** Flag draped arms within a circle of arms **Rev:** Man on horse with condor in background, date at left, denomination below **Edge:** Reeded

Date	Mintage	VF20	XF40	MS60	MS63	MS65
1999	—	PF60 25.00	PF63 40.00	PF65 60.00		

KM# 74 CONDOR (Un)
8.36 g., 0.900 Gold 0.2419 oz. AGW **Obv:** Head of Bolivar left, date below **Rev:** Flag draped arms, denomination above, mint name below **Rev. Legend:** BIRMINGHAM at bottom **Note:** 5,000 were released into circulation; the remainder are held as the Central Bank gold reserve.

Date	Mintage	F12	VF20	XF40	MS60	MS63
1928	20,000	—	310	450	500	675

REFORM COINAGE

100 Centavos = 1 Dollar

KM# 104 CENTAVO (Un)
2.52 g., Brass, 19 mm. **Obv:** Map of the Americas within circle **Rev:** Denomination **Edge:** Plain

Date	Mintage	VF20	XF40	MS60	MS63	MS65
2000	—	—	—	0.20	0.40	0.50

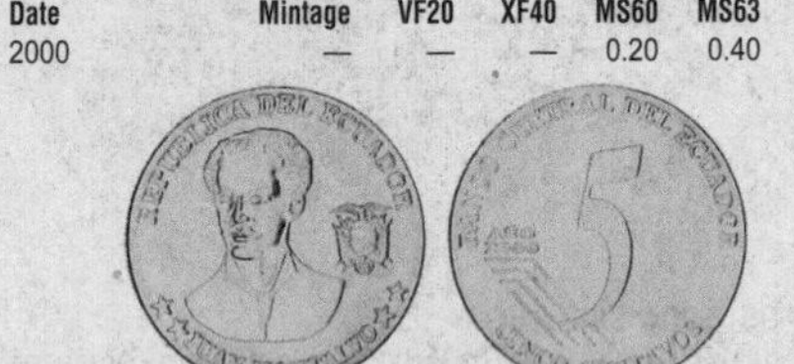

KM# 105 5 CENTAVOS (Cinco)
5.00 g., Steel, 21.2 mm. **Subject:** Juan Montalvo **Obv:** Bust 3/4 facing and arms **Rev:** Denomination **Edge:** Plain

Date	Mintage	VF20	XF40	MS60	MS63	MS65
2000	—	—	—	0.50	0.75	1.00

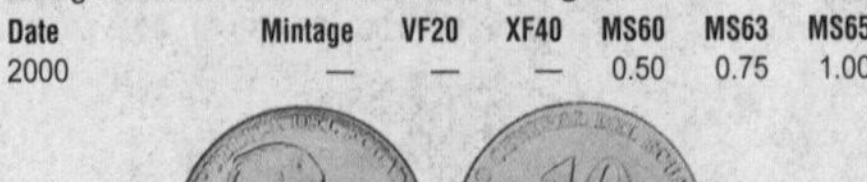

KM# 106 10 CENTAVOS (Diez)
2.24 g., Steel, 17.9 mm. **Subject:** Eugenio Espejo **Obv:** Bust 3/4 left and arms **Rev:** Denomination **Edge:** Reeded

Date	Mintage	VF20	XF40	MS60	MS63	MS65
2000	—	—	—	0.25	0.50	0.65

KM# 107 25 CENTAVOS
5.65 g., Steel, 24.2 mm. **Subject:** Jose Joaquin De Olmedo **Obv:** Bust facing and arms **Rev:** Denomination **Edge:** Reeded

Date	Mintage	VF20	XF40	MS60	MS63	MS65
2000	—	—	—	0.25	0.50	0.65

KM# 108 50 CENTAVOS (Cincuenta)
11.32 g., Steel, 30.6 mm. **Subject:** Eloy Alfaro **Obv:** Head at left 3/4 facing and arms **Rev:** Denomination **Edge:** Reeded

Date	Mintage	VF20	XF40	MS60	MS63	MS65
2000	—	—	0.50	1.25	1.75	3.00

KM# 110 SUCRE (Un)
11.25 g., Nickel Clad Steel, 30.5 mm. **Obv:** Denomination **Rev:** Antonio Jose De Sucre and small national arms **Edge:** Reeded

Date	Mintage	VF20	XF40	MS60	MS63	MS65
2000	—	—	0.50	1.25	1.75	3.00

PATTERNS

Including off metal strikes

KM#	Date	Mintage	Identification	Mkt Val
Pn11	1928	—	Condor. Copper-Nickel. KM#74.	—
Pn12	1928	—	Condor. Copper. KM#74.	—
PnA13	1970	—	20 Centavos. Brass. KM#75c, non-magnetic, issued in a commemorative set from Monnaies et Medailles du Monde in Paris (1977).	225
Pn13	1974	—	20 Centavos. Brass. KM#77.2, non-magnetic, issued in a commemorative set from Monnaies et Medailles du Monde in Paris (1977).	225
Pn14	1975	—	50 Centavos. Brass. KM#81, non-magnetic, issued in a commemorative set from Monnaies et Medailles du Monde in Paris (1977).	225
Pn15	1975	—	Sucre. Brass. KM#83, non-magnetic, issued in a commemorative set from Monnaies et Medailles du Monde in Paris (1977).	225
Pn16	1976	—	10 Centavos. Brass. KM#76d, non-magnetic, issued in a commemorative set from Monnaies et Medailles du Monde in Paris (1977).	225

PIEDFORT

KM#	Date	Mintage	Identification	Mkt Val
P1	1915H	—	1/2 Decimo. Copper-Nickel.	750
P2	1915H	—	Decimo. Copper-Nickel.	750

MINT SETS

KM#	Date	Mintage	Identification	Issue Price	Mkt Val
MS35	1975 (0)	10,000	8 circulating coins and 1 commemorative dollar Polo	30.00	25.00
MSA36	1977 (5)	—	KM#PnA13, Pn13-Pn16 Commemorative set struck in brass by Monnaies et Medailles du Monde, Paris in 1977	—	1,000
MS36	2000 (5)	—	KM#104-108	30.00	20.00

PROOF SETS

KM#	Date	Mintage	Identification	Issue Price	Mkt Val
PS3	1988 (6)	25	KM#89-94	—	—

EGYPT

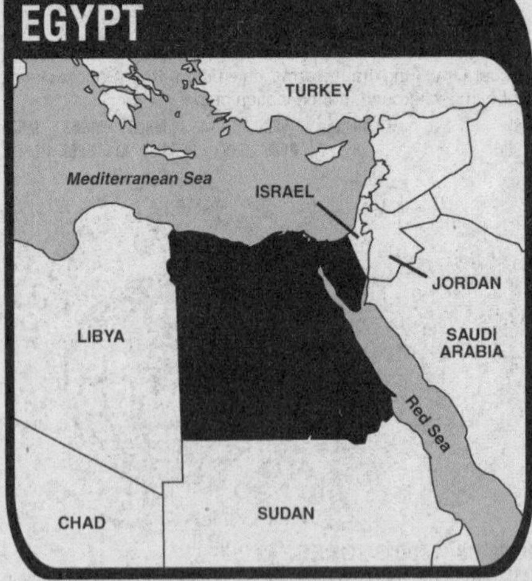

The Arab Republic of Egypt, located on the northeastern corner of Africa, has an area of 385,229 sq. mi. (1,1001,450 sq. km.) and a population of 62.4 million. Capital: Cairo. Although Egypt is an almost rainless expanse of desert, its economy is predominantly agricultural. Cotton, rice and petroleum are exported. Other main sources of income are revenues from the Suez Canal, remittances of Egyptian workers abroad and tourism.

Egyptian history dates back to about 3000 B.C. when the empire was established by uniting the upper and lower kingdoms. Following its 'Golden Age' (16th to 13th centuries B.C.), Egypt was conquered by Persia (525 B.C.) and Alexander the Great (332 B.C.). The Ptolemies, descended from one of Alexander's generals, ruled until the suicide of Cleopatra (30 B.C.) when Egypt became the private domain of the Roman emperor, and subsequently part of the Byzantine world. Various Muslim dynasties ruled Egypt from 641 on, including Ayyubid Sultans to 1250 and Mamluks to 1517, when it was conquered by the Ottoman Turks, interrupted by the occupation of Napoleon (1798-1801). A semi-independent dynasty was founded by Muhammad Ali in 1805 which lasted until 1952. Turkish rule became increasingly casual, permitting Great Britain to inject its influence by purchasing shares in the Suez Canal. British troops occupied Egypt in 1882, becoming the de facto rulers. On Dec. 14, 1914, Egypt was made a protectorate of Britain. British occupation ended on Feb. 28, 1922, when Egypt became a sovereign, independent kingdom. The monarchy was abolished and a republic proclaimed on June 18, 1953.

On Feb. 1, 1958, Egypt and Syria formed the United Arab Republic. Yemen joined on March 8 in an association known as the United Arab States. Syria withdrew from the United Arab Republic on Sept. 29, 1961, and on Dec. 26 Egypt dissolved its ties with Yemen in the United Arab States. On Sept. 2, 1971, Egypt finally shed the name United Arab Republic in favor of the Arab Republic of Egypt.

RULERS

British, 1882-1922

Kingdom, 1922-1953

Ahmed Fuad I, 1922-1936
Farouk, 1936-1952
Fuad II, 1952-1953

Republic, 1953-

MONETARY SYSTEM

(1885-1916)
10 Ushr-al-Qirsh = 1 Piastre
(Commencing 1916)
10 Milliemes = 1 Piastre (Qirsh)
100 Piastres = 1 Pound (Gunayh)

MINT MARKS

Egyptian coins issued prior to the advent of the British Protectorate series of Sultan Hussein Kamil introduced in 1916 were very similar to Turkish coins of the same period. They can best be distinguished by the presence of the Arabic word *Misr* Egypt) on the reverse, which generally appears immediately above the Muslim accession date of the ruler, which is presented in Arabic numerals. Each coin is individually dated according to the regnal years.

BP - Budapest, Hungary
H - Birmingham, England
KN - King's Norton, England

ENGRAVER

W - Emil Weigand, Berlin

REGNAL YEAR IDENTIFICATION

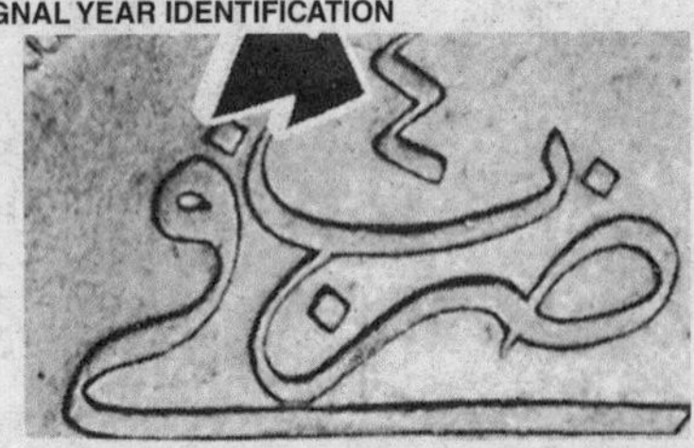

4
Duriba fi

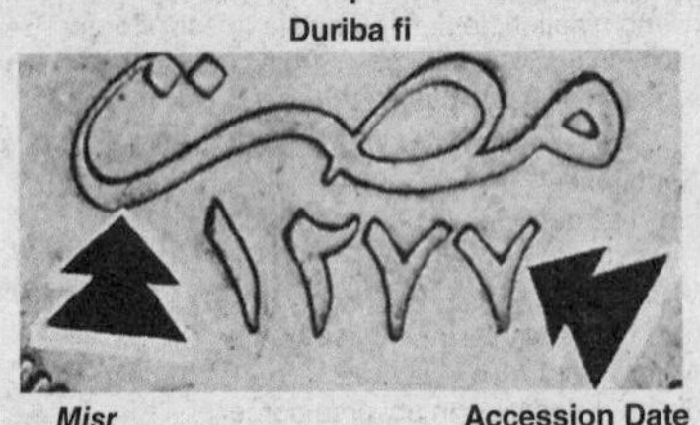

Misr **Accession Date**

DENOMINATIONS

Para

Qirsh

NOTE: The unit of value on coins of this period is generally presented on the obverse immediately below the toughra, as shown in the illustrations above.

Piastres **1916-1933**

Milliemes

Piastres **1934 –**

TITLES

al-Mamlaka al-Misriya

(The Kingdom of Egypt)

U.A.R. EGYPT

The legend illustrated is *Jumhuriyat Misr al-Arabiyya* which translates to 'The Arab Republic of Egypt'. Similar legends are found on the modern issues of Syria.

OTTOMAN EMPIRE

Abdul Hamid II

AH1293-1327/1876-1909AD

REFORM COINAGE

KM# 287 1/40 QIRSH

Bronze **Obv:** Toughra **Rev:** Legend **Mint:** Misr

Date	Mintage	VF20	XF40	MS60	MS63	MS65
AH1293/27	1,200,000	1.50	4.00	12.00	20.00	—
AH1293/29	2,000,000	1.00	3.00	6.00	17.00	—
AH1293/31	2,400,000	1.00	3.00	6.00	17.00	—
AH1293/32	Inc. below	1.00	4.00	12.00	20.00	—
AH1293/33	1,200,000	1.00	4.00	12.00	20.00	—
AH1293/35	1,200,000	3.00	8.00	15.00	25.00	—

KM# 288 1/20 QIRSH

3.12 g., Bronze **Obv:** Toughra **Rev:** Legend **Note:** Misir or Heaton mint.

Date	Mintage	VF20	XF40	MS60	MS63	MS65
AH1293/26	1,405,000	1.00	2.00	3.00	12.00	—
AH1293/27	1,402,000	1.00	3.00	5.00	12.00	—
AH1293/29	3,200,000	1.00	3.00	5.00	14.00	—
AH1293/31 H	3,000,000	1.00	3.00	5.00	14.00	—
AH1293/32 H	Inc. below	1.00	3.00	5.00	14.00	—
AH1293/33 H	1,400,000	2.00	3.00	7.00	16.00	—
AH1293/35 H	1,400,000	3.00	6.00	12.00	20.00	—

KM# 289 1/10 QIRSH

1.75 g., Copper-Nickel, 14.7 mm. **Obv:** Toughra **Rev:** Denomination **Mint:** Misr

Date	Mintage	VF20	XF40	MS60	MS63	MS65
AH1293/27-35	—	PF63 100				
Note: Above value for common date proof						
AH1293/27	3,010,000	1.00	2.00	5.00	10.00	—
AH1293/28	6,000,000	1.00	2.00	5.00	10.00	—
AH1293/29	1,500,000	1.00	3.00	6.00	15.00	—
AH1293/30	1,000,000	1.00	3.00	6.00	15.00	—
AH1293/31	3,000,000	1.00	3.00	6.00	15.00	—
AH1293/32	Inc. below	1.00	3.00	6.00	15.00	—
AH1293/33	2,000,000	1.00	3.00	5.00	10.00	—
AH1293/35	2,000,000	1.25	5.00	12.00	20.00	—

KM# 290 2/10 QIRSH

2.39 g., Copper-Nickel **Obv:** Toughra **Rev:** Denomination **Mint:** Misr

Date	Mintage	VF20	XF40	MS60	MS63	MS65
AH1293/27	1,002,000	1.00	5.00	12.00	20.00	—
AH1293/28	2,000,000	1.00	5.00	12.00	20.00	—
AH1293/29	1,500,000	1.00	5.00	12.00	20.00	—
AH1293/30	—	3.00	12.00	22.00	42.00	—
AH1293/31 H	1,000,000	1.00	5.00	12.00	20.00	—
AH1293/33 H	1,500,000	1.00	5.00	12.00	20.00	—
AH1293/35 H	750,000	2.00	10.00	20.00	35.00	—

KM# 291 5/10 QIRSH

3.71 g., Copper-Nickel, 21 mm. **Mint:** Misr

Date	Mintage	VF20	XF40	MS60	MS63	MS65
AH1293/27	4,999,000	0.30	5.00	11.00	20.00	—
AH1293/29	12,000,000	0.30	2.00	6.00	12.00	—
AH1293/30	2,000,000	0.50	4.00	12.00	25.00	—
AH1293/33	1,000,000	2.00	9.00	22.50	40.00	—
AH1293/27-33	—	PF63 145				
Note: Above value for common date proof						

KM# 292 QIRSH

1.40 g., 0.833 Silver 0.0375 oz. ASW **Obv:** Toughra **Mint:** Misr

Date	Mintage	VF20	XF40	MS60	MS63	MS65
AH1293/27-33	—	PF63 155				
Note: Above value for common date proof						
AH1293/27 W	200,000	1.50	8.00	17.00	32.50	—
AH1293/29 W	100,000	1.75	8.00	18.00	35.00	—
AH1293/29 H	100,000	1.50	6.00	14.00	30.00	—
AH1293/33	100,000	1.50	6.00	14.00	30.00	—

KM# 299 QIRSH

Copper-Nickel **Obv:** Toughra **Rev:** Stars surround legend **Mint:** Misr

Date	Mintage	VF20	XF40	MS60	MS63	MS65
AH1293/27	999,000	2.00	12.00	32.00	50.00	—
AH1293/29	3,500,000	2.00	5.00	15.00	30.00	—
AH1293/30	500,000	2.50	14.00	35.00	55.00	—
AH1293/33	1,000,000	2.00	8.00	22.00	45.00	—

KM# 293 2 QIRSH

2.80 g., 0.833 Silver 0.075 oz. ASW, 19 mm. **Obv:** Flower to right of toughra **Rev:** Denomination **Mint:** Misr

Date	Mintage	VF20	XF40	MS60	MS63	MS65
AH1293/17-33	—	PF63 165				
Note: Above value for common date of proof						
AH1293/27 W	1,000,000	3.50	9.00	25.00	45.00	—
AH1293/29 W	450,000	4.00	12.00	30.00	50.00	—
AH1293/29	1,250,000	3.00	7.00	17.00	35.00	—
AH1293/30	500,000	4.00	12.00	25.00	46.00	—
AH1293/31	Inc. above	4.00	12.00	25.00	46.00	—
AH1293/33	450,000	4.00	12.00	25.00	45.00	—

KM# 294 5 QIRSH

7.00 g., 0.833 Silver 0.1875 oz. ASW **Obv:** Flower at right of toughra

Date	Mintage	VF20	XF40	MS60	MS63	MS65
AH1293/27 W	448,000	8.00	17.00	32.50	60.00	—
AH1293/29 W	600,000	8.00	17.00	32.50	60.00	—
AH1293/29 H	3,465,000	8.00	17.00	32.50	60.00	—
AH1293/30 H	1,213,000	8.00	17.00	37.50	70.00	—
AH1293/31 H	1,959,000	8.00	17.00	37.50	70.00	—
AH1293/32 H	Inc. above	8.00	17.00	32.50	60.00	—
AH1293/33 H	2,800,000	8.00	14.00	32.50	60.00	—

KM# 298 5 QIRSH

0.42 g., 0.875 Gold 0.0118 oz. AGW **Obv:** "Al-Ghazi" at right of toughra **Rev:** Denomination

Date	Mintage	VF20	XF40	MS60	MS63	MS65
AH1293//26	—	50.00	140	175	250	—
AH1293//34	8,000	50.00	140	175	250	—

KM# 295 10 QIRSH

14.00 g., 0.833 Silver 0.3749 oz. ASW **Obv:** Flower at right of toughra **Rev:** Denomination **Mint:** Misr

Date	Mintage	VF20	XF40	MS60	MS63	MS65
AH1293/27-33	—	PF63 435				
Note: Above value for common date of proof						
AH1293/27 W	250,000	18.00	50.00	95.00	150	—
AH1293/29 W	Est. 2450000	15.00	35.00	70.00	115	—
AH1293/29	2,950,000	15.00	35.00	70.00	115	—
AH1293/30	1,000,000	15.00	35.00	70.00	115	—
AH1293/31	1,250,000	15.00	35.00	70.00	150	—
AH1293/32	Inc. below	14.00	30.00	65.00	100	—
AH1293/33	2,400,000	14.00	30.00	65.00	100	—

KM# 282 10 QIRSH

0.85 g., 0.875 Gold 0.024 oz. AGW **Obv:** Al-Ghazi at right of toughra **Rev:** Denomination **Mint:** Misr

Date	Mintage	VF20	XF40	MS60	MS63	MS65
AH1293/34	5,000	100	250	300	525	—

KM# 296 20 QIRSH

28.00 g., 0.833 Silver 0.7499 oz. ASW **Obv:** Toughra **Rev:** Legend within wreath **Mint:** Misr

Date	Mintage	VF20	XF40	MS60	MS63	MS65
AH1293/27-33	—	PF63 950				
Note: Above value for common date of proof						
AH1293/27 W	25,000	42.00	125	290	575	—
AH1293/29 W	50,000	50.00	125	230	500	—
AH1293/29	425,000	50.00	125	205	450	—
AH1293/30	200,000	50.00	115	230	450	—
AH1293/31	250,000	50.00	115	230	450	—
AH1293/32	Inc. below	50.00	115	230	450	—
AH1293/33	300,000	50.00	100	200	400	—

Muhammad V

AH1327-1332/1909-1914AD

MILLED COINAGE

KM# 300 1/40 QIRSH

Bronze **Obv:** Tughra **Rev:** Denomination **Mint:** Misr

Date	Mintage	VF20	XF40	MS60	MS63	MS65
AH1327/2	2,000,000	1.50	5.00	10.00	25.00	—
AH1327/3	2,000,000	1.50	5.00	10.00	25.00	—
AH1327/4	1,200,000	1.50	5.00	10.00	25.00	—
AH1327/6	1,200,000	1.00	4.00	8.00	20.00	—

KM# 301 1/20 QIRSH
Bronze **Obv:** Tughra **Rev:** Denomination **Mint:** Misr

Date	Mintage	VF20	XF40	MS60	MS63	MS65
AH1327/2 H	2,000,000	1.00	5.00	11.00	18.00	—
AH1327/3 H	2,000,000	1.50	5.00	15.00	25.00	—
AH1327/4 H	2,400,000	1.00	5.00	11.00	18.00	—
AH1327/6 H	1,400,000	0.75	4.00	11.00	18.00	—

KM# 302 1/10 QIRSH
Copper-Nickel **Obv:** Tughra **Rev:** Denomination **Mint:** Misr

Date	Mintage	VF20	XF40	MS60	MS63	MS65
AH1327/2-6 H	—	PF63 110				
Note: Above value for common date of proof						
AH1327/2 H	3,000,000	3.00	6.00	15.00	25.00	—
AH1327/3	1,000,000	5.00	12.00	30.00	50.00	—
AH1327/4 H	3,000,000	1.00	2.00	5.00	14.00	—
AH1327/6 H	3,000,000	0.75	1.50	3.00	12.50	—

KM# 303 2/10 QIRSH
2.42 g., Copper-Nickel **Obv:** Tughra within wreath **Rev:** Denomination **Mint:** Misr

Date	Mintage	VF20	XF40	MS60	MS63	MS65
AH1327/2 H	1,000,000	2.00	6.00	15.00	25.00	—
AH1327/3	500,000	3.00	10.00	20.00	35.00	—
AH1327/4 H	1,000,000	2.00	6.00	15.00	25.00	—
AH1327/6 H	1,000,000	1.25	6.00	15.00	25.00	—
AH1327/2-6 H	—	PF63 120				
Note: Above value for common date of proof						

KM# 304 5/10 QIRSH
Copper-Nickel **Obv:** Tughra within wreath **Rev:** Denomination **Mint:** Misr

Date	Mintage	VF20	XF40	MS60	MS63	MS65
AH1327/2	2,131,000	2.50	12.00	20.00	50.00	—
AH1327/3	1,000,000	5.00	22.00	45.00	75.00	—
AH1327/4	3,327,000	1.00	7.00	11.00	25.00	—
AH1327/6	3,000,000	1.00	7.00	11.00	25.00	—

KM# 305 QIRSH
1.40 g., 0.833 Silver 0.0375 oz. ASW **Obv:** Tughra **Rev:** Denomination **Mint:** Misr

Date	Mintage	VF20	XF40	MS60	MS63	MS65
AH1327/2	251,000	5.00	20.00	20.00	60.00	—
AH1327/3	171,000	5.00	20.00	35.00	70.00	—

KM# 306 QIRSH
Copper-Nickel **Obv:** Tughra within wreath **Rev:** Denomination within circle of stars **Mint:** Misr

Date	Mintage	VF20	XF40	MS60	MS63	MS65
AH1327/2	1,000,000	2.00	7.00	18.00	35.00	—
AH1327/3	300,000	20.00	40.00	95.00	150	—
AH1327/4	500,000	4.00	15.00	40.00	75.00	—
AH1327/6	2,500,000	2.00	6.00	8.00	20.00	—

KM# 307 2 QIRSH
2.80 g., 0.833 Silver 0.075 oz. ASW **Obv:** Tughra, spray below **Rev:** Denomination within wreath **Mint:** Misr

Date	Mintage	VF20	XF40	MS60	MS63	MS65
AH1327/2	250,000	8.00	25.00	50.00	110	—
AH1327/3	300,000	8.00	25.00	50.00	110	—

KM# 308 5 QIRSH
7.00 g., 0.833 Silver 0.1875 oz. ASW **Obv:** Tughra above spray **Rev:** Denomination within wreath **Mint:** Misr

Date	Mintage	VF20	XF40	MS60	MS63	MS65
AH1327/2-6	—	PF63 400				
Note: Above value for common date of proof						
AH1327/2	574,000	12.00	46.00	100	175	—
AH1327/3	2,400,000	8.00	22.50	46.00	80.00	—
AH1327/4	1,351,000	9.00	25.00	50.00	100	—
AH1327/6	7,400,000	7.00	20.00	40.00	65.00	—

KM# 309 10 QIRSH
14.00 g., 0.833 Silver 0.3749 oz. ASW **Obv:** Tughra, spray below **Rev:** Denomination within wreath

Date	Mintage	VF20	XF40	MS60	MS63	MS65
AH1327/2-6 H	—	PF63 550				
Note: Above value for common date of proof						
AH1327/2 H	300,000	22.50	60.00	125	230	—
AH1327/3 H	1,300,000	17.00	40.00	85.00	130	—
AH1327/4 H	300,000	20.00	60.00	125	230	—
AH1327/6 H	4,212,000	15.00	35.00	48.00	90.00	—

KM# 310 20 QIRSH
28.00 g., 0.833 Silver 0.7499 oz. ASW, 40 mm. **Obv:** Tughra, spray below **Rev:** Denomination within wreath **Mint:** Misr

Date	Mintage	VF20	XF40	MS60	MS63	MS65
AH1327/2-6	—	PF63 1,100				
Note: Above value for common date of proof						
AH1327/2	75,000	60.00	85.00	240	575	—
AH1327/3	600,000	45.00	85.00	115	375	—
AH1327/4 H	100,000	45.00	95.00	155	500	—
AH1327/6 H	875,000	40.00	75.00	95.00	350	—

BRITISH PROTECTORATE

AH1333-1341 / 1914-1922AD

Hussein Kamil

As Sultan, AH1333-1336/1914-1917AD

OCCUPATION COINAGE

KM# 312 1/2 MILLIEME
Bronze **Obv:** Tughra, date below **Rev:** Dates below denominations **Note:** Accession date: AH1333.

Date	Mintage	VF20	XF40	MS60	MS63	MS65
AH1335-1917	4,000,000	2.00	8.00	15.00	25.00	—

KM# 313 MILLIEME
Copper-Nickel **Obv:** Center hole divides date and legend **Rev:** Center hole divides denomination, date below **Note:** Accession date: AH1333.

Date	Mintage	VF20	XF40	MS60	MS63	MS65
AH1335-1917	4,002,000	1.25	4.00	11.00	20.00	—
AH1335-1917 H	12,000,000	0.40	2.00	7.00	12.00	—

KM# 314 2 MILLIEMES
Copper-Nickel **Obv:** Center hole divides date **Rev:** Center hole divides denomination, date below **Note:** Accession date: AH1333.

Date	Mintage	VF20	XF40	MS60	MS63	MS65
AH1335-1916 H	300,000	1.25	8.00	15.00	30.00	—
AH1335-1917	3,006,000	1.00	4.00	12.00	22.00	—
AH1335-1917 H	9,000,000	0.40	2.00	5.00	14.00	—

KM# 315 5 MILLIEMES
4.75 g., Copper-Nickel **Obv:** Center hole divides dates **Rev:** Center hole divides denomination **Note:** Accession date: AH1333.

Date	Mintage	VF20	XF40	MS60	MS63	MS65
AH1335-1916	3,000,000	2.00	5.00	25.00	50.00	—
AH1335-1916 H	3,000,000	1.35	5.50	25.00	50.00	—
AH1335-1917	6,776,000	1.00	2.50	6.00	15.00	—
AH1335-1917 H	37,000,000	0.60	1.50	2.50	8.00	—

KM# 316 10 MILLIEMES
Copper-Nickel **Obv:** Center hole divides dates **Rev:** Center hole divides denomination **Note:** Accession date: AH1333.

Date	Mintage	VF20	XF40	MS60	MS63	MS65
AH1335-1916	1,006,999	2.00	6.00	40.00	100	—
AH1335-1916 H	1,000,000	1.50	6.00	40.00	100	—
AH1335-1917	1,010,999	2.00	6.00	18.00	35.00	—
AH1335-1917 H	6,000,000	0.75	2.00	7.00	16.00	—
AH1335-1917 KN	4,000,000	1.25	3.00	8.00	20.00	—

KM# 317.1 2 PIASTRES
2.80 g., 0.833 Silver 0.075 oz. ASW, 19 mm. **Obv:** Text above date and sprays **Rev:** Denomination, legend within wreath **Note:** Accession date: AH1333.

Date	Mintage	VF20	XF40	MS60	MS63	MS65
AH1335-1916	2,505,000	4.00	7.00	17.00	35.00	—
AH1335-1917	4,461,000	3.00	6.00	12.00	22.50	—

KM# 317.2 2 PIASTRES
2.80 g., 0.833 Silver 0.075 oz. ASW **Obv:** Without inner circle **Rev:** Without inner circle **Note:** Accession date: AH1333.

Date	Mintage	VF20	XF40	MS60	MS63	MS65
AH1335-1917 H	2,180,000	3.00	5.00	10.00	20.00	—

KM# 318.1 5 PIASTRES
7.00 g., 0.833 Silver 0.1875 oz. ASW, 26 mm. **Obv:** Text within wreath **Rev:** Denomination within wreath **Edge:** Reeded **Note:** Accession date: AH1333.

Date	Mintage	VF20	XF40	MS60	MS63	MS65
AH1335-1916	6,000,000	8.00	14.00	22.50	42.00	—
AH1335-1917	9,218,000	8.00	14.00	20.00	37.50	—

KM# 318.2 5 PIASTRES
7.00 g., 0.833 Silver 0.1875 oz. ASW **Obv:** Without inner circle **Rev:** Without inner circle **Note:** Accession date: AH1333.

Date	Mintage	VF20	XF40	MS60	MS63	MS65
AH1335-1917 H	5,036,000	8.00	14.00	25.00	50.00	—
AH1335-1917 H	—	PF63 375				

KM# 319 10 PIASTRES
14.00 g., 0.833 Silver 0.3749 oz. ASW **Obv:** Text above date within wreath **Rev:** Denomination within wreath, dates below **Note:** Accession date: AH1333.

Date	Mintage	VF20	XF40	MS60	MS63	MS65
AH1335-1916	2,900,000	14.00	22.50	46.00	75.00	—
AH1335-1917	4,859,000	14.00	20.00	25.00	50.00	—

KM# 320 10 PIASTRES
14.00 g., 0.833 Silver 0.3749 oz. ASW **Obv:** Text above date within wreath, without inner circle **Rev:** Denomination within wreath, without inner circle **Note:** Accession date: AH1333.

Date	Mintage	VF20	XF40	MS60	MS63	MS65
AH1335-1917 H	2,000,000	14.00	22.50	50.00	80.00	—

KM# 321 20 PIASTRES
28.00 g., 0.833 Silver 0.7499 oz. ASW, 40 mm. **Obv:** Text above date within wreath **Rev:** Denomination within wreath, dates below **Note:** Accession date: AH1333.

Date	Mintage	VF20	XF40	MS60	MS63	MS65
AH1335-1916	1,500,000	45.00	75.00	150	200	—
AH1335-1917	840,000	45.00	75.00	150	200	—
AH1335-1917	—	PF63 875				

KM# 322 20 PIASTRES
28.00 g., 0.833 Silver 0.7499 oz. ASW **Obv:** Without inner circle **Rev:** Without inner circle **Note:** Accession date: AH1333.

Date	Mintage	VF20	XF40	MS60	MS63	MS65
AH1335-1917 H	250,000	45.00	95.00	175	230	—

KM# 324 100 PIASTRES
8.50 g., 0.875 Gold 0.2391 oz. AGW **Obv:** Text above date within wreath **Rev:** Denomination within wreath, dates below **Note:** Accession date: AH1333.

Date	Mintage	VF20	XF40	MS60	MS63	MS65
AH1335-1916	10,000	—	305	425	525	—
AH1335-1916 Prooflike	—					

Note: Restrikes may exist

Fuad I

As Sultan, AH1336-1341/1917-1922AD

KM# 325 2 PIASTRES
2.80 g., 0.833 Silver 0.075 oz. ASW **Obv:** Text above date **Rev:** Denomination and dates **Note:** Accession date: AH1335.

Date	Mintage	VF20	XF40	MS60	MS63	MS65
AH1338-1920 H	2,820,000	30.00	80.00	225	350	—

KM# 326 5 PIASTRES
7.00 g., 0.833 Silver 0.1875 oz. ASW **Obv:** Text above date **Rev:** Denomination and dates **Note:** Accession date: AH1335.

Date	Mintage	VF20	XF40	MS60	MS63	MS65
AH1338-1920 H	1,000,000	20.00	70.00	200	325	—

KM# 327 10 PIASTRES
14.00 g., 0.833 Silver 0.3749 oz. ASW **Obv:** Text above date **Rev:** Denomination and dates **Note:** Accession date: AH1335.

Date	Mintage	VF20	XF40	MS60	MS63	MS65
AH1338-1920 H	500,000	40.00	90.00	180	300	—

KM# 328 20 PIASTRES
28.00 g., 0.833 Silver 0.7499 oz. ASW **Obv:** Text above date **Rev:** Denomination and dates **Note:** Accession date: AH1335.

Date	Mintage	VF20	XF40	MS60	MS63	MS65
AH1338-1920 H Rare	2	—	—	—	—	—

KINGDOM

AH1341-1372 / 1922-1952AD

Fuad I

As King, AH1341-1355/1922-1936AD

DECIMAL COINAGE

KM# 330 1/2 MILLIEME
Bronze **Obv:** Bust right **Rev:** Denomination, dates above

Date	Mintage	VF20	XF40	MS60	MS63	MS65
AH1342-1924 H	3,000,000	2.00	5.00	14.00	25.00	—
AH1342-1924 H	—	PF63 120				

KM# 343 1/2 MILLIEME
Bronze **Obv:** Uniformed bust left **Rev:** Dates above denomination **Mint:** British Royal Mint

Date	Mintage	VF20	XF40	MS60	MS63	MS65
AH1348-1929	1,000,000	6.00	20.00	30.00	50.00	—
AH1351-1932	1,000,000	3.00	20.00	30.00	50.00	—
AH1351-1932	—	PF63 160				

KM# 331 MILLIEME
Bronze **Obv:** Bust right. **Rev:** Denomination divides dates

Date	Mintage	VF20	XF40	MS60	MS63	MS65
AH1342-1924 H	6,500,000	1.25	3.00	6.00	15.00	—

KM# 344 MILLIEME
4.24 g., Bronze **Obv:** Uniformed bust left **Rev:** Denomination divides dates

Date	Mintage	VF20	XF40	MS60	MS63	MS65
AH1348-1929 BP	4,500,000	1.50	4.00	10.00	20.00	—
AH1351-1932 H	2,500,000	0.50	1.25	6.00	15.00	—
AH1351-1932 H	—	PF63 120				
AH1352-1933 H	5,110,000	1.25	3.00	15.00	40.00	—
AH1354-1935 H	18,000,000	0.20	0.50	2.00	8.00	—

KM# 332 2 MILLIEMES
Copper-Nickel **Obv:** Bust right **Rev:** Denomination divides dates

Date	Mintage	VF20	XF40	MS60	MS63	MS65
AH1342-1924 H	4,500,000	1.25	3.00	10.00	20.00	—
AH1342-1924 H	—	PF63 120				

KM# 345 2 MILLIEMES
Copper-Nickel **Obv:** Uniformed bust left **Rev:** Denomination divides dates

Date	Mintage	VF20	XF40	MS60	MS63	MS65
AH1348-1929 BP	Est. 3500000	0.40	1.00	5.00	10.00	—

KM# 356 2-1/2 MILLIEMES
Copper-Nickel **Obv:** Uniformed bust left **Rev:** Denomination divides dates **Shape:** 8-sided **Mint:** British Royal Mint

Date	Mintage	VF20	XF40	MS60	MS63	MS65
AH1352-1933	4,000,000	1.25	7.00	10.00	30.00	—

KM# 333 5 MILLIEMES
Copper-Nickel **Obv:** Bust right **Rev:** Denomination divides dates

Date	Mintage	VF20	XF40	MS60	MS63	MS65
AH1342-1924	6,000,000	1.25	6.00	17.50	28.00	—

KM# 346 5 MILLIEMES
3.80 g., Copper-Nickel, 21 mm. **Obv:** Uniformed bust left **Rev:** Denomination divides dates

Date	Mintage	VF20	XF40	MS60	MS63	MS65
AH1348-1929 BP	4,000,000	0.75	5.00	14.00	25.00	—
AH1352-1933 H	3,000,000	1.50	4.00	18.00	35.00	—
AH1354-1935 H	8,000,000	0.80	1.00	6.00	12.50	—
AH1354-1935 H	—	PF63 120				

KM# 334 10 MILLIEMES
5.19 g., Copper-Nickel **Obv:** Bust right **Rev:** Denomination divides dates

Date	Mintage	VF20	XF40	MS60	MS63	MS65
AH1342-1924	2,000,000	2.00	15.00	30.00	100	—

KM# 347 10 MILLIEMES
5.22 g., Copper-Nickel **Obv:** Uniformed bust left **Rev:** Denomination divides dates

Date	Mintage	VF20	XF40	MS60	MS63	MS65
AH1348-1929 BP	1,500,000	1.35	8.50	20.00	38.00	—
AH1352-1933 H	1,500,000	1.35	8.50	25.00	45.00	—
AH1354-1935 H	4,000,000	0.75	3.00	11.50	20.00	—

KM# 335 2 PIASTRES
2.80 g., 0.833 Silver 0.075 oz. ASW **Obv:** Bust right **Rev:** Denomination above center circle, dates flank below

Date	Mintage	VF20	XF40	MS60	MS63	MS65
AH1342-1923 H	2,500,000	4.00	9.00	12.00	25.00	—

KM# 348 2 PIASTRES
2.80 g., 0.833 Silver 0.075 oz. ASW **Obv:** Uniformed bust left **Rev:** Denomination above center circle, dates flank below **Mint:** British Royal Mint

Date	Mintage	VF20	XF40	MS60	MS63	MS65
AH1348-1929	500,000	4.00	9.00	12.00	20.00	—

Note: Edge varieties exist

KM# 336 5 PIASTRES
7.00 g., 0.833 Silver 0.1875 oz. ASW **Obv:** Bust right **Rev:** Denomination above center circle, dates flank below

Date	Mintage	VF20	XF40	MS60	MS63	MS65
AH1341-1923	800,000	9.00	17.00	37.50	70.00	—
AH1341-1923 H	1,800,000	8.00	13.00	32.00	65.00	—
AH1341-1923 H	—	PF63 275				

KM# 349 5 PIASTRES
7.00 g., 0.833 Silver 0.1875 oz. ASW **Obv:** Uniformed bust left **Rev:** Denomination above center circle, dates flank below **Mint:** British Royal Mint

Date	Mintage	VF20	XF40	MS60	MS63	MS65
AH1348-1929	800,000	9.00	17.00	37.50	70.00	—
AH1352-1933	1,300,000	8.00	13.00	27.50	60.00	—
AH1352-1933	—	PF63 275				

KM# 337 10 PIASTRES
14.00 g., 0.833 Silver 0.3749 oz. ASW, 32.5 mm. **Obv:** Bust right **Rev:** Denomination above center circle, dates flank below

Date	Mintage	VF20	XF40	MS60	MS63	MS65
AH1341-1923	400,000	14.00	27.50	75.00	130	—
AH1341-1923 H	1,000,000	13.00	25.00	65.00	120	—
AH1341-1923 H	—	PF63 500				

KM# 350 10 PIASTRES
14.00 g., 0.833 Silver 0.3749 oz. ASW **Obv:** Uniformed bust left **Rev:** Denomination above center circle, dates flank below **Mint:** British Royal Mint

Date	Mintage	VF20	XF40	MS60	MS63	MS65
AH1348-1929	400,000	13.00	22.50	60.00	110	—
AH1352-1933	Est. 350000	13.00	22.50	60.00	110	—
AH1352-1933	—	PF63 525				

KM# 338 20 PIASTRES
28.00 g., 0.833 Silver 0.7499 oz. ASW, 40 mm. **Obv:** Bust right **Rev:** Denomination above center circle, dates flank below

Date	Mintage	VF20	XF40	MS60	MS63	MS65
AH1341-1923	100,000	27.50	65.00	230	475	—
AH1341-1923 H	50,000	30.00	75.00	265	500	—
AH1341-1923 H	—	PF63 975				

KM# 339 20 PIASTRES
1.70 g., 0.875 Gold 0.0478 oz. AGW **Obv:** Bust right **Rev:** Denomination above center inscription, dates flank below **Mint:** British Royal Mint

Date	Mintage	VF20	XF40	MS60	MS63	MS65
AH1341-1923	72,500	85.00	115	180	225	—

Note: 65,000 struck in 1923 and an additional 7,500 struck in 1928. Coins were struck in both red and yellow gold.

KM# 351 20 PIASTRES
1.70 g., 0.875 Gold 0.0478 oz. AGW **Obv:** Bust left **Mint:** British Royal Mint

Date	Mintage	VF20	XF40	MS60	MS63	MS65
AH1348-1929	20,000	95.00	115	180	235	—
AH1349-1930	30,000	95.00	115	180	235	—

Note: Mint records indicate no proofs were struck, however these "early strikes" are considered to have proof qualities.

KM# 352 20 PIASTRES
28.00 g., 0.833 Silver 0.7499 oz. ASW, 40 mm. **Obv:** Uniformed bust left **Rev:** Denomination above center circle, dates flank below **Mint:** British Royal Mint

Date	Mintage	VF20	XF40	MS60	MS63	MS65
AH1348-1929	50,000	30.00	80.00	190	400	—
AH1352-1933	25,000	30.00	80.00	175	350	—
AH1352-1933 Proof	—	—	—	—	—	—

KM# 340 50 PIASTRES
4.25 g., 0.875 Gold 0.1196 oz. AGW **Obv:** Bust right **Rev:** Denomination above inscription, dates flank **Mint:** British Royal Mint

Date	Mintage	VF20	XF40	MS60	MS63	MS65
AH1341-1923	19,000	152	210	225	250	—

Note: 18,000 struck in 1923 and an additional 1,000 struck in 1928. Coins were struck in both red and yellow gold.

KM# 353 50 PIASTRES
4.25 g., 0.875 Gold 0.1196 oz. AGW **Obv:** Bust left **Rev:** Denomination above inscription, dates flank below **Mint:** British Royal Mint

Date	Mintage	VF20	XF40	MS60	MS63	MS65
AH1348-1929	6,000	152	215	235	265	—
AH1349-1930	10,000	152	210	225	250	—

Note: Mint records indicate no proofs were struck, however these "early strikes" are considered to have proof qualities.

KM# 341 100 PIASTRES
8.50 g., 0.875 Gold 0.2391 oz. AGW **Obv:** Bust right **Rev:** Denomination above center circle, dates flank below **Mint:** British Royal Mint

Date	Mintage	VF20	XF40	MS60	MS63	MS65
AH1340-1922	25,000	305	425	450	500	—

Note: Coins were struck in both red and yellow gold.

KM# 354 100 PIASTRES
8.50 g., 0.875 Gold 0.2391 oz. AGW **Obv:** Bust left **Mint:** British Royal Mint

Date	Mintage	VF20	XF40	MS60	MS63	MS65
AH1348-1929	3,000	305	425	450	500	—
AH1349-1930	6,000	305	425	450	500	—

Note: Mint records indicate no proofs were struck, however these "early strikes" are considered to have proof qualities.

KM# 342 500 PIASTRES
42.50 g., 0.875 Gold 1.1956 oz. AGW **Obv:** Bust right **Rev:** Denomination above center circle, dates flank below **Mint:** British Royal Mint

Date	Mintage	VF20	XF40	MS60	MS63	MS65
AH1340-1922	1,800	—	—	2,100	2,250	—

Note: Coins were struck in both red and yellow gold.

Date	Mintage					
AH1340-1922	—	PF63 2,800				

Note: Circulation coins were struck in both red and yellow gold

KM# 355 500 PIASTRES
42.50 g., 0.875 Gold 1.1956 oz. AGW **Obv:** Uniformed bust left **Rev:** Denomination above center circle, dates flank below **Mint:** British Royal Mint

Date	Mintage	VF20	XF40	MS60	MS63	MS65
AH1348-1929	400	—	—	2,100	2,200	—
AH1351-1932	300	—	—	2,100	2,200	—
AH1351-1932	—	PF63 2,600				

Note: Mint records indicate no proofs were struck, however these "early strikes" are considered to have proof qualities.

Farouk
AH1355-1372/1936-1952AD

KM# 357 1/2 MILLIEME
Bronze **Obv:** Uniformed bust looking left **Rev:** Denomination, dates below **Mint:** British Royal Mint

Date	Mintage	VF20	XF40	MS60	MS63	MS65
AH1357-1938	4,000,000	1.50	5.00	9.00	18.00	—
AH1357-1938	—	PF63 100				

KM# 358 MILLIEME
Bronze **Obv:** Uniformed bust looking left **Rev:** Denomination, dates below **Mint:** British Royal Mint

Date	Mintage	VF20	XF40	MS60	MS63	MS65
AH1357-1938	26,240,000	0.20	0.50	2.00	7.00	—
AH1357-1938	—	PF63 120				
AH1364-1945	10,000,000	1.25	7.00	26.00	50.00	—
AH1366-1947	—	1.25	7.00	26.00	50.00	—
AH1369-1950	5,000,000	0.40	1.00	3.00	10.00	—
AH1369-1950	—	PF63 85.00				

KM# 362 MILLIEME
3.96 g., Copper-Nickel, 18.1 mm. **Mint:** British Royal Mint

Date	Mintage	VF20	XF40	MS60	MS63	MS65
AH1357-1938	3,500,000	1.00	3.50	8.00	15.00	—

KM# 359 2 MILLIEMES
2.51 g., Copper-Nickel **Obv:** Uniformed bust looking left **Rev:** Denomination divides dates **Mint:** British Royal Mint

Date	Mintage	VF20	XF40	MS60	MS63	MS65
AH1357-1938	2,500,000	1.50	4.00	14.00	25.00	—
AH1357-1938	—	PF63 140				

KM# 360 5 MILLIEMES
Bronze **Obv:** Uniformed bust looking left **Rev:** Denomination divides dates **Shape:** Scalloped **Mint:** British Royal Mint

Date	Mintage	VF20	XF40	MS60	MS63	MS65
AH1357-1938	—	0.40	1.00	3.00	10.00	—
AH1357-1938	—	PF63 65.00				
AH1362-1943	—	0.40	1.00	3.00	10.00	—

KM# 363 5 MILLIEMES
4.00 g., Copper-Nickel **Obv:** Uniformed bust looking left **Rev:** Denomination divides dates **Mint:** British Royal Mint

Date	Mintage	VF20	XF40	MS60	MS63	MS65
AH1357-1938	7,000,000	0.40	1.00	4.00	10.00	—
AH1357-1938	—	PF63 75.00				
AH1360-1941	11,500,000	0.20	1.00	4.00	8.00	—

KM# 361 10 MILLIEMES
5.70 g., Bronze **Obv:** Uniformed bust looking left **Rev:** Denomination divides dates **Shape:** Scalloped **Mint:** British Royal Mint

Date	Mintage	VF20	XF40	MS60	MS63	MS65
AH1357-1938	—	0.40	1.00	4.00	10.00	—
AH1357-1938	—	PF63 140				
AH1362-1943	—	—	0.75	4.00	10.00	—

KM# 364 10 MILLIEMES
5.50 g., Copper-Nickel, 23 mm. **Obv:** Uniformed bust looking left **Rev:** Denomination divides dates **Mint:** British Royal Mint

Date	Mintage	VF20	XF40	MS60	MS63	MS65
AH1357-1938	3,500,000	0.40	1.00	5.00	12.50	—
AH1357-1938	—	PF63 85.00				
AH1360-1941	5,322,000	0.40	1.00	5.00	12.50	—

KM# 365 2 PIASTRES
2.80 g., 0.833 Silver 0.075 oz. ASW **Mint:** British Royal Mint

Date	Mintage	VF20	XF40	MS60	MS63	MS65
AH1356-1937	500,000	1.40	3.00	5.00	10.00	—

Note: Fine and coarse edge reeding exist

Date	Mintage	VF20	XF40	MS60	MS63	MS65
AH1356-1937	—	PF63 350				
AH1358-1939	500,000	1.40	5.00	12.00	85.00	—
AH1358-1939	—	PF63 230				

Date	Mintage	VF20	XF40	MS60	MS63	MS65
AH1361-1942	10,000,000	1.40	3.00	5.00	12.00	—

Note: Normal and flat rim varieties exist for AH1361 coins

KM# 369 2 PIASTRES

2.80 g., 0.500 Silver 0.045 oz. ASW **Obv:** Uniformed bust left **Rev:** Denomination and dates within tasseled wreath **Shape:** 6-sided **Mint:** British Royal Mint

Date	Mintage	VF20	XF40	MS60	MS63	MS65
AH1363-1944	32,000	1.00	3.00	5.00	9.00	—

KM# 366 5 PIASTRES

7.00 g., 0.833 Silver 0.1875 oz. ASW, 25.92 mm. **Obv:** Uniformed bust left **Edge:** Security **Mint:** British Royal Mint

Date	Mintage	VF20	XF40	MS60	MS63	MS65
AH1356-1937	—	8.00	12.00	14.00	20.00	40.00
AH1356-1937	—	PF63 325				
AH1358-1939	8,000,000	8.00	12.00	14.00	20.00	40.00
AH1358-1939	—	PF63 325				

KM# 367 10 PIASTRES

14.00 g., 0.833 Silver 0.3749 oz. ASW, 33 mm. **Mint:** British Royal Mint

Date	Mintage	VF20	XF40	MS60	MS63	MS65
AH1356-1937	2,800,000	14.00	17.00	22.50	35.00	65.00
AH1356-1937	—	PF63 425				
AH1358-1939	2,850,000	13.00	17.00	22.50	35.00	65.00
AH1358-1939	—	PF63 350				

KM# 368 20 PIASTRES

28.00 g., 0.833 Silver 0.7499 oz. ASW, 40 mm. **Obv:** Uniformed bust looking left **Rev:** Denomination and dates within tasseled wreath **Mint:** British Royal Mint

Date	Mintage	VF20	XF40	MS60	MS63	MS65
AH1356-1937	—	30.00	35.00	65.00	90.00	150
AH1356-1937	—	PF63 1,150				
AH1358-1939	—	30.00	35.00	65.00	90.00	150
AH1358-1939	—	PF63 1,400				

KM# 370 20 PIASTRES

1.70 g., 0.875 Gold 0.0478 oz. AGW **Subject:** Royal Wedding **Obv:** Uniformed bust looking left **Rev:** Dates within circle, denomination above, decorative vine surrounds **Mint:** British Royal Mint

Date	Mintage	VF20	XF40	MS60	MS63	MS65
AH1357-1938	20,000	85.00	115	175	200	—

KM# 371 50 PIASTRES

4.25 g., 0.875 Gold 0.1196 oz. AGW **Subject:** Royal Wedding **Obv:** Uniformed bust looking left **Rev:** Dates within circle, denomination above, decorative vine surrounds **Mint:** British Royal Mint

Date	Mintage	VF20	XF40	MS60	MS63	MS65
AH1357-1938	10,000	210	230	350	425	—

KM# 372 100 PIASTRES

8.50 g., 0.875 Gold 0.2391 oz. AGW **Subject:** Royal Wedding **Obv:** Uniformed bust looking left **Rev:** Dates within circle, denomination above, decorative vine surrounds **Mint:** British Royal Mint

Date	Mintage	VF20	XF40	MS60	MS63	MS65
AH1357-1938	5,000	420	450	475	550	—

Note: Circulation coins were struck in both red and yellow gold

KM# 373 500 PIASTRES

42.50 g., 0.875 Gold 1.1956 oz. AGW **Subject:** Royal Wedding **Obv:** Uniformed bust looking left **Rev:** Dates within circle, denomination above, decorative vine surrounds **Mint:** British Royal Mint

Date	Mintage	VF20	XF40	MS60	MS63	MS65
AH1357-1938	—	—	2,150	2,800	3,250	—
AH1357-1938	—	PF63 3,400				

FIRST REPUBLIC

AH1373-1378 / 1953-1958AD

KM# 375 MILLIEME

1.80 g., Aluminum-Bronze **Obv:** Denomination divides dates **Rev:** Small sphinx with outlined base

Date	Mintage	VF20	XF40	MS60	MS63	MS65
AH1373-1954	—	20.00	60.00	100	250	—
AH1374-1954	—	3.25	6.00	10.00	12.00	20.00
AH1374-1955	—	2.00	5.00	7.00	9.00	12.00
AH1375-1956	—	2.00	5.00	7.00	9.00	12.00

KM# 376 MILLIEME

1.80 g., Aluminum-Bronze **Obv:** Denomination divides dates **Rev:** Small sphinx without base outlined

Date	Mintage	VF20	XF40	MS60	MS63	MS65
AH1373-1954	—	12.50	25.00	35.00	50.00	—
AH1374-1954	—	3.25	6.00	10.00	12.00	20.00
AH1374-1955	—	1.50	3.00	5.00	7.00	9.00
AH1375-1956	—	1.50	3.00	5.00	7.00	9.00
AH1376-1957	—	40.00	70.00	100	150	—

KM# 377 MILLIEME

1.80 g., Aluminum-Bronze **Rev:** Large sphinx with outlined base

Date	Mintage	VF20	XF40	MS60	MS63	MS65
AH1375-1956	—	0.25	0.50	0.75	1.25	2.50
AH1376-1957	—	0.25	0.50	0.75	1.25	2.50
AH1377-1958	—	0.25	0.50	0.75	1.25	2.50

KM# 378 5 MILLIEMES

Aluminum-Bronze **Obv:** Denomination divides dates **Rev:** Small sphinx with outlined base

Date	Mintage	VF20	XF40	MS60	MS63	MS65
AH1373-1954	—	5.00	7.00	10.00	20.00	35.00
AH1374-1954	—	4.00	6.00	9.00	15.00	25.00
AH1374-1955	—	10.00	15.00	20.00	35.00	50.00
AH1375-1956	—	3.00	5.00	7.00	10.00	15.00

KM# 379 5 MILLIEMES

4.84 g., Aluminum-Bronze, 23 mm. **Obv:** Denomination divides dates **Rev:** Large sphinx

Date	Mintage	VF20	XF40	MS60	MS63	MS65
AH1376-1957	—	2.00	3.00	5.00	7.00	9.00
AH1377-1957	—	2.00	3.00	5.00	7.00	9.00
AH1377-1958	—	2.00	3.00	5.00	7.00	9.00

KM# 380.1 10 MILLIEMES

Aluminum-Bronze **Obv:** Denomination divides dates **Rev:** Small sphinx with base outlined **Note:** Thin milliemes.

Date	Mintage	VF20	XF40	MS60	MS63	MS65
AH1373-1954	—	4.00	7.00	12.00	15.00	25.00

KM# 380.2 10 MILLIEMES

Aluminum-Bronze **Obv:** Denomination divides date **Rev:** Small sphinx with base outlined **Note:** Thick Milliemes.

Date	Mintage	VF20	XF40	MS60	MS63	MS65
AH1374-1954	—	4.00	7.00	12.00	15.00	22.00
AH1374-1955	—	3.00	5.00	7.00	10.00	15.00

KM# 381 10 MILLIEMES

4.74 g., Aluminum-Bronze, 23.0 mm. **Rev:** Large sphinx **Note:** Exists also with eagle, 2 stars.

Date	Mintage	VF20	XF40	MS60	MS63	MS65
AH1374-1955	—	50.00	75.00	100	150	—
AH1375-1956	—	1.50	4.00	6.00	10.00	12.00
AH1376-1957	—	1.50	3.00	5.00	7.00	10.00
AH1377-1958	—	1.50	3.00	5.00	7.00	10.00

KM# 382 5 PIASTRES
3.50 g., 0.720 Silver 0.081 oz. ASW **Obv:** Denomination within wings **Rev:** Small Sphinx with outlined base **Note:** Die varieties exist which appear to be lacking outlined base of Sphinx.

Date	Mintage	VF20	XF40	MS60	MS63	MS65
AH1375-1956	—	1.50	4.00	6.00	8.00	12.00
AH1376-1956	—	1.50	4.00	6.00	8.00	12.00
AH1376-1957	—	1.50	4.00	6.00	8.00	12.00

KM# 383 10 PIASTRES
7.00 g., 0.625 Silver 0.1407 oz. ASW **Obv:** Denomination within wings **Rev:** Large sphinx

Date	Mintage	VF20	XF40	MS60	MS63	MS65
AH1374-1955	1,408,000	2.50	7.50	10.00	12.00	18.00

Note: Varieties in date sizes exist

KM# 383a 10 PIASTRES
7.00 g., 0.720 Silver 0.162 oz. ASW **Obv:** Denomination within wings **Rev:** Sphinx, dates

Date	Mintage	VF20	XF40	MS60	MS63	MS65
AH1375-1956	—	3.00	6.00	8.00	10.00	15.00
AH1376-1957	—	3.00	6.00	8.00	10.00	13.00

KM# 384 20 PIASTRES
14.00 g., 0.720 Silver 0.3241 oz. ASW, 33 mm. **Obv:** Denomination within wings

Date	Mintage	VF20	XF40	MS60	MS63	MS65
AH1375-1956	—	6.00	8.00	11.00	14.00	20.00

KM# 385 25 PIASTRES
17.50 g., 0.720 Silver 0.4051 oz. ASW, 35 mm. **Subject:** Suez Canal Nationalization **Obv:** Denomination and dates above wings **Rev:** Headquarter building in Port Said

Date	Mintage	VF20	XF40	MS60	MS63	MS65
AH1375-1956	258,000	7.50	9.00	12.00	15.00	20.00

KM# 389 25 PIASTRES
17.50 g., 0.720 Silver 0.4051 oz. ASW, 35 mm. **Subject:** National Assembly Inauguration **Obv:** Denomination and dates above wings **Rev:** Radiant sun behind building

Date	Mintage	VF20	XF40	MS60	MS63	MS65
AH1376-1957	246,000	7.50	9.00	12.00	15.00	20.00

KM# 386 50 PIASTRES
28.00 g., 0.900 Silver 0.8102 oz. ASW, 40 mm. **Subject:** Evacuation of the British **Obv:** Denomination and dates above wings **Rev:** Figure with torch and broken chains

Date	Mintage	VF20	XF40	MS60	MS63	MS65
AH1375-1956	250,000	—	15.00	18.00	20.00	25.00

KM# 387 POUND
8.50 g., 0.875 Gold 0.2391 oz. AGW **Subject:** 3rd and 5th Anniversaries of Revolution **Obv:** Denomination and dates above wings **Rev:** Pharoah Ramses II in a war chariot

Date	Mintage	VF20	XF40	MS60	MS63	MS65
AH1374-1955	16,000	—	305	350	395	415
AH1377-1957	10,000	—	305	350	400	425

Note: Struck in red and yellow gold

KM# 388 5 POUNDS
42.50 g., 0.875 Gold 1.1956 oz. AGW **Subject:** 3rd and 5th Anniversaries of Revolution **Obv:** Denomination and dates above wings **Rev:** Horse, chariot, and archer

Date	Mintage	VF20	XF40	MS60	MS63	MS65
AH1374-1955	—	—	1,525	1,550	2,000	2,200
AH1377-1957	—	—	1,525	1,600	2,100	2,300

Note: Struck in red and yellow gold

UNITED ARAB REPUBLIC

AH1378-1391 / 1958-1971AD

KM# 393 MILLIEME
Aluminum-Bronze **Obv:** Denomination divides dates, legend above **Rev:** Eagle with shield on breast

Date	Mintage	VF20	XF40	MS60	MS63	MS65
AH1380-1960	—	0.10	0.15	0.30	0.50	1.00
AH1386-1966	—	PF65 3.00				

KM# 403 2 MILLIEMES
Aluminum-Bronze **Obv:** Denomination divides dates, legend above **Rev:** Eagle with shield on breast

Date	Mintage	VF20	XF40	MS60	MS63	MS65
AH1381-1962	—	0.15	0.35	0.50	0.65	1.25
AH1386-1966	—	PF65 3.00				

KM# 394 5 MILLIEMES
Aluminum-Bronze **Obv:** Denomination divides dates, legend above **Rev:** Eagle with shield on breast

Date	Mintage	VF20	XF40	MS60	MS63	MS65
AH1380-1960	—	0.15	0.35	0.65	0.85	1.50
AH1386-1966	—	PF65 3.00				

KM# 410 5 MILLIEMES
Aluminum

Date	Mintage	VF20	XF40	MS60	MS63	MS65
AH1386-1967	—	0.15	0.35	0.50	0.75	1.50

KM# 395 10 MILLIEMES
Aluminum-Bronze **Obv:** Denomination divides dates, legend above **Obv. Legend:** Misr **Rev:** Eagle with shield on breast

Date	Mintage	VF20	XF40	MS60	MS63	MS65
AH1378-1958	—	15.00	20.00	35.00	45.00	75.00
AH1380-1960	16,079,999	0.25	0.50	0.75	1.00	1.50
AH1386-1966	—	PF65 4.00				

KM# 396 10 MILLIEMES
Aluminum-Bronze **Obv:** Denomination divides dates, legend above, without Misr above denomination **Rev:** Eagle with shield on breast

Date	Mintage	VF20	XF40	MS60	MS63	MS65
AH1378-1958	—	15.00	25.00	40.00	65.00	—
AH1378-1958	—	PF65 300				

KM# 411 10 MILLIEMES
Aluminum **Obv:** Denomination divides dates **Rev:** Eagle with shield on breast

Date	Mintage	VF20	XF40	MS60	MS63	MS65
AH1386-1967	—	0.15	0.35	0.50	0.75	1.00

KM# 390 20 MILLIEMES

Aluminum-Bronze, 24 mm. **Subject:** Agriculture and Industrial Fair in Cairo **Obv:** Denomination divides dates, legend above **Rev:** Symbols of agriculture and industry

Date	Mintage	VF20	XF40	MS60	MS63	MS65
AH1378-1958	—	—	0.75	1.25	2.00	5.00

KM# 397 5 PIASTRES

3.50 g., 0.720 Silver 0.081 oz. ASW **Obv:** Denomination divides dates, legend above **Rev:** Eagle with shield on breast

Date	Mintage	VF20	XF40	MS60	MS63	MS65
AH1380-1960	—	—	2.50	3.00	4.00	7.00
AH1386-1966	—	PF65 12.00				

KM# 404 5 PIASTRES

2.50 g., 0.720 Silver 0.0579 oz. ASW **Subject:** Diversion of the Nile **Obv:** Denomination divides dates, legend above **Rev:** Sadd el-Ali Dam, Nile River basin scene

Date	Mintage	VF20	XF40	MS60	MS63	MS65
AH1384-1964	500,000	—	1.75	2.25	3.00	6.00
AH1384-1964	2,000	PF65 10.00				

KM# 412 5 PIASTRES

Copper-Nickel, 25 mm. **Obv:** Denomination divides dates, legend above **Rev:** Eagle with shield on breast

Date	Mintage	VF20	XF40	MS60	MS63	MS65
AH1387-1967	10,800,000	—	0.50	0.75	1.50	2.00

Note: Edge varieties, narrow and gapped milling, exist

KM# 414 5 PIASTRES

Copper-Nickel **Subject:** International Industrial Fair **Obv:** Denomination, legend above **Rev:** Globe with cogwheel section around, dates below

Date	Mintage	VF20	XF40	MS60	MS63	MS65
AH1388-1968	500,000	—	0.75	1.00	1.25	2.50

KM# 417 5 PIASTRES

Copper-Nickel, 25 mm. **Subject:** 50th Anniversary - International Labor Organization **Obv:** Denomination, legend **Rev:** Hands holding open-ended wrenches within wreath, dates divided below

Date	Mintage	VF20	XF40	MS60	MS63	MS65
AH1389-1969	500,000	—	0.75	1.00	1.25	2.50

KM# 392 10 PIASTRES

7.00 g., 0.720 Silver 0.162 oz. ASW, 24 mm. **Subject:** First Anniversary of U.A.R. Founding **Obv:** Denomination divides dates, legend above **Rev:** Eagle with shield on breast

Date	Mintage	VF20	XF40	MS60	MS63	MS65
AH1378-1959	—	3.00	5.00	10.00	12.00	15.00

KM# 398 10 PIASTRES

7.00 g., 0.720 Silver 0.162 oz. ASW **Obv:** Denomination divides dates, legend above **Rev:** Eagle with shield on breast

Date	Mintage	VF20	XF40	MS60	MS63	MS65
AH1380-1960	500,000	—	3.00	5.00	7.50	10.00
AH1386-1966	—	PF65 17.00				

KM# 405 10 PIASTRES

5.00 g., 0.720 Silver 0.1157 oz. ASW **Subject:** Diversion of the Nile **Obv:** Denomination divides dates, legend above **Rev:** Sadd el-Ali Dam, Nile River basin scene

Date	Mintage	VF20	XF40	MS60	MS63	MS65
AH1384-1964	500,000	—	2.25	3.50	5.00	7.00
AH1384-1964	2,000	PF65 16.00				

KM# 413 10 PIASTRES

Copper-Nickel, 27 mm. **Obv:** Denomination divides dates, legend above **Rev:** Eagle with shield on breast

Date	Mintage	VF20	XF40	MS60	MS63	MS65
AH1387-1967	13,200,000	—	0.50	0.75	1.25	2.00

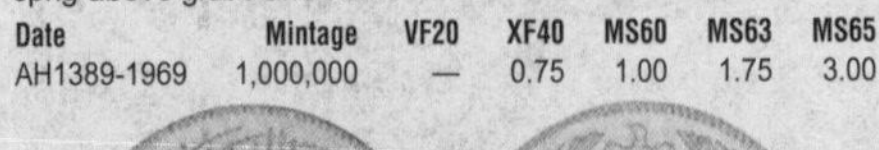

KM# 419 10 PIASTRES

Copper-Nickel **Subject:** Cairo International Agricultural Fair **Obv:** Denomination divides dates, legend above **Rev:** Grain sprig above globe and name

Date	Mintage	VF20	XF40	MS60	MS63	MS65
AH1389-1969	1,000,000	—	0.75	1.00	1.75	3.00

KM# 418 10 PIASTRES

Copper-Nickel **Series:** F.A.O. **Obv:** Denomination divides dates, legend above **Rev:** People with oxen, eagle above, logo below

Date	Mintage	VF20	XF40	MS60	MS63	MS65
ND-1970	500,000	—	0.75	1.25	2.00	4.00

KM# 420 10 PIASTRES

Copper-Nickel **Subject:** 50 Years - Banque Misr **Obv:** Crowned head within wreath left of denomination and date **Rev:** Sun above building

Date	Mintage	VF20	XF40	MS60	MS63	MS65
AH1390-1970	500,000	—	0.50	0.75	1.25	2.00

KM# 421.1 10 PIASTRES

Copper-Nickel **Subject:** Cairo International Industrial Fair **Obv:** Denomination **Rev:** Ship within cogwheel, dates in box below

Date	Mintage	VF20	XF40	MS60	MS63	MS65
AH1390-1970	500,000	—	0.75	1.25	2.00	3.50

KM# 421.2 10 PIASTRES

6.02 g., Copper-Nickel, 27 mm. **Subject:** Cairo International Industrial Fair **Obv:** New shorter Arabic inscriptions, denomination at center **Rev:** Ship within cogwheel, dates in box below

Date	Mintage	VF20	XF40	MS60	MS63	MS65
AH1391-1971	500,000	—	0.50	0.75	1.25	2.50

KM# 399 20 PIASTRES

14.00 g., 0.720 Silver 0.3241 oz. ASW, 33 mm. **Obv:** Denomination divides dates, legend above **Rev:** Eagle with shield on breast

Date	Mintage	VF20	XF40	MS60	MS63	MS65
AH1380-1960	400,000	—	6.00	9.00	12.00	18.00
AH1386-1966	—	PF65 37.50				

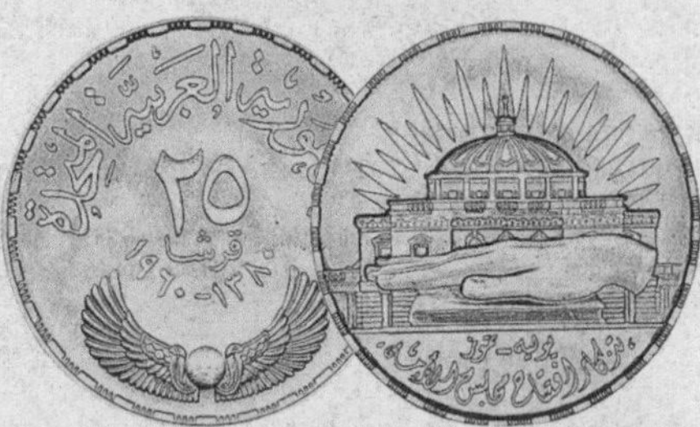

KM# 400 25 PIASTRES

17.50 g., 0.720 Silver 0.4051 oz. ASW, 35 mm. **Subject:** 3rd Year of National Assembly **Obv:** Denomination and dates above wings **Rev:** Radiant sun back of building, hand on book in front

Date	Mintage	VF20	XF40	MS60	MS63	MS65
AH1380-1960	250,000	—	7.50	9.00	12.00	18.00

KM# 406 25 PIASTRES

10.00 g., 0.720 Silver 0.2315 oz. ASW **Subject:** Diversion of the Nile **Obv:** Denomination divides dates, legend above **Rev:** Sadd el-Ali Dam, Nile River basin scene

Date	Mintage	VF20	XF40	MS60	MS63	MS65
AH1384-1964	250,000	—	4.25	7.00	9.00	12.00
AH1384-1964	2,000	PF65 40.00				

KM# 422 25 PIASTRES
6.00 g., 0.720 Silver 0.1389 oz. ASW **Subject:** President Nasser **Obv:** Head of President Nasser right

Date	Mintage	VF20	XF40	MS60	MS63	MS65
AH1390-1970	700,000	—	2.50	5.00	7.00	10.00

KM# 407 50 PIASTRES
20.00 g., 0.720 Silver 0.463 oz. ASW **Subject:** Diversion of the Nile **Rev:** Nile River basin scene

Date	Mintage	VF20	XF40	MS60	MS63	MS65
AH1384-1964	250,000	—	8.50	9.00	13.00	20.00
AH1384-1964	2,000	PF65 50.00				

KM# 423 50 PIASTRES
12.50 g., 0.720 Silver 0.2894 oz. ASW, 33 mm. **Subject:** President Nasser **Obv:** Head of President Nasser right **Rev:** Denomination and dates

Date	Mintage	VF20	XF40	MS60	MS63	MS65
AH1390-1970	400,000	—	5.25	8.00	12.00	16.00

KM# 391 1/2 POUND
4.25 g., 0.875 Gold 0.1196 oz. AGW, 20 mm. **Subject:** U.A.R. Founding **Obv:** Denomination and dates above wings **Rev:** Pharoah Ramses II in a war chariot

Date	Mintage	VF20	XF40	MS60	MS63	MS65
AH1378-1958	30,000	—	—	—	220	245

KM# 401 POUND
8.50 g., 0.875 Gold 0.2391 oz. AGW **Rev:** Aswan Dam

Date	Mintage	VF20	XF40	MS60	MS63	MS65
AH1379-1960	252,000	—	—	—	420	440

KM# 415 POUND
25.00 g., 0.720 Silver 0.5787 oz. ASW, 40 mm. **Obv:** Denomination and dates **Rev:** Power station for Aswan Dam, grain sprigs flank

Date	Mintage	VF20	XF40	MS60	MS63	MS65
AH1387-1968	100,000	—	11.00	15.00	18.00	22.00

KM# 424 POUND
25.00 g., 0.720 Silver 0.5787 oz. ASW, 40 mm. **Subject:** 1000th Anniversary - Al Azhar Mosque **Obv:** Center circle divides dates **Rev:** Al Azhar Mosque

Date	Mintage	VF20	XF40	MS60	MS63	MS65
AH1359-1361 - 1970-1972	100,000	—	11.00	15.00	18.00	22.00

KM# 425 POUND
25.00 g., 0.720 Silver 0.5787 oz. ASW, 40 mm. **Subject:** President Nasser **Obv:** Head of President Nasser right **Rev:** Denomination divides dates, legend above

Date	Mintage	VF20	XF40	MS60	MS63	MS65
AH1390-1970	400,000	—	11.00	15.00	18.00	21.00

KM# 426 POUND
8.00 g., 0.875 Gold 0.2251 oz. AGW **Subject:** President Nasser **Obv:** Head of President Nasser right **Rev:** Denomination divides dates, legend above

Date	Mintage	VF20	XF40	MS60	MS63	MS65
AH1390-1970	10,000	—	—	—	350	370

KM# 402 5 POUNDS
42.50 g., 0.875 Gold 1.1956 oz. AGW **Obv:** Denomination and dates above wings **Rev:** Aswan Dam

Date	Mintage	VF20	XF40	MS60	MS63	MS65
AH1379-1960	5,000	—	—	—	1,800	2,000

KM# 408 5 POUNDS
26.00 g., 0.875 Gold 0.7314 oz. AGW **Subject:** Diversion of the Nile **Obv:** Denomination divides dates, legend above **Rev:** Nile River basin scene

Date	Mintage	VF20	XF40	MS60	MS63	MS65
AH1384-1964	—	—	—	—	1,050	1,250

KM# 416 5 POUNDS
26.00 g., 0.875 Gold 0.7314 oz. AGW **Subject:** 1400th Anniversary of the Koran **Obv:** Denomination and dates within center circle **Rev:** Open Koran book above globe with radiant sun in back

Date	Mintage	VF20	XF40	MS60	MS63	MS65
AH1388-1968	10,000	—	—	—	1,050	1,250

KM# 427 5 POUNDS
26.00 g., 0.875 Gold 0.7314 oz. AGW **Subject:** 1000th Anniversary - Al Azhar Mosque **Rev:** Al Azhar Mosque

Date	Mintage	VF20	XF40	MS60	MS63	MS65
AH1390-1970	—	—	—	—	1,200	1,350

KM# 428 5 POUNDS
26.00 g., 0.875 Gold 0.7314 oz. AGW **Subject:** President Nasser **Obv:** Head of President Nasser right

Date	Mintage	VF20	XF40	MS60	MS63	MS65
AH1390-1970	3,000	—	—	—	1,200	1,350

KM# 409 10 POUNDS
52.00 g., 0.875 Gold 1.4629 oz. AGW **Subject:** Diversion of the Nile **Obv:** Denomination divides dates **Rev:** Nile River basin scene

Date	Mintage	VF20	XF40	MS60	MS63	MS65
AH1384-1964	2,000	—	—	—	2,250	2,450

ARAB REPUBLIC

AH1391- / 1971- AD

KM# A423 MILLIEME

Aluminum **Obv:** Denomination divides dates, legend above **Rev:** Eagle with shield on breast

Date	Mintage	VF20	XF40	MS60	MS63	MS65
AH1392-1972	—	—	0.10	0.30	0.50	0.75

KM# A424 5 MILLIEMES

Aluminum **Obv:** Denomination divides dates, legend above **Rev:** Corn ears and grain sprigs encircle figure below sun **Note:** Mule - Obverse of KM#A425 and reverse of KM#433.

Date	Mintage	VF20	XF40	MS60	MS63	MS65
AH1392-1972	—	10.00	15.00	25.00	45.00	—

KM# A425 5 MILLIEMES

Aluminum **Obv:** Denomination divides dates, legend above **Rev:** Eagle with shield on breast

Date	Mintage	VF20	XF40	MS60	MS63	MS65
AH1392-1972	16,000,000	—	0.20	0.50	1.00	2.50

KM# 432 5 MILLIEMES

2.00 g., Brass, 18 mm. **Obv:** Denomination divides dates, legend above **Rev:** Eagle with shield on breast

Date	Mintage	VF20	XF40	MS60	MS63	MS65
AH1393-1973	—	—	0.10	0.15	0.30	0.50

KM# A433 5 MILLIEMES

Aluminum, 18 mm. **Obv:** Denomination divides dates, legend above **Rev:** Eagle with shield on breast **Note:** Mule - Obverse of KM#433 and reverse of KM#A425.

Date	Mintage	VF20	XF40	MS60	MS63	MS65
AH1393-1973	—	—	10.00	20.00	45.00	—

KM# 433 5 MILLIEMES

Aluminum **Series:** F.A.O. **Obv:** Denomination divides dates, legend above **Rev:** Corn ears and grain sprigs flank Aswan Dam

Date	Mintage	VF20	XF40	MS60	MS63	MS65
AH1393-1973	10,000,000	—	0.25	0.50	0.75	1.25

KM# 434 5 MILLIEMES

2.00 g., Brass, 18 mm. **Obv:** Denomination divides dates, legend above **Rev:** Nefertiti head right and grain sprig **Note:** Mule.

Date	Mintage	VF20	XF40	MS60	MS63	MS65
AH1393-1973	—	7.00	15.00	25.00	40.00	—

KM# 445 5 MILLIEMES

4.00 g., Brass, 18 mm. **Series:** International Women's Year **Obv:** Denomination divides dates, legend above **Rev:** Nefertiti head right and grain sprig

Date	Mintage	VF20	XF40	MS60	MS63	MS65
AH1395-1975	10,000,000	—	0.15	0.25	0.50	0.75

KM# 462 5 MILLIEMES

Brass, 18 mm. **Series:** F.A.O. **Obv:** Denomination divides dates, legend above **Rev:** People, animals, and building

Date	Mintage	VF20	XF40	MS60	MS63	MS65
AH1397-1977	5,000,000	—	0.15	0.25	0.75	1.00

KM# 463 5 MILLIEMES

Brass **Subject:** 1971 Corrective Revolution **Obv:** Denomination divides dates, legend above **Rev:** City scene

Date	Mintage	VF20	XF40	MS60	MS63	MS65
AH1397-1977	2,500,000	—	0.15	0.25	0.75	1.00
AH1399-1979	2,500,000	—	0.15	0.25	0.75	1.00

KM# A426 10 MILLIEMES

Aluminum, 21 mm.

Date	Mintage	VF20	XF40	MS60	MS63	MS65
AH1392-1972	20,000,000	—	0.75	1.50	2.50	4.00

Note: Two varieties of edge letterings exist

KM# 435 10 MILLIEMES

3.20 g., Brass, 21 mm.

Date	Mintage	VF20	XF40	MS60	MS63	MS65
AH1393-1973	—	—	0.10	0.25	0.50	0.75
AH1396-1976	—	—	0.50	1.00	1.50	2.50

KM# 446 10 MILLIEMES

3.20 g., Brass, 21 mm. **Series:** F.A.O. **Obv:** Denomination divides dates, legend above **Rev:** Family scene

Date	Mintage	VF20	XF40	MS60	MS63	MS65
AH1395-1975	10,000,000	—	0.10	0.20	0.35	0.50

KM# 449 10 MILLIEMES

3.11 g., Brass, 21 mm. **Series:** F.A.O. **Obv:** Denomination divides dates, legend above **Rev:** Osiris seated, wheat ear at right

Date	Mintage	VF20	XF40	MS60	MS63	MS65
AH1396-1976	10,000,000	—	0.10	0.20	0.30	0.50

KM# 464 10 MILLIEMES

3.28 g., Brass, 21 mm. **Series:** F.A.O. **Obv:** Denomination divides dates, legend above **Rev:** Various laborers surround center design

Date	Mintage	VF20	XF40	MS60	MS63	MS65
AH1397-1977	10,000,000	—	0.10	0.20	0.85	1.25

KM# 465 10 MILLIEMES

Brass, 21 mm. **Subject:** 1971 Corrective Revolution **Obv:** Denomination divides dates, legend above **Rev:** Date and denomination left of head

Date	Mintage	VF20	XF40	MS60	MS63	MS65
AH1397-1977	2,500,000	—	0.10	0.20	0.65	1.00
AH1399-1979	2,500,000	—	0.20	0.40	1.00	1.50

KM# 476 10 MILLIEMES

Brass, 21 mm. **Series:** F.A.O. **Obv:** Denomination divides dates, legend above **Rev:** Woman looking into microscope

Date	Mintage	VF20	XF40	MS60	MS63	MS65
AH1398-1978	2,000,000	—	0.10	0.20	0.80	1.25

KM# 483 10 MILLIEMES

Brass, 21 mm. **Series:** International Year of the Child **Obv:** Denomination divides dates, legend above **Rev:** Seated woman and child

Date	Mintage	VF20	XF40	MS60	MS63	MS65
AH1399-1979	2,000,000	—	0.10	0.20	0.65	1.00

KM# 498 10 MILLIEMES

Aluminum-Bronze, 21 mm. **Subject:** Sadat's Corrective Revolution **Obv:** Fist raised holding grain stalk **Rev:** Denomination divides dates, legend above

Date	Mintage	VF20	XF40	MS60	MS63	MS65
AH1400-1980	2,500,000	—	0.10	0.25	1.00	1.50

KM# 499 10 MILLIEMES

Aluminum-Bronze, 21 mm. **Series:** F.A.O.

Date	Mintage	VF20	XF40	MS60	MS63	MS65
AH1400-1980	2,000,000	—	0.10	0.20	0.60	1.00

KM# 553.1 PIASTRE

Aluminum-Bronze, 18 mm. **Obv:** Christian date left of denomination, tughra above **Rev:** Pyramids

Date	Mintage	VF20	XF40	MS60	MS63	MS65
AH1404-1984	—	—	—	0.15	0.35	0.50

KM# 553.2 PIASTRE

Aluminum-Bronze, 18 mm. **Obv:** Islamic date left of denomination, tughra above **Rev:** Pyramids

Date	Mintage	VF20	XF40	MS60	MS63	MS65
AH1404-1984	—	—	—	0.15	0.35	0.50

KM# 500 2 PIASTRES

4.90 g., Aluminum-Bronze, 23 mm.

Date	Mintage	VF20	XF40	MS60	MS63	MS65
AH1400-1980	—	—	0.20	0.30	0.60	1.00

KM# 554.1 2 PIASTRES

4.90 g., Aluminum-Bronze, 21 mm. **Obv:** Christian date left of denomination

Date	Mintage	VF20	XF40	MS60	MS63	MS65
AH1404-1984	—	—	—	0.20	0.50	0.75

KM# 554.2 2 PIASTRES
4.90 g., Aluminum-Bronze, 21 mm. **Obv:** Islamic date left of denomination

Date	Mintage	VF20	XF40	MS60	MS63	MS65
AH1404-1984	—	—	—	0.20	0.50	0.75

KM# A427 5 PIASTRES
4.51 g., Copper-Nickel, 24.5 mm. **Subject:** 25th Anniversary of UNICEF

Date	Mintage	VF20	XF40	MS60	MS63	MS65
AH1392-1972	500,000	—	0.75	1.00	1.75	3.00

Note: Error in spelling "UNICFE".

KM# A428 5 PIASTRES
4.50 g., Copper-Nickel, 25 mm. **Obv:** Denomination divides dates, legend above **Rev:** Islamic falcon

Date	Mintage	VF20	XF40	MS60	MS63	MS65
AH1392-1972	—	—	0.50	0.75	1.25	1.75

KM# 436 5 PIASTRES
Copper-Nickel, 25 mm. **Subject:** Cairo State Fair **Obv:** Denomination divides dates, legend above **Rev:** Stylized design

Date	Mintage	VF20	XF40	MS60	MS63	MS65
AH1393-1973	500,000	—	0.60	0.75	1.25	1.75

KM# 437 5 PIASTRES
4.52 g., Copper-Nickel, 25 mm. **Subject:** 75th Anniversary - National Bank of Egypt **Obv:** Denomination divides dates, legend above **Rev:** Bank building in front of globe at left

Date	Mintage	VF20	XF40	MS60	MS63	MS65
AH1393-1973	1,000,000	—	0.60	0.75	1.25	1.75

KM# A441 5 PIASTRES
4.55 g., Copper-Nickel, 25 mm. **Subject:** First Anniversary - October War **Obv:** Denomination divides dates, legend above **Rev:** Soldier with gun facing right

Date	Mintage	VF20	XF40	MS60	MS63	MS65
AH1394-1974	2,000,000	—	0.60	0.75	1.25	1.75

KM# 447 5 PIASTRES
4.46 g., Copper-Nickel, 25 mm. **Series:** International Women's Year **Obv:** Denomination divides dates, legend above **Rev:** Bust of Nefertiti right, grain sprig at left

Date	Mintage	VF20	XF40	MS60	MS63	MS65
AH1395-1975	2,000,000	—	0.50	0.65	1.25	1.75

KM# 450 5 PIASTRES
Copper-Nickel, 25 mm. **Obv:** Denomination divides dates, legend above **Rev:** Islamic falcon **Note:** Mule.

Date	Mintage	VF20	XF40	MS60	MS63	MS65
AH1396-1976	—	—	4.00	7.00	18.00	22.00

KM# 451 5 PIASTRES
Copper-Nickel, 25 mm. **Subject:** 1976 Cairo Trade Fair **Obv:** Denomination divides dates, legend above **Rev:** Legend forms square around design, florals flank

Date	Mintage	VF20	XF40	MS60	MS63	MS65
AH1396-1976	500,000	—	0.60	0.75	1.25	1.75

KM# 466 5 PIASTRES
Copper-Nickel, 25 mm. **Subject:** 1971 Corrective Revolution

Date	Mintage	VF20	XF40	MS60	MS63	MS65
AH1397-1977	1,000,000	—	0.50	0.60	1.00	1.50
AH1399-1979	—	—	0.50	0.60	1.00	1.50

KM# 467 5 PIASTRES
Copper-Nickel, 25 mm. **Subject:** 50th Anniversary - Textile Industry **Obv:** Crowned head within wreath at right of denomination and dates **Rev:** Figure between dates

Date	Mintage	VF20	XF40	MS60	MS63	MS65
AH1397-1977	1,000,000	—	0.50	0.75	1.25	1.75

KM# 468 5 PIASTRES
Copper-Nickel, 25 mm. **Series:** F.A.O. **Obv:** Denomination divides dates, legend above **Rev:** People, animals, and building

Date	Mintage	VF20	XF40	MS60	MS63	MS65
AH1397-1977	—	—	0.50	0.75	1.25	1.75

Note: Edge varieties exist with narrow and wide milling

KM# 477 5 PIASTRES
Copper-Nickel, 25 mm. **Subject:** Portland Cement **Obv:** Denomination divides dates, legend above **Rev:** Cement factory, dates at top

Date	Mintage	VF20	XF40	MS60	MS63	MS65
AH1398-1978	500,000	—	0.50	0.75	1.25	1.75

KM# 478 5 PIASTRES
4.46 g., Copper-Nickel, 25 mm. **Series:** F.A.O. **Obv:** Denomination divides dates, legend above **Rev:** Woman looking into microscope

Date	Mintage	VF20	XF40	MS60	MS63	MS65
AH1398-1978	1,000,000	—	0.50	0.75	1.25	1.75

KM# 484 5 PIASTRES
Copper-Nickel, 25 mm. **Series:** International Year of the Child **Obv:** Denomination divides dates, legend above **Rev:** Woman seated with child

Date	Mintage	VF20	XF40	MS60	MS63	MS65
AH1399-1979	1,000,000	—	0.50	0.75	1.25	1.75

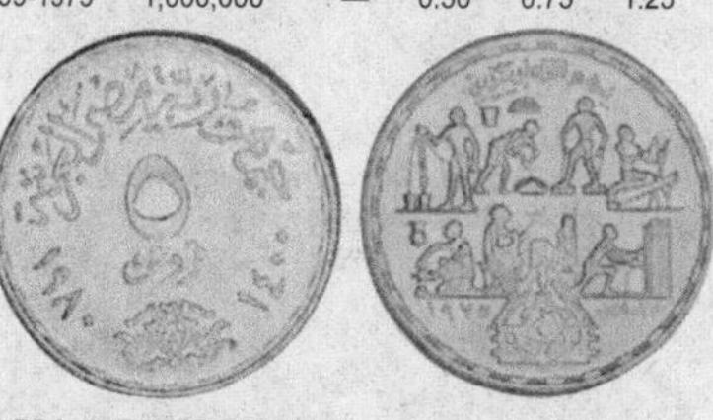

KM# 501 5 PIASTRES
Copper-Nickel, 25 mm. **Subject:** Applied Professions **Obv:** Denomination divides dates, legend above **Rev:** Various professions depicted, date and shield below

Date	Mintage	VF20	XF40	MS60	MS63	MS65
AH1400-1980	500,000	—	0.50	0.75	1.25	1.75

KM# 502 5 PIASTRES
Copper-Nickel, 25 mm. **Subject:** Sadat's Corrective Revolution of May 15, 1971 **Obv:** Denomination divides dates, legend above **Rev:** Raised fist holding stalk of grain

Date	Mintage	VF20	XF40	MS60	MS63	MS65
AH1400-1980	1,000,000	—	0.25	0.60	1.00	1.50

KM# 555.1 5 PIASTRES
Aluminum-Bronze **Obv:** Christian date left of denomination, tughra above **Rev:** Pyramids

Date	Mintage	VF20	XF40	MS60	MS63	MS65
AH1404-1984	—	—	—	0.25	0.75	1.25

Note: Varieties exist with wide and narrow rims

KM# 555.2 5 PIASTRES
Aluminum-Bronze **Obv:** Islamic date left of denomination, tughra above **Rev:** Pyramids

Date	Mintage	VF20	XF40	MS60	MS63	MS65
AH1404-1984	—	—	—	0.25	0.75	1.25

KM# 622.1 5 PIASTRES
4.91 g., Aluminum-Bronze, 23.39 mm. **Obv:** Tughra below dates and denomination, denomination not shaded **Rev:** Pyramids **Edge:** Reeded

Date	Mintage	VF20	XF40	MS60	MS63	MS65
AH1404-1984	—	—	—	0.25	0.85	1.50

KM# 622.2 5 PIASTRES
Aluminum-Bronze, 23 mm. **Obv:** Denomination shaded, tughra below **Rev:** Pyramids

Date	Mintage	VF20	XF40	MS60	MS63	MS65
AH1404-1984	—	—	—	0.25	0.85	1.50

KM# 731 5 PIASTRES
2.00 g., Brass, 21 mm. **Obv:** Denomination divides dates, legend above **Rev:** Decorated vase

Date	Mintage	VF20	XF40	MS60	MS63	MS65
AH1413-1992	—	—	—	0.50	0.75	1.25

KM# 429 10 PIASTRES
Copper-Nickel, 27 mm. **Subject:** Cairo International Fair **Obv:** Denomination, legend **Rev:** Dates in box below ship with mast

Date	Mintage	VF20	XF40	MS60	MS63	MS65
AH1392-1972	500,000	—	0.60	0.75	1.25	2.50

KM# 430 10 PIASTRES
Copper-Nickel, 27 mm. **Rev:** Islamic falcon

Date	Mintage	VF20	XF40	MS60	MS63	MS65
AH1392-1972	—	—	0.60	0.75	1.25	2.50

KM# 431 10 PIASTRES
Copper-Nickel, 27 mm. **Obv:** Denomination divides dates, legend above **Rev:** Islamic falcon **Note:** Mule.

Date	Mintage	VF20	XF40	MS60	MS63	MS65
AH1392-1972	—	—	5.50	10.00	17.50	27.50

Note: Wide and narrow inscriptions exist for obverse

KM# 442 10 PIASTRES
Copper-Nickel, 27 mm. **Subject:** First Anniversary - October War **Obv:** Denomination divides dates, legend above **Rev:** Wreath above 3/4 figure of soldier, dates below

Date	Mintage	VF20	XF40	MS60	MS63	MS65
AH1394-1974	2,000,000	—	0.60	0.75	1.25	2.00

KM# 448 10 PIASTRES
6.00 g., Copper-Nickel, 27 mm. **Series:** F.A.O. **Obv:** Denomination divides dates, legend above **Rev:** Family scene

Date	Mintage	VF20	XF40	MS60	MS63	MS65
AH1395-1975	2,000,000	—	0.60	0.75	1.25	2.00

KM# 452 10 PIASTRES
6.00 g., Copper-Nickel, 27 mm. **Subject:** Reopening of the Suez Canal **Obv:** Denomination divides dates, legend above **Rev:** Canal scene

Date	Mintage	VF20	XF40	MS60	MS63	MS65
AH1396-1976	5,000,000	—	0.60	0.75	1.25	2.00

Note: Wide and narrow inscriptions exist for the obverse

KM# 469 10 PIASTRES
Copper-Nickel, 27 mm. **Series:** F.A.O. **Obv:** Denomination divides dates, legend above **Rev:** Various laborers surround center design

Date	Mintage	VF20	XF40	MS60	MS63	MS65
AH1397-1977	1,000,000	—	0.60	0.75	1.25	2.00

KM# 470 10 PIASTRES
4.54 g., Copper-Nickel, 27 mm. **Subject:** 1971 Corrective Revolution **Obv:** Denomination divides dates, legend above **Rev:** Date and denomination left of head

Date	Mintage	VF20	XF40	MS60	MS63	MS65
AH1397-1977	1,000,000	—	0.50	0.65	0.85	1.75
AH1399-1979	1,000,000	—	0.50	0.65	0.85	1.75

KM# 471 10 PIASTRES
Copper-Nickel, 27 mm. **Subject:** 20th Anniversary - Economic Union

Date	Mintage	VF20	XF40	MS60	MS63	MS65
AH1397-1977	1,000,000	—	0.50	0.65	0.85	1.75

KM# 479 10 PIASTRES
Copper-Nickel, 27 mm. **Subject:** Cairo International Fair **Obv:** Denomination divides dates, legend above **Rev:** Legend forms square around design at top

Date	Mintage	VF20	XF40	MS60	MS63	MS65
AH1398-1978	—	—	0.50	0.75	1.25	2.00

KM# 485 10 PIASTRES
Copper-Nickel, 27 mm. **Subject:** 25th Anniversary of Abbasia Mint **Obv:** Denomination divides dates, legend above **Rev:** Dates at top corners of building, cogwheel design above

Date	Mintage	VF20	XF40	MS60	MS63	MS65
AH1399-1979	1,000,000	—	0.50	0.65	0.85	1.75

KM# 486 10 PIASTRES
5.96 g., Copper-Nickel, 27 mm. **Subject:** National Education Day **Obv:** Denomination divides dates, legend above **Rev:** Teachers, back to back and students, wreath in background

Date	Mintage	VF20	XF40	MS60	MS63	MS65
AH1399-1979	1,000,000	—	0.50	0.65	0.85	1.75

KM# 503 10 PIASTRES
Copper-Nickel, 27 mm. **Subject:** Doctor's Day **Obv:** Denomination divides dates, legend above. **Rev:** Seated Egyptian healer with staff left

Date	Mintage	VF20	XF40	MS60	MS63	MS65
AH1400-1980	1,000,000	—	0.50	0.75	1.25	2.00

KM# 504 10 PIASTRES
Copper-Nickel, 27 mm. **Subject:** Egyptian-Israeli Peace Treaty **Obv:** Denomination divides dates, legend above **Rev:** Anwar Sadat at right facing left, dove of peace, hand with quill signing treaty

Date	Mintage	VF20	XF40	MS60	MS63	MS65
AH1400-1980	1,000,000	—	0.75	1.25	2.00	3.00

KM# 505 10 PIASTRES
Copper-Nickel, 27 mm. **Series:** F.A.O.

Date	Mintage	VF20	XF40	MS60	MS63	MS65
AH1400-1980	1,000,000	—	0.50	0.75	1.25	2.00

KM# 506 10 PIASTRES
Copper-Nickel, 27 mm. **Series:** F.A.O. **Subject:** Sadat's Corrective Revolution of May 15, 1971 **Obv:** Denomination divides dates, legend above **Rev:** Raised fist with grain stalk

Date	Mintage	VF20	XF40	MS60	MS63	MS65
AH1400-1980	1,000,000	—	0.50	0.75	1.25	2.00
AH1401-1981	—	—	0.60	0.75	1.25	2.50

KM# 520 10 PIASTRES
Copper-Nickel, 27 mm. **Subject:** Scientist's Day **Obv:** Denomination, seated figure at left **Rev:** Cogwheel center of spray below sun and satellite dish

Date	Mintage	VF20	XF40	MS60	MS63	MS65
AH1401-1981	—	—	0.50	0.75	1.25	2.00

KM# 521 10 PIASTRES
6.12 g., Copper-Nickel, 27 mm. **Subject:** 25th Anniversary - Trade Unions **Obv:** Denomination divides dates, legend above **Rev:** Half cogwheel above shield

Date	Mintage	VF20	XF40	MS60	MS63	MS65
AH1402-1981	—	—	0.75	1.25	2.00	3.00

KM# 599 10 PIASTRES
Copper-Nickel, 27 mm. **Subject:** 50th Anniversary of Egyptian Products Co. **Obv:** Denomination divides dates, legend above **Rev:** Head within crowned wreath at top, triangle in background

Date	Mintage	VF20	XF40	MS60	MS63	MS65
AH1402-1982	—	—	0.50	0.75	1.25	2.00

KM# 556 10 PIASTRES
4.49 g., Copper-Nickel, 24.81 mm. **Obv:** Denomination divides dates, legend above **Rev:** Mohammad Ali Mosque **Edge:** Reeded

Date	Mintage	VF20	XF40	MS60	MS63	MS65
AH1404-1984	—	—	—	0.50	0.75	1.25

KM# 570 10 PIASTRES
Copper-Nickel, 25 mm. **Subject:** 25th Anniversary - National Planning Institute **Obv:** Arabic legends, dates below **Rev:** Shield divides dates

Date	Mintage	VF20	XF40	MS60	MS63	MS65
AH1405-1985	100,000	—	—	0.50	0.75	1.25

KM# 573 10 PIASTRES
Copper-Nickel, 25 mm. **Subject:** 60th Anniversary - Egyptian Parliament **Obv:** Arabic legends, dates below **Rev:** Dates above building

Date	Mintage	VF20	XF40	MS60	MS63	MS65
AH1405-1985	250,000	—	—	0.50	0.75	1.25

KM# 675 10 PIASTRES
Copper-Nickel, 25 mm. **Subject:** 1973 October War **Obv:** Tughra below dates, denomination at right **Rev:** Figure with flag left, building at right, dates below

Date	Mintage	VF20	XF40	MS60	MS63	MS65
AH1410-1989	250,000	—	—	0.50	0.75	1.25

KM# 732 10 PIASTRES
Brass, 23 mm. **Obv:** Denomination divides dates, legend above **Rev:** Mohammad Ali Mosque

Date	Mintage	VF20	XF40	MS60	MS63	MS65
AH1413-1992	—	—	—	0.50	0.75	1.25

KM# 507 20 PIASTRES
10.05 g., Copper-Nickel, 30.04 mm. **Obv:** Denomination divides dates, legend above **Rev:** Eagle with shield on breast **Edge:** Reeded

Date	Mintage	VF20	XF40	MS60	MS63	MS65
AH1400-1980	—	—	0.75	1.00	1.50	2.50

KM# 557 20 PIASTRES
6.00 g., Copper-Nickel, 27 mm. **Obv:** Denomination divides dates, legend above **Obv. Legend:** Mohammad Ali Mosque **Rev:** Mohammad Ali Mosque

Date	Mintage	VF20	XF40	MS60	MS63	MS65
AH1404-1984	—	—	0.50	0.85	1.25	2.00

KM# 596 20 PIASTRES
6.00 g., Copper-Nickel, 27 mm. **Subject:** 25th Anniversary - Cairo International Airport **Obv:** Arabic legends, dates below **Rev:** Birds in flight, wings and tails form diamond at center

Date	Mintage	VF20	XF40	MS60	MS63	MS65
AH1405-1985	50,000	—	—	0.75	1.00	1.50

KM# 597 20 PIASTRES
Copper-Nickel, 27 mm. **Subject:** Professions **Obv:** Arabic legends, dates below **Rev:** People doing various jobs

Date	Mintage	VF20	XF40	MS60	MS63	MS65
AH1406-1985	100,000	—	—	0.75	1.00	1.50

KM# 606 20 PIASTRES
Copper-Nickel, 27 mm. **Subject:** Warrior's Day **Obv:** Arabic legends, dates below **Rev:** Torch on crossed swords within wreath

Date	Mintage	VF20	XF40	MS60	MS63	MS65
AH1406-1986	50,000	—	—	1.00	1.50	2.50

KM# 607 20 PIASTRES
Copper-Nickel, 27 mm. **Subject:** Census **Obv:** Arabic legends, dates below **Rev:** City scene

Date	Mintage	VF20	XF40	MS60	MS63	MS65
AH1407-1986	500,000	—	—	0.75	1.00	1.50

KM# 652 20 PIASTRES
Copper-Nickel, 27 mm. **Subject:** Investment Bank **Obv:** Tughra divides dates **Rev:** Design in center of toothed circle, within circle

Date	Mintage	VF20	XF40	MS60	MS63	MS65
AH1407-1987	250,000	—	—	1.00	1.50	2.50

KM# 646 20 PIASTRES
Copper-Nickel, 27 mm. **Subject:** Police Day **Obv:** Arabic legends, dates below **Rev:** Eagle with wings spread on pedestal within wreath

Date	Mintage	VF20	XF40	MS60	MS63	MS65
AH1408-1988	250,000	—	—	1.00	1.50	2.50

KM# 650 20 PIASTRES
Copper-Nickel, 27 mm. **Subject:** Dedication of Cairo Opera House **Obv:** Arabic legends, dates below **Rev:** Building

Date	Mintage	VF20	XF40	MS60	MS63	MS65
AH1409-1988	250,000	—	—	1.00	1.50	2.50

KM# 676 20 PIASTRES
6.00 g., Copper-Nickel, 27 mm. **Subject:** 1973 October War **Obv:** Tughra below denomination and dates **Rev:** Figure with

flag at left, building at right, dates below **Edge:** Reeded

Date	Mintage	VF20	XF40	MS60	MS63	MS65
AH1410-1989	250,000	—	—	1.00	1.50	2.50

KM# 685 20 PIASTRES
Copper-Nickel, 27 mm. **Subject:** National Health Insurance **Obv:** Denomination and dates within circle at top **Rev:** People within half moon design at left, rock in background, dates below

Date	Mintage	VF20	XF40	MS60	MS63	MS65
AH1409-1989	250,000	—	—	1.00	1.50	2.50

KM# 690 20 PIASTRES
Copper-Nickel, 25 mm. **Subject:** Cairo Subway **Obv:** Four patterned tiles divide dates **Rev:** Designs within circles flank 3/4 wreath surrounding train

Date	Mintage	VF20	XF40	MS60	MS63	MS65
AH1409-1989	250,000	—	—	1.00	1.50	2.50

KM# 733 20 PIASTRES
Copper-Nickel, 25 mm. **Subject:** Mosque **Obv:** Denomination divides dates

Date	Mintage	VF20	XF40	MS60	MS63	MS65
AH1413-1992	—	—	—	0.75	1.00	1.50

KM# 438 25 PIASTRES
6.00 g., 0.720 Silver 0.1389 oz. ASW **Subject:** 75th Anniversary - National Bank of Egypt **Obv:** Denomination divides dates **Rev:** National Bank building, globe at back, divides dates

Date	Mintage	VF20	XF40	MS60	MS63	MS65
AH1393-1973	100,000	—	2.75	3.50	5.00	7.00

KM# 734 25 PIASTRES
Copper-Nickel **Obv:** Chain surrounds center hole, dates below **Rev:** Chain surrounds center hole, denomination below

Date	Mintage	VF20	XF40	MS60	MS63	MS65
AH1413-1993	—	—	—	0.75	1.25	2.00

KM# 834 1/2 POUND
4.00 g., 0.875 Gold 0.1125 oz. AGW **Subject:** El Akkad **Obv:** Legend and vase **Rev:** Portrait

Date	Mintage	VF20	XF40	MS60	MS63	MS65
AH1413-1992	600	—	—	—	275	300

KM# 809 1/2 POUND
4.00 g., 0.875 Gold 0.1125 oz. AGW **Subject:** 20th Anniversary - October War **Obv:** Smoking chimney text **Rev:** Soldier with flag

Date	Mintage	VF20	XF40	MS60	MS63	MS65
AH1414-1993	—	—	—	—	265	285

KM# 760 1/2 POUND
4.00 g., 0.875 Gold 0.1125 oz. AGW **Subject:** Salah El Din El-Ayubi **Obv:** Denomination **Rev:** Portrait

Date	Mintage	VF20	XF40	MS60	MS63	MS65
AH1414-1994	500	—	—	—	275	300

KM# 439 POUND
25.00 g., 0.720 Silver 0.5787 oz. ASW, 40 mm. **Series:** F.A.O. **Obv:** Denomination divides dates, legend above **Rev:** Corn ears and grain sprigs flank Aswan Dam

Date	Mintage	VF20	XF40	MS60	MS63	MS65
AH1393-1973	50,000	—	13.00	16.00	18.00	21.00

KM# 440 POUND
8.00 g., 0.875 Gold 0.2251 oz. AGW **Subject:** 75th Anniversary - National Bank of Egypt **Obv:** Denomination divides dates **Rev:** National Bank of Egypt building, globe at back, divides dates

Date	Mintage	VF20	XF40	MS60	MS63	MS65
AH1393-1973	7,000	—	—	—	—	400

KM# 443 POUND
15.00 g., 0.720 Silver 0.3472 oz. ASW **Subject:** First Anniversary - October War **Obv:** Denomination divides dates **Rev:** Half-figure of soldier within 3/4 wreath above

Date	Mintage	VF20	XF40	MS60	MS63	MS65
AH1394-1974	50,000	—	—	—	8.25	9.75

KM# 453 POUND
15.00 g., 0.720 Silver 0.3472 oz. ASW **Series:** F.A.O. **Obv:** Denomination divides dates **Rev:** Osiris seated, wheat sprig at right

Date	Mintage	VF20	XF40	MS60	MS63	MS65
AH1396-1976	50,000	—	—	—	7.75	9.25

KM# 454 POUND
15.00 g., 0.720 Silver 0.3472 oz. ASW **Subject:** Reopening of Suez Canal **Obv:** Denomination divides dates **Rev:** Sun above canal scene

Date	Mintage	VF20	XF40	MS60	MS63	MS65
AH1396-1976	250,000	—	—	—	7.75	9.25

KM# 455 POUND
15.00 g., 0.720 Silver 0.3472 oz. ASW **Rev:** Om Kalsoum right, singer, music symbol in hair

Date	Mintage	VF20	XF40	MS60	MS63	MS65
AH1396-1976	250,000	—	—	—	7.75	9.25

KM# 456 POUND
8.00 g., 0.875 Gold 0.2251 oz. AGW **Rev:** Om Kalsoum right

Date	Mintage	VF20	XF40	MS60	MS63	MS65
AH1396-1976	5,000	—	—	—	—	400

KM# 457 POUND
15.00 g., 0.720 Silver 0.3472 oz. ASW **Obv:** Denomination divides dates **Rev:** Bust of King Faisal half right

Date	Mintage	VF20	XF40	MS60	MS63	MS65
AH1396-1976	100,000	—	—	—	7.75	9.25

KM# 458 POUND
8.00 g., 0.875 Gold 0.2251 oz. AGW **Obv:** Denomination divides dates **Rev:** Bust of King Faisal half right

Date	Mintage	VF20	XF40	MS60	MS63	MS65
AH1396-1976	8,000	—	—	—	—	410

KM# 472 POUND
15.00 g., 0.720 Silver 0.3472 oz. ASW **Series:** F.A.O. **Obv:** Denomination divides dates **Rev:** Various laborers surround center design

Date	Mintage	VF20	XF40	MS60	MS63	MS65
AH1397-1977	50,000	—	—	—	7.75	9.25

KM# 473 POUND
15.00 g., 0.720 Silver 0.3472 oz. ASW **Subject:** 1971 Corrective Revolution **Obv:** Denomination divides dates **Rev:** Sun above head at right, date and denomination at left

Date	Mintage	VF20	XF40	MS60	MS63	MS65
AH1397-1977	50,000	—	—	—	7.75	9.25
AH1399-1979	49,000	—	—	—	7.75	9.25
AH1399-1979	1,500	**PF65** 30.00				

KM# 474 POUND
15.00 g., 0.720 Silver 0.3472 oz. ASW **Subject:** 20th Anniversary - Economic Union **Obv:** Denomination divides dates **Rev:** Design above grasped hands divides dates, grain stalks divided by cogwheel below flank

Date	Mintage	VF20	XF40	MS60	MS63	MS65
AH1397-1977	50,000	—	—	—	7.75	9.25

KM# 475 POUND
8.00 g., 0.875 Gold 0.2251 oz. AGW **Subject:** 20th Anniversary - Economic Union

Date	Mintage	VF20	XF40	MS60	MS63	MS65
AH1397-1977	5,000	—	—	—	—	400

KM# 480 POUND
15.00 g., 0.720 Silver 0.3472 oz. ASW **Subject:** Portland Cement **Obv:** Denomination divides dates **Rev:** Cement factory

Date	Mintage	VF20	XF40	MS60	MS63	MS65
AH1398-1978	50,000	—	—	—	7.75	9.25

KM# 481 POUND
15.00 g., 0.720 Silver 0.3472 oz. ASW **Subject:** 25th Anniversary - Ain Shams University **Obv:** Denomination divides dates **Rev:** Birds flank center design, dates below

Date	Mintage	VF20	XF40	MS60	MS63	MS65
AH1398-1978	50,000	—	—	—	7.75	9.25

KM# 482 POUND
15.00 g., 0.720 Silver 0.3472 oz. ASW **Series:** F.A.O. **Rev:** Female looking into microscope

Date	Mintage	VF20	XF40	MS60	MS63	MS65
AH1398-1978	50,000	—	—	—	7.75	9.25

KM# 488 POUND
15.00 g., 0.720 Silver 0.3472 oz. ASW **Subject:** 25th Anniversary - Abbasia Mint **Obv:** Denomination divides dates **Rev:** Dates above building at corners, cogwheel at top

Date	Mintage	VF20	XF40	MS60	MS63	MS65
AH1399-1979	23,000	—	—	—	9.75	13.50
AH1399-1979	2,000	**PF65** 25.00				

KM# 489 POUND
15.00 g., 0.720 Silver 0.3472 oz. ASW **Series:** F.A.O. and I.Y.C. **Obv:** Denomination divides dates **Rev:** Seated woman with child, logo and designs at right, FAO below chair

Date	Mintage	VF20	XF40	MS60	MS63	MS65
AH1399-1979	48,000	—	—	—	7.75	9.25
AH1399-1979	2,500	**PF65** 22.00				

KM# 490 POUND
15.00 g., 0.720 Silver 0.3472 oz. ASW **Subject:** National Education Day **Obv:** Denomination divides dates **Rev:** Back to back teachers and students, wreath in background

Date	Mintage	VF20	XF40	MS60	MS63	MS65
AH1399-1979	98,000	—	—	—	7.75	9.25
AH1399-1979	2,000	**PF65** 22.00				

KM# 491 POUND
15.00 g., 0.720 Silver 0.3472 oz. ASW **Subject:** 100th Anniversary - Bank of Land Reform **Rev:** Seated figure, workers harvesting grain at back, farmers and oxen above

Date	Mintage	VF20	XF40	MS60	MS63	MS65
AH1399-1979	98,000	—	—	—	7.75	9.25
AH1399-1979	2,000	**PF65** 22.00				

KM# 492 POUND
8.00 g., 0.875 Gold 0.2251 oz. AGW **Subject:** 100th Anniversary - Bank of Land Reform

Date	Mintage	VF20	XF40	MS60	MS63	MS65
AH1399-1979	4,200	—	—	—	—	400
AH1399-1979	800	**PF65** 420				

KM# 493 POUND
15.00 g., 0.720 Silver 0.3472 oz. ASW **Subject:** 1400th Anniversary - Mohammed's Flight **Obv:** Denomination divides dates **Rev:** Birds and eggs in front of web design

Date	Mintage	VF20	XF40	MS60	MS63	MS65
AH1400-1979	97,000	—	—	—	7.75	9.25
AH1400-1979	3,000	**PF65** 22.00				

KM# 494 POUND
8.00 g., 0.875 Gold 0.2251 oz. AGW **Subject:** 1400th Anniversary - Mohammed's Flight

Date	Mintage	VF20	XF40	MS60	MS63	MS65
AH1400-1979	2,000	—	—	—	—	400
AH1400-1979	2,000	**PF65** 420				

KM# 508 POUND
15.00 g., 0.720 Silver 0.3472 oz. ASW **Subject:** Egyptian-Israeli Peace Treaty **Obv:** Denomination divides dates **Rev:** Head of Anwar Sadat at right facing left, with dove of peace at left

Date	Mintage	VF20	XF40	MS60	MS63	MS65
AH1400-1980	95,000	—	—	—	7.75	9.25
AH1400-1980	5,000	**PF65** 20.00				

KM# 509 POUND
8.00 g., 0.875 Gold 0.2251 oz. AGW **Subject:** Egyptian-Israeli Peace Treaty **Obv:** Denomination divides dates **Rev:** Head of Anwar Sadat left, with dove of peace at left

Date	Mintage	VF20	XF40	MS60	MS63	MS65
AH1400-1980	9,500	—	—	—	—	400
AH1400-1980	500	**PF65** 420				

KM# 510 POUND
15.00 g., 0.720 Silver 0.3472 oz. ASW **Subject:** Applied Professions in Egypt **Obv:** Denomination divides dates **Rev:** Various professions depicted, date and shield below

Date	Mintage	VF20	XF40	MS60	MS63	MS65
AH1400-1980	22,000	—	—	—	9.75	13.50
AH1400-1980	3,000	**PF65** 22.00				

KM# 511 POUND
15.00 g., 0.720 Silver 0.3472 oz. ASW **Subject:** Doctor's Day **Obv:** Denomination divides dates **Rev:** Seated healer with staff facing left

Date	Mintage	VF20	XF40	MS60	MS63	MS65
AH1400-1980	97,000	—	—	—	7.75	9.25
AH1400-1980	3,000	**PF65** 22.00				

KM# 512 POUND
8.00 g., 0.875 Gold 0.2251 oz. AGW **Subject:** Doctor's Day **Rev:** Seated healer with staff facing left

Date	Mintage	VF20	XF40	MS60	MS63	MS65
AH1400-1980	5,000	PF65 400				

KM# 513 POUND
15.00 g., 0.720 Silver 0.3472 oz. ASW **Series:** F.A.O. **Obv:** Denomination divides dates **Rev:** Kneeling figure with book and birds, city scene at right, pyramids and tractor at left

Date	Mintage	VF20	XF40	MS60	MS63	MS65
AH1400-1980	97,000	—	—	—	7.75	9.25
AH1400-1980	3,000	PF65 25.00				

KM# 514 POUND
15.00 g., 0.720 Silver 0.3472 oz. ASW **Subject:** Sadat's Corrective Revolution of May 15, 1971 **Obv:** Denomination divides dates **Rev:** Raised clenched fist holding grain sprig

Date	Mintage	VF20	XF40	MS60	MS63	MS65
AH1400-1980	47,000	—	—	—	7.75	9.25
AH1400-1980	3,000	PF65 22.00				

KM# 515 POUND
15.00 g., 0.720 Silver 0.3472 oz. ASW **Obv:** Denomination divides dates **Rev:** Cairo University Law facility

Date	Mintage	VF20	XF40	MS60	MS63	MS65
AH1400-1980	47,000	—	—	—	7.75	9.25
AH1400-1980	3,000	PF65 22.00				

KM# 516 POUND
8.00 g., 0.875 Gold 0.2251 oz. AGW **Obv:** Denomination divides dates **Rev:** Cairo University Law facility

Date	Mintage	VF20	XF40	MS60	MS63	MS65
AH1400-1980	2,000	—	—	—	—	400
AH1400-1980	—	PF65 425				

KM# 522 POUND
15.00 g., 0.720 Silver 0.3472 oz. ASW **Subject:** Scientists' Day **Obv:** Denomination within circle, seated figure at left **Rev:** Sun above satellite dish, cogwheel divides spray below

Date	Mintage	VF20	XF40	MS60	MS63	MS65
AH1401-1981	25,000	—	—	—	8.75	11.50

KM# 523 POUND
15.00 g., 0.720 Silver 0.3472 oz. ASW **Series:** World Food Day **Obv:** Denomination divides dates **Rev:** Standing figure with food tray, animals at right, figure harvesting grain at left

Date	Mintage	VF20	XF40	MS60	MS63	MS65
AH1401-1981	50,000	—	—	—	7.75	9.25
AH1401-1981	1,500	PF65 45.00				

KM# 524 POUND
15.00 g., 0.720 Silver 0.3472 oz. ASW **Subject:** 3rd Anniversary - Suez Canal Reopening **Obv:** Denomination divides dates **Rev:** Grain stalk right of canal scene

Date	Mintage	VF20	XF40	MS60	MS63	MS65
AH1401-1981	50,000	—	—	—	7.75	9.25
AH1401-1981	2,000	PF65 25.00				

KM# 525 POUND
8.00 g., 0.875 Gold 0.2251 oz. AGW **Subject:** 3rd Anniversary - Suez Canal Reopening

Date	Mintage	VF20	XF40	MS60	MS63	MS65
AH1401-1981	150	PF65 425				

KM# 526 POUND
15.00 g., 0.720 Silver 0.3472 oz. ASW **Subject:** 25th Anniversary - Egyptian Industry

Date	Mintage	VF20	XF40	MS60	MS63	MS65
AH1402-1981	25,000	—	—	—	8.75	11.50

KM# 527 POUND
15.00 g., 0.720 Silver 0.3472 oz. ASW **Subject:** 25th Anniversary - Trade Unions **Obv:** Denomination divides dates **Rev:** Hands holding up factories, flower below, all within oval on shield with 1/2 cogwheel above, dates at left

Date	Mintage	VF20	XF40	MS60	MS63	MS65
AH1402-1981	25,000	—	—	—	8.75	11.50

KM# 528 POUND
15.00 g., 0.720 Silver 0.3472 oz. ASW **Subject:** 25th Anniversary - Nationalization of Suez Canal **Obv:** Denomination divides dates **Rev:** Central design divides dates, grain spray below

Date	Mintage	VF20	XF40	MS60	MS63	MS65
AH1401-1981	25,000	—	—	—	8.75	11.50
AH1401-1981	1,500	PF65 30.00				

KM# 529 POUND
8.00 g., 0.875 Gold 0.2251 oz. AGW **Subject:** 25th Anniversary - Nationalization of Suez Canal **Obv:** Denomination divides dates **Rev:** Central design divides dates, grain spray below

Date	Mintage	VF20	XF40	MS60	MS63	MS65
AH1401-1981	3,000	—	—	—	—	400

KM# 530 POUND
15.00 g., 0.720 Silver 0.3472 oz. ASW **Subject:** 100th Anniversary - Revolt by Arabi Pasha **Rev:** Pasha mounted on horse in front of his followers

Date	Mintage	VF20	XF40	MS60	MS63	MS65
AH1402-1981	50,000	—	—	—	7.75	9.25
AH1402-1981	1,500	PF65 30.00				

KM# 531 POUND
8.00 g., 0.875 Gold 0.2251 oz. AGW **Subject:** 100th Anniversary - Revolt by Arabi Pasha **Rev:** Pasha mounted on horse in front of his followers

Date	Mintage	VF20	XF40	MS60	MS63	MS65
AH1402-1981	3,000	—	—	—	—	400

KM# 532 POUND
15.00 g., 0.720 Silver 0.3472 oz. ASW **Series:** F.A.O. **Obv:** Denomination divides dates **Rev:** Figures flank design at center

Date	Mintage	VF20	XF40	MS60	MS63	MS65
AH1401-1981	50,000	—	—	—	7.75	9.25

KM# 539 POUND

15.00 g., 0.720 Silver 0.3472 oz. ASW **Subject:** Golden Jubilee - Egypt Air **Obv:** Denomination divides dates **Rev:** Stylized bird on globe, dates above

Date	Mintage	VF20	XF40	MS60	MS63	MS65
AH1402-1982	20,000	—	—	—	8.75	11.50

KM# 540 POUND

15.00 g., 0.720 Silver 0.3472 oz. ASW **Subject:** 1000th Anniversary - Al Azhar Mosque **Obv:** Denomination within circle, divides dates **Rev:** Mosque

Date	Mintage	VF20	XF40	MS60	MS63	MS65
AH1402-1982	23,000	—	—	—	8.75	11.50
AH1402-1982	4,000	PF65 22.00				

KM# 541 POUND

8.00 g., 0.875 Gold 0.2251 oz. AGW **Subject:** 1000th Anniversary - Al Azhar Mosque **Rev:** Mosque

Date	Mintage	VF20	XF40	MS60	MS63	MS65
AH1402-1982	2,000	PF65 400				

KM# 542 POUND

15.00 g., 0.720 Silver 0.3472 oz. ASW **Subject:** 50th Anniversary of Air Force **Rev:** Air Force insignia within wreath

Date	Mintage	VF20	XF40	MS60	MS63	MS65
AH1403-1982	10,000	—	—	—	9.75	13.50
AH1403-1982	2,260	PF65 25.00				

KM# 543 POUND

8.00 g., 0.875 Gold 0.2251 oz. AGW **Subject:** 50th Anniversary of Air Force **Rev:** Air Force insignia within wreath

Date	Mintage	VF20	XF40	MS60	MS63	MS65
AH1403-1982	2,000	PF65 400				

KM# 544 POUND

15.00 g., 0.720 Silver 0.3472 oz. ASW **Subject:** 50th Anniversary - Egyptian Products Co. **Obv:** Denomination divides dates **Rev:** Head within crowned wreath at top, triangle in background

Date	Mintage	VF20	XF40	MS60	MS63	MS65
AH1402-1982	5,000	—	—	—	9.75	13.50
AH1402-1982	2,000	PF65 25.00				

KM# 545 POUND

15.00 g., 0.720 Silver 0.3472 oz. ASW **Subject:** Return of Sinai to Egypt **Obv:** Denomination divides dates **Rev:** Grain sprigs form 'V', bird above

Date	Mintage	VF20	XF40	MS60	MS63	MS65
AH1402-1982(1983)	50,000	—	—	—	7.75	9.25
AH1402-1982(1983)	2,000	PF65 25.00				

KM# 549 POUND

15.00 g., 0.720 Silver 0.3472 oz. ASW **Subject:** 50th Anniversary - Deaths of Shawky and Hafez **Obv:** Denomination divides dates **Rev:** Two busts, flowers flank

Date	Mintage	VF20	XF40	MS60	MS63	MS65
AH1403-1983	25,000	—	—	—	8.75	11.50

KM# 551 POUND

15.00 g., 0.720 Silver 0.3472 oz. ASW **Subject:** Misr Insurance Company **Obv:** Denomination divides dates **Rev:** Design within center oval divides dates

Date	Mintage	VF20	XF40	MS60	MS63	MS65
AH1404-1984	20,000	—	—	—	8.75	11.50

KM# 559 POUND

15.00 g., 0.720 Silver 0.3472 oz. ASW **Subject:** Helwan University Faculty of Fine Arts **Obv:** Flower head at top, denomination and dates **Rev:** Artist's tools within design

Date	Mintage	VF20	XF40	MS60	MS63	MS65
AH1404-1984	25,000	—	—	—	8.75	11.50
AH1404-1984	Est. 25	PF65 200				

KM# 583 POUND

8.00 g., 0.875 Gold 0.2251 oz. AGW **Subject:** 50th Anniversary - Egyptian Radio Broadcasting

Date	Mintage	VF20	XF40	MS60	MS63	MS65
AH1404-1984	2,000	—	—	—	—	375

KM# 571 POUND

8.00 g., 0.875 Gold 0.2251 oz. AGW **Subject:** 25th Anniversary - National Planning Institute

Date	Mintage	VF20	XF40	MS60	MS63	MS65
AH1405-1985	200	—	—	—	—	420

KM# 574 POUND

8.00 g., 0.875 Gold 0.2251 oz. AGW **Subject:** 60th Anniversary - Egyptian Parliament **Rev:** Parliament building

Date	Mintage	VF20	XF40	MS60	MS63	MS65
AH1405-1985	1,000	—	—	—	—	385

KM# 577 POUND

8.00 g., 0.875 Gold 0.2251 oz. AGW **Subject:** 25th Anniversary - Cairo Stadium **Rev:** Stadium

Date	Mintage	VF20	XF40	MS60	MS63	MS65
AH1405-1985	300	—	—	—	—	420

KM# 580 POUND

8.00 g., 0.875 Gold 0.2251 oz. AGW **Subject:** 25th Anniversary - Egyptian Television

Date	Mintage	VF20	XF40	MS60	MS63	MS65
AH1405-1985	150	—	—	—	—	445

KM# 604 POUND

8.00 g., 0.875 Gold 0.2251 oz. AGW **Subject:** Commerce Day **Rev:** Stylized depictions of commercial activity

Date	Mintage	VF20	XF40	MS60	MS63	MS65
AH1405-1985	2,000	PF65 375				

KM# 605 POUND

8.00 g., 0.875 Gold 0.2251 oz. AGW **Subject:** Faculty of Economics and Political Science **Obv:** Arabic legends, seals, and date **Rev:** Graph within wreath, partial gear wheel

Date	Mintage	VF20	XF40	MS60	MS63	MS65
AH1405-1985	250	PF65 420				

KM# 632 POUND

8.00 g., 0.875 Gold 0.2251 oz. AGW **Subject:** Prophet's Mosque **Obv:** Minaret, globe, denomination, legends **Rev:** Crescent, mosque, minaret below legend arch

Date	Mintage	VF20	XF40	MS60	MS63	MS65
AH1406-1985	800	—	—	—	—	375

KM# 635 POUND

8.00 g., 0.875 Gold 0.2251 oz. AGW **Subject:** 25th Anniversary - Cairo International Airport **Obv:** Stylized legend above dates, dividing two seals **Rev:** Two circling vultures within Arabic and English legends

Date	Mintage	VF20	XF40	MS60	MS63	MS65
AH1405-1985	200	—	—	—	—	420

KM# 636 POUND

8.00 g., 0.875 Gold 0.2251 oz. AGW **Subject:** Cairo University Faculty of Commerce **Obv:** Stylized legend above dates, dividing two seals **Rev:** Ancient Egyptian commerce related scenes

Date	Mintage	VF20	XF40	MS60	MS63	MS65
AH1406-1986	200	—	—	—	—	420

KM# 637 POUND

8.00 g., 0.875 Gold 0.2251 oz. AGW **Subject:** 25th Anniversary - Egyptian Central Bank **Obv:** Stylized flowers, gear wheel and cotton within legend **Rev:** Ancient Egyptian sculptures, legends above and below within ornamental border

Date	Mintage	VF20	XF40	MS60	MS63	MS65
AH1406-1986	200	—	—	—	—	420

KM# 638 POUND

8.00 g., 0.875 Gold 0.2251 oz. AGW **Subject:** 100th Anniversary - Petroleum Industry **Obv:** Stylized legend above dates, dividing two seals **Rev:** Oil well and landscape within ornamental circle

Date	Mintage	VF20	XF40	MS60	MS63	MS65
AH1406-1986	800	—	—	—	—	375

KM# 639 POUND

8.00 g., 0.875 Gold 0.2251 oz. AGW **Subject:** Census **Obv:** Arabic legends, seals, date **Rev:** City view with paper doll cutout human figures

Date	Mintage	VF20	XF40	MS60	MS63	MS65
AH1407-1986	200	—	—	—	—	400

KM# 640 POUND

8.00 g., 0.875 Gold 0.2251 oz. AGW **Subject:** 50th Anniversary - National Theater **Obv:** Stylized stage curtain, legend within **Rev:** Large building, two masks in foreground, legend above

Date	Mintage	VF20	XF40	MS60	MS63	MS65
AH1406-1986	250	—	—	—	—	415

KM# 643 POUND

8.00 g., 0.875 Gold 0.2251 oz. AGW **Subject:** 40th Anniversary - Engineer's Syndicate **Obv:** Arabic legends, seals, dates **Rev:** Three triangles, legend, ornamentation

Date	Mintage	VF20	XF40	MS60	MS63	MS65
AH1407-1986	400	—	—	—	—	390

KM# 644 POUND

8.00 g., 0.875 Gold 0.2251 oz. AGW **Subject:** Restoration of Parliament Building **Obv:** Arabic legends **Rev:** Dome and tower with scaffolding

Date	Mintage	VF20	XF40	MS60	MS63	MS65
AH1406-1986	400	—	—	—	—	390

KM# 645 POUND

8.00 g., 0.875 Gold 0.2251 oz. AGW **Subject:** Parliament Museum **Obv:** Arabic legends, seals, dates **Rev:** Documents, quill, carriage, building with national emblem

Date	Mintage	VF20	XF40	MS60	MS63	MS65
AH1407-1987	400	—	—	—	—	390

KM# 653 POUND
8.00 g., 0.875 Gold 0.2251 oz. AGW **Subject:** Investment Bank **Obv:** Toughra, legends above and below, dates **Rev:** Symbol within stylized circle, legend around

Date	Mintage	VF20	XF40	MS60	MS63	MS65
AH1407-1987	600	—	—	—	—	390

KM# 673 POUND
8.00 g., 0.875 Gold 0.2251 oz. AGW **Subject:** First African Subway **Obv:** Stylized legends and denomination **Rev:** Subway emerging from tunnel with legend around rim

Date	Mintage	VF20	XF40	MS60	MS63	MS65
AH1408-1987	500	PF65 390				

KM# 647 POUND
8.00 g., 0.875 Gold 0.2251 oz. AGW **Subject:** Police Day **Obv:** Arabic and English legends, seals, dates **Rev:** Police emblem - eagle in wreath, legends

Date	Mintage	VF20	XF40	MS60	MS63	MS65
AH1408-1988	500	—	—	—	—	390

KM# 654 POUND
8.00 g., 0.875 Gold 0.2251 oz. AGW **Subject:** Dedication of Cairo Opera House **Obv:** Arabic legends, seals, dates **Rev:** Opera house, legends above and below

Date	Mintage	VF20	XF40	MS60	MS63	MS65
AH1409-1988	1,500	—	—	—	—	395

KM# 661 POUND
8.00 g., 0.875 Gold 0.2251 oz. AGW **Subject:** Naquib Mahfouz, Nobel Laureate **Obv:** Stylized quill ink and paper design with legend above **Rev:** Head of Mahfouz left

Date	Mintage	VF20	XF40	MS60	MS63	MS65
AH1409-1988	1,000	PF65 395				

KM# 664 POUND
8.00 g., 0.875 Gold 0.2251 oz. AGW **Subject:** United Parliamentary Union **Obv:** Kufic legend above denomination and dates **Rev:** Anniversary dates, map in wreath above domed building, and legend

Date	Mintage	VF20	XF40	MS60	MS63	MS65
AH1409-1989	200	PF65 420				

KM# 666 POUND
8.00 g., 0.875 Gold 0.2251 oz. AGW **Subject:** First Arab Olympics **Obv:** Kufic legend above denomination and dates **Rev:** 5 Olympic rings and map as part of torch held by hand within wreath and legend

Date	Mintage	VF20	XF40	MS60	MS63	MS65
AH1409-1989	300	PF65 400				

KM# 668 POUND
8.00 g., 0.875 Gold 0.2251 oz. AGW **Subject:** National Research Center **Obv:** Kufic legend above denomination and dates **Rev:** Stylized ancient and modern research elements

Date	Mintage	VF20	XF40	MS60	MS63	MS65
AH1409-1989	250	PF65 400				

KM# 677 POUND
8.00 g., 0.875 Gold 0.2251 oz. AGW **Subject:** University of Cairo, School of Agriculture **Obv:** Denomination between wheat ears above legend **Rev:** Ancient farming scene and coat of arms, building in background

Date	Mintage	VF20	XF40	MS60	MS63	MS65
AH1410-1989	200	PF65 420				

KM# 695 POUND
8.00 g., 0.875 Gold 0.2251 oz. AGW **Subject:** Export Trade Show **Obv:** Toughra, inscription above **Rev:** Display of symbols

Date	Mintage	VF20	XF40	MS60	MS63	MS65
AH1410-1989	200	PF65 420				

KM# 696 POUND
8.00 g., 0.875 Gold 0.2251 oz. AGW **Subject:** Union of African Parliament **Obv:** Toughra, denomination, date within circle and legend **Rev:** Map of Africa, laurel branch and Parliament building

Date	Mintage	VF20	XF40	MS60	MS63	MS65
AH1410-1990	200	PF65 420				

KM# 699 POUND
8.00 g., 0.875 Gold 0.2251 oz. AGW **Subject:** 5th African Games - Cairo **Obv:** Torch with legend and inscription **Rev:** Logo above rings within legend

Date	Mintage	VF20	XF40	MS60	MS63	MS65
AH1411-1991	200	PF65 420				

KM# 726 POUND
8.00 g., 0.875 Gold 0.2251 oz. AGW **Subject:** Mohamed Abdel Wahab **Rev:** Bust of Mohamed Abdel Wahab left with music sheet in background

Date	Mintage	VF20	XF40	MS60	MS63	MS65
AH1412-1991	1,000	—	—	—	—	385

KM# 832 POUND
8.00 g., 0.875 Gold 0.2251 oz. AGW **Subject:** Library of Alexandria **Obv:** Legend and inscription **Rev:** Waterfront building with tower

Date	Mintage	VF20	XF40	MS60	MS63	MS65
AH1411-1991	300	—	—	—	—	425

KM# 835 POUND
15.00 g., 0.720 Silver 0.3472 oz. ASW **Subject:** Gorgui Zidane **Obv:** Legend and vase **Rev:** Portrait **Edge:** Reeded

Date	Mintage	VF20	XF40	MS60	MS63	MS65
AH1413-1992	3,000	—	—	—	—	20.00

KM# 836 POUND
8.00 g., 0.875 Gold 0.2251 oz. AGW **Subject:** Rifa'a El Tahtaoui **Obv:** Legend and vase **Rev:** Portrait

Date	Mintage	VF20	XF40	MS60	MS63	MS65
AH1413-1992	800	—	—	—	—	425

KM# 810 POUND
15.00 g., 0.720 Silver 0.3472 oz. ASW **Subject:** 20th Anniversary - October War **Obv:** Smoking chimneys divide dates, text **Rev:** Soldier with flag

Date	Mintage	VF20	XF40	MS60	MS63	MS65
AH1414-1993	Est. 25000	—	—	—	8.75	11.00

KM# 811 POUND
8.00 g., 0.875 Gold 0.2251 oz. AGW **Subject:** 20th Anniversary - October War **Obv:** Smoking chimney, text **Rev:** Soldier with flag

Date	Mintage	VF20	XF40	MS60	MS63	MS65
AH1414-1993	Est. 3000	—	—	—	—	425

KM# 761 POUND
15.00 g., 0.720 Silver 0.3472 oz. ASW **Subject:** Salah El Din El-Ayubi **Obv:** Denomination **Rev:** Portrait

Date	Mintage	VF20	XF40	MS60	MS63	MS65
AH1414-1994	5,000	—	—	—	8.75	11.00

KM# 762 POUND
8.00 g., 0.875 Gold 0.2251 oz. AGW **Subject:** Salah El Din El-Ayubi **Obv:** Denomination **Rev:** Portrait

Date	Mintage	VF20	XF40	MS60	MS63	MS65
AH1414-1994	300	—	—	—	—	425

KM# 764 POUND
15.00 g., 0.720 Silver 0.3472 oz. ASW **Subject:** 125 Years - Suez Canal **Obv:** Toughra **Rev:** Building and canal scenes

Date	Mintage	VF20	XF40	MS60	MS63	MS65
AH1415-1994	3,000	—	—	—	9.75	14.00

KM# 766 POUND
15.00 g., 0.720 Silver 0.3472 oz. ASW **Subject:** 75 Years - Bank of Misr **Obv:** Inscription **Rev:** Bank building and emblem, dates upper left

Date	Mintage	VF20	XF40	MS60	MS63	MS65
AH1415-1994	2,500	—	—	—	8.75	11.00

KM# 767 POUND
8.00 g., 0.875 Gold 0.2251 oz. AGW **Subject:** 75 Years - Bank of Misr

Date	Mintage	VF20	XF40	MS60	MS63	MS65
AH1415-1995	1,000	—	—	—	390	410

KM# 769 POUND
15.00 g., 0.720 Silver 0.3472 oz. ASW **Series:** F.A.O. **Rev:** Workers

Date	Mintage	VF20	XF40	MS60	MS63	MS65
AH1415-1995	3,000	—	—	—	9.75	14.00

KM# 771 POUND
8.00 g., 0.875 Gold 0.2251 oz. AGW **Subject:** Pediatrics International Conference **Obv:** Tughra divides dates and denomination **Rev:** Children and pyramids on globe, dates divided below

Date	Mintage	VF20	XF40	MS60	MS63	MS65
AH1416-1995	300	—	—	—	—	425

KM# 839 POUND
15.00 g., 0.720 Silver 0.3472 oz. ASW **Subject:** Abd Al Halem Hafez **Obv:** Tughra, date and denomination **Rev:** Head left

Date	Mintage	VF20	XF40	MS60	MS63	MS65
AH1416-1995	3,000	—	—	—	8.75	11.00

KM# 840 POUND
8.00 g., 0.875 Gold 0.2251 oz. AGW **Obv:** Denomination **Rev:** Abd Al Halem Hafez

Date	Mintage	VF20	XF40	MS60	MS63	MS65
AH1416-1995	500	—	—	—	—	425

KM# 844 POUND
15.00 g., 0.720 Silver 0.3472 oz. ASW **Subject:** Centennial - Electrification **Obv:** Legend and inscription **Rev:** Electric bolt on Pyramid

Date	Mintage	VF20	XF40	MS60	MS63	MS65
AH1417-1996	3,000	—	—	—	8.75	11.00

KM# 937 POUND
8.00 g., 0.875 Gold 0.2251 oz. AGW, 24 mm. **Subject:** Centennial of the Geological Survey Authority **Obv:** Toughra, value **Rev:** Ancient dig **Edge:** Reeded **Mint:** Cairo

Date	Mintage	VF20	XF40	MS60	MS63	MS65
AH1416-1996	250	—	—	—	—	450

KM# 946 POUND
8.00 g., 0.875 Gold 0.2251 oz. AGW, 24 mm. **Subject:** Diamond Jubilee Electricity in Egypt **Obv:** Value **Rev:** Prism, gear teeth below **Edge:** Reeded **Mint:** Cairo

Date	Mintage	VF20	XF40	MS60	MS63	MS65
AH1417-1996	1,000	—	—	—	—	385

KM# 845 POUND
15.00 g., 0.720 Silver 0.3472 oz. ASW **Subject:** 65 Years - Egyptian Air Force **Obv:** Denomination **Rev:** Flying eagle in wreath

Date	Mintage	VF20	XF40	MS60	MS63	MS65
AH1418-1997	Est. 226	—	—	—	35.00	65.00

KM# 847 POUND
15.00 g., 0.720 Silver 0.3472 oz. ASW **Subject:** 50 Years Arab Land Bank **Obv:** Denomination **Rev:** Arab Real Estate domed Bank building

Date	Mintage	VF20	XF40	MS60	MS63	MS65
AH1418-1997	3,000	—	—	—	8.75	11.00

KM# 849 POUND
15.00 g., 0.720 Silver 0.3472 oz. ASW **Subject:** 95th Interparliamentary Union Conference **Obv:** Circular design above inscription **Rev:** Pyramids in wreath

Date	Mintage	VF20	XF40	MS60	MS63	MS65
AH1418-1997	Est. 375	—	—	—	35.00	65.00

KM# 926 POUND
15.00 g., 0.720 Silver 0.3472 oz. ASW, 35 mm. **Subject:** Soccer FIFA-JVC Cup **Obv:** Value, ornamental design and inscription **Rev:** Games logo **Edge:** Reeded **Mint:** Cairo

Date	Mintage	VF20	XF40	MS60	MS63	MS65
AH1418-1997	—	—	—	—	35.00	65.00

KM# 947 POUND
8.00 g., 0.875 Gold 0.2251 oz. AGW, 24 mm. **Series:** 4th World Youth Cup **Obv:** Ornamental doorway, value **Rev:** Stylized player on soccer ball **Rev. Legend:** WORLD CHAMPIONSHIP / FOR THE FIFA/IYC CUP EGYPT **Edge:** Reeded **Mint:** Cairo

Date	Mintage	VF20	XF40	MS60	MS63	MS65
AH1418-1997	130	—	—	—	—	425

KM# 948 POUND
8.00 g., 0.875 Gold 0.2251 oz. AGW, 24 mm. **Subject:** Air Force Day **Obv:** Value **Rev:** Air Force emblem **Edge:** Reeded **Mint:** Cairo

Date	Mintage	VF20	XF40	MS60	MS63	MS65
AH1418-1997	1,250	—	—	—	—	385

KM# 851 POUND
15.00 g., 0.720 Silver 0.3472 oz. ASW **Subject:** Centennial - Chemical Department **Obv:** Denomination **Rev:** Symbolic design

Date	Mintage	VF20	XF40	MS60	MS63	MS65
AH1419-1998	1,000	—	—	—	15.00	30.00

KM# 855 POUND
15.00 g., 0.720 Silver 0.3472 oz. ASW **Series:** Centennial - National Bank **Obv:** Denomination **Rev:** Large "100"

Date	Mintage	VF20	XF40	MS60	MS63	MS65
AH1419-1998	2,000	—	—	—	20.00	40.00

KM# 857 POUND
15.00 g., 0.720 Silver 0.3472 oz. ASW **Subject:** 25th Anniversary - October War **Obv:** Denomination **Rev:** Symbolic design

Date	Mintage	VF20	XF40	MS60	MS63	MS65
AH1419-1998	2,000	—	—	—	15.00	30.00

KM# 859 POUND
15.00 g., 0.720 Silver 0.3472 oz. ASW **Subject:** Death of Imam Metwaly El Sharawi **Obv:** Open book **Rev:** Bust of El Sharawi facing

Date	Mintage	VF20	XF40	MS60	MS63	MS65
AH1419-1998	2,000	—	—	—	15.00	30.00

KM# 861 POUND
15.00 g., 0.720 Silver 0.3472 oz. ASW **Subject:** Centennial - Land Surveying **Obv:** Denomination **Rev:** "100" above ancient surveyors

Date	Mintage	VF20	XF40	MS60	MS63	MS65
AH1419-1998	1,000	—	—	—	15.00	30.00

KM# 863 POUND
15.00 g., 0.720 Silver 0.3472 oz. ASW **Series:** Centennial - Solidarity **Obv:** Denomination **Rev:** Symbolic design

Date	Mintage	VF20	XF40	MS60	MS63	MS65
AH1419-1998	2,000	—	—	—	15.00	30.00

KM# 949 POUND
8.00 g., 0.875 Gold 0.2251 oz. AGW, 224 mm. **Subject:** Centennial National Bank of Egypt **Obv:** Value **Rev:** Sprig though large "100" **Edge:** Reeded **Mint:** Cairo

Date	Mintage	VF20	XF40	MS60	MS63	MS65
AH1419-1998	1,000	—	—	—	—	390

KM# 950 POUND
8.00 g., 0.875 Gold 0.2251 oz. AGW, 24 mm. **Subject:** Silver Jubilee October War **Obv:** Value **Rev:** Monument **Edge:** Reeded **Mint:** Cairo

Date	Mintage	VF20	XF40	MS60	MS63	MS65
AH1419-1998	1,000	—	—	—	—	390

KM# 951 POUND
8.00 g., 0.875 Gold 0.2251 oz. AGW, 24 mm. **Subject:** Sheikh Mohamed Metwally El-Shaarawi **Obv:** Open book with rays, value below **Rev:** Bust of shiekh facing holding open book **Edge:** Reeded **Mint:** Cairo

Date	Mintage	VF20	XF40	MS60	MS63	MS65
AH1419-1998	1,200	—	—	—	—	390

KM# 952 POUND
8.00 g., 0.875 Gold 0.2251 oz. AGW, 24 mm. **Subject:** Nilesat **Obv:** Value **Rev:** Sphinx at lower right **Edge:** Reeded **Mint:** Cairo

Date	Mintage	VF20	XF40	MS60	MS63	MS65
AH1419-1998	1,500	—	—	—	—	390

KM# 953 POUND
8.00 g., 0.875 Gold 0.2251 oz. AGW, 24 mm. **Subject:** Restoration of Al Azhar Mosque **Obv:** Value **Rev:** Mosque **Edge:** Reeded **Mint:** Cairo

Date	Mintage	VF20	XF40	MS60	MS63	MS65
AH1419-1998	1,000	—	—	—	—	390

KM# 865 POUND
15.00 g., 0.720 Silver 0.3472 oz. ASW **Subject:** Golden Jubilee of Ash Shanns University **Obv:** Denomination **Rev:** Monument

Date	Mintage	VF20	XF40	MS60	MS63	MS65
AH1420-1999	1,000	—	—	—	15.00	30.00

KM# 954 POUND
8.00 g., 0.875 Gold 0.2251 oz. AGW, 24 mm. **Subject:** Cairo Metro Tunnel under Nile River **Obv:** Value **Rev:** Water, Metro train below **Edge:** Reeded **Mint:** Cairo

Date	Mintage	VF20	XF40	MS60	MS63	MS65
AH1420-1999	550	—	—	—	—	425

KM# 928 POUND
15.00 g., 0.720 Silver 0.3472 oz. ASW, 35 mm. **Subject:** National Insurance Company Centennial **Obv:** Value **Rev:** Ancient seated figure with "100" **Edge:** Reeded **Mint:** Cairo

Date	Mintage	VF20	XF40	MS60	MS63	MS65
AH1421-2000	2,500	—	—	—	8.75	11.00

KM# 441 5 POUNDS
26.00 g., 0.875 Gold 0.7314 oz. AGW **Subject:** 75th Anniveresary - National Bank of Egypt **Obv:** Denomination and dates **Rev:** World globe back of bank building divides dates

Date	Mintage	VF20	XF40	MS60	MS63	MS65
AH1393-1973	1,000	—	—	—	—	1,200
AH1393-1973	—	PF65 1,250				

KM# 444 5 POUNDS
26.00 g., 0.875 Gold 0.7314 oz. AGW **Subject:** 1973 October War **Obv:** Denomination, dates, and legend **Rev:** Half-figure of soldier, 3/4 wreath surrounds above

Date	Mintage	VF20	XF40	MS60	MS63	MS65
AH1394-1974	1,000	—	—	—	—	1,250

KM# 459 5 POUNDS
26.00 g., 0.875 Gold 0.7314 oz. AGW **Subject:** King Faisal of Saudi Arabia **Obv:** Denomination divides dates **Rev:** Head 3/4 right

Date	Mintage	VF20	XF40	MS60	MS63	MS65
AH1396-1976	2,500	—	—	—	—	1,300

KM# 460 5 POUNDS
26.00 g., 0.875 Gold 0.7314 oz. AGW **Subject:** Reopening of Suez Canal

Date	Mintage	VF20	XF40	MS60	MS63	MS65
AH1396-1976	2,000	—	—	—	—	1,175

KM# 461 5 POUNDS
26.00 g., 0.875 Gold 0.7314 oz. AGW **Subject:** Om Kalsoum **Obv:** Denomination divides dates **Rev:** Head right, music symbol in hair

Date	Mintage	VF20	XF40	MS60	MS63	MS65
AH1396-1976	1,000	—	—	—	—	1,250

KM# 495 5 POUNDS
26.00 g., 0.875 Gold 0.7314 oz. AGW **Subject:** 100th Anniversary - Bank of Land Reform **Rev:** Seated man, farmer tilling soil with three oxen behind, mural showing workers cutting grain sheaves

Date	Mintage	VF20	XF40	MS60	MS63	MS65
AH1399-1979	1,750	—	—	—	—	1,175
AH1399-1979	250	PF65 1,250				

KM# 496 5 POUNDS
26.00 g., 0.875 Gold 0.7314 oz. AGW **Subject:** 1400th

Anniversary - Mohammed's Flight **Obv:** Denomination divides dates, legend above **Rev:** Two doves with eggs in front of spider web

Date	Mintage	VF20	XF40	MS60	MS63	MS65
AH1400-1979	2,000	—	—	—	—	1,175

KM# 517 5 POUNDS
26.00 g., 0.875 Gold 0.7314 oz. AGW **Subject:** Egyptian-Israeli Peace Treaty **Obv:** Denomination divides dates, legend above **Rev:** Head of Anwar Sadat at right facing left, dove of peace at left behind

Date	Mintage	VF20	XF40	MS60	MS63	MS65
AH1400-1980	2,375	—	—	—	—	1,175
AH1400-1980	125	PF65 1,300				

KM# 518 5 POUNDS
26.00 g., 0.875 Gold 0.7314 oz. AGW **Subject:** Doctors' Day

Date	Mintage	VF20	XF40	MS60	MS63	MS65
AH1400-1980	1,000	—	—	—	—	1,200

KM# 533 5 POUNDS
24.00 g., 0.925 Silver 0.7137 oz. ASW **Series:** International Year of the Child **Rev:** Children holding hands and dancing around stylistic globe

Date	Mintage	VF20	XF40	MS60	MS63	MS65
AH1401-1981	10,000	PF63 15.00	PF65 20.00			

KM# 534 5 POUNDS
26.00 g., 0.875 Gold 0.7314 oz. AGW **Subject:** 3rd Anniversary - Suez Canal Reopening

Date	Mintage	VF20	XF40	MS60	MS63	MS65
AH1401-1981	75	PF65 1,350				
AH1401-1981	925	—	—	—	—	1,200

KM# 535 5 POUNDS
26.00 g., 0.875 Gold 0.7314 oz. AGW **Subject:** 25th Anniversary - Ministry of Industry

Date	Mintage	VF20	XF40	MS60	MS63	MS65
AH1402-1981	1,500	PF65 1,175				

KM# 536 5 POUNDS
26.00 g., 0.875 Gold 0.7314 oz. AGW **Subject:** 100th Anniversary - Revolt by Arabi Pasha **Rev:** Pasha mounted on horse in front of his followers

Date	Mintage	VF20	XF40	MS60	MS63	MS65
AH1402-1981	1,000	—	—	—	—	1,175

KM# 537 5 POUNDS
26.00 g., 0.875 Gold 0.7314 oz. AGW **Subject:** 25th Anniversary - Nationalization of Suez Canal **Obv:** Denomination divides dates, legend above **Rev:** Design at center, grain spray below

Date	Mintage	VF20	XF40	MS60	MS63	MS65
AH1401-1981	1,000	—	—	—	—	1,175

KM# 546 5 POUNDS
26.00 g., 0.875 Gold 0.7314 oz. AGW **Subject:** 1000th Anniversary - Al Azhar Mosque **Rev:** Mosque

Date	Mintage	VF20	XF40	MS60	MS63	MS65
AH1402-1982	1,500	—	—	—	—	1,175

KM# 547 5 POUNDS
26.00 g., 0.875 Gold 0.7314 oz. AGW **Subject:** 50th Anniversary - Air Force **Rev:** Air Force insignia within wreath

Date	Mintage	VF20	XF40	MS60	MS63	MS65
AH1403-1982	1,000	—	—	—	—	1,175

KM# 552 5 POUNDS
17.50 g., 0.720 Silver 0.4051 oz. ASW **Subject:** 75th Anniversary - Cairo University **Obv:** Denomination within circle divides dates **Rev:** Buildings, shield within wreath at right

Date	Mintage	VF20	XF40	MS60	MS63	MS65
AH1404-1983	25,000	—	—	—	9.50	15.50

KM# 558 5 POUNDS
17.50 g., 0.720 Silver 0.4051 oz. ASW **Subject:** Los Angeles Olympics **Obv:** Torch above Olympic rings, dates below **Rev:** Athletes above symbols

Date	Mintage	VF20	XF40	MS60	MS63	MS65
AH1404-1984	20,000	—	—	—	9.50	13.50

KM# 560 5 POUNDS
17.50 g., 0.720 Silver 0.4051 oz. ASW **Subject:** Academy of Arabic Languages **Obv:** Denomination within circle divides dates **Rev:** World globe above book

Date	Mintage	VF20	XF40	MS60	MS63	MS65
AH1404-1984	25,000	—	—	—	9.50	13.50

KM# 561 5 POUNDS
17.50 g., 0.720 Silver 0.4051 oz. ASW **Subject:** 50th Anniversary - Egyptian Radio Broadcasting **Obv:** Designs within small circles flank design at top, dates below **Rev:** Radio tower divides dates

Date	Mintage	VF20	XF40	MS60	MS63	MS65
AH1404-1984	25,000	—	—	—	9.50	15.50

KM# 565 5 POUNDS
17.50 g., 0.720 Silver 0.4051 oz. ASW **Subject:** Sculptor Mahmoud Mokhtar **Obv:** Denomination within circle divides dates **Rev:** Bust left

Date	Mintage	VF20	XF40	MS60	MS63	MS65
AH1404-1984	10,000	—	—	—	9.50	16.50

KM# 566 5 POUNDS
17.50 g., 0.720 Silver 0.4051 oz. ASW **Subject:** Golden Jubilee of Petroleum Industry **Obv:** Denomination within circle divides dates **Rev:** Radiant flame above three rings

Date	Mintage	VF20	XF40	MS60	MS63	MS65
AH1404-1984	10,000	—	—	—	9.50	15.50

KM# 567 5 POUNDS
17.50 g., 0.720 Silver 0.4051 oz. ASW **Subject:** Diamond Jubilee of Cooperation **Obv:** Arabic legends, dates below **Rev:** Seven joined hexagons with different scenes

Date	Mintage	VF20	XF40	MS60	MS63	MS65
AH1404-1984	10,000	—	—	—	9.50	16.50

KM# 671 5 POUNDS
26.00 g., 0.875 Gold 0.7314 oz. AGW **Subject:** 50th Anniversary - Egyptian Radio **Obv:** Arabic legends **Rev:** Tall buildings with transmitter

Date	Mintage	VF20	XF40	MS60	MS63	MS65
AH1404-1984	500	PF65 1,175				

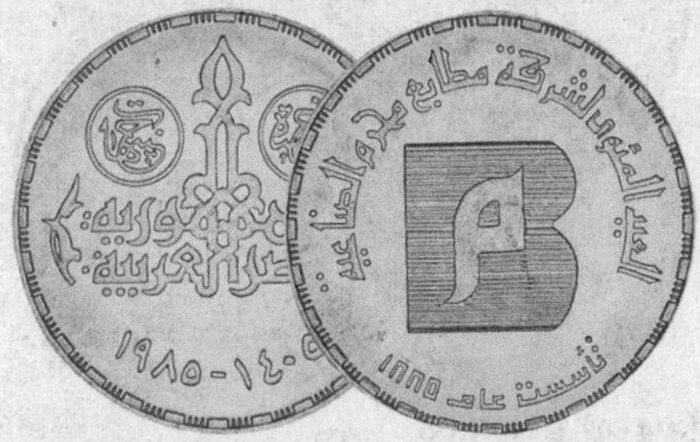

KM# 563 5 POUNDS
17.50 g., 0.720 Silver 0.4051 oz. ASW **Subject:** 100th Anniversary - Moharram Printing Press Co. **Obv:** Arabic legends, date below **Rev:** Printing design on shaded field that resembles the letter 'B'

Date	Mintage	VF20	XF40	MS60	MS63	MS65
AH1405-1985	20,000	—	—	—	9.50	15.50

KM# 564 5 POUNDS
40.00 g., 0.875 Gold 1.1253 oz. AGW **Subject:** 100th Anniversary - Moharram Printing Press Co.

Date	Mintage	VF20	XF40	MS60	MS63	MS65
AH1405-1985	200	—	—	—	—	2,000

KM# 572 5 POUNDS
17.50 g., 0.720 Silver 0.4051 oz. ASW **Subject:** 25th Anniversary - National Planning Institute **Obv:** Arabic legends, dates below **Rev:** Design on shield divides dates

Date	Mintage	VF20	XF40	MS60	MS63	MS65
AH1405-1985	15,000	—	—	—	9.50	16.50

KM# 575 5 POUNDS
17.50 g., 0.720 Silver 0.4051 oz. ASW **Subject:** 60th Anniversary - Egyptian Parliament **Obv:** Arabic legends, dates below **Rev:** Parliament building, dates above

Date	Mintage	VF20	XF40	MS60	MS63	MS65
AH1405-1985	25,000	—	—	—	9.50	15.50

KM# 576 5 POUNDS
26.00 g., 0.875 Gold 0.7314 oz. AGW **Subject:** 60th Anniversary - Egyptian Parliament **Rev:** Parliament building

Date	Mintage	VF20	XF40	MS60	MS63	MS65
AH1405-1985	500	—	—	—	—	1,750

KM# 578 5 POUNDS
17.50 g., 0.720 Silver 0.4051 oz. ASW **Subject:** 25th Anniversary - Cairo Stadium **Obv:** Arabic legends, dates below **Rev:** Stadium

Date	Mintage	VF20	XF40	MS60	MS63	MS65
AH1405-1985	25,000	—	—	—	9.50	15.50

KM# 579 5 POUNDS
26.00 g., 0.875 Gold 0.7314 oz. AGW **Subject:** 25th Anniversary - Cairo Stadium **Rev:** Stadium

Date	Mintage	VF20	XF40	MS60	MS63	MS65
AH1405-1985	200	—	—	—	—	1,850

KM# 581 5 POUNDS
17.50 g., 0.720 Silver 0.4051 oz. ASW **Subject:** 25th Anniversary - Egyptian Television **Obv:** Arabic legends, dates below **Rev:** Television tower emitting signal divides dates

Date	Mintage	VF20	XF40	MS60	MS63	MS65
AH1405-1985	5,000	—	—	—	9.50	18.50

KM# 582 5 POUNDS
26.00 g., 0.875 Gold 0.7314 oz. AGW **Subject:** 25th Anniversary - Egyptian Television **Obv:** Arabic legends, dates below **Rev:** Television tower emitting signal divides dates

Date	Mintage	VF20	XF40	MS60	MS63	MS65
AH1405-1985	100	—	—	—	—	1,400

KM# 584 5 POUNDS
17.50 g., 0.720 Silver 0.4051 oz. ASW **Subject:** The Prophet's Mosque **Obv:** Towers at left of stylized globe **Rev:** Mosque

Date	Mintage	VF20	XF40	MS60	MS63	MS65
AH1406-1985	25,000	—	—	—	9.50	15.50
AH1406-1985	1,000	PF65 37.00				

KM# 585 5 POUNDS
17.50 g., 0.720 Silver 0.4051 oz. ASW **Subject:** 25th Anniversary - Cairo International Airport **Rev:** Buzzards in flight adapted from ancient Egyptian art

Date	Mintage	VF20	XF40	MS60	MS63	MS65
AH1405-1985	20,000	—	—	—	9.50	13.50

KM# 587 5 POUNDS
17.50 g., 0.720 Silver 0.4051 oz. ASW **Subject:** Professions **Obv:** Arabic legends, dates below **Rev:** Various professions illustrated on coin

Date	Mintage	VF20	XF40	MS60	MS63	MS65
AH1406-1985	8,000	—	—	—	9.50	17.50

KM# 592 5 POUNDS
17.50 g., 0.720 Silver 0.4051 oz. ASW **Subject:** Tutankhamen **Obv:** Arabic legends, dates below **Rev:** Bust left

Date	Mintage	VF20	XF40	MS60	MS63	MS65
AH1405-1985	6,000	—	—	—	9.50	16.50
AH1405-1985	2,000	PF65 32.50				

KM# 593 5 POUNDS
17.50 g., 0.720 Silver 0.4051 oz. ASW **Subject:** XV UIA Congress **Obv:** Arabic legends, dates below **Rev:** Pyramid

Date	Mintage	VF20	XF40	MS60	MS63	MS65
AH1405-1985	10,000	—	—	—	9.50	16.50
AH1405-1985	Est. 500	PF65 30.00				

KM# 598 5 POUNDS
17.50 g., 0.720 Silver 0.4051 oz. ASW **Subject:** Faculty of Economics and Political Science **Obv:** Arabic legends, dates below **Rev:** Grid on globe, dentiled arch above, spray below, divides dates above

Date	Mintage	VF20	XF40	MS60	MS63	MS65
AH1405-1985	8,000	—	—	—	9.50	17.50

KM# 600 5 POUNDS
17.50 g., 0.720 Silver 0.4051 oz. ASW **Subject:** Commerce Day **Obv:** Arabic legends, dates below **Rev:** Ship above head on grid, vendors and shoppers flank

Date	Mintage	VF20	XF40	MS60	MS63	MS65
AH1405-1985	20,000	—	—	—	9.50	15.50
AH1405-1985	1,000	PF65 37.00				

KM# 633 5 POUNDS
26.00 g., 0.875 Gold 0.7314 oz. AGW **Subject:** Prophet's Mosque **Obv:** Minaret, globe, denomination, legends **Rev:** Crescent, mosque, minaret below legend arch

Date	Mintage	VF20	XF40	MS60	MS63	MS65
AH1406-1985	400	—	—	—	—	1,200

KM# 586 5 POUNDS
17.50 g., 0.720 Silver 0.4051 oz. ASW **Subject:** Cairo University Faculty of Commerce **Obv:** Arabic legends, dates below **Rev:** Scribes and merchant vessel

Date	Mintage	VF20	XF40	MS60	MS63	MS65
AH1406-1986	20,000	—	—	—	9.50	15.50

KM# 588 5 POUNDS
17.50 g., 0.720 Silver 0.4051 oz. ASW **Subject:** 25th Anniversary - Egyptian National Bank **Obv:** Denomination divides dates, buds above, cogwheel at left **Rev:** Monument divides dates

Date	Mintage	VF20	XF40	MS60	MS63	MS65
AH1406-1986	6,000	—	—	—	9.50	17.50

KM# 589 5 POUNDS
17.68 g., 0.720 Silver 0.4093 oz. ASW **Subject:** World Soccer Championships **Obv:** Grain heads above denomination and dates **Rev:** Soccer ball, three pyramids

Date	Mintage	VF20	XF40	MS60	MS63	MS65
AH1406-1986	5,000	—	—	—	9.50	18.50
Prooflike						
AH1406-1986	2,150	PF65 30.00				

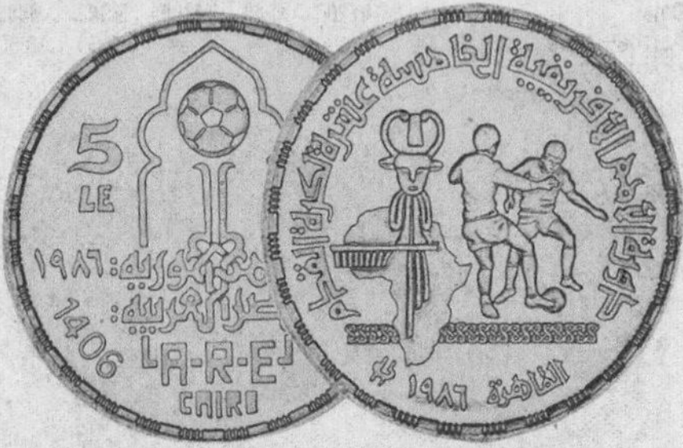

KM# 590 5 POUNDS
17.50 g., 0.720 Silver 0.4051 oz. ASW **Subject:** African Soccer Championship Games **Rev:** Two soccer players at right

Date	Mintage	VF20	XF40	MS60	MS63	MS65
AH1406-1986	15,000	—	—	—	9.50	17.50
AH1406-1986	2,000	PF65 30.00				

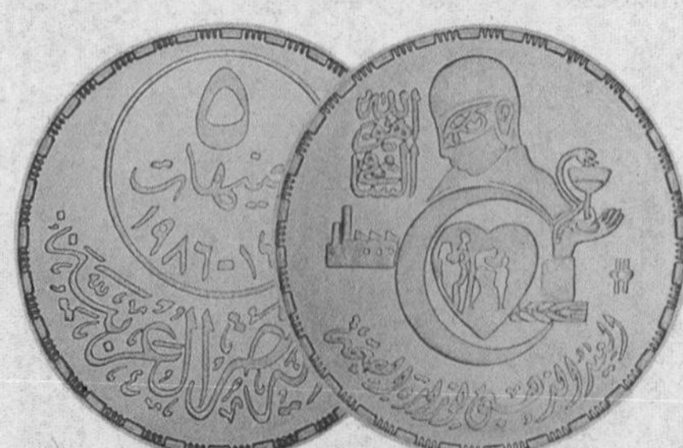

KM# 594 5 POUNDS
17.50 g., 0.720 Silver 0.4051 oz. ASW **Subject:** 50th Anniversary - Ministry of Health **Obv:** Denomination and dates within circle **Rev:** Figures on heart, within half moon design, below surgeon holding snake and glass

Date	Mintage	VF20	XF40	MS60	MS63	MS65
AH1406-1986	10,000	—	—	—	9.50	16.50
AH1406-1986	Est. 500	PF65 55.00				

KM# 601 5 POUNDS
17.50 g., 0.720 Silver 0.4051 oz. ASW **Subject:** Warrior's Day **Rev:** Crossed swords within wreath

Date	Mintage	VF20	XF40	MS60	MS63	MS65
AH1406-1986	16,000	—	—	—	9.50	17.50

KM# 602 5 POUNDS
17.50 g., 0.720 Silver 0.4051 oz. ASW **Subject:** 100th Anniversary - Petroleum Industry **Obv:** Arabic legends, dates below **Rev:** Oil derrick with building behind

Date	Mintage	VF20	XF40	MS60	MS63	MS65
AH1406-1986	6,000	—	—	—	9.50	17.50

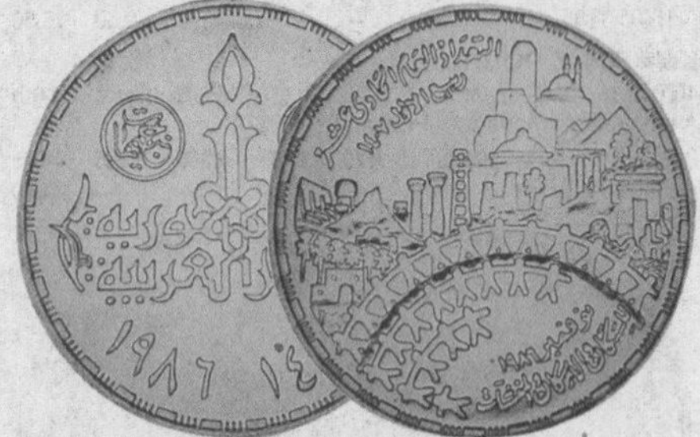

KM# 603 5 POUNDS
17.50 g., 0.720 Silver 0.4051 oz. ASW **Subject:** Census **Obv:** Arabic legends, dates below **Rev:** Joined figures below city scene

Date	Mintage	VF20	XF40	MS60	MS63	MS65
AH1407-1986	6,000	—	—	—	9.50	17.50

KM# 608 5 POUNDS
17.50 g., 0.720 Silver 0.4051 oz. ASW **Subject:** 50th Anniversary - National Theater **Obv:** Drapes enclose text **Rev:** Theater building, masks below

Date	Mintage	VF20	XF40	MS60	MS63	MS65
AH1406-1986	6,000	—	—	—	9.50	17.50

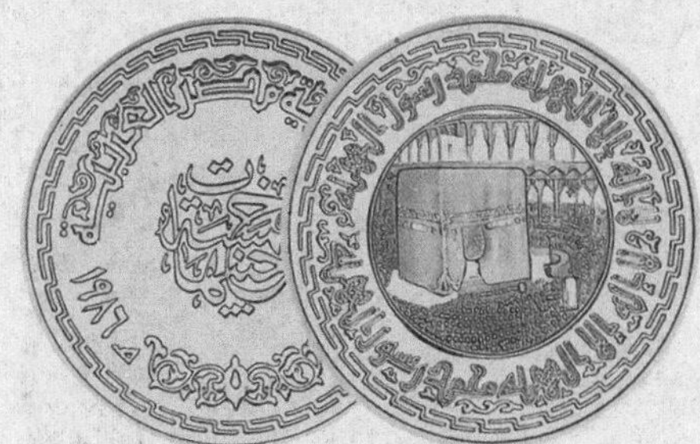

KM# 609 5 POUNDS
17.50 g., 0.720 Silver 0.4051 oz. ASW **Subject:** Mecca **Obv:** Denomination and dates **Rev:** Building within circle

Date	Mintage	VF20	XF40	MS60	MS63	MS65
AH1406-1986	30,000	—	—	—	9.50	13.50
AH1406-1986	—	PF65 22.00				

KM# 609a 5 POUNDS
26.00 g., 0.875 Gold 0.7314 oz. AGW **Subject:** Mecca **Obv:** Denomination and dates **Rev:** Building within circle

Date	Mintage	VF20	XF40	MS60	MS63	MS65
AH1406-1986	1,400	PF65 1,175				

KM# 610 5 POUNDS
17.50 g., 0.720 Silver 0.4051 oz. ASW **Subject:** 40th Anniversary - Engineer's Syndicate **Obv:** Arabic legends, dates below **Rev:** Stylized train and pyramids within square formed by outer designs

Date	Mintage	VF20	XF40	MS60	MS63	MS65
AH1407-1986	6,000	—	—	—	9.50	17.50

KM# 614 5 POUNDS
17.50 g., 0.720 Silver 0.4051 oz. ASW **Subject:** Restoration of Parliament Building **Obv:** Arabic legends, dates below **Rev:** Dome and tower with scaffolding

Date	Mintage	VF20	XF40	MS60	MS63	MS65
AH1406-1986	5,000	—	—	—	9.50	18.50

KM# 614a 5 POUNDS
26.00 g., 0.875 Gold 0.7314 oz. AGW **Subject:** Restoration of Parliament Building **Obv:** Arabic legends **Rev:** Dome and tower with scaffolding

Date	Mintage	VF20	XF40	MS60	MS63	MS65
AH1406-1986	300	—	—	—	—	1,200

KM# 615 5 POUNDS
17.50 g., 0.720 Silver 0.4051 oz. ASW **Subject:** 30th Anniversary - Atomic Energy Organization **Obv:** Arabic legends, dates below **Rev:** Atoms within circle above center design, figures flank

Date	Mintage	VF20	XF40	MS60	MS63	MS65
AH1406-1986	5,000	—	—	—	9.50	18.50

KM# 616 5 POUNDS
17.50 g., 0.720 Silver 0.4051 oz. ASW **Subject:** 30th Anniversary - Egyptian Industry **Obv:** Arabic legends, dates below **Rev:** Split dentiled design at center

Date	Mintage	VF20	XF40	MS60	MS63	MS65
AH1407-1986	5,000	—	—	—	9.50	18.50

KM# 611 5 POUNDS
17.50 g., 0.720 Silver 0.4051 oz. ASW **Subject:** Aida Opera **Obv:** Towers, sun, date, names and inscriptions **Rev:** Scene from the opera, 'AIDA'

Date	Mintage	VF20	XF40	MS60	MS63	MS65
ND(1407-1987)	25,000	—	—	—	9.50	19.50

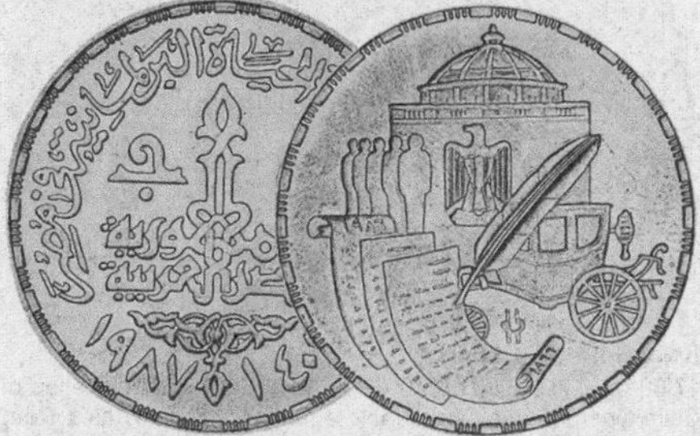

KM# 617 5 POUNDS
17.50 g., 0.720 Silver 0.4051 oz. ASW **Subject:** Parliament Museum **Obv:** Arabic legends, seals and dates **Rev:** Documents, quill, carriage, building with national emblem

Date	Mintage	VF20	XF40	MS60	MS63	MS65
AH1407-1987	5,000	—	—	—	9.50	18.50

KM# 617a 5 POUNDS
26.00 g., 0.875 Gold 0.7314 oz. AGW **Subject:** Parliament Museum **Obv:** Arabic legends, seals and dates **Rev:** Documents, quill, carriage, building with national emblem

Date	Mintage	VF20	XF40	MS60	MS63	MS65
AH1407-1987	300	—	—	—	—	1,175

KM# 618 5 POUNDS
17.50 g., 0.720 Silver 0.4051 oz. ASW **Subject:** Veterinarian Day **Obv:** Arabic legends, dates below **Rev:** Squatting figure with ox, caduceus within large 'V' above ox at left

Date	Mintage	VF20	XF40	MS60	MS63	MS65
AH1407-1987	5,000	—	—	—	9.50	18.50

KM# 619 5 POUNDS
17.50 g., 0.720 Silver 0.4051 oz. ASW **Subject:** 75th Anniversary - Misr Petroleum Company **Obv:** Arabic legends, dates below **Rev:** Pyramids within circle divides dates

Date	Mintage	VF20	XF40	MS60	MS63	MS65
AH1407-1987	10,000	—	—	—	9.50	16.50

KM# 620 5 POUNDS
17.50 g., 0.720 Silver 0.4051 oz. ASW **Subject:** First African Subway **Obv:** Four square designs divide dates **Rev:** Train leaving tunnel

Date	Mintage	VF20	XF40	MS60	MS63	MS65
AH1408-1987	15,000	—	—	—	9.50	15.50

KM# 623 5 POUNDS
17.50 g., 0.720 Silver 0.4051 oz. ASW **Subject:** 25th Anniversary - Hellwan Company **Obv:** Circles flank smoking towers at top, dates below **Rev:** Design within inner circle, legends and dentiled circle surrounds

Date	Mintage	VF20	XF40	MS60	MS63	MS65
AH1408-1987	8,000	—	—	—	9.50	17.50

KM# 630 5 POUNDS
17.50 g., 0.720 Silver 0.4051 oz. ASW **Subject:** Faculty of Fine Arts **Obv:** Denomination, dates and legend **Rev:** Design above dates

Date	Mintage	VF20	XF40	MS60	MS63	MS65
AH1407-1987	5,000	—	—	—	9.50	19.50

KM# 651 5 POUNDS
17.78 g., 0.720 Silver 0.4116 oz. ASW **Subject:** Investment Bank **Obv:** Tughra divides dates **Rev:** Design within inner dentiled circle

Date	Mintage	VF20	XF40	MS60	MS63	MS65
AH1407-1987	8,000	—	—	—	9.75	17.50

KM# 674 5 POUNDS
26.00 g., 0.875 Gold 0.7314 oz. AGW **Subject:** First African Subway **Obv:** Stylized legends and denomination **Rev:** Subway emerging from tunnel with legend around rim

Date	Mintage	VF20	XF40	MS60	MS63	MS65
AH1408-1987	200	PF65 1,300				

KM# 621 5 POUNDS
17.50 g., 0.720 Silver 0.4051 oz. ASW **Subject:** Police Day **Obv:** Arabic legends **Rev:** Eagle with wings spread within oval wreath

Date	Mintage	VF20	XF40	MS60	MS63	MS65
AH1408-1988	35,000	—	—	—	9.50	13.50

KM# 624 5 POUNDS
17.50 g., 0.720 Silver 0.4051 oz. ASW **Series:** Summer Olympics **Obv:** Denomination and date above design and legend **Rev:** Pharoah and athletes

Date	Mintage	VF20	XF40	MS60	MS63	MS65
AH1408-1988	—	—	—	—	—	55.00
Matte						
AH1408-1988	30,000	—	—	—	9.50	13.50
AH1408-1988	2,000	PF65 30.00				

KM# 626 5 POUNDS
17.50 g., 0.720 Silver 0.4051 oz. ASW **Series:** Summer Olympics **Obv:** Denomination and date above design and legend **Rev:** Athletes and mythological figures, dates below

Date	Mintage	VF20	XF40	MS60	MS63	MS65
AH1408-1988	24,000	—	—	—	9.50	14.50
AH1408-1988	—	—	—	—	—	55.00
Matte						
AH1408-1988	5,000	PF65 22.00				

KM# 628 5 POUNDS
17.50 g., 0.720 Silver 0.4051 oz. ASW **Series:** Winter Olympics **Rev:** Ski jumper and figure skater

Date	Mintage	VF20	XF40	MS60	MS63	MS65
AH1408-1988	8,000	—	—	—	9.50	17.50
AH1408-1988	—	—	—	—	—	55.00
Matte						
AH1408-1988	2,000	PF65 25.00				

KM# 631 5 POUNDS
17.50 g., 0.720 Silver 0.4051 oz. ASW **Subject:** 50th Anniversary of Air Travel **Obv:** Torch above shield within eagles wings **Rev:** Stylized airplane above text divides dates

Date	Mintage	VF20	XF40	MS60	MS63	MS65
AH1408-1988	5,000	—	—	—	9.50	18.50

KM# 649 5 POUNDS
17.50 g., 0.720 Silver 0.4051 oz. ASW **Subject:** Dedication of Cairo Opera House **Obv:** Arabic legends, seals and dates **Rev:** Opera house

Date	Mintage	VF20	XF40	MS60	MS63	MS65
AH1409-1988	30,000	—	—	—	9.50	13.50

KM# 655 5 POUNDS
26.00 g., 0.875 Gold 0.7314 oz. AGW **Subject:** Dedication of Cairo Opera House **Obv:** Arabic legends, seals, dates **Rev:** Opera house, legends above and below

Date	Mintage	VF20	XF40	MS60	MS63	MS65
AH1409-1988	200	—	—	—	—	1,700

KM# 660 5 POUNDS
17.50 g., 0.720 Silver 0.4051 oz. ASW **Subject:** Ministry of Agriculture **Obv:** Tughra divides dates and denomination **Rev:** Tractor above corn ears, within grain sprigs and flowers

Date	Mintage	VF20	XF40	MS60	MS63	MS65
AH1409-1988	5,000	—	—	—	9.50	18.50

KM# 662 5 POUNDS
17.50 g., 0.720 Silver 0.4051 oz. ASW **Subject:** Naguib Mahfouz, Nobel Laureate **Obv:** Quill in inkwell designed as globe, divides date and denomination **Rev:** Head left

Date	Mintage	VF20	XF40	MS60	MS63	MS65
AH1409-1988	15,000	—	—	—	9.50	16.50

KM# 669 5 POUNDS
17.50 g., 0.720 Silver 0.4051 oz. ASW **Subject:** National Research Center **Rev:** Stylized ancient and modern research elements

Date	Mintage	VF20	XF40	MS60	MS63	MS65
AH1408-1988	5,000	—	—	—	9.50	18.50

KM# 670 5 POUNDS
26.00 g., 0.875 Gold 0.7314 oz. AGW **Subject:** National Research Center **Obv:** Kufic legend above denomination and date **Rev:** Stylized ancient and modern research elements

Date	Mintage	VF20	XF40	MS60	MS63	MS65
AH1408-1988	—	PF65 1,300				
AH1409-1989	200	PF65 1,300				

KM# 663 5 POUNDS
17.50 g., 0.720 Silver 0.4051 oz. ASW **Subject:** Advista Arabia II **Obv:** Arabic legends, seals and dates **Rev:** Head with art tools left, date at right

Date	Mintage	VF20	XF40	MS60	MS63	MS65
AH1409-1989	5,000	—	—	—	9.50	19.50

KM# 665 5 POUNDS
17.50 g., 0.720 Silver 0.4051 oz. ASW **Subject:** United Parliamentary Union **Obv:** Denomination divides dates below text **Rev:** Globe within wreath divides buildings, date on top building

Date	Mintage	VF20	XF40	MS60	MS63	MS65
AH1409-1989	5,000	—	—	—	9.50	18.50

KM# 667 5 POUNDS
17.50 g., 0.720 Silver 0.4051 oz. ASW **Subject:** First Arab Olympics **Obv:** Kufic legend below denomination and date within circle **Rev:** Wreath surrounds hand holding pillar with map and rings on top

Date	Mintage	VF20	XF40	MS60	MS63	MS65
AH1409-1989	8,000	—	—	—	9.50	17.50

KM# 678 5 POUNDS
17.50 g., 0.720 Silver 0.4051 oz. ASW **Subject:** University of Cairo - School of Agriculture **Obv:** Denomination and dates within wreath of grain sprigs, text below **Rev:** Shield to right of farmers and oxen, building in background

Date	Mintage	VF20	XF40	MS60	MS63	MS65
AH1410-1989	4,000	—	—	—	9.50	19.50

KM# 686 5 POUNDS
17.50 g., 0.720 Silver 0.4051 oz. ASW **Subject:** National Health Insurance **Obv:** Dates and denomination within circle, text below **Rev:** Figures within half moon design on rock, dates below

Date	Mintage	VF20	XF40	MS60	MS63	MS65
AH1409-1989	3,000	—	—	—	9.50	19.50

KM# 687 5 POUNDS
17.50 g., 0.720 Silver 0.4051 oz. ASW **Subject:** Export Drive **Obv:** Tughra, date and text **Rev:** Stylized symbols

Date	Mintage	VF20	XF40	MS60	MS63	MS65
AH1410-1989	4,000	—	—	—	9.50	19.50

KM# 679 5 POUNDS
17.50 g., 0.720 Silver 0.4051 oz. ASW **Series:** Soccer World Championship - Italy **Obv:** Circle of text at center of wings, denomination and dates above **Rev:** Ancient gods in front of pyramid with soccer ball above

Date	Mintage	VF20	XF40	MS60	MS63	MS65
AH1410-1990	600	—	—	—	100	125
AH1410-1990	8,000	PF65 22.00				

KM# 682 5 POUNDS
17.50 g., 0.720 Silver 0.4051 oz. ASW **Series:** Soccer World Championship - Italy **Obv:** Text within circle at center of wings, denomination and dates above **Rev:** Player chasing ball

Date	Mintage	VF20	XF40	MS60	MS63	MS65
AH1410-1990	400	—	—	—	125	150
Matte						
AH1410-1990	4,000	PF65 32.50				

KM# 688 5 POUNDS
17.50 g., 0.720 Silver 0.4051 oz. ASW **Subject:** National Population Center **Obv:** Tughra below dates **Rev:** Repeated design of people forms square at center, which holds text

Date	Mintage	VF20	XF40	MS60	MS63	MS65
AH1410-1990	5,000	—	—	—	9.50	18.50

KM# 689 5 POUNDS
17.50 g., 0.720 Silver 0.4051 oz. ASW **Subject:** Union of African Parliaments **Obv:** Tughra below dates and denomination, within circle **Rev:** Map in background divides grain sprig and building

Date	Mintage	VF20	XF40	MS60	MS63	MS65
AH1410-1990	5,000	—	—	—	9.50	18.50

KM# 691 5 POUNDS
17.82 g., 0.900 Silver 0.5156 oz. ASW **Subject:** Dar-el-Eloun Faculty **Obv:** Denomination and dates within circle above text **Rev:** Bust and shield left of dates, text below

Date	Mintage	VF20	XF40	MS60	MS63	MS65
AH1410-1990	5,000	—	—	—	12.00	21.00

KM# 697 5 POUNDS
17.50 g., 0.720 Silver 0.4051 oz. ASW **Subject:** Newly Populated Areas Organization

Date	Mintage	VF20	XF40	MS60	MS63	MS65
AH1410-1990	2,000	—	—	—	20.00	35.00

KM# 698 5 POUNDS
17.50 g., 0.720 Silver 0.4051 oz. ASW **Subject:** Alexandria Sports Club **Obv:** Denomination and dates within circle above text **Rev:** Athletes surround center circles with text and designs

Date	Mintage	VF20	XF40	MS60	MS63	MS65
AH1411-1990	5,000	—	—	—	9.50	18.50

KM# 692 5 POUNDS
17.82 g., 0.900 Silver 0.5156 oz. ASW **Subject:** Islamic Development Bank **Obv:** Globe back of towered buildings above grasped hands, dentiled design below, grain stalks flank **Rev:** Tughra divided dates above inscription and denomination

Date	Mintage	VF20	XF40	MS60	MS63	MS65
AH1411-1991	5,000	—	—	—	12.00	21.00

KM# 700 5 POUNDS
17.82 g., 0.900 Silver 0.5156 oz. ASW **Subject:** 5th African Games - Cairo

Date	Mintage	VF20	XF40	MS60	MS63	MS65
AH1411-1991	3,000	—	—	—	18.00	25.00

KM# 727 5 POUNDS
17.50 g., 0.720 Silver 0.4051 oz. ASW **Subject:** Muhamed Abdel Wahab **Obv:** Arabic legends and inscriptions **Rev:** Bust left with music sheet in background

Date	Mintage	VF20	XF40	MS60	MS63	MS65
AH1412-1991	30,000	—	—	—	9.50	13.50

KM# 728 5 POUNDS
26.00 g., 0.875 Gold 0.7314 oz. AGW **Subject:** Muhamed Abdel Wahab **Obv:** Arabic legends and inscriptions **Rev:** Bust left with music sheet in background

Date	Mintage	VF20	XF40	MS60	MS63	MS65
AH1412-1991 Proof	400	—	—	—	—	1,300

KM# 791 5 POUNDS
17.42 g., 0.720 Silver 0.4032 oz. ASW **Subject:** National Zoo **Obv:** Zoo entrance, dates and denomination **Rev:** Five zoo animals

Date	Mintage	VF20	XF40	MS60	MS63	MS65
AH1411-1991	—	—	—	—	12.00	19.50

KM# 804 5 POUNDS
17.50 g., 0.720 Silver 0.4051 oz. ASW **Subject:** Atomic Energy **Obv:** Denomination **Rev:** Ancient statue and pyramid within rings

Date	Mintage	VF20	XF40	MS60	MS63	MS65
AH1411-1991	Est. 5000	—	—	—	9.50	19.50

KM# 805 5 POUNDS
17.50 g., 0.720 Silver 0.4051 oz. ASW **Subject:** Library of Alexandria **Obv:** Arabic inscription, dates **Rev:** Library building complex

Date	Mintage	VF20	XF40	MS60	MS63	MS65
AH1411-1991	Est. 8000	—	—	—	9.50	17.50

KM# 805a 5 POUNDS
26.00 g., 0.875 Gold 0.7314 oz. AGW **Subject:** Library of Alexandria **Obv:** Arabic inscription **Rev:** Library building complex **Edge:** Reeded **Note:** Struck at Cairo.

Date	Mintage	VF20	XF40	MS60	MS63	MS65
AH1411-1991 Proof	200	—	—	—	—	1,200

KM# 833 5 POUNDS
26.00 g., 0.875 Gold 0.7314 oz. AGW **Subject:** Library of Alexandria **Obv:** Legend and inscription **Rev:** Waterfront building with tower

Date	Mintage	VF20	XF40	MS60	MS63	MS65
AH1411-1991	200	—	—	—	—	1,200

KM# 701 5 POUNDS
17.50 g., 0.720 Silver 0.4051 oz. ASW **Series:** Summer Olympics **Obv:** Text within circle at center of wings, denomination and dates above **Rev:** Two men fencing

Date	Mintage	VF20	XF40	MS60	MS63	MS65
AH1412-1992	999	—	—	—	20.00	35.00
AH1412-1992	2,999	**PF65** 37.50				

KM# 702 5 POUNDS
17.50 g., 0.720 Silver 0.4051 oz. ASW **Series:** Summer Olympics **Obv:** Text within circle at center of wings, denomination and dates above **Rev:** Pairs wrestling, half globe below

Date	Mintage	VF20	XF40	MS60	MS63	MS65
AH1412-1992	999	—	—	—	65.00	90.00
AH1412-1992	2,999	**PF65** 37.50				

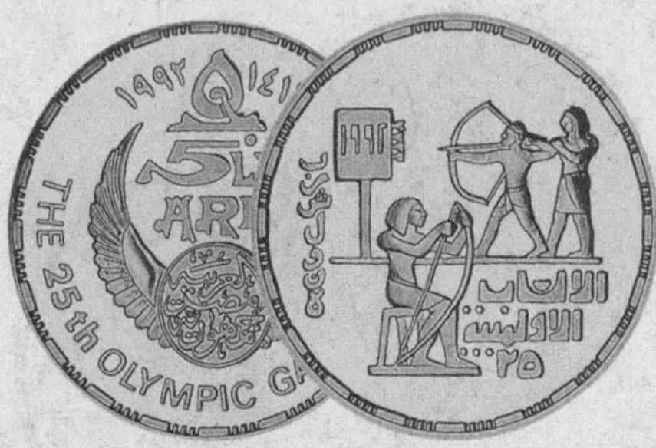

KM# 703 5 POUNDS
17.50 g., 0.720 Silver 0.4051 oz. ASW **Series:** Summer Olympics **Obv:** Text within circle at center of wings, denomination and dates above **Rev:** Archery demonstrated

Date	Mintage	VF20	XF40	MS60	MS63	MS65
AH1412-1992	999	—	—	—	65.00	90.00
AH1412-1992	2,999	**PF65** 37.50				

KM# 704 5 POUNDS
17.50 g., 0.720 Silver 0.4051 oz. ASW **Series:** Summer Olympics **Obv:** Text within circle at center of wings, denomination and dates above **Rev:** Many men wrestling an ox

Date	Mintage	VF20	XF40	MS60	MS63	MS65
AH1412-1992	999	—	—	—	65.00	90.00
AH1412-1992	2,999	**PF65** 37.50				

KM# 705 5 POUNDS
17.50 g., 0.720 Silver 0.4051 oz. ASW **Series:** Summer Olympics **Obv:** Text within circle at center of wings, denomination and dates above **Rev:** Swimmer stalking a duck

Date	Mintage	VF20	XF40	MS60	MS63	MS65
AH1412-1992	999	—	—	—	65.00	90.00
AH1412-1992	2,999	**PF65** 37.50				

KM# 706 5 POUNDS
17.50 g., 0.720 Silver 0.4051 oz. ASW **Series:** Summer Olympics **Rev:** Handball player

Date	Mintage	VF20	XF40	MS60	MS63	MS65
AH1412-1992	999	—	—	—	65.00	90.00
AH1412-1992	25,000	**PF65** 19.50				

KM# 707 5 POUNDS
17.50 g., 0.720 Silver 0.4051 oz. ASW **Series:** Summer Olympics **Rev:** Field hockey player

Date	Mintage	VF20	XF40	MS60	MS63	MS65
AH1412-1992	999	—	—	—	65.00	90.00
AH1412-1992	25,000	**PF65** 19.50				

KM# 708 5 POUNDS
17.50 g., 0.720 Silver 0.4051 oz. ASW **Series:** Summer Olympics **Obv:** Text within circle at center of wings, denomination and dates above **Rev:** Soccer player kicking ball

Date	Mintage	VF20	XF40	MS60	MS63	MS65
AH1412-1992	999	—	—	—	65.00	90.00
AH1412-1992	25,000	**PF65** 19.50				

KM# 806 5 POUNDS
17.50 g., 0.720 Silver 0.4051 oz. ASW **Subject:** Lighthouse of Alexandria **Obv:** Denomination and dates within circle above text **Rev:** Ancient tower and Egyptian

Date	Mintage	VF20	XF40	MS60	MS63	MS65
AH1412-1992	—	—	—	—	9.50	18.50

KM# 807 5 POUNDS
17.50 g., 0.720 Silver 0.4051 oz. ASW **Subject:** 50 Years - University of Alexandria **Obv:** Arabic inscription, dates **Rev:** University emblem divides dates

Date	Mintage	VF20	XF40	MS60	MS63	MS65
AH1413-1992	—	—	—	—	9.50	18.50

KM# 808 5 POUNDS
17.50 g., 0.720 Silver 0.4051 oz. ASW **Subject:** Naguib Mahfouz, Nobel Laureate **Obv:** Vase and inscriptions, dates below **Rev:** Bust right

Date	Mintage	VF20	XF40	MS60	MS63	MS65
AH1413-1992	Est. 6000	—	—	—	9.50	17.50

KM# 735 5 POUNDS
22.50 g., 0.999 Silver 0.7227 oz. ASW **Subject:** Cleopatra - queen and statesperson, 69-30BC **Obv:** Vulture, denomination above and dates below **Rev:** Bust in formal headdress left

Date	Mintage	VF20	XF40	MS60	MS63	MS65
AH1413-1993	50,000	**PF63** 25.00	**PF65** 31.50			

KM# 740 5 POUNDS
22.50 g., 0.999 Silver 0.7227 oz. ASW **Subject:** Pyramids **Obv:** Vulture, denomination above and dates below **Rev:** Three pyramids

Date	Mintage	VF20	XF40	MS60	MS63	MS65
AH1414-1993	50,000	**PF63** 24.00	**PF65** 31.50			

KM# 741 5 POUNDS
22.50 g., 0.999 Silver 0.7227 oz. ASW **Obv:** Vulture, denomination above and dates below **Rev:** Sphinx

Date	Mintage	VF20	XF40	MS60	MS63	MS65
AH1414-1993	50,000	**PF63** 24.00	**PF65** 31.50			

KM# 742 5 POUNDS
22.50 g., 0.999 Silver 0.7227 oz. ASW **Subject:** King Narmur Smiting a Foe **Obv:** Vulture, denomination above and dates below **Rev:** Decorative vase depicting punishment scene

Date	Mintage	VF20	XF40	MS60	MS63	MS65
AH1414-1993	50,000	**PF63** 24.00	**PF65** 31.50			

KM# 743 5 POUNDS
22.50 g., 0.999 Silver 0.7227 oz. ASW **Obv:** Vulture, denomination above and dates below **Rev:** Guardian Goddess Serket

Date	Mintage	VF20	XF40	MS60	MS63	MS65
AH1414-1993	50,000	**PF63** 24.00	**PF65** 31.50			

KM# 744 5 POUNDS
22.50 g., 0.999 Silver 0.7227 oz. ASW **Subject:** Amulet of Hathor **Obv:** Vulture, denomination above and dates below **Rev:** Sculpture of head

Date	Mintage	VF20	XF40	MS60	MS63	MS65
AH1414-1993	50,000	**PF63** 24.00	**PF65** 31.50			

KM# 745 5 POUNDS
22.50 g., 0.999 Silver 0.7227 oz. ASW **Obv:** Vulture, denomination above and dates below **Rev:** Standing Ramses II

Date	Mintage	VF20	XF40	MS60	MS63	MS65
AH1414-1993	50,000	**PF63** 24.00	**PF65** 31.50			

KM# 746 5 POUNDS
22.50 g., 0.999 Silver 0.7227 oz. ASW **Subject:** Menkaure Triad **Obv:** Vulture, denomination above and dates below **Rev:** Three figures

Date	Mintage	VF20	XF40	MS60	MS63	MS65
AH1414-1993	50,000	**PF63** 24.00	**PF65** 31.50			

KM# 747 5 POUNDS
22.50 g., 0.999 Silver 0.7227 oz. ASW **Subject:** Symbol of Unification **Obv:** Vulture, denomination above and dates below **Rev:** Two females representing the upper and lower Nile

Date	Mintage	VF20	XF40	MS60	MS63	MS65
AH1414-1993	50,000	**PF63** 24.00	**PF65** 31.50			

KM# 748 5 POUNDS
22.50 g., 0.999 Silver 0.7227 oz. ASW **Series:** World Cup Soccer **Obv:** Vulture, denomination above and dates below **Rev:** Kneeling King Pepi I facing

Date	Mintage	VF20	XF40	MS60	MS63	MS65
AH1414-1993	—	PF63 30.00		PF65 40.00		
AH1415-1994	50,000	PF63 24.00		PF65 31.50		

KM# 759 5 POUNDS
17.50 g., 0.720 Silver 0.4051 oz. ASW **Subject:** Beram El Tunsi, Poet **Obv:** Inscription and seals, dates below **Rev:** Bust 3/4 left

Date	Mintage	VF20	XF40	MS60	MS63	MS65
AH1413-1993	3,000	—	—	—	25.00	35.00

KM# 793 5 POUNDS
22.50 g., 0.999 Silver 0.7227 oz. ASW **Obv:** Vulture, denomination above and dates below **Rev:** Tutankhamen's burial mask

Date	Mintage	VF20	XF40	MS60	MS63	MS65
AH1414-1993	—	PF63 26.00		PF65 33.50		

KM# 812 5 POUNDS
17.50 g., 0.720 Silver 0.4051 oz. ASW **Subject:** 20th Anniversary - October War **Obv:** Smoking towers divide dates **Rev:** Soldier with flag

Date	Mintage	VF20	XF40	MS60	MS63	MS65
AH1414-1993	—	—	—	—	9.50	19.50

KM# 837 5 POUNDS
17.50 g., 0.720 Silver 0.4051 oz. ASW **Subject:** 125th Anniversary of Taalat Harb Birth **Obv:** Denomination and date in circle above inscription **Rev:** Taalat Harb wearing fez **Edge:** Reeded

Date	Mintage	VF20	XF40	MS60	MS63	MS65
AH1413-1993	5,000	—	—	—	9.50	17.50

KM# 869 5 POUNDS
22.55 g., 0.999 Silver 0.7243 oz. ASW **Subject:** King Kha-Sekhem **Obv:** Vulture, denomination above and dates below **Rev:** Seated figure **Edge:** Reeded

Date	Mintage	VF20	XF40	MS60	MS63	MS65
AH1414-1993 Proof	15,000	—	—	—	16.50	25.50

KM# 879 5 POUNDS
26.00 g., 0.875 Gold 0.7314 oz. AGW **Subject:** Symbol of Unification **Obv:** Vulture, denomination above and dates below **Rev:** Two females representing the upper and lower Nile

Date	Mintage	VF20	XF40	MS60	MS63	MS65
AH1414-1993 Proof	3,000	—	—	—	—	1,175

KM# 736 5 POUNDS
17.50 g., 0.925 Silver 0.5204 oz. ASW **Series:** World Cup Soccer **Obv:** Text within circle at center of wings, dates above divided by oval shield **Rev:** Two players, pyramid with Statue of Liberty at left

Date	Mintage	VF20	XF40	MS60	MS63	MS65
AH1415-1994	499	—	—	—	125	160
AH1415-1994	15,000	PF63 30.00		PF65 40.00		

KM# 738 5 POUNDS
17.50 g., 0.925 Silver 0.5204 oz. ASW **Series:** World Cup Soccer **Rev:** Stylized player

Date	Mintage	VF20	XF40	MS60	MS63	MS65
AH1415-1994	499	—	—	—	125	160
AH1415-1994	15,000	PF63 30.00		PF65 40.00		

KM# 749 5 POUNDS
22.50 g., 0.999 Silver 0.7227 oz. ASW **Obv:** Vulture, denomination above and dates below **Rev:** Sphinx and pyramids

Date	Mintage	VF20	XF40	MS60	MS63	MS65
AH1414-1994	50,000	PF63 24.00		PF65 31.50		

KM# 750 5 POUNDS
22.50 g., 0.999 Silver 0.7227 oz. ASW **Obv:** Vulture, denomination above and dates below **Rev:** King Djoser wearing the Red Crown right

Date	Mintage	VF20	XF40	MS60	MS63	MS65
AH1415-1994	50,000	PF63 24.00		PF65 31.50		

KM# 751 5 POUNDS
22.50 g., 0.999 Silver 0.7227 oz. ASW **Obv:** Vulture, denomination above and dates below **Rev:** King Khonsu facing

Date	Mintage	VF20	XF40	MS60	MS63	MS65
AH1415-1994	50,000	PF63 24.00		PF65 31.50		

KM# 752 5 POUNDS
22.50 g., 0.999 Silver 0.7227 oz. ASW **Obv:** Vulture, denomination above and dates below **Rev:** RE (Sun God) presenting the Ankh (Symbol of Life) to Sesostris I wearing Double Crown

Date	Mintage	VF20	XF40	MS60	MS63	MS65
AH1415-1994	50,000	PF63 24.00		PF65 31.50		

KM# 753 5 POUNDS
22.50 g., 0.999 Silver 0.7227 oz. ASW **Obv:** Vulture, denomination above and dates below **Rev:** God Horus wearing Double Crown

Date	Mintage	VF20	XF40	MS60	MS63	MS65
AH1415-1994	50,000	PF63 24.00		PF65 31.50		

KM# 754 5 POUNDS
22.50 g., 0.999 Silver 0.7227 oz. ASW **Obv:** Vulture, denomination above and dates below **Rev:** Standing god Seth left

Date	Mintage	VF20	XF40	MS60	MS63	MS65
AH1415-1994	50,000	PF63 24.00		PF65 31.50		

KM# 757 5 POUNDS
22.50 g., 0.999 Silver 0.7227 oz. ASW **Obv:** Vulture, denomination above and dates below **Rev:** Queen Nefretari, wife of Ramses II kneeling right

Date	Mintage	VF20	XF40	MS60	MS63	MS65
AH1415-1994	—	PF63 24.00	PF65 31.50			

KM# 763 5 POUNDS
17.50 g., 0.720 Silver 0.4051 oz. ASW **Subject:** Salah El Din El-Ayubi **Obv:** Dates and denomination within circle above text **Rev:** Bust at center, mosque behind at left, mounted rider with sword at right

Date	Mintage	VF20	XF40	MS60	MS63	MS65
AH1414-1994	5,000	—	—	—	27.00	37.00

KM# 783 5 POUNDS
22.50 g., 0.999 Silver 0.7227 oz. ASW **Obv:** Ancient style vulture **Rev:** Bust of Nefertiti right

Date	Mintage	VF20	XF40	MS60	MS63	MS65
AH1415-1994	50,000	PF63 24.00	PF65 31.50			

KM# 784 5 POUNDS
22.50 g., 0.999 Silver 0.7227 oz. ASW **Obv:** Vulture, denomination above and dates below **Rev:** Archer in chariot

Date	Mintage	VF20	XF40	MS60	MS63	MS65
AH1415-1994	50,000	PF63 24.00	PF65 31.50			

KM# 785 5 POUNDS
22.50 g., 0.999 Silver 0.7227 oz. ASW **Obv:** Vulture, denomination above and dates below **Rev:** Five birds

Date	Mintage	VF20	XF40	MS60	MS63	MS65
AH1415-1994	50,000	PF63 24.00	PF65 31.50			

KM# 786 5 POUNDS
22.50 g., 0.999 Silver 0.7227 oz. ASW **Obv:** Vulture, denomination above and dates below **Rev:** Hippopotamus right

Date	Mintage	VF20	XF40	MS60	MS63	MS65
AH1415-1994	50,000	PF63 24.00	PF65 31.50			

KM# 787 5 POUNDS
22.50 g., 0.999 Silver 0.7227 oz. ASW **Obv:** Vulture, denomination above and dates below **Rev:** Ruins of Karnak

Date	Mintage	VF20	XF40	MS60	MS63	MS65
AH1415-1994	50,000	PF63 24.00	PF65 31.50			

KM# 788 5 POUNDS
22.50 g., 0.999 Silver 0.7227 oz. ASW **Obv:** Vulture, denomination above and dates below **Rev:** Standing Goddess Neith wearing the Red Crown

Date	Mintage	VF20	XF40	MS60	MS63	MS65
AH1415-1994	50,000	PF63 24.00	PF65 31.50			

KM# 789 5 POUNDS
22.50 g., 0.999 Silver 0.7227 oz. ASW **Obv:** Vulture, denomination above and dates below **Rev:** Statue of King Amenemhat III

Date	Mintage	VF20	XF40	MS60	MS63	MS65
AH1415-1994	50,000	PF63 24.00	PF65 31.50			

KM# 790 5 POUNDS
22.50 g., 0.999 Silver 0.7227 oz. ASW **Obv:** Vulture, denomination above and dates below **Rev:** Ritual mask of Queen Hatshepsut, female Pharoah, peacemaker, died 1468BC

Date	Mintage	VF20	XF40	MS60	MS63	MS65
AH1415-1994	50,000	PF63 24.00	PF65 31.50			

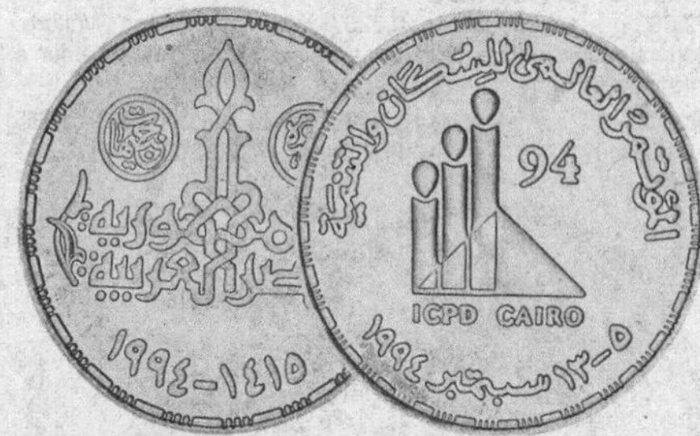

KM# 792 5 POUNDS
15.00 g., 0.720 Silver 0.3472 oz. ASW **Subject:** ICPD Cairo **Obv:** Inscription and seals **Rev:** Stylized design

Date	Mintage	VF20	XF40	MS60	MS63	MS65
AH1415-1994	—	—	—	—	8.25	14.00

KM# 794 5 POUNDS
22.60 g., 0.999 Silver 0.7257 oz. ASW **Obv:** Vulture, denomination above and dates below **Rev:** Seated, jeweled cat

Date	Mintage	VF20	XF40	MS60	MS63	MS65
AH1415-1994	—	PF63 26.00	PF65 34.00			

KM# 795 5 POUNDS
22.60 g., 0.999 Silver 0.7257 oz. ASW **Obv:** Vulture, denomination above and dates below **Rev:** Sacred falcon at Edfu

Date	Mintage	VF20	XF40	MS60	MS63	MS65
AH1415-1994	—	PF63 26.00	PF65 34.00			

KM# 797 5 POUNDS
22.60 g., 0.999 Silver 0.7257 oz. ASW **Obv:** Vulture, denomination above and dates below **Rev:** Tutankhamen's throne

Date	Mintage	VF20	XF40	MS60	MS63	MS65
AH1415-1994	—	**PF63** 24.00	**PF65** 32.00			

KM# 798 5 POUNDS
22.60 g., 0.999 Silver 0.7257 oz. ASW **Obv:** Vulture, denomination above and dates below **Rev:** King Au as high priest

Date	Mintage	VF20	XF40	MS60	MS63	MS65
AH1415-1994	—	**PF63** 24.00	**PF65** 32.00			

KM# 799 5 POUNDS
22.60 g., 0.999 Silver 0.7257 oz. ASW **Obv:** Vulture, denomination above and dates below **Rev:** Akhnaton

Date	Mintage	VF20	XF40	MS60	MS63	MS65
AH1415-1994	—	**PF63** 24.00	**PF65** 32.00			

KM# 800 5 POUNDS
22.60 g., 0.999 Silver 0.7257 oz. ASW **Obv:** Vulture, denomination above and dates below **Rev:** Osiris, seated right

Date	Mintage	VF20	XF40	MS60	MS63	MS65
AH1415-1994	—	**PF63** 24.00	**PF65** 32.00			

KM# 801 5 POUNDS
22.60 g., 0.999 Silver 0.7257 oz. ASW **Obv:** Vulture, denomination above and dates below **Rev:** RE, the sun god, walking left

Date	Mintage	VF20	XF40	MS60	MS63	MS65
AH1415-1994	—	**PF63** 24.00	**PF65** 32.00			

KM# 802 5 POUNDS
22.60 g., 0.999 Silver 0.7257 oz. ASW **Obv:** Vulture, denomination above and dates below **Rev:** The God Khnoum, walking right

Date	Mintage	VF20	XF40	MS60	MS63	MS65
AH1415-1994	—	**PF63** 24.00	**PF65** 32.00			

KM# 803 5 POUNDS
22.60 g., 0.999 Silver 0.7257 oz. ASW **Obv:** Vulture, denomination above and dates below **Rev:** Sobek, Crocodile God, walking left

Date	Mintage	VF20	XF40	MS60	MS63	MS65
AH1415-1994	—	**PF63** 24.00	**PF65** 32.00			

KM# 813 5 POUNDS
22.55 g., 0.999 Silver 0.7243 oz. ASW **Obv:** Vulture, denomination above and dates below **Rev:** Ancient seated scribe **Edge:** Reeded

Date	Mintage	VF20	XF40	MS60	MS63	MS65
AH1415-1994	—	**PF63** 24.00	**PF65** 31.50			

KM# 823 5 POUNDS
22.50 g., 0.999 Silver 0.7227 oz. ASW **Obv:** Vulture, denomination above and dates below **Rev:** Temple of Ramses II

Date	Mintage	VF20	XF40	MS60	MS63	MS65
AH1415-1994	—	**PF63** 24.00	**PF65** 31.50			

KM# 824 5 POUNDS
22.50 g., 0.999 Silver 0.7227 oz. ASW **Obv:** Vulture, denomination above and dates below **Rev:** Ancient ruins

Date	Mintage	VF20	XF40	MS60	MS63	MS65
AH1415-1994	—	**PF63** 24.00	**PF65** 31.50			

KM# 825 5 POUNDS
22.50 g., 0.999 Silver 0.7227 oz. ASW **Obv:** Vulture, denomination above and dates below **Rev:** Egyptian gazelle right

Date	Mintage	VF20	XF40	MS60	MS63	MS65
AH1415-1994	—	**PF63** 24.00	**PF65** 31.50			

KM# 826 5 POUNDS
22.50 g., 0.999 Silver 0.7227 oz. ASW **Obv:** Vulture, denomination above and dates below **Rev:** King Thoutmosis III, kneeling, left

Date	Mintage	VF20	XF40	MS60	MS63	MS65
AH1415-1994	—	**PF63** 24.00	**PF65** 31.50			

KM# 827 5 POUNDS
22.50 g., 0.999 Silver 0.7227 oz. ASW **Obv:** Vulture, denomination above and dates below **Rev:** Seated King Khufu

Date	Mintage	VF20	XF40	MS60	MS63	MS65
AH1415-1994	—	PF63 24.00	PF65 31.50			

KM# 828 5 POUNDS
22.50 g., 0.999 Silver 0.7227 oz. ASW **Obv:** Vulture, denomination above and dates below **Rev:** Standing Goddess Hathor left

Date	Mintage	VF20	XF40	MS60	MS63	MS65
AH1415-1994	—	PF63 24.00	PF65 31.50			

KM# 829 5 POUNDS
22.50 g., 0.999 Silver 0.7227 oz. ASW **Obv:** Vulture, denomination above and dates below **Rev:** Standing God Ptah of Memphis right

Date	Mintage	VF20	XF40	MS60	MS63	MS65
AH1415-1994	—	PF63 24.00	PF65 31.50			

KM# 830 5 POUNDS
22.50 g., 0.999 Silver 0.7227 oz. ASW **Obv:** Vulture, denomination above and dates below **Rev:** Seated Goddess Isis nursing child

Date	Mintage	VF20	XF40	MS60	MS63	MS65
AH1415-1994	—	PF63 24.00	PF65 31.50			

KM# 831 5 POUNDS
22.50 g., 0.999 Silver 0.7227 oz. ASW **Obv:** Vulture, denomination above and dates below **Rev:** Dwarf Seneb and family

Date	Mintage	VF20	XF40	MS60	MS63	MS65
AH1415-1994	—	PF63 24.00	PF65 31.50			

KM# 874 5 POUNDS
26.00 g., 0.875 Gold 0.7314 oz. AGW **Rev:** Sphinx and pyramids

Date	Mintage	VF20	XF40	MS60	MS63	MS65
AH1415-1994	5,000	PF65 1,175				

KM# 875 5 POUNDS
22.50 g., 0.999 Silver 0.7227 oz. ASW **Rev:** 3/4-length standing Sheikh El Balad

Date	Mintage	VF20	XF40	MS60	MS63	MS65
AH1415-1994	15,000	PF63 24.00	PF65 31.50			

KM# 876 5 POUNDS
26.00 g., 0.875 Gold 0.7314 oz. AGW **Rev:** 3/4-length standing Sheikh El Balad

Date	Mintage	VF20	XF40	MS60	MS63	MS65
AH1415-1994	3,000	PF65 1,175				

KM# 878 5 POUNDS
26.00 g., 0.875 Gold 0.7314 oz. AGW **Obv:** Vulture, denomination above and dates below **Rev:** Dwarf Seneb and family

Date	Mintage	VF20	XF40	MS60	MS63	MS65
AH1415-1994	3,000	PF65 1,175				

KM# 880 5 POUNDS
26.00 g., 0.875 Gold 0.7314 oz. AGW **Rev:** Kneeling King Pepi I facing

Date	Mintage	VF20	XF40	MS60	MS63	MS65
AH1415-1994	3,000	PF65 1,175				

KM# 881 5 POUNDS
26.00 g., 0.875 Gold 0.7314 oz. AGW **Rev:** Statue of King Amenemhat III

Date	Mintage	VF20	XF40	MS60	MS63	MS65
AH1415-1994	3,000	PF65 1,175				

KM# 883 5 POUNDS
22.50 g., 0.999 Silver 0.7227 oz. ASW **Rev:** Seated King Horemheb

Date	Mintage	VF20	XF40	MS60	MS63	MS65
AH1415-1994	15,000	PF63 24.00	PF65 31.50			

KM# 889 5 POUNDS
22.50 g., 0.999 Silver 0.7227 oz. ASW **Obv:** Vulture, denomination above and dates below **Rev:** Akhnaton and family

Date	Mintage	VF20	XF40	MS60	MS63	MS65
AH1415-1994	15,000	PF63 24.00	PF65 31.50			

KM# 894 5 POUNDS
22.50 g., 0.999 Silver 0.7227 oz. ASW **Obv:** Vulture, denomination above and dates below **Rev:** Bust amulet of Hathor

Date	Mintage	VF20	XF40	MS60	MS63	MS65
AH1415-1994	15,000	PF63 24.00	PF65 31.50			

KM# 896 5 POUNDS
22.50 g., 0.999 Silver 0.7227 oz. ASW **Rev:** Pair of geese

Date	Mintage	VF20	XF40	MS60	MS63	MS65
AH1415-1994	15,000	PF63 24.00	PF65 31.50			

KM# 969 5 POUNDS
17.50 g., 0.925 Silver 0.5204 oz. ASW, 37 mm. **Series:** Protect Our world **Obv:** Sculpture above winged inscription in circle **Rev:** Relief stone carving of 4 seated royalty **Edge:** Reeded **Mint:** Cairo

Date	Mintage	VF20	XF40	MS60	MS63	MS65
AH1415-1994 Matte	5,000	—	—	—	—	65.00

KM# 970 5 POUNDS
17.50 g., 0.925 Silver 0.5204 oz. ASW, 37 mm. **Series:** Protect Our world **Obv:** Sculpture above winged inscription in circle **Rev:** Sphinx, pyramids **Edge:** Reeded **Mint:** Cairo

Date	Mintage	VF20	XF40	MS60	MS63	MS65
AH1415-1994 Matte	—	—	—	—	—	65.00

KM# 971 5 POUNDS
17.50 g., 0.925 Silver 0.5204 oz. ASW, 37 mm. **Obv:** Relief stone sculpture above winged circle with inscription **Rev:** Ancient boat of Queen Chnemtamun **Edge:** Reeded **Mint:** Cairo

Date	Mintage	VF20	XF40	MS60	MS63	MS65
AH1415-1994 Matte	—	—	—	—	—	65.00

KM# 972 5 POUNDS
17.50 g., 0.925 Silver 0.5204 oz. ASW, 37 mm. **Obv:** Relief stone sculpture above winged circle with inscription **Rev:** Suez canal scene, pyramids in background **Edge:** Reeded **Mint:** Cairo

Date	Mintage	VF20	XF40	MS60	MS63	MS65
AH1415-1994 Matte	—	—	—	—	—	65.00

KM# 765 5 POUNDS
17.50 g., 0.720 Silver 0.4051 oz. ASW **Subject:** 50 Years - Arab League **Obv:** Dates and denomination within circle above text **Rev:** Buildings and emblem

Date	Mintage	VF20	XF40	MS60	MS63	MS65
AH1415-1995	5,000	—	—	—	9.50	18.50

KM# 768 5 POUNDS
17.50 g., 0.720 Silver 0.4051 oz. ASW **Subject:** 75 Years - Bank of Misr

Date	Mintage	VF20	XF40	MS60	MS63	MS65
AH1415-1995	2,500	—	—	—	9.50	19.50

KM# 770 5 POUNDS
17.50 g., 0.720 Silver 0.4051 oz. ASW **Series:** F.A.O. **Obv:** Tughra above logo **Rev:** People working

Date	Mintage	VF20	XF40	MS60	MS63	MS65
AH1415-1995	5,000	—	—	—	18.00	24.50

KM# 772 5 POUNDS
17.50 g., 0.720 Silver 0.4051 oz. ASW **Subject:** Pediatrics International Conference

Date	Mintage	VF20	XF40	MS60	MS63	MS65
AH1416-1995	4,000	—	—	—	9.50	18.50

KM# 773 5 POUNDS
17.50 g., 0.720 Silver 0.4051 oz. ASW **Subject:** 75 Years - Architects Association **Obv:** Outline of building divides dates **Rev:** Seated statue

Date	Mintage	VF20	XF40	MS60	MS63	MS65
AH1416-1995	3,000	—	—	—	16.00	21.50

KM# 774 5 POUNDS
26.00 g., 0.875 Gold 0.7314 oz. AGW **Subject:** 75 Years - Architects Association **Obv:** Tughra **Rev:** Head left

Date	Mintage	VF20	XF40	MS60	MS63	MS65
AH1416-1995	300	—	—	—	—	1,250

KM# 838 5 POUNDS
17.50 g., 0.720 Silver 0.4051 oz. ASW **Subject:** 75 Years - American University in Cairo **Rev:** Design in center surrounded by inscriptions and border

Date	Mintage	VF20	XF40	MS60	MS63	MS65
AH1415-1995	3,000	—	—	—	9.50	18.50

KM# 841 5 POUNDS
17.50 g., 0.720 Silver 0.4051 oz. ASW **Obv:** Tughra **Rev:** Abd Al Halem Hafez left

Date	Mintage	VF20	XF40	MS60	MS63	MS65
AH1416-1995	5,000	—	—	—	9.50	17.50

KM# 842 5 POUNDS
26.00 g., 0.875 Gold 0.7314 oz. AGW **Rev:** Abd Al Halem Hafez

Date	Mintage	VF20	XF40	MS60	MS63	MS65
AH1416-1995	500	—	—	—	—	1,200

KM# 843 5 POUNDS
17.50 g., 0.900 Silver 0.5064 oz. ASW **Subject:** Centennial - Mining and Geology **Obv:** Denomination with toughra **Rev:** Building in circle

Date	Mintage	VF20	XF40	MS60	MS63	MS65
AH1416-1996	700	—	—	—	50.00	75.00

KM# 846 5 POUNDS
17.50 g., 0.900 Silver 0.5064 oz. ASW **Subject:** 65 Years - Egyptian Air Force **Rev:** Flying eagle in wreath

Date	Mintage	VF20	XF40	MS60	MS63	MS65
AH1418-1997	300	—	—	—	75.00	125

KM# 848 5 POUNDS
17.50 g., 0.900 Silver 0.5064 oz. ASW **Subject:** 50 Years Arab Land Bank **Rev:** Arab Real Estate domed Bank building

Date	Mintage	VF20	XF40	MS60	MS63	MS65
AH1418-1997	3,000	—	—	—	11.50	20.50

KM# 850 5 POUNDS
17.50 g., 0.900 Silver 0.5064 oz. ASW **Subject:** 95th Interparliamentary Union Conference **Obv:** Circular design above inscription **Rev:** Pyramids in wreath

Date	Mintage	VF20	XF40	MS60	MS63	MS65
AH1418-1997	375	—	—	—	75.00	125

KM# 973 5 POUNDS
17.50 g., 0.720 Silver 0.4051 oz. ASW, 37 mm. **Subject:** 4th World Youth Cup **Obv:** Ornate doorway **Rev:** Stylized player on soccer ball **Rev. Inscription:** 4th U.17 WORLD CHAMPIONSHIP / FOR THE FIFA / IYC CUP EGYPT 1997 **Edge:** Reeded **Mint:** Cairo

Date	Mintage	VF20	XF40	MS60	MS63	MS65
AH1418-1997	850	—	—	—	135	150

KM# 852 5 POUNDS
17.50 g., 0.900 Silver 0.5064 oz. ASW **Subject:** Centennial - Chemical Department **Rev:** Symbolic design

Date	Mintage	VF20	XF40	MS60	MS63	MS65
AH1419-1998	1,000	—	—	—	35.00	50.00

KM# 853 5 POUNDS
17.50 g., 0.900 Silver 0.5064 oz. ASW **Subject:** Restoration of Al Azhar Mosque

Date	Mintage	VF20	XF40	MS60	MS63	MS65
AH1419-1998	4,000	—	—	—	11.50	19.50

KM# 856 5 POUNDS
17.50 g., 0.900 Silver 0.5064 oz. ASW **Subject:** Centennial of National Bank **Rev:** Large "100"

Date	Mintage	VF20	XF40	MS60	MS63	MS65
AH1419-1998	2,000	—	—	—	35.00	50.00

KM# 858 5 POUNDS
17.50 g., 0.900 Silver 0.5064 oz. ASW **Subject:** 25th Anniversary - October War **Rev:** Symbolic design

Date	Mintage	VF20	XF40	MS60	MS63	MS65
AH1419-1998	1,500	—	—	—	35.00	50.00

KM# 860 5 POUNDS
17.50 g., 0.900 Silver 0.5064 oz. ASW **Subject:** Death of El Sheikh M. Metwaly El Sharawy **Rev:** Bust of Imam Metwaly El Sharawi facing

Date	Mintage	VF20	XF40	MS60	MS63	MS65
AH1419-1998	3,000	—	—	—	11.50	20.50

KM# 862 5 POUNDS
17.50 g., 0.900 Silver 0.5064 oz. ASW **Subject:** Centennial - Land Surveying **Rev:** "100" above ancient surveyors

Date	Mintage	VF20	XF40	MS60	MS63	MS65
AH1419-1998	6,000	—	—	—	11.50	19.50

KM# 864 5 POUNDS
17.50 g., 0.900 Silver 0.5064 oz. ASW **Subject:** Centennial - Solidarity **Rev:** Symbolic design

Date	Mintage	VF20	XF40	MS60	MS63	MS65
AH1419-1998	9,500	—	—	—	11.50	19.50

KM# 854 5 POUNDS
17.50 g., 0.900 Silver 0.5064 oz. ASW **Subject:** 16th Men's World Handball Championship **Obv:** Denomination and dates **Rev:** Handball game

Date	Mintage	VF20	XF40	MS60	MS63	MS65
AH1420-1999	6,500	—	—	—	11.50	19.50

KM# 867 5 POUNDS
17.50 g., 0.900 Silver 0.5064 oz. ASW **Subject:** 50 Years Cairo Metropolitan Mass Transit System **Rev:** Water above subway train

Date	Mintage	VF20	XF40	MS60	MS63	MS65
AH1420-1999	2,000	—	—	—	11.50	20.50

KM# 897 5 POUNDS
17.50 g., 0.900 Silver 0.5064 oz. ASW **Subject:** 75 Years - Dar El-Eloum University

Date	Mintage	VF20	XF40	MS60	MS63	MS65
AH1420-1999	2,000	—	—	—	11.50	20.50

KM# 898 5 POUNDS
17.33 g., 0.975 Silver 0.5432 oz. ASW, 37 mm. **Subject:** Sacred falcon **Obv:** Denomination and inscription **Rev:** Ancient sacred falcon **Edge:** Reeded **Mint:** Franklin Mint

Date	Mintage	VF20	XF40	MS60	MS63	MS65
AH1420-1999	—	**PF63** 20.00	**PF65** 27.50			

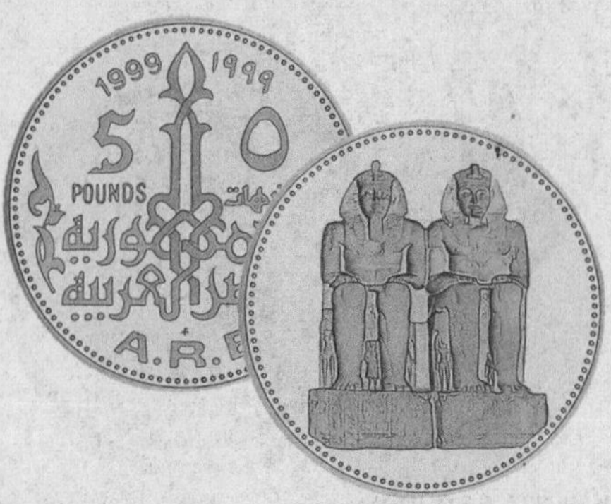

KM# 899 5 POUNDS
17.33 g., 0.975 Silver 0.5432 oz. ASW, 37 mm. **Obv:** Denomination and inscription **Rev:** Two statues of Ramses II **Edge:** Reeded **Mint:** Franklin Mint

Date	Mintage	VF20	XF40	MS60	MS63	MS65
AH1420-1999	—	**PF63** 20.00	**PF65** 27.50			

KM# 900 5 POUNDS
17.33 g., 0.975 Silver 0.5432 oz. ASW, 37 mm. **Obv:** Denomination and inscription **Rev:** Tutankhamen's Death Mask **Edge:** Reeded **Mint:** Franklin Mint

Date	Mintage	VF20	XF40	MS60	MS63	MS65
AH1420-1999	—	**PF63** 20.00	**PF65** 27.50			

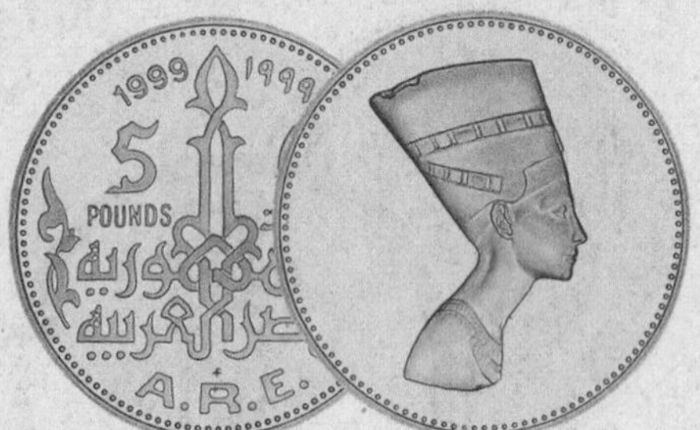

KM# 901 5 POUNDS
17.33 g., 0.975 Silver 0.5432 oz. ASW, 37 mm. **Obv:** Denomination and inscription **Rev:** Bust of Nefertiti right **Edge:** Reeded **Mint:** Franklin Mint

Date	Mintage	VF20	XF40	MS60	MS63	MS65
AH1420-1999	—	**PF63** 20.00	**PF65** 27.50			

KM# 902 5 POUNDS
17.33 g., 0.975 Silver 0.5432 oz. ASW, 37 mm. **Obv:** Denomination and inscription **Rev:** Imaginary bust of Cleopatra left **Edge:** Reeded **Mint:** Franklin Mint

Date	Mintage	VF20	XF40	MS60	MS63	MS65
AH1420-1999	—	**PF63** 20.00	**PF65** 27.50			

KM# 927 5 POUNDS
17.50 g., 0.720 Silver 0.4051 oz. ASW, 37 mm. **Subject:** Ain Shams University **Obv:** Value **Rev:** Shams University logo above anniversary dates 2000-1950 **Edge:** Reeded **Mint:** Cairo

Date	Mintage	VF20	XF40	MS60	MS63	MS65
AH1420-1999	1,000	—	—	—	50.00	75.00

KM# 929 5 POUNDS
17.50 g., 0.720 Silver 0.4051 oz. ASW, 37 mm. **Subject:** National Insurance Company Centennial **Obv:** Value **Rev:** Ancient seated figure with "100" **Edge:** Reeded **Mint:** Cairo

Date	Mintage	VF20	XF40	MS60	MS63	MS65
AH1421-2000	2,500	—	—	—	35.00	50.00

KM# 519 10 POUNDS
40.00 g., 0.875 Gold 1.1253 oz. AGW **Subject:** Egyptian-Israeli Peace Treaty **Obv:** Denomination divides dates **Rev:** Head at right facing left, dove with olive branch at left

Date	Mintage	VF20	XF40	MS60	MS63	MS65
AH1400-1980	950	—	—	—	1,900	2,100
AH1400-1980	50	PF65 2,150				

KM# 538 10 POUNDS
40.00 g., 0.875 Gold 1.1253 oz. AGW **Subject:** 25th Anniversary - Ministry of Industry **Obv:** Text, denomination and dates **Rev:** Factory building, cogwheel at right

Date	Mintage	VF20	XF40	MS60	MS63	MS65
AH1402-1981	18	—	—	—	—	2,400
AH1402-1981	1,000	PF65 1,900				

KM# 548 10 POUNDS
40.00 g., 0.875 Gold 1.1253 oz. AGW **Subject:** 1000th Anniversary - Al Azhar Mosque **Obv:** Text within circle divides dates **Rev:** Mosque

Date	Mintage	VF20	XF40	MS60	MS63	MS65
AH1402-1982	1,322	PF65 1,875				

KM# 634 10 POUNDS
40.00 g., 0.875 Gold 1.1253 oz. AGW **Subject:** Prophet's Mosque **Obv:** Minaret, globe, denomination, legends **Rev:** Crescent, mosque, minaret below legend arch

Date	Mintage	VF20	XF40	MS60	MS63	MS65
AH1406-1985	300	PF65 2,000				

KM# 641 50 POUNDS
8.50 g., 0.900 Gold 0.246 oz. AGW **Subject:** Mecca **Obv:** Arabic legend, ornamentation **Rev:** Interior view of the Kaaba

Date	Mintage	VF20	XF40	MS60	MS63	MS65
AH1406-1986	14,000	—	—	—	—	375

KM# 672 50 POUNDS
8.50 g., 0.900 Gold 0.246 oz. AGW **Series:** World Soccer Championships **Obv:** Stylized flowers, denomination, date and legends **Rev:** Soccer ball on road between Mexican and Egyptian pyramids

Date	Mintage	VF20	XF40	MS60	MS63	MS65
AH1406-1986	250	—	—	—	—	425
AH1406-1986	250	PF65 475				

KM# 612 50 POUNDS
8.50 g., 0.900 Gold 0.246 oz. AGW **Subject:** Aida Opera **Obv:** Radiant sun, pillars and inscriptions **Rev:** Ancient figures among ruins

Date	Mintage	VF20	XF40	MS60	MS63	MS65
AH1407-1987	40,000	—	—	—	—	375

KM# 625 50 POUNDS
8.50 g., 0.900 Gold 0.246 oz. AGW **Series:** Summer Olympics **Obv:** Arabic legend and ornamentation within English legend **Rev:** Pharoah and athletes

Date	Mintage	VF20	XF40	MS60	MS63	MS65
AH1408-1988	150	—	—	—	—	450
AH1408-1988	50	PF65 550				

KM# 627 50 POUNDS
8.50 g., 0.900 Gold 0.246 oz. AGW **Series:** Summer Olympics **Rev:** Athletes and mythological figures

Date	Mintage	VF20	XF40	MS60	MS63	MS65
AH1408-1988	750	—	—	—	—	425
AH1408-1988	250	PF65 475				

KM# 629 50 POUNDS
8.50 g., 0.900 Gold 0.246 oz. AGW **Series:** Winter Olympics **Obv:** Winged design, English legend, Arabic inscription **Rev:** Ski jumper and figure skater within Arabic legend

Date	Mintage	VF20	XF40	MS60	MS63	MS65
AH1408-1988	150	—	—	—	—	450
AH1408-1988	50	PF65 550				

KM# 680 50 POUNDS
8.50 g., 0.900 Gold 0.246 oz. AGW **Subject:** Soccer World Championship - Italy **Obv:** Text within circle at center of wings, denomination and dates above **Rev:** Ancient gods

Date	Mintage	VF20	XF40	MS60	MS63	MS65
AH1410-1990	225	PF65 550				

KM# 683 50 POUNDS
8.50 g., 0.900 Gold 0.246 oz. AGW **Subject:** Soccer World Championship **Rev:** Player chasing ball

Date	Mintage	VF20	XF40	MS60	MS63	MS65
AH1410-1990	75	PF65 600				

KM# 709 50 POUNDS
8.50 g., 0.900 Gold 0.246 oz. AGW **Series:** Summer Olympics **Obv:** Text within circle at center of wings, denomination and dates above **Rev:** Fencing

Date	Mintage	VF20	XF40	MS60	MS63	MS65
AH1412-1992	49	—	—	—	—	625
AH1412-1992	99	PF65 600				

KM# 710 50 POUNDS
8.50 g., 0.900 Gold 0.246 oz. AGW **Series:** Summer Olympics **Obv:** Text within circle at center of wings, denomination and dates above **Rev:** Wrestling, half globe below

Date	Mintage	VF20	XF40	MS60	MS63	MS65
AH1412-1992	49	—	—	—	—	625
AH1412-1992	99	PF65 600				

KM# 711 50 POUNDS
8.50 g., 0.900 Gold 0.246 oz. AGW **Series:** Summer Olympics **Obv:** Text within circle at center of wings, denomination and dates above **Rev:** Archery

Date	Mintage	VF20	XF40	MS60	MS63	MS65
AH1412-1992	49	—	—	—	—	625
AH1412-1992	99	PF65 600				

KM# 712 50 POUNDS
8.50 g., 0.900 Gold 0.246 oz. AGW **Series:** Summer Olympics **Obv:** Text within circle at center of wings, denomination and dates above **Rev:** Many men wrestling an ox

Date	Mintage	VF20	XF40	MS60	MS63	MS65
AH1412-1992	49	—	—	—	—	625
AH1412-1992	99	PF65 600				

KM# 713 50 POUNDS
8.50 g., 0.900 Gold 0.246 oz. AGW **Series:** Summer Olympics **Obv:** Text within circle at center of wings, denomination and dates above **Rev:** Swimmer stalking a duck

Date	Mintage	VF20	XF40	MS60	MS63	MS65
AH1412-1992	49	—	—	—	—	625
AH1412-1992	99	PF65 600				

KM# 714 50 POUNDS
8.50 g., 0.900 Gold 0.246 oz. AGW **Series:** Summer Olympics **Obv:** Text within circle at center of wings, denomination and dates above **Rev:** Handball player

Date	Mintage	VF20	XF40	MS60	MS63	MS65
AH1412-1992	49	—	—	—	—	625
AH1412-1992	99	PF65 600				

KM# 715 50 POUNDS
8.50 g., 0.900 Gold 0.246 oz. AGW **Series:** Summer Olympics **Obv:** Text within circle at center of wings, denomination and dates above **Rev:** Field hockey player

Date	Mintage	VF20	XF40	MS60	MS63	MS65
AH1412-1992	49	—	—	—	—	625
AH1412-1992	99	PF65 600				

KM# 716 50 POUNDS
8.50 g., 0.900 Gold 0.246 oz. AGW **Series:** Summer Olympics **Obv:** Text within circle at center of wings, denomination and

dates above **Rev:** Soccer player kicking ball

Date	Mintage	VF20	XF40	MS60	MS63	MS65
AH1412-1992	49	—	—	—	—	625
AH1412-1992	115	PF65 600				

KM# 755 50 POUNDS
8.50 g., 0.900 Gold 0.246 oz. AGW **Obv:** Vulture, denomination above and dates below **Rev:** King Tutankhamen's burial mask

Date	Mintage	VF20	XF40	MS60	MS63	MS65
AH1414-1993	—	PF65 425				

KM# 756 50 POUNDS
8.50 g., 0.900 Gold 0.246 oz. AGW **Subject:** Cleopatra **Obv:** Vulture, denomination above and dates below **Rev:** Bust left

Date	Mintage	VF20	XF40	MS60	MS63	MS65
AH1414-1993	—	PF65 400				

KM# 775 50 POUNDS
8.50 g., 0.900 Gold 0.246 oz. AGW **Obv:** Vulture, denomination above and dates below **Rev:** Three pyramids

Date	Mintage	VF20	XF40	MS60	MS63	MS65
AH1414-1993	—	PF65 400				

KM# 776 50 POUNDS
8.50 g., 0.900 Gold 0.246 oz. AGW **Obv:** Vulture, denomination above and dates below **Rev:** Sphinx head

Date	Mintage	VF20	XF40	MS60	MS63	MS65
AH1414-1993	—	PF65 400				

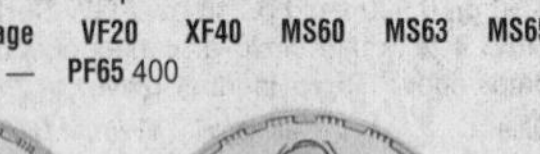

KM# 777 50 POUNDS
8.50 g., 0.900 Gold 0.246 oz. AGW **Obv:** Vulture, denomination above and dates below **Rev:** Standing Ramses II

Date	Mintage	VF20	XF40	MS60	MS63	MS65
AH1414-1993	—	PF65 400				

KM# 868 50 POUNDS
8.50 g., 0.900 Gold 0.246 oz. AGW **Subject:** King Narmer Palette **Obv:** Vulture, denomination above and dates below **Rev:** King killing a wounded foe

Date	Mintage	VF20	XF40	MS60	MS63	MS65
AH1414-1993	3,000	PF65 400				

KM# 870 50 POUNDS
8.50 g., 0.900 Gold 0.246 oz. AGW **Subject:** King Kna-Sekhem **Obv:** Vulture, denomination above and dates below **Rev:** Seated king

Date	Mintage	VF20	XF40	MS60	MS63	MS65
AH1414-1993	3,000	PF65 400				

KM# 873 50 POUNDS
8.50 g., 0.900 Gold 0.246 oz. AGW **Subject:** Menkaure Triad **Obv:** Vulture, denomination above and dates below **Rev:** Three carved figurines

Date	Mintage	VF20	XF40	MS60	MS63	MS65
AH1414-1993	3,000	PF65 400				

KM# 885 50 POUNDS
8.50 g., 0.900 Gold 0.246 oz. AGW **Subject:** Thoutmosis III **Obv:** Vulture, denomination above and dates below **Rev:** Kneeling figure holding jar

Date	Mintage	VF20	XF40	MS60	MS63	MS65
AH1414-1993	3,000	PF65 400				

KM# 737 50 POUNDS
8.50 g., 0.900 Gold 0.246 oz. AGW **Series:** World Cup Soccer **Obv:** Text within circle at center of wings, oval shield above divides dates **Rev:** Two players, pyramid and Statue of Liberty

Date	Mintage	VF20	XF40	MS60	MS63	MS65
AH1415-1994	99	—	—	—	—	475
AH1415-1994	99	PF65 475				

KM# 739 50 POUNDS
8.50 g., 0.900 Gold 0.246 oz. AGW **Series:** World Cup Soccer **Obv:** Text within circle at center of wings, oval shield above divides dates **Rev:** Stylized player

Date	Mintage	VF20	XF40	MS60	MS63	MS65
AH1415-1994	99	—	—	—	—	475
AH1415-1994	99	PF65 475				

KM# 778 50 POUNDS
8.50 g., 0.900 Gold 0.246 oz. AGW **Obv:** Vulture, denomination above and dates below **Rev:** Crowned falcon left **Mint:** Cairo

Date	Mintage	VF20	XF40	MS60	MS63	MS65
AH1415-1994	—	PF65 400				

KM# 779 50 POUNDS
8.50 g., 0.900 Gold 0.246 oz. AGW **Subject:** Queen Nefertiti **Obv:** Vulture, denomination above and dates below **Rev:** Bust right

Date	Mintage	VF20	XF40	MS60	MS63	MS65
AH1415-1994	—	PF65 400				

KM# 780 50 POUNDS
8.50 g., 0.900 Gold 0.246 oz. AGW **Obv:** Vulture, denomination above and dates below **Rev:** Seated cat right

Date	Mintage	VF20	XF40	MS60	MS63	MS65
AH1415-1994	—	PF65 400				

KM# 781 50 POUNDS
8.50 g., 0.900 Gold 0.246 oz. AGW **Obv:** Vulture, denomination above and dates below **Rev:** Archer in chariot

Date	Mintage	VF20	XF40	MS60	MS63	MS65
AH1415-1994	—	PF65 400				

KM# 782 50 POUNDS
8.50 g., 0.900 Gold 0.246 oz. AGW **Obv:** Vulture, denomination above and dates below **Rev:** Standing God Seth left

Date	Mintage	VF20	XF40	MS60	MS63	MS65
AH1415-1994	—	PF65 400				

KM# 814 50 POUNDS
8.50 g., 0.900 Gold 0.246 oz. AGW **Obv:** Vulture, denomination above and dates below **Rev:** Hippopotamus

Date	Mintage	VF20	XF40	MS60	MS63	MS65
AH1415-1994	—	PF65 400				

KM# 815 50 POUNDS
8.50 g., 0.900 Gold 0.246 oz. AGW **Obv:** Vulture, denomination above and dates below **Rev:** Egyptian gazelle

Date	Mintage	VF20	XF40	MS60	MS63	MS65
AH1415-1994	—	PF65 400				

KM# 816 50 POUNDS
8.50 g., 0.900 Gold 0.246 oz. AGW **Obv:** Vulture, denomination above and dates below **Rev:** Phoenix birds

Date	Mintage	VF20	XF40	MS60	MS63	MS65
AH1415-1994	—	PF65 400				

KM# 817 50 POUNDS
8.50 g., 0.900 Gold 0.246 oz. AGW **Obv:** Vulture, denomination above and dates below **Rev:** Egyptian geese

Date	Mintage	VF20	XF40	MS60	MS63	MS65
AH1415-1994	—	PF65 400				

KM# 818 50 POUNDS
8.50 g., 0.900 Gold 0.246 oz. AGW **Obv:** Vulture, denomination above and dates below **Rev:** King Taharqa

Date	Mintage	VF20	XF40	MS60	MS63	MS65
AH1415-1994	—	PF65 400				

KM# 819 50 POUNDS
8.50 g., 0.900 Gold 0.246 oz. AGW **Obv:** Vulture, denomination above and dates below **Rev:** Amenhotep Temple

Date	Mintage	VF20	XF40	MS60	MS63	MS65
AH1415-1994	—	PF65 400				

KM# 820 50 POUNDS
8.50 g., 0.900 Gold 0.246 oz. AGW **Obv:** Vulture, denomination above and dates below **Rev:** Karnak Temple

Date	Mintage	VF20	XF40	MS60	MS63	MS65
AH1415-1994	—	PF65 400				

KM# 821 50 POUNDS
8.50 g., 0.900 Gold 0.246 oz. AGW **Obv:** Vulture, denomination above and dates below **Rev:** Philae Temple

Date	Mintage	VF20	XF40	MS60	MS63	MS65
AH1415-1994	—	PF65 400				

KM# 822 50 POUNDS
8.50 g., 0.900 Gold 0.246 oz. AGW **Obv:** Vulture, denomination above and dates below **Rev:** Khonsu Temple

Date	Mintage	VF20	XF40	MS60	MS63	MS65
AH1415-1994	—	PF65 400				

KM# 871 50 POUNDS
8.50 g., 0.900 Gold 0.246 oz. AGW **Obv:** Vulture, denomination above and dates below **Rev:** King Djoser wearing the Red Crown

Date	Mintage	VF20	XF40	MS60	MS63	MS65
AH1415-1994	3,000	PF65 400				

KM# 872 50 POUNDS
8.50 g., 0.900 Gold 0.246 oz. AGW **Obv:** Vulture, denomination above and dates below **Rev:** Seated King Khufu with flat-top hat

Date	Mintage	VF20	XF40	MS60	MS63	MS65
AH1415-1994	3,000	PF65 400				

KM# 877 50 POUNDS
26.00 g., 0.875 Gold 0.7314 oz. AGW **Obv:** Vulture, denomination above and dates below **Rev:** Ancient seated scribe

Date	Mintage	VF20	XF40	MS60	MS63	MS65
AH1415-1994	3,000	PF65 1,175				

KM# 882 50 POUNDS
8.50 g., 0.900 Gold 0.246 oz. AGW **Subject:** King Sesostris I **Obv:** Vulture, denomination above and dates below **Rev:** RE (sun god) presenting the ANKH (symbol of life) to the king wearing the Double Crown

Date	Mintage	VF20	XF40	MS60	MS63	MS65
AH1415-1994	3,000	PF65 400				

KM# 884 50 POUNDS
8.50 g., 0.900 Gold 0.246 oz. AGW **Subject:** King Horemheb **Obv:** Vulture, denomination above and dates below **Rev:** Seated King Horemheb

Date	Mintage	VF20	XF40	MS60	MS63	MS65
AH1415-1994	3,000	PF65 400				

KM# 886 50 POUNDS
8.50 g., 0.900 Gold 0.246 oz. AGW **Subject:** King Khonsu **Obv:** Vulture, denomination above and dates below **Rev:** 1/2-length King Khonsu

Date	Mintage	VF20	XF40	MS60	MS63	MS65
AH1415-1994	3,000	PF65 400				

KM# 887 50 POUNDS
8.50 g., 0.900 Gold 0.246 oz. AGW **Subject:** Tutankhamen's Throne **Obv:** Vulture, denomination above and dates below **Rev:** King Tut seated on throne with servant

Date	Mintage	VF20	XF40	MS60	MS63	MS65
AH1415-1994	3,000	PF65 420				

KM# 888 50 POUNDS
8.50 g., 0.900 Gold 0.246 oz. AGW **Subject:** Queen Hatshepsut **Obv:** Vulture, denomination above and dates below **Rev:** Queen's facial sculpture

Date	Mintage	VF20	XF40	MS60	MS63	MS65
AH1415-1994	3,000	PF65 400				

KM# 890 50 POUNDS
8.50 g., 0.900 Gold 0.246 oz. AGW **Subject:** Akhnaton and Family **Obv:** Vulture, denomination above and dates below **Rev:** Family scene

Date	Mintage	VF20	XF40	MS60	MS63	MS65
AH1415-1994	3,000	PF65 400				

KM# 891 50 POUNDS
8.50 g., 0.900 Gold 0.246 oz. AGW **Obv:** Vulture, denomination above and dates below **Rev:** Akhnaton

Date	Mintage	VF20	XF40	MS60	MS63	MS65
AH1415-1994	3,000	PF65 400				

KM# 892 50 POUNDS
8.50 g., 0.900 Gold 0.246 oz. AGW **Subject:** Queen Nefertari **Obv:** Vulture, denomination above and dates below **Rev:** Kneeling Queen Nefertari

Date	Mintage	VF20	XF40	MS60	MS63	MS65
AH1415-1994	5,000	PF65 400				

KM# 893 50 POUNDS
8.50 g., 0.900 Gold 0.246 oz. AGW **Subject:** Ramses III **Obv:** Vulture, denomination above and dates below **Rev:** 3/4-length Ramses III

Date	Mintage	VF20	XF40	MS60	MS63	MS65
AH1415-1994	3,000	PF65 420				

KM# 895 50 POUNDS
8.50 g., 0.900 Gold 0.246 oz. AGW **Obv:** Vulture, denomination above and dates below **Rev:** Amulet of Hathor

Date	Mintage	VF20	XF40	MS60	MS63	MS65
AH1415-1994	3,000	PF65 400				

KM# 921 50 POUNDS
11.80 g., 0.900 Gold 0.3414 oz. AGW, 26 mm. **Obv:** Value and inscription **Rev:** Statue of Ramses II seated **Edge:** Reeded **Mint:** Franklin Mint

Date	Mintage	VF20	XF40	MS60	MS63	MS65
AH1420-1999	—	PF65 550				

KM# 550 100 POUNDS
17.15 g., 0.900 Gold 0.4962 oz. AGW **Obv:** Denomination, dates and text **Rev:** Bust of Queen Nefertiti right

Date	Mintage	VF20	XF40	MS60	MS63	MS65
AH1404-1983	16,000	PF65 850				

KM# 562 100 POUNDS
17.15 g., 0.900 Gold 0.4962 oz. AGW **Obv:** Denomination, dates and text **Rev:** Bust of Cleopatra VII in formal headdress left 69-30BC, Queen and statesperson

Date	Mintage	VF20	XF40	MS60	MS63	MS65
AH1404-1984	2,121	PF65 900				

KM# 569 100 POUNDS
17.15 g., 0.900 Gold 0.4962 oz. AGW **Obv:** Denomination, dates and text **Rev:** The golden falcon, from an ancient breastplate found in King Tutankhamen's tomb

Date	Mintage	VF20	XF40	MS60	MS63	MS65
AH1405-1985	1,800	PF65 825				

KM# 591 100 POUNDS
17.15 g., 0.900 Gold 0.4962 oz. AGW **Rev:** Tutankhamen

Date	Mintage	VF20	XF40	MS60	MS63	MS65
AH1406-1986	7,500	PF65 875				

KM# 642 100 POUNDS
17.00 g., 0.900 Gold 0.4919 oz. AGW **Subject:** Mecca **Obv:** Arabic legend, ornamentation **Rev:** Interior view of the Kaaba

Date	Mintage	VF20	XF40	MS60	MS63	MS65
AH1406-1986	700	—	—	—	—	850

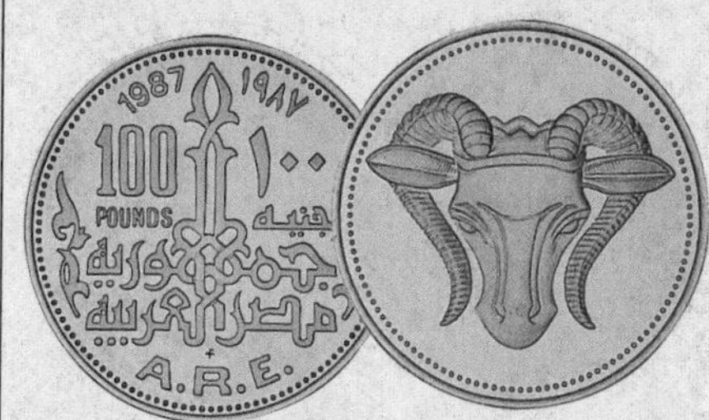

KM# 613 100 POUNDS
17.00 g., 0.900 Gold 0.4919 oz. AGW **Obv:** Denomination, dates and text **Rev:** The golden ram

Date	Mintage	VF20	XF40	MS60	MS63	MS65
AH1407-1987	7,500	PF65 800				

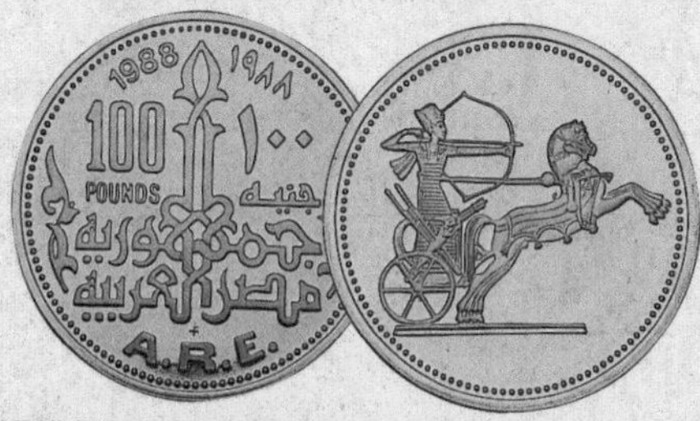

KM# 648 100 POUNDS
17.00 g., 0.900 Gold 0.4919 oz. AGW **Obv:** Denomination, dates and text **Rev:** The golden warrior

Date	Mintage	VF20	XF40	MS60	MS63	MS65
AH1408-1988	5,500	PF65 800				

KM# 656 100 POUNDS
17.15 g., 0.900 Gold 0.4962 oz. AGW **Obv:** Denomination, dates and text **Rev:** The golden cat

Date	Mintage	VF20	XF40	MS60	MS63	MS65
AH1409-1989 FM	Est. 7500	PF65 800				

KM# 681 100 POUNDS
17.00 g., 0.900 Gold 0.4919 oz. AGW **Series:** World Soccer Championship - Italy **Rev:** Ancient gods

Date	Mintage	VF20	XF40	MS60	MS63	MS65
AH1410-1990	125	PF65 900				

KM# 684 100 POUNDS
17.00 g., 0.900 Gold 0.4919 oz. AGW **Series:** World Soccer Championship - Italy **Rev:** Player chasing ball

Date	Mintage	VF20	XF40	MS60	MS63	MS65
AH1410-1990	75	PF65 925				

KM# 693 100 POUNDS
17.00 g., 0.900 Gold 0.4919 oz. AGW **Series:** Ancient Egyptian Culture **Obv:** Denomination, dates and text **Rev:** Sphinx

Date	Mintage	VF20	XF40	MS60	MS63	MS65
AH1410-1990 FM	Est. 5000	PF65 800				

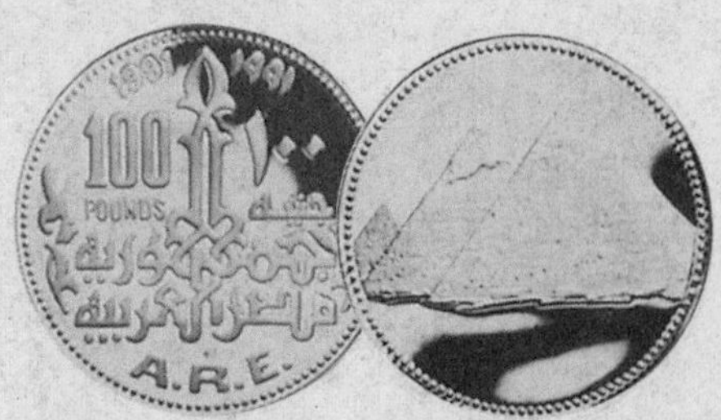

KM# 729 100 POUNDS
17.00 g., 0.900 Gold 0.4919 oz. AGW **Series:** Ancient Egyptian Culture **Obv:** Denomination, dates and text **Rev:** Pyramids of Giza

Date	Mintage	VF20	XF40	MS60	MS63	MS65
AH1411-1991	—	PF65 800				

KM# 717 100 POUNDS
17.00 g., 0.900 Gold 0.4919 oz. AGW **Series:** Summer Olympics **Rev:** Fencing

Date	Mintage	VF20	XF40	MS60	MS63	MS65
AH1412-1992	49	—	—	—	—	925
AH1412-1992	99	PF65 900				

KM# 718 100 POUNDS
17.00 g., 0.900 Gold 0.4919 oz. AGW **Series:** Summer Olympics **Obv:** Text within circle at center of wings, denomination and dates above **Rev:** Wrestling matches

Date	Mintage	VF20	XF40	MS60	MS63	MS65
AH1412-1992	49	—	—	—	—	925
AH1412-1992	99	PF65 900				

KM# 719 100 POUNDS
17.00 g., 0.900 Gold 0.4919 oz. AGW **Series:** Summer Olympics **Obv:** Text within circle at center of wings, denomination and dates above **Rev:** Archery demonstration

Date	Mintage	VF20	XF40	MS60	MS63	MS65
AH1412-1992	49	—	—	—	—	925
AH1412-1992	99	PF65 900				

KM# 720 100 POUNDS
17.00 g., 0.900 Gold 0.4919 oz. AGW **Series:** Summer Olympics **Obv:** Text within circle at center of wings, denomination and dates above **Rev:** Many men wrestling an ox

Date	Mintage	VF20	XF40	MS60	MS63	MS65
AH1412-1992	49	—	—	—	—	925
AH1412-1992	99	PF65 900				

KM# 721 100 POUNDS
17.00 g., 0.900 Gold 0.4919 oz. AGW **Series:** Summer Olympics **Rev:** Swimmer stalking a duck

Date	Mintage	VF20	XF40	MS60	MS63	MS65
AH1412-1992	49	—	—	—	—	925
AH1412-1992	99	PF65 900				

KM# 722 100 POUNDS
17.00 g., 0.900 Gold 0.4919 oz. AGW **Series:** Summer Olympics **Rev:** Handball player

Date	Mintage	VF20	XF40	MS60	MS63	MS65
AH1412-1992	49	—	—	—	—	925
AH1412-1992	99	PF65 900				

KM# 723 100 POUNDS
17.00 g., 0.900 Gold 0.4919 oz. AGW **Series:** Summer Olympics **Rev:** Field hockey player

Date	Mintage	VF20	XF40	MS60	MS63	MS65
AH1412-1992	49	—	—	—	—	925
AH1412-1992	99	PF65 900				

KM# 724 100 POUNDS
17.00 g., 0.900 Gold 0.4919 oz. AGW **Series:** Summer Olympics **Rev:** Soccer player

Date	Mintage	VF20	XF40	MS60	MS63	MS65
AH1412-1992	49	—	—	—	—	925
AH1412-1992	115	PF65 900				

KM# 730 100 POUNDS
17.15 g., 0.900 Gold 0.4962 oz. AGW **Subject:** The Golden Guardians **Obv:** Denomination, dates and text **Rev:** Two statues of Ramses II

Date	Mintage	VF20	XF40	MS60	MS63	MS65
1992	Est. 5000	PF65 800				

PATTERNS

Including off metal strikes

KM#	Date	Mintage	Identification	Mkt Val
Pn26	1917	—	1/2 Millieme. Copper-Nickel.	500
Pn27	1942	—	2 Piastres. Platinum. KM#365.	—
Pn28	1960	—	25 Piastres. Silver. KM#400 but with hand pointing to right.	—
Pn29	1962	—	5 Piastres. Bronze. ESSAi.	—
Pn30	1962	—	5 Piastres. Brass or Aluminum-Bronze.	1,650
Pn31	1964	—	10 Piastres. Copper-Nickel.	—
Pn32	1917	—	10 Milliemes. Copper-Nickel. Design of KM-316 obverse. Blank. Plain. Obverse die trial of KM-316.	—
Pn33	ND (1917) KN	—	10 Milliemes. Copper-Nickel. Blank. Design of KM-316 reverse. Plain. Reverse die trial of KM-316.	—

PIEDFORT

KM#	Date	Mintage	Identification	Mkt Val
P1	1981	152	5 Pounds. 0.900. Silver. KM533.	350

PROOF SETS

KM#	Date	Mintage	Identification	Issue Price	Mkt Val
PS1	1938 (4)	—	KM#370, 371, 372, 373	4,200	4,500
PS2	1964 (4)	2,000	KM#404, 405, 406, 407	18.00	115
PS3	1966 (7)	2,500	KM#393, 394, 395, 397, 398, 399, 403	9.00	80.00
PS4	1980 (4)	—	KM#508, 509, 517, 519	—	4,100
PS5	1980 (3)	—	KM#509, 517, 519	—	4,100

SPECIMEN SETS (SS)

KM#	Date	Mintage	Identification	Issue Price	Mkt Val
SS1	1916/7 (10)	—	KM#312-316, 317.1, 318.1, 319, 321, 324	—	1,700

EL SALVADOR

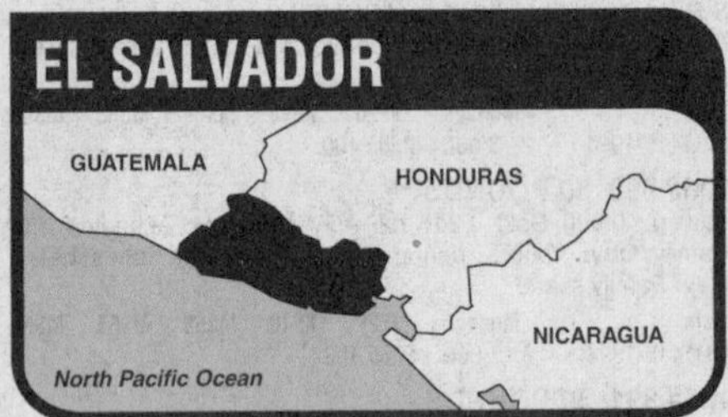

The Republic of El Salvador, a Central American country bordered by Guatemala, Honduras and the Pacific Ocean, has an area of 8,124 sq. mi. (21,040 sq. km.) and a population of 6.0 million. Capital: San Salvador. This most intensely cultivated of Latin America countries produces coffee (the major crop), sugar and balsam for export. Gold, silver and other metals are largely unexploited.

The first Spanish attempt to subjugate the area was undertaken in 1523 by Pedro de Alvarado, Cortes' lieutenant. He was forced to retreat by Indian forces, but returned in 1525 and succeeded in bringing the region under control of the Captaincy General of Guatemala. In 1821, El Salvador and the other Central American provinces jointly declared independence from Spain. In 1823, the Republic of Central America was formed by the five Central American states; this federation dissolved in 1839. El Salvador then became an independent republic in 1841.

Since 1960, El Salvador has been a part of the Central American Common Market. During the 1980's El Salvador went through a 12 year Civil War that ended in 1992 with the signing of a United Nations-sponsored Peace Accord. Free elections, with full participation of all political parties, were held in 1994, 1997 and 1999. Armando Calderon-Sol was elected president in 1994 for a 5-year term and Francisco Flores was elected in 1999 for a 5-year term as well.

MINT MARK
C.A.M. - Central American Mint, San Salvador

MONETARY SYSTEM
100 Centavos = 1 Peso

REPUBLIC OF EL SALVADOR

DECIMAL COINAGE

100 Centavos = 1 Peso

KM# 120 1/4 REAL

3.20 g., Bronze, 19 mm. **Obv:** Flag draped arms within wreath, liberty cap on top, swords above cap **Rev:** Denomination and date within wreath **Note:** The decimal value of this coin was about 3 Centavos. It was apparently struck in response to the continuing use of the Reales monetary system in rural areas.

Date	Mintage	F12	VF20	XF40	MS60	MS63
1909	—	—	—	60.00	120	—

KM# 106 CENTAVO

2.50 g., Copper-Nickel **Obv:** Head of Francisco Morazan left, date below **Obv. Legend:** REPUBLICA DEL SALVADOR **Rev:** Denomination within wreath **Note:** Medal rotation.

Date	Mintage	F12	VF20	XF40	MS60	MS63
1913 H	2,500,000	0.50	1.00	3.00	30.00	60.00

KM# 127 CENTAVO

2.50 g., Copper-Nickel **Obv:** Head of Francisco Morazan left, date below **Rev:** Denomination within wreath **Note:** Medal rotation.

Date	Mintage	F12	VF20	XF40	MS60	MS63
1915 (P)	5,000,000	0.50	1.00	7.00	25.00	40.00
1919 (P)	1,000,000	1.00	2.00	12.00	30.00	60.00
1920 (P)	1,490,000	1.00	2.00	9.00	30.00	60.00
1925 (f)	200,000	2.00	5.00	15.00	50.00	75.00
1926 (f)	400,000	1.00	4.00	12.00	35.00	70.00
1928 S	5,000,000	0.50	1.00	7.00	25.00	40.00
Note: Varieties exist with large or small "S"						
1936 (P)	2,500,000	0.50	1.00	7.00	25.00	40.00

KM# 107 3 CENTAVOS

3.30 g., Copper-Nickel, 20 mm. **Obv:** Head of Francisco Morazan left **Obv. Legend:** REPUBLICA DEL SALVADOR **Rev:** Denomination within wreath **Note:** Medal rotation.

Date	Mintage	F12	VF20	XF40	MS60	MS63
1913 H	1,000,000	1.00	6.00	12.00	50.00	125
1913 H	—	PF63 750				

KM# 128 3 CENTAVOS

3.50 g., Copper-Nickel, 20 mm. **Obv:** Head of Francisco Morazan left, date below **Rev:** Denomination within wreath **Note:** Medal rotation.

Date	Mintage	F12	VF20	XF40	MS60	MS63
1915 (P)	2,700,000	1.00	3.00	15.00	85.00	200

KM# 121 5 CENTAVOS

1.25 g., 0.835 Silver 0.0336 oz. ASW, 14 mm. **Obv:** Arms **Rev:** Denomination within wreath

Date	Mintage	F12	VF20	XF40	MS60	MS63
1911	1,000,000	2.00	4.00	10.00	35.00	70.00

KM# 124 5 CENTAVOS

1.25 g., 0.835 Silver 0.0336 oz. ASW, 14 mm. **Obv:** Flag draped triangular arms within wreath **Rev:** Denomination within wreath

Date	Mintage	F12	VF20	XF40	MS60	MS63
1914 (P)	2,000,000	2.00	4.00	10.00	25.00	50.00
1914 (P)	20	PF63 650				

KM# 129 5 CENTAVOS

5.00 g., Copper-Nickel **Obv:** Head of Francisco Morazan left, date below **Rev:** Denomination within wreath **Note:** Medal rotation.

Date	Mintage	F12	VF20	XF40	MS60	MS63
1915 (P)	2,500,000	1.00	3.00	10.00	35.00	75.00
1916 (P)	1,500,000	1.00	3.00	10.00	35.00	75.00
1917 (P)	1,000,000	1.00	3.00	10.00	35.00	75.00
1918/7 (P)	1,000,000	1.00	3.00	10.00	35.00	75.00
1918 (P)	Inc. above	1.00	3.00	10.00	35.00	75.00
1919/8 (P)	—	1.00	3.00	10.00	35.00	75.00
1919 (P)	2,000,000	1.00	3.00	10.00	35.00	75.00
1920 (P)	2,000,000	1.00	3.00	8.00	30.00	60.00
1921 (f)	1,780,000	1.00	3.00	8.00	30.00	60.00
1925 (f)	4,000,000	1.00	2.00	5.00	25.00	60.00

KM# 122 10 CENTAVOS

2.50 g., 0.835 Silver 0.0671 oz. ASW, 18 mm. **Obv:** Flag draped arms, liberty cap on top, dates below **Rev:** Denomination within wreath

Date	Mintage	F12	VF20	XF40	MS60	MS63
1911	1,000,000	2.00	4.00	10.00	35.00	70.00

KM# 125 10 CENTAVOS

2.50 g., 0.835 Silver 0.0671 oz. ASW, 18 mm. **Obv:** Flag draped triangular arms within wreath, dates below **Rev:** Denomination within wreath

Date	Mintage	F12	VF20	XF40	MS60	MS63
1914 (P)	1,500,000	2.00	3.00	8.00	30.00	60.00
1914 (P)	20	PF63 750				

KM# 123 25 CENTAVOS

6.25 g., 0.835 Silver 0.1678 oz. ASW, 24 mm. **Obv:** Flag draped arms, liberty cap above, dates below **Rev:** Denomination within wreath

Date	Mintage	F12	VF20	XF40	MS60	MS63
1911	600,000	5.00	8.00	12.00	35.00	75.00

KM# 126 25 CENTAVOS

6.25 g., 0.835 Silver 0.1678 oz. ASW, 24 mm. **Obv:** Flag draped triangular arms within wreath, dates below **Rev:** Denomination within wreath

Date	Mintage	F12	VF20	XF40	MS60	MS63
1914 (P) 15 DE SEPT DE 1821	1,400,000	5.00	8.00	8.00	30.00	60.00
1914 (P) 15 SET DE 1821	Inc. above	5.00	8.00	12.00	25.00	40.00
1914 (P)	20	PF63 1,500				

KM# 115.1 PESO (Colon)

25.00 g., 0.900 Silver 0.7234 oz. ASW **Obv:** Arms **Obv. Legend:** REPUBLICA DEL SALVADOR **Rev:** Columbus bust left

Date	Mintage	F12	VF20	XF40	MS60	MS63
1904 C.A.M.	600,000	14.00	20.00	30.00	100	200
1908 C.A.M.	1,600,000	14.00	20.00	30.00	100	200
1911 C.A.M.	500,000	14.00	20.00	30.00	100	200
1914 C.A.M.	700,000	—	—	—	—	—
Note: 1914 struck at the Brussels mint, but then remelted						

KM# 115.2 PESO (Colon)

25.00 g., 0.900 Silver 0.7234 oz. ASW **Obv:** Flag draped arms, liberty cap and swords above, dates below **Rev:** Columbus bust left, denomination below, heavier portrait (wider right shoulder) **Note:** Struck at United States mints.

Date	Mintage	F12	VF20	XF40	MS60	MS63
1904 C.A.M. (f)	400,000	13.50	20.00	30.00	125	350
1909 C.A.M. (f)	690,000	13.50	20.00	30.00	125	275
1911 C.A.M. (P) (S)	1,020,000	13.50	20.00	30.00	100	275
Note: Of the total mintage, 510, 993 struck at Philadelphia Mint (P), and 511,108 were struck at San Francisco Mint (f)						
1914 C.A.M. (P)	2,100,000	13.50	20.00	30.00	100	250
1914 C.A.M.	Est. 20	PF63 3,500				

REFORM COINAGE

100 Centavos = 1 Colon

KM# 133 CENTAVO

2.50 g., Copper-Nickel **Obv:** Head of Francisco Morazan left **Rev:** Denomination within wreath **Note:** Medal rotation.

Date	Mintage	F12	VF20	XF40	MS60	MS63
1940 (P)	1,000,000	0.50	2.00	6.00	12.00	20.00

KM# 135.1 CENTAVO

2.50 g., Bronze, 15 mm. **Obv:** Head of Francisco Morazan left, date below **Rev:** Denomination within wreath

Date	Mintage	F12	VF20	XF40	MS60	MS63
1942 (P)	5,000,000	0.20	0.50	1.00	2.00	3.00
Note: Struck in 1943						
1943 (f)	5,000,000	0.20	0.50	1.00	2.00	3.00
Note: Struck in 1944						
1945 (P)	5,000,000	0.20	0.40	0.75	1.50	3.00
1947 (P)	5,000,000	0.20	0.50	1.00	1.25	2.00
1951 (f)	10,000,000	0.10	0.30	0.75	1.00	1.25
1952 (f)	10,000,000	0.10	0.20	0.40	0.75	1.00
Note: Struck in 1953						
1956 (P)	10,000,000	0.10	0.20	0.40	0.75	1.00
Note: Struck in 1957						
1966	5,000,000	—	—	0.10	0.35	0.75
1968 (f)	5,000,000	—	—	0.10	0.35	0.75
1969 (b)	5,000,000	—	—	0.10	0.35	0.75
1972 (f)	20,000,000	—	—	0.10	0.25	0.50

KM# 135.1a CENTAVO
2.50 g., Bronze Clad Steel **Obv:** Head of Francisco Morazan left **Rev:** Denomination within wreath **Note:** Prev. KM#135d. Medal rotation.

Date	Mintage	VF20	XF40	MS60	MS63	MS65
1989 (h)	36,000,000	—	0.10	0.20	0.35	0.50
1992 (h)	—	—	0.10	0.20	0.35	0.50

KM# 135.2 CENTAVO
2.50 g., Brass **Obv:** Head of Francisco Morazan left **Rev:** Denomination within wreath **Note:** Prev. KM#135a. Medal rotation.

Date	Mintage	VF20	XF40	MS60	MS63	MS65
1976	20,000,000	—	0.10	0.20	0.35	0.50
1977	40,000,000	—	0.10	0.20	0.35	0.50

KM# 135.2a CENTAVO
2.50 g., Brass **Obv:** DH monogram at truncation, smaller Morazan portrait **Rev:** Denomination in wreath, SM at right base of 1 **Note:** Previously KM#135c.

Date	Mintage	VF20	XF40	MS60	MS63	MS65
1981 (d)	50,000,000	—	0.10	0.20	0.35	0.50

KM# 135.2b CENTAVO
2.50 g., Copper Clad Steel **Obv:** DH monogram at truncation, smaller Morazan portrait **Rev:** Denomination in wreath, SM at right base of 1 **Note:** Prev. KM#135b.

Date	Mintage	VF20	XF40	MS60	MS63	MS65
1986 (a)	30,000,000	—	0.10	0.20	0.35	0.50

KM# A154 CENTAVO
1.50 g., Brass Plated Steel, 15 mm. **Obv:** Head of Francisco Morazan left **Rev:** Denomination in wreath

Date	Mintage	VF20	XF40	MS60	MS63	MS65
1988 (h)	—	PF65 50.00				

KM# 135.2c CENTAVO
2.50 g., Brass Clad Steel **Obv:** DH monogram at truncation, smaller portrait **Rev:** Denomination in wreath, SM at right base of 1

Date	Mintage	VF20	XF40	MS60	MS63	MS65
1995 (a)	—	—	0.10	0.20	0.35	0.50

KM# 147 2 CENTAVOS
2.60 g., Nickel-Brass **Obv:** Head of Francisco Morazan left **Rev:** Denomination within wreath **Note:** Medal rotation.

Date	Mintage	F12	VF20	XF40	MS60	MS63
1974 (a)	10,002,000	—	0.10	0.20	0.50	1.00
1974 (a)	2,000	PF65 30.00				

Note: In proof sets only

KM# 148 3 CENTAVOS
4.00 g., Nickel-Brass, 19 mm. **Obv:** Head of Francisco Morazan left **Rev:** Denomination within wreath **Note:** Medal rotation.

Date	Mintage	VF20	XF40	MS60	MS63	MS65
1974 (a)	10,002,000	0.15	0.20	0.50	1.00	1.50
1974 (a)	2,000	PF65 35.00				

Note: In proof sets only

KM# 134 5 CENTAVOS
5.00 g., Copper-Nickel, 23 mm. **Obv:** Head of Francisco Morazan left **Rev:** Denomination within wreath **Note:** Medal rotation.

Date	Mintage	F12	VF20	XF40	MS60	MS63
1939	—	—	—	—	—	—
1940 (P)	800,000	0.50	1.00	3.00	12.00	30.00
1951 S	2,000,000	0.25	0.75	2.50	5.00	10.00
1956 (P)	8,000,000	0.10	0.15	0.25	0.50	0.75
1959 (P)	6,000,000	0.10	0.15	0.25	0.50	0.75
1963 (P)	10,000,000	—	0.10	0.15	0.35	0.50
1966	6,000,000	0.10	0.15	0.25	0.50	0.75
1967 (f)	10,000,000	—	0.10	0.15	0.35	0.75
1972 (f)	10,000,000	—	0.10	0.15	0.35	0.75
1974 (g)	10,002,000	—	0.10	0.15	0.35	0.75
1974 (g)	2,000	PF65 35.00				

Note: In proof sets only

KM# 134a 5 CENTAVOS
5.00 g., Nickel-Silver, 23 mm. **Obv:** Head of Francisco Morazan left, date below **Rev:** Denomination within wreath

Date	Mintage	VF20	XF40	MS60	MS63	MS65
1944 (f)	5,000,000	1.00	3.00	5.00	7.00	10.00
1948 (f)	3,000,000	1.00	2.00	4.00	6.00	10.00
1950 (f)	2,000,000	1.00	3.00	5.00	7.00	10.00
1952 (f)	4,000,000	0.50	0.75	1.50	3.00	6.00

Note: Half the total mintage was struck in 1952, the remainder in 1953

KM# 149 5 CENTAVOS
5.00 g., Copper-Nickel Clad Steel, 23 mm. **Obv:** Head of Francisco Morazan left, date below **Rev:** Denomination within wreath **Note:** Medal rotation.

Date	Mintage	VF20	XF40	MS60	MS63	MS65
1975 (a)	15,000,000	0.10	0.15	0.30	0.50	0.75
1975	2,000	PF65 40.00				
Note: In proof sets only						
1986 (h)	30,000,000	0.10	0.15	0.30	0.50	0.75

KM# 149a 5 CENTAVOS
5.00 g., Nickel Clad Steel, 23 mm. **Obv:** Head of Francisco Morazan left **Rev:** Denomination within wreath

Date	Mintage	VF20	XF40	MS60	MS63	MS65
1976 (g)	15,000,000	0.10	0.15	0.30	0.50	0.75
1984 (a)	15,000,000	0.10	0.15	0.30	0.50	0.75

KM# 149b 5 CENTAVOS
5.00 g., Copper-Nickel-Zinc, 23 mm. **Obv:** Head of Francisco Morazan left **Rev:** Denomination within wreath **Note:** Previously KM#149a.

Date	Mintage	VF20	XF40	MS60	MS63	MS65
1977 (h)	26,000,000	0.10	0.15	0.30	0.50	0.75

KM# 154 5 CENTAVOS
2.00 g., Stainless Steel, 17 mm. **Obv:** Head of Francisco Morazan left, date below **Rev:** Denomination within wreath

Date	Mintage	VF20	XF40	MS60	MS63	MS65
1987 (h)	30,000,000	0.10	0.15	0.30	0.50	0.75
1987 (h)	—	PF65 50.00				
1999 (h)	—	0.10	0.15	0.30	0.50	0.75

KM# 154a 5 CENTAVOS
2.00 g., Copper-Nickel Clad Steel **Obv:** Head of Francisco Morazan left **Rev:** Denomination within wreath **Note:** Medal rotation.

Date	Mintage	VF20	XF40	MS60	MS63	MS65
1991 (h)	—	0.10	0.15	0.30	0.50	0.75
1998 (c)	—	0.10	0.15	0.30	0.50	0.75

KM# 154b 5 CENTAVOS
2.00 g., Nickel Clad Steel, 17 mm. **Obv:** Head of Francisco Morazan left, date below **Rev:** Denomination within wreath **Note:** Medal rotation.

Date	Mintage	VF20	XF40	MS60	MS63	MS65
1992 (g)	—	0.10	0.15	0.30	0.50	0.75
1993 (g)	—	0.10	0.15	0.30	0.50	0.75
1994 (h)	—	0.10	0.15	0.30	0.50	0.75
1994 (h)	—	PF65 40.00				
1995 (g)	—	0.10	0.15	0.30	0.50	0.75
1998	—	0.10	0.15	0.30	0.50	0.75
1999	—	0.10	0.15	0.30	0.50	0.75

KM# 130 10 CENTAVOS
7.00 g., Copper-Nickel, 26 mm. **Obv:** Head of Francisco Morazan left, date below **Rev:** Denomination within wreath **Note:** Medal rotation.

Date	Mintage	F12	VF20	XF40	MS60	MS63
1921 (f)	2,000,000	2.00	5.00	20.00	125	225
1925 (f)	2,000,000	3.00	7.00	50.00	225	350
1940 (f)	500,000	2.00	5.00	20.00	75.00	150
1951 (f)	1,000,000	0.25	1.00	5.00	10.00	15.00
1967 (f)	2,000,000	—	0.10	0.50	0.75	1.00
1968 (b)	3,000,000	—	0.10	0.40	0.75	1.00
1969 (b)	3,000,000	—	0.10	0.40	0.75	1.00
1972 (f)	7,000,000	—	0.10	0.25	0.75	1.00

KM# 130a 10 CENTAVOS
7.00 g., Copper-Nickel-Zinc, 26 mm. **Obv:** Head of Francisco Morazan left **Rev:** Denomination within wreath

Date	Mintage	VF20	XF40	MS60	MS63	MS65
1952 (f)	2,000,000	0.25	0.75	1.25	2.00	4.00
Note: Of the 2,000,000 struck, 336,000 were struck in 1952 and the remaining 1,664,000 struck in 1953						
1985 Mo	15,000,000	0.10	0.15	0.30	0.50	0.75

KM# 150 10 CENTAVOS
7.00 g., Copper-Nickel Clad Steel, 26 mm. **Obv:** Head of Francisco Morazan left date below **Rev:** Denomination within wreath **Note:** Medal rotation.

Date	Mintage	VF20	XF40	MS60	MS63	MS65
1975 (a)	15,000,000	0.15	0.25	0.50	0.75	1.00
1975 (a)	2,000	PF65 35.00				

Note: In proof sets only

KM# 150a 10 CENTAVOS
7.00 g., Copper-Nickel-Zinc, 26 mm. **Obv:** Head of Francisco Morazan left **Rev:** Denomination within wreath **Note:** Medal rotation.

Date	Mintage	VF20	XF40	MS60	MS63	MS65
1977 (h)	24,000,000	0.10	0.20	0.45	0.75	1.00
1977 (h)	—	PF65 40.00				

KM# 155 10 CENTAVOS

3.00 g., Stainless Steel, 20 mm. **Obv:** Head of Francisco Morazan left date below **Rev:** Denomination within wreath **Note:** Medal rotation.

Date	Mintage	VF20	XF40	MS60	MS63	MS65
1987 (h)	30,000,000	0.10	0.20	0.35	0.50	0.75
1987 (h)	—	PF65 50.00				
1999 (i)	—	0.10	0.20	0.35	0.50	0.75

KM# 155a 10 CENTAVOS

Nickel Clad Steel **Obv:** Head of Francisco Morazan left **Rev:** Denomination within wreath **Note:** Medal rotation.

Date	Mintage	VF20	XF40	MS60	MS63	MS65
1992 (a)	—	0.10	0.20	0.35	0.50	0.75
1993 (g)	—	0.10	0.20	0.35	0.50	0.75
1994 (h)	—	0.10	0.20	0.35	0.50	0.75
1994	—	PF65 40.00				

KM# 155b 10 CENTAVOS

Copper-Nickel Clad Steel **Obv:** Head of Francisco Morazan left **Rev:** Denomination within wreath

Date	Mintage	VF20	XF40	MS60	MS63	MS65
1995 (c)	—	0.10	0.20	0.35	0.50	0.75
1998 (c)	—	0.10	0.20	0.35	0.50	0.75
1999	—	0.10	0.20	0.35	0.50	0.75

KM# 136 25 CENTAVOS

7.50 g., 0.900 Silver 0.217 oz. ASW, 29 mm. **Obv:** Head of Francisco Morazan left, date below **Rev:** Denomination within wreath

Date	Mintage	F12	VF20	XF40	MS60	MS63
1943 (f)	1,200,000	4.00	6.00	8.00	12.00	15.00
1944	1,000,000	4.25	6.00	8.00	12.00	15.00

KM# 137 25 CENTAVOS

2.50 g., 0.900 Silver 0.0723 oz. ASW, 18 mm. **Obv:** Head of Jose Matias Delgado left, date below **Rev:** Denomination within wreath

Date	Mintage	VF20	XF40	MS60	MS63	MS65
1953	14,000,000	—	1.50	3.00	6.00	9.00

KM# 139 25 CENTAVOS

2.50 g., Nickel, 17.8 mm. **Obv:** Head of Jose Matias Delgado left, date below **Rev:** Denomination within wreath **Edge:** Reeded

Date	Mintage	VF20	XF40	MS60	MS63	MS65
1970 (a)	14,000,000	0.10	0.20	0.40	0.60	0.80
1973 (g)	28,000,000	0.10	0.20	0.35	0.50	0.75
1975 (g)	20,000,000	0.10	0.20	0.35	0.50	0.75
1977 (a)	22,400,000	0.10	0.20	0.35	0.50	0.75

KM# 139a 25 CENTAVOS

2.50 g., Copper-Nickel **Obv:** Head of Jose Matias Delgado left **Rev:** Denomination within wreath

Date	Mintage	VF20	XF40	MS60	MS63	MS65
1986 Mo	21,000,000	0.10	0.20	0.35	0.50	0.75
1986 Mo	—	PF65 50.00				

KM# 157 25 CENTAVOS

4.00 g., Stainless Steel, 22.5 mm. **Obv:** Head of Jose Matias Delgado left, date below **Rev:** Denomination within wreath **Note:** Medal rotation.

Date	Mintage	VF20	XF40	MS60	MS63	MS65
1988 (h)	20,000,000	0.10	0.20	0.35	0.50	0.75
1988 (h)	—	PF65 50.00				
1999 (i)	—	0.10	0.20	0.35	0.50	0.75

KM# 157a 25 CENTAVOS

4.00 g., Copper-Nickel Clad Steel **Obv:** Bust of Jose Matias Delgado left **Rev:** Denomination

Date	Mintage	VF20	XF40	MS60	MS63	MS65
1992	—	0.10	0.20	0.35	0.50	0.75
1995	—	0.10	0.20	0.35	0.50	0.75

KM# 158b 25 CENTAVOS

4.00 g., Nickel Clad Steel **Obv:** Head of Jose Matias Delgado left, date below **Rev:** Denomination within wreath **Note:** Medal rotation.

Date	Mintage	VF20	XF40	MS60	MS63	MS65
1993 (a)	—	0.10	0.20	0.35	0.50	0.75
1994 (g)	—	0.10	0.20	0.35	0.50	0.75
1998	—	0.10	0.20	0.35	0.50	0.75
1999	—	0.10	0.20	0.35	0.50	0.75

KM# 138 50 CENTAVOS

5.00 g., 0.900 Silver 0.1447 oz. ASW, 21 mm. **Obv:** Head of Jose Matias Delgado left, date below **Rev:** Denomination within wreath

Date	Mintage	VF20	XF40	MS60	MS63	MS65
1953 (f)	3,000,000	—	2.75	4.00	6.00	8.00

KM# 140.1 50 CENTAVOS

5.00 g., Nickel, 20 mm. **Obv:** Head of Jose Matias Delgado left, date below **Rev:** Denomination within wreath **Note:** 1.65 millimeters thick.

Date	Mintage	VF20	XF40	MS60	MS63	MS65
1970 (a)	3,000,000	0.20	0.30	0.40	0.60	0.80

KM# 140.2 50 CENTAVOS

5.10 g., Nickel, 20 mm. **Obv:** Head of Jose Matias Delgado left **Rev:** Denomination **Note:** Two millimeters thick.

Date	Mintage	VF20	XF40	MS60	MS63	MS65
1977 (a)	1,500,000	0.20	0.30	0.40	0.60	0.80

KM# 131 COLON

25.00 g., 0.900 Silver 0.7234 oz. ASW, 37 mm. **Subject:** 400th Anniversary - San Salvador **Obv:** Flags flank triangular arms within wreath, denomination below **Rev:** Alvarado and Quinonez busts left, dates above

Date	Mintage	VF20	XF40	MS60	MS63	MS65
ND-1925 Mo	2,000	—	—	120	190	275

KM# 141 COLON

2.30 g., 0.999 Silver 0.0739 oz. ASW **Subject:** 150th Anniversary of Independence **Obv:** Flags flank triangular arms within wreath, bust at right **Rev:** Salvador Dali image, "La Fecundida" within circle, denomination below

Date	Mintage	VF20	XF40	MS60	MS63	MS65
1971	21,000	PF63 7.00	PF65 9.00	PF67 12.00		

KM# 153 COLON

9.25 g., Copper-Nickel, 29 mm. **Obv:** Head of Christopher Columbus left, date below **Rev:** Denomination within wreath

Date	Mintage	VF20	XF40	MS60	MS63	MS65
1984 Mo	10,000,000	0.50	0.75	1.25	2.00	2.50
1984 Mo	—	PF65 125				
1985 Mo	20,000,000	0.50	0.75	1.25	2.00	2.50
1985 Mo	—	PF65 200				

KM# 156 COLON

6.00 g., Stainless Steel, 25 mm. **Obv:** Head of Christopher Columbus left, date below **Rev:** Denomination within wreath

Date	Mintage	VF20	XF40	MS60	MS63	MS65
1988 (h)	30,000,000	0.40	0.75	1.00	1.25	2.00
1988 (h)	—	PF65 50.00				
1999 (i)	—	0.40	0.75	1.00	1.25	2.00

KM# 156a COLON

6.00 g., Copper-Nickel Clad Steel, 25 mm. **Obv:** Head of Christopher Columbus left **Rev:** Denomination within wreath **Note:** Medal rotation.

Date	Mintage	VF20	XF40	MS60	MS63	MS65
1991 (h)	—	0.40	0.75	1.00	1.25	2.00

KM# 156b COLON

6.00 g., Nickel Clad Steel, 25 mm. **Obv:** Head of Christopher Columbus left **Rev:** Denomination within wreath **Note:** Medal rotation.

Date	Mintage	VF20	XF40	MS60	MS63	MS65
1993 (a)	—	0.40	0.75	1.00	1.25	2.00
1994 (g)	—	0.40	0.75	1.00	1.25	2.00
1995 (h)	—	0.40	0.75	1.00	1.25	2.00
1998	—	0.40	0.75	1.00	1.25	2.00
1999	—	0.40	0.75	1.00	1.25	2.00

KM# 142 5 COLONES

11.50 g., 0.999 Silver 0.3694 oz. ASW **Subject:** 150th Anniversary of Independence **Obv:** Flags flank triangular arms within wreath, date below **Rev:** Liberty statue, Cañas bust at right, dates at left, denomination below

Date	Mintage	F12	VF20	XF40	MS60	MS63
1971	18,000	PF60 10.00	PF63 14.00	PF65 16.00		

KM# 162 5 COLONES
7.50 g., Bi-Metallic Bronze Plated Steel center in Nickel-plated Steel ring, 26 mm. **Obv:** Columbus' ships sailing west on world map within circle, date below **Rev:** Denomination within circle, wreath surrounds **Edge:** Segmented reeding **Note:** Viridian mint. Not released for circulation.

Date	Mintage	VF20	XF40	MS60	MS63	MS65
1997	—	—	—	—	—	—

KM# 163 5 COLONES
7.50 g., Bi-Metallic, 25.9 mm. **Obv:** Y2K motif **Rev:** Denomination **Note:** Not released for circulation.

Date	Mintage	VF20	XF40	MS60	MS63	MS65
2000	—	—	—	—	1,500	—

KM# 132 20 COLONES
16.71 g., 0.900 Gold 0.4835 oz. AGW, 27 mm. **Subject:** 400th Anniversary - San Salvador **Obv:** Flags flank triangular arms within wreath, denomination below **Rev:** Alvarado and Quinonez busts left, dates above

Date	Mintage	VF20	XF40	MS60	MS63	MS65
ND-1925 Mo	200	950	1,650	2,750	4,000	5,500

KM# 143 25 COLONES
2.94 g., 0.900 Gold 0.0851 oz. AGW **Subject:** 150th Anniversary of Independence **Obv:** Flags flank triangular arms within wreath **Rev:** Salvador Dali image, "La Fecundida" within circle, denomination below

Date	Mintage	F12	VF20	XF40	MS60	MS63
1971	7,650	PF65 175				

KM# 151 25 COLONES
25.00 g., 0.900 Silver 0.7234 oz. ASW **Subject:** 18th Annual Governors' Assembly **Obv:** Flags flank triangular arms within wreath, denomination below **Rev:** First coin of C.A. Federation 1874, date below **Note:** Medal rotation.

Date	Mintage	VF20	XF40	MS60	MS63	MS65
1977	2,000	—	—	20.00	25.00	35.00
1977	20,000	PF65 22.00	PF67 30.00			

KM# 144 50 COLONES
5.90 g., 0.900 Gold 0.1707 oz. AGW **Subject:** 150th Anniversary of Independence **Obv:** Flags flank triangular arms within wreath **Rev:** Liberty statue, Cañas bust at right, dates at left, denomination below

Date	Mintage	F12	VF20	XF40	MS60	MS63
1971	3,530	PF65 325				

KM# 145 100 COLONES
11.80 g., 0.900 Gold 0.3414 oz. AGW **Subject:** 150th Anniversary of Independence **Obv:** Flags flank triangular arms within wreath **Rev:** Map of El Salvador, denomination below

Date	Mintage	F12	VF20	XF40	MS60	MS63
1971	2,750	PF65 625				

KM# 158 150 COLONES
25.00 g., 0.900 Silver 0.7234 oz. ASW, 37 mm. **Subject:** Union for Peace **Obv:** Four clasped hands, date below **Rev:** Denomination within wreath **Edge:** Lettered

Date	Mintage	VF20	XF40	MS60	MS63	MS65
1992	—	—	—	20.00	25.00	35.00

KM# 160 150 COLONES
25.00 g., 0.900 Silver 0.7234 oz. ASW, 37 mm. **Subject:** Discovery of America **Obv:** Columbus' ships and world map, date below **Rev:** Denomination within wreath **Edge:** Lettered

Date	Mintage	VF20	XF40	MS60	MS63	MS65
1992	—	—	—	20.00	25.00	35.00

KM# 146 200 COLONES
23.60 g., 0.900 Gold 0.6829 oz. AGW **Subject:** 150th Anniversary of Independence **Obv:** Flags flank triangular arms within wreath, bust at right, date below **Rev:** Panchimalco Church, denomination below

Date	Mintage	F12	VF20	XF40	MS60	MS63
1971	2,245	PF65 1,250				

KM# 152 250 COLONES
16.00 g., 0.917 Gold 0.4717 oz. AGW **Subject:** 18th Annual Governors' Assembly **Obv:** Flags flank triangular arms within wreath, denomination below **Rev:** First coin of C.A. Federation 1824, dates below

Date	Mintage	VF20	XF40	MS60	MS63	MS65
1977	4,000	—	—	—	825	850
1977	400	PF65 950	PF67 1,000			

KM# 159 2500 COLONES
16.00 g., 0.917 Gold 0.4717 oz. AGW **Subject:** Union for Peace **Obv:** Four clasped hands, date below **Rev:** Denomination within wreath

Date	Mintage	VF20	XF40	MS60	MS63	MS65
1992	—	—	—	—	—	825
1992	—	PF65 900	PF67 950			

KM# 161 2500 COLONES
16.00 g., 0.917 Gold 0.4717 oz. AGW **Subject:** Discovery of America **Obv:** Columbus' ships and world map, date below **Rev:** Denomination within wreath

Date	Mintage	VF20	XF40	MS60	MS63	MS65
1992	—	—	—	—	—	825
1992	—	PF65 900	PF67 950			

PATTERNS

Including off metal strikes

KM#	Date	Mintage	Identification	Mkt Val
Pn51	1996 (1997)	—	5 Colones. Nickel Plated Steel. Columbus' ships and world map, date below. Denomination within wreath. Prev.KM#Pn15..	450

PROOF SETS

KM#	Date	Mintage	Identification	Issue Price	Mkt Val
PS3	1914 (4)	—	KM#115.2, 124-126	—	6,500
PS4	1971 (6)	—	KM#141-146	—	2,450
PS5	1971 (4)	—	KM#143-146	250	2,400
PS6	1971 (2)	—	KM#141-142	6.00	18.00
PS7	1974 (3)	2,000	KM#134, 147-148	—	100
PS8	1975 (2)	2,000	KM#149.1, 150	—	70.00
PS9	1987-88 (5)	—	KM#A154, 154-157	—	250

EQUATORIAL AFRICAN STATES

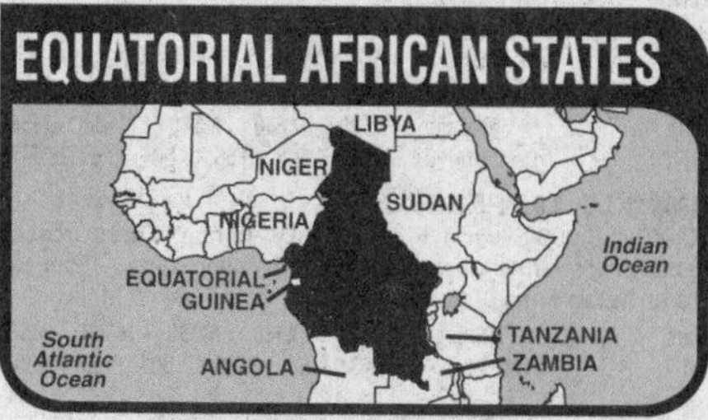

For historical background, see the introduction to Central African States.

CURRENCY UNION

DECIMAL COINAGE

100 Centimes = 1 Franc

KM# 6 FRANC
Aluminum **Obv:** Three giant eland left, date below **Rev:** Denomination within wreath

Date	Mintage	VF20	XF40	MS60	MS63	MS65
1969 (a)	2,500,000	0.35	0.65	1.00	2.25	4.00
1971 (a)	3,000,000	0.35	0.65	1.00	2.25	4.00

KM# 1 5 FRANCS
Aluminum-Bronze **Obv:** Three giant eland left **Rev:** Denomination within wreath

Date	Mintage	VF20	XF40	MS60	MS63	MS65
1961 (a)	10,000,000	0.50	1.00	1.50	2.50	4.00
1962 (a)	5,000,000	0.50	1.00	1.50	2.50	4.00

KM# 1a 5 FRANCS
Aluminum-Nickel-Bronze **Obv:** Three giant eland left, date below **Rev:** Denomination within wreath

Date	Mintage	VF20	XF40	MS60	MS63	MS65
1965 (a)	7,000,000	0.50	1.00	1.50	3.00	5.00
1967 (a)	4,000,000	0.50	1.00	1.25	2.50	4.00
1968 (a)	5,000,000	0.50	1.00	1.25	2.50	4.00
1970 (a)	9,000,000	0.50	1.00	1.25	2.50	4.00
1972 (a)	5,000,000	0.50	1.00	1.25	2.50	4.00
1973 (a)	5,010,000	0.50	1.00	1.25	2.50	4.00

KM# 2 10 FRANCS
Aluminum-Bronze **Obv:** Three giant eland left **Rev:** Denomination within wreath

Date	Mintage	VF20	XF40	MS60	MS63	MS65
1961 (a)	10,000,000	0.50	1.00	1.75	3.00	4.50
1962 (a)	5,000,000	0.50	1.00	1.75	3.00	4.50

KM# 2a 10 FRANCS
Aluminum-Nickel-Bronze **Obv:** Three giant eland left, date below **Rev:** Denomination within wreath

Date	Mintage	VF20	XF40	MS60	MS63	MS65
1965 (a)	7,000,000	1.00	1.75	2.75	5.00	8.00
1967 (a)	10,000,000	0.50	1.00	1.75	3.00	5.00
1968 (a)	2,000,000	1.50	2.25	3.50	6.00	10.00
1969 (a)	10,000,000	0.50	1.00	1.75	3.00	5.00
1972 (a)	5,000,000	0.50	1.00	1.75	3.00	5.00
1973 (a)	5,000,000	0.75	1.50	2.50	4.50	7.00

KM# 4 25 FRANCS
Aluminum-Bronze **Obv:** Three giant eland left, date below **Rev:** Denomination within wreath

Date	Mintage	VF20	XF40	MS60	MS63	MS65
1962 (a)	6,000,000	0.60	1.25	2.25	4.00	7.00

KM# 4a 25 FRANCS
Aluminum-Nickel-Bronze **Obv:** Three giant eland left, date below **Rev:** Denomination, within wreath

Date	Mintage	VF20	XF40	MS60	MS63	MS65
1970 (a)	3,019,000	0.60	1.25	2.25	4.00	7.00
1972 (a)	5,000,000	0.60	1.25	2.00	3.00	6.00

KM# 3 50 FRANCS
12.00 g., Copper-Nickel, 31 mm. **Obv:** Three giant eland left, date below **Rev:** Denomination within wreath

Date	Mintage	VF20	XF40	MS60	MS63	MS65
1961 (a)	5,000,000	2.00	4.00	6.00	12.00	20.00
1963 (a)	5,000,000	2.00	4.00	6.00	12.00	20.00

KM# 5 100 FRANCS
11.71 g., Nickel, 25.2 mm. **Obv:** Three giant eland left **Rev:** Denomination, date above **Note:** KM#5 was issued double thick and should not be considered a piefort.

Date	Mintage	VF20	XF40	MS60	MS63	MS65
1966 (a)	6,000,000	2.00	4.00	7.00	15.00	30.00
1967 (a)	5,800,000	2.00	4.00	7.00	15.00	30.00
1968 (a)	6,200,000	2.00	4.00	7.00	15.00	30.00

ESSAIS

Standard metals unless otherwise noted

KM#	Date	Mintage	Identification	Mkt Val
E1	1961(a)	—	5 Francs. KM#1.	20.00
E2	1961(a)	—	10 Francs. KM#2.	25.00
E3	1961(a)	—	50 Francs. Three Giant Eland, left, date below. Denomination within wreath. KM#3.	120
E4	1961(a)	—	50 Francs. Gold. KM#4.	1,750
E5	1962(a)	—	25 Francs. KM#4. This is a mule, having an old reverse die with a wing privy mark.	185
E6	1966(a)	—	100 Francs. KM#5.	55.00
E7	1969(a)	—	Franc. KM#6.	25.00

PIEDFORT

KM#	Date	Mintage	Identification	Mkt Val
P1	1965(a)	—	100 Francs. Gold. Three Giant Eland, left. Denomination, date above. KM#5. With ESSAI.	2,475

EQUATORIAL GUINEA

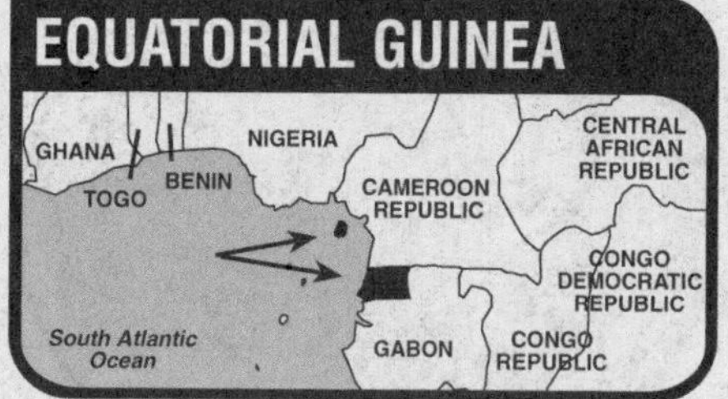

The Republic of Equatorial Guinea (formerly Spanish Guinea) consists of Rio Muni, located on the coast of West-Central Africa between Cameroon and Gabon, and the off-shore islands of Fernando Po, Annobon, Corisco, Elobey Grande and Elobey Chico. The equatorial country has an area of 10,831 sq. mi. (28,050 sq. km.) and a population of 420,293. Capital: Malabo. The economy is based on agriculture and forestry. Cacao, wood and coffee are exported.

Fernando Po was discovered between 1474 and 1496 by Portuguese navigators charting a route to the spice islands of the Far East. Portugal retained control of it and the adjacent islands until 1778 when they, together with trading rights to the African coast between the Ogooue and Niger Rivers, were ceded to Spain. Fernando Po was administered, with Spanish consent, by the British from 1827 to 1844 when it was reclaimed by Spain. Mainland Rio Muni was granted to Spain by the Berlin Conference of 1885. The name of the colony was changed from Spanish Guinea to Equatorial Guinea in Dec. of 1963. Independence was attained on Oct. 12, 1968.

Equatorial Guinea converted to the CFA currency system as issued for the Central African States issuing its first 100 Franc denomination in 1985.

NOTE: The 1969 coinage carries the actual minting date in the stars at the sides of the large date.

MINT MARK
(a) - Paris, privy marks only

REPUBLIC

PESETA COINAGE

KM# 1 PESETA
3.42 g., Aluminum-Bronze, 19.5 mm. **Edge:** Reeded

Date	Mintage	VF20	XF40	MS60	MS63	MS65
1969(69)	—	0.35	0.75	1.25	2.50	—

KM# 2 5 PESETAS
4.90 g., Copper-Nickel, 22 mm. **Edge:** Reeded

Date	Mintage	VF20	XF40	MS60	MS63	MS65
1969(69)	—	0.75	1.50	2.50	8.00	—

KM# 3 25 PESETAS
Copper-Nickel, 24 mm. **Obv:** Crossed tusks, date below **Rev:** Denomination at left, shielded arms at right, stars above arms

Date	Mintage	VF20	XF40	MS60	MS63	MS65
1969(69)	—	1.50	2.50	6.50	12.00	—

KM# 5 25 PESETAS
5.00 g., 0.999 Silver 0.1606 oz. ASW **Subject:** World Bank **Obv:** Crossed tusks divide arms above and denomination below **Rev:** Banner crosses globe

Date	Mintage	VF20	XF40	MS60	MS63	MS65
1970	2,475	PF63 15.00	PF65 22.00	PF67 25.00		

KM# 6 25 PESETAS
5.00 g., 0.999 Silver 0.1606 oz. ASW **Subject:** United Nations **Obv:** Crossed tusks divide arms above and denomination below **Rev:** UN logo

Date	Mintage	VF20	XF40	MS60	MS63	MS65
1970	2,475	PF63 15.00	PF65 22.00	PF67 25.00		

KM# 4 50 PESETAS
Copper-Nickel **Obv:** Head right, date below **Rev:** Denomination at left, arms at right

Date	Mintage	VF20	XF40	MS60	MS63	MS65
1969(69)	—	2.00	3.00	7.50	16.50	—

KM# 7 50 PESETAS
10.00 g., 0.999 Silver 0.3212 oz. ASW **Obv:** Crossed tusks divide arms above and denomination below **Rev:** Durer's Praying Hands

Date	Mintage	VF20	XF40	MS60	MS63	MS65
1970	3,840	PF63 15.00	PF65 20.00	PF67 22.00		

KM# 8 75 PESETAS
15.00 g., 0.999 Silver 0.4818 oz. ASW **Obv:** Crossed tusks divide arms above and denomination below **Rev:** Pope John XXIII bust left

Date	Mintage	VF20	XF40	MS60	MS63	MS65
1970	4,000	PF63 20.00	PF65 30.00	PF67 35.00		

KM# 9.1 75 PESETAS
15.00 g., 0.999 Silver 0.4818 oz. ASW **Subject:** Centennial - Birth of Vladimir Ilyich Lenin **Obv:** Crossed tusks divide arms above and denomination below, fineness stamp in field behind denomination **Rev:** Head left divides dates **Note:** Prev. KM#9.

Date	Mintage	VF20	XF40	MS60	MS63	MS65
1970	4,000	PF63 25.00	PF65 35.00	PF67 40.00		

KM# 9.2 75 PESETAS
15.14 g., 1.000 Silver 0.4868 oz. ASW, 35.8 mm. **Subject:** Centennial of Lenin's birth **Obv:** Crossed tusks divide arms above and denomination below, fineness stamp at truncation of left tusk **Rev:** Head left divides dates

Date	Mintage	VF20	XF40	MS60	MS63	MS65
1970	—	PF63 12.00	PF65 15.00	PF67 18.00		

KM# 10.1 75 PESETAS
15.00 g., 0.999 Silver 0.4818 oz. ASW **Subject:** Abraham Lincoln **Obv:** Crossed tusks divide arms above and denomination below, hallmark "1000" in oval at left tusk base **Rev:** Bust facing divides dates

Date	Mintage	VF20	XF40	MS60	MS63	MS65
1970	—	PF63 38.00	PF65 45.00	PF67 50.00		

KM# 10.2 75 PESETAS
15.00 g., 0.999 Silver 0.4818 oz. ASW **Obv:** "1 AR" Hallmark above "E" in "Pesetas"

Date	Mintage	VF20	XF40	MS60	MS63	MS65
1970	—	PF63 15.00	PF65 20.00	PF67 22.00		

KM# 11 75 PESETAS
15.00 g., 0.999 Silver 0.4818 oz. ASW **Subject:** Centennial - Birth of Mahatma Gandhi **Obv:** Crossed tusks divide arms above and denomination below **Rev:** Bust looking right divides dates

Date	Mintage	VF20	XF40	MS60	MS63	MS65
1970	4,000	PF63 35.00	PF65 50.00	PF67 55.00		

KM# 12.1 100 PESETAS
20.00 g., 0.999 Silver 0.6424 oz. ASW, 40 mm. **Obv:** Crossed tusk divide arms above and denomination below **Rev:** Durer's Praying Hands

Date	Mintage	VF20	XF40	MS60	MS63	MS65
1970	—	PF63 17.50	PF65 20.50	PF67 23.50		

KM# 12.2 100 PESETAS
20.00 g., 0.999 Silver 0.6424 oz. ASW, 40 mm. **Obv:** Crossed tusks divide arms above and denomination below, "1 AR" hallmark **Rev:** Durer's Praying Hands

Date	Mintage	VF20	XF40	MS60	MS63	MS65
1970	—	PF63 17.50	PF65 20.50	PF67 23.50		

KM# 13.1 100 PESETAS
20.00 g., 0.999 Silver 0.6424 oz. ASW, 40 mm. **Obv:** Crossed tusks divide arms above and denomination below **Rev:** Goya's Naked Maja

Date	Mintage	VF20	XF40	MS60	MS63	MS65
1970	30,000	PF63 17.50	PF65 22.50	PF67 25.50		

KM# 13.2 100 PESETAS
20.00 g., 0.999 Silver 0.6424 oz. ASW, 40 mm. **Obv:** Crossed tusks divide arms above and denomination below, fineness stamp at base of right tusk **Rev:** Goya's Naked Maja

Date	Mintage	VF20	XF40	MS60	MS63	MS65
1970	Inc. above	PF63 17.50	PF65 22.50	PF67 25.50		

KM# 13.3 100 PESETAS
20.00 g., 0.999 Silver 0.6424 oz. ASW, 40 mm. **Obv:** Crossed tusks divide arms above and denomination below, fineness stamp below base of right tusk **Rev:** Goya's Naked Maja

Date	Mintage	VF20	XF40	MS60	MS63	MS65
1970	Inc. above	PF63 17.50	PF65 22.50	PF67 25.50		

KM# 13.4 100 PESETAS
20.00 g., 0.999 Silver 0.6424 oz. ASW, 40 mm. **Obv:** Crossed tusks divide arms above and denomination below, fineness stamp above letters AN **Rev:** Goya's Naked Maja

Date	Mintage	VF20	XF40	MS60	MS63	MS65
1970	Inc. above	PF63 17.50	PF65 22.50	PF67 25.50		

KM# 13.5 100 PESETAS
20.00 g., 0.999 Silver 0.6424 oz. ASW, 40 mm. **Obv:** Crossed tusks divide arms above and denomination below, 1000 in oval at base of right tusk **Rev:** Goya's Naked Maja

Date	Mintage	VF20	XF40	MS60	MS63	MS65
1970	Inc. above	PF63 17.50	PF65 22.50	PF67 25.50		

KM# 14 150 PESETAS
30.00 g., 0.999 Silver 0.9636 oz. ASW, 45 mm. **Subject:** Centennial of the Capital Rome **Obv:** Crossed tusks divide arms above and denomination below **Rev:** Symbols of Rome, dates at left

Date	Mintage	VF20	XF40	MS60	MS63	MS65
1970	3,520	PF63 35.00	PF65 55.00	PF67 75.00		

KM# 15 150 PESETAS
30.00 g., 0.999 Silver 0.9636 oz. ASW, 45 mm. **Subject:** Centennial of the Capital Rome **Obv:** Crossed tusks divide arms above and denomination below **Rev:** Coliseum

Date	Mintage	VF20	XF40	MS60	MS63	MS65
1970	3,520	PF63 35.00	PF65 55.00	PF67 75.00		

KM# 16 150 PESETAS
30.00 g., 0.999 Silver 0.9636 oz. ASW, 45 mm. **Subject:** Centennial of the Capital Rome **Obv:** Crossed tusks divide arms above and denomination below **Rev:** Athena divides dates and buildings

Date	Mintage	VF20	XF40	MS60	MS63	MS65
1970	3,520	PF63 35.00	PF65 55.00	PF67 75.00		

KM# 17 150 PESETAS
30.00 g., 0.999 Silver 0.9636 oz. ASW, 45 mm. **Subject:** Centennial of the Capital Rome **Obv:** Crossed tusks divide arms above and denomination below **Rev:** Mercury left, dates lower left

Date	Mintage	VF20	XF40	MS60	MS63	MS65
1970	3,520	PF63 40.00	PF65 60.00	PF67 80.00		

KM# 18.1 200 PESETAS
40.00 g., 0.999 Silver 1.2847 oz. ASW, 52 mm. **Subject:** World Soccer Championship in Mexico **Obv:** Crossed tusks divide arms above and denomination below **Rev:** Statue flanked by countries with dates, four on each side

Date	Mintage	VF20	XF40	MS60	MS63	MS65
1970	—	PF63 50.00	PF65 70.00	PF67 90.00		

KM# 18.2 200 PESETAS
40.00 g., 0.999 Silver 1.2847 oz. ASW, 52 mm. **Subject:** World Soccer Championship in Mexico **Obv:** Fineness stamp in oval at base of right tusk; mint mark stamp "1 AR" at base of left tusk; incuse serial number below denomination **Rev:** Statue flanked by countries with dates, four on each side

Date	Mintage	VF20	XF40	MS60	MS63	MS65
1970	—	PF63 60.00	PF65 80.00	PF67 100		

KM# 19 200 PESETAS
40.00 g., 0.999 Silver 1.2847 oz. ASW, 52 mm. **Subject:** First President Francisco Macias **Obv:** Crossed tusks divide arms above and denomination below **Rev:** Head 3/4 right

Date	Mintage	VF20	XF40	MS60	MS63	MS65
1970	4,000	PF63 45.00	PF65 65.00	PF67 85.00		

KM# 20.1 250 PESETAS
3.52 g., 0.900 Gold 0.1019 oz. AGW **Obv:** Crossed tusks divide arms above and denomination below, fineness countermark at 8 o'clock by tusk base **Rev:** Goya's Naked Maja **Note:** Prev. KM#20.

Date	Mintage	VF20	XF40	MS60	MS63	MS65
1970	3,500	PF63 150	PF65 180	PF67 200		

KM# 20.2 250 PESETAS
3.52 g., 0.900 Gold 0.1019 oz. AGW **Obv:** Crossed tusks divide arms above and denomination below, fineness countermark at 4 o'clock by tusk base **Rev:** Goya's Naked Maja

Date	Mintage	VF20	XF40	MS60	MS63	MS65
1970	—	PF63 150	PF65 180	PF67 200		

KM# 21 250 PESETAS
3.52 g., 0.900 Gold 0.1019 oz. AGW **Obv:** Crossed tusks divide arms above and denomination below **Rev:** Durer's Praying Hands

Date	Mintage	VF20	XF40	MS60	MS63	MS65
1970	2,000	PF63 150	PF65 180	PF67 200		

KM# 22 500 PESETAS
7.05 g., 0.900 Gold 0.204 oz. AGW **Obv:** Crossed tusks divide arms above and denomination below **Rev:** Bust of Pope John XXIII

Date	Mintage	VF20	XF40	MS60	MS63	MS65
1970	1,680	PF63 325	PF65 350	PF67 375		

KM# 23 500 PESETAS
7.05 g., 0.900 Gold 0.204 oz. AGW **Subject:** Vladimer Illyich Lenin **Obv:** Crossed tusks divide arms above and denomination below **Rev:** Head left divides dates

Date	Mintage	VF20	XF40	MS60	MS63	MS65
1970	1,680	PF63 325	PF65 350	PF67 375		

KM# 24 500 PESETAS
7.05 g., 0.900 Gold 0.204 oz. AGW **Obv:** Crossed tusks divide arms above and denomination below **Rev:** President Abraham Lincoln

Date	Mintage	VF20	XF40	MS60	MS63	MS65
1970	1,700	PF63 325	PF65 350	PF67 375		

KM# 25 500 PESETAS
7.05 g., 0.900 Gold 0.204 oz. AGW **Subject:** Centennial - Birth of Mahatma Gandhi **Obv:** Crossed tusks divide arms above and denomination below **Rev:** Portrait of Gandhi

Date	Mintage	VF20	XF40	MS60	MS63	MS65
1970	1,680	PF63 325	PF65 350	PF67 375		

KM# 26 750 PESETAS
10.57 g., 0.900 Gold 0.3058 oz. AGW **Subject:** Centennial of the Capital Rome **Obv:** Crossed tusks divide arms above and denomination below **Rev:** Symbols of Rome

Date	Mintage	VF20	XF40	MS60	MS63	MS65
1970	1,650	PF63 450	PF65 500	PF67 550		

KM# 27 750 PESETAS
10.57 g., 0.900 Gold 0.3058 oz. AGW **Subject:** Centennial of the Capital Rome **Obv:** Crossed tusks divide arms above and denomination below **Rev:** Coliseum

Date	Mintage	VF20	XF40	MS60	MS63	MS65
1970	1,550	PF63 450	PF65 500	PF67 550		

KM# 28 750 PESETAS
10.57 g., 0.900 Gold 0.3058 oz. AGW **Subject:** Centennial of the Capital Rome **Obv:** Crossed tusks divide arms above and denomination below **Rev:** Athena divides dates and buildings

Date	Mintage	VF20	XF40	MS60	MS63	MS65
1970	1,550	PF63 450	PF65 500	PF67 550		

KM# 29 750 PESETAS
10.57 g., 0.900 Gold 0.3058 oz. AGW **Subject:** Centennial of the Capital Rome **Obv:** Crossed tusks divide arms above and denomination below **Rev:** Head of Mercury left

Date	Mintage	VF20	XF40	MS60	MS63	MS65
1970	1,550	PF63 450	PF65 500	PF67 550		

KM# 30 1000 PESETAS
14.10 g., 0.900 Gold 0.408 oz. AGW **Subject:** World Soccer Championship in Mexico **Obv:** Crossed tusks divide arms above and denomination below **Rev:** Statue flanked by countries with dates, four on each side

Date	Mintage	VF20	XF40	MS60	MS63	MS65
1970	1,190	PF63 625	PF65 675	PF67 750		

KM# 31 5000 PESETAS
70.52 g., 0.900 Gold 2.0405 oz. AGW **Subject:** First President - Francisco Macias **Obv:** Crossed tusks divide arms above and denomination below **Rev:** Head 3/4 right

Date	Mintage	VF20	XF40	MS60	MS63	MS65
1970	330	PF63 3,350	PF65 3,550	PF67 3,750		

REFORM COINAGE

1975-1980

KM# 32 EKUELE
Brass **Obv:** Head left, date below **Rev:** Assorted tools divide denomination **Note:** Withdrawn from circulation.

Date	Mintage	VF20	XF40	MS60	MS63	MS65
1975	3,000,000	0.50	1.00	1.50	3.00	5.00

KM# 33 5 EKUELE
Copper-Nickel **Obv:** Head left, date below **Rev:** Figures on split shields divide denomination **Note:** Withdrawn from circulation.

Date	Mintage	VF20	XF40	MS60	MS63	MS65
1975	2,800,000	0.50	1.00	1.50	3.00	5.00

KM# 34 10 EKUELE
Copper-Nickel **Obv:** Head left, date below **Rev:** Rooster within shield divides denomination **Note:** Withdrawn from circulation.

Date	Mintage	VF20	XF40	MS60	MS63	MS65
1975	1,300,000	0.75	1.50	2.00	4.00	7.00

KM# 35 1000 EKUELE
21.43 g., 0.925 Silver 0.6373 oz. ASW **Obv:** Bank building, denomination below **Rev:** Head right, date below

Date	Mintage	VF20	XF40	MS60	MS63	MS65
1978	31,000	PF63 25.00	PF65 35.00	PF67 45.00		

KM# 36 2000 EKUELE
42.87 g., 0.925 Silver 1.2749 oz. ASW **Obv:** Assorted tools, denomination below, rooster above **Rev:** President Masie Nguema Biyogo head, right, date below

Date	Mintage	VF20	XF40	MS60	MS63	MS65
1978	31,000	PF63 40.00	PF65 50.00	PF67 60.00		

KM# 37 2000 EKUELE
31.10 g., 0.927 Silver 0.9269 oz. ASW **Subject:** XXII Olympics **Rev:** Discus thrower, building at left, Olympic logo at right

Date	Mintage	VF20	XF40	MS60	MS63	MS65
ND-1979	11,000	PF63 25.00	PF65 30.00	PF67 35.00		

KM# 38 2000 EKUELE
42.87 g., 0.925 Silver 1.2749 oz. ASW **Subject:** Soccer Games - Argentina 1978

Date	Mintage	VF20	XF40	MS60	MS63	MS65
ND-1979	195	PF63 125	PF65 150	PF67 185		

KM# 55 2000 EKUELE
31.00 g., 0.927 Silver 0.9239 oz. ASW **Rev:** Burchell's zebra

Date	Mintage	VF20	XF40	MS60	MS63	MS65
1980 (1983)	EST. 1000	PF63 25.00	PF65 35.00	PF67 45.00		

KM# 56 2000 EKUELE
31.00 g., 0.927 Silver 0.9239 oz. ASW **Rev:** Impalas

Date	Mintage	VF20	XF40	MS60	MS63	MS65
1980 (1983)	EST. 1000	PF63 25.00	PF65 35.00	PF67 45.00		

KM# 57 2000 EKUELE
31.00 g., 0.927 Silver 0.9239 oz. ASW **Obv:** Bank building, denomination below **Rev:** Tiger's head 3/4 left, date below

Date	Mintage	VF20	XF40	MS60	MS63	MS65
1980 (1983)	EST. 1000	PF63 27.00	PF65 37.50	PF67 50.00		

KM# 58 2000 EKUELE
31.00 g., 0.927 Silver 0.9239 oz. ASW **Rev:** Cheetah running left, date below

Date	Mintage	VF20	XF40	MS60	MS63	MS65
1980 (1983)	EST. 1000	PF63 27.00	PF65 37.50	PF67 50.00		

KM# 39 5000 EKUELE
6.96 g., 0.917 Gold 0.2052 oz. AGW **Obv:** Bank building, denomination below **Rev:** Head right, date below

Date	Mintage	VF20	XF40	MS60	MS63	MS65
1978	31,000	PF63 300	PF65 350	PF67 400		

KM# 40 10000 EKUELE
13.92 g., 0.917 Gold 0.4104 oz. AGW **Obv:** Assorted tools, denomination below, rooster above **Rev:** Head right, date below

Date	Mintage	VF20	XF40	MS60	MS63	MS65
1978	31,000	PF63 625	PF65 675	PF67 725		

KM# 41 10000 EKUELE
13.92 g., 0.917 Gold 0.4104 oz. AGW **Subject:** Soccer Games - Argentina 1978 **Obv:** Assorted tools, denomination below, rooster above **Rev:** Country name and map at center, soccer players flank, shields above and below

Date	Mintage	VF20	XF40	MS60	MS63	MS65
ND-1979	121	PF63 725	PF65 775	PF67 850		

KM# 153 1000 BIPKWELE
0.925 Silver, 39 mm. **Obv:** Arms, denomination below **Rev:** Bust of President Obiang

Date	Mintage	VF20	XF40	MS60	MS63	MS65
1979	—	PF63 35.00	PF65 45.00	PF67 55.00		

KM# 154 1000 BIPKWELE
0.925 Silver, 39 mm. **Obv:** Arms, denomination below **Rev:** Juan Carlos I head left

Date	Mintage	VF20	XF40	MS60	MS63	MS65
1979	—	PF63 35.00		PF65 45.00		PF67 55.00

REFORM COINAGE

1980-1982

KM# 50 EKUELE
Aluminum-Bronze **Obv:** T. E. Nkogo head right, date below **Rev:** Denomination at left, shielded arms at right, stars above arms **Note:** Two digit incuse date within star to left of date on obverse

Date	Mintage	VF20	XF40	MS60	MS63	MS65
1980(80)	Est. 200000	—	—	15.00	35.00	70.00

KM# 54 EKUELE
62.29 g., 0.999 Gold 2.0007 oz. AGW **Obv:** Coat of arms **Rev:** Pope John Paul II

Date	Mintage	VF20	XF40	MS60	MS63	MS65
1982	—	—	—	—	3,750	—

KM# 51 5 BIPKWELE
Copper-Nickel **Obv:** T. E. Nkogo right **Rev:** Value and arms **Edge:** Reeded **Note:** The date is on the stars flanking the date. (19) to the left and (80) to the right.

Date	Mintage	VF20	XF40	MS60	MS63	MS65
1980(80)	Est. 200000	—	35.00	75.00	120	—

KM# 52 25 BIPKWELE
6.38 g., Copper-Nickel **Obv:** T. E. Nkogo head right, date below **Rev;** Denomination at left, arms at right **Note:** Two digit incuse date within star to left of date on obverse

Date	Mintage	VF20	XF40	MS60	MS63	MS65
1980(80)	Est. 200000	—	5.00	15.00	35.00	50.00
1981	—	—	—	—	—	—

KM# 53 50 BIPKWELE
Copper-Nickel **Obv:** T. E. Nkogo right **Rev:** Value and arms **Note:** Two digit incuse date within star to left of date on obverse

Date	Mintage	VF20	XF40	MS60	MS63	MS65
1980(80)	Est. 200000	—	5.00	15.00	40.00	60.00
1981	Est. 500000	—	—	—	—	—

REFORM COINAGE

1985

KM# 62 5 FRANCOS
Aluminum-Bronze **Obv:** Three Giant Eland left **Rev:** Denomination above date

Date	Mintage	VF20	XF40	MS60	MS63	MS65
1985 (a)	—	—	1.50	3.00	5.00	7.00

KM# 60 25 FRANCOS
Aluminum-Bronze **Obv:** Three Giant Eland left **Rev:** Denomination above date

Date	Mintage	VF20	XF40	MS60	MS63	MS65
1985 (a)	—	—	2.00	5.00	10.00	15.00

KM# 64 50 FRANCOS
4.70 g., Nickel, 21.5 mm. **Obv:** Three Giant Eland left **Rev:** Denomination above date

Date	Mintage	VF20	XF40	MS60	MS63	MS65
1985 (a)	—	—	4.00	7.00	12.00	20.00
1986 (a)	—	—	3.00	5.00	10.00	15.00

KM# 59 100 FRANCOS
7.00 g., Nickel, 25.5 mm. **Obv:** Three Giant Eland left **Rev:** Denomination above date

Date	Mintage	VF20	XF40	MS60	MS63	MS65
1985 (a)	—	—	7.00	12.00	20.00	35.00
1986 (a)	—	—	5.00	10.00	15.00	25.00

KM# 68 1000 FRANCOS
Copper-Nickel **Obv:** Arms above denomination **Rev:** Brandenburg Gate, dates below

Date	Mintage	VF20	XF40	MS60	MS63	MS65
1991 Proof, Rare	5,150	PF65 15.00				

KM# 81 1000 FRANCOS
Copper-Nickel **Subject:** Jurassic Dinosaurs **Obv:** Arms divide date, denomination below **Rev:** Diplodocus **Note:** Multicolored.

Date	Mintage	VF20	XF40	MS60	MS63	MS65
1993	—	—	—	—	—	12.00

KM# 82 1000 FRANCOS
Copper-Nickel **Subject:** Jurassic Dinosaurs **Obv:** Arms divide date, denomination below **Rev:** Styracosaurus

Date	Mintage	VF20	XF40	MS60	MS63	MS65
1993	—	—	—	—	—	12.00

KM# 83 1000 FRANCOS
Copper-Nickel **Subject:** Jurassic Dinosaurs **Obv:** Arms divide date, denomination below **Rev:** Tyrannosaurus

Date	Mintage	VF20	XF40	MS60	MS63	MS65
1993	—	—	—	—	—	15.00

KM# 88 1000 FRANCOS
Copper-Nickel **Subject:** Jurassic Dinosaurs **Obv:** Arms divide date, denomination below **Rev:** Plateosaurus

Date	Mintage	VF20	XF40	MS60	MS63	MS65
1993	—	—	—	—	—	12.00

KM# 115 1000 FRANCOS
25.56 g., Copper-Nickel, 38 mm. **Subject:** Jurassic Dinosaurs **Obv:** Arms divide date, denomination below **Rev:** Multicolor stegosaurus **Edge:** Reeded

Date	Mintage	VF20	XF40	MS60	MS63	MS65
1993	—	—	—	—	—	12.00

KM# 130 1000 FRANCOS
Copper-Nickel-Zinc **Obv:** National arms divide date, denomination below **Rev:** Lucerne city view **Rev. Legend:** LUGARES FAMOSOS DEL MUNDO

Date	Mintage	VF20	XF40	MS60	MS63	MS65
1993	—	PF65 15.00				

KM# 131 1000 FRANCOS
Copper-Nickel **Subject:** XV World Soccer Cup - USA 1994 **Obv:** National arms **Rev:** Playing field **Rev. Inscription:** 999 CuNi

Date	Mintage	VF20	XF40	MS60	MS63	MS65
1993	—	PF65 15.00				

KM# 132 1000 FRANCOS
Copper-Nickel **Subject:** XV World Soccer Cup - USA 1994 **Obv:** National arms **Rev:** Soccer net and players **Rev. Inscription:** 999

Date	Mintage	VF20	XF40	MS60	MS63	MS65
1993	—	PF65 15.00				
1994	—	PF65 15.00				

KM# 87 1000 FRANCOS
Copper-Nickel, 39 mm. **Subject:** Jurassic Dinosaurs **Obv:** Arms divide date, denomination below **Rev:** Allosaurus in color

Date	Mintage	VF20	XF40	MS60	MS63	MS65
1994	—	—	—	—	—	12.00

KM# 89 1000 FRANCOS
Copper-Nickel **Subject:** African Bird Wildlife - Kingfisher **Obv:** Arms divide date, denomination below **Rev:** Pair of multicolored kingfishers

Date	Mintage	VF20	XF40	MS60	MS63	MS65
1994	10,000	—	—	—	—	12.00

KM# 90 1000 FRANCOS
Copper-Nickel **Subject:** FIFA - XV World Soccer Championship - USA 1994 **Obv:** National arms divide date, denomination below **Rev:** Brazilian champion soccer players with trophy

Date	Mintage	VF20	XF40	MS60	MS63	MS65
1994	—	PF65 15.00				

KM# 91 1000 FRANCOS
Copper-Nickel-Zinc **Series:** World's Famous Dogs **Obv:** Arms divide date, denomination below **Rev:** St. Bernards **Note:** Multicolored.

Date	Mintage	VF20	XF40	MS60	MS63	MS65
1994	10,000	—	—	—	—	12.00

KM# 92 1000 FRANCOS
Copper-Nickel **Subject:** 25th Anniversary - Moon Landing **Obv:** Arms divide date, denomination below **Rev:** Placing the flag

Date	Mintage	VF20	XF40	MS60	MS63	MS65
1994	15,000	—	—	—	—	12.00

KM# 93 1000 FRANCOS
Copper-Nickel-Zinc **Subject:** World's Famous Stamps **Obv:** National arms divide date, denomination below **Rev:** Swiss stamp of Jean Tinguely, multicolor

Date	Mintage	VF20	XF40	MS60	MS63	MS65
1994	15,000	—	—	—	—	12.00
1995	Inc. above	—	—	—	—	12.00

KM# 112 1000 FRANCOS
26.00 g., Copper-Nickel, 38 mm. **Obv:** Arms divide date, denomination below **Rev:** Multicolor Spanish Salvador Dali stamp design **Edge:** Reeded

Date	Mintage	VF20	XF40	MS60	MS63	MS65
1994	15,000	PF65 15.00				

KM# 136 1000 FRANCOS
Copper-Nickel-Zinc **Series:** Famous World Places **Obv:** National arms **Rev:** Ruins of the Kaiser Wilhelm Gedächtnis Church, Berlin, multicolor

Date	Mintage	VF20	XF40	MS60	MS63	MS65
1994	15,000	PF65 15.00				

KM# 138 1000 FRANCOS
Copper-Nickel **Subject:** FIFA - XV World Soccer Championship - USA 1994 **Obv:** National arms divide date, denomination below **Rev:** Brazilian champion soccer player's arms holding trophy, soccer ball outline in background

Date	Mintage	VF20	XF40	MS60	MS63	MS65
1994	—	PF65 15.00				

KM# 139 1000 FRANCOS
Copper-Nickel-Zinc **Subject:** World's Famous Dogs **Obv:** National arms **Rev:** Dalmation, multicolor

Date	Mintage	VF20	XF40	MS60	MS63	MS65
1994	—	—	—	—	—	12.00

KM# 84.1 1000 FRANCOS
Copper-Nickel **Subject:** 150th Anniversary - Basel "Taube" Stamp **Obv:** Arms divide date, denomination below **Rev:** Stamp within circle **Note:** Multicolored.

Date	Mintage	VF20	XF40	MS60	MS63	MS65
1995	15,000	—	—	—	—	12.00

KM# 84.2 1000 FRANCOS
Copper-Nickel **Subject:** 150th Anniversary - Basel "Taube" Stamp **Obv:** Arms divide date, denomination below **Rev. Legend:** Stamp within circle, error, "TAUBER" **Note:** Multicolored.

Date	Mintage	VF20	XF40	MS60	MS63	MS65
1995	Inc. above	—	—	—	—	12.00

KM# 95 1000 FRANCOS
Copper-Nickel **Subject:** Famous Places in the World - Altdorf **Obv:** Arms divide date, denomination below **Rev:** Multicolor applique of Wilhelm Tell

Date	Mintage	VF20	XF40	MS60	MS63	MS65
1996	—	PF65 15.00				

KM# 96 1000 FRANCOS
Copper-Nickel **Subject:** Famous Stamps of the World - Pintores Famosos dei Mundo - Rolf Knie **Obv:** Arms divide date, denomination below **Rev:** Multicolor applique of Swiss circus stamp design

Date	Mintage	VF20	XF40	MS60	MS63	MS65
1996	—	PF65 18.00				

KM# 97 1000 FRANCOS
Copper-Nickel **Subject:** Famous Stamps of the World - XXVI Juegos Olimpicos de Verano **Obv:** Arms divide date, denomination below **Rev:** Stamp with downhill skier

Date	Mintage	VF20	XF40	MS60	MS63	MS65
1996	—	PF65 18.00				

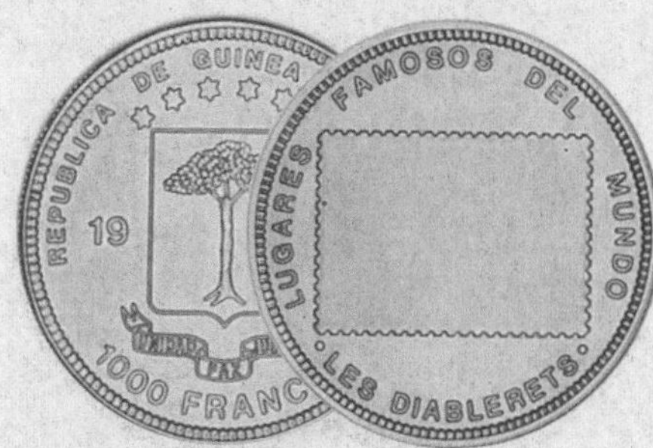

KM# 118 1000 FRANCOS
29.50 g., Copper-Nickel, 38 mm. **Subject:** Famous Places - les Diablerets **Obv:** Arms divide date, denomination below **Rev:** Multicolor stamp design **Edge:** Reeded

Date	Mintage	VF20	XF40	MS60	MS63	MS65
1996	—	PF65 18.00				

KM# 142 1000 FRANCOS
Copper-Nickel, 39 mm. **Subject:** Piz Palau **Rev:** Swiss stamp applique in center

Date	Mintage	VF20	XF40	MS60	MS63	MS65
1996	—	—	—	—	—	10.00

KM# 143 1000 FRANCOS
Copper-Nickel, 39 mm. **Subject:** Gottardo **Obv:** Arms divide date, denomination below **Rev:** Swiss stamp applique at center

Date	Mintage	VF20	XF40	MS60	MS63	MS65
1996	—	—	—	—	—	10.00

KM# 144 1000 FRANCOS
Copper-Nickel, 39 mm. **Subject:** Olympics Centennial, Athens to Atlanta **Obv:** Arms divide date, denomination below **Rev:** French Olympic stamp

Date	Mintage	VF20	XF40	MS60	MS63	MS65
1996	—	—	—	—	—	10.00

KM# 145 1000 FRANCOS
Copper-Nickel, 39 mm. **Subject:** Tokyo Olympics, 1964 **Obv:** Arms divide date, denomination below **Rev:** Japanese postage stamp

Date	Mintage	VF20	XF40	MS60	MS63	MS65
1996	—	—	—	—	—	10.00

KM# 134 3000 FRANCOS
1.55 g., 0.999 Gold 0.0498 oz. AGW **Series:** Zodiac **Subject:** Year of the Dog **Obv:** Flower blossom in sprays **Rev:** Dog standing left

Date	Mintage	VF20	XF40	MS60	MS63	MS65
1994	—	PF65 85.00				

KM# 66 7000 FRANCOS
26.30 g., 0.999 Silver 0.8447 oz. ASW **Obv:** Arms above denomination **Rev:** President Mbasogo bust above three shields

Date	Mintage	VF20	XF40	MS60	MS63	MS65
1991	—	PF65 32.00				

KM# 67 7000 FRANCOS
25.70 g., 0.999 Silver 0.8254 oz. ASW **Subject:** Soccer - Italy 1990 **Obv:** Arms above denomination **Rev:** Soccer players, small statue at left

Date	Mintage	VF20	XF40	MS60	MS63	MS65
1991	6,000	PF65 35.00				

KM# 69 7000 FRANCOS
20.00 g., 0.999 Silver 0.6424 oz. ASW **Subject:** Discovery of America **Obv:** Arms above denomination **Rev:** Santa Maria, date below

Date	Mintage	VF20	XF40	MS60	MS63	MS65
1991	15,000	PF65 25.00				

KM# 70 7000 FRANCOS
20.00 g., 0.999 Silver 0.6424 oz. ASW **Subject:** Seville Expo **Obv:** Arms above denomination **Rev:** Symbols from expo

Date	Mintage	VF20	XF40	MS60	MS63	MS65
1991	15,000	PF65 25.00				

KM# 71 7000 FRANCOS
20.00 g., 0.999 Silver 0.6424 oz. ASW **Subject:** Barcelona Olympics **Obv:** Arms above denomination **Rev:** Athletes covering Olympic rings

Date	Mintage	VF20	XF40	MS60	MS63	MS65
1991	15,000	PF65 27.50				

KM# 76 7000 FRANCOS
510.30 g., 0.999 Silver 16.3901 oz. ASW, 75.1 mm. **Subject:** Endangered Wildlife **Obv:** Arms at lower left, figures and wildlife scene **Rev:** Lions, denomination below **Note:** Illustration reduced.

Date	Mintage	VF20	XF40	MS60	MS63	MS65
1992	1,700	PF65 450				

KM# 80 7000 FRANCOS
10.48 g., 0.999 Silver 0.3366 oz. ASW **Subject:** Barcelona Olympics - 1992 **Obv:** Arms above denomination **Rev:** Katrin Krabbe, German sprinter

Date	Mintage	VF20	XF40	MS60	MS63	MS65
1992	15,000	PF65 12.00				

KM# 105 7000 FRANCOS
7.77 g., 0.900 Gold 0.2248 oz. AGW **Subject:** Endangered Wildlife **Obv:** Arms above denomination **Rev:** Lions

Date	Mintage	VF20	XF40	MS60	MS63	MS65
1992	450	PF65 400				

KM# 77 7000 FRANCOS
10.51 g., 0.999 Silver 0.3376 oz. ASW **Subject:** African Elephant Protection **Obv:** National arms divide date, denomination below **Rev:** Elephant

Date	Mintage	VF20	XF40	MS60	MS63	MS65
1993	Est. 25000	PF65 15.00				

KM# 78 7000 FRANCOS
20.00 g., 0.999 Silver 0.6424 oz. ASW **Subject:** Barcelona Olympics **Obv:** Arms divide date, denomination below **Rev:** Athletes covering Olympic rings

Date	Mintage	VF20	XF40	MS60	MS63	MS65
1993	—	PF65 35.00				

KM# 94 7000 FRANCOS
20.17 g., 0.999 Silver 0.6478 oz. ASW **Subject:** Jurassic Dinosaurs **Obv:** Arms divide date, denomination below **Rev:** Multicolor stegosaurus scene applique

Date	Mintage	VF20	XF40	MS60	MS63	MS65
1993	—	PF65 35.00				

KM# 114 7000 FRANCOS
9.93 g., 0.740 Silver 0.2362 oz. ASW, 34.8 mm. **Subject:** Endangered Wildlife **Obv:** Arms divide date, denomination below **Rev:** Giraffe family **Edge:** Reeded

Date	Mintage	VF20	XF40	MS60	MS63	MS65
1993	—	PF65 35.00				

KM# 119 7000 FRANCOS
20.00 g., 0.999 Silver 0.6424 oz. ASW **Obv:** Arms divide date, denomination below **Rev:** Zebras

Date	Mintage	VF20	XF40	MS60	MS63	MS65
1993	—	PF65 35.00				

KM# 121 7000 FRANCOS
10.51 g., 0.999 Silver 0.3376 oz. ASW, 34.9 mm. **Obv:** National armsabove denomination **Rev:** Elephant in profile, no trees or fineness statement in background **Edge:** Reeded

Date	Mintage	VF20	XF40	MS60	MS63	MS65
1993	—	PF65 40.00				

KM# 122 7000 FRANCOS
10.27 g., 0.999 Silver 0.3299 oz. ASW, 34.8 mm. **Subject:** Protection of Endangered Wildlife **Obv:** Arms divide date, denomination below **Rev:** Two gorillas **Edge:** Reeded

Date	Mintage	VF20	XF40	MS60	MS63	MS65
1993	—	PF65 40.00				

KM# 123 7000 FRANCOS
19.73 g., 0.999 Silver 0.6337 oz. ASW, 38.1 mm. **Obv:** National arms divide date, denomination below **Rev:** Lucerne city view **Rev. Legend:** LUGARES FAMOSOS DEL MUNDO **Edge:** Reeded

Date	Mintage	VF20	XF40	MS60	MS63	MS65
1993	—	PF65 30.00				

KM# 126 7000 FRANCOS
0.999 Silver, 34.8 mm. **Subject:** Endangered Wildlife **Obv:** Arms divide date, denomination below **Rev:** Rhino **Edge:** Reeded

Date	Mintage	VF20	XF40	MS60	MS63	MS65
1993	—	PF65 45.00				

KM# 127 7000 FRANCOS
0.999 Silver, 34.8 mm. **Subject:** Endangered Wildlife **Obv:** Arms divide date, denomination below **Rev:** Buffalo **Edge:** Reeded

Date	Mintage	VF20	XF40	MS60	MS63	MS65
1993	—	PF65 35.00				

KM# 128 7000 FRANCOS
0.999 Silver, 34.8 mm. **Subject:** Endangered Wildlife **Obv:** Arms divide date, denomination below **Rev:** Lion **Edge:** Reeded

Date	Mintage	VF20	XF40	MS60	MS63	MS65
1993	—	PF65 45.00				

KM# 129 7000 FRANCOS
0.999 Silver, 34.8 mm. **Subject:** Endangered Wildlife **Obv:** Arms divide date, denomination below **Rev:** Springbok **Edge:** Reeded

Date	Mintage	VF20	XF40	MS60	MS63	MS65
1993	—	PF65 35.00				

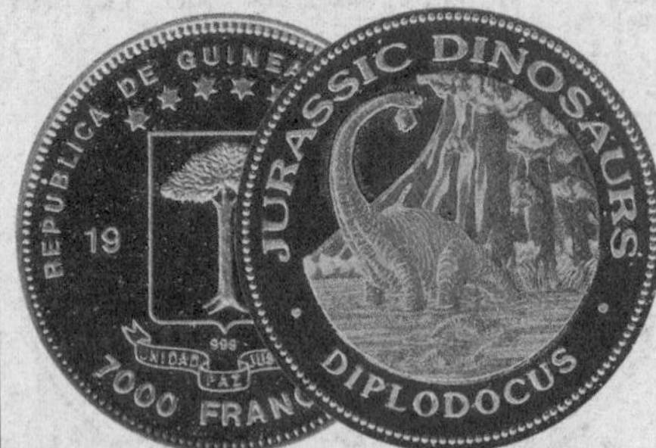

KM# 146 7000 FRANCOS
0.999 Silver, 39 mm. **Obv:** Arms divide date, denomination below **Rev:** Diplodocus in color

Date	Mintage	VF20	XF40	MS60	MS63	MS65
1993	—	PF65 25.00				

KM# 147 7000 FRANCOS
0.999 Silver, 39 mm. **Obv:** Arms divide date, denomination below **Rev:** Plateosaurus in color

Date	Mintage	VF20	XF40	MS60	MS63	MS65
1993	—	PF65 25.00				

KM# 148 7000 FRANCOS
0.999 Silver, 39 mm. **Obv:** Arms divide date, denomination below **Rev:** Allosaurus in color

Date	Mintage	VF20	XF40	MS60	MS63	MS65
1993	—	PF65 25.00				

KM# 149 7000 FRANCOS
0.999 Silver, 39 mm. **Obv:** Arms divide date, denomination below **Rev:** Tyrannosaurus in color

Date	Mintage	VF20	XF40	MS60	MS63	MS65
1993	—	PF65 25.00				

KM# 150 7000 FRANCOS
0.999 Silver, 39 mm. **Obv:** Arms divide date, denomination below **Rev:** Styraccosaurus in color

Date	Mintage	VF20	XF40	MS60	MS63	MS65
1993	—	PF65 25.00				

KM# 86 7000 FRANCOS
20.17 g., 0.999 Silver 0.6478 oz. ASW **Subject:** XV World Cup Soccer - USA 1994 **Obv:** Arms divide date, denomination below **Rev:** Soccer net and players

Date	Mintage	VF20	XF40	MS60	MS63	MS65
1994	—	PF65 27.50				

KM# 98 7000 FRANCOS
20.35 g., 0.999 Silver 0.6536 oz. ASW **Subject:** African Bird Wildlife - Kingfisher **Obv:** Arms divide date, denomination below **Rev:** Pair of multicolor kingfishers

Date	Mintage	VF20	XF40	MS60	MS63	MS65
1994	—	PF65 30.00				

KM# 99 7000 FRANCOS
20.35 g., 0.999 Silver 0.6536 oz. ASW **Series:** World's Famous Dogs **Obv:** Arms divide date, denomination below **Rev:** Pair of St. Bernards, multicolor

Date	Mintage	VF20	XF40	MS60	MS63	MS65
1994	7,500	PF65 35.00				

KM# 108 7000 FRANCOS
20.35 g., 0.999 Silver 0.6536 oz. ASW **Subject:** 25th Anniversary - Moon Landing **Obv:** Arms divide date, denomination below **Rev:** Multicolor moon landing scene

Date	Mintage	VF20	XF40	MS60	MS63	MS65
1994	10,000	PF65 27.50				

KM# 113 7000 FRANCOS
20.35 g., 0.999 Silver 0.6536 oz. ASW, 38 mm. **Obv:** Arms divide date, denomination below **Rev:** Multicolor Spanish Salvador Dali stamp design **Edge:** Reeded

Date	Mintage	VF20	XF40	MS60	MS63	MS65
1994	—	PF65 35.00				

KM# 125 7000 FRANCOS
20.35 g., 0.999 Silver 0.6536 oz. ASW, 38.1 mm. **Obv:** Arms divide date, denomination below **Rev:** Multicolor Bulldog on cross **Edge:** Reeded

Date	Mintage	VF20	XF40	MS60	MS63	MS65
1994	—	PF65 30.00				

KM# 133 7000 FRANCOS
20.00 g., 0.999 Silver 0.6424 oz. ASW **Subject:** XV World Soccer Cup - USA 1994 **Obv:** National arms **Rev:** Playing field

Date	Mintage	VF20	XF40	MS60	MS63	MS65
1994	—	PF65 27.50				

KM# 137 7000 FRANCOS
20.00 g., 0.999 Silver 0.6424 oz. ASW **Series:** Famous World Places **Obv:** National arms **Rev:** Ruins of the Kaiser Wilhelm Gedächtnis Church - Berlin, multicolor

Date	Mintage	VF20	XF40	MS60	MS63	MS65
1994	10,000	PF65 27.50				

KM# 140 7000 FRANCOS
20.00 g., 0.999 Silver 0.6424 oz. ASW **Subject:** World's Famous Dogs **Obv:** National arms **Rev:** Dalmation, multicolor

Date	Mintage	VF20	XF40	MS60	MS63	MS65
1994	—	PF65 35.00				

KM# 151 7000 FRANCOS
0.999 Silver, 39 mm. **Obv:** Arms divide date, denomination below **Rev:** Swiss stamp of Rolf Knie

Date	Mintage	VF20	XF40	MS60	MS63	MS65
1994	—	PF65 25.00				

KM# 85 7000 FRANCOS
21.00 g., 0.999 Silver 0.6745 oz. ASW **Subject:** 50th Anniversary - United Nations **Obv:** Arms divide date, denomination below **Rev:** Building and laurel sprigs, dates below

Date	Mintage	VF20	XF40	MS60	MS63	MS65
1995	—	PF65 22.50				

KM# 100 7000 FRANCOS
157.55 g., 0.999 Silver 5.0603 oz. ASW, 64.9 mm. **Subject:** Endangered wildlife **Obv:** Topical map of Africa **Rev:** Elephant head facing, denomination below **Note:** Illustration reduced.

Date	Mintage	VF20	XF40	MS60	MS63	MS65
1995	555	PF65 175	PF67 225			

KM# 101 7000 FRANCOS
157.55 g., 0.999 Silver 5.0603 oz. ASW **Subject:** Endangered wildlife **Obv:** Topical map of Africa **Rev:** Mother elephant with calf, denomination below **Note:** Illustration reduced.

Date	Mintage	VF20	XF40	MS60	MS63	MS65
1995	555	PF65 175	PF67 225			

KM# 102 7000 FRANCOS
157.55 g., 0.999 Silver 5.0603 oz. ASW **Subject:** Endangered wildlife **Obv:** Topical map of Africa **Rev:** Elephants at watering hole, denomination below **Note:** Illustration reduced.

Date	Mintage	VF20	XF40	MS60	MS63	MS65
1995	555	PF65 175	PF67 225			

KM# 103 7000 FRANCOS
157.55 g., 0.999 Silver 5.0603 oz. ASW **Subject:** Endangered wildlife **Obv:** Topical map of Africa **Rev:** Elephant family, denomination below **Note:** Illustration reduced.

Date	Mintage	VF20	XF40	MS60	MS63	MS65
1995	555	PF65 175	PF67 225			

KM# 104 7000 FRANCOS
157.55 g., 0.999 Silver 5.0603 oz. ASW **Subject:** Endangered wildlife **Obv:** Topical map of Africa **Rev:** Adolescent elephant with adult **Note:** Illustration reduced.

Date	Mintage	VF20	XF40	MS60	MS63	MS65
1995	555	PF65 175	PF67 225			

KM# 109 7000 FRANCOS
20.35 g., 0.999 Silver 0.6536 oz. ASW **Subject:** 150th Anniversary - Basel "Taube" Stamp **Obv:** Arms divide date, denomination below **Rev:** Multicolored stamp

Date	Mintage	VF20	XF40	MS60	MS63	MS65
1995	—	PF65 20.00				

KM# 141 7000 FRANCOS
20.00 g., 0.999 Silver 0.6424 oz. ASW **Subject:** World's Famous Stamps **Obv:** National arms divide date, denomination below **Rev:** Swiss stamp of Jean Tinguely, multicolor

Date	Mintage	VF20	XF40	MS60	MS63	MS65
1995	7,500	PF65 35.00				

KM# 152 7000 FRANCOS
0.999 Silver, 39 mm. **Obv:** Arms divide date, denomination below **Rev:** Swiss stamp Spannorter

Date	Mintage	VF20	XF40	MS60	MS63	MS65
1996	—	PF65 22.00				

KM# 120 7000 FRANCOS
19.60 g., 0.9999 Silver 0.6301 oz. ASW, 37.9 mm. **Subject:** Charlemagne **Obv:** Arms divide date, denomination below **Rev:** King on horse **Edge:** Reeded

Date	Mintage	VF20	XF40	MS60	MS63	MS65
1997	—	PF65 20.00	PF67 25.00			

KM# 116 8000 FRANCOS
7.77 g., 0.999 Gold 0.2496 oz. AGW, 26.9 mm. **Subject:** World's Famous Dogs **Obv:** Arms divide date, denomination below **Rev:** Pekingese dog and Chinese building **Edge:** Reeded

Date	Mintage	VF20	XF40	MS60	MS63	MS65
1994	—	PF65 400	PF67 450			

KM# 72 15000 FRANCOS
7.00 g., 0.917 Gold 0.2064 oz. AGW **Subject:** Discovery of America - Columbus **Obv:** Arms above denomination

Date	Mintage	VF20	XF40	MS60	MS63	MS65
1991	1,500	PF65 325	PF67 375			

KM# 73 15000 FRANCOS
7.00 g., 0.917 Gold 0.2064 oz. AGW **Subject:** Expo Seville **Obv:** Arms above denomination **Rev:** Ship and Space Shuttle, dates below

Date	Mintage	VF20	XF40	MS60	MS63	MS65
1991	1,500	PF65 325	PF67 375			

KM# 74 15000 FRANCOS
7.00 g., 0.917 Gold 0.2064 oz. AGW **Series:** Barcelona Olympics **Obv:** Arms above denomination **Rev:** Equestrian jumping

Date	Mintage	VF20	XF40	MS60	MS63	MS65
1991	1,500	PF65 325	PF67 375			

KM# 74a 15000 FRANCOS
20.33 g., 0.999 Silver 0.653 oz. ASW **Series:** Barcelona Olympics **Obv:** Arms above denomination **Rev:** Equestrian jumping

Date	Mintage	VF20	XF40	MS60	MS63	MS65
1992	—	PF65 30.00	PF67 35.00			

KM# 79 15000 FRANCOS
855.34 g., 0.999 Silver 27.4724 oz. ASW, 106 mm. **Subject:** Endangered Wildlife **Obv:** Topical map of Africa **Rev:** Elephant mother and calf, denomination below **Note:** Illustration reduced.

Date	Mintage	VF20	XF40	MS60	MS63	MS65
1992	2,200	PF65 575	PF67 600			

KM# 106 15000 FRANCOS
15.55 g., 0.900 Gold 0.4499 oz. AGW **Subject:** Endangered Wildlife **Obv:** Topical map of Africa **Rev:** Elephant

Date	Mintage	VF20	XF40	MS60	MS63	MS65
1992	450	PF65 675	PF67 700			

KM# 135 15000 FRANCOS
31.10 g., 0.999 Gold 0.9989 oz. AGW **Series:** Zodiac **Subject:** Year of the Dog **Obv:** Flower blossom in sprays **Rev:** Dog standing left

Date	Mintage	VF20	XF40	MS60	MS63	MS65
1994	—	PF65 1,650	PF67 1,750			

KM# 107 30000 FRANCOS
33.93 g., 0.917 Gold 1.0003 oz. AGW, 32.8 mm. **Subject:** Elephant Protection **Obv:** Arms above denomination **Rev:** Elephant **Edge:** Reeded

Date	Mintage	VF20	XF40	MS60	MS63	MS65
1993	700	PF65 1,650	PF67 1,750			

Note: 400 pieces remelted at mint

ESSAIS

KM#	Date	Mintage	Identification	Mkt Val
E1	1978	25	1000 Ekuele. Aluminum. KM#35.	65.00
E2	1978	20	1000 Ekuele. Copper. KM#35.	70.00
E3	1978	25	2000 Ekuele. Aluminum. KM#36.	75.00
E4	1978	Est. 20	2000 Ekuele. Copper. KM#36.	80.00
E5	1978	Est. 25	5000 Ekuele. Aluminum. KM#39.	55.00
E6	1978	—	5000 Ekuele. Copper. KM#39.	60.00
E7	1978	—	10000 Ekuele. Aluminum. KM#40.	65.00
E8	1978	Est. 20	10000 Ekuele. Copper. KM#40.	70.00
E9	ND-1979	Est. 25	2000 Ekuele. Aluminum. KM#38.	45.00
E10	ND-1979	Est. 20	2000 Ekuele. Copper. KM#38.	110
E11	ND-1979	Est. 25	10000 Ekuele. Aluminum. KM#41.	45.00
E12	ND-1979	Est. 20	10000 Ekuele. Copper. KM#41.	80.00
E13	1980	—	Bipkwele. Copper. KM#5.	40.00
E28	1985	—	5 Francos. Aluminum-Bronze. KM#62.	55.00
E29	1985	—	25 Francos. Aluminum-Bronze. Three Giant Eland, left. Denomination above date. KM#60.	60.00
E30	1985	—	50 Francos. Nickel. KM#64.	75.00
E31	1985	—	100 Francos. Nickel. Three Giant Eland, left. Denomination above date. KM#59.	50.00

PATTERNS

Including off metal strikes

KM#	Date	Mintage	Identification	Mkt Val
Pn31	1992	—	15000 Francos. 0.999. Silver Gilt.	—
Pn32	1993	—	1000 Francos. Copper-Nickel. Soccer scene.	70.00
Pn33	1993	—	1000 Francos. Copper-Nickel. Soccer players through net.	70.00
Pn34	1994	—	1000 Francos. Copper-Nickel. Hands holding FIFA cup.	60.00
Pn35	1994	—	1000 Francos. Copper-Nickel. Three players holding cup.	60.00
Pn36	1994	—	7000 Francos. 0.999. Silver. Dalmations.	85.00
Pn17	1995	—	1000 Francos. Copper-Nickel. National arms. Large "UN" letters with German inscription on UN logo. Reeded. First reported in World Coin News Round-up in August 2003.	135
Pn37	1995	—	1000 Francos. Copper-Nickel. National arms. "UN" letters with German inscription and the UN logo in background. Reeded.	—
Pn38	1996	—	1000 Francos. Brass. National arms. French postage stamp design. Reeded.	325

PIEDFORT

KM#	Date	Mintage	Identification	Mkt Val
P1	1978	Est. 5	1000 Ekuele. Copper. KM#35.	225
P2	1978	Est. 10	1000 Ekuele. 0.925. Silver. KM#35.	275
P3	1978	Est. 5	2000 Ekuele. Copper. Plain. KM#36.	325
P4	1978	Est. 5	5000 Ekuele. Copper. Milled. KM#39.	200
P5	1978	—	5000 Ekuele. Copper. Plain.	175
P6	1978	Est. 5	10000 Ekuele. Copper. Milled. KM#41.	125
P7	ND-1979	—	2000 Ekuele. Copper. KM#38.	225
P8	ND-1979	Est. 16	2000 Ekuele. 0.925. Silver. KM#38.	325

P9	ND-1979	—	2000 Ekuele. Copper Gilt.	225
P10	ND-1979	Est. 5	10000 Ekuele. Copper. KM#41.	250
P11	ND-1979	—	10000 Ekuele. Gold. KM#41.	1,650
P12	ND-1979	—	10000 Ekuele. Copper Gilt. KM#41.	225

TRIAL STRIKES

KM#	Date	Mintage	Identification	Mkt Val
TS1	1978	—	2000 Ekuele. Copper. KM#36. PRUEBA.	185
TS2	1978	—	2000 Ekuele. Copper. PRUEBA. KM#36.	185
TS3	1978	—	5000 Ekuele. Copper. KM39. PRUEBA.	110
TS4	1978	—	5000 Ekuele. Copper. KM39. PRUEBA.	110
TS5	1978	—	10000 Ekuele. Copper. KM40. PRUEBA.	110
TS6	1978	—	10000 Ekuele. Copper. PRUEBA. KM#40.	110
TS7	1978(80) (1978)	—	2000 Bipkwele. 0.925. Silver. M2. PRUEBA.	185
TS8	1978(80) (1980)	—	2000 Bipkwele. 0.925. Silver. PRUEBA. M3.	185

MINT SETS

KM#	Date	Mintage	Identification	Issue Price	Mkt Val
MS1	1975 (3)	—	KM#32-34	—	50.00

PROOF SETS

KM#	Date	Mintage	Identification	Issue Price	Mkt Val
PS1	1970 (27)	330	KM#5-31	—	9,350
PS2	1970 (15)	2,475	KM#5-19	126	725
PS3	1970 (12)	330	KM#20-31	—	8,600

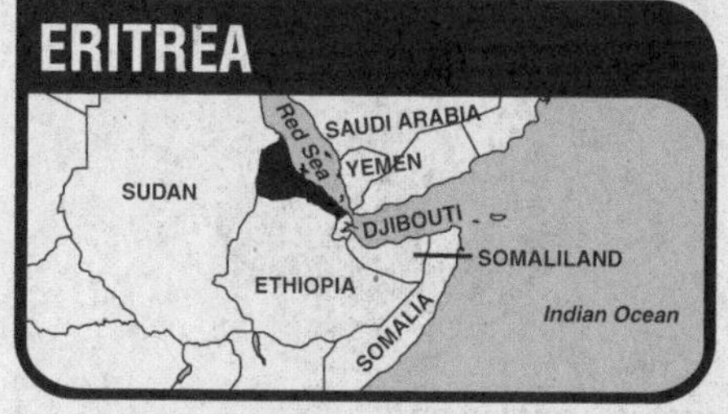

The State of Eritrea, a former Ethiopian province fronting on the Red Sea, has an area of 45,300 sq. mi. (117,600 sq. km.) and a population of 3.6 million. It was an Italian colony from 1889 until its incorporation into Italian East Africa in 1936. It was under the British Military Administration from 1941 to Sept. 15, 1952, when the United Nations designated it an autonomous unit within the federation of Ethiopia and Eritrea. On Nov. 14, 1962, it was annexed with Ethiopia. In 1991 the Eritrean Peoples Liberation Front extended its control over the entire territory of Eritrea. Following 2 years of provisional government, Eritrea held a referendum on independence in May 1993. Overwhelming popular approval led to the proclamation of an independent Republic of Eritrea on May 24.

RULERS

Vittorio Emanuele III, 1900-1945

MINT MARKS

M - Milan
PM - Pobjoy
R – Rome

MONETARY SYSTEM

100 Centesimi = 1 Lira
5 Lire = 1 Tallero

ITALIAN COLONY

COLONIAL COINAGE

KM# 5 TALLERO

28.07 g., 0.835 Silver 0.7535 oz. ASW, 40 mm. **Ruler:** Vittorio Emanuele III **Obv:** Bust with loose hair right, date at right **Rev:** Crowned imperial eagle with shield on breast

Date	Mintage	F12	VF20	XF40	MS60	MS63
1918 R	510,000	40.00	100	300	650	1,000

REPUBLIC

DECIMAL COINAGE

100 Cents = 1 Dollar

KM# 43 CENT

2.20 g., Nickel Clad Steel, 17 mm. **Obv:** Red-fronted gazelle right, divides denomination **Rev:** Soldiers with flag, date at left

Date	Mintage	VF20	XF40	MS60	MS63	MS65
1997	—	—	—	0.25	0.50	1.00

KM# 44 5 CENTS

2.70 g., Nickel Clad Steel, 18.9 mm. **Obv:** Leopard on log divides denomination **Rev:** Soldiers with flag, date at left

Date	Mintage	VF20	XF40	MS60	MS63	MS65
1997	—	—	—	0.35	0.75	1.50

KM# 45 10 CENTS

3.30 g., Nickel Clad Steel, 20.95 mm. **Obv:** Ostrich left divides denomination **Rev:** Soldiers with flag, date at left **Edge:** Reeded

Date	Mintage	VF20	XF40	MS60	MS63	MS65
1997	—	—	—	0.50	1.00	1.75

KM# 46 25 CENTS

5.80 g., Nickel Clad Steel, 23 mm. **Obv:** Grevy's zebra left divides denomination **Rev:** Soldiers with flag, date at left

Date	Mintage	VF20	XF40	MS60	MS63	MS65
1997	—	—	—	0.65	1.25	2.00

KM# 47 50 CENTS

7.80 g., Nickel Clad Steel, 24.95 mm. **Obv:** Greater Kudu left divides denomination **Rev:** Soldiers with flag, date at left

Date	Mintage	VF20	XF40	MS60	MS63	MS65
1997	—	—	—	0.75	1.50	2.25

KM# 48 100 CENTS

10.30 g., Nickel Clad Steel, 26.2 mm. **Obv:** African elephant and calf left, divide denomination **Rev:** Soldiers with flag, date at left

Date	Mintage	VF20	XF40	MS60	MS63	MS65
1997	—	—	—	1.00	2.00	3.00

KM# 6 DOLLAR

Copper-Nickel **Subject:** Independence Day **Obv:** Dhow, camel and palm tree, date below, all within circle **Rev:** Tree within laurel wreath, dates below, circle surrounds, denomination below

Date	Mintage	VF20	XF40	MS60	MS63	MS65
1993	—	—	—	—	7.00	10.00

KM# 10 DOLLAR

Copper-Nickel **Subject:** Preserve Planet Earth **Obv:** Dhow, camel and palm tree, date below, all within circle **Rev:** Triceratops, denomination below

Date	Mintage	VF20	XF40	MS60	MS63	MS65
1993	—	—	—	—	6.00	9.00

KM# 13 DOLLAR

Copper-Nickel **Subject:** Preserve Planet Earth **Obv:** Dhow, camel and palm tree, date below, all within circle **Rev:** Ankylosaurus, denomination below

Date	Mintage	VF20	XF40	MS60	MS63	MS65
1993	—	—	—	—	6.00	9.00

KM# 14 DOLLAR

Copper-Nickel **Subject:** Preserve Planet Earth **Obv:** Dhow, camel and palm tree, date below, all within circle **Rev:** Pteranodon, denomination below

Date	Mintage	VF20	XF40	MS60	MS63	MS65
1993	—	—	—	—	6.00	9.00

KM# 15 DOLLAR
Copper-Nickel **Subject:** Preserve Planet Earth **Obv:** Dhow, camel and palm tree, date below, all within circle **Rev:** Cheetah, denomination below

Date	Mintage	VF20	XF40	MS60	MS63	MS65
1994	—	—	—	—	6.00	9.00

KM# 16 DOLLAR
Copper-Nickel **Subject:** Preserve Planet Earth **Obv:** Dhow, camel and palm tree, date below, all within circle **Rev:** Black Rhinoceros, denomination below

Date	Mintage	VF20	XF40	MS60	MS63	MS65
1994	—	—	—	—	6.00	9.00

KM# 17 DOLLAR
Copper-Nickel **Subject:** Preserve Planet Earth **Obv:** Dhow, camel and palm tree, date below, all within circle **Rev:** Black and White Colobus Monkey, denomination below

Date	Mintage	VF20	XF40	MS60	MS63	MS65
1994	—	—	—	—	6.00	9.00

KM# 28 DOLLAR
Copper-Nickel **Subject:** Preserve Planet Earth **Obv:** Dhow, camel and palm tree, date below, all within circle **Rev:** Lions

Date	Mintage	VF20	XF40	MS60	MS63	MS65
1995 PM	—	—	—	—	6.00	9.00

KM# 31 DOLLAR
Copper-Nickel **Subject:** Preserve Planet Earth **Obv:** Dhow, camel and palm tree, date below, all within circle **Rev:** Cape Eagle owl

Date	Mintage	VF20	XF40	MS60	MS63	MS65
1995 PM	—	—	—	—	6.00	9.00

KM# 34 DOLLAR
Copper-Nickel **Subject:** Preserve Planet Earth **Obv:** Dhow, camel and palm tree, date below, all within circle **Rev:** Wattled Cranes

Date	Mintage	VF20	XF40	MS60	MS63	MS65
1996	—	—	—	—	6.00	9.00

KM# 37 DOLLAR
Copper-Nickel **Subject:** Preserve Planet Earth **Obv:** Dhow, camel and palm tree, date below, all within circle **Rev:** Laner falcon

Date	Mintage	VF20	XF40	MS60	MS63	MS65
1996	—	—	—	—	6.00	9.00

KM# 40 DOLLAR
Copper-Nickel **Subject:** Jurassic Park **Obv:** Dhow, camel and palm tree, date below, all within circle **Rev:** Triceratops, Jurassic Park logo

Date	Mintage	VF20	XF40	MS60	MS63	MS65
1997	—	—	—	—	6.00	9.00

KM# 7 10 DOLLARS
31.10 g., 0.9999 Silver 0.9999 oz. ASW **Subject:** Independence Day **Obv:** Dhow, camel and palm tree, date below, within circle **Rev:** Tree within laurel wreath, dates below, circle surrounds, denomination below

Date	Mintage	VF20	XF40	MS60	MS63	MS65
1993	—	PF65 23.00	PF67 28.00			

KM# 11 10 DOLLARS
28.28 g., 0.925 Silver 0.841 oz. ASW **Subject:** Preserve Planet Earth **Obv:** Dhow, camel and palm tree, date below, all within circle **Rev:** Triceratops, denomination below

Date	Mintage	VF20	XF40	MS60	MS63	MS65
1993	Est. 30000	PF65 23.00	PF67 28.00			

KM# 24 10 DOLLARS
28.28 g., 0.925 Silver 0.841 oz. ASW **Subject:** Preserve Planet Earth **Obv:** Dhow, camel and palm tree, date below, all within circle **Rev:** Ankylosaurus

Date	Mintage	VF20	XF40	MS60	MS63	MS65
1993	Est. 30000	PF65 23.00	PF67 28.00			

KM# 25 10 DOLLARS
28.28 g., 0.925 Silver 0.841 oz. ASW **Subject:** Preserve Planet Earth **Obv:** Dhow, camel and palm tree, date below, all within circle **Rev:** Pteranodon

Date	Mintage	VF20	XF40	MS60	MS63	MS65
1993	Est. 30000	PF65 23.00	PF67 28.00			

KM# 18 10 DOLLARS
28.28 g., 0.925 Silver 0.841 oz. ASW **Subject:** Preserve Planet Earth **Obv:** Dhow, camel and palm tree, date below, all within circle **Rev:** Cheetah, denomination below

Date	Mintage	VF20	XF40	MS60	MS63	MS65
1994	Est. 30000	PF65 23.00	PF67 28.00			

KM# 19 10 DOLLARS
28.28 g., 0.925 Silver 0.841 oz. ASW **Subject:** Preserve Planet Earth **Obv:** Dhow, camel and palm tree, date below, all within circle **Rev:** Black rhinoceros, denomination below

Date	Mintage	VF20	XF40	MS60	MS63	MS65
1994	Est. 30000	PF65 23.00	PF67 28.00			

KM# 20 10 DOLLARS
28.28 g., 0.925 Silver 0.841 oz. ASW **Subject:** Preserve Planet Earth **Obv:** Dhow, camel and palm tree, date below, all within circle **Rev:** Colobus monkey, denomination below

Date	Mintage	VF20	XF40	MS60	MS63	MS65
1994	Est. 30000	PF65 23.00	PF67 28.00			

KM# 29 10 DOLLARS
28.28 g., 0.925 Silver 0.841 oz. ASW **Subject:** Preserve Planet Earth **Obv:** Dhow, camel and palm tree, date below, all within circle **Rev:** Lions, denomination below

Date	Mintage	VF20	XF40	MS60	MS63	MS65
1995 PM	5,000	PF65 25.00	PF67 30.00			

KM# 32 10 DOLLARS
28.28 g., 0.925 Silver 0.841 oz. ASW **Subject:** Preserve Planet Earth **Obv:** Dhow, camel and palm tree, date below, all within circle **Rev:** Cape Eagle owl, denomination below

Date	Mintage	VF20	XF40	MS60	MS63	MS65
1995 PM	Est. 30000	PF65 23.00	PF67 28.00			

KM# 35 10 DOLLARS
28.28 g., 0.925 Silver 0.841 oz. ASW **Subject:** Preserve Planet Earth **Obv:** Dhow, camel and palm tree, date below, all within circle **Rev:** Wattled cranes, denomination below

Date	Mintage	VF20	XF40	MS60	MS63	MS65
1996	—	PF65 23.00	PF67 28.00			

KM# 38 10 DOLLARS
28.28 g., 0.925 Silver 0.841 oz. ASW **Subject:** Preserve Planet Earth **Obv:** Dhow, camel and palm tree, date below, all within circle **Rev:** Laner falcon, denomination below

Date	Mintage	VF20	XF40	MS60	MS63	MS65
1996	—	PF65 23.00	PF67 28.00			

KM# 41 10 DOLLARS
28.28 g., 0.925 Silver 0.841 oz. ASW **Subject:** Jurassic Park **Obv:** Dhow, camel and palm tree, date below, all within circle **Rev:** Triceratops, Jurassic Park logo, denomination below

Date	Mintage	VF20	XF40	MS60	MS63	MS65
1997	Est. 10000	PF65 23.00	PF67 28.00			

KM# 8 50 DOLLARS
3.11 g., 0.999 Gold 0.0999 oz. AGW **Subject:** Independence Day **Obv:** Dhow, camel and tree within circle, denomination below **Rev:** Tree within laurel wreath, dates below, circle surrounds, denomination below

Date	Mintage	VF20	XF40	MS60	MS63	MS65
1993	Est. 20000	PF65 160	PF67 175			

KM# 9 100 DOLLARS
6.22 g., 0.999 Gold 0.1998 oz. AGW **Subject:** Independence Day **Obv:** Dhow, camel and palm tree, date below, all within circle **Rev:** Tree within laurel wreath, dates below, circle surrounds, denomination below

Date	Mintage	VF20	XF40	MS60	MS63	MS65
1993	Est. 5000	PF65 320	PF67 340			

KM# 12 100 DOLLARS
6.22 g., 0.999 Gold 0.1998 oz. AGW **Subject:** Preserve Planet Earth **Obv:** Dhow, camel and tree within circle, denomination below **Rev:** Triceratops, denomination below

Date	Mintage	VF20	XF40	MS60	MS63	MS65
1993	Est. 5000	PF65 320	PF67 340			

KM# 26 100 DOLLARS
6.22 g., 0.999 Gold 0.1998 oz. AGW **Subject:** Preserve Planet Earth **Obv:** Dhow, camel and palm tree, date below, all within circle **Rev:** Ankylosaurus

Date	Mintage	VF20	XF40	MS60	MS63	MS65
1993	Est. 5000	PF65 320	PF67 340			

KM# 27 100 DOLLARS
6.22 g., 0.999 Gold 0.1998 oz. AGW **Subject:** Preserve Planet Earth **Obv:** Dhow, camel and palm tree, date below, all within circle **Rev:** Pteranodon

Date	Mintage	VF20	XF40	MS60	MS63	MS65
1993	—	PF65 320	PF67 340			

KM# 21 100 DOLLARS
6.22 g., 0.999 Gold 0.1998 oz. AGW **Subject:** Preserve Planet Earth **Obv:** Dhow, camel and palm tree, date below, all within circle **Rev:** Mother and baby cheetah

Date	Mintage	VF20	XF40	MS60	MS63	MS65
1994	5,000	PF65 320	PF67 340			

KM# 22 100 DOLLARS
6.22 g., 0.999 Gold 0.1998 oz. AGW **Subject:** Preserve Planet Earth **Obv:** Dhow, camel and palm tree, date below, all within circle **Rev:** Rhinoceros head right

Date	Mintage	VF20	XF40	MS60	MS63	MS65
1994	5,000	PF65 320	PF67 340			

KM# 23 100 DOLLARS
6.22 g., 0.999 Gold 0.1998 oz. AGW **Subject:** Preserve Planet Earth **Obv:** Dhow, camel and palm tree, date below, all within circle **Rev:** Colobus monkey

Date	Mintage	VF20	XF40	MS60	MS63	MS65
1994	5,000	PF65 320	PF67 340			

KM# 30 100 DOLLARS
6.22 g., 0.999 Gold 0.1998 oz. AGW **Subject:** Preserve Planet Earth **Obv:** Dhow, camel and palm tree, date below, all within circle **Rev:** Female lion and cub

Date	Mintage	VF20	XF40	MS60	MS63	MS65
1995	Est. 5000	PF65 320	PF67 340			

KM# 33 100 DOLLARS
6.22 g., 0.999 Gold 0.1998 oz. AGW **Subject:** Preserve Planet Earth **Obv:** Dhow, camel and palm tree, date below, all within circle **Rev:** Cape eagle owl

Date	Mintage	VF20	XF40	MS60	MS63	MS65
1995	Est. 5000	PF65 320	PF67 340			

KM# 36 100 DOLLARS
6.22 g., 0.999 Gold 0.1998 oz. AGW **Subject:** Preserve Planet Earth **Obv:** Dhow, camel and palm tree, date below, all within circle **Rev:** Wattled cranes

Date	Mintage	VF20	XF40	MS60	MS63	MS65
1996	Est. 5000	PF65 320	PF67 340			

KM# 39 100 DOLLARS
6.22 g., 0.999 Gold 0.1998 oz. AGW **Subject:** Preserve Planet Earth **Obv:** Dhow, camel and palm tree, date below, all within circle **Rev:** Laner falcon

Date	Mintage	VF20	XF40	MS60	MS63	MS65
1996	Est. 5000	PF65 320	PF67 340			

KM# 42 100 DOLLARS
6.22 g., 0.999 Gold 0.1998 oz. AGW **Subject:** Jurassic Park **Obv:** Dhow, camel and tree within circle, denomination below **Rev:** Triceratops, Jurassic Park logo

Date	Mintage	VF20	XF40	MS60	MS63	MS65
1997	Est. 2500	PF65 340	PF67 360			

PROVAS

KM#	Date	Mintage	Identification	Mkt Val
Pr1	1918R	—	Tallero. Bust with loose hair right. Crowned imperial eagle, shield on breast. KM5..	1,250

The Republic of Estonia (formerly the Estonian Soviet Socialist Republic of the U.S.S.R.) is the northernmost of the three Baltic States in Eastern Europe. It has an area of 17,462 sq. mi. (45,100 sq. km.) and a population of 1.6 million. Capital: Tallinn. Agriculture and dairy farming are the principal industries. Butter, eggs, bacon, timber and petroleum are exported.

This small and ancient Baltic state had enjoyed but two decades of independence since the 13th century until the present time. After having been conquered by the Danes, the Livonian Knights, the Teutonic Knights of Germany (who reduced the people to serfdom), the Swedes, the Poles and Russia, Estonia declared itself an independent republic on Feb. 24, 1918 but was not freed until Feb. 1919. The peace treaty was signed Feb. 2, 1920. Shortly after the start of World War II, it was again occupied by Russia and incorporated as the 16th state of the U.S.S.R Germany occupied the tiny state from 1941 to 1944, after which it was retaken by Russia. Most of the nations of the world, including the United States and Great Britain, did not recognize Estonia's incorporation into the Soviet Union.

The coinage, issued during the country's brief independence, is obsolete.

On August 20, 1991, the Parliament of the Estonian Soviet Socialist Republic voted to reassert the republic's independence.

REPUBLIC

1918 - 1941

REPUBLIC COINAGE

KM# 1 MARK
Copper-Nickel, 18 mm. **Obv:** Three leopards left divide date **Rev:** Denomination **Edge:** Milled

Date	Mintage	F12	VF20	XF40	MS60	MS63
1922	5,025,000	4.00	5.00	9.00	15.00	25.00

KM# 1a MARK
2.60 g., Nickel-Bronze, 18 mm. **Obv:** Three leopards left divide date **Rev:** Denomination **Edge:** Milled

Date	Mintage	F12	VF20	XF40	MS60	MS63
1924	1,985,000	5.00	7.00	12.00	25.00	35.00

KM# 5 MARK
Nickel-Bronze **Obv:** National arms within wreath **Rev:** Denomination

Date	Mintage	F12	VF20	XF40	MS60	MS63
1926	3,979,000	3.00	5.00	9.00	20.00	35.00

KM# 2 3 MARKA
Copper-Nickel **Obv:** Three leopards left divide date **Rev:** Denomination

Date	Mintage	F12	VF20	XF40	MS60	MS63
1922	2,089,000	3.00	5.00	9.00	20.00	30.00

KM# 2a 3 MARKA
Nickel-Bronze **Obv:** Three leopards left divide date **Rev:** Denomination

Date	Mintage	F12	VF20	XF40	MS60	MS63
1925	1,134,000	5.00	9.00	18.00	35.00	55.00

KM# 6 3 MARKA
Nickel-Bronze **Obv:** National arms within wreath **Rev:** Denomination, date below

Date	Mintage	F12	VF20	XF40	MS60	MS63
1926	903,000	25.00	40.00	65.00	120	165

KM# 3 5 MARKA
5.00 g., Copper-Nickel, 23 mm. **Obv:** Three leopards left divide date **Rev:** Denomination **Edge:** Milled

Date	Mintage	F12	VF20	XF40	MS60	MS63
1922	3,983,000	4.00	6.00	10.00	20.00	30.00

KM# 3a 5 MARKA
5.00 g., Nickel-Bronze, 23 mm. **Obv:** Three leopards left divide date **Rev:** Denomination **Edge:** Milled

Date	Mintage	F12	VF20	XF40	MS60	MS63
1924	1,335,000	5.00	8.00	15.00	25.00	35.00

KM# 7 5 MARKA
Nickel-Bronze **Obv:** National arms within wreath **Rev:** Denomination above date

Date	Mintage	F12	VF20	XF40	MS60	MS63
1926	1,038,000	75.00	100	150	300	500

KM# 4 10 MARKA
6.00 g., Nickel-Bronze, 26 mm. **Obv:** Three leopards left divide date **Rev:** Denomination **Edge:** Milled

Date	Mintage	F12	VF20	XF40	MS60	MS63
1925	2,200,000	5.00	8.00	15.00	25.00	40.00

KM# 8 10 MARKA
Nickel-Bronze **Obv:** National arms within wreath **Rev:** Denomination above date

Date	Mintage	F12	VF20	XF40	MS60	MS63
1926	2,789,000	—	—	—	1,500	2,000

Note: Most of this issue was melted down; Not released to circulation

REFORM COINAGE

100 Senti = 1 Kroon

KM# 10 SENT
2.00 g., Bronze, 17 mm. **Obv:** Three leopards left above date **Rev:** Denomination, oak leaves in background **Edge:** Plain

Date	Mintage	F12	VF20	XF40	MS60	MS63
1929	23,553,000	2.00	3.00	5.00	8.00	12.00

KM# 19.1 SENT
2.00 g., Bronze, 16 mm. **Obv:** Three leopards left above date **Rev:** Denomination **Edge:** Plain **Note:** 1mm thick planchet.

Date	Mintage	F12	VF20	XF40	MS60	MS63
1939	5,000,000	—	3.00	6.00	20.00	40.00

KM# 19.2 SENT
Bronze **Obv:** Three leopards left divide date **Rev:** Denomination **Note:** 0.9mm thick planchet.

Date	Mintage	F12	VF20	XF40	MS60	MS63
1939	Inc. above	—	3.00	6.00	20.00	40.00

KM# 15 2 SENTI
3.50 g., Bronze, 19 mm. **Obv:** Three leopards left above date **Rev:** Denomination **Edge:** Plain

Date	Mintage	F12	VF20	XF40	MS60	MS63
1934	5,838,000	3.00	5.00	8.00	15.00	25.00

KM# 11 5 SENTI
3.50 g., Bronze, 23.3 mm. **Obv:** Three leopards left above date **Rev:** Denomination **Edge:** Plain

Date	Mintage	F12	VF20	XF40	MS60	MS63
1931	11,000,000	4.00	5.00	10.00	20.00	35.00

KM# 12 10 SENTI
2.50 g., Nickel-Bronze, 18 mm. **Obv:** National arms divide date **Rev:** Denomination **Edge:** Plain

Date	Mintage	F12	VF20	XF40	MS60	MS63
1931	4,089,000	4.50	6.00	12.00	22.00	37.00

KM# 17 20 SENTI
3.92 g., Nickel-Bronze, 21 mm. **Obv:** National arms divide date **Rev:** Denomination **Edge:** Plain

Date	Mintage	F12	VF20	XF40	MS60	MS63
1935	4,250,000	4.50	6.00	12.00	22.00	37.00

KM# 9 25 SENTI
Nickel-Bronze **Obv:** National arms, wreath surrounds **Rev:** Denomination above date

Date	Mintage	F12	VF20	XF40	MS60	MS63
1928	2,025,000	6.00	12.00	25.00	40.00	65.00

KM# 18 50 SENTI
7.50 g., Nickel-Bronze, 27.5 mm. **Obv:** National arms divide date **Rev:** Denomination **Edge:** Plain

Date	Mintage	F12	VF20	XF40	MS60	MS63
1936	1,256,000	5.00	10.00	20.00	30.00	45.00

KM# 14 KROON
6.00 g., 0.500 Silver 0.0965 oz. ASW, 26 mm. **Subject:** 10th Singing Festival **Obv:** National arms, wreath surrounds, date below **Rev:** Harp divides dates, denomination below

Date	Mintage	F12	VF20	XF40	MS60	MS63
1933	350,000	20.00	25.00	35.00	50.00	75.00

KM# 16 KROON
5.96 g., Aluminum-Bronze, 25 mm. **Obv:** National arms, wreath surrounds, date below **Rev:** Ship of Vikings, denomination below **Edge:** Plain **Note:** 1990 restrikes which exist are private issues.

Date	Mintage	F12	VF20	XF40	MS60	MS63
1934	3,304,000	4.50	9.00	18.00	35.00	60.00

KM# 20 2 KROONI
12.00 g., 0.500 Silver 0.1929 oz. ASW, 30 mm. **Subject:**

Toompea Fortress at Tallinn **Obv:** National arms, wreath surrounds, date below **Rev:** Castle denomination below **Edge:** Milled

Date	Mintage	F12	VF20	XF40	MS60	MS63
1930	1,276,000	7.00	12.00	20.00	38.00	65.00

KM# 13 2 KROONI
12.00 g., 0.500 Silver 0.1929 oz. ASW, 30 mm. **Subject:** Tercentenary - University of Tartu **Obv:** National arms, wreath surrounds, date below **Rev:** University building, denomination below **Edge:** Plain

Date	Mintage	F12	VF20	XF40	MS60	MS63
1932	100,000	12.00	20.00	35.00	50.00	75.00

MODERN REPUBLIC

1991 - present

STANDARD COINAGE

KM# 21 5 SENTI
1.29 g., Aluminum-Bronze, 15.9 mm. **Obv:** Three leopards left divide date **Rev:** Denomination **Edge:** Plain

Date	Mintage	VF20	XF40	MS60	MS63	MS65
1991	Inc. below	—	—	0.50	1.00	1.50
1992	38,790,000	—	—	0.50	1.00	1.50
1995	5,000,000	—	—	0.50	1.00	1.50

KM# 22 10 SENTI
1.85 g., Aluminum-Bronze, 17.1 mm. **Obv:** Three lions left divide date **Rev:** Denomination **Rev. Legend:** EESTI VABARIIK **Edge:** Plain

Date	Mintage	VF20	XF40	MS60	MS63	MS65
1991	Inc. below	—	0.20	0.50	1.00	1.50
1992	31,280,000	—	0.20	0.50	1.00	1.50
1994	10,020,000	—	0.20	0.50	1.00	1.50
1996	10,110,000	—	0.20	0.50	1.00	1.50
1997	15,000,000	—	0.20	0.50	1.00	1.50
1998	30,980,000	—	0.20	0.50	1.00	1.50

KM# 23 20 SENTI
2.27 g., Aluminum-Bronze, 18.95 mm. **Obv:** The leopards left divide date **Rev:** Denomination **Edge:** Plain

Date	Mintage	VF20	XF40	MS60	MS63	MS65
1992	31,540,000	—	—	1.00	1.50	2.00
1996	10,740,000	—	—	1.00	1.50	2.00

KM# 23a 20 SENTI
2.00 g., Nickel Plated Steel, 18.9 mm. **Obv:** National arms divide date **Rev:** Denomination **Rev. Legend:** EESTI VABARIIK **Edge:** Plain

Date	Mintage	VF20	XF40	MS60	MS63	MS65
1997	10,500,000	—	0.50	1.00	1.50	2.00
1999	20,330,000	—	0.50	1.00	1.50	2.00

KM# 24 50 SENTI
2.90 g., Aluminum-Bronze, 19.5 mm. **Obv:** National arms divide date **Rev:** Denomination **Rev. Legend:** EESTI VABARIIK **Edge:** Plain

Date	Mintage	VF20	XF40	MS60	MS63	MS65
1992	31,200,000	—	0.60	1.50	2.00	2.50

KM# 28 KROON
5.44 g., Copper-Nickel, 23.5 mm. **Obv:** National arms divide date **Rev:** Large, thick denomination **Edge:** Plain

Date	Mintage	VF20	XF40	MS60	MS63	MS65
1992	20,000	—	—	—	—	30.00
Note: In sets only						
1993	8,300,000	—	—	1.50	2.00	2.50
1995	19,900,000	—	—	1.50	2.00	2.50

KM# 35 KROON
5.00 g., Aluminum-Bronze, 23.5 mm. **Obv:** National arms **Rev:** Large, thick denomination **Rev. Legend:** EESTI VABARIIK **Edge:** Segmented reeding

Date	Mintage	VF20	XF40	MS60	MS63	MS65
1998	15,000,000	—	0.60	1.50	2.00	2.50
1999 In sets only	50,000	—	—	—	—	5.00
2000	15,000,000	—	0.60	1.50	2.00	2.50

KM# 36 KROON
0.50 g., Aluminum-Bronze, 23.25 mm. **Obv:** Bird above date **Rev:** Festival building and denomination **Edge:** Segmented reeding

Date	Mintage	VF20	XF40	MS60	MS63	MS65
1999	100,000	—	—	—	—	6.00

KM# 29 5 KROONI
7.10 g., Aluminum-Bronze, 26.2 mm. **Subject:** 75th Anniversary - Declaration of Independence **Obv:** National arms divide date **Rev:** Small deer right, denomination at right **Edge:** Plain

Date	Mintage	VF20	XF40	MS60	MS63	MS65
1993	1,500,000	—	—	3.00	5.00	7.00
1993	10,000	PF65 7.00				

KM# 30 5 KROONI
7.10 g., Aluminum-Bronze, 26.1 mm. **Subject:** 75th Anniversary - Bank of Estonia **Obv:** National arms divide date **Rev:** Denomination on design **Edge:** Plain

Date	Mintage	VF20	XF40	MS60	MS63	MS65
1994	10,180,000	—	—	3.00	5.00	7.00

KM# 25 10 KROONI
28.28 g., 0.925 Silver 0.841 oz. ASW **Series:** Olympics **Obv:** National arms, wreath surrounds, date below **Rev:** Two sail boats, denomination below

Date	Mintage	VF20	XF40	MS60	MS63	MS65
1992	Est. 20000	PF63 30.00		PF65 40.00		PF67 50.00

KM# 26 10 KROONI
28.28 g., 0.925 Silver 0.841 oz. ASW **Obv:** National arms, wreath surrounds, date below **Rev:** Barn Swallow, denomination below

Date	Mintage	VF20	XF40	MS60	MS63	MS65
1992	Est. 10000	PF63 35.00		PF65 45.00		PF67 55.00

KM# 32 10 KROONI
16.00 g., 0.925 Silver 0.4758 oz. ASW, 31 mm. **Subject:** 80th Anniversary of Nation **Obv:** Framed dates **Rev:** Farmer plowing field, denomination above

Date	Mintage	VF20	XF40	MS60	MS63	MS65
ND(1998)	Est. 15000	PF63 20.00		PF65 30.00		PF67 40.00

KM# 37 15.65 KROONI
1.73 g., 0.900 Gold 0.0501 oz. AGW **Subject:** Estonia's Euro Equivalent **Obv:** National arms, wreath surrounds, date below **Rev:** Cross and stars design, denomination below

Date	Mintage	VF20	XF40	MS60	MS63	MS65
1999	Est. 5000	PF65 165	PF67 185			

KM# 27 100 KROONI
24.00 g., 0.925 Silver 0.7137 oz. ASW **Obv:** National arms **Rev:** Barn Swallows, date below, denomination above

Date	Mintage	VF20	XF40	MS60	MS63	MS65
1992	Est. 50000	PF63 25.00		PF65 35.00		PF67 45.00

KM# 31 100 KROONI

28.28 g., 0.925 Silver 0.841 oz. ASW **Obv:** National arms, wreath surrounds, date below **Rev:** Olympics - Nike crowning Wrestler, denomination below

Date	Mintage	VF20	XF40	MS60	MS63	MS65
1996	—	—	—	—	17.00	30.00
1996	10,000	PF63 25.00	PF65 35.00	PF67 45.00		

KM# 33 100 KROONI

27.00 g., 0.925 Silver 0.803 oz. ASW **Subject:** 80th Anniversary of Nation **Obv:** Framed dates **Rev:** Male figure and stylized eagle head, denomination below

Date	Mintage	VF20	XF40	MS60	MS63	MS65
ND-1998	Est. 12000	PF63 20.00	PF65 30.00	PF67 40.00		
ND(1998)	—	—	—	—	—	30.00

KM# 34 500 KROONI

8.64 g., 0.900 Gold 0.250 oz. AGW **Subject:** 80th Anniversary of Nation **Obv:** Framed dates **Rev:** Male figure on horse, denomination above

Date	Mintage	VF20	XF40	MS60	MS63	MS65
ND-1998	Est. 3000	PF65 425	PF67 450			

MINT SETS

KM#	Date	Mintage	Identification	Issue Price	Mkt Val
MS1	1992 (5)	20,000	KM#21-24, 28	—	32.00

ETHIOPIA

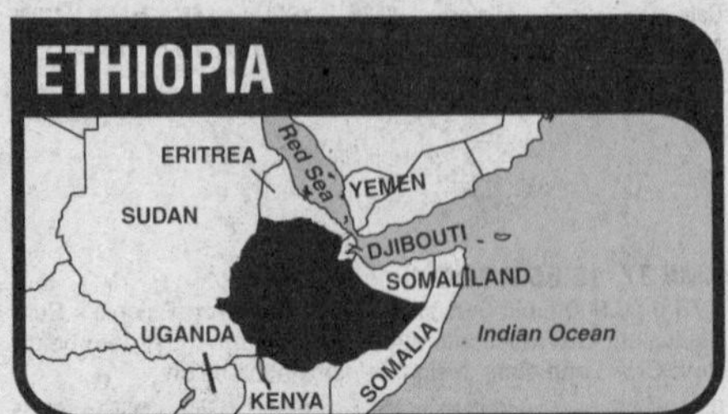

The People's Federal Republic of Ethiopia (formerly the Peoples Democratic Republic and the Empire of Ethiopia), Africa's oldest independent nation, faces the Red Sea in East-Central Africa. The country has an area of 424,214 sq. mi. (1,004,390 sq. km.) and a population of 56 million people who are divided among 40 tribes that speak some 270 languages and dialects. Capital: Addis Ababa. The economy is predominantly agricultural and pastoral. Gold and platinum are mined and petroleum fields are being developed. Coffee, oilseeds, hides and cereals are exported.

Legend claims that Menelik I, the son born to Solomon, King of Israel, by the Queen of Sheba, settled in Axum in North Ethiopia to establish the dynasty, which reigned with only brief interruptions until 1974. Modern Ethiopian history began with the reign of Emperor Menelik II (1889-1913) under whose guidance the country emerged from medieval isolation. Progress continued throughout the reigns of Menelik's daughter, Empress Zauditu, and her successor Emperor Haile Selassie I who was coronated in 1930. Ethiopia was invaded by Italy in 1935, and together with Italian Somaliland and Eritrea became part of Italian East Africa. Victor Emmanuel III, as declared by Mussolini, would be Ethiopia's emperor as well as a king of Italy. Liberated by British and Ethiopian troops in 1941, Ethiopia reinstated Haile Selassie I to the throne. The 225th consecutive Solomonic ruler was deposed by a military committee on Sept 12, 1974. In July 1976 Ethiopia's military provisional government referred to the country as Socialist Ethiopia. After establishing a new regime in 1991, Ethiopia became a federated state and is now the Federal Republic of Ethiopia. Following 2 years of provisional government, the province of Eritrea held a referendum on independence in May 1993 leading to the proclamation of its independence on May 24.

No coins, patterns or presentation pieces are known bearing Emperor Lij Yasu's likeness or titles. Coins of Menelik II were struck during this period with dates frozen.

RULERS

Menelik II, 1889-1913
Lij Yasu, 1913-1916
Zauditu, Empress, 1916-1930
Haile Selassie I, 1930-36, 1941-1974
Victor Emmanuel III, of Italy 1936-1941

MINT MARKS

A - Paris
(a) - Paris, privy marks only
(b)

Coinage of Menelik II, 1889-1913

NOTE: The first national issue coinage, dated 1887 and 1888 E.E., carried a cornucopia, A, and fasces on the reverse. Subsequent dates have a torch substituted for the fasces, the A being dropped. All issues bearing these marks were struck at the Paris Mint. Coins without mint marks were struck in Addis Ababa.

MONETARY SYSTEM

(Until about 1903)
40 Besa = 20 Gersh = 1 Birr
(After 1903)
32 Besa = 16 Gersh = 1 Birr

DATING

Ethiopian coinage is dated by the Ethiopian Era calendar (E.E.), which commenced 7 years and 8 months after the advent of A.D. dating.

EXAMPLE

1900 (10 and 9 = 19 x 100)
36 (Add 30 and 6)
1936 E.E.
8 (Add)
1943/4 AD

PEOPLES DEMOCRATIC REPUBLIC

We have two varieties for KM#43.1 to KM#46.1. One was minted at the British Royal Mint, the other at the Berlin Mint. The main difference is where the lion's chin whiskers end above the date (easiest to see on the 2nd, 3rd and 4th characters).

British Royal Mint

Berlin Mint

EMPIRE OF ETHIOPIA

REFORM COINAGE

KM# 12 GERSH

1.40 g., 0.835 Silver 0.0377 oz. ASW, 16.5 mm. **Ruler:** Menelik II **Obv:** Crowned bust right **Rev:** Crowned lion left, left foreleg raised holding ribboned cross

Date	Mintage	F12	VF20	XF40	MS60	MS63
EE1895 (1902-03) A	44,789,000	2.00	3.50	12.50	25.00	35.00

Note: Struck between 1903-1928

KM# 3 1/4 BIRR

7.11 g., 0.835 Silver 0.1908 oz. ASW, 25 mm. **Ruler:** Menelik II **Obv:** Crowned bust right **Rev:** Crowned lion left, left foreleg raised holding ribboned cross

Date	Mintage	F12	VF20	XF40	MS60	MS63
EE1895 (1902-03) A	821,000	7.00	15.00	50.00	150	250

Note: Struck between 1903 and 1925

KM# 19 BIRR

28.08 g., 0.835 Silver 0.7537 oz. ASW, 40 mm. **Ruler:** Menelik II **Obv:** Crowned bust right **Rev:** Crowned lion left, right foreleg raised holding ribboned cross

Date	Mintage	F12	VF20	XF40	MS60	MS63
EE1895 (1902-03)	459,000	25.00	65.00	140	350	500
Note: Struck in 1901, 1903 and 1904						
EE1895 (1902-03)	—	PF63 1,250				

KM# 20 1/2 WERK

3.50 g., 0.900 Gold 0.1013 oz. AGW, 18 mm. **Ruler:** Haile Selassie I **Obv:** Crowned bust left, laurels below **Rev:** St. George on horseback slaying the dragon

Date	Mintage	F12	VF20	XF40	MS60	MS63
EE1923 (1930-31)	—	220	480	750	1,350	—

KM# 21 WERK

7.00 g., 0.900 Gold 0.2025 oz. AGW, 21 mm. **Ruler:** Haile Selassie I **Obv:** Crowned bust left, laurels below **Rev:** St. George on horseback slaying the dragon

Date	Mintage	F12	VF20	XF40	MS60	MS63
EE1923 (1930-31)	—	500	1,000	1,650	3,500	—

DECIMAL COINAGE

100 Santeems (Cents) = 1 Birr (Dollar)
100 Matonas = 100 Santeems

KM# 27 MATONA

Copper **Ruler:** Haile Selassie I **Obv:** Crowned head right **Rev:** Crowned lion right, right foreleg raised holding ribboned cross

Date	Mintage	F12	VF20	XF40	MS60	MS63
EE1923 (1930-31)	1,250,000	1.50	2.50	8.00	16.00	22.00

Note: Struck by ICI in Birmingham, England. Other denominations in the Matona series were struck in Addis Ababa

KM# 32 CENT (Ande Santeem)

Copper, 17 mm. **Ruler:** Haile Selassie I **Obv:** Bust left, date below **Rev:** Crowned lion right, right foreleg raised holding ribboned cross

Date	Mintage	F12	VF20	XF40	MS60	MS63
EE1936 (1943-44)	20,000,000	—	0.10	0.20	1.00	2.00

Note: Struck at Philadelphia, Birmingham and the Royal Mint, London between 1944 and 1975 with the date EE1936 frozen

KM# 28.1 5 MATONAS

Copper **Ruler:** Haile Selassie I **Obv:** Crowned head right **Rev:** Crowned lion right, right foreleg raised holding ribboned cross **Edge:** Plain

Date	Mintage	F12	VF20	XF40	MS60	MS63
EE1923 (1930-31)	1,363,000	2.00	3.50	6.00	20.00	25.00

KM# 28.2 5 MATONAS

Copper **Ruler:** Haile Selassie I **Obv:** Crowned head right **Rev:** Crowned lion right, right foreleg raised holding ribboned cross **Edge:** Reeded

Date	Mintage	F12	VF20	XF40	MS60	MS63
EE1923 (1930-31)	Inc. above	3.00	4.50	8.00	25.00	40.00

KM# 33 5 CENTS (Amist Santeem)

Copper, 20 mm. **Ruler:** Haile Selassie I **Obv:** Bust left, date below **Rev:** Crowned lion right, right foreleg raised holding ribboned cross

Date	Mintage	F12	VF20	XF40	MS60	MS63
EE1936 (1943-44)	219,000,000	—	0.10	0.20	0.50	1.50

Note: Struck between 1944-1962 in Philadelphia and 1964-1966 in Birmingham

KM# 29 10 MATONAS

Nickel **Ruler:** Haile Selassie I **Obv:** Crowned bust right **Rev:** Crowned lion right, right foreleg raised holding ribboned cross

Date	Mintage	F12	VF20	XF40	MS60	MS63
EE1923 (1930-31)	936,000	1.50	2.50	4.50	12.50	—

KM# 34 10 CENTS (Assir Santeem)

Copper, 23 mm. **Ruler:** Haile Selassie I **Obv:** Bust left, date below **Rev:** Crowned lion right, right foreleg raised holding ribboned cross

Date	Mintage	F12	VF20	XF40	MS60	MS63
EE1936 (1943-44)	348,998,000	—	0.10	0.25	1.00	2.00

Note: Struck between 1945-1963 in Philadelphia, 1964-1966 in Birmingham and 1974-1975 in London

KM# 30 25 MATONAS

Nickel **Ruler:** Haile Selassie I **Obv:** Crowned head right **Rev:** Crowned lion right, right foreleg raised holding ribboned cross

Date	Mintage	F12	VF20	XF40	MS60	MS63
EE1923 (1930-31)	2,742,000	1.25	2.00	5.00	10.00	—

KM# 35 25 CENTS (Haya Amist Santeem)

Copper, 26 mm. **Ruler:** Haile Selassie I **Obv:** Bust left, date below **Rev:** Crowned lion right, right foreleg raised holding ribboned cross

Date	Mintage	F12	VF20	XF40	MS60	MS63
EE1936 (1943-44)	10,000,000	5.00	10.00	20.00	45.00	60.00

Note: 421,500 issued and 1952 withdrawn and replaced by KM#36

KM# 36 25 CENTS (Haya Amist Santeem)

Copper, 25.5 mm. **Ruler:** Haile Selassie I **Obv:** Bust left, date below **Rev:** Crowned lion right, right foreleg raised holding ribboned cross **Shape:** Scalloped

Date	Mintage	F12	VF20	XF40	MS60	MS63
EE1936 (1943-44)	30,000,000	0.25	0.50	1.00	4.00	10.00

Note: Issued in 1952 and 1953. Crude and refined edges

KM# 31 50 MATONAS

7.11 g., Nickel **Ruler:** Haile Selassie I **Obv:** Crowned head right **Rev:** Crowned lion right, right foreleg raised holding ribboned cross

Date	Mintage	F12	VF20	XF40	MS60	MS63
EE1923 (1930-31)	1,621,000	1.50	3.00	8.00	15.00	—

KM# 37 50 CENTS (Hamsa Santeem)

7.03 g., 0.800 Silver 0.1808 oz. ASW **Ruler:** Haile Selassie I **Obv:** Bust left, date below **Rev:** Crowned lion right, right foreleg raised holding ribboned cross

Date	Mintage	F12	VF20	XF40	MS60	MS63
EE1936 (1943-44)	30,000,000	6.50	8.50	15.00	30.00	—

Note: Struck in 1944-1945

KM# 37a 50 CENTS (Hamsa Santeem)

7.03 g., 0.700 Silver 0.1582 oz. ASW **Ruler:** Haile Selassie I **Obv:** Bust left, date below **Rev:** Crowned lion right, right foreleg raised holding ribboned cross

Date	Mintage	VF20	XF40	MS60	MS63	MS65
EE1936 (1943-44)	20,434,000	7.50	12.50	25.00	—	—

Note: Struck in 1947

KM# 48 5 DOLLARS

20.00 g., 0.925 Silver 0.5948 oz. ASW **Ruler:** Haile Selassie **Obv:** Bust half left of Emperor Theodros II (1855-1868) **Rev:** Bust facing, dates below

Date	Mintage	VF20	XF40	MS60	MS63	MS65
EE1964 F-NI	—	—	—	—	—	65.00
EE1964 (1973-74) NI	55,000	PF65 45.00				

KM# 49 5 DOLLARS

20.00 g., 0.925 Silver 0.5948 oz. ASW **Ruler:** Haile Selassie **Rev:** Crowned bust of Emperor Johannes IV (1872-1889), facing, dates below

Date	Mintage	VF20	XF40	MS60	MS63	MS65
EE1964 F-NI	—	—	—	—	—	65.00
EE1964 (1971-72) NI	55,000	PF65 45.00				

KM# 50 5 DOLLARS

20.00 g., 0.925 Silver 0.5948 oz. ASW **Ruler:** Haile Selassie **Obv:** Ayers: crowned bust of Emperor Menelik II right (1889-1913) **Rev:** Crowned lion right, right foreleg raised holding ribboned cross

Date	Mintage	VF20	XF40	MS60	MS63	MS65
EE1964 (1971-72) F-NI	—	—	—	—	—	75.00
EE1964 (1971-72) NI	60,000	PF65 45.00				

KM# 51 5 DOLLARS

20.00 g., 0.925 Silver 0.5948 oz. ASW **Ruler:** Haile Selassie **Rev:** Veiled bust of Empress Zauditu right (1916-30), left, dates at right

Date	Mintage	VF20	XF40	MS60	MS63	MS65
EE1964 (1971-72) F-NI	—	—	—	—	—	80.00
EE1964 (1971-72) NI	60,000	PF65 45.00				

KM# 52 5 DOLLARS
25.00 g., 0.9999 Silver 0.8037 oz. ASW **Ruler:** Haile Selassie **Obv:** Uniformed bust right, crown at left, shield at right **Rev:** Crowned lion right, right foreleg raised holding ribboned cross

Date	Mintage	VF20	XF40	MS60	MS63	MS65
1972 HF	100,000	PF63 20.50	PF65 25.00	PF67 27.50		

KM# 38 10 DOLLARS
4.00 g., 0.900 Gold 0.1157 oz. AGW **Ruler:** Haile Selassie **Subject:** 75th Anniverary of Birth and 50th Jubilee of Reign of Emperor Haile Selassie I **Obv:** Bust 3/4 left divides crown and shield **Rev:** Crowned lion right, right foreleg raised holding ribboned cross

Date	Mintage	F12	VF20	XF40	MS60	MS63
EE1958 NI	28,000	PF63 200	PF65 245			

KM# 53 10 DOLLARS
40.00 g., 0.925 Silver 1.1896 oz. ASW **Ruler:** Haile Selassie **Obv:** Uniformed bust 3/4 facing **Rev:** Crowned lion right, right foreleg raised holding ribboned cross

Date	Mintage	VF20	XF40	MS60	MS63	MS65
EE1964 F-NI	—	—	—	—	175	—
EE1964 NI	50,000	PF63 85.00	PF65 100			

KM# 39 20 DOLLARS
8.00 g., 0.900 Gold 0.2315 oz. AGW **Ruler:** Haile Selassie **Subject:** 75th Anniversary of Birth and 50th Jubilee of Reign of Emperor Haile Selassie I **Obv:** Bust 3/4 left divides crown and shield **Rev:** Crowned lion right, right foreleg raised holding ribboned cross

Date	Mintage	F12	VF20	XF40	MS60	MS63
EE1958 NI	25,000	PF63 375	PF65 400			

KM# 40 50 DOLLARS
20.00 g., 0.900 Gold 0.5787 oz. AGW **Ruler:** Haile Selassie **Subject:** 75th Anniversary of Birth and 50th Jubilee of Reign of Emperor Haile Selassie I **Obv:** Bust 3/4 left divides crown and shield **Rev:** Crowned lion right, right foreleg raised holding ribboned cross

Date	Mintage	F12	VF20	XF40	MS60	MS63
EE1958 NI	15,000	PF63 900	PF65 950			

KM# 55 50 DOLLARS
20.00 g., 0.900 Gold 0.5787 oz. AGW **Ruler:** Haile Selassie **Obv:** Bust of Theodros II, Emperor 1855-1866AD **Rev:** Lion

Date	Mintage	VF20	XF40	MS60	MS63	MS65
EE1964 NI	12,000	PF63 900	PF65 950			

KM# 56 50 DOLLARS
20.00 g., 0.900 Gold 0.5787 oz. AGW **Ruler:** Haile Selassie **Obv:** Bust of Yohannes IV, Emperor, 1872-1889AD

Date	Mintage	VF20	XF40	MS60	MS63	MS65
EE1964 NI	12,000	PF63 900	PF65 950			

KM# 57 50 DOLLARS
20.00 g., 0.900 Gold 0.5787 oz. AGW **Ruler:** Haile Selassie **Obv:** Bust of Menelik II, Emperor, 1889-1913AD

Date	Mintage	VF20	XF40	MS60	MS63	MS65
EE1964 NI	20,000	PF63 900	PF65 950			

KM# 58 50 DOLLARS
20.00 g., 0.900 Gold 0.5787 oz. AGW **Ruler:** Haile Selassie **Obv:** Bust of Empress Zauditu, 1916-1930AD

Date	Mintage	VF20	XF40	MS60	MS63	MS65
EE1964 NI	16,000	PF63 900	PF65 950			

KM# 41 100 DOLLARS
40.00 g., 0.900 Gold 1.1574 oz. AGW **Ruler:** Haile Selassie **Subject:** 75th Anniversary of Birth and 50th Jubilee of Reign of Emperor Haile Selassie I **Rev:** Crowned lion right, right foreleg raised holding ribboned cross

Date	Mintage	F12	VF20	XF40	MS60	MS63
EE1958 NI	11,000	PF63 1,750	PF65 1,850			

KM# 59 100 DOLLARS
40.00 g., 0.900 Gold 1.1574 oz. AGW **Ruler:** Haile Selassie **Obv:** Uniformed bust 3/4 facing **Rev:** Crowned lion right, right foreleg raised holding ribboned cross

Date	Mintage	VF20	XF40	MS60	MS63	MS65
EE1964 NI	10,000	PF63 1,750	PF65 1,850			

KM# 42 200 DOLLARS
80.00 g., 0.900 Gold 2.3149 oz. AGW **Ruler:** Haile Selassie **Subject:** 75th Anniversary of Birth and 50th Jubilee of Reign of Emperor Haile Selassie I **Rev:** Crowned lion right, right foreleg raised holding ribboned cross

Date	Mintage	F12	VF20	XF40	MS60	MS63
EE1958 NI	8,823	PF63 3,500	PF65 3,750			

TOKEN COINAGE

KM# Tn1 PIASTRE (1/16 Thaler)
Aluminum, 21 mm. **Ruler:** Empress Zauditu **Obv:** Seven line inscription **Rev:** Denomination and date

Date	Mintage	VG8	F12	VF20	XF40	MS60
1922	—	12.00	25.00	40.00	85.00	—

Note: Issued by a Syndicat Des Commercants in Dire Dawa

KM# Tn2 PIASTRE (1/16 Thaler)
Aluminum, 23.5 mm. **Obv:** Legend within circle and surrounding **Rev:** Denomination

Date	Mintage	VG8	F12	VF20	XF40	MS60
ND	—	10.00	20.00	35.00	75.00	—

Note: Issued by P. P. Trohalis in Addis Ababa

KM# Tn3 PIASTRE (1/16 Thaler)
Copper-Nickel-Zinc, 20 mm. **Obv:** Legend surrounds center **Rev:** Denomination

Date	Mintage	VG8	F12	VF20	XF40	MS60
ND	—	25.00	40.00	65.00	115	—

Note: Issued by Magdalinos Freres in Addis Ababa

KM# Tn4 PIASTRE (1/16 Thaler)
Aluminum, 21 mm. **Obv:** PRASSO within beaded circle, legend surrounds **Rev:** Denomination

Date	Mintage	VG8	F12	VF20	XF40	MS60
ND	—	20.00	35.00	60.00	110	—

Note: Issued by Prasso Concessions En Abyssinie

KM# Tn5 PIASTRE (1/16 Thaler)
Aluminum **Note:** Uniface

Date	Mintage	VG8	F12	VF20	XF40	MS60
ND	—	25.00	45.00	75.00	125	—

Note: Issued by F. L. in Addis Abada

PEOPLES DEMOCRATIC REPUBLIC

DECIMAL COINAGE

100 Santeems (Cents) = 1 Birr (Dollar)
100 Matonas = 100 Santeems

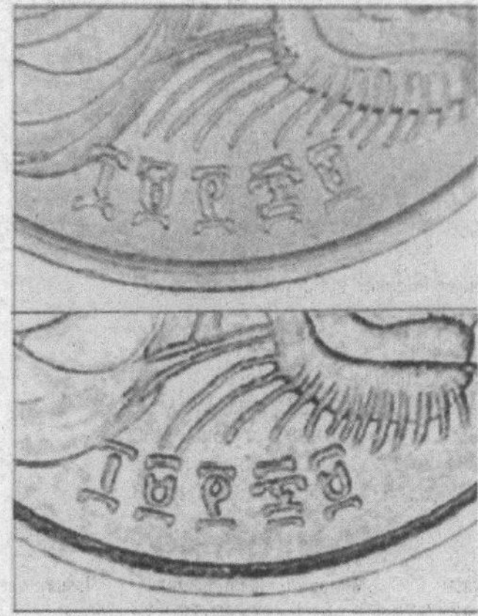

KM# 43.1 CENT
0.60 g., Aluminum, 17 mm. **Series:** F.A.O. **Obv:** Small lion head right, uniform chin whiskers **Rev:** Farmer with two oxen, denomination above

Date	Mintage	VF20	XF40	MS60	MS63	MS65
EE1969 (1977)	35,034,000	0.30	0.50	1.00	1.50	2.00

KM# 43.2 CENT
0.60 g., Aluminum, 17 mm. **Obv:** Small lion head right, two long chin whiskers at left nearly touch date **Rev:** Farmer with two oxen, denomination above

Date	Mintage	VF20	XF40	MS60	MS63	MS65
EE1969 (1977)	Inc. above	0.35	0.65	1.25	2.00	2.50

KM# 43.3 CENT
0.60 g., Aluminum, 17 mm. **Obv:** Large lion head right **Rev:** Farmer with two oxen, denomination above

Date	Mintage	VF20	XF40	MS60	MS63	MS65
EE1969 (1977) FM	12,000	PF65 3.00				

KM# 44.1 5 CENTS
3.00 g., Brass, 20 mm. **Obv:** Small lion head right, uniform chin whiskers **Rev:** Denomination left of figure

Date	Mintage	VF20	XF40	MS60	MS63	MS65
EE1969 (1977)	201,275,000	0.30	0.50	1.25	2.00	2.50

KM# 44.2 5 CENTS
3.00 g., Brass, 20 mm. **Obv:** Lion head right, date below **Rev:** Denomination left of figure

Date	Mintage	VF20	XF40	MS60	MS63	MS65
EE1969 (1977)	Inc. above	0.35	0.65	1.50	2.50	3.00

KM# 44.3 5 CENTS
3.00 g., Brass Plated Steel, 20 mm. **Obv:** Large lion head, right **Rev:** Denomination left of figure

Date	Mintage	VF20	XF40	MS60	MS63	MS65
EE1969 (1977) FM	12,000	PF65 2.50				

KM# 45.1 10 CENTS
4.50 g., Brass, 23 mm. **Obv:** Small lion head right, uniform chin whiskers **Rev:** Mountain Nyala, denomination at right

Date	Mintage	VF20	XF40	MS60	MS63	MS65
EE1969 (1977)	202,722,000	0.30	0.60	1.50	2.50	3.00

KM# 45.2 10 CENTS
4.50 g., Brass, 23 mm. **Obv:** Small lion head, two long chin whiskers at left nearly touch date **Rev:** Mountain Nyala and denomination

Date	Mintage	VF20	XF40	MS60	MS63	MS65
EE1969 (1977)	Inc. above	0.40	0.75	1.75	2.75	3.25

KM# 45.3 10 CENTS
4.50 g., Brass Plated Steel, 23 mm. **Obv:** Large lion head right **Rev:** Mountain Nyala, denomination at right

Date	Mintage	VF20	XF40	MS60	MS63	MS65
EE1969 (1977) FM	—	—	—	2.00	3.00	3.50
EE1969 (1977) FM	12,000	PF65 4.00				

KM# 46.1 25 CENTS
3.70 g., Copper-Nickel, 21.45 mm. **Obv:** Small lion head right, uniform chin whiskers **Rev:** Man and woman with arms raised divide denomination **Edge:** Reeded

Date	Mintage	VF20	XF40	MS60	MS63	MS65
EE1969 (1977)	44,983,000	0.30	0.60	1.25	2.00	2.50

KM# 46.2 25 CENTS
3.70 g., Copper-Nickel, 21.45 mm. **Obv:** Small lion head, two long chin whiskers at left nearly touch date **Rev:** Man and woman with arms raised divide denomination

Date	Mintage	VF20	XF40	MS60	MS63	MS65
EE1969 (1977)	Inc. above	0.40	0.75	1.50	2.50	—

KM# 46.3 25 CENTS
3.70 g., Copper-Nickel Plated Steel, 21.45 mm. **Obv:** Large lion head right **Rev:** Man and woman with arms raised divide denomination

Date	Mintage	VF20	XF40	MS60	MS63	MS65
EE1969 (1977) FM	12,000	PF65 4.50				

KM# 47.1 50 CENTS
6.00 g., Copper-Nickel, 25 mm. **Obv:** Small lion head right, uniform chin whiskers **Rev:** People of the Republic, denomination above

Date	Mintage	VF20	XF40	MS60	MS63	MS65
EE1969 (1977)	27,772,000	0.75	1.25	3.00	—	—

KM# 47.2 50 CENTS
6.00 g., Copper-Nickel Plated Steel, 25 mm. **Obv:** Small lion head, two long chin whiskers at left nearly touch date **Rev:** People of the republic, denomination above

Date	Mintage	VF20	XF40	MS60	MS63	MS65
EE1969 (1977)	Inc. above	0.85	1.50	3.00	4.00	—

KM# 47.3 50 CENTS
6.00 g., Copper-Nickel, 25 mm. **Obv:** Large lion head **Rev:** People of the republic, denomination above **Note:** Prev. KM#47.2.

Date	Mintage	VF20	XF40	MS60	MS63	MS65
EE1969 (1977) FM	12,000	PF65 7.50				

KM# 64 2 BIRR
Copper-Nickel **Subject:** World Soccer Games 1982 **Obv:** Lion head right **Rev:** Soccer players in front of two joined globes, denomination above

Date	Mintage	VF20	XF40	MS60	MS63	MS65
EE1964 (error)	7	—	—	—	145	—
EE1974 (1982)	—	—	—	—	8.00	12.00

KM# 61 10 BIRR
25.31 g., 0.925 Silver 0.7527 oz. ASW **Subject:** Conservation **Obv:** Lion within circle divides wreath surrounding symbols in center **Rev:** Bearded vulture

Date	Mintage	VF20	XF40	MS60	MS63	MS65
EE1970 (1977-78)	4,002	—	—	—	27.00	35.00

KM# 61a 10 BIRR
28.28 g., 0.925 Silver 0.841 oz. ASW **Obv:** Lion within circle divides wreath surrounding symbols in center **Rev:** Bearded vulture

Date	Mintage	VF20	XF40	MS60	MS63	MS65
EE1970 (1977-78)	3,460	PF63 40.00	PF65 60.00			

KM# 54 20 BIRR
23.33 g., 0.925 Silver 0.6938 oz. ASW **Subject:** International Year of the Child **Obv:** Silhouette of child flanked by laurels, logo above **Rev:** Children, logo above, denomination below

Date	Mintage	VF20	XF40	MS60	MS63	MS65
EE1972 (1979)	16,000	PF63 25.00	PF65 30.00			

KM# 65 20 BIRR
23.33 g., 0.925 Silver 0.6938 oz. ASW **Subject:** World Soccer Games 1982 **Obv:** Lion head right **Rev:** Soccer players in front of two joined globes, denomination above

Date	Mintage	VF20	XF40	MS60	MS63	MS65
EE1974 (1982)	10,000	PF63 37.00	PF65 50.00			

KM# 73 20 BIRR

23.33 g., 0.925 Silver 0.6938 oz. ASW **Subject:** Decade for Women **Rev:** Woman in field

Date	Mintage	VF20	XF40	MS60	MS63	MS65
1984	372	PF65 175				

KM# 74 20 BIRR

23.33 g., 0.925 Silver 0.6938 oz. ASW **Subject:** 50th Anniversary UNICEF - Folk Dance **Obv:** Two dancing girls in front of huts, denomination below **Rev:** UNICEF logo divides date **Edge:** Reeded

Date	Mintage	VF20	XF40	MS60	MS63	MS65
1998	—	PF63 45.00	PF65 55.00			

KM# 62 25 BIRR

31.65 g., 0.925 Silver 0.9413 oz. ASW **Subject:** Conservation **Obv:** Lion within circle divides wreath surrounding symbols in center **Rev:** Mountain Nyala left, right foreleg raised

Date	Mintage	VF20	XF40	MS60	MS63	MS65
EE1970 (1977)	4,002	—	—	—	32.00	45.00

KM# 62a 25 BIRR

35.00 g., 0.925 Silver 1.0409 oz. ASW **Obv:** Lion within circle divides wreath surrounding symbols in center **Rev:** Mountain Nyala left, right foreleg raised

Date	Mintage	VF20	XF40	MS60	MS63	MS65
EE1970 (1977)	3,295	PF63 40.00	PF65 45.00			

KM# 66 50 BIRR

28.50 g., 0.925 Silver 0.8476 oz. ASW, 38 mm. **Subject:** International Year of Disabled Persons **Obv:** Symbol within wreath **Rev:** Hand grasping wrist, denomination below, initials above

Date	Mintage	VF20	XF40	MS60	MS63	MS65
EE1974 (1982)	11,000	—	—	—	—	55.00
EE1974 (1982)	10,000	PF63 55.00	PF65 65.00			

KM# 75 50 BIRR

28.28 g., 0.925 Silver 0.841 oz. ASW, 38.61 mm. **Subject:** Revolution, 10th Anniversary **Obv:** Large lion head right **Rev:** Landscape, wheat stalk, star above

Date	Mintage	VF20	XF40	MS60	MS63	MS65
EE1976/1984	Est. 1000	PF65 150				

KM# 67 200 BIRR

7.13 g., 0.900 Gold 0.2063 oz. AGW **Subject:** World Soccer Games 1982 **Obv:** Lion head right **Rev:** Soccer players in front of two joined globes, denomination above

Date	Mintage	VF20	XF40	MS60	MS63	MS65
1982	1,310	PF65 350	PF67 375			

KM# 72 200 BIRR

7.13 g., 0.900 Gold 0.2063 oz. AGW **Subject:** Decade for Women **Obv:** Small lion head right, denomination below **Rev:** Woman with child, writing

Date	Mintage	VF20	XF40	MS60	MS63	MS65
1984	298	PF67 425				

KM# 60 400 BIRR

17.17 g., 0.900 Gold 0.4968 oz. AGW **Subject:** International Year of the Child **Obv:** Silhouette of child, laurels flanking, logo above **Rev:** Children playing, denomination below, logo above

Date	Mintage	VF20	XF40	MS60	MS63	MS65
EE1972 (1979)	3,387	PF65 835	PF67 865			

KM# 68 500 BIRR

15.98 g., 0.917 Gold 0.4711 oz. AGW **Subject:** International Year of the Disabled Persons **Obv:** Symbol within wreath **Rev:** Flanking figures on steps holding arms of central figure, denomination below

Date	Mintage	VF20	XF40	MS60	MS63	MS65
EE1974	2,007	—	—	—	—	800
EE1974 (1982)	2,042	PF65 825	PF67 850			

KM# 63 600 BIRR

33.44 g., 0.900 Gold 0.9675 oz. AGW **Subject:** Conservation **Obv:** Lion within circle divides wreath surrounding symbols at center **Rev:** Walia Ibex right

Date	Mintage	VF20	XF40	MS60	MS63	MS65
EE1970 (1977)	547	—	—	—	—	1,650
EE1970 (1977)	160	PF65 1,750	PF67 1,850			

PATTERNS

Including off metal strikes

KM#	Date	Mintage	Identification	Mkt Val
Pn7	EE1921 (1928)	—	1/2 Werk. Gold. Similar to KM20 (proof).	—
Pn8	EE1921 (1928)	—	Werk. Gold. Similar to KM21 (proof).	—

TRIAL STRIKES

KM#	Date	Mintage	Identification	Mkt Val
TS9	EE1917 (1925)	—	1/2 Birr. Pewter. KM M3. (thin).	350
TS10	EE1917 (1925)	—	Birr. Pewter. KM M4. (thin).	550
TS11	1966	—	10 Dollars. Bronze Gilt. KM38.	50.00
TS12	1966	—	20 Dollars. Bronze Gilt. KM39.	80.00
TS13	1966	—	50 Dollars. Bronze Gilt. KM40.	150
TS14	1966	—	100 Dollars. Bronze Gilt. KM41.	250
TS15	1966	—	200 Dollars. Bronze Gilt. KM42.	450

Note: Issued in cased set of five pieces

PIEDFORT

KM#	Date	Mintage	Identification	Mkt Val
P1	1980	39	20 Birr. Silver. KM54.	175
P2	1980	8	400 Birr. Gold. KM60.	1,850
P3	1981	1,100	50 Birr. Silver. KM66.	125
P4	1982	520	500 Birr. Gold. KM68.	1,650

MINT SETS

KM#	Date	Mintage	Identification	Issue Price	Mkt Val
MS1	1972 (5)	—	KM48-51, 53	—	500

PROOF SETS

KM#	Date	Mintage	Identification	Issue Price	Mkt Val
PS2	1966 (5)	8,823	KM38-42	—	7,650
PS3	1972 (10)	—	KM48-51, 53, 55-59	—	6,250
PS5	1972 (5)	10,000	KM55-59	—	6,000
PS6	1972 (5)	50,000	KM48-51, 53	46.00	250
PS7	1977 (5)	11,724	KM43.2-47.2	25.00	25.00
PS8	1979 (2)	—	KM61a-62a	—	90.00

FAEROE ISLANDS

The Faeroe Islands, a self-governing community within the kingdom of Denmark, are situated in the North Atlantic between Iceland and the Shetland Islands. The 17 inhabited islands and numerous islets and reefs have an area of 540 sq. mi. (1,400 sq. km.)and a population of 46,000. Capital: Thorshavn. The principal industries are fishing and livestock. Fish and fish products are exported.

While it is thought that Irish hermits lived on the islands in the 7th and 8th centuries, the present inhabitants are descended from 6th century Norse settlers. The Faeroe Islands became a Norwegian fief in 1035 and became Danish in 1380 when Norway and Denmark were united. They have ever since remained in Danish possession and were granted self-government (except for an appointed governor-general) with their own legislature, executive and flag in 1948.

The islands were occupied by British troops during World War II, after the German occupation of Denmark. The Faeroe island coinage was struck in London during World War II.

RULER

Danish

MONETARY SYSTEM

100 Øre = 1 Krone

DANISH STATE

DECIMAL COINAGE

KM# 1 ØRE

Bronze, 15.5 mm. **Obv:** Center hole divides date and denomination **Rev:** Center hole within crowned monogram

Date	Mintage	VF20	XF40	MS60	MS63	MS65
1941	—	25.00	45.00	85.00	125	150

Note: Also struck in 1942 with 1941 dies

Date	Mintage	VF20	XF40	MS60	MS63	MS65
1941	—	PF63 500				

KM# 2 2 ØRE

Bronze, 20.5 mm. **Obv:** Center hole divides date and denomination **Rev:** Center hole within crowned monogram

Date	Mintage	VF20	XF40	MS60	MS63	MS65
1941	Est. 200000	20.00	35.00	65.00	90.00	135

Note: Also struck in 1942 with 1941 dies

Date	Mintage	VF20	XF40	MS60	MS63	MS65
1941	—	PF63 500				

KM# 3 5 ØRE

Bronze, 27 mm. **Obv:** Center hole divides date and denomination **Rev:** Center hole within crowned monogram

Date	Mintage	VF20	XF40	MS60	MS63	MS65
1941	—	12.00	25.00	45.00	75.00	125

Note: Also struck in 1942 with 1941 dies

Date	Mintage	VF20	XF40	MS60	MS63	MS65
1941	—	PF63 500				

KM# 4 10 ØRE

Copper-Nickel, 17.5 mm. **Obv:** Center hole divides crowned monogram, date below **Rev:** Center hole with ornaments divides denomination

Date	Mintage	VF20	XF40	MS60	MS63	MS65
1941	—	15.00	30.00	60.00	85.00	130

Note: Also struck in 1942 with 1941 dies

Date	Mintage	VF20	XF40	MS60	MS63	MS65
1941	—	PF63 500				

KM# 5 25 ØRE

Copper-Nickel, 22.5 mm. **Obv:** Center hole divides crowned monogram, date below **Rev:** Center hole with ornaments divides denomination

Date	Mintage	VF20	XF40	MS60	MS63	MS65
1941	Est. 250000	15.00	30.00	60.00	90.00	140

Note: Also struck in 1942 with 1941 dies

Date	Mintage	VF20	XF40	MS60	MS63	MS65
1941	—	PF63 500				

PROOF SETS

KM#	Date	Mintage	Identification	Issue Price	Mkt Val
PS1	1941 (5)	—	KM1-5	—	3,000

FALKLAND ISLANDS

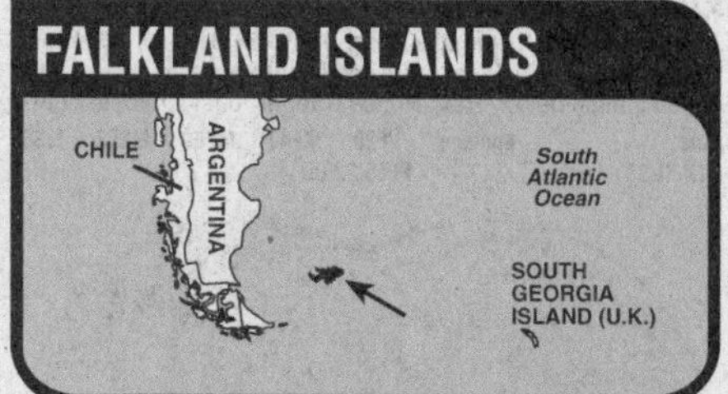

The Colony of the Falkland Islands and Dependencies, a British colony located in the South Atlantic about 500 miles northeast of Cape Horn, has an area of 4,700 sq. mi. (12,170 sq. km.) and a population of 2,121. East Falkland, West Falkland, South Georgia, and South Sandwich are the largest of the 200 islands. Capital: Stanley. Sheep grazing is the main industry. Wool, whale oil, and seal oil are exported.

The Falklands were discovered by British navigator John Davis (Davys) in 1592, and named by Capt. John Strong - for Viscount Falkland, treasurer of the British navy - in 1690. French navigator Louis De Bougainville established the first settlement, at Port Louis, in 1764. The following year Capt. John Byron claimed the islands for Britain and left a small party at Saunders Island. Spain later forced the French and British to abandon their settlements but did not implement its claim to the islands. In 1829 the Republic of Buenos Aires, which claimed to have inherited the Spanish rights, sent Louis Vernet to develop a colony on the islands. In 1831 he seized three American sealing vessels, whereupon the men of the corvette, the U.S.S. Lexington, destroyed his settlement and proclaimed the Falklands to be 'free of all governance'. Britain, which had never renounced its claim, then re-established its settlement in 1833.

RULER
British

MONETARY SYSTEM
100 Pence = 1 Pound

BRITISH COLONY

DECIMAL COINAGE

KM# 1 1/2 PENNY

1.78 g., Bronze, 17.14 mm. **Ruler:** Elizabeth II **Obv:** Young bust right **Rev:** Salmon behind denomination, date at right

Date	Mintage	VF20	XF40	MS60	MS63	MS65
1974	23,000	PF65 1.50				
1974	140,000	—	0.10	0.25	0.35	0.50
1980	10,000	PF65 1.50				
1980	—	—	0.10	0.15	0.25	0.50
1982	—	—	0.10	0.15	0.25	0.50
1982	—	PF65 1.50				
1983	—	—	0.10	0.15	0.25	0.50

KM# 2 PENNY

3.56 g., Bronze, 20.32 mm. **Ruler:** Elizabeth II **Obv:** Young bust right **Rev:** Gentoo penguins flank denomination, date below

Date	Mintage	VF20	XF40	MS60	MS63	MS65
1974	23,000	PF65 2.00				
1974	96,000	0.10	0.20	0.35	0.60	1.00
1980	10,000	PF65 2.00				
1980	—	0.10	0.20	0.35	0.60	1.00
1982	—	0.10	0.20	0.35	0.60	1.00
1982	—	PF65 2.00				
1983	—	0.10	0.20	0.35	0.60	1.00
1985	—	0.10	0.20	0.35	0.60	1.00
1987	111,000	—	0.20	0.35	0.60	1.00
1987	—	PF65 2.50				
1992	—	0.10	0.20	0.35	0.60	1.00
1992	—	PF65 2.50				

KM# 2a PENNY

3.56 g., Copper Plated Steel, 20.32 mm. **Ruler:** Elizabeth II **Obv:** Young bust right **Rev:** Denomination divides penguins, date below

Date	Mintage	VF20	XF40	MS60	MS63	MS65
1998	2,500	—	—	0.25	0.50	0.75
1999	—	—	—	0.25	0.50	0.75
1999	2,500	PF65 2.00				

KM# 3 2 PENCE

7.12 g., Bronze, 25.91 mm. **Ruler:** Elizabeth II **Obv:** Young bust right **Rev:** Upland goose, wings open, denomination above, date at right

Date	Mintage	VF20	XF40	MS60	MS63	MS65
1974	23,000	PF65 3.00				
1974	72,000	0.10	0.15	0.25	0.50	2.00
1980	—	0.10	0.15	0.25	0.50	2.00
1980	10,000	PF65 3.00				
1982	—	0.10	0.15	0.25	0.50	2.00
1982	—	PF65 3.00				
1983	—	0.10	0.15	0.25	0.50	2.00
1985	—	0.10	0.15	0.25	0.50	2.00
1987	106,000	—	0.15	0.25	0.50	2.00
1987	—	PF65 3.50				
1992	—	PF65 3.50				
1992	—	0.10	0.15	0.25	0.50	2.00

KM# 3a 2 PENCE

7.12 g., Copper Plated Steel, 25.91 mm. **Ruler:** Elizabeth II **Obv:** Young bust right **Rev:** Upland goose, wings open, denomination above, date at right

Date	Mintage	VF20	XF40	MS60	MS63	MS65
1998	—	—	—	0.20	0.35	1.00
1999	2,500	PF65 3.00				
1999	—	—	—	0.20	0.35	1.00

KM# 4.1 5 PENCE

5.65 g., Copper-Nickel, 23.6 mm. **Ruler:** Elizabeth II **Obv:** Young bust right **Rev:** Blackbrowed albatross in flight, denomination and date below

Date	Mintage	VF20	XF40	MS60	MS63	MS65
1974	67,000	0.10	0.25	0.35	0.75	1.00
1974	23,000	PF65 3.50				
1980	10,000	PF65 4.00				
1980	—	0.10	0.25	0.35	0.75	1.00
1982	—	0.10	0.25	0.35	0.75	1.00
1982	—	PF65 4.00				
1983	—	0.10	0.25	0.35	0.75	1.00
1985	—	0.10	0.25	0.35	0.75	1.00
1987	5,000	—	0.25	0.35	0.75	1.00
1987	—	PF65 4.50				
1992	—	0.10	0.25	0.35	0.75	1.00
1992	—	PF65 4.50				

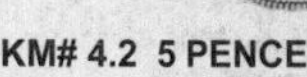

KM# 4.2 5 PENCE

3.25 g., Copper-Nickel, 18 mm. **Ruler:** Elizabeth II **Obv:** Young bust right **Rev:** Blackbrowed albatross in flight, denomination and date below **Edge:** Reeded

Date	Mintage	VF20	XF40	MS60	MS63	MS65
1998	—	—	—	0.35	0.75	1.00
1999	—	—	—	0.35	0.75	1.00
1999	2,500	PF65 4.00				

KM# 5.1 10 PENCE

11.31 g., Copper-Nickel, 28.5 mm. **Ruler:** Elizabeth II **Obv:** Young bust right **Rev:** Ursine seal with cub, denomination below, date at left

Date	Mintage	VF20	XF40	MS60	MS63	MS65
1974	23,000	PF65 5.00				
1974	87,000	0.20	0.40	0.75	1.50	3.50
1980	10,000	PF65 5.00				
1980	—	0.20	0.40	0.75	1.50	3.50
1982	—	PF65 5.00				
1982	—	0.20	0.40	0.75	1.50	3.50
1983	—	0.20	0.40	0.75	1.50	3.50
1985	—	0.20	0.40	0.75	1.50	3.50
1987	4,000	—	0.40	0.75	1.50	3.50
1987	—	PF65 5.50				
1992	—	0.20	0.40	0.75	1.50	3.50
1992	—	PF65 5.50				

KM# 5.2 10 PENCE

6.50 g., Copper-Nickel, 24.5 mm. **Ruler:** Elizabeth II **Obv:** Young bust right **Rev:** Ursine seal with cub, denomination below, date at left **Edge:** Reeded

Date	Mintage	VF20	XF40	MS60	MS63	MS65
1998	—	—	—	0.75	1.50	3.00
1999	2,500	PF65 5.00				
1999	—	—	—	0.75	1.50	3.00

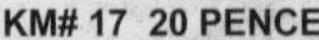

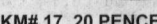

KM# 17 20 PENCE

5.00 g., Copper-Nickel, 21.4 mm. **Ruler:** Elizabeth II **Obv:** Young bust right **Rev:** Romney marsh sheep left, denomination above **Shape:** 7-sided

Date	Mintage	VF20	XF40	MS60	MS63	MS65
1982	—	0.40	0.65	1.00	2.00	4.00
1982	—	PF65 5.00				
1983	—	0.40	0.65	1.00	2.00	4.00
1985	—	0.40	0.65	1.00	2.00	4.00
1987	—	PF65 5.50				
1987	4,250	0.40	0.65	1.00	2.00	4.00
1992	—	PF65 5.50				
1992	—	0.40	0.65	1.00	2.00	4.00
1998	—	0.40	0.65	1.00	2.00	4.00
1999	2,500	PF65 5.00				
1999	—	—	—	1.00	2.00	4.00

KM# 10 50 PENCE

28.28 g., Copper-Nickel, 38.61 mm. **Ruler:** Elizabeth II **Subject:** Queen's Silver Jubilee **Obv:** Young bust right, dates at left **Rev:** Sheep above ship on shield within wreath, denomination below

Date	Mintage	VF20	XF40	MS60	MS63	MS65
ND-1977	100,000	1.00	1.50	2.00	3.00	4.50

KM# 10a 50 PENCE

28.28 g., 0.925 Silver 0.841 oz. ASW, 38.5 mm. **Ruler:** Elizabeth II **Obv:** Young bust right **Rev:** Sheep above ship on shield within wreath, denomination below

Date	Mintage	VF20	XF40	MS60	MS63	MS65
ND-1977	22,000	PF65 22.00				

KM# 14.1 50 PENCE

13.50 g., Copper-Nickel, 30 mm. **Ruler:** Elizabeth II **Obv:** Young bust right **Rev:** Falkland Island fox (extinct), date at right, denomination above **Shape:** 7-sided

Date	Mintage	VF20	XF40	MS60	MS63	MS65
1980	—	PF65 8.00				
1980	—	1.00	2.00	3.50	5.00	7.50
1982	—	1.00	2.00	3.50	5.00	7.50
1982	—	PF65 8.00				
1983	—	1.00	2.00	3.50	5.00	7.50
1985	—	1.00	2.00	3.50	5.00	7.50
1987	—	PF65 9.00				
1987	4,000	1.00	2.00	3.50	5.00	7.50
1992	—	1.00	2.00	3.50	5.00	7.50
1992	—	PF65 9.00				
1995	—	—	2.00	3.50	5.00	7.50

KM# 14.2 50 PENCE

8.00 g., Copper-Nickel, 27.3 mm. **Ruler:** Elizabeth II **Obv:** Young bust right **Rev:** Falkland Island fox (extinct) **Shape:** 7-sided **Note:** Reduced size.

Date	Mintage	VF20	XF40	MS60	MS63	MS65
1998	—	—	2.00	3.50	5.00	7.50
1999	—	—	2.00	3.50	5.00	7.50
1999	2,500	PF65 8.00				

KM# 15 50 PENCE

Copper-Nickel, 38.5 mm. **Ruler:** Elizabeth II **Subject:** 80th Anniversary - Birth of Queen Mother **Obv:** Young bust right **Rev:** Queen Mother's bust left

Date	Mintage	VF20	XF40	MS60	MS63	MS65
ND-1980	—	1.00	1.50	2.50	3.50	6.00

KM# 15a 50 PENCE

28.28 g., 0.925 Silver 0.841 oz. ASW, 38.5 mm. **Ruler:** Elizabeth II **Subject:** 80th Anniversary-Birth of Queen Mother **Obv:** Young bust right **Rev:** Queen Mother's bust left

Date	Mintage	VF20	XF40	MS60	MS63	MS65
ND-1980	—	PF65 22.00				

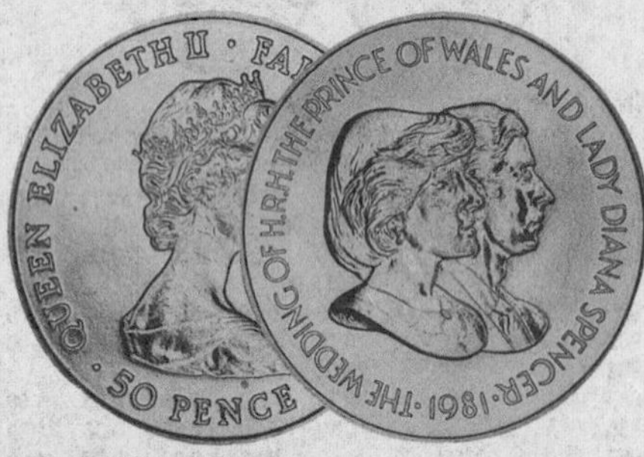

KM# 16 50 PENCE

Copper-Nickel, 38.5 mm. **Ruler:** Elizabeth II **Subject:** Wedding of Prince Charles and Lady Diana **Obv:** Young bust right **Rev:** Conjoined busts of royal couple right

Date	Mintage	VF20	XF40	MS60	MS63	MS65
1981	—	1.00	1.50	2.00	3.00	4.50

KM# 16a 50 PENCE

28.28 g., 0.925 Silver 0.841 oz. ASW, 38.5 mm. **Ruler:** Elizabeth II **Subject:** Wedding of Prince Charles and Lady Diana **Obv:** Young bust right **Rev:** Conjoined busts of royal couple right

Date	Mintage	VF20	XF40	MS60	MS63	MS65
1981	40,000	PF65 22.00				

KM# 18 50 PENCE

Copper-Nickel, 38.5 mm. **Subject:** Liberation from Argentina Forces **Obv:** Young bust right, denomination below **Rev:** Flag design in background, state shield at left, date below

Date	Mintage	VF20	XF40	MS60	MS63	MS65
ND-1982	—	1.00	1.50	2.00	3.00	4.50

KM# 18a 50 PENCE

28.28 g., 0.925 Silver 0.841 oz. ASW, 38.5 mm. **Ruler:** Elizabeth II **Obv:** Young bust right, denomination below **Rev:** Flag design in background, state shield at left, date below

Date	Mintage	VF20	XF40	MS60	MS63	MS65
ND-1982	Est. 25000	PF65 22.00				

KM# 18b 50 PENCE

47.54 g., 0.917 Gold 1.4016 oz. AGW, 38.5 mm. **Ruler:** Elizabeth II **Subject:** Liberation From Argentina Forces **Obv:** Young bust right, denomination below **Rev:** Flag design in background, state shield at left, date below

Date	Mintage	VF20	XF40	MS60	MS63	MS65
ND-1982	25	PF67 5,000				

KM# 19 50 PENCE

28.28 g., Copper-Nickel, 38.61 mm. **Ruler:** Elizabeth II **Subject:** 150th Anniversary of British Rule **Obv:** Young bust right **Rev:** Ship divides dates

Date	Mintage	VF20	XF40	MS60	MS63	MS65
ND-1983	Est. 50000	1.00	2.00	3.50	5.00	7.00

KM# 19a 50 PENCE

28.28 g., 0.925 Silver 0.841 oz. ASW, 38.61 mm. **Ruler:** Elizabeth II **Subject:** 150th Anniversary of British rule **Obv:** Young bust right **Rev:** Ship divides dates

Date	Mintage	VF20	XF40	MS60	MS63	MS65
ND-1983	Est. 10000	PF65 22.00				

KM# 19b 50 PENCE

47.54 g., 0.917 Gold 1.4016 oz. AGW, 38.61 mm. **Ruler:** Elizabeth II **Subject:** 150th Anniversary of British Rule **Obv:** Young bust right **Rev:** Ship divides dates

Date	Mintage	VF20	XF40	MS60	MS63	MS65
ND-1983	150	PF67 2,000				

KM# 21 50 PENCE

Copper-Nickel, 38.5 mm. **Ruler:** Elizabeth II **Subject:** Opening of Mount Pleasant Airport **Obv:** Crowned bust right, denomination below **Rev:** Prince Charles' bust left, date at right

Date	Mintage	VF20	XF40	MS60	MS63	MS65
ND-1985	—	—	—	2.00	3.00	4.50

KM# 21a 50 PENCE

28.28 g., 0.925 Silver 0.841 oz. ASW, 38.61 mm. **Subject:** Opening of Mount Pleasant Airport **Obv:** Crowned bust right, denomination below **Rev:** Prince Charles' bust left, date right

Date	Mintage	VF20	XF40	MS60	MS63	MS65
ND (1985)	—	PF65 22.00				

KM# 25 50 PENCE

Copper-Nickel, 38.5 mm. **Ruler:** Elizabeth II **Subject:** World Wildlife Fund **Obv:** Crowned bust right **Rev:** King penguins, denomination and date

Date	Mintage	VF20	XF40	MS60	MS63	MS65
1987	—	—	—	3.00	5.00	9.00

KM# 25a 50 PENCE

28.28 g., 0.925 Silver 0.841 oz. ASW, 38.5 mm. **Ruler:** Elizabeth II **Subject:** World Wildlife Fund **Obv:** Crowned bust right **Rev:** King Penguins, denomination and date

Date	Mintage	VF20	XF40	MS60	MS63	MS65
1987	Est. 25000	PF65 28.00				

KM# 26 50 PENCE

Copper-Nickel, 38.5 mm. **Ruler:** Elizabeth II **Subject:** Children's Fund **Obv:** Crowned bust right **Rev:** Woman on horseback, dog herding animals, denomination below

Date	Mintage	VF20	XF40	MS60	MS63	MS65
1990	Est. 20000	—	—	3.00	5.00	9.00

KM# 26a 50 PENCE

28.28 g., 0.925 Silver 0.841 oz. ASW, 38.5 mm. **Ruler:** Elizabeth II **Subject:** Children's Fund **Obv:** Crowned bust right **Rev:** Woman on horseback, dog herding animals, denomination below

Date	Mintage	VF20	XF40	MS60	MS63	MS65
1990	—	PF65 25.00				

KM# 34 50 PENCE

28.28 g., Copper-Nickel, 38.61 mm. **Ruler:** Elizabeth II **Subject:** 40th Anniversary - Reign of Queen Elizabeth II **Obv:** Crowned bust right **Rev:** Three figures, one at left is silhouette, dates below

Date	Mintage	VF20	XF40	MS60	MS63	MS65
ND-1992	—	—	—	2.50	4.50	6.50

KM# 34a 50 PENCE

28.28 g., 0.925 Silver 0.841 oz. ASW, 38.61 mm. **Ruler:** Elizabeth II **Subject:** 40th Anniversary - Reign of Queen Elizabeth II **Obv:** Crowned bust right **Rev:** Three figures, one at left is silhouette, dates below

Date	Mintage	VF20	XF40	MS60	MS63	MS65
ND-1992	5,000	PF65 35.00				

KM# 34b 50 PENCE

47.54 g., 0.917 Gold 1.4016 oz. AGW, 38.61 mm. **Ruler:** Elizabeth II **Subject:** Queen Elizabeth, 40th Anniversary of reign **Obv:** Crowned bust right **Rev:** Three figures, one at left is silhouette, dates below

Date	Mintage	VF20	XF40	MS60	MS63	MS65
ND-1992	150	PF67 2,000				

KM# 43 50 PENCE

Copper-Nickel, 38.5 mm. **Ruler:** Elizabeth II **Subject:** 40th Anniversary - Coronation of Queen Elizabeth II **Obv:** Crowned bust right **Rev:** Queen on horseback, dates and denomination below

Date	Mintage	VF20	XF40	MS60	MS63	MS65
ND-1993	—	—	—	2.50	4.50	6.50

KM# 43a 50 PENCE

28.28 g., 0.925 Silver 0.841 oz. ASW, 38.5 mm. **Ruler:** Elizabeth II **Subject:** 40th Anniversary - Coronation of Queen Elizabeth II **Obv:** Crowned bust right **Rev:** Queen on horseback, dates and denomination below

Date	Mintage	VF20	XF40	MS60	MS63	MS65
ND-1993	Est. 10000	PF65 28.00				

KM# 45 50 PENCE

Copper-Nickel, 38.5 mm. **Ruler:** Elizabeth II **Subject:** V. E. Day - 50th Anniversary **Obv:** Crowned bust right **Rev:** Denomination and dove divide flags, date below

Date	Mintage	VF20	XF40	MS60	MS63	MS65
1995	—	—	—	2.50	4.50	6.50

KM# 45a 50 PENCE

28.28 g., 0.925 Silver 0.841 oz. ASW, 38.5 mm. **Ruler:** Elizabeth II **Subject:** V. E. Day - 50th Anniversary **Obv:** Crowned bust right **Rev:** Denomination and dove divide flags, date below

Date	Mintage	VF20	XF40	MS60	MS63	MS65
1995	Est. 10000	PF65 25.00				

KM# 45b 50 PENCE

47.54 g., 0.917 Gold 1.4016 oz. AGW, 38.5 mm. **Ruler:** Elizabeth II **Subject:** V.E. Day - 50th Anniversary **Obv:** Crowned bust right **Rev:** Denomination and dove divide flags, date below

Date	Mintage	VF20	XF40	MS60	MS63	MS65
1995	Est. 100	PF67 2,000				

KM# 72 50 PENCE

28.28 g., Copper-Nickel, 38.6 mm. **Ruler:** Elizabeth II **Obv:** Crowned bust right, date below **Rev:** Queen Mother holding infant on lap, date below, circle surrounds, denmination below **Edge:** Reeded

Date	Mintage	VF20	XF40	MS60	MS63	MS65
1995	—	—	—	2.50	4.50	6.50

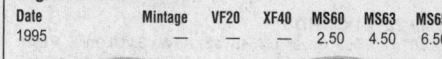

KM# 72a.1 50 PENCE

15.92 g., 0.925 Silver 0.4735 oz. ASW, 28.3 mm. **Ruler:** Elizabeth II **Obv:** Crowned bust right, date below **Rev:** Queen Mother holding the baby, date below, circle surrounds, denomination below **Edge:** Reeded

Date	Mintage	VF20	XF40	MS60	MS63	MS65
1997	—	PF65 15.00				

KM# 72a 50 PENCE

28.28 g., 0.925 Silver 0.841 oz. ASW, 38.6 mm. **Ruler:** Elizabeth II **Obv:** Crowned bust right, date below **Rev:** Queen Mother holding infant on lap, date below, circle surrounds, denomination below

Date	Mintage	VF20	XF40	MS60	MS63	MS65
1995	—	PF65 25.00				

KM# 46 50 PENCE

Copper-Nickel, 38.5 mm. **Ruler:** Elizabeth II **Subject:** Queen Elizabeth II's 70th Birthday **Obv:** Crowned bust right **Rev:** Queen and Prince Philip as young adults, denomination and date below

Date	Mintage	VF20	XF40	MS60	MS63	MS65
1996	—	—	—	2.50	4.50	6.50

KM# 46a 50 PENCE

28.28 g., 0.925 Silver 0.841 oz. ASW, 38.5 mm. **Ruler:** Elizabeth II **Subject:** Queen Elizabeth II's 70th Birthday **Obv:** Crowned bust right **Rev:** Queen and Prince Philip as young adults, denomination and date below

Date	Mintage	VF20	XF40	MS60	MS63	MS65
1996	—	PF65 25.00				

KM# 59 50 PENCE

Copper-Nickel, 38.5 mm. **Ruler:** Elizabeth II **Subject:** WWF - Conserving Nature **Obv:** Crowned bust right **Rev:** Pair of Black-browed Albatross, date above

Date	Mintage	VF20	XF40	MS60	MS63	MS65
1997	—	—	—	—	10.00	12.00

KM# 59a 50 PENCE

28.28 g., 0.925 Silver 0.841 oz. ASW, 38.5 mm. **Ruler:** Elizabeth II **Subject:** WWF - Conserving Nature **Obv:** Crowned bust right **Rev:** Pair of Black-browed Albatross, date above

Date	Mintage	VF20	XF40	MS60	MS63	MS65
1997	Est. 15000	PF65 20.00				

KM# 60 50 PENCE
Copper-Nickel, 38.5 mm. **Ruler:** Elizabeth II **Subject:** WWF - Conserving Nature **Obv:** Crowned bust right **Rev:** Peale's dolphin, date above

Date	Mintage	VF20	XF40	MS60	MS63	MS65
1998	—	—	—	—	10.00	12.00

KM# 60a 50 PENCE
28.28 g., 0.925 Silver 0.841 oz. ASW, 38.5 mm. **Ruler:** Elizabeth II **Subject:** WWF - Conserving Nature **Obv:** Crowned bust right **Rev:** Peale's dolphin

Date	Mintage	VF20	XF40	MS60	MS63	MS65
1998	—	PF65 20.00				

KM# 66 50 PENCE
28.28 g., Copper-Nickel, 38.5 mm. **Ruler:** Elizabeth II **Subject:** Winston Churchill **Obv:** Crowned bust right **Rev:** Churchill in Admiral's uniform, date below ship at left

Date	Mintage	VF20	XF40	MS60	MS63	MS65
1999	—	—	—	2.50	4.50	6.50

KM# 66a 50 PENCE
28.28 g., 0.925 Silver 0.841 oz. ASW, 38.5 mm. **Ruler:** Elizabeth II **Subject:** Winston Churchill **Obv:** Crowned bust right **Rev:** Churchill in Admiral's uniform

Date	Mintage	VF20	XF40	MS60	MS63	MS65
1999	2,500	PF65 20.00				

KM# 66b 50 PENCE
47.54 g., 0.917 Gold 1.4016 oz. AGW, 38.61 mm. **Ruler:** Elizabeth II **Obv:** Crowned bust right **Rev:** Churchill in Admiral's uniform

Date	Mintage	VF20	XF40	MS60	MS63	MS65
1999	125	PF67 2,000				

KM# 6 1/2 POUND
3.99 g., 0.917 Gold 0.1176 oz. AGW **Ruler:** Elizabeth II **Obv:** Young bust right **Rev:** Romney marsh sheep left, date above

Date	Mintage	VF20	XF40	MS60	MS63	MS65
1974	2,673	PF65 225	PF67 250			

KM# 7 POUND
7.99 g., 0.917 Gold 0.2356 oz. AGW **Ruler:** Elizabeth II **Obv:** Young bust right **Rev:** Romney marsh sheep left, date above

Date	Mintage	VF20	XF40	MS60	MS63	MS65
1974	2,675	PF65 450	PF67 475			

KM# 24 POUND
9.50 g., Nickel-Brass, 22.5 mm. **Ruler:** Elizabeth II **Obv:** Crowned bust right **Rev:** State shield, date and denomination **Edge Lettering:** DESIRE THE RIGHT

Date	Mintage	VF20	XF40	MS60	MS63	MS65
1987	2,500	PF65 12.50				
1987	—	—	—	—	2.00	3.50
1992	—	PF65 12.50				
1992	—	—	—	—	2.00	3.50
1999	—	—	—	—	2.00	3.50
1999	2,500	PF65 12.50				
2000	—	—	—	—	2.00	3.50

KM# 24a POUND
9.50 g., 0.925 Silver 0.2825 oz. ASW, 22.5 mm. **Ruler:** Elizabeth II **Obv:** Crowned bust right **Rev:** State shield, date and denomination

Date	Mintage	VF20	XF40	MS60	MS63	MS65
1987	Est. 5000	PF65 12.50				

KM# 24b POUND
19.65 g., 0.917 Gold 0.5793 oz. AGW, 22.5 mm. **Ruler:** Elizabeth II **Obv:** Crowned bust right **Rev:** State shield, date and denomination

Date	Mintage	VF20	XF40	MS60	MS63	MS65
1987	Est. 200	PF67 900				

KM# 8 2 POUNDS
15.98 g., 0.917 Gold 0.4711 oz. AGW **Ruler:** Elizabeth II **Obv:** Young bust right **Rev:** Romney marsh sheep left, date above

Date	Mintage	VF20	XF40	MS60	MS63	MS65
1974	2,158	PF65 775	PF67 800			

KM# 22 2 POUNDS
28.28 g., 0.500 Silver 0.4546 oz. ASW, 38.61 mm. **Ruler:** Elizabeth II **Subject:** Commonweatlth Games **Obv:** Crowned bust right, denomination below **Rev:** Marksman

Date	Mintage	VF20	XF40	MS60	MS63	MS65
1986	Est. 50000	—	—	—	—	18.00

KM# 22a 2 POUNDS
28.28 g., 0.925 Silver 0.841 oz. ASW, 38.61 mm. **Ruler:** Elizabeth II **Obv:** Crowned bust right, denomination below **Rev:** Marksman

Date	Mintage	VF20	XF40	MS60	MS63	MS65
1986	Est. 20000	PF65 30.00				

KM# 32 2 POUNDS
28.28 g., 0.925 Silver 0.841 oz. ASW, 38.61 mm. **Ruler:** Elizabeth II **Subject:** 10th Wedding Anniversary - Prince Charles and Lady Diana **Obv:** Crowned bust right **Rev:** Facing cameos divide cathedral and crown design, wreath surrounds

Date	Mintage	VF20	XF40	MS60	MS63	MS65
1991	Est. 10000	PF65 30.00				

KM# 35 2 POUNDS
28.28 g., Copper-Nickel, 38.61 mm. **Ruler:** Elizabeth II **Subject:** Heritage Year **Obv:** Crowned bust right **Rev:** State shield below flowers, ferns flank

Date	Mintage	VF20	XF40	MS60	MS63	MS65
1992	—	—	—	—	5.00	7.50

KM# 35a 2 POUNDS
28.28 g., 0.925 Silver 0.841 oz. ASW, 38.61 mm. **Ruler:** Elizabeth II **Subject:** Heritage Year **Obv:** Crowned bust right **Rev:** State shield below flowers, ferns flank

Date	Mintage	VF20	XF40	MS60	MS63	MS65
1992	Est. 7500	PF65 25.00				

KM# 47 2 POUNDS
28.28 g., 0.925 Silver 0.841 oz. ASW, 38.61 mm. **Ruler:** Elizabeth II **Subject:** Royal Heritage - Egbert of Wessex **Obv:** Crowned bust right **Rev:** Egbert in archway, dates divided

Date	Mintage	VF20	XF40	MS60	MS63	MS65
1996	10,000	PF65 35.00				

KM# 47a 2 POUNDS
28.15 g., 0.925 Bi-Metallic 0.8372 oz. Silver center in Gold-plated Silver ring, 38.61 mm. **Ruler:** Elizabeth II **Subject:** Royal Heritage - Egbert of Wessex **Obv:** Crowned bust right **Rev:** Egbert in archway, dates divided

Date	Mintage	VF20	XF40	MS60	MS63	MS65
1996	Est. 10000	PF65 30.00				

KM# 47b 2 POUNDS
28.28 g., Copper-Nickel, 38.6 mm. **Ruler:** Elizabeth II **Subject:** Royal Heritage - Egbert of Wessex **Obv:** Crowned bust right **Rev:** Egbert in archway, dates divided **Edge:** Reeded

Date	Mintage	VF20	XF40	MS60	MS63	MS65
1996	—	—	—	—	4.50	6.50

KM# 48 2 POUNDS
28.28 g., 0.925 Silver 0.841 oz. ASW, 38.61 mm. **Ruler:** Elizabeth II **Subject:** Royal Heritage - Alfred the Great **Obv:** Crowned bust right **Rev:** Alfred with axe, scroll, ancient coin, dates divided

Date	Mintage	VF20	XF40	MS60	MS63	MS65
1996	10,000	PF65 35.00				

KM# 48a 2 POUNDS
28.15 g., 0.925 Bi-Metallic 0.8372 oz. Silver center in Gold-plated Silver ring, 38.61 mm. **Ruler:** Elizabeth II **Subject:** Royal Heritage - Alfred the Great **Obv:** Crowned bust right **Rev:** Alfred with axe, scroll, ancient coin, dates divided

Date	Mintage	VF20	XF40	MS60	MS63	MS65
1996	Est. 10000	PF65 22.50				

KM# 48b 2 POUNDS
28.28 g., Copper-Nickel, 38.6 mm. **Ruler:** Elizabeth II **Subject:** Royal Heritage - Alfred the Great **Obv:** Crowned bust right **Rev:** Alfred with axe, scroll, ancient coin, dates divided **Edge:** Reeded

Date	Mintage	VF20	XF40	MS60	MS63	MS65
1996	—	—	—	—	4.50	6.50

KM# 49 2 POUNDS
28.28 g., 0.925 Silver 0.841 oz. ASW, 38.61 mm. **Ruler:** Elizabeth II **Subject:** Royal Heritage - Edward the Confessor **Obv:** Crowned bust right **Rev:** Edward with halo offering miniature church within wreath, dates divided

Date	Mintage	VF20	XF40	MS60	MS63	MS65
1996	10,000	PF65 35.00				

KM# 49a 2 POUNDS
28.15 g., 0.925 Bi-Metallic 0.8372 oz. Silver center in Gold-plated Silver ring, 38.61 mm. **Ruler:** Elizabeth II **Subject:** Royal Heritage - Edward the Confessor **Obv:** Crowned bust right **Rev:** Edward with halo offering miniature church; dates divided

Date	Mintage	VF20	XF40	MS60	MS63	MS65
1996	Est. 10000	PF65 22.50				

KM# 49b 2 POUNDS
28.28 g., Copper-Nickel, 38.6 mm. **Ruler:** Elizabeth II **Subject:** Royal Heritage - Edward the Confessor 1042-66 **Obv:** Crowned bust right **Rev:** Edward with halo offering miniature church within wreath, dates divided **Edge:** Reeded

Date	Mintage	VF20	XF40	MS60	MS63	MS65
1996	—	—	—	—	4.50	6.50

KM# 50 2 POUNDS
28.28 g., 0.925 Silver 0.841 oz. ASW, 38.61 mm. **Ruler:** Elizabeth II **Subject:** Royal Heritage - William I **Obv:** Crowned bust right **Rev:** Seated William holding miniature church, Doomsday Book at left, shield at right, dates below

Date	Mintage	VF20	XF40	MS60	MS63	MS65
1996	10,000	PF65 35.00				

KM# 50a 2 POUNDS
28.15 g., 0.925 Bi-Metallic 0.8372 oz. Silver center in Gold-plated ring, 38.61 mm. **Ruler:** Elizabeth II **Subject:** Royal Heritage - William I **Obv:** Crowned bust right **Rev:** Seated William holding miniature church, Doomsday Book at left, shield at right, dates below

Date	Mintage	VF20	XF40	MS60	MS63	MS65
1996	Est. 10000	PF65 22.50				

KM# 50b 2 POUNDS
28.28 g., Copper-Nickel, 38.6 mm. **Ruler:** Elizabeth II **Subject:** Royal Heritage - William I the Conqueror 1066-87 **Obv:** Crowned bust right **Rev:** Seated William holding miniature church, Doomsday Book at left, shield at right, dates below **Edge:** Reeded

Date	Mintage	VF20	XF40	MS60	MS63	MS65
1996	—	—	—	—	4.50	6.50

KM# 51 2 POUNDS
28.28 g., 0.925 Silver 0.841 oz. ASW, 38.61 mm. **Ruler:** Elizabeth II **Subject:** Royal Heritage - Henry II 1154-89 **Obv:** Crowned bust right **Rev:** Crowned bust of Henry II 3/4 facing, dates at right

Date	Mintage	VF20	XF40	MS60	MS63	MS65
1996	10,000	PF65 35.00				

KM# 51a 2 POUNDS
28.15 g., 0.925 Bi-Metallic 0.8372 oz. Silver center in Gold-plated Silver ring, 38.61 mm. **Ruler:** Elizabeth II **Subject:** Royal Heritage - Henry II 1154-89 **Obv:** Crowned bust right **Rev:** Crowned bust of Henry II 3/4 facing, dates at right

Date	Mintage	VF20	XF40	MS60	MS63	MS65
1996	Est. 10000	PF65 22.50				

KM# 51b 2 POUNDS
28.28 g., Copper-Nickel, 38.6 mm. **Ruler:** Elizabeth II **Subject:** Royal Heritage - Henry II 1154-89 **Obv:** Crowned bust right **Rev:** Crowned bust of Henry II 3/4 facing, dates at right **Edge:** Reeded

Date	Mintage	VF20	XF40	MS60	MS63	MS65
1996	—	—	—	—	4.50	6.50

KM# 52 2 POUNDS
28.28 g., 0.925 Silver 0.841 oz. ASW, 38.61 mm. **Ruler:** Elizabeth II **Subject:** Royal Heritage - Richard I The Lionheart 1189-99 **Obv:** Crowned bust right **Rev:** Seated Richard flanked by sun and crescent moon, dates divided

Date	Mintage	VF20	XF40	MS60	MS63	MS65
1996	10,000	PF65 35.00				

KM# 52a 2 POUNDS
28.15 g., 0.925 Bi-Metallic 0.8372 oz. Silver center in Gold-plated Silver ring, 38.61 mm. **Ruler:** Elizabeth II **Subject:** Royal Heritage - Richard I The Lionheart 1189-99 **Obv:** Crowned bust right **Rev:** Seated Richard flanked by sun and crescent moon; dates divided

Date	Mintage	VF20	XF40	MS60	MS63	MS65
1996	Est. 10000	PF65 20.00				

KM# 52b 2 POUNDS
28.28 g., Copper-Nickel, 38.6 mm. **Ruler:** Elizabeth II **Subject:** Royal Heritage - Richard the Lionheart 1189-99 **Obv:** Crowned bust right **Rev:** Seated Richard flanked by sun and crescent moon, dates divided **Edge:** Reeded

Date	Mintage	VF20	XF40	MS60	MS63	MS65
1996	—	—	—	—	4.50	6.50

KM# 53 2 POUNDS
28.28 g., 0.925 Silver 0.841 oz. ASW, 38.61 mm. **Ruler:** Elizabeth II **Subject:** Royal Heritage - Henry IV 1399-1413 **Obv:** Crowned bust right **Rev:** Portrait of Henry in crown and cape right, dates below

Date	Mintage	VF20	XF40	MS60	MS63	MS65
1996	—	PF65 35.00				

KM# 53a 2 POUNDS
28.15 g., 0.925 Bi-Metallic 0.8372 oz. Silver center in Gold-plated Silver ring, 38.61 mm. **Ruler:** Elizabeth II **Subject:** Royal Heritage - Henry IV 1399-1413 **Obv:** Crowned bust right **Rev:** Portrait of Henry in crown and cape right, dates below

Date	Mintage	VF20	XF40	MS60	MS63	MS65
1996	Est. 10000	PF65 22.50				

KM# 53b 2 POUNDS
28.28 g., Copper-Nickel, 38.6 mm. **Ruler:** Elizabeth II **Subject:** Royal Heritage - Henry IV 1399-1413 **Obv:** Crowned bust right **Rev:** Portrait of Henry in crown and cape right, dates below **Edge:** Reeded

Date	Mintage	VF20	XF40	MS60	MS63	MS65
1996	—	—	—	—	4.50	6.50

KM# 54 2 POUNDS
28.28 g., 0.925 Silver 0.841 oz. ASW, 38.61 mm. **Ruler:** Elizabeth II **Subject:** Royal Heritage - Edward IV 1461-83 **Obv:** Crowned bust right **Rev:** Youthful Edward bust looking left, castle and ship at left, dates divided

Date	Mintage	VF20	XF40	MS60	MS63	MS65
1996	10,000	PF65 35.00				

KM# 54a 2 POUNDS
28.15 g., 0.925 Bi-Metallic 0.8372 oz. Silver center in Gold-plated Silver ring, 38.61 mm. **Ruler:** Elizabeth II **Subject:** Royal Heritage - Edward IV 1461-83 **Obv:** Crowned bust right **Rev:** Youthful Edward bust looking left, castle and ship at left, dates divided

Date	Mintage	VF20	XF40	MS60	MS63	MS65
1996	Est. 10000	PF65 22.50				

KM# 54b 2 POUNDS
28.28 g., Copper-Nickel, 38.6 mm. **Ruler:** Elizabeth II **Subject:** Royal Heritage - Edward IV 1461-83 **Obv:** Crowned bust right **Rev:** Youthful Edward bust looking left, castle and ship at left, dates divided **Edge:** Reeded

Date	Mintage	VF20	XF40	MS60	MS63	MS65
1996	—	—	—	—	4.50	6.50

KM# 55 2 POUNDS
28.28 g., 0.925 Silver 0.841 oz. ASW, 38.61 mm. **Ruler:** Elizabeth II **Subject:** Royal Heritage - Henry VIII 1509-47 **Obv:** Crowned bust right **Rev:** Standing Henry with shield; dates below at left

Date	Mintage	VF20	XF40	MS60	MS63	MS65
1996	10,000	PF65 35.00				

KM# 55a 2 POUNDS
28.15 g., 0.925 Bi-Metallic 0.8372 oz. Silver center in Gold-plated Silver ring, 38.61 mm. **Ruler:** Elizabeth II **Subject:** Royal Heritage - Henry VIII 1509-47 **Obv:** Crowned bust right **Rev:** Standing Henry with shield; dates

Date	Mintage	VF20	XF40	MS60	MS63	MS65
1996	Est. 10000	PF65 22.50				

KM# 55b 2 POUNDS
28.28 g., Copper-Nickel, 38.6 mm. **Ruler:** Elizabeth II **Subject:** Royal Heritage - Henry VIII 1509-47 **Obv:** Crowned bust right **Rev:** Standing Henry with shield; dates below at left **Edge:** Reeded

Date	Mintage	VF20	XF40	MS60	MS63	MS65
1996	—	—	—	—	4.50	6.50

KM# 56 2 POUNDS
28.28 g., 0.925 Silver 0.841 oz. ASW, 38.61 mm. **Ruler:** Elizabeth II **Subject:** Royal Heritage - Elizabeth I 1558-1603 **Obv:** Crowned bust right **Rev:** Bust with high ruffled collar 3/4 facing, dates below

Date	Mintage	VF20	XF40	MS60	MS63	MS65
1996	—	PF65 35.00				

KM# 56a 2 POUNDS
28.15 g., 0.925 Bi-Metallic 0.8372 oz. Silver center in Gold-plated Silver ring, 38.61 mm. **Ruler:** Elizabeth II **Subject:** Royal Heritage - Elizabeth I 1558-1603 **Obv:** Crowned bust right **Rev:** Bust with high ruffled collar 3/4 facing, dates below

Date	Mintage	VF20	XF40	MS60	MS63	MS65
1996	Est. 10000	PF65 22.50				

KM# 56b 2 POUNDS
28.28 g., Copper-Nickel, 38.6 mm. **Ruler:** Elizabeth II **Subject:** Royal Heritage - Elizabeth I 1558-1603 **Obv:** Crowned bust right **Rev:** Bust with high ruffled collar 3/4 facing, dates below **Edge:** Reeded

Date	Mintage	VF20	XF40	MS60	MS63	MS65
1996	—	—	—	—	4.50	6.50

KM# 57 2 POUNDS
28.28 g., 0.925 Silver 0.841 oz. ASW, 38.61 mm. **Ruler:** Elizabeth II **Subject:** Royal Heritage - Charles I 1625-49 **Obv:** Crowned bust right **Rev:** Smiling portrait of Charles 3/4 right, small shield and dates at right

Date	Mintage	VF20	XF40	MS60	MS63	MS65
1996	10,000	PF65 35.00				

KM# 57a 2 POUNDS
28.15 g., 0.925 Bi-Metallic 0.8372 oz. Silver center in Gold-plated Silver ring, 38.61 mm. **Ruler:** Elizabeth II **Subject:** Royal Heritage - Charles I 1625-49 **Obv:** Crowned bust right **Rev:** Smiling portrait of Charles 3/4 right, small shield and dates at right

Date	Mintage	VF20	XF40	MS60	MS63	MS65
1996	Est. 10000	PF65 22.50				

KM# 57b 2 POUNDS
28.28 g., Copper-Nickel, 38.6 mm. **Ruler:** Elizabeth II **Subject:** Royal Heritage - Charles I 1625-49 **Obv:** Crowned bust right **Rev:** Smiling portrait of Charles 3/4 right, small shield and dates at right **Edge:** Reeded

Date	Mintage	VF20	XF40	MS60	MS63	MS65
1996	—	—	—	—	4.50	6.50

KM# 58 2 POUNDS
28.28 g., 0.925 Silver 0.841 oz. ASW, 38.61 mm. **Ruler:** Elizabeth II **Subject:** Royal Heritage - Victoria 1837-1901 **Obv:** Crowned bust right **Rev:** Seated Queen Victoria with scepter and shield, dates at right

Date	Mintage	VF20	XF40	MS60	MS63	MS65
1996	10,000	PF65 35.00				

KM# 58a 2 POUNDS
28.15 g., 0.925 Bi-Metallic 0.8372 oz. Silver center in Gold-plated Silver ring, 38.61 mm. **Ruler:** Elizabeth II **Subject:** Royal Heritage - Victoria 1837-1901 **Obv:** Crowned bust right **Rev:** Seated Queen Victoria with sceptre and shield, dates at right

Date	Mintage	VF20	XF40	MS60	MS63	MS65
1996	Est. 10000	PF65 22.50				

KM# 58b 2 POUNDS
28.28 g., Copper-Nickel, 38.6 mm. **Ruler:** Elizabeth II **Subject:** Royal Heritage - Victoria 1837-1901 **Obv:** Crowned bust right **Rev:** Seated Queen Victoria with scepter and shield, dates at right **Edge:** Reeded

Date	Mintage	VF20	XF40	MS60	MS63	MS65
1996	—	—	—	—	4.50	6.50

KM# 104 2 POUNDS
1.24 g., 0.999 Gold 0.0399 oz. AGW, 14 mm. **Ruler:** Elizabeth II **Obv:** Crowned bust right **Rev:** Egbert of Wessex 802-839 **Edge:** Reeded

Date	Mintage	VF20	XF40	MS60	MS63	MS65
1997	—	PF65 60.00	PF67 70.00			

KM# 105 2 POUNDS
1.24 g., 0.999 Gold 0.0399 oz. AGW, 14 mm. **Ruler:** Elizabeth II **Obv:** Crowned bust right **Rev:** Alfred the Great 871-899 **Edge:** Reeded

Date	Mintage	VF20	XF40	MS60	MS63	MS65
1997	—	PF65 60.00	PF67 70.00			

KM# 106 2 POUNDS
1.24 g., 0.999 Gold 0.0399 oz. AGW, 14 mm. **Ruler:** Elizabeth II **Obv:** Crowned bust right **Rev:** Edward the Confessor **Edge:** Reeded

Date	Mintage	VF20	XF40	MS60	MS63	MS65
1997	—	PF65 60.00	PF67 70.00			

KM# 107 2 POUNDS
1.24 g., 0.999 Gold 0.0399 oz. AGW, 14 mm. **Ruler:** Elizabeth II **Obv:** Crowned bust right **Rev:** William I the Conqueror 1066-87 **Edge:** Reeded

Date	Mintage	VF20	XF40	MS60	MS63	MS65
1997	—	PF65 60.00	PF67 70.00			

KM# 108 2 POUNDS
1.24 g., 0.999 Gold 0.0399 oz. AGW, 14 mm. **Ruler:** Elizabeth II **Obv:** Crowned bust right **Rev:** Henry II 1154-89 **Edge:** Reeded

Date	Mintage	VF20	XF40	MS60	MS63	MS65
1997	—	PF65 60.00	PF67 70.00			

KM# 109 2 POUNDS
1.24 g., 0.999 Gold 0.0399 oz. AGW, 14 mm. **Ruler:** Elizabeth II **Obv:** Crowned bust right **Rev:** Richard I the Lion Hearted, 1189-99 **Edge:** Reeded

Date	Mintage	VF20	XF40	MS60	MS63	MS65
1997	—	PF65 60.00	PF67 70.00			

KM# 110 2 POUNDS
1.24 g., 0.999 Gold 0.0399 oz. AGW, 14 mm. **Ruler:** Elizabeth II **Obv:** Crowned bust right **Rev:** Henry IV 1399-1413 **Edge:** Reeded

Date	Mintage	VF20	XF40	MS60	MS63	MS65
1997	—	PF65 60.00	PF67 70.00			

KM# 111 2 POUNDS
1.24 g., 0.999 Gold 0.0399 oz. AGW, 14 mm. **Ruler:** Elizabeth II **Obv:** Crowned bust right **Rev:** Edward IV 1461-83 **Edge:** Reeded

Date	Mintage	VF20	XF40	MS60	MS63	MS65
1997	—	PF65 60.00	PF67 70.00			

KM# 112 2 POUNDS
1.24 g., 0.999 Gold 0.0399 oz. AGW, 14 mm. **Ruler:** Elizabeth II **Obv:** Crowned bust right **Rev:** Henry VIII 1509-47 **Edge:** Reeded

Date	Mintage	VF20	XF40	MS60	MS63	MS65
1997	—	PF65 60.00	PF67 70.00			

KM# 113 2 POUNDS
1.24 g., 0.999 Gold 0.0399 oz. AGW, 14 mm. **Ruler:** Elizabeth II **Obv:** Crowned bust right **Rev:** Elizabeth I 1558-1603 **Edge:** Reeded

Date	Mintage	VF20	XF40	MS60	MS63	MS65
1997	—	PF65 60.00	PF67 70.00			

KM# 114 2 POUNDS
1.24 g., 0.999 Gold 0.0399 oz. AGW, 14 mm. **Ruler:** Elizabeth II **Obv:** Crowned bust right **Rev:** Charles I 1625-49 **Edge:** Reeded

Date	Mintage	VF20	XF40	MS60	MS63	MS65
1997	—	PF65 60.00	PF67 70.00			

KM# 115 2 POUNDS
1.24 g., 0.999 Gold 0.0399 oz. AGW, 14 mm. **Ruler:** Elizabeth II **Obv:** Crowned bust right **Rev:** Victoria 1837-1901 **Edge:** Reeded

Date	Mintage	VF20	XF40	MS60	MS63	MS65
1998	—	PF65 60.00	PF67 70.00			

KM# 116 2 POUNDS
7.80 g., 0.583 Gold 0.1462 oz. AGW, 24.9 mm. **Ruler:** Elizabeth II **Subject:** Royal Heritage - Egbert of Wessex 802-839 **Obv:** Crowned bust right **Rev:** Egbert in archway, dates divided **Edge:** Reeded

Date	Mintage	VF20	XF40	MS60	MS63	MS65
1997	—	PF65 220	PF67 240			

KM# 117 2 POUNDS
7.80 g., 0.583 Gold 0.1462 oz. AGW, 24.9 mm. **Ruler:** Elizabeth II **Obv:** Crowned bust right **Rev:** Alfred the Great 871-899 **Edge:** Reeded

Date	Mintage	VF20	XF40	MS60	MS63	MS65
1997	—	PF65 220	PF67 240			

KM# 118 2 POUNDS
7.80 g., 0.583 Gold 0.1462 oz. AGW, 24.9 mm. **Ruler:** Elizabeth II **Obv:** Crowned bust right **Rev:** Edward the Confessor 1042-66 **Edge:** Reeded

Date	Mintage	VF20	XF40	MS60	MS63	MS65
1997	—	PF65 220	PF67 240			

KM# 119 2 POUNDS
7.80 g., 0.583 Gold 0.1462 oz. AGW, 24.9 mm. **Ruler:** Elizabeth II **Obv:** Crowned bust right **Rev:** William I the Conqueror 1066-87 **Edge:** Reeded

Date	Mintage	VF20	XF40	MS60	MS63	MS65
1997	—	PF65 220	PF67 240			

KM# 120 2 POUNDS
7.80 g., 0.583 Gold 0.1462 oz. AGW, 24.9 mm. **Ruler:** Elizabeth II **Obv:** Crowned bust right **Rev:** Henry II 1154-89 **Edge:** Reeded

Date	Mintage	VF20	XF40	MS60	MS63	MS65
1997	—	PF65 220	PF67 240			

KM# 121 2 POUNDS
7.80 g., 0.583 Gold 0.1462 oz. AGW, 24.9 mm. **Ruler:** Elizabeth II **Obv:** Crowned bust right **Rev:** Richard I the Lion Hearted 1189-99 **Edge:** Reeded

Date	Mintage	VF20	XF40	MS60	MS63	MS65
1997	—	PF65 220	PF67 240			

KM# 122 2 POUNDS
7.80 g., 0.583 Gold 0.1462 oz. AGW, 24.9 mm. **Ruler:** Elizabeth II **Obv:** Crowned bust right **Rev:** Henry IV 1399-1413 **Edge:** Reeded

Date	Mintage	VF20	XF40	MS60	MS63	MS65
1997	—	PF65 220	PF67 240			

KM# 123 2 POUNDS
7.80 g., 0.583 Gold 0.1462 oz. AGW, 24.9 mm. **Ruler:** Elizabeth II **Obv:** Crowned bust right **Rev:** Edward IV 1461-83 **Edge:** Reeded

Date	Mintage	VF20	XF40	MS60	MS63	MS65
1997	—	PF65 220	PF67 240			

KM# 124 2 POUNDS
7.87 g., 0.583 Gold 0.1475 oz. AGW, 24.9 mm. **Ruler:** Elizabeth II **Obv:** Crowned bust right **Rev:** Henry VIII 1509-47, shield at right, dates at left **Edge:** Reeded

Date	Mintage	VF20	XF40	MS60	MS63	MS65
1997	—	PF65 220	PF67 240			

KM# 125 2 POUNDS
7.80 g., 0.583 Gold 0.1462 oz. AGW, 24.9 mm. **Ruler:** Elizabeth II **Subject:** Royal Heritage - Elizabeth I 1558-1603 **Obv:** Crowned bust right **Rev:** Bust with high ruffled collar 3/4 facing, dates below **Edge:** Reeded

Date	Mintage	VF20	XF40	MS60	MS63	MS65
1998	—	PF65 220	PF67 240			

KM# 126 2 POUNDS
7.80 g., 0.583 Gold 0.1462 oz. AGW, 24.9 mm. **Ruler:** Elizabeth II **Obv:** Crowned bust right **Rev:** Charles I 1625-49 **Edge:** Reeded

Date	Mintage	VF20	XF40	MS60	MS63	MS65
1998	—	PF65 220	PF67 240			

KM# 127 2 POUNDS
7.80 g., 0.583 Gold 0.1462 oz. AGW, 24.9 mm. **Ruler:** Elizabeth II **Obv:** Crowned bust right **Rev:** Victoria 1837-1901 **Edge:** Reeded

Date	Mintage	VF20	XF40	MS60	MS63	MS65
1998	—	PF65 220	PF67 240			

KM# 61 2 POUNDS
28.28 g., Copper-Nickel, 38.61 mm. **Ruler:** Elizabeth II **Subject:** Flying Doctor Service **Obv:** Crowned bust right **Rev:** Two airplanes in flight, denomination below

Date	Mintage	VF20	XF40	MS60	MS63	MS65
1998	—	—	—	—	4.50	6.50

KM# 61a 2 POUNDS
28.28 g., 0.925 Silver 0.841 oz. ASW **Ruler:** Elizabeth II **Subject:** Flying Doctor Service **Obv:** Crowned bust right **Rev:** Two airplanes in flight

Date	Mintage	VF20	XF40	MS60	MS63	MS65
1998	Est. 10000	PF65 35.00				

KM# 128 2 POUNDS
7.67 g., 0.583 Gold 0.1438 oz. AGW, 24.9 mm. **Ruler:** Elizabeth II **Obv:** Crowned bust right, date below **Rev:** Queen Mother holding the baby within circle, denomination below **Edge:** Reeded

Date	Mintage	VF20	XF40	MS60	MS63	MS65
1998	—	PF65 220	PF67 240			

KM# 64 2 POUNDS
Copper-Nickel **Ruler:** Elizabeth II **Subject:** Sir Ernest Henry Shackleton **Obv:** Crowned bust right **Rev:** Cameo portrait and icebound ship "Endurance", denomination below divides dates

Date	Mintage	VF20	XF40	MS60	MS63	MS65
1999	—	—	—	—	4.50	6.50

KM# 64a 2 POUNDS
28.28 g., 0.925 Silver 0.841 oz. ASW **Ruler:** Elizabeth II **Subject:** Sir Ernest Henry Shackleton **Obv:** Crowned bust right **Rev:** Cameo portrait and icebound ship "Endurance"

Date	Mintage	VF20	XF40	MS60	MS63	MS65
1999	Est. 10000	PF65 35.00				

KM# 69 2 POUNDS
28.28 g., Bi-Metallic Copper-Nickel center in Nickel-Brass ring, 38.61 mm. **Ruler:** Elizabeth II **Obv:** Crowned bust right **Rev:** Island map, radiant sun and denomination within circle of wildlife **Edge:** Plain

Date	Mintage	VF20	XF40	MS60	MS63	MS65
1999	—	—	—	—	6.00	8.00
1999	2,500	PF65 20.00				

KM# 67 2 POUNDS
28.28 g., Copper-Nickel, 38.61 mm. **Ruler:** Elizabeth II **Subject:** The Gold Rush - "Vicar of Bray" Ship **Obv:** Crowned bust right, date below **Rev:** Ship in harbor, denomination below **Edge:** Reeded

Date	Mintage	VF20	XF40	MS60	MS63	MS65
2000	—	—	—	—	4.50	6.50

KM# 67a 2 POUNDS
28.28 g., 0.925 Silver 0.841 oz. ASW **Ruler:** Elizabeth II **Subject:** The Gold Rush - "Vicar of Bray" Ship **Obv:** Crowned bust right **Rev:** Ship in harbor, denomination below **Edge:** Reeded

Date	Mintage	VF20	XF40	MS60	MS63	MS65
2000	10,000	PF65 32.50				

KM# 69a 2 POUNDS
28.15 g., 0.925 Bi-Metallic 0.8372 oz. Silver center in Gold-plated Silver ring, 38.61 mm. **Ruler:** Elizabeth II **Obv:** Crowned bust right within circle, dates below **Rev:** Islands map, radiant sun, and denomination within circle of local wildlife **Edge:** Reeded

Date	Mintage	VF20	XF40	MS60	MS63	MS65
1999-2000	—	PF65 40.00				

KM# 85 2 POUNDS
28.40 g., 0.925 Silver 0.8446 oz. ASW with gold gilt outer ring, 38.4 mm. **Ruler:** Elizabeth II **Subject:** Queen Mother **Obv:** Crowned bust right within beaded circle, date below **Rev:** Queen Mother holding baby and date within beaded circle, denomination below **Edge:** Reeded

Date	Mintage	VF20	XF40	MS60	MS63	MS65
2000	10,000	PF65 35.00				

KM# 9 5 POUNDS
39.94 g., 0.917 Gold 1.1775 oz. AGW **Ruler:** Elizabeth II **Obv:** Young bust right **Rev:** Romney marsh sheep left, date above

Date	Mintage	VF20	XF40	MS60	MS63	MS65
1974	2,158	PF65 1,850	PF67 2,000			

KM# 11 5 POUNDS
28.28 g., 0.925 Silver 0.841 oz. ASW **Ruler:** Elizabeth II **Subject:** Conservation **Obv:** Young bust right **Rev:** Humpback whale

Date	Mintage	VF20	XF40	MS60	MS63	MS65
1979	3,998	—	—	—	25.00	35.00
1979	3,432	PF65 45.00				

KM# 27 5 POUNDS
28.28 g., Copper-Nickel, 38.61 mm. **Ruler:** Elizabeth II **Subject:** 90th Birthday of Queen Mother **Obv:** Crowned bust right, denomination below **Rev:** Crowned monogram, flowers flank, dates below

Date	Mintage	VF20	XF40	MS60	MS63	MS65
1990	—	—	—	—	12.00	14.00

KM# 27a 5 POUNDS
28.28 g., 0.925 Silver 0.841 oz. ASW **Ruler:** Elizabeth II **Subject:** 90th Birthday of Queen Mother **Obv:** Crowned bust right, denomination below **Rev:** Flowers flank crowned monogram, dates below

Date	Mintage	VF20	XF40	MS60	MS63	MS65
1990	Est. 10000	PF65 22.50				

KM# 33 5 POUNDS
39.94 g., 0.917 Gold 1.1775 oz. AGW **Ruler:** Elizabeth II **Subject:** 10th Wedding Anniversary - Prince Charles and Lady Diana **Obv:** Crowned bust right **Rev:** Facing cameo portraits of Prince Charles and Princess Diana

Date	Mintage	VF20	XF40	MS60	MS63	MS65
1991	—	PF67 2,000				

KM# 36 5 POUNDS
28.28 g., Copper-Nickel, 38.61 mm. **Ruler:** Elizabeth II **Subject:** 10th Anniversary of Liberation **Obv:** Crowned bust right **Rev:** Statue at center, inscription at right within 1/2 wreath

Date	Mintage	VF20	XF40	MS60	MS63	MS65
1992	—	—	—	—	9.00	12.00

KM# 36a 5 POUNDS
28.28 g., 0.925 Silver 0.841 oz. ASW, 38.61 mm. **Ruler:** Elizabeth II **Subject:** 10th Anniversary of Liberation **Obv:** Crowned bust right **Rev:** Statue at center, inscription at right

Date	Mintage	VF20	XF40	MS60	MS63	MS65
1992	Est. 5000	PF65 27.50				

KM# 36b 5 POUNDS
39.94 g., 0.917 Gold 1.1775 oz. AGW **Ruler:** Elizabeth II **Subject:** 10th Anniversary of Liberation **Obv:** Crowned bust right **Rev:** Statue at center, inscription at right

Date	Mintage	VF20	XF40	MS60	MS63	MS65
1992	100	PF67 2,000				

KM# 37 5 POUNDS
28.28 g., 0.925 Silver 0.841 oz. ASW **Ruler:** Elizabeth II **Subject:** 400th Anniversary of Discovery - Ship "Desire" **Obv:** Crowned bust right **Rev:** Map above ship, "Desire" at sea, dates at right

Date	Mintage	VF20	XF40	MS60	MS63	MS65
ND-1992	—	PF65 25.00				

KM# 63 5 POUNDS
28.28 g., Copper-Nickel, 38.61 mm. **Ruler:** Elizabeth II **Subject:** Queen's Golden Wedding Anniversary **Obv:** Crowned bust right **Rev:** Royal couple with gold inlay shield, dates at right

Date	Mintage	VF20	XF40	MS60	MS63	MS65
1997	—	—	—	—	14.00	17.00

KM# 63a 5 POUNDS
28.28 g., 0.925 Silver 0.841 oz. ASW, 38.6 mm. **Ruler:** Elizabeth II **Subject:** Queen's Golden Wedding Anniversary **Obv:** Crowned bust right **Rev:** Royal couple with gold inlay shield **Edge:** Reeded

Date	Mintage	VF20	XF40	MS60	MS63	MS65
1997	—	PF65 30.00				

KM# 12 10 POUNDS
35.00 g., 0.925 Silver 1.0409 oz. ASW **Ruler:** Elizabeth II **Subject:** Conservation **Obv:** Young bust right **Rev:** Flightless steamer ducks, denomination below, date at right

Date	Mintage	VF20	XF40	MS60	MS63	MS65
1979	3,996	—	—	—	35.00	45.00
1979	3,247	PF65 50.00				

KM# 28 10 POUNDS
3.13 g., 0.999 Gold 0.1005 oz. AGW **Ruler:** Elizabeth II **Subject:** 90th Birthday of Queen Mother **Obv:** Crowned bust right **Rev:** Crowned arms with supporters, dates below

Date	Mintage	VF20	XF40	MS60	MS63	MS65
ND-1990	Est. 750	PF65 150	PF67 175			

KM# 38 10 POUNDS
3.13 g., 0.999 Gold 0.1005 oz. AGW **Ruler:** Elizabeth II **Subject:** 400th Anniversary of Discovery - Ship "Desire" **Obv:** Crowned bust right **Rev:** Map above ship "Desire" at sea, dates at right

Date	Mintage	VF20	XF40	MS60	MS63	MS65
ND-1992	Est. 400	PF65 150	PF67 175			

KM# 62 20 POUNDS
6.22 g., 0.999 Gold 0.1998 oz. AGW **Ruler:** Elizabeth II **Subject:** Flying Doctor Service **Obv:** Crowned bust right **Rev:** Two airplanes in flight

Date	Mintage	VF20	XF40	MS60	MS63	MS65
1998	Est. 1000	PF65 300	PF67 350			

KM# 65 20 POUNDS
6.22 g., 0.999 Gold 0.1998 oz. AGW **Ruler:** Elizabeth II **Subject:** Sir Ernest H. Shackleton **Obv:** Crowned bust right **Rev:** Cameo portrait and icebound ship

Date	Mintage	VF20	XF40	MS60	MS63	MS65
1999	Est. 1000	PF65 300	PF67 350			

KM# 68 20 POUNDS
6.22 g., 0.999 Gold 0.1998 oz. AGW **Ruler:** Elizabeth II **Subject:** The Gold Rush **Obv:** Crowned bust right **Rev:** "Vicar of Bray" in harbor **Edge:** Reeded

Date	Mintage	VF20	XF40	MS60	MS63	MS65
2000 PM	1,000	PF65 300	PF67 350			

KM# 20 25 POUNDS
150.00 g., 0.925 Silver 4.4609 oz. ASW, 65 mm. **Ruler:** Elizabeth II **Subject:** 100 Years of Self Sufficiency **Obv:** Crowned bust right **Rev:** S.S. Great Britain a steam and sailing ship which was scuttled in the Falkland Islands (and since raised and returned to Great Britian), dates below **Edge:** Reeded

Date	Mintage	VF20	XF40	MS60	MS63	MS65
ND-1985	Est. 20000	PF65 150	PF67 165			

KM# 23 25 POUNDS
150.00 g., 0.925 Silver 4.4609 oz. ASW **Ruler:** Elizabeth II **Subject:** Prince Andrew's Wedding **Obv:** Crowned bust right **Rev:** Profiles of Prince Andrew and Sarah Ferguson facing, date above

Date	Mintage	VF20	XF40	MS60	MS63	MS65
1986	Est. 20000	PF65 135	PF67 150			

KM# 29 25 POUNDS
7.81 g., 0.999 Gold 0.2508 oz. AGW **Ruler:** Elizabeth II **Subject:** 90th Birthday of Queen Mother **Obv:** Crowned bust right **Rev:** Queen Mother head left, within wreath and flowers, dates below

Date	Mintage	VF20	XF40	MS60	MS63	MS65
ND-1990	—	PF65 375	PF67 400			

KM# 39 25 POUNDS
155.58 g., 0.925 Silver 4.6269 oz. ASW, 65 mm. **Ruler:** Elizabeth II **Subject:** 400th Anniversary - First Sighting of Falkland Islands **Obv:** Crowned bust right **Rev:** Map above ship "Desire" at sea, dates at right

Date	Mintage	VF20	XF40	MS60	MS63	MS65
ND-1992	Est. 3000	PF65 175	PF67 190			

KM# 40 25 POUNDS
7.81 g., 0.999 Gold 0.2508 oz. AGW, 22 mm. **Ruler:** Elizabeth II **Subject:** 100th Anniversary of Christchurch Cathedral **Obv:** Crowned bust right, denomination below **Rev:** Cathedral, cross, scepter, and mitre, dates at left

Date	Mintage	VF20	XF40	MS60	MS63	MS65
1992	Est. 400	PF65 375	PF67 400			

KM# 30 50 POUNDS
15.61 g., 0.999 Gold 0.5014 oz. AGW **Ruler:** Elizabeth II **Subject:** 90th Birthday of Queen Mother **Obv:** Crowned bust right

Date	Mintage	VF20	XF40	MS60	MS63	MS65
ND-1990	—	PF65 775	PF67 825			

KM# 41 50 POUNDS
15.61 g., 0.999 Gold 0.5014 oz. AGW, 27 mm. **Ruler:** Elizabeth II **Subject:** 100th Anniversary of Defense Force **Obv:** Crowned bust right **Rev:** Soldier with shield, dates at right

Date	Mintage	VF20	XF40	MS60	MS63	MS65
ND-1992	Est. 400	PF65 775	PF67 825			

KM# 44 50 POUNDS
47.54 g., 0.917 Gold 1.4016 oz. AGW **Ruler:** Elizabeth II **Subject:** 40th Anniversary - Coronation of Queen Elizabeth II

Date	Mintage	VF20	XF40	MS60	MS63	MS65
ND-1993	Est. 100	PF67 2,250				

KM# 31 100 POUNDS

31.21 g., 0.999 Gold 1.0024 oz. AGW **Ruler:** Elizabeth II **Subject:** 90th Birthday of Queen Mother **Obv:** Crowned bust right **Rev:** Queen Mother's head left, within wreath and flowers, dates below

Date	Mintage	VF20	XF40	MS60	MS63	MS65
ND-1990	Est. 750	PF67 1,600				

KM# 42 100 POUNDS

31.21 g., 0.999 Gold 1.0024 oz. AGW, 32.69 mm. **Ruler:** Elizabeth II **Subject:** 400th Anniversary of Discovery - Ship "Desire" **Obv:** Crowned bust right **Rev:** Map above ship "Desire" at sea, dates at right

Date	Mintage	VF20	XF40	MS60	MS63	MS65
ND-1992	Est. 400	PF67 1,600				

KM# 13 150 POUNDS

33.44 g., 0.900 Gold 0.9675 oz. AGW **Ruler:** Elizabeth II **Subject:** Conservation **Obv:** Young bust right **Rev:** Falkland Fur Seal, denomination below, date at right

Date	Mintage	VF20	XF40	MS60	MS63	MS65
1979	488	—	—	—	1,600	1,700
1979	164	PF65 1,850	PF67 1,950			

PIEDFORT

KM#	Date	Mintage	Identification	Mkt Val
P1	1987	2,500	Pound. 0.925. Silver. KM24a.	45.00
P2	1992	750	50 Pence. 0.925. Silver. KM34a.	75.00
P3	1995	Est. 750	50 Pence. 0.925. Silver. KM45a.	100

MINT SETS

KM#	Date	Mintage	Identification	Issue Price	Mkt Val
MS1	1987 (7)	—	KM2-3, 4.1-5.1, 14.1, 17, 24	10.00	18.50
MS2	1992 (8)	—	KM2-3, 4.1-5.1, 14.1, 17, 24, 35	24.50	30.00
MS3	1999 (8)	—	KM2a-3a, 4.2-5.2, 14.2, 17, 24, 69	20.00	30.00

PROOF SETS

KM#	Date	Mintage	Identification	Issue Price	Mkt Val
PS1	1974 (4)	—	KM1, 3, 4.1, 5.1	12.00	12.50
PS2	1974 (4)	2,000	KM6-9	1,100	3,500
PS3	1979 (2)	10,000	KM11-12	—	100
PS4	1980 (6)	10,000	KM1-3, 4.1-5.1, 14.1	35.00	25.00
PS5	1982 (8)	5,000	KM1-3, 4.1-5.1, 14.1, 17, 18a	—	50.00
PS6	1982 (7)	5,000	KM1-3, 4.1-5.1, 14.1, 17	—	22.00
PS7	1987 (7)	2,500	KM2-3, 4.1-5.1, 14.1, 17, 24	35.00	37.00
PS8	1990 (4)	750	KM28-31	1,595	3,200
PS9	1992 (8)	2,500	KM2-3, 4.1-5.1, 14.1, 17, 24, 35a	89.50	90.00
PS10	1992 (4)	400	KM38, 40-42	1,595	3,200
PS11	1992 (6)	—	KM#35a, 36a, 39, 40-42	—	3,250
PS12	1999 (8)	2,500	KM2a-3a, 4.2-5.2, 14.2, 17, 24, 69	50.00	60.00

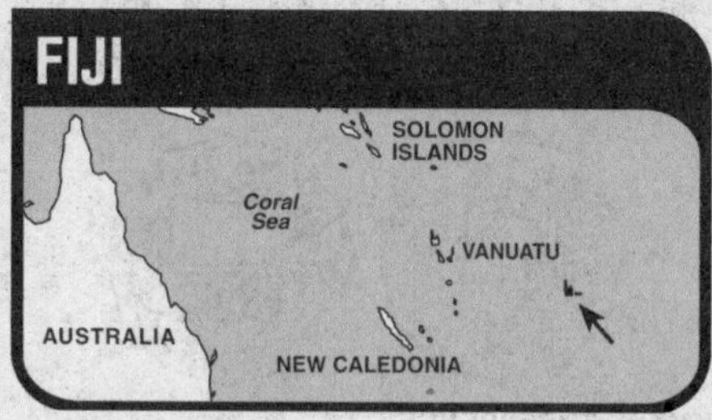

The Republic of Fiji, consists of about 320 islands located in the southwestern Pacific 1,100 miles (1,770 km.) north of New Zealand. The islands have a combined area of 7,056 sq. mi. (18,274 sq. km.) and a population of 772,891. Capital: Suva. Fiji's economy is based on agriculture and mining. Sugar, coconut products, manganese, and gold are exported.

The first European to sight Fiji was the Dutch navigator Abel Tasman in 1643 and the islands were visited by British naval captain James Cook in 1774. The first complete survey of the island was conducted by the United States in 1840. Settlement by mercenaries from Tonga, and traders attracted by the sandalwood trade, began in 1801. Following a lengthy period of intertribal warfare, the islands were unconditionally ceded to Great Britain in 1874 by King Cakobau. Fiji became a sovereign and independent nation on Oct. 10, 1970, the 96th anniversary of the cession of the islands to Queen Victoria.

Fiji was declared a Republic in 1987 following two military coups. It left the British Commonwealth and Queen Elizabeth ceased to be the Head of State. A new constitution was introduced in 1991. The country returned to the Commonwealth in 1997 with a revised constitution. Fiji is a member of the Commonwealth of Nations, but has been subject to periodic short suspensions.

RULER
British until 1970

MINT MARKS
(c) - Australian Mint, Canberra
(H) – The Mint, Birmingham
(I) – Royal Mint, Llatrisant
(o) - Royal Canadian Mint, Ottawa
S - San Francisco, U.S.A.

MONETARY SYSTEM
12 Pence = 1 Shilling
2 Shillings = 1 Florin
20 Shillings = 1 Pound

REPUBLIC

British Administration until 1970

POUND STERLING COINAGE

KM# 1 1/2 PENNY

Copper-Nickel **Ruler:** George V **Obv:** Crown above center hole **Rev:** Center hole divides date, denomination above

Date	Mintage	F12	VF20	XF40	MS60	MS63
1934	96,000	0.75	1.75	4.00	18.00	25.00
1934	—	PF63 1,200				

KM# 14 1/2 PENNY

Copper-Nickel **Ruler:** George VI **Obv:** Crown above center hole **Rev:** Center hole divides date, denomination above

Date	Mintage	F12	VF20	XF40	MS60	MS63
1940	24,000	2.50	7.50	12.50	36.00	60.00
1940	—	PF63 450				
1941	—	PF63 300				
1941	96,000	0.75	1.50	4.00	12.00	25.00

KM# 14a 1/2 PENNY

Brass **Ruler:** George VI **Obv:** Crown above center hole **Rev:** Center hole divides date, denomination above

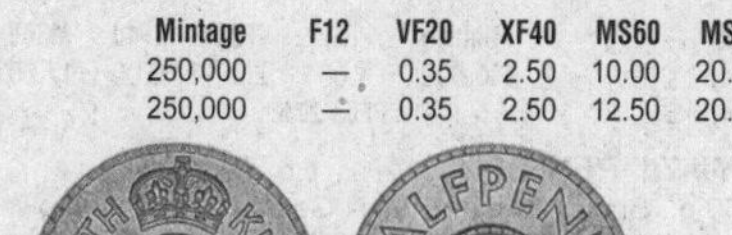

Date	Mintage	F12	VF20	XF40	MS60	MS63
1942 S	250,000	—	0.35	2.50	10.00	20.00
1943 S	250,000	—	0.35	2.50	12.50	20.00

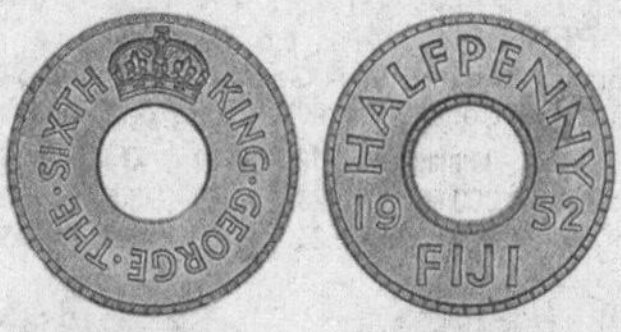

KM# 16 1/2 PENNY

Copper-Nickel **Ruler:** George VI **Obv:** Crown above center hole, EMPEROR dropped from legend **Rev:** Center hole divides date, denomination above

Date	Mintage	F12	VF20	XF40	MS60	MS63
1949	—	PF63 250				
1949	96,000	—	0.50	2.00	7.50	12.50
1950	115,000	—	0.35	1.50	6.00	10.00
1950	—	PF63 275				
1951	115,000	—	0.35	1.50	5.00	7.50
1951	—	PF63 225				
1952 Proof	—	—	—	—	—	—
1952	228,000	—	0.25	0.75	1.50	2.00

KM# 20 1/2 PENNY

Copper-Nickel **Ruler:** Elizabeth II **Obv:** Crown above center hole **Rev:** Center hole divides date, denomination above

Date	Mintage	F12	VF20	XF40	MS60	MS63
1954	228,000	—	0.25	0.50	1.00	1.50
1954	—	PF60 250	PF63 450	PF65 850		

KM# 2 PENNY

Copper-Nickel, 26 mm. **Ruler:** George V **Obv:** Crown above center hole **Rev:** Center hole divides date, denomination below

Date	Mintage	F12	VF20	XF40	MS60	MS63
1934	480,000	0.50	1.00	5.00	15.00	27.50
1934	—	PF63 1,200				
1935	240,000	0.65	1.25	5.00	18.00	30.00
1935	—	PF63 1,200				
1936	—	PF63 1,200				
1936	240,000	0.65	1.25	5.00	20.00	33.00

KM# 6 PENNY

Copper-Nickel, 26 mm. **Ruler:** Edward VIII **Obv:** Crown above center hole **Rev:** Center hole divides date, denomination below

Date	Mintage	F12	VF20	XF40	MS60	MS63
1936	—	PF63 275				
1936	120,000	0.50	1.00	2.00	4.00	8.00

KM# 7 PENNY

Copper-Nickel, 26 mm. **Ruler:** George VI **Obv:** Crown above center hole **Rev:** Center hole divides date, denomination below

Date	Mintage	F12	VF20	XF40	MS60	MS63
1937	—	PF63 275				
1937	360,000	0.50	1.00	3.00	8.00	14.00
1940	144,000	1.50	3.00	15.00	49.50	85.00
1940	—	PF63 275				
1941	228,000	0.50	1.00	2.00	11.00	17.00
1941	—	PF63 275				

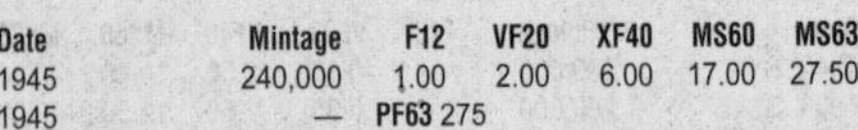

Date	Mintage	F12	VF20	XF40	MS60	MS63
1945	240,000	1.00	2.00	6.00	17.00	27.50
1945	—	PF63 275				

KM# 7a PENNY

6.50 g., Brass, 26 mm. **Ruler:** George VI **Obv:** Crown above center hole **Rev:** Center hole divides date, denomination below

Date	Mintage	F12	VF20	XF40	MS60	MS63
1942 S	1,000,000	0.25	1.00	3.50	10.00	20.00
1943 S	1,000,000	0.25	1.00	3.50	7.50	20.00

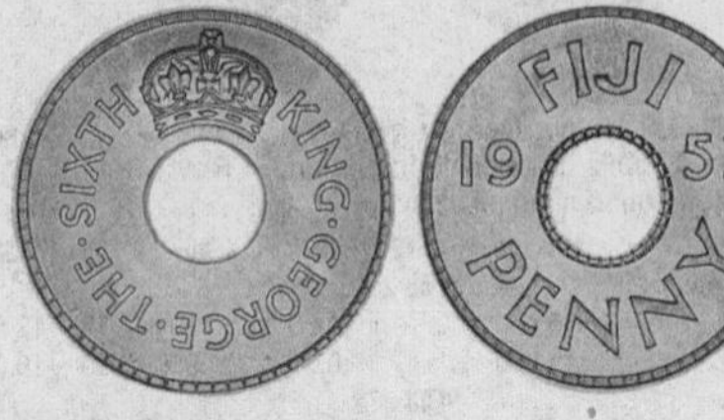

KM# 17 PENNY

6.50 g., Copper-Nickel, 26 mm. **Ruler:** George VI **Obv:** Crown above center hole, "EMPEROR" dropped from legend **Rev:** Center hole divides date, denomination below

Date	Mintage	F12	VF20	XF40	MS60	MS63
1949	—	PF63 350				
1949	120,000	0.25	0.50	1.00	4.50	7.50
1950	—	PF63 250				
1950	58,000	1.50	3.50	12.50	65.00	100
1952	230,000	0.25	0.50	1.00	3.75	7.00
1952	—	PF63 225				

KM# 21 PENNY

6.64 g., Copper-Nickel, 26 mm. **Ruler:** Elizabeth II **Obv:** Crown above center hole **Rev:** Center hole divides date, denomination below

Date	Mintage	F12	VF20	XF40	MS60	MS63
1954	511,000	0.20	0.50	1.00	3.00	4.50
1954	—	PF63 200				
1955	230,000	0.20	0.50	1.25	5.00	9.00
1955	—	PF63 200				
1956	—	PF63 200				
1956	230,000	0.20	0.50	1.25	3.50	7.50
1957	—	PF63 200				
1957	360,000	0.10	0.25	0.75	3.00	7.00
1959	—	PF63 200				
1959	864,000	—	0.20	0.35	2.00	3.50
1961	432,000	0.15	0.35	0.50	1.25	3.00
1961	—	PF63 200				
1963	432,000	0.15	0.35	0.50	1.25	3.00
1963	—	PF63 200				
1964	—	PF63 175				
1964	864,000	—	0.15	0.25	0.85	2.00
1965	1,440,000	—	—	0.20	0.75	2.00
1966	720,000	—	—	0.20	0.85	2.50
1967	720,000	—	—	0.20	0.75	1.50
1968	720,000	—	—	0.20	0.75	1.50

KM# 15 THREEPENCE

6.17 g., Nickel-Brass, 21.19 mm. **Ruler:** George VI **Obv:** Crowned head left **Rev:** Native dwelling, date above, denomination below **Shape:** 12-sided

Date	Mintage	F12	VF20	XF40	MS60	MS63
1947	450,000	1.50	2.50	6.00	22.50	49.50
1947	—	PF63 250				

KM# 18 THREEPENCE

Nickel-Brass **Ruler:** George VI **Obv:** Crowned head left, EMPEROR dropped from legend **Rev:** Native dwelling, date above, denomination below **Shape:** 12-sided

Date	Mintage	F12	VF20	XF40	MS60	MS63
1950	—	PF63 250				
1950	450,000	0.50	1.00	4.00	15.00	25.00
1952	400,000	0.50	1.00	5.00	22.50	35.00
1952	—	PF63 250				

KM# 22 THREEPENCE

Nickel-Brass **Ruler:** Elizabeth II **Obv:** Crowned head right **Rev:** Native dwelling, date above, denomination below **Shape:** 12-sided

Date	Mintage	F12	VF20	XF40	MS60	MS63
1955	400,000	0.50	1.00	4.00	17.50	35.00
1955	—	PF63 150				
1956	200,000	0.50	1.00	4.00	20.00	40.00
1956	—	PF63 175				
1958	—	PF63 160				
1958	200,000	0.50	1.00	4.00	20.00	40.00
1960	240,000	0.25	0.50	3.00	8.50	15.00
1960	—	PF63 145				
1961	240,000	0.25	0.50	1.25	6.00	12.50
1961	—	PF63 145				
1963	240,000	0.15	0.30	0.75	5.00	10.00
1963	—	PF63 135				
1964	240,000	0.15	0.30	0.50	2.00	5.00
1965	800,000	—	0.15	0.25	1.50	3.50
1967	800,000	—	0.15	0.25	1.50	3.50

KM# 3 SIXPENCE

2.83 g., 0.500 Silver 0.0455 oz. ASW, 19.5 mm. **Ruler:** George V **Obv:** Crowned bust left **Rev:** Sea turtle divides date, denomination below

Date	Mintage	F12	VF20	XF40	MS60	MS63
1934	160,000	1.50	2.50	10.00	42.00	55.00
1934	—	PF63 650				
1935	—	PF63 550				
1935	120,000	1.75	3.50	12.50	55.00	65.00
1936	—	PF63 550				
1936	40,000	2.00	4.00	15.00	65.00	85.00

KM# 8 SIXPENCE

2.83 g., 0.500 Silver 0.0455 oz. ASW, 19.5 mm. **Ruler:** George VI **Obv:** Crowned head left **Rev:** Sea turtle divides date, denomination below

Date	Mintage	F12	VF20	XF40	MS60	MS63
1937	—	PF63 500				
1937	40,000	2.00	4.00	16.00	55.00	85.00

KM# 11 SIXPENCE

2.83 g., 0.500 Silver 0.0455 oz. ASW, 19.5 mm. **Ruler:** George VI **Obv:** Smaller head **Rev:** Sea turtle divides date, denomination below

Date	Mintage	F12	VF20	XF40	MS60	MS63
1938	40,000	2.00	4.00	13.50	49.50	65.00
1938	—	PF63 600				
1940	40,000	2.00	4.00	13.50	49.50	65.00
1940	—	PF63 450				
1941	40,000	3.00	8.00	20.00	65.00	95.00
1941	—	PF63 450				

KM# 11a SIXPENCE

2.83 g., 0.900 Silver 0.0818 oz. ASW, 19.5 mm. **Ruler:** George VI **Obv:** Crowned head left **Rev:** Sea turtle divides date, denomination below

Date	Mintage	F12	VF20	XF40	MS60	MS63
1942 S	400,000	—	3.00	4.00	8.50	11.50
1943 S	400,000	—	3.00	4.00	8.50	11.50

KM# 19 SIXPENCE

2.80 g., Copper-Nickel, 19.5 mm. **Ruler:** Elizabeth II **Obv:** Crowned head right **Rev:** Sea turtle divides date, denomination below **Edge:** Reeded

Date	Mintage	F12	VF20	XF40	MS60	MS63
1953	—	PF63 250				
1953	800,000	0.25	0.50	1.00	3.00	7.50
1958	400,000	0.25	0.50	1.50	4.50	8.00
1958	—	PF63 250				
1961	400,000	0.25	0.50	1.00	3.50	7.00
1961	—	PF63 250				
1962	400,000	0.25	0.50	1.00	3.00	7.00
1962	—	PF63 250				
1965	800,000	0.15	0.30	1.00	2.50	6.00
1967	800,000	0.15	0.30	1.00	2.50	6.00

KM# 4 SHILLING

5.66 g., 0.500 Silver 0.0909 oz. ASW, 23.5 mm. **Ruler:** George V **Obv:** Crowned bust left **Rev:** Outrigger divides dates, denomination above

Date	Mintage	F12	VF20	XF40	MS60	MS63
1934	360,000	3.50	5.00	14.50	70.00	90.00
1934	—	PF63 850				
1935	—	PF63 750				
1935	180,000	3.50	5.00	15.50	90.00	110
1936	140,000	4.50	7.00	16.50	90.00	110
1936	—	PF63 750				

KM# 9 SHILLING

5.66 g., 0.500 Silver 0.0909 oz. ASW, 23.5 mm. **Ruler:** George VI **Obv:** Crowned head left **Rev:** Outrigger divides dates, denomination above

Date	Mintage	F12	VF20	XF40	MS60	MS63
1937	40,000	3.50	8.00	18.50	85.00	110
1937	—	PF63 600				

KM# 12 SHILLING

5.66 g., 0.500 Silver 0.0909 oz. ASW, 23.5 mm. **Ruler:** George VI **Obv:** Smaller head **Rev:** Outrigger divides date, denomination above

Date	Mintage	F12	VF20	XF40	MS60	MS63
1938	40,000	3.50	8.00	18.50	85.00	110
1938	—	PF63 550				
1941	40,000	3.50	8.00	18.50	85.00	110
1941	—	PF63 550				

KM# 12a SHILLING

5.66 g., 0.900 Silver 0.1636 oz. ASW, 23.5 mm. **Ruler:** George VI **Obv:** Crowned head left **Rev:** Outrigger divides date, denomination above

Date	Mintage	F12	VF20	XF40	MS60	MS63
1942 S	500,000	—	6.00	7.00	10.00	14.00
1943 S	500,000	—	6.00	7.00	10.00	14.00

KM# 23 SHILLING

5.60 g., Copper-Nickel, 23.5 mm. **Ruler:** Elizabeth II **Obv:** Crowned head right **Rev:** Outrigger divides date, denomination above

Date	Mintage	F12	VF20	XF40	MS60	MS63
1957	400,000	0.50	0.75	2.00	10.00	12.50
1957	—	PF63 375				
1958	400,000	0.50	0.75	2.25	10.00	12.50
1958	—	PF63 325				
1961	200,000	0.75	1.00	2.25	7.50	10.00
1961	—	PF63 300				
1962	400,000	0.35	0.75	1.25	4.00	6.50
1962	—	PF63 275				
1965	800,000	0.25	0.50	0.75	2.00	3.50

KM# 5 FLORIN

11.31 g., 0.500 Silver 0.1818 oz. ASW **Ruler:** George V **Obv:** Crowned bust left **Rev:** Shield of arms divides date, denomination below

Date	Mintage	F12	VF20	XF40	MS60	MS63
1934	200,000	6.50	7.50	17.50	150	175
1934	—	PF63 950				
1935	50,000	6.50	9.00	20.00	220	250
1935	—	PF63 900				
1936	65,000	6.50	9.00	20.00	205	230
1936	—	PF63 925				

KM# 10 FLORIN

11.31 g., 0.500 Silver 0.1818 oz. ASW **Ruler:** George VI **Obv:** Crowned head left **Rev:** Shield of arms divides date, denomination below

Date	Mintage	F12	VF20	XF40	MS60	MS63
1937	30,000	6.50	8.00	17.50	165	185
1937	—	PF63 950				

KM# 13 FLORIN

11.31 g., 0.500 Silver 0.1818 oz. ASW **Ruler:** George VI **Obv:** Smaller head **Rev:** Shield of arms divides dates, denomination below

Date	Mintage	F12	VF20	XF40	MS60	MS63
1938	20,000	6.50	12.00	25.00	210	235
1938	—	PF63 850				
1941	20,000	6.50	12.00	25.00	210	235
1941	—	PF63 875				
1945	100,000	9.00	20.00	35.00	255	300
1945	—	PF63 850				

KM# 13a FLORIN

11.31 g., 0.900 Silver 0.3273 oz. ASW **Ruler:** George VI **Obv:** Crowned head left **Rev:** Shield of arms divides date, denomination below

Date	Mintage	F12	VF20	XF40	MS60	MS63
1942 S	250,000	—	12.00	13.50	16.00	22.50
1943 S	250,000	—	12.00	14.50	17.50	27.50

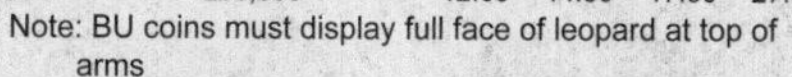

Note: BU coins must display full face of leopard at top of arms

KM# 24 FLORIN

11.20 g., Copper-Nickel, 28.3 mm. **Ruler:** Elizabeth II **Obv:** Crowned head right **Rev:** Shield of arms divides date, denomination below

Date	Mintage	F12	VF20	XF40	MS60	MS63
1957	300,000	0.50	1.00	4.00	15.00	20.00
1957	—	PF63 400				
1958	220,000	0.50	1.00	4.00	15.00	20.00
1958	—	PF63 400				
1962	200,000	0.25	0.50	2.00	10.00	15.00
1962	—	PF63 400				
1964	200,000	0.25	0.50	1.50	5.00	10.00
1964	—	PF63 425				
1965	400,000	0.25	0.50	1.00	3.00	5.00

DECIMAL COINAGE

100 Cents = 1 Dollar

KM# 27 CENT

1.90 g., Bronze, 17.5 mm. **Ruler:** Elizabeth II **Obv:** Young bust right **Rev:** Tanoa kava bowl divides denomination

Date	Mintage	VF20	XF40	MS60	MS63	MS65
1969	10,000	PF65 0.50				
1969 (h)	11,000,000	—	0.10	0.20	0.50	1.00
1973	3,000,000	—	0.10	0.50	1.00	2.00
1975	2,064,000	—	0.10	0.50	0.75	1.00
1976	—	—	0.10	0.50	0.75	1.00
1976	2,005,000	—	0.10	0.50	0.75	1.00
1983	3,000	PF65 1.00				
1983	3,000,000	—	0.10	0.50	0.75	1.00
1984	2,295,000	—	0.10	0.35	0.70	1.00
1985	—	—	0.10	0.35	0.70	1.00

KM# 27a CENT

2.26 g., 0.925 Silver 0.0672 oz. ASW, 17.5 mm. **Ruler:** Elizabeth II **Obv:** Young bust right **Rev:** Tanoa kava bowl divides denomination

Date	Mintage	VF20	XF40	MS60	MS63	MS65
1976	3,012	PF65 4.00				

KM# 39 CENT

1.90 g., Bronze, 17.5 mm. **Ruler:** Elizabeth II **Series:** F.A.O. **Obv:** Young bust right **Rev:** Rice plant at left, denomination at right

Date	Mintage	VF20	XF40	MS60	MS63	MS65
1977	3,000,000	—	0.10	0.50	1.00	1.50
1978	3,032,000	—	0.10	0.50	1.00	1.50
1978	2,000	PF65 2.50				
1979	2,500,000	—	0.10	2.00	3.00	4.00
1980	314,000	—	0.10	0.50	1.00	1.50
1980	2,500	PF65 1.50				
1981	4,040,000	—	0.10	0.50	0.75	1.00
1982	3,000	PF65 1.00				
1982	5,000,000	—	0.10	0.50	0.75	1.00

KM# 49 CENT

1.90 g., Bronze, 17.5 mm. **Ruler:** Elizabeth II **Obv:** Crowned head right, date at right **Rev:** Tanoa kava bowl divides denomination

Date	Mintage	VF20	XF40	MS60	MS63	MS65
1986	3,400,000	—	0.10	0.50	0.75	1.00
1987	3,400,000	—	0.15	0.50	0.75	1.00

KM# 49a CENT

1.58 g., Copper Plated Zinc, 17.53 mm. **Ruler:** Elizabeth II **Obv:** Crowned head right, date at right **Rev:** Tanoa kava bowl divides denomination

Date	Mintage	VF20	XF40	MS60	MS63	MS65
1990 (o)	8,500,000	—	0.10	0.25	0.45	0.75
1992 (o)	16,200,000	—	0.10	0.25	0.45	0.75

Date	Mintage	VF20	XF40	MS60	MS63	MS65
1994 (o)	7,800,000	—	—	0.25	0.45	0.75
1995 (o)	6,000,000	—	—	0.25	1.00	2.00
1997 (o)	12,000,000	—	—	0.25	0.50	1.00
1999 (o)	14,000,000	—	—	0.25	0.45	0.75

KM# 28 2 CENTS

3.85 g., Bronze, 21.1 mm. **Ruler:** Elizabeth II **Obv:** Young bust right, date at right **Rev:** Palm fan and denomination

Date	Mintage	VF20	XF40	MS60	MS63	MS65
1969	10,000	PF65 0.75				
1969 (h)	8,000,000	—	0.10	0.35	0.50	0.75
1973	2,110,000	0.10	0.15	0.75	1.25	2.50
1975	1,500,000	0.10	0.15	0.75	1.00	1.50
1976	1,004,999	0.10	0.15	0.75	1.00	1.50
1977	1,250,000	—	0.10	0.75	1.00	1.50
1978	2,000	PF65 3.50				
1978	1,502,000	—	0.10	0.75	1.00	1.50
1979	500,000	—	0.10	2.50	3.50	5.00
1980	2,500	PF65 2.50				
1980	4,019,999	—	0.10	1.00	1.25	1.75
1981	3,250,000	—	0.10	1.00	1.50	2.00
1982	3,000	PF65 2.00				
1982	4,000,000	—	0.10	1.00	1.25	1.75
1983	3,000	PF65 1.50				
1983	3,000,000	—	0.10	0.75	1.25	1.75
1984	1,845,000	—	0.10	0.75	1.25	1.75
1985	1,700,000	—	0.10	0.75	1.00	2.00

KM# 28a 2 CENTS

4.53 g., 0.925 Silver 0.1347 oz. ASW, 21.1 mm. **Ruler:** Elizabeth II **Obv:** Young bust right **Rev:** Palm fan and denomination

Date	Mintage	VF20	XF40	MS60	MS63	MS65
1976	3,012	PF65 6.00				

KM# 50 2 CENTS

3.85 g., Bronze, 21.1 mm. **Ruler:** Elizabeth II **Obv:** Crowned head right, date at right **Rev:** Palm fan and denomination

Date	Mintage	VF20	XF40	MS60	MS63	MS65
1986	1,700,000	—	0.15	0.75	1.00	1.50
1987	1,700,000	—	0.15	0.75	1.00	1.50

KM# 50a 2 CENTS

3.16 g., Copper Plated Zinc, 21.08 mm. **Ruler:** Elizabeth II **Obv:** Crowned head right, date at right **Rev:** Palm fan and denomination

Date	Mintage	VF20	XF40	MS60	MS63	MS65
1990 (o)	5,500,000	—	—	0.50	0.75	1.00
1992 (o)	10,000,000	—	—	0.50	0.75	1.00
1994 (o)	6,000,000	—	—	0.35	1.00	2.00
1995 (o)	5,000,000	—	—	0.35	0.50	1.00

KM# 29 5 CENTS

2.83 g., Copper-Nickel, 19.41 mm. **Ruler:** Elizabeth II **Obv:** Young bust right **Rev:** Fijian drum - lali divides denomination **Edge:** Reeded

Date	Mintage	VF20	XF40	MS60	MS63	MS65
1969	10,000	PF65 0.75				
1969 (l)	9,200,000	0.10	0.20	0.50	0.75	1.00
1973	600,000	0.10	0.30	1.00	1.50	2.00
1974	608,000	0.10	0.30	1.00	1.25	2.00
1975	1,008,000	0.10	0.20	1.00	1.25	2.00
1976	1,205,000	0.10	0.20	1.00	1.25	2.00
1977	960,000	0.10	0.20	1.00	1.25	2.00
1978	2,000	PF65 5.00				
1978	880,000	0.10	0.20	1.00	1.50	2.00
1979	1,500,000	0.10	0.25	2.00	3.00	4.50
1980	2,500	PF65 3.50				
1980	2,506,000	0.10	0.15	0.50	1.00	1.50
1981	1,980,000	0.10	0.15	0.50	1.00	1.50
1982	3,000	PF65 3.00				
1982	2,700,000	0.10	0.15	0.50	1.00	1.50
1983	3,000,000	0.10	0.15	0.50	1.00	1.50
1983	3,000	PF65 2.00				
1984	5,005,000	0.10	0.20	0.50	1.00	1.50

KM# 29a 5 CENTS

3.28 g., 0.925 Silver 0.0975 oz. ASW, 19.35 mm. **Ruler:** Elizabeth II **Series:** F.A.O. **Obv:** Young bust right **Rev:** Fijian drum - lali divides denomination

Date	Mintage	VF20	XF40	MS60	MS63	MS65
1976	3,012	PF65 7.00				

KM# 51 5 CENTS

2.83 g., Copper-Nickel, 19.41 mm. **Ruler:** Elizabeth II **Obv:** Crowned head right **Rev:** Fijian drum - lali divides denomination **Edge:** Reeded

Date	Mintage	VF20	XF40	MS60	MS63	MS65
1986	1,200,000	0.10	0.20	0.50	1.00	1.50
1987	1,200,000	0.10	0.20	0.50	1.00	2.00

KM# 51a 5 CENTS

2.34 g., Nickel Plated Steel, 19.41 mm. **Ruler:** Elizabeth II **Obv:** Crowned head right **Rev:** Fijian drum - lali divides denomination **Edge:** Reeded

Date	Mintage	VF20	XF40	MS60	MS63	MS65
1990 (o)	4,000,000	—	—	0.50	1.00	1.50
1992 (o)	7,700,000	—	—	0.50	0.75	1.00
1994 (o)	500,000	—	—	0.50	0.75	1.00
1995	—	—	—	0.75	1.25	2.50
1997 (l)	4,000,000	—	—	0.50	0.75	1.00
1998 (l)	3,000,000	—	—	0.50	0.75	1.00
1999 (l)	3,000,000	—	—	0.50	0.75	1.00
2000 (l)	3,000,000	—	—	0.50	0.75	1.00

KM# 77 5 CENTS

2.34 g., Nickel Plated Steel, 19.41 mm. **Ruler:** Elizabeth II **Series:** F.A.O. **Subject:** Harvest From the Sea **Obv:** Crowned head right, date at right **Rev:** Fish, F.A.O. logo below denomination **Edge:** Reeded

Date	Mintage	VF20	XF40	MS60	MS63	MS65
1995 (o)	300,000	—	—	0.75	1.00	1.50

KM# 30 10 CENTS

5.65 g., Copper-Nickel, 23.6 mm. **Ruler:** Elizabeth II **Obv:** Young bust right **Rev:** Throwing club - ula tava tava divides value **Edge:** Reeded

Date	Mintage	VF20	XF40	MS60	MS63	MS65
1969	10,000	PF65 1.00				
1969	3,500,000	0.20	0.35	0.50	0.75	1.50
1973	750,000	0.20	0.50	2.50	3.25	4.00
1975	752,000	0.20	0.50	1.75	2.25	3.00
1976	805,000	0.20	0.50	1.50	2.00	2.50
1977	240,000	0.25	0.65	1.50	2.00	2.50
1978	664,000	0.20	0.50	1.50	2.00	2.50
1978	2,000	PF65 6.00				
1979	702,000	0.20	0.50	1.50	2.00	2.50
1980	2,500	PF65 4.50				
1980	1,000,000	0.15	0.30	1.50	2.00	2.50
1981	1,200,000	0.20	0.50	1.25	1.50	2.00
1982	1,500,000	0.20	0.50	1.25	1.50	2.00
1982	3,000	PF65 4.00				
1983	3,003,000	0.25	0.65	1.25	1.50	2.00
1983	3,000	PF65 3.00				
1984	5,000,000	0.25	0.65	1.25	1.50	2.00
1985	660,000	0.20	0.50	1.25	1.50	2.00

KM# 30a 10 CENTS

6.55 g., 0.925 Silver 0.1948 oz. ASW, 23.6 mm. **Ruler:** Elizabeth II **Obv:** Young bust right **Rev:** Throwing club - ula tava tava divides value

Date	Mintage	VF20	XF40	MS60	MS63	MS65
1976	3,012	PF65 9.00				

KM# 52 10 CENTS

5.65 g., Copper-Nickel, 23.6 mm. **Ruler:** Elizabeth II **Obv:** Crowned head right, date at right **Rev:** Throwing club - ula tava tava divides value **Edge:** Reeded

Date	Mintage	VF20	XF40	MS60	MS63	MS65
1986	740,000	0.20	0.40	0.75	1.50	2.25
1987	740,000	0.20	0.40	0.75	1.50	2.25

KM# 52a 10 CENTS

4.75 g., Nickel Plated Steel, 23.6 mm. **Ruler:** Elizabeth II **Obv:** Crowned head right **Rev:** Throwing club - ula tava tava divides value **Edge:** Reeded

Date	Mintage	VF20	XF40	MS60	MS63	MS65
1990	2,000,000	—	—	0.65	1.25	1.75
1992	31,640,000	—	—	0.65	1.25	1.75
1994	1,000,000	—	—	0.65	1.25	1.75
1995	736,000	—	—	0.65	1.25	2.00
1996	1,000,000	—	—	0.65	1.25	2.50
1997	2,000,000	—	—	0.50	1.00	1.50
1998 (l)	2,000,000	—	—	0.50	1.00	1.25
1999 (l)	2,000,000	—	—	0.50	1.00	1.25
2000 (l)	1,340,000	—	—	0.50	1.00	1.25

KM# 31 20 CENTS

11.31 g., Copper-Nickel, 28.5 mm. **Ruler:** Elizabeth II **Obv:** Young bust right, date at right **Rev:** Tabua on braided sennit cord divides value **Edge:** Reeded

Date	Mintage	VF20	XF40	MS60	MS63	MS65
1969	2,000,000	0.30	0.80	1.50	1.75	2.25
1969	10,000	PF65 1.75				
1973	250,000	0.35	1.00	2.25	2.50	3.00
1974	252,000	0.35	0.75	2.00	2.50	3.00
1975	352,000	0.35	0.75	3.00	3.75	4.50
1976	405,000	0.25	0.65	1.75	2.00	2.25
1977	200,000	0.35	0.75	3.00	3.50	4.00
1978	406,000	0.25	0.50	1.75	2.00	2.25
1978	2,000	PF65 8.00				
1979	500,000	0.25	0.60	1.75	2.00	2.25
1980	1,014,000	0.25	0.60	1.75	2.00	2.25
1980	2,500	PF65 6.50				
1981	1,200,000	0.25	0.60	1.75	2.00	2.25
1982	1,500,000	0.25	0.60	1.25	1.50	2.00
1982	3,000	PF65 6.00				
1983	3,003,000	0.35	0.75	1.25	1.50	2.00
1983	3,000	PF65 5.00				
1984	5,005,000	0.35	0.75	1.25	1.50	2.00
1985	240,000	0.20	0.35	1.75	2.00	2.25

KM# 31a 20 CENTS

13.09 g., 0.925 Silver 0.3893 oz. ASW, 28.5 mm. **Ruler:** Elizabeth II **Obv:** Young bust right **Rev:** Tabua on braided sennit cord divides denomination

Date	Mintage	VF20	XF40	MS60	MS63	MS65
1976	3,012	PF65 15.00				

KM# 53 20 CENTS

11.31 g., Copper-Nickel, 28.5 mm. **Ruler:** Elizabeth II **Obv:** Crowned head right **Rev:** Tabua on braided sennit cord divides denomination **Edge:** Reeded

Date	Mintage	VF20	XF40	MS60	MS63	MS65
1986	360,000	0.25	0.60	1.50	2.00	2.50
1987	360,000	0.25	0.60	1.50	2.00	2.50

KM# 53a 20 CENTS

10.50 g., Nickel Plated Steel, 28.5 mm. **Ruler:** Elizabeth II **Obv:** Crowned head right **Rev:** Tabua on braided sennit cord divides denomination **Edge:** Reeded

Date	Mintage	VF20	XF40	MS60	MS63	MS65
1990	1,500,000	0.20	0.35	1.00	1.50	2.00
1992	1,000,000	0.20	0.35	1.75	2.25	3.50
1994	500,000	0.20	0.35	1.50	2.00	3.00
1995	200,000	0.20	0.35	1.25	1.50	2.00
1996 (l)	1,000,000	0.20	0.35	0.75	1.25	1.50
1997 (l)	153,000	0.20	0.35	0.75	1.50	3.00
1998	1,000,000	0.20	0.35	0.75	1.25	1.50
1999 (l)	1,000,000	0.20	0.35	0.75	1.25	1.50
2000 (l)	1,000,000	0.20	0.35	0.75	1.25	1.50

KM# 36 50 CENTS

15.55 g., Copper-Nickel, 31.5 mm. **Ruler:** Elizabeth II **Obv:** Young bust right, date at right **Rev:** Sailing canoe - Takia, denomination below **Shape:** 12-sided

Date	Mintage	VF20	XF40	MS60	MS63	MS65
1975	1,000,000	0.75	1.50	2.00	4.00	6.50
1976	805,000	0.50	1.00	1.50	2.00	3.50
1978	4,006	1.25	2.00	3.00	5.00	6.50
1978	2,000	PF65 13.00				
1979	258,000	0.75	1.00	3.00	4.50	6.50
1980	316,000	0.75	1.00	1.50	2.00	3.50
1980	2,500	PF65 11.50				
1981	511,000	0.75	1.00	2.25	4.00	7.00
1982	1,000,000	0.75	1.00	1.75	3.00	5.00
1982	3,000	PF65 10.00				
1983	3,000,000	0.65	1.00	1.50	2.50	4.00
1983	3,000	PF65 9.00				
1984	5,000,000	0.65	1.00	1.50	2.25	3.50

KM# 36a 50 CENTS

18.00 g., 0.925 Silver 0.5353 oz. ASW, 31.5 mm. **Ruler:** Elizabeth II **Obv:** Young bust right **Rev:** Sailing canoe - Takia, denomination below **Shape:** 12-sided

Date	Mintage	VF20	XF40	MS60	MS63	MS65
1976	3,012	PF65 20.00				

KM# 44 50 CENTS

15.55 g., Copper-Nickel, 31.5 mm. **Ruler:** Elizabeth II **Series:** F.A.O. **Subject:** First Indians in Fiji Centennial **Obv:** Young bust right, date at right **Rev:** Rice plants, denomination and date at right **Shape:** 12-sided

Date	Mintage	VF20	XF40	MS60	MS63	MS65
1979	258,000	—	—	1.50	2.50	3.75
1979	6,004	PF65 7.50				

KM# 45 50 CENTS

15.55 g., Copper-Nickel, 31.5 mm. **Ruler:** Elizabeth II **Subject:** 10th Anniversary of Independence **Obv:** Arms with supporters, date below **Rev:** Prince Charles 3/4 facing, denomination below **Shape:** 12-sided

Date	Mintage	VF20	XF40	MS60	MS63	MS65
1980	10,000	—	—	1.50	2.50	3.75

KM# 54 50 CENTS

15.55 g., Copper-Nickel, 31.5 mm. **Ruler:** Elizabeth II **Obv:** Crowned head right, date at right **Rev:** Sailing canoe - Takia, denomination below **Shape:** 12-sided

Date	Mintage	VF20	XF40	MS60	MS63	MS65
1986	160,000	0.75	1.00	1.50	2.00	4.00
1987	160,000	0.50	0.75	1.50	2.00	4.00

KM# 54a 50 CENTS

13.44 g., Nickel Bonded Steel, 31.51 mm. **Ruler:** Elizabeth II **Obv:** Crowned head right **Rev:** Sailing canoe - Takia, denomination below **Shape:** 12-sided

Date	Mintage	VF20	XF40	MS60	MS63	MS65
1990 (o)	800,000	—	0.60	1.25	1.75	2.50
1992 (o)	280,000	—	0.60	1.25	1.75	2.50
1994 (o)	480,000	—	0.60	1.00	1.50	2.50
1995 (l)	480,000	—	0.60	1.00	1.50	2.50
1996 (l)	560,000	—	0.60	1.00	1.50	2.50
1997 (l)	536,000	—	0.60	1.00	1.50	2.50
1998 (l)	536,000	—	0.60	1.00	1.50	2.50
1999 (l)	536,000	—	0.60	1.00	1.50	2.50
2000 (l)	536,000	—	0.60	1.00	1.50	2.50

KM# 32 DOLLAR

Copper-Nickel, 38.5 mm. **Ruler:** Elizabeth II **Obv:** Young bust right **Rev:** Arms with supporters, date below

Date	Mintage	VF20	XF40	MS60	MS63	MS65
1969	70,000	—	—	1.00	2.00	3.75
1969	10,000	PF65 5.00				
1976	5,007	1.00	1.50	2.50	5.00	7.50

KM# 32a DOLLAR

28.28 g., 0.925 Silver 0.841 oz. ASW **Ruler:** Elizabeth II **Obv:** Young bust right **Rev:** Arms with supporters divide denomination

Date	Mintage	VF20	XF40	MS60	MS63	MS65
1976	3,012	PF65 30.00				

KM# 33 DOLLAR

Copper-Nickel **Ruler:** Elizabeth II **Subject:** Independence Commemorative **Obv:** Young bust right, date at right **Rev:** Dove with olive branch on shield, crown above, palm trees flank

Date	Mintage	VF20	XF40	MS60	MS63	MS65
1970	15,000	—	—	1.00	2.00	3.75
1970	15,000	PF65 5.00				

Note: Variety with medallic alignment exists; Value: $100

KM# 33a DOLLAR

28.28 g., 0.925 Silver 0.841 oz. ASW **Ruler:** Elizabeth II **Subject:** Independence Commemorative **Obv:** Young bust right **Rev:** Crown above dove on shield, palm trees flank

Date	Mintage	VF20	XF40	MS60	MS63	MS65
1970	1,000	PF65 65.00				

KM# 71 DOLLAR

Copper-Nickel **Ruler:** Elizabeth II **Subject:** Move to Buckingham Palace **Obv:** Crowned head right **Rev:** Buckingham Palace and soldier within circle, denomination below

Date	Mintage	VF20	XF40	MS60	MS63	MS65
1995	Est. 300000	—	—	—	3.00	4.50

KM# 73 DOLLAR

8.00 g., Aluminum-Bronze, 23 mm. **Ruler:** Elizabeth II **Obv:** Crowned head right, date at right **Rev:** A saqamoli, native rattle, denomination above **Edge:** Reeded

Date	Mintage	VF20	XF40	MS60	MS63	MS65
1995	5,000,000	—	—	1.00	2.00	3.75
1996 (l)	1,000,000	—	—	1.00	2.00	3.50
1997 (l)	1,000,000	—	—	1.00	2.00	3.50
1998 (l)	1,000,000	—	—	1.00	2.00	3.50
1999 (l)	1,000,000	—	—	1.00	2.00	3.50
2000 (l)	1,000,000	—	—	1.00	2.00	3.50

KM# 78 2 DOLLARS

42.41 g., 0.925 Silver 1.2614 oz. ASW **Ruler:** Elizabeth II **Subject:** Soft Coral Capital of the World **Obv:** Crowned head at left facing right **Rev:** Denomination at right, coral industry scenes **Shape:** 1/3 circle segment

Date	Mintage	VF20	XF40	MS60	MS63	MS65
1998	20,000	PF65 50.00				

Note: Part of a tri-nation, three coin matching set with Cook Islands and Samoa

KM# 81 5 DOLLARS

20.00 g., 0.500 Silver 0.3215 oz. ASW **Ruler:** Elizabeth II **Subject:** Protect Our World **Obv:** Crowned head right **Rev:** Reef-heron, fish and tree, denomination below **Edge:** Reeded

Date	Mintage	VF20	XF40	MS60	MS63	MS65
1993	25,000	PF63 9.00	PF65 12.00			

KM# 69 5 DOLLARS

20.00 g., 0.500 Silver 0.3215 oz. ASW **Ruler:** Elizabeth II **Subject:** Queen Mother's London House **Obv:** Crowned head right **Rev:** Clarence House within circle, denomination below **Edge:** Reeded

Date	Mintage	VF20	XF40	MS60	MS63	MS65
1994	50,000	PF63 9.00	PF65 12.00			

KM# 80 5 DOLLARS

31.44 g., 0.925 Silver 0.935 oz. ASW **Ruler:** Elizabeth II **Subject:** Millennium 2000 **Obv:** Crowned head right, date at right **Rev:** Woman, map of Tavenui with 180 meridian and branch, denomination above **Shape:** 5-sided

Date	Mintage	VF20	XF40	MS60	MS63	MS65
1999	10,000	PF63 20.00	PF65 30.00			

KM# 40 10 DOLLARS

30.30 g., 0.925 Silver 0.9011 oz. ASW **Ruler:** Elizabeth II **Subject:** Queen's Silver Jubilee **Obv:** Young bust right, date at right **Rev:** Arms with supporters, crown divides dates above, denomination below

Date	Mintage	VF20	XF40	MS60	MS63	MS65
1977	3,010	PF63 27.00	PF65 35.00			

KM# 41 10 DOLLARS

28.28 g., 0.500 Silver 0.4546 oz. ASW **Ruler:** Elizabeth II **Subject:** Conservation **Obv:** Young bust right **Rev:** Pink-billed parrot finch on branch right

Date	Mintage	VF20	XF40	MS60	MS63	MS65
1978	3,582	—	—	15.00	25.00	35.00

KM# 41a 10 DOLLARS

28.28 g., 0.925 Silver 0.841 oz. ASW **Ruler:** Elizabeth II **Subject:** Conservation **Obv:** Young bust right **Rev:** Pink-billed parrot finch

Date	Mintage	VF20	XF40	MS60	MS63	MS65
1978	4,026	PF65 32.00				

KM# 46 10 DOLLARS

28.44 g., 0.500 Silver 0.4572 oz. ASW **Ruler:** Elizabeth II **Subject:** 10th Anniversary of Independence **Obv:** Arms with supporters, date below **Rev:** Bust 3/4 left, denomination below

Date	Mintage	VF20	XF40	MS60	MS63	MS65
1980	5,001	—	—	10.00	12.00	15.00

KM# 46a 10 DOLLARS

30.48 g., 0.925 Silver 0.9065 oz. ASW **Ruler:** Elizabeth II **Subject:** 10th Anniversary of Independence **Obv:** Arms with supporters **Rev:** Bust of Prince Charles 3/4 left

Date	Mintage	VF20	XF40	MS60	MS63	MS65
1980	3,001	PF65 25.00				

KM# 48 10 DOLLARS

30.00 g., 0.925 Silver 0.8922 oz. ASW **Ruler:** Elizabeth II **Subject:** Wedding of Prince Charles and Lady Diana **Obv:** Young bust right **Rev:** Head 3/4 left

Date	Mintage	VF20	XF40	MS60	MS63	MS65
1981	5,000	PF65 25.00				

KM# 55 10 DOLLARS

28.28 g., 0.925 Silver 0.841 oz. ASW **Ruler:** Elizabeth II **Subject:** 25th Anniversary - World Wildlife Fund **Obv:** Crowned head right **Rev:** Fijian ground frog, denomination at right

Date	Mintage	VF20	XF40	MS60	MS63	MS65
1986	25,000	PF65 30.00				

KM# 60 10 DOLLARS

28.28 g., 0.925 Silver 0.841 oz. ASW **Ruler:** Elizabeth II **Subject:** Save the Children Fund **Obv:** Crowned head right **Rev:** Children reading by lantern light, denomination upper right

Date	Mintage	VF20	XF40	MS60	MS63	MS65
1991	20,000	PF65 35.00				

KM# 62 10 DOLLARS

28.28 g., 0.925 Silver 0.841 oz. ASW **Ruler:** Elizabeth II **Subject:** 40th Anniversary - Coronation of Queen Elizabeth II **Obv:** Crowned head right **Rev:** Queen seated on throne flanked by church figures

Date	Mintage	VF20	XF40	MS60	MS63	MS65
1993	10,000	PF65 22.00				

KM# 63 10 DOLLARS

31.10 g., 0.925 Silver 0.925 oz. ASW **Ruler:** Elizabeth II **Subject:** Discovery of Fiji **Obv:** Crowned head right **Rev:** Cameo of Abel J. Tasman upper right, ships below

Date	Mintage	VF20	XF40	MS60	MS63	MS65
1993	10,000	PF65 25.00				

KM# 64 10 DOLLARS

31.10 g., 0.925 Silver 0.925 oz. ASW **Ruler:** Elizabeth II **Subject:** Discovery of Fiji **Obv:** Crowned head right **Rev:** Cameo of William Bligh upper right, long boat with sailors, denomination below

Date	Mintage	VF20	XF40	MS60	MS63	MS65
1993	10,000	PF65 22.00				

KM# 66 10 DOLLARS

31.46 g., 0.925 Silver 0.9356 oz. ASW **Ruler:** Elizabeth II **Subject:** Protect Our World **Obv:** Crowned head right **Rev:** Island scene within palm of hand, denomination below

Date	Mintage	VF20	XF40	MS60	MS63	MS65
1993	—	PF65 22.00				

KM# 67 10 DOLLARS

31.46 g., 0.925 Silver 0.9356 oz. ASW **Ruler:** Elizabeth II **Series:** 1996 Olympics **Obv:** Crowned head right **Rev:** Judo match, denomination below

Date	Mintage	VF20	XF40	MS60	MS63	MS65
1993	20,000	PF65 22.00				

KM# 68 10 DOLLARS

31.64 g., 0.925 Silver 0.941 oz. ASW **Ruler:** Elizabeth II **Subject:** World Cup Soccer **Obv:** Crowned head right **Rev:** Soccer player

Date	Mintage	VF20	XF40	MS60	MS63	MS65
(1993)	—	PF65 22.00				

KM# 70 10 DOLLARS

31.47 g., 0.925 Silver 0.9359 oz. ASW **Ruler:** Elizabeth II **Subject:** Lunar Module "Eagle" **Obv:** Crowned head right **Rev:** Lunar module on moon, eagle outline in background, denomination below

Date	Mintage	VF20	XF40	MS60	MS63	MS65
1994	Est. 10000	PF65 22.00				

KM# 74 10 DOLLARS

31.37 g., 0.925 Silver 0.9329 oz. ASW **Ruler:** Elizabeth II **Subject:** Endangered Wildlife **Obv:** Crowned head right **Rev:** Streaked Fantail on branch, denomination below

Date	Mintage	VF20	XF40	MS60	MS63	MS65
1995	—	PF65 25.00				

KM# 75 10 DOLLARS

34.46 g., 0.925 Silver 1.0248 oz. ASW **Ruler:** Elizabeth II **Subject:** Silver Jubilee of Independence **Obv:** Crowned head right **Rev:** Arms with supporters, crown above divides dates, denomination below

Date	Mintage	VF20	XF40	MS60	MS63	MS65
1995	—	PF65 30.00				

KM# 79 10 DOLLARS

31.52 g., 0.925 Silver 0.9374 oz. ASW **Ruler:** Elizabeth II **Series:** Olympic Games 1996 **Obv:** Crowned head right **Rev:** Two sailboarders, denomination at right

Date	Mintage	VF20	XF40	MS60	MS63	MS65
1995	—	PF65 25.00				

KM# 86 10 DOLLARS
31.35 g., 0.925 Silver 0.9323 oz. ASW, 38.7 mm. **Ruler:** Elizabeth II **Subject:** Queen Elizabeth II and The Queen Mother - Move to Buckingham Palace **Obv:** Crowned head right **Rev:** 1/2 bust of soldier at right in front of Buckingham Palace within circle, denomination below **Edge:** Reeded

Date	Mintage	VF20	XF40	MS60	MS63	MS65
1995	—	PF65 22.00				

KM# 90 10 DOLLARS
28.50 g., 0.925 Silver 0.8476 oz. ASW, 38.5 mm. **Ruler:** Elizabeth II **Subject:** Queen's 70th Birthday **Obv:** Crowned head right **Rev:** Native dancer, denomination divides dates below **Edge:** Reeded

Date	Mintage	VF20	XF40	MS60	MS63	MS65
1996	—	PF65 25.00				

KM# 100 10 DOLLARS
31.47 g., 0.925 Silver 0.9359 oz. ASW, 38.61 mm. **Ruler:** Elizabeth II **Subject:** Victorian Age - Queen Victoria's Coronation, 28 June 1838 **Obv:** Crowned head right **Rev:** Crowned Queen Victoria **Edge:** Reeded

Date	Mintage	VF20	XF40	MS60	MS63	MS65
1996	10,000	PF65 25.00				

KM# 76 10 DOLLARS
31.33 g., 0.925 Silver 0.9317 oz. ASW **Ruler:** Elizabeth II **Subject:** Endangered Wildlife **Obv:** Crowned head right **Rev:** Banded iguana left

Date	Mintage	VF20	XF40	MS60	MS63	MS65
1997	—	PF65 27.00				

KM# 85 10 DOLLARS
28.28 g., 0.925 Silver 0.841 oz. ASW, 38.6 mm. **Ruler:** Elizabeth II **Subject:** UNICEF **Obv:** Crowned head right **Rev:** Two young folk dancers, denomination below **Edge:** Reeded

Date	Mintage	VF20	XF40	MS60	MS63	MS65
1997	25,000	PF65 25.00				

KM# 87 10 DOLLARS
19.70 g., 0.925 Silver 0.5859 oz. ASW, 33.9 mm. **Ruler:** Elizabeth II **Subject:** Queen Elizabeth II's Golden Jubilee **Obv:** Crowned head right **Rev:** The royal couple, shield and treehouse **Edge:** Reeded

Date	Mintage	VF20	XF40	MS60	MS63	MS65
1997	—	PF65 16.00				

KM# 92 10 DOLLARS
31.60 g., 0.925 Silver 0.9398 oz. ASW, 38.6 mm. **Ruler:** Elizabeth II **Subject:** Princess Diana **Obv:** Crowned head right **Rev:** Diana with sick child **Edge:** Reeded

Date	Mintage	VF20	XF40	MS60	MS63	MS65
1997	—	PF65 28.00				

KM# 96 10 DOLLARS
34.47 g., 0.925 Silver 1.0251 oz. ASW, 38.6 mm. **Ruler:** Elizabeth II **Subject:** HM Barge [sic] "Endeavour" **Obv:** Crowned head right **Rev:** Endeavour **Edge:** Reeded

Date	Mintage	VF20	XF40	MS60	MS63	MS65
1998 (o)	20,000	PF65 28.00				

KM# 97 10 DOLLARS
1.25 g., 0.999 Gold 0.0401 oz. AGW **Ruler:** Elizabeth II **Subject:** Discovery of Gold in Fiji - 1932 **Obv:** Crowned head right **Rev:** Gold panning

Date	Mintage	VF20	XF40	MS60	MS63	MS65
1998	—	PF65 70.00				

KM# 174 10 DOLLARS
Silver, 38 mm. **Ruler:** Elizabeth II **Subject:** Queen Mother's birthday **Rev:** Launch of the Cunard liner: R.M.S. Queen Elizabeth **Edge:** Reeded

Date	Mintage	VF20	XF40	MS60	MS63	MS65
1998	—	PF65 35.00				

KM# 91 10 DOLLARS
28.10 g., 0.925 Silver 0.8357 oz. ASW Gold plated outer ring, 38.6 mm. **Ruler:** Elizabeth II **Subject:** Queen Mother's Centennial **Obv:** Crowned head right within beaded circle, date at right **Rev:** Elizabeth and David as children within beaded circle, denomination below **Edge:** Reeded

Date	Mintage	VF20	XF40	MS60	MS63	MS65
2000	10,000	PF65 22.00				

KM# 103 10 DOLLARS
1.24 g., 0.999 Gold 0.0398 oz. AGW **Ruler:** Elizabeth II **Obv:** Crowned head right **Obv. Legend:** ELIZABETH II - FIJI **Rev:** Dakuwaqa - Shark god

Date	Mintage	VF20	XF40	MS60	MS63	MS65
2000	—	PF65 70.00				

KM# 42 20 DOLLARS
35.00 g., 0.500 Silver 0.5626 oz. ASW **Ruler:** Elizabeth II **Subject:** Conservation **Obv:** Young bust right **Rev:** Golden cowrie, denomination below

Date	Mintage	VF20	XF40	MS60	MS63	MS65
1978	3,584	—	—	12.00	15.00	20.00

KM# 42a 20 DOLLARS
35.00 g., 0.925 Silver 1.0409 oz. ASW **Ruler:** Elizabeth II **Subject:** Conservation **Obv:** Young bust right **Rev:** Golden cowrie

Date	Mintage	VF20	XF40	MS60	MS63	MS65
1978	3,869	PF63 25.00	PF65 35.00			

KM# 102 20 DOLLARS
3.11 g., 0.585 Gold 0.0585 oz. AGW **Ruler:** Elizabeth II **Subject:** XXVII Summer Olympics - Sydney 2000 **Obv:** Crowned head right **Obv. Legend:** ELIZABETH II - FIJI **Rev:** Sprinter

Date	Mintage	VF20	XF40	MS60	MS63	MS65
1998	—	PF63 125	PF65 150			

KM# 34 25 DOLLARS
48.60 g., 0.925 Silver 1.4453 oz. ASW **Ruler:** Elizabeth II **Subject:** 100th Anniversary - Cession to Great Britian **Obv:** Young bust right **Rev:** Bust of King Cakobau, facing, denomination below, dates in legend at right **Edge:** Reeded

Date	Mintage	XF40	MS60	MS63	MS65	MS66
1974	2,400	—	35.00	40.00	50.00	65.00
1974	8,299	PF65 45.00	PF67 60.00			

KM# 37 25 DOLLARS
48.60 g., 0.925 Silver 1.4453 oz. ASW **Ruler:** Elizabeth II **Obv:** Young bust right **Rev:** King Cakobau bust facing, denomination below, dates above

Date	Mintage	XF40	MS60	MS63	MS65	MS66
1975	5,157	PF65 45.00	PF67 60.00			
1975	836	—	50.00	55.00	65.00	80.00

KM# 57 25 DOLLARS
7.78 g., 0.750 Gold 0.1875 oz. AGW **Ruler:** Elizabeth II **Obv:** Denomination at center of designs **Rev:** Balikula mint mark of Pacific Sovereign Mint, Fijian thatched temple

Date	Mintage	XF40	MS60	MS63	MS65	MS66
ND-1990	443	—	—	325	400	450
Note: Boar tusks						
ND-1991	512	—	—	325	400	450
Note: War fan						
ND-1992	50	—	—	375	450	500

KM# 58 50 DOLLARS
15.55 g., 0.750 Gold 0.375 oz. AGW **Ruler:** Elizabeth II **Obv:** Denomination at center of patterns **Rev:** Balikula mint mark of Pacific Sovereign Mint, Fijian warrior

Date	Mintage	XF40	MS60	MS63	MS65	MS66
ND-1990	168	—	—	650	700	750
Note: Boar tusks						
ND-1991	141	—	—	650	700	750
Note: War fan						
ND-1992	43	—	—	700	750	800

KM# 72 50 DOLLARS
7.78 g., 0.5833 Gold 0.1458 oz. AGW **Ruler:** Elizabeth II **Subject:** Olympics **Obv:** Crowned head right, date at right **Rev:** Two field hockey players, denomination below

Date	Mintage	VF20	XF40	MS60	MS63	MS65
1996	Est. 3000	—	—	—	275	300

KM# 88 50 DOLLARS
1000.00 g., 0.999 Silver 32.1186 oz. ASW, 100 mm. **Ruler:** Elizabeth II **Subject:** 70th Birthday of Queen Elizabeth II **Obv:** Crowned head right **Rev:** Queen and Queen mother side by side facing **Edge:** Reeded **Note:** Illustration reduced.

Date	Mintage	VF20	XF40	MS60	MS63	MS65
1996	99	PF65 750	PF67 950			

KM# 35 100 DOLLARS
31.36 g., 0.500 Gold 0.5041 oz. AGW **Ruler:** Elizabeth II **Subject:** 100th Anniversary - Cession to Great Britain **Obv:** Young bust right **Rev:** Bust of King Cakobau facing, denomination below

Date	Mintage	XF40	MS60	MS63	MS65	MS66
1974	1,109	—	—	—	950	1,000
1974	2,321	PF65 925	PF67 950			

KM# 38 100 DOLLARS
31.30 g., 0.500 Gold 0.5032 oz. AGW **Ruler:** Elizabeth II **Obv:** Young bust right **Rev:** King Cakobau facing, denomination below

Date	Mintage	XF40	MS60	MS63	MS65	MS66
1975	3,197	PF65 925	PF67 950			
1975	593	—	—	—	950	1,000

KM# 59 100 DOLLARS
31.10 g., 0.750 Gold 0.7499 oz. AGW **Ruler:** Elizabeth II **Obv:** Denomination within center, diamonds on pattern at top, bottom, right and left **Rev:** Balikula mint mark of Pacific Sovereign Mint **Note:** Dates are privy marks; 1990 - Boar Tusks; 1991 - War Fan; 1992 - ?.

Date	Mintage	XF40	MS60	MS63	MS65	MS66
ND-1990	161	—	—	1,300	1,350	1,400
ND-1991	131	—	—	1,300	1,350	1,400
ND-1992	41	—	—	1,400	1,450	1,500

KM# 65 100 DOLLARS
7.50 g., 0.917 Gold 0.2211 oz. AGW **Ruler:** Elizabeth II **Subject:** Discovery of Fiji **Obv:** Crowned head right, date at right **Rev:** James Cook in cameo right of sailing ship, denomination below

Date	Mintage	VF20	XF40	MS60	MS63	MS65
1993	3,000	PF65 425	PF67 475			

KM# 98 100 DOLLARS
0.999 Gold **Ruler:** Elizabeth II **Subject:** Silver Jubilee of Independence **Obv:** Crowned head right **Rev:** Arms

Date	Mintage	VF20	XF40	MS60	MS63	MS65
1995	—	PF65 400	PF67 450			

KM# 47 200 DOLLARS
15.98 g., 0.917 Gold 0.4711 oz. AGW **Ruler:** Elizabeth II **Subject:** 10th Anniversary of Independence **Obv:** Arms with supporters, date below **Rev:** Bust 3/4 facing, denomination below

Date	Mintage	VF20	XF40	MS60	MS63	MS65
1980	1,166	PF63 900	PF65 950			
1980	500	—	—	—	875	900

KM# 56 200 DOLLARS
15.98 g., 0.917 Gold 0.4711 oz. AGW **Ruler:** Elizabeth II **Subject:** 25th Anniversary - World Wildlife Fund **Obv:** Young bust right **Rev:** Ogmodon

Date	Mintage	VF20	XF40	MS60	MS63	MS65
1986	5,000	PF63 875	PF65 925			

KM# 61 200 DOLLARS
10.00 g., 0.917 Gold 0.2948 oz. AGW **Ruler:** Elizabeth II **Subject:** Save the Children Fund **Obv:** King Cakobau facing divides date **Rev:** Child with toy boat, figure in background with spear, denomination below

Date	Mintage	VF20	XF40	MS60	MS63	MS65
1991	32,000	PF63 550	PF65 600			

KM# 43 250 DOLLARS
33.44 g., 0.900 Gold 0.9675 oz. AGW **Ruler:** Elizabeth II **Subject:** Conservation **Obv:** Young bust right **Rev:** Banded iguana, denomination at right

Date	Mintage	VF20	XF40	MS60	MS63	MS65
1978	252	PF65 1,900	PF67 2,000			
1978	810	—	—	—	1,750	1,800

TRIAL STRIKES

KM#	Date	Mintage	Identification	Mkt Val
TS1	1974	—	100 Dollars. Bronze. KM35.	950
TS2	1974	—	Cent. Bronze. Fijian planting taro.	275
TS3	1974	—	Cent. Copper-Nickel. Fijian planting taro.	325

MINT SETS

KM#	Date	Mintage	Identification	Issue Price	Mkt Val
MS1	1976 (7)	5,001	KM27-32, 36	9.00	18.00
MS2	1976 (6)	—	KM27-31, 36	—	13.00
MS3	1978 (6)	4,000	KM28-31,36,39	4.50	17.00
MS4	1978 (3)	—	KM41-43	444	1,450
MS5	1978 (2)	—	KM41-42	44.00	45.00
MS6	1983 (6)	3,000	KM27-31, 36	5.00	12.50
MS7	1984 (6)	5,000	KM27-31, 36	3.60	12.00
MS8	1990 (6)	—	KM49a-54a	—	10.00
MS9	1990 (3)	—	KM57-59	905	2,500
MSA1	1934 (3)	—	KM3-5	—	800
MSB1	1969 (6)	—	KM27-32	—	10.00

PROOF SETS

KM#	Date	Mintage	Identification	Issue Price	Mkt Val
PS1	1969 (6)	10,000	KM#27-32	7.20	8.50
PS2	1976 (7)	3,023	KM#27a-32a, 36a	87.50	80.00
PS3	1978 (6)	2,000	KM#28-31, 36, 39	31.00	35.00
PS4	1978 (2)	—	KM#41a, 42a	76.00	60.00
PS5	1978 (3)	—	KM#41a, 42a, 43	726	1,600
PS6	1980 (6)	2,500	KM#28-31, 36, 39	45.00	30.00
PS7	1982 (7)	3,000	KM#28-31, 36, 39	32.00	27.00
PS8	1983 (6)	3,000	KM#27-31, 36	27.00	30.00
PS9	1993 (3)	—	KM#63-65	370	400

The Republic of Finland, the third northernmost state of the European continent, has an area of 130,559 sq. mi. (338,127 sq. km.) and a population of 5.1 million. Capital: Helsinki. Lumbering, shipbuilding, metal and woodworking are the leading industries. Paper, timber, wood pulp, plywood and metal products are exported.

The Finns, who probably originated in the Volga region of Russia, took Finland from the Lapps late in the 7th century. They were conquered in the 12th century by Eric IX of Sweden, and brought into contact with Western Christendom. In 1809, Sweden was conquered by Alexander I of Russia, and the peace terms gave Finland to Russia which became a grand duchy, with autonomy, within the Russian Empire until Dec. 6, 1917, when, shortly after the Bolshevik revolution it declared its independence. After a brief but bitter civil war between the Russian communists and Finnish nationalists in which the Whites (nationalists) were victorious, a new constitution was adopted, and on Dec. 6, 1917 Finland was established as a republic. In 1939 Soviet troops attacked Finland over disputed territorial concessions which were later granted in the peace treaty of 1940. When the Germans invaded Russia, Finland became involved and in the Armistice of 1944 lost the Petsamo area to the Soviets.

RULER

Nicholas II, 1894-1917

MONETARY SYSTEM

100 Pennia = 1 Markka
Commencing 1963
100 Old Markka = 1 New Markka

MINT MARKS

H - Birmingham 1921
Heart (h) - Copenhagen 1922
No mm – Helsinki

MINT OFFICIALS' INITIALS

Letter	Date	Name
H	1948-1958	Peppo Uolevi Helle
H-M	1990	Raimo Heino & Raimo Makkonen
K	1976-1983	Timo Koivuranta
K-H	1977, 1979	Timo Koivuranta & Heikki Halvaola (Designer)
K-M	1983	Timo Koivuranta & Pertti Makinen
K-N	1978	Timo Koivuranta & Antti Neuvonen
K-T	1982	Timo Koivuranta & Eria Tielinen
L	1885-1912	Johan Conrad Lihr
L	1948	Vesa Uolevi Liuhto
L-M	1991	Arto Lappalainen & Raimo Makkonen
L-M	2000	Maija Lavonen & Raimo Makkonen
M	1987	Raimo Makkonen & Henrik Gummerus
M-G	1998	Raimo Makkonen & Henrik Gummerus
M-L	1997	Raimo Makkonen & Tero Lounas
M-L-L	1995	Raimo Makkonen & Arto Lappalainen & Marita Lappalainen
M-L-M	1989	Marjo Lahtinen & Raimo Makkonen
M-O	1998	Raimo Makkonen & Harri Ojala
M-S	1992, 1997	Raimo Makkonen & Erikki Salmela
N	1983-1987	Tapio Nevalainen
P-M	1989-1991, 1994-1995, 1997, 2000	Reijo Paavilainen & Raimo Makkonen
P-N	1985	Reijo Paavilainen & Tapio Nevalainen
P-V-M	1999	Juhani Pallasmaa, Jukka Veistola & Raimo Makkonen
R-M	1999	Jarkko Roth & Raimo Makkonen
S	1912-1947	Isak Gustaf Sundell
S	1958-1975	Allan Alarik Soiniemi
S-H	1967-1971	Allan Alarik Soiniemi & Heikki Halvaola (Designer)
S-J	1960	Allan Alarik Soiniemi & Tolvo Jaatinen
S-M	1995	Terho Sakki & Raimo Makkonen
T-M	1996, 2000	Eria Tielinen & Raimo Makkonen

GRAND DUCHY

DECIMAL COINAGE

KM# 13 PENNI

1.28 g., Copper, 15 mm. **Ruler:** Nicholas II **Obv:** Crowned monogram **Rev:** Denomination and date

Date	Mintage	F12	VF20	XF40	MS60	MS63
1901	1,520,000	1.00	2.00	10.00	20.00	—
1902	1,000,000	2.00	8.00	12.00	20.00	—
1903	1,145,000	2.00	8.00	12.00	20.00	—
Note: Small 3						
1903	Inc. above	3.00	12.00	25.00	40.00	—
Note: Large 3						
1904	500,000	3.00	12.00	20.00	30.00	—
1905	1,390,000	0.75	1.50	6.00	10.00	—
1906	1,020,000	0.75	1.50	6.00	10.00	—
1907	2,490,000	0.50	1.00	2.50	8.00	—
Note: Normal 7						
1907	Inc. above	0.50	1.00	2.50	8.00	—
Note: Without serif on 7 arm						
1908	950,000	1.00	3.00	8.00	15.00	—
1909	3,060,000	0.25	0.75	2.00	3.00	5.00
1911	2,550,000	0.25	0.75	2.00	3.00	5.00
1912	2,450,000	0.25	0.75	2.00	3.00	5.00
1913	1,650,000	0.25	0.75	2.00	3.00	5.00
1914	1,900,000	0.25	0.75	2.00	3.50	6.00
1915	2,250,000	0.25	0.75	2.00	3.00	5.00
1916	3,040,000	0.25	0.75	2.00	3.00	5.00

KM# 15 5 PENNIÄ

6.50 g., Copper, 25 mm. **Ruler:** Nicholas II **Obv:** Crowned monogram **Rev:** Denomination and date

Date	Mintage	F12	VF20	XF40	MS60	MS63
1901	625,000	1.00	12.00	80.00	150	—
1905	620,000	3.00	20.00	100	200	—
1906	960,000	2.00	12.00	75.00	175	—
1907	770,000	3.00	15.00	150	300	—
1908	1,660,000	1.50	7.00	50.00	100	—
1910	60,000	50.00	100	300	600	—
1911	1,050,000	1.00	6.00	50.00	120	—
1912	460,000	3.00	10.00	90.00	200	—
1913	1,060,000	0.75	5.00	20.00	55.00	85.00
1914	820,000	0.75	5.00	20.00	50.00	75.00
1915	2,080,000	0.30	1.00	8.00	20.00	45.00
1916	4,470,000	0.30	1.00	5.00	15.00	30.00
1917	4,070,000	0.30	1.00	5.00	15.00	30.00

KM# 14 10 PENNIÄ

12.80 g., Copper, 30 mm. **Ruler:** Nicholas II **Obv:** Crowned monogram **Rev:** Denomination and date within wreath

Date	Mintage	F12	VF20	XF40	MS60	MS63
1905	500,000	5.00	25.00	200	550	—
1907	503,000	5.00	25.00	180	500	—
1908	320,000	5.00	25.00	120	240	—
1909	180,000	7.00	35.00	300	650	—
1910	241,000	5.00	25.00	85.00	200	—
1911	370,000	3.00	12.00	50.00	100	—
1912	191,000	5.00	20.00	75.00	200	—
1913	150,000	10.00	30.00	200	520	—
1914	605,000	2.00	5.00	30.00	75.00	—
1915	420,000	2.00	3.00	15.00	30.00	50.00
1916	1,952,000	1.00	2.00	10.00	20.00	35.00
1917	1,600,000	2.00	5.00	20.00	40.00	75.00

KM# 6.2 25 PENNIÄ

1.27 g., 0.750 Silver 0.0307 oz. ASW, 16 mm. **Ruler:** Nicholas II **Obv:** Crowned imperial double eagle with scepter and orb **Rev:** Denomination and date within wreath **Note:** Dentilated border.

Date	Mintage	F12	VF20	XF40	MS60	MS63
1901 L	993,900	1.50	5.00	25.00	60.00	—
1902 L	210,000	6.00	20.00	80.00	250	—
1906 L	281,000	3.00	12.00	50.00	150	—
1907 L	590,000	2.50	5.00	25.00	50.00	—
1908 L	340,000	3.00	12.00	45.00	120	—
1909 L	1,099,000	1.25	2.50	15.00	30.00	50.00
1910 L	392,000	5.00	20.00	50.00	150	—
1913 S	832,000	1.25	2.50	5.00	10.00	20.00
1915 S	2,400,000	0.60	1.25	1.50	3.00	5.00
1916 S	6,392,000	0.60	1.25	1.50	3.00	5.00
1917 S	5,820,000	0.60	1.25	1.50	3.00	5.00

KM# 2.2 50 PENNIÄ

2.55 g., 0.750 Silver 0.0615 oz. ASW, 18.6 mm. **Ruler:** Nicholas II **Obv:** Crowned imperial double eagle with scepter and orb **Rev:** Denomination and date within wreath **Note:** Dentilated border.

Date	Mintage	F12	VF20	XF40	MS60	MS63
1907 L	260,000	3.00	12.00	60.00	175	—
1908 L	353,000	2.25	5.00	22.50	70.00	—
1911 L	616,000	2.25	3.00	6.00	12.00	20.00
1914 S	600,000	2.25	3.00	5.00	8.00	15.00
1915 S	1,000,000	1.10	2.25	3.00	5.00	7.50
1916 S	4,752,000	1.10	2.25	3.00	5.00	7.50
1917 S	3,972,000	1.10	2.25	3.00	5.00	7.50

KM# 3.2 MARKKA

5.18 g., 0.868 Silver 0.1446 oz. ASW, 24 mm. **Ruler:** Nicholas II **Obv:** Crowned imperial double eagle holding orb and scepter, fineness around (text in Finnish) **Rev:** Denomination and date within wreath **Note:** Obverse text translates to: "94.48 pieces from one pound of fine silver." Dentilated border.

Date	Mintage	F12	VF20	XF40	MS60	MS63
1907 L	350,000	10.00	12.00	30.00	60.00	85.00
1908 L	153,000	15.00	25.00	70.00	200	—
1915 S	1,212,000	7.50	10.00	20.00	30.00	50.00

KM# 7.2 2 MARKKAA

10.37 g., 0.868 Silver 0.2893 oz. ASW, 27.5 mm. **Ruler:** Nicholas II **Obv:** Crowned imperial double eagle holding orb and scepter, fineness around (Finnish text) **Rev:** Denomination and date within wreath **Note:** Obverse text translates to: "47.24 pieces from one pound of fine silver." Dentilated border.

Date	Mintage	F12	VF20	XF40	MS60	MS63
1905 L	24,000	250	350	850	3,000	—
1906 L	225,000	20.00	35.00	125	200	—
1907 L	125,000	25.00	50.00	150	300	—
1908 L	124,000	20.00	40.00	60.00	150	225

KM# 8.2 10 MARKKAA

3.23 g., 0.900 Gold 0.0933 oz. AGW, 18.9 mm. **Ruler:** Nicholas II **Obv:** Crowned imperial double eagle holding orb and scepter **Rev:** Denomination and date within circle, fineness around **Note:** Regal issues

Date	Mintage	F12	VF20	XF40	MS60	MS63
1904 L	102,000	600	800	1,100	1,350	—
1905 L	43,000	2,500	4,000	5,500	7,000	—
1913 S	396,000	190	300	350	450	500

KM# 9.2 20 MARKKAA

6.45 g., 0.900 Gold 0.1867 oz. AGW, 21.3 mm. **Ruler:** Nicholas II **Obv:** Crowned imperial double eagle holding orb and scepter **Rev:** Denomination and date within circle, fineness around **Note:** Regal issues.

Date	Mintage	F12	VF20	XF40	MS60	MS63
1903 L	112,000	335	425	550	700	800
1904 L	188,000	325	400	475	650	700
1910 L	201,000	325	400	475	650	700
1911 L	161,000	325	400	475	650	700
1912 L	881,000	7,800	12,000	20,000	24,000	—
1912 S	Inc. above	325	400	450	600	700
1913 S	214,000	325	400	475	650	700

CIVIL WAR COINAGE

Kerenski Government Issue

KM# 16 PENNI

1.28 g., Copper, 15 mm. **Ruler:** Nicholas II

Date	Mintage	F12	VF20	XF40	MS60	MS63
1917	1,650,000	0.25	0.75	1.00	2.00	3.00

KM# 17 5 PENNIÄ

6.40 g., Copper, 25 mm. **Ruler:** Nicholas II **Obv:** Imperial double eagle holding royal orb and scepter, shield on breast within circle **Rev:** Denomination above date

Date	Mintage	F12	VF20	XF40	MS60	MS63
1917	Inc. above	0.30	0.75	3.00	7.00	10.00

KM# 18 10 PENNIÄ

12.80 g., Copper, 30 mm. **Ruler:** Nicholas II

Date	Mintage	F12	VF20	XF40	MS60	MS63
1917	Inc. above	0.50	1.50	5.00	9.00	15.00

KM# 19 25 PENNIÄ

1.27 g., 0.750 Silver 0.0307 oz. ASW, 16 mm. **Ruler:** Nicholas II **Obv:** Crown above eagle removed

Date	Mintage	F12	VF20	XF40	MS60	MS63
1917 S	2,310,000	—	0.60	1.25	2.50	4.00

KM# 20 50 PENNIÄ

2.55 g., 0.750 Silver 0.0615 oz. ASW, 18.6 mm. **Ruler:** Nicholas II **Obv:** Imperial double eagle holding royal orb and scepter, shield on breast **Rev:** Denomination and date within wreath **Note:** No crown above eagle

Date	Mintage	F12	VF20	XF40	MS60	MS63
1917 S	570,000	—	1.25	2.25	3.50	6.00

CIVIL WAR COINAGE

Liberated Finnish Government Issue

KM# 21 5 PENNIÄ

2.50 g., Copper, 17.9 mm. **Obv:** Flag and 3 trumpets within wreath, wreath knot centered between 9 and 1 of date below **Obv. Legend:** • KANSAN TYÖ, KANSAN VALTA • - SUOMI - FINLAND **Rev:** Large value flanked by flower heads **Note:** Prev. KM#21.1. For previously listed KM#21.2, refer to Unusual World Coins, X#B1.

Date	Mintage	F12	VF20	XF40	MS60	MS63
1918	34,880	40.00	60.00	90.00	120	150

REPUBLIC

DECIMAL COINAGE

KM# 23 PENNI

1.00 g., Copper, 14 mm. **Rev:** Denomination flanked by rosettes

Date	Mintage	F12	VF20	XF40	MS60	MS63
1919	1,200,000	0.25	0.65	1.25	1.75	3.00
1920	720,000	0.25	0.65	1.25	1.75	3.00
1921	510,000	0.35	1.00	1.50	2.00	4.00
1922	1,060,000	0.25	0.65	1.25	1.75	3.00
1923	990,000	0.25	0.65	1.25	1.75	3.00
1924	2,180,000	0.25	0.65	1.25	1.75	3.00

KM# 22 5 PENNIÄ

2.50 g., Copper, 18 mm. **Obv:** Rampant lion left with sword divides date **Rev:** Rosettes flank denomination

Date	Mintage	F12	VF20	XF40	MS60	MS63
1918	4,270,000	0.10	0.25	0.50	1.00	4.00
1919	4,640,000	0.10	0.25	0.50	1.00	4.00
1920	7,710,000	0.10	0.25	0.50	1.00	3.00
1921	5,910,000	0.10	0.25	0.50	1.00	3.00
1922	8,540,000	0.10	0.25	0.50	1.00	3.00
1927	1,520,000	0.75	1.50	2.50	5.00	20.00
1928	2,110,000	0.25	0.50	1.00	2.00	10.00
1929	1,500,000	0.25	0.50	1.00	2.00	10.00
1930	2,140,000	0.75	1.25	2.00	3.00	12.00
1932	2,130,000	0.15	0.50	1.00	1.50	6.00
1934	2,180,000	0.15	0.50	0.75	1.00	6.00
1935	1,610,000	0.15	0.35	1.00	2.00	7.00
1936	2,610,000	0.15	0.35	0.75	1.50	4.00
1937	3,830,000	0.10	0.25	0.50	1.00	3.00
1938	4,300,000	0.10	0.25	0.50	1.00	3.00
1939	2,270,000	0.10	0.25	0.50	1.00	3.00
1940	1,610,000	0.25	0.50	1.00	1.50	5.00

KM# 64.1 5 PENNIÄ

1.27 g., Copper, 16 mm. **Obv:** Rosette above center hole flanked by leaves dividing date below **Rev:** Center hole divides denomination, rosettes flank **Note:** Punched center hole.

Date	Mintage	F12	VF20	XF40	MS60	MS63
1941	5,950,000	0.10	0.20	0.30	0.50	1.25
1942	4,280,000	0.10	0.20	0.30	0.50	1.25
1943	1,530,000	0.10	0.50	0.75	1.25	2.50

KM# 64.2 5 PENNIÄ

Copper, 16 mm. **Note:** Without punched center hole. These issues were not authorized by the government and any that exist were illegally removed from the mint.

Date	Mintage	F12	VF20	XF40	MS60	MS63
1941	Inc. above	25.00	30.00	50.00	100	150
1942	Inc. above	25.00	30.00	50.00	100	150
1943	Inc. above	50.00	70.00	90.00	120	175

KM# 24 10 PENNIÄ

5.00 g., Copper, 22 mm. **Obv:** Rampant lion left, holding sword, divides date **Rev:** Value flanked by rosettes **Edge:** Plain

Date	Mintage	F12	VF20	XF40	MS60	MS63
1919	3,670,000	0.10	0.25	0.50	1.00	5.00
1920	2,380,000	0.10	0.25	0.50	1.00	5.00
1921	3,970,000	0.10	0.25	0.50	1.00	5.00
1922	2,180,000	0.10	0.25	0.50	2.00	7.00
1923	910,000	2.00	5.00	10.00	20.00	60.00
1924	1,350,000	0.25	0.50	2.50	5.00	20.00
1926	1,690,000	0.25	0.50	1.50	3.50	15.00
1927	1,330,000	0.50	2.00	7.00	15.00	50.00
1928	1,006,000	0.50	2.00	5.00	10.00	30.00
1929	1,560,000	0.35	0.85	2.50	5.00	20.00
1930	650,000	0.75	1.50	5.50	12.50	25.00
1931	1,040,000	2.00	5.00	10.00	20.00	60.00
1934	1,680,000	0.35	0.85	2.50	5.00	12.00
1935	1,690,000	0.15	0.25	1.00	2.00	10.00

Date	Mintage	F12	VF20	XF40	MS60	MS63
1936	2,009,999	0.15	0.25	0.50	1.00	7.50
1937	2,420,000	0.10	0.25	0.35	0.75	3.50
1938	2,940,000	0.10	0.25	0.35	0.75	3.50
1939	2,100,000	0.10	0.25	0.35	0.75	3.50
1940	2,009,999	0.25	0.50	0.75	1.50	5.00

KM# 33.1 10 PENNIÄ

2.55 g., Copper, 18.5 mm. **Obv:** Rosette above center hole flanked by leaves dividing date below **Rev:** Center hole divides denomination, rosettes flank

Date	Mintage	F12	VF20	XF40	MS60	MS63
1941	3,610,000	0.10	0.25	0.35	0.50	1.25
1942	4,970,000	0.10	0.25	0.35	0.50	1.25
1943	1,860,000	0.25	0.75	1.25	1.50	2.50

KM# 33.2 10 PENNIÄ

2.60 g., Copper, 18.5 mm. **Obv:** Rosette above center hole flanked by leaves dividing date below **Rev:** Center hole divides denomination, rosettes flank **Note:** Without punched center hole. These issues were not authorized by the government and any that exist were illegally removed from the mint.

Date	Mintage	F12	VF20	XF40	MS60	MS63
1941	Inc. above	30.00	50.00	70.00	100	150
1942	Inc. above	30.00	50.00	70.00	100	150
1943	Inc. above	35.00	75.00	95.00	120	175

KM# 34.1 10 PENNIÄ

1.12 g., Iron, 16 mm. **Obv:** Rosette above center hole flanked by leaves dividing date below **Rev:** Center hole flanked by rosettes divides denomination **Note:** Reduced planchet size.

Date	Mintage	F12	VF20	XF40	MS60	MS63
1943	1,430,000	0.10	0.25	0.50	1.00	5.00
1944	3,040,000	0.10	0.25	0.50	1.00	5.00
1945	1,810,000	0.25	0.50	1.00	2.00	10.00

KM# 34.2 10 PENNIÄ

Iron, 16 mm. **Obv:** Sprigs divide date, rosette above **Rev:** Rosettes and denomination **Note:** Without punched center hole. These issues were not authorized by the government and any that exist were illegally removed from the mint.

Date	Mintage	F12	VF20	XF40	MS60	MS63
1943	Inc. above	50.00	75.00	95.00	120	150
1944	Inc. above	50.00	75.00	95.00	120	150
1945	Inc. above	70.00	100	150	200	250

KM# 25 25 PENNIÄ

1.27 g., Copper-Nickel, 16 mm. **Obv:** Rampant lion left holding sword divides date **Rev:** Denomination flanked by grain sprigs

Date	Mintage	F12	VF20	XF40	MS60	MS63
1921 H	20,096,000	0.10	0.25	0.50	1.00	3.00
1925 S	1,250,000	0.50	1.50	10.00	20.00	30.00
1926 S	2,820,000	0.40	1.25	3.00	7.00	15.00
1927 S	1,120,000	0.50	1.50	7.00	15.00	25.00
1928 S	2,920,000	0.40	1.00	5.00	10.00	18.00
1929 S	200,000	3.00	6.50	15.00	45.00	80.00
1930 S	1,090,000	1.00	3.00	5.00	10.00	20.00
1934 S	1,260,000	0.40	0.75	1.50	3.00	12.00
1935 S	2,190,000	0.30	0.50	1.00	2.00	8.00
1936 S	2,300,000	0.20	0.40	1.00	2.00	7.50
1937 S	4,019,999	0.20	0.40	0.75	1.00	5.00
1938 S	4,500,000	0.20	0.40	0.75	1.00	3.00
1939 S	2,712,000	0.20	0.40	0.75	1.00	3.00
1940 S	4,840,000	0.15	0.30	0.50	0.75	2.00

KM# 25a 25 PENNIÄ

1.27 g., Copper, 16 mm. **Obv:** Rampant lion left divides date **Rev:** Grain sprigs flank denomination

Date	Mintage	F12	VF20	XF40	MS60	MS63
1940 S	72,000	1.00	2.00	3.50	7.50	20.00
1941 S	5,980,000	0.10	0.35	1.00	2.00	5.00
1942 S	6,464,000	0.10	0.35	1.00	2.00	5.00
1943 S	4,912,000	0.25	0.50	1.50	3.00	7.00

KM# 25b 25 PENNIÄ

1.10 g., Iron, 16 mm. **Obv:** Rampant lion left divides dates **Rev:** Grain sprigs flank denomination

Date	Mintage	F12	VF20	XF40	MS60	MS63
1943 S	2,700,000	0.15	0.50	1.50	3.00	12.00
1944 S	5,480,000	0.15	0.50	1.50	2.00	8.00

Note: Small closed 4s

Date	Mintage	F12	VF20	XF40	MS60	MS63
1944 S	Inc. above	0.15	0.50	1.50	2.00	8.00
Note: Large open 4's						
1945 S	6,810,000	0.25	0.75	1.75	3.00	12.00

KM# 26 50 PENNIÄ

2.55 g., Copper-Nickel, 18.5 mm. **Obv:** Rampant lion left divides date

Date	Mintage	F12	VF20	XF40	MS60	MS63
1921 H	10,072,000	0.15	0.30	0.50	1.00	3.00
1923 S	6,000,000	0.25	1.00	2.00	3.00	12.00
1929 S	984,000	1.00	2.00	10.00	20.00	65.00
1934 S	612,000	1.00	2.00	10.00	20.00	65.00
1935 S	610,000	1.00	2.00	8.00	15.00	50.00
1936 S	1,520,000	0.30	0.50	1.50	3.00	15.00
1937 S	2,350,000	0.15	0.25	0.50	1.00	7.50
1938 S	2,330,000	0.15	0.25	0.50	1.00	5.00
1939 S	1,280,000	0.15	0.25	0.50	1.00	5.00
1940 S	3,152,000	0.15	0.25	0.50	1.00	3.00

KM# 26a 50 PENNIÄ

2.55 g., Copper, 18.5 mm. **Obv:** Rampant lion left divides date **Rev:** Grain sprigs flank denomination

Date	Mintage	F12	VF20	XF40	MS60	MS63
1940 S	480,000	1.25	2.50	4.50	8.00	20.00
1941 S	3,860,000	0.15	0.40	1.50	3.00	8.00
1942 S	5,900,000	0.15	0.40	1.50	3.00	8.00
1943 S	3,140,000	0.25	0.50	1.50	3.00	8.00

KM# 26b 50 PENNIÄ

2.25 g., Iron, 18.5 mm. **Obv:** Rampant lion left divides date **Rev:** Grain sprigs flank denomination

Date	Mintage	F12	VF20	XF40	MS60	MS63
1943 S	1,580,000	0.25	0.50	2.00	5.00	20.00
1944 S	7,600,000	0.15	0.40	1.50	3.00	12.00
1945 S	4,700,000	0.15	0.40	1.50	3.00	15.00
1946 S	2,632,000	0.30	0.50	1.50	3.00	15.00
1947 S	1,748,000	0.50	2.00	5.00	10.00	25.00
1948 L	1,112,000	3.00	10.00	15.00	25.00	40.00

KM# 27 MARKKA

5.10 g., Copper-Nickel, 24 mm.

Date	Mintage	F12	VF20	XF40	MS60	MS63
1921 H	10,048,000	1.00	2.00	3.00	5.00	15.00
1922 Heart	10,000,000	1.00	2.00	5.00	7.00	20.00
1923 S	1,780,000	10.00	20.00	30.00	50.00	100
1924 S	3,270,000	5.00	10.00	20.00	35.00	75.00

KM# 30 MARKKA

4.00 g., Copper-Nickel, 21 mm. **Obv:** Rampant lion left divides date **Rev:** Denomination flanked by branches **Edge:** Reeded **Note:** Reduced size.

Date	Mintage	F12	VF20	XF40	MS60	MS63
1928 S	3,000,000	0.15	1.00	2.50	5.00	20.00
1929 S	3,862,000	0.15	1.00	2.50	5.00	20.00
1930 S	10,284,000	0.15	1.00	2.50	5.00	20.00
1931 S	2,830,000	0.15	1.00	4.00	8.00	25.00
1932 S	4,140,000	0.15	1.00	4.00	8.00	25.00
1933 S	4,032,000	0.15	1.00	2.50	5.00	20.00
1936 S	562,000	1.00	3.00	12.00	25.00	75.00
1937 S	4,930,000	0.15	1.00	1.50	3.00	6.00
1938 S	4,410,000	0.15	1.00	1.50	3.00	6.00
1939 S	3,070,000	0.15	1.00	1.50	3.00	6.00
1940 S	3,372,000	0.15	1.00	1.50	3.00	6.00

Note: Coins dated 1928S, 1929S and 1930S are known to be restruck on 1921-24, KM#27 coins; 1928S: 2 or 3 known

KM# 30a MARKKA

4.00 g., Copper, 21 mm. **Obv:** Rampant lion left divides date **Rev:** Denomination flanked by branches

Date	Mintage	F12	VF20	XF40	MS60	MS63
1940 S	84,000	1.50	3.50	7.00	12.00	25.00
1941 S	8,970,000	0.15	0.50	1.00	2.00	8.00
1942 S	11,200,000	0.15	0.50	1.00	2.00	8.00
1943 S	7,460,000	0.15	0.50	1.00	2.00	8.00
1949 H	250	6,000	9,000	10,000	11,500	15,000
Note: Counterfeits exist						
1950 H	320,000	0.50	1.00	2.00	3.00	10.00
1951 H	4,630,000	0.25	0.50	1.00	2.00	8.00

KM# 30b MARKKA

3.50 g., Iron, 21 mm. **Obv:** Rampant lion left divides date **Rev:** Branches flank denomination **Edge:** Reeded

Date	Mintage	F12	VF20	XF40	MS60	MS63
1943 S	7,460,000	0.15	0.25	2.00	5.00	20.00
1944 S	12,830,000	0.15	0.25	2.00	5.00	20.00
1945 S	21,950,000	0.15	0.25	2.00	5.00	20.00
1946 S	2,630,000	0.15	0.30	2.00	5.00	20.00
1947 S	1,750,000	0.25	0.50	2.50	7.00	25.00
1948 L	20,500,000	0.15	0.25	1.50	3.00	10.00
1949 H	17,358,000	0.15	0.25	1.50	3.00	10.00
1950 H	14,654,000	0.15	0.25	1.00	2.00	7.00
1951 H	21,414,000	0.15	0.25	1.00	2.00	7.00
1952 H	5,410,000	0.25	0.50	2.00	5.00	20.00

KM# 36 MARKKA

1.15 g., Iron, 16 mm. **Obv:** Four joined loops form design, date below **Rev:** Grasped hands flank denomination

Date	Mintage	F12	VF20	XF40	MS60	MS63
1952	22,050,000	0.15	0.35	0.50	1.00	7.00
1953	28,618,000	0.15	0.35	0.50	1.00	7.00

KM# 36a MARKKA

1.15 g., Nickel Plated Iron, 16 mm. **Obv:** Four joined loops form design, date below **Rev:** Grasped hands flank denomination

Date	Mintage	F12	VF20	XF40	MS60	MS63
1953	6,000,000	5.00	7.00	10.00	15.00	25.00
1954	36,400,000	—	0.10	0.15	0.25	0.50
1955	38,100,000	—	0.10	0.15	0.25	0.50
1956	35,600,000	—	0.10	0.15	0.25	1.00
1957	29,100,000	—	0.10	0.15	0.25	0.50
1958	19,940,000	0.10	0.20	0.30	0.35	0.70
1959	Inc. above	—	0.10	0.15	0.25	1.00
Note: Thin letters						
1959	23,920,000	—	0.10	0.15	0.25	0.50
Note: Thick letters						
1960	22,020,000	—	0.10	0.15	0.25	0.50
1961	32,220,000	—	0.10	0.15	0.25	0.50
1962	29,040,000	—	0.10	0.15	0.25	0.50

KM# 31 5 MARKKAA

4.55 g., Aluminum-Bronze, 23 mm. **Obv:** Wreath divides denomination **Rev:** Shielded arms within wreath divide date

Date	Mintage	F12	VF20	XF40	MS60	MS63
1928 S	580,000	70.00	100	150	200	400
1929 S	Inc. above	60.00	90.00	120	200	500
1930 S	592,000	1.00	3.00	20.00	50.00	120
1931 S	3,090,000	1.00	2.00	15.00	35.00	60.00
1932 S	964,000	12.00	40.00	120	250	500
1933 S	1,050,000	1.00	5.00	25.00	50.00	120
1935 S	440,000	2.00	10.00	30.00	55.00	130
1936 S	470,000	2.00	10.00	35.00	60.00	170
1937 S	1,032,000	1.00	5.00	12.00	25.00	60.00
1938 S	912,000	1.00	5.00	12.00	25.00	60.00
1939 S	752,000	1.00	5.00	12.00	25.00	60.00
1940 S	820,000	2.00	7.00	15.00	35.00	80.00
1941 S	1,452,000	1.00	3.00	7.00	12.00	20.00
1942 S	1,390,000	1.00	3.00	8.00	15.00	30.00
1946 S	618,000	5.00	10.00	20.00	30.00	100

KM# 31a 5 MARKKAA

4.55 g., Brass, 23 mm. **Obv:** Denomination divided by wreath **Rev:** Shielded arms within wreath divides date below

Date	Mintage	F12	VF20	XF40	MS60	MS63
1946 S	5,538,000	0.50	1.00	2.00	3.00	10.00
1947 S	6,550,000	1.00	2.00	4.00	7.00	15.00
1948 L	8,210,000	0.50	1.00	3.00	5.00	12.00
1949 H	Inc. above	1.00	2.00	3.50	5.00	10.00
Note: Wide H						
1949 H	11,014,000	2.00	5.00	7.00	10.00	20.00
Note: Thin H						
1950 H	4,760,000	0.50	1.00	3.00	5.00	10.00
1951 H	7,800,000	0.50	1.00	2.00	3.00	8.00
1952 H	1,210,000	3.00	10.00	15.00	20.00	35.00

KM# 37 5 MARKKAA

2.55 g., Iron, 18 mm. **Obv:** Four joined loops form design, date below **Rev:** Grasped hands flank denomination

Date	Mintage	F12	VF20	XF40	MS60	MS63
1952	10,820,000	0.20	0.35	1.25	2.00	8.00
1953	9,772,000	0.20	0.35	1.50	3.00	10.00

KM# 37a 5 MARKKAA

2.55 g., Nickel Plated Iron, 18 mm. **Obv:** Four joined loops form design, date below **Rev:** Grasped hands flank denomination

Date	Mintage	F12	VF20	XF40	MS60	MS63
1953	Inc. above	100	150	200	250	350
1954	6,696,000	—	0.20	0.50	1.00	5.00
1955	9,894,000	—	0.20	0.50	1.00	5.00
1956	8,220,000	—	0.20	0.50	1.00	5.00
1957	4,276,000	—	0.20	0.50	1.00	5.00
1958	3,300,000	—	0.20	0.50	1.00	7.00
1959	5,874,000	—	0.20	0.50	1.00	5.00
1960	3,066,000	0.10	0.25	0.75	1.25	7.00
1961	7,254,000	0.10	0.25	0.75	1.25	5.00
1962	4,542,000	0.50	2.00	3.00	5.00	8.00

KM# A32 10 MARKKAA

8.00 g., Aluminum-Bronze, 27 mm. **Obv:** Wreath divides denomination **Rev:** Shielded arms within wreath divide date below **Note:** Prev. KM#63.

Date	Mintage	F12	VF20	XF40	MS60	MS63
1928 S	730,000	5.00	25.00	50.00	100	250
1929 S	Inc. above	3.00	15.00	40.00	80.00	200
1930 S	260,000	2.00	10.00	25.00	50.00	150
1931 S	1,530,000	2.00	10.00	25.00	50.00	175
1932 S	1,010,000	2.00	7.50	20.00	35.00	120
1934 S	154,000	2.00	12.00	45.00	75.00	200
1935 S	81,000	5.00	20.00	60.00	120	250
1936 S	304,000	5.00	15.00	35.00	75.00	150
1937 S	181,000	3.00	10.00	25.00	50.00	120
1938 S	631,000	2.00	5.00	12.00	25.00	75.00
1939 S	133,000	5.00	15.00	22.00	40.00	90.00

KM# 38 10 MARKKAA

3.00 g., Aluminum-Bronze, 20 mm. **Obv:** Rampant lion left within circle, date below **Rev:** Tree right of denomination **Edge:** Reeded

Date	Mintage	F12	VF20	XF40	MS60	MS63
1952 H	6,390,000	0.20	1.00	3.00	5.00	12.00
1953 H	22,650,000	0.15	0.35	0.50	1.00	5.00
1954 H	2,452,000	0.50	1.00	2.50	5.00	15.00
1955 H	2,342,000	0.20	0.50	2.00	5.00	12.00
1956 H	4,240,000	0.20	0.40	1.50	3.00	10.00
1958 H	3,292,000	3.00	10.00	15.00	25.00	40.00
Note: Thin 1						

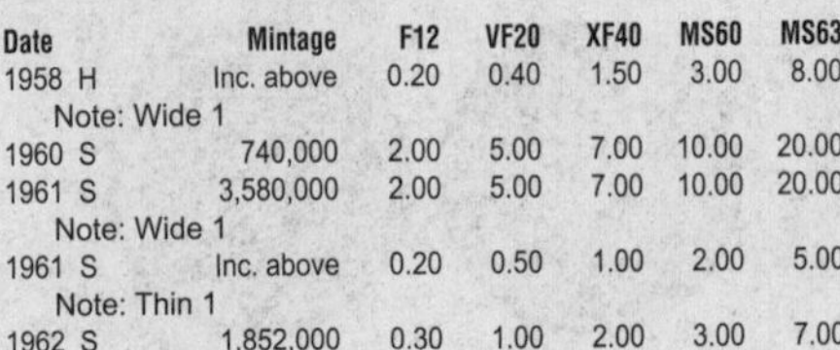

Date	Mintage	F12	VF20	XF40	MS60	MS63
1958 H	Inc. above	0.20	0.40	1.50	3.00	8.00
Note: Wide 1						
1960 S	740,000	2.00	5.00	7.00	10.00	20.00
1961 S	3,580,000	2.00	5.00	7.00	10.00	20.00
Note: Wide 1						
1961 S	Inc. above	0.20	0.50	1.00	2.00	5.00
Note: Thin 1						
1962 S	1,852,000	0.30	1.00	2.00	3.00	7.00

Note: The "1" in the denomination on all 1952 to 1956 issues is the thin variety; 1960 issues are the wide variety, and 1961s and 1962s are thin; Varieties exist in root length of tree

KM# 32 20 MARKKAA

13.00 g., Aluminum-Bronze, 31 mm. **Obv:** Wreath divides denomination **Rev:** Shielded arms within wreath divide date below

Date	Mintage	F12	VF20	XF40	MS60	MS63
1931 S	16,000	20.00	40.00	50.00	65.00	100
1932 S	14,000	30.00	50.00	60.00	85.00	120
1934 S	390,000	3.00	12.00	35.00	70.00	120
1935 S	250,000	3.00	15.00	40.00	80.00	160
1936 S	110,000	5.00	20.00	50.00	100	250
1937 S	510,000	3.00	10.00	20.00	40.00	100
1938 S	360,000	3.00	10.00	20.00	40.00	100
1939 S	960,000	2.00	3.00	7.00	15.00	30.00

KM# 39 20 MARKKAA

4.50 g., Aluminum-Bronze, 25.5 mm. **Obv:** Rampant lion left within circle, date below **Rev:** Tree right of denomination **Edge:** Reeded

Date	Mintage	F12	VF20	XF40	MS60	MS63
1952 H	83,000	7.00	10.00	15.00	20.00	40.00
1953 H	2,880,000	0.25	0.50	2.00	3.00	15.00
1954 H	17,034,000	0.15	0.50	1.00	2.00	10.00
1955 H	2,800,000	0.25	0.50	3.00	5.00	15.00
1956 H	2,540,000	0.25	0.50	3.00	5.00	15.00
1957 H	1,050,000	0.50	1.00	4.00	8.00	20.00
1958 H	515,000	2.50	5.00	10.00	20.00	40.00
1959 S	1,580,000	0.25	0.50	2.50	5.00	15.00
1960 S	3,850,000	0.15	0.50	1.00	3.00	10.00
1961 S	4,430,000	0.15	0.50	1.00	3.00	10.00
1962 S	2,280,000	0.15	0.50	1.00	3.00	8.00

KM# 40 50 MARKKAA

5.50 g., Aluminum-Bronze, 25 mm. **Obv:** Rampant lion left within circle, date below **Rev:** Tree right of denomination

Date	Mintage	F12	VF20	XF40	MS60	MS63
1952 H	991,000	2.00	5.00	12.00	25.00	50.00
1953 H	10,300,000	0.25	1.00	3.00	7.00	15.00
1954 H	1,170,000	3.00	8.00	15.00	28.00	55.00
1955 H	583,000	5.00	15.00	22.00	35.00	75.00
1956 H	792,000	3.00	10.00	20.00	30.00	50.00
1958 H	242,000	25.00	40.00	55.00	70.00	80.00
1960 S	110,000	25.00	50.00	60.00	75.00	100
1961 S	1,811,000	1.00	3.00	7.00	10.00	20.00
1962 S	405,000	5.00	15.00	20.00	25.00	35.00

KM# 28 100 MARKKAA

4.21 g., 0.900 Gold 0.1218 oz. AGW, 18.5 mm. **Obv:** Rampant lion left divides date **Rev:** Denomination flanked by sprigs

Date	Mintage	F12	VF20	XF40	MS60	MS63
1926 S	50,000	—	1,000	1,200	1,300	1,850

KM# 41 100 MARKKAA

5.20 g., 0.500 Silver 0.0836 oz. ASW, 24 mm. **Obv:** Shielded arms above date **Rev:** Denomination surrounded by trees and tree tops

Date	Mintage	F12	VF20	XF40	MS60	MS63
1956 H	3,012,000	—	1.50	2.50	3.00	5.00
1957 H	3,012,000	—	1.50	2.50	3.00	5.00
1958 H	1,704,000	1.50	3.00	4.00	5.00	7.00
1959 S	1,270,000	5.00	7.50	12.00	16.00	20.00
1960 S	290,000	3.50	7.00	10.00	15.00	20.00

KM# 29 200 MARKKAA

8.42 g., 0.900 Gold 0.2437 oz. AGW, 22.5 mm. **Obv:** Rampant lion left divides date **Rev:** Denomination flanked by sprigs

Date	Mintage	F12	VF20	XF40	MS60	MS63
1926 S	50,000	—	1,350	1,650	2,250	2,800

KM# 42 200 MARKKAA

8.30 g., 0.500 Silver 0.1334 oz. ASW, 27.5 mm. **Obv:** Shielded arms above date **Rev:** Denomination surrounded by trees and tree tops

Date	Mintage	F12	VF20	XF40	MS60	MS63
1956 H	1,552,000	—	2.50	3.50	5.00	8.00
1957 H	2,157,000	—	2.50	3.50	5.00	9.00
1958 H	1,477,000	2.50	4.50	5.00	6.00	10.00
1958 S	34,000	400	500	600	700	800
1959 S	70,000	25.00	30.00	40.00	55.00	70.00

KM# 35 500 MARKKAA

12.00 g., 0.500 Silver 0.1929 oz. ASW, 32 mm. **Obv:** Wreath divides denomination **Rev:** Olympic logo above date

Date	Mintage	F12	VF20	XF40	MS60	MS63
1951 H	19,000	100	120	150	200	300
1952 H	586,000	10.00	12.00	15.00	20.00	28.00

KM# 43 1000 MARKKAA

14.00 g., 0.875 Silver 0.3938 oz. ASW, 32 mm. **Subject:** Markka Currency System Centennial - Snellman **Obv:** Head left, date below **Rev:** Denomination within wreath

Date	Mintage	F12	VF20	XF40	MS60	MS63
1960 S-J	201,000	14.00	16.00	20.00	25.00	35.00

REFORM COINAGE

100 Old Markkaa = 1 New Markkaa 1963

KM# 44 PENNI

1.60 g., Copper, 15.8 mm. **Obv:** Four joined loops form design, date below **Rev:** Grasped hands flank denomination

Date	Mintage	VF20	XF40	MS60	MS63	MS65
1963	171,333,000	—	0.15	0.25	0.50	1.50
Note: Struck at Leningrad Mint						
1964	49,300,000	—	0.15	0.25	0.50	2.00
1965	43,112,000	—	0.15	0.25	0.50	2.00
1966	36,880,000	—	0.15	0.25	0.50	2.00
1967	62,792,000	—	0.15	0.25	0.50	2.00
1968	73,416,000	—	—	0.25	0.50	2.00
1969	51,748,000	—	—	0.25	0.50	2.00

KM# 44a PENNI

0.45 g., Aluminum, 15.8 mm. **Obv:** Four joined loops form design, date below **Rev:** Grasped hands flank denomination

Date	Mintage	VF20	XF40	MS60	MS63	MS65
1969	28,524,000	—	—	0.25	0.50	2.00
1970	85,140,000	—	—	—	0.20	1.00
1971	70,240,000	—	—	—	0.20	1.00
1972	95,096,000	—	—	—	0.20	1.00
1973	115,532,000	—	—	—	0.20	0.50
1974	100,132,000	—	—	—	0.20	0.50
1975	111,906,000	—	—	—	0.20	0.50
1976	34,965,000	—	—	—	0.20	0.50
1977	61,393,000	—	—	—	0.20	0.50
1978	90,132,000	—	—	—	0.20	0.50
1979	33,388,000	—	—	—	0.20	0.50

KM# 45 5 PENNIÄ

2.60 g., Copper, 18.5 mm. **Obv:** Four joined loops form design, date below **Rev:** Grasped hands flank denomination

Date	Mintage	VF20	XF40	MS60	MS63	MS65
1963	60,320,000	—	0.15	0.25	0.50	1.50
1964	4,634,000	0.50	1.00	2.00	5.00	15.00
1965	10,264,000	—	0.15	0.25	0.50	2.00
1966	8,064,000	—	0.15	0.25	0.50	3.00
1967	9,968,000	—	0.15	0.25	0.50	2.00
1968	6,144,000	—	0.15	0.25	0.50	2.00
1969	3,598,000	—	0.15	0.25	0.50	2.00
1970	13,772,000	—	—	—	0.25	1.00
1971	20,010,000	—	—	—	0.25	1.00
1972	24,122,000	—	—	—	0.25	1.00
1973	25,644,000	—	—	—	0.25	1.00
1974	21,530,000	—	—	—	0.25	1.00
1975	25,010,000	—	—	—	0.25	1.00
1976	25,551,000	—	—	—	0.25	1.00
1977	1,489,000	—	0.10	0.25	0.50	1.50

KM# 45a 5 PENNIÄ

0.80 g., Aluminum, 18 mm. **Obv:** Four joined loops form design, date below **Rev:** Grasped hands flank denomination

Date	Mintage	VF20	XF40	MS60	MS63	MS65
1977	30,552,000	—	—	—	0.15	0.50
1978	26,112,000	—	—	—	0.15	0.50
1979	40,042,000	—	—	—	0.15	0.50
1980	60,026,000	—	—	—	0.15	0.50
1981	2,044,000	—	0.20	0.30	0.40	1.00
1982	10,012,000	—	—	—	0.25	0.75
1983	33,885,000	—	—	—	—	0.25
1984	25,001,000	—	—	—	—	0.25
1985	25,000,000	—	—	—	—	0.25
1986	20,000,000	—	—	—	—	0.25
1987	2,020,000	—	—	—	—	0.25
1988	33,005,000	—	—	—	—	0.15
1989	2,200,000	—	—	—	—	0.50
1990	2,506,000	—	—	—	—	0.50

KM# 46 10 PENNIÄ

3.00 g., Aluminum-Bronze, 20 mm. **Obv:** Rampant lion left, date below **Rev:** Tree right of denomination **Edge:** Reeded

Date	Mintage	VF20	XF40	MS60	MS63	MS65
1963 S	38,420,000	—	0.15	0.25	0.50	1.50
1964 S	6,926,000	—	0.15	0.50	1.00	3.00
1965 S	4,524,000	—	0.15	0.25	0.50	3.00
1966 S	3,094,000	—	0.15	0.25	0.50	2.00
1967 S	1,050,000	0.15	0.30	1.00	3.00	10.00
1968 S	3,004,000	—	—	0.15	0.25	1.50
1969 S	5,046,000	—	—	0.15	0.20	1.50
1970 S	3,996,000	—	—	0.15	0.20	1.50
1971 S	15,026,000	—	—	—	0.10	1.00
1972 S	19,900,000	—	—	—	0.10	1.00
1973 S	9,196,000	—	—	—	0.10	1.00
1974 S	8,930,000	—	—	—	0.10	1.00
1975 S	15,064,000	—	—	—	0.10	0.50
1976 K	10,063,000	—	—	—	0.10	0.50
1977 K	10,043,000	—	—	—	0.10	0.50
1978 K	10,062,000	—	—	—	0.10	0.50
1979 K	13,072,000	—	—	—	0.10	0.50
1980 K	23,654,000	—	—	—	0.10	0.50
1981 K	30,036,000	—	—	—	0.10	0.50
1982 K	35,548,000	—	—	—	0.10	0.50

KM# 46a 10 PENNIÄ

1.00 g., Aluminum, 20 mm. **Obv:** Rampant lion left, date below **Rev:** Tree right of denomination

Date	Mintage	VF20	XF40	MS60	MS63	MS65
1983 K	6,320,000	—	—	0.15	0.25	1.00
1983 N	4,191,000	—	—	0.15	0.25	1.00
1984 N	20,061,000	—	—	—	0.10	0.50
1985 N	20,000,000	—	—	—	0.10	0.50
1986 N	15,000,000	—	—	—	0.10	0.50
1987 N	1,400,000	—	—	0.15	0.25	1.00
1987 M	8,654,000	—	—	0.15	0.25	1.00
1988 M	23,197,000	—	—	—	0.10	0.50
1989 M	2,400,000	—	—	0.15	0.25	0.50
1990 M	2,254,000	—	—	0.15	0.25	0.50

KM# 65 10 PENNI'A'

1.80 g., Copper-Nickel, 16.3 mm. **Obv:** Flower pods and stems, date at right **Rev:** Denomination to right of honeycombs

Date	Mintage	VF20	XF40	MS60	MS63	MS65
1990 M	338,100,000	—	—	—	0.10	0.15
1991 M	263,899,000	—	—	—	0.10	0.15
1992 M	136,131,000	—	—	—	0.10	0.15
1993 M	56,206,000	—	—	—	0.10	0.15
1994 M	59,946,000	—	—	—	0.10	0.15
1994 M	5,000	PF65 7.00				
1995 M	85,000,000	—	—	—	0.10	0.15
1995 M	3,000	PF65 7.00				
1996 M	123,000,000	—	—	—	0.10	0.15
1996 M	1,200	PF65 7.00				
1997 M	43,406,000	—	—	—	0.10	0.15
1997 M	2,000	PF65 7.00				
1998 M	95,322,000	—	—	—	0.10	0.15
1998 M	2,000	PF65 7.00				
1999 M	46,375,000	—	—	—	0.10	0.15
1999 M	—	PF65 7.00				
2000 M	114,903,000	—	—	—	—	0.15
2000 M	—	PF65 7.00				

KM# 47 20 PENNIÄ

4.50 g., Aluminum-Bronze, 22.5 mm. **Obv:** Rampant lion left, date below **Rev:** Tree right of denomination **Edge:** Reeded

Date	Mintage	VF20	XF40	MS60	MS63	MS65
1963 S	39,970,000	0.15	0.20	0.50	1.00	1.50
1964 S	4,248,000	1.00	1.50	2.50	3.50	5.00
1965 S	5,704,000	0.50	0.65	1.00	2.00	3.00
1966 S	4,085,000	0.50	0.65	1.00	2.00	3.00
1967 S	1,716,000	0.50	0.65	1.00	2.00	3.00
1968 S	1,330,000	0.50	0.65	1.00	2.00	3.00
1969 S	201,000	1.00	1.25	2.00	3.00	4.00
1970 S	230,000	1.00	1.25	2.00	2.50	3.50
1971 S	5,150,000	0.25	0.35	0.50	0.75	1.00

Note: Some coins dated 1971 are magnetic and command a higher premium

Date	Mintage	VF20	XF40	MS60	MS63	MS65
1972 S	10,001,000	0.25	0.35	0.50	0.75	1.00
1973 S	9,462,000	0.25	0.35	0.50	0.75	1.00
1974 S	12,705,000	0.25	0.35	0.50	0.75	1.00
1975 S	12,068,000	0.25	0.35	0.50	0.75	1.00
1976 K	20,058,000	0.25	0.35	0.50	0.75	1.00
1977 K	10,063,000	0.25	0.35	0.50	0.75	1.00
1978 K	10,014,000	0.25	0.35	0.50	0.75	1.00
1979 K	7,513,000	0.25	0.35	0.50	0.75	1.00
1980 K	20,047,000	—	—	0.25	0.50	0.75
1981 K	30,002,000	—	—	0.25	0.50	0.75
1982 K	35,050,000	—	—	0.25	0.50	0.75
1983 N	12,889,000	—	—	0.25	0.50	0.75
1983 K	7,113,000	—	—	0.25	0.50	0.75
1984 N	20,029,000	—	—	0.25	0.50	0.75
1985 N	15,004,000	—	—	0.25	0.50	0.75
1986 N	20,001,000	—	—	0.25	0.50	0.75
1987 M	25,670,000	—	—	0.25	0.50	0.75
1987 N	1,200,000	0.25	0.35	0.50	1.00	1.50
1988 M	13,853,000	—	—	0.25	0.50	0.75
1989 M	40,695,000	—	—	0.25	0.50	0.75
1990 M	9,168,000	—	—	0.25	0.50	0.75

KM# 48 50 PENNIÄ

5.50 g., Aluminum-Bronze, 25.0 mm. **Obv:** Rampant lion left, date below **Rev:** Tree right of denomination **Edge:** Reeded

Date	Mintage	VF20	XF40	MS60	MS63	MS65
1963 S	17,316,000	0.20	0.30	0.50	2.00	3.00
1964 S	3,101,000	0.25	1.00	3.00	5.00	10.00
1965 S	1,667,000	0.20	0.75	2.00	3.50	5.00
1966 S	1,051,000	0.20	0.75	2.00	4.00	7.50
1967 S	400,000	0.50	1.00	2.25	4.00	7.00
1968 S	816,000	0.25	0.50	1.00	2.50	4.00
1969 S	1,341,000	0.20	0.30	0.50	1.50	3.00
1970 S	2,250,000	0.20	0.30	0.50	1.00	2.00
1971 S	10,003,000	0.20	0.30	0.50	1.00	1.50

Note: Some coins dated 1971 are magnetic and command a higher premium

Date	Mintage	VF20	XF40	MS60	MS63	MS65
1972 S	7,892,000	0.20	0.30	0.50	1.00	1.50
1973 S	5,428,000	0.20	0.30	0.50	1.00	1.50
1974 S	5,049,000	0.20	0.30	0.50	1.00	1.50
1975 S	4,305,000	0.20	0.30	0.50	1.00	1.50
1976 K	7,022,000	0.20	0.30	0.50	1.00	1.50
1977 K	8,077,000	0.20	0.30	0.50	1.00	1.50
1978 K	8,048,000	0.20	0.30	0.50	1.00	1.50
1979 K	8,004,000	0.20	0.30	0.50	1.00	1.50
1980 K	5,349,000	0.20	0.30	0.50	1.00	1.50
1981 K	20,031,000	0.20	0.30	0.50	1.00	1.50
1982 K	5,042,000	0.20	0.30	0.50	1.00	1.50
1983 N	1,016,000	0.20	0.30	0.50	1.00	1.50
1983 K	4,043,999	—	—	0.25	1.00	1.60
1984 N	3,006,000	—	—	0.25	1.00	1.50
1985 N	10,000,000	—	—	0.25	1.00	1.50
1986 N	9,002,000	—	—	0.25	1.00	1.50
1987 N	700,000	0.30	0.50	0.75	1.50	2.00
1987 M	4,305,000	—	—	0.25	1.00	1.50
1988 M	14,735,000	—	—	0.25	1.00	1.50
1989 M	10,651,000	—	—	0.25	1.00	1.50
1990 M	5,391,000	—	0.25	0.50	1.50	2.00

KM# 66 50 PENNI'A'

3.30 g., Copper-Nickel, 19.7 mm. **Obv:** Polar bear, date below **Rev:** Denomination above flower heads **Edge:** Reeded

Date	Mintage	VF20	XF40	MS60	MS63	MS65
1990 M	70,459,000	—	—	0.20	0.75	1.25
1991 M	90,480,000	—	—	0.20	0.75	1.25
1992 M	58,996,000	—	—	0.20	0.75	1.25
1993 M	10,066,000	—	—	0.20	0.75	1.25
1994 M	3,005,000	—	—	0.20	0.75	1.25
1994 M	5,000	PF65 8.00				
1995 M	1,048,000	—	—	0.20	0.75	1.25
1995 M	3,000	PF65 8.00				
1996 M	17,000,000	—	—	0.20	0.75	1.25
1996 M	1,200	PF65 8.00				
1997 M	524,000	—	—	0.20	0.75	1.25
1997 M	2,000	PF65 8.00				
1998 M	3,345,500	—	—	0.20	0.75	1.25
1998 M	2,000	PF65 8.00				
1999 M	100,000	—	—	0.20	1.00	1.50
1999 M	—	PF65 8.00				
2000 M	100,000	—	—	0.20	1.00	1.50
2000 M	—	PF65 8.00				

KM# 49 MARKKA

6.40 g., 0.350 Silver 0.072 oz. ASW, 24 mm. **Obv:** Rampant lion left, date below **Rev:** Stylized fir trees with denomination in center **Edge Lettering:** SUOMI FINLAND

Date	Mintage	VF20	XF40	MS60	MS63	MS65
1964 S	9,999,000	2.50	3.00	3.50	5.00	6.00
1965 S	15,107,000	1.30	2.25	2.75	3.50	5.00
1966 S	15,183,000	1.30	2.25	2.75	3.50	5.00
1967 S	6,249,000	1.30	2.25	2.75	3.50	5.00
1968 S	3,063,000	1.30	2.25	2.75	3.50	5.00

KM# 49a MARKKA

6.10 g., Copper-Nickel, 24 mm. **Obv:** Rampant lion left, date below **Rev:** Denomination flanked by stylized fir trees **Edge Lettering:** SUOMI FINLAND

Date	Mintage	VF20	XF40	MS60	MS63	MS65
1969 S	1,308,000	0.50	0.75	1.00	2.00	2.50
1970 S	12,255,000	0.35	0.50	0.65	1.00	1.25
1971 S	19,676,000	0.35	0.50	0.65	1.00	1.25
1972 S	19,885,000	0.35	0.50	0.65	1.00	1.25
1973 S	17,060,000	0.35	0.50	0.65	1.00	1.25
1974 S	18,065,000	0.35	0.50	0.65	1.00	1.25
1975 S	11,523,000	0.35	0.50	0.65	1.00	1.25
1976 K	12,048,000	0.35	0.50	0.65	1.00	1.25
1977 K	10,077,000	0.35	0.50	0.65	1.00	1.25
1978 K	10,022,000	0.35	0.50	0.65	1.00	1.25
1979 K	11,311,000	0.35	0.50	0.65	1.00	1.25
1980 K	19,306,000	—	0.25	0.35	0.75	1.00
1981 K	32,003,000	—	0.25	0.35	0.75	1.00
1982 K	30,001,000	—	0.25	0.35	0.75	1.00
1983 N	11,927,000	—	0.25	0.35	0.75	1.00
1983 K	8,074,999	—	0.25	0.35	0.75	1.00
1984 N	15,000,000	—	0.25	0.35	0.75	1.00
1985 N	19,001,000	—	0.25	0.35	0.75	1.00
1986 N	10,000,000	—	0.25	0.35	0.75	1.00
1987 N	700,000	0.50	0.75	1.00	2.00	2.50
1987 M	9,303,000	—	0.25	0.35	0.75	1.00
1988 M	27,535,000	—	0.25	0.35	0.75	1.00
1989 M	37,520,000	—	0.25	0.35	0.75	1.00
1990 M	50,305,000	—	0.25	0.35	0.75	1.00
1991 M	15,026,000	—	0.25	0.35	0.75	1.00
1992 M	3,628,000	—	0.25	0.35	0.75	1.00
1993 M	1,036,000	—	0.25	0.50	1.00	—

KM# 76 MARKKA

5.00 g., Aluminum-Bronze, 22.2 mm. **Obv:** Rampant lion left within circle, date below **Rev:** Ornaments flank denomination within circle

Date	Mintage	VF20	XF40	MS60	MS63	MS65
1993 M	91,588,000	—	0.25	0.35	0.75	1.00
1994 M	152,011,000	—	0.25	0.35	0.75	1.00
1994 M	5,000	PF65 10.00				
1995 M	40,008,000	—	0.25	0.35	0.75	1.00
1995 M	3,000	PF65 10.00				
1996 M	21,000,000	—	0.25	0.35	0.75	1.00
1996 M	1,200	PF65 10.00				
1997 M	23,775,200	—	0.25	0.35	0.75	1.00
1997 M	2,000	PF65 10.00				
1998 M	33,955,200	—	0.25	0.35	0.75	1.00
1998 M	2,000	PF65 10.00				
1999 M	100,000	—	0.25	0.50	1.00	1.50
1999 M	—	PF65 10.00				
2000 M	100,000	—	0.25	0.50	1.00	1.50
2000 M	—	PF65 10.00				

KM# 76a MARKKA

Copper-Nickel **Obv:** Rampant lion left within circle, date below **Rev:** Ornaments flank denomination

Date	Mintage	VF20	XF40	MS60	MS63	MS65
1993 M Sets only	100,000	—	—	—	—	10.00

KM# 53 5 MARKKAA

8.00 g., Aluminum-Bronze, 26.3 mm. **Obv:** Icebreaker "Varma", date below **Rev:** Stylized flock of birds **Edge Lettering:** REPUBLIKEN FINLAND SUOMEN TASAVALTA

Date	Mintage	VF20	XF40	MS60	MS63	MS65
1972 S	400,000	2.00	2.25	2.50	3.50	5.00
1973 S	2,188,000	1.00	1.25	1.50	2.00	2.50
1974 S	300,000	1.00	1.25	1.50	2.00	2.50
1975 S	300,000	1.00	1.25	1.50	2.00	2.50
1976 K	400,000	1.00	1.25	1.50	2.00	2.50
1977 K	300,000	1.00	1.25	1.50	2.00	2.50
1978 K	300,000	1.00	1.25	1.50	2.00	2.50

KM# 57 5 MARKKAA

8.20 g., Aluminum-Bronze, 26.3 mm. **Obv:** Icebreaker "Urho", date below **Rev:** Stylized flock of birds with denomination at top

Date	Mintage	VF20	XF40	MS60	MS63	MS65
1979 K	2,005,000	—	—	1.00	2.00	2.50
1980 K	501,000	1.00	1.25	1.50	2.00	2.50
1981 K	1,009,000	—	—	1.00	1.50	2.00
1982 K	3,004,000	—	—	1.00	1.50	2.00
1983 K	8,776,000	—	—	1.00	1.50	2.00
1983 N	11,230,000	—	—	1.00	1.50	2.00
1984 N	15,001,000	—	—	1.00	1.50	2.00
1985 N	8,005,000	—	—	1.00	1.50	2.00
1986 N	5,006,000	—	—	1.00	1.50	2.00
1987 N	660,000	1.00	1.25	1.50	2.00	2.50
1987 M	2,348,000	—	—	1.00	1.50	2.00
1988 M	3,042,000	—	—	1.00	1.50	2.00
1989 M	10,175,000	—	—	1.00	1.50	2.00
1990 M	9,925,000	—	—	1.00	1.50	2.00
1991 M	9,910,000	—	—	1.00	1.50	2.00
1992 M	547,000	—	—	1.50	2.50	3.00
1993 M	911,000	—	—	1.50	2.50	3.00

KM# 73 5 MARKKAA

5.50 g., Copper-Aluminum-Nickel, 24.5 mm. **Obv:** Lake Saimaa ringed seal, date below **Rev:** Denomination, dragonfly and lily pad leaves

Date	Mintage	VF20	XF40	MS60	MS63	MS65
1992 M	800,000	—	—	1.50	2.50	3.00
1993 M	46,034,000	—	—	1.50	2.50	3.00
1994 M	19,003,000	—	—	1.50	1.50	2.00
1994 M	5,000	PF65 12.00				
1995 M	9,016,000	—	—	1.00	1.50	2.00
1995 M	3,000	PF65 12.00				
1996 M	7,000,000	—	—	1.50	2.00	2.50
1996 M	1,200	PF65 12.00				
1997 M	537,700	—	1.00	2.00	3.00	3.50
1997 M	2,000	PF65 12.00				
1998 M	813,650	—	1.00	2.00	2.50	3.00
1998 M	2,000	PF65 12.00				
1999 M	100,000	—	1.50	2.00	3.00	3.50
1999 M	—	PF65 12.00				
2000 M	100,000	—	1.50	2.00	3.00	3.50
2000 M	—	PF65 12.00				

KM# 50 10 MARKKAA

23.75 g., 0.900 Silver 0.6872 oz. ASW, 35 mm. **Subject:** 50th Anniversary of Independence **Obv:** Five Whooper swans in flight, date above **Rev:** Design above denomination **Edge Lettering:** ITSENAINEN SUOMI 50 FINLAND SJALVSTANDIGT 50

Date	Mintage	VF20	XF40	MS60	MS63	MS65
1967 S-H	1,000,000	—	12.50	15.00	16.50	18.50

KM# 51 10 MARKKAA

22.75 g., 0.500 Silver 0.3657 oz. ASW, 35 mm. **Subject:** Centennial - Birth of President Paasikivi **Obv:** Denomination below date, brick wall background **Rev:** Head facing

Date	Mintage	VF20	XF40	MS60	MS63	MS65
1970 S-H	600,000	—	6.75	8.50	10.00	11.50

KM# 52 10 MARKKAA

24.20 g., 0.500 Silver 0.389 oz. ASW, 35 mm. **Subject:** 10th European Athletic Championships **Obv:** Denomination above city scene **Rev:** Runners on track, date lower right

Date	Mintage	VF20	XF40	MS60	MS63	MS65
1971 S-H	1,000,000	—	7.25	9.00	10.50	12.00

KM# 54 10 MARKKAA

23.50 g., 0.500 Silver 0.3778 oz. ASW, 35 mm. **Subject:** 75th Birthday of President Kekkonen **Obv:** Denomination below trees, hills in background **Rev:** Head facing

Date	Mintage	VF20	XF40	MS60	MS63	MS65
1975 S-H	1,000,000	—	7.00	8.75	10.00	11.50

KM# 55 10 MARKKAA

21.78 g., 0.500 Silver 0.3501 oz. ASW, 35 mm. **Subject:** 60th Anniversary of Independence **Obv:** Four line inscription superimposed over five line inscription, date at left **Rev:** Crowds of people, denomination upper right

Date	Mintage	VF20	XF40	MS60	MS63	MS65
1977 K-H	400,000	—	6.50	8.00	9.50	11.00

KM# 77 10 MARKKAA

8.80 g., Bi-Metallic Brass center in Copper-Nickel ring, 27.25 mm. **Obv:** Capercaillie bird within circle, date above **Rev:** Denomination and branches

Date	Mintage	VF20	XF40	MS60	MS63	MS65
1993 M	30,002,000	—	—	2.00	2.50	2.75
1994 M	19,979,000	—	—	2.00	2.50	2.75
1994 M	5,000	PF65 18.00				
1995 M	4,008,000	—	—	2.00	2.50	2.75
1995 M	3,000	PF65 18.00				
1996 M	3,300,000	—	—	2.00	3.00	3.50
1996 M	1,200	PF65 18.00				
1997 M	917,607	—	—	2.00	3.00	3.50
1997 M	2,000	PF65 18.00				
1998 M	797,713	—	—	2.00	3.00	3.50
1998 M	2,000	PF65 18.00				
1999 M	100,000	—	2.00	3.00	4.00	5.00
1999 M	—	PF65 18.00				
2000 M	100,000	—	2.00	3.00	4.00	5.00
2000 M	—	PF65 18.00				

KM# 82 10 MARKKAA

8.00 g., Bi-Metallic Brass center in Copper-Nickel ring, 27.25 mm. **Subject:** European Unity **Obv:** Swan in flight within circle, date upper right **Rev:** Denomination and branches

Date	Mintage	VF20	XF40	MS60	MS63	MS65
1995 M	500,000	—	2.00	3.00	4.00	5.00

KM# 82a 10 MARKKAA

Bi-Metallic Gold center in Silver ring, 27.25 mm. **Subject:** European Unity **Obv:** Swan in flight left within circle **Rev:** Denomination and branches **Note:** Total weight 12.200 grams.

Date	Mintage	VF20	XF40	MS60	MS63	MS65
1995 M	2,000	PF65 2,000				

KM# 91 10 MARKKAA

8.82 g., Bi-Metallic Copper-Nickel center in Brass ring, 27.25 mm. **Subject:** Finnish Presidency of the EU. **Obv:** Fire breathing profile left, date at right **Rev:** Denomination and branches

Date	Mintage	VF20	XF40	MS60	MS63	MS65
1999 M	100,000	—	—	3.00	5.00	7.00

KM# 91a 10 MARKKAA

13.20 g., Bi-Metallic .925 Silver center in .75 Gold ring, 27.25 mm. **Obv:** Fire breathing profile left **Rev:** Denomination and branches **Edge:** Lettered **Note:** Total weight 13.200 grams.

Date	Mintage	VF20	XF40	MS60	MS63	MS65
1999	3,000	—	—	—	1,000	1,150

KM# 56 25 MARKKAA

26.30 g., 0.500 Silver 0.4228 oz. ASW, 37 mm. **Subject:** Winter Games in Lahti **Obv:** Ski trail, denomination at left

Date	Mintage	VF20	XF40	MS60	MS63	MS65
1978 K-N	500,000	—	—	10.00	11.00	12.00

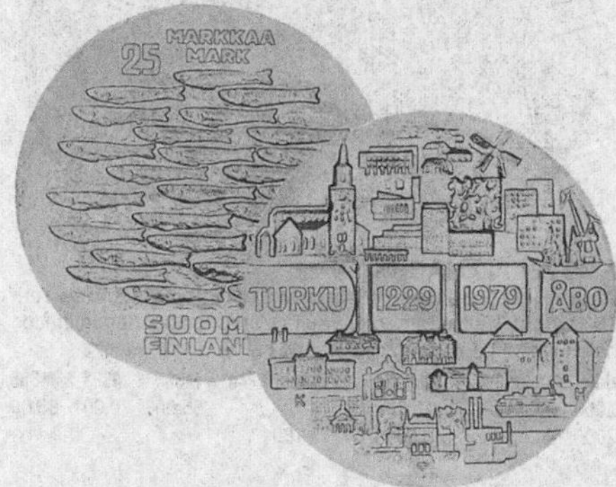

KM# 58 25 MARKKAA

26.30 g., 0.500 Silver 0.4228 oz. ASW, 37 mm. **Subject:** 750th Anniversary of Turku **Obv:** School of fish, denomination above **Rev:** City scene with dates

Date	Mintage	VF20	XF40	MS60	MS63	MS65
1979 K-H	300,000	—	—	10.00	12.00	15.00

KM# 85 25 MARKKAA

20.20 g., Bi-Metallic Brass center in Copper-Nickel ring, 35 mm. **Subject:** 80th Anniversary of Independence **Obv:** Stylized landscape, dates below **Rev:** Stylized city view, denomination below

Date	Mintage	VF20	XF40	MS60	MS63	MS65
ND-1997 M-L	100,000	—	—	12.50	15.00	—
ND-1997 M-L	2,000	PF65 16.50				

Note: Sets only

KM# 59 50 MARKKAA

20.00 g., 0.500 Silver 0.3215 oz. ASW, 30 mm. **Subject:** 80th Birthday of President Kekkonen **Obv:** Head 3/4 facing **Rev:** Horses, denomination above

Date	Mintage	VF20	XF40	MS60	MS63	MS65
1981 K	500,000	—	—	9.00	10.00	12.00

KM# 60 50 MARKKAA

23.10 g., 0.500 Silver 0.3713 oz. ASW, 35 mm. **Subject:** World Ice Hockey Championship Games **Obv:** Denomination **Rev:** Hockey player, date at right

Date	Mintage	VF20	XF40	MS60	MS63	MS65
1982 K-T	400,000	—	—	10.00	12.00	13.00

KM# 61 50 MARKKAA

21.80 g., 0.500 Silver 0.3504 oz. ASW, 35 mm. **Subject:** 1st World Athletics Championships **Obv:** Trees divide denomination **Rev:** Hurdler, date at right

Date	Mintage	VF20	XF40	MS60	MS63	MS65
1983 K-M	450,000	—	—	10.00	12.00	13.00

KM# 62 50 MARKKAA

19.90 g., 0.500 Silver 0.3199 oz. ASW, 35 mm. **Subject:** National Epic - The Kalevala **Obv:** Trees with reflections, denomination at right **Rev:** Stylized waves with figure, dates below

Date	Mintage	VF20	XF40	MS60	MS63	MS65
1985 P-N	300,000	—	—	11.00	12.00	13.00

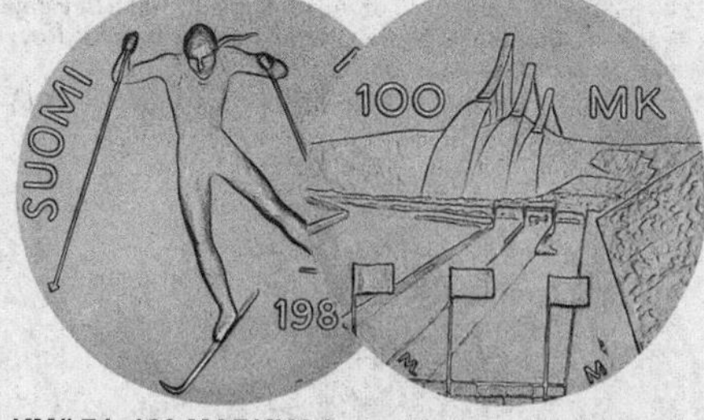

KM# 74 100 MARKKAA

24.00 g., 0.830 Silver 0.6404 oz. ASW **Subject:** World Nordic Skiing Championships, Lahti, Finland 1989 **Obv:** Marjo Matikainen (5 km ski champion in 1988 Calgary Olympics)

Date	Mintage	VF20	XF40	MS60	MS63	MS65
1989 M-L-M	100,000	—	—	16.00	18.00	—

KM# 75 100 MARKKAA

24.00 g., 0.830 Silver 0.6404 oz. ASW **Subject:** Pictorial Arts of Finland **Obv:** Artistic design, denomination above **Rev:** Two figures holding artists palette, date at right

Date	Mintage	VF20	XF40	MS60	MS63	MS65
1989 P-M	100,000	—	—	16.00	18.00	20.00

KM# 67 100 MARKKAA

24.00 g., 0.830 Silver 0.6404 oz. ASW **Subject:** 50th Anniversary of Disabled War Veterans Association **Obv:** Home and landscape scene, denomination above **Rev:** Cross superimposed on people, date below

Date	Mintage	VF20	XF40	MS60	MS63	MS65
1990 P-M	100,000	—	—	18.00	20.00	22.00

KM# 68 100 MARKKAA

24.00 g., 0.830 Silver 0.6404 oz. ASW **Subject:** 350th Anniversary - University of Helsinki **Obv:** Owl, denomination below **Rev:** Harp within square, dates below

Date	Mintage	VF20	XF40	MS60	MS63	MS65
1990 H-M	150,000	—	—	18.00	20.00	22.00

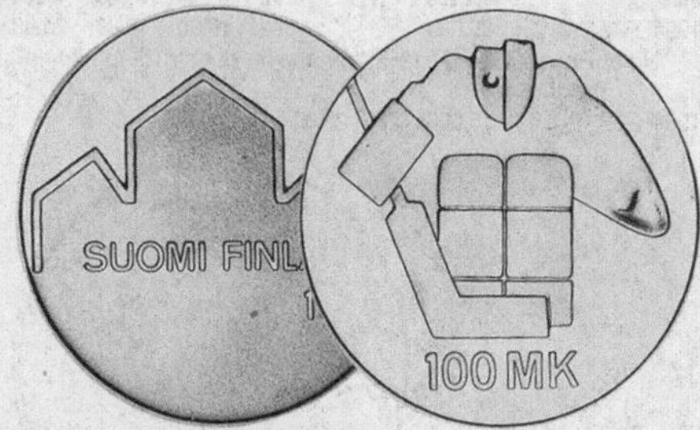

KM# 69 100 MARKKAA

24.00 g., 0.830 Silver 0.6404 oz. ASW, 35 mm. **Subject:** Ice Hockey World Championship Games **Obv:** Stylized design, date lower right **Rev:** Stylized hockey player, denomination below

Date	Mintage	VF20	XF40	MS60	MS63	MS65
1991 L-M	150,000	—	—	18.00	20.00	22.00
1991 L-M	200	PF65 500				

Note: Struck with polished dies to prooflike quality and encapsulated in hard plastic 60 mm x 83 mm square; these pieces were given out as business gifts to selected mint visitors

KM# 70 100 MARKKAA

24.00 g., 0.925 Silver 0.7137 oz. ASW **Subject:** 70th Anniversary - Autonomy of Åland **Obv:** Masted ship at sea, denomination above **Rev:** Stag on crowned shield, dates below

Date	Mintage	VF20	XF40	MS60	MS63	MS65
1991 P-M	Est. 700	PF65 700				

Note: Encapsulated as KM#69 above, but struck to higher prooflike quality

Date	Mintage	VF20	XF40	MS60	MS63	MS65
1991 P-M	100,000	—	—	18.00	20.00	22.00

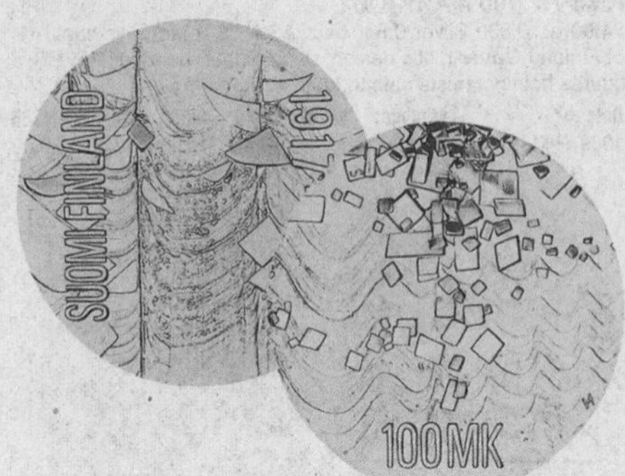

KM# 71 100 MARKKAA
24.00 g., 0.925 Silver 0.7137 oz. ASW **Subject:** 75th Anniversary of Independence **Obv:** Pine trees **Rev:** Artistic design, denomination below

Date	Mintage	VF20	XF40	MS60	MS63	MS65
1992 M-S	300,000	—	—	16.00	18.00	20.00

KM# 78 100 MARKKAA
24.00 g., 0.925 Silver 0.7137 oz. ASW **Subject:** Stadium of Friendship **Obv:** Laurel sprig, stylized stadium, denomination above **Rev:** Sprinters, date above

Date	Mintage	VF20	XF40	MS60	MS63	MS65
1994 P-M	80,000	—	—	16.00	18.00	20.00
Note: Encapsulated as KM#69 above, but struck to higher proof quality						
1994 P-M	15,000	PF65 25.00				

KM# 80 100 MARKKAA
24.00 g., 0.925 Silver 0.7137 oz. ASW **Subject:** 100th Birthday - Artturi Ilmari Virtanen **Obv:** Budding branch, denomination below **Rev:** Head right

Date	Mintage	VF20	XF40	MS60	MS63	MS65
1995 S-M	40,000	—	—	16.00	18.00	20.00
1995 S-M	3,000	PF65 45.00				

KM# 81 100 MARKKAA
24.00 g., 0.925 Silver 0.7137 oz. ASW **Subject:** 50th Anniversary - United Nations **Obv:** Design, denomination at left, date below **Rev:** Face foreward, dates at right

Date	Mintage	VF20	XF40	MS60	MS63	MS65
1995 P-M	40,000	—	—	16.00	18.00	20.00
1995 P-M	3,000	PF65 55.00				

KM# 83 100 MARKKAA
24.00 g., 0.925 Silver 0.7137 oz. ASW **Subject:** Helene Schjerfbeck - Painter - 50th Anniversary of Her Death

Date	Mintage	VF20	XF40	MS60	MS63	MS65
1996 T-M	300,000	—	—	—	50.00	65.00
1996 T-M	3,000	PF65 125				

KM# 84 100 MARKKAA
22.00 g., 0.925 Silver 0.6543 oz. ASW **Subject:** 100th Birthday - Paavo Nurmi **Obv:** Two gymnasts **Rev:** Facial portrait and running Paavo Nurmi, denomination below

Date	Mintage	VF20	XF40	MS60	MS63	MS65
1997 M-S	45,000	—	—	16.00	18.00	20.00
1997 M-S	6,500	PF65 35.00				

KM# 87 100 MARKKAA
22.00 g., 0.925 Silver 0.6543 oz. ASW **Subject:** 100th Birthday - Alvar Aalto **Obv:** Walls above cliffs and denominations **Rev:** Mature rye plants, dates in vertical at right

Date	Mintage	VF20	XF40	MS60	MS63	MS65
1998 M-G	Est. 44000	—	—	—	18.00	20.00
1998 M-G	4,000	PF65 40.00				

KM# 88 100 MARKKAA
22.00 g., 0.925 Silver 0.6543 oz. ASW **Subject:** Suomenlinna Fortress **Obv:** Stylized island view, denomination below **Rev:** Sailship and fortress gate, dates at right

Date	Mintage	VF20	XF40	MS60	MS63	MS65
1998 M-O	30,000	—	—	16.00	18.00	20.00
1998 M-O	3,300	PF65 45.00				

KM# 89 100 MARKKAA
22.00 g., 0.925 Silver 0.6543 oz. ASW **Subject:** Jean Sibelius - Composer **Obv:** Head left **Rev:** Finlandia musical score divides date and denomination

Date	Mintage	VF20	XF40	MS60	MS63	MS65
1999 P-V-M	30,000	—	—	18.00	20.00	22.00
1999 P-V-M	6,000	PF65 40.00				

KM# 92 100 MARKKAA
22.00 g., 0.925 Silver 0.6543 oz. ASW **Subject:** Jubilee Year 2000 **Obv:** Turku Cathedral vault ceiling design, denomination below **Rev:** Leaf within circle, date below **Edge:** Plain

Date	Mintage	VF20	XF40	MS60	MS63	MS65
2000 M L-M	15,000	—	—	55.00	70.00	85.00
2000 M L-M	3,000	PF65 100				

KM# 93 100 MARKKAA
22.00 g., 0.925 Silver 0.6543 oz. ASW **Subject:** 450th Anniversary - Helsinki Cultural Capital **Obv:** Symbolic column design **Rev:** Carved city view, denomination upper left **Edge:** Plain

Date	Mintage	VF20	XF40	MS60	MS63	MS65
2000 P-M	10,000	—	—	15.00	30.00	40.00
2000 P-M	8,000	PF65 45.00				

KM# 94 100 MARKKAA
22.00 g., 0.925 Silver 0.6543 oz. ASW, 35 mm. **Subject:** Aleksis Kivi **Obv:** Books on shelves, denomination below **Rev:** Portrait on partial disc, facing left, date at left **Edge:** Plain

Date	Mintage	VF20	XF40	MS60	MS63	MS65
2000 FI T-M	10,000	—	—	—	25.00	35.00
2000 FI T-M	6,000	PF65 60.00				

KM# 72 1000 MARKKAA

9.00 g., 0.900 Gold 0.2604 oz. AGW, 22.1 mm. **Subject:** 75th Anniversary of Independence **Obv:** Dates above design **Rev:** Denomination below design

Date	Mintage	VF20	XF40	MS60	MS63	MS65
1992 M-S	35,000	—	—	—	375	400

KM# 86 1000 MARKKAA

8.64 g., 0.900 Gold 0.250 oz. AGW **Subject:** 80th Anniversary of Independence **Obv:** New shoot growing from tree stump, denomination above **Rev:** Symbolic design separating dates

Date	Mintage	VF20	XF40	MS60	MS63	MS65
ND (1997) M-P	20,000	PF65 400				

KM# 90 1000 MARKKAA

8.64 g., 0.900 Gold 0.250 oz. AGW **Subject:** Jean Sibelius - Composer **Obv:** Head left **Rev:** Finlandia musical score, denomination above, date below

Date	Mintage	VF20	XF40	MS60	MS63	MS65
1999 P-V-M	25,000	PF65 400				

KM# 79 2000 MARKKAA

16.97 g., 0.900 Gold 0.491 oz. AGW, 28 mm. **Subject:** 50 Years of Peace **Obv:** Design at center, date below **Rev:** Design above denomination

Date	Mintage	VF20	XF40	MS60	MS63	MS65
1995 M-L-L	6,900	PF65 850				

EURO COINAGE

European Union Issues

KM# 98 EURO CENT

2.30 g., Copper Plated Steel, 16.25 mm. **Obv:** Rampant lion left surrounded by stars, date at left **Rev:** Denomination and globe **Edge:** Plain

Date	Mintage	VF20	XF40	MS60	MS63	MS65
1999 M	8,100,000	—	—	—	—	1.25
1999 M Proof	15,000	—	—	—	—	—
2000 M	7,600,000	—	—	—	—	2.50
2000 M Proof	15,000	—	—	—	—	—

KM# 99 2 EURO CENT

3.06 g., Copper Plated Steel, 18.75 mm. **Obv:** Rampant lion surrounded by stars, date at left **Rev:** Denomination and globe **Edge:** Grooved

Date	Mintage	VF20	XF40	MS60	MS63	MS65
1999 M	1,785,000	—	—	—	—	3.00
1999 M	15,000	PF65 15.00				
2000 M	13,937,000	—	—	—	—	2.00
2000 M	15,000	PF65 15.00				

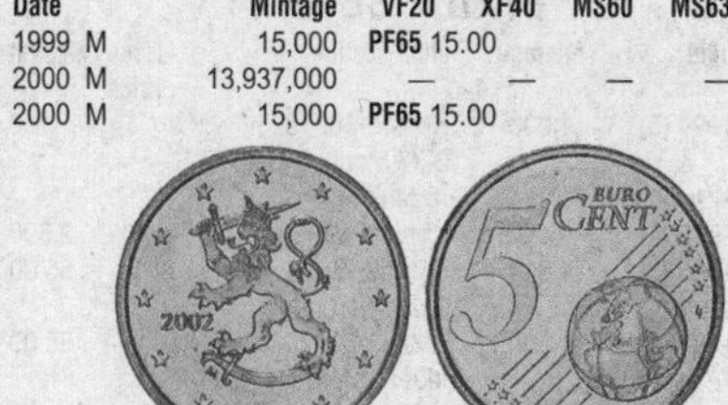

KM# 100 5 EURO CENT

3.92 g., Copper Plated Steel, 21.25 mm. **Obv:** Rampant lion left surrounded by stars, date at left **Rev:** Denomination and globe **Edge:** Plain

Date	Mintage	VF20	XF40	MS60	MS63	MS65
1999 M	63,380,000	—	—	—	—	1.00
1999 M	15,000	PF65 15.00				
2000 M	56,660,000	—	—	—	—	1.00
2000 M	15,000	PF65 15.00				

KM# 101 10 EURO CENT

4.10 g., Brass, 19.75 mm. **Obv:** Rampant lion left surrounded by stars, date at left **Rev:** Denomination and map **Edge:** Reeded

Date	Mintage	VF20	XF40	MS60	MS63	MS65
1999 M	133,520,000	—	—	—	—	1.25
1999 M	15,000	PF65 18.00				
2000 M	167,449,000	—	—	—	—	1.75
2000 M	15,000	PF65 18.00				

KM# 102 20 EURO CENT

5.74 g., Brass, 22.25 mm. **Obv:** Rampant lion left surrounded by stars, date at left **Rev:** Denomination and map **Edge:** Notched

Date	Mintage	VF20	XF40	MS60	MS63	MS65
1999 M	42,350,000	—	—	—	—	2.00
1999 M	15,000	PF65 20.00				
2000 M	500,000	—	—	—	—	20.00
2000 M	15,000	PF65 20.00				

KM# 103 50 EURO CENT

7.80 g., Brass, 24.25 mm. **Obv:** Rampant lion left surrounded by stars, date at left **Rev:** Denomination and map **Edge:** Reeded

Date	Mintage	VF20	XF40	MS60	MS63	MS65
1999 M	20,696,000	—	—	—	—	3.00
1999 M	15,000	PF65 22.00				
2000 M	67,097,000	—	—	—	—	2.50
2000 M	15,000	PF65 22.00				

KM# 104 EURO

7.50 g., Bi-Metallic Copper-Nickel center in Nickel-Brass ring, 23.25 mm. **Obv:** 2 flying swans, date below, surrounded by stars on outer ring **Rev:** Denomination and map **Edge:** Segmented reeding

Date	Mintage	VF20	XF40	MS60	MS63	MS65
1999 M	16,210,000	—	—	—	—	5.00
1999 M	15,000	PF65 25.00				
2000 M	36,639,000	—	—	—	—	5.00
2000 M	15,000	PF65 25.00				

KM# 105 2 EURO

8.50 g., Bi-Metallic Nickel-Brass center in Copper-Nickel ring, 25.75 mm. **Obv:** 2 cloudberry flowers surrounded by stars on outer ring **Rev:** Denomination and map **Edge:** Reeded and lettered **Edge Lettering:** SUOMI FINLAND

Date	Mintage	VF20	XF40	MS60	MS63	MS65
1999 M	16,090,000	—	—	—	—	5.00
1999 M	15,000	PF65 30.00				
2000 M	8,680,000	—	—	—	—	10.00
2000 M	15,000	PF65 30.00				

PATTERNS

Including off metal strikes

KM#	Date	Mintage	Identification	Mkt Val
Pn11	1918	—	5 Penniä. Silver.	3,500
Pn12	1919	—	Penni. Nickel.	—
Pn13	1921	—	10 Penniä. Iron.	—
Pn14	1922	—	5 Penniä. Silver.	—
Pn15	1923	—	50 Penniä. Copper.	—
Pn16	1923	—	Markkaa. Copper.	—
Pn17	1924	—	10 Penniä. Nickel.	—
Pn18	1926	—	200 Markkaa. Copper.	—
Pn19	1927	—	10 Penniä. Copper.	—
Pn20	1936	—	25 Penniä. Copper.	—
Pn21	1936	—	Markkaa. Iron.	—
Pn22	1941	—	10 Penniä. Iron.	250
Pn23	1942	—	25 Penniä. Aluminum.	—
Pn24	1942	—	50 Penniä. Aluminum.	—
Pn25	1942	—	Markkaa. Aluminum.	—
Pn26	1942	—	Markka. Iron.	—
Pn27	1942	—	5 Markkaa. Brass.	—
Pn28	1945	—	Markkaa. Brass.	3,000
Pn29	1946	—	5 Markkaa. Nickel.	—
Pn30	1947	—	5 Markkaa. Iron.	—
Pn31	1948	—	Markkaa. Aluminum.	—
Pn32	1948	—	Markkaa. Bronze.	—
Pn33	1948	—	5 Markkaa. Nickel.	—
Pn34	1949	—	Markkaa. Copper.	5,000
Pn35	1949	—	5 Markkaa. Iron.	—
Pn36	1950 H	—	Markkaa. Brass.	2,500
Pn37	1951	—	500 Markkaa. Aluminum.	—
Pn38	1952	—	Markkaa. Iron.	—
Pn39	1952	—	5 Markkaa. Iron.	—
Pn40	1952	—	10 Markkaa. Iron.	500
Pn41	1952	—	10 Markkaa. Copper.	—
Pn42	1953	—	Markka. Aluminum. With pearls.	—
Pn43	1953	—	Markka. Iron. Lion head.	—
Pn44	1953	—	Markka. Iron. With pearls.	—
Pn45	1953	—	5 Markkaa. Iron.	—
Pn46	1953	—	50 Markkaa. Nickel.	—
Pn47	1954	—	Markkaa. Nickel Plated Iron.	1,000
Pn48	1954	—	Markkaa. Iron. With pearls.	—
Pn49	1954	—	5 Markkaa. Iron. With pearls.	—
Pn50	1954	—	20 Markkaa. Nickel.	—
Pn51	1956	—	20 Markkaa. Nickel.	—
Pn52	1956	—	20 Markkaa. Silver.	—
Pn53	1956	—	500 Markkaa. Silver. With waves.	—
Pn54	1956	—	500 Markkaa. Silver. With plain field.	—
Pn55	1969	—	5 Markkaa. Copper-Nickel.	—

TRIAL STRIKES

KM#	Date	Mintage	Identification	Mkt Val
TS6	1918	—	5 Penniä. Iron.	2,000
TS7	1960	—	(1000 Markkaa). Brass.	—
TS8	1960	—	(1000 Markkaa). Brass.	—

MINT SETS

KM#	Date	Mintage	Identification	Issue Price	Mkt Val
MS1	1973 (7)	9,978	KM#44a, 45-48, 49a, 53 Soft plastic holder	10.00	50.00
MS2	1973 (7)	10,029	KM#44a, 45-48, 49a, 53 Hard plastic holder	5.00	15.00
MS3	1974 (7)	79,258	KM#44a, 45-48, 49a, 53	3.75	8.00
MS4	1975 (7)	58,820	KM#44a, 45-48, 49a, 53	3.75	9.00
MS5	1976 (7)	45,263	KM#44a, 45-48, 49a, 53	3.75	9.00
MS6	1977 (7)	40,392	KM#44a, 45-48, 49a, 53	4.00	8.00
MS7	1978 (7)	39,745	KM#44a-45a, 46-48, 49a, 53	4.45	6.00
MS8	1979 (7)	36,000	KM#44a-45a, 46-48, 49a, 57	4.85	8.00
MS9	1980 (6)	33,805	KM#45a, 46-48, 49a, 57	5.00	6.00
MS10	1981 (6)	63,100	KM#45a, 46-48, 49a, 57	5.25	6.00
MS11	1982 (6)	35,500	KM#45a, 46-48, 49a, 57	5.50	6.00
MS12	1983 (6)	30,100	KM#45a-46a, 47-48, 49a, 57	3.25	6.00

MS13	1983 (6)	9,250	KM#45a-46a, 47-48, 49a, 57	3.25	15.00
MS14	1984 (6)	30,500	KM#45a-46a, 47-48, 49a, 57	3.25	6.00
MS15	1984 (6)	600	KM#45a-46a, 47-48, 49a, 57 Russian text	3.75	35.00
MS16	1985 (6)	38,385	KM#45a-46a, 47-48, 49a, 57 Finnish text	3.25	6.00
MS17	1985 (6)	1,500	KM#45a-46a, 47-48, 49a, 57 Russian text	4.65	20.00
MS18	1985 (6)	1,560	KM#45a-46a, 47-48, 49a, 57 English text	3.75	20.00
MS19	1986 (6)	37,100	KM#45a-46a, 47-48, 49a, 57 Finnish text	3.25	6.00
MS20	1986 (6)	1,300	KM#45a-46a, 47-48, 49a, 57 Russian text	5.00	20.00
MS21	1986 (6)	1,780	KM#45a-46a, 47-48, 49a, 57 English text	4.25	20.00
MS22	1987 (6)	34,300	KM#45a-46a, 47-48, 49a, 57 Finnish text	—	6.00
MS23	1987 (6)	1,120	KM#45a-46a, 47-48, 49a, 57 Russian text	—	20.00
MS24	1987 (6)	1,400	KM#45a-46a, 47-48, 49a, 57 English text	—	20.00
MS25	1987 (6)	15,900	KM#45a-46a, 47-48, 49a, 57 Finnish text	—	7.00
MS26	1987 (6)	300	KM#45a-46a, 47-48, 57 Russian text	—	50.00
MS27	1987 (6)	180	KM#45a-46a, 47-48, 49a, 57 English text	—	50.00
MS28	1988 (6)	35,750	KM#45a-46a, 47-48, 49a, 57 Finnish text	—	6.00
MS29	1988 (6)	1,450	KM#45a-46a, 47-48, 49a, 57 English text	—	15.00
MS30	1988 (6)	1,220	KM#45a-46a, 47-48, 49a, 57 Russian text	—	15.00
MS31	1989 (6)	33,000	KM#45a-46a, 47-48, 49a, 57 Finnish text, bronze medal	—	6.00
MS32	1989 (6)	1,450	KM#45a-46a, 47-48, 49a, 57 English text, bronze medal	—	10.00
MS33	1989 (6)	1,700	KM#45a-46a, 47-48, 49a, 57 Russian text, bronze medal	—	10.00
MS34	1989 (6)	15,982	KM#45a-46a, 47-48, 49a, 57 Finnish text, silver medal	—	22.00
MS35	1989 (6)	1,000	KM#45a-46a, 47-48, 49a, 57 English text, silver medal	—	35.00
MS36	1989 (6)	1,150	KM#45a-46a, 47-48, 49a, 57 Russian text, silver medal	—	35.00
MS37	1990 (6)	29,400	KM#45a-46a, 47-48, 49a, 57 Finnish text	—	7.50
MS38	1990 (6)	1,000	KM#45a-46a, 47-48, 49a, 57 English text	—	10.00
MS39	1990 (6)	1,500	KM#45a-46a, 47-48, 49a, 57 Russian text	—	10.00
MS40	1990 (4)	41,750	KM#49a, 57, 65-66 Finnish text	—	7.00
MS41	1990 (4)	3,500	KM#49a, 57, 65-66 English text	—	10.00
MS42	1991 (4)	30,000	KM#49a, 57, 65-66 Finnish-Swedish text	—	8.00
MS43	1991 (4)	5,000	KM#49a, 57, 65-66 English text	—	10.00
MS44	1992 (5)	28,000	KM#49a, 57, 65-55, 73	—	10.00
MS45	1993 (5)	100,000	KM#49a, 65-66, 73, 76a, 77	—	18.00
MS46	1993 (5)	—	KM#65-66, 73, 76-77	13.30	16.00
MS47	1993 (4)	20,000	KM#49a, 65-66, 73 Silver medal	—	15.00
MS48	1994 (5)	25,000	KM#65-66, 73, 76-77 Medal (August Frederick Soldan)	—	18.00
MS49	1995 (5)	23,190	KM#65-66, 73, 76-77 Ecu medal	—	20.00
MS50	1995 (5)	15,000	KM#65-66, 73, 76-77 Medal (John Conrad Lihr)	—	22.50
MS51	1996 (5)	16,300	KM#65-66, 73, 76-77 Medal (Isak Gustaf Sundell)	—	20.00
MS52	1997 (5)	18,000	KM#65-66, 73, 76-77 Medal (Peippo Uolevi Helle)	—	20.00
MS53	1998 (5)	18,000	KM#65-66, 73, 76-77 Medal, (Allan Alarik Soiniemi)	—	20.00
MS54	1999 (5)	—	KM#65-66, 73, 76-77 Medal (Euro Summit)	—	20.00
MS55	1999 (5)	—	KM#65-66, 73, 76-77 Medal , Finnish presidency of the EU	12.50	20.00
MS56	2000 (5)	—	KM#65-66, 73, 76-77 Medal (Byzantine imitation coin found in Finland)	12.50	25.00
MS57	2000 (6)	—	KM#65-66, 73, 76-77 Medal (Time)	12.50	25.00

PROOF SETS

KM#	Date	Mintage	Identification	Issue Price	Mkt Val
PS1	1994 (5)	1,000	KM#65-66, 73, 76-77 Medal (August Frederik Soldan)	—	150
PS2	1995 (2)	500	KM#80, 82a	802	2,600
PS3	1995 (5)	1,810	KM#65-66, 73, 76-77 Medal (Ecu)	—	55.00
PS4	1996 (5)	1,200	KM#65-66, 73, 76-77 Medal (Johan Conrad Lihr)	—	55.00
PS5	1997 (6)	2,000	KM#65-66, 73, 76-77, 85	67.50	72.50
PS6	1998 (5)	1,600	KM#65-66, 73, 76-77 Medal (10 Euro Suomenlinna Fortress)	—	55.00
PS7	1999 (5)	—	KM#65-66, 73, 76-77 Medal (Euro Summit)	—	55.00
PS8	2000 (6)	—	KM#65-66, 73, 76-77, medal (Nykyaika)	—	55.00

The French Republic, largest of the West European nations, has an area of 210,026 sq. mi. (547,030 sq. km.) and a population of 58.1 million. Capital: Paris. Agriculture, manufacturing, tourist industry and financial services are the most important elements of France's diversified economy. Textiles and clothing, steel products, machinery and transportation equipment, chemicals, pharmaceuticals, nuclear electricity, agricultural products and wine are exported.

The monarchy was ousted by the Revolution of 1848 and the Second Republic proclaimed. Louis Napoleon Bonaparte (nephew of Napoleon I) was elected president of the Second Republic. He was proclaimed emperor in 1852. As Napoleon III, he gave France two decades of prosperity under a stable, autocratic regime, but led it to defeat in the Franco-Prussian War of 1870, after which the Third Republic was established.

The Third Republic endured until 1940 and the capitulation of France to the swiftly maneuvering German forces. Marshal Philippe Petain formed a puppet government that sued for peace and ruled unoccupied France until 1942 from Vichy. Meanwhile, General Charles de Gaulle escaped to London where he formed a wartime government in exile and the Free French army. De Gaulle's provisional exile government was officially recognized by the Allies after the liberation of Paris in 1944, and De Gaulle, who had been serving as head of the provisional government, tacitly maintained that position. In October 1945, the people overwhelmingly rejected a return to the prewar government, thus paving the way for the formation of the Fourth Republic in 1947 just after the dismissal of De Gaulle, at grips with a coalition of rival parties, the Communists especially.

In actual operation, the Fourth Republic was remarkably like the Third, with the National Assembly the focus of power causing a constant governmental instability. The later years of the Fourth Republic were marked by a burst of industrial expansion unmatched in modern French history. The growth rate, however, was marred by a two colonial wars, nagging inflationary trend that weakened the franc and undermined the betterment of the people's buying power. This and the Algerian conflict led to the recall of De Gaulle to power, the adoption of a new constitution vesting strong powers in the executive, and the establishment in 1959 of the current Fifth Republic.

RULERS

Third Republic, 1871-1940
Vichy State, 1940-1944
De Gaulle's Provisional Govt., 1944-1946
Fourth Republic, 1947-1958
Fifth Republic, 1959—

MINT MARKS AND PRIVY MARKS

In addition to the date and mint mark which are customary on western civilization coinage, most coins manufactured by the French Mints contain two or three small 'Marks or Differents' as the French call them. These privy marks represent the men responsible for the dies which struck the coins. One privy mark is sometimes for the Engraver General (since 1880 the title is Chief Engraver). The other privy mark is the signature of the Mint Director of each mint; another one is the different' of the local engraver. Three other marks appeared at the end of Louis XIV's reign: one for the Director General of Mints, one for the General Engineer of Mechanical edge-marking, one identifying over struck coins in 1690-1705 and in 1715-1723. Equally amazing and unique is that sometimes the local assayer's or Judge-custody's 'different' or 'secret pellet' appears. Since 1880 this privy mark has represented the office rather than the personage of both the Administration of Coins & Medals and the Mint Director, and a standard privy mark has been used (cornucopia).

For most dates these privy marks are important though minor features for advanced collectors or local researchers. During some issue dates, however, the marks changed. To be even more accurate sometimes the marks changed when the date didn't, even though it should have. These coins can be attributed to the proper mintage report only by considering the privy marks. Previous references (before G. Sobin and F. Droulers) have by and large ignored these privy marks. It is entirely possible that unattributed varieties may exist for any privy mark transition. All transition years which may have two or three varieties or combinations of privy marks have the known attribution indicated after the date (if it has been confirmed).

ENGRAVER GENERAL'S PRIVY MARKS

Mark	Desc.	Date	Name
	Torch	1896-1930	Henry Patey
	Wing	1931-57	Lucien Bazor
	Owl	1957-74	Raymond Joly
	Dolphin	1974-94	Emile Rousseau
	Bee	1994-2000	Pierre Rodier

MINT DIRECTORS' PRIVY MARKS

Some modern coins struck from dies produced at the Paris Mint have the 'A' mint mark. In the absence of a mint mark, the cornucopia privy mark serves to attribute a coin to Paris design.

A – Paris, Central Mint

B – Beaumont – Le Roger

Mark	Desc.	Date
	Cornucopia	1943-58

(b) – Brussels

Legend ending BD, see PAU

C - Castelsarrasin

Mark	Desc.	Date
C	Cornucopia	1914, 1943-46

Thunderbolt (tb) - Poissy

Mark	Desc.	Date
	Cornucopia	1922-24

Star (s) - Madrid

Mark	Date
★	1916

MONETARY SYSTEM

(Commencing 1960)
1 Old Franc = 1 New Centime
100 New Centimes = 1 New Franc

MODERN REPUBLICS

1870-present

DECIMAL COINAGE

KM# 840 CENTIME

1.00 g., Bronze, 15 mm. **Obv:** Liberty head right **Rev:** Denomination above date within wreath **Mint:** Paris **Note:** Without mint mark or privy mark.

Date	Mintage	F12	VF20	XF40	MS60	MS63
1901	1,000,000	1.00	2.00	15.00	25.00	50.00
1902	1,000,000	0.75	1.50	4.00	15.00	25.00
1903	2,000,000	0.50	1.50	3.00	15.00	25.00
1904	1,000,000	0.75	1.50	4.00	15.00	25.00
1908	4,500,000	2.00	4.00	10.00	15.00	35.00
1909	1,500,000	3.00	5.00	12.00	20.00	50.00
1910	1,500,000	10.00	20.00	40.00	100	185
1911	5,000,000	0.25	0.75	1.50	5.00	10.00
1912	2,000,000	0.50	1.00	2.00	7.00	12.00
1913	1,500,000	0.50	1.00	2.00	5.00	12.00
1914	1,000,000	0.75	1.50	3.00	7.00	15.00

Date	Mintage	F12	VF20	XF40	MS60	MS63
1916	1,996,000	0.50	1.00	2.00	5.00	12.00
1919	2,407,000	0.25	0.75	1.50	5.00	12.00
1920	2,594,000	0.25	0.75	1.50	5.00	12.00

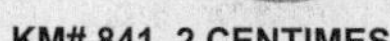

KM# 841 2 CENTIMES

2.00 g., Bronze, 20.2 mm. **Obv:** Liberty head right **Rev:** Denomination and date within wreath **Mint:** Paris **Note:** Without mint mark or privy mark.

Date	Mintage	F12	VF20	XF40	MS60	MS63
1901	1,000,000	1.00	2.50	4.00	10.00	35.00
1902	750,000	1.50	3.50	5.50	15.00	55.00
1903	750,000	1.50	3.50	5.50	16.50	55.00
1904	500,000	2.00	4.50	7.50	18.50	60.00
1907	250,000	10.00	25.00	55.00	130	200
1908	3,500,000	0.35	0.75	2.00	6.00	20.00
1909	1,750,000	6.00	12.00	30.00	50.00	90.00
1910	1,750,000	0.50	1.00	5.00	12.50	40.00
1911	5,000,000	0.15	0.50	1.25	5.00	15.00
1912	1,500,000	0.25	1.00	2.00	7.00	20.00
1913	1,750,000	0.25	1.00	2.00	5.00	15.00
1914	2,000,000	0.15	0.50	1.25	5.00	15.00
1916	500,000	0.75	1.50	3.00	9.00	30.00
1919	902,000	0.50	1.00	2.00	6.00	20.00
1920	598,000	0.75	1.50	3.00	8.00	25.00

KM# 842 5 CENTIMES

5.00 g., Bronze, 25.1 mm. **Obv:** Liberty head right **Rev:** Republic protecting her child, denomination at right, date below **Mint:** Paris **Note:** Without mint mark.

Date	Mintage	F12	VF20	XF40	MS60	MS63
1901 (c)	6,000,000	1.75	3.50	15.00	40.00	75.00
1902	7,900,000	1.75	3.50	10.00	40.00	70.00
1903	2,879,000	5.00	10.00	25.00	75.00	100
1904	8,000,000	1.00	3.00	6.50	20.00	50.00
1905	2,100,000	6.00	16.00	45.00	100	225
1906	8,394,000	0.75	2.50	6.00	20.00	50.00
1907	7,900,000	0.75	2.50	6.00	20.00	50.00
1908	6,090,000	2.00	4.00	12.00	25.00	75.00
1909	8,000,000	0.75	2.50	6.00	20.00	50.00
1910	4,000,000	1.50	2.50	9.00	35.00	85.00
1911	15,386,000	0.25	0.75	1.75	7.00	15.00
1912	20,000,000	0.25	0.75	1.75	7.00	15.00
1913	12,603,000	0.25	0.75	1.75	7.00	15.00
1914	7,000,000	0.25	0.75	1.75	7.00	15.00
1915	6,032,000	0.25	0.75	1.75	7.00	15.00
1916	41,531,000	0.25	0.75	1.75	5.00	12.50
1916 (s)	Inc. above	0.25	0.75	1.75	5.00	12.50
1917	16,963,000	0.25	0.75	1.75	5.00	12.50
1920	8,151,999	2.00	4.00	9.00	28.00	55.00
1921	142,000	200	325	500	1,300	—

KM# 865 5 CENTIMES

3.00 g., Nickel, 19 mm. **Obv:** Monogram within wreath divided by center hole, liberty cap above **Rev:** Denomination divided by plant and center hole, dash under MES

Date	Mintage	F12	VF20	XF40	MS60	MS63
1914 Rare	—	—	—	—	—	—

KM# 865a 5 CENTIMES

3.00 g., Copper-Nickel, 19 mm. **Obv:** Monogram within wreath divided by center hole, liberty cap above **Rev:** Denomination divided by plant and center hole

Date	Mintage	VF20	XF40	MS60	MS63	MS65
1917	10,458,000	1.75	4.00	18.00	40.00	—
1918	35,592,000	0.75	1.75	4.50	10.00	—
1919	43,848,000	0.75	1.75	4.00	9.00	—
1920	51,321,000	0.50	1.75	3.50	8.00	—

KM# 875 5 CENTIMES

2.00 g., Copper-Nickel, 17 mm. **Obv:** Monogram divided by center hole, liberty cap above, wreath surrounds **Rev:** Denomination divided by plant and center hole, date below

Date	Mintage	F12	VF20	XF40	MS60	MS63
1920	Inc. above	5.00	15.00	28.00	75.00	150
1921	32,908,000	0.25	0.50	1.75	4.00	9.00
1922	31,700,000	0.25	0.50	1.75	4.00	9.00
1922 (tb)	17,717,000	1.50	2.50	5.00	13.50	28.00
1923	23,322,000	0.50	1.50	2.00	6.50	12.00
1923 (tb)	45,097,000	0.25	0.50	1.00	3.50	8.00
1924	47,018,000	0.25	0.50	1.00	3.50	8.00
1924 (tb)	21,210,000	0.50	1.50	2.00	5.50	10.00
1925	66,837,999	0.25	0.50	1.00	2.50	6.00
1926	19,820,000	0.25	1.50	2.00	5.50	10.00
1927	6,066,000	2.50	8.50	25.00	60.00	180
1930	31,902,000	0.20	0.50	1.00	2.25	5.00
1931	34,711,000	0.20	0.50	1.00	2.25	5.00
1932	31,112,000	0.20	0.50	1.00	2.25	5.00
1933	12,970,000	1.00	1.75	4.00	10.00	20.00
1934	27,144,000	0.30	0.65	2.00	5.00	10.00
1935	57,221,000	0.25	0.50	1.00	2.25	5.00
1936	64,340,999	0.15	0.25	0.75	2.25	5.00
1937	26,329,000	0.15	0.25	0.75	2.25	5.00
1938	21,614,000	0.15	0.25	0.75	2.25	5.00

KM# 875a 5 CENTIMES

1.50 g., Nickel-Bronze, 17 mm. **Obv:** Center hole divides monogram, liberty cap above, wreath surrounds **Rev:** Center hole and plant divide denomination, date below

Date	Mintage	VF20	XF40	MS60	MS63	MS65
.1938.	26,330,000	0.50	1.00	8.00	15.00	—
.1938. Star	Inc. above	100	200	400	600	—
.1939.	52,673,000	0.25	0.75	6.00	15.00	—

KM# 843 10 CENTIMES

10.00 g., Bronze, 30 mm. **Obv:** Liberty head right **Rev:** Republic protecting her child **Mint:** Paris **Note:** Without mint mark.

Date	Mintage	F12	VF20	XF40	MS60	MS63
1901 (c)	2,700,000	1.50	3.00	20.00	50.00	75.00
1902	3,800,000	0.75	1.75	6.50	20.00	45.00
1903	3,650,000	0.75	1.75	6.50	20.00	45.00
1904	3,800,000	0.75	1.75	6.50	26.00	45.00
1905	950,000	25.00	50.00	100	250	475
1906	3,000,000	2.00	5.00	12.00	40.00	65.00
1907	4,000,000	0.75	1.75	4.50	20.00	35.00
1908	3,500,000	0.75	1.75	4.50	20.00	35.00
1909	2,933,000	0.75	1.75	4.50	20.00	40.00
1910	3,567,000	0.75	1.75	4.50	15.00	35.00
1911	7,903,000	0.50	1.25	2.75	12.00	20.00
1912	9,500,000	0.50	1.25	2.75	12.00	20.00
1913	9,000,000	0.50	1.25	2.75	12.00	20.00
1914	6,000,000	0.75	1.75	3.50	12.00	25.00
1915	4,362,000	0.50	1.25	2.75	10.00	20.00
1916	22,477,000	0.25	0.75	1.50	7.00	12.00
1916 (s)	Inc. above	0.25	0.75	1.50	7.00	12.00
1917	11,914,000	0.25	0.75	1.50	7.00	12.00
1920	4,119,000	1.50	3.00	10.00	40.00	65.00
1921	1,896,000	8.00	16.00	30.00	65.00	140

KM# 866 10 CENTIMES

4.00 g., Nickel, 21.3 mm. **Obv:** Monogram divided by center hole, liberty cap above, wreath surrounds **Rev:** Denomination divided by plant and center hole, date below

Date	Mintage	F12	VF20	XF40	MS60	MS63
1914 dash	3,972	—	—	—	2,000	3,500

KM# 866a 10 CENTIMES

4.00 g., Copper-Nickel, 21.3 mm. **Obv:** Center hole divides monogram, liberty cap above, wreath surrounds **Rev:** Center hole and plant divides denomination, date below **Note:** Varieties with small and large hole exist.

Date	Mintage	VF20	XF40	MS60	MS63	MS65
1917	8,170,999	1.50	3.50	20.00	35.00	—
1918	30,605,000	0.50	1.00	3.50	6.50	—
1919	33,488,999	0.50	1.00	3.50	6.50	—
1920	38,845,000	0.50	1.00	3.50	6.50	—
1921	42,768,000	0.35	0.75	2.50	6.50	—
1922	23,033,000	0.75	1.25	4.00	7.00	—
1922 (tb)	12,412,000	1.50	2.50	6.50	12.00	—
1923	18,701,000	1.00	2.00	4.50	8.00	—
1923 (tb)	30,016,000	0.50	1.00	3.00	5.00	—
1924	43,949,000	0.35	0.75	2.00	3.00	—
1924 (tb)	13,591,000	4.50	12.50	40.00	65.00	—
1925	46,266,000	0.35	0.75	2.00	3.00	—
1926	25,660,000	0.50	1.00	3.00	5.00	—
1927	16,203,000	0.75	1.25	4.00	7.00	—
1928	6,967,000	2.50	8.00	28.00	55.00	—
1929	24,531,000	0.35	1.00	2.00	3.00	—
1930	22,146,000	0.35	1.00	2.00	3.00	—
1931	49,107,000	0.35	1.00	2.00	3.00	—
1932	30,317,000	0.35	1.00	2.00	3.00	—
1933	13,042,000	0.75	1.50	4.00	7.00	—
1934	24,067,000	0.50	1.00	2.00	3.00	—
1935	47,487,000	0.50	1.00	2.00	3.00	—
1936	57,738,000	0.50	1.00	2.00	3.00	—
1937	25,308,000	0.50	1.00	2.00	3.00	—
1938	17,063,000	0.75	1.75	4.50	8.00	—

KM# 889.1 10 CENTIMES

3.00 g., Nickel-Bronze, 21.3 mm. **Obv:** Monogram divided by center hole, liberty cap above, wreath surrounds **Rev:** Denomination divided by plant and center hole, date below

Date	Mintage	F12	VF20	XF40	MS60	MS63
.1938.	24,151,000	0.25	0.50	1.00	2.00	6.00
.1939.	62,269,000	0.15	0.30	0.65	1.75	5.00

KM# 889.2 10 CENTIMES

Nickel-Bronze, 21.3 mm. **Obv:** Center hole divides monogram, liberty cap above **Rev:** Center hole and plant divide denomination **Note:** Thin flan: 1.35-1.45mm thickness

Date	Mintage	F12	VF20	XF40	MS60	MS63
.1939.	Inc. above	0.10	0.20	0.50	1.25	4.00

KM# 895 10 CENTIMES

Zinc **Rev:** Without dash below MES in C MES

Date	Mintage	F12	VF20	XF40	MS60	MS63
1941	235,875,000	1.00	2.00	6.00	15.00	25.00

KM# 896 10 CENTIMES

Zinc **Obv:** Monogram within wreath divided by center hole, liberty cap above **Rev:** Center hole within wreath divides denomination, date below, dash below MES in C MES

Date	Mintage	F12	VF20	XF40	MS60	MS63
1941	Inc. above	0.75	1.25	4.00	10.00	20.00

KM# 897 10 CENTIMES

2.50 g., Zinc, 21 mm. **Obv:** Monogram within wreath divided by center hole, liberty cap above **Rev:** Center hole within wreath divides denomination, dot before and after date below **Edge:** Reeded

Date	Mintage	F12	VF20	XF40	MS60	MS63
.1941.	Inc. above	0.25	0.50	1.00	4.00	8.00

KM# 898.1 10 CENTIMES

Zinc, 21 mm. **Obv:** Grain sprigs flank center hole **Rev:** Center hole divides denomination, oak leaves flank, date below **Edge:** Reeded **Note:** Issued for Vichy French State, thickness 1.5 mm. Varieties exist w/o hole.

Date	Mintage	F12	VF20	XF40	MS60	MS63
1941	70,860,000	0.35	0.65	1.50	6.00	10.00
1942	139,598,000	0.30	0.60	1.25	4.00	8.00
1943	48,957,600	1.00	2.00	4.00	15.00	25.00

KM# 898.2 10 CENTIMES

2.50 g., Zinc, 21.3 mm. **Obv:** Grain sprigs flank center hole **Rev:** Center hole divides denomination, oak leaves flank, date below **Edge:** Reeded **Mint:** Paris **Note:** Thin flan, 1.3mm.

Date	Mintage	F12	VF20	XF40	MS60	MS63
1941	Inc. above	0.25	0.50	1.25	3.00	8.00
1942	Inc. above	0.20	0.40	1.00	2.25	6.00
1943	Inc. above	0.75	1.50	2.75	6.00	10.00

KM# 903 10 CENTIMES

1.50 g., Zinc, 17 mm. **Obv:** Grain sprigs flank center hole **Rev:** Center hole divides denomination, oak leaves flank, date below **Note:** Reduced size.

Date	Mintage	F12	VF20	XF40	MS60	MS63
1943	24,638,000	0.25	0.75	2.50	7.00	10.00
1944	58,463,000	0.25	0.50	2.00	5.00	9.00

KM# 906.1 10 CENTIMES

Zinc, 17 mm. **Obv:** Monogram divided by center hole, liberty cap above, wreath surrounds **Rev:** Center hole and plant divide denomination, date below **Note:** Reduced size.

Date	Mintage	F12	VF20	XF40	MS60	MS63
1945	38,174,000	1.00	1.75	3.25	12.00	20.00

KM# 906.2 10 CENTIMES

Zinc **Obv:** Monogram divided by center hole, liberty cap above, wreath surrounds **Rev:** Center hole and plant divide denomination **Mint:** Beaumont - Le Roger

Date	Mintage	F12	VF20	XF40	MS60	MS63
1945 B	7,246,000	1.50	3.00	6.00	16.00	25.00
1946 B	10,566,000	2.50	5.00	10.00	25.00	60.00

KM# 906.3 10 CENTIMES

Zinc **Obv:** Monogram divided by center hole, liberty cap above, wreath surrounds **Rev:** Center hole and plant divide denomination **Mint:** Castelsarrasin

Date	Mintage	F12	VF20	XF40	MS60	MS63
1945 C	8,379,000	2.00	4.00	8.00	20.00	45.00

KM# 899 20 CENTIMES

3.50 g., Zinc, 24 mm. **Obv:** Grain sprigs flank center hole **Rev:** Center hole divides denomination, oak leaves flank, date below **Edge:** Reeded **Note:** Issued for Vichy French State.

Date	Mintage	F12	VF20	XF40	MS60	MS63
1941	54,044,000	1.00	2.00	4.00	17.00	30.00

KM# 900.1 20 CENTIMES

3.50 g., Zinc **Obv:** Grain sprigs flank center hole **Rev:** Center hole divides denomination, oak leaves flank, date below **Edge:** Reeded **Mint:** Paris **Note:** Thick flan.

Date	Mintage	F12	VF20	XF40	MS60	MS63
1941 A	31,397,000	1.00	2.00	4.00	15.00	25.00
1942 A	112,868,000	0.50	1.00	2.00	7.00	10.00
1943 A	64,138,000	0.75	1.50	2.50	8.50	14.00

KM# 900.2 20 CENTIMES

3.00 g., Zinc **Obv:** Grain sprigs flank center hole **Rev:** Center hole divides denomination, leaves flank **Edge:** Reeded **Mint:** Paris **Note:** Thin flan. Struck at Paris Mint.

Date	Mintage	F12	VF20	XF40	MS60	MS63
1941	Inc. above	0.50	0.75	2.00	8.50	14.00
1942	Inc. above	0.50	0.75	2.00	7.50	10.00
1943	Inc. above	0.50	0.75	2.00	6.50	10.00
1944	5,250,000	15.00	30.00	80.00	200	375

KM# 900.2a 20 CENTIMES

3.00 g., Iron **Obv:** Grain sprigs flank center hole **Rev:** Center hole divides denomination, leaves flank

Date	Mintage	VF20	XF40	MS60	MS63	MS65
1944	695,000	50.00	100	125	500	—

KM# 907.1 20 CENTIMES

Zinc **Obv:** Monogram divided by center hole, liberty cap above, wreath surrounds **Rev:** Center hole and plant divide denomination, date below **Note:** Fourth Republic.

Date	Mintage	F12	VF20	XF40	MS60	MS63
1945	6,003,000	2.00	4.00	9.00	22.00	45.00
1946	2,662,000	8.00	18.00	35.00	85.00	160

KM# 907.2 20 CENTIMES

3.00 g., Zinc, 24 mm. **Obv:** Monogram divided by center hole, liberty cap above, wreath surrounds **Rev:** Center hole and plant divide denomination, date below **Mint:** Beaumont - Le Roger

Date	Mintage	F12	VF20	XF40	MS60	MS63
1945 B	100,000	50.00	100	225	425	900
1946 B Rare	5,525,000	75.00	150	260	450	950

KM# 907.3 20 CENTIMES

Zinc **Obv:** Monogram divided by center hole, liberty cap above, wreath surrounds **Rev:** Center hole and plant divide denomination, date below **Mint:** Castelsarrasin

Date	Mintage	F12	VF20	XF40	MS60	MS63
1945 C	299,000	20.00	40.00	85.00	150	220

KM# 855 25 CENTIMES

7.00 g., Nickel, 24 mm. **Obv:** Laureate liberty head left **Rev:** Denomination and date flanked by cornucopias **Mint:** Paris **Note:** Without mint mark.

Date	Mintage	F12	VF20	XF40	MS60	MS63
1903	16,000,000	0.25	1.00	2.00	11.50	20.00

KM# 856 25 CENTIMES

7.00 g., Nickel, 24 mm. **Obv:** Laureate bust left **Rev:** Oak leaves divide date and denomination, column with axe head on top at left **Shape:** 22-sided

Date	Mintage	F12	VF20	XF40	MS60	MS63
1904	16,000,000	0.25	0.75	2.00	13.50	20.00
1905	8,000,000	0.50	1.50	3.50	20.00	30.00

KM# 867 25 CENTIMES

5.04 g., Nickel, 24 mm. **Obv:** Monogram divided by center hole, liberty cap above, wreath surrounds **Rev:** Center hole and plant divide denomination, dash under "MES" in denomination

Date	Mintage	F12	VF20	XF40	MS60	MS63
1914	941,000	1.50	3.00	7.00	22.50	40.00
1915	535,000	2.50	4.00	8.00	32.00	60.00
1916	100,000	15.00	30.00	60.00	120	245
1917	65,000	30.00	50.00	85.00	185	375

KM# 867a 25 CENTIMES

5.00 g., Copper-Nickel, 24 mm. **Obv:** Monogram divided by center hole, liberty cap above, wreath surrounds **Rev:** Without dash under "MES" in denomination **Edge:** Plain **Note:** Varieties: Edges reeded on 1920, 1929, 1931, different hole.

Date	Mintage	VF20	XF40	MS60	MS63	MS65
1917	3,085,000	4.00	12.00	22.00	40.00	—
1918	18,330,000	0.50	1.50	3.50	6.00	—
1919	5,106,000	2.00	3.00	7.00	12.00	—
1920	18,108,000	0.50	1.00	3.00	5.00	—
1921	18,531,000	0.50	1.00	3.00	5.00	—
1922	17,766,000	0.50	1.00	3.00	5.00	—
1923	19,718,000	0.50	1.00	3.00	5.00	—
1924	24,535,000	0.50	1.00	3.00	5.00	—
1925	17,807,000	0.50	1.00	3.00	5.00	—
1926	13,226,000	0.50	1.00	3.00	5.00	—
1927	13,465,000	0.50	1.00	3.00	5.00	—
1928	9,960,000	0.50	1.50	3.50	6.50	—
1929	12,887,000	0.50	1.00	2.50	4.00	—
1930	28,363,000	0.50	1.00	2.50	4.00	—
1931	22,121,000	0.50	1.00	2.50	4.00	—
1932	30,364,000	0.50	1.00	2.50	4.00	—
1933	28,562,000	0.50	1.00	2.50	4.00	—
1936	4,657,000	3.00	8.00	18.00	35.00	—
1937	7,780,000	0.50	1.50	3.50	6.00	—

KM# 867b 25 CENTIMES

4.16 g., Nickel-Bronze, 24 mm. **Rev:** Center hole and plant divide denomination, date below **Edge:** Plain **Note:** Listings below appear with a period before and after the date.

Date	Mintage	VF20	XF40	MS60	MS63	MS65
1938	5,170,000	0.50	1.00	2.50	3.50	—
1939	42,964,000	0.35	0.75	1.50	2.50	—
Note: Thick flan (1.55mm)						
1939	Inc. above	0.35	0.75	1.50	2.50	—
Note: Thin flan (1.35mm)						
1940	3,446,000	12.00	18.00	45.00	65.00	—

KM# 854 50 CENTIMES

2.50 g., 0.835 Silver 0.0671 oz. ASW, 18.1 mm. **Obv:** Figure sowing seed **Rev:** Leafy branch divides date and denomination **Edge:** Reeded **Mint:** Paris **Note:** Without mint mark.

Date	Mintage	F12	VF20	XF40	MS60	MS63
1901	4,960,000	1.20	4.00	12.00	45.00	90.00
1902	3,778,000	1.20	5.00	15.00	55.00	80.00
1903	2,222,000	1.20	25.00	50.00	165	250
1904	4,000,000	1.20	3.50	10.00	45.00	90.00
1905	2,381,000	1.20	9.00	20.00	75.00	200
1906	2,679,000	1.20	5.00	15.00	45.00	85.00
1907	7,332,000	1.20	3.50	10.00	30.00	50.00
1908	14,304,000	1.20	2.75	4.00	15.00	30.00
1909	9,900,000	1.20	2.75	4.00	15.00	30.00
1910	15,923,000	1.20	1.35	3.00	10.00	20.00
1911	1,330,000	1.20	20.00	70.00	250	450
1912	16,000,000	—	1.20	2.50	5.00	9.00
1913	14,000,000	—	1.20	2.50	5.00	9.00
1914	9,657,000	—	1.20	2.50	6.00	10.00
1915	20,893,000	—	1.20	2.50	3.00	7.00
1916	52,963,000	—	1.20	2.50	2.75	5.00
1917	48,629,000	—	1.20	2.50	2.75	5.00
1918	36,492,000	—	1.20	2.50	2.75	5.00
1919	24,299,000	—	1.20	2.50	2.75	5.00
1920	8,509,000	—	1.20	3.00	6.00	10.00

KM# 884 50 CENTIMES

2.00 g., Aluminum-Bronze, 18 mm. **Obv:** Denomination within circle **Rev:** Mercury seated left, caduceus at left, shield on right, date below **Edge:** Reeded **Note:** Varieties for 1924: Closed and open 4's.

Date	Mintage	F12	VF20	XF40	MS60	MS63
1921	8,692,000	0.75	2.00	6.00	18.00	55.00
1922	86,226,000	0.15	0.25	1.00	4.00	8.00
1923	119,584,000	0.15	0.25	0.75	2.50	5.00
1924	97,036,000	0.15	0.25	1.00	3.00	6.00
1925	48,017,000	0.25	0.50	1.25	5.00	10.00
1926	46,447,000	0.25	0.50	1.25	5.00	10.00
1927	23,703,000	0.75	1.50	3.00	8.50	16.50
1928	10,329,000	0.75	2.00	5.00	16.00	30.00
1929	6,669,000	2.50	6.00	12.50	20.00	70.00

KM# 894.1 50 CENTIMES

2.00 g., Aluminum-Bronze, 18 mm. **Obv:** Laureate head left **Rev:** Denomination above date, cornucopias flank

Date	Mintage	F12	VF20	XF40	MS60	MS63
1931	62,775,000	0.15	0.25	1.00	3.00	5.00
1932 Open 9	108,839,000	0.15	0.25	0.50	2.00	3.50
1932 Closed 9	Inc. above	0.15	0.25	0.50	2.00	3.50
1933 Closed 9	Inc. above	0.15	0.25	0.75	3.00	5.00
1933 Open 9	41,937,000	0.15	0.25	0.75	3.00	5.00
1936	16,602,000	0.50	1.00	2.00	5.00	9.00
1937	43,950,000	0.15	0.25	0.75	3.00	5.00
1938	55,707,000	0.15	0.25	0.75	3.00	5.00
1939	96,594,000	0.15	0.25	0.50	2.00	3.50
1940	10,854,000	0.50	1.00	2.00	5.00	9.00
1941	82,958,000	0.15	0.25	1.00	3.00	5.00
1947	—	60.00	125	225	450	700

Note: 1947 date was struck for colonial use in Africa

KM# 894.1a 50 CENTIMES

0.75 g., Aluminum, 18 mm. **Obv:** Laureate liberty head left **Rev:** Cornucopias flank denomination and date **Mint:** Paris **Note:** Without mint mark. Thick and thin planchets exist.

Date	Mintage	VF20	XF40	MS60	MS63	MS65
1941	129,758,000	0.25	0.50	2.00	3.00	—
1944	9,898,000	1.00	2.50	6.00	9.00	—
1945	26,224,000	0.25	1.00	3.00	5.00	—
1946	24,605,000	0.25	1.00	3.00	5.00	—
1947	51,744,000	0.25	0.60	2.00	3.00	—

KM# 894.2a 50 CENTIMES

0.75 g., Aluminum, 18 mm. **Obv:** Laureate liberty head left **Rev:** Cornucopias flank denomination and date **Mint:** Beaumont - Le Roger

Date	Mintage	VF20	XF40	MS60	MS63	MS65
1944 B	20,000	—	—	—	—	—
Note: No known examples exist						
1945 B	6,357,000	1.00	3.00	8.00	15.00	—
1946 B	29,344,000	0.25	1.00	4.00	7.00	—
1947 B	18,504,000	5.00	10.00	20.00	35.00	—

KM# 894.2 50 CENTIMES

2.00 g., Aluminum-Bronze, 18 mm. **Obv:** Laureate liberty head left **Rev:** Cornucopias flank denomination and date **Note:** Struck at Brussels.

Date	Mintage	F12	VF20	XF40	MS60	MS63
1939 B	6,200,000	0.50	1.00	2.50	10.00	18.00

KM# 914.1 50 CENTIMES

Aluminum, 18 mm. **Obv:** Double bit axe, grain sprigs flank **Rev:** Denomination above date, oak leaves flank **Mint:** Paris **Note:** Without mint mark. Vichy French State. Thick flan.

Date	Mintage	F12	VF20	XF40	MS60	MS63
1942	50,134,000	0.15	0.25	0.75	2.00	4.00
1943	84,462,000	0.15	0.25	0.75	2.00	4.00
1944	57,410,000	1.50	3.00	6.00	18.00	32.50

KM# 914.2 50 CENTIMES

0.80 g., Aluminum, 18 mm. **Obv:** Grain sprigs flank double bit axe **Rev:** Denomination above date, oak leaves flank **Mint:** Beaumont - Le Roger

Date	Mintage	F12	VF20	XF40	MS60	MS63
1943 B	21,916,000	5.00	10.00	28.00	50.00	70.00
1944 B	27,334,000	1.50	3.00	7.00	15.00	25.00

KM# 914.3 50 CENTIMES

Aluminum, 18 mm. **Obv:** Grain sprigs flank double bit axe **Rev:** Denomination above date, oak leaves flank **Mint:** Castelsarrasin

Date	Mintage	F12	VF20	XF40	MS60	MS63
1944 C	27,213,000	2.00	4.00	8.00	26.00	40.00

KM# 914.4 50 CENTIMES

Aluminum, 18 mm. **Obv:** Grain sprigs flank double bit axe **Rev:** Denomination above date, oak leaves flank **Mint:** Paris **Note:** Without mint mark. Thin flan. Struck at Paris Mint.

Date	Mintage	F12	VF20	XF40	MS60	MS63
1942	—	0.15	0.25	1.00	2.50	4.50
1943	—	0.15	0.25	0.50	1.25	2.00

KM# 894.3a 50 CENTIMES

0.75 g., Aluminum, 18 mm. **Obv:** Laureate liberty head left **Rev:** Cornucopias flank denomination and date **Mint:** Castelsarrasin

Date	Mintage	VF20	XF40	MS60	MS63	MS65
1945 C	2,968,000	3.00	6.00	12.00	25.00	—

KM# 844.1 FRANC

5.00 g., 0.835 Silver 0.1342 oz. ASW, 23 mm. **Obv:** Figure sowing seed **Rev:** Leafy branch divides date and denomination **Edge:** Reeded **Mint:** Paris **Note:** Without mint mark.

Date	Mintage	F12	VF20	XF40	MS60	MS63
1901	6,200,000	2.50	15.00	30.00	100	130
1902	6,000,000	2.50	6.00	20.00	65.00	140
1903	472,000	2.50	40.00	100	750	1,200
1904	7,000,000	2.50	6.00	17.50	65.00	130
1905	6,004,000	2.50	6.00	15.00	65.00	110
1906	1,908,000	2.50	20.00	40.00	85.00	175
1907	2,563,000	2.50	14.00	30.00	90.00	150
1908	3,961,000	2.50	8.00	20.00	65.00	110
1909	10,924,000	2.50	5.00	8.00	22.00	75.00
1910	7,725,000	2.50	5.00	8.00	22.00	75.00
1911	5,542,000	2.50	5.00	12.00	45.00	90.00
1912	10,001,000	2.50	5.00	8.00	22.00	75.00
1913	13,654,000	2.50	5.00	6.00	18.00	50.00
1914	14,361,000	—	2.50	5.00	15.00	45.00
1915	47,955,000	—	2.50	5.00	8.00	10.00
1916	92,029,000	—	—	2.50	5.00	9.00
1917	57,153,000	—	—	2.50	5.00	9.00
1918	50,112,000	—	—	2.50	5.00	9.00
1919	46,112,000	—	—	2.50	5.00	9.00
1920	19,322,000	—	—	5.00	8.00	10.00

KM# 844.2 FRANC

5.00 g., 0.835 Silver 0.1342 oz. ASW, 23 mm. **Obv:** Figure sowing seed **Rev:** Leafy branch divides date and denomination **Edge:** Reeded **Mint:** Castelsarrasin

Date	Mintage	F12	VF20	XF40	MS60	MS63
1914 C	43,000	—	—	350	500	900

KM# 876 FRANC

4.09 g., Aluminum-Bronze, 23 mm. **Obv:** Value **Obv. Legend:** CHAMBRES • DE • COMMERCE • DE • FRANCE **Rev:** Mercury seated left **Rev. Legend:** COMMERCE - INDUSTRIE **Edge:** Reeded **Mint:** Paris **Note:** Without mint mark. Chamber of Commerce.

Date	Mintage	F12	VF20	XF40	MS60	MS63
1920	590,000	3.00	5.00	12.50	32.00	55.00
1921	54,572,000	0.25	0.50	1.50	5.50	9.00
1922	111,343,000	0.15	0.25	1.00	4.50	8.00
1923	140,138,000	0.15	0.25	1.00	3.50	7.00
1924 Open 4	87,715,000	0.15	0.25	1.00	4.50	12.00
1924 Closed 4	Inc. above	0.35	0.60	2.00	6.50	8.00
1925	36,523,000	0.25	0.50	1.50	5.50	9.00
1926	1,580,000	3.00	8.00	20.00	45.00	75.00
1927	11,330,000	0.50	1.50	3.50	8.50	16.00

KM# 885 FRANC

4.00 g., Aluminum-Bronze, 23 mm. **Obv:** Laureate head left **Rev:** Cornucopias flank denomination and date **Edge:** Plain

Date	Mintage	F12	VF20	XF40	MS60	MS63
1931	15,504,000	0.25	0.50	2.00	6.50	10.00
1932	29,768,000	0.15	0.25	1.00	4.00	7.00
1933	15,356,000	0.25	0.50	2.00	6.50	10.00
1934	17,286,000	0.25	0.50	2.00	5.00	9.00
1935	1,166,000	6.00	15.00	20.00	70.00	140
1936	23,817,000	0.15	0.25	1.00	4.00	7.00
1937	30,940,000	0.15	0.25	1.00	3.00	5.00
1938	66,165,000	0.15	0.25	1.00	2.50	4.50
1939	48,434,000	0.15	0.25	1.00	3.00	5.00
1940	25,525,000	0.15	0.25	1.00	3.50	6.00
1941	34,705,000	0.15	0.25	1.00	3.00	5.00

KM# 885a.1 FRANC

1.50 g., Aluminum, 23 mm. **Obv:** Laureate head left **Rev:** Cornucopias flank denomination and date **Edge:** Plain **Note:** Thick and thin planchets exist.

Date	Mintage	VF20	XF40	MS60	MS63	MS65
1941	60,877,000	0.20	1.00	4.00	6.00	—
1943	4,400	1,500	2,250	4,000	6,000	—
Note: Struck for colonial use in Africa.						
1944	22,608,000	0.20	1.50	5.00	8.00	—
1945	61,780,000	0.15	0.50	2.00	3.00	—
1946	52,516,000	0.15	0.25	2.00	3.00	—
1947	110,448,000	0.15	0.25	2.00	3.00	—
1948	96,092,000	0.15	0.25	2.00	3.00	—
1949	41,090,000	0.15	0.25	2.00	3.00	—
1950	27,882,000	0.15	0.50	2.50	4.00	—
1957	16,497,000	0.15	0.75	3.00	5.00	—
1958	21,197,000	0.15	0.75	3.00	5.00	—
1959	41,985,000	0.15	0.25	1.25	2.00	—

KM# 902.1 FRANC

Aluminum, 23 mm. **Obv:** Double bit axe, grain sprigs flank **Rev:** Denomination above date, oak leaves flank **Mint:** Paris **Note:** Without mint mark. Vichy French State Issues. Thick and thin planchets exist.

Date	Mintage	F12	VF20	XF40	MS60	MS63
1942	152,144,000	0.25	0.50	1.50	4.00	6.00
1942 Without LB	Inc. above	—	—	—	—	—
1943	205,564,000	0.10	0.25	1.00	2.50	3.50
1943 No known thin flan examples exist	Inc. above	—	—	—	—	—
1944	50,605,000	0.50	1.25	2.00	10.00	15.00

KM# 885b FRANC

Zinc, 23 mm. **Obv:** Laureate head left **Rev:** Cornucopias flank denomination and date **Mint:** Paris **Note:** Struck for colonial use in Africa.

Date	Mintage	VF20	XF40	MS60	MS63	MS65
1943 A	Est. 17000	1,100	1,700	3,200	4,400	—

KM# 902.2 FRANC

1.28 g., Aluminum, 23 mm. **Obv:** Grain sprigs flank double bit axe **Rev:** Leaves flank denomination, date below **Mint:** Rouen

Date	Mintage	F12	VF20	XF40	MS60	MS63
1943 B	68,082,000	5.00	9.00	28.00	80.00	120

Date	Mintage	F12	VF20	XF40	MS60	MS63
1944 B	13,622,000	1.50	3.00	12.00	25.00	40.00

KM# 885a.3 FRANC

1.50 g., Aluminum, 23 mm. **Obv:** Laureate head left **Rev:** Cornucopias flank denomination and date **Mint:** Castelsarrasin

Date	Mintage	VF20	XF40	MS60	MS63	MS65
1944 C	33,600,000	1.50	3.50	12.00	20.00	—
1945 C	5,220,000	3.50	9.00	25.00	60.00	—

KM# 902.3 FRANC

Aluminum, 23 mm. **Obv:** Grain sprigs flank double bit axe **Rev:** Leaves flank denomination, date below **Mint:** Castelsarrasin

Date	Mintage	F12	VF20	XF40	MS60	MS63
1944 Large C	74,859,000	0.50	1.50	3.50	12.50	20.00
1944 Small C	Inc. above	50.00	100	200	400	840

KM# 885a.2 FRANC

1.50 g., Aluminum, 23 mm. **Obv:** Laureate head left **Rev:** Cornucopias flank denomination and date **Mint:** Beaumont - Le Roger

Date	Mintage	VF20	XF40	MS60	MS63	MS65
1945 B	4,251,000	3.50	9.00	20.00	75.00	—
1946 B	26,493,000	0.20	1.50	5.00	8.00	—
1947 B	31,562,000	0.20	1.00	4.00	7.00	—
1948 B	45,481,000	0.20	1.00	3.50	5.00	—
1949 B	35,840,000	0.20	1.00	4.00	7.00	—
1950 B	18,800,000	2.00	3.50	15.00	22.00	—
1957 B	63,976,000	0.20	1.00	4.00	7.00	—
1958 B	13,412,000	0.75	2.00	5.50	9.00	—

KM# 845.1 2 FRANCS

10.00 g., 0.835 Silver 0.2685 oz. ASW, 27 mm. **Obv:** Figure sowing seed **Rev:** Leafy branch divides denomination and date **Edge:** Reeded **Mint:** Paris **Note:** Without mint mark.

Date	Mintage	F12	VF20	XF40	MS60	MS63
1901	1,860,000	10.00	18.00	50.00	125	275
1902	2,000,000	10.00	18.00	50.00	125	210
1904	1,500,000	12.00	18.00	40.00	150	250
1905	2,000,000	10.00	18.00	50.00	150	225
1908	2,502,000	10.00	11.00	20.00	75.00	100
1909	1,000,000	13.00	18.00	35.00	175	250
1910	2,190,000	10.00	11.00	20.00	75.00	100
1912	1,000,000	11.00	18.00	40.00	125	200
1913	500,000	15.00	25.00	50.00	100	200
1914	5,719,000	5.00	9.00	11.00	20.00	50.00
1915	13,963,000	—	5.00	9.00	15.00	25.00
1916	17,887,000	—	5.00	9.00	15.00	25.00
1917	16,555,000	—	5.00	9.00	15.00	25.00
1918	12,026,000	—	5.00	9.00	15.00	25.00
1919	9,261,000	—	5.00	9.00	12.00	22.00
1920	3,014,000	5.00	9.00	11.00	15.00	35.00

KM# 845.2 2 FRANCS

10.00 g., 0.8352 Silver 0.2685 oz. ASW, 27 mm. **Obv:** Figure sowing seed **Rev:** Leafy branch divides date and denomination **Edge:** Reeded **Mint:** Castelsarrasin

Date	Mintage	F12	VF20	XF40	MS60	MS63
1914 C	462,000	—	10.00	20.00	30.00	110

KM# 877 2 FRANCS

8.00 g., Aluminum-Bronze, 27 mm. **Subject:** French Chamber of Commerce **Obv:** Denomination within circle **Rev:** Mercury seated left, caduceus at left, shield on right, date below **Edge:** Reeded **Mint:** Paris **Note:** Without mint mark.

Date	Mintage	F12	VF20	XF40	MS60	MS63
1920	14,363,000	6.00	15.00	40.00	100	175
1921	Inc. above	0.75	1.50	3.00	12.50	20.00
1922	29,463,000	0.50	1.00	2.00	7.50	12.00
1923	43,960,000	0.50	1.00	2.00	7.50	12.00
1924 Open 4	29,631,000	0.50	1.00	2.00	7.50	12.00
1924 Closed 4	Inc. above	0.65	1.50	3.00	10.00	18.00
1925/3	31,607,000	0.75	1.75	4.00	15.00	30.00
1925	Inc. above	0.50	1.00	2.00	8.00	14.00
1926	2,962,000	7.00	18.00	30.00	100	150
1927	1,678,000	50.00	150	300	600	1,000

KM# 886 2 FRANCS

8.00 g., Aluminum-Bronze, 27 mm. **Obv:** Laureate head left **Rev:** Denomination and date flanked by cornucopias

Date	Mintage	F12	VF20	XF40	MS60	MS63
1931	1,717,000	3.00	6.00	12.00	35.00	50.00
1932	8,943,000	0.75	1.50	3.00	10.00	18.00
1933	8,413,000	0.75	1.50	3.00	10.00	18.00
1934	6,896,000	1.25	2.50	6.00	12.00	20.00
1935	298,000	12.00	20.00	40.00	90.00	125
1936	12,394,000	0.25	1.00	2.00	6.00	10.00
1937	11,055,000	0.25	1.00	2.00	6.00	10.00
1938	28,072,000	0.20	0.50	1.00	5.00	9.00
1939	25,403,000	0.20	0.50	1.00	5.00	9.00
1940	9,716,000	1.00	2.00	3.50	10.00	18.00
1941	16,684,000	0.25	1.00	2.00	6.00	10.00

KM# 886a.1 2 FRANCS

2.20 g., Aluminum, 27 mm. **Obv:** Laureate head left **Rev:** Denomination and date flanked by cornucopias

Date	Mintage	VF20	XF40	MS60	MS63	MS65
1941	Inc. above	0.50	1.00	3.00	5.00	—
1944	7,224,000	1.50	4.00	12.00	20.00	—
1945	16,636,000	1.00	2.50	7.00	10.00	—
1946	34,930,000	0.50	1.00	3.50	5.00	—
1947	78,984,000	0.30	1.00	2.50	4.00	—
1948	32,354,000	0.50	1.00	3.50	5.00	—
1949	13,683,000	0.50	1.00	2.50	4.00	—
1950	12,191,000	0.50	1.00	2.50	4.00	—
1958	9,906,000	0.50	1.00	3.50	5.00	—
1959	17,774,000	0.50	1.00	3.50	5.00	—

KM# 904.1 2 FRANCS

2.20 g., Aluminum, 27 mm. **Obv:** Double bit axe, grain sprigs flank **Rev:** Oak leaves flank denomination, date below **Mint:** Paris **Note:** Without mint mark. Issued for Vichy French State.

Date	Mintage	F12	VF20	XF40	MS60	MS63
1943	106,997,000	0.20	0.50	1.00	10.00	25.00
1944	25,546,000	0.75	1.50	3.50	12.00	25.00

KM# 904.2 2 FRANCS

2.20 g., Aluminum, 27 mm. **Obv:** Grain sprigs flank double bit axe **Rev:** Oak leaves flank denomination, date below **Mint:** Beaumont - Le Roger

Date	Mintage	F12	VF20	XF40	MS60	MS63
1943 B	34,131,000	3.50	7.00	12.00	20.00	40.00
1944 B	10,298,000	1.50	3.00	6.00	14.00	35.00

KM# 886a.2 2 FRANCS

2.20 g., Aluminum, 27 mm. **Obv:** Laureate head left **Rev:** Denomination and date flanked by cornucopias **Mint:** Beaumont - Le Roger

Date	Mintage	VF20	XF40	MS60	MS63	MS65
1944 B	170,000	—	—	—	—	—
1945 B	1,726,000	7.00	15.00	35.00	50.00	—
1946 B	6,018,000	4.00	8.00	20.00	30.00	—
1947 B	26,220,000	0.50	1.00	3.50	5.00	—
1948 B	39,090,000	0.50	1.00	3.00	5.00	—
1949 B	23,955,000	0.50	1.00	3.50	5.00	—
1950 B	18,185,000	1.00	3.00	5.00	8.00	—

KM# 904.3 2 FRANCS

2.20 g., Aluminum, 27 mm. **Obv:** Grain sprigs flank double bit axe **Rev:** Oak leaves flank denomination, date below **Mint:** Castelsarrasin

Date	Mintage	F12	VF20	XF40	MS60	MS63
1944 C	19,470,000	1.25	2.50	5.00	18.00	30.00

KM# 905 2 FRANCS

8.15 g., Brass, 27 mm. **Obv:** FRANCE within wreath **Rev:** Large denomination above date **Mint:** Philadelphia **Note:** Without mint mark. Issued during Allied Occupation for circulation in Algeria and France.

Date	Mintage	F12	VF20	XF40	MS60	MS63
1944	50,000,000	1.00	2.00	6.00	75.00	300

KM# 886a.3 2 FRANCS

2.20 g., Aluminum, 27 mm. **Obv:** Laureate head left **Rev:** Denomination and date flanked by cornucopias **Mint:** Castelsarrasin

Date	Mintage	VF20	XF40	MS60	MS63	MS65
1945 C	1,165,000	10.00	25.00	65.00	110	—

KM# 887 5 FRANCS

6.00 g., Nickel, 23.7 mm. **Obv:** Head right, date below **Rev:** Denomination flanked by grain sprigs **Mint:** Paris **Note:** Without mint mark.

Date	Mintage	F12	VF20	XF40	MS60	MS63
1933 (a)	105,029,373	0.75	1.50	3.50	20.00	50.00

KM# 888 5 FRANCS

12.00 g., Nickel, 31 mm. **Obv:** Laureate head left **Rev:** Denomination above date within sectioned wreath **Mint:** Paris **Note:** Without mint mark.

Date	Mintage	F12	VF20	XF40	MS60	MS63
1933 (a)	56,686,000	0.25	0.75	2.50	8.00	14.00
1935 (a)	54,164,000	0.25	0.75	2.50	8.00	14.00
1936 (a)	117,000	400	700	1,200	1,850	2,100
1937 (a)	157,000	45.00	75.00	140	300	600
1938 (a)	4,977,000	12.00	25.00	50.00	120	230
1939 (a)	—	700	1,200	2,000	4,000	—

KM# 888a.1 5 FRANCS

12.00 g., Aluminum-Bronze, 31 mm. **Obv:** Laureate head left **Rev:** Denomination above date within sectioned wreath **Note:** Struck for Colonial use in Algeria.

Date	Mintage	VF20	XF40	MS60	MS63	MS65
1938 (a)	10,144,000	10.00	18.00	85.00	120	—
1939 (a)	Inc. above	5.00	12.00	30.00	60.00	—
1940 (a)	38,758,000	2.00	3.50	10.00	40.00	—

KM# 901 5 FRANCS

4.00 g., Copper-Nickel, 22 mm. **Obv:** Double bit axe divides denomination, date below **Rev:** Head with collar left **Mint:** Paris **Note:** Without mint mark.

Date	Mintage	F12	VF20	XF40	MS60	MS63
1941 (a)	13,782,000	75.00	120	250	415	750

Note: Never released into circulation.

KM# 888a.2 5 FRANCS

12.00 g., Aluminum-Bronze, 31 mm. **Obv:** Laureate head left **Rev:** Denomination above date within sectioned wreath **Note:** Struck for Colonial use in Africa.

Date	Mintage	VF20	XF40	MS60	MS63	MS65
1945 (a) Open 9	13,044,000	2.00	4.00	11.00	18.00	—
1946 (a) Open 9	21,790,000	2.00	4.00	11.00	18.00	—
1947 (a)	2,662,000	200	500	1,000	1,875	2,100

Note: Date exists with both open and closed 9s.

KM# 888a.3 5 FRANCS

12.00 g., Aluminum-Bronze, 31 mm. **Obv:** Laureate head left **Rev:** Denomination above date within sectioned wreath **Mint:** Castelsarrasin

Date	Mintage	VF20	XF40	MS60	MS63	MS65
1945 C Open 9	Inc. above	7.00	15.00	30.00	50.00	—
1946 C Open 9	Inc. above	15.00	30.00	60.00	125	—

KM# 888b.1 5 FRANCS

3.75 g., Aluminum, 31 mm. **Obv:** Laureate head left **Rev:** Denomination above date within sectioned wreath **Edge:** Plain **Mint:** Paris **Note:** Without mint mark.

Date	Mintage	VF20	XF40	MS60	MS63	MS65
1945 (a) Open 9	95,399,000	0.35	1.50	6.00	9.00	—
1946 (a) Open 9	61,332,000	0.35	1.50	6.00	9.00	—
1947 (a) Open 9	46,576,000	0.35	1.50	6.00	9.00	—
1947 (a) Closed 9	Inc. above	0.35	1.50	6.00	9.00	—
1948 (a) Open 9	104,473,000	3.00	6.00	12.50	25.00	—
1948 (a) Closed 9	Inc. above	10.00	30.00	50.00	80.00	—
1949 (a) Closed 9	203,252,000	0.35	0.75	3.00	5.00	—
1950 (a) Closed 9	128,372,000	0.35	0.75	3.00	5.00	—
1952 (a) Closed 9	4,000,000	40.00	100	225	450	—

KM# 888b.2 5 FRANCS

3.75 g., Aluminum, 31 mm. **Obv:** Laureate head left **Rev:** Denomination above date within sectioned wreath **Mint:** Beaumont - Le Roger

Date	Mintage	VF20	XF40	MS60	MS63	MS65
1945 B Open 9	6,043,000	3.00	5.00	15.00	28.00	—
1946 B Open 9	13,360,000	1.50	3.00	12.00	20.00	—
1947 B Open 9	30,839,000	1.00	2.50	8.00	14.00	—
1947 B Closed 9	Inc. above	1.00	2.50	8.00	14.00	—
1948 B Open 9	28,047,000	40.00	100	275	450	840
1949 B Closed 9	48,414,000	1.00	2.50	8.00	14.00	—
1950 B Closed 9	28,952,000	1.50	3.50	9.00	16.00	—

KM# 888b.3 5 FRANCS

3.75 g., Aluminum, 31 mm. **Obv:** Laureate head left **Rev:** Denomination above date within sectioned wreath **Mint:** Castelsarrasin

Date	Mintage	VF20	XF40	MS60	MS63	MS65
1945 C Open 9	2,208,000	15.00	28.00	60.00	85.00	—
1946 C Open 9	1,269,000	18.00	38.00	75.00	95.00	—

KM# 846 10 FRANCS

3.23 g., 0.900 Gold 0.0933 oz. AGW **Mint:** Paris

Date	Mintage	F12	VF20	XF40	MS60	MS63
1901	2,100,000	—	—	120	175	200
1905	1,426,000	—	—	120	175	200
1906	3,665,000	—	—	120	175	200
1907	3,364,000	—	—	120	175	200
1908	1,650,000	—	—	120	175	200
1909	599,000	—	120	175	250	410
1910	2,110,000	—	—	120	150	160
1911	1,881,000	—	—	120	150	160
1912	1,756,000	—	—	120	150	160
1914	3,041,000	—	—	120	150	160

KM# 878 10 FRANCS

10.00 g., 0.680 Silver 0.2186 oz. ASW, 28 mm. **Mint:** Paris **Note:** Without mint mark letters, but with mint symbols

Date	Mintage	F12	VF20	XF40	MS60	MS63
1929	16,292,000	4.00	8.00	9.00	15.00	25.00
1930	36,986,000	—	4.00	8.00	12.00	19.00
1931	35,468,000	—	4.00	8.00	12.00	19.00
1932	40,288,000	—	4.00	8.00	10.00	15.00
1933	31,146,000	—	4.00	8.00	10.00	15.00
1934	52,001,000	—	4.00	8.00	10.00	15.00
1936	—	—	—	—	—	—
1937	52,000	40.00	70.00	150	500	900
1938	14,090,000	4.00	8.00	9.00	16.00	27.50
1939	8,298,999	4.00	8.00	11.00	20.00	35.00

KM# 908.1 10 FRANCS

7.00 g., Copper-Nickel, 26 mm. **Obv:** Laureate head right, long leaves and short leaves **Rev:** Denomination above date, inscription below, grain columns flank **Edge:** Reeded **Note:** Large head.

Date	Mintage	F12	VF20	XF40	MS60	MS63
1945 (ll)	6,557,000	0.25	0.75	2.00	6.00	9.00
1945 (sl)	Inc. above	15.00	30.00	50.00	90.00	140
1946 (ll)	24,409,000	185	300	400	900	1,350
1946 (sl)	Inc. above	0.25	0.50	2.00	5.00	8.00
1947	41,627,000	0.25	0.50	1.00	3.00	5.00

KM# 908.2 10 FRANCS

7.00 g., Copper-Nickel, 26 mm. **Obv:** Laureate head right **Rev:** Denomination above date, inscription below, grain columns flank **Edge:** Reeded **Mint:** Beaumont - Le Roger **Note:** Large head

Date	Mintage	F12	VF20	XF40	MS60	MS63
1946 B (ll)	8,452,000	20.00	35.00	50.00	85.00	125
1946 B (sl)	Inc. above	0.25	0.75	2.00	9.00	16.00
1947 B	17,188,000	0.25	0.50	2.00	8.00	14.00

KM# 909.1 10 FRANCS

7.00 g., Copper-Nickel, 26 mm. **Obv:** Laureate head right, small head **Rev:** Denomination above date, inscription below, grain columns flank **Edge:** Reeded **Mint:** Paris **Note:** Without mint mark.

Date	Mintage	F12	VF20	XF40	MS60	MS63
1947	Inc. above	0.30	0.75	1.50	3.50	5.00
1948	155,945,000	0.20	0.35	0.75	2.00	3.50
1949	118,149,000	0.20	0.35	0.75	2.00	3.50

KM# 909.2 10 FRANCS

7.00 g., Copper-Nickel, 26 mm. **Obv:** Large head **Rev:** Denomination above date, inscription below, grain columns flank **Edge:** Reeded **Mint:** Beaumont - Le Roger

Date	Mintage	F12	VF20	XF40	MS60	MS63
1947 B	Inc. above	1.00	2.50	6.00	30.00	50.00
1948 B	40,500,000	0.35	0.75	2.00	7.00	10.00
1949 B	29,518,000	0.35	0.75	2.00	7.00	10.00

KM# 915.1 10 FRANCS

3.00 g., Aluminum-Bronze, 20 mm. **Obv:** Head left **Rev:** Denomination above date at right, rooster above laurel leaves at left **Edge:** Plain **Mint:** Paris **Note:** Without mint mark.

Date	Mintage	F12	VF20	XF40	MS60	MS63
1950	13,534,000	0.35	0.65	1.50	5.00	8.00
1951	153,689,000	0.20	0.35	0.75	2.00	3.50
1952	76,810,000	0.20	0.35	0.75	2.00	3.50
1953	46,272,000	0.25	0.50	0.75	2.50	4.00
1954	2,207,000	4.00	12.00	20.00	35.00	60.00
1955	47,466,000	0.20	0.35	0.75	2.50	4.00
1956	2,570,000	—	—	—	—	—
Note: Requires Confirmation.						
1957	26,351,000	0.50	1.00	2.00	4.50	7.50
1958 (w)	27,213,000	0.50	1.00	2.00	4.50	7.50
1959	125,000	—	—	—	—	—
Note: Requires Confirmation.						

KM# 915.2 10 FRANCS

3.00 g., Aluminum-Bronze, 20 mm. **Obv:** Head left **Rev:** Rooster above laurel sprig, denominaton at right **Mint:** Beaumont - Le Roger

Date	Mintage	F12	VF20	XF40	MS60	MS63
1950 B	4,808,000	1.00	3.00	6.00	17.50	30.00
1951 B	106,866,000	0.20	0.35	0.75	2.00	3.00
1952 B	72,346,000	0.20	0.35	0.75	2.00	3.00
1953 B	36,466,000	0.25	0.50	1.00	3.00	4.50
1954 B	21,634,000	0.75	1.50	3.50	7.00	10.00
1958 B	1,500,000	—	—	—	—	—
Note: Requires Confirmation.						

KM# 847 20 FRANCS

6.45 g., 0.900 Gold 0.1867 oz. AGW **Edge Lettering:** DIEU PROTEGE LA FRANCE

Date	Mintage	F12	VF20	XF40	MS60	MS63
1901 A	2,643,000	—	—	237	300	320
1902 A	2,394,000	—	—	237	300	320
1903 A	4,405,000	—	—	237	300	320
1904 A	7,706,000	—	—	237	300	320
1905 A	9,158,000	—	—	237	300	320
1906 A	14,613,000	—	—	237	300	320

KM# 857 20 FRANCS

6.45 g., 0.900 Gold 0.1867 oz. AGW **Obv:** Oak leaf wreath encircles liberty head right **Rev:** Rooster divides denomination, date below **Edge Lettering:** LIBERTE EGALITE FRATERNITE **Note:** All dates from 1907-1914 have been officially restruck.

Date	Mintage	F12	VF20	XF40	MS60	MS63
1906	—	—	—	237	300	320
1907	17,716,000	—	—	237	300	320
1908	6,721,000	—	—	237	300	320
1909	9,637,000	—	—	237	300	320
1910	5,779,000	—	—	237	300	320
1911	5,346,000	—	—	237	300	320
1912	10,332,000	—	—	237	300	320
1913	12,163,000	—	—	237	300	320
1914	6,518,000	—	—	237	300	320

KM# 879 20 FRANCS

20.00 g., 0.680 Silver 0.4372 oz. ASW, 35 mm. **Obv:** Laureate head right, long and short leaves **Rev:** Denomination above date, inscription below, grain columns flank **Mint:** Paris **Note:** Without mint mark.

Date	Mintage	F12	VF20	XF40	MS60	MS63
1929 (ll)	3,234,000	—	8.00	15.00	40.00	90.00
1933 (sl)	24,449,048	—	8.00	15.00	22.50	45.00
Note: Counterfeits exist in bronze-aluminum with thin silver sheath.						
1933 (ll)	Inc. above	—	8.00	15.00	22.50	45.00
1934 (sl)	11,785,000	—	8.00	15.00	25.00	50.00
1936 (sl)	48,000	—	200	450	600	—
1937 (sl)	1,189,000	—	8.00	15.00	25.00	50.00
1938 (sl)	10,910,000	—	8.00	15.00	25.00	40.00
1939 (sl)	3,918	—	—	—	4,000	—

KM# 916.1 20 FRANCS

4.00 g., Aluminum-Bronze, 23 mm. **Obv:** Head left, "GEORGES GUIRAUD" behind head **Rev:** Denomination above date at right, rooster above laurel branch at left **Edge:** Plain **Mint:** Paris **Note:** The 4-plume variety has been identified as a counterfeit.

Date	Mintage	F12	VF20	XF40	MS60	MS63
1950	5,779,000	0.50	1.00	2.50	7.00	12.00

KM# 916.2 20 FRANCS

4.00 g., Aluminum-Bronze, 23 mm. **Obv:** Head left **Rev:** Rooster above laurel sprig, denomination at right **Mint:** Beaumont - Le Roger **Note:** The 4-plume variety has been identified as a counterfeit.

Date	Mintage	F12	VF20	XF40	MS60	MS63
1950 B	—	1.50	3.00	7.00	20.00	35.00
Note: 3 plumes						
1950 B	—	40.00	85.00	150	160	200
Note: 4 plumes						

KM# 917.1 20 FRANCS

4.00 g., Aluminum-Bronze, 23 mm. **Obv:** Head left, "G. GUIRAUD" behind head **Rev:** Denomination above date at right, rooster above laurel branch at left **Mint:** Paris **Note:** Without mint mark.

Date	Mintage	F12	VF20	XF40	MS60	MS63
1950	120,656,000	2.00	6.00	12.00	30.00	75.00

Date	Mintage	F12	VF20	XF40	MS60	MS63
Note: 3 plumes						
1950	Inc. above	0.25	0.40	1.00	2.50	3.50
Note: 4 plumes						
1951	97,922,000	0.25	0.40	1.00	2.50	3.50
Note: 4 plumes						
1952	130,281,000	0.25	0.40	1.00	2.50	3.50
Note: 4 plumes						
1953	60,158,000	0.30	0.50	1.00	2.50	3.50
Note: 4 plumes						

KM# 917.2 20 FRANCS

4.00 g., Aluminum-Bronze, 23 mm. **Obv:** "G. GUIRAUD" behind head **Rev:** Rooster above laurel sprig, denomination at right **Mint:** Beaumont - Le Roger

Date	Mintage	F12	VF20	XF40	MS60	MS63
1950 B	43,355,000	25.00	35.00	45.00	100	200
Note: 3 plumes						
1950 B	Inc. above	0.50	1.00	3.00	6.50	10.00
Note: 4 plumes						
1951 B	46,815,000	0.30	0.50	1.75	3.50	5.00
Note: 4 plumes						
1952 B	54,381,000	0.30	0.50	1.75	3.50	5.00
Note: 4 plumes						
1953 B	42,410,000	0.30	0.50	1.75	3.50	5.00
Note: 4 plumes						
1954 B	1,573,000	85.00	125	250	600	—
Note: 4 plumes						

KM# 831 50 FRANCS

16.13 g., 0.900 Gold 0.4667 oz. AGW **Obv:** Standing Genius writing the Constitution, rooster at right, fasces at left **Rev:** Denomination above date within circular wreath **Mint:** Paris

Date	Mintage	F12	VF20	XF40	MS60	MS63
1904 A	20,000	600	850	1,000	1,650	3,000

KM# 918.1 50 FRANCS

8.00 g., Aluminum-Bronze, 27 mm. **Obv:** Head left **Rev:** Denomination above date at right, rooster above laurel branch at left **Edge:** Plain **Mint:** Paris **Note:** Without mint mark.

Date	Mintage	F12	VF20	XF40	MS60	MS63
1950	600,000	100	200	225	600	—
1951	68,630,000	0.50	1.00	2.25	5.50	9.00
1952	74,212,000	0.50	1.00	2.25	5.50	9.00
1953	63,172,000	0.50	1.00	2.25	5.50	9.00
1954	997,000	15.00	35.00	65.00	110	225
1958 (w)	501,000	25.00	50.00	85.00	240	400

KM# 918.2 50 FRANCS

Aluminum-Bronze, 27 mm. **Obv:** Head left **Rev:** Rooster above laurel, denomination at right **Mint:** Beaumont - Le Roger

Date	Mintage	F12	VF20	XF40	MS60	MS63
1950 B Rare	—	—	1,000	3,000	—	—
1951 B	11,829,000	0.75	1.50	3.00	9.00	16.00
1952 B	13,432,000	1.00	2.00	5.00	10.00	28.00
1953 B	23,376,000	0.65	1.25	2.50	8.00	14.00
1954 B	6,531,000	3.00	5.50	11.50	30.00	50.00

KM# 832 100 FRANCS

32.26 g., 0.900 Gold 0.9334 oz. AGW **Obv:** Standing Genius writing the Constitution, rooster on right, fasces on left **Rev:** Denomination above date within circular wreath **Edge Lettering:** DIEU PROTEGE LA FRANCE **Mint:** Paris

Date	Mintage	F12	VF20	XF40	MS60	MS63
1901 A	10,000	—	—	1,250	1,700	2,300
1902 A	10,000	—	—	1,250	1,700	2,300
1903 A	10,000	—	—	1,250	1,700	2,300
1904 A	20,000	—	—	1,250	1,700	2,300
1905 A	10,000	—	—	1,250	1,700	2,300
1906 A	30,000	—	—	1,250	1,700	2,300

KM# 858 100 FRANCS

32.26 g., 0.900 Gold 0.9334 oz. AGW **Obv:** Standing Genius writing the constitution, rooster on right, column on the left **Rev:** Denomination and date within wreath **Edge Lettering:** LIBERTE EGALITE FRATERNITE

Date	Mintage	F12	VF20	XF40	MS60	MS63
1907 A	20,000	—	—	1,250	1,700	2,200
1908 A	23,000	—	—	1,250	1,700	2,200
1909 A	20,000	—	—	1,250	1,700	2,200
1910 A	20,000	—	—	1,250	1,700	2,200
1911 A	30,000	—	—	1,250	1,700	2,200
1912 A	20,000	—	—	1,250	1,700	2,200
1913 A	30,000	—	—	1,250	1,700	2,200
1914 A No known examples exist	1,281	—	—	—	—	—

KM# 880 100 FRANCS

6.55 g., 0.900 Gold 0.1895 oz. AGW **Obv:** Winged head left **Rev:** Denomination above grain sprig, date below, laurel and oak branches flank **Mint:** Paris **Note:** Without mint mark.

Date	Mintage	F12	VF20	XF40	MS60	MS63
1929	50	—	—	7,000	9,000	—
1932	—	—	—	6,000	7,500	—
1933	Est. 300	—	—	4,000	6,000	—
1934 Rare	—	—	—	—	—	—
1935	6,102,000	—	242	800	1,700	2,100
1936	7,689,000	—	242	800	1,700	2,100

KM# 919.1 100 FRANCS

6.00 g., Copper-Nickel, 24 mm. **Obv:** Liberty bust with torch right **Rev:** Denomination above date at left, grain sprigs at right **Edge:** Reeded

Date	Mintage	F12	VF20	XF40	MS60	MS63
1954	97,285,000	—	1.00	2.50	7.00	10.00
1955	152,517,000	—	0.75	1.50	4.50	6.00
1956	7,578,000	—	5.00	12.00	35.00	70.00
1957	11,312,000	—	3.00	6.00	18.00	30.00
1958 (w)	3,256,000	—	5.50	10.00	25.00	60.00
1958 (o)	Inc. above	—	20.00	30.00	100	150

KM# 919.2 100 FRANCS

6.00 g., Copper-Nickel, 24 mm. **Obv:** Liberty bust with torch right **Rev:** Denomination and date left of grain sprigs **Edge:** Reeded **Mint:** Beaumont - Le Roger

Date	Mintage	F12	VF20	XF40	MS60	MS63
1954 B	86,261,000	—	1.25	2.50	5.00	8.00
1955 B	136,585,000	—	0.75	1.50	3.50	5.00
1956 B	19,154,000	—	2.00	4.50	10.00	15.00
1957 B	25,702,000	—	2.00	4.50	12.50	22.00
1958 B	54,072,000	—	2.00	4.50	11.50	20.00

REFORM COINAGE

1 Old Franc = 1 New Centime;
100 New Centimes = 1 New Franc
Commencing 1960

KM# 928 CENTIME

1.65 g., Stainless Steel, 15 mm. **Obv:** Cursive legend surrounds grain sprig **Rev:** Cursive denomination, date at top **Edge:** Plain **Mint:** Paris **Note:** 1991-1993 dated coins, non-Proof, exist in both coin and medal alignment. Values given here are for medal alignment examples. Pieces struck in coin alignment have been traded for as much as $50.00.

Date	Mintage	VF20	XF40	MS60	MS63	MS65
1962	34,200,000	—	0.10	0.25	0.35	0.50
1963	16,811,000	0.10	0.15	0.35	0.50	0.65
1964	22,654,000	—	0.10	0.25	0.35	0.50
1965	47,799,000	—	0.10	0.25	0.35	0.50
1966	19,688,000	—	0.10	0.25	0.35	0.50
1967	52,308,000	—	0.10	0.25	0.35	0.50
1968	40,890,000	—	0.10	0.25	0.35	0.50
1969	35,430,000	—	0.10	0.25	0.35	0.50
1970	29,600,000	—	0.10	0.25	0.35	0.50
1971	3,082,000	—	0.10	0.25	0.35	0.50
1972	1,014,999	0.10	0.15	0.35	0.50	0.65
1973	1,806,000	0.10	0.15	0.35	0.50	0.65
1974	7,949,000	—	0.10	0.25	0.35	0.50
1975	771,000	0.10	0.25	0.50	1.00	1.50
1976	4,482,000	—	0.10	0.25	0.35	0.50
1977	6,425,000	—	0.10	0.25	0.35	0.50
1978	1,236,000	0.10	0.15	0.35	0.50	0.65
1979	2,213,000	—	0.10	0.25	0.35	0.50
1980	60,000	—	—	—	1.00	1.50
1981	50,000	—	—	—	1.00	1.50
1982	69,000	—	—	—	1.00	1.50
1983	101,000	—	—	—	1.00	1.50
1984	50,000	—	—	—	1.00	1.50
1985	20,000	—	—	—	1.00	1.50
1986 In sets only	48,000	—	—	—	1.00	1.50
1987	100,000	—	—	—	1.00	1.50
1988	100,000	—	—	—	1.00	1.50
1989	83,000	—	—	—	1.00	1.50
1990	15,000	—	—	—	1.00	1.50
1991	2,511	—	—	—	600	800
1991	10,000	**PF65** 2.00				
1991 Medallic rotation	2,500	—	—	—	400	600
1992	85,000	—	—	20.00	22.00	32.00
1992	15,000	**PF65** 2.00				
1992 Medallic rotation	2,698	—	—	35.00	50.00	60.00
1993	40,000	—	—	15.00	20.00	30.00
1993	10,000	**PF65** 2.00				
1993 Medallic rotation	3,095	—	—	35.00	50.00	60.00
1994 bee	20,000	—	—	15.00	20.00	30.00
1994 fish	10,000	—	—	20.00	30.00	50.00
1995	25,000	—	—	—	1.00	1.50
1995	10,000	**PF65** 2.00				
1996	17,000	—	—	—	1.00	1.50
1996	8,000	**PF65** 2.00				
1997 In sets only	15,000	—	—	—	—	1.50
1997	10,000	**PF65** 2.00				
1998 In sets only	—	—	—	—	—	1.50
1998	—	**PF65** 2.00				
1999 In sets only	—	—	—	—	—	1.50
1999	—	**PF65** 2.00				
2000 In sets only	—	—	—	—	—	1.50
2000	—	**PF65** 2.00				

KM# 928a CENTIME

2.50 g., 0.750 Gold 0.0603 oz. AGW **Obv:** Cursive legend surrounds grain sprig, medallic alignment **Rev:** Cursive denomination, date above, medallic alignment **Edge:** Plain **Mint:** Paris **Note:** Last Centime.

Date	Mintage	VF20	XF40	MS60	MS63	MS65
2000	25,000	—	—	—	—	185

KM# 927 5 CENTIMES

3.50 g., Stainless Steel **Obv:** Cursive legend surrounds grain sprig **Rev:** Cursive denomination, date above **Mint:** Paris

Date	Mintage	VF20	XF40	MS60	MS63	MS65
1961	39,000,000	0.20	0.50	2.00	3.00	4.00
1962	166,360,000	0.15	0.20	0.75	1.00	1.25
1963	71,900,000	0.20	0.40	1.00	1.50	0.25
1964	126,480,000	0.15	0.30	0.75	1.00	1.25

KM# 933 5 CENTIMES

2.00 g., Aluminum-Bronze, 17 mm. **Obv:** Liberty bust left **Rev:** Denomination above date, grain sprig below, laurel branch at left **Edge:** Plain **Mint:** Paris **Note:** 1991-1993 dated coins, non-Proof exist in both coin and medal alignment.

Date	Mintage	VF20	XF40	MS60	MS63	MS65
1966	502,512,000	—	—	0.10	0.15	0.25
1967	11,747,000	—	5.00	15.00	25.00	40.00
1968	110,395,000	—	—	0.10	0.15	0.25
1969	94,955,000	—	—	0.10	0.15	0.25
1970	58,900,000	—	—	0.10	0.15	0.25
1971	93,190,000	—	—	0.10	0.15	0.25
1972	100,515,000	—	—	0.10	0.15	0.25
1973	100,344,000	—	—	0.10	0.15	0.25
1974	103,890,000	—	—	0.10	0.15	0.25
1975	95,835,000	—	—	0.10	0.15	0.25
1976	148,395,000	—	—	0.10	0.15	0.25
1977	115,285,000	—	—	0.10	0.15	0.25
1978	189,804,000	—	—	0.10	0.15	0.25
1979	180,000,000	—	—	0.10	0.15	0.25
1980	180,010,000	—	—	0.10	0.15	0.25
1981	134,974,000	—	—	0.10	0.15	0.25
1982	138,000,000	—	—	0.10	0.15	0.25
1983	132,000,000	—	—	0.10	0.15	0.25
1984	150,000,000	—	—	0.10	0.15	0.25
1985	170,000,000	—	—	0.10	0.15	0.25
1986	280,000,000	—	—	0.10	0.15	0.25
1987	310,000,000	—	—	0.10	0.15	0.25
1988	200,000,000	—	—	0.10	0.15	0.25
1989	84,000	—	—	10.00	20.00	25.00
1990	79,992,000	—	—	0.20	0.30	0.40
1991	49,994,000	—	—	0.20	0.30	0.40
1991	10,000	PF65 1.00				
1992	179,996,000	—	—	0.20	0.30	0.40
1992	15,000	PF65 1.00				
1993	154,988,000	—	—	0.20	0.30	0.40
1993	10,000	PF65 1.00				
1994	—	—	—	0.20	0.30	0.40
1994 fish	60,000,000	—	—	0.20	0.30	0.40
1994 fish Proof	10,000	—	—	—	—	—
1994 bee	59,996,000	—	—	0.20	0.30	0.40
1995	129,991,999	—	—	0.20	0.30	0.40
1995	10,000	PF65 1.00				
1996	139,990,000	—	—	0.20	0.30	0.40
1996	8,000	PF65 1.00				
1997	199,995,000	—	—	0.20	0.30	0.40
1997	10,000	PF65 1.00				
1998	300,084,000	—	—	0.20	0.30	0.40
1998	—	PF65 1.00				
1999 In sets only	—	—	—	—	—	2.50
1999	—	PF65 1.00				
2000 In sets only	—	—	—	—	—	2.50
2000	—	PF65 1.00				

KM# 929 10 CENTIMES

3.00 g., Aluminum-Bronze, 20 mm. **Obv:** Liberty bust left **Rev:** Denomination above date, grain sprig below, laurel branch at left **Edge:** Plain **Mint:** Paris **Note:** Without mint mark. 1991-1993 dated coins, non-Proof, exist in both coin and medal alignment.

Date	Mintage	VF20	XF40	MS60	MS63	MS65
1962	29,100,000	—	—	0.40	0.60	0.75
1963	217,601,000	—	—	0.10	0.15	0.25
1964	93,409,000	—	—	0.20	0.30	0.40
1965	41,220,000	—	—	0.30	0.50	0.65
1966	16,428,999	—	—	0.40	0.60	0.75
1967	196,728,000	—	—	0.10	0.15	0.25
1968	111,700,000	—	—	0.10	0.15	0.25
1969	129,530,000	—	—	0.10	0.15	0.25
1970	77,020,000	—	—	0.10	0.15	0.25
1971	26,280,000	—	—	0.10	0.15	0.25
1972	45,700,000	—	—	0.10	0.15	0.25
1973	58,000,000	—	—	0.10	0.15	0.25
1974	91,990,000	—	—	0.10	0.15	0.25
1975	74,450,000	—	—	0.10	0.15	0.25
1976	137,320,000	—	—	0.10	0.15	0.25
1977	140,110,000	—	—	0.10	0.15	0.25
1978	154,360,000	—	—	0.10	0.15	0.25
1979	140,000,000	—	—	0.10	0.15	0.25
1980	140,010,000	—	—	0.10	0.15	0.25
1981	135,000,000	—	—	0.10	0.15	0.25
1982	110,000,000	—	—	0.10	0.15	0.25
1983	150,000,000	—	—	0.10	0.15	0.25
1984	200,000,000	—	—	0.10	0.15	0.25
1985	170,000,000	—	—	0.10	0.15	0.25
1986	150,000,000	—	—	0.10	0.15	0.25
1987	150,000,000	—	—	0.10	0.15	0.25
1988	145,000,000	—	—	0.10	0.15	0.25
1989	179,984,000	—	—	0.10	0.15	0.25
1990	179,992,000	—	—	0.10	0.15	0.25
1991	179,986,000	—	—	0.10	0.15	0.25
1991	10,000	PF65 1.00				
1992	179,996,000	—	—	0.10	0.15	0.25
1992	15,000	PF65 1.00				
1993	154,988,000	—	—	0.10	0.15	0.25
1993	10,000	PF65 1.00				
1994 Fish	103,000,000	—	—	0.10	0.15	0.25
1994 Fish	10,000	PF65 1.00				
1994 Bee	76,988,000	—	—	0.10	0.15	0.25
1995	169,996,000	—	—	0.10	0.15	0.25
1995	10,000	PF65 1.00				
1996	179,981,000	—	—	0.10	0.15	0.25
1996	8,000	PF65 1.00				
1997	551,991,000	—	—	0.10	0.15	0.25
1997	10,000	PF65 1.00				
1998	350,000,000	—	—	0.10	0.15	0.25
1998	—	PF65 1.00				
1999 In sets only	—	—	—	—	—	3.00
1999	—	PF65 1.00				
2000	60,000,000	—	—	0.10	0.15	0.25
2000	—	PF65 1.00				

KM# 930 20 CENTIMES

4.00 g., Aluminum-Bronze, 23.5 mm. **Obv:** Liberty bust left **Rev:** Denomination above date, grain sprig below, laurel branch at left **Edge:** Plain **Mint:** Paris **Note:** Without mint mark. 1991-1993 dated coins, non-Proof, exist in both coin and medal alignment.

Date	Mintage	VF20	XF40	MS60	MS63	MS65
1962	48,200,000	—	—	0.25	0.50	0.65
1963	190,330,000	—	—	0.30	0.50	0.65
1964	127,521,000	—	—	0.30	0.50	0.65
1965	27,024,000	—	—	0.40	0.60	0.75
1966	21,762,000	—	—	0.40	0.60	0.75
1967	138,780,000	—	—	0.15	0.25	0.35
1968	77,408,000	—	—	0.20	0.30	0.40
1969	50,570,000	—	—	0.20	0.30	0.40
1970	70,040,000	—	—	0.15	0.25	0.35
1971	31,080,000	—	—	0.15	0.25	0.35
1972	39,740,000	—	—	0.15	0.25	0.35
1973	45,240,000	—	—	0.15	0.25	0.35
1974	54,250,000	—	—	0.15	0.25	0.35
1975	40,570,000	—	—	0.15	0.25	0.35
1976	117,610,000	—	—	0.10	0.15	0.25
1977	100,340,000	—	—	0.10	0.15	0.25
1978	125,015,000	—	—	0.10	0.15	0.25
1979	70,000,000	—	—	0.10	0.15	0.25
1980	20,010,000	—	—	0.15	0.25	0.35
1981	125,000,000	—	—	0.10	0.15	0.25
1982	150,000,000	—	—	0.10	0.15	0.25
1983	110,000,000	—	—	0.10	0.15	0.25
1984	200,000,000	—	—	0.10	0.15	0.25
1985	150,000,000	—	—	0.10	0.15	0.25
1986	40,000,000	—	—	0.10	0.15	0.25
1987	60,000,000	—	—	0.10	0.15	0.25
1988	220,000,000	—	—	0.10	0.15	0.25
1989	139,985,000	—	—	0.10	0.15	0.25
1990	49,990,000	—	—	0.10	0.15	0.25
1991 1	10,000	PF65 1.00				
1991	39,992,000	—	—	0.10	0.15	0.25
1992	89,985,000	—	—	0.10	0.15	0.25
1992 1	15,000	PF65 1.00				
1993	10,990,000	—	—	0.10	0.15	0.25
1993 1	10,000	PF65 1.00				
1994	—	—	—	0.10	0.15	0.25
1994 Fish	60,000,000	—	—	0.10	0.15	0.25
1994 Fish	10,000	PF65 1.00				
1994 Bee	79,900,000	—	—	0.10	0.15	0.25
1995	109,995,000	—	—	0.10	0.15	0.25
1995	10,000	PF65 1.00				
1996	139,987,000	—	—	0.10	0.15	0.25
1996	8,000	PF65 1.00				
1997	436,216,500	—	—	0.10	0.15	0.25
1997	10,000	PF65 1.00				
1998 In sets only	—	—	—	—	—	3.00
1998	—	PF65 1.00				
1999 In sets only	—	—	—	—	—	3.00
1999	—	PF65 1.00				
2000	85,385,000	—	—	0.10	0.15	0.25
2000	—	PF65 1.00				

KM# 939.1 50 CENTIMES

7.00 g., Aluminum-Bronze, 25 mm. **Obv:** Liberty bust left, 3 folds in collar **Rev:** Denomination above date, grain sprig below, laurel branch at left **Edge:** Plain

Date	Mintage	VF20	XF40	MS60	MS63	MS65
1962	37,560,000	0.60	1.50	2.00	3.00	5.00
1963	62,482,000	0.40	1.00	1.50	2.00	3.00

KM# 939.2 50 CENTIMES

7.00 g., Aluminum-Bronze, 25 mm. **Obv:** Liberty bust left, 4 folds in collar **Rev:** Denomination above grain sprig, laurel at left **Edge:** Plain

Date	Mintage	VF20	XF40	MS60	MS63	MS65
1962	Inc. above	30.00	70.00	90.00	120	150
1963	Inc. above	0.40	1.00	1.50	2.00	3.00
1964	41,471,000	0.90	2.00	3.50	6.00	9.00

KM# 931.1 1/2 FRANC

4.50 g., Nickel, 19.5 mm. **Obv:** The Seed Sower **Rev:** Laurel divides denomination and date **Edge:** Reeded **Mint:** Paris **Note:** Without mint mark.

Date	Mintage	VF20	XF40	MS60	MS63	MS65
1965	184,834,000	—	0.15	0.20	0.30	0.50
Note: Small legends						
1965	Inc. above	—	0.15	0.20	0.30	0.50
Note: Large legends						
1966	88,890,000	—	0.15	0.20	0.30	0.50
1967	28,394,000	—	0.15	0.20	0.40	0.60
1968	57,548,000	—	0.15	0.20	0.30	0.50
1969	47,144,000	—	0.15	0.20	0.30	0.50
1970	42,298,000	—	0.15	0.20	0.30	0.50
1971	36,068,000	—	0.15	0.20	0.30	0.50
1972	42,302,000	—	0.15	0.20	0.30	0.50
1972	Inc. above	50.00	100	125	150	200
Note: Without "O. ROTY"						
1973	48,372,000	—	0.15	0.20	0.30	0.60
1974	37,072,000	—	0.15	0.20	0.30	0.50
1975	22,803,000	—	0.15	0.20	0.40	0.60
1976	115,314,000	—	0.15	0.20	0.30	0.50
1977	131,644,000	—	0.15	0.20	0.30	0.50
1978	63,360,000	—	0.15	0.20	0.30	0.50
1979	51,000	—	—	0.25	0.50	0.75
1980 In sets only	60,000	—	—	0.25	0.50	0.75
1981	50,000	—	—	0.25	0.50	0.75
1982	78,000	—	—	0.25	0.50	0.75
1983	50,000,000	—	0.15	0.20	0.30	0.50
1984	80,000,000	—	0.15	0.20	0.30	0.50
1985	50,000,000	—	—	1.00	1.50	2.50
1986	110,000,000	—	—	1.00	1.50	2.50
1987	50,000,000	—	—	0.20	0.30	0.50
1988	100,000	—	—	0.25	0.40	0.60
1989	83,000	—	—	0.25	0.40	0.60
1990	15,000	—	—	0.35	0.50	0.75
1991	49,988,000	—	—	0.25	0.40	0.60
Note: Exists in both coin and medal alignment						
1992	29,968,000	—	—	0.25	0.40	0.60
Note: Exists in both coin and medal alignment						
1993	24,972,000	—	—	0.25	0.40	0.60
1994 Fish	10,000,000	—	—	0.25	0.40	0.60
1994 Bee	29,972,000	—	—	0.25	0.40	0.60
1995	29,976,000	—	—	0.25	0.40	0.60
1996	55,978,000	—	—	0.25	0.40	0.60
1997	99,976,000	—	—	0.25	0.40	0.60
1998 In sets only	—	—	—	1.00	2.00	3.00
1999 In sets only	—	—	—	1.00	2.00	3.00
2000	75,000,000	—	—	0.25	0.40	0.60

KM# 931.2 1/2 FRANC

4.50 g., Nickel, 19.5 mm. **Obv:** Modified sower, engraver's signature: "O. ROTY" preceded by "D'AP" **Rev:** Laurel divides date and denomination **Edge:** Plain

Date	Mintage	VF20	XF40	MS60	MS63	MS65
1991	—	—	—	0.25	0.40	0.60
1991	10,000	PF65 1.50				
1992	—	—	—	0.25	0.40	0.60

Date	Mintage	VF20	XF40	MS60	MS63	MS65
1992	15,000	PF65 1.50				
1993	—	—	—	0.25	0.40	0.60
1993	10,000	PF65 1.50				
1994 Fish	—	—	—	0.25	0.40	0.60
1994 Fish	10,000	PF65 1.50				
1994 Bee	—	—	—	0.25	0.40	0.60
1995	—	—	—	0.25	0.40	0.60
1995	10,000	PF65 1.50				
1996	—	—	—	0.25	0.40	0.60
1996	8,000	PF65 1.50				
1997	—	—	—	0.25	0.40	0.60
1997	10,000	PF65 1.50				
1998	—	PF65 1.50				
1999	—	PF65 1.50				
2000	—	—	—	0.25	0.40	0.60
2000	—	PF65 1.50				

KM# 925.1 FRANC

6.00 g., Nickel, 24 mm. **Obv:** The Seed Sower **Rev:** Laurel branch divides denomination and date **Edge:** Reeded **Mint:** Paris **Note:** Without mint mark.

Date	Mintage	VF20	XF40	MS60	MS63	MS65
1960	406,375,000	—	—	0.30	0.40	1.00
1961	119,611,000	—	—	0.30	0.40	0.60
1962	14,014,000	—	—	0.35	0.50	0.75
1964	77,425,000	—	—	0.30	0.40	0.60
1965	44,252,000	—	—	0.30	0.40	0.60
1966	38,038,000	—	—	0.30	0.40	0.60
1967	11,322,000	—	—	0.35	0.50	0.75
1968	51,550,000	—	—	0.30	0.40	0.60
1969	70,595,000	—	—	0.30	0.40	0.60
1970	42,560,000	—	—	0.30	0.40	0.60
1971	42,475,000	—	—	0.30	0.40	0.60
1972	48,250,000	—	—	0.30	0.40	0.60
1973	70,000,000	—	—	0.30	0.40	0.60
1974	82,235,000	—	—	0.30	0.40	0.60
1975	101,685,000	—	—	0.30	0.40	0.60
1976	192,520,000	—	—	0.30	0.40	0.60
1977	230,085,000	—	—	0.30	0.40	0.60
1978	136,580,000	—	—	0.30	0.40	0.60
1979	51,000	—	—	2.00	3.00	5.00
1980 In sets only	60,000	—	—	2.00	3.00	5.00
1981	50,000	—	—	2.00	3.00	5.00
1982	92,000	—	—	2.00	3.00	5.00
1983	101,000	—	—	2.00	3.00	5.00
1984	50,000	—	—	2.00	3.00	5.00
1985	7,002,000	—	—	1.00	2.00	3.00
1986	48,000	—	—	2.00	3.00	5.00
1987	100,000	—	—	1.25	2.50	4.00
1988	100,000	—	—	1.25	2.50	4.00
1989	83,000	—	—	2.00	3.00	5.00
1990	15,000	—	—	12.00	15.00	30.00
1991	54,988,000	—	—	0.25	0.40	0.60
Note: Exists in both coin and medal alignment						
1992	30,000,000	—	—	0.25	0.40	0.60
Note: Exists in both coin and medal alignment						
1993	20,000	—	—	2.50	4.00	6.00
1994 Bee	4,792,000	—	—	0.25	0.40	0.60
1995	15,000	—	—	0.25	0.40	0.60
1996 In sets only	—	—	—	2.00	3.00	5.00
1997 In sets only	—	—	—	2.00	3.00	5.00
1998 In sets only	—	—	—	2.00	3.00	5.00
1999	80,432,000	—	—	0.25	0.40	0.60
2000 In sets only	—	—	—	2.00	3.00	5.00

KM# 963 FRANC

6.00 g., Nickel, 24 mm. **Subject:** 30th Anniversary of Fifth Republic **Obv:** Head right **Rev:** Denomination within six-sided wreath, dates below **Edge:** Reeded **Mint:** Paris

Date	Mintage	VF20	XF40	MS60	MS63	MS65
1988	49,921,000	—	—	0.50	1.00	2.00

KM# 978 FRANC

22.20 g., 0.900 Silver 0.6424 oz. ASW, 24 mm. **Subject:** 30th Anniversary of Fifth Republic

Date	Mintage	VF20	XF40	MS60	MS63	MS65
1988	60,000	PF65 30.00				

KM# 979 FRANC

9.00 g., 0.920 Gold 0.2662 oz. AGW, 24 mm. **Subject:** 30th Anniversary of Fifth Republic

Date	Mintage	VF20	XF40	MS60	MS63	MS65
1988	20,000	PF65 500				

KM# 967 FRANC

6.00 g., Nickel, 24 mm. **Subject:** 200th Anniversary of Estates General **Obv:** Denomination within wreath, date below **Rev:** Three figure monument

Date	Mintage	VF20	XF40	MS60	MS63	MS65
1989	5,010,000	—	—	1.25	2.50	4.50

KM# 925.2 FRANC

6.00 g., Nickel, 24 mm. **Obv:** Modified sower, engraver's signature: O. ROTY, preceded by D'AP **Rev:** Laurel divides date and denomination **Edge:** Plain

Date	Mintage	VF20	XF40	MS60	MS63	MS65
1991	—	—	—	2.50	0.40	0.60
1991	10,000	PF65 2.50				
1992	—	—	—	0.25	0.40	0.60
1992	15,000	PF65 2.50				
1993	—	—	—	0.25	0.40	0.60
1993	10,000	PF65 2.50				
1994 Bee	—	—	—	0.25	0.40	0.60
1994 Fish	10,000	PF65 2.50				
1995	35,000	—	—	0.25	0.40	0.60
1995	10,000	PF65 2.50				
1996	5,000	—	—	2.50	0.40	0.60
1996	8,000	PF65 2.50				
1997	15,000	—	—	0.25	0.40	0.60
1997	—	PF65 2.50				
1998	—	PF65 2.50				
1999	—	PF65 2.50				
2000	—	—	—	0.25	0.40	0.60
2000	—	PF65 2.50				

KM# 1004.1 FRANC

6.00 g., Nickel, 24 mm. **Subject:** 200th Anniversary of French Republic **Obv:** Liberty bust left **Rev:** Denomination within wreath, date below **Edge:** Reeded **Mint:** Paris

Date	Mintage	VF20	XF40	MS60	MS63	MS65
1992	30,000,000	—	—	1.00	1.25	2.00

KM# 1004.1a FRANC

9.00 g., 0.920 Gold 0.2662 oz. AGW, 24 mm. **Subject:** 200th Anniversary of the French Republic **Obv:** Liberty bust left **Rev:** Denomination within wreath

Date	Mintage	VF20	XF40	MS60	MS63	MS65
1992	5,000	PF65 450				

KM# 1004.1b FRANC

11.00 g., 0.999 Platinum 0.3533 oz. APW, 24 mm. **Obv:** Liberty bust left **Rev:** Denomination within wreath

Date	Mintage	VF20	XF40	MS60	MS63	MS65
1992	2,000	PF65 700				

KM# 1005 FRANC

15.55 g., 0.900 Silver 0.4499 oz. ASW **Obv:** Liberty bust left **Rev:** Denomination within wreath, date below

Date	Mintage	VF20	XF40	MS60	MS63	MS65
1992	—	—	—	18.00	20.00	25.00
1992	30,000	PF65 35.00				

KM# 1014 FRANC

22.20 g., 0.900 Silver 0.6424 oz. ASW **Obv:** American soldiers storming Omaha Beach **Rev:** Head of Liberty Statue, flags, denomination and date

Date	Mintage	VF20	XF40	MS60	MS63	MS65
1993	1,000,000	—	—	20.00	22.50	27.50
1993	150,000	PF65 35.00				

KM# 1015 FRANC

17.00 g., 0.925 Gold 0.5056 oz. AGW **Subject:** Normandy Invasion **Obv:** American soldiers storming Omaha beach **Rev:** Head of Liberty Statue, flags, denomination and date

Date	Mintage	VF20	XF40	MS60	MS63	MS65
1993	Est. 20000	PF65 900				

KM# 1133 FRANC

6.00 g., Nickel, 24 mm. **Subject:** 200th Anniversary of Institute of France **Obv:** Institut de France building divides denomination, date below **Rev:** Framed arms, date below, branches flank three sides

Date	Mintage	VF20	XF40	MS60	MS63	MS65
1995	4,976,000	—	—	1.25	1.50	2.00

KM# 1160 FRANC

6.00 g., Nickel, 24 mm. **Subject:** 100th Anniversary - Birth of Jacques Rueff **Obv:** Head at right facing **Rev:** Figure at center, flanked by branches, divides denomination

Date	Mintage	VF20	XF40	MS60	MS63	MS65
1996	2,976,000	—	—	1.25	1.50	2.50

KM# 1211 FRANC

12.00 g., 0.900 Silver 0.3472 oz. ASW **Subject:** 1998 World Cup Soccer Ga mes **Obv:** Games logo above denomination **Rev:** Soccer ball on world globe

Date	Mintage	VF20	XF40	MS60	MS63	MS65
1997	250,000	—	—	—	25.00	30.00

KM# 1214 FRANC

11.94 g., 0.900 Silver 0.3455 oz. ASW **Subject:** 125th Anniversary - Universal Postal Union **Obv:** Partial stamp design, monograms, dates above denomination **Rev:** Head left on stamp design, patterned coin background **Edge:** Reeded **Mint:** Paris

Date	Mintage	VF20	XF40	MS60	MS63	MS65
ND-1999	—	—	—	18.00	20.00	25.00

KM# 1291 FRANC

13.00 g., 0.900 Silver 0.3762 oz. ASW, 30 mm. **Subject:** Rugby **Obv:** Players in a scrum, date above **Rev:** Players jumping for a ball, denomination below **Edge:** Plain **Mint:** Paris

Date	Mintage	VF20	XF40	MS60	MS63	MS65
1999	50,000	—	—	22.00	25.00	30.00

KM# 925.1a FRANC

8.00 g., 0.750 Gold 0.1929 oz. AGW, 24 mm. **Obv:** The Seed Sower **Rev:** Laurel divides date and denomination **Edge:** Reeded **Mint:** Paris **Note:** Medallic alignment.

Date	Mintage	VF20	XF40	MS60	MS63	MS65
2000	5,000	—	—	245	285	385

KM# 1262 FRANC

13.00 g., 0.900 Silver 0.3762 oz. ASW **Subject:** World Soccer Championship **Obv:** Soccer ball design, denomination on ball divides "R" and "F", date below **Rev:** Soccer player **Edge:** Reeded **Mint:** Paris

Date	Mintage	VF20	XF40	MS60	MS63	MS65
2000	10,000	—	—	22.00	25.00	30.00

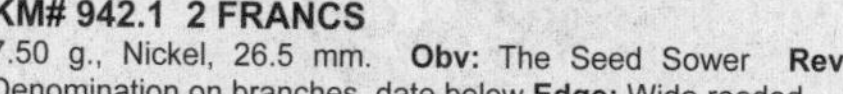

KM# 942.1 2 FRANCS

7.50 g., Nickel, 26.5 mm. **Obv:** The Seed Sower **Rev:** Denomination on branches, date below **Edge:** Wide reeded

Date	Mintage	VF20	XF40	MS60	MS63	MS65
1979	130,000,000	—	—	0.65	1.00	1.50
1980	100,010,000	—	—	0.65	1.00	1.50
1981	120,000,000	—	—	0.65	1.00	1.50
1982	90,000,000	—	—	0.65	1.00	1.50
1983	90,000,000	—	—	0.65	1.00	1.50
1984	50,000	—	—	0.50	0.75	1.25
1985	20,000	—	—	1.50	2.00	3.00
1986	48,000	—	—	1.50	2.00	3.00
1987	100,000	—	—	0.50	0.75	1.25
1988	100,000	—	—	0.50	0.75	1.25
1989	83,000	—	—	0.50	0.75	1.25
1990	15,000	—	—	0.50	0.75	1.25
1991	2,500	—	—	100	150	200
1992	6,500	—	—	—	1.00	2.00
1994 Fish	—	—	—	0.50	0.75	1.25
1994 Bee	—	—	—	12.00	14.00	20.00
1995	—	—	—	0.50	0.75	1.25
1996	—	—	—	0.50	0.75	1.25
1997	—	—	—	0.50	0.75	1.25
1998	—	—	—	0.50	0.75	1.25
1999	—	—	—	0.50	0.75	1.25
2000	—	—	—	0.50	0.75	1.25

KM# 942.2 2 FRANCS

7.50 g., Nickel, 26.5 mm. **Obv:** The Seed Sower **Rev:** Denomination on branches, date below **Edge:** Plain

Date	Mintage	VF20	XF40	MS60	MS63	MS65
1991	5,000	—	—	75.00	100	175
1991	10,000	PF65 90.00				
1992	15,000	—	—	0.50	0.75	1.25
1992	85,000	PF65 3.50				
1993	40,000	—	—	0.50	0.75	1.25

Date	Mintage	VF20	XF40	MS60	MS63	MS65
1993	10,000	PF65 3.50				
1994 Fish	9,870,000	—	—	0.50	0.75	1.25
1994 Fish	10,000	PF65 3.50				
1994 Bee	20,000	—	—	0.50	0.75	1.25
1995	20,000	—	—	0.50	0.75	1.25
1995	10,000	PF65 3.50				
1996	11,980,000	—	—	0.50	0.75	1,25
1996	8,000	PF65 3.50				
1997	9,990,000	—	—	0.50	0.75	1.25
1997	10,000	PF65 3.50				
1998	45,000,000	—	—	0.50	0.75	1.25
1998	—	PF65 3.50				
1999	—	PF65 3.50				
2000	25,000,000	—	—	0.50	0.75	1.25
2000	—	PF65 3.50				

KM# 1062 2 FRANCS

7.50 g., Nickel, 26.5 mm. **Obv:** Bust with hat facing, double cross in background **Rev:** Denomination on branches, date below **Edge:** Reeded

Date	Mintage	VF20	XF40	MS60	MS63	MS65
1993	30,000,000	—	—	0.65	1.00	1.50

KM# 1119 2 FRANCS

7.50 g., Nickel, 26.5 mm. **Obv:** Head of Louis Pasteur facing, building at left **Rev:** Denomination to right of bottles, date below

Date	Mintage	VF20	XF40	MS60	MS63	MS65
1995	9,975,000	—	—	1.50	2.00	2.75

KM# 1187 2 FRANCS

7.50 g., Nickel, 26.5 mm. **Obv:** Georges Guynemer, WWI ace fighter pilot, looking left, date below **Rev:** Guynemer's stork emblem below denomination

Date	Mintage	VF20	XF40	MS60	MS63	MS65
1997	—	—	—	2.00	2.25	3.00

KM# 1213 2 FRANCS

7.50 g., Nickel, 26.5 mm. **Subject:** 50th Anniversary-Declaration of Human Rights **Obv:** Rene Cassin head right, initials above inscription, dates and building below **Rev:** Denomination on world globe, laurel spray and date below

Date	Mintage	VF20	XF40	MS60	MS63	MS65
1998	—	—	—	2.00	2.25	3.00

KM# 926 5 FRANCS

12.00 g., 0.835 Silver 0.3222 oz. ASW, 29 mm. **Obv:** Figure sowing seed **Rev:** Branches divide denomination and date **Edge Lettering:** LIBERTE EGALITE FRATERNITE

Date	Mintage	VF20	XF40	MS60	MS63	MS65
1960	55,182,000	—	6.00	7.25	14.00	16.00
1961	15,630,000	—	6.00	7.25	14.00	16.00
1962	42,500,000	—	6.00	7.25	14.00	16.00
1963	37,936,000	—	6.00	7.25	14.00	16.00
1964	32,378,000	—	6.00	7.25	14.00	16.00
1965	5,156,000	—	6.00	7.25	14.00	16.00
1966	5,017,000	—	6.00	7.25	14.00	16.00
1967	502,000	6.00	13.00	16.00	18.00	
1968	557,000	—	6.00	7.25	14.00	16.00
1969	504,000	—	6.00	12.00	14.00	16.00

KM# 926a.1 5 FRANCS

10.00 g., Nickel Clad Copper-Nickel, 29 mm. **Obv:** The Seed Sower **Rev:** Branches divide denomination and date **Edge:** Reeded **Mint:** Paris

Date	Mintage	VF20	XF40	MS60	MS63	MS65
1970	57,890,000	—	—	1.25	1.75	2.00
1971	142,204,000	—	—	1.25	1.75	2.00
1972	45,492,000	—	—	1.50	2.25	2.50
1973	45,079,000	—	—	1.25	1.75	2.00
1974	26,888,000	—	—	1.25	1.75	2.00
1975	16,712,000	—	—	1.25	1.75	2.00
1976	1,662,000	—	—	2.00	3.00	5.00
1977	485,000	1.00	1.50	2.25	3.50	5.00
1978	30,022,000	—	—	1.25	1.75	2.00
1979	51,000	—	—	2.50	3.50	5.50
1980 In sets only	60,000	—	—	3.00	5.00	7.50
1981	50,000	—	—	2.50	3.00	5.50
1982	60,000	—	—	2.50	3.50	5.50
1983	101,000	—	—	2.50	3.50	5.50
1984	49,000	—	—	12.00	25.00	60.00
1985	20,000	—	—	15.00	30.00	70.00
1986 In sets only	48,000	—	—	3.00	5.00	7.50
1987	20,000,000	—	—	1.25	1.65	2.50
1988	100,000	—	—	1.25	1.65	2.85
1989	83,000	—	—	1.25	1.65	3.00
1990	14,990,000	—	—	1.25	1.65	2.50
1991	7,488,000	—	—	1.25	1.65	2.50
1992	9,966,000	—	—	1.25	1.65	2.50
1993	14,970,000	—	—	1.25	1.65	2.50
1994 Bee	6,000,000	—	—	1.25	1.65	2.50
1994 Fish	3,990,000	—	—	1.25	1.65	2.50
1995	19,986,000	—	—	1.25	1.65	2.50
1996	12,000	—	—	7.00	15.00	20.00
1997 In sets only	15,000	—	—	3.50	5.00	7.50
1998 In sets only	25,000	—	—	3.50	5.00	7.50
1999 In sets only	25,500	—	—	3.50	5.00	7.50
2000 In sets only	100,000	—	—	3.50	5.00	7.50

KM# 968 5 FRANCS

10.00 g., Nickel, 29 mm. **Subject:** Centennial - Erection of Eiffel Tower **Obv:** Base of tower, denomination above **Rev:** Eiffel Tower, dates at right **Mint:** Paris

Date	Mintage	VF20	XF40	MS60	MS63	MS65
1989	9,774,000	—	—	4.00	6.50	9.00

KM# 968a 5 FRANCS

12.00 g., 0.900 Silver 0.3472 oz. ASW, 29 mm. **Subject:** Centennial - Erection of Eiffel Tower **Obv:** Denomination above tower base **Rev:** Tower view from bottom

Date	Mintage	VF20	XF40	MS60	MS63	MS65
1989	80,000	PF65 28.00				

KM# 968b 5 FRANCS

14.00 g., 0.925 Gold 0.4164 oz. AGW, 29 mm. **Subject:** Centennial - Erection of Eiffel Tower **Obv:** Denomination above tower base **Rev:** Tower view from bottom

Date	Mintage	VF20	XF40	MS60	MS63	MS65
1989	30,000	PF65 775				

KM# 968c 5 FRANCS

16.00 g., 0.999 Platinum 0.5139 oz. APW, 29 mm. **Subject:** Centennial - Erection of Eiffel Tower **Obv:** Denomination above base **Rev:** Tower view from base

Date	Mintage	VF20	XF40	MS60	MS63	MS65
1989	Est. 3000	PF65 1,000				

Note: 1,800 pieces were melted by MTB Banking

KM# 926a.2 5 FRANCS
10.00 g., Nickel Clad Copper-Nickel, 29 mm. **Obv:** Modified sower, engraver's signature: "O. ROTY" preceded by "D'AP" **Rev:** Branches divide date and denomination **Edge:** Plain **Mint:** Paris

Date	Mintage	VF20	XF40	MS60	MS63	MS65
1991	7,490,000	—	—	1.25	1.65	2.50
1991	10,000	PF65 6.50				
1992	9,986,000	—	—	1.25	1.65	2.50
1992	15,000	PF65 6.50				
1993	14,990,000	—	—	1.25	1.65	2.50
1993	10,000	PF65 6.50				
1994 Fish	6,000,000	—	—	1.25	1.65	2.50
1994 Fish	10,000	PF65 6.50				
1994 Bee	3,990,000	—	—	1.25	1.65	2.50
1995	20,006,000	—	—	1.25	1.65	2.50
1995	—	PF65 6.50				
1996	17,000	—	—	1.25	1.65	2.50
1996	8,000	PF65 6.50				
1997	15,000	—	—	1.25	1.65	2.50
1997	—	PF65 6.50				
1998	—	PF65 6.50				
1999	—	PF65 6.50				
2000	—	—	—	1.25	1.65	2.50
2000	—	PF65 6.50				

KM# 1006 5 FRANCS
10.00 g., Nickel, 29 mm. **Obv:** Denomination within design **Rev:** Bust of Pierre Mendes France facing **Mint:** Paris

Date	Mintage	VF20	XF40	MS60	MS63	MS65
1992	10,000,000	—	—	3.00	4.50	6.00

KM# 1006a 5 FRANCS
12.00 g., 0.900 Silver 0.3472 oz. ASW, 29 mm. **Obv:** Denomination within design **Rev:** Bust of Pierre Mendes France facing

Date	Mintage	VF20	XF40	MS60	MS63	MS65
1992	10,000	PF65 30.00				

KM# 1006b 5 FRANCS
14.00 g., 0.920 Gold 0.4141 oz. AGW, 29 mm. **Obv:** Denomination within design **Rev:** Bust of Pierre Mendes France facing

Date	Mintage	VF20	XF40	MS60	MS63	MS65
1992	1,000	PF65 775				

KM# 1007 5 FRANCS
12.00 g., 0.900 Silver 0.3472 oz. ASW, 29 mm. **Subject:** French Antarctic Territories **Rev:** 3 albatross in flight

Date	Mintage	VF20	XF40	MS60	MS63	MS65
1992	15,000	PF65 50.00				

KM# 1063 5 FRANCS
10.00 g., Nickel, 29 mm. **Obv:** Head of Voltaire the poet 3/4 facing **Rev:** Quill divides building and date from denomination **Edge:** Reeded **Mint:** Paris

Date	Mintage	VF20	XF40	MS60	MS63	MS65
1994	15,000,000	—	—	3.00	4.00	5.00

KM# 1118 5 FRANCS
12.00 g., 0.900 Silver 0.3472 oz. ASW, 29 mm. **Subject:** 50th Anniversary - United Nations **Obv:** Dove and branch at left, denomination at right **Rev:** UN logo, dates below

Date	Mintage	VF20	XF40	MS60	MS63	MS65
1995	250,000	PF65 27.50				

KM# 1118a 5 FRANCS
14.00 g., 0.920 Gold 0.4141 oz. AGW, 29 mm. **Obv:** Dove and branch left of denomination **Rev:** UN logo and dates

Date	Mintage	VF20	XF40	MS60	MS63	MS65
1995	125,000	PF65 775				

KM# 1155 5 FRANCS
10.00 g., Nickel, 29 mm. **Obv:** Denomination and date within wreath **Rev:** Hercules group design **Edge:** Reeded **Mint:** Paris

Date	Mintage	VF20	XF40	MS60	MS63	MS65
1996	4,976,000	—	—	3.00	4.50	6.00

KM# 1212 5 FRANCS
12.00 g., 0.900 Silver 0.3472 oz. ASW, 29 mm. **Subject:** 1998 World Cup Soccer Games: French Victory **Obv:** Game logo above denomination **Rev:** Handheld trophy with stadium in background

Date	Mintage	VF20	XF40	MS60	MS63	MS65
1998	Est. 100000	PF65 45.00				

KM# 1215 5 FRANCS
12.00 g., 0.900 Silver 0.3472 oz. ASW, 29 mm. **Subject:** Yves St. Laurent **Obv:** RF monogram within entwined snake design, denomination below **Rev:** Fashion show scene **Mint:** Paris

Date	Mintage	VF20	XF40	MS60	MS63	MS65
2000	—	—	—	—	30.00	—

KM# 1222 5 FRANCS
10.00 g., Copper-Nickel Plated Nickel, 29 mm. **Subject:** 2000 Years of French Coinage **Obv:** Denomination and date within wreath **Rev:** 1st century B.C. Celtic Parisii Stater coin design **Edge:** Reeded **Mint:** Paris

Date	Mintage	VF20	XF40	MS60	MS63	MS65
2000	50,000	—	—	—	10.00	12.00

KM# 1223 5 FRANCS
10.00 g., Copper-Nickel Plated Nickel, 29 mm. **Subject:** 2000 Years of French Coinage **Obv:** Denomination and date within wreath **Rev:** Charlemagne Denar coin design **Edge:** Reeded **Mint:** Paris

Date	Mintage	VF20	XF40	MS60	MS63	MS65
2000	50,000	—	—	—	10.00	12.00

KM# 1224 5 FRANCS
10.00 g., Copper-Nickel Plated Nickel, 29 mm. **Subject:** 2000 Years of French Coinage **Obv:** Denomination and date within wreath **Rev:** Louis IX Gold Ecu design **Edge:** Reeded **Mint:** Paris

Date	Mintage	VF20	XF40	MS60	MS63	MS65
2000	50,000	—	—	—	9.50	11.50

KM# 1962 5 FRANCS
Copper-Nickel Plated Nickel **Rev:** Gold Frank of John II (the Good) (1360)

Date	Mintage	VF20	XF40	MS60	MS63	MS65
2000	7,932	—	—	—	—	27.50

KM# 1963 5 FRANCS
Copper-Nickel Plated Nickel **Rev:** Franc of Henry III (1577) **Mint:** Paris

Date	Mintage	VF20	XF40	MS60	MS63	MS65
2000	7,932	—	—	—	—	27.50

KM# 1964 5 FRANCS
Copper-Nickel Plated Nickel **Rev:** Pistole of Louis XIII (1640) **Mint:** Paris

Date	Mintage	VF20	XF40	MS60	MS63	MS65
2000	7,932	—	—	—	—	27.50

KM# 1965 5 FRANCS
Copper-Nickel Plated Nickel **Rev:** Marianne (Bonnet type) **Mint:** Paris

Date	Mintage	VF20	XF40	MS60	MS63	MS65
2000	9,863	—	—	—	—	27.50

KM# 1966 5 FRANCS
Copper-Nickel Plated Nickel **Rev:** Marianne (Chaplain type) **Mint:** Paris

Date	Mintage	VF20	XF40	MS60	MS63	MS65
2000	9,863	—	—	—	—	27.50

KM# 1967 5 FRANCS
Copper-Nickel Plated Nickel **Rev:** Marianne (Lagriffoul type) **Mint:** Paris

Date	Mintage	VF20	XF40	MS60	MS63	MS65
2000	9,863	—	—	—	—	27.50

KM# 1968 5 FRANCS
Silver **Rev:** Gold Franc of John II **Mint:** Paris

Date	Mintage	VF20	XF40	MS60	MS63	MS65
2000	1,662	PF65 80.00				

KM# 1254 6.55957 FRANCS
13.00 g., 0.900 Silver 0.3762 oz. ASW **Subject:** Euro Conversion Series **Obv:** Europa allegorical portrait, denomination and date at left **Rev:** Country names and euro-currency equivalents around "RF" and denomination in center **Edge:** Plain **Mint:** Paris **Note:** Struck at Paris Mint.

Date	Mintage	VF20	XF40	MS60	MS63	MS65
1999	200,000	—	—	—	30.00	80.00

KM# 1255 6.55957 FRANCS
22.20 g., 0.900 Silver 0.6424 oz. ASW **Obv:** Europa allegorical portrait **Rev:** Country names and euro-currency equivalents around RF and denomination in center plus French coin designs **Edge:** Reeded

Date	Mintage	VF20	XF40	MS60	MS63	MS65
1999	20,000	—	—	—	—	80.00

KM# 1225 6.55957 FRANCS
22.20 g., 0.900 Silver 0.6424 oz. ASW **Subject:** European Art Styles - Renaissance **Obv:** Europa allegorical portrait, denomination and date at left **Rev:** Renaissance style buildings **Edge Lettering:** " Europa" repeated four times **Mint:** Paris

Date	Mintage	VF20	XF40	MS60	MS63	MS65
2000	15,000	PF65 80.00				

KM# 1226 6.55957 FRANCS
22.20 g., 0.900 Silver 0.6424 oz. ASW **Series:** European Art Styles - Classical and Baroque **Obv:** Europa allegorical portrait, denomination and date at left **Rev:** Buildings, top and left of artistic design **Mint:** Paris

Date	Mintage	VF20	XF40	MS60	MS63	MS65
2000	15,000	PF65 80.00				

KM# 1227 6.55957 FRANCS
22.20 g., 0.900 Silver 0.6424 oz. ASW **Series:** European Art Styles - Art Nouveau **Rev:** Artistic designs **Mint:** Paris

Date	Mintage	VF20	XF40	MS60	MS63	MS65
2000	15,000	PF65 80.00				

KM# 1228 6.55957 FRANCS
22.20 g., 0.900 Silver 0.6424 oz. ASW **Series:** European Art Styles - Modern **Obv:** Europa allegorical portrait, denomination and date at left **Rev:** Modern artistic designs **Mint:** Paris

Date	Mintage	VF20	XF40	MS60	MS63	MS65
2000	15,000	PF65 80.00				

KM# 1244 6.55957 FRANCS
22.20 g., 0.900 Silver 0.6424 oz. ASW **Series:** European Art Styles - Greek and Roman **Rev:** Greek and Roman architecture **Mint:** Paris

Date	Mintage	VF20	XF40	MS60	MS63	MS65
2000	15,000	PF65 80.00				

KM# 1245 6.55957 FRANCS
22.20 g., 0.900 Silver 0.6424 oz. ASW **Series:** European Art Styles - Romanesque Art **Rev:** Figure on shield, columns in background **Mint:** Paris

Date	Mintage	VF20	XF40	MS60	MS63	MS65
2000	15,000	PF65 80.00				

KM# 1246 6.55957 FRANCS
22.20 g., 0.900 Silver 0.6424 oz. ASW **Series:** European Art Styles - Gothic **Rev:** Religious figure in foreground, designs in background **Mint:** Paris

Date	Mintage	VF20	XF40	MS60	MS63	MS65
2000	15,000	PF65 80.00				

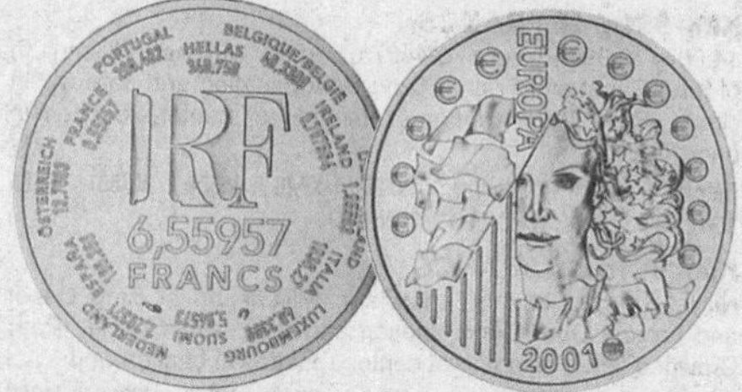

KM# 1258 6.55957 FRANCS
13.00 g., 0.900 Silver 0.3762 oz. ASW **Obv:** Country names and euro-currency equivalents around "RF" and denomination **Rev:** Europa allegorical portrait, date below **Edge:** Plain

Date	Mintage	VF20	XF40	MS60	MS63	MS65
2000	200,000	—	—	—	30.00	80.00

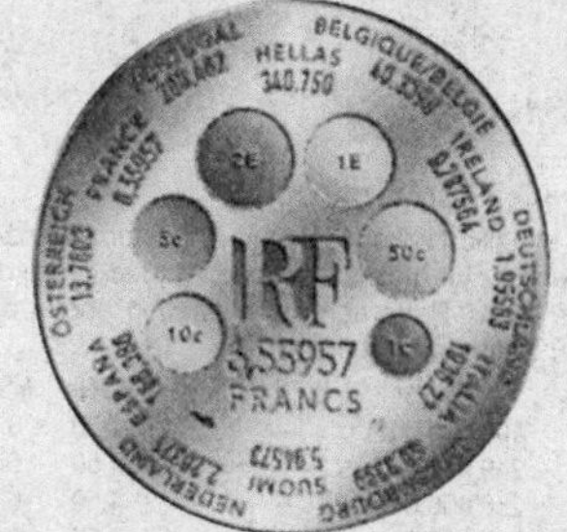

KM# 1259 6.55957 FRANCS
22.20 g., 0.900 Silver 0.6424 oz. ASW **Obv:** Country names and euro-currency equivalents around "RF", denomination and French euro coin designs **Edge:** Plain

Date	Mintage	VF20	XF40	MS60	MS63	MS65
2000	10,000	PF65 80.00				

KM# 932 10 FRANCS
25.00 g., 0.900 Silver 0.7234 oz. ASW, 37 mm. **Obv:** Denomination and date within wreath **Rev:** Hercules group **Mint:** Paris **Note:** Without mint mark.

Date	Mintage	VF20	XF40	MS60	MS63	MS65
1965	8,051,000	—	13.50	16.00	17.50	30.00
1966	9,800,000	—	—	14.50	16.00	28.00
1967	10,100,000	—	—	14.50	16.00	28.00
1968	3,887,000	—	13.50	16.00	18.00	35.00
1969	761,000	13.50	14.50	27.50	35.00	40.00
1970	5,013,000	—	13.50	16.00	17.50	32.00
1971	513,000	13.50	14.50	27.50	35.00	40.00
1972	915,000	—	13.50	25.00	30.00	35.00
1973	207,000	13.50	15.50	30.00	38.00	45.00

KM# 940 10 FRANCS
10.00 g., Nickel-Brass, 26 mm. **Obv:** Stylized map of france **Rev:** High tension towers and electric transmission wires, denomination at center **Edge Lettering:** LIBERTÉ, EGALITÉ, FRATERNITÉ, incuse

Date	Mintage	VF20	XF40	MS60	MS63	MS65
1974	22,447,000	—	—	1.75	2.00	2.50
1975	59,013,000	—	—	1.75	2.00	2.50
1976	104,093,000	—	—	1.75	2.00	2.50
1977	100,028,000	—	—	1.75	2.00	2.50
1978	97,590,000	—	—	1.75	2.00	2.50
1979	110,000,000	—	—	1.75	2.00	2.50
1980	80,010,000	—	—	1.75	2.00	2.50
1981	50,000	—	—	2.25	2.75	3.75
1982	74,000	—	—	2.25	2.75	3.75
1983	101,000	—	—	2.25	2.75	3.75
1984	39,988,000	—	—	1.75	2.00	2.50
1985	30,000,000	—	—	1.75	2.00	2.50
1987	Est. 50000000	—	—	2.00	2.50	3.00

KM# 950 10 FRANCS
10.00 g., Nickel-Bronze, 26 mm. **Subject:** 100th Anniversary - Death of Leon Gambetta **Obv:** Denomination and date, flags in background **Rev:** Head left

Date	Mintage	VF20	XF40	MS60	MS63	MS65
1982	3,045,000	—	—	3.00	4.00	5.00

KM# 952 10 FRANCS
Nickel-Bronze, 26 mm. **Subject:** 200th Anniversary - Montgolfier Balloon **Obv:** Denomination and date below balloon basket **Rev:** Balloon, figures and date below

Date	Mintage	VF20	XF40	MS60	MS63	MS65
1983	3,001,000	—	—	3.00	4.00	5.00

KM# 953 10 FRANCS
Nickel-Bronze, 26 mm. **Subject:** 200th Anniversary - Birth of Stendhal **Obv:** Head 3/4 facing **Rev:** Quill, branch, book, and buildings divide date and denomination

Date	Mintage	VF20	XF40	MS60	MS63	MS65
1983	2,951,000	—	—	3.00	4.00	5.00

KM# 954 10 FRANCS
Nickel-Bronze, 26 mm. **Subject:** 200th Anniversary - Birth of Francois Rude **Obv:** Head 3/4 right, RF below **Rev:** Armed figure divides denomination and date

Date	Mintage	VF20	XF40	MS60	MS63	MS65
1984	10,000,000	—	—	2.75	3.50	4.50

KM# 956 10 FRANCS
Nickel-Bronze, 26 mm. **Subject:** Centennial - Death of Victor Hugo **Obv:** Denomination above armed figures, quill and book at right, date below **Rev:** Head facing

Date	Mintage	VF20	XF40	MS60	MS63	MS65
1985	10,000,000	—	—	2.75	3.50	4.50

KM# 956a 10 FRANCS
12.00 g., 0.900 Silver 0.3472 oz. ASW, 26 mm. **Subject:** Centennial - Death of Victor Hugo **Obv:** Figures left of quill and book, denomination above **Rev:** Head facing

Date	Mintage	VF20	XF40	MS60	MS63	MS65
1985	20,000	—	—	20.00	22.00	25.00

KM# 956b 10 FRANCS
12.00 g., 0.999 Silver 0.3854 oz. ASW, 26 mm. **Subject:** Centennial - Death of Victor Hugo **Obv:** Figures left of quill and book, denomination above **Rev:** Head facing

Date	Mintage	VF20	XF40	MS60	MS63	MS65
1985	8,000	PF65 35.00				

KM# 958 10 FRANCS
6.50 g., Nickel, 21 mm. **Subject:** 100th Anniversary - Birth of Robert Schuman **Obv:** Rooster at left, denomination right **Rev:** Half head right

Date	Mintage	VF20	XF40	MS60	MS63	MS65
1986	9,961,000	—	—	10.00	20.00	25.00

KM# 958a 10 FRANCS
7.00 g., 0.900 Silver 0.2025 oz. ASW, 21 mm. **Obv:** Rooster at left, denomination right **Rev:** Half head right

Date	Mintage	VF20	XF40	MS60	MS63	MS65
1986	20,000	—	—	18.50	22.50	25.00

KM# 958b 10 FRANCS
7.00 g., 0.950 Silver 0.2138 oz. ASW, 21 mm. **Obv:** Rooster at left, denomination right **Rev:** Half head right

Date	Mintage	VF20	XF40	MS60	MS63	MS65
1986	6,000	PF65 45.00				

KM# 958c 10 FRANCS
7.00 g., 0.920 Gold 0.2071 oz. AGW, 21 mm. **Subject:** 100th Anniversary - Birth of Robert Schuman **Obv:** Rooster at left, denomination right **Rev:** Half head right

Date	Mintage	VF20	XF40	MS60	MS63	MS65
1986	5,000	PF65 400				

KM# 959 10 FRANCS
6.50 g., Nickel, 21 mm. **Obv:** Designs divide denomination and date **Rev:** Madam Republic head, map in background

Date	Mintage	VF20	XF40	MS60	MS63	MS65
1986	110,015,000	—	3.00	5.00	10.00	15.00

Note: Recalled and melted, no longer legal tender

KM# 961 10 FRANCS
12.00 g., 0.900 Silver 0.3472 oz. ASW **Subject:** Millennium of King Hugo Capet first King of France **Obv:** Denomination and date within circle **Rev:** Crowned figure standing at center divides dates below, rosettes in background

Date	Mintage	VF20	XF40	MS60	MS63	MS65
1987	20,000	—	—	18.50	22.50	25.00

KM# 961a 10 FRANCS
12.00 g., 0.950 Silver 0.3665 oz. ASW **Subject:** Millennium of King Capet and France **Obv:** Denomination and date within circle **Rev:** Crowned figure standing at center, rosettes in background

Date	Mintage	VF20	XF40	MS60	MS63	MS65
1987	10,000	PF65 40.00				

KM# 961b 10 FRANCS
12.00 g., 0.920 Gold 0.3549 oz. AGW **Subject:** Millennium of King Capet and France **Obv:** Denomination and date within circle **Rev:** Crowned figure standing at center, rosettes in background

Date	Mintage	VF20	XF40	MS60	MS63	MS65
1987	6,000	PF65 680				

KM# 961c 10 FRANCS
14.00 g., 0.999 Platinum 0.4497 oz. APW **Subject:** Millennium of King Capet and France **Obv:** Denomination and date within circle **Rev:** Crowned figure standing at center, rosettes in background

Date	Mintage	VF20	XF40	MS60	MS63	MS65
1987	1,000	PF65 850				

KM# 961d 10 FRANCS
Nickel-Bronze, 21 mm. **Subject:** Millennium of King Capet and France **Obv:** Denomination and date within circle **Rev:** Crowned figure standing at center, rosettes in background

Date	Mintage	VF20	XF40	MS60	MS63	MS65
1987	70,000,000	—	—	5.00	6.50	9.00

KM# 964.1 10 FRANCS
6.50 g., Bi-Metallic Nickel center in Aluminum-Bronze ring, 23 mm. **Subject:** Spirit of Bastille **Obv:** Winged figure divides RF within circle **Rev:** Patterned denomination above date within circle **Edge:** Segmented reeding

Date	Mintage	VF20	XF40	MS60	MS63	MS65
1988	100,000,000	—	—	4.50	6.00	7.50
1989	249,980,000	—	—	4.50	6.00	7.50
1990	250,000,000	—	—	4.50	6.00	7.50
1991	249,987,000	—	—	4.50	6.00	7.50
Note: Exist in both medal and coin alignment						
1992	99,966,000	—	—	4.50	6.00	7.50
Note: Exist in both medal and coin alignment						
1995	15,000	—	6.00	8.00	10.00	12.50
1996	12,000	—	6.00	8.00	10.00	12.50
2000	28,065,000	—	2.50	4.50	6.00	7.50

KM# 964.1a 10 FRANCS
Bi-Metallic .920 Gold center in Gold with Palladium and Silver alloy ring, 23 mm. **Subject:** Spirit of Bastille **Obv:** Winged figure divides RF **Rev:** Patterned denomination above date

Date	Mintage	VF20	XF40	MS60	MS63	MS65
1988	5,000	PF65 700				

KM# 965 10 FRANCS
Aluminum-Bronze, 26 mm. **Subject:** 100th Anniversary - Birth of Roland Garros **Obv:** Denomination below wings **Rev:** Dates and plane above head right

Date	Mintage	VF20	XF40	MS60	MS63	MS65
1988	30,000,000	—	—	3.00	4.00	5.00

KM# 965a 10 FRANCS
12.00 g., 0.900 Silver 0.3472 oz. ASW, 26 mm. **Obv:** Wings above denomination **Rev:** Airplane above head right

Date	Mintage	VF20	XF40	MS60	MS63	MS65
1988	10,000	—	—	18.50	22.50	25.00

KM# 965b 10 FRANCS
12.00 g., 0.950 Silver 0.3665 oz. ASW, 26 mm. **Obv:** Wings above denomination **Rev:** Airplane above head right

Date	Mintage	VF20	XF40	MS60	MS63	MS65
1988	10,000	PF65 35.00				

KM# 965c 10 FRANCS
12.00 g., 0.920 Gold 0.3549 oz. AGW, 26 mm. **Subject:** 100th Anniversary - Birth of Roland Garros **Obv:** Wings above denomination **Rev:** Airplane above head right

Date	Mintage	VF20	XF40	MS60	MS63	MS65
1988	3,000	PF65 680				

KM# 969 10 FRANCS
Bi-Metallic Steel center in Aluminum-Bronze ring, 23 mm. **Subject:** 300th Anniversary - Birth of Montesquieu **Obv:** Bust right **Rev:** Patterned denomination above date

Date	Mintage	VF20	XF40	MS60	MS63	MS65
1989	15,000	—	100	150	200	300

KM# 969a 10 FRANCS
Bi-Metallic Gold, Palladium and Silver alloy center in .920 Gold ring, 23 mm. **Subject:** 300th Anniversary - Birth of Montesquieu **Obv:** Bust right **Rev:** Patterned denomination above date

Date	Mintage	VF20	XF40	MS60	MS63	MS65
1989	5,000	PF65 700				

KM# 964.2 10 FRANCS
Aluminum-Bronze, 23 mm. **Obv:** Winged figure divides RF **Rev:** Patterned denomination above date **Edge:** Plain

Date	Mintage	VF20	XF40	MS60	MS63	MS65
1991	—	—	—	—	—	—
Note: Exists in both medal and coin alignment.						
1991	10,000	PF65 15.00				
1992	—	—	—	4.00	6.00	7.50
Note: Exists in both medal and coin alignment.						
1992	15,000	PF65 15.00				
1993	20,000	—	—	4.00	6.00	7.50
1993	10,000	PF65 15.00				
1994 Bee	20,000	—	—	4.00	6.00	7.50
1994 Fish	10,000	PF65 15.00				
1995	25,000	—	—	4.00	6.00	7.50
1995	10,000	PF65 15.00				
1996	17,000	—	—	4.00	6.00	7.50
1996	8,000	PF65 15.00				
1997	15,000	—	—	4.00	6.00	7.50
1997	10,000	PF65 15.00				
1998	—	—	—	4.00	6.00	7.50
1998	—	PF65 15.00				
1999	—	—	—	4.00	6.00	7.50
1999	—	PF65 15.00				
2000	—	—	—	4.00	6.00	7.50
2000	—	PF65 15.00				

KM# 1144 10 FRANCS
21.16 g., 0.900 Silver 0.6123 oz. ASW **Subject:** World Cup - Coupe du Monde 1998 **Obv:** World Cup 1998 logo above denomination **Rev:** Soccer ball breaking net, stylized dove, date upper right

Date	Mintage	VF20	XF40	MS60	MS63	MS65
1996	—	PF65 40.00				

KM# 1166 10 FRANCS
21.16 g., 0.900 Silver 0.6123 oz. ASW **Subject:** World Cup - Uruguay 1930 1958 **Obv:** World Cup 1998 logo above denomination **Rev:** Stylized gaucho and soccer player, date below

Date	Mintage	VF20	XF40	MS60	MS63	MS65
1996	100,000	PF65 35.00				

KM# 1161 10 FRANCS
21.16 g., 0.900 Silver 0.6123 oz. ASW **Subject:** World Cup - Argentina 1978 1986 **Obv:** World Cup 1998 logo above denomination **Rev:** Stylized bull and soccer player, date below

Date	Mintage	VF20	XF40	MS60	MS63	MS65
1997	100,000	PF65 35.00				

KM# 1163 10 FRANCS
21.16 g., 0.900 Silver 0.6123 oz. ASW **Subject:** World Cup - England 1966 **Obv:** World Cup 1998 logo above denomination **Rev:** Big Ben and soccer player, date below

Date	Mintage	VF20	XF40	MS60	MS63	MS65
1997	100,000	PF65 35.00				

KM# 1164 10 FRANCS
21.16 g., 0.900 Silver 0.6123 oz. ASW **Subject:** World Cup - Germany 1954 1974 1990 **Obv:** World Cup 1998 logo above denomination **Rev:** Brandenburg gate, soccer player, date below

Date	Mintage	VF20	XF40	MS60	MS63	MS65
1997	100,000	PF65 35.00				

KM# 1165 10 FRANCS
21.16 g., 0.900 Silver 0.6123 oz. ASW **Subject:** World Cup - Italy 1934 1938 1982 **Obv:** World Cup 1998 logo above denomination and date **Rev:** Colosseum and soccer player, date below

Date	Mintage	VF20	XF40	MS60	MS63	MS65
1997	100,000	PF65 35.00				

KM# 1162 10 FRANCS
21.16 g., 0.900 Silver 0.6123 oz. ASW **Subject:** World Cup - Brazil 1958 1968 1970 1994 **Obv:** World Cup 1998 logo above denomination **Rev:** Pavilion and soccer player, date below

Date	Mintage	VF20	XF40	MS60	MS63	MS65
1998	100,000	PF65 35.00				

KM# 1167 10 FRANCS
21.16 g., 0.900 Silver 0.6123 oz. ASW **Subject:** World Cup - Coupe du Monte **Obv:** World Cup 1998 logo above denomination and date **Rev:** World Cup trophy and 10 French city arms

Date	Mintage	VF20	XF40	MS60	MS63	MS65
1998	100,000	PF65 37.50				

KM# 1205 10 FRANCS
22.20 g., 0.900 Silver 0.6424 oz. ASW **Series:** Treasures of the Nile - J.F. Champollion **Obv:** Portrait and obelisk **Rev:** Sphinx and pyramids, date at left, denomination below

Date	Mintage	VF20	XF40	MS60	MS63	MS65
1998	15,000	PF65 45.00				

KM# 1206 10 FRANCS
22.20 g., 0.900 Silver 0.6424 oz. ASW **Series:** Treasures of the Nile **Subject:** Nefertiti 1372-1350BC, Queen and monotheist **Obv:** Crowned bust 3/4 right **Rev:** Sphinx and pyramids, date at left, denomination below

Date	Mintage	VF20	XF40	MS60	MS63	MS65
1998	15,000	PF65 50.00				

KM# 1207 10 FRANCS
22.20 g., 0.900 Silver 0.6424 oz. ASW **Series:** Treasures of the Nile **Subject:** Ramses II **Rev:** Kneeling figure right

Date	Mintage	VF20	XF40	MS60	MS63	MS65
1998	15,000	PF65 45.00				

KM# 1294 10 FRANCS
22.23 g., 0.900 Silver 0.6432 oz. ASW, 36.9 mm. **Subject:** Rugby **Obv:** Players in a "scrum" **Rev:** Players jumping for a ball **Edge:** Plain **Mint:** Paris

Date	Mintage	VF20	XF40	MS60	MS63	MS65
1999 A	10,000	PF65 35.00				

KM# 1398 10 FRANCS
22.20 g., 0.900 Silver 0.6424 oz. ASW, 37 mm. **Obv:** Partial postage stamp with denomination below, Initials, "RF" on wavy field **Rev:** First French postage stamp **Edge:** Plain **Mint:** Paris

Date	Mintage	VF20	XF40	MS60	MS63	MS65
ND (1999) A	—	PF65 45.00				

KM# 1216 10 FRANCS
22.23 g., 0.900 Silver 0.6432 oz. ASW **Series:** XXth Century - Biology and Medicine **Obv:** Double X design divides date and denomination **Rev:** Parents, fetus, hands **Edge:** Plain **Mint:** Paris

Date	Mintage	VF20	XF40	MS60	MS63	MS65
2000	10,000	PF65 40.00				

KM# 1217 10 FRANCS
22.23 g., 0.900 Silver 0.6432 oz. ASW **Series:** XXth Century - Physical Sciences **Rev:** Einstein's portrait, atom and planets **Mint:** Paris

Date	Mintage	VF20	XF40	MS60	MS63	MS65
2000	10,000	PF65 40.00				

KM# 1218 10 FRANCS
22.23 g., 0.900 Silver 0.6432 oz. ASW **Series:** XXth Century - Communications **Rev:** World, satellites and keyboard **Mint:** Paris

Date	Mintage	VF20	XF40	MS60	MS63	MS65
2000	10,000	PF65 40.00				

KM# 1219 10 FRANCS
22.23 g., 0.900 Silver 0.6432 oz. ASW **Series:** XXth Century - The Automobile **Rev:** Race cars above horse **Mint:** Paris

Date	Mintage	VF20	XF40	MS60	MS63	MS65
2000	10,000	PF65 40.00				

KM# 1220 10 FRANCS
22.23 g., 0.900 Silver 0.6432 oz. ASW **Series:** XXth Century - Flight **Rev:** Icarus in flight above Bleriot monoplane **Mint:** Paris

Date	Mintage	VF20	XF40	MS60	MS63	MS65
2000	10,000	PF65 40.00				

KM# 1221 10 FRANCS
22.23 g., 0.900 Silver 0.6432 oz. ASW **Series:** XXth Century - Space Travel **Rev:** Astronaut weightless in space amidst planets **Mint:** Paris

Date	Mintage	VF20	XF40	MS60	MS63	MS65
2000	10,000	PF65 40.00				

KM# 1229 10 FRANCS
22.20 g., 0.900 Silver 0.6424 oz. ASW **Subject:** 2000 Years - French Coinage **Obv:** Denomination and date within wreath **Rev:** 1st century B.C. Celtic Parisii Stater coin design **Edge:** Plain **Mint:** Paris

Date	Mintage	VF20	XF40	MS60	MS63	MS65
2000	10,000	PF65 40.00				

KM# 1230 10 FRANCS
22.20 g., 0.900 Silver 0.6424 oz. ASW **Rev:** Charlemagne Denar coin design, laureate head right **Mint:** Paris

Date	Mintage	VF20	XF40	MS60	MS63	MS65
2000	10,000	PF65 42.00				

KM# 1231 10 FRANCS
22.20 g., 0.900 Silver 0.6424 oz. ASW **Subject:** 2000 Years of French Coinage **Obv:** Denomination **Rev:** Louis IX gold ecu coin design, arms on shield within scalloped wreath **Edge:** Plain **Mint:** Paris

Date	Mintage	VF20	XF40	MS60	MS63	MS65
2000	10,000	PF65 42.00				

KM# 1235 10 FRANCS
22.20 g., 0.900 Silver 0.6424 oz. ASW **Subject:** Yves St. Laurent **Obv:** RF monogram within entwined snake design, date above, denomination lower right **Rev:** Fashion show scene **Mint:** Paris

Date	Mintage	VF20	XF40	MS60	MS63	MS65
2000	30,000	PF65 37.50				

KM# 1263 10 FRANCS
22.20 g., 0.900 Silver 0.6424 oz. ASW **Subject:** Antoine de St. Exupery **Obv:** RF Monogram, portrait and bi-plane **Rev:** Multicolor "Little Prince" character, denomination at left, date below **Mint:** Paris

Date	Mintage	VF20	XF40	MS60	MS63	MS65
2000	10,000	PF65 47.50				

KM# 1400 10 FRANCS
22.20 g., 0.900 Silver 0.6424 oz. ASW, 36.9 mm. **Obv:** Liberty bust by Dupre **Rev:** Value **Edge:** Plain **Mint:** Paris

Date	Mintage	VF20	XF40	MS60	MS63	MS65
2000	—	PF65 50.00				

KM# 1401 10 FRANCS
22.20 g., 0.900 Silver 0.6424 oz. ASW, 36.9 mm. **Obv:** Liberty bust by Lagriffoul **Rev:** Value **Edge:** Plain **Mint:** Paris

Date	Mintage	VF20	XF40	MS60	MS63	MS65
2000	—	PF65 50.00				

KM# 1969 10 FRANCS
Silver **Rev:** Franken of Henry III (1577) **Mint:** Paris

Date	Mintage	VF20	XF40	MS60	MS63	MS65
2000	1,471	PF65 80.00				

KM# 1970 10 FRANCS
Silver **Rev:** Pistol of Louis XIII (1640) **Mint:** Paris

Date	Mintage	VF20	XF40	MS60	MS63	MS65
2000	1,467	PF65 80.00				

KM# 1971 10 FRANCS
Silver **Rev:** Marianne (Chaplain type) **Mint:** Paris

Date	Mintage	VF20	XF40	MS60	MS63	MS65
2000	6,949	PF65 40.00				

KM# 1008.1 20 FRANCS
Tri-Metallic Copper-Aluminum-Nickel center, Nickel inner ring, Copper-Aluminum-Nickel outer ring, 27 mm. **Obv:** Mont St. Michel **Rev:** Patterned denomination above date within circle **Edge:** 4 milled bands

Date	Mintage	VF20	XF40	MS60	MS63	MS65
1992	Inc. above	—	—	12.00	15.00	18.00
Note: Open V in outer ring						
1992	60,000,000	—	—	12.00	15.00	18.00
Note: Closed V in outer ring						

KM# 1008.2 20 FRANCS
9.00 g., Tri-Metallic Copper-Aluminum-Nickel center, Nickel inner ring, Copper-Aluminum-Nickel outer ring, 27 mm. **Obv:** Mont St. Michel **Rev:** Patterned denomination above date **Edge:** 5 milled bands, reeded or plain

Date	Mintage	VF20	XF40	MS60	MS63	MS65
1992	15,000	PF65 25.00				
1992	Inc. above	—	—	5.00	6.50	8.50
Note: Open V in outer ring, exist in both coin and medal alignment						
1992	59,986,000	—	—	5.00	6.50	8.50
Note: Closed V in outer ring, exist in both coin and medal alignment						
1993	54,990,000	—	—	5.00	7.00	9.00
Note: Exist in both coin and medal alignment						
1993	10,000	PF65 25.00				
1994	—	—	—	6.00	8.00	10.00
1994	—	PF65 25.00				
1994 Fish	5,000,000	—	—	7.00	10.00	12.50
1994 Fish	10,000	PF65 25.00				
1994 Bee	9,990,000	—	—	6.00	9.00	11.00
1995	9,996,000	—	—	6.00	9.00	11.00
1995	10,000	PF65 25.00				
1996	17,000	—	—	5.00	6.50	8.50
1996	8,000	PF65 25.00				
1997	15,000	—	—	6.00	8.00	10.00
1997	10,000	PF65 25.00				
1998	—	—	—	6.00	8.00	10.00
1998	—	PF65 25.00				
1999	—	—	—	6.00	8.00	10.00
1999	—	PF65 25.00				
2000	—	—	—	6.00	8.00	10.00
2000	—	PF65 25.00				

KM# 1008.2a 20 FRANCS
12.66 g., Tri-Metallic .720 Gold center, .950 Silver inner ring, .750 Gold outer ring, 27 mm. **Obv:** Mont St. Michel; 5 bands of stripes in outer ring **Rev:** Patterned denomination above date

Date	Mintage	VF20	XF40	MS60	MS63	MS65
1992	15,000	PF65 500				

KM# 1008.2b 20 FRANCS
16.46 g., Tri-Metallic .920 Gold center, .750 Gold inner ring, .920 Gold outer ring, 27 mm. **Obv:** Mont St. Michel **Rev:** Patterned denomination above date

Date	Mintage	VF20	XF40	MS60	MS63	MS65
1992	5,000	PF65 800				

KM# 1016 20 FRANCS
Tri-Metallic Aluminum-Bronze center, Nickel inner ring, Copper-Aluminum-Nickel outer ring, 27 mm. **Subject:** Mediterranean Games **Obv:** Tower of Adge **Rev:** Denomination flanked by laurels, wavy design below, rings divide date at bottom

Date	Mintage	VF20	XF40	MS60	MS63	MS65
1993	5,001,000	—	—	8.00	10.00	12.00

KM# 1036 20 FRANCS
Tri-Metallic Aluminum-Bronze center, Nickel inner ring, Copper-Aluminum-Nickel outer ring, 26.8 mm. **Subject:** Founder of Modern Day Olympics - Pierre de Coubertin **Obv:** Head left, 'RF' below, torch at right **Rev:** Building at left, denomination and date divided by Olympic logo at right

Date	Mintage	VF20	XF40	MS60	MS63	MS65
1994	15,000,000	—	—	8.00	10.00	12.00

KM# 941.1 50 FRANCS
30.00 g., 0.900 Silver 0.8681 oz. ASW, 41 mm. **Obv:** Denomination within wreath **Rev:** Hercules group **Mint:** Paris **Note:** Without mint mark.

Date	Mintage	VF20	XF40	MS60	MS63	MS65
1974	4,299,000	—	16.00	17.50	30.00	40.00
1975	4,551,000	—	16.00	17.50	30.00	40.00
1976	7,739,000	—	16.00	17.50	30.00	40.00
1977	7,884,000	—	16.00	17.50	30.00	40.00
1978	12,028,000	—	16.00	17.50	30.00	40.00
1979	12,041,000	—	16.00	17.50	30.00	40.00
1980	60,000	—	30.00	40.00	50.00	70.00
Note: In sets only						

KM# 941.2 50 FRANCS
30.00 g., 0.900 Silver 0.8681 oz. ASW, 41 mm. **Obv:** Denomination within wreath **Rev:** Legend begins at the level of the beltline of the goddess of Hercules' at left

Date	Mintage	VF20	XF40	MS60	MS63	MS65
1974	—	32.50	45.00	55.00	70.00	90.00

KM# 1145 50 FRANCS
8.45 g., 0.920 Gold 0.250 oz. AGW **Subject:** World Class Soccer **Obv:** Soccer ball, denomination and date below **Rev:** Stylized dove, soccer ball

Date	Mintage	VF20	XF40	MS60	MS63	MS65
1996	Est. 10000	PF65 475				

KM# 1208 50 FRANCS
8.45 g., 0.920 Gold 0.250 oz. AGW **Subject:** Treasures of the Nile **Obv:** Portrait above 'RF', obelisk at right **Rev:** Sphinx and pyramids, date at left, denomination below

Date	Mintage	VF20	XF40	MS60	MS63	MS65
1998	3,000	PF65 475				

KM# 1958 50 FRANCS
8.45 g., 0.920 Gold 0.2499 oz. AGW **Subject:** French Postage Stamps, 150th Anniversary **Mint:** Paris

Date	Mintage	VF20	XF40	MS60	MS63	MS65
1999	1,000	PF65 475				

KM# 1236 50 FRANCS
8.45 g., 0.920 Gold 0.250 oz. AGW **Subject:** Yves St. Laurent **Obv:** RF monogram, denomination **Rev:** Fashion show scene **Edge:** Plain **Mint:** Paris

Date	Mintage	VF20	XF40	MS60	MS63	MS65
2000	2,000	PF65 475				

KM# 1256 65.5997 FRANCS
8.45 g., 0.925 Gold 0.2513 oz. AGW **Series:** Euro Conversion Series **Obv:** Country names with euro currency equivalents around "RF", denomination and French coin designs **Rev:** Europa allegorical portrait **Edge:** Plain **Mint:** Paris

Date	Mintage	VF20	XF40	MS60	MS63	MS65
1999	10,000	PF65 700				

KM# 1260 65.5997 FRANCS
8.45 g., 0.925 Gold 0.2513 oz. AGW **Obv:** Country names with euro-currency equivalents around "RF", denomination and French euro coin designs **Mint:** Paris

Date	Mintage	VF20	XF40	MS60	MS63	MS65
2000	3,000	PF65 700				

KM# 951.1 100 FRANCS
15.00 g., 0.900 Silver 0.434 oz. ASW **Obv:** Pantheon, date below **Rev:** Leafy design above denomination **Mint:** Paris **Note:** Without mint mark.

Date	Mintage	VF20	XF40	MS60	MS63	MS65
1982	3,030,000	—	15.00	22.00	27.50	37.50
1982	25,000	PF65 45.00				
1983	5,001,000	—	15.00	22.00	27.50	37.50
1983	17,000	PF65 45.00				
1984	5,000,000	—	15.00	22.00	27.50	37.50
1985	999,000	—	15.00	25.00	30.00	50.00
1985	13,000	PF65 45.00				
1986	519,000	—	15.00	25.00	30.00	45.00
1987	100,000	—	16.00	25.00	30.00	40.00
1988	100,000	—	16.00	25.00	30.00	40.00
1989	83,000	—	20.00	25.00	30.00	40.00
1990	15,000	—	20.00	28.00	35.00	45.00
1991	5,000	—	30.00	50.00	100	200
1991	10,000	PF65 55.00				
1992	15,000	PF65 45.00				
1993	15,000	PF65 45.00				
1994	15,000	PF65 45.00				
1995	4,011	—	30.00	50.00	100	220
1995	10,000	PF65 48.00				
1996	2,013	—	85.00	125	250	500
1996	8,000	PF65 60.00				
1997	—	—	20.00	30.00	40.00	50.00
1997	—	PF65 60.00				
1998	—	—	20.00	30.00	40.00	50.00
1998	—	PF65 60.00				
1999	—	—	20.00	30.00	40.00	50.00
1999	—	PF65 60.00				
2000	—	—	20.00	30.00	40.00	50.00
2000	—	PF65 60.00				

KM# 955 100 FRANCS
15.00 g., 0.900 Silver 0.434 oz. ASW **Subject:** 50th Anniversary - Death of Marie Curie **Obv:** Leafy branches divide date and denomination **Rev:** Head right, dates below

Date	Mintage	VF20	XF40	MS60	MS63	MS65
1984	3,964,000	—	20.00	22.00	25.00	30.00

KM# 955a 100 FRANCS
15.00 g., 0.950 Silver 0.4581 oz. ASW **Obv:** Leafy branches divide date and denomination **Rev:** Head right, two dates

Date	Mintage	VF20	XF40	MS60	MS63	MS65
1984	1,000	PF65 200				

KM# 955b 100 FRANCS
17.00 g., 0.920 Gold 0.5028 oz. AGW **Subject:** 50th Anniversary - Death of Marie Curie **Obv:** Leafy branches divide date and denomination **Rev:** Head right, two dates

Date	Mintage	VF20	XF40	MS60	MS63	MS65
1984	5,000	PF65 950				

KM# 957 100 FRANCS
15.00 g., 0.900 Silver 0.434 oz. ASW **Subject:** Centennial of Emile Zola's Novel **Rev:** Head right

Date	Mintage	VF20	XF40	MS60	MS63	MS65
1985	3,980,000	—	15.00	18.00	28.00	35.00
1985	13,000	PF65 55.00				

KM# 957a 100 FRANCS
15.00 g., 0.950 Silver 0.4581 oz. ASW **Subject:** Centennial of Emile Zola's Novel **Rev:** Head right

Date	Mintage	VF20	XF40	MS60	MS63	MS65
1985	5,000	PF65 115				

KM# 957b 100 FRANCS
17.00 g., 0.920 Gold 0.5028 oz. AGW **Subject:** Centennial of Emile Zola's Novel **Rev:** Head right

Date	Mintage	VF20	XF40	MS60	MS63	MS65
1985	5,000	PF65 950				

KM# 960 100 FRANCS
15.00 g., 0.900 Silver 0.434 oz. ASW, 31 mm. **Subject:** Centennial - Statue of Liberty **Obv:** Top of statue facing, dates at right **Rev:** Liberty cap over inscription above denomination, date below

Date	Mintage	VF20	XF40	MS60	MS63	MS65
1986	4,427,000	—	—	—	14.50	18.50

KM# 960a 100 FRANCS
15.00 g., 0.950 Silver 0.4581 oz. ASW **Subject:** Centennial of Statue of Liberty **Obv:** Top of statue facing **Rev:** Liberty cap over inscription above denomination, date below

Date	Mintage	VF20	XF40	MS60	MS63	MS65
1986	18,000	PF65 45.00				

KM# 960b 100 FRANCS
17.00 g., 0.920 Gold 0.5028 oz. AGW **Subject:** Centennial - Statue of Liberty **Obv:** Top of statue facing **Rev:** Liberty cap over inscription above denomination, date below

Date	Mintage	VF20	XF40	MS60	MS63	MS65
1986	13,000	—	—	—	875	900
1986	17,000	PF65 950				

KM# 960c 100 FRANCS
20.00 g., 0.999 Platinum 0.6424 oz. APW **Subject:** Centennial - Statue of Liberty **Obv:** Top of statue facing **Rev:** Liberty cap over inscription above denomination, date below

Date	Mintage	VF20	XF40	MS60	MS63	MS65
1986	9,500	PF65 1,500				

KM# 960d 100 FRANCS
17.00 g., 0.900 Palladium 0.4919 oz. APW **Subject:** Centennial - Statue of Liberty **Obv:** Top of statue facing **Rev:** Liberty cap over inscription above denomination, date below

Date	Mintage	VF20	XF40	MS60	MS63	MS65
1986	1,250	PF65 450				

KM# 962 100 FRANCS
15.00 g., 0.900 Silver 0.434 oz. ASW, 31 mm. **Subject:** 230th Anniversary - Birth of General Lafayette **Obv:** Bust left **Rev:** Liberty cap over inscription above denomination, date below

Date	Mintage	VF20	XF40	MS60	MS63	MS65
1987	4,801,000	—	—	—	20.00	25.00

KM# 962a 100 FRANCS
15.00 g., 0.950 Silver 0.4581 oz. ASW **Subject:** 230th Anniversary - Birth of General Lafayette **Obv:** Bust left **Rev:** Liberty cap over inscription above denomination, date below

Date	Mintage	VF20	XF40	MS60	MS63	MS65
1987	30,000	PF65 35.00				

KM# 962b 100 FRANCS
17.00 g., 0.920 Gold 0.5028 oz. AGW **Subject:** 230th Anniversary - Birth of General Lafayette **Obv:** Bust left **Rev:** Liberty cap over inscription above denomination, date below

Date	Mintage	VF20	XF40	MS60	MS63	MS65
1987	10,000	—	—	—	875	950
1987	20,000	PF65 950				

KM# 962c 100 FRANCS
20.00 g., 0.999 Platinum 0.6424 oz. APW **Subject:** 230th Anniversary - Birth of General Lafayette **Obv:** Bust left **Rev:** Liberty cap over inscription above denomination, date below

Date	Mintage	VF20	XF40	MS60	MS63	MS65
1987	8,500	PF65 1,350				

KM# 962d 100 FRANCS
17.00 g., 0.900 Palladium 0.4919 oz. APW **Subject:** 230th Anniversary - Birth of General Lafayette **Obv:** Bust left **Rev:** Liberty cap over inscription above denomination, date below

Date	Mintage	VF20	XF40	MS60	MS63	MS65
1987	7,000	PF65 450				

KM# 966 100 FRANCS
15.00 g., 0.900 Silver 0.434 oz. ASW **Subject:** Fraternity **Obv:** Radiant head left with crown of cherubs **Rev:** Liberty cap over inscription above denomination, date below

Date	Mintage	VF20	XF40	MS60	MS63	MS65
1988	4,853,000	—	15.00	18.00	26.50	32.50

KM# 966a 100 FRANCS
15.00 g., 0.950 Silver 0.4581 oz. ASW **Subject:** Fraternity **Obv:** Radiant head left with crown of cherubs

Date	Mintage	VF20	XF40	MS60	MS63	MS65
1988	20,000	PF65 40.00				

KM# 966b 100 FRANCS
17.00 g., 0.920 Gold 0.5028 oz. AGW **Subject:** Fraternity **Obv:** Radiant head left with crown of cherubs **Rev:** Liberty cap over inscription above denomination, date below

Date	Mintage	VF20	XF40	MS60	MS63	MS65
1988	3,000	—	—	—	875	950
1988	12,000	PF65 950				

KM# 966c 100 FRANCS
20.00 g., 0.999 Platinum 0.6424 oz. APW **Subject:** Fraternity **Obv:** Radiant head left with crown of cherubs **Rev:** Liberty cap over inscription above denomination, date below

Date	Mintage	VF20	XF40	MS60	MS63	MS65
1988	5,000	PF65 1,450				

KM# 966d 100 FRANCS
17.00 g., 0.900 Palladium 0.4919 oz. APW **Subject:** Fraternity **Obv:** Radiant head left with crown of cherubs **Rev:** Liberty cap over inscription above denomination, date below

Date	Mintage	VF20	XF40	MS60	MS63	MS65
1988	7,000	PF65 450				

KM# 970 100 FRANCS
15.00 g., 0.900 Silver 0.434 oz. ASW **Subject:** Human Rights **Obv:** Standing Genius writing the constitution **Rev:** Liberty cap over inscription above denomination, date below

Date	Mintage	VF20	XF40	MS60	MS63	MS65
1989	4,823,000	—	15.00	20.00	32.50	37.50

KM# 970a 100 FRANCS
15.00 g., 0.950 Silver 0.4581 oz. ASW **Subject:** Human Rights **Obv:** Standing Genius writing the constitution **Rev:** Liberty cap over inscription above denomination, date below

Date	Mintage	VF20	XF40	MS60	MS63	MS65
1989	40,000	PF65 40.00				

KM# 970b 100 FRANCS
17.00 g., 0.920 Gold 0.5028 oz. AGW **Subject:** Human Rights **Obv:** Standing Genius writing the constitution **Rev:** Liberty cap over inscription above denomination, date below

Date	Mintage	VF20	XF40	MS60	MS63	MS65
1989	1,000	—	—	—	—	950
1989	20,000	PF65 950				

KM# 970c 100 FRANCS
20.00 g., 0.999 Platinum 0.6424 oz. APW **Subject:** Human Rights **Obv:** Standing Genius writing the constitution **Rev:** Liberty cap over inscription above denomination, date below

Date	Mintage	VF20	XF40	MS60	MS63	MS65
1989	1,000	PF65 1,350				

KM# 970d 100 FRANCS
17.00 g., 0.900 Palladium 0.4919 oz. APW **Subject:** Human Rights **Obv:** Standing Genius writing the constitution **Rev:** Liberty cap over inscription above denomination, date below

Date	Mintage	VF20	XF40	MS60	MS63	MS65
1989	1,250	PF65 450				

KM# 971 100 FRANCS
22.20 g., 0.900 Silver 0.6424 oz. ASW **Subject:** 1992 Olympics **Obv:** Alpine skiing **Rev:** Cross on flame, date and denomination, logo below

Date	Mintage	VF20	XF40	MS60	MS63	MS65
1989	136,000	PF65 30.00				

KM# 972 100 FRANCS
22.20 g., 0.900 Silver 0.6424 oz. ASW **Subject:** 1992 Olympics **Obv:** Ice Skating Couple **Rev:** Cross on flame, date and denomination, logo below

Date	Mintage	VF20	XF40	MS60	MS63	MS65
1989	179,000	PF65 27.50				

KM# 980 100 FRANCS
22.20 g., 0.900 Silver 0.6424 oz. ASW **Series:** 1992 Olympics **Obv:** Speed skaters and alpine marmot **Rev:** Crossed flame divides date and denomination, Olympic logo below

Date	Mintage	VF20	XF40	MS60	MS63	MS65
1990	137,000	PF65 30.00				

KM# 981 100 FRANCS
22.20 g., 0.900 Silver 0.6424 oz. ASW **Series:** 1992 Olympics **Obv:** Bobsledding **Rev:** Games logo, value and legend

Date	Mintage	VF20	XF40	MS60	MS63	MS65
1990	127,000	PF65 30.00				

KM# 982 100 FRANCS
15.01 g., 0.900 Silver 0.4343 oz. ASW **Subject:** Charlemagne **Obv:** Date and denomination divided by monogram, laurel spray below, circle surrounds **Rev:** Stylized head facing

Date	Mintage	VF20	XF40	MS60	MS63	MS65
1990	4,950,000	—	20.00	30.00	37.50	42.50

KM# 983 100 FRANCS
22.20 g., 0.900 Silver 0.6424 oz. ASW **Series:** 1992 Olympics **Obv:** Free-style skier and chamois **Rev:** Crossed flame, date and denomination, logo below

Date	Mintage	VF20	XF40	MS60	MS63	MS65
1990	110,000	PF65 32.50				

KM# 984 100 FRANCS

22.20 g., 0.900 Silver 0.6424 oz. ASW **Subject:** 1992 Olympics **Obv:** Slalom skiers **Rev:** Crossed flame, date and denomination, logo below

Date	Mintage	VF20	XF40	MS60	MS63	MS65
1990	110,000	PF65 30.00				

KM# 991 100 FRANCS

22.20 g., 0.900 Silver 0.6424 oz. ASW **Subject:** 100th Anniversary of Basketball **Obv:** 2 players **Rev:** Star, ring, and globe above denomination and date

Date	Mintage	VF20	XF40	MS60	MS63	MS65
1991	13,000	PF65 50.00				

KM# 992 100 FRANCS

22.20 g., 0.900 Silver 0.6424 oz. ASW **Subject:** 100th Anniversary of Basketball **Obv:** 1 player, hoops in background

Date	Mintage	VF20	XF40	MS60	MS63	MS65
1991	13,000	PF65 50.00				

KM# 993 100 FRANCS

22.20 g., 0.900 Silver 0.6424 oz. ASW **Series:** 1992 Olympics **Obv:** Hockey players and Ibex **Rev:** Crossed flame divides date and denomination, Olympic logo below

Date	Mintage	VF20	XF40	MS60	MS63	MS65
1991	93,000	PF65 40.00				

KM# 994 100 FRANCS

22.20 g., 0.900 Silver 0.6424 oz. ASW **Series:** 1992 Olympics **Obv:** Cross-country skier, building at left **Rev:** Crossed flame, date and denomination, logo below

Date	Mintage	VF20	XF40	MS60	MS63	MS65
1991	93,000	PF65 35.00				

KM# 995 100 FRANCS

22.20 g., 0.900 Silver 0.6424 oz. ASW **Series:** 1992 Olympics **Obv:** Ski jumpers **Rev:** Crossed flame, date and denomination, logo below

Date	Mintage	VF20	XF40	MS60	MS63	MS65
1991	90,000	PF65 37.50				

KM# 996 100 FRANCS

15.01 g., 0.900 Silver 0.4343 oz. ASW **Obv:** Finger pointing on starred paper, denomination below **Rev:** Head 3/4 facing, date below

Date	Mintage	VF20	XF40	MS60	MS63	MS65
1991	3,985,000	—	—	—	32.50	35.00

KM# 1009 100 FRANCS

22.20 g., 0.900 Silver 0.6424 oz. ASW **Subject:** Paralympics **Obv:** Segmented flying birds, denomination and date below **Rev:** Designs

Date	Mintage	VF20	XF40	MS60	MS63	MS65
1992	5,000	PF65 60.00				

KM# 1010 100 FRANCS

22.20 g., 0.900 Silver 0.6424 oz. ASW **Subject:** French Antarctic Territories **Obv:** Head at left facing, ship, mountains and "RF" in background, denomination below **Rev:** Fur seals above date

Date	Mintage	VF20	XF40	MS60	MS63	MS65
1992	15,000	PF65 75.00				

KM# 1011 100 FRANCS

22.20 g., 0.900 Silver 0.6424 oz. ASW **Subject:** French Antarctic Territories **Rev:** Emperor Penguins, date below

Date	Mintage	VF20	XF40	MS60	MS63	MS65
1992	15,000	PF65 75.00				

KM# 1120 100 FRANCS

15.01 g., 0.900 Silver 0.4343 oz. ASW **Subject:** Jean Monet **Rev:** Denomination above date within legend, rings surround, RF at bottom

Date	Mintage	VF20	XF40	MS60	MS63	MS65
1992	3,925,000	—	20.00	28.00	35.00	37.50

KM# 1017 100 FRANCS

22.20 g., 0.900 Silver 0.6424 oz. ASW **Series:** Bicentennial of the Louvre **Obv:** Mona Lisa **Rev:** Patterned pyramids front museum, date and denomination below

Date	Mintage	VF20	XF40	MS60	MS63	MS65
1993	200,000	PF65 45.00				

KM# 1018.1 100 FRANCS

15.00 g., 0.900 Silver 0.434 oz. ASW, 31 mm. **Series:** Bicentennial of the Louvre **Obv:** Liberty **Rev:** Patterned pyramids front museum, date and denomination below

Date	Mintage	VF20	XF40	MS60	MS63	MS65
1993	—	—	—	28.00	35.00	40.00

KM# 1018.2 100 FRANCS

22.20 g., 0.900 Silver 0.6424 oz. ASW **Series:** Bicentennial of the Louvre **Obv:** Liberty **Rev:** Patterned pyramids front museum, date and denomination below

Date	Mintage	VF20	XF40	MS60	MS63	MS65
1993	20,000	PF65 37.50				

KM# 1018.2a 100 FRANCS

17.00 g., 0.920 Gold 0.5028 oz. AGW **Series:** Bicentennial of the Louvre **Obv:** Liberty **Rev:** Patterned pyramids front museum, date and denomination below

Date	Mintage	VF20	XF40	MS60	MS63	MS65
1993	5,000	PF65 950				

KM# 1019 100 FRANCS

22.20 g., 0.900 Silver 0.6424 oz. ASW **Series:** Bicentennial of the Louvre **Obv:** Victory **Rev:** Patterned pyramids front museum, date and denomination below

Date	Mintage	VF20	XF40	MS60	MS63	MS65
1993	20,000	PF65 37.50				

KM# 1019a 100 FRANCS

17.00 g., 0.920 Gold 0.5028 oz. AGW **Series:** Bicentennial of the Louvre **Obv:** Victory **Rev:** Patterned pyramids front museum, date and denomination below

Date	Mintage	VF20	XF40	MS60	MS63	MS65
1993	5,000	PF65 950				

KM# 1020 100 FRANCS

22.26 g., 0.900 Silver 0.6441 oz. ASW **Series:** Bicentennial of the Louvre **Obv:** Venus de Milo **Rev:** Patterned pyramids front museum, date and denomination below

Date	Mintage	VF20	XF40	MS60	MS63	MS65
1993	20,000	PF65 40.00				

KM# 1021 100 FRANCS

22.26 g., 0.900 Silver 0.6441 oz. ASW **Series:** Bicentennial of the Louvre **Obv:** Marie-Marguerite **Rev:** Patterned pyramids front museum, date and denomination below

Date	Mintage	VF20	XF40	MS60	MS63	MS65
1993	20,000	PF65 35.00				

KM# 1021a 100 FRANCS

17.00 g., 0.920 Gold 0.5028 oz. AGW **Series:** Bicentennial of the Louvre **Obv:** Marie-Marguerite **Rev:** Patterned pyramids front museum, date and denomination below

Date	Mintage	VF20	XF40	MS60	MS63	MS65
1993	5,000	PF65 950				

KM# 1022 100 FRANCS

22.26 g., 0.900 Silver 0.6441 oz. ASW **Series:** Bicentennial of the Louvre **Obv:** Napoleon crowning Josephine as Empress, 1763-1814 **Rev:** Patterned pyramids front museum, date and denomination below

Date	Mintage	VF20	XF40	MS60	MS63	MS65
1993	20,000	PF65 50.00				

KM# 1022a 100 FRANCS

17.00 g., 0.920 Gold 0.5028 oz. AGW **Series:** Bicentennial of the Louvre **Obv:** Napoleon crowning Josephine **Rev:** Patterned pyramids front museum, date and denomination below

Date	Mintage	VF20	XF40	MS60	MS63	MS65
1993	5,000	PF65 950				

KM# 1023 100 FRANCS

22.20 g., 0.900 Silver 0.6424 oz. ASW **Obv:** Head with hat facing **Rev:** Flaming torch, denomination below

Date	Mintage	VF20	XF40	MS60	MS63	MS65
1993	100,000	—	—	—	28.00	32.00
1993	50,000	PF65 45.00				

KM# 1037 100 FRANCS

22.20 g., 0.900 Silver 0.6424 oz. ASW **Subject:** Winston Churchill **Obv:** Uniformed bust right

Date	Mintage	VF20	XF40	MS60	MS63	MS65
1994	Est. 30000	PF65 45.00				

KM# 1038 100 FRANCS

22.20 g., 0.900 Silver 0.6424 oz. ASW **Subject:** General de Gaulle **Obv:** Bust right at microphone **Rev:** Map of France, inscription overlay

Date	Mintage	VF20	XF40	MS60	MS63	MS65
1994	Est. 30000	PF65 47.50				

KM# 1039 100 FRANCS

22.20 g., 0.900 Silver 0.6424 oz. ASW **Subject:** General Leclerc **Obv:** Bust facing **Rev:** Flag, inscription, fort, denomination

Date	Mintage	VF20	XF40	MS60	MS63	MS65
1994	Est. 30000	PF65 45.00				

KM# 1040 100 FRANCS

22.20 g., 0.900 Silver 0.6424 oz. ASW **Subject:** General Marie Pierre Koenig **Obv:** Bust facing looking left **Rev:** Battle scene

Date	Mintage	VF20	XF40	MS60	MS63	MS65
1994	Est. 30000	PF65 47.50				

KM# 1041 100 FRANCS

22.20 g., 0.900 Silver 0.6424 oz. ASW **Subject:** General Juin **Obv:** Mountaintop building **Rev:** Uniformed bust right, map of Italy at right

Date	Mintage	VF20	XF40	MS60	MS63	MS65
1994	Est. 30000	PF65 45.00				

KM# 1042 100 FRANCS

22.20 g., 0.900 Silver 0.6424 oz. ASW **Subject:** General Dwight David Eisenhower **Obv:** Bust 3/4 left **Rev:** Flags representing allied countries under Supreme Commander Eisenhower

Date	Mintage	VF20	XF40	MS60	MS63	MS65
1994	Est. 30000	PF65 45.00				

KM# 1043 100 FRANCS

22.20 g., 0.900 Silver 0.6424 oz. ASW **Subject:** Sainte - Mere - Eglise **Rev:** Church, parachute behind

Date	Mintage	VF20	XF40	MS60	MS63	MS65
1994	Est. 30000	PF65 45.00				

KM# 1044 100 FRANCS
22.20 g., 0.900 Silver 0.6424 oz. ASW **Subject:** General de Lattre de Tassigny **Obv:** Face in profile right **Rev:** Waving flags below denomination

Date	Mintage	VF20	XF40	MS60	MS63	MS65
1994	Est. 30000	PF65 45.00				

KM# 1045.1 100 FRANCS
15.00 g., 0.900 Silver 0.434 oz. ASW, 31 mm. **Subject:** Liberation of Paris **Obv:** Battle scene, denomination below **Rev:** Triumphant troops marching down Champs Elysees **Note:** Smaller size.

Date	Mintage	VF20	XF40	MS60	MS63	MS65
1994	1,598,000	—	16.00	25.00	32.00	40.00

KM# 1045.2 100 FRANCS
22.20 g., 0.900 Silver 0.6424 oz. ASW **Subject:** Liberation of Paris **Obv:** Battle scene, denomination **Rev:** Triumphant troops marching down Champs Elysees

Date	Mintage	VF20	XF40	MS60	MS63	MS65
1994	Est. 30000	PF65 45.00				

KM# 1046 100 FRANCS
22.20 g., 0.900 Silver 0.6424 oz. ASW **Subject:** De Gaulle and Adenauer **Obv:** Facing busts, date below **Rev:** Two hands joined in handshake

Date	Mintage	VF20	XF40	MS60	MS63	MS65
1994	Est. 30000	PF65 45.00				

KM# 1047 100 FRANCS
33.63 g., 0.925 Silver 1.0001 oz. ASW **Series:** 1996 Olympics **Obv:** Head facing, denomination and date below **Rev:** Discus thrower **Edge Lettering:** CITIUS ALTIUS FORTIUS

Date	Mintage	VF20	XF40	MS60	MS63	MS65
1994	250,000	PF65 35.00				

KM# 1048 100 FRANCS
33.63 g., 0.925 Silver 1.0001 oz. ASW **Subject:** 1996 Olympics **Obv:** Head facing, denomination and date below **Rev:** Javelin Thrower **Edge:** CITIUS ALTIUS FORTIUS

Date	Mintage	VF20	XF40	MS60	MS63	MS65
1994	250,000	PF65 35.00				

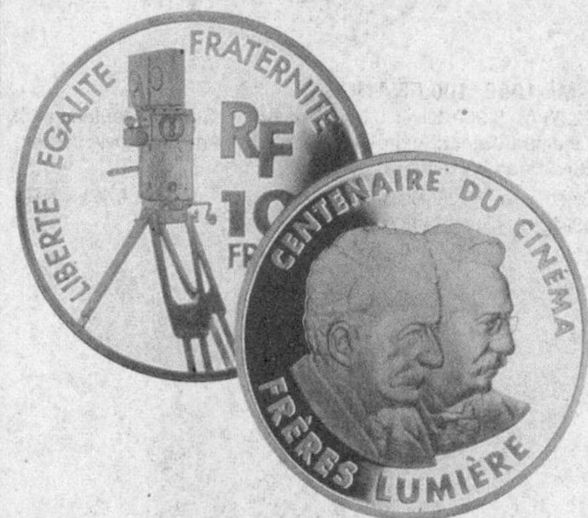

KM# 1072 100 FRANCS
22.20 g., 0.900 Silver 0.6424 oz. ASW **Series:** Centennial of Cinema **Subject:** Lumiere Brothers **Obv:** Antique movie camera, denomination at right **Rev:** Conjoined busts right

Date	Mintage	VF20	XF40	MS60	MS63	MS65
1994	15,000	PF65 35.00				
1995	—	PF65 35.00				

KM# 1073 100 FRANCS
17.00 g., 0.920 Gold 0.5028 oz. AGW **Series:** Centennial of Cinema **Subject:** Lumiere Brothers **Obv:** Antique movie camera **Rev:** Conjoined busts right

Date	Mintage	VF20	XF40	MS60	MS63	MS65
1994	5,000	PF65 950				
1995	—	PF65 950				

KM# 1076 100 FRANCS
22.20 g., 0.900 Silver 0.6424 oz. ASW **Series:** Centennial of Cinema **Subject:** Charlie Chaplin **Obv:** Antique movie camera **Rev:** Head facing

Date	Mintage	VF20	XF40	MS60	MS63	MS65
1994	15,000	PF65 45.00				
1995	—	PF65 45.00				

KM# 1077 100 FRANCS
17.00 g., 0.920 Gold 0.5028 oz. AGW **Series:** Centennial of Cinema **Subject:** Charlie Chaplin **Obv:** Antique movie camera **Rev:** Head facing

Date	Mintage	VF20	XF40	MS60	MS63	MS65
1994	5,000	PF65 875				
1995	—	PF65 875				

KM# 1105 100 FRANCS
17.00 g., 0.920 Gold 0.5028 oz. AGW **Series:** Centennial of Cinema **Subject:** Yves Montand **Obv:** Antique movie camera **Rev:** Bust 3/4 facing

Date	Mintage	VF20	XF40	MS60	MS63	MS65
1994	5,000	PF65 950				
1995	—	PF65 950				

KM# 1182 100 FRANCS
22.20 g., 0.900 Silver 0.6424 oz. ASW **Rev:** Voltaire

Date	Mintage	VF20	XF40	MS60	MS63	MS65
1994	3,000	PF65 60.00				

KM# 1929 100 FRANCS
22.20 g., 0.900 Silver 0.6424 oz. ASW, 37 mm. **Rev:** Female with flag and rifle **Mint:** Paris

Date	Mintage	VF20	XF40	MS60	MS63	MS65
1994	—	PF65 70.00				

KM# 1930 100 FRANCS
22.20 g., 0.900 Silver 0.6424 oz. ASW, 37 mm. **Subject:** Treasurers of the Louvre **Rev:** Nike of Samothrace **Mint:** Paris

Date	Mintage	VF20	XF40	MS60	MS63	MS65
1994	—	PF65 70.00				

KM# 1931 100 FRANCS
22.20 g., 0.900 Silver 0.6424 oz. ASW, 37 mm. **Subject:** Treasurers of the Louvre **Rev:** La Gioconda **Mint:** Paris

Date	Mintage	VF20	XF40	MS60	MS63	MS65
1994	—	PF65 70.00				

KM# 1932 100 FRANCS
17.00 g., 0.920 Gold 0.5028 oz. AGW, 31 mm. **Subject:** Treasurers of the Louvre **Rev:** Female with flag and rifle **Mint:** Paris

Date	Mintage	VF20	XF40	MS60	MS63	MS65
1994	—	PF65 1,000				

KM# 1933 100 FRANCS
17.00 g., 0.920 Gold 0.5028 oz. AGW, 31 mm. **Subject:** Treasurers of the Louvre **Rev:** Nike of Samothrace **Mint:** Paris

Date	Mintage	VF20	XF40	MS60	MS63	MS65
1994	—	PF65 1,000				

KM# 1935 100 FRANCS
22.20 g., 0.900 Silver 0.6424 oz. ASW, 37 mm. **Subject:** Treasurers of the Louvre **Rev:** Napoleon crowning Josephine **Mint:** Paris

Date	Mintage	VF20	XF40	MS60	MS63	MS65
1994	—	PF65 70.00				

KM# 1936 100 FRANCS
22.20 g., 0.900 Silver 0.6424 oz. ASW, 37 mm. **Subject:** Treasurers of the Louvre **Rev:** Marie-Marguerite **Mint:** Paris

Date	Mintage	VF20	XF40	MS60	MS63	MS65
1994	—	PF65 70.00				

KM# 1937 100 FRANCS
22.20 g., 0.900 Silver 0.6424 oz. ASW, 37 mm. **Subject:** Treasurers of the Louvre **Rev:** Venus de Milo **Mint:** Paris

Date	Mintage	VF20	XF40	MS60	MS63	MS65
1994	—	PF65 70.00				

KM# 1938 100 FRANCS
17.00 g., 0.920 Gold 0.5028 oz. AGW, 31 mm. **Rev:** Napoleon crowning Josephine **Mint:** Paris

Date	Mintage	VF20	XF40	MS60	MS63	MS65
1994	—	PF65 1,000				

KM# 1939 100 FRANCS
17.00 g., 0.920 Gold 0.5028 oz. AGW, 31 mm. **Subject:** Treasurers of the Louvre **Rev:** Marie-Marguerite **Mint:** Paris

Date	Mintage	VF20	XF40	MS60	MS63	MS65
1994	—	PF65 1,000				

KM# 1080 100 FRANCS
22.20 g., 0.900 Silver 0.6424 oz. ASW **Series:** Centennial of

Cinema **Subject:** Leon Gaumont **Obv:** Antique movie camera **Rev:** Head facing

Date	Mintage	VF20	XF40	MS60	MS63	MS65
1995	15,000	PF65 40.00				

KM# 1081 100 FRANCS
17.00 g., 0.920 Gold 0.5028 oz. AGW **Series:** Centennial of Cinema **Subject:** Leon Gaumont **Obv:** Antique movie camera **Rev:** Head facing

Date	Mintage	VF20	XF40	MS60	MS63	MS65
1995	5,000	PF65 875				

KM# 1084 100 FRANCS
22.20 g., 0.900 Silver 0.6424 oz. ASW **Series:** Centennial of Cinema **Subject:** Jean Renoir **Obv:** Antique movie camera **Rev:** Head right

Date	Mintage	VF20	XF40	MS60	MS63	MS65
1995	15,000	PF65 30.00				

KM# 1085 100 FRANCS
17.00 g., 0.920 Gold 0.5028 oz. AGW **Series:** Centennial of Cinema **Subject:** Jean Renoir **Obv:** Antique movie camera **Rev:** Head right

Date	Mintage	VF20	XF40	MS60	MS63	MS65
1995	5,000	PF65 950				

KM# 1088 100 FRANCS
22.20 g., 0.900 Silver 0.6424 oz. ASW **Series:** Centennial of Cinema **Subject:** Alfred Hitchcock **Obv:** Antique movie camera **Rev:** Head 1/4 left

Date	Mintage	VF20	XF40	MS60	MS63	MS65
1995	15,000	PF65 40.00				

KM# 1089 100 FRANCS
17.00 g., 0.920 Gold 0.5028 oz. AGW **Series:** Centennial of Cinema **Subject:** Alfred Hitchcock **Obv:** Antique movie camera **Rev:** Head 1/4 left

Date	Mintage	VF20	XF40	MS60	MS63	MS65
1995	5,000	PF65 950				

KM# 1092 100 FRANCS
22.20 g., 0.900 Silver 0.6424 oz. ASW **Series:** Centennial of Cinema **Subject:** Greta Garbo **Obv:** Antique movie camera **Rev:** Head right

Date	Mintage	VF20	XF40	MS60	MS63	MS65
1995	15,000	PF65 40.00				

KM# 1093 100 FRANCS
17.00 g., 0.920 Gold 0.5028 oz. AGW **Series:** Centennial of Cinema **Subject:** Greta Garbo 1905-1990, actress in "Camille & Ninotchka" **Obv:** Antique movie camera **Rev:** Head right

Date	Mintage	VF20	XF40	MS60	MS63	MS65
1995	5,000	PF65 950				

KM# 1096 100 FRANCS
22.20 g., 0.900 Silver 0.6424 oz. ASW **Series:** Centennial of Cinema **Subject:** Audrey Hepburn **Obv:** Antique movie camera **Rev:** Head 3/4 left

Date	Mintage	VF20	XF40	MS60	MS63	MS65
1994	15,000	PF65 38.00				

KM# 1097 100 FRANCS
17.00 g., 0.920 Gold 0.5028 oz. AGW **Series:** Centennial of Cinema **Subject:** Audrey Hepburn **Obv:** Antique movie camera **Rev:** Head 3/4 left

Date	Mintage	VF20	XF40	MS60	MS63	MS65
1995	—	PF65 950				
1994	5,000	PF65 950				

KM# 1100 100 FRANCS
22.20 g., 0.900 Silver 0.6424 oz. ASW **Series:** Centennial of Cinema **Subject:** Federico Fellini **Obv:** Antique movie camera **Rev:** Bust 3/4 right

Date	Mintage	VF20	XF40	MS60	MS63	MS65
1995	15,000	PF65 30.00				

KM# 1101 100 FRANCS
17.00 g., 0.920 Gold 0.5028 oz. AGW **Series:** Centennial of Cinema **Subject:** Federico Fellini **Obv:** Antique movie camera **Rev:** Bust 3/4 right

Date	Mintage	VF20	XF40	MS60	MS63	MS65
1995	5,000	PF65 875				

KM# 1104 100 FRANCS
22.20 g., 0.900 Silver 0.6424 oz. ASW **Series:** Centennial of Cinema **Subject:** Yves Montand **Obv:** Antique movie camera **Rev:** Bust 3/4 facing

Date	Mintage	VF20	XF40	MS60	MS63	MS65
1994	15,000	PF65 30.00				

KM# 1108 100 FRANCS
22.20 g., 0.900 Silver 0.6424 oz. ASW **Series:** Centennial of Cinema **Subject:** Romy Schneider **Obv:** Antique movie camera **Rev:** Bust 3/4 left

Date	Mintage	VF20	XF40	MS60	MS63	MS65
1995	15,000	PF65 35.00				

KM# 1109 100 FRANCS
17.00 g., 0.920 Gold 0.5028 oz. AGW **Series:** Centennial of Cinema **Subject:** Romy Schneider **Obv:** Antique movie camera **Rev:** Bust 3/4 left

Date	Mintage	VF20	XF40	MS60	MS63	MS65
1995	5,000	PF65 950				

KM# 1116.1 100 FRANCS
15.00 g., 0.900 Silver 0.434 oz. ASW, 31 mm. **Subject:** V.E. Day **Obv:** Victory in Europe date, May 8, 1945 **Rev:** Birds in flight above banners, PAX below

Date	Mintage	VF20	XF40	MS60	MS63	MS65
1995	1,990,000	—	—	—	40.00	45.00

KM# 1116.2 100 FRANCS
22.20 g., 0.900 Silver 0.6424 oz. ASW, 37 mm. **Obv:** Victory in Europe date, May 8,1945 **Rev:** Birds in flight above banners, PAX below

Date	Mintage	VF20	XF40	MS60	MS63	MS65
1995	30,000	PF65 45.00				

KM# 1134 100 FRANCS
22.20 g., 0.900 Silver 0.6424 oz. ASW **Obv:** Bust facing **Rev:** Lab bottles, denomination and date

Date	Mintage	VF20	XF40	MS60	MS63	MS65
1995	10,000	PF65 45.00				

KM# 1136 100 FRANCS
22.20 g., 0.900 Silver 0.6424 oz. ASW **Obv:** Bust 1/4 left **Rev:** Bird in tree, denomination at right, fox and date below

Date	Mintage	VF20	XF40	MS60	MS63	MS65
1995	10,000	PF65 45.00				

KM# 1498 100 FRANCS
22.20 g., 0.900 Silver 0.6424 oz. ASW, 37 mm. **Subject:** Allies in Europe, 50th Anniversary **Rev:** Flags **Mint:** Paris

Date	Mintage	VF20	XF40	MS60	MS63	MS65
1995	1,990,400	—	—	22.00	27.00	—

KM# 1942 100 FRANCS
22.20 g., 0.900 Silver 0.6424 oz. ASW, 37 mm. **Subject:** Georges Melies **Mint:** Paris

Date	Mintage	VF20	XF40	MS60	MS63	MS65
1995	—	PF65 35.00				

KM# 1943 100 FRANCS
22.20 g., 0.900 Silver 0.6424 oz. ASW, 37 mm. **Subject:** Gerard Philippe **Mint:** Paris

Date	Mintage	VF20	XF40	MS60	MS63	MS65
1995	—	PF65 35.00				

KM# 1944 100 FRANCS
22.20 g., 0.900 Silver 0.6424 oz. ASW, 37 mm. **Subject:** Marcel Pagnol **Mint:** Paris

Date	Mintage	VF20	XF40	MS60	MS63	MS65
1995	—	PF65 35.00				

KM# 1945 100 FRANCS
22.20 g., 0.900 Silver 0.6424 oz. ASW, 37 mm. **Subject:** Leonie Bathiat (Arletty) **Mint:** Paris

Date	Mintage	VF20	XF40	MS60	MS63	MS65
1995	—	PF65 35.00				

KM# 1946 100 FRANCS
17.00 g., 0.920 Gold 0.5028 oz. AGW, 31 mm. **Subject:** Georges Melies **Mint:** Paris

Date	Mintage	VF20	XF40	MS60	MS63	MS65
1995	—	PF65 950				

KM# 1947 100 FRANCS
17.00 g., 0.920 Gold 0.5028 oz. AGW, 31 mm. **Subject:** Gerard Philippe **Mint:** Paris

Date	Mintage	VF20	XF40	MS60	MS63	MS65
1995	—	PF65 950				

KM# 1948 100 FRANCS
17.00 g., 0.920 Gold 0.5028 oz. AGW, 31 mm. **Subject:** Marcel Pagnol **Mint:** Paris

Date	Mintage	VF20	XF40	MS60	MS63	MS65
1995	—	PF65 950				

KM# 1949 100 FRANCS
17.00 g., 0.920 Gold 0.5028 oz. AGW, 31 mm. **Subject:** Leonie Bathiat (Arletty) **Mint:** Paris

Date	Mintage	VF20	XF40	MS60	MS63	MS65
1995	—	PF65 950				

KM# 1138 100 FRANCS
22.20 g., 0.900 Silver 0.6424 oz. ASW **Subject:** 300th Anniversary of the Death of Marie de Sevigne; letter writer, 1626-1696 **Obv:** Bust 1/4 left **Rev:** Crowned double arms with supporters divide date and denomination

Date	Mintage	VF20	XF40	MS60	MS63	MS65
1996	5,000	PF65 65.00				

KM# 1172 100 FRANCS
17.00 g., 0.920 Gold 0.5028 oz. AGW **Subject:** Coupe du Monde 1998 - France **Obv:** World Cup 1998 logo above denomination and date **Rev:** Segment of Eiffel tower, soccer player

Date	Mintage	VF20	XF40	MS60	MS63	MS65
1996	25,000	PF65 950				

KM# 1180 100 FRANCS
15.05 g., 0.900 Silver 0.4355 oz. ASW **Subject:** King Clovis I **Obv:** Bust facing **Rev:** Baptism scene, date and denomination below

Date	Mintage	VF20	XF40	MS60	MS63	MS65
1996	2,000,000	—	16.00	25.00	32.50	37.50
1996	—	PF65 60.00				

KM# 1951 100 FRANCS
22.20 g., 0.900 Silver 0.6424 oz. ASW, 37 mm. **Subject:** French Christianity, 1500th Anniversary **Obv:** Covis **Rev:** Bishop of Reims **Mint:** Paris

Date	Mintage	VF20	XF40	MS60	MS63	MS65
1996	Est. 2500	PF65 125				

KM# 1168 100 FRANCS
17.00 g., 0.920 Gold 0.5028 oz. AGW **Subject:** Coupe du Monde 1998 - Africa **Obv:** World Cup 1998 logo above denomination and date **Rev:** Soccer player and map of Africa, date below

Date	Mintage	VF20	XF40	MS60	MS63	MS65
1997	25,000	PF65 950				

KM# 1169 100 FRANCS
17.00 g., 0.920 Gold 0.5028 oz. AGW **Subject:** Coupe du Monde 1998 - America **Obv:** World Cup 1998 logo above denomination and date below **Rev:** Soccer player and map of North & South America

Date	Mintage	VF20	XF40	MS60	MS63	MS65
1997	25,000	PF65 950				

KM# 1170 100 FRANCS
17.00 g., 0.920 Gold 0.5028 oz. AGW **Subject:** Coupe du Monde 1998 - Asia **Rev:** Soccer player and map of Asia, date below

Date	Mintage	VF20	XF40	MS60	MS63	MS65
1997	25,000	PF65 900				

KM# 1173 100 FRANCS
17.00 g., 0.920 Gold 0.5028 oz. AGW **Subject:** Coupe du Monde 1998 - Oceania **Rev:** Soccer player and map of the Pacific, with Australia highlighted in a box, date below

Date	Mintage	VF20	XF40	MS60	MS63	MS65
1997	25,000	PF65 950				

KM# 1188 100 FRANCS
15.00 g., 0.900 Silver 0.434 oz. ASW, 31 mm. **Obv:** André Melraux head facing **Rev:** Two cats flanking denomination

Date	Mintage	VF20	XF40	MS60	MS63	MS65
1997	494,000	—	20.00	30.00	40.00	70.00

KM# 1195 100 FRANCS
8.45 g., 0.920 Gold 0.2499 oz. AGW **Obv:** Pantheon, date below **Rev:** Denomination and tree design

Date	Mintage	VF20	XF40	MS60	MS63	MS65
1997	500	PF65 475				
1998	500	PF65 475				
1999	500	PF65 475				
2000	131	PF65 475				

KM# 1196 100 FRANCS
22.20 g., 0.900 Silver 0.6424 oz. ASW **Subject:** Georges Guynemer **Obv:** Bust 3/4 facing **Rev:** Guynemer's stork and denomination

Date	Mintage	VF20	XF40	MS60	MS63	MS65
1997	3,000	PF65 50.00				

KM# 1198 100 FRANCS
22.20 g., 0.900 Silver 0.6424 oz. ASW **Subject:** Pierre and

Marie Curie, 1867-1934, physicist - chemist **Obv:** Conjoined busts left **Rev:** Denomination

Date	Mintage	VF20	XF40	MS60	MS63	MS65
1997	3,000	PF65 50.00				

KM# 1952 100 FRANCS
22.20 g., 0.900 Silver 0.6424 oz. ASW, 37 mm. **Subject:** Andre Malraux **Mint:** Paris

Date	Mintage	VF20	XF40	MS60	MS63	MS65
1997	—	PF65 125				

KM# 1171 100 FRANCS
17.00 g., 0.920 Gold 0.5028 oz. AGW **Subject:** Coupe du Monte 1998 - Europe **Obv:** World Cup 1998 logo, denomination and date below **Rev:** Soccer player and map of Europe, date below

Date	Mintage	VF20	XF40	MS60	MS63	MS65
1998	25,000	PF65 950				

KM# 1201 100 FRANCS
22.20 g., 0.900 Silver 0.6424 oz. ASW **Subject:** Marie Caritat Marquis de Condorcet **Obv:** Bust 3/4 right **Rev:** Denomination

Date	Mintage	VF20	XF40	MS60	MS63	MS65
1998	3,000	PF65 50.00				

KM# 1203 100 FRANCS
22.20 g., 0.900 Silver 0.6424 oz. ASW **Subject:** Gaspard Monge **Obv:** Bust 3/4 right, building at right **Rev:** Denomination

Date	Mintage	VF20	XF40	MS60	MS63	MS65
1998	3,000	PF65 50.00				

KM# 1209 100 FRANCS
17.00 g., 0.920 Gold 0.5028 oz. AGW **Subject:** Treasures of the Nile - King Tutankhamon **Obv:** Burial mask and dog **Rev:** Sphinx and pyramids

Date	Mintage	VF20	XF40	MS60	MS63	MS65
1998	2,000	PF65 1,100				

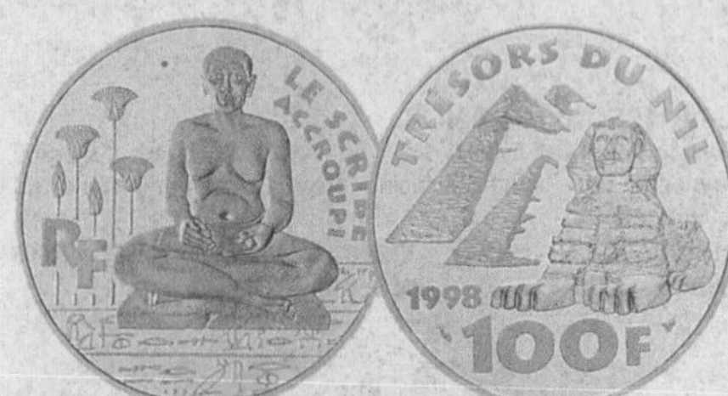

KM# 1210 100 FRANCS
17.00 g., 0.920 Gold 0.5028 oz. AGW **Subject:** Treasures of the Nile - The Scribe Accroupi **Obv:** Seated scribe **Rev:** Pyramids, Sphinx, date at left, denomination below

Date	Mintage	VF20	XF40	MS60	MS63	MS65
1998	2,000	PF65 1,100				

KM# 1397 100 FRANCS
22.14 g., 0.900 Silver 0.6406 oz. ASW, 37 mm. **Subject:** Human Rights Declaration **Obv:** Bust right, building and dates below **Rev:** Denomination on globe, laurel spray below **Edge:** Plain **Mint:** Paris

Date	Mintage	VF20	XF40	MS60	MS63	MS65
1998 A	—	PF65 50.00				

KM# 1295 100 FRANCS
22.30 g., 0.900 Silver 0.6453 oz. ASW, 36.7 mm. **Subject:** Louis Braille **Obv:** Portrait, dots and fingers **Rev:** Braille text, tools and fingers **Edge:** Plain **Mint:** Paris

Date	Mintage	VF20	XF40	MS60	MS63	MS65
1999	3,000	PF65 50.00				

KM# 1296 100 FRANCS
22.30 g., 0.900 Silver 0.6453 oz. ASW, 36.7 mm. **Subject:** Jean Jaures **Obv:** Bearded portrait **Rev:** Floor plan and dome **Edge:** Plain **Mint:** Paris

Date	Mintage	VF20	XF40	MS60	MS63	MS65
1999	3,000	PF65 50.00				

KM# 1959 100 FRANCS
17.00 g., 0.920 Gold 0.5028 oz. AGW **Subject:** World Rugby Championship **Mint:** Paris

Date	Mintage	VF20	XF40	MS60	MS63	MS65
1999	1,000	PF65 950				

KM# 1232 100 FRANCS
17.00 g., 0.920 Gold 0.5028 oz. AGW **Subject:** 2000 Years - French Coinage **Obv:** Denomination **Rev:** 1st century B.C. Celtic Parisii Stater coin design **Edge:** Plain **Mint:** Paris

Date	Mintage	VF20	XF40	MS60	MS63	MS65
2000	1,000	PF65 950				

KM# 1233 100 FRANCS
17.00 g., 0.920 Gold 0.5028 oz. AGW **Subject:** 2000 Years - French Coinage **Rev:** Charlemagne Denar coin design **Mint:** Paris

Date	Mintage	VF20	XF40	MS60	MS63	MS65
2000	1,000	PF65 950				

KM# 1234 100 FRANCS
17.00 g., 0.920 Gold 0.5028 oz. AGW **Subject:** 2000 Years - French Coinage **Rev:** Louis IX gold Ecu coin design **Mint:** Paris

Date	Mintage	VF20	XF40	MS60	MS63	MS65
2000	1,000	PF65 950				

KM# 1238 100 FRANCS
17.00 g., 0.920 Gold 0.5028 oz. AGW **Series:** XXth Century **Subject:** Biology and Medicine **Obv:** Double X design **Rev:** Parents, fetus, hands **Mint:** Paris

Date	Mintage	VF20	XF40	MS60	MS63	MS65
2000	1,000	PF65 950				

KM# 1239 100 FRANCS
17.00 g., 0.920 Gold 0.5028 oz. AGW **Series:** XXth Century **Subject:** Physics **Rev:** Einstein's portrait, atom and formula **Mint:** Paris

Date	Mintage	VF20	XF40	MS60	MS63	MS65
2000	1,000	PF65 950				

KM# 1240 100 FRANCS
17.00 g., 0.920 Gold 0.5028 oz. AGW **Series:** XXth Century **Subject:** Communications **Rev:** World, satellites, keyboard **Mint:** Paris

Date	Mintage	VF20	XF40	MS60	MS63	MS65
2000	1,000	PF65 950				

KM# 1241 100 FRANCS
17.00 g., 0.920 Gold 0.5028 oz. AGW **Series:** XXth Century **Subject:** Automobile **Rev:** Race cars above horse **Mint:** Paris

Date	Mintage	VF20	XF40	MS60	MS63	MS65
2000	1,000	PF65 950				

KM# 1242 100 FRANCS
17.00 g., 0.920 Gold 0.5028 oz. AGW **Series:** XXth Century **Subject:** Flight **Rev:** Icarus in flight above Bleriot monoplane **Mint:** Paris

Date	Mintage	VF20	XF40	MS60	MS63	MS65
2000	1,000	PF65 950				

KM# 1243 100 FRANCS
17.00 g., 0.920 Gold 0.5028 oz. AGW **Series:** XXth Century **Subject:** Space Travel **Rev:** Astronaut, footprint on moon, planets **Mint:** Paris

Date	Mintage	VF20	XF40	MS60	MS63	MS65
2000	1,000	PF65 950				

KM# 1264 100 FRANCS
17.00 g., 0.920 Gold 0.5028 oz. AGW **Subject:** Antoine de St. Exupery **Obv:** Portrait, bi-plane **Rev:** The "Little Prince" standing on a small planet **Mint:** Paris

Date	Mintage	VF20	XF40	MS60	MS63	MS65
2000	1,000	PF65 950				

KM# 1972 100 FRANCS
17.00 g., 0.920 Gold 0.5028 oz. AGW **Rev:** Gold Franc of John II **Mint:** Paris

Date	Mintage	VF20	XF40	MS60	MS63	MS65
2000	643	PF65 975				

KM# 1973 100 FRANCS
17.00 g., 0.920 Gold 0.5028 oz. AGW **Rev:** Franc of Henry III **Mint:** Paris

Date	Mintage	VF20	XF40	MS60	MS63	MS65
2000	100	PF65 1,400				

KM# 1974 100 FRANCS
17.00 g., 0.920 Gold 0.5028 oz. AGW **Rev:** Pistole of Louis XIII **Mint:** Paris

Date	Mintage	VF20	XF40	MS60	MS63	MS65
2000	134	PF65 1,400				

KM# 1975 100 FRANCS
17.00 g., 0.920 Gold 0.5028 oz. AGW **Rev:** Marianne (Bonnet type) **Mint:** Paris

Date	Mintage	VF20	XF40	MS60	MS63	MS65
2000	147	PF65 1,400				

KM# 1976 100 FRANCS
17.00 g., 0.920 Gold 0.5028 oz. AGW **Rev:** Marianne (Chaplain type) **Mint:** Paris

Date	Mintage	VF20	XF40	MS60	MS63	MS65
2000	846	PF65 1,000				

KM# 1977 100 FRANCS
17.00 g., 0.920 Gold 0.5028 oz. AGW **Rev:** Marianne (Lagriffoul type) **Mint:** Paris

Date	Mintage	VF20	XF40	MS60	MS63	MS65
2000	1,000	PF65 1,000				

KM# 1978 100 FRANCS
22.20 g., 0.900 Silver 0.6424 oz. ASW **Subject:** Jacques Germain Soufflot **Rev:** Pantheon in skyline **Mint:** Paris

Date	Mintage	VF20	XF40	MS60	MS63	MS65
2000	833	PF65 750				

KM# 1979 100 FRANCS
17.00 g., 0.920 Gold 0.5028 oz. AGW **Subject:** Jacques Germain Soufflot **Rev:** Pantheon in skyline view **Mint:** Paris

Date	Mintage	VF20	XF40	MS60	MS63	MS65
2000	71	PF65 1,600				

KM# 1980 100 FRANCS
22.20 g., 0.900 Silver 0.6424 oz. ASW **Subject:** Jean Jacques Rousseau **Mint:** Paris

Date	Mintage	VF20	XF40	MS60	MS63	MS65
2000	864	PF65 750				

KM# 973 500 FRANCS
17.00 g., 0.920 Gold 0.5028 oz. AGW **Series:** 1992 Olympics **Obv:** Alpine skiing **Rev:** Cross on flame, date and denomination, Olympic logo below **Mint:** Paris **Note:** Without mint mark.

Date	Mintage	VF20	XF40	MS60	MS63	MS65
1989	19,000	PF65 950				

KM# 974 500 FRANCS

17.00 g., 0.920 Gold 0.5028 oz. AGW **Series:** 1992 Olympics **Obv:** Ice skating couple **Rev:** Cross on flame divides date and denomination, Olympic logo below **Mint:** Paris

Date	Mintage	VF20	XF40	MS60	MS63	MS65
1989	Est. 17000	PF65 950				

KM# 985 500 FRANCS

17.00 g., 0.920 Gold 0.5028 oz. AGW **Series:** 1992 Olympics **Obv:** Speed skating **Rev:** Crossed flame, date and denomination, logo below **Mint:** Paris

Date	Mintage	VF20	XF40	MS60	MS63	MS65
1990	13,000	PF65 950				

KM# 986 500 FRANCS

17.00 g., 0.920 Gold 0.5028 oz. AGW **Series:** 1992 Olympics **Obv:** Bobsledding **Rev:** Games logo, value and legend **Mint:** Paris

Date	Mintage	VF20	XF40	MS60	MS63	MS65
1990	13,000	PF65 950				

KM# 987 500 FRANCS

17.00 g., 0.920 Gold 0.5028 oz. AGW **Series:** 1992 Olympics **Subject:** Pierre de Coubertin **Obv:** Free-style skier watched by chamois **Rev:** Head facing **Mint:** Paris

Date	Mintage	VF20	XF40	MS60	MS63	MS65
1990	8,000	PF65 950				

KM# 988 500 FRANCS

17.00 g., 0.920 Gold 0.5028 oz. AGW **Series:** 1992 Olympics **Obv:** Modern and old style slalom skiers **Mint:** Paris

Date	Mintage	VF20	XF40	MS60	MS63	MS65
1990	8,000	PF65 950				

KM# 977 500 FRANCS

17.00 g., 0.920 Gold 0.5028 oz. AGW **Subject:** 100th Anniversary of Basketball **Obv:** Player jumping for lay-up shot, hoop behind **Rev:** Star, ring, and globe, denomination and date below **Mint:** Paris

Date	Mintage	VF20	XF40	MS60	MS63	MS65
1991	5,000	PF65 950				

KM# 997 500 FRANCS

17.00 g., 0.920 Gold 0.5028 oz. AGW **Series:** 1992 Olympics **Obv:** 2 hockey players and large ibex ram **Mint:** Paris

Date	Mintage	VF20	XF40	MS60	MS63	MS65
1991	8,000	PF65 1,100				

KM# 998 500 FRANCS

17.00 g., 0.920 Gold 0.5028 oz. AGW **Subject:** 1992 Olympics **Mint:** Paris

Date	Mintage	VF20	XF40	MS60	MS63	MS65
1991	8,000	PF65 950				

KM# 999 500 FRANCS

17.00 g., 0.920 Gold 0.5028 oz. AGW **Series:** 1992 Olympics **Obv:** Old style and modern ski jumpers **Mint:** Paris

Date	Mintage	VF20	XF40	MS60	MS63	MS65
1991	8,000	PF65 950				

KM# 1000 500 FRANCS

17.00 g., 0.920 Gold 0.5028 oz. AGW **Series:** 1992 Olympics **Subject:** Pierre de Coubertin **Obv:** Head facing **Rev:** Cross on flame divides date and denomination, Olympic logo below **Mint:** Paris

Date	Mintage	VF20	XF40	MS60	MS63	MS65
1991	28,000	PF65 950				

KM# 1001 500 FRANCS

17.00 g., 0.920 Gold 0.5028 oz. AGW **Obv:** Building, denomination and date below **Rev:** Mozart in Paris at piano **Mint:** Paris

Date	Mintage	VF20	XF40	MS60	MS63	MS65
1991	Est. 5000	PF65 950				

KM# 1024 500 FRANCS

31.10 g., 0.999 Gold 0.999 oz. AGW **Series:** Bicentennial of the Louvre **Obv:** Mona Lisa **Rev:** Pyramids front building, date and denomination below **Mint:** Paris

Date	Mintage	VF20	XF40	MS60	MS63	MS65
1993	5,000	PF65 1,850				

KM# 1025.1 500 FRANCS

31.10 g., 0.999 Gold 0.999 oz. AGW **Series:** Bicentennial of the Louvre **Obv:** Venus de Milo **Mint:** Paris

Date	Mintage	VF20	XF40	MS60	MS63	MS65
1993	5,000	PF65 1,850				

KM# 1025.2 500 FRANCS

155.50 g., 0.999 Gold 4.9944 oz. AGW, 50 mm. **Obv:** Venus de Milo **Rev:** The Louvre Building entrance above value **Mint:** Paris

Date	Mintage	VF20	XF40	MS60	MS63	MS65
1993	99	PF65 9,500				

KM# 1026 500 FRANCS

155.52 g., 0.999 Gold 4.995 oz. AGW **Series:** Bicentennial of the Louvre **Obv:** Liberty **Rev:** Pyramids front building, date and denomination below **Mint:** Paris

Date	Mintage	VF20	XF40	MS60	MS63	MS65
1993	99	PF65 9,500				

KM# 1027 500 FRANCS

155.52 g., 0.999 Gold 4.995 oz. AGW **Series:** Bicentennial of the Louvre **Obv:** Mona Lisa **Rev:** Patterned pyramids front building **Mint:** Paris

Date	Mintage	VF20	XF40	MS60	MS63	MS65
1993	99	PF65 9,500				

KM# 1028 500 FRANCS

17.00 g., 0.920 Gold 0.5028 oz. AGW **Subject:** Jean Moulin **Obv:** Head facing **Mint:** Paris

Date	Mintage	VF20	XF40	MS60	MS63	MS65
1993	5,000	PF65 950				

KM# 1183 500 FRANCS

155.52 g., 0.999 Gold 4.995 oz. AGW **Series:** Bicentennial of the Louvre **Obv:** Victory **Mint:** Paris

Date	Mintage	VF20	XF40	MS60	MS63	MS65
1993	99	PF65 9,500				

KM# 1184 500 FRANCS

155.52 g., 0.999 Gold 4.995 oz. AGW **Series:** Bicentennial of the Louvre **Obv:** Napoleon and Josephine **Mint:** Paris

Date	Mintage	VF20	XF40	MS60	MS63	MS65
1993	99	PF65 9,500				

KM# 1185 500 FRANCS

155.52 g., 0.999 Gold 4.995 oz. AGW **Series:** Bicentennial of the Louvre **Obv:** Marie Marguerite **Mint:** Paris

Date	Mintage	VF20	XF40	MS60	MS63	MS65
1993	99	PF65 9,500				

KM# 1399 500 FRANCS

155.52 g., 0.999 Gold 4.995 oz. AGW, 50 mm. **Subject:** Venus De Milo **Edge:** Plain **Mint:** Paris

Date	Mintage	VF20	XF40	MS60	MS63	MS65
1993 A	99	PF65 9,500				

KM# 1049 500 FRANCS

17.00 g., 0.920 Gold 0.5028 oz. AGW **Subject:** Winston Churchill **Obv:** Bust right, denomination and date **Rev:** Eleven line inscription on flag design, rampant lion at right **Mint:** Paris

Date	Mintage	VF20	XF40	MS60	MS63	MS65
1994	Est. 2000	PF65 950				

KM# 1050 500 FRANCS

17.00 g., 0.920 Gold 0.5028 oz. AGW **Subject:** General de Gaulle **Obv:** 3/4 bust of General de Gaulle in front of microphone **Mint:** Paris

Date	Mintage	VF20	XF40	MS60	MS63	MS65
1994	—	PF65 950				

KM# 1051 500 FRANCS
17.00 g., 0.920 Gold 0.5028 oz. AGW **Subject:** General Leclerc **Obv:** Bust facing **Mint:** Paris

Date	Mintage	VF20	XF40	MS60	MS63	MS65
1994	Est. 2000	PF65 950				

KM# 1052 500 FRANCS
17.00 g., 0.920 Gold 0.5028 oz. AGW **Subject:** General Marie Pierre Koenig **Obv:** Bust looking left **Mint:** Paris

Date	Mintage	VF20	XF40	MS60	MS63	MS65
1994	Est. 2000	PF65 950				

KM# 1053 500 FRANCS
17.00 g., 0.920 Gold 0.5028 oz. AGW **Subject:** General Juin **Obv:** Bust right, map of Italy at right **Mint:** Paris

Date	Mintage	VF20	XF40	MS60	MS63	MS65
1994	Est. 2000	PF65 950				

KM# 1054 500 FRANCS
17.00 g., 0.920 Gold 0.5028 oz. AGW **Subject:** Dwight David Eisenhower **Obv:** Uniformed bust left **Mint:** Paris

Date	Mintage	VF20	XF40	MS60	MS63	MS65
1994	Est. 2000	PF65 950				

KM# 1055 500 FRANCS
17.00 g., 0.920 Gold 0.5028 oz. AGW **Rev:** Church of Sainte - Mere - Eglise, parachute behind **Mint:** Paris

Date	Mintage	VF20	XF40	MS60	MS63	MS65
1994	Est. 2000	PF65 950				

KM# 1056 500 FRANCS
17.00 g., 0.920 Gold 0.5028 oz. AGW **Subject:** General de Lattre de Tassigny **Obv:** Head right **Mint:** Paris

Date	Mintage	VF20	XF40	MS60	MS63	MS65
1994	Est. 2000	PF65 950				

KM# 1057 500 FRANCS
17.00 g., 0.920 Gold 0.5028 oz. AGW **Subject:** Liberation of Paris **Obv:** Triumphant troops marching down Champs Elysees **Mint:** Paris

Date	Mintage	VF20	XF40	MS60	MS63	MS65
1994	Est. 5000	PF65 950				

KM# 1058 500 FRANCS
17.00 g., 0.920 Gold 0.5028 oz. AGW **Obv:** Heads of de Gaulle and Adenauer facing the center, date below **Mint:** Paris

Date	Mintage	VF20	XF40	MS60	MS63	MS65
1994	—	PF65 950				

KM# 1059 500 FRANCS
16.97 g., 0.917 Gold 0.5003 oz. AGW **Subject:** 1996 Olympics **Obv:** Head facing, date and denomination **Rev:** Archer in front of Eiffel Tower **Edge Lettering:** CITIUS ALTIUS FORTTUS **Mint:** Paris

Date	Mintage	VF20	XF40	MS60	MS63	MS65
1994	60,000	PF65 950				

KM# 1074 500 FRANCS
31.04 g., 0.999 Gold 0.9968 oz. AGW **Series:** Centennial of Cinema **Subject:** Lumiere Brothers **Obv:** Antique camera **Rev:** Conjoined busts right **Mint:** Paris

Date	Mintage	VF20	XF40	MS60	MS63	MS65
1994	3,000	PF65 1,850				

KM# 1078 500 FRANCS
31.04 g., 0.999 Gold 0.9968 oz. AGW **Series:** Centennial of Cinema **Subject:** Charlie Chaplin **Obv:** Antique movie camera **Rev:** Head facing **Mint:** Paris

Date	Mintage	VF20	XF40	MS60	MS63	MS65
1994	3,000	PF65 1,850				
1995	—	PF65 1,850				

KM# 1079 500 FRANCS
155.52 g., 0.999 Gold 4,995 oz. AGW **Series:** Centennial of Cinema **Subject:** Charlie Chaplin **Obv:** Antique movie camera **Rev:** Head facing **Mint:** Paris

Date	Mintage	VF20	XF40	MS60	MS63	MS65
1994	99	PF65 9,500				
1995	—	PF65 9,500				

KM# 1098 500 FRANCS
31.04 g., 0.999 Gold 0.9968 oz. AGW **Series:** Centennial of Cinema **Subject:** Audrey Hepburn **Obv:** Antique movie camera **Rev:** Head 3/4 left **Mint:** Paris

Date	Mintage	VF20	XF40	MS60	MS63	MS65
1994	3,000	PF65 1,850				
1995	—	PF65 1,850				

KM# 1099 500 FRANCS
155.52 g., 0.999 Gold 4.995 oz. AGW **Series:** Centennial of Cinema **Subject:** Audrey Hepburn **Obv:** Antique movie camera **Rev:** Head 3/4 left **Mint:** Paris

Date	Mintage	VF20	XF40	MS60	MS63	MS65
1994	99	PF65 9,500				
1995	—	PF65 9,500				

KM# 1106 500 FRANCS
31.04 g., 0.999 Gold 0.9968 oz. AGW **Series:** Centennial of Cinema **Subject:** Yves Montand **Obv:** Antique movie camera **Rev:** Bust 3/4 facing **Mint:** Paris

Date	Mintage	VF20	XF40	MS60	MS63	MS65
1994	3,000	PF65 1,850				
1995	—	PF65 1,850				

KM# 1107 500 FRANCS
155.52 g., 0.999 Gold 4.995 oz. AGW **Series:** Centennial of Cinema **Subject:** Yves Montand **Obv:** Antique movie camera **Rev:** Bust 3/4 facing **Mint:** Paris

Date	Mintage	VF20	XF40	MS60	MS63	MS65
1994	99	PF65 9,500				
1995	—	PF65 9,500				

KM# 1186 500 FRANCS
17.00 g., 0.920 Gold 0.5028 oz. AGW **Series:** Centennial of Cinema **Rev:** Voltaire **Mint:** Paris

Date	Mintage	VF20	XF40	MS60	MS63	MS65
1994	350	PF65 950				

KM# 1934 500 FRANCS
31.11 g., 0.999 Gold 0.999 oz. AGW, 37 mm. **Subject:** Treasurers of the Louvre **Rev:** La Gioconda **Mint:** Paris

Date	Mintage	VF20	XF40	MS60	MS63	MS65
1994	—	PF65 1,800				

KM# 1940 500 FRANCS
31.10 g., 0.999 Gold 0.9989 oz. AGW, 37 mm. **Subject:** Treasurers of the Louvre **Rev:** Venus de Milo **Mint:** Paris

Date	Mintage	VF20	XF40	MS60	MS63	MS65
1994	—	PF65 1,800				

KM# 1950 500 FRANCS
155.50 g., 0.999 Gold 4.9944 oz. AGW, 50 mm. **Subject:** Charles Chaplin **Mint:** Paris

Date	Mintage	VF20	XF40	MS60	MS63	MS65
1994	99	PF65 9,500				
1995	99	PF65 9,500				

KM# 1082 500 FRANCS
31.04 g., 0.999 Gold 0.9968 oz. AGW **Series:** Centennial of Cinema **Subject:** Leon Gaumont **Obv:** Antique movie camera **Rev:** Head facing **Mint:** Paris

Date	Mintage	VF20	XF40	MS60	MS63	MS65
1995	3,000	PF65 1,850				

KM# 1083 500 FRANCS
155.52 g., 0.999 Gold 4.995 oz. AGW **Series:** Centennial of Cinema **Subject:** Leon Gaumont **Obv:** Antique movie camera **Rev:** Head facing **Mint:** Paris

Date	Mintage	VF20	XF40	MS60	MS63	MS65
1995	99	PF65 9,500				

KM# 1086 500 FRANCS
31.04 g., 0.999 Gold 0.9968 oz. AGW **Series:** Centennial of Cinema **Subject:** Jean Renoir **Obv:** Antique movie camera **Rev:** Head 3/4 right **Mint:** Paris

Date	Mintage	VF20	XF40	MS60	MS63	MS65
1995	3,000	PF65 1,850				

KM# 1087 500 FRANCS
155.52 g., 0.999 Gold 4.995 oz. AGW **Series:** Centennial of Cinema **Subject:** Jean Renoir **Obv:** Antique movie camera **Rev:** Head 3/4 right **Mint:** Paris

Date	Mintage	VF20	XF40	MS60	MS63	MS65
1995	99	PF65 9,500				

KM# 1090 500 FRANCS
31.04 g., 0.999 Gold 0.9968 oz. AGW **Series:** Centennial of Cinema **Subject:** Alfred Hitchcock **Obv:** Antique movie camera **Rev:** Bust 3/4 facing **Mint:** Paris

Date	Mintage	VF20	XF40	MS60	MS63	MS65
1995	3,000	PF65 1,850				

KM# 1091 500 FRANCS
155.52 g., 0.999 Gold 4.995 oz. AGW **Series:** Centennial of Cinema **Subject:** Alfred Hitchcock **Obv:** Antique movie camera **Rev:** Bust 3/4 facing **Mint:** Paris

Date	Mintage	VF20	XF40	MS60	MS63	MS65
1995	99	PF65 9,500				

KM# 1094 500 FRANCS
31.04 g., 0.999 Gold 0.9968 oz. AGW **Series:** Centennial of Cinema **Subject:** Greta Garbo 1905-1990; actress in "Camille & Ninotchka" **Obv:** Antique movie camera **Rev:** Head with high collar right **Mint:** Paris

Date	Mintage	VF20	XF40	MS60	MS63	MS65
1995	3,000	PF65 1,850				

KM# 1095 500 FRANCS
155.52 g., 0.999 Gold 4.995 oz. AGW **Series:** Centennial of Cinema **Subject:** Greta Garbo 1905-1990; actress in "Camille & Ninotchka" **Obv:** Antique movie camera **Rev:** Head with high collar right **Mint:** Paris

Date	Mintage	VF20	XF40	MS60	MS63	MS65
1995	99	PF65 9,500				

KM# 1102 500 FRANCS
31.04 g., 0.999 Gold 0.9968 oz. AGW **Series:** Centennial of Cinema **Subject:** Federico Fellini **Obv:** Antique movie camera **Rev:** Bust 3/4 right **Mint:** Paris

Date	Mintage	VF20	XF40	MS60	MS63	MS65
1995	3,000	PF65 1,850				

KM# 1103 500 FRANCS
155.52 g., 0.999 Gold 4.995 oz. AGW **Series:** Centennial of Cinema **Subject:** Federico Fellini **Obv:** Antique movie camera **Rev:** Bust 3/4 right **Mint:** Paris

Date	Mintage	VF20	XF40	MS60	MS63	MS65
1995	99	PF65 9,500				

KM# 1110 500 FRANCS
31.04 g., 0.999 Gold 0.9968 oz. AGW **Series:** Centennial of Cinema **Subject:** Romy Schneider **Obv:** Antique movie camera **Rev:** Bust 3/4 left **Mint:** Paris

Date	Mintage	VF20	XF40	MS60	MS63	MS65
1995	3,000	PF65 1,850				

KM# 1111 500 FRANCS
155.52 g., 0.999 Gold 4.995 oz. AGW **Series:** Centennial of Cinema **Subject:** Romy Schneider **Obv:** Antique movie camera **Rev:** Bust 3/4 left **Mint:** Paris

Date	Mintage	VF20	XF40	MS60	MS63	MS65
1995	99	PF65 9,500				

KM# 1117 500 FRANCS
17.00 g., 0.920 Gold 0.5028 oz. AGW **Subject:** V.E. Day **Obv:** Victory in Europe date May 8, 1945, denomination **Rev:** Birds in flight above banners, PAX below **Mint:** Paris

Date	Mintage	VF20	XF40	MS60	MS63	MS65
1995	5,000	PF65 950				

KM# 1135 500 FRANCS
17.00 g., 0.920 Gold 0.5028 oz. AGW **Obv:** Louis Pasteur **Mint:** Paris

Date	Mintage	VF20	XF40	MS60	MS63	MS65
1995	1,000	PF65 950				

KM# 1137 500 FRANCS
17.00 g., 0.920 Gold 0.5028 oz. AGW **Obv:** Jean de la Fountain **Mint:** Paris

Date	Mintage	VF20	XF40	MS60	MS63	MS65
1995	1,000	PF65 950				

KM# 1311 500 FRANCS
155.50 g., 0.999 Gold 4.9944 oz. AGW, 50 mm. **Series:** Centennial of Cinema **Subject:** Gerard Philipe **Obv:** Antique movie camera **Rev:** Bust 3/4 facing **Mint:** Paris

Date	Mintage	VF20	XF40	MS60	MS63	MS65
1995	99	PF65 9,500				

KM# 1312 500 FRANCS
155.50 g., 0.999 Gold 4.9944 oz. AGW, 50 mm. **Series:** Centennial of Cinema **Subject:** George Melies **Obv:** Antique movie camera **Rev:** Head facing **Mint:** Paris

Date	Mintage	VF20	XF40	MS60	MS63	MS65
1995	99	PF65 9,500				

KM# 1313 500 FRANCS
155.50 g., 0.999 Gold 4.9944 oz. AGW, 50 mm. **Series:** Centennial of Cinema **Subject:** Arletty **Obv:** Antique movie camera **Rev:** Head left **Mint:** Paris

Date	Mintage	VF20	XF40	MS60	MS63	MS65
1995	99	PF65 9,500				

KM# 1314 500 FRANCS
155.50 g., 0.999 Gold 4.9944 oz. AGW, 50 mm. **Series:** Centennial of Cinema **Subject:** Marcel Pagnol **Obv:** Antique movie camera **Rev:** Head 3/4 left **Mint:** Paris

Date	Mintage	VF20	XF40	MS60	MS63	MS65
1995	—	PF65 9,500				

KM# 1499 500 FRANCS
155.50 g., 0.999 Gold 4.9944 oz. AGW, 50 mm. **Rev:** Leonie Bathiat **Mint:** Paris

Date	Mintage	VF20	XF40	MS60	MS63	MS65
1995	—	PF65 8,000				

KM# 1546 500 FRANCS
155.50 g., 0.999 Gold 4.9944 oz. AGW, 50 mm. **Rev:** Gerard Philippe **Mint:** Paris

Date	Mintage	VF20	XF40	MS60	MS63	MS65
1995	—	PF65 8,000				

KM# 1547 500 FRANCS
155.50 g., 0.999 Gold 4.9944 oz. AGW, 50 mm. **Rev:** Marcel Pagnol **Mint:** Paris

Date	Mintage	VF20	XF40	MS60	MS63	MS65
1995	—	PF65 8,000				

KM# 1139 500 FRANCS
17.00 g., 0.920 Gold 0.5028 oz. AGW **Subject:** 300th Anniversary - Death of Marie de Sevigne; letter writer, 1626-1696 **Obv:** Bust 1/2 left **Mint:** Paris

Date	Mintage	VF20	XF40	MS60	MS63	MS65
1996	500	PF65 950				

KM# 1181 500 FRANCS
17.00 g., 0.920 Gold 0.5028 oz. AGW **Subject:** King Clovis I **Obv:** Bust facing **Mint:** Paris

Date	Mintage	VF20	XF40	MS60	MS63	MS65
1996	250	PF65 950				

KM# 1197 500 FRANCS
17.00 g., 0.920 Gold 0.5028 oz. AGW **Subject:** Georges Guynemer **Obv:** Bust 3/4 facing **Rev:** Stork emblem and denomination **Mint:** Paris

Date	Mintage	VF20	XF40	MS60	MS63	MS65
1997	300	PF65 950				

KM# 1199 500 FRANCS
17.00 g., 0.920 Gold 0.5028 oz. AGW **Subject:** Pierre and Marie Curie 1867-1934, physicist - chemist **Obv:** Conjoined busts left **Rev:** Denomination **Mint:** Paris

Date	Mintage	VF20	XF40	MS60	MS63	MS65
1997	300	PF65 950				

KM# 1200 500 FRANCS
17.00 g., 0.920 Gold 0.5028 oz. AGW **Subject:** Andre Malraux **Obv:** Head facing **Rev:** Cats flanking denomination **Mint:** Paris

Date	Mintage	VF20	XF40	MS60	MS63	MS65
1997	300	PF65 950				

KM# 1202 500 FRANCS
17.00 g., 0.920 Gold 0.5028 oz. AGW **Subject:** Marquis de Condorcet **Obv:** Head right **Rev:** Denomination **Mint:** Paris

Date	Mintage	VF20	XF40	MS60	MS63	MS65
1998	300	PF65 950				

KM# 1204 500 FRANCS
17.00 g., 0.920 Gold 0.5028 oz. AGW **Subject:** Gaspard Monge **Obv:** Head 1/2 right **Rev:** Denomination **Mint:** Paris

Date	Mintage	VF20	XF40	MS60	MS63	MS65
1998	300	PF65 950				

KM# 1957 500 FRANCS
17.00 g., 0.920 Gold 0.5028 oz. AGW **Subject:** Rene Samuel Cassin **Mint:** Paris

Date	Mintage	VF20	XF40	MS60	MS63	MS65
1998	Est. 3000	PF65 950				

KM# 1960 500 FRANCS
17.00 g., 0.920 Gold 0.5028 oz. AGW **Subject:** Louis Braille, 190th Anniversary of Birth **Mint:** Paris

Date	Mintage	VF20	XF40	MS60	MS63	MS65
1999	Est. 300	PF65 1,000				

KM# 1961 500 FRANCS
17.00 g., 0.920 Gold 0.5028 oz. AGW **Subject:** Jean Jaures, 140th Anniversary of Birth **Mint:** Paris

Date	Mintage	VF20	XF40	MS60	MS63	MS65
1999	300	PF65 1,400				

KM# 1237 500 FRANCS
31.10 g., 0.999 Gold 0.999 oz. AGW **Subject:** Yves St. Laurent **Obv:** RF monogram within entwined snake design divides denomination and date **Rev:** Fashion show scene **Edge:** Plain **Mint:** Paris

Date	Mintage	VF20	XF40	MS60	MS63	MS65
2000	1,000	PF65 1,850				

KM# 1981 500 FRANCS
17.00 g., 0.920 Gold 0.5028 oz. AGW **Subject:** Jean Jacques Rousseau **Mint:** Paris

Date	Mintage	VF20	XF40	MS60	MS63	MS65
2000	70	PF65 1,600				

KM# 1257 655.957 FRANCS
31.10 g., 0.999 Gold 0.999 oz. AGW **Series:** Euro conversion **Obv:** Country names with euro-currency equivalents around "RF", denomination and French coin designs **Rev:** Europa allegorical portrait **Edge:** Plain **Mint:** Paris

Date	Mintage	VF20	XF40	MS60	MS63	MS65
1999	2,000	PF65 1,850				

KM# 1247 655.957 FRANCS
15.55 g., 0.999 Gold 0.4995 oz. AGW **Series:** European Art Styles - Renaissance **Obv:** Europe allegorical portrait **Rev:** Greek and Roman style buildings **Mint:** Paris

Date	Mintage	VF20	XF40	MS60	MS63	MS65
2000	2,000	PF65 1,850				

KM# 1248 655.957 FRANCS
15.55 g., 0.999 Gold 0.4995 oz. AGW **Series:** European Art Styles - Roman **Rev:** Roman sculpture and ancient buildings **Mint:** Paris

Date	Mintage	VF20	XF40	MS60	MS63	MS65
2000	2,000	PF65 1,850				

KM# 1249 655.957 FRANCS
15.55 g., 0.999 Gold 0.4995 oz. AGW **Series:** European Art Styles - Gothic **Rev:** Gothic sculpture and buildings **Mint:** Paris

Date	Mintage	VF20	XF40	MS60	MS63	MS65
2000	2,000	PF65 1,850				

KM# 1250 655.957 FRANCS
15.55 g., 0.999 Gold 0.4995 oz. AGW **Series:** European Art Styles - Renaissance **Rev:** Renaissance buildings **Mint:** Paris

Date	Mintage	VF20	XF40	MS60	MS63	MS65
2000	2,000	PF65 1,850				

KM# 1251 655.957 FRANCS
15.55 g., 0.999 Gold 0.4995 oz. AGW **Series:** European Art Styles - Classic and Baroque **Rev:** Classic and Baroque art **Mint:** Paris

Date	Mintage	VF20	XF40	MS60	MS63	MS65
2000	2,000	PF65 1,850				

KM# 1252 655.957 FRANCS
15.55 g., 0.999 Gold 0.4995 oz. AGW **Series:** European Art Styles - Art Nouveau **Rev:** Arches and scrollwork **Mint:** Paris

Date	Mintage	VF20	XF40	MS60	MS63	MS65
2000	2,000	PF65 1,850				

KM# 1253 655.957 FRANCS
15.55 g., 0.999 Gold 0.4995 oz. AGW **Series:** European Art Styles - Modern **Rev:** Modern artistic designs **Mint:** Paris

Date	Mintage	VF20	XF40	MS60	MS63	MS65
2000	2,000	PF65 1,850				

KM# 1261 655.957 FRANCS
31.10 g., 0.999 Gold 0.999 oz. AGW **Obv:** Country names with euro-currency equivalents around "RF", denomination and French euro coin design **Mint:** Paris

Date	Mintage	VF20	XF40	MS60	MS63	MS65
2000	2,000	PF65 2,200				

ECU / FRANCS COINAGE

European Currency Units

KM# 989 100 FRANCS-15 ECUS
22.20 g., 0.900 Silver 0.6424 oz. ASW **Obv:** Center monogram divides date and denomination, laurel spray below **Rev:** Stylized head facing, denomination below

Date	Mintage	VF20	XF40	MS60	MS63	MS65
1990	30,000	PF65 85.00				

KM# 1002 100 FRANCS-15 ECUS
22.20 g., 0.900 Silver 0.6424 oz. ASW **Subject:** Descartes **Obv:** Finger pointing to starred paper, denomination below **Rev:** Head 3/4 facing, denomination and date below

Date	Mintage	VF20	XF40	MS60	MS63	MS65
1991	20,000	PF65 65.00				

KM# 1012 100 FRANCS-15 ECUS
22.20 g., 0.900 Silver 0.6424 oz. ASW **Subject:** Jean Monet **Obv:** Denomination in center within legend and chain above RF **Rev:** Head left, denomination at right

Date	Mintage	VF20	XF40	MS60	MS63	MS65
1992	30,000	PF65 55.00				

KM# 1029 100 FRANCS-15 ECUS
22.20 g., 0.900 Silver 0.6424 oz. ASW **Subject:** Mediterranean Games **Obv:** Head left, denomination below **Rev:** Swimming, denomination below, rings divide date below

Date	Mintage	VF20	XF40	MS60	MS63	MS65
1993	15,000	PF65 47.50				

KM# 1030 100 FRANCS-15 ECUS
22.20 g., 0.900 Silver 0.6424 oz. ASW **Subject:** Mediterranean Games **Obv:** Head left, denomination below **Rev:** Soccer, denomination below, rings divide date below

Date	Mintage	VF20	XF40	MS60	MS63	MS65
1993	15,000	PF65 47.50				

KM# 1031 100 FRANCS-15 ECUS
22.20 g., 0.900 Silver 0.6424 oz. ASW **Rev:** Arc de Triumph

Date	Mintage	VF20	XF40	MS60	MS63	MS65
1993	20,000	PF65 42.50				

KM# 1032 100 FRANCS-15 ECUS
22.20 g., 0.900 Silver 0.6424 oz. ASW **Rev:** Brandenburg Gate

Date	Mintage	VF20	XF40	MS60	MS63	MS65
1993	20,000	PF65 42.50				

KM# 1060 100 FRANCS-15 ECUS
22.20 g., 0.900 Silver 0.6424 oz. ASW **Rev:** Stylized Tunnel View - Map

Date	Mintage	VF20	XF40	MS60	MS63	MS65
1994	20,000	PF65 32.50				

KM# 1068 100 FRANCS-15 ECUS
22.20 g., 0.900 Silver 0.6424 oz. ASW **Obv:** Denominations-(francs/ecus) **Rev:** St. Mark's Cathedral, Venice

Date	Mintage	VF20	XF40	MS60	MS63	MS65
1994	20,000	PF65 32.50				

KM# 1070 100 FRANCS-15 ECUS
22.20 g., 0.900 Silver 0.6424 oz. ASW **Obv:** Stars surround denominations, (francs/euros) **Rev:** Big Ben, London, date below

Date	Mintage	VF20	XF40	MS60	MS63	MS65
1994	20,000	PF65 32.50				

KM# 1112 100 FRANCS-15 ECUS
22.20 g., 0.900 Silver 0.6424 oz. ASW **Rev:** The Alhambra, Granada, date below

Date	Mintage	VF20	XF40	MS60	MS63	MS65
1995	20,000	PF65 35.00				

KM# 1114 100 FRANCS-15 ECUS
22.20 g., 0.900 Silver 0.6424 oz. ASW **Rev:** The Parthenon, Greece, date below

Date	Mintage	VF20	XF40	MS60	MS63	MS65
1995	20,000	PF65 35.00				

KM# 990 500 FRANCS-70 ECUS
17.00 g., 0.920 Gold 0.5028 oz. AGW **Obv:** Center monogram divides date and denomination, laurel spray below **Rev:** Stylized head facing above denomination

Date	Mintage	VF20	XF40	MS60	MS63	MS65
1990	5,000	PF65 950				

KM# 990a 500 FRANCS-70 ECUS
20.00 g., 0.999 Platinum 0.6424 oz. APW **Obv:** Monogram divides denomination and date, spray below **Rev:** Stylized head facing, denomintion below

Date	Mintage	VF20	XF40	MS60	MS63	MS65
1990	2,000	PF65 1,250				

KM# 1003 500 FRANCS-70 ECUS
17.00 g., 0.920 Gold 0.5028 oz. AGW **Subject:** Descartes **Obv:** Finger pointing to page with stars **Rev:** Head 3/4 facing

Date	Mintage	VF20	XF40	MS60	MS63	MS65
1991	3,000	PF65 950				

KM# 1003a 500 FRANCS-70 ECUS
20.00 g., 0.999 Platinum 0.6424 oz. APW **Subject:** Descartes **Obv:** Finger pointing to page with stars, denomination **Rev:** Head 3/4 facing

Date	Mintage	VF20	XF40	MS60	MS63	MS65
1991	1,000	PF65 1,250				

KM# 1013 500 FRANCS-70 ECUS
17.00 g., 0.920 Gold 0.5028 oz. AGW **Subject:** Jean Monet **Obv:** Denomination and date within legend at center, chain surrounds, RF below **Rev:** Head left, denomination at right

Date	Mintage	VF20	XF40	MS60	MS63	MS65
1992	5,000	PF65 950				

KM# 1013a 500 FRANCS-70 ECUS
20.00 g., 0.999 Platinum 0.6424 oz. APW **Subject:** Jean Monet **Obv:** Denomination and date within legend at center, chain surrounds, RF below **Rev:** Head 3/4 left

Date	Mintage	VF20	XF40	MS60	MS63	MS65
1992	2,000	PF65 1,250				

KM# 1033 500 FRANCS-70 ECUS
17.00 g., 0.920 Gold 0.5028 oz. AGW **Subject:** Mediterranean Games **Obv:** Head left, denomination below **Rev:** Statue divides denomination above, rings divide date below

Date	Mintage	VF20	XF40	MS60	MS63	MS65
1993	3,000	PF65 950				

KM# 1034 500 FRANCS-70 ECUS
17.00 g., 0.920 Gold 0.5028 oz. AGW **Obv:** Denominations-(francs/ecus) **Rev:** Arc de Triumph, date below

Date	Mintage	VF20	XF40	MS60	MS63	MS65
1993	5,000	PF65 950				

KM# 1034a 500 FRANCS-70 ECUS
19.80 g., 0.990 Platinum 0.6302 oz. APW **Obv:** Denominations-(francs/ecus) **Rev:** Arc de Triumph

Date	Mintage	VF20	XF40	MS60	MS63	MS65
1993	2,000	PF65 1,250				

KM# 1035 500 FRANCS-70 ECUS
17.00 g., 0.920 Gold 0.5028 oz. AGW **Obv:** Denominations-(francs/ecus) **Rev:** Brandenburg Gate, date above

Date	Mintage	VF20	XF40	MS60	MS63	MS65
1993	5,000	PF65 950				

KM# 1035a 500 FRANCS-70 ECUS
19.80 g., 0.990 Platinum 0.6302 oz. APW **Obv:** Denominations-(francs/ecus) **Rev:** Brandenburg Gate

Date	Mintage	VF20	XF40	MS60	MS63	MS65
1993	2,000	PF65 1,250				

KM# 1061 500 FRANCS-70 ECUS
17.00 g., 0.920 Gold 0.5028 oz. AGW **Obv:** Stars surround denominations, (francs/euros) **Rev:** Channel Tunnel

Date	Mintage	VF20	XF40	MS60	MS63	MS65
1994	5,000	PF65 950				

KM# 1069 500 FRANCS-70 ECUS
17.00 g., 0.920 Gold 0.5028 oz. AGW **Obv:** Stars surround denominations, (francs/euros) **Rev:** St. Mark's Cathedral, Venice, date below

Date	Mintage	VF20	XF40	MS60	MS63	MS65
1994	5,000	PF65 950				

KM# 1069a 500 FRANCS-70 ECUS
20.00 g., 0.999 Platinum 0.6424 oz. APW **Obv:** Stars surround denominations, (francs/euros) **Rev:** St. Mark's Cathedral, Venice

Date	Mintage	VF20	XF40	MS60	MS63	MS65
1994	2,000	PF65 1,250				

KM# 1071 500 FRANCS-70 ECUS
17.00 g., 0.920 Gold 0.5028 oz. AGW **Obv:** Stars surround denominations, (francs/euros) **Rev:** Big Ben, London, date below

Date	Mintage	VF20	XF40	MS60	MS63	MS65
1994	5,000	PF65 950				

KM# 1071a 500 FRANCS-70 ECUS
20.00 g., 0.999 Platinum 0.6424 oz. APW **Obv:** Stars surround denominations, (francs/euros) **Rev:** Big Ben, London

Date	Mintage	VF20	XF40	MS60	MS63	MS65
1994	2,000	PF65 1,250				

KM# 1113 500 FRANCS-70 ECUS
17.00 g., 0.920 Gold 0.5028 oz. AGW **Obv:** Stars surround denominations, (francs/euros) **Rev:** The Alhambra, Granada

Date	Mintage	VF20	XF40	MS60	MS63	MS65
1995	5,000	PF65 950				

KM# 1113a 500 FRANCS-70 ECUS
20.00 g., 0.999 Platinum 0.6424 oz. APW **Obv:** Stars surround denominations, (francs/euros) **Rev:** The Alhambra, Granada

Date	Mintage	VF20	XF40	MS60	MS63	MS65
1995	2,000	PF65 1,250				

KM# 1115 500 FRANCS-70 ECUS
17.00 g., 0.920 Gold 0.5028 oz. AGW **Obv:** Stars surround denominations, (francs/euros) **Rev:** The Parthenon, Athens

Date	Mintage	VF20	XF40	MS60	MS63	MS65
1995	5,000	PF65 950				

KM# 1115a 500 FRANCS-70 ECUS
20.00 g., 0.999 Platinum 0.6424 oz. APW **Obv:** Stars surround denominations, (francs/euros) **Rev:** The Parthenon, Athens

Date	Mintage	VF20	XF40	MS60	MS63	MS65
1995	2,000	PF65 1,250				

MEDALLIC COINAGE

KM# M27 20 FRANCS
Silver **Subject:** President of Rene Coty Visit **Obv:** Head of Republic **Rev:** Coin press **Mint:** Paris

Date	Mintage	F12	VF20	XF40	MS60	MS63
1955	—	—	65.00	125	250	300

KM# M27a 20 FRANCS
Gold **Subject:** President of Rene Coty Visit **Obv:** Head of Republic **Rev:** Coin press **Mint:** Paris

Date	Mintage	F12	VF20	XF40	MS60	MS63
1955	—	—	—	1,250	1,500	1,800

KM# M28 20 FRANCS
Silver **Subject:** Visit by President of Rene Coty **Obv:** Head of Republic **Rev:** Coin press

Date	Mintage	F12	VF20	XF40	MS60	MS63
1955	—	—	65.00	125	250	300

KM# M28a 20 FRANCS
Gold **Subject:** Visit by President of Rene Coty **Obv:** Head of Republic **Rev:** Coin press

Date	Mintage	F12	VF20	XF40	MS60	MS63
1955	—	—	—	1,250	1,500	1,800

EURO / FRANCS COINAGE

KM# 1121 10 FRANCS-1.5 EURO
22.20 g., 0.900 Silver 0.6424 oz. ASW, 37 mm. **Series:** Museum Treasures **Subject:** La Source by Raphael Jean A.D. Ingres **Obv:** Standing nude facing, RF and date at left **Rev:** Denominations, (francs/euros), on lined field, stars surround

Date	Mintage	VF20	XF40	MS60	MS63	MS65
1996	15,000	PF65 35.00				

KM# 1122 10 FRANCS-1.5 EURO
22.20 g., 0.900 Silver 0.6424 oz. ASW **Series:** Museum Treasures **Subject:** Fife player by Edouard Manet **Obv:** Standing figure facing, RF and date at left **Rev:** Denominations, (francs/euros), on lined field, stars surround

Date	Mintage	VF20	XF40	MS60	MS63	MS65
1996	15,000	PF65 40.00				

KM# 1123 10 FRANCS-1.5 EURO
22.20 g., 0.900 Silver 0.6424 oz. ASW, 37 mm. **Series:** Museum Treasures **Subject:** Shang Dynasty Elephant **Obv:** Elephant left, RF and date at left **Rev:** Denominations, (francs/euros), on lined field, stars surround

Date	Mintage	VF20	XF40	MS60	MS63	MS65
1996	15,000	PF65 30.00				

KM# 1124 10 FRANCS-1.5 EURO
22.20 g., 0.900 Silver 0.6424 oz. ASW **Series:** Museum Treasures **Subject:** "The Thinker" by Auguste Rodin **Obv:** Seated statue left, RF and date at left **Rev:** Denominations, (francs/euros), on lined field, stars surround **Note:** Silver coins sold as a set only.

Date	Mintage	VF20	XF40	MS60	MS63	MS65
1996	15,000	PF65 50.00				

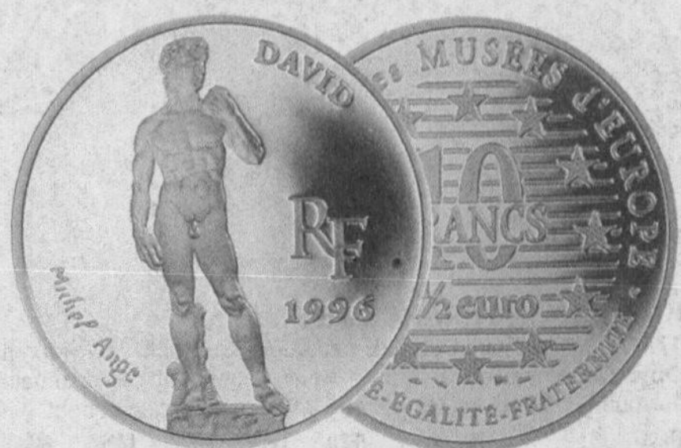

KM# 1146 10 FRANCS-1.5 EURO
22.20 g., 0.900 Silver 0.6424 oz. ASW **Series:** Museum Treasures **Subject:** David by Michaelangelo **Obv:** Standing nude facing, RF and date at right **Rev:** Denominations, (francs/euros), on lined field, stars surround

Date	Mintage	VF20	XF40	MS60	MS63	MS65
1996	15,000	PF65 40.00				

KM# 1147 10 FRANCS-1.5 EURO
22.20 g., 0.900 Silver 0.6424 oz. ASW **Series:** Museum Treasures **Subject:** Vincent Van Gogh, self portrait **Obv:** Bust 3/4 left, RF and date at left **Rev:** Denominations, (francs/euros), on lined field, stars surround

Date	Mintage	VF20	XF40	MS60	MS63	MS65
1996	15,000	PF65 50.00				

KM# 1148 10 FRANCS-1.5 EURO
22.20 g., 0.900 Silver 0.6424 oz. ASW **Series:** Museum Treasures **Subject:** Clothed Maya by Goya **Obv:** Reclining figure, RF and date at left **Rev:** Denominations, (francs/euros), on lined field, stars surround

Date	Mintage	VF20	XF40	MS60	MS63	MS65
1996	15,000	PF65 40.00				

KM# 1158 10 FRANCS-1.5 EURO
22.20 g., 0.900 Silver 0.6424 oz. ASW **Series:** Museum Treasures **Subject:** Chinese Horseman **Obv:** Equestrian statue right, RF and date at right **Rev:** Denominations, (francs/euros), on lined field, stars surround

Date	Mintage	VF20	XF40	MS60	MS63	MS65
1996	15,000	PF65 30.00				

KM# 1292 10 FRANCS-1.5 EURO
22.22 g., 0.900 Silver 0.643 oz. ASW, 36.9 mm. **Subject:** Museum Treasures **Obv:** Figure wearing tutu left, RF and date at right **Rev:** Denominations, (francs/euros), on lined field, stars surround **Edge:** Plain **Mint:** Paris

Date	Mintage	VF20	XF40	MS60	MS63	MS65
1997	15,000	PF65 30.00				

KM# 1297 10 FRANCS-1.5 EURO
22.22 g., 0.900 Silver 0.643 oz. ASW **Series:** Museum Treasures **Obv:** Japanese woman carrying a glass box **Rev:** Denominations, (francs/euros), on lined field, stars surround

Date	Mintage	VF20	XF40	MS60	MS63	MS65
1997	15,000	PF65 30.00				

KM# 1298 10 FRANCS-1.5 EURO

22.22 g., 0.900 Silver 0.643 oz. ASW **Series:** Museum Treasures **Subject:** Durer's "Self Portrait" **Obv:** Bust facing **Rev:** Denominations, (francs/euros), on lined field, stars surround

Date	Mintage	VF20	XF40	MS60	MS63	MS65
1997	15,000	PF65 50.00				

KM# 1299 10 FRANCS-1.5 EURO

22.22 g., 0.900 Silver 0.643 oz. ASW **Series:** Museum Treasures **Subject:** Klimt's "The Kiss" **Obv:** Two figures embraced **Rev:** Denominations, (francs/euros), on lined field, stars surround

Date	Mintage	VF20	XF40	MS60	MS63	MS65
1997	15,000	PF65 50.00				

KM# 1125 100 FRANCS-15 EURO

17.00 g., 0.920 Gold 0.5028 oz. AGW **Series:** Museum Treasures **Subject:** La Source by Raphael Jean A.D. Ingres **Obv:** Standing nude facing **Rev:** Denominations, (francs/euros), on lined field, stars surround

Date	Mintage	VF20	XF40	MS60	MS63	MS65
1996	5,000	PF65 950				

KM# 1126 100 FRANCS-15 EURO

17.00 g., 0.920 Gold 0.5028 oz. AGW **Series:** Museum Treasures **Subject:** Fife Player by Edouard Manet **Obv:** Standing figure facing **Rev:** Denominations, (francs/euros), on lined field, stars surround

Date	Mintage	VF20	XF40	MS60	MS63	MS65
1996	5,000	PF65 950				

KM# 1127 100 FRANCS-15 EURO

17.00 g., 0.920 Gold 0.5028 oz. AGW **Series:** Museum Treasures **Subject:** Shang Dynasty Elephant **Obv:** Elephant left **Rev:** Denominations, (francs/euros), on lined field, stars surround

Date	Mintage	VF20	XF40	MS60	MS63	MS65
1996	5,000	PF65 950				

KM# 1140 100 FRANCS-15 EURO

22.20 g., 0.900 Silver 0.6424 oz. ASW **Obv:** Stars surround denominations, (francs/euros) **Rev:** St. Stephen's Cathedral, Vienna, date at right

Date	Mintage	VF20	XF40	MS60	MS63	MS65
1996	20,000	PF65 50.00				

KM# 1142 100 FRANCS-15 EURO

22.20 g., 0.900 Silver 0.6424 oz. ASW **Obv:** Stars surround denominations, (francs/euros) **Rev:** Grand Place, Bruxelles, date below

Date	Mintage	VF20	XF40	MS60	MS63	MS65
1996	20,000	PF65 37.50				

KM# 1149 100 FRANCS-15 EURO

17.00 g., 0.920 Gold 0.5028 oz. AGW **Series:** Museum Treasures **Subject:** Van Gogh, Self Portrait **Obv:** Bust 3/4 left **Rev:** Denominations, (francs/euros), on lined field, stars surround

Date	Mintage	VF20	XF40	MS60	MS63	MS65
1996	5,000	PF65 950				

KM# 1150 100 FRANCS-15 EURO

17.00 g., 0.920 Gold 0.5028 oz. AGW **Series:** Museum Treasures **Subject:** Clothed Maya by Goya **Obv:** Reclined figure **Rev:** Stars surround denominations, (francs/euros), on lined field

Date	Mintage	VF20	XF40	MS60	MS63	MS65
1996	5,000	PF65 900				

KM# 1156 100 FRANCS-15 EURO

22.20 g., 0.900 Silver 0.6424 oz. ASW **Subject:** Amsterdam - Magere Brug **Obv:** Denominations, (francs/euros), on field of stars **Rev:** Bridge, date below

Date	Mintage	VF20	XF40	MS60	MS63	MS65
1996	20,000	PF65 37.50				

KM# 1159 100 FRANCS-15 EURO

17.00 g., 0.920 Gold 0.5028 oz. AGW **Series:** Museum Treasures **Subject:** Chinese Horseman **Obv:** Equestrian statue **Rev:** Stars surround denominations, (francs/euros), on lined field

Date	Mintage	VF20	XF40	MS60	MS63	MS65
1996	5,000	PF65 950				

KM# 1174 100 FRANCS-15 EURO

22.20 g., 0.900 Silver 0.6424 oz. ASW **Subject:** Lisbon **Obv:** Denominations-(francs/ecus), on field of stars **Rev:** Castle-like building Tour de Belem, date below

Date	Mintage	VF20	XF40	MS60	MS63	MS65
1997	20,000	PF65 50.00				

KM# 1176 100 FRANCS-15 EURO

22.20 g., 0.900 Silver 0.6424 oz. ASW **Subject:** Helsinki **Obv:** Denominations-(francs/ecus) **Rev:** Cathedral, Cathedrale Saint - Nicolas, date below

Date	Mintage	VF20	XF40	MS60	MS63	MS65
1997	20,000	PF65 50.00				

KM# 1178 100 FRANCS-15 EURO

22.20 g., 0.900 Silver 0.6424 oz. ASW **Subject:** Copenhagen **Obv:** Denominations-(francs/ecus) **Rev:** Statue of the Copenhagen mermaid, Petite Sirene, date at right

Date	Mintage	VF20	XF40	MS60	MS63	MS65
1997	20,000	PF65 55.00				

KM# 1189 100 FRANCS-15 EURO

22.20 g., 0.900 Silver 0.6424 oz. ASW **Subject:** Irlande - Rock of Cashel **Obv:** Denomination **Rev:** Celtic cross and castle, date below

Date	Mintage	VF20	XF40	MS60	MS63	MS65
1997	20,000	PF65 50.00				

KM# 1191 100 FRANCS-15 EURO

22.20 g., 0.900 Silver 0.6424 oz. ASW **Subject:** Luxembourg - Wenceslaus Wall **Obv:** Denomination **Rev:** Walled palace, date above

Date	Mintage	VF20	XF40	MS60	MS63	MS65
1997	20,000	PF65 50.00				

KM# 1193 100 FRANCS-15 EURO

22.20 g., 0.900 Silver 0.6424 oz. ASW **Subject:** Stockholm - Hotel de Ville **Obv:** Denomination **Rev:** Tower and building, date at right

Date	Mintage	VF20	XF40	MS60	MS63	MS65
1997	20,000	PF65 50.00				

KM# 1953 100 FRANCS-15 EURO

17.00 g., 0.920 Gold 0.5028 oz. AGW **Subject:** Albert Durer, self-portrait **Mint:** Paris

Date	Mintage	VF20	XF40	MS60	MS63	MS65
1997	Est. 5000	PF65 1,000				

KM# 1954 100 FRANCS-15 EURO

17.00 g., 0.920 Gold 0.5028 oz. AGW **Subject:** The Kiss by Gustav Klimt **Mint:** Paris

Date	Mintage	VF20	XF40	MS60	MS63	MS65
1997	—	PF65 1,000				

KM# 1955 100 FRANCS-15 EURO

17.00 g., 0.920 Gold 0.5028 oz. AGW **Subject:** Kitagara Utamaro's Lady with satchel **Mint:** Paris

Date	Mintage	VF20	XF40	MS60	MS63	MS65
1997 Proof	—	—	—	—	—	950

KM# 1941 500 FRANCS-75 EURO

20.00 g., 0.999 Platinum 0.6424 oz. APW **Rev:** Parthenon in Athens **Mint:** Paris

Date	Mintage	VF20	XF40	MS60	MS63	MS65
1995	30	PF65 1,300				

KM# 1128 500 FRANCS-75 EURO

31.10 g., 0.999 Gold 0.999 oz. AGW **Series:** Museum Treasures **Subject:** "The Thinker", by Auguste Rodin **Obv:** Seated statue left **Rev:** Stars surround denominations, (francs/euros), on lined field

Date	Mintage	VF20	XF40	MS60	MS63	MS65
1996	5,000	PF65 1,850				

KM# 1129 500 FRANCS-75 EURO
155.52 g., 0.999 Gold 4.995 oz. AGW **Series:** Museum Treasures **Subject:** La Source by Raphael Jean A.D. Ingres **Obv:** Standing nude facing **Rev:** Stars surround denominations, (francs/euros), on lined field

Date	Mintage	VF20	XF40	MS60	MS63	MS65
1996 Prof	99	PF65 9,500				

KM# 1130 500 FRANCS-75 EURO
155.52 g., 0.999 Gold 4.995 oz. AGW **Series:** Museum Treasures **Subject:** Fife Player by Edouard Manet **Obv:** Standing figure facing **Rev:** Stars surround denominations, (francs/euros), on lined field

Date	Mintage	VF20	XF40	MS60	MS63	MS65
1996	99	PF65 9,500				

KM# 1131 500 FRANCS-75 EURO
155.52 g., 0.999 Gold 4.995 oz. AGW **Series:** Museum Treasures **Subject:** Shang Dynasty Elephant **Obv:** Elephant left **Rev:** Stars surround denominations, (francs/euros), on lined field

Date	Mintage	VF20	XF40	MS60	MS63	MS65
1996	99	PF65 9,500				

KM# 1141 500 FRANCS-75 EURO
17.00 g., 0.920 Gold 0.5028 oz. AGW **Subject:** St. Stephen's Cathedral, Vienna **Obv:** Denominations, (francs/euro), on field of stars **Rev:** Cathedral, date at right

Date	Mintage	VF20	XF40	MS60	MS63	MS65
1996	5,000	PF65 950				

KM# 1141a 500 FRANCS-75 EURO
20.00 g., 0.999 Platinum 0.6424 oz. APW **Subject:** St. Stephen's Cathedral, Vienna **Obv:** Denominations-(francs/ecus) **Rev:** Cathedral

Date	Mintage	VF20	XF40	MS60	MS63	MS65
1996 Prof	2,000	PF65 1,250				

KM# 1143 500 FRANCS-75 EURO
17.00 g., 0.920 Gold 0.5028 oz. AGW **Subject:** Grand Place, Bruxelles **Obv:** Denominations-(francs/ecus) **Rev:** Buildings with tower, date below

Date	Mintage	VF20	XF40	MS60	MS63	MS65
1996	5,000	PF65 950				

KM# 1143a 500 FRANCS-75 EURO
20.00 g., 0.999 Platinum 0.6424 oz. APW **Subject:** Grand Place, Bruxelles **Obv:** Denominations-(francs/ecus) **Rev:** Buildings with tower

Date	Mintage	VF20	XF40	MS60	MS63	MS65
1996	2,000	PF65 1,250				

KM# 1151 500 FRANCS-75 EURO
31.10 g., 0.999 Gold 0.999 oz. AGW **Series:** Museum Treasures **Subject:** David by Michaelangelo **Obv:** Standing nude **Rev:** Denominations, (francs/euros), on lined field, stars surround

Date	Mintage	VF20	XF40	MS60	MS63	MS65
1996	5,000	PF65 1,900				

KM# 1152 500 FRANCS-75 EURO
155.52 g., 0.999 Gold 4.995 oz. AGW **Series:** Museum Treasures **Subject:** David by Michaelangelo **Obv:** Standing nude **Rev:** Denominations-(francs/ecus), on lined field, stars surround

Date	Mintage	VF20	XF40	MS60	MS63	MS65
1996	99	PF65 9,500				

KM# 1153 500 FRANCS-75 EURO
155.52 g., 0.999 Gold 4.995 oz. AGW **Series:** Museum Treasures **Subject:** Vincent Van Gogh, Self Portrait **Obv:** Bust 3/4 left, RF and date at left **Rev:** Denominations-(francs/ecus), on lined field, stars surround

Date	Mintage	VF20	XF40	MS60	MS63	MS65
1996	99	PF65 9,500				

KM# 1154 500 FRANCS-75 EURO
155.52 g., 0.999 Gold 4.995 oz. AGW **Series:** Museum Treasures **Subject:** Clothed Maya by Goya **Obv:** Reclined figure, RF and date at left **Rev:** Denominations-(francs/ecus), on lined field, stars surround

Date	Mintage	VF20	XF40	MS60	MS63	MS65
1996	99	PF65 9,500				

KM# 1157 500 FRANCS-75 EURO
17.00 g., 0.920 Gold 0.5028 oz. AGW **Subject:** Amsterdam Magere Brug

Date	Mintage	VF20	XF40	MS60	MS63	MS65
1996	5,000	PF65 950				

KM# 1157a 500 FRANCS-75 EURO
20.00 g., 0.999 Platinum 0.6424 oz. APW **Subject:** Amsterdam Magere Brug

Date	Mintage	VF20	XF40	MS60	MS63	MS65
1996	2,000	PF65 1,250				

KM# 1315 500 FRANCS-75 EURO
155.50 g., 0.999 Gold 4.9944 oz. AGW, 50 mm. **Subject:** "The Thinker" by Auguste Rodin **Obv:** Seated statue left **Rev:** Denominations-(francs and euros) **Mint:** Paris

Date	Mintage	VF20	XF40	MS60	MS63	MS65
1996	99	PF65 9,500				

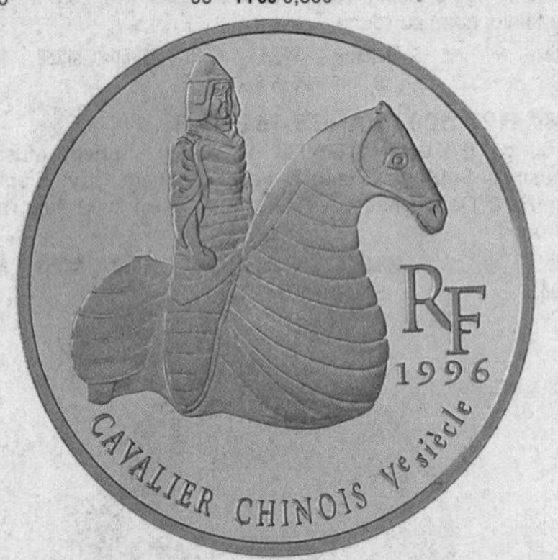

KM# 1316 500 FRANCS-75 EURO
155.50 g., 0.999 Gold 4.9944 oz. AGW, 50 mm. **Subject:** Chinese Horseman **Obv:** Equestrian statue **Rev:** Denominations-(francs and euros) **Mint:** Paris

Date	Mintage	VF20	XF40	MS60	MS63	MS65
1996	99	PF65 9,500				

KM# 1175 500 FRANCS-75 EURO
17.00 g., 0.920 Gold 0.5028 oz. AGW **Subject:** Lisbon **Obv:** Denominations **Rev:** Castle-like building Tour de Belem, date below

Date	Mintage	VF20	XF40	MS60	MS63	MS65
1997	5,000	PF65 950				

KM# 1175a 500 FRANCS-75 EURO
20.00 g., 0.999 Platinum 0.6424 oz. APW **Subject:** Lisbon **Obv:** Denominations **Rev:** Castle-like building Tour de Belem

Date	Mintage	VF20	XF40	MS60	MS63	MS65
1997	2,000	PF65 1,250				

KM# 1177 500 FRANCS-75 EURO
17.00 g., 0.920 Gold 0.5028 oz. AGW **Subject:** Helsinki **Obv:** Denominations **Rev:** Cathedrale Saint Nicholas, date below

Date	Mintage	VF20	XF40	MS60	MS63	MS65
1997	5,000	PF65 950				

KM# 1177a 500 FRANCS-75 EURO
20.00 g., 0.999 Platinum 0.6424 oz. APW **Subject:** Helsinki **Obv:** Denominations **Rev:** Cathedral, Cathedrale Saint Nicholas

Date	Mintage	VF20	XF40	MS60	MS63	MS65
1997	2,000	PF65 1,250				

KM# 1179 500 FRANCS-75 EURO
17.00 g., 0.920 Gold 0.5028 oz. AGW **Subject:** Copenhagen **Obv:** Denominations, (francs/euros), on field of stars **Rev:** Statue of Copenhagen's Little Mermaid, Petite Siren, date at right

Date	Mintage	VF20	XF40	MS60	MS63	MS65
1997	5,000	PF65 950				

KM# 1179a 500 FRANCS-75 EURO
20.00 g., 0.999 Platinum 0.6424 oz. APW **Subject:** Copenhagen **Obv:** Denominations **Rev:** Statue of Copenhagen's Little Mermaid, Petite Siren

Date	Mintage	VF20	XF40	MS60	MS63	MS65
1997	2,000	PF65 1,250				

KM# 1190 500 FRANCS-75 EURO
17.00 g., 0.920 Gold 0.5028 oz. AGW **Subject:** Ireland - Rock of Cashel **Obv:** Denomination **Rev:** Celtic cross and castle

Date	Mintage	VF20	XF40	MS60	MS63	MS65
1997	5,000	PF65 950				

KM# 1190a 500 FRANCS-75 EURO
20.00 g., 0.999 Platinum 0.6424 oz. APW **Subject:** Ireland - Rock of Cashel **Obv:** Denomination **Rev:** Celtic cross and castle

Date	Mintage	VF20	XF40	MS60	MS63	MS65
1997	2,000	PF65 1,250				

KM# 1192 500 FRANCS-75 EURO
17.00 g., 0.920 Gold 0.5028 oz. AGW **Subject:** Luxembourg - Wenceslas Wall **Obv:** Denomination **Rev:** Walled palace

Date	Mintage	VF20	XF40	MS60	MS63	MS65
1997	5,000	PF65 950				

KM# 1192a 500 FRANCS-75 EURO
20.00 g., 0.999 Platinum 0.6424 oz. APW **Subject:** Luxembourg-Wenceslas Wall **Obv:** Denomination **Rev:** Walled palace

Date	Mintage	VF20	XF40	MS60	MS63	MS65
1997	2,000	PF65 1,250				

KM# 1194 500 FRANCS-75 EURO
17.00 g., 0.999 Gold 0.546 oz. AGW **Subject:** Stockholm - Hotel de Ville **Obv:** Denomination **Rev:** Tower and building

Date	Mintage	VF20	XF40	MS60	MS63	MS65
1997	5,000	PF65 975				

KM# 1194a 500 FRANCS-75 EURO
20.00 g., 0.999 Platinum 0.6424 oz. APW **Subject:** Stockholm - Hotel de Ville **Obv:** Denomination **Rev:** Tower and building

Date	Mintage	VF20	XF40	MS60	MS63	MS65
1997	2,000	PF65 1,250				

KM# 1317 500 FRANCS-75 EURO
155.50 g., 0.999 Gold 4.9944 oz. AGW, 50 mm. **Subject:** Klimt's "The Kiss" **Obv:** Two figures embraced **Rev:** Denominations-(francs and euros) **Mint:** Paris

Date	Mintage	VF20	XF40	MS60	MS63	MS65
1997	—	PF65 9,500				

KM# 1318 500 FRANCS-75 EURO
155.50 g., 0.999 Gold 4.9944 oz. AGW, 50 mm. **Subject:** Durer's Self Portrait **Obv:** Bust facing **Rev:** Denominations-(francs and euros) **Mint:** Paris

Date	Mintage	VF20	XF40	MS60	MS63	MS65
1997	99	PF65 9,500				

KM# 1319 500 FRANCS-75 EURO
155.50 g., 0.999 Gold 4.9944 oz. AGW, 50 mm. **Obv:** Japanese woman carrying a case **Rev:** Denominations-(francs and euros) **Mint:** Paris

Date	Mintage	VF20	XF40	MS60	MS63	MS65
1997	99	PF65 9,500				

KM# 1320 500 FRANCS-75 EURO
155.50 g., 0.999 Gold 4.9944 oz. AGW, 50 mm. **Subject:** The "Little Dancer" by Degas **Obv:** Figure in tutu left **Rev:** Denominations-(francs and euros) **Mint:** Paris

Date	Mintage	VF20	XF40	MS60	MS63	MS65
1997	99	PF65 9,500				

KM# 1956 500 FRANCS-75 EURO
31.10 g., 0.999 Gold 0.9989 oz. AGW, 50 mm. **Subject:** Hilaire Germain Degas' Ballet Dancer **Mint:** Paris

Date	Mintage	VF20	XF40	MS60	MS63	MS65
1997	—	PF65 1,800				

EURO COINAGE

European Union Issues

KM# 1282 EURO CENT
2.27 g., Copper Plated Steel, 16.3 mm. **Obv:** Human face **Rev:** Denomination and globe **Edge:** Plain **Mint:** Paris

Date	Mintage	VF20	XF40	MS60	MS63	MS65
1999	794,054,000	—	—	0.35	0.50	0.75
1999	15,000	PF65 10.00				
2000	605,267,000	—	—	0.35	0.50	0.75
2000	15,000	PF65 10.00				

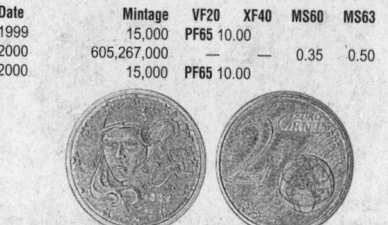

KM# 1283 2 EURO CENT
3.03 g., Copper Plated Steel, 18.7 mm. **Obv:** Human face **Rev:** Denomination and globe **Edge:** Grooved **Mint:** Paris

Date	Mintage	VF20	XF40	MS60	MS63	MS65
1999	702,104,000	—	—	0.50	0.75	1.00
1999	15,000	PF65 10.00				
2000	510,155,000	—	—	0.50	0.75	1.00
2000	15,000	PF65 10.00				

KM# 1284 5 EURO CENT
3.86 g., Copper Plated Steel, 21.2 mm. **Obv:** Human face **Rev:** Denomination and globe **Edge:** Plain **Mint:** Paris

Date	Mintage	VF20	XF40	MS60	MS63	MS65
1999	616,227,000	—	—	0.75	1.25	1.50
1999	15,000	PF65 12.00				
2000	280,099,000	—	—	0.75	1.25	1.50
2000	15,000	PF65 12.00				

KM# 1285 10 EURO CENT
4.07 g., Brass, 19.7 mm. **Obv:** The seed sower divides date and RF **Rev:** Denomination and map **Edge:** Reeded **Mint:** Paris

Date	Mintage	VF20	XF40	MS60	MS63	MS65
1999	447,284,600	—	—	0.75	1.25	1.50
1999	15,000	PF65 12.00				
2000	297,467,000	—	—	0.75	1.25	1.50
2000	15,000	PF65 12.00				

KM# 1286 20 EURO CENT
5.73 g., Brass, 22.2 mm. **Obv:** The seed sower divides date and RF **Rev:** Denomination and map **Edge:** Notched **Mint:** Paris

Date	Mintage	VF20	XF40	MS60	MS63	MS65
1999	454,326,200	—	—	1.00	1.50	2.00
1999	15,000	PF65 14.00				
2000	148,988,600	—	—	1.25	2.00	2.50
2000	15,000	PF65 14.00				

KM# 1287 50 EURO CENT
7.81 g., Brass, 24.2 mm. **Obv:** The Seed Sower divides date and RF **Rev:** Denomination and map **Edge:** Reeded **Mint:** Paris

Date	Mintage	VF20	XF40	MS60	MS63	MS65
1999	150,788,600	—	—	—	1.50	2.25
1999	15,000	PF65 15.00				
2000	179,531,000	—	—	—	1.25	2.00
2000	15,000	PF65 15.00				

KM# 1288 EURO
7.50 g., Bi-Metallic Copper-Nickel center in Nickel-Brass ring, 23.25 mm. **Obv:** Stylized tree divides RF within circle, date below **Rev:** Denomination and map **Edge:** Segmented reeding **Mint:** Paris

Date	Mintage	VF20	XF40	MS60	MS63	MS65
1999	301,085,000	—	—	—	2.50	3.75
1999	15,000	**PF65** 18.00				
2000	297,305,000	—	—	—	2.50	3.75
2000	15,000	**PF65** 18.00				

KM# 1289 2 EURO
8.50 g., Bi-Metallic Nickel-Brass center in Copper-Nickel ring, 25.75 mm. **Obv:** Stylized tree divides RF within circle, date below **Rev:** Denomination and map **Edge:** Reeded with 2s and stars **Mint:** Paris

Date	Mintage	VF20	XF40	MS60	MS63	MS65
1999	56,730,000	—	—	—	4.50	7.00
1999	15,000	**PF65** 20.00				
2000	171,155,000	—	—	—	3.75	6.00
2000	15,000	**PF65** 20.00				

ESSAIS

Standard metals unless otherwise noted

KM#	Date	Mintage	Identification	Mkt Val
E38	1903 (a)	—	25 Centimes. Nickel. Denomination within square, date below. KM#855.	225
AE39	1904 (a)	—	25 Centimes. Nickel. Laureate bust left. Denomination above date. Without square around denomination, 22 sided flan.	200
E39	1904 (a)	—	25 Centimes. Nickel. Laureate bust left. Leafy branch divides denomination and date, axe on column at left. KM#856.	125
AE40	1904 (a)	—	25 Centimes. Nickel. 22 sided flan, KM#856.	200
EB40	1904 (a)	—	25 Centimes. Nickel. 18 sided flan, KM#856.	200
E40	1908 (a)	—	10 Centimes. Aluminum. KM#843.	150
EC40	1908 (a)	—	5 Centimes. Bronze. Head right. Woman and child, denomination at right, date below. KM#842.	110
E41	1910 (a)	—	5 Centimes. Bronze. KM#842.	100
E42	1913 (a)	—	25 Centimes. Nickel. KM#867.	150
E43	1914 (a)	104	5 Centimes. Copper-Nickel. KM#865.	900
E44	1914 (a)	—	25 Centimes. Nickel. KM#867.	150
E45	1929 (a)	—	10 Francs. Silver. Delannoy.	600
E46	1929 (a)	—	10 Francs. Aluminum-Bronze. Republic above denomination and date. Laureate head right.	60.00
E47	1929 (a)	—	10 Francs. Aluminum-Bronze. Oak leaves on head right, date at right. Hand holding supported torch divides denomination.	60.00
E48	1929 (a)	—	10 Francs. Silver. KM#878.	700
E49	1929 (a)	—	20 Francs. Silver. KM#879.	850
E50	1929 (a)	—	20 Francs. Aluminum-Bronze. KM#879.	100
E51	1929 (a)	15	100 Francs. Gold. Winged head left. Leafy branches flank grain sprig, denomination above, date below.	6,500
E52	1929	15	100 Francs. Gold. Map of France with sprays flanking, denomination below.	3,850
E53	1929 (a)	15	100 Francs. Gold. Laureate head left. Grain sprig left and branch right divide denomination and date.	4,500
E54	1929 (a)	15	100 Francs. Gold. Laureate bust left. Ribboned branches and torch divide RF above denomination and date.	4,500
E55	1929 (a)	15	100 Francs. Gold. Braided head left. Caduceus divides denomination, cornucopias, and date below.	4,500
E56	1929 (a)	15	100 Francs. Gold. Laureate head left. Denomination and date within wreath.	4,500
E57	1929 (a)	15	100 Francs. Gold. Laureate head left. Denomination and date within wreath.	4,500
E58	1929 (a)	15	100 Francs. Gold. Laureate head left. Five grain sprigs divide denomination and date below.	4,500
E59	1929 (a)	15	100 Francs. Gold. Head left. Oak tree divides denomination.	4,500
E60	1929 (a)	15	100 Francs. Gold. Head left, hair in bun. Three grain sprigs divide date and denomination.	4,500
E62	1929 (a)	15	100 Francs. Gold. With Essai, KM#880.	4,800
AE64	1931	—	50 Centimes. Aluminum-Bronze. KM#894.1, Morlon.	125
E64	1931	—	2 Francs. Aluminum-Bronze. KM#886.	125
EB64	1931	—	Franc. Aluminum-Bronze. KM#885, Morlon.	125
AE65	1933	—	5 Francs. Nickel. KM#887, Bazor.	225
E65	1933	—	5 Francs. Nickel. KM#888.	200
E66	1933	—	5 Francs. Seated Liberty, date below. 5 FRANCS at center, legend and wheat spears around.	200
AE67	1933	—	5 Francs. Silver. Laureate head right. Denomination and date above inscription, grain columns flank. Turin.	700
E67	1934 (a)	—	5 Francs. Nickel. KM#888.	—
E68	1938 (a)	—	25 Centimes. Nickel-Bronze. KM#867b.	130
E69	1938 (a)	—	10 Francs. Nickel. KM#908.1.	225
E70	1938 (a)	—	20 Francs. Nickel. KM#879.	250
E71	1938 (a)	—	20 Francs. Aluminum. KM#879.	200
E72	1939 (a)	—	20 Francs. Copper-Nickel. KM#879.	175
E73	1940 (a)	—	25 Centimes. Zinc. KM#867b.	150
E74	1941 (a)	—	10 Centimes. Zinc. KM#898.1.	150
E75	1941 (a)	—	20 Centimes. Zinc. KM#899.	150
E76	1941 (a)	—	20 Centimes. Zinc. KM#900.1.	150
AE77	1941	—	2 Francs. Iron. KM#886, Morlon.	285
E77	1941	—	5 Francs. Copper-Nickel. Head left. Cross divides denomination. Bazor.	350
E78	1941	—	10 Francs. Aluminum. Head left. Shield divides denomination and date. Delannoy.	350
E79	1941	—	10 Francs. Nickel.	550
AE80	1941	—	10 Francs. Aluminum. Head left. Grain sprig divides denomination, date below, wreath surrounds. Simon.	325
E80	1941 (a)	—	10 Francs. Nickel.	525
E81	1941	—	10 Francs. Copper-Nickel. Face and inscription left. Denomination and date on center shield, family scenes flank. Galle.	375
E82	1941	—	20 Francs. Aluminum. Head left, date below. Leaves at center of grain sheaf divide denomination. Cochet.	285
AE92	1941	—	20 Francs. Aluminum. Denomination and date below center inscription. Bouchard.	365
E83	1942	—	Franc. Aluminum. KM#902.1.	200
E83a	1942	300	50 Centimes. Aluminum. KM#914.1.	200
E84	1943 (a)	300	10 Centimes. Zinc. KM#903.	110
E85	1943 (a)	300	2 Francs. Aluminum. KM#904.	200
E86	1943	—	10 Francs. Copper-Nickel. Bazor.	200
E86a	1943	—	10 Francs. Aluminum. Head left. Statues below denomination, date at bottom. Bazor.	320
E87	1944 (a)	300	10 Centimes. Zinc. KM#906.	165
E88	1945 (a)	40	20 Centimes. Zinc. KM#907.	475
E89	1945 (a)	1,100	5 Francs. KM#888b.	110
E90	1945 (a)	1,100	10 Francs. Copper-Nickel. KM#909.	140
E91	1950 (g)	1,700	10 Francs. Aluminum-Bronze. KM#915.	110
E92	1950 (a)	25	20 Francs. Aluminum-Bronze. Georges Guiraud, KM#916.	400
E93	1950 (a)	1,700	20 Francs. Aluminum-Bronze. G. Guiraud, KM#971.	100
E94	1950 (a)	1,700	50 Francs. Aluminum-Bronze. KM#918.	125
E95	1950 (a)	50	100 Francs.	300
AE96	1950	—	100 Francs. Copper-Nickel. KM#919.1.	4,000
E96	1951 (a)	28	20 Francs. Aluminum-Bronze. KM#917.	625
E97	1954 (a)	1,200	100 Francs. Copper-Nickel. KM#919.	200
E98	1959 (a)	4,000	Franc. Nickel. KM#925.	300
E99	1959 (a)	4,000	Franc. Nickel. KM#925.	300
E100	1959	—	2 Francs. Silver. KM#845.1.	1,200
E101	1959 (a)	4,000	5 Francs. Silver. KM#926.	200
E102	1959 (a)	Inc. above	5 Francs. Silver. Small 5 in date, KM#926.	200
E103	1961 (a)	3,500	Centime. Chrome-Steel. KM#928.	85.00
E103.1	1961	3,500	2 Centimes. Chrome-Steel.	500
E104	1961 (a)	3,500	5 Centimes. Chrome-Steel. KM#927.	40.00
E105	1961	—	20 Centimes. Aluminum-Bronze. KM#930.	35.00
E106	1961	—	20 Centimes. Laureate head with short hair left. Denomination and date within wreath.	40.00
E107	1961	—	20 Centimes. Head with long hair left. Denomination above date within wreath.	75.00
E108	1962 (a)	3,500	10 Centimes. Aluminum-Bronze. KM#929.	25.00
E109	1962 (a)	3,500	20 Centimes. Aluminum-Bronze. KM#930.	25.00
E110	1962 (a)	3,500	50 Centimes. Aluminum-Bronze. KM#939.	30.00
E111	1964 (a)	3,500	10 Francs. Silver. KM#932.	200
E112	1965 (a)	4,700	1/2 Franc. Nickel. KM#931.	50.00
E113	1966 (a)	4,128	5 Centimes. Aluminum-Bronze. KM#933.	30.00
E114	1970 (a)	5,000	5 Francs. Silver. KM#926a.	50.00
E115	1974	7,300	10 Francs. Nickel-Brass. KM#940.	35.00
E116	1974	9	10 Francs. Gold. KM#940.	3,600
E117	1974	13,800	50 Francs. Silver. KM#941.	80.00
E118	1974	5	50 Francs. Gold. KM#941.	4,000
E119	1978	6,000	2 Francs. Nickel. KM#942.	200
E120	1978	22	2 Francs. Silver. KM#942.	450
E121	1978	12	2 Francs. Gold. KM#942.	1,350
E122	1982	—	10 Francs. Copper-Nickel. Gambetta, KM#950.	50.00
E123	1982	—	100 Francs. Silver. KM#951.	75.00
E124	1983	4,000	10 Francs. Nickel-Bronze. Baloon, KM#952.	40.00
E125	1983	9	10 Francs. Gold. Baloon, KM#952.	2,400
E126	1983	4,000	10 Francs. Nickel-Bronze. Stendhal, KM#953.	40.00
E127	1983	9	10 Francs. Gold. Stendhal, KM#953.	2,400
E128	1984	—	10 Francs. Nickel-Bronze. Rude, KM#954.	45.00
E129	1984	—	100 Francs. Silver. Curie, KM#955.	75.00
E130	1985	1,700	10 Francs. Nickel-Bronze. Hugo, KM#956.	35.00
E131	1985	1,700	100 Francs. Silver. Zola, KM#957.	50.00
E132	1986	1,750	10 Francs. Nickel. KM#959.	35.00
E133	1986	9	10 Francs. Gold. KM#959.	2,200
E134	1986	1,750	10 Francs. Nickel. Schuman, KM#958d.	35.00
E135	1986	1,750	100 Francs. Silver. Liberty, KM#960.	100
E136	1987	1,850	10 Francs. Nickel-Bronze. Capet, KM#916.1.	40.00
E137	1987	1,850	100 Francs. Silver. Lafayette, KM#962.	100
E138	1988	1,850	Franc. Nickel. KM#963.	60.00

KM#	Date	Mintage	Identification	Mkt Val
E139	1988	1,850	10 Francs. Aluminum-Bronze. Garros, KM#965.	30.00
E140	1988	1,850	10 Francs. Bi-Metallic. Bastille, KM#964.	100
E141	1988	1,850	100 Francs. Silver. Fraternity, KM#966.	50.00
E142	1989	—	Franc. Nickel. KM#967.	40.00
E143	1989	—	5 Francs. Nickel. Eiffel TOwer, KM#968.	50.00
E144	1989	—	10 Francs. Bi-Metallic. Montesquien, KM#969.	200
E145	1989	—	100 Francs. Silver. Human Rights, KM#970.	65.00
E146	1994	—	20 Francs. Tri-Metallic. KM#1036.	75.00

PATTERNS

Including off metal strikes

KM#	Date	Mintage	Identification	Mkt Val
Pn102	1929	—	100 Francs. Aluminum-Bronze. Bust left. Date.	140
Pn103	1933	—	5 Francs. Liberty bust left. Legend above, date below.	180
Pn104	1939	—	20 Francs. Copper-Nickel.	600
Pn105	1941	—	10 Francs. Copper-Nickel. Petain bust left, legend in front. People working at sides. TRAVAIL / FAMILLE / PATRIE / 10 / FRANCS / 1941.	425
Pn106	1941	—	20 Francs. Copper-Nickel. Petain bust left. Sheaves of wheat bent outward divide denomination, legend above.	325
Pn107	1941	—	20 Francs. Copper-Nickel. Petain bust left. Famlly group above FAMILLE divide 20-FR.	325
Pn108	1941	—	20 Francs. Nickel. Petain bust left. 3 figures, 2 standing, 1 sitting.	325
Pn109	1942	—	5 Francs. Copper-Nickel. Petain bust left. TRAVAIL / FAMILLE / PATRIE / 5 / FRANCS / 1942.	325
Pn110	1943	—	10 Francs. Copper-Nickel. Petain bust left. 3 figures, 2 standing, 1 sitting.	325
Pn111	1950	—	20 Francs. Liberty left. 20-FR divided by symbol.	55.00
Pn112	1950	—	20 Francs. Liberty left. Inscription above 20 dividing flowers, FRANCS and date below.	55.00
Pn113	1950	—	20 Francs. Liberty bust left. 20 over branch at left, FRANCS in center at right, date below.	55.00
Pn114	1950	—	20 Francs. Liberty bust left. 20 in small circle of branches, 4 branches to edge of coin.	55.00
Pn115	1950	—	100 Francs. Copper-Nickel.	250
Pn116	1964	131	10 Francs. Silver. KM#756. KM#932.	1,200
Pn117	1964	3,500	10 Francs. Silver. KM#932.	250
Pn118	1977	253	2 Francs. Nickel. KM#942.	900

PIEDFORT

Standard metals unless otherwise noted

KM#	Date	Mintage	Identification	Mkt Val
P251	1903	—	25 Centimes. Copper-Nickel-Zinc.	250
P270	1914	—	10 Centimes. Nickel. KM#866.	1,200
P272	1914	—	25 Centimes. Nickel. KM#867.	265
P280	1920	—	5 Centimes. Copper-Nickel. KM#875.	235
PA297	1920	—	2 Francs. Aluminum-Bronze. KM#877.	300
P297	1928	—	2 Francs. Silver. KM#845.	320
P300	1929	—	100 Francs. Gold. KM#880.	5,300
P305	1941	—	10 Centimes. Zinc. KM#895.	220
P341	1962	500	Centime. Chrome-Steel. KM#928.	25.00
P342	1962	50	Centime. Silver. KM#928.	65.00
P343	1962	20	Centime. Gold. KM#928.	700
P344	1962	500	10 Centimes. Aluminum-Bronze. KM#929.	25.00
P345	1962	50	10 Centimes. Silver. KM#929.	85.00
P346	1962	20	10 Centimes. Gold. KM#929.	750
P347	1962	500	20 Centimes. Aluminum-Bronze. KM#930.	25.00
P348	1962	50	20 Centimes. Silver. KM#930.	120
P349	1962	20	20 Centimes. Gold. KM#930.	800
P350	1962	500	50 Centimes. Aluminum-Bronze. KM#939.	25.00
P351	1962	50	50 Centimes. Silver. KM#939.	130
P352	1962	20	50 Centimes. Gold. KM#939.	1,000
P353	1965	500	1/2 Franc. Nickel. KM#931.	30.00
P354	1965	50	1/2 Franc. Silver. KM#931.	75.00
P355	1965	20	1/2 Franc. Gold. KM#931.	800
P356	1965	500	10 Francs. Silver. KM#932.	75.00
P357	1965	50	10 Francs. Gold. KM#932.	3,750
P358	1966	500	5 Centimes. Aluminum-Bronze. KM#933.	20.00
P359	1966	50	5 Centimes. Silver. KM#933.	80.00
P360	1966	20	5 Centimes. Gold. KM#933.	700
P361	1967	500	Centime. Chrome Plated Steel. KM#928.	20.00
P362	1967	50	Centime. Silver. KM#928.	35.00
P363	1967	20	Centime. Gold. KM#928.	750
P364	1967	500	5 Centimes. Aluminum-Bronze. KM#933.	20.00
P365	1967	50	5 Centimes. Silver. KM#933.	50.00
P366	1967	20	5 Centimes. Gold. KM#933.	700
P367	1967	500	10 Centimes. Aluminum-Bronze. KM#929.	20.00
P368	1967	50	10 Centimes. Silver. KM#929.	65.00
P369	1967	20	10 Centimes. Gold. KM#929.	700
P370	1967	500	20 Centimes. Aluminum-Bronze. KM#930.	20.00
P371	1967	50	20 Centimes. Silver. KM#930.	125
P372	1967	20	20 Centimes. Gold. KM#930.	800
P373	1967	500	25 Centimes. Aluminum-Bronze. KM#939.	20.00
P374	1967	50	50 Centimes. Silver. KM#939.	125
P375	1967	20	50 Centimes. Gold. KM#939.	1,350
P376	1967	500	1/2 Franc. Nickel. KM#931.	25.00
P377	1967	50	1/2 Franc. Silver. KM#931.	85.00
P378	1967	20	1/2 Franc. Gold. KM#931.	900
P379	1967	500	Franc. Nickel. KM#925.	25.00
P380	1967	50	Franc. Silver. KM#925.	85.00
P382	1967	500	5 Francs. Silver. KM#926.	35.00
P383	1967	50	5 Francs. Gold. KM#926.	1,700
P384	1967	500	10 Francs. Silver. KM#932.	50.00
P385	1967	50	10 Francs. Gold. KM#932.	3,000
P386	1968	500	Centime. Chrome-Steel. KM#928.	35.00
P387	1968	50	Centime. Silver. KM#928.	60.00
P388	1968	20	Centime. Gold. KM#928.	750
P389	1968	500	5 Centimes. Aluminum-Bronze. KM#933.	35.00
P390	1968	50	5 Centimes. Silver. KM#933.	60.00
P391	1968	20	5 Centimes. Gold. KM#933.	450
P392	1968	500	10 Centimes. Aluminum-Bronze. KM#929.	35.00
P393	1968	50	10 Centimes. Silver. KM#929.	60.00
P394	1968	20	10 Centimes. Gold. KM#929.	650
P395	1968	500	20 Centimes. Aluminum-Bronze. KM#930.	35.00
P396	1968	50	20 Centimes. Silver. KM#930.	60.00
P397	1968	20	20 Centimes. Gold. KM#930.	850
P398	1968	500	1/2 Franc. Nickel. KM#931.	35.00
P399	1968	50	1/2 Franc. Silver. KM#931.	65.00
P400	1968	20	1/2 Franc. Gold. KM#931.	850
P401	1968	500	Franc. Nickel. KM#925.	35.00
P402	1968	50	Franc. Silver. KM#925.	65.00
P404	1968	500	5 Francs. Silver. KM#926.	35.00
P405	1968	50	5 Francs. Gold. KM#926.	1,750
P406	1968	500	10 Francs. Silver. KM#932.	45.00
P407	1968	50	10 Francs. Gold. KM#932.	3,750
P408	1970	500	5 Francs. Nickel Clad Copper-Nickel. KM#926a.	40.00
P409	1970	200	5 Francs. Silver. KM#926a.	60.00
P410	1970	100	5 Francs. Gold. KM#926a.	1,750
P411	1970	100	5 Francs. Platinum. KM#926a.	2,250
P412	1971	500	Centime. Chrome-Steel. KM#928.	20.00
P413	1971	250	Centime. Silver. KM#928.	30.00
P414	1971	100	Centime. Gold. KM#928.	300
P415	1971	500	5 Centimes. Aluminum-Bronze. KM#933.	20.00
P416	1971	250	5 Centimes. Silver. KM#933.	30.00
P417	1971	100	5 Centimes. Gold. KM#933.	425
P418	1971	500	10 Centimes. Aluminum-Bronze. KM#929.	20.00
P419	1971	250	10 Centimes. Silver. KM#929.	35.00
P420	1971	100	10 Centimes. Gold. KM#929.	500
P421	1971	500	20 Centimes. Aluminum-Bronze. KM#930.	20.00
P422	1971	250	20 Centimes. Silver. KM#930.	35.00
P423	1971	100	20 Centimes. Gold. KM#930.	750
P424	1971	500	1/2 Franc. Nickel. KM#931.	20.00
P425	1971	250	1/2 Franc. Silver. KM#931.	35.00
P426	1971	100	1/2 Franc. Gold. KM#931.	725
P427	1971	500	Franc. Nickel. KM#925.	25.00
P428	1971	250	Franc. Silver. KM#925.	35.00
P429	1971	100	Franc. Gold. KM#925.	900
P430	1971	1,000	5 Francs. Nickel Clad Copper-Nickel. KM#926a.	20.00
P431	1971	500	5 Francs. Silver. KM#926a.	30.00
P432	1971	250	5 Francs. Gold. KM#926a.	1,750
P433	1971	100	5 Francs. Platinum. KM#926a.	2,500
P435	1971	500	10 Francs. Silver. KM#932.	50.00
P436	1971	250	10 Francs. Gold. KM#932.	3,600
P437	1972	250	Centime. Chrome-Steel. KM#928.	20.00
P438	1972	150	Centime. Silver. KM#928.	25.00
P439	1972	75	Centime. Gold. KM#928.	300
P440	1972	250	5 Centimes. Aluminum-Bronze. KM#933.	20.00
P441	1972	150	5 Centimes. Silver. KM#933.	25.00
P442	1972	75	5 Centimes. Gold. KM#933.	400
P443	1972	250	10 Centimes. Aluminum-Bronze. KM#929.	20.00
P444	1972	150	10 Centimes. Silver. KM#929.	25.00
P445	1972	75	10 Centimes. Gold. KM#929.	575
P446	1972	250	20 Centimes. Aluminum-Bronze. KM#930.	25.00
P447	1972	150	20 Centimes. Silver. KM#930.	35.00
P448	1972	75	20 Centimes. Gold. KM#930.	700
P449	1972	250	1/2 Franc. Nickel. KM#931.	25.00
P450	1972	150	1/2 Franc. Silver. KM#931.	35.00
P451	1972	75	1/2 Franc. Gold. KM#931.	750
P452	1972	250	Franc. Nickel. KM#925.	25.00
P453	1972	150	Franc. Silver. KM#925.	40.00
P454	1972	75	Franc. Gold. KM#925.	1,000
P455	1972	500	5 Francs. Nickel Clad Copper-Nickel. KM#926a.	25.00
P456	1972	250	5 Francs. Silver. KM#926a.	35.00
P457	1972	200	5 Francs. Gold. KM#926a.	1,750
P458	1972	500	10 Francs. Silver. KM#932.	70.00
P459	1972	200	10 Francs. Gold. KM#932.	3,600
P460	1972	20	10 Francs. Platinum. KM#932.	5,900
P461	1973	250	Centime. Chrome-Steel. KM#928.	20.00
P462	1973	150	Centime. Silver. KM#928.	25.00
P463	1973	75	Centime. Gold. KM#928.	350
P464	1973	250	5 Centimes. Aluminum-Bronze. KM#933.	20.00
P465	1973	150	5 Centimes. Silver. KM#933.	25.00
P466	1973	75	5 Centimes. Gold. KM#933.	400
P467	1973	250	10 Centimes. Aluminum-Bronze. KM#929.	20.00
P468	1973	150	10 Centimes. Silver. KM#929.	25.00
P469	1973	75	10 Centimes. Gold. KM#929.	450
P470	1973	250	20 Centimes. Aluminum-Bronze. KM#930.	20.00
P471	1973	150	20 Centimes. Silver. KM#930.	25.00
P472	1973	75	20 Centimes. Gold. KM#930.	650
P473	1973	250	1/2 Franc. Nickel. KM#931.	20.00
P474	1973	150	1/2 Franc. Silver. KM#931.	25.00
P475	1973	75	1/2 Franc. Gold. KM#931.	650
P476	1973	250	Franc. Nickel. KM#925.	20.00
P477	1973	150	Franc. Silver. KM#925.	25.00
P478	1973	75	Franc. Gold. KM#925.	900
P479	1973	500	5 Francs. Nickel Clad Copper-Nickel. KM#926a.	20.00
P480	1973	250	5 Francs. Silver. KM#926a.	35.00
P481	1973	200	5 Francs. Gold. KM#926a.	1,450
P482	1973	500	10 Francs. Silver. KM#932.	25.00
P483	1973	200	10 Francs. Gold. KM#932.	3,750
P484	1973	20	10 Francs. Platinum. KM#932.	4,500
P485	1974	127	Centime. Chrome-Steel. KM#928.	30.00
P486	1974	242	Centime. Silver. KM#928.	35.00
P487	1974	96	Centime. Gold. KM#928.	325
P488	1974	98	5 Centimes. Aluminum-Bronze. KM#933.	30.00
P489	1974	247	5 Centimes. Silver. KM#933.	35.00
P490	1974	96	5 Centimes. Gold. KM#933.	450
P491	1974	97	10 Centimes. Aluminum-Bronze. KM#929.	30.00
P492	1974	246	10 Centimes. Silver. KM#929.	35.00
P493	1974	94	10 Centimes. Gold. KM#929.	550
P494	1974	101	20 Centimes. Aluminum-Bronze. KM#930.	30.00
P495	1974	247	20 Centimes. Silver. KM#930.	35.00
P496	1974	98	20 Centimes. Gold. KM#930.	725
P497	1974	102	1/2 Franc. Nickel. KM#931.	30.00
P498	1974	241	1/2 Franc. Silver. KM#931.	35.00
P499	1974	91	1/2 Franc. Gold. KM#931.	750
P500	1974	118	Franc. Nickel. KM#925.	35.00
P501	1974	246	Franc. Silver. KM#925.	40.00
P502	1974	95	Franc. Gold. KM#925.	975
P503	1974	162	5 Francs. Nickel Clad Copper-Nickel. KM#926a.	35.00
P504	1974	245	5 Francs. Silver. KM#926a.	40.00
P505	1974	107	5 Francs. Gold. KM#926a.	1,750
P506	1974	493	10 Francs. Nickel-Brass. KM#940.	35.00
P507	1974	491	10 Francs. Silver. KM#940.	40.00
P508	1974	172	10 Francs. Gold. KM#940.	1,750
P509	1974	982	50 Francs. Silver. KM#941.	125
P510	1974	241	50 Francs. Gold. KM#941.	6,800
P511	1974	18	50 Francs. Platinum. KM#941.	11,000
P512	1975	147	Centime. Chrome-Steel. KM#928.	20.00
P513	1975	228	Centime. Silver. KM#928.	25.00
P514	1975	67	Centime. Gold. KM#928.	450
P515	1975	129	5 Centimes. Aluminum-Bronze. KM#933.	20.00
P516	1975	203	5 Centimes. Silver. KM#933.	25.00
P517	1975	44	5 Centimes. Gold. KM#933.	400
P518	1975	127	10 Centimes. Aluminum-Bronze. KM#929.	20.00
P519	1975	198	10 Centimes. Silver. KM#929.	25.00
P520	1975	39	10 Centimes. Gold. KM#929.	750

P521	1975	133	20 Centimes. Aluminum-Bronze. KM#930.	20.00
P522	1975	212	20 Centimes. Silver. KM#930.	25.00
P523	1975	42	20 Centimes. Gold. KM#930.	950
P524	1975	131	1/2 Franc. Nickel. KM#931.	20.00
P525	1975	213	1/2 Franc. Silver. KM#931.	25.00
P526	1975	40	1/2 Franc. Gold. KM#931.	800
P527	1975	145	Franc. Nickel. KM#925.	20.00
P528	1975	250	Franc. Silver. KM#925.	25.00
P529	1975	51	Franc. Gold. KM#925.	1,250
P530	1975	202	5 Francs. Nickel Clad Copper-Nickel. KM#926a.	20.00
P531	1975	250	5 Francs. Silver. KM#926a.	30.00
P532	1975	60	5 Francs. Gold. KM#926a.	1,950
P533	1975	356	10 Francs. Nickel-Brass. KM#940.	25.00
P534	1975	500	10 Francs. Silver. KM#940.	35.00
P535	1975	62	10 Francs. Gold. KM#940.	1,950
P536	1975	955	50 Francs. Silver. KM#941.	125
P537	1975	74	50 Francs. Gold. KM#941.	6,000
P538	1975	10	50 Francs. Platinum. KM#941.	10,000
P539	1976	200	Centime. Chrome-Steel. KM#928.	20.00
P540	1976	300	Centime. Silver. KM#928.	25.00
P541	1976	100	Centime. Gold. KM#928.	400
P542	1976	200	5 Centimes. Aluminum-Bronze. KM#933.	20.00
P543	1976	300	5 Centimes. Silver. KM#933.	25.00
P544	1976	100	5 Centimes. Gold. KM#933.	450
P545	1976	200	10 Centimes. Aluminum-Bronze. KM#929.	20.00
P546	1976	300	10 Centimes. Silver. KM#929.	25.00
P547	1976	100	10 Centimes. Gold. KM#929.	550
P548	1976	200	20 Centimes. Aluminum-Bronze. KM#930.	20.00
P549	1976	300	20 Centimes. Silver. KM#930.	25.00
P550	1976	100	20 Centimes. Gold. KM#930.	725
P551	1976	200	1/2 Franc. Nickel. KM#931.	20.00
P552	1976	250	1/2 Franc. Silver. KM#931.	25.00
P553	1976	100	1/2 Franc. Gold. KM#931.	1,000
P554	1976	126	Franc. Nickel. KM#925.	30.00
P555	1976	88	Franc. Silver. KM#925.	35.00
P556	1976	38	Franc. Gold. KM#925.	1,000
P557	1976	178	5 Francs. Nickel Clad Copper-Nickel. KM#926a.	30.00
P558	1976	104	5 Francs. Silver. KM#926a.	37.50
P559	1976	26	5 Francs. Gold. KM#926a.	1,750
P560	1976	175	10 Francs. Nickel-Brass. KM#940.	30.00
P561	1976	121	10 Francs. Silver. KM#940.	40.00
P562	1976	36	10 Francs. Gold. KM#940.	1,750
P563	1976	213	50 Francs. Silver. KM#941.	150
P564	1976	54	50 Francs. Gold. KM#941.	8,900
P565	1976	6	50 Francs. Platinum. KM#941.	14,000
P566	1977	118	Centime. Chrome-Steel. KM#928.	25.00
P567	1977	247	Centime. Silver. KM#928.	30.00
P568	1977	53	Centime. Gold. KM#928.	325
P569	1977	89	5 Centimes. Aluminum-Bronze. KM#933.	25.00
P570	1977	232	5 Centimes. Silver. KM#933.	30.00
P571	1977	41	5 Centimes. Gold. KM#933.	400
P572	1977	85	10 Centimes. Aluminum-Bronze. KM#929.	25.00
P573	1977	231	10 Centimes. Silver. KM#929.	30.00
P574	1977	32	10 Centimes. Gold. KM#929.	475
P575	1977	88	20 Centimes. Aluminum-Bronze. KM#930.	30.00
P576	1977	243	20 Centimes. Silver. KM#930.	35.00
P577	1977	32	20 Centimes. Gold. KM#930.	725
P578	1977	89	1/2 Franc. Nickel. KM#931.	30.00
P579	1977	234	1/2 Franc. Silver. KM#931.	35.00
P580	1977	32	1/2 Franc. Gold. KM#931.	800
P581	1977	100	Franc. Nickel. KM#925.	30.00
P582	1977	259	Franc. Silver. KM#925.	35.00
P583	1977	42	Franc. Gold. KM#925.	1,450
P584	1977	139	5 Francs. Nickel Clad Copper-Nickel. KM#926a.	30.00
P585	1977	282	5 Francs. Silver. KM#926a.	35.00
P586	1977	35	5 Francs. Gold. KM#926a.	1,750
P587	1977	146	10 Francs. Nickel-Brass. KM#940.	30.00
P588	1977	296	10 Francs. Silver. KM#940.	40.00
P589	1977	43	10 Francs. Gold. KM#940.	1,750
P590	1977	465	50 Francs. Silver. KM#941.	250
P591	1977	50	50 Francs. Gold. KM#941.	7,700
P592	1977	19	50 Francs. Platinum. KM#941.	8,500
P593	1978	150	Centime. Chrome-Steel. KM#928.	20.00
P594	1978	294	Centime. Silver. KM#928.	25.00
P595	1978	144	Centime. Gold. KM#928.	350
P596	1978	148	5 Centimes. Aluminum-Bronze. KM#933.	20.00
P597	1978	295	5 Centimes. Silver. KM#933.	25.00
P598	1978	144	5 Centimes. Gold. KM#933.	400
P599	1978	147	10 Centimes. Aluminum-Bronze. KM#929.	20.00
P600	1978	290	10 Centimes. Silver. KM#929.	25.00
P601	1978	139	10 Centimes. Gold. KM#929.	475
P602	1978	148	20 Centimes. Aluminum-Bronze. KM#930.	20.00
P603	1978	296	20 Centimes. Silver. KM#930.	25.00
P604	1978	141	20 Centimes. Gold. KM#930.	725
P605	1978	149	1/2 Franc. Nickel. KM#931.	20.00
P606	1978	296	1/2 Franc. Silver. KM#931.	25.00
P607	1978	141	1/2 Franc. Gold. KM#931.	800
P608	1978	149	Franc. Nickel. KM#925.	20.00
P609	1978	297	Franc. Silver. KM#925.	25.00
P610	1978	142	Franc. Gold. KM#925.	1,000
P611	1978	350	2 Francs. Silver. KM#942.	30.00
P612	1978	—	2 Francs. Nickel. KM#942.	100
P613	1978	150	5 Francs. Nickel Clad Copper-Nickel. KM#926a.	20.00
P614	1978	306	5 Francs. Silver. KM#926a.	25.00
P615	1978	143	5 Francs. Gold. KM#926a.	1,750
P616	1978	174	10 Francs. Nickel-Brass. KM#940.	25.00
P617	1978	345	10 Francs. Silver. KM#940.	35.00
P618	1978	144	10 Francs. Gold. KM#940.	1,650
P619	1978	599	50 Francs. Silver. KM#941.	120
P620	1978	149	50 Francs. Gold. KM#941.	7,700
P621	1978	25	50 Francs. Platinum. KM#941.	8,500
P622	1979	300	Centime. Chrome-Steel. KM#928.	15.00
P623	1979	600	Centime. Silver. KM#928.	20.00
P624	1979	300	Centime. Gold. KM#928.	325
P625	1979	299	5 Centimes. KM#935.	15.00
P626	1979	600	5 Centimes. Silver. KM#933.	20.00
P627	1979	300	5 Centimes. Gold. KM#933.	325
P628	1979	300	10 Centimes. Aluminum-Bronze. KM#929.	15.00
P629	1979	600	10 Centimes. Silver. KM#929.	20.00
P630	1979	300	10 Centimes. Gold. KM#929.	550
P631	1979	300	20 Centimes. Aluminum-Bronze. KM#930.	15.00
P632	1979	600	20 Centimes. Silver. KM#930.	20.00
P633	1979	300	20 Centimes. Gold. KM#930.	650
P634	1979	300	1/2 Franc. Nickel. KM#931.	15.00
P635	1979	600	1/2 Franc. Silver. KM#931.	20.00
P636	1979	300	1/2 Franc. Gold. KM#931.	800
P637	1979	500	Franc. Nickel. KM#925.	20.00
P638	1979	1,250	Franc. Silver. KM#925.	85.00
P639	1979	600	Franc. Gold. KM#925.	1,000
P640	1979	500	2 Francs. Nickel. KM#942.	20.00
P641	1979	1,250	2 Francs. Silver. KM#942.	30.00
P642	1979	600	2 Francs. Gold. KM#942.	1,100
P643	1979	40	2 Francs. Platinum. KM#942.	2,000
P644	1979	300	5 Francs. Nickel Clad Copper-Nickel. KM#926a.	20.00
P645	1979	600	5 Francs. Silver. KM#926a.	30.00
P646	1979	300	5 Francs. Gold. KM#926a.	1,750
P647	1979	349	10 Francs. Nickel-Brass. KM#940.	25.00
P648	1979	700	10 Francs. Silver. KM#940.	35.00
P649	1979	300	10 Francs. Gold. KM#940.	1,450
P650	1979	2,250	50 Francs. Silver. KM#941.	125
P651	1979	400	50 Francs. Gold. KM#941.	6,800
P652	1979	30	50 Francs. Platinum. KM#941.	7,500
P653	1980	155	Centime. Chrome Plated Steel. KM#928.	15.00
P654	1980	570	Centime. Silver. KM#928.	20.00
P655	1980	176	Centime. Gold. KM#928.	325
P656	1980	142	5 Centimes. Aluminum-Bronze. KM#933.	15.00
P657	1980	547	5 Centimes. Silver. KM#933.	20.00
P658	1980	137	5 Centimes. Gold. KM#933.	400
P659	1980	148	10 Centimes. Aluminum-Bronze. KM#929.	15.00
P660	1980	528	10 Centimes. Silver. KM#929.	20.00
P661	1980	127	10 Centimes. Gold. KM#929.	550
P662	1980	140	20 Centimes. Aluminum-Bronze. KM#930.	15.00
P663	1980	569	20 Centimes. Silver. KM#930.	20.00
P664	1980	136	20 Centimes. Gold. KM#930.	650
P665	1980	156	1/2 Franc. Nickel. KM#931.	15.00
P666	1980	537	1/2 Franc. Silver. KM#931.	20.00
P667	1980	118	1/2 Franc. Gold. KM#931.	800
P668	1980	132	Franc. Nickel. KM#925.	15.00
P669	1980	563	Franc. Silver. KM#925.	20.00
P670	1980	193	Franc. Gold. KM#925.	1,000
P671	1980	194	2 Francs. Nickel. KM#942.	15.00
P672	1980	772	2 Francs. Silver. KM#942.	20.00
P673	1980	130	2 Francs. Gold. KM#942.	1,400
P674	1980	271	5 Francs. Nickel Clad Copper-Nickel. KM#926a.	15.00
P675	1980	580	5 Francs. Silver. KM#926a.	20.00
P676	1980	213	5 Francs. Gold. KM#926a.	1,800
P677	1980	148	10 Francs. Nickel-Brass. KM#940.	15.00
P678	1980	730	10 Francs. Silver. KM#940.	20.00
P679	1980	157	10 Francs. Gold. KM#940.	1,800
P680	1980	2,500	50 Francs. Silver. KM#941.	130
P681	1980	500	50 Francs. Gold. KM#941.	7,700
P682	1980	34	50 Francs. Platinum. KM#941.	8,700
P683	1981	150	Centime. Chrome-Steel. KM#928.	15.00
P684	1981	362	Centime. Silver. KM#928.	20.00
P685	1981	69	Centime. Gold. KM#928.	325
P686	1981	105	5 Centimes. Aluminum-Bronze. KM#933.	15.00
P687	1981	358	5 Centimes. Silver. KM#933.	20.00
P688	1981	42	5 Centimes. Gold. KM#933.	400
P689	1981	104	10 Centimes. Aluminum-Bronze. KM#929.	15.00
P690	1981	357	10 Centimes. Silver. KM#929.	20.00
P691	1981	32	10 Centimes. Gold. KM#929.	500
P692	1981	106	20 Centimes. Aluminum-Bronze. KM#930.	15.00
P693	1981	359	20 Centimes. Silver. KM#930.	20.00
P694	1981	30	20 Centimes. Gold. KM#930.	725
P695	1981	110	1/2 Franc. Nickel. KM#931.	15.00
P696	1981	358	1/2 Franc. Silver. KM#931.	20.00
P697	1981	33	1/2 Franc. Gold. KM#931.	800
P698	1981	16	1/2 Franc. Platinum. KM#931.	1,500
P699	1981	122	Franc. Nickel. KM#925.	15.00
P700	1981	358	Franc. Silver. KM#925.	20.00
P701	1981	42	Franc. Gold. KM#925.	950
P702	1981	16	Franc. Platinum. KM#925.	2,050
P703	1981	131	2 Francs. Nickel. KM#942.	15.00
P704	1981	359	2 Francs. Silver. KM#942.	25.00
P705	1981	37	2 Francs. Gold. KM#942.	1,400
P706	1981	16	2 Francs. Platinum. KM#942.	2,500
P707	1981	150	5 Francs. Nickel Clad Copper-Nickel. KM#926a.	15.00
P708	1981	261	5 Francs. Silver. KM#926a.	20.00
P709	1981	52	5 Francs. Gold. KM#926a.	1,800
P710	1981	16	5 Francs. Platinum. KM#926a.	2,650
P711	1981	150	10 Francs. Nickel-Brass. KM#940.	15.00
P712	1981	365	10 Francs. Silver. KM#940.	30.00
P713	1981	52	10 Francs. Gold. KM#940.	1,800
P714	1981	17	10 Francs. Platinum. KM#940.	2,800
P715	1982	70	Centime. Steel. KM#928.	20.00
P716	1982	195	Centime. Silver. KM#928.	25.00
P717	1982	36	Centime. Gold. KM#928.	450
P718	1982	53	5 Centimes. Aluminum-Bronze. KM#933.	25.00
P719	1982	164	5 Centimes. Silver. KM#933.	25.00
P720	1982	26	5 Centimes. Gold. KM#933.	500
P721	1982	53	10 Centimes. Aluminum-Bronze. KM#929.	25.00
P722	1982	163	10 Centimes. Silver. KM#929.	25.00
P723	1982	29	10 Centimes. Gold. KM#929.	550
P724	1982	53	20 Centimes. Aluminum-Bronze. KM#930.	25.00
P725	1982	171	20 Centimes. Silver. KM#930.	25.00
P726	1982	26	20 Centimes. Gold. KM#930.	775
P727	1982	54	1/2 Franc. Nickel. KM#931.	25.00
P728	1982	165	1/2 Franc. Silver. KM#931.	25.00
P729	1982	26	1/2 Franc. Gold. KM#931.	775
P730	1982	4	1/2 Franc. Platinum. KM#931.	5,000
P731	1982	57	Franc. Nickel. KM#925.	25.00
P732	1982	252	Franc. Silver. KM#925.	25.00
P733	1982	29	Franc. Gold. KM#925.	900
P734	1982	6	Franc. Platinum. KM#925.	3,800
P735	1982	62	2 Francs. Nickel. KM#942.	25.00
P736	1982	203	2 Francs. Silver. KM#942.	25.00
P737	1982	27	2 Francs. Gold. KM#942.	1,400
P738	1982	4	2 Francs. Platinum. KM#942.	6,400
P739	1982	69	5 Francs. Nickel Clad Copper-Nickel. KM#926a.	25.00
P740	1982	188	5 Francs. Silver. KM#926a.	25.00
P741	1982	27	5 Francs. Gold. KM#926a.	1,450
P742	1982	4	5 Francs. Platinum. KM#926a.	7,000
P743	1982	80	10 Francs. Nickel-Brass. KM#940.	25.00
P744	1982	239	10 Francs. Silver. KM#940.	30.00
P745	1982	33	10 Francs. Gold. KM#940.	1,800
P746	1982	4	10 Francs. Platinum. KM#940.	6,000
P747	1982	326	10 Francs. Nickel-Bronze. KM#950.	20.00
P748	1982	812	10 Francs. Silver. KM#950.	30.00
P749	1982	87	10 Francs. Gold. KM#950.	1,475
P750	1982	14	10 Francs. Platinum. KM#950.	2,550
P751	1982	999	100 Francs. Silver. KM#951.	75.00
P752	1982	93	100 Francs. Gold. KM#951.	2,000
P753	1982	16	100 Francs. Platinum. KM#951.	3,600
P754	1983	50	Centime. Steel. KM#928.	20.00
P755	1983	98	Centime. Silver. KM#928.	25.00
P756	1983	17	Centime. Gold. KM#928.	450
P757	1983	42	Centime. Aluminum-Bronze. KM#933.	20.00
P758	1983	90	5 Centimes. Silver. KM#933.	25.00
P759	1983	7	5 Centimes. Gold. KM#933.	2,400
P760	1983	42	10 Centimes. Aluminum-Bronze. KM#929.	25.00
P761	1983	90	10 Centimes. Silver. KM#929.	30.00
P762	1983	6	10 Centimes. Gold. KM#929.	2,800
P763	1983	44	20 Centimes. Aluminum-Bronze. KM#930.	25.00
P764	1983	95	20 Centimes. Silver. KM#930.	30.00
P765	1983	5	20 Centimes. Gold. KM#930.	3,200
P766	1983	43	1/2 Franc. Nickel. KM#931.	25.00
P767	1983	89	1/2 Franc. Silver. KM#931.	35.00
P768	1983	5	1/2 Franc. Gold. KM#931.	1,650

KM#	Date	Mintage	Identification	Mkt Val
P769	1983	3	1/2 Franc. Platinum. KM#931.	11,000
P770	1983	46	Franc. Nickel. KM#925.	25.00
P771	1983	98	Franc. Silver. KM#925.	35.00
P772	1983	11	Franc. Gold. KM#925.	1,200
P773	1983	3	Franc. Platinum. KM#925.	11,000
P774	1983	51	2 Francs. Nickel. KM#942.	25.00
P775	1983	121	2 Francs. Silver. KM#942.	35.00
P776	1983	9	2 Francs. Gold. KM#942.	2,500
P777	1983	3	2 Francs. Platinum. KM#942.	11,000
P778	1983	58	5 Francs. Nickel Clad Copper-Nickel. KM#926a.	25.00
P779	1983	97	5 Francs. Silver. KM#926a.	35.00
P780	1983	8	5 Francs. Gold. KM#926a.	3,400
P781	1983	3	5 Francs. Platinum. KM#926a.	11,000
P782	1983	286	10 Francs. Nickel-Bronze. KM#952.	20.00
P783	1983	454	10 Francs. Silver. KM#952.	35.00
P784	1983	34	10 Francs. Gold. KM#952.	1,500
P785	1983	13	10 Francs. Platinum. KM#952.	3,550
P786	1983	74	10 Francs. Nickel-Brass. KM#940.	25.00
P787	1983	118	10 Francs. Silver. KM#940.	45.00
P788	1983	12	10 Francs. Gold. KM#940.	1,600
P789	1983	5	10 Francs. Platinum. KM#940.	4,200
P790	1983	206	10 Francs. Nickel-Bronze. KM#953.	20.00
P791	1983	314	10 Francs. Silver. KM#953.	45.00
P792	1983	29	10 Francs. Gold. KM#953.	1,600
P793	1983	5	10 Francs. Platinum. KM#953.	4,200
P794	1983	242	100 Francs. Silver. KM#951.	55.00
P795	1983	14	100 Francs. Gold. KM#951.	2,900
P796	1983	7	100 Francs. Platinum. KM#951.	4,000
P797	1984	56	Centime. Steel. KM#928.	25.00
P798	1984	64	Centime. Silver. KM#928.	25.00
P799	1984	10	Centime. Gold. KM#928.	450
P800	1984	36	5 Centimes. Aluminum-Bronze. KM#933.	30.00
P801	1984	49	5 Centimes. Silver. KM#933.	25.00
P802	1984	6	5 Centimes. Gold. KM#933.	2,400
P803	1984	34	10 Centimes. Copper-Nickel. KM#929.	30.00
P804	1984	54	10 Centimes. Silver. KM#929.	25.00
P805	1984	4	10 Centimes. Gold. KM#929.	3,400
P806	1984	34	20 Centimes. Copper-Nickel. KM#930.	30.00
P807	1984	60	20 Centimes. Silver. KM#930.	25.00
P808	1984	4	20 Centimes. Gold. KM#930.	3,750
P809	1984	34	1/2 Franc. Nickel. KM#931.	30.00
P900	1984	59	1/2 Franc. Silver. KM#931.	25.00
P901	1984	8	1/2 Franc. Gold. KM#931.	1,800
P902	1984	5	1/2 Franc. Platinum. KM#931.	3,200
P903	1984	40	Franc. Nickel. KM#925.	30.00
P904	1984	69	Franc. Silver. KM#925.	25.00
P905	1984	6	Franc. Gold. KM#925.	3,100
P906	1984	5	Franc. Platinum. KM#925.	3,850
P907	1984	42	2 Francs. Nickel. KM#942.	30.00
P908	1984	79	2 Francs. Silver. KM#942.	25.00
P909	1984	9	2 Francs. Gold. KM#942.	2,500
P910	1984	5	2 Francs. Platinum. KM#942.	3,200
P911	1984	55	5 Francs. Nickel Clad Copper-Nickel. KM#926a.	30.00
P912	1984	59	5 Francs. Silver. KM#926a.	30.00
P913	1984	4	5 Francs. Gold. KM#926a.	3,900
P914	1984	5	5 Francs. Platinum. KM#926a.	4,050
P915	1984	50	10 Francs. Copper-Nickel-Aluminum. KM#940.	30.00
P916	1984	79	10 Francs. Silver. KM#940.	30.00
P917	1984	6	10 Francs. Gold. KM#940.	3,000
P918	1984	5	10 Francs. Platinum. KM#940.	3,750
P919	1984	184	10 Francs. Copper-Nickel-Aluminum. KM#954.	25.00
P920	1984	244	10 Francs. Silver. KM#954.	30.00
P921	1984	18	10 Francs. Gold. KM#954.	1,450
P922	1984	5	10 Francs. Platinum. KM#954.	3,300
P923	1984	500	100 Francs. Silver. KM#955.	50.00
P924	1984	34	100 Francs. Gold. KM#955.	2,500
P925	1984	9	100 Francs. Platinum. KM#955.	3,000
P926	1984	100	100 Francs. Silver. KM#951.	65.00
P927	1984	10	100 Francs. Gold. KM#951.	2,500
P928	1984	5	100 Francs. Platinum. KM#951.	4,800
P929	1985	100	Centime. 0.925. Silver. KM#928.	20.00
P930	1985	18	Centime. 0.920. Gold. KM#928.	450
P931	1985	60	5 Centimes. 0.925. Silver. KM#933.	30.00
P932	1985	6	5 Centimes. 0.920. Gold. KM#933.	1,800
P933	1985	65	10 Centimes. 0.925. Silver. KM#929.	32.00
P934	1985	4	10 Centimes. 0.920. Gold. KM#929.	2,000
P935	1985	85	20 Centimes. 0.925. Silver. KM#930.	35.00
P936	1985	4	20 Centimes. 0.920. Gold. KM#930.	2,400
P937	1985	80	1/2 Franc. 0.925. Silver. KM#931.	35.00
P938	1985	16	1/2 Franc. 0.920. Gold. KM#931.	750
P939	1985	5	1/2 Franc. Platinum. KM#931.	3,000
P940	1985	90	Franc. 0.925. Silver. KM#925.	35.00
P941	1985	5	Franc. 0.920. Gold. KM#925.	1,500
P942	1985	5	Franc. Platinum. KM#925.	2,400
P943	1985	90	2 Francs. 0.925. Silver. KM#942.	35.00
P944	1985	17	2 Francs. 0.920. Gold. KM#942.	1,500
P945	1985	5	2 Francs. Platinum. KM#942.	2,400
P946	1985	70	5 Francs. 0.925. Silver. KM#926a.	50.00
P947	1985	4	5 Francs. 0.920. Gold. KM#926a.	3,750
P948	1985	5	5 Francs. Platinum. KM#926a.	3,400
P949	1985	120	10 Francs. 0.925. Silver. KM#940.	45.00
P950	1985	12	10 Francs. 0.920. Gold. KM#940.	1,800
P951	1985	5	10 Francs. Platinum. KM#940.	3,250
P952	1985	8	10 Francs. 0.920. Gold. KM#952.	1,800
P953	1985	8	10 Francs. 0.920. Gold. KM#953.	1,800
P954	1985	45	10 Francs. 0.925. Silver. KM#954.	60.00
P955	1985	8	10 Francs. 0.920. Gold. KM#954.	2,000
P956	1985	215	10 Francs. 0.925. Silver. KM#956.	45.00
P957	1985	17	10 Francs. 0.920. Gold. KM#956.	1,800
P958	1985	15	10 Francs. Platinum. KM#956.	3,600
P959	1985	100	100 Francs. 0.925. Silver. KM#951.	65.00
P960	1985	18	100 Francs. 0.920. Gold. KM#951.	2,500
P961	1985	10	100 Francs. Platinum. KM#951.	4,300
P962	1985	200	100 Francs. 0.925. Silver. KM#955a.	55.00
P963	1985	8	100 Francs. 0.920. Gold. KM#955b.	2,650
P964	1985	440	100 Francs. 0.925. Silver. KM#957.	45.00
P965	1985	30	100 Francs. 0.920. Gold. KM#957.	2,500
P966	1985	15	100 Francs. Platinum. KM#957.	3,600
P967	1986	10	10 Francs. Platinum. KM#958.	2,900
P968	1986	200	10 Francs. 0.950. Silver. KM#959.	50.00
P969	1986	5	10 Francs. Platinum. KM#959.	3,500
P970	1986	5	100 Francs. Platinum. KM#951.	4,500
P971	1986	250	100 Francs. Silver. KM#951.	50.00
P972	1986	5,000	100 Francs. 0.900. Silver. KM#960.	22.50
P973	1986	15	100 Francs. Platinum. KM#960.	3,500
P973b	1986	50	100 Francs. Gold. KM#960b.	2,900
P974	1987	50	Centime. 0.950. Silver. KM#928.	45.00
P975	1987	50	5 Centimes. 0.950. Silver. KM#933.	50.00
P976	1987	50	10 Centimes. 0.950. Silver. KM#929.	50.00
P977	1987	50	20 Centimes. 0.950. Silver. KM#930.	50.00
P978	1987	50	1/2 Franc. 0.950. Silver. KM#931.	50.00
P979	1987	50	Franc. 0.950. Silver. KM#925.	40.00
P980	1987	50	2 Francs. 0.950. Silver. KM#942.	50.00
P981	1987	50	5 Francs. 0.950. Silver. KM#926a.	65.00
P982	1987	50	10 Francs. 0.950. Silver. KM#940.	65.00
P983	1987	15	10 Francs. 0.920. Gold. KM#940.	1,600
P984	1987	5	10 Francs. 0.999. Platinum. KM#940.	3,300
P985	1987	1,000	10 Francs. 0.950. Silver. KM#961.	45.00
P986	1987	25	10 Francs. 0.920. Gold. KM#961.	2,750
P987	1987	10	10 Francs. 0.999. Platinum. KM#961.	3,000
P988	1987	30	100 Francs. 0.900. Silver. KM#951.	65.00
P989	1987	15	100 Francs. 0.920. Gold. KM#951.	2,900
P990	1987	5	100 Francs. 0.999. Platinum. KM#951.	4,300
P991	1987	51,000	100 Francs. 0.950. Silver. KM#962, Proof.	20.00
P991a	1987	100,000	100 Francs. 0.900. Silver. KM#962, Unc.	12.50
P992	1987	50	100 Francs. 0.920. Gold. KM#962.	2,900
P993	1987	15	100 Francs. 0.999. Platinum. KM#962.	3,800
P994	1988	5	Centime. Platinum. KM#928.	780
P995	1988	—	10 Francs. 0.900. Silver. KM#965a, Proof.	100
P996	1988	—	10 Francs. Gold. KM#965c, Proof.	1,950
P997	1988	10	10 Francs. Platinum. KM#965.	3,000
P998	1988	5	100 Francs. Platinum. KM#951.	3,500
P999	1988	20,000	100 Francs. 0.900. Silver. KM#966, Unc.	14.00
PSA999	1988	—	100 Francs. 0.900. Silver. KM#966, Proof.	2,200
P1000	1988	10	100 Francs. Platinum. KM#966.	3,600
P1001	1989	5	Centime. Platinum. KM#928.	950
P1002	1989	10	Franc. Platinum. KM#925.	3,000
P1003	1989	300	Franc. Silver. KM#967.	225
P1004	1989	25	Franc. Gold. KM#967.	1,200
P1005	1989	10	Franc. Platinum. KM#967.	3,000
P1006	1989	10	5 Francs. Platinum. KM#968.	3,000
P1007	1989	5	100 Francs. Platinum. KM#951.	4,000
P1008	1989	10,000	100 Francs. 0.900. Silver. KM#970, Unc.	45.00
PA1008	1989	—	100 Francs. 0.900. Silver. KM#970, Proof.	125
P1009	1989	10	100 Francs. Platinum. KM#970.	4,250
P1010	1990	50	Centime. Silver. KM#928.	80.00
P1011	1990	10	Centime. Gold. KM#928.	650
P1012	1990	5	Centime. Platinum. KM#928.	1,000
P1013	1990	50	5 Centimes. Silver. KM#933.	80.00
P1014	1990	50	10 Centimes. Silver. KM#929.	80.00
P1015	1990	50	20 Centimes. Silver. KM#930.	80.00
P1016	1990	5	20 Centimes. Gold. KM#930.	1,050
P1017	1990	50	1/2 Franc. Silver. KM#931.	80.00
P1018	1990	50	Franc. Silver. KM#925.	80.00
P1019	1990	50	2 Francs. Silver. KM#942.	80.00
P1020	1990	5	2 Francs. Gold. KM#942.	1,650
P1021	1990	50	5 Francs. Silver. KM#926a.	90.00
P1022	1990	10	10 Francs. Gold. Gold Alloy Spirit of Bastille.	1,600
P1023	1990	50	100 Francs. Silver. KM#951.	250
P1024	1990	10	100 Francs. Gold. KM#951.	2,900
P1025	1990	5	100 Francs. Platinum. KM#951.	4,000
P1026	1990	100	100 Francs. Silver. KM#982.	175
P1027	1990	10	100 Francs. Gold. KM#982.	2,800
P1028	1990	5	100 Francs. Platinum. KM#982.	4,000
P1029	1991	—	100 Francs. Silver. KM#951.	100
P1030	1991	—	100 Francs. Silver. KM#996.	100

PIEDFORT WITH ESSAI

Double thickness; standard metals unless otherwise noted

KM#	Date	Mintage	Identification	Mkt Val
PE271	1914	—	10 Centimes. Nickel. Center hole divides RF within wreath, liberty cap above. Denomination divided by plant and center hole, date below. KM#866.	1,200
PE272	1914	—	25 Centimes. Nickel. KM#867.	550
PE281	1920	—	50 Centimes. Aluminum-Bronze. Denomination within circle, legend surrounds. Mercury seated left, caduceus on left, shield on right, date below. KM#875.	120
PRA281	1920	—	5 Centimes. Copper-Nickel. KM#875.	220
PE282	1920	—	Franc. Bronze-Aluminum. Denomination within circle, legend surrounds. Mercury seated left, caduceus on left, shield on right, date below.	120
PE298	1929	—	10 Francs. Silver. KM#878.	1,200
PE299	1929	—	20 Francs. Silver. KM#879.	1,200
PE301	1931	—	50 Centimes. Aluminum-Bronze. KM#894.1.	—
PE302	1931	—	Franc. Aluminum-Bronze. KM#885.	—
PE303	1931	—	2 Francs. Aluminum-Bronze. KM#886.	—
PE304	1941	—	20 Centimes. Zinc. KM#899.	140
PE306	1941	—	10 Centimes. Zinc. KM#898.	120
PE307	1941	—	20 Centimes. Zinc. KM#900.	120
PE308	1941	—	5 Francs. Copper-Nickel. KM#901.	500
PE309	1943	—	2 Francs. Aluminum. KM#904.	150

KM#	Date	Mintage	Identification	Mkt Val
PE310	1945	104	20 Centimes. Zinc. KM#907.	165
PE311	1945	104	5 Francs. Aluminum. KM#888.	120
PE312	1945	104	20 Francs. Copper-Nickel. KM#879.	185
PE313	1946	104	50 Centimes. Aluminum. KM#894.1a.	90.00
PE314	1946	104	Franc. Aluminum. KM#885a.	100
PE315	1946	104	2 Francs. Aluminum. KM#886a.	120
PE316	1946	104	10 Francs. Copper-Nickel. Laureate head right. Denomination above date, inscription below, grain columns flank. KM#909.	175
PE317	1950	—	10 Francs. Aluminum-Bronze. KM#915.	70.00
PE318	1950	—	20 Francs. Aluminum-Bronze. KM#916.	85.00
PE319	1950	—	50 Francs. Aluminum-Bronze. KM#918.	135
PE320	1952	104	10 Francs. Aluminum-Bronze. KM#915.	70.00
PE321	1952	104	20 Francs. Aluminum-Bronze. KM#917.	85.00
PE322	1952	104	50 Francs. Aluminum-Bronze. KM#918.	115
PE323	1954	104	100 Francs. Copper-Nickel. KM#919.	115
PE324	1958	65	100 Francs. Silver. KM#919.	550
PE325	1959	104	Franc. Nickel. KM#925.	400
PE326	1959	104	5 Francs. Silver. KM#926, Small 5.	300
PE327	1959	104	5 Francs. Silver. KM#926, Large 5.	400
PE328	1960	50	Franc. Silver. KM#925.	165
PE329	1960	20	Franc. Gold. KM#925.	1,200
PE330	1960	500	Franc. Nickel. KM#925.	45.00
PE331	1960	500	5 Francs. Silver. KM#926.	115
PE332	1960	50	5 Francs. Gold. KM#926.	2,400
PE333	1961	104	Centime. Chrome-Steel. KM#928.	200
PE334	1961	104	5 Centimes. Chrome-Steel. KM#927.	65.00
PE335	1961	500	5 Centimes. Chrome-Steel. KM#927.	60.00
PE336	1961	50	5 Centimes. Silver. KM#927.	120
PE337	1961	20	5 Centimes. Gold. KM#927.	1,000
PE338	1962	104	10 Centimes. Aluminum-Bronze. KM#929.	50.00
PE339	1962	104	20 Centimes. Aluminum-Bronze. KM#930.	50.00
PE340	1962	104	50 Centimes. Aluminum-Bronze. KM#939.	85.00
PE434	1971	100	5 Francs. Platinum. KM#926a.	2,500

MINT SETS

KM#	Date	Mintage	Identification	Issue Price	Mkt Val
MS1	1986 (10)	20,000	KM#925.1, 926a, 928-931, 933, 942, 951.1, 959 (sets with perfect case and no PVC damage on coins command a 25% premium)	—	100
MS2	1987 (10)	4,000	KM#925.1, 926a, 928-931, 933, 940, 942, 961d	—	60.00
MS3	1988 (10)	2,000	KM#925.1, 926a, 928-931, 933, 942, 964-965	—	65.00
MS4	1989 (10)	2,000	KM#925.1, 926a, 928-931, 933, 942, 964, 969	—	175
MS6	1991 (9)	2,500	KM#925.1, 926a.1, 928-930, 931.1, 933, 942.1, 964.1, medal rotation	50.00	400
MS7	1992 (10)	20,000	KM#925.1, 926a.1, 928-930, 931.1, 933, 942.1, 964.1, 1008.2, medal rotation	—	50.00
MS8	1993 (10)	20,000	KM#925.1, 926a.1, 928-930, 931.1, 933, 942.1, 964.1, 1008.2, medal rotation	—	55.00
MS9	1994 (10)	20,000	KM#925.1, 926a.1, 928-930, 931.1, 933, 942.1, 964.2, 1008.2 bee privy mark	—	50.00
MS10	1995 (9)	20,000	KM#925.1, 926a.1, 928, 930, 931.1, 933, 942.1, 964.2, 1008.2	—	55.00
MS11	1996 (10)	5,000	KM#925.1, 926a.1, 928-930, 931.1, 933, 942.1, 964.2, 1008.2	—	70.00
MS12	1996 (3)	2,500	KM#1155, 1160, 1180	—	70.00
MS13	1997 (10)	15,000	KM#925.1, 926a.1, 928-930, 931.1, 933, 942.1, 964.2, 1008.2	—	60.00
MS14	1998 (10)	—	KM#925.1, 926a.1, 928-930, 931.1, 933, 942.1, 964.2, 1008.2	—	50.00
MS15	1999 (10)	—	KM#925.1, 926a.1, 928-930, 931.1, 933, 942.1, 964.2, 1008.2	—	55.00
MS16	2000 (3)	—	KM#1222-1224	—	37.50
MS17	2000 (10)	50,000	KM#925, 926a, 928-931, 933, 942, 964.2, 1008.2	—	60.00
MS18	1999 (8)	35,000	KM#1282-1289	20.25	110
MS19	2000 (8)	35,000	KM#1282-1289	20.25	50.00

PROOF SETS

KM#	Date	Mintage	Identification	Issue Price	Mkt Val
PS6	1990-91 (9)	—	KM#971-972, 980-981, 983-984, 993-995	—	300
PS7	1991 (10)	10,000	KM#925.2, 926a.2, 928-930, 931.2, 933, 942.2, 951.2, 964.2	175	175
PS8	1991 (3)	15,000	KM#977, 991-992	—	1,000
PS9	1992 (11)	15,000	KM#925.2, 926a.2, 928-930, 931-2, 933, 942.2, 951.1, 964.2, 1008.2	—	125
PS10	1992 (3)	2,000	KM#1007, 1010-1011	—	200
PS11	1993 (11)	10,000	KM#925.1, 926a.1, 928-930, 931.2, 933, 942.1, 964.1, 961.1, 1008.2	—	135
PS12	1994 (11)	10,000	KM#925.2, 926a.2, 928-930, 931.2, 933, 942.2, 951.1, 964.2, 1008.2, fish privy mark	—	135
PS13	1995 (11)	10,000	KM#925.2, 926a.2, 928-930, 931.2, 933, 942.2, 951.1, 964.2, 1008.2	—	135
PS14	1996 (11)	8,000	KM#925.2, 926a.2, 928-930, 931.2, 933, 942.2, 951.1, 964.2, 1008.2	—	140
PS15	1997 (11)	10,000	KM#925.2, 926a.2, 928, 930, 931.2, 933, 942.2, 951.1, 964.2, 1008.2	—	135
PS16	1998 (11)	—	KM#925.2, 926a.2, 928, 930, 931.2, 933, 942.2, 951.1, 964.2, 1008.2	—	135
PS17	1999 (11)	—	KM#925.2, 926a.2, 928, 930, 941.2, 933, 942.2, 951.1, 964.2, 1008.2	—	135
PS18	2000 (11)	—	KM#925.2, 926a.2, 928, 930, 931.2, 933, 942.2, 951.1, 964.2, 1008.2	—	135
PS19	1999 (8)	15,000	KM#1282-1289	59.00	110
PS20	2000 (8)	15,000	KM#1282-1289	59.00	110

SPECIMEN FDC SETS (FLEUR DE COIN)

KM#	Date	Mintage	Identification	Issue Price	Mkt Val
SS1	1964 (7)	25,600	KM#925-930, 939	4.00	100
SS2	1965 (7)	35,000	KM#925-926, 928-932	7.60	100
SS3	1966 (8)	7,171	KM#925-926, 928-933	9.00	200
SS4	1967 (8)	2,305	KM#925-926, 928-933	10.00	300
SS5	1968 (8)	3,000	With perfect box KM#925-926, 928-933	10.00	400
SS5A	1968 (8)	Inc. above	KM#925-926, 928-933 without box	—	100
SS6	1969 (8)	6,050	KM#925-926, 928-933	10.00	120
SS7	1970 (8)	10,000	KM#925, 926a, 928-933	9.00	50.00
SS8	1971 (8)	12,000	KM#925, 926a, 928-933	9.00	48.00
SS9	1972 (8)	15,000	KM#925, 926a, 928-933	9.00	50.00
SS10	1973 (8)	79,000	KM#925, 926a, 928-933	12.00	35.00
SS11	1974 (9)	98,800	KM#925, 926a, 928-931, 933, 940-941	31.00	35.00
SS12	1975 (9)	52,000	KM#925, 926a, 928-931, 933, 940-941	35.00	40.00
SS13	1976 (9)	35,700	KM#925, 926a, 928-931, 933, 940-941	35.00	40.00
SS14	1977 (9)	25,000	KM#925, 926a, 928-931, 933, 940-941	36.00	45.00
SS15	1978 (9)	24,000	KM#925, 926a, 928-931, 933, 940-941	39.00	45.00
SS16	1979 (10)	40,500	KM#925, 926a, 928-931, 933, 940--942	55.00	50.00
SS17	1980 (10)	60,000	KM#925, 926a, 928-931, 933, 940-942	90.00	75.00
SS18	1981 (9)	26,000	KM#925, 926a, 928-931, 933, 940, 942	—	50.00
SS19	1982 (11)	27,500	KM#925, 926a, 928-931, 933, 940, 942, 950-951	—	65.00
SS20	1983 (12)	16,561	KM#925, 926a, 928-931, 933, 940, 942, 951-953	—	100
SS21	1984 (12)	13,388	KM#825, 926a, 928-931, 933, 940, 942, 951, 954, 955	—	150
SS22	1985 (12)	12,224	KM#925, 926a, 928-931, 933, 940, 942, 951, 956-957	—	125
SS23	1986 (12)	13,000	KM#925.1, 926a.1, 928-931.1, 933, 942.1, 951, 958, 959, 960	—	180
SS24	1987 (12)	15,000	KM#925.1, 926a.1, 928-931.1, 933, 940, 942.1, 951, 961, 962	68.00	150
SS25	1987 (2)	—	KMP991-991a, Proof and BU	120	50.00
SS26	1988 (13)	13,000	KM#925.1, 926a.1, 928-931.1, 933, 941.1, 951, 963-966	—	150
SS27	1989 (14)	10,000	KM#925.1, 926a.1, 928-931.1, 933, 942.1, 951, 964, 967-970	—	245
SS28	1990 (13)	10,000	KM#925.1, 926a.1, 928-931.1, 933, 942.1, 951, 964, 980-982	—	190
SS29	1990 (11)	10,000	KM#925.1, 926a.1, 928-931.1, 933, 942.1, 951, 964, 982	—	150

FRENCH AFARS & ISSAS

MINT MARK
(a) - Paris (privy marks only)

MONETARY SYSTEM
100 Centimes = 1 Franc

NOTE
For later coinage, see Djibouti
For earlier coinage, see French Somaliland

FRENCH COLONY

DECIMAL COINAGE

KM# 16 FRANC
1.30 g., Aluminum, 24 mm. **Obv:** Winged bust left, date below **Rev:** Lyre antelope divides denomination

Date	Mintage	VF20	XF40	MS60	MS63	MS65
1969 (a)	100,000	2.00	3.50	6.00	10.00	15.00
1971 (a)	100,000	2.00	3.50	6.00	10.00	15.00
1975 (a)	300,000	1.25	2.00	3.00	10.00	15.00

KM# 13 2 FRANCS
2.20 g., Aluminum, 27 mm. **Obv:** Winged bust left, date below **Rev:** Lyre antelope divides denomination

Date	Mintage	VF20	XF40	MS60	MS63	MS65
1968 (a)	100,000	2.00	3.50	6.00	10.00	15.00
1975 (a)	180,000	1.50	2.50	5.00	10.00	15.00

KM# 14 5 FRANCS
3.80 g., Aluminum, 31.1 mm. **Obv:** Winged bust left, date below **Rev:** Lyre antelope divides denomination

Date	Mintage	VF20	XF40	MS60	MS63	MS65
1968 (a)	100,000	2.00	3.50	6.00	10.00	15.00
1975 (a)	300,000	1.25	2.00	4.00	8.00	15.00

KM# 17 10 FRANCS
3.00 g., Aluminum-Bronze, 20 mm. **Obv:** Winged bust left, date below **Rev:** Dhow, ocean liner, denomination above

Date	Mintage	VF20	XF40	MS60	MS63	MS65
1969 (a)	100,000	3.00	6.00	9.00	18.00	28.00
1970 (a)	300,000	2.00	4.00	7.00	14.00	20.00
1975 (a)	360,000	1.50	3.00	5.00	10.00	15.00

KM# 15 20 FRANCS
4.10 g., Aluminum-Bronze, 23.6 mm. **Obv:** Winged bust left, date below **Rev:** Dhow, ocean liner, denomination above

Date	Mintage	VF20	XF40	MS60	MS63	MS65
1968 (a)	300,000	2.50	4.50	8.00	15.00	25.00
1975 (a)	300,000	2.00	4.00	7.00	14.00	20.00

KM# 18 50 FRANCS
7.00 g., Copper-Nickel, 25.5 mm. **Obv:** Hooded head left, date below **Rev:** Pair of dromedary camels, denomination above

Date	Mintage	VF20	XF40	MS60	MS63	MS65
1970 (a)	600,000	3.00	6.00	10.00	15.00	30.00
1975 (a)	180,000	3.00	6.00	10.00	15.00	30.00

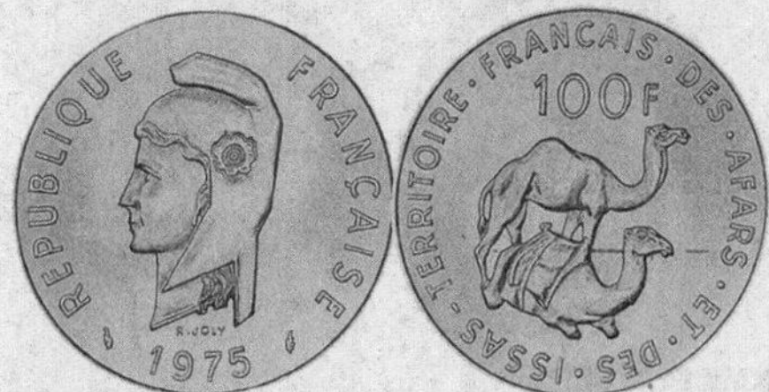

KM# 19 100 FRANCS
11.90 g., Copper-Nickel, 30 mm. **Obv:** Hooded head left, date below **Rev:** Pair of dromedary camels, denomination above

Date	Mintage	VF20	XF40	MS60	MS63	MS65
1970 (a)	600,000	4.00	7.00	11.50	18.50	35.00
1975 (a)	400,000	4.50	7.50	12.50	20.00	35.00

ESSAIS

Standard metals unless otherwise noted

KM#	Date	Mintage	Identification	Mkt Val
E1	1968(a)	1,700	2 Francs. KM13.	25.00
E2	1968(a)	1,700	5 Francs. KM14.	25.00
E3	1968(a)	1,700	20 Francs. KM15.	25.00
E4	1969(a)	1,700	Franc. KM16.	25.00
E5	1969(a)	1,700	10 Francs. KM17.	25.00
E6	1970(a)	1,700	50 Francs. KM18.	45.00
E7	1970(a)	1,700	100 Francs. KM19.	50.00

FRENCH EQUATORIAL AFRICA

French Equatorial Africa, an area consisting of four self governing dependencies (Middle Congo, Ubangi-Shari, Chad and Gabon) in West-Central Africa, had an area of 969,111 sq. mi. (2,509,987 sq. km.). Capital: Brazzaville. The area, rich in natural resources, exported cotton, timber, coffee, cacao, diamonds and gold.

Little is known of the history of these parts of Africa prior to French occupation - which began with no thought of territorial acquisition. France's initial intent was simply to establish a few supply stations along the west coast of Africa to service the warships assigned to combat the slave trade in the early part of the 19th century. French settlement began in 1839. Gabon (then Gabun) and the Middle Congo were secured between 1885 and 1891; Chad and Ubangi-Shari between 1894 and 1897. The four colonies were joined to form French Equatorial Africa in 1910. The dependencies were changed from colonies to territories within the French Union in 1946, and all the inhabitants were made French citizens. In 1958 they voted to become autonomous republics within the new French Community, and attained full independence in 1960.

For later coinage see Central African States, Congo Peoples Republic, Gabon and Chad.

RULER
French, until 1960

MINT MARKS
(a) - Paris, privy marks only
(t) - Poissy, privy marks only, thunderbolt
SA - Pretoria (1942-1943)

ENGRAVERS' INITIALS
GLS – Steynberg

MONETARY SYSTEM
100 Centimes = 1 Franc

FRENCH COLONY
DECIMAL COINAGE

KM# 3 5 CENTIMES
Aluminum-Bronze **Note:** Similar to 10 Centimes, KM#4.

Date	Mintage	F12	VF20	XF40	MS60	MS63
1943	Est. 44000000	90.00	150	325	600	1,000

Note: Not released for circulation

KM# 4 10 CENTIMES
Aluminum-Bronze

Date	Mintage	F12	VF20	XF40	MS60	MS63
1943	Est. 13000000	75.00	100	160	400	625

Note: Not released for circulation

KM# 5 25 CENTIMES
Aluminum-Bronze **Note:** Similar to 10 Centimes, KM#4.

Date	Mintage	F12	VF20	XF40	MS60	MS63
1943	Est. 4160000	200	350	550	900	1,500

Note: Not released for circulation

KM# 1 50 CENTIMES
Brass **Rev:** Double cross divides denomination, date below

Date	Mintage	F12	VF20	XF40	MS60	MS63
1942 SA	8,000,000	1.50	3.00	8.00	20.00	30.00

KM# 1a 50 CENTIMES
Bronze **Rev:** Double cross divides denomination

Date	Mintage	F12	VF20	XF40	MS60	MS63
1943 SA	16,000,000	1.25	2.50	7.00	18.00	25.00

KM# 2 FRANC
Brass **Obv:** Rooster, small shield above **Rev:** Double cross divides denomination, date below

Date	Mintage	F12	VF20	XF40	MS60	MS63
1942 SA	3,000,000	2.00	3.50	10.00	22.50	30.00

KM# 2a FRANC
Bronze **Obv:** Rooster left, small shield above **Rev:** Double cross divides denomination

Date	Mintage	F12	VF20	XF40	MS60	MS63
1943 SA	6,000,000	1.75	2.75	9.00	20.00	30.00

KM# 6 FRANC
Aluminum, 23 mm. **Obv:** Winged bust left, date below **Rev:** Loder's gazelle divides denomination

Date	Mintage	VF20	XF40	MS60	MS63	MS65
1948 (a)	15,000,000	0.25	0.50	2.00	10.00	15.00

KM# 7 2 FRANCS
Aluminum **Obv:** Winged bust left, date below **Rev:** Loder's gazelle divides denomination

Date	Mintage	VF20	XF40	MS60	MS63	MS65
1948 (a)	5,040,000	0.50	1.50	4.00	10.00	15.00

TOKEN COINAGE

Middle Congo

KM# TnA1 NON-DENOMINATED
Aluminum **Obv:** Center hole, date below, MC above **Rev:** Center hole within Elephant walking left **Note:** Prev. KM#Tn1.

Date	Mintage	F12	VF20	XF40	MS60	MS63
1925 (t)	—	35.00	65.00	115	320	500

KM# TnA2 NON-DENOMINATED
Aluminum **Rev:** Center hole within Leopard walking left **Note:** Previous KM#Tn2.

Date	Mintage	F12	VF20	XF40	MS60	MS63
1926	—	40.00	75.00	150	325	500

ESSAIS

Standard metals unless otherwise noted

KM#	Date	Mintage	Identification	Mkt Val
E1	1948(a)	2,000	Franc. Copper-Nickel. KM#7.	35.00
E2	1948(a)	2,000	2 Francs. Copper-Nickel. KM#7.	40.00

PIEDFORT WITH ESSAI

Standard metals unless otherwise noted

KM#	Date	Mintage	Identification	Mkt Val
PE1	1948(a)	104	Franc. Aluminum. KM#6.	160
PE2	1948(a)	104	2 Francs. Aluminum. KM#7.	220

FRENCH INDO-CHINA

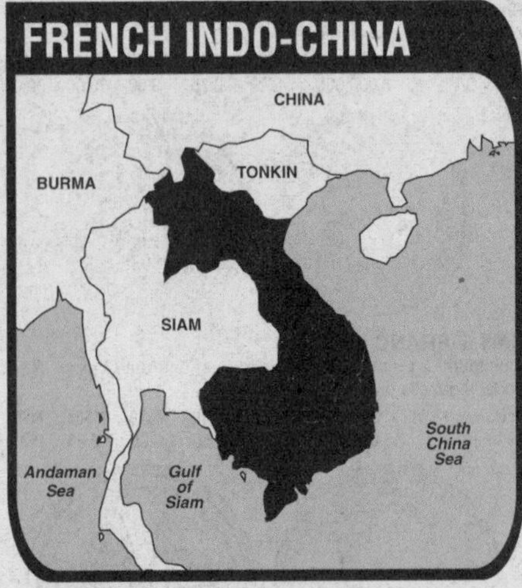

French Indo-China, made up of the protectorates of Annam, Tonkin, Cambodia and Laos and the colony of Cochin-China was located on the Indo-Chinese peninsula of Southeast Asia. The colony had an area of 286,194 sq. mi. (741,242 sq. km.). and a population of 30 million. Principal cities: Saigon, Haiphong, Vientiane, Pnom-Penh and Hanoi.

The forebears of the modern Indo-Chinese people originated in the Yellow River Valley of Northern China. From there, they were driven into the Indo-Chinese peninsula by the Han Chinese. The Chinese followed southward in the second century B.C., conquering the peninsula and ruling it until 938, leaving a lingering heritage of Chinese learning and culture. Indo-Chinese independence was basically maintained until the arrival of the French in the mid-19th century who established control over all of Vietnam, Laos and Cambodia. Activities directed toward obtaining self-determination accelerated during the Japanese occupation of World War II. The dependencies were changed from colonies to territories within the French Union in 1946, and all the inhabitants were made French citizens.

In Aug. of 1945, an uprising erupted involving the French and Vietnamese Nationalists, culminated in the French military disaster at Dien Bien Phu (May, 1954) and the subsequent Geneva Conference that brought an end to French colonial rule in Indo-China.

For later coinage see Kampuchea, Laos and Vietnam.

RULER

French, until 1954

MINT MARKS

A - Paris
(a) - Paris, privy marks only
B - Beaumont-le-Roger
C - Castlesarrasin
H - Heaton, Birmingham
(p) - Thunderbolt - Poissy
S - San Francisco, U.S.A.
None - Osaka, Japan
None - Hanoi, Tonkin

MONETARY SYSTEM

5 Sapeques = 1 Cent
100 Cents = 1 Piastre

FRENCH COLONY

STANDARD COINAGE

KM# 6 2 SAPEQUE

Bronze

Date	Mintage	F12	VF20	XF40	MS60	MS63
1901 A	4,843,000	2.50	7.50	15.00	45.00	100
1902 A	2,500,000	7.50	20.00	40.00	125	250

KM# 25 1/4 CENT

Zinc **Obv:** Square surrounds center hole, grain sprigs flank, date below **Rev:** Square around center hole, corners section coin, denomination divided by hole **Note:** Lead counterfeits dated 1941 and 1942 are known.

Date	Mintage	F12	VF20	XF40	MS60	MS63
1941	—	12.00	25.00	35.00	80.00	110
1942	221,800,000	8.00	15.00	35.00	75.00	100
1943	279,450,000	15.00	35.00	55.00	125	150
1944	46,122,000	100	180	250	750	1,300

KM# 20 1/2 CENT

Bronze, 21 mm. **Obv:** Center hole divides RF, liberty cap above, wreath surrounds **Rev:** Denomination divided by grain sprigs around center hole, date below

Date	Mintage	VF20	XF40	MS60	MS63	MS65
1935 (a)	26,365,000	0.50	2.00	10.00	25.00	—
1936 (a)	23,635,000	0.50	2.00	10.00	25.00	—
1937 (a)	10,244,000	1.50	5.00	15.00	40.00	—
1938 (a)	16,665,000	0.75	2.50	12.00	29.00	—
1939 (a)	17,305,000	0.75	2.50	12.00	29.00	—
1940 (a)	11,218,000	8.00	20.00	40.00	75.00	—

KM# 20a 1/2 CENT

Zinc, 21 mm. **Obv:** Center hole divides RF, liberty cap above, wreath surrounds **Rev:** Denomination divided by center hole and grain sprigs

Date	Mintage	F12	VF20	XF40	MS60	MS63
1939 (a)	185,000	200	400	600	900	—
1940 (a)	Inc. above	350	500	800	1,200	—

KM# 8 CENT

7.51 g., Bronze, 27.5 mm. **Obv:** Center hole within statue, denomination below **Rev:** Symbols at four sides of center hole within circle, date below

Date	Mintage	F12	VF20	XF40	MS60	MS63
1901	9,750,000	2.00	3.00	7.50	25.00	50.00
1902	6,050,000	4.00	7.00	15.00	50.00	75.00
1903	8,000,000	2.50	4.00	8.00	30.00	60.00
1906	2,000,000	15.00	20.00	35.00	120	200

KM# 12.1 CENT

Bronze, 26 mm. **Obv:** Center hole within statue, denomination below, mint mark "A" for Paris mint **Rev:** Symbols at four sides of center hole within circle, date below

Date	Mintage	VF20	XF40	MS60	MS63	MS65
1908	3,000,000	20.00	55.00	140	235	350
1909	5,000,000	40.00	80.00	165	275	400
1910	7,703,000	5.00	15.00	22.00	35.00	60.00
1911	15,234,000	3.00	7.00	12.00	20.00	40.00
1912	17,027,000	2.00	6.50	12.00	20.00	40.00
1913	3,945,000	7.00	15.00	27.00	45.00	75.00
1914	11,027,000	3.00	9.00	18.00	30.00	60.00
1916	1,312,000	12.00	20.00	35.00	65.00	90.00
1917	9,762,000	4.00	7.00	12.00	20.00	30.00
1918	2,372,000	11.00	18.00	30.00	50.00	75.00
1919	9,148,000	4.00	7.00	12.00	20.00	30.00
1920	18,305,000	2.50	4.00	7.50	12.50	22.00
1921	14,272,000	2.00	3.00	6.00	10.00	22.00
1922	8,850,000	3.00	5.00	12.00	20.00	30.00
1923	1,079,000	35.00	75.00	100	150	350
1926	11,672,000	2.00	4.00	8.00	15.00	25.00
1927	3,328,000	15.00	25.00	40.00	70.00	100
1930	4,682,000	2.50	4.50	9.00	15.00	25.00
1931	5,318,000	65.00	125	150	235	550
Note: Torch privy mark						
1931	Inc. above	95.00	185	250	400	800
Note: Wing privy mark						
1937	8,902,000	2.50	4.50	7.50	12.00	20.00
1938	15,499,000	1.00	2.00	3.50	7.00	15.00
1939	17,589,000	1.00	2.00	3.50	7.00	15.00

KM# 12.2 CENT

Bronze, 26 mm. **Obv:** No mint mark at bottom, (San Francisco mint) **Rev:** Four symbols surround center hole **Note:** Without mint mark.

Date	Mintage	VF20	XF40	MS60	MS63	MS65
1920	13,290,000	4.00	8.00	15.00	25.00	45.00
1921	1,710,000	60.00	125	210	350	500

KM# 12.3 CENT

Bronze, 26 mm. **Obv:** Center hole within statue, denomination below **Rev:** Four symbols surround center hole

Date	Mintage	VF20	XF40	MS60	MS63	MS65
1922 (p)	9,476,000	1.75	3.50	7.50	12.00	30.00
1923 (p)	35,524,000	0.75	1.50	4.50	7.50	12.00

KM# 24.1 CENT

Zinc **Obv:** Wreath surrounds center hole, liberty cap above, denomination below **Rev:** Center hole divides denomination, wreath surrounds, date below **Note:** Vichy Government issue. Type 1: Circles on Phrygian cap.

Date	Mintage	F12	VF20	XF40	MS60	MS63
1940	1,990,000	9.00	18.00	35.00	75.00	—

KM# 24.2 CENT

Zinc **Obv:** Wreath surrounds center hole, liberty cap above, denomination below **Rev:** Center hole divides denomination, wreath surrounds, date below **Note:** Vichy Government issue. Type 2: Rosette on Phrygian cap, variety 2 with 12 petals.

Date	Mintage	F12	VF20	XF40	MS60	MS63
1940	150,000	18.00	35.00	70.00	140	—

KM# 24.3 CENT

Zinc **Obv:** Wreath surrounds, cap above, denomination below **Rev:** Wreath surrounds center hole, denomination divided **Note:** Vichy Government issue. Type 2: Rosette on Phrygian cap. Variety 2: 11 petals.

Date	Mintage	F12	VF20	XF40	MS60	MS63
1940	2,360,000	7.00	15.00	30.00	60.00	—
1941	2,500,000	6.00	12.00	20.00	60.00	—

KM# 26 CENT

Aluminum **Obv:** Center hole flanked by leafy sprays, date below **Rev:** Denomination left and top of center hole **Note:** Edge varieties exist - plain, grooved, and partially grooved.

Date	Mintage	F12	VF20	XF40	MS60	MS63
1943	15,000,000	0.75	2.00	4.00	7.00	12.00

KM# 18 5 CENTS

5.20 g., Copper-Nickel, 24 mm. **Obv:** Cornucopias flank center hole, laureate head left above **Rev:** Center hole within wreath divides denomination, date below **Note:** 1.6 mm thick; prev. KM#18.1.

Date	Mintage	VF20	XF40	MS60	MS63	MS65
1923 (a)	1,611,000	10.00	20.00	35.00	55.00	80.00
1924 (a)	3,389,000	12.00	22.00	40.00	60.00	85.00
1925 (a)	6,000,000	10.00	20.00	35.00	60.00	100
1930 (a) Torch	4,000,000	10.00	20.00	35.00	60.00	100
1937 (a) Wing	10,000,000	4.00	8.00	12.00	15.00	20.00
1938 (a)	1,480,000	20.00	45.00	75.00	125	200
1938 (a)	—	PF63 300				

KM# 18.1a 5 CENTS

4.00 g., Nickel-Brass, 24 mm. **Obv:** Cornucopias flank center hole, laureate head left above **Rev:** Center hole divides denomination, wreath surrounds, date below **Note:** 1.3 mm thick.

Date	Mintage	VF20	XF40	MS60	MS63	MS65
1938 (a)	50,569,000	2.00	5.00	7.00	10.00	16.00
1939 (a)	38,501,000	2.00	5.00	7.00	10.00	16.00

KM# 27 5 CENTS

Aluminum **Note:** Vichy Government issue. Edge varieties exist: reeded - rare, plain, grooved, and partially grooved.

Date	Mintage	VF20	XF40	MS60	MS63	MS65
1943 A	10,000,000	2.00	3.00	5.00	7.00	10.00

KM# 30.1 5 CENTS

Aluminum **Obv:** Bust right holding laurel, date below **Rev:** Plant divides denomination

Date	Mintage	VF20	XF40	MS60	MS63	MS65
1946 (a)	28,000,000	0.60	1.00	3.00	5.00	7.00

KM# 30.2 5 CENTS

Aluminum **Obv:** Bust right holding laurel, date below **Rev:** Plant divide denomination

Date	Mintage	VF20	XF40	MS60	MS63	MS65
1946 B	22,000,000	0.60	1.00	3.00	5.00	7.00

KM# 9 10 CENTS

2.70 g., 0.835 Silver 0.0725 oz. ASW **Obv:** Liberty seated left with fasces **Rev:** Denomination within wreath **Rev. Legend:** TITRE 0.835. POIDS 2 GR. 7

Date	Mintage	F12	VF20	XF40	MS60	MS63
1901	2,950,000	8.00	27.50	65.00	220	375
1902	7,050,000	4.00	13.00	35.00	145	—
1903	1,300,000	13.00	33.00	90.00	350	—
1908	1,000,000	55.00	110	220	625	800
1909	1,000,000	33.00	85.00	145	475	775
1910	2,689,000	27.50	65.00	110	375	—
1911	2,311,000	27.50	45.00	95.00	350	—
1912	2,500,000	27.50	38.50	75.00	300	—
1913	4,847,000	8.00	14.00	35.00	145	—
1914	2,667,000	11.00	33.00	65.00	200	—
1916	2,000,000	11.00	33.00	65.00	215	—
1917	1,500,000	27.50	55.00	110	325	550
1919	1,500,000	33.00	65.00	140	375	600

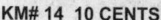

KM# 14 10 CENTS

3.00 g., 0.400 Silver 0.0386 oz. ASW **Obv:** Liberty seated, date below **Rev:** Denomination within wreath, without fineness indicated **Note:** Without mint mark.

Date	Mintage	F12	VF20	XF40	MS60	MS63
1920	10,000,000	10.00	20.00	50.00	150	200

KM# 16.1 10 CENTS

2.70 g., 0.680 Silver 0.059 oz. ASW **Obv:** Liberty seated, date below **Rev:** Denomination within wreath **Rev. Legend:** TITRE 0.680 POIDS 2 GR. 7

Date	Mintage	F12	VF20	XF40	MS60	MS63
1921 A	12,516,000	2.50	4.00	12.00	30.00	35.00
1922 A	22,381,000	2.50	4.00	10.00	22.50	30.00
1923 A	21,755,000	2.50	4.00	10.00	22.50	30.00
1924 A	2,816,000	6.00	12.00	30.00	70.00	90.00
1925 A	4,909,000	2.75	6.00	17.00	40.00	65.00
1927 A	6,471,000	3.50	8.00	20.00	46.00	75.00
1928 A	1,593,000	46.00	115	230	550	875
1929 A	5,831,000	2.50	4.00	12.00	35.00	60.00
1930 A	6,608,000	2.50	4.00	9.00	35.00	60.00
1931 A	100	PF60 400				

KM# 16.2 10 CENTS

2.70 g., 0.680 Silver 0.059 oz. ASW **Obv:** Liberty seated left, date below **Rev:** Denomination within wreath **Rev. Legend:** TITRE 0.680 POIDS 2 GR. 7

Date	Mintage	VF20	XF40	MS60	MS63	MS65
1937 (a)	25,000,000	3.50	5.00	7.00	9.00	14.00

KM# 21.1 10 CENTS

3.00 g., Nickel, 18 mm. **Obv:** Bust right holding laurel, date without dots **Rev:** Plant divides denomination **Edge:** Reeded **Note:** These coins are magnetic.

Date	Mintage	VF20	XF40	MS60	MS63	MS65
1939 (a)	16,841,000	1.00	2.00	4.00	8.00	12.00
1940 (a)	25,505,000	1.00	2.00	4.00	8.00	12.00

KM# 21.1a 10 CENTS

3.00 g., Copper-Nickel, 18 mm. **Obv:** Date without dots **Rev:** Plant divides denomination **Edge:** Reeded **Note:** These coins are not magnetic.

Date	Mintage	F12	VF20	XF40	MS60	MS63
1939 (a)	—	45.00	100	100	375	700
Note: Mintage included in KM#21.2						
1941 S	50,000,000	0.50	1.00	2.00	4.00	8.00

KM# 21.2 10 CENTS

3.00 g., Copper-Nickel, 18 mm. **Obv:** Date between two dots **Rev:** Plant divides denomination **Edge:** Reeded **Note:** These coins are not magnetic.

Date	Mintage	F12	VF20	XF40	MS60	MS63
.1939. (a)	2,237,000	50.00	125	175	275	475

KM# 28.1 10 CENTS

Aluminum, 23 mm. **Obv:** Bust right holding laurel, date below **Rev:** Plant divides denomination

Date	Mintage	VF20	XF40	MS60	MS63	MS65
1945 (a)	40,170,000	0.50	1.00	3.00	4.50	6.00

KM# 28.2 10 CENTS

Aluminum, 23 mm. **Obv:** Bust right holding laurel, date below **Rev:** Plant divides denomination

Date	Mintage	VF20	XF40	MS60	MS63	MS65
1945 B	9,830,000	2.00	5.00	7.50	12.50	22.50

KM# 10 20 CENTS

5.40 g., 0.835 Silver 0.145 oz. ASW

Date	Mintage	F12	VF20	XF40	MS60	MS63
1901	1,375,000	22.50	55.00	110	225	325
1902	3,525,000	8.00	17.00	45.00	100	195
1903	675,000	55.00	110	175	450	650
1908	500,000	110	275	450	650	925
1909	500,000	110	220	375	600	925
1911	2,340,000	8.00	17.00	38.00	75.00	140
1912	160,000	110	220	450	700	1,000
1913	1,252,000	55.00	110	165	285	450
1914	2,500,000	8.00	17.00	28.00	65.00	135
1916	1,000,000	22.50	49.50	130	200	300

KM# 13 20 CENTS

0.835 Silver **Obv:** KM#10 **Rev:** KM#3a **Note:** Mule.

Date	Mintage	F12	VF20	XF40	MS60	MS63
1909	—	100	250	650	1,000	1,400

KM# 15 20 CENTS

6.00 g., 0.400 Silver 0.0772 oz. ASW **Rev:** Without fineness indicated **Note:** Without mint mark.

Date	Mintage	F12	VF20	XF40	MS60	MS63
1920	4,000,000	14.00	27.50	55.00	200	300

KM# 17.1 20 CENTS

4.50 g., 0.680 Silver 0.0984 oz. ASW, 25.9 mm. **Obv:** Seated liberty left, date below **Rev:** Denomination within wreath **Rev. Legend:** TITRE O.680 POIDS 5 GR. 4

Date	Mintage	F12	VF20	XF40	MS60	MS63
1921 A	3,663,000	6.00	10.00	20.00	30.00	50.00
1922 A	5,812,000	4.00	6.00	12.00	20.00	35.00
1923 A	7,109,000	4.00	6.00	12.00	20.00	35.00
1924 A	1,400,000	10.00	22.50	45.00	65.00	100
1925 A	2,556,000	8.00	17.00	35.00	55.00	85.00
1927 A	3,245,000	6.00	10.00	20.00	30.00	50.00
1928 A	794,000	17.00	45.00	95.00	175	300
1929 A	644,000	22.50	55.00	110	200	325
1930 A	5,576,000	4.00	6.00	12.00	20.00	35.00

Note: An overdate of 1930/20 also exists.

KM# 17.2 20 CENTS

5.40 g., 0.680 Silver 0.1181 oz. ASW **Obv:** Liberty seated, date below **Rev:** Denomination within wreath **Rev. Legend:** TITRE O.680 POIDS 5 GR. 4

Date	Mintage	VF20	XF40	MS60	MS63	MS65
1937 (a)	17,500,000	6.00	10.00	15.00	18.00	30.00

KM# 23 20 CENTS

Nickel, 24 mm. **Obv:** Bust right holding laurel, date below **Rev:** Plant divides denomination **Note:** Magnetic coin with security edge.

Date	Mintage	F12	VF20	XF40	MS60	MS63
1939 (a)	344,500	15.00	30.00	40.00	125	260

KM# 23a.1 20 CENTS

Copper-Nickel, 24 mm. **Obv:** Bust right holding laurel, date below **Rev:** Plant divides denomination **Edge:** Reeded **Note:** Non-magnetic coin.

Date	Mintage	VF20	XF40	MS60	MS63	MS65
1939 (a)	14,676,000	1.00	2.00	10.00	20.00	—

Note: Date between dots

KM# 23a.2 20 CENTS

Copper-Nickel, 24 mm. **Obv:** Bust right holding laurel, date below **Rev:** Plant divides denomination **Edge:** Reeded **Note:** Non-magnetic coin.

Date	Mintage	VF20	XF40	MS60	MS63	MS65
1941 S	25,000,000	1.00	2.00	4.00	6.00	9.00

Note: Date between dots

KM# 29.1 20 CENTS

Aluminum **Obv:** Bust right holding laurel, date below **Rev:** Plant divides denomination

Date	Mintage	VF20	XF40	MS60	MS63	MS65
1945 (a)	15,412,000	1.00	2.50	4.50	7.00	10.00

KM# 29.2 20 CENTS

Aluminum **Obv:** Bust right holding laurel, date below **Rev:** Plant divides denomination

Date	Mintage	VF20	XF40	MS60	MS63	MS65
1945 B	6,665,000	3.00	6.00	8.00	12.00	25.00

KM# 29.3 20 CENTS

Aluminum **Obv:** Bust right holding laurel, date below **Rev:** Plant divides denomination

Date	Mintage	VF20	XF40	MS60	MS63	MS65
1945 C	22,423,000	1.00	3.00	5.00	8.00	16.00

KM# 4a.2 50 CENTS

13.50 g., 0.900 Silver 0.3906 oz. ASW **Obv:** Liberty seated, date below **Rev:** Denomination within wreath **Rev. Legend:** TITRE 0.900. POIDS 13 GR. 5

Date	Mintage	VF20	XF40	MS60	MS63	MS65
1936 (a)	4,000,000	16.00	20.00	35.00	70.00	120

KM# 31 50 CENTS

12.47 g., Copper-Nickel **Obv:** Liberty seated, date below **Rev:** Denomination within wreath **Rev. Legend:** BRONZE DE NICKEL

Date	Mintage	F12	VF20	XF40	MS60	MS63
1946 (a)	32,292,000	2.00	4.00	9.00	30.00	65.00

KM# 5a.1 PIASTRE

27.00 g., 0.900 Silver 0.7813 oz. ASW **Obv:** Liberty seated left with fasces **Rev:** Denomination within wreath **Rev. Legend:** TITRE 0.900 POIDS 27 GR.

Date	Mintage	F12	VF20	XF40	MS60	MS63
1901 A	3,150,000	30.00	35.00	50.00	230	325
1902 A	3,327,000	30.00	35.00	50.00	230	325
1903 A	10,077,000	30.00	35.00	40.00	200	300
1904 A	5,751,000	30.00	35.00	40.00	200	300
1905 A	3,561,000	30.00	35.00	40.00	200	300
1906 A	10,194,000	30.00	35.00	40.00	200	300
1907 A	14,062,000	30.00	35.00	40.00	200	300
1908 A	13,986,000	30.00	35.00	40.00	200	300
1909 A	9,201,000	30.00	35.00	40.00	200	300
1910 A	761,000	45.00	75.00	220	450	600
1913 A	3,244,000	30.00	35.00	40.00	200	300
1924 A	2,831,000	30.00	35.00	50.00	230	325
1925 A	2,882,000	30.00	35.00	50.00	230	325
1926 A	6,383,000	30.00	35.00	40.00	200	300
1927 A	8,183,999	30.00	35.00	40.00	200	300
1928 A	5,290,000	30.00	35.00	50.00	290	375

KM# 5a.2 PIASTRE

27.00 g., 0.900 Silver 0.7813 oz. ASW **Rev:** Denomination within wreath **Note:** Without mint mark.

Date	Mintage	F12	VF20	XF40	MS60	MS63
1921	4,850,000	30.00	35.00	75.00	230	425
1922	1,150,000	30.00	50.00	135	400	550

KM# 5a.3 PIASTRE

27.00 g., 0.900 Silver 0.7813 oz. ASW **Rev:** Denomination within wreath

Date	Mintage	F12	VF20	XF40	MS60	MS63
1921 H	3,580,000	28.00	35.00	60.00	250	300
1922 H	7,420,000	28.00	32.00	40.00	180	250

KM# 19 PIASTRE

20.00 g., 0.900 Silver 0.5787 oz. ASW **Obv:** Laureate head left **Rev:** Denomination and date within keyhole shape wreath

Date	Mintage	VF20	XF40	MS60	MS63	MS65
1931 (a)	16,000,000	25.00	45.00	125	200	375

FEDERATED STATES

French Union

KM# 32.1 PIASTRE

Copper-Nickel, 34.5 mm. **Obv:** Bust right holding laurel, date below **Rev:** Grain sprigs below denomination **Note:** Security edge.

Date	Mintage	F12	VF20	XF40	MS60	MS63
1946 (a)	2,520,000	7.50	12.50	20.00	85.00	135
1947 (a)	261,000	15.00	35.00	75.00	160	300

KM# 32.2 PIASTRE

18.13 g., Copper-Nickel, 34.5 mm. **Obv:** Bust right holding laurel, date below **Rev:** Denomination above plants **Edge:** Reeded **Note:** Similar coins dated 1946 with reverse legend: INDOCHINE - FRANCAISE are Essais.

Date	Mintage	F12	VF20	XF40	MS60	MS63
1947 (a)	54,480,000	2.00	4.00	7.50	10.00	35.00

ESSAIS

Standard metals unless otherwise noted

KM#	Date	Mintage	Identification	Mkt Val
E7	1910	—	Cent. Copper-Nickel. ESSAI. KM#12.1.	450
E8	1919	—	10 Cents. Silver. Fineness 0.700/0.835 incuse plus 0.700 incuse on field on reverse; KM#9.	1,000
E9	ND (1920)	—	20 Cents. Silver. Mule. Two reverses. KM#3.	500
E10	1923(p)	—	Cent. Bronze. ESSAI in field; KM#12.1.	550
E11	1923(p)	—	Cent. Bronze. ESSAI at rim; KM#12.1.	550
E12	1923(a)	—	5 Cents. Cornucopias flank center hole, laureate liberty, left, above. Center hole within wreath divides denomination. KM#18.1.	180
E13	1928	—	20 Cents. Brass. Plain. KM#17.1.	250
E14	1928(a)	—	20 Cents. Bronze. KM#17.1.	500
E15	19(30a) (1930)	—	Cent. Silver. KM#12.1.	750
E16	19(30a) (1930)	—	Cent. Aluminum-Bronze. KM#12.1.	600
E17	1930(a)	—	Piastre. Silver. Uniface.	4,650
E18	19(31) (1931)	—	10 Cents. Silver.	850
E19	19(31a) (1931)	—	10 Cents. Silver-Bronze. KM#16.1, medallic alignment.	900
E20	19(31) (1931)	—	20 Cents. Silver.	700
E21	19(31a) (1931)	—	20 Cents. Silver-Bronze. KM#17.1, medallic alignment.	1,000
E22	1(931) (1931)	—	50 Cents. Medallic alignment.	—
E23	1(931a) (1931)	—	50 Cents. Silver-Bronze. Liberty seated, date below. Denomination within wreath.	1,000
E24	19(31a) (1931)	—	Piastre. Silver. KM#19.	9,000
E25	19(31a) (1931)	—	Piastre. Silver-Bronze. KM#19.	400
EA26	1931(a)	—	Piastre. Aluminum. Unique.	—
E26	1931(a)	—	Piastre. Silver. KM#19.	475
E27	1935(a)	—	1/2 Cent. Bronze. KM#20.	90.00
E28	1936(a)	—	50 Cents. Aluminum. Liberty seated, date below. Denomination within wreath.	250
E29	1937(a)	—	10 Cents. Nickel. KM#16.2.	200
E30	1937(a)	—	20 Cents. Silver. KM#17.2.	340
E31	1937(a)	—	20 Cents. Nickel. KM#17.2.	250
E32	1939(a)	—	10 Cents. Nickel. KM#21.	110
E33	1939(a)	—	20 Cents. Nickel. Plain. KM#23.	225
E34	1939(a)	—	20 Cents. Nickel. Security edge; KM#23.	200
E35	1939(a)	—	20 Cents. Copper-Nickel. Reeded. KM#23a.1.	260
E36	1940(a)	—	Cent. Zinc. KM#24.1.	150
E37	1940(a)	—	Cent. Aluminum-Bronze. KM#24.1.	450
E45	ND(1943)	—	Tael. Silver. KM#2.	—
E46	ND(1943)	—	1/2 Tael. Silver. KM#1.	—
E38	1945(a)	1,100	10 Cents. Aluminum. KM#28.1.	55.00
E39	1945(a)	1,100	20 Cents. Aluminum. KM#29.	65.00
E40	1946(a)	1,100	5 Cents. Aluminum. KM#30.1.	40.00
E41	1946(a)	1,100	50 Cents. Copper-Nickel. KM#31.	90.00
E42	1946(a)	1,100	Piastre. Federation.	185
E43	1946(a)	1,100	Piastre. Copper-Nickel. Indochina. KM#32.1.	310
E44	1947(a)	104	Piastre. Bust right holding laurel, date below. Grain sprigs below denomination. Federation.	770

PIEDFORT

KM#	Date	Mintage	Identification	Mkt Val
P2	1908	—	Cent. Bronze. KM#12.1.	725
P3	1920	—	20 Cents. Brass. Reeded. Medallic alignment. KM#15.	400
P4	1923	—	Cent. Bronze. Filled center hole. KM#12.1.	—

P5	19(30) (1930)	—	Cent. Bronze. France Y#81. Filled center hole; KM#12.1.	—
P6	19(30) (1930)	—	Cent. Aluminum-Bronze. France Y#81. Filled center hole; KM#12.1.	1,150
P7	19(31) (1931)	—	20 Cents. Medallic alignment.	750
P8	1939	—	1/2 Cent. Zinc. KM#20a.	500

PIEDFORT WITH ESSAI

Double thickness -
Standard metals unless otherwise noted

KM#	Date	Mintage	Identification	Mkt Val
PE1	1908	—	Cent. Bronze. KM#12.1.	700
PE2	1923	—	5 Cents. Nickel-Brass. KM#18.1.	1,100
PE3	1931(a)	—	Piastre. Silver. Laureate head left. Denomination and date within keyhole shape wreath. KM#19.	6,000
PE4	1945(a)	104	10 Cents. Aluminum. KM#28.1.	550
PE5	1945(a)	104	20 Cents. Aluminum. KM#29.1.	600
PE6	1946(a)	104	5 Cents. Aluminum. KM#30.1.	375
PE7	1946(a)	104	50 Cents. Copper-Nickel. KM#31.	900
PE8	1947(a)	104	Piastre. Copper-Nickel. KM#32.	1,350

TRIAL STRIKES

KM#	Date	Mintage	Identification	Mkt Val
TS1	1921	—	Piastre. 0.900. Silver. Without collar.	600
TS2	ND(1931)	—	Piastre. Uniface.	1,200
TS3	1931	—	Piastre. Uniface, denomination and date within keyhole shape wreath.	650
TS4	1931	—	Piastre. KM#19 but struck in aluminum.	375

FRENCH OCEANIA

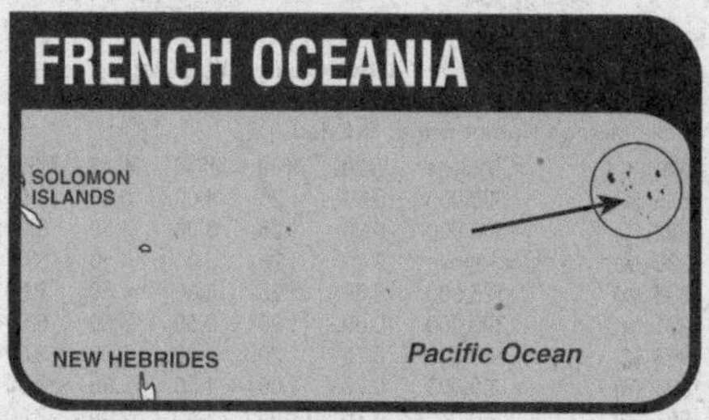

The Colony of French Oceania (now the Territory of French Polynesia), comprising 130 basalt and coral islands scattered among five archipelagoes in the South Pacific, had an area of 1,544 sq. mi. (3,999 sq. km.). Capital: Papeete. The colony produced phosphates, copra and vanilla.

Tahiti of the Society Islands, the hub of French Oceania, was visited by Capt. Cook in 1769 and by Capt. Bligh on the Bounty 1788-89. The Society Islands were claimed by France in 1768, and in 1903 grouped with the Marquesas Islands, the Tuamotu Archipelago, the Gambier Islands and the Austral Islands under a single administrative head located at Papeete, Tahiti, to form the colony of French Oceania.

RULER
French

MINT MARKS
(a) - Paris, privy marks only
(b)

MONETARY SYSTEM
100 Centimes = 1 Franc

FRENCH OVERSEAS TERRITORY

DECIMAL COINAGE

KM# 1 50 CENTIMES

0.75 g., Aluminum, 18 mm. **Obv:** Seated Liberty with torch and cornucopia right, date below **Rev:** Inscription and island scene divide denomination **Edge:** Plain

Date	Mintage	VF20	XF40	MS60	MS63	MS65
1949 (a)	795,000	0.75	1.50	5.00	10.00	20.00

KM# 2 FRANC

1.31 g., Aluminum, 23.4 mm. **Obv:** Seated Liberty with torch and cornucopia right, date below **Rev:** Inscription and island scene divide denomination **Edge:** Plain

Date	Mintage	VF20	XF40	MS60	MS63	MS65
1949 (a)	2,000,000	0.35	1.00	4.00	10.00	20.00

KM# 3 2 FRANCS

2.25 g., Aluminum, 27 mm. **Obv:** Seated Liberty with torch and cornucopia right, date below **Rev:** Inscription and island scene divide denomination **Edge:** Plain

Date	Mintage	VF20	XF40	MS60	MS63	MS65
1949 (a)	1,000,000	0.60	1.25	5.00	10.00	20.00

KM# 4 5 FRANCS

3.75 g., Aluminum, 31 mm. **Obv:** Seated Liberty with torch and cornucopia right, date below **Rev:** Inscription and island scene divide denomination **Edge:** Plain

Date	Mintage	VF20	XF40	MS60	MS63	MS65
1952	2,000,000	0.75	1.50	6.00	12.00	25.00

ESSAIS

Standard metals unless otherwise noted

KM#	Date	Mintage	Identification	Mkt Val
E1	1948	1,100	50 Centimes. Incuse design.	40.00
E2	1948	1,100	50 Centimes. Raised design.	40.00
E3	1948	1,100	Franc. Incuse design.	50.00
E4	1948	1,100	Franc. Raised design.	50.00
E5	1948	1,100	2 Francs. Copper-Nickel. Republic seated with grain spray and shield. Dhow divides denomination and date. Plain. Incuse design.	60.00
E6	1948	1,100	2 Francs. Copper-Nickel. Raised design.	45.00
E7	1949(a)	2,000	50 Centimes. Copper-Nickel. KM1.	40.00
E8	1949(a)	2,000	Franc. Copper-Nickel. KM2.	35.00
E9	1949(a)	2,000	2 Francs. Copper-Nickel. KM3.	40.00
E10	1952(a)	1,200	5 Francs. Aluminum. KM4.	45.00

PIEDFORT WITH ESSAI

Double thickness -
Standard metals unless otherwise noted

KM#	Date	Mintage	Identification	Mkt Val
PE1	1949(a)	104	50 Centimes.	200
PE2	1949(a)	104	Franc.	225
PE3	1949(a)	104	2 Francs.	240
PE4	1952(a)	104	5 Francs.	250

FRENCH POLYNESIA

The Territory of French Polynesia (formerly French Oceania) has an area of 1,544 sq. mi. (3,941 sq. km.) and a population of 220,000. It is comprised of the same five archipelagoes that were grouped administratively to form French Oceania.

The colony of French Oceania became the Territory of French Polynesia by act of the French National Assembly in March, 1957. In Sept. of 1958 it voted in favor of the new constitution of the Fifth Republic, thereby electing to remain within the new French Community.

Picturesque, mountainous Tahiti, the setting of many tales of adventure and romance, is one of the most inspiringly beautiful islands in the world. Robert Louis Stevenson called it 'God's sweetest works'. It was there that Paul Gaugin, one of the pioneers of the Impressionist movement, painted the brilliant, exotic pictures that later made him famous. The arid coral atolls of Tuamotu comprise the most economically valuable area of French Polynesia. Pearl oysters thrive in the warm, limpid lagoons, and extensive portions of the atolls are valuable phosphate rock.

RULER
French

MINT MARKS
(a) - Paris, privy marks only
(b)

MONETARY SYSTEM
100 Centimes = 1 Franc

FRENCH OVERSEAS TERRITORY

DECIMAL COINAGE

KM# 1 50 CENTIMES

Aluminum **Obv:** Seated Liberty with torch and cornucopia right, date below **Rev:** Legend and island scene divides denomination

Date	Mintage	VF20	XF40	MS60	MS63	MS65
1965 (a)	400,000	0.25	0.50	1.50	2.50	4.50

KM# 2 FRANC

1.30 g., Aluminum, 23 mm. **Obv:** Seated Liberty with torch and cornucopia right, date below **Rev:** Legend and island scene divide denomination

Date	Mintage	VF20	XF40	MS60	MS63	MS65
1965 (a)	3,300,000	0.10	0.20	0.75	1.25	2.50

KM# 11 FRANC

1.30 g., Aluminum, 23 mm. **Obv:** Seated Liberty with torch and cornucopia right, date below, legend added flanking figure's feet **Obv. Legend:** I. E. O. M. **Rev:** Legend and island scene divide denomination

Date	Mintage	VF20	XF40	MS60	MS63	MS65
1975 (a)	2,000,000	0.10	0.15	0.45	1.25	2.50
1977 (a)	2,000,000	0.10	0.15	0.45	1.00	1.75
1979 (a)	1,500,000	0.10	0.15	0.45	0.75	1.25
1981 (a)	2,000,000	0.10	0.15	0.45	0.75	1.25
1982 (a)	1,000,000	0.10	0.15	0.45	0.75	1.25
1983 (a)	2,200,000	0.10	0.15	0.45	0.75	1.25
1984 (a)	1,500,000	0.10	0.15	0.45	0.75	1.25
1985 (a)	2,000,000	0.10	0.15	0.45	0.75	1.25
1986 (a)	2,000,000	0.10	0.15	0.45	0.75	1.25
1987 (a)	2,000,000	0.10	0.15	0.45	0.75	1.25
1989 (a)	1,000,000	0.10	0.15	0.45	0.75	1.25
1990 (a)	1,500,000	0.10	0.15	0.45	0.65	1.00
1991 (a)	1,400,000	0.10	0.15	0.35	0.50	1.00
1992 (a)	800,000	0.10	0.15	0.35	0.50	1.00
1993 (a)	2,300,000	0.10	0.15	0.35	0.50	1.00
1994 (a)	1,000,000	0.10	0.15	0.30	0.50	1.00
1995 (a)	1,000,000	0.10	0.15	0.30	0.50	1.00
1996 (a)	2,700,000	0.10	0.15	0.30	0.50	1.00
1997 (a)	1,100,000	0.10	0.15	0.25	0.45	0.75
1998 (a)	1,600,000	0.10	0.15	0.25	0.45	0.75
1999 (a)	2,600,000	0.10	0.15	0.25	0.45	0.75
2000 (a)	3,000,000	0.10	0.15	0.25	0.45	0.75

KM# 3 2 FRANCS
2.70 g., Aluminum, 27 mm. **Obv:** Seated Liberty with torch and cornucopia right, date below **Rev:** Legend and island scene divide denomination

Date	Mintage	VF20	XF40	MS60	MS63	MS65
1965 (a)	1,750,000	0.10	0.25	1.00	1.50	2.50

KM# 10 2 FRANCS
2.30 g., Aluminum, 27 mm. **Obv:** Seated Liberty with torch and cornucopia right, date below, legend added flanking figure's feet **Obv. Legend:** I. E. O. M. **Rev:** Legend and island scene divide denomination

Date	Mintage	VF20	XF40	MS60	MS63	MS65
1973 (a)	400,000	0.10	0.25	0.75	1.75	3.00
1975 (a)	1,000,000	0.10	0.25	0.75	1.50	2.00
1977 (a)	1,000,000	0.10	0.25	0.75	1.50	2.00
1979 (a)	2,000,000	0.10	0.25	0.75	1.25	1.75
1982 (a)	1,000,000	0.10	0.25	0.75	1.25	1.75
1983 (a)	1,500,000	0.10	0.25	0.75	1.25	1.75
1984 (a)	1,200,000	0.10	0.25	0.75	1.25	1.75
1985 (a)	1,400,000	0.10	0.25	0.75	1.00	1.50
1986 (a)	1,500,000	0.10	0.25	0.75	1.00	1.50
1987 (a)	1,000,000	0.10	0.25	0.75	1.00	1.50
1988 (a)	500,000	0.10	0.25	0.75	1.00	1.50
1989 (a)	1,000,000	0.10	0.25	0.75	1.00	1.50
1990 (a)	1,500,000	0.10	0.25	0.75	1.00	1.50
1991 (a)	1,500,000	0.10	0.25	0.60	0.75	1.50
1992 (a)	—	0.10	0.25	0.60	1.00	1.25
1993 (a)	1,400,000	0.10	0.25	0.50	1.00	1.25
1995 (a)	1,200,000	0.10	0.20	0.40	0.75	1.25
1996 (a)	2,200,000	0.10	0.20	0.40	0.75	1.25
1997 (a)	1,300,000	0.10	0.20	0.40	0.75	1.25
1998 (a)	600,000	0.10	0.20	0.40	0.75	1.25
1999 (a)	2,800,000	0.10	0.20	0.40	0.75	1.00
2000 (a)	1,600,000	0.10	0.20	0.40	0.75	1.00

KM# 4 5 FRANCS
3.75 g., Aluminum, 31 mm. **Obv:** Seated Liberty with torch and cornucopia right, date below **Rev:** Legend and island scene divide denomination

Date	Mintage	VF20	XF40	MS60	MS63	MS65
1965 (a)	1,520,000	0.25	0.50	1.75	2.50	3.50

KM# 12 5 FRANCS
3.75 g., Aluminum, 31 mm. **Obv:** Seated Liberty with torch and cornucopia right, date below, legend added flanking figure's feet **Obv. Legend:** I. E. O. M. **Rev:** Legend and island divide denomination

Date	Mintage	VF20	XF40	MS60	MS63	MS65
1975 (a)	500,000	0.20	0.40	1.25	2.25	3.25
1977 (a)	500,000	0.20	0.40	1.25	1.75	2.25
1982 (a)	500,000	0.20	0.40	1.25	1.75	2.25
1983 (a)	800,000	0.20	0.40	1.25	1.50	2.00
1984 (a)	600,000	0.20	0.40	1.25	1.50	2.00
1985 (a)	—	0.20	0.40	1.25	1.50	2.00
1986 (a)	600,000	0.20	0.40	1.25	1.50	2.00
1987 (a)	400,000	0.20	0.40	1.00	1.25	1.75
1988 (a)	400,000	0.20	0.40	1.00	1.25	1.75
1989 (a)	—	0.20	0.40	1.00	1.25	1.75
1990 (a)	500,000	0.20	0.40	1.00	1.25	1.75
1991 (a)	700,000	0.20	0.40	1.00	1.25	1.50
1992 (a)	500,000	0.20	0.40	1.00	1.25	1.50
1993 (a)	400,000	0.20	0.35	0.50	0.75	1.25
1994 (a)	500,000	0.20	0.35	0.50	0.75	1.25
1996 (a)	100,000	0.20	0.35	0.50	0.75	1.25
1997 (a)	500,000	0.20	0.35	0.50	0.75	1.25
1998 (a)	800,000	0.20	0.35	0.50	0.75	1.25
1999 (a)	600,000	0.20	0.35	0.50	0.75	1.25
2000 (a)	900,000	—	—	0.50	0.75	1.00

KM# 5 10 FRANCS
6.00 g., Nickel, 24 mm. **Obv:** Capped head left, date below **Rev:** Native art above denomination **Edge:** Reeded

Date	Mintage	VF20	XF40	MS60	MS63	MS65
1967 (a)	1,000,000	0.50	0.75	1.85	2.75	4.75

KM# 8 10 FRANCS
6.00 g., Nickel, 24 mm. **Obv:** Capped head left, date and legend below **Obv. Legend:** I. E. O. M. **Rev:** Native art, denomination below **Edge:** Reeded

Date	Mintage	VF20	XF40	MS60	MS63	MS65
1972 (a)	300,000	0.50	0.75	2.75	3.25	4.50
1973 (a)	400,000	0.50	0.75	2.00	2.50	3.00
1975 (a)	1,000,000	0.50	0.75	1.75	2.25	2.75
1979 (a)	500,000	0.50	0.75	1.75	2.25	2.75
1982 (a)	500,000	0.50	0.75	1.75	2.25	2.75
1983 (a)	1,000,000	0.50	0.75	1.75	2.25	2.75
1984 (a)	800,000	0.50	0.75	1.75	2.25	2.75
1985 (a)	800,000	0.50	0.75	1.75	2.25	2.75
1986 (a)	800,000	0.50	0.75	1.75	2.25	2.75
1991 (a)	600,000	0.50	0.75	1.50	2.25	2.75
1992 (a)	400,000	0.50	0.75	1.25	2.25	2.75
1993 (a)	600,000	0.50	0.75	1.25	2.25	2.75
1995 (a)	500,000	0.50	0.70	1.00	1.50	2.00
1996 (a)	300,000	0.50	0.70	1.00	1.50	2.00
1997 (a)	300,000	0.50	0.70	1.00	1.50	2.00
1998 (a)	1,000,000	0.45	0.65	0.85	1.25	1.75
1999 (a)	2,000,000	0.45	0.65	0.85	1.25	1.75
2000 (a)	1,200,000	0.45	0.65	0.85	1.25	1.75

KM# 6 20 FRANCS
10.00 g., Nickel, 28.3 mm. **Obv:** Capped head left, date below **Rev:** Flowers, vanilla shoots, bread fruit **Edge:** Reeded

Date	Mintage	VF20	XF40	MS60	MS63	MS65
1967	750,000	0.75	1.25	2.75	3.75	4.50
1969	250,000	1.00	2.00	5.00	7.00	9.00
1970	500,000	0.75	1.25	2.50	3.00	3.75

KM# 9 20 FRANCS
10.00 g., Nickel, 28.3 mm. **Obv:** Capped head left, date and legend below **Obv. Legend:** I. E. O. M. **Rev:** Flowers, vanilla shoots, bread fruit **Edge:** Reeded

Date	Mintage	VF20	XF40	MS60	MS63	MS65
1972 (a)	300,000	0.50	1.00	3.00	4.00	5.50
1973 (a)	300,000	0.50	1.00	2.75	3.50	4.50
1975 (a)	700,000	0.50	1.00	2.25	2.75	3.50
1977 (a)	350,000	0.75	1.50	4.50	5.50	7.50
1979 (a)	500,000	0.50	1.00	2.25	2.75	3.50
1983 (a)	800,000	0.50	1.00	2.25	2.75	3.50
1984 (a)	600,000	0.50	1.00	2.25	2.75	3.50
1986 (a)	400,000	0.50	1.00	2.25	2.75	3.00
1988 (a)	250,000	0.50	1.00	2.25	2.75	3.00
1991 (a)	500,000	0.50	1.00	2.00	2.50	3.00
1992 (a)	250,000	0.50	1.00	2.00	2.50	3.00
1993 (a)	120,000	0.50	1.00	1.75	2.00	2.50
1995 (a)	260,000	0.50	1.00	1.75	2.00	2.50
1996 (a)	220,000	0.50	0.85	1.50	1.75	2.25
1997 (a)	400,000	0.50	0.85	1.50	1.75	2.25
1998 (a)	400,000	0.50	0.85	1.25	1.50	2.00
1999 (a)	450,000	0.50	0.85	1.25	1.50	2.00
2000 (a)	460,000	—	—	1.00	1.25	1.75

KM# 7 50 FRANCS
15.00 g., Nickel, 33 mm. **Obv:** Capped head left, date below **Rev:** Denomination above Morea Harbor **Edge:** Reeded

Date	Mintage	VF20	XF40	MS60	MS63	MS65
1967 (a)	600,000	1.00	2.00	5.00	7.00	10.00

KM# 13 50 FRANCS
15.00 g., Nickel, 33 mm. **Obv:** Capped head left, date and legend below **Obv. Legend:** I. E. O. M. **Rev:** Denomination above Moorea Harbor **Edge:** Reeded

Date	Mintage	VF20	XF40	MS60	MS63	MS65
1975 (a)	500,000	0.80	1.25	4.00	5.50	7.50
1982 (a)	500,000	0.80	1.25	3.00	4.50	6.00
1985 (a)	Inc. above	0.80	1.25	3.00	4.50	6.00
1988 (a)	125,000	0.80	1.25	3.00	4.50	7.00
1991 (a)	300,000	0.80	1.25	2.50	3.50	5.00
1995 (a)	150,000	0.75	1.20	2.00	2.50	3.50
1996 (a)	60,000	0.75	1.00	1.50	2.00	2.50
1997 (a)	60,000	0.75	1.00	1.50	2.00	2.50
1998 (a)	260,000	0.75	1.00	1.50	2.00	2.50
1999 (a)	190,000	0.75	1.00	1.50	2.00	2.50
2000 (a)	170,000	—	—	1.50	2.00	2.50

KM# 14 100 FRANCS
10.00 g., Nickel-Bronze, 30 mm. **Obv:** Capped head left, date below **Rev:** Denomination above Moorea Harbor **Edge:** Reeded

Date	Mintage	VF20	XF40	MS60	MS63	MS65
1976 (a)	2,000,000	1.50	2.00	4.00	6.00	9.00
1979 (a)	150	—	—	—	—	—
1982 (a)	1,000,000	1.50	2.25	5.00	6.50	8.50
1984 (a)	500,000	1.50	2.25	4.00	6.00	8.00
1986 (a)	400,000	1.50	2.25	4.00	6.00	8.00
1987 (a)	500,000	1.50	2.25	4.00	6.00	8.00
1988 (a)	500,000	1.50	2.25	3.50	5.50	7.50
1991 (a)	—	1.50	2.25	4.25	5.75	7.50
1992 (a)	—	1.50	2.25	4.00	5.50	7.50
1995 (a)	—	1.50	2.25	3.50	4.50	6.50
1996 (a)	—	1.50	2.00	3.00	4.50	6.50
1997 (a)	—	1.50	2.00	3.00	5.00	6.00
1998 (a)	—	1.25	1.75	2.50	3.50	5.00
1999 (a)	—	—	—	2.50	3.50	5.00
2000 (a)	—	—	—	2.00	2.75	3.50

ESSAIS

Standard metals unless otherwise noted

KM#	Date	Mintage	Identification	Mkt Val
E1	1967(a)	1,700	10 Francs. Nickel. KM5.	30.00
E2	1967(a)	1,700	20 Francs. Nickel. KM6.	35.00
E3	1967(a)	1,700	50 Francs. Nickel. KM7.	40.00
E4	1976(a)	1,900	100 Francs. Nickel-Bronze. KM14.	45.00

PIEDFORT

KM#	Date	Mintage	Identification	Mkt Val
P1	1967(a)	500	10 Francs. Nickel. KM5.	40.00
P2	1967(a)	50	10 Francs. 0.950. Silver. KM5.	175
P3	1967(a)	20	10 Francs. 0.920. Gold. KM5.	1,950
P4	1967(a)	500	20 Francs. Nickel. KM6.	45.00
P5	1967(a)	50	20 Francs. 0.950. Silver. KM6.	200
P6	1967(a)	20	20 Francs. 0.920. Gold. KM6.	2,250
P7	1967(a)	500	50 Francs. Nickel. KM7.	50.00
P8	1967(a)	50	50 Francs. 0.950. Silver. KM7.	300
P9	1967(a)	20	50 Francs. 0.920. Gold. KM7.	3,500
P10	1979(a)	150	Franc. Aluminum. KM11.	200
P11	1979(a)	250	Franc. 0.925. Silver. KM11.	275
P12	1979(a)	93	Franc. 0.920. Gold. KM11.	1,350
P13	1979(a)	150	2 Francs. Aluminum. KM10.	225
P14	1979(a)	250	2 Francs. 0.925. Silver. KM10.	275
P15	1979(a)	94	2 Francs. 0.920. Gold. KM10.	1,900
P16	1979(a)	150	5 Francs. Aluminum. KM12.	225
P17	1979(a)	250	5 Francs. 0.925. Silver. KM12.	275
P18	1979(a)	95	5 Francs. 0.920. Gold. KM12.	2,950
P19	1979(a)	150	10 Francs. Nickel. KM8.	225
P20	1979(a)	250	10 Francs. 0.925. Silver. KM8.	300
P21	1979(a)	94	10 Francs. 0.920. Gold. KM8.	1,900
P22	1979(a)	150	20 Francs. Nickel. KM9.	225
P23	1979(a)	250	20 Francs. 0.925. Silver. KM9.	300
P24	1979(a)	93	20 Francs. 0.920. Gold. KM9.	3,000
P25	1979(a)	150	50 Francs. Nickel. KM13.	225
P26	1979(a)	250	50 Francs. 0.925. Silver. KM13.	400
P27	1979(a)	94	50 Francs. 0.920. Gold. KM13.	4,100
P28	1979(a)	150	100 Francs. Nickel-Bronze. KM14.	300
P29	1979(a)	350	100 Francs. 0.925. Silver. KM14.	375
P30	1979(a)	98	100 Francs. 0.920. Gold. KM14.	3,600

FDC SETS

KM#	Date	Mintage	Identification	Issue Price	Mkt Val
SS1	1965 (4)	2,200	KM1-4	—	15.00
SS2	1967 (3)	2,200	K5-7	10.00	18.00

FRENCH SOMALILAND

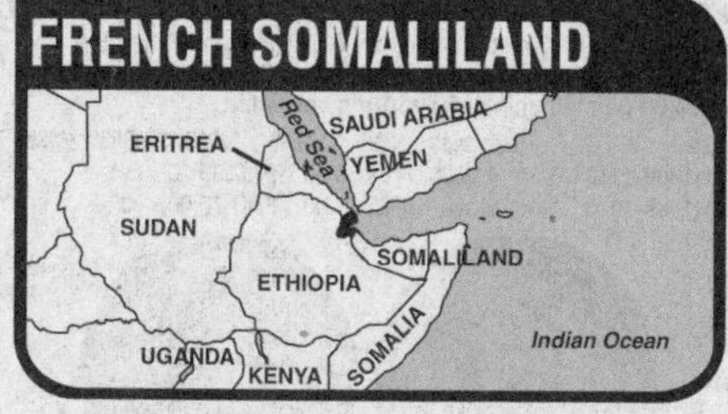

French Somaliland is located in northeast Africa at the Bab el Mandeb Strait connecting the Suez Canal and the Red Sea with the Gulf of Aden and the Indian Ocean. French interest in French Somaliland began in 1839 with concessions obtained by a French naval lieutenant from the provincial sultans. French Somaliland was made a protectorate in 1884 and its boundaries were delimited by the Franco-British and Ethiopian accords of 1887 and 1897. It became a colony in 1896 and a territory within the French Union in 1946.

NOTE: For later coinage see French Afars & Issas.

MINT MARK

(a) - Paris (privy marks only)

MONETARY SYSTEM

100 Centimes = 1 Franc

FRENCH OVERSEAS TERRITORY

DECIMAL COINAGE

KM# 4 FRANC

Aluminum **Obv:** Winged head left, date below **Rev:** Lyre antelope divides denomination

Date	Mintage	VF20	XF40	MS60	MS63	MS65
1948 (a)	200,000	12.50	25.00	45.00	90.00	—
1949 (a)	Inc. above	15.00	30.00	60.00	110	—

KM# 8 FRANC

1.30 g., Aluminum, 22.8 mm. **Obv:** Winged head left, date below **Rev:** Lyre antelope divides denomination

Date	Mintage	VF20	XF40	MS60	MS63	MS65
1959 (a)	500,000	0.50	1.50	3.00	5.00	7.00
1965 (a)	200,000	0.60	2.00	4.00	6.00	9.00

KM# 5 2 FRANCS

Aluminum **Obv:** Winged head left, date below **Rev:** Lyre antelope divides denomination

Date	Mintage	VF20	XF40	MS60	MS63	MS65
1948 (a)	200,000	12.50	25.00	60.00	80.00	—
1949 (a)	Inc. above	15.00	30.00	70.00	95.00	—

KM# 9 2 FRANCS

2.20 g., Aluminum **Obv:** Winged head left, date below **Rev:** Lyre antelope divides denomination

Date	Mintage	VF20	XF40	MS60	MS63	MS65
1959 (a)	200,000	0.75	2.50	5.00	7.00	10.00
1965 (a)	240,000	0.75	2.50	5.00	7.00	10.00

KM# 6 5 FRANCS

Aluminum **Obv:** Winged head left, date below **Rev:** Lyre antelope divides denomination

Date	Mintage	VF20	XF40	MS60	MS63	MS65
1948 (a)	500,000	10.00	25.00	45.00	85.00	—

KM# 10 5 FRANCS

3.66 g., Aluminum, 31 mm. **Obv:** Winged head left, date below **Rev:** Lyre antelope divides denomination

Date	Mintage	VF20	XF40	MS60	MS63	MS65
1959 (a)	500,000	0.75	2.50	5.50	7.50	12.00
1965 (a)	200,000	0.75	3.00	6.50	8.50	15.00

KM# 11 10 FRANCS

Aluminum-Bronze **Obv:** Winged head left, date below **Rev:** Dhow, ocean liner, denomination above

Date	Mintage	VF20	XF40	MS60	MS63	MS65
1965 (a)	250,000	1.00	3.00	6.00	8.00	14.00

KM# 7 20 FRANCS

3.96 g., Aluminum-Bronze **Obv:** Winged head left, date below **Rev:** Dhow, ocean liner, denomination above

Date	Mintage	VF20	XF40	MS60	MS63	MS65
1952 (a)	500,000	2.50	4.50	10.00	12.00	20.00

KM# 12 20 FRANCS

Aluminum-Bronze **Obv:** Winged head left, date below **Rev:** Dhow, ocean liner, denomination above

Date	Mintage	VF20	XF40	MS60	MS63	MS65
1965 (a)	200,000	2.00	4.00	8.00	10.00	18.00

ESSAIS

Standard metals unless otherwise noted

KM#	Date	Mintage	Identification	Mkt Val
E1	1948(a)	2,000	Franc. Copper-Nickel. KM4.	22.00
E2	1948(a)	2,000	2 Francs. Copper-Nickel. KM5.	25.00
E3	1948(a)	2,000	5 Francs. Copper-Nickel. KM6.	35.00
E4	1952(a)	1,200	20 Francs. Aluminum-Bronze. KM7.	29.00
E5	1965(a)	2,000	10 Francs. Aluminum-Bronze. KM11.	30.00

PIEDFORT WITH ESSAI

Standard metals unless otherwise noted

KM#	Date	Mintage	Identification	Mkt Val
PE1	1948(a)	104	Franc.	225
PE2	1948(a)	104	2 Francs.	245
PE3	1948(a)	104	5 Francs.	250
PE4	1952(a)	104	20 Francs.	230

FDC SETS

KM#	Date	Mintage	Identification	Issue Price	Mkt Val
SS1	1965 (5)	1,898	KM#8-12; Issued with French Polynesia	—	40.00

FRENCH WEST AFRICA

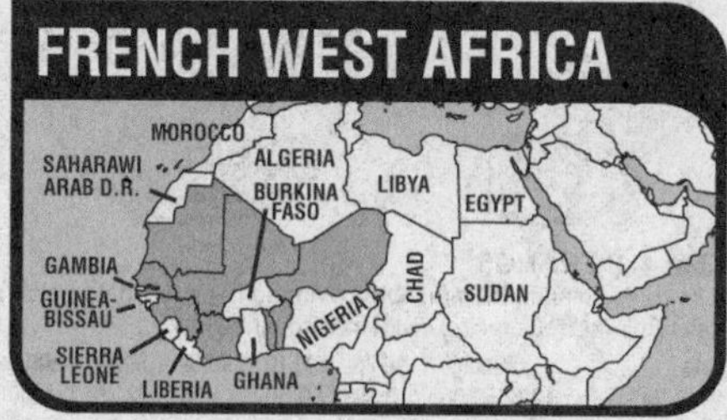

French West Africa (Afrique Occidentale Francaise), a former federation of French colonial territories on the northwest coast of Africa, had an area of 1,831,079 sq. mi. (4,742,495 sq. km.) and a population of about 17.4 million. Capital: Dakar. The constituent territories were Mauritania, Senegal, Dahomey, French Sudan, Ivory Coast, Upper Volta, Niger, French Guinea, and later on the mandated area of Togo. Peanuts, palm kernels, cacao, coffee and bananas were exported.

Prior to the mid-19th century, France, as the other European states, maintained establishments on the west coast of Africa for the purpose of trading in slaves and gum, but made no serious attempt at colonization. From 1854 onward, the coastal settlements were gradually extended into the interior until, by the opening of the 20th century, acquisition ended and organization and development began. French West Africa was formed in 1895 by grouping the several colonies under one administration (at Dakar) while retaining a large measure of autonomy to each of the constituent territories. The inhabitants of French West Africa were made French citizens in 1946. With the exception of French Guinea, all of the colonies voted in 1958 to become autonomous members of the new French Community. French Guinea voted to become the fully independent Republic of Guinea. The present-day independent states are members of the "Union Monetaire Ouest-Africaine". For later coinage see West African States.

RULERS
French

MINT MARKS
(a) - Paris, privy marks only
(L) – London

MONETARY SYSTEM
100 Centimes = 1 Franc
5 Francs = 1 Unit

FRENCH COLONIES

COLONIAL COINAGE

KM# 1 50 CENTIMES
Aluminum-Bronze, 18 mm. **Obv:** Laureate head left **Rev:** Cornucopias flank denomination and date

Date	Mintage	VF20	XF40	MS60	MS63	MS65
1944 (L)	10,000,000	4.00	8.00	16.00	27.00	50.00
1944 (L)	—	PF63 300				

KM# 2 FRANC
Aluminum-Bronze, 23 mm. **Obv:** Laureate head left **Rev:** Cornucopias flank denomination and date

Date	Mintage	VF20	XF40	MS60	MS63	MS65
1944 (L)	15,000,000	2.00	7.00	15.00	25.00	45.00
1944 (L)	—	PF63 350				

KM# 3 FRANC
Aluminum, 23 mm. **Obv:** Winged head left, date below **Rev:** Rhim gazelle facing divides denomination

Date	Mintage	VF20	XF40	MS60	MS63	MS65
1948 (a)	30,110,000	0.20	2.00	4.00	5.00	7.00
1955 (a)	5,200,000	0.35	1.00	3.00	4.00	6.00

KM# 4 2 FRANCS
2.24 g., Aluminum, 27 mm. **Obv:** Winged head left, date below **Rev:** Rhim gazelle facing divides denomination

Date	Mintage	VF20	XF40	MS60	MS63	MS65
1948 (a)	12,665,000	0.30	0.50	1.75	2.75	5.00
1955 (a)	1,400,000	0.40	5.00	10.00	15.00	25.00

KM# 5 5 FRANCS
Aluminum-Bronze, 19 mm. **Obv:** Head left divides date above **Rev:** Rhim gazelle facing, divides denomination

Date	Mintage	VF20	XF40	MS60	MS63	MS65
1956 (a)	85,000,000	0.50	1.00	2.50	5.00	7.00

KM# 6 10 FRANCS
Aluminum-Bronze, 23.5 mm. **Obv:** Head left, divides date above **Rev:** Rhim gazelle facing divides denomination

Date	Mintage	VF20	XF40	MS60	MS63	MS65
1956 (a)	20,000,000	1.00	1.50	3.50	6.00	9.00

KM# 8 10 FRANCS
3.92 g., Aluminum-Bronze, 23.9 mm. **Obv:** Fish divides denomination **Rev:** Rhim gazelle facing, date below **Note:** Issued for circulation in French West Africa, including Togo.

Date	Mintage	VF20	XF40	MS60	MS63	MS65
1957 (a)	30,000,000	1.00	1.50	3.00	5.00	7.00

KM# 7 25 FRANCS
Aluminum-Bronze, 27 mm. **Obv:** Head left divides date above **Rev:** Rhim gazelle facing, divides denomination

Date	Mintage	VF20	XF40	MS60	MS63	MS65
1956 (a)	37,877,000	1.00	2.00	5.50	8.00	12.00

KM# 9 25 FRANCS
Aluminum-Bronze, 27 mm. **Obv:** Fish divides denomination **Rev:** Rhim gazelle facing, date below **Note:** Also issued for circulation in Togo

Date	Mintage	VF20	XF40	MS60	MS63	MS65
1957 (a)	30,000,000	1.00	2.00	5.00	7.00	10.00

ESSAIS

Standard metals unless otherwise noted

KM#	Date	Mintage	Identification	Mkt Val
E1	1948(a)	2,000	Franc. Copper-Nickel. KM3.	35.00
E2	1948	2,000	2 Francs. Copper-Nickel. KM4.	40.00
E3	1956(a)	2,300	5 Francs. Aluminum-Bronze. KM5.	26.00
E4	1956(a)	2,300	10 Francs. Aluminum-Bronze. KM6.	30.00
E5	1956(a)	2,300	25 Francs. Aluminum-Bronze. KM7.	32.00
E6	1957(a)	—	10 Francs. Aluminum-Bronze. KM8.	30.00
E7	1957(a)	—	25 Francs. Aluminum-Bronze. KM9.	32.00

PIEDFORT WITH ESSAI

Double thickness -
Standard metals unless otherwise noted

KM#	Date	Mintage	Identification	Mkt Val
PE1	1948(a)	104	Franc. Aluminum. KM3.	200
PE2	1948(a)	104	2 Francs. Aluminum. KM4.	225

FUJAIRAH

An original member of the United Arab Emirates, Fujairah is the only emirate that does not have territory on the Persian Gulf. It is on the eastern side of the "horn" of Oman. It has an estimated area of 450 sq. mi. (1200 sq. km.) and a population of 27,000. Fujairah has been, historically a frequent rival of Sharjah. As recently as 1952 Great Britain recognized Fujairah as an autonomous state.

TITLES

الفجيرة

al Fujaira(t)

RULERS
Muhammad bin Hamad al-Sharqi, 1952-74
Hamad bin Muhammad al-Sharqi, 1974--

EMIRATE

NON-CIRCULATING LEGAL TENDER COINAGE

KM# 1 RIYAL
3.00 g., 1.000 Silver 0.0965 oz. ASW **Ruler:** Muhammad bin Hamad al-Sharqi **Subject:** Desert Fort **Obv:** Arms-flags above rifles on pointed shield **Rev:** Arms below fort

Date	Mintage	VF20	XF40	MS60	MS63	MS65
AH1388-1969	4,050	PF65 50.00	PF67 65.00			
AH1389-1970	Inc. above	PF65 55.00	PF67 70.00			

KM# 2 2 RIYALS
6.00 g., 1.000 Silver 0.1929 oz. ASW **Ruler:** Muhammad bin Hamad al-Sharqi **Subject:** President Richard Nixon **Obv:** Arms-flags above rifles on pointed shield **Rev:** Head 3/4 right

Date	Mintage	VF20	XF40	MS60	MS63	MS65
AH1388-1969	6,250	PF65 45.00	PF67 60.00			
AH1389-1970	Inc. above	PF65 50.00	PF67 65.00			

KM# 3 5 RIYALS
15.00 g., 1.000 Silver 0.4823 oz. ASW **Ruler:** Muhammad bin Hamad al-Sharqi **Series:** 1972 Munich Olympics **Obv:** Arms-flags above rifles on pointed shield **Rev:** Olympic rings, logo and torch

Date	Mintage	VF20	XF40	MS60	MS63	MS65
AH1388-1969	3,550	PF65 145	PF67 165			
AH1389-1970	1,300	PF65 175	PF67 200			

KM# 4.1 10 RIYALS

30.00 g., 1.000 Silver 0.9645 oz. ASW, 45 mm. **Ruler:** Muhammad bin Hamad al-Sharqi **Subject:** Apollo XI **Obv:** Arms, fineness in oval at lower left, mintage figure at lower right **Rev:** Astronauts, moon and stars, dates at upper left

Date	Mintage	VF20	XF40	MS60	MS63	MS65
AH1388-1969	14,000	PF65 95.00	PF67 135			

KM# 4.2 10 RIYALS

30.00 g., 1.000 Silver 0.9645 oz. ASW, 45 mm. **Ruler:** Muhammad bin Hamad al-Sharqi **Obv:** Arms, mintage figure stamped at lower left, fineness in oval at lower right **Rev:** Astronauts, moon and stars, dates upper left

Date	Mintage	VF20	XF40	MS60	MS63	MS65
AH1389-1969	—	PF65 95.00	PF67 135			

KM# 5 10 RIYALS

30.00 g., 1.000 Silver 0.9645 oz. ASW, 45 mm. **Ruler:** Muhammad bin Hamad al-Sharqi **Subject:** Apollo XII **Obv:** Arms **Rev:** Four shields on moon background at left, astronauts aligned on large shield at right

Date	Mintage	VF20	XF40	MS60	MS63	MS65
AH1388-1969	15,000	PF65 95.00	PF67 135			
AH1389-1970	15,000	PF65 95.00	PF67 135			

KM# 19 10 RIYALS

30.00 g., 1.000 Silver 0.9645 oz. ASW, 45 mm. **Ruler:** Muhammad bin Hamad al-Sharqi **Subject:** Apollo XIII **Obv:** Arms **Rev:** Five shields at left, Arab riders and sun at right

Date	Mintage	VF20	XF40	MS60	MS63	MS65
AH1389-1969	15,000	PF65 120	PF67 170			

KM# 20 10 RIYALS

30.00 g., 1.000 Silver 0.9645 oz. ASW **Ruler:** Muhammad bin Hamad al-Sharqi **Subject:** Visit of Pope Paul VI to Philippines **Obv:** Arms-flags above rifles on pointed shield **Rev:** Buildings, Pope's profile at right

Date	Mintage	VF20	XF40	MS60	MS63	MS65
AH1389-1969	300	PF65 200	PF67 250			

KM# 21 10 RIYALS

30.00 g., 1.000 Silver 0.9645 oz. ASW **Ruler:** Muhammad bin Hamad al-Sharqi **Subject:** Visit of Pope Paul VI to Australia **Obv:** Arms-flags above rifles on pointed shield **Rev:** Pope's profile at left, crown with keys and kangaroo on map at right

Date	Mintage	VF20	XF40	MS60	MS63	MS65
AH1389-1969	12,000	PF65 165	PF67 215			

KM# 22 10 RIYALS

30.00 g., 1.000 Silver 0.9645 oz. ASW, 45 mm. **Ruler:** Muhammad bin Hamad al-Sharqi **Subject:** Apollo XIV **Obv:** Arms-flags above rifles on pointed shield **Rev:** Moon above shooting star within ring, planet lower left

Date	Mintage	VF20	XF40	MS60	MS63	MS65
AH1389-1969	14,000	PF65 135	PF67 185			

KM# 7 25 RIYALS

5.18 g., 0.900 Gold 0.1499 oz. AGW **Ruler:** Muhammad bin Hamad al-Sharqi **Subject:** U.S. President Richard Nixon **Obv:** Arms-flags above rifles on pointed shield **Rev:** Head 3/4 right

Date	Mintage	VF20	XF40	MS60	MS63	MS65
AH1388-1969	3,280	PF65 350	PF67 400			
Note: Fineness incuse						
AH1389-1970	Inc. above	PF65 350	PF67 400			
Note: Fineness both raised and incuse						

KM# 8 50 RIYALS

10.36 g., 0.900 Gold 0.2998 oz. AGW **Ruler:** Muhammad bin Hamad al-Sharqi **Series:** 1972 Munich Olympics **Obv:** Arms-flags above rifles on pointed shield **Rev:** Olympic logo and symbols with date

Date	Mintage	VF20	XF40	MS60	MS63	MS65
AH1388-1969	1,230	PF65 675	PF67 725			
AH1389-1970	400	PF65 700	PF67 750			

KM# 9 100 RIYALS

20.73 g., 0.900 Gold 0.5998 oz. AGW **Ruler:** Muhammad bin Hamad al-Sharqi **Subject:** Apollo X **Obv:** Arms-flags above rifles on pointed shield **Rev:** Three astronauts and moon

Date	Mintage	VF20	XF40	MS60	MS63	MS65
AH1388-1969	2,140	PF65 1,350	PF67 1,450			

KM# 10 100 RIYALS
20.73 g., 0.900 Gold 0.5998 oz. AGW **Ruler:** Muhammad bin Hamad al-Sharqi **Subject:** Apollo XII **Obv:** Arms-flags above rifles on pointed shield **Rev:** Four shields on moon surface at left, three astronauts on shield at right

Date	Mintage	VF20	XF40	MS60	MS63	MS65
AH1388-1969	3,040	PF65 1,350	PF67 1,450			
AH1389-1970	—	PF65 1,350	PF67 1,450			

KM# 23 100 RIYALS
20.73 g., 0.900 Gold 0.5998 oz. AGW **Ruler:** Muhammad bin Hamad al-Sharqi **Subject:** Apollo XIII **Obv:** Arms-flags above rifles on pointed shield **Rev:** Five shields at left, Arab riders and sun at right

Date	Mintage	VF20	XF40	MS60	MS63	MS65
AH1389-1970	600	PF65 1,350	PF67 1,450			

KM# 24 100 RIYALS
20.73 g., 0.900 Gold 0.5998 oz. AGW **Ruler:** Muhammad bin Hamad al-Sharqi **Subject:** Visit of Pope Paul VI to Philippines **Obv:** Arms-flags above rifles on pointed shield **Rev:** Buildings, Pope's profile at right

Date	Mintage	VF20	XF40	MS60	MS63	MS65
AH1389-1970	290	PF65 1,400	PF67 1,500			

KM# 26 100 RIYALS
20.73 g., 0.900 Gold 0.5998 oz. AGW **Ruler:** Muhammad bin Hamad al-Sharqi **Subject:** Visit of Pope Paul VI to Australia **Obv:** Arms-flags above rifles on pointed shield **Rev:** Pope's profile at left, crown with keys and kangaroo on map at right

Date	Mintage	VF20	XF40	MS60	MS63	MS65
AH1389-1970	250	PF65 1,500	PF67 1,600			

KM# 25 100 RIYALS
20.73 g., 0.900 Gold 0.5998 oz. AGW **Ruler:** Muhammad bin Hamad al-Sharqi **Subject:** Apollo XIV **Obv:** Arms-flags above rifles on pointed shield **Rev:** Moon above shooting star within ring, planet lower left

Date	Mintage	VF20	XF40	MS60	MS63	MS65
AH1389-1971	550	PF65 1,350	PF67 1,450			

KM# 11 200 RIYALS
41.46 g., 0.900 Gold 1.1997 oz. AGW **Ruler:** Muhammad bin Hamad al-Sharqi **Subject:** Mohamad bin Hamad al-Sharqi **Obv:** Arms-flags above rifles on pointed shield **Rev:** Bust left

Date	Mintage	VF20	XF40	MS60	MS63	MS65
AH1388-1969	680	PF65 2,800	PF67 2,900			

Note: Serially numbered on the obverse

PROOF SETS

KM#	Date	Mintage	Identification	Issue Price	Mkt Val
PS4	1969 (8)	—	KM#1-3, 4.2, 7-9, 11	—	5,550
PS5	1969 (5)	2,550	KM#1-3, 4.2, 5	40.00	450
PS6	1969 (5)	5,000	KM#7-11	280	6,550
PS7	1969 (4)	—	KM#1-3, 4.2	—	350
PS8	1970 (5)	200	KM#1-3, 4.2, 5	40.00	315

GABON

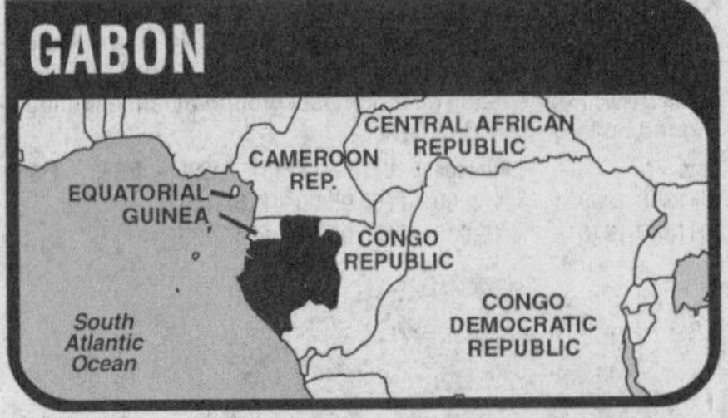

The Gabonese Republic, a member of the French Community, straddles the equator on the west coast of Africa. The hot and humid rain forest country has an area of 103,347 sq. mi. (267,670 sq. km.) and a population of 1.2 million, almost all of Bantu origin. Capital: Libreville. Extravagantly rich in resources, Gabon exports crude oil, manganese ore, gold and timbers.

Gabon was first visited by Portuguese navigator Diego Cam in the 15th century. Dutch, French and British traders, lured by the rich stands of hard woods and oil palms, quickly followed. The French founded their first settlement on the left bank of the Gabon River in 1839 and established their presence by signing treaties with the tribal chiefs. After gradually extending their influence into the interior during the last half of the 19th century, France occupied Gabon in 1885 and, in 1910, organized it as one of the four territories of French Equatorial Africa. It became an autonomous republic within the French Union in 1946, and on Aug. 17, 1960, became a completely independent republic within the new French Community.

For earlier coinage see French Equatorial Africa, Central African States and the Equatorial African States.

MINT MARKS
(a) - Paris, privy marks only
(t) - Poissy, privy marks only, thunderbolt

FRENCH EQUATORIAL AFRICAN TERRITORY

TOKEN COINAGE

Believed to be initially used for payment of taxes. These tokens do not show a denomination, but circulated until 1930 with varying values corresponding to the animals shown. All have center hole.

KM# Tn1 NON-DENOMINATED
Aluminum **Obv:** Date below center hole, "GABON" above **Rev:** Hole within elephant walking left

Date	Mintage	F12	VF20	XF40	MS60	MS63
1925 (t)	—	75.00	150	300	700	1,500

KM# Tn2 NON-DENOMINATED
Aluminum **Obv:** Date below center hole, "GABON" above **Rev:** Center hole within leopard walking left

Date	Mintage	F12	VF20	XF40	MS60	MS63
1926	—	120	200	350	750	1,650

KM# Tn3 NON-DENOMINATED
Aluminum **Obv:** Date below center hole, "GABON" above **Rev:** Center hole within ox head facing

Date	Mintage	F12	VF20	XF40	MS60	MS63
1927 (t)	—	100	175	275	600	1,250

KM# Tn4 NON-DENOMINATED
Aluminum **Obv:** Date below center hole, "GABON" above **Rev:** Center hole within pelican right

Date	Mintage	F12	VF20	XF40	MS60	MS63
1928	—	150	250	400	750	1,650

KM# Tn5 NON-DENOMINATED
Aluminum **Obv:** "Gabon" above center hole, date below **Rev:** Rhinoceros walking left

Date	Mintage	F12	VF20	XF40	MS60	MS63
1929	—	—	3,000	4,000	—	—

REPUBLIC

DECIMAL COINAGE

KM# 1 10 FRANCS
4.20 g., 0.900 Gold 0.1215 oz. AGW **Subject:** Independence **Obv:** Head of Mba right, date below **Rev:** Arms with supporters, denomination below

Date	Mintage	VF20	XF40	MS60	MS63	MS65
1960	500	PF65 225	PF67 250			

KM# 2 25 FRANCS
8.00 g., 0.900 Gold 0.2315 oz. AGW **Subject:** Independence **Obv:** Head of Mba right, date below **Rev:** Arms with supporters, denomination below

Date	Mintage	VF20	XF40	MS60	MS63	MS65
1960	10,000	—	—	—	—	420
1960	500	PF65 500	PF67 550			

KM# 3 50 FRANCS
16.00 g., 0.900 Gold 0.463 oz. AGW **Subject:** Independence **Obv:** Head of Mba right, date below **Rev:** Arms with supporters, denomination below

Date	Mintage	VF20	XF40	MS60	MS63	MS65
1960	500	PF65 1,100	PF67 1,200			

KM# 4 100 FRANCS
32.00 g., 0.900 Gold 0.9259 oz. AGW **Subject:** Independence **Obv:** Head of Mba right, date below **Rev:** Arms with supporters, denomination

Date	Mintage	VF20	XF40	MS60	MS63	MS65
1960	500	PF65 2,000	PF67 2,200			

KM# 12 100 FRANCS
Nickel, 25 mm. **Obv:** Three great eland left **Rev:** Denomination within circle, date below

Date	Mintage	VF20	XF40	MS60	MS63	MS65
1971 (a)	1,300,000	1.00	1.50	3.00	6.00	12.00
1972 (a)	2,000,000	1.00	1.50	3.00	6.00	12.00

KM# 13 100 FRANCS
7.00 g., Nickel, 25.5 mm. **Obv:** Three great eland left **Rev:** Denomination within circle, date below

Date	Mintage	VF20	XF40	MS60	MS63	MS65
1975 (a)	—	1.00	1.50	3.00	6.00	12.00
1977 (a)	—	1.50	2.50	4.50	9.00	18.00
1978 (a)	—	1.25	2.00	3.50	7.50	15.00
1982 (a)	—	1.00	1.50	3.00	5.00	10.00
1983 (a)	—	1.00	1.50	3.00	5.00	10.00
1984 (a)	—	1.00	1.50	3.00	5.00	10.00
1985 (a)	—	1.00	1.50	3.00	5.00	10.00

KM# 14 500 FRANCS
Copper-Nickel **Obv:** Leafy plants divide denomination and date **Rev:** Head left, inscription at right

Date	Mintage	VF20	XF40	MS60	MS63	MS65
1985 (a)	—	3.00	5.00	10.00	12.00	25.00

KM# 6 1000 FRANCS
3.50 g., 0.900 Gold 0.1013 oz. AGW **Obv:** Head of Bongo left **Rev:** Stump of okume tree, denomination below, arms above

Date	Mintage	VF20	XF40	MS60	MS63	MS65
1969	4,000	PF65 185	PF67 210			

KM# 7 3000 FRANCS
10.50 g., 0.900 Gold 0.3038 oz. AGW **Obv:** Head of Bongo left **Rev:** Arms with supporters, denomination below

Date	Mintage	VF20	XF40	MS60	MS63	MS65
1969	4,000	PF65 525	PF67 575			

KM# 8 5000 FRANCS
17.50 g., 0.900 Gold 0.5064 oz. AGW **Obv:** Head of Bongo left **Rev:** Reliquary figure of Bakota, denomination below, arms above

Date	Mintage	VF20	XF40	MS60	MS63	MS65
1969	4,000	PF65 875	PF67 950			

KM# 11 5000 FRANCS
17.50 g., 0.900 Gold 0.5064 oz. AGW **Subject:** Visit of French President Georges Pompidou **Rev:** Head left

Date	Mintage	VF20	XF40	MS60	MS63	MS65
1971	—	PF65 950	PF67 1,100			

KM# 9 10000 FRANCS
35.00 g., 0.900 Gold 1.0127 oz. AGW **Subject:** 1st Moon landing **Obv:** Head of Bongo left **Rev:** Lunar module, denomination below

Date	Mintage	VF20	XF40	MS60	MS63	MS65
1969	4,000	PF65 1,550	PF67 1,850			

KM# 10 20000 FRANCS
70.00 g., 0.900 Gold 2.0255 oz. AGW **Subject:** 1st Moon landing - Cape Kennedy **Obv:** Head of Bongo left **Rev:** Apollo XI at launching pad, denomination below

Date	Mintage	VF20	XF40	MS60	MS63	MS65
1969	4,000	PF65 3,150	PF67 3,600			

ESSAIS

Standard metals unless otherwise noted

KM#	Date	Mintage	Identification	Mkt Val
E1	1960	10	25 Francs. Gold. KM2.	2,200
E2	1960	—	25 Francs. Silver. KM2.	250
E3	1971(a)	1,450	100 Francs. KM12.	50.00
E4	1971(a)	4	100 Francs. Gold. KM12.	2,500
E5	1971(a)	—	5000 Francs. Copper-Aluminum-Nickel. KM11.	250
E6	1975(a)	1,700	100 Francs. Three great eland left. Denomination within circle, date below. KM13.	40.00
E7	1985(a)	1,700	500 Francs. Plants divide denomination and date. Head left, inscription at right. KM14.	50.00

PROOF SETS

KM#	Date	Mintage	Identification	Issue Price	Mkt Val
PS1	1960 (4)	500	KM1-4	—	3,850
PS2	1969 (5)	4,000	KM6-10	—	6,850

GAMBIA

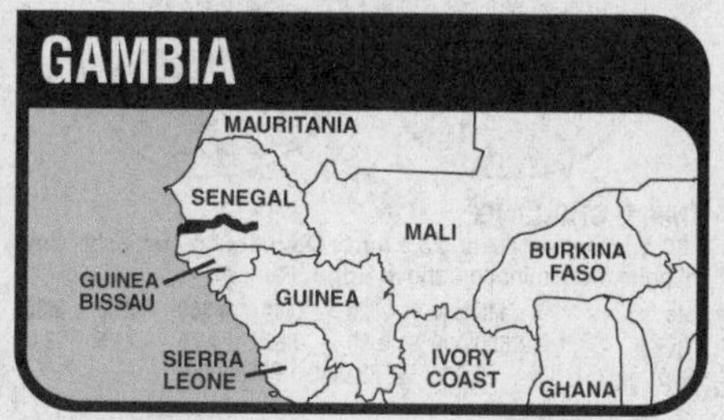

The Republic of The Gambia, occupies a strip of land 7 miles (11km.) to 20 miles (32 km.) wide and 200 miles (322 km.) long encompassing both sides of West Africa's Gambia River, and completely surrounded by Senegal. The republic, one of Africa's smallest countries, has an area of 4,127 sq. mi. (11,300 sq. km.) and a population of 989,273. Capital: Banjul. Agriculture and tourism are the principal industries. Peanuts constitute 95 per cent of export earnings.

The Gambia was once part of the great empires of Ghana and Songhay. When Portuguese gold seekers and slave traders visited The Gambia in the 15th century, it was part of the Kingdom of Mali. In 1588 the territory became, through purchase, the first British colony in Africa. English slavers established Fort James, the first settlement, on a small island a dozen miles up the Gambia River in 1664. After alternate periods of union with Sierra Leone and existence as a separate colony The Gambia became a British colony in 1888. On Feb. 18, 1965, The Gambia achieved independence as a constitutional monarchy within the Commonwealth of Nations, with Elizabeth II as Head of State as Queen of The Gambia. It became a republic on April 24, 1970, remaining a member of the Commonwealth, but with the president as Chief of State and Head of Government.

Together with Senegal, The Gambia formed a confederation on February 1, 1982. This confederation was officially dissolved on September 21, 1989. In July, 1994 a military junta took control of The Gambia and disbanded its elected government.

For earlier coinage see British West Africa.

RULER
British until 1970

COLONIAL

STERLING COINAGE

12 Pence = 1 Shilling

KM# 1 PENNY
Bronze, 25.5 mm. **Obv:** Young bust right **Rev:** Sailing vessel, denomination at right **Edge:** Smooth

Date	Mintage	VF20	XF40	MS60	MS63	MS65
1966	3,600,000	0.20	0.40	0.75	1.00	1.50
1966	6,600	PF63 1.00	PF65 1.50			

KM# 2 3 PENCE
Nickel-Brass, 21.5 mm. **Obv:** Young bust right **Rev:** Double-spurred francolin, denomination above **Edge:** Smooth

Date	Mintage	VF20	XF40	MS60	MS63	MS65
1966	2,000,000	0.30	0.50	1.50	2.00	2.50
1966	6,600	PF63 1.50	PF65 2.50			

KM# 3 6 PENCE

2.77 g., Copper-Nickel, 19.5 mm. **Obv:** Young bust right **Rev:** Peanuts divide denomination **Edge:** Reeded

Date	Mintage	VF20	XF40	MS60	MS63	MS65
1966	1,500,000	0.30	0.50	1.50	2.00	2.50
1966	6,600	PF63 1.75	PF65 2.75			

KM# 4 SHILLING

5.80 g., Copper-Nickel, 23.5 mm. **Obv:** Young bust right **Rev:** Oil palm, denomination above **Edge:** Reeded

Date	Mintage	VF20	XF40	MS60	MS63	MS65
1966	2,500,000	0.50	0.80	1.75	2.25	3.00
1966	6,600	PF63 2.00	PF65 3.00			

KM# 5 2 SHILLINGS

Copper-Nickel, 28.3 mm. **Obv:** Young bust right **Rev:** African domestic ox divides denomination **Edge:** Reeded

Date	Mintage	VF20	XF40	MS60	MS63	MS65
1966	1,600,000	0.75	1.50	2.50	3.00	4.00
1966	6,600	PF63 2.50	PF65 3.50			

KM# 6 4 SHILLINGS

Copper-Nickel, 34 mm. **Obv:** Young bust right **Rev:** Slender-snouted crocodile, denomination at right **Edge:** Reeded

Date	Mintage	VF20	XF40	MS60	MS63	MS65
1966	800,000	1.50	2.50	3.50	5.50	9.00
1966	6,600	PF63 10.00	PF65 12.00			

KM# 7 8 SHILLINGS

Copper-Nickel, 41 mm. **Obv:** Young bust right **Rev:** Hippopotamus, denomination above

Date	Mintage	VF20	XF40	MS60	MS63	MS65
1970	25,000	2.00	4.00	8.00	12.00	16.00

KM# 7a 8 SHILLINGS

32.40 g., 0.925 Silver 0.9636 oz. ASW **Obv:** Young bust right **Rev:** Hippopotamus, denomination above

Date	Mintage	VF20	XF40	MS60	MS63	MS65
1970	4,500	PF63 25.00	PF65 40.00			

Note: VIP issued proofs have a frosted relief, value: $175.

REPUBLIC

DECIMAL COINAGE

100 Bututs = 1 Dalasi

KM# 8 BUTUT

1.80 g., Bronze, 17.15 mm. **Obv:** President's bust left **Rev:** Peanuts, denomination at right

Date	Mintage	VF20	XF40	MS60	MS63	MS65
1971	12,449,000	—	0.10	0.20	0.30	0.50
1971	32,000	PF65 0.50				
1973	3,000,000	—	0.10	0.25	0.35	0.60
1974	19,060,000	0.25	0.50	0.75	1.25	2.00

KM# 14 BUTUT

1.80 g., Bronze, 17.15 mm. **Series:** F.A.O. **Obv:** President's bust left **Rev:** Peanuts, denomination at right

Date	Mintage	VF20	XF40	MS60	MS63	MS65
1974	26,062,000	—	0.10	0.20	0.30	0.50
1985	4,500,000	—	0.15	0.25	0.35	0.60

KM# 54 BUTUT

Copper Plated Steel, 17.6 mm. **Obv:** National arms, date below **Rev:** Peanuts, denomination at right

Date	Mintage	VF20	XF40	MS60	MS63	MS65
1998	—	—	—	0.20	0.30	0.50

KM# 9 5 BUTUTS

3.55 g., Bronze, 20.3 mm. **Obv:** President's bust left **Rev:** Sailing vessel, denomination at right

Date	Mintage	VF20	XF40	MS60	MS63	MS65
1971	5,400,000	—	0.10	0.35	0.50	0.75
1971	32,000	PF65 0.60				

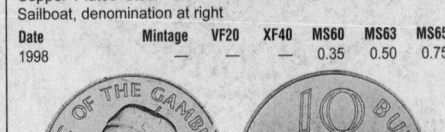

KM# 55 5 BUTUTS

Copper Plated Steel **Obv:** National arms, date below **Rev:** Sailboat, denomination at right

Date	Mintage	VF20	XF40	MS60	MS63	MS65
1998	—	—	—	0.35	0.50	0.75

KM# 10 10 BUTUTS

6.20 g., Nickel-Brass, 25.9 mm. **Obv:** President's bust left **Rev:** Double-spurred francolin, denomination at right

Date	Mintage	VF20	XF40	MS60	MS63	MS65
1971	3,000,000	0.15	0.35	0.75	1.25	2.00
1971	32,000	PF65 2.00				

KM# 64 10 BUTUTS

24.70 g., Copper-Nickel, 38.5 mm. **Subject:** Marine Life Protection **Obv:** National arms **Rev:** Multicolor fish scene **Edge:** Reeded

Date	Mintage	VF20	XF40	MS60	MS63	MS65
1997	—	—	—	—	—	27.50

KM# 56 10 BUTUTS

Brass Plated Steel, 26 mm. **Obv:** National arms, date below **Rev:** Double-spurred francolin, denomination at right

Date	Mintage	VF20	XF40	MS60	MS63	MS65
1998	—	—	—	0.75	1.00	1.50

KM# 11 25 BUTUTS

5.65 g., Copper-Nickel, 23.6 mm. **Obv:** President's bust left **Rev:** Oil palm, denomination above

Date	Mintage	VF20	XF40	MS60	MS63	MS65
1971	3,040,000	0.15	0.30	0.50	0.75	1.00
1971	32,000	PF65 1.25				

KM# 57 25 BUTUTS

4.97 g., Copper-Nickel, 23.9 mm. **Obv:** National arms, date below **Rev:** Oil palm, denomination above

Date	Mintage	VF20	XF40	MS60	MS63	MS65
1998	—	—	—	0.75	1.00	1.25

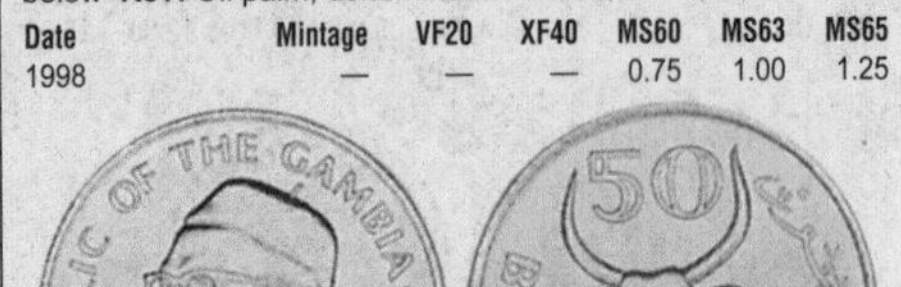

KM# 12 50 BUTUTS

11.30 g., Copper-Nickel, 28.5 mm. **Obv:** President's bust left **Rev:** African domestic ox divides denomination

Date	Mintage	VF20	XF40	MS60	MS63	MS65
1971	1,700,000	0.35	0.65	1.25	1.75	2.50
1971	32,000	PF65 1.75				

KM# 60 50 BUTUTS

24.97 g., 0.980 Silver 0.7867 oz. ASW **Subject:** Marine Life Protection **Obv:** National arms, date and denomination below **Rev:** Pair of multicolor fish

Date	Mintage	VF20	XF40	MS60	MS63	MS65
1997	—	PF65 25.00				

KM# 58 50 BUTUTS

9.84 g., Nickel Plated Steel, 28.8 mm. **Obv:** National arms date below **Rev:** African domestic ox divides denomination

Date	Mintage	VF20	XF40	MS60	MS63	MS65
1998	—	—	—	1.00	1.50	2.00

KM# 62 2000 BUTUTS

28.28 g., 0.925 Silver 0.841 oz. ASW, 38.6 mm. **Subject:** Millennium **Obv:** National arms, dates below **Rev:** Gambian map on radiant sun, denomination below **Edge:** Reeded **Shape:** 10-sided **Note:** Struck at British Royal Mint.

Date	Mintage	VF20	XF40	MS60	MS63	MS65
ND-1999	—	PF63 25.00	PF65 35.00			

KM# 13 DALASI

Copper-Nickel **Obv:** President's bust left **Rev:** Slender-snouted crocodile, denomination at right

Date	Mintage	VF20	XF40	MS60	MS63	MS65
1971	1,300,000	2.00	3.50	5.00	7.00	10.00
1971	32,000	PF65 5.00				

KM# 29 DALASI

12.20 g., Copper-Nickel, 30.8 mm. **Obv:** President's bust left **Rev:** Slender-snouted crocodile, denomination at right **Edge:** Reeded, smooth alternating edge **Shape:** 7-sided

Date	Mintage	VF20	XF40	MS60	MS63	MS65
1987	—	1.75	2.75	4.00	6.00	7.50

KM# 65 DALASI

28.11 g., Copper-Nickel, 38.6 mm. **Subject:** Queen Mother **Obv:** National arms, date below **Rev:** Oval portraits of George V, Edward VIII and George VI within circle, denomination below **Edge:** Reeded

Date	Mintage	VF20	XF40	MS60	MS63	MS65
1996	30,000	—	—	—	7.00	9.00

KM# 59 DALASI

8.81 g., Copper-Nickel, 28 mm. **Obv:** National arms, date below **Rev:** Slender-snouted crocodile, denomination at right **Shape:** 7-sided

Date	Mintage	VF20	XF40	MS60	MS63	MS65
1998	—	—	2.75	4.00	6.00	7.50

KM# 46 2 DALASIS

9.92 g., 0.500 Silver 0.1595 oz. ASW **Subject:** Olympic Games 1996 **Obv:** National arms, date below **Rev:** Two runners crossing a finish line, denomination at right

Date	Mintage	VF20	XF40	MS60	MS63	MS65
1996	Est. 10000	PF63 10.00	PF65 15.00			

KM# 49 2 DALASIS

Copper-Nickel **Subject:** 70th Birthday of Queen Elizabeth II **Obv:** National arms

Date	Mintage	VF20	XF40	MS60	MS63	MS65
1996	5,000	—	—	4.00	6.00	9.00

KM# 70 5 DALASIS

Copper-Nickel **Subject:** Return of Hong Kong to China

Date	Mintage	VF20	XF40	MS60	MS63	MS65
1997	—	—	—	4.00	6.00	9.00

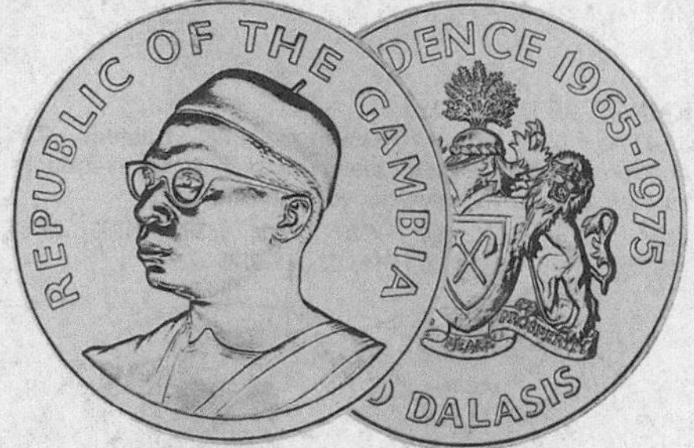

KM# 16 10 DALASIS

28.28 g., 0.500 Silver 0.4546 oz. ASW, 38.6 mm. **Subject:** 10th Anniversary of Independence **Obv:** President's bust left **Rev:** National arms, denomination below

Date	Mintage	VF20	XF40	MS60	MS63	MS65
1975	50,000	—	—	—	10.00	12.00

KM# 16a 10 DALASIS

28.28 g., 0.925 Silver 0.841 oz. ASW, 38.6 mm. **Subject:** 10th Anniversary of Independence **Obv:** President's bust left **Rev:** National arms, denomination

Date	Mintage	VF20	XF40	MS60	MS63	MS65
1975	20,000	PF63 17.00	PF65 25.00			

KM# 23 10 DALASIS

28.28 g., 0.500 Silver 0.4546 oz. ASW, 38.61 mm. **Subject:** Commonwealth Games **Obv:** President's bust left **Rev:** Hurdlers, denomination below

Date	Mintage	VF20	XF40	MS60	MS63	MS65
1986	Est. 50000	—	—	—	10.00	12.00

KM# 23a 10 DALASIS

28.28 g., 0.925 Silver 0.841 oz. ASW, 38.61 mm. **Subject:** Commonwealth Games **Obv:** President's bust left **Rev:** Hurdlers, denomination

Date	Mintage	VF20	XF40	MS60	MS63	MS65
1986	Est. 20000	PF63 15.00	PF65 25.00			

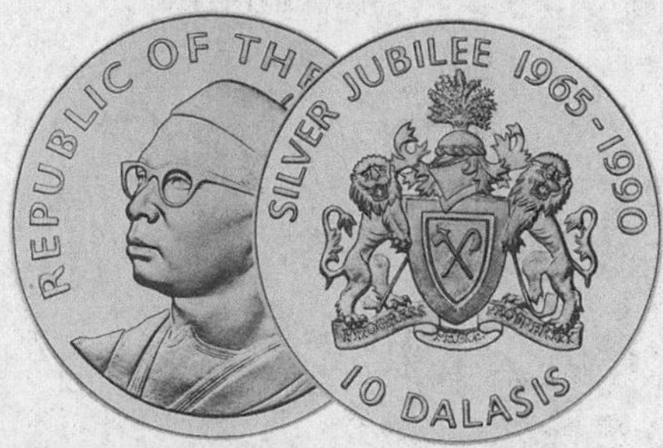

KM# 28 10 DALASIS

28.28 g., 0.925 Silver 0.841 oz. ASW **Subject:** Silver Jubilee of Independence **Obv:** President's bust left **Rev:** National arms, denomination below

Date	Mintage	VF20	XF40	MS60	MS63	MS65
1990	2,000	PF65 42.50				

KM# 30 10 DALASIS

Copper-Nickel **Subject:** Papal Visit **Obv:** National arms, denomination below **Rev:** Half-figure of Pope 3/4 facing, right arm raised

Date	Mintage	VF20	XF40	MS60	MS63	MS65
1992	—	—	—	3.00	4.00	6.00

KM# 30a 10 DALASIS

28.28 g., 0.925 Silver 0.841 oz. ASW **Subject:** Papal Visit **Obv:** National arms, denomination **Rev:** Half figure of Pope 3/4 facing with right arm raised

Date	Mintage	VF20	XF40	MS60	MS63	MS65
1992	5,000	PF63 35.00	PF65 45.00			

KM# 50 10 DALASIS

Copper-Nickel **Subject:** 70th Birthday of H.M. Queen Elizabeth II **Obv:** National arms, date **Rev:** Queen inspecting guard, denomination

Date	Mintage	VF20	XF40	MS60	MS63	MS65
1996	—	—	—	3.00	4.00	6.00

KM# 50a 10 DALASIS

28.28 g., 0.925 Silver 0.841 oz. ASW **Subject:** 70th Birthday of H.M. Queen Elizabeth II **Obv:** National arms, date below **Rev:** Queen inspecting guard, denomination divides dates

Date	Mintage	VF20	XF40	MS60	MS63	MS65
1996	70,000	PF63 17.00	PF65 25.00			

KM# 71 10 DALASIS
28.28 g., 0.925 Silver 0.841 oz. ASW partially gilt, 38.61 mm. **Subject:** Elizabeth II and Prince Philip, 50th Wedding Anniversary **Obv:** National arms **Rev:** Elizabeth in corronation robes, carriage in backgorund, gilt shield at left

Date	Mintage	VF20	XF40	MS60	MS63	MS65
1997	—	PF63 22.00	PF65 35.00			

KM# 17 20 DALASIS
28.63 g., 0.925 Silver 0.8514 oz. ASW **Subject:** Conservation **Obv:** President's bust left **Rev:** Spur-winged goose divides denomination

Date	Mintage	VF20	XF40	MS60	MS63	MS65
1977	4,302	—	—	—	20.00	25.00

KM# 17a 20 DALASIS
28.28 g., 0.925 Silver 0.841 oz. ASW **Subject:** Conservation **Obv:** President's bust left **Rev:** Spur-winged goose divides denomination

Date	Mintage	VF20	XF40	MS60	MS63	MS65
1977	4,404	PF65 28.00				

KM# 20 20 DALASIS
28.28 g., 0.925 Silver 0.841 oz. ASW **Subject:** World Food Day **Obv:** President's bust left **Rev:** Logo above field worker, denomination below

Date	Mintage	VF20	XF40	MS60	MS63	MS65
1981	10,000	—	—	—	20.00	25.00
1981	5,000	PF63 25.00	PF65 35.00			

KM# 21 20 DALASIS
28.28 g., 0.925 Silver 0.841 oz. ASW **Subject:** Year of the Scout **Obv:** President's bust in beret left **Rev:** Scout emblem above motto, denomination

Date	Mintage	VF20	XF40	MS60	MS63	MS65
1983	Est. 10000	—	—	—	20.00	25.00
1983	Inc. above	PF63 25.00	PF65 35.00			

KM# 24 20 DALASIS
28.34 g., 0.925 Silver 0.8428 oz. ASW, 38.66 mm. **Subject:** World Wildlife Fund **Obv:** Bust of President Kairaba Jawara 3/4 left **Rev:** Temminck's colobus monkey divides denomination **Edge:** Reeded

Date	Mintage	VF20	XF40	MS60	MS63	MS65
1987	Est. 25000	PF63 25.00	PF65 35.00			
1989	—	PF65 65.00				

KM# 26 20 DALASIS
28.28 g., 0.925 Silver 0.841 oz. ASW **Subject:** Save the Children Fund **Obv:** Bust of President Alhaji Sir Dawda Dairaba Jawara **Rev:** Girls playing "akara" (rythmic clapping and dancing game), denomination below

Date	Mintage	VF20	XF40	MS60	MS63	MS65
1989	Est. 20000	PF63 25.00	PF65 30.00			

KM# 32 20 DALASIS
31.47 g., 0.925 Silver 0.9359 oz. ASW **Subject:** 40th Anniversary - Coronation of Queen Elizabeth II **Obv:** President's bust left **Rev:** Royal crown above denomination

Date	Mintage	VF20	XF40	MS60	MS63	MS65
1993	Est. 10000	PF63 27.00	PF65 37.00			

KM# 33 20 DALASIS
31.26 g., 0.925 Silver 0.9297 oz. ASW **Series:** Olympics **Obv:** President's bust left **Rev:** Wrestlers, denomination below

Date	Mintage	VF20	XF40	MS60	MS63	MS65
1993	Est. 40000	PF63 18.00	PF65 20.00			

KM# 34 20 DALASIS
31.47 g., 0.925 Silver 0.9359 oz. ASW **Subject:** Prince Henry the Navigator **Obv:** President's bust left **Rev:** Ship at sea at left, 3/4 figure at right above denomination

Date	Mintage	VF20	XF40	MS60	MS63	MS65
1993	Est. 15000	PF63 18.00	PF65 20.00			

KM# 36 20 DALASIS
31.47 g., 0.925 Silver 0.9359 oz. ASW **Subject:** Rendezvous in Space **Obv:** President's bust left **Rev:** Space Shuttle at left, astronauts at right, denomination below

Date	Mintage	VF20	XF40	MS60	MS63	MS65
1993	Est. 10000	PF63 18.00	PF65 20.00			

KM# 38 20 DALASIS
31.47 g., 0.925 Silver 0.9359 oz. ASW **Subject:** Endangered Wildlife **Obv:** President's bust left **Rev:** Chimpanzee, denomination below

Date	Mintage	VF20	XF40	MS60	MS63	MS65
1993	Est. 15000	PF63 18.00	PF65 20.00			
1994	—	PF63 20.00	PF65 25.00			

KM# 35 20 DALASIS
31.47 g., 0.925 Silver 0.9359 oz. ASW **Subject:** Soccer - World Cup 1994 **Obv:** President's bust left **Rev:** Maps on globe, soccer ball and players, denomination below

Date	Mintage	VF20	XF40	MS60	MS63	MS65
1994	Est. 15000	PF63 18.00	PF65 20.00			

KM# 39 20 DALASIS
31.47 g., 0.925 Silver 0.9359 oz. ASW **Subject:** Mungo Park **Obv:** President's bust left **Rev:** Bust left at right, figures piloting raft at left, denomination above

Date	Mintage	VF20	XF40	MS60	MS63	MS65
1994	Est. 10000	PF63 18.00	PF65 20.00			

KM# 40 20 DALASIS
31.47 g., 0.925 Silver 0.9359 oz. ASW **Subject:** Elizabeth, the Queen Mother **Obv:** National arms, date below **Rev:** Busts of Edward VIII, George V and George VI facing within circles, inscription above **Rev. Inscription:** Year of the Three Kings

Date	Mintage	VF20	XF40	MS60	MS63	MS65
1994	Est. 30000	PF63 18.00	PF65 20.00			

KM# 47 20 DALASIS
31.47 g., 0.925 Silver 0.9359 oz. ASW **Subject:** Olympic Games 1996 **Obv:** National arms, date below **Rev:** Two runners crossing a finish line, denomination at right

Date	Mintage	VF20	XF40	MS60	MS63	MS65
1994	—	PF63 18.00	PF65 20.00			

KM# 37 20 DALASIS
Copper-Nickel **Subject:** 50th Anniversary - United Nations **Obv:** National arms, date below **Rev:** Dove with olive branch above UN logo, map in background, denomination below

Date	Mintage	VF20	XF40	MS60	MS63	MS65
1995	—	—	—	3.00	4.00	6.00

KM# 37a 20 DALASIS
28.28 g., 0.925 Silver 0.841 oz. ASW **Subject:** 50th Anniversary - United Nations **Obv:** National arms, date **Rev:** Dove with olive branch above logo, map in background

Date	Mintage	VF20	XF40	MS60	MS63	MS65
1995	—	PF63 16.00	PF65 20.00			

KM# 41 20 DALASIS
31.47 g., 0.925 Silver 0.9359 oz. ASW **Subject:** Protect Our World **Obv:** National arms, date below **Rev:** Nudes in forest, birds and snake in trees, denomination below

Date	Mintage	VF20	XF40	MS60	MS63	MS65
1995	Est. 10000	PF63 20.00	PF65 25.00			

KM# 42 20 DALASIS
7.78 g., 0.5833 Gold 0.1458 oz. AGW **Subject:** Endangered Wildife **Obv:** National arms, date below **Rev:** Black rhinoceros, denomination below

Date	Mintage	VF20	XF40	MS60	MS63	MS65
1995	Est. 2000	—	—	—	245	265

KM# 43 20 DALASIS
7.78 g., 0.5833 Gold 0.1458 oz. AGW **Subject:** Endangered Wildife **Obv:** National arms, date below **Rev:** African elephant, denomination below

Date	Mintage	VF20	XF40	MS60	MS63	MS65
1995	Est. 2000	—	—	—	245	265

KM# 44 20 DALASIS
31.47 g., 0.925 Silver 0.9359 oz. ASW **Subject:** Victorian Age **Obv:** National arms, date below **Rev:** Queen Victoria with first steam locomotive in background within circle, denomination below

Date	Mintage	VF20	XF40	MS60	MS63	MS65
1996	Est. 10000	—	—	—	20.00	25.00

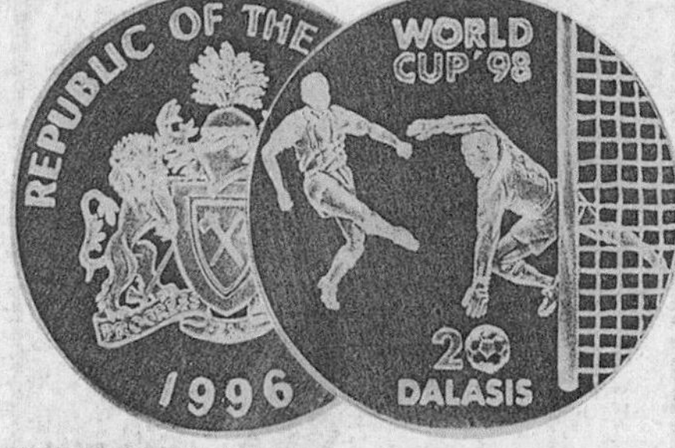

KM# 51 20 DALASIS
31.47 g., 0.999 Silver 1.0108 oz. ASW **Subject:** World Cup 1998 **Obv:** National arms, date below **Rev:** Two soccer players, denomination below

Date	Mintage	VF20	XF40	MS60	MS63	MS65
1996	10,000	PF63 20.00	PF65 25.00			

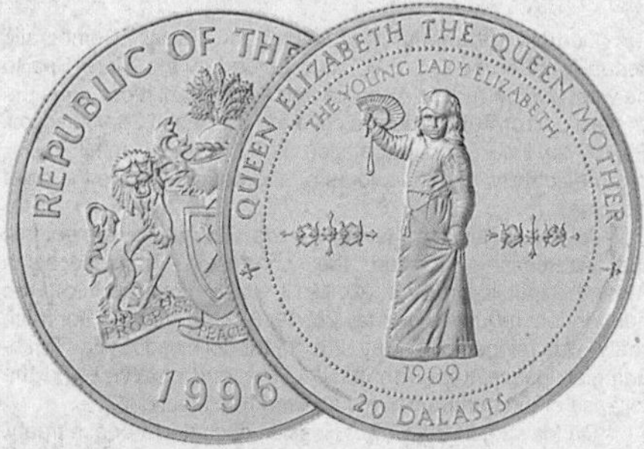

KM# 63 20 DALASIS
31.36 g., 0.925 Silver 0.9326 oz. ASW, 38.5 mm. **Subject:** British Queen Mother **Obv:** National arms, date below **Rev:** 1909 Portrait of the Queen Mother, denomination below **Edge:** Reeded

Date	Mintage	VF20	XF40	MS60	MS63	MS65
1996	—	PF63 18.00	PF65 25.00			

KM# 18 40 DALASIS
35.29 g., 0.925 Silver 1.0495 oz. ASW **Subject:** Conservation **Obv:** President's bust left **Rev:** Aardvark divides denomination

Date	Mintage	VF20	XF40	MS60	MS63	MS65
1977	4,304	—	—	22.00	25.00	28.00

KM# 18a 40 DALASIS
35.00 g., 0.925 Silver 1.0409 oz. ASW **Subject:** Conservation **Obv:** President's bust left **Rev:** Aardvark divides denomination

Date	Mintage	VF20	XF40	MS60	MS63	MS65
1977	4,183	PF65 35.00				

KM# 67 50 DALASIS
500.00 g., 0.999 Silver 16.0593 oz. ASW, 90 mm. **Rev:** Cheetah

Date	Mintage	VF20	XF40	MS60	MS63	MS65
1995	Est. 1000	PF65 450	PF67 500			

KM# 52 50 DALASIS
1.24 g., 0.999 Gold 0.040 oz. AGW **Subject:** Kankan Manga Musa **Obv:** National arms, date below **Rev:** Seated king and supplicant, denomination below

Date	Mintage	VF20	XF40	MS60	MS63	MS65
1997	—	PF65 65.00	PF67 75.00			

KM# 68 100 DALASIS
1000.00 g., 0.999 Silver 32.1186 oz. ASW, 100 mm. **Rev:** Eland

Date	Mintage	VF20	XF40	MS60	MS63	MS65
1995	Est. 1000	PF65 950	PF67 1,000			

KM# 45 100 DALASIS
1000.00 g., 0.999 Silver 32.1186 oz. ASW, 100 mm. **Subject:** Endangered Wildlife **Obv:** National arms, date below **Rev:** Lion family within circle, denomination below **Note:** Illustration reduced.

Date	Mintage	VF20	XF40	MS60	MS63	MS65
1996	1,000	PF65 750	PF67 850			

KM# 53 100 DALASIS
3.11 g., 0.5833 Gold 0.0583 oz. AGW **Series:** Olympic Games 2000 **Obv:** National arms, date below **Rev:** Silhouette of three runners, denomination below

Date	Mintage	VF20	XF40	MS60	MS63	MS65
1997	5,000	PF65 90.00	PF67 100			

KM# 61 150 DALASIS
7.78 g., 0.583 Gold 0.1458 oz. AGW **Subject:** British Year of 3 Kings and Queen Mother **Obv:** National arms, date below **Rev:** Busts of Edward VIII, George V and George VI facing within circles

Date	Mintage	VF20	XF40	MS60	MS63	MS65
1996	—	PF65 225	PF67 250			

KM# 48 200 DALASIS
31.10 g., 0.999 Gold 0.999 oz. AGW **Subject:** Endangered Wildlife **Rev:** Lion right, denomination below

Date	Mintage	VF20	XF40	MS60	MS63	MS65
1996	1,000	PF65 1,650	PF67 1,800			

KM# 22 250 DALASIS
15.98 g., 0.917 Gold 0.4711 oz. AGW **Subject:** Year of the Scout **Obv:** President's bust in beret left **Rev:** Scout emblem above motto, denomination below

Date	Mintage	VF20	XF40	MS60	MS63	MS65
1983	2,000	—	—	—	750	775
1983	2,000	PF65 800				

KM# 66 250 DALASIS
47.54 g., 0.916 Gold 1.4001 oz. AGW, 38.61 mm. **Subject:** 25th Anniversary of Statehood **Rev:** State arms

Date	Mintage	VF20	XF40	MS60	MS63	MS65
1990	Est. 50	PF67 2,400				

KM# 31 250 DALASIS
47.54 g., 0.917 Gold 1.4016 oz. AGW **Subject:** Papal Visit **Obv:** National arms **Rev:** Pope John Paul II giving a blessing

Date	Mintage	VF20	XF40	MS60	MS63	MS65
1992	100	PF67 1,350				

KM# 19 500 DALASIS
33.44 g., 0.900 Gold 0.9675 oz. AGW **Subject:** Conservation **Obv:** President's bust left **Rev:** Sitatunga divides denomination

Date	Mintage	VF20	XF40	MS60	MS63	MS65
1977	699	—	—	—	1,600	1,650
1977	285	PF65 1,700	PF67 1,800			

KM# 25 1000 DALASIS
10.00 g., 0.917 Gold 0.2948 oz. AGW **Subject:** World Wildlife Fund **Obv:** President's bust left **Rev:** Gambian puffback bird divides denomination

Date	Mintage	VF20	XF40	MS60	MS63	MS65
1987	Est. 5000	PF65 500	PF67 550			

KM# 27 1000 DALASIS
10.00 g., 0.917 Gold 0.2948 oz. AGW **Subject:** Save the Children Fund **Obv:** President's bust left

Date	Mintage	VF20	XF40	MS60	MS63	MS65
1989	Est. 3000	PF65 525	PF67 575			

KM# 69 1000 DALASIS
155.50 g., 0.999 Gold 4.9944 oz. AGW, 63 mm. **Obv:** Arms **Rev:** Lion family

Date	Mintage	VF20	XF40	MS60	MS63	MS65
1996	99	PF65 7,650	PF67 8,250			

PROOF SETS

KM#	Date	Mintage	Identification	Issue Price	Mkt Val
PS1	1966 (6)	5,100	KM1-6	13.00	17.50
PS2	1966; 1970 (7)	1,500	KM1-6, 7a	25.00	55.00
PS3	1971 (6)	26,249	KM8-13	—	11.50
PS4	1977 (2)	—	KM17a, 18a	60.00	60.00

GEORGIA

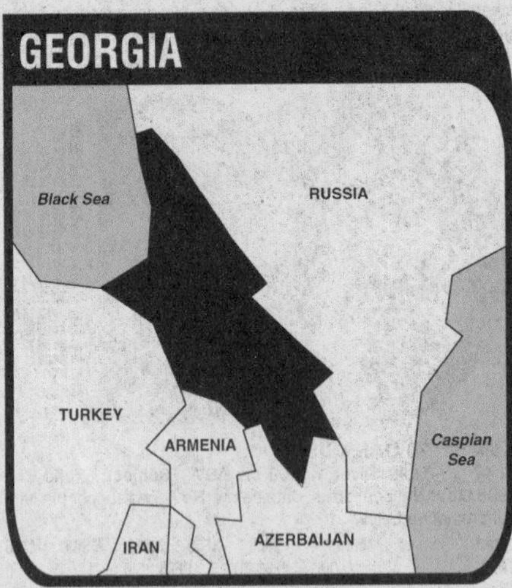

Georgia (formerly the Georgian Social Democratic Republic under the U.S.S.R.), is bounded by the Black Sea to the west and by Turkey, Armenia and Azerbaijan. It occupies the western part of Transcaucasia covering an area of 26,900 sq. mi. (69,700 sq. km.) and a population of 5.7 million. Capitol: Tbilisi. Hydro-electricity, minerals, forestry and agriculture are the chief industries.

After the Russian Revolution the Georgians, Armenians, and Azerbaijanis formed the short-lived Transcaucasian Federal Republic on Sept. 20, 1917, which broke up into three independent republics on May 26, 1918. A Germano-- Georgian treaty was signed on May 28, 1918, followed by a Turko-Georgian peace treaty on June 4. The end of WW I and the collapse of the central powers allowed free elections.

On May 20, 1920, Soviet Russia concluded a peace treaty, recognizing its independen ce, but later invaded on Feb. 11, 1921 and a soviet republic was proclaimed. On March 12, 1922 Stalin included Georgia in a newly formed Transcaucasian Soviet Federated Socialist Republic. On Dec. 5, 1936 the T.S.F.S.R. was dissolved and Georgia became a direct member of the U.S.S.R. The collapse of the U.S.S.R. allowed full transition to independence and on April 9, 1991 a unanimous vote declared the republic an independent state based on its original treaty of independence of May 1918.

INDEPENDENT STATE (C.I.S.)

STANDARD COINAGE

100 Thetri = 1 Lari

KM# 76 THETRI
1.38 g., Stainless Steel, 15 mm. **Obv:** Stylized candelabra design divides date within circle **Rev:** Denomination above grapes **Edge:** Plain

Date	Mintage	VF20	XF40	MS60	MS63	MS65
1993	—	—	—	0.25	0.35	0.50

KM# 77 2 THETRI
1.90 g., Stainless Steel, 17.5 mm. **Obv:** Stylized candelabra divides date within circle **Rev:** Stylized eagle above denomination **Edge:** Plain

Date	Mintage	VF20	XF40	MS60	MS63	MS65
1993	—	—	—	0.35	0.50	0.65

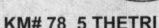

KM# 78 5 THETRI
2.50 g., Stainless Steel, 20 mm. **Obv:** Stylized candelabra divides date within circle **Rev:** Stylized lion above denomination **Edge:** Plain

Date	Mintage	VF20	XF40	MS60	MS63	MS65
1993	—	—	—	0.75	1.00	1.25

KM# 79 10 THETRI
3.00 g., Stainless Steel, 22 mm. **Obv:** Stylized candelabra divides date within circle **Rev:** St. Mamas riding lion right, denomination **Edge:** Plain

Date	Mintage	VF20	XF40	MS60	MS63	MS65
1993	—	—	—	1.25	1.50	1.75

KM# 80 20 THETRI
5.00 g., Stainless Steel, 25 mm. **Obv:** Stylized candelabra divides date within circle **Rev:** Red Deer left, denomination **Edge:** Plain

Date	Mintage	VF20	XF40	MS60	MS63	MS65
1993	—	—	—	1.50	1.75	2.00

KM# 81 50 THETRI
2.50 g., Brass, 19 mm. **Obv:** Stylized candelabra divides date within circle **Rev:** Stylized griffin left, above denomination **Edge:** Plain

Date	Mintage	VF20	XF40	MS60	MS63	MS65
1993	—	—	—	2.00	2.25	2.50

KM# 83 10 LARI
28.28 g., 0.925 Silver 0.841 oz. ASW, 38.61 mm. **Subject:** State System 3,000 Years **Obv:** Denomination within circle **Rev:** Eagle and lion within circle **Edge:** Reeded

Date	Mintage	VF20	XF40	MS60	MS63	MS65
2000	1,000	PF65 55.00	PF67 70.00			

KM# 84 10 LARI
28.28 g., 0.925 Silver 0.841 oz. ASW, 38.61 mm. **Subject:** Birth of Jesus 2,000th Anniversary **Obv:** Denomination within circle **Rev:** Christian arms within circle

Date	Mintage	VF20	XF40	MS60	MS63	MS65
2000	1,000	PF65 55.00	PF67 70.00			

KM# 85 10 LARI
10.60 g., Bi-Metallic Copper-Nickel center in Nickel-Brass ring, 26 mm. **Subject:** State System: 3000 Years **Obv:** Denomination within circle **Rev:** Eagle above lion within circle **Edge Lettering:** Reeding over incuse "GEORGIA • TEN LARI"

Date	Mintage	VF20	XF40	MS60	MS63	MS65
2000	Est. 1000	—	—	12.00	15.00	18.00

KM# 86 10 LARI
10.60 g., Bi-Metallic Copper-Nickel center in Brass ring, 25.9 mm. **Subject:** Christianity: 2000 Years **Obv:** Denomination within circle **Rev:** Christian arms within circle **Edge:** Reeding over "GEORGIA • TEN LARI"

Date	Mintage	VF20	XF40	MS60	MS63	MS65
2000	25,000	—	—	5.00	7.00	9.00

KM# 86a 10 LARI
16.00 g., 0.900 Silver 0.463 oz. ASW, 28.3 mm. **Obv:** Denomination **Rev:** Christian arms **Edge:** Reeded and lettered **Edge Lettering:** GEORGIA TEN LARI

Date	Mintage	VF20	XF40	MS60	MS63	MS65
2000	—	PF63 45.00	PF65 60.00			

KM# 87 10 LARI
28.28 g., Copper-Nickel, 38.61 mm. **Subject:** 300th Anniversary of Statehood **Obv:** Eagle above lion **Rev:** Denomination

Date	Mintage	VF20	XF40	MS60	MS63	MS65
2000	2,000	—	—	10.00	14.00	18.00

KM# 88 10 LARI
28.28 g., Copper-Nickel, 38.61 mm. **Subject:** 2000th Anniversary of the Birth of Christ

Date	Mintage	VF20	XF40	MS60	MS63	MS65
2000	2,000	—	—	10.00	14.00	18.00

KM# 82 500 LARI
17.00 g., 0.917 Gold 0.5012 oz. AGW **Subject:** 50th Anniversary - Defeat of Fascism **Obv:** Stylized candelabra divides date above denomination **Rev:** Profiles of Stalin, Roosevelt, Churchill and de Gaulle left, date below

Date	Mintage	VF20	XF40	MS60	MS63	MS65
1995	2,000	PF65 850	PF67 925			

MINT SETS

KM#	Date	Mintage	Identification	Issue Price	Mkt Val
MS1	1993 (6)	—	KM76-81	—	8.00

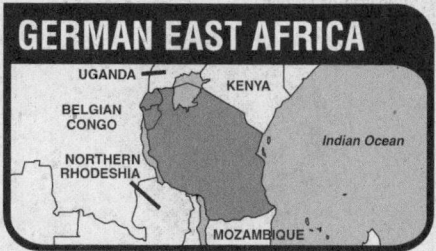

GERMAN EAST AFRICA

German East Africa (Tanganyika), located on the coast of east-central Africa between British East Africa (now Kenya) and Portuguese East Africa (now Mozambique), had an area of 362,284 sq. mi. (938,216 sq. km.) and a population of about 6 million. Capital: Dar es Salaam. Chief produ cts prior to German control were ivory and slaves; after German control, sisal, coffee, and rubber. Germany acquired control of the area by treaties with coastal chiefs in 1884, established it as a protectorate in 1891, and proclaimed it the Colony of German East Africa in 1897. After World War I, Tanganyika was entrusted to Great Britain as a League of Nations mandate, and after World War II as a United Nations trust territory. Tanganyika became an independent nation within the British Commonwealth on Dec. 9, 1961. Coins dated up until 1902 were issued by the German East Africa Company. From 1904 onwards, the government issued coins.

NOTE: For later coinage see East Africa.

RULER
Wilhelm II, 1888-1918

MINT MARKS
A - Berlin
J - Hamburg
T - Tabora

MONETARY SYSTEM
Until 1904
64 Pesa = 1 Rupie
Commencing 1904
100 Heller = 1 Rupie

COLONY

STANDARD COINAGE

German East Africa Company; 1891-1902

KM# 3 1/4 RUPIE
2.92 g., 0.917 Silver 0.086 oz. ASW **Ruler:** Wihelm II **Obv:** Armored bust left **Rev:** Shielded arms, denomination below

Date	Mintage	F12	VF20	XF40	MS60	MS63
1901	350,000	8.00	25.00	65.00	195	220

KM# 4 1/2 RUPIE
5.83 g., 0.917 Silver 0.1719 oz. ASW, 25 mm. **Ruler:** Wihelm II **Obv:** Armored bust left **Rev:** Shielded arms, denomination below **Edge:** Reeded

Date	Mintage	F12	VF20	XF40	MS60	MS63
1901	215,000	20.00	55.00	140	350	450

KM# 2 RUPIE
11.66 g., 0.917 Silver 0.3439 oz. ASW **Ruler:** Wihelm II **Obv:** Armored bust left **Rev:** Shielded arms, denomination below

Date	Mintage	F12	VF20	XF40	MS60	MS63
1901	319,000	18.00	36.00	110	210	270
1902	151,000	30.00	60.00	180	550	700

STANDARD COINAGE

After 1904

KM# 6 1/2 HELLER
Bronze **Ruler:** Wihelm II **Obv:** Crown with ribbon above date **Rev:** Denomination within wreath

Date	Mintage	F12	VF20	XF40	MS60	MS63
1904 A	1,201,000	3.00	8.00	14.00	48.00	70.00
1904 A	—	PF63 300	PF65 600			
1905 A	7,192,000	3.00	7.00	13.00	45.00	65.00
1905 J	4,000,000	3.00	7.00	13.00	45.00	65.00
1906 J	6,000,000	1.75	5.00	9.00	38.50	55.00
1906 J	—	PF63 300	PF65 600			

KM# 7 HELLER
Bronze **Ruler:** Wihelm II **Obv:** Crown with ribbon above date **Rev:** Denomination within wreath

Date	Mintage	F12	VF20	XF40	MS60	MS63
1904 A	10,256,000	1.75	6.00	9.00	46.00	70.00
1904 A	—	PF60 145	PF63 300			
1904 J	2,500,000	1.75	6.00	16.00	60.00	80.00
1905 A	3,760,000	1.75	6.00	16.00	60.00	80.00
1905 A	—	PF60 145	PF63 300			
1905 J	7,556,000	1.75	6.00	9.00	60.00	80.00
1906 A	3,004,000	1.75	6.00	16.00	60.00	90.00
1906 A	—	PF60 230	PF63 550			
1906 J	1,962,000	1.75	6.00	16.00	70.00	115
1907 J	17,790,000	1.75	3.50	9.00	46.00	60.00
1907 J	—	PF60 175	PF63 350	PF65 700		
1908 J	12,205,000	1.75	3.50	9.00	46.00	60.00

Date	Mintage	F12	VF20	XF40	MS60	MS63
1908 J	—	PF60 155	PF63 325			
1909 J	1,698,000	6.00	17.00	34.50	80.00	115
1909 J	—	PF60 155	PF63 325			
1910 J	5,096,000	1.75	3.50	9.00	46.00	60.00
1910 J	—	PF60 155	PF63 325			
1911 J	6,420,000	1.75	3.50	9.00	46.00	60.00
1911 J	—	PF60 155	PF63 325			
1912 J	7,012,000	1.75	3.50	9.00	60.00	90.00
1912 J	—	PF60 155	PF63 325			
1913 A	—	1.75	3.50	9.00	46.00	70.00
1913 A	—	PF60 155	PF63 325			
1913 J	5,186,000	1.75	3.50	9.00	46.00	70.00
1913 J	—	PF60 175	PF63 350			

KM# 11 5 HELLER

Bronze, 37 mm. **Ruler:** Wihelm II **Obv:** Crown with ribbon above date **Rev:** Denomination within wreath **Edge:** Plain

Date	Mintage	F12	VF20	XF40	MS60	MS63
1908 J	600,000	25.00	55.00	110	625	775
1908 J	—	PF60 1,250	PF63 2,250			
1909 J	756,000	30.00	65.00	115	625	775
1909 J	60	PF60 1,250	PF63 2,250			

KM# 13 5 HELLER

Copper-Nickel **Ruler:** Wihelm II **Obv:** Center hole divides date, crown with ribbon above, legend below **Rev:** Center hole divides denomination, sprigs flank

Date	Mintage	F12	VF20	XF40	MS60	MS63
1913 A	1,000,000	7.00	17.00	30.00	65.00	115
1913 A	—	PF63 290				
1913 J	1,000,000	7.00	17.00	30.00	70.00	115
1913 J	—	PF63 290				
1914 J	1,000,000	6.00	14.00	25.00	60.00	115
1914 J	—	PF63 290				

KM# 14.1 5 HELLER

Brass **Ruler:** Wihelm II **Obv:** Crown with ribbon above date, oval base on crown **Rev:** Denomination within wreath **Note:** 1-1/2 -2mm thick. Tabora emergency issue.

Date	Mintage	F12	VF20	XF40	MS60	MS63
1916 T	30,000	14.00	30.00	55.00	110	210

KM# 14.2 5 HELLER

Brass **Ruler:** Wihelm II **Obv:** Crown with ribbon above date, flat base on crown **Rev:** Denomination within wreath **Note:** 1mm or less thick.

Date	Mintage	F12	VF20	XF40	MS60	MS63
1916 T	Inc. above	6.00	16.00	42.00	80.00	140

KM# 12 10 HELLER

Copper-Nickel **Ruler:** Wihelm II **Obv:** Center hole divides date, crown with ribbon above, legend below **Rev:** Center hole divides denomination, sprigs flank

Date	Mintage	F12	VF20	XF40	MS60	MS63
1908 J	—	6.00	17.00	34.50	105	145
1908 J	—	PF60 400	PF63 700	PF65 1,200		
1909 J	1,990,000	3.50	12.00	22.50	90.00	145
1909 J	—	PF60 325	PF63 650	PF65 1,100		
1910 J	500,000	3.50	12.00	22.50	90.00	175
1910 J	—	PF60 325	PF63 650	PF65 1,100		
1911 A	500,000	6.00	17.00	40.25	115	175
1911 A	—	PF60 350	PF63 675	PF65 1,150		
1914 J	200,000	12.00	34.50	70.00	145	230
1914	—	PF60 325	PF63 650	PF65 1,100		

Obverse A
Large Crown

Obverse B
Small Crown

Reverse A
Curled tip on second L

Reverse B
Pointed tips on L's

Reverse C
Curled tips on L's

KM# 15 20 HELLER

Copper **Ruler:** Wihelm II **Obv:** Crown with ribbon above date **Rev:** Denomination within wreath **Note:** Tabora Emergency Coinage.

Date	Mintage	F12	VF20	XF40	MS60	MS63
1916 T	300,000	8.00	14.00	30.00	115	140
Note: Obverse A and reverse A						
1916 T	Inc. above	175	275	500	—	—
Note: Obverse A and reverse B						
1916 T	Inc. above	80.00	115	195	—	—
Note: Obverse B and reverse A						
1916 T	Inc. above	8.00	14.00	30.00	80.00	110
Note: Obverse B and reverse B						
1916 T Rare	Inc. above	—	—	—	—	—
Note: Obverse A and reverse C						
1916 T Rare	Inc. above	—	—	—	—	—
Note: Obverse B and reverse C						

KM# 15a 20 HELLER

Brass, 28 mm. **Ruler:** Wihelm II **Obv:** Crown with ribbon above date **Rev:** Denomination within wreath **Edge:** Plain **Note:** Tabora Emergency Issue.

Date	Mintage	F12	VF20	XF40	MS60	MS63
1916 T	1,600,000	8.00	14.00	30.00	105	125
Note: Obverse A and reverse A; Curled tip on second L						
1916 T	Inc. above	9.00	17.00	35.00	115	140
Note: Obverse A and reverse B; Pointed tips on L's						
1916 T	Inc. above	9.00	17.00	35.00	115	140
Note: Obverse B and reverse A; Curled tip on second L						

Date	Mintage	F12	VF20	XF40	MS60	MS63
1916 T	Inc. above	8.00	14.00	30.00	90.00	110
Note: Obverse B and reverse B; Pointed tips on Ls						
1916 T	Inc. above	14.00	42.00	65.00	175	210
Note: Obverse A and reverse C; Curled tips on Ls						
1916 T	Inc. above	16.00	48.00	70.00	185	210
Note: Obverse B and reverse C; Curled tips on Ls						

KM# 8 1/4 RUPIE

2.92 g., 0.917 Silver 0.086 oz. ASW **Ruler:** Wihelm II **Obv:** Armored bust left **Rev:** Denomination and date within wreath

Date	Mintage	F12	VF20	XF40	MS60	MS63
1904 A	300,000	7.00	16.00	50.00	150	215
1904 A	—	PF63 350				
1906 A	300,000	7.00	16.00	50.00	150	215
1906 A	—	PF63 350				
1906 J	100,000	30.00	80.00	175	400	550
1907 J	200,000	14.00	34.50	105	275	375
1907 J	—	PF63 425				
1909 A	300,000	8.00	18.00	55.00	255	300
1910 J	600,000	7.00	16.00	50.00	150	200
1910 J	—	PF63 400				
1912 J	400,000	8.00	18.00	55.00	165	240
1912 J	—	PF63 400				
1913 A	200,000	9.00	20.00	60.00	185	300
1913 A	—	PF63 400				
1913 J	400,000	7.00	16.00	50.00	150	200
1913 J	—	PF63 350				
1914 J	200,000	9.00	20.00	60.00	175	275
1914 J	—	PF63 350				

KM# 9 1/2 RUPIE

5.83 g., 0.917 Silver 0.1719 oz. ASW **Ruler:** Wihelm II **Obv:** Armored bust left **Rev:** Denomination and date within wreath

Date	Mintage	F12	VF20	XF40	MS60	MS63
1904 A	400,000	17.00	46.00	110	325	375
1904 A	—	PF60 300	PF63 525	PF65 950		
1906 A	50,000	145	260	400	875	1,150
1906 A	—	PF60 375	PF63 650	PF65 1,150		
1906 J	50,000	145	260	400	875	1,150
1907 J	140,000	22.50	60.00	145	350	400
1907 J	—	PF60 350	PF63 625	PF65 1,100		
1909 A	100,000	34.50	75.00	175	400	575
1910 J	300,000	22.50	46.00	115	290	325
1910 J	—	PF60 300	PF63 525	PF65 950		
1912 J	200,000	17.00	46.00	110	290	350
1913 A	100,000	22.50	50.00	125	350	450
1913 J	200,000	17.00	46.00	110	230	290
1914 J	100,000	22.50	50.00	115	325	400

KM# 10 RUPIE

11.66 g., 0.917 Silver 0.3439 oz. ASW **Ruler:** Wihelm II **Obv:** Armored bust left **Rev:** Denomination and date within wreath

Date	Mintage	F12	VF20	XF40	MS60	MS63
1904 A	1,000,000	16.00	32.00	65.00	150	175
1904 A	—	PF60 200	PF63 500	PF65 850		
1905 A	300,000	20.00	38.00	80.00	215	290
1905 A	—	PF60 225	PF63 525	PF65 900		
1905 J	1,000,000	16.00	32.00	65.00	150	185
1905 J	—	PF60 175	PF63 450	PF65 750		
1906 A	950,000	16.00	32.00	65.00	150	185
1906 J	700,000	20.00	40.00	90.00	200	230
1907 J	880,000	14.00	20.00	65.00	205	230
1908 J	500,000	17.00	35.00	75.00	220	260
1908 J	—	PF60 225	PF63 525	PF65 900		
1909 A	200,000	20.00	38.00	90.00	325	400

Date	Mintage	F12	VF20	XF40	MS60	MS63
1910 J	270,000	14.00	20.00	65.00	230	325
1910 J	—	PF60 300	PF63 700	PF65 1,200		
1911 A	300,000	17.00	34.50	75.00	200	290
1911 A	—	PF60 225	PF63 525	PF65 900		
1911 J	1,400,000	14.00	20.00	65.00	175	200
1911 J	—	PF60 175	PF63 450	PF65 750		
1912 J	300,000	17.00	35.00	75.00	190	290
1912 J	—	PF60 225	PF63 525	PF65 900		
1913 A	400,000	17.00	35.00	75.00	185	260
1913 J	1,400,000	14.00	20.00	65.00	175	200
1913 J	—	PF60 175	PF63 450	PF65 750		
1914 J	500,000	16.00	32.00	70.00	200	290

KM# 16.1 15 RUPIEN
7.17 g., 0.750 Gold 0.1728 oz. AGW **Ruler:** Wihelm II **Obv:** Crowned imperial eagle, right arabesque ends below "T" of "OSTAFRIKA" **Rev:** Elephant roaring right above date **Note:** Tabora Emergency Issue.

Date	Mintage	F12	VF20	XF40	MS60	MS63
1916 T	9,803	800	1,750	3,450	4,300	5,000

KM# 16.2 15 RUPIEN
7.17 g., 0.750 Gold 0.1728 oz. AGW **Ruler:** Wihelm II **Obv:** Crowned imperial eagle above denomination, right arabesque ends below first "A" of "OSTAFRIKA" **Rev:** Elephant roaring right above date **Note:** Tabora Emergency Issue.

Date	Mintage	F12	VF20	XF40	MS60	MS63
1916 T	6,395	825	1,750	3,450	4,300	5,000

PATTERNS

Including off metal strikes

KM#	Date	Mintage	Identification	Mkt Val
Pn1	1908	—	5 Heller. Bronze.	1,300
Pn2	1908	—	10 Heller. Copper-Nickel. Crown with ribbon above center hole dividing date. Center hole divides denomination.	425
Pn2a	1908/1908	—	10 Heller. Copper-Nickel. Two obverses.	450
Pn5	ND (1908)	—	5 Rupien. White Metal. Uniface.	575
Pn6	1913A	—	Rupie. Aluminum.	—
Pn7	1916	—	Heller. Zinc. Imperial crown divides D - O above 3-line inscription. Date in large numeral in center of plain field.	—

GERMAN STATES

Although the origin of the German Empire can be traced to the Treaty of Verdun that ceded Charlemagne's lands east of the Rhine to German Prince Louis, it was for centuries little more than a geographic expression, con- sisting of hundreds of effectively autonomous big and little states. Nominally the states owed their allegiance to the Holy Roman Emperor, who was also a German king, but as the Emperors exhibited less and less concern for Germany the actual power devolved on the lords of the individual states. The fragmentation of the empire climaxed with the tragic denouement of the Thirty Years War, 1618-48, which devastated much of Germany, destroyed its agriculture and medieval commercial eminence and ended the attempt of the Hapsburgs to unify Germany. Deprived of administrative capacity by a lack of resources, the imperial authority became utterly powerless. At this time Germany contained an estimated 1,800 individual states, some with a population of as little as 300. The German Empire of recent history (the creation of Bismarck) was formed on April 14, 1871, when the king of Prussia became German Emperor William I. The new empire comprised 4 kingdoms, 6 grand duchies, 12 duchies and principalities, 3 free cities and the nonautonomous province of Alsace-Lorraine. The states had the right to issue gold and silver coins of higher value than 1 Mark; coins of 1 Mark and under were general issues of the empire.

MINT MARKS

A - Berlin, 1750-date
D - Munich (Germany), 1872-date
E - Muldenhutten (Germany), 1887-1953
F - Stuttgart (Germany) 1872-date
G - Karlsruhe (Germany) 1872-date
J - Hamburg (Germany) 1873-date

MONETARY SYSTEM

After the German unification in 1871 when the old Thaler system was abandoned in favor of the Mark system (100 Pfennig = 1 Mark) the Vereinsthaler continued to circulate as a legal tender 3 Mark coin, and the double Thaler as a 6 Mark coin until 1908. In 1908 the Vereinsthalers were officially demonetized and the Thaler coinage was replaced by the new 3 Mark coin which had the same specifications as the old Vereinsthaler. The double Thaler coinage was not replaced as there was no great demand for a 6 Mark coin. Until the 1930's the German public continued to refer to the 3 Mark piece as a "Thaler."

Commencing 1871

100 Pfennig = 1 Mark

VERRECHNUNGS & GUTSCHRIFTS TOKENS

These were metallic indebtedness receipts used for commercial and banking purposes due to the lack of available subsidiary coinage. These tokens could be redeemed in sufficient quantities.

ANHALT-DESSAU

Anhalt-Dessau was part of the 1252 division that included Zerbst and Köthen. In 1396, Anhalt-Zerbst was divided into Anhalt-Zerbst and Anhalt-Dessau. In 1508, Anhalt-Zerbst was absorbed into Anhalt-Dessau. The latter was given to the eldest son of Joachim Ernst in the division of 1603. As other lines became extinct, they fell to Anhalt-Dessau, which united all territories of the dynasty in 1863. The last ruler was forced to give up power at the end of World War I. Anhalt area: 2314 km. Capital: Dessau.

RULERS

Friedrich I, 1871-1904
Friedrich II, 1904-1918
Ernst, 1918

MINT MARK

A – Berlin Mint, 1839-1914

DUCHY

REFORM COINAGE

KM# 27 2 MARK
11.11 g., 0.900 Silver 0.3215 oz. ASW, 28 mm. **Ruler:** Friedrich II **Obv:** Head left **Rev:** Crowned imperial German eagle, shield on breast **Edge:** Reeded **Mint:** Berlin

Date	Mintage	F12	VF20	XF40	MS60	MS63
1901 A	—	120	260	440	1,200	1,650
1904 A	50,000	120	300	440	1,100	1,500
1904 A	150	PF63 1,850				

KM# 29 3 MARK
16.67 g., 0.900 Silver 0.4823 oz. ASW, 33 mm. **Ruler:** Friedrich II **Obv:** Head left **Rev:** Crowned imperial German eagle, shield on breast **Edge Lettering:** GOTT MIT UNS **Mint:** Berlin

Date	Mintage	F12	VF20	XF40	MS60	MS63
1909 A	100,000	28.00	60.00	120	250	400
1911 A	100,000	32.00	68.00	132	250	420
Common date	—	PF63 550				
Common date	—	PF63 400				

KM# 30 3 MARK
16.67 g., 0.900 Silver 0.4823 oz. ASW, 33 mm. **Ruler:** Friedrich II **Subject:** Silver Wedding Anniversary **Obv:** Jugate heads left **Rev:** Crowned imperial German eagle, shield on breast **Edge Lettering:** GOTT MIT UNS **Mint:** Berlin

Date	Mintage	F12	VF20	XF40	MS60	MS63
1914 A	200,000	20.00	48.00	68.00	120	170
1914 A	1,000	PF63 325				

KM# 31 5 MARK
27.78 g., 0.900 Silver 0.8037 oz. ASW, 38 mm. **Ruler:** Friedrich II **Subject:** Silver Wedding Anniversary **Obv:** Jugate heads left **Rev:** Crowned imperial German eagle, shield on breast **Edge Lettering:** GOTT MIT UNS **Mint:** Berlin

Date	Mintage	F12	VF20	XF40	MS60	MS63
1901 A	—	360	640	1,000	2,700	4,000
1914 A	30,000	52.00	144	228	450	650
1914 A	1,000	PF63 1,000				

KM# 25 10 MARK
3.98 g., 0.900 Gold 0.1152 oz. AGW **Ruler:** Friedrich I **Obv:** Head right **Obv. Legend:** FRIEDRICH HERZOG VON ANHALT **Rev:** Crowned imperial German eagle **Rev. Legend:** DEUTSCHES REICH date 10 MARK **Edge:** GOTT MIT UNS **Mint:** Berlin

Date	Mintage	F12	VF20	XF40	MS60	MS63
1901 A	20,000	600	1,000	1,440	2,700	3,500
1901 A	200	**PF63** 4,250				

KM# 26 20 MARK
7.97 g., 0.900 Gold 0.2305 oz. AGW **Ruler:** Friedrich I **Obv:** Small head right **Obv. Legend:** FRIEDRICH HERZOG VON ANHALT **Rev:** Crowned imperial German eagle **Rev. Legend:** DEUTSCHES REICH date ZWEI MARK **Mint:** Berlin

Date	Mintage	F12	VF20	XF40	MS60	MS63
1901 A	15,000	600	1,000	1,440	2,700	3,500
1901 A	200	**PF63** 4,250				

KM# 28 20 MARK
7.97 g., 0.900 Gold 0.2305 oz. AGW **Ruler:** Friedrich II **Obv:** Head left **Rev:** Crowned imperial German eagle, shield on breast **Edge Lettering:** GOTT MIT UNS **Mint:** Berlin

Date	Mintage	F12	VF20	XF40	MS60	MS63
1904 A	25,000	480	800	1,120	2,500	3,500
1904 A	200	**PF63** 3,750				

PATTERNS

Including off metal strikes

KM#	Date	Mintage	Identification	Mkt Val
Pn1	1901A	—	2 Mark. Silver. KM23.	3,500
Pn2	1901A	—	5 Mark. Silver. KM24.	5,000
Pn3	1914	—	3 Mark. Silver. Wreath around rim. KM30.	—
Pn4	1914	—	3 Mark. Brass.	—
Pn5	1914	—	5 Mark. Silver. Pn6. KM31.	2,000
Pn6	1914	—	5 Mark. Silver. Lettered.	2,000
Pn7	1914	—	5 Mark. Silver. Plain.	2,000

BADEN

The earliest rulers of Baden, in the southwestern part of Germany along the Rhine, descended from the dukes of Zähringen in the late 11th century. The first division of the territory occurred in 1190, when separate lines of margraves were established in Baden and in Hachberg. Immediately prior to its extinction in 1418, Hachberg was sold back to Baden, which underwent several minor divisions itself during the next century. Baden acquired most of the countship of Sponheim from Electoral Pfalz near the end of the 15th century. In 1515, the most significant division of the patrimony took place, in which the Baden-Baden and Baden-(Pforzheim) Durlach lines were established.

Although Baden-Durlach was founded upon the division of Baden in 1515, the youngest son of Christoph I did not begin ruling in his own right until the demise of his father. This part of Baden was called Pforzheim until 1565, when the margrave moved his seat from the former to Durlach, located to the west and nearer the Rhine. After the male line of Baden-Baden failed in 1771 and the two parts of Baden were reunited, the fortunes of the margraviate continued to grow. Karlsruhe, near Durlach, was developed into a well-planned capital city. The ruler was given the rank of elector in 1803, only to be raised to grand duke three years later. The grand duchy came to an end in 1918, but had by this time become one of the largest states in Germany.

RULERS
Friedrich I, Prince Regent 1852-1856,
Grand Duke 1856-1907
Friedrich II, 1907-1918
Karlsruhe, 1979

BADEN

Grand Duchy

REFORM COINAGE

KM# 269 2 MARK
11.11 g., 0.900 Silver 0.3215 oz. ASW, 28 mm. **Ruler:** Friedrich I **Obv:** Head left **Obv. Legend:** FRIEDRICH GROSHERZOG VON BADEN **Rev:** Crowned imperial German eagle **Rev. Legend:** DEUTSCHES REICH date ZWEI MARK **Mint:** Stuttgart

Date	Mintage	F12	VF20	XF40	MS60	MS63
1901 G	401,322	32.00	72.00	220	1,200	2,250
1901 G	—	**PF63** 3,000				
1902 G	5,368	275	700	1,500	4,000	6,000
1902 G Proof, rare	—	**PF63** 7,500				

KM# 271 2 MARK
11.11 g., 0.900 Silver 0.3215 oz. ASW, 28 mm. **Ruler:** Friedrich I **Subject:** 50th Year of Reign **Obv:** Head right **Rev:** Crowned imperial German eagle, shield on breast

Date	Mintage	F12	VF20	XF40	MS60	MS63
1902	375,018	9.50	20.00	28.00	50.00	70.00

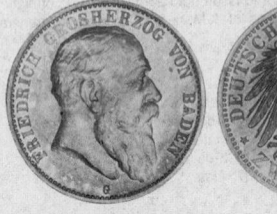

KM# 272 2 MARK
11.11 g., 0.900 Silver 0.3215 oz. ASW, 28 mm. **Ruler:** Friedrich I **Obv:** Head right **Rev:** Crowned imperial German eagle, shield on breast **Mint:** Stuttgart

Date	Mintage	F12	VF20	XF40	MS60	MS63
1902 G	198,250	20.00	44.00	72.00	250	500
1903 G	493,989	16.00	36.00	72.00	250	350
1904 G	1,121,754	16.00	32.00	64.00	250	350
1905 G	609,835	16.00	36.00	56.00	175	300
1906 G Rare	107,549	36.00	72.00	180	700	1,400
1907 G	913,024	16.00	32.00	52.00	150	225

KM# 276 2 MARK
11.11 g., 0.900 Silver 0.3215 oz. ASW, 28 mm. **Ruler:** Friedrich I **Subject:** Golden Wedding Anniversary **Obv:** Heads of royal couple right **Rev:** Crowned imperial German eagle, shield on breast

Date	Mintage	F12	VF20	XF40	MS60	MS63
1906	350,000	12.00	20.00	28.00	60.00	70.00
1906 Matte proof	200	—	—	—	—	—

KM# 278 2 MARK
11.11 g., 0.900 Silver 0.3215 oz. ASW, 28 mm. **Ruler:** Friedrich I **Subject:** Death of Friedrich **Obv:** Head right **Rev:** Crowned imperial German eagle, shield on breast

Date	Mintage	F12	VF20	XF40	MS60	MS63
1907	350,000	16.00	40.00	56.00	90.00	100
1907	—	**PF63** 175				

KM# 283 2 MARK
11.11 g., 0.900 Silver 0.3215 oz. ASW, 28 mm. **Ruler:** Friedrich II **Obv:** Head left **Rev:** Crowned imperial German eagle, shield on breast **Mint:** Stuttgart

Date	Mintage	F12	VF20	XF40	MS60	MS63
1911 G	72,000	100	200	320	750	1,200
1913 G	937,050	80.00	175	300	700	1,200
Common date	—	**PF63** 1,500				

KM# 280 3 MARK
16.67 g., 0.900 Silver 0.4823 oz. ASW, 33 mm. **Ruler:** Friedrich II **Obv:** Head left **Rev:** Crowned imperial German eagle, shield on breast **Mint:** Stuttgart

Date	Mintage	F12	VF20	XF40	MS60	MS63
1908 G	304,927	15.00	22.00	35.00	100	160
1909 G	760,716	13.50	20.00	28.00	75.00	160
1910 G	674,640	13.50	20.00	28.00	75.00	160
1911 G	382,033	13.50	20.00	28.00	75.00	160
1912 G	835,199	13.50	20.00	28.00	75.00	160
1914 G	412,804	13.50	20.00	28.00	70.00	160
1915 G	169,533	20.00	45.00	75.00	225	300
Common date	—	**PF63** 250				

KM# 268 5 MARK
27.78 g., 0.900 Silver 0.8037 oz. ASW, 38 mm. **Ruler:** Friedrich I **Obv:** Head left **Obv. Legend:** FRIEDRICH GROSHERZOG VON BADEN **Rev:** Crowned imperial German eagle **Rev. Legend:** DEUTSCHES REICH date FUNF MARK **Mint:** Karlsruhe

Date	Mintage	F12	VF20	XF40	MS60	MS63
1901 G	128,131	24.00	72.00	400	2,000	4,000
1902 G	42,708	28.00	72.00	400	2,000	4,250
Common date	—	**PF63** 5,000				

KM# 273 5 MARK
27.78 g., 0.900 Silver 0.8037 oz. ASW, 38 mm. **Ruler:** Friedrich I **Subject:** 50th Year of Reign **Obv:** Head right **Rev:** Crowned imperial German eagle, shield on breast

Date	Mintage	F12	VF20	XF40	MS60	MS63
1902	50,024	40.00	80.00	135	225	300
1902	—	PF63 625				

KM# 274 5 MARK
27.78 g., 0.900 Silver 0.8037 oz. ASW, 38 mm. **Ruler:** Friedrich I **Obv:** Head right **Rev:** Crowned imperial German eagle, shield on breast **Edge Lettering:** GOTT MIT UNS **Note:** Varieties exist.

Date	Mintage	F12	VF20	XF40	MS60	MS63
1902 G	128,100	32.00	54.00	135	600	1,200
1903 G	439,105	25.00	45.00	126	600	1,000
1904 G	237,914	25.00	45.00	126	600	1,000
1907 G	243,821	25.00	45.00	126	600	850
Common date	—	PF63 1,250				

KM# 277 5 MARK
27.78 g., 0.900 Silver 0.8037 oz. ASW, 38 mm. **Ruler:** Friedrich I **Subject:** Golden Wedding Anniversary **Obv:** Jugate busts right **Rev:** Crowned imperial German eagle, shield on breast

Date	Mintage	F12	VF20	XF40	MS60	MS63
1906	60,000	36.00	72.00	130	220	325
1906	—	PF63 400				

KM# 279 5 MARK
27.78 g., 0.900 Silver 0.8037 oz. ASW, 38 mm. **Ruler:** Friedrich I **Subject:** Death of Friedrich **Obv:** Head right **Rev:** Crowned imperial German eagle, shield on breast

Date	Mintage	F12	VF20	XF40	MS60	MS63
1907	60,000	55.00	115	160	250	350
1907	—	PF63 425				

KM# 281 5 MARK
27.78 g., 0.900 Silver 0.8037 oz. ASW, 38 mm. **Ruler:** Friedrich II **Obv:** Head left **Rev:** Crowned imperial German eagle, shield on breast **Mint:** Stuttgart

Date	Mintage	F12	VF20	XF40	MS60	MS63
1908 G	184,000	36.00	54.00	180	600	1,100
1913 G	244,000	27.00	45.00	160	400	900
Common date	—	PF63 1,500				

KM# 267 10 MARK
3.98 g., 0.900 Gold 0.1152 oz. AGW **Ruler:** Friedrich I **Obv:** Head left **Obv. Legend:** FRIEDRICH GROSHERZOG VON BADEN **Rev:** Crowned imperial German eagle **Rev. Legend:** DEUTSCHES REICH date 10 MARK **Mint:** Stuttgart

Date	Mintage	F12	VF20	XF40	MS60	MS63
1901 G	91,248	180	200	270	500	700
1901 G	—	PF63 2,000				

KM# 275 10 MARK
3.98 g., 0.900 Gold 0.1152 oz. AGW **Ruler:** Friedrich I **Obv:** Head right **Rev:** Crowned imperial German eagle, shield on breast **Mint:** Stuttgart

Date	Mintage	F12	VF20	XF40	MS60	MS63
1902 G	30,409	180	270	400	750	1,250
1903 G	109,450	175	195	250	450	700
1904 G	149,240	175	195	250	400	700
1905 G	95,932	175	195	250	500	750
1906 G	120,902	175	195	250	400	700
1907 G	121,902	175	195	250	400	700
Common date	—	PF63 2,000				

KM# 282 10 MARK
3.98 g., 0.900 Gold 0.1152 oz. AGW **Ruler:** Friedrich II **Obv:** Head right **Rev:** Crowned imperial German eagle, shield on breast **Mint:** Stuttgart

Date	Mintage	F12	VF20	XF40	MS60	MS63
1909 G	86,000	200	450	630	950	1,300
1910 G	60,649	200	450	630	950	1,300
1911 G	29,488	2,000	4,000	5,000	6,750	8,000
1912 G	25,975	700	850	1,400	2,000	3,000
1913 G	41,567	500	700	850	1,250	2,000
Common date	—	PF63 2,000				

KM# 284 20 MARK
7.97 g., 0.900 Gold 0.2305 oz. AGW **Ruler:** Friedrich II **Obv:** Head left **Rev:** Crowned imperial German eagle, shield on breast **Mint:** Stuttgart

Date	Mintage	F12	VF20	XF40	MS60	MS63
1911 G	190,836	295	400	415	425	475
1912 G	311,063	295	400	415	425	475
1913 G	85,374	295	400	415	425	475
1914 G	280,520	295	400	415	425	475
Common date	—	PF63 1,750				

BAVARIA

(Bayern)

Located in south Germany. In 1180 the Duchy of Bavaria was given to the Count of Wittelsbach by the emperor. He is the ancestor of all who ruled in Bavaria until 1918. Primogeniture was proclaimed in 1506 and in 1623 the dukes of Bavaria were given the electoral right. Bavaria, which had been divided for the various heirs, was reunited in 1799. The title of king was granted to Bavaria in 1805. Captial: München, population-- 1905: 6,524,372.

RULERS
Otto, 1886-1913, Prince Regent Luitpold, 1886-1912
Ludwig III, 1913-1918

MINT MARKS
D - Munich

KINGDOM

REFORM COINAGE

KM# 913 2 MARK
11.11 g., 0.900 Silver 0.3215 oz. ASW, 28 mm. **Ruler:** Otto **Obv:** Head left **Obv. Legend:** OTTO KOENIG VON BAYERN **Rev:** Crowned imperial German eagle **Rev. Legend:** DEUTSCHES REICH, ZWEI MARK **Edge:** Reeded **Mint:** Munich **Note:** Open and closed curl varieties exist. Prev. KM#511. Varieites exist

Date	Mintage	F12	VF20	XF40	MS60	MS63
1901 D	829,064	11.50	22.50	44.00	135	300
1902 D	1,340,789	9.50	17.50	36.00	120	300
1903 D	1,406,067	9.50	17.50	36.00	110	275
1904 D	2,320,238	8.50	16.00	32.00	100	275
1905 D	1,406,100	9.50	17.50	36.00	100	275
1906 D	1,054,500	9.50	17.50	44.00	120	325
1907 D	2,106,712	8.50	16.00	28.00	100	275
1908 D	632,700	9.50	17.50	36.00	95.00	300
1912 D	213,652	11.50	22.50	48.00	125	400
1913 D	97,698	40.00	80.00	160	250	475

KM# 997 2 MARK
11.11 g., 0.900 Silver 0.3215 oz. ASW **Ruler:** Otto **Subject:** 90th Birthday of Prince Regent Luitpold **Obv:** Head right **Rev:** Crowned imperial German eagle, shield on breast **Edge:** Reeded **Mint:** Munich **Note:** Prev. KM#516.

Date	Mintage	F12	VF20	XF40	MS60	MS63
1911 D	640,000	11.20	17.60	28.00	55.00	75.00
1911 D	—	PF63 125				

KM# 1002 2 MARK
11.11 g., 0.900 Silver 0.3215 oz. ASW, 28 mm. **Ruler:** Ludwig III **Obv:** Head left **Rev:** Crowned imperial eagle, shield on breast **Mint:** Munich **Note:** Prev. KM#519.

Date	Mintage	F12	VF20	XF40	MS60	MS63
1914 D	573,533	24.00	40.00	88.00	160	250
1914 D	—	PF63 450				

KM# 996 3 MARK
16.67 g., 0.900 Silver 0.4823 oz. ASW, 33 mm. **Ruler:** Otto **Obv:** Head left **Rev:** Crowned imperial eagle, shield on breast **Edge Lettering:** GOTT MIT UNS **Mint:** Munich **Note:** Prev. KM#515

Date	Mintage	F12	VF20	XF40	MS60	MS63
1908 D	680,529	13.50	16.00	28.00	60.00	125
1909 D	827,460	12.50	14.50	24.00	50.00	125
1910 D	1,496,091	12.50	14.50	24.00	50.00	125
1911 D	843,437	13.50	16.00	28.00	60.00	125
1912 D	1,013,650	13.50	16.00	28.00	60.00	125
1913 D	713,275	13.50	16.00	28.00	60.00	125
1913 D	—	PF63 250				

KM# 998 3 MARK

16.67 g., 0.900 Silver 0.4823 oz. ASW, 33 mm. **Ruler:** Otto **Subject:** 90th Birthday of Prince Regent Luitpold **Obv:** Head right **Rev:** Crowned imperial eagle, shield on breast **Edge Lettering:** GOTT MIT UNS **Mint:** Munich **Note:** Prev. KM#517.

Date	Mintage	F12	VF20	XF40	MS60	MS63
1911 D	639,721	14.50	17.50	28.00	50.00	65.00
1911 D	—	PF63 125				

KM# 1005 3 MARK

16.67 g., 0.900 Silver 0.4823 oz. ASW, 33 mm. **Ruler:** Ludwig III **Obv:** Head left **Rev:** Crowned imperial eagle, shield on breast **Edge Lettering:** GOTT MIT UNS **Mint:** Munich **Note:** Prev. KM#520.

Date	Mintage	F12	VF20	XF40	MS60	MS63
1914 D	717,460	20.00	32.50	50.00	75.00	130
1914 D	—	PF63 250				

KM# 1010 3 MARK

16.67 g., 0.900 Silver 0.4823 oz. ASW, 33 mm. **Ruler:** Ludwig III **Subject:** Golden Wedding Anniversary **Obv:** Jugate heads right **Rev:** Crowned imperial eagle, shield on breast **Mint:** Munich **Note:** Prev. KM#523.

Date	Mintage	F12	VF20	XF40	MS60	MS63
1918 D	130	—	12,500	26,000	32,000	45,000

KM# 915 5 MARK

27.78 g., 0.900 Silver 0.8037 oz. ASW, 38 mm. **Ruler:** Otto **Obv:** Head left **Obv. Legend:** OTTO KOENIG VON BAYERN **Rev:** Crowned imperial German eagle **Rev. Legend:** DEUTSCHES REICH, FUNF MARK **Edge Lettering:** GOTT MIT UNS **Mint:** Munich **Note:** Varieties in the hair locks and curls exist. Prev. KM#512.1-512.4.

Date	Mintage	F12	VF20	XF40	MS60	MS63
1901 D	295,371	25.00	35.00	85.00	300	550
1902 D	506,049	25.00	35.00	70.00	250	500
1903 D	1,012,097	25.00	35.00	70.00	250	450
1904 D	548,340	27.00	37.00	72.00	250	450
1906 D	70,249	35.00	70.00	180	1,100	2,000
1907 D	752,653	25.00	28.00	54.00	200	425
1908 D	576,579	25.00	28.00	54.00	200	425
1913 D	520,000	25.00	28.00	45.00	120	275
Common date	—	PF63 800				

KM# 999 5 MARK

27.78 g., 0.900 Silver 0.8037 oz. ASW, 38 mm. **Ruler:** Otto **Subject:** 90th Birthday of Prince Regent Luitpold **Obv:** Head right **Rev:** Crowned imperial eagle, shield on breast **Mint:** Munich **Note:** Prev. KM#518.

Date	Mintage	F12	VF20	XF40	MS60	MS63
1911 D	160,000	32.00	58.00	85.00	170	225
1911 D	—	PF63 275				

KM# 1007 5 MARK

27.78 g., 0.900 Silver 0.8037 oz. ASW, 38 mm. **Ruler:** Ludwig III **Obv:** Head left **Mint:** Munich **Note:** Prev. KM#521.

Date	Mintage	F12	VF20	XF40	MS60	MS63
1914 D	142,600	40.00	80.00	160	250	375

KM# 994 10 MARK

3.98 g., 0.900 Gold 0.1152 oz. AGW **Ruler:** Otto **Obv:** Head left **Obv. Legend:** OTTO KOENIG V. BAYERN **Rev:** Crowned imperial German eagle **Rev. Legend:** DEUTSCHES REICH **Mint:** Munich **Note:** Prev. KM#514.

Date	Mintage	F12	VF20	XF40	MS60	MS63
1901 D	140,639	180	200	220	275	425
1902 D	70,308	180	200	220	275	425
1903 D	534,426	180	200	220	275	425
1904 D	210,112	180	200	220	275	425
1905 D	281,231	180	200	220	275	425
1906 D	140,512	180	200	225	300	425
1907 D	211,211	180	200	220	275	425
1909 D	208,970	180	200	220	275	425
1910 D	140,753	180	200	220	275	425
1911 D	71,616	180	200	235	325	425
1912 D	140,874	180	200	225	300	425
Common date	—	PF63 1,000				

KM# 920 20 MARK

7.97 g., 0.900 Gold 0.2305 oz. AGW **Ruler:** Otto **Obv:** Head left **Obv. Legend:** OTTO KOENIG VON BAYERN **Rev:** Type III **Rev. Legend:** DEUTSCHES REICH **Edge Lettering:** GOTT MIT UNS **Mint:** Munich **Note:** Prev. KM#513.

Date	Mintage	F12	VF20	XF40	MS60	MS63
1905 D	501,000	295	375	390	410	425
1905 D	—	PF63 1,600				
1913 D	310,778	—	15,000	22,500	25,000	—
1913 D	—	PF63 35,000				

KM# 1009 20 MARK

7.97 g., 0.900 Gold 0.2305 oz. AGW **Ruler:** Ludwig III **Obv:** Head left **Rev:** Crowned imperial eagle, shield on breast **Mint:** Munich **Note:** Prev. KM#522. Never officially released.

Date	Mintage	F12	VF20	XF40	MS60	MS63
1914 D	532,851	—	2,000	3,000	3,500	4,500
1914 D	—	PF63 5,000				

PATTERNS

Including off metal strikes

KM#	Date	Mintage	Identification	Mkt Val
Pn14	1904	—	5 Mark. Silver. Eagle in ring. Reeded.	—
Pn15	1904D	—	5 Mark. Silver. Eagle in ring. Lettered.	—
Pn16	1904D	—	5 Mark. Silver. Without inner circle.	3,000
Pn17	1905D	—	5 Mark. Copper. KM915.	—
Pn18	1911	—	3 Mark. Silver.	—
Pn19	1911D	—	3 Mark. Copper.	—
Pn25	1913D	—	3 Mark. Silver. Plain.	—
Pn35	1914D	—	3 Mark. Silver. Bust faces right.	2,000
Pn36	1914D	—	5 Mark. Silver. Larger lettering. KM#1007.	2,500
Pn37	1914D	—	5 Mark. Silver. Plain. KM1007.	—
Pn38	1914D	—	20 Mark. Gold. Lettered.	10,000
Pn39	1914D	—	20 Mark. Silver Gilt. Hallmarked, plain.	150
Pn40	1914D	—	20 Mark. Silver Gilt. Hallmarked, plain. KM1009.	—
Pn41	1914D	—	20 Mark. Gold. Denticled rim. Plain. KM#1009.	9,000
Pn42	1914D	—	20 Mark. Silver Gilt. Denticled rim. KM522. Hallmarked, plain.	—
Pn43	1914D	—	20 Mark. Gold. 18-millimeter bust. KM522. Lettered.	8,000
Pn44	1914D	—	20 Mark. Silver Gilt. 18mm bust. Hallmarked, plain. KM#1009.	—
Pn45	1914D	—	20 Mark. Gold. Plain rim. Plain. KM#1009.	9,000
Pn46	1914D	—	20 Mark. Gold. Plain rim. Lettered. KM#1009.	9,000
Pn47	1914D	—	20 Mark. Gold. Round "O" in KOENIG. Lettered.	9,000
Pn48	1914D	—	20 Mark. Silver Gilt. Round "O" in KOENIG. Hallmarked, plain. KM#1009.	—
Pn49	ND (1914) J	—	Gulden. Gold. Bust of Ludwig III in uniform. Main bridge of Wurzburger.	—

BREMEN

Established at about the same time as the bishopric in 787, Bremen was under the control of the bishops and archbishops until joining the Hanseatic League in 1276. Archbishop Albrecht II granted the mint right to the city in 1369, but this was not formalized by imperial decree until 1541. In 1646, Bremen was raised to free imperial status and continued to strike its own coins into the early 20th century. The city lost its free imperial status in 1803 and was controlled by France from 1806 until 1813. Regaining it independence in 1815, Bremen joined the North German Confederation in 1867 and the German Empire in 1871. Since 1369, there was practically continuous coinage until 1907.

FREE CITY

REGULAR COINAGE

KM# 250 2 MARK

11.11 g., 0.900 Silver 0.3215 oz. ASW, 28 mm. **Obv:** Key on crowned shield with supporters **Rev:** Crowned imperial eagle, shield on breast, date at right, denomination below **Edge:** Reeded

Date	Mintage	F12	VF20	XF40	MS60	MS63
1904 J	100,000	25.00	90.00	100	150	225
1904 J	200	PF63 400				

KM# 251 5 MARK
27.78 g., 0.900 Silver 0.8037 oz. ASW, 38 mm. **Obv:** Key on crowned shield with supporters **Rev:** Crowned imperial eagle, shield on breast, date at right, denomination below **Edge Lettering:** GOTT MIT UNS

Date	Mintage	F12	VF20	XF40	MS60	MS63
1906 J	40,846	75.00	185	300	450	550
1906 J	600	PF63 1,000				

KM# 253 10 MARK
3.98 g., 0.900 Gold 0.1152 oz. AGW **Obv:** Key on crowned shield with supporters **Rev:** Crowned imperial eagle, shield on breast, date at right, denomination below

Date	Mintage	F12	VF20	XF40	MS60	MS63
1907 J	20,006	425	1,000	1,400	1,800	2,500
1907 J	—	PF63 2,800				

KM# 252 20 MARK
7.97 g., 0.900 Gold 0.2305 oz. AGW **Edge Lettering:** GOTT MIT UNS

Date	Mintage	F12	VF20	XF40	MS60	MS63
1906 J	20,122	475	1,000	1,400	1,850	2,600
1906 J	—	PF63 2,850				

TOKEN COINAGE

These vouchers, issued March 18, 1924, were based on the American dollar. Issued in conjunction with Bremens issue of treasury. Due to monies being held to purchase Bremens 5% Dollar Bond, they rarely circulated. The tokens were withdrawn September 30 of that same year.

Reckoning Tokens

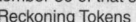

KM# Tn1 2 VERRECHNUNGS-PFENNIG
Brass **Obv:** State arms-key within circle **Rev:** Denomination within circle **Mint:** Nürnberg

Date	Mintage	F12	VF20	XF40	MS60	MS63
ND-1924	501,000	8.00	23.00	45.00	85.00	130

KM# Tn2 5 VERRECHNUNGS-PFENNIG
Aluminum **Obv:** State arms-key within circle **Rev:** Denomination within circle **Mint:** Nürnberg

Date	Mintage	F12	VF20	XF40	MS60	MS63
ND-1924	669,000	7.00	16.00	30.00	70.00	125

KM# Tn3 10 VERRECHNUNGS-PFENNIG
Aluminum **Obv:** State arms-key within circle **Rev:** Denomination within circle **Mint:** Nürnberg

Date	Mintage	F12	VF20	XF40	MS60	MS63
ND-1924	695,000	8.00	18.00	35.00	75.00	125

KM# Tn4 20 VERRECHNUNGS-PFENNIG
Aluminum **Obv:** State arms-key within circle **Rev:** Denomination within circle **Mint:** Nürnberg

Date	Mintage	F12	VF20	XF40	MS60	MS63
ND-1924	382,000	15.00	33.00	60.00	120	200

KM# Tn5 50 VERRECHNUNGS-PFENNIG
Aluminum **Obv:** Key on crowned shield with supporters **Rev:** Denomination within circle **Mint:** Hamburg

Date	Mintage	F12	VF20	XF40	MS60	MS63
ND-1924	483,000	28.00	73.00	125	200	300

KM# Tn6 VERRECHNUNGSMARK
Aluminum **Obv:** Crowned shield with supporters on pedestal, key on shield **Rev:** Large, thick denomination **Mint:** Menden
Note: This coin is listed in Jaeger & Funck as struck in aluminum. Kunker has listed it as having an iron core but doesn't indicate what metal clads or plates the piece.

Date	Mintage	F12	VF20	XF40	MS60	MS63
ND-1924	382,000	75.00	150	275	500	—

PATTERNS

Including off metal strikes

KM#	Date	Mintage	Identification	Mkt Val
Pn40	1904 J	—	5 Mark. KM251.	25,000
Pn41	1905 J	—	2 Mark. KM250.	5,000
Pn42	1905 J	—	5 Mark. Silver. Larger lettering without beaded rim. KM251.	20,000
Pn43	1905 J	—	5 Mark. Tin.	2,000
Pn44	1906	—	5 Mark. Bronze.	5,000
Pn45	1906	—	5 Mark. Silver.	5,000
Pn46	1906	—	5 Mark. Tin.	—
Pn47	ND (1906)	—	S.m. Copper.	—

BRUNSWICK-WOLFENBÜTTEL

(Braunschweig-Wolfenbüttel)

Located in north-central Germany. Wolfenbüttel was annexed to Brunswick in 1257. One of the five surviving sons of Albrecht II founded the first line in Wolfenbüttel in 1318. A further division in Wolfenbüttel and Lüneburg was undertaken in 1373. Another division occurred in 1495, but the Wolfenbüttel duchy survived in the younger line. Heinrich IX was forced out of his territory during the religious wars of the mid-sixteenth century by Duke Johann Friedrich I of Saxony and Landgrave Philipp of Hessen in 1542, but was restored to his possessions in 1547. Duke Friedrich Ulrich was forced to cede the Grubenhagen lands, which had been acquired by Wolfenbüttel in 1596, to Lüneburg in 1617. When the succession died out in 1634, the lands and titles fell to the cadet line in Dannenberg. The line became extinct once again and passed to Brunswick-Bevern in 1735 from which a new succession of Wolfenbüttel dukes descended. The ducal family was beset by continual personal and political tragedy during the nineteenth century. Two of the dukes were killed in battles with Napoleon, the territories were occupied by the French and became part of the Kingdom of Westphalia, another duke was forced out by a revolt in 1823. From 1884 until 1913, Brunswick-Wolfenbüttel was governed by Prussia and then turned over to the only surviving (of 3) prince of Brunswick who married the only daughter of Kaiser Wilhelm II. His reign was short, however, as he was forced to abdicate at the end of World War I.

RULERS
Prussian rule, 1884-1913
Ernst August, 1913-1918

DUCHY

REFORM COINAGE

KM# 1161 3 MARK
16.67 g., 0.900 Silver 0.4823 oz. ASW, 33 mm. **Ruler:** Ernst August **Subject:** Ernst August Wedding and Accession **Obv:** Jugate heads right **Rev:** Crowned imperial eagle, shield on breast **Edge Lettering:** GOTT MIT UNS **Mint:** Berlin

Date	Mintage	F12	VF20	XF40	MS60	MS63
1915 A	1,700	480	960	2,000	2,750	3,500
1915 A	—	PF63 3,750				

KM# 1162 3 MARK
16.67 g., 0.900 Silver 0.4823 oz. ASW, 33 mm. **Ruler:** Ernst August **Subject:** Ernst August Wedding and Accession **Obv:** Jugate heads right **Obv. Legend:** U LUNEB added **Rev:** Crowned imperial eagle, shield on breast **Mint:** Berlin

Date	Mintage	F12	VF20	XF40	MS60	MS63
1915 A	31,634	40.00	95.00	200	275	375
1915 A	—	PF63 450				

KM# 1163 5 MARK
27.78 g., 0.900 Silver 0.8037 oz. ASW, 38 mm. **Ruler:** Ernst August **Subject:** Ernst August Wedding and Accession **Obv:** Jugate heads right **Rev:** Crowned imperial eagle, shield on breast **Edge Lettering:** GOTT MIT UNS **Mint:** Berlin

Date	Mintage	F12	VF20	XF40	MS60	MS63
1915 A	1,400	640	1,400	3,000	3,750	4,500
1915 A	—	PF63 4,750				

KM# 1164 5 MARK
27.78 g., 0.900 Silver 0.8037 oz. ASW, 38 mm. **Ruler:** Ernst August **Subject:** Ernst August Wedding and Accession **Obv:** Jugate heads right **Obv. Legend:** U. LUNEB added **Rev:** Crowned imperial eagle, shield on breast **Mint:** Berlin

Date	Mintage	F12	VF20	XF40	MS60	MS63
1915 A	8,600	150	320	700	1,200	1,500
1915 A	—	PF63 1,600				

PATTERNS

Including off metal strikes

KM#	Date	Mintage	Identification	Mkt Val
Pn54	1913	—	3 Mark. Silver.	3,500
Pn55	1913	—	5 Mark. Silver.	5,000
Pn56	1915A	—	3 Mark. Silver. Plain. KM1161.	—
Pn57	1915A	—	3 Mark. Silver. Beaded rim. Weak 5 in date. Plain. KM1162.	—
Pn58	191x (1915)	—	5 Mark. Silver. Beaded rim, wedding portraits facing left. Partial date. Plain.	—

HAMBURG

The city of Hamburg is located on the Elbe River about 75 miles (125 kilometers) from the North Sea. Tradition states that it was founded by Charlemagne in the early 9th century. At first, the town was controlled by the archbishopric of Bremen and Hamburg (see Bremen). In 1110, Hamburg and the territory of Holstein came under the rule of Count Adolf I of Schauenburg (Schaumburg, ruled 1106-1128), which inaugurated a period stretching for four centuries in which the Holstein dynasty exercised authority over the city. Hamburg joined with Lübeck in 1241 to form the first partnership in what was to become the Hanseatic League. Count Adolf VI of Schauenburg (1290-1315) gave civic autonomy to Hamburg in 1292 and leased the mint right to the citizens the next year. Local *hohlpfennige* had already been struck fifty years previous. From this early time, the city struck an almost continuous series of coins throughout the centuries up to World War I. In 1510, Hamburg was granted the status of a Free City of the Empire, although it had actually been free for about 250 years. It was occupied by the French during the period of the Napoleonic Wars. In 1866, Hamburg joined the North German Confederation and became a part of the German Empire in 1871.

FREE CITY

REFORM COINAGE

KM# 612 2 MARK

11.11 g., 0.900 Silver 0.3215 oz. ASW, 28 mm. **Obv:** Helmeted arms with lion supporters **Obv. Legend:** FREIE UND HANSESTADT HAMBURG **Rev:** Crowned imperial eagle **Rev. Legend:** DEUTSCHES REICH 1899, ZWEI MARK below **Edge:** Reeded **Mint:** Hamburg **Note:** Prev. KM#294.

Date	Mintage	F12	VF20	XF40	MS60	MS63
1901 J	482,408	12.00	20.00	48.00	200	300
1902 J	778,880	10.00	20.00	48.00	200	300
1903 J	817,215	10.00	20.00	40.00	200	300
1904 J	1,248,330	10.00	20.00	40.00	180	300
1905 J	204,040	28.00	52.00	100	550	1,000
1906 J	1,224,910	10.00	20.00	40.00	180	300
1907 J	1,225,503	10.00	20.00	40.00	180	300
1908 J	367,750	10.00	24.00	44.00	180	325
1911 J	204,250	10.00	24.00	44.00	180	325
1912 J	78,500	16.00	40.00	90.00	300	600
1913 J	105,325	10.00	24.00	52.00	180	550
1914 J	327,758	9.50	20.00	40.00	140	300
Common date	—	PF63 400				

KM# 620 3 MARK

16.67 g., 0.900 Silver 0.4823 oz. ASW, 33 mm. **Obv:** Three tower castle on helmeted shield with supporters **Rev:** Crowned imperial eagle, shield on breast **Edge Lettering:** GOTT MIT UNS **Mint:** Hamburg **Note:** Prev. KM#296.

Date	Mintage	F12	VF20	XF40	MS60	MS63
1908 J	408,475	13.50	20.00	36.00	85.00	135
1909 J	1,388,892	13.50	20.00	36.00	85.00	135
1910 J	525,500	13.50	20.00	36.00	85.00	135
1911 J	922,000	13.50	20.00	36.00	85.00	135
1912 J	491,088	13.50	20.00	36.00	85.00	135
1913 J	343,200	13.50	20.00	36.00	85.00	135
1914 J	575,111	13.50	20.00	36.00	85.00	135
Common date	—	PF63 250				

KM# 610 5 MARK

27.78 g., 0.900 Silver 0.8037 oz. ASW, 38 mm. **Obv:** Helmeted arms with lion supporters **Obv. Legend:** FREIE UND HANSESTADT HAMBURG **Rev:** Crowned imperial eagle **Rev. Legend:** DEUTSCHES REICH 1907, FUNF MARK below **Edge Lettering:** GOTT MIT UNS **Mint:** Hamburg **Note:** Prev. KM#293.

Date	Mintage	F12	VF20	XF40	MS60	MS63
1901 J	171,603	24.00	37.50	80.00	500	900
1902 J	294,034	22.50	32.00	64.00	400	800
1903 J	588,535	22.50	32.00	60.00	275	450
1904 J	318,640	22.00	30.00	60.00	275	550
1907 J	325,534	22.00	30.00	60.00	275	550
1908 J	457,794	22.00	30.00	60.00	200	325
1913 J	326,800	22.00	30.00	48.00	165	225
Common date	—	PF63 1,500				

KM# 608 10 MARK

3.98 g., 0.900 Gold 0.1152 oz. AGW **Obv:** Helmeted arms with lion supporters **Obv. Legend:** FREIE UND HANSESTADT HAMBURG **Rev:** Crowned imperial eagle, type II **Rev. Legend:** DEUTSCHES REICH **Mint:** Hamburg **Note:** Prev. KM#292.

Date	Mintage	F12	VF20	XF40	MS60	MS63
1901 J	81,891	190	200	225	385	500
1902 J	40,763	215	255	400	650	1,000
1903 J	229,786	190	200	225	350	500
1905 J	164,000	190	200	225	350	500
1906 J	163,347	190	200	225	350	500
1907 J	111,373	190	200	225	350	500
1908 J	31,685	215	340	500	800	1,300
1909 J	122,245	190	200	225	350	500
1909 J	—	PF63 1,600				
1910 J	40,598	190	255	350	620	1,000
1910 J	—	PF63 2,000				
1911 J	75,000	190	210	290	330	800
1911 J	—	PF63 3,500				
1912 J	47,775	200	275	400	520	1,000
1912 J	—	PF63 2,000				
1913 J	40,937	200	275	350	430	1,000
1913 J	—	PF63 2,000				

KM# 618 20 MARK

7.97 g., 0.900 Gold 0.2305 oz. AGW **Obv:** Helmeted arms with lion supporters **Obv. Legend:** FREIE UND HANSESTADT HAMBURG **Rev:** Crowned imperial eagle, type III **Rev. Legend:** DEUTSCHES REICH **Edge Lettering:** GOTT MIT UNS **Mint:** Hamburg **Note:** Prev. KM#295.

Date	Mintage	F12	VF20	XF40	MS60	MS63
1908 J Rare	14	—	—	—	75,000	—
1913 J	491,133	—	—	295	375	400
1913 J	—	PF63 1,000				

TOKEN COINAGE

Reckoning Tokens

KM# TS1 1/100 VERRECHNUNGSMARKE

Aluminum, 20.5 mm. **Issuer:** Hamburg Bank **Obv:** City arms-three tower castle on helmeted shield with supporters **Rev:** Denomination within circle

Date	Mintage	F12	VF20	XF40	MS60	MS63
1923	9,128,000	3.00	5.00	7.50	12.50	25.00

KM# TS2 5/100 VERRECHNUNGSMARKE

Aluminum, 23 mm. **Issuer:** Hamburg Bank **Obv:** City arms-three tower castle on helmeted shield with supporters **Rev:** Denomination within circle

Date	Mintage	F12	VF20	XF40	MS60	MS63
1923	8,100,000	2.75	3.50	5.00	9.00	18.00

KM# TS3 1/10 VERRECHNUNGSMARKE

Aluminum, 26.5 mm. **Issuer:** Hamburg Bank **Obv:** City arms-three tower castle on helmeted shield with supporters **Rev:** Denomination within circle

Date	Mintage	F12	VF20	XF40	MS60	MS63
1923	8,600,000	2.75	3.50	6.00	10.00	20.00

PATTERNS

Including off metal strikes

KM#	Date	Mintage	Identification	Mkt Val
Pn20	1906J	—	5 Mark. Copper. Plain. KM#610.	—
Pn21	1913	—	5 Mark. Silver. Plain. KM#610.	1,100
Pn22	1913J	—	5 Mark. Silver. Plain. KM#610.	—
Pn23	1914J	—	3 Mark. Silver. Plain. KM#620.	1,250
Pn24	1922J	—	1/2 Mark. Aluminum. Plain.	—
Pn25	1922J	—	1/2 Mark. Iron. Plain.	—
Pn26	1922J	—	1/2 Mark. Nickel. Plain.	—
Pn27	1922J	—	1/2 Mark. Copper. Plain. 19 mm.	225
Pn28	1922J	—	Mark. Aluminum. Plain.	—
Pn29	1922J	—	Mark. Copper. Plain.	—
Pn30	1922J	—	Mark. Nickel. Plain.	—
Pn31	1922J	—	Mark. Iron. Plain.	—
Pn32	1922J	—	2 Mark. Nickel. Plain.	—
Pn33	1922J	—	2 Mark. Aluminum. Plain.	—
Pn34	1922J	—	2 Mark. Zinc. Plain.	—
Pn35	1922J	—	3 Mark. Iron. Plain. Copper-nickel plated.	—
Pn36	1922J	—	3 Mark. Aluminum. Plain.	—
Pn37	1922J	—	3 Mark. Nickel. Plain.	—
Pn38	1922J	—	5 Mark. Nickel Plated Iron. Plain.	—
Pn39	1922J	—	5 Mark. Aluminum. Plain.	—
Pn40	1922J	—	5 Mark. Nickel. Plain.	—
Pn41	1922J	—	5 Mark. Zinc. Plain.	—

HESSE-DARMSTADT

(Hessen-Darmstadt)

Founded by the youngest of Philipp I's four sons upon the death of their father in 1567, Hesse-Darmstadt was one of the two main branches of the family which survived past the beginning of the 17th century. The Countship of Hanau-Lichtenberg was through marriage when the male line failed in 1736. Ludwig X was forced to cede that territory to France in 1801. In 1803, Darmstadt acquired part of the Palatinate, the city of Friedberg, part of the city of Mainz, and the Duchy of Westphalia in a general settlement with France. The Landgrave was elevated to the status of Grand Duke in 1806 and reacquired Hesse-Homburg, which got its souveranity back in 1816. In 1815 the Congress of Vienna awarded Hesse-Darmstadt the city of Worms and all of Mainz. These were relinquished, along with Hesse-Homburg, to Prussia in 1866 and Hesse-Darmstadt was called just Hesse from 1867 onwards. Hesse became part of the German Empire in 1871, but ceased to exist as a semi-sovereign state at the end of World War I.

RULER

Ernst Ludwig, 1892-1918

GRAND DUCHY

REFORM COINAGE

Grossherzogtum within the German Empire

KM# 372 2 MARK
11.11 g., 0.900 Silver 0.3215 oz. ASW, 28 mm. **Ruler:** Ernst Ludwig **Subject:** 400th Birthday of Philipp the Magnanimous **Obv:** Jugate heads left, dates below **Rev:** Crowned imperial eagle with shield on breast **Edge:** Reeded

Date	Mintage	F12	VF20	XF40	MS60	MS63
1904	100,000	27.00	60.00	85.00	120	160
1904	2,250	PF63 300				

Note: Obverse matte, reverse polished

KM# 375 3 MARK
16.67 g., 0.900 Silver 0.4823 oz. ASW, 33 mm. **Ruler:** Ernst Ludwig **Obv:** Head left **Rev:** Crowned imperial eagle, shield on breast **Edge Lettering:** GOTT MIT UNS **Mint:** Berlin

Date	Mintage	F12	VF20	XF40	MS60	MS63
1910 A	200,000	45.00	90.00	125	240	500
1910 A	—	PF63 600				

KM# 376 3 MARK
16.67 g., 0.900 Silver 0.4823 oz. ASW, 33 mm. **Ruler:** Ernst Ludwig **Subject:** 25-Year Jubilee **Obv:** Head left **Rev:** Crowned imperial eagle, shield on breast **Mint:** Berlin **Note:** All minted pieces are proof. Values in circulated grades are for impaired proofs.

Date	Mintage	F12	VF20	XF40	MS60	MS63
1917 A	1,333	PF60 6,500	PF63 7,500	PF65 9,000		

KM# 373 5 MARK
27.78 g., 0.900 Silver 0.8037 oz. ASW, 38 mm. **Ruler:** Ernst Ludwig **Subject:** 400th birthday of Philipp the Magnanimous **Obv:** Jugate heads left, dates below **Rev:** Crowned imperial eagle, shield on breast **Edge Lettering:** GOTT MIT UNS

Date	Mintage	F12	VF20	XF40	MS60	MS63
1904	40,000	55.00	120	180	300	450
1904	700	PF63 600				

Note: Obverse matte, reverse polished

KM# 371 20 MARK
7.97 g., 0.900 Gold 0.2305 oz. AGW **Ruler:** Ernst Ludwig **Obv:** Head left **Obv. Legend:** ERNST LUDWIG GROSHERZOG VON HESSEN **Rev:** Crowned imperial eagle, shield on breast **Rev. Legend:** DEUTSCHES REICH (date), 20 MARK below **Edge Lettering:** GOTT MIT UNS **Mint:** Berlin

Date	Mintage	F12	VF20	XF40	MS60	MS63
1901 A	80,000	295	320	480	800	1,280
1901 A	600	PF63 2,720				
1903 A	40,000	295	320	560	800	1,280
1903 A	100	PF63 2,400				

KM# 374 20 MARK
7.97 g., 0.900 Gold 0.2305 oz. AGW **Ruler:** Ernst Ludwig **Obv:** Head left **Obv. Legend:** ERNST LUDWIG GROSSHERZOG VON HESSEN **Rev:** Crowned imperial eagle, shield on breast **Rev. Legend:** DEUTSCHES REICH date, 20 MARK below **Edge Lettering:** GOTT MIT UNS **Mint:** Berlin

Date	Mintage	F12	VF20	XF40	MS60	MS63
1905 A	45,000	300	380	580	750	1,000
1905 A	200	PF63 1,100				
1906 A	85,000	300	340	430	700	900
1906 A	199	PF63 1,000				
1908 A	40,000	300	380	580	750	1,000
1908 A	—	PF63 1,100				
1911 A	150,000	300	330	400	700	900
1911 A	—	PF63 900				

PATTERNS

Including off metal strikes

KM#	Date	Mintage	Identification	Mkt Val
Pn31	1910A	—	3 Mark. Silver.	1,800
Pn32	1917	—	3 Mark. Silver.	—
Pn33	1917A	—	3 Mark. Silver. Plain. Y82.	10,000

LIPPE-DETMOLD

After the division of 1613, the Counts of Lippe-Detmold, as the senior branch of the family, ruled over the largest portion of Lippe (see), a small patrimony in northwestern Germany. In 1620, Lippe-Sternberg became extinct and its lands and titles reverted to Lippe-Detmold. The younger brother of Hermann Adolf founded the line of Lippe-Sternberg-Schwalenberg (Biesterfeld) in 1652, which lasted into the 20th century. In 1720, the count was raised to the rank of prince, but did not use the title until 1789. Lippe joined the North German Confederation in 1866 and became part of the German Empire in 1871. Prince Alexander was declared insane and placed under a regency during his entire reign. There ensued a ten-year testamentary dispute between the Lippe-Biesterfeld and the Schaumburg-Lippe lines over the succession to the childless Alexander - a Wilhelmine cause célèbre. Leopold (V) of the Biesterfeld line gained the principality in 1905, but was forced to abdicate in 1918, at the end of World War I. In 1947, Lippe was absorbed by the German state of North Rhine-Westphalia.

RULERS
Alexander, 1895-1905
Leopold IV, 1905-1918

MINT MARK
A - Berlin mint, 1843-1918

PRINCIPALITY

REFORM COINAGE

KM# 270 2 MARK
11.11 g., 0.900 Silver 0.3215 oz. ASW, 28 mm. **Ruler:** Leopold IV **Obv:** Head left **Rev:** Crowned imperial eagle, shield on breast **Edge:** Reeded **Mint:** Berlin

Date	Mintage	F12	VF20	XF40	MS60	MS63
1906 A	20,000	110	200	350	500	650
1906 A	1,100	PF63 750				

KM# 275 3 MARK
16.67 g., 0.900 Silver 0.4823 oz. ASW, 33 mm. **Ruler:** Leopold IV **Obv:** Head left **Rev:** Crowned imperial eagle, shield on breast **Edge Lettering:** GOTT MIT UNS **Mint:** Berlin

Date	Mintage	F12	VF20	XF40	MS60	MS63
1913 A	15,000	135	295	450	600	750
1913 A	100	PF63 1,100				

LÜBECK

The original settlement was called Liubice, the capital of a Slavic principality. It was located at the confluence of the Schwartau with the Trave Rivers and contained a castle with a merchant town on a harbor. The town was burned down in 1138 and Count Adolf II of Holstein (1128-64) refounded the city four miles (6.5 kilometers) up the Trave in 1143. Duke Heinirich III the Lion of Saxony (1153-80) forced Adolf II to relinquish Lübeck to him as his feudal overlord. Heinrich III no sooner had the city in his possession when a fire destroyed it. Heinrich III began rebuilding it in 1159 and this is now considered the traditional date of it founding. As the city and its trade on the Baltic grew in importance, special rights and privileges were granted to it in 1188 by Emperor Friedrich I Barbarossa. In 1226, Friedrich II raised Lübeck to the status of a free imperial city and a long period of self-government began. From about 1190 and into the 13th century, an imperial mint operated in the town. Although Lübeck was granted the mint right in 1188, reiterated in 1226 and 1340, its earliest civic coinage only began about 1350. The commercial importance of the city became even greater when it joined with Hamburg in 1241 to form the nucleus of what was to become the Hanseatic League. In 1358, the member cities of the League, which had grown very powerful during the preceding century, elected Lübeck as the administrative capital. By the beginning of the 15th century, the city was second only to Cologne as the largest in northern Germany.

The Protestant Reformation swept through Lübeck in 1529-30 (see Bishopric) and changes came rapidly as the governing city council was removed from office, only to be replaced by a revolutionary *burgomeister*, Jürgen Wullenwever. An unsuccessful war ensued against Denmark, Sweden and the Netherlands and caused the city to lose its powerful position in northern Europe. This began the dismemberment of the Hanseatic League and even a victorious war against Sweden during 1563-1570 was not enough to prevent the decline of Lübeck's fortunes. The demise of the League in 1630, during the Thirty Years' War, may have actually been beneficial to the city as it was able to remain neutral during the long years of struggle throughout Germany. The city was able to regain much of its lost economic power during the 18th century, partly due to increased trade with Russia through its new Baltic port of St. Petersburg. Lübeck's economy was completely ruined, however, during the Napoleonic Wars (1792-1815). Occupied by the French from 1811 to 1813, it was restored as a free city in the latter year. After 1815, the city was a member of the German Confederation and joined the North German Confederation in 1866. It remained a free city as part of the German Empire from 1871 until the end of World War I in 1918. However, its status as a self-governing entity, which had begun in 1226, did not end until 1937, when it was made a part of the province of Schleswig-Holstein.

FREE CITY

REFORM COINAGE

KM# 210 2 MARK
11.11 g., 0.900 Silver 0.3215 oz. ASW, 28 mm. **Obv:** Double imperial eagle with divided shield on breast **Rev:** Crowned imperial eagle, shield on breast **Edge:** Reeded **Mint:** Berlin

Date	Mintage	F12	VF20	XF40	MS60	MS63
1901 A	25,000	90.00	215	300	475	700
1901 A	—	PF63 900				

KM# 212 2 MARK
11.11 g., 0.900 Silver 0.3215 oz. ASW, 28 mm. **Obv:** Double imperial eagle with divided shield on breast **Edge:** Reeded **Mint:** Berlin

Date	Mintage	F12	VF20	XF40	MS60	MS63
1904 A	25,000	35.00	90.00	150	225	375
1904 A	200	PF63 500				

Date	Mintage	F12	VF20	XF40	MS60	MS63
1905 A	25,000	35.00	90.00	150	225	325
1905 A	178	PF63 500				
1906 A	25,000	35.00	90.00	150	225	325
1906 A	200	PF63 500				
1907 A	25,000	35.00	90.00	150	225	325
1907 A	—	PF63 500				
1911 A	25,000	35.00	90.00	150	225	325
1911 A	—	PF63 500				
1912 A	25,000	35.00	90.00	150	225	325
1912 A	—	PF63 500				

KM# 215 3 MARK
16.67 g., 0.900 Silver 0.4823 oz. ASW, 33 mm. **Obv:** Double imperial eagle with divided shield on breast **Rev:** Crowned imperial eagle, shield on breast **Edge Lettering:** GOTT MIT UNS **Mint:** Berlin

Date	Mintage	F12	VF20	XF40	MS60	MS63
1908 A	33,334	20.00	65.00	125	200	350
1909 A	33,334	20.00	65.00	125	200	350
1910 A	33,334	20.00	65.00	125	200	350
1911 A	33,334	20.00	65.00	125	200	350
1912 A	34,000	20.00	65.00	125	200	350
1913 A	30,000	20.00	65.00	125	200	350
1914 A	10,000	30.00	80.00	150	250	350
Common date	—	PF63 400				

KM# 213 5 MARK
27.78 g., 0.900 Silver 0.8037 oz. ASW, 38 mm. **Obv:** Double imperial eagle with divided shield on breast **Rev:** Crowned imperial eagle, shield on breast **Mint:** Berlin

Date	Mintage	F12	VF20	XF40	MS60	MS63
1904 A	10,000	110	315	425	550	1,100
1904 A	200	PF63 1,500				
1907 A	10,000	110	315	450	575	1,100
1907	—	PF63 1,700				
1908 A	10,000	110	315	450	600	1,100
1908	—	PF63 1,600				
1913 A	6,000	110	315	450	650	1,100
1913	—	PF63 1,750				

KM# 211 10 MARK
3.98 g., 0.900 Gold 0.1152 oz. AGW **Obv:** Double imperial eagle with divided shield on breast **Rev:** Crowned imperial eagle, shield on breast **Edge Lettering:** ~ * ~ **Mint:** Berlin

Date	Mintage	F12	VF20	XF40	MS60	MS63
1901 A	10,000	340	975	1,350	1,650	2,700
1901 A	200	PF63 3,000				
1904 A	10,000	340	975	1,350	1,650	2,700
1904 A	130	PF63 3,000				

KM# 214 10 MARK
3.98 g., 0.900 Gold 0.1152 oz. AGW **Obv:** Double imperial eagle with divided shield on breast **Rev:** Crowned imperial eagle, shield on breast **Edge:** ~ * ~ **Mint:** Berlin

Date	Mintage	F12	VF20	XF40	MS60	MS63
1905 A	10,000	340	945	1,300	1,650	2,500
1905 A	247	PF63 3,250				
1906 A	10,000	340	945	1,300	1,650	2,500
1906 A	216	PF63 3,250				
1909 A	10,000	340	945	1,300	1,650	2,000
1909 A	—	PF63 2,750				
1910 A	10,000	275	720	1,200	1,650	2,250
1910 A	—	PF63 3,000				

PATTERNS

Including off metal strikes

KM#	Date	Mintage	Identification	Mkt Val
Pn38	1915A	—	3 Mark. Copper. Aluminum plated.	—
Pn39	1915A	—	3 Mark. Zinc. Aluminum-plated.	—
Pn40	1915A	—	3 Mark. Silver.	3,000

MECKLENBURG-SCHWERIN

The Duchy of Mecklenburg was divided in 1592 to form the branches of Mecklenburg-Schwerin and Mecklenburg-Güstrow. During the Thirty Years' War, the several dukes of the Mecklenburg states sided with the Protestant forces against the emperor. Albrecht von Wallenstein, Duke of Friedland and imperial general, ousted the Mecklenburg dukes from their territories in 1628. The rightful rulers were each restored to their lands in 1632. In 1658, Mecklenburg-Schwerin was divided by the four sons of Adolf Friedrich into the lines of Mecklenburg-Schwerin, Mecklenburg-Grabow, Mecklenburg-Mirow (extinct in 1675) and Mecklenburg-Strelitz (see). Mecklenburg-Schwerin and Mecklenburg-Güstrow fell extinct in the male line in 1692 and 1695 respectively, becoming a source of dispute between Mecklenburg-Grabow and Mecklenburg-Strelitz. Both parties finally agreed to a settlement in 1701 which awarded about eighty percent of all Mecklenburg territory to Grabow, which became the main Schwerin line, and the rest to Strelitz. No coinage was produced for Mecklenburg-Schwerin from 1708 until 1750. In 1815, the Congress of Vienna elevated the ruler to the rank of Grand Duke. Mecklenburg-Schwerin became a part of the German Empire in 1871. The last grand duke abdicated at the end of World War I in 1918.

RULER
Friedrich Franz IV, 1897-1918

MINT MARKS
A - Berlin mint, 1852-1915

GRAND DUCHY

REFORM COINAGE

KM# 330 2 MARK
11.11 g., 0.900 Silver 0.3215 oz. ASW, 28 mm. **Ruler:** Friedrich Franz IV **Subject:** Grand Duke Coming of Age **Obv:** Head right **Rev:** Crowned imperial eagle, shield on breast **Edge:** Reeded **Mint:** Berlin

Date	Mintage	F12	VF20	XF40	MS60	MS63
1901 A	50,000	110	315	450	1,100	1,600
1901 A	1,000	PF63 2,000				

KM# 333 2 MARK
11.11 g., 0.900 Silver 0.3215 oz. ASW, 28 mm. **Ruler:** Friedrich Franz IV **Subject:** Friedrich Franz IV Wedding **Obv:** Jugate heads left **Rev:** Crowned imperial eagle, shield on breast **Edge:** Reeded **Mint:** Berlin

Date	Mintage	F12	VF20	XF40	MS60	MS63
1904 A	100,000	18.00	36.00	60.00	100	150
1904 A	6,000	PF63 225				

KM# 340 3 MARK
16.67 g., 0.900 Silver 0.4823 oz. ASW, 33 mm. **Ruler:** Friedrich Franz IV **Subject:** 100 Years as Grand Duchy **Obv:** Uniformed jugate busts left **Rev:** Crowned imperial eagle, shield on breast within circle **Edge Lettering:** GOTT MIT UNS **Mint:** Berlin

Date	Mintage	F12	VF20	XF40	MS60	MS63
1915 A	33,334	45.00	90.00	160	250	350
1915 A	—	PF63 500				

KM# 334 5 MARK
27.78 g., 0.900 Silver 0.8037 oz. ASW, 38 mm. **Ruler:** Friedrich Franz IV **Subject:** Friedrich Franz IV Wedding **Obv:** Jugate heads left **Rev:** Crowned imperial eagle, shield on breast **Edge Lettering:** GOTT MIT UNS **Mint:** Berlin

Date	Mintage	F12	VF20	XF40	MS60	MS63
1904 A	40,000	42.00	90.00	160	250	375
1904 A	2,500	PF63 600				

KM# 341 5 MARK
27.78 g., 0.900 Silver 0.8037 oz. ASW, 38 mm. **Ruler:** Friedrich Franz IV **Subject:** 100 Years as Grand Duchy **Obv:** Uniformed jugate busts left **Rev:** Crowned imperial eagle, shield on breast within circle **Edge Lettering:** GOTT MIT UNS **Mint:** Berlin

Date	Mintage	F12	VF20	XF40	MS60	MS63
1915 A	10,000	120	335	450	900	1,500
1915 A	—	PF63 1,600				

KM# 331 10 MARK
3.98 g., 0.900 Gold 0.1152 oz. AGW **Ruler:** Friedrich Franz IV **Subject:** Grand Duke Coming of Age **Obv:** Head right **Rev:** Crowned imperial eagle, shield on breast, type III **Edge:** ~ * ~ **Mint:** Berlin

Date	Mintage	F12	VF20	XF40	MS60	MS63
1901 A	10,000	1,150	2,000	2,950	4,500	7,000
1901 A	200	PF63 8,000				

KM# 332 20 MARK
7.97 g., 0.900 Gold 0.2305 oz. AGW **Ruler:** Friedrich Franz IV **Subject:** Grand Duke Coming of Age **Obv:** Head right **Rev:** Crowned imperial eagle, shield on breast, type III **Edge Lettering:** GOTT MIT UNS **Mint:** Berlin

Date	Mintage	F12	VF20	XF40	MS60	MS63
1901 A	5,000	1,500	2,900	4,000	6,250	9,000
1901 A	200	PF63 10,000				

PATTERNS

Including off metal strikes

KM#	Date	Mintage	Identification	Mkt Val
Pn26	1915A	—	3 Mark. Silver. Plain. KM340.	2,000
Pn27	1915A	—	3 Mark. Silver.	—
Pn28	1915A	—	5 Mark. Silver. KM341.	3,000

MECKLENBURG-STRELITZ

The Duchy of Mecklenburg-Strelitz was the youngest branch of the dynasty established when Mecklenburg-Schwerin was divided in 1658. Like its parent senior line, Mecklenburg-Strelitz became a grand duchy in 1815 as enacted by the Congress of Vienna. It became a constituent part of the German Empire in 1871, but all sovereignty ended with the conclusion of World War I in 1918.

RULERS
Friedrich Wilhelm, 1860-1904
Adolf Friedrich V, 1904-1914
Adolf Friedrich VI, 1914-1918

GRAND DUCHY

REFORM COINAGE

KM# 115 2 MARK
11.11 g., 0.900 Silver 0.3215 oz. ASW, 28 mm. **Ruler:** Adolph Friedrich V **Obv:** Head left **Rev:** Crowned imperial eagle, shield on breast **Edge:** Reeded **Mint:** Berlin

Date	Mintage	F12	VF20	XF40	MS60	MS63
1905	10,000	135	360	520	1,000	1,400
1905	2,500	PF63 1,500				

KM# 120 3 MARK
16.67 g., 0.900 Silver 0.4823 oz. ASW, 33 mm. **Ruler:** Adolph Friedrich V **Obv:** Head left **Rev:** Crowned imperial eagle, shield on breast **Edge Lettering:** GOTT MIT UNS **Mint:** Berlin

Date	Mintage	F12	VF20	XF40	MS60	MS63
1913	7,000	225	540	850	1,600	2,400
1913	—	PF63 2,800				

KM# 116 10 MARK
3.98 g., 0.900 Gold 0.1152 oz. AGW **Ruler:** Adolph Friedrich V **Obv:** Head left **Rev:** Crowned imperial eagle, shield on breast **Edge:** ~ * ~ **Mint:** Berlin

Date	Mintage	F12	VF20	XF40	MS60	MS63
1905	1,000	1,750	3,750	6,000	7,500	9,000
1905	150	PF63 10,000				

KM# 117 20 MARK
7.97 g., 0.900 Gold 0.2305 oz. AGW **Ruler:** Adolph Friedrich V **Obv:** Head left **Rev:** Crowned imperial eagle, shield on breast, type III **Edge Lettering:** GOTT MIT UNS **Mint:** Berlin

Date	Mintage	F12	VF20	XF40	MS60	MS63
1905	1,000	3,000	5,500	8,000	11,500	15,000
1905	160	PF63 17,500				

PATTERNS

Including off metal strikes

KM#	Date	Mintage	Identification	Mkt Val
Pn41	1913	—	3 Mark. Silver. KM120.	3,000

OLDENBURG

The countship of Oldenburg was situated on the North Seacoast, to the east of the principality of East Friesland. It was originally part of the old duchy of Saxony and the first recorded lord ruled from the beginning of the 11th century. The first count was named in 1091 and had already acquired the countship of Delmenhorst prior to that time. The first identifiable Oldenburg coinage was struck in the first half of the 13th century. Oldenburg was divided into Oldenburg and Delmenhorst in 1270, but the two lines were reunited by marriage five generations later. Through another marriage to the heiress of the duchy of Schleswig and countship of Holstein, the royal house of Denmark descended through the Oldenburg line beginning in 1448, while a junior branch continued as counts of Oldenburg. The lordship of Jever was added to the county's domains in 1575. One of the sons of Johann V, Christoph, studied for the priesthood, but became involved in the War of the Counts against King Christian III of Denmark (1534-59). Christoph issued field campaign money, invoking the name of Christian III's deceased cousin, King Christian II (1513-23). In 1667, the last count died without a direct heir and Oldenburg reverted to Denmark until 1773. In the following year, Oldenburg was given to the bishop of Lübeck, of the Holstein-Gottorp line, and raised to the status of a duchy. Oldenburg was occupied several times during the Napoleonic Wars and became a grand duchy in 1829. In 1817, Oldenburg acquired the principality of Birkenfeld from Prussia and struck coins in denominations used there. World War I spelled the end of temporal power for the grand duke in 1918, but the title has continued up to the present time. Grand Duke Anton Günther was born in 1923.

RULER
Friedrich August, 1900-1918

MINT MARK
A - Berlin mint, 1891-1901

GRAND DUCHY

REFORM COINAGE

KM# 202 2 MARK
11.11 g., 0.900 Silver 0.3215 oz. ASW, 28 mm. **Ruler:** Friedrich August **Obv:** Head left **Obv. Legend:** FRIEDRICH AUGUST GROSSHERZOG V. OLDENBURG **Rev:** Crowned imperial eagle with wreathed arms on breast **Rev. Legend:** DEUTSCHES REICH date, ZWEI MARK below **Edge:** Reeded **Mint:** Berlin

Date	Mintage	F12	VF20	XF40	MS60	MS63
1901 A	75,000	90.00	200	360	900	1,500
1901 A	260	PF63 2,500				

KM# 203 5 MARK
27.78 g., 0.900 Silver 0.8037 oz. ASW, 38 mm. **Ruler:** Friedrich August **Obv:** Head left **Obv. Legend:** FRIEDRICH AUGUST GROSSHERZOG V. OLDENBURG **Rev:** Crowned imperial eagle with wreathed arms on breast **Rev. Legend:** DEUTSCHES REICH date, FUNF MARK below **Edge Lettering:** GOTT ~ MIT ~ UNS **Mint:** Berlin

Date	Mintage	F12	VF20	XF40	MS60	MS63
1901 A	10,000	350	900	1,500	3,750	7,000
1901 A	170	PF63 8,000				

PRUSSIA

(Preussen)

Elector Friedrich III of Brandenburg-Prussia (1688-1713) was accorded the title of "King in Prussia" in 1701 as a reward for his support of Austria during the War of the Spanish Succession. Under successive strong leaders, Prussia gained increasing importance and added to its territories to become one of the leading countries of Europe in the course of the 18th century. As part of the reforms instituted by Friedrich II, the system of single letter mintmarks representing specific mints replaced the traditional incorporation of mint officials' symbols and/or initials as part of coin designs. Some of these very same mintmarks are still in use on modern German coins up to the present day. During the Napoleonic Wars (1792-1815), Prussia was allied with Saxony and they were soundly defeated at Jena in 1806. Prussia was forced to cede large portions of its territory at the time, but played a large part in the final defeat of Napoleon. The Congress of Vienna awarded Prussia part of Pomerania, the northern half of Saxony, much of Westphalia and the Rhineland, thus making it the largest state in Germany and a major power in European affairs. After defeating Denmark in 1864 and Austria in 1866, Prussia acquired Schleswig-Holstein, Hannover, Hesse-Cassel, Nassau and Frankfurt am Main. By this time, Prussia encompassed a large part of German territory and its population included two-thirds of all the German people. By winning the Franco-Prussian War (1870-71), Prussia became the pivotal state in the unification of Germany in 1871. King Wilhelm I was proclaimed Kaiser (Emperor) of all Germany, but World War I brought an end to both the Empire and the Kingdom of Prussia in 1918.

RULER
Wilhelm II, 1888-1918

MINT MARK
A - Berlin = Prussia, East Friesland, East Prussia, Posen

KINGDOM

REFORM COINAGE

A series of counterfeit Prussian 5, 10 and 20 Mark gold pieces all dated 1887A were being marketed in the early 1970's. They were created by a dentist in Bonn, West Germany and the previously unknown date listed above aroused the curiousity of the numismatic community and eventually exposed the scam.

KM# 522 2 MARK
11.11 g., 0.900 Silver 0.3215 oz. ASW, 28 mm. **Ruler:** Wilhelm II **Obv:** Head right **Obv. Legend:** WILHELM II DEUTSCHER KAISER KONIG V. PREUSSEN **Rev:** Crowned imperial eagle **Rev. Legend:** DEUTSCHES REICH date, ZWEI MARK below **Edge:** Reeded

Date	Mintage	F12	VF20	XF40	MS60	MS63
1901 A	398,486	70.00	160	300	1,000	2,250
1901 A	—	PF63 3,000				
1902 A	3,948,323	9.00	16.00	45.00	100	275
1903 A	4,078,709	9.00	16.00	45.00	100	275
1904 A	9,981,031	9.00	16.00	45.00	100	250
1905 A	6,493,135	9.00	15.00	40.00	100	275
1905 A	620	PF63 600				
1906 A	4,019,250	9.00	15.00	40.00	100	300

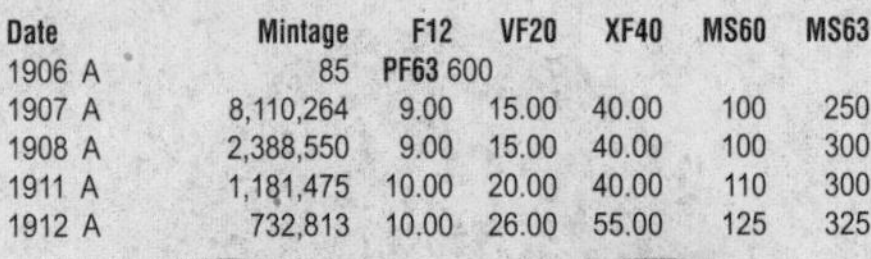

Date	Mintage	F12	VF20	XF40	MS60	MS63
1906 A	85	PF63 600				
1907 A	8,110,264	9.00	15.00	40.00	100	250
1908 A	2,388,550	9.00	15.00	40.00	100	300
1911 A	1,181,475	10.00	20.00	40.00	110	300
1912 A	732,813	10.00	26.00	55.00	125	325

KM# 525 2 MARK

11.11 g., 0.900 Silver 0.3215 oz. ASW, 28 mm. **Ruler:** Wilhelm II **Subject:** 200th Anniversary - Kingdom of Prussia **Obv:** Friedrich I, Wilhelm II left **Rev:** Crowned imperial eagle with shield on breast **Edge:** Reeded

Date	Mintage	F12	VF20	XF40	MS60	MS63
1901 A	2,600,000	9.00	14.00	20.00	35.00	50.00
1901 A	—	PF63 125				

KM# 532 2 MARK

11.11 g., 0.900 Silver 0.3215 oz. ASW, 28 mm. **Ruler:** Wilhelm II **Subject:** 100th Anniversary - victory over Napoleon at Leipzig **Obv:** Eagle with snake in talons, denomination below **Rev:** Figure on horseback surrounded by people **Edge:** Reeded

Date	Mintage	F12	VF20	XF40	MS60	MS63
1913 A	1,500,000	9.00	14.00	20.00	45.00	60.00
1913 A	—	PF63 125				

KM# 533 2 MARK

11.11 g., 0.900 Silver 0.3215 oz. ASW, 28 mm. **Ruler:** Wilhelm II **Subject:** 25th Year of Reign **Obv:** Uniformed bust right **Rev:** Crowned imperial eagle with shield on breast **Edge:** Reeded

Date	Mintage	F12	VF20	XF40	MS60	MS63
1913 A	1,500,000	9.00	14.00	20.00	45.00	60.00
1913 A	5,000	PF63 125				

KM# 527 3 MARK

16.67 g., 0.900 Silver 0.4823 oz. ASW, 33 mm. **Ruler:** Wilhelm II **Obv:** Head right **Rev:** Crowned imperial eagle with shield on breast **Edge Lettering:** GOTT MIT UNS

Date	Mintage	F12	VF20	XF40	MS60	MS63
1908 A	2,858,666	15.00	18.00	30.00	90.00	150
1909 A	6,343,745	15.00	18.00	30.00	90.00	150
1910 A	5,590,624	15.00	18.00	30.00	90.00	150
1911 A	3,241,710	15.00	18.00	30.00	90.00	150
1912 A	4,625,724	15.00	18.00	30.00	85.00	150
Common date	—	PF63 250				

KM# 530 3 MARK

16.67 g., 0.900 Silver 0.4823 oz. ASW, 33 mm. **Ruler:** Wilhelm II **Subject:** Berlin University **Obv:** Friedrich Wilhelm III and Wilhelm II left divide dates **Rev:** Crowned imperial eagle with shield on breast **Edge Lettering:** GOTT MIT UNS

Date	Mintage	F12	VF20	XF40	MS60	MS63
1910 A	200,000	20.00	50.00	80.00	125	225
1910 A	2,000	PF63 375				

KM# 531 3 MARK

16.67 g., 0.900 Silver 0.4823 oz. ASW, 33 mm. **Ruler:** Wilhelm II **Subject:** Breslau University **Obv:** Friedrich Wilhelm III, Wilhelm II left within circle **Rev:** Crowned imperial eagle with shield on breast **Edge Lettering:** GOTT MIT UNS

Date	Mintage	F12	VF20	XF40	MS60	MS63
1911 A	400,000	18.00	42.00	65.00	85.00	200
1911 A	—	PF63 300				

KM# 534 3 MARK

16.67 g., 0.900 Silver 0.4823 oz. ASW, 33 mm. **Ruler:** Wilhelm II **Subject:** 100 Years - Defeat of Napoleon **Obv:** Eagle with snake in talons, denomination below **Rev:** Figure on horseback surrounded by people **Edge Lettering:** GOTT MIT UNS

Date	Mintage	F12	VF20	XF40	MS60	MS63
1913 A	3,000,000	15.00	20.00	26.00	45.00	65.00
1913 A	—	PF63 150				

KM# 535 3 MARK

16.67 g., 0.900 Silver 0.4823 oz. ASW, 33 mm. **Ruler:** Wilhelm II **Subject:** 25th Year of Reign **Obv:** Uniformed bust right **Rev:** Crowned imperial eagle with shield on breast **Edge Lettering:** GOTT MIT UNS

Date	Mintage	F12	VF20	XF40	MS60	MS63
1913 A	1,000,000	15.00	20.00	26.00	45.00	65.00
1913 A	6,000	PF63 130				

KM# 538 3 MARK

16.67 g., 0.900 Silver 0.4823 oz. ASW, 33 mm. **Ruler:** Wilhelm II **Obv:** Uniformed bust right **Rev:** Crowned imperial eagle with shield on breast **Edge Lettering:** GOTT MIT UNS

Date	Mintage	F12	VF20	XF40	MS60	MS63
1914 A	2,022,000	15.00	20.00	26.00	70.00	300
1914 A	—	PF63 600				

KM# 539 3 MARK

16.67 g., 0.900 Silver 0.4823 oz. ASW, 33 mm. **Ruler:** Wilhelm II **Subject:** Centenary - Absorption of Mansfeld **Obv:** St. George slaying the dragon **Rev:** Crowned imperial eagle with shield on breast **Edge Lettering:** GOTT MIT UNS

Date	Mintage	F12	VF20	XF40	MS60	MS63
1915 A	30,000	220	400	600	1,100	1,300
1915 A	—	PF63 1,500				

KM# 523 5 MARK

27.78 g., 0.900 Silver 0.8037 oz. ASW, 38 mm. **Ruler:** Wilhelm II **Obv:** Head right **Obv. Legend:** WILHELM II DEUTSCHER KAISER KONIG V. PREUSSEN **Rev:** Crowned imperial eagle, type III **Rev. Legend:** DEUTSCHES REICH date, FUNF MARK below **Edge Lettering:** GOTT MIT UNS

Date	Mintage	F12	VF20	XF40	MS60	MS63
1901 A	667,990	15.00	32.50	80.00	450	1,250
1902 A	1,950,840	15.00	30.00	80.00	300	1,250
1903 A	3,855,795	15.00	30.00	80.00	300	110
1904 A	2,060,410	15.00	30.00	95.00	300	1,100
1906 A	230,963	30.00	50.00	130	1,000	2,200
1907 A	2,902,338	15.00	27.50	65.00	200	600
1908 A	2,230,579	15.00	27.50	60.00	250	600
Common date	—	PF63 1,500				

KM# 526 5 MARK

27.78 g., 0.900 Silver 0.8037 oz. ASW, 38 mm. **Ruler:** Wilhelm II **Subject:** 200 Years - Kingdom of Prussia **Obv:** Friedrich I, Wilhelm II left **Rev:** Crowned imperial eagle with shield on breast **Edge Lettering:** GOTT MIT UNS

Date	Mintage	F12	VF20	XF40	MS60	MS63
1901 A	460,000	27.00	45.00	75.00	110	150
1901 A	—	PF63 275				

KM# 536 5 MARK

27.78 g., 0.900 Silver 0.8037 oz. ASW, 38 mm. **Ruler:** Wilhelm II **Obv:** Uniformed bust right **Rev:** Crowned imperial eagle, shield on breast

Date	Mintage	F12	VF20	XF40	MS60	MS63
1913 A	1,961,712	30.00	35.00	50.00	150	350
1914 A	1,587,179	30.00	32.00	45.00	150	400
Common date	—	PF63 1,500				

KM# 520 10 MARK

3.98 g., 0.900 Gold 0.1152 oz. AGW **Ruler:** Wilhelm II **Obv:** Head right **Obv. Legend:** WILHELM II DEUTSCHER KAISER KONIG V. PREUSSEN **Rev:** Crowned imperial eagle, type III **Rev. Legend:** DEUTSCHES REICH date, 10 MARK below **Edge:** ~ * ~

Date	Mintage	F12	VF20	XF40	MS60	MS63
1901 A	701,930	147	190	215	250	500
1901 A	—	PF63 1,600				
1902 A	270,911	147	210	275	275	500
1902 A	—	PF63 1,600				
1903 A	1,684,979	147	190	215	250	450
1903 A	—	PF63 1,600				
1904 A	1,178,129	147	190	215	250	400
1905 A	1,062,513	147	190	215	250	400
1905 A	117	PF63 1,200				
1906 A	531,970	147	190	220	265	425
1906 A	150	PF63 1,200				
1907 A	812,698	147	190	215	250	400
1907 A	—	PF63 1,600				
1909 A	531,934	147	190	220	265	425
1909 A	—	PF63 1,600				
1910 A	803,111	147	190	215	250	400
1910	—	PF63 1,600				
1911 A	270,798	147	200	270	295	420
1911 A	—	PF63 1,600				
1912 A	542,372	147	190	215	250	400
1912 A	—	PF63 1,600				

KM# 521 20 MARK

7.97 g., 0.900 Gold 0.2305 oz. AGW **Ruler:** Wilhelm II **Obv:** Head right **Obv. Legend:** WILHELM II DEUTSCHER KAISER KONIG V. PREUSSEN **Rev:** Crowned imperial eagle, type III **Rev. Legend:** DEUTSCHES REICH date, 20 MARK below

Date	Mintage	F12	VF20	XF40	MS60	MS63
1901 A	5,188,340	—	—	325	395	450
1901 A	—	PF63 1,500				
1902 A	4,138,128	—	—	325	395	450
1902 A	—	PF63 1,500				
1903 A	2,870,073	—	—	325	395	450
1903 A	—	PF63 1,500				
1904 A	3,452,625	—	—	325	395	450
1904 A	—	PF63 1,500				
1905 A	4,175,793	—	—	325	395	450
1905 A	287	PF63 1,500				
1905 J	920,784	305	310	325	410	475
1906 A	7,788,122	—	—	325	395	450
1906 A	124	PF63 1,500				
1906 J	81,686	310	325	340	470	650
1907 A	2,576,286	—	—	325	395	450
1907 A	—	PF63 1,500				
1908 A	3,274,168	—	—	325	395	450
1908 A	—	PF63 1,500				
1909 A	5,212,836	—	—	325	395	450
1909 A	—	PF63 1,500				
1909 J	350,128	—	—	325	410	475
1909 J	—	PF63 1,750				
1910 A	8,645,549	—	—	325	395	450
1910 A	—	PF63 1,500				
1910 J	753,217	—	—	325	395	450
1911 A	4,745,790	—	—	325	395	450
1911 A	—	PF63 1,500				
1912 A	5,569,398	—	—	325	395	450
1912 A	—	PF63 1,500				
1912 J	502,530	305	310	325	410	475
1913 A	6,102,730	—	—	325	395	450
1913 A	—	PF63 1,500				

KM# 537 20 MARK

7.97 g., 0.900 Gold 0.2305 oz. AGW **Ruler:** Wilhelm II **Obv:** Uniformed bust right **Rev:** Crowned imperial eagle with shield on breast

Date	Mintage	F12	VF20	XF40	MS60	MS63
1913 A	—	295	310	325	395	425
1913 A	—	PF63 1,500				
1914 A	2,136,861	295	310	325	395	425
1914 A	—	PF63 1,500				
1915 A	1,268,055	—	1,100	1,400	2,000	2,500

PATTERNS

Including off metal strikes

KM#	Date	Mintage	Identification	Mkt Val
Pn28	1901	—	5 Mark. Silver. Larger design. KM526.	3,000
Pn29	1901A	—	5 Mark. Silver. Larger design. KM526.	3,000
PnA30	1901A	—	20 Mark. Silver. Plain.	350
Pn30	1904A	—	2 Mark. Silver. Plain. Broader rim. KM522.	1,000
Pn31	1904A	—	5 Mark. Silver.	—
Pn32	1904A	—	5 Mark. Copper. N.A." countermarked.	—
Pn33	1904A	—	5 Mark. Silver. Reeded. Without beaded rims. KM523.	—
Pn34	1904A	—	5 Mark. Silver. Smaller lettering. KM523.	—
Pn35	1904A	—	5 Mark. Silver. Eagle in ornamental in inner border.	3,000
Pn36	1905A	—	3 Mark. Silver.	3,500
Pn37	1905A	—	3 Mark. Silver. Legend in different position.	3,500
Pn38	1905A	—	3 Mark. Copper.	—
Pn39	1905A	—	3 Mark. Silver. KM527.	—
PnA40	1907A	—	20 Mark. Copper.	—
Pn40	1908A	—	5 Mark. Silver.	—
Pn41	1908A	—	5 Mark. Brass.	—
Pn42	1908J	—	20 Mark. Gold. KM521.2. Extra rare.	—
Pn43	1909A	—	2 Mark. Nickel. KM522.	—
Pn44	1910	—	3 Mark. Silver.	2,000
Pn45	1910	—	3 Mark. Copper.	—
Pn46	1911	—	3 Mark. Silver. KM531.	2,000
Pn47	1911	—	3 Mark. Silver.	—
Pn48	1911A	—	3 Mark. Silver. KM531.	1,000
Pn49	1912A	—	2 Mark. Silver. KM533.	1,000
Pn51	1912	—	3 Mark. Bronze.	—
Pn52	1912A	—	3 Mark. Silver.	1,500
Pn53	1912A	—	3 Mark. Bronze.	—
Pn54	1913A	—	2 Mark. Silver. Dots above "O" in KONIG. KM533.	2,500
Pn55	1913	—	3 Mark. Silver.	2,000
Pn56	1913	—	3 Mark. Bronze.	—
Pn57	1913A	—	3 Mark. Silver.	2,500
Pn58	1913A	—	3 Mark. Bronze.	—
Pn59	1913A	—	3 Mark. Silver. Dots above O in KONIG. KM535.	2,500
Pn60	1913A	—	3 Mark. Copper.	—
Pn61	1913A	—	5 Mark. Silver. Extra sharp design. KM536.	—
Pn62	1914A	—	3 Mark. Silver. Extra sharp design. KM538.	—
Pn63	1915	—	3 Mark. Silver. Gothic script. KM539.	3,500
Pn64	1915	—	3 Mark. White Metal.	—
Pn65	1915	—	3 Mark. Iron, Tinned. Tin-iron.	—

REUSS

The Reuss family, whose lands were located in Thuringia, was founded c. 1035. By the end of the 12th century, the custom of naming all males in the ruling house Heinrich had been established. The Elder Line modified this strange practice in the late 17th century to numbering all males from 1 to 100, then beginning over again. The Younger Line, meanwhile, decided to start the numbering of Heinrichs with the first male born in each century. Greiz was founded in1303. Upper and Lower Greiz lines were founded in 1535 and the territories were divided until 1768. In 1778 the ruler was made a prince of the Holy Roman Empire. The principality endured until 1918.

MINT MARKS

A - Berlin
B - Hannover

REUSS-OBERGREIZ

The other branch of the division of 1635, Obergreiz went through a number of consolidations and further divisions. Upon the extinction of the Ruess-Untergreiz line in 1768, the latter passed to Reuss-Obergreiz and this line continued on into the 20th century, obtaining the rank of count back in 1673 and that of prince in 1778.

RULERS

Heinrich XXII, 1859-1902
Heinrich XXIV, 1902-1918

PRINCIPALITY

REFORM COINAGE

KM# 128 2 MARK

11.11 g., 0.900 Silver 0.3215 oz. ASW, 28 mm. **Ruler:** Heinrich XXII **Obv:** Head right **Obv. Legend:** HEINRICH XXII v. G. G. ALT. L. SOUV. FÜRST REUSS **Rev:** Crowned imperial eagle with shield on breast **Rev. Legend:** DEUTSCHES REICH date, ZWEI MARK below **Edge:** Reeded **Mint:** Berlin

Date	Mintage	F12	VF20	XF40	MS60	MS63
1901 A	10,000	125	250	375	700	1,100
1901 A	—	PF63 1,200				

KM# 130 3 MARK

16.67 g., 0.900 Silver 0.4823 oz. ASW, 33 mm. **Ruler:** Heinrich XXIV **Obv:** Head right **Rev:** Crowned imperial eagle with shield on breast **Mint:** Berlin

Date	Mintage	F12	VF20	XF40	MS60	MS63
1909 A	10,000	140	325	450	800	1,300
1909 A	400	PF63 1,500				

PATTERNS

Including off metal strikes

KM#	Date	Mintage	Identification	Mkt Val
Pn4	1909A	—	3 Mark. Silver. Head faces left. KM130, Rare.	—

SAXONY

(Sachsen)

From about the time of Charlemagne, the term Saxony covered most of what is the northwestern part of modern day Germany. It roughly covered the area between the River Ems, the North Sea, the Eider and Elbe Rivers, extending to the southern slopes of the Harz Mountains, bordering Franconia, but not as far as the Rhine. The early Saxon tribes were pagans who, upon conquest by the Franks, became the nucleus of a buffer state between that empire and the heathen Slav peoples to the east.

The first Margrave of Saxony was Ludolf, named in 850 to defend the frontier, and recognized as founder of the Liudolfinger dynasty. His grandson acquired Thuringia (Thüringen) in 908 and was raised to the rank of duke in 911. The dynasty furnished the Saxon line of German kings and emperors beginning with Heinrich I the Fowler in 919 and up to Heinrich II, who died in 1024. A relative of the dynasty was delegated to rule Saxony and founded the Billung dynasty of dukes in 961. In 1260, Saxony was divided into Saxe-Lauenburg (Northern or Lower Saxony, which see) and Saxe-Wittenberg, also known as Upper Saxony, the southern part of the territory ruled by the Billungers.

SAXONY-ALBERTINE

(Sachsen-Albertinische Linie)

The younger of the two branches of the Billung dynasty, which ruled in Upper Saxony and Meissen, this line founded by Friedrich II's son, Albrecht, in 1485, first ruled in Meissen as dukes of Saxony. As a result of the conflict between Johann Friedrich I and Emperor Karl V (see Ernestine Line), the Albertine Line acquired the electoral dignity in 1547. The elector also became King of Poland in 1696 and permanently in 1709. As a result of the Napoleonic Wars (1792-1815), the elector was made King of Saxony in 1806, but lost half his territory to Prussia in 1813. The last king was forced to abdicate at the end of World War I.

RULERS

Albert, 1873-1902
Georg, 1902-1904
Friedrich August III, 1904-1918

MINT MARK

L - Leipzig

KINGDOM

REFORM COINAGE

KM# 1245 2 MARK

11.11 g., 0.900 Silver 0.3215 oz. ASW **Ruler:** Albert **Edge:** Reeded **Mint:** Muldenhutten **Note:** Similar to KM#185.

Date	Mintage	F12	VF20	XF40	MS60	MS63
1901 E	439,724	15.00	55.00	110	300	1,000
1902 E	542,762	12.50	55.00	110	275	800
1902 E	—	PF63 1,750				

KM# 1255 2 MARK

11.11 g., 0.900 Silver 0.3215 oz. ASW, 28 mm. **Ruler:** Georg **Subject:** Death of Albert **Obv:** Head right **Rev:** Crowned imperial eagle with shield on breast **Edge:** Reeded **Mint:** Muldenhutten

Date	Mintage	F12	VF20	XF40	MS60	MS63
1902 E	167,625	16.00	40.00	65.00	125	175
1902 E	250	PF63 225				

KM# 1257 2 MARK

11.11 g., 0.900 Silver 0.3215 oz. ASW, 28 mm. **Ruler:** Georg **Obv:** Head right **Rev:** Crowned imperial eagle with shield on breast **Mint:** Muldenhutten

Date	Mintage	F12	VF20	XF40	MS60	MS63
1903 E	745,551	30.00	60.00	140	250	600
1903 E	50	PF63 1,100				
1904 E	1,265,533	18.00	50.00	100	200	600
1904 E	—	PF63 900				

KM# 1261 2 MARK

11.11 g., 0.900 Silver 0.3215 oz. ASW, 28 mm. **Ruler:** Friedrich August III **Subject:** Death of Georg **Obv:** Head right **Rev:** Crowned imperial eagle with shield on breast **Edge:** Reeded **Mint:** Muldenhutten

Date	Mintage	F12	VF20	XF40	MS60	MS63
1904 E	150,000	16.00	40.00	90.00	120	160
1904 E	55	PF63 250				

KM# 1263 2 MARK

11.11 g., 0.900 Silver 0.3215 oz. ASW, 28 mm. **Ruler:** Friedrich August III **Obv:** Head right **Rev:** Crowned imperial eagle with shield on breast **Edge:** Reeded **Mint:** Muldenhutten

Date	Mintage	F12	VF20	XF40	MS60	MS63
1905 E	558,951	20.00	45.00	75.00	160	350
1905 E	100	PF63 650				
1906 E	558,750	20.00	45.00	75.00	160	350
1907 E	1,112,519	20.00	45.00	70.00	155	350
1908 E	335,689	20.00	45.00	70.00	155	350
1911 E	186,250	20.00	45.00	75.00	200	350
1912 E	167,625	20.00	45.00	75.00	200	350
1914 E	298,000	20.00	45.00	70.00	125	350
Common date	—	PF63 500				

KM# 1268 2 MARK

11.11 g., 0.900 Silver 0.3215 oz. ASW, 28 mm. **Ruler:** Friedrich August III **Subject:** 500th Anniversary - Leipzig University **Obv:** Crown Prince Friedrich the Pugnacious and Friedrich August III left **Rev:** Crowned imperial eagle with shield on breast **Edge:** Reeded

Date	Mintage	F12	VF20	XF40	MS60	MS63
1909	125,000	16.00	35.00	65.00	100	130
1909	300	PF63 225				

KM# 1267 3 MARK

16.67 g., 0.900 Silver 0.4823 oz. ASW, 33 mm. **Ruler:** Friedrich August III **Obv:** Head right **Rev:** Crowned imperial eagle with shield on breast **Edge Lettering:** GOTT MIT UNS **Mint:** Muldenhutten

Date	Mintage	F12	VF20	XF40	MS60	MS63
1908 E	276,073	17.00	22.00	40.00	100	150
1909 E	1,196,719	17.00	20.00	35.00	80.00	150
1910 E	745,000	17.00	20.00	35.00	90.00	150
1911 E	581,250	17.00	20.00	35.00	90.00	150
1912 E	378,750	17.00	20.00	35.00	90.00	150
1913 E	306,500	17.00	20.00	35.00	90.00	150
Common date	—	PF63 450				

KM# 1275 3 MARK

16.67 g., 0.900 Silver 0.4823 oz. ASW, 33 mm. **Ruler:** Friedrich August III **Subject:** Battle of Leipzig Centennial **Obv:** Monument divides date above **Rev:** Crowned imperial eagle with shield on breast **Edge Lettering:** GOTT MIT UNS **Mint:** Muldenhutten

Date	Mintage	F12	VF20	XF40	MS60	MS63
1913 E	999,999	9.00	18.00	28.00	40.00	55.00
1913 E	17,000	PF63 200				

KM# 1276 3 MARK

16.67 g., 0.900 Silver 0.4823 oz. ASW, 33 mm. **Ruler:** Friedrich August III **Subject:** Jubilee of Reformation **Obv:** Friederich the Wise right, Protector of Martin Luther **Rev:** Crowned imperial eagle with shield on breast **Edge Lettering:** GOTT MIT UNS **Mint:** Muldenhutten

Date	Mintage	F12	VF20	XF40	MS60	MS63
1917 E	100	PF63 75,000				

KM# 1246 5 MARK

27.78 g., 0.900 Silver 0.8037 oz. ASW, 38 mm. **Ruler:** Albert **Obv:** Head right **Obv. Legend:** ALBERT KOENIG VON SACHSEN **Rev:** Crowned imperial eagle **Rev. Legend:** DEUTSCHES REICH date, FUNF MARK below **Edge Lettering:** GOTT MIT UNS **Mint:** Muldenhutten

Date	Mintage	F12	VF20	XF40	MS60	MS63
1901 E	—	30.00	55.00	300	750	1,500
1901 E	—	PF63 2,750				
1902 E	168,200	28.00	45.00	275	650	1,200
1902 E	—	PF63 2,750				

KM# 1256 5 MARK

27.78 g., 0.900 Silver 0.8037 oz. ASW, 38 mm. **Ruler:** Georg **Subject:** Death of Albert **Obv:** Head right **Rev:** Crowned imperial eagle with shield on breast **Edge Lettering:** GOTT MIT UNS **Mint:** Muldenhutten

Date	Mintage	F12	VF20	XF40	MS60	MS63
1902 E	100,000	37.00	65.00	125	300	345
1902 E	250	PF63 750				

KM# 1258 5 MARK
27.78 g., 0.900 Silver 0.8037 oz. ASW, 38 mm. **Ruler:** Georg **Obv:** Head right **Rev:** Crowned imperial eagle with shield on breast **Edge Lettering:** GOTT MIT UNS **Mint:** Muldenhutten

Date	Mintage	F12	VF20	XF40	MS60	MS63
1903 E	536,298	30.00	50.00	175	550	1,000
1903 E	50	PF63 2,000				
1904 E	290,643	35.00	60.00	175	650	1,000
1904 E	—	PF63 1,500				

KM# 1262 5 MARK
27.78 g., 0.900 Silver 0.8037 oz. ASW, 38 mm. **Ruler:** Friedrich August III **Subject:** Death of Georg **Obv:** Head right **Rev:** Crowned imperial eagle with shield on breast **Edge Lettering:** GOTT MIT UNS **Mint:** Muldenhutten

Date	Mintage	F12	VF20	XF40	MS60	MS63
1904 E	37,200	45.00	150	225	350	450
1904 E	70	PF63 800				

KM# 1266 5 MARK
27.78 g., 0.900 Silver 0.8037 oz. ASW, 38 mm. **Ruler:** Friedrich August III **Obv:** Head right **Rev:** Crowned imperial eagle with shield on breast **Mint:** Muldenhutten

Date	Mintage	F12	VF20	XF40	MS60	MS63
1907 E	398,043	30.00	50.00	90.00	300	525
1908 E	317,301	30.00	45.00	85.00	250	500
1914 E	298,000	28.00	40.00	80.00	200	325
1914 E	—	PF63 1,500				

KM# 1269 5 MARK
27.78 g., 0.900 Silver 0.8037 oz. ASW, 38 mm. **Ruler:** Friedrich August III **Subject:** 500th Anniversary - Leipzig University **Obv:** Crown Prince Friedrich the Pugracious and Friederich August III left **Rev:** Crowned imperial eagle with shield on breast **Edge Lettering:** GOTT MIT UNS

Date	Mintage	F12	VF20	XF40	MS60	MS63
1909	50,000	50.00	100	190	275	350
1909	300	PF63 600				

KM# 1247 10 MARK
3.98 g., 0.900 Gold 0.1152 oz. AGW **Ruler:** Albert **Rev:** Crowned imperial eagle, type III **Edge:** ~ * ~ **Mint:** Muldenhutten

Date	Mintage	F12	VF20	XF40	MS60	MS63
1901 E	74,767	200	215	260	500	800
1902 E	37,413	200	215	260	500	800
1902 E	—	PF63 2,000				

KM# 1259 10 MARK
3.98 g., 0.900 Gold 0.1152 oz. AGW **Ruler:** Georg **Obv:** Head right **Rev:** Crowned imperial eagle with shield on breast **Edge:** ~ * ~ **Mint:** Muldenhutten

Date	Mintage	F12	VF20	XF40	MS60	MS63
1903 E	283,822	200	260	350	600	1,200
1903 E	100	PF63 2,750				
1904 E	149,260	200	260	350	600	1,200
1904 E	—	PF63 2,250				

KM# 1264 10 MARK
3.98 g., 0.900 Gold 0.1152 oz. AGW **Ruler:** Friedrich August III **Obv:** Head right **Rev:** Crowned imperial eagle with shield on breast **Edge:** ~ * ~ **Mint:** Muldenhutten

Date	Mintage	F12	VF20	XF40	MS60	MS63
1905 E	111,994	200	300	360	500	750
1905 E	100	PF63 2,500				
1906 E	75,093	200	300	360	500	850
1906 E	—	PF63 2,500				
1907 E	112,000	200	300	360	500	750
1907 E	111,878	PF63 2,500				
1909 E	112,070	200	300	360	500	750
1910 E	75,185	200	300	360	500	900
1910 E	—	PF63 2,500				
1911 E	37,622	200	300	360	500	900
1912 E	75,252	200	300	360	500	800
1912 E	—	PF63 2,500				

KM# 1260 20 MARK
7.97 g., 0.900 Gold 0.2305 oz. AGW **Ruler:** Georg **Obv:** Head right **Rev:** Crowned imperial eagle with shield on breast, type III **Edge Lettering:** GOTT MIT UNS **Mint:** Muldenhutten

Date	Mintage	F12	VF20	XF40	MS60	MS63
1903 E	250,000	295	400	425	450	550
1903 E	—	PF63 2,500				

KM# 1265 20 MARK
7.97 g., 0.900 Gold 0.2305 oz. AGW **Ruler:** Friedrich August III **Obv:** Head right **Rev:** Crowned imperial eagle with shield on breast **Mint:** Muldenhutten

Date	Mintage	F12	VF20	XF40	MS60	MS63
1905 E	500,173	295	400	420	500	650
1905 E	86	PF63 2,750				
1913 E	121,002	295	400	425	600	800
1914 E	325,246	295	400	415	475	650
1914 E	—	PF63 2,500				

PATTERNS

Including off metal strikes

KM#	Date	Mintage	Identification	Mkt Val
Pn78	1902 E	—	5 Mark. Silver. KM1258.	—
PnA78	1905E	—	20 Mark. Copper.	—
PnB78	1905E	—	20 Mark. Copper. Bust in uniform.	—
Pn79	1913	—	3 Mark. Silver.	—
Pn80	1917 E	—	3 Mark. Aluminum. KM1267.	—

SAXE-ALTENBURG

(Sachsen-(New)-Altenburg)

A new line was established at Altenburg when the Duke of Saxe-Hildburghausen exchanged Hildburghausen for Altenburg in 1826. This line lasted until the end of World War I, when the last duke was forced to abdicate.

RULERS
Ernst I, 1853-1908
Ernst II, 1908-1918

MINT MARKS
Berlin - A

DUCHY

REGULAR COINAGE

KM# 36 2 MARK
11.11 g., 0.900 Silver 0.3215 oz. ASW **Ruler:** Ernst I **Subject:** Ernst's 75th Birthday **Obv:** Head right **Rev:** Crowned imperial eagle with shield on breast **Edge:** Reeded **Mint:** Berlin **Note:** Prev. Saxe-Old-Altenburg KM#144.

Date	Mintage	F12	VF20	XF40	MS60	MS63
1901 A	500	PF63 1,400				
1901 A	50,000	95.00	200	360	750	1,200

KM# 38 5 MARK
27.77 g., 0.900 Silver 0.8035 oz. ASW **Ruler:** Ernst I **Subject:** Ernst's 75th Birthday **Obv:** Head right **Rev:** Crowned imperial eagle with shield on breast **Edge:** GOTT MIT UNS **Mint:** Berlin **Note:** Prev. Saxe-Old-Altenburg KM#145.

Date	Mintage	F12	VF20	XF40	MS60	MS63
1901 A	500	PF63 2,500				
1901 A	20,000	160	400	600	1,450	2,300

KM# 40 5 MARK
27.77 g., 0.900 Silver 0.8035 oz. ASW **Ruler:** Ernst I **Subject:** Ernst's 50th Year of Reign **Obv:** Head right, date and sprays below **Rev:** Crowned imperial eagle with shield on breast **Edge:** GOTT MIT UNS **Mint:** Berlin **Note:** Prev. Saxe-Old-Altenburg KM#147.

Date	Mintage	F12	VF20	XF40	MS60	MS63
1903 A	—	PF63 1,000				
1903 A	—	80.00	160	260	700	500

SAXE-COBURG-GOTHA

(Sachsen-Coburg-Gotha)

Upon the extinction of the ducal line in Saxe-Gotha-Altenburg in 1826, Gotha was assigned to Saxe-Coburg-Saalfeld and Saxe-Meiningen received Saalfeld. The resulting duchy became called Saxe-Coburg-Gotha. Albert, the son of Ernst I and younger brother of Ernst II, married Queen Victoria of Great Britain and the British royal dynastic name was that of Saxe-Coburg-Gotha. Their son, Alfred was made the Duke of Edinburgh and succeeded his uncle, Ernst II, as Duke of Saxe-Coburg-Gotha. Alfred's older brother, Eduard Albert, followed their mother as King Edward VII (1901-1910). The last duke of Saxe-Coburg-Gotha was Alfred's nephew, Karl Eduard, forced to abdicate in 1918 as a result of World War I, which was fought in part against his cousin, King George V.

RULER

Karl Eduard, 1900-1918

MINT MARK

A – Berlin Mint, 1886-1911

DUCHY

REFORM COINAGE

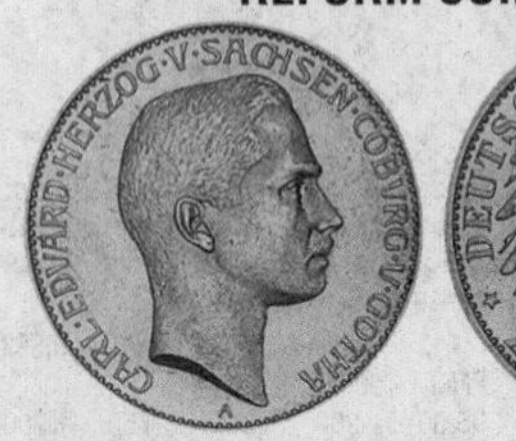

KM# 166 2 MARK

11.11 g., 0.900 Silver 0.3215 oz. ASW, 28 mm. **Ruler:** Karl Eduard **Obv:** Head right **Edge:** Reeded **Note:** Prev. KM#152.

Date	Mintage	F12	VF20	XF40	MS60	MS63
1905 A	10,000	110	280	480	1,100	1,300
1905 A	—	**PF63** 1,400				
1911 A	100	**PF63** 14,000				

KM# 174 5 MARK

27.78 g., 0.900 Silver 0.8038 oz. ASW, 38 mm. **Ruler:** Karl Eduard **Obv:** Head right **Rev:** Crowned imperial eagle with shield on breast **Edge Lettering:** GOTT MIT UNS **Note:** Prev. KM#153.

Date	Mintage	F12	VF20	XF40	MS60	MS63
1907 A	10,000	260	680	920	1,750	2,400
1907 A	—	**PF63** 3,250				

KM# 169 10 MARK

3.98 g., 0.900 Gold 0.1152 oz. AGW **Ruler:** Karl Eduard **Obv:** Head right **Rev:** Crowned imperial eagle with shield on breast **Edge:** ~ * ~ **Note:** Prev. KM#154.

Date	Mintage	F12	VF20	XF40	MS60	MS63
1905 A	10,000	800	1,280	1,600	2,600	3,750
1905 A	—	**PF63** 4,250				

KM# 172 20 MARK

7.97 g., 0.900 Gold 0.2305 oz. AGW **Ruler:** Karl Eduard **Obv:** Head, right **Rev:** Crowned imperial eagle with shield on breast, type I **Edge Lettering:** GOTT MIT UNS **Note:** Prev. KM#155.

Date	Mintage	F12	VF20	XF40	MS60	MS63
1905 A	10,000	800	1,280	1,600	2,850	3,700
1905 A	—	**PF63** 5,000				

SAXE-MEININGEN

(Sachsen-Meiningen)

The duchy of Saxe-Meiningen was located in Thuringia (Thüringen), sandwiched between Saxe-Weimar-Eisenach on the west and north and the enclave of Schmalkalden belonging to Hesse-Cassel on the east. It was founded upon the division of the Ernestine line in Saxe-Gotha in 1680. In 1735, due to an exchange of some territory, the duchy became known as Saxe-Coburg-Meiningen. In 1826, Saxe-Coburg-Gotha assigned Saalfeld to Saxe-Meiningen. The duchy came under the strong influence of Prussia from 1866, when Bernhard II was forced to abdicate because of his support of Austria. The last duke was forced to give up his sovereign power at the end of World War I in 1918.

RULERS

Georg II, 1866-1914
Bernhard III, 1914-1918

DUCHY

REFORM COINAGE

KM# 196 2 MARK

11.11 g., 0.900 Silver 0.3215 oz. ASW, 28 mm. **Ruler:** Georg II **Subject:** Duke's 75th Birthday **Obv:** Head right **Rev:** Crowned imperial eagle with shield on breast **Edge:** Reeded **Mint:** Munich

Date	Mintage	F12	VF20	XF40	MS60	MS63
1901 D	20,000	80.00	200	320	750	1,000
1901 D	—	**PF63** 1,250				

KM# 198 2 MARK

11.11 g., 0.900 Silver 0.3215 oz. ASW, 28 mm. **Ruler:** Georg II **Obv:** Head left, long beard **Rev:** Crowned imperial eagle with shield on breast **Edge:** Reeded **Mint:** Munich

Date	Mintage	F12	VF20	XF40	MS60	MS63
1902 D	20,000	200	640	920	2,200	3,250

KM# 199 2 MARK

11.11 g., 0.900 Silver 0.3215 oz. ASW, 28 mm. **Ruler:** Georg II **Obv:** Head left, short beard **Rev:** Crowned imperial eagle with shield on breast **Mint:** Munich

Date	Mintage	F12	VF20	XF40	MS60	MS63
1902 D	Inc. above	80.00	160	280	750	1,250
1913 D	5,000	120	220	480	1,250	1,750
1913 D	—	**PF63** 1,800				

KM# 206 2 MARK

11.11 g., 0.900 Silver 0.3215 oz. ASW, 28 mm. **Ruler:** Bernhard III **Subject:** Death of Georg II **Obv:** Head left, long beard **Rev:** Crowned imperial eagle with shield on breast **Edge:** Reeded

Date	Mintage	F12	VF20	XF40	MS60	MS63
1915	30,000	28.00	60.00	120	220	325
1915	—	**PF63** 400				

KM# 203 3 MARK

16.67 g., 0.900 Silver 0.4823 oz. ASW, 33 mm. **Ruler:** Georg II **Obv:** Head left, long beard **Rev:** Crowned imperial eagle with shield on breast **Edge Lettering:** GOTT MIT UNS **Mint:** Munich

Date	Mintage	F12	VF20	XF40	MS60	MS63
1908 D	35,000	28.00	85.00	130	250	350
1908 D	—	**PF63** 600				
1913 D	20,000	28.00	85.00	135	300	400
1913 D	—	**PF63** 600				

KM# 207 3 MARK

16.67 g., 0.900 Silver 0.4823 oz. ASW, 33 mm. **Ruler:** Bernhard III **Subject:** Death of Georg II **Obv:** Head left, long beard **Rev:** Crowned imperial eagle with shield on breast **Edge Lettering:** GOTT MIT UNS

Date	Mintage	F12	VF20	XF40	MS60	MS63
1915	30,000	24.00	55.00	120	220	325
1915	—	**PF63** 500				

KM# 197 5 MARK

27.78 g., 0.900 Silver 0.8037 oz. ASW, 38 mm. **Ruler:** Georg II **Subject:** Duke's 75th Birthday **Obv:** Head right, long beard **Rev:** Crowned imperial eagle with shield on breast **Edge Lettering:** GOTT MIT UNS **Mint:** Munich

Date	Mintage	F12	VF20	XF40	MS60	MS63
1901 D	20,000	70.00	260	440	1,000	1,600
1901 D	—	**PF63** 2,000				

KM# 200 5 MARK

27.78 g., 0.900 Silver 0.8037 oz. ASW, 38 mm. **Ruler:** Georg II **Obv:** Long beard **Rev:** Crowned imperial eagle with shield on breast **Edge Lettering:** GOTT MIT UNS **Mint:** Munich

Date	Mintage	F12	VF20	XF40	MS60	MS63
1902 D	20,000	48.00	160	280	1,000	1,500

KM# 201 5 MARK

27.78 g., 0.900 Silver 0.8037 oz. ASW, 38 mm. **Ruler:** Georg II **Obv:** Head left, short beard **Rev:** Crowned imperial eagle with shield on breast **Mint:** Munich

Date	Mintage	F12	VF20	XF40	MS60	MS63
1902 D	Inc. above	48.00	140	380	1,200	1,800
1908 D	60,000	40.00	128	220	850	1,350

KM# 202 10 MARK

3.98 g., 0.900 Gold 0.1152 oz. AGW **Ruler:** Georg II **Obv:** Head left, long beard **Rev:** Crowned imperial eagle with shield on breast **Edge:** ~ * ~ **Mint:** Munich

Date	Mintage	F12	VF20	XF40	MS60	MS63
1902 D	2,000	1,125	2,250	3,375	4,500	6,250
1902 D	—	**PF63** 8,000				
1909 D	2,000	1,125	2,250	3,375	4,500	6,250

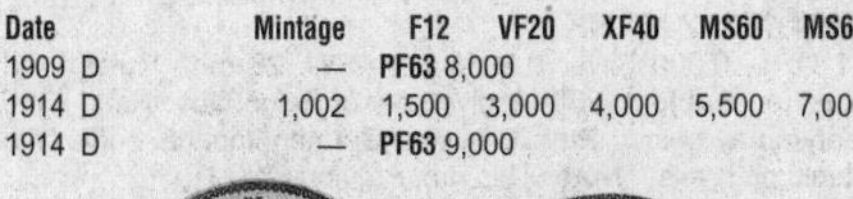

Date	Mintage	F12	VF20	XF40	MS60	MS63
1909 D	—	PF63 8,000				
1914 D	1,002	1,500	3,000	4,000	5,500	7,000
1914 D	—	PF63 9,000				

KM# 195 20 MARK
7.97 g., 0.900 Gold 0.2305 oz. AGW **Ruler:** Georg II **Obv:** Head left, short beard **Obv. Legend:** GEORG HERZOG VON SACHSEN MEININGEN **Rev:** Crowned imperial eagle, type III **Rev. Legend:** DEUTSCHES REICH date, 20 MARK below **Edge:** GOTT MIT UNS **Mint:** Munich

Date	Mintage	F12	VF20	XF40	MS60	MS63
1905 D	1,000	3,000	6,000	8,500	12,500	17,000
1905 D	—	PF63 17,500				
1910 D	1,004	—	—	—	—	—
1914 D	1,001	—	—	—	—	—

KM# 205 20 MARK
7.97 g., 0.900 Gold 0.2305 oz. AGW **Ruler:** Georg II **Obv:** Head left, long beard **Rev:** Crowned imperial eagle with shield on breast **Edge Lettering:** GOTT MIT UNS **Mint:** Munich

Date	Mintage	F12	VF20	XF40	MS60	MS63
1910 D	1,004	2,000	3,750	5,500	7,000	9,000
1910 D	—	PF63 10,000				
1914 D	1,000	2,000	3,750	5,500	7,000	9,000
1914 D	—	PF63 10,000				

PATTERNS

Including off metal strikes

KM#	Date	Mintage	Identification	Mkt Val
Pn16	1901D	—	10 Mark. Gold. With neck and beard variety. KM202. Extra rare.	—
Pn17	1901D	—	10 Mark. Gold. KM202.	—
Pn18	1915D	—	2 Mark. KM206.	1,250
Pn19	1915D	—	3 Mark. KM207.	1,250

SAXE-WEIMAR-EISENACH

(Sachsen-Weimar-Eisenach)

When the death of the duke of Saxe-Eisenach in 1741 heralded the extinction of that line, its possessions reverted to Saxe-Weimar, which henceforth was known as Saxe-Weimar-Eisenach. Because of the strong role played by the duke during the Napoleonic Wars, Saxe-Weimar-Eisenach was raised to the rank of a grand duchy in 1814 and granted the territory of Neustadt, taken from Saxony. The last grand duke abdicated at the end of World War I.

RULERS
Karl Alexander, 1853-1901
Wilhelm Ernst, 1901-1918

MINT MARK
A – Berlin Mint, 1840-1915

GRAND DUCHY

REFORM COINAGE

KM# 215 2 MARK
11.11 g., 0.900 Silver 0.3215 oz. ASW, 28 mm. **Ruler:** Wilhelm Ernst **Obv:** Head left **Rev:** Crowned imperial eagle with shield on breast **Edge:** Reeded **Note:** Prev. Y#170.

Date	Mintage	F12	VF20	XF40	MS60	MS63
1901 A	100,000	100	260	360	850	1,500
1901 A	—	PF63 2,000				

KM# 217 2 MARK
11.11 g., 0.900 Silver 0.3215 oz. ASW, 28 mm. **Ruler:** Wilhelm Ernst **Subject:** Grand Duke's First Marriage - Caroline **Obv:** Jugate heads left **Rev:** Crowned imperial eagle with shield on breast **Edge:** Reeded **Note:** Prev. Y#172.

Date	Mintage	F12	VF20	XF40	MS60	MS63
1903 A	40,000	28.00	48.00	80.00	160	225
1903 A	Est. 1000	PF63 250				

KM# 219 2 MARK
11.11 g., 0.900 Silver 0.3215 oz. ASW, 28 mm. **Ruler:** Wilhelm Ernst **Subject:** Jena University 350th Anniversary **Obv:** Johan Friedrich I the Magnanimous 3/4 right **Rev:** Crowned imperial eagle with shield on breast **Edge:** Reeded **Note:** Prev. Y#174.

Date	Mintage	F12	VF20	XF40	MS60	MS63
1908	50,000	20.00	45.00	90.00	135	200

KM# 221 3 MARK
16.67 g., 0.900 Silver 0.4823 oz. ASW, 33 mm. **Ruler:** Wilhelm Ernst **Subject:** Grand Duke's Second Marriage - Feodora **Obv:** Jugate heads left **Rev:** Crowned imperial eagle with shield on breast **Edge Lettering:** GOTT MIT UNS **Note:** Prev. Y#176.

Date	Mintage	F12	VF20	XF40	MS60	MS63
1910 A	133,000	20.00	35.00	65.00	125	170
1910 A	—	PF63 250				

KM# 222 3 MARK
16.67 g., 0.900 Silver 0.4823 oz. ASW, 33 mm. **Ruler:** Wilhelm Ernst **Subject:** Centenary of Grand Duchy **Obv:** Wilhelm Ernst and Carl August right **Rev:** Crowned imperial eagle with shield on breast **Edge Lettering:** GOTT MIT UNS **Note:** Prev. Y#177.

Date	Mintage	F12	VF20	XF40	MS60	MS63
1915 A	50,000	22.50	40.00	110	150	250
1915 A	—	PF63 400				

KM# 218 5 MARK
27.78 g., 0.900 Silver 0.8037 oz. ASW, 38 mm. **Ruler:** Wilhelm Ernst **Subject:** Grand Duke's First Marriage - Caroline **Obv:** Jugate heads left **Rev:** Crowned imperial eagle with shield on breast **Edge Lettering:** GOTT MIT UNS **Note:** Prev. Y#173.

Date	Mintage	F12	VF20	XF40	MS60	MS63
1903 A	24,000	48.00	100	180	375	500
1903 A	Est. 1000	PF63 750				

KM# 220 5 MARK
27.78 g., 0.900 Silver 0.8037 oz. ASW, 38 mm. **Ruler:** Wilhelm Ernst **Subject:** Jena University 350th Anniversary **Obv:** Johan Friedrich I the Magnanimous 3/4 right **Rev:** Crowned imperial eagle with shield on breast **Edge Lettering:** GOTT MIT UNS **Note:** Prev. Y#175.

Date	Mintage	F12	VF20	XF40	MS60	MS63
1908 A	40,000	45.00	85.00	160	300	425
1908 A	—	PF63 750				

KM# 216 20 MARK
7.97 g., 0.900 Gold 0.2305 oz. AGW **Ruler:** Wilhelm Ernst **Subject:** Golden Wedding of Carl Alexander **Obv:** Head left **Rev:** Crowned imperial eagle with shield on breast **Edge Lettering:** GOTT MIT UNS **Note:** Prev. Y#171.

Date	Mintage	F12	VF20	XF40	MS60	MS63
1901 A	5,000	1,250	2,000	3,500	5,500	7,000
1901 A	—	PF63 10,000				

PATTERNS

Including off metal strikes

KM#	Date	Mintage	Identification	Mkt Val
Pn46	1908	—	5 Mark. Silver. Figure smaller. Y#175. Rare.	—
Pn47	1910	—	3 Mark. Silver. Prev. KM#Pn2.	2,000
Pn48	1910	—	3 Mark. Brass. Prev. Pn#3.	—

SCHAUMBURG-LIPPE

The tiny countship of Schaumburg-Lippe, with an area of only 131 square miles (218 square kilometers) in northwest Germany, was surrounded by the larger states of Brunswick-Lüneburg-Calenberg, an enclave of Hesse-Cassel, and the bishopric of Minden (part of Brandenburg-Prussia from 1648). It was founded in 1640 when Schaumburg-Gehmen was divided between Hesse-Cassel and Lippe-Alverdissen. The two became known as Schaumburg-Hessen and Schaumburg-Lippe. Philipp II, the youngest son of Count Simon VI of Lippe came into the possession of Alverdissen and Lipperode upon his father's death in 1613. In 1640, he also inherited half of Schaumburg-Bückeburg, becoming the first Count of Schaumburg-Lippe. A separate line of Schaumburg-Alverdissen was established in 1681 and, upon the extinction of the elder line in 1777, the lands and titles devolved onto Alverdissen, becoming the ruling line in the countship. In 1807, the count was raised to the rank of prince and Schaumburg-Lippe was incorporated into the Rhine Confederation. It became a part of the German Confederation in 1815 and joined the North German Confederation in 1866. The principality became a member state in the German Empire in 1871. The last sovereign prince resigned as a result of World War I.

RULERS
Albrecht Georg, 1893-1911
Adolf II Bernhard, 1911-1918

MINT MARK
A - Berlin mint, 1858-1911

PRINCIPALITY

REFORM COINAGE

KM# 49 2 MARK
11.11 g., 0.900 Silver 0.3215 oz. ASW, 28 mm. **Ruler:** Albrecht Georg **Obv:** Head left **Obv. Legend:** GEORG FURST ZU SCHAUMBURG-LIPPE **Rev:** Crowned imperial eagle with shield on breast **Rev. Legend:** DEUTSCHES REICH date, ZWEI MARK below **Edge:** Reeded **Mint:** Berlin **Note:** Prev. Y#203.

Date	Mintage	F12	VF20	XF40	MS60	MS63
1904 A	5,000	200	475	550	850	1,100
1904 A	—	**PF63** 1,750				

KM# 55 3 MARK
16.67 g., 0.900 Silver 0.4823 oz. ASW, 33 mm. **Ruler:** Albrecht Georg **Subject:** Death of Prince Georg **Obv:** Head left **Rev:** Crowned imperial eagle with shield on breast **Edge Lettering:** GOTT MIT UNS **Mint:** Berlin **Note:** Prev. Y#206.

Date	Mintage	F12	VF20	XF40	MS60	MS63
1911 A	50,000	30.00	65.00	100	250	300
1911 A	—	**PF63** 375				

KM# 50 5 MARK
27.78 g., 0.900 Silver 0.8037 oz. ASW, 38 mm. **Ruler:** Albrecht Georg **Obv:** Head left **Obv. Legend:** GEORG FURST ZU SCHAUMBURG-LIPPE **Rev:** Crowned imperial eagle with shield on breast **Rev. Legend:** DEUTSCHES REICH date, FUNF MARK below **Edge Lettering:** GOTT MIT UNS **Mint:** Berlin **Note:** Prev. Y#204.

Date	Mintage	F12	VF20	XF40	MS60	MS63
1904 A	3,000	350	900	1,250	2,400	3,250
1904 A	—	**PF63** 3,750				

KM# 51 20 MARK
7.97 g., 0.900 Gold 0.2305 oz. AGW **Ruler:** Albrecht Georg **Obv:** Head left **Obv. Legend:** GEORG FURST ZU SCHAUMBURG-LIPPE **Rev:** Crowned imperial eagle with shield on breast **Rev. Legend:** DEUTSCHES REICH date, 20 MARK below **Edge Lettering:** GOTT MIT UNS **Mint:** Berlin **Note:** Prev. Y#205.

Date	Mintage	F12	VF20	XF40	MS60	MS63
1904 A	5,500	1,250	2,200	3,000	4,000	5,250
1904 A	132	**PF63** 6,000				

SCHLESWIG-HOLSTEIN

Schleswig-Holstein is located along the border area between Denmark and Germany. The Duchy of Schleswig was predominantly Danish while the Duchy of Holstein was mostly German. Holstein-Gottorp was the ruling line in most of the territory from 1533 and lost Schleswig to Denmark permanently in 1721. Holstein-Gottorp was transferred by the 1773 Treaty of Zarskoje Selo to Denmark in exchange for Oldenburg. There was a great deal of trouble in the area during the 19th century and as a result of a war with Denmark, Prussia annexed the territory in 1864. After World War I, a plebiscite was held and the area was divided in 1920. North Slesvig went to Denmark while South Schleswig and Holstein became a permanent part of Germany.

STATE

GUTSCHRIFTSMARKE COINAGE

KM# Tn1 5/100 GUTSCHRIFTSMARKE
Aluminum, 23 mm. **Obv:** Provincial arms **Rev:** Denomination **Mint:** (no Mint Information)

Date	Mintage	F12	VF20	XF40	MS60	MS63
1923	3,330,000	3.00	7.00	14.00	20.00	25.00

KM# Tn2 10/100 GUTSCHRIFTSMARKE
Aluminum, 27 mm. **Obv:** Provincial arms **Rev:** Denomination **Mint:** (no Mint Information)

Date	Mintage	F12	VF20	XF40	MS60	MS63
1923	4,500,000	4.00	8.00	16.00	20.00	25.00

SCHWARZBURG-RUDOLSTADT

Established upon the division of Schwarzburg-Sondershausen in 1552, the younger main branch of Schwarzburg, centered on the castle and town of Rudolstadt, 17 miles (29 kilometers) south of Weimar, flourished until the end of World War I. The count was raised to the rank of prince in 1711. The three sons of Albrecht VII, the first Count of Schwarzburg-Rudolstadt, ruled and issued coinage jointly, followed by a long succession of sole rulers descended from the middle son, Ludwig Günther I.

RULER
Günther Viktor, 1890-1918 (died 1925)

MINT MARK
A - Berlin mint, 1841-1901

PATTERNS

Including off metal strikes

KM#	Date	Mintage	Identification	Mkt Val
Pn9	1901 A	—	2 Mark. Silver. Y207. Extra rare. Prev. KM#Pn3.	—

SCHWARZBURG-SONDERSHAUSEN

As the elder main line of Schwarzburg established in 1552, the counts of Schwarzburg-Sondershausen controlled their scattered territories from the castle of Sondershausen in northern Thuringia (Thüringen), 10 miles (16 kilometers) southeast of Nordhausen. Count Christian Wilheim I was raised to the rank of prince in 1697 and the line descended from him until it finally became extinct in 1909. All titles and territories then passed to Schwarzburg-Rudolstadt.

RULER
Karl Günther, 1880-1909

ARMS
(See under Schwarzburg)

MINT MARK
A - Berlin mint, 1846-1909

PRINCIPALITY

REFORM COINAGE

KM# 152 2 MARK
11.11 g., 0.900 Silver 0.3215 oz. ASW, 28 mm. **Ruler:** Karl Günther **Subject:** 25th Anniversary of Reign **Obv:** Head right, leafy spray below **Rev:** Crowned German imperial eagle with shield on breast **Edge:** Reeded **Note:** Thick rim. Prev. Y#211.

Date	Mintage	F12	VF20	XF40	MS60	MS63
1905	13,000	35.00	70.00	125	250	325
1905	—	**PF63** 400				

KM# 153 2 MARK
11.11 g., 0.900 Silver 0.3215 oz. ASW, 28 mm. **Ruler:** Karl Günther **Subject:** 25th Anniversary of Reign **Obv:** Head right, leafy spray below **Rev:** Crowned German imperial eagle with shield on breast **Note:** Thin rim. Previous Y#211a.

Date	Mintage	F12	VF20	XF40	MS60	MS63
1905	62,000	20.00	55.00	75.00	150	275
1905	—	**PF63** 400				

KM# 154 3 MARK
16.67 g., 0.900 Silver 0.4823 oz. ASW, 33 mm. **Ruler:** Karl Günther **Subject:** Death of Karl Gunther **Obv:** Head right **Rev:** Crowned German imperial eagle with shield on breast **Edge Lettering:** GOTT MIT UNS **Mint:** Arnstadt **Note:** Previous Y#212.

Date	Mintage	F12	VF20	XF40	MS60	MS63
1909 A	70,000	24.00	48.00	80.00	175	325
1909 A	200	**PF63** 500				

PATTERNS

Including off metal strikes

KM#	Date	Mintage	Identification	Mkt Val
Pn2	1901A	—	2 Mark. Silver. Y209.	3,000
Pn3	1901A	—	2 Mark. Silver. Y211.	3,000
Pn4	1909A	—	3 Mark. Silver.	3,500

WALDECK-PYRMONT

The Count of Waldeck-Eisenberg inherited the Countship of Pyrmont, located between Lippe and Hannover, in 1625, thus creating an entity which encompassed about 672 square miles (1120 square kilometers). Waldeck and Pyrmont were permanently united in 1668, thus continuing the Eisenberg line as Waldeck-Pyrmont from that date. The count was raised to the rank of prince in 1712 and the unification of the two territories was confirmed in 1812. Waldeck-Pyrmont joined the German Confederation in 1815 and the North German Confederation in 1867. The prince renounced his sovereignty on 1 October of that year and Waldeck-Pyrmont was incorporated into Prussia. However, coinage was struck into the early 20th century for Waldeck-Pyrmont as a member of the German Empire. The hereditary territorial titles were lost along with the war in 1918. Some coins were struck for issue in Pyrmont only in the 18th through 20th centuries and those are listed separately under that name.

RULER
Friedrich, 1893-1918 (d.1946)

MINT MARKS
A - Berlin mint, 1842-1903

PRINCIPALITY

REFORM COINAGE

KM# 192 5 MARK
27.78 g., 0.900 Silver 0.8037 oz. ASW, 38 mm. **Ruler:** Friedrich **Obv:** Head left **Rev:** Crowned imperial eagle with shield on breast **Edge Lettering:** GOTT MIT UNS **Mint:** Hannover **Note:** Prev. Y#213.

Date	Mintage	F12	VF20	XF40	MS60	MS63
1903 A	2,000	—	2,800	3,750	5,000	7,500
1903 A	—	**PF63** 8,000				

KM# 195 20 MARK
7.97 g., 0.900 Gold 0.2305 oz. AGW **Ruler:** Friedrich **Obv:** Head left **Rev:** Crowned imperial eagle with shield on breast **Edge Lettering:** GOTT MIT UNS **Mint:** Hannover **Note:** Prev. Y#214.

Date	Mintage	F12	VF20	XF40	MS60	MS63
1903 A	2,000	2,750	4,500	7,500	11,000	14,000
1903 A	150	PF63 16,000				

WÜRTTEMBERG

Located in South Germany, between Baden and Bavaria, Württemberg takes its name from the ancestral castle of the ruling dynasty. The early countship was located in the old duchy of Swabia, most of which was given to Count Ulrich II (1265-79) in 1268 by Conradin von Hohenstaufen. Ulrich's son, Eberhard II (1279-1325) moved the seat of his rule to Stuttgart. Württemberg obtained the mint right in 1374 and joined the Swabian monetary union two years later. The countship was divided into the lines of Württemberg-Urach and Württemberg-Stuttgart in 1441 and the elder Urach branch was raised to the rank of duke in 1495. It became extinct in the following year and the younger line in Württemberg-Stuttgart inherited the lands and ducal title. A cadet line of the family had been established in Mömpelgard in 1473 and, when the Württemberg-Stuttgart line fell extinct in 1593, the primacy of the dynasty fell to Württemberg-Mömpelgard. The latter took the Stuttgart title and spun off several cadet branches in Neustadt, Neuenburg and Weiltingen-Brenz. Meanwhile, the duke in Stuttgart succumbed to the French advances under Napoleon. Land west of the Rhine was exchanged with France for territories in and around Reutlingen, Heilbronn and seven other towns in 1802. More territories were added in Swabia at the expense of Austria in 1805. Napoleon elevated the duke to the status of elector in 1803 and then to king in 1806. Even more land was given to Württemberg that year, doubling the kingdom's size, and it joined the Confederation of the Rhine. At the close of the Napoleonic Wars (1792-1815), Württemberg joined the German Confederation, but sided with Austria in its war with Prussia in 1866. It sided with Prussia against France in 1870 and became a member of the German Empire in 1871. King Wilhelm II was forced to abdicate at the end of World War I in 1918.

RULER
Wilhelm II, 1891-1918

MINT MARKS
F - Freudenstadt Mint

KINGDOM

REFORM COINAGE

KM# 631 2 MARK
11.11 g., 0.900 Silver 0.3215 oz. ASW, 28 mm. **Ruler:** Wilhelm II **Obv:** Head right **Obv. Legend:** WILHELM II KOENIG VON WUERTTEMBERG **Rev:** Crowned imperial eagle with shield on breast **Rev. Legend:** DEUTSCHES REICH (date) / ZWEI MARK **Edge:** Reeded **Mint:** Freudenstadt

Date	Mintage	F12	VF20	XF40	MS60	MS63
1901 F	591,927	10.00	17.00	40.00	125	300
1902 F	815,620	10.00	15.00	40.00	125	350
1903 F	811,383	10.00	17.00	40.00	125	350
1904 F	1,988,177	10.00	13.00	30.00	100	300
1905 F	609,835	10.00	18.00	35.00	100	300
1906 F	1,504,620	10.00	18.00	35.00	100	375
1907 F	1,504,497	10.00	13.00	30.00	100	300
1908 F	451,370	10.00	20.00	40.00	125	275
1912 F	251,224	10.00	13.00	30.00	100	200
1913 F	5,675	10.00	15.00	40.00	125	350
1914 F	5,962	10.00	15.00	35.00	100	225
Common date	—	PF63 275				

KM# 635 3 MARK
16.67 g., 0.900 Silver 0.4823 oz. ASW, 33 mm. **Ruler:** Wilhelm II **Obv:** Head right **Rev:** Crowned imperial eagle with shield on breast **Edge Lettering:** GOTT MIT UNS **Mint:** Freudenstadt

Date	Mintage	F12	VF20	XF40	MS60	MS63
1908 F	300,000	15.00	18.00	28.00	70.00	150
1909 F	1,906,698	15.00	18.00	28.00	65.00	150
1910 F	837,230	15.00	18.00	28.00	65.00	150
1911 F	424,820	15.00	18.00	28.00	65.00	150
1912 F	849,100	15.00	17.00	23.00	60.00	150
1913 F	267,700	15.00	18.00	28.00	75.00	150
1914 F	733,121	15.00	17.00	23.00	60.00	125
Common date	—	PF63 300				

KM# 636 3 MARK
16.67 g., 0.900 Silver 0.4823 oz. ASW, 33 mm. **Ruler:** Wilhelm II **Subject:** Silver Wedding Anniversary **Obv:** Conjoined heads right, normal bar in "H" of "CHARLOTTE" **Rev:** Crowned imperial eagle with shield on breast **Edge Lettering:** GOTT MIT UNS **Mint:** Freudenstadt

Date	Mintage	F12	VF20	XF40	MS60	MS63
1911 F	493,000	15.00	17.00	22.00	45.00	65.00
1911 F	—	PF63 175				

KM# 637 3 MARK
16.67 g., 0.900 Silver 0.4823 oz. ASW, 33 mm. **Ruler:** Wilhelm II **Subject:** Silver Wedding Anniversary **Obv:** High bar in "H" of "CHARLOTTE" **Rev:** Crowned imperial eagle with shield on breast **Edge Lettering:** GOTT MIT UNS **Mint:** Freudenstadt

Date	Mintage	F12	VF20	XF40	MS60	MS63
1911 F	7,000	110	240	380	700	1,100
1911 F	—	PF63 1,250				

KM# 638 3 MARK
16.67 g., 0.900 Silver 0.4823 oz. ASW, 33 mm. **Ruler:** Wilhelm II **Subject:** 25th Year of Reign **Obv:** Head right **Rev:** Crowned imperial eagle with shield on breast **Edge Lettering:** GOTT MIT UNS **Mint:** Freudenstadt **Note:** 5,650 were melted.

Date	Mintage	F12	VF20	XF40	MS60	MS63
1916 F	1,000	PF63 8,500				

KM# 632 5 MARK
27.78 g., 0.900 Silver 0.8037 oz. ASW, 38 mm. **Ruler:** Wilhelm II **Obv:** Head right **Obv. Legend:** WILHELM II KOENIG VON WUERTTEMBERG **Rev:** Crowned imperial eagle with shield on breast **Rev. Legend:** DEUTSCHES REICH (date) / FUNF MARK **Edge Lettering:** GOTT MIT UNS **Mint:** Freudenstadt

Date	Mintage	F12	VF20	XF40	MS60	MS63
1901 F	210,700	28.00	37.00	90.00	600	1,250
1902 F	360,889	28.00	37.00	90.00	400	1,400
1903 F	722,182	28.00	35.00	75.00	375	1,100
1904 F	391,317	28.00	35.00	75.00	375	1,100
1906 F	45,000	30.00	65.00	200	1,200	2,500
1906 F	50	PF63 3,500				
1907 F	436,321	28.00	35.00	65.00	300	800
1908 F	521,716	28.00	32.00	55.00	250	500
1913 F	341,200	28.00	32.00	50.00	200	375
Common date	—	PF63 1,300				

KM# 633 10 MARK
3.98 g., 0.900 Gold 0.1152 oz. AGW **Ruler:** Wilhelm II **Obv:** Head right **Obv. Legend:** WILHELM II KOENIG VON WUERTTEMBERG **Rev:** Crowned imperial eagle with shield on breast **Rev. Legend:** DEUTSCHES REICH **Edge:** ~ * ~ **Mint:** Freudenstadt

Date	Mintage	F12	VF20	XF40	MS60	MS63
1901 F	110,262	190	210	230	400	725
1902 F	50,112	190	230	255	525	900
1903 F	180,402	190	210	230	400	725
1903 F	—	PF63 2,200				
1904 F	349,631	190	210	230	400	725
1904 F	—	PF63 2,200				
1905 F	199,312	190	210	230	400	650
1905 F	—	PF63 2,200				
1906 F	100,164	190	210	230	400	725
1906 F	50	PF63 2,200				
1907 F	149,921	190	210	230	400	650
1907 F	—	PF63 2,200				
1909 F	100,189	190	210	230	400	650
1909 F	—	PF63 2,500				
1910 F	150,229	200	220	240	400	650
1910 F	—	PF63 2,500				
1911 F	50,337	190	315	440	775	1,050
1911 F	—	PF63 2,500				
1912 F	49,353	190	315	415	775	1,300
1912 F	—	PF63 2,500				
1913 F	50,038	190	315	465	775	1,300
1913 F	—	PF63 2,500				

KM# 634 20 MARK
7.97 g., 0.900 Gold 0.2305 oz. AGW **Ruler:** Wilhelm II **Obv:** Head right **Obv. Legend:** WILHELM II KOENIG VON WUERTTEMBERG **Rev:** Crowned imperial eagle with shield on breast **Rev. Legend:** DEUTSCHES REICH (date) / 20 MARK **Edge Lettering:** GOTT MIT UNS **Mint:** Freudenstadt

Date	Mintage	F12	VF20	XF40	MS60	MS63
1905 F	500,594	—	295	410	450	525
1905 F	—	PF63 2,300				
1913 F	42,687	5,000	16,000	25,000	50,000	81,500
1913 F	—	PF63 95,000				
1914 F	552,684	1,750	2,750	3,750	5,000	6,500
1914 F	—	PF63 9,200				

PATTERNS

Including off metal strikes

KM#	Date	Mintage	Identification	Mkt Val
Pn42	19xx (1904) F	—	5 Mark. Copper. Lettered.	—
Pn43	1904	—	5 Mark. Silver.	2,500
Pn44	1904F	—	5 Mark. Copper. Y222. Eagle within irregular inner circle, countermarked "N.A.	—
Pn45	1905	—	5 Mark. Silver.	3,500
Pn46	1905	—	5 Mark. Silver. Beaded rim.	5,500
Pn47	1905F	—	5 Mark. Silver. Lettered.	3,500
Pn48	1905F	—	5 Mark. Silver. Reeded.	3,500
Pn49	1910F	—	3 Mark. Silver. Irregular "LH" under neck. Y225a.	—
Pn50	1911	—	3 Mark. Silver.	—
Pn51	1911	—	3 Mark. Silver. Busts divide date.	—
Pn52	1911F	—	3 Mark. Aluminum.	—
PnA53	1911F	—	3 Mark. Iron. Aluminum-plated.	—
Pn54	1911F	—	3 Mark. Silver.	—
Pn55	1911F	—	3 Mark. Copper.	—
Pn56	1911F	—	3 Mark. Silver.	—
Pn57	1911F	—	3 Mark. Copper.	—
Pn58	1911F	—	3 Mark. Silver.	3,500
Pn59	1911F	—	3 Mark. Copper.	—
Pn60	1913F	—	2 Mark. Aluminum.	—

Pn61	1913	—	5 Mark. Nickel.	—
Pn62	1916F	—	3 Mark. Aluminum.	6,000
Pn63	1916F	—	3 Mark. Silver.	12,500

TRIAL STRIKES

KM#	Date	Mintage	Identification	Mkt Val
TS3	1905	—	3 Mark. Silver. Uniface.	—
TS4	19xx (1905)	—	5 Mark. Silver. Uniface.	225

1871-1918

Germany, a nation of north-central Europe which from1871 to 1945 was, successively, an empire, a republic and a totalitarian state, attained its territorial peak as an empire when it comprised a 208,780 sq. mi. (540,740 sq. km.) homeland and an overseas colonial empire.

As the power of the Roman Empire waned, several warlike tribes residing in northern Germany moved south and west, invading France, Belgium, England, Italy and Spain. In 800 A.D. the Frankish king Charlemagne, who ruled most of France and Germany, was crowned Emperor of the Holy Roman Empire, a loose federation of an estimated 1,800 German States that lasted until 1806. Modern Germany was formed from the eastern part of Charlemagne's empire.

After 1812, the German States were reduced to a federation of 32, of which Prussia was the strongest. In 1871, Prussian chancellor Otto von Bismarck united the German States into an empire ruled by William I, the Prussian king. The empire initiated a colonial endeavor and became one of the world's greatest powers. Germany disintegrated as a result of World War I.

It was reestablished as the Weimar Republic. The humiliation of defeat, economic depression, poverty and discontent gave rise to Adolf Hitler, 1933, who reconstituted Germany as the Third Reich and after initial diplomatic and military triumphs, expanded his goals beyond Europe into Africa and USSR which led it into final disaster in World War II, ending on VE Day, May 7, 1945.

RULERS

Wilhelm II, 1888-1918

MINT MARKS

A - Berlin
D - Munich
E - Muldenhutten (1887-1953)
F - Stuttgart
G - Karlsruhe
J - Hamburg

MONETARY SYSTEM

(Until 1923)

100 Pfennig = 1 Mark

(Commencing 1945)

100 Pfennig = 1 Mark

EMPIRE

STANDARD COINAGE

KM# 10 PFENNIG

2.00 g., Copper, 17.5 mm. **Ruler:** Wilhelm II **Obv:** Denomination, date at right **Rev:** Large crowned imperial eagle with shield on breast **Note:** Struck from 1890-1916.

Date	Mintage	F12	VF20	XF40	MS60	MS63
1901 A	21,045,000	0.20	1.25	4.00	22.00	25.00
1901 D	5,337,000	0.50	2.00	9.00	40.00	45.00
1901 E	1,397,000	1.00	6.00	27.00	80.00	100
1901 F	2,925,000	0.60	4.00	17.00	60.00	80.00
1901 G	1,977,000	2.50	9.00	32.00	100	130
1901 J	2,011,000	4.00	12.50	40.00	170	225
1902 A	7,474,000	0.50	2.00	4.00	22.00	30.00
1902 D	2,811,000	0.60	3.50	6.00	35.00	45.00
1902 E	1,183,000	1.00	6.00	25.00	85.00	125
1902 F	1,250,000	1.00	6.00	20.00	75.00	120
1902 G	881,000	4.00	22.50	60.00	190	230
1902 J	150	450	1,500	2,200	4,750	6,000
1903 A	12,690,000	0.20	1.00	4.00	25.00	35.00
1903 D	3,140,000	0.80	2.00	8.00	35.00	50.00
1903 E	1,956,000	1.50	3.00	10.00	45.00	60.00
1903 F	2,945,000	0.80	2.00	10.00	40.00	55.00
1903 G	1,377,000	3.00	6.00	25.00	95.00	125
1903 J	2,832,000	1.00	4.00	20.00	55.00	80.00
1904 A	28,625,000	0.20	1.00	3.00	15.00	30.00
1904 D	4,118,000	0.80	2.00	8.00	30.00	45.00
1904 E	2,778,000	1.00	3.00	9.00	30.00	50.00
1904 F	4,520,000	1.00	3.00	8.00	30.00	50.00
1904 G	3,232,000	2.00	6.00	18.00	70.00	90.00
1904 J	4,467,000	1.00	2.50	10.00	30.00	50.00
1905 A	19,631,000	0.20	1.00	3.50	16.00	22.00
1905 D	6,084,000	0.50	2.00	5.50	25.00	35.00
1905 E	3,564,000	0.50	2.00	5.50	25.00	35.00
1905 E	Inc. above	—	—	2,500	—	—
Note: Cross under denomination						
1905 F	4,153,000	0.80	3.00	6.50	35.00	45.00
1905 G	3,051,000	0.80	3.00	18.00	65.00	80.00
1905 J	4,085,000	1.00	5.00	12.00	50.00	65.00
1906 A	46,921,000	0.20	0.80	2.50	16.00	20.00
1906 D	5,633,000	0.20	0.80	5.00	25.00	35.00
1906 E	7,278,000	0.20	0.80	5.00	15.00	25.00
1906 F	7,173,000	0.20	0.80	5.00	20.00	30.00
1906 G	5,194,000	0.20	0.80	5.00	35.00	45.00
1906 J	3,622,000	0.20	1.00	6.00	40.00	55.00
1907 A	33,711,000	0.20	0.80	1.50	12.00	16.00
1907 D	14,691,000	0.20	1.00	2.00	18.00	23.00
1907 E	3,719,000	0.20	1.50	5.00	18.00	25.00
1907 F	7,026,000	0.20	1.00	3.00	18.00	23.00
1907 G	3,052,000	0.20	1.50	6.00	28.00	35.00
1907 J	6,722,000	0.20	1.50	6.00	18.00	25.00
1908 A	21,922,000	0.20	0.60	1.25	10.00	15.00
1908 D	10,629,000	0.20	0.80	2.25	18.00	23.00
1908 E	3,400,000	0.20	1.50	5.00	20.00	26.00
1908 F	6,112,000	0.20	1.50	5.00	20.00	26.00
1908 G	3,663,000	0.20	2.00	6.00	35.00	45.00
1908 J	5,581,000	0.20	1.50	5.00	20.00	26.00
1909 A	21,430,000	0.20	0.75	3.00	18.00	23.00
1909 D	2,814,000	0.20	1.25	7.00	50.00	65.00
1909 E	2,562,000	1.00	3.00	8.00	40.00	50.00
1909 F	2,425,000	1.50	4.00	10.00	45.00	60.00
1909 G	1,220,000	1.50	5.00	12.00	75.00	90.00
1909 J	1,634,000	1.50	5.00	11.00	75.00	90.00
1910 A	10,761,000	0.20	0.75	2.50	13.00	18.00
1910 D	4,221,000	0.20	1.00	3.00	18.00	24.00
1910 E	1,600,000	0.50	3.00	5.00	36.00	42.00
1910 F	3,009,000	0.30	2.00	6.00	28.00	35.00
1910 G	1,834,000	0.50	3.00	16.00	80.00	95.00
1910 J	2,450,000	0.50	3.00	9.00	55.00	70.00
1911 A	38,172,000	0.20	0.75	2.00	12.00	16.00
1911 D	8,657,000	0.20	1.00	3.00	18.00	23.00
1911 E	5,236,000	0.20	1.00	3.00	18.00	23.00
1911 F	5,780,000	0.20	1.00	3.00	18.00	23.00
1911 G	2,075,000	0.20	1.50	5.00	30.00	40.00
1911 J	5,594,000	0.20	1.00	3.00	13.00	18.00
1912 A	42,693,000	0.10	0.75	1.50	8.00	13.00
1912 D	10,173,000	0.10	0.80	2.00	10.00	15.00
1912 E	5,689,000	0.10	0.80	2.50	11.00	16.00
1912 F	7,441,000	0.10	0.80	3.00	11.00	16.00
1912 G	5,526,000	0.10	0.80	3.00	13.00	20.00
1912 J	5,615,000	0.10	0.80	3.00	23.00	30.00
1913 A	32,671,000	0.10	0.50	2.00	8.00	13.00
1913 D	8,161,000	0.20	1.00	3.00	10.00	15.00
1913 E	2,258,000	1.00	2.00	4.00	18.00	23.00
1913 F	6,620,000	0.20	1.00	3.00	12.00	16.00
1913 G	3,209,000	0.20	1.00	2.00	22.00	30.00
1913 J	1,456,000	0.10	5.00	10.00	42.00	50.00
1914 A	9,976,000	0.20	0.80	2.00	6.00	10.00
1914 D	1,842,000	0.20	1.25	2.50	12.00	17.00
1914 E	2,926,000	0.30	2.00	3.00	13.00	18.00
1914 F	3,316,000	0.20	1.00	2.00	13.00	18.00
1914 G	2,100,000	0.20	1.75	2.50	13.00	18.00
1914 J	4,368,000	0.20	1.75	2.50	13.00	18.00
1915 A	14,738,000	0.10	0.75	1.50	6.00	10.00
1915 D	1,771,000	0.20	1.00	2.50	17.00	22.00
1915 E	2,779,000	0.20	1.00	3.50	18.00	22.00
1915 F	1,411,000	0.20	1.00	4.00	22.00	30.00
1915 G	2,041,000	0.20	1.00	4.00	22.00	30.00
1915 J	2,981,000	0.20	1.00	4.00	18.00	25.00
1916 A	5,960,000	0.20	0.75	2.50	8.00	12.00
1916 D	5,401,000	0.20	1.00	4.00	20.00	30.00
1916 E	818,000	1.00	6.00	8.00	30.00	40.00
1916 F	1,104,000	0.80	3.00	8.00	30.00	40.00
1916 G	671,000	1.50	6.00	20.00	55.00	70.00
1916 J	898,000	1.00	5.00	10.00	45.00	55.00
1901-16 Common date proof	—	PF63 100	PF65 150			

KM# 24 PFENNIG

0.50 g., Aluminum **Ruler:** Wilhelm II **Obv:** Denomination, date at right **Rev:** Crowned imperial eagle with shield on breast

Date	Mintage	F12	VF20	XF40	MS60	MS63
1916 G	—	—	260	380	750	1,000
1917 A	27,159,000	0.15	0.75	2.00	6.00	8.00
1917 A	—	PF63 90.00				
1917 D	6,940,000	0.15	0.75	2.50	8.00	12.00
1917 E	3,862,000	0.50	2.00	5.00	13.00	18.00
1917 E	—	PF63 90.00				
1917 F	5,125,000	0.25	2.00	3.00	8.00	12.00
1917 G	3,139,000	0.25	2.00	4.00	9.00	14.00
1917 G	—	PF63 90.00				
1917 J	4,182,000	0.50	2.50	3.00	22.00	28.00
1917 J	—	PF63 90.00				
1918 A	—	—	2,000	3,000	4,000	5,000
1918 D	318,000	10.00	20.00	45.00	100	125
1918 F	—	—	1,800	3,500	—	—
Note: The 1918F 1 Pfennigs are from the burned-out ruins of the Stuttgart Mint destroyed in World War II						
1916-18 Common date proof	—	PF63 90.00				

KM# 16 2 PFENNIG

3.25 g., Copper, 20 mm. **Ruler:** Wilhelm II **Obv:** Denomination, date at right **Rev:** Large crowned imperial eagle with shield on breast

Date	Mintage	F12	VF20	XF40	MS60	MS63
1904 A	5,414,000	0.20	1.00	5.00	20.00	30.00
1904 D	1,404,000	0.50	2.00	10.00	25.00	35.00
1904 E	744,000	2.00	6.00	16.00	62.00	80.00
1904 F	1,002,000	0.20	3.50	12.00	40.00	55.00
1904 G	495,000	3.00	7.00	28.00	130	160
1904 J	44,000	2.00	11.00	25.00	170	200
1905 A	5,172,000	0.10	0.50	2.50	15.00	22.00
1905 D	1,570,000	0.20	2.00	10.00	25.00	35.00
1905 E	924,000	0.40	3.50	12.00	50.00	65.00
1905 F	1,115,000	0.40	3.00	10.00	55.00	70.00
1905 G	1,030,000	0.40	3.50	16.00	70.00	100
1905 J	1,609,000	0.40	3.00	12.00	80.00	100
1906 A	8,459,000	0.20	1.00	5.00	25.00	35.00
1906 D	3,539,000	0.20	1.75	6.00	30.00	40.00
1906 E	2,055,000	0.20	1.50	7.50	35.00	45.00
1906 F	2,840,000	0.20	1.50	6.50	30.00	40.00
1906 G	1,527,000	0.40	2.00	12.00	70.00	90.00
1906 J	1,908,000	0.40	2.00	12.00	55.00	75.00
1907 A	13,468,000	0.10	0.50	3.00	14.00	20.00
1907 D	1,921,000	0.20	0.75	4.50	26.00	30.00
1907 E	744,000	0.50	2.50	8.00	50.00	65.00
1907 F	1,059,000	0.20	2.50	12.00	60.00	80.00
1907 G	610,000	0.50	3.00	12.00	62.00	85.00
1907 J	952,000	0.20	2.50	10.00	50.00	65.00
1908 A	5,421,000	0.10	1.00	4.00	18.00	25.00
1908 D	1,407,000	0.10	2.00	7.00	23.00	30.00
1908 E	745,000	1.00	3.00	10.00	42.00	55.00
1908 F	1,003,000	0.10	3.00	10.00	42.00	55.00
1908 G	610,000	0.25	4.00	14.00	62.00	80.00
1908 J	817,000	0.10	3.00	12.00	55.00	70.00
1910 A	5,421,000	0.20	1.00	5.00	16.00	22.00
1910 D	1,407,000	0.50	2.00	8.00	25.00	35.00
1910 E	745,000	1.00	4.50	10.00	45.00	60.00
1910 F	1,003,000	0.40	2.00	8.00	40.00	55.00
1910 G	517,000	0.40	3.00	15.00	85.00	110
1910 J	568,000	0.40	3.00	15.00	75.00	95.00
1911 A	8,187,000	0.20	1.00	3.00	15.00	20.00
1911 D	2,100,000	0.20	2.00	4.00	20.00	26.00
1911 E	1,133,000	0.50	3.00	5.00	22.00	30.00
1911 F	1,490,000	0.40	2.00	4.00	20.00	26.00
1911 G	1,313,000	0.40	2.00	6.00	25.00	35.00
1911 J	1,883,000	0.40	2.00	4.00	20.00	26.00
1912 A	13,580,000	0.20	0.75	3.00	16.00	20.00
1912 D	3,109,000	0.30	1.00	4.00	20.00	26.00
1912 E	1,808,000	0.30	2.00	5.00	20.00	26.00
1912 F	2,366,000	0.30	1.00	6.00	20.00	26.00
1912 G	1,395,000	0.50	2.50	7.50	45.00	60.00
1912 J	1,605,000	0.50	2.00	6.00	25.00	35.00
1913 A	4,212,000	0.20	0.75	3.00	14.00	18.00
1913 D	2,525,000	0.20	1.00	6.00	22.00	28.00
1913 E	413,000	0.50	3.00	12.00	60.00	75.00
1913 F	1,602,000	0.40	2.00	12.00	55.00	70.00
1913 G	741,000	1.50	9.00	13.00	65.00	80.00
1913 J	1,254,000	0.40	2.00	9.00	55.00	70.00
1914 A	5,350,000	0.10	1.00	3.00	12.00	16.00
1914 E	1,201,000	1.00	5.00	8.00	35.00	45.00

Date	Mintage	F12	VF20	XF40	MS60	MS63
1914 F	158,000	12.00	45.00	90.00	275	320
1914 G	610,000	2.00	9.00	25.00	95.00	135
1914 J	817,000	0.10	6.00	17.00	60.00	80.00
1915 A	3,897,000	0.40	1.00	3.00	10.00	15.00
1915 D	1,407,000	0.40	2.00	6.00	18.00	25.00
1915 E	288,000	3.00	15.00	28.00	42.00	60.00
1915 F	904,000	0.20	2.00	7.00	20.00	30.00
1916 A	3,524,000	0.20	1.00	3.00	10.00	14.00
1916 D	915,000	0.40	1.50	8.00	16.00	22.00
1916 E	484,000	1.00	3.50	10.00	28.00	36.00
1916 F	651,000	0.25	1.50	5.00	18.00	25.00
1916 G	397,000	1.00	3.50	14.00	42.00	60.00
1916 J	531,000	0.50	2.50	12.00	32.00	50.00
1904-16 Common date proof	—	PF63 150				

KM# 11 5 PFENNIG

2.50 g., Copper-Nickel, 18 mm. **Ruler:** Wilhelm II **Obv:** Denomination, date at right **Rev:** Large crowned imperial eagle with shield on breast **Note:** Struck from 1890-1915.

Date	Mintage	F12	VF20	XF40	MS60	MS63
1901 A	8,155,000	0.20	0.60	5.00	30.00	50.00
1901 D	2,779,000	0.20	1.50	12.00	65.00	85.00
1901 E	1,492,000	0.40	2.50	12.00	90.00	120
1901 F	1,810,000	0.40	2.50	10.00	80.00	110
1901 G	915,000	0.50	3.50	35.00	290	350
1901 J	1,226,000	0.50	3.50	25.00	140	170
1902 A	8,949,000	0.20	0.75	5.00	30.00	50.00
1902 D	2,812,000	0.40	2.50	12.00	80.00	110
1902 E	1,120,000	1.00	3.50	12.00	60.00	80.00
1902 F	1,800,000	1.00	3.00	11.00	50.00	70.00
1902 G	1,220,000	1.50	6.00	25.00	140	170
1902 J	1,636,000	1.50	6.00	20.00	120	150
1903 A	5,932,000	0.20	4.00	6.00	60.00	80.00
1903 D	1,406,000	0.60	2.00	15.00	90.00	120
1903 E	1,114,000	0.80	3.50	18.00	70.00	100
1903 F	1,209,000	1.00	4.00	20.00	165	225
1903 G	610,000	2.00	9.00	55.00	265	300
1903 J	817,000	1.00	6.00	45.00	215	250
1904 A	6,791,000	0.20	6.00	10.00	55.00	75.00
1904 D	1,408,000	1.00	2.50	15.00	70.00	100
1904 E	746,000	1.50	6.00	20.00	120	150
1904 F	1,006,000	1.00	3.50	20.00	90.00	120
1904 G	610,000	2.00	8.00	25.00	290	350
1904 J	818,000	1.00	5.00	28.00	190	225
1905 A	8,129,000	0.20	0.75	2.50	25.00	45.00
1905 D	2,109,000	0.20	1.00	6.00	70.00	90.00
1905 E	1,117,000	0.40	1.75	7.00	50.00	70.00
1905 F	1,505,000	0.20	1.00	6.00	60.00	80.00
1905 G	915,000	1.00	3.00	16.00	120	145
1905 J	1,226,000	0.60	2.50	12.00	110	135
1906 A	18,970,000	0.20	0.75	2.00	20.00	35.00
1906 D	4,922,000	0.20	1.00	5.00	30.00	50.00
1906 E	2,605,000	0.20	1.25	5.00	35.00	55.00
1906 F	3,512,000	0.20	1.00	5.00	40.00	60.00
1906 G	2,136,000	0.50	2.00	15.00	120	150
1906 J	2,859,000	0.20	1.75	13.00	120	150
1907 A	11,930,000	0.20	0.75	2.25	12.00	25.00
1907 D	2,113,000	0.20	1.00	5.00	30.00	50.00
1907 E	1,517,000	0.30	1.75	5.00	30.00	50.00
1907 F	1,845,000	0.30	1.75	5.00	30.00	45.00
1907 G	915,000	1.00	2.50	6.00	55.00	80.00
1907 J	1,636,000	0.50	2.00	5.00	35.00	50.00
1908 A	22,114,000	0.20	0.50	2.50	12.00	20.00
1908 D	4,991,000	0.20	1.00	3.00	14.00	25.00
1908 E	2,919,000	0.30	1.50	5.00	25.00	40.00
1908/7 F	5,124,000	30.00	60.00	80.00	120	150
1908 F	Inc. above	0.50	1.50	5.00	30.00	50.00
1908 G	3,357,000	0.50	2.00	8.00	60.00	80.00
1908 J	3,264,000	0.50	2.00	10.00	95.00	125
1909 A	5,797,000	0.40	1.50	9.00	50.00	70.00
1909 D	2,753,000	0.60	2.50	14.00	95.00	125
1909 E	984,000	1.50	4.50	18.00	110	140
1909 F	252,000	2.00	18.00	50.00	240	300
1909/8 J	1,632,000	1.00	5.00	5.00	35.00	50.00
1909 J	Inc. above	1.00	9.00	28.00	160	190
1910 A	7,344,000	0.20	0.50	3.00	20.00	30.00
1910 D	2,814,000	0.20	0.80	6.00	30.00	50.00
1910 E	1,290,000	0.20	1.00	9.00	50.00	70.00
1910 F	1,721,000	0.20	1.50	11.00	55.00	75.00
1910 G	1,222,000	0.30	1.75	20.00	110	130
1910 J	152,000	30.00	42.00	70.00	140	175
1911 A	15,660,000	0.20	0.50	1.50	8.00	12.00
1911 D	2,221,000	0.20	1.00	2.50	12.00	18.00
1911 E	1,770,000	0.40	2.00	3.00	12.00	18.00
1911 F	2,714,000	0.40	2.00	3.00	12.00	18.00
1911 G	1,833,000	0.40	1.00	2.50	12.00	18.00
1911 J	3,116,000	0.20	1.00	2.00	15.00	22.00
1912 A	19,320,000	0.20	0.80	2.00	9.00	15.00
1912 D	4,015,000	0.20	0.80	2.50	13.00	18.00
1912 E	2,568,000	0.20	1.00	2.50	17.00	25.00
1912 F	3,679,000	0.20	1.00	2.50	17.00	25.00
1912 G	2,440,000	0.20	1.00	3.00	27.00	35.00
1912 J	3,020,000	0.20	1.00	2.50	17.00	25.00
1913 A	15,506,000	0.20	0.50	1.50	9.00	15.00
1913 D	5,519,000	0.20	0.50	2.00	12.00	18.00
1913 E	2,373,000	0.50	2.00	3.00	14.00	20.00
1913 F	2,054,000	0.50	2.00	3.00	14.00	20.00
1913 G	1,221,000	1.00	5.00	9.00	60.00	80.00
1913 J	253,000	10.00	16.00	35.00	145	180
1914 A	23,605,000	0.20	0.50	1.00	7.00	10.00
1914 D	3,014,000	0.20	0.80	1.50	9.00	15.00
1914 E	1,710,000	0.20	1.00	3.50	12.00	16.00
1914 F	2,206,000	0.20	1.00	2.50	15.00	22.00
1914 G	1,218,000	0.20	1.00	3.00	17.00	25.00
1914 J	3,235,000	0.20	1.00	2.50	17.00	25.00
1915 D	3,516,000	0.10	1.00	2.00	15.00	22.00
1915 E	834,000	1.00	8.00	13.00	50.00	70.00
1915 F	1,894,000	0.10	2.00	5.00	25.00	40.00
1915 G	894,000	0.50	7.00	18.00	60.00	80.00
1915 J	1,669,000	0.10	6.00	14.00	50.00	70.00
1901-15 Common date proof	—	PF63 120	PF65 165			

KM# 19 5 PFENNIG

2.51 g., Iron, 17.8 mm. **Obv:** Denomination, date below **Rev:** Crowned imperial eagle with shield on breast

Date	Mintage	F12	VF20	XF40	MS60	MS63
1915 A	34,631,000	0.20	0.50	3.00	12.00	20.00
1915 D	2,021,000	2.00	7.00	13.00	52.00	70.00
1915 E	4,670,000	1.00	4.00	9.00	32.00	45.00
1915 F	3,500,000	0.80	3.00	6.00	30.00	40.00
1915 G	3,676,000	0.80	3.00	6.00	30.00	40.00
1915 J	2,100,000	1.50	6.00	12.00	45.00	60.00
1916 A	51,003,000	0.20	0.50	2.50	10.00	15.00
1916 D	19,590,000	0.20	0.50	3.00	16.00	22.00
1916 E	2,271,000	2.00	6.00	15.00	45.00	60.00
1916 F	10,479,000	0.20	0.80	5.00	22.00	30.00
1916 G	5,599,000	0.50	1.50	5.50	30.00	40.00
1916 J	10,253,000	0.30	1.00	4.00	27.00	35.00
1917 A	87,315,000	0.10	0.30	1.50	10.00	15.00
1917 D	19,581,000	0.20	1.00	2.50	12.00	17.00
1917 E	11,092,000	0.50	1.00	3.00	16.00	20.00
1917 F	10,930,000	0.20	0.50	3.50	18.00	22.00
1917 F	—	600	1,000	1,600	2,250	2,500
Note: Mule with Polish reverse of Y#5, see Poland						
1917 G	6,720,000	0.20	1.00	4.00	16.00	22.00
1917 J	11,686,000	0.20	1.00	4.50	18.00	25.00
1918 A	223,516,000	0.10	0.50	1.00	5.00	8.00
1918 D	29,130,000	0.10	0.50	1.00	7.00	10.00
1918 E	23,600,000	0.20	1.00	2.00	8.00	14.00
1918 F	24,598,000	0.10	0.30	1.25	7.00	12.00
1918 G	12,697,000	0.20	1.00	2.00	8.00	14.00
1918 J	20,240,000	0.10	0.50	1.00	7.00	10.00
1919 A	112,102,000	0.10	0.50	0.75	5.00	8.00
1919 D	41,163,000	0.10	0.50	1.00	7.00	10.00
1919 E	20,608,000	0.10	0.50	1.00	7.00	10.00
1919 F	32,700,000	0.10	0.50	1.00	7.00	10.00
1919 G	13,925,000	0.20	1.00	2.00	12.00	20.00
1919 J	16,249,000	0.50	1.50	6.00	14.00	22.00
1920 A	80,300,000	0.10	0.40	1.00	5.00	8.00
1920 D	25,502,000	0.10	0.50	1.00	6.00	9.00
1920 E	11,646,000	0.50	1.00	3.00	22.00	30.00
1920 F	24,300,000	0.10	0.40	1.00	8.00	12.00
1920 G	10,244,000	0.10	0.50	1.25	14.00	18.00
1920 J	16,857,000	0.20	0.30	1.00	12.00	16.00
1921 A	143,418,000	0.10	0.20	0.75	6.00	9.00
1921 D	38,133,000	0.10	0.20	1.00	7.00	10.00
1921 E	21,104,000	0.50	1.00	3.50	22.00	30.00
1921 F	24,800,000	0.10	0.20	1.00	7.00	10.00
1921 G	21,289,000	0.10	0.20	1.00	7.00	10.00
1921 J	28,928,000	0.15	1.00	2.50	7.00	10.00
1922 A Rare	89,062,000	—	—	—	—	—
1922 D	31,240,000	0.10	0.20	0.50	10.00	14.00
1922 E	19,156,000	0.50	1.00	8.00	18.00	25.00
1922 F	16,436,000	0.10	0.20	1.00	10.00	14.00
1922 G	19,708,000	0.10	0.25	1.00	7.00	10.00
1922 J	16,820,000	0.10	0.20	1.25	13.00	18.00
1915-22 Common date proof	—	PF63 110				

KM# 12 10 PFENNIG

4.00 g., Copper-Nickel, 21 mm. **Ruler:** Wilhelm II **Obv:** Denomination, date at right **Rev:** Large crowned imperial eagle with shield on breast **Note:** Struck from 1890-1916.

Date	Mintage	F12	VF20	XF40	MS60	MS63
1901 A	10,200,000	0.20	1.00	8.00	50.00	75.00
1901 D	3,259,000	1.00	4.00	22.00	145	200
1901 E	1,863,000	1.00	5.00	20.00	165	250
1901 F	2,594,000	1.00	5.00	16.00	135	200
1901 G	1,527,000	2.00	17.00	60.00	275	350
1901 J	1,225,000	2.00	14.00	60.00	275	350
1902 A	5,878,000	0.20	1.00	4.00	55.00	80.00
1902 D	1,406,000	0.20	1.00	15.00	115	150
1902 E	502,000	1.00	5.00	35.00	220	325
1902 F	1,003,000	0.20	1.00	15.00	105	145
1902 G	610,000	0.20	10.00	50.00	275	375
1902 J	815,000	1.50	8.00	30.00	215	300
1903 A	5,131,000	0.20	0.50	5.00	85.00	120
1903 D	1,406,000	0.40	1.00	15.00	145	200
1903 E	988,000	0.40	1.00	15.00	115	160
1903 F	1,003,000	0.50	2.00	22.00	170	225
1903 G	610,000	2.00	8.00	50.00	245	325
1903 J	816,000	1.50	6.00	45.00	245	325
1904 A	5,189,000	0.20	0.50	4.00	65.00	95.00
1904 D	1,056,000	0.20	1.50	14.00	135	185
1904 E	559,000	0.20	1.50	14.00	125	175
1904 F	753,000	0.20	1.50	16.00	175	240
1904 G	457,000	2.00	10.00	50.00	275	375
1904 J	612,000	2.00	8.00	40.00	245	325
1905 A	8,650,000	0.20	0.50	3.00	45.00	65.00
1905 A	250	PF63 150	PF65 225			
1905 D	1,846,000	0.20	1.00	6.00	85.00	120
1905 E	980,000	0.40	1.50	16.00	145	200
1905 F	1,310,000	0.40	1.50	16.00	145	200
1905 G	642,000	1.50	8.00	50.00	245	325
1905 J	1,430,000	1.50	8.00	40.00	215	290
1906 A	14,470,000	0.20	0.50	4.00	45.00	65.00
1906 D	4,132,000	0.20	1.00	5.00	75.00	110
1906 E	2,189,000	0.20	1.00	6.00	75.00	110
1906 F	2,953,000	0.20	1.00	6.00	70.00	105
1906 G	1,952,000	1.00	5.00	40.00	255	350
1906 J	2,042,000	1.00	5.00	30.00	215	290
1907 A	17,971,000	0.20	0.50	2.00	20.00	35.00
1907 D	2,813,000	0.20	1.00	3.00	35.00	55.00
1907 E	2,291,000	0.20	1.00	3.00	40.00	60.00
1907 F	3,206,000	0.20	1.00	6.00	55.00	80.00
1907 G	1,889,000	0.50	2.00	15.00	135	190
1907 J	2,750,000	0.40	1.00	12.00	85.00	130
1908 A	20,410,000	0.20	0.50	2.00	30.00	45.00
1908 D	6,773,000	0.20	1.00	2.00	25.00	35.00
1908 E	2,490,000	0.20	1.00	5.00	75.00	100
1908 F	3,535,000	0.20	1.00	5.00	75.00	100
1908 G	1,708,000	0.40	2.00	15.00	125	175
1908 J	2,649,000	0.20	1.00	12.00	85.00	120
1909 A	2,270,000	0.40	1.00	8.00	75.00	110
1909 D	966,000	0.60	2.00	15.00	115	160
1909 E	806,000	1.00	3.00	13.00	125	175
1909 F	780,000	3.00	12.00	36.00	175	240
1909 G	980,000	2.00	9.00	40.00	235	320
1909 J	725,000	3.00	15.00	60.00	345	475
1910 A	3,734,000	0.20	6.00	2.00	25.00	40.00
1910 D	1,406,000	0.30	1.00	4.00	30.00	45.00
1910 E	300,000	2.50	10.00	28.00	155	215
1910 F	1,003,000	0.50	2.00	12.00	55.00	80.00
1910 G	610,000	2.50	10.00	33.00	215	290
1911 A	13,554,000	0.10	0.50	1.50	20.00	35.00
1911 D	2,508,000	0.20	0.80	2.50	20.00	35.00
1911 E	2,246,000	0.30	0.80	3.00	25.00	40.00
1911 F	2,235,000	0.30	0.80	3.00	25.00	40.00
1911 G	1,678,000	0.20	1.50	6.00	40.00	55.00
1911 J	3,062,000	0.20	0.80	3.00	35.00	50.00
1912 A	21,312,000	0.10	0.40	2.00	16.00	25.00
1912 D	6,988,000	0.20	0.80	2.00	22.00	30.00
1912 E	2,649,000	0.20	0.80	3.00	26.00	37.00
1912 F	3,787,000	0.10	0.40	3.00	20.00	29.00
1912 G	2,441,000	0.40	0.40	4.00	28.00	40.00
1912 J	2,730,000	0.10	0.40	4.00	28.00	40.00
1913 A	13,466,000	0.10	0.50	1.00	16.00	25.00
1913 D	3,164,000	0.20	0.80	2.00	20.00	29.00
1913 E	1,478,000	0.20	1.00	2.50	23.00	33.00
1913 F	1,991,000	0.20	1.00	2.50	28.00	40.00
1913 G	1,373,000	0.20	1.50	4.00	32.00	45.00
1913 J	1,550,000	0.20	1.50	4.00	32.00	45.00
1914 A	18,570,000	0.10	0.50	2.00	16.00	25.00
1914 D	2,301,000	0.10	0.50	2.00	20.00	29.00
1914 E	3,478,000	0.10	0.60	3.00	20.00	29.00
1914 F	4,515,000	0.20	1.00	2.50	23.00	33.00
1914 G	2,689,000	0.20	1.00	3.00	28.00	40.00
1914 J	1,589,000	0.20	0.50	3.00	26.00	35.00
1915 A	10,639,000	0.10	0.50	2.00	16.00	25.00
1915 D	2,277,000	0.10	0.50	3.00	20.00	29.00
1915 E	1,027,000	0.20	1.00	3.00	28.00	40.00
1915 F	1,508,000	0.20	1.00	3.00	28.00	40.00
1915 G	363,000	30.00	90.00	175	375	525
1915 J	2,677,000	0.50	1.00	5.00	28.00	40.00
1916 D	1,128,000	0.50	1.00	5.00	28.00	40.00
1901-16 Common date proof	—	PF63 125	PF65 175			

KM# 20 10 PFENNIG

3.60 g., Iron **Obv:** Denomination, date below **Rev:** Crowned imperial eagle with shield on breast, beaded border

Date	Mintage	F12	VF20	XF40	MS60	MS63
1916 A	69,143,000	0.20	0.60	1.50	8.00	—
1916 D	11,609,000	0.20	0.60	1.50	12.00	—
1916 E	8,280,000	0.30	1.00	2.50	12.00	—
1916 F	7,473,000	0.30	2.00	4.50	15.00	—
1916 G	5,878,000	0.30	2.00	4.50	18.00	—
1916 J	11,683,000	0.30	1.00	2.50	15.00	—
1916 Rare	—	180	220	—	—	—
1917 A	53,198,000	0.20	0.60	1.50	4.00	—
1917 D	16,370,000	0.20	0.60	1.50	5.00	—
1917 E	9,182,000	0.30	1.00	3.00	7.00	—
1917 F	11,341,000	0.20	1.50	3.00	7.00	—
1917 F	—	—	—	—	—	—
Note: Mule with Polish reverse of Y#6, see Poland						
1917 G	7,088,000	0.30	1.50	8.00	25.00	—
1917 J	9,205,000	0.30	1.00	8.00	25.00	—
1918 D	42,000	—	1,250	2,400	—	—
1921 A	16,265,000	0.80	3.00	8.00	33.00	—
1922 D	—	2.00	6.00	12.00	45.00	—
1922 E	2,235,000	10.00	30.00	60.00	200	—
1922 F	1,928,000	2.00	6.00	12.00	45.00	—
1922 G	1,358,000	10.00	30.00	60.00	200	—
1922 J	2,420,000	2.00	6.00	15.00	60.00	—
1922	—	40.00	130	200	—	—
Note: There are several 1915A patterns for this type						
1916-22 Common date proof	—	PF63 150				

KM# 25 10 PFENNIG

Zinc **Ruler:** Wilhelm II **Rev:** Crowned imperial eagle with shield on breast, beaded border

Date	Mintage	F12	VF20	XF40	MS60	MS63
1917	—	90.00	180	425	750	1,200

KM# 26 10 PFENNIG

Zinc **Obv:** Denomination, date below **Rev:** Crowned imperial eagle with shield on breast **Note:** Weight varies: 3.10-3.60 grams. Without mint mark. Variations in planchet thickness exist.

Date	Mintage	F12	VF20	XF40	MS60	MS63
1917	75,073,000	0.10	0.20	1.00	8.00	—
1918	202,008,000	0.10	0.20	1.00	8.00	—
1918	28	PF63 300				
1919	147,800,000	0.10	0.20	1.00	8.00	—
1919	50	PF63 100				
1920	223,019,000	0.10	0.20	1.00	6.00	—
1920	40	PF63 100				
1921	319,334,000	0.10	0.20	1.00	4.00	—
1921	24	PF63 300				
1922	274,499,000	0.10	0.20	1.00	8.00	—
1922	12	PF63 400				

KM# 18 25 PFENNIG

4.10 g., Nickel, 23 mm. **Ruler:** Wilhelm II **Obv:** Crowned imperial eagle with shield on breast **Rev:** Denomination within wreath

Date	Mintage	F12	VF20	XF40	MS60	MS63
1909 A	962,000	3.00	9.00	15.00	30.00	50.00
1909 D	1,406,000	3.00	9.00	12.00	25.00	40.00
1909 E	250,000	15.00	32.00	45.00	100	145
1909 F	400,000	3.00	11.00	20.00	45.00	80.00
1909 G	610,000	5.00	13.00	20.00	45.00	80.00
1909 J	10,000	220	500	1,250	2,500	3,500
1910 A	9,522,000	2.00	6.00	10.00	20.00	30.00
1910 D	1,408,000	4.00	11.00	22.00	65.00	90.00
1910 E	1,242,000	5.00	14.00	23.00	70.00	100
1910 F	1,605,000	3.00	9.00	20.00	55.00	85.00
1910 G	330,000	3.00	9.00	20.00	65.00	100
1910 J	1,561,000	3.00	9.00	17.00	45.00	65.00
1911 A	3,179,000	2.50	8.00	14.00	20.00	30.00
1911 D	506,000	5.00	14.00	28.00	50.00	80.00
1911 E	747,000	4.00	11.00	22.00	65.00	90.00
1911 G	892,000	4.00	11.00	22.00	65.00	90.00
1911 J	516,000	6.00	11.00	26.00	75.00	110
1912 A	2,590,000	3.00	9.00	12.00	30.00	50.00
1912 D	900,000	4.50	12.00	15.00	40.00	60.00
1912 F	1,003,000	4.50	12.00	15.00	40.00	60.00
1912 J	362,000	12.50	25.00	35.00	85.00	125
1909-12 Common date proof	—	PF63 250				

KM# 15 50 PFENNIG

2.78 g., 0.900 Silver 0.0804 oz. ASW **Ruler:** Wilhelm II **Obv:** Denomination within wreath **Rev:** Small eagle with long wing feathers, shield of arms on breast, all within wreath

Date	Mintage	F12	VF20	XF40	MS60	MS63
1901 A	194,000	160	300	400	625	800
1902 F	95,000	250	300	500	825	1,100
1902 F	—	PF63 1,000	PF65 1,500			
1903 A	384,000	130	220	280	500	675
1901-03 Common date proof	—	PF63 550	PF65 775			

KM# 17 1/2 MARK

2.77 g., 0.900 Silver 0.0802 oz. ASW, 20 mm. **Obv:** Denomination within wreath **Rev:** Crowned imperial eagle with shield on breast within wreath **Edge:** Reeded **Note:** Some coins dated from 1918-19 were issued with a black finish to prevent hoarding.

Date	Mintage	F12	VF20	XF40	MS60	MS63
1905 A	37,766,000	3.00	3.50	5.00	25.00	40.00
1905 D	7,636,000	3.00	3.50	5.00	35.00	50.00
1905 E	4,908,000	3.00	3.50	5.00	30.00	50.00
1905 F	6,310,000	3.00	3.50	7.00	35.00	50.00
1905 G	3,886,000	3.00	7.50	9.00	45.00	70.00
1905 J	6,316,000	3.00	8.00	15.00	65.00	90.00
1906 A	29,754,000	3.00	3.50	5.00	25.00	42.00
1906 D	11,977,000	3.00	5.00	7.00	27.00	46.00
1906 E	5,821,000	3.00	5.00	7.00	27.00	46.00
1906 F	8,036,000	3.00	8.00	9.00	27.00	46.00
1906 G	4,273,000	3.00	8.00	9.00	60.00	80.00
1906 J	2,179,000	7.00	20.00	40.00	285	400
1907 A	14,168,000	3.00	3.50	5.00	40.00	65.00
1907 D	2,884,000	3.00	3.50	7.00	35.00	50.00
1907 E	600,000	7.00	22.50	45.00	110	160
1907 F	1,202,000	5.00	13.00	32.00	170	230
1907 G	927,000	5.00	9.00	48.00	195	260
1907 J	3,268,000	3.00	8.00	30.00	110	160
1908 A	5,018,000	3.00	8.00	22.50	100	140
1908 D	400,000	8.00	22.50	75.00	225	325
1908 E	591,000	5.00	16.00	30.00	180	240
1908 F	1,000	2,000	5,000	8,000	11,000	15,000
1908 G	675,000	5.00	48.00	100	600	800
1908 J	Inc. above	5.00	42.00	160	1,500	2,000
1808/7 J	1,309,000	5.00	48.00	100	600	800
1909 A	5,404,000	3.00	5.00	15.00	110	160
1909/5 D	1,001,000	3.00	9.00	32.00	145	195
1909 D	Inc. above	3.00	9.00	32.00	145	195
1909 E	745,000	5.00	15.00	32.00	145	195
1909 F	999,000	3.00	9.00	32.00	140	210
1909 G	607,000	7.00	22.50	65.00	420	575
1909 J	816,000	5.00	16.00	32.00	190	260
1911 A	2,710,000	3.00	5.00	15.00	80.00	115
1911 D	Inc. above	3.00	8.00	20.00	80.00	115
1911/05 D	703,000	3.00	8.00	20.00	80.00	115
1911 E	376,000	3.00	9.00	22.50	85.00	125
1911 F	502,000	5.00	15.00	35.00	135	185
1911 G	610,000	5.00	15.00	35.00	120	175
1911 J	418,000	8.00	22.50	65.00	400	550
1912 A	2,709,000	3.00	8.00	15.00	40.00	65.00
1912 D	Inc. above	5.00	16.00	32.00	80.00	115
1912/5 D	703,000	5.00	16.00	32.00	80.00	115
1912 E	369,000	5.00	16.00	48.00	170	230
1912 F	501,000	7.00	20.00	35.00	155	215
1912 J	399,000	15.00	42.00	85.00	285	400
1913 A	5,419,000	3.00	5.00	12.00	30.00	45.00
1913 D	Inc. above	3.00	8.00	15.00	32.00	50.00
1913/05 D	1,406,000	3.00	8.00	15.00	32.00	50.00
1913 E	745,000	3.00	8.00	16.00	45.00	70.00
1913 F	1,003,000	5.00	9.00	13.00	40.00	60.00
1913 G	610,000	5.00	15.00	30.00	80.00	115
1913 J	817,000	5.00	16.00	32.00	120	175
1914 A	13,525,000	3.00	3.50	7.00	20.00	35.00
1914 D	Inc. above	5.00	16.00	40.00	65.00	90.00
1914/05 D	328,000	5.00	16.00	40.00	65.00	90.00
1914 J	2,292,000	3.00	8.00	16.00	55.00	75.00
1915 A	13,015,000	3.00	3.50	7.00	15.00	22.50
1915 D	Inc. above	3.00	3.50	8.00	20.00	30.00
1915/05 D	5,117,000	3.00	3.50	5.00	20.00	30.00
1915 E	3,308,000	3.00	3.50	5.00	20.00	30.00
1915 F	5,309,000	3.00	3.50	5.00	20.00	30.00
1915 G	2,730,000	3.00	5.00	9.00	22.00	35.00
1915 J	2,285,000	3.00	5.00	7.00	22.00	35.00
1916 A	9,750,000	3.00	3.50	5.00	22.00	35.00
1916 D	Inc. above	3.00	5.00	12.00	22.00	35.00
1916/616 D	4,397,000	3.00	3.50	5.00	15.00	22.50
1916/05 D	Inc. above	3.00	3.50	5.00	15.00	22.50
1916/5 D	Inc. above	3.00	3.50	5.00	15.00	22.50
1916 E	1,640,000	3.00	5.00	12.00	15.00	22.50
1916 F	2,410,000	3.00	5.00	12.00	22.00	35.00
1916 G	1,779,000	3.00	8.00	13.00	28.00	40.00
1916 J	1,464,000	3.00	8.00	13.00	37.00	55.00
1917 A	14,692,000	3.00	3.50	5.00	14.00	20.00
1917 D	Inc. above	3.00	5.00	8.00	18.00	30.00
1917/05 D	979,000	3.00	5.00	8.00	18.00	30.00
1917 E	1,561,000	3.00	3.50	5.00	22.00	35.00
1917 F	450,000	5.00	16.00	48.00	250	350
1917 G	619,000	5.00	16.00	48.00	165	230
1917 J	1,039,000	5.00	13.00	16.00	35.00	50.00
1918 A	14,622,000	3.00	3.50	5.00	15.00	25.00
1918 D	Inc. above	3.00	3.50	5.00	15.00	25.00
1918/05 D	3,670,000	3.00	3.50	5.00	15.00	25.00
1918 E	2,807,000	5.00	13.00	20.00	28.00	40.00
1918 F	4,010,000	9.00	12.00	14.00	18.00	30.00
1918 G	1,032,000	7.00	12.00	22.50	65.00	90.00
1918 J	3,452,000	5.00	12.00	20.00	35.00	50.00
1919 A	9,124,000	3.00	3.50	7.00	18.00	30.00
1919 D	Inc. above	7.00	12.00	20.00	60.00	80.00
1919/05 D	Inc. above	3.00	3.50	8.00	22.00	35.00
1919/1619 D	2,195,000	3.00	3.50	8.00	22.00	35.00
1919 E	1,767,000	7.00	12.00	20.00	35.00	50.00
1919 F	1,559,000	9.00	17.00	30.00	80.00	115
1919 J	1,875,000	7.00	12.00	32.00	45.00	65.00
1905-19 Common date proof	—	PF63 175				

KM# 14 MARK

5.55 g., 0.900 Silver 0.1606 oz. ASW, 24 mm. **Ruler:** Wilhelm II **Obv:** Denomination within wreath **Rev:** Crowned imperial eagle with shield on breast **Note:** Struck from 1890-1916.

Date	Mintage	F12	VF20	XF40	MS60	MS63
1901 D	Inc. above	6.00	12.00	32.50	80.00	125
1901 A	3,821,000	6.00	12.00	32.50	80.00	125
1901/800 D	914,000	7.00	9.00	20.00	80.00	125
1901/801 D	915,000	7.00	9.00	20.00	80.00	125
1901 E	484,000	9.00	18.00	40.00	225	300
1901 F	802,000	6.00	12.00	35.00	195	250
1901 G	579,000	9.00	18.00	70.00	345	425
1901 J	531,000	9.00	22.50	80.00	345	425
1902 A	5,222,000	7.00	15.00	22.50	140	225
1902 D	1,546,000	7.00	12.00	22.50	110	150
1902 E	819,000	7.00	16.00	50.00	285	400
1902 F	953,000	6.00	13.00	50.00	225	300
1902 G	270,000	13.00	32.00	90.00	745	1,200
1902 J	898,000	8.00	16.00	60.00	695	1,100
1903 A	3,965,000	6.00	12.00	20.00	105	145
1903/803 D	914,000	7.00	15.00	20.00	80.00	110
1903 D	Inc. above	7.00	15.00	20.00	80.00	110
1903 E	485,000	8.00	14.00	49.50	320	425
1903 F	652,000	8.00	13.00	37.50	320	425
1903 G	614,000	8.00	13.00	70.00	270	350
1903 J	531,000	8.00	16.00	45.00	1,100	1,500
1904 A	3,243,000	6.00	9.00	20.00	170	200
1904 D	1,761,000	6.00	9.00	30.00	75.00	100
1904 E	931,000	6.00	12.00	34.50	225	300
1904 F	1,255,000	6.00	12.00	31.75	105	140
1904 G	664,000	7.00	15.00	44.75	225	300
1904 J	1,021,000	7.00	15.00	65.00	1,100	1,500
1905 A	10,303,000	6.00	9.00	22.50	60.00	75.00
1905 D	1,759,000	6.00	12.00	25.00	95.00	115
1905 E	931,000	6.00	15.00	38.00	180	225
1905 F	Inc. above	8,000	12,500	20,000	35,000	50,000
1905 G	860,000	6.00	16.00	35.00	300	350
1905 J	1,021,000	7.00	20.00	65.00	700	1,000
1906 A	5,414,000	6.00	9.00	20.00	145	175
1906 D	1,412,000	6.00	12.00	20.00	110	130
1906 E	745,000	7.00	16.00	38.00	225	300
1906 F	2,257,000	7.00	15.00	30.00	110	150
1906 G	609,000	9.00	20.00	70.00	400	500

Date	Mintage	F12	VF20	XF40	MS60	MS63
1906 J	372,000	13.00	25.00	75.00	1,500	2,000
1907 A	9,201,000	6.00	7.00	9.00	60.00	75.00
1907 D	2,387,000	6.00	7.00	16.00	55.00	70.00
1907 E	1,265,000	6.00	9.00	20.00	100	120
1907 F	1,704,000	6.00	9.00	14.00	80.00	100
1907 G	1,035,000	5.00	12.00	20.00	120	150
1907 J	1,833,000	7.00	15.00	43.25	320	375
1908 A	4,338,000	6.00	9.00	16.00	80.00	100
1908 D	1,126,000	6.00	9.00	16.00	70.00	90.00
1908 E	596,000	7.00	13.00	31.75	170	200
1908 F	802,000	6.00	15.00	25.00	100	125
1908 G	488,000	7.00	25.00	41.50	215	250
1908 J	653,000	7.00	22.50	50.00	400	550
1909 A	4,151,000	6.00	15.00	22.50	185	225
1909 D	1,968,000	6.00	15.00	20.00	80.00	100
1909 E	Inc. below	65.00	190	270	475	625
1909 G	854,000	8.00	16.00	36.00	150	200
1909 J	53,000	135	280	425	1,250	2,500
1910 A	5,870,000	6.00	9.00	20.00	60.00	75.00
1910 D	1,406,000	7.00	12.00	10.00	55.00	70.00
1910 E	1,050,000	7.00	15.00	20.00	85.00	110
1910 F	1,631,000	7.00	15.00	17.00	75.00	100
1910 G	610,000	6.00	13.00	38.00	170	200
1910 J	1,094,000	7.00	15.00	50.00	325	400
1911 A	5,693,000	6.00	9.00	16.00	55.00	70.00
1911 D	126,000	13.00	48.00	70.00	270	300
1911 E	738,000	7.00	15.00	14.00	60.00	75.00
1911 F	773,000	7.00	16.00	85.00	1,000	1,350
1911 G	305,000	9.00	20.00	70.00	150	180
1911 J	812,000	7.00	16.00	65.00	825	1,000
1912 A	2,439,000	6.00	7.00	10.00	65.00	80.00
1912 D	632,000	7.00	12.00	17.00	80.00	100
1912 E	708,000	6.00	9.00	17.00	80.00	100
1912 F	502,000	6.00	12.00	30.00	170	200
1912 J	409,000	8.00	40.00	75.00	450	850
1913 F	450,000	9.00	30.00	50.00	255	250
1913 G	275,000	25.00	65.00	90.00	280	325
1913 J	368,000	11.00	32.00	60.00	295	400
1914 A	11,304,000	6.00	6.50	7.00	18.00	25.00
1914/9 D	3,515,000	6.00	7.00	10.00	22.00	30.00
1914 D	Inc. above	6.00	7.00	10.00	22.00	30.00
1914 E	2,235,000	6.00	9.00	13.00	22.00	30.00
1914 F	2,300,000	6.00	7.00	10.00	18.00	25.00
1914 G	1,911,000	6.00	12.00	14.00	22.00	30.00
1914 J	2,978,000	6.00	12.00	14.00	22.00	30.00
1915 A	13,817,000	6.00	7.00	10.00	18.00	25.00
1915 D	4,218,000	6.00	9.00	14.00	22.00	30.00
1915 E	2,235,000	6.00	9.00	14.00	22.00	30.00
1915 F	2,911,000	6.00	9.00	16.00	22.00	30.00
1915 G	1,749,000	6.00	9.00	16.00	22.00	30.00
1915 J	1,634,000	7.00	12.00	14.00	22.00	30.00
1916 F	306,000	16.00	48.00	70.00	125	175
1901-16 Common date proof	—	**PF63** 165	**PF65** 265			

MILITARY COINAGE - WWI

Issued under the authority of the German Military Commander of the East for use in Estonia, Latvia, Lithuania, Poland, and Northwest Russia.

KM# 21 KOPEK

Iron **Ruler:** Wilhelm II **Obv:** Inscription **Rev:** Denomination and date within iron cross

Date	Mintage	F12	VF20	XF40	MS60	MS63
1916 A	11,942,000	2.00	6.00	15.00	50.00	100
1916 A	—	**PF63** 250				
1916 J	8,000,000	2.50	7.00	20.00	50.00	100
1916 J	—	**PF63** 250				

KM# 22 2 KOPEKS

Iron **Ruler:** Wilhelm II **Obv:** Inscription **Rev:** Denomination and date within iron cross

Date	Mintage	F12	VF20	XF40	MS60	MS63
1916 A	6,973,000	2.00	6.00	15.00	50.00	100
1916 A	—	**PF63** 250				
1916 J	8,000,000	2.50	6.00	15.00	50.00	100
1916 J	—	**PF63** 250				

KM# 23 3 KOPEKS

Iron **Ruler:** Wilhelm II **Obv:** Inscription **Rev:** Denomination and date within iron cross

Date	Mintage	F12	VF20	XF40	MS60	MS63
1916 A	8,670,000	2.50	6.00	18.00	50.00	100
1916 A	—	**PF63** 250				
1916 J	8,000,000	2.50	6.00	18.00	50,00	100
1916 J	—	**PF63** 250				

PATTERNS

Including off metal strikes

KM#	Date	Mintage	Identification	Mkt Val
Pn66	1901A	—	50 Pfennig. Silver. Plain 2mm edge. KM#15.	250
Pn67	1901A	—	50 Pfennig. Silver. Plain 3.5mm edge. KM#15.	250
Pn68	1901A	—	50 Pfennig. Silver. Coarse reeding. KM#15.	250
Pn69	1901A	—	50 Pfennig. Silver. Coarse wavy reeding. KM#15.	250
Pn70	1901A	—	1/2 Mark. Silver.	450
Pn71	1901D	—	1/2 Mark. Silver. Date.	450
Pn72	1901D	—	1/2 Mark. Silver. Incuse diamond.	450
Pn73	1901D	—	1/2 Mark. Brass. Incuse diamond.	250
Pn74	1901D	—	1/2 Mark. Brass. Incuse diamond, beaded circle.	250
Pn75	1901D	—	1/2 Mark. Silver. Diamond within beads.	425
Pn76	1901D	—	1/2 Mark. Brass. Beaded diamond.	250
Pn77	1901D	—	1/2 Mark. Silver. Beaded diamond.	425
Pn78	1901D	—	1/2 Mark. Silver. Beaded circle.	425
Pn79	1901D	—	1/2 Mark. Brass. Beaded circle.	250
Pn80	1901D	—	1/2 Mark. Silver. Diamond within beads.	425
Pn81	1901D	—	1/2 Mark. Silver. Incuse diamond.	425
Pn82	1901D	—	1/2 Mark. Brass. Incuse diamond.	250
Pn83	1901D	—	1/2 Mark. Silver. Date.	425
Pn84	1901D	—	1/2 Mark. Silver. Beaded circle.	425
Pn85	1901D	—	1/2 Mark. Brass. Beaded circle.	250
Pn86	1902A	—	50 Pfennig. Silver. Without beaded rims, coarse reeding; KM#15.	425
Pn87	1902A	—	50 Pfennig. Silver. Without beaded rims, reeded edge; KM#15.	425
Pn88	1902A	—	50 Pfennig. 0.710. Silver. Incuse circle.	525
Pn89	1902A	—	1/2 Mark. Silver. Incuse circle.	425
Pn90	1903A	—	50 Pfennig. Silver. Without beaded rim, coarse reeding; KM#15.	425
Pn91	1903A	—	50 Pfennig. Silver. Coarse reeding; KM#15.	425
Pn92	1903D	—	50 Pfennig. Silver. Crown.	450
Pn93	1903D	—	50 Pfennig. Eagle.	425
Pn94	1903D	—	50 Pfennig. Brass. Otto of Bavaria.	425
Pn95	1903D	—	50 Pfennig. Copper. Otto of Bavaria.	425
Pn96	1903	—	50 Pfennig. Brass. Crown. Otto of Bavaria.	425
Pn97	1903D	—	50 Pfennig. Brass. Germania.	400
Pn98	1904A	—	1/2 Mark. Silver. KM#17.	450
Pn99	ND (1904)A	—	25 Pfennig. Nickel-Silver. Value within beaded circle.	250
Pn100	ND (1904)A	—	25 Pfennig. Copper-Nickel. Beaded circle.	250
Pn101	ND (1904)A	—	25 Pfennig. Tin Alloy. Beaded circle.	250
Pn102	1907	—	25 Pfennig. Nickel. Germania.	200
Pn103	1907A	—	25 Pfennig. Copper. Crown.	200
Pn104	1907A	—	25 Pfennig. Nickel. Crown.	200
Pn105	1907D	—	1/2 Mark. Silver. Coarse reeding; KM#17.	250
Pn106	1908A	—	25 Pfennig. Nickel.	350
Pn107	1908A	—	25 Pfennig. Nickel-Silver. Eagle plain.	250
Pn108	1908A	—	25 Pfennig. Silver. Eagle plain.	350
Pn109	1908A	—	25 Pfennig. Nickel-Silver. Eagle within beads.	250
Pn110	1908A	—	25 Pfennig. Nickel-Silver. Eagle within beads.	250
Pn111	1908A	—	25 Pfennig. Eagle plain.	250
Pn112	1908A	—	25 Pfennig. Copper-Nickel.	250
Pn113	1908A	—	25 Pfennig. Nickel-Silver.	250
Pn114	1908A	—	25 Pfennig. Nickel.	250
Pn115	1908A	—	25 Pfennig. Nickel-Silver.	250
Pn116	1908A	—	25 Pfennig. Aluminum.	250
Pn117	1908A	—	25 Pfennig. Copper-Nickel.	200
Pn118	1908A	—	25 Pfennig. Silver.	300
Pn119	1908A	—	25 Pfennig. Bronze.	200
Pn120	1908A	—	25 Pfennig. Copper.	200
Pn121	1908A	—	25 Pfennig. Silver. Eagle in crown.	450
Pn122	1908A	—	25 Pfennig. Silver. Cross in crown.	450
Pn123	1908A	—	25 Pfennig. Silver.	450
Pn124	1908A	—	25 Pfennig. Copper-Nickel.	250
Pn125	1908A	—	25 Pfennig. Silver.	450
Pn126	1908A	—	25 Pfennig. Nickel.	250
Pn127	1908A	—	25 Pfennig. Copper-Nickel.	300
Pn128	1908A	—	25 Pfennig. Nickel.	300
Pn129	1908A	—	25 Pfennig. Nickel. Germania.	300
Pn130	1908A	—	25 Pfennig. Nickel. Kaiser Wilhelm.	275
Pn131	1908A	—	25 Pfennig. Iron. Kaiser Wilhelm.	250
Pn132	1908A	—	25 Pfennig. Copper. Kaiser Wilhelm.	300
PnA133	1908D	—	25 Pfennig. Copper. Eagle head in order collar.	150
Pn133	1908D	—	25 Pfennig. Silver Plated Copper.	200
Pn134	1908D	—	25 Pfennig. Silver Plated Copper.	200
Pn135	1908A	—	25 Pfennig. Lead. Without circle around eagle, or crown above value.	200
PnA136	1908D	—	25 Pfennig. Nickel.	200
PnB136	1908J	—	25 Pfennig. Nickel. Previous German East Africa Pn3; with sprigs.	300
PnC136	1908J	—	25 Pfennig. Nickel. Previous German East Africa Pn4; with sprigs.	—
Pn136	1908J	—	25 Pfennig. Copper-Nickel. Gothic style.	300
Pn137	1908J	—	25 Pfennig. Copper-Nickel. Block style.	300
Pn138	1908A	—	25 Pfennig. Copper-Nickel. Crown.	300
Pn139	1908A	—	25 Pfennig. Tin. Crown.	250
Pn140	1908A	—	25 Pfennig. Aluminum. Crown.	250
Pn141	1908	—	25 Pfennig. Silver. Eagle within beads.	400
Pn142	1908/09	—	25 Pfennig. Nickel-Silver. Eagle within beads.	300
Pn143	1909A	—	25 Pfennig. Silver. Large eagle.	350
Pn144	1909A	—	10 Pfennig. Nickel. 2mm rims, KM#12.	300
Pn145	1909	—	25 Pfennig. Nickel.	250
Pn146	1909	—	25 Pfennig. Bronze.	250
Pn147	1909A	—	25 Pfennig. Silver-Copper.	225
Pn148	1909A	—	25 Pfennig. Cast.	250
Pn149	1909A	—	25 Pfennig. Copper-Nickel.	250
Pn150	1909A	—	25 Pfennig. Nickel.	250
Pn151	1909A	—	25 Pfennig. Nickel.	250
Pn152	1909A	—	25 Pfennig. Nickel-Silver.	250
Pn153	1909A	—	25 Pfennig. Nickel.	250
Pn154	1909A	—	25 Pfennig. Iron.	225
Pn155	1909A	—	25 Pfennig. Nickel.	250
Pn156	1909A	—	25 Pfennig. Nickel.	250
Pn157	1909A	—	25 Pfennig. Silver.	400
Pn158	1909A	—	25 Pfennig. Silver. Standing eagle right.	400
Pn159	1909A	—	25 Pfennig. Silver.	400
Pn160	1909A	—	25 Pfennig. Silver. Standing eagle right.	400
Pn161	1909A	—	25 Pfennig. Silver.	350
Pn162	1909A	—	25 Pfennig. Nickel.	250
Pn163	1909A	—	25 Pfennig. Copper-Nickel.	250

KM#	Date	Mintage	Identification	Mkt Val
Pn168	1909A	—	25 Pfennig. Silver. Eagle within legend.	350
Pn169	1909A	—	25 Pfennig. Silver. Large eagle, legend above crowned value.	350
Pn170	1909A	—	25 Pfennig. Silver.	400
PnA171	1909A	—	25 Pfennig.	300
Pn171	1909A	—	25 Pfennig. Silver.	350
Pn172	1909A	—	25 Pfennig. Silver.	350
Pn173	1909A	—	25 Pfennig. Nickel. GOTT MITUNS above crowned eagle with spread wings. DEUTSCHES REICH above large numerals.	300
Pn174	1909A	—	25 Pfennig. Nickel. Stockier eagle, countermarked mm. Large munerals and countermarked date.	300
Pn175	1909A	—	25 Pfennig.	300
Pn176	1909E	—	25 Pfennig. Silver or Copper-Nickel.	350
Pn177	1909A	—	25 Pfennig. Silver Plated Copper.	300
Pn178	ND (1909)A	—	25 Pfennig. Silver. Large eagle.	400
Pn179	1910E	—	25 Pfennig. Silver. Eagle within legend.	300
Pn180	1910A	—	1/2 Mark. Silver. KM#17.	400
Pn181	1910	—	Mark. Silver. Without mint mark, KM#7.	—
PnD182	1910A	—	3 Mark. Ernst Ludwig.	—
PnA182	1911D	—	Mark. Aluminum Clad Zinc.	—
PnB182	1911D	—	2 Mark. Aluminum Clad Zinc. Bavaria.	—
PnC182	1912D	—	3 Mark. Aluminum Clad Zinc. Bavaria.	—
PnE182	1913	—	3 Mark. Silver. Without mint mark, Kaiser on horseback.	—
PnF182	1913	—	3 Mark. Copper.	—
Pn182	1914A	—	5 Pfennig. Unknown Metal. Reeded. KM#11.	—
PnA183	1915	—	Non-Denominated. Bronze Gilt.	—
Pn183	1915A	—	Pfennig. Zinc. Reeded. KM#10.	—
Pn184	1915A	—	Pfennig. Iron. Date below value, KM#24.	—
Pn185	1915A	—	Pfennig. Aluminum.	—
Pn186	1915	—	5 Pfennig. Copper-Nickel. Without mint mark, KM#11.	—
Pn187	1915A	—	10 Pfennig. Brass. KM#17. KM#12.	—
Pn188	1915A	—	10 Pfennig. Brass. Broad rims, KM#12.	—
Pn189	1915A	—	10 Pfennig. Nickel. Broad rims.	—
Pn190	1915A	—	10 Pfennig. Copper-Nickel. Broad rims.	—
Pn191	1915A	—	10 Pfennig. Rusted Iron. Broad rims.	150
Pn192	1915A	—	10 Pfennig. Brass. Date above value.	—
Pn193	1915A	—	10 Pfennig. Nickel. Date above value.	—
Pn194	1915A	—	10 Pfennig. Iron. Date above value.	—
Pn195	1915A	—	10 Pfennig. Small "10".	—
Pn196	1915A	—	10 Pfennig. Large "10".	—
Pn197	1915A	—	10 Pfennig. Brass. Small "10", KM#20.	—
Pn198	1915A	—	10 Pfennig. Nickel. Small "10", KM#20.	—
Pn199	1915A	—	10 Pfennig. Iron. 67 beads on rim.	—
Pn200	1915A	—	10 Pfennig. Nickel. 67 beads on rim.	—
Pn201	1915A	—	10 Pfennig. Copper-Nickel. KM#20.	—
Pn202	1915A	—	10 Pfennig. Iron. KM#20.	550
Pn203	1915A	—	1/2 Mark. Silver. Large eagle.	—
Pn204	1915A	—	Mark. Aluminum. GOTT MIT UNS on rim, KM#14.	—
PnA205	ND (1915)	—	Pfennig. Copper. KM#24.	—
Pn205	1916A	—	Pfennig. Aluminum. KM#24.	1,500
Pn206	1916F	—	Pfennig. Aluminum. KM#24.	—
Pn207	1917	—	Pfennig. Aluminum. Without mint mark, KM#24.	—
Pn208	1917	—	10 Pfennig. Iron. Without mint mark, KM#20.	—
Pn209	1917A	—	10 Pfennig. Zinc. Mint mark, KM#26.	—

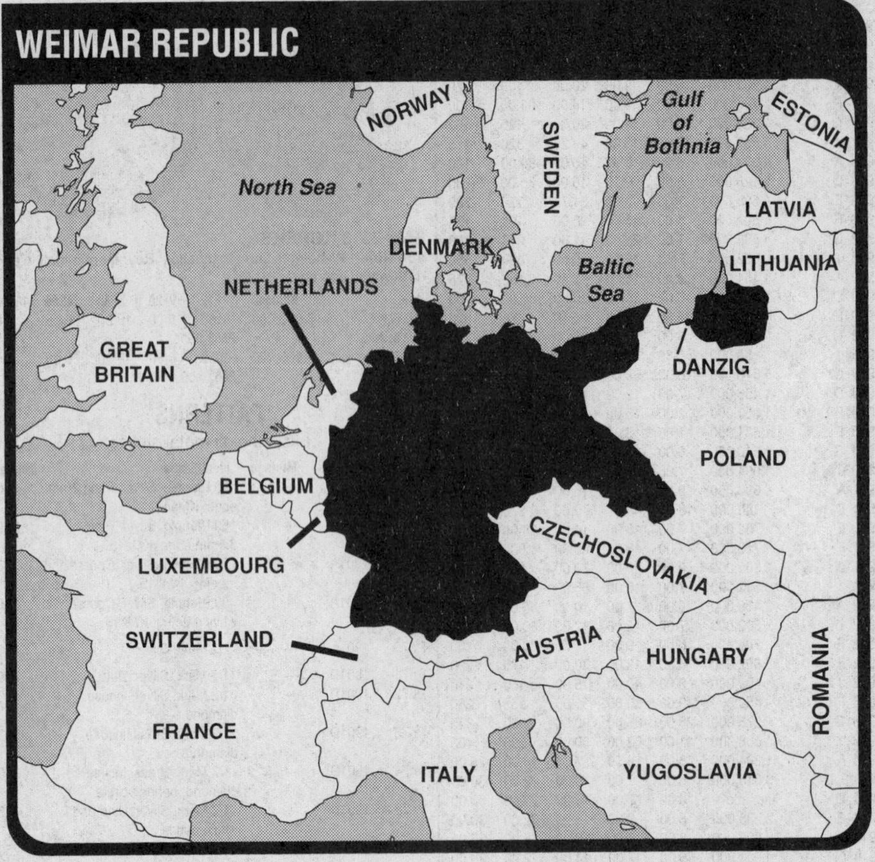

1919-1933

The Imperial German government disintegrated in a flurry of royal abdications as World War I ended. Desperate German parliamentarians, fearful of impending anarchy and civil war, hastily declared a German Republic. The new National Assembly, which was convened Feb. 6, 1919 in Weimar had to establish a legal government, draft a constitution, and then conclude a peace treaty with the Allies. Friedrich Ebert was elected as Reichs President. The harsh terms of the peace treaty imposed on Germany were economically and psychologically unacceptable to the German population regardless of political persuasion and the problem of German treaty compliance was to plague the Republic until the worldwide Great Depression of 1929. The new constitution paid less attention to fundamental individual rights and concentrated more power in the President and Central Government to insure a more stable social and economic order. The German bureaucracy survived the transition intact and had a stifling effect on the democratic process. The army started training large numbers of reservists in conjunction with the U.S.S.R. thereby circumventing treaty limitations on the size of the German military.

New anti-democratic ideologies were forming. Communism and Fascism were spreading. The National Socialist German Workers Party, under Hitler's leadership, incorporated the ever-present anti-Semitism into a new virulent Nazi Catechism.

In spite of the historic German inflation, the French occupation of the Rhineland, and the loss of vast territories and resources, the republic survived. By 1929 the German economy had been restored to its pre-war level. Much of the economic gains however were dependent on the extensive assistance provided by the U.S.A. and collapsed along with the world economy in 1929. Even during the good times, the Republic was never able to muster any loyal public support or patriotism. By 1930, Nationalists, Nazis, and Communists held nearly half of the Reichstag seats and the government was forced to rely more and more on presidential decrees as the only means to effectuate policy. In 1932, the Nazis won 230 Reichstag seats. As head of the largest party, Hitler claimed the right to form the next government. President Hindenburg's opposition forced a second election in which the Nazis lost 34 seats. Von Papen, however, convinced Hindenburg to name Hitler Chancellor by arguing that Hitler could be controlled! Hitler formed his cabinet and immediately began consolidating his power and laying the groundwork for the Third Reich.

MONETARY SYSTEM

(During 1923-1924)

100 Rentenpfennig = 1 Rentenmark

(Commencing 1924)

100 Reichspfennig = 1 Reichsmark

WEIMAR REPUBLIC

MARK COINAGE

1922-1923

KM# 27 50 PFENNIG

1.60 g., Aluminum, 23 mm. **Obv:** Denomination above date **Rev:** Sheaf behind inscription **Edge:** Reeded

Date	Mintage	F12	VF20	XF40	MS60	MS63
1919 A	7,173,000	0.25	1.00	3.50	20.00	25.00
1919 D	791,000	5.00	15.00	30.00	80.00	100
1919 E	930,000	2.00	20.00	40.00	400	450
1919 E	35	**PF63** 350				
1919 F	160,000	10.00	25.00	50.00	150	200
1919 G	660,000	2.00	6.00	45.00	60.00	75.00
1919 J	800,000	5.00	15.00	30.00	100	120
1920 A	119,793,000	0.10	0.50	2.00	8.00	12.00
1920 D	28,306,000	0.10	0.50	2.00	10.00	14.00
1920 E	14,400,000	0.25	1.50	3.00	15.00	18.00
1920 E	226	**PF63** 150				
1920 F	10,932,000	0.25	1.50	3.00	15.00	18.00
1920 G	5,040,000	0.25	2.00	4.00	30.00	35.00
1920 J	15,423,000	0.25	2.00	4.00	18.00	25.00
1921 A	184,468,000	0.10	0.15	0.50	5.00	7.00
1921 D	48,729,000	0.10	0.15	0.75	7.00	10.00
1921 E	31,210,000	0.15	1.50	2.50	12.00	15.00
1921 E	332	**PF63** 115				
1921 F	46,950,000	0.10	0.15	0.75	12.00	15.00
1921 G	19,107,000	0.10	0.25	1.00	8.00	12.00
1921 J	28,013,000	0.10	0.25	1.00	8.00	12.00
1922 A	145,215,000	0.10	0.25	2.00	8.00	10.00
1922 D	58,019,000	0.10	0.25	2.00	10.00	13.00
1922 E	33,930,000	0.15	1.00	3.00	15.00	20.00
1922 E	333	**PF63** 115				
1922 F	33,000,000	0.10	0.25	2.00	10.00	13.00
1922 G	36,745,000	0.10	0.25	2.00	10.00	13.00
1922 J	36,202,000	0.10	0.25	2.00	10.00	13.00

KM# 28 3 MARK
Aluminum **Obv:** Denomination above date **Rev:** Eagle **Edge:** Reeded

Date	Mintage	F12	VF20	XF40	MS60	MS63
1922 A	15,497,000	1.50	6.00	12.00	30.00	40.00
1922 A	—	PF63 85.00				
1922 E	2,000	60.00	130	500	1,000	1,200
1922 E	1,000	PF63 1,500				
1922 F Rare	—	—	—	—	—	—

KM# 29 3 MARK
2.03 g., Aluminum **Subject:** 3rd Anniversary Weimar Constitution **Obv:** Around eagle, VERFASSUNGSTAG "AUGUST 1922"

Date	Mintage	F12	VF20	XF40	MS60	MS63
1922 A	32,514,000	0.50	2.50	5.00	25.00	30.00
1922 D	8,441,000	140	300	450	1,200	1,400
1922 D	—	PF63 1,500				
1922 E	2,440,000	0.50	2.50	5.00	25.00	30.00
1922 E	22,000	PF63 50.00				
1922 F	6,023,000	2.00	6.00	18.00	50.00	60.00
1922 G	3,655,000	0.50	2.50	5.00	25.00	30.00
1922 J	4,896,000	0.50	2.50	5.00	25.00	30.00
1923 E	2,060,000	8.00	18.00	35.00	130	150
1923 E	2,291	PF63 150				
1923 F Rare	—	—	—	—	—	—

Note: The 1923F 3 Mark pieces are from the burned-out ruin of the Stuttgart Mint, destroyed in World War II. Most known examples are in bad condition, yet quite expensive

KM# 35 200 MARK
1.00 g., Aluminum, 23 mm. **Obv:** Denomination above date **Rev:** Eagle **Edge:** Reeded

Date	Mintage	F12	VF20	XF40	MS60	MS63
1923 A	174,900,000	0.15	0.50	0.75	3.00	6.00
1923 A	—	PF63 125				
1923 D	35,189,000	0.20	0.50	1.50	4.00	5.00
1923 D Proof, unique	—	—	—	—	—	—
1923 E	11,250,000	0.20	1.00	4.00	15.00	18.00
1923 E	4,095	PF63 100				
1923 F	20,090,000	0.25	0.75	3.00	6.00	8.00
1923 F	—	PF63 125				
1923 G	24,923,000	0.25	1.00	3.00	6.00	8.00
1923 G	—	PF63 125				
1923 J	16,258,000	0.20	1.00	4.00	15.00	18.00
1923 J	—	PF63 125				

KM# 36 500 MARK
1.67 g., Aluminum, 27.1 mm. **Obv:** Denomination above date **Rev:** Eagle

Date	Mintage	F12	VF20	XF40	MS60	MS63
1923 A	59,278,000	0.25	2.00	3.00	12.00	15.00
1923 A	—	PF63 125				
1923 D	13,683,000	0.25	2.00	6.00	25.00	30.00
1923 D	—	PF63 125				
1923 E	2,128,000	2.50	7.00	18.00	50.00	60.00
1923 E	2,053	PF63 100				
1923 F	7,963,000	0.25	2.00	9.00	20.00	22.00
1923 F	—	PF63 125				
1923 G	4,404,000	0.50	4.00	8.00	25.00	30.00
1923 G	—	PF63 125				
1923 J	1,008,000	10.00	25.00	60.00	100	120
1923 J	—	PF63 250				

RENTENMARK COINAGE

1923-1929

KM# 30 RENTENPFENNIG
2.00 g., Bronze **Obv:** Denomination within circle **Rev:** Wheat sheaf divides date

Date	Mintage	F12	VF20	XF40	MS60	MS63
1923 A	12,629,000	0.25	1.50	4.00	15.00	16.00
1923 D	Est. 2314000	0.25	3.00	9.00	30.00	33.00
1923 E	2,200,000	1.00	3.00	9.00	30.00	33.00
1923 F	160,000	3.00	12.00	28.00	90.00	100
1923 G	1,004,000	1.00	4.00	8.00	30.00	33.00
1923 J	1,470,000	2.00	10.00	25.00	90.00	100
1924 A	55,273,000	0.25	1.50	4.00	15.00	17.00
1924 D	17,540,000	0.25	1.50	4.00	15.00	17.00
1924 E	6,838,000	1.00	2.50	8.00	25.00	27.00
1924 F	10,347,000	1.00	2.50	8.00	25.00	27.00
1924 G	7,366,000	1.00	3.00	10.00	35.00	40.00
1924 J	11,024,000	1.00	2.50	8.00	25.00	28.00
1925 A	—	800	1,300	2,600	—	—
1929 F	—	150	300	600	1,200	—
Common date	—	PF63 120				

KM# 31 2 RENTENPFENNIG
3.30 g., Bronze, 20 mm. **Obv:** Denomination within circle **Rev:** Wheat sheaf divides date

Date	Mintage	F12	VF20	XF40	MS60	MS63
1923 A	8,587,000	0.50	2.00	4.00	20.00	22.00
1923 D	1,490,000	0.50	2.00	7.00	35.00	40.00
1923 F	Inc. above	1.50	4.00	12.00	50.00	60.00
1923 G	Inc. above	1.00	3.00	10.00	45.00	55.00
1923 J	Inc. above	2.00	7.00	15.00	80.00	90.00
1924 A	80,864,000	0.20	0.50	1.50	8.00	10.00
1924 D	19,899,000	0.25	1.00	3.00	16.00	18.00
1924 E	6,595,000	0.25	1.00	3.00	16.00	18.00
1924 F	14,969,000	0.25	1.00	3.00	16.00	18.00
1924 G	10,349,000	0.25	1.00	4.00	25.00	28.00
1924 J	21,196,000	0.25	1.00	3.00	12.00	15.00
Common date	—	PF63 140				

KM# 32 5 RENTENPFENNIG
2.50 g., Aluminum-Bronze, 18 mm. **Obv:** Denomination within square, oak leaf on each side **Rev:** Six grain sprigs form center triangle above date

Date	Mintage	F12	VF20	XF40	MS60	MS63
1923 A	3,083,000	1.00	4.00	10.00	50.00	55.00
1923 D	Inc. below	1.00	4.00	12.00	60.00	65.00
1923 F	Inc. below	35.00	70.00	120	350	400
1923 G	Inc. below	10.00	25.00	50.00	250	280
1924 A	171,966,000	0.25	1.50	4.00	20.00	24.00
1924 D	31,163,000	0.25	1.50	6.00	30.00	33.00
1924 E	12,206,000	0.25	1.50	9.00	35.00	38.00
1924 F	29,032,000	0.25	1.50	6.00	30.00	33.00
1924 G	19,217,000	0.25	1.50	6.00	35.00	38.00
1924 J	32,332,000	0.25	1.50	6.00	28.00	30.00
1925 F	—	—	—	—	—	—

Note: The 1925F is only known as a counterfeit.

Date	Mintage	F12	VF20	XF40	MS60	MS63
Common date	—	PF63 160				

KM# 33 10 RENTENPFENNIG
3.92 g., Aluminum-Bronze, 21 mm. **Obv:** Denomination within square, oak leaf on each side **Rev:** Six grain sprigs form center triangle above date

Date	Mintage	F12	VF20	XF40	MS60	MS63
1923 A	Inc. below	0.50	5.00	12.00	35.00	40.00
1923 D	Inc. below	0.50	8.00	15.00	55.00	60.00
1923 F	Inc. below	30.00	100	200	450	480
1923 G	Inc. below	3.00	18.00	35.00	130	150
1924 A	169,956,000	0.50	2.00	5.00	20.00	25.00
1924 D	33,894,000	0.50	2.00	5.00	25.00	30.00
1924 E	18,679,000	0.50	2.00	6.00	30.00	35.00
1924 F	42,237,000	0.50	2.00	6.00	30.00	35.00
1924 F	—	PF63 160				
1924 G	18,758,000	0.50	2.00	8.00	27.00	32.00
1924 J	33,928,000	0.50	2.00	8.00	35.00	40.00
1925 F	13,000	800	1,500	2,500	—	—
1923-1925 Common date proof	—	PF63 160				

KM# 34 50 RENTENPFENNIG
5.17 g., Aluminum-Bronze **Obv:** Denomination within square, oak leaf on each side **Rev:** Six grain sprigs form center triangle above date

Date	Mintage	F12	VF20	XF40	MS60	MS63
1923 A	451,000	10.00	22.00	35.00	80.00	100
1923 D	192,000	15.00	40.00	60.00	200	225
1923 F	120,000	40.00	120	160	500	550
1923 G	120,000	20.00	50.00	70.00	300	350
1923 J	4,000	400	800	1,600	3,000	3,500
1924 A	117,365,000	6.00	16.00	25.00	75.00	90.00
1924 D	30,971,000	7.00	20.00	30.00	100	120
1924 E	14,668,000	7.00	20.00	30.00	100	120
1924 F	21,968,000	7.00	20.00	30.00	100	120
1924 G	13,349,000	15.00	30.00	50.00	160	180
1924 J	17,252,000	10.00	20.00	45.00	130	150
Common date	—	PF63 225				

REICHSMARK COINAGE

1924-1938

KM# 37 REICHSPFENNIG
2.00 g., Bronze **Obv:** Denomination within circle **Rev:** Wheat sheaf divides date

Date	Mintage	F12	VF20	XF40	MS60	MS63
1924 A	13,496,000	0.20	0.50	1.00	10.00	11.00
1924 D	6,206,000	0.20	0.50	1.00	12.00	13.00
1924 E	1,100,000	100	250	450	900	1,000
1924 F	2,650,000	0.20	0.50	1.00	12.00	13.00
1924 G	5,100,000	0.25	0.75	3.00	18.00	20.00
1924 J	24,400,000	0.20	0.50	1.00	12.00	13.00
1925 A	40,925,000	0.20	0.50	1.00	5.00	10.00
1925 D	1,558,000	5.00	15.00	35.00	110	150
1925 E	10,460,000	0.20	0.50	1.00	10.00	11.00
1925 F	5,673,000	0.20	0.50	1.00	10.00	11.00
1925 G	13,502,000	0.20	0.50	1.00	10.00	11.00
1925 J	30,300,000	0.20	0.50	1.00	10.00	11.00
1927 A	4,671,000	0.30	1.50	3.50	20.00	22.00
1927 D	4,203,000	0.30	1.50	3.50	20.00	22.00
1927 E	8,000,000	0.30	1.50	3.50	20.00	22.00
1927 F	2,350,000	0.50	2.50	10.00	40.00	45.00
1927 G	3,236,000	0.50	2.00	8.00	35.00	40.00
1928 A	19,300,000	0.20	0.50	2.00	10.00	11.00
1928 D	10,200,000	0.20	0.50	2.00	12.00	15.00
1928 F	8,672,000	0.20	0.50	2.00	15.00	18.00
1928 G	3,764,000	0.50	2.00	5.00	30.00	35.00
1929 A	37,170,000	0.20	1.00	2.55	10.00	12.00
1929 D	9,337,000	0.20	1.00	2.50	10.00	12.00
1929 E	6,600,000	0.20	1.00	2.50	12.00	15.00
1929 F	3,150,000	0.20	1.00	2.50	12.00	15.00
1929 G	1,986,000	0.50	1.50	4.00	16.00	20.00
1930 A	40,997,000	0.20	0.50	2.00	10.00	12.00
1930 D	6,441,000	0.20	0.50	2.00	12.00	14.00
1930 E	1,412,000	6.00	20.00	50.00	160	190
1930 F	6,415,000	0.20	2.00	4.00	14.00	17.00
1930 G	5,017,000	0.20	2.00	4.00	14.00	17.00
1931 A	38,481,000	0.20	2.00	4.00	10.00	12.00
1931 D	5,998,000	0.20	2.00	3.00	14.00	17.00
1931 E	12,800,000	0.20	2.00	4.00	18.00	20.00
1931 F	12,591,000	0.50	2.00	4.00	14.00	17.00
1931 G	2,622,000	0.50	4.00	7.00	35.00	40.00
1932 A	17,096,000	0.50	2.00	4.00	25.00	30.00
1933 A	37,846,000	0.20	0.50	2.00	8.00	10.00
1933 E	2,945,000	0.30	3.00	8.00	35.00	40.00
1933 F	5,023,000	0.20	2.00	4.00	12.00	15.00
1934 A	51,214,000	0.20	2.00	4.00	8.00	10.00
1934 D	7,408,000	0.20	0.50	2.50	10.00	12.00
1934 E	4,628,000	0.50	4.00	10.00	38.00	45.00
1934 F	5,667,000	0.20	0.50	3.00	15.00	18.00
1934 G	2,450,000	0.20	0.50	3.00	20.00	22.00
1934 J	4,271,000	0.20	0.50	3.00	20.00	22.00
1935 A	35,894,000	0.20	0.50	1.00	8.00	10.00

Date	Mintage	F12	VF20	XF40	MS60	MS63
1935 D	15,489,000	0.20	0.50	1.00	10.00	12.00
1935 E	8,351,000	0.20	0.50	2.00	14.00	17.00
1935 F	12,094,000	0.20	0.50	1.50	10.00	12.00
1935 G	7,454,000	0.20	0.50	1.00	14.00	17.00
1935 J	8,505,000	0.20	0.50	1.00	12.00	15.00
1936 A	—	0.20	0.50	2.00	8.00	10.00
1936 D	12,262,000	0.20	0.50	2.00	10.00	12.00
1936 E	2,576,000	0.50	4.00	8.00	35.00	40.00
1936 F	6,915,000	0.20	0.50	2.00	12.00	15.00
1936 G	Est. 2940000	0.20	2.00	4.00	14.00	17.00
1936 J	Est. 5421000	0.20	2.00	4.00	14.00	17.00
Common date	—	PF63 90.00				

KM# 38 2 REICHSPFENNIG

3.34 g., Bronze **Obv:** Denomination within circle **Rev:** Wheat sheaf divides date

Date	Mintage	F12	VF20	XF40	MS60	MS63
1923 F	—	PF63 4,500				
1924 A	19,620,000	0.20	0.50	2.00	12.00	15.00
1924 D	3,482,000	0.30	2.00	4.00	22.00	25.00
1924 E	4,253,000	0.30	2.00	5.00	25.00	28.00
1924 F	4,567,000	0.30	0.60	2.00	15.00	17.00
1924 G	7,560,000	0.30	2.00	4.00	15.00	17.00
1924 J	7,489,000	0.30	2.00	4.00	15.00	17.00
1925 A	22,433,000	0.20	0.50	2.00	8.00	10.00
1925 D	2,412,000	0.20	2.00	4.00	30.00	33.00
1925 E	5,414,000	0.30	2.00	4.00	20.00	22.00
1925 F	4,851,000	0.30	2.00	4.00	20.00	22.00
1925 G	2,456,000	2.00	8.00	16.00	90.00	120
1936 A	3,220,000	0.50	2.00	5.00	24.00	26.00
1936 D	6,525,000	0.20	0.50	2.00	8.00	10.00
1936 E	573,000	4.00	12.00	25.00	100	125
1936 F	3,100,000	0.20	0.60	4.00	23.00	25.00
Common date	—	PF63 90.00				

KM# 75 4 REICHSPFENNIG

Bronze **Obv:** Large denomination within circle, date at right **Rev:** Eagle

Date	Mintage	F12	VF20	XF40	MS60	MS63
1932 A	27,101,000	—	9.00	15.00	35.00	40.00
1932 A	—	PF63 150				
1932 D	7,055,000	—	12.00	18.00	45.00	55.00
1932 D	—	PF63 150				
1932 E	3,729,000	—	15.00	25.00	60.00	75.00
1932 E	—	PF63 150				
1932 F	5,022,000	—	12.00	20.00	55.00	70.00
1932 F	—	PF63 150				
1932 G	3,050,000	—	20.00	30.00	90.00	120
1932 G	—	PF63 150				
1932 J	4,094,000	—	12.00	25.00	75.00	90.00
1932 J	—	PF63 150				

KM# 39 5 REICHSPFENNIG

2.54 g., Aluminum-Bronze **Obv:** Denomination within square, oak leaf on each side **Rev:** Six grain sprigs form center triangle above date

Date	Mintage	F12	VF20	XF40	MS60	MS63
1924 A	14,469,000	0.30	0.60	3.00	20.00	22.00
1924 D	8,139,000	0.50	1.00	3.00	20.00	23.00
1924 E	5,976,000	0.50	2.00	4.00	25.00	28.00
1924 E Proof, Rare	166	—	—	—	—	—
1924 F	3,134,000	0.50	2.00	4.00	20.00	25.00
1924 G	4,790,000	0.50	2.00	7.00	30.00	33.00
1924 J	2,200,000	0.50	2.00	10.00	40.00	44.00
1925 A	85,239,000	0.20	0.50	2.50	15.00	18.00
1925 D	39,750,000	0.20	0.50	2.50	18.00	20.00
1925 E	17,554,000	0.20	1.00	5.00	20.00	22.00
1925 E Proof, Rare	61	—	—	—	—	—
1925 F Large 5	20,990,000	6.00	16.00	32.00	130	150
1925 F Small 5	Inc. above	0.20	0.50	5.00	25.00	28.00
1925 G	10,232,000	0.20	1.00	5.00	30.00	35.00
1925 J	10,950,000	0.50	4.00	10.00	45.00	50.00
1926 A	22,377,000	0.50	2.00	6.00	30.00	35.00
1926 E	5,990,000	10.00	30.00	60.00	250	290
1926 E Proof, Rare	33	—	—	—	—	—
1926 F	2,871,000	5.00	16.00	40.00	190	220
1930 A	7,418,000	0.30	3.00	6.00	25.00	30.00
1935 A	19,178,000	0.20	2.00	4.00	12.00	14.00
1935 D	5,480,000	0.20	0.50	3.00	20.00	24.00
1935 E	2,384,000	0.30	0.60	3.00	25.00	28.00
1935 F	4,585,000	0.20	0.50	2.00	25.00	28.00
1935 G	2,652,000	0.30	2.00	4.00	25.00	28.00
1935 J	2,614,000	0.30	2.00	4.00	25.00	28.00
1936 A	36,992,000	0.20	0.30	2.00	15.00	18.00
1936 D	8,108,000	0.20	0.50	2.00	15.00	18.00
1936 E	2,981,000	0.20	0.60	3.00	22.00	25.00
1936 F	6,643,000	0.20	0.60	2.00	20.00	24.00
1936 G	2,274,000	0.20	0.60	2.00	25.00	30.00
1936 J	4,470,000	0.20	0.60	2.00	25.00	30.00
Common date	—	PF63 100				

KM# 40 10 REICHSPFENNIG

4.05 g., Aluminum-Bronze, 21 mm. **Obv:** Denomination within square, oak leaf on each side **Rev:** Six grain sprigs form center triangle above date

Date	Mintage	F12	VF20	XF40	MS60	MS63
1924 A	20,883,000	0.20	1.00	6.00	40.00	50.00
1924 D	9,639,000	0.20	1.00	9.00	70.00	85.00
1924 E	5,185,000	0.20	1.00	6.00	40.00	50.00
1924 E Proof, Rare	166	—	—	—	—	—
1924 F	2,758,000	3.00	12.00	40.00	200	250
1924 G	4,363,000	0.50	2.00	15.00	80.00	90.00
1924 J	3,993,000	0.50	2.00	15.00	80.00	90.00
1925 A	102,319,000	0.20	0.50	3.00	15.00	20.00
1925 D	36,853,000	0.20	1.00	12.00	36.00	45.00
1925 E	18,700,000	0.30	2.00	18.00	45.00	52.00
1925 E Proof, Rare	61	—	—	—	—	—
1925 F	12,516,000	0.20	3.00	18.00	50.00	60.00
1925 G	10,360,000	0.30	4.00	18.00	55.00	65.00
1925 J	8,755,000	1.00	5.00	18.00	80.00	90.00
1926 A	14,390,000	0.30	3.00	15.00	60.00	70.00
1926 G	1,481,000	2.00	12.00	40.00	160	180
1928 A	2,308,000	2.00	5.00	15.00	75.00	90.00
1928 G	Inc. below	50.00	150	250	700	750
1929 A	25,712,000	0.20	1.00	2.00	30.00	35.00
1929 D	7,049,000	0.20	1.00	2.00	40.00	48.00
1929 E	3,138,000	0.30	2.00	15.00	90.00	105
1929 F	3,740,000	0.30	2.00	15.00	90.00	105
1929 G	2,729,000	0.30	4.00	25.00	120	140
1929 J	4,086,000	0.30	2.00	15.00	90.00	105
1930 A	7,540,000	0.20	1.00	3.00	25.00	30.00
1930 D	2,148,000	0.30	2.00	5.00	40.00	50.00
1930 E	2,090,000	1.00	4.00	15.00	90.00	110
1930 F	2,006,000	1.00	4.00	15.00	80.00	100
1930 G	1,542,000	2.00	6.00	25.00	120	135
1930 J	1,637,000	2.00	4.00	15.00	100	120
1931 A	9,661,000	0.30	2.00	4.00	25.00	35.00
1931 D	664,000	15.00	45.00	90.00	200	240
1931 F	1,482,000	7.50	25.00	50.00	150	180
1931 G	38,000	150	260	480	1,600	2,000
1932 A	4,528,000	0.30	2.00	4.00	24.00	28.00
1932 D	2,812,000	0.50	4.00	15.00	50.00	60.00
1932 E	1,491,000	2.50	4.00	15.00	80.00	100
1932 F	1,806,000	2.00	6.00	20.00	100	125
1932 G	137,000	350	850	1,500	—	—
1933 A	1,349,000	15.00	35.00	55.00	180	220
1933 G	1,046,000	6.00	20.00	40.00	90.00	110
1933 J	1,634,000	4.00	15.00	30.00	70.00	85.00
1934 A	3,200,000	0.30	1.00	6.00	30.00	35.00
1934 D	1,252,000	2.00	7.00	18.00	110	125
1934 E	Inc. below	18.00	35.00	65.00	180	215
1934 F	100,000	12.00	30.00	55.00	170	205
1934 G	150,000	15.00	40.00	75.00	290	335
1935 A	35,890,000	0.20	0.50	3.00	15.00	18.00
1935 D	8,960,000	0.20	0.50	3.00	18.00	22.00
1935 E	5,966,000	0.20	0.50	3.00	20.00	25.00
1935 F	7,944,000	0.20	0.30	2.00	18.00	22.00
1935 G	4,847,000	0.20	0.50	4.00	24.00	28.00
1935 J	8,995,000	0.20	0.50	4.00	24.00	28.00
1936 A	24,527,000	0.20	0.80	2.00	20.00	24.00
1936 D	8,092,000	0.20	2.00	4.00	25.00	30.00
1936 E	2,441,000	0.20	2.00	8.00	30.00	35.00
1936 F	4,889,000	0.20	2.00	4.00	26.00	30.00
1936 G	1,715,000	0.50	4.00	10.00	50.00	60.00
1936 J	1,632,000	0.50	6.00	20.00	80.00	100
Common date	—	PF63 100				

KM# 41 50 REICHSPFENNIG

Aluminum-Bronze **Obv:** Denomination within square, oak leaf on each side **Rev:** Six grain sprigs form center triangle above date

Date	Mintage	F12	VF20	XF40	MS60	MS63
1924 A	801,000	700	1,200	2,000	3,200	3,800
1924 A	—	PF63 4,000				
1924 E Rare	Inc. below	—	—	—	—	—
1924 F	55,000	—	—	—	—	—
1924 F	—	PF63 25,000				

Note: Peus Auction #324 4-89 proof realized $10,360

Date	Mintage	F12	VF20	XF40	MS60	MS63
1924 G Rare	11,000	—	—	—	—	—
1924 G	—	PF63 15,000				
1925 E	1,805,000	700	1,200	2,000	3,200	4,000
1925 E	196	PF63 5,500				
1925 F Rare	—	—	—	—	—	—
1925 F	—	PF63 35,000				

Note: Peus Auction #324 4-89 proof realized $23,830. Kurdfälzische Munzhandlung Mannheim 6-91 proof realized $37,600

KM# 49 50 REICHSPFENNIG

3.50 g., Nickel, 20 mm. **Obv:** Eagle within circle, leaf spray below **Rev:** Denomination within lined circle, oak leaves and acorns above

Date	Mintage	F12	VF20	XF40	MS60	MS63
1927 A	16,309,000	2.00	5.00	10.00	25.00	35.00
1927 D	2,228,000	3.00	10.00	20.00	75.00	90.00
1927 E	1,070,000	4.00	10.00	20.00	75.00	90.00
1927 F	1,940,000	3.00	8.00	16.00	60.00	80.00
1927 G	1,756,000	6.00	18.00	30.00	120	150
1927 J	4,056,000	3.00	8.00	16.00	60.00	80.00
1928 A	43,864,000	0.80	4.00	8.00	20.00	25.00
1928 D	14,088,000	1.00	3.00	6.00	35.00	40.00
1928 E	8,618,000	1.00	3.00	6.00	35.00	40.00
1928 F	9,954,000	1.00	3.00	6.00	35.00	40.00
1928 G	6,177,000	1.00	3.50	7.00	40.00	50.00
1928 J	6,565,000	1.00	3.00	6.00	40.00	50.00
1929 A	10,298,000	1.00	5.00	10.00	45.00	60.00
1929 D	1,965,000	2.00	6.00	18.00	80.00	100
1929 F	1,162,000	10.00	30.00	50.00	150	180
1930 A	4,128,000	1.00	5.00	9.00	50.00	60.00
1930 D	1,406,000	3.00	8.00	12.00	75.00	88.00
1930 E	745,000	10.00	30.00	70.00	220	250
1930 F	320,000	40.00	70.00	140	400	450
1930 G	610,000	20.00	50.00	100	250	280
1930 J	526,000	20.00	50.00	100	280	320
1931 A	5,624,000	1.00	5.00	9.00	40.00	50.00
1931 D	1,125,000	2.00	7.00	16.00	70.00	85.00
1931 F	1,484,000	2.00	6.00	12.00	40.00	50.00
1931 G	60,000	190	300	420	1,200	1,400
1931 J	291,000	45.00	120	200	500	600
1932 E	598,000	40.00	90.00	200	500	600
1932 G	96,000	800	1,300	1,900	—	—
1933 G	333,000	55.00	120	200	500	600
1933 J	654,000	45.00	100	155	400	500
1935 A	6,390,000	1.00	5.00	12.00	32.00	36.00
1935 D	2,812,000	3.00	8.00	16.00	45.00	52.00
1935 E	745,000	10.00	25.00	40.00	130	150
1935 F	2,006,000	3.00	8.00	15.00	45.00	52.00
1935 G	650,000	15.00	35.00	60.00	160	190
1935 J	1,635,000	3.00	14.00	36.00	120	150
1936 A	7,696,000	2.00	4.00	12.00	25.00	35.00
1936 D	844,000	7.00	24.00	50.00	180	220
1936 E	1,190,000	7.00	24.00	50.00	180	220
1936 F	602,000	10.00	30.00	60.00	200	250
1936 G	936,000	7.00	24.00	50.00	180	220
1936 J	490,000	30.00	70.00	140	350	450
1937 A	10,842,000	1.00	4.00	8.00	20.00	25.00
1937 D	2,814,000	2.00	8.00	16.00	45.00	60.00
1937 F	1,700,000	2.00	8.00	16.00	45.00	60.00
1937 J	300,000	60.00	130	250	450	550
1938 E	1,200,000	8.00	15.00	35.00	110	125
1938 G	1,299,000	7.00	15.00	35.00	110	125
1938 J	1,333,000	7.00	15.00	35.00	110	125
Common date	—	PF63 200				

KM# 42 MARK

5.00 g., 0.500 Silver 0.0804 oz. ASW, 23 mm. **Obv:** Denomination above date **Rev:** Eagle

Date	Mintage	F12	VF20	XF40	MS60	MS63
1924 A	75,536,000	6.00	15.00	30.00	65.00	80.00
1924 D	17,099,000	6.00	18.00	35.00	75.00	90.00
1924 E	12,293,000	7.00	20.00	40.00	140	180
1924 E	115	PF63 275				
1924 F	16,550,000	—	18.00	35.00	130	160
1924 G	10,065,000	7.00	18.00	35.00	180	220
1924 J	13,481,000	6.00	15.00	30.00	130	160
1925 A	13,878,000	18.00	40.00	80.00	160	220
1925 D	6,100,000	10.00	25.00	50.00	130	160
Common date	—	PF63 250				

KM# 43 3 MARK

15.00 g., 0.500 Silver 0.2411 oz. ASW, 30 mm. **Obv:** Denomination above date **Rev:** Eagle

Date	Mintage	F12	VF20	XF40	MS60	MS63
1924 A	24,386,000	15.00	32.00	65.00	150	180
1924 D	3,769,000	25.00	65.00	110	700	400
1924 E	3,353,000	25.00	65.00	110	300	400
1924 E	115	PF63 450				
1924 F	4,518,000	25.00	65.00	110	300	400
1924 G	2,745,000	25.00	65.00	130	350	450
1924 J	3,677,000	25.00	65.00	130	300	400
1925 D	2,558,000	50.00	130	260	600	800
Common date	—	PF63 280				

KM# 44 REICHSMARK

5.00 g., 0.500 Silver 0.0804 oz. ASW **Obv:** Eagle above date **Rev:** Denomination within wreath

Date	Mintage	F12	VF20	XF40	MS60	MS63
1925 A	34,527,000	5.00	15.00	30.00	60.00	65.00
1925 A	600	PF63 380				
1925 D	13,854,000	6.00	20.00	40.00	80.00	110
1925 E	6,460,000	8.00	25.00	50.00	100	130
1925 F	8,035,000	8.00	20.00	50.00	150	190
1925 G	4,520,000	9.00	25.00	50.00	130	160
1925 J	6,800,000	9.00	25.00	50.00	130	160
1926 A	35,555,000	8.00	20.00	35.00	110	140
1926 D	4,424,000	10.00	25.00	40.00	150	190
1926 E	3,225,000	14.00	30.00	70.00	280	320
1926 E	31	PF63 450				
1926 F	3,045,000	12.00	30.00	50.00	200	250
1926 G	3,410,000	14.00	35.00	80.00	230	280
1926 J	1,290,000	60.00	150	300	500	600
1927 A	364,000	250	450	700	1,500	2,000
1927 F	1,959,000	35.00	70.00	130	360	450
1927 J	2,451,000	25.00	55.00	120	300	360

KM# 45 2 REICHSMARK

10.00 g., 0.500 Silver 0.1608 oz. ASW, 28 mm. **Obv:** Eagle above date **Rev:** Denomination within wreath

Date	Mintage	F12	VF20	XF40	MS60	MS63
1925 A	16,145,000	8.00	20.00	35.00	100	130
1925 D	2,272,000	12.00	30.00	40.00	180	225
1925 E	1,971,000	12.00	30.00	50.00	180	225
1925 E	101	PF63 350				
1925 F	2,414,000	12.00	30.00	50.00	150	190
1925 G	929,000	16.00	40.00	80.00	170	210
1925 J	2,326,000	12.00	30.00	50.00	150	225
1926 A	31,645,000	8.00	20.00	35.00	110	140
1926 D	11,322,000	8.00	20.00	35.00	120	150
1926 E	5,107,000	12.00	30.00	60.00	180	225
1926 E Proof	30	—	750	—	—	—
1926 F	7,115,000	12.00	30.00	55.00	170	210
1926 G	5,171,000	12.00	30.00	60.00	180	225
1926 J	5,305,000	12.00	30.00	60.00	180	225
1927 A	6,399,000	12.00	30.00	60.00	180	220
1927 D	466,000	800	1,300	2,200	6,000	6,500
1927 E	373,000	220	550	1,200	3,000	3,300
1927 E	53	PF63 3,000				
1927 F	502,000	60.00	200	350	1,100	1,300
1927 J	540,000	60.00	160	260	600	700
1931 D	2,109,000	20.00	50.00	70.00	200	260
1931 E	1,118,000	26.00	60.00	90.00	300	380
1931 F	1,505,000	22.00	50.00	90.00	300	380
1931 G	915,000	30.00	70.00	130	300	450
1931 J	1,226,000	30.00	70.00	130	800	1,200
Common date	—	PF63 300				

KM# 46 3 REICHSMARK

15.00 g., 0.500 Silver 0.2411 oz. ASW, 30 mm. **Subject:** 1000th Year of the Rhineland **Obv:** Armored figure behind shield divides date, right arm raised **Rev:** Denomination within wreath

Date	Mintage	F12	VF20	XF40	MS60	MS63
1925 A	3,052,000	25.00	55.00	75.00	120	150
1925 A	—	PF63 320				
1925 D	1,123,000	25.00	55.00	75.00	120	150
1925 D	—	PF63 400				
1925 E	441,000	25.00	60.00	85.00	140	175
1925 E	229	PF63 400				
1925 F	173,000	35.00	80.00	110	160	200
1925 F	—	PF63 500				
1925 G	300,000	30.00	60.00	85.00	140	175
1925 G	—	PF63 400				
1925 J	492,000	25.00	55.00	75.00	130	160
1925 J	—	PF63 400				

KM# 48 3 REICHSMARK

15.00 g., 0.500 Silver 0.2411 oz. ASW, 30 mm. **Subject:** 700 Years of Freedom for Lubeck **Obv:** Denomination within circle, leaf spray below **Rev:** Double-headed eagle on shield within circle, dates above

Date	Mintage	F12	VF20	XF40	MS60	MS63
1926 A	200,000	60.00	140	250	300	350
1926 A	—	PF63 300				

KM# 50 3 REICHSMARK

15.00 g., 0.500 Silver 0.2411 oz. ASW, 30 mm. **Subject:** 100th Anniversary of Bremerhaven **Obv:** Eagle on shield within scalloped design **Rev:** Shield divides date below ship

Date	Mintage	F12	VF20	XF40	MS60	MS63
1927 A	150,000	70.00	150	300	500	580
1927 A	—	PF63 300				

KM# 52 3 REICHSMARK

15.00 g., 0.500 Silver 0.2411 oz. ASW, 30 mm. **Subject:** 1000th Anniversary - Founding of Nordhausen **Obv:** Large denomination within scalloped design **Rev:** Heinrich I and Mathilde

Date	Mintage	F12	VF20	XF40	MS60	MS63
1927 A	100,000	70.00	150	300	550	650
1927 A	—	PF63 650				

KM# 53 3 REICHSMARK

15.00 g., 0.500 Silver 0.2411 oz. ASW, 30 mm. **Subject:** 400th Anniversary - Philipps University in Marburg **Obv:** Eagle, denomination below **Rev:** Arms of Philip I the Magnanimous

Date	Mintage	F12	VF20	XF40	MS60	MS63
1927 A	130,000	70.00	150	260	400	450
1927 A	—	PF63 500				

KM# 54 3 REICHSMARK

15.00 g., 0.500 Silver 0.2411 oz. ASW, 30 mm. **Subject:** 450th Anniversary - Tubingen University **Obv:** Eagle, denomination below **Rev:** Count Eberhard the Bearded left

Date	Mintage	F12	VF20	XF40	MS60	MS63
1927 F	50,000	190	400	800	1,200	1,300
1927 F	—	PF63 1,350				

KM# 57 3 REICHSMARK

15.00 g., 0.500 Silver 0.2411 oz. ASW, 30 mm. **Subject:** 900th Anniversary - Founding of Naumburg **Obv:** Eagle above denomination **Rev:** Margrave Hermann, City Founder

Date	Mintage	F12	VF20	XF40	MS60	MS63
1928 A	100,000	80.00	180	280	400	480
1928 A Matte proof	—	PF63 600				

KM# 58 3 REICHSMARK

15.00 g., 0.500 Silver 0.2411 oz. ASW, 30 mm. **Subject:** 400th Anniversary - Death of Albrecht Dürer **Obv:** Eagle above denomination **Rev:** Head left within circle, date below

Date	Mintage	F12	VF20	XF40	MS60	MS63
1928 D	50,000	165	350	700	1,050	1,200
1928 D Matte proof	—	PF63 1,200				

KM# 59 3 REICHSMARK
15.00 g., 0.500 Silver 0.2411 oz. ASW, 30 mm. **Subject:** 1000th Anniversary - Founding of Dinkelsbühl **Obv:** Eagle above denomination **Rev:** Shield below figure holding sickle and sheaf, towers flank, date is divided in fourths by the above

Date	Mintage	F12	VF20	XF40	MS60	MS63
1928 D	40,000	250	600	900	1,300	1,500
1928 D	—	**PF63** 1,700				
1928 D Matte proof	—	**PF63** 2,250				

KM# 60 3 REICHSMARK
15.00 g., 0.500 Silver 0.2411 oz. ASW, 30 mm. **Subject:** 200th Anniversary - Birth of Gotthold Lessing **Obv:** Small eagle, denomination below **Rev:** Head left divides dates

Date	Mintage	F12	VF20	XF40	MS60	MS63
1929 A	217,000	30.00	70.00	140	280	350
1929 A	—	**PF63** 500				
1929 D	56,000	35.00	80.00	160	300	350
1929 D	—	**PF63** 600				
1929 E	30,000	40.00	90.00	180	350	400
1929 E	—	**PF63** 600				
1929 F	40,000	35.00	80.00	160	320	370
1929 F	—	**PF63** 60.00				
1929 G	24,000	12.00	100	150	300	370
1929 G	—	**PF63** 600				
1929 J	33,000	40.00	90.00	180	300	370
1929 J	—	**PF63** 600				

KM# 62 3 REICHSMARK
15.00 g., 0.500 Silver 0.2411 oz. ASW, 30 mm. **Subject:** Waldeck-Prussia Union **Obv:** Eagle above denomination **Rev:** Eagle with wings lowered holds shield at left, date below

Date	Mintage	F12	VF20	XF40	MS60	MS63
1929 A	170,000	60.00	140	260	300	350
1929 A	—	**PF63** 600				

KM# 63 3 REICHSMARK
15.00 g., 0.500 Silver 0.2411 oz. ASW, 30 mm. **Subject:** 10th Anniversary - Weimar Constitution **Obv:** President Paul von Hindenburg **Rev:** Hand with two fingers raised within circle, dates below

Date	Mintage	F12	VF20	XF40	MS60	MS63
1929 A	1,421,000	20.00	50.00	75.00	100	120
1929 A	—	**PF63** 320				
1929 A Matte proof	—	—	—	—	—	—
1929 D	499,000	25.00	60.00	100	140	150
1929 D	—	**PF63** 320				
1929 E	122,000	30.00	75.00	150	200	220
1929 E	—	**PF63** 400				
1929 F	370,000	25.00	60.00	120	160	185
1929 F	—	**PF63** 400				
1929 G	256,000	25.00	60.00	120	160	185
1929 G	—	**PF63** 400				
1929 J	342,000	25.00	60.00	120	160	185
1929 J	—	**PF63** 400				

KM# 65 3 REICHSMARK
15.00 g., 0.500 Silver 0.2411 oz. ASW, 30 mm. **Subject:** 1000th Anniversary - Meissen **Obv:** Eagle within circle, denomination below **Rev:** Central figure holding shields on poles divides date, five crosses above

Date	Mintage	F12	VF20	XF40	MS60	MS63
1929 E	200,000	40.00	90.00	180	260	290
1929 E	—	**PF63** 500				

KM# 67 3 REICHSMARK
15.00 g., 0.500 Silver 0.2411 oz. ASW, 30 mm. **Subject:** Graf Zeppelin Flight **Obv:** Eagle, denomination below **Rev:** Zeppelin across globe, date below

Date	Mintage	F12	VF20	XF40	MS60	MS63
1930 A	542,000	55.00	120	150	230	280
1930 A	—	**PF63** 500				
1930 D	141,000	45.00	100	150	250	300
1930 D	—	**PF63** 550				
1930 E	75,000	70.00	150	200	260	300
1930 E	—	**PF63** 550				
1930 F	100,000	55.00	120	160	230	280
1930 F	—	**PF63** 500				
1930 G	61,000	70.00	150	200	260	300
1930 G	—	**PF63** 550				
1930 J	82,000	70.00	150	180	250	290
1930 J	—	**PF63** 550				

KM# 69 3 REICHSMARK
15.00 g., 0.500 Silver 0.2411 oz. ASW, 30 mm. **Subject:** 700th Anniversary - Death of Von Der Vogelweide **Obv:** Eagle on shield, design in background **Rev:** Figure of Walther von der Vogelweide sitting, left, with doves, harp on lower left. date at bottom **Note:** Same reverse used on Austria 2 schillings. KM# 2845

Date	Mintage	F12	VF20	XF40	MS60	MS63
1930 A	163,000	35.00	75.00	150	220	250
1930 A	—	**PF63** 450				
1930 A Matte proof	—	**PF63** 500				
1930 D	42,000	45.00	100	180	230	260
1930 D	—	**PF63** 450				
1930 E	22,000	55.00	120	200	260	320
1930 E	—	**PF63** 500				
1930 F	30,000	45.00	100	180	230	260
1930 F	—	**PF63** 500				
1930 G	18,000	55.00	120	200	260	320
1930 G	—	**PF63** 500				
1930 J	25,000	55.00	120	200	260	320
1930 J	—	**PF63** 500				

KM# 70 3 REICHSMARK
15.00 g., 0.500 Silver 0.2411 oz. ASW, 30 mm. **Subject:** Liberation of Rhineland **Obv:** Eagle on shield, design in background **Rev:** Eagle left on bridge divides date

Date	Mintage	F12	VF20	XF40	MS60	MS63
1930 A	1,734,000	35.00	75.00	110	200	250
1930 A	—	**PF63** 400				
1930 A Matte proof	—	—	—	—	—	—
1930 D	450,000	40.00	90.00	130	250	300
1930 D	—	**PF63** 400				
1930 E	38,000	70.00	150	300	600	700
1930 E	—	**PF63** 750				
1930 F	321,000	60.00	130	200	300	360
1930 F	—	**PF63** 400				
1930 G	195,000	60.00	130	200	320	380
1930 G	—	**PF63** 400				
1930 J	261,000	60.00	130	200	300	360
1930 J	—	**PF63** 400				

KM# 72 3 REICHSMARK
15.00 g., 0.500 Silver 0.2411 oz. ASW, 30 mm. **Subject:** 300th Anniversary - Magdeburg Rebuilding **Obv:** Eagle on shield, scalloped design in background **Rev:** Shield divides dates above city scene

Date	Mintage	F12	VF20	XF40	MS60	MS63
1931 A	100,000	120	250	480	650	750
1931 A	—	**PF63** 800				

KM# 73 3 REICHSMARK
15.00 g., 0.500 Silver 0.2411 oz. ASW, 30 mm. **Subject:** Centenary - Death of von Stein **Obv:** Eagle divides dates, denomination below **Rev:** Head left, name below

Date	Mintage	F12	VF20	XF40	MS60	MS63
1931 A	150,000	70.00	150	240	350	450
1931 A	—	**PF63** 500				

KM# 74 3 REICHSMARK
15.00 g., 0.500 Silver 0.2411 oz. ASW, 30 mm. **Obv:** Eagle above date **Rev:** Denomination within wreath

Date	Mintage	F12	VF20	XF40	MS60	MS63
1931 A	13,324,000	140	300	500	900	1,100
1931 D	2,232,000	170	360	500	1,200	1,400
1931 E	2,235,000	200	420	600	1,400	1,700
1931 F	2,357,000	170	360	500	1,200	1,400
1931 G	1,468,000	200	420	650	1,200	2,200
1931 J	1,115,000	200	400	600	1,500	2,000
1932 A	2,933,000	160	360	600	1,100	1,300
1932 D	1,986,000	160	360	650	1,600	1,900
1932 F	653,000	250	600	1,200	2,500	2,900
1932 G	210,000	600	1,300	2,500	6,500	7,500
1932 J	1,336,000	190	400	850	1,600	1,900

Date	Mintage	F12	VF20	XF40	MS60	MS63
1933 G	152,000	1,100	2,500	4,000	10,000	13,000

Note: Less than 10 percent of issue was released

Date	Mintage	F12	VF20	XF40	MS60	MS63
Common date	—	PF63 1,400				

KM# 76 3 REICHSMARK

15.00 g., 0.500 Silver 0.2411 oz. ASW, 30 mm. **Subject:** Centenary - Death of Goethe **Obv:** Eagle divides dates, denomination below **Rev:** Head left, name below

Date	Mintage	F12	VF20	XF40	MS60	MS63
1932 A	217,000	35.00	125	180	250	300
1932 A	—	PF63 400				
1932 D	56,000	40.00	130	200	280	350
1932 D	—	PF63 400				
1932 E	30,000	45.00	140	220	300	380
1932 E	—	PF63 450				
1932 F	40,000	35.00	130	200	280	350
1932 F	—	PF63 400				
1932 F Matte proof	—	PF63 600				
1932 G	24,000	45.00	140	220	300	380
1932 G	—	PF63 500				
1932 J	33,000	45.00	130	200	280	350
1932 J	—	PF63 450				

KM# 47 5 REICHSMARK

25.00 g., 0.500 Silver 0.4019 oz. ASW, 37 mm. **Subject:** 1000th Year of the Rhineland **Obv:** Armored figure behind shield divides date, right arm raised **Rev:** Denomination within wreath

Date	Mintage	F12	VF20	XF40	MS60	MS63
1925 A	684,000	60.00	125	200	350	600
1925 A	—	PF63 600				
1925 D	452,000	65.00	130	220	400	660
1925 D	—	PF63 1,150				
1925 E	204,000	70.00	150	250	450	550
1925 E	226	PF63 1,150				
1925 F	212,000	70.00	150	260	450	550
1925 F	—	PF63 1,150				
1925 G	89,000	90.00	200	380	530	650
1925 G	—	PF63 1,150				
1925 J	43,000	120	250	500	750	900
1925 J	—	PF63 1,300				

KM# 51 5 REICHSMARK

25.00 g., 0.500 Silver 0.4019 oz. ASW, 37 mm. **Subject:** 100th Anniversary - Bremerhaven **Obv:** Eagle on shield, scalloped design in background **Rev:** Crowned shield divides date below ship

Date	Mintage	F12	VF20	XF40	MS60	MS63
1927 A	50,000	300	600	800	1,100	1,250
1927 A	—	PF63 1,300				

KM# 55 5 REICHSMARK

25.00 g., 0.500 Silver 0.4019 oz. ASW, 37 mm. **Subject:** 450th Anniversary - University of Tübingen **Rev:** Bust left within circle

Date	Mintage	F12	VF20	XF40	MS60	MS63
1927 F	40,000	130	500	850	1,200	1,350
1927 F	—	PF63 1,500				

KM# 56 5 REICHSMARK

25.00 g., 0.500 Silver 0.4019 oz. ASW, 37 mm. **Obv:** Eagle within circle, denomination below **Rev:** Oaktree divides date

Date	Mintage	F12	VF20	XF40	MS60	MS63
1927 A	7,926,000	70.00	150	225	500	600
1927 D	1,471,000	80.00	170	240	600	750
1927 E	1,100,000	90.00	190	260	800	950
1927 F	700,000	100	200	280	1,000	1,150
1927 G	759,000	90.00	190	270	1,200	1,500
1927 J	1,006,000	80.00	160	240	1,000	1,150
1928 A	15,466,000	60.00	120	220	500	600
1928 D	4,613,000	75.00	150	250	600	750
1928 E	2,310,000	90.00	160	250	700	900
1928 F	3,771,000	75.00	160	250	600	720
1928 G	1,923,000	75.00	160	250	600	720
1928 J	2,450,000	75.00	160	250	600	720
1929 A	6,730,000	75.00	140	240	600	750
1929 D	2,020,000	75.00	160	280	700	850
1929 E	860,000	160	300	600	1,900	2,400
1929 F	814,000	90.00	200	400	800	1,000
1929 G	950,000	110	220	420	1,000	1,300
1929 J	779,000	100	210	420	800	1,200
1930 A	3,790,000	70.00	140	250	800	1,000
1930 D	606,000	300	600	1,200	2,400	2,700
1930 E Rare	354,000	—	—	—	—	—
1930 F	630,000	350	700	950	1,800	2,200
1930 G	367,000	700	1,500	2,500	6,000	7,500
1930 J	740,000	350	700	1,100	2,200	2,600
1931 A	14,651,000	60.00	130	250	460	600
1931 D	3,254,000	70.00	140	270	520	650
1931 E	2,245,000	70.00	140	280	750	850
1931 F	4,152,000	70.00	140	300	550	700
1931 G	1,620,000	110	250	430	1,400	1,600
1931 J	3,092,000	90.00	200	400	800	950
1932 A	32,303,000	60.00	130	260	500	600
1932 D	8,556,000	60.00	130	300	600	720
1932 E	4,013,000	60.00	130	300	600	720
1932 F	5,019,000	60.00	130	300	600	720
1932 G	3,504,000	70.00	140	320	700	850
1932 J	3,752,000	80.00	190	320	750	900
1933 J Rare	423,000	—	—	—	—	—
1933 J	—	PF63 6,500				
Common date	—	PF63 1,500				

KM# 61 5 REICHSMARK

25.00 g., 0.500 Silver 0.4019 oz. ASW, 37 mm. **Subject:** 200th Anniversary - Birth of Gotthold Lessing **Obv:** Small eagle, denomination below **Rev:** Head left divides date

Date	Mintage	F12	VF20	XF40	MS60	MS63
1929 A	87,000	70.00	150	280	380	440
1929 A	—	PF63 750				
1929 D	22,000	70.00	180	320	430	500
1929 D	—	PF63 900				
1929 E	12,000	90.00	200	350	430	500
1929 E	—	PF63 900				
1929 F	16,000	90.00	200	350	430	500
1929 F	—	PF63 500				
1929 G	9,760	120	250	380	500	600
1929 G	—	PF63 1,000				
1929 J	13,000	90.00	200	350	430	500
1929 J	—	PF63 900				

KM# 64 5 REICHSMARK

25.00 g., 0.500 Silver 0.4019 oz. ASW, 37 mm. **Subject:** 10th Anniversary - Weimar Constitution **Obv:** Hand with two fingers raised, dates below **Rev:** Head left, denomination above

Date	Mintage	F12	VF20	XF40	MS60	MS63
1929 A	325,000	60.00	125	250	380	520
1929 A	—	PF63 550				
1929 D	84,000	70.00	140	280	430	520
1929 D	—	PF63 550				
1929 E	45,000	80.00	150	300	430	520
1929 E	—	PF63 550				
1929 F	60,000	80.00	150	300	430	520
1929 F	—	PF63 550				
1929 G	37,000	80.00	170	320	500	620
1929 G	—	PF63 550				
1929 J	49,000	70.00	150	300	430	520
1929 J	—	PF63 550				

KM# 66 5 REICHSMARK

25.00 g., 0.500 Silver 0.4019 oz. ASW, 37 mm. **Subject:** 1000th Anniversary - Meissen **Obv:** Eagle **Rev:** Central figure holding shields on poles divides date, five crosses above

Date	Mintage	F12	VF20	XF40	MS60	MS63
1929 E	120,000	220	450	700	1,000	1,200
1929 E	—	PF63 1,500				

KM# 68 5 REICHSMARK
25.00 g., 0.500 Silver 0.4019 oz. ASW, 37 mm. **Subject:** Graf Zeppelin Flight **Obv:** Eagle, denomination below **Rev:** Zeppelin across globe, date below

Date	Mintage	F12	VF20	XF40	MS60	MS63
1930 A	217,000	70.00	150	270	400	480
1930 A	—	**PF63** 500				
1930 A Matte proof	—	—	—	—	—	—
1930 D	56,000	75.00	160	280	420	500
1930 D	—	**PF63** 650				
1930 E	30,000	80.00	180	300	500	600
1930 E	—	**PF63** 650				
1930 F	40,000	75.00	160	280	480	580
1930 F	—	**PF63** 650				
1930 G	24,000	90.00	200	300	500	600
1930 G	—	**PF63** 660				
1930 J	33,000	90.00	180	280	480	580
1930 J	—	**PF63** 660				

KM# 71 5 REICHSMARK
25.00 g., 0.500 Silver 0.4019 oz. ASW, 37 mm. **Subject:** Liberation of Rhineland **Obv:** Eagle on shield, design in background **Rev:** Eagle left on bridge divides date

Date	Mintage	F12	VF20	XF40	MS60	MS63
1930 A	325,000	70.00	140	280	440	520
1930 A	—	**PF63** 600				
1930 D	84,000	75.00	160	320	500	600
1930 D	—	**PF63** 700				
1930 E	45,000	85.00	175	340	550	320
1930 E	—	**PF63** 700				
1930 F	60,000	75.00	160	340	550	620
1930 F	—	**PF63** 600				
1930 G	37,000	120	250	380	600	750
1930 G	—	**PF63** 900				
1930 J	49,000	120	250	350	550	620
1930 J	—	**PF63** 800				

KM# 77 5 REICHSMARK
25.00 g., 0.500 Silver 0.4019 oz. ASW, 37 mm. **Subject:** Centenary - Death of Goethe **Obv:** Eagle divides dates, denomination below **Rev:** Head left, name below

Date	Mintage	F12	VF20	XF40	MS60	MS63
1932 A	11,000	1,100	2,750	3,600	5,000	6,000
1932 A	—	**PF63** 5,600				
1932 D	2,812	1,200	2,850	4,300	5,600	6,500
1932 D	—	**PF63** 6,000				
1932 E	1,490	1,200	3,000	4,400	6,000	7,000
1932 E	—	**PF63** 6,000				
1932 F	2,006	1,200	3,000	4,400	6,000	7,000
1932 F	—	**PF63** 6,000				
1932 G	1,220	1,200	3,000	4,400	6,000	7,000
1932 G	—	**PF63** 6,000				
1932 J	1,634	1,200	3,000	4,400	6,000	7,000
1932 J	—	**PF63** 6,000				

PATTERNS

Including off metal strikes

KM#	Date	Mintage	Identification	Mkt Val
Pn212	1919A	—	50 Pfennig. Brass.	275
Pn213	1919A	—	50 Pfennig. Silver.	375
Pn214	1919A	—	50 Pfennig. Nickel.	200
Pn215	1919A	—	50 Pfennig. Aluminum.	200
Pn216	1919A	—	50 Pfennig. Zinc.	200
Pn217	1919A	—	50 Pfennig. Zinc. Reeded.	—
Pn218	1919A	—	50 Pfennig. Aluminum. Reeded.	150
Pn219	1919A	—	50 Pfennig. Aluminum. Plain.	—
Pn220	1919A	—	50 Pfennig. Aluminum. Ornamental.	—
Pn221	1919A	—	50 Pfennig. Zinc. Ornamental.	—
Pn222	1919G	—	1/2 Mark. KM#17.	—
Pn223	1919G	—	Mark. Copper. KM#14.	—
Pn224	19xx (1919)A	—	Mark. Aluminum.	—
Pn225	1921A	—	Mark. Brass Plated Aluminum.	—
Pn226	1921A	—	Mark. Zinc.	—
Pn227	1921A	—	Mark.	—
Pn228	1921A	—	Mark. Aluminum Plated Steel.	—
Pn229	1921A	—	Mark. Nickel.	175
Pn230	1921A	—	Mark. Silver.	—
Pn231	1921A	—	Mark. Iron.	—
Pn232	1921A	—	Mark. Copper Strips inlaid in Silver or Copper-Nickel.	—
Pn233	1921A	—	Mark. Copper Strips inlaid in Aluminum.	—
PnA234	1922A	—	10 Pfennig. Iron.	250
Pn234	1922A	—	50 Pfennig. Iron. Plain with 6 ridges. KM#27.	—
Pn235	1922F	—	3 Mark. Aluminum. KM#28; GOTT MIT UNS.	875

Note: Most 1922F lettered-edge 3 Marks were recovered from the burned out ruins of the Stuttgart Mint destroyed in World War II; the above value is for the one known perfect example, blackened VF examples are valued between $200 and $400

KM#	Date	Mintage	Identification	Mkt Val
Pn236	1922F	—	3 Mark. Aluminum. Reeded. KM#28.	—
Pn237	1922F	—	3 Mark. Aluminum. Plain. KM#28.	—
Pn238	1922G	—	3 Mark. Aluminum. Reeded. KM#28.	—
Pn239	1922A	—	5 Mark. Aluminum.	150
Pn239a	1922A	—	5 Mark. Aluminum Plated Copper.	775
Pn240	1922A	—	5 Mark. Roman lettering.	—
Pn241	1923	—	2 Pfennig. Bronze. Without mintmark; KM#31.	—
Pn242	1923	—	50 Pfennig. Aluminum-Bronze. Without mintmark; KM#34.	—
Pn243	1923F	—	3 Mark. KM#29.4.	275

Note: All pattern 1923F 3 Marks were recovered from the burned out ruins of the Stuttgart Mint destroyed in World War II; blackened VF examples range in value from $250 to $450

KM#	Date	Mintage	Identification	Mkt Val
Pn244	1923A	—	20 Mark. Aluminum.	—
Pn245	1923A	—	100 Mark. Aluminum.	—
Pn246	1923F	—	200 Mark. Aluminum. Doubled reeding; KM#35.	—
Pn247	1923F	—	1000 Mark. Aluminum. Reeded.	350
Pn248	1923F	—	1000 Mark. Silver. Reeded.	—
Pn249	1923F	—	1000 Mark. Aluminum. Plain.	—
PnA250	1924	—	2 Pfennig. Brass. KM#31.	175
Pn250	1924E	—	2 Pfennig. Copper. Eagle head left.	—
Pn251	1924E	—	10 Pfennig. Copper.	—
Pn252	1924E	—	10 Pfennig. Aluminum.	—
Pn253	1924E	—	10 Pfennig. Copper. Full eagle.	—
Pn254	1924E	—	10 Pfennig. Aluminum. Full eagle.	—
Pn255	1924E	—	10 Pfennig. Nickel. Full eagle.	—
Pn256	1924D	—	50 Pfennig. Lead. KM#41.	—
Pn257	1924A	—	Mark. Silver. Reeded, lettered.	—
Pn258	1924A	—	3 Mark. 0.500. Silver. Ornamental.	—
Pn259	1924E	—	5 Mark. Silver.	—
Pn260	1925E	—	Pfennig. Copper.	—
Pn261	1925E	—	2 Pfennig. Copper.	—
Pn262	1925E	—	5 Pfennig. Copper-Nickel.	—
Pn263	1925E	—	5 Pfennig. Copper-Nickel. Larger eagle head.	—
Pn264	1925E	—	10 Pfennig. Copper-Nickel.	—
Pn265	1925	6	50 Pfennig. Aluminum-Bronze. KM#41.	17,500

Note: An XF-AU example brought $15,957, Emporium Hamburg 1987 sale

KM#	Date	Mintage	Identification	Mkt Val
Pn266	1925F	—	50 Pfennig. Brass. Bundle.	150
Pn267	1925F	—	50 Pfennig. Bronze. Bundle.	150
Pn268	1925F	—	50 Pfennig. Copper-Nickel. Bundle.	150
Pn269	1925F	—	50 Pfennig. Nickel. Bundle.	150
Pn270	1925F	—	50 Pfennig. Nickel-Silver. Mercury.	175
Pn271	1925F	—	50 Pfennig. Nickel. Mercury.	175
Pn272	1925F	—	50 Pfennig. Brass. Mercury.	—
Pn273	1925E	—	Mark. Silver. Thick wreath.	—
Pn274	1925E	—	Mark. Nickel. Thick wreath.	—
Pn275	1925E	—	Mark. 0.450. Silver. Thin wreath.	—
PnA276	1925F	—	3 Mark. Brass.	—
Pn276	1925E	—	2 Mark. 0.500. Silver. Thick wreath.	200
PnA277	1925	—	3 Mark. Brass. Woman's head.	—
Pn277	1925J	—	3 Mark. Iron. KM#46.	—
Pn278	1925E	—	3 Mark. Silver.	475
Pn279	1925E	—	5 Reichsmark. Silver.	875
Pn280	1925E	—	5 Mark. Silver.	875
Pn281	1925F	—	5 Mark. Silver.	1,850
Pn281a	1925F	—	5 Mark. Silver Plated Bronze.	200
Pn282	1925E	—	5 Mark. Silver.	1,500
Pn283	1925E	—	20 Mark. Gold.	7,750
Pn284	1925E	—	20 Mark. Brass.	—
Pn285	1926E	—	50 Pfennig. Copper-Nickel.	—
Pn286	1926	—	50 Pfennig.	—
Pn287	1926E	—	50 Pfennig. Copper-Nickel. Leaves through value.	175
Pn288	1926A	—	50 Pfennig. Leaves below value.	—
Pn289	1926E	—	50 Pfennig. Copper-Nickel. Leaves below value.	—
Pn290	1926	—	50 Pfennig. Leaves below value.	—
Pn291	1926E	—	50 Pfennig. Copper-Nickel. Cornucopia.	175
Pn292	1926E	—	50 Pfennig. Copper-Nickel. Two leaves.	—
Pn293	1926E	—	50 Pfennig. Copper-Nickel. Wreath.	—
Pn294	1926E	—	50 Pfennig. Copper-Nickel. Wheat.	—
Pn295	1926E	—	50 Pfennig. Copper-Nickel. Eagle.	—
Pn296	1926E	—	50 Pfennig. Copper-Nickel. Two leaves.	—
Pn297	1926E	—	50 Pfennig. Copper-Nickel. Eagle.	—
Pn298	1926E	—	50 Pfennig. Copper-Nickel. Wheat.	—
Pn299	1926E	—	50 Pfennig. Copper-Nickel. Two leaves.	—
Pn300	1926E	—	50 Pfennig. Copper-Nickel. Eagle.	—
Pn301	1926E	—	50 Pfennig. Copper-Nickel. Reichspfennig.	—
Pn302	1926E	—	50 Pfennig. Copper-Nickel.	—
Pn303	1926A	—	50 Pfennig. Nickel.	—
Pn304	1926E	—	50 Pfennig. Copper-Nickel.	—
Pn305	1926J	—	50 Pfennig. Nickel.	150
Pn306	1926J	—	50 Pfennig. Nickel. Smaller eagle.	—
Pn307	1926A	—	Mark. Brass.	150
Pn307a	1926A	—	Mark. Silver.	—
PnA308	1926	—	3 Mark.	—
Pn308	1926A	—	5 Mark. Silver.	—
Pn309	1926	—	5 Mark. Silver. Wreath aar-ound eagle.	—
Pn310	1926A	—	5 Mark. Silver.	875
Pn311	1926A	—	5 Mark. Silver.	875
Pn312	1926A	—	5 Mark. Silver.	1,000
Pn312a	1926D	—	5 Mark. Silver. Ship sailing right.	650
Pn313	1926E	—	5 Mark. Silver. Large eagle, small mint mark.	650
Pn314	1926	—	5 Mark. Silver. Small eagle, large mint mark.	650
Pn315	1926E	—	5 Mark. Silver.	900
Pn316	1926E	—	5 Mark. Silver.	900
Pn317	1926F	—	5 Mark. Silver. PROBE"; with motto.	—
Pn318	1926F	—	5 Mark. Silver. With motto.	750
Pn319	1926F	—	5 Mark. Silver. PROBE" without motto.	—
Pn320	1926F	—	5 Mark. Silver. Without motto.	900
Pn321	1927A	—	50 Pfennig. Nickel. Deeper relief, KM#49.	—
Pn322	1927E	—	50 Pfennig. Silver.	—
Pn323	1927F	—	50 Pfennig. Copper-Nickel.	200
Pn324	1927	—	Mark. Brass. Pn307.	—
Pn325	1927F	—	Mark. 0.500. Silver. Ornamental.	225
Pn326	1927F	—	Mark. 0.993. Silver. Plain.	275
Pn327	1927A	—	3 Mark. 0.993. Silver.	—
Pn327a	1927A	—	3 Mark. Copper-Nickel.	1,000
Pn328	1927F	—	3 Mark. Silver. Lettered. PROBE.	—
Pn329	1927F	—	3 Mark. Silver. Lettered.	—

Pn330	1927F	—	3 Mark. Plain.	900
PnA331	1927F	—	3 Mark. Silver. Justus Von Liebig; never issued.	—

Note: An XF-AU example brought $15,957 at the Emporium Hamburg 1987 sale.

Pn331	1927A	—	5 Mark. Silver. Large eagle.	—
Pn332	ND (1927)A	—	5 Mark. Silver Plated Tin. Small eagle.	—
Pn334	1927A	—	5 Mark. Silver. 50 stars; KM#56.	—
Pn335	1927A	—	5 Mark. Silver. 47 stars; KM#56.	—
Pn336	1927A	—	5 Mark. Silver. 73 stars; KM#56.	—
Pn337	1929A	—	3 Mark. Silver. Script on edge; KM#60.	900
Pn338	1929A	—	3 Mark. Silver. PROBE"; KM#62.	—
Pn339	1929A	—	5 Mark. Silver. Plain rims; "PROBE".	—
Pn340	1929A	—	5 Mark. Silver. Star rims; "PROBE".	—
Pn341	1929A	—	5 Mark. Silver. PROBE".	1,850
Pn342	1929A	—	5 Mark. Silver. Pn346.	—
PnA343	1929E	—	3 Mark. PROBE.	—
Pn343	1930	—	3 Mark. Silver. PROBE"; KM#70.	—
Pn344	1930	—	3 Mark. Silver. PROBE.	950
Pn345	1930A	—	3 Mark. Silver. PROBE"; KM#69.	950
Pn346	1930A	—	5 Mark. Silver. PROBE"; KM#68.	—
Pn347	1930	—	5 Mark. Silver.	—
PnA347	1931G	—	Pfennig. Brass.	150
Pn348	1931A	—	3 Mark.	—
Pn349	1931	—	5 Mark.	—
Pn350	1932A	—	4 Pfennig. Silver Plated Copper. PROBE.	—
PnA351	1932	—	3 Mark. Silver.	—
Pn351	1932D	—	3 Mark. 0.750. Silver. KM#74.	775
Pn352	1932F	—	3 Mark. Silver. Reeded. PROBE"; KM#74.	—
Pn353	1932F	—	3 Mark. Silver. Reeded. Without "PROBE"; KM#74.	—
Pn353a	1932A	—	5 Mark. Nickel. PROBE. KM#76.	450

1933-1945

A wide range of factors, such as humiliation of defeat, economic depression, poverty, and a pervasive feeling of discontent aided Hitler in his climb to power. After the unsuccessful Putsch (uprising against the Bavarian Government) in 1923, Hitler was imprisoned in Landsberg Fortress. While imprisoned Hitler dictated his book *"Mein Kampf"* which became the cornerstone of Nazism espousing Hitler's irrational ideology and the manipulation of power without moral constraint as the basis of strategy.

Master propagandist Josef Goebbels tried to attract the sympathetic attention of the German public. The usual tactic was to have Hitler promise all things to all people provided that they in turn would pledge to him their complete faith and obedience.

Once in power, coercion was used to elicit the appearance of unanimous endorsement. Public works and military rearmament helped overcome the depression. It took the Nazis only about two years to consolidate their system politically. The combined terrorism of the storm troops and the police forces, including the Gestapo, stifled potential opposition. By 1935, Nazi affiliated organizations controlled all German cultural, professional, and economic fields, assuring strict compliance with the party line.

With the passage of the Nurnberg Laws in 1935, the more ominous aspects of Nazi anti-Semitism came to light. Jews were deprived of their citizenship and forbidden to marry non-Jews. This was followed by confiscation of property and the required wearing of the Star of David for identification purposes, eventually culminating in the mass deportation to concentration and death camps.

By 1936, unemployment was virtually eliminated and economic production was up to 1929 levels. All sources of information were under the control of Josef Goebbels, while all police power was in the hands of Heinrich Himmler. Himmler's Gestapo would silence Germans who were not convinced by Goebbel's propaganda machine. Usually the implied threat was enough. The majority of Germans did not suffer any ill effects at first and national pride stirred once again.

Hitler's audacity in foreign affairs met with success due to the trend of appeasement by the western powers. First, Germany withdrew from the League of Nations and the World Disarmament Council. In 1935, the Saar voted to return to Germany and Hitler renounced the reviled 1921 peace treaty and related pacts. In 1936, German forces reoccupied the Rhineland. In 1938, Austria was annexed and at the Munich Conference, which excluded Czechoslovakia, Great Britain and France agreed that the Sudetenland was to become German territory. In 1939, Slovakia became an independent Nazi Puppet State and the "Protectorate" of Bohemia and Moravia was established. Next came the German-Soviet non-aggression pact, which secretly divided up Poland between the two totalitarian powers. Great Britain and France finally declared war when Poland was invaded. The years of 1939-1942 were a period of impressive victories for Germany's well-trained and equipped forces. However, when Hitler expanded his war beyond Western Europe by invading Africa and Russia and declaring war on the U.S.A., it started the chain of events, which would culminate in the total and final German defeat on May 8, 1945, VE Day, ending the European theater of the Second World War and The Third Reich.

MINT MARKS

A - Berlin
B - Vienna, 1938-1944
D - Munich
E - Muldenhutten
F - Stuttgart
G - Karlsruhe
J - Hamburg

MONETARY SYSTEMS

(During 1923-1924)
100 Rentenpfennig = 1 Rentenmark
(Commencing 1924)
100 Reichspfennig = 1 Reichsmark

THIRD REICH

STANDARD COINAGE

KM# 89 REICHSPFENNIG

2.01 g., Bronze, 17.43 mm. **Obv:** Eagle above swastika within wreath **Rev:** Denomination, oak leaves below

Date	Mintage	VF20	XF40	MS60	MS63	MS65
1936 A	—	6.00	16.50	50.00	80.00	100
Note: Mintage included with KM#37						
1936 E	150,000	60.00	120	200	250	300
1936 F	4,600,000	50.00	100	175	225	275
1936 G	—	30.00	65.00	120	210	265
Note: Mintage included with KM#37						
1936 J	—	25.00	55.00	110	175	250
Note: Mintage included with KM#37						
1937 A	67,180,000	1.00	1.25	3.50	6.50	12.50
1937 D	14,060,000	1.00	1.50	6.00	13.50	15.00
1937 E	10,700,000	1.00	1.50	6.50	13.50	15.00
1937 F	11,058,000	1.00	1.50	6.50	13.50	15.00
1937 G	4,250,000	1.25	3.00	7.50	16.00	25.00
1937 J	6,714,000	1.00	1.50	6.50	13.50	15.00
1938 A	75,707,000	1.00	1.25	5.00	10.00	12.50
1938 B	2,378,000	4.00	7.50	16.00	25.00	35.00
1938 D	13,930,000	1.00	1.25	6.00	10.00	15.00
1938 E	14,503,000	1.00	1.25	6.00	10.00	15.00
1938 F	11,714,000	1.00	1.25	6.00	10.00	15.00
1938 G	8,390,000	1.00	1.50	6.50	11.00	15.00
1938 J	15,458,000	1.00	1.25	6.00	10.00	15.00
1939 A	97,541,000	1.00	1.25	4.00	9.00	15.00
1939 B	22,732,000	1.00	1.25	6.00	11.00	15.00
1939 D	20,760,000	1.00	1.25	5.00	10.00	15.00
1939 E	12,478,000	1.00	1.25	6.00	11.00	15.00
1939 F	12,482,000	1.00	1.25	5.00	10.00	15.00
1939 G	12,250,000	1.00	1.25	5.00	10.00	15.00
1939 J	8,368,000	1.00	1.25	6.00	11.00	15.00
1940 A	27,094,000	1.00	1.25	5.00	11.00	15.00
1940 F	7,850,000	1.00	1.25	7.00	13.50	20.00
1940 G	3,875,000	5.00	12.00	22.50	40.00	60.00
1940 J	7,450,000	2.50	4.00	11.00	22.00	30.00
Common date	—	**PF63** 150				

KM# 97 REICHSPFENNIG

1.85 g., Zinc, 17 mm. **Obv:** Eagle above swastika within wreath **Rev:** Denomination, oak leaves below

Date	Mintage	VF20	XF40	MS60	MS63	MS65
1940 A	223,948,000	0.50	1.25	5.50	9.00	12.00
1940 B	62,198,000	0.50	1.25	5.50	9.00	15.00
1940 D	43,951,000	0.50	1.25	5.50	9.00	15.00
1940 E	20,749,000	1.00	5.00	12.25	18.00	20.00
1940 F	33,854,000	0.50	1.25	6.50	11.00	15.00
1940 G	20,165,000	0.50	1.25	6.50	12.00	15.00
1940 J	24,459,000	0.50	1.25	6.50	11.00	15.00
1941 A	281,618,000	0.50	1.25	4.50	8.00	15.00
1941 B	62,285,000	1.00	1.50	5.50	8.00	15.00
1941 D	73,745,000	0.50	1.25	5.50	8.00	15.00
1941 E	49,041,000	0.50	1.50	9.50	12.00	15.00
1941 F	51,017,000	0.50	1.25	5.50	9.00	15.00
1941 G	44,810,000	0.50	1.25	8.25	11.00	15.00
1941 J	57,625,000	0.50	1.25	6.50	11.00	20.00
1942 A	558,877,000	0.50	1.25	5.00	6.50	15.00
1942 B	124,740,000	0.50	1.25	6.00	7.75	15.00
1942 D	134,145,000	0.50	1.25	6.00	7.75	15.00
1942 E	84,674,000	1.25	2.00	8.00	10.00	15.00
1942 F	90,788,000	0.50	1.25	6.00	7.75	15.00
1942 G	59,858,000	0.50	1.25	6.00	9.00	15.00
1942 J	122,934,000	0.50	1.25	6.00	7.75	15.00
1943 A	372,401,000	0.50	1.25	6.00	7.75	15.00
1943 B	79,315,000	0.50	1.25	6.00	7.75	15.00
1943 D	91,629,000	0.50	1.25	6.00	7.75	15.00
1943 E	34,191,000	2.25	6.50	13.00	18.00	22.50
1943 F	70,269,000	0.50	1.25	6.00	7.75	15.00
1943 G	24,688,000	1.25	2.25	8.00	12.25	15.00
1943 J	37,695,000	1.25	2.25	6.00	7.75	15.00
1944 A	124,421,000	0.50	1.75	5.00	7.75	15.00
1944 B	87,850,000	1.00	2.00	6.50	10.00	15.00
1944 D	56,755,000	1.00	2.00	7.00	11.00	15.00
1944 E	41,729,000	2.00	4.50	13.00	20.00	25.00
1944 F	15,580,000	3.50	7.25	16.00	25.00	30.00

Date	Mintage	VF20	XF40	MS60	MS63	MS65
1944 G	34,967,000	0.60	1.65	6.50	12.25	15.00
1945 A	17,145,000	2.75	8.00	20.00	25.00	35.00
1945 E	6,800,000	60.00	110	100	150	250
Common date	—	PF63 200				

KM# 90 2 REICHSPFENNIG

3.31 g., Bronze, 20.2 mm. **Obv:** Eagle above swastika within wreath **Rev:** Denomination, oak leaves below

Date	Mintage	VF20	XF40	MS60	MS63	MS65
1936 A	Inc. below	4.00	11.00	40.00	55.00	75.00
1936 D	Inc. below	4.00	9.00	30.00	37.50	50.00
1936 F	3,100,000	16.50	30.00	75.00	120	150
1937 A	34,404,000	1.00	1.35	7.00	11.00	15.00
1937 D	9,016,000	1.00	1.35	7.00	12.00	15.00
1937 E	Inc. below	19.00	40.00	77.50	100	120
1937 F	7,487,000	1.00	2.00	8.00	13.50	20.00
1937 G	490,000	8.25	15.50	40.00	55.00	75.00
1937 J	450,000	8.25	15.50	30.00	37.50	60.00
1938 A	27,264,000	—	1.00	6.00	9.00	15.00
1938 B	2,714,000	3.50	9.00	30.00	40.00	60.00
1938 D	8,770,000	1.00	1.25	6.00	10.00	15.00
1938 E	5,450,000	1.00	2.25	7.00	11.00	15.00
1938 F	10,090,000	1.00	1.25	6.00	10.00	15.00
1938 G	3,685,000	1.00	6.00	15.00	24.00	40.00
1938 J	7,243,000	1.00	1.50	7.00	14.50	17.50
1939 A	37,348,000	1.00	1.25	6.00	9.00	15.00
1939 B	9,361,000	1.00	1.25	6.00	9.00	15.00
1939 D	7,555,000	1.00	1.25	6.00	9.00	15.00
1939 E	6,650,000	1.00	2.25	7.00	12.25	15.00
1939 F	7,019,000	1.00	1.25	6.00	11.00	15.00
1939 G	4,885,000	1.00	1.50	9.00	15.00	20.00
1939 J	6,996,000	1.00	1.50	7.00	11.00	15.00
1940 A	22,681,000	1.00	1.25	8.00	13.25	16.00
1940 D	3,855,000	2.75	6.00	20.00	27.50	35.00
1940 E	3,412,000	8.00	12.50	20.00	32.50	40.00
1940 G	1,161,000	90.00	130	250	300	350
1940 J	2,357,000	7.75	14.50	35.00	50.00	60.00
Common date	—	PF63 225				

KM# 91 5 REICHSPFENNIG

2.44 g., Aluminum-Bronze, 18.1 mm. **Obv:** Eagle above swastika within wreath **Rev:** Denomination, oak leaves below **Edge:** Reeded

Date	Mintage	VF20	XF40	MS60	MS63	MS65
1936 A	Inc. below	75.00	100	140	175	250
1936 D	Inc. below	75.00	100	175	250	350
1936 G	Inc. below	100	165	300	375	450
1937 A	29,700,000	1.50	2.25	7.00	11.00	25.00
1937 D	4,992,000	1.50	2.25	13.00	22.50	30.00
1937 E	4,474,000	1.50	4.00	22.50	30.00	50.00
1937 F	2,092,000	1.50	7.00	22.50	40.00	60.00
1937 G	2,749,000	6.50	13.00	31.50	50.00	75.00
1937 J	6,991,000	2.50	5.00	18.00	30.00	50.00
1938 A	54,012,000	2.50	4.00	9.00	13.50	25.00
1938 B	3,447,000	2.25	5.00	16.50	22.50	30.00
1938 D	17,708,000	1.50	2.25	8.00	11.00	25.00
1938 E	8,602,000	1.50	4.50	12.00	22.50	30.00
1938 F	8,147,000	1.50	2.25	10.00	22.50	30.00
1938 G	7,323,000	1.50	2.25	10.00	22.50	30.00
1938 J	7,646,000	1.50	2.25	10.00	20.00	30.00
1939 A	35,337,000	1.50	2.00	7.00	10.00	25.00
1939 B	8,313,000	1.50	2.00	7.00	11.00	25.00
1939 D	8,304,000	1.50	2.25	7.50	13.50	25.00
1939 E	5,138,000	1.50	2.25	7.50	13.50	25.00
1939 F	10,339,000	1.50	2.00	7.00	11.00	25.00
1939 G	4,266,000	1.50	7.00	15.00	25.00	30.00
1939 J	4,177,000	2.50	6.50	13.00	25.00	30.00
Common date	—	PF63 200				

KM# 100 5 REICHSPFENNIG

2.50 g., Zinc, 19 mm. **Obv:** Eagle above swastika within wreath **Rev:** Denomination, oak leaves below **Edge:** Reeded

Date	Mintage	VF20	XF40	MS60	MS63	MS65
1940 A	174,684,000	0.25	0.75	6.00	8.00	25.00
1940 B	63,469,000	1.00	1.50	6.00	8.00	25.00
1940 D	44,364,000	1.00	1.50	6.00	8.00	25.00
1940 E	25,800,000	1.00	3.50	7.00	10.00	25.00
1940 F	31,381,000	1.00	2.00	7.00	10.00	25.00
1940 G	24,148,000	1.00	2.75	8.00	15.00	25.00
1940 J	30,518,000	1.00	2.00	7.00	10.00	25.00
1941 A	246,216,000	0.25	0.75	5.00	7.00	25.00
1941 B	60,297,000	0.40	1.75	7.50	10.00	25.00
1941 D	51,100,000	0.40	1.75	7.50	10.00	25.00
1941 E	26,354,000	0.40	1.75	7.50	10.00	25.00
1941 F	36,725,000	0.40	1.75	7.50	10.00	25.00
1941 G	21,276,000	0.40	2.00	8.50	12.00	25.00
1941 J	52,872,000	0.40	2.00	7.50	10.00	25.00
1942 A	161,042,000	0.25	0.75	6.00	9.00	25.00
1942 B	12,405,000	1.50	4.50	10.00	15.00	25.00
1942 D	15,486,000	0.45	2.25	8.00	12.00	25.00
1942 E	8,800,000	15.00	20.00	40.00	50.00	75.00
1942 F	24,662,000	0.35	1.50	8.00	12.00	25.00
1942 G	12,749,000	0.40	2.25	10.00	15.00	25.00
1943 A	46,830,000	0.50	1.75	7.00	10.00	25.00
1943 B	833,000	50.00	75.00	160	200	250
1943 D	13,650,000	0.50	3.50	9.00	13.00	25.00
1943 E	16,581,000	6.00	10.00	20.00	25.00	50.00
1943 F	9,891,000	1.00	2.50	8.00	12.00	25.00
1943 G	7,237,000	0.75	2.25	9.00	15.00	30.00
1944 A	23,699,000	12.50	25.00	40.00	50.00	75.00
1944 D	26,340,000	1.25	2.50	7.00	10.00	25.00
1944 E	19,720,000	2.50	5.00	10.00	14.00	25.00
1944 F	6,853,000	1.50	2.75	8.00	12.00	25.00
1944 G	3,540,000	200	275	400	500	650
Common date	—	PF63 250				

KM# 92 10 REICHSPFENNIG

4.00 g., Aluminum-Bronze, 21 mm. **Obv:** Eagle above swastika within wreath **Rev:** Denomination, oak leaves below **Edge:** Reeded

Date	Mintage	VF20	XF40	MS60	MS63	MS65
1936 A	Inc. below	40.00	60.00	100	120	150
1936 E	245,000	150	200	300	375	450
1936 G	129,000	225	300	450	650	800
1937 A	36,830,000	2.00	2.25	12.00	20.00	30.00
1937 D	6,882,000	2.00	3.50	12.00	22.00	30.00
1937 E	3,786,000	9.00	18.00	45.00	60.00	75.00
1937 F	5,934,000	2.50	6.00	25.00	40.00	60.00
1937 G	2,131,000	5.50	9.00	30.00	60.00	75.00
1937 J	4,439,000	2.00	5.00	20.00	30.00	50.00
1938 A	70,068,000	1.00	2.00	7.00	12.00	30.00
1938 B	7,852,000	2.00	4.50	15.00	20.00	30.00
1938 D	16,990,000	1.00	2.00	9.00	16.00	30.00
1938 E	10,739,000	2.00	2.50	10.00	18.00	30.00
1938 F	12,307,000	2.00	2.75	11.00	18.00	30.00
1938 G	8,584,000	2.00	3.00	12.00	22.00	30.00
1938 J	10,389,000	2.00	2.75	12.00	20.00	30.00
1939 A	40,171,000	2.00	2.25	9.00	15.00	30.00
1939 B	7,814,000	2.00	2.25	10.00	16.00	30.00
1939 D	11,307,000	2.00	2.25	12.00	20.00	30.00
1939 E	5,079,000	2.00	6.50	15.00	20.00	30.00
1939 F	6,993,000	2.00	3.00	12.00	20.00	30.00
1939 G	5,532,000	4.50	9.00	16.00	22.00	30.00
1939 J	5,557,000	2.00	2.50	12.00	20.00	30.00
Common date	—	PF63 250				

KM# 101 10 REICHSPFENNIG

3.52 g., Zinc, 21 mm. **Obv:** Eagle above swastika within wreath **Rev:** Denomination, oak leaves below

Date	Mintage	VF20	XF40	MS60	MS63	MS65
1940 A	212,948,000	0.40	1.75	8.00	15.00	25.00
1940 B	76,274,000	0.75	3.00	12.00	20.00	30.00
1940 D	45,434,000	0.75	2.50	12.00	20.00	30.00
1940 E	34,350,000	0.75	2.50	12.00	25.00	35.00
1940 F	27,603,000	1.50	6.00	17.50	40.00	55.00
1940 G	27,308,000	1.50	8.00	25.00	50.00	75.00
1940 J	41,678,000	1.25	2.50	12.00	25.00	35.00
1941 A	240,284,000	0.40	1.50	7.00	14.00	25.00
1941 B	70,747,000	0.75	3.00	9.00	15.00	25.00
1941 D	77,560,000	0.75	3.50	12.00	20.00	30.00
1941 E	36,548,000	0.75	3.50	12.00	20.00	30.00
1941 F	42,834,000	0.75	3.50	12.00	20.00	30.00
1941 G	28,765,000	2.25	9.00	25.00	40.00	55.00
1941 J	30,525,000	0.75	2.50	12.00	25.00	35.00
1942 A	184,545,000	0.30	0.75	9.00	15.00	25.00
1942 B	16,329,000	3.00	12.00	30.00	50.00	65.00
1942 D	40,852,000	1.25	3.50	12.00	25.00	35.00
1942 E	18,334,000	2.00	12.00	30.00	50.00	65.00
1942 F	32,690,000	0.50	3.50	12.00	25.00	35.00
1942 G	20,295,000	2.00	12.00	35.00	60.00	75.00
1942 J	29,957,000	1.75	3.50	12.00	25.00	35.00
1943 A	157,357,000	1.50	2.50	9.00	15.00	25.00
1943 B	11,940,000	7.50	14.00	30.00	60.00	75.00
1943 D	17,304,000	1.75	4.50	16.00	25.00	35.00
1943 E	10,445,000	7.50	14.00	35.00	60.00	75.00
1943 F	24,804,000	2.50	5.00	20.00	25.00	35.00
1943 G	3,618,000	14.00	35.00	80.00	150	200
1943 J	1,821,000	45.00	85.00	200	250	350
1944 A	84,164,000	1.00	2.50	10.00	15.00	25.00
1944 B	40,781,000	1.50	2.50	12.00	20.00	30.00
1944 D	30,369,000	1.50	2.50	12.00	20.00	30.00
1944 E	29,963,000	2.00	4.50	12.00	20.00	30.00
1944 F	19,639,000	2.50	5.00	14.00	25.00	35.00
1944 G	13,023,000	3.50	10.00	30.00	50.00	65.00
1945 A	7,112,000	12.50	30.00	100	150	225
1945 E	4,897,000	35.00	80.00	140	200	300
Common date	—	PF63 400	PF65 650			

KM# 87 50 REICHSPFENNIG

Aluminum **Obv:** Eagle above date **Rev:** Denomination, oak leaves below

Date	Mintage	VF20	XF40	MS60	MS63	MS65
1935 A	75,912,000	2.25	9.00	35.00	80.00	125
1935 A	—	PF63 400	PF65 650			
1935 D	19,688,000	2.25	12.00	60.00	100	125
1935 D	—	PF63 400	PF65 650			
1935 E	10,418,000	3.50	12.00	60.00	100	150
1935 E	—	PF63 400	PF65 650			
1935 F	14,061,000	2.25	12.00	60.00	100	150
1935 F	—	PF63 400	PF65 650			
1935 G	8,540,000	4.50	14.00	65.00	110	150
1935 G	—	PF63 400	PF65 650			
1935 J	11,438,000	4.50	14.00	65.00	80.00	125
1935 J	—	PF63 400	PF65 650			

KM# 95 50 REICHSPFENNIG

3.50 g., Nickel, 20 mm. **Obv:** Eagle above swastika within wreath **Rev:** Denomination within circle, oak leaves and acorns below

Date	Mintage	VF20	XF40	MS60	MS63	MS65
1938 A	5,051,000	32.50	42.50	55.00	75.00	125
1938 B	1,124,000	40.00	50.00	80.00	100	150
1938 D	1,260,000	40.00	55.00	80.00	100	150
1938 E	949,000	40.00	60.00	100	125	175
1938 F	1,210,000	30.00	50.00	90.00	125	175
1938 G	460,000	60.00	80.00	160	225	275
1938 J	730,000	90.00	120	225	275	325
1939 A	15,037,000	30.00	40.00	50.00	60.00	125
1939 B	2,826,000	35.00	45.00	60.00	90.00	125
1939 D	3,648,000	35.00	45.00	60.00	90.00	125
1939 E	1,924,000	35.00	50.00	85.00	100	150
1939 F	2,602,000	35.00	50.00	70.00	90.00	125
1939 G	1,565,000	35.00	75.00	130	170	225
1939 J	2,114,000	35.00	60.00	100	120	175
Common date	—	PF63 275				

KM# 96 50 REICHSPFENNIG

1.35 g., Aluminum, 22.7 mm. **Obv:** Eagle above swastika within wreath **Rev:** Denomination, oak leaves below **Edge:** Reeded

Date	Mintage	VF20	XF40	MS60	MS63	MS65
1939 A	5,000,000	6.00	20.00	65.00	100	125
1939 B	5,482,000	6.00	20.00	65.00	100	125
1939 D	600,000	16.00	35.00	120	170	225
1939 E	2,000,000	6.00	25.00	70.00	110	150
1939 F	3,600,000	11.00	30.00	70.00	120	150
1939 G	560,000	22.50	60.00	150	200	250
1939 J	1,000,000	22.50	50.00	150	200	250
1940 A	56,128,000	4.50	11.00	35.00	50.00	100
1940 B	10,016,000	9.00	25.00	70.00	100	125

Date	Mintage	VF20	XF40	MS60	MS63	MS65
1940 D	13,800,000	15.00	30.00	100	150	200
1940 E	5,618,000	15.00	30.00	100	150	200
1940 F	6,663,000	10.00	25.00	65.00	100	125
1940 G	5,616,000	27.00	55.00	130	200	250
1940 J	7,335,000	15.00	30.00	100	150	200
1941 A	31,263,000	9.00	20.00	65.00	100	125
1941 B	4,291,000	10.00	25.00	80.00	110	150
1941 D	7,200,000	10.00	25.00	80.00	110	150
1941 E	3,806,000	15.00	27.50	85.00	125	175
1941 F	5,128,000	10.00	25.00	65.00	100	125
1941 G	3,091,000	20.00	40.00	110	150	200
1941 J	4,165,000	20.00	35.00	110	150	200
1942 A	11,580,000	5.00	10.00	30.00	50.00	100
1942 B	2,876,000	12.00	25.00	70.00	100	125
1942 D	2,247,000	20.00	35.00	80.00	120	150
1942 E	3,810,000	20.00	40.00	110	150	200
1942 F	5,133,000	15.00	30.00	80.00	120	150
1942 G	1,400,000	25.00	70.00	125	200	250
1943 A	29,325,000	5.00	10.00	30.00	40.00	100
1943 B	8,229,000	5.00	10.00	25.00	40.00	100
1943 D	5,315,000	7.00	16.00	50.00	75.00	125
1943 G	2,892,000	20.00	50.00	110	180	225
1943 J	4,166,000	9.00	14.00	30.00	45.00	100
1944 B	5,622,000	8.00	12.00	50.00	70.00	100
1944 D	4,886,000	16.00	40.00	100	130	175
1944 F	3,739,000	10.00	20.00	75.00	100	125
1944 G	1,190,000	100	180	400	600	800
Common date	—	PF63 275				

KM# 78 REICHSMARK

4.85 g., Nickel, 23 mm. **Obv:** Denomination within wreath, date below **Rev:** Eagle

Date	Mintage	VF20	XF40	MS60	MS63	MS65
1933 A	6,030,000	6.00	10.00	35.00	50.00	75.00
1933 D	4,562,000	6.00	10.00	35.00	50.00	75.00
1933 E	3,500,000	8.50	10.00	27.50	50.00	75.00
1933 F	1,400,000	9.50	17.50	45.00	72.50	100
1933 G	2,000,000	11.00	22.00	90.00	145	200
1934 A	52,345,000	6.00	10.00	11.00	16.50	40.00
1934 D	30,597,000	6.00	10.00	16.00	24.00	50.00
1934 E	15,135,000	6.00	10.00	17.50	24.00	50.00
1934 F	23,672,000	6.00	10.00	15.00	22.50	45.00
1934 G	13,252,000	6.00	10.00	20.00	27.50	55.00
1934 J	16,820,000	6.00	10.00	16.00	22.50	45.00
1935 A	57,896,000	6.00	10.00	13.50	16.50	40.00
1935 J	3,621,000	16.50	32.50	100	150	200
1936 A	20,287,000	6.00	10.00	22.50	27.50	40.00
1936 D	4,940,000	8.50	16.50	45.00	55.00	75.00
1936 E	3,200,000	16.50	38.00	110	160	200
1936 F	2,075,000	32.50	55.00	120	160	200
1936 G	620,000	85.00	160	225	300	350
1936 J	2,975,000	16.50	32.50	110	165	200
1937 A	49,976,000	6.00	10.00	11.00	14.50	40.00
1937 D	10,529,000	6.00	10.00	20.00	32.50	60.00
1937 E	2,926,000	13.50	25.00	50.00	75.00	100
1937 F	6,221,000	13.50	25.00	65.00	90.00	125
1937 G	2,143,000	10.00	18.00	45.00	75.00	100
1937 J	4,721,000	10.00	18.00	60.00	95.00	125
1938 A	9,829,000	6.00	13.50	32.50	50.00	75.00
1938 E	2,073,000	20.00	40.00	95.00	145	175
1938 F	2,739,000	22.00	27.50	80.00	120	150
1938 G	4,381,000	40.00	70.00	155	250	300
1938 J	1,269,000	75.00	100	160	275	325
1939 A	52,150,000	13.50	17.50	42.50	55.00	75.00
1939 B	9,836,000	120	170	300	350	400
1939 D	12,522,000	25.00	40.00	80.00	110	150
1939 E	6,570,000	45.00	70.00	145	175	225
1939 F	10,033,000	30.00	50.00	120	160	200
1939 G	5,475,000	150	200	375	475	550
1939 J	8,478,000	45.00	65.00	125	150	200
Common date	—	PF63 350	PF65 500			

KM# 79 2 REICHSMARK

8.00 g., 0.625 Silver 0.1608 oz. ASW, 27 mm. **Subject:** 450th Anniversary - Birth of Martin Luther **Obv:** Eagle above denomination **Rev:** Head left, dates below

Date	Mintage	VF20	XF40	MS60	MS63	MS65
1933 A	542,000	25.00	32.50	50.00	100	150
1933 A	—	PF63 250	PF65 350			
1933 D	141,000	27.50	37.50	60.00	100	200
1933 D	—	PF63 250	PF65 350			
1933 E	75,000	32.50	45.00	70.00	100	200
1933 E	—	PF63 300	PF65 400			
1933 F	100,000	27.50	40.00	65.00	100	200
1933 F	—	PF63 300	PF65 400			
1933 G	61,000	32.50	45.00	85.00	120	250
1933 G	—	PF63 250	PF65 350			
1933 J	82,000	27.50	45.00	70.00	100	200
1933 J	—	PF63 350	PF65 500			

KM# 81 2 REICHSMARK

8.00 g., 0.625 Silver 0.1608 oz. ASW, 27 mm. **Subject:** 1st Anniversary - Nazi Rule March 21, 1933 **Obv:** Eagle divides dates, denomination below **Rev:** Potsdam Garrison Church

Date	Mintage	VF20	XF40	MS60	MS63	MS65
1934 A	2,710,000	12.00	22.00	50.00	100	200
1934 A	—	PF63 250				
1934 D	703,000	14.00	28.00	70.00	100	225
1934 D	—	PF63 250				
1934 E	373,000	19.00	40.00	75.00	150	250
1934 E	—	PF63 250				
1934 F	502,000	14.00	32.50	75.00	150	250
1934 F	—	PF63 250				
1934 G	305,000	17.00	45.00	75.00	150	250
1934 G	—	PF63 250				
1934 J	409,000	17.00	40.00	100	175	300
1934 J	—	PF63 250				

KM# 84 2 REICHSMARK

8.00 g., 0.625 Silver 0.1608 oz. ASW, 27 mm. **Subject:** 175th Anniversary - Birth of Schiller **Obv:** Eagle, oak leaves flank, denomination below **Rev:** Head left, date below

Date	Mintage	VF20	XF40	MS60	MS63	MS65
1934 F	300,000	70.00	90.00	75.00	175	250
1934 F	—	PF63 250				

KM# 93 2 REICHSMARK

8.00 g., 0.625 Silver 0.1608 oz. ASW, 25 mm. **Subject:** Swastika-Hindenburg Issue **Obv:** Eagle above swastika within wreath **Rev:** Large head, right

Date	Mintage	VF20	XF40	MS60	MS63	MS65
1936 D	840,000	12.00	25.00	65.00	95.00	200
1936 E	Inc. below	32.00	49.00	125	250	350
1936 G	Inc. below	22.50	34.00	85.00	150	250
1936 J	Inc. below	70.00	160	300	400	500
1937 A	23,425,000	8.00	9.00	20.00	40.00	100
1937 D	6,190,000	8.00	9.00	25.00	50.00	150
1937 E	3,725,000	8.00	11.00	25.00	45.00	175
1937 F	5,015,000	8.00	11.00	35.00	65.00	200
1937 G	1,913,000	9.00	16.00	45.00	60.00	175
1937 J	2,756,000	8.00	11.00	25.00	50.00	175
1938 A	13,201,000	8.00	10.00	20.00	40.00	100
1938 B	13,163,000	8.00	10.00	30.00	45.00	125
1938 D	3,711,000	8.00	10.00	30.00	50.00	150
1938 E	4,731,000	8.00	10.00	35.00	60.00	175
1938 F	1,882,000	9.00	12.00	35.00	75.00	200
1938 G	2,313,000	8.00	11.00	35.00	75.00	200
1938 J	2,306,000	8.00	11.00	35.00	75.00	200
1939 A	26,855,000	8.00	9.00	20.00	35.00	100
1939 B	3,522,000	8.00	11.00	25.00	45.00	125
1939 D	5,357,000	8.00	10.00	20.00	40.00	150
1939 E	251,000	32.00	47.00	80.00	135	250
1939 F	3,180,000	8.00	11.00	25.00	65.00	200
1939 G	2,305,000	8.00	13.00	35.00	50.00	150
1939 J	3,414,000	8.00	12.00	22.50	60.00	200
Common date	—	PF63 275				

KM# 80 5 REICHSMARK

13.88 g., 0.900 Silver 0.4016 oz. ASW, 29 mm. **Subject:** 450th Anniversary - Birth of Martin Luther **Obv:** Eagle, denomination below **Rev:** Head left, dates below

Date	Mintage	VF20	XF40	MS60	MS63	MS65
1933 A	108,000	100	150	200	250	400
1933 A	—	PF63 450				
1933 D	28,000	125	175	200	350	450
1933 D	—	PF63 500				
1933 E	12,000	145	190	225	350	500
1933 E	—	PF63 500				
1933 F	20,000	125	160	200	250	400
1933 F	—	PF63 575				
1933 G	12,000	175	250	300	400	600
1933 G	—	PF63 600				
1933 J	16,000	145	180	250	400	650
1933 J	—	PF63 600				

KM# 82 5 REICHSMARK

13.88 g., 0.900 Silver 0.4016 oz. ASW, 29 mm. **Subject:** 1st Anniversary - Nazi Rule **Obv:** Eagle divides date, denomination below **Rev:** Potsdam Garrison Church divides date

Date	Mintage	VF20	XF40	MS60	MS63	MS65
1934 A	2,168,000	18.00	40.00	100	120	250
1934 D	562,000	22.00	45.00	110	140	300
1934 E	298,000	24.00	50.00	120	200	400
1934 F	401,000	20.00	40.00	110	140	300
1934 G	244,000	24.00	50.00	110	140	300
1934 J	327,000	24.00	45.00	120	250	500
1934	—	PF63 350				

Note: Impaired proofs are common and valued around $200

KM# 83 5 REICHSMARK

13.88 g., 0.900 Silver 0.4016 oz. ASW, 29 mm. **Subject:** 1st Anniversary - Nazi Rule **Obv:** Eagle divides date, denomination below **Rev:** Potsdam Garrison Church, date 21 MARZ 1933 dropped

Date	Mintage	VF20	XF40	MS60	MS63	MS65
1934 A	14,526,000	17.00	20.00	40.00	60.00	200
1934 D	6,303,000	17.00	25.00	45.00	75.00	275
1934 E	2,739,000	17.00	27.50	50.00	80.00	300
1934 F	4,844,000	17.00	25.00	45.00	75.00	350
1934 G	2,304,000	17.00	27.50	50.00	100	400
1934 J	4,294,000	17.00	25.00	45.00	75.00	350
1935 A	23,407,000	17.00	19.00	35.00	45.00	200
1935 D	3,539,000	17.00	25.00	40.00	75.00	225
1935 E	2,476,000	17.00	27.50	50.00	60.00	175
1935 F	2,177,000	17.00	32.50	55.00	70.00	200
1935 G	1,966,000	17.00	30.00	70.00	150	400
1935 J	1,425,000	17.00	38.75	100	175	500
Common date	—	PF63 350				

KM# 85 5 REICHSMARK

13.88 g., 0.900 Silver 0.4016 oz. ASW, 29 mm. **Subject:** 175th Anniversary - Birth of Schiller **Obv:** Eagle, oak leaves flank, denomination below **Rev:** Head left, dates below

Date	Mintage	VF20	XF40	MS60	MS63	MS65
1934 F	100,000	200	285	350	450	750
1934 F	—	PF63 600	PF65 1,000			

KM# 86 5 REICHSMARK

13.88 g., 0.900 Silver 0.4016 oz. ASW, 29 mm. **Subject:** Hindenburg issue **Obv:** Eagle divides date, denomination below **Rev:** Large head, right

Date	Mintage	VF20	XF40	MS60	MS63	MS65
1935 A	19,325,000	16.00	20.00	25.00	40.00	175
1935 D	6,596,000	17.00	20.00	30.00	50.00	200
1935 E	3,260,000	17.00	23.50	40.00	55.00	200
1935 F	4,372,000	17.00	20.00	40.00	55.00	200
1935 G	2,371,000	18.00	26.00	40.00	55.00	200
1935 J	2,830,000	18.00	26.00	40.00	55.00	200
1936 A	30,611,000	16.00	20.00	25.00	40.00	175
1936 D	7,032,000	17.00	20.00	30.00	45.00	200
1936 E	3,320,000	17.00	23.00	40.00	55.00	200
1936 F	4,926,000	17.00	23.50	40.00	55.00	200
1936 G	2,734,000	18.00	28.50	50.00	80.00	300
1936 J	3,706,000	18.00	26.00	45.00	75.00	225
Common date	—	PF63 300				

KM# 94 5 REICHSMARK

13.88 g., 0.900 Silver 0.4016 oz. ASW, 29 mm. **Subject:** Swastika-Hindenburg Issue **Obv:** Eagle above swastika within wreath **Rev:** Large head, right

Date	Mintage	VF20	XF40	MS60	MS63	MS65
1936 A	8,430,000	18.00	21.00	30.00	50.00	200
1936 D	1,872,000	20.00	26.00	50.00	75.00	225
1936 E	870,000	20.00	31.00	50.00	85.00	250
1936 F	1,732,000	20.00	26.00	45.00	80.00	225
1936 G	743,000	22.50	36.00	80.00	110	250
1936 J	640,000	36.50	51.00	110	160	300
1937 A	6,662,000	18.00	20.00	30.00	50.00	200
1937 D	2,173,000	18.00	21.00	40.00	60.00	225
1937 E	1,490,000	20.00	26.00	45.00	80.00	250
1937 F	1,578,000	20.00	26.00	40.00	60.00	225
1937 G	1,472,000	20.00	26.00	45.00	80.00	250
1937 J	2,191,000	18.00	26.00	45.00	80.00	250
1938 A	6,789,000	18.00	20.00	30.00	50.00	200
1938 D	1,304,000	18.00	26.00	40.00	60.00	225
1938 E	425,000	20.00	26.00	50.00	100	250
1938 F	740,000	19.00	26.00	40.00	80.00	250
1938 G	861,000	20.00	26.00	50.00	80.00	200
1938 J	1,302,000	19.00	26.00	40.00	65.00	225
1939 A	3,428,000	20.00	26.00	30.00	50.00	200
1939 B	1,942,000	20.00	26.00	35.00	70.00	200
1939 D	1,216,000	25.00	33.50	50.00	75.00	200
1939 E	1,320,000	39.00	50.00	60.00	150	300
1939 F	1,060,000	27.50	40.00	50.00	125	300
1939 G	567,000	39.00	60.00	100	180	325
1939 J	1,710,000	22.50	36.00	60.00	100	250
Common date	—	PF63 300				

MILITARY COINAGE

WWII

KM# 98 5 REICHSPFENNIG

Zinc **Rev:** Eagle head above center hole, denomination below **Note:** Circulated only in occupied territories.

Date	Mintage	F12	VF20	XF40	MS60	MS63
1940 A	—	15.00	20.00	30.00	60.00	150
1940 B	3,020,000	100	160	325	550	900
1940 D	—	30.00	45.00	75.00	120	300
1940 E	2,445,000	100	200	325	550	750
1940 F	—	200	300	425	675	1,000
1940 G	—	6,000	10,000	—	—	—
1940 J	—	100	225	325	500	750
1941 A	—	300	500	800	1,500	2,500
1941 F	—	5,000	10,000	—	—	—
Common date	—	PF60 850	PF63 950			

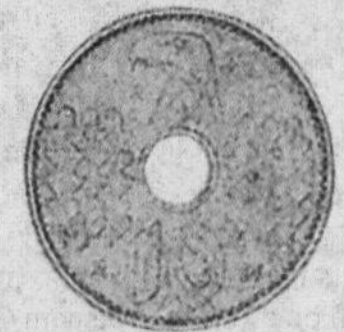

KM# 99 10 REICHSPFENNIG

Zinc **Rev:** Eagle head above center hole, denomination below **Note:** Circulated only in occupied territories.

Date	Mintage	F12	VF20	XF40	MS60	MS63
1940 A	—	15.00	20.00	30.00	100	200
1940 B	840,000	200	325	650	950	1,250
1940 D	—	5,000	6,000	10,000	15,000	20,000
1940 E	5,100,000	3,000	4,500	6,000	10,000	12,000
1940 F	—	300	450	1,250	1,750	2,250
1940 G	150,000	100	125	225	400	550
1940 J	—	400	900	1,400	2,500	3,500
1941 A	—	600	1,000	1,800	2,500	3,500
1941 F 2 known	—	—	12,000	—	15,000	—
1940-1941	—	PF60 1,150	PF63 1,250			

ALLIED OCCUPATION

POST WW II COINAGE

KM# A102 REICHSPFENNIG

Zinc **Obv:** Modified design, swastika and wreath removed **Rev:** Eagle missing tail feathers

Date	Mintage	F12	VF20	XF40	MS60	MS63
1944 D	—	—	—	10,000	—	—

Note: Possibly a pattern, only one known

KM# A103 REICHSPFENNIG

Zinc **Obv:** Eagle above date **Rev:** Denomination

Date	Mintage	F12	VF20	XF40	MS60	MS63
1945 F	2,984,000	6.00	12.00	20.00	40.00	60.00
1946 F	1,633,000	20.00	40.00	70.00	140	180
1946 G	1,500,000	40.00	70.00	110	170	225
Common date	—	PF60 250	PF63 300			

KM# A105 5 REICHSPFENNIG

Zinc **Obv:** Eagle, date below **Rev:** Denomination

Date	Mintage	F12	VF20	XF40	MS60	MS63
1947 A	—	3.00	7.50	15.00	40.00	55.00
1947 D	16,528,000	3.00	5.00	7.00	25.00	40.00
1948 A	—	5.00	12.50	20.00	45.00	70.00
1948 E	7,666,000	150	300	400	600	800
1947-1948	—	PF60 250	PF63 300			

KM# A104 10 REICHSPFENNIG

Zinc **Obv:** Eagle **Rev:** Denomination

Date	Mintage	F12	VF20	XF40	MS60	MS63
1945 F	5,942,000	4.50	7.50	15.00	35.00	80.00
1946 F	3,738,000	15.00	25.00	35.00	90.00	120
1946 G	1,600,000	40.00	70.00	120	150	250
1947 A	—	4.50	10.00	20.00	35.00	65.00
1947 E	2,612,000	250	350	575	775	950
1947 F	1,269,000	2.00	4.00	9.00	30.00	60.00
1948 A	—	5.00	18.00	22.50	35.00	55.00
1948 F	19,579,000	2.00	4.00	9.00	30.00	50.00
Common date	—	PF60 225	PF63 300			

PATTERNS

Including off metal strikes

KM#	Date	Mintage	Identification	Mkt Val
Pn354	1933	—	Mark. Nickel. Legend above eagle.	325
Pn355	1933A	—	Mark. Nickel. PROBE.	325
Pn356	1933A	—	Mark. Nickel. Rays above eagle.	325
Pn357	1933A	—	Mark. Nickel. Plain above eagle.	325
Pn358	1933A	—	Mark. Nickel. Large 1 with rays. PROBE.	325
Pn359	1933A	—	Mark. Nickel. PROBE.	325
Pn360	1933J	—	Mark. Nickel. KM78.	325
PnA361	1933/6	—	5 Mark. Copper-Nickel. Martin Luther. Eagle. KM94.	—
Pn361	1934	—	2 Mark. KM79. KM81.	—
Pn362	1934A	—	2 Mark. Silver. KM84.	—
Pn363	ND (1934)D	—	5 Mark. Silver. Similar to Pn351. KM80.	—
Pn364	1934A	—	5 Mark. Silver. KM85. "PROBE".	—
Pn365	1934A	—	5 Pfennig. Brass. KM91.	—
Pn366	1934A	—	5 Pfennig. Aluminum-Bronze. KM91.1. "PROBE.	—
Pn367	1935A	—	50 Pfennig. Aluminum.	—
Pn368	1935A	—	50 Pfennig. Oak leaves next to date. Wavy.	—
Pn369	1935E	—	Mark. Nickel. KM78.	—
Pn370	1935A	—	5 Mark. Silver. PROBE.	—
Pn371	1935A	—	5 Mark. Silver. PROBE.	—
Pn372	1935A	—	5 Mark. Silver. Masses entering. PROBE.	—
Pn373	1935A	—	5 Mark. 0.900. Silver. Family entering. PROBE.	—
Pn374	1935A	—	5 Mark. Electrotype.	—
PnA375	1936D	—	Reichspfennig. Copper Plated Iron. KM30.	—
Pn375	1936D	—	Pfennig. Copper Plated Iron. KM89.	—
Pn376	1937	—	5 Pfennig. Iron. KM91. Hindenburg.	—
Pn377	1937A	—	50 Pfennig. Nickel. KM95. "PROBE.	—
Pn378	1939A	—	5 Pfennig. Zinc. KM100.	—
Pn379	1939A	—	Mark. Nickel. PROBE" on rim.	—
Pn380	1939A	—	Mark. Pn379. Pn381.	—
Pn381	1939A	—	Mark.	250
Pn382	1939A	—	Mark. Aluminum. KM78. Pn381.	—
Pn383	1939/1940 (1939)	—	Mark. Iron. PROBE." Copper-nickel plated.	325
Pn384	1940	—	Mark. Silver.	425
Pn385	1942	—	5 Reichsmark. Silver Plated Copper.	—
Pn386	1942	—	5 Reichsmark. Copper. Klippe.	—
Pn387	1942	—	5 Reichsmark. Silver. Klippe.	6,500
Pn388	1942A	—	5 Mark. Silver Plated Copper. Steel helmet in laurel wreath.	—
PnA389	1946G	—	Pfennig. Aluminum.	—
PnB389	1947J	—	5 Pfennig. Zinc. without swastika. KM100.	3,350
PnC389	1947D	—	5 Pfennig. Aluminum. Reeded.	—
PnD389	1947A	—	10 Pfennig. Zinc. with slavic 7. KM104.	6,000
Pn389	1947J	—	10 Pfennig. Zinc. Without swastika. KM101.	3,350
PnA390	1947D	—	10 Pfennig. Aluminum. Plain.	—
PnB390	1946G	—	10 Pfennig. Brass.	900
PnC390	1947A	—	10 Pfennig. Dur-Aluminum.	—
Pn390	1947J	—	50 Pfennig. Aluminum.	—
Pn391	1947D	—	5 Pfennig. Aluminum.	—
Pn392	1947	—	5 Pfennig. Brass Plated Aluminum.	—
Pn393	1947D	—	5 Pfennig. Copper-Nickel Plated Iron. Copper-nickel plated.	—
Pn394	1947D	—	10 Pfennig. Aluminum.	—
Pn395	1947D	—	10 Pfennig. Iron. Copper-nickel plated.	—
Pn396	1948F	—	10 Pfennig. Zinc.	—

1949-1990

The German Democratic Republic, formerly East Germany, was located on the great north European plain, had an area of 41,768 sq. mi. (108,330 sq. km.) and a population of 16.6 million. The figures included East Berlin, which had been incorporated into the G.D.R. Capital: East Berlin. The economy was highly industrialized. Machinery, transport equipment chemicals, and lignite were exported.

During the closing days of World War II in Europe, Soviet troops advancing into Germany from the east occupied the German provinces of Mecklenburg, Brandenburg, Lusatia, Saxony and Thuringia. These five provinces comprised the occupation zone administered by the Soviet Union after the cessation of hostilities. The other three zones were administered by the U.S., Great Britain and France. Under the Potsdam agreement, questions affecting Germany as a whole were to be settled by the commanders of the occupation zones acting jointly and by unanimous decision. When Soviet intransigence rendered the quadripartite commission inoperable, the three western zones were united to form the Federal Republic of Germany, May 23, 1949. Thereupon the Soviet Union dissolved its occupation zone and established it as the Democratic Republic of Germany, Oct. 7, 1949.

The post-WW II division of Germany was ended Oct. 3,1990, when the German Democratic Republic (East Germany) ceased to exist and its five constituent provinces were formally admitted to the Federal Republic of Germany. An election Dec. 2, 1990, chose representatives to the united federal parliament (Bundestag), which then conducted its opening session in Berlin in the old Reichstag building.

MARKS

A - Berlin

E - Muldenhutten

MONETARY SYSTEM

100 Pfennig = 1 Mark

DEMOCRATIC REPUBLIC

STANDARD COINAGE

KM# 1 PFENNIG

Aluminum **Obv:** Denomination **Rev:** Cogwheel back of grain sprig

Date	Mintage	VF20	XF40	MS60	MS63	MS65
1948 A	243,000,000	0.45	0.75	1.50	5.00	25.00
1949 A	Inc. above	0.45	0.75	1.50	5.00	25.00
1949 E	55,200,000	2.00	4.00	10.00	20.00	100
1950 A	—	0.45	0.75	1.50	5.00	25.00
1950 E	—	1.00	2.00	5.00	15.00	75.00

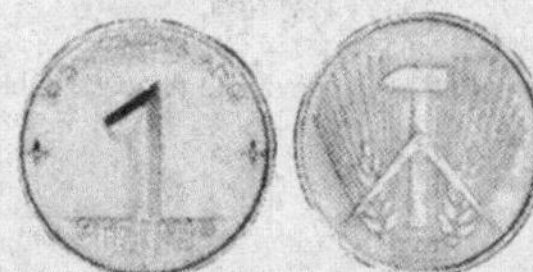

KM# 5 PFENNIG

0.70 g., Aluminum **Obv:** Denomination **Rev:** Grain sprigs back of hammer and protractor

Date	Mintage	VF20	XF40	MS60	MS63	MS65
1952 A	297,213,000	0.25	0.50	1.50	3.00	15.00
1952 E	49,296,000	0.50	1.00	2.50	7.50	35.00
1953 A	114,002,000	0.25	0.50	1.50	3.00	15.00
1953 E	50,876,000	1.50	3.00	7.00	15.00	75.00

KM# 8.1 PFENNIG

0.70 g., Aluminum, 17 mm. **Obv:** State emblem **Rev:** Denomination flanked by oak leaves, date below

Date	Mintage	VF20	XF40	MS60	MS63	MS65
1960 A	101,808,000	0.25	0.35	0.75	1.50	3.00
1961 A	101,776,000	0.25	0.35	0.75	1.50	3.00
1962 A	81,459,000	0.25	0.35	0.75	1.50	3.00
1963 A	101,402,000	0.25	0.35	0.75	1.50	3.00
1964 A	98,967,000	0.25	0.35	0.75	1.50	3.00
1965 A	38,585,000	1.00	2.00	4.00	10.00	50.00
1968 A	813,680,000	0.25	0.35	0.75	1.50	3.00
1972 A	4,801,000	0.50	1.00	2.50	5.00	25.00
1973 A	5,518,000	0.50	1.00	2.50	5.00	25.00
1975 A	202,752,000	0.25	0.35	0.75	1.50	3.00

KM# 8.2 PFENNIG

0.70 g., Aluminum, 17 mm. **Obv:** State emblem, smaller design features **Rev:** Denomination flanked by leaves, smaller design features

Date	Mintage	VF20	XF40	MS60	MS63	MS65
1977 A	61,560,000	0.10	0.25	0.50	1.00	2.00
1978 A	200,050,000	0.10	0.20	0.35	0.75	1.50
1979 A	100,640,000	0.10	0.20	0.35	0.75	1.50
1979 A	—	PF63 25.00				
1980 A	153,000,000	0.10	0.20	0.35	0.75	1.50
1980 A	—	PF63 25.00				
1981 A	200,436,000	0.10	0.20	0.35	0.75	1.50
1981 A Proof	40	—	—	—	—	—
1982 A	99,200,000	0.10	0.20	0.35	0.75	1.50
1982 A	2,500	PF63 5.00				
1983 A	150,000,000	0.10	0.20	0.35	0.75	1.50
1983 A	2,550	PF63 5.00				
1984 A	137,600,000	0.10	0.20	0.35	0.75	1.50
1984 A	3,015	PF63 3.00				
1985 A	125,060,000	0.10	0.20	0.35	0.75	1.50
1985 A	2,816	PF63 3.00				
1986 A	73,900,000	0.10	0.20	0.35	0.75	1.50
1986 A	2,800	PF63 3.00				
1987 A	50,015,000	0.10	0.20	0.35	0.75	1.50
1987 A	2,345	PF63 3.00				
1988 A	75,450,000	0.10	0.20	0.35	0.75	1.50
1988 A	2,300	PF63 3.00				
1989 A	84,410,000	0.10	0.20	0.35	0.75	1.50
1989 A	2,300	PF63 3.00				
1990 A	15,670,000	0.35	0.75	1.50	3.00	7.00

KM# 2 5 PFENNIG

1.20 g., Aluminum **Obv:** Denomination **Rev:** Cogwheel back of grain sprig

Date	Mintage	VF20	XF40	MS60	MS63	MS65
1948 A	205,072,000	0.25	0.50	2.00	5.00	25.00
1949 A	Inc. above	0.35	0.75	2.50	6.00	30.00
1950 A	Inc. above	0.50	1.00	3.00	7.00	35.00

KM# 6 5 PFENNIG

Aluminum **Obv:** Denomination **Rev:** Grain sprigs flank hammer and protractor, date below

Date	Mintage	VF20	XF40	MS60	MS63	MS65
1952 A	113,397,000	0.50	1.00	1.75	3.50	18.00
1952 E	24,024,000	0.75	1.50	3.50	7.50	38.00
1953 A	40,994,000	0.50	1.00	1.75	3.50	18.00
1953 E	28,665,000	1.00	2.00	5.00	10.00	50.00

KM# 9.1 5 PFENNIG

1.00 g., Aluminum, 19 mm. **Obv:** State emblem **Rev:** Denomination flanked by oak leaves, date below

Date	Mintage	VF20	XF40	MS60	MS63	MS65
1968 A	282,303,000	0.25	0.50	1.00	2.00	3.00
1972 A	51,462,000	0.25	0.50	1.00	2.00	3.00
1975 A	84,710,000	0.25	0.50	1.00	2.00	3.00

KM# 9.2 5 PFENNIG

1.00 g., Aluminum, 19 mm. **Obv:** State emblem, smaller design features **Rev:** Denomination flanked by oak leaves, smaller design features **Note:** Varieties exist.

Date	Mintage	VF20	XF40	MS60	MS63	MS65
1976 A 2 known	—	—	—	—	—	—
1978 A	43,257,000	0.15	0.25	0.50	1.00	2.00
1979 A	46,194,000	0.15	0.25	0.50	1.00	2.00
1979 A	—	PF63 25.00				
1980 A	31,977,000	0.15	0.25	0.50	1.00	2.00
1980 A	—	PF63 25.00				
1981 A	33,101,999	0.15	0.25	0.50	1.00	2.00
1981 A Proof	40	—	—	—	—	—
1982 A	916,000	3.00	7.00	20.00	30.00	75.00
1982 A	2,500	PF63 5.00				
1983 A	100,890,000	0.15	0.25	0.50	1.00	2.00
1983 A	2,550	PF63 7.00				
1984 A	Est. 6000	—	—	7.00	15.00	30.00
1984 A	3,015	PF63 3.00				
1985 A	1,000,000	1.25	2.50	5.00	7.50	15.00
1985 A	2,816	PF63 3.00				
1986 A	1,000,000	1.25	2.50	5.00	7.50	15.00
1986 A	2,800	PF63 3.00				
1987 A	Est. 20000	—	—	5.00	9.00	20.00
1987 A	2,345	PF63 3.00				
1988 A	35,930,000	0.15	0.25	0.50	1.00	2.00
1988 A	2,300	PF63 3.00				
1989 A	21,550,000	0.15	0.25	0.50	1.00	2.00
1989 A	2,300	PF63 3.00				
1990 A	50,640,000	0.15	0.25	0.50	1.00	2.00

KM# 3 10 PFENNIG

1.00 g., Aluminum **Obv:** Denomination **Rev:** Cogwheel back of grain sprigs

Date	Mintage	VF20	XF40	MS60	MS63	MS65
1948 A	216,537,000	0.65	1.25	2.50	5.00	25.00
1949 A	Inc. above	0.65	1.25	2.50	5.00	25.00
1950 A	Inc. above	0.65	1.25	2.50	5.00	25.00
1950 E	16,000,000	2.50	7.00	25.00	75.00	375

KM# 7 10 PFENNIG

Aluminum **Obv:** Denomination **Rev:** Grain sprigs flank hammer and protractor, date below

Date	Mintage	VF20	XF40	MS60	MS63	MS65
1952 A	70,427,000	0.65	1.25	2.50	5.00	25.00
1952 E	21,498,000	1.50	3.00	10.00	25.00	125
1953 A	18,611,000	0.65	1.25	2.50	5.00	25.00
1953 E	11,500,000	2.00	4.00	7.50	15.00	75.00

KM# 10 10 PFENNIG

1.50 g., Aluminum, 21 mm. **Obv:** State emblem **Rev:** Denomination divides leaf and date

Date	Mintage	VF20	XF40	MS60	MS63	MS65
1963 A	21,063,000	1.50	3.00	10.00	25.00	85.00
1965 A	55,313,000	0.25	0.50	1.00	2.00	4.00
1967 A	96,955,000	0.15	0.35	0.75	1.50	3.50
1968 A	207,461,000	0.15	0.35	0.75	1.50	3.50
1970 A	13,387,000	0.25	0.75	1.50	3.00	5.00
1971 A	66,617,999	0.15	0.35	0.75	1.50	3.50

Date	Mintage	VF20	XF40	MS60	MS63	MS65
1972 A	5,702,000	0.75	1.50	3.00	5.00	10.00
1973 A	11,257,000	0.25	0.50	1.00	2.00	4.00
1978 A	40,000,000	0.15	0.35	0.75	1.50	3.50
1979 A	54,665,000	0.15	0.35	0.75	1.50	3.50
1979 A	—	PF63 20.00				
1980 A	20,664,000	0.25	0.50	1.00	2.00	4.00
1980 A	—	PF63 20.00				
1981 A	40,704,000	0.15	0.35	0.75	1.50	3.50
1981 A Proof	40	—	—	—	—	—
1982 A	40,212,000	0.25	0.50	1.00	2.00	4.00
1982 A	2,500	PF63 5.00				
1983 A	40,699,000	0.25	0.75	1.50	3.00	5.00
1983 A	2,550	PF63 7.00				
1984 A	Est. 12000	—	3.00	5.00	10.00	35.00
Note: Issued Sets only, remainder unaccountable						
1984 A	3,015	PF63 3.00				
1985 A	1,010,000	0.35	1.50	3.00	5.00	15.00
1985 A	2,816	PF63 3.00				
1986 A	1,000,000	0.35	1.50	3.00	5.00	15.00
1986 A	2,800	PF63 3.00				
1987 A	Est. 20000	—	2.00	4.00	7.50	22.00
Note: Issued Sets only, remainder unaccountable						
1987 A	2,345	PF63 3.00				
1988 A	10,705,000	0.15	0.35	0.75	1.50	3.50
1988 A	2,300	PF63 3.00				
1989 A	37,640,000	0.15	0.35	0.75	1.50	3.50
1989 A	2,300	PF63 3.00				
1990 A	Est. 14000	—	—	—	8.00	25.00
Note: Issued Sets only, remainder unaccountable						

KM# 11 20 PFENNIG

5.40 g., Brass, 22.3 mm. **Obv:** State emblem **Rev:** Denomination above date **Note:** Ribbon width varieties exist.

Date	Mintage	VF20	XF40	MS60	MS63	MS65
1969	167,168,000	0.25	0.50	1.00	3.00	7.00
1971	24,563,000	0.25	0.50	1.00	3.00	7.00
1972 A	5,007,000	0.45	0.75	3.00	5.00	12.00
1973 A	2,524,000	0.45	0.75	3.00	5.00	12.00
1974 A	7,458,000	0.35	0.65	2.50	3.50	10.00
1979 A	293,000	0.50	1.00	3.50	6.50	12.50
1979 A	—	PF63 15.00				
1980 A	2,190,000	0.45	0.75	3.00	5.00	12.00
1980 A	—	PF63 15.00				
1981 A	983,000	0.45	0.75	3.00	5.00	12.00
1981 A Proof	40	—	—	—	—	—
1982 A	10,458,000	0.45	0.75	3.00	5.00	12.00
1982 A	2,500	PF63 5.00				
1983 A	25,809,000	0.25	0.50	1.00	3.00	7.00
1983 A	2,550	PF63 7.00				
1984 A	25,009,000	0.25	0.50	1.00	3.00	7.00
1984 A	3,015	PF63 3.00				
1985 A	1,559,000	0.45	0.75	3.00	5.00	12.00
1985 A	2,816	PF63 3.00				
1986 A	1,147,000	0.45	0.75	3.00	6.00	15.00
1986 A	2,800	PF63 3.00				
1987 A	Est. 20000	—	—	—	10.00	20.00
Note: Issued Sets only, remainder unaccountable						
1987 A	2,345	PF63 3.00				
1988 A	Est. 15000	—	—	—	12.00	25.00
Note: Issued Sets only, remainder unaccountable						
1988 A	2,300	PF63 3.00				
1989 A	14,690,000	0.20	0.50	1.00	2.00	3.00
1989 A	2,300	PF63 3.00				
1990 A	Est. 14000	—	—	—	8.00	16.00
Note: Issued Sets only, remainder unaccountable						

KM# 4 50 PFENNIG

3.38 g., Aluminum-Bronze, 20 mm. **Obv:** Denomination above date **Rev:** Man and plow in front of buildings with tall smokestacks

Date	Mintage	VF20	XF40	MS60	MS63	MS65
1949 A	Inc. below	—	7,500	8,500	10,000	—
1950 A	67,703,000	7.50	25.00	75.00	225	—

Note: Some authorities believe the 1949-dated piece is a pattern

KM# 12.1 50 PFENNIG

2.00 g., Aluminum, 23 mm. **Obv:** Small state emblem **Rev:** Denomination divides leaf and date **Edge:** Reeded

Date	Mintage	VF20	XF40	MS60	MS63	MS65
1958 A	101,606,000	0.25	0.50	1.50	3.00	10.00

KM# 12.2 50 PFENNIG

2.00 g., Aluminum, 23 mm. **Obv:** Large state emblem **Rev:** Denomination divides date and leaf **Edge:** Reeded **Note:** Inscription varieties exist.

Date	Mintage	VF20	XF40	MS60	MS63	MS65
1968 A	19,860,000	0.25	0.50	1.50	4.00	8.00
1971 A	35,829,000	0.25	0.50	1.50	3.00	6.00
1972 A	8,117,000	0.25	0.50	1.50	4.50	9.00
1973 A	6,530,000	0.25	0.50	1.50	6.00	12.00
1979 A	1,026,999	0.25	0.50	1.50	6.00	12.00
1979 A Proof	—	—	—	—	—	—
1980 A	1,118,000	0.75	1.50	3.00	9.00	20.00
1980 A Proof	—	—	—	—	—	—
1981 A	10,546,000	0.35	0.75	1.50	5.00	10.00
1981 A Proof	40	—	—	—	—	—
1982 A	79,832,000	—	0.35	0.75	2.50	5.00
1982 A	2,500	PF63 12.50				
1983 A	1,309,000	0.35	0.75	1.50	5.00	10.00
1983 A	2,550	PF63 25.00				
1984 A	Est. 5000	—	—	—	15.00	30.00
1984 A	3,015	PF63 5.50				
1985 A	1,565,000	0.35	0.75	1.50	5.00	10.00
1985 A	2,816	PF63 5.50				
1986 A	776,000	0.35	0.75	1.50	5.00	10.00
1986 A	2,800	PF63 5.50				
1987 A	Est. 21000	0.75	1.50	3.00	8.00	16.00
Note: Issued Sets only, remainder unaccountable						
1987 A	2,345	PF63 5.50				
1988 A	Est. 15000	0.75	1.50	3.00	8.00	16.00
Note: Issued Sets only, remainder unaccountable						
1988 A	2,300	PF63 5.50				
1989 A	31,000	0.35	0.75	1.50	5.00	10.00
1989 A	2,300	PF63 5.50				
1990 A	Est. 14000	—	—	—	10.00	20.00
Note: Issued Sets only, remainder unaccountable						

KM# 13 MARK

2.40 g., Aluminum **Obv:** State emblem **Rev:** Large, thick denomination flanked by leaves, date below

Date	Mintage	VF20	XF40	MS60	MS63	MS65
1956 A	112,108,000	0.65	1.25	2.50	6.00	12.00
1962 A	45,920,000	0.50	1.00	2.00	5.00	10.00
1963 A	31,910,000	0.50	1.00	2.00	5.00	10.00

KM# 35.1 MARK

Aluminum **Obv:** State emblem **Rev:** Large 1 flanked by oak leaves

Date	Mintage	VF20	XF40	MS60	MS63	MS65
1972 A	30,288,000	0.35	0.75	1.50	5.00	10.00

KM# 35.2 MARK

2.40 g., Aluminum, 25 mm. **Obv:** State emblem **Rev:** Large, thick denomination flanked by leaves, small date below

Date	Mintage	VF20	XF40	MS60	MS63	MS65
1973 A	6,972,000	0.50	1.00	3.00	7.50	15.00
1975 A	32,094,000	0.35	0.75	1.50	5.00	10.00
1977 A	119,813,000	0.25	0.50	1.00	2.00	4.00
1978 A	18,824,000	0.25	0.50	1.00	2.00	4.00
1979 A	1,002,999	0.50	1.00	3.00	7.50	15.00
1979 A Proof	—	—	—	—	—	—
1980 A	1,069,000	1.00	2.00	3.50	9.00	20.00
1980 A Proof	—	—	—	—	—	—
1981 A	1,006,000	0.50	1.00	3.00	7.50	15.00
1981 A Proof	40	—	—	—	—	—
1982 A	51,619,000	0.25	0.50	1.00	2.00	4.00
1982 A	2,500	PF63 12.00				
1983 A	1,065,000	0.25	0.50	1.00	5.00	10.00
1983 A	2,550	PF63 15.00				
1984 A	Est. 5000	—	—	—	20.00	40.00
1984 A	3,015	PF63 6.00				
1985 A	1,128,000	0.50	1.00	2.00	5.00	10.00
1985 A	2,816	PF63 7.50				
1986 A	1,000,000	0.50	1.00	2.00	5.00	10.00
1986 A	2,800	PF63 7.50				
1987 A	Est. 21000	0.50	1.00	3.00	7.50	15.00
Note: Issued Sets only, remainder unaccountable						
1987 A	2,345	PF63 7.50				
1988 A	Est. 15000	—	—	—	10.00	20.00
Note: Issued Sets only, remainder unaccountable						
1988 A	2,300	PF63 7.50				
1989 A	33,000	1.00	2.00	4.00	9.00	18.00
1989 A	2,300	PF63 7.50				
1990 A	Est. 14000	—	—	—	10.00	20.00
Note: Issued Sets only, remainder unaccountable						

KM# 14 2 MARK

Aluminum **Obv:** State emblem **Rev:** Large denomination flanked by leaves, date below

Date	Mintage	VF20	XF40	MS60	MS63	MS65
1957 A	77,961,000	0.35	0.75	1.50	3.00	6.00

KM# 48 2 MARK

3.00 g., Aluminum, 27 mm. **Obv:** State emblem **Rev:** Large denomination flanked by leaves, date below

Date	Mintage	VF20	XF40	MS60	MS63	MS65
1972 A	—	—	—	—	—	—
Note: 3 pieces known						
1974 A	5,790,000	1.00	2.00	5.00	10.00	20.00
1975 A	32,464,000	0.50	1.00	2.00	5.00	10.00
1977 A	27,859,000	0.50	1.00	2.00	5.00	10.00
1978 A	23,415,000	0.50	1.00	2.00	5.00	10.00
1979 A	985,000	0.50	1.00	2.00	5.00	10.00
1979 A Proof	—	—	—	—	—	—
1980 A	1,018,999	0.50	1.00	2.00	5.00	15.00
1980 A Proof	—	—	—	—	—	—
1981 A	939,000	0.50	1.00	2.00	5.00	12.00
1981 A Proof	40	—	—	—	—	—
1982 A	60,488,000	0.25	0.50	1.00	2.00	4.00
1982 A	2,500	PF63 25.00				
1983 A	1,030,000	0.50	1.00	2.00	4.00	8.00
1983 A	2,550	PF63 30.00				
1984 A	Est. 6000	—	—	—	20.00	40.00
1984 A	3,015	PF63 10.00				
1985 A	1,310,000	0.75	1.50	3.00	7.00	15.00
1985 A	2,816	PF63 10.00				
1986 A	1,000,000	0.75	1.50	3.00	7.00	15.00
1986 A	2,800	PF63 10.00				
1987 A	Est. 30000	—	—	—	10.00	20.00
Note: Issued Sets only, remainder unaccountable						
1987 A	2,345	PF63 10.00				
1988 A	Est. 15000	—	—	—	12.00	22.00
Note: Issued Sets only, remainder unaccountable						
1988 A	2,300	PF63 10.00				
1989 A	46,000	1.00	2.00	5.00	10.00	20.00
1989 A	2,300	PF63 10.00				
1990 A	Est. 14000	—	—	—	7.00	12.00
Note: Issued Sets only, remainder unaccountable						

KM# 19.1 5 MARK

9.70 g., Copper-Nickel, 29 mm. **Subject:** 125th Anniversary of Birth of Robert Koch, doctor **Obv:** State emblem **Rev:** Head left

Edge Lettering: 5 MARK 5 MARK 5 MARK

Date	Mintage	VF20	XF40	MS60	MS63	MS65
1968	100,000	—	—	4.50	7.50	15.00

KM# 19.2 5 MARK

9.70 g., Copper-Nickel, 29 mm. **Obv:** State emblem **Rev:** Head left **Note:** Error: plain edge.

Date	Mintage	VF20	XF40	MS60	MS63	MS65
1968	—	—	—	420	700	1,350

KM# 22.1 5 MARK

Nickel-Bronze, 29 mm. **Subject:** 20th Anniversary D.D.R **Obv:** State emblem **Rev:** Denomination, date at left **Edge Lettering:** 5 Mark (repeated)

Date	Mintage	VF20	XF40	MS60	MS63	MS65
1969	50,222,000	—	—	1.50	2.50	5.50

Note: 10% nickel and 90% copper

KM# 22.1a 5 MARK

Copper-Nickel, 29 mm. **Obv:** State emblem **Rev:** Denomination, date at left **Edge Lettering:** 5 Mark (repeated)

Date	Mintage	VF20	XF40	MS60	MS63	MS65
1969	12,741	—	—	15.00	25.00	45.00

Note: 25% nickel and 75% copper

KM# 22.2 5 MARK

Nickel-Bronze, 29 mm. **Obv:** State emblem **Rev:** Denomination, date at left **Note:** Error: plain edge.

Date	Mintage	VF20	XF40	MS60	MS63	MS65
1969	—	—	—	30.00	50.00	100

KM# 22.3 5 MARK

Nickel-Bronze, 29 mm. **Obv:** State emblem **Rev:** Denomination, date at left **Note:** Error: Mongolian inscription and dates on edge.

Date	Mintage	VF20	XF40	MS60	MS63	MS65
1969	—	—	—	—	—	—

KM# 23 5 MARK

9.70 g., Copper-Nickel, 29 mm. **Subject:** Heinrich Hertz, physicist **Obv:** State emblem, denomination **Rev:** Head right, dates below **Edge Lettering:** 5 Mark (repeated)

Date	Mintage	VF20	XF40	MS60	MS63	MS65
1969	100,000	—	—	5.50	9.00	20.00

KM# 26 5 MARK

9.70 g., Copper-Nickel, 29 mm. **Subject:** Wilhelm Conrad Rontgen, physicist **Edge Lettering:** 5 Mark (repeated)

Date	Mintage	VF20	XF40	MS60	MS63	MS65
1970	100,000	—	—	4.50	7.50	12.00

KM# 29 5 MARK

9.70 g., Copper-Nickel, 29 mm. **Subject:** Brandenburg Gate **Edge Lettering:** 5 Mark (repeated)

Date	Mintage	VF20	XF40	MS60	MS63	MS65
1971 A	4,000,000	—	—	2.50	4.00	18.00
1979 A	32,000	—	—	7.50	12.00	22.00
1979 A	2,500	PF63 220	PF65 350			
1980 A	30,000	—	—	7.50	12.00	22.00
1980 A Proof	2,500	—	—	—	—	—
1981 A	30,000	—	—	6.00	10.00	20.00
1981 A Proof	2,500	—	—	—	—	—
1982 A	28,000	—	—	6.00	10.00	20.00
1982 A	2,500	PF63 220	PF65 350			
1983 A	3,000	—	—	228	380	700
1984 A	28,000	—	—	10.00	18.00	40.00
1984 A	3,015	PF63 80.00	PF65 135			
1985 A	3,000	—	—	215	360	660
1986 A	28,000	—	—	25.00	40.00	70.00
1986 A	2,800	PF63 100	PF65 165			
1987 A	220,000	—	—	3.50	6.00	15.00
1987 A	6,424	PF63 42.00	PF65 70.00			
1988 A	28,000	—	—	4.50	7.00	17.00
1988 A	2,300	PF63 120	PF65 200			
1989 A	28,000	—	—	7.50	12.00	24.00
1989 A	2,405	PF63 100	PF65 175			
1990 A	50,000	—	—	6.00	10.00	25.00

KM# 30 5 MARK

9.70 g., Copper-Nickel, 29 mm. **Subject:** Johannes Kepler, 400th Anniversary of Birth **Edge Lettering:** 5 Mark (repeated)

Date	Mintage	VF20	XF40	MS60	MS63	MS65
1971	100,000	—	—	4.50	7.00	24.00

KM# 36.1 5 MARK

9.70 g., Copper-Nickel, 29 mm. **Subject:** 75th Anniversary - Death of Johannes Brahms **Obv:** State emblem, denomination **Rev:** Name, musical score, dates **Edge Lettering:** 5 Mark 5 Mark 5 Mark 5 Mark

Date	Mintage	VF20	XF40	MS60	MS63	MS65
1972	55,000	—	—	5.00	8.00	17.00

KM# 36.2 5 MARK

9.70 g., Copper-Nickel, 29 mm. **Obv:** State emblem, denomination **Rev:** Musical score, name and dates **Note:** Error: Double edge inscription.

Date	Mintage	VF20	XF40	MS60	MS63	MS65
1972	—	—	—	360	600	1,000

KM# 37 5 MARK

9.70 g., Copper-Nickel, 29 mm. **Subject:** City of Meissen **Obv:** State emblem, denomination **Rev:** City scene **Edge Lettering:** 5 Mark (repeated)

Date	Mintage	VF20	XF40	MS60	MS63	MS65
1972 A	3,500,000	—	—	2.50	4.00	9.00
1981 A	40	PF63 1,650	PF65 2,750			
1983 A	28,000	—	—	35.00	65.00	145
1983 A	2,550	PF63 200	PF65 350			

KM# 43 5 MARK

9.70 g., Copper-Nickel, 29 mm. **Subject:** 125th Anniversary - Birth of Otto Lilienthal, aviation pioneer **Obv:** State emblem, denomination **Rev:** Plane divides dates **Edge Lettering:** 5 Mark (repeated)

Date	Mintage	VF20	XF40	MS60	MS63	MS65
1973	100,000	—	—	8.50	14.00	27.00

KM# 49 5 MARK

9.70 g., Copper-Nickel, 29 mm. **Subject:** Centenary - Death of Philipp Reis, physicist, telephone inventor **Obv:** State emblem, denomination **Rev:** Telephone and telegraph divided by name, dates at bottom **Edge Lettering:** 5 Mark (repeated)

Date	Mintage	VF20	XF40	MS60	MS63	MS65
1974	100,000	—	—	5.00	8.00	15.00

KM# 54 5 MARK

9.70 g., Copper-Nickel, 29 mm. **Subject:** 100th Anniversary - Birth of Thomas Mann, writer **Obv:** State emblem, denomination **Rev:** Head left, dates below **Edge Lettering:** 5 Mark (repeated)

Date	Mintage	VF20	XF40	MS60	MS63	MS65
1975	100,000	—	—	3.50	6.00	10.00

KM# 55 5 MARK

9.70 g., Copper-Nickel, 29 mm. **Subject:** International Women's Year **Obv:** State emblem, denomination **Rev:** Profiles of three women right **Edge Lettering:** 5 Mark (repeated)

Date	Mintage	VF20	XF40	MS60	MS63	MS65
1975	250,000	—	—	3.00	5.00	9.00

KM# 60 5 MARK

9.70 g., Copper-Nickel, 29 mm. **Subject:** 200th Anniversary - Birth of Ferdinand von Schill, military officer **Obv:** State emblem, denomination **Rev:** Hat divides dates above sword and name **Edge Lettering:** 5 Mark (repeated)

Date	Mintage	VF20	XF40	MS60	MS63	MS65
1976	100,000	—	—	5.50	9.00	17.00

KM# 64 5 MARK

9.70 g., Copper-Nickel, 29 mm. **Subject:** 125th Anniversary - Death of Friedrich Ludwig Jahn, father of German gymnastics **Obv:** State emblem, denomination **Rev:** Bust 3/4 facing, dates below **Edge Lettering:** 5 Mark (repeated)

Date	Mintage	VF20	XF40	MS60	MS63	MS65
1977	10,000	PF63 32.00	PF65 55.00			
1977	90,000	—	—	7.50	12.00	20.00

KM# 67 5 MARK

9.70 g., Copper-Nickel, 29 mm. **Subject:** 175th Anniversary - Death of Friedrich Klopstock, poet **Obv:** State emblem, denomination **Rev:** Bust left **Edge Lettering:** 5 Mark (repeated)

Date	Mintage	VF20	XF40	MS60	MS63	MS65
1978	96,000	—	—	7.20	12.00	20.00
1978	4,500	PF63 42.00	PF65 70.00			

KM# 68 5 MARK
9.70 g., Copper-Nickel, 29 mm. **Subject:** Anti-Apartheid Year **Obv:** Denomination, date below small state emblem at left **Rev:** Raised clenched fist

Date	Mintage	VF20	XF40	MS60	MS63	MS65
1978 A	4,000	PF63 45.00	PF65 75.00			
1978 A	196,000	—	—	4.00	6.50	12.00

KM# 72 5 MARK
9.70 g., Copper-Nickel, 29 mm. **Subject:** 100th Anniversary - Birth of Albert Einstein, physicist **Obv:** State emblem, denomination **Rev:** Head 3/4 right

Date	Mintage	VF20	XF40	MS60	MS63	MS65
1979	56,000	—	—	12.00	20.00	40.00
1979	4,500	PF63 55.00	PF65 90.00			

KM# 76 5 MARK
9.70 g., Copper-Nickel, 29 mm. **Subject:** 75th Anniversary - Death of Adolph von Menzel **Obv:** State emblem, denomination **Rev:** Bust left divides dates

Date	Mintage	VF20	XF40	MS60	MS63	MS65
1980	55,000	—	—	7.50	12.00	24.00
1980	5,500	PF63 42.00	PF65 70.00			

KM# 79 5 MARK
9.70 g., Copper-Nickel, 29 mm. **Subject:** 450th Anniversary - Death of Tilman Riemenschneider, sculptor **Obv:** State emblem, denomination **Rev:** Bust 3/4 facing, divides dates

Date	Mintage	VF20	XF40	MS60	MS63	MS65
1981	55,000	—	—	9.50	16.00	32.00
1981	5,500	PF63 50.00	PF65 80.00			

KM# 84 5 MARK
9.70 g., Copper-Nickel, 29 mm. **Subject:** 200th Anniversary - Birth of Friedrich Frobel **Obv:** State emblem, denomination **Rev:** Three children with building blocks, dates below

Date	Mintage	VF20	XF40	MS60	MS63	MS65
1982	55,000	—	—	9.50	16.00	28.00
1982	5,500	PF63 45.00	PF65 75.00			

KM# 85 5 MARK
9.70 g., Copper-Nickel-Zinc, 29 mm. **Subject:** Goethe's Weimar Cottage **Obv:** Small state emblem, denomination **Rev:** Cottage

Date	Mintage	VF20	XF40	MS60	MS63	MS65
1982 A	245,000	—	—	6.00	10.00	20.00
1982 A	5,500	PF63 35.00	PF65 65.00			
Note: House and trees frosted						
1982 A	210	PF63 1,800	PF65 3,000			
Note: House only frosted						

KM# 86 5 MARK
9.70 g., Copper-Nickel-Zinc, 29 mm. **Subject:** Wartburg Castle **Obv:** State emblem, denomination **Rev:** Castle

Date	Mintage	VF20	XF40	MS60	MS63	MS65
1982 A	245,000	—	—	6.00	10.00	18.00
1982 A	5,500	PF63 35.00	PF65 65.00			
1983 A	10,000	—	—	65.00	100	170

KM# 89 5 MARK
9.70 g., Copper-Nickel, 29 mm. **Subject:** Wittenberg Church **Obv:** Small state emblem, denomination **Rev:** Church

Date	Mintage	VF20	XF40	MS60	MS63	MS65
1983 A	245,000	—	—	6.00	10.00	20.00
1983 A	5,500	PF63 42.00	PF65 70.00			

KM# 90 5 MARK
9.70 g., Copper-Nickel, 29 mm. **Subject:** Martin Luther's birthplace **Obv:** State emblem, denomination **Rev:** House

Date	Mintage	VF20	XF40	MS60	MS63	MS65
1983 A	245,000	—	—	6.00	10.00	18.00
1983 A	5,500	PF63 35.00	PF65 65.00			

KM# 91 5 MARK
Copper-Nickel-Zinc, 29 mm. **Subject:** 125th Anniversary - Birth of Max Planck **Obv:** State emblem, denomination **Rev:** Head right, dates below

Date	Mintage	VF20	XF40	MS60	MS63	MS65
1983	56,000	—	—	9.00	15.00	28.00
1983	4,200	PF63 50.00	PF65 85.00			

KM# 96 5 MARK
9.70 g., Copper-Nickel, 29 mm. **Subject:** Leipzig Old City Hall **Obv:** State emblem, denomination **Rev:** City hall building

Date	Mintage	VF20	XF40	MS60	MS63	MS65
1984 A	245,000	—	—	5.00	8.00	17.00
1984 A	5,500	PF63 30.00	PF65 50.00			

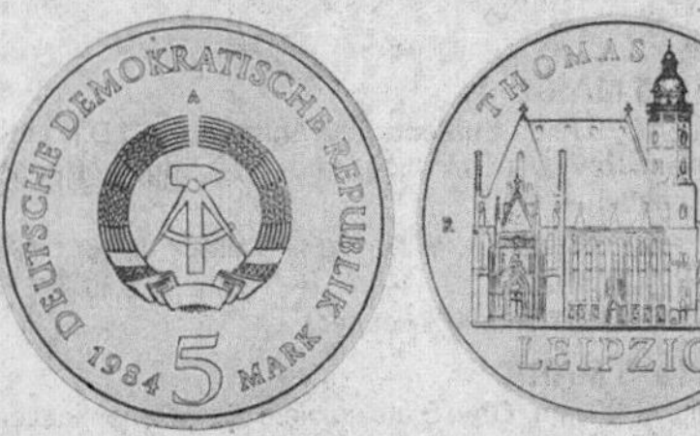

KM# 97 5 MARK
9.70 g., Copper-Nickel, 29 mm. **Subject:** Thomas Church of Leipzig **Obv:** State emblem, denomination **Rev:** Church

Date	Mintage	VF20	XF40	MS60	MS63	MS65
1984 A	245,000	—	—	5.00	8.00	17.00
1984 A	5,500	PF63 30.00	PF65 50.00			

KM# 98 5 MARK
9.70 g., Copper-Nickel, 29 mm. **Subject:** 150th Anniversary - Death of Adolf Freiherr von Lutzow **Obv:** State emblem, denomination **Rev:** Three uniformed figures on horses

Date	Mintage	VF20	XF40	MS60	MS63	MS65
1984 A	55,000	—	—	12.00	20.00	35.00
1984 A	5,000	PF63 50.00	PF65 85.00			

KM# 102 5 MARK
9.70 g., Copper-Nickel, 29 mm. **Subject:** Restoration of Dresden Women's Church **Obv:** State emblem divides date above six line inscription, denomination below **Rev:** Church buildings, date above

Date	Mintage	VF20	XF40	MS60	MS63	MS65
1985 A	245,000	—	—	6.00	10.00	20.00
1985 A	8,476	PF63 32.00	PF65 55.00			

KM# 103 5 MARK
9.70 g., Copper-Nickel, 29 mm. **Subject:** Restoration of Dresden Zwinger **Obv:** State emblem, denomination **Rev:** Building

Date	Mintage	VF20	XF40	MS60	MS63	MS65
1985 A	245,000	—	—	5.50	9.00	18.00
1985 A	5,500	PF63 32.00	PF65 55.00			

KM# 104 5 MARK

9.70 g., Copper-Nickel, 29 mm. **Subject:** 225th Anniversary - Death of Caroline Neuber **Obv:** State emblem, denomination **Rev:** Caroline on stage, 1697-1760

Date	Mintage	VF20	XF40	MS60	MS63	MS65
1985 A	56,000	—	—	14.50	24.00	42.00
1985 A	4,000	PF63 65.00	PF65 110			

KM# 110 5 MARK

9.70 g., Copper-Nickel, 29 mm. **Subject:** Potsdam - Sanssouci Palace **Obv:** State emblem, denomination **Rev:** Palace

Date	Mintage	VF20	XF40	MS60	MS63	MS65
1986 A	296,000	—	—	3.00	5.00	10.00
1986 A	4,200	PF63 45.00	PF65 75.00			

KM# 111 5 MARK

9.70 g., Copper-Nickel, 29 mm. **Subject:** Potsdam - New Palace **Obv:** State emblem, denomination **Rev:** Palace buildings

Date	Mintage	VF20	XF40	MS60	MS63	MS65
1986 A	296,000	—	—	2.50	4.00	9.00
1986 A	4,200	PF63 50.00	PF65 80.00			

KM# 112 5 MARK

9.70 g., Copper-Nickel, 29 mm. **Subject:** 175th Anniversary - Death of Heinrich von Kleist **Obv:** State emblem, denomination **Rev:** Bust left looking forward divides dates

Date	Mintage	VF20	XF40	MS60	MS63	MS65
1986 A	56,000	—	—	27.00	45.00	75.00
1986 A	4,000	PF63 115	PF65 190			

KM# 114 5 MARK

9.70 g., Copper-Nickel-Zinc, 29 mm. **Subject:** Berlin - Nikolai Quarter **Obv:** State emblem, denomination **Rev:** Buildings with two towers

Date	Mintage	VF20	XF40	MS60	MS63	MS65
1987 A	496,000	—	—	2.00	3.50	7.50
1987 A	4,200	PF63 40.00	PF65 65.00			

KM# 115 5 MARK

9.70 g., Copper-Nickel-Zinc, 29 mm. **Subject:** Berlin - Red City Hall **Obv:** State emblem, denomination **Rev:** City hall building

Date	Mintage	VF20	XF40	MS60	MS63	MS65
1987 A	496,000	—	—	2.00	3.50	7.50
1987 A	4,200	PF63 40.00	PF65 65.00			

KM# 116 5 MARK

9.70 g., Copper-Nickel-Zinc, 29 mm. **Subject:** Berlin - Universal Time Clock **Obv:** State emblem, denomination **Rev:** Universal clock

Date	Mintage	VF20	XF40	MS60	MS63	MS65
1987 A	496,000	—	—	2.00	3.50	7.50
1987 A	4,200	PF63 40.00	PF65 65.00			

KM# 120 5 MARK

9.70 g., Copper-Nickel, 29 mm. **Subject:** Germany's First Railroad **Obv:** State emblem, denomination **Rev:** Train engine, tower in background

Date	Mintage	VF20	XF40	MS60	MS63	MS65
1988 A	496,000	—	—	2.50	4.00	8.00
1988 A	4,200	PF63 70.00	PF65 120			

KM# 121 5 MARK

9.70 g., Copper-Nickel, 29 mm. **Subject:** Port City of Rostock **Obv:** State emblem, denomination **Rev:** Ships in port

Date	Mintage	VF20	XF40	MS60	MS63	MS65
1988 A	496,000	—	—	2.00	3.50	7.50
1988 A	4,200	PF63 65.00	PF65 110			

KM# 122 5 MARK

9.70 g., Copper-Nickel, 29 mm. **Subject:** 50th Anniversary - Death of Ernst Barlach **Obv:** State emblem, denomination **Rev:** Full-length figure playing horn, dates at right

Date	Mintage	VF20	XF40	MS60	MS63	MS65
1988 A	56,000	—	—	14.50	24.00	45.00
1988 A	4,000	PF63 110	PF65 185			

KM# 129 5 MARK

9.70 g., Copper-Nickel-Zinc, 29 mm. **Subject:** Katharinen Kirche in Zwickau **Obv:** State emblem, denomination **Rev:** Church

Date	Mintage	VF20	XF40	MS60	MS63	MS65
1989 A	496,000	—	—	2.75	4.50	9.00
1989 A	4,200	PF63 55.00	PF65 90.00			

KM# 130 5 MARK

9.70 g., Copper-Nickel-Zinc, 29 mm. **Subject:** Marien Kirche in Mühlhausen **Obv:** State emblem, denomination **Rev:** Church and city scene

Date	Mintage	VF20	XF40	MS60	MS63	MS65
1989 A	496,000	—	—	2.75	4.50	9.00
1989 A	4,200	PF63 55.00	PF65 90.00			

KM# 131 5 MARK

9.70 g., Copper-Nickel-Zinc, 29 mm. **Subject:** 100th Anniversary - Birth of Carl von Ossietzky, publisher **Obv:** State emblem, denomination **Rev:** Bust left, dates at right

Date	Mintage	VF20	XF40	MS60	MS63	MS65
1989 A	56,000	—	—	12.00	20.00	35.00
1989 A	4,000	PF63 100	PF65 170			

KM# 133 5 MARK

9.70 g., Copper-Nickel-Zinc, 29 mm. **Subject:** 100th Anniversary - Birth of Kurt Tucholsky **Obv:** State emblem, denomination **Rev:** Head facing, dates below

Date	Mintage	VF20	XF40	MS60	MS63	MS65
1990 A	51,000	—	—	9.50	16.00	30.00
1990 A	4,000	PF63 70.00	PF65 120			

KM# 134 5 MARK

9.70 g., Copper-Nickel-Zinc, 29 mm. **Subject:** 500 Years of Postal Service **Obv:** State emblem, denomination **Rev:** Antique car

Date	Mintage	VF20	XF40	MS60	MS63	MS65
1990 A	496,000	—	—	2.00	3.50	7.00
1990 A	4,200	PF63 45.00	PF65 75.00			

KM# 135 5 MARK
9.70 g., Copper-Nickel-Zinc, 29 mm. **Subject:** Zeughaus Museum in Berlin **Obv:** State emblem, denomination **Rev:** Museum

Date	Mintage	VF20	XF40	MS60	MS63	MS65
1990 A	496,000	—	—	2.00	3.00	6.00
1990 A	4,200	PF63 42.00	PF65 70.00			

KM# 15.1 10 MARK
17.00 g., 0.800 Silver 0.4372 oz. ASW, 31 mm. **Subject:** 125th Anniversary - Death of Karl Friedrich Schinkel, artist, painter **Obv:** State emblem, denomination **Rev:** Head right, dates below **Edge Lettering:** 10 MARK DER DEUTSCHEN NOTEN BANK

Date	Mintage	VF20	XF40	MS60	MS63	MS65
1966	50,000	—	—	70.00	115	195
1966 Proof, extremely rare	—	—	—	—	—	—

KM# 15.2 10 MARK
17.00 g., 0.800 Silver 0.4372 oz. ASW, 31 mm. **Obv:** State emblem, denomination **Rev:** Head right, dates below **Note:** Error: Plain edge.

Date	Mintage	VF20	XF40	MS60	MS63	MS65
1966	—	—	—	—	—	—

KM# 17.1 10 MARK
17.00 g., 0.800 Silver 0.4372 oz. ASW, 31 mm. **Subject:** 100th Anniversary - Birth of Käthe Kollwitz, artist **Obv:** State emblem, denomination **Rev:** Head left, dates below **Edge Lettering:** 10 MARK DER DEUTSCHEN NOTENBANK

Date	Mintage	VF20	XF40	MS60	MS63	MS65
1967	97,000	—	—	20.00	37.00	75.00
1967 Proof, extrememly rare	—	—	—	—	—	—

KM# 17.2 10 MARK
17.00 g., 0.800 Silver 0.4372 oz. ASW, 31 mm. **Subject:** 100th Anniversary - Birth of Kathe Kollwitz **Obv:** State emblem, denomination **Rev:** Head left, dates below **Note:** Error, edge: 10 MARK*10 MARK*10 MARK*

Date	Mintage	VF20	XF40	MS60	MS63	MS65
1967	3,000	—	—	60.00	100	190

KM# 20.1 10 MARK
17.00 g., 0.625 Silver 0.3416 oz. ASW, 31 mm. **Subject:** 500th Anniversary - Death of Johann Gutenberg, printer

Date	Mintage	VF20	XF40	MS60	MS63	MS65
1968	100,000	—	—	10.00	18.00	32.00

KM# 20.2 10 MARK
17.00 g., 0.625 Silver 0.3416 oz. ASW, 31 mm. **Subject:** 500th Anniversary - Death of Johann Gutenberg, printer **Note:** Error: Plain edge.

Date	Mintage	VF20	XF40	MS60	MS63	MS65
1968	—	—	—	100	170	285

KM# 24 10 MARK
17.00 g., 0.625 Silver 0.3416 oz. ASW, 31 mm. **Subject:** 250th Anniversary - Death of Johann Friedrich Böttger, German Porcelain **Obv:** State emblem, denomination **Rev:** Pitcher, dates divided above

Date	Mintage	VF20	XF40	MS60	MS63	MS65
1969	100,000	—	—	9.50	16.00	32.00
1969 Proof, extremely rare	—	—	—	—	—	—

KM# 27.1 10 MARK
17.00 g., 0.625 Silver 0.3416 oz. ASW, 31 mm. **Subject:** Ludwig Van Beethoven, composer **Obv:** State emblem, denomination **Rev:** Head left, dates below

Date	Mintage	VF20	XF40	MS60	MS63	MS65
1970	100,000	—	—	9.50	16.00	32.00
1970 Proof, extremely rare	—	—	—	—	—	—

KM# 27.2 10 MARK
17.00 g., 0.625 Silver 0.3416 oz. ASW, 31 mm. **Obv:** State emblem, denomination **Rev:** Head left **Note:** Error: Plain edge.

Date	Mintage	VF20	XF40	MS60	MS63	MS65
1970	—	—	—	—	—	390

KM# 31 10 MARK
17.00 g., 0.625 Silver 0.3416 oz. ASW, 31 mm. **Subject:** Albrecht Durer, artist **Obv:** State emblem, denomination **Rev:** Durer's monogram

Date	Mintage	VF20	XF40	MS60	MS63	MS65
1971	100,000	—	—	9.50	16.00	32.00
1971 Proof, extremely rare	—	—	—	—	—	—

KM# 38 10 MARK
Copper-Nickel, 31 mm. **Subject:** Buchenwald Memorial **Obv:** State emblem, denomination **Rev:** Monument

Date	Mintage	VF20	XF40	MS60	MS63	MS65
1972 A	2,500,000	—	—	2.00	3.50	7.00
1972 A Prooflike	—	—	—	5.00	8.00	18.00

KM# 39 10 MARK
17.00 g., 0.625 Silver 0.3416 oz. ASW, 31 mm. **Subject:** 175th Anniversary - Birth of Heinrich Heine, poet **Obv:** Hammer and protractor within wreath, (state emblem), denomination and date below **Rev:** Bust 3/4 left, divides dates

Date	Mintage	VF20	XF40	MS60	MS63	MS65
1972	100,000	—	—	12.00	22.00	45.00

KM# 44 10 MARK
Copper-Nickel, 31 mm. **Subject:** 10th Youth Festival Games **Obv:** State emblem below date and denomination **Rev:** Games symbol **Edge:** Reeded

Date	Mintage	VF20	XF40	MS60	MS63	MS65
1973 A	1,500,000	—	—	2.00	3.00	6.00
1973 A Prooflike	—	—	—	4.50	7.50	15.00

KM# 45 10 MARK
17.00 g., 0.625 Silver 0.3416 oz. ASW, 31 mm. **Subject:** 75th Anniversary - Birth of Bertolt Brecht, poet **Obv:** State emblem, denomination **Rev:** Head left, dates below

Date	Mintage	VF20	XF40	MS60	MS63	MS65
1973	100,000	—	—	10.00	18.00	32.00
1973 Proof, extremely rare	—	—	—	—	—	—

KM# 50 10 MARK
Copper-Nickel, 31 mm. **Subject:** 25th Anniversary (with state motto) **Obv:** Date and denomination below legend **Rev:** Dates above state emblem **Edge:** Reeded

Date	Mintage	VF20	XF40	MS60	MS63	MS65
1974 A	3,000,000	—	—	2.00	3.00	8.00
1974 A Prooflike	—	—	—	4.50	7.50	15.00

KM# 51 10 MARK
17.00 g., 0.625 Silver 0.3416 oz. ASW, 31 mm. **Subject:** 25th

Anniversary D.D.R. **Obv:** State emblem, denomination **Rev:** City scene

Date	Mintage	VF20	XF40	MS60	MS63	MS65
1974	70,000	—	—	10.00	18.00	32.00
1974	200	PF63 2,250	PF65 3,750			

KM# 52 10 MARK
17.00 g., 0.625 Silver 0.3416 oz. ASW, 31 mm. **Subject:** 200th Anniversary - Birth of Caspar David Friedrich, painter **Obv:** State emblem, denomination **Rev:** Bust right within inner circle, dates below

Date	Mintage	VF20	XF40	MS60	MS63	MS65
1974	75,000	—	—	10.00	18.00	32.00
1974	100	PF63 3,300	PF65 5,500			

KM# 56 10 MARK
17.00 g., 0.625 Silver 0.3416 oz. ASW, 31 mm. **Subject:** Centenary - Birth of Albert Schweitzer, doctor and philosopher **Obv:** State emblem, denomination **Rev:** Head left, dates below

Date	Mintage	VF20	XF40	MS60	MS63	MS65
1975	99,000	—	—	12.00	22.00	45.00
1975	1,040	PF63 750	PF65 1,250			

KM# 57 10 MARK
17.00 g., 0.500 Silver 0.2733 oz. ASW, 31 mm. **Subject:** Mule **Obv:** State emblem below denomination, date **Rev:** Head left, dates below **Edge:** Plain

Date	Mintage	VF20	XF40	MS60	MS63	MS65
1975 A	6,700	—	—	—	—	110

KM# 58 10 MARK
Copper-Nickel, 31 mm. **Subject:** 20th Anniversary - Warsaw Pact **Obv:** State emblem below denomination, date **Rev:** Roman numerals, 'XX' divide seven shields **Edge:** Reeded

Date	Mintage	VF20	XF40	MS60	MS63	MS65
1975 A	2,500,000	—	—	2.00	3.50	7.50
1975 A Prooflike	—	—	—	5.00	8.00	18.00

KM# 61 10 MARK
Copper-Nickel, 31 mm. **Subject:** 20th Anniversary - National People's Army **Obv:** State emblem below denomination, date **Rev:** Bust of soldier 3/4 facing **Edge:** Reeded

Date	Mintage	VF20	XF40	MS60	MS63	MS65
1976 A	750,000	—	—	2.50	4.00	9.00
1976 A Prooflike	—	—	—	5.50	9.00	20.00

KM# 62 10 MARK
17.00 g., 0.500 Silver 0.2733 oz. ASW, 31 mm. **Subject:** 150th Anniversary - Death of Carl Maria von Weber, composer **Obv:** State emblem, denomination **Rev:** Bust right divides dates **Edge Lettering:** 10 Mark (repeated)

Date	Mintage	VF20	XF40	MS60	MS63	MS65
1976	94,000	—	—	13.50	24.00	45.00
1976	6,037	PF63 70.00	PF65 115			

KM# 65 10 MARK
17.00 g., 0.500 Silver 0.2733 oz. ASW, 31 mm. **Subject:** 375th Anniversary - Birth of Otto von Guericke **Obv:** State emblem, denomination **Rev:** Vacuum pump below and castle above divide dates **Edge Lettering:** 10 Mark (repeated)

Date	Mintage	VF20	XF40	MS60	MS63	MS65
1977	69,000	—	—	18.00	30.00	55.00
1977	6,000	PF63 75.00	PF65 125			

KM# 69 10 MARK
17.00 g., 0.500 Silver 0.2733 oz. ASW, 31 mm. **Subject:** 175th Anniversary - Birth of Justus von Liebig, chemist **Obv:** State emblem, denomination **Rev:** Bust 3/4 facing, dates at left **Edge Lettering:** 10 Mark (repeated)

Date	Mintage	VF20	XF40	MS60	MS63	MS65
1978	71,000	—	—	12.00	20.00	35.00
1978	4,500	PF63 70.00	PF65 115			

KM# 70 10 MARK
Copper-Nickel, 31 mm. **Subject:** Joint USSR-DDR Orbital Flight **Obv:** State emblem below denomination, date **Edge Lettering:** 10 Mark (repeated)

Date	Mintage	VF20	XF40	MS60	MS63	MS65
1978 A	748,000	—	—	5.00	8.00	20.00
1978 A	2,200	PF63 270	PF65 450			

KM# 73 10 MARK
17.00 g., 0.500 Silver 0.2733 oz. ASW, 31 mm. **Subject:** 175th Anniversary - Birth of Ludwig Feuerbach, philosopher **Obv:** State emblem below denomination, date **Rev:** Bust 3/4 right, dates and name below **Edge Lettering:** 10 Mark (repeated)

Date	Mintage	VF20	XF40	MS60	MS63	MS65
1979	51,000	—	—	30.00	50.00	90.00
1979	4,500	PF63 100	PF65 175			

KM# 77 10 MARK
17.00 g., 0.500 Silver 0.2733 oz. ASW, 31 mm. **Subject:** 225th Anniversary - Birth of Gerhard von Scharnhorst, General & Politician in Prussia **Obv:** State emblem below denomination, date **Rev:** Bust left divides dates **Edge Lettering:** 10 Mark (repeated)

Date	Mintage	VF20	XF40	MS60	MS63	MS65
1980	55,000	—	—	9.50	16.00	30.00
1980	5,500	PF63 50.00	PF65 80.00			

KM# 80 10 MARK
Copper-Nickel, 31 mm. **Subject:** 25th Anniversary - National People's Army **Obv:** State emblem and denomination divide date **Rev:** Plane above ship at center, tank below, dates at sides **Edge Lettering:** 10 Mark (repeated)

Date	Mintage	VF20	XF40	MS60	MS63	MS65
1981 A	745,000	—	—	4.50	7.50	12.00
1981 A	5,500	PF63 35.00	PF65 60.00			

KM# 81 10 MARK
17.00 g., 0.500 Silver 0.2733 oz. ASW, 31 mm. **Subject:** 150th Anniversary - Death of Georg Hegel, philosopher **Obv:** Date and denomination above legend, state emblem below **Rev:** Head right divides dates **Edge Lettering:** 10 Mark (repeated)

Date	Mintage	VF20	XF40	MS60	MS63	MS65
1981	50,000	—	—	9.50	16.00	30.00
1981	5,500	PF63 42.00	PF65 70.00			

KM# 82 10 MARK

Copper-Nickel, 31 mm. **Subject:** 700th Anniversary - Berlin Mint **Obv:** State emblem and denomination divide date **Rev:** Berlin Pfennig 1369 at center **Edge Lettering:** 10 Mark (repeated)

Date	Mintage	VF20	XF40	MS60	MS63	MS65
1981	55,000	—	—	7.50	12.50	27.00
1981	5,500	**PF63** 55.00	**PF65** 90.00			

KM# 87 10 MARK

17.00 g., 0.500 Silver 0.2733 oz. ASW, 31 mm. **Subject:** Leipzig Gewandhaus **Obv:** Legend divides denomination and state emblem **Rev:** Design above building **Edge Lettering:** 10 Mark (repeated)

Date	Mintage	VF20	XF40	MS60	MS63	MS65
1982	50,000	—	—	8.50	14.00	30.00
1982	5,500	**PF63** 45.00	**PF65** 75.00			

KM# 92 10 MARK

17.11 g., 0.500 Silver 0.275 oz. ASW, 31 mm. **Subject:** 100th Anniversary - Death of Richard Wagner, Composer **Obv:** Legend divides state emblem and denomination **Rev:** Tannhaeuser & Singer in an opera by Wegner, dates below **Edge Lettering:** 10 Mark (repeated)

Date	Mintage	VF20	XF40	MS60	MS63	MS65
1983	44,000	—	—	8.50	14.00	32.00
1983	5,500	**PF63** 50.00	**PF65** 80.00			

KM# 93 10 MARK

Copper-Nickel-Zinc, 31 mm. **Subject:** 30th Anniversary - Worker's Militia **Obv:** Legend divides state emblem and denomination **Rev:** Worker and soldier facing left **Edge Lettering:** 10 Mark (repeated)

Date	Mintage	VF20	XF40	MS60	MS63	MS65
1983 A	495,000	—	—	3.50	6.00	14.00
1983 A	5,000	**PF63** 42.00	**PF65** 70.00			

KM# 99 10 MARK

17.00 g., 0.500 Silver 0.2733 oz. ASW, 31 mm. **Subject:** 100th Anniversary - Death of Zoologe Alfred Brehm **Obv:** State emblem, denomination **Rev:** Marabou stork left **Edge Lettering:** 10 Mark (repeated)

Date	Mintage	VF20	XF40	MS60	MS63	MS65
1984 A	50,000	—	—	14.00	24.00	45.00
1984 A	5,000	**PF63** 60.00	**PF65** 100			

KM# 101 10 MARK

17.00 g., 0.500 Silver 0.2733 oz. ASW, 31 mm. **Subject:** Restoration of Semper Opera in Dresden **Obv:** Legend divides state emblem and denomination **Rev:** Opera House **Edge Lettering:** * 1841 * 1878 * 1945 * 1985

Date	Mintage	VF20	XF40	MS60	MS63	MS65
1985 A	50,000	—	—	12.50	22.00	40.00
1985 A	5,000	**PF63** 70.00	**PF65** 115			

KM# 106 10 MARK

Copper-Nickel-Zinc, 31 mm. **Subject:** 40th Anniversary - Liberation from Fascism **Obv:** State emblem, denomination **Rev:** Statue divides inscription **Edge Lettering:** 10 Mark (repeated)

Date	Mintage	VF20	XF40	MS60	MS63	MS65
1985 A	745,000	—	—	3.00	5.00	9.00
1985 A	5,500	**PF63** 42.00	**PF65** 70.00			

KM# 107 10 MARK

17.00 g., 0.500 Silver 0.2733 oz. ASW, 31 mm. **Subject:** 175th Anniversary - Humboldt University in Berlin **Obv:** Legend divides state emblem and denomination **Rev:** Seated statues in front of Berlin University **Edge Lettering:** 10 Mark (repeated)

Date	Mintage	VF20	XF40	MS60	MS63	MS65
1985 A	51,000	—	—	14.00	24.00	45.00
1985 A	4,000	**PF63** 55.00	**PF65** 90.00			

KM# 109 10 MARK

Copper-Nickel, 31 mm. **Subject:** 100th Anniversary - Birth of Ernst Thalmann, Communist Polition, 1886-1944 **Obv:** State emblem below denomination, date **Rev:** People behind front figure with right fist raised **Edge Lettering:** 10 Mark (repeated)

Date	Mintage	VF20	XF40	MS60	MS63	MS65
1986 A	746,000	—	—	3.00	5.00	9.00
1986 A	4,000	**PF63** 42.00	**PF65** 70.00			

KM# 113 10 MARK

17.00 g., 0.500 Silver 0.2733 oz. ASW, 31 mm. **Subject:** Charité - Berlin **Obv:** State emblem divides date below legend, denomination above **Rev:** Building **Edge Lettering:** 10 Mark (repeated)

Date	Mintage	VF20	XF40	MS60	MS63	MS65
1986 A	51,000	—	—	14.00	24.00	45.00
1986 A	4,000	**PF63** 65.00	**PF65** 110			

KM# 118 10 MARK

17.00 g., 0.500 Silver 0.2733 oz. ASW, 31 mm. **Subject:** Berlin - Theater **Obv:** State emblem and denomination divide date **Rev:** Theater building **Edge Lettering:** 10 Mark (repeated)

Date	Mintage	VF20	XF40	MS60	MS63	MS65
1987 A	51,000	—	—	10.00	18.00	32.00
1987 A	4,000	**PF63** 70.00	**PF65** 115			

KM# 123 10 MARK

17.00 g., 0.500 Silver 0.2733 oz. ASW, 31 mm. **Subject:** 500th Anniversary - Birth of Ulrich von Hutten, warrior **Obv:** State emblem, denomination **Rev:** Half figure left divides dates **Edge Lettering:** 10 Mark (repeated)

Date	Mintage	VF20	XF40	MS60	MS63	MS65
1988 A	52,000	—	—	18.00	30.00	60.00
1988 A	3,500	**PF63** 100	**PF65** 165			

KM# 125 10 MARK

Copper-Nickel, 31 mm. **Subject:** 40 Years of East German Sports **Obv:** State emblem, denomination **Rev:** Three women running left, dates below **Edge Lettering:** 10 Mark (repeated)

Date	Mintage	VF20	XF40	MS60	MS63	MS65
1988 A	747,000	—	—	3.50	6.00	10.00
1988 A	3,200	**PF63** 75.00	**PF65** 125			

KM# 126 10 MARK

Copper-Nickel, 31 mm. **Subject:** Council of Mutual Economic Aid **Obv:** State emblem, denomination **Rev:** Tall building, dates at right **Edge Lettering:** 10 Mark (repeated)

Date	Mintage	VF20	XF40	MS60	MS63	MS65
1989 A	96,000	—	—	7.50	12.00	24.00
1989 A	4,000	**PF63** 150	**PF65** 260			

KM# 128 10 MARK

17.00 g., 0.500 Silver 0.2733 oz. ASW, 31 mm. **Subject:** 225th Anniversary - Birth of Johann Gottfried Schadow **Obv:** State emblem, denomination **Rev:** Winged figure in chariot (monument on top of Bradenbury Gate in Berlin), dates below **Edge Lettering:** 10 Mark (repeated)

Date	Mintage	VF20	XF40	MS60	MS63	MS65
1989 A	51,000	—	—	25.00	40.00	70.00
1989 A	4,000	PF63 170	PF65 285			

KM# 132 10 MARK

Copper-Nickel-Zinc, 31 mm. **Subject:** 40th Anniversary - East German Government **Obv:** State emblem divides dates above inscription, denomination below **Rev:** Fifteen shields on right, legend at left **Edge Lettering:** 10 MARK (repeated)

Date	Mintage	VF20	XF40	MS60	MS63	MS65
1989 A	746,000	—	—	2.50	4.00	9.00
1989 A	3,080	PF63 125	PF65 210			

KM# 136 10 MARK

Copper-Nickel-Zinc, 31 mm. **Subject:** International Labor Day **Obv:** State emblem below date and denomination **Rev:** Stylized lettering divides dates **Edge Lettering:** 10 MARK (repeated)

Date	Mintage	VF20	XF40	MS60	MS63	MS65
1990 A	747,000	—	—	2.00	3.00	7.00
1990 A	4,367	PF63 60.00	PF65 95.00			

KM# 137 10 MARK

17.00 g., 0.500 Silver 0.2733 oz. ASW, 31 mm. **Subject:** Johann Gottlieb Fichte, philosopher **Obv:** State emblem, denomination **Rev:** Figure at lectering facing left **Edge Lettering:** 10 Mark (repeated)

Date	Mintage	VF20	XF40	MS60	MS63	MS65
1990 A	37,000	—	—	18.00	30.00	50.00
1990 A	4,900	PF63 100	PF65 165			

KM# 16.1 20 MARK

20.90 g., 0.800 Silver 0.5376 oz. ASW, 33 mm. **Subject:** 250th Anniversary - Death of Gottfried Wilhelm Leibniz **Obv:** State emblem, denomination **Rev:** Bust right, dates below **Edge Lettering:** 20 MARK DER DEUTSCHEN NOTEN BANK

Date	Mintage	VF20	XF40	MS60	MS63	MS65
1966	50,000	—	—	42.00	70.00	120
1966 Proof, extremely rare	—	—	—	—	—	—

KM# 16.2 20 MARK

20.90 g., 0.800 Silver 0.5376 oz. ASW, 33 mm. **Subject:** 250th Anniversary - Death of Gottfried Wilhelm Leibniz **Obv:** State emblem, denomination **Rev:** Bust right **Edge:** Error: In inscription **Edge Lettering:** 10 MARK DER DEUTSCHEN NOTEN BANK

Date	Mintage	VF20	XF40	MS60	MS63	MS65
1966	—	—	—	—	—	—

KM# 18.1 20 MARK

20.90 g., 0.800 Silver 0.5376 oz. ASW, 33 mm. **Subject:** 200th Anniversary - Birth of Wilhelm von Humboldt **Obv:** State emblem, denomination **Rev:** Head with high collar left, dates below **Edge Lettering:** 20 MARK DER DEUTSCHEN NOTENBANK

Date	Mintage	VF20	XF40	MS60	MS63	MS65
1967	97,000	—	—	32.00	55.00	95.00
1967 Proof, extremely rare	—	—	—	—	—	—

KM# 18.2 20 MARK

20.90 g., 0.800 Silver 0.5376 oz. ASW, 33 mm. **Obv:** State emblem, denomination **Rev:** Head with high collar left, dates below **Edge:** Error: In inscription **Edge Lettering:** 20 MARK*20 MARK*20 MARK*20 MARK

Date	Mintage	VF20	XF40	MS60	MS63	MS65
1967	3,000	—	—	—	—	165

KM# 21 20 MARK

20.90 g., 0.800 Silver 0.5376 oz. ASW, 33 mm. **Subject:** 150th Anniversary - Birth of Karl Marx **Obv:** State emblem, denomination **Rev:** Head left, dates below **Edge Lettering:** 20 Mark (repeated)

Date	Mintage	VF20	XF40	MS60	MS63	MS65
1968	100,000	—	—	20.00	32.00	55.00
1968 Proof, extremely rare	—	—	—	—	—	—

KM# 25 20 MARK

20.90 g., 0.625 Silver 0.420 oz. ASW, 33 mm. **Subject:** 220th Birth Anniversary - Johann Wolfgang von Goethe, poet **Obv:** State emblem, denomination **Rev:** Head left, dates below **Edge Lettering:** 20 Mark (repeated)

Date	Mintage	VF20	XF40	MS60	MS63	MS65
1969	100,000	—	—	27.00	45.00	80.00
1969 Proof, extremely rare	—	—	—	—	—	—

KM# 28 20 MARK

20.90 g., 0.625 Silver 0.420 oz. ASW, 33 mm. **Subject:** 150th Anniversary - Birth of Friedrich Engels **Obv:** State emblem, denomination **Rev:** Head left, dates at right **Edge Lettering:** 20 Mark (repeated)

Date	Mintage	VF20	XF40	MS60	MS63	MS65
1970	100,000	—	—	20.00	32.00	60.00
1970 Proof, extremely rare	—	—	—	—	—	—

KM# 32 20 MARK

20.90 g., 0.625 Silver 0.420 oz. ASW, 33 mm. **Subject:** Karl Liebknecht - Rosa Luxemburg **Obv:** State emblem, denomination **Rev:** Jugate busts left, dates below **Edge Lettering:** 20 MARK (repeated)

Date	Mintage	VF20	XF40	MS60	MS63	MS65
1971	100,000	—	—	18.00	30.00	55.00
1971 Proof, extremely rare	—	—	—	—	—	—

KM# 33 20 MARK

Copper-Nickel, 33 mm. **Subject:** 100th Anniversary - Birth of Heinrich Mann, writer **Obv:** State emblem, denomination **Rev:** Head left, dates below **Edge Lettering:** 20 MARK (repeated)

Date	Mintage	VF20	XF40	MS60	MS63	MS65
1971	2,000,000	—	—	2.50	4.00	9.00
(1971) Prooflike	—	—	—	7.50	12.00	25.00

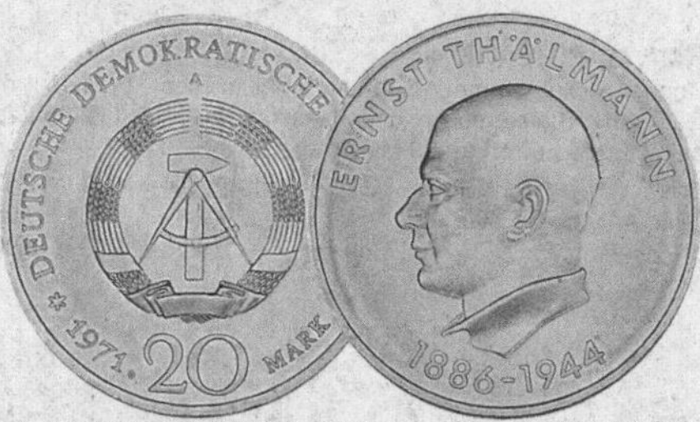

KM# 34 20 MARK

Copper-Nickel, 33 mm. **Subject:** 85th Birthday of Ernst Thälmann **Obv:** State emblem, denomination **Rev:** Head left, dates below **Edge Lettering:** 20 MARK (repeated) **Note:** Edge varieties exist.

Date	Mintage	VF20	XF40	MS60	MS63	MS65
1971 A	2,500,000	—	—	2.00	3.50	8.00
1971 A Prooflike	—	—	—	5.50	9.00	20.00

KM# 40 20 MARK

Copper-Nickel, 33 mm. **Subject:** Friedrich von Schiller, poet **Obv:** State emblem, denomination **Rev:** Head right divides dates

Date	Mintage	VF20	XF40	MS60	MS63	MS65
1972 A	3,000,000	—	—	2.00	3.50	8.00
1972 A Prooflike	—	—	—	7.50	12.50	25.00

KM# 41 20 MARK

20.90 g., 0.625 Silver 0.420 oz. ASW, 33 mm. **Subject:** 500th Anniversary - Birth of Lucas Cranach, painter **Obv:** State emblem, denomination **Rev:** Crowned snake with ring and wings, wings divide dates above **Edge Lettering:** 20 MARK (repeated)

Date	Mintage	VF20	XF40	MS60	MS63	MS65
1972	100,000	—	—	18.00	30.00	55.00
1972 Proof, extremely rare	—	—	—	—	—	—

KM# 42 20 MARK

Copper-Nickel, 33 mm. **Subject:** Wilhelm Pieck, President of GDR **Obv:** State emblem, denomination **Rev:** Head left, dates below **Edge Lettering:** 20 Mark (repeated)

Date	Mintage	VF20	XF40	MS60	MS63	MS65
1972 A	2,500,000	—	—	2.00	3.50	9.00
1972 A Prooflike	—	—	—	5.50	9.00	18.00

KM# 46 20 MARK

20.90 g., 0.625 Silver 0.420 oz. ASW, 33 mm. **Subject:** 60th Anniversary - Death of August Bebel, Socialist **Obv:** State emblem, denomination **Rev:** Bust half facing, dates at left **Edge Lettering:** 20 Mark (repeated)

Date	Mintage	VF20	XF40	MS60	MS63	MS65
1973	100,000	—	—	14.00	24.00	45.00
1973 Proof, extremely rare	—	—	—	—	—	—

KM# 47 20 MARK

Copper-Nickel, 33 mm. **Subject:** Otto Grotewohl, Politician **Obv:** State emblem, denomination **Rev:** Head left, dates below **Edge Lettering:** 20 MARK (repeated)

Date	Mintage	VF20	XF40	MS60	MS63	MS65
1973 A	2,500,000	—	—	2.00	3.50	8.00
1973 A Prooflike	—	—	—	6.00	10.00	22.00

KM# 53 20 MARK

20.90 g., 0.625 Silver 0.420 oz. ASW, 33 mm. **Subject:** 250th Anniversary - Death of Immanuel Kant, philosopher **Obv:** State emblem, denomination **Rev:** Bust 3/4 facing, dates at left **Edge Lettering:** 20 Mark (repeated)

Date	Mintage	VF20	XF40	MS60	MS63	MS65
1974	96,000	—	—	18.00	30.00	55.00
1974	4,221	PF63 85.00	PF65 145			

KM# 59 20 MARK

20.90 g., 0.625 Silver 0.420 oz. ASW, 33 mm. **Subject:** 225th Anniversary - Death of Johann Sebastian Bach, composer **Obv:** State emblem, denomination **Rev:** Musical score, dates upper left **Edge Lettering:** 20 Mark (repeated)

Date	Mintage	VF20	XF40	MS60	MS63	MS65
1975	100,000	—	—	20.00	35.00	65.00
1975 Proof, extremely rare	Inc. above	—	—	—	—	—

KM# 63 20 MARK

20.90 g., 0.625 Silver 0.420 oz. ASW, 33 mm. **Subject:** 150th Anniversary - Birth of Wilhelm Liebknecht (socialist member of Reichstag Parliament) **Obv:** State emblem, denomination **Rev:** Bust 3/4 left divides dates **Edge Lettering:** 20 Mark (repeated)

Date	Mintage	VF20	XF40	MS60	MS63	MS65
1976	96,000	—	—	18.00	30.00	55.00
1976	4,000	PF63 80.00	PF65 135			

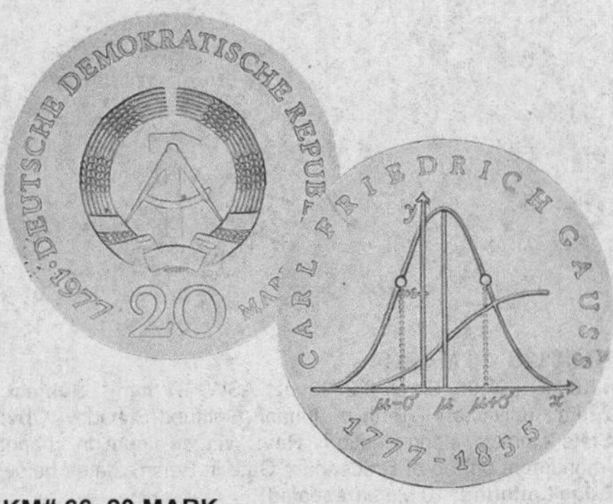

KM# 66 20 MARK

20.90 g., 0.500 Silver 0.336 oz. ASW, 33 mm. **Subject:** 200th Anniversary - Birth of Carl Friedrich Gauss, scientist **Obv:** State emblem, denomination **Rev:** Lines and arrows form graph, dates below **Edge Lettering:** 20 Mark (repeated)

Date	Mintage	VF20	XF40	MS60	MS63	MS65
1977	55,000	—	—	24.00	40.00	70.00

KM# 71 20 MARK

20.90 g., 0.500 Silver 0.336 oz. ASW, 33 mm. **Subject:** 175th Anniversary - Death of Johann von Herder, philosopher **Obv:** State emblem, denomination **Rev:** Head 3/4 left, dates at right **Edge Lettering:** 20 Mark (repeated)

Date	Mintage	VF20	XF40	MS60	MS63	MS65
1978	51,000	—	—	22.00	38.00	65.00
1978	4,500	PF63 75.00	PF65 125			

KM# 74 20 MARK

20.90 g., 0.500 Silver 0.336 oz. ASW, 33 mm. **Subject:** 250th Anniversary - Birth of Gotthold Ephraim Lessing, poet **Obv:** State emblem, denomination **Rev:** Three figures and two palm trees, dates above **Edge Lettering:** 20 Mark (repeated)

Date	Mintage	VF20	XF40	MS60	MS63	MS65
1979	41,000	—	—	22.00	38.00	65.00
1979	4,500	PF63 85.00	PF65 145			

KM# 75 20 MARK

Copper-Nickel, 33 mm. **Subject:** 30th Anniversary - East German Regime **Obv:** Large denomination above date, state emblem below **Rev:** Two jugate heads; front head facing, back head left, chemical factory at left **Edge Lettering:** 20 Mark (repeated)

Date	Mintage	VF20	XF40	MS60	MS63	MS65
1979 A	1,000,000	—	—	3.50	6.00	12.00
1979 A Prooflike	—	—	—	6.00	10.00	22.00

KM# 78 20 MARK
20.92 g., 0.500 Silver 0.3363 oz. ASW, 33 mm. **Subject:** 75th Anniversary - Death of Ernst Abbe, physicist **Obv:** Legend divides state emblem and denomination **Rev:** Early optical instrument, dates below **Edge Lettering:** 20 Mark (repeated)

Date	Mintage	VF20	XF40	MS60	MS63	MS65
1980	40,000	—	—	22.00	38.00	65.00
1980	5,500	PF63 70.00	PF65 120			

KM# 83 20 MARK
20.92 g., 0.500 Silver 0.3363 oz. ASW, 33 mm. **Subject:** 150th Anniversary - Death of vom Stein, Statesman and Reformer **Obv:** Legend divides state emblem and denomination **Rev:** Small bust half left below name **Edge Lettering:** 20 Mark (repeated)

Date	Mintage	VF20	XF40	MS60	MS63	MS65
1981	40,000	—	—	18.00	30.00	55.00
1981	5,500	PF63 70.00	PF65 120			

KM# 88 20 MARK
20.92 g., 0.500 Silver 0.3363 oz. ASW, 33 mm. **Subject:** 125th Anniversary - Birth of Clara Zetkin, Communist leader murdered in Berlin in 1920 **Obv:** State emblem, denomination **Rev:** Bust 3/4 left, dates at left **Edge Lettering:** 20 Mark (repeated)

Date	Mintage	VF20	XF40	MS60	MS63	MS65
1982	40,000	—	—	18.00	30.00	55.00
1982	5,500	PF63 70.00	PF65 120			

KM# 94 20 MARK
20.92 g., 0.500 Silver 0.3363 oz. ASW, 33 mm. **Subject:** 500th Anniversary - Birth of Martin Luther, Reformer **Obv:** State emblem divides date, denomination below **Rev:** Bust holding bible looking left **Edge Lettering:** 20 Mark (repeated)

Date	Mintage	VF20	XF40	MS60	MS63	MS65
1983	45,000	—	—	110	180	315
1983	5,000	PF63 300	PF65 500			

KM# 95 20 MARK
Copper-Nickel, 33 mm. **Subject:** 100th Anniversary - Death of Karl Marx **Obv:** State emblem above inscription, date and denomination below **Rev:** Head 3/4 facing, name and dates below **Edge Lettering:** 20 Mark (repeated)

Date	Mintage	VF20	XF40	MS60	MS63	MS65
1983 A	995,000	—	—	3.00	5.00	12.00
1983 A	5,000	PF63 40.00	PF65 65.00			

KM# 100 20 MARK
20.92 g., 0.500 Silver 0.3363 oz. ASW, 33 mm. **Subject:** 225th Anniversary - Death of Georg Friedrich Händel, Composer **Obv:** State emblem, denomination **Rev:** Bust looking right, dates below **Edge Lettering:** 20 Mark (repeated)

Date	Mintage	VF20	XF40	MS60	MS63	MS65
1984 A	41,000	—	—	32.00	55.00	95.00
1984 A	4,500	PF63 120	PF65 200			

KM# 105 20 MARK
20.92 g., 0.500 Silver 0.3363 oz. ASW, 33 mm. **Subject:** 125th Anniversary - Death of Ernst Moritz Arndt, Poet and Reformer **Obv:** State emblem, denomination **Rev:** Bust 3/4 right divides dates **Edge Lettering:** 20 Mark (repeated)

Date	Mintage	VF20	XF40	MS60	MS63	MS65
1985 A	41,000	—	—	25.00	42,00	75.00
1985 A	4,000	PF63 110	PF65 185			

KM# 108 20 MARK
20.90 g., 0.625 Silver 0.420 oz. ASW, 33 mm. **Subject:** 200th Anniversary - Birth of Jacob and Wilhelm Grimm, Writers **Obv:** State emblem, denomination **Rev:** "Puss 'n Boots" divides dates **Edge Lettering:** 20 Mark (repeated)

Date	Mintage	VF20	XF40	MS60	MS63	MS65
1986 A	37,000	—	—	60.00	95.00	170
1986 A	3,500	PF63 225	PF65 375			

KM# 119.1 20 MARK
20.90 g., 0.625 Silver 0.420 oz. ASW, 33 mm. **Subject:** 700 Years Berlin - City Seal **Obv:** State emblem, denomination **Rev:** Helmeted shield with supporters within circle **Edge Lettering:** 20 Mark (repeated)

Date	Mintage	VF20	XF40	MS60	MS63	MS65
1987 A	42,000	—	—	85.00	145	240
1987 A	2,100	PF63 900	PF65 1,500			

Note: Seal on reverse totally frosted on proof coins

KM# 119.2 20 MARK
20.90 g., 0.625 Silver 0.420 oz. ASW, 33 mm. **Obv:** State emblem, denomination **Rev:** Fields in seal polished

Date	Mintage	VF20	XF40	MS60	MS63	MS65
1987 A	2,100	PF63 900	PF65 1,500			

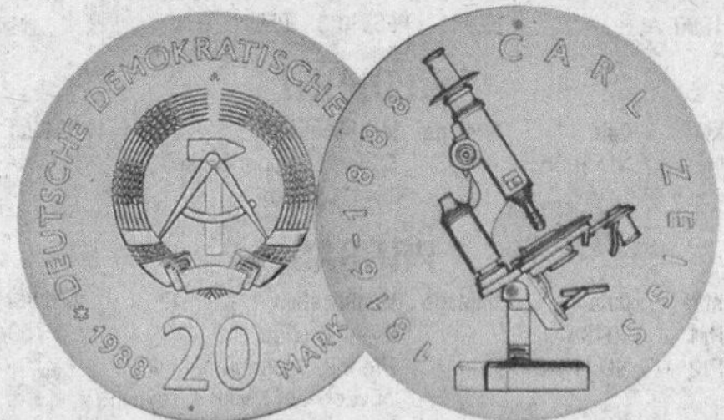

KM# 124 20 MARK
20.90 g., 0.625 Silver 0.420 oz. ASW, 33 mm. **Subject:** 100th Anniversary - Death of Carl Zeiss, Glass Scientist **Obv:** State emblem, denomination **Rev:** Microscope, dates at left **Edge Lettering:** 20 Mark (repeated)

Date	Mintage	VF20	XF40	MS60	MS63	MS65
1988 A	37,000	—	—	55.00	90.00	150
1988 A	3,500	PF63 225	PF65 375			

KM# 127 20 MARK
20.90 g., 0.625 Silver 0.420 oz. ASW, 33 mm. **Subject:** 500th Anniversary - Birth of Thomas Muntzer, Religious Reformer **Obv:** State emblem, denomination **Rev:** Head left divides dates **Edge Lettering:** 20 Mark (repeated)

Date	Mintage	VF20	XF40	MS60	MS63	MS65
1989 A	37,000	—	—	22.00	35.00	65.00
1989 A	3,500	PF63 150	PF65 250			

KM# 138 20 MARK
20.90 g., 0.625 Silver 0.420 oz. ASW, 33 mm. **Subject:** Andreas Schlüter **Obv:** State emblem, denomination **Rev:** Head right on decorative shield divides dates **Edge Lettering:** 20 Mark (repeated)

Date	Mintage	VF20	XF40	MS60	MS63	MS65
1990 A	37,000	—	—	27.00	45.00	75.00
1990 A	3,500	PF63 140	PF65 230			

KM# 139 20 MARK
Copper-Nickel, 33 mm. **Subject:** Opening of Brandenburg Gate **Obv:** State emblem, denomination **Rev:** Brandenburg Gate **Edge Lettering:** 20 Mark (repeated)

Date	Mintage	VF20	XF40	MS60	MS63	MS65
1990 A	300,000	—	—	3.00	5.00	10.00

KM# 139a 20 MARK
18.20 g., 0.999 Silver 0.5846 oz. ASW, 33 mm. **Subject:** Opening of Brandenburg Gate **Obv:** State emblem, denomination **Edge Lettering:** 20 Mark (repeated)

Date	Mintage	VF20	XF40	MS60	MS63	MS65
1990 A	145,000	—	—	7.50	12.00	22.00
1990 A	5,000	PF63 100	PF65 175			

PIEDFORT

KM#	Date	Mintage	Identification	Mkt Val
P1	ND-1985	—	5 Mark. Copper-Nickel-Zinc. KM#110, Unc.	—

PROBAS

KM#	Date	Mintage	Identification	Mkt Val
Pr1	1948A	—	Pfennig. Zinc.	1,750
Pr2	ND (1948)	—	Pfennig. Aluminum. Mule - obv: obv. of KM#8.1, rev: obverse of KM#5.	—
Pr3	ND-1967	—	10 Mark. Silver. Neubauer.	3,750
Pr4	1968A	—	5 Pfennig. Brass. KM#9.1.	—
Pr5	1968A	—	10 Pfennig. Brass Plated Steel. KM#10.1.	375
Pr6	1968A	—	50 Pfennig. Brass. KM#12.	475
Pr7	1968	—	20 Mark. 0.999. Gold. KM#21.	—
Pr8	ND-1969	—	20 Pfennig. Brass. Mule - 2 obverses of KM#11.	—
Pr9	1969	—	20 Pfennig. Nickel. KM#11.	—
Pr10	1969	12,741	5 Mark. Copper-Nickel-Zinc. PROBE.	150
Pr11	1972A	—	10 Pfennig. Steel. KM#10.1.	—
PrA12	1972A	—	2 Mark. Aluminum. KM#48.	—
Pr12	1973A	—	10 Mark. Copper-Nickel. Edge: 10 MARK* 10 MARK * 10 MARK *, KM#44.	350
Pr13	1974A	1,500	10 Mark. 0.500. Silver. KM#50.	750
Pr14	1974A	100	10 Mark. 0.625. Silver. Mintage numbered on lead seal, PROBE, KM#52.	7,500
Pr15	1975A	—	5 Pfennig. Nickel. KM#9.1,.	—
Pr16	1975	10,261	20 Mark. Silver. Incuse notes, Unc, KM#59.	175
Pr17	1975	Inc. above	20 Mark. Silver. Incuse notes, matte fields, proof, KM#59.	4,500
Pr18	1975	8,810	10 Mark. Silver. PROBE, KM#57.	150
PrA19	1976A	—	5 Pfennig. Aluminum. KM#9.2.	—
Pr19	ND-1977	6,000	10 Mark. Silver. State emblem, denomination. Ancient vacuum pump above horses, dates below. Guericke.	200
Pr20	1978A	100	10 Mark. Silver. KM#70.	—
Pr21	1979A	—	20 Mark. Copper-Nickel-Zinc. Obverse: PROBA instead of date, KM#75.	—
Pr22	1979A	10,000	20 Mark. Copper-Nickel-Zinc. Large denomination above state emblem. Dates above split leaf design.	75.00
Pr23	1981	Inc. below	10 Mark. 0.500. Silver. State emblem divides date, denomination below. Shields within inner circle form cross. PROBE on obverse, Unc.	2,000
Pr24	1981	2,250	10 Mark. 0.500. Silver. PROBE on obverse, Proof.	1,250
Pr25	1982A	—	5 Pfennig. Aluminum. Reeded edge, PROBA, KM#9.2.	375
Pr26	1982A	—	20 Pfennig. Brass Plated Steel. KM#11.	550
Pr27	1982A	210	5 Mark. Copper-Nickel-Zinc. House frosted on reverse, K#85, Proof.	6,000
Pr28	1982	90	20 Mark. Silver. State emblem, denomination. Head 1/4 right, dates at right. Countermark number of issue right of date, KM#88, Unc.	8,500
PrA29	1983A	—	5 Pfennig. Nickel. KM#9.2.	—
Pr29	1983A	100	10 Mark. Copper-Nickel-Zinc. Countermark PROBE and number on obverse, KM#93, Unc.	2,000
Pr30	1983	100	20 Mark. Copper-Nickel-Zinc. PROBE and number below date, KM#94, Unc.	3,750
Pr31	1983	100	20 Mark. Copper-Nickel-Zinc. PROBE and issue number left and right of denomination, KM#95, Unc.	3,500
Pr32	ND-1985	300	5 Mark. Copper-Nickel-Zinc. Incusely numbered, PROBA, Unc.	—
Pr33	1985A	112	10 Mark. Silver. Denomination above state emblem. Building within circle.	8,000
Pr34	1985A	50	10 Mark. Copper-Nickel-Zinc. Reverse large design size, KM#106, Unc.	5,000
Pr35	1985A	—	10 Mark. 0.500. Silver. KM#106, Unc.	—
Pr36	1985A	—	10 Mark. 0.500. Silver. KM#106, Proof.	12,500
Pr37	1985A	266	10 Mark. 0.333. Gold. Alloyed with silver, KM#16, Proof.	5,500
Pr38	1986A	—	Mark. Copper-Nickel-Zinc. PROBE, KM#35.	—
Pr39	1986A	—	2 Mark. Copper-Nickel-Zinc. PROBE, KM#48.	—
Pr40	1986A	110	5 Mark. Copper-Nickel-Zinc. P below tower, Unc.	—
Pr41	1986A	107	10 Mark. 0.500. Silver. P next to state emblem, KM#109, Unc.	3,000
Pr42	1988A	1,000	10 Mark. 0.500. Silver. P below value, KM#125, Proof.	1,100
Pr43	1988A	15	20 Mark. Silver. PROBE, large inscription, KM#124, Unc.	9,500
Pr44	1989A	—	10 Mark. 0.500. Silver. KM#132, Proof.	11,500

TRIAL STRIKES

KM#	Date	Mintage	Identification	Mkt Val
TS1	ND-1966	300	10 Mark. Aluminum. Uniface, Reverse of KM#15.	270
TS2	ND-1966	300	20 Mark. Aluminum. Uniface, Reverse of KM#16.	280
TS3	ND-1967	400	10 Mark. Aluminum. Uniface, Reverse of KM#17.	250
TS4	ND-1967	400	20 Mark. Aluminum. Uniface, Reverse of KM#18.	280
TS5	1968A	350	5 Mark. Aluminum. Uniface, Reverse of KM#19.	175
TS6	ND-1968	300	10 Mark. Aluminum. Uniface, Reverse of KM#20.	200
TS7	ND-1968	300	20 Mark. Aluminum. Uniface, Reverse of KM#21.	285
TS8	ND-1969	—	5 Mark. Nickel-Bronze. Uniface, obverse of KM#14, edge 5 MARK * 5 MARK * 5 MARK *.	—
TS9	ND-1969	350	5 Mark. Aluminum. Uniface, reverse of KM#23.	175
TS10	ND-1969	300	10 Mark. Aluminum. Uniface, reverse of KM#24.	200
TS11	ND-1969	300	20 Mark. Aluminum. Uniface, reverse of KM#25.	200
TS12	ND-1970	350	5 Mark. Aluminum. Uniface, reverse of KM#26.	175
TS13	ND-1970	300	10 Mark. Aluminum. Uniface, reverse of KM#27.	200
TS14	ND-1970	330	20 Mark. Aluminum. Uniface, reverse of KM#28.	225
TS15	ND-1971	450	5 Mark. Aluminum. Uniface, reverse of KM#30.	165
TS16	ND-1971	300	10 Mark. Aluminum. Uniface, reverse of KM#31.	225
TS17	ND-1971	410	20 Mark. Aluminum. Uniface, reverse of KM#32.	200
TS18	ND-1972	300	5 Mark. Aluminum. Uniface, reverse of KM#36.	175
TS19	ND-1972	300	10 Mark. Aluminum. Uniface, reverse of KM#39.	200
TS20	ND-1972	300	20 Mark. Aluminum. Uniface, reverse of KM#41.	225
TS21	ND-1973	300	5 Mark. Aluminum. Uniface, reverse of KM#43.	200
TS22	ND-1973	—	20 Mark. Copper-Nickel-Zinc. Uniface, reverse of KM#47.	—
TS23	ND-1973	—	20 Mark. Copper-Nickel-Zinc. Uniface, reverse with portrait within circular legend, KM#47.	—
TS24	ND-1975	306	10 Mark. Aluminum. Uniface, reverse of KM#56.	240
TS25	1979	—	20 Mark. Copper-Nickel-Zinc. Uniface, reverse of PR22.	—

MINT SETS

KM#	Date	Mintage	Identification	Issue Price	Mkt Val
MS1	1979A (8)	26,000	KM#8.2, 9.2, 10, 11, 12.2, 29, 35.2, 48	—	85.00
MS2	1980A (8)	25,000	KM#8.2, 9.2, 10, 11, 12.2, 35.2, 48	—	110
MS3	1981 (8)	25,000	KM#8.2, 9.2, 10, 11, 12.2, 29, 35.2, 48	—	90.00
MS4	1982 (8)	21,000	KM#8.2, 9.2, 10, 11, 12.2, 29, 35.2, 48	—	150
MS5	1982 (7)	4,500	KM#8.2, 9.2, 10, 11, 12.2, 35.2, 48	—	125
MS6	1983 (8)	19,000	KM#8.2, 9.2, 10, 11, 12.2, 35.2, 37, 48	—	235
MS7	1983 (7)	4,500	KM#8.2, 9.2, 10, 11, 12.2, 35.2, 48	—	150
MS8	1984 (8)	19,000	KM#8.2, 9.2, 10, 11, 12.2, 29, 35.2, 48	—	300
MS9	1984 (7)	4,500	KM#8.2, 9.2, 10, 11, 12.2, 35.2, 48	—	220
MS10	1985 (8)	6,000	KM#8.2, 9.2, 10, 11, 12.2, 35.2, 48, 102	—	135
MS11	1985 (7)	4,500	KM#8.2, 9.2, 10, 11, 12.2, 35.2, 48	—	85.00
MS12	1986 (8)	7,000	KM#8.2, 9.2, 10, 11, 12, 29, 35.2, 48	—	175
MS13	1986 (7)	4,500	KM#8.2, 9.2, 10, 11, 12.2, 35.2, 48	—	90.00
MS14	1987 (8)	8,000	KM#8.2, 9.2, 10, 11, 12.2, 29, 35.2, 48	—	115
MS15	1987 (7)	4,500	KM#8.2-10, 11-12.2, 35.2, 48	—	110
MSA16	1987 (4)	—	KM#29, 114-116	—	75.00
MS16	1988 (8)	11,000	KM#8.2-10, 11-12.2, 29, 35.2, 48	—	115
MS17	1988 (7)	4,500	KM#8.2, 9.2, 10, 11, 12.2, 35.2, 48	—	100
MS18	1989 (8)	11,000	KM8.2, 9.2, 10, 11, 12.2, 29, 35.2, 48	—	115
MS19	1989 (7)	4,500	KM#8.2, 9.2, 10, 11, 12.2, 35.2, 48	—	80.00
MS20	1990 (8)	11,000	KM#8.2, 9.2, 10, 11, 12.2, 29, 35.2, 48	—	220
MS21	1990 (7)	4,500	KM#8.2, 9.2, 10, 11, 12.2, 35.2, 48	—	185

PROOF SETS

KM#	Date	Mintage	Identification	Issue Price	Mkt Val
PS1	1981 (8)	20	KM#8.2, 9.2, 10, 11, 12.2, 35.2, 48, 79	—	—
PS2	1981 (8)	20	KM#8.2, 9.2, 10, 11, 12.2, 35.2, 37, 48	—	—
PS3	1982 (8)	2,500	KM#8.2, 9.2, 10, 11, 12.2, 29, 35.2, 48	—	375
PS4	1983 (8)	2,550	KM#8.2, 9.2, 10, 11, 12.2, 35.2, 37, 48	—	700
PS5	1984 (8)	3,015	KM#8.2, 9.2, 10, 11, 12.2, 29, 35.2, 48	—	200
PS6	1985 (8)	2,816	KM#8.2, 9.2, 10, 11, 12.2, 35.2, 48, 102	—	130
PS7	1986 (8)	2,800	KM#8.2, 9.2, 10, 11, 12.2, 29, 35.2, 48	—	200
PS8	1987 (8)	2,345	KM#8.2, 9.2, 10, 11, 12.2, 29, 35.2, 48	—	150
PS9	1988 (8)	2,300	KM#8.2, 9.2, 10, 11, 12.2, 28, 35.2, 48	—	180
PS10	1989 (8)	2,300	KM#8.2, 9.2, 10, 11, 12.2, 28, 35.2, 48	—	225

The Federal Republic of Germany, located in north-central Europe, has an area of 137,744 sq. mi. (356,910sq. km.) and a population of 81.1 million. Capital: Berlin. The economy centers about one of the world's foremost industrial establishments. Machinery, motor vehicles, iron, steel, yarns and fabrics are exported.

During the post-Normandy phase of World War II, Allied troops occupied the western German provinces of Schleswig-Holstein, Hamburg, Lower Saxony, Bremen, North Rhine-Westphalia, Hesse, Rhineland-Palatinate, Baden-Wurttemberg, Bavaria and Saarland. The conquered provinces were divided into American, British and French occupation zones. Five eastern German provinces were occupied and administered by the forces of the Soviet Union.

The post-World War II division of Germany was ended Oct. 3, 1990, when the German Democratic Republic (East Germany) ceased to exist and its five constituent provinces were formally admitted to the Federal Republic of Germany. An election Dec. 2, 1990, chose representatives to the united federal parliament (Bundestag), which then conducted its opening session in Berlin in the old Reichstag building. Berlin is again the capital of a United Germany.

MINT MARKS

A - Berlin
D - Munich
F - Stuttgart
G - Karlsruhe
J - Hamburg

MONETARY SYSTEM

100 Pfennig = 1 Deutsche Mark (DM)

FEDERAL REPUBLIC

STANDARD COINAGE

KM# A101 PFENNIG

2.00 g., Copper Plated Steel, 16.5 mm. **Obv:** Five oak leaves, date below **Obv. Legend:** BANK DEUTSCHER LÄNDER **Rev:** Denomination

Date	Mintage	F12	VF20	XF40	MS60	MS63
1948 D	46,325,000	—	0.50	15.00	40.00	45.00
1948 F	68,203,000	—	0.50	8.00	32.50	40.00
1948 F	250	**PF63** 150				
1948 G	45,604,000	—	0.50	15.00	60.00	75.00
1948 J	79,304,000	—	0.50	15.00	50.00	65.00
1949 D	99,863,000	—	0.50	6.00	27.50	35.00
1949 D	—	**PF63** 100				
1949 F	70,900,000	—	0.50	6.00	22.50	30.00
1949 F	250	**PF63** 60.00				
1949 G	70,950,000	—	0.50	10.00	40.00	45.00
1949 J	101,932,000	—	0.50	6.00	27.50	35.00
1949 J	—	**PF63** 85.00				

KM# 105 PFENNIG

2.00 g., Copper Plated Steel, 16.5 mm. **Obv:** Five oak leaves, date below **Obv. Legend:** BUNDESREPUBLIK DEUTSCHLAND **Rev:** Denomination

Date	Mintage	F12	VF20	XF40	MS60	MS63
1950 D	772,592,000	—	—	0.10	1.00	2.00
1950 F	898,277,000	—	—	0.10	1.00	2.00
1950 F	620	**PF63** 27.50				
1950 G	515,673,000	—	—	0.10	2.00	3.00
1950 G	1,800	**PF63** 5.00				
1950 J	784,424,000	—	—	0.10	1.00	2.00
1950 J	—	**PF63** 12.00				
1966 D	65,063,000	—	—	0.10	2.00	3.00
1966 F	75,031,000	—	—	0.10	2.00	3.00
1966 F	100	**PF65** 35.00				
1966 G	48,261,000	—	—	0.10	3.00	5.00
1966 G	3,070	**PF65** 4.00				
1966 J	66,842,000	—	—	0.10	2.00	3.00
1966 J	1,000	**PF65** 8.00				
1967 D	39,082,000	—	0.10	2.00	5.00	9.00
1967 F	45,003,000	—	0.10	1.50	4.00	8.00
1967 F	1,500	**PF65** 6.00				
1967 G	20,787,000	—	0.20	4.50	12.00	17.00
1967 G	4,500	**PF65** 3.50				
1967 J	42,583,000	—	0.10	1.50	4.00	8.00
1967 J	1,500	**PF65** 8.00				
1968 D	32,796,999	—	0.10	1.50	3.50	7.00
1968 F	26,338,000	—	0.10	1.50	3.50	7.00
1968 F	3,000	**PF65** 5.00				
1968 G	20,382,000	—	0.10	1.50	4.00	8.00
1968 G	6,023	**PF65** 4.00				
1968 J	23,414,000	—	0.10	1.50	4.00	8.00
1968 J	2,000	**PF65** 6.50				
1969 D	78,177,000	—	—	0.10	0.50	1.00
1969 F	90,172,000	—	—	0.10	0.50	1.00
1969 F	5,100	**PF65** 1.50				
1969 G	61,836,000	—	—	0.10	1.00	2.00
1969 G	8,700	**PF65** 1.25				
1969 J	80,221,000	—	—	0.10	0.50	1.00
1969 J	5,000	**PF65** 1.50				
1970 D	91,151,000	—	—	0.10	0.50	1.00
1970 F	105,236,000	—	—	0.10	0.50	1.00
1970 F	5,240	**PF65** 1.50				
1970 G	82,421,000	—	—	0.10	0.50	1.00
1970 G	10,200	**PF65** 1.00				
1970 Small J	93,455,000	—	—	0.10	0.50	1.00
1970 Large J	Inc. above	—	—	0.10	0.50	1.00
1970 J	5,000	**PF65** 1.50				
1971 D	116,612,000	—	—	0.10	0.50	1.00
1971 D	8,000	**PF65** 1.00				
1971 F	157,393,000	—	—	0.10	0.50	1.00
1971 F	8,000	**PF65** 1.00				
1971 G	77,674,000	—	—	0.10	1.00	2.00
1971 G	10,200	**PF65** 1.00				
1971 J	120,218,000	—	—	0.10	0.50	1.00
1971 J	8,000	**PF65** 1.00				
1972 D	90,696,000	—	—	0.10	0.25	0.50
1972 D	8,000	**PF65** 1.00				
1972 F	105,006,000	—	—	0.10	0.25	0.50
1972 F	8,000	**PF65** 1.00				
1972 G	60,660,000	—	—	0.10	0.25	0.50
1972 G	10,000	**PF65** 1.00				
1972 J	93,492,000	—	—	0.10	0.25	0.50
1972 J	8,000	**PF65** 1.00				
1973 D	38,976,000	—	—	0.10	0.25	0.50
1973 D	9,000	**PF65** 1.00				
1973 F	45,006,000	—	—	0.10	0.25	0.50
1973 F	9,000	**PF65** 1.00				
1973 G	25,811,000	—	—	0.10	0.25	0.50
1973 G	9,000	**PF65** 1.00				
1973 J	40,057,000	—	—	0.10	0.25	0.50
1973 J	9,000	**PF65** 1.00				
1974 D	90,951,000	—	—	0.10	0.25	0.50
1974 D	35,000	**PF65** 0.75				
1974 F	105,091,000	—	—	0.10	0.25	0.50
1974 F	35,000	**PF65** 0.70				
1974 G	60,548,000	—	—	0.10	0.25	0.50
1974 G	35,000	**PF65** 0.75				
1974 J	93,527,000	—	—	0.10	0.25	0.50
1974 J	35,000	**PF65** 0.70				
1975 D	91,053,000	—	—	0.10	0.25	0.50
1975 D	43,000	**PF65** 0.75				
1975 F	105,007,000	—	—	0.10	0.25	0.50
1975 F	43,000	**PF65** 0.75				
1975 G	60,704,000	—	—	0.10	0.25	0.50
1975 G	43,000	**PF65** 0.75				
1975 J	93,495,000	—	—	0.10	0.25	0.50
1975 J	43,000	**PF65** 0.75				
1976 D	130,227,000	—	—	0.10	0.25	0.50
1976 D	43,000	**PF65** 0.75				
1976 F	150,037,000	—	—	0.10	0.25	0.50
1976 F	43,000	**PF65** 0.75				
1976 G	86,586,000	—	—	0.10	0.25	0.50
1976 G	43,000	**PF65** 0.75				
1976 J	133,500,000	—	—	0.10	0.25	0.50
1976 J	43,000	**PF65** 0.75				
1977 D	143,000,000	—	—	0.10	0.25	0.50
1977 D	52,000	**PF65** 0.75				
1977 F	165,000,000	—	—	0.10	0.25	0.50
1977 F	51,000	**PF65** 0.75				
1977 G	95,201,000	—	—	0.10	0.25	0.50
1977 G	51,000	**PF65** 0.75				
1977 J	146,788,000	—	—	0.10	0.25	0.50
1977 J	51,000	**PF65** 0.75				
1978 D	156,000,000	—	—	0.10	0.25	0.50
1978 D	54,000	**PF65** 0.75				
1978 F	180,000,000	—	—	0.10	0.25	0.50
1978 F	54,000	**PF65** 0.75				
1978 G	103,800,000	—	—	0.10	0.25	0.50
1978 G	54,000	**PF65** 0.75				
1978 J	160,200,000	—	—	0.10	0.25	0.50
1978 J	54,000	**PF65** 0.75				
1979 D	156,000,000	—	—	0.10	0.25	0.50
1979 D	89,000	**PF65** 0.75				
1979 F	180,000,000	—	—	0.10	0.25	0.50
1979 F	89,000	**PF65** 0.75				
1979 G	103,800,000	—	—	0.10	0.25	0.50
1979 G	89,000	**PF65** 0.75				
1979 J	160,200,000	—	—	0.10	0.25	0.50
1979 J	89,000	**PF65** 0.75				
1980 D	200,080,000	—	—	0.10	0.25	0.50
1980 D	110,000	**PF65** 0.75				
1980 F	200,620,000	—	—	0.10	0.25	0.50
1980 F	110,000	**PF65** 0.75				
1980 G	71,940,000	—	—	0.10	0.25	0.50
1980 G	110,000	**PF65** 0.75				
1980 J	143,110,000	—	—	0.10	0.25	0.50
1980 J	110,000	**PF65** 0.75				
1981 D	169,550,000	—	—	0.10	0.25	0.50
1981 D	91,000	**PF65** 0.75				
1981 F	274,010,000	—	—	0.10	0.25	0.50
1981 F	91,000	**PF65** 0.75				
1981 G	178,010,000	—	—	0.10	0.25	0.50
1981 G	91,000	**PF65** 0.75				
1981 J	189,090,000	—	—	0.10	0.25	0.50
1981 J	91,000	**PF65** 0.75				
1982 D	130,090,000	—	—	0.10	0.20	0.40
1982 D	78,000	**PF65** 0.60				
1982 F	108,390,000	—	—	0.10	0.20	0.40
1982 F	78,000	**PF65** 0.60				
1982 G	77,740,000	—	—	0.10	0.20	0.40
1982 G	78,000	**PF65** 0.60				
1982 J	124,720,000	—	—	0.10	0.20	0.40
1982 J	78,000	**PF65** 0.60				
1983 D	46,800,000	—	—	0.10	0.20	0.40
1983 D	75,000	**PF65** 0.60				
1983 F	54,000,000	—	—	0.10	0.20	0.40
1983 F	75,000	**PF65** 0.60				
1983 G	31,140,000	—	—	0.10	0.20	0.40
1983 G	75,000	**PF65** 0.60				
1983 J	48,060,000	—	—	0.10	0.20	0.40
1983 J	75,000	**PF65** 0.60				
1984 D	58,500,000	—	—	0.10	0.20	0.40
1984 D	64,000	**PF65** 0.60				
1984 F	67,500,000	—	—	0.10	0.20	0.40
1984 F	64,000	**PF65** 0.60				
1984 G	38,900,000	—	—	0.10	0.20	0.40
1984 G	64,000	**PF65** 0.60				
1984 J	60,100,000	—	—	0.10	0.20	0.40
1984 J	64,000	**PF65** 0.60				
1985 D	19,500,000	—	—	0.10	0.20	0.40
1985 D	56,000	**PF65** 0.60				
1985 F	22,500,000	—	—	0.10	0.20	0.40
1985 F	54,000	**PF65** 0.40				
1985 G	13,000,000	—	—	—	0.10	0.20
1985 G	55,000	**PF65** 0.40				
1985 J	20,000,000	—	—	—	0.10	0.20
1985 J	54,000	**PF65** 0.40				
1986 D	39,000,000	—	—	—	0.10	0.20
1986 D	44,000	**PF65** 0.40				
1986 F	45,000,000	—	—	—	0.10	0.20
1986 F	44,000	**PF65** 0.40				
1986 G	25,900,000	—	—	—	0.10	0.20
1986 G	44,000	**PF65** 0.40				
1986 J	40,100,000	—	—	—	0.10	0.20
1986 J	44,000	**PF65** 0.40				
1987 D	6,500,000	—	—	—	0.10	0.20
1987 D	45,000	**PF65** 0.40				
1987 F	7,500,000	—	—	—	0.10	0.20
1987 F	45,000	**PF65** 0.40				
1987 G	4,330,000	—	—	—	0.10	0.20
1987 G	45,000	**PF65** 0.40				
1987 J	6,680,000	—	—	—	0.10	0.20
1987 J	45,000	**PF65** 0.40				
1988 D	52,000,000	—	—	—	0.10	0.20
1988 D	45,000	**PF65** 0.40				
1988 F	60,000,000	—	—	—	0.10	0.20
1988 F	45,000	**PF65** 0.40				
1988 G	34,600,000	—	—	—	0.10	0.20
1988 G	45,000	**PF65** 0.40				
1988 J	53,400,000	—	—	—	0.10	0.20
1988 J	45,000	**PF65** 0.40				
1989 D	104,000,000	—	—	—	0.10	0.20
1989 D	45,000	**PF65** 0.40				
1989 F	120,000,000	—	—	—	0.10	0.20
1989 F	45,000	**PF65** 0.40				
1989 G	69,200,000	—	—	—	0.10	0.20
1989 G	45,000	**PF65** 0.40				
1989 J	106,800,000	—	—	—	0.10	0.20
1989 J	45,000	**PF65** 0.40				
1990 D	169,000,000	—	—	—	0.10	0.20

Date	Mintage	F12	VF20	XF40	MS60	MS63
1990 D	45,000	PF65 0.40				
1990 F	195,000,000	—	—	—	0.10	0.20
1990 F	45,000	PF65 0.40				
1990 G	112,450,000	—	—	—	0.10	0.20
1990 G	45,000	PF65 0.40				
1990 J	173,550,000	—	—	—	0.10	0.20
1990 J	45,000	PF65 0.40				
1991 A	260,000,000	—	—	—	0.10	0.20
1991 A	45,000	PF65 0.40				
1991 D	273,000,000	—	—	—	0.10	0.20
1991 D	45,000	PF65 0.40				
1991 F	312,000,000	—	—	—	0.10	0.20
1991 F	45,000	PF65 0.40				
1991 G	182,000,000	—	—	—	0.10	0.20
1991 G	45,000	PF65 0.40				
1991 J	273,000,000	—	—	—	0.10	0.20
1991 J	45,000	PF65 0.40				
1992 A	40,000,000	—	—	—	0.10	0.20
1992 A	45,000	PF65 0.40				
1992 D	42,000,000	—	—	—	0.10	0.20
1992 D	45,000	PF65 0.40				
1992 F	48,000,000	—	—	—	0.10	0.20
1992 F	45,000	PF65 0.40				
1992 G	28,000,000	—	—	—	0.10	0.20
1992 G	45,000	PF65 0.40				
1992 J	42,000,000	—	—	—	0.10	0.20
1992 J	45,000	PF65 0.40				
1993 A	40,000,000	—	—	—	0.10	0.20
1993 A	45,000	PF65 0.40				
1993 D	42,000,000	—	—	—	0.10	0.20
1993 D	45,000	PF65 0.40				
1993 F	48,000,000	—	—	—	0.10	0.20
1993 F	45,000	PF65 0.40				
1993 G	28,000,000	—	—	—	0.10	0.20
1993 G	45,000	PF65 0.40				
1993 J	42,000,000	—	—	—	0.10	0.20
1993 J	45,000	PF65 0.40				
1994 A	100,000,000	—	—	—	0.10	0.20
1994 A	45,000	PF65 0.40				
1994 D	105,000,000	—	—	—	0.10	0.20
1994 D	45,000	PF65 0.40				
1994 F	120,000,000	—	—	—	0.10	0.20
1994 F	45,000	PF65 0.40				
1994 G	70,000,000	—	—	—	0.10	0.20
1994 G	45,000	PF65 0.40				
1994 J	105,000,000	—	—	—	0.10	0.20
1994 J	45,000	PF65 0.40				
1995 A	100,000,000	—	—	—	0.15	0.25
1995 A	45,000	PF65 0.45				
1995 D	105,000,000	—	—	—	0.15	0.25
1995 D	45,000	PF65 0.45				
1995 F	120,000,000	—	—	—	0.15	0.25
1995 F	45,000	PF65 0.45				
1995 G	70,000,000	—	—	—	0.15	0.25
1995 G	45,000	PF65 0.45				
1995 J	105,000,000	—	—	—	0.15	0.25
1995 J	45,000	PF65 0.45				
1996 A	80,000,000	—	—	—	0.20	0.30
1996 A	45,000	PF65 0.50				
1996 D	84,000,000	—	—	—	0.20	0.30
1996 D	45,000	PF65 0.50				
1996 F	96,000,000	—	—	—	0.20	0.30
1996 F	45,000	PF65 0.50				
1996 G	56,000,000	—	—	—	0.20	0.30
1996 G	45,000	PF65 0.50				
1996 J	84,000,000	—	—	—	0.20	0.30
1996 J	45,000	PF65 0.50				
1997 A Sets only	70,000	—	—	—	—	1.75
1997 A	45,000	PF65 2.00				
1997 D Sets only	70,000	—	—	—	—	1.75
1997 D	45,000	PF65 2.00				
1997 F Sets only	70,000	—	—	—	—	1.75
1997 F	45,000	PF65 2.00				
1997 G Sets only	70,000	—	—	—	—	1.75
1997 G	45,000	PF65 2.00				
1997 J Sets only	70,000	—	—	—	—	1.75
1997 J	45,000	PF65 2.00				
1998 A Sets only	70,000	—	—	—	—	1.75
1998 A	45,000	PF65 2.00				
1998 D Sets only	70,000	—	—	—	—	1.75
1998 D	45,000	PF65 2.00				
1998 F Sets only	70,000	—	—	—	—	1.75
1998 F	—	PF65 2.00				
1998 G Sets only	70,000	—	—	—	—	1.75
1998 G	45,000	PF65 2.00				
1998 J Sets only	70,000	—	—	—	—	1.75
1998 J	45,000	PF65 2.00				
1999 A Sets only	70,000	—	—	—	—	1.75
1999 A	45,000	PF65 2.00				
1999 D Sets only	70,000	—	—	—	—	1.75
1999 D	45,000	PF65 2.00				
1999 F Sets only	70,000	—	—	—	—	1.75
1999 F	—	PF65 2.00				
1999 G Sets only	70,000	—	—	—	—	1.75
1999 G	45,000	PF65 2.00				
1999 J Sets only	70,000	—	—	—	—	1.75
1999 J	45,000	PF65 2.00				
2000 A Sets only	20,000	—	—	—	—	1.75
2000 A	45,000	PF65 2.00				
2000 D Sets only	20,000	—	—	—	—	1.75
2000 D	45,000	PF65 2.00				
2000 F Sets only	20,000	—	—	—	—	1.75
2000 F	45,000	PF65 2.00				
2000 G Sets only	20,000	—	—	—	—	1.75
2000 G	45,000	PF65 2.00				
2000 J Sets only	20,000	—	—	—	—	1.75
2000 J	45,000	PF65 2.00				

KM# 106 2 PFENNIG

3.25 g., Bronze, 19.25 mm. **Obv:** Five oak leaves, date below **Rev:** Denomination

Date	Mintage	F12	VF20	XF40	MS60	MS63
1950 D	26,263,000	—	0.10	2.50	10.00	12.00
1950 D	—	PF63 50.00				
1950 F	30,278,000	—	0.10	2.00	8.00	10.00
1950 F Proof	200	—	—	—	—	—
1950 G	17,151,000	—	0.10	2.50	10.00	12.50
1950 G	—	PF63 90.00				
1950 J	27,216,000	—	0.10	2.50	10.00	12.00
1950 J	—	PF63 40.00				
1958 D	19,440,000	—	0.10	3.00	12.00	14.00
1958 F	24,122,000	—	0.10	2.00	8.00	10.00
1958 F Proof	100	—	—	—	—	—
1958 G	15,255,000	—	0.10	4.00	16.00	18.00
1958 J	21,250,000	—	0.10	2.00	8.00	10.00
1959 D	19,690,000	—	0.10	2.00	8.00	10.00
1959 F	25,017,000	—	0.10	1.50	8.00	10.00
1959 F Proof	75	—	—	—	—	—
1959 G	12,899,000	—	0.10	3.00	12.00	14.00
1959 J	25,482,000	—	0.10	2.00	8.00	10.00
1960 D	21,979,000	—	0.10	1.50	7.00	9.00
1960 F	13,060,000	—	—	0.10	8.00	10.00
1960 F Proof	75	—	—	—	—	—
1960 G	5,657,000	—	0.10	2.00	16.00	18.00
1960 J	17,799,000	—	0.10	2.00	8.00	10.00
1961 D	26,662,000	—	0.10	1.50	7.00	9.00
1961 F	24,990,000	—	0.10	1.50	6.00	8.00
1961 G	18,060,000	—	0.10	1.50	7.00	9.00
1961 J	22,147,000	—	0.10	1.50	6.00	8.00
1962 D	21,297,000	—	0.10	1.50	7.00	9.00
1962 F	42,189,000	—	0.10	1.00	4.00	6.00
1962 G	17,297,000	—	0.10	2.00	10.00	12.00
1962 J	30,706,000	—	0.10	1.00	6.00	8.00
1963 D	7,648,000	—	0.10	2.00	8.00	10.00
1963 F	18,299,000	—	0.10	1.50	7.00	9.00
1963 G	35,838,000	—	0.10	1.50	6.00	8.00
1963 G Proof		—	—	—	—	—
1963 J	42,884,000	—	0.10	1.50	4.00	6.00
1964 D	20,336,000	—	0.10	1.50	8.00	10.00
1964 F	31,400,000	—	0.10	1.50	5.00	7.00
1964 G	18,431,000	—	0.10	1.50	6.00	8.00
1964 G	Est. 600	PF65 12.00				
1964 J	13,370,000	—	0.10	1.50	6.00	8.00
1965 D	48,541,000	—	0.10	1.00	2.00	4.00
1965 F	27,000,000	—	0.10	1.00	4.00	6.00
1965 F	Est. 80	PF65 70.00				
1965 G	13,584,000	—	0.10	1.50	5.00	7.00
1965 G	1,200	PF65 5.00				
1965 J	33,397,000	—	0.10	1.00	2.00	4.00
1966 D	65,077,000	—	—	0.50	1.00	3.00
1966 F	52,543,000	—	—	0.50	1.00	3.00
1966 F	100	PF65 80.00				
1966 G	40,804,000	—	—	0.50	1.00	3.00
1966 G	3,070	PF65 5.50				
1966 J	46,754,000	—	—	0.50	1.00	3.00
1966 J	1,000	PF65 40.00				
1967 D	25,997,000	—	0.10	1.00	4.00	6.00
1967 F	30,004,000	—	0.10	1.00	3.00	5.00
1967 F	1,500	PF65 7.00				
1967 G	6,280,000	—	0.10	1.50	8.00	10.00
1967 G	4,500	PF65 4.50				
1967 J	26,725,000	—	0.10	1.00	4.00	6.00
1967 J	1,500	PF65 10.00				
1968 D	19,523,000	—	0.10	1.00	3.00	5.00
1968 G	15,357,000	—	0.10	1.00	4.00	6.00
1968 G	3,651	PF65 4.00				
1968 J	—	—	200	350	500	650

Note: A 1968J error of 1963J exists with coin alignment

Date	Mintage	F12	VF20	XF40	MS60	MS63
1969 J	—	—	200	350	500	650

KM# 106a 2 PFENNIG

2.90 g., Copper Plated Steel, 19.25 mm. **Obv:** Five oak leaves, date below **Rev:** Denomination

Date	Mintage	F12	VF20	XF40	MS60	MS63
1967 G	520	PF65 950				
1968 D	19,523,000	—	—	0.50	1.25	2.50
1968 F	30,000,000	—	—	0.50	1.25	2.50
1968 F	3,000	PF65 6.00				
1968 G	13,004,000	—	—	0.50	1.25	2.50
1968 G	2,372	PF65 4.00				
1968 J	20,026,000	—	—	0.25	1.00	2.00
1968 J	2,000	PF65 7.50				
1969 D	39,012,000	—	—	0.25	0.50	1.00
1969 D	—	PF65 1.25				
1969 F	45,029,000	—	—	0.25	0.50	1.00
1969 F	5,100	PF65 1.25				
1969 G	32,156,999	—	—	0.25	0.50	1.00
1969 G	8,700	PF65 1.25				
1969 J	40,102,000	—	—	0.25	0.50	1.00
1969 J	5,000	PF65 2.50				
1970 D	45,525,000	—	—	0.10	0.25	0.50
1970 F	73,851,000	—	—	0.10	0.25	0.50
1970 F	5,140	PF65 1.25				
1970 G	30,330,000	—	—	0.10	0.25	0.50
1970 G	10,200	PF65 1.25				
1970 Small J	46,730,000	—	—	0.10	0.25	0.50
1970 Large J	Inc. above	—	—	0.10	0.25	0.50
1970 J	5,000	PF65 1.75				
1971 D	71,755,000	—	—	0.10	0.25	0.50
1971 D	8,000	PF65 1.25				
1971 F	82,765,000	—	—	0.10	0.25	0.50
1971 F	8,000	PF65 1.25				
1971 G	47,850,000	—	—	0.10	0.25	0.50
1971 G	10,000	PF65 1.25				
1971 J	73,641,000	—	—	0.10	0.25	0.50
1971 J	8,000	PF65 1.25				
1972 D	52,403,000	—	—	0.10	0.25	0.50
1972 D	8,000	PF65 1.00				
1972 F	60,272,000	—	—	0.10	0.25	0.50
1972 F	8,000	PF65 1.00				
1972 G	34,864,000	—	—	0.10	0.25	0.50
1972 G	10,000	PF65 1.00				
1972 J	53,673,000	—	—	0.10	0.25	0.50
1972 J	8,000	PF65 1.00				
1973 D	26,190,000	—	—	0.10	0.25	0.50
1973 D	9,000	PF65 1.00				
1973 F	30,160,000	—	—	0.10	0.25	0.50
1973 F	9,000	PF65 1.00				
1973 G	17,379,000	—	—	0.10	0.25	0.50
1973 G	9,000	PF65 1.00				
1973 J	26,830,000	—	—	0.10	0.25	0.50
1973 J	9,000	PF65 1.00				
1974 D	58,667,000	—	—	0.10	0.25	0.35
1974 D	35,000	PF65 0.50				
1974 F	67,596,000	—	—	0.10	0.25	0.35
1974 F	35,000	PF65 0.50				
1974 G	39,007,000	—	—	0.10	0.25	0.35
1974 G	35,000	PF65 0.50				
1974 J	60,195,000	—	—	0.10	0.25	0.35
1974 J	35,000	PF65 0.50				
1975 D	58,634,000	—	—	0.10	0.25	0.35
1975 D	43,000	PF65 0.50				
1975 F	67,685,000	—	—	0.10	0.25	0.35
1975 F	43,000	PF65 0.50				
1975 G	39,391,000	—	—	0.10	0.25	0.35
1975 G	43,000	PF65 0.50				
1975 J	60,207,000	—	—	0.10	0.25	0.35
1975 J	43,000	PF65 0.50				
1976 D	78,074,000	—	—	0.10	0.25	0.35
1976 D	43,000	PF65 0.50				
1976 F	90,130,000	—	—	0.10	0.25	0.35
1976 F	43,000	PF65 0.50				
1976 G	51,988,000	—	—	0.10	0.25	0.35
1976 G	43,000	PF65 0.50				
1976 J	80,145,000	—	—	0.10	0.25	0.35
1976 J	43,000	PF65 0.50				
1977 D	84,516,000	—	—	0.10	0.20	0.30
1977 D	51,000	PF65 0.40				
1977 F	97,504,000	—	—	0.10	0.20	0.30
1977 F	51,000	PF65 0.40				
1977 G	56,276,000	—	—	0.10	0.20	0.30
1977 G	51,000	PF65 0.40				
1977 J	86,888,000	—	—	0.10	0.20	0.30
1977 J	51,000	PF65 0.40				
1978 D	84,500,000	—	—	0.10	0.20	0.30
1978 D	54,000	PF65 0.40				
1978 F	97,500,000	—	—	0.10	0.20	0.30
1978 F	54,000	PF65 0.40				
1978 G	56,225,000	—	—	0.10	0.20	0.30
1978 G	54,000	PF65 0.40				

Date	Mintage	F12	VF20	XF40	MS60	MS63
1978 J	86,775,000	—	—	0.10	0.20	0.30
1978 J	54,000	PF65 0.40				
1979 D	91,000,000	—	—	0.10	0.20	0.30
1979 D	89,000	PF65 0.40				
1979 F	105,000,000	—	—	0.10	0.20	0.30
1979 F	89,000	PF65 0.40				
1979 G	60,550,000	—	—	0.10	0.20	0.30
1979 G	89,000	PF65 0.40				
1979 J	93,480,000	—	—	0.10	0.20	0.30
1979 J	89,000	PF65 0.40				
1980 D	93,360,000	—	—	0.10	0.20	0.30
1980 D	110,000	PF65 0.40				
1980 F	120,360,000	—	—	0.10	0.20	0.30
1980 F	110,000	PF65 0.40				
1980 G	50,830,000	—	—	0.10	0.20	0.30
1980 G	110,000	PF65 0.40				
1980 J	102,260,000	—	—	0.10	0.20	0.30
1980 J	110,000	PF65 0.40				
1981 D	93,910,000	—	—	0.10	0.20	0.30
1981 D	91,000	PF65 0.40				
1981 F	83,710,000	—	—	0.10	0.20	0.30
1981 F	91,000	PF65 0.40				
1981 G	89,850,000	—	—	0.10	0.20	0.30
1981 G	91,000	PF65 0.40				
1981 J	87,250,000	—	—	0.10	0.20	0.30
1981 J	91,000	PF65 0.40				
1982 D	64,390,000	—	—	0.10	0.20	0.30
1982 D	78,000	PF65 0.40				
1982 F	36,870,000	—	—	0.10	0.20	0.30
1982 F	78,000	PF65 0.40				
1982 G	58,590,000	—	—	0.10	0.20	0.30
1982 G	78,000	PF65 0.40				
1982 J	57,690,000	—	—	0.10	0.20	0.30
1982 J	78,000	PF65 0.40				
1983 D	71,500,000	—	—	0.10	0.20	0.30
1983 D	75,000	PF65 0.40				
1983 F	82,500,000	—	—	0.10	0.20	0.30
1983 F	75,000	PF65 0.40				
1983 G	47,575,000	—	—	0.10	0.20	0.30
1983 G	75,000	PF65 0.40				
1983 J	73,425,000	—	—	0.10	0.20	0.30
1983 J	75,000	PF65 0.40				
1984 D	58,500,000	—	—	0.10	0.20	0.30
1984 D	64,000	PF65 0.40				
1984 F	67,500,000	—	—	0.10	0.20	0.30
1984 F	64,000	PF65 0.40				
1984 G	38,900,000	—	—	0.10	0.20	0.30
1984 G	64,000	PF65 0.40				
1984 J	60,100,000	—	—	0.10	0.20	0.30
1984 J	64,000	PF65 0.40				
1985 D	19,500,000	—	0.10	1.00	2.00	3.00
1985 D	56,000	PF65 0.40				
1985 F	22,500,000	—	0.25	1.00	2.00	3.00
1985 F	54,000	PF65 0.40				
1985 G	13,000,000	0.25	0.75	2.50	5.00	8.00
1985 G	55,000	PF65 0.40				
1985 J	20,000,000	0.25	0.50	2.00	4.00	7.00
1985 J	54,000	PF65 0.40				
1986 D	39,000,000	—	—	—	0.25	0.35
1986 D	44,000	PF65 0.40				
1986 F	45,000,000	—	—	—	0.25	0.35
1986 F	44,000	PF65 0.40				
1986 G	25,900,000	—	—	—	0.25	0.35
1986 G	44,000	PF65 0.40				
1986 J	40,100,000	—	—	—	0.25	0.35
1986 J	44,000	PF65 0.40				
1987 D	6,500,000	0.50	1.00	2.50	3.50	5.00
1987 D	45,000	PF65 0.40				
1987 F	7,500,000	0.50	1.00	2.50	3.50	5.00
1987 F	45,000	PF65 0.40				
1987 G	4,330,000	0.75	1.25	2.75	4.00	6.00
1987 G	45,000	PF65 0.40				
1987 J	6,680,000	0.50	1.00	2.50	3.50	5.00
1987 J	45,000	PF65 0.40				
1988 D	52,000,000	—	—	—	0.25	0.35
1988 D	45,000	PF65 0.40				
1988 F	60,000,000	—	—	—	0.25	0.35
1988 F	45,000	PF65 0.40				
1988 G	34,600,000	—	—	—	0.25	0.35
1988 G	45,000	PF65 0.40				
1988 J	53,400,000	—	—	—	0.25	0.35
1988 J	45,000	PF65 0.40				
1989 D	52,000,000	—	—	—	0.25	0.35
1989 D	45,000	PF65 0.40				
1989 F	60,000,000	—	—	—	0.25	0.35
1989 F	45,000	PF65 0.40				
1989 G	34,600,000	—	—	—	0.25	0.35
1989 G	45,000	PF65 0.40				
1989 J	53,400,000	—	—	—	0.25	0.35
1989 J	45,000	PF65 0.40				
1990 D	71,500,000	—	—	—	0.25	0.35
1990 D	45,000	PF65 0.40				
1990 F	82,500,000	—	—	—	0.25	0.35
1990 F	45,000	PF65 0.40				
1990 G	47,570,000	—	—	—	0.25	0.35
1990 G	45,000	PF65 0.40				
1990 J	73,420,000	—	—	—	0.25	0.35
1990 J	45,000	PF65 0.40				
1991 A	115,000,000	—	—	—	0.25	0.35
1991 A	45,000	PF65 0.40				
1991 D	120,750,000	—	—	—	0.25	0.35
1991 D	45,000	PF65 0.40				
1991 F	138,000,000	—	—	—	0.25	0.35
1991 F	45,000	PF65 0.40				
1991 G	80,500,000	—	—	—	0.25	0.35
1991 G	45,000	PF65 0.40				
1991 J	120,750,000	—	—	—	0.25	0.35
1991 J	45,000	PF65 0.40				
1992 A	60,000,000	—	—	—	0.25	0.35
1992 A	45,000	PF65 0.40				
1992 D	63,000,000	—	—	—	0.25	0.35
1992 D	45,000	PF65 0.40				
1992 F	72,000,000	—	—	—	0.25	0.35
1992 F	45,000	PF65 0.40				
1992 G	42,000,000	—	—	—	0.25	0.35
1992 G	45,000	PF65 0.40				
1992 J	63,000,000	—	—	—	0.25	0.35
1992 J	45,000	PF65 0.40				
1993 A	10,000,000	—	0.25	1.00	2.00	4.00
1993 A	45,000	PF65 0.40				
1993 D	10,500,000	—	0.25	1.00	2.00	4.00
1993 D	45,000	PF65 0.40				
1993 F	12,000,000	—	0.25	1.00	2.00	4.00
1993 F	45,000	PF65 0.40				
1993 G	7,000,000	—	0.25	1.00	2.00	4.00
1993 G	45,000	PF65 0.40				
1993 J	10,000,000	—	0.25	1.00	2.00	4.00
1993 J	45,000	PF65 0.40				
1994 A	55,000,000	—	—	—	0.15	0.25
1994 A	45,000	PF65 0.40				
1994 D	57,750,000	—	—	—	0.15	0.25
1994 D	45,000	PF65 0.40				
1994 F	66,000,000	—	—	—	0.15	0.25
1994 F	45,000	PF65 0.40				
1994 G	38,500,000	—	—	—	0.25	0.35
1994 G	45,000	PF65 0.40				
1994 J	57,750,000	—	—	—	0.15	0.25
1994 J	45,000	PF65 0.40				
1995 A	1,000,000,000	—	—	—	0.15	0.25
1995 A	45,000	PF65 0.45				
1995 D	105,000,000	—	—	—	0.15	0.25
1995 D	45,000	PF65 0.45				
1995 F	120,000,000	—	—	—	0.15	0.25
1995 F	45,000	PF65 0.45				
1995 G	70,000,000	—	—	—	0.25	0.35
1995 G	45,000	PF65 0.45				
1995 J	105,000,000	—	—	—	0.15	0.25
1995 J	45,000	PF65 0.45				
1996 A	40,000,000	—	—	—	0.20	0.30
1996 A	45,000	PF65 0.50				
1996 D	42,000,000	—	—	—	0.20	0.30
1996 D	45,000	PF65 0.50				
1996 F	48,000,000	—	—	—	0.20	0.30
1996 F	45,000	PF65 0.50				
1996 G	28,000,000	—	—	—	0.25	0.35
1996 G	45,000	PF65 0.50				
1996 J	42,000,000	—	—	—	0.20	0.30
1996 J	45,000	PF65 0.50				
1997 A Sets only	70,000	—	—	—	—	1.75
1997 A	45,000	PF65 2.00				
1997 D Sets only	70,000	—	—	—	—	1.75
1997 D	45,000	PF65 2.00				
1997 F Sets only	70,000	—	—	—	—	1.75
1997 F	45,000	PF65 2.00				
1997 G Sets only	70,000	—	—	—	—	1.75
1997 G	45,000	PF65 2.00				
1997 J Sets only	70,000	—	—	—	—	1.75
1997 J	45,000	PF65 2.00				
1998 A Sets only	70,000	—	—	—	—	1.75
1998 A	45,000	PF65 2.00				
1998 D Sets only	70,000	—	—	—	—	1.75
1998 D	45,000	PF65 2.00				
1998 F Sets only	70,000	—	—	—	—	1.75
1998 F	45,000	PF65 2.00				
1998 G Sets only	70,000	—	—	—	—	1.75
1998 G	45,000	PF65 2.00				
1998 J Sets only	70,000	—	—	—	—	1.75
1998 J	45,000	PF65 2.00				
1999 A Sets only	70,000	—	—	—	—	1.75
1999 A	45,000	PF65 2.00				
1999 D Sets only	70,000	—	—	—	—	1.75
1999 D	45,000	PF65 2.00				
1999 F Sets only	70,000	—	—	—	—	1.75
1999 F	45,000	PF65 2.00				
1999 G Sets only	70,000	—	—	—	—	1.75
1999 G	45,000	PF65 2.00				
1999 J Sets only	70,000	—	—	—	—	1.75
1999 J	45,000	PF65 2.00				
2000 A Sets only	70,000	—	—	—	—	1.75
2000 A	45,000	PF65 2.00				
2000 D Sets only	70,000	—	—	—	—	1.75
2000 D	45,000	PF65 2.00				
2000 F Sets only	70,000	—	—	—	—	1.75
2000 F	45,000	PF65 2.00				
2000 G Sets only	70,000	—	—	—	—	1.75
2000 G	45,000	PF65 2.00				
2000 J Sets only	70,000	—	—	—	—	1.75
2000 J	45,000	PF65 2.00				

KM# 102 5 PFENNIG

3.00 g., Brass Clad Steel, 18.5 mm. **Obv:** Five oak leaves, date below **Obv. Legend:** BANK DEUTSCHER LÄNDER **Rev:** Denomination

Date	Mintage	F12	VF20	XF40	MS60	MS63
1949 D	60,026,000	0.25	1.00	10.00	45.00	50.00
1949 D	—	PF63 150				
1949 F	66,081,999	0.25	1.00	7.50	35.00	40.00
1949 F	250	PF63 85.00				
1949 G	57,356,000	0.25	1.50	12.50	50.00	55.00
1949 J	68,977,000	0.25	1.00	10.00	40.00	45.00
1949 J	—	PF63 85.00				

KM# 107 5 PFENNIG

3.00 g., Brass Clad Steel, 18.5 mm. **Obv:** Five oak leaves, date below **Obv. Legend:** BUNDESREPUBLIK DEUTSCHLAND **Rev:** Denomination

Date	Mintage	F12	VF20	XF40	MS60	MS63
1950 D	271,962,000	—	—	1.50	2.50	5.00
1950 F	362,880,000	—	—	1.50	2.50	5.00
1950 F	500	PF63 65.00				
1950 G	180,492,000	—	—	1.50	2.50	5.00
1950 G	1,800	PF63 25.00				
1950 J Large J	285,283,000	—	—	1.50	2.50	5.00
1950 J Small J	Inc. above	—	—	1.50	2.50	5.00
1950 J Proof.		—	—	—	—	—
1966 D	26,036,000	—	—	1.50	4.00	8.50
1966 F	30,047,000	—	—	1.50	4.00	8.50
1966 F	100	PF65 60.00				
1966 G	17,333,000	—	—	1.50	4.00	8.50
1966 G	3,070	PF65 7.50				
1966 J	26,741,000	—	—	1.50	4.00	8.50
1966 J	1,000	PF65 17.50				
1967 D	10,418,000	—	—	1.50	4.00	8.50
1967 F	12,012,000	—	—	1.50	4.00	8.50
1967 F	1,500	PF65 15.00				
1967 G	1,736,000	0.50	2.50	7.00	15.00	25.00
1967 G	4,500	PF65 7.50				
1967 J	10,706,000	—	—	1.50	4.00	8.50
1967 J	1,500	PF65 15.00				
1968 D	13,047,000	—	—	1.00	3.00	6.00
1968 F	15,026,000	—	—	1.00	2.50	5.00
1968 F	3,000	PF65 9.00				
1968 G	13,855,000	—	—	1.00	3.50	7.00
1968 G	6,023	PF65 6.00				
1968 J	13,362,000	—	—	1.00	3.50	7.00
1968 J	2,000	PF65 15.00				
1969 D	23,488,000	—	—	0.50	1.25	2.50
1969 F	27,046,000	—	—	0.50	1.25	2.50
1969 F	5,000	PF65 3.00				
1969 G	15,631,000	—	—	0.50	1.50	3.00
1969 G	8,700	PF65 2.50				
1969 J	24,120,000	—	—	0.50	1.25	2.50
1969 J	5,000	PF65 2.00				
1970 D	39,940,000	—	—	0.10	0.50	1.00
1970 F	45,517,000	—	—	0.10	0.50	1.00
1970 F	5,140	PF65 2.50				
1970 G	27,638,000	—	—	0.10	0.50	1.00
1970 G	10,200	PF65 1.50				
1970 J	40,873,000	—	—	0.10	0.50	1.00
1970 J	5,000	PF65 2.50				
1971 D	57,345,000	—	—	0.10	0.50	1.00
1971 D	8,000	PF65 1.50				
1971 F	66,426,000	—	—	0.10	0.50	1.00
1971 F	8,000	PF65 1.50				
1971 G	38,284,000	—	—	0.10	0.50	1.00
1971 G	10,000	PF65 1.50				
1971 J	58,566,000	—	—	0.10	0.50	1.00
1971 J	8,000	PF65 1.50				
1972 D	52,325,000	—	—	0.10	0.50	1.00
1972 D	8,000	PF65 1.50				
1972 F	60,292,000	—	—	0.10	0.50	1.00
1972 F	8,000	PF65 1.50				
1972 G	34,719,000	—	—	0.10	0.50	1.00
1972 G	10,000	PF65 1.50				
1972 J	54,218,000	—	—	0.10	0.50	1.00
1972 J	8,000	PF65 1.50				
1973 D	15,596,000	—	—	0.10	0.50	1.00

Date	Mintage	F12	VF20	XF40	MS60	MS63
1973 D	9,000	PF65 1.50				
1973 F	18,039,000	—	—	0.10	0.50	1.00
1973 F	9,000	PF65 1.50				
1973 G	10,391,000	—	—	0.10	0.50	1.00
1973 G	9,000	PF65 1.50				
1973 J	16,035,000	—	—	0.10	0.50	1.00
1973 J	9,000	PF65 1.50				
1974 D	15,769,000	—	—	0.10	0.50	1.00
1974 D	35,000	PF65 0.50				
1974 F	18,143,000	—	—	0.10	0.50	1.00
1974 F	35,000	PF65 0.50				
1974 G	10,508,000	—	—	0.10	0.50	1.00
1974 G	35,000	PF65 0.50				
1974 J	16,055,000	—	—	0.10	0.50	1.00
1974 J	35,000	PF65 0.50				
1975 D	15,715,000	—	—	0.10	0.50	1.00
1975 D	43,000	PF65 0.50				
1975 F	18,013,000	—	—	0.10	0.35	0.75
1975 F	43,000	PF65 0.50				
1975 G	10,466,000	—	—	0.10	0.35	0.75
1975 G	43,000	PF65 0.50				
1975 J	16,201,000	—	—	0.10	0.35	0.75
1975 J	43,000	PF65 0.50				
1976 D	47,091,000	—	—	0.10	0.35	0.75
1976 D	43,000	PF65 0.50				
1976 F	54,370,000	—	—	0.10	0.35	0.75
1976 F	43,000	PF65 0.50				
1976 G	31,367,000	—	—	0.10	0.35	0.75
1976 G	43,000	PF65 0.50				
1976 J	48,321,000	—	—	0.10	0.35	0.75
1976 J	43,000	PF65 0.50				
1977 D	52,159,000	—	—	0.10	0.35	0.75
1977 D	51,000	PF65 0.45				
1977 F	60,124,000	—	—	0.10	0.35	0.75
1977 F	51,000	PF65 0.45				
1977 G	34,600,000	—	—	0.10	0.35	0.75
1977 G	51,000	PF65 0.45				
1977 J	53,481,000	—	—	0.10	0.35	0.75
1977 J	51,000	PF65 0.45				
1978 D	41,600,000	—	—	0.10	0.35	0.75
1978 D	54,000	PF65 0.45				
1978 F	48,000,000	—	—	0.10	0.35	0.75
1978 F	54,000	PF65 0.45				
1978 G	27,680,000	—	—	0.10	0.35	0.75
1978 G	54,000	PF65 0.45				
1978 J	42,720,000	—	—	0.10	0.35	0.75
1978 J	54,000	PF65 0.45				
1979 D	41,600,000	—	—	0.10	0.20	0.40
1979 D	89,000	PF65 0.40				
1979 F	48,000,000	—	—	0.10	0.20	0.40
1979 F	89,000	PF65 0.40				
1979 G	27,680,000	—	—	0.10	0.20	0.40
1979 G	89,000	PF65 0.40				
1979 J	42,711,000	—	—	0.10	0.20	0.40
1979 J	89,000	PF65 0.40				
1980 D	39,880,000	—	—	0.10	0.20	0.40
1980 D	110,000	PF65 0.40				
1980 F	53,270,000	—	—	0.10	0.20	0.40
1980 F	110,000	PF65 0.40				
1980 G	43,070,000	—	—	0.10	0.20	0.40
1980 G	110,000	PF65 0.40				
1980 J	59,130,000	—	—	0.10	0.20	0.40
1980 J	110,000	PF65 0.40				
1981 D	82,250,000	—	—	0.10	0.20	0.40
1981 D	91,000	PF65 0.40				
1981 F	84,910,000	—	—	0.10	0.20	0.40
1981 F	91,000	PF65 0.40				
1981 G	41,910,000	—	—	0.10	0.20	0.40
1981 G	91,000	PF65 0.40				
1981 J	49,290,000	—	—	0.10	0.20	0.40
1981 J	91,000	PF65 0.40				
1982 D	57,500,000	—	—	0.10	0.20	0.40
1982 D	78,000	PF65 0.40				
1982 F	53,290,000	—	—	0.10	0.20	0.40
1982 F	78,000	PF65 0.40				
1982 G	23,750,000	—	—	0.10	0.20	0.40
1982 G	78,000	PF65 0.40				
1982 J	62,000,000	—	—	0.10	0.20	0.40
1982 J	78,000	PF65 0.40				
1983 D	46,800,000	—	—	0.10	0.20	0.40
1983 D	75,000	PF65 0.40				
1983 F	54,000,000	—	—	0.10	0.20	0.40
1983 F	75,000	PF65 0.40				
1983 G	31,140,000	—	—	0.10	0.20	0.40
1983 G	75,000	PF65 0.40				
1983 J	48,060,000	—	—	0.10	0.20	0.40
1983 J	75,000	PF65 0.40				
1984 D	36,400,000	—	—	0.10	0.20	0.40
1984 D	64,000	PF65 0.40				
1984 F	42,000,000	—	—	0.10	0.20	0.40
1984 F	64,000	PF65 0.40				
1984 G	24,200,000	—	—	0.10	0.20	0.40
1984 G	64,000	PF65 0.40				
1984 J	37,400,000	—	—	0.10	0.20	0.40
1984 J	64,000	PF65 0.40				
1985 D	15,600,000	—	—	0.10	0.50	1.00
1985 D	56,000	PF65 0.50				
1985 F	18,000,000	—	—	0.10	0.50	1.00
1985 F	54,000	PF65 0.50				
1985 G	10,400,000	—	—	0.10	0.50	1.00
1985 G	55,000	PF65 0.50				
1985 J	16,000,000	—	—	0.10	0.50	1.00
1985 J	54,000	PF65 0.50				
1986 D	36,400,000	—	—	—	0.25	0.50
1986 D	44,000	PF65 0.40				
1986 F	42,000,000	—	—	—	0.25	0.50
1986 F	44,000	PF65 0.40				
1986 G	24,200,000	—	—	—	0.25	0.50
1986 G	44,000	PF65 0.40				
1986 J	37,400,000	—	—	—	0.25	0.50
1986 J	44,000	PF65 0.40				
1987 D	52,000,000	—	—	—	0.25	0.50
1987 D	45,000	PF65 0.40				
1987 F	60,000,000	—	—	—	0.25	0.50
1987 F	45,000	PF65 0.40				
1987 G	34,600,000	—	—	—	0.25	0.50
1987 G	45,000	PF65 0.40				
1987 J	53,400,000	—	—	—	0.25	0.50
1987 J	45,000	PF65 0.40				
1988 D	52,400,000	—	—	—	0.25	0.50
1988 D	45,000	PF65 0.40				
1988 F	72,000,000	—	—	—	0.25	0.50
1988 F	45,000	PF65 0.40				
1988 G	41,500,000	—	—	—	0.25	0.50
1988 G	45,000	PF65 0.40				
1988 J	64,099,999	—	—	—	0.25	0.50
1988 J	45,000	PF65 0.40				
1989 D	93,600,000	—	—	—	0.25	0.50
1989 D	45,000	PF65 0.40				
1989 F	108,000,000	—	—	—	0.25	0.50
1989 F	45,000	PF65 0.40				
1989 G	62,280,000	—	—	—	0.25	0.50
1989 G	45,000	PF65 0.40				
1989 J	96,120,000	—	—	—	0.25	0.50
1989 J	45,000	PF65 0.40				
1990 A	70,000,000	—	—	—	0.10	0.20
1990 D	93,600,000	—	—	—	0.10	0.20
1990 D	45,000	PF65 0.40				
1990 F	108,000,000	—	—	—	0.10	0.20
1990 F	45,000	PF65 0.40				
1990 G	62,280,000	—	—	—	0.10	0.20
1990 G	45,000	PF65 0.40				
1990 J	96,120,000	—	—	—	0.10	0.20
1990 J	45,000	PF65 0.40				
1991 A	128,000,000	—	—	—	0.10	0.20
1991 A	45,000	PF65 0.40				
1991 D	134,400,000	—	—	—	0.10	0.20
1991 D	45,000	PF65 0.40				
1991 F	153,600,000	—	—	—	0.10	0.20
1991 F	45,000	PF65 0.40				
1991 G	89,600,000	—	—	—	0.10	0.20
1991 G	45,000	PF65 0.40				
1991 J	134,400,000	—	—	—	0.10	0.20
1991 J	45,000	PF65 0.40				
1992 A	28,000,000	—	—	—	0.10	0.20
1992 A	45,000	PF65 0.40				
1992 D	29,400,000	—	—	—	0.10	0.20
1992 D	45,000	PF65 0.40				
1992 F	33,600,000	—	—	—	0.10	0.20
1992 F	45,000	PF65 0.40				
1992 G	19,600,000	—	—	—	0.10	0.20
1992 G	45,000	PF65 0.40				
1992 J	29,400,000	—	—	—	0.10	0.20
1992 J	45,000	PF65 0.40				
1993 A	36,000,000	—	—	—	0.10	0.20
1993 A	45,000	PF65 0.40				
1993 D	37,800,000	—	—	—	0.10	0.20
1993 D	45,000	PF65 0.40				
1993 F	43,200,000	—	—	—	0.10	0.20
1993 F	45,000	PF65 0.40				
1993 G	25,200,000	—	—	—	0.10	0.20
1993 G	45,000	PF65 0.40				
1993 J	37,800,000	—	—	—	0.10	0.20
1993 J	45,000	PF65 0.40				
1994 A	38,000,000	—	—	—	0.10	0.20
1994 A	45,000	PF65 0.40				
1994 D	39,900,000	—	—	—	0.10	0.20
1994 D	45,000	PF65 0.40				
1994 F	45,600,000	—	—	—	0.10	0.20
1994 F	45,000	PF65 0.40				
1994 G	26,600,000	—	—	—	0.10	0.20
1994 G	45,000	PF65 0.40				
1994 J	39,900,000	—	—	—	0.10	0.20
1994 J	45,000	PF65 0.40				
1995 A	48,000,000	—	—	—	0.15	0.30
1995 A	45,000	PF65 0.45				
1995 D	50,400,000	—	—	—	0.15	0.30
1995 D	45,000	PF65 0.45				
1995 F	57,600,000	—	—	—	0.15	0.30
1995 F	45,000	PF65 0.45				
1995 G	33,600,000	—	—	—	0.15	0.30
1995 G	45,000	PF65 0.45				
1995 J	50,400,000	—	—	—	0.15	0.30
1995 J	45,000	PF65 0.45				
1996 A	48,000,000	—	—	—	0.20	0.40
1996 A	45,000	PF65 0.50				
1996 D	50,400,000	—	—	—	0.20	0.40
1996 D	45,000	PF65 0.50				
1996 F	57,600,000	—	—	—	0.20	0.40
1996 F	45,000	PF65 0.50				
1996 G	33,600,000	—	—	—	0.20	0.40
1996 G	45,000	PF65 0.50				
1996 J	50,400,000	—	—	—	0.20	0.40
1996 J	45,000	PF65 0.50				
1997 A Sets only	70,000	—	—	—	—	1.75
1997 A	45,000	PF65 2.00				
1997 D Sets only	70,000	—	—	—	—	1.75
1997 D	45,000	PF65 2.00				
1997 F Sets only	70,000	—	—	—	—	1.75
1997 F	45,000	PF65 2.00				
1997 G Sets only	70,000	—	—	—	—	1.75
1997 G	45,000	PF65 2.00				
1997 J Sets only	70,000	—	—	—	—	1.75
1997 J	45,000	PF65 2.00				
1998 A Sets only	70,000	—	—	—	—	1.75
1998 A	45,000	PF65 2.00				
1998 D Sets only	70,000	—	—	—	—	1.75
1998 D	45,000	PF65 2.00				
1998 F Sets only	70,000	—	—	—	—	1.75
1998 F	45,000	PF65 2.00				
1998 G Sets only	70,000	—	—	—	—	1.75
1998 G	45,000	PF65 2.00				
1998 J Sets only	70,000	—	—	—	—	1.75
1998 J	45,000	PF65 2.00				
1999 A Sets only	70,000	—	—	—	—	1.75
1999 A	45,000	PF65 2.00				
1999 D Sets only	70,000	—	—	—	—	1.75
1999 D	45,000	PF65 2.00				
1999 F Sets only	70,000	—	—	—	—	1.75
1999 F	45,000	PF65 2.00				
1999 G Sets only	70,000	—	—	—	—	1.75
1999 G	45,000	PF65 2.00				
1999 J Sets only	70,000	—	—	—	—	1.75
1999 J	45,000	PF65 2.00				
2000 A Sets only	45,000	—	—	—	—	1.75
2000 A	70,000	PF65 2.00				
2000 D Sets only	45,000	—	—	—	—	1.75
2000 D	70,000	PF65 2.00				
2000 F Sets only	45,000	—	—	—	—	1.75
2000 F	70,000	PF65 2.00				
2000 G Sets only	45,000	—	—	—	—	1.75
2000 G	70,000	PF65 2.00				
2000 J Sets only	45,000	—	—	—	—	1.75
2000 J	70,000	PF65 2.00				

KM# 103 10 PFENNIG

4.00 g., Brass Clad Steel, 21.5 mm. **Obv:** Five oak leaves, date below **Obv. Legend:** BANK DEUTSCHER LÄNDER **Rev:** Denomination

Date	Mintage	F12	VF20	XF40	MS60	MS63
1949 D	140,558,000	—	0.50	7.50	30.00	35.00
1949 D	—	PF63 150				
1949 F	120,932,000	—	0.50	10.00	35.00	42.00
1949 F	250	PF63 140				
1949 G	82,933,000	—	1.00	10.00	40.00	45.00
1949 J Large J	154,095,000	—	0.50	7.50	30.00	35.00
1949 J	—	PF63 60.00				
1949 J Small J	Inc. above	—	0.50	7.50	32.00	38.00
1949 J	—	PF63 60.00				

KM# 108 10 PFENNIG

4.00 g., Brass Clad Steel, 21.5 mm. **Obv:** Five oak leaves, date below **Obv. Legend:** BUNDESREPUBLIK DEUTSCHLAND **Rev:** Denomination **Edge:** Plain

Date	Mintage	F12	VF20	XF40	MS60	MS63
1950 D	393,209,000	—	—	0.50	2.00	4.00
1950 F	584,340,000	—	—	0.50	2.00	4.00
1950 F	500	PF63 45.00				
1950 G	309,045,000	—	0.20	1.00	4.00	8.00
1950 G	1,800	PF63 5.00				
1950 J	402,452,000	—	—	0.50	2.00	4.00
1950 J	—	PF63 20.00				
1966 D	31,220,000	—	0.20	1.50	4.00	8.00
1966 F	36,097,000	—	0.20	1.50	4.00	8.00
1966 F	100	PF65 75.00				

Date	Mintage	F12	VF20	XF40	MS60	MS63
1966 G	25,338,000	—	0.20	1.50	4.50	9.00
1966 G	3,070	PF65	7.50			
1966 J	32,116,000	—	0.20	1.50	4.00	8.00
1966 J	1,000	PF65	12.50			
1967 D	15,632,000	—	0.20	3.00	5.00	10.00
1967 F	18,049,000	—	0.20	2.00	4.50	9.00
1967 F	1,500	PF65	15.00			
1967 G	1,518,000	0.20	2.00	7.00	15.00	30.00
1967 G	4,500	PF65	7.50			
1967 J	16,050,999	—	0.20	3.00	5.00	10.00
1967 J	1,500	PF65	12.50			
1968 D	5,207,000	—	0.20	2.00	5.00	10.00
1968 F	6,010,000	—	0.20	2.00	4.00	8.00
1968 F	3,000	PF65	10.00			
1968 G	12,384,000	—	0.15	1.50	3.50	7.00
1968 G	6,023	PF65	5.00			
1968 J	5,422,000	—	0.20	2.00	5.00	10.00
1968 J	2,000	PF65	10.00			
1969 D	41,693,000	—	—	0.15	1.00	2.00
1969 F	48,084,000	—	—	0.15	1.00	2.00
1969 F	5,000	PF65	3.00			
1969 G	48,760,000	—	—	0.15	1.00	2.00
1969 G	8,700	PF65	2.50			
1969 J	42,756,000	—	—	0.15	1.00	2.00
1969 J	5,000	PF65	2.50			
1970 D	54,085,000	—	—	0.15	1.00	2.00
1970 F	60,086,000	—	—	0.15	1.00	2.00
1970 F	5,140	PF65	3.00			
1970 G	35,900,000	—	—	0.15	0.50	1.00
1970 G	10,200	PF65	2.00			
1970 J	40,115,000	—	—	0.15	0.50	1.00
1970 J	5,000	PF65	2.50			
1971 D	54,022,000	—	—	0.15	0.25	0.50
1971 D	8,000	PF65	2.50			
1971 F	92,534,000	—	—	0.15	0.25	0.50
1971 F	8,000	PF65	2.50			
1971 G	88,614,000	—	—	0.15	0.25	0.50
1971 G	10,000	PF65	2.00			
1971 Small J	65,622,000	—	—	0.15	0.25	0.50
1971 Large J	Inc. above	—	—	0.15	0.25	0.50
1971 J	8,000	PF65	1.50			
1972 D	104,345,000	—	—	0.15	0.25	0.50
1972 D	8,000	PF65	1.50			
1972 F	110,177,000	—	—	0.15	0.25	0.50
1972 F	8,000	PF65	1.50			
1972 G	71,766,000	—	—	0.15	0.25	0.50
1972 G	10,000	PF65	1.50			
1972 J	96,991,000	—	—	0.15	0.25	0.50
1972 J	8,000	PF65	1.50			
1973 D	26,052,000	—	—	0.15	0.25	0.50
1973 D	9,000	PF65	1.50			
1973 F	30,070,000	—	—	0.15	0.25	0.50
1973 F	9,000	PF65	1.50			
1973 G	17,294,000	—	—	0.15	0.25	0.50
1973 G	9,000	PF65	1.50			
1973 J	26,774,000	—	—	0.15	0.25	0.50
1973 J	9,000	PF65	1.50			
1974 D	15,707,000	—	—	0.15	0.25	0.50
1974 D	35,000	PF65	0.75			
1974 F	18,135,000	—	—	0.15	0.25	0.50
1974 F	35,000	PF65	0.75			
1974 G	10,450,000	—	—	0.15	0.25	0.50
1974 G	35,000	PF65	0.75			
1974 J	16,056,000	—	—	0.15	0.25	0.50
1974 J	35,000	PF65	0.75			
1975 D	15,654,000	—	—	0.15	0.25	0.50
1975 D	43,000	PF65	0.75			
1975 F	18,043,000	—	—	0.15	0.25	0.50
1975 F	43,000	PF65	0.75			
1975 G	10,403,000	—	—	0.15	0.25	0.50
1975 G	43,000	PF65	0.75			
1975 J	16,111,000	—	—	0.15	0.25	0.50
1975 J	43,000	PF65	0.75			
1976 D	65,200,000	—	—	0.15	0.25	0.50
1976 D	43,000	PF65	0.75			
1976 F	75,282,000	—	—	0.15	0.25	0.50
1976 F	43,000	PF65	0.75			
1976 G	43,372,000	—	—	0.15	0.25	0.50
1976 G	43,000	PF65	0.75			
1976 J	66,930,000	—	—	0.15	0.25	0.50
1976 J	43,000	PF65	0.75			
1977 D	64,989,000	—	—	0.10	0.20	0.40
1977 D	51,000	PF65	0.50			
1977 F	75,052,000	—	—	0.10	0.20	0.40
1977 F	51,000	PF65	0.50			
1977 G	43,300,000	—	—	0.10	0.20	0.40
1977 G	51,000	PF65	0.50			
1977 J	66,800,000	—	—	0.10	0.20	0.40
1977 J	51,000	PF65	0.50			
1978 D	91,000,000	—	—	0.10	0.20	0.40
1978 D	54,000	PF65	0.50			
1978 F	105,000,000	—	—	0.10	0.20	0.40
1978 F	54,000	PF65	0.50			
1978 G	60,590,000	—	—	0.10	0.20	0.40
1978 G	54,000	PF65	0.50			
1978 J	93,490,000	—	—	0.10	0.20	0.40
1978 J	54,000	PF65	0.50			
1979 D	104,000,000	—	—	0.10	0.20	0.40
1979 D	89,000	PF65	0.50			
1979 F	120,000,000	—	—	0.10	0.20	0.40
1979 F	89,000	PF65	0.50			
1979 G	69,200,000	—	—	0.10	0.20	0.40
1979 G	89,000	PF65	0.50			
1979 J	106,800,000	—	—	0.10	0.20	0.40
1979 J	89,000	PF65	0.50			
1980 D	65,450,000	—	—	0.10	0.20	0.40
1980 D	110,000	PF65	0.50			
1980 F	122,780,000	—	—	0.10	0.20	0.40
1980 F	110,000	PF65	0.50			
1980 G	75,410,000	—	—	0.10	0.20	0.40
1980 G	110,000	PF65	0.50			
1980 J	70,960,000	—	—	0.10	0.20	0.40
1980 J	110,000	PF65	0.50			
1981 D	135,200,000	—	—	0.10	0.20	0.40
1981 D	91,000	PF65	0.50			
1981 F	117,410,000	—	—	0.10	0.20	0.40
1981 F	91,000	PF65	0.50			
1981 G	69,440,000	—	—	0.10	0.20	0.40
1981 G	91,000	PF65	0.50			
1981 J	138,360,000	—	—	0.10	0.20	0.40
1981 J	91,000	PF65	0.50			
1982 D	74,690,000	—	—	0.10	0.20	0.40
1982 D	78,000	PF65	0.50			
1982 F	85,140,000	—	—	0.10	0.20	0.40
1982 F	78,000	PF65	0.50			
1982 G	50,840,000	—	—	0.10	0.20	0.40
1982 G	78,000	PF65	0.50			
1982 J	80,620,000	—	—	0.10	0.20	0.40
1982 J	78,000	PF65	0.50			
1983 D	33,800,000	—	—	0.10	0.20	0.40
1983 D	75,000	PF65	0.50			
1983 F	39,000,000	—	—	0.10	0.20	0.40
1983 F	75,000	PF65	0.50			
1983 G	22,490,000	—	—	0.10	0.20	0.40
1983 G	75,000	PF65	0.50			
1983 J	34,710,000	—	—	0.10	0.20	0.40
1983 J	75,000	PF65	0.50			
1984 D	52,000,000	—	—	0.10	0.20	0.40
1984 D	64,000	PF65	0.50			
1984 F	60,000,000	—	—	0.10	0.20	0.40
1984 F	64,000	PF65	0.50			
1984 G	34,600,000	—	—	0.10	0.20	0.40
1984 G	64,000	PF65	0.50			
1984 J	53,400,000	—	—	0.10	0.20	0.40
1984 J	64,000	PF65	0.50			
1985 D	78,000,000	—	—	—	0.15	0.30
1985 D	56,000	PF65	0.50			
1985 F	90,000,000	—	—	—	0.15	0.30
1985 F	54,000	PF65	0.50			
1985 G	51,900,000	—	—	—	0.15	0.30
1985 G	55,000	PF65	0.50			
1985 J	80,100,000	—	—	—	0.15	0.30
1985 J	54,000	PF65	0.50			
1986 D	41,600,000	—	—	—	0.15	0.30
1986 D	44,000	PF65	0.50			
1986 F	48,000,000	—	—	—	0.15	0.30
1986 F	44,000	PF65	0.50			
1986 G	27,700,000	—	—	—	0.15	0.30
1986 G	44,000	PF65	0.50			
1986 J	42,700,000	—	—	—	0.15	0.30
1986 J	44,000	PF65	0.50			
1987 D	58,500,000	—	—	—	0.10	0.20
1987 D	45,000	PF65	0.30			
1987 F	67,500,000	—	—	—	0.10	0.20
1987 F	45,000	PF65	0.30			
1987 G	38,900,000	—	—	—	0.10	0.20
1987 G	45,000	PF65	0.30			
1987 J	60,100,000	—	—	—	0.15	0.30
1987 J	45,000	PF65	0.50			
1988 D	109,200,000	—	—	—	0.15	0.30
1988 D	45,000	PF65	0.50			
1988 F	126,000,000	—	—	—	0.15	0.30
1988 F	45,000	PF65	0.50			
1988 G	72,700,000	—	—	—	0.15	0.30
1988 G	45,000	PF65	0.50			
1988 J	112,100,000	—	—	—	0.15	0.30
1988 J	45,000	PF65	0.50			
1989 D	119,600,000	—	—	—	0.15	0.30
1989 D	45,000	PF65	0.50			
1989 F	138,000,000	—	—	—	0.15	0.30
1989 F	45,000	PF65	0.50			
1989 G	79,580,000	—	—	—	0.15	0.30
1989 G	45,000	PF65	0.50			
1989 J	122,820,000	—	—	—	0.15	0.30
1989 J	45,000	PF65	0.50			
1990 A	100,000,000	—	—	—	0.15	0.30
1990 D	156,000,000	—	—	—	0.15	0.30
1990 D	45,000	PF65	0.50			
1990 F	180,000,000	—	—	—	0.15	0.30
1990 F	45,000	PF65	0.50			
1990 G	103,800,000	—	—	—	0.15	0.30
1990 G	45,000	PF65	0.50			
1990 J	160,200,000	—	—	—	0.15	0.30
1990 J	45,000	PF65	0.50			
1991 A	170,000,000	—	—	—	0.15	0.30
1991 A	45,000	PF65	0.40			
1991 D	178,550,000	—	—	—	0.15	0.30
1991 D	45,000	PF65	0.40			
1991 F	204,000,000	—	—	—	0.15	0.30
1991 F	45,000	PF65	0.40			
1991 G	119,000,000	—	—	—	0.15	0.30
1991 G	45,000	PF65	0.40			
1991 J	178,500,000	—	—	—	0.15	0.30
1991 J	45,000	PF65	0.40			
1992 A	80,000,000	—	—	—	0.10	0.20
1992 A	45,000	PF65	0.40			
1992 D	84,000,000	—	—	—	0.10	0.20
1992 D	45,000	PF65	0.40			
1992 F	96,000,000	—	—	—	0.10	0.20
1992 F	45,000	PF65	0.40			
1992 G	56,000,000	—	—	—	0.10	0.20
1992 G	45,000	PF65	0.40			
1992 J	84,000,000	—	—	—	0.10	0.20
1992 J	45,000	PF65	0.40			
1993 A	80,000,000	—	—	—	0.10	0.20
1993 A	45,000	PF65	0.40			
1993 D	84,000,000	—	—	—	0.10	0.20
1993 D	45,000	PF65	0.40			
1993 F	96,000,000	—	—	—	0.10	0.20
1993 F	45,000	PF65	0.40			
1993 G	56,000,000	—	—	—	0.10	0.20
1993 G	45,000	PF65	0.40			
1993 J	84,000,000	—	—	—	0.10	0.20
1993 J	45,000	PF65	0.40			
1994 A	100,000,000	—	—	—	0.10	0.20
1994 A	45,000	PF65	0.40			
1994 D	105,000,000	—	—	—	0.10	0.20
1994 D	45,000	PF65	0.40			
1994 F	120,000,000	—	—	—	0.10	0.20
1994 F	45,000	PF65	0.40			
1994 G	70,000,000	—	—	—	0.10	0.20
1994 G	45,000	PF65	0.40			
1994 J	105,000,000	—	—	—	0.10	0.20
1994 J	45,000	PF65	0.40			
1995 A	110,000,000	—	—	—	0.15	0.30
1995 A	45,000	PF65	0.45			
1995 D	115,000,000	—	—	—	0.15	0.30
1995 D	45,000	PF65	0.45			
1995 F	132,000,000	—	—	—	0.15	0.30
1995 F	45,000	PF65	0.45			
1995 G	77,000,000	—	—	—	0.15	0.30
1995 G	45,000	PF65	0.45			
1995 J	115,500,000	—	—	—	0.15	0.30
1995 J	45,000	PF65	0.45			
1996 A	90,000,000	—	—	—	0.20	0.40
1996 A	45,000	PF65	0.50			
1996 D	94,500,000	—	—	—	0.20	0.40
1996 D	45,000	PF65	0.50			
1996 F	108,000,000	—	—	—	0.20	0.40
1996 F	45,000	PF65	0.50			
1996 G	63,000,000	—	—	—	0.20	0.40
1996 G	45,000	PF65	0.50			
1996 J	94,500,000	—	—	—	0.20	0.40
1996 J	45,000	PF65	0.50			
1997 A Sets only	70,000	—	—	—	—	1.75
1997 A	45,000	PF65	2.00			
1997 D Sets only	70,000	—	—	—	—	1.75
1997 D	45,000	PF65	2.00			
1997 F Sets only	70,000	—	—	—	—	1.75
1997 F	45,000	PF65	2.00			
1997 G Sets only	70,000	—	—	—	—	1.75
1997 G	45,000	PF65	2.00			
1997 J Sets only	70,000	—	—	—	—	1.75
1997 J	45,000	PF65	2.00			
1998 A Sets only	70,000	—	—	—	—	1.75
1998 A	45,000	PF65	2.00			
1998 D Sets only	70,000	—	—	—	—	1.75
1998 D	45,000	PF65	2.00			
1998 F Sets only	70,000	—	—	—	—	1.75
1998 F	45,000	PF65	2.00			
1998 G Sets only	70,000	—	—	—	—	1.75
1998 G	45,000	PF65	2.00			
1998 J Sets only	79,000	—	—	—	—	1.75
1998 J	—	PF65	2.00			
1999 A Sets only	70,000	—	—	—	—	1.75
1999 A	45,000	PF65	2.00			
1999 D Sets only	70,000	—	—	—	—	1.75
1999 D	—	PF65	2.00			
1999 F Sets only	70,000	—	—	—	—	1.75
1999 F	45,000	PF65	2.00			
1999 G Sets only	70,000	—	—	—	—	1.75
1999 G	45,000	PF65	2.00			
1999 J Sets only	70,000	—	—	—	—	1.75
1999 J	45,000	PF65	2.00			
2000 A Sets only	70,000	—	—	—	—	1.75
2000 A	45,000	PF65	2.00			
2000 D Sets only	70,000	—	—	—	—	1.75
2000 D	45,000	PF65	2.00			
2000 F Sets only	70,000	—	—	—	—	1.75
2000 F	45,000	PF65	2.00			
2000 G Sets only	70,000	—	—	—	—	1.75
2000 G	45,000	PF65	2.00			
2000 J Sets only	70,000	—	—	—	—	1.75
2000 J	45,000	PF65	2.00			

KM# 104 50 PFENNIG

3.50 g., Copper-Nickel, 20 mm. **Obv:** Denomination **Obv. Legend:** BANK DEUTSCHER LÄNDER **Rev:** Woman planting an oak seedling, date below **Edge:** Reeded

Date	Mintage	F12	VF20	XF40	MS60	MS63
1949 D	39,108,000	—	0.75	4.50	45.00	55.00
1949 F	45,118,000	—	0.50	3.00	35.00	45.00
1949 F	200	PF63 125				
1949 G	25,924,000	—	0.75	5.00	55.00	65.00
1949 J	42,303,000	—	0.75	3.50	35.00	45.00
1949 J	—	PF63 135				
1950 G	30,000	—	350	450	600	800

Note: The 1950G dated coin was restruck without authorization by a mint official using genuine dies - quantity unknown. Mintmark J also with year "9" (instead of 1949)- Rare.

KM# 109.1 50 PFENNIG

3.50 g., Copper-Nickel, 20 mm. **Obv:** Denomination **Obv. Legend:** BUNDESREPUBLIK DEUTSCHLAND **Rev:** Woman planting an oak seedling **Edge:** Reeded

Date	Mintage	F12	VF20	XF40	MS60	MS63
1950 D	100,735,000	—	0.50	0.75	3.50	7.00
1950 F	143,510,000	—	0.50	0.75	3.50	7.00
1950 F	450	PF63 85.00				
1950 G	66,421,000	—	0.50	1.50	6.00	12.00
1950 G	1,800	PF63 5.00				
1950 J	102,736,000	—	0.50	0.75	4.50	9.00
1950 J	—	PF63 25.00				
1966 D	8,327,999	—	0.50	1.00	7.00	15.00
1966 F	9,605,000	—	0.50	1.00	7.00	15.00
1966 F	100	PF65 125				
1966 G	5,543,000	—	0.50	1.50	7.50	16.00
1966 G	3,070	PF65 10.00				
1966 J	8,569,000	—	1.00	7.00	18.00	35.00
1966 J	1,000	PF65 20.00				
1967 D	5,207,000	—	0.50	1.00	7.00	15.00
1967 F	6,005,000	—	0.50	1.00	7.00	15.00
1967 F	1,500	PF65 18.00				
1967 G	1,843,000	—	1.00	5.00	10.00	22.00
1967 G	4,500	PF65 15.00				
1967 J	10,684,000	—	0.50	1.50	9.00	20.00
1967 J	1,500	PF65 18.00				
1968 D	7,809,000	—	0.50	1.50	6.00	12.00
1968 F	3,000,000	—	0.50	1.50	6.00	12.00
1968 F	3,000	PF65 15.00				
1968 G	6,818,000	—	0.50	1.50	6.00	12.00
1968 G	6,023	PF65 8.00				
1968 J	2,672,000	—	1.00	5.00	15.00	30.00
1968 J	2,000	PF65 15.00				
1969 D	14,561,000	—	0.45	0.55	1.25	2.50
1969 F	16,804,000	—	0.45	0.55	1.25	2.50
1969 F	5,000	PF65 4.00				
1969 G	9,704,000	—	0.45	0.55	1.25	2.50
1969 G	8,700	PF65 3.50				
1969 J	14,969,000	—	0.45	0.55	1.25	2.50
1969 J	5,000	PF65 10.00				
1970 D	25,294,000	—	0.45	0.55	0.75	1.50
1970 F	26,455,000	—	0.45	0.55	0.75	1.50
1970 F	5,140	PF65 3.50				
1970 G	11,955,000	—	0.45	0.55	0.75	1.50
1970 G	10,200	PF65 3.00				
1970 J	10,683,000	—	0.45	0.55	0.75	1.50
1970 J	5,000	PF65 3.50				
1971 D	23,393,000	—	0.45	0.55	0.65	1.25
1971 D	8,000	PF65 3.00				
1971 F	29,746,000	—	0.45	0.55	0.65	1.25
1971 F	8,000	PF65 3.00				
1971 G	15,556,000	—	0.45	0.55	0.65	1.25
1971 G	10,000	PF65 3.00				
1971 Large J	24,044,000	—	0.45	0.55	0.65	1.25
1971 Small J	Inc. above	—	0.45	0.55	0.65	1.25
1971 J	8,000	PF65 3.00				

KM# 109.2 50 PFENNIG

3.50 g., Copper-Nickel, 20 mm. **Obv:** Denomination **Obv. Legend:** BUNDESREPUBLIK DEUTSCHLAND **Rev:** Woman planting an oak seedling **Edge:** Plain

Date	Mintage	F12	VF20	XF40	MS60	MS63
1972 D	26,008,000	—	—	0.45	0.60	1.20
1972 D	8,000	PF65 2.00				
1972 F	30,043,000	—	—	0.45	0.60	1.20
1972 F	8,000	PF65 2.00				
1972 G	17,337,000	—	—	0.45	0.60	1.20
1972 G	10,000	PF65 2.00				
1972 J	26,707,000	—	—	0.45	0.60	1.20
1972 J	8,000	PF65 2.00				
1973 D	7,810,000	—	—	0.45	1.00	2.00
1973 D	9,000	PF65 2.00				
1973 F	8,994,000	—	—	0.45	0.60	1.20
1973 F	9,000	PF65 2.00				
1973 G	5,201,000	—	—	0.45	0.60	1.20
1973 G	9,000	PF65 2.00				
1973 J	8,010,999	—	—	0.45	0.60	1.20
1973 J	9,000	PF65 2.00				
1974 D	18,264,000	—	—	0.45	1.00	2.00
1974 D	35,000	PF65 1.00				
1974 Large F	21,036,000	—	—	0.45	1.00	2.00
1974 Small F	Inc. above	—	—	0.45	1.00	2.00
1974 F	35,000	PF65 1.00				
1974 G	12,159,000	—	—	0.45	1.50	3.00
1974 G	35,000	PF65 1.00				
1974 J	18,752,000	—	—	0.45	1.00	2.00
1974 J	35,000	PF65 1.00				
1975 D	13,055,000	—	—	0.45	1.00	2.00
1975 D	43,000	PF65 1.00				
1975 F	15,003,000	—	—	0.45	1.00	2.00
1975 F	43,000	PF65 1.00				
1975 G	8,675,000	—	—	0.45	1.50	3.00
1975 G	43,000	PF65 1.00				
1975 J	13,379,000	—	—	0.45	1.00	2.00
1975 J	43,000	PF65 1.00				
1976 D	10,411,000	—	—	0.45	0.60	1.20
1976 D	43,000	PF65 1.00				
1976 F	12,048,000	—	—	0.45	0.60	1.20
1976 F	43,000	PF65 1.00				
1976 G	6,653,000	—	—	0.45	1.25	2.50
1976 G	43,000	PF65 1.00				
1976 J	10,716,000	—	—	0.45	0.60	1.20
1976 J	43,000	PF65 1.00				
1977 D	10,400,000	—	—	0.45	0.60	1.20
1977 D	51,000	PF65 0.75				
1977 F	12,000,000	—	—	0.45	0.60	1.20
1977 F	51,000	PF65 0.75				
1977 G	6,921,000	—	—	0.45	1.00	2.00
1977 G	51,000	PF65 0.75				
1977 J	10,708,000	—	—	0.45	0.60	1.20
1977 J	51,000	PF65 0.75				
1978 D	10,400,000	—	—	0.45	1.00	2.00
1978 D	54,000	PF65 0.75				
1978 F	12,000,000	—	—	0.45	0.60	1.20
1978 F	54,000	PF65 0.75				
1978 G	6,640,000	—	—	0.45	1.00	2.00
1978 G	54,000	PF65 0.75				
1978 J	10,680,000	—	—	0.45	0.60	1.20
1978 J	54,000	PF65 0.75				
1979 D	10,400,000	—	—	0.45	1.00	2.00
1979 D	89,000	PF65 0.75				
1979 F	12,000,000	—	—	0.45	0.60	1.20
1979 F	89,000	PF65 0.75				
1979 G	6,920,000	—	—	0.45	1.00	2.00
1979 G	89,000	PF65 0.75				
1979 J	10,680,000	—	—	0.45	0.60	1.20
1979 J	89,000	PF65 0.75				
1980 D	23,250,000	—	—	0.45	0.60	1.20
1980 D	110,000	PF65 0.75				
1980 F	17,440,000	—	—	0.45	0.60	1.20
1980 F	110,000	PF65 0.75				
1980 G	22,460,000	—	—	0.45	0.60	1.20
1980 G	110,000	PF65 0.75				
1980 J	24,030,000	—	—	0.45	0.60	1.20
1980 J	110,000	PF65 0.75				
1981 D	17,900,000	—	—	0.45	0.65	1.25
1981 D	91,000	PF65 0.75				
1981 F	29,810,000	—	—	0.45	0.65	1.25
1981 F	91,000	PF65 0.75				
1981 G	10,880,000	—	—	0.45	0.75	1.50
1981 G	91,000	PF65 0.75				
1981 J	24,140,000	—	—	0.45	0.65	1.25
1981 J	91,000	PF65 0.75				
1982 D	21,540,000	—	—	0.45	0.65	1.25
1982 D	78,000	PF65 0.75				
1982 F	28,900,000	—	—	0.45	0.65	1.25
1982 F	78,000	PF65 0.75				
1982 G	19,710,000	—	—	0.45	0.75	1.50
1982 G	78,000	PF65 0.75				
1982 J	17,210,000	—	—	0.45	0.65	1.25
1982 J	78,000	PF65 0.75				
1983 D	20,800,000	—	—	0.45	0.65	1.25
1983 D	75,000	PF65 0.75				
1983 F	24,000,000	—	—	0.45	0.65	1.25
1983 F	75,000	PF65 0.75				
1983 G	13,840,000	—	—	0.45	0.75	1.50
1983 G	75,000	PF65 0.75				
1983 J	21,360,000	—	—	0.45	0.65	1.25
1983 J	75,000	PF65 0.75				
1984 D	11,700,000	—	—	0.45	0.75	1.50
1984 D	64,000	PF65 0.75				
1984 F	13,500,000	—	—	0.45	0.75	1.50
1984 F	64,000	PF65 0.75				
1984 G	7,800,000	—	—	0.45	0.75	1.50
1984 G	64,000	PF65 0.75				
1984 J	12,000,000	—	—	0.45	0.75	1.50
1984 J	64,000	PF65 0.75				
1985 D	15,700,000	—	—	0.45	0.75	1.50
1985 D	56,000	PF65 0.75				
1985 F	18,000,000	—	—	0.45	0.75	1.50
1985 F	54,000	PF65 0.75				
1985 G	10,400,000	—	—	0.45	0.75	1.50
1985 G	55,000	PF65 0.75				
1985 J	16,100,000	—	—	0.45	0.75	1.50
1985 J	54,000	PF65 0.75				
1986 D	2,100,000	—	1.00	2.00	4.00	8.00
1986 D	44,000	PF65 0.75				
1986 F	2,400,000	—	1.00	2.00	3.50	7.00
1986 F	44,000	PF65 0.75				
1986 G	1,400,000	1.00	2.00	4.00	6.00	10.00
1986 G	44,000	PF65 0.75				
1986 J	2,100,000	—	1.50	3.50	7.00	12.50
1986 J	44,000	PF65 0.75				
1987 D	520,000	2.00	5.00	10.00	18.00	30.00
1987 D	45,000	PF65 0.75				
1987 F	600,000	1.00	3.00	6.00	9.00	15.00
1987 F	45,000	PF65 0.75				
1987 G	350,000	2.50	5.00	8.00	15.00	28.00
1987 G	45,000	PF65 0.75				
1987 J	530,000	1.00	3.00	6.00	9.00	15.00
1987 J	45,000	PF65 0.75				
1988 D	4,160,000	—	—	0.50	1.00	2.00
1988 D	45,000	PF65 0.75				
1988 F	4,800,000	—	—	0.50	1.00	2.00
1988 F	45,000	PF65 0.75				
1988 G	2,770,000	—	—	1.00	1.50	3.00
1988 G	45,000	PF65 0.75				
1988 J	4,300,000	—	—	0.50	1.00	2.00
1988 J	45,000	PF65 0.75				
1989 D	36,400,000	—	—	—	0.50	1.00
1989 D	45,000	PF65 0.75				
1989 F	42,000,000	—	—	—	0.50	1.00
1989 F	45,000	PF65 0.75				
1989 G	24,220,000	—	—	—	0.50	1.00
1989 G	45,000	PF65 0.75				
1989 J	37,380,000	—	—	—	0.50	1.00
1989 J	45,000	PF65 0.75				
1990 A	150,000,000	—	—	—	0.50	1.00
1990 D	58,500,000	—	—	—	0.50	1.00
1990 D	45,000	PF65 0.75				
1990 F	67,500,000	—	—	—	0.50	1.00
1990 F	45,000	PF65 0.75				
1990 G	38,920,000	—	—	—	0.50	1.00
1990 G	45,000	PF65 0.75				
1990 J	60,070,000	—	—	—	0.50	1.00
1990 J	45,000	PF65 0.75				
1991 A	22,000,000	—	—	—	0.50	1.00
1991 A	45,000	PF65 0.75				
1991 D	23,100,000	—	—	—	0.50	1.00
1991 D	45,000	PF65 0.75				
1991 F	26,400,000	—	—	—	0.50	1.00
1991 F	45,000	PF65 0.75				
1991 G	15,400,000	—	—	—	0.50	1.00
1991 G	45,000	PF65 0.75				
1991 J	23,100,000	—	—	—	0.50	1.00
1991 J	45,000	PF65 0.75				
1992 A	18,000,000	—	—	—	0.50	1.00
1992 A	45,000	PF65 0.75				
1992 D	18,900,000	—	—	—	0.50	1.00
1992 D	45,000	PF65 0.75				
1992 F	21,600,000	—	—	—	0.50	1.00
1992 F	45,000	PF65 0.75				
1992 G	12,600,000	—	—	—	0.50	1.00
1992 G	45,000	PF65 0.75				
1992 J	18,900,000	—	—	—	0.50	1.00
1992 J	45,000	PF65 0.75				
1993 A	16,000,000	—	—	—	0.50	1.00
1993 A	45,000	PF65 0.75				
1993 D	16,800,000	—	—	—	0.50	1.00
1993 D	45,000	PF65 0.75				
1993 F	19,200,000	—	—	—	0.50	1.00
1993 F	45,000	PF65 0.75				
1993 G	11,200,000	—	—	—	0.75	1.50
1993 G	45,000	PF65 0.75				
1993 J	16,800,000	—	—	—	0.50	1.00
1993 J	45,000	PF65 0.75				
1994 A	7,500,000	—	—	—	1.00	2.00
1994 A	45,000	PF65 0.75				
1994 D	7,875,000	—	—	—	1.50	3.00
1994 D	45,000	PF65 0.75				
1994 F	9,000,000	—	—	—	1.50	3.00
1994 F	45,000	PF65 0.75				
1994 G	5,250,000	—	—	—	1.50	3.00
1994 G	45,000	PF65 0.75				
1994 J	7,875,000	—	—	—	1.00	2.00
1994 J	45,000	PF65 0.75				

Date	Mintage	F12	VF20	XF40	MS60	MS63
1995 A	1,300,000	—	—	—	2.25	4.50
1995 A	45,000	PF65 6.00				
1995 D	1,365,000	—	—	—	2.25	4.50
1995 D	45,000	PF65 6.00				
1995 F	20,000	—	—	—	50.00	90.00
1995 F	45,000	PF65 12.00				
1995 G	20,000	—	—	—	60.00	100
1995 G	45,000	PF65 12.00				
1995 J	150,000	—	—	—	8.00	15.00
1995 J	45,000	PF65 12.00				
1996 A Sets only	50,000	—	—	—	—	12.00
1996 A	45,000	PF65 13.50				
1996 D Sets only	50,000	—	—	—	—	12.00
1996 D	45,000	PF65 13.50				
1996 F Sets only	50,000	—	—	—	—	12.00
1996 F	45,000	PF65 13.50				
1996 G Sets only	50,000	—	—	—	—	12.00
1996 G	45,000	PF65 13.50				
1996 J Sets only	50,000	—	—	—	—	12.00
1996 J	45,000	PF65 13.50				
1997 A Sets only	70,000	—	—	—	—	4.75
1997 A	45,000	PF65 5.00				
1997 D Sets only	70,000	—	—	—	—	4.75
1997 D	45,000	PF65 5.00				
1997 F Sets only	70,000	—	—	—	—	4.75
1997 F	45,000	PF65 5.00				
1997 G Sets only	70,000	—	—	—	—	4.75
1997 G	45,000	PF65 5.00				
1997 J Sets only	70,000	—	—	—	—	4.75
1997 J	45,000	PF65 5.00				
1998 A Sets only	70,000	—	—	—	—	4.75
1998 A	45,000	PF65 5.00				
1998 D Sets only	70,000	—	—	—	—	4.75
1998 D	45,000	PF65 5.00				
1998 F Sets only	70,000	—	—	—	—	4.75
1998 F	45,000	PF65 5.00				
1998 G Sets only	70,000	—	—	—	—	4.75
1998 G	45,000	PF65 5.00				
1998 J Sets only	70,000	—	—	—	—	4.75
1998 J	45,000	PF65 5.00				
1999 A Sets only	70,000	—	—	—	—	4.75
1999 A	45,000	PF65 5.00				
1999 D Sets only	70,000	—	—	—	—	4.75
1999 D	45,000	PF65 5.00				
1999 F Sets only	70,000	—	—	—	—	4.75
1999 F	45,000	PF65 5.00				
1999 G Sets only	70,000	—	—	—	—	4.75
1999 G	45,000	PF65 5.00				
1999 J Sets only	70,000	—	—	—	—	4.75
1999 J	45,000	PF65 5.00				
2000 A Sets only	70,000	—	—	—	—	5.00
2000 A	45,000	PF65 5.00				
2000 D Sets only	70,000	—	—	—	—	5.00
2000 D	45,000	PF65 5.00				
2000 F Sets only	70,000	—	—	—	—	5.00
2000 F	45,000	PF65 5.00				
2000 G Sets only	70,000	—	—	—	—	5.00
2000 G	45,000	PF65 5.00				
2000 J Sets only	70,000	—	—	—	—	5.00
2000 J	45,000	PF65 5.00				

KM# 110 MARK

5.50 g., Copper-Nickel, 23.5 mm. **Obv:** Eagle **Rev:** Denomination flanked by oak leaves, date below

Date	Mintage	F12	VF20	XF40	MS60	MS63
1950 D	60,467,000	—	1.50	12.00	40.00	75.00
1950 D	—	PF63 200				
1950 F	69,183,000	—	1.50	12.00	35.00	70.00
1950 F	150	PF63 450				
1950 G	39,826,000	—	2.00	15.00	55.00	110
1950 G	Est. 200	PF63 375				
1950 J	61,483,000	—	1.00	10.00	35.00	65.00
1950 J	—	PF63 200				
1954 D	5,202,000	2.00	8.00	100	220	425
1954 D	—	PF63 925				
1954 F	6,000,000	2.50	10.00	200	325	650
1954 F	175	PF63 1,000				
1954 G	3,459,000	4.00	25.00	450	800	1,900
1954 G	15	PF63 2,250				
1954 J	5,341,000	1.50	7.00	55.00	200	400
1954 J	—	PF63 1,000				
1955 D	3,093,000	2.00	9.00	125	275	550
1955 D	—	PF63 900				
1955 F	4,909,000	1.00	6.00	50.00	250	500
1955 F	Est. 20	PF63 750				
1955 G	2,500,000	4.00	40.00	400	850	1,650
1955 G	—	PF63 2,750				
1955 J	5,294,000	1.00	6.00	50.00	110	220
1955 J	—	PF63 650				
1956 D	13,231,000	1.00	4.00	35.00	175	325
1956 D	—	PF63 525				
1956 F	14,700,000	1.00	4.00	35.00	200	375
1956 F	100	PF63 500				
1956 G	8,362,000	1.00	4.00	35.00	145	275
1956 G	—	PF63 650				
1956 J	11,478,000	1.00	5.00	40.00	110	220
1956 J	—	PF63 850				
1957 D	6,820,000	1.00	5.00	75.00	175	325
1957 D	100	PF63 475				
1957 F	6,390,000	1.00	5.00	75.00	175	325
1957 F	100	PF63 485				
1957 G	3,841,000	2.50	10.00	145	400	800
1957 G	27	PF63 1,350				
1957 J	6,632,000	1.00	6.00	100	250	500
1957 J	200	PF63 385				
1958 D	4,150,000	1.00	4.00	40.00	145	275
1958 D	200	PF63 400				
1958 F	4,109,000	1.00	5.00	45.00	200	375
1958 F	100	PF63 525				
1958 G	3,460,000	2.50	8.00	135	550	1,100
1958 G	20	PF63 2,100				
1958 J	4,656,000	1.00	5.00	50.00	250	500
1958 J	37	PF63 850				
1959 D	10,409,000	—	2.00	20.00	115	225
1959 D	40	PF63 850				
1959 F	11,972,000	—	2.00	20.00	115	225
1959 F	100	PF63 475				
1959 G	6,921,000	1.00	5.00	40.00	200	375
1959 G	20	PF63 2,100				
1959 J	10,691,000	1.00	4.00	35.00	325	650
1959 J	25	PF63 1,250				
1960 D	5,453,000	—	2.00	25.00	375	750
1960 D	100	PF63 550				
1960 F	5,709,000	—	2.00	25.00	125	250
1960 F	100	PF63 800				
1960 G	3,632,000	1.00	6.00	50.00	300	600
1960 G	100	PF63 650				
1960 J	5,612,000	2.50	8.00	200	375	750
1960 J	36	PF63 1,650				
1961 D	7,536,000	—	2.00	20.00	145	275
1961 D	60	PF63 800				
1961 F	6,029,000	—	2.00	20.00	85.00	175
1961 F	50	PF63 800				
1961 G	4,843,000	1.00	6.00	50.00	245	475
1961 G	70	PF63 700				
1961 J	7,483,000	1.50	7.00	75.00	425	850
1961 J	28	PF63 1,000				
1962 D	10,327,000	—	1.50	15.00	200	400
1962 D	40	PF63 800				
1962 F	11,122,000	—	1.50	10.00	65.00	125
1962 F	45	PF63 750				
1962 G	6,054,000	—	2.00	25.00	400	800
1962 G	100	PF63 550				
1962 J	10,822,000	—	2.00	17.50	110	220
1962 J	28	PF63 1,100				
1963 D	12,624,000	—	1.00	10.00	55.00	110
1963 D	40	PF63 550				
1963 F	18,292,000	—	1.50	15.00	70.00	135
1963 F	45	PF63 650				
1963 G	11,253,000	—	1.50	12.50	85.00	165
1963 G	200	PF63 300				
1963 J	15,906,000	—	1.50	15.00	100	200
1963 J	28	PF63 1,200				
1964 D	8,048,000	—	0.85	4.00	50.00	100
1964 D	30	PF65 1,000				
1964 F	12,796,000	—	0.85	4.00	45.00	90.00
1964 F	25	PF65 1,900				
1964 G	3,465,000	—	2.00	20.00	125	250
1964 G	368	PF65 275				
1964 J	6,958,000	—	0.85	4.00	42.00	85.00
1964 J	33	PF65 900				
1965 D	9,388,000	—	0.75	3.00	18.50	37.50
1965 F	9,013,000	—	0.75	3.00	20.00	40.00
1965 F	Est. 80	PF65 175				
1965 G	6,232,000	—	0.75	3.00	25.00	47.50
1965 G	1,200	PF65 65.00				
1965 J	8,023,999	—	0.75	3.00	27.00	55.00
1966 D	11,717,000	—	0.75	3.00	22.00	42.50
1966 F	11,368,000	—	0.75	3.00	22.00	42.50
1966 F	100	PF65 200				
1966 G	7,799,000	—	0.75	3.00	27.00	55.00
1966 G	3,070	PF65 45.00				
1966 J	12,030,000	—	0.75	3.00	22.00	42.50
1966 J	1,000	PF65 85.00				
1967 D	13,017,000	—	0.75	3.00	17.00	32.50
1967 F	7,500,000	—	0.75	5.00	50.00	100
1967 F	1,500	PF65 95.00				
1967 G	4,324,000	—	0.75	3.00	28.00	55.00
1967 G	4,500	PF65 50.00				
1967 J	13,357,000	—	0.75	3.00	20.00	40.00
1967 J	1,500	PF65 85.00				
1968 D	1,303,000	—	1.00	10.00	32.00	65.00
1968 F	1,500,000	—	0.75	4.00	20.00	40.00
1968 F	3,000	PF65 65.00				
1968 G	5,198,000	—	1.50	7.00	30.00	60.00
1968 G	6,023	PF65 35.00				
1968 J	1,338,000	1.00	12.50	145	200	375
1968 J	2,000	PF65 85.00				
1969 D	13,025,000	—	0.75	1.50	12.00	22.00
1969 F	15,021,000	—	0.75	1.50	10.00	20.00
1969 F	5,000	PF65 15.00				
1969 G	8,665,000	—	0.75	1.50	17.00	32.50
1969 G	8,700	PF65 14.50				
1969 J	13,370,000	—	0.75	1.50	12.00	25.00
1969 J	5,000	PF65 18.00				
1970 D	17,928,000	—	0.75	1.00	10.00	20.00
1970 F	19,408,000	—	0.75	1.00	12.00	25.00
1970 F	5,140	PF65 15.00				
1970 G	20,386,000	—	0.75	1.00	17.00	32.50
1970 G	10,200	PF65 9.00				
1970 J	10,707,000	—	0.75	1.00	10.00	20.00
1970 J	5,000	PF65 15.00				
1971 D	24,513,000	—	0.75	1.00	5.00	10.00
1971 D	8,000	PF65 8.00				
1971 F	28,275,000	—	0.75	1.00	5.00	10.00
1971 F	8,000	PF65 8.00				
1971 G	16,375,000	—	0.75	1.00	6.50	12.50
1971 G	10,000	PF65 8.00				
1971 J	25,214,000	—	0.75	1.00	5.00	10.00
1971 J	8,000	PF65 8.00				
1972 D	20,904,000	—	0.75	1.00	5.00	10.00
1972 D	8,000	PF65 7.00				
1972 F	24,086,000	—	0.75	1.00	5.00	10.00
1972 F	8,000	PF65 7.00				
1972 G	13,868,000	—	0.75	1.00	5.00	10.00
1972 G	10,000	PF65 7.00				
1972 J	21,360,000	—	0.75	1.00	5.00	10.00
1972 J	8,000	PF65 7.00				
1973 D	14,327,000	—	0.75	1.00	3.00	6.00
1973 D	9,000	PF65 5.00				
1973 F	16,591,999	—	0.75	1.00	3.00	6.00
1973 F	9,000	PF65 5.00				
1973 G	10,409,000	—	0.75	1.00	3.00	6.00
1973 G	9,000	PF65 5.00				
1973 J	14,704,000	—	0.75	1.00	3.00	6.00
1973 J	9,000	PF65 5.00				
1974 D	20,876,000	—	0.75	1.00	3.00	6.00
1974 D	35,000	PF65 4.00				
1974 F	24,057,000	—	0.75	1.00	3.00	6.00
1974 F	35,000	PF65 4.00				
1974 G	13,931,000	—	0.75	1.00	3.00	6.00
1974 G	35,000	PF65 4.00				
1974 J	21,440,000	—	0.75	1.00	3.00	6.00
1974 J	35,000	PF65 4.00				
1975 D	18,241,000	—	0.75	1.00	3.00	6.00
1975 D	43,000	PF65 4.00				
1975 F	21,059,000	—	0.75	1.00	3.00	6.00
1975 F	43,000	PF65 4.00				
1975 G	12,142,000	—	0.75	1.00	3.25	6.50
1975 G	43,000	PF65 4.00				
1975 J	18,770,000	—	0.75	1.00	3.00	6.00
1975 J	43,000	PF65 4.00				
1976 D	15,670,000	—	0.75	1.00	3.00	6.00
1976 D	43,000	PF65 4.00				
1976 F	18,105,000	—	0.75	1.00	3.00	6.00
1976 F	43,000	PF65 4.00				
1976 G	10,382,000	—	0.75	1.00	3.00	6.00
1976 G	43,000	PF65 4.00				
1976 J	16,046,000	—	0.75	1.00	3.00	6.00
1976 J	43,000	PF65 4.00				
1977 D	20,801,000	—	0.75	0.85	1.50	3.00
1977 D	51,000	PF65 2.00				
1977 F	24,026,000	—	0.75	0.85	1.50	3.00
1977 F	51,000	PF65 2.00				
1977 G	13,849,000	—	0.75	0.85	1.50	3.00
1977 G	51,000	PF65 2.00				
1977 J	21,416,000	—	0.75	0.85	1.50	3.00
1977 J	51,000	PF65 2.00				
1978 D	15,600,000	—	0.75	0.85	1.00	2.00
1978 D	54,000	PF65 1.25				
1978 F	18,000,000	—	0.75	0.85	1.00	2.00
1978 F	54,000	PF65 1.25				
1978 G	10,380,000	—	0.75	0.85	1.00	2.00
1978 G	54,000	PF65 1.25				
1978 J	16,020,000	—	0.75	0.85	1.00	2.00
Note: Error with coin alignment exists						
1978 J	54,000	PF65 1.25				
1979 D	18,200,000	—	0.75	0.85	1.00	2.00
1979 D	89,000	PF65 1.25				
1979 F	21,000,000	—	0.75	0.85	1.00	2.00
1979 F	89,000	PF65 1.25				
1979 G	12,110,000	—	0.75	0.85	1.00	2.00
1979 G	89,000	PF65 1.25				
1979 J	18,690,000	—	0.75	0.85	1.00	2.00
1979 J	89,000	PF65 1.25				
1980 D	24,330,000	—	—	0.75	0.90	2.00
1980 D	110,000	PF65 1.00				
1980 F	9,670,000	—	—	0.75	0.90	2.00
1980 F	110,000	PF65 1.00				
1980 G	8,540,000	—	—	0.75	0.90	2.00
1980 G	110,000	PF65 1.00				
1980 J	16,010,000	—	—	0.75	0.90	2.00
1980 J	110,000	PF65 1.00				
1981 D	21,150,000	—	—	1.50	3.00	5.00

Date	Mintage	F12	VF20	XF40	MS60	MS63
1981 D	91,000	PF65 1.00				
1981 F	25,910,000	—	—	1.50	3.00	5.00
1981 F	91,000	PF65 1.00				
1981 G	14,090,000	—	—	1.50	3.00	5.00
1981 G	91,000	PF65 1.00				
1981 J	18,800,000	—	—	1.50	3.00	5.00
1981 J	91,000	PF65 1.00				
1982 D	20,590,000	—	—	1.50	3.00	5.00
1982 D	78,000	PF65 1.00				
1982 F	22,990,000	—	—	1.50	3.00	5.00
1982 F	78,000	PF65 1.00				
1982 G	14,900,000	—	—	1.50	3.00	5.00
1982 G	78,000	PF65 1.00				
1982 J	11,520,000	—	—	1.50	3.00	5.00
1982 J	78,000	PF65 1.00				
1983 D	18,200,000	—	—	1.50	3.00	5.00
1983 D	75,000	PF65 1.00				
1983 F	21,000,000	—	—	1.50	3.00	5.00
1983 F	75,000	PF65 1.00				
1983 G	12,100,000	—	—	1.50	3.00	5.00
1983 G	75,000	PF65 1.00				
1983 J	18,690,000	—	—	1.50	3.00	5.00
1983 J	75,000	PF65 1.00				
1984 D	8,400,000	—	—	1.50	3.00	5.00
1984 D	64,000	PF65 1.50				
1984 F	9,700,000	—	—	1.50	3.00	5.00
1984 F	64,000	PF65 1.50				
1984 G	5,600,000	—	—	1.50	3.00	5.00
1984 G	64,000	PF65 1.50				
1984 J	8,700,000	—	—	1.50	3.00	5.00
1984 J	64,000	PF65 1.50				
1985 D	11,700,000	—	—	1.50	3.00	5.00
1985 D	56,000	PF65 1.50				
1985 F	13,500,000	—	—	1.50	3.00	5.00
1985 F	54,000	PF65 1.50				
1985 G	7,800,000	—	—	1.50	3.00	5.00
1985 G	55,000	PF65 1.50				
1985 J	12,000,000	—	—	1.50	3.00	5.00
1985 J	54,000	PF65 1.50				
1986 D	10,400,000	—	—	1.50	3.00	5.00
1986 D	44,000	PF65 1.50				
1986 F	12,000,000	—	—	1.50	3.00	5.00
1986 F	44,000	PF65 1.50				
1986 G	6,900,000	—	—	1.50	3.00	5.00
1986 G	44,000	PF65 1.50				
1986 J	10,700,000	—	—	1.50	3.00	5.00
1986 J	44,000	PF65 1.50				
1987 D	3,120,000	—	3.50	7.50	12.00	15.00
1987 D	45,000	PF65 1.50				
1987 F	3,600,000	—	3.50	7.50	12.00	15.00
1987 F	45,000	PF65 1.50				
1987 G	2,080,000	—	3.50	7.50	12.00	15.00
1987 G	45,000	PF65 1.50				
1987 J	3,200,000	—	3.50	7.50	12.00	15.00
1987 J	45,000	PF65 1.50				
1988 D	20,800,000	—	—	0.75	1.50	3.00
1988 D	45,000	PF65 1.50				
1988 F	24,000,000	—	—	0.75	1.50	3.00
1988 F	45,000	PF65 1.50				
1988 G	13,800,000	—	—	0.75	1.50	3.00
1988 G	45,000	PF65 1.50				
1988 J	21,400,000	—	—	0.75	1.50	3.00
1988 J	45,000	PF65 1.50				
1989 D	39,000,000	—	—	—	1.00	2.00
1989 D	45,000	PF65 1.50				
1989 F	45,000,000	—	—	—	1.00	2.00
1989 F	45,000	PF65 1.50				
1989 G	25,950,000	—	—	—	1.00	2.00
1989 G	45,000	PF65 1.50				
1989 J	40,050,000	—	—	—	1.00	2.00
1989 J	45,000	PF65 1.50				
1990 A	55,000,000	—	—	—	1.00	2.00
1990 D	77,740,000	—	—	—	1.00	2.00
1990 D	45,000	PF65 1.50				
1990 F	89,700,000	—	—	—	1.00	2.00
1990 F	45,000	PF65 1.50				
1990 G	51,720,000	—	—	—	1.00	2.00
1990 G	45,000	PF65 1.50				
1990 J	79,830,000	—	—	—	1.00	2.00
1990 J	45,000	PF65 1.50				
1991 A	30,000,000	—	—	—	1.00	2.00
1991 A	45,000	PF65 1.50				
1991 D	31,500,000	—	—	—	1.00	2.00
1991 D	45,000	PF65 1.50				
1991 F	36,000,000	—	—	—	1.00	2.00
1991 F	45,000	PF65 1.50				
1991 G	21,000,000	—	—	—	1.00	2.00
1991 G	45,000	PF65 1.50				
1991 J	31,500,000	—	—	—	1.00	2.00
1991 J	45,000	PF65 1.50				
1992 A	30,000,000	—	—	—	1.00	2.00
1992 A	45,000	PF65 1.50				
1992 D	31,500,000	—	—	—	1.00	2.00
1992 D	45,000	PF65 1.50				
1992 F	36,000,000	—	—	—	1.00	2.00
1992 F	45,000	PF65 1.50				
1992 G	21,000,000	—	—	—	1.00	2.00
1992 G	45,000	PF65 1.50				
1992 J	31,500,000	—	—	—	1.00	2.00
1992 J	45,000	PF65 1.50				
1993 A	8,000,000	—	—	—	1.00	2.00
1993 A	45,000	PF65 1.50				
1993 D	8,400,000	—	—	—	1.00	2.00
1993 D	45,000	PF65 1.50				
1993 F	9,600,000	—	—	—	1.00	2.00
1993 F	45,000	PF65 1.50				
1993 G	5,600,000	—	—	—	1.00	2.00
1993 G	45,000	PF65 1.50				
1993 J	8,400,000	—	—	—	1.00	2.00
1993 J	45,000	PF65 1.50				
1994 A	18,000,000	—	—	—	1.00	2.00
1994 A	45,000	PF65 1.50				
1994 D	18,900,000	—	—	—	1.00	2.00
1994 D	45,000	PF65 1.50				
1994 F	21,800,000	—	—	—	1.00	2.00
1994 F	45,000	PF65 1.50				
1994 G	12,800,000	—	—	—	1.00	2.00
1994 G	45,000	PF65 1.50				
1994 J	18,900,000	—	—	—	1.00	2.00
1994 J	45,000	PF65 1.50				
1995 A Sets only	20,000	—	—	—	—	70.00
1995 A	45,000	PF65 20.00				
1995 D Sets only	20,000	—	—	—	—	70.00
1995 D	45,000	PF65 20.00				
1995 F Sets only	20,000	—	—	—	—	70.00
1995 F	45,000	PF65 20.00				
1995 G Sets only	20,000	—	—	—	—	70.00
1995 G	45,000	PF65 20.00				
1995 J	100,000	—	—	—	—	18.00
1995 J	45,000	PF65 20.00				
1996 A Sets only	50,000	—	—	—	—	12.50
1996 A	45,000	PF65 14.00				
1996 D Sets only	50,000	—	—	—	—	12.50
1996 D	45,000	PF65 14.00				
1996 F Sets only	50,000	—	—	—	—	12.50
1996 F	45,000	PF65 14.00				
1996 G Sets only	50,000	—	—	—	—	12.50
1996 G	45,000	PF65 14.00				
1996 J Sets only	50,000	—	—	—	—	12.50
1996 J	45,000	PF65 14.00				
1997 A Sets only	70,000	—	—	—	—	4.75
1997 A	45,000	PF65 5.00				
1997 D Sets only	70,000	—	—	—	—	4.75
1997 D	45,000	PF65 5.00				
1997 F Sets only	70,000	—	—	—	—	4.75
1997 F	45,000	PF65 5.00				
1997 G Sets only	70,000	—	—	—	—	4.75
1997 G	45,000	PF65 5.00				
1997 J Sets only	70,000	—	—	—	—	4.75
1997 J	45,000	PF65 5.00				
1998 A Sets only	70,000	—	—	—	—	4.75
1998 A	45,000	PF65 5.00				
1998 D Sets only	70,000	—	—	—	—	4.75
1998 D	45,000	PF65 5.00				
1998 F Sets only	70,000	—	—	—	—	4.75
1998 F	45,000	PF65 5.00				
1998 G Sets only	70,000	—	—	—	—	4.75
1998 G	45,000	PF65 5.00				
1998 J Sets only	70,000	—	—	—	—	4.75
1998 J	45,000	PF65 5.00				
1999 A Sets only	70,000	—	—	—	—	4.75
1999 A	45,000	PF65 5.00				
1999 D Sets only	70,000	—	—	—	—	4.75
1999 D	45,000	PF65 5.00				
1999 F Sets only	70,000	—	—	—	—	4.75
1999 F	45,000	PF65 5.00				
1999 G Sets only	70,000	—	—	—	—	4.75
1999 G	45,000	PF65 5.00				
1999 J Sets only	70,000	—	—	—	—	4.75
1999 J	45,000	PF65 5.00				
2000 A Sets only	70,000	—	—	—	—	5.00
2000 A	45,000	PF65 5.00				
2000 D Sets only	70,000	—	—	—	—	5.00
2000 D	45,000	PF65 5.00				
2000 F Sets only	70,000	—	—	—	—	5.00
2000 F	45,000	PF65 5.00				
2000 G Sets only	70,000	—	—	—	—	5.00
2000 G	45,000	PF65 5.00				
2000 J Sets only	70,000	—	—	—	—	5.00
2000 J	45,000	PF65 5.00				

KM# 111 2 MARK

7.00 g., Copper-Nickel, 26.75 mm. **Obv:** Eagle **Rev:** Denomination flanked by leaves, grapes, and grain sprigs, date above **Edge:** EINIGKEIT UND RECHT UND FREIHEIT

Date	Mintage	F12	VF20	XF40	MS60	MS63
1951 D	19,564,000	—	25.00	30.00	75.00	150
1951 D	200	PF63 450				
1951 F	22,609,000	—	25.00	30.00	75.00	150
1951 F	150	PF63 500				
1951 G	Est. 13012000	—	50.00	75.00	150	300

Note: The 1951G dated coin was restruck without authorization by a mint official using genuine dies - quantity unknown

Date	Mintage	F12	VF20	XF40	MS60	MS63
1951 G	33	PF63 1,200				
1951 J	20,104,000	—	25.00	30.00	75.00	150
1951 J	180	PF63 450				

KM# 116 2 MARK

7.00 g., Copper-Nickel, 26.75 mm. **Subject:** Max Planck **Obv:** Eagle above denomination **Rev:** Head left, dates below **Edge Lettering:** EINIGKEIT UND RECHT UND FREIHEIT

Date	Mintage	VF20	XF40	MS60	MS63	MS65
1957 D	7,452,000	2.00	6.00	20.00	35.00	75.00
1957 D	350	PF63 235				
1957 F	6,337,000	2.00	6.00	20.00	35.00	75.00
1957 F	100	PF63 325				
1957 G	2,598,000	3.00	7.50	35.00	65.00	135
1957 G	56	PF63 600				
1957 J	11,210,000	2.00	6.00	18.00	30.00	60.00
1957 J	370	PF63 175				
1958 D	12,623,000	1.50	5.00	15.00	25.00	50.00
1958 D	1,240	PF63 85.00				
1958 F	16,825,000	1.50	4.00	12.50	22.00	45.00
1958 F	300	PF63 200				
1958 G	10,744,000	1.50	4.00	12.50	22.00	45.00
1958 G	45	PF63 700				
1958 J	9,408,000	1.50	4.00	12.50	22.00	45.00
1958 J	100	PF63 400				
1959 D	1,020,000	4.00	15.00	70.00	120	240
1959 D	38	PF63 1,150				
1959 F	203,000	15.00	60.00	130	220	450
1959 F	24	PF63 1,850				
1960 D	3,535,000	1.50	4.00	10.00	17.00	35.00
1960 D	100	PF63 325				
1960 F	3,692,000	1.50	4.00	1.00	17.00	35.00
1960 F	50	PF63 600				
1960 G	2,695,000	2.00	4.00	10.00	17.00	35.00
1960 G	130	PF63 300				
1960 J	4,676,000	1.50	4.00	10.00	17.00	35.00
1960 J	36	PF63 800				
1961 D	3,918,000	1.50	4.00	10.00	17.00	35.00
1961 D	50	PF63 600				
1961 F	3,872,000	1.50	4.00	10.00	17.00	35.00
1961 F	46	PF63 650				
1961 G	2,776,000	2.00	4.00	10.00	17.00	35.00
1961 G	100	PF63 325				
1961 J	2,940,000	1.50	4.00	10.00	17.00	35.00
1961 J	28	PF63 800				
1962 D	4,105,000	2.00	5.00	10.00	17.00	35.00
1962 D	50	PF63 600				
1962 F	3,344,000	2.00	5.00	10.00	17.00	35.00
1962 F	42	PF63 625				
1962 G	1,800,000	2.00	6.00	12.50	22.00	45.00
1962 G	130	PF63 300				
1962 J	3,609,000	2.00	3.50	7.00	12.00	25.00
1962 J	28	PF63 750				
1963 D	4,411,000	1.50	4.00	7.00	12.00	25.00
1963 D	40	PF63 650				
1963 F	3,752,000	1.50	4.00	7.00	12.00	25.00
1963 F	47	PF63 600				
1963 G	3,448,000	1.50	4.00	7.00	12.00	25.00
1963 G	200	PF63 350				
1963 J	7,348,000	1.50	4.00	7.00	12.00	25.00
1963 J	32	PF63 700				
1964 D	5,205,000	1.50	4.00	6.00	10.00	20.00
1964 D	40	PF65 650				
1964 F	4,834,000	1.50	4.00	6.00	10.00	20.00
1964 F	36	PF65 800				
1964 G	3,044,000	10.00	25.00	35.00	65.00	125
1964 G	368	PF65 150				
1964 J	2,681,000	1.50	4.00	6.00	10.00	20.00
1964 J	43	PF65 600				
1965 D	3,903,000	1.50	2.50	4.00	7.50	15.00
1965 D	35	PF65 800				
1965 F	4,045,000	1.50	2.50	4.00	7.50	15.00
1965 F	300	PF65 250				
1965 G	2,599,000	1.50	2.50	4.00	7.50	15.00
1965 G	8,233	PF65 5.00				
1965 J	4,006,999	1.50	2.50	4.00	7.50	15.00

Note: Error exists without edge inscription

Date	Mintage	VF20	XF40	MS60	MS63	MS65
1965 J	36	PF65 750				

Date	Mintage	VF20	XF40	MS60	MS63	MS65
1966 D	5,855,000	1.50	2.50	3.50	6.00	12.00
1966 D	20	PF65 900				
1966 F	3,750,000	1.50	2.50	3.50	6.00	12.00
1966 F	450	PF65 250				
1966 G	3,895,000	1.50	2.50	3.50	6.00	12.00
1966 G	3,070	PF65 20.00				
1966 J	6,014,000	1.50	2.50	3.50	6.00	12.00
1966 J	1,000	PF65 35.00				
1967 D	3,254,000	1.50	2.50	3.50	6.00	12.00
1967 D	20	PF65 900				
1967 F	3,758,000	1.50	2.50	3.50	6.00	12.00
1967 F	1,600	PF65 32.00				
1967 G	1,878,000	1.50	3.00	4.50	8.00	16.00
1967 G	5,363	PF65 28.00				
1967 J	6,684,000	1.25	2.50	3.50	6.00	12.00
1967 J	1,500	PF65 32.00				
1968 D	4,166,000	1.25	2.50	4.00	7.50	15.00
1968 D	30	PF65 850				
1968 F	1,050,000	2.00	3.50	6.00	10.00	20.00
1968 F	3,100	PF65 22.00				
1968 G	3,060,000	2.00	2.50	3.50	6.00	12.00
1968 G	6,023	PF65 15.00				
1968 J	939,000	2.00	3.50	6.00	10.00	20.00
1968 J	2,000	PF65 28.00				
1969 D	2,602,000	1.50	2.50	4.00	7.50	15.00
1969 F	3,005,000	1.50	2.50	4.00	7.50	15.00
1969 F	5,100	PF65 6.00				
1969 G	1,754,000	1.50	2.50	4.50	8.00	16.00
1969 G	8,700	PF65 6.00				
1969 J	2,680,000	1.50	2.50	3.00	5.00	10.00
1969 J	5,000	PF65 6.00				
1970 D	5,203,000	1.25	2.00	2.50	4.00	8.00
1970 F	6,018,000	1.25	2.00	2.50	4.00	8.00
1970 F	5,140	PF65 7.50				
1970 G	3,461,000	1.25	2.00	2.50	4.00	8.00
1970 G	10,000	PF65 5.00				
1970 J	5,691,000	1.25	2.00	2.50	4.00	8.00
1970 J	5,000	PF65 6.00				
1971 D	8,451,000	—	1.00	1.50	3.00	6.00
1971 D	8,000	PF65 5.00				
1971 F	10,017,000	—	1.00	1.50	3.00	6.00
1971 F	8,000	PF65 5.00				
1971 G	5,631,000	—	1.00	1.50	3.00	6.00
1971 G	10,000	PF65 5.00				
1971 J	8,786,000	—	1.00	1.50	3.00	6.00
1971 J	8,000	PF65 6.00				

KM# 124 2 MARK

7.00 g., Copper-Nickel Clad Nickel, 26.75 mm. **Subject:** Konrad Adenauer **Obv:** Eagle above denomination **Rev:** Head left, dates below **Edge Lettering:** EINIGKEIT UND RECHT UND FREIHEIT

Date	Mintage	VF20	XF40	MS60	MS63	MS65
1969 D	7,001,000	—	—	1.50	3.00	6.00
1969 F	7,006,000	—	—	1.50	3.00	6.00
1969 G	7,010,000	—	—	1.50	3.00	6.00
1969 J	7,000,000	—	—	1.50	3.00	6.00
1970 D	7,318,000	—	—	1.50	3.00	6.00
1970 F	8,422,000	—	—	1.50	3.00	6.00
1970 G	4,844,000	—	—	1.50	3.00	6.00
1970 J	7,476,000	—	—	1.50	3.00	6.00
1971 D	7,287,000	—	—	1.50	3.00	6.00
1971 F	8,400,000	—	—	1.50	3.00	6.00
1971 G	4,848,000	—	—	1.50	3.00	6.00
1971 J	7,476,000	—	—	1.50	3.00	6.00
1972 D	7,286,000	—	—	1.50	3.00	6.00
1972 D	8,000	PF65 4.50				
1972 F	8,392,000	—	—	1.50	3.00	6.00
1972 F	8,000	PF65 4.50				
1972 G	4,848,000	—	—	1.50	3.00	6.00
1972 G	10,000	PF65 4.50				
1972 J	7,476,000	—	—	1.50	3.00	6.00
1972 J	8,000	PF65 4.50				
1973 D	10,393,000	—	—	1.50	3.00	6.00
1973 D	9,000	PF65 4.50				
1973 F	11,015,000	—	—	1.50	3.00	6.00
Note: Errors exist without edge inscription						
1973 F	9,000	PF65 4.50				
1973 G	9,022,000	—	—	1.50	3.00	6.00
1973 G	9,000	PF65 4.50				
1973 J	12,272,000	—	—	1.50	3.00	6.00
Note: Errors with coin alignment exist						
1973 J	9,000	PF65 4.50				
1974 D	5,151,000	—	—	1.50	3.00	6.00
1974 D	35,000	PF65 2.25				
1974 F	5,894,000	—	—	1.50	3.00	6.00
1974 F	35,000	PF65 2.25				
1974 G	3,790,000	—	—	1.50	3.00	6.00
1974 G	35,000	PF65 2.25				
1974 J	5,282,000	—	—	1.50	3.00	6.00
1974 J	35,000	PF65 2.25				
1975 D	4,553,000	—	—	1.50	2.50	5.00
1975 D	43,000	PF65 2.25				
1975 F	5,270,000	—	—	1.50	2.50	5.00
1975 F	43,000	PF65 2.25				
1975 G	3,035,000	—	—	1.50	2.50	5.00
1975 G	43,000	PF65 2.25				
1975 J	4,673,000	—	—	1.50	2.50	5.00
1975 J	43,000	PF65 2.25				
1976 D	4,576,000	—	—	1.50	2.50	5.00
1976 D	43,000	PF65 2.25				
1976 F	5,257,000	—	—	1.50	2.50	5.00
1976 F	43,000	PF65 2.25				
1976 G	3,028,000	—	—	1.50	2.50	5.00
1976 G	43,000	PF65 2.25				
1976 J	4,673,000	—	—	1.50	2.50	5.00
1976 J	43,000	PF65 2.25				
1977 D	5,906,000	—	—	1.50	2.50	5.00
1977 D	51,000	PF65 2.00				
1977 F	6,765,000	—	—	1.50	2.50	5.00
1977 F	51,000	PF65 2.00				
1977 G	3,892,000	—	—	1.50	2.50	5.00
1977 G	51,000	PF65 2.00				
1977 J	6,007,000	—	—	1.50	2.50	5.00
1977 J	51,000	PF65 2.00				
1978 D	3,304,000	—	—	1.50	2.50	5.00
1978 D	54,000	PF65 2.00				
1978 F	3,804	—	—	1.50	2.50	5.00
1978 F	54,000	PF65 2.00				
1978 G	2,217,000	—	—	1.50	2.50	5.00
1978 G	54,000	PF65 2.00				
1978 J	3,392,000	—	—	1.50	2.50	5.00
1978 J	54,000	PF65 2.00				
1979 D	3,209,000	—	—	1.50	2.50	5.00
1979 D	89,000	PF65 2.00				
1979 F	3,689,000	—	—	1.50	2.50	5.00
1979 F	89,000	PF65 2.00				
1979 G	2,165,000	—	—	1.50	2.50	5.00
1979 G	89,000	PF65 2.00				
1979 J	3,293,000	—	—	1.50	2.50	5.00
1979 J	89,000	PF65 2.00				
1980 D	10,810,000	—	—	1.50	2.00	4.00
1980 D	110,000	PF65 2.00				
1980 F	8,910,000	—	—	1.50	2.00	4.00
1980 F	110,000	PF65 2.00				
1980 G	1,170,000	—	—	1.50	2.00	4.00
1980 G	110,000	PF65 2.00				
1980 J	4,670,000	—	—	1.50	2.00	4.00
1980 J	110,000	PF65 2.00				
1981 D	8,180,000	—	—	1.50	2.00	4.00
1981 D	91,000	PF65 2.00				
1981 F	7,690,000	—	—	1.50	2.00	4.00
1981 F	91,000	PF65 2.00				
1981 G	7,070,000	—	—	1.50	2.00	4.00
1981 G	91,000	PF65 2.00				
1981 J	8,289,999	—	—	1.50	2.00	4.00
1981 J	91,000	PF65 2.00				
1982 D	9,220,000	—	—	1.50	2.00	4.00
1982 D	78,000	PF65 2.00				
1982 F	11,260,000	—	—	1.50	2.00	4.00
1982 F	78,000	PF65 2.00				
1982 G	6,640,000	—	—	1.50	2.00	4.00
1982 G	78,000	PF65 2.00				
1982 J	9,790,000	—	—	1.50	2.00	4.00
1982 J	78,000	PF65 2.00				
1983 D	1,560,000	—	—	1.50	2.00	4.00
1983 D	75,000	PF65 2.00				
1983 F	1,800,000	—	—	1.50	2.00	4.00
1983 F	75,000	PF65 2.00				
1983 G	1,030,000	—	—	1.50	2.00	4.00
1983 G	75,000	PF65 2.00				
1983 J	1,600,000	—	—	1.50	2.00	4.00
1983 J	75,000	PF65 2.00				
1984 D	52,000	2.00	3.00	4.50	8.00	16.00
1984 D	64,000	PF65 2.00				
1984 F	60,000	2.00	3.00	4.50	8.00	16.00
1984 F	64,000	PF65 2.00				
1984 G	35,000	3.00	5.00	7.00	12.00	25.00
1984 G	64,000	PF65 2.00				
1984 J	53,000	2.00	3.00	4.50	8.00	16.00
1984 J	64,000	PF65 2.00				
1985 D	2,600,000	—	—	—	2.00	4.00
1985 D	56,000	PF65 2.25				
1985 F	3,000,000	—	—	1.25	1.75	3.50
1985 F	54,000	PF65 2.25				
1985 G	1,730,000	—	—	1.25	1.75	3.50
1985 G	55,000	PF65 2.25				
1985 J	2,670,000	—	—	1.25	1.75	3.50
1985 J	54,000	PF65 2.25				
1986 D	2,600,000	—	—	1.25	1.75	3.50
1986 D	44,000	PF65 2.25				
1986 F	3,000,000	—	—	1.25	1.75	3.50
1986 F	44,000	PF65 2.25				
1986 G	1,730,000	—	—	1.25	1.75	3.50
1986 G	44,000	PF65 2.25				
1986 J	2,670,000	—	—	1.25	1.75	3.50
1986 J	44,000	PF65 2.25				
1987 D	4,420,000	—	—	1.25	1.75	3.50
1987 D	45,000	PF65 2.25				
1987 F	5,100,000	—	—	1.25	1.75	3.50
1987 F	45,000	PF65 2.25				
1987 G	2,940,000	—	—	1.25	1.75	3.50
1987 G	45,000	PF65 2.25				
1987 J	4,540,000	—	—	1.25	1.75	3.50
1987 J	45,000	PF65 2.25				

KM# A127 2 MARK

7.00 g., Copper-Nickel Clad Nickel, 26.75 mm. **Subject:** Theodor Heuss **Obv:** Eagle above denomination **Rev:** Head left, dates below **Edge Lettering:** EINIGKEIT UND RECHT UND FREIHEIT

Date	Mintage	VF20	XF40	MS60	MS63	MS65
1970 D	7,317,000	—	—	1.50	3.00	5.00
1970 F	8,426,000	—	—	1.50	3.00	5.00
1970 G	4,844,000	—	—	1.50	3.00	5.00
1970 J	7,476,000	—	—	1.50	3.00	5.00
1971 D	7,280,000	—	—	1.50	3.00	5.00
1971 F	8,403,000	—	—	1.50	3.00	5.00
1971 G	4,841,000	—	—	1.50	3.00	5.00
1971 J	7,476,000	—	—	1.50	3.00	5.00
1972 D	7,288,000	—	—	1.50	3.00	5.00
1972 D	8,000	PF65 4.50				
1972 F	8,401,000	—	—	1.50	3.00	5.00
1972 F	8,000	PF65 4.50				
1972 G	4,859,000	—	—	1.50	3.00	5.00
1972 G	10,000	PF65 4.50				
1972 J	7,476,000	—	—	1.50	3.00	5.00
1972 J	8,000	PF65 4.50				
1973 D	10,379,000	—	—	1.50	3.00	5.00
1973 D	9,000	PF65 4.50				
1973 F	11,018,000	—	—	1.50	3.00	5.00
1973 F	9,000	PF65 4.50				
1973 G	8,975,000	—	—	1.50	3.00	5.00
1973 G	9,000	PF65 4.50				
1973 J	12,360,000	—	—	1.50	3.00	5.00
1973 J	9,000	PF65 4.50				
1974 D	5,147,000	—	—	1.50	3.00	5.00
1974 D	35,000	PF65 2.00				
1974 F	5,899,000	—	—	1.50	3.00	5.00
1974 F	35,000	PF65 2.00				
1974 G	3,820,000	—	—	1.50	3.00	5.00
1974 G	35,000	PF65 2.00				
1974 J	5,280,000	—	—	1.50	3.00	5.00
1974 J	35,000	PF65 2.00				
1975 D	4,623,000	—	—	1.50	2.00	3.50
1975 D	43,000	PF65 2.00				
1975 F	5,251,000	—	—	1.50	2.00	3.50
1975 F	43,000	PF65 2.00				
1975 G	3,034,000	—	—	1.50	2.00	3.50
1975 G	43,000	PF65 2.00				
1975 J	4,675,000	—	—	1.50	2.00	3.50
1975 J	43,000	PF65 2.00				
1976 D	4,546,000	—	—	1.50	2.00	3.50
1976 D	43,000	PF65 2.00				
1976 F	5,259,000	—	—	1.50	2.00	3.50
1976 F	43,000	PF65 2.00				
1976 G	3,028,000	—	—	1.50	2.00	3.50
1976 G	43,000	PF65 2.00				
1976 J	4,681,000	—	—	1.50	2.00	3.50
1976 J	43,000	PF65 2.00				
1977 D	5,857,000	—	—	1.50	2.00	3.50
1977 D	51,000	PF65 1.75				
1977 F	6,752,000	—	—	1.50	2.00	3.50
1977 F	51,000	PF65 1.75				
1977 G	3,892,000	—	—	1.50	2.00	3.50
1977 G	51,000	PF65 1.75				
1977 J	6,009,000	—	—	1.50	2.00	3.50
1977 J	51,000	PF65 1.75				
1978 D	3,804,000	—	—	1.50	2.00	3.50
Note: Errors without edge inscription exist						
1978 D	54,000	PF65 1.75				
1978 F	3,804,000	—	—	1.50	2.00	3.50
1978 F	54,000	PF65 1.75				
1978 G	2,217,000	—	—	1.50	2.00	3.50
1978 G	54,000	PF65 1.75				
1978 J	3,392,000	—	—	1.50	2.00	3.50
1978 J	54,000	PF65 1.75				
1979 D	3,209,000	—	—	1.50	2.00	3.50
1979 D	89,000	PF65 1.75				
1979 F	3,689,000	—	—	1.50	2.00	3.50
1979 F	89,000	PF65 1.75				

Date	Mintage	VF20	XF40	MS60	MS63	MS65
1979 G	2,165,000	—	—	1.50	2.00	3.50
1979 G	89,000	PF65 1.75				
1979 J	3,293,000	—	—	1.50	2.00	3.50
1979 J	89,000	PF65 1.75				
1980 D	2,000,000	—	—	1.25	1.75	3.00
1980 D	110,000	PF65 1.75				
1980 F	2,300,000	—	—	1.25	1.75	3.00
1980 F	110,000	PF65 1.75				
1980 G	1,300,000	—	—	1.25	1.75	3.00
1980 G	110,000	PF65 1.75				
1980 J	2,000,000	—	—	1.25	1.75	3.00
1980 J	110,000	PF65 1.75				
1981 D	2,000,000	—	—	1.25	1.75	3.00
1981 D	91,000	PF65 1.75				
1981 F	2,300,000	—	—	1.25	1.75	3.00
1981 F	91,000	PF65 1.75				
1981 G	1,300,000	—	—	1.25	1.75	3.00
1981 G	91,000	PF65 1.75				
1981 J	2,000,000	—	—	1.25	1.75	3.00
1981 J	91,000	PF65 1.75				
1982 D	3,100,000	—	—	1.25	1.75	3.00
1982 D	78,000	PF65 1.75				
1982 F	3,600,000	—	—	1.25	1.75	3.00
1982 F	78,000	PF65 1.75				
1982 G	2,100,000	—	—	1.25	1.75	3.00
1982 G	78,000	PF65 1.75				
1982 J	3,200,000	—	—	1.25	1.75	3.00
1982 J	78,000	PF65 1.75				
1983 D	1,560,000	—	—	1.25	1.75	3.00
1983 D	75,000	PF65 1.75				
1983 F	1,800,000	—	—	1.25	1.75	3.00
1983 F	75,000	PF65 1.75				
1983 G	1,030,000	—	—	1.25	1.75	3.00
1983 G	75,000	PF65 1.75				
1983 J	1,600,000	—	—	1.25	1.75	3.00
1983 J	75,000	PF65 1.75				
1984 D	52,000	2.00	3.50	5.50	8.50	16.00
1984 D	64,000	PF65 2.00				
1984 F	60,000	2.00	3.50	5.50	8.50	16.00
1984 F	64,000	PF65 2.00				
1984 G	35,000	2.50	4.00	6.00	10.00	18.00
1984 G	64,000	PF65 2.00				
1984 J	53,000	2.00	3.50	5.50	8.50	16.00
1984 J	64,000	PF65 2.00				
1985 D	2,600,000	—	—	—	1.75	3.00
1985 D	56,000	PF65 2.25				
1985 F	3,000,000	—	—	—	1.75	3.00
1985 F	54,000	PF65 2.25				
1985 G	1,730,000	—	—	—	1.75	3.00
1985 G	55,000	PF65 2.25				
1985 J	2,670,000	—	—	—	1.75	3.00
1985 J	54,000	PF65 2.25				
1986 D	2,600,000	—	—	—	1.75	3.00
1986 D	44,000	PF65 2.25				
1986 F	3,000,000	—	—	—	1.75	3.00
1986 F	44,000	PF65 2.25				
1986 G	1,730,000	—	—	—	1.75	3.00
1986 G	44,000	PF65 2.25				
1986 J	2,670,000	—	—	—	1.75	3.00
1986 J	44,000	PF65 2.25				
1987 D	4,420,000	—	—	—	1.75	3.00
1987 D	45,000	PF65 2.25				
1987 F	5,100,000	—	—	—	1.75	3.00
1987 F	45,000	PF65 2.25				
1987 G	2,940,000	—	—	—	1.75	3.00
1987 G	45,000	PF65 2.25				
1987 J	4,540,000	—	—	—	1.75	3.00
1987 J	45,000	PF65 2.25				

KM# 149 2 MARK

7.00 g., Copper-Nickel Clad Nickel, 26.75 mm. **Subject:** Dr. Kurt Schumacher **Obv:** Eagle above denomination **Rev:** Head 3/4 left divides dates **Edge Lettering:** EINIGKEIT UND RECHT UND FREIHEIT

Date	Mintage	VF20	XF40	MS60	MS63	MS65
1979 D	3,209,000	—	—	1.50	2.00	3.50
1979 D	89,000	PF65 1.75				
1979 F	3,689,000	—	—	1.50	2.00	3.50
1979 F	89,000	PF65 1.75				
1979 G	2,165,000	—	—	1.50	2.00	3.50
1979 G	89,000	PF65 1.75				
1979 J	3,293,000	—	—	1.50	2.00	3.50
1979 J	89,000	PF65 1.75				
1980 D	2,000,000	—	—	1.50	2.00	3.50
1980 D	110,000	PF65 1.75				
1980 F	2,300,000	—	—	1.50	2.00	3.50
1980 F	110,000	PF65 1.75				
1980 G	1,300,000	—	—	1.50	2.00	3.50
1980 G	110,000	PF65 1.75				
1980 J	2,000,000	—	—	1.50	2.00	3.50
1980 J	110,000	PF65 1.75				
1981 D	2,000,000	—	—	1.50	2.00	3.50
1981 D	91,000	PF65 1.75				
1981 F	2,000,000	—	—	1.50	2.00	3.50
Note: Errors without edge inscription exist						
1981 F	91,000	PF65 1.75				
1981 G	1,300,000	—	—	1.50	2.00	3.50
1981 G	91,000	PF65 1.75				
1981 J	2,000,000	—	—	1.50	2.00	3.50
1981 J	91,000	PF65 1.75				
1982 D	3,100,000	—	—	1.50	2.00	3.50
1982 D	78,000	PF65 1.75				
1982 F	3,600,000	—	—	1.50	2.00	3.50
1982 F	78,000	PF65 1.75				
1982 G	2,100,000	—	—	1.50	2.00	3.50
1982 G	78,000	PF65 1.75				
1982 J	3,200,000	—	—	1.50	2.00	3.50
1982 J	78,000	PF65 1.75				
1983 D	1,560,000	—	—	1.50	2.00	3.50
1983 D	75,000	PF65 1.75				
1983 F	1,800,000	—	—	1.50	2.00	3.50
1983 F	75,000	PF65 1.75				
1983 G	1,030,000	—	—	1.50	2.00	3.50
1983 G	75,000	PF65 1.75				
1983 J	1,600,000	—	—	1.50	2.00	3.50
1983 J	75,000	PF65 1.75				
1984 D	52,000	2.00	3.50	5.50	8.50	15.00
1984 D	64,000	PF65 1.75				
1984 F	60,000	2.00	3.50	5.50	8.50	15.00
1984 F	64,000	PF65 1.75				
1984 G	35,000	3.00	5.00	7.00	11.50	20.00
1984 G	64,000	PF65 1.75				
1984 J	53,000	2.00	3.50	5.50	8.50	15.00
1984 J	64,000	PF65 1.75				
1985 D	2,600,000	—	—	—	1.75	2.50
1985 D	56,000	PF65 2.25				
1985 F	3,000,000	—	—	—	1.75	2.50
1985 F	54,000	PF65 2.25				
1985 G	1,730,000	—	—	—	1.75	2.50
1985 G	55,000	PF65 2.25				
1985 J	2,670,000	—	—	—	1.75	2.50
1985 J	54,000	PF65 2.25				
1986 D	2,600,000	—	—	—	1.75	2.50
1986 D	44,000	PF65 2.25				
1986 F	3,000,000	—	—	—	1.75	2.50
1986 F	44,000	PF65 2.25				
1986 G	1,730,000	—	—	—	1.75	2.50
1986 G	44,000	PF65 2.25				
1986 J	2,670,000	—	—	—	1.75	2.50
1986 J	44,000	PF65 2.25				
1987 D	4,420,000	—	—	—	1.75	2.50
1987 D	45,000	PF65 2.25				
1987 F	5,100,000	—	—	—	1.75	2.50
1987 F	45,000	PF65 2.25				
1987 G	2,940,000	—	—	—	1.75	2.50
1987 G	45,000	PF65 2.25				
1987 J	4,540,000	—	—	—	1.75	2.50
1987 J	45,000	PF65 2.25				
1988 D	5,850,000	—	—	—	1.75	2.50
1988 D	45,000	PF65 2.25				
1988 F	6,750,000	—	—	—	1.75	2.50
1988 F	45,000	PF65 2.25				
1988 G	3,890,000	—	—	—	1.75	2.50
1988 G	45,000	PF65 2.25				
1988 J	6,010,000	—	—	—	1.75	2.50
1988 J	45,000	PF65 2.25				
1989 D	10,400,000	—	—	—	1.75	2.50
1989 D	45,000	PF65 2.25				
1989 F	12,000,000	—	—	—	1.75	2.50
1989 F	45,000	PF65 2.25				
1989 G	6,920,000	—	—	—	1.75	2.50
1989 G	45,000	PF65 2.25				
1989 J	10,680,000	—	—	—	1.75	2.50
1989 J	45,000	PF65 2.25				
1990 D	18,370,000	—	—	—	1.75	2.50
1990 D	45,000	PF65 2.25				
1990 F	21,200,000	—	—	—	1.75	2.50
1990 F	45,000	PF65 2.25				
1990 G	12,220,000	—	—	—	1.75	2.50
1990 G	45,000	PF65 2.25				
1990 J	18,870,000	—	—	—	1.75	2.50
1990 J	45,000	PF65 2.25				
1991 A	4,000,000	—	—	—	1.75	2.50
1991 A	45,000	PF65 2.25				
1991 D	4,200,000	—	—	—	1.75	2.50
1991 D	45,000	PF65 2.25				
1991 F	4,800,000	—	—	—	1.75	2.50
1991 F	45,000	PF65 2.25				
1991 G	2,800,000	—	—	—	1.75	2.50
1991 G	45,000	PF65 2.25				
1991 J	4,200,000	—	—	—	1.75	2.50
1991 J	45,000	PF65 2.25				
1992 A	7,330,000	—	—	—	1.75	2.50
1992 A	45,000	PF65 2.25				
1992 D	7,700,000	—	—	—	1.75	2.50
1992 D	45,000	PF65 2.25				
1992 F	8,800,000	—	—	—	1.75	2.50
1992 F	45,000	PF65 2.25				
1992 G	5,130,000	—	—	—	1.75	2.50
1992 G	45,000	PF65 2.25				
1992 J	7,700,000	—	—	—	1.75	2.50
1992 J	45,000	PF65 2.25				
1993 A	600,000	—	3.00	4.50	7.00	12.00
1993 A	45,000	PF65 2.25				
1993 D	630,000	—	3.00	4.50	7.00	12.00
1993 D	45,000	PF65 2.25				
1993 F	720,000	—	3.00	4.50	7.00	12.00
1993 F	45,000	PF65 2.25				
1993 G	420,000	—	4.00	6.00	10.00	15.00
1993 G	45,000	PF65 2.25				
1993 J	630,000	—	3.00	4.50	7.00	12.00
1993 J	45,000	PF65 2.25				

KM# 170 2 MARK

7.00 g., Copper-Nickel Clad Nickel, 26.75 mm. **Subject:** Ludwig Erhard **Obv:** Eagle above denomination **Rev:** Head facing divides dates **Edge Lettering:** EINIGKEIT UND RECHT UND FREIHEIT

Date	Mintage	VF20	XF40	MS60	MS63	MS65
1988 D	5,850,000	—	—	—	1.65	2.25
1988 D	45,000	PF65 2.00				
1988 F	6,750,000	—	—	—	1.65	2.25
1988 F	45,000	PF65 2.00				
1988 G	3,890,000	—	—	—	1.65	2.25
1988 G	45,000	PF65 2.00				
1988 J	6,010,000	—	—	—	1.65	2.25
1988 J	45,000	PF65 2.00				
1989 D	10,400,000	—	—	—	1.65	2.25
1989 D	45,000	PF65 2.00				
1989 F	12,000,000	—	—	—	1.65	2.25
1989 F	45,000	PF65 2.00				
1989 G	6,920,000	—	—	—	1.65	2.25
1989 G	45,000	PF65 2.00				
1989 J	10,680,000	—	—	—	1.65	2.25
1989 J	45,000	PF65 2.00				
1990 D	18,370,000	—	—	—	1.65	2.25
1990 D	45,000	PF65 2.00				
1990 F	21,200,000	—	—	—	1.65	2.25
1990 F	45,000	PF65 2.00				
1990 G	12,220,000	—	—	—	1.65	2.25
1990 G	45,000	PF65 2.00				
1990 J	18,870,000	—	—	—	1.65	2.25
1990 J	45,000	PF65 2.00				
1991 A	4,000,000	—	—	—	1.65	2.25
1991 A	45,000	PF65 2.00				
1991 D	4,200,000	—	—	—	1.65	2.25
1991 D	45,000	PF65 2.00				
1991 F	4,800,000	—	—	—	1.65	2.25
1991 F	45,000	PF65 2.00				
1991 G	2,800,000	—	—	—	1.65	2.25
Note: Errors without edge inscription exist						
1991 G	45,000	PF65 2.00				
1991 J	4,200,000	—	—	—	1.65	2.25
1991 J	45,000	PF65 2.00				
1992 A	7,330,000	—	—	—	1.75	2.50
1992 A	45,000	PF65 2.25				
1992 D	7,700,000	—	—	—	1.75	2.50
1992 D	45,000	PF65 2.25				
1992 F	8,800,000	—	—	—	1.75	2.50
1992 F	45,000	PF65 2.25				
1992 G	5,130,000	—	—	—	1.75	2.50
1992 G	45,000	PF65 2.25				
1992 J	7,700,000	—	—	—	1.75	2.50
1992 J	45,000	PF65 2.25				
1993 A	600,000	—	3.00	4.50	7.00	12.00
1993 A	45,000	PF65 2.25				
1993 D	630,000	—	3.00	4.50	7.00	12.00
1993 D	45,000	PF65 2.25				
1993 F	720,000	—	3.00	4.50	7.00	12.00
1993 F	45,000	PF65 2.25				
1993 G	420,000	—	4.00	6.00	10.00	15.00
1993 G	45,000	PF65 2.25				
1993 J	630,000	—	3.00	4.50	7.00	12.00
1993 J	45,000	PF65 2.25				
1994 A	5,000,000	—	—	—	1.75	2.50
1994 A	45,000	PF65 2.25				
1994 D	5,250,000	—	—	—	1.75	2.50
1994 D	45,000	PF65 2.25				
1994 F	6,000,000	—	—	—	1.75	2.50
1994 F	45,000	PF65 2.25				
1994 G	3,500,000	—	—	—	1.75	2.50

Date	Mintage	VF20	XF40	MS60	MS63	MS65
1994 G	45,000	PF65 2.25				
1994 J	5,250,000	—	—	—	1.75	2.50
1994 J	45,000	PF65 2.25				
1995 A	1,595,000	—	—	—	3.50	5.00
1995 A	45,000	PF65 17.50				
1995 D Sets only	20,000	—	—	—	—	60.00
1995 D	45,000	PF65 17.50				
1995 F Sets only	20,000	—	—	—	—	60.00
1995 F	45,000	PF65 17.50				
1995 G	920,000	—	—	—	6.00	10.00
1995 G	45,000	PF65 17.50				
1995 J Sets only	20,000	—	—	—	—	60.00
1995 J	45,000	PF65 17.50				
1996 A	—	—	—	—	5.00	8.00
1996 A	45,000	PF65 6.00				
1996 D	—	—	—	—	5.00	8.00
1996 D	45,000	PF65 6.00				
1996 F	—	—	—	—	5.00	8.00
1996 F	45,000	PF65 6.00				
1996 G	—	—	—	—	5.00	8.00
1996 G	45,000	PF65 6.00				
1996 J	—	—	—	—	5.00	8.00
1996 J	45,000	PF65 6.00				
1997 A Sets only	70,000	—	—	—	—	4.25
1997 A	45,000	PF65 5.00				
1997 D Sets only	70,000	—	—	—	—	4.25
1997 D	45,000	PF65 5.00				
1997 F Sets only	70,000	—	—	—	—	4.25
1997 F	45,000	PF65 5.00				
1997 G Sets only	70,000	—	—	—	—	4.25
1997 G	45,000	PF65 5.00				
1997 J Sets only	70,000	—	—	—	—	4.25
1997 J	45,000	PF65 5.00				
1998 A Sets only	70,000	—	—	—	—	4.25
1998 A	45,000	PF65 5.00				
1998 D Sets only	70,000	—	—	—	—	4.25
1998 D	45,000	PF65 5.00				
1998 F Sets only	70,000	—	—	—	—	4.25
1998 F	45,000	PF65 5.00				
1998 G Sets only	70,000	—	—	—	—	4.25
1998 G	45,000	PF65 5.00				
1998 J Sets only	70,000	—	—	—	—	4.25
1998 J	45,000	PF65 5.00				
1999 A Sets only	70,000	—	—	—	—	4.25
1999 A	45,000	PF65 5.00				
1999 D Sets only	70,000	—	—	—	—	4.25
1999 D	45,000	PF65 5.00				
1999 F Sets only	70,000	—	—	—	—	4.25
1999 F	45,000	PF65 5.00				
1999 G Sets only	70,000	—	—	—	—	4.75
1999 G	45,000	PF65 5.00				
1999 J Sets only	70,000	—	—	—	—	4.75
1999 J	45,000	PF65 5.00				
2000 A Sets only	70,000	—	—	—	—	5.00
2000 A	45,000	PF65 5.00				
2000 D Sets only	70,000	—	—	—	—	5.00
2000 D	45,000	PF65 5.00				
2000 F Sets only	70,000	—	—	—	—	5.00
2000 F	45,000	PF65 5.00				
2000 G Sets only	70,000	—	—	—	—	5.00
2000 G	45,000	PF65 5.00				
2000 J Sets only	70,000	—	—	—	—	5.00
2000 J	45,000	PF65 5.00				

KM# 175 2 MARK

7.04 g., Copper-Nickel Clad Nickel, 26.8 mm. **Subject:** Franz Joseph Strauss **Obv:** Eagle above denomination **Rev:** Head left divides dates **Edge Lettering:** EINIGKEIT UND RECHT UND FREIHEIT

Date	Mintage	VF20	XF40	MS60	MS63	MS65
1990 D	18,370,000	—	—	—	1.75	2.50
1990 D	45,000	PF65 2.25				
1990 F	21,200,000	—	—	—	1.75	2.50
1990 F	45,000	PF65 2.25				
1990 G	12,220,000	—	—	—	1.75	2.50
1990 G	45,000	PF65 2.25				
1990 J	18,870,000	—	—	—	1.75	2.50
1990 J	45,000	PF65 2.25				
1991 A	4,000,000	—	—	—	1.75	2.50
1991 A	45,000	PF65 2.25				
1991 D	4,200,000	—	—	—	1.75	2.50
1991 D	45,000	PF65 2.25				
1991 F	4,800,000	—	—	—	1.75	2.50
1991 F	45,000	PF65 2.25				
1991 G	2,800,000	—	—	—	1.75	2.50
1991 G	45,000	PF65 2.25				
1991 J	4,200,000	—	—	—	1.75	2.50
1991 J	45,000	PF65 2.25				
1992 A	7,330,000	—	—	—	1.75	2.50
1992 A	45,000	PF65 2.25				
1992 D	7,700,000	—	—	—	1.75	2.50
1992 D	45,000	PF65 2.25				
1992 F	8,800,000	—	—	—	1.75	2.50
1992 F	45,000	PF65 2.25				
1992 G	5,130,000	—	—	—	1.75	2.50
1992 G	45,000	PF65 2.25				
1992 J	7,700,000	—	—	—	1.75	2.50
1992 J	45,000	PF65 2.25				
1993 A	600,000	—	3.00	4.50	7.00	12.00
1993 A	45,000	PF65 2.25				
1993 D	630,000	—	3.00	4.50	7.00	12.00
1993 D	45,000	PF65 2.25				
1993 F	720,000	—	3.00	4.50	7.00	12.00
1993 F	45,000	PF65 2.25				
1993 G	420,000	—	4.00	6.00	10.00	15.00
1993 G	45,000	PF65 2.25				
1993 J	630,000	—	3.00	4.50	7.00	12.00
1993 J	45,000	PF65 2.25				
1994 A	5,000,000	—	—	—	1.75	2.50
1994 A	45,000	PF65 2.25				
1994 D	5,250,000	—	—	—	1.75	2.50
1994 D	45,000	PF65 2.25				
1994 F	6,000,000	—	—	—	1.75	2.50
1994 F	45,000	PF65 2.25				
1994 G	3,500,000	—	—	—	1.75	2.50
1994 G	45,000	PF65 2.25				
1994 J	5,250,000	—	—	—	1.75	2.50
1994 J	45,000	PF65 2.25				
1995 A	1,595,000	—	—	—	3.50	5.00
1995 A	45,000	PF65 17.50				
1995 D Sets only	20,000	—	—	—	—	60.00
1995 D	45,000	PF65 17.50				
1995 F Sets only	20,000	—	—	—	—	60.00
1995 F	45,000	PF65 17.50				
1995 G	620,000	—	—	—	7.00	12.00
1995 G	45,000	PF65 17.50				
1995 J Sets only	20,000	—	—	—	—	60.00
1995 J	45,000	PF65 17.50				
1996 A	—	—	—	—	5.00	8.00
1996 A	45,000	PF65 6.00				
1996 D	—	—	—	—	5.00	8.00
1996 D	45,000	PF65 6.00				
1996 F	—	—	—	—	5.00	8.00
1996 F	45,000	PF65 6.00				
1996 G	—	—	—	—	5.00	8.00
1996 G	45,000	PF65 6.00				
1996 J	—	—	—	—	5.00	8.00
1996 J	45,000	PF65 6.00				
1997 A Sets only	70,000	—	—	—	—	4.25
1997 A	45,000	PF65 5.00				
1997 D Sets only	70,000	—	—	—	—	4.25
1997 D	45,000	PF65 5.00				
1997 F Sets only	70,000	—	—	—	—	4.25
1997 F	45,000	PF65 5.00				
1997 G Sets only	70,000	—	—	—	—	4.25
1997 G	45,000	PF65 5.00				
1997 J Sets only	70,000	—	—	—	—	4.25
1997 J	45,000	PF65 5.00				
1998 A Sets only	70,000	—	—	—	—	4.25
1998 A	45,000	PF65 5.00				
1998 D Sets only	70,000	—	—	—	—	4.25
1998 D	45,000	PF65 5.00				
1998 F Sets only	70,000	—	—	—	—	4.25
1998 F	45,000	PF65 5.00				
1998 G Sets only	70,000	—	—	—	—	4.25
1998 G	45,000	PF65 5.00				
1998 J Sets only	70,000	—	—	—	—	4.25
1998 J	45,000	PF65 5.00				
1999 A Sets only	70,000	—	—	—	—	4.25
1999 A	45,000	PF65 5.00				
1999 D Sets only	70,000	—	—	—	—	4.25
1999 D	45,000	PF65 5.00				
1999 F Sets only	70,000	—	—	—	—	4.25
1999 F	45,000	PF65 5.00				
1999 G Sets only	70,000	—	—	—	—	4.25
1999 G	45,000	PF65 5.00				
1999 J Sets only	70,000	—	—	—	—	4.25
1999 J	45,000	PF65 5.00				
2000 A Sets only	70,000	—	—	—	—	5.00
2000 A	45,000	PF65 5.00				
2000 D Sets only	70,000	—	—	—	—	5.00
2000 D	45,000	PF65 5.00				
2000 F Sets only	70,000	—	—	—	—	5.00
2000 F	45,000	PF65 5.00				
2000 G Sets only	70,000	—	—	—	—	5.00
2000 G	45,000	PF65 5.00				
2000 J Sets only	70,000	—	—	—	—	5.00
2000 J	45,000	PF65 5.00				

KM# 183 2 MARK

7.00 g., Copper-Nickel Clad Nickel, 26.75 mm. **Subject:** Willy Brandt **Obv:** Eagle above denomination **Rev:** Head facing divides dates **Edge Lettering:** EINIGKEIT UND RECHT UND FREIHEIT

Date	Mintage	VF20	XF40	MS60	MS63	MS65
1994 A	5,000,000	—	—	—	2.00	3.00
1994 A	45,000	PF65 2.50				
1994 D	5,250,000	—	—	—	2.00	3.00
1994 D	45,000	PF65 2.50				
1994 F	6,000,000	—	—	—	2.00	3.00
1994 F	45,000	PF65 2.50				
1994 G	3,600,000	—	—	—	2.00	3.00
1994 G	45,000	PF65 2.50				
1994 J	5,250,000	—	—	—	2.00	3.00
1994 J	45,000	PF65 2.50				
1995 A	1,595,000	—	—	—	3.50	5.00
1995 A	45,000	PF65 17.50				
1995 D	20,000	—	—	—	—	65.00
Note: Sets only						
1995 D	45,000	PF65 17.50				
1995 F	20,000	—	—	—	—	65.00
Note: Sets only						
1995 F	45,000	PF65 17.50				
1995 G	1,220,000	—	—	—	4.50	7.00
1995 G	45,000	PF65 17.50				
1995 J	75,000	—	—	—	15.00	30.00
1995 J	45,000	PF65 17.50				
1996 A	—	—	—	—	5.50	9.00
1996 A	45,000	PF65 6.50				
1996 D	—	—	—	—	5.50	9.00
1996 D	45,000	PF65 6.50				
1996 F	—	—	—	—	5.50	9.00
1996 F	45,000	PF65 6.50				
1996 G	—	—	—	—	5.50	9.00
1996 G	45,000	PF65 6.50				
1996 J	—	—	—	—	5.50	9.00
1996 J	45,000	PF65 6.50				
1997 A Sets only	70,000	—	—	—	—	4.25
1997 A	45,000	PF65 5.00				
1997 D Sets only	70,000	—	—	—	—	4.25
1997 D	45,000	PF65 5.00				
1997 F Sets only	70,000	—	—	—	—	4.25
1997 F	45,000	PF65 5.00				
1997 G Sets only	70,000	—	—	—	—	4.25
1997 G	45,000	PF65 5.00				
1997 J Sets only	70,000	—	—	—	—	4.25
1997 J	45,000	PF65 5.00				
1998 A Sets only	70,000	—	—	—	—	4.25
1998 A	45,000	PF65 5.00				
1998 D Sets only	70,000	—	—	—	—	4.25
1998 D	45,000	PF65 5.00				
1998 F Sets only	70,000	—	—	—	—	4.25
1998 F	45,000	PF65 5.00				
1998 G Sets only	70,000	—	—	—	—	4.25
1998 G	45,000	PF65 5.00				
1998 J Sets only	70,000	—	—	—	—	4.25
1998 J	45,000	PF65 5.00				
1999 A Sets only	70,000	—	—	—	—	4.25
1999 A	45,000	PF65 5.00				
1999 D Sets only	70,000	—	—	—	—	4.25
1999 D	45,000	PF65 5.00				
1999 F Sets only	70,000	—	—	—	—	4.25
1999 F	45,000	PF65 5.00				
1999 G Sets only	70,000	—	—	—	—	4.25
1999 G	45,000	PF65 5.00				
1999 J Sets only	70,000	—	—	—	—	4.25
1999 J	45,000	PF65 5.00				
2000 A Sets only	70,000	—	—	—	—	5.00
2000 A	45,000	PF65 5.00				
2000 D Sets only	70,000	—	—	—	—	5.00
2000 D	45,000	PF65 5.00				
2000 F Sets only	70,000	—	—	—	—	5.00
2000 F	45,000	PF65 5.00				
2000 G Sets only	70,000	—	—	—	—	5.00
2000 G	45,000	PF65 5.00				
2000 J Sets only	70,000	—	—	—	—	5.00
2000 J	45,000	PF65 5.00				

KM# 112.1 5 MARK

11.20 g., 0.625 Silver 0.2251 oz. ASW, 29 mm. **Obv:** Denomination above date **Rev:** Large eagle **Edge Lettering:** EINIGKEIT UND RECHT UND FREIHEIT

Date	Mintage	VF20	XF40	MS60	MS63	MS65
1951 D	20,600,000	8.00	15.00	35.00	75.00	—
1951 D	—	PF63 425				
1951 F	24,000,000	8.00	15.00	40.00	85.00	—
1951 F	280	PF63 350				
1951 G	13,840,000	8.00	20.00	65.00	135	—
1951 G	—	PF63 950				
1951 J	21,360,000	8.00	15.00	30.00	60.00	—
1951 J	—	PF63 245				
1956 D	1,092,000	25.00	60.00	145	185	—
1956 D	—	PF63 1,500				
1956 F	1,200,000	16.00	75.00	225	475	—
1956 F	23	PF63 2,500				
1956 J	1,068,000	16.00	50.00	125	250	—
1956 J	—	PF63 2,750				
1957 D	566,000	16.00	65.00	150	300	—
1957 D Proof	—	—	—	—	—	—
1957 F	2,100,000	12.00	50.00	150	300	—
1957 F	—	PF63 2,500				
1957 G	692,000	16.00	75.00	325	650	—
1957 G	—	PF63 3,500				
1957 J	1,630,000	12.00	35.00	120	245	—
1957 J Proof	—	—	—	—	—	—
1958 D	1,226,000	12.00	30.00	75.00	150	—
1958 D Proof	—	—	—	—	—	—
1958 F	600,000	32.00	145	400	800	—
1958 F	100	PF63 1,350				
1958 G	1,557,000	12.00	28.00	70.00	140	—
1958 G Proof	—	—	—	—	—	—
1958 J	60,000	1,750	2,250	3,250	4,500	—
1958 J	—	PF63 7,000				
1959 D	496,000	16.00	45.00	165	325	—
1959 D	—	PF63 1,250				
1959 G	692,000	25.00	45.00	140	285	—
1959 G	—	PF63 1,500				
1959 J	713,000	13.00	40.00	150	300	—
1959 J	—	PF63 2,000				
1960 D	1,040,000	11.00	20.00	60.00	120	—
1960 D	—	PF63 1,250				
1960 F	1,576,000	11.00	20.00	70.00	135	—
1960 F	50	PF63 1,250				
1960 G	692,000	11.00	22.00	65.00	125	—
1960 G	—	PF63 750				
1960 J	1,618,000	11.00	18.00	45.00	90.00	—
1960 J Proof	—	—	—	—	—	—
1961 D	1,040,000	9.00	20.00	50.00	100	—
1961 D	—	PF63 450				
1961 F	824,000	9.00	22.00	100	200	—
1961 F	—	PF63 2,200				
1961 J	518,000	10.00	28.00	85.00	165	—
1961 J	—	PF63 3,000				
1963 D	2,080,000	9.00	15.00	30.00	60.00	—
1963 D Proof	—	—	—	—	—	—
1963 F	1,254,000	9.00	18.00	38.00	75.00	—
1963 F	—	PF63 2,500				
1963 G	600,000	12.00	20.00	45.00	90.00	—
1963 G	Est. 100	PF63 500				
1963 J	2,136,000	9.00	15.00	30.00	60.00	—
1963 J	—	PF63 3,000				
1964 D	456,000	25.00	50.00	85.00	175	285
1964 D	—	PF65 3,250				
1964 F	2,646,000	9.00	15.00	30.00	60.00	100
1964 F	—	PF65 2,500				
1964 G	1,649,000	9.00	15.00	30.00	60.00	100
1964 G	—	PF65 450				
1964 J	1,335,000	8.00	15.00	32.00	65.00	120
1964 J	—	PF65 2,750				
1965 D	4,354,000	8.00	12.50	30.00	50.00	90.00
1965 D	—	PF65 4,000				
1965 F	4,050,000	8.00	11.50	30.00	50.00	90.00
1965 F	Est. 80	PF65 1,000				
1965 G	2,335,000	8.00	11.50	25.00	45.00	85.00
1965 G	8,233	PF65 55.00				
1965 J	3,605,000	8.00	11.50	25.00	45.00	85.00
1965 J	—	PF65 3,250				
1966 D	5,200,000	8.00	11.50	22.50	40.00	75.00
1966 D	—	PF65 4,000				
1966 F	6,000,000	8.00	11.50	22.50	40.00	75.00
1966 F	100	PF65 1,000				
1966 G	3,460,000	8.00	11.50	22.50	40.00	75.00
1966 G	3,070	PF65 50.00				
1966 J	5,340,000	8.00	11.50	22.50	40.00	75.00
1966 J	1,000	PF65 125				
1967 D	3,120,000	8.00	11.50	22.50	40.00	75.00
1967 D	—	PF65 4,000				
1967 F	3,598,000	8.00	11.50	22.50	40.00	75.00
1967 F	1,500	PF65 110				
1967 G	1,406,000	8.00	11.50	25.00	45.00	75.00
1967 G	4,500	PF65 50.00				
1967 J	3,204,000	8.00	11.50	22.50	40.00	75.00
Note: Errors exist with coin alignment						
1967 J	1,500	PF65 100				
1968 D	1,300,000	8.00	14.00	35.00	55.00	100
1968 D	—	PF65 4,000				
1968 F	1,497,000	8.00	14.00	35.00	55.00	100
1968 F	3,000	PF65 125				
1968 G	1,535,000	8.00	14.00	35.00	55.00	100
1968 G	6,023	PF65 65.00				
1968 J	1,335,000	8.00	14.00	35.00	55.00	100
1968 J	2,000	PF65 125				
1969 D	2,080,000	8.00	11.50	22.00	30.00	55.00
1969 D	—	PF65 35.00				
1969 F	2,395,000	8.00	11.50	22.00	30.00	55.00
1969 F	5,000	PF65 35.00				
1969 G	3,484,000	8.00	11.50	22.00	30.00	55.00
1969 G	8,700	PF65 32.00				
1969 J	2,136,000	8.00	11.50	22.00	30.00	55.00
1969 J	5,000	PF65 32.00				
1970 D	2,000,000	8.00	11.50	22.00	30.00	55.00
1970 D	—	PF65 32.00				
1970 F	1,995,000	8.00	11.50	22.00	30.00	55.00
1970 F	5,140	PF65 32.00				
1970 G	6,000,000	8.00	10.00	14.00	18.00	28.00
1970 G	10,200	PF65 22.00				
1970 J	4,000,000	8.00	10.00	14.00	18.00	28.00
1970 J	5,000	PF65 25.00				
1971 D	4,000,000	8.00	10.00	14.00	18.00	28.00
1971 D	8,000	PF65 22.00				
1971 F	3,993,000	8.00	10.00	14.00	18.00	28.00
1971 F	8,000	PF65 22.00				
1971 G	6,010,000	8.00	10.00	14.00	18.00	28.00
1971 G	10,000	PF65 22.00				
1971 J	6,000,000	8.00	10.00	14.00	18.00	28.00
1971 J	8,000	PF65 22.00				
1972 D	3,000,000	8.00	10.00	14.00	18.00	28.00
1972 D	8,000	PF65 22.00				
1972 F	8,992,000	8.00	10.00	14.00	18.00	28.00
1972 F	8,100	PF65 22.00				
1972 G	4,999,000	8.00	10.00	14.00	18.00	28.00
1972 G	10,000	PF65 22.00				
1972 J	6,000,000	8.00	10.00	14.00	18.00	28.00
1972 J	8,000	PF65 22.00				
1973 D	3,380,000	8.00	10.00	14.00	18.00	28.00
1973 D	9,000	PF65 22.00				
1973 F	3,891,000	8.00	10.00	14.00	18.00	28.00
1973 F	9,100	PF65 22.00				
1973 G	2,240,000	8.00	10.00	14.00	18.00	28.00
1973 G	9,000	PF65 22.00				
1973 J	5,571,000	8.00	10.00	14.00	18.00	28.00
1973 J	9,000	PF65 22.00				
1974 D	4,594,000	8.00	10.00	14.00	18.00	28.00
1974 D	35,000	PF65 22.00				
1974 F	6,514,000	8.00	10.00	14.00	18.00	28.00
1974 F	35,000	PF65 22.00				
1974 G	3,708,000	8.00	10.00	14.00	18.00	28.00
1974 G	35,000	PF65 22.00				
1974 J	2,968,000	8.00	10.00	14.00	18.00	28.00
1974 J	35,000	PF65 22.00				

KM# 112.3 5 MARK

11.20 g., 0.625 Silver 0.2251 oz. ASW, 29 mm. **Obv:** Denomination **Rev:** Large eagle **Note:** Error. With edge lettering: GRUSS DICH DEUTSCHLAND AUS HERZENSGRUND.

Date	Mintage	VF20	XF40	MS60	MS63	MS65
1957 J	Inc. above	1,250	1,650	2,250	3,000	—

KM# 112.2 5 MARK

11.20 g., 0.625 Silver 0.2251 oz. ASW, 29 mm. **Obv:** Denomination **Rev:** Large eagle **Note:** Uninscribed plain edge errors. Mintages are included with same dates of KM #112.1.

Date	Mintage	VF20	XF40	MS60	MS63	MS65
1959 D	Inc. above	65.00	125	200	300	—
1959 J	Inc. above	65.00	125	200	300	—
1963 J	Inc. above	65.00	125	200	300	—
1964 F	Inc. above	65.00	125	200	300	—
1964 G	Inc. above	—	—	—	—	—
1965 F	Inc. above	65.00	125	200	300	—
1965 J	Inc. above	—	—	—	—	—
1965 G	Inc. above	65.00	125	200	300	—
1966 F	Inc. above	125	250	350	500	—
1966 G	Inc. above	65.00	125	200	300	—
Note: Errors without edge inscription exist with coin alignment						
1967 D	Inc. above	125	250	350	500	—
1967 G	Inc. above	65.00	125	200	300	—
1969 F	Inc. above	—	—	—	—	—
1970 F	Inc. above	—	—	—	—	—
1970 G	Inc. above	—	—	—	—	—
1971 F	Inc. above	—	—	—	—	—
1972 F	Inc. above	—	—	—	—	—
1973 F	Inc. above	—	—	—	—	—
1974 F	Inc. above	—	—	—	—	—

KM# 112.4 5 MARK

11.20 g., 0.625 Silver 0.2251 oz. ASW, 29 mm. **Obv:** Denomination **Rev:** Large eagle **Note:** Error. With edge lettering: ALLE MENSCHEN WERDEN BRÜDER.

Date	Mintage	VF20	XF40	MS60	MS63	MS65
1970 F	—	1,250	1,650	2,250	3,000	—

KM# 140.1 5 MARK

10.00 g., Copper-Nickel Clad Nickel, 29 mm. **Obv:** Denomination within rounded square therefore nicknamed "TV-Fives **Rev:** Eagle above date **Edge Lettering:** EINIGKEIT UND RECHT UND FREIHEIT

Date	Mintage	VF20	XF40	MS60	MS63	MS65
1975 D	65,663,000	—	3.50	4.50	6.50	9.00
Note: Error strikes exist without edge inscription						
1975 D	43,000	PF65 7.00				
1975 F	75,002,000	—	3.50	4.50	6.50	9.00
Note: Error strikes exist without edge inscription						
1975 F	43,000	PF65 7.00				
1975 G	43,297,000	—	3.50	4.50	6.50	9.00
1975 G	43,000	PF65 7.00				
1975 J	67,372,000	—	3.50	4.50	6.50	9.00
1975 J	43,000	PF65 7.00				
1976 D	7,821,000	—	3.50	5.00	7.00	10.00
1976 D	43,000	PF65 7.00				
1976 F	9,072,000	—	3.50	5.00	7.00	10.00
1976 F	43,000	PF65 7.00				
1976 G	5,784,000	—	3.50	5.00	7.00	10.00
1976 G	43,000	PF65 7.00				
1976 J	8,068,000	—	3.50	5.00	7.00	10.00
1976 J	43,000	PF65 7.00				
1977 D	8,321,000	—	3.50	5.00	7.00	10.00
1977 D	51,000	PF65 6.00				
1977 F	9,612,000	—	3.50	5.00	7.00	10.00
1977 F	51,000	PF65 6.00				
1977 G	5,746,000	—	3.50	5.00	7.00	10.00
1977 G	51,000	PF65 6.00				
1977 J	8,577,000	—	3.50	5.00	7.00	10.00
1977 J	51,000	PF65 6.00				
1978 D	7,854,000	—	3.50	5.00	7.00	10.00
1978 D	54,000	PF65 6.00				
1978 F	9,054,000	—	3.50	5.00	7.00	10.00
1978 F	54,000	PF65 6.00				
1978 G	5,244,000	—	3.50	5.00	7.00	10.00
1978 G	54,000	PF65 6.00				
1978 J	8,064,000	—	3.50	5.00	7.00	10.00
1978 J	54,000	PF65 6.00				
1979 D	7,889,000	—	3.50	5.00	7.00	10.00
1979 D	89,000	PF65 6.00				
1979 F	9,089,000	—	3.50	5.00	7.00	10.00
1979 F	89,000	PF65 6.00				
1979 G	5,279,000	—	3.50	5.00	7.00	10.00
1979 G	89,000	PF65 6.00				
1979 J	8,099,000	—	3.50	5.00	7.00	10.00
1979 J	89,000	PF65 6.00				
1980 D	8,300,000	—	3.50	5.00	7.00	10.00
1980 D	110,000	PF65 6.00				
1980 F	9,640,000	—	3.50	5.00	7.00	10.00
1980 F	110,000	PF65 6.00				
1980 G	5,500,000	—	3.50	5.00	7.00	10.00
1980 G	110,000	PF65 6.00				
1980 J	8,500,000	—	3.50	5.00	7.00	10.00
1980 J	110,000	PF65 6.00				
1981 D	8,300,000	—	3.50	5.00	7.00	10.00
1981 D	91,000	PF65 7.00				
1981 F	9,600,000	—	3.50	5.00	7.00	10.00
1981 F	91,000	PF65 7.00				
1981 G	5,500,000	—	3.50	5.00	7.00	10.00
1981 G	91,000	PF65 7.00				
1981 J	8,500,000	—	3.50	5.00	7.00	10.00
1981 J	91,000	PF65 7.00				
1982 D	8,900,000	—	3.50	5.00	7.00	10.00
1982 D	78,000	PF65 7.00				
1982 F	10,300,000	—	3.50	5.00	7.00	10.00
1982 F	78,000	PF65 7.00				
1982 G	5,990,000	—	3.50	5.00	7.00	10.00
1982 G	78,000	PF65 7.00				
1982 J	9,100,000	—	3.50	5.00	7.00	10.00
1982 J	78,000	PF65 7.00				
1983 D	6,240,000	—	3.50	5.00	7.00	10.00
1983 D	75,000	PF65 9.00				
1983 F	7,200,000	—	3.50	5.00	7.00	10.00
1983 F	75,000	PF65 9.00				
1983 G	4,152,000	—	3.50	5.00	7.00	10.00
1983 G	75,000	PF65 9.00				
1983 J	6,408,000	—	3.50	5.00	7.00	10.00
1983 J	75,000	PF65 9.00				
1984 D	6,000,000	—	3.50	5.00	7.00	10.00

Date	Mintage	VF20	XF40	MS60	MS63	MS65
1984 D	64,000	PF65 9.00				
1984 F	6,900,000	—	3.50	5.00	7.00	10.00
1984 F	64,000	PF65 9.00				
1984 G	4,000,000	—	3.50	5.00	7.00	10.00
1984 G	64,000	PF65 9.00				
1984 J	6,100,000	—	3.50	5.00	7.00	10.00
1984 J	64,000	PF65 9.00				
1985 D	4,900,000	—	3.50	6.00	8.00	11.00
1985 D	56,000	PF65 10.00				
1985 F	5,700,000	—	3.50	6.00	8.00	11.00
1985 F	54,000	PF65 10.00				
1985 G	3,300,000	—	3.50	6.00	8.00	11.00
1985 G	55,000	PF65 10.00				
1985 J	5,100,000	—	3.50	6.00	8.00	11.00
1985 J	54,000	PF65 10.00				
1986 D	4,900,000	—	3.50	7.00	10.00	12.00
1986 D	44,000	PF65 20.00				
1986 F	5,700,000	—	3.50	7.00	10.00	12.00
1986 F	44,000	PF65 20.00				
1986 G	3,300,000	—	3.50	7.00	10.00	12.00
1986 G	44,000	PF65 25.00				
1986 J	5,100,000	—	3.50	7.00	10.00	12.00
1986 J	44,000	PF65 20.00				
1987 D	6,760,000	—	3.50	6.00	8.00	11.00
1987 D	45,000	PF65 10.00				
1987 F	7,800,000	—	3.50	6.00	8.00	11.00
1987 F	45,000	PF65 10.00				
1987 G	4,500,000	—	3.50	6.00	8.00	11.00
1987 G	45,000	PF65 10.00				
1987 J	6,940,000	—	3.50	6.00	8.00	11.00
1987 J	45,000	PF65 10.00				
1988 D	11,960,000	—	—	5.00	7.00	10.00
1988 D	45,000	PF65 12.00				
1988 F	13,800,000	—	—	5.00	7.00	10.00
1988 F	45,000	PF65 12.00				
1988 G	7,960,000	—	—	5.00	7.00	10.00
1988 G	45,000	PF65 12.00				
1988 J	12,280,000	—	—	5.00	7.00	10.00
1988 J	45,000	PF65 12.00				
1989 D	17,160,000	—	—	5.00	7.00	10.00
1989 D	45,000	PF65 12.00				
1989 F	19,800,000	—	—	5.00	7.00	10.00
1989 F	45,000	PF65 12.00				
1989 G	11,420,000	—	—	5.00	7.00	10.00
1989 G	45,000	PF65 12.00				
1989 J	17,620,000	—	—	5.00	7.00	10.00
1989 J	45,000	PF65 12.00				
1990 D	20,900,000	—	—	5.00	7.00	10.00
1990 D	45,000	PF65 10.00				
1990 F	24,120,000	—	—	5.00	7.00	10.00
1990 F	45,000	PF65 10.00				
1990 G	13,910,000	—	—	5.00	7.00	10.00
1990 G	45,000	PF65 10.00				
1990 J	21,470,000	—	—	5.00	7.00	10.00
1990 J	45,000	PF65 10.00				
1991 A	18,000,000	—	—	5.00	7.00	10.00
1991 A	45,000	PF65 7.00				
1991 D	18,900,000	—	—	5.00	7.00	10.00
1991 D	45,000	PF65 7.00				
1991 F	21,600,000	—	—	5.00	7.00	10.00
1991 F	45,000	PF65 7.00				
1991 G	12,600,000	—	—	5.00	7.00	10.00
1991 G	45,000	PF65 7.00				
1991 J	18,900,000	—	—	5.00	7.00	10.00
1991 J	45,000	PF65 7.00				
1992 A	16,000,000	—	—	5.00	7.00	10.00
1992 A	45,000	PF65 7.00				
1992 D	16,800,000	—	—	5.00	7.00	10.00
1992 D	45,000	PF65 7.00				
1992 F	19,200,000	—	—	5.00	7.00	10.00
1992 F	45,000	PF65 7.00				
1992 G	11,200,000	—	—	5.00	7.00	10.00
1992 G	45,000	PF65 7.00				
1992 J	16,800,000	—	—	5.00	7.00	10.00
1992 J	45,000	PF65 7.00				
1993 A	3,200,000	—	—	6.00	8.00	11.00
1993 A	45,000	PF65 10.00				
1993 D	3,380,000	—	—	6.00	8.00	11.00
1993 D	45,000	PF65 10.00				
1993 F	3,840,000	—	—	6.00	8.00	11.00
1993 F	45,000	PF65 10.00				
1993 G	2,240,000	—	—	6.00	8.00	11.00
1993 G	45,000	PF65 10.00				
1993 J	3,360,000	—	—	6.00	8.00	11.00
1993 J	45,000	PF65 10.00				
1994 A	4,000,000	—	—	5.00	7.00	10.00
1994 A	45,000	PF65 10.00				
1994 D	4,200,000	—	—	5.00	7.00	10.00
1994 D	45,000	PF65 10.00				
1994 F	4,800,000	—	—	5.00	7.00	10.00
1994 F	45,000	PF65 10.00				
1994 G	2,800,000	—	—	5.00	7.00	10.00
1994 G	45,000	PF65 10.00				
1994 J	4,200,000	—	—	5.00	7.00	10.00
1994 J	45,000	PF65 10.00				
1995 A Sets only	20,000	—	—	—	—	80.00
1995 A	45,000	PF65 30.00				
1995 D Sets only	20,000	—	—	—	—	80.00
1995 D	45,000	PF65 30.00				
1995 F Sets only	20,000	—	—	—	—	80.00
1995 F	45,000	PF65 30.00				
1995 G Sets only	20,000	—	—	—	—	80.00
1995 G	45,000	PF65 30.00				
1995 J Sets only	20,000	—	—	—	—	80.00
1995 J	45,000	PF65 30.00				
1996 A Sets only	50,000	—	—	—	—	15.00
1996 A	45,000	PF65 17.50				
1996 D Sets only	50,000	—	—	—	—	15.00
1996 D	45,000	PF65 17.50				
1996 F Sets only	50,000	—	—	—	—	15.00
1996 F	45,000	PF65 17.50				
1996 G Sets only	50,000	—	—	—	—	15.00
1996 G	45,000	PF65 17.50				
1996 J Sets only	50,000	—	—	—	—	15.00
1996 J	45,000	PF65 17.50				
1997 A Sets only	70,000	—	—	—	—	6.00
1997 A	45,000	PF65 7.00				
1997 D Sets only	70,000	—	—	—	—	6.00
1997 D	45,000	PF65 7.00				
1997 F Sets only	70,000	—	—	—	—	6.00
1997 F	45,000	PF65 7.00				
1997 G Sets only	70,000	—	—	—	—	6.00
1997 G	45,000	PF65 7.00				
1997 J Sets only	70,000	—	—	—	—	6.00
1997 J	45,000	PF65 7.00				
1998 A Sets only	70,000	—	—	—	—	6.00
1998 A	45,000	PF65 7.00				
1998 D Sets only	70,000	—	—	—	—	6.00
1998 D	45,000	PF65 7.00				
1998 F Sets only	70,000	—	—	—	—	6.00
1998 F	45,000	PF65 7.00				
1998 G Sets only	70,000	—	—	—	—	6.00
1998 G	45,000	PF65 7.00				
1998 J Sets only	70,000	—	—	—	—	6.00
1998 J	45,000	PF65 7.00				
1999 A Sets only	70,000	—	—	—	—	6.00
1999 A	45,000	PF65 7.00				
1999 D Sets only	70,000	—	—	—	—	6.00
1999 D	45,000	PF65 7.00				
1999 F Sets only	70,000	—	—	—	—	6.00
1999 F	45,000	PF65 7.00				
1999 G Sets only	70,000	—	—	—	—	6.00
1999 G	45,000	PF65 7.00				
1999 J Sets only	70,000	—	—	—	—	6.00
1999 J	45,000	PF65 7.00				
2000 A Sets only	70,000	—	—	—	—	15.00
2000 A	45,000	PF65 15.00				
2000 D Sets only	70,000	—	—	—	—	15.00
2000 D	45,000	PF65 15.00				
2000 F Sets only	70,000	—	—	—	—	15.00
2000 F	45,000	PF65 15.00				
2000 G Sets only	70,000	—	—	—	—	15.00
2000 G	45,000	PF65 15.00				
2000 J Sets only	70,000	—	—	—	—	15.00
2000 J	45,000	PF65 15.00				

KM# 140.2 5 MARK

5.44 g., Copper-Nickel Clad Nickel, 29 mm. **Obv:** Denomination within rounded square **Rev:** Eagle **Note:** Thin variety.

Date	Mintage	VF20	XF40	MS60	MS63	MS65
1975 J	—	—	70.00	100	175	250

Note: Illegally produced by a German Mint official

KM# 140.3 5 MARK

10.00 g., Copper-Nickel Clad Nickel, 29 mm. **Obv:** Denomination within rounded square **Rev:** Eagle **Note:** Errors without edge inscription.

Date	Mintage	VF20	XF40	MS60	MS63	MS65
1975 D	—	—	—	—	—	—
1975 F	—	—	—	—	—	—

COMMEMORATIVE COINAGE

KM# 113 5 MARK

11.20 g., 0.625 Silver 0.2251 oz. ASW, 29 mm. **Subject:** Centenary - Nürnberg Museum **Obv:** Eagle below legend **Rev:** East-Gothic eagle-brooch from the 5th Century AD, between museum dates **Edge Lettering:** EINIGKEIT UND RECHT UND FREIHEIT

Date	Mintage	VF20	XF40	MS60	MS63	MS65
1952 D	199,000	500	700	800	1,200	—
1952 D	1,240	PF65 4,000				

KM# 114 5 MARK

11.20 g., 0.625 Silver 0.2251 oz. ASW, 29 mm. **Subject:** 150th Anniversary - Death of Friedrich von Schiller **Obv:** Eagle above denomination **Rev:** Head with high collar right **Edge Lettering:** SEID EINIG EINIG EINIG

Date	Mintage	VF20	XF40	MS60	MS63	MS65
1955 F	199,000	260	450	725	850	—
1955 F	1,217	PF65 2,150				

KM# 115 5 MARK

11.20 g., 0.625 Silver 0.2251 oz. ASW, 29 mm. **Subject:** 300th Anniversary - Birth of Ludwig von Baden **Obv:** In front of palace, eagle above denomination, date below **Rev:** Bust, right **Edge Lettering:** SCHILD DES REICHES

Date	Mintage	VF20	XF40	MS60	MS63	MS65
1955 G	198,000	260	420	650	800	—
1955 G	—	PF65 1,950				

Note: This coin was restruck without authorization by a mint official using genuine dies - quantity unknown

KM# 117 5 MARK

11.20 g., 0.625 Silver 0.2251 oz. ASW, 29 mm. **Subject:** Centenary - Death of Joseph Freiherr von Eichendorff, poet **Obv:** Eagle divides date at top, denomination below **Rev:** Head with high collar left, dates below **Edge Lettering:** GRÜSS . DICH . DEUTSCHLAND . AUS . HERZENSGRUND .

Date	Mintage	VF20	XF40	MS60	MS63	MS65
1957 J	198,000	200	380	550	725	—
1957 J	2,000	PF65 1,950				

KM# 118.1 5 MARK

11.20 g., 0.625 Silver 0.2251 oz. ASW, 29 mm. **Subject:** 150th Anniversary - Death of Johann Gottlieb Fichte, philosopher **Obv:** Eagle divides date above denomination **Rev:** Head with high collar left, dates below **Edge Lettering:** NUR DAS MACHT GLÜCKSELIG WAS GUT IST

Date	Mintage	VF20	XF40	MS60	MS63	MS65
1964 J	495,000	50.00	75.00	125	150	175
1964 J	5,000	PF65 850				

KM# 118.2 5 MARK

11.20 g., 0.625 Silver 0.2251 oz. ASW, 29 mm. **Obv:** Eagle above denomination **Rev:** Head with high collar left **Note:** Error. Plain edge.

Date	Mintage	VF20	XF40	MS60	MS63	MS65
1964 J	—	250	500	700	850	1,000

KM# 119.1 5 MARK
11.20 g., 0.625 Silver 0.2251 oz. ASW, 29 mm. **Subject:** 250th Anniversary - Death of Gottfried Wilhelm Leibniz, philosopher **Obv:** Eagle divides date above, denomination below **Rev:** Head 3/4 facing, dates below **Edge Lettering:** MAGNUM TOTUS GERMANIAE DECUS

Date	Mintage	VF20	XF40	MS60	MS63	MS65
1966 D	1,925,000	9.00	12.00	15.00	20.00	30.00
1966 D	75,000	PF65 115				

KM# 119.2 5 MARK
11.20 g., 0.625 Silver 0.2251 oz. ASW, 29 mm. **Obv:** Eagle divides date, denomination below **Rev:** Head 3/4 facing, dates **Note:** Error. Plain edge.

Date	Mintage	VF20	XF40	MS60	MS63	MS65
1966 D	Inc. above	225	425	700	—	—

KM# 120.1 5 MARK
11.20 g., 0.625 Silver 0.2251 oz. ASW, 29 mm. **Subject:** Wilhelm and Alexander von Humboldt **Obv:** Eagle above denomination dividing date **Rev:** Conjoined heads; one left and one facing **Edge Lettering:** FREIHEIT ERHÖHT, ZWANG ERSTICKT UNSERE KRAFT

Date	Mintage	VF20	XF40	MS60	MS63	MS65
1967 F	1,940,000	9.00	12.00	15.00	20.00	30.00
1967 F	60,000	PF65 160				

KM# 120.2 5 MARK
11.20 g., 0.625 Silver 0.2251 oz. ASW, 29 mm. **Obv:** Eagle **Rev:** Conjoined heads; one left and one facing **Note:** Error. Plain edge.

Date	Mintage	VF20	XF40	MS60	MS63	MS65
1967 F	Inc. above	225	425	700	—	—

KM# 121 5 MARK
11.20 g., 0.625 Silver 0.2251 oz. ASW, 29 mm. **Subject:** 150th Anniversary - Birth of Friedrich Raiffeisen, (social reformer) **Obv:** Eagle above denomination and date **Rev:** Bust 3/4 facing, dates below **Edge Lettering:** EINER FÜR ALLE - ALLE FÜR EINEN

Date	Mintage	VF20	XF40	MS60	MS63	MS65
1968 J	3,942,500	7.00	8.00	10.00	12.00	14.00
1968 J	140,000	PF65 50.00				

KM# 122 5 MARK
11.20 g., 0.625 Silver 0.2251 oz. ASW, 29 mm. **Subject:** 500th Anniversary - Death of Johannes Gutenberg, (first German printer) **Obv:** Denomination divides date, eagle above **Rev:** Bust 3/4 right, dates below **Edge Lettering:** GESEGNET SEI WER DIE SCHRIFT ERFAND

Date	Mintage	VF20	XF40	MS60	MS63	MS65
1968 G	2,930,000	7.00	8.00	10.00	12.00	14.00
1968 G	100,000	PF65 65.00				

KM# 123.1 5 MARK
11.20 g., 0.625 Silver 0.2251 oz. ASW, 29 mm. **Subject:** 150th Anniversary - Birth of Max von Pettenkofer **Obv:** Stylized eagle, denomination above **Rev:** Face 3/4 left, dates below **Edge Lettering:** HYGIENE STREBT DER ÜBEL WURZEL AUSZUROTTEN

Date	Mintage	VF20	XF40	MS60	MS63	MS65
1968 D	2,930,000	7.00	8.00	10.00	12.00	14.00
1968 D	100,000	PF65 50.00				

KM# 123.2 5 MARK
11.20 g., 0.625 Silver 0.2251 oz. ASW, 29 mm. **Obv:** Stylized eagle, denomination above **Rev:** Face 3/4 left **Note:** Polished devices.

Date	Mintage	VF20	XF40	MS60	MS63	MS65
1968 D	—	PF65 300				

KM# 125.1 5 MARK
11.20 g., 0.625 Silver 0.2251 oz. ASW, 29 mm. **Subject:** 150th Anniversary - Birth of Theodor Fontane, writer, poet **Obv:** Eagle divides date, denomination below **Rev:** Head left **Edge:** DER FREIE NUR IST TREU

Date	Mintage	VF20	XF40	MS60	MS63	MS65
1969 G	2,900,000	7.00	8.00	10.00	12.00	14.00
1969 G	170,000	PF65 35.00				

KM# 125.2 5 MARK
11.20 g., 0.625 Silver 0.2251 oz. ASW, 29 mm. **Obv:** Eagle divides date, denomination below **Rev:** Head left **Note:** Error. Incomplete nose and hair.

Date	Mintage	VF20	XF40	MS60	MS63	MS65
1969 G	Inc. above	PF65 145				

KM# 126.1 5 MARK
11.20 g., 0.625 Silver 0.2251 oz. ASW, 29 mm. **Subject:** 375th Anniversary - Death of Gerhard Mercator (cartographer) **Obv:** Eagle, denomination divides date below **Rev:** Bust with long beard 3/4 right **Edge Lettering:** TERRAE DESCRIPTIO AD USUM NAVIGANTIUM

Date	Mintage	VF20	XF40	MS60	MS63	MS65
1969 F	4,804,000	—	—	8.00	9.00	10.00
1969 F	200,000	PF65 20.00				

KM# 126.2 5 MARK
11.20 g., 0.625 Silver 0.2251 oz. ASW, 29 mm. **Obv:** Eagle, denomination divides date below **Rev:** Bust with long beard 3/4 right **Note:** Error. Plain edge.

Date	Mintage	VF20	XF40	MS60	MS63	MS65
1969 F	Inc. above	250	450	750	—	—

KM# 126.3 5 MARK
11.20 g., 0.625 Silver 0.2251 oz. ASW, 29 mm. **Obv:** Eagle, denomination divides date below **Rev:** Bust with long beard 3/4 right **Note:** Error. With edge lettering: Einigkeit und Recht und Freiheit.

Date	Mintage	VF20	XF40	MS60	MS63	MS65
1969 F	Inc. above	600	1,000	1,600	—	—

KM# 126.4 5 MARK
11.20 g., 0.625 Silver 0.2251 oz. ASW, 29 mm. **Obv:** Eagle, denomination divides date below **Rev:** Bust with long beard 3/4 right **Note:** Error. With long "R" in "MERCATOR".

Date	Mintage	VF20	XF40	MS60	MS63	MS65
1969 F	Inc. above	25.00	55.00	100	—	—

KM# 127 5 MARK
11.20 g., 0.625 Silver 0.2251 oz. ASW, 29 mm. **Subject:** 200th Anniversary - Birth of Ludwig van Beethoven, composer **Obv:** Eagle, denomination divides date below **Rev:** Head left, dates below **Edge Lettering:** ALLE MENSCHEN WERDEN BRÜDER

Date	Mintage	VF20	XF40	MS60	MS63	MS65
1970 F	4,800,000	—	7.00	8.00	10.00	12.00
1970 F	200,000	PF65 18.00				

KM# 128.1 5 MARK
11.20 g., 0.625 Silver 0.2251 oz. ASW, 29 mm. **Subject:** Foundation of German Empire, 1871 **Obv:** Eagle divides date above legend, denomination below **Rev:** Reichstag building, in Berlin **Edge Lettering:** EINIGKEIT UND RECHT UND FREIHEIT

Date	Mintage	VF20	XF40	MS60	MS63	MS65
1971 G	4,800,000	7.00	8.00	10.00	11.00	13.00
1971 G	200,000	PF65 22.00				

KM# 128.2 5 MARK®
11.20 g., 0.625 Silver 0.2251 oz. ASW, 29 mm. **Obv:** Eagle divides date above legend **Rev:** Reichstag building **Note:** Error. With weak window details.

Date	Mintage	VF20	XF40	MS60	MS63	MS65
1971 F	—	PF65 100				

KM# 129 5 MARK
11.20 g., 0.625 Silver 0.2251 oz. ASW, 29 mm. **Subject:** 500th Anniversary - Birth of Albrecht Dürer, (painter) **Obv:** Eagle above inscription, date and denomination below **Rev:** Initials above name and dates **Edge Lettering:** DER ALLER EDELST SINN DER MENSCHEN IST SEHEN

Date	Mintage	VF20	XF40	MS60	MS63	MS65
1971 D	7,800,000	—	—	7.00	8.00	10.00
1971 D	200,000	PF65 27.50				

KM# 136 5 MARK
11.20 g., 0.625 Silver 0.2251 oz. ASW, 29 mm. **Subject:** 500th Anniversary - Birth of Nicholas Copernicus **Obv:** Eagle in grid form, denomination divides date below **Rev:** Sun at center of rings, planet names descend from top towards center **Edge Lettering:** IN MEDIO OMNIUM RESIDET SOL

Date	Mintage	VF20	XF40	MS60	MS63	MS65
1973 J	7,750,000	—	—	8.00	10.00	12.00
1973 J	250,000	PF65 15.00				

KM# 137 5 MARK
11.20 g., 0.625 Silver 0.2251 oz. ASW, 29 mm. **Subject:** 125th Anniversary - Frankfurt Parliament **Obv:** Denomination below stylized eagle divides date **Rev:** Date at center of Parliament building **Edge Lettering:** EINIGKEIT RECHT FREIHEIT

Date	Mintage	VF20	XF40	MS60	MS63	MS65
1973 G	7,750,000	—	—	8.00	10.00	12.00
1973 G	250,000	PF65 15.00				

KM# 138 5 MARK
11.20 g., 0.625 Silver 0.2251 oz. ASW, 29 mm. **Subject:** 25th Anniversary - Constitutional Law **Obv:** Fat eagle above date divided by denomination **Rev:** Symbol of the 11 countries forming the Federal Republic **Edge Lettering:** DIE MENSCHENWÜRDE IST UNANTASTBAR

Date	Mintage	VF20	XF40	MS60	MS63	MS65
1974 F	7,750,000	—	—	8.00	10.00	12.00
1974 F	250,000	PF65 15.00				

KM# 139 5 MARK
11.20 g., 0.625 Silver 0.2251 oz. ASW, 29 mm. **Subject:** 250th Anniversary - Birth of Immanuel Kant, philosopher **Obv:** Legend divides eagle and denomination **Rev:** Bust at left facing right, name and dates at right **Edge Lettering:** ACHTUNG FUERS MORALISCHE GESETZ

Date	Mintage	VF20	XF40	MS60	MS63	MS65
1974 D	7,750,000	—	—	8.00	10.00	12.00
1974 D	250,000	PF65 18.00				

KM# 141 5 MARK
11.20 g., 0.625 Silver 0.2251 oz. ASW, 29 mm. **Subject:** 50th Anniversary - Death of Friedrich Ebert **Obv:** Eagle above denomination, date at right **Rev:** Head left, dates at left **Edge Lettering:** DES VOLKES WOHL IST MEINER ARBEIT ZIEL

Date	Mintage	VF20	XF40	MS60	MS63	MS65
1975 J	7,750,000	—	—	8.00	10.00	12.00
1975 J	250,000	PF65 15.00				

KM# 142.1 5 MARK
11.20 g., 0.625 Silver 0.2251 oz. ASW, 29 mm. **Subject:** European Monument Protection Year **Obv:** Eagle divides date at top, denomination below **Rev:** Patterned designs and two line inscription with date **Edge Lettering:** ZUKUNFT FÜR UNSERE VERGANGENHEIT **Note:** 2.1 mm thick.

Date	Mintage	VF20	XF40	MS60	MS63	MS65
1975 F	7,750,000	—	—	8.00	10.00	12.00
1975 F	250,000	PF65 15.00				

KM# 142.2 5 MARK
5.30 g., 0.625 Silver 0.1065 oz. ASW, 29 mm. **Subject:** Intensifying Protection of old monuments and buildings **Obv:** Eagle divides date at top **Rev:** Front of houses **Note:** 1.4 mm thick.

Date	Mintage	VF20	XF40	MS60	MS63	MS65
1975 F	Inc. above	—	—	12.00	14.00	16.00

KM# 143 5 MARK
11.20 g., 0.625 Silver 0.2251 oz. ASW, 29 mm. **Subject:** Centenary - Birth of Albert Schweitzer **Obv:** Eagle above denomination **Rev:** Head facing, dates at right **Edge Lettering:** EHRFURCHT VOR DEM LEBEN

Date	Mintage	VF20	XF40	MS60	MS63	MS65
1975 G	7,750,000	—	—	8.00	10.00	12.00
1975 G	250,000	PF65 15.00				

KM# 144 5 MARK
11.20 g., 0.625 Silver 0.2251 oz. ASW, 29 mm. **Subject:** 300th Anniversary - Death of von Grimmelshausen, writer. **Obv:** Eagle above denomination, date at left **Rev:** Mythic figure with book left, dates divided above **Edge Lettering:** DER ABENTHEURLICHE SIMPLICISSIMUS

Date	Mintage	VF20	XF40	MS60	MS63	MS65
1976 D	7,750,000	—	—	8.00	10.00	12.00
1976 D	250,000	PF65 18.00				

KM# 145 5 MARK
11.20 g., 0.625 Silver 0.2251 oz. ASW, 29 mm. **Subject:** 200th Anniversary - Birth of Carl Friedrich Gauss **Obv:** Eagle above date and denomination **Rev:** Head 3/4 facing, dates at right **Edge Lettering:** PAUCA SED NATURA

Date	Mintage	VF20	XF40	MS60	MS63	MS65
1977 J	7,750,000	—	—	8.00	10.00	12.00
1977 J	250,000	PF65 18.00				

KM# 146 5 MARK
11.20 g., 0.625 Silver 0.2251 oz. ASW, 29 mm. **Subject:** 200th Anniversary - Birth of Heinrich von Kleist **Obv:** Eagle above denomination **Rev:** Bust 3/4 left, dates below **Edge Lettering:** FRIEDEN IST DIE BEDINGUNG DOCH VON ALLEM

Date	Mintage	VF20	XF40	MS60	MS63	MS65
1977 G	7,741,080	—	—	8.00	10.00	12.00
1977 G	258,920	PF65 17.00				

KM# 147 5 MARK
11.20 g., 0.625 Silver 0.2251 oz. ASW, 29 mm. **Subject:** 100th Anniversary - Birth of Gustav Stresemann **Obv:** Eagle above denomination **Rev:** Head left, dates at left **Edge Lettering:** DURCH FRIEDEN UND VERSTÄNDIGUNG SIEGEN

Date	Mintage	VF20	XF40	MS60	MS63	MS65
1978 D	7,740,880	—	—	8.00	10.00	12.00
1978 D	259,120	PF65 15.00				

KM# 148 5 MARK
11.20 g., 0.625 Silver 0.2251 oz. ASW, 29 mm. **Subject:** 225th Anniversary - Death of Balthasar Neumann, architect **Obv:** Eagle above denomination **Rev:** Interior of church Vierzehnheiligen **Edge Lettering:** WALLFAHRTSKIRCHE VIERZEHNHEILIGEN 1743 - 1772

Date	Mintage	VF20	XF40	MS60	MS63	MS65
1978 F	7,740,880	—	—	8.00	10.00	12.00
1978 F	259,120	PF65 15.00				

KM# 150 5 MARK
11.20 g., 0.625 Silver 0.2251 oz. ASW, 29 mm. **Subject:** 150th Anniversary - German Archaeological Institute **Obv:** Denomination divides date, eagle above **Edge Lettering:** MONUMENTIS AC LITTERIS

Date	Mintage	VF20	XF40	MS60	MS63	MS65
1979 J	7,740,880	—	—	8.00	10.00	12.00
1979 J	259,120	PF65 15.00				

KM# 151 5 MARK
10.00 g., Copper-Nickel Clad Nickel, 29 mm. **Subject:** 100th Anniversary - Birth of Otto Hahn **Obv:** Stylized eagle above legend **Rev:** Symbols of Hahn's studies in chemistry, name and dates below **Edge Lettering:** 1938 ERSTE SPALTUNG DES URANKERNS

Date	Mintage	VF20	XF40	MS60	MS63	MS65
1979 G	5,000,000	—	3.00	5.00	6.00	7.00
1979 G	350,000	PF65 11.50				

KM# 151a 5 MARK
11.20 g., 0.625 Silver 0.2251 oz. ASW, 29 mm. **Obv:** Stylized eagle above legend **Rev:** Chemistry symbols, name and date below **Edge Lettering:** 1938 ERSTE SPALTUNG DES URANKERNS

Date	Mintage	VF20	XF40	MS60	MS63	MS65
1979 G	18	—	—	22,500	—	—

KM# 152 5 MARK

10.00 g., Copper-Nickel Clad Nickel, 29 mm. **Subject:** 750th Anniversary - Death of von der Vogelweide **Obv:** Eagle above date divided by denomination **Rev:** Reading half figure with paper, dates below **Edge Lettering:** WOL VIERZEG JAR HAB ICH GESUNGEN ODER ME

Date	Mintage	VF20	XF40	MS60	MS63	MS65
1980 D	5,000,000	—	3.00	5.00	6.00	7.00
1980 D	350,000	PF65 11.50				

KM# 153 5 MARK

10.00 g., Copper-Nickel Clad Nickel, 29 mm. **Subject:** 100th Anniversary - Cologne Cathedral **Obv:** Eagle, narrow design **Rev:** Cathedral **Edge Lettering:** ZEUGNIS DES GLAUBENS - ZEICHEN DER EINHEIT

Date	Mintage	VF20	XF40	MS60	MS63	MS65
1980 F	5,000,000	—	3.00	5.00	6.00	7.00
1980 F	350,000	PF65 13.50				

KM# 154 5 MARK

10.00 g., Copper-Nickel Clad Nickel, 29 mm. **Subject:** 200th Anniversary - Death of Gotthold Ephraim Lessing **Obv:** Denomination divides date below eagle **Rev:** Bust in silhouette left **Edge Lettering:** SIEH ÜBERALL MIT DEINEN EIGENEN AUGEN

Date	Mintage	VF20	XF40	MS60	MS63	MS65
1981 J	6,500,000	—	3.00	4.00	5.00	6.00
1981 J	350,000	PF65 11.00				

KM# 155 5 MARK

10.00 g., Copper-Nickel Clad Nickel, 29 mm. **Subject:** 150th Anniversary - Death of Carl vom Stein **Obv:** Eagle in relief, denomination divides date below **Rev:** Bust 3/4 facing, dates at right **Edge Lettering:** ICH HABE NUR EIN VATERLAND - DEUTSCHLAND

Date	Mintage	VF20	XF40	MS60	MS63	MS65
1981 G	6,500,000	—	3.00	4.00	5.00	6.00
1981 G	350,000	PF65 11.00				

KM# 156 5 MARK

10.00 g., Copper-Nickel Clad Nickel, 29 mm. **Subject:** 150th Anniversary - Death of Johann Wolfgang von Goethe **Obv:** Eagle above denomination, date at right **Rev:** Head right, dates below **Edge Lettering:** ZWISCHEN UNS SEI WAHRHEIT

Date	Mintage	VF20	XF40	MS60	MS63	MS65
1982 D	8,000,000	—	3.00	4.00	5.00	6.00
1982 D	350,000	PF65 11.50				

KM# 157 5 MARK

10.00 g., Copper-Nickel Clad Nickel, 29 mm. **Subject:** 10th Anniversary - U.N. Environmental Conference **Obv:** Eagle above denomination **Rev:** Stylized figure in center of design, date above **Edge Lettering:** DIE EINE ERDE SCHUETZEN

Date	Mintage	VF20	XF40	MS60	MS63	MS65
1982 F	8,000,000	—	3.00	4.00	5.00	6.00
1982 F	350,000	PF65 11.00				

KM# 158 5 MARK

10.00 g., Copper-Nickel Clad Nickel, 29 mm. **Subject:** 100th Anniversary - Death of Karl Marx **Obv:** Eagle in relief above denomination **Rev:** Head 3/4 facing, dates below **Edge Lettering:** WAHRHEIT ALS WIRKLICHKEIT UND MACHT

Date	Mintage	VF20	XF40	MS60	MS63	MS65
1983 J	8,000,000	—	3.00	4.00	5.00	6.00
1983 J	350,000	PF65 11.00				

KM# 159 5 MARK

10.00 g., Copper-Nickel Clad Nickel, 29 mm. **Subject:** 500th Anniversary - Birth of Martin Luther **Obv:** Eagle, denomination below divides date **Rev:** Inscription covers head 3/4 right **Edge Lettering:** GOTTES WORT BLEIBT IN EWIGKEIT

Date	Mintage	VF20	XF40	MS60	MS63	MS65
1983 G	8,000,000	—	3.00	4.00	5.00	6.00
1983 G	350,000	PF65 12.00				

KM# 160 5 MARK

10.00 g., Copper-Nickel Clad Nickel, 29 mm. **Subject:** 150th Anniversary - German Customs Union **Obv:** Eagle, denomination divides date below **Rev:** Horses and carriage passing under open customs barrier **Edge Lettering:** ZOLLVEREIN DEUTSCHLAND * EWG EUROPA

Date	Mintage	VF20	XF40	MS60	MS63	MS65
1984 D	8,000,000	—	3.00	4.00	5.00	6.00
1984 D	350,000	PF65 11.50				

KM# 161 5 MARK

10.00 g., Copper-Nickel Clad Nickel, 29 mm. **Subject:** 175th Anniversary - Birth of Felix Bartholdy **Obv:** Eagle above denomination **Rev:** 3/4 figure looking left, left hand on hip, music score in background **Edge Lettering:** IHR TÖNE SCHWINGT EUCH FREUDIG DURCH DIE SAITEN

Date	Mintage	VF20	XF40	MS60	MS63	MS65
1984 J	8,000,000	—	3.00	4.00	5.00	6.00
1984 J	350,000	PF65 12.50				

KM# 162 5 MARK

10.00 g., Copper-Nickel Clad Nickel, 29 mm. **Subject:** European Year of Music **Obv:** Stylized eagle in circle at left, denomination at right, date above **Rev:** Circle at left holds stars and outline of face in harp, music notes at right **Edge Lettering:** SCHÜTZ BACH HÄNDEL SCARLATTI BERG

Date	Mintage	VF20	XF40	MS60	MS63	MS65
1985 F	8,000,000	—	3.00	4.00	5.00	6.00
1985 F	350,000	PF65 11.50				

KM# 163 5 MARK

10.00 g., Copper-Nickel Clad Nickel, 29 mm. **Subject:** 150th Anniversary - German Railroad **Obv:** Stylized eagle above denomination **Rev:** Spoked wheel design **Edge Lettering:** EISENBAHN NÜRNBERG - FÜHRT 7. DEZEMBER 1835

Date	Mintage	VF20	XF40	MS60	MS63	MS65
1985 G	8,000,000	—	3.00	4.00	5.00	6.00
1985 G	350,000	PF65 11.00				

KM# 164 5 MARK

10.00 g., Copper-Nickel Clad Nickel, 29 mm. **Subject:** 600th Anniversary - Heidelberg University **Obv:** Denomination divides date below eagle **Rev:** Crowned rampant lion left within legend **Edge Lettering:** AUS TRADITION IN DIE ZUKUNFT

Date	Mintage	VF20	XF40	MS60	MS63	MS65
1986 D	8,000,000	—	3.00	4.00	5.00	6.00
1986 D	350,000	PF65 11.00				

KM# 165 5 MARK

10.00 g., Copper-Nickel Clad Nickel, 29 mm. **Subject:** 200th Anniversary - Death of Frederick the Great **Obv:** Eagle above denomination **Rev:** Uniformed bust left, dates below **Edge Lettering:** ICH BIN DER ERSTE DIENER MEINES STAATES

Date	Mintage	VF20	XF40	MS60	MS63	MS65
1986 F	8,000,000	—	3.00	4.00	5.00	6.00
1986 F	350,000	PF65 12.50				

KM# 130 10 MARK

15.50 g., 0.625 Silver 0.3115 oz. ASW, 32.5 mm. **Series:** Munich Olympics **Obv:** Artistic eagle, denomination below **Rev:** "In Deutschland" with spiraling symbol **Edge Lettering:** FORTIVS CITIVS ALTIVS **Note:** Issued 1970.

Date	Mintage	VF20	XF40	MS60	MS63	MS65
1972 D	2,375,000	—	—	8.00	10.00	12.00
1972 D	125,000	PF65 26.00				
1972 F	2,375,000	—	—	8.00	10.00	12.00
1972 F	125,000	PF65 26.00				
1972 G	2,375,000	—	—	8.00	10.00	12.00
1972 G	125,000	PF65 26.00				
1972 J	2,375,000	—	—	8.00	10.00	12.00
1972 J	125,000	PF65 26.00				

KM# 131 10 MARK

15.50 g., 0.625 Silver 0.3115 oz. ASW, 32.5 mm. **Series:** Munich Olympics **Obv:** Eagle above denomination **Rev:** Schleife (knot) **Edge Lettering:** FORTIVS CITIVS ALTIVS **Note:** Issued 1971.

Date	Mintage	VF20	XF40	MS60	MS63	MS65
1972 D	4,875,000	—	—	8.00	10.00	12.00
1972 D	125,000	PF65 20.00				
1972 F	4,875,000	—	—	8.00	10.00	12.00
1972 F	125,000	PF65 20.00				
1972 G	4,875,000	—	—	8.00	10.00	12.00
1972 G	125,000	PF65 20.00				
1972 J	4,875,000	—	—	8.00	10.00	12.00
1972 J	125,000	PF65 20.00				

KM# 132 10 MARK

15.50 g., 0.625 Silver 0.3115 oz. ASW, 32.5 mm. **Series:** Munich Olympics **Obv:** Eagle above denomination **Rev:** Athletes kneeling **Edge Lettering:** FORTIVS CITIVS ALTIVS **Note:** Issued 1971.

Date	Mintage	VF20	XF40	MS60	MS63	MS65
1972 D	4,850,000	—	—	8.00	10.00	12.00
1972 D	150,000	PF65 16.50				
1972 F	4,850,000	—	—	8.00	10.00	12.00
1972 F	150,000	PF65 16.50				
1972 G	4,850,000	—	—	8.00	10.00	12.00
1972 G	150,000	PF65 16.50				
1972 J	4,850,000	—	—	8.00	10.00	12.00
1972 J	150,000	PF65 16.50				

KM# 133 10 MARK

15.50 g., 0.625 Silver 0.3115 oz. ASW, 32.5 mm. **Series:** Munich Olympics **Obv:** Eagle above denomination **Rev:** Stadium - aerial view **Edge Lettering:** FORTIVS CITIVS ALTIVS

Date	Mintage	VF20	XF40	MS60	MS63	MS65
1972 D	4,350,000	—	—	8.00	10.00	12.00
1972 D	150,000	PF65 17.50				
1972 F	7,345,000	—	—	8.00	10.00	12.00
1972 F	150,000	PF65 17.50				
1972 G	4,350,000	—	—	8.00	10.00	12.00
1972 G	150,000	PF65 17.50				
1972 J	4,350,000	—	—	8.00	10.00	12.00
1972 J	150,000	PF65 17.50				

KM# 134.1 10 MARK

15.50 g., 0.625 Silver 0.3115 oz. ASW, 32.5 mm. **Series:** Munich Olympics **Obv:** Eagle above denomination **Rev:** "In Munchen" - with spiral symbol **Edge:** Lettering separated by periods **Edge Lettering:** FORTIVS CITIVS ALTIVS

Date	Mintage	VF20	XF40	MS60	MS63	MS65
1972 D	2,350,000	—	—	8.00	10.00	12.00
1972 D	150,000	PF65 20.00				
1972 F	2,350,000	—	—	8.00	10.00	12.00
1972 F	150,000	PF65 20.00				
1972 G	2,350,000	—	—	8.00	10.00	12.00
1972 G	150,000	PF65 20.00				
1972 J	2,350,000	—	—	8.00	10.00	12.00
1972 J	150,000	PF65 20.00				

KM# 134.2 10 MARK

15.50 g., 0.625 Silver 0.3115 oz. ASW, 32.5 mm. **Obv:** Eagle above denomination **Rev:** Spiral design **Edge:** Lettering separated by arabesques **Edge Lettering:** FORTIVS CITIVS ALTIVS **Note:** Error.

Date	Mintage	VF20	XF40	MS60	MS63	MS65
1972 D Inc. above	—	—	—	—	2,760	—
1972 F Inc. above	—	—	—	—	2,760	—
1972 G Inc. above	—	—	—	—	2,760	—
1972 J	600	200	300	500	650	—

KM# 135 10 MARK

15.50 g., 0.625 Silver 0.3115 oz. ASW, 32.5 mm. **Series:** Munich Olympics **Obv:** Eagle above denomination **Rev:** Olympic Flame, spiral symbol above, rings divide date below **Edge Lettering:** FORTIVS CITIVS ALTIVS

Date	Mintage	VF20	XF40	MS60	MS63	MS65
1972 D	4,850,000	—	—	8.00	10.00	12.00
1972 D	150,000	PF65 17.50				
1972 F	4,850,000	—	—	8.00	10.00	12.00
1972 F	150,000	PF65 17.50				
1972 G	4,850,000	—	—	8.00	10.00	12.00
1972 G	150,000	PF65 17.50				
1972 J	4,850,000	—	—	8.00	10.00	12.00
1972 J	150,000	PF65 17.50				

KM# 166 10 MARK

15.50 g., 0.625 Silver 0.3115 oz. ASW, 32.5 mm. **Subject:** 750th Anniversary - Berlin **Obv:** Eagle above denomination **Rev:** Bear at right holding circular shield **Edge Lettering:** EINIGKEIT UND RECHT UND FREIHEIT

Date	Mintage	VF20	XF40	MS60	MS63	MS65
1987 J	8,000,000	—	—	8.00	10.00	12.00
1987 J	350,000	PF65 50.00				

KM# 167 10 MARK

15.50 g., 0.625 Silver 0.3115 oz. ASW, 32.5 mm. **Subject:** 30 Years of European Unity **Obv:** Eagle above denomination **Rev:** Horses pulling 30 year symbol, dates at right **Edge Lettering:** ADENAUER . BECH . DE GASPERI . LUNS . SCHUMANN . SPAAK .

Date	Mintage	VF20	XF40	MS60	MS63	MS65
1987 G	8,000,000	—	—	8.00	10.00	12.00
1987 G	350,000	PF65 30.00				

KM# 168 10 MARK

15.50 g., 0.625 Silver 0.3115 oz. ASW, 32.5 mm. **Subject:** 200th Anniversary - Birth of Arthur Schopenhauer **Obv:** Eagle above denomination **Rev:** Head facing, dates below left **Edge Lettering:** DIE WELT ALS WILLE UND VORSTELLUNG

Date	Mintage	VF20	XF40	MS60	MS63	MS65
1988 D	8,000,000	—	—	8.00	10.00	12.00
1988 D	350,000	PF65 27.50				

KM# 169 10 MARK

15.50 g., 0.625 Silver 0.3115 oz. ASW, 32.5 mm. **Subject:** 100th Anniversary - Death of Carl Zeiss **Obv:** Eagle above denomination **Rev:** Head at left, looking right **Edge Lettering:** OPTIK FÜR WISSENSCHAFT UND TECHNIK

Date	Mintage	VF20	XF40	MS60	MS63	MS65
1988 F	8,000,000	—	—	8.00	10.00	12.00
1988 F	350,000	PF65 25.00				

KM# 171 10 MARK
15.50 g., 0.625 Silver 0.3115 oz. ASW, 32.5 mm. **Subject:** 800th Year - Port of Hamburg **Obv:** Small eagle above denomination **Rev:** Three towered city gate, waves below **Edge Lettering:** HAMBURG TOR ZUR WELT

Date	Mintage	VF20	XF40	MS60	MS63	MS65
1989 J	8,000,000	—	—	8.00	10.00	12.00
1989 J	350,000	PF65 25.00				

KM# 172 10 MARK
15.50 g., 0.625 Silver 0.3115 oz. ASW, 32.5 mm. **Subject:** 2000th Anniversary - City of Bonn **Obv:** Eagle above denomination **Rev:** Building left of sun design **Edge Lettering:** BONN BLÜHE UND BLEIBE

Date	Mintage	VF20	XF40	MS60	MS63	MS65
1989 D	8,000,000	—	—	8.00	10.00	12.00
1989 D	350,000	PF65 25.00				

KM# 173 10 MARK
15.50 g., 0.625 Silver 0.3115 oz. ASW, 32.5 mm. **Subject:** 40th Anniversary - Republic **Obv:** Linear eagle above date and denomination **Rev:** Eleven shields form a circle **Edge Lettering:** 40 JAHRE FRIEDEN UND FREIHEIT

Date	Mintage	VF20	XF40	MS60	MS63	MS65
1989 G	8,000,000	—	—	8.00	10.00	12.00
1989 G	350,000	PF65 28.00				

KM# 174 10 MARK
15.50 g., 0.625 Silver 0.3115 oz. ASW, 32.5 mm. **Subject:** 800th Anniversary - Death of Kaiser Friedrich Barbarossa **Obv:** Eagle above denomination **Rev:** Crowned figure with royal orb and scepter rising above castle walls, dates below **Edge Lettering:** E HONOR IMPERII

Date	Mintage	VF20	XF40	MS60	MS63	MS65
1990 F	7,450,000	—	—	8.00	10.00	12.00
1990 F	400,000	PF65 18.00				

KM# 176 10 MARK
15.50 g., 0.625 Silver 0.3115 oz. ASW, 32.5 mm. **Subject:** 800th Anniversary - The Teutonic Order **Obv:** Eagle above denomination **Rev:** Wrinkled page with Madonna and child pictured, shield upper left **Edge Lettering:** ES LEB IM GEDÄCHTNIS SO LANG GOTT WILL

Date	Mintage	VF20	XF40	MS60	MS63	MS65
1990 J	8,400,000	—	—	8.00	10.00	12.00
1990 J	450,000	PF65 15.00				

KM# 177 10 MARK
15.50 g., 0.625 Silver 0.3115 oz. ASW, 32.5 mm. **Subject:** German Unity **Obv:** Eagle above denomination **Rev:** Brandenburg Gate in Berlin **Edge Lettering:** DEUTSCHLAND EINIG VATERLAND

Date	Mintage	VF20	XF40	MS60	MS63	MS65
1991 A	8,400,000	—	—	8.00	10.00	12.00
1991 A	450,000	PF65 17.50				

KM# 178 10 MARK
15.50 g., 0.625 Silver 0.3115 oz. ASW, 32.5 mm. **Subject:** 125th Anniversary - Birth of Kathe Kollwitz - Artist and Sculptor **Obv:** Denomination divides date below eagle **Rev:** Figure at easel drawing, dates below **Edge Lettering:** ICH WILL WIRKEN IN DIESER ZEIT

Date	Mintage	VF20	XF40	MS60	MS63	MS65
1992 G	8,000,000	—	—	8.00	10.00	12.00
1992 G	450,000	PF65 15.00				

KM# 179 10 MARK
15.50 g., 0.625 Silver 0.3115 oz. ASW, 32.5 mm. **Subject:** 150th Anniversary - Civil Pour-le-Merite Order **Obv:** Eagle above denomination, date at left **Rev:** Alexander von Humbolt, 1st chancellor of the Order **Edge Lettering:** GEMEINSCHAFT VON GELEHRTEN UND KÜNSTLERN

Date	Mintage	VF20	XF40	MS60	MS63	MS65
1992 D	8,000,000	—	—	8.00	10.00	12.00
1992 D	450,000	PF65 15.00				

KM# 180 10 MARK
15.50 g., 0.625 Silver 0.3115 oz. ASW, 32.5 mm. **Subject:** 1000th Anniversary - Potsdam **Obv:** Eagle above denomination, date at left **Rev:** Palace of Sanssouci and Nicolai Church **Edge Lettering:** DAS GANZE EILAND MUSS EIN PARADIES WERDEN

Date	Mintage	VF20	XF40	MS60	MS63	MS65
1993 F	7,500,000	—	—	8.00	10.00	12.00
1993 F	450,000	PF65 15.00				

KM# 181 10 MARK
15.50 g., 0.625 Silver 0.3115 oz. ASW, 32.5 mm. **Subject:** 150th Birth Anniversary of Robert Koch **Obv:** Eagle above denomination **Rev:** Head 3/4 facing **Edge Lettering:** MITBEGRUENDER DER BAKTERIOLOGIE

Date	Mintage	VF20	XF40	MS60	MS63	MS65
1993 J	7,000,000	—	—	8.00	10.00	12.00
1993 J	450,000	PF65 15.00				

KM# 182 10 MARK
15.50 g., 0.625 Silver 0.3115 oz. ASW, 32.5 mm. **Subject:** Attempt on Hitler's Life, July 20, 1944 **Obv:** Eagle above denomination **Rev:** Wing with chain surrounding, date below **Edge Lettering:** WIDERSTAND GEGEN DEN NATIONALSOZIALIMUS

Date	Mintage	VF20	XF40	MS60	MS63	MS65
1994 A	7,000,000	—	—	8.00	10.00	12.00
1994 A	450,000	PF65 20.00				

KM# 184 10 MARK
15.50 g., 0.625 Silver 0.3115 oz. ASW, 32.5 mm. **Subject:** 250th Birth Anniversary- Johann Gottfried Herder **Obv:** Eagle, denomination at left and below **Rev:** Head looking right, shadow head behind **Edge Lettering:** HUMANITÄT 1ST DER ZWECK DER MENSCHHEIT

Date	Mintage	VF20	XF40	MS60	MS63	MS65
1994 G	7,000,000	—	—	8.00	10.00	12.00
1994 G	400,000	PF65 15.00				

KM# 185 10 MARK
15.50 g., 0.625 Silver 0.3115 oz. ASW, 32.5 mm. **Subject:** 50th Anniversary of Peace and Reconciliation **Obv:** Eagle above denomination and date **Rev:** Ruins of Frauen Kirche in Dresden **Edge Lettering:** STEINERNE GLOCKE SYMBOL FUER TOLERANZ

Date	Mintage	VF20	XF40	MS60	MS63	MS65
1995 J	7,000,000	—	—	8.00	10.00	12.00
1995 J	450,000	PF65 15.00				

KM# 186 10 MARK
15.50 g., 0.625 Silver 0.3115 oz. ASW, 32.5 mm. **Subject:** 500th Anniversary of death - Henry the Lion **Obv:** Thin eagle divides date and denomination **Rev:** Artistic rampant lion, left **Edge Lettering:** HEINRICH DER LOEWE AUS KAISERLICHEM STAMM

Date	Mintage	VF20	XF40	MS60	MS63	MS65
1995 F	6,500,000	—	—	8.00	10.00	12.00
1995 F	400,000	PF65 15.00				

KM# 187 10 MARK
15.50 g., 0.625 Silver 0.3115 oz. ASW, 32.5 mm. **Subject:** 150th Birth Anniversary - Wilhelm Conrad Röntgen; 100th Anniversary of x-ray **Obv:** Eagle divides date and denomination **Rev:** Hand and X-rayed hand **Edge Lettering:** ERSTER NOBEL PREIS FUER PHYSIK

Date	Mintage	VF20	XF40	MS60	MS63	MS65
1995 D	6,500,000	—	—	8.00	10.00	12.00
1995 D	400,000	PF65 15.00				

KM# 188 10 MARK
15.50 g., 0.625 Silver 0.3115 oz. ASW, 32.5 mm. **Subject:** 150th Anniversary of founding - Kolpingwerk **Obv:** Eagle, denomination at left and below **Rev:** Globe in background, face in triangle at right, three pictures in rectangle at left **Edge Lettering:** TAETIGE LIEBE HEILT ALLE WUNDEN

Date	Mintage	VF20	XF40	MS60	MS63	MS65
1996 A	5,600,000	—	—	8.00	10.00	12.00
1996 A	400,000	PF65 15.00				

KM# 189.1 10 MARK
15.50 g., 0.625 Silver 0.3115 oz. ASW, 32.5 mm. **Subject:** 500th Birth Anniversary - Philipp Melanchthon **Obv:** Stylized eagle above denomination **Rev:** Bust left, dates at right **Edge Lettering:** ZUM GESPRAECH GEBOREN

Date	Mintage	VF20	XF40	MS60	MS63	MS65
1997 A	150,000	PF65 18.00				
1997 D	150,000	PF65 18.00				
1997 F	150,000	PF65 18.00				
1997 G	150,000	PF65 18.00				
1997 J	3,010,000	—	—	8.00	10.00	12.00
1997 J	150,000	PF65 18.00				

KM# 189.2 10 MARK
15.50 g., 0.625 Silver 0.3115 oz. ASW, 32.5 mm. **Subject:** 500th Birth Anniversary - Philipp Melanchthon **Obv:** Stylized eagle, denomination **Rev:** Different forelock on portrait **Edge Lettering:** ZUM GESPRAECH GEBOREN

Date	Mintage	VF20	XF40	MS60	MS63	MS65
1997 J	Inc. above	—	—	8.00	10.00	12.00
1997 J	Inc. above	PF65 20.00				

KM# 190 10 MARK
15.50 g., 0.625 Silver 0.3115 oz. ASW, 32.5 mm. **Subject:** 200th Birth Anniversary - Heinrich Heine **Obv:** Stylized eagle, denomination below **Rev:** Half figure 3/4 left with handwritten text in background **Edge Lettering:** DEUTSCHLAND DAS SIND WIR SELBER

Date	Mintage	VF20	XF40	MS60	MS63	MS65
1997 A	150,000	PF65 22.50				
1997 D	3,000,000	—	—	8.00	10.00	12.00
1997 D	750,000	PF65 22.50				
1997 F	150,000	PF65 22.50				
1997 G	150,000	PF65 22.50				
1997 J	150,000	PF65 22.50				

KM# 192 10 MARK
15.50 g., 0.625 Silver 0.3115 oz. ASW, 32.5 mm. **Subject:** Diesel Engine Centennial **Obv:** Stylized eagle above denomination **Rev:** First diesel engine **Edge Lettering:** GEDANKEN SIND DER MOTOR DER WELT

Date	Mintage	VF20	XF40	MS60	MS63	MS65
1997 A	150,000	PF65 17.00				
1997 D	150,000	PF65 17.00				
1997 F	3,000,000	—	—	8.00	10.00	12.00
1997 F	150,000	PF65 17.00				
1997 G	150,000	PF65 17.00				
1997 J	150,000	PF65 17.00				

KM# 191 10 MARK
15.50 g., 0.925 Silver 0.461 oz. ASW, 32.5 mm. **Subject:** 300th Anniversary end of 30 Years War - Peace of Westphalia **Obv:** Stylized eagle above denomination **Rev:** Clasped hands, dove and quill **Edge Lettering:** FRIED ERNAEHRT UNFRIED VERAEHRT

Date	Mintage	VF20	XF40	MS60	MS63	MS65
1998 A	200,000	PF65 20.00				
1998 D	200,000	PF65 20.00				
1998 F	200,000	PF65 20.00				
1998 G	200,000	PF65 20.00				
1998 J	3,500,000	—	—	12.00	14.00	16.00
1998 J	200,000	PF65 20.00				

Note: A 1997 strike of this coin does not exist

KM# 193 10 MARK
15.50 g., 0.925 Silver 0.461 oz. ASW, 32.5 mm. **Subject:** 900th Anniversary - Birth of Hildegard von Bingen (1098-1178AD), abbess and scholar **Obv:** Stylized eagle above denomination **Rev:** Seated figure writing, small hand above left **Edge Lettering:** WISSE DIE WEGE DES HERRN

Date	Mintage	VF20	XF40	MS60	MS63	MS65
1998 A	200,000	PF65 20.00				
1998 D	200,000	PF65 20.00				
1998 F	200,000	PF65 20.00				
1998 G	3,500,000	—	—	12.00	14.00	16.00
1998 G	200,000	PF65 20.00				
1998 J	200,000	PF65 20.00				

KM# 194 10 MARK
15.50 g., 0.925 Silver 0.461 oz. ASW, 32.5 mm. **Subject:** 300th Anniversary Franckesche Charitable Endowment **Edge Lettering:** ER VERTRAUTE GOTT

Date	Mintage	VF20	XF40	MS60	MS63	MS65
1998 A	3,500,000	—	—	12.00	14.00	16.00
1998 A	200,000	PF65 20.00				
1998 D	200,000	PF65 20.00				
1998 F	200,000	PF65 20.00				
1998 G	200,000	PF65 20.00				
1998 J	200,000	PF65 20.00				

KM# 195 10 MARK
15.50 g., 0.925 Silver 0.461 oz. ASW, 32.5 mm. **Subject:** 50 Years of the Deutsche Mark **Obv:** Denomination above eagle **Rev:** Seven coin designs **Edge Lettering:** EINIGKEIT UND RECHT UND FREIHEIT

Date	Mintage	VF20	XF40	MS60	MS63	MS65
1998 A	195,000	PF65 22.00				
1998 D	195,000	PF65 22.00				
1998 F	3,525,000	—	—	12.00	14.00	16.00
1998 F	175,000	PF65 22.00				
1998 G	195,000	PF65 22.00				
1998 J	195,000	PF65 22.00				

KM# 196 10 MARK

15.50 g., 0.925 Silver 0.461 oz. ASW, 32.5 mm. **Subject:** 50th Anniversary - Bundes Republic Constitution **Obv:** Small eagle above denomination **Rev:** German constitution **Edge Lettering:** FÜR DAS GESAMTE DEUTSCHE VOLK

Date	Mintage	VF20	XF40	MS60	MS63	MS65
1999 A	160,000	PF65 22.00				
1999 D	3,000,000	—	—	12.00	14.00	16.00
1999 D	160,000	PF65 22.00				
1999 F	160,000	PF65 22.00				
1999 G	160,000	PF65 22.00				
1999 J	160,000	PF65 22.00				

KM# 197 10 MARK

15.50 g., 0.925 Silver 0.461 oz. ASW, 32.5 mm. **Subject:** 250th Anniversary - Birth of J.W. von Goethe **Obv:** Eagle above denomination **Rev:** Bust at left facing inscribed field right **Edge Lettering:** WIRKE GUT SO WIRKST DU LÄNGER

Date	Mintage	VF20	XF40	MS60	MS63	MS65
1999 A	160,000	PF65 20.00				
1999 D	160,000	PF65 20.00				
1999 F	3,000,000	—	—	12.00	14.00	16.00
1999 F	160,000	PF65 20.00				
1999 G	160,000	PF65 20.00				
1999 J	160,000	PF65 20.00				

KM# 198 10 MARK

15.50 g., 0.925 Silver 0.461 oz. ASW, 32.5 mm. **Subject:** Charity for children without parents all over the world **Obv:** Stylized eagle, denomination divides date below **Rev:** Stylized globe, children playing **Edge Lettering:** SOS - KINDERDÖRFER - EINE IDEE FÜR DIE WELT

Date	Mintage	VF20	XF40	MS60	MS63	MS65
1999 A	160,000	PF65 20.00				
1999 D	160,000	PF65 20.00				
1999 F	160,000	PF65 20.00				
1999 G	160,000	PF65 20.00				
1999 J	3,000,000	—	—	12.00	14.00	16.00
1999 J	160,000	PF65 20.00				

Note: NOTE: A 1997 strike of this coin does not exist.

KM# 199 10 MARK

15.50 g., 0.925 Silver 0.461 oz. ASW, 32.5 mm. **Subject:** Expo 2000 **Obv:** Stylized eagle **Rev:** Childlike drawing of human balance scale **Edge Lettering:** WELTAUSSTELLUNG EXPO 2000 HANNOVER

Date	Mintage	VF20	XF40	MS60	MS63	MS65
2000 A	3,000,000	—	—	12.00	14.00	16.00
2000 A	163,000	PF65 22.00				
2000 D	163,000	PF65 22.00				
2000 F	163,000	PF65 22.00				
2000 G	163,000	PF65 22.00				
2000 J	163,000	PF65 22.00				

KM# 200 10 MARK

15.50 g., 0.925 Silver 0.461 oz. ASW, 32.5 mm. **Subject:** 1200th Anniversary - Founding of the Church in Aachen by Charlemagne **Obv:** Stylized eagle **Rev:** Charlemagne handing church model to Madonna and child **Edge Lettering:** URBS AQUENSIS - URBS REGALIS

Date	Mintage	VF20	XF40	MS60	MS63	MS65
2000 A	163,000	PF65 20.00				
2000 D	163,000	PF65 20.00				
2000 F	163,000	PF65 20.00				
2000 G	3,000,000	—	—	12.00	14.00	16.00
2000 G	163,000	PF65 20.00				
2000 J	163,000	PF65 20.00				

KM# 201 10 MARK

15.50 g., 0.925 Silver 0.461 oz. ASW, 32.5 mm. **Subject:** 10th Anniversary of Reunification **Obv:** Eagle and denomination **Rev:** Parliament building **Edge Lettering:** WIR SIND DAS VOLK WIR SIND EIN VOLK

Date	Mintage	VF20	XF40	MS60	MS63	MS65
2000 A	163,000	PF65 20.00				
2000 D	3,000,000	—	—	12.00	14.00	16.00
2000 D	163,000	PF65 20.00				
2000 F	163,000	PF65 20.00				
2000 G	163,000	PF65 20.00				
2000 J	163,000	PF65 20.00				

KM# 202 10 MARK

15.50 g., 0.925 Silver 0.461 oz. ASW, 32.5 mm. **Subject:** 250th anniversary of the death of Bach **Obv:** Eagle above denomination **Rev:** Face on inscribed background, dates below **Edge Lettering:** JOHANN SEBASTIAN BACH 250 TODESTAG

Date	Mintage	VF20	XF40	MS60	MS63	MS65
2000 A	163,000	PF65 20.00				
2000 D	163,000	PF65 20.00				
2000 F	3,000,000	—	—	12.00	14.00	16.00
2000 F	163,000	PF65 20.00				
2000 G	163,000	PF65 20.00				
2000 J	163,000	PF65 20.00				

PATTERNS

Including off metal strikes

KM#	Date	Mintage	Identification	Mkt Val
Pn397	1950D	—	2 Mark. Copper-Nickel. With Hole, PN#400..	—
Pn398	1951D	—	2 Mark. Copper-Nickel. Max Planck..	—
Pn399	1951F	—	2 Mark. Copper-Nickel. Max Planck..	—
Pn400	1955J	—	2 Mark.	—
Pn401	1959F	—	2 Pfennig. Brass.	—
Pn402	1960F	—	2 Pfennig. Zinc.	—

TRIAL STRIKES

KM#	Date	Mintage	Identification	Mkt Val
TS1	ND (1947)J	—	10 Pfennig. KM#4. Uniface..	—
TS2	ND (1948)J	—	2 Mark. Silver. Pn400. Uniface..	—
TS3	1950J	—	2 Mark. Silver. Pn400. Uniface..	—
TS4	ND (1950)J	—	2 Mark. Lead. Pn400. Uniface..	—
TS5	1950J	—	2 Mark. Lead. Pn400. Uniface..	—
TS6	1951F	—	2 Mark. Lead. Max Planck. Uniface..	—
TS7	ND (1951)F	—	2 Mark. Lead. Max Planck. Uniface..	—
TS8	1951J	—	2 Mark. Iron. Max Planck. Uniface..	—
TS9	ND (1951)J	—	2 Mark. Iron. Max Planck. Uniface..	—
TS10	1951J	—	2 Mark. Lead. Max Planck. Uniface..	—
TS11	ND (1951)J	—	2 Mark. Lead. Max Planck. Uniface..	—

MINT SETS

KM#	Date	Mintage	Identification	Issue Price	Mkt Val
MS1	1974D (9)	20,000	KM#105, 106a, 107-108, 109.2, 110, 112.1, 124, A127	—	40.00
MS2	1974F (9)	20,000	KM#105, 106a, 107-108, 109.2, 110, 112.1, 124, A127	—	40.00
MS3	1974G (9)	20,000	KM#105, 106a, 107-108, 109.2, 110, 112.1, 124, A127	—	40.00
MS4	1974J (9)	20,000	KM#105, 106a, 107-108, 109.2, 110, 112.1, 124, A127	—	40.00
MS5	1975D (9)	26,000	KM#105, 106a, 107-108, 109.2, 110, 124, A127, 140.1	—	15.00
MS6	1975F (9)	26,000	KM#105, 106a, 107-108, 109.2, 110, 124, A127, 140.1	—	15.00
MS7	1975G (9)	26,000	KM#105, 106a, 107-108, 109.2, 110, 124, A127, 140.1	—	15.00
MS8	1975J (9)	26,000	KM#105, 106a, 107-108, 109.2, 110, 124, A127, 140.1	—	15.00
MS9	1976D (9)	26,000	KM#105, 106a, 107-108, 109.2, 110, 124, A127, 140.1	—	23.00
MS10	1976F (9)	26,000	KM#105, 106a, 107-108, 1092., 110, 124, A127, 140.1	—	23.00
MS11	1976G (9)	26,000	KM#105, 106a, 107-108, 109.2, 110, 124, A127, 140.1	—	23.00
MS12	1976J (9)	26,000	KM#105, 106a, 107-108, 109.2, 110, 124, A127, 140.1	—	23.00
MS13	1977D (9)	29,000	KM#105, 106a, 107-108, 109.2, 110, 124, A127, 140.1	—	15.00
MS14	1977F (9)	29,000	KM#105, 106a, 107-108, 109.2, 110, 124, A127, 140.1	—	15.00
MS15	1977G (9)	29,000	KM#105, 106a, 107-108, 109.2, 110, 124, A127, 140.1	—	15.00
MS16	1977J (9)	29,000	KM#105, 106a, 107-108, 109.2, 110, 124, A127, 140.1	—	15.00
MS17	1978D (9)	30,000	KM#105, 106a, 107-108, 109.2, 110, 124, A127, 140.1	—	15.00
MS18	1978F (9)	30,000	KM#105, 106a, 107-108, 109.2, 110, 124, A127, 140.1	—	15.00
MS19	1978g (9)	30,000	KM#105, 106a, 107-108, 109.2, 110, 124, A127, 140.1	—	15.00
MS20	1978J (9)	30,000	KM#105, 106a, 107-108, 109.2, 110, 124, A127, 140.1	—	15.00
MS21	1979D (10)	34,000	KM105, 106a, 107-108, 109.2, 110, 124, A127, 140.1, 149	11.00	15.00
MS22	1979F (10)	34,000	KM105, 106a, 107-108, 109.2, 110, 124, A127, 140.1, 149	11.00	15.00
MS23	1979G (10)	34,000	KM105, 106a, 107-108, 109.2, 110, 124, A127, 140.1, 149	11.00	15.00
MS24	1979J (10)	34,000	KM105, 106a, 107-108, 109.2, 110, 124, A127, 140.1, 149	11.00	15.00
MS25	1980D (10)	36,000	KM105, 106a, 107-108, 109.2, 110, 124, A127, 140.1, 149	11.00	15.00
MS26	1980F (10)	36,000	KM105, 106a, 107-108, 109.2, 110, 124, A127, 140.1, 149	11.00	15.00
MS27	1980G (10)	36,000	KM105, 106a, 107-108, 109.2, 110, 124, A127, 140.1, 149	11.00	15.00
MS28	1980J (10)	36,000	KM105, 106a, 107-108, 109.2, 110, 124, A127, 140.1, 149	11.00	15.00
MS29	1981D (10)	38,000	KM105, 106a, 107-108, 109.2, 110, 124, A127, 140.1, 149	11.00	15.00
MS30	1981F (10)	38,000	KM105, 106a, 107-108, 109.2, 110, 124, A127, 140.1, 149	11.00	15.00
MS31	1981G (10)	38,000	KM105, 106a, 107-108, 109.2, 110, 124, A127, 140.1, 149	11.00	15.00
MS32	1981J (10)	38,000	KM105, 106a, 107-108, 109.2, 110, 124, A127, 140.1, 149	11.00	15.00
MS33	1982D (10)	33,000	KM105, 106a, 107-108, 109.2, 110, 124, A127, 140.1, 149	11.00	15.00
MS34	1982F (10)	33,000	KM105, 106a, 107-108, 109.2, 110, 124, A127, 140.1, 149	11.00	15.00
MS35	1982G (10)	33,000	KM105, 106a, 107-108, 109.2, 110, 124, A127, 140.1, 149	11.00	15.00
MS36	1982J (10)	33,000	KM105, 106a, 107-108, 109.2, 110, 124, A127, 140.1, 149	11.00	15.00

KM#	Date	Mintage	Identification	Issue Price	Mkt Val
MS37	1983D (10)	31,000	KM105, 106a, 107-108, 109.2, 110, 124, A127, 140.1, 149	11.00	15.00
MS38	1983F (10)	31,000	KM105, 106a, 107-108, 109.2, 110, 124, A127, 140.1, 149	11.00	15.00
MS39	1983G (10)	31,000	KM105, 106a, 107-108, 109.2, 110, 124, A127, 140.1, 149	11.00	15.00
MS40	1983J (10)	31,000	KM105, 106a, 107-108, 109.2, 110, 124, A127, 140.1, 149	11.00	15.00
MS41	1984D (10)	25,000	KM105, 106a, 107-108, 109.2, 110, 124, A127, 140.1, 149	11.00	45.00
MS42	1984F (10)	25,000	KM105, 106a, 107-108, 109.2, 110, 124, A127, 140.1, 149	11.00	45.00
MS43	1984G (10)	25,000	KM105, 106a, 107-108, 109.2, 110, 124, A127, 140.1, 149	11.00	45.00
MS44	1984J (10)	25,000	KM105, 106a, 107-108, 109.2, 110, 124, A127, 140.1, 149	11.00	45.00
MS45	1985D (10)	23,000	KM105, 106a, 107-108, 109.2, 110, 124, A127, 140.1, 149	11.00	15.00
MS46	1985F (10)	23,000	KM105, 106a, 107-108, 109.2, 110, 124, A127, 140.1, 149	11.00	15.00
MS47	1985G (10)	23,000	KM105, 106a, 107-108, 109.2, 110, 124, A127, 140.1, 149	11.00	15.00
MS48	1985J (10)	23,000	KM105, 106a, 107-108, 109.2, 110, 124, A127, 140.1, 149	11.00	15.00
MS49	1986D (10)	15,000	KM105, 106a, 107-108, 109.2, 110, 124, A127, 140.1, 149	11.00	100
MS50	1986F (10)	15,000	KM105, 106a, 107-108, 109.2, 110, 124, A127, 140.1, 149	11.00	100
MS51	1986G (10)	15,000	KM105, 106a, 107-108, 109.2, 110, 124, A127, 140.1, 149	11.00	100
MS52	1986J (10)	15,000	KM105, 106a, 107-108, 109.2, 110, 124, A127, 140.1, 149	11.00	100
MS53	1987D (10)	18,000	KM105, 106a, 107-108, 109.2, 110, 124, A127, 140.1, 149	11.00	40.00
MS54	1987F (10)	18,000	KM105, 106a, 107-108, 109.2, 110, 124, A127, 140.1, 149	11.00	40.00
MS55	1987G (10)	18,000	KM105, 106a, 107-108, 109.2, 110, 124, A127, 140.1, 149	11.00	40.00
MS56	1987J (10)	18,000	KM105, 106a, 107-108, 109.2, 110, 124, A127, 140.1, 149	11.00	40.00
MS57	1988D (9)	18,000	KM105, 106a, 107-108, 109.2, 110, 140.1, 149, 170	—	22.50
MS58	1988F (9)	18,000	KM105, 106a, 107-108, 109.2, 110, 140.1, 149, 170	—	22.50
MS59	1988G (9)	18,000	KM105, 106a, 107-108, 109.2, 110, 140.1, 149, 170	—	22.50
MS60	1988J (9)	18,000	KM105, 106a, 107-108, 109.2, 110, 140.1, 149, 170	—	22.50
MS61	1989D (9)	18,000	KM105, 106a, 107-108, 109.2, 110, 140.1, 149, 170	—	22.50
MS62	1989F (9)	18,000	KM105, 106a, 107-108, 109.2, 110, 140.1, 149, 170	—	22.50
MS63	1989G (9)	18,000	KM105, 106a, 107-108, 109.2, 110, 140.1, 149, 170	—	22.50
MS64	1989J (9)	18,000	KM105, 106a, 107-108, 109.2, 110, 140.1, 149, 170	—	22.50
MS65	1990D (10)	20,000	KM105, 106a, 107-108, 109.2, 110, 140.1, 149, 170, 175	—	20.00
MS66	1990F (10)	20,000	KM105, 106a, 107-108, 109.2, 110, 140.1, 149, 170, 175	—	20.00
MS67	1990G (10)	20,000	KM105, 106a, 107-108, 109.2, 110, 140.1, 149, 170, 175	—	20.00
MS68	1990J (10)	20,000	KM105, 106a, 107-108, 109.2, 110, 140.1, 149, 170, 175	—	20.00
MS69	1991A (10)	20,000	KM105, 106a, 107-108, 109.2, 110, 140.1, 149, 170, 175	—	25.00
MS70	1991D (10)	20,000	KM105, 106a, 107-108, 109.2, 110, 140.1, 149, 170, 175	—	25.00
MS71	1991F (10)	20,000	KM105, 106a, 107-108, 109.2, 110, 140.1, 149, 170, 175	—	25.00
MS72	1991G (10)	20,000	KM105, 106a, 107-108, 109.2, 110, 140.1, 149, 170, 175	—	25.00
MS73	1991J (10)	20,000	KM105, 106a, 107-108, 109.2, 110, 140.1, 149, 170, 175	—	25.00
MS74	1992A (10)	20,000	KM105, 106a, 107-108, 109.2, 110, 140.1, 149, 170, 175	—	25.00
MS75	1992D (10)	20,000	KM105, 106a, 107-108, 109.2, 110, 140.1, 149, 170, 175	—	25.00
MS76	1992F (10)	20,000	KM105, 106a, 107-108, 109.2, 110, 140.1, 149, 170, 175	—	25.00
MS77	1992G (10)	20,000	KM105, 106a, 107-108, 109.2, 110, 140.1, 149, 170, 175	—	25.00
MS78	1992J (10)	20,000	KM105, 106a, 107-108, 109.2, 110, 140.1, 149, 170, 175	—	25.00
MS79	1993A (10)	20,000	KM105, 106a, 107-108, 109.2, 110, 140.1, 149, 170, 175	—	35.00
MS80	1993D (10)	20,000	KM105, 106a, 107-108, 109.2, 110, 140.1, 149, 170, 175	—	35.00
MS81	1993F (10)	20,000	KM105, 106a, 107-108, 109.2, 110, 140.1, 149, 170, 175	—	35.00
MS82	1993G (10)	20,000	KM105, 106a, 107-108, 109.2, 110, 140.1, 149, 170, 175	—	35.00
MS83	1993J (10)	20,000	KM105, 106a, 107-108, 109.2, 110, 140.1, 149, 170, 175	—	35.00
MS84	1994A (10)	10,000	KM105, 106A, 107-108, 109.2, 110, 140.1, 170, 175, 183	—	25.00
MS85	1994D (10)	20,000	KM105, 106a, 107-108, 109.2, 110, 140.1, 170, 175, 183	—	25.00
MS86	1994F (10)	20,000	KM105, 106a, 107-108, 109.2, 110, 140.1, 170, 175, 183	—	25.00
MS87	1994G (10)	20,000	KM105, 106a, 107-108, 109.2, 110, 140.1, 170, 175, 183	—	25.00
MS88	1994J (10)	20,000	KM105, 106a, 107-108, 109.2, 110, 140.1, 170, 175, 183	—	25.00
MS89	1995A (10)	20,000	KM105, 106a, 107-108, 109.2, 110, 140.1, 170, 175, 183	—	300
MS90	1995D (10)	20,000	KM105, 106a, 107-108, 109.2, 110, 140.1, 170, 175, 183	—	300
MS91	1995F (10)	20,000	KM105, 106a, 107-108, 109.2, 110, 140.1, 170, 175, 183	—	300
MS92	1995G (10)	20,000	KM105, 106a, 107-108, 109.2, 110, 140.1, 170, 175, 183	—	300
MS93	1995J (10)	20,000	KM105, 106A, 107-108, 109.2, 110, 140.1, 170, 175, 183	—	300
MS94	1996A (10)	50,000	KM105, 106a, 107-108, 109.2, 110, 140.1, 170, 175, 183	—	45.00
MS95	1996D (10)	50,000	KM105, 106a, 107-108, 109.2, 110, 140.1, 170, 175, 183	—	45.00
MS96	1996F (10)	50,000	KM105, 106a, 107-108, 109.2, 110, 140.1, 170, 175, 183	—	45.00
MS97	1996G (10)	50,000	KM105, 106a, 107-108, 109.2, 110, 140.1, 170, 175, 183	—	45.00
MS98	1996J (10)	50,000	KM105, 106a, 107-108, 109.2, 110, 140.1, 170, 175, 183	—	45.00
MS99	1997A (9)	70,000	KM105, 106a, 108, 109.2, 110, 140.1, 170, 175, 183	—	25.00
MS100	1997D (10)	70,000	KM105, 106a, 107-108, 109.2, 110, 140.1, 170, 175, 183	—	25.00
MS101	1997F (10)	70,000	KM105, 106a, 107-108, 109.2, 110, 140.1, 170, 175, 183	—	25.00
MS102	1997G (10)	70,000	KM105, 106a, 107-108, 109.2, 110, 140.1, 170, 175, 183	—	25.00
MS103	1997J (10)	70,000	KM105, 106a, 107-108, 109.2, 110, 140.1, 170, 175, 183	—	25.00
MS104	1998A (10)	70,000	KM105, 106a, 107-108, 109.2, 110, 140.1, 170, 175, 183	—	25.00
MS105	1998D (10)	70,000	KM105, 106a, 107-108, 109.2, 110, 140.1, 170, 175, 183	—	25.00
MS106	1998F (10)	70,000	KM105, 106a, 107-108, 109.2, 110, 140.1, 170, 175, 183	—	25.00
MS107	1998G (10)	70,000	KM105, 106a, 107-108, 109.2, 110, 140.1, 170, 175, 183	—	25.00
MS108	1998J (10)	70,000	KM105, 106a, 107-108, 109.2, 110, 140.1, 170, 175, 183	—	25.00
MS109	1999A (10)	70,000	KM105, 106a, 107-108, 109.2, 110, 140.1, 170, 175, 183	—	25.00
MS110	1999D (10)	70,000	km105, 106A, 107-108, 109.2, 110, 140.1, 170, 175, 183	—	25.00
MS112	1999G (10)	70,000	KM105, 106a, 107-108, 109.2, 110, 140.1, 170, 175, 183	—	25.00
MS114	1999J (10)	70,000	KM105, 106a, 107-108, 109.2, 110, 140.1, 170, 175, 183	—	25.00
MS115	2000D (10)	20,000	KM105, 106a, 107-108, 109.2, 110, 140.1, 170, 175, 183	—	40.00
MS116	2000F (10)	20,000	KM105, 160a, 107-108, 109.2, 110, 140.1, 170, 175, 183	—	40.00
MS117	2000G (10)	20,000	KM105, 106a, 107-108, 109.2, 110, 140.1, 170, 175, 183	—	40.00
MS118	2000J (10)	20,000	KM105, 106a, 107-108, 109.2, 110, 140.1, 170, 175, 183	—	40.00

PROOF SETS

KM#	Date	Mintage	Identification	Issue Price	Mkt Val
PS4	1966F (8)	450	KM105-108, 109.1, 110, 112.1, 116	—	3,500
PS5	1966G (8)	3,070	KM105-108, 109.1, 110, 112.1, 116	—	550
PS6	1966J (8)	1,000	KM105-108, 109.1, 110, 112.1, 116	—	900
PS7	1967F (8)	1,600	KM105-108, 109.1, 110, 112.1, 116	—	600
PS8	1967G (8)	3,630	KM105-108, 109.1, 110, 112.1, 116	—	400
PS9	1967G (8)	520	KM105, 106a*, 107-108, 109.1, 110, 112.1, 116	—	3,500
PS10	1967J (8)	1,500	KM105, 106a, 107-108, 109.1, 110, 112.1, 116	—	800
PS11	1968F (8)	3,000	KM105, 106a, 107-108, 109.1, 110, 112.1, 116	—	550
PS12	1968G (8)	3,651	KM105, 106, 107-108, 109.1, 110, 112.1, 116	—	325
PS12a	1968G (8)	2,372	KM105, 106a, 107-108, 109.1, 110, 112.1, 116	—	400
PS13	1968J (8)	2,000	KM105, 106a, 107-108, 109.1, 110, 112.1, 116	—	550
PS14	1969F (8)	5,000	KM105, 106a, 107-108, 109.1, 110, 112.1, 116	—	100
PS15	1969G (8)	8,700	KM105, 106a, 107-108, 109.1, 110, 112.1, 116	—	100
PS16	1969J (8)	5,000	KM105, 106a, 107-108, 109.1, 110, 112.1, 116	—	100
PS17	1970F (8)	5,140	KM105, 106a, 107-108, 109.1, 110, 112.1, 116	—	140
PS18	1970G (8)	10,200	KM105, 106a, 107-108, 109.1, 110, 112.1, 116	—	100
PS19	1970J (8)	5,000	KM105, 106a, 107-108, 109.1, 110, 112.1, 116	—	100
PS20	1971D (8)	8,000	KM105, 106a, 107-108, 109.1, 110, 112.1, 116	—	95.00
PS21	1971F (8)	8,000	KM105, 106a, 107-108, 109.1, 110, 112.1, 116	—	95.00

PS22	1971G (8)	10,200	KM105, 106a, 107-108, 109.1, 110, 112.1, 116	—	95.00
PS23	1971J (8)	8,000	KM105, 106a, 107-108, 109.1, 110, 112.1, 116	—	95.00
PS24	1972D (9)	8,000	KM105, 106a, 107-108, 109.2, 110, 112.1, 124, A127	—	95.00
PS25	1972F (9)	8,000	KM105, 106a, 107-108, 109.2, 110, 112.1, 124, A127	—	95.00
PS26	1972G (9)	10,000	KM105, 106a, 107-108, 109.2, 110, 112.1, 124, A127	—	95.00
PS27	1972J (9)	8,000	KM105, 106a, 107-108, 109.2, 110, 112.1, 124, A127	—	95.00
PS28	1973D (9)	9,000	KM105, 106a, 107-108, 109.2, 110, 112.1, 124, A127	—	95.00
PS29	1973F (9)	9,000	KM105, 106a, 107-108, 109.2, 110, 112.1, 124, A127	—	95.00
PS30	1973G (9)	9,000	KM105, 106a, 107-108, 109.2, 110, 112.1, 124, A127	—	95.00
PS31	1973J (9)	9,000	KM105, 106a, 107-108, 109.2, 110, 112.1, 124, A127	—	95.00
PS32	1974D (9)	35,000	KM105, 106a, 107-108, 109.2, 110, 112.1, 124, A127	10.00	35.00
PS33	1974F (9)	35,000	KM105, 106a, 107-108, 109.2, 110, 112.1, 124, A127	10.00	35.00
PS34	1974G (9)	35,000	KM105, 106a, 107-108, 109.2, 110, 112.1, 124, A127	10.00	35.00
PS35	1974J (9)	35,000	KM105, 106a, 107-108, 109.2, 110, 112.1, 124, A127	10.00	35.00
PS36	1975D (9)	43,120	KM105, 106a, 107-108, 109.2, 110, 124, A127, 140.1	10.00	17.00
PS37	1975F (9)	43,100	KM105, 106a, 107-108, 109.2, 110, 124, A127, 140.1	10.00	17.00
PS38	1975G (9)	43,100	KM105, 106a, 107-108, 109.2, 110, 124, A127, 140.1	10.00	17.00
PS39	1975J (9)	43,120	KM105, 106a, 107-108, 109.2, 110, 124, A127, 140.1	10.00	17.00
PS40	1976D (9)	43,120	KM105, 106a, 107-108, 109.2, 110, 124, A127, 140.1	10.00	20.00
PS41	1976F (9)	43,100	KM105, 106a, 107-108, 109.2, 110, 124, A127, 140.1	10.00	20.00
PS42	1976G (9)	43,100	KM105, 106a, 107-108, 109.2, 110, 124, A127, 140.1	10.00	20.00
PS43	1976J (9)	43,120	KM105, 106a, 107-108, 109.2, 110, 124, A127, 140.1	10.00	20.00
PS44	1977D (9)	50,620	KM105, 106a, 107-108, 109.2, 110, 124, A127, 140.1	12.50	25.00
PS45	1977F (9)	50,600	KM105, 106a, 107-108, 109.2, 110, 124, A127, 140.1	12.50	25.00
PS46	1977G (9)	50,600	KM105, 106a, 107-108, 109.2, 110, 124, A127, 140.1	12.50	25.00
PS47	1977J (9)	50,620	KM105, 106a, 107-108, 109.2, 110, 124, A127, 140.1	12.50	25.00
PS48	1978D (9)	54,000	KM105, 106A, 107-108, 109.2, 110, 124, A127, 140.1	13.00	17.00
PS49	1978F (9)	54,000	KM105, 106a, 107-108, 109.2, 110, 124, A127, 140.1	13.00	17.00
PS50	1978G (9)	54,000	KM105, 106a, 107-108, 109.2, 110, 124, A127, 140.1	13.00	17.00
PS51	1978J (9)	54,000	KM105, 106a, 107-108, 109.2, 110, 124, A127, 140.1	13.00	17.00
PS52	1979D (10)	89,000	KM105, 106a, 107-108, 109.2, 110, 124, A127, 140.1, 149	15.00	17.00
PS53	1979F (10)	89,000	KM105, 106a, 107-108, 109.2, 110, 124, A127, 140.1, 149	15.00	17.00
PS54	1979G (10)	89,000	KM105, 106a, 107-108, 109.2, 110, 124, A127, 140.1, 149	15.00	20.00
PS55	1979J (10)	89,000	KM105, 106a, 107-108, 109.2, 110, 124, A127, 140.1, 149	15.00	17.00
PS56	1980D (10)	60,000	KM105, 106a, 107-108, 109.2, 110, 124, A127, 140.1, 149	15.00	20.00
PS57	1980F (10)	60,000	KM105, 106a, 107-108, 109.2, 110, 124, A127, 140.1, 149	15.00	17.00
PS58	1980G (10)	60,000	KM105, 106a, 107-108, 109.2, 110, 124, A127, 140.1, 149	15.00	17.00
PS59	1980J (10)	60,000	KM105, 106a, 107-108, 109.2, 110, 124, A127, 140.1, 149	15.00	17.00
PS60	1981D (10)	60,000	KM105, 106a, 107-108, 109.2, 110, 124, A127, 140.1, 149	15.00	17.00
PS61	1981F (10)	91,000	KM105, 106a, 107-108, 109.2, 110, 124, A127, 140.1, 149	15.00	17.00
PS62	1981G (10)	91,000	KM105, 106a, 107-108, 109.2, 110, 124, A127, 140.1, 149	15.00	17.00
PS63	1981J (10)	45,000	KM105, 106a, 107-108, 109.2, 110, 124, A127, 140.1, 149	15.00	18.00
PS64	1982D (10)	40,000	KM105, 106a, 107-108, 109.2, 110, 124, A127, 140.1, 149	15.00	15.00
PS65	1982F (10)	40,000	KM105, 106a, 107-108, 109.2, 110, 124, A127, 140.1, 149	15.00	15.00
PS66	1982G (10)	40,000	KM105, 106a, 107-108, 109.2, 110, 124, A127, 140.1, 149	15.00	15.00
PS67	1982J (10)	78,000	KM105, 106a, 107-108, 109.2, 110, 124, A127, 140.1, 149	15.00	15.00
PS68	1983D (10)	40,000	KM105, 106a, 107-108, 109.2, 110, 124, A127, 140.1, 149	15.00	17.00
PS69	1983F (10)	47,000	KM105, 106a, 107-108, 109.2, 110, 124, A127, 140.1, 149	15.00	17.00
PS70	1983G (10)	75,000	KM105, 106a, 107-108, 109.2, 110, 124, A127, 140.1, 149	15.00	17.00
PS71	1983J (10)	75,000	KM105, 106a, 107-108, 109.2, 110, 124, A127, 140.1, 149	15.00	17.00
PS72	1984D (10)	64,000	KM105, 106a, 107-108, 109.2, 110, 124, A127, 140.1, 149	15.00	25.00
PS73	1984F (10)	64,000	KM105, 106a, 107-108, 109.2, 110, 124, A127, 140.1, 149	15.00	20.00
PS74	1984G (10)	64,000	KM105, 106a, 107-108, 109.2, 110, 124, A127, 140.1, 149	15.00	20.00
PS75	1984J (10)	64,000	KM105, 106a, 107-108, 109.2, 110, 124, A127, 140.1, 149	15.00	20.00
PS76	1985D (0)	56,000	KM105, 106a, 107-108, 109.2, 110, 124, A127, 140.1, 149	15.00	20.00
PS77	1985F (10)	54,000	KM105, 106a, 107-108, 109.2, 110, 124, A127, 140.1, 149	15.00	20.00
PS78	1985G (10)	55,000	KM105, 106a, 107-108, 109.2, 110, 124, A127, 140.1, 149	15.00	20.00
PS79	1985J (10)	54,000	KM105, 106a, 107-108, 109.2, 110, 124, A127, 140.1, 149	15.00	20.00
PS80	1986D (10)	44,000	KM105, 106a, 107-108, 109.2, 110, 124, A127, 140.1, 149	15.00	22.50
PS81	1986F (10)	44,000	KM105, 106a, 107-108, 109.2, 110, 124, A127, 140.1, 149	15.00	22.50
PS82	1986G (10)	44,000	KM105, 106a, 107-108, 109.2, 110, 124, A127, 140.1, 149	15.00	22.50
PS83	1986J (10)	44,000	KM105, 106a, 107-108, 109.2, 110, 124, A127, 140.1, 149	15.00	22.50
PS84	1987D (10)	45,000	KM105, 106a, 107-108, 109.2, 110, 124, A127, 140.1, 149	15.00	30.00
PS85	1987F (10)	45,000	KM105, 106a, 107-108, 109.2, 110, 124, A127, 140.1, 149	15.00	30.00
PS86	1987G (10)	45,000	KM105, 106a, 107-108, 109.2, 110, 124, A127, 140.1, 149	15.00	30.00
PS87	1987J (10)	45,000	KM105, 106a, 107-108, 109.2, 110, 124, A127, 140.1, 149	15.00	30.00
PS88	1988D (9)	45,000	KM105, 106a, 107-108, 109.2, 110, 140.1, 149, 170	—	20.00
PS89	1988F (9)	45,000	KM105, 106a, 107-108, 109.2, 110, 140.1, 149, 170	—	20.00
PS90	1988G (9)	45,000	KM105, 106a, 107-108, 109.2, 110, 140.1, 149, 170	—	20.00
PS91	1988J (9)	45,000	KM105, 106a, 107-108, 109.2, 110, 140.1, 149, 170	—	20.00
PS92	1989D (9)	45,000	KM105, 106a, 107-108, 109.2, 110, 140.1, 149, 170	—	20.00
PS93	1989F (9)	45,000	KM105, 106a, 107-108, 109.2, 110, 140.1, 149, 170	—	20.00
PS94	1989G (9)	45,000	KM105-106a, 107-108, 109.2, 110, 140.1, 149, 170	—	20.00
PS95	1989J (9)	45,000	KM105-106a, 107-108, 109.2, 110, 140.1, 149, 170	—	20.00
PS96	1990D (10)	45,000	KM105, 106a, 107-108, 109.2, 110, 140.1, 149, 170, 175	—	20.00
PS97	1990F (10)	45,000	KM105, 106a, 107-108, 109.2, 110, 140.1, 149, 170, 175	—	20.00
PS98	1990G (10)	45,000	KM105, 106a, 107-180, 109.2, 110, 140.1, 149, 170, 175	—	20.00
PS99	1990J (10)	45,000	KM105, 106a, 107-108, 109.2, 110, 140.1, 149, 170, 175	—	20.00
PS100	1991A (10)	45,000	KM105, 106a, 107-108, 109.2, 110, 140.1, 149, 170, 175	—	22.50
PS101	1991D (10)	45,000	KM105, 106a, 107-108, 109.2, 110, 140.1, 149, 170, 175	—	22.50
PS102	1991F (10)	45,000	KM105, 106a, 107-108, 109.2, 110, 140.1, 149, 170, 175	—	22.50
PS103	1991G (10)	45,000	KM105, 106a, 107-108, 109.2, 110, 140.1, 149, 170, 175	—	22.50
PS104	1991J (10)	45,000	KM105, 106a, 107-108, 109.2, 110, 140.1, 149, 170, 175	—	22.50
PS105	1992A (10)	45,000	KM105, 106a, 107-108, 109.2, 110, 140.1, 149, 170, 175	—	22.50
PS106	1992D (10)	45,000	KM105, 106a, 107-108, 109.2, 110, 140.1, 149, 170, 175	—	22.50
PS107	1992F (10)	45,000	KM105, 106a, 107-108, 109.2, 110, 140.1, 149, 170, 175	—	22.50
PS108	1992G (10)	45,000	KM105, 106a, 107, 109.2, 110, 140.1, 149, 170, 175	—	22.50
PS109	1992J (10)	45,000	KM105, 106a, 107-108, 109.2, 110, 140.1, 149, 170, 175	—	22.50
PS110	1993A (10)	45,000	KM105, 106a, 107-108, 109.2, 110, 140.1, 149, 170, 175	—	30.00
PS111	1993D (10)	45,000	KM105, 106a, 107-108, 109.2, 110, 140.1, 149, 170, 175	—	30.00
PS112	1993F (10)	45,000	KM105, 106a, 107-108, 109.2, 110, 140.1, 149, 170, 175	—	30.00
PS113	1993G (10)	45,000	KM105, 106a, 107-108, 109.2, 110, 140.1, 149, 170, 175	—	30.00
PS114	1993J (10)	45,000	KM105, 106a, 107-108, 109.2, 110, 140.1, 149, 170, 175	—	30.00
PS115	1994A (10)	45,000	KM105, 106a, 107-108, 109.2, 110, 140.1, 170, 175, 183	—	20.00
PS116	1994D (10)	45,000	KM105, 106a, 107-108, 109.2, 110, 140.1, 170, 175, 183	—	20.00
PS117	1994F (10)	45,000	KM105, 106a, 107-108, 109.2, 110, 140, 1, 170, 175, 183	—	20.00
PS118	1994G (10)	45,000	KM105, 106a, 107-108, 109.2, 110, 140.1, 170, 175, 183	—	20.00
PS119	1994J (10)	45,000	KM105, 106a, 107-108, 109.2, 110, 140.1, 170, 175, 183	—	20.00
PS120	1995A (10)	45,000	KM105, 106a, 107-108, 109.2, 110, 140.1, 170, 175, 183	—	200

PS121	1995D (10)	45,000	KM105, 106a, 107-108, 109.2, 110, 140.1, 170, 175, 183	—	200
PS122	1995F (10)	45,000	KM105, 106a, 107-108, 109.2, 110, 140.1, 170, 175, 183	—	225
PS123	1995G (10)	45,000	KM105, 106a, 107-108, 109.2, 110, 140.1, 170, 175, 183	—	225
PS124	1995J (10)	45,000	KM105, 106a, 107-108, 109.2, 110, 140.1, 170, 175, 183	—	200
PS125	1996A (10)	45,000	KM105, 106a, 107-108, 109.2, 110, 140.1, 170, 175, 183	—	45.00
PS126	1996D (10)	45,000	KM105, 106a, 107-108, 109.2, 110, 140.1, 170, 175, 183	—	45.00
PS127	1996F (10)	45,000	KM105, 106a, 107-108, 109.2, 110, 140.1, 170, 175, 183	—	45.00
PS128	1996G (10)	45,000	KM105, 106a, 107-108, 109.2, 110, 140.1, 170, 175, 183	—	45.00
PS129	1996J (10)	45,000	KM105, 106a, 107-108, 109.2, 110, 140.1, 170, 175, 183	—	45.00
PS130	1997A (10)	45,000	KM105, 106a, 107-108, 109.2, 110, 140.1, 170, 175, 183	—	30.00
PS131	1997D (11)	45,000	KM105, 106a, 107-108, 109.2, 110, 140.1, 170, 175, 183	—	30.00
PS132	1997F (10)	45,000	KM105, 106a, 107-108, 109.2, 110, 140.1, 170, 175, 183	—	30.00
PS133	1997G (10)	45,000	KM105, 106a, 107-108, 109.2, 110, 140.1, 170, 175, 183	—	30.00
PS134	1997J (10)	45,000	KM105, 106a, 107-108, 109.2, 110, 140.1, 170, 175, 183	—	30.00
PS135	1998A (10)	45,000	KM105, 106a, 107-108, 109.2, 110, 140.1, 170, 175, 183	—	30.00
PS136	1998D (10)	45,000	KM105, 106a, 107-108, 109.2, 110, 140.1, 170, 175, 183	—	30.00
PS137	1998F (10)	45,000	KM105, 106a, 107-108, 109.2, 110, 140.1, 170, 175, 183	—	30.00
PS138	1998G (10)	45,000	KM105, 106a, 107-108, 109.2, 110, 140.1, 170, 175, 183	—	30.00
PS139	1998J (10)	45,000	KM105, 106a, 107-108, 109.2, 110, 140.1, 170, 175, 183	—	30.00
PS140	1999A (10)	45,000	KM105, 106a, 107-108, 109.2, 110, 140.1, 170, 175, 183	—	30.00
PS141	1999D (10)	45,000	KM105, 106a, 107-108, 109.2, 110, 140.1, 170, 175, 183	—	30.00
PS142	1999F (10)	45,000	KM105, 106a, 107-108, 109.2, 110, 140.1, 170, 175, 183	—	30.00
PS143	1999G (10)	45,000	KM105, 106a, 107-108, 109.2, 110, 140.1, 170, 175, 183	—	30.00
PS144	1999J (10)	45,000	KM105, 106a, 107-108, 109.2, 110, 140.1, 170, 175, 183	—	30.00
PS145	2000A (10)	45,000	KM105, 106a, 107-108, 109.2, 110, 140.1, 170, 175, 183	—	55.00
PS146	2000D (10)	45,000	KM105, 106a, 107-108, 109.2, 110, 140.1, 170, 175, 183	—	45.00
PS147	2000F (10)	45,000	KM105, 106a, 107, 108, 109.2, 110, 140.1, 170, 175, 183	—	45.00
PS148	2000G (10)	45,000	KM105, 106a, 107-108, 109.2, 110, 140.1, 170, 175, 183	—	45.00
PS149	2000J (10)	45,000	KM105, 106a, 107-108, 109.2, 110, 140.1, 170, 175, 183	—	45.00

GHANA

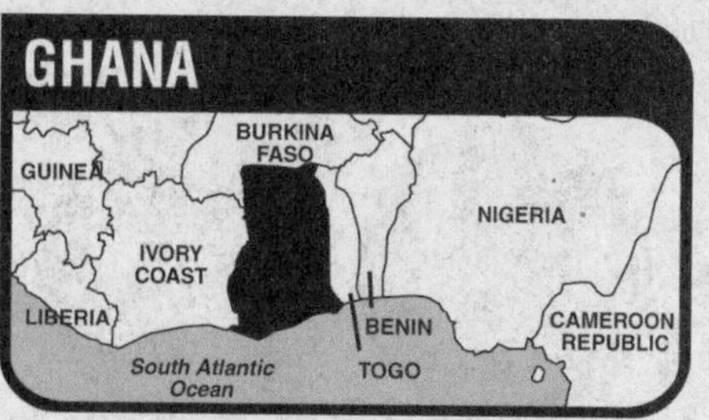

The Republic of Ghana, a member of the Commonwealth of Nations situated on the West Coast of Africa between Ivory Coast and Togo, has an area of 92,100 sq. mi. (238,540 sq. km.) and a population of 14 million, almost entirely African. Capital: Accra. Cocoa (the major crop), coconuts, palm kernels and coffee are exported. Mining, second in importance to agriculture, is concentrated on gold, manganese and industrial diamonds.

The state of Ghana, comprising the Gold Coast and British Togoland, obtained independence on March 6, 1957, becoming the first Negro African colony to do so. On July I, 1960, Ghana adopted a republican constitution, changing from a ministerial to a presidential form of government. The government was overthrown, the constitution suspended and the National Assembly dissolved by the Ghanaian army and police on Feb. 24, 1966. The government was returned to civilian authority in Oct. 1969, but was again seized by military officers in a bloodless coup on Jan. 13, 1972, but 3 further coups occurred in 1978, 1979 and 1981. The latter 2 coups were followed by suspension of the constitution and banning of political parties. A new constitution, which allowed multiparty politics, was approved in April 1992.

Ghana's monetary denomination of Cedi' is derived from the word 'sedie' meaning cowrie, a shell money commonly employed by coastal tribes.

MONETARY SYSTEM
12 Pence = 1 Shilling

REPUBLIC

STANDARD COINAGE

KM# 1 1/2 PENNY
Bronze **Obv:** Dr. Kwame Nkrumah head right **Rev:** Date divided by star, denomination below

Date	Mintage	VF20	XF40	MS60	MS63	MS65
1958	32,200,000	0.10	0.25	0.50	1.00	1.50
1958	20,000	PF65 0.75				

KM# 2 PENNY
Bronze **Obv:** Dr. Kwame Nkrumah head right **Rev:** Date divided by star, denomination below

Date	Mintage	VF20	XF40	MS60	MS63	MS65
1958	60,000,000	0.15	0.35	0.75	1.25	1.75
1958	20,000	PF65 1.00				

KM# 3 3 PENCE
3.23 g., Copper-Nickel, 19.5 mm. **Obv:** Dr. Kwame Nkrumah head right **Rev:** Date divided by star, denomination below **Shape:** Scalloped

Date	Mintage	VF20	XF40	MS60	MS63	MS65
1958	25,200,000	0.20	0.45	1.00	1.50	2.00
1958	20,000	PF65 1.50				

KM# 4 6 PENCE
2.26 g., Copper-Nickel **Obv:** Head of Dr. Kwame Nkrumah right **Rev:** Date divided by star, denomination below

Date	Mintage	VF20	XF40	MS60	MS63	MS65
1958	15,200,000	0.20	0.45	1.00	1.50	2.00
1958	—	PF65 1.50				

KM# 5 SHILLING
Copper-Nickel, 21 mm. **Obv:** Dr. Kwame Nkrumah head right **Rev:** Date divided by star, denomination below

Date	Mintage	VF20	XF40	MS60	MS63	MS65
1958	34,400,000	0.25	0.50	1.75	2.25	3.50
1958	20,000	PF65 2.50				

KM# 6 2 SHILLINGS
Copper-Nickel, 26.5 mm. **Obv:** Dr. Kwame Nkrumah head right **Rev:** Date divided by star, denomination below

Date	Mintage	VF20	XF40	MS60	MS63	MS65
1958	72,700,000	0.35	0.75	2.25	3.25	4.75
1958	20,000	PF65 3.50				

KM# 7 10 SHILLINGS
28.28 g., 0.925 Silver 0.841 oz. ASW, 38 mm. **Obv:** Dr. Kwame Nkrumah head right **Rev:** Date divided by star, denomination below **Edge Lettering:** 6 MARCH 1957 - INDEPENDENCE OF GHANA

Date	Mintage	VF20	XF40	MS60	MS63	MS65
1958	11,000	PF63 30.00	PF65 35.00			

DECIMAL COINAGE

KM# 12 1/2 PESEWA
Bronze, 20.3 mm. **Obv:** Bush drums **Rev:** Star divides date and denomination

Date	Mintage	VF20	XF40	MS60	MS63	MS65
1967	30,000,000	0.10	0.20	0.50	0.75	1.00
1967	2,000	PF65 1.50				

KM# 13 PESEWA
5.70 g., Bronze, 25.5 mm. **Obv:** Bush drums **Rev:** Star divides date and denomination

Date	Mintage	VF20	XF40	MS60	MS63	MS65
1967	30,000,000	0.15	0.25	0.60	0.85	1.25
1967	2,000	PF65 1.50				
1975	50,250,000	0.10	0.20	0.50	0.75	1.00
1979	50,000,000	0.10	0.20	0.50	0.75	1.00

KM# 14 2-1/2 PESEWAS
3.20 g., Copper-Nickel, 19.5 mm. **Obv:** Cocoa beans within circle **Rev:** Rampant lion at center of quartered shield dividing date and denomination **Shape:** Scalloped

Date	Mintage	VF20	XF40	MS60	MS63	MS65
1967	6,000,000	0.10	0.20	0.75	1.25	1.50
1967	2,000	PF65 1.75				

KM# 8 5 PESEWAS
4.13 g., Copper-Nickel, 22 mm. **Obv:** Dr. Kwame Nkrumah head right **Rev:** Star divides date and denomination **Shape:** Scalloped

Date	Mintage	VF20	XF40	MS60	MS63	MS65
1965	30,000,000	0.20	0.35	1.25	2.00	2.50

KM# 15 5 PESEWAS
Copper-Nickel, 19.5 mm. **Obv:** Cocoa beans within circle **Rev:** Rampant lion at center of quartered shield dividing date and denomination

Date	Mintage	VF20	XF40	MS60	MS63	MS65
1967	30,000,000	0.15	0.25	0.75	1.25	1.50
1967	2,000	PF65 2.00				
1973	8,000,000	0.15	0.25	0.75	1.25	1.50
1975	20,000,000	0.15	0.25	0.75	1.25	1.50

KM# 9 10 PESEWAS
Copper-Nickel **Obv:** Dr. Kwame Nkrumah head right **Rev:** Star divides date and denomination

Date	Mintage	VF20	XF40	MS60	MS63	MS65
1965	50,000,000	0.25	0.50	1.25	2.00	2.50

KM# 16 10 PESEWAS
5.57 g., Copper-Nickel, 23.6 mm. **Obv:** Cocoa beans within circle **Rev:** Rampant lion at center of quartered shield dividing date and denomination

Date	Mintage	VF20	XF40	MS60	MS63	MS65
1967	13,200,000	0.20	0.40	1.50	2.25	2.75
1967	2,000	PF65 3.00				
1975	20,000,000	0.20	0.40	1.25	1.75	2.00
1979	5,500,000	0.20	0.40	1.25	1.75	2.00

KM# 17 20 PESEWAS
Copper-Nickel, 28.5 mm. **Obv:** Cocoa beans within circle **Rev:** Rampant lion at center of quartered shield dividing date and denomination

Date	Mintage	VF20	XF40	MS60	MS63	MS65
1967	25,800,000	0.25	0.50	1.75	2.50	3.00
1967	2,000	PF65 3.50				
1979	5,000,000	0.25	0.50	1.75	2.50	3.00

KM# 10 25 PESEWAS
8.65 g., Copper-Nickel **Obv:** Head of Dr. Kwame Nkrumah right **Rev:** Star divides date and denomination

Date	Mintage	VF20	XF40	MS60	MS63	MS65
1965	60,100,000	0.35	0.75	2.00	3.00	3.50

KM# 11 50 PESEWAS
Copper-Nickel **Obv:** Dr. Kwame Nkrumah head right **Rev:** Star divides date and denomination

Date	Mintage	VF20	XF40	MS60	MS63	MS65
1965	18,200,000	0.75	1.50	3.50	5.00	6.50

KM# 18 50 PESEWAS
12.36 g., Brass **Series:** F.A.O. **Obv:** Cocoa beans within circle **Rev:** Rampant lion at center of quartered shield dividing date and denomination

Date	Mintage	VF20	XF40	MS60	MS63	MS65
1979	60,000,000	0.45	0.75	2.25	3.50	5.00

KM# 24 50 PESEWAS
Brass **Obv:** Cocoa beans within circle **Rev:** Rampant lion at center of quartered shield dividing date and denomination

Date	Mintage	VF20	XF40	MS60	MS63	MS65
1984	10,000,000	0.10	0.25	0.60	1.00	1.25

KM# 19 CEDI
11.90 g., Brass, 30 mm. **Series:** F.A.O. **Obv:** Cowrie shell **Rev:** Rampant lion at center of quartered shield dividing date and denomination

Date	Mintage	VF20	XF40	MS60	MS63	MS65
1979	160,000,000	0.35	0.85	3.00	5.00	7.00

KM# 25 CEDI
2.24 g., Brass, 19.2 mm. **Obv:** Cowrie shell **Rev:** Rampant lion at center of quartered shield dividing date and denomination

Date	Mintage	VF20	XF40	MS60	MS63	MS65
1984	40,000,000	0.10	0.25	1.50	3.50	5.00

KM# 26 5 CEDIS
Brass **Obv:** Bush drums **Rev:** Rampant lion at center of quartered shield dividing date and denomination

Date	Mintage	VF20	XF40	MS60	MS63	MS65
1984	88,920,000	0.10	0.20	0.50	0.75	1.00

KM# 33 5 CEDIS
Brass Plated Steel **Obv:** Bush drums **Rev:** Rampant lion at center of quartered shield dividing date and denomination

Date	Mintage	VF20	XF40	MS60	MS63	MS65
1991	—	0.10	0.20	0.50	0.75	1.00

KM# 29 10 CEDIS
3.50 g., Nickel Clad Steel, 21.8 mm. **Obv:** Cocoa beans within circle **Rev:** Rampant lion at center of quartered shield dividing date and denomination **Shape:** 7-sided

Date	Mintage	VF20	XF40	MS60	MS63	MS65
1991	—	—	0.35	0.75	1.25	1.50

KM# 30 20 CEDIS
5.40 g., Nickel Clad Steel, 24.5 mm. **Obv:** Cowrie shell **Rev:** Rampant lion at center of quartered shield dividing date and denomination

Date	Mintage	VF20	XF40	MS60	MS63	MS65
1991	—	—	0.35	1.50	3.00	3.50
1995	—	—	0.35	1.50	3.00	3.50

KM# 20 50 CEDIS
28.28 g., 0.925 Silver 0.841 oz. ASW **Subject:** International Year of Disabled Persons **Obv:** Triangular symbol within wreath, date above **Rev:** Person in wheelchair divides dates, denomination below

Date	Mintage	VF20	XF40	MS60	MS63	MS65
1981	10,000	—	—	—	16.00	20.00
1981	10,000	PF63 20.00	PF65 25.00			

KM# 21 50 CEDIS
Copper-Nickel **Series:** F.A.O. **Subject:** World Fisheries Conference **Obv:** Bush drums **Rev:** People in boat on water, denomination

Date	Mintage	VF20	XF40	MS60	MS63	MS65
ND-1984	100,000	—	—	5.00	7.00	9.00

KM# 21a 50 CEDIS
28.28 g., 0.925 Silver 0.841 oz. ASW **Series:** F.A.O. **Subject:** World Fisheries Conference **Obv:** Bust drums **Rev:** People in boat on water, denomination

Date	Mintage	VF20	XF40	MS60	MS63	MS65
ND-1984	21,000	PF63 22.00	PF65 28.00			

KM# 21b 50 CEDIS
47.54 g., 0.917 Gold 1.4016 oz. AGW **Series:** F.A.O. **Subject:** World Fisheries Conference **Obv:** Bush drums **Rev:** People in boat on water, denomination

Date	Mintage	VF20	XF40	MS60	MS63	MS65
ND-1984	105	PF63 1,950	PF65 2,450			

KM# 22 50 CEDIS
28.28 g., 0.925 Silver 0.841 oz. ASW **Subject:** Year of the Scout **Obv:** Rampant lion at center of quartered shield, denomination below, rope encircles **Rev:** Two scouts planting trees, dates at left

Date	Mintage	VF20	XF40	MS60	MS63	MS65
ND-1984	10,000	—	—	—	20.00	25.00
ND-1984	Inc. above	PF65 55.00				

KM# 31 50 CEDIS
Copper-Nickel, 27.4 mm. **Obv:** Bush drums **Rev:** Rampant lion at center of quartered shield dividing date and denomination

Date	Mintage	VF20	XF40	MS60	MS63	MS65
1991	—	—	1.00	2.25	3.25	3.75

KM# 31a 50 CEDIS
7.40 g., Nickel Plated Steel, 27.4 mm. **Obv:** Bush drums **Rev:** Rampant lion at center of quartered shield dividing date and denomination

Date	Mintage	VF20	XF40	MS60	MS63	MS65
1995	—	—	1.00	2.25	3.25	3.75
1997	—	—	1.00	2.25	3.25	3.75
1999	—	—	1.00	2.25	3.25	3.75

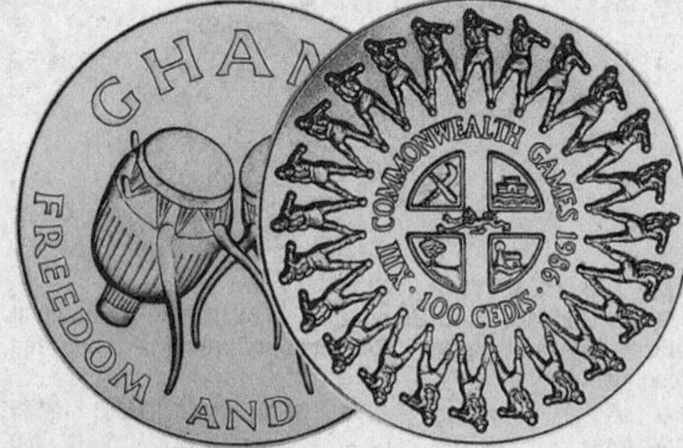

KM# 27 100 CEDIS
28.28 g., 0.500 Silver 0.4546 oz. ASW **Subject:** Commonwealth Games **Obv:** Bush drums **Rev:** Game design, denomination and date within ring of boxers

Date	Mintage	VF20	XF40	MS60	MS63	MS65
1986	50,000	—	—	—	10.00	12.00

KM# 27a 100 CEDIS
28.28 g., 0.925 Silver 0.841 oz. ASW **Subject:** Commonwealth Games **Obv:** Bush drums **Rev:** Game design, denomination and date within ring of boxers

Date	Mintage	VF20	XF40	MS60	MS63	MS65
1986	20,000	PF65 20.00				

KM# 32 100 CEDIS
6.90 g., Bi-Metallic Brass center in Copper-Nickel ring, 26 mm. **Obv:** Cocoa beans within circle **Rev:** Rampant lion at center of quartered shield dividing date and denomination, circle surrounds

Date	Mintage	VF20	XF40	MS60	MS63	MS65
1991	—	—	1.50	2.00	3.50	4.50
1997	—	—	1.25	1.75	3.00	4.00
1999	—	—	1.25	1.75	3.00	4.00

KM# 35 200 CEDIS
Nickel Plated Steel **Obv:** Cowrie shell **Rev:** Rampant lion at center of quartered shield dividing date and denomination **Shape:** 7-sided

Date	Mintage	VF20	XF40	MS60	MS63	MS65
1996	—	—	—	3.00	4.00	5.00
1998	—	—	—	3.00	4.00	5.00

Note: Fields frosted but not center design

KM# 28 500 CEDIS
15.98 g., 0.917 Gold 0.4711 oz. AGW **Subject:** International Year of Disabled Persons **Obv:** Triangular symbol within wreath, date above **Rev:** Bust 3/4 left divides dates, denomination below

Date	Mintage	VF20	XF40	MS60	MS63	MS65
1981	—	—	—	725	775	850
1981	—	PF63 850	PF65 950			

KM# 23 500 CEDIS
15.98 g., 0.917 Gold 0.4711 oz. AGW **Subject:** Year of the Scout **Obv:** Rampant lion at center of quartered shield, denomination below, rope encircles **Rev:** Scouting symbol within rope, dates below

Date	Mintage	VF20	XF40	MS60	MS63	MS65
ND-1984	2,000	—	—	725	775	850
ND-1984	2,000	PF63 850	PF65 950			

KM# 34 500 CEDIS
9.17 g., Nickel-Brass **Obv:** Bush drums **Rev:** Rampant lion at center of quartered shield dividing date and denomination

Date	Mintage	VF20	XF40	MS60	MS63	MS65
1996	—	—	—	3.50	4.50	6.00
1998	—	—	—	3.50	4.50	6.00

PIEDFORT

KM#	Date	Mintage	Identification	Mkt Val
P1	1981	1,050	50 Cedis. Silver. KM20.	75.00
P2	1981	—	500 Cedis. Gold. KM28.	1,750
P3	ND-1984	520	50 Cedis. Silver. KM21a.	90.00

PROOF SETS

KM#	Date	Mintage	Identification	Issue Price	Mkt Val
PS1	1958 (7)	6,431	KM1-7	—	45.00
PS2	1967 (6)	100	KM12-17	8.53	11.50

GIBRALTAR

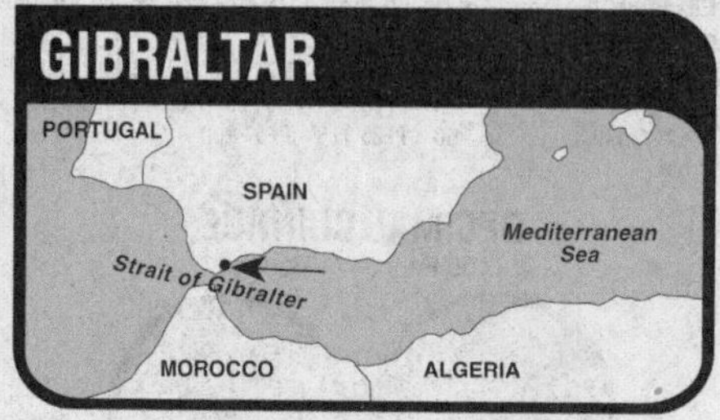

The British Colony of Gibraltar, located at the southernmost point of the Iberian Peninsula, has an area of 2.25 sq. mi. (6.5 sq. km.) and a population of 29,651. Capital (and only town): Gibraltar. Aside from its strategic importance as guardian of the western entrance to the Mediterranean Sea, Gibraltar is also a free port and a British naval base.

Gibraltar, rooted in Greek mythology as one of the Pillars of Hercules, has long been a coveted stronghold. Moslems took it from Spain and fortified it in 711. Spain retook it in 1309, lost it again to the Moors in 1333 and retook it in 1462. After 1540 Spain strengthened its defenses and held it until the War of the Spanish Succession when it was captured by a combined British and Dutch force in 1704. Britain held it against the Franco-Spanish attacks of 1704-05 and through the historic Great Siege of 1779-83.Recently Spain has attempted to discourage British occupancy by harassment and economic devices. In 1967, Gibraltar's inhabitants voted 12,138 to 44 to remain under British rule.

Gibraltar's celebrated Barbary Ape, the last monkey to be found in a wild state in Europe, is featured on the colony's first decimal crown, released in 1971.

RULERS
British

MINT MARKS
PM - Pobjoy Mint
PMM – Pobjoy Mint (only appears on coins dated 2000)

NOTE: ALL coins for 1988 –2003 include the PM mint mark except the 2000 dated circulation pieces which instead have PMM.

MINT PRIVY MARKS
U - Unc finish

DIE MARKS
1988: AA-AE
1989: AA-AF
1990: AA-AB
1991: AA
1992: AA-BB
1993: AA-BB
1994-1999: AA

MONETARY SYSTEM
4 Farthings = 1 Penny
12 Pence = 1 Shilling
2 Shillings = 1 Florin
5 Shillings = 1 Crown
20 Shillings = 1 Pound

BRITISH COLONY

CROWN COINAGE

1967-1970

KM# 4 CROWN

Copper-Nickel, 38.5 mm. **Ruler:** Elizabeth II **Obv:** Young bust right **Rev:** Key below castle divides date, denomination below

Date	Mintage	VF20	XF40	MS60	MS63	MS65
1967	125,000	1.25	2.25	3.00	5.00	6.50
1968	40,000	1.50	2.50	3.50	6.00	7.50
1969	40,000	1.50	2.50	3.50	6.00	7.50
1970	45,000	1.50	2.50	3.50	6.00	7.50

KM# 4a CROWN

28.28 g., 0.500 Silver 0.4546 oz. ASW, 38.5 mm. **Ruler:** Elizabeth II **Obv:** Young bust right **Rev:** Key below castle divides date

Date	Mintage	VF20	XF40	MS60	MS63	MS65
1967	10,000	PF63 15.00		PF65 17.00	PF67 20.00	
1967 Frosted Proof	50	PF65 175		PF67 200		

DECIMAL COINAGE

100 Pence = 1 Pound

KM# 20 PENNY

3.56 g., Bronze, 20.32 mm. **Ruler:** Elizabeth II **Obv:** Crowned head right **Rev:** Barbary partridge divides denomination

Date	Mintage	VF20	XF40	MS60	MS63	MS65
1988 AA	—	—	—	0.15	0.35	0.75
1988 AB	—	—	—	0.15	0.35	0.75
1988 AC	—	—	—	0.15	0.35	0.75
1988 AD	—	—	—	0.15	0.35	0.75
1988 AE	—	—	—	0.15	0.35	0.75
1989 AA	—	—	—	0.15	0.35	0.75
1989 AB	—	—	—	0.15	0.35	0.75
1989 AC	—	—	—	0.15	0.35	0.75
1989 AD	—	—	—	0.15	0.35	0.75
1989 AE	—	—	—	0.15	0.35	0.75
1989 AF	—	—	—	0.15	0.35	0.75
1990 AA	—	—	—	0.15	0.35	0.75
1990 AB	—	—	—	0.15	0.35	0.75
1991 AA	—	—	—	0.15	0.35	0.75
1992 AA	—	—	—	0.15	0.35	0.75
1992 BB	—	—	—	0.15	0.35	0.75
1993 AA	—	—	—	0.15	0.35	0.75
1993 BB	—	—	—	0.15	0.35	0.75
1994 AA	—	—	—	0.15	0.35	0.75
1995 AB	—	—	—	0.15	0.35	0.75
1995 AA	—	—	—	0.15	0.35	0.75

KM# 20a PENNY

3.56 g., Copper Plated Steel, 20.32 mm. **Ruler:** Elizabeth II **Obv:** Crowned head right **Rev:** Barbary partridge left divides denomination **Edge:** Plain

Date	Mintage	VF20	XF40	MS60	MS63	MS65
1995 AA	—	—	—	0.15	0.35	0.50
1995 PM AB	—	—	—	0.15	0.35	0.50
1996 AA	—	—	—	0.15	0.35	0.50
1997 AA	—	—	—	0.15	0.35	0.50

KM# 773 PENNY

3.56 g., Copper Plated Steel, 20.32 mm. **Ruler:** Elizabeth II **Obv:** Head with tiara right **Rev:** Barbary partridge left divides denomination

Date	Mintage	VF20	XF40	MS60	MS63	MS65
1998 AA	—	—	—	0.15	0.35	0.50
1999 AA	—	—	—	0.15	0.35	0.50
2000 PMM AA	—	—	—	0.15	0.35	0.50

KM# 21 2 PENCE

7.12 g., Bronze, 25.91 mm. **Ruler:** Elizabeth II **Obv:** Crowned head right **Rev:** Lighthouse on Europa Point, denomination **Edge:** Plain

Date	Mintage	VF20	XF40	MS60	MS63	MS65
1988 AA	—	—	—	0.20	0.50	0.75
1988 AB	—	—	—	0.20	0.50	0.75
1988 AC	—	—	—	0.20	0.50	0.75
1988 AD	—	—	—	0.20	0.50	0.75
1988 AE	—	—	—	0.20	0.50	0.75
1989 AA	—	—	—	0.20	0.50	0.75
1989 AB	—	—	—	0.20	0.50	0.75
1989 AC	—	—	—	0.20	0.50	0.75
1989 AD	—	—	—	0.20	0.50	0.75
1989 AE	—	—	—	0.20	0.50	0.75
1989 AF	—	—	—	0.20	0.50	0.75
1990 AA	—	—	—	0.20	0.50	0.75
1990 AB	—	—	—	0.20	0.50	0.75
1991 AA	—	—	—	0.20	0.50	0.75
1991 AB	—	—	—	0.20	0.50	0.75
1992 AA	—	—	—	0.20	0.50	0.75
1992 BB	—	—	—	0.20	0.50	0.75
1993 AA	—	—	—	0.20	0.50	0.75
1993 BB	—	—	—	0.20	0.50	0.75
1994 AA	—	—	—	0.20	0.50	0.75
1995 AA	—	—	—	0.20	0.50	0.75

KM# 21a 2 PENCE

7.12 g., Copper Plated Steel, 25.91 mm. **Ruler:** Elizabeth II **Obv:** Crowned head right **Rev:** Lighthouse on Europa Point, denomination

Date	Mintage	VF20	XF40	MS60	MS63	MS65
1995 AB	—	—	—	0.20	0.50	0.65
1995 AA	—	—	—	0.20	0.50	0.75
1996 AA	—	—	—	0.20	0.50	0.75
1997 AA	—	—	—	0.20	0.50	0.75

KM# 774 2 PENCE

7.12 g., Copper Plated Steel, 25.91 mm. **Ruler:** Elizabeth II **Obv:** Head with tiara right

Date	Mintage	VF20	XF40	MS60	MS63	MS65
1998 AA	—	—	—	0.20	0.50	0.85
1999 AA	—	—	—	0.20	0.50	0.85
1999 AB	—	—	—	0.20	0.50	0.85
2000 AA	—	—	—	0.20	0.50	0.85

KM# 22.1 5 PENCE

5.65 g., Copper-Nickel, 23.6 mm. **Ruler:** Elizabeth II **Obv:** Crowned head right **Rev:** Barbary ape divides denomination

Date	Mintage	VF20	XF40	MS60	MS63	MS65
1988 AA	—	—	—	0.45	0.85	1.50
1988 AB	—	—	—	0.45	0.85	1.50
1989 AA	—	—	—	0.45	0.85	1.50
1989 AB	—	—	—	0.45	0.85	1.50
1989 PM AC	—	—	—	0.45	0.85	1.50
1990 AA	—	—	—	0.45	0.85	1.50
1990 AB	—	—	—	0.45	0.85	1.50

KM# 22.2 5 PENCE

3.25 g., Copper-Nickel, 18 mm. **Ruler:** Elizabeth II **Obv:** Crowned head right **Rev:** Barbary ape divides denomination **Edge:** Reeded **Note:** Reduced size.

Date	Mintage	VF20	XF40	MS60	MS63	MS65
1990 AA	—	—	—	0.25	0.60	1.00
1990 AB	—	—	—	0.25	0.60	1.00
1991 AA	—	—	—	0.25	0.60	1.00
1991 AB	—	—	—	0.25	0.60	1.00
1992 AA	—	—	—	0.25	0.60	1.00
1992 AB	—	—	—	0.25	0.60	1.00
1993 AA	—	—	—	0.25	0.60	1.00
1993 AB	—	—	—	0.25	0.60	1.00
1994 AA	—	—	—	0.25	0.60	1.00
1995 AA	—	—	—	0.25	0.60	1.00
1996 AA	—	—	—	0.25	0.60	1.00
1997 AA	—	—	—	0.25	0.60	1.00

KM# 22.2a 5 PENCE

3.25 g., 0.925 Silver 0.0967 oz. ASW, 18 mm. **Ruler:** Elizabeth II **Obv:** Crowned head right **Rev:** Barbary ape left divides denomination

Date	Mintage	VF20	XF40	MS60	MS63	MS65
1990	5,000	PF65 25.00				

KM# 22.2b 5 PENCE

3.25 g., 0.917 Gold 0.0958 oz. AGW, 18 mm. **Ruler:** Elizabeth II **Obv:** Crowned head right **Rev:** Barbary ape left divides denomination

Date	Mintage	VF20	XF40	MS60	MS63	MS65
1990	1,000	PF65 175				

KM# 775 5 PENCE

3.25 g., Copper-Nickel, 18 mm. **Ruler:** Elizabeth II **Obv:** Head with tiara right **Rev:** Barbary Ape left divides denomination **Edge:** Reeded

Date	Mintage	VF20	XF40	MS60	MS63	MS65
1998 AA	—	—	—	0.25	0.60	0.75
1999 AA	—	—	—	0.25	0.60	0.75
2000	—	—	—	0.25	0.60	0.75

KM# 23.1 10 PENCE

11.31 g., Copper-Nickel, 28.5 mm. **Ruler:** Elizabeth II **Obv:** Crowned head right **Rev:** Moorish castle, denomination **Edge:** Reeded

Date	Mintage	VF20	XF40	MS60	MS63	MS65
1988 AA	—	—	—	0.50	1.00	1.25
1988 AB	—	—	—	0.50	1.00	1.25
1989 AA	—	—	—	0.50	1.00	1.25
1989 PM AB	—	—	—	0.50	1.00	1.25
1989 PM AC	—	—	—	0.50	1.00	1.25
1989 PM AD	—	—	—	0.50	1.00	1.25
1990 AA	—	—	—	0.50	1.00	1.25
1990 AB	—	—	—	0.50	1.00	1.25
1990 AC	—	—	—	0.50	1.00	1.25
1991 AA	—	—	—	0.50	1.00	1.25
1991 AB	—	—	—	0.50	1.00	1.25

KM# 112 10 PENCE

6.50 g., Copper-Nickel, 24.5 mm. **Ruler:** Elizabeth II **Obv:** Crowned head right **Rev:** Europort **Edge:** Reeded

Date	Mintage	VF20	XF40	MS60	MS63	MS65
1992 AA	—	—	—	0.35	0.75	1.00
1993 AA	—	—	—	0.35	0.75	1.00

Date	Mintage	VF20	XF40	MS60	MS63	MS65
1995 AA	—	—	—	0.35	0.75	1.00
1996 AA	—	—	—	0.35	0.75	1.00
1996 PM BB	—	—	—	0.35	0.75	1.00
1997 AA	—	—	—	0.35	0.75	1.00

KM# 112a 10 PENCE

6.50 g., 0.925 Silver 0.1933 oz. ASW, 24.5 mm. **Ruler:** Elizabeth II **Obv:** Crowned head right **Rev:** Europort **Edge:** Reeded

Date	Mintage	VF20	XF40	MS60	MS63	MS65
1992	25,000	PF65 25.00				

KM# 112b 10 PENCE

6.50 g., 0.917 Gold 0.1916 oz. AGW, 24.5 mm. **Ruler:** Elizabeth II **Obv:** Crowned head right **Rev:** Europort **Edge:** Reeded

Date	Mintage	VF20	XF40	MS60	MS63	MS65
1992	3,500	PF65 350				

KM# 112c 10 PENCE

6.50 g., 0.950 Platinum 0.1985 oz. APW, 24.5 mm. **Ruler:** Elizabeth II **Obv:** Crowned head right **Rev:** Europort **Edge:** Reeded

Date	Mintage	VF20	XF40	MS60	MS63	MS65
1992	3,500	PF65 375				

KM# 23.2 10 PENCE

6.50 g., Copper-Nickel, 24.5 mm. **Ruler:** Elizabeth II **Obv:** Crowned head right **Rev:** Moorish castle, denomination **Edge:** Reeded **Note:** Reduced size.

Date	Mintage	VF20	XF40	MS60	MS63	MS65
1994 AA	—	—	—	0.50	1.00	1.25

KM# 776 10 PENCE

6.50 g., Copper-Nickel, 24.5 mm. **Ruler:** Elizabeth II **Obv:** Head with tiara right, date below **Rev:** Denomination below building **Edge:** Reeded

Date	Mintage	VF20	XF40	MS60	MS63	MS65
1998 AA	—	—	—	0.50	1.00	1.25
1999 AA	—	—	—	0.50	1.00	1.25
2000	—	—	—	0.50	1.00	1.25

KM# 16 20 PENCE

5.00 g., Copper-Nickel, 21.4 mm. **Ruler:** Elizabeth II **Obv:** Crowned head right **Rev:** Our Lady of Europa, a polychrome wood statue, two-feet tall, from the 16th century **Shape:** 7-sided

Date	Mintage	VF20	XF40	MS60	MS63	MS65
1988 AA	—	—	—	0.70	1.50	2.00
1988 AB	—	—	—	0.70	1.50	2.00
1988 AC	—	—	—	0.70	1.50	2.00
1988 AA Proof	—	—	—	—	—	—
1989 AA	—	—	—	0.70	1.50	2.00
1990 AA	—	—	—	0.70	1.50	2.00
1991 AA	—	—	—	0.70	1.50	2.00
1992 AA	—	—	—	0.70	1.50	2.00
1993 AA	—	—	—	0.70	1.50	2.00
1994 AA	—	—	—	0.70	1.50	2.00
1995 AA	—	—	—	0.70	1.50	2.00
1995 AA Proof	—	—	—	—	—	—
1996 AA	—	—	—	0.70	1.50	2.00
1997 AA	—	—	—	0.70	1.50	2.00

KM# 777 20 PENCE

5.00 g., Copper-Nickel, 21.4 mm. **Ruler:** Elizabeth II **Obv:** Head with tiara right, date below **Rev:** Our Lady of Europa, denomination below and right **Shape:** 7-sided

Date	Mintage	VF20	XF40	MS60	MS63	MS65
1998 AA	—	—	—	0.70	1.50	2.00
1999 AA	—	—	—	0.70	1.50	2.00
2000 AA	—	—	—	0.70	1.50	2.00

KM# 5 25 NEW PENCE

Copper-Nickel, 38.5 mm. **Ruler:** Elizabeth II **Obv:** Young bust right, date below **Rev:** Barbary ape left, denomination below

Date	Mintage	VF20	XF40	MS60	MS63	MS65
1971	75,000	—	3.00	9.00	14.00	—

KM# 5a 25 NEW PENCE

28.28 g., 0.500 Silver 0.4546 oz. ASW, 38.5 mm. **Ruler:** Elizabeth II **Obv:** Young bust right, date below **Rev:** Barbary ape left, denomination

Date	Mintage	VF20	XF40	MS60	MS63	MS65
1971 Frosted Proof	50	PF65 200	PF67 225			
1971	20,000	PF65 20.00	PF67 25.00			

KM# 6 25 NEW PENCE

Copper-Nickel, 38.5 mm. **Ruler:** Elizabeth II **Subject:** 25th Wedding Anniversary **Obv:** Young bust right **Rev:** Arms of Queen Elizabeth II and Prince Philip, date and denomination below

Date	Mintage	VF20	XF40	MS60	MS63	MS65
1972	70,000	—	2.00	4.00	8.00	—

KM# 6a 25 NEW PENCE

28.28 g., 0.925 Silver 0.841 oz. ASW, 38.5 mm. **Ruler:** Elizabeth II **Subject:** 25th Wedding Anniversary **Obv:** Young bust right

Date	Mintage	VF20	XF40	MS60	MS63	MS65
1972	15,000	PF65 28.00	PF67 30.00			

KM# 10 25 NEW PENCE

Copper-Nickel, 38.5 mm. **Ruler:** Elizabeth II **Subject:** Queen's Silver Jubilee **Obv:** Young bust right **Rev:** Shield within wreath of apes and laurel, denomination below

Date	Mintage	VF20	XF40	MS60	MS63	MS65
1977	65,000	—	2.50	5.00	7.00	—

KM# 10a 25 NEW PENCE

28.28 g., 0.925 Silver 0.841 oz. ASW, 38.5 mm. **Ruler:** Elizabeth II **Subject:** Queen's Silver Jubilee **Obv:** Young bust right

Date	Mintage	VF20	XF40	MS60	MS63	MS65
1977	24,000	PF65 28.00	PF67 30.00			

KM# 17 50 PENCE

13.50 g., Copper-Nickel, 30 mm. **Ruler:** Elizabeth II **Obv:** Crowned head right **Rev:** Denomination in wreath of Candytuft flowers (Iberis Gibraltarica) **Shape:** 7-sided

Date	Mintage	VF20	XF40	MS60	MS63	MS65
1988 AA	30,000	—	—	—	2.00	2.50
1988 AB	—	—	—	—	2.00	2.50
1989 AA	—	—	—	—	2.00	2.50
1989 AB	—	—	—	—	2.00	2.50

KM# 19 50 PENCE

13.50 g., Copper-Nickel, 30 mm. **Ruler:** Elizabeth II **Subject:** Christmas **Obv:** Crowned head right **Rev:** The Three Wise Men

Date	Mintage	VF20	XF40	MS60	MS63	MS65
1988 AA	—	—	—	—	4.00	5.00
1988	Est. 30000	PF65 15.00				

KM# 19a 50 PENCE

15.50 g., 0.925 Silver 0.461 oz. ASW, 30 mm. **Ruler:** Elizabeth II **Subject:** Christmas **Obv:** Crowned head right **Rev:** The Three Wise Men

Date	Mintage	VF20	XF40	MS60	MS63	MS65
1988	Est. 5000	PF65 17.00				

KM# 19b 50 PENCE

26.00 g., 0.917 Gold 0.7665 oz. AGW, 30 mm. **Ruler:** Elizabeth II **Subject:** Christmas **Obv:** Crowned head right **Rev:** The Three Wise Men

Date	Mintage	VF20	XF40	MS60	MS63	MS65
1988	250	PF65 1,250				

KM# 19c 50 PENCE

30.40 g., 0.995 Platinum 0.9725 oz. APW, 30 mm. **Ruler:** Elizabeth II **Subject:** Christmas **Obv:** Crowned head right **Rev:** The Three Wise Men

Date	Mintage	VF20	XF40	MS60	MS63	MS65
1988	50	PF65 1,750				

KM# 31 50 PENCE

13.50 g., Copper-Nickel, 30 mm. **Ruler:** Elizabeth II **Subject:** Christmas **Obv:** Crowned head right **Rev:** Choir boy, denomination below **Shape:** 7-sided

Date	Mintage	VF20	XF40	MS60	MS63	MS65
1989 AA	—	—	—	—	6.00	8.00
1989 AA	Est. 30000	PF65 7.50				

KM# 31a 50 PENCE

15.50 g., 0.925 Silver 0.461 oz. ASW, 30 mm. **Ruler:** Elizabeth II **Subject:** Christmas **Obv:** Crowned head right **Rev:** Choir boy

Date	Mintage	VF20	XF40	MS60	MS63	MS65
1989	Est. 5000	PF65 45.00				

KM# 31b 50 PENCE
26.00 g., 0.917 Gold 0.7665 oz. AGW, 30 mm. **Ruler:** Elizabeth II **Subject:** Christmas **Obv:** Crowned head right **Rev:** Choir boy

Date	Mintage	VF20	XF40	MS60	MS63	MS65
1989	Est. 250	PF65 1,250				

KM# 31c 50 PENCE
30.40 g., 0.995 Platinum 0.9725 oz. APW, 30 mm. **Ruler:** Elizabeth II **Subject:** Christmas **Obv:** Crowned head right **Rev:** Choir boy

Date	Mintage	VF20	XF40	MS60	MS63	MS65
1989	Est. 50	PF65 1,750				

KM# 39 50 PENCE
13.50 g., Copper-Nickel, 30 mm. **Ruler:** Elizabeth II **Obv:** Crowned head right **Rev:** Dolphins surround denomination **Shape:** 7-sided

Date	Mintage	VF20	XF40	MS60	MS63	MS65
1990 AA	—	—	—	—	4.50	7.00
1991 AA	—	—	—	—	4.50	7.00
1992 AA	—	—	—	—	4.50	7.00
1993 AA	—	—	—	—	4.50	7.00
1994 AA	—	—	—	—	4.50	7.00
1995 AA	—	—	—	—	4.50	7.00
1995 AD	—	—	—	—	4.50	7.00
1996 AA	—	—	—	—	4.50	7.00
1997	—	—	—	—	4.00	7.00

KM# 39a 50 PENCE
15.50 g., 0.925 Silver 0.461 oz. ASW **Ruler:** Elizabeth II **Obv:** Crowned head right **Rev:** Dolphins **Shape:** 7-sided

Date	Mintage	VF20	XF40	MS60	MS63	MS65
1990	—	PF65 47.50				
1993	—	PF65 50.00				

KM# 39b 50 PENCE
26.00 g., 0.917 Gold 0.7665 oz. AGW, 30 mm. **Ruler:** Elizabeth II **Obv:** Crowned head right **Rev:** Dolphins

Date	Mintage	VF20	XF40	MS60	MS63	MS65
1990	250	PF65 1,250				

KM# 47 50 PENCE
13.50 g., Copper-Nickel, 30 mm. **Ruler:** Elizabeth II **Subject:** Christmas **Obv:** Crowned head right **Rev:** Mary and Joseph with child, denomination below **Shape:** 7-sided

Date	Mintage	VF20	XF40	MS60	MS63	MS65
1990 AA	—	—	—	—	4.00	5.00
1990 BB	Est. 30000	PF65 8.00				

KM# 47a 50 PENCE
15.50 g., 0.925 Silver 0.461 oz. ASW, 30 mm. **Ruler:** Elizabeth II **Subject:** Christmas **Obv:** Crowned head right **Rev:** Mary and Joseph with child **Shape:** 7-sided

Date	Mintage	VF20	XF40	MS60	MS63	MS65
1990	5,000	PF65 45.00				

KM# 47b 50 PENCE
26.00 g., 0.917 Gold 0.7665 oz. AGW, 30 mm. **Ruler:** Elizabeth II **Subject:** Christmas **Obv:** Crowned head right **Rev:** Mary and Joseph with child **Shape:** 7-sided

Date	Mintage	VF20	XF40	MS60	MS63	MS65
1990	250	PF65 1,250				

KM# 47c 50 PENCE
30.40 g., 0.995 Platinum 0.9725 oz. APW, 30 mm. **Ruler:** Elizabeth II **Subject:** Christmas **Obv:** Crowned head right **Rev:** Mary and Joseph with child **Shape:** 7-sided

Date	Mintage	VF20	XF40	MS60	MS63	MS65
1990	50	PF65 1,750				

KM# 83 50 PENCE
13.50 g., Copper-Nickel, 30 mm. **Ruler:** Elizabeth II **Subject:** Christmas **Obv:** Crowned head right **Rev:** Family caroling, denomination below **Shape:** 7-sided

Date	Mintage	VF20	XF40	MS60	MS63	MS65
1991 AA	—	—	—	—	4.00	5.00
1991 AA	—	PF65 7.50				
1991 BB	—	—	—	—	4.00	5.00

KM# 83a 50 PENCE
15.50 g., 0.925 Silver 0.461 oz. ASW, 30 mm. **Ruler:** Elizabeth II **Subject:** Christmas **Obv:** Crowned head right **Rev:** Family caroling **Shape:** 7-sided

Date	Mintage	VF20	XF40	MS60	MS63	MS65
1991	Est. 5000	PF65 40.00				

KM# 83b 50 PENCE
26.00 g., 0.917 Gold 0.7665 oz. AGW, 30 mm. **Ruler:** Elizabeth II **Subject:** Christmas **Obv:** Crowned head right **Rev:** Family caroling **Shape:** 7-sided

Date	Mintage	VF20	XF40	MS60	MS63	MS65
1991	250	PF65 1,250				

KM# 83c 50 PENCE
30.40 g., 0.995 Platinum 0.9725 oz. APW, 30 mm. **Ruler:** Elizabeth II **Subject:** Christmas **Obv:** Crowned head right **Rev:** Family caroling **Shape:** 7-sided

Date	Mintage	VF20	XF40	MS60	MS63	MS65
1991	50	PF65 1,750				

KM# 108 50 PENCE
13.50 g., Copper-Nickel, 30 mm. **Ruler:** Elizabeth II **Subject:** Christmas **Obv:** Crowned head right **Rev:** Bust of Santa facing, denomination below **Shape:** 7-sided

Date	Mintage	VF20	XF40	MS60	MS63	MS65
1992 AA	—	PF65 6.50				
1992 AA	Est. 30000	—	—	—	3.50	4.50

KM# 108a 50 PENCE
15.50 g., 0.925 Silver 0.461 oz. ASW, 30 mm. **Ruler:** Elizabeth II **Subject:** Christmas **Obv:** Crowned head right **Rev:** Bust of Santa facing **Shape:** 7-sided

Date	Mintage	VF20	XF40	MS60	MS63	MS65
1992	Est. 5000	PF65 40.00				

KM# 108b 50 PENCE
26.00 g., 0.917 Gold 0.7665 oz. AGW, 30 mm. **Ruler:** Elizabeth II **Subject:** Christmas **Obv:** Crowned head right **Rev:** Bust of Santa facing **Shape:** 7-sided

Date	Mintage	VF20	XF40	MS60	MS63	MS65
1992	250	PF65 1,250				

KM# 108c 50 PENCE
30.40 g., 0.995 Platinum 0.9725 oz. APW, 30 mm. **Ruler:** Elizabeth II **Subject:** Christmas **Obv:** Crowned head right **Rev:** Bust of Santa facing **Shape:** 7-sided

Date	Mintage	VF20	XF40	MS60	MS63	MS65
1992	50	PF65 1,750				

KM# 190 50 PENCE
13.50 g., Copper-Nickel, 30 mm. **Ruler:** Elizabeth II **Subject:** Christmas **Obv:** Crowned head right **Rev:** Santa in automobile, denomination below **Shape:** 7-sided

Date	Mintage	VF20	XF40	MS60	MS63	MS65
1993 AA	30,000	—	—	—	3.50	4.50

KM# 190a 50 PENCE
15.50 g., 0.925 Silver 0.461 oz. ASW, 30 mm. **Ruler:** Elizabeth II **Subject:** Christmas **Obv:** Crowned head right **Rev:** Santa in automobile **Shape:** 7-sided

Date	Mintage	VF20	XF40	MS60	MS63	MS65
1993	Est. 5000	PF65 40.00				

KM# 190b 50 PENCE
26.00 g., 0.917 Gold 0.7665 oz. AGW, 30 mm. **Ruler:** Elizabeth II **Subject:** Christmas **Obv:** Crowned head right **Rev:** Santa in automobile **Shape:** 7-sided

Date	Mintage	VF20	XF40	MS60	MS63	MS65
1993	Est. 250	PF65 1,250				

KM# 190c 50 PENCE
30.40 g., 0.995 Platinum 0.9725 oz. APW, 30 mm. **Ruler:** Elizabeth II **Subject:** Christmas **Obv:** Crowned head right **Rev:** Santa in automobile **Shape:** 7-sided

Date	Mintage	VF20	XF40	MS60	MS63	MS65
1993	Est. 50	PF65 1,750				

KM# 294 50 PENCE
13.50 g., Copper-Nickel, 30 mm. **Ruler:** Elizabeth II **Subject:** Christmas **Obv:** Crowned head right **Rev:** Santa with sack and hot air balloon **Shape:** 7-sided

Date	Mintage	VF20	XF40	MS60	MS63	MS65
1994 AA	30,000	—	—	—	3.50	4.50
1994 PM Prooflike	—	—	—	—	—	6.00

KM# 294a 50 PENCE
15.50 g., 0.925 Silver 0.461 oz. ASW **Ruler:** Elizabeth II **Subject:** Christmas **Obv:** Crowned head right **Rev:** Santa with sack and hot air balloon **Shape:** 7-sided

Date	Mintage	VF20	XF40	MS60	MS63	MS65
1994	Est. 5000	PF65 40.00				

KM# 294b 50 PENCE
26.00 g., 0.917 Gold 0.7665 oz. AGW, 30 mm. **Ruler:** Elizabeth II **Subject:** Christmas **Obv:** Crowned head right **Rev:** Santa with sack and hot air balloon **Shape:** 7-sided

Date	Mintage	VF20	XF40	MS60	MS63	MS65
1994	Est. 250	PF65 1,250				

KM# 294c 50 PENCE
30.40 g., 0.995 Platinum 0.9725 oz. APW, 30 mm. **Ruler:** Elizabeth II **Subject:** Christmas **Obv:** Crowned head right **Rev:** Santa with sack and hot air balloon **Shape:** 7-sided

Date	Mintage	VF20	XF40	MS60	MS63	MS65
1994	—	PF65 1,750				

KM# 336 50 PENCE
13.50 g., Copper-Nickel, 30 mm. **Ruler:** Elizabeth II **Subject:** Christmas **Obv:** Crowned head right **Rev:** Penguins parading, denomination below **Shape:** 7-sided

Date	Mintage	VF20	XF40	MS60	MS63	MS65
1995 AA	Est. 30000	—	—	—	4.00	5.00

KM# 336a 50 PENCE
15.50 g., 0.925 Silver 0.461 oz. ASW, 30 mm. **Ruler:** Elizabeth II **Subject:** Christmas **Obv:** Crowned head right **Rev:** Penguins parading **Shape:** 7-sided

Date	Mintage	VF20	XF40	MS60	MS63	MS65
1995	Est. 5000	PF65 40.00				

KM# 336b 50 PENCE
26.00 g., 0.917 Gold 0.7665 oz. AGW, 30 mm. **Ruler:** Elizabeth II **Subject:** Christmas **Obv:** Crowned head right **Rev:** Penguins parading **Shape:** 7-sided

Date	Mintage	VF20	XF40	MS60	MS63	MS65
1995	Est. 250	PF65 1,250				

KM# 336c 50 PENCE
30.40 g., 0.995 Platinum 0.9725 oz. APW, 30 mm. **Ruler:** Elizabeth II **Subject:** Christmas **Obv:** Crowned head right **Rev:** Penguins parading **Shape:** 7-sided

Date	Mintage	VF20	XF40	MS60	MS63	MS65
1995	50	PF65 1,750				

KM# 453 50 PENCE
13.50 g., Copper-Nickel, 30 mm. **Ruler:** Elizabeth II **Subject:** Christmas **Obv:** Crowned head right **Rev:** Santa Claus and biplane **Shape:** 7-sided

Date	Mintage	VF20	XF40	MS60	MS63	MS65
1996 No die letters	—	—	—	—	—	—
1996 AA	Est. 30000	—	—	—	4.00	5.00

KM# 453a 50 PENCE
15.00 g., 0.925 Silver 0.4461 oz. ASW, 30 mm. **Ruler:** Elizabeth II **Subject:** Christmas **Obv:** Crowned head right **Rev:** Santa Claus and biplane **Shape:** 7-sided

Date	Mintage	VF20	XF40	MS60	MS63	MS65
1996	Est. 5000	PF65 35.00				

KM# 453b 50 PENCE
26.00 g., 0.917 Gold 0.7665 oz. AGW, 30 mm. **Ruler:** Elizabeth II **Subject:** Christmas **Obv:** Crowned head right **Rev:** Santa Claus and biplane **Shape:** 7-sided

Date	Mintage	VF20	XF40	MS60	MS63	MS65
1996	—	PF65 1,250				

KM# 39.1 50 PENCE
8.00 g., Copper-Nickel, 27.3 mm. **Ruler:** Elizabeth II **Obv:** Crowned head right **Rev:** Dolphins surround denomination **Shape:** 7-sided

Date	Mintage	VF20	XF40	MS60	MS63	MS65
1997 AA	—	—	—	—	4.50	5.00
1998	—	—	—	—	4.50	5.00

KM# 39.1a 50 PENCE
8.00 g., 0.925 Silver 0.2379 oz. ASW, 27.3 mm. **Ruler:** Elizabeth II **Obv:** Crowned head right **Rev:** Dolphins surround denomination **Shape:** 7-sided

Date	Mintage	VF20	XF40	MS60	MS63	MS65
1997	Est. 5000	PF65 35.00				

KM# 39.1b 50 PENCE
8.00 g., 0.9999 Gold 0.2572 oz. AGW, 27.3 mm. **Ruler:** Elizabeth II **Obv:** Crowned head right **Rev:** Dolphins surround denomination **Shape:** 7-sided

Date	Mintage	VF20	XF40	MS60	MS63	MS65
1997	—	PF65 450				

KM# 606 50 PENCE
8.00 g., Copper-Nickel, 27.3 mm. **Ruler:** Elizabeth II **Subject:** Christmas **Obv:** Crowned head right **Rev:** Santa Claus in sleigh **Shape:** 7-sided

Date	Mintage	VF20	XF40	MS60	MS63	MS65
1997	Est. 30000	—	—	—	4.00	5.00

KM# 606a 50 PENCE
8.00 g., 0.925 Silver 0.2379 oz. ASW, 27.3 mm. **Ruler:** Elizabeth II **Subject:** Christmas **Obv:** Crowned head right **Rev:** Santa Claus in sleigh **Shape:** 7-sided

Date	Mintage	VF20	XF40	MS60	MS63	MS65
1997	—	PF65 35.00				

KM# 606b 50 PENCE
8.00 g., 0.917 Gold 0.2359 oz. AGW, 27.3 mm. **Ruler:** Elizabeth II **Subject:** Christmas **Obv:** Crowned head right **Rev:** Santa in sleigh **Shape:** 7-sided

Date	Mintage	VF20	XF40	MS60	MS63	MS65
1997	Est. 250	PF65 450				

KM# 769 50 PENCE
8.00 g., Copper-Nickel, 27.3 mm. **Ruler:** Elizabeth II **Obv:** Head with tiara right, date below **Rev:** Santa Claus in chimney **Shape:** 7-sided

Date	Mintage	VF20	XF40	MS60	MS63	MS65
1998 PM	Est. 30000	—	—	—	4.00	5.00

Note: Some examples have the PM over AA

KM# 769a 50 PENCE
8.00 g., 0.925 Silver 0.2379 oz. ASW, 27.3 mm. **Ruler:** Elizabeth II **Obv:** Head with tiara right **Rev:** Santa Claus in chimney **Shape:** 7-sided

Date	Mintage	VF20	XF40	MS60	MS63	MS65
1998	Est. 5000	PF65 35.00				

KM# 769b 50 PENCE
8.00 g., 0.917 Gold 0.2359 oz. AGW, 27.3 mm. **Ruler:** Elizabeth II **Obv:** Head with tiara right **Rev:** Santa Claus in chimney **Shape:** 7-sided

Date	Mintage	VF20	XF40	MS60	MS63	MS65
1998	Est. 250	PF65 450				

KM# 778 50 PENCE
8.00 g., Copper-Nickel, 27.3 mm. **Ruler:** Elizabeth II **Obv:** Head with tiara right **Rev:** Dolphins surround denomination **Edge:** Plain **Shape:** 7-sided

Date	Mintage	VF20	XF40	MS60	MS63	MS65
1998 PM AA	—	—	—	—	4.50	5.50
1999 PM AA	—	—	—	—	4.50	5.50
2000 PM AA	—	—	—	—	4.50	5.50

KM# 866 50 PENCE
8.00 g., Copper-Nickel, 27.3 mm. **Ruler:** Elizabeth II **Series:** Christmas **Obv:** Head with tiara right, date below **Rev:** Santa with pair of Barbary Apes **Edge:** Plain **Shape:** 7-sided

Date	Mintage	VF20	XF40	MS60	MS63	MS65
1999 BB Prooflike	Est. 30000	—	—	—	4.00	5.00

KM# 866a 50 PENCE
8.00 g., 0.925 Silver 0.2379 oz. ASW, 27.3 mm. **Ruler:** Elizabeth II **Obv:** Head with tiara right **Rev:** Santa with pair of monkeys **Shape:** 7-sided

Date	Mintage	VF20	XF40	MS60	MS63	MS65
1999	Est. 5000	PF65 35.00				

KM# 866b 50 PENCE
8.00 g., 0.917 Gold 0.2359 oz. AGW, 27.3 mm. **Ruler:** Elizabeth II **Obv:** Head with tiara right **Rev:** Santa with pair of monkeys **Shape:** 7-sided

Date	Mintage	VF20	XF40	MS60	MS63	MS65
1999	Est. 250	PF65 450				

KM# 887 50 PENCE
8.00 g., Copper-Nickel, 27.3 mm. **Ruler:** Elizabeth II **Subject:** Christmas **Obv:** Head with tiara right, date below **Rev:** Madonna and child with angels **Edge:** Plain **Shape:** 7-sided

Date	Mintage	VF20	XF40	MS60	MS63	MS65
2000 AA	30,000	—	—	—	4.00	5.00

KM# 887a 50 PENCE
8.00 g., 0.925 Silver 0.2379 oz. ASW, 27.3 mm. **Ruler:** Elizabeth II **Subject:** Christmas **Obv:** Head with tiara right **Rev:** Madonna and child with angels **Shape:** 7-sided

Date	Mintage	VF20	XF40	MS60	MS63	MS65
2000	5,000	PF65 35.00				

KM# 887b 50 PENCE
8.00 g., 0.916 Gold 0.2356 oz. AGW, 27.3 mm. **Ruler:** Elizabeth II **Subject:** Christmas **Obv:** Head with tiara **Rev:** Madonna and child with angels **Shape:** 7-sided **Note:** KM#310-317 previously listed here do not exist and have been removed.

Date	Mintage	VF20	XF40	MS60	MS63	MS65
2000	250	PF65 450				

KM# 18 POUND
9.50 g., Nickel-Brass, 22.5 mm. **Ruler:** Elizabeth II **Obv:** Crowned head right **Rev:** Gibraltar castle and key

Date	Mintage	VF20	XF40	MS60	MS63	MS65
1988 AA	—	—	—	3.50	4.50	6.00
1988 PM AB	—	—	—	3.50	4.50	6.00
1990 AA	—	—	—	3.50	4.50	6.00
1991 AC	—	—	—	3.50	4.50	6.00
1991 AA	—	—	—	3.50	4.50	6.00
1992 AA	—	—	—	3.50	4.50	6.00
1993 AA	—	—	—	3.50	4.50	6.00
1996 AA	—	—	—	3.50	4.50	6.00
1997 AA	—	—	—	3.50	4.50	6.00

KM# 18a POUND
9.50 g., 0.925 Silver 0.2825 oz. ASW, 22.5 mm. **Ruler:** Elizabeth II **Obv:** Crowned head right **Rev:** Gibraltar castle and key

Date	Mintage	VF20	XF40	MS60	MS63	MS65
1988	—	PF65 16.00				

KM# 18b POUND
9.50 g., 0.917 Gold 0.2801 oz. AGW, 22.5 mm. **Ruler:** Elizabeth II **Obv:** Crowned head right **Rev:** Gibraltar castle and key

Date	Mintage	VF20	XF40	MS60	MS63	MS65
1988	—	PF65 450				

KM# 32 POUND
9.50 g., Nickel-Brass, 22.5 mm. **Ruler:** Elizabeth II **Subject:** 150th Anniversary of Gibraltar Coinage **Obv:** Crowned head right **Rev:** Gibraltar castle and key within circle

Date	Mintage	VF20	XF40	MS60	MS63	MS65
1989 AA	—	—	—	4.00	5.00	7.00

KM# 32a POUND
9.50 g., 0.925 Silver 0.2825 oz. ASW, 22.5 mm. **Ruler:** Elizabeth II **Subject:** 150th Anniversary of Gibraltar Coinage **Obv:** Crowned head right **Rev:** Gibraltar castle and key

Date	Mintage	VF20	XF40	MS60	MS63	MS65
1989	—	PF65 35.00				

KM# 32b POUND
9.50 g., 0.917 Gold 0.2801 oz. AGW, 22.5 mm. **Ruler:** Elizabeth II **Subject:** 150th Anniversary of Gibraltar Coinage **Obv:** Crowned head right **Rev:** Gibraltar castle and key

Date	Mintage	VF20	XF40	MS60	MS63	MS65
1989	150	PF65 450				

KM# 32c POUND
9.00 g., 0.950 Platinum 0.2749 oz. APW, 22.5 mm. **Ruler:** Elizabeth II **Obv:** Crowned head right **Rev:** Gibraltar castle and key

Date	Mintage	VF20	XF40	MS60	MS63	MS65
1989	100	PF65 475				

KM# 191 POUND
9.50 g., Nickel-Brass, 22.5 mm. **Ruler:** Elizabeth II **Subject:** Referendum of 1967 **Obv:** Crowned head right **Rev:** Gibraltar arms above Rock of Gibraltar with Union Jack background

Date	Mintage	VF20	XF40	MS60	MS63	MS65
1993 AA	—	—	—	4.50	5.50	7.50

KM# 191a POUND
9.50 g., 0.925 Silver 0.2825 oz. ASW, 22.5 mm. **Ruler:** Elizabeth II **Subject:** Referendum of 1967 **Obv:** Crowned head right **Rev:** Gibraltar arms above Rock of Gibraltar with Union Jack background

Date	Mintage	VF20	XF40	MS60	MS63	MS65
1993	—	PF65 35.00				

KM# 191b POUND

9.50 g., 0.917 Gold 0.2801 oz. AGW, 22.5 mm. **Ruler:** Elizabeth II **Subject:** Referendum of 1967 **Obv:** Crowned head right **Rev:** Gibraltar arms above Rock of Gibraltar with Union Jack background

Date	Mintage	VF20	XF40	MS60	MS63	MS65
1993	Est. 3500	PF65 450				

KM# 324 POUND

9.50 g., Nickel-Brass, 22.5 mm. **Ruler:** Elizabeth II **Subject:** 40th Anniversary - Queen Elizabeth II's 1st Royal Visit to Gibraltar **Obv:** Crowned head right **Rev:** Luxury liner at sea

Date	Mintage	VF20	XF40	MS60	MS63	MS65
1994 AA	—	—	—	7.50	9.00	11.00

KM# 340 POUND

9.50 g., Nickel-Brass, 22.5 mm. **Ruler:** Elizabeth II **Subject:** National Day, 50th Anniversary of the U.N. **Obv:** Crowned head right **Rev:** Rock of Gibraltar

Date	Mintage	VF20	XF40	MS60	MS63	MS65
1995 AA	—	—	—	3.50	5.00	7.00

KM# 340a POUND

9.50 g., 0.925 Silver 0.2825 oz. ASW, 22.5 mm. **Ruler:** Elizabeth II **Obv:** Crowned head right **Rev:** Rock of Gibraltar

Date	Mintage	VF20	XF40	MS60	MS63	MS65
1995	3,500	PF65 35.00				

KM# 869 POUND

9.50 g., Nickel-Brass, 22.5 mm. **Ruler:** Elizabeth II **Obv:** Head with tiara right **Rev:** Gibraltar coat of arms - castle and key

Date	Mintage	VF20	XF40	MS60	MS63	MS65
1998 AA	—	—	—	3.50	4.50	6.00
1999 AA	—	—	—	3.50	4.50	6.00
2000 PMM AA	—	—	—	3.50	4.50	6.00

KM# 24 2 POUNDS

Virenium **Ruler:** Elizabeth II **Obv:** Crowned head right **Rev:** Cannon in fortress tunnel

Date	Mintage	VF20	XF40	MS60	MS63	MS65
1988 AA	—	—	—	7.50	8.50	10.00
1989 AA	—	—	—	7.50	8.50	10.00
1990 AA	—	—	—	7.50	8.50	10.00
1991 AA	—	—	—	7.50	8.50	10.00
1993 AA	—	—	—	7.50	8.50	10.00
1995 AA	—	—	—	7.50	8.50	10.00
1995 AB	—	—	—	7.50	8.50	10.00
1995 AC	—	—	—	7.50	8.50	10.00
1996 AA	—	—	—	7.50	8.50	10.00
1997 AA	—	—	—	7.50	8.50	10.00

KM# 98 2 POUNDS

Virenium **Ruler:** Elizabeth II **Obv:** Crowned head right **Rev:** Columbus and ship

Date	Mintage	VF20	XF40	MS60	MS63	MS65
1992 AA	—	—	—	6.50	7.50	9.00

KM# 98a 2 POUNDS

9.30 g., 0.925 Silver 0.2766 oz. ASW **Ruler:** Elizabeth II **Obv:** Crowned head right **Rev:** Columbus and ship

Date	Mintage	VF20	XF40	MS60	MS63	MS65
1992	Est. 5000	PF65 40.00				

KM# 98b 2 POUNDS

15.94 g., 0.917 Gold 0.4699 oz. AGW **Ruler:** Elizabeth II **Obv:** Crowned head right **Rev:** Columbus and ship

Date	Mintage	VF20	XF40	MS60	MS63	MS65
1992	Est. 5000	PF65 725				

KM# 98c 2 POUNDS

18.00 g., 0.950 Platinum 0.5498 oz. APW **Ruler:** Elizabeth II **Obv:** Crowned head right **Rev:** Columbus and ship

Date	Mintage	VF20	XF40	MS60	MS63	MS65
1992	Est. 1000	PF65 1,150				

KM# 325 2 POUNDS

Virenium **Ruler:** Elizabeth II **Subject:** 40th Anniversary - Queen Elizabeth II's 1st Royal Visit to Gibraltar **Obv:** Crowned head right **Rev:** Luxury liner at sea

Date	Mintage	VF20	XF40	MS60	MS63	MS65
1994 AA	Est. 5000	—	—	6.50	7.50	9.00

KM# 755 2 POUNDS

12.00 g., Bi-Metallic Copper-Nickel center in Nickel-Brass ring, 28.4 mm. **Ruler:** Elizabeth II **Subject:** The Labours of Hercules **Obv:** Crowned head right **Rev:** Hercules wrestling the Nimean Lion

Date	Mintage	VF20	XF40	MS60	MS63	MS65
1997	—	—	—	—	—	35.00
1997 AA	—	—	—	—	—	35.00

KM# 755a 2 POUNDS

12.00 g., 0.999 Silver Gilt 0.3854 oz. **Ruler:** Elizabeth II **Subject:** The Labours of Hercules **Obv:** Crowned head right **Rev:** Hercules wrestling the Nimean Lion

Date	Mintage	VF20	XF40	MS60	MS63	MS65
1997	Est. 7500	PF65 65.00				

KM# 756a 2 POUNDS

12.00 g., 0.999 Silver Gilt 0.3854 oz. **Ruler:** Elizabeth II **Subject:** The Labours of Hercules **Obv:** Crowned head right **Rev:** Hercules fighting the Hydra

Date	Mintage	VF20	XF40	MS60	MS63	MS65
1997	Est. 7500	PF65 65.00				

KM# 757a 2 POUNDS

12.00 g., 0.999 Silver Gilt 0.3854 oz. **Ruler:** Elizabeth II **Subject:** The Labours of Hercules **Obv:** Crowned head right **Rev:** Hercules and the Ceryneian Hind

Date	Mintage	VF20	XF40	MS60	MS63	MS65
1997	Est. 7500	PF65 65.00				

KM# 758a 2 POUNDS

0.999 Silver Gilt **Ruler:** Elizabeth II **Subject:** The Labours of Hercules **Obv:** Crowned head right **Rev:** Hercules wrestles the Erymanthian Boar

Date	Mintage	VF20	XF40	MS60	MS63	MS65
1997	7,500	PF65 65.00				

KM# 756 2 POUNDS

12.00 g., Bi-Metallic Copper-Nickel center in Nickel-Brass ring, 28.4 mm. **Ruler:** Elizabeth II **Subject:** The Labours of Hercules **Obv:** Crowned head right **Rev:** Hercules fighting the Hydra

Date	Mintage	VF20	XF40	MS60	MS63	MS65
1998 AA	—	—	—	—	—	35.00

KM# 757 2 POUNDS

12.00 g., Bi-Metallic Copper-Nickel center in Nickel-Brass ring, 28.4 mm. **Ruler:** Elizabeth II **Subject:** The Labours of Hercules **Obv:** Crowned head right **Rev:** Hercules and the Ceryneian Hind

Date	Mintage	VF20	XF40	MS60	MS63	MS65
1998 AA	—	—	—	—	—	35.00

KM# 758 2 POUNDS

12.00 g., Bi-Metallic Copper-Nickel center in Nickel-Brass ring, 28.4 mm. **Ruler:** Elizabeth II **Subject:** The Labours of Hercules **Obv:** Crowned head right **Rev:** Hercules wrestles the Erymanthian Boar

Date	Mintage	VF20	XF40	MS60	MS63	MS65
1998 AA	—	—	—	—	—	35.00

KM# 759 2 POUNDS

12.00 g., Bi-Metallic Copper-Nickel center in Nickel-Brass ring, 28.4 mm. **Ruler:** Elizabeth II **Subject:** The Labours of Hercules **Obv:** Crowned head right **Rev:** Hercules and the Augean Stables

Date	Mintage	VF20	XF40	MS60	MS63	MS65
1999 AA	—	—	—	—	—	35.00

KM# 759a 2 POUNDS

10.00 g., 0.999 Silver Gilt 0.3212 oz. **Ruler:** Elizabeth II **Subject:** The Labours of Hercules **Obv:** Crowned head right **Rev:** Hercules and the Augean Stables

Date	Mintage	VF20	XF40	MS60	MS63	MS65
1999	Est. 25000	PF65 65.00				

KM# 760 2 POUNDS

Bi-Metallic Copper-Nickel center in Nickel-Brass ring, 28.4 mm. **Ruler:** Elizabeth II **Subject:** The Labours of Hercules **Obv:** Crowned head right **Rev:** Hercules and the Cretan Bull

Date	Mintage	VF20	XF40	MS60	MS63	MS65
1999 AA	—	—	—	—	—	35.00
1999 No die letters	—	—	—	—	—	35.00

KM# 760a 2 POUNDS

10.00 g., 0.999 Silver Gilt 0.3212 oz. **Subject:** The Labours of Hercules **Obv:** Crowned head right **Rev:** Hercules and the Cretan Bull

Date	Mintage	VF20	XF40	MS60	MS63	MS65
1999	Est. 25000	PF65 65.00				

KM# 761 2 POUNDS
12.00 g., Bi-Metallic Copper-Nickel center in Nickel-Brass ring, 28.4 mm. **Ruler:** Elizabeth II **Subject:** The Labours of Hercules **Obv:** Crowned head right **Rev:** Hercules and the Stymphalian Birds

Date	Mintage	VF20	XF40	MS60	MS63	MS65
1999 AA	—	—	—	—	—	35.00

KM# 761a 2 POUNDS
10.00 g., 0.999 Silver Gilt 0.3212 oz. **Ruler:** Elizabeth II **Subject:** The Labours of Hercules **Obv:** Crowned head right **Rev:** Hercules and the Stymphalian Birds

Date	Mintage	VF20	XF40	MS60	MS63	MS65
1999	Est. 25000	PF65 65.00				

KM# 762 2 POUNDS
12.00 g., Bi-Metallic Copper-Nickel center in Nickel-Brass ring, 28.4 mm. **Ruler:** Elizabeth II **Subject:** The Labours of Hercules **Obv:** Crowned head right **Rev:** Hercules and the Mares of Diomedes

Date	Mintage	VF20	XF40	MS60	MS63	MS65
1999 AA	—	—	—	—	—	35.00
1999 No die letters	—	—	—	—	—	35.00

KM# 762a 2 POUNDS
10.00 g., 0.999 Silver Gilt 0.3212 oz. **Ruler:** Elizabeth II **Subject:** The Labours of Hercules **Obv:** Crowned head right **Rev:** Hercules and the Mares of Diomedes

Date	Mintage	VF20	XF40	MS60	MS63	MS65
1999	Est. 25000	PF65 65.00				

KM# 763 2 POUNDS
12.00 g., Bi-Metallic Copper-Nickel center in Nickel-Brass ring, 28.4 mm. **Ruler:** Elizabeth II **Subject:** The Labours of Hercules **Obv:** Head with tiara right **Rev:** Hercules and Hippolyta's Girdle **Edge:** Reeded

Date	Mintage	VF20	XF40	MS60	MS63	MS65
2000 AA	Est. 2000	—	—	—	—	45.00
2000 No die letters	—	—	—	—	—	45.00

KM# 763a 2 POUNDS
12.00 g., 0.999 Silver 0.3854 oz. ASW, 28.4 mm. **Ruler:** Elizabeth II **Subject:** The Labours of Hercules **Obv:** Crowned head right **Rev:** Hercules and Hippolyta's Girdle **Edge:** Reeded **Note:** Partially gold plated.

Date	Mintage	VF20	XF40	MS60	MS63	MS65
2000	7,500	PF65 60.00				

KM# 764 2 POUNDS
12.00 g., Bi-Metallic Copper-Nickel center in Nickel-Brass ring, 28.4 mm. **Ruler:** Elizabeth II **Subject:** The Labours of Hercules - Geryon's Cattle **Obv:** Head with tiara right **Rev:** Hercules with cow and three devils shot by one arrow **Edge:** Reeded

Date	Mintage	VF20	XF40	MS60	MS63	MS65
2000 No die letters	—	—	—	—	—	45.00
2000 AA	—	—	—	—	—	45.00

KM# 764a 2 POUNDS
12.00 g., 0.999 Silver 0.3854 oz. ASW, 28.4 mm. **Ruler:** Elizabeth II **Subject:** The Labours of Hercules **Obv:** Head with tiara right **Rev:** Hercules with cow and three devils shot by one arrow **Edge:** Reeded **Note:** Partially gold plated.

Date	Mintage	VF20	XF40	MS60	MS63	MS65
2000	7,500	PF65 60.00				

KM# 765 2 POUNDS
12.00 g., Bi-Metallic Copper-Nickel center in Nickel-Brass ring, 28.4 mm. **Ruler:** Elizabeth II **Subject:** The Labours of Hercules **Obv:** Head with tiara right **Rev:** Hercules carrying the world while facing a man with a bushel of apples **Edge:** Reeded

Date	Mintage	VF20	XF40	MS60	MS63	MS65
2000 AA	—	—	—	—	—	45.00
2000 No die letters	—	—	—	—	—	45.00

KM# 765a 2 POUNDS
12.00 g., 0.999 Silver 0.3854 oz. ASW, 28.4 mm. **Ruler:** Elizabeth II **Subject:** The Labours of Hercules **Obv:** Head with tiara right **Rev:** Hercules carrying the world while facing a man with a bushel of apples **Edge:** Reeded **Note:** Partially gold plated.

Date	Mintage	VF20	XF40	MS60	MS63	MS65
2000	7,500	PF65 60.00				

KM# 766 2 POUNDS
12.00 g., Bi-Metallic Copper-Nickel center in Nickel-Brass ring, 28.4 mm. **Ruler:** Elizabeth II **Subject:** The Labours of Hercules **Obv:** Head with tiara right **Rev:** Hercules chaining Cerberus

Date	Mintage	VF20	XF40	MS60	MS63	MS65
2000 No die letters	—	—	—	—	—	45.00
2000 AA	—	—	—	—	—	45.00

KM# 766a 2 POUNDS
12.00 g., 0.999 Silver 0.3854 oz. ASW, 28.4 mm. **Ruler:** Elizabeth II **Subject:** The Labours of Hercules **Obv:** Head with tiara right **Rev:** Hercules chaining Cerberus **Note:** Partially gold plated.

Date	Mintage	VF20	XF40	MS60	MS63	MS65
2000	7,500	PF65 60.00				

KM# 25 5 POUNDS
Virenium, 36 mm. **Ruler:** Elizabeth II **Obv:** Crowned head right **Rev:** Hercules statue standing

Date	Mintage	VF20	XF40	MS60	MS63	MS65
1988 AA	—	—	—	15.00	17.00	25.00
1989 AA	—	—	—	15.00	17.00	25.00
1989 No die letters	—	—	—	15.00	17.00	25.00
1990 AA	—	—	—	15.00	17.00	25.00
1991 AA	—	—	—	15.00	17.00	25.00
1992 AA	—	—	—	15.00	17.00	25.00
1993 AA	—	—	—	15.00	17.00	25.00

KM# 309 5 POUNDS
Virenium, 36 mm. **Ruler:** Elizabeth II **Obv:** Crowned bust right **Rev:** D-Day - Soldier, sailor and pilot above tank, plane, and ship

Date	Mintage	VF20	XF40	MS60	MS63	MS65
1994 AA	—	—	—	—	17.50	22.00
1994 AA	—	PF65 25.00				

KM# 309a 5 POUNDS
23.50 g., 0.925 Silver 0.6989 oz. ASW, 36 mm. **Ruler:** Elizabeth II **Obv:** Crowned bust right **Rev:** D-Day - Soldier, sailor and pilot above tank, plane, and ship

Date	Mintage	VF20	XF40	MS60	MS63	MS65
1994	Est. 5000	PF65 45.00				

KM# 309b 5 POUNDS
39.83 g., 0.917 Gold 1.1743 oz. AGW, 36 mm. **Ruler:** Elizabeth II **Obv:** Crowned bust right **Rev:** D-Day - Soldier, sailor and pilot above tank, plane, and ship

Date	Mintage	VF20	XF40	MS60	MS63	MS65
1994	Est. 850	PF65 1,650				

KM# 332 5 POUNDS
Virenium, 36 mm. **Ruler:** Elizabeth II **Obv:** Crowned head right **Rev:** 50th Anniversary - VE Day

Date	Mintage	VF20	XF40	MS60	MS63	MS65
1995 AA	—	—	—	—	17.50	22.00
1995	Est. 5000	PF65 25.00				

KM# 332a 5 POUNDS
23.50 g., 0.925 Silver 0.6989 oz. ASW, 36 mm. **Ruler:** Elizabeth II **Obv:** Crowned head right **Rev:** 50th Anniversary - VE Day

Date	Mintage	VF20	XF40	MS60	MS63	MS65
1995	—	PF65 45.00				

KM# 332b 5 POUNDS
39.83 g., 0.917 Gold 1.1743 oz. AGW, 36 mm. **Ruler:** Elizabeth II **Obv:** Crowned head right **Rev:** 50th Anniversary - VE Day

Date	Mintage	VF20	XF40	MS60	MS63	MS65
1995	Est. 850	PF65 1,650				

KM# 334 5 POUNDS
Virenium, 36 mm. **Ruler:** Elizabeth II **Obv:** Crowned head right **Rev:** Queen Mother viewing bomb-damaged Buckingham Palace

Date	Mintage	VF20	XF40	MS60	MS63	MS65
1995 AA	—	—	—	—	16.00	20.00

KM# 334a 5 POUNDS
25.50 g., 0.925 Silver 0.7584 oz. ASW, 36 mm. **Ruler:** Elizabeth II **Obv:** Crowned head right **Rev:** Queen Mother viewing bomb-damaged Buckingham Palace

Date	Mintage	VF20	XF40	MS60	MS63	MS65
1995	Est. 5000	PF65 45.00				

KM# 334b 5 POUNDS
39.83 g., 0.917 Gold 1.1743 oz. AGW, 36 mm. **Ruler:** Elizabeth II **Obv:** Crowned head right **Rev:** Queen Mother viewing bomb-damaged Buckingham Palace

Date	Mintage	VF20	XF40	MS60	MS63	MS65
1995	Est. 850	PF65 1,650				

KM# 335 5 POUNDS
Virenium, 36 mm. **Ruler:** Elizabeth II **Obv:** Crowned head right **Rev:** VJ Day - Flag Raising

Date	Mintage	VF20	XF40	MS60	MS63	MS65
1995 AA	—	—	—	—	17.50	22.00
1995	Est. 5000	PF65 25.00				

KM# 335a 5 POUNDS
23.50 g., 0.925 Silver 0.6989 oz. ASW, 36 mm. **Ruler:** Elizabeth II **Obv:** Crowned head right **Rev:** VJ Day - Flag Raising

Date	Mintage	VF20	XF40	MS60	MS63	MS65
1995	Est. 5000	PF65 40.00				

KM# 335b 5 POUNDS
39.83 g., 0.917 Gold 1.1743 oz. AGW, 36 mm. **Ruler:** Elizabeth II **Obv:** Crowned head right **Rev:** VJ Day - Flag Raising

Date	Mintage	VF20	XF40	MS60	MS63	MS65
1995	Est. 850	PF65 1,650				

KM# 341 5 POUNDS
Virenium, 36 mm. **Ruler:** Elizabeth II **Subject:** 190th Anniversary - Death Of Admiral Nelson **Obv:** Crowned head right **Rev:** Bust at right facing left, ship at left

Date	Mintage	VF20	XF40	MS60	MS63	MS65
1995 AA	—	—	—	—	16.00	20.00

KM# 341a 5 POUNDS
23.50 g., 0.925 Silver 0.6989 oz. ASW, 36 mm. **Ruler:** Elizabeth II **Subject:** 190th Anniversary - Death of Admiral Nelson **Obv:** Crowned head right **Rev:** Bust at right facing left, ship at left

Date	Mintage	VF20	XF40	MS60	MS63	MS65
1995	Est. 5000	PF65 45.00				

KM# 341b 5 POUNDS
39.83 g., 0.917 Gold 1.1743 oz. AGW, 36 mm. **Ruler:** Elizabeth II **Subject:** 190th Anniversary - Death of Admiral Nelson **Obv:** Crowned head right **Rev:** Bust at right facing left, ship at left

Date	Mintage	VF20	XF40	MS60	MS63	MS65
1995	Est. 850	PF65 1,650				

KM# 354 5 POUNDS
Virenium, 36 mm. **Ruler:** Elizabeth II **Subject:** 70th Birthday of Queen Elizabeth II **Obv:** Crowned head right **Rev:** Monogram and castle within ribbon

Date	Mintage	VF20	XF40	MS60	MS63	MS65
1996 AA	—	—	—	—	17.50	22.00

KM# 354a 5 POUNDS
23.50 g., 0.925 Silver 0.6989 oz. ASW, 36 mm. **Ruler:** Elizabeth II **Subject:** 70th Birthday of Queen Elizabeth II **Obv:** Crowned head right **Rev:** Monogram and castle within ribbon

Date	Mintage	VF20	XF40	MS60	MS63	MS65
1996	Est. 5000	PF65 45.00				

KM# 354b 5 POUNDS
39.83 g., 0.917 Gold 1.1743 oz. AGW, 36 mm. **Ruler:** Elizabeth II **Subject:** 70th Birthday of Queen Elizabeth II **Obv:** Crowned head right **Rev:** Monogram and castle within ribbon

Date	Mintage	VF20	XF40	MS60	MS63	MS65
1996	Est. 850	PF65 1,650				

KM# 355 5 POUNDS
Virenium, 36 mm. **Ruler:** Elizabeth II **Subject:** Centennial Olympics **Obv:** Crowned head right **Rev:** Zeus on Throne, various athletes flank

Date	Mintage	VF20	XF40	MS60	MS63	MS65
1996 AA	—	—	—	—	17.50	22.00

KM# 355a 5 POUNDS
23.50 g., 0.925 Silver 0.6989 oz. ASW, 36 mm. **Ruler:** Elizabeth II **Subject:** Centennial Olympics **Obv:** Crowned head right **Rev:** Zeus on Throne, various athletes flank

Date	Mintage	VF20	XF40	MS60	MS63	MS65
1996	Est. 5000	PF65 45.00				

KM# 355b 5 POUNDS
39.83 g., 0.917 Gold 1.1743 oz. AGW, 36 mm. **Ruler:** Elizabeth II **Subject:** Centennial Olympics **Obv:** Crowned head right **Rev:** Zeus on Throne, various athletes flank

Date	Mintage	VF20	XF40	MS60	MS63	MS65
1996	Est. 850	PF65 1,650				

KM# 527 5 POUNDS
Virenium, 36 mm. **Ruler:** Elizabeth II **Subject:** Queen Elizabeth II's Golden Wedding Anniversary **Obv:** Crowned head right **Rev:** Two hands within wreath of ribbon

Date	Mintage	VF20	XF40	MS60	MS63	MS65
1997 AA	—	—	—	—	17.50	22.00

KM# 527a 5 POUNDS
25.50 g., 0.925 Silver 0.7584 oz. ASW, 36 mm. **Ruler:** Elizabeth II **Subject:** Queen Elizabeth II's Golden Wedding Anniversary **Obv:** Crowned head right **Rev:** Two hands within wreath of ribbon

Date	Mintage	VF20	XF40	MS60	MS63	MS65
1997	Est. 10000	PF65 45.00				

KM# 527b 5 POUNDS
39.83 g., 0.917 Gold 1.1743 oz. AGW, 36 mm. **Ruler:** Elizabeth II **Subject:** Queen Elizabeth II's Golden Wedding Anniversary **Obv:** Crowned head right **Rev:** Two hands within wreath of ribbon

Date	Mintage	VF20	XF40	MS60	MS63	MS65
1997	Est. 850	PF65 1,650				

KM# 605 5 POUNDS
Virenium, 36 mm. **Ruler:** Elizabeth II **Subject:** Bicentennial - Arrival of Commodore Nelson **Obv:** Crowned head right **Rev:** Cameo left of full masted ship

Date	Mintage	VF20	XF40	MS60	MS63	MS65
1997 AA	—	—	—	—	17.50	22.00

KM# 605a 5 POUNDS
23.50 g., 0.925 Silver 0.6989 oz. ASW, 36 mm. **Ruler:** Elizabeth II **Subject:** Bicentennial - Arrival of Commodore Nelson **Obv:** Crowned head right **Rev:** Cameo left of full masted ship

Date	Mintage	VF20	XF40	MS60	MS63	MS65
1997	Est. 10000	PF65 45.00				

KM# 605b 5 POUNDS
39.83 g., 0.917 Gold 1.1743 oz. AGW, 36 mm. **Ruler:** Elizabeth II **Subject:** Bicentennial - Arrival of Commodore Nelson **Obv:** Crowned head right **Rev:** Cameo left of full masted ship

Date	Mintage	VF20	XF40	MS60	MS63	MS65
1997	Est. 850	PF65 1,650				

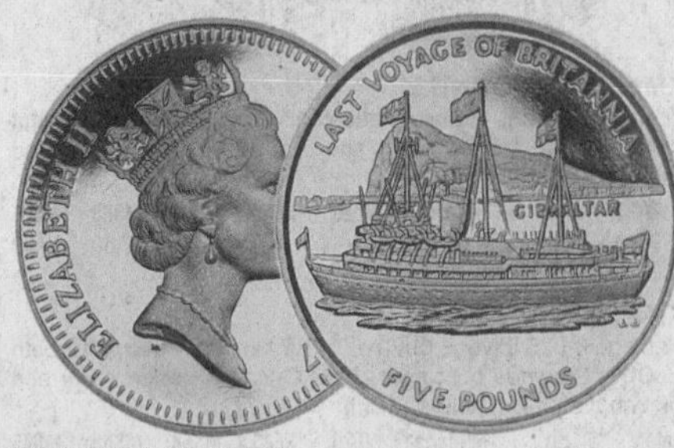

KM# 607 5 POUNDS
Virenium, 36 mm. **Ruler:** Elizabeth II **Subject:** Last Voyage of Britannia **Obv:** Crowned head right **Rev:** Ship sailing past Gibraltar

Date	Mintage	VF20	XF40	MS60	MS63	MS65
1997 AA	—	—	—	—	17.50	22.00

KM# 607a 5 POUNDS
23.50 g., 0.925 Silver 0.6989 oz. ASW, 36 mm. **Ruler:** Elizabeth II **Subject:** Last Voyage of Britannia **Obv:** Crowned head right **Rev:** Ship sailing past Gibraltar

Date	Mintage	VF20	XF40	MS60	MS63	MS65
1997	—	PF65 50.00				

KM# 607b 5 POUNDS
39.83 g., 0.917 Gold 1.1743 oz. AGW, 36 mm. **Ruler:** Elizabeth II **Subject:** Last Voyage of Britannia **Obv:** Crowned head right **Rev:** Ship sailing past Gibraltar

Date	Mintage	VF20	XF40	MS60	MS63	MS65
1997	Est. 850	PF65 1,650				

KM# 740 5 POUNDS
Virenium, 36 mm. **Ruler:** Elizabeth II **Subject:** 40th Anniversary of Radio Gibraltar **Obv:** Head with tiara right **Rev:** Radio broadcaster, rock in background

Date	Mintage	VF20	XF40	MS60	MS63	MS65
1998 AA	—	—	—	—	17.50	22.00

KM# 740a 5 POUNDS
23.50 g., 0.925 Silver 0.6989 oz. ASW, 36 mm. **Ruler:** Elizabeth II **Subject:** 40th Anniversary of Radio Gibraltar **Obv:** Head with tiara right **Rev:** Radio broadcaster, rock in background

Date	Mintage	VF20	XF40	MS60	MS63	MS65
1998	Est. 5000	PF65 45.00				

KM# 740b 5 POUNDS
39.83 g., 0.917 Gold 1.1743 oz. AGW, 36 mm. **Ruler:** Elizabeth II **Subject:** 40th Anniversary of Radio Gibraltar **Obv:** Head with tiara right **Rev:** Radio broadcaster, rock in background

Date	Mintage	VF20	XF40	MS60	MS63	MS65
1998	Est. 850	PF65 1,650				

KM# 770 5 POUNDS
Virenium, 36 mm. **Ruler:** Elizabeth II **Subject:** 80th Anniversary of the RAF **Obv:** Crowned head right **Rev:** Eurofighter over map

Date	Mintage	VF20	XF40	MS60	MS63	MS65
1998	—	—	—	—	17.50	22.00

KM# 770a 5 POUNDS
23.50 g., 0.925 Silver 0.6989 oz. ASW, 36 mm. **Ruler:** Elizabeth II **Subject:** 80th Anniversary of the RAF **Obv:** Crowned head right **Rev:** Eurofighter over map

Date	Mintage	VF20	XF40	MS60	MS63	MS65
1998	Est. 5000	PF65 50.00				

KM# 770b 5 POUNDS
39.83 g., 0.917 Gold 1.1743 oz. AGW, 36 mm. **Ruler:** Elizabeth II **Subject:** 80th Anniversary of the RAF **Obv:** Crowned head right **Rev:** Eurofighter over map

Date	Mintage	VF20	XF40	MS60	MS63	MS65
1998	Est. 850	PF65 1,650				

KM# 771 5 POUNDS
Virenium, 36 mm. **Ruler:** Elizabeth II **Subject:** Millennium 2000 **Obv:** Head with tiara right **Rev:** Landmarks of London

Date	Mintage	VF20	XF40	MS60	MS63	MS65
1998 AA	—	—	—	—	17.50	22.00

KM# 771a 5 POUNDS
23.50 g., 0.925 Silver 0.6989 oz. ASW, 36 mm. **Ruler:** Elizabeth II **Subject:** Millennium 2000 **Obv:** Head with tiara right **Rev:** Landmarks of London

Date	Mintage	VF20	XF40	MS60	MS63	MS65
1998	Est. 5000	PF65 50.00				

KM# 771b 5 POUNDS
39.83 g., 0.917 Gold 1.1743 oz. AGW, 36 mm. **Ruler:** Elizabeth II **Obv:** Head with tiara right **Rev:** Landmarks of London

Date	Mintage	VF20	XF40	MS60	MS63	MS65
1998	Est. 850	PF65 1,650				

KM# 772 5 POUNDS
Virenium, 36 mm. **Ruler:** Elizabeth II **Subject:** 50th Birthday of Prince Charles **Obv:** Crowned head right **Rev:** Heads of Prince Charles and sons William and Harry left

Date	Mintage	VF20	XF40	MS60	MS63	MS65
1998 AA	—	—	—	—	17.50	22.00

KM# 772a 5 POUNDS
23.50 g., 0.925 Silver 0.6989 oz. ASW, 36 mm. **Ruler:** Elizabeth II **Subject:** 50th Birthday of Prince Charles **Obv:** Crowned head right **Rev:** Heads of Prince Charles and sons William and Harry

Date	Mintage	VF20	XF40	MS60	MS63	MS65
1998	5,000	PF65 50.00				

KM# 772b 5 POUNDS
39.83 g., 0.917 Gold 1.1743 oz. AGW, 36 mm. **Ruler:** Elizabeth II **Subject:** 50th Birthday of Prince Charles **Obv:** Crowned head right **Rev:** Heads of Prince Charles and sons William and Harry

Date	Mintage	VF20	XF40	MS60	MS63	MS65
1998	Est. 850	PF65 1,650				

KM# 797 5 POUNDS
Virenium, 36 mm. **Ruler:** Elizabeth II **Subject:** Millennium 2000 **Obv:** Head with tiara right **Rev:** Sundial, digital clock face, candle and traditional clock face

Date	Mintage	VF20	XF40	MS60	MS63	MS65
1999 AA	—	—	—	—	17.50	22.00

KM# 797a 5 POUNDS
10.00 g., Titanium, 36.1 mm. **Ruler:** Elizabeth II **Subject:** Millennium 2000 **Obv:** Head with tiara right **Rev:** Sundial, digital clock face, candle and traditional clock face

Date	Mintage	VF20	XF40	MS60	MS63	MS65
1999	—	PF65 85.00				

KM# 797b 5 POUNDS
28.28 g., 0.925 Silver 0.841 oz. ASW, 36 mm. **Ruler:** Elizabeth II **Subject:** Millennium 2000 **Obv:** Head with tiara right **Rev:** Sundial, digital clock face, candle and traditional clock face

Date	Mintage	VF20	XF40	MS60	MS63	MS65
1999	Est. 5000	PF65 65.00				

KM# 867 5 POUNDS
Virenium, 36 mm. **Ruler:** Elizabeth II **Subject:** Mediterranean Rowing Club **Obv:** Head with tiara right **Rev:** A one-man and a four-man row boat

Date	Mintage	VF20	XF40	MS60	MS63	MS65
1999	—	—	—	—	17.50	22.00

KM# 867a 5 POUNDS
23.50 g., 0.925 Silver 0.6989 oz. ASW, 36 mm. **Ruler:** Elizabeth II **Subject:** Mediterranean Rowing Club **Obv:** Head with tiara right **Rev:** A one-man and a four-man row boat

Date	Mintage	VF20	XF40	MS60	MS63	MS65
1999	Est. 5000	PF65 65.00				

KM# 867b 5 POUNDS
39.83 g., 0.917 Gold 1.1743 oz. AGW, 36 mm. **Ruler:** Elizabeth II **Subject:** Mediterranean Rowing Club **Obv:** Head with tiara right **Rev:** A one-man and a four-man row boat

Date	Mintage	VF20	XF40	MS60	MS63	MS65
1999	Est. 850	PF65 1,650				

KM# 878 5 POUNDS
Virenium, 36 mm. **Ruler:** Elizabeth II **Subject:** Battle of Britain **Obv:** Head with tiara right **Rev:** Spitfire in flight

Date	Mintage	VF20	XF40	MS60	MS63	MS65
2000 AA	—	—	—	—	16.00	20.00

KM# 878a 5 POUNDS
23.50 g., 0.925 Silver 0.6989 oz. ASW, 36 mm. **Ruler:** Elizabeth II **Subject:** Battle of Britain **Obv:** Head with tiara right **Rev:** Spitfire in flight

Date	Mintage	VF20	XF40	MS60	MS63	MS65
2000	Est. 10000	PF65 50.00				

KM# 878b 5 POUNDS
39.83 g., 0.916 Gold 1.173 oz. AGW, 36 mm. **Ruler:** Elizabeth II **Subject:** Battle of Britain **Obv:** Head with tiara right **Rev:** Spitfire in flight

Date	Mintage	VF20	XF40	MS60	MS63	MS65
2000	Est. 850	PF65 1,650				

KM# 885 5 POUNDS
10.00 g., Titanium blue tone. **Ruler:** Elizabeth II **Subject:** 160th Anniversary - Uniform Penny Post **Obv:** Head with tiara right **Rev:** Postage stamp design **Edge:** Reeded

Date	Mintage	VF20	XF40	MS60	MS63	MS65
2000	15,000	PF65 55.00				

KM# 7 25 POUNDS
7.77 g., 0.917 Gold 0.2291 oz. AGW **Ruler:** Elizabeth II **Subject:** 250th Anniversary - Introduction of British Sterling **Obv:** Young bust right **Rev:** Lion and key

Date	Mintage	VF20	XF40	MS60	MS63	MS65
1975	2,395	—	—	—	—	400
1975	750	PF65 425				

KM# 8 50 POUNDS
15.55 g., 0.917 Gold 0.4584 oz. AGW **Ruler:** Elizabeth II **Subject:** 250th Anniversary - Introduction of British Sterling **Obv:** Young bust right **Rev:** Our Lady of Europa

Date	Mintage	VF20	XF40	MS60	MS63	MS65
1975	1,625	—	—	—	—	700
1975	750	PF65 725				

KM# 13 50 POUNDS
15.98 g., 0.917 Gold 0.471 oz. AGW **Ruler:** Elizabeth II **Subject:** 175th Anniversary - Death of Admiral Nelson **Obv:** Young bust right **Rev:** Bust right of ship at left looking left

Date	Mintage	VF20	XF40	MS60	MS63	MS65
1980	Est. 7500	—	—	—	—	725
1980	Est. 5000	PF65 750				

KM# 15 50 POUNDS
15.98 g., 0.917 Gold 0.471 oz. AGW **Ruler:** Elizabeth II **Subject:** Wedding of Prince Charles and Lady Diana **Rev:** The royal couple

Date	Mintage	VF20	XF40	MS60	MS63	MS65
1981	—	—	—	—	—	725
1981	—	PF65 750				

KM# 9 100 POUNDS
31.10 g., 0.917 Gold 0.9169 oz. AGW **Ruler:** Elizabeth II **Subject:** 250th Anniversary - Introduction of British Sterling **Rev:** Coat of arms

Date	Mintage	VF20	XF40	MS60	MS63	MS65
1975	1,625	—	—	—	—	1,450
1975	750	PF65 1,550				

SOVEREIGN COINAGE

KM# 26 1/4 SOVEREIGN
1.99 g., 0.917 Gold 0.0587 oz. AGW **Ruler:** Elizabeth II **Subject:** 150th Anniversary of Regal Coinage **Obv:** Crowned bust right **Rev:** Queen and lion left

Date	Mintage	VF20	XF40	MS60	MS63	MS65
1989 U	—	—	—	—	—	95.00
1989	Est. 1989	PF65 100				

KM# 41 1/4 SOVEREIGN
1.99 g., 0.917 Gold 0.0587 oz. AGW **Ruler:** Elizabeth II **Subject:** 21st Anniversary - Constitution **Obv:** Crowned bust right **Rev:** Standing figure with key and trident, shield lower right

Date	Mintage	VF20	XF40	MS60	MS63	MS65
1990	Est. 1000	PF65 100				

KM# 515 1/4 SOVEREIGN
1.22 g., 0.9999 Gold 0.0394 oz. AGW **Ruler:** Elizabeth II **Obv:** Crowned bust right **Rev:** Queen and lion left

Date	Mintage	VF20	XF40	MS60	MS63	MS65
1997	—	PF65 100				

KM# 27 1/2 SOVEREIGN
3.98 g., 0.917 Gold 0.1173 oz. AGW **Ruler:** Elizabeth II **Subject:** 150th Anniversary of Regal Coinage **Obv:** Crowned bust right **Rev:** Queen and lion left

Date	Mintage	VF20	XF40	MS60	MS63	MS65
1989 U	—	—	—	—	—	185
1989	Est. 1989	PF65 200				

KM# 42 1/2 SOVEREIGN
3.98 g., 0.917 Gold 0.1173 oz. AGW **Ruler:** Elizabeth II **Subject:** 21st Anniversary - Constitution **Obv:** Crowned bust right **Rev:** Standing figure with key and trident, shield lower right

Date	Mintage	VF20	XF40	MS60	MS63	MS65
1990	1,000	PF65 200				

KM# 516 1/2 SOVEREIGN
3.11 g., 0.9999 Gold 0.100 oz. AGW **Ruler:** Elizabeth II **Obv:** Crowned bust right **Rev:** Queen and lion left

Date	Mintage	VF20	XF40	MS60	MS63	MS65
1997	—	PF65 160				

KM# 28 SOVEREIGN
7.96 g., 0.917 Gold 0.2347 oz. AGW **Ruler:** Elizabeth II **Subject:** 150th Anniversary of Regal Coinage **Obv:** Crowned bust right **Rev:** Queen and lion left

Date	Mintage	VF20	XF40	MS60	MS63	MS65
1989 U	—	—	—	—	—	350
1989	Est. 1989	PF65 375				

KM# 43 SOVEREIGN
7.96 g., 0.917 Gold 0.2347 oz. AGW **Ruler:** Elizabeth II **Subject:** 21st Anniversary - Constitution **Obv:** Crowned bust right **Rev:** Standing figure with key and trident, shield at lower right

Date	Mintage	VF20	XF40	MS60	MS63	MS65
1990	Est. 1000	PF65 375				

KM# 517 SOVEREIGN

6.22 g., 0.9999 Gold 0.200 oz. AGW, 22 mm. **Ruler:** Elizabeth II **Obv:** Crowned bust right **Rev:** Queen and lion left

Date	Mintage	VF20	XF40	MS60	MS63	MS65
1997	—	PF65 300				

KM# 29 2 SOVEREIGNS

15.94 g., 0.917 Gold 0.4699 oz. AGW **Ruler:** Elizabeth II **Subject:** 150th Anniversary of Regal Coinage **Obv:** Crowned bust right **Rev:** Queen and lion left

Date	Mintage	VF20	XF40	MS60	MS63	MS65
1989	1,989	PF65 725				

KM# 44 2 SOVEREIGNS

15.94 g., 0.917 Gold 0.4699 oz. AGW **Ruler:** Elizabeth II **Subject:** 21st Anniversary - Constitution **Obv:** Crowned bust right **Rev:** Standing figure with key and trident, shield lower right

Date	Mintage	VF20	XF40	MS60	MS63	MS65
1990	1,000	PF65 725				

KM# 30 5 SOVEREIGNS

39.83 g., 0.917 Gold 1.1743 oz. AGW **Ruler:** Elizabeth II **Subject:** 150th Anniversary of Regal Coinage **Obv:** Crowned bust right **Rev:** Queen and lion left

Date	Mintage	VF20	XF40	MS60	MS63	MS65
1989	1,989	PF65 1,650				

KM# 45 5 SOVEREIGNS

39.83 g., 0.917 Gold 1.1743 oz. AGW **Ruler:** Elizabeth II **Subject:** 21st Anniversary - Constitution **Obv:** Crowned bust right **Rev:** Standing figure with key and trident, shield lower right

Date	Mintage	VF20	XF40	MS60	MS63	MS65
1990	Est. 1000	PF65 1,650				

CROWN SERIES

1980 -

KM# 310 1/25 CROWN

1.24 g., 0.999 Gold 0.040 oz. AGW, 13.9 mm. **Ruler:** Elizabeth II **Subject:** Barcelona Olympics **Obv:** Crowned bust right **Rev:** Ancient discus thrower within circle, denomination below **Edge:** Reeded

Date	Mintage	VF20	XF40	MS60	MS63	MS65
1991	—	PF65 69.00				

KM# 311 1/25 CROWN

1.24 g., 0.999 Gold 0.040 oz. AGW, 13.9 mm. **Ruler:** Elizabeth II **Subject:** Barcelona Olympics **Obv:** Crowned bust right **Rev:** Ancient chariot racers within circle, denomination below **Edge:** Reeded

Date	Mintage	VF20	XF40	MS60	MS63	MS65
1991	—	PF65 69.00				

KM# 312 1/25 CROWN

1.24 g., 0.999 Gold 0.040 oz. AGW, 13.9 mm. **Ruler:** Elizabeth II **Subject:** Barcelona Olympics **Obv:** Crowned bust right **Rev:** Ancient runners within circle, denomination below **Edge:** Reeded

Date	Mintage	VF20	XF40	MS60	MS63	MS65
1991	—	PF65 69.00				

KM# 313 1/25 CROWN

1.24 g., 0.999 Gold 0.040 oz. AGW, 13.9 mm. **Ruler:** Elizabeth II **Subject:** Barcelona Olympics **Obv:** Crowned bust right **Rev:** Ancient javelin thrower within circle, denomination below **Edge:** Reeded

Date	Mintage	VF20	XF40	MS60	MS63	MS65
1991	—	PF65 69.00				

KM# 314 1/25 CROWN

1.24 g., 0.999 Gold 0.040 oz. AGW, 13.9 mm. **Ruler:** Elizabeth II **Subject:** Barcelona Olympics **Obv:** Crowned bust right **Rev:** Ancient wrestlers, head at left looking right, circle surrounds **Edge:** Reeded

Date	Mintage	VF20	XF40	MS60	MS63	MS65
1991	—	PF65 69.00				

KM# 315 1/25 CROWN

1.24 g., 0.999 Gold 0.040 oz. AGW, 13.9 mm. **Ruler:** Elizabeth II **Subject:** Barcelona Olympics **Obv:** Crowned bust right **Rev:** Ancient boxer within circle, denomination below **Edge:** Reeded

Date	Mintage	VF20	XF40	MS60	MS63	MS65
1991	—	PF65 69.00				

KM# 316 1/25 CROWN

1.24 g., 0.999 Gold 0.040 oz. AGW, 13.9 mm. **Ruler:** Elizabeth II **Subject:** Barcelona Olympics **Obv:** Crowned bust right **Rev:** Long jumper within circle, denomination below **Edge:** Reeded

Date	Mintage	VF20	XF40	MS60	MS63	MS65
1991	—	PF65 69.00				

KM# 317 1/25 CROWN

1.24 g., 0.999 Gold 0.040 oz. AGW, 13.9 mm. **Ruler:** Elizabeth II **Subject:** Barcelona Olympics **Obv:** Crowned bust right **Rev:** Ancient victor wearing laurels, denomination below **Edge:** Reeded

Date	Mintage	VF20	XF40	MS60	MS63	MS65
1991	—	PF65 69.00				

KM# 124 1/25 CROWN

1.24 g., 0.9999 Gold 0.040 oz. AGW, 13.9 mm. **Ruler:** Elizabeth II **Rev:** Japanese Royal Wedding

Date	Mintage	VF20	XF40	MS60	MS63	MS65
1993	Est. 25000	PF65 69.00				

KM# 183 1/25 CROWN

1.24 g., 0.999 Gold 0.040 oz. AGW, 13.9 mm. **Ruler:** Elizabeth II **Obv:** Crowned bust right **Rev:** Stylized panda **Edge:** Reeded

Date	Mintage	VF20	XF40	MS60	MS63	MS65
1993	—	PF65 69.00				

KM# 187 1/25 CROWN

1.24 g., 0.999 Gold 0.040 oz. AGW, 13.9 mm. **Ruler:** Elizabeth II **Obv:** Crowned bust right **Rev:** Natural panda amongst bamboo shoots **Edge:** Reeded

Date	Mintage	VF20	XF40	MS60	MS63	MS65
1993	—	PF65 69.00				

KM# 202 1/25 CROWN

1.24 g., 0.9999 Gold 0.040 oz. AGW, 13.9 mm. **Ruler:** Elizabeth II **Series:** Peter Rabbit Centennial **Subject:** The Tale of Peter Rabbit **Obv:** Crowned bust right **Rev:** Peter Rabbit eating carrots

Date	Mintage	VF20	XF40	MS60	MS63	MS65
1993	Est. 25000	PF65 69.00				

KM# 202a 1/25 CROWN

1.24 g., 0.995 Platinum 0.0398 oz. APW, 13.9 mm. **Ruler:** Elizabeth II **Series:** Peter Rabbit Centennial **Subject:** The Tale of Peter Rabbit **Obv:** Crowned bust right **Rev:** Peter Rabbit eating carrots

Date	Mintage	VF20	XF40	MS60	MS63	MS65
1993	7,500	PF65 58.00				

KM# 206 1/25 CROWN

1.24 g., 0.9999 Gold 0.040 oz. AGW, 13.9 mm. **Ruler:** Elizabeth II **Series:** Peter Rabbit Centennial **Subject:** The Tale of Peter Rabbit **Obv:** Crowned bust right **Rev:** Mrs. Tiggy-Winkel ironing

Date	Mintage	VF20	XF40	MS60	MS63	MS65
1993	Est. 25000	PF65 69.00				

KM# 210 1/25 CROWN

1.24 g., 0.9999 Gold 0.040 oz. AGW, 13.9 mm. **Ruler:** Elizabeth II **Series:** Peter Rabbit Centennial **Subject:** The Tale of Peter Rabbit **Obv:** Crowned bust right **Rev:** Jeremy Fisher fishing

Date	Mintage	VF20	XF40	MS60	MS63	MS65
1993	Est. 25000	PF65 69.00				

KM# 214 1/25 CROWN

1.24 g., 0.9999 Gold 0.040 oz. AGW, 13.9 mm. **Ruler:** Elizabeth II **Series:** Peter Rabbit Centennial **Subject:** The Tale of Peter Rabbit **Obv:** Crowned bust right **Rev:** Tom Kitten with mother cat

Date	Mintage	VF20	XF40	MS60	MS63	MS65
1993	Est. 25000	PF65 69.00				

KM# 218 1/25 CROWN

1.24 g., 0.9999 Gold 0.040 oz. AGW, 13.9 mm. **Ruler:** Elizabeth II **Series:** Peter Rabbit Centennial **Subject:** The Tale of Peter Rabbit **Obv:** Crowned bust right **Rev:** Benjamin Bunny wearing hat and holding coat

Date	Mintage	VF20	XF40	MS60	MS63	MS65
1993	Est. 25000	PF65 69.00				

KM# 222 1/25 CROWN

1.24 g., 0.9999 Gold 0.040 oz. AGW, 13.9 mm. **Ruler:** Elizabeth II **Series:** Peter Rabbit Centennial **Subject:** The Tale of Peter Rabbit **Obv:** Crowned bust right **Rev:** Jemima Puddle Duck talking with fox

Date	Mintage	VF20	XF40	MS60	MS63	MS65
1993	Est. 25000	PF65 69.00				

KM# 437 1/25 CROWN

1.24 g., 0.9999 Gold 0.040 oz. AGW, 13.9 mm. **Ruler:** Elizabeth II **Series:** Peter Rabbit Centennial **Subject:** The Tale of Peter Rabbit **Obv:** Crowned bust right **Rev:** Mother and bunnies

Date	Mintage	VF20	XF40	MS60	MS63	MS65
1994	25,000	PF65 69.00				

KM# 437a 1/25 CROWN

1.24 g., 0.995 Platinum 0.0398 oz. APW, 13.9 mm. **Ruler:** Elizabeth II **Series:** Peter Rabbit Centennial **Subject:** The Tale of Peter Rabbit **Obv:** Crowned bust right **Rev:** Mother and bunnies

Date	Mintage	VF20	XF40	MS60	MS63	MS65
1994	Est. 7500	PF65 58.00				

KM# 368 1/25 CROWN

1.24 g., 0.9999 Gold 0.040 oz. AGW, 13.9 mm. **Ruler:** Elizabeth II **Obv:** Crowned bust right **Rev:** Roses

Date	Mintage	VF20	XF40	MS60	MS63	MS65
1996	Est. 25000	PF65 69.00				

KM# 375 1/25 CROWN

1.24 g., 0.9999 Gold 0.040 oz. AGW, 13.9 mm. **Ruler:** Elizabeth II **Series:** Peter Rabbit Centennial **Subject:** The Tale of Peter Rabbit **Obv:** Crowned bust right **Rev:** Rabbit escaping the garden

Date	Mintage	VF20	XF40	MS60	MS63	MS65
1996	—	PF65 69.00				

KM# 375a 1/25 CROWN

1.25 g., 0.995 Platinum 0.040 oz. APW, 13.9 mm. **Ruler:** Elizabeth II **Series:** Peter Rabbit Centennial **Subject:** The Tale of Peter Rabbit **Obv:** Crowned bust right **Rev:** Rabbit escaping the garden

Date	Mintage	VF20	XF40	MS60	MS63	MS65
1996	Est. 7500	PF65 59.00				

KM# 390 1/25 CROWN
1.24 g., 0.9999 Gold 0.040 oz. AGW, 13.9 mm. **Ruler:** Elizabeth II **Series:** Centenary of the Cinema **Subject:** Grace Kelly - actress, 1929-82 **Obv:** Crowned bust right **Rev:** Bust 3/4 facing, denomination

Date	Mintage	VF20	XF40	MS60	MS63	MS65
1996	Est. 25000	PF65 69.00				

KM# 395 1/25 CROWN
1.24 g., 0.9999 Gold 0.040 oz. AGW, 13.9 mm. **Ruler:** Elizabeth II **Series:** Centenary of the Cinema **Subject:** James Dean **Obv:** Crowned bust right **Rev:** Standing central figure, dates at right

Date	Mintage	VF20	XF40	MS60	MS63	MS65
1996	Est. 25000	PF65 69.00				

KM# 400 1/25 CROWN
1.24 g., 0.9999 Gold 0.040 oz. AGW, 13.9 mm. **Ruler:** Elizabeth II **Series:** Centenary of the Cinema **Subject:** Marilyn Monroe - actress, 1926-62 **Obv:** Crowned bust right **Rev:** Bust looking back over shoulder

Date	Mintage	VF20	XF40	MS60	MS63	MS65
1996	Est. 25000	PF65 69.00				

KM# 405 1/25 CROWN
1.24 g., 0.9999 Gold 0.040 oz. AGW, 13.9 mm. **Ruler:** Elizabeth II **Series:** Centenary of the Cinema **Subject:** Audrey Hepburn - actress, 1929-93 **Obv:** Crowned bust right **Rev:** Head 3/4 facing

Date	Mintage	VF20	XF40	MS60	MS63	MS65
1996	25,000	PF65 69.00				

KM# 405a 1/25 CROWN
1.25 g., 0.995 Platinum 0.040 oz. APW, 13.9 mm. **Ruler:** Elizabeth II **Series:** Centenary of the Cinema **Subject:** Audrey Hepburn - actress, 1929-93 **Obv:** Crowned bust right **Rev:** Head 3/4 facing

Date	Mintage	VF20	XF40	MS60	MS63	MS65
1996	Est. 1000	PF65 59.00				

KM# 410 1/25 CROWN
1.24 g., 0.9999 Gold 0.040 oz. AGW, 13.9 mm. **Ruler:** Elizabeth II **Series:** Centenary of the Cinema **Subject:** Bruce Lee - actor, 1940-73 **Obv:** Crowned bust right **Rev:** Kickboxer and chinese dragon

Date	Mintage	VF20	XF40	MS60	MS63	MS65
1996	Est. 25000	PF65 69.00				

KM# 415 1/25 CROWN
1.24 g., 0.9999 Gold 0.040 oz. AGW, 13.9 mm. **Ruler:** Elizabeth II **Series:** Centenary of the Cinema **Subject:** Charlie Chaplan - actor, 1889-1977 **Obv:** Crowned bust right **Rev:** Standing central figure with cane, dates

Date	Mintage	VF20	XF40	MS60	MS63	MS65
1996	Est. 25000	PF65 69.00				

KM# 420 1/25 CROWN
1.24 g., 0.9999 Gold 0.040 oz. AGW, 13.9 mm. **Ruler:** Elizabeth II **Series:** Centenary of the Cinema **Subject:** Gone With The Wind **Obv:** Crowned bust right **Rev:** Rhett Butler and Scarlett O'Hara

Date	Mintage	VF20	XF40	MS60	MS63	MS65
1996	Est. 25000	PF65 69.00				

KM# 425 1/25 CROWN
1.24 g., 0.9999 Gold 0.040 oz. AGW, 13.9 mm. **Ruler:** Elizabeth II **Series:** Centenary of the Cinema **Obv:** Crowned bust right **Rev:** The Flintstones

Date	Mintage	VF20	XF40	MS60	MS63	MS65
1996	Est. 25000	PF65 69.00				

KM# 452 1/25 CROWN
1.24 g., 0.9999 Gold 0.040 oz. AGW, 13.9 mm. **Ruler:** Elizabeth II **Series:** Centenary of the Cinema **Subject:** James Dean - actor, 1931-55 **Obv:** Crowned bust right **Rev:** Standing central figure, dates

Date	Mintage	VF20	XF40	MS60	MS63	MS65
1996	Est. 25000	PF65 69.00				

KM# 454 1/25 CROWN
1.24 g., 0.9999 Gold 0.040 oz. AGW, 13.9 mm. **Ruler:** Elizabeth II **Series:** Centenary of the Cinema **Subject:** Wizard of Oz **Obv:** Crowned bust right **Rev:** Characters of Oz

Date	Mintage	VF20	XF40	MS60	MS63	MS65
1996	—	PF65 69.00				

KM# 458 1/25 CROWN
1.24 g., 0.9999 Gold 0.040 oz. AGW, 13.9 mm. **Ruler:** Elizabeth II **Series:** Centenary of the Cinema **Subject:** The Marx Brothers - actors **Obv:** Crowned bust right **Rev:** Three busts 3/4 left

Date	Mintage	VF20	XF40	MS60	MS63	MS65
1996	Est. 25000	PF65 69.00				

KM# 462 1/25 CROWN
1.24 g., 0.9999 Gold 0.040 oz. AGW, 13.9 mm. **Ruler:** Elizabeth II **Series:** Centenary of the Cinema **Subject:** Elvis Presley - actor/entertainer, 1935-77 **Obv:** Crowned bust right **Rev:** Guitar beneath and behind bust 3/4 left

Date	Mintage	VF20	XF40	MS60	MS63	MS65
1996	—	PF65 69.00				

KM# 466 1/25 CROWN
1.24 g., 0.9999 Gold 0.040 oz. AGW, 13.9 mm. **Ruler:** Elizabeth II **Series:** Centenary of the Cinema **Subject:** Casablanca **Obv:** Crowned bust right **Rev:** Bogart and Bergman

Date	Mintage	VF20	XF40	MS60	MS63	MS65
1996	—	PF65 69.00				

KM# 470 1/25 CROWN
1.24 g., 0.9999 Gold 0.040 oz. AGW, 13.9 mm. **Ruler:** Elizabeth II **Series:** Centenary of the Cinema **Obv:** Crowned bust right **Rev:** E.T.

Date	Mintage	VF20	XF40	MS60	MS63	MS65
1996	Est. 25000	PF65 69.00				

KM# 474 1/25 CROWN
1.24 g., 0.9999 Gold 0.040 oz. AGW, 13.9 mm. **Ruler:** Elizabeth II **Series:** Centenary of the Cinema **Subject:** Alfred Hitchcock - Producer/Director, 1899-1980 **Obv:** Crowned bust right **Rev:** Bust facing looking at bird on left shoulder

Date	Mintage	VF20	XF40	MS60	MS63	MS65
1996	Est. 25000	PF65 69.00				

KM# 518 1/25 CROWN
1.24 g., 0.9999 Gold 0.040 oz. AGW, 13.9 mm. **Ruler:** Elizabeth II **Subject:** The Tale of Peter Rabbit **Obv:** Crowned bust right **Rev:** Standing rabbit

Date	Mintage	VF20	XF40	MS60	MS63	MS65
1997	Est. 25000	PF65 69.00				

KM# 518a 1/25 CROWN
1.25 g., 0.995 Platinum 0.040 oz. APW, 13.9 mm. **Ruler:** Elizabeth II **Subject:** The Tale of Peter Rabbit **Obv:** Crowned bust right **Rev:** Standing rabbit

Date	Mintage	VF20	XF40	MS60	MS63	MS65
1997	—	PF65 59.00				

KM# 537 1/25 CROWN
1.24 g., 0.9999 Gold 0.040 oz. AGW, 13.9 mm. **Ruler:** Elizabeth II **Obv:** Crowned bust right **Rev:** Peonies

Date	Mintage	VF20	XF40	MS60	MS63	MS65
1997	—	PF65 69.00				

KM# 541 1/25 CROWN
1.24 g., 0.9999 Gold 0.040 oz. AGW, 13.9 mm. **Ruler:** Elizabeth II **Subject:** Nefertiti **Obv:** Crowned bust right **Rev:** Head right

Date	Mintage	VF20	XF40	MS60	MS63	MS65
1997	Est. 10000	PF65 69.00				

KM# 545 1/25 CROWN
1.24 g., 0.9999 Gold 0.040 oz. AGW, 13.9 mm. **Ruler:** Elizabeth II **Subject:** Cleopatra **Obv:** Crowned bust right **Rev:** Head facing

Date	Mintage	VF20	XF40	MS60	MS63	MS65
1997	Est. 10000	PF65 69.00				

KM# 549 1/25 CROWN
1.24 g., 0.9999 Gold 0.040 oz. AGW, 13.9 mm. **Ruler:** Elizabeth II **Subject:** Europa **Obv:** Crowned bust right **Rev:** Head 1/4 left

Date	Mintage	VF20	XF40	MS60	MS63	MS65
1997	Est. 10000	PF65 69.00				

KM# 553 1/25 CROWN
1.24 g., 0.9999 Gold 0.040 oz. AGW, 13.9 mm. **Ruler:** Elizabeth II **Subject:** Liberty **Obv:** Crowned bust right **Rev:** Laureate head right

Date	Mintage	VF20	XF40	MS60	MS63	MS65
1997	Est. 10000	PF65 69.00				

KM# 581 1/25 CROWN
1.24 g., 0.9999 Gold 0.040 oz. AGW, 13.9 mm. **Ruler:** Elizabeth II **Series:** Evolution of Mankind **Subject:** Egypt **Obv:** Crowned bust right **Rev:** Three ancient Egyptians, pyramids, hieroglyphics

Date	Mintage	VF20	XF40	MS60	MS63	MS65
1997	Est. 15000	PF65 69.00				

KM# 583 1/25 CROWN
1.24 g., 0.9999 Gold 0.040 oz. AGW, 13.9 mm. **Ruler:** Elizabeth II **Series:** Evolution of Mankind **Subject:** Israel **Obv:** Crowned bust right **Rev:** Star of David, Moses and Temple of Solomon

Date	Mintage	VF20	XF40	MS60	MS63	MS65
1997	Est. 15000	PF65 69.00				

KM# 585 1/25 CROWN
1.24 g., 0.9999 Gold 0.040 oz. AGW, 13.9 mm. **Ruler:** Elizabeth II **Series:** Evolution of Mankind **Subject:** China **Obv:** Crowned bust right **Rev:** Emperor and the Great Wall

Date	Mintage	VF20	XF40	MS60	MS63	MS65
1997	Est. 15000	PF65 69.00				

KM# 587 1/25 CROWN
1.24 g., 0.9999 Gold 0.040 oz. AGW, 13.9 mm. **Ruler:** Elizabeth II **Series:** Evolution of Mankind **Subject:** Greece **Obv:** Crowned bust right **Rev:** Aristotle, classic Greek building

Date	Mintage	VF20	XF40	MS60	MS63	MS65
1997	Est. 15000	PF65 69.00				

KM# 589 1/25 CROWN
1.24 g., 0.9999 Gold 0.040 oz. AGW, 13.9 mm. **Ruler:** Elizabeth II **Series:** Evolution of Mankind **Subject:** Rome **Obv:** Crowned bust right **Rev:** Julius Caesar and Stonehenge

Date	Mintage	VF20	XF40	MS60	MS63	MS65
1997	Est. 15000	PF65 69.00				

KM# 591 1/25 CROWN
1.24 g., 0.9999 Gold 0.040 oz. AGW, 13.9 mm. **Ruler:** Elizabeth II **Series:** Evolution of Mankind **Subject:** India **Obv:** Crowned bust right **Rev:** Krishna playing flute by a temple

Date	Mintage	VF20	XF40	MS60	MS63	MS65
1997	Est. 15000	PF65 69.00				

KM# 593 1/25 CROWN
1.24 g., 0.9999 Gold 0.040 oz. AGW, 13.9 mm. **Ruler:** Elizabeth II **Series:** Evolution of Mankind **Subject:** Holy Roman Empire **Obv:** Crowned bust right **Rev:** Charlemagne and soldiers on horseback

Date	Mintage	VF20	XF40	MS60	MS63	MS65
1997	Est. 15000	PF65 69.00				

KM# 595 1/25 CROWN
1.24 g., 0.9999 Gold 0.040 oz. AGW, 13.9 mm. **Ruler:** Elizabeth II **Series:** Evolution of Mankind **Subject:** Macedonia **Obv:** Crowned bust right **Rev:** Alexander the Great on horseback

Date	Mintage	VF20	XF40	MS60	MS63	MS65
1997	Est. 15000	PF65 69.00				

KM# 597 1/25 CROWN
1.24 g., 0.9999 Gold 0.040 oz. AGW, 13.9 mm. **Ruler:** Elizabeth II **Series:** Evolution of Mankind **Subject:** Native America **Obv:** Crowned bust right **Rev:** Native american on horseback, totem pole at left

Date	Mintage	VF20	XF40	MS60	MS63	MS65
1997	Est. 15000	PF65 69.00				

KM# 599 1/25 CROWN
1.24 g., 0.9999 Gold 0.040 oz. AGW, 13.9 mm. **Ruler:** Elizabeth II **Series:** Evolution of Mankind **Subject:** Asia **Obv:** Crowned bust right **Rev:** Buddha and temple

Date	Mintage	VF20	XF40	MS60	MS63	MS65
1997	Est. 15000	PF65 69.00				

KM# 601 1/25 CROWN
1.24 g., 0.9999 Gold 0.040 oz. AGW, 13.9 mm. **Ruler:** Elizabeth II **Series:** Evolution of Mankind **Subject:** Inca Empire **Obv:** Crowned bust right **Rev:** Incan Emperor and Machu Picchu

Date	Mintage	VF20	XF40	MS60	MS63	MS65
1997	Est. 15000	PF65 69.00				

KM# 603 1/25 CROWN
1.24 g., 0.9999 Gold 0.040 oz. AGW, 13.9 mm. **Ruler:** Elizabeth II **Series:** Evolution of Mankind **Subject:** Islamic Civilization **Obv:** Crowned bust right **Rev:** General Tariq Ibn Ziyad and building

Date	Mintage	VF20	XF40	MS60	MS63	MS65
1997	Est. 15000	PF65 69.00				

KM# 608 1/25 CROWN
1.24 g., 0.9999 Gold 0.040 oz. AGW, 13.9 mm. **Ruler:** Elizabeth II **Series:** Traders of the World **Subject:** Sir Francis Drake **Obv:** Crowned bust right **Rev:** Bust at right, ship and beach

Date	Mintage	VF20	XF40	MS60	MS63	MS65
1997	Est. 15000	PF65 69.00				

KM# 610 1/25 CROWN
1.24 g., 0.9999 Gold 0.040 oz. AGW, 13.9 mm. **Ruler:** Elizabeth II **Series:** Traders of the World **Subject:** Romans **Obv:** Crowned bust right **Rev:** Lion, lioness, ship, map

Date	Mintage	VF20	XF40	MS60	MS63	MS65
1997	Est. 15000	PF65 69.00				

KM# 612 1/25 CROWN
1.24 g., 0.9999 Gold 0.040 oz. AGW, 13.9 mm. **Ruler:** Elizabeth II **Series:** Traders of the World **Subject:** Venetians **Obv:** Crowned bust right **Rev:** Pair of oysters with pearls, Venetian canal scene

Date	Mintage	VF20	XF40	MS60	MS63	MS65
1997	Est. 15000	PF65 69.00				

KM# 614 1/25 CROWN
1.24 g., 0.9999 Gold 0.040 oz. AGW, 13.9 mm. **Ruler:** Elizabeth II **Series:** Traders of the World **Subject:** Portuguese **Obv:** Crowned bust right **Rev:** Gold ingots and Portuguese ship

Date	Mintage	VF20	XF40	MS60	MS63	MS65
1997	Est. 15000	PF65 69.00				

KM# 616 1/25 CROWN
1.24 g., 0.9999 Gold 0.040 oz. AGW, 13.9 mm. **Ruler:** Elizabeth II **Series:** Traders of the World **Subject:** Spanish **Obv:** Crowned bust right **Rev:** Tobacco leaves, ship, map and gems

Date	Mintage	VF20	XF40	MS60	MS63	MS65
1997	Est. 15000	PF65 69.00				

KM# 618 1/25 CROWN
1.24 g., 0.9999 Gold 0.040 oz. AGW, 13.9 mm. **Ruler:** Elizabeth II **Series:** Traders of the World **Subject:** English **Obv:** Crowned bust right **Rev:** Profile of Queen above fighting ships

Date	Mintage	VF20	XF40	MS60	MS63	MS65
1997	Est. 15000	PF65 69.00				

KM# 620 1/25 CROWN
1.24 g., 0.9999 Gold 0.040 oz. AGW, 13.9 mm. **Ruler:** Elizabeth II **Series:** Traders of the World **Subject:** Captain Bligh **Obv:** Crowned bust right **Rev:** Figure sitting on rock on beach, ship in background

Date	Mintage	VF20	XF40	MS60	MS63	MS65
1997	Est. 15000	PF65 69.00				

KM# 622 1/25 CROWN
1.24 g., 0.9999 Gold 0.040 oz. AGW **Series:** Traders of the World **Subject:** Captain Cook **Obv:** Crowned bust right **Rev:** Beaver on rock, ship, bust in background

Date	Mintage	VF20	XF40	MS60	MS63	MS65
1997	Est. 15000	PF65 69.00				

KM# 649 1/25 CROWN
1.24 g., 0.9999 Gold 0.040 oz. AGW, 13.9 mm. **Ruler:** Elizabeth II **Subject:** The Tale of Peter Rabbit **Obv:** Crowned bust right **Rev:** Standing rabbit facing

Date	Mintage	VF20	XF40	MS60	MS63	MS65
1998	Est. 25000	PF65 69.00				

KM# 649a 1/25 CROWN
1.24 g., 0.995 Platinum 0.0398 oz. APW, 13.9 mm. **Ruler:** Elizabeth II **Subject:** The Tale of Peter Rabbit **Obv:** Crowned bust right **Rev:** Standing rabbit facing

Date	Mintage	VF20	XF40	MS60	MS63	MS65
1998	Est. 7500	PF65 59.00				

KM# 657 1/25 CROWN
1.24 g., 0.9999 Gold 0.040 oz. AGW, 13.9 mm. **Ruler:** Elizabeth II **Subject:** Chrysanthemum **Obv:** Crowned bust right **Rev:** Three blossoms

Date	Mintage	VF20	XF40	MS60	MS63	MS65
1998	Est. 25000	PF65 69.00				

KM# 662 1/25 CROWN
1.24 g., 0.9999 Gold 0.040 oz. AGW, 13.9 mm. **Ruler:** Elizabeth II **Subject:** Britannia **Obv:** Crowned bust right **Rev:** Helmeted head right

Date	Mintage	VF20	XF40	MS60	MS63	MS65
1998	Est. 10000	PF65 69.00				

KM# 663 1/25 CROWN
1.24 g., 0.9999 Gold 0.040 oz. AGW, 13.9 mm. **Ruler:** Elizabeth II **Subject:** Juno **Obv:** Crowned bust right **Rev:** Head facing

Date	Mintage	VF20	XF40	MS60	MS63	MS65
1998	Est. 10000	PF65 69.00				

KM# 664 1/25 CROWN
1.24 g., 0.9999 Gold 0.040 oz. AGW, 13.9 mm. **Ruler:** Elizabeth II **Subject:** Athena **Obv:** Crowned bust right **Rev:** Helmeted head right

Date	Mintage	VF20	XF40	MS60	MS63	MS65
1998	Est. 10000	PF65 69.00				

KM# 665 1/25 CROWN
1.24 g., 0.9999 Gold 0.040 oz. AGW, 13.9 mm. **Subject:** Arethusa **Obv:** Crowned bust right **Rev:** Head left with dolphins

Date	Mintage	VF20	XF40	MS60	MS63	MS65
1998	Est. 10000	PF65 69.00				

KM# 678 1/25 CROWN
1.24 g., 0.9999 Gold 0.040 oz. AGW, 13.9 mm. **Ruler:** Elizabeth II **Obv:** Crowned bust right **Rev:** Paddington with suitcase

Date	Mintage	VF20	XF40	MS60	MS63	MS65
1998	—	PF65 69.00				

KM# 678a 1/25 CROWN
1.24 g., 0.995 Platinum 0.0398 oz. APW, 13.9 mm. **Ruler:** Elizabeth II **Obv:** Crowned bust right **Rev:** Paddington with suitcase

Date	Mintage	VF20	XF40	MS60	MS63	MS65
1998	Est. 5000	PF65 58.00				

KM# 691 1/25 CROWN
1.24 g., 0.9999 Gold 0.040 oz. AGW, 13.9 mm. **Ruler:** Elizabeth II **Series:** Traders of the World **Subject:** Phoenecians, 200BC-600AD **Obv:** Crowned bust right **Rev:** Phoenician Galley, shells below

Date	Mintage	VF20	XF40	MS60	MS63	MS65
1998	Est. 10000	PF65 69.00				

KM# 693 1/25 CROWN
1.24 g., 0.9999 Gold 0.040 oz. AGW, 13.9 mm. **Ruler:** Elizabeth II **Series:** Traders of the World **Subject:** Vikings **Obv:** Crowned bust right **Rev:** Viking ship (900 AD), pair of fish

Date	Mintage	VF20	XF40	MS60	MS63	MS65
1998	Est. 10000	PF65 69.00				

KM# 695 1/25 CROWN
1.24 g., 0.9999 Gold 0.040 oz. AGW, 13.9 mm. **Ruler:** Elizabeth II **Series:** Traders of the World **Subject:** Marco Polo, 1254-1324 **Obv:** Crowned bust right **Rev:** Bust at right facing, ship at left

Date	Mintage	VF20	XF40	MS60	MS63	MS65
1998	Est. 10000	PF65 69.00				

KM# 697 1/25 CROWN
1.24 g., 0.9999 Gold 0.040 oz. AGW, 13.9 mm. **Ruler:** Elizabeth II **Series:** Traders of the World **Subject:** Hanseatic League Nations **Obv:** Crowned bust right **Rev:** Hanseatic Kogge (circa 1350), coins above ship

Date	Mintage	VF20	XF40	MS60	MS63	MS65
1998	Est. 10000	PF65 69.00				

KM# 699 1/25 CROWN
1.24 g., 0.9999 Gold 0.040 oz. AGW, 13.9 mm. **Ruler:** Elizabeth II **Series:** Traders of the World **Subject:** Chinese **Obv:** Crowned bust right **Rev:** Chinese Junk (1400s)

Date	Mintage	VF20	XF40	MS60	MS63	MS65
1998	Est. 10000	PF65 69.00				

KM# 701 1/25 CROWN
1.24 g., 0.9999 Gold 0.040 oz. AGW, 13.9 mm. **Ruler:** Elizabeth II **Series:** Traders of the World **Subject:** Christopher Columbus, 1451-1506 **Obv:** Crowned bust right **Rev:** Bust at left looking right and ship

Date	Mintage	VF20	XF40	MS60	MS63	MS65
1998	Est. 10000	PF65 69.00				

KM# 703 1/25 CROWN
1.24 g., 0.9999 Gold 0.040 oz. AGW, 13.9 mm. **Ruler:** Elizabeth II **Series:** Traders of the World **Subject:** Sir Walter Raleigh, 1552-1618 **Obv:** Crowned bust right **Rev:** Figure standing on beach, ship in background

Date	Mintage	VF20	XF40	MS60	MS63	MS65
1998	Est. 10000	PF65 69.00				

KM# 705 1/25 CROWN
1.24 g., 0.9999 Gold 0.040 oz. AGW, 13.9 mm. **Ruler:** Elizabeth II **Series:** Traders of the World **Obv:** Crowned bust right **Rev:** Sinking ships at the Boston Tea Party (1773), tea leaf

Date	Mintage	VF20	XF40	MS60	MS63	MS65
1998	Est. 10000	PF65 69.00				

KM# 707 1/25 CROWN
1.24 g., 0.9999 Gold 0.040 oz. AGW **Ruler:** Elizabeth II **Series:** Evolution of Mankind **Subject:** Australopithecus - Lucy **Obv:** Crowned head right **Rev:** Upright figure left, brain depiction at left

Date	Mintage	VF20	XF40	MS60	MS63	MS65
1998	Est. 15000	PF65 69.00				

KM# 709 1/25 CROWN
1.24 g., 0.9999 Gold 0.040 oz. AGW, 13.9 mm. **Ruler:** Elizabeth II **Series:** Traders of the World **Subject:** Homo Habilis **Obv:** Crowned head right **Rev:** Squatting figure using tools

Date	Mintage	VF20	XF40	MS60	MS63	MS65
1998	Est. 15000	PF65 69.00				

KM# 711 1/25 CROWN
1.24 g., 0.9999 Gold 0.040 oz. AGW, 13.9 mm. **Ruler:** Elizabeth II **Series:** Traders of the World **Subject:** Homo Erectus **Obv:** Crowned bust right **Rev:** Cave people using fire

Date	Mintage	VF20	XF40	MS60	MS63	MS65
1998	Est. 15000	PF65 69.00				

KM# 713 1/25 CROWN
1.24 g., 0.9999 Gold 0.040 oz. AGW, 13.9 mm. **Ruler:** Elizabeth II **Series:** Evolution of Mankind **Subject:** Gibraltar Skull **Obv:** Crowned bust right **Rev:** Caveman, skull and 'the rock'

Date	Mintage	VF20	XF40	MS60	MS63	MS65
1998	Est. 15000	PF65 69.00				

KM# 715 1/25 CROWN
1.24 g., 0.9999 Gold 0.040 oz. AGW, 13.9 mm. **Ruler:** Elizabeth II **Series:** Evolution of Mankind **Subject:** Neanderthal Man **Obv:** Crowned bust right **Rev:** Early man at burial scene, skull

Date	Mintage	VF20	XF40	MS60	MS63	MS65
1998	Est. 15000	PF65 69.00				

KM# 717 1/25 CROWN
1.24 g., 0.9999 Gold 0.040 oz. AGW, 13.9 mm. **Ruler:** Elizabeth II **Series:** Evolution of Mankind **Subject:** Homo Sapiens **Obv:** Crowned bust right **Rev:** Early man doing cave painting

Date	Mintage	VF20	XF40	MS60	MS63	MS65
1998	Est. 15000	PF65 69.00				

KM# 719 1/25 CROWN
1.24 g., 0.9999 Gold 0.040 oz. AGW, 13.9 mm. **Ruler:** Elizabeth II **Series:** Evolution of Mankind **Subject:** Homo Sapiens Hunting Mammoth **Obv:** Crowned bust right **Rev:** Figures spearing mammoth

Date	Mintage	VF20	XF40	MS60	MS63	MS65
1998	Est. 15000	PF65 69.00				

KM# 722 1/25 CROWN
1.24 g., 0.9999 Gold 0.040 oz. AGW, 13.9 mm. **Ruler:** Elizabeth II **Series:** Evolution of Mankind **Subject:** Theory of Evolution **Obv:** Crowned bust right **Rev:** Illustrated theory of evolution

Date	Mintage	VF20	XF40	MS60	MS63	MS65
1998	Est. 15000	PF65 69.00				

KM# 723 1/25 CROWN
1.24 g., 0.9999 Gold 0.040 oz. AGW, 13.9 mm. **Ruler:** Elizabeth II **Series:** Evolution of Mankind **Subject:** The Common Ancestry of Man and Ape **Obv:** Crowned bust right **Rev:** Human and primate mothers with young

Date	Mintage	VF20	XF40	MS60	MS63	MS65
1998	Est. 15000	PF65 69.00				

KM# 725 1/25 CROWN
1.24 g., 0.9999 Gold 0.040 oz. AGW, 13.9 mm. **Ruler:** Elizabeth II **Series:** Evolution of Mankind **Subject:** Charles Darwin **Obv:** Crowned bust right **Rev:** Bust facing, neanderthal and space shuttle

Date	Mintage	VF20	XF40	MS60	MS63	MS65
1998	Est. 15000	PF65 69.00				

KM# 727 1/25 CROWN
1.24 g., 0.9999 Gold 0.040 oz. AGW, 13.9 mm. **Ruler:** Elizabeth II **Series:** Evolution of Mankind **Subject:** Raymond Dart **Obv:** Crowned bust right **Rev:** Bust at left looking at skull on right

Date	Mintage	VF20	XF40	MS60	MS63	MS65
1998	Est. 15000	PF65 69.00				

KM# 729 1/25 CROWN
1.24 g., 0.9999 Gold 0.040 oz. AGW, 13.9 mm. **Ruler:** Elizabeth II **Series:** Evolution of Mankind **Subject:** 20th Century Homo Sapiens **Obv:** Crowned bust right **Rev:** Five depictions of evolution

Date	Mintage	VF20	XF40	MS60	MS63	MS65
1998	Est. 15000	PF65 69.00				

KM# 779.1 1/25 CROWN
1.24 g., 0.9999 Gold 0.040 oz. AGW, 13.9 mm. **Ruler:** Elizabeth II **Subject:** 1999 The Year of the Rabbit **Obv:** Crowned bust right **Rev:** Rabbit reading, sparrow and chinese characters

Date	Mintage	VF20	XF40	MS60	MS63	MS65
1999	Est. 5000	PF65 69.00				

KM# 779.1a 1/25 CROWN
1.24 g., 0.995 Platinum 0.0397 oz. APW, 13.9 mm. **Ruler:** Elizabeth II **Subject:** 1999 The Year of the Rabbit **Obv:** Crowned bust right **Rev:** Rabbit reading, sparrow and chinese characters

Date	Mintage	VF20	XF40	MS60	MS63	MS65
1999	Est. 3000	PF65 58.00				

KM# 779.2 1/25 CROWN
1.24 g., 0.9999 Gold 0.040 oz. AGW, 13.9 mm. **Ruler:** Elizabeth II **Subject:** The Year of the Rabbit **Obv:** Crowned bust right **Rev:** Rabbit reading, sparrow; without Chinese characters

Date	Mintage	VF20	XF40	MS60	MS63	MS65
1999	Inc. above	PF65 69.00				

KM# 779.2a 1/25 CROWN
1.24 g., 0.995 Platinum 0.0397 oz. APW **Ruler:** Elizabeth II **Subject:** The Year of the Rabbit **Obv:** Crowned bust right **Rev:** Rabbit reading, sparrow; without Chinese characters

Date	Mintage	VF20	XF40	MS60	MS63	MS65
1999	Inc. above	PF65 58.00				

KM# 1092 1/25 CROWN
1.24 g., 0.999 Gold 0.0398 oz. AGW, 13.92 mm. **Ruler:** Elizabeth II **Subject:** Millennium **Rev:** Candle and clock

Date	Mintage	VF20	XF40	MS60	MS63	MS65
1999	Est. 10000	PF63 85.00				

KM# 50 1/10 CROWN
3.11 g., 0.9999 Gold 0.100 oz. AGW, 17.95 mm. **Ruler:** Elizabeth II **Series:** Barcelona Olympics **Obv:** Crowned bust right **Rev:** Discus thrower

Date	Mintage	VF20	XF40	MS60	MS63	MS65
1991	—	PF65 172				
1992	—	PF65 172				

KM# 51 1/10 CROWN
3.11 g., 0.9999 Gold 0.100 oz. AGW, 17.95 mm. **Ruler:** Elizabeth II **Series:** Barcelona Olympics **Obv:** Crowned bust right **Rev:** Chariot racing

Date	Mintage	VF20	XF40	MS60	MS63	MS65
1991	Est. 20000	PF65 172				
1992	Est. 20000	PF65 172				

KM# 52 1/10 CROWN
3.11 g., 0.9999 Gold 0.100 oz. AGW, 17.95 mm. **Ruler:** Elizabeth II **Series:** Barcelona Olympics **Obv:** Crowned bust right **Rev:** Runners

Date	Mintage	VF20	XF40	MS60	MS63	MS65
1991	Est. 20000	PF65 172				
1992	Est. 20000	PF65 172				

KM# 53 1/10 CROWN
3.11 g., 0.9999 Gold 0.100 oz. AGW, 17.95 mm. **Ruler:** Elizabeth II **Series:** Barcelona Olympics **Obv:** Crowned bust right **Rev:** Javelin thrower

Date	Mintage	VF20	XF40	MS60	MS63	MS65
1991	Est. 20000	PF65 172				
1992	Est. 20000	PF65 172				

KM# 54 1/10 CROWN
3.11 g., 0.9999 Gold 0.100 oz. AGW, 17.95 mm. **Ruler:** Elizabeth II **Series:** Barcelona Olympics **Obv:** Crowned bust right **Rev:** Wrestlers

Date	Mintage	VF20	XF40	MS60	MS63	MS65
1991	—	PF65 172				
1992	Est. 20000	PF65 172				

KM# 55 1/10 CROWN
3.11 g., 0.9999 Gold 0.100 oz. AGW, 17.95 mm. **Ruler:** Elizabeth II **Series:** Barcelona Olympics **Obv:** Crowned bust right **Rev:** Boxers

Date	Mintage	VF20	XF40	MS60	MS63	MS65
1991	Est. 20000	PF65 172				
1992	Est. 20000	PF65 172				

KM# 56 1/10 CROWN
3.11 g., 0.9999 Gold 0.100 oz. AGW, 17.95 mm. **Ruler:** Elizabeth II **Series:** Barcelona Olympics **Obv:** Crowned bust right **Rev:** Long jumper

Date	Mintage	VF20	XF40	MS60	MS63	MS65
1991	Est. 20000	PF65 172				
1992	—	PF65 172				

KM# 57 1/10 CROWN
3.11 g., 0.9999 Gold 0.100 oz. AGW, 17.95 mm. **Ruler:** Elizabeth II **Series:** Barcelona Olympics **Obv:** Crowned bust right **Rev:** Olympic victor

Date	Mintage	VF20	XF40	MS60	MS63	MS65
1991	Est. 20000	PF65 172				
1992	Est. 20000	PF65 172				

KM# 125 1/10 CROWN
3.11 g., 0.9999 Gold 0.100 oz. AGW, 17.95 mm. **Ruler:** Elizabeth II **Subject:** Japanese Royal Wedding

Date	Mintage	VF20	XF40	MS60	MS63	MS65
1993	Est. 10000	PF65 172				

KM# 203 1/10 CROWN
3.11 g., 0.9999 Gold 0.100 oz. AGW, 17.95 mm. **Ruler:** Elizabeth II **Series:** Peter Rabbit Centennial **Subject:** The Tale of Peter Rabbit **Obv:** Crowned bust right **Rev:** Rabbit eating carrots, sparrow on handle

Date	Mintage	VF20	XF40	MS60	MS63	MS65
1993	Est. 20000	PF65 172				

KM# 203a 1/10 CROWN
3.11 g., 0.999 Platinum 0.0999 oz. APW **Ruler:** Elizabeth II **Series:** Peter Rabbit Centennial **Subject:** The Tale of Peter Rabbit **Obv:** Crowned bust right **Rev:** Rabbit eating carrots, sparrow on handle

Date	Mintage	VF20	XF40	MS60	MS63	MS65
1993	Est. 5000	PF65 147				

KM# 207 1/10 CROWN
3.11 g., 0.999 Platinum 0.0999 oz. APW **Ruler:** Elizabeth II **Series:** Peter Rabbit Centennial **Subject:** The Tale of Peter Rabbit **Obv:** Crowned bust right **Rev:** Mrs. Tiggy-Winkel ironing

Date	Mintage	VF20	XF40	MS60	MS63	MS65
1993	Est. 20000	PF65 147				

KM# 211 1/10 CROWN
3.11 g., 0.999 Platinum 0.0999 oz. APW **Ruler:** Elizabeth II **Series:** Peter Rabbit Centennial **Subject:** The Tale of Peter Rabbit **Obv:** Crowned bust right **Rev:** Jeremy Fisher fishing

Date	Mintage	VF20	XF40	MS60	MS63	MS65
1993	Est. 20000	PF65 147				

KM# 215 1/10 CROWN
3.11 g., 0.999 Platinum 0.0999 oz. APW **Ruler:** Elizabeth II **Series:** Peter Rabbit Centennial **Subject:** The Tale of Peter Rabbit **Obv:** Crowned bust right **Rev:** Tom Kitten with mother cat

Date	Mintage	VF20	XF40	MS60	MS63	MS65
1993	Est. 20000	PF65 147				

KM# 219 1/10 CROWN
3.11 g., 0.999 Platinum 0.0999 oz. APW **Ruler:** Elizabeth II **Series:** Peter Rabbit Centennial **Subject:** The Tale of Peter Rabbit **Obv:** Crowned bust right **Rev:** Benjamin Bunny wearing hat and holding coat

Date	Mintage	VF20	XF40	MS60	MS63	MS65
1993	Est. 20000	PF65 147				

KM# 223 1/10 CROWN
3.11 g., 0.999 Platinum 0.0999 oz. APW **Ruler:** Elizabeth II **Series:** Peter Rabbit Centennial **Subject:** The Tale of Peter Rabbit **Obv:** Crowned bust right **Rev:** Jemima Puddle Duck talking with fox

Date	Mintage	VF20	XF40	MS60	MS63	MS65
1993	Est. 20000	PF65 147				

KM# 439 1/10 CROWN
3.11 g., 0.999 Platinum 0.0999 oz. APW **Ruler:** Elizabeth II **Series:** Peter Rabbit Centennial **Subject:** The Tale of Peter Rabbit **Obv:** Crowned bust right **Rev:** Mother Rabbit and bunnies

Date	Mintage	VF20	XF40	MS60	MS63	MS65
1994	—	PF65 147				

KM# 439a 1/10 CROWN
3.11 g., 0.995 Platinum 0.0995 oz. APW **Ruler:** Elizabeth II **Series:** Peter Rabbit Centennial **Obv:** Crowned bust right **Rev:** Mother Rabbit and bunnies

Date	Mintage	VF20	XF40	MS60	MS63	MS65
1994	—	PF65 147				

KM# 369 1/10 CROWN
3.11 g., 0.9999 Gold 0.100 oz. AGW, 17.95 mm. **Ruler:** Elizabeth II **Subject:** Roses **Obv:** Crowned bust right

Date	Mintage	VF20	XF40	MS60	MS63	MS65
1996	Est. 20000	PF65 172				

KM# 377 1/10 CROWN
3.11 g., 0.9999 Gold 0.100 oz. AGW, 17.95 mm. **Ruler:** Elizabeth II **Series:** Peter Rabbit Centennial **Subject:** The Tale of Peter Rabbit **Obv:** Crowned bust right **Rev:** Rabbit escaping the garden

Date	Mintage	VF20	XF40	MS60	MS63	MS65
1996	Est. 20000	PF65 172				

KM# 377a 1/10 CROWN
3.13 g., 0.995 Platinum 0.100 oz. APW **Ruler:** Elizabeth II **Series:** Peter Rabbit Centennial **Subject:** The Tale of Peter Rabbit **Obv:** Crowned bust right **Rev:** Rabbit escaping the garden

Date	Mintage	VF20	XF40	MS60	MS63	MS65
1996	Est. 10000	PF65 147				

KM# 391 1/10 CROWN
3.11 g., 0.9999 Gold 0.100 oz. AGW, 17.95 mm. **Ruler:** Elizabeth II **Series:** Centenary of the Cinema **Subject:** Grace Kelly - actress, 1929-82 **Obv:** Crowned bust right **Rev:** Bust 3/4 facing, dates

Date	Mintage	VF20	XF40	MS60	MS63	MS65
1996	Est. 20000	PF65 172				

KM# 396 1/10 CROWN
3.11 g., 0.9999 Gold 0.100 oz. AGW, 17.95 mm. **Ruler:** Elizabeth II **Series:** Centenary of the Cinema **Subject:** James Dean - actor, 1931-55 **Obv:** Crowned bust right **Rev:** Bust facing, dates

Date	Mintage	VF20	XF40	MS60	MS63	MS65
1996	20,000	PF65 172				

KM# 401 1/10 CROWN
3.11 g., 0.9999 Gold 0.100 oz. AGW, 17.95 mm. **Ruler:** Elizabeth II **Series:** Centenary of the Cinema **Subject:** Marilyn Monroe - actress, 1926-62 **Obv:** Crowned bust right **Rev:** Bust looking back over shoulder, dates

Date	Mintage	VF20	XF40	MS60	MS63	MS65
1996	Est. 20000	PF65 172				

KM# 406 1/10 CROWN
3.11 g., 0.9999 Gold 0.100 oz. AGW, 17.95 mm. **Ruler:** Elizabeth II **Series:** Centenary of the Cinema **Subject:** Audrey Hepburn - actress, 1929-93 **Obv:** Crowned bust right **Rev:** Bust facing, dates

Date	Mintage	VF20	XF40	MS60	MS63	MS65
1996	—	PF65 172				

KM# 406a 1/10 CROWN
3.11 g., 0.995 Platinum 0.0995 oz. APW **Ruler:** Elizabeth II **Series:** Centenary of the Cinema **Subject:** Audrey Hepburn - actress, 1929-93 **Obv:** Crowned bust right **Rev:** Bust facing, dates

Date	Mintage	VF20	XF40	MS60	MS63	MS65
1996	Est. 1000	PF65 147				

KM# 411 1/10 CROWN
3.11 g., 0.9999 Gold 0.100 oz. AGW, 17.95 mm. **Ruler:** Elizabeth II **Series:** Centenary of the Cinema **Subject:** Bruce Lee **Obv:** Crowned bust right **Rev:** Kickboxer and chinese dragon

Date	Mintage	VF20	XF40	MS60	MS63	MS65
1996	—	PF65 172				

KM# 416 1/10 CROWN
3.11 g., 0.9999 Gold 0.100 oz. AGW, 17.95 mm. **Ruler:** Elizabeth II **Series:** Centenary of the Cinema **Subject:** Charlie Chaplan - actor, 1889-1977 **Obv:** Crowned bust right **Rev:** Standing central figure with cane, dates

Date	Mintage	VF20	XF40	MS60	MS63	MS65
1996	Est. 20000	PF65 172				

KM# 421 1/10 CROWN
3.11 g., 0.9999 Gold 0.100 oz. AGW, 17.95 mm. **Ruler:** Elizabeth II **Series:** Centenary of the Cinema **Subject:** Gone With The Wind **Obv:** Crowned bust right **Rev:** Rhett Butler and Scarlett O'Hara

Date	Mintage	VF20	XF40	MS60	MS63	MS65
1996	Est. 20000	PF65 172				

KM# 426 1/10 CROWN
3.11 g., 0.9999 Gold 0.100 oz. AGW, 17.95 mm. **Ruler:** Elizabeth II **Series:** Centenary of the Cinema **Obv:** Crowned bust right **Rev:** The Flintstones

Date	Mintage	VF20	XF40	MS60	MS63	MS65
1996	Est. 20000	PF65 172				

KM# 446 1/10 CROWN
3.11 g., 0.9999 Gold 0.100 oz. AGW, 17.95 mm. **Ruler:** Elizabeth II **Subject:** Lord Buddha **Rev:** Seated figure facing

Date	Mintage	VF20	XF40	MS60	MS63	MS65
1996	Est. 10000	PF65 172				

KM# 455 1/10 CROWN
3.11 g., 0.9999 Gold 0.100 oz. AGW, 17.95 mm. **Ruler:** Elizabeth II **Series:** Centenary of the Cinema **Subject:** Wizard of Oz **Obv:** Crowned bust right **Rev:** Wizard of Oz characters

Date	Mintage	VF20	XF40	MS60	MS63	MS65
1996	—	PF65 172				

KM# 459 1/10 CROWN
3.11 g., 0.9999 Gold 0.100 oz. AGW, 17.95 mm. **Ruler:** Elizabeth II **Series:** Centenary of the Cinema **Subject:** Marx Brothers **Obv:** Crowned bust right **Rev:** Three busts left

Date	Mintage	VF20	XF40	MS60	MS63	MS65
1996	Est. 20000	PF65 172				

KM# 463 1/10 CROWN
3.11 g., 0.9999 Gold 0.100 oz. AGW, 17.95 mm. **Ruler:** Elizabeth II **Series:** Centenary of the Cinema **Subject:** Elvis Presley **Obv:** Crowned bust right **Rev:** Guitar beneath and behind bust 3/4 left

Date	Mintage	VF20	XF40	MS60	MS63	MS65
1996	Est. 20000	PF65 172				

KM# 467 1/10 CROWN
3.11 g., 0.9999 Gold 0.100 oz. AGW, 17.95 mm. **Ruler:** Elizabeth II **Series:** Centenary of the Cinema **Subject:** Casablanca **Obv:** Crowned bust right **Rev:** Bogart and Bergman

Date	Mintage	VF20	XF40	MS60	MS63	MS65
1996	Est. 20000	PF65 172				

KM# 471 1/10 CROWN
3.11 g., 0.9999 Gold 0.100 oz. AGW, 17.95 mm. **Ruler:** Elizabeth II **Series:** Centenary of the Cinema **Obv:** Crowned bust right **Rev:** E.T.

Date	Mintage	VF20	XF40	MS60	MS63	MS65
1996	Est. 20000	PF65 172				

KM# 475 1/10 CROWN
3.11 g., 0.9999 Gold 0.100 oz. AGW, 17.95 mm. **Ruler:** Elizabeth II **Series:** Centenary of the Cinema **Subject:** Alfred Hitchcock - Producer/Director, 1899-1980 **Obv:** Crowned bust right **Rev:** Bust facing looking at bird on left shoulder

Date	Mintage	VF20	XF40	MS60	MS63	MS65
1996	Est. 20000	PF65 172				

KM# 520 1/10 CROWN
3.11 g., 0.9999 Gold 0.100 oz. AGW, 17.95 mm. **Ruler:** Elizabeth II **Subject:** Tale of Peter Rabbit **Obv:** Crowned bust right **Rev:** Standing rabbit facing

Date	Mintage	VF20	XF40	MS60	MS63	MS65
1997	—	PF65 172				

KM# 520a 1/10 CROWN
3.13 g., 0.995 Platinum 0.100 oz. APW **Ruler:** Elizabeth II **Subject:** Tale of Peter Rabbit **Obv:** Crowned bust right **Rev:** Standing rabbit facing

Date	Mintage	VF20	XF40	MS60	MS63	MS65
1997	Est. 5000	PF65 147				

KM# 538 1/10 CROWN
3.11 g., 0.9999 Gold 0.100 oz. AGW, 17.95 mm. **Ruler:** Elizabeth II **Obv:** Crowned bust right **Rev:** Peonies

Date	Mintage	VF20	XF40	MS60	MS63	MS65
1997	Est. 20000	PF65 172				

KM# 542 1/10 CROWN
3.11 g., 0.9999 Gold 0.100 oz. AGW, 17.95 mm. **Ruler:** Elizabeth II **Subject:** Nefertiti **Obv:** Crowned bust right **Rev:** Head right

Date	Mintage	VF20	XF40	MS60	MS63	MS65
1997	Est. 7500	PF65 172				

KM# 546 1/10 CROWN
3.11 g., 0.9999 Gold 0.100 oz. AGW, 17.95 mm. **Ruler:** Elizabeth II **Subject:** Cleopatra **Obv:** Crowned bust right **Rev:** Head facing

Date	Mintage	VF20	XF40	MS60	MS63	MS65
1997	Est. 7500	PF65 172				

KM# 550 1/10 CROWN
3.11 g., 0.9999 Gold 0.100 oz. AGW, 17.95 mm. **Ruler:** Elizabeth II **Subject:** Europa **Obv:** Crowned bust right **Rev:** Head 3/4 left

Date	Mintage	VF20	XF40	MS60	MS63	MS65
1997	Est. 7500	PF65 172				

KM# 554 1/10 CROWN
3.11 g., 0.9999 Gold 0.100 oz. AGW, 17.95 mm. **Ruler:** Elizabeth II **Subject:** Liberty **Obv:** Crowned bust right **Rev:** Laureate head right

Date	Mintage	VF20	XF40	MS60	MS63	MS65
1997	Est. 7500	PF65 172				

KM# 651 1/10 CROWN
3.11 g., 0.9999 Gold 0.100 oz. AGW, 17.95 mm. **Ruler:** Elizabeth II **Subject:** Tale of Peter Rabbit **Obv:** Crowned bust right **Rev:** Standing rabbit facing, sparrow

Date	Mintage	VF20	XF40	MS60	MS63	MS65
1998	—	PF65 172				

KM# 651a 1/10 CROWN
3.11 g., 0.995 Platinum 0.0995 oz. APW **Ruler:** Elizabeth II **Subject:** Tale of Peter Rabbit **Obv:** Crowned bust right **Rev:** Standing rabbit facing, sparrow

Date	Mintage	VF20	XF40	MS60	MS63	MS65
1998	Est. 5000	PF65 147				

KM# 658 1/10 CROWN
3.11 g., 0.9999 Gold 0.100 oz. AGW, 17.95 mm. **Ruler:** Elizabeth II **Subject:** Chrysanthemum **Obv:** Crowned bust right **Rev:** Three blossoms

Date	Mintage	VF20	XF40	MS60	MS63	MS65
1998	Est. 20000	PF65 172				

KM# 666 1/10 CROWN
3.11 g., 0.9999 Gold 0.100 oz. AGW, 17.95 mm. **Ruler:** Elizabeth II **Subject:** Brittania **Obv:** Crowned bust right **Rev:** Helmeted head right

Date	Mintage	VF20	XF40	MS60	MS63	MS65
1998	Est. 7500	PF65 172				

KM# 667 1/10 CROWN
3.11 g., 0.9999 Gold 0.100 oz. AGW, 17.95 mm. **Ruler:** Elizabeth II **Subject:** Juno **Obv:** Crowned bust right **Rev:** Head 3/4 facing

Date	Mintage	VF20	XF40	MS60	MS63	MS65
1998	Est. 7500	PF65 172				

KM# 668 1/10 CROWN
3.11 g., 0.9999 Gold 0.100 oz. AGW, 17.95 mm. **Ruler:** Elizabeth II **Subject:** Athena **Obv:** Crowned bust right **Rev:** Helmeted head right

Date	Mintage	VF20	XF40	MS60	MS63	MS65
1998	—	PF65 172				

KM# 669 1/10 CROWN

3.11 g., 0.9999 Gold 0.100 oz. AGW, 17.95 mm. **Ruler:** Elizabeth II **Subject:** Arethusa **Obv:** Crowned bust right **Rev:** Head left with dolphins

Date	Mintage	VF20	XF40	MS60	MS63	MS65
1998	Est. 7500	PF65 172				

KM# 679 1/10 CROWN

3.11 g., 0.9999 Gold 0.100 oz. AGW, 17.95 mm. **Ruler:** Elizabeth II **Subject:** Paddington Bear **Obv:** Crowned bust right **Rev:** Bear with suitcase

Date	Mintage	VF20	XF40	MS60	MS63	MS65
1998	Est. 7500	PF65 172				

KM# 679a 1/10 CROWN

3.11 g., 0.995 Platinum 0.0995 oz. APW **Ruler:** Elizabeth II **Subject:** Paddington Bear **Obv:** Crowned bust right **Rev:** Bear with suitcase

Date	Mintage	VF20	XF40	MS60	MS63	MS65
1998	Est. 5000	PF65 147				

KM# 1107 1/10 CROWN

3.11 g., 0.999 Gold 0.0999 oz. AGW, 17.95 mm. **Ruler:** Elizabeth II **Subject:** Millennium **Rev:** Candle and clock

Date	Mintage	VF20	XF40	MS60	MS63	MS65
1999	Est. 7500	PF65 200				

KM# 1109 1/10 CROWN

3.11 g., 0.999 Gold 0.0999 oz. AGW, 17.95 mm. **Ruler:** Elizabeth II **Subject:** 2000 Summer Olympics, Sydney **Rev:** Sydney Opera House

Date	Mintage	VF20	XF40	MS60	MS63	MS65
2000	Est. 5000	PF65 200				

KM# 1110 1/10 CROWN

3.11 g., 0.999 Gold 0.0999 oz. AGW, 17.95 mm. **Ruler:** Elizabeth II **Subject:** 2000 Summer Olympics, Sydney **Rev:** Ayers Rock

Date	Mintage	VF20	XF40	MS60	MS63	MS65
2000	Est. 5000	PF65 200				

KM# 1111 1/10 CROWN

3.11 g., 0.999 Gold 0.0999 oz. AGW, 17.95 mm. **Ruler:** Elizabeth II **Subject:** 2000 Summer Olympics **Rev:** Koala and freestyle swimmer

Date	Mintage	VF20	XF40	MS60	MS63	MS65
2000	Est. 5000	PF65 200				

KM# 1112 1/10 CROWN

3.11 g., 0.999 Gold 0.0999 oz. AGW, 17.95 mm. **Ruler:** Elizabeth II **Subject:** 2000 Summer Olympics, Sydney **Rev:** Rower

Date	Mintage	VF20	XF40	MS60	MS63	MS65
2000	Est. 5000	PF65 200				

KM# 1113 1/10 CROWN

3.11 g., 0.999 Gold 0.0999 oz. AGW, 17.95 mm. **Ruler:** Elizabeth II **Subject:** 2000 Summer Olympics, Sydney **Rev:** Kangaroo and long jumper

Date	Mintage	VF20	XF40	MS60	MS63	MS65
2000	Est. 5000	PF65 200				

KM# 1114 1/10 CROWN

3.11 g., 0.999 Gold 0.0999 oz. AGW, 17.95 mm. **Ruler:** Elizabeth II **Subject:** 2000 Summer Olympics, Sydney **Rev:** Dingo and torch runners

Date	Mintage	VF20	XF40	MS60	MS63	MS65
2000	Est. 5000	PF65 200				

KM# 48 1/5 CROWN

6.22 g., 0.999 Gold 0.1998 oz. AGW, 22 mm. **Ruler:** Elizabeth II **Series:** 150th Anniversary of the First Adhesive Postage Stamp **Subject:** Penny Black Stamp **Obv:** Crowned bust right **Rev:** Heads flank stamp design

Date	Mintage	VF20	XF40	MS60	MS63	MS65
1990	Est. 5000	PF65 320				

KM# 76 1/5 CROWN

6.22 g., 0.999 Gold 0.1998 oz. AGW, 22 mm. **Ruler:** Elizabeth II **Series:** World Cup Soccer **Obv:** Crowned bust right **Rev:** Italian flag

Date	Mintage	VF20	XF40	MS60	MS63	MS65
1990	Est. 5000	PF65 320				

KM# 76a 1/5 CROWN

6.22 g., 0.995 Platinum 0.199 oz. APW **Ruler:** Elizabeth II **Series:** World Cup Soccer **Obv:** Crowned bust right **Rev:** Italian flag

Date	Mintage	VF20	XF40	MS60	MS63	MS65
1990	Est. 1000	PF65 280				

KM# 77 1/5 CROWN

6.22 g., 0.9999 Gold 0.200 oz. AGW, 22 mm. **Ruler:** Elizabeth II **Series:** World Cup Soccer **Obv:** Crowned bust right **Rev:** Map of Italy

Date	Mintage	VF20	XF40	MS60	MS63	MS65
1990	Est. 5000	PF65 320				

KM# 77a 1/5 CROWN

6.22 g., 0.995 Platinum 0.199 oz. APW, 22 mm. **Ruler:** Elizabeth II **Series:** World Cup Soccer **Obv:** Crowned bust right **Rev:** Map of Italy

Date	Mintage	VF20	XF40	MS60	MS63	MS65
1990	Est. 1000	PF65 280				

KM# 78 1/5 CROWN

6.22 g., 0.9999 Gold 0.200 oz. AGW, 22 mm. **Ruler:** Elizabeth II **Series:** World Cup Soccer **Obv:** Crowned bust right **Rev:** Goalie catching ball

Date	Mintage	VF20	XF40	MS60	MS63	MS65
1990	Est. 5000	PF65 320				

KM# 78a 1/5 CROWN

6.22 g., 0.995 Platinum 0.199 oz. APW **Ruler:** Elizabeth II **Series:** World Cup Soccer **Obv:** Crowned bust right **Rev:** Goalie catching ball

Date	Mintage	VF20	XF40	MS60	MS63	MS65
1990	Est. 1000	PF65 280				

KM# 79 1/5 CROWN

6.22 g., 0.9999 Gold 0.200 oz. AGW, 22 mm. **Ruler:** Elizabeth II **Series:** World Cup Soccer **Obv:** Crowned bust right **Rev:** One player

Date	Mintage	VF20	XF40	MS60	MS63	MS65
1990	—	PF65 320				

KM# 79a 1/5 CROWN

6.22 g., 0.995 Platinum 0.199 oz. APW **Ruler:** Elizabeth II **Series:** World Cup Soccer **Obv:** Crowned bust right **Rev:** One player

Date	Mintage	VF20	XF40	MS60	MS63	MS65
1990	Est. 1000	PF65 280				

KM# 80 1/5 CROWN

6.22 g., 0.9999 Gold 0.200 oz. AGW, 22 mm. **Ruler:** Elizabeth II **Series:** World Cup Soccer **Obv:** Crowned bust right **Rev:** Two players

Date	Mintage	VF20	XF40	MS60	MS63	MS65
1990	Est. 5000	PF65 320				

KM# 80a 1/5 CROWN

6.22 g., 0.995 Platinum 0.199 oz. APW **Ruler:** Elizabeth II **Series:** World Cup Soccer **Obv:** Crowned bust right **Rev:** Two players

Date	Mintage	VF20	XF40	MS60	MS63	MS65
1990	Est. 1000	PF65 280				

KM# 81 1/5 CROWN

6.22 g., 0.9999 Gold 0.200 oz. AGW, 22 mm. **Ruler:** Elizabeth II **Series:** World Cup Soccer **Obv:** Crowned bust right **Rev:** Three players

Date	Mintage	VF20	XF40	MS60	MS63	MS65
1990	Est. 5000	PF65 320				

KM# 81a 1/5 CROWN

6.22 g., 0.995 Platinum 0.199 oz. APW **Ruler:** Elizabeth II **Series:** World Cup Soccer **Obv:** Crowned bust right **Rev:** Three players

Date	Mintage	VF20	XF40	MS60	MS63	MS65
1990	Est. 1000	PF65 280				

KM# 58 1/5 CROWN

6.22 g., 0.9999 Gold 0.200 oz. AGW, 22 mm. **Ruler:** Elizabeth II **Series:** Barcelona Olympics **Obv:** Crowned bust right **Rev:** Discus thrower

Date	Mintage	VF20	XF40	MS60	MS63	MS65
1991	Est. 5000	PF65 320				
1992	Est. 5000	PF65 320				

KM# 58a 1/5 CROWN

6.22 g., 0.995 Platinum 0.199 oz. APW **Ruler:** Elizabeth II **Series:** Barcelona Olympics **Obv:** Crowned bust right **Rev:** Discus thrower

Date	Mintage	VF20	XF40	MS60	MS63	MS65
1991	Est. 1000	PF65 280				

KM# 59 1/5 CROWN

6.22 g., 0.9999 Gold 0.200 oz. AGW, 22 mm. **Ruler:** Elizabeth II **Series:** Barcelona Olympics **Obv:** Crowned bust right **Rev:** Chariot racing

Date	Mintage	VF20	XF40	MS60	MS63	MS65
1991	Est. 5000	PF65 320				
1992	Est. 5000	PF65 320				

KM# 59a 1/5 CROWN

6.22 g., 0.995 Platinum 0.199 oz. APW **Ruler:** Elizabeth II **Series:** Barcelona Olympics **Obv:** Crowned bust right **Rev:** Chariot racing

Date	Mintage	VF20	XF40	MS60	MS63	MS65
1991	Est. 1000	PF65 280				

KM# 60 1/5 CROWN

6.22 g., 0.9999 Gold 0.200 oz. AGW, 22 mm. **Ruler:** Elizabeth II **Series:** Barcelona Olympics **Obv:** Crowned bust right **Rev:** Runners

Date	Mintage	VF20	XF40	MS60	MS63	MS65
1991	—	PF65 320				
1992	—	PF65 320				

KM# 60a 1/5 CROWN

6.22 g., 0.995 Platinum 0.199 oz. APW **Ruler:** Elizabeth II **Series:** Barcelona Olympics **Obv:** Crowned bust right **Rev:** Runners

Date	Mintage	VF20	XF40	MS60	MS63	MS65
1991	Est. 1000	PF65 280				

KM# 61 1/5 CROWN

6.22 g., 0.9999 Gold 0.200 oz. AGW, 22 mm. **Ruler:** Elizabeth II **Series:** Barcelona Olympics **Obv:** Crowned bust right **Rev:** Javelin thrower

Date	Mintage	VF20	XF40	MS60	MS63	MS65
1991	Est. 5000	PF65 320				
1992	Est. 5000	PF65 320				

KM# 61a 1/5 CROWN

6.22 g., 0.995 Platinum 0.199 oz. APW **Ruler:** Elizabeth II **Series:** Barcelona Olympics **Obv:** Crowned bust right **Rev:** Javelin thrower

Date	Mintage	VF20	XF40	MS60	MS63	MS65
1991	Est. 1000	PF65 280				

KM# 62 1/5 CROWN

6.22 g., 0.9999 Gold 0.200 oz. AGW, 22 mm. **Ruler:** Elizabeth II **Series:** Barcelona Olympics **Obv:** Crowned bust right **Rev:** Wrestlers

Date	Mintage	VF20	XF40	MS60	MS63	MS65
1991	—	PF65 320				
1992	Est. 5000	PF65 320				

KM# 62a 1/5 CROWN

6.22 g., 0.995 Platinum 0.199 oz. APW **Ruler:** Elizabeth II **Series:** Barcelona Olympics **Obv:** Crowned bust right **Rev:** Wrestlers

Date	Mintage	VF20	XF40	MS60	MS63	MS65
1991	Est. 1000	PF65 280				

KM# 63 1/5 CROWN

6.22 g., 0.9999 Gold 0.200 oz. AGW, 22 mm. **Ruler:** Elizabeth II **Series:** Barcelona Olympics **Obv:** Crowned bust right **Rev:** Boxers

Date	Mintage	VF20	XF40	MS60	MS63	MS65
1991	Est. 5000	PF65 320				
1992	Est. 5000	PF65 320				

KM# 63a 1/5 CROWN

6.22 g., 0.995 Platinum 0.199 oz. APW **Ruler:** Elizabeth II **Series:** Barcelona Olympics **Obv:** Crowned bust right **Rev:** Boxers

Date	Mintage	VF20	XF40	MS60	MS63	MS65
1991	Est. 1000	PF65 280				

KM# 64 1/5 CROWN

6.22 g., 0.9999 Gold 0.200 oz. AGW, 22 mm. **Ruler:** Elizabeth II **Series:** Barcelona Olympics **Obv:** Crowned bust right **Rev:** Long jumper

Date	Mintage	VF20	XF40	MS60	MS63	MS65
1991	Est. 5000	PF65 320				
1992	Est. 5000	PF65 320				

KM# 64a 1/5 CROWN

6.22 g., 0.995 Platinum 0.199 oz. APW **Ruler:** Elizabeth II **Series:** Barcelona Olympics **Obv:** Crowned bust right **Rev:** Long jumper

Date	Mintage	VF20	XF40	MS60	MS63	MS65
1991	Est. 1000	PF65 280				

KM# 65 1/5 CROWN

6.22 g., 0.9999 Gold 0.200 oz. AGW, 22 mm. **Ruler:** Elizabeth II **Series:** Barcelona Olympics **Obv:** Crowned bust right **Rev:** Olympic victor

Date	Mintage	VF20	XF40	MS60	MS63	MS65
1991	Est. 5000	PF65 320				
1992	—	PF65 320				

KM# 65a 1/5 CROWN

6.22 g., 0.995 Platinum 0.199 oz. APW **Ruler:** Elizabeth II **Series:** Barcelona Olympics **Obv:** Crowned bust right **Rev:** Olympic victor

Date	Mintage	VF20	XF40	MS60	MS63	MS65
1991	Est. 1000	PF65 280				

KM# 126 1/5 CROWN

6.22 g., 0.9999 Gold 0.200 oz. AGW, 22 mm. **Ruler:** Elizabeth II **Rev:** Japanese Royal Wedding **Note:** Similar to 1/2 Crown, KM#127.

Date	Mintage	VF20	XF40	MS60	MS63	MS65
1993	Est. 10000	PF65 320				

KM# 150 1/5 CROWN

6.22 g., 0.9999 Gold 0.200 oz. AGW **Ruler:** Elizabeth II **Series:** Preserve Planet Earth **Subject:** Cetiosaurus **Obv:** Crowned bust right **Rev:** Long-necked dinosaur

Date	Mintage	VF20	XF40	MS60	MS63	MS65
1993	Est. 5000	PF65 320				

KM# 152 1/5 CROWN
6.22 g., 0.9999 Gold 0.200 oz. AGW, 22 mm. **Ruler:** Elizabeth II **Series:** Preserve Planet Earth **Subject:** Stegosaurus **Obv:** Crowned bust right **Rev:** Dinosaur with pointed plates along spine

Date	Mintage	VF20	XF40	MS60	MS63	MS65
1993	Est. 5000	PF65 320				

KM# 153 1/5 CROWN
6.22 g., 0.9999 Gold 0.200 oz. AGW, 22 mm. **Ruler:** Elizabeth II **Series:** WWII Warships **Obv:** Crowned bust right **Rev:** USS Philadelphia

Date	Mintage	VF20	XF40	MS60	MS63	MS65
1993	Est. 5000	PF65 320				

KM# 154 1/5 CROWN
6.22 g., 0.9999 Gold 0.200 oz. AGW, 22 mm. **Ruler:** Elizabeth II **Series:** WWII Warships **Obv:** Crowned bust right **Rev:** USS McLanahan

Date	Mintage	VF20	XF40	MS60	MS63	MS65
1993	Est. 5000	PF65 320				

KM# 155 1/5 CROWN
6.22 g., 0.9999 Gold 0.200 oz. AGW, 22 mm. **Ruler:** Elizabeth II **Series:** WWII Warships **Obv:** Crowned bust right **Rev:** HNLMS Isaac Sweers

Date	Mintage	VF20	XF40	MS60	MS63	MS65
1993	Est. 5000	PF65 320				

KM# 156 1/5 CROWN
6.22 g., 0.9999 Gold 0.200 oz. AGW, 22 mm. **Ruler:** Elizabeth II **Series:** WWII Warships **Obv:** Crowned bust right **Rev:** USS Weehawken

Date	Mintage	VF20	XF40	MS60	MS63	MS65
1993	—	PF65 320				

KM# 157 1/5 CROWN
6.22 g., 0.9999 Gold 0.200 oz. AGW, 22 mm. **Ruler:** Elizabeth II **Series:** WWII Warships **Obv:** Crowned bust right **Rev:** HMS Warspite

Date	Mintage	VF20	XF40	MS60	MS63	MS65
1993	—	PF65 320				

KM# 158 1/5 CROWN
6.22 g., 0.9999 Gold 0.200 oz. AGW, 22 mm. **Ruler:** Elizabeth II **Series:** WWII Warships **Obv:** Crowned bust right **Rev:** HMS Hood

Date	Mintage	VF20	XF40	MS60	MS63	MS65
1993	—	PF65 320				

KM# 159 1/5 CROWN
6.22 g., 0.9999 Gold 0.200 oz. AGW, 22 mm. **Ruler:** Elizabeth II **Series:** WWII Warships **Obv:** Crowned bust right **Rev:** HMS Penelope

Date	Mintage	VF20	XF40	MS60	MS63	MS65
1993	Est. 5000	PF65 320				

KM# 160 1/5 CROWN
6.22 g., 0.9999 Gold 0.200 oz. AGW, 22 mm. **Ruler:** Elizabeth II **Series:** WWII Warships **Obv:** Crowned bust right **Rev:** HMCS Prescott

Date	Mintage	VF20	XF40	MS60	MS63	MS65
1993	Est. 5000	PF65 320				

KM# 161 1/5 CROWN
6.22 g., 0.9999 Gold 0.200 oz. AGW, 22 mm. **Ruler:** Elizabeth II **Series:** WWII Warships **Obv:** Crowned bust right **Rev:** HMS Ark Royal

Date	Mintage	VF20	XF40	MS60	MS63	MS65
1993	Est. 5000	PF65 320				

KM# 162 1/5 CROWN
6.22 g., 0.9999 Gold 0.200 oz. AGW, 22 mm. **Ruler:** Elizabeth II **Series:** WWII Warships **Obv:** Crowned bust right **Rev:** USS Gleaves

Date	Mintage	VF20	XF40	MS60	MS63	MS65
1993	Est. 5000	PF65 320				

KM# 163 1/5 CROWN
6.22 g., 0.9999 Gold 0.200 oz. AGW, 22 mm. **Ruler:** Elizabeth II **Series:** WWII Warships **Obv:** Crowned bust right **Rev:** HMAS Waterhen

Date	Mintage	VF20	XF40	MS60	MS63	MS65
1993	—	PF65 320				

KM# 164 1/5 CROWN
6.22 g., 0.9999 Gold 0.200 oz. AGW, 22 mm. **Ruler:** Elizabeth II **Series:** WWII Warships **Obv:** Crowned bust right **Rev:** FSS Savorgnan de Brazza

Date	Mintage	VF20	XF40	MS60	MS63	MS65
1993	Est. 5000	PF65 320				

KM# 165 1/5 CROWN
6.22 g., 0.9999 Gold 0.200 oz. AGW, 22 mm. **Ruler:** Elizabeth II **Series:** House of Stuart **Subject:** Queen Anne, 1702-1714 **Obv:** Young bust right **Rev:** Bust left

Date	Mintage	VF20	XF40	MS60	MS63	MS65
1993	—	PF65 320				

KM# 166 1/5 CROWN
6.22 g., 0.9999 Gold 0.200 oz. AGW, 22 mm. **Ruler:** Elizabeth II **Series:** House of Hanover **Subject:** King George I, 1714-1727 **Obv:** Young bust right **Rev:** Laureate bust right

Date	Mintage	VF20	XF40	MS60	MS63	MS65
1993	Est. 5000	PF65 320				

KM# 167 1/5 CROWN
6.22 g., 0.9999 Gold 0.200 oz. AGW, 22 mm. **Ruler:** Elizabeth II **Series:** House of Hanover **Subject:** King George II, 1727-1760 **Obv:** Young bust right **Rev:** Bust left

Date	Mintage	VF20	XF40	MS60	MS63	MS65
1993	Est. 5000	PF65 320				

KM# 168 1/5 CROWN
6.22 g., 0.9999 Gold 0.200 oz. AGW, 22 mm. **Ruler:** Elizabeth II **Series:** House of Hanover **Subject:** King George III, 1760-1820 **Obv:** Young bust right **Rev:** Bust right

Date	Mintage	VF20	XF40	MS60	MS63	MS65
1993	—	PF65 320				

KM# 169 1/5 CROWN
6.22 g., 0.9999 Gold 0.200 oz. AGW, 22 mm. **Ruler:** Elizabeth II **Series:** House of Hanover **Subject:** King George IV, 1820-1830 **Obv:** Young bust right **Rev:** Bust left

Date	Mintage	VF20	XF40	MS60	MS63	MS65
1993	Est. 5000	PF65 320				

KM# 170 1/5 CROWN
6.22 g., 0.9999 Gold 0.200 oz. AGW, 22 mm. **Ruler:** Elizabeth II **Series:** House of Hanover **Subject:** King William IV, 1830-1837 **Obv:** Young bust right **Rev:** Bust right

Date	Mintage	VF20	XF40	MS60	MS63	MS65
1993	Est. 5000	PF65 320				

KM# 171 1/5 CROWN
6.22 g., 0.9999 Gold 0.200 oz. AGW, 22 mm. **Ruler:** Elizabeth II **Series:** House of Hanover **Subject:** Queen Victoria, 1837-1901 **Obv:** Young bust right **Rev:** Bust left

Date	Mintage	VF20	XF40	MS60	MS63	MS65
1993	Est. 5000	PF65 320				

KM# 172 1/5 CROWN
6.22 g., 0.9999 Gold 0.200 oz. AGW, 22 mm. **Ruler:** Elizabeth II **Series:** House of Saxe-Coburg **Subject:** King Edward VII, 1901-1910 **Obv:** Young bust right **Rev:** Uniformed bust right

Date	Mintage	VF20	XF40	MS60	MS63	MS65
1993	Est. 5000	PF65 320				

KM# 173 1/5 CROWN
6.22 g., 0.9999 Gold 0.200 oz. AGW, 22 mm. **Ruler:** Elizabeth II **Series:** House of Windsor **Subject:** King George V, 1910-1936 **Obv:** Young bust right **Rev:** Uniformed bust left

Date	Mintage	VF20	XF40	MS60	MS63	MS65
1993	Est. 5000	PF65 320				

KM# 174 1/5 CROWN

6.22 g., 0.9999 Gold 0.200 oz. AGW, 22 mm. **Ruler:** Elizabeth II **Series:** House of Windsor **Subject:** King Edward VIII, 1936 **Obv:** Young bust right **Rev:** Bust left

Date	Mintage	VF20	XF40	MS60	MS63	MS65
1993	Est. 5000	PF65 320				

KM# 175 1/5 CROWN

6.22 g., 0.9999 Gold 0.200 oz. AGW, 22 mm. **Ruler:** Elizabeth II **Series:** House of Windsor **Subject:** King George VI, 1936-1952 **Obv:** Young bust right **Rev:** Bust left

Date	Mintage	VF20	XF40	MS60	MS63	MS65
1993	Est. 5000	PF65 320				

KM# 176 1/5 CROWN

6.22 g., 0.9999 Gold 0.200 oz. AGW, 22 mm. **Ruler:** Elizabeth II **Subject:** 40th Anniversary of Coronation **Obv:** Crowned bust right **Rev:** Queen Elizabeth II bust left

Date	Mintage	VF20	XF40	MS60	MS63	MS65
1993	—	PF65 320				

KM# 181 1/5 CROWN

6.22 g., 0.9999 Gold 0.200 oz. AGW, 22 mm. **Ruler:** Elizabeth II **Series:** International Friendship **Obv:** Crowned bust right **Rev:** Stylized panda

Date	Mintage	VF20	XF40	MS60	MS63	MS65
1993	Est. 5000	PF65 320				

KM# 185 1/5 CROWN

6.22 g., 0.9999 Gold 0.200 oz. AGW, 22 mm. **Ruler:** Elizabeth II **Series:** International Friendship **Obv:** Crowned bust right **Rev:** Natural panda

Date	Mintage	VF20	XF40	MS60	MS63	MS65
1993	—	PF65 320				

KM# 189 1/5 CROWN

6.22 g., 0.9999 Gold 0.200 oz. AGW **Ruler:** Elizabeth II **Series:** International Friendship **Obv:** Crowned bust right **Rev:** General Sikarski portrait above B-24 bomber with Rock of Gibraltar in background

Date	Mintage	VF20	XF40	MS60	MS63	MS65
1993	Est. 5000	PF65 320				

KM# 199 1/5 CROWN

6.21 g., 0.9999 Gold 0.1998 oz. AGW **Ruler:** Elizabeth II **Subject:** Dependent Territories Conference **Obv:** Crowned bust right **Rev:** 7 shields, 2 in center, 5 around with rope loops

Date	Mintage	VF20	XF40	MS60	MS63	MS65
1993	Est. 5000	PF65 320				

KM# 204 1/5 CROWN

6.22 g., 0.9999 Gold 0.200 oz. AGW, 22 mm. **Ruler:** Elizabeth II **Series:** Peter Rabbit Centennial **Subject:** The Tale of Peter Rabbit **Obv:** Crowned bust right **Rev:** Rabbit eating carrots, sparrow on handle

Date	Mintage	VF20	XF40	MS60	MS63	MS65
1993	Est. 5000	PF65 320				

KM# 204a 1/5 CROWN

6.22 g., 0.995 Platinum 0.199 oz. APW **Ruler:** Elizabeth II **Series:** Peter Rabbit Centennial **Subject:** The Tale of Peter Rabbit **Obv:** Crowned bust right **Rev:** Rabbit eating carrots, sparrow on handle

Date	Mintage	VF20	XF40	MS60	MS63	MS65
1993	Est. 5000	PF65 280				

KM# 208 1/5 CROWN

6.22 g., 0.9999 Gold 0.200 oz. AGW, 22 mm. **Ruler:** Elizabeth II **Series:** Peter Rabbit Centennial **Subject:** The Tale of Peter Rabbit **Obv:** Crowned bust right **Rev:** Mrs. Tiggy-Winkel ironing

Date	Mintage	VF20	XF40	MS60	MS63	MS65
1993	Est. 5000	PF65 320				

KM# 212 1/5 CROWN

6.22 g., 0.9999 Gold 0.200 oz. AGW, 22 mm. **Ruler:** Elizabeth II **Series:** Peter Rabbit Centennial **Subject:** The Tale of Peter Rabbit **Obv:** Crowned bust right **Rev:** Jeremy Fisher fishing

Date	Mintage	VF20	XF40	MS60	MS63	MS65
1993	Est. 5000	PF65 320				

KM# 216 1/5 CROWN

6.22 g., 0.9999 Gold 0.200 oz. AGW, 22 mm. **Ruler:** Elizabeth II **Series:** Peter Rabbit Centennial **Subject:** The Tale of Peter Rabbit **Obv:** Crowned bust right **Rev:** Tom Kitten with mother cat

Date	Mintage	VF20	XF40	MS60	MS63	MS65
1993	—	PF65 320				

KM# 220 1/5 CROWN

6.22 g., 0.9999 Gold 0.200 oz. AGW, 22 mm. **Ruler:** Elizabeth II **Series:** Peter Rabbit Centennial **Subject:** The Tale of Peter Rabbit **Obv:** Crowned bust right **Rev:** Benjamin Bunny wearing hat and holding coat

Date	Mintage	VF20	XF40	MS60	MS63	MS65
1993	—	PF65 320				

KM# 224 1/5 CROWN

6.22 g., 0.9999 Gold 0.200 oz. AGW, 22 mm. **Ruler:** Elizabeth II **Series:** Peter Rabbit Centennial **Subject:** The Tale of Peter Rabbit **Obv:** Crowned bust right **Rev:** Jemima Puddle-Duck talking with fox

Date	Mintage	VF20	XF40	MS60	MS63	MS65
1993	Est. 5000	PF65 320				

KM# 643 1/5 CROWN

6.22 g., 0.9999 Gold 0.200 oz. AGW, 22 mm. **Ruler:** Elizabeth II **Series:** XVII Winter Olympics **Obv:** Crowned bust right **Rev:** Figure skaters

Date	Mintage	VF20	XF40	MS60	MS63	MS65
1993	Est. 5000	PF65 320				

KM# 644 1/5 CROWN

6.22 g., 0.9999 Gold 0.200 oz. AGW, 22 mm. **Ruler:** Elizabeth II **Series:** XVII Winter Olympics **Obv:** Crowned bust right **Rev:** Ice hockey

Date	Mintage	VF20	XF40	MS60	MS63	MS65
1993	—	PF65 320				

KM# 645 1/5 CROWN

6.22 g., 0.9999 Gold 0.200 oz. AGW, 22 mm. **Ruler:** Elizabeth II **Series:** XVII Winter Olympics **Obv:** Crowned bust right **Rev:** Bobsledding

Date	Mintage	VF20	XF40	MS60	MS63	MS65
1993	—	PF65 320				

KM# 646 1/5 CROWN

6.22 g., 0.9999 Gold 0.200 oz. AGW, 22 mm. **Ruler:** Elizabeth II **Series:** XVII Winter Olympics **Obv:** Crowned bust right **Rev:** Skiers

Date	Mintage	VF20	XF40	MS60	MS63	MS65
1993	Est. 5000	PF65 320				

KM# 226 1/5 CROWN

6.22 g., 0.9999 Gold 0.200 oz. AGW, 22 mm. **Ruler:** Elizabeth II **Series:** World Cup Soccer **Obv:** Crowned bust right **Rev:** 3 players kicking ball up field

Date	Mintage	VF20	XF40	MS60	MS63	MS65
1994	Est. 5000	PF65 320				

KM# 228 1/5 CROWN

6.22 g., 0.9999 Gold 0.200 oz. AGW, 22 mm. **Ruler:** Elizabeth II **Series:** World Cup Soccer **Obv:** Crowned bust right **Rev:** 2 players facing; 1 kicking and 1 defending

Date	Mintage	VF20	XF40	MS60	MS63	MS65
1994	Est. 5000	PF65 320				

KM# 230 1/5 CROWN

6.22 g., 0.9999 Gold 0.200 oz. AGW, 22 mm. **Ruler:** Elizabeth II **Series:** World Cup Soccer **Obv:** Crowned bust right **Rev:** 2 players; 1 goalie and 1 player trying to score

Date	Mintage	VF20	XF40	MS60	MS63	MS65
1994	Est. 5000	PF65 320				

KM# 232 1/5 CROWN

6.22 g., 0.9999 Gold 0.200 oz. AGW, 22 mm. **Ruler:** Elizabeth II **Series:** World Cup Soccer **Obv:** Crowned bust right **Rev:** 1 player looking up

Date	Mintage	VF20	XF40	MS60	MS63	MS65
1994	Est. 5000	PF65 320				

KM# 234 1/5 CROWN

6.22 g., 0.9999 Gold 0.200 oz. AGW, 22 mm. **Ruler:** Elizabeth II **Series:** World Cup Soccer **Obv:** Crowned bust right **Rev:** 1 player kicking, 1 player running forward

Date	Mintage	VF20	XF40	MS60	MS63	MS65
1994	Est. 5000	PF65 320				

KM# 236 1/5 CROWN

6.22 g., 0.9999 Gold 0.200 oz. AGW, 22 mm. **Ruler:** Elizabeth II **Series:** World Cup Soccer **Obv:** Crowned bust right **Rev:** Player in foreground heading ball to player

Date	Mintage	VF20	XF40	MS60	MS63	MS65
1994	Est. 5000	PF65 320				

KM# 238 1/5 CROWN

6.22 g., 0.9999 Gold 0.200 oz. AGW, 22 mm. **Ruler:** Elizabeth II **Series:** Preserve Planet Earth **Obv:** Crowned bust right **Rev:** Sabre Tooth Tiger

Date	Mintage	VF20	XF40	MS60	MS63	MS65
1994	Est. 5000	PF65 320				

KM# 240 1/5 CROWN

6.22 g., 0.9999 Gold 0.200 oz. AGW, 22 mm. **Ruler:** Elizabeth II **Series:** Preserve Planet Earth **Obv:** Crowned bust right **Rev:** Spanish Eagle flying above island

Date	Mintage	VF20	XF40	MS60	MS63	MS65
1994	Est. 5000	PF65 320				

KM# 242 1/5 CROWN

6.22 g., 0.9999 Gold 0.200 oz. AGW, 22 mm. **Ruler:** Elizabeth II **Series:** Preserve Planet Earth **Obv:** Crowned bust right **Rev:** Three Striped Dolphins

Date	Mintage	VF20	XF40	MS60	MS63	MS65
1994	Est. 5000	PF65 320				

KM# 244 1/5 CROWN

6.22 g., 0.9999 Gold 0.200 oz. AGW, 22 mm. **Ruler:** Elizabeth II **Series:** Preserve Planet Earth **Obv:** Crowned bust right **Rev:** Mother and baby elephants

Date	Mintage	VF20	XF40	MS60	MS63	MS65
1994	—	PF65 320				

KM# 253 1/5 CROWN

6.22 g., 0.9999 Gold 0.200 oz. AGW, 22 mm. **Ruler:** Elizabeth II **Series:** World War II **Obv:** Crowned bust right **Rev:** Maltese convoy of ships

Date	Mintage	VF20	XF40	MS60	MS63	MS65
1994	Est. 5000	PF65 320				

KM# 254 1/5 CROWN

6.22 g., 0.9999 Gold 0.200 oz. AGW, 22 mm. **Ruler:** Elizabeth II **Series:** World War II **Obv:** Crowned bust right **Rev:** Squadron 202 flying, Rock of Gibraltar in background

Date	Mintage	VF20	XF40	MS60	MS63	MS65
1994	—	PF65 320				

KM# 255 1/5 CROWN

6.22 g., 0.9999 Gold 0.200 oz. AGW, 22 mm. **Ruler:** Elizabeth II **Series:** World War II **Obv:** Crowned bust right **Rev:** Admiral Somerville, ship in background

Date	Mintage	VF20	XF40	MS60	MS63	MS65
1994	Est. 5000	PF65 320				

KM# 256 1/5 CROWN

6.22 g., 0.9999 Gold 0.200 oz. AGW, 22 mm. **Ruler:** Elizabeth II **Series:** World War II **Obv:** Crowned bust right **Rev:** Glen Miller and band

Date	Mintage	VF20	XF40	MS60	MS63	MS65
1994	—	PF65 320				

KM# 257 1/5 CROWN

6.22 g., 0.9999 Gold 0.200 oz. AGW, 22 mm. **Ruler:** Elizabeth II **Series:** World War II **Obv:** Crowned bust right **Rev:** King George VI congratulating pilots

Date	Mintage	VF20	XF40	MS60	MS63	MS65
1994	Est. 5000	PF65 320				

KM# 258 1/5 CROWN

6.22 g., 0.9999 Gold 0.200 oz. AGW, 22 mm. **Ruler:** Elizabeth II **Series:** World War II **Obv:** Crowned bust right **Rev:** General Eisenhower, planes and ships in background

Date	Mintage	VF20	XF40	MS60	MS63	MS65
1994	—	PF65 320				

KM# 265 1/5 CROWN

6.22 g., 0.9999 Gold 0.200 oz. AGW, 22 mm. **Ruler:** Elizabeth II **Series:** First Man on Moon **Obv:** Crowned bust right **Rev:** Dr. Wernher von Braun with replica of rocket

Date	Mintage	VF20	XF40	MS60	MS63	MS65
1994	Est. 5000	PF65 320				

KM# 266 1/5 CROWN

6.22 g., 0.9999 Gold 0.200 oz. AGW, 22 mm. **Ruler:** Elizabeth II **Series:** First Man on Moon **Obv:** Crowned bust right **Rev:** Rocket on pad before lift-off

Date	Mintage	VF20	XF40	MS60	MS63	MS65
1994	—	PF65 320				

KM# 267 1/5 CROWN

6.22 g., 0.9999 Gold 0.200 oz. AGW, 22 mm. **Ruler:** Elizabeth II **Series:** First Man on Moon **Obv:** Crowned bust right **Rev:** Recovering space capsule after splashdown

Date	Mintage	VF20	XF40	MS60	MS63	MS65
1994	Est. 5000	PF65 320				

KM# 268 1/5 CROWN

6.22 g., 0.9999 Gold 0.200 oz. AGW, 22 mm. **Ruler:** Elizabeth II **Series:** First Man on Moon **Obv:** Crowned bust right **Rev:** Lunar Module landing on the moon

Date	Mintage	VF20	XF40	MS60	MS63	MS65
1994	Est. 5000	PF65 320				

KM# 269 1/5 CROWN

6.22 g., 0.9999 Gold 0.200 oz. AGW, 22 mm. **Ruler:** Elizabeth II **Series:** First Man on Moon **Obv:** Crowned bust right **Rev:** Astronaut stepping on the moon

Date	Mintage	VF20	XF40	MS60	MS63	MS65
1994	—	PF65 320				

KM# 270 1/5 CROWN

6.22 g., 0.9999 Gold 0.200 oz. AGW, 22 mm. **Ruler:** Elizabeth II **Series:** First Man on Moon **Obv:** Crowned bust right **Rev:** Astronaut setting up flag on the moon

Date	Mintage	VF20	XF40	MS60	MS63	MS65
1994	—	PF65 320				

KM# 277 1/5 CROWN

6.22 g., 0.9999 Gold 0.200 oz. AGW, 22 mm. **Ruler:** Elizabeth II **Series:** Sherlock Holmes **Obv:** Crowned bust right **Rev:** Holmes sitting with pipe in hand

Date	Mintage	VF20	XF40	MS60	MS63	MS65
1994	Est. 5000	PF65 320				

KM# 278 1/5 CROWN

6.22 g., 0.9999 Gold 0.200 oz. AGW, 22 mm. **Ruler:** Elizabeth II **Series:** Sherlock Holmes **Obv:** Crowned bust right **Rev:** Holmes playing violin, Dr. Watson watching

Date	Mintage	VF20	XF40	MS60	MS63	MS65
1994	Est. 5000	PF65 320				

KM# 279 1/5 CROWN

6.22 g., 0.9999 Gold 0.200 oz. AGW, 22 mm. **Ruler:** Elizabeth II **Series:** Sherlock Holmes **Obv:** Crowned bust right **Rev:** People talking before 221 B Baker St.

Date	Mintage	VF20	XF40	MS60	MS63	MS65
1994	Est. 5000	PF65 320				

KM# 280 1/5 CROWN

6.22 g., 0.9999 Gold 0.200 oz. AGW, 22 mm. **Ruler:** Elizabeth II **Series:** Sherlock Holmes **Obv:** Crowned bust right **Rev:** Scene from book "The Empty House"

Date	Mintage	VF20	XF40	MS60	MS63	MS65
1994	Est. 5000	PF65 320				

KM# 281 1/5 CROWN

6.22 g., 0.9999 Gold 0.200 oz. AGW, 22 mm. **Ruler:** Elizabeth II **Series:** Sherlock Holmes **Obv:** Crowned bust right **Rev:** Sailing ship "Mary Celeste"

Date	Mintage	VF20	XF40	MS60	MS63	MS65
1994	Est. 5000	PF65 320				

KM# 282 1/5 CROWN

6.22 g., 0.9999 Gold 0.200 oz. AGW, 22 mm. **Ruler:** Elizabeth II **Series:** Sherlock Holmes **Obv:** Crowned bust right **Rev:** Scene from the "Hound of the Baskervilles"

Date	Mintage	VF20	XF40	MS60	MS63	MS65
1994	Est. 5000	PF65 320				

KM# 283 1/5 CROWN

6.22 g., 0.9999 Gold 0.200 oz. AGW, 22 mm. **Ruler:** Elizabeth II **Series:** Sherlock Holmes **Obv:** Crowned bust right **Rev:** Scene from the "Three Garriders"

Date	Mintage	VF20	XF40	MS60	MS63	MS65
1994	Est. 5000	PF65 320				

KM# 284 1/5 CROWN

6.22 g., 0.9999 Gold 0.200 oz. AGW, 22 mm. **Ruler:** Elizabeth II **Series:** Sherlock Holmes **Obv:** Crowned bust right **Rev:** Scene from the "Final Problem"

Date	Mintage	VF20	XF40	MS60	MS63	MS65
1994	Est. 5000	PF65 320				

KM# 441 1/5 CROWN

6.22 g., 0.9999 Gold 0.200 oz. AGW, 22 mm. **Ruler:** Elizabeth II **Subject:** The Tale of Peter Rabbit **Obv:** Crowned bust right **Rev:** Peter rabbit with four little bunnies

Date	Mintage	VF20	XF40	MS60	MS63	MS65
1994	Est. 10000	PF65 320				

KM# 442 1/5 CROWN

6.22 g., 0.995 Platinum 0.199 oz. APW, 22 mm. **Ruler:** Elizabeth II

Date	Mintage	VF20	XF40	MS60	MS63	MS65
1994	Est. 2500	PF65 280				

KM# 295 1/5 CROWN

6.22 g., 0.9999 Gold 0.200 oz. AGW, 22 mm. **Ruler:** Elizabeth II **Series:** Atlanta Olympics **Obv:** Crowned bust right **Rev:** Long jumpers

Date	Mintage	VF20	XF40	MS60	MS63	MS65
1995	Est. 5000	PF65 320				

KM# 296 1/5 CROWN

6.22 g., 0.9999 Gold 0.200 oz. AGW, 22 mm. **Ruler:** Elizabeth II **Series:** Atlanta Olympics **Obv:** Crowned bust right **Rev:** Discus throwers

Date	Mintage	VF20	XF40	MS60	MS63	MS65
1995	Est. 5000	PF65 320				

KM# 297 1/5 CROWN

6.22 g., 0.9999 Gold 0.200 oz. AGW, 22 mm. **Ruler:** Elizabeth II **Series:** Atlanta Olympics **Obv:** Crowned bust right **Rev:** Relay racers

Date	Mintage	VF20	XF40	MS60	MS63	MS65
1995	Est. 5000	PF65 320				

KM# 298 1/5 CROWN

6.22 g., 0.9999 Gold 0.200 oz. AGW, 22 mm. **Ruler:** Elizabeth II **Series:** Atlanta Olympics **Obv:** Crowned bust right **Rev:** Javelin throwers

Date	Mintage	VF20	XF40	MS60	MS63	MS65
1995	Est. 5000	PF65 320				

KM# 303 1/5 CROWN

6.22 g., 0.9999 Gold 0.200 oz. AGW, 22 mm. **Ruler:** Elizabeth II **Obv:** Crowned bust right **Rev:** Rock of Gibraltar and rising sun

Date	Mintage	VF20	XF40	MS60	MS63	MS65
1995	Est. 5000	PF65 320				

KM# 326 1/5 CROWN

6.22 g., 0.9999 Gold 0.200 oz. AGW, 22 mm. **Ruler:** Elizabeth II **Subject:** The Tale of Peter Rabbit **Obv:** Crowned bust right **Rev:** Peter Rabbit running right

Date	Mintage	VF20	XF40	MS60	MS63	MS65
1995	Est. 5000	PF65 320				

KM# 326a 1/5 CROWN

6.22 g., 0.995 Platinum 0.199 oz. APW **Ruler:** Elizabeth II **Subject:** The Tale of Peter Rabbit **Obv:** Crowned bust right **Rev:** Peter Rabbit running right

Date	Mintage	VF20	XF40	MS60	MS63	MS65
1995	Est. 2500	PF65 280				

KM# 328 1/5 CROWN

6.22 g., 0.9999 Gold 0.200 oz. AGW, 22 mm. **Ruler:** Elizabeth II **Series:** Island Games **Obv:** Crowned bust right **Rev:** Circle of athletes with shield at center

Date	Mintage	VF20	XF40	MS60	MS63	MS65
1995	Est. 5000	PF65 320				

KM# 330 1/5 CROWN

6.22 g., 0.9999 Gold 0.200 oz. AGW, 22 mm. **Ruler:** Elizabeth II **Series:** Island Games **Obv:** Crowned bust right **Rev:** Circle of athletes with shield at center

Date	Mintage	VF20	XF40	MS60	MS63	MS65
1995	Est. 5000	PF65 320				

KM# 342 1/5 CROWN

6.22 g., 0.9999 Gold 0.200 oz. AGW, 22 mm. **Ruler:** Elizabeth II **Series:** Olympics **Obv:** Crowned bust right **Rev:** Tennis player

Date	Mintage	VF20	XF40	MS60	MS63	MS65
1996	Est. 5000	PF65 320				

KM# 343 1/5 CROWN

6.22 g., 0.9999 Gold 0.200 oz. AGW, 22 mm. **Ruler:** Elizabeth II **Series:** Olympics **Obv:** Crowned bust right **Rev:** Wrestlers

Date	Mintage	VF20	XF40	MS60	MS63	MS65
1996	—	PF65 320				

KM# 344 1/5 CROWN

6.22 g., 0.9999 Gold 0.200 oz. AGW, 22 mm. **Ruler:** Elizabeth II **Series:** Olympics **Obv:** Crowned bust right **Rev:** Baseball players

Date	Mintage	VF20	XF40	MS60	MS63	MS65
1996	Est. 5000	PF65 320				

KM# 345 1/5 CROWN

6.22 g., 0.9999 Gold 0.200 oz. AGW, 22 mm. **Ruler:** Elizabeth II **Series:** Olympics **Obv:** Crowned bust right **Rev:** Flame

Date	Mintage	VF20	XF40	MS60	MS63	MS65
1996	Est. 5000	PF65 320				

KM# 346 1/5 CROWN

6.22 g., 0.9999 Gold 0.200 oz. AGW, 22 mm. **Ruler:** Elizabeth II **Series:** Olympics **Obv:** Crowned bust right **Rev:** Volleyball game

Date	Mintage	VF20	XF40	MS60	MS63	MS65
1996	Est. 5000	PF65 320				

KM# 347 1/5 CROWN

6.22 g., 0.9999 Gold 0.200 oz. AGW, 22 mm. **Ruler:** Elizabeth II **Series:** Olympics **Obv:** Crowned bust right **Rev:** Basketball game

Date	Mintage	VF20	XF40	MS60	MS63	MS65
1996	Est. 5000	PF65 320				

KM# 357 1/5 CROWN

6.22 g., 0.9999 Gold 0.200 oz. AGW, 22 mm. **Ruler:** Elizabeth II **Subject:** Nefusat Yehuda Synagogue Renovation **Obv:** Crowned bust right **Rev:** Hebrew symbol, rock, arms and building

Date	Mintage	VF20	XF40	MS60	MS63	MS65
1996	Est. 5000	PF65 320				

KM# 360 1/5 CROWN

6.22 g., 0.9999 Gold 0.200 oz. AGW, 22 mm. **Ruler:** Elizabeth II **Series:** Euro 96 **Rev:** England

Date	Mintage	VF20	XF40	MS60	MS63	MS65
1996	—	PF65 320				

KM# 370 1/5 CROWN

6.22 g., 0.9999 Gold 0.200 oz. AGW, 22 mm. **Ruler:** Elizabeth II **Obv:** Crowned bust right **Rev:** Roses

Date	Mintage	VF20	XF40	MS60	MS63	MS65
1996	Est. 5000	PF65 320				

KM# 370a 1/5 CROWN

6.25 g., 0.995 Platinum 0.200 oz. APW **Ruler:** Elizabeth II **Obv:** Crowned bust right **Rev:** Roses

Date	Mintage	VF20	XF40	MS60	MS63	MS65
1996	Est. 1000	PF65 285				

KM# 379 1/5 CROWN

6.22 g., 0.9999 Gold 0.200 oz. AGW, 22 mm. **Ruler:** Elizabeth II **Series:** Peter Rabbit Centennial **Subject:** The Tale of Peter Rabbit **Obv:** Crowned bust right **Rev:** Peter Rabbit escaping garden

Date	Mintage	VF20	XF40	MS60	MS63	MS65
1996	Est. 7500	PF65 320				

KM# 379a 1/5 CROWN

6.22 g., 0.995 Platinum 0.199 oz. APW **Ruler:** Elizabeth II **Series:** Peter Rabbit Centennial **Subject:** The Tale of Peter Rabbit **Obv:** Crowned bust right **Rev:** Peter Rabbit escaping garden

Date	Mintage	VF20	XF40	MS60	MS63	MS65
1996	Est. 5000	PF65 280				

KM# 384 1/5 CROWN

6.22 g., 0.9999 Gold 0.200 oz. AGW, 22 mm. **Ruler:** Elizabeth II **Series:** Preserve Planet Earth **Obv:** Crowned bust right **Rev:** Shag Birds

Date	Mintage	VF20	XF40	MS60	MS63	MS65
1996	Est. 5000	PF65 320				

KM# 385 1/5 CROWN

6.22 g., 0.9999 Gold 0.200 oz. AGW, 22 mm. **Ruler:** Elizabeth II **Series:** Preserve Planet Earth **Obv:** Crowned bust right **Rev:** Puffins

Date	Mintage	VF20	XF40	MS60	MS63	MS65
1996	Est. 5000	PF65 320				

KM# 392 1/5 CROWN

6.22 g., 0.9999 Gold 0.200 oz. AGW, 22 mm. **Ruler:** Elizabeth II **Series:** Cinema Centennial **Subject:** Grace Kelly - actress, 1929-82 **Obv:** Crowned bust right **Rev:** Bust 3/4 facing, dates

Date	Mintage	VF20	XF40	MS60	MS63	MS65
1996	Est. 5000	PF65 320				

KM# 392a 1/5 CROWN

6.22 g., 0.995 Platinum 0.199 oz. APW **Ruler:** Elizabeth II **Series:** Cinema Centennial **Subject:** Grace Kelly - actress, 1929-82 **Obv:** Crowned bust right **Rev:** Bust 3/4 facing

Date	Mintage	VF20	XF40	MS60	MS63	MS65
1996	Est. 1000	PF65 280				

KM# 397 1/5 CROWN
6.22 g., 0.9999 Gold 0.200 oz. AGW, 22 mm. **Ruler:** Elizabeth II **Series:** Centenary of the Cinema **Subject:** James Dean - actor, 1931-55 **Obv:** Crowned bust right **Rev:** Standing central figure, dates

Date	Mintage	VF20	XF40	MS60	MS63	MS65
1996	Est. 5000	PF65 320				

KM# 397a 1/5 CROWN
6.22 g., 0.995 Platinum 0.199 oz. APW **Ruler:** Elizabeth II **Series:** Centenary of the Cinema **Subject:** James Dean - actor, 1931-55 **Obv:** Crowned bust right **Rev:** Standing central figure, dates

Date	Mintage	VF20	XF40	MS60	MS63	MS65
1996	Est. 1000	PF65 280				

KM# 402 1/5 CROWN
6.22 g., 0.9999 Gold 0.200 oz. AGW, 22 mm. **Ruler:** Elizabeth II **Series:** Centenary of the Cinema **Subject:** Marilyn Monroe - actress, 1926-62 **Obv:** Crowned bust right **Rev:** Bust looking back over shoulder

Date	Mintage	VF20	XF40	MS60	MS63	MS65
1996	Est. 5000	PF65 320				

KM# 402a 1/5 CROWN
6.22 g., 0.995 Platinum 0.199 oz. APW **Ruler:** Elizabeth II **Series:** Centenary of the Cinema **Subject:** Marilyn Monroe - actress, 1926-62 **Obv:** Crowned bust right **Rev:** Bust looking back over shoulder

Date	Mintage	VF20	XF40	MS60	MS63	MS65
1996	Est. 1000	PF65 280				

KM# 407 1/5 CROWN
6.22 g., 0.9999 Gold 0.200 oz. AGW, 22 mm. **Ruler:** Elizabeth II **Series:** Centenary of the Cinema **Subject:** Audrey Hepburn - actress, 1929-93 **Obv:** Crowned bust right **Rev:** Bust 3/4 facing, dates

Date	Mintage	VF20	XF40	MS60	MS63	MS65
1996	Est. 5000	PF65 320				

KM# 407a 1/5 CROWN
6.22 g., 0.995 Platinum 0.199 oz. APW **Ruler:** Elizabeth II **Series:** Centenary of the Cinema **Subject:** Audrey Hepburn - actress, 1929-93 **Obv:** Crowned bust right **Rev:** Bust 3/4 facing, dates

Date	Mintage	VF20	XF40	MS60	MS63	MS65
1996	Est. 1000	PF65 280				

KM# 412 1/5 CROWN
6.22 g., 0.9999 Gold 0.200 oz. AGW, 22 mm. **Ruler:** Elizabeth II **Series:** Centenary of the Cinema **Subject:** Bruce Lee - actor, 1940-73 **Obv:** Crowned bust right **Rev:** Kickboxer and chinese dragon, dates

Date	Mintage	VF20	XF40	MS60	MS63	MS65
1996	Est. 5000	PF65 320				

KM# 417 1/5 CROWN
6.22 g., 0.9999 Gold 0.200 oz. AGW, 22 mm. **Ruler:** Elizabeth II **Series:** Centenary of the Cinema **Subject:** Charlie Chaplan - actor, 1889-1977 **Obv:** Crowned bust right **Rev:** Standing central figure with cane, dates

Date	Mintage	VF20	XF40	MS60	MS63	MS65
1996	Est. 5000	PF65 320				

KM# 422 1/5 CROWN
6.22 g., 0.9999 Gold 0.200 oz. AGW, 22 mm. **Ruler:** Elizabeth II **Series:** Centenary of the Cinema **Subject:** Gone With the Wind **Obv:** Crowned bust right **Rev:** Rhett Butler and Scarlett O'Hara

Date	Mintage	VF20	XF40	MS60	MS63	MS65
1996	—	PF65 320				

KM# 427 1/5 CROWN
6.22 g., 0.9999 Gold 0.200 oz. AGW, 22 mm. **Ruler:** Elizabeth II **Series:** Centenary of the Cinema **Obv:** Crowned bust right **Rev:** The Flintstones

Date	Mintage	VF20	XF40	MS60	MS63	MS65
1996	Est. 5000	PF65 320				

KM# 431 1/5 CROWN
6.22 g., 0.9999 Gold 0.200 oz. AGW, 22 mm. **Ruler:** Elizabeth II **Series:** Duke of Edinburgh Awards Scheme **Obv:** Crowned bust right **Rev:** 7 Events surround central crowned arms

Date	Mintage	VF20	XF40	MS60	MS63	MS65
1996	Est. 5000	PF65 320				

KM# 434 1/5 CROWN
6.22 g., 0.9999 Gold 0.200 oz. AGW, 22 mm. **Ruler:** Elizabeth II **Series:** Duke of Edinburgh Awards Scheme **Obv:** Crowned bust right **Rev:** Cameo above team of horses pulling wagon

Date	Mintage	VF20	XF40	MS60	MS63	MS65
1996	Est. 5000	PF65 320				

KM# 447 1/5 CROWN
6.22 g., 0.9999 Gold 0.200 oz. AGW, 22 mm. **Ruler:** Elizabeth II **Subject:** Lord Buddha **Obv:** Crowned bust right **Rev:** Seated facing figure

Date	Mintage	VF20	XF40	MS60	MS63	MS65
1996	Est. 8000	PF65 320				

KM# 456 1/5 CROWN
6.22 g., 0.9999 Gold 0.200 oz. AGW, 22 mm. **Ruler:** Elizabeth II **Series:** Centenary of the Cinema **Subject:** Wizard of Oz **Obv:** Crowned bust right **Rev:** Wizard of Oz characters

Date	Mintage	VF20	XF40	MS60	MS63	MS65
1996	Est. 5000	PF65 320				

KM# 460 1/5 CROWN
6.22 g., 0.9999 Gold 0.200 oz. AGW, 22 mm. **Ruler:** Elizabeth II **Series:** Centenary of the Cinema **Subject:** Marx Brothers **Obv:** Crowned bust right **Rev:** Three busts 3/4 left

Date	Mintage	VF20	XF40	MS60	MS63	MS65
1996	—	PF65 320				

KM# 464 1/5 CROWN
6.22 g., 0.9999 Gold 0.200 oz. AGW, 22 mm. **Ruler:** Elizabeth II **Series:** Centenary of the Cinema **Subject:** Elvis Presley - actor/entertainer, 1935-77 **Obv:** Crowned bust right **Rev:** Guitar below and behind bust 3/4 left, dates

Date	Mintage	VF20	XF40	MS60	MS63	MS65
1996	Est. 5000	PF65 320				

KM# 468 1/5 CROWN
6.22 g., 0.9999 Gold 0.200 oz. AGW, 22 mm. **Ruler:** Elizabeth II **Series:** Centenary of the Cinema **Subject:** Casablanca **Obv:** Crowned bust right **Rev:** Bogart and Bergman

Date	Mintage	VF20	XF40	MS60	MS63	MS65
1996	—	PF65 320				

KM# 472 1/5 CROWN
6.22 g., 0.9999 Gold 0.200 oz. AGW, 22 mm. **Ruler:** Elizabeth II **Series:** Centenary of the Cinema **Obv:** Crowned bust right **Rev:** E.T.

Date	Mintage	VF20	XF40	MS60	MS63	MS65
1996	Est. 5000	PF65 320				

KM# 476 1/5 CROWN
6.22 g., 0.9999 Gold 0.200 oz. AGW, 22 mm. **Ruler:** Elizabeth II **Series:** Centenary of the Cinema **Subject:** Alfred Hitchcock - Producer/Director, 1899-1980 **Obv:** Crowned bust right **Rev:** Bust facing looking at bird on left shoulder

Date	Mintage	VF20	XF40	MS60	MS63	MS65
1996	Est. 5000	PF65 320				

KM# 513 1/5 CROWN
6.22 g., 0.9999 Gold 0.200 oz. AGW, 22 mm. **Ruler:** Elizabeth II **Obv:** Crowned bust right **Rev:** Peacocks, one with tail spread

Date	Mintage	VF20	XF40	MS60	MS63	MS65
1997	—	PF65 320				

KM# 522 1/5 CROWN
6.22 g., 0.9999 Gold 0.200 oz. AGW, 22 mm. **Ruler:** Elizabeth II **Subject:** The Tale of Peter Rabbit **Obv:** Crowned bust right **Rev:** Standing rabbit 3/4 right

Date	Mintage	VF20	XF40	MS60	MS63	MS65
1997	Est. 10000	PF65 320				

KM# 522a 1/5 CROWN
6.25 g., 0.995 Platinum 0.200 oz. APW **Ruler:** Elizabeth II **Subject:** The Tale of Peter Rabbit **Obv:** Crowned bust right **Rev:** Standing rabbit 3/4 right

Date	Mintage	VF20	XF40	MS60	MS63	MS65
1997	Est. 2500	PF65 285				

KM# 529 1/5 CROWN
6.22 g., 0.9999 Gold 0.200 oz. AGW, 22 mm. **Ruler:** Elizabeth II **Series:** Golden Wedding Anniversary **Subject:** Queen Elizabeth and Prince Philip **Obv:** Crowned bust right **Rev:** Engagement portrait

Date	Mintage	VF20	XF40	MS60	MS63	MS65
1997	Est. 3500	PF65 320				

KM# 531 1/5 CROWN
6.22 g., 0.9999 Gold 0.200 oz. AGW, 22 mm. **Ruler:** Elizabeth II **Series:** Golden Wedding Anniversary **Subject:** Queen Elizabeth and Prince Philip **Obv:** Crowned bust right **Rev:** Queen with her first born, Prince Charles

Date	Mintage	VF20	XF40	MS60	MS63	MS65
1997	Est. 3500	PF65 320				

KM# 533 1/5 CROWN
6.22 g., 0.9999 Gold 0.200 oz. AGW, 22 mm. **Ruler:** Elizabeth II **Series:** Golden Wedding Anniversary **Subject:** Queen Elizabeth and Prince Philip **Obv:** Crowned bust right **Rev:** the Queen, two children and a monkey

Date	Mintage	VF20	XF40	MS60	MS63	MS65
1997	Est. 3500	PF65 320				

KM# 535 1/5 CROWN
6.22 g., 0.9999 Gold 0.200 oz. AGW, 22 mm. **Ruler:** Elizabeth II **Series:** Golden Wedding Anniversary **Subject:** Queen Elizabeth and Prince Philip **Obv:** Crowned bust right **Rev:** Queen and adoring crowd

Date	Mintage	VF20	XF40	MS60	MS63	MS65
1997	Est. 3500	PF65 320				

KM# 539 1/5 CROWN
6.22 g., 0.9999 Gold 0.200 oz. AGW, 22 mm. **Ruler:** Elizabeth II **Obv:** Crowned bust right **Rev:** Peonies

Date	Mintage	VF20	XF40	MS60	MS63	MS65
1997	Est. 5000	PF65 320				

KM# 539a 1/5 CROWN
6.22 g., 0.995 Platinum 0.199 oz. APW **Ruler:** Elizabeth II **Obv:** Crowned bust right **Rev:** Peonies

Date	Mintage	VF20	XF40	MS60	MS63	MS65
1997	Est. 1000	PF65 280				

KM# 543 1/5 CROWN
6.22 g., 0.9999 Gold 0.200 oz. AGW, 22 mm. **Ruler:** Elizabeth II **Subject:** Nefertiti **Obv:** Crowned bust right **Rev:** Head right

Date	Mintage	VF20	XF40	MS60	MS63	MS65
1997	Est. 5000	PF65 320				

KM# 543a 1/5 CROWN
6.22 g., 0.995 Platinum 0.199 oz. APW **Ruler:** Elizabeth II **Subject:** Nefertiti **Obv:** Crowned bust right **Rev:** Head right

Date	Mintage	VF20	XF40	MS60	MS63	MS65
1997	Est. 1000	PF65 280				

KM# 547 1/5 CROWN
6.22 g., 0.9999 Gold 0.200 oz. AGW, 22 mm. **Ruler:** Elizabeth II **Subject:** Cleopatra **Obv:** Crowned bust right **Rev:** Head facing

Date	Mintage	VF20	XF40	MS60	MS63	MS65
1997	Est. 5000	PF65 320				

KM# 547a 1/5 CROWN
6.22 g., 0.995 Platinum 0.199 oz. APW **Ruler:** Elizabeth II **Subject:** Cleopatra **Obv:** Crowned bust right **Rev:** Head facing

Date	Mintage	VF20	XF40	MS60	MS63	MS65
1997	Est. 1000	PF65 280				

KM# 551 1/5 CROWN
6.22 g., 0.9999 Gold 0.200 oz. AGW, 22 mm. **Ruler:** Elizabeth II **Subject:** Europa **Obv:** Crowned bust right **Rev:** Head 3/4 left

Date	Mintage	VF20	XF40	MS60	MS63	MS65
1997	—	PF65 320				

KM# 551a 1/5 CROWN
6.22 g., 0.995 Platinum 0.199 oz. APW **Ruler:** Elizabeth II **Subject:** Europa **Obv:** Crowned bust right **Rev:** Head 3/4 left

Date	Mintage	VF20	XF40	MS60	MS63	MS65
1997	Est. 1000	PF65 280				

KM# 555 1/5 CROWN
6.22 g., 0.9999 Gold 0.200 oz. AGW, 22 mm. **Ruler:** Elizabeth II **Subject:** Liberty **Obv:** Crowned bust right **Rev:** Laureate head right

Date	Mintage	VF20	XF40	MS60	MS63	MS65
1997	—	PF65 320				

KM# 555a 1/5 CROWN
6.22 g., 0.995 Platinum 0.199 oz. APW **Ruler:** Elizabeth II **Subject:** Liberty **Obv:** Crowned bust right **Rev:** Laureate head right

Date	Mintage	VF20	XF40	MS60	MS63	MS65
1997	Est. 1000	PF65 280				

KM# 562 1/5 CROWN
6.22 g., 0.9999 Gold 0.200 oz. AGW, 22 mm. **Ruler:** Elizabeth II **Series:** Queen's Birthday **Obv:** Crowned bust right **Rev:** Queen on horseback left

Date	Mintage	VF20	XF40	MS60	MS63	MS65
1997	Est. 5000	PF65 320				

KM# 563 1/5 CROWN
6.22 g., 0.9999 Gold 0.200 oz. AGW, 22 mm. **Ruler:** Elizabeth II **Series:** Queen's Birthday **Obv:** Crowned bust right **Rev:** Queen on horseback returning salute

Date	Mintage	VF20	XF40	MS60	MS63	MS65
1997	—	PF65 320				

KM# 564 1/5 CROWN
6.22 g., 0.9999 Gold 0.200 oz. AGW, 22 mm. **Ruler:** Elizabeth II **Series:** Queen's Birthday **Obv:** Crowned bust right **Rev:** Trooping the Colors scene, cameo above

Date	Mintage	VF20	XF40	MS60	MS63	MS65
1997	Est. 5000	PF65 320				

KM# 565 1/5 CROWN
6.22 g., 0.9999 Gold 0.200 oz. AGW, 22 mm. **Ruler:** Elizabeth II **Series:** Queen's Birthday **Obv:** Crowned bust right **Rev:** Gurkha troops with dragons

Date	Mintage	VF20	XF40	MS60	MS63	MS65
1997	Est. 5000	PF65 320				

KM# 570 1/5 CROWN
6.22 g., 0.9999 Gold 0.200 oz. AGW, 22 mm. **Ruler:** Elizabeth II **Subject:** The New Mosque **Obv:** Crowned bust right **Rev:** Two cavalry riders with mosque in background

Date	Mintage	VF20	XF40	MS60	MS63	MS65
1997	Est. 5000	PF65 320				

KM# 635 1/5 CROWN
6.22 g., 0.9999 Gold 0.200 oz. AGW, 22 mm. **Ruler:** Elizabeth II **Subject:** Winter Olympics Japan **Obv:** Crowned bust right **Rev:** Speed skater and "Bullet Train"

Date	Mintage	VF20	XF40	MS60	MS63	MS65
1998	Est. 5000	PF65 320				

KM# 637 1/5 CROWN
6.22 g., 0.9999 Gold 0.200 oz. AGW, 22 mm. **Ruler:** Elizabeth II **Series:** Winter Olympics Japan **Obv:** Crowned bust right **Rev:** Ski jumper and Buddha

Date	Mintage	VF20	XF40	MS60	MS63	MS65
1998	Est. 5000	PF65 320				

KM# 639 1/5 CROWN
6.22 g., 0.9999 Gold 0.200 oz. AGW, 22 mm. **Ruler:** Elizabeth II **Series:** Winter Olympics Japan **Obv:** Crowned bust right **Rev:** Cross-country skiers

Date	Mintage	VF20	XF40	MS60	MS63	MS65
1998	—	PF65 320				

KM# 641 1/5 CROWN
6.22 g., 0.9999 Gold 0.200 oz. AGW, 22 mm. **Ruler:** Elizabeth II **Series:** Winter Olympics Japan **Obv:** Crowned bust right **Rev:** Slalom skier and Zenkoji temple

Date	Mintage	VF20	XF40	MS60	MS63	MS65
1998	Est. 5000	PF65 320				

KM# 653 1/5 CROWN

6.22 g., 0.9999 Gold 0.200 oz. AGW, 22 mm. **Ruler:** Elizabeth II **Subject:** The Tale of Peter Rabbit **Obv:** Crowned bust right **Rev:** Standing rabbit facing with sparrow at left

Date	Mintage	VF20	XF40	MS60	MS63	MS65
1998	Est. 10000	PF65 320				

KM# 653a 1/5 CROWN

6.22 g., 0.995 Platinum 0.199 oz. APW **Ruler:** Elizabeth II **Subject:** The Tale of Peter Rabbit **Obv:** Crowned bust right **Rev:** Standing rabbit facing with sparrow at left

Date	Mintage	VF20	XF40	MS60	MS63	MS65
1998	—	PF65 280				

KM# 659 1/5 CROWN

6.22 g., 0.9999 Gold 0.200 oz. AGW, 22 mm. **Ruler:** Elizabeth II **Obv:** Crowned bust right **Rev:** Chrysanthemum

Date	Mintage	VF20	XF40	MS60	MS63	MS65
1998	—	PF65 320				

KM# 659a 1/5 CROWN

6.22 g., 0.995 Platinum 0.199 oz. APW **Ruler:** Elizabeth II **Obv:** Crowned bust right **Rev:** Chrysanthemum

Date	Mintage	VF20	XF40	MS60	MS63	MS65
1998	Est. 1000	PF65 280				

KM# 671 1/5 CROWN

6.22 g., 0.9999 Gold 0.200 oz. AGW, 22 mm. **Ruler:** Elizabeth II **Subject:** Juno **Obv:** Crowned bust right **Rev:** Head 3/4 facing

Date	Mintage	VF20	XF40	MS60	MS63	MS65
1998	Est. 5000	PF65 320				

KM# 671a 1/5 CROWN

6.22 g., 0.995 Platinum 0.199 oz. APW **Ruler:** Elizabeth II **Subject:** Juno **Obv:** Crowned bust right **Rev:** Head 3/4 facing

Date	Mintage	VF20	XF40	MS60	MS63	MS65
1998	Est. 1000	PF65 280				

KM# 672 1/5 CROWN

6.22 g., 0.9999 Gold 0.200 oz. AGW, 22 mm. **Ruler:** Elizabeth II **Subject:** Athena **Obv:** Crowned bust right **Rev:** Helmeted head right

Date	Mintage	VF20	XF40	MS60	MS63	MS65
1998	Est. 5000	PF65 320				

KM# 672a 1/5 CROWN

6.22 g., 0.995 Platinum 0.199 oz. APW **Ruler:** Elizabeth II **Subject:** Athena **Obv:** Crowned bust right **Rev:** Helmeted head right

Date	Mintage	VF20	XF40	MS60	MS63	MS65
1998	Est. 1000	PF65 280				

KM# 673 1/5 CROWN

6.22 g., 0.9999 Gold 0.200 oz. AGW, 22 mm. **Ruler:** Elizabeth II **Subject:** Arethusa **Obv:** Crowned bust right **Rev:** Head left with dolphins

Date	Mintage	VF20	XF40	MS60	MS63	MS65
1998	Est. 5000	PF65 320				

KM# 673a 1/5 CROWN

6.22 g., 0.995 Platinum 0.199 oz. APW **Ruler:** Elizabeth II **Subject:** Arethusa **Obv:** Crowned bust right **Rev:** Head left with dolphins

Date	Mintage	VF20	XF40	MS60	MS63	MS65
1998	Est. 1000	PF65 280				

KM# 680 1/5 CROWN

6.22 g., 0.9999 Gold 0.200 oz. AGW, 22 mm. **Ruler:** Elizabeth II **Subject:** Paddington Bear **Obv:** Crowned bust right **Rev:** Bear with suitcase

Date	Mintage	VF20	XF40	MS60	MS63	MS65
1998	—	PF65 320				

KM# 680a 1/5 CROWN

6.22 g., 0.995 Platinum 0.199 oz. APW **Ruler:** Elizabeth II **Subject:** Paddington Bear **Obv:** Crowned bust right **Rev:** Bear with suitcase

Date	Mintage	VF20	XF40	MS60	MS63	MS65
1998	Est. 2000	PF65 280				

KM# 683 1/5 CROWN

6.22 g., 0.9999 Gold 0.200 oz. AGW, 22 mm. **Ruler:** Elizabeth II **Subject:** World Cup France 1998 **Obv:** Crowned bust right **Rev:** Goalie, map of Europe

Date	Mintage	VF20	XF40	MS60	MS63	MS65
1998	Est. 5000	PF65 320				

KM# 684 1/5 CROWN

6.22 g., 0.9999 Gold 0.200 oz. AGW, 22 mm. **Ruler:** Elizabeth II **Subject:** World Cup France 1998 **Obv:** Crowned bust right **Rev:** Player kicking to left

Date	Mintage	VF20	XF40	MS60	MS63	MS65
1998	Est. 5000	PF65 320				

KM# 685 1/5 CROWN

6.22 g., 0.9999 Gold 0.200 oz. AGW, 22 mm. **Ruler:** Elizabeth II **Subject:** World Cup France 1998 **Obv:** Crowned bust right **Rev:** Player dribbling ball

Date	Mintage	VF20	XF40	MS60	MS63	MS65
1998	Est. 5000	PF65 320				

KM# 686 1/5 CROWN

6.22 g., 0.9999 Gold 0.200 oz. AGW, 22 mm. **Ruler:** Elizabeth II **Subject:** World Cup France 1998 **Obv:** Crowned bust right **Rev:** Two players, map of Europe

Date	Mintage	VF20	XF40	MS60	MS63	MS65
1998	Est. 5000	PF65 320				

KM# 731 1/5 CROWN

6.22 g., 0.9999 Gold 0.200 oz. AGW, 22 mm. **Ruler:** Elizabeth II **Obv:** Crowned bust right **Rev:** Cupid with hologram heart

Date	Mintage	VF20	XF40	MS60	MS63	MS65
1998	Est. 5000	PF65 320				

KM# 741 1/5 CROWN

6.22 g., 0.9999 Gold 0.200 oz. AGW, 22 mm. **Ruler:** Elizabeth II **Subject:** Year of the Ocean **Obv:** Crowned bust right **Rev:** Polar bear and walrus

Date	Mintage	VF20	XF40	MS60	MS63	MS65
1998	Est. 5000	PF65 320				

KM# 742 1/5 CROWN

6.22 g., 0.9999 Gold 0.200 oz. AGW, 22 mm. **Ruler:** Elizabeth II **Subject:** Year of the Ocean **Obv:** Crowned bust right **Rev:** Seals and penguins

Date	Mintage	VF20	XF40	MS60	MS63	MS65
1998	Est. 5000	PF65 320				

KM# 743 1/5 CROWN

6.22 g., 0.9999 Gold 0.200 oz. AGW, 22 mm. **Ruler:** Elizabeth II **Subject:** Year of the Ocean **Obv:** Crowned bust right **Rev:** Sea cow with calf

Date	Mintage	VF20	XF40	MS60	MS63	MS65
1998	Est. 5000	PF65 320				

KM# 744 1/5 CROWN

6.22 g., 0.9999 Gold 0.200 oz. AGW, 22 mm. **Ruler:** Elizabeth II **Subject:** Year of the Ocean **Obv:** Crowned bust right **Rev:** Surfer

Date	Mintage	VF20	XF40	MS60	MS63	MS65
1998	—	PF65 320				

KM# 767 1/5 CROWN

6.22 g., 0.9999 Gold 0.200 oz. AGW, 22 mm. **Ruler:** Elizabeth II **Subject:** Gibraltar Regiment New Colours **Obv:** Crowned bust right **Rev:** Soldiers presenting keys

Date	Mintage	VF20	XF40	MS60	MS63	MS65
1998	Est. 5000	PF65 320				

KM# 798 1/5 CROWN

6.22 g., 0.9999 Gold 0.200 oz. AGW, 22 mm. **Ruler:** Elizabeth II **Series:** The World At War **Subject:** General D.D. Eisenhower **Obv:** Crowned bust right **Rev:** Bust facing and North African invasion scene

Date	Mintage	VF20	XF40	MS60	MS63	MS65
1998	Est. 5000	PF65 320				

KM# 781.1 1/5 CROWN

6.22 g., 0.9999 Gold 0.200 oz. AGW, 22 mm. **Ruler:** Elizabeth II **Subject:** 1999 Year of the Rabbit **Obv:** Crowned bust right **Rev:** Rabbit reading, sparrow, Chinese characters

Date	Mintage	VF20	XF40	MS60	MS63	MS65
1999	Est. 3500	PF65 320				

KM# 781.1a 1/5 CROWN

6.22 g., 0.995 Platinum 0.199 oz. APW **Ruler:** Elizabeth II **Subject:** 1999 Year of the Rabbit **Obv:** Crowned bust right **Rev:** Rabbit reading, sparrow, Chinese characters

Date	Mintage	VF20	XF40	MS60	MS63	MS65
1999	Est. 1500	PF65 280				

KM# 781.2 1/5 CROWN

6.22 g., 0.9999 Gold 0.200 oz. AGW, 22 mm. **Ruler:** Elizabeth II **Obv:** Crowned bust right **Rev:** Rabbit reading, sparrow, without Chinese characters

Date	Mintage	VF20	XF40	MS60	MS63	MS65
1999	Inc. above	PF65 320				

KM# 781.2a 1/5 CROWN

6.22 g., 0.995 Platinum 0.199 oz. APW **Ruler:** Elizabeth II **Obv:** Crowned bust right **Rev:** Rabbit reading, sparrow; without Chinese characters

Date	Mintage	VF20	XF40	MS60	MS63	MS65
1999	Inc. above	PF65 280				

KM# 784 1/5 CROWN

6.22 g., 0.9999 Gold 0.200 oz. AGW, 22 mm. **Ruler:** Elizabeth II **Series:** Summer Olympics - Sydney **Obv:** Crowned bust right **Rev:** Broad jumper with kangaroo

Date	Mintage	VF20	XF40	MS60	MS63	MS65
1999	—	PF65 320				

KM# 786 1/5 CROWN

6.22 g., 0.9999 Gold 0.200 oz. AGW, 22 mm. **Ruler:** Elizabeth II **Series:** Summer Olympics - Sydney **Obv:** Crowned bust right **Rev:** Sailboats and platypus

Date	Mintage	VF20	XF40	MS60	MS63	MS65
1999	Est. 5000	PF65 320				

KM# 788 1/5 CROWN

6.22 g., 0.9999 Gold 0.200 oz. AGW, 22 mm. **Ruler:** Elizabeth II **Series:** Summer Olympics - Sydney **Obv:** Crowned bust right **Rev:** Swimmer and koala bear

Date	Mintage	VF20	XF40	MS60	MS63	MS65
1999	—	PF65 320				

KM# 790 1/5 CROWN

6.22 g., 0.9999 Gold 0.200 oz. AGW, 22 mm. **Ruler:** Elizabeth II **Series:** Summer Olympics - Sydney **Obv:** Crowned bust right **Rev:** Two oarsmen and cockatoos

Date	Mintage	VF20	XF40	MS60	MS63	MS65
1999	Est. 5000	PF65 320				

KM# 792 1/5 CROWN

6.22 g., 0.9999 Gold 0.200 oz. AGW, 22 mm. **Ruler:** Elizabeth II **Series:** Summer Olympics - Sydney **Obv:** Crowned bust right **Rev:** Man with torch and dog

Date	Mintage	VF20	XF40	MS60	MS63	MS65
1999	—	PF65 320				

KM# 794 1/5 CROWN

6.22 g., 0.9999 Gold 0.200 oz. AGW, 22 mm. **Ruler:** Elizabeth II **Series:** Summer Olympics - Sydney **Obv:** Crowned bust right **Rev:** Torch runner, portrait of Aborigini and Ayers Rock

Date	Mintage	VF20	XF40	MS60	MS63	MS65
1999	Est. 5000	PF65 320				

KM# 796 1/5 CROWN

6.22 g., 0.9999 Gold 0.200 oz. AGW, 22 mm. **Ruler:** Elizabeth II **Subject:** Millennium 2000 **Obv:** Head with tiara right **Rev:** Sundial, digital clock face, candle and traditional clock face

Date	Mintage	VF20	XF40	MS60	MS63	MS65
1999	Est. 5000	PF65 320				

KM# 800 1/5 CROWN

6.22 g., 0.9999 Gold 0.200 oz. AGW, 22 mm. **Ruler:** Elizabeth II **Subject:** King Alfred the Great, 871-899 **Obv:** Crowned bust right **Rev:** Crowned bust left

Date	Mintage	VF20	XF40	MS60	MS63	MS65
1999	Est. 5000	PF65 320				

KM# 802 1/5 CROWN
6.22 g., 0.9999 Gold 0.200 oz. AGW, 22 mm. **Ruler:** Elizabeth II **Subject:** King Canute, 1016-1035 **Obv:** Crowned bust right **Rev:** Crowned bust left

Date	Mintage	VF20	XF40	MS60	MS63	MS65
1999	Est. 5000	PF65 320				

KM# 804 1/5 CROWN
6.22 g., 0.9999 Gold 0.200 oz. AGW, 22 mm. **Ruler:** Elizabeth II **Subject:** King Edward the Confessor, 1042-1066 **Obv:** Crowned bust right **Rev:** Crowned bust left

Date	Mintage	VF20	XF40	MS60	MS63	MS65
1999	Est. 5000	PF65 320				

KM# 806 1/5 CROWN
6.22 g., 0.9999 Gold 0.200 oz. AGW, 22 mm. **Ruler:** Elizabeth II **Series:** House of Normandy **Subject:** King William I, 1066-1087 **Obv:** Crowned bust right **Rev:** Crowned bust left

Date	Mintage	VF20	XF40	MS60	MS63	MS65
1999	Est. 5000	PF65 320				

KM# 808 1/5 CROWN
6.22 g., 0.9999 Gold 0.200 oz. AGW, 22 mm. **Ruler:** Elizabeth II **Series:** House of Plantagenet **Subject:** King Richard I, 1189-1199 **Obv:** Crowned bust right **Rev:** Crowned bust right

Date	Mintage	VF20	XF40	MS60	MS63	MS65
1999	Est. 5000	PF65 320				

KM# 810 1/5 CROWN
6.22 g., 0.9999 Gold 0.200 oz. AGW, 22 mm. **Ruler:** Elizabeth II **Series:** House of Plantagenet **Subject:** King John, 1199-1216 **Obv:** Crowned bust right **Rev:** Crowned bust left

Date	Mintage	VF20	XF40	MS60	MS63	MS65
1999	—	PF65 320				

KM# 812 1/5 CROWN
6.22 g., 0.9999 Gold 0.200 oz. AGW, 22 mm. **Ruler:** Elizabeth II **Series:** House of Lancaster **Subject:** King Henry V, 1413-1422 **Obv:** Crowned bust right **Rev:** Bust right

Date	Mintage	VF20	XF40	MS60	MS63	MS65
1999	—	PF65 320				

KM# 814 1/5 CROWN
6.22 g., 0.9999 Gold 0.200 oz. AGW, 22 mm. **Ruler:** Elizabeth II **Series:** House of York **Subject:** King Richard III, 1483-1485 **Obv:** Crowned bust right **Rev:** Bust with hat right

Date	Mintage	VF20	XF40	MS60	MS63	MS65
1999	Est. 5000	PF65 320				

KM# 816 1/5 CROWN
6.22 g., 0.9999 Gold 0.200 oz. AGW, 22 mm. **Ruler:** Elizabeth II **Series:** House of Tudor **Subject:** King Henry VIII, 1509-1547 **Obv:** Crowned bust right **Rev:** Bust with hat right

Date	Mintage	VF20	XF40	MS60	MS63	MS65
1999	—	PF65 320				

KM# 818 1/5 CROWN
6.22 g., 0.9999 Gold 0.200 oz. AGW, 22 mm. **Ruler:** Elizabeth II **Series:** House of Tudor **Subject:** Queen Elizabeth, 1558-1603 **Obv:** Crowned bust right **Rev:** Crowned bust with high ruffled collar left

Date	Mintage	VF20	XF40	MS60	MS63	MS65
1999	Est. 5000	PF65 320				

KM# 820 1/5 CROWN
6.22 g., 0.9999 Gold 0.200 oz. AGW, 22 mm. **Ruler:** Elizabeth II **Series:** House of Stuart **Subject:** King Charles I, 1625-1649 **Obv:** Crowned bust right **Rev:** Bust right

Date	Mintage	VF20	XF40	MS60	MS63	MS65
1999	Est. 5000	PF65 320				

KM# 822 1/5 CROWN
6.22 g., 0.9999 Gold 0.200 oz. AGW, 22 mm. **Ruler:** Elizabeth II **Series:** House of Stuart **Subject:** King Charles II, 1660-1685 **Obv:** Crowned bust right **Rev:** Laureate bust right

Date	Mintage	VF20	XF40	MS60	MS63	MS65
1999	Est. 5000	PF65 320				

KM# 824 1/5 CROWN
6.22 g., 0.9999 Gold 0.200 oz. AGW, 22 mm. **Ruler:** Elizabeth II **Subject:** The Wedding of Prince Edward and Miss Sophie Rhys-Jones **Obv:** Crowned bust right **Rev:** Heads facing above banner and wedding bells

Date	Mintage	VF20	XF40	MS60	MS63	MS65
1999	—	PF65 320				

KM# A826 1/5 CROWN
6.22 g., 0.9999 Gold 0.200 oz. AGW, 22 mm. **Ruler:** Elizabeth II **Subject:** The Wedding of Prince Edward and Miss Sophie Rhys-Jones **Obv:** Crowned bust right **Rev:** St. George's Chapel

Date	Mintage	VF20	XF40	MS60	MS63	MS65
1999	Est. 5000	PF65 320				

KM# 834 1/5 CROWN
6.22 g., 0.9999 Gold 0.200 oz. AGW, 22 mm. **Ruler:** Elizabeth II **Subject:** The Life of Queen Elizabeth **Obv:** Crowned bust right **Rev:** 1905 portrait of Queen Mother as a girl

Date	Mintage	VF20	XF40	MS60	MS63	MS65
1999	Est. 5000	PF65 320				

KM# 836 1/5 CROWN
6.22 g., 0.9999 Gold 0.200 oz. AGW, 22 mm. **Ruler:** Elizabeth II **Subject:** The Life of Queen Elizabeth **Obv:** Crowned bust right **Rev:** 1918 portrait of Queen Mother with wounded veteran

Date	Mintage	VF20	XF40	MS60	MS63	MS65
1999	Est. 5000	PF65 320				

KM# 838 1/5 CROWN
6.22 g., 0.9999 Gold 0.200 oz. AGW, 22 mm. **Ruler:** Elizabeth II **Subject:** The Life of Queen Elizabeth **Obv:** Crowned bust right **Rev:** 1923 wedding portrait

Date	Mintage	VF20	XF40	MS60	MS63	MS65
1999	Est. 5000	PF65 320				

KM# 840 1/5 CROWN
6.22 g., 0.9999 Gold 0.200 oz. AGW, 22 mm. **Ruler:** Elizabeth II **Subject:** The Life of Queen Elizabeth **Obv:** Crowned bust right **Rev:** 1936 family portrait

Date	Mintage	VF20	XF40	MS60	MS63	MS65
1999	Est. 5000	PF65 320				

KM# 843 1/5 CROWN
6.22 g., 0.9999 Gold 0.200 oz. AGW, 22 mm. **Ruler:** Elizabeth II **Series:** The World At War **Subject:** Franklin D. Roosevelt **Obv:** Crowned bust right **Rev:** Bust writing at left, Zero fighter at right

Date	Mintage	VF20	XF40	MS60	MS63	MS65
1999	—	PF65 320				

KM# 844 1/5 CROWN
6.22 g., 0.9999 Gold 0.200 oz. AGW, 22 mm. **Ruler:** Elizabeth II **Subject:** Operation Manna **Obv:** Crowned bust right **Rev:** Bomber dropping food packets

Date	Mintage	VF20	XF40	MS60	MS63	MS65
1999	Est. 5000	PF65 320				

KM# 847 1/5 CROWN
6.22 g., 0.9999 Gold 0.200 oz. AGW, 22 mm. **Ruler:** Elizabeth II **Subject:** The World At War **Obv:** Crowned bust right **Rev:** B-29, mushroom cloud and bust at right

Date	Mintage	VF20	XF40	MS60	MS63	MS65
1999	Est. 5000	PF65 320				

KM# 848 1/5 CROWN
6.22 g., 0.9999 Gold 0.200 oz. AGW, 22 mm. **Ruler:** Elizabeth II **Subject:** Barnes Wallis **Obv:** Crowned bust right **Rev:** Bust at left reading, bomber above dam

Date	Mintage	VF20	XF40	MS60	MS63	MS65
1999	Est. 5000	PF65 320				

KM# 850 1/5 CROWN
6.22 g., 0.9999 Gold 0.200 oz. AGW, 22 mm. **Ruler:** Elizabeth II **Subject:** The World At War **Obv:** Crowned bust right **Rev:** Bust at left facing, planes in combat

Date	Mintage	VF20	XF40	MS60	MS63	MS65
1999	Est. 5000	PF65 320				

KM# 852 1/5 CROWN
6.22 g., 0.9999 Gold 0.200 oz. AGW, 22 mm. **Ruler:** Elizabeth II **Subject:** Winston Churchill **Obv:** Crowned bust right **Rev:** Bust with hand showing 'V' sign, crowd in background

Date	Mintage	VF20	XF40	MS60	MS63	MS65
1999	Est. 5000	PF65 320				

KM# 854 1/5 CROWN
6.22 g., 0.9999 Gold 0.200 oz. AGW, 22 mm. **Ruler:** Elizabeth II **Subject:** The World At War **Obv:** Crowned bust right **Rev:** Battleship and sailor

Date	Mintage	VF20	XF40	MS60	MS63	MS65
1999	Est. 5000	PF65 320				

KM# 856 1/5 CROWN
6.22 g., 0.9999 Gold 0.200 oz. AGW, 22 mm. **Ruler:** Elizabeth II **Subject:** War Babies **Obv:** Crowned bust right **Rev:** Soldier kissing child

Date	Mintage	VF20	XF40	MS60	MS63	MS65
1999	Est. 5000	PF65 320				

KM# 858 1/5 CROWN
6.22 g., 0.9999 Gold 0.200 oz. AGW, 22 mm. **Ruler:** Elizabeth II **Subject:** The World At War **Obv:** Crowned bust right **Rev:** 2 firemen in action after air raid

Date	Mintage	VF20	XF40	MS60	MS63	MS65
1999	Est. 5000	PF65 320				

KM# 860 1/5 CROWN
6.22 g., 0.9999 Gold 0.200 oz. AGW, 22 mm. **Ruler:** Elizabeth II **Subject:** The World At War **Obv:** Crowned bust right **Rev:** Landing scene

Date	Mintage	VF20	XF40	MS60	MS63	MS65
1999	Est. 5000	PF65 320				

KM# 862 1/5 CROWN
6.22 g., 0.9999 Gold 0.200 oz. AGW, 22 mm. **Ruler:** Elizabeth II **Subject:** Operation Heavywater **Obv:** Crowned bust right **Rev:** Military skier

Date	Mintage	VF20	XF40	MS60	MS63	MS65
1999	Est. 5000	PF65 320				

KM# 864 1/5 CROWN
6.22 g., 0.9999 Gold 0.200 oz. AGW, 22 mm. **Ruler:** Elizabeth II **Subject:** The World At War **Obv:** Crowned bust right **Rev:** German tanks in Russia

Date	Mintage	VF20	XF40	MS60	MS63	MS65
1999	Est. 5000	PF65 320				

KM# 870 1/5 CROWN
6.22 g., 0.9999 Gold 0.200 oz. AGW, 22 mm. **Ruler:** Elizabeth II **Series:** Queen Mother **Obv:** Head with tiara right **Rev:** 1937 Coronation scene

Date	Mintage	VF20	XF40	MS60	MS63	MS65
2000	5,000	PF65 320				

KM# 872 1/5 CROWN
6.22 g., 0.9999 Gold 0.200 oz. AGW, 22 mm. **Ruler:** Elizabeth II **Series:** Queen Mother **Obv:** Crowned bust right **Rev:** 1938 Visit to France

Date	Mintage	VF20	XF40	MS60	MS63	MS65
2000	5,000	PF65 320				

KM# 874 1/5 CROWN
6.22 g., 0.9999 Gold 0.200 oz. AGW, 22 mm. **Ruler:** Elizabeth II **Series:** Queen Mother **Obv:** Crowned bust right **Rev:** 1940 Bomb damage

Date	Mintage	VF20	XF40	MS60	MS63	MS65
2000	5,000	PF65 320				

KM# 876 1/5 CROWN
6.22 g., 0.9999 Gold 0.200 oz. AGW, 22 mm. **Ruler:** Elizabeth II **Series:** Queen Mother **Obv:** Crowned bust right

Date	Mintage	VF20	XF40	MS60	MS63	MS65
2000	5,000	PF65 320				

KM# 879 1/5 CROWN
6.22 g., 0.9999 Gold 0.200 oz. AGW, 22 mm. **Ruler:** Elizabeth II **Subject:** 18th Birthday of Prince William **Obv:** Crowned bust right **Rev:** Bust facing **Edge:** Reeded

Date	Mintage	VF20	XF40	MS60	MS63	MS65
2000	5,000	PF65 320				

KM# 881 1/5 CROWN
6.22 g., 0.9999 Gold 0.200 oz. AGW, 22 mm. **Ruler:** Elizabeth II **Series:** 100th Birthday of the Queen Mother **Obv:** Crowned bust right **Rev:** Bust facing **Note:** Queen Mother's portrait has a real diamond chip (.015) set in her crown.

Date	Mintage	VF20	XF40	MS60	MS63	MS65
2000	2,000	PF65 320				

KM# 868.1 1/4 CROWN
7.78 g., 0.925 Silver 0.2314 oz. ASW **Ruler:** Elizabeth II **Subject:** 1999 The Year of the Rabbit **Obv:** Crowned bust right **Rev:** Peter Rabbit reading, sparrow, Chinese characters

Date	Mintage	VF20	XF40	MS60	MS63	MS65
1999	Est. 25000	PF65 35.00				

KM# 868.2 1/4 CROWN
7.78 g., 0.925 Silver 0.2314 oz. ASW **Ruler:** Elizabeth II **Obv:** Crowned bust right **Rev:** Rabbit reading, sparrow; without Chinese characters

Date	Mintage	VF20	XF40	MS60	MS63	MS65
1999	Inc. above	PF65 35.00				

KM# 886 1/2 CROWN
15.55 g., 0.9999 Gold 0.4999 oz. AGW, 30 mm. **Ruler:** Elizabeth II **Subject:** Rotary Club of Gibraltar

Date	Mintage	VF20	XF40	MS60	MS63	MS65
1991	5,000	PF65 775				

KM# 127 1/2 CROWN
15.55 g., 0.9999 Gold 0.4999 oz. AGW, 30 mm. **Ruler:** Elizabeth II **Subject:** Japanese Royal Wedding **Obv:** Crowned bust right **Rev:** Peacocks

Date	Mintage	VF20	XF40	MS60	MS63	MS65
1993	5,000	PF65 775				

KM# 177 1/2 CROWN
15.55 g., 0.999 Silver 0.4994 oz. ASW **Ruler:** Elizabeth II **Series:** WWII Warships **Obv:** Crowned bust right **Rev:** HMS Hood

Date	Mintage	VF20	XF40	MS60	MS63	MS65
1993	Est. 30000	—	—	—	—	35.00

KM# 198 1/2 CROWN
15.55 g., 0.999 Silver 0.4994 oz. ASW **Ruler:** Elizabeth II **Subject:** King Edward VIII, House of Windsor **Obv:** Young bust right **Rev:** Bust left

Date	Mintage	VF20	XF40	MS60	MS63	MS65
1993	Est. 30000	PF65 27.50				

KM# 443 1/2 CROWN
15.55 g., 0.9999 Gold 0.4999 oz. AGW, 30 mm. **Ruler:** Elizabeth II **Series:** Peter Rabbit Centennial **Subject:** The Tale of Peter Rabbit **Obv:** Crowned bust right **Rev:** Mother and bunnies

Date	Mintage	VF20	XF40	MS60	MS63	MS65
1994	—	PF65 775				

KM# 572 1/2 CROWN
15.55 g., 0.999 Silver 0.4994 oz. ASW **Ruler:** Elizabeth II **Obv:** Crowned bust right **Rev:** Sherlock Holmes smoking pipe left

Date	Mintage	VF20	XF40	MS60	MS63	MS65
1994	Est. 30000	PF65 25.00				

KM# 372 1/2 CROWN
15.55 g., 0.9999 Gold 0.4999 oz. AGW, 30 mm. **Ruler:** Elizabeth II **Obv:** Crowned bust right **Rev:** Roses

Date	Mintage	VF20	XF40	MS60	MS63	MS65
1996	Est. 3000	PF65 775				

KM# 381 1/2 CROWN
15.55 g., 0.9999 Gold 0.4999 oz. AGW, 30 mm. **Ruler:** Elizabeth II **Series:** Peter Rabbit Centennial **Subject:** The Tale of Peter Rabbit **Obv:** Crowned bust right **Rev:** Peter Rabbit escaping garden

Date	Mintage	VF20	XF40	MS60	MS63	MS65
1996	Est. 5000	PF65 775				

KM# 448 1/2 CROWN
15.55 g., 0.9999 Gold 0.4999 oz. AGW, 30 mm. **Ruler:** Elizabeth II **Subject:** Lord Buddha **Obv:** Crowned bust right **Rev:** Seated figure facing

Date	Mintage	VF20	XF40	MS60	MS63	MS65
1996	Est. 5000	PF65 775				

KM# 524 1/2 CROWN
15.55 g., 0.9999 Gold 0.4999 oz. AGW, 30 mm. **Ruler:** Elizabeth II **Subject:** The Tale of Peter Rabbit **Obv:** Crowned bust right **Rev:** Standing rabbit 3/4 right

Date	Mintage	VF20	XF40	MS60	MS63	MS65
1997	Est. 2500	PF65 775				

KM# 647 1/2 CROWN
15.55 g., 0.9999 Gold 0.4999 oz. AGW, 30 mm. **Ruler:** Elizabeth II **Obv:** Crowned bust right **Rev:** Cupid with hologram heart

Date	Mintage	VF20	XF40	MS60	MS63	MS65
1998	Est. 3500	PF65 775				

KM# 655 1/2 CROWN
15.55 g., 0.9999 Gold 0.4999 oz. AGW, 30 mm. **Ruler:** Elizabeth II **Subject:** The Tale of Peter Rabbit **Obv:** Crowned bust right **Rev:** Standing rabbit facing, sparrow at left

Date	Mintage	VF20	XF40	MS60	MS63	MS65
1998	Est. 2500	PF65 775				

KM# 681 1/2 CROWN
15.55 g., 0.9999 Gold 0.4999 oz. AGW, 30 mm. **Ruler:** Elizabeth II **Subject:** Paddington Bear **Obv:** Crowned bust right **Rev:** Bear with suitcase

Date	Mintage	VF20	XF40	MS60	MS63	MS65
1998	Est. 2500	PF65 775				

KM# 732 1/2 CROWN
15.55 g., 0.9999 Gold 0.4999 oz. AGW, 30 mm. **Ruler:** Elizabeth II **Subject:** Peacocks **Obv:** Crowned bust right **Rev:** Pair of peacocks, one with full display in hologram, denomination below

Date	Mintage	VF20	XF40	MS60	MS63	MS65
1998	—	PF65 775				

KM# 895 1/2 CROWN
15.78 g., 0.999 Silver 0.5068 oz. ASW, 32.25 mm. **Ruler:** Elizabeth II **Subject:** Cupid **Obv:** Crowned bust right **Rev:** Cupid with multicolor holographic heart similar to 1/2 crown KM#-647 but without the metal content statement, denomination below **Edge:** Reeded

Date	Mintage	VF20	XF40	MS60	MS63	MS65
1998	10,000	PF65 50.00				

KM# 782.1 1/2 CROWN
15.55 g., 0.9999 Gold 0.4999 oz. AGW, 30 mm. **Ruler:** Elizabeth II **Subject:** 1999 The Year of the Rabbit **Obv:** Crowned bust right **Rev:** Rabbit reading, sparrow, Chinese characters

Date	Mintage	VF20	XF40	MS60	MS63	MS65
1999	Est. 1000	PF65 775				

KM# 782.2 1/2 CROWN
15.55 g., 0.9999 Gold 0.4999 oz. AGW, 30 mm. **Ruler:** Elizabeth II **Obv:** Crowned bust right **Rev:** Rabbit reading, sparrow; without Chinese characters

Date	Mintage	VF20	XF40	MS60	MS63	MS65
1999	Inc. above	PF65 775				

KM# 1108 1/2 CROWN
15.55 g., 0.999 Gold 0.4994 oz. AGW, 30 mm. **Ruler:** Elizabeth II **Subject:** Millennium **Rev:** Candle and clock

Date	Mintage	VF20	XF40	MS60	MS63	MS65
1999	Est. 1000	PF65 900				

KM# 1116 1/2 CROWN
15.55 g., 0.999 Gold 0.4994 oz. AGW, 30 mm. **Ruler:** Elizabeth II **Subject:** English Monarchs **Rev:** Elizabeth I

Date	Mintage	VF20	XF40	MS60	MS63	MS65
1999	—	PF65 900				

KM# 883 1/2 CROWN
Bi-Metallic Titanium center in Gold ring. .9g Gold .289 AGW. **Ruler:** Elizabeth II **Subject:** 160th Anniversary of the Uniform Penny Post **Obv:** Crowned bust right **Rev:** Postage stamp design, blue center **Edge:** Reeded

Date	Mintage	VF20	XF40	MS60	MS63	MS65
2000	5,000	PF65 475				

KM# 894 1/2 CROWN
15.55 g., 0.999 Gold 0.4995 oz. AGW, 30 mm. **Ruler:** Elizabeth II **Obv:** Crowned bust right **Rev:** Postage stamp design **Edge:** Reeded

Date	Mintage	VF20	XF40	MS60	MS63	MS65
2000	999	PF65 775				

KM# 11 CROWN
Copper-Nickel, 38.8 mm. **Ruler:** Elizabeth II **Subject:** 80th Birthday of Queen Mother **Rev:** Bust left, mountain and water in background

Date	Mintage	VF20	XF40	MS60	MS63	MS65
1980	—	—	1.50	3.00	4.00	5.00

KM# 11a CROWN
28.28 g., 0.925 Silver 0.841 oz. ASW, 38.8 mm. **Ruler:** Elizabeth II **Subject:** 80th Birthday of Queen Mother **Rev:** Bust left, mountains and water in background

Date	Mintage	VF20	XF40	MS60	MS63	MS65
1980	Est. 25000	PF65 30.00				

KM# 12 CROWN
Copper-Nickel, 38.8 mm. **Ruler:** Elizabeth II **Subject:** 175th Anniversary - Death of Nelson **Obv:** Young bust right **Rev:** Head at right looking left, ship in background

Date	Mintage	VF20	XF40	MS60	MS63	MS65
1980	Est. 100000	—	2.00	4.00	7.00	9.00

KM# 12a CROWN
28.28 g., 0.925 Silver 0.841 oz. ASW, 38.8 mm. **Ruler:** Elizabeth II **Subject:** 175th Anniversary - Death of Nelson **Obv:** Bust right

Date	Mintage	VF20	XF40	MS60	MS63	MS65
1980	Est. 15000	PF65 35.00				

KM# 14 CROWN
Copper-Nickel, 38.8 mm. **Ruler:** Elizabeth II **Subject:** Wedding of Prince Charles and Lady Diana **Rev:** The royal couple facing

Date	Mintage	VF20	XF40	MS60	MS63	MS65
1981	—	—	1.00	2.50	3.50	5.00

KM# 14a CROWN
28.28 g., 0.925 Silver 0.841 oz. ASW, 38.8 mm. **Ruler:** Elizabeth II **Subject:** The Wedding of Prince Charles and Lady Diana **Rev:** The royal couple facing

Date	Mintage	VF20	XF40	MS60	MS63	MS65
1981	Est. 30000	PF65 25.00				

KM# 33 CROWN

Copper-Nickel, 38.8 mm. **Ruler:** Elizabeth II **Series:** World Cup Soccer **Obv:** Crowned bust right **Rev:** Italian flag, soccer player and globe

Date	Mintage	VF20	XF40	MS60	MS63	MS65
1990	—	—	—	3.50	5.00	7.50

KM# 33a CROWN

28.28 g., 0.925 Silver 0.841 oz. ASW, 38.8 mm. **Ruler:** Elizabeth II **Series:** World Cup Soccer **Obv:** Crowned bust right **Rev:** Italian flag, soccer player and globe

Date	Mintage	VF20	XF40	MS60	MS63	MS65
1990	Est. 30000	PF65 32.50				

KM# 34 CROWN

Copper-Nickel, 38.8 mm. **Ruler:** Elizabeth II **Series:** World Cup Soccer **Obv:** Crowned bust right **Rev:** Map of Italy on soccer ball background

Date	Mintage	VF20	XF40	MS60	MS63	MS65
1990	—	—	—	3.50	5.00	7.50

KM# 34a CROWN

28.28 g., 0.925 Silver 0.841 oz. ASW, 38.8 mm. **Ruler:** Elizabeth II **Series:** World Cup Soccer **Obv:** Crowned bust right **Rev:** Map of Italy on soccer ball background

Date	Mintage	VF20	XF40	MS60	MS63	MS65
1990	Est. 30000	PF65 27.50				

KM# 35 CROWN

Copper-Nickel, 38.8 mm. **Ruler:** Elizabeth II **Series:** World Cup Soccer **Obv:** Crowned bust right **Rev:** Goalie catching ball

Date	Mintage	VF20	XF40	MS60	MS63	MS65
1990	—	—	—	3.50	5.00	7.50

KM# 35a CROWN

28.28 g., 0.925 Silver 0.841 oz. ASW, 38.8 mm. **Ruler:** Elizabeth II **Series:** World Cup Soccer **Obv:** Crowned bust right **Rev:** Goalie catching ball

Date	Mintage	VF20	XF40	MS60	MS63	MS65
1990	—	PF65 27.50				

KM# 36 CROWN

Copper-Nickel, 38.8 mm. **Ruler:** Elizabeth II **Series:** World Cup Soccer **Obv:** Crowned bust right **Rev:** Ball at head

Date	Mintage	VF20	XF40	MS60	MS63	MS65
1990	—	—	—	3.50	5.00	7.50

KM# 36a CROWN

28.28 g., 0.925 Silver 0.841 oz. ASW, 38.8 mm. **Ruler:** Elizabeth II **Series:** World Cup Soccer **Obv:** Crowned bust right **Rev:** Ball at head

Date	Mintage	VF20	XF40	MS60	MS63	MS65
1990	Est. 30000	PF65 27.50				

KM# 37 CROWN

Copper-Nickel, 38.8 mm. **Ruler:** Elizabeth II **Series:** World Cup Soccer **Obv:** Crowned bust right **Rev:** Ball at feet

Date	Mintage	VF20	XF40	MS60	MS63	MS65
1990	—	—	—	3.50	5.00	7.50

KM# 37a CROWN

28.28 g., 0.925 Silver 0.841 oz. ASW, 38.8 mm. **Ruler:** Elizabeth II **Series:** World Cup Soccer **Obv:** Crowned bust right **Rev:** Ball at feet

Date	Mintage	VF20	XF40	MS60	MS63	MS65
1990	Est. 30000	PF65 27.50				

KM# 38 CROWN

Copper-Nickel, 38.8 mm. **Ruler:** Elizabeth II **Series:** World Cup Soccer **Obv:** Crowned bust right **Rev:** Three players

Date	Mintage	VF20	XF40	MS60	MS63	MS65
1990	—	—	—	3.50	5.00	7.50

KM# 38a CROWN

28.28 g., 0.925 Silver 0.841 oz. ASW, 38.8 mm. **Ruler:** Elizabeth II **Series:** World Cup Soccer **Obv:** Crowned bust right **Rev:** Three players

Date	Mintage	VF20	XF40	MS60	MS63	MS65
1990	Est. 30000	PF65 27.50				

KM# 40 CROWN

Copper-Nickel, 38.8 mm. **Ruler:** Elizabeth II **Subject:** 21st Anniversary - Constitution **Obv:** Crowned bust right **Rev:** Standing figure with key, shield and spear

Date	Mintage	VF20	XF40	MS60	MS63	MS65
1990	—	—	—	—	6.50	8.50

KM# 40a CROWN

28.28 g., 0.925 Silver 0.841 oz. ASW, 38.8 mm. **Ruler:** Elizabeth II **Subject:** 21st Anniversary - Constitution **Obv:** Crowned bust right **Rev:** Standing figure with key, spear and shield

Date	Mintage	VF20	XF40	MS60	MS63	MS65
1990	Est. 30000	PF65 45.00				

KM# 46 CROWN

Copper-Nickel, 38.6 mm. **Ruler:** Elizabeth II **Obv:** Crowned bust right **Rev:** Head 3/4 left divides dates

Date	Mintage	VF20	XF40	MS60	MS63	MS65
1990	—	—	—	—	4.50	6.00

KM# 46a CROWN

28.28 g., 0.925 Silver 0.841 oz. ASW, 38.6 mm. **Ruler:** Elizabeth II **Obv:** Crowned bust right **Rev:** Head 3/4 left divides dates

Date	Mintage	VF20	XF40	MS60	MS63	MS65
1990	—	PF65 25.00				

KM# 46b CROWN

6.22 g., 0.9999 Gold 0.200 oz. AGW **Ruler:** Elizabeth II **Obv:** Crowned bust right **Rev:** Head 3/4 left divides date

Date	Mintage	VF20	XF40	MS60	MS63	MS65
1990	Est. 5000	PF65 350				

KM# 46c CROWN

6.22 g., 0.995 Platinum 0.199 oz. APW **Ruler:** Elizabeth II **Obv:** Crowned bust right **Rev:** Head 3/4 left divides dates

Date	Mintage	VF20	XF40	MS60	MS63	MS65
1990	Est. 1000	PF65 375				

KM# 49 CROWN

Copper-Nickel, 38.8 mm. **Ruler:** Elizabeth II **Series:** 150th Anniversary of the First Adhesive Postage Stamp **Subject:** Penny Black Stamp **Obv:** Crowned bust right **Rev:** Heads flank stamp design

Date	Mintage	VF20	XF40	MS60	MS63	MS65
1990	Est. 50000	PF65 18.00				
1990	—	—	—	7.50	9.00	12.00

KM# 49a CROWN

28.28 g., 0.925 Silver 0.841 oz. ASW **Ruler:** Elizabeth II **Series:** 150th Anniversary of the First Adhesive Postage Stamp **Subject:** Penny Black Stamp **Obv:** Crowned bust right **Rev:** Heads flank stamp design

Date	Mintage	VF20	XF40	MS60	MS63	MS65
1990	Est. 30000	PF65 40.00				

KM# 49b CROWN

31.10 g., 0.9999 Gold 0.9998 oz. AGW **Ruler:** Elizabeth II **Series:** 150th Anniversary of the First Adhesive Postage Stamp **Subject:** Penny Black Stamp **Obv:** Crowned bust right **Rev:** Heads flank stamp design

Date	Mintage	VF20	XF40	MS60	MS63	MS65
1990	Est. 1000	PF65 1,650				

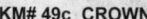

KM# 49c CROWN

15.55 g., 0.9999 Gold 0.4999 oz. AGW **Ruler:** Elizabeth II **Series:** 150th Anniversary of the First Adhesive Postage Stamp **Subject:** Penny Black Stamp **Obv:** Crowned bust right **Rev:** Heads flank stamp design

Date	Mintage	VF20	XF40	MS60	MS63	MS65
1990	—	PF65 865				

KM# 66 CROWN

Copper-Nickel, 38.8 mm. **Ruler:** Elizabeth II **Series:** Barcelona Olympics **Obv:** Crowned bust right **Rev:** Discus thrower

Date	Mintage	VF20	XF40	MS60	MS63	MS65
1991	—	—	—	—	4.50	5.50
1991	Est. 8000	PF65 20.00				
1992	—	—	—	—	5.00	6.00

KM# 66a CROWN

28.28 g., 0.925 Silver 0.841 oz. ASW, 38.8 mm. **Ruler:** Elizabeth II **Series:** Barcelona Olympics **Obv:** Crowned bust right **Rev:** Discus thrower

Date	Mintage	VF20	XF40	MS60	MS63	MS65
1991	Est. 30000	PF65 25.00				
1992	—	PF65 90.00				

KM# 67 CROWN

Copper-Nickel, 38.8 mm. **Ruler:** Elizabeth II **Series:** Barcelona Olympics **Obv:** Crowned bust right **Rev:** Chariot racing

Date	Mintage	VF20	XF40	MS60	MS63	MS65
1991	—	—	—	—	5.00	6.00
1991	Est. 8000	PF65 20.00				
1992	—	—	—	—	5.00	6.00

KM# 67a CROWN

28.28 g., 0.925 Silver 0.841 oz. ASW, 38.8 mm. **Ruler:** Elizabeth II **Series:** Barcelona Olympics **Obv:** Crowned bust right **Rev:** Chariot racing

Date	Mintage	VF20	XF40	MS60	MS63	MS65
1991	Est. 30000	PF65 25.00				

KM# 68 CROWN

Copper-Nickel, 38.8 mm. **Ruler:** Elizabeth II **Series:** Barcelona Olympics **Obv:** Crowned bust right **Rev:** Runners

Date	Mintage	VF20	XF40	MS60	MS63	MS65
1991	—	—	—	—	4.50	5.50
1991	Est. 8000	PF65 20.00				
1992	—	—	—	—	5.00	6.00

KM# 68a CROWN

28.28 g., 0.925 Silver 0.841 oz. ASW, 38.8 mm. **Ruler:** Elizabeth II **Series:** Barcelona Olympics **Obv:** Crowned bust right **Rev:** Runners

Date	Mintage	VF20	XF40	MS60	MS63	MS65
1991	Est. 30000	PF65 25.00				

KM# 69 CROWN

Copper-Nickel, 38.8 mm. **Ruler:** Elizabeth II **Series:** Barcelona Olympics **Obv:** Crowned bust right **Rev:** Javelin thrower

Date	Mintage	VF20	XF40	MS60	MS63	MS65
1991	—	—	—	—	4.50	5.50
1991	Est. 8000	PF65 20.00				
1992	—	—	—	—	5.00	6.00

KM# 69a CROWN

28.28 g., 0.925 Silver 0.841 oz. ASW, 38.8 mm. **Ruler:** Elizabeth II **Series:** Barcelona Olympics **Obv:** Crowned bust right **Rev:** Javelin thrower

Date	Mintage	VF20	XF40	MS60	MS63	MS65
1991	Est. 30000	PF65 25.00				
1992	—	PF65 60.00				

KM# 70 CROWN

Copper-Nickel, 38.8 mm. **Ruler:** Elizabeth II **Series:** Barcelona Olympics **Obv:** Crowned bust right **Rev:** Head facing at left, wrestlers at right

Date	Mintage	VF20	XF40	MS60	MS63	MS65
1991	—	—	—	—	4.50	5.50
1991	Est. 8000	PF65 20.00				
1992	—	—	—	—	5.00	6.00

KM# 70a CROWN

28.28 g., 0.925 Silver 0.841 oz. ASW, 38.8 mm. **Ruler:** Elizabeth II **Series:** Barcelona Olympics **Obv:** Crowned bust right **Rev:** Head facing at left, wrestlers at right

Date	Mintage	VF20	XF40	MS60	MS63	MS65
1991	—	PF65 25.00				

KM# 71 CROWN

Copper-Nickel, 38.8 mm. **Ruler:** Elizabeth II **Series:** Barcelona Olympics **Obv:** Crowned bust right **Rev:** Seated figure at left, boxers at right

Date	Mintage	VF20	XF40	MS60	MS63	MS65
1991	—	—	—	—	4.50	5.50
1991	Est. 8000	PF65 20.00				
1992	—	—	—	—	5.00	6.00

KM# 71a CROWN

28.28 g., 0.925 Silver 0.841 oz. ASW, 38.8 mm. **Ruler:** Elizabeth II **Series:** Barcelona Olympics **Obv:** Crowned bust right **Rev:** Seated figure at left, boxers at right

Date	Mintage	VF20	XF40	MS60	MS63	MS65
1991	Est. 30000	PF65 25.00				

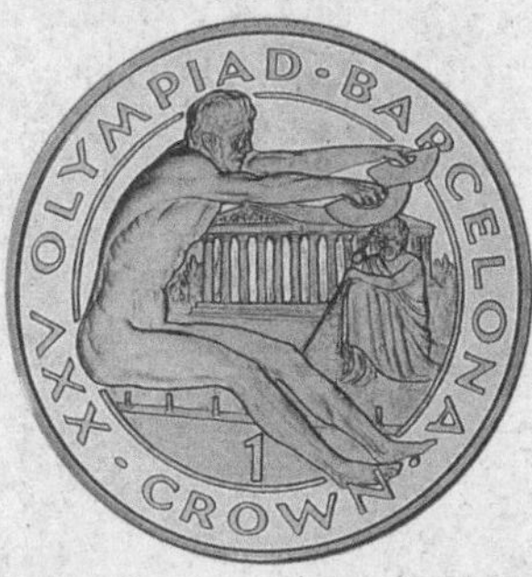

KM# 72 CROWN

Copper-Nickel, 38.8 mm. **Ruler:** Elizabeth II **Series:** Barcelona Olympics **Obv:** Crowned bust right **Rev:** Long jumper

Date	Mintage	VF20	XF40	MS60	MS63	MS65
1991	—	PF65 20.00				
1991	—	—	—	—	4.50	5.50
1992	—	—	—	—	5.00	6.00

KM# 72a CROWN

28.28 g., 0.925 Silver 0.841 oz. ASW, 38.8 mm. **Ruler:** Elizabeth II **Series:** Barcelona Olympics **Obv:** Crowned bust right **Rev:** Long jumper

Date	Mintage	VF20	XF40	MS60	MS63	MS65
1991	—	PF65 25.00				

KM# 73 CROWN

Copper-Nickel **Ruler:** Elizabeth II **Series:** Barcelona Olympics **Obv:** Crowned bust right **Rev:** Olympic victor

Date	Mintage	VF20	XF40	MS60	MS63	MS65
1991	—	PF65 20.00				
1991	—	—	—	—	4.50	5.50
1992	—	—	—	—	5.00	6.00

KM# 73a CROWN

28.28 g., 0.925 Silver 0.841 oz. ASW, 38.8 mm. **Ruler:** Elizabeth II **Series:** Barcelona Olympics **Obv:** Crowned bust right **Rev:** Olympic victor

Date	Mintage	VF20	XF40	MS60	MS63	MS65
1991	Est. 30000	PF65 28.00				

KM# 74 CROWN

Copper-Nickel, 38.8 mm. **Ruler:** Elizabeth II **Subject:** Rotary Club of Gibraltar **Obv:** Crowned bust right **Rev:** Cogwheel design on globe

Date	Mintage	VF20	XF40	MS60	MS63	MS65
1991	—	—	—	—	5.00	7.00

KM# 74a CROWN

28.28 g., 0.925 Silver 0.841 oz. ASW, 38.8 mm. **Ruler:** Elizabeth II **Subject:** Rotary Club of Gibraltar **Obv:** Crowned bust right **Rev:** Cogwheel design on globe

Date	Mintage	VF20	XF40	MS60	MS63	MS65
1991	Est. 30000	PF65 22.00				

KM# 74b CROWN

15.55 g., 0.999 Gold 0.4994 oz. AGW, 32.25 mm. **Ruler:** Elizabeth II **Subject:** Rotary Club of Gibraltar **Obv:** Crowned bust right **Rev:** Cogwheel design (Rotary logo) on globe

Date	Mintage	VF20	XF40	MS60	MS63	MS65
1991	—	PF65 865				

KM# 84 CROWN

Copper-Nickel, 38.5 mm. **Ruler:** Elizabeth II **Series:** 10th Wedding Anniversary **Subject:** Prince Charles **Rev:** Head 3/4 left

Date	Mintage	VF20	XF40	MS60	MS63	MS65
1991	—	—	—	—	4.00	5.00

KM# 84a CROWN

28.28 g., 0.925 Silver 0.841 oz. ASW, 38.5 mm. **Ruler:** Elizabeth II **Series:** 10th Wedding Anniversary **Subject:** Prince Charles **Rev:** Head 3/4 left

Date	Mintage	VF20	XF40	MS60	MS63	MS65
1991	Est. 30000	PF65 30.00				

KM# 84b CROWN

6.22 g., 0.9999 Gold 0.200 oz. AGW **Ruler:** Elizabeth II **Series:** 10th Wedding Anniversary **Subject:** Prince Charles **Rev:** Head 3/4 left

Date	Mintage	VF20	XF40	MS60	MS63	MS65
1991	Est. 5000	PF65 345				

KM# 85 CROWN

Copper-Nickel, 38.5 mm. **Ruler:** Elizabeth II **Series:** 10th Wedding Anniversary **Subject:** Princess Diana **Rev:** Head 3/4 right

Date	Mintage	VF20	XF40	MS60	MS63	MS65
1991	—	—	—	—	4.00	5.00

KM# 85a CROWN

28.28 g., 0.925 Silver 0.841 oz. ASW, 38.5 mm. **Ruler:** Elizabeth II **Series:** 10th Wedding Anniversary **Subject:** Princess Diana **Rev:** Head 3/4 right

Date	Mintage	VF20	XF40	MS60	MS63	MS65
1991	—	PF65 32.50				

KM# 85b CROWN

6.22 g., 0.9999 Gold 0.200 oz. AGW **Ruler:** Elizabeth II **Series:** 10th Wedding Anniversary **Subject:** Princess Diana **Rev:** Head 3/4 right

Date	Mintage	VF20	XF40	MS60	MS63	MS65
1991	—	PF65 345				

KM# 86 CROWN

Copper-Nickel, 38.5 mm. **Ruler:** Elizabeth II **Series:** 10th Wedding Anniversary **Subject:** Royal Yacht 'Brittannia' **Rev:** Luxury liner at sea

Date	Mintage	VF20	XF40	MS60	MS63	MS65
1991	—	—	—	—	4.00	5.00

KM# 86a CROWN

28.28 g., 0.925 Silver 0.841 oz. ASW, 38.5 mm. **Ruler:** Elizabeth II **Series:** 10th Wedding Anniversary **Subject:** Royal Yacht 'Britannia' **Rev:** Luxury liner at sea

Date	Mintage	VF20	XF40	MS60	MS63	MS65
1991	Est. 30000	PF65 30.00				

KM# 86b CROWN

6.22 g., 0.9999 Gold 0.200 oz. AGW **Ruler:** Elizabeth II **Series:** 10th Wedding Anniversary **Subject:** Royal Yacht 'Britannia' **Rev:** Liner at sea

Date	Mintage	VF20	XF40	MS60	MS63	MS65
1991	—	PF65 345				

KM# 95 CROWN

Copper-Nickel, 38.8 mm. **Ruler:** Elizabeth II **Obv:** Crowned bust right **Rev:** Corgi

Date	Mintage	VF20	XF40	MS60	MS63	MS65
1991	—	—	—	—	12.50	20.00

KM# 95a CROWN

31.10 g., 0.999 Silver 0.999 oz. ASW, 38.8 mm. **Ruler:** Elizabeth II **Obv:** Crowned bust right **Rev:** Corgi

Date	Mintage	VF20	XF40	MS60	MS63	MS65
1991	—	PF65 30.00				

KM# 103 CROWN

Copper-Nickel, 38.8 mm. **Ruler:** Elizabeth II **Obv:** Crowned bust right **Rev:** Cocker Spaniel

Date	Mintage	VF20	XF40	MS60	MS63	MS65
1992	—	—	—	—	12.50	20.00

KM# 103a CROWN

31.11 g., 0.999 Silver 0.999 oz. ASW, 38.8 mm. **Ruler:** Elizabeth II **Obv:** Crowned bust right **Rev:** Cocker Spaniel

Date	Mintage	VF20	XF40	MS60	MS63	MS65
1992	—	PF65 45.00				

KM# 178 CROWN

Copper-Nickel, 38.8 mm. **Ruler:** Elizabeth II **Subject:** Gibraltar City Charter **Obv:** Crowned bust right **Rev:** Bust left at right, building at left

Date	Mintage	VF20	XF40	MS60	MS63	MS65
1992	—	—	—	—	5.00	6.50

KM# 178a CROWN

28.28 g., 0.925 Silver 0.841 oz. ASW, 38.8 mm. **Ruler:** Elizabeth II **Subject:** Gibraltar City Charter **Obv:** Crowned bust right **Rev:** Bust left at right, building at left

Date	Mintage	VF20	XF40	MS60	MS63	MS65
1992	Est. 30000	PF65 30.00				

KM# 113 CROWN

Copper-Nickel, 38.8 mm. **Ruler:** Elizabeth II **Series:** WWII Warships **Obv:** Crowned bust right **Rev:** USS Philadelphia

Date	Mintage	VF20	XF40	MS60	MS63	MS65
1993	—	—	—	—	4.00	5.00

KM# 113a CROWN

28.28 g., 0.925 Silver 0.841 oz. ASW, 38.8 mm. **Ruler:** Elizabeth II **Series:** WWII Warships **Obv:** Crowned bust right **Rev:** USS Philadelphia

Date	Mintage	VF20	XF40	MS60	MS63	MS65
1993	Est. 30000	PF65 25.00				

KM# 114 CROWN

Copper-Nickel, 38.8 mm. **Ruler:** Elizabeth II **Series:** WWII Warships **Obv:** Crowned bust right **Rev:** USS McLanahan

Date	Mintage	VF20	XF40	MS60	MS63	MS65
1993	—	—	—	—	10.00	12.00

KM# 114a CROWN

28.28 g., 0.925 Silver 0.841 oz. ASW, 38.8 mm. **Ruler:** Elizabeth II **Series:** WWII Warships **Obv:** Crowned bust right **Rev:** USS McLanahan

Date	Mintage	VF20	XF40	MS60	MS63	MS65
1993	Est. 30000	PF65 25.00				

KM# 115 CROWN

Copper-Nickel, 38.8 mm. **Ruler:** Elizabeth II **Series:** WWII Warships **Obv:** Crowned bust right **Rev:** HNLMS Isaac Sweers

Date	Mintage	VF20	XF40	MS60	MS63	MS65
1993	—	—	—	—	4.00	5.00

KM# 115a CROWN

28.28 g., 0.925 Silver 0.841 oz. ASW, 38.8 mm. **Ruler:** Elizabeth II **Series:** WWII Warships **Obv:** Crowned bust right **Rev:** HNLMS Isaac Sweers

Date	Mintage	VF20	XF40	MS60	MS63	MS65
1993	Est. 30000	PF65 25.00				

KM# 116 CROWN

Copper-Nickel, 38.8 mm. **Ruler:** Elizabeth II **Series:** WWII Warships **Obv:** Crowned bust right **Rev:** USS Weehawken

Date	Mintage	VF20	XF40	MS60	MS63	MS65
1993	—	—	—	—	4.00	5.00

KM# 116a CROWN

28.28 g., 0.925 Silver 0.841 oz. ASW, 38.8 mm. **Ruler:** Elizabeth II **Series:** WWII Warships **Obv:** Crowned bust right **Rev:** USS Weehawken

Date	Mintage	VF20	XF40	MS60	MS63	MS65
1993	Est. 30000	PF65 25.00				

KM# 117 CROWN

Copper-Nickel, 38.8 mm. **Ruler:** Elizabeth II **Series:** WWII Warships **Obv:** Crowned bust right **Rev:** HMS Warspite

Date	Mintage	VF20	XF40	MS60	MS63	MS65
1993	—	—	—	—	4.00	5.00

KM# 117a CROWN

28.28 g., 0.925 Silver 0.841 oz. ASW, 38.8 mm. **Ruler:** Elizabeth II **Series:** WWII Warships **Obv:** Crowned bust right **Rev:** HMS Warspite

Date	Mintage	VF20	XF40	MS60	MS63	MS65
1993	—	PF65 25.00				

KM# 118 CROWN

Copper-Nickel, 38.8 mm. **Ruler:** Elizabeth II **Series:** WWII Warships **Obv:** Crowned bust right **Rev:** HMS Hood

Date	Mintage	VF20	XF40	MS60	MS63	MS65
1993	—	—	—	—	4.00	5.00

KM# 118a CROWN

28.28 g., 0.925 Silver 0.841 oz. ASW, 38.8 mm. **Ruler:** Elizabeth II **Series:** WWII Warships **Obv:** Crowned bust right **Rev:** HMS Hood

Date	Mintage	VF20	XF40	MS60	MS63	MS65
1993	Est. 30000	PF65 25.00				

KM# 119 CROWN

Copper-Nickel, 38.8 mm. **Ruler:** Elizabeth II **Series:** WWII Warships **Obv:** Crowned bust right **Rev:** HMS Penelope

Date	Mintage	VF20	XF40	MS60	MS63	MS65
1993	—	—	—	—	4.00	5.00

KM# 119a CROWN

28.28 g., 0.925 Silver 0.841 oz. ASW, 38.8 mm. **Ruler:** Elizabeth II **Series:** WWII Warships **Obv:** Crowned bust right **Rev:** HMS Penelope

Date	Mintage	VF20	XF40	MS60	MS63	MS65
1993	—	PF65 25.00				

KM# 120 CROWN

Copper-Nickel, 38.8 mm. **Ruler:** Elizabeth II **Series:** WWII Warships **Obv:** Crowned bust right **Rev:** HMCS Prescott

Date	Mintage	VF20	XF40	MS60	MS63	MS65
1993	—	—	—	—	10.00	12.00

KM# 120a CROWN

28.28 g., 0.925 Silver 0.841 oz. ASW, 38.8 mm. **Ruler:** Elizabeth II **Series:** WWII Warships **Obv:** Crowned bust right **Rev:** HMCS Prescott

Date	Mintage	VF20	XF40	MS60	MS63	MS65
1993	Est. 30000	PF65 25.00				

KM# 121 CROWN

Copper-Nickel, 38.8 mm. **Ruler:** Elizabeth II **Series:** WWII Warships **Obv:** Crowned bust right **Rev:** HMS Ark Royal

Date	Mintage	VF20	XF40	MS60	MS63	MS65
1993	—	—	—	—	4.00	5.00

KM# 121a CROWN

28.28 g., 0.925 Silver 0.841 oz. ASW, 38.8 mm. **Ruler:** Elizabeth II **Series:** WWII Warships **Obv:** Crowned bust right **Rev:** HMS Ark Royal

Date	Mintage	VF20	XF40	MS60	MS63	MS65
1993	—	PF65 25.00				

KM# 122 CROWN

Copper-Nickel, 38.8 mm. **Ruler:** Elizabeth II **Series:** WWII Warships **Obv:** Crowned bust right **Rev:** USS Gleaves

Date	Mintage	VF20	XF40	MS60	MS63	MS65
1993	—	—	—	—	4.00	5.00

KM# 122a CROWN

28.28 g., 0.925 Silver 0.841 oz. ASW, 38.8 mm. **Ruler:** Elizabeth II **Series:** WWII Warships **Obv:** Crowned bust right **Rev:** USS Gleaves

Date	Mintage	VF20	XF40	MS60	MS63	MS65
1993	Est. 30000	PF65 25.00				

KM# 123 CROWN

Copper-Nickel, 38.8 mm. **Ruler:** Elizabeth II **Series:** WWII Warships **Obv:** Crowned bust right **Rev:** HMAS Waterhen

Date	Mintage	VF20	XF40	MS60	MS63	MS65
1993	—	—	—	—	4.00	5.00

KM# 123a CROWN

28.28 g., 0.925 Silver 0.841 oz. ASW, 38.8 mm. **Ruler:** Elizabeth II **Series:** WWII Warships **Obv:** Crowned bust right **Rev:** HMAS Waterhen

Date	Mintage	VF20	XF40	MS60	MS63	MS65
1993	Est. 30000	PF65 25.00				

KM# 132 CROWN

Copper-Nickel, 38.8 mm. **Ruler:** Elizabeth II **Series:** House of - Stuart **Subject:** Queen Anne, 1702-1714 **Obv:** Young bust right **Rev:** Bust left

Date	Mintage	VF20	XF40	MS60	MS63	MS65
1993 Prooflike	—	—	—	—	4.00	5.00

KM# 132a CROWN

28.28 g., 0.925 Silver 0.841 oz. ASW, 38.8 mm. **Ruler:** Elizabeth II **Series:** House of - Stuart **Subject:** Queen Anne, 1702-1714 **Obv:** Young bust right **Rev:** Bust left

Date	Mintage	VF20	XF40	MS60	MS63	MS65
1993	Est. 30000	PF65 30.00				

KM# 133 CROWN

Copper-Nickel, 38.8 mm. **Ruler:** Elizabeth II **Series:** House of - Hanover **Subject:** King GeorgeI, 1714-1727 **Obv:** Young bust right **Rev:** Laureate bust right

Date	Mintage	VF20	XF40	MS60	MS63	MS65
1993 Prooflike	—	—	—	—	4.00	5.00

KM# 133a CROWN

28.28 g., 0.925 Silver 0.841 oz. ASW, 38.8 mm. **Ruler:** Elizabeth II **Series:** House of - Hanover **Subject:** King George I, 1714-1727 **Obv:** Young bust right **Rev:** Laureate bust right

Date	Mintage	VF20	XF40	MS60	MS63	MS65
1993	—	PF65 30.00				

KM# 134 CROWN

Copper-Nickel, 38.8 mm. **Ruler:** Elizabeth II **Series:** House of - Hanover **Subject:** King George II, 1727-1760 **Obv:** Young bust right **Rev:** Uniformed bust left

Date	Mintage	VF20	XF40	MS60	MS63	MS65
1993 Prooflike	—	—	—	—	4.00	5.00

KM# 134a CROWN

28.28 g., 0.925 Silver 0.841 oz. ASW, 38.8 mm. **Ruler:** Elizabeth II **Series:** House of - Hanover **Subject:** King George II, 1727-1760 **Obv:** Young bust right **Rev:** Uniformed bust left

Date	Mintage	VF20	XF40	MS60	MS63	MS65
1993	—	PF65 28.00				

KM# 135 CROWN
Copper-Nickel, 38.8 mm. **Ruler:** Elizabeth II **Series:** House of - Hanover **Subject:** King George III, 1760-1820 **Obv:** Young bust right **Rev:** Bust right

Date	Mintage	VF20	XF40	MS60	MS63	MS65
1993 Prooflike	—	—	—	—	4.00	5.00

KM# 135a CROWN
28.28 g., 0.925 Silver 0.841 oz. ASW, 38.8 mm. **Ruler:** Elizabeth II **Series:** House of - Hanover **Subject:** King George III, 1760-1820 **Obv:** Young bust right **Rev:** Bust right

Date	Mintage	VF20	XF40	MS60	MS63	MS65
1993	Est. 30000	PF65 28.00				

KM# 136 CROWN
Copper-Nickel, 38.8 mm. **Ruler:** Elizabeth II **Series:** House of - Hanover **Subject:** King George IV, 1820-1830 **Obv:** Young bust right **Rev:** Bust left

Date	Mintage	VF20	XF40	MS60	MS63	MS65
1993 Prooflike	—	—	—	—	4.00	5.00

KM# 136a CROWN
28.28 g., 0.925 Silver 0.841 oz. ASW, 38.8 mm. **Ruler:** Elizabeth II **Series:** House of - Hanover **Subject:** King George IV, 1820-1830 **Obv:** Young bust right **Rev:** Bust left

Date	Mintage	VF20	XF40	MS60	MS63	MS65
1993	Est. 30000	PF65 30.00				

KM# 137 CROWN
Copper-Nickel, 38.8 mm. **Ruler:** Elizabeth II **Series:** House of - Hanover **Subject:** King William IV, 1830-1837 **Obv:** Young bust right **Rev:** Bust right

Date	Mintage	VF20	XF40	MS60	MS63	MS65
1993 Prooflike	—	—	—	—	4.00	5.00

KM# 137a CROWN
28.28 g., 0.925 Silver 0.841 oz. ASW, 38.8 mm. **Ruler:** Elizabeth II **Series:** House of - Hanover **Subject:** King William IV, 1830-1837 **Obv:** Young bust right **Rev:** Bust right

Date	Mintage	VF20	XF40	MS60	MS63	MS65
1993	Est. 30000	PF65 30.00				

KM# 138 CROWN
Copper-Nickel, 38.8 mm. **Ruler:** Elizabeth II **Series:** House of - Hanover **Subject:** Queen Victoria, 1837-1901 **Obv:** Young bust right **Rev:** Bust left

Date	Mintage	VF20	XF40	MS60	MS63	MS65
1993 Prooflike	—	—	—	—	4.00	5.00

KM# 138a CROWN
28.28 g., 0.925 Silver 0.841 oz. ASW, 38.8 mm. **Ruler:** Elizabeth II **Series:** House of - Hanover **Subject:** Queen Victoria, 1837-1901 **Obv:** Young bust right **Rev:** Bust left

Date	Mintage	VF20	XF40	MS60	MS63	MS65
1993	Est. 30000	PF65 30.00				

KM# 139 CROWN
Copper-Nickel, 38.8 mm. **Ruler:** Elizabeth II **Series:** House of - Saxe-Coburg **Subject:** King Edward VII, 1901-1910 **Obv:** Young bust right **Rev:** Uniformed bust right

Date	Mintage	VF20	XF40	MS60	MS63	MS65
1993 Prooflike	—	—	—	—	4.00	5.00

KM# 139a CROWN
28.28 g., 0.925 Silver 0.841 oz. ASW, 38.8 mm. **Ruler:** Elizabeth II **Series:** House of - Saxe-Coburg **Subject:** King Edward VII, 1901-1910 **Obv:** Young bust right **Rev:** Uniformed bust right

Date	Mintage	VF20	XF40	MS60	MS63	MS65
1993	Est. 30000	PF65 32.00				

KM# 140 CROWN
Copper-Nickel, 38.8 mm. **Ruler:** Elizabeth II **Series:** House of - Windsor **Subject:** King George V, 1910-1936 **Obv:** Young bust right **Rev:** Uniformed bust left

Date	Mintage	VF20	XF40	MS60	MS63	MS65
1993 Prooflike	—	—	—	—	4.00	5.00

KM# 140a CROWN
28.28 g., 0.925 Silver 0.841 oz. ASW, 38.8 mm. **Ruler:** Elizabeth II **Series:** House of - Windsor **Subject:** King George V, 1910-1936 **Obv:** Young bust right **Rev:** Uniformed bust left

Date	Mintage	VF20	XF40	MS60	MS63	MS65
1993	Est. 30000	PF65 30.00				

KM# 141 CROWN
Copper-Nickel, 38.8 mm. **Ruler:** Elizabeth II **Series:** House of - Windsor **Subject:** King Edward VIII, 1936 **Obv:** Young bust right **Rev:** Bust left

Date	Mintage	VF20	XF40	MS60	MS63	MS65
1993 Prooflike	—	—	—	—	4.00	5.00

KM# 141a CROWN
28.28 g., 0.925 Silver 0.841 oz. ASW, 38.8 mm. **Ruler:** Elizabeth II **Series:** House of - Windsor **Subject:** King Edward VIII, 1936 **Obv:** Young bust right **Rev:** Bust left

Date	Mintage	VF20	XF40	MS60	MS63	MS65
1993	Est. 30000	PF65 30.00				

KM# 142 CROWN
Copper-Nickel, 38.8 mm. **Ruler:** Elizabeth II **Series:** House of - Windsor **Subject:** King George VI, 1936-1952 **Obv:** Young bust right **Rev:** Bust left

Date	Mintage	VF20	XF40	MS60	MS63	MS65
1993 Prooflike	—	—	—	—	4.00	5.00

KM# 142a CROWN
28.28 g., 0.925 Silver 0.841 oz. ASW, 38.8 mm. **Ruler:** Elizabeth II **Series:** House of - Windsor **Subject:** King George VI, 1936-1952 **Obv:** Young bust right **Rev:** Bust left

Date	Mintage	VF20	XF40	MS60	MS63	MS65
1993	Est. 30000	PF65 30.00				

KM# 143 CROWN
Copper-Nickel, 38.8 mm. **Ruler:** Elizabeth II **Subject:** Coronation of Queen Elizabeth II **Rev:** Crowned half figure left with scepter divides dates

Date	Mintage	VF20	XF40	MS60	MS63	MS65
1993	—	—	—	—	4.00	5.00

KM# 143a CROWN
28.28 g., 0.925 Silver 0.841 oz. ASW **Subject:** Coronation of Queen Elizabeth II **Rev:** Crowned half figure left with scepter divides dates

Date	Mintage	VF20	XF40	MS60	MS63	MS65
1993	Est. 30000	PF65 30.00				

KM# 144 CROWN

Copper-Nickel, 38.8 mm. **Ruler:** Elizabeth II **Series:** WWII Warships **Obv:** Crowned bust right **Rev:** FSS Savorgnan de Brazza

Date	Mintage	VF20	XF40	MS60	MS63	MS65
1993	—	—	—	—	4.00	5.00

KM# 144a CROWN

28.28 g., 0.925 Silver 0.841 oz. ASW, 38.8 mm. **Ruler:** Elizabeth II **Subject:** WWII Warships **Obv:** Crowned bust right **Rev:** FSS Savorgnan de Brazza

Date	Mintage	VF20	XF40	MS60	MS63	MS65
1993	Est. 30000	PF65 22.00				

KM# 145 CROWN

Copper-Nickel, 38.8 mm. **Ruler:** Elizabeth II **Series:** XVII Winter Olympics **Rev:** Skaters

Date	Mintage	VF20	XF40	MS60	MS63	MS65
1993	—	PF65 5.00				

KM# 145a CROWN

28.28 g., 0.925 Silver 0.841 oz. ASW, 38.8 mm. **Ruler:** Elizabeth II **Series:** XVII Winter Olympics **Rev:** Skaters

Date	Mintage	VF20	XF40	MS60	MS63	MS65
1993	Est. 30000	PF65 30.00				

KM# 145b CROWN

6.22 g., 0.9999 Gold 0.200 oz. AGW **Ruler:** Elizabeth II **Series:** XVII Winter Olympics **Rev:** Skaters

Date	Mintage	VF20	XF40	MS60	MS63	MS65
1993	Est. 5000	PF65 325				

KM# 146 CROWN

Copper-Nickel, 38.8 mm. **Ruler:** Elizabeth II **Series:** XVII Winter Olympics **Rev:** Ice hockey

Date	Mintage	VF20	XF40	MS60	MS63	MS65
1993	—	PF65 5.00				

KM# 146a CROWN

28.28 g., 0.925 Silver 0.841 oz. ASW, 38.8 mm. **Ruler:** Elizabeth II **Series:** XVII Winter Olympics **Rev:** Ice hockey

Date	Mintage	VF20	XF40	MS60	MS63	MS65
1993	Est. 30000	PF65 30.00				

KM# 146b CROWN

6.22 g., 0.9999 Gold 0.200 oz. AGW **Ruler:** Elizabeth II **Series:** XVII Winter Olympics **Rev:** Ice hockey

Date	Mintage	VF20	XF40	MS60	MS63	MS65
1993	Est. 5000	PF65 325				

KM# 147 CROWN

Copper-Nickel, 38.8 mm. **Ruler:** Elizabeth II **Series:** XVII Winter Olympics **Rev:** Bobsledding

Date	Mintage	VF20	XF40	MS60	MS63	MS65
1993	—	PF65 5.00				

KM# 147a CROWN

28.28 g., 0.925 Silver 0.841 oz. ASW, 38.8 mm. **Ruler:** Elizabeth II **Series:** XVII Winter Olympics **Rev:** Bobsledding

Date	Mintage	VF20	XF40	MS60	MS63	MS65
1993	Est. 30000	PF65 30.00				

KM# 147b CROWN

6.22 g., 0.9999 Gold 0.200 oz. AGW **Ruler:** Elizabeth II **Series:** XVII Winter Olympics **Rev:** Bobsledding

Date	Mintage	VF20	XF40	MS60	MS63	MS65
1993	Est. 5000	PF65 325				

KM# 148 CROWN

Copper-Nickel, 38.8 mm. **Ruler:** Elizabeth II **Series:** XVII Winter Olympics **Rev:** Skiers

Date	Mintage	VF20	XF40	MS60	MS63	MS65
1993	—	PF65 5.00				

KM# 148a CROWN

28.28 g., 0.925 Silver 0.841 oz. ASW, 38.8 mm. **Ruler:** Elizabeth II **Series:** XVII Winter Olympics **Rev:** Skiers

Date	Mintage	VF20	XF40	MS60	MS63	MS65
1993	—	PF65 30.00				

KM# 148b CROWN

6.22 g., 0.9999 Gold 0.200 oz. AGW **Ruler:** Elizabeth II **Rev:** XVII Winter Olympics

Date	Mintage	VF20	XF40	MS60	MS63	MS65
1993	Est. 5000	PF65 325				

KM# 149 CROWN

Copper-Nickel, 38.8 mm. **Ruler:** Elizabeth II **Series:** Preserve Planet Earth **Obv:** Crowned bust right **Rev:** Cetiosaurus

Date	Mintage	VF20	XF40	MS60	MS63	MS65
1993	—	—	—	—	10.00	14.00

KM# 149a CROWN

28.28 g., 0.925 Silver 0.841 oz. ASW, 38.8 mm. **Ruler:** Elizabeth II **Series:** Preserve Planet Earth **Obv:** Crowned bust right **Rev:** Cetiosaurus

Date	Mintage	VF20	XF40	MS60	MS63	MS65
1993	Est. 30000	PF65 30.00				

KM# 151 CROWN

Copper-Nickel, 38.8 mm. **Ruler:** Elizabeth II **Series:** Preserve Planet Earth **Obv:** Crowned bust right **Rev:** Stegosaurus

Date	Mintage	VF20	XF40	MS60	MS63	MS65
1993	—	—	—	—	10.00	14.00

KM# 151a CROWN

28.28 g., 0.925 Silver 0.841 oz. ASW, 38.8 mm. **Ruler:** Elizabeth II **Series:** Preserve Planet Earth **Obv:** Crowned bust right **Rev:** Stegosaurus

Date	Mintage	VF20	XF40	MS60	MS63	MS65
1993	—	PF65 30.00				

KM# 180 CROWN

Copper-Nickel, 38.8 mm. **Ruler:** Elizabeth II **Series:** International Friendship **Obv:** Crowned bust right **Rev:** Stylized panda

Date	Mintage	VF20	XF40	MS60	MS63	MS65
1993	—	—	—	—	8.50	15.00

KM# 180a CROWN

28.28 g., 0.925 Silver 0.841 oz. ASW, 38.8 mm. **Ruler:** Elizabeth II **Series:** International Friendship **Obv:** Crowned bust right **Rev:** Stylized panda

Date	Mintage	VF20	XF40	MS60	MS63	MS65
1993	Est. 30000	PF65 30.00				

KM# 184 CROWN

Copper-Nickel, 38.8 mm. **Ruler:** Elizabeth II **Series:** International Friendship **Obv:** Crowned bust right **Rev:** Natural panda

Date	Mintage	VF20	XF40	MS60	MS63	MS65
1993	—	—	—	—	8.50	15.00

KM# 184a CROWN

28.28 g., 0.925 Silver 0.841 oz. ASW, 38.8 mm. **Ruler:** Elizabeth II **Series:** International Friendship **Obv:** Crowned bust right **Rev:** Natural panda

Date	Mintage	VF20	XF40	MS60	MS63	MS65
1993	—	PF65 30.00				

KM# 188 CROWN

Copper-Nickel, 38.8 mm. **Ruler:** Elizabeth II **Series:** International Friendship **Subject:** General Sikorski **Obv:** Crowned bust right **Rev:** Uniformed bust above plane, mountains in background

Date	Mintage	VF20	XF40	MS60	MS63	MS65
1993	—	—	—	—	5.00	6.50

KM# 188a CROWN

28.28 g., 0.925 Silver 0.841 oz. ASW, 38.8 mm. **Ruler:** Elizabeth II **Series:** International Friendship **Subject:** General Sikorski **Obv:** Crowned bust right **Rev:** Uniformed bust above plane, mountains in background

Date	Mintage	VF20	XF40	MS60	MS63	MS65
1993	Est. 30000	PF65 30.00				

KM# 192.1 CROWN

Copper-Nickel, 38.8 mm. **Ruler:** Elizabeth II **Obv:** Crowned bust right **Rev:** Long-haired Dachshund

Date	Mintage	VF20	XF40	MS60	MS63	MS65
1993	—	—	—	—	10.00	15.00
1993	Est. 250	PF65 22.00				

KM# 192.1a CROWN

31.10 g., 0.925 Silver 0.925 oz. ASW, 38.8 mm. **Ruler:** Elizabeth II **Obv:** Crowned bust right **Rev:** Long-haired Dachshund

Date	Mintage	VF20	XF40	MS60	MS63	MS65
1993	Est. 50000	PF65 28.00				

KM# 192.2 CROWN

Copper-Nickel, 38.8 mm. **Ruler:** Elizabeth II **Obv:** Crowned bust right **Rev:** Long-haired Dachshund, mint mark left of dog

Date	Mintage	VF20	XF40	MS60	MS63	MS65
1993 (c)	—	—	—	—	10.00	15.00
1993	—	PF65 20.00				

KM# 192.2a CROWN

28.28 g., 0.925 Silver 0.841 oz. ASW, 38.8 mm. **Ruler:** Elizabeth II **Obv:** Crowned bust right **Rev:** Mint mark left of dog

Date	Mintage	VF20	XF40	MS60	MS63	MS65
1993	—	—	—	—	30.00	32.00

KM# 200 CROWN

Copper-Nickel, 38.8 mm. **Ruler:** Elizabeth II **Subject:** Dependent Territories Conference **Obv:** Crowned bust right **Rev:** Two shields at center surrounded by five shields

Date	Mintage	VF20	XF40	MS60	MS63	MS65
1993	—	—	—	—	5.50	7.00

KM# 200a CROWN

28.28 g., 0.925 Silver 0.841 oz. ASW, 38.8 mm. **Ruler:** Elizabeth II **Subject:** Dependent Territories Conference **Obv:** Crowned bust right **Rev:** Two center shields surrounded by five shields

Date	Mintage	VF20	XF40	MS60	MS63	MS65
1993	Est. 30000	PF65 30.00				

KM# 201 CROWN

Copper-Nickel, 38.8 mm. **Ruler:** Elizabeth II **Series:** Peter Rabbit Centennial **Subject:** The Tale of Peter Rabbit **Obv:** Crowned bust right **Rev:** Peter Rabbit, sparrow on handle

Date	Mintage	VF20	XF40	MS60	MS63	MS65
1993	—	—	—	—	7.50	9.00

KM# 201a CROWN

28.28 g., 0.925 Silver 0.841 oz. ASW, 38.8 mm. **Ruler:** Elizabeth II **Series:** Peter Rabbit Centennial **Subject:** The Tale of Peter Rabbit **Obv:** Crowned bust right **Rev:** Peter Rabbit, sparrow on handle

Date	Mintage	VF20	XF40	MS60	MS63	MS65
1993	Est. 30000	PF65 32.00				

KM# 205 CROWN

Copper-Nickel, 38.8 mm. **Ruler:** Elizabeth II **Series:** Peter Rabbit Centennial **Subject:** The Tale of Peter Rabbit **Obv:** Crowned bust right **Rev:** Mrs. Tiggy-Winkel ironing

Date	Mintage	VF20	XF40	MS60	MS63	MS65
1993	—	—	—	—	7.50	9.00

KM# 205a CROWN

28.28 g., 0.925 Silver 0.841 oz. ASW, 38.8 mm. **Ruler:** Elizabeth II **Series:** Peter Rabbit Centennial **Subject:** The Tale of Peter Rabbit **Obv:** Crowned bust right **Rev:** Mrs. Tiggy-Winkel ironing

Date	Mintage	VF20	XF40	MS60	MS63	MS65
1993	Est. 30000	PF65 28.00				

KM# 209 CROWN

Copper-Nickel, 38.8 mm. **Ruler:** Elizabeth II **Series:** Peter Rabbit Centennial **Subject:** The Tale of Peter Rabbit **Obv:** Crowned bust right **Rev:** Jeremy Fisher fishing

Date	Mintage	VF20	XF40	MS60	MS63	MS65
1993	—	—	—	—	7.50	9.00

KM# 209a CROWN

28.28 g., 0.925 Silver 0.841 oz. ASW, 38.8 mm. **Ruler:** Elizabeth II **Series:** Peter Rabbit Centennial **Subject:** The Tale of Peter Rabbit **Obv:** Crowned bust right **Rev:** Jeremy Fisher fishing

Date	Mintage	VF20	XF40	MS60	MS63	MS65
1993	Est. 30000	PF65 28.00				

KM# 213 CROWN

Copper-Nickel, 38.8 mm. **Ruler:** Elizabeth II **Series:** Peter Rabbit Centennial **Subject:** The Tale of Peter Rabbit **Obv:** Crowned bust right **Rev:** Tom Kitten with mother cat

Date	Mintage	VF20	XF40	MS60	MS63	MS65
1993	—	—	—	—	7.50	9.00

KM# 213a CROWN

28.28 g., 0.925 Silver 0.841 oz. ASW, 38.8 mm. **Ruler:** Elizabeth II **Series:** Peter Rabbit Centennial **Subject:** The Tale of Peter Rabbit **Obv:** Crowned bust right **Rev:** Tom Kitten with mother cat

Date	Mintage	VF20	XF40	MS60	MS63	MS65
1993	Est. 30000	PF65 28.00				

KM# 217 CROWN

Copper-Nickel, 38.8 mm. **Ruler:** Elizabeth II **Series:** Peter Rabbit Centennial **Subject:** The Tale of Peter Rabbit **Obv:** Crowned bust right **Rev:** Benjamin Bunny with hat, holding coat

Date	Mintage	VF20	XF40	MS60	MS63	MS65
1993	—	—	—	—	7.50	9.00

KM# 217a CROWN

28.28 g., 0.925 Silver 0.841 oz. ASW, 38.8 mm. **Ruler:** Elizabeth II **Series:** Peter Rabbit Centennial **Subject:** The Tale of Peter Rabbit **Obv:** Crowned bust right **Rev:** Benjamin Bunny with hat holding coat

Date	Mintage	VF20	XF40	MS60	MS63	MS65
1993	Est. 30000	PF65 28.00				

KM# 221 CROWN
Copper-Nickel, 38.8 mm. **Ruler:** Elizabeth II **Series:** Peter Rabbit Centennial **Subject:** The Tale of Peter Rabbit **Obv:** Crowned bust right **Rev:** Jemima Puddle-Duck talking to fox

Date	Mintage	VF20	XF40	MS60	MS63	MS65
1993	—	—	—	—	7.50	9.00

KM# 221a CROWN
28.28 g., 0.925 Silver 0.841 oz. ASW, 38.8 mm. **Ruler:** Elizabeth II **Series:** Peter Rabbit Centennial **Subject:** The Tale of Peter Rabbit **Obv:** Crowned bust right **Rev:** Jemima Puddle-Duck talking to fox

Date	Mintage	VF20	XF40	MS60	MS63	MS65
1993	Est. 30000	PF65 28.00				

KM# 342c CROWN
Copper-Nickel, 38.8 mm. **Ruler:** Elizabeth II **Subject:** Year of the Cockerel **Obv:** Crowned bust right **Rev:** Cockerel (rooster)

Date	Mintage	VF20	XF40	MS60	MS63	MS65
1993	—	—	—	—	9.00	11.00

KM# 225 CROWN
Copper-Nickel, 38.8 mm. **Ruler:** Elizabeth II **Subject:** World Cup Soccer **Obv:** Crowned bust right **Rev:** Three players

Date	Mintage	VF20	XF40	MS60	MS63	MS65
1994	—	—	—	—	4.75	6.00

KM# 225a CROWN
28.28 g., 0.925 Silver 0.841 oz. ASW, 38.8 mm. **Ruler:** Elizabeth II **Subject:** World Cup Soccer **Obv:** Crowned bust right **Rev:** Three players

Date	Mintage	VF20	XF40	MS60	MS63	MS65
1994	—	PF65 28.00				

KM# 227 CROWN
Copper-Nickel, 38.8 mm. **Ruler:** Elizabeth II **Subject:** World Cup Soccer **Obv:** Crowned bust right **Rev:** Two players

Date	Mintage	VF20	XF40	MS60	MS63	MS65
1994	—	—	—	—	4.75	6.00

KM# 227a CROWN
28.28 g., 0.925 Silver 0.841 oz. ASW, 38.8 mm. **Ruler:** Elizabeth II **Subject:** World Cup Soccer **Obv:** Crowned bust right **Rev:** Two players facing

Date	Mintage	VF20	XF40	MS60	MS63	MS65
1994	Est. 30000	PF65 28.00				

KM# 229 CROWN
Copper-Nickel, 38.8 mm. **Ruler:** Elizabeth II **Subject:** World Cup Soccer **Obv:** Crowned bust right **Rev:** Goalie and scorer

Date	Mintage	VF20	XF40	MS60	MS63	MS65
1994	—	—	—	—	4.75	6.00

KM# 229a CROWN
28.28 g., 0.925 Silver 0.841 oz. ASW, 38.8 mm. **Ruler:** Elizabeth II **Subject:** World Cup Soccer **Obv:** Crowned bust right **Rev:** Goalie and scorer

Date	Mintage	VF20	XF40	MS60	MS63	MS65
1994	Est. 30000	PF65 28.00				

KM# 231 CROWN
Copper-Nickel, 38.8 mm. **Ruler:** Elizabeth II **Subject:** World Cup Soccer **Obv:** Crowned bust right **Rev:** One player

Date	Mintage	VF20	XF40	MS60	MS63	MS65
1994	—	—	—	—	4.75	6.00

KM# 231a CROWN
28.28 g., 0.925 Silver 0.841 oz. ASW, 38.8 mm. **Ruler:** Elizabeth II **Subject:** World Cup Soccer **Obv:** Crowned bust right **Rev:** One player

Date	Mintage	VF20	XF40	MS60	MS63	MS65
1994	Est. 30000	PF65 28.00				

KM# 233 CROWN
Copper-Nickel, 38.8 mm. **Ruler:** Elizabeth II **Subject:** World Cup Soccer **Obv:** Crowned bust right **Rev:** Two players, one kicking

Date	Mintage	VF20	XF40	MS60	MS63	MS65
1994	—	—	—	—	4.75	6.00

KM# 233a CROWN
28.28 g., 0.925 Silver 0.841 oz. ASW, 38.8 mm. **Ruler:** Elizabeth II **Subject:** World Cup Soccer **Obv:** Crowned bust right **Rev:** Two players, one kicking

Date	Mintage	VF20	XF40	MS60	MS63	MS65
1994	Est. 30000	PF65 28.00				

KM# 235 CROWN
Copper-Nickel, 38.8 mm. **Ruler:** Elizabeth II **Subject:** World Cup Soccer **Obv:** Crowned bust right **Rev:** Two players sideways

Date	Mintage	VF20	XF40	MS60	MS63	MS65
1994	—	—	—	—	4.75	6.00

KM# 235a CROWN
28.28 g., 0.925 Silver 0.841 oz. ASW, 38.8 mm. **Ruler:** Elizabeth II **Subject:** World Cup Soccer **Obv:** Crowned bust right **Rev:** Two players sideways

Date	Mintage	VF20	XF40	MS60	MS63	MS65
1994	Est. 30000	PF65 28.00				

KM# 239 CROWN
Copper-Nickel, 38.8 mm. **Ruler:** Elizabeth II **Series:** Preserve Planet Earth **Obv:** Crowned bust right **Rev:** Sabre-tooth Tiger

Date	Mintage	VF20	XF40	MS60	MS63	MS65
1994	—	—	—	—	7.00	15.00

KM# 239a CROWN
28.28 g., 0.925 Silver 0.841 oz. ASW, 38.8 mm. **Ruler:** Elizabeth II **Series:** Preserve Planet Earth **Obv:** Crowned bust right **Rev:** Sabre-tooth Tiger

Date	Mintage	VF20	XF40	MS60	MS63	MS65
1994	Est. 30000	PF65 32.00				

KM# 241 CROWN
Copper-Nickel, 38.8 mm. **Ruler:** Elizabeth II **Series:** Preserve Planet Earth **Obv:** Crowned bust right **Rev:** Spanish Eagle

Date	Mintage	VF20	XF40	MS60	MS63	MS65
1994	—	—	—	—	9.00	14.00

KM# 241a CROWN
28.28 g., 0.925 Silver 0.841 oz. ASW **Series:** Preserve Planet Earth **Obv:** Crowned bust right **Rev:** Spanish Eagle

Date	Mintage	VF20	XF40	MS60	MS63	MS65
1994	Est. 30000	PF65 32.00				

KM# 243 CROWN
Copper-Nickel, 38.8 mm. **Ruler:** Elizabeth II **Series:** Preserve Planet Earth **Obv:** Crowned bust right **Rev:** Striped Dolphins

Date	Mintage	VF20	XF40	MS60	MS63	MS65
1994	—	—	—	—	9.00	14.00

KM# 243a CROWN
28.28 g., 0.925 Silver 0.841 oz. ASW, 38.8 mm. **Ruler:** Elizabeth II **Series:** Preserve Planet Earth **Obv:** Crowned bust right **Rev:** Striped Dolphins

Date	Mintage	VF20	XF40	MS60	MS63	MS65
1994	Est. 30000	PF65 32.00				

KM# 245 CROWN
Copper-Nickel, 38.8 mm. **Ruler:** Elizabeth II **Series:** Preserve Planet Earth **Obv:** Crowned bust right **Rev:** African Elephants

Date	Mintage	VF20	XF40	MS60	MS63	MS65
1994	—	—	—	—	9.00	14.00

KM# 245a CROWN
28.28 g., 0.925 Silver 0.841 oz. ASW, 38.8 mm. **Ruler:** Elizabeth II **Series:** Preserve Planet Earth **Obv:** Crowned bust right **Rev:** African Elephants

Date	Mintage	VF20	XF40	MS60	MS63	MS65
1994	Est. 30000	PF65 32.00				

KM# 259 CROWN
Copper-Nickel, 38.8 mm. **Ruler:** Elizabeth II **Series:** World War II **Obv:** Crowned bust right **Rev:** Maltese convoy

Date	Mintage	VF20	XF40	MS60	MS63	MS65
1994	—	—	—	—	6.00	8.00

KM# 259a CROWN
28.28 g., 0.925 Silver 0.841 oz. ASW, 38.8 mm. **Ruler:** Elizabeth II **Series:** World War II **Obv:** Crowned bust right **Rev:** Maltese convoy

Date	Mintage	VF20	XF40	MS60	MS63	MS65
1994	Est. 30000	PF65 28.00				

KM# 260 CROWN
Copper-Nickel, 38.8 mm. **Ruler:** Elizabeth II **Series:** World War II **Obv:** Crowned bust right **Rev:** Squadron 202 in Gibraltar

Date	Mintage	VF20	XF40	MS60	MS63	MS65
1994	—	—	—	—	6.00	8.00

KM# 260a CROWN
28.28 g., 0.925 Silver 0.841 oz. ASW, 38.8 mm. **Ruler:** Elizabeth II **Series:** World War II **Obv:** Crowned bust right **Rev:** Squadron 202 in Gibraltar

Date	Mintage	VF20	XF40	MS60	MS63	MS65
1994	Est. 30000	PF65 28.00				

KM# 261 CROWN
Copper-Nickel, 38.8 mm. **Ruler:** Elizabeth II **Series:** World War II **Obv:** Crowned bust right **Rev:** Admiral Somerville

Date	Mintage	VF20	XF40	MS60	MS63	MS65
1994	—	—	—	—	6.00	8.00

KM# 261a CROWN
28.28 g., 0.925 Silver 0.841 oz. ASW, 38.8 mm. **Ruler:** Elizabeth II **Series:** World War II **Obv:** Crowned bust right **Rev:** Admiral Somerville

Date	Mintage	VF20	XF40	MS60	MS63	MS65
1994	Est. 30000	PF65 28.00				

KM# 262 CROWN
Copper-Nickel, 38.8 mm. **Ruler:** Elizabeth II **Series:** World War II **Obv:** Crowned bust right **Rev:** Glen Miller and band

Date	Mintage	VF20	XF40	MS60	MS63	MS65
1994	—	—	—	—	6.00	8.00

KM# 262a CROWN
28.28 g., 0.925 Silver 0.841 oz. ASW, 38.8 mm. **Ruler:** Elizabeth II **Series:** World War II **Obv:** Crowned bust right **Rev:** Glen Miller and band

Date	Mintage	VF20	XF40	MS60	MS63	MS65
1994	—	PF65 28.00				

KM# 263 CROWN
Copper-Nickel, 38.8 mm. **Ruler:** Elizabeth II **Series:** World War II **Obv:** Crowned bust right **Rev:** King George VI and pilots

Date	Mintage	VF20	XF40	MS60	MS63	MS65
1994	—	—	—	—	6.00	8.00

KM# 263a CROWN
28.28 g., 0.925 Silver 0.841 oz. ASW, 38.8 mm. **Ruler:** Elizabeth II **Series:** World War II **Obv:** Crowned bust right **Rev:** King George VI and pilots

Date	Mintage	VF20	XF40	MS60	MS63	MS65
1994	Est. 30000	PF65 30.00				

KM# 264 CROWN
Copper-Nickel, 38.8 mm. **Ruler:** Elizabeth II **Series:** World War II **Obv:** Crowned bust right **Rev:** General Eisenhower

Date	Mintage	VF20	XF40	MS60	MS63	MS65
1994	—	—	—	—	6.00	8.00

KM# 264a CROWN
28.28 g., 0.925 Silver 0.841 oz. ASW, 38.8 mm. **Ruler:** Elizabeth II **Series:** World War II **Obv:** Crowned bust right **Rev:** General Eisenhower

Date	Mintage	VF20	XF40	MS60	MS63	MS65
1994	—	PF65 30.00				

KM# 271 CROWN
Copper-Nickel, 38.8 mm. **Ruler:** Elizabeth II **Series:** First Man on Moon **Obv:** Crowned bust right **Rev:** Dr. Wernher von Braun with model of shuttle

Date	Mintage	VF20	XF40	MS60	MS63	MS65
1994	—	—	—	—	5.75	6.50

KM# 271a CROWN
, 38.8 mm. **Ruler:** Elizabeth II **Series:** First Man on Moon **Obv:** Crowned bust right **Rev:** Dr. Wernher von Braun with model of shuttle

Date	Mintage	VF20	XF40	MS60	MS63	MS65
1994	Est. 30000	PF65 25.00				

KM# 272 CROWN
Copper-Nickel, 38.8 mm. **Ruler:** Elizabeth II **Series:** First Man on Moon **Obv:** Crowned bust right **Rev:** Rocket launching

Date	Mintage	VF20	XF40	MS60	MS63	MS65
1994	—	—	—	—	5.75	6.50

KM# 272a CROWN
28.28 g., 0.925 Silver 0.841 oz. ASW, 38.8 mm. **Ruler:** Elizabeth II **Series:** First Man on Moon **Obv:** Crowned bust right **Rev:** Rocket launching

Date	Mintage	VF20	XF40	MS60	MS63	MS65
1994	Est. 30000	PF65 25.00				

KM# 273 CROWN
Copper-Nickel, 38.8 mm. **Ruler:** Elizabeth II **Series:** First Man on Moon **Obv:** Crowned bust right **Rev:** Space capsule recovery

Date	Mintage	VF20	XF40	MS60	MS63	MS65
1994	—	—	—	—	5.75	6.50

KM# 273a CROWN
28.28 g., 0.925 Silver 0.841 oz. ASW, 38.8 mm. **Ruler:** Elizabeth II **Series:** First Man on Moon **Obv:** Crowned bust right **Rev:** Space capsule recovery

Date	Mintage	VF20	XF40	MS60	MS63	MS65
1994	—	PF65 25.00				

KM# 274 CROWN
Copper-Nickel, 38.8 mm. **Ruler:** Elizabeth II **Series:** First Man on Moon **Obv:** Crowned bust right **Rev:** First manned lunar landing

Date	Mintage	VF20	XF40	MS60	MS63	MS65
1994	—	—	—	—	5.75	6.50

KM# 274a CROWN
28.28 g., 0.925 Silver 0.841 oz. ASW, 38.8 mm. **Ruler:** Elizabeth II **Series:** First Man on Moon **Obv:** Crowned bust right **Rev:** First manned lunar landing

Date	Mintage	VF20	XF40	MS60	MS63	MS65
1994	Est. 30000	PF65 25.00				

KM# 275 CROWN
Copper-Nickel, 38.8 mm. **Ruler:** Elizabeth II **Series:** First Man on Moon **Obv:** Crowned bust right **Rev:** First step on moon

Date	Mintage	VF20	XF40	MS60	MS63	MS65
1994	—	—	—	—	5.75	6.50

KM# 275a CROWN
28.28 g., 0.925 Silver 0.841 oz. ASW, 38.8 mm. **Ruler:** Elizabeth II **Series:** First Man on Moon **Obv:** Crowned bust right **Rev:** First step on moon

Date	Mintage	VF20	XF40	MS60	MS63	MS65
1994	Est. 30000	PF65 25.00				

KM# 276 CROWN
Copper-Nickel, 38.8 mm. **Ruler:** Elizabeth II **Series:** First Man on Moon **Obv:** Crowned bust right **Rev:** First flag planted on moon

Date	Mintage	VF20	XF40	MS60	MS63	MS65
1994	—	—	—	—	5.75	6.50

KM# 276a CROWN
28.28 g., 0.925 Silver 0.841 oz. ASW, 38.8 mm. **Ruler:** Elizabeth II **Series:** First Man on Moon **Obv:** Crowned bust right **Rev:** First flag planted on moon

Date	Mintage	VF20	XF40	MS60	MS63	MS65
1994	Est. 30000	PF65 25.00				

KM# 285 CROWN
Copper-Nickel, 38.8 mm. **Ruler:** Elizabeth II **Series:** 100th Anniversary of The Return of Sherlock Holmes **Subject:** Sherlock Holmes **Obv:** Crowned bust right **Rev:** Bust with pipe left

Date	Mintage	VF20	XF40	MS60	MS63	MS65
1994	—	—	—	—	8.00	9.00

KM# 285a CROWN
28.28 g., 0.925 Silver 0.841 oz. ASW, 38.8 mm. **Ruler:** Elizabeth II **Series:** 100th Anniversary of The Return of Sherlock Holmes **Subject:** Sherlock Holmes **Obv:** Crowned bust right **Rev:** Bust with pipe left

Date	Mintage	VF20	XF40	MS60	MS63	MS65
1994	Est. 30000	PF65 25.00				

KM# 286 CROWN
Copper-Nickel, 38.8 mm. **Ruler:** Elizabeth II **Series:** 100th Anniversary of The Return of Sherlock Holmes **Obv:** Crowned bust right **Rev:** Sherlock Holmes playing violin for Dr. Watson

Date	Mintage	VF20	XF40	MS60	MS63	MS65
1994	—	—	—	—	8.00	9.00

KM# 286a CROWN
28.28 g., 0.925 Silver 0.841 oz. ASW, 38.8 mm. **Ruler:** Elizabeth II **Series:** 100th Anniversary of The Return of Sherlock Holmes **Obv:** Crowned bust right **Rev:** Sherlock Holmes playing violin for Dr. Watson

Date	Mintage	VF20	XF40	MS60	MS63	MS65
1994	Est. 30000	PF65 25.00				

KM# 287 CROWN
Copper-Nickel, 38.8 mm. **Ruler:** Elizabeth II **Series:** 100th Anniversary of The Return of Sherlock Holmes **Subject:** 221 B Baker Street **Obv:** Crowned bust right **Rev:** Figures in front of building

Date	Mintage	VF20	XF40	MS60	MS63	MS65
1994	—	—	—	—	8.00	9.00

KM# 287a CROWN
28.28 g., 0.925 Silver 0.841 oz. ASW, 38.8 mm. **Ruler:** Elizabeth II **Series:** 100th Anniversary of The Return of Sherlock Holmes **Subject:** 221 B Baker Street **Obv:** Crowned bust right **Rev:** Figures in front of building

Date	Mintage	VF20	XF40	MS60	MS63	MS65
1994	—	PF65 25.00				

KM# 288 CROWN
Copper-Nickel, 38.8 mm. **Ruler:** Elizabeth II **Series:** 100th Anniversary of The Return of Sherlock Holmes **Subject:** The Empty House **Obv:** Crowned bust right **Rev:** Three figures

Date	Mintage	VF20	XF40	MS60	MS63	MS65
1994	—	—	—	—	8.00	9.00

KM# 288a CROWN
28.28 g., 0.925 Silver 0.841 oz. ASW, 38.8 mm. **Ruler:** Elizabeth II **Series:** 100th Anniversary of The Return of Sherlock Holmes **Subject:** The Empty House **Obv:** Crowned bust right **Rev:** Three figures

Date	Mintage	VF20	XF40	MS60	MS63	MS65
1994	Est. 30000	PF65 25.00				

KM# 289 CROWN
Copper-Nickel, 38.8 mm. **Ruler:** Elizabeth II **Series:** 100th Anniversary of The Return of Sherlock Holmes **Subject:** The Mary Celeste **Obv:** Crowned bust right **Rev:** Cameo left of masted ship at sea

Date	Mintage	VF20	XF40	MS60	MS63	MS65
1994	—	—	—	—	8.00	9.00

KM# 289a CROWN
28.28 g., 0.925 Silver 0.841 oz. ASW, 38.8 mm. **Ruler:** Elizabeth II **Series:** 100th Anniversary of The Return of Sherlock Holmes **Subject:** The Mary Celeste **Obv:** Crowned bust right **Rev:** Cameo left of masted ship at sea

Date	Mintage	VF20	XF40	MS60	MS63	MS65
1994	Est. 30000	PF65 32.00				

KM# 290 CROWN

Copper-Nickel, 38.8 mm. **Ruler:** Elizabeth II **Series:** 100th Anniversary of The Return of Sherlock Holmes **Subject:** The Hound of the Baskervilles **Obv:** Crowned bust right **Rev:** Two figures back and right of large dog at front

Date	Mintage	VF20	XF40	MS60	MS63	MS65
1994	—	—	—	—	8.00	9.00

KM# 290a CROWN

28.28 g., 0.925 Silver 0.841 oz. ASW, 38.8 mm. **Ruler:** Elizabeth II **Series:** 100th Anniversary of The Return of Sherlock Holmes **Subject:** The Hound of the Baskervilles **Obv:** Crowned bust right **Rev:** Two figures back and right of large dog at front

Date	Mintage	VF20	XF40	MS60	MS63	MS65
1994	—	PF65 30.00				

KM# 291 CROWN

Copper-Nickel, 38.8 mm. **Ruler:** Elizabeth II **Series:** 100th Anniversary of The Return of Sherlock Holmes **Subject:** The Three Garriders **Obv:** Crowned bust right **Rev:** Two seated figures **Note:** Variety exists with spelling error: GARRIDEBS.

Date	Mintage	VF20	XF40	MS60	MS63	MS65
1994	—	—	—	—	8.00	9.00

KM# 291a CROWN

28.28 g., 0.925 Silver 0.841 oz. ASW, 38.8 mm. **Ruler:** Elizabeth II **Series:** 100th Anniversary of The Return of Sherlock Holmes **Subject:** The Three Garriders **Obv:** Crowned bust right **Rev:** Two seated figures

Date	Mintage	VF20	XF40	MS60	MS63	MS65
1994	Est. 30000	PF65 25.00				

KM# 292 CROWN

Copper-Nickel, 38.8 mm. **Ruler:** Elizabeth II **Series:** 100th Anniversary of The Return of Sherlock Holmes **Subject:** The Final Problem **Obv:** Crowned bust right **Rev:** Two figures and waterfall

Date	Mintage	VF20	XF40	MS60	MS63	MS65
1994	—	—	—	—	8.00	9.00

KM# 292a CROWN

28.28 g., 0.925 Silver 0.841 oz. ASW, 38.8 mm. **Ruler:** Elizabeth II **Series:** 100th Anniversary of The Return of Sherlock Holmes **Subject:** The Final Problem **Obv:** Crowned bust right **Rev:** Two figures and waterfall

Date	Mintage	VF20	XF40	MS60	MS63	MS65
1994	Est. 30000	PF65 25.00				

KM# 444 CROWN

Copper-Nickel, 38.8 mm. **Ruler:** Elizabeth II **Subject:** The Tale of Peter Rabbit **Obv:** Crowned bust right **Rev:** Mother rabbit with bunnies

Date	Mintage	VF20	XF40	MS60	MS63	MS65
1994	—	—	—	—	7.50	10.00

KM# 444a CROWN

28.28 g., 0.925 Silver 0.841 oz. ASW, 38.8 mm. **Ruler:** Elizabeth II **Subject:** The Tale of Peter Rabbit **Obv:** Crowned bust right **Rev:** Mother rabbit with bunnies

Date	Mintage	VF20	XF40	MS60	MS63	MS65
1994	Est. 30000	PF65 35.00				

KM# 299 CROWN

Copper-Nickel, 38.8 mm. **Ruler:** Elizabeth II **Series:** Atlanta Olympics **Obv:** Crowned bust right **Rev:** Long jumper

Date	Mintage	VF20	XF40	MS60	MS63	MS65
1995	—	PF65 7.00				

KM# 299a CROWN

28.28 g., 0.925 Silver 0.841 oz. ASW, 38.8 mm. **Ruler:** Elizabeth II **Series:** Atlanta Olympics **Obv:** Crowned bust right **Rev:** Long jumper

Date	Mintage	VF20	XF40	MS60	MS63	MS65
1995	Est. 30000	PF65 25.00				

KM# 300 CROWN

Copper-Nickel, 38.8 mm. **Ruler:** Elizabeth II **Series:** Atlanta Olympics **Obv:** Crowned bust right **Rev:** Discus thrower

Date	Mintage	VF20	XF40	MS60	MS63	MS65
1995	—	—	—	—	5.50	6.00

KM# 300a CROWN

28.28 g., 0.925 Silver 0.841 oz. ASW, 38.8 mm. **Ruler:** Elizabeth II **Series:** Atlanta Olympics **Obv:** Crowned bust right **Rev:** Discus thrower

Date	Mintage	VF20	XF40	MS60	MS63	MS65
1995	Est. 30000	PF65 25.00				

KM# 301 CROWN

Copper-Nickel, 38.8 mm. **Ruler:** Elizabeth II **Obv:** Crowned bust right **Rev:** Relay runners

Date	Mintage	VF20	XF40	MS60	MS63	MS65
1995	—	—	—	—	5.50	6.00

KM# 301a CROWN

28.28 g., 0.925 Silver 0.841 oz. ASW, 38.8 mm. **Ruler:** Elizabeth II **Obv:** Crowned bust right **Rev:** Relay runners

Date	Mintage	VF20	XF40	MS60	MS63	MS65
1995	Est. 30000	PF65 25.00				

KM# 302 CROWN

Copper-Nickel, 38.8 mm. **Ruler:** Elizabeth II **Series:** Atlanta Olympics **Obv:** Crowned bust right **Rev:** Javelin throwers

Date	Mintage	VF20	XF40	MS60	MS63	MS65
1995	—	—	—	—	5.50	6.00

KM# 302a CROWN

28.28 g., 0.925 Silver 0.841 oz. ASW, 38.8 mm. **Ruler:** Elizabeth II **Series:** Atlanta Olympics **Obv:** Crowned bust right **Rev:** Javelin throwers

Date	Mintage	VF20	XF40	MS60	MS63	MS65
1995	—	PF65 25.00				

KM# 304 CROWN

Copper-Nickel, 38.8 mm. **Ruler:** Elizabeth II **Obv:** Crowned bust right **Rev:** Sun rising over Rock of Gibraltar

Date	Mintage	VF20	XF40	MS60	MS63	MS65
1995	—	—	—	—	6.50	7.50

KM# 304a CROWN

28.28 g., 0.925 Silver 0.841 oz. ASW, 38.8 mm. **Ruler:** Elizabeth II **Obv:** Crowned bust right **Rev:** Sun rising over Rock of Gibraltar

Date	Mintage	VF20	XF40	MS60	MS63	MS65
1995	Est. 30000	PF65 35.00				

KM# 306 CROWN

Copper-Nickel, 38.8 mm. **Ruler:** Elizabeth II **Series:** Preserve Planet Earth **Obv:** Crowned bust right **Rev:** Monkeys

Date	Mintage	VF20	XF40	MS60	MS63	MS65
1995	—	—	—	—	10.00	14.00

KM# 306a CROWN

28.28 g., 0.925 Silver 0.841 oz. ASW, 38.8 mm. **Series:** Preserve Planet Earth **Obv:** Crowned bust right **Rev:** Monkeys

Date	Mintage	VF20	XF40	MS60	MS63	MS65
1995	Est. 30000	PF65 35.00				

KM# 308 CROWN

Copper-Nickel, 38.8 mm. **Ruler:** Elizabeth II **Series:** Preserve Planet Earth **Obv:** Crowned bust right **Rev:** Sperm whale

Date	Mintage	VF20	XF40	MS60	MS63	MS65
1995	—	—	—	—	10.00	14.00

KM# 308a CROWN

28.28 g., 0.925 Silver 0.841 oz. ASW, 38.8 mm. **Ruler:** Elizabeth II **Series:** Preserve Planet Earth **Obv:** Crowned bust right **Rev:** Sperm whale

Date	Mintage	VF20	XF40	MS60	MS63	MS65
1995	Est. 30000	PF65 35.00				

KM# 327 CROWN

Copper-Nickel, 38.8 mm. **Ruler:** Elizabeth II **Subject:** The Tale of Peter Rabbit **Obv:** Crowned bust right **Rev:** Rabbit running right

Date	Mintage	VF20	XF40	MS60	MS63	MS65
1995	—	—	—	—	6.50	8.00

KM# 327a CROWN

28.28 g., 0.925 Silver 0.841 oz. ASW, 38.8 mm. **Ruler:** Elizabeth II **Subject:** The Tale of Peter Rabbit **Obv:** Crowned bust right **Rev:** Rabbit running right

Date	Mintage	VF20	XF40	MS60	MS63	MS65
1995	Est. 30000	PF65 32.00				

KM# 329 CROWN

Copper-Nickel, 38.8 mm. **Ruler:** Elizabeth II **Series:** Island Games **Obv:** Crowned bust right **Rev:** Various athletes around shield

Date	Mintage	VF20	XF40	MS60	MS63	MS65
1995	—	—	—	—	6.00	7.50

KM# 329a CROWN

28.28 g., 0.925 Silver 0.841 oz. ASW, 38.8 mm. **Ruler:** Elizabeth II **Series:** Island Games **Obv:** Crowned bust right **Rev:** Various athletes around shield

Date	Mintage	VF20	XF40	MS60	MS63	MS65
1995	Est. 30000	PF65 30.00				

KM# 331 CROWN

Copper-Nickel, 38.8 mm. **Ruler:** Elizabeth II **Series:** Island Games **Obv:** Crowned bust right **Rev:** Various athletes around shield

Date	Mintage	VF20	XF40	MS60	MS63	MS65
1995	—	—	—	—	6.00	7.50

KM# 331a CROWN

28.28 g., 0.925 Silver 0.841 oz. ASW, 38.8 mm. **Ruler:** Elizabeth II **Series:** Island Games **Obv:** Crowned bust right **Rev:** Various athletes around shield

Date	Mintage	VF20	XF40	MS60	MS63	MS65
1995	Est. 30000	PF65 30.00				

KM# 348 CROWN

Copper-Nickel, 38.8 mm. **Ruler:** Elizabeth II **Series:** Atlanta Olympics **Obv:** Crowned bust right **Rev:** Tennis player

Date	Mintage	VF20	XF40	MS60	MS63	MS65
1996	—	—	—	—	6.00	7.50

KM# 348a CROWN

28.28 g., 0.925 Silver 0.841 oz. ASW, 38.8 mm. **Ruler:** Elizabeth II **Series:** Atlanta Olympics **Obv:** Crowned bust right **Rev:** Tennis player

Date	Mintage	VF20	XF40	MS60	MS63	MS65
1996	Est. 30000	PF65 38.00				

KM# 349 CROWN

28.28 g., Copper-Nickel, 38.8 mm. **Ruler:** Elizabeth II **Series:** 1996 Atlanta Olympics **Obv:** Crowned bust right **Rev:** Wrestlers

Date	Mintage	VF20	XF40	MS60	MS63	MS65
1996	—	—	—	—	6.00	7.50

KM# 349a CROWN

28.28 g., 0.925 Silver 0.841 oz. ASW, 38.8 mm. **Ruler:** Elizabeth II **Series:** 1996 Atlanta Olympics **Obv:** Crowned bust right **Rev:** Wrestlers

Date	Mintage	VF20	XF40	MS60	MS63	MS65
1996	Est. 30000	PF65 38.00				

KM# 350 CROWN

Copper-Nickel, 38.8 mm. **Ruler:** Elizabeth II **Series:** 1996 Atlanta Olympics **Obv:** Crowned bust right **Rev:** Flag at center of baseball game

Date	Mintage	VF20	XF40	MS60	MS63	MS65
1996	—	—	—	—	6.00	7.50

KM# 350a CROWN

28.28 g., 0.925 Silver 0.841 oz. ASW, 38.8 mm. **Ruler:** Elizabeth II **Series:** 1996 Atlanta Olympics **Obv:** Crowned bust right **Rev:** Flag at center of baseball game

Date	Mintage	VF20	XF40	MS60	MS63	MS65
1996	Est. 30000	PF65 38.00				

KM# 351 CROWN

Copper-Nickel, 38.8 mm. **Ruler:** Elizabeth II **Series:** 1996 Atlanta Olympics **Obv:** Crowned bust right **Rev:** Olympic Flame

Date	Mintage	VF20	XF40	MS60	MS63	MS65
1996	—	—	—	—	6.00	7.50

KM# 351a CROWN

28.28 g., 0.925 Silver 0.841 oz. ASW, 38.8 mm. **Ruler:** Elizabeth II **Series:** 1996 Atlanta Olympics **Obv:** Crowned bust right **Rev:** Olympic Flame

Date	Mintage	VF20	XF40	MS60	MS63	MS65
1996	Est. 30000	PF65 38.00				

KM# 352 CROWN

Copper-Nickel, 38.8 mm. **Ruler:** Elizabeth II **Series:** 1996 Atlanta Olympics **Obv:** Crowned bust right **Rev:** Volleyball game

Date	Mintage	VF20	XF40	MS60	MS63	MS65
1996	—	—	—	—	6.00	7.50

KM# 352a CROWN

28.28 g., 0.925 Silver 0.841 oz. ASW, 38.8 mm. **Ruler:** Elizabeth II **Series:** 1996 Atlanta Olympics **Obv:** Crowned bust right **Rev:** Volleyball game

Date	Mintage	VF20	XF40	MS60	MS63	MS65
1996	Est. 30000	PF65 38.00				

KM# 353 CROWN

Copper-Nickel, 38.8 mm. **Ruler:** Elizabeth II **Series:** 1996 Atlanta Olympics **Obv:** Crowned bust right **Rev:** Basketball game

Date	Mintage	VF20	XF40	MS60	MS63	MS65
1996	—	—	—	—	6.00	7.50

KM# 353a CROWN

28.28 g., 0.925 Silver 0.841 oz. ASW, 38.8 mm. **Ruler:** Elizabeth II **Series:** 1996 Atlanta Olympics **Obv:** Crowned bust right **Rev:** Basketball game

Date	Mintage	VF20	XF40	MS60	MS63	MS65
1996	—	PF65 38.00				

KM# 358 CROWN

Copper-Nickel, 38.8 mm. **Ruler:** Elizabeth II **Obv:** Crowned bust right **Rev:** Nefusot Yehuda Synagogue Renovation, denomination below

Date	Mintage	VF20	XF40	MS60	MS63	MS65
1996	—	—	—	—	7.00	9.00

KM# 358a CROWN

28.28 g., 0.925 Silver 0.841 oz. ASW, 38.8 mm. **Ruler:** Elizabeth II **Obv:** Crowned bust right **Rev:** Nefusot Yehuda Synagogue Renovation

Date	Mintage	VF20	XF40	MS60	MS63	MS65
1996	Est. 30000	PF65 35.00				

KM# 359 CROWN
Copper-Nickel, 38.8 mm. **Ruler:** Elizabeth II **Subject:** Euro Soccer 96 **Obv:** Crowned bust right **Rev:** Net and soccer player

Date	Mintage	VF20	XF40	MS60	MS63	MS65
1996	—	—	—	—	8.00	9.50

KM# 359a CROWN
28.28 g., 0.925 Silver 0.841 oz. ASW, 38.8 mm. **Ruler:** Elizabeth II **Subject:** Euro Soccer 96 **Obv:** Crowned bust right **Rev:** Soccer player and net

Date	Mintage	VF20	XF40	MS60	MS63	MS65
1996	Est. 30000	PF65 40.00				

KM# 373 CROWN
Copper-Nickel, 38.8 mm. **Ruler:** Elizabeth II **Obv:** Crowned bust right **Rev:** Roses

Date	Mintage	VF20	XF40	MS60	MS63	MS65
1996	—	—	—	—	8.00	9.50

KM# 373a CROWN
28.28 g., 0.925 Silver 0.841 oz. ASW, 38.8 mm. **Ruler:** Elizabeth II **Obv:** Crowned bust right **Rev:** Roses

Date	Mintage	VF20	XF40	MS60	MS63	MS65
1996	Est. 30000	PF65 35.00				

KM# 382 CROWN
Copper-Nickel, 38.8 mm. **Ruler:** Elizabeth II **Subject:** The Tale of Peter Rabbit **Obv:** Crowned bust right **Rev:** Rabbit escaping the garden

Date	Mintage	VF20	XF40	MS60	MS63	MS65
1996	—	—	—	—	6.50	8.00

KM# 382a CROWN
28.28 g., 0.925 Silver 0.841 oz. ASW, 38.8 mm. **Ruler:** Elizabeth II **Subject:** The Tale of Peter Rabbit **Obv:** Crowned bust right **Rev:** Rabbit escaping the garden

Date	Mintage	VF20	XF40	MS60	MS63	MS65
1996	Est. 30000	PF65 35.00				

KM# 386 CROWN
Copper-Nickel, 38.8 mm. **Ruler:** Elizabeth II **Series:** Preserve Planet Earth **Obv:** Crowned bust right **Rev:** Shag Birds

Date	Mintage	VF20	XF40	MS60	MS63	MS65
1996	—	—	—	—	10.00	14.00

KM# 386a CROWN
28.28 g., 0.925 Silver 0.841 oz. ASW, 38.8 mm. **Ruler:** Elizabeth II **Series:** Preserve Planet Earth **Obv:** Crowned bust right **Rev:** Shag Birds

Date	Mintage	VF20	XF40	MS60	MS63	MS65
1996	—	PF65 35.00				

KM# 387 CROWN
Copper-Nickel, 38.8 mm. **Ruler:** Elizabeth II **Series:** Preserve Planet Earth **Obv:** Crowned bust right **Rev:** Atlantic Puffins

Date	Mintage	VF20	XF40	MS60	MS63	MS65
1996	—	—	—	—	10.00	14.00

KM# 387a CROWN
28.28 g., 0.925 Silver 0.841 oz. ASW, 38.8 mm. **Ruler:** Elizabeth II **Series:** Preserve Planet Earth **Obv:** Crowned bust right **Rev:** Atlantic Puffins

Date	Mintage	VF20	XF40	MS60	MS63	MS65
1996	Est. 30000	PF65 35.00				

KM# 393 CROWN
Copper-Nickel, 38.8 mm. **Ruler:** Elizabeth II **Series:** Centenary of the Cinema **Subject:** Grace Kelly - actress, 1929-82 **Obv:** Crowned bust right **Rev:** Bust 3/4 facing, dates

Date	Mintage	VF20	XF40	MS60	MS63	MS65
1996	—	—	—	—	8.00	9.50

KM# 393a CROWN
28.28 g., 0.925 Silver 0.841 oz. ASW, 38.8 mm. **Ruler:** Elizabeth II **Series:** Centenary of the Cinema **Subject:** Grace Kelly - actress, 1929-82 **Obv:** Crowned bust right **Rev:** Bust 3/4 facing, dates

Date	Mintage	VF20	XF40	MS60	MS63	MS65
1996	—	PF65 32.00				

KM# 398 CROWN
Copper-Nickel, 38.8 mm. **Ruler:** Elizabeth II **Series:** Centenary of the Cinema **Subject:** James Dean - actor, 1931-55 **Obv:** Crowned bust right **Rev:** Standing central figure, dates

Date	Mintage	VF20	XF40	MS60	MS63	MS65
1996	—	—	—	—	8.00	9.50

KM# 398a CROWN
28.28 g., 0.925 Silver 0.841 oz. ASW, 38.8 mm. **Ruler:** Elizabeth II **Series:** Centenary of the Cinema **Subject:** James Dean - actor, 1931-55 **Obv:** Crowned bust right **Rev:** Standing central figure, dates

Date	Mintage	VF20	XF40	MS60	MS63	MS65
1996	Est. 30000	PF65 35.00				

KM# 403 CROWN
Copper-Nickel, 38.8 mm. **Ruler:** Elizabeth II **Series:** Centenary of the Cinema **Subject:** Marilyn Monroe - actress, 1926-62 **Obv:** Crowned bust right **Rev:** Bust looking back over shoulder, dates

Date	Mintage	VF20	XF40	MS60	MS63	MS65
1996	—	—	—	—	8.00	9.50

KM# 403a CROWN
28.28 g., 0.925 Silver 0.841 oz. ASW, 38.8 mm. **Ruler:** Elizabeth II **Series:** Centenary of the Cinema **Subject:** Marilyn Monroe - actress, 1926-62 **Obv:** Crowned bust right **Rev:** Bust looking back over shoulder, dates

Date	Mintage	VF20	XF40	MS60	MS63	MS65
1996	—	PF65 35.00				

KM# 408 CROWN
Copper-Nickel, 38.8 mm. **Ruler:** Elizabeth II **Series:** Centenary of the Cinema **Subject:** Audrey Hepburn - actress, 1929-93 **Obv:** Crowned bust right **Rev:** Bust 3/4 facing, dates

Date	Mintage	VF20	XF40	MS60	MS63	MS65
1996	—	—	—	—	8.00	9.50

KM# 408a CROWN
28.28 g., 0.925 Silver 0.841 oz. ASW, 38.8 mm. **Ruler:** Elizabeth II **Series:** Centenary of the Cinema **Subject:** Audrey Hepburn - actress, 1929-93 **Obv:** Crowned bust right **Rev:** Bust 3/4 facing, dates

Date	Mintage	VF20	XF40	MS60	MS63	MS65
1996	—	PF65 32.00				

KM# 413 CROWN
Copper-Nickel, 38.8 mm. **Ruler:** Elizabeth II **Series:** Centenary of the Cinema **Subject:** Bruce Lee - actor, 1940-73 **Obv:** Crowned bust right **Rev:** Kickboxer and chinese dragon

Date	Mintage	VF20	XF40	MS60	MS63	MS65
1996	—	—	—	—	8.00	9.50

KM# 413a CROWN
28.28 g., 0.925 Silver 0.841 oz. ASW, 38.8 mm. **Ruler:** Elizabeth II **Series:** Centenary of the Cinema **Subject:** Bruce Lee - actor, 1940-73 **Obv:** Crowned bust right **Rev:** Kickboxer and chinese dragon

Date	Mintage	VF20	XF40	MS60	MS63	MS65
1996	Est. 30000	PF65 35.00				

KM# 418 CROWN
Copper-Nickel, 38.8 mm. **Ruler:** Elizabeth II **Series:** Centenary of the Cinema **Subject:** Charlie Chaplan - actor, 1889-1977 **Obv:** Crowned bust right **Rev:** Standing central figure with cane, dates

Date	Mintage	VF20	XF40	MS60	MS63	MS65
1996	—	—	—	—	8.00	9.50

KM# 418a CROWN
28.28 g., 0.925 Silver 0.841 oz. ASW, 38.8 mm. **Ruler:** Elizabeth II **Series:** Centenary of the Cinema **Subject:** Charlie Chaplan - actor, 1889-1977 **Obv:** Crowned bust right **Rev:** Standing central figure with cane, dates

Date	Mintage	VF20	XF40	MS60	MS63	MS65
1996	Est. 30000	PF65 32.00				

KM# 423 CROWN
Copper-Nickel, 38.8 mm. **Ruler:** Elizabeth II **Series:** Centenary of the Cinema **Subject:** Gone With The Wind **Obv:** Crowned bust right **Rev:** Rhett Butler and Scarlett O'Hara

Date	Mintage	VF20	XF40	MS60	MS63	MS65
1996	—	—	—	—	8.00	9.50

KM# 423a CROWN
28.28 g., 0.925 Silver 0.841 oz. ASW, 38.8 mm. **Ruler:** Elizabeth II **Series:** Centenary of the Cinema **Subject:** Gone With The Wind **Obv:** Crowned bust right **Rev:** Rhett Butler and Scarlett O'Hara

Date	Mintage	VF20	XF40	MS60	MS63	MS65
1996	Est. 30000	PF65 35.00				

KM# 428 CROWN
Copper-Nickel, 38.8 mm. **Ruler:** Elizabeth II **Series:** Centenary of the Cinema **Obv:** Crowned bust right **Rev:** The Flintstones

Date	Mintage	VF20	XF40	MS60	MS63	MS65
1996	—	—	—	—	8.00	9.50

KM# 428a CROWN
28.28 g., 0.925 Silver 0.841 oz. ASW, 38.8 mm. **Ruler:** Elizabeth II **Series:** Centenary of the Cinema **Obv:** Crowned bust right **Rev:** The Flintstones

Date	Mintage	VF20	XF40	MS60	MS63	MS65
1996	Est. 30000	PF65 35.00				

KM# 430 CROWN
28.28 g., 0.925 Silver 0.841 oz. ASW, 38.8 mm. **Ruler:** Elizabeth II **Series:** European Football Championship **Subject:** Goliath **Obv:** Crowned bust right **Rev:** Cartoon lion with football

Date	Mintage	VF20	XF40	MS60	MS63	MS65
1996	Est. 10000	PF65 28.00				

KM# 432 CROWN
Copper-Nickel, 38.8 mm. **Ruler:** Elizabeth II **Series:** Duke of Edinburgh Awards Scheme **Obv:** Crowned bust right **Rev:** 7 scenes surround center crowned arms

Date	Mintage	VF20	XF40	MS60	MS63	MS65
1996	—	—	—	—	8.00	9.00

KM# 432a CROWN
28.28 g., 0.925 Silver 0.841 oz. ASW, 38.8 mm. **Ruler:** Elizabeth II **Series:** Duke of Edinburgh Awards Scheme **Obv:** Crowned bust right **Rev:** 7 scenes surround center crowned arms

Date	Mintage	VF20	XF40	MS60	MS63	MS65
1996	—	PF65 35.00				

KM# 435 CROWN
Copper-Nickel, 38.8 mm. **Ruler:** Elizabeth II **Subject:** Duke of Edinburgh 75th Birthday **Obv:** Crowned bust right **Rev:** Cameo above team of horses pulling wagon

Date	Mintage	VF20	XF40	MS60	MS63	MS65
1996	—	—	—	—	8.00	9.00

KM# 435a CROWN
28.28 g., 0.925 Silver 0.841 oz. ASW, 38.8 mm. **Ruler:** Elizabeth II **Series:** Duke of Edinburgh Awards Scheme **Obv:** Duke of Edinburgh Awards Scheme **Rev:** Cameo above team of horses pulling wagon

Date	Mintage	VF20	XF40	MS60	MS63	MS65
1996	Est. 30000	PF65 35.00				

KM# 449 CROWN
Copper-Nickel, 38.8 mm. **Ruler:** Elizabeth II **Subject:** Lord Buddha **Obv:** Crowned bust right **Rev:** Seated figure facing

Date	Mintage	VF20	XF40	MS60	MS63	MS65
1996	—	—	—	—	7.50	8.50

KM# 449a CROWN
28.28 g., 0.925 Silver 0.841 oz. ASW, 38.8 mm. **Ruler:** Elizabeth II **Subject:** Lord Buddha **Obv:** Crowned bust right **Rev:** Seated figure facing

Date	Mintage	VF20	XF40	MS60	MS63	MS65
1996	Est. 15000	PF65 25.00				

KM# 457 CROWN
Copper-Nickel, 38.8 mm. **Ruler:** Elizabeth II **Series:** Centenary of the Cinema **Subject:** Wizard of Oz **Obv:** Crowned bust right **Rev:** Characters of Oz

Date	Mintage	VF20	XF40	MS60	MS63	MS65
1996	—	—	—	—	7.75	9.00

KM# 457a CROWN
28.28 g., 0.925 Silver 0.841 oz. ASW, 38.8 mm. **Ruler:** Elizabeth II **Series:** Centenary of the Cinema **Subject:** Wizard of Oz **Obv:** Crowned bust right **Rev:** Characters of Oz

Date	Mintage	VF20	XF40	MS60	MS63	MS65
1996	Est. 30000	PF65 35.00				

KM# 461 CROWN
Copper-Nickel, 38.8 mm. **Ruler:** Elizabeth II **Series:** Centenary of the Cinema **Subject:** The Marx Brothers **Obv:** Crowned bust right **Rev:** Three busts 3/4 left

Date	Mintage	VF20	XF40	MS60	MS63	MS65
1996	—	—	—	—	7.75	9.00

KM# 461a CROWN
28.28 g., 0.925 Silver 0.841 oz. ASW, 38.8 mm. **Ruler:** Elizabeth II **Series:** Centenary of the Cinema **Subject:** The Marx Brothers **Obv:** Crowned bust right **Rev:** Three busts 3/4 left

Date	Mintage	VF20	XF40	MS60	MS63	MS65
1996	Est. 30000	PF65 32.00				

KM# 465 CROWN
Copper-Nickel, 38.8 mm. **Ruler:** Elizabeth II **Series:** Centenary of the Cinema **Subject:** Elvis Presley - actor/entertainer, 1935-77 **Obv:** Crowned bust right **Rev:** Guitar beneath and behind bust 3/4 left

Date	Mintage	VF20	XF40	MS60	MS63	MS65
1996	—	—	—	—	7.75	9.00

KM# 465a CROWN
28.00 g., 0.925 Silver 0.8327 oz. ASW, 38.8 mm. **Ruler:** Elizabeth II **Series:** Centenary of the Cinema **Subject:** Elvis Presley - actor/entertainer, 1935-77 **Obv:** Crowned bust right **Rev:** Guitar beneath and behind bust 3/4 left

Date	Mintage	VF20	XF40	MS60	MS63	MS65
1996	Est. 30000	PF65 35.00				

KM# 469 CROWN

Copper-Nickel, 38.8 mm. **Ruler:** Elizabeth II **Series:** Centenary of the Cinema **Subject:** Casablanca **Obv:** Crowned bust right **Rev:** Bogart and Bergman

Date	Mintage	VF20	XF40	MS60	MS63	MS65
1996	—	—	—	—	7.75	9.00

KM# 469a CROWN

28.00 g., 0.925 Silver 0.8327 oz. ASW, 38.8 mm. **Ruler:** Elizabeth II **Series:** Centenary of the Cinema **Subject:** Casablanca **Obv:** Crowned bust right **Rev:** Bogart and Bergman

Date	Mintage	VF20	XF40	MS60	MS63	MS65
1996	Est. 30000	PF65 32.00				

KM# 473 CROWN

Copper-Nickel, 38.8 mm. **Ruler:** Elizabeth II **Series:** Centenary of the Cinema **Obv:** Crowned bust right **Rev:** E.T.

Date	Mintage	VF20	XF40	MS60	MS63	MS65
1996	—	—	—	—	7.75	9.00

KM# 473a CROWN

28.00 g., 0.925 Silver 0.8327 oz. ASW, 38.8 mm. **Ruler:** Elizabeth II **Series:** Centenary of the Cinema **Obv:** Crowned bust right **Rev:** E.T.

Date	Mintage	VF20	XF40	MS60	MS63	MS65
1996	Est. 30000	PF65 32.00				

KM# 477 CROWN

Copper-Nickel, 38.8 mm. **Ruler:** Elizabeth II **Series:** Centenary of the Cinema **Subject:** Alfred Hitchcock - Director/Producer, 1899-1980 **Obv:** Crowned bust right **Rev:** Bust facing looking at bird on left shoulder

Date	Mintage	VF20	XF40	MS60	MS63	MS65
1996	—	—	—	—	7.75	9.00

KM# 477a CROWN

28.00 g., 0.925 Silver 0.8327 oz. ASW, 38.8 mm. **Ruler:** Elizabeth II **Series:** Centenary of the Cinema **Subject:** Alfred Hitchcock - Director/Producer, 1899-1980 **Obv:** Crowned bust right **Rev:** Bust facing looking at bird on left shoulder

Date	Mintage	VF20	XF40	MS60	MS63	MS65
1996	Est. 30000	PF65 32.00				

KM# 514 CROWN

Copper-Nickel, 38.8 mm. **Ruler:** Elizabeth II **Obv:** Crowned bust right **Rev:** Two peacocks, one with tail spread

Date	Mintage	VF20	XF40	MS60	MS63	MS65
1997	—	—	—	—	12.00	17.50

KM# 514a CROWN

28.28 g., 0.925 Silver 0.841 oz. ASW, 38.8 mm. **Ruler:** Elizabeth II **Obv:** Crowned bust right **Rev:** Two peacocks, one with tail spread

Date	Mintage	VF20	XF40	MS60	MS63	MS65
1997	Est. 30000	PF65 40.00				

KM# 525 CROWN

Copper-Nickel, 38.8 mm. **Ruler:** Elizabeth II **Subject:** The Tale of Peter Rabbit **Obv:** Crowned bust right **Rev:** Rabbit standing 3/4 right

Date	Mintage	VF20	XF40	MS60	MS63	MS65
1997	—	—	—	—	10.00	15.00

KM# 526 CROWN

28.28 g., 0.925 Silver 0.841 oz. ASW, 38.8 mm. **Ruler:** Elizabeth II

Date	Mintage	VF20	XF40	MS60	MS63	MS65
1997	Est. 30000	PF65 35.00				

KM# 530 CROWN

Copper-Nickel, 38.8 mm. **Ruler:** Elizabeth II **Series:** Golden Wedding Anniversary **Subject:** Queen Elizabeth and Prince Phillip **Obv:** Crowned bust right **Rev:** Royal couple facing

Date	Mintage	VF20	XF40	MS60	MS63	MS65
1997	—	—	—	—	7.50	9.00

KM# 530a CROWN

28.28 g., 0.925 Gold Clad Silver 0.841 oz., 38.8 mm. **Ruler:** Elizabeth II **Series:** Golden Wedding Anniversary **Subject:** Queen Elizabeth and Prince Phillip **Obv:** Crowned bust right **Rev:** Royal couple facing

Date	Mintage	VF20	XF40	MS60	MS63	MS65
1997	Est. 10000	PF65 40.00				

KM# 532 CROWN

Copper-Nickel, 38.8 mm. **Ruler:** Elizabeth II **Series:** Golden Wedding Anniversary **Subject:** Queen Elizabeth and Prince Philip **Obv:** Crowned bust right **Rev:** The Queen with her first-born, Prince Charles

Date	Mintage	VF20	XF40	MS60	MS63	MS65
1997	—	—	—	—	7.50	9.00

KM# 532a CROWN

28.28 g., 0.925 Gold Clad Silver 0.841 oz., 38.8 mm. **Ruler:** Elizabeth II **Series:** Golden Wedding Anniversary **Subject:** Queen Elizabeth and Prince Philip **Obv:** Crowned bust right **Rev:** The Queen with her first-born, Prince Charles

Date	Mintage	VF20	XF40	MS60	MS63	MS65
1997	Est. 10000	PF65 40.00				

KM# 534 CROWN

Copper-Nickel, 38.8 mm. **Ruler:** Elizabeth II **Series:** Golden Wedding Anniversary **Subject:** Queen Elizabeth and Prince Philip **Obv:** Crowned bust right **Rev:** The Queen, two children and a monkey

Date	Mintage	VF20	XF40	MS60	MS63	MS65
1997	—	—	—	—	7.50	9.00

KM# 534a CROWN

28.28 g., 0.925 Gold Clad Silver 0.841 oz., 38.8 mm. **Ruler:** Elizabeth II **Series:** Golden Wedding Anniversary **Subject:** Queen Elizabeth and Prince Philip **Obv:** Crowned bust right **Rev:** The Queen, two children and a monkey

Date	Mintage	VF20	XF40	MS60	MS63	MS65
1997	Est. 10000	PF65 40.00				

KM# 536 CROWN

Copper-Nickel, 38.8 mm. **Ruler:** Elizabeth II **Series:** Golden Wedding Anniversary **Subject:** Queen Elizabeth and Prince Philip **Obv:** Crowned bust right **Rev:** The Queen and adoring crowd

Date	Mintage	VF20	XF40	MS60	MS63	MS65
1997	—	—	—	—	7.50	9.00

KM# 536a CROWN

28.28 g., 0.925 Gold Clad Silver 0.841 oz., 38.8 mm. **Ruler:** Elizabeth II **Series:** Golden Wedding Anniversary **Subject:** Queen Elizabeth and Prince Philip **Obv:** Crowned bust right **Rev:** The Queen and adoring crowd

Date	Mintage	VF20	XF40	MS60	MS63	MS65
1997	Est. 10000	PF65 40.00				

KM# 540 CROWN

Copper-Nickel, 38.8 mm. **Ruler:** Elizabeth II **Obv:** Crowned bust right **Rev:** Peonies

Date	Mintage	VF20	XF40	MS60	MS63	MS65
1997	—	—	—	—	8.00	9.00

KM# 540a CROWN

28.28 g., 0.925 Silver 0.841 oz. ASW, 38.8 mm. **Ruler:** Elizabeth II **Obv:** Crowned bust right **Rev:** Peonies

Date	Mintage	VF20	XF40	MS60	MS63	MS65
1997	Est. 30000	PF65 35.00				

KM# 544 CROWN

28.28 g., 0.925 Silver 0.841 oz. ASW, 38.8 mm. **Ruler:** Elizabeth II **Subject:** Nefertiti **Obv:** Crowned bust right **Rev:** Head right

Date	Mintage	VF20	XF40	MS60	MS63	MS65
1997	Est. 10000	PF65 38.00				

KM# 548 CROWN

28.28 g., 0.925 Silver 0.841 oz. ASW, 38.8 mm. **Ruler:** Elizabeth II **Subject:** Cleopatra **Obv:** Crowned bust right **Rev:** Head facing

Date	Mintage	VF20	XF40	MS60	MS63	MS65
1997	Est. 10000	PF65 38.00				

KM# 552 CROWN

28.28 g., 0.925 Silver 0.841 oz. ASW, 38.8 mm. **Ruler:** Elizabeth II **Subject:** Europa **Obv:** Crowned bust right **Rev:** Head 3/4 left

Date	Mintage	VF20	XF40	MS60	MS63	MS65
1997	Est. 10000	PF65 38.00				

KM# 556 CROWN

28.28 g., 0.925 Silver 0.841 oz. ASW, 38.8 mm. **Ruler:** Elizabeth II **Subject:** Liberty **Obv:** Crowned bust right **Rev:** Laureate head right

Date	Mintage	VF20	XF40	MS60	MS63	MS65
1997	Est. 10000	PF65 38.00				

KM# 561 CROWN

Copper-Nickel, 38.8 mm. **Ruler:** Elizabeth II **Subject:** Yorkshire Terrier **Obv:** Crowned bust right

Date	Mintage	VF20	XF40	MS60	MS63	MS65
1997	—	—	—	—	10.00	12.00

KM# 566 CROWN

Copper-Nickel, 38.8 mm. **Ruler:** Elizabeth II **Series:** Queen's Birthday **Obv:** Crowned bust right **Rev:** Queen on horseback, Rock of Gibraltar in background

Date	Mintage	VF20	XF40	MS60	MS63	MS65
1997	—	—	—	—	8.50	9.50

KM# 566a CROWN

28.28 g., 0.925 Silver 0.841 oz. ASW, 38.8 mm. **Ruler:** Elizabeth II **Series:** Queen's Birthday **Obv:** Crowned bust right **Rev:** Queen on horseback, Rock of Gibraltar in background

Date	Mintage	VF20	XF40	MS60	MS63	MS65
1997	Est. 30000	PF65 35.00				

KM# 567 CROWN

Copper-Nickel, 38.8 mm. **Ruler:** Elizabeth II **Series:** Queen's Birthday **Obv:** Crowned bust right **Rev:** Queen on horseback returning salute

Date	Mintage	VF20	XF40	MS60	MS63	MS65
1997	—	—	—	—	8.50	9.50

KM# 567a CROWN

28.28 g., 0.925 Silver 0.841 oz. ASW, 38.8 mm. **Ruler:** Elizabeth II **Series:** Queen's Birthday **Obv:** Crowned bust right **Rev:** Queen on horseback returning salute

Date	Mintage	VF20	XF40	MS60	MS63	MS65
1997	—	PF65 35.00				

KM# 568 CROWN

Copper-Nickel, 38.8 mm. **Ruler:** Elizabeth II **Series:** Queen's Birthday **Obv:** Crowned bust right **Rev:** Cameo above Trooping the Colors scene

Date	Mintage	VF20	XF40	MS60	MS63	MS65
1997	—	—	—	—	8.50	9.50

KM# 568a CROWN

28.28 g., 0.925 Silver 0.841 oz. ASW, 38.8 mm. **Ruler:** Elizabeth II **Series:** Queen's Birthday **Obv:** Crowned bust right **Rev:** Cameo above Trooping the Colors scene

Date	Mintage	VF20	XF40	MS60	MS63	MS65
1997	Est. 30000	PF65 35.00				

KM# 569 CROWN

Copper-Nickel, 38.8 mm. **Ruler:** Elizabeth II **Series:** Queen's Birthday **Obv:** Crowned bust right **Rev:** Gurkha troops with dragons

Date	Mintage	VF20	XF40	MS60	MS63	MS65
1997	—	—	—	—	8.50	9.50

KM# 569a CROWN

28.28 g., 0.925 Silver 0.841 oz. ASW, 38.8 mm. **Ruler:** Elizabeth II **Series:** Queen's Birthday **Obv:** Crowned bust right **Rev:** Gurkha troops with dragons

Date	Mintage	VF20	XF40	MS60	MS63	MS65
1997	—	PF65 35.00				

KM# 571 CROWN

Copper-Nickel, 38.8 mm. **Ruler:** Elizabeth II **Subject:** The New Mosque **Obv:** Crowned bust right **Rev:** Two Moorish cavalry riders with mosque in background

Date	Mintage	VF20	XF40	MS60	MS63	MS65
1997	—	—	—	—	8.00	9.00

KM# 571a CROWN

28.28 g., 0.925 Silver 0.841 oz. ASW, 38.8 mm. **Ruler:** Elizabeth II **Subject:** The New Mosque **Obv:** Crowned bust right **Rev:** Two Moorish cavalry riders with mosque in background

Date	Mintage	VF20	XF40	MS60	MS63	MS65
1997	Est. 30000	PF65 35.00				

KM# 573 CROWN
28.28 g., 0.925 Silver 0.841 oz. ASW with Gold inset., 38.8 mm. **Ruler:** Elizabeth II **Series:** Wonders of the World **Subject:** Mausoleum at Halicarnassus **Obv:** Crowned bust right **Rev:** Gold coin design inset on mausoleum

Date	Mintage	VF20	XF40	MS60	MS63	MS65
1997	Est. 7500	PF65 50.00				

KM# 574 CROWN
28.28 g., 0.925 Silver 0.841 oz. ASW with Gold inset., 38.8 mm. **Ruler:** Elizabeth II **Series:** Wonders of the World **Subject:** Statue of Zeus at Olympia **Obv:** Crowned bust right **Rev:** Gold coin design inset on statue of Zeus

Date	Mintage	VF20	XF40	MS60	MS63	MS65
1997	Est. 7500	PF65 50.00				

KM# 575 CROWN
28.28 g., 0.925 Silver 0.841 oz. ASW with Gold inset., 38.8 mm. **Ruler:** Elizabeth II **Series:** Wonders of the World **Subject:** The Pharos of Alexandria **Obv:** Crowned bust right **Rev:** Gold coin design inset on lighthouse

Date	Mintage	VF20	XF40	MS60	MS63	MS65
1997	Est. 7500	PF65 50.00				

KM# 576 CROWN
28.28 g., 0.925 Silver 0.841 oz. ASW with Gold inset., 38.8 mm. **Ruler:** Elizabeth II **Series:** Wonders of the World **Subject:** The Pillars of Hercules **Obv:** Crowned bust right **Rev:** Gold coin design inset on the Rock of Gibraltar

Date	Mintage	VF20	XF40	MS60	MS63	MS65
1997	Est. 7500	PF65 50.00				

KM# 577 CROWN
28.28 g., 0.925 Silver 0.841 oz. ASW with Gold inset., 38.8 mm. **Ruler:** Elizabeth II **Series:** Wonders of the World **Subject:** The Colossus of Rhodes **Obv:** Crowned bust right **Rev:** Gold coin design inset on large statue

Date	Mintage	VF20	XF40	MS60	MS63	MS65
1997	Est. 7500	PF65 50.00				

KM# 578 CROWN
28.28 g., 0.925 Silver 0.841 oz. ASW with Gold inset., 38.8 mm. **Ruler:** Elizabeth II **Series:** Wonders of the World **Subject:** The Pyramids of Egypt **Obv:** Crowned bust right **Rev:** Gold coin design inset on pyramids

Date	Mintage	VF20	XF40	MS60	MS63	MS65
1997	Est. 7500	PF65 50.00				

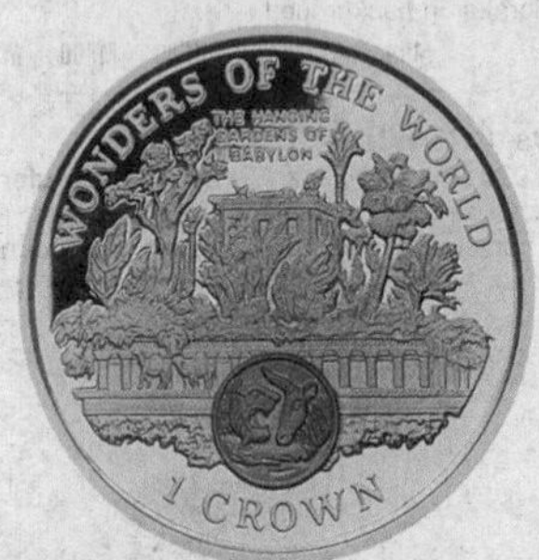

KM# 579 CROWN
28.28 g., 0.925 Silver 0.841 oz. ASW with Gold inset., 38.8 mm. **Ruler:** Elizabeth II **Series:** Wonders of the World **Subject:** The Hanging Gardens of Babylon **Obv:** Crowned bust right **Rev:** Gold coin design inset on an overgrown building

Date	Mintage	VF20	XF40	MS60	MS63	MS65
1997	Est. 7500	PF65 50.00				

KM# 580 CROWN
28.28 g., 0.925 Silver 0.841 oz. ASW with Gold inset., 38.8 mm. **Ruler:** Elizabeth II **Series:** Wonders of the World **Subject:** The Temple of Artemis at Ephesus **Obv:** Crowned bust right **Rev:** Gold coin design inset on classic Greek building

Date	Mintage	VF20	XF40	MS60	MS63	MS65
1997	Est. 7500	PF65 50.00				

KM# 582 CROWN
28.28 g., 0.925 Silver 0.841 oz. ASW with Gold inset., 38.8 mm. **Ruler:** Elizabeth II **Series:** Evolution of Mankind **Subject:** Egypt **Obv:** Crowned bust right **Rev:** Three ancient Egyptians, pyramids, hieroglyphics

Date	Mintage	VF20	XF40	MS60	MS63	MS65
1997	Est. 10000	PF65 40.00				

KM# 584 CROWN
28.28 g., 0.925 Silver 0.841 oz. ASW with Gold inset., 38.8 mm. **Ruler:** Elizabeth II **Series:** Evolution of Mankind **Subject:** Israel **Obv:** Crowned bust right **Rev:** Star of David, Moses and Temple of Solomon

Date	Mintage	VF20	XF40	MS60	MS63	MS65
1997	Est. 10000	PF65 40.00				

KM# 586 CROWN
28.28 g., 0.925 Silver 0.841 oz. ASW with Gold inset., 38.8 mm. **Ruler:** Elizabeth II **Series:** Evolution of Mankind **Subject:** China **Obv:** Crowned bust right **Rev:** Emperor and the Great Wall

Date	Mintage	VF20	XF40	MS60	MS63	MS65
1997	Est. 10000	PF65 40.00				

KM# 586a CROWN
28.34 g., Copper-Nickel, 38.5 mm. **Ruler:** Elizabeth II **Obv:** Crowned bust right **Rev:** Chinese Emperor Shih Huang Ti and Great Wall **Edge:** Reeded

Date	Mintage	VF20	XF40	MS60	MS63	MS65
1997	—	—	—	—	10.00	14.00

KM# 588 CROWN
28.28 g., 0.925 Silver 0.841 oz. ASW with Gold inset., 38.8 mm. **Ruler:** Elizabeth II **Series:** Evolution of Mankind **Subject:** Greece **Obv:** Crowned bust right **Rev:** Aristotle, classic Greek building

Date	Mintage	VF20	XF40	MS60	MS63	MS65
1997	Est. 10000	PF65 40.00				

KM# 590 CROWN
28.28 g., 0.925 Silver 0.841 oz. ASW with Gold inset., 38.8 mm. **Ruler:** Elizabeth II **Series:** Evolution of Mankind **Subject:** Rome **Obv:** Crowned bust right **Rev:** Julius Caesar and Stonehenge

Date	Mintage	VF20	XF40	MS60	MS63	MS65
1997	Est. 10000	PF65 40.00				

KM# 590a CROWN
Copper-Nickel **Ruler:** Elizabeth II **Series:** Evolution of mankind **Subject:** Rome

Date	Mintage	VF20	XF40	MS60	MS63	MS65
1997 PM	—	—	—	—	—	12.50

KM# 592 CROWN
28.28 g., 0.925 Silver 0.841 oz. ASW with Gold inset., 38.8 mm. **Ruler:** Elizabeth II **Series:** Evolution of Mankind **Subject:** India **Obv:** Crowned bust right **Rev:** Krishna playing flute by a temple

Date	Mintage	VF20	XF40	MS60	MS63	MS65
1997	Est. 10000	PF65 40.00				

KM# 594 CROWN
28.28 g., 0.925 Silver 0.841 oz. ASW with Gold inset., 38.8 mm. **Ruler:** Elizabeth II **Series:** Evolution of Mankind **Subject:** Holy Roman Empire **Obv:** Crowned bust right **Rev:** Charlemagne and soldiers on horseback

Date	Mintage	VF20	XF40	MS60	MS63	MS65
1997	Est. 10000	PF65 40.00				

KM# 596 CROWN
28.28 g., 0.925 Silver 0.841 oz. ASW with Gold inset., 38.8 mm. **Ruler:** Elizabeth II **Series:** Evolution of Mankind **Subject:** Macedonia **Obv:** Crowned bust right **Rev:** Alexander the Great on horseback

Date	Mintage	VF20	XF40	MS60	MS63	MS65
1997	Est. 10000	PF65 40.00				

KM# 598 CROWN
28.28 g., 0.925 Silver 0.841 oz. ASW with Gold inset., 38.8 mm. **Ruler:** Elizabeth II **Series:** Evolution of Mankind **Subject:** Native America **Obv:** Crowned bust right **Rev:** North American native on horseback and totem pole

Date	Mintage	VF20	XF40	MS60	MS63	MS65
1997	Est. 10000	PF65 40.00				

KM# 600 CROWN
28.28 g., 0.925 Silver 0.841 oz. ASW with Gold inset., 38.8 mm. **Ruler:** Elizabeth II **Series:** Evolution of Mankind **Subject:** Asia **Obv:** Crowned bust right **Rev:** Buddha and temple

Date	Mintage	VF20	XF40	MS60	MS63	MS65
1997	Est. 10000	PF65 40.00				

KM# 602 CROWN
28.28 g., 0.925 Silver 0.841 oz. ASW with Gold inset., 38.8 mm. **Ruler:** Elizabeth II **Series:** Evolution of Mankind **Subject:** Inca Empire **Obv:** Crowned bust right **Rev:** Incan Emperor and Machu Picchu

Date	Mintage	VF20	XF40	MS60	MS63	MS65
1997	Est. 10000	PF65 40.00				

KM# 604 CROWN
28.28 g., 0.925 Silver 0.841 oz. ASW with Gold inset., 38.8 mm. **Ruler:** Elizabeth II **Series:** Evolution of Mankind **Subject:** Islamic Civilization **Obv:** Crowned bust right **Rev:** General Tariq Ibn Ziyad and building

Date	Mintage	VF20	XF40	MS60	MS63	MS65
1997	Est. 10000	PF65 40.00				

KM# 609 CROWN
28.28 g., 0.925 Silver 0.841 oz. ASW, 38.8 mm. **Ruler:** Elizabeth II **Series:** Traders of the World **Subject:** Sir Francis Drake **Obv:** Crowned bust right **Rev:** Sir Francis Drake, ship and beach

Date	Mintage	VF20	XF40	MS60	MS63	MS65
1997	Est. 10000	PF65 42.50				

KM# 611 CROWN
28.28 g., 0.925 Silver 0.841 oz. ASW, 38.8 mm. **Ruler:** Elizabeth II **Series:** Traders of the World **Subject:** Romans **Obv:** Crowned bust right **Rev:** Lion, lioness, ship and map

Date	Mintage	VF20	XF40	MS60	MS63	MS65
1997	Est. 10000	PF65 42.50				

KM# 613 CROWN
28.28 g., 0.925 Silver 0.841 oz. ASW, 38.8 mm. **Ruler:** Elizabeth II **Series:** Traders of the World **Subject:** Venetians **Obv:** Crowned bust right **Rev:** Pair of oysters with pearls, Venetian canal scene

Date	Mintage	VF20	XF40	MS60	MS63	MS65
1997	Est. 10000	PF65 42.50				

KM# 615 CROWN
28.28 g., 0.925 Silver 0.841 oz. ASW, 38.8 mm. **Ruler:** Elizabeth II **Series:** Traders of the World **Subject:** Portuguese **Obv:** Crowned bust right **Rev:** Gold ingots and Portuguese ship

Date	Mintage	VF20	XF40	MS60	MS63	MS65
1997	Est. 10000	PF65 42.50				

KM# 617 CROWN
28.28 g., 0.925 Silver 0.841 oz. ASW, 38.8 mm. **Ruler:** Elizabeth II **Series:** Traders of the World **Subject:** Spanish **Obv:** Crowned bust right **Rev:** Tobacco leaves, ship, map, gems

Date	Mintage	VF20	XF40	MS60	MS63	MS65
1997	Est. 10000	PF65 42.50				

KM# 619 CROWN
28.28 g., 0.925 Silver 0.841 oz. ASW, 38.8 mm. **Ruler:** Elizabeth II **Series:** Traders of the World **Subject:** English **Obv:** Crowned bust right **Rev:** Profile of Queen Elizabeth I above fighting ships

Date	Mintage	VF20	XF40	MS60	MS63	MS65
1997	Est. 10000	PF65 42.50				

KM# 621 CROWN
28.28 g., 0.925 Silver 0.841 oz. ASW, 38.8 mm. **Ruler:** Elizabeth II **Series:** Traders of the World **Subject:** Captain Bligh **Obv:** Queen's portrait **Rev:** Figure seated on rock, ship at right

Date	Mintage	VF20	XF40	MS60	MS63	MS65
1997	Est. 10000	PF65 42.50				

KM# 623 CROWN
28.28 g., 0.925 Silver 0.841 oz. ASW, 38.8 mm. **Ruler:** Elizabeth II **Series:** Traders of the World **Subject:** Captain Cook **Obv:** Crowned bust right **Rev:** Beaver on rock, ship at right, bust facing in background

Date	Mintage	VF20	XF40	MS60	MS63	MS65
1997	Est. 10000	PF65 42.50				

KM# 636 CROWN
Copper-Nickel, 38.8 mm. **Ruler:** Elizabeth II **Series:** Winter Olympics - Japan **Obv:** Crowned bust right **Rev:** Speed skater and Bullet Train

Date	Mintage	VF20	XF40	MS60	MS63	MS65
1998	—	—	—	—	8.00	10.00

KM# 636a CROWN
28.28 g., 0.925 Silver 0.841 oz. ASW, 38.8 mm. **Ruler:** Elizabeth II **Series:** Winter Olympics - Japan **Obv:** Crowned bust right **Rev:** Speed skater and Bullet Train

Date	Mintage	VF20	XF40	MS60	MS63	MS65
1998	—	PF65 40.00				

KM# 638 CROWN
Copper-Nickel, 38.8 mm. **Ruler:** Elizabeth II **Series:** Winter Olympics - Japan **Obv:** Crowned bust right **Rev:** Ski jumper and Buddha

Date	Mintage	VF20	XF40	MS60	MS63	MS65
1998	—	—	—	—	8.00	10.00

KM# 638a CROWN
28.28 g., 0.925 Silver 0.841 oz. ASW, 38.8 mm. **Ruler:** Elizabeth II **Subject:** Winter Olympics - Japan **Obv:** Crowned bust right **Rev:** Ski jumper and Buddha

Date	Mintage	VF20	XF40	MS60	MS63	MS65
1998	Est. 30000	PF65 40.00				

KM# 640 CROWN
Copper-Nickel, 38.8 mm. **Ruler:** Elizabeth II **Series:** Winter Olympics - Japan **Obv:** Crowned bust right **Rev:** Cross-country skiers

Date	Mintage	VF20	XF40	MS60	MS63	MS65
1998	—	—	—	—	8.00	10.00

KM# 640a CROWN
28.28 g., 0.925 Silver 0.841 oz. ASW, 38.8 mm. **Ruler:** Elizabeth II **Series:** Winter Olympics - Japan **Obv:** Crowned bust right **Rev:** Cross-country skiers

Date	Mintage	VF20	XF40	MS60	MS63	MS65
1998	Est. 30000	PF65 40.00				

KM# 642 CROWN
Copper-Nickel, 38.8 mm. **Ruler:** Elizabeth II **Series:** Winter Olympics - Japan **Obv:** Crowned bust right **Rev:** Slalom skier, Zenkoji temple

Date	Mintage	VF20	XF40	MS60	MS63	MS65
1998	—	—	—	—	8.00	10.00

KM# 642a CROWN
28.28 g., 0.925 Silver 0.841 oz. ASW, 38.8 mm. **Ruler:** Elizabeth II **Series:** Winter Olympics - Japan **Obv:** Crowned bust right **Rev:** Slalom skier, Zenkoji temple

Date	Mintage	VF20	XF40	MS60	MS63	MS65
1998	Est. 30000	PF65 40.00				

KM# 656 CROWN
Copper-Nickel, 38.8 mm. **Ruler:** Elizabeth II **Subject:** The Tale of Peter Rabbit **Obv:** Crowned bust right **Rev:** Standing rabbit facing, sparrow at left

Date	Mintage	VF20	XF40	MS60	MS63	MS65
1998	—	—	—	—	10.00	12.00

KM# 656a CROWN
28.28 g., 0.925 Silver 0.841 oz. ASW, 38.8 mm. **Ruler:** Elizabeth II **Subject:** The Tale of Peter Rabbit **Obv:** Crowned bust right **Rev:** Standing rabbit facing, sparrow at left

Date	Mintage	VF20	XF40	MS60	MS63	MS65
1998	Est. 30000	PF65 45.00				

KM# 661 CROWN
Copper-Nickel, 38.8 mm. **Ruler:** Elizabeth II **Subject:** Chrysanthemum **Obv:** Crowned bust right **Rev:** Three blossoms

Date	Mintage	VF20	XF40	MS60	MS63	MS65
1998	—	—	—	—	8.50	9.50

KM# 661a CROWN

28.28 g., 0.925 Silver 0.841 oz. ASW, 38.8 mm. **Ruler:** Elizabeth II **Subject:** Chrysanthemum **Obv:** Crowned bust right **Rev:** Three blossoms

Date	Mintage	VF20	XF40	MS60	MS63	MS65
1998	Est. 30000	PF65 45.00				

KM# 674 CROWN

28.28 g., 0.925 Silver 0.841 oz. ASW, 38.8 mm. **Ruler:** Elizabeth II **Subject:** Britannia **Obv:** Crowned bust right **Rev:** Helmeted head right

Date	Mintage	VF20	XF40	MS60	MS63	MS65
1998	Est. 10000	PF65 50.00				

KM# 675 CROWN

28.28 g., 0.925 Silver 0.841 oz. ASW, 38.8 mm. **Ruler:** Elizabeth II **Subject:** Juno **Obv:** Crowned bust right **Rev:** Head 3/4 facing

Date	Mintage	VF20	XF40	MS60	MS63	MS65
1998	Est. 10000	PF65 50.00				

KM# 676 CROWN

28.28 g., 0.925 Silver 0.841 oz. ASW, 38.8 mm. **Ruler:** Elizabeth II **Subject:** Athena **Obv:** Crowned bust right **Rev:** Helmeted head right

Date	Mintage	VF20	XF40	MS60	MS63	MS65
1998	Est. 10000	PF65 50.00				

KM# 677 CROWN

28.28 g., 0.925 Silver 0.841 oz. ASW, 38.8 mm. **Ruler:** Elizabeth II **Subject:** Arethusa **Obv:** Crowned bust right **Rev:** Head left with dolphins

Date	Mintage	VF20	XF40	MS60	MS63	MS65
1998	Est. 10000	PF65 50.00				

KM# 682 CROWN

Copper-Nickel, 38.8 mm. **Ruler:** Elizabeth II **Subject:** Paddington Bear **Obv:** Crowned bust right **Rev:** Bear with suitcase

Date	Mintage	VF20	XF40	MS60	MS63	MS65
1998	—	—	—	—	10.00	15.00

KM# 682a CROWN

28.28 g., 0.925 Silver 0.841 oz. ASW, 38.8 mm. **Ruler:** Elizabeth II **Subject:** Paddington Bear **Obv:** Crowned bust right **Rev:** Bear with suitcase

Date	Mintage	VF20	XF40	MS60	MS63	MS65
1998	Est. 30000	PF65 45.00				

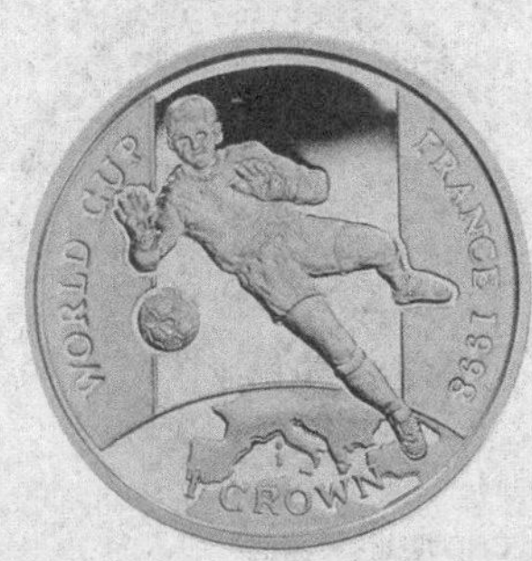

KM# 687 CROWN

Copper-Nickel, 38.8 mm. **Ruler:** Elizabeth II **Series:** World Cup France 1998 **Obv:** Crowned bust right **Rev:** Goalie

Date	Mintage	VF20	XF40	MS60	MS63	MS65
1998	—	—	—	—	8.00	9.00

KM# 687a CROWN

28.28 g., 0.925 Silver 0.841 oz. ASW, 38.8 mm. **Ruler:** Elizabeth II **Series:** World Cup France 1998 **Obv:** Crowned bust right **Rev:** Goalie

Date	Mintage	VF20	XF40	MS60	MS63	MS65
1998	Est. 30000	PF65 45.00				

KM# 688 CROWN

Copper-Nickel, 38.8 mm. **Ruler:** Elizabeth II **Series:** World Cup France 1998 **Obv:** Crowned bust right **Rev:** Player kicking to the left

Date	Mintage	VF20	XF40	MS60	MS63	MS65
1998	—	—	—	—	8.00	9.00

KM# 688a CROWN

28.28 g., 0.925 Silver 0.841 oz. ASW, 38.8 mm. **Ruler:** Elizabeth II **Series:** World Cup France 1998 **Obv. Inscription:** Crowned bust right **Rev:** Player kicking to the left

Date	Mintage	VF20	XF40	MS60	MS63	MS65
1998	Est. 30000	PF65 45.00				

KM# 689 CROWN

Copper-Nickel, 38.8 mm. **Ruler:** Elizabeth II **Series:** World Cup France 1998 **Obv:** Crowned bust right **Rev:** Player advancing ball

Date	Mintage	VF20	XF40	MS60	MS63	MS65
1998	—	—	—	—	8.00	9.00

KM# 689a CROWN

28.28 g., 0.925 Silver 0.841 oz. ASW, 38.8 mm. **Ruler:** Elizabeth II **Series:** World Cup France 1998 **Obv:** Crowned bust right **Rev:** Player advancing ball

Date	Mintage	VF20	XF40	MS60	MS63	MS65
1998	Est. 30000	PF65 45.00				

KM# 690 CROWN

Copper-Nickel, 38.8 mm. **Ruler:** Elizabeth II **Series:** World Cup France 1998 **Obv:** Crowned bust right **Rev:** Two players

Date	Mintage	VF20	XF40	MS60	MS63	MS65
1998	—	—	—	—	8.00	9.00

KM# 690a CROWN

28.28 g., 0.925 Silver 0.841 oz. ASW, 38.8 mm. **Ruler:** Elizabeth II **Series:** World Cup France 1998 **Obv:** Crowned bust right **Rev:** Two players

Date	Mintage	VF20	XF40	MS60	MS63	MS65
1998	Est. 30000	PF65 45.00				

KM# 692 CROWN

28.28 g., 0.925 Silver 0.841 oz. ASW, 38.8 mm. **Ruler:** Elizabeth II **Series:** Traders of the World **Subject:** Phoenecians **Obv:** Crowned bust right **Rev:** Galley (200BC-600AD) above shells

Date	Mintage	VF20	XF40	MS60	MS63	MS65
1998	Est. 10000	PF65 45.00				

KM# 694 CROWN

28.28 g., 0.925 Silver 0.841 oz. ASW, 38.8 mm. **Ruler:** Elizabeth II **Series:** Traders of the World **Subject:** Vikings, 900AD **Obv:**

Crowned bust right **Rev:** Ship (900AD), pair of fish and walrus tusks

Date	Mintage	VF20	XF40	MS60	MS63	MS65
1998	Est. 10000	PF65 45.00				

KM# 696 CROWN

28.28 g., 0.925 Silver 0.841 oz. ASW, 38.8 mm. **Ruler:** Elizabeth II **Series:** Traders of the World **Subject:** Marco Polo, 1254-1324 **Obv:** Crowned bust right **Rev:** Chopsticks with noodles below bust at right, ship at left

Date	Mintage	VF20	XF40	MS60	MS63	MS65
1998	Est. 10000	PF65 45.00				

KM# 698 CROWN

28.28 g., 0.925 Silver 0.841 oz. ASW, 38.8 mm. **Ruler:** Elizabeth II **Series:** Traders of the World **Subject:** Hanseatic League Nations **Obv:** Queen's portrait **Rev:** Coins of the nations above Hanseatic Kogge (circa 1350), map at right

Date	Mintage	VF20	XF40	MS60	MS63	MS65
1998	Est. 10000	PF65 45.00				

KM# 700 CROWN

28.28 g., 0.925 Silver 0.841 oz. ASW, 38.8 mm. **Ruler:** Elizabeth II **Series:** Traders of the World **Subject:** Chinese **Obv:** Crowned bust right **Rev:** Chinese Junk (1400s), silk worm and pottery

Date	Mintage	VF20	XF40	MS60	MS63	MS65
1998	Est. 10000	PF65 45.00				

KM# 702 CROWN

28.28 g., 0.925 Silver 0.841 oz. ASW, 38.8 mm. **Ruler:** Elizabeth II **Series:** Traders of the World **Subject:** Christopher Columbus, 1451-1506 **Obv:** Crowned bust right **Rev:** Bust at left looking right, ship at right

Date	Mintage	VF20	XF40	MS60	MS63	MS65
1998	Est. 10000	PF65 45.00				

KM# 704 CROWN

Copper-Nickel, 38.8 mm. **Ruler:** Elizabeth II **Series:** Traders of the World **Subject:** Sir Walter Raleigh, 1552-1618 **Obv:** Crowned bust right **Rev:** Standing figure, ship in background

Date	Mintage	VF20	XF40	MS60	MS63	MS65
1998	—	—	—	—	10.00	14.00

KM# 704a CROWN

28.28 g., 0.925 Silver 0.841 oz. ASW, 38.8 mm. **Ruler:** Elizabeth II **Series:** Traders of the World **Subject:** Sir Walter Raleigh, 1552-1618 **Obv:** Crowned bust right **Rev:** Standing figure, ship in background

Date	Mintage	VF20	XF40	MS60	MS63	MS65
1998	Est. 10000	PF65 45.00				

KM# 706 CROWN

28.28 g., 0.925 Silver 0.841 oz. ASW, 38.8 mm. **Ruler:** Elizabeth II **Series:** Traders of the World **Obv:** Crowned bust right **Rev:** Boston Tea Party (1773) scene, tea leaf above

Date	Mintage	VF20	XF40	MS60	MS63	MS65
1998	Est. 10000	PF65 45.00				

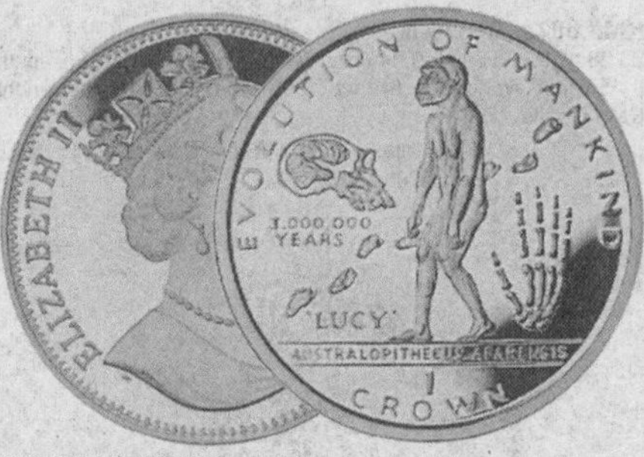

KM# 708 CROWN

Copper-Nickel, 38.8 mm. **Ruler:** Elizabeth II **Series:** Evolution of Mankind **Subject:** Australopithecus, Lucy **Obv:** Crowned bust right **Rev:** Upright figure left, brain depiction at left

Date	Mintage	VF20	XF40	MS60	MS63	MS65
1998	—	—	—	—	12.00	15.00

KM# 708a CROWN

28.28 g., 0.925 Silver 0.841 oz. ASW, 38.8 mm. **Ruler:** Elizabeth II **Series:** Evolution of Mankind **Subject:** Australopithecus, Lucy **Obv:** Crowned bust right **Rev:** Upright figure left, brain depiction at left

Date	Mintage	VF20	XF40	MS60	MS63	MS65
1998	Est. 10000	PF65 45.00				

KM# 710 CROWN

Copper-Nickel, 38.8 mm. **Ruler:** Elizabeth II **Series:** Evolution of Mankind **Subject:** Homo Habilis **Obv:** Crowned bust right **Rev:** Squatted figure right using tools

Date	Mintage	VF20	XF40	MS60	MS63	MS65
1998	—	—	—	—	12.00	15.00

KM# 710a CROWN

28.28 g., 0.925 Silver 0.841 oz. ASW, 38.8 mm. **Ruler:** Elizabeth II **Series:** Evolution of Mankind **Subject:** Homo Habilis **Obv:** Crowned bust right **Rev:** Squatted figure right using tools

Date	Mintage	VF20	XF40	MS60	MS63	MS65
1998	Est. 10000	PF65 45.00				

KM# 712 CROWN

Copper-Nickel, 38.8 mm. **Ruler:** Elizabeth II **Series:** Evolution of Mankind **Subject:** Homo Erectus **Obv:** Crowned bust right **Rev:** Three figures with fire

Date	Mintage	VF20	XF40	MS60	MS63	MS65
1998	—	—	—	—	12.00	15.00

KM# 712a CROWN

28.28 g., 0.925 Silver 0.841 oz. ASW, 38.8 mm. **Ruler:** Elizabeth II **Series:** Evolution of Mankind **Subject:** Homo Erectus **Obv:** Crowned bust right **Rev:** Three figures with fire

Date	Mintage	VF20	XF40	MS60	MS63	MS65
1998	Est. 10000	PF65 45.00				

KM# 714 CROWN

Copper-Nickel, 38.8 mm. **Ruler:** Elizabeth II **Series:** Evolution of Mankind **Subject:** Gibraltar Skull **Obv:** Crowned bust right **Rev:** Skull, rock and caveman

Date	Mintage	VF20	XF40	MS60	MS63	MS65
1998	—	—	—	—	12.00	15.00

KM# 714a CROWN

28.28 g., 0.925 Silver 0.841 oz. ASW, 38.8 mm. **Ruler:** Elizabeth II **Series:** Evolution of Mankind **Subject:** Gibraltar Skull **Obv:** Crowned bust right **Rev:** Skull, rock and caveman

Date	Mintage	VF20	XF40	MS60	MS63	MS65
1998	Est. 10000	PF65 45.00				

KM# 716 CROWN

Copper-Nickel, 38.8 mm. **Ruler:** Elizabeth II **Series:** Evolution of Mankind **Subject:** Neanderthal Man **Obv:** Crowned bust right **Rev:** Skull left of burial scene

Date	Mintage	VF20	XF40	MS60	MS63	MS65
1998	—	—	—	—	12.00	15.00

KM# 716a CROWN

28.28 g., 0.925 Silver 0.841 oz. ASW, 38.8 mm. **Ruler:** Elizabeth II **Series:** Evolution of Mankind **Subject:** Neanderthal Man **Obv:** Crowned bust right **Rev:** Skull left of burial scene

Date	Mintage	VF20	XF40	MS60	MS63	MS65
1998	Est. 10000	PF65 45.00				

KM# 718 CROWN

Copper-Nickel, 38.8 mm. **Ruler:** Elizabeth II **Series:** Evolution of Mankind **Subject:** Homo Sapiens **Obv:** Crowned bust right **Rev:** Figure doing cave painting

Date	Mintage	VF20	XF40	MS60	MS63	MS65
1998	—	—	—	—	12.00	15.00

KM# 718a CROWN

28.28 g., 0.925 Silver 0.841 oz. ASW, 38.8 mm. **Ruler:** Elizabeth II **Series:** Evolution of Mankind **Subject:** Homo Sapiens **Obv:** Crowned bust right **Rev:** Figure doing cave painting

Date	Mintage	VF20	XF40	MS60	MS63	MS65
1998	Est. 10000	PF65 45.00				

KM# 720 CROWN

Copper-Nickel, 38.8 mm. **Ruler:** Elizabeth II **Series:** Evolution of Mankind **Subject:** Homo Sapiens Hunting Mammoth **Obv:** Crowned bust right **Rev:** Figures spearing mammoth

Date	Mintage	VF20	XF40	MS60	MS63	MS65
1998	—	—	—	—	12.00	20.00

KM# 720a CROWN

28.28 g., 0.925 Silver 0.841 oz. ASW, 38.8 mm. **Ruler:** Elizabeth II **Series:** Evolution of Mankind **Subject:** Homo Sapiens Hunting Mammoth **Obv:** Crowned bust right **Rev:** Figures spearing mammoth

Date	Mintage	VF20	XF40	MS60	MS63	MS65
1998	Est. 10000	PF65 45.00				

KM# 722.1 CROWN

Copper-Nickel, 38.8 mm. **Ruler:** Elizabeth II **Series:** Evolution of Mankind **Obv:** Queen's portrait **Rev:** Pictorial representation of theory of evolution, denomination below

Date	Mintage	VF20	XF40	MS60	MS63	MS65
1998	—	—	—	—	12.00	15.00

KM# 722a CROWN

28.28 g., 0.925 Silver 0.841 oz. ASW, 38.8 mm. **Ruler:** Elizabeth II **Series:** Evolution of Mankind **Obv:** Queen's portrait **Rev:** Illustrated theory of evolution

Date	Mintage	VF20	XF40	MS60	MS63	MS65
1998	Est. 10000	PF65 45.00				

KM# 724 CROWN

Copper-Nickel, 38.8 mm. **Ruler:** Elizabeth II **Series:** Evolution of Mankind **Subject:** The Common Ancestry of Ape and Man **Obv:** Crowned bust right **Rev:** Human and primate mothers with young

Date	Mintage	VF20	XF40	MS60	MS63	MS65
1998	—	—	—	—	12.00	15.00

KM# 724a CROWN

28.28 g., 0.925 Silver 0.841 oz. ASW, 38.8 mm. **Ruler:** Elizabeth II **Series:** Evolution of Mankind **Subject:** The Common Ancestry of Ape and Man **Obv:** Crowned bust right **Rev:** Human and primate mothers with young

Date	Mintage	VF20	XF40	MS60	MS63	MS65
1998	Est. 10000	PF65 45.00				

KM# 726 CROWN

Copper-Nickel, 38.8 mm. **Ruler:** Elizabeth II **Series:** Evolution of Mankind **Subject:** Charles Darwin, 1809-1882 **Obv:** Homo Sapiens Hunting Mammoth **Rev:** Bust facing, caveman and space shuttle at right

Date	Mintage	VF20	XF40	MS60	MS63	MS65
1998	—	—	—	—	12.00	15.00

KM# 726a CROWN

28.28 g., 0.925 Silver 0.841 oz. ASW, 38.8 mm. **Ruler:** Elizabeth II **Series:** Evolution of Mankind **Subject:** Charles Darwin, 1809-1882 **Obv:** Crowned bust right **Rev:** Bust facing, caveman and space shuttle at right

Date	Mintage	VF20	XF40	MS60	MS63	MS65
1998	Est. 10000	PF65 45.00				

KM# 728 CROWN

Copper-Nickel, 38.8 mm. **Ruler:** Elizabeth II **Series:** Evolution of Mankind **Subject:** Raymond Dart **Obv:** Crowned bust right **Rev:** Bust at left looking at skull

Date	Mintage	VF20	XF40	MS60	MS63	MS65
1998	—	—	—	—	12.00	15.00

KM# 728a CROWN

28.28 g., 0.925 Silver 0.841 oz. ASW, 38.8 mm. **Ruler:** Elizabeth II **Series:** Evolution of Mankind **Subject:** Raymond Dart **Obv:** Crowned bust right **Rev:** Bust at left looking at skull on right

Date	Mintage	VF20	XF40	MS60	MS63	MS65
1998	Est. 10000	PF65 45.00				

KM# 730 CROWN

Copper-Nickel, 38.8 mm. **Ruler:** Elizabeth II **Series:** Evolution of Mankind **Subject:** 20th Century Homo Sapiens **Obv:** Crowned bust right **Rev:** Five depictions of evolution

Date	Mintage	VF20	XF40	MS60	MS63	MS65
1998	—	—	—	—	12.00	15.00

KM# 730a CROWN

28.28 g., 0.925 Silver 0.841 oz. ASW, 38.8 mm. **Ruler:** Elizabeth II **Series:** Evolution of Mankind **Subject:** 20th Century Homo Sapiens **Obv:** Crowned bust right **Rev:** Five depictions of evolution

Date	Mintage	VF20	XF40	MS60	MS63	MS65
1998	Est. 10000	PF65 45.00				

KM# 733 CROWN

28.28 g., 0.925 Silver 0.841 oz. ASW with Gold inset., 38.8 mm. **Ruler:** Elizabeth II **Series:** Wonders of the World **Subject:** Guilin Hills, China **Obv:** Crowned bust right **Rev:** Chinese coin design inlay below hill scene

Date	Mintage	VF20	XF40	MS60	MS63	MS65
1998	Est. 7500	PF65 60.00				

KM# 734 CROWN

28.28 g., 0.925 Silver 0.841 oz. ASW with Gold inset., 38.8 mm. **Ruler:** Elizabeth II **Series:** Wonders of the World **Subject:** Victoria Falls, Africa **Obv:** Crowned bust right **Rev:** South African coin design inlay below falls scene

Date	Mintage	VF20	XF40	MS60	MS63	MS65
1998	Est. 7500	PF65 60.00				

KM# 735 CROWN

28.28 g., 0.925 Silver 0.841 oz. ASW with Gold inset., 38.8 mm. **Ruler:** Elizabeth II **Series:** Wonders of the World **Subject:** The Materhorn, Switzerland, Italy **Obv:** Crowned bust right **Rev:** Swiss coin design inlay below mountain

Date	Mintage	VF20	XF40	MS60	MS63	MS65
1998	Est. 7500	PF65 60.00				

KM# 736 CROWN

28.28 g., 0.925 Silver 0.841 oz. ASW with Gold inset., 38.8 mm. **Ruler:** Elizabeth II **Series:** Wonders of the World **Subject:** Taroko Gorge, Taiwan **Obv:** Crowned bust right **Rev:** Taiwanese coin design inlay below gorge scene

Date	Mintage	VF20	XF40	MS60	MS63	MS65
1998	—	PF65 60.00				

KM# 737 CROWN

28.28 g., 0.925 Silver 0.841 oz. ASW with Gold inset., 38.8 mm. **Ruler:** Elizabeth II **Series:** Wonders of the World **Subject:** Niagara Falls, Canada, USA **Obv:** Crowned bust right **Rev:** American coin design inlay below falls scene

Date	Mintage	VF20	XF40	MS60	MS63	MS65
1998	—	PF65 60.00				

KM# 738 CROWN

28.28 g., 0.925 Silver 0.841 oz. ASW with Gold inset., 38.8 mm. **Ruler:** Elizabeth II **Series:** Wonders of the World **Subject:** Mount Fuji, Japan **Obv:** Crowned bust right **Rev:** Japanese coin design inlay below plants and mountain

Date	Mintage	VF20	XF40	MS60	MS63	MS65
1998	Est. 7500	PF65 60.00				

KM# 739 CROWN

28.28 g., 0.925 Silver 0.841 oz. ASW with Gold inset., 38.8 mm. **Ruler:** Elizabeth II **Series:** Wonders of the World **Subject:** Uluru, Australia **Obv:** Crowned bust right **Rev:** Australian coin design inlay below mountain

Date	Mintage	VF20	XF40	MS60	MS63	MS65
1998	—	PF65 60.00				

KM# 745 CROWN

Copper-Nickel, 38.8 mm. **Ruler:** Elizabeth II **Series:** Year of the Ocean **Obv:** Crowned bust right **Rev:** Mermaid and dolphin

Date	Mintage	VF20	XF40	MS60	MS63	MS65
1998	—	—	—	—	10.00	14.00

KM# 745a CROWN

28.28 g., 0.925 Silver 0.841 oz. ASW, 38.8 mm. **Ruler:** Elizabeth II **Series:** Year of the Ocean **Obv:** Crowned bust right **Rev:** Mermaid and dolphin

Date	Mintage	VF20	XF40	MS60	MS63	MS65
1998	Est. 30000	PF65 45.00				

KM# 746 CROWN

Copper-Nickel, 38.8 mm. **Ruler:** Elizabeth II **Series:** Year of the Ocean **Obv:** Crowned bust right **Rev:** Octopus, fish and coral

Date	Mintage	VF20	XF40	MS60	MS63	MS65
1998	—	—	—	—	10.00	14.00

KM# 746a CROWN

28.28 g., 0.925 Silver 0.841 oz. ASW, 38.8 mm. **Ruler:** Elizabeth II **Series:** Year of the Ocean **Obv:** Crowned bust right **Rev:** Octopus, fish and coral

Date	Mintage	VF20	XF40	MS60	MS63	MS65
1998	Est. 30000	PF65 45.00				

KM# 747 CROWN

Copper-Nickel, 38.8 mm. **Ruler:** Elizabeth II **Series:** Year of the Ocean **Obv:** Crowned bust right **Rev:** Jellyfish, stingray and fish

Date	Mintage	VF20	XF40	MS60	MS63	MS65
1998	—	—	—	—	10.00	14.00

KM# 747a CROWN

28.28 g., 0.925 Silver 0.841 oz. ASW, 38.8 mm. **Ruler:** Elizabeth II **Series:** Year of the Ocean **Obv:** Crowned bust right **Rev:** Jellyfish, stingray and fish

Date	Mintage	VF20	XF40	MS60	MS63	MS65
1998	Est. 30000	PF65 55.00				

KM# 748 CROWN

Copper-Nickel, 38.8 mm. **Ruler:** Elizabeth II **Series:** Year of the Ocean **Obv:** Crowned bust right **Rev:** Two wind surfers

Date	Mintage	VF20	XF40	MS60	MS63	MS65
1998	—	—	—	—	9.50	12.00

KM# 748a CROWN

28.28 g., 0.925 Silver 0.841 oz. ASW, 38.8 mm. **Ruler:** Elizabeth II **Series:** Year of the Ocean **Obv:** Crowned bust right **Rev:** Two wind surfers

Date	Mintage	VF20	XF40	MS60	MS63	MS65
1998	Est. 30000	PF65 55.00				

KM# 768 CROWN

Copper-Nickel, 38.8 mm. **Ruler:** Elizabeth II **Subject:** The Gibraltar Regiment New Colors **Obv:** Crowned bust right **Rev:** Soldier presenting keys, flags and crowned arms

Date	Mintage	VF20	XF40	MS60	MS63	MS65
1998	—	—	—	—	10.00	12.50

KM# 768a CROWN

28.28 g., 0.925 Silver 0.841 oz. ASW, 38.8 mm. **Ruler:** Elizabeth II **Subject:** The Gibraltar Regiment New Colors **Obv:** Crowned bust right **Rev:** Soldier presenting keys, flags and crowned arms

Date	Mintage	VF20	XF40	MS60	MS63	MS65
1998	Est. 30000	PF65 45.00				

KM# 799 CROWN

Copper-Nickel, 38.8 mm. **Ruler:** Elizabeth II **Series:** The World At War **Subject:** General D.D. Eisenhower **Obv:** Crowned bust right **Rev:** North African invasion scene

Date	Mintage	VF20	XF40	MS60	MS63	MS65
1998	—	—	—	—	8.00	10.00

KM# 799a CROWN

28.28 g., 0.925 Silver 0.841 oz. ASW, 38.8 mm. **Ruler:** Elizabeth II **Series:** The World At War **Subject:** General D.D. Eisenhower **Obv:** Crowned bust right **Rev:** North African invasion scene

Date	Mintage	VF20	XF40	MS60	MS63	MS65
1998	Est. 10000	PF65 45.00				

KM# 1097 CROWN

38.80 g., Copper-Nickel, 38.8 mm. **Ruler:** Elizabeth II **Series:** Year of the Ocean **Obv:** Crowned bust right **Rev:** Humpback whale

Date	Mintage	VF20	XF40	MS60	MS63	MS65
1998	—	—	—	—	—	14.00

KM# 783.1 CROWN

Copper-Nickel, 38.8 mm. **Ruler:** Elizabeth II **Subject:** 1999 The Year of the Rabbit **Obv:** Crowned bust right **Rev:** Rabbit reading, sparrow, Chinese characters

Date	Mintage	VF20	XF40	MS60	MS63	MS65
1999	—	—	—	—	10.00	12.00

KM# 783.1a CROWN

28.28 g., 0.925 Silver 0.841 oz. ASW, 38.8 mm. **Ruler:** Elizabeth II **Subject:** 1999 The Year of the Rabbit **Obv:** Crowned bust right **Rev:** Rabbit reading, sparrow, Chinese characters

Date	Mintage	VF20	XF40	MS60	MS63	MS65
1999	Est. 10000	PF65 45.00				

KM# 783.2 CROWN

Copper-Nickel, 38.8 mm. **Ruler:** Elizabeth II **Obv:** Crowned bust right **Rev:** Rabbit reading, sparrow; without Chinese characters

Date	Mintage	VF20	XF40	MS60	MS63	MS65
1999	Inc. above	—	—	—	10.00	12.00

KM# 783.2a CROWN

28.28 g., 0.925 Silver 0.841 oz. ASW, 38.8 mm. **Ruler:** Elizabeth II **Obv:** Crowned bust right **Rev:** Rabbit reading, sparrow; without Chinese characters

Date	Mintage	VF20	XF40	MS60	MS63	MS65
1999	Inc. above	PF65 45.00				

KM# 785 CROWN

28.28 g., Copper-Nickel, 38.8 mm. **Ruler:** Elizabeth II **Series:** Summer Olympics - Sydney **Obv:** Crowned bust right **Rev:** Broad jumper and kangaroo

Date	Mintage	VF20	XF40	MS60	MS63	MS65
1999	—	—	—	—	8.00	10.00
2000 PM	—	—	—	—	8.00	10.00

KM# 785a CROWN

28.28 g., 0.925 Silver 0.841 oz. ASW, 38.8 mm. **Ruler:** Elizabeth II **Series:** Summer Olympics - Sydney **Obv:** Crowned bust right **Rev:** Broad jumper and kangaroo

Date	Mintage	VF20	XF40	MS60	MS63	MS65
1999	Est. 30000	PF65 45.00				

KM# 787 CROWN

28.28 g., Copper-Nickel, 38.8 mm. **Ruler:** Elizabeth II **Series:** Summer Olympics - Sydney **Obv:** Crowned bust right **Rev:** Sailboats and platypus

Date	Mintage	VF20	XF40	MS60	MS63	MS65
1999	—	—	—	—	8.00	10.00
2000 PM	—	—	—	—	8.00	10.00

KM# 787a CROWN

28.28 g., 0.925 Silver 0.841 oz. ASW, 38.8 mm. **Ruler:** Elizabeth II **Series:** Summer Olympics - Sydney **Obv:** Crowned bust right **Rev:** Sailboats and platypus

Date	Mintage	VF20	XF40	MS60	MS63	MS65
1999	Est. 30000	PF65 45.00				

KM# 789 CROWN

28.28 g., Copper-Nickel, 38.8 mm. **Ruler:** Elizabeth II **Series:** Summer Olympics - Sydney **Obv:** Crowned bust right **Rev:** Swimmer and koala bear

Date	Mintage	VF20	XF40	MS60	MS63	MS65
1999	—	—	—	—	8.00	10.00
2000 PM	—	—	—	—	8.00	10.00

KM# 789a CROWN

28.28 g., 0.925 Silver 0.841 oz. ASW, 38.8 mm. **Ruler:** Elizabeth II **Series:** Summer Olympics - Sydney **Obv:** Crowned bust right **Rev:** Swimmer and koala bear

Date	Mintage	VF20	XF40	MS60	MS63	MS65
1999	Est. 30000	PF65 45.00				

KM# 791 CROWN

28.28 g., Copper-Nickel, 38.8 mm. **Ruler:** Elizabeth II **Series:** Summer Olympics - Sydney **Obv:** Crowned bust right **Rev:** Two oarsmen below cockatoos

Date	Mintage	VF20	XF40	MS60	MS63	MS65
1999	—	—	—	—	8.00	10.00
2000 PM	—	—	—	—	8.00	10.00

KM# 791a CROWN

28.28 g., 0.925 Silver 0.841 oz. ASW, 38.8 mm. **Ruler:** Elizabeth II **Series:** Summer Olympics - Sydney **Obv:** Crowned bust right **Rev:** Two oarsmen below cockatoos **Note:** Prev. KM791.1

Date	Mintage	VF20	XF40	MS60	MS63	MS65
1999	Est. 30000	PF65 45.00				

KM# 793 CROWN

28.28 g., Copper-Nickel, 38.8 mm. **Ruler:** Elizabeth II **Series:** Summer Olympics - Sydney **Obv:** Crowned bust right **Rev:** Man with torch and dingo, denomination below

Date	Mintage	VF20	XF40	MS60	MS63	MS65
1999	—	—	—	—	8.00	10.00
2000 PM	—	—	—	—	8.00	10.00

KM# 793a CROWN

28.28 g., 0.925 Silver 0.841 oz. ASW, 38.8 mm. **Ruler:** Elizabeth II **Series:** Summer Olympics - Sydney **Obv:** Crowned bust right **Rev:** Man with torch and dingo

Date	Mintage	VF20	XF40	MS60	MS63	MS65
1999	Est. 30000	PF65 45.00				

KM# 795 CROWN

28.28 g., Copper-Nickel, 38.8 mm. **Ruler:** Elizabeth II **Series:** Summer Olympics - Sydney **Obv:** Crowned bust right **Rev:** Runner with torch, Aboriginal portrait and Ayer's Rock

Date	Mintage	VF20	XF40	MS60	MS63	MS65
1999	—	—	—	—	8.00	10.00
2000 PM	—	—	—	—	8.00	10.00

KM# 795a CROWN

28.28 g., 0.925 Silver 0.841 oz. ASW, 38.8 mm. **Ruler:** Elizabeth II **Series:** Summer Olympics - Sydney **Obv:** Crowned bust right **Rev:** Runner with torch, Aboriginal portrait and Ayer's Rock

Date	Mintage	VF20	XF40	MS60	MS63	MS65
1999	—	PF65 45.00				

KM# 796.1 CROWN

6.22 g., 0.9999 Gold 0.200 oz. AGW **Ruler:** Elizabeth II **Subject:** Millennium 2000 **Obv:** Head with tiara right **Rev:** Sundial, digital clock face, candle and traditional clock face

Date	Mintage	VF20	XF40	MS60	MS63	MS65
1999	5,000	PF65 325				

KM# 801 CROWN

Copper-Nickel, 38.8 mm. **Ruler:** Elizabeth II **Subject:** King Alfred the Great, 871-899 **Obv:** Crowned bust right **Rev:** Crowned bust left, dates

Date	Mintage	VF20	XF40	MS60	MS63	MS65
1999	—	—	—	—	7.50	9.00

KM# 801a CROWN

28.28 g., 0.925 Silver 0.841 oz. ASW, 38.8 mm. **Ruler:** Elizabeth II **Subject:** King Alfred the Great, 871-899 **Obv:** Crowned bust right **Rev:** Crowned bust left, dates

Date	Mintage	VF20	XF40	MS60	MS63	MS65
1999	Est. 10000	PF65 42.00				

KM# 803 CROWN

Copper-Nickel, 38.8 mm. **Ruler:** Elizabeth II **Subject:** King Canute, 1016-1035 **Obv:** Crowned bust right **Rev:** Crowned bust left, dates

Date	Mintage	VF20	XF40	MS60	MS63	MS65
1999	—	—	—	—	7.50	9.00

KM# 803a CROWN

28.28 g., 0.925 Silver 0.841 oz. ASW, 38.8 mm. **Ruler:** Elizabeth II **Subject:** King Canute, 1016-1035 **Obv:** Crowned bust right **Rev:** Crowned bust left, dates

Date	Mintage	VF20	XF40	MS60	MS63	MS65
1999	Est. 10000	PF65 42.00				

KM# 805 CROWN
Copper-Nickel, 38.8 mm. **Ruler:** Elizabeth II **Subject:** King Edward the Confessor, 1042-1066 **Obv:** Crowned bust right **Rev:** Crowned bust left, dates

Date	Mintage	VF20	XF40	MS60	MS63	MS65
1999	—	—	—	—	7.50	9.00

KM# 805a CROWN
28.28 g., 0.925 Silver 0.841 oz. ASW, 38.8 mm. **Ruler:** Elizabeth II **Subject:** King Edward the Confessor, 1042-1066 **Obv:** Crowned bust right **Rev:** Crowned bust left, dates

Date	Mintage	VF20	XF40	MS60	MS63	MS65
1999	Est. 10000	**PF65** 42.00				

KM# 807 CROWN
Copper-Nickel, 38.8 mm. **Ruler:** Elizabeth II **Series:** House - Normandy **Subject:** King William I, 1066-1087 **Obv:** Crowned bust right **Rev:** Crowned bust left, dates

Date	Mintage	VF20	XF40	MS60	MS63	MS65
1999	—	—	—	—	7.50	9.00

KM# 807a CROWN
28.28 g., 0.925 Silver 0.841 oz. ASW, 38.8 mm. **Ruler:** Elizabeth II **Series:** House of - Normandy **Subject:** King William I, 1066-1087 **Obv:** Crowned bust right **Rev:** Crowned bust left, dates

Date	Mintage	VF20	XF40	MS60	MS63	MS65
1999	Est. 10000	**PF65** 42.00				

KM# 809 CROWN
Copper-Nickel, 38.8 mm. **Ruler:** Elizabeth II **Series:** House of - Plantagenet **Subject:** King Richard I, 1189-1199 **Obv:** Crowned bust right **Rev:** Crowned bust right, dates

Date	Mintage	VF20	XF40	MS60	MS63	MS65
1999	—	—	—	—	7.50	9.00

KM# 809a CROWN
28.28 g., 0.925 Silver 0.841 oz. ASW, 38.8 mm. **Ruler:** Elizabeth II **Series:** House of - Plantagenet **Subject:** King Richard I, 1189-1199 **Obv:** Crowned bust right **Rev:** Crowned bust right, dates

Date	Mintage	VF20	XF40	MS60	MS63	MS65
1999	Est. 10000	**PF65** 42.00				

KM# 811 CROWN
Copper-Nickel, 38.8 mm. **Ruler:** Elizabeth II **Series:** House of - Plantagenet **Subject:** King John, 1199-1216 **Obv:** Crowned bust right **Rev:** Crowned bust left, dates

Date	Mintage	VF20	XF40	MS60	MS63	MS65
1999	—	—	—	—	7.50	9.00

KM# 811a CROWN
28.28 g., 0.925 Silver 0.841 oz. ASW, 38.8 mm. **Ruler:** Elizabeth II **Series:** House of - Plantagenet **Subject:** King John, 1199-1216 **Obv:** Crowned bust right **Rev:** Crowned bust left, dates

Date	Mintage	VF20	XF40	MS60	MS63	MS65
1999	Est. 10000	**PF65** 42.00				

KM# 813 CROWN
Copper-Nickel, 38.8 mm. **Ruler:** Elizabeth II **Series:** House of - Lancaster **Subject:** King Henry V, 1413-1422 **Obv:** Crowned bust right **Rev:** Bust right, dates

Date	Mintage	VF20	XF40	MS60	MS63	MS65
1999	—	—	—	—	7.50	9.00

KM# 813a CROWN
28.28 g., 0.925 Silver 0.841 oz. ASW, 38.8 mm. **Ruler:** Elizabeth II **Series:** House of - Lancaster **Subject:** King Henry V, 1413-1422 **Obv:** Crowned bust right **Rev:** Bust right, dates

Date	Mintage	VF20	XF40	MS60	MS63	MS65
1999	Est. 10000	**PF65** 42.00				

KM# 815 CROWN
Copper-Nickel, 38.8 mm. **Ruler:** Elizabeth II **Series:** House of - York **Subject:** King Richard III, 1483-1485 **Obv:** Crowned bust right **Rev:** Bust with hat right, dates

Date	Mintage	VF20	XF40	MS60	MS63	MS65
1999	—	—	—	—	7.50	9.00

KM# 815a CROWN
28.28 g., 0.925 Silver 0.841 oz. ASW, 38.8 mm. **Ruler:** Elizabeth II **Series:** House of - York **Subject:** King Richard III, 1483-1485 **Obv:** Crowned bust right **Rev:** Bust with hat right, dates

Date	Mintage	VF20	XF40	MS60	MS63	MS65
1999	Est. 10000	**PF65** 42.00				

KM# 817 CROWN
Copper-Nickel, 38.8 mm. **Ruler:** Elizabeth II **Series:** House of - Tudor **Subject:** King Henry VIII, 1509-1547 **Obv:** Crowned bust right **Rev:** Bust with flat hat right, dates

Date	Mintage	VF20	XF40	MS60	MS63	MS65
1999	—	—	—	—	7.50	9.00

KM# 817a CROWN
28.28 g., 0.925 Silver 0.841 oz. ASW, 38.8 mm. **Ruler:** Elizabeth II **Series:** House of - Tudor **Subject:** King Henry VIII, 1509-1547 **Obv:** Crowned bust right **Rev:** Bust with flat hat right, dates

Date	Mintage	VF20	XF40	MS60	MS63	MS65
1999	Est. 10000	**PF65** 42.00				

KM# 819 CROWN
Copper-Nickel, 38.8 mm. **Ruler:** Elizabeth II **Series:** Tudor **Subject:** Queen Elizabeth I, 1558-1603 **Obv:** Crowned bust right **Rev:** Crowned bust with high ruffled collar left, dates

Date	Mintage	VF20	XF40	MS60	MS63	MS65
1999	—	—	—	—	7.50	9.00

KM# 819a CROWN
28.28 g., 0.925 Silver 0.841 oz. ASW, 38.8 mm. **Ruler:** Elizabeth II **Series:** House of - Tudor **Subject:** Queen Elizabeth I, 1558-1603 **Obv:** Crowned bust right **Rev:** Crowned bust with high ruffled collar left, dates

Date	Mintage	VF20	XF40	MS60	MS63	MS65
1999	Est. 10000	**PF65** 42.00				

KM# 821 CROWN
Copper-Nickel, 38.8 mm. **Ruler:** Elizabeth II **Series:** House of - Stuart **Subject:** King Charles I, 1625-1649 **Obv:** Crowned bust right **Rev:** Bust right, dates

Date	Mintage	VF20	XF40	MS60	MS63	MS65
1999	—	—	—	—	7.50	9.00

KM# 821a CROWN
28.28 g., 0.925 Silver 0.841 oz. ASW, 38.8 mm. **Ruler:** Elizabeth II **Series:** House of - Stuart **Subject:** King Charles I, 1625-1649 **Obv:** Crowned bust right **Rev:** Bust right, dates

Date	Mintage	VF20	XF40	MS60	MS63	MS65
1999	Est. 10000	**PF65** 42.00				

KM# 823 CROWN
Copper-Nickel, 38.8 mm. **Ruler:** Elizabeth II **Series:** House of - Stuart **Subject:** King Charles II, 1660-1685 **Obv:** Crowned bust right **Rev:** Laureate bust right, dates

Date	Mintage	VF20	XF40	MS60	MS63	MS65
1999	—	—	—	—	7.50	9.00

KM# 823a CROWN
28.28 g., 0.925 Silver 0.841 oz. ASW, 38.8 mm. **Ruler:** Elizabeth II **Series:** House of - Stuart **Subject:** King Charles II, 1660-1685 **Obv:** Crowned bust right **Rev:** Laureate bust right, dates

Date	Mintage	VF20	XF40	MS60	MS63	MS65
1999	Est. 10000	PF65 40.00				

KM# 826 CROWN
Copper-Nickel, 38.8 mm. **Ruler:** Elizabeth II **Subject:** The Wedding of Prince Edward and Miss Sophie Rhys-Jones **Obv:** Crowned bust right **Rev:** Two heads facing above banner and wedding bells **Note:** Prev. KM#826.1.

Date	Mintage	VF20	XF40	MS60	MS63	MS65
1999	—	—	—	—	8.00	9.50

KM# 826a CROWN
28.28 g., 0.925 Silver 0.841 oz. ASW, 38.8 mm. **Ruler:** Elizabeth II **Subject:** The Wedding of Prince Edward and Miss Sophie Rhys-Jones **Obv:** Crowned bust right **Rev:** St. George's Chapel

Date	Mintage	VF20	XF40	MS60	MS63	MS65
1999	10,000	PF65 42.00				

KM# 827 CROWN
Copper-Nickel, 38.8 mm. **Ruler:** Elizabeth II **Subject:** The Wedding of Prince Edward and Miss Sophie Rhys-Jones **Obv:** Crowned bust right **Rev:** St. George's Chapel

Date	Mintage	VF20	XF40	MS60	MS63	MS65
1999	—	—	—	—	8.00	9.50

KM# 827a CROWN
28.28 g., 0.925 Silver 0.841 oz. ASW, 38.8 mm. **Ruler:** Elizabeth II **Subject:** The Wedding of Prince Edward and Miss Sophie Rhys-Jones **Obv:** Crowned bust right **Rev:** St. George's Chapel

Date	Mintage	VF20	XF40	MS60	MS63	MS65
1999	Est. 10000	PF65 45.00				

KM# 835 CROWN
Copper-Nickel, 38.8 mm. **Ruler:** Elizabeth II **Series:** The Life Of Queen Elizabeth The Queen Mother **Subject:** Queen's childhood **Obv:** Crowned bust right **Rev:** 1903 portrait of Queen Mother as a girl

Date	Mintage	VF20	XF40	MS60	MS63	MS65
1999	—	—	—	—	8.00	9.50

KM# 835a CROWN
28.28 g., 0.925 Silver 0.841 oz. ASW, 38.8 mm. **Ruler:** Elizabeth II **Series:** The Life Of Queen Elizabeth The Queen Mother **Subject:** Queen's childhood **Obv:** Crowned bust right **Rev:** 1903 portrait of Queen Mother as a girl

Date	Mintage	VF20	XF40	MS60	MS63	MS65
1999	Est. 10000	PF65 45.00				

KM# 835b CROWN
28.46 g., 0.925 Silver Gilt 0.8464 oz., 38.5 mm. **Ruler:** Elizabeth II **Series:** The Life Of Queen Elizabeth The Queen Mother **Subject:** Queen's childhood **Obv:** Crowned bust right **Rev:** Queen Mother as a young girl **Edge:** Reeded

Date	Mintage	VF20	XF40	MS60	MS63	MS65
1999 PM	—	PF65 45.00				

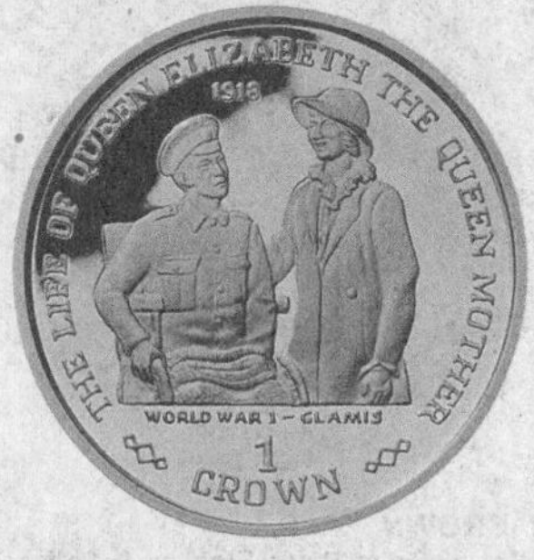

KM# 837 CROWN
Copper-Nickel, 38.8 mm. **Ruler:** Elizabeth II **Series:** The Life Of Queen Elizabeth The Queen Mother **Subject:** World War I - Glamis **Obv:** Crowned bust right **Rev:** 1918 portrait with wounded soldier

Date	Mintage	VF20	XF40	MS60	MS63	MS65
1999	—	—	—	—	8.00	9.50

KM# 837a CROWN
28.28 g., 0.925 Silver 0.841 oz. ASW, 38.8 mm. **Ruler:** Elizabeth II **Series:** The Life Of Queen Elizabeth The Queen Mother **Subject:** World War I - Glamis **Obv:** Crowned bust right **Rev:** 1918 portrait with wounded soldier

Date	Mintage	VF20	XF40	MS60	MS63	MS65
1999	Est. 10000	PF65 45.00				

KM# 837b CROWN
28.46 g., 0.925 Silver Gilt 0.8464 oz., 38.5 mm. **Ruler:** Elizabeth II **Series:** The Life Of Queen Elizabeth The Queen Mother **Subject:** World War I - Glamis **Obv:** Crowned bust right **Rev:** Queen Mother with wounded soldier in 1918 **Edge:** Reeded

Date	Mintage	VF20	XF40	MS60	MS63	MS65
1999 PM	—	PF65 45.00				

KM# 839 CROWN
Copper-Nickel, 38.8 mm. **Ruler:** Elizabeth II **Subject:** A Royal Marriage **Obv:** Crowned bust right **Rev:** 1923 wedding portrait

Date	Mintage	VF20	XF40	MS60	MS63	MS65
1999	—	—	—	—	8.00	9.50

KM# 839a CROWN
28.28 g., 0.925 Silver 0.841 oz. ASW, 38.8 mm. **Ruler:** Elizabeth II **Series:** The Life Of Queen Elizabeth The Queen Mother **Subject:** A Royal Marriage **Obv:** Crowned bust right **Rev:** 1923 wedding portrait

Date	Mintage	VF20	XF40	MS60	MS63	MS65
1999	Est. 10000	PF65 45.00				

KM# 839b CROWN
28.46 g., 0.925 Silver Gilt 0.8464 oz., 38.5 mm. **Ruler:** Elizabeth II **Series:** The Life Of Queen Elizabeth The Queen Mother **Subject:** A Royal Marriage **Obv:** Crowned bust right **Rev:** Queen Mother's 1923 wedding portrait **Edge:** Reeded

Date	Mintage	VF20	XF40	MS60	MS63	MS65
1999 PM	—	PF65 45.00				

KM# 841 CROWN
Copper-Nickel, 38.8 mm. **Ruler:** Elizabeth II **Series:** The Life Of Queen Elizabeth The Queen Mother **Subject:** A Royal Family **Obv:** Crowned bust right **Rev:** 1936 family portrait

Date	Mintage	VF20	XF40	MS60	MS63	MS65
1999	—	—	—	—	8.00	9.50

KM# 841a CROWN

28.28 g., 0.925 Silver 0.841 oz. ASW, 38.8 mm. **Ruler:** Elizabeth II **Series:** The Life Of Queen Elizabeth The Queen Mother **Subject:** A Royal Family **Obv:** Crowned bust right **Rev:** 1936 family portrait

Date	Mintage	VF20	XF40	MS60	MS63	MS65
1999	Est. 10000	PF65 45.00				

KM# 841b CROWN

28.46 g., 0.925 Silver Gilt 0.8464 oz., 38.5 mm. **Ruler:** Elizabeth II **Series:** The Life Of Queen Elizabeth The Queen Mother **Subject:** A Royal Family **Obv:** Crowned bust right **Rev:** 1936 Queen Mother's family portrait **Edge:** Reeded

Date	Mintage	VF20	XF40	MS60	MS63	MS65
1999 PM	—	PF65 45.00				

KM# 843.1 CROWN

28.28 g., 0.925 Silver 0.841 oz. ASW **Subject:** The World at War **Obv:** Queen's portrait **Rev:** Franklin Roosevelt and Zero fighter

Date	Mintage	VF20	XF40	MS60	MS63	MS65
1999	—	—	—	—	10.00	12.00

KM# 843a CROWN

28.28 g., 0.925 Silver 0.841 oz. ASW, 38.8 mm. **Ruler:** Elizabeth II **Series:** The World At War **Subject:** Franklin D. Roosevelt **Obv:** Crowned bust right **Rev:** Bust writing at left, Zero fighter plane at right

Date	Mintage	VF20	XF40	MS60	MS63	MS65
1999	Est. 10000	PF65 45.00				

KM# 845 CROWN

Copper-Nickel, 38.8 mm. **Ruler:** Elizabeth II **Series:** The World At War **Subject:** Operation Manna **Obv:** Crowned bust right **Rev:** Bomber dropping food packets

Date	Mintage	VF20	XF40	MS60	MS63	MS65
1999	—	—	—	—	10.00	12.00

KM# 845a CROWN

28.28 g., 0.925 Silver 0.841 oz. ASW, 38.8 mm. **Ruler:** Elizabeth II **Series:** The World At **Subject:** Operation Manna **Obv:** Crowned bust right **Rev:** Bomber dropping food packets

Date	Mintage	VF20	XF40	MS60	MS63	MS65
1999	Est. 10000	PF65 45.00				

KM# 847.1 CROWN

Copper-Nickel, 38.8 mm. **Ruler:** Elizabeth II **Series:** The World At War **Subject:** J. Robert Oppenheimer **Obv:** Crowned bust right **Rev:** Bust at right looking left, B-29 and mushroom cloud

Date	Mintage	VF20	XF40	MS60	MS63	MS65
1999	—	—	—	—	10.00	12.00

KM# 847a CROWN

28.28 g., 0.925 Silver 0.841 oz. ASW, 38.8 mm. **Ruler:** Elizabeth II **Series:** The World At War **Subject:** J. Robert Oppenheimer **Obv:** Crowned bust right **Rev:** Bust at right looking left, B-29 and mushroom cloud

Date	Mintage	VF20	XF40	MS60	MS63	MS65
1999	Est. 10000	PF65 45.00				

KM# 849 CROWN

Copper-Nickel, 38.8 mm. **Ruler:** Elizabeth II **Series:** The World At War **Subject:** Barnes Wallis **Obv:** Crowned bust right **Rev:** Seated figure at left reading, bomber above dam at right

Date	Mintage	VF20	XF40	MS60	MS63	MS65
1999	—	—	—	—	10.00	12.00

KM# 849a CROWN

28.28 g., 0.925 Silver 0.841 oz. ASW, 38.8 mm. **Ruler:** Elizabeth II **Series:** The World At War **Subject:** Barnes Wallis **Obv:** Crowned bust right **Rev:** Seated figure at left reading, bomber above dam at right

Date	Mintage	VF20	XF40	MS60	MS63	MS65
1999	Est. 10000	PF65 45.00				

KM# 851 CROWN

Copper-Nickel, 38.8 mm. **Ruler:** Elizabeth II **Series:** The World At War **Subject:** Douglas Bader **Obv:** Crowned bust right **Rev:** Bust facing at left, planes in combat

Date	Mintage	VF20	XF40	MS60	MS63	MS65
1999	—	—	—	—	10.00	12.00

KM# 851a CROWN

28.28 g., 0.925 Silver 0.841 oz. ASW, 38.8 mm. **Ruler:** Elizabeth II **Series:** The World At War **Subject:** Douglas Bader **Obv:** Crowned bust right **Rev:** Bust facing at left, planes in combat

Date	Mintage	VF20	XF40	MS60	MS63	MS65
1999	Est. 10000	PF65 45.00				

KM# 853 CROWN

Copper-Nickel, 38.8 mm. **Ruler:** Elizabeth II **Series:** The World At War **Subject:** Winston Churchill **Obv:** Crowned bust right **Rev:** Bust facing with hand raised in "V" sign and crowd

Date	Mintage	VF20	XF40	MS60	MS63	MS65
1999	—	—	—	—	10.00	12.00

KM# 853a CROWN

28.28 g., 0.925 Silver 0.841 oz. ASW, 38.8 mm. **Ruler:** Elizabeth II **Series:** The World At War **Subject:** Winston Churchill **Obv:** Crowned bust right **Rev:** Bust facing with hand raised in "V" sign and crowd

Date	Mintage	VF20	XF40	MS60	MS63	MS65
1999	Est. 10000	PF65 45.00				

KM# 855 CROWN

Copper-Nickel, 38.8 mm. **Ruler:** Elizabeth II **Series:** The World At War **Subject:** Tirpitz **Obv:** Crowned bust right **Rev:** Battleship and sailor

Date	Mintage	VF20	XF40	MS60	MS63	MS65
1999	—	—	—	—	10.00	12.00

KM# 855a CROWN

28.28 g., 0.925 Silver 0.841 oz. ASW, 38.8 mm. **Ruler:** Elizabeth II **Series:** The World At War **Subject:** Tirpitz **Obv:** Crowned bust right **Rev:** Battleship and sailor

Date	Mintage	VF20	XF40	MS60	MS63	MS65
1999	Est. 10000	PF65 45.00				

KM# 857 CROWN

Copper-Nickel, 38.8 mm. **Ruler:** Elizabeth II **Series:** The World At War **Subject:** War Babies **Obv:** Crowned bust right **Rev:** Soldier kissing child

Date	Mintage	VF20	XF40	MS60	MS63	MS65
1999	—	—	—	—	10.00	12.00

KM# 857a CROWN

28.28 g., 0.925 Silver 0.841 oz. ASW, 38.8 mm. **Ruler:** Elizabeth II **Series:** The World At War **Subject:** War Babies **Obv:** Crowned bust right **Rev:** Soldier kissing child

Date	Mintage	VF20	XF40	MS60	MS63	MS65
1999	Est. 10000	PF65 45.00				

KM# 859 CROWN
Copper-Nickel, 38.8 mm. **Ruler:** Elizabeth II **Series:** The World At War **Subject:** The Blitz **Obv:** Crowned bust right **Rev:** Firefighters in action after air raid

Date	Mintage	VF20	XF40	MS60	MS63	MS65
1999	—	—	—	—	10.00	12.00

KM# 859a CROWN
28.28 g., 0.925 Silver 0.841 oz. ASW, 38.8 mm. **Ruler:** Elizabeth II **Series:** The World At War **Subject:** The Blitz **Obv:** Crowned bust right **Rev:** Firefighters in action after air raid

Date	Mintage	VF20	XF40	MS60	MS63	MS65
1999	Est. 10000	PF65 45.00				

KM# 861 CROWN
Copper-Nickel, 38.8 mm. **Ruler:** Elizabeth II **Series:** The World At War **Subject:** D-Day **Obv:** Crowned bust right **Rev:** D-Day landing scene

Date	Mintage	VF20	XF40	MS60	MS63	MS65
1999	—	—	—	—	10.00	12.00

KM# 861a CROWN
28.28 g., 0.925 Silver 0.841 oz. ASW, 38.8 mm. **Ruler:** Elizabeth II **Series:** The World At War **Subject:** D-Day **Obv:** Crowned bust right **Rev:** D-Day landing scene

Date	Mintage	VF20	XF40	MS60	MS63	MS65
1999	Est. 10000	PF65 45.00				

KM# 863 CROWN
Copper-Nickel, 38.8 mm. **Ruler:** Elizabeth II **Series:** The World At War **Subject:** Operation Heavywater **Obv:** Crowned bust right **Rev:** Military skier

Date	Mintage	VF20	XF40	MS60	MS63	MS65
1999	—	—	—	—	10.00	12.00

KM# 863a CROWN
28.28 g., 0.925 Silver 0.841 oz. ASW, 38.8 mm. **Ruler:** Elizabeth II **Series:** The World At War **Subject:** Operation Heavywater **Obv:** Crowned bust right **Rev:** Military skier

Date	Mintage	VF20	XF40	MS60	MS63	MS65
1999	Est. 10000	PF65 45.00				

KM# 865 CROWN
Copper-Nickel, 38.8 mm. **Ruler:** Elizabeth II **Series:** The World At War **Subject:** Barbarossa **Obv:** Crowned bust right **Rev:** German tanks in Russia

Date	Mintage	VF20	XF40	MS60	MS63	MS65
1999	—	—	—	—	10.00	12.00

KM# 865a CROWN
28.28 g., 0.925 Silver 0.841 oz. ASW, 38.8 mm. **Ruler:** Elizabeth II **Series:** The World At War **Subject:** Barbarossa **Obv:** Crowned bust right **Rev:** German tanks in Russia

Date	Mintage	VF20	XF40	MS60	MS63	MS65
1999	Est. 10000	PF65 45.00				

KM# 871 CROWN
28.28 g., Copper-Nickel, 38.8 mm. **Ruler:** Elizabeth II **Series:** The Life Of Queen Elizabeth The Queen Mother **Subject:** Crowned Queen Consort **Obv:** Head with tiara right **Rev:** 1937 crowning of the Queen consort

Date	Mintage	VF20	XF40	MS60	MS63	MS65
2000	—	—	—	—	10.00	12.00

KM# 871a CROWN
28.28 g., 0.925 Silver 0.841 oz. ASW, 38.8 mm. **Ruler:** Elizabeth II **Series:** The Life Of Queen Elizabeth The Queen Mother **Subject:** Crowned Queen Consort **Obv:** Head with tiara right **Rev:** 1937 coronation scene

Date	Mintage	VF20	XF40	MS60	MS63	MS65
2000	10,000	PF65 45.00				

KM# 873 CROWN
Copper-Nickel, 38.8 mm. **Ruler:** Elizabeth II **Series:** The Life Of Queen Elizabeth The Queen Mother **Subject:** State Visit To France **Obv:** Crowned bust right **Rev:** Seated figure looking left

Date	Mintage	VF20	XF40	MS60	MS63	MS65
2000	—	—	—	—	10.00	12.00

KM# 873a CROWN
28.28 g., 0.925 Silver 0.841 oz. ASW, 38.8 mm. **Ruler:** Elizabeth II **Series:** The Life Of Queen Elizabeth The Queen Mother **Subject:** State Visit To France **Obv:** Crowned bust right **Rev:** Seated figure looking left

Date	Mintage	VF20	XF40	MS60	MS63	MS65
2000	10,000	PF65 45.00				

KM# 875 CROWN
Copper-Nickel, 38.8 mm. **Ruler:** Elizabeth II **Series:** The Life Of Queen Elizabeth The Queen Mother **Subject:** London Bombings **Obv:** Crowned bust right **Rev:** Royals looking at bomb damage

Date	Mintage	VF20	XF40	MS60	MS63	MS65
2000	—	—	—	—	10.00	12.00

KM# 875a CROWN
28.28 g., 0.925 Silver 0.841 oz. ASW, 38.8 mm. **Ruler:** Elizabeth II **Series:** The Life Of Queen Elizabeth The Queen Mother **Subject:** London Bombings **Obv:** Crowned bust right **Rev:** Royals looking at bomb damage

Date	Mintage	VF20	XF40	MS60	MS63	MS65
2000	10,000	PF65 45.00				

KM# 877 CROWN
Copper-Nickel, 38.8 mm. **Ruler:** Elizabeth II **Series:** The Life Of Queen Elizabeth The Queen Mother **Subject:** Victory **Obv:** Crowned bust right **Rev:** Portrait of royal family

Date	Mintage	VF20	XF40	MS60	MS63	MS65
2000	—	—	—	—	10.00	12.00

KM# 877a CROWN
28.28 g., 0.925 Silver 0.841 oz. ASW, 38.8 mm. **Ruler:** Elizabeth II **Series:** The Life Of Queen Elizabeth The Queen Mother **Subject:** Victory **Obv:** Crowned bust right **Rev:** Portrait of royal family

Date	Mintage	VF20	XF40	MS60	MS63	MS65
2000	10,000	PF65 45.00				

KM# 880 CROWN
28.28 g., Copper-Nickel, 38.8 mm. **Ruler:** Elizabeth II **Subject:** 18th Birthday - H.R.H. The Prince William **Obv:** Crowned bust right **Rev:** Bust 3/4 right

Date	Mintage	VF20	XF40	MS60	MS63	MS65
2000	—	—	—	—	10.00	12.00

KM# 880a CROWN
28.28 g., 0.925 Silver 0.841 oz. ASW, 38.8 mm. **Ruler:** Elizabeth II **Subject:** 18th Birthday - H.R.H. The Prince William **Obv:** Crowned bust right **Rev:** Bust 3/4 right

Date	Mintage	VF20	XF40	MS60	MS63	MS65
2000	10,000	PF65 45.00				

KM# 882 CROWN
Copper-Nickel, 38.8 mm. **Ruler:** Elizabeth II **Subject:** Queen Mother **Obv:** Queen's portrait **Rev:** Queen Mother's portrait

Date	Mintage	VF20	XF40	MS60	MS63	MS65
2000	—	—	—	—	10.00	12.00

KM# 882a CROWN
28.28 g., 0.925 Silver 0.841 oz. ASW, 38.8 mm. **Ruler:** Elizabeth II **Obv:** Queen's portrait

Date	Mintage	VF20	XF40	MS60	MS63	MS65
2000	10,000	PF65 45.00				

KM# 884 CROWN
Bi-Metallic Titanium center in Gold ring, 38.8 mm. **Ruler:** Elizabeth II **Subject:** 160th Anniversary - Uniform Penny Post **Obv:** Queen's portrait **Rev:** Postage stamp design, blue center **Edge:** Reeded

Date	Mintage	VF20	XF40	MS60	MS63	MS65
2000	999	PF65 750				

KM# 128 2 CROWN
62.21 g., 0.999 Silver 1.998 oz. ASW **Ruler:** Elizabeth II **Subject:** Japanese Royal Wedding **Obv:** Crowned bust right **Rev:** Pair of peacocks

Date	Mintage	VF20	XF40	MS60	MS63	MS65
1993	Est. 20000	PF65 85.00				

KM# 128a 2 CROWN
62.21 g., 0.9999 Gold 1.9998 oz. AGW **Ruler:** Elizabeth II **Subject:** Japanese Royal Wedding **Obv:** Crowned bust right **Rev:** Pair of peacocks

Date	Mintage	VF20	XF40	MS60	MS63	MS65
1993	Est. 2500	PF65 3,500				

KM# 129 2 CROWN
62.21 g., 0.999 Silver 1.998 oz. ASW **Ruler:** Elizabeth II **Subject:** Japanese Royal Wedding **Obv:** Crowned bust right **Rev:** Two peacocks, one in full display

Date	Mintage	VF20	XF40	MS60	MS63	MS65
1993	Est. 20000	PF65 85.00				

KM# 129a 2 CROWN
62.21 g., 0.9999 Gold 1.9998 oz. AGW **Ruler:** Elizabeth II **Subject:** Japanese Royal Wedding **Obv:** Crowned bust right **Rev:** Two peacocks, one in full display

Date	Mintage	VF20	XF40	MS60	MS63	MS65
1993	Est. 2500	PF65 3,500				

KM# 106 5 CROWN
155.92 g., 0.999 Silver 5.008 oz. ASW, 65 mm. **Ruler:** Elizabeth II **Series:** Olympics - Barcelona **Obv:** Crowned bust right **Rev:** Discus thrower

Date	Mintage	VF20	XF40	MS60	MS63	MS65
1991	Est. 1000	PF65 225				

KM# 451 5 CROWN
155.52 g., 0.9999 Gold 4.9995 oz. AGW **Ruler:** Elizabeth II **Subject:** Lord Buddha **Rev:** Seated figure facing

Date	Mintage	VF20	XF40	MS60	MS63	MS65
1996	Est. 250	PF65 8,500				

KM# 107 10 CROWN
311.85 g., 0.999 Silver 10.016 oz. ASW, 73 mm. **Ruler:** Elizabeth II **Series:** Olympics - Barcelona **Obv:** Crowned bust right **Rev:** Ancient runners

Date	Mintage	VF20	XF40	MS60	MS63	MS65
1991	Est. 1000	PF65 350				

KM# 130 10 CROWN
311.85 g., 0.999 Silver 10.016 oz. ASW, 73 mm. **Ruler:** Elizabeth II **Subject:** Japanese Royal Wedding **Obv:** Crowned bust right **Rev:** Pair of peacocks

Date	Mintage	VF20	XF40	MS60	MS63	MS65
1993	Est. 5000	PF65 350				

KM# 131 32 CROWNS
1000.00 g., 0.999 Silver 32.1186 oz. ASW, 85 mm. **Ruler:** Elizabeth II **Subject:** Japanese Royal Wedding **Obv:** Crowned bust right **Rev:** Two peacocks, one in full display

Date	Mintage	VF20	XF40	MS60	MS63	MS65
1993	Est. 1000	PF65 1,000				

KM# 333 40 CROWN
1244.14 g., 0.999 Silver 39.960 oz. ASW, 100 mm. **Ruler:** Elizabeth II **Rev:** Rock of Gibraltar and rising sun

Date	Mintage	VF20	XF40	MS60	MS63	MS65
1994	Est. 1500	PF65 1,200				

ROYAL COINAGE

KM# 91 1/25 ROYAL
1.24 g., 0.9999 Gold 0.0399 oz. AGW **Ruler:** Elizabeth II **Subject:** Dogs **Obv:** Crowned bust right **Rev:** Corgi

Date	Mintage	VF20	XF40	MS60	MS63	MS65
1991	—	—	—	—	—	60.00
1991	Est. 1000	PF65 65.00				

KM# 99 1/25 ROYAL
1.24 g., 0.9999 Gold 0.0399 oz. AGW **Ruler:** Elizabeth II **Subject:** Dogs **Obv:** Crowned bust right **Rev:** Cocker Spaniel

Date	Mintage	VF20	XF40	MS60	MS63	MS65
1992	—	—	—	—	—	60.00
1992	Est. 1000	PF65 65.00				

KM# 193 1/25 ROYAL
1.24 g., 0.9999 Gold 0.0399 oz. AGW **Ruler:** Elizabeth II **Subject:** Dogs **Obv:** Crowned bust right **Rev:** Long-haired Dachshund

Date	Mintage	VF20	XF40	MS60	MS63	MS65
1993	—	—	—	—	—	60.00
1993	Est. 1000	PF65 65.00				

KM# 248 1/25 ROYAL
1.24 g., 0.9999 Gold 0.0399 oz. AGW **Ruler:** Elizabeth II **Subject:** Dogs **Obv:** Crowned bust right **Rev:** Pekingese

Date	Mintage	VF20	XF40	MS60	MS63	MS65
1994	—	—	—	—	—	60.00
1994	Est. 1000	PF65 65.00				

KM# 319 1/25 ROYAL
1.24 g., 0.9999 Gold 0.0399 oz. AGW **Ruler:** Elizabeth II **Subject:** Crowned bust right **Obv:** Crowned bust right **Rev:** Collie

Date	Mintage	VF20	XF40	MS60	MS63	MS65
1995	—	—	—	—	—	60.00
1995	Est. 1000	PF65 65.00				

KM# 361 1/25 ROYAL
1.24 g., 0.9999 Gold 0.0399 oz. AGW **Ruler:** Elizabeth II **Subject:** Dogs **Obv:** Crowned bust right **Rev:** Bulldog

Date	Mintage	VF20	XF40	MS60	MS63	MS65
1996	—	—	—	—	—	60.00
1996	Est. 1000	PF65 65.00				

KM# 557 1/25 ROYAL
1.24 g., 0.9999 Gold 0.0399 oz. AGW **Ruler:** Elizabeth II **Subject:** Dogs **Obv:** Crowned bust right **Rev:** Yorkshire Terrier

Date	Mintage	VF20	XF40	MS60	MS63	MS65
1997	—	—	—	—	—	60.00
1997	Est. 1000	PF65 65.00				

KM# 749 1/25 ROYAL
1.24 g., 0.9999 Gold 0.0399 oz. AGW **Ruler:** Elizabeth II **Obv:** Crowned bust right **Rev:** Kissing cherubs

Date	Mintage	VF20	XF40	MS60	MS63	MS65
1998	—	—	—	—	—	60.00
1998	Est. 1000	PF65 65.00				

KM# 749a 1/25 ROYAL
1.24 g., 0.995 Platinum 0.0397 oz. APW **Ruler:** Elizabeth II **Obv:** Crowned bust right **Rev:** Kissing cherubs

Date	Mintage	VF20	XF40	MS60	MS63	MS65
1998	—	PF65 75.00				

KM# 828 1/25 ROYAL
1.24 g., 0.999 Gold 0.0398 oz. AGW **Ruler:** Elizabeth II **Obv:** Crowned bust right **Rev:** Cherub

Date	Mintage	VF20	XF40	MS60	MS63	MS65
1999 U	—	—	—	—	—	60.00
1999 U Y2K	—	—	—	—	—	60.00
1999	Est. 1000	PF65 65.00				

KM# 828a 1/25 ROYAL
1.24 g., 0.995 Platinum 0.0397 oz. APW **Ruler:** Elizabeth II **Obv:** Crowned bust right **Rev:** One cherub

Date	Mintage	VF20	XF40	MS60	MS63	MS65
1999	Est. 1000	PF65 75.00				

KM# 888 1/25 ROYAL
1.24 g., 0.999 Gold 0.040 oz. AGW, 13.92 mm. **Ruler:** Elizabeth II **Subject:** Bullion **Obv:** Crowned bust right **Rev:** 2 cherubs **Edge:** Reeded

Date	Mintage	VF20	XF40	MS60	MS63	MS65
2000	—	—	—	—	—	60.00
2000	1,000	PF65 65.00				

Note: In proof sets only

KM# 92 1/10 ROYAL
3.11 g., 0.9999 Gold 0.100 oz. AGW **Ruler:** Elizabeth II **Subject:** Dogs **Obv:** Crowned bust right **Rev:** Corgi

Date	Mintage	VF20	XF40	MS60	MS63	MS65
1991	—	—	—	—	—	150
1991	Est. 1000	PF65 155				

KM# 100 1/10 ROYAL
3.11 g., 0.9999 Gold 0.100 oz. AGW **Ruler:** Elizabeth II **Subject:** Dogs **Obv:** Crowned bust right **Rev:** Cocker Spaniel

Date	Mintage	VF20	XF40	MS60	MS63	MS65
1992	—	—	—	—	—	150
1992	Est. 1000	PF65 155				

KM# 194 1/10 ROYAL
3.11 g., 0.9999 Gold 0.100 oz. AGW **Ruler:** Elizabeth II **Obv:** Crowned bust right **Rev:** Long-haired Dachshund

Date	Mintage	VF20	XF40	MS60	MS63	MS65
1993	—	—	—	—	—	150
1993	Est. 1000	PF65 155				

KM# 249 1/10 ROYAL
3.11 g., 0.9999 Gold 0.100 oz. AGW **Ruler:** Elizabeth II **Subject:** Dogs **Obv:** Crowned bust right **Rev:** Pekingese

Date	Mintage	VF20	XF40	MS60	MS63	MS65
1994	—	—	—	—	—	150
1994	Est. 1000	PF65 155				

KM# 320 1/10 ROYAL
3.11 g., 0.9999 Gold 0.100 oz. AGW **Ruler:** Elizabeth II **Subject:** Dogs **Obv:** Crowned bust right **Rev:** Collie

Date	Mintage	VF20	XF40	MS60	MS63	MS65
1995	—	—	—	—	—	150
1995	Est. 1000	PF65 155				

KM# 362 1/10 ROYAL
3.11 g., 0.9999 Gold 0.100 oz. AGW **Ruler:** Elizabeth II **Subject:** Dogs **Obv:** Crowned bust right **Rev:** Bulldog

Date	Mintage	VF20	XF40	MS60	MS63	MS65
1996	—	—	—	—	—	150
1996	Est. 1000	PF65 155				

KM# 558 1/10 ROYAL
3.11 g., 0.9999 Gold 0.100 oz. AGW **Ruler:** Elizabeth II **Subject:** Dogs **Obv:** Crowned bust right **Rev:** Yorkshire Terrier

Date	Mintage	VF20	XF40	MS60	MS63	MS65
1997	—	—	—	—	—	150
1997	Est. 1000	PF65 155				

KM# 750 1/10 ROYAL
3.11 g., 0.9999 Gold 0.100 oz. AGW **Ruler:** Elizabeth II **Obv:** Crowned bust right **Rev:** Kissing cherubs

Date	Mintage	VF20	XF40	MS60	MS63	MS65
1998	—	—	—	—	—	150
1998	Est. 1000	PF65 155				

KM# 829 1/10 ROYAL
3.11 g., 0.9999 Gold 0.100 oz. AGW **Ruler:** Elizabeth II **Obv:** Crowned bust right **Rev:** Cherub

Date	Mintage	VF20	XF40	MS60	MS63	MS65
1999 U Y2K	Est. 10000	—	—	—	—	150
1999 U	—	—	—	—	—	150
1999	—	PF65 155				

KM# 829a 1/10 ROYAL
3.11 g., 0.995 Platinum 0.0995 oz. APW **Ruler:** Elizabeth II **Obv:** Crowned bust right **Rev:** Cherub

Date	Mintage	VF20	XF40	MS60	MS63	MS65
1999	Est. 1000	PF65 155				

KM# 889 1/10 ROYAL
3.11 g., 0.999 Gold 0.0999 oz. AGW **Ruler:** Elizabeth II **Obv:** Crowned bust right **Rev:** Two cherubs **Edge:** Reeded

Date	Mintage	VF20	XF40	MS60	MS63	MS65
2000	—	—	—	—	—	150
2000	1,000	PF65 155				

KM# 93 1/5 ROYAL
6.22 g., 0.9999 Gold 0.200 oz. AGW **Ruler:** Elizabeth II **Subject:** Dogs **Obv:** Crowned bust right **Rev:** Corgi

Date	Mintage	VF20	XF40	MS60	MS63	MS65
1991	—	—	—	—	—	295
1991	Est. 1000	PF65 300				

KM# 101 1/5 ROYAL
6.22 g., 0.9999 Gold 0.200 oz. AGW **Ruler:** Elizabeth II **Subject:** Dogs **Obv:** Crowned bust right **Rev:** Cocker Spaniel

Date	Mintage	VF20	XF40	MS60	MS63	MS65
1992	—	—	—	—	—	295
1992	Est. 1000	PF65 300				

KM# 195 1/5 ROYAL
6.22 g., 0.9999 Gold 0.200 oz. AGW **Ruler:** Elizabeth II **Subject:** Dogs **Obv:** Crowned bust right **Rev:** Long-haired Dachshund

Date	Mintage	VF20	XF40	MS60	MS63	MS65
1993	—	—	—	—	—	295
1993	Est. 1000	PF65 300				

KM# 250 1/5 ROYAL
6.22 g., 0.9999 Gold 0.200 oz. AGW **Ruler:** Elizabeth II **Subject:** Dogs **Obv:** Crowned bust right **Rev:** Pekingese

Date	Mintage	VF20	XF40	MS60	MS63	MS65
1994	—	—	—	—	—	295
1994	Est. 1000	PF65 300				

KM# 321 1/5 ROYAL
6.22 g., 0.9999 Gold 0.200 oz. AGW **Ruler:** Elizabeth II **Subject:** Dogs **Obv:** Crowned bust right **Rev:** Collie

Date	Mintage	VF20	XF40	MS60	MS63	MS65
1995	—	—	—	—	—	295
1995	Est. 1000	PF65 300				

KM# 363 1/5 ROYAL
6.22 g., 0.9999 Gold 0.200 oz. AGW **Ruler:** Elizabeth II **Subject:** Dogs **Obv:** Crowned bust right **Rev:** Bulldog

Date	Mintage	VF20	XF40	MS60	MS63	MS65
1996	—	—	—	—	—	295
1996	Est. 1000	PF65 300				

KM# 559 1/5 ROYAL
6.22 g., 0.9999 Gold 0.200 oz. AGW **Ruler:** Elizabeth II **Subject:** Dogs **Obv:** Crowned bust right **Rev:** Yorkshire Terrier

Date	Mintage	VF20	XF40	MS60	MS63	MS65
1997	—	—	—	—	—	295
1997	Est. 1000	PF65 300				

KM# 751 1/5 ROYAL
6.22 g., 0.9999 Gold 0.200 oz. AGW **Ruler:** Elizabeth II **Obv:** Crowned bust right **Rev:** Kissing cherubs

Date	Mintage	VF20	XF40	MS60	MS63	MS65
1998	—	—	—	—	—	295
1998	Est. 1000	PF65 300				

KM# 830 1/5 ROYAL
6.22 g., 0.9999 Gold 0.200 oz. AGW **Ruler:** Elizabeth II **Obv:** Crowned bust right **Rev:** Four cherubs

Date	Mintage	VF20	XF40	MS60	MS63	MS65
1999 U Y2K	—	—	—	—	—	295
1999	—	PF65 300				
1999 U	—	—	—	—	—	295

KM# 830a 1/5 ROYAL
6.22 g., 0.995 Platinum 0.199 oz. APW **Ruler:** Elizabeth II **Obv:** Crowned bust right **Rev:** Four cherubs

Date	Mintage	VF20	XF40	MS60	MS63	MS65
1999	Est. 1000	PF65 300				

KM# 890 1/5 ROYAL
6.22 g., 0.999 Gold 0.1998 oz. AGW **Ruler:** Elizabeth II **Obv:** Crowned bust right **Rev:** 2 cherubs **Edge:** Reeded

Date	Mintage	VF20	XF40	MS60	MS63	MS65
2000	—	—	—	—	—	295
2000	1,000	PF65 300				

KM# 94 1/2 ROYAL
15.55 g., 0.9999 Gold 0.4999 oz. AGW **Ruler:** Elizabeth II **Subject:** Dogs **Obv:** Crowned bust right **Rev:** Corgi

Date	Mintage	VF20	XF40	MS60	MS63	MS65
1991	—	—	—	—	—	695
1991	Est. 1000	PF65 700				

KM# 102 1/2 ROYAL
15.55 g., 0.9999 Gold 0.4999 oz. AGW **Ruler:** Elizabeth II **Subject:** Dogs **Obv:** Crowned bust right **Rev:** Cocker Spaniel

Date	Mintage	VF20	XF40	MS60	MS63	MS65
1992	—	—	—	—	—	695
1992	Est. 1000	PF65 700				

KM# 196 1/2 ROYAL
15.55 g., 0.9999 Gold 0.4999 oz. AGW **Ruler:** Elizabeth II **Subject:** Dogs **Obv:** Crowned bust right **Rev:** Long-haired Dachshund

Date	Mintage	VF20	XF40	MS60	MS63	MS65
1993	—	—	—	—	—	695
1993	Est. 1000	PF65 700				

KM# 251 1/2 ROYAL
15.55 g., 0.9999 Gold 0.4999 oz. AGW **Ruler:** Elizabeth II **Subject:** Dogs **Obv:** Crowned bust right **Rev:** Pekingese

Date	Mintage	VF20	XF40	MS60	MS63	MS65
1994	—	—	—	—	—	695
1994	Est. 1000	PF65 700				

KM# 322 1/2 ROYAL
15.55 g., 0.9999 Gold 0.4999 oz. AGW **Ruler:** Elizabeth II **Subject:** Dogs **Obv:** Crowned bust right **Rev:** Collie

Date	Mintage	VF20	XF40	MS60	MS63	MS65
1995	—	—	—	—	—	695
1995	Est. 1000	PF65 700				

KM# 364 1/2 ROYAL
15.55 g., 0.9999 Gold 0.4999 oz. AGW **Ruler:** Elizabeth II **Subject:** Dogs **Obv:** Crowned bust right **Rev:** Bulldog

Date	Mintage	VF20	XF40	MS60	MS63	MS65
1996	—	—	—	—	—	695
1996	Est. 1000	PF65 700				

KM# 560 1/2 ROYAL
15.55 g., 0.9999 Gold 0.4999 oz. AGW **Ruler:** Elizabeth II **Subject:** Dogs **Obv:** Crowned bust right **Rev:** Yorkshire Terrier

Date	Mintage	VF20	XF40	MS60	MS63	MS65
1997	—	—	—	—	—	695
1997	Est. 1000	PF65 700				

KM# 752 1/2 ROYAL
15.55 g., 0.9999 Gold 0.4999 oz. AGW **Ruler:** Elizabeth II **Obv:** Crowned bust right **Rev:** Kissing cherubs

Date	Mintage	VF20	XF40	MS60	MS63	MS65
1998	—	—	—	—	—	695
1998	Est. 1000	PF65 700				

KM# 831 1/2 ROYAL
15.55 g., 0.9999 Gold 0.4999 oz. AGW **Ruler:** Elizabeth II **Obv:** Crowned bust right **Rev:** Four cherubs

Date	Mintage	VF20	XF40	MS60	MS63	MS65
1999	—	—	—	—	—	695
1999	—	PF65 700				

KM# 891 1/2 ROYAL
15.55 g., 0.9999 Gold 0.4999 oz. AGW **Ruler:** Elizabeth II **Obv:** Crowned bust right **Rev:** Two cherubs **Edge:** Reeded

Date	Mintage	VF20	XF40	MS60	MS63	MS65
2000	—	—	—	—	—	695
2000	1,000	PF65 700				

KM# 97 ROYAL
31.10 g., 0.9999 Gold 0.9999 oz. AGW **Ruler:** Elizabeth II **Obv:** Crowned bust right **Rev:** Corgi

Date	Mintage	VF20	XF40	MS60	MS63	MS65
1991	—	—	—	—	—	1,425
1991	Est. 1000	PF65 1,450				

KM# 105 ROYAL
31.10 g., 0.9999 Gold 0.9999 oz. AGW **Ruler:** Elizabeth II **Obv:** Crowned bust right **Rev:** Cocker Spaniel

Date	Mintage	VF20	XF40	MS60	MS63	MS65
1992	—	—	—	—	—	1,425
1992	Est. 1000	PF65 1,450				

KM# 197 ROYAL
31.10 g., 0.9999 Gold 0.9999 oz. AGW **Ruler:** Elizabeth II **Obv:** Crowned bust right **Rev:** Long-haired Dachshund

Date	Mintage	VF20	XF40	MS60	MS63	MS65
1993	—	—	—	—	—	1,425
1993	Est. 1000	PF65 1,450				

KM# 246 ROYAL
Copper-Nickel **Ruler:** Elizabeth II **Subject:** Dogs **Obv:** Crowned bust right **Rev:** Pekingese Dog

Date	Mintage	VF20	XF40	MS60	MS63	MS65
1994 PM	250	PF65 25.00				
1994	—	—	—	—	7.00	14.00

KM# 252 ROYAL
31.10 g., 0.999 Silver 0.9989 oz. ASW **Ruler:** Elizabeth II **Subject:** Dogs **Obv:** Crowned bust right **Rev:** Pekingese

Date	Mintage	VF20	XF40	MS60	MS63	MS65
1994	—	PF65 50.00				

KM# 252a ROYAL
31.10 g., 0.9999 Gold 0.9999 oz. AGW **Ruler:** Elizabeth II **Subject:** Dogs **Obv:** Crowned bust right **Rev:** Pekingese

Date	Mintage	VF20	XF40	MS60	MS63	MS65
1994	—	—	—	—	—	1,425
1994	Est. 1000	PF65 1,450				

KM# 318 ROYAL
28.62 g., Copper-Nickel, 38.8 mm. **Ruler:** Elizabeth II **Subject:** Collie **Obv:** Crowned bust right **Rev:** Collie **Edge:** Reeded

Date	Mintage	VF20	XF40	MS60	MS63	MS65
1995	—	—	—	—	12.00	15.00
1995	Est. 250	PF65 25.00				

KM# 318a ROYAL
31.10 g., 0.999 Silver 0.999 oz. ASW **Ruler:** Elizabeth II **Subject:** Dogs **Obv:** Crowned bust right **Rev:** Collie

Date	Mintage	VF20	XF40	MS60	MS63	MS65
1995	Est. 50000	PF65 50.00				

KM# 318b ROYAL
31.10 g., 0.9999 Gold 0.9999 oz. AGW **Ruler:** Elizabeth II **Subject:** Dogs **Obv:** Crowned bust right **Rev:** Collie

Date	Mintage	VF20	XF40	MS60	MS63	MS65
1995	—	—	—	—	—	1,425
1995	Est. 1000	PF65 1,450				

KM# 365 ROYAL
Copper-Nickel **Ruler:** Elizabeth II **Subject:** Dogs **Obv:** Crowned bust right **Rev:** Bulldog

Date	Mintage	VF20	XF40	MS60	MS63	MS65
1996 P/L	—	—	—	—	—	15.00

KM# 365a ROYAL
31.10 g., 0.999 Silver 0.999 oz. ASW **Ruler:** Elizabeth II **Subject:** Dogs **Obv:** Crowned bust right **Rev:** Bulldog

Date	Mintage	VF20	XF40	MS60	MS63	MS65
1996	Est. 50000	PF65 50.00				

KM# 365b ROYAL
31.10 g., 0.9999 Gold 0.9999 oz. AGW **Ruler:** Elizabeth II **Subject:** Dogs **Obv:** Crowned bust right **Rev:** Bulldog

Date	Mintage	VF20	XF40	MS60	MS63	MS65
1996	—	—	—	—	—	1,425
1996	Est. 1000	PF65 1,450				

KM# 561a ROYAL
31.10 g., 0.999 Silver 0.999 oz. ASW **Ruler:** Elizabeth II **Subject:** Dogs **Obv:** Crowned bust right **Rev:** Yorkshire terrier

Date	Mintage	VF20	XF40	MS60	MS63	MS65
1997	Est. 50000	PF65 50.00				

KM# 561a.1 ROYAL
31.30 g., 0.999 Silver 1.0053 oz. ASW, 38.5 mm. **Ruler:** Elizabeth II **Subject:** Dogs **Obv:** Crowned bust right **Rev:** Gold-plated Yorkshire Terrier **Edge:** Reeded

Date	Mintage	VF20	XF40	MS60	MS63	MS65
1997 Proof	—	—	—	—	—	55.00

KM# 561b ROYAL
31.10 g., 0.9999 Gold 0.9999 oz. AGW **Ruler:** Elizabeth II **Subject:** Dogs **Obv:** Crowned bust right **Rev:** Yorkshire terrier

Date	Mintage	VF20	XF40	MS60	MS63	MS65
1997	—	—	—	—	—	1,425
1997	Est. 1000	PF65 1,450				

KM# 753 ROYAL
Copper-Nickel **Ruler:** Elizabeth II **Obv:** Crowned bust right **Rev:** Kissing cherubs

Date	Mintage	VF20	XF40	MS60	MS63	MS65
1998	—	—	—	—	10.00	12.00

KM# 753a ROYAL
28.28 g., 0.999 Silver 0.9083 oz. ASW **Ruler:** Elizabeth II **Obv:** Crowned bust right **Rev:** Kissing cherubs

Date	Mintage	VF20	XF40	MS60	MS63	MS65
1998	Est. 20000	PF65 50.00				

KM# 754 ROYAL
31.10 g., 0.9999 Gold 0.9999 oz. AGW **Ruler:** Elizabeth II **Obv:** Crowned bust right **Rev:** Kissing cherubs

Date	Mintage	VF20	XF40	MS60	MS63	MS65
1998	—	—	—	—	—	1,425
1998	Est. 1000	PF65 1,450				

KM# 832 ROYAL
Copper-Nickel **Ruler:** Elizabeth II **Obv:** Crowned bust right **Rev:** Four cherubs

Date	Mintage	VF20	XF40	MS60	MS63	MS65
1999	—	—	—	—	10.00	12.00

KM# 832a ROYAL
31.10 g., 0.999 Silver 0.999 oz. ASW **Ruler:** Elizabeth II **Obv:** Crowned bust right **Rev:** Four cherubs

Date	Mintage	VF20	XF40	MS60	MS63	MS65
1999	—	PF65 50.00				

KM# 833 ROYAL
31.10 g., 0.9999 Gold 0.9999 oz. AGW **Ruler:** Elizabeth II **Obv:** Crowned bust right **Rev:** Four cherubs

Date	Mintage	VF20	XF40	MS60	MS63	MS65
1999	—	PF65 1,450				
1999 U	—	—	—	—	—	1,425

KM# 892 ROYAL
28.28 g., Copper-Nickel **Ruler:** Elizabeth II **Obv:** Crowned bust right **Rev:** 2 cherubs **Edge:** Reeded

Date	Mintage	VF20	XF40	MS60	MS63	MS65
2000	—	—	—	—	12.00	14.00

KM# 892a ROYAL
31.10 g., 0.999 Silver 0.999 oz. ASW **Ruler:** Elizabeth II **Obv:** Crowned bust right **Rev:** 2 cherubs **Edge:** Reeded

Date	Mintage	VF20	XF40	MS60	MS63	MS65
2000	10,000	PF65 50.00				

KM# 893 ROYAL
31.10 g., 0.999 Gold 0.999 oz. AGW **Ruler:** Elizabeth II **Obv:** Crowned bust right **Rev:** Two cherubs **Edge:** Reeded

Date	Mintage	VF20	XF40	MS60	MS63	MS65
2000	—	—	—	—	—	1,425
2000	1,000	PF65 1,450				

Note: In proof sets only

EUROPEAN CURRENCY UNITS

Dual Denomination Coinage

KM# 293 2.8 ECUS-2 POUNDS
Copper-Nickel **Ruler:** Elizabeth II **Obv:** Crowned bust right **Rev:** Knight on horseback jumping left, stars encircle

Date	Mintage	VF20	XF40	MS60	MS63	MS65
1992	—	—	—	—	11.50	13.50

KM# 87 14 ECUS-10 POUNDS
10.00 g., 0.925 Silver 0.2974 oz. ASW **Ruler:** Elizabeth II **Subject:** European Currency Unit **Obv:** Crowned bust right **Rev:** Knight on horseback jumping left, stars encircle

Date	Mintage	VF20	XF40	MS60	MS63	MS65
1991	Est. 10000	PF65 18.00				
1992	Est. 5000	PF65 28.00				
1993	—	—	—	—	70.00	75.00
1994	—	—	—	—	70.00	75.00

KM# 89 14 ECUS-10 POUNDS
10.00 g., 0.925 Silver 0.2974 oz. ASW **Ruler:** Elizabeth II **Obv:** Crowned bust right **Rev:** Knight on horse jumping right

Date	Mintage	VF20	XF40	MS60	MS63	MS65
1992 A Matte	—	—	—	—	17.50	20.00

KM# 109 14 ECUS-10 POUNDS
10.00 g., 0.925 Silver 0.2974 oz. ASW **Ruler:** Elizabeth II **Obv:** Uncouped portrait **Rev:** Mounted rider right

Date	Mintage	VF20	XF40	MS60	MS63	MS65
1992	—	—	—	—	12.50	15.00
1992	—	PF65 25.00				
1993	—	PF65 30.00				

KM# 337 14 ECUS-10 POUNDS
10.00 g., 0.925 Silver 0.2974 oz. ASW **Ruler:** Elizabeth II **Obv:** Crowned bust right **Rev:** Torch shield

Date	Mintage	VF20	XF40	MS60	MS63	MS65
1992	—	PF65 20.00				

KM# 624 14 ECUS-10 POUNDS
10.00 g., 0.925 Silver 0.2974 oz. ASW **Ruler:** Elizabeth II **Obv:** Crowned bust right **Rev:** Knight on horseback jumping left, stars encircle

Date	Mintage	VF20	XF40	MS60	MS63	MS65
1992	Est. 2500	PF65 20.00				

KM# 627 14 ECUS-10 POUNDS
10.00 g., 0.925 Silver 0.2974 oz. ASW **Ruler:** Elizabeth II **Obv:** Crowned bust right **Rev:** Knight on horseback jumping right, stars encircle

Date	Mintage	VF20	XF40	MS60	MS63	MS65
1993	Est. 2500	PF65 20.00				

KM# 88 35 ECUS-25 POUNDS
28.28 g., 0.925 Silver 0.841 oz. ASW **Ruler:** Elizabeth II **Obv:** Crowned bust right **Rev:** Knight on horseback jumping left, stars encircle

Date	Mintage	VF20	XF40	MS60	MS63	MS65
1991	Est. 10000	PF65 60.00				
1992	—	—	—	—	40.00	45.00
1992	Est. 15000	PF65 60.00				

KM# 110 35 ECUS-25 POUNDS
28.28 g., 0.925 Silver 0.841 oz. ASW **Ruler:** Elizabeth II **Obv:** Crowned bust right **Rev:** Knight on horseback jumping right, stars encircle

Date	Mintage	VF20	XF40	MS60	MS63	MS65
1992	Est. 15000	PF65 50.00				
1993	—	PF65 70.00				

KM# 338 35 ECUS-25 POUNDS
28.28 g., 0.925 Silver 0.841 oz. ASW **Ruler:** Elizabeth II **Obv:** Crowned bust right **Rev:** Knight on horseback jumping left, stars encircle

Date	Mintage	VF20	XF40	MS60	MS63	MS65
1992	Est. 2000	PF65 85.00				

KM# 625 35 ECUS-25 POUNDS
28.28 g., 0.925 Silver 0.841 oz. ASW **Ruler:** Elizabeth II **Obv:** Crowned bust right **Rev:** Knight on horseback jumping left, stars encircle

Date	Mintage	VF20	XF40	MS60	MS63	MS65
1992	Est. 2000	PF65 100				

KM# 628 35 ECUS-25 POUNDS
28.28 g., 0.925 Silver 0.841 oz. ASW **Ruler:** Elizabeth II **Obv:** Crowned bust right **Rev:** Knight on horseback jumping right, three lions on shield

Date	Mintage	VF20	XF40	MS60	MS63	MS65
1993	—	PF65 75.00				

KM# 75 70 ECUS-50 POUNDS
6.12 g., 0.500 Gold 0.0984 oz. AGW **Ruler:** Elizabeth II **Obv:** Crowned bust right **Rev:** Knight on horseback jumping left, stars encircle

Date	Mintage	VF20	XF40	MS60	MS63	MS65
1991	Est. 5000	PF65 200				
1991	—	—	—	—	—	175
1992	—	—	—	—	—	175
1992	—	PF65 215				
1994	—	—	—	—	240	260

KM# 111 70 ECUS-50 POUNDS
6.12 g., 0.500 Gold 0.0984 oz. AGW **Ruler:** Elizabeth II **Obv:** Crowned bust right **Rev:** Knight on horseback jumping right, stars encircle

Date	Mintage	VF20	XF40	MS60	MS63	MS65
1992	Est. 2000	PF65 170				
1993	Est. 1000	PF65 190				

KM# 339 70 ECUS-50 POUNDS
6.12 g., 0.500 Gold 0.0984 oz. AGW **Ruler:** Elizabeth II **Obv:** Crowned bust right **Rev:** Knight on horseback jumping left, stars encircle

Date	Mintage	VF20	XF40	MS60	MS63	MS65
1992	Est. 1000	PF65 190				

KM# 626 70 ECUS-50 POUNDS
6.12 g., 0.500 Gold 0.0984 oz. AGW **Ruler:** Elizabeth II **Obv:** Crowned bust right **Rev:** Knight on horseback jumping left, stars encircle

Date	Mintage	VF20	XF40	MS60	MS63	MS65
1992	Est. 1000	PF65 190				

KM# 629 70 ECUS-50 POUNDS
6.12 g., 0.500 Gold 0.0984 oz. AGW **Ruler:** Elizabeth II **Obv:** Crowned bust right **Rev:** Knight on horseback jumping right, stars encircle

Date	Mintage	VF20	XF40	MS60	MS63	MS65
1993	Est. 1000	PF65 170				

STERLING ECU

KM# 478 2.8 ECUS
Copper-Nickel **Ruler:** Elizabeth II **Subject:** Euro Tunnel **Obv:** Crowned bust right **Rev:** Train exiting tunnel

Date	Mintage	VF20	XF40	MS60	MS63	MS65
1993	—	—	—	—	9.00	11.00

KM# 630 2.8 ECUS
Copper-Nickel **Ruler:** Elizabeth II **Subject:** A'riane - European Space Programme **Obv:** Crowned bust right **Rev:** Rocket orbiting earth

Date	Mintage	VF20	XF40	MS60	MS63	MS65
1993	—	—	—	—	7.00	8.50

KM# 1062 2.8 ECUS
28.10 g., Copper-Nickel, 38.47 mm. **Ruler:** Elizabeth II **Subject:** Euro Tunnel **Obv:** Crowned bust right **Rev:** Partial tunnels connecting England and France, Euro train emerging, Gibraltar below **Edge:** Reeded

Date	Mintage	VF20	XF40	MS60	MS63	MS65
1993 PM	—	—	—	—	9.50	12.00

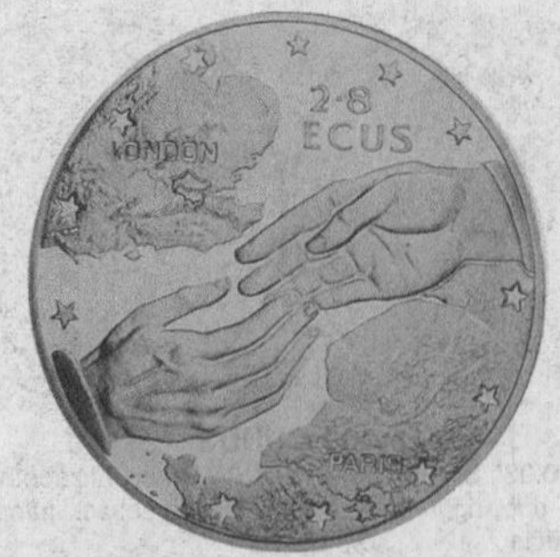

KM# 484 2.8 ECUS
Copper-Nickel **Ruler:** Elizabeth II **Subject:** Euro Tunnel **Obv:** Crowned bust right **Rev:** Clasping hands

Date	Mintage	VF20	XF40	MS60	MS63	MS65
1994	—	—	—	—	8.50	10.50

KM# 489 2.8 ECUS
Copper-Nickel **Ruler:** Elizabeth II **Subject:** Mythology **Obv:** Crowned bust right **Rev:** Winged Victory above chariot

Date	Mintage	VF20	XF40	MS60	MS63	MS65
1994	—	—	—	—	8.00	9.50

KM# 1022 2.8 ECUS
Copper-Nickel **Ruler:** Elizabeth II **Obv:** Crowned bust right **Rev:** Europa sowing seeds

Date	Mintage	VF20	XF40	MS60	MS63	MS65
1994	—	—	—	—	8.50	10.50

KM# 494 2.8 ECUS
Copper-Nickel **Ruler:** Elizabeth II **Subject:** 190th Anniversary of Admiral Nelson's Death **Obv:** Crowned bust right **Rev:** Bust at right of ship looking left

Date	Mintage	VF20	XF40	MS60	MS63	MS65
1995	—	—	—	—	8.00	9.50

KM# 508 2.8 ECUS
Copper-Nickel **Ruler:** Elizabeth II **Obv:** Crowned bust right **Rev:** Austrian knight on rearing horse within circle of shields and stars

Date	Mintage	VF20	XF40	MS60	MS63	MS65
1996	—	—	—	—	8.00	9.50

KM# 1033 4.2 ECUS
7.44 g., Bi-Metallic Brass center in Copper-Nickel ring, 26.25 mm. **Ruler:** Elizabeth II **Obv:** Crowned bust right **Rev:** Knight on horseback jumping left, stars encircle **Edge:** Segmented reeding

Date	Mintage	VF20	XF40	MS60	MS63	MS65
1994 PM Prooflike	10,000	—	—	—	12.00	14.50

KM# 479 14 ECUS
10.00 g., 0.925 Silver 0.2974 oz. ASW **Ruler:** Elizabeth II **Subject:** Euro Tunnel **Obv:** Crowned bust right **Rev:** Train exiting tunnel

Date	Mintage	VF20	XF40	MS60	MS63	MS65
1993	30,000	PF65 14.00				

KM# 631 14 ECUS
10.00 g., 0.925 Silver 0.2974 oz. ASW **Ruler:** Elizabeth II **Subject:** Sir Winston Churchill **Obv:** Crowned bust right **Rev:** Uniformed bust at left looking right

Date	Mintage	VF20	XF40	MS60	MS63	MS65
1993	Est. 20000	PF65 15.00				

KM# 483 14 ECUS
10.00 g., 0.925 Silver 0.2974 oz. ASW **Ruler:** Elizabeth II **Subject:** International Aid for Europe **Obv:** Crowned bust right **Rev:** Two faces facing each other

Date	Mintage	VF20	XF40	MS60	MS63	MS65
1994	Est. 30000	PF65 17.50				

KM# 485 14 ECUS
10.00 g., 0.925 Silver 0.2974 oz. ASW **Ruler:** Elizabeth II **Subject:** Euro Tunnel **Obv:** Crowned bust right **Rev:** Train exiting tunnel

Date	Mintage	VF20	XF40	MS60	MS63	MS65
1994	Est. 30000	PF65 18.00				

KM# 490 14 ECUS
10.00 g., 0.925 Silver 0.2974 oz. ASW **Ruler:** Elizabeth II **Obv:** Crowned bust right **Rev:** Parthenon and Brandenburg Gate

Date	Mintage	VF20	XF40	MS60	MS63	MS65
1994	Est. 30000	PF65 14.00				

KM# 495 14 ECUS
10.00 g., 0.925 Silver 0.2974 oz. ASW, 30 mm. **Ruler:** Elizabeth II **Obv:** Crowned bust right **Rev:** L'Arc de Triumph, Ceres

Date	Mintage	VF20	XF40	MS60	MS63	MS65
1995	Est. 30000	PF65 17.50				

KM# 496 14 ECUS
10.00 g., 0.925 Silver 0.2974 oz. ASW **Ruler:** Elizabeth II **Obv:** Crowned bust right **Rev:** Richard the Lionheart

Date	Mintage	VF20	XF40	MS60	MS63	MS65
1995	Est. 30000	PF65 17.50				

KM# 509 14 ECUS
10.00 g., 0.925 Silver 0.2974 oz. ASW, 30 mm. **Ruler:** Elizabeth II **Obv:** Crowned bust right **Rev:** Napoleon above map of Europe and battle scene

Date	Mintage	VF20	XF40	MS60	MS63	MS65
1996	—	PF65 16.50				

KM# 510 14 ECUS
10.00 g., 0.925 Silver 0.2974 oz. ASW **Ruler:** Elizabeth II **Obv:** Crowned bust right **Rev:** Leaning Tower of Pisa, Irish Harp

Date	Mintage	VF20	XF40	MS60	MS63	MS65
1996	—	PF65 16.50				

KM# 497 15 ECUS
1.24 g., 0.9999 Gold 0.0399 oz. AGW **Ruler:** Elizabeth II **Obv:** Crowned bust right **Rev:** Knight with shield and banner

Date	Mintage	VF20	XF40	MS60	MS63	MS65
1995	15,000	PF65 70.00				

KM# 504 15 ECUS
1.24 g., 0.9999 Gold 0.0399 oz. AGW **Ruler:** Elizabeth II **Obv:** Crowned bust right **Rev:** Sir Francis Drake's ship "Golden Hind"

Date	Mintage	VF20	XF40	MS60	MS63	MS65
1996	Est. 1500	PF65 70.00				

KM# 480 21 ECUS
19.20 g., 0.925 Silver 0.571 oz. ASW **Ruler:** Elizabeth II **Subject:** Euro Tunnel **Obv:** Crowned bust right **Rev:** Trains exiting tunnel

Date	Mintage	VF20	XF40	MS60	MS63	MS65
1993	Est. 15000	PF65 30.00				

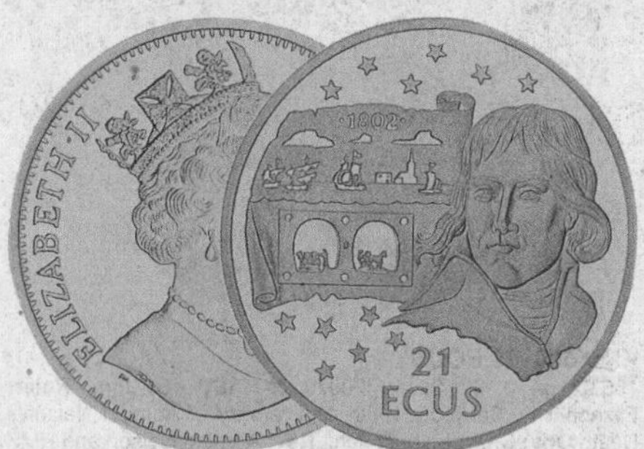

KM# 482 21 ECUS
19.20 g., 0.925 Silver 0.571 oz. ASW **Ruler:** Elizabeth II **Subject:** Euro Tunnel **Obv:** Crowned bust right **Rev:** Tunnel view and Napoleon

Date	Mintage	VF20	XF40	MS60	MS63	MS65
1993	Est. 15000	PF65 20.00				

KM# 632 21 ECUS
19.20 g., 0.925 Silver 0.571 oz. ASW **Ruler:** Elizabeth II **Subject:** European Economic Community **Obv:** Crowned bust right **Rev:** European coins within circle

Date	Mintage	VF20	XF40	MS60	MS63	MS65
1993	Est. 15000	PF65 25.00				

KM# 486 21 ECUS
19.20 g., 0.925 Silver 0.571 oz. ASW **Ruler:** Elizabeth II **Subject:** Euro Tunnel **Obv:** Crowned bust right **Rev:** Two trains and motor vehicle

Date	Mintage	VF20	XF40	MS60	MS63	MS65
1994	Est. 15000	PF65 25.00				

KM# 491 21 ECUS
19.20 g., 0.925 Silver 0.571 oz. ASW **Ruler:** Elizabeth II **Subject:** 21 Years - European Community Membership **Obv:** Crowned bust right **Rev:** Europa on bull holding starred rope

Date	Mintage	VF20	XF40	MS60	MS63	MS65
1994	Est. 15000	PF65 32.50				

KM# 498 21 ECUS
19.20 g., 0.925 Silver 0.571 oz. ASW **Ruler:** Elizabeth II **Obv:** Crowned bust right **Rev:** Europa with Shields of Austria, Sweden and Finland

Date	Mintage	VF20	XF40	MS60	MS63	MS65
1995	Est. 15000	PF65 32.50				

KM# 499 21 ECUS
19.20 g., 0.925 Silver 0.571 oz. ASW **Ruler:** Elizabeth II **Subject:** Agreement of Cooperation between Russia and the European Union **Obv:** Crowned bust right **Rev:** European landmark buildings and arrows

Date	Mintage	VF20	XF40	MS60	MS63	MS65
1995	Est. 15000	PF65 30.00				

KM# 505 35 ECUS
3.11 g., 0.9999 Gold 0.100 oz. AGW **Ruler:** Elizabeth II **Obv:** Crowned bust right **Rev:** Ship "Hanseatic Kogge"

Date	Mintage	VF20	XF40	MS60	MS63	MS65
1996	Est. 1500	PF65 170				

KM# 633 70 ECUS
155.52 g., 0.999 Silver 4.995 oz. ASW **Ruler:** Elizabeth II **Subject:** Ariane - European Space Programme **Obv:** Crowned bust right **Rev:** Rocket orbiting Earth

Date	Mintage	VF20	XF40	MS60	MS63	MS65
1993	—	PF65 165				

KM# 634 70 ECUS
6.22 g., 0.9999 Gold 0.200 oz. AGW **Ruler:** Elizabeth II **Subject:** Ariane - European Space Programme **Obv:** Crowned bust right **Rev:** Rocket orbiting Earth, stars encircle

Date	Mintage	VF20	XF40	MS60	MS63	MS65
1993	Est. 2000	PF65 345				
1994	Est. 1000	PF65 365				

KM# 1023 70 ECUS
155.52 g., 0.999 Silver 4.995 oz. ASW, 65 mm. **Ruler:** Elizabeth II **Obv:** Crowned bust right **Rev:** European coins

Date	Mintage	VF20	XF40	MS60	MS63	MS65
1993	Est. 2000	PF65 165				

KM# 487 70 ECUS
155.52 g., 0.999 Silver 4.995 oz. ASW, 65 mm. **Ruler:** Elizabeth II **Subject:** Euro Tunnel **Obv:** Crowned bust right **Rev:** Tunnel view and Napoleon bust

Date	Mintage	VF20	XF40	MS60	MS63	MS65
1994	Est. 2000	PF65 165				

KM# 488 70 ECUS
6.22 g., 0.9999 Gold 0.200 oz. AGW **Ruler:** Elizabeth II **Subject:** Euro Tunnel **Obv:** Crowned bust right **Rev:** Outreached hands above English Channel

Date	Mintage	VF20	XF40	MS60	MS63	MS65
1994	Est. 2000	PF65 345				

KM# 492 70 ECUS
155.52 g., 0.999 Silver 4.995 oz. ASW, 65 mm. **Ruler:** Elizabeth II **Subject:** European Unity **Obv:** Crowned bust right **Rev:** Goddess with quadriga

Date	Mintage	VF20	XF40	MS60	MS63	MS65
1994	Est. 2000	PF65 165				

KM# 493 70 ECUS
6.22 g., 0.9999 Gold 0.200 oz. AGW **Ruler:** Elizabeth II **Subject:** Mythology **Obv:** Crowned bust right **Rev:** Europa sowing seeds

Date	Mintage	VF20	XF40	MS60	MS63	MS65
1994	—	PF65 345				

KM# 1024 70 ECUS
155.52 g., 0.999 Silver 4.995 oz. ASW, 65 mm. **Ruler:** Elizabeth II **Obv:** Crowned bust right **Rev:** Train exiting tunnel

Date	Mintage	VF20	XF40	MS60	MS63	MS65
1994	—	PF65 165				

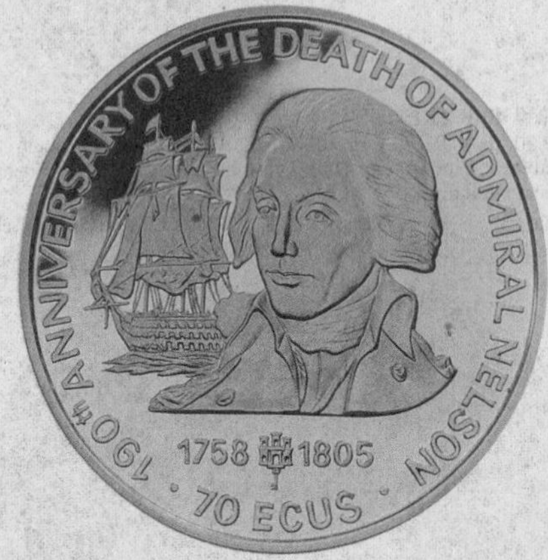

KM# 500 70 ECUS
155.92 g., 0.999 Silver 5.0079 oz. ASW, 65 mm. **Ruler:** Elizabeth II **Subject:** 190th Anniversary of Admiral Nelson's Death **Obv:** Crowned bust right **Rev:** Admiral Nelson and HMS Victory

Date	Mintage	VF20	XF40	MS60	MS63	MS65
1995	2,000	PF65 165				

KM# 501 70 ECUS
155.92 g., 0.999 Silver 5.0079 oz. ASW, 65 mm. **Ruler:** Elizabeth II **Obv:** Crowned bust right **Rev:** Liberty and Brittania seated above Euro Tunnel

Date	Mintage	VF20	XF40	MS60	MS63	MS65
1995	Est. 2000	PF65 165				

KM# 502 70 ECUS
6.22 g., 0.9999 Gold 0.200 oz. AGW **Ruler:** Elizabeth II **Obv:** Crowned bust right **Rev:** Mercury above ship

Date	Mintage	VF20	XF40	MS60	MS63	MS65
1995	Est. 2000	PF65 345				

KM# 503 70 ECUS
6.22 g., 0.9999 Gold 0.200 oz. AGW **Ruler:** Elizabeth II **Obv:** Crowned bust right **Rev:** Richard the Lionheart

Date	Mintage	VF20	XF40	MS60	MS63	MS65
1995	Est. 2000	PF65 345				

KM# 506 70 ECUS
6.22 g., 0.9999 Gold 0.200 oz. AGW **Ruler:** Elizabeth II **Obv:** Crowned bust right **Rev:** HMS Victory

Date	Mintage	VF20	XF40	MS60	MS63	MS65
1996	Est. 1500	PF65 345				

KM# 511 70 ECUS
155.52 g., 0.999 Silver 4.995 oz. ASW, 65 mm. **Ruler:** Elizabeth II **Obv:** Crowned bust right **Rev:** Sir Francis Drake and the "Golden Hind"

Date	Mintage	VF20	XF40	MS60	MS63	MS65
1996	Est. 2000	PF65 165				

KM# 512 70 ECUS
6.22 g., 0.9999 Gold 0.200 oz. AGW **Ruler:** Elizabeth II **Obv:** Crowned bust right **Rev:** Austrian Knight within circle of stars and shields

Date	Mintage	VF20	XF40	MS60	MS63	MS65
1996	2,000	PF65 490				

KM# 528 75 ECUS
3.89 g., 0.9995 Bi-Metallic 0.1249 oz. Platinum center in Gold ring **Ruler:** Elizabeth II **Subject:** Austrian Centennial **Obv:** Crowned bust right **Rev:** Standing allegorical figure with shield and trident

Date	Mintage	VF20	XF40	MS60	MS63	MS65
1996	1,500	PF65 440				

KM# 507 140 ECUS
15.55 g., 0.9999 Gold 0.4999 oz. AGW **Ruler:** Elizabeth II **Obv:** Crowned bust right **Rev:** Viking Longship

Date	Mintage	VF20	XF40	MS60	MS63	MS65
1996	Est. 1500	PF65 865				

PATTERNS

Including off metal strikes

KM#	Date	Mintage	Identification	Mkt Val
Pn4	1989	—	1/4 Sovereign. Gold. Similar to Pn8.	—
Pn5	1989	—	1/2 Sovereign. Gold. Similar to Pn8.	—
Pn6	1989	—	Sovereign. Gold. Similar to Pn8.	—
Pn7	1989	—	2 Sovereigns. Gold. Similar to Pn8.	—
Pn8	1989	—	5 Sovereigns. Gold. Una and the lion with the Rock of Gibraltar in background.	—

PIEDFORT

KM#	Date	Mintage	Identification	Mkt Val
P1	1990	5,000	5 Pence. 0.925. Silver. KM#22b.	85.00
P2	1990	1,000	5 Pence. 0.916. Gold. KM#22c.	—
P3	1993	5,000	14 ECUs. 0.925. Silver. KM#631.	75.00

MINT SETS

KM#	Date	Mintage	Identification	Issue Price	Mkt Val
MS1	1975 (3)	1,625	KM#7-9	—	2,950
MS2	1988 (9)	—	KM#16-18, 20-25	21.00	40.00
MS3	1989 (9)	—	KM#16-17, 20-25, 32	—	40.00
MS4	1990 (9)	—	km#16, 18, 20-21, 22A, 23-25, 39	25.00	45.00
MS5	1991 (9)	—	KM#16, 18, 20-21, 22a, 23-25, 39	25.00	45.00
MS7	1995 (7)	—	KM#16, 20-21, 22A, 24, 39, 112, 334, 340	—	42.50
MS8	1996 (9)	—	KM#16, 18, 20a-22a, 24, 39, 112, 355	—	46.00
MS9	1997 (9)	—	KM#16, 18, 20a-22a, 24, 39, 112, 527	—	50.00
MS10	1998 (9)	—	KM#777, 869, 773-75, 778, 776, 756 & 740	—	45.00
MS11	1999 (9)	—	KM#777, 869, 773-75, 778, 776, 759 & 797	—	45.00

PROOF SETS

KM#	Date	Mintage	Identification	Issue Price	Mkt Val
PS1	1975 (3)	750	KM#7-9	875	2,975
PS2	1989 (5)	—	KM#26-30	—	3,750
PS3	1989 (2)	—	KM#29-30	—	2,975
PS4	1990 (6)	500	KM#76-81	—	2,150
PS5	1990 (6)	250	KM#76a-81a	—	2,350
PS6	1990 (5)	1,000	KM#41-45	1,800	3,750
PS7	1991 (8)	20,000	KM#50-57	—	1,475
PS8	1991 (8)	5,000	KM#58-65	—	2,875
PS9	1991 (8)	1,000	KM#58a-65a	—	3,100
PS10	1991 (8)	50	KM#66-73	120	180
PS11	1991 (5)	1,000	KM#91-94, 97	—	3,250
PS12	1992 (5)	1,000	KM#99-102, 105	—	3,250
PS13	1993 (5)	1,000	KM#193-197	—	3,250
PS14	1993 (5)	300	KM#124-128	—	1,600
PS15	1994 (5)	1,000	KM#248-251, 252a	—	3,250
PS19	1995 (5)	1,000	KM#318b, 319-322	—	3,250
PS21	1996 (5)	1,000	KM#361-364, 365b	—	3,250
PS22	1996 (4)	1,500	KM#504-507	—	1,525
PS23	1997 (5)	1,000	KM#557-560, 561b	—	3,250
PS24	1998 (5)	1,000	KM#749-752, 754	1,309	3,250
PS25	1999 (5)	1,000	KM#828-831, 833	1,310	3,250
PS26	2000 (5)	1,000	KM#888-891, 893	—	3,250

PROOF-LIKE SETS (PL)

KM#	Date	Mintage	Identification	Issue Price	Mkt Val
PL1	1992 (8)	—	KM#66-73	—	100

GREAT BRITAIN

The United Kingdom of Great Britain and Northern Ireland, located off the northwest coast of the European continent, has an area of 94,227 sq. mi. (244,820 sq. km.) and a population of 54 million. Capital: London. The economy is based on industrial activity and trading. Machinery, motor vehicles, chemicals, and textile yarns and fabrics are exported.

After the departure of the Romans, who brought Britain into a more active relationship with Europe, it fell prey to invaders from Scandinavia and the Low Countries who drove the original Britons into Scotland and Wales, and established a profusion of kingdoms that finally united in the 11th century under the Danish King Canute. Norman rule, following the conquest of 1066, stimulated the development of those institutions, which have since distinguished British life. Henry VIII (1509-47) turned Britain from continental adventuring and faced it to the sea - a decision that made Britain a world power during the reign of Elizabeth I (1558-1603). Strengthened by the Industrial Revolution and the defeat of Napoleon, 19th century Britain turned to the remote parts of the world and established a colonial empire of such extent and prosperity that the world has never seen its like. World Wars I and II sealed the fate of the Empire and relegated Britain to a lesser role in world affairs by draining her resources and inaugurating a worldwide movement toward national self-determination in her former colonies.

By the mid-20th century, most of the territories formerly comprising the British Empire had gained independence, and the empire had evolved into the Commonwealth of Nations, an association of equal and autonomous states, which enjoy special trade interests. The Commonwealth is presently composed of 54 member nations, including the United Kingdom. All recognize the British monarch as head of the Commonwealth. Sixteen continue to recognize the British monarch as Head of State. They are: United Kingdom, Antigua and Barbuda, Australia, Bahamas, Barbados, Belize, Canada, Grenada, Jamaica, New Zealand, Papua New Guinea, St. Christopher & Nevis, Saint Lucia, Saint Vincent and the Grenadines, Solomon Islands, and Tuvalu. Elizabeth II is personally, and separately, the Queen of the sovereign, independent countries just mentioned. There is no other British connection between the several individual, national sovereignties, except that High Commissioners represent them each instead of ambassadors in each others' countries.

RULERS
Victoria, 1837-1901
Edward VII, 1901-1910
George V, 1910-1936
Edward VIII, 1936
George VI, 1936-1952
Elizabeth II, 1952-

MINT MARKS
H - Heaton
KN - King's Norton

MONETARY SYSTEM

(Until 1970)

4 Farthings = 1 Penny
12 Pence = 1 Shilling
2 Shillings = 1 Florin
5 Shillings = 1 Crown
20 Shillings = 1 Pound (Sovereign)
21 Shillings = 1 Guinea
½ Sovereign = 10 Shillings (i.e. ½ Pound)
1 Sovereign = 1 Pound

NOTE: Proofs exist for many dates of British coins in the 19th and early 20th centuries and for virtually all coins between 1926 and 1964. Those not specifically listed here are extremely rare.

NOTE: Pound Coinage - Strictly red, original mint luster coins in the copper series command premiums.

KINGDOM

PRE-DECIMAL COINAGE

KM# 791 1/3 FARTHING
0.95 g., Bronze **Ruler:** Edward VII **Obv:** Head right **Rev:** Denomination and date within crowned oak wreath **Note:** Homeland style struck for Malta.

Date	Mintage	F12	VF20	XF40	MS60	MS63
1902	288,000	4.00	10.00	30.00	65.00	90.00

KM# 823 1/3 FARTHING
0.95 g., Bronze, 15.3 mm. **Ruler:** George V **Obv:** Head left **Rev:** Crowned value within oak wreath **Note:** Homeland style struck for Malta.

Date	Mintage	F12	VF20	XF40	MS60	MS63
1913	288,000	3.50	9.00	25.00	55.00	80.00

KM# 788.2 FARTHING
2.80 g., Bronze, 20 mm. **Ruler:** Victoria **Obv:** Mature draped bust left **Obv. Legend:** VICTORIA • DEI • GRA • BRITT • REGINA • FID • DEF • IND • IMP • **Rev:** Britannia seated right **Note:** Blackened finish.

Date	Mintage	F12	VF20	XF40	MS60	MS63
1901	8,016,000	0.75	2.50	6.00	25.00	45.00

KM# 792 FARTHING
2.80 g., Bronze, 20 mm. **Ruler:** Edward VII **Obv:** Head right **Rev:** Britannia seated right

Date	Mintage	F12	VF20	XF40	MS60	MS63
1902	5,125,000	1.00	5.00	15.00	35.00	—
1903	5,331,000	1.50	6.00	18.00	40.00	—
1903	—	PF63 1,800				
Note: Shield heraldically colored						
1904	3,629,000	3.50	6.50	18.00	40.00	—
1905	4,077,000	1.50	6.00	18.00	40.00	—
1906	5,340,000	1.50	5.00	15.00	40.00	—
1907	4,399,000	1.50	5.00	15.00	40.00	—
1908	4,265,000	1.50	5.00	15.00	40.00	—
1909	8,852,000	1.50	5.00	15.00	40.00	—
1910	2,598,000	5.00	10.00	25.00	50.00	—

KM# 808.1 FARTHING
2.80 g., Bronze, 20 mm. **Ruler:** George V **Obv:** Head left **Rev:** Britannia seated right

Date	Mintage	F12	VF20	XF40	MS60	MS63
1911	5,197,000	0.60	1.50	4.00	24.00	—
1912	7,670,000	0.35	0.75	3.00	22.00	—
1913	4,184,000	0.50	0.75	4.00	22.00	—
1914	6,127,000	0.35	0.75	3.00	22.00	—
1915	7,129,000	0.50	0.75	5.00	25.00	—
1916	10,993,000	0.35	0.75	3.00	25.00	—
1917	21,435,000	0.35	0.75	3.00	25.00	—
1918	19,363,000	0.75	1.50	10.00	45.00	—

KM# 808.2 FARTHING
2.80 g., Bronze, 20 mm. **Ruler:** George V **Obv:** Head left **Rev:** Britannia seated right **Note:** Bright finish.

Date	Mintage	F12	VF20	XF40	MS60	MS63
1918	Inc. above	0.50	1.00	5.00	22.00	—
1919	15,089,000	0.50	1.00	5.00	22.00	—
1920	11,481,000	0.50	1.00	5.00	22.00	—
1921	9,469,000	0.50	1.00	5.00	22.00	—
1922	9,957,000	0.50	1.00	5.00	22.00	—
1923	8,034,000	0.50	1.00	5.00	22.00	—
1924	8,733,000	0.50	1.00	5.00	22.00	—
1924 Specimen	2	—	—	—	—	2,000
1925	12,635,000	0.50	1.00	5.00	22.00	—

KM# 825 FARTHING

2.80 g., Bronze, 20 mm. **Ruler:** George V **Obv:** Head left, modified effigy **Rev:** Britannia seated right

Date	Mintage	F12	VF20	XF40	MS60	MS63
1926	9,792,000	0.25	1.00	2.00	18.00	—
1926	—	PF63 1,000				
1927	7,868,000	0.25	1.00	2.00	18.00	—
1927	—	PF63 850				
1928	11,626,000	0.25	1.00	2.00	18.00	—
1928	—	PF63 700				
1929	8,419,000	0.25	1.00	2.00	18.00	—
1929	—	PF63 700				
1930	4,195,000	0.50	1.50	3.00	25.00	—
1930	—	PF63 700				
1931	6,595,000	0.25	1.00	2.00	18.00	—
1931	—	PF63 700				
1932	9,293,000	0.25	1.00	2.00	18.00	—
1932	—	PF63 700				
1933	4,560,000	0.25	1.00	2.00	18.00	—
1933	—	PF63 700				
1934	3,053,000	0.50	1.25	2.50	20.00	—
1934	—	PF63 700				
1935	2,227,000	1.00	2.00	5.00	32.00	—
1935	—	PF63 725				
1936	9,734,000	0.25	1.00	2.00	18.00	—
1936	—	PF63 700				

KM# 843 FARTHING

2.80 g., Bronze, 20 mm. **Ruler:** George VI **Obv:** Head left **Rev:** Wren left

Date	Mintage	F12	VF20	XF40	MS60	MS63
1937	8,131,000	0.15	0.25	1.00	8.00	—
1937	26,000	PF63 15.00				
1937 Matte Proof	—	PF63 1,800				

Note: There are reportedly 3-4 pieces known of this variety struck specifically for use in photographs

Date	Mintage	F12	VF20	XF40	MS60	MS63
1938	7,450,000	0.25	1.00	2.00	15.00	—
1938	—	PF63 700				
1939	31,440,000	0.10	0.25	1.00	10.00	—
1939	—	PF63 700				
1940	18,360,000	0.10	0.25	1.00	8.00	—
1940	—	PF63 700				
1941	27,312,000	0.10	0.25	1.00	8.00	—
1941	—	PF63 700				
1942	28,858,000	0.10	0.20	1.00	8.00	—
1942	—	PF63 700				
1943	33,345,999	0.10	0.15	1.00	8.00	—
1943	—	PF63 700				
1944	25,138,000	0.10	0.15	1.00	8.00	—
1944	—	PF63 850				
1945	23,736,000	0.10	0.20	1.00	8.00	—
1945	—	PF63 850				
1946	24,365,000	0.10	0.20	1.00	8.00	—
1946	—	PF63 850				
1947	14,746,000	0.10	0.20	1.00	8.00	—
1947	—	PF63 850				
1948	16,622,000	0.10	0.20	1.00	8.00	—
1948	—	PF63 850				

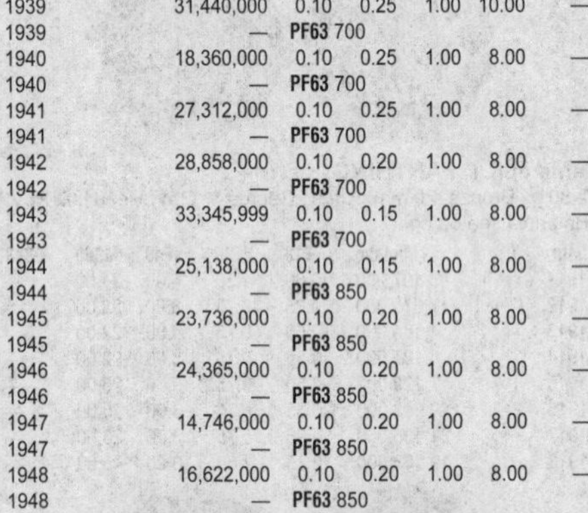

KM# 867 FARTHING

Bronze, 20 mm. **Ruler:** George VI **Obv:** Head left **Obv. Legend:** Without IND IMP **Rev:** Wren left

Date	Mintage	F12	VF20	XF40	MS60	MS63
1949	8,424,000	0.25	0.50	1.50	8.00	—
1949	—	PF63 850				
1950	10,325,000	0.25	0.50	1.50	8.00	—
1950	18,000	PF63 16.00				
1950 Matte Proof	—	PF63 1,800				

Note: There are reportedly 3-4 known of this variety, struck specifically for use in photographs

Date	Mintage	F12	VF20	XF40	MS60	MS63
1951	14,016,000	0.50	1.00	2.50	10.00	—
1951	20,000	PF63 20.00				
1951 Matte Proof	—	PF63 1,800				

Note: There are reportedly 3-4 known of this variety, struck specifically for use in photographs

Date	Mintage	F12	VF20	XF40	MS60	MS63
1952	5,251,000	0.10	0.20	1.00	8.00	—
1952	—	PF63 750				

KM# 881 FARTHING

Bronze, 20 mm. **Ruler:** Elizabeth II **Obv:** Laureate bust right **Rev:** Wren left

Date	Mintage	F12	VF20	XF40	MS60	MS63
1953	6,131,000	0.15	0.25	0.50	3.00	—
1953	40,000	PF63 10.00				
1953 Matte Proof	—	PF63 1,800				

Note: There are reportedly 1-2 known of this variety, struck specifically for use in photographs

KM# 895 FARTHING

Bronze, 20 mm. **Ruler:** Elizabeth II **Obv:** Laureate bust right **Obv. Legend:** Without BRITT OMN **Rev:** Wren left

Date	Mintage	F12	VF20	XF40	MS60	MS63
1954	6,566,000	0.10	0.15	1.00	6.00	—
1954	—	PF63 650				
1955	5,779,000	0.10	0.15	1.00	6.00	—
1955	—	PF63 650				
1956	1,997,000	0.25	0.50	3.00	10.00	—
1956	—	PF63 650				

KM# 789 1/2 PENNY

5.70 g., Bronze, 25.5 mm. **Ruler:** Victoria **Obv:** Mature draped bust left **Obv. Legend:** VICTORIA • DEI • GRA • BRITT • REGINA • FID • DEF • IND • IMP • **Rev:** Britannia seated right

Date	Mintage	F12	VF20	XF40	MS60	MS63
1901	11,127,000	2.00	5.00	10.00	60.00	85.00
1901	—	PF63 1,600				

KM# 793.1 1/2 PENNY

Bronze, 25.5 mm. **Ruler:** Edward VII **Obv:** Head right **Rev:** Britannia seated right, low horizon line

Date	Mintage	F12	VF20	XF40	MS60	MS63
1902	13,673,000	20.00	85.00	175	425	—

KM# 793.2 1/2 PENNY

5.20 g., Bronze, 25.5 mm. **Ruler:** Edward VII **Obv:** Head right **Rev:** Britannia seated right, high horizon line

Date	Mintage	F12	VF20	XF40	MS60	MS63
1902	Inc. above	1.00	3.00	18.00	55.00	—
1903	11,451,000	3.00	6.00	20.00	80.00	—
1904	8,131,000	4.00	10.00	28.00	120	—
1905	10,125,000	3.00	5.00	25.00	95.00	—
1906	11,101,000	2.00	6.00	25.00	90.00	—
1907	16,849,000	1.50	4.00	20.00	85.00	—
1908	16,620,999	2.00	4.00	20.00	85.00	—
1909	8,279,000	5.00	8.00	25.00	95.00	—
1910	10,770,000	3.00	5.00	20.00	85.00	—

KM# 809 1/2 PENNY

5.40 g., Bronze, 25.5 mm. **Ruler:** George V **Obv:** Head left **Rev:** Britannia seated right

Date	Mintage	F12	VF20	XF40	MS60	MS63
1911	12,571,000	2.00	5.00	10.00	50.00	—
1912	21,186,000	1.50	4.00	12.00	55.00	—
1913	17,476,000	3.00	7.50	12.00	55.00	—
1914	20,289,000	2.00	5.00	14.00	60.00	—
1915	21,563,000	0.75	4.00	15.00	65.00	—
1916	39,386,000	0.75	2.50	15.00	65.00	—
1917	38,245,000	0.75	2.50	12.00	55.00	—
1918	22,321,000	0.75	2.50	12.00	55.00	—
1919	28,104,000	0.75	2.50	12.00	55.00	—
1920	35,147,000	0.75	4.00	15.00	65.00	—
1921	28,027,000	0.75	2.50	12.00	55.00	—
1922	10,735,000	2.00	7.00	25.00	90.00	—
1923	12,266,000	1.00	5.00	12.00	55.00	—
1924	13,971,000	1.00	3.50	12.00	55.00	—
1924 Specimen	2	—	—	—	—	1,800
1925	12,216,000	3.00	5.00	12.00	55.00	—

KM# 824 1/2 PENNY

Bronze, 25.5 mm. **Ruler:** George V **Obv:** Head left, modified effigy **Rev:** Britannia seated right

Date	Mintage	F12	VF20	XF40	MS60	MS63
1925	Inc. above	4.00	9.50	20.00	75.00	—
1926	6,712,000	2.50	4.00	12.00	55.00	—
1926	—	PF63 1,200				
1927	15,590,000	1.00	3.00	10.00	50.00	—
1927	—	PF63 900				

KM# 837 1/2 PENNY

Bronze, 25.5 mm. **Ruler:** George V **Obv:** Smaller head left **Rev:** Britannia seated right

Date	Mintage	F12	VF20	XF40	MS60	MS63
1928	20,935,000	0.50	2.00	8.00	45.00	—
1928	—	PF63 800				
1929	25,680,000	0.50	2.00	8.00	45.00	—
1929	—	PF63 800				
1930	12,533,000	1.50	4.00	15.00	50.00	—
1930	—	PF63 800				
1931	16,138,000	0.50	2.00	8.00	45.00	—
1931	—	PF63 800				
1932	14,448,000	0.50	2.00	8.00	45.00	—
1932	—	PF63 800				
1933	10,560,000	1.00	2.50	8.00	45.00	—
1933	—	PF63 900				
1934	7,704,000	3.00	4.50	14.00	50.00	—
1934	—	PF63 900				
1935	12,180,000	1.00	2.50	8.00	45.00	—
1935	—	PF63 800				
1936	23,009,000	0.50	1.50	7.00	30.00	—
1936	—	PF63 800				

KM# 844 1/2 PENNY

Bronze, 25.5 mm. **Ruler:** George VI **Obv:** Head left **Rev:** The Golden Hind

Date	Mintage	F12	VF20	XF40	MS60	MS63
1937	24,504,000	0.50	0.75	2.00	10.00	—
1937	26,000	PF63 18.00				
1937 Matte Proof	Est. 4	PF63 1,800				
1938	40,320,000	0.25	0.50	2.00	15.00	—
1938	—	PF63 700				
1939	28,925,000	0.25	0.50	3.00	28.00	—
1939	—	PF63 700				
1940	32,162,000	0.25	0.50	3.00	28.00	—
1940	—	PF63 700				

Date	Mintage	F12	VF20	XF40	MS60	MS63
1941	45,120,000	0.25	0.50	2.00	12.00	—
1941	—	**PF63** 700				
1942	71,909,000	0.25	0.50	1.00	10.00	—
1942	—	**PF63** 700				
1943	76,200,000	0.25	0.50	1.00	10.00	—
1943	—	**PF63** 850				
1944	81,840,000	0.25	0.50	1.00	10.00	—
1944	—	**PF63** 1,000				
1945	57,000,000	0.25	0.50	1.50	12.00	—
1945	—	**PF63** 850				
1946	22,726,000	0.50	1.50	5.00	22.00	—
1946	—	**PF63** 850				
1947	21,266,000	0.25	0.50	2.50	12.00	—
1947	—	**PF63** 900				
1948	26,947,000	0.25	0.50	2.50	12.00	—
1948	—	**PF63** 900				

KM# 868 1/2 PENNY

Bronze, 25.5 mm. **Ruler:** George VI **Obv:** Head left **Obv. Legend:** Without IND IMP **Rev:** The Golden Hind

Date	Mintage	F12	VF20	XF40	MS60	MS63
1949	24,744,000	0.50	1.00	4.00	20.00	—
1949	—	**PF63** 1,000				
1950	24,154,000	0.50	1.00	3.00	15.00	—
1950	18,000	**PF63** 15.00				
1950 Matte Proof	—	**PF63** 1,600				
Note: There are reportedly 1-2 known of this variety, struck specifically for use in photographs						
1951	14,868,000	1.00	2.00	5.00	30.00	—
1951	20,000	**PF63** 18.00				
1951 Matte Proof	—	**PF63** 1,600				
Note: There are reportedly 1-2 known of this variety, struck specifically for use in photographs						
1952	33,278,000	0.25	0.50	2.00	12.00	—
1952	—	**PF63** 950				

KM# 882 1/2 PENNY

Bronze, 25.5 mm. **Ruler:** Elizabeth II **Obv:** Laureate bust right **Rev:** The Golden Hind

Date	Mintage	F12	VF20	XF40	MS60	MS63
1953	8,926,000	0.25	0.50	1.50	3.00	5.00
1953	40,000	**PF63** 13.00				
1953 Matte Proof	—	**PF63** 1,600				
Note: There are reportedly 1-2 known of this variety, struck specifically for use in photographs						

KM# 896 1/2 PENNY

5.60 g., Bronze, 25.44 mm. **Ruler:** Elizabeth II **Obv:** Laureate bust right **Obv. Legend:** Without BRITT OMN **Rev:** The Golden Hind **Edge:** Plain

Date	Mintage	F12	VF20	XF40	MS60	MS63
1954	19,375,000	0.10	0.50	1.50	8.00	—
1954	—	**PF63** 700				
1955	18,799,000	0.10	0.25	1.50	6.00	—
1955	—	**PF63** 700				
1956	21,799,000	0.15	0.50	1.50	8.00	—
1956	—	**PF63** 700				
1957	43,684,000	0.10	0.25	1.00	4.00	—
1957	—	**PF63** 600				
1958	62,318,000	—	0.10	0.50	3.00	—
1958	—	**PF63** 600				
1959	79,176,000	—	0.10	0.50	2.00	—
1959	—	**PF63** 600				
1960	41,340,000	—	0.10	0.35	1.50	—
1960	—	**PF63** 600				
1962	41,779,000	—	—	0.15	1.00	—
1962	—	**PF63** 700				
1963	45,036,000	—	—	0.15	1.00	—
1963	—	**PF63** 700				
1964	78,583,000	—	—	0.15	1.00	—
1964	—	**PF63** 800				
1965	98,083,000	—	—	0.15	1.00	—
1965 Proof	—	—	—	—	—	—
Note: Requires Confirmation						
1966	95,289,000	—	—	0.15	1.00	—
1966 Proof	—	—	—	—	—	—
Note: Requires Confirmation						
1967	146,491,000	—	—	0.15	1.00	—
1967 Proof	—	—	—	—	—	—
Note: Requires Confirmation						
1970	750,000	**PF63** 4.00				

KM# 775 PENNY

0.47 g., 0.925 Silver 0.014 oz. ASW, 11 mm. **Ruler:** Victoria **Obv:** Mature draped bust left **Rev:** Crowned denomination divides date within oak wreath

Date	Mintage	F12	VF20	XF40	MS60	MS63
1901 Prooflike	18,000	—	—	30.00	45.00	55.00

KM# 790 PENNY

9.40 g., Bronze, 31 mm. **Ruler:** Victoria **Obv:** Mature draped bust left **Obv. Legend:** VICTORIA • DEI • GRA • BRITT • REGINA • FID • DEF • IND • IMP • **Rev:** Britannia seated right

Date	Mintage	F12	VF20	XF40	MS60	MS63
1901	22,206,000	1.00	3.00	25.00	60.00	90.00
1901 Proof	—	—	—	—	—	—

KM# 794.1 PENNY

9.40 g., Bronze, 31 mm. **Ruler:** Edward VII **Obv:** Head right **Rev:** Britannia seated right, low sea level

Date	Mintage	F12	VF20	XF40	MS60	MS63
1902	26,977,000	10.00	55.00	185	350	375

KM# 794.2 PENNY

9.40 g., Bronze, 31 mm. **Ruler:** Edward VII **Obv:** Head right **Rev:** Britannia seated right, high sea level

Date	Mintage	F12	VF20	XF40	MS60	MS63
1902	Inc. above	1.25	3.50	20.00	65.00	—
1903	21,415,000	1.25	5.00	26.00	95.00	—
1904	12,913,000	3.00	10.00	55.00	150	—
1905	17,784,000	2.00	8.00	50.00	135	—
1906	37,990,000	1.50	6.00	30.00	110	—
1907	47,322,000	1.50	5.00	35.00	120	—
1908	31,506,000	2.00	6.00	30.00	110	—
1908 Matte Proof; Rare	3	—	—	—	—	—
1909	19,617,000	3.00	8.00	35.00	120	—
1910	29,549,000	1.00	4.50	25.00	100	—

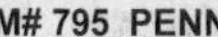

KM# 795 PENNY

0.47 g., 0.925 Silver 0.014 oz. ASW **Ruler:** Edward VII **Obv:** Head right **Rev:** Crowned denomination divides date within oak wreath

Date	Mintage	F12	VF20	XF40	MS60	MS63
1902 Prooflike	21,000	—	—	25.00	40.00	50.00
1903 Prooflike	17,000	—	—	25.00	40.00	50.00
1904 Prooflike	19,000	—	—	25.00	40.00	50.00
1905 Prooflike	18,000	—	—	25.00	40.00	50.00
1906 Prooflike	19,000	—	—	25.00	40.00	50.00
1907 Prooflike	18,000	—	—	25.00	40.00	50.00
1908 Prooflike	18,000	—	—	25.00	40.00	50.00
1909 Prooflike	2,948	—	—	35.00	55.00	70.00
1910 Prooflike	3,392	—	—	40.00	60.00	75.00

KM# 810 PENNY

9.40 g., Bronze, 31 mm. **Ruler:** George V **Obv:** Head left **Obv. Legend:** GEORGIVS V DEI GRA: BRITT: OMN: REX FID: DEF: IND: IMP: **Rev:** Britannia seated right **Note:** Fully struck and orginal mint lustre coins command a premium.

Date	Mintage	F12	VF20	XF40	MS60	MS63
1911	23,079,000	1.00	2.50	18.00	65.00	—
1912	48,306,000	0.80	3.00	28.00	75.00	—
1912 H	16,800,000	2.50	18.00	125	350	—
1913	65,497,000	1.00	5.00	30.00	90.00	—
1914	50,821,000	1.00	3.00	25.00	70.00	—
1915	47,311,000	1.00	3.00	28.00	75.00	—
1916	86,411,000	1.00	3.00	25.00	70.00	—
1917	107,905,000	1.00	3.00	25.00	70.00	—
1918	84,227,000	1.00	3.00	25.00	70.00	—
1918 H	2,573,000	4.00	30.00	300	800	—
1918 KN	Inc. above	5.00	75.00	425	1,600	—
1919	113,761,000	1.00	3.00	25.00	70.00	—
1919 H	4,526,000	3.00	35.00	350	1,100	—
1919 KN	Inc. above	8.00	95.00	950	2,400	—
1920	124,693,000	1.00	3.00	28.00	80.00	—
1921	129,717,999	1.00	3.00	25.00	70.00	—
1922	16,347,000	1.50	5.00	35.00	125	—
1922	—	2,250	7,000	—	10,000	—
Note: Reverse of 1927						
1922 Specimen	2	—	—	—	—	25,000
Note: Reverse of 1927						
1926	4,499,000	2.50	7.50	40.00	130	—
1926	—	**PF63** 2,500				

KM# 811 PENNY

0.47 g., 0.925 Silver 0.014 oz. ASW **Ruler:** George V **Obv:** Head left **Rev:** Crowned denomination divides date within oak wreath

Date	Mintage	F12	VF20	XF40	MS60	MS63
1911 Prooflike	1,913	—	—	30.00	45.00	55.00
1912 Prooflike	1,616	—	—	30.00	45.00	55.00
1913 Prooflike	1,590	—	—	30.00	45.00	55.00
1914 Prooflike	1,818	—	—	30.00	45.00	55.00
1915 Prooflike	2,072	—	—	30.00	45.00	55.00
1916 Prooflike	1,647	—	—	30.00	45.00	55.00
1917 Prooflike	1,820	—	—	30.00	45.00	55.00
1918 Prooflike	1,911	—	—	30.00	45.00	55.00
1919 Prooflike	1,699	—	—	30.00	45.00	55.00
1920 Prooflike	1,715	—	—	30.00	45.00	55.00

KM# 811a PENNY

0.47 g., 0.500 Silver 0.0076 oz. ASW **Ruler:** George V **Obv:** Head left **Rev:** Crowned denomination divides date within oak wreath

Date	Mintage	F12	VF20	XF40	MS60	MS63
1921 Prooflike	1,847	—	—	30.00	45.00	55.00
1922 Prooflike	1,758	—	—	30.00	45.00	55.00
1923 Prooflike	1,840	—	—	30.00	45.00	55.00
1924 Prooflike	1,619	—	—	30.00	45.00	55.00
1925 Prooflike	1,890	—	—	30.00	45.00	55.00
1926 Prooflike	2,180	—	—	30.00	45.00	55.00
1927 Prooflike	1,647	—	—	30.00	45.00	55.00

KM# 826 PENNY

9.40 g., Bronze, 31 mm. **Ruler:** George V **Obv:** Modified head left **Rev:** Britannia seated right

Date	Mintage	F12	VF20	XF40	MS60	MS63
1926	—	65.00	325	1,500	3,750	—
1926 Proof	—	—	—	—	—	—
Note: Requires Confirmation						
1927	60,990,000	0.50	2.00	18.00	55.00	—
1927	—	PF63 1,800				

KM# 838 PENNY

9.40 g., Bronze, 31 mm. **Ruler:** George V **Obv:** Smaller head left **Rev:** Britannia seated right

Date	Mintage	F12	VF20	XF40	MS60	MS63
1928	50,178,000	0.50	2.00	18.00	50.00	—
1928	—	PF63 1,800				
1929	49,133,000	0.50	2.00	18.00	60.00	—
1929	—	PF63 1,800				
1930	29,098,000	1.50	5.00	30.00	80.00	—
1930	—	PF63 1,800				
1931	19,843,000	1.00	3.00	25.00	65.00	—
1931	—	PF63 1,800				
1932	8,278,000	1.50	5.00	40.00	175	—
1932	—	PF63 2,250				
1933 Rare	Est. 7	—	—	—	100,000	—
1933 Proof	—	—	—	—	—	—
Note: Requires Confirmation, probably prooflike, early strike						
1934	13,966,000	1.00	4.00	30.00	80.00	—
1934	—	PF63 2,000				
1935	56,070,000	0.50	1.50	10.00	45.00	—
1935	—	PF63 1,750				
1936	154,296,000	0.50	1.00	8.00	30.00	—
1936	—	PF63 1,750				

KM# 839 PENNY

0.47 g., 0.500 Silver 0.0076 oz. ASW **Ruler:** George V **Obv:** Modified head left **Rev:** Crowned denomination divides date within oak wreath

Date	Mintage	F12	VF20	XF40	MS60	MS63
1928 Prooflike	1,846	—	—	35.00	50.00	60.00
1929 Prooflike	1,837	—	—	35.00	50.00	60.00
1930 Prooflike	1,724	—	—	35.00	50.00	60.00
1931 Prooflike	1,759	—	—	35.00	50.00	60.00
1932 Prooflike	1,835	—	—	35.00	50.00	60.00
1933 Prooflike	1,872	—	—	35.00	50.00	60.00
1934 Prooflike	1,919	—	—	35.00	50.00	60.00
1935 Prooflike	1,975	—	—	35.00	50.00	60.00
1936 Prooflike	1,329	—	—	40.00	55.00	65.00

KM# 845 PENNY

9.40 g., Bronze, 31 mm. **Ruler:** George VI **Obv:** Head left **Rev:** Britannia seated right

Date	Mintage	F12	VF20	XF40	MS60	MS63
1937	88,896,000	0.50	1.00	3.00	10.00	—
1937	26,000	PF63 25.00				
1937 Matte Proof	Est. 4	PF63 4,000				
1938	121,560,000	0.25	0.50	2.00	15.00	—
1938	—	PF63 1,600				
1939	55,560,000	0.50	1.50	4.00	20.00	—
1939	—	PF63 1,600				
1940	42,284,000	0.50	1.50	10.00	60.00	—
1940	—	PF63 1,800				
1944	42,600,000	1.00	2.50	6.00	35.00	—
1944	—	PF63 1,700				
1945	79,531,000	1.00	2.00	5.00	28.00	—
1945	—	PF63 1,700				
1946	66,855,999	0.20	0.75	5.00	19.00	—
1946	—	PF63 1,700				
1947	52,220,000	0.15	0.50	1.50	10.00	—
1947	—	PF63 2,250				
1948	63,961,000	0.15	0.25	1.00	10.00	—
1948	—	PF63 2,250				

KM# 846 PENNY

0.47 g., 0.500 Silver 0.0076 oz. ASW **Ruler:** George VI **Obv:** Head left **Rev:** Crowned denomination divides date within oak wreath

Date	Mintage	F12	VF20	XF40	MS60	MS63
1937 Prooflike	1,329	—	—	25.00	40.00	50.00
1938 Prooflike	1,275	—	—	30.00	45.00	55.00
1939 Prooflike	1,253	—	—	30.00	45.00	55.00
1940 Prooflike	1,375	—	—	30.00	45.00	55.00
1941 Prooflike	1,255	—	—	30.00	45.00	55.00
1942 Prooflike	1,243	—	—	30.00	45.00	55.00
1943 Prooflike	1,347	—	—	30.00	45.00	55.00
1944 Prooflike	1,259	—	—	30.00	45.00	55.00
1945 Prooflike	1,367	—	—	30.00	45.00	55.00
1946 Prooflike	1,479	—	—	30.00	45.00	55.00

KM# 846a PENNY

0.47 g., 0.925 Silver 0.014 oz. ASW **Ruler:** George VI **Obv:** Head left **Rev:** Crowned denomination divides date within oak wreath

Date	Mintage	F12	VF20	XF40	MS60	MS63
1947 Prooflike	1,387	—	—	30.00	45.00	55.00
1948 Prooflike	1,397	—	—	30.00	45.00	55.00

KM# 869 PENNY

9.40 g., Bronze, 31 mm. **Ruler:** George VI **Obv:** Head left **Obv. Legend:** without IND: IMP: **Rev:** Britannia seated right

Date	Mintage	F12	VF20	XF40	MS60	MS63
1949	14,324,000	0.25	0.50	1.00	10.00	—
1949	—	PF63 2,000				
1950	240,000	3.00	6.00	20.00	75.00	90.00
1950 Matte Proof	—	PF63 3,000				
Note: There are reportedly 1-2 known of this variety, struck specifically for use in photography						
1950	18,000	PF63 50.00				
1951	120,000	15.00	25.00	40.00	65.00	80.00
1951 Matte Proof	—	PF63 3,000				
Note: There are reportedly 1-2 known of this variety, struck specifically for use in photography						
1951	20,000	PF63 60.00				
1952 Proof, Unique	—	PF63 100,000				

KM# 870 PENNY

0.47 g., 0.925 Silver 0.014 oz. ASW **Ruler:** George VI **Obv:** Head left **Obv. Legend:** without IND: IMP: **Rev:** Crowned denomination divides date within oak wreath

Date	Mintage	F12	VF20	XF40	MS60	MS63
1949 Prooflike	1,407	—	—	35.00	50.00	60.00
1950 Prooflike	1,527	—	—	35.00	50.00	60.00
1951 Prooflike	1,480	—	—	35.00	50.00	60.00
1952 Prooflike	1,024	—	—	40.00	55.00	65.00

KM# 883 PENNY

9.40 g., Bronze, 31 mm. **Ruler:** Elizabeth II **Obv:** Laureate bust right **Rev:** Britannia seated right

Date	Mintage	F12	VF20	XF40	MS60	MS63
1953	1,308,000	1.50	3.00	5.00	14.00	18.00
1953	40,000	PF63 25.00				
1953 Matte Proof; Rare	—	PF63 3,500				
Note: There are reportedly 1-2 known of this variety, struck specifically for use in photography						

KM# 884 PENNY

0.47 g., 0.925 Silver 0.014 oz. ASW **Ruler:** Elizabeth II **Obv:** Laureate bust right **Rev:** Britannia seated right

Date	Mintage	F12	VF20	XF40	MS60	MS63
1953 Prooflike	1,050	—	—	250	285	325

KM# 897 PENNY

9.40 g., Bronze, 31 mm. **Ruler:** Elizabeth II **Obv:** Laureate bust right **Obv. Legend:** without BRITT: OMN: **Rev:** Britannia seated right **Edge:** Plain

Date	Mintage	F12	VF20	XF40	MS60	MS63
1954 1 Known	—	—	—	—	—	100,000
1961	48,313,000	—	—	0.25	3.00	4.50
1961	—	PF63 1,500				
1962	143,309,000	—	—	0.15	1.00	1.50
1962	—	PF63 1,500				
1963	125,236,000	—	—	0.15	1.00	1.50
1963	—	PF63 1,500				
1964	153,294,000	—	—	0.15	1.00	1.50
1964	—	PF63 2,000				
1965	121,310,000	—	—	0.15	1.00	1.50
1966	165,739,000	—	—	0.15	1.00	1.50
1967	654,564,000	—	—	0.15	1.00	1.50
1970	750,000	PF63 10.00				

KM# 898 PENNY

0.47 g., 0.925 Silver 0.014 oz. ASW, 11 mm. **Ruler:** Elizabeth II **Obv:** Laureate bust right **Rev:** Crowned value in sprays divides date within wreath **Edge:** Reeded **Mint:** British Royal Mint

Date	Mintage	F12	VF20	XF40	MS60	MS63
1954 Prooflike	1,088	—	—	30.00	40.00	50.00
1955 Prooflike	1,036	—	—	30.00	40.00	50.00
1955 Matte	—	—	—	—	—	—
1956 Prooflike	1,100	—	—	30.00	40.00	50.00
1957 Prooflike	1,168	—	—	30.00	40.00	50.00
1958 Prooflike	1,112	—	—	30.00	40.00	50.00
1959 Prooflike	1,118	—	—	30.00	40.00	50.00
1960 Prooflike	1,124	—	—	30.00	40.00	50.00
1961 Prooflike	1,200	—	—	30.00	40.00	50.00
1962 Prooflike	1,127	—	—	30.00	40.00	50.00
1963 Prooflike	1,133	—	—	30.00	40.00	50.00
1964 Prooflike	1,215	—	—	30.00	40.00	50.00
1965 Prooflike	1,143	—	—	30.00	40.00	50.00
1966 Prooflike	1,206	—	—	30.00	40.00	55.00
1967 Prooflike	1,068	—	—	35.00	45.00	55.00
1968 Prooflike	964	—	—	35.00	45.00	55.00
1969 Prooflike	1,002	—	—	35.00	45.00	55.00
1970 Prooflike	980	—	—	35.00	45.00	55.00
1971 Prooflike	1,108	—	—	35.00	45.00	55.00
1972 Prooflike	1,026	—	—	35.00	45.00	55.00
1973 Prooflike	1,004	—	—	35.00	45.00	55.00
1974 Prooflike	1,138	—	—	35.00	45.00	55.00
1975 Prooflike	1,050	—	—	35.00	45.00	55.00
1976 Prooflike	1,158	—	—	35.00	45.00	55.00
1977 Prooflike	1,240	—	—	35.00	45.00	55.00
1978 Prooflike	1,178	—	—	35.00	45.00	55.00
1979 Prooflike	1,188	—	—	35.00	45.00	55.00
1980 Prooflike	1,198	—	—	35.00	45.00	55.00
1981 Prooflike	1,288	—	—	35.00	45.00	55.00
1982 Prooflike	1,218	—	—	35.00	45.00	55.00
1983 Prooflike	1,228	—	—	35.00	45.00	55.00
1984 Prooflike	1,354	—	—	35.00	45.00	55.00
1985 Prooflike	1,248	—	—	35.00	45.00	55.00
1986 Prooflike	1,378	—	—	35.00	45.00	55.00
1987 Prooflike	1,512	—	—	35.00	45.00	55.00
1988 Prooflike	1,402	—	—	35.00	45.00	55.00
1989 Prooflike	1,353	—	—	35.00	45.00	55.00
1990 Prooflike	1,523	—	—	35.00	45.00	55.00
1991 Prooflike	1,514	—	—	35.00	45.00	55.00
1992 Prooflike	1,556	—	—	35.00	45.00	55.00
1993 Prooflike	1,440	—	—	35.00	45.00	55.00
1994 Prooflike	1,443	—	—	35.00	45.00	55.00
1995 Prooflike	1,466	—	—	35.00	45.00	55.00
1996 Prooflike	1,629	—	—	37.00	50.00	60.00
1997 Prooflike	1,786	—	—	37.00	50.00	60.00
1998 Prooflike	1,654	—	—	37.00	50.00	60.00
1999 Prooflike	1,676	—	—	37.00	50.00	60.00
2000 Prooflike	1,686	—	—	45.00	55.00	65.00

KM# 776 2 PENCE

0.94 g., 0.925 Silver 0.028 oz. ASW **Ruler:** Victoria **Obv:** Mature draped bust left **Rev:** Crowned denomination divides date within oak wreath

Date	Mintage	F12	VF20	XF40	MS60	MS63
1901 Prooflike	14,000	—	—	30.00	50.00	60.00

KM# 796 2 PENCE

0.94 g., 0.925 Silver 0.028 oz. ASW **Ruler:** Edward VII **Obv:** Head right **Rev:** Crowned denomination divides date within oak wreath

Date	Mintage	F12	VF20	XF40	MS60	MS63
1902 Prooflike	14,000	—	—	25.00	40.00	50.00
1903 Prooflike	13,000	—	—	25.00	40.00	50.00
1904 Prooflike	14,000	—	—	25.00	40.00	50.00
1905 Prooflike	11,000	—	—	25.00	40.00	50.00
1906 Prooflike	11,000	—	—	25.00	40.00	50.00
1907 Prooflike	8,760	—	—	25.00	40.00	50.00
1908 Prooflike	15,000	—	—	25.00	40.00	50.00
1909 Prooflike	2,695	—	—	45.00	70.00	80.00
1910 Prooflike	2,998	—	—	50.00	80.00	90.00

KM# 812 2 PENCE

0.94 g., 0.925 Silver 0.028 oz. ASW **Ruler:** George V **Obv:** Head left **Rev:** Crowned denomination divides date within oak wreath

Date	Mintage	F12	VF20	XF40	MS60	MS63
1911 Prooflike	1,635	—	—	35.00	50.00	60.00
1912 Prooflike	1,678	—	—	35.00	50.00	60.00
1913 Prooflike	1,880	—	—	35.00	50.00	60.00
1914 Prooflike	1,659	—	—	35.00	50.00	60.00
1915 Prooflike	1,465	—	—	35.00	50.00	60.00
1916 Prooflike	1,509	—	—	35.00	50.00	60.00
1917 Prooflike	1,506	—	—	35.00	50.00	60.00
1918 Prooflike	1,547	—	—	35.00	50.00	60.00
1919 Prooflike	1,567	—	—	35.00	50.00	60.00
1920 Prooflike	1,630	—	—	35.00	50.00	60.00

KM# 812a 2 PENCE

0.94 g., 0.500 Silver 0.0152 oz. ASW **Ruler:** George V **Obv:** Head left **Rev:** Crowned denomination divides date within oak wreath

Date	Mintage	F12	VF20	XF40	MS60	MS63
1921 Prooflike	1,794	—	—	35.00	50.00	60.00
1922 Prooflike	3,074	—	—	35.00	50.00	60.00
1923 Prooflike	1,527	—	—	35.00	50.00	60.00
1924 Prooflike	1,602	—	—	35.00	50.00	60.00
1925 Prooflike	1,670	—	—	35.00	50.00	60.00
1926 Prooflike	1,902	—	—	35.00	50.00	60.00
1927 Prooflike	1,766	—	—	35.00	50.00	60.00

KM# 840 2 PENCE

0.94 g., 0.500 Silver 0.0152 oz. ASW **Ruler:** George V **Obv:** Modified head left **Rev:** Crowned denomination divides date within oak wreath

Date	Mintage	F12	VF20	XF40	MS60	MS63
1928 Prooflike	1,706	—	—	35.00	50.00	60.00
1929 Prooflike	1,862	—	—	35.00	50.00	60.00
1930 Prooflike	1,901	—	—	35.00	50.00	60.00
1931 Prooflike	1,897	—	—	35.00	50.00	60.00
1932 Prooflike	1,960	—	—	35.00	50.00	60.00
1933 Prooflike	2,066	—	—	35.00	50.00	60.00
1934 Prooflike	1,927	—	—	35.00	50.00	60.00
1935 Prooflike	1,928	—	—	35.00	50.00	60.00
1936 Prooflike	1,365	—	—	35.00	55.00	65.00

KM# 847 2 PENCE

0.94 g., 0.500 Silver 0.0152 oz. ASW **Ruler:** George VI **Obv:** Head left **Rev:** Crowned denomination divides date within oak wreath

Date	Mintage	F12	VF20	XF40	MS60	MS63
1937 Prooflike	1,472	—	—	30.00	45.00	55.00
1938 Prooflike	1,374	—	—	30.00	45.00	55.00
1939 Prooflike	1,436	—	—	30.00	45.00	55.00
1940 Prooflike	1,277	—	—	30.00	45.00	55.00
1941 Prooflike	1,345	—	—	30.00	45.00	55.00
1942 Prooflike	1,231	—	—	30.00	45.00	55.00
1943 Prooflike	1,239	—	—	30.00	45.00	55.00
1944 Prooflike	1,345	—	—	30.00	45.00	55.00
1945 Prooflike	1,355	—	—	30.00	45.00	55.00
1946 Prooflike	1,365	—	—	30.00	45.00	55.00

KM# 847a 2 PENCE

0.94 g., 0.925 Silver 0.028 oz. ASW **Ruler:** George VI **Obv:** Head left **Rev:** Crowned denomination divides date within oak wreath

Date	Mintage	F12	VF20	XF40	MS60	MS63
1947 Prooflike	1,479	—	—	30.00	45.00	55.00
1948 Prooflike	1,385	—	—	30.00	45.00	55.00

KM# 871 2 PENCE

0.94 g., 0.925 Silver 0.028 oz. ASW **Ruler:** George VI **Obv:** Head left **Obv. Legend:** without IND IMP **Rev:** Crowned denomination divides date within oak wreath

Date	Mintage	F12	VF20	XF40	MS60	MS63
1949 Prooflike	1,395	—	—	35.00	50.00	60.00
1950 Prooflike	1,405	—	—	35.00	50.00	60.00
1951 Prooflike	1,580	—	—	35.00	50.00	60.00
1952 Prooflike	1,064	—	—	45.00	60.00	70.00

KM# 885 2 PENCE

0.94 g., 0.925 Silver 0.028 oz. ASW **Ruler:** Elizabeth II **Obv:** Laureate bust right **Rev:** Crowned denomination divides date within oak wreath

Date	Mintage	F12	VF20	XF40	MS60	MS63
1953 Prooflike	1,025	—	—	150	180	200

KM# 899 2 PENCE

0.94 g., 0.925 Silver 0.028 oz. ASW, 13 mm. **Ruler:** Elizabeth II **Obv:** Laureate bust right **Obv. Legend:** Without BRITT OMN **Rev:** Crowned value in sprays divides date within wreath **Edge:** Reeded **Mint:** British Royal Mint

Date	Mintage	F12	VF20	XF40	MS60	MS63
1954 Prooflike	1,020	—	—	25.00	50.00	40.00
1955 Prooflike	1,082	—	—	25.00	50.00	40.00
1955 Matte	—	—	—	—	—	—
1956 Prooflike	1,088	—	—	25.00	50.00	40.00
1957 Prooflike	1,094	—	—	25.00	50.00	40.00
1958 Prooflike	1,164	—	—	25.00	50.00	40.00
1959 Prooflike	1,106	—	—	25.00	50.00	40.00
1960 Prooflike	1,112	—	—	25.00	50.00	40.00
1961 Prooflike	1,118	—	—	25.00	50.00	40.00
1962 Prooflike	1,197	—	—	25.00	50.00	40.00
1963 Prooflike	1,131	—	—	25.00	50.00	40.00
1964 Prooflike	1,137	—	—	25.00	50.00	40.00
1965 Prooflike	1,221	—	—	25.00	50.00	40.00
1966 Prooflike	1,206	—	—	25.00	50.00	40.00
1967 Prooflike	986	—	—	35.00	55.00	45.00
1968 Prooflike	1,048	—	—	35.00	55.00	45.00
1969 Prooflike	1,002	—	—	35.00	55.00	45.00
1970 Prooflike	980	—	—	35.00	55.00	45.00
1971 Prooflike	1,018	—	—	35.00	55.00	45.00
1972 Prooflike	1,026	—	—	35.00	55.00	45.00
1973 Prooflike	1,004	—	—	35.00	55.00	45.00
1974 Prooflike	1,042	—	—	35.00	55.00	45.00
1975 Prooflike	1,148	—	—	35.00	55.00	45.00
1976 Prooflike	1,158	—	—	35.00	55.00	45.00
1977 Prooflike	1,138	—	—	35.00	55.00	45.00
1978 Prooflike	1,282	—	—	35.00	55.00	45.00
1979 Prooflike	1,188	—	—	30.00	55.00	45.00
1980 Prooflike	1,198	—	—	30.00	55.00	45.00
1981 Prooflike	1,178	—	—	30.00	55.00	45.00
1982 Prooflike	1,330	—	—	30.00	55.00	45.00
1983 Prooflike	1,228	—	—	30.00	55.00	45.00
1984 Prooflike	1,238	—	—	30.00	55.00	45.00
1985 Prooflike	1,366	—	—	30.00	55.00	45.00
1986 Prooflike	1,378	—	—	30.00	55.00	45.00
1987 Prooflike	1,390	—	—	30.00	55.00	45.00
1988 Prooflike	1,526	—	—	30.00	55.00	45.00
1989 Prooflike	1,353	—	—	30.00	55.00	45.00
1990 Prooflike	1,523	—	—	30.00	55.00	45.00
1991 Prooflike	1,384	—	—	30.00	55.00	45.00
1992 Prooflike	1,424	—	—	30.00	55.00	45.00
1993 Prooflike	1,440	—	—	30.00	55.00	45.00
1994 Prooflike	1,443	—	—	30.00	55.00	45.00
1995 Prooflike	1,466	—	—	30.00	55.00	45.00
1996 Prooflike	1,629	—	—	35.00	60.00	50.00
1997 Prooflike	1,786	—	—	35.00	60.00	50.00
1998 Prooflike	1,654	—	—	35.00	60.00	50.00
1999 Prooflike	1,676	—	—	35.00	60.00	50.00
2000 Prooflike	1,686	—	—	45.00	70.00	60.00

KM# 777 3 PENCE

1.41 g., 0.925 Silver 0.042 oz. ASW, 16 mm. **Ruler:** Victoria **Obv:** Mature draped bust left **Rev:** Crowned denomination divides date within oak wreath

Date	Mintage	F12	VF20	XF40	MS60	MS63
1901	6,100,000	5.00	10.00	20.00	40.00	50.00
1901 Prooflike	8,976	—	—	—	65.00	75.00

KM# 797.1 3 PENCE

1.30 g., 0.925 Silver 0.0387 oz. ASW, 16.1 mm. **Ruler:** Edward VII **Obv:** Head right **Rev:** Crowned denomination divides date within oak wreath **Note:** The prooflike coins come with a mirror or satin finish.

Date	Mintage	F12	VF20	XF40	MS60	MS63
1902	8,287,000	2.00	5.00	20.00	40.00	50.00
1902 Prooflike	8,976	—	—	—	55.00	65.00
1902 Matte Proof	15,000	**PF63** 60.00				
1903	5,235,000	3.00	10.00	30.00	90.00	110
1903 Prooflike	8,976	—	—	—	55.00	65.00
1904	3,630,000	6.00	15.00	60.00	240	275
1904 Prooflike	8,876	—	—	—	55.00	65.00

KM# 797.2 3 PENCE

1.41 g., 0.925 Silver 0.042 oz. ASW, 16 mm. **Ruler:** Edward VII **Obv:** Head right **Rev:** Crowned denomination divides date within oak wreath **Note:** The below Prooflike listings can be of mirror or satin-like finish, which are more difficult to separate from the currency strikes, especially for the years 1903-1906.

Date	Mintage	F12	VF20	XF40	MS60	MS63
1904	Inc. above	6.00	15.00	42.00	150	175
1905	3,563,000	4.00	11.00	35.00	90.00	110
1905 Prooflike	8,976	—	—	—	55.00	65.00
1906	3,174,000	5.00	13.00	42.00	115	135
1906 Prooflike	8,800	—	—	—	55.00	65.00
1907	4,841,000	3.00	11.00	30.00	60.00	70.00
1907 Prooflike	11,000	—	—	—	55.00	65.00
1908	8,176,000	3.00	5.00	18.00	60.00	70.00
1908 Prooflike	8,760	—	—	—	55.00	65.00
1909	4,054,999	3.00	11.00	32.50	85.00	95.00
1909 Prooflike	1,983	—	—	—	85.00	95.00
1910	4,565,000	2.00	5.00	18.00	50.00	60.00
1910 Prooflike	1,140	—	—	—	90.00	100

KM# 813 3 PENCE

1.41 g., 0.925 Silver 0.042 oz. ASW, 16 mm. **Ruler:** George V **Obv:** Head left **Rev:** Crowned denomination divides date within oak wreath

Date	Mintage	F12	VF20	XF40	MS60	MS63
1911	5,843,000	2.40	5.00	7.00	30.00	40.00
1911 Prooflike	1,991	—	—	—	70.00	85.00
1911	6,007	**PF63** 75.00				
1912	8,934,000	2.00	5.00	7.00	30.00	40.00
1912 Prooflike	1,246	—	—	—	70.00	85.00
1913	7,144,000	2.00	5.00	7.00	30.00	40.00
1913 Prooflike	1,228	—	—	—	70.00	85.00
1914	6,735,000	1.50	3.00	7.00	27.50	35.00
1914 Prooflike	982	—	—	—	70.00	85.00
1915	5,452,000	1.50	3.00	7.00	32.00	45.00
1915 Prooflike	1,293	—	—	—	70.00	85.00
1916	18,556,000	1.50	3.00	4.00	22.00	28.00
1916 Prooflike	1,128	—	—	—	70.00	85.00
1917	21,664,000	1.50	3.00	4.00	22.00	28.00
1917 Prooflike	1,237	—	—	—	70.00	85.00
1918	20,632,000	1.50	3.00	6.00	22.00	28.00
1918 Prooflike	1,375	—	—	—	70.00	85.00
1919	16,846,000	1.50	3.00	6.00	22.00	28.00
1919 Prooflike	1,258	—	—	—	70.00	85.00
1920	16,704,999	2.50	5.00	10.00	32.00	38.00
1920 Prooflike	1,399	—	—	—	70.00	85.00

KM# 813a 3 PENCE

1.41 g., 0.500 Silver 0.0227 oz. ASW, 16.1 mm. **Ruler:** George V **Obv:** Head left **Rev:** Crowned denomination divides date within oak wreath

Date	Mintage	F12	VF20	XF40	MS60	MS63
1920	Inc. above	1.00	1.50	5.00	25.00	30.00
1921	8,751,000	1.00	1.50	5.00	33.00	38.00
1921 Prooflike	1,386	—	—	—	55.00	65.00
1922	7,981,000	1.00	3.00	20.00	80.00	90.00
1922 Prooflike	1,373	—	—	—	65.00	85.00
1923 Prooflike	1,430	—	—	—	65.00	85.00
1924 Prooflike	1,515	—	—	—	65.00	85.00
1924 Satin specimen	2	—	—	—	—	2,750
1925	3,733,000	1.25	2.25	25.00	70.00	80.00
1925 Prooflike	1,438	—	—	—	65.00	85.00
1926	4,109,000	3.00	8.00	45.00	140	165
1926 Prooflike	1,504	—	—	—	100	125
1927 Prooflike	1,690	—	—	—	65.00	85.00

KM# 827 3 PENCE

1.41 g., 0.500 Silver 0.0227 oz. ASW, 16 mm. **Ruler:** George V **Obv:** Modified head left **Rev:** Crowned denomination divides date within oak wreath

Date	Mintage	F12	VF20	XF40	MS60	MS63
1926	Inc. above	1.50	3.00	15.00	50.00	60.00
1928 Prooflike	1,835	—	—	—	50.00	60.00
1929 Prooflike	1,761	—	—	—	50.00	60.00
1930 Prooflike	1,948	—	—	—	50.00	60.00
1931 Prooflike	1,818	—	—	—	50.00	60.00
1932 Prooflike	2,042	—	—	—	50.00	60.00
1933 Prooflike	1,920	—	—	—	50.00	60.00
1934 Prooflike	1,887	—	—	—	50.00	60.00
1935 Prooflike	2,007	—	—	—	50.00	60.00
1936 Prooflike	1,307	—	—	—	55.00	65.00

KM# 831 3 PENCE

1.41 g., 0.500 Silver 0.0227 oz. ASW, 16 mm. **Ruler:** George V **Obv:** Head left **Rev:** Three oak leaves and acorns divided

Date	Mintage	F12	VF20	XF40	MS60	MS63
1927	15,000	PF63 150				
1927 Matte Proof	—	PF63 2,000				

Note: There are reportedly 3-4 known of this variety, struck specifically for use in photographs

Date	Mintage	F12	VF20	XF40	MS60	MS63
1928	1,302,000	2.00	3.00	15.00	55.00	65.00
1928	—	PF63 800				
1930	1,319,000	3.00	8.00	20.00	65.00	75.00
1930	—	PF63 800				
1931	6,252,000	0.40	1.00	2.00	20.00	25.00
1931	—	PF63 800				
1932	5,887,000	0.40	1.00	2.25	20.00	25.00
1932	—	PF63 800				
1933	5,579,000	0.40	1.00	2.25	20.00	25.00
1933	—	PF63 800				
1934	7,406,000	0.40	1.00	2.00	18.00	22.00
1934	—	PF63 800				
1935	7,028,000	0.40	1.00	2.00	20.00	25.00
1935	—	PF63 800				
1936	3,239,000	0.40	1.00	2.25	15.00	20.00
1936	—	PF63 800				

KM# 848 3 PENCE

1.41 g., 0.500 Silver 0.0227 oz. ASW, 16 mm. **Ruler:** George VI **Obv:** Head left **Rev:** St. George shield on Tudor rose divides date

Date	Mintage	F12	VF20	XF40	MS60	MS63
1937	8,148,000	0.40	1.50	3.00	15.00	20.00
1937	26,000	PF63 20.00				
1937 Matte Proof; Rare	—	—	—	—	—	—

Note: There are reportedly 2-4 known of this variety, struck specifically for use in photography

Date	Mintage	F12	VF20	XF40	MS60	MS63
1938	6,402,000	0.40	1.00	2.00	15.00	20.00
1938	—	PF63 700				
1939	1,356,000	0.40	1.50	10.00	35.00	45.00
1939	—	PF63 700				
1940	7,914,000	0.40	2.00	5.00	25.00	30.00
1940	—	PF63 700				
1941	7,979,000	0.40	1.50	4.00	25.00	30.00
1941	—	PF63 700				
1942	4,144,000	4.00	8.00	20.00	50.00	60.00
1942	—	PF63 700				
1943	1,379,000	4.00	8.00	25.00	60.00	70.00
1943	—	PF63 700				
1944	2,005,999	5.00	15.00	40.00	100	125
1944	—	PF63 800				
1945 Rare	320,000	—	—	—	—	—

Note: Issue melted, only one known

KM# 849 3 PENCE

Nickel-Brass **Ruler:** George VI **Obv:** Head left **Rev:** Thrift plant (allium porrum) **Shape:** 12-sided

Date	Mintage	F12	VF20	XF40	MS60	MS63
1937	45,708,000	0.25	0.50	2.00	12.00	15.00
1937	26,000	PF63 20.00				
1937 Matte Proof; Rare	—	—	—	—	—	—

Note: There are reportedly 2-4 known of this variety, struck specifically for use in photography

Date	Mintage	F12	VF20	XF40	MS60	MS63
1938	14,532,000	1.00	2.50	6.00	28.00	35.00
1938	—	PF63 600				
1939	5,603,000	2.00	6.00	10.00	50.00	60.00
1939	—	PF63 600				
1940	12,636,000	0.75	3.00	6.00	30.00	35.00
1940	—	PF63 600				
1941	60,239,000	0.50	1.00	3.00	15.00	18.00
1941	—	PF63 600				
1942	103,214,000	0.50	1.00	2.50	12.00	15.00
1942 Proof	—	—	—	—	—	—
1943	101,702,000	0.50	1.00	2.50	12.00	15.00
1943 Proof	—	—	—	—	—	—
1944	69,760,000	0.50	1.00	2.50	15.00	18.00
1944 Proof	—	—	—	—	—	—
1945	33,942,000	0.75	2.00	5.00	20.00	25.00
1945 Proof	—	—	—	—	—	—
1946	621,000	6.00	30.00	250	850	950
1946	—	PF63 1,200				
1948	4,230,000	2.50	3.00	10.00	65.00	75.00
1948	—	PF63 850				

KM# 850 3 PENCE

1.41 g., 0.500 Silver 0.0227 oz. ASW, 16 mm. **Ruler:** George VI **Obv:** Head left **Rev:** Crowned denomination divides date within oak wreath

Date	Mintage	F12	VF20	XF40	MS60	MS63
1937 Prooflike	1,351	—	—	35.00	50.00	60.00
1938 Prooflike	1,350	—	—	35.00	50.00	60.00
1939 Prooflike	1,234	—	—	35.00	50.00	60.00
1940 Prooflike	1,290	—	—	35.00	50.00	60.00
1941 Prooflike	1,253	—	—	35.00	50.00	60.00
1942 Prooflike	1,325	—	—	35.00	50.00	60.00
1943 Prooflike	1,335	—	—	35.00	50.00	60.00
1944 Prooflike	1,345	—	—	35.00	50.00	60.00
1945 Prooflike	1,355	—	—	35.00	50.00	60.00
1946 Prooflike	1,365	—	—	35.00	50.00	60.00

KM# 850a 3 PENCE

1.41 g., 0.925 Silver 0.042 oz. ASW, 16 mm. **Ruler:** George VI **Obv:** Head left **Rev:** Crowned denomination divides date within oak wreath

Date	Mintage	F12	VF20	XF40	MS60	MS63
1947 Prooflike	1,375	—	—	35.00	50.00	60.00
1948 Prooflike	1,491	—	—	35.00	50.00	60.00

KM# 872 3 PENCE

1.41 g., 0.925 Silver 0.042 oz. ASW, 16 mm. **Ruler:** George VI **Obv:** Head left **Obv. Legend:** without IND IMP **Rev:** Crowned denomination divides date within oak wreath

Date	Mintage	F12	VF20	XF40	MS60	MS63
1949 Prooflike	1,395	—	—	35.00	50.00	60.00
1950 Prooflike	1,405	—	—	35.00	50.00	60.00
1951 Prooflike	1,468	—	—	35.00	50.00	60.00
1952 Prooflike	1,012	—	—	45.00	60.00	70.00

KM# 873 3 PENCE

6.80 g., Nickel-Brass **Ruler:** George VI **Obv:** Head left **Obv. Legend:** without IND IMP **Rev:** Thrift plant (allium porrum)

Date	Mintage	F12	VF20	XF40	MS60	MS63
1949	464,000	12.00	30.00	200	675	775
1949	—	PF63 1,000				
1950	1,600,000	2.50	5.00	25.00	135	150
1950	18,000	PF63 50.00				
1950 Matte Proof; Rare	—	—	—	—	—	—

Note: There are reportedly 2-4 known of this variety, struck specifically for use in photography

Date	Mintage	F12	VF20	XF40	MS60	MS63
1951	1,184,000	1.00	3.00	30.00	150	165
1951	20,000	PF63 50.00				
1951 Matte Proof; Rare	—	PF63 1,800				

Note: There are reportedly 2-4 known of this variety, struck specifically for use in photography

Date	Mintage	F12	VF20	XF40	MS60	MS63
1952	25,494,000	1.00	2.00	5.00	25.00	30.00
1952	—	PF63 800				

KM# 886 3 PENCE

Nickel-Brass **Ruler:** Elizabeth II **Obv:** Laureate bust right **Rev:** Crowned portcullis

Date	Mintage	F12	VF20	XF40	MS60	MS63
1953	30,618,000	0.50	1.00	3.00	6.00	7.50
1953	40,000	PF63 12.00				
1953 Matte Proof; Rare	—	PF63 1,800				

Note: There are reportedly 2-4 known of this variety, struck specifically for use in photography

KM# 887 3 PENCE

1.41 g., 0.925 Silver 0.042 oz. ASW **Ruler:** Elizabeth II **Obv:** Laureate bust right **Rev:** Crowned portcullis

Date	Mintage	F12	VF20	XF40	MS60	MS63
1953 Prooflike	1,078	—	—	175	225	250

KM# 900 3 PENCE

Nickel-Brass **Ruler:** Elizabeth II **Obv:** Laureate bust right **Obv. Legend:** without BRITT OMN **Rev:** Crowned portcullis **Shape:** 12-sided

Date	Mintage	F12	VF20	XF40	MS60	MS63
1954	41,720,000	—	1.00	2.50	8.00	10.00
1954	—	PF63 600				
1955	41,075,000	—	0.50	1.00	10.00	12.00
1955	—	PF63 600				
1956	36,902,000	—	0.50	1.00	10.00	12.00
1956	—	PF63 600				
1957	24,294,000	—	—	1.00	6.00	7.50
1957	—	PF63 600				
1958	20,504,000	—	1.00	2.25	15.00	18.00
1958	—	PF63 600				
1959	28,499,000	—	0.50	1.00	6.00	7.50
1959	—	PF63 600				
1960	83,078,000	—	1.00	2.00	7.00	9.00
1960	—	PF63 600				
1961	41,102,000	—	—	0.50	3.00	4.50
1961	—	PF63 600				
1962	47,242,000	—	0.25	0.50	2.00	3.00
1962	—	PF63 600				
1963	35,280,000	—	0.25	0.35	2.00	3.00
1963	—	PF63 600				
1964	47,440,000	—	0.25	0.35	2.00	3.00
1964 Proof	—	—	—	—	—	—
1965	23,907,000	—	0.25	0.35	2.00	3.00
1965 Proof	—	—	—	—	—	—
1966	55,320,000	—	0.25	0.35	1.00	2.00
1966 Proof	—	—	—	—	—	—
1967	49,000,000	—	0.25	0.35	1.00	2.00
1967 Proof	—	—	—	—	—	—
1970	750,000	PF63 10.00				

KM# 901 3 PENCE

1.41 g., 0.925 Silver 0.042 oz. ASW, 16 mm. **Ruler:** Elizabeth II **Obv:** Laureate bust right **Obv. Legend:** without BRITT OMN **Rev:** Crowned value in sprays divides date within wreath **Edge:** Reeded **Mint:** British Royal Mint

Date	Mintage	F12	VF20	XF40	MS60	MS63
1954 Prooflike	1,076	—	—	35.00	60.00	50.00
1955 Prooflike	1,082	—	—	35.00	60.00	50.00
1956 Prooflike	1,088	—	—	35.00	60.00	50.00
1957 Prooflike	1,094	—	—	35.00	60.00	50.00
1958 Prooflike	1,100	—	—	35.00	60.00	50.00
1959 Prooflike	1,172	—	—	35.00	60.00	50.00
1960 Prooflike	1,112	—	—	35.00	60.00	50.00
1961 Prooflike	1,118	—	—	35.00	60.00	50.00
1962 Prooflike	1,125	—	—	35.00	60.00	50.00
1963 Prooflike	1,205	—	—	35.00	60.00	50.00
1964 Prooflike	1,213	—	—	35.00	60.00	50.00
1965 Prooflike	1,221	—	—	35.00	60.00	50.00
1966 Prooflike	1,206	—	—	35.00	60.00	50.00
1967 Prooflike	986	—	—	40.00	65.00	55.00
1968 Prooflike	964	—	—	40.00	65.00	55.00
1969 Prooflike	1,088	—	—	40.00	65.00	55.00
1970 Prooflike	980	—	—	40.00	65.00	55.00
1971 Prooflike	1,018	—	—	40.00	65.00	55.00
1972 Prooflike	1,026	—	—	40.00	65.00	55.00
1973 Prooflike	1,098	—	—	40.00	65.00	55.00
1974 Prooflike	1,138	—	—	40.00	65.00	55.00
1975 Prooflike	1,148	—	—	40.00	65.00	55.00
1976 Prooflike	1,158	—	—	40.00	65.00	55.00
1977 Prooflike	1,138	—	—	40.00	65.00	55.00
1978 Prooflike	1,178	—	—	40.00	65.00	55.00
1979 Prooflike	1,294	—	—	40.00	65.00	55.00
1980 Prooflike	1,198	—	—	40.00	65.00	55.00
1981 Prooflike	1,178	—	—	40.00	65.00	55.00
1982 Prooflike	1,218	—	—	40.00	65.00	55.00
1983 Prooflike	1,342	—	—	40.00	65.00	55.00
1984 Prooflike	1,354	—	—	40.00	65.00	55.00
1985 Prooflike	1,366	—	—	40.00	65.00	55.00
1986 Prooflike	1,378	—	—	40.00	65.00	55.00
1987 Prooflike	1,390	—	—	40.00	65.00	55.00
1988 Prooflike	1,528	—	—	40.00	65.00	55.00
1989 Prooflike	1,353	—	—	40.00	65.00	55.00
1990 Prooflike	1,523	—	—	40.00	65.00	55.00
1991 Prooflike	1,384	—	—	40.00	65.00	55.00
1992 Prooflike	1,424	—	—	40.00	65.00	55.00
1993 Prooflike	1,440	—	—	40.00	65.00	55.00
1994 Prooflike	1,433	—	—	40.00	65.00	55.00
1995 Prooflike	1,466	—	—	40.00	65.00	55.00
1996 Prooflike	1,629	—	—	45.00	70.00	60.00
1997 Prooflike	1,786	—	—	45.00	70.00	60.00
1998 Prooflike	1,654	—	—	45.00	70.00	60.00
1999 Prooflike	1,676	—	—	45.00	70.00	60.00
2000 Prooflike	1,686	—	—	50.00	75.00	65.00

KM# 778 4 PENCE (Groat)

1.89 g., 0.925 Silver 0.0561 oz. ASW **Ruler:** Victoria **Obv:** Mature draped bust left **Obv. Legend:** VICTORIA • DEI • GRA • BRITT • REGINA • FID • DEF • IND • IMP • **Rev:** Crowned denomination divides date within oak wreath

Date	Mintage	F12	VF20	XF40	MS60	MS63
1901 Prooflike	12,000	—	—	35.00	50.00	60.00

KM# 798 4 PENCE (Groat)

1.89 g., 0.925 Silver 0.0561 oz. ASW **Ruler:** Edward VII **Obv:** Head left **Rev:** Crowned denomination divides date within oak wreath

Date	Mintage	F12	VF20	XF40	MS60	MS63
1902 Prooflike	10,000	—	—	30.00	45.00	55.00
1903 Prooflike	9,729	—	—	30.00	45.00	55.00
1904 Prooflike	12,000	—	—	30.00	45.00	55.00
1905 Prooflike	11,000	—	—	30.00	45.00	55.00
1906 Prooflike	11,000	—	—	30.00	45.00	55.00
1907 Prooflike	11,000	—	—	30.00	45.00	55.00
1908 Prooflike	9,929	—	—	30.00	45.00	55.00
1909 Prooflike	2,428	—	—	55.00	70.00	80.00
1910 Prooflike	2,755	—	—	60.00	75.00	85.00

KM# 814 4 PENCE (Groat)

1.89 g., 0.925 Silver 0.0561 oz. ASW **Ruler:** George V **Obv:** Head left **Rev:** Crowned denomination divides date within oak wreath

Date	Mintage	F12	VF20	XF40	MS60	MS63
1911 Prooflike	1,768	—	—	35.00	50.00	60.00
1912 Prooflike	1,700	—	—	35.00	50.00	60.00
1913 Prooflike	1,798	—	—	35.00	50.00	60.00
1914 Prooflike	1,651	—	—	35.00	50.00	60.00
1915 Prooflike	1,441	—	—	35.00	50.00	60.00
1916 Prooflike	1,499	—	—	35.00	50.00	60.00
1917 Prooflike	1,478	—	—	35.00	50.00	60.00
1918 Prooflike	1,479	—	—	35.00	50.00	60.00
1919 Prooflike	1,524	—	—	35.00	50.00	60.00
1920 Prooflike	1,460	—	—	35.00	50.00	60.00

KM# 814a 4 PENCE (Groat)

1.89 g., 0.500 Silver 0.0303 oz. ASW **Ruler:** George V **Obv:** Head left **Rev:** Crowned denomination divides date within oak wreath

Date	Mintage	F12	VF20	XF40	MS60	MS63
1921 Prooflike	1,542	—	—	35.00	50.00	60.00
1922 Prooflike	1,609	—	—	35.00	50.00	60.00
1923 Prooflike	1,635	—	—	35.00	50.00	60.00
1924 Prooflike	1,665	—	—	35.00	50.00	60.00
1925 Prooflike	1,786	—	—	35.00	50.00	60.00
1926 Prooflike	1,762	—	—	35.00	50.00	60.00
1927 Prooflike	1,681	—	—	35.00	50.00	60.00

KM# 841 4 PENCE (Groat)

1.89 g., 0.500 Silver 0.0303 oz. ASW **Ruler:** George V **Obv:** Modified head left **Rev:** Crowned denomination divides date within oak wreath

Date	Mintage	F12	VF20	XF40	MS60	MS63
1928 Prooflike	1,642	—	—	35.00	50.00	60.00
1929 Prooflike	1,969	—	—	35.00	50.00	60.00
1930 Prooflike	1,744	—	—	35.00	50.00	60.00
1931 Prooflike	1,915	—	—	35.00	50.00	60.00
1932 Prooflike	1,937	—	—	35.00	50.00	60.00
1933 Prooflike	1,931	—	—	35.00	50.00	60.00
1934 Prooflike	1,893	—	—	35.00	50.00	60.00
1935 Prooflike	1,995	—	—	35.00	50.00	60.00
1936 Prooflike	1,323	—	—	40.00	55.00	65.00

KM# 851 4 PENCE (Groat)

1.89 g., 0.500 Silver 0.0303 oz. ASW **Ruler:** George VI **Obv:** Head left **Rev:** Crowned denomination divides date within oak wreath

Date	Mintage	F12	VF20	XF40	MS60	MS63
1937 Prooflike	1,325	—	—	35.00	50.00	60.00
1938 Prooflike	1,424	—	—	40.00	55.00	65.00
1939 Prooflike	1,332	—	—	40.00	55.00	65.00
1940 Prooflike	1,367	—	—	40.00	55.00	65.00
1941 Prooflike	1,345	—	—	40.00	55.00	65.00
1942 Prooflike	1,325	—	—	40.00	55.00	65.00
1943 Prooflike	1,335	—	—	40.00	55.00	65.00
1944 Prooflike	1,345	—	—	40.00	55.00	65.00
1945 Prooflike	1,355	—	—	40.00	55.00	65.00
1946 Prooflike	1,365	—	—	40.00	55.00	65.00

KM# 851a 4 PENCE (Groat)

1.89 g., 0.925 Silver 0.0561 oz. ASW **Ruler:** George VI **Obv:** Head left **Rev:** Crowned denomination divides date within oak wreath

Date	Mintage	F12	VF20	XF40	MS60	MS63
1947 Prooflike	1,375	—	—	40.00	55.00	65.00
1948 Prooflike	1,385	—	—	40.00	55.00	65.00

KM# 874 4 PENCE (Groat)

1.89 g., 0.925 Silver 0.0561 oz. ASW **Ruler:** George VI **Obv:** Head left **Obv. Legend:** without IND IMP **Rev:** Crowned denomination divides date within oak wreath

Date	Mintage	F12	VF20	XF40	MS60	MS63
1949 Prooflike	1,503	—	—	40.00	55.00	65.00
1950 Prooflike	1,515	—	—	40.00	55.00	65.00
1951 Prooflike	1,580	—	—	40.00	55.00	65.00
1952 Prooflike	1,064	—	—	45.00	60.00	70.00

KM# 888 4 PENCE (Groat)

1.89 g., 0.925 Silver 0.0561 oz. ASW **Ruler:** Elizabeth II **Obv:** Bust right **Rev:** Crowned denomination divides date within oak wreath

Date	Mintage	F12	VF20	XF40	MS60	MS63
1953 Prooflike	1,078	—	—	150	180	200

KM# 902 4 PENCE (Groat)

1.89 g., 0.925 Silver 0.0561 oz. ASW, 18 mm. **Ruler:** Elizabeth II **Obv:** Laureate bust right **Obv. Legend:** without BRITT OMN **Rev:** Crowned denomination divides date within wreath **Edge:** Reeded **Mint:** British Royal Mint

Date	Mintage	F12	VF20	XF40	MS60	MS63
1954 Prooflike	1,076	—	—	35.00	60.00	50.00
1955 Prooflike	1,082	—	—	35.00	60.00	50.00
1955 Matte	—	—	—	—	—	—
1956 Prooflike	1,088	—	—	35.00	60.00	50.00
1957 Prooflike	1,094	—	—	35.00	60.00	50.00
1958 Prooflike	1,100	—	—	35.00	60.00	50.00
1959 Prooflike	1,106	—	—	35.00	60.00	50.00
1960 Prooflike	1,180	—	—	35.00	60.00	50.00
1961 Prooflike	1,118	—	—	35.00	60.00	50.00
1962 Prooflike	1,197	—	—	35.00	60.00	50.00
1963 Prooflike	1,205	—	—	35.00	60.00	50.00
1964 Prooflike	1,213	—	—	35.00	60.00	50.00
1965 Prooflike	1,221	—	—	35.00	60.00	50.00
1966 Prooflike	1,206	—	—	35.00	60.00	50.00
1967 Prooflike	986	—	—	40.00	65.00	55.00
1968 Prooflike	964	—	—	40.00	65.00	55.00
1969 Prooflike	1,002	—	—	40.00	65.00	55.00
1970 Prooflike	1,068	—	—	40.00	65.00	55.00
1971 Prooflike	1,108	—	—	40.00	65.00	55.00
1972 Prooflike	1,118	—	—	40.00	65.00	55.00
1973 Prooflike	1,098	—	—	40.00	65.00	55.00
1974 Prooflike	1,138	—	—	40.00	65.00	55.00
1975 Prooflike	1,148	—	—	40.00	65.00	55.00
1976 Prooflike	1,158	—	—	40.00	65.00	55.00
1977 Prooflike	1,138	—	—	40.00	65.00	55.00
1978 Prooflike	1,178	—	—	40.00	65.00	55.00
1979 Prooflike	1,188	—	—	40.00	65.00	55.00
1980 Prooflike	1,306	—	—	40.00	65.00	55.00
1981 Prooflike	1,288	—	—	40.00	65.00	55.00
1982 Prooflike	1,330	—	—	40.00	65.00	55.00
1983 Prooflike	1,342	—	—	40.00	65.00	55.00
1984 Prooflike	1,354	—	—	40.00	65.00	55.00
1985 Prooflike	1,366	—	—	40.00	65.00	55.00
1986 Prooflike	1,378	—	—	40.00	65.00	55.00
1987 Prooflike	1,390	—	—	40.00	65.00	55.00
1988 Prooflike	1,402	—	—	40.00	65.00	55.00
1989 Prooflike	1,353	—	—	40.00	65.00	55.00
1990 Prooflike	1,523	—	—	40.00	65.00	55.00
1991 Prooflike	1,514	—	—	40.00	65.00	55.00
1992 Prooflike	1,556	—	—	40.00	65.00	55.00
1993 Prooflike	1,440	—	—	40.00	65.00	55.00
1994 Prooflike	1,433	—	—	40.00	65.00	55.00
1995 Prooflike	1,466	—	—	40.00	65.00	55.00
1996 Prooflike	1,629	—	—	45.00	70.00	60.00
1997 Prooflike	1,786	—	—	45.00	70.00	60.00
1998 Prooflike	1,654	—	—	45.00	70.00	60.00
1999 Prooflike	1,676	—	—	45.00	70.00	60.00
2000 Prooflike	1,686	—	—	50.00	75.00	65.00

KM# 779 6 PENCE

2.83 g., 0.925 Silver 0.0841 oz. ASW, 19.5 mm. **Ruler:** Victoria **Obv:** Mature draped bust left **Obv. Legend:** VICTORIA • DEI • GRA • BRITT • REGINA • FID • DEF • IND • IMP • **Rev:** Crowned denomination within oak wreath **Edge:** Reeded

Date	Mintage	F12	VF20	XF40	MS60	MS63
1901	5,109,000	13.50	22.00	50.00	110	160

KM# 799 6 PENCE

3.01 g., 0.925 Silver 0.0895 oz. ASW, 19.5 mm. **Ruler:** Edward

VII **Obv:** Head right **Rev:** Crowned denomination within oak wreath, date below

Date	Mintage	F12	VF20	XF40	MS60	MS63
1902	6,356,000	8.00	15.00	55.00	90.00	115
1902 Matte Proof	15,000	PF63 125				
1903	5,411,000	5.00	15.00	60.00	135	160
1904	4,487,000	10.00	30.00	125	300	350
1905	4,236,000	8.00	25.00	90.00	225	275
1906	7,641,000	5.00	15.00	60.00	130	155
1907	8,734,000	8.00	15.00	65.00	135	160
1908	6,739,000	8.00	16.00	70.00	175	200
1909	6,584,000	5.00	15.00	65.00	130	155
1910	12,491,000	5.00	10.00	50.00	90.00	115

KM# 815 6 PENCE

2.83 g., 0.925 Silver 0.0841 oz. ASW, 19.5 mm. **Ruler:** George V **Obv:** Head left **Rev:** Lion atop crown dividing date **Edge:** Reeded

Date	Mintage	F12	VF20	XF40	MS60	MS63
1911	9,165,000	3.00	10.00	30.00	60.00	85.00
1911	6,007	PF63 95.00				
1912	10,984,000	5.00	12.00	40.00	75.00	100
1913	7,500,000	6.00	15.00	45.00	80.00	105
1914	22,715,000	3.00	10.00	30.00	60.00	85.00
1915	15,695,000	3.00	10.00	30.00	70.00	95.00
1916	22,207,000	3.00	10.00	30.00	60.00	85.00
1917	7,725,000	6.00	18.00	55.00	150	175
1918	27,559,000	3.00	10.00	30.00	60.00	85.00
1919	13,375,000	5.00	12.00	35.00	70.00	95.00
1920	14,136,000	6.00	15.00	45.00	85.00	110

KM# 815a.1 6 PENCE

2.83 g., 0.500 Silver 0.0455 oz. ASW, 19.5 mm. **Ruler:** George V **Obv:** Head left **Rev:** Lion atop crown dividing date **Edge:** Reeded **Note:** Narrow rim.

Date	Mintage	F12	VF20	XF40	MS60	MS63
1920	Inc. above	3.00	7.00	30.00	80.00	105
1921	30,340,000	2.00	4.00	25.00	75.00	100
1922	16,879,000	2.00	5.00	25.00	75.00	100
1923	6,383,000	3.00	6.00	30.00	85.00	110
1924	17,444,000	2.00	4.00	20.00	60.00	85.00
1924 Satin specimen	2	—	—	—	—	1,800
1925	12,721,000	2.00	4.00	30.00	65.00	90.00

KM# 815a.2 6 PENCE

2.83 g., 0.500 Silver 0.0455 oz. ASW, 19.5 mm. **Ruler:** George V **Obv:** Head left **Rev:** Lion atop crown dividing date **Edge:** Reeded **Note:** Wide rim.

Date	Mintage	F12	VF20	XF40	MS60	MS63
1925	Inc. above	2.00	4.00	30.00	55.00	65.00
1926	21,810,000	2.00	4.00	30.00	55.00	65.00

KM# 828 6 PENCE

2.83 g., 0.500 Silver 0.0455 oz. ASW, 19.5 mm. **Ruler:** George V **Obv:** Modified head left **Rev:** Lion atop crown divides date

Date	Mintage	F12	VF20	XF40	MS60	MS63
1926	Inc. above	0.80	5.00	20.00	50.00	60.00
1927	8,925,000	2.00	4.00	25.00	55.00	65.00
1927	—	PF63 1,000				

KM# 832 6 PENCE

2.83 g., 0.500 Silver 0.0455 oz. ASW, 19.5 mm. **Ruler:** George V **Obv:** Head left **Rev:** Six oak leaves and acorns divided **Note:** Varieties in edge milling exist.

Date	Mintage	F12	VF20	XF40	MS60	MS63
1927	15,000	PF63 65.00				
1927 Matte Proof; Rare	—	PF63 2,000				

Note: There are reportedly 3-4 known of this variety, struck specifically for use in photographs

Date	Mintage	F12	VF20	XF40	MS60	MS63
1928	23,123,000	0.80	3.00	10.00	35.00	45.00
1928	—	PF63 700				
1929	28,319,000	0.80	3.00	10.00	35.00	45.00
1929	—	PF63 700				
1930	16,990,000	0.80	4.00	16.00	40.00	50.00
1930	—	PF63 700				
1931	16,873,000	2.00	3.00	10.00	40.00	50.00
1931	—	PF63 700				
1932	9,406,000	3.00	5.00	18.00	60.00	70.00
1932	—	PF63 750				
1933	22,185,000	2.00	3.00	10.00	40.00	50.00
1933	—	PF63 700				
1934	9,304,000	2.00	3.00	12.00	50.00	60.00
1934	—	PF63 700				
1935	13,996,000	0.80	2.00	8.00	30.00	40.00
1935	—	PF63 700				
1936	24,380,000	0.80	2.00	7.50	25.00	35.00
1936	—	PF63 700				

KM# 852 6 PENCE

2.83 g., 0.500 Silver 0.0455 oz. ASW, 19.5 mm. **Ruler:** George VI **Obv:** Head left **Rev:** Crowned monogram divides date **Edge:** Reeded

Date	Mintage	F12	VF20	XF40	MS60	MS63
1937	22,303,000	—	2.00	5.00	15.00	20.00
1937	26,000	PF63 18.00				
1937 Matte Proof; Rare	—	—	—	—	—	—

Note: There are reportedly 3-4 known of this variety, struck specifically for use in photographs

Date	Mintage	F12	VF20	XF40	MS60	MS63
1938	13,403,000	2.50	3.50	7.00	25.00	30.00
1938	—	PF63 600				
1939	28,670,000	3.00	4.00	6.00	25.00	30.00
1939	—	PF63 600				
1940	20,875,000	2.00	2.50	6.00	25.00	30.00
1940	—	PF63 600				
1941	23,087,000	2.00	2.50	4.00	20.00	25.00
1941	—	PF63 600				
1942	44,943,000	2.00	2.50	4.00	15.00	20.00
1942	—	PF63 600				
1943	46,927,000	2.00	2.50	4.00	15.00	20.00
1943	—	PF63 600				
1944	36,953,000	2.00	2.50	4.00	15.00	20.00
1944	—	PF63 600				
1945	39,939,000	2.00	2.50	4.00	15.00	20.00
1945	—	PF63 750				
1946	43,466,000	2.00	2.50	4.00	15.00	20.00
1946	—	PF63 750				

KM# 862 6 PENCE

2.83 g., Copper-Nickel, 19.5 mm. **Ruler:** George VI **Obv:** Head left **Rev:** Crowned monogram divides date **Edge:** Reeded

Date	Mintage	F12	VF20	XF40	MS60	MS63
1947	29,993,000	—	0.50	2.00	10.00	12.50
1947	—	PF63 600				
1948	88,324,000	—	0.50	2.00	10.00	12.50
1948	—	PF63 850				

KM# 875 6 PENCE

2.83 g., Copper-Nickel, 19.5 mm. **Ruler:** George VI **Obv:** Head left **Rev:** Crowned monogram divides date **Rev. Legend:** without IND IMP **Edge:** Reeded

Date	Mintage	F12	VF20	XF40	MS60	MS63
1949	41,336,000	—	0.50	1.50	12.00	15.00
1949	—	PF63 700				
1950	32,741,999	—	1.00	3.00	15.00	18.00
1950	18,000	PF63 22.00				
1950 Matte Proof; Rare	—	—	—	—	—	—

Note: There are reportedly 3-4 known of this variety, struck specifically for use in photographs

Date	Mintage	F12	VF20	XF40	MS60	MS63
1951	40,399,000	—	2.00	5.00	20.00	25.00
1951	20,000	PF63 20.00				
1951 Matte Proof; Rare	—	—	—	—	—	—

Note: There are reportedly 3-4 known of this variety, struck specifically for use in photographs

Date	Mintage	F12	VF20	XF40	MS60	MS63
1952	1,012,999	4.00	7.50	40.00	125	150
1952	—	PF63 1,500				

KM# 889 6 PENCE

2.83 g., Copper-Nickel, 19.5 mm. **Ruler:** Elizabeth II **Obv:** Laureate bust right **Rev:** Flora; leek, rose, thistle and shamrock **Edge:** Reeded

Date	Mintage	F12	VF20	XF40	MS60	MS63
1953	70,324,000	—	0.75	1.50	4.00	5.00
1953	40,000	PF63 8.00				
1953 Matte Proof; Rare	—	—	—	—	—	—

Note: There are reportedly 3-4 known of this variety, struck specifically for use in photographs

KM# 903 6 PENCE

2.83 g., Copper-Nickel, 19.5 mm. **Ruler:** Elizabeth II **Obv:** Laureate bust right **Obv. Legend:** Without BRITT OMN **Rev:** Flora; leek, rose, thistle and shamrock **Edge:** Reeded

Date	Mintage	F12	VF20	XF40	MS60	MS63
1954	105,241,000	—	0.75	1.50	8.00	10.00
1954	—	PF63 600				
1955	109,930,000	—	0.75	1.50	4.00	5.00
1955	—	PF63 600				
1956	109,842,000	—	0.75	1.50	5.00	7.50
1956	—	PF63 600				
1957	105,654,000	—	0.75	1.50	4.00	5.00
1957	—	PF63 600				
1958	123,519,000	—	0.75	2.50	10.00	12.50
1958	—	PF63 600				
1959	93,089,000	—	0.75	1.50	3.00	4.00
1959	—	PF63 600				
1960	103,283,000	—	0.75	2.50	7.00	8.00
1960	—	PF63 600				
1961	115,052,000	—	0.75	1.50	6.00	7.50
1961	—	PF63 600				
1962	166,484,000	—	0.15	0.75	2.00	3.00
1962	—	PF63 600				
1963	120,056,000	—	0.15	0.75	2.00	3.00
1963	—	PF63 600				
1964	152,336,000	—	0.10	0.75	2.00	3.00
1964 Proof	—	—	—	—	—	—
Note: Requires Confirmation						
1965	129,644,000	—	0.10	0.75	1.50	2.50
1965 Proof	—	—	—	—	—	—
Note: Requires Confirmation						
1966	175,676,000	—	0.10	0.75	1.50	2.50
1966 Proof	—	—	—	—	—	—
Note: Requires Confirmation						
1967 Proof	—	—	—	—	—	—
Note: Requires Confirmation						
1967	240,788,000	—	0.10	0.75	1.50	2.50
1970	750,000	PF63 10.00				

KM# 780 SHILLING

5.66 g., 0.925 Silver 0.1682 oz. ASW, 23.5 mm. **Ruler:** Victoria **Obv:** Mature draped bust left **Obv. Legend:** VICTORIA • DEI • GRA • BRITT • REGINA • FID • DEF • IND • IMP • **Rev:** Crowned shields of England, Scotland and Ireland

Date	Mintage	F12	VF20	XF40	MS60	MS63
1901	3,426,000	18.00	27.00	75.00	165	215

KM# 800 SHILLING
5.66 g., 0.925 Silver 0.1682 oz. ASW, 23.5 mm. **Ruler:** Edward VII **Obv:** Head right **Rev:** Lion atop crown dividing date

Date	Mintage	F12	VF20	XF40	MS60	MS63
1902	7,890,000	8.00	16.00	65.00	110	135
1902 Matte Proof	15,000	PF63 115				
1903	2,061,999	10.00	25.00	175	550	600
1904	2,040,000	10.00	20.00	150	450	500
1905	488,000	125	350	1,350	3,000	3,500
1906	10,791,000	8.00	15.00	80.00	250	300
1907	14,083,000	8.00	15.00	90.00	275	375
1908	3,807,000	15.00	30.00	190	600	650
1909	5,665,000	15.00	30.00	190	600	650
1910	26,547,000	6.00	15.00	75.00	150	175

KM# 816 SHILLING
5.66 g., 0.925 Silver 0.1682 oz. ASW, 23.5 mm. **Ruler:** George V **Obv:** Head left **Rev:** Lion atop crown dividing date **Note:** Fully struck 1914-1918 pieces command a premium.

Date	Mintage	F12	VF20	XF40	MS60	MS63
1911	20,066,000	5.75	12.00	40.00	80.00	105
1911	6,007	PF63 100				
1912	15,594,000	6.00	15.00	45.00	125	150
1913	9,002,000	9.50	20.00	75.00	200	225
1914	23,416,000	5.75	12.00	40.00	85.00	110
1915	39,279,000	5.50	6.50	35.00	80.00	105
1916	35,862,000	5.50	6.50	35.00	80.00	105
1917	22,203,000	5.50	6.50	40.00	110	135
1918	34,916,000	5.50	6.50	35.00	80.00	105
1919	10,824,000	5.50	10.00	45.00	95.00	120

KM# 816a SHILLING
5.66 g., 0.500 Silver 0.0909 oz. ASW, 23.5 mm. **Ruler:** George V **Obv:** Head left **Rev:** Lion atop crown dividing date

Date	Mintage	F12	VF20	XF40	MS60	MS63
1920	22,825,000	5.00	15.00	45.00	90.00	115
1921	22,649,000	5.00	20.00	65.00	150	175
1922	27,216,000	4.00	6.00	45.00	85.00	110
1923	14,575,000	4.00	6.00	30.00	85.00	110
1924	2	—	—	—	—	2,500
Note: Satin specimen						
1924	9,250,000	4.00	12.00	55.00	90.00	115
1925	5,419,000	5.00	15.00	65.00	150	175
1926	22,516,000	4.00	10.00	35.00	85.00	110

KM# 829 SHILLING
5.66 g., 0.500 Silver 0.0909 oz. ASW, 23.5 mm. **Ruler:** George V **Obv:** Modified head left **Rev:** Lion atop crown dividing date

Date	Mintage	F12	VF20	XF40	MS60	MS63
1926	Inc. above	3.00	4.50	30.00	60.00	75.00
1927	9,262,000	3.25	6.00	40.00	70.00	85.00

KM# 833 SHILLING
5.66 g., 0.500 Silver 0.0909 oz. ASW, 23.5 mm. **Ruler:** George V **Obv:** Head left **Rev:** Lion atop crown

Date	Mintage	F12	VF20	XF40	MS60	MS63
1927	Inc. above	3.00	4.50	20.00	60.00	—
1927	15,000	PF63 75.00				
1927 Matte Proof	—	PF63 3,000				
Note: There are reportedly 1-2 of this variety, struck specifically for use in photographs						

Date	Mintage	F12	VF20	XF40	MS60	MS63
1928	18,137,000	3.00	3.50	15.00	45.00	55.00
1928	—	PF63 1,000				
1929	19,343,000	3.00	3.50	15.00	45.00	55.00
1929	—	PF63 1,000				
1930	3,137,000	5.00	16.00	50.00	125	150
1930	—	PF63 1,000				
1931	6,994,000	3.00	4.00	15.00	50.00	60.00
1931	—	PF63 1,000				
1932	12,168,000	3.00	4.00	15.00	50.00	60.00
1932	—	PF63 1,000				
1933	11,512,000	3.00	3.50	15.00	50.00	60.00
1933	—	PF63 1,000				
1934	6,138,000	3.25	5.50	20.00	60.00	75.00
1934	—	PF63 1,000				
1935	9,183,000	3.00	3.50	15.00	45.00	55.00
1935	—	PF63 1,000				
1936	11,911,000	3.00	3.50	10.00	35.00	45.00
1936	—	PF63 1,000				

KM# 853 SHILLING
5.66 g., 0.500 Silver 0.0909 oz. ASW, 23.5 mm. **Ruler:** George VI **Obv:** Head left **Rev:** Lion atop crown dividing date

Date	Mintage	F12	VF20	XF40	MS60	MS63
1937	8,359,000	3.00	5.00	7.00	22.00	25.00
1937	26,000	PF63 22.00				
1937 Matte Proof	—	PF63 2,500				
Note: There are reportedly 1-2 known of this variety, struck specifically for use in photographs						
1938	4,833,000	3.00	5.00	8.00	45.00	55.00
1938	—	PF63 850				
1939	11,053,000	1.70	3.00	4.50	20.00	25.00
1939	—	PF63 800				
1940	11,099,000	1.70	3.50	5.00	25.00	30.00
1940	—	PF63 800				
1941	11,392,000	1.70	3.00	5.00	20.00	25.00
1941	—	PF63 800				
1942	17,454,000	1.70	3.00	5.00	20.00	25.00
1942	—	PF63 800				
1943	11,404,000	1.70	3.00	5.00	20.00	25.00
1943	—	PF63 800				
1944	11,587,000	1.70	3.00	5.00	20.00	25.00
1944	—	PF63 850				
1945	15,143,000	1.70	3.00	4.00	15.00	20.00
1945	—	PF63 1,000				
1946	18,664,000	1.70	3.00	4.00	15.00	20.00
1946	—	PF63 1,200				

KM# 854 SHILLING
5.66 g., 0.500 Silver 0.0909 oz. ASW, 23.5 mm. **Ruler:** George VI **Obv:** Head left **Rev:** Scottish crest; lion seated atop crown holding sword and scepter divides date, shields flank **Edge:** Reeded

Date	Mintage	F12	VF20	XF40	MS60	MS63
1937	6,749,000	3.00	4.00	6.00	15.00	20.00
1937	26,000	PF63 22.00				
1937 Matte Proof	—	PF63 2,500				
Note: There are reportedly 1-2 known of this variety, struck specifically for use in photographs						
1938	4,798,000	3.00	5.00	9.00	40.00	45.00
1938	—	PF63 850				
1939	10,264,000	3.00	4.00	5.00	20.00	25.00
1939	—	PF63 800				
1940	9,913,000	3.00	4.00	6.00	25.00	30.00
1940	—	PF63 800				
1941	8,086,000	3.00	4.00	6.00	25.00	30.00
1941	—	PF63 800				
1942	13,677,000	3.00	4.00	6.00	25.00	30.00
1942	—	PF63 800				
1943	9,824,000	3.00	4.00	6.00	20.00	25.00
1943	—	PF63 800				
1944	10,990,000	3.00	4.00	6.00	20.00	25.00
1944	—	PF63 850				
1945	15,106,000	3.00	4.00	6.00	15.00	20.00
1945	—	PF63 1,200				
1946	16,382,000	3.00	4.00	6.00	15.00	20.00
1946	—	PF63 1,200				

KM# 863 SHILLING
5.65 g., Copper-Nickel, 23.5 mm. **Ruler:** George VI **Obv:** Head left **Rev:** English crest; lion atop crown dividing date **Edge:** Reeded

Date	Mintage	F12	VF20	XF40	MS60	MS63
1947	12,121,000	0.50	1.00	2.50	12.00	15.00
1947	—	PF63 800				
1948	45,577,000	0.50	1.00	2.50	12.00	15.00
1948	—	PF63 1,200				

KM# 864 SHILLING
5.65 g., Copper-Nickel, 23.5 mm. **Ruler:** George VI **Obv:** Head left **Rev:** Scottish crest; lion seated atop crown holding sword and scepter divides date, shields flank **Edge:** Reeded

Date	Mintage	F12	VF20	XF40	MS60	MS63
1947	12,283,000	0.50	1.00	2.50	12.00	15.00
1947	—	PF63 800				
1948	45,352,000	0.50	1.00	2.50	12.00	15.00
1948	—	PF63 1,200				

KM# 876 SHILLING
5.65 g., Copper-Nickel, 23.5 mm. **Ruler:** George VI **Obv:** Head left **Rev:** English crest; lion atop crown dividing date **Edge:** Reeded

Date	Mintage	F12	VF20	XF40	MS60	MS63
1949	19,328,000	1.00	2.50	5.00	30.00	35.00
1949	—	PF63 850				
1950	19,244,000	1.00	2.00	5.00	30.00	35.00
1950	18,000	PF63 30.00				
1950 Matte Proof	—	PF63 1,800				
Note: There are reportedly 1-2 known of this variety, struck specifically for use in photographs						
1951	9,957,000	1.00	3.00	6.00	30.00	35.00
1951	20,000	PF63 25.00				
1951 Matte Proof	—	PF63 1,800				
Note: There are reportedly 1-2 known of this variety, struck specifically for use in photographs						
1952 Proof; Rare	—	—	—	—	—	—
Note: There are reportedly 1-2 known of this variety.						

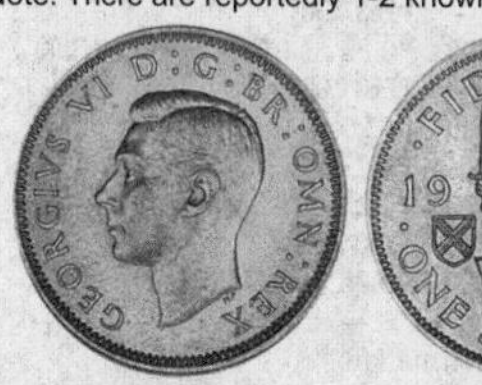

KM# 877 SHILLING
5.65 g., Copper-Nickel, 23.5 mm. **Ruler:** George VI **Obv:** Head left **Rev:** Scottish crest; lion seated atop crown holding sword and scepter divides date, shields flank **Edge:** Reeded

Date	Mintage	F12	VF20	XF40	MS60	MS63
1949	21,243,000	1.00	2.50	5.00	30.00	35.00
1949	—	PF63 850				
1950	14,300,000	1.00	2.00	8.00	30.00	35.00
1950	18,000	PF63 30.00				
1950 Matte Proof	—	PF63 1,800				
Note: There are reportedly 1-2 known of this variety, struck specifically for use in photographs						
1951	10,961,000	1.00	3.00	6.00	30.00	35.00
1951	20,000	PF63 25.00				
1951 Matte Proof	—	PF63 1,600				
Note: There are reportedly 1-2 known of this variety, struck specifically for use in photographs						

KM# 890 SHILLING

5.65 g., Copper-Nickel, 23.5 mm. **Ruler:** Elizabeth II **Obv:** Laureate bust right **Rev:** Crowned English shield divides date **Edge:** Reeded

Date	Mintage	F12	VF20	XF40	MS60	MS63
1953	41,943,000	0.50	1.00	2.00	7.00	9.00
1953	40,000	**PF63** 14.00				
1953 Matte Proof	—	**PF63** 1,800				

Note: There are reportedly 1-2 known of this variety, struck specifically for use in photographs

KM# 891 SHILLING

5.65 g., Copper-Nickel, 23.5 mm. **Ruler:** Elizabeth II **Obv:** Laureate bust right **Rev:** Crowned Scottish shield divides date **Edge:** Reeded

Date	Mintage	F12	VF20	XF40	MS60	MS63
1953	20,664,000	0.50	1.00	2.00	7.50	9.50
1953	40,000	**PF63** 14.00				
1953 Matte Proof	—	**PF63** 1,800				

Note: There are reportedly 1-2 known of this variety, struck specifically for use in photographs

KM# 904 SHILLING

5.65 g., Copper-Nickel, 23.5 mm. **Ruler:** Elizabeth II **Obv:** Laureate bust right **Obv. Legend:** without BRITT OMN **Rev:** Crowned English shield divides date **Edge:** Reeded

Date	Mintage	F12	VF20	XF40	MS60	MS63
1954	30,162,000	0.25	0.50	1.00	6.50	8.00
1954	—	**PF63** 700				
1955	45,260,000	0.25	0.50	1.00	6.50	8.00
1955	—	**PF63** 700				
1956	44,970,000	0.50	1.00	2.00	12.00	15.00
1956	—	**PF63** 700				
1957	42,774,000	0.25	0.50	1.00	6.00	7.50
1957	—	**PF63** 700				
1958	14,392,000	2.00	3.50	8.00	65.00	75.00
1958	—	**PF63** 800				
1959	19,443,000	0.25	0.50	1.00	6.00	7.50
1959	—	**PF63** 700				
1960	27,028,000	0.50	1.00	2.00	10.00	12.50
1960	—	**PF63** 700				
1961	39,817,000	0.25	0.35	0.50	3.00	4.00
1961	—	**PF63** 700				
1962	36,704,000	0.25	0.35	0.50	2.00	3.00
1962	—	**PF63** 700				
1963	49,434,000	0.25	0.35	0.50	2.00	3.00
1963	—	**PF63** 750				
1964	8,591,000	0.25	0.35	0.50	2.00	3.00
1964 Proof	—	—	—	—	—	—

Note: Requires Confirmation

Date	Mintage	F12	VF20	XF40	MS60	MS63
1965	9,216,000	0.25	0.35	0.50	2.00	3.00
1965 Proof	—	—	—	—	—	—

Note: Requires Confirmation

Date	Mintage	F12	VF20	XF40	MS60	MS63
1966	15,002,000	0.25	0.35	0.50	2.00	3.00
1966 Proof	—	—	—	—	—	—

Note: Requires Confirmation

Date	Mintage	F12	VF20	XF40	MS60	MS63
1970	750,000	**PF63** 10.00				

KM# 905 SHILLING

5.65 g., Copper-Nickel, 23.5 mm. **Ruler:** Elizabeth II **Obv:** Laureate bust right **Rev:** Crowned Scottish shield divides date **Edge:** Reeded

Date	Mintage	F12	VF20	XF40	MS60	MS63
1954	26,772,000	0.25	0.50	1.00	6.50	8.00
1954	—	**PF63** 700				
1954 Matte Proof; Rare	Est. 2	—	—	—	—	—
1955	27,951,000	0.25	0.50	1.00	8.00	10.00
1955	—	**PF63** 700				
1956	42,854,000	0.25	0.50	2.00	12.00	15.00
1956	—	**PF63** 700				
1957	17,960,000	1.00	2.00	5.00	35.00	40.00
1957	—	**PF63** 800				
1958	40,823,000	0.25	0.50	1.00	6.00	7.50
1958	—	**PF63** 700				
1959	1,012,999	2.00	5.00	10.00	90.00	100
1959	—	**PF63** 800				
1960	14,376,000	0.50	1.00	2.00	10.00	12.50
1960	—	**PF63** 700				
1961	2,763,000	1.00	2.00	3.00	20.00	25.00
1961	—	**PF63** 700				
1962	17,475,000	0.25	0.50	0.75	5.00	6.50
1962	—	**PF63** 700				
1963	32,299,999	0.25	0.35	0.50	2.00	3.00
1963	—	**PF63** 750				
1964	5,239,000	0.25	0.35	0.50	2.00	3.00
1964 Proof	—	—	—	—	—	—

Note: Requires Confirmation

Date	Mintage	F12	VF20	XF40	MS60	MS63
1965	2,774,000	0.25	0.35	0.50	2.00	3.00
1965 Proof	—	—	—	—	—	—

Note: Requires Confirmation

Date	Mintage	F12	VF20	XF40	MS60	MS63
1966	15,604,000	0.25	0.35	0.50	2.00	3.00
1966 Proof	—	—	—	—	—	—

Note: Requires Confirmation

Date	Mintage	F12	VF20	XF40	MS60	MS63
1970	750,000	**PF63** 8.00				

KM# 781 FLORIN (Two Shillings)

11.31 g., 0.925 Silver 0.3364 oz. ASW, 28.3 mm. **Ruler:** Victoria **Obv:** Mature draped bust left **Obv. Legend:** VICTORIA • DEI • GRA • BRITT • REGINA • FID • DEF • IND • IMP • **Rev:** Crowned shields of England, Scotland and Ireland **Edge:** Reeded

Date	Mintage	F12	VF20	XF40	MS60	MS63
1901	2,649,000	12.00	25.00	70.00	150	200

KM# 801 FLORIN (Two Shillings)

11.31 g., 0.925 Silver 0.3364 oz. ASW, 28.3 mm. **Ruler:** Edward VII **Obv:** Head right **Rev:** Britannia standing looking right **Edge:** Reeded

Date	Mintage	F12	VF20	XF40	MS60	MS63
1902	2,190,000	11.00	25.00	75.00	135	160
1902 Matte Proof	15,000	**PF63** 150				
1903	995,000	18.00	40.00	175	450	500
1904	2,770,000	20.00	50.00	250	575	650
1905	1,188,000	70.00	200	800	1,750	2,100
1906	6,910,000	15.00	35.00	175	500	575
1907	5,948,000	15.00	45.00	200	525	600
1908	3,280,000	20.00	55.00	335	800	900
1909	3,483,000	20.00	55.00	315	750	850
1910	5,651,000	15.00	30.00	135	375	425

KM# 817 FLORIN (Two Shillings)

11.31 g., 0.925 Silver 0.3364 oz. ASW, 28.3 mm. **Ruler:** George V **Obv:** Head left **Rev:** Cross of crowned shield, sceptres in angles **Edge:** Reeded **Note:** Fully struck examples are scarce

Date	Mintage	F12	VF20	XF40	MS60	MS63
1911	5,951,000	11.00	17.00	60.00	145	170
1911	6,007	**PF63** 165				
1912	8,572,000	11.00	20.00	75.00	200	225
1913	4,545,000	12.00	35.00	105	250	300
1914	21,253,000	11.00	15.00	50.00	105	135
1915	12,358,000	12.00	27.50	65.00	190	220
1916	21,064,000	11.00	15.00	50.00	100	125
1917	11,182,000	11.00	18.00	55.00	120	150
1918	29,212,000	11.00	15.00	45.00	100	125
1919	9,469,000	11.00	18.00	55.00	120	150

KM# 817a FLORIN (Two Shillings)

11.31 g., 0.500 Silver 0.1818 oz. ASW, 28.3 mm. **Ruler:** George V **Obv:** Head left **Rev:** Cross of crowned shields, sceptres in angles **Edge:** Reeded

Date	Mintage	F12	VF20	XF40	MS60	MS63
1920	15,388,000	7.00	15.00	60.00	150	175
1921	34,864,000	6.00	10.00	55.00	110	135
1922	23,861,000	6.00	9.00	50.00	95.00	120
1923	21,547,000	6.00	9.00	40.00	85.00	110
1924	4,582,000	7.00	15.00	65.00	140	165
1924 Satin specimen	2	—	—	—	—	2,500
1925	1,404,000	30.00	60.00	275	625	725
1926	5,125,000	7.00	15.00	65.00	140	165

KM# 834 FLORIN (Two Shillings)

11.31 g., 0.500 Silver 0.1818 oz. ASW, 28.3 mm. **Ruler:** George V **Obv:** Head left **Rev:** Cross of crowned sceptres, shields in angles **Edge:** Reeded

Date	Mintage	F12	VF20	XF40	MS60	MS63
1927	15,000	**PF63** 120				
1927 Matte Proof	—	**PF63** 3,500				

Note: There are reportedly 3-4 known of this variety, struck specifically for use in photographs

Date	Mintage	F12	VF20	XF40	MS60	MS63
1928	11,088,000	3.25	6.00	14.00	35.00	45.00
1928	—	**PF63** 1,000				
1929	16,397,000	3.25	6.00	18.00	50.00	60.00
1929	—	**PF63** 1,000				
1930	5,734,000	7.00	12.00	40.00	90.00	100
1930	—	**PF63** 1,350				
1931	6,556,000	6.00	7.00	20.00	65.00	75.00
1931	—	**PF63** 1,000				
1932	717,000	22.00	87.00	425	1,000	1,100
1932	—	**PF63** 3,000				
1933	8,685,000	6.00	7.00	15.00	60.00	70.00
1933	—	**PF63** 1,000				
1935	7,541,000	6.00	7.00	15.00	50.00	60.00
1935	—	**PF63** 1,000				
1936	9,897,000	6.00	7.00	10.00	35.00	45.00
1936	—	**PF63** 1,000				

KM# 855 FLORIN (Two Shillings)

11.31 g., 0.500 Silver 0.1818 oz. ASW, 28.3 mm. **Ruler:** George VI **Obv:** Head left **Rev:** Crowned tudor rose, thistle, letter 'G', and shamrock, letter 'R' flanking **Edge:** Reeded

Date	Mintage	F12	VF20	XF40	MS60	MS63
1937	13,007,000	—	6.00	7.00	20.00	25.00
1937	26,000	**PF63** 25.00				
1937 Matte Proof; Rare	—	—	—	—	—	—

Note: There are reportedly 1-2 known of this variety, struck specifically for use in photographs

Date	Mintage	F12	VF20	XF40	MS60	MS63
1938	7,909,000	6.00	7.00	10.00	45.00	55.00
1938	—	**PF63** 850				
1939	20,851,000	6.00	7.00	8.00	20.00	25.00
1939	—	**PF63** 800				
1940	18,700,000	6.00	7.00	8.00	25.00	30.00
1940	—	**PF63** 800				
1941	24,451,000	6.00	7.00	8.00	20.00	25.00
1941	—	**PF63** 800				
1942	39,895,000	—	7.00	8.00	20.00	25.00
1942	—	**PF63** 750				
1943	26,712,000	6.00	7.00	8.00	20.00	25.00
1943	—	**PF63** 650				
1944	27,560,000	—	7.00	8.00	20.00	25.00

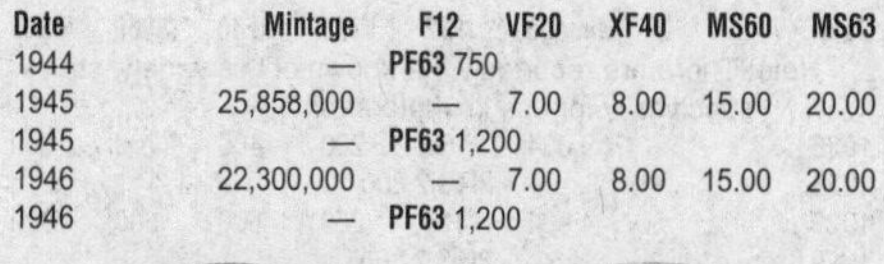

Date	Mintage	F12	VF20	XF40	MS60	MS63
1944	—	PF63 750				
1945	25,858,000	—	7.00	8.00	15.00	20.00
1945	—	PF63 1,200				
1946	22,300,000	—	7.00	8.00	15.00	20.00
1946	—	PF63 1,200				

KM# 865 FLORIN (Two Shillings)

11.31 g., Copper-Nickel, 28.3 mm. **Ruler:** George VI **Obv:** Head left **Rev:** Crowned tudor rose, thistle, letter 'G', and shamrock, letter 'R' flanking **Edge:** Reeded

Date	Mintage	F12	VF20	XF40	MS60	MS63
1947	22,910,000	0.20	0.50	2.00	12.00	15.00
1947	—	PF63 750				
1948	67,554,000	0.20	0.50	2.00	12.00	15.00
1948	—	PF63 1,000				

KM# 878 FLORIN (Two Shillings)

11.31 g., Copper-Nickel, 28.3 mm. **Ruler:** George VI **Obv:** Head left **Obv. Legend:** without IND IMP **Rev:** Crowned tudor rose, thistle, letter 'G', and shamrock, letter 'R' flanking **Edge:** Reeded

Date	Mintage	F12	VF20	XF40	MS60	MS63
1949	28,615,000	0.50	0.75	5.00	30.00	35.00
1949	—	PF63 800				
1950	24,357,000	0.50	0.75	8.00	30.00	35.00
1950	18,000	PF63 30.00				
1950 Matte Proof; Rare	—	—	—	—	—	—

Note: There are reportedly 1-2 known of this variety, struck specifically for use in photographs

Date	Mintage	F12	VF20	XF40	MS60	MS63
1951	27,412,000	0.50	0.75	8.00	35.00	40.00
1951	20,000	PF63 35.00				
1951 Matte Proof; Rare	—	—	—	—	—	—

Note: There are reportedly 1-2 known of this variety, struck specifically for use in photographs

KM# 892 FLORIN (Two Shillings)

11.31 g., Copper-Nickel, 28.3 mm. **Ruler:** Elizabeth II **Obv:** Laureate bust right **Rev:** Tudor rose at center, thistle and shamrock wreath surround **Edge:** Reeded

Date	Mintage	F12	VF20	XF40	MS60	MS63
1953	11,959,000	0.25	0.50	1.00	8.00	10.00
1953	40,000	PF63 15.00				
1953 Matte Proof; Rare	—	—	—	—	—	—

Note: There are reportedly 1-2 known of this variety, struck specifically for use in photographs

KM# 906 FLORIN (Two Shillings)

11.31 g., Copper-Nickel, 28.3 mm. **Ruler:** Elizabeth II **Obv:** Laureate bust right **Obv. Legend:** without BRITT OMN **Rev:** Tudor rose at center, thistle and shamrock wreath surround **Edge:** Reeded

Date	Mintage	F12	VF20	XF40	MS60	MS63
1954	13,085,000	1.00	2.50	8.00	50.00	60.00
1954	—	PF63 700				
1955	25,887,000	0.20	0.50	2.00	12.00	15.00
1955	—	PF63 700				
1956	47,824,000	0.20	0.30	1.00	12.00	15.00
1956	—	PF63 700				
1957	33,070,999	0.50	1.00	8.00	50.00	60.00
1957	—	PF63 750				
1958	9,565,000	1.00	2.50	10.00	50.00	60.00
1958	—	PF63 750				
1959	14,080,000	2.00	4.00	30.00	60.00	70.00
1959	—	PF63 700				
1960	13,832,000	0.50	1.00	3.00	15.00	20.00
1960	—	PF63 700				
1961	37,735,000	0.25	0.50	1.00	12.00	15.00
1961	—	PF63 700				
1962	35,148,000	0.25	0.50	1.50	5.00	7.50
1962	—	PF63 700				
1963	26,471,000	0.25	0.35	0.75	4.00	5.00
1963	—	PF63 700				
1964	16,539,000	0.25	0.35	0.75	4.00	5.00
1965	48,163,000	0.25	0.35	0.75	4.00	5.00
1966	83,999,000	—	0.25	0.50	3.00	4.00
1967	39,718,000	—	0.25	0.50	3.00	4.00
1970	750,000	PF63 8.00				

KM# 782 1/2 CROWN

14.14 g., 0.925 Silver 0.4205 oz. ASW, 32.3 mm. **Ruler:** Victoria **Obv:** Mature draped bust left **Rev:** Crowned and quartered spade shield within wreath **Rev. Legend:** FID • DEF • IND • IMP • around top, HALF date CROWN below **Edge:** Reeded

Date	Mintage	F12	VF20	XF40	MS60	MS63
1901	1,577,000	18.00	35.00	75.00	190	240

KM# 802 1/2 CROWN

14.14 g., 0.925 Silver 0.4205 oz. ASW, 32.3 mm. **Ruler:** Edward VII **Obv:** Head right **Rev:** Crowned and quartered shield within Garter band **Edge:** Reeded **Note:** Particular attention should be given to quality of detail in hair and beard on obverse.

Date	Mintage	F12	VF20	XF40	MS60	MS63
1902	1,316,000	20.00	40.00	100	250	300
1902 Matte Proof	15,000	PF63 200				
1903	275,000	200	625	2,500	5,000	5,500
1904	710,000	70.00	325	1,000	3,750	3,250
1905	166,000	600	1,750	5,000	10,500	12,500
1906	2,886,000	20.00	65.00	325	950	1,050
1907	3,694,000	20.00	60.00	300	900	1,000
1908	1,759,000	25.00	60.00	500	1,400	1,750
1909	3,052,000	20.00	55.00	400	1,150	1,350
1910	2,558,000	20.00	45.00	275	700	800

KM# 818.1 1/2 CROWN

14.14 g., 0.925 Silver 0.4205 oz. ASW, 32.3 mm. **Ruler:** George V **Obv:** Head left **Rev:** Crowned and quartered shield within Garter band **Edge:** Reeded **Note:** Fully struck World War I (1914-1918) specimens command a premium.

Date	Mintage	F12	VF20	XF40	MS60	MS63
1911	2,915,000	7.75	30.00	85.00	230	275
1911	6,007	PF63 250				
1912	4,701,000	7.75	30.00	80.00	300	350
1913	4,090,000	7.75	36.00	90.00	300	350
1914	18,333,000	7.75	15.00	45.00	120	150
1915	32,433,000	7.75	15.00	40.00	115	135
1916	29,530,000	7.75	15.00	40.00	115	135
1917	11,172,000	7.75	20.00	60.00	135	165
1918	29,080,000	7.75	15.00	45.00	110	135
1919	10,267,000	7.75	20.00	55.00	135	165

KM# 818.1a 1/2 CROWN

14.14 g., 0.500 Silver 0.2273 oz. ASW, 32.3 mm. **Ruler:** George V **Obv:** Head left **Rev:** Crowned shield within Garter rose, crown touches shield **Edge:** Reeded **Note:** Fully struck coins command a premium.

Date	Mintage	F12	VF20	XF40	MS60	MS63
1920	17,983,000	8.00	15.00	55.00	165	190
1921	23,678,000	8.00	15.00	60.00	150	175
1922	16,396,999	8.00	12.00	60.00	150	175

KM# 818.2 1/2 CROWN

14.14 g., 0.500 Silver 0.2273 oz. ASW, 32.3 mm. **Ruler:** George V **Obv:** Head left **Rev:** Crowned shield within Garter band, groove between crown and shield **Edge:** Reeded **Note:** Fully struck coins command a premium.

Date	Mintage	F12	VF20	XF40	MS60	MS63
1922	Inc. above	8.00	12.00	60.00	150	195
1923	26,309,000	4.25	8.00	40.00	85.00	100
1924	5,866,000	8.00	12.00	60.00	150	175
1924 Satin specimen	Est. 2	—	—	—	—	3,500
1925	1,413,000	30.00	80.00	375	975	1,075
1926	4,474,000	8.00	20.00	85.00	185	210

KM# 830 1/2 CROWN

14.14 g., 0.500 Silver 0.2273 oz. ASW, 32.3 mm. **Ruler:** George V **Obv:** Modified head left, larger beads **Rev:** Crowned shield within Garter band **Edge:** Reeded

Date	Mintage	F12	VF20	XF40	MS60	MS63
1926	Inc. above	8.00	25.00	85.00	220	245
1927	6,838,000	8.00	12.00	45.00	100	125

KM# 835 1/2 CROWN

14.14 g., 0.500 Silver 0.2273 oz. ASW, 32.3 mm. **Ruler:** George V **Obv:** Head left **Rev:** Quartered shield flanked by crowned monograms **Edge:** Reeded

Date	Mintage	F12	VF20	XF40	MS60	MS63
1927	15,000	PF63 120				
1927 Matte Proof; Rare	—	PF63 2,250				

Note: There are reportedly 1-2 known of this variety, struck specifically for use in photographs

Date	Mintage	F12	VF20	XF40	MS60	MS63
1928	18,763,000	4.25	8.00	18.00	45.00	55.00
1928	—	PF63 1,250				
1929	17,633,000	4.25	8.00	20.00	50.00	60.00
1929	—	PF63 1,250				
1930	810,000	25.00	90.00	375	1,000	1,100
1930	—	PF63 1,500				
1931	11,264,000	4.25	8.00	25.00	70.00	80.00
1931	—	PF63 1,250				
1932	4,794,000	4.25	10.00	25.00	90.00	100
1932	—	PF63 1,350				
1933	10,311,000	4.25	8.00	15.00	70.00	80.00
1933	—	PF63 2,150				
1934	2,422,000	8.00	12.00	75.00	195	215
1934	—	PF63 1,350				
1935	7,022,000	4.25	8.00	15.00	45.00	55.00
1935	—	PF63 1,200				
1936	7,039,000	4.25	8.00	12.00	35.00	45.00
1936	—	PF63 1,200				

KM# 856 1/2 CROWN

14.14 g., 0.500 Silver 0.2273 oz. ASW, 32.3 mm. **Ruler:** George VI **Obv:** Head left **Rev:** Quartered shield flanked by crowned monograms **Edge:** Reeded

Date	Mintage	F12	VF20	XF40	MS60	MS63
1937	9,106,000	4.25	8.00	10.00	25.00	30.00

Date	Mintage	F12	VF20	XF40	MS60	MS63
1937	26,000	**PF63** 35.00				
1937 Matte Proof; Rare	—	—	—	—	—	—

Note: There are reportedly 1-2 known of this variety, struck specifically for use in photographs

Date	Mintage	F12	VF20	XF40	MS60	MS63
1938	6,426,000	4.25	9.00	10.00	50.00	60.00
1938	—	**PF63** 1,250				
1939	15,479,000	4.25	8.00	10.00	25.00	30.00
1939	—	**PF63** 1,000				
1940	17,948,000	4.25	9.00	10.00	30.00	35.00
1940	—	**PF63** 1,000				
1941	15,774,000	4.25	8.00	10.00	25.00	30.00
1941	—	**PF63** 1,000				
1942	31,220,000	4.25	8.00	10.00	20.00	25.00
1942	—	**PF63** 1,000				
1943	15,463,000	4.25	8.00	10.00	25.00	30.00
1943	—	**PF63** 900				
1944	15,255,000	4.25	8.00	10.00	20.00	25.00
1944	—	**PF63** 900				
1945	19,849,000	4.25	8.00	10.00	20.00	25.00
1945	—	**PF63** 1,200				
1946	22,725,000	4.25	8.00	10.00	20.00	25.00
1946	—	**PF63** 1,200				

KM# 866 1/2 CROWN

14.14 g., Copper-Nickel, 32.3 mm. **Ruler:** George VI **Obv:** Head left **Rev:** Quartered shield flanked by crowned monograms **Edge:** Reeded

Date	Mintage	F12	VF20	XF40	MS60	MS63
1947	21,910,000	0.50	0.85	2.00	12.00	15.00
1947	—	**PF63** 900				
1948	71,165,000	0.50	0.75	1.50	10.00	12.50
1948	—	**PF63** 1,350				

KM# 879 1/2 CROWN

14.14 g., Copper-Nickel, 32.3 mm. **Ruler:** George VI **Obv:** Head left **Rev:** Quartered shield flanked by crowned monograms **Rev. Legend:** without IND IMP **Edge:** Reeded

Date	Mintage	F12	VF20	XF40	MS60	MS63
1949	28,273,000	0.50	1.50	5.00	25.00	30.00
1949	—	**PF63** 1,200				
1950	28,336,000	0.50	1.50	8.00	35.00	40.00
1950	18,000	**PF63** 40.00				
1950 Matte Proof; Rare	—	—	—	—	—	—

Note: There are reportedly 1-2 known of this variety, struck specifically for use in photographs

Date	Mintage	F12	VF20	XF40	MS60	MS63
1951	9,004,000	1.00	2.50	8.00	35.00	40.00
1951	20,000	**PF63** 35.00				
1951 Matte Proof; Rare	—	**PF63** 2,750				

Note: There are reportedly 1-2 known of this variety, struck specifically for use in photographs

Date	Mintage	F12	VF20	XF40	MS60	MS63
1952	Est. 1	—	80,000	—	—	—
1952	Est. 1	**PF63** 100,000				

KM# 893 1/2 CROWN

14.14 g., Copper-Nickel, 32.3 mm. **Ruler:** Elizabeth II **Obv:** Laureate bust right **Rev:** Crowned quartered shield flanked by initials, 'ER' **Edge:** Reeded

Date	Mintage	F12	VF20	XF40	MS60	MS63
1953	4,333,000	0.50	1.00	4.00	11.00	13.00
1953	40,000	**PF63** 20.00				
1953 Matte Proof; Rare	—	—	—	—	—	—

Note: There are reportedly 1-2 known of this variety, struck specifically for use in photographs

KM# 907 1/2 CROWN

14.14 g., Copper-Nickel, 32.3 mm. **Ruler:** Elizabeth II **Obv:** Laureate bust right **Obv. Legend:** without BRITT OMN **Rev:** Crowned quartered shield flanked by initials, 'ER' **Edge:** Reeded

Date	Mintage	F12	VF20	XF40	MS60	MS63
1954	11,615,000	1.00	2.50	8.00	50.00	60.00
1954	—	**PF63** 900				
1955	23,629,000	0.25	0.50	3.00	12.00	15.00
1955	—	**PF63** 900				
1956	33,935,000	0.25	1.00	4.50	18.00	22.00
1956	—	**PF63** 900				
1957	34,201,000	0.25	0.50	2.50	8.50	10.00
1957	—	**PF63** 900				
1958	15,746,000	1.00	2.50	8.00	40.00	45.00
1958	—	**PF63** 1,000				
1959	9,029,000	1.00	2.00	8.00	60.00	70.00
1959	—	**PF63** 1,000				
1960	19,929,000	0.25	0.50	1.00	20.00	25.00
1960	—	**PF63** 900				
1961	25,888,000	0.25	0.50	0.75	6.00	7.50
1961 Prooflike	—	—	—	—	25.00	30.00
1961	—	**PF63** 1,000				
1962	24,013,000	0.25	0.50	0.75	6.00	7.50
1962 Proof	—	—	—	—	—	—
1963	17,625,000	0.25	0.50	0.75	6.00	7.50
1963 Proof	—	—	—	—	—	—
1964	5,974,000	0.25	0.50	1.00	8.00	10.00
1965	9,778,000	0.20	0.30	0.50	6.00	7.50
1966	13,375,000	0.20	0.30	0.50	3.00	4.00
1967	33,058,000	0.20	0.30	0.50	3.00	4.00
1970	750,000	**PF63** 12.00				

KM# 803 CROWN

28.28 g., 0.925 Silver 0.8409 oz. ASW, 38.61 mm. **Ruler:** Edward VII **Obv:** Head right **Rev:** St. George slaying the dragon **Edge:** Lettered

Date	Mintage	F12	VF20	XF40	MS60	MS63
1902	256,000	80.00	140	240	375	425
1902 Matte Proof	15,000	**PF63** 325				

KM# 836 CROWN

28.28 g., 0.500 Silver 0.4545 oz. ASW, 38.61 mm. **Ruler:** George V **Obv:** Head left **Rev:** Date divided above crown within wreath

Date	Mintage	F12	VF20	XF40	MS60	MS63
1927	15,000	**PF63** 375				
1927 Matte Proof; Rare	—	**PF63** 12,500				

Note: There are reportedly 1-2 known of this variety, struck specifically for use in photographs

Date	Mintage	F12	VF20	XF40	MS60	MS63
1928	9,034	100	200	400	700	800
1928	—	**PF63** 2,800				
1929	4,994	115	250	500	800	900
1929	—	**PF63** 2,800				
1930	4,847	100	225	450	750	850
1930	—	**PF63** 2,800				
1931	4,056	110	250	475	725	825
1931	—	**PF63** 2,800				
1932	2,395	180	350	750	1,050	1,150
1932	—	**PF63** 3,500				
1933	7,132	100	200	425	700	800
1933	—	**PF63** 2,500				
1934	932	1,500	2,500	4,000	5,500	6,000
1934	—	**PF63** 10,000				
1936	2,473	175	350	775	1,100	1,200
1936	—	**PF63** 4,000				

KM# 842 CROWN

28.28 g., 0.500 Silver 0.4545 oz. ASW, 38.61 mm. **Ruler:** George V **Subject:** Silver Jubilee **Obv:** Head left **Rev:** St. George slaying the dragon

Date	Mintage	F12	VF20	XF40	MS60	MS63
1935	715,000	8.50	20.00	30.00	50.00	60.00

Note: Incused edge lettering

Date	Mintage	F12	VF20	XF40	MS60	MS63
1935	—	**PF63** 625				

Note: Raised edge lettering

Date	Mintage	F12	VF20	XF40	MS60	MS63
1935	—	—	—	—	85.00	—

Note: Specimen in box of issue

Date	Mintage	F12	VF20	XF40	MS60	MS63
1935	Inc. above	—	250	500	1,000	—

Note: (Error) Edge lettering: MEN.ANNO-REGNIXXV

KM# 842a CROWN

28.28 g., 0.925 Silver 0.8409 oz. ASW, 38.61 mm. **Ruler:** George V **Subject:** Silver Jubilee **Obv:** Head left **Rev:** St. George slaying the dragon **Edge:** Lettered

Date	Mintage	F12	VF20	XF40	MS60	MS63
1935	2,500	—	—	—	—	2,400

Note: Raised edge lettering

Date	Mintage	F12	VF20	XF40	MS60	MS63
1935	—	**PF63** 24,000				

Note: (Error) Edge lettering: DECUS ANNO REGNI TUTAMEN•XXV•

KM# 842b CROWN

47.83 g., 0.917 Gold 1.4101 oz. AGW, 38.61 mm. **Ruler:** George V **Subject:** Silver Jubilee **Obv:** Head left **Rev:** St. George slaying the dragon

Date	Mintage	F12	VF20	XF40	MS60	MS63
1935	28	**PF63** 32,500				

KM# 857 CROWN

28.28 g., 0.500 Silver 0.4545 oz. ASW, 38.61 mm. **Ruler:** George VI **Obv:** Head left **Rev:** Crowned, quartered shield with supporters **Edge:** Reeded

Date	Mintage	F12	VF20	XF40	MS60	MS63
1937	419,000	8.50	16.00	30.00	65.00	90.00
1937	26,000	PF63 85.00				
1937 Proof, VIP accentuated device cameo	—	PF63 1,100				

Note: Frosted cameo relief; V.I.P. issue

Date	Mintage	F12	VF20	XF40	MS60	MS63
1937 Matte Proof; Rare	—	PF63 6,000				

Note: 1-2 pieces known

KM# 880 CROWN

28.28 g., Copper-Nickel, 38.61 mm. **Ruler:** George VI **Subject:** Festival of Britain **Obv:** Head left **Rev:** St. George slaying the dragon

Date	Mintage	F12	VF20	XF40	MS60	MS63
1951 Prooflike	2,004,000	—	—	6.00	15.00	20.00
1951	—	PF63 25.00				
1951	—	PF63 900				

Note: Frosted cameo relief; V.I.P. issue; 30-50 pieces known

Date	Mintage	F12	VF20	XF40	MS60	MS63
1951 Matte Proof	—	PF63 4,000				

Note: 1-2 pieces known

KM# 894 CROWN

28.28 g., Copper-Nickel, 38.61 mm. **Ruler:** Elizabeth II **Subject:** Coronation of Queen Elizabeth II **Obv:** Queen on horseback left, crowned monograms flank **Rev:** Crown at center of cross formed by rose, shamrock, leek and thistle, shields in angles **Edge Lettering:** FAITH AND TRUTH I WILL BEAR UNTO YOU

Date	Mintage	F12	VF20	XF40	MS60	MS63
1953	5,963,000	—	—	7.50	12.00	15.00
1953	40,000	PF63 45.00				
1953	—	PF63 750				

Note: 20-30 pieces; V.I.P. issue

Date	Mintage	F12	VF20	XF40	MS60	MS63
1953 Matte Proof	—	PF63 4,000				

Note: 1-2 pieces

KM# 909 CROWN

28.28 g., Copper-Nickel, 38.61 mm. **Ruler:** Elizabeth II **Subject:** British Exhibition in New York **Obv:** Laureate bust right **Rev:** Crown at center of cross formed by rose, shamrock, leek and thistle, shields in angles **Edge:** Reeded

Date	Mintage	F12	VF20	XF40	MS60	MS63
1960	1,024,000	—	—	6.00	10.00	12.00
1960 Prooflike	70,000	—	—	10.00	25.00	35.00
1960	—	PF63 800				

Note: V.I.P. issue; 30-50 pieces

KM# 910 CROWN

28.28 g., Copper-Nickel, 38.61 mm. **Ruler:** Elizabeth II **Obv:** Laureate bust right **Rev:** Sir. Winston Churchill head right **Rev. Legend:** CHURCHILL **Edge:** Reeded

Date	Mintage	F12	VF20	XF40	MS60	MS63
1965	9,640,000	—	—	1.00	2.00	3.00
1965 Specimen	—	—	—	—	1,650	—

Note: Satin finish

DECIMAL COINAGE

1971-1981: 100 New Pence = 1 Pound;
1982-present: 100 Pence = 1 Pound

KM# 914 1/2 NEW PENNY

1.78 g., Bronze, 17.14 mm. **Ruler:** Elizabeth II **Obv:** Young bust right **Rev:** NEW PENNY above crown and value fraction

Date	Mintage	VF20	XF40	MS60	MS63	MS65
1971	1,394,188,250	—	0.15	0.75	1.25	1.75
1971	350,000	PF65 1.75				
1972	150,000	PF65 3.00				
1973	365,680,000	—	0.15	0.75	1.25	1.75
1973	100,000	PF65 2.50				
1974	365,448,000	—	0.15	0.75	1.25	1.75
1974	100,000	PF65 2.00				
1975	197,600,000	—	0.15	0.75	1.25	1.75
1975	100,000	PF65 2.00				
1976	412,172,000	—	0.15	0.75	1.25	1.75
1976	100,000	PF65 2.00				
1977	66,368,000	—	0.15	1.00	1.75	2.50
1977	193,000	PF65 2.00				
1978	59,532,000	—	0.15	1.00	1.75	2.50
1978	86,100	PF65 2.50				
1979	219,132,000	—	0.15	0.75	1.25	1.75
1979	81,000	PF65 2.50				
1980	202,788,000	—	0.15	0.75	1.25	1.75
1980	143,000	PF65 2.00				
1981	46,748,000	—	0.15	1.00	1.75	2.50
1981	100,300	PF65 2.50				

KM# 926 1/2 PENNY

1.78 g., Bronze, 17.14 mm. **Ruler:** Elizabeth II **Obv:** Young bust right **Rev:** HALF PENNY above crown and fraction

Date	Mintage	VF20	XF40	MS60	MS63	MS65
1982	190,752,000	—	0.15	0.75	1.25	1.75
1982	106,800	PF65 2.00				
1983	7,600,000	—	0.15	2.00	2.50	3.00
1983	107,800	PF65 3.00				
1984 Sets only	158,820	—	—	—	—	3.50
1984	106,520	PF65 3.50				

KM# 915 NEW PENNY

3.56 g., Bronze, 20.32 mm. **Ruler:** Elizabeth II **Obv:** Young bust right **Rev:** Crowned portocullis

Date	Mintage	VF20	XF40	MS60	MS63	MS65
1971	1,521,666,250	—	0.15	0.75	1.25	1.75
1971	350,000	PF65 2.00				
1972	150,000	PF65 3.50				
1973	280,196,000	—	0.15	1.00	1.75	2.50
1973	100,000	PF65 2.50				
1974	330,892,000	—	0.15	1.00	1.75	2.50
1974	100,000	PF65 2.50				
1975	221,604,000	—	0.15	1.00	1.75	2.50
1975	100,000	PF65 2.50				
1976	300,160,000	—	0.15	1.00	1.75	2.50
1976	100,000	PF65 2.50				
1977	285,430,000	—	0.15	1.00	1.75	2.50
1977	193,000	PF65 2.50				
1978	292,770,000	—	0.15	1.00	1.75	2.50
1978	86,100	PF65 2.50				
1979	459,000,000	—	0.15	1.00	1.75	2.50
1979	81,000	PF65 2.50				
1980	416,304,000	—	0.15	1.00	1.75	2.50
1980	143,000	PF65 2.50				
1981	301,800,000	—	0.15	1.00	1.75	2.50
1981	100,300	PF65 2.50				

KM# 927 PENNY

3.56 g., Bronze, 20.32 mm. **Ruler:** Elizabeth II **Obv:** Young bust right **Rev:** Crowned portcullis

Date	Mintage	VF20	XF40	MS60	MS63	MS65
1982	100,292,000	—	0.15	1.00	1.75	2.50
1982	106,800	PF65 2.50				
1983	243,002,000	—	0.15	1.00	1.75	2.50
1983	107,800	PF65 2.50				
1984	154,759,625	—	0.20	1.00	1.75	2.50
1984	106,520	PF65 2.50				

KM# 935 PENNY

3.56 g., Bronze, 20.32 mm. **Ruler:** Elizabeth II **Obv:** Crowned head right **Rev:** Crowned portcullis

Date	Mintage	VF20	XF40	MS60	MS63	MS65
1985	200,605,245	—	0.15	1.00	1.75	2.50
1985	102,015	PF65 2.50				
1986	369,989,130	—	0.15	1.00	1.75	2.50
1986	104,597	PF65 2.50				
1987	499,946,000	—	0.15	1.00	1.75	2.50
1987	88,659	PF65 2.50				
1988	793,492,000	—	0.15	1.00	1.75	2.50
1988	79,314	PF65 2.50				
1989	658,142,000	—	0.15	1.00	1.75	2.50
1989	85,704	PF65 2.50				
1990	529,047,500	—	0.15	1.00	1.75	2.50
1990	79,052	PF65 2.50				
1991	206,457,600	—	0.15	1.00	1.75	2.50
1991	55,144	PF65 2.50				
1992 Sets only	—	—	—	—	—	3.50
1992	44,337	PF65 3.50				

KM# 935a PENNY

3.56 g., Copper Plated Steel, 20.32 mm. **Ruler:** Elizabeth II **Obv:** Crowned head right **Rev:** Crowned portcullis

Date	Mintage	VF20	XF40	MS60	MS63	MS65
1992	253,867,000	—	0.15	0.20	1.00	1.50
1993	602,590,000	—	0.15	0.20	1.00	1.50
1993	66,080	PF65 1.25				
1994	843,834,000	—	0.15	0.20	1.00	1.50
1994	44,643	PF65 1.25				
1995	303,314,000	—	0.15	0.20	1.00	1.50
1995	42,842	PF65 1.25				
1996	723,840,060	—	—	0.20	1.00	1.50
1996	46,295	PF65 1.25				
1997	396,874,000	—	—	0.20	1.00	1.50
1997	80,748	PF65 1.25				

KM# 935b PENNY

3.56 g., 0.925 Silver 0.1059 oz. ASW, 20.32 mm. **Ruler:** Elizabeth II **Obv:** Crowned head right **Rev:** Crowned portcullis

Date	Mintage	VF20	XF40	MS60	MS63	MS65
1996	—	PF65 16.00				

KM# 986 PENNY

3.56 g., Copper Plated Steel, 20.32 mm. **Ruler:** Elizabeth II **Subject:** Badge of Henry VII **Obv:** Head with tiara right **Rev:** Crowned portcullis with chains **Edge:** Plain

Date	Mintage	VF20	XF40	MS60	MS63	MS65
1998	739,770,000	—	0.15	1.00	1.75	2.50
1998	63,670	PF65 3.25				
1999	891,392,000	—	0.15	1.00	1.75	2.50
2000	1,060,420,000	—	0.15	1.00	1.75	2.50
2000	72,469	PF65 3.25				

KM# 986a PENNY

3.50 g., Bronze, 20.3 mm. **Ruler:** Elizabeth II **Obv:** Head with tiara right **Rev:** Crowned portcullis **Edge:** Plain **Mint:** British Royal Mint

Date	Mintage	VF20	XF40	MS60	MS63	MS65
1999	80,144	PF65 3.25				
1999 Sets only	916,000,000	—	0.15	1.00	1.75	2.50

KM# 986b PENNY

3.56 g., 0.925 Silver 0.1059 oz. ASW, 20.3 mm. **Ruler:** Elizabeth II **Obv:** Head with tiara right **Rev:** Crowned portcullis **Edge:** Plain **Mint:** British Royal Mint

Date	Mintage	VF20	XF40	MS60	MS63	MS65
2000	15,000	PF65 16.50				

KM# 916 2 NEW PENCE

7.12 g., Bronze, 25.91 mm. **Ruler:** Elizabeth II **Obv:** Young bust right **Rev:** Welsh plumes and crown

Date	Mintage	VF20	XF40	MS60	MS63	MS65
1971	1,454,856,250	—	0.15	0.20	0.35	0.50
1971	350,000	PF65 1.50				
1972	150,000	PF65 1.50				
1973	100,000	PF65 1.50				
1974	100,000	PF65 1.50				
1975	145,545,000	—	0.15	0.20	0.35	0.50
1975	100,000	PF65 1.50				
1976	181,379,000	—	0.15	0.20	0.35	0.50
1976	100,000	PF65 1.50				
1977	109,281,000	—	0.15	0.20	0.35	0.50
1977	193,000	PF65 1.50				
1978	189,658,000	—	0.15	0.20	0.35	0.50
1978	86,100	PF65 1.50				
1979	260,200,000	—	0.15	0.20	0.35	0.50
1979	81,000	PF65 1.50				
1980	408,527,000	—	0.15	0.20	0.35	0.50
1980	143,000	PF65 1.50				
1981	353,191,000	—	0.15	0.20	0.35	0.50
1981	100,300	PF65 1.50				
1983	—	—	—	—	—	1,950

Note: An old reverse die was used in the production of 1983 Uncirculated sets. The "mule" has been found in a small number of these sets.

KM# 928 2 PENCE

7.12 g., Bronze, 25.91 mm. **Ruler:** Elizabeth II **Obv:** Young bust right **Rev:** Welsh plumes and crown **Note:** In sets only

Date	Mintage	VF20	XF40	MS60	MS63	MS65
1982	205,000	—	—	0.50	1.00	2.00
1982	106,800	PF65 1.50				
1983	631,000	—	—	0.50	1.00	2.00
1983	107,800	PF65 1.50				
1984	159,000	—	—	0.50	1.00	2.00
1984	106,520	PF65 1.50				

KM# 936 2 PENCE

7.12 g., Bronze, 25.91 mm. **Ruler:** Elizabeth II **Obv:** Crowned head right **Rev:** Welsh plumes and crown

Date	Mintage	VF20	XF40	MS60	MS63	MS65
1985	107,113,000	—	0.15	0.20	0.50	1.00
1985	102,015	PF65 1.50				
1986	168,967,500	—	0.15	0.20	0.50	1.00
1986	104,597	PF65 1.50				
1987	218,100,750	—	0.15	0.20	0.50	1.00
1987	88,659	PF65 1.50				
1988	419,889,000	—	0.15	0.20	0.50	1.00
1988	79,314	PF65 1.50				
1989	359,226,000	—	0.15	0.20	0.50	1.00
1989	85,704	PF65 1.50				
1990	204,499,700	—	0.15	0.20	0.50	1.00
1990	79,052	PF65 1.50				
1991	86,625,250	—	0.15	0.20	0.50	1.00
1991	55,144	PF65 1.50				
1992 Sets only	—	—	—	—	—	1.00
1992	62,326	PF65 1.50				

KM# 936a 2 PENCE

Copper Plated Steel, 25.91 mm. **Ruler:** Elizabeth II **Obv:** Crowned head right **Rev:** Welsh plumes and crown

Date	Mintage	VF20	XF40	MS60	MS63	MS65
1992	102,247,000	—	0.15	1.00	1.75	2.50
1993	235,674,000	—	0.15	1.00	1.75	2.50
1993	66,080	PF65 2.50				
1994	531,628,000	—	0.15	1.00	1.75	2.50
1994	66,721	PF65 3.00				
1995	124,482,000	—	0.15	1.00	1.75	2.50
1995	60,639	PF65 3.00				
1996	296,278,000	—	0.15	1.00	1.75	2.50
1996	67,581	PF65 3.00				
1997	496,116,000	—	0.15	1.00	1.75	2.50
1997	80,748	PF65 2.50				

KM# 936b 2 PENCE

7.12 g., 0.925 Silver 0.2117 oz. ASW, 25.91 mm. **Ruler:** Elizabeth II **Obv:** Crowned head right **Rev:** Welsh plumes and crown

Date	Mintage	VF20	XF40	MS60	MS63	MS65
1996	—	PF65 17.00				

KM# 987 2 PENCE

7.14 g., Copper Plated Steel, 25.86 mm. **Ruler:** Elizabeth II **Obv:** Head with tiara right **Rev:** Welsh plumes and crown **Edge:** Plain

Date	Mintage	VF20	XF40	MS60	MS63	MS65
1998	115,154,000	—	0.15	1.00	1.75	2.50
1998	63,670	PF65 2.50				
1999	353,816,000	—	0.15	1.00	1.75	2.50
1999	80,144	PF65 2.50				
2000	536,659,000	—	0.15	1.00	1.75	2.50
2000	72,469	PF65 2.50				

KM# 987a 2 PENCE

Bronze, 25.91 mm. **Ruler:** Elizabeth II **Obv:** Head with tiara right **Rev:** Welsh plumes and crown

Date	Mintage	VF20	XF40	MS60	MS63	MS65
1998	98,676,000	—	0.15	1.00	1.75	2.50
1998	63,670	PF65 2.50				
1999	460,000,000	—	0.15	1.00	1.75	2.50
1999	80,144	PF65 2.50				

KM# 987b 2 PENCE

7.12 g., 0.925 Silver 0.2117 oz. ASW, 25.9 mm. **Ruler:** Elizabeth II **Obv:** Head with tiara right **Rev:** Welsh plumes and crown **Edge:** Plain **Mint:** British Royal Mint

Date	Mintage	VF20	XF40	MS60	MS63	MS65
2000	15,000	PF65 18.50				

KM# 911 5 NEW PENCE

5.65 g., Copper-Nickel, 23.6 mm. **Ruler:** Elizabeth II **Obv:** Young bust right **Rev:** Crowned thistle **Edge:** Reeded

Date	Mintage	VF20	XF40	MS60	MS63	MS65
1968	98,868,250	—	0.25	0.50	1.00	1.75
1969	120,270,000	—	0.25	0.50	1.00	1.75
1970	225,948,525	—	0.25	0.75	1.50	1.75
1971	81,783,475	—	0.25	0.75	1.50	1.75
1971	350,000	PF65 2.50				
1972	150,000	PF65 4.00				
1973	100,000	PF65 4.50				
1974	100,000	PF65 4.50				
1975	141,539,000	—	0.25	0.75	1.50	2.00
1975	100,000	PF65 2.50				
1976	100,000	PF65 4.50				
1977	24,308,000	—	0.25	1.00	2.00	2.50
1977	193,000	PF65 3.00				
1978	61,094,000	—	0.25	0.75	1.50	2.00
1978	86,100	PF65 3.50				
1979	155,456,000	—	0.25	0.75	1.50	2.00
1979	81,000	PF65 3.50				
1980	220,566,000	—	0.25	0.75	1.50	2.00
1980	143,000	PF65 2.50				
1981	100,300	PF65 3.50				

KM# 929 5 PENCE

5.65 g., Copper-Nickel, 23.59 mm. **Ruler:** Elizabeth II **Obv:** Young bust right **Rev:** Crowned thistle **Note:** In sets only

Date	Mintage	VF20	XF40	MS60	MS63	MS65
1982	205,000	—	—	—	3.00	3.50
1982	106,800	PF65 3.00				
1983	637,000	—	—	—	2.50	3.00
1983	107,800	PF65 3.00				
1984	159,000	—	—	—	3.50	4.00
1984	106,520	PF65 3.50				

KM# 937 5 PENCE

5.65 g., Copper-Nickel, 23.6 mm. **Ruler:** Elizabeth II **Obv:** Crowned head right **Rev:** Modified design, Five Pence is away from the edge **Edge:** Reeded

Date	Mintage	VF20	XF40	MS60	MS63	MS65
1985 Sets only	178,000	—	—	—	3.00	3.50
1985	102,015	PF65 3.00				
1986 Sets only	167,000	—	—	—	3.00	3.50
1986	104,597	PF65 3.00				
1987	48,220,000	—	0.25	1.00	2.00	2.50
1987	88,659	PF65 3.00				
1988	120,744,610	—	0.25	1.00	2.00	2.50
1988	79,314	PF65 3.00				
1989	101,406,000	—	0.25	1.00	2.00	2.50
1989	85,704	PF65 3.00				
1990 Sets only	—	—	—	—	3.00	—
1990	79,052	PF65 3.00				

KM# 937a 5 PENCE

5.60 g., 0.925 Silver 0.1665 oz. ASW, 23.59 mm. **Ruler:** Elizabeth II **Obv:** Crowned head right **Rev:** Crowned thistle

Date	Mintage	VF20	XF40	MS60	MS63	MS65
1990	35,000	PF65 22.00				

KM# 937b 5 PENCE

3.25 g., Copper-Nickel, 18 mm. **Ruler:** Elizabeth II **Obv:** Crowned head right **Rev:** Crowned thistle **Note:** Reduced size. Varieties in thickness and edge milling exist.

Date	Mintage	VF20	XF40	MS60	MS63	MS65
1990	1,634,976,005	—	0.25	1.00	2.00	2.50
1990	79,052	PF65 2.50				
1991	724,979,000	—	0.25	1.00	2.00	2.50
1991	55,144	PF65 2.50				
1992	453,173,500	—	0.25	1.00	2.00	2.50
1992	62,326	PF65 2.50				

Date	Mintage	VF20	XF40	MS60	MS63	MS65
1993 Sets only	56,945	—	0.25	1.00	2.00	2.50
1993	66,080	PF65 2.50				
1994	93,602,000	—	0.25	1.00	2.00	2.50
1994	44,649	PF65 2.50				
1995	183,384,000	—	0.25	1.00	2.00	2.50
1995	60,639	PF65 2.50				
1996	302,902,000	—	0.25	1.00	2.00	2.50
1996	67,581	PF65 2.50				
1997	236,596,000	—	0.25	1.00	2.00	2.50
1997	80,748	PF65 2.50				

KM# 937c 5 PENCE

3.25 g., 0.925 Silver 0.0967 oz. ASW, 18 mm. **Ruler:** Elizabeth II **Obv:** Crowned head right **Rev:** Crowned thistle

Date	Mintage	VF20	XF40	MS60	MS63	MS65
1990	35,000	PF65 16.00				
Note: Also exists as a Piedfort, P12.						
1996	—	PF65 16.00				

KM# 988 5 PENCE

3.25 g., Copper-Nickel, 18 mm. **Ruler:** Elizabeth II **Obv:** Head with tiara right **Rev:** Crowned thistle

Date	Mintage	VF20	XF40	MS60	MS63	MS65
1998	217,376,000	—	0.25	1.00	2.00	2.50
1998	63,670	PF65 3.00				
1999	195,490,000	—	0.25	1.00	2.00	2.50
1999	80,144	PF65 3.00				
2000	388,512,000	—	0.25	1.00	2.00	2.50
2000	72,469	PF65 3.00				

KM# 988a 5 PENCE

3.25 g., 0.925 Silver 0.0967 oz. ASW, 18 mm. **Ruler:** Elizabeth II **Obv:** Head with tiara right **Rev:** Crowned thistle **Edge:** Reeded **Mint:** British Royal Mint

Date	Mintage	VF20	XF40	MS60	MS63	MS65
2000	15,000	PF65 22.50				

KM# 912 10 NEW PENCE

11.31 g., Copper-Nickel, 28.5 mm. **Ruler:** Elizabeth II **Obv:** Young bust right **Rev:** Crowned lion prancing left **Edge:** Reeded

Date	Mintage	VF20	XF40	MS60	MS63	MS65
1968	336,143,250	—	0.35	0.75	1.50	2.00
1969	314,008,000	—	0.35	0.75	1.50	2.00
1970	133,571,000	—	0.50	1.00	2.00	2.50
1971	63,205,000	—	0.50	1.50	3.00	3.50
1971 Proof	350,000	—	—	—	—	—
1972	150,000	PF65 5.00				
1973	152,174,000	—	0.50	1.00	2.00	2.50
1973	100,000	PF65 2.50				
1974	92,741,000	—	0.50	1.00	2.00	2.50
1974	100,000	PF65 2.50				
1975	181,559,000	—	0.50	1.00	2.00	2.50
1975	100,000	PF65 2.50				
1976	228,220,000	—	0.50	1.00	2.00	2.50
1976	100,000	PF65 2.50				
1977	59,323,000	—	0.50	1.25	2.50	3.00
1977	193,000	PF65 2.50				
1978	86,100	PF65 5.25				
1979	115,457,000	—	0.50	1.00	2.00	2.50
1979	81,000	PF65 3.00				
1980	88,650,000	—	0.50	1.00	2.00	2.50
1980	143,000	PF65 2.50				
1981	3,487,000	0.25	0.50	1.50	3.00	3.50
1981	100,300	PF65 3.00				

KM# 930 10 PENCE

11.31 g., Copper-Nickel, 28.5 mm. **Ruler:** Elizabeth II **Obv:** Young bust right **Rev:** Crowned lion prancing left **Note:** In sets only

Date	Mintage	VF20	XF40	MS60	MS63	MS65
1982	205,000	—	0.50	1.75	3.50	4.00
1982	106,800	PF65 3.00				
1983	637,000	—	0.50	1.50	3.00	3.50
1983	107,800	PF65 3.00				
1984	159,000	—	—	1.75	3.50	4.00
1984	106,520	PF65 3.00				

KM# 938 10 PENCE

11.31 g., Copper-Nickel, 28.5 mm. **Ruler:** Elizabeth II **Obv:** Crowned head right **Rev:** Modified design, TEN PENCE is away from the edge **Note:** In sets only

Date	Mintage	VF20	XF40	MS60	MS63	MS65
1985	178,000	—	0.50	1.75	3.50	4.00
1985	102,015	PF65 3.00				
1986	167,000	—	0.50	1.75	3.50	4.00
1986	104,597	PF65 3.00				
1987	172,000	—	0.50	1.75	3.50	4.00
1987	88,659	PF65 3.00				
1988	134,000	—	0.50	1.75	3.50	4.00
1988	79,314	PF65 3.00				
1989	78,000	—	0.50	1.75	3.50	4.00
1989	85,704	PF65 3.00				
1990	—	—	0.50	1.75	3.50	4.00
1990	79,052	PF65 3.00				
1991	—	—	0.50	1.75	3.50	4.00
1991	—	PF65 3.00				
1992	—	—	0.50	1.75	3.50	4.00
1992	—	PF65 3.00				

KM# 938a 10 PENCE

11.31 g., 0.925 Silver 0.3364 oz. ASW, 28.5 mm. **Ruler:** Elizabeth II **Obv:** Crowned head right **Rev:** Crowned lion prancing left **Note:** Date varieties exist.

Date	Mintage	VF20	XF40	MS60	MS63	MS65
1992	35,000	PF65 25.00				
Note: Also exists as a Piedfort, P13.						

KM# 938b 10 PENCE

6.50 g., Copper-Nickel, 24.5 mm. **Ruler:** Elizabeth II **Obv:** Crowned head right **Rev:** Crowned lion prancing left **Note:** Reduced size. Varieties in thickness and edge milling exist.

Date	Mintage	VF20	XF40	MS60	MS63	MS65
1992	1,413,455,170	—	0.50	1.75	3.50	4.00
1992	62,326	PF65 3.50				
1993 Sets only	—	—	0.50	1.75	3.50	4.00
1993	66,080	PF65 3.50				
1994 Sets only	—	—	0.50	1.75	3.50	4.00
1994	44,649	PF65 3.50				
1995	43,259,000	—	0.50	1.75	3.50	4.00
1995	60,639	PF65 3.50				
1996	118,738,000	—	0.50	1.75	3.50	4.00
1996	67,581	PF65 3.50				
1997	99,196,000	—	0.50	1.75	3.50	4.00
1997	80,748	PF65 3.50				

KM# 938c 10 PENCE

6.50 g., 0.925 Silver 0.1933 oz. ASW, 28.5 mm. **Ruler:** Elizabeth II **Obv:** Crowned head right **Rev:** Crowned lion prancing left

Date	Mintage	VF20	XF40	MS60	MS63	MS65
1992	35,000	PF65 16.00				
1996	—	PF65 16.00				

KM# 989 10 PENCE

6.50 g., Copper-Nickel, 24.5 mm. **Ruler:** Elizabeth II **Obv:** Head with tiara right **Rev:** Crowned lion passant left

Date	Mintage	VF20	XF40	MS60	MS63	MS65
1998 Sets only	—	—	0.50	1.75	3.50	4.00
1998	63,670	PF65 3.50				
1999 Sets only	136,492	—	0.50	1.75	3.50	4.00
1999	80,144	PF65 3.50				
2000	134,733,000	—	0.50	1.75	3.50	4.00
2000	72,469	PF65 3.50				

KM# 989a 10 PENCE

6.50 g., 0.925 Silver 0.1933 oz. ASW, 24.5 mm. **Ruler:** Elizabeth II **Obv:** Head with tiara right **Rev:** Crowned lion prancing left **Edge:** Reeded **Mint:** British Royal Mint

Date	Mintage	VF20	XF40	MS60	MS63	MS65
2000	15,000	PF65 20.00				

KM# 931 20 PENCE

5.00 g., Copper-Nickel, 21.4 mm. **Ruler:** Elizabeth II **Obv:** Young bust right **Rev:** Crowned rose **Shape:** 7-sided

Date	Mintage	VF20	XF40	MS60	MS63	MS65
1982	740,815,000	—	0.50	1.00	2.00	2.50
1982	106,800	PF65 3.00				
Note: Also exists as a Piedfort, P2.						
1983	158,463,000	—	0.50	1.25	2.50	3.00
1983	107,800	PF65 3.00				
1984	65,350,965	—	0.50	1.25	2.50	3.00
1984	106,520	PF65 3.00				

KM# 939 20 PENCE

5.00 g., Copper-Nickel, 21.4 mm. **Ruler:** Elizabeth II **Obv:** Crowned head right **Rev:** Crowned rose **Shape:** 7-sided

Date	Mintage	VF20	XF40	MS60	MS63	MS65
1985	74,273,699	—	0.50	1.25	2.50	3.00
1985	102,015	PF65 4.50				
1986 Sets only	167,000	—	0.50	1.50	3.00	3.50
1986	104,597	PF65 4.50				
1987	137,450,000	—	0.50	1.50	3.00	3.50
1987	88,659	PF65 4.50				
1988	38,038,344	—	0.50	1.75	3.50	4.00
1988	79,314	PF65 5.00				
1989	132,013,890	—	0.50	1.75	3.50	4.00
1989	85,704	PF65 5.00				
1990	88,097,500	—	0.50	1.50	3.00	4.00
1990	79,052	PF65 5.00				
1991	35,901,250	—	0.50	2.00	4.00	4.50
1991	55,144	PF65 5.00				
1992	31,205,000	—	0.50	2.00	4.00	4.50
1992	62,326	PF65 5.00				
1993	123,123,750	—	0.50	1.75	3.50	4.00
1993	66,080	PF65 5.00				
1994	67,131,250	—	0.50	2.00	4.00	4.50
1994	44,649	PF65 5.00				
1995	102,005,000	—	0.50	1.75	3.50	4.00
1995	60,639	PF65 5.00				
1996	83,163,750	—	0.50	1.75	3.50	4.00
1996	67,581	PF65 5.00				
1997	89,518,750	—	0.50	1.75	3.50	4.00

Date	Mintage	VF20	XF40	MS60	MS63	MS65
Note: Variations in portrait exist						
1997	80,748	PF65 5.00				

KM# 939a 20 PENCE

5.00 g., 0.925 Silver 0.1487 oz. ASW, 21.4 mm. **Ruler:** Elizabeth II **Obv:** Crowned head right **Rev:** Crowned rose **Shape:** 7-sided

Date	Mintage	VF20	XF40	MS60	MS63	MS65
1996	—	PF65 18.50				

KM# 990 20 PENCE

5.00 g., Copper-Nickel, 21.4 mm. **Ruler:** Elizabeth II **Obv:** Head with tiara right **Rev:** Crowned double rose **Shape:** 7-sided

Date	Mintage	VF20	XF40	MS60	MS63	MS65
1998	76,965,000	—	0.50	1.75	3.50	4.00
1998	63,670	PF65 4.50				
1999	73,478,750	—	0.50	1.75	3.50	4.00
1999	80,144	PF65 4.50				
2000	136,428,750	—	0.50	1.75	3.50	4.00
2000	72,469	PF65 4.50				

KM# 990a 20 PENCE

5.00 g., 0.925 Silver 0.1487 oz. ASW, 21.4 mm. **Ruler:** Elizabeth II **Obv:** Head with tiara right **Rev:** Crowned double rose **Edge:** Plain **Shape:** 7-sided **Mint:** British Royal Mint

Date	Mintage	VF20	XF40	MS60	MS63	MS65
2000	15,000	PF65 22.50				

KM# 917 25 NEW PENCE

28.28 g., Copper-Nickel, 38.6 mm. **Ruler:** Elizabeth II **Subject:** Royal Silver Wedding Anniversary **Obv:** Young bust right **Rev:** Crowned EP monogram **Edge:** Reeded

Date	Mintage	VF20	XF40	MS60	MS63	MS65
ND-1972	7,452,000	—	1.00	1.75	2.50	3.00
ND-1972	150,000	PF65 6.00				

KM# 917a 25 NEW PENCE

28.28 g., 0.925 Silver 0.8409 oz. ASW, 38.61 mm. **Ruler:** Elizabeth II **Obv:** Young bust right **Rev:** Crowned EP monogram

Date	Mintage	VF20	XF40	MS60	MS63	MS65
ND-1972	100,000	PF65 32.00				

KM# 920 25 NEW PENCE

28.28 g., Copper-Nickel, 38.61 mm. **Ruler:** Elizabeth II **Subject:** Silver Jubilee of Reign **Obv:** Queen on horseback left **Rev:** Eagle over spoon within circle, crown above **Edge:** Reeded

Date	Mintage	VF20	XF40	MS60	MS63	MS65
1977	37,061,000	—	1.00	1.25	1.50	2.00
1977 Special Unc	—	—	—	—	—	4.00
Note: Sealed in Royal Mint Folder and First Day Covers						
1977	194,000	PF65 6.00				

KM# 920a 25 NEW PENCE

28.28 g., 0.925 Silver 0.8409 oz. ASW, 38.61 mm. **Ruler:** Elizabeth II **Obv:** Queen on horseback left **Rev:** Eagle over spoon within circle, crown above

Date	Mintage	VF20	XF40	MS60	MS63	MS65
1977	377,000	PF65 30.00				

KM# 921 25 NEW PENCE

28.28 g., Copper-Nickel, 38.61 mm. **Ruler:** Elizabeth II **Subject:** 80th Birthday of Queen Mother **Obv:** Young bust right **Rev:** Queen Mother's profile left within circle of rampant lions and banners **Edge:** Reeded

Date	Mintage	VF20	XF40	MS60	MS63	MS65
ND-1980	9,306,000	—	1.00	1.25	1.50	2.00

KM# 921a 25 NEW PENCE

28.28 g., 0.925 Silver 0.8409 oz. ASW, 38.61 mm. **Ruler:** Elizabeth II **Obv:** Young bust right **Rev:** Queen Mother's profile left in circle of rampant lions and banners

Date	Mintage	VF20	XF40	MS60	MS63	MS65
ND-1980	84,000	PF65 55.00				

KM# 925 25 NEW PENCE

28.28 g., Copper-Nickel, 38.61 mm. **Ruler:** Elizabeth II **Subject:** Wedding of Prince Charles and Lady Diana **Obv:** Young bust right **Rev:** Jugate heads left **Edge:** Reeded

Date	Mintage	VF20	XF40	MS60	MS63	MS65
1981	26,773,000	—	1.00	1.75	2.50	3.50

KM# 925a 25 NEW PENCE

28.28 g., 0.925 Silver 0.8409 oz. ASW, 38.61 mm. **Ruler:** Elizabeth II **Subject:** Wedding of Prince Charles and Lady Diana **Obv:** Young bust right **Rev:** Conjoined busts left

Date	Mintage	VF20	XF40	MS60	MS63	MS65
1981	218,000	PF65 35.00				

KM# 913 50 NEW PENCE

13.50 g., Copper-Nickel, 30 mm. **Ruler:** Elizabeth II **Obv:** Young bust right **Rev:** Britannia seated right **Shape:** 7-sided

Date	Mintage	VF20	XF40	MS60	MS63	MS65
1969	188,400,000	—	1.50	2.00	2.50	3.00
1970	19,462,000	—	1.50	3.00	3.50	4.00
1971	350,000	PF65 4.00				
1972	150,000	PF65 7.00				
1974	100,000	PF65 6.00				
1975	100,000	PF65 6.00				
1976	43,746,500	—	1.50	3.00	3.50	4.00
1976	100,000	PF65 4.00				
1977	49,536,000	—	1.50	3.00	3.50	4.00
1977	193,000	PF65 3.50				
1978	72,005,500	—	1.50	3.00	3.50	4.00
1978	86,100	PF65 4.00				
1979	58,680,000	—	1.50	2.00	2.50	3.00
1979	81,000	PF65 4.00				
1980	89,086,000	—	1.50	2.00	2.50	3.00
1980	143,000	PF65 3.50				
1981	74,002,000	—	1.50	2.00	2.50	3.00
1981	100,300	PF65 4.00				

KM# 918 50 PENCE

13.50 g., Copper-Nickel, 30 mm. **Ruler:** Elizabeth II **Subject:** Britain's entry into E.E.C **Obv:** Young bust right **Rev:** Denomination and date at center of nine clasped hands **Shape:** 7-sided

Date	Mintage	VF20	XF40	MS60	MS63	MS65
1973	89,775,000	—	1.50	3.50	4.50	5.00
1973	357,000	PF65 5.00				
Note: Also exists as a Piedfort, P1.						

KM# 932 50 PENCE

13.50 g., Copper-Nickel, 30 mm. **Ruler:** Elizabeth II **Obv:** Young bust right **Rev:** Britannia seated right **Shape:** 7-sided

Date	Mintage	VF20	XF40	MS60	MS63	MS65
1982	51,312,000	—	1.00	1.50	2.00	2.50
1982	106,800	PF65 2.50				
1983	62,825,000	—	1.00	1.50	2.00	2.50
1983	107,800	PF65 2.50				
1984 Sets only	Est. 107,000	—	—	—	—	3.50
1984	106,520	PF65 3.50				

KM# 940.1 50 PENCE

13.50 g., Copper-Nickel, 30 mm. **Ruler:** Elizabeth II **Obv:** Crowned head right **Rev:** Britannia seated right **Shape:** 7-sided

Date	Mintage	VF20	XF40	MS60	MS63	MS65
1985	682,103	—	1.50	3.50	5.50	6.50
1985	102,015	PF65 5.00				
1986 Sets only	167,000	—	—	—	—	3.50
1986	104,597	PF65 3.50				
1987 Sets only	172,000	—	—	—	—	3.50
1987	88,659	PF65 3.50				
1988 Sets only	134,000	—	—	—	—	3.50
1988	79,314	PF65 3.50				
1989 Sets only	78,000	—	—	—	—	4.00
1989	85,704	PF65 3.50				
1990 Sets only	—	—	—	—	—	4.00
1990	79,052	PF65 6.00				
1991 Sets only	—	—	—	—	—	4.00
1991	55,144	PF65 6.00				
1992 Sets only	—	—	—	—	—	4.00
1992	62,326	PF65 6.00				
1993 Sets only	—	—	—	—	—	4.00
1993	66,080	PF65 6.00				
1995 Sets only	—	—	—	—	—	4.00
1995	60,639	PF65 6.00				
1996 Sets only	—	—	—	—	—	4.00
1996	67,581	PF65 6.00				
1997 Sets only	—	—	—	—	—	3.50
1997	80,748	PF65 6.00				

KM# 963 50 PENCE
13.50 g., Copper-Nickel, 30 mm. **Ruler:** Elizabeth II **Subject:** British Presidency of European Council of Ministers **Obv:** Crowned head right **Rev:** Stars on conference table **Shape:** 7-sided

Date	Mintage	VF20	XF40	MS60	MS63	MS65
ND-1992	109,000	—	—	—	12.00	15.00
ND-1992	Est. 100000	PF65 15.00				

KM# 963a 50 PENCE
13.50 g., 0.925 Silver 0.4015 oz. ASW, 30 mm. **Ruler:** Elizabeth II **Obv:** Crowned head right **Rev:** Stars on conference table

Date	Mintage	VF20	XF40	MS60	MS63	MS65
ND-1992	Est. 35000	PF65 35.00				

Note: Also exists as a Piedfort, P15.

KM# 963b 50 PENCE
26.32 g., 0.917 Gold 0.776 oz. AGW, 30 mm. **Ruler:** Elizabeth II **Subject:** British Presidency of European Council of Ministers **Obv:** Crowned head right **Rev:** Stars on conference table

Date	Mintage	VF20	XF40	MS60	MS63	MS65
ND-1992	—	PF65 1,250				

KM# 966 50 PENCE
13.50 g., Copper-Nickel, 30 mm. **Ruler:** Elizabeth II **Subject:** 50th Anniversary of Normandy Invasion **Obv:** Crowned head right **Rev:** Boats and planes **Shape:** 7-sided

Date	Mintage	VF20	XF40	MS60	MS63	MS65
1994	6,705,520	—	—	—	5.00	6.00
1994	44,649	PF65 7.00				

KM# 966a 50 PENCE
13.50 g., 0.925 Silver 0.4015 oz. ASW, 30 mm. **Ruler:** Elizabeth II **Obv:** Crowned head right **Rev:** Boats and planes

Date	Mintage	VF20	XF40	MS60	MS63	MS65
1994	—	PF65 45.00				

Note: Also exists as a Piedfort, P17.

KM# 966b 50 PENCE
26.32 g., 0.917 Gold 0.776 oz. AGW, 30 mm. **Ruler:** Elizabeth II **Obv:** Crowned head right **Rev:** Boats and planes

Date	Mintage	VF20	XF40	MS60	MS63	MS65
1994	—	PF65 1,250				

KM# 940.1a 50 PENCE
13.50 g., 0.925 Silver 0.4015 oz. ASW, 30 mm. **Ruler:** Elizabeth II **Obv:** Crowned head right **Rev:** Britannia seated

Date	Mintage	VF20	XF40	MS60	MS63	MS65
1996	—	PF65 30.00				

KM# 940.2 50 PENCE
8.00 g., Copper-Nickel, 27.3 mm. **Ruler:** Elizabeth II **Obv:** Crowned head right **Rev:** Britannia seated right **Shape:** 7-sided **Note:** Reduced size.

Date	Mintage	VF20	XF40	MS60	MS63	MS65
1997	456,364,100	—	—	—	3.50	4.00
1997	—	PF65 4.00				

KM# 940.2a 50 PENCE
8.00 g., 0.925 Silver 0.2379 oz. ASW **Ruler:** Elizabeth II **Obv:** Crowned head right **Rev:** Britannia seated right **Shape:** 7-sided

Date	Mintage	VF20	XF40	MS60	MS63	MS65
1997	1,000	PF65 25.00				

Note: Also exists as a Piedfort, P24.

KM# 991 50 PENCE
8.00 g., Copper-Nickel, 27.3 mm. **Ruler:** Elizabeth II **Obv:** Head with tiara right **Rev:** Britannia seated right with shield, spear and lion **Shape:** 7-sided

Date	Mintage	VF20	XF40	MS60	MS63	MS65
1998	64,306,500	—	1.00	2.50	3.50	4.00
1998	63,670	PF65 4.00				
1999	24,905,000	—	1.00	2.50	3.50	4.00
1999	80,144	PF65 4.00				
2000	27,915,500	—	1.00	2.50	3.50	4.00
2000	72,469	PF65 4.00				

KM# 992 50 PENCE
8.00 g., Copper-Nickel, 27.3 mm. **Ruler:** Elizabeth II **Subject:** 25th Anniversary - Britain in the Common Market **Obv:** Head with tiara right **Rev:** Bouquet of stars **Shape:** 7-sided

Date	Mintage	VF20	XF40	MS60	MS63	MS65
1998	5,043,000	—	1.00	2.50	3.50	4.00
1998	Est. 100000	PF65 9.50				

KM# 992a 50 PENCE
8.00 g., 0.925 Silver 0.2379 oz. ASW, 27.3 mm. **Ruler:** Elizabeth II **Obv:** Head with tiara right **Rev:** Bouquet of stars

Date	Mintage	VF20	XF40	MS60	MS63	MS65
1998	8,859	PF65 40.00				

Note: Also exists as a Piedfort, P28.

KM# 996 50 PENCE
8.00 g., Copper-Nickel, 27.3 mm. **Ruler:** Elizabeth II **Subject:** National Health Service **Obv:** Head with tiara right **Rev:** Radiant hands within circle **Shape:** 7-sided

Date	Mintage	VF20	XF40	MS60	MS63	MS65
1998	5,001,000	—	1.00	2.50	3.50	4.00
1998 In folder	—	—	—	—	7.00	8.50
1998	—	PF65 12.00				

KM# 996a 50 PENCE
8.00 g., 0.925 Silver 0.2379 oz. ASW, 27.3 mm. **Ruler:** Elizabeth II **Subject:** National Health Service **Obv:** Head with tiara right **Rev:** Radiant hands **Shape:** 7-sided

Date	Mintage	VF20	XF40	MS60	MS63	MS65
1998	9,032	PF65 40.00				

Note: Also exists as a Piedfort, P29.

KM# 996b 50 PENCE
15.50 g., 0.9167 Gold 0.4568 oz. AGW, 27.3 mm. **Ruler:** Elizabeth II **Subject:** National Health Service **Obv:** Head with tiara right **Rev:** Radiant hands **Shape:** 7-sided

Date	Mintage	VF20	XF40	MS60	MS63	MS65
1998	Est. 1500	PF65 700				

KM# 1083 50 PENCE
8.11 g., 0.9854 Silver 0.2569 oz. ASW, 22 mm. **Ruler:** Elizabeth II **Obv:** Head with tiara right **Rev:** Britannia in chariot right **Edge:** Reeded **Mint:** British Royal Mint

Date	Mintage	VF20	XF40	MS60	MS63	MS65
1999	—	PF65 35.00				

KM# 991a 50 PENCE
8.00 g., 0.925 Silver 0.2379 oz. ASW, 27.3 mm. **Ruler:** Elizabeth II **Obv:** Head with tiara right **Rev:** Britannia seated right with shield, spear and lion **Edge:** Plain **Shape:** 7-sided **Mint:** British Royal Mint

Date	Mintage	VF20	XF40	MS60	MS63	MS65
2000	15,000	PF65 24.00				

KM# 1004 50 PENCE
8.00 g., Copper-Nickel, 27.3 mm. **Ruler:** Elizabeth II **Subject:** Public Library **Obv:** Head with tiara right **Rev:** Open book above building, CDs in pediment **Edge:** Plain edge **Shape:** 7-sided **Mint:** British Royal Mint

Date	Mintage	VF20	XF40	MS60	MS63	MS65
2000	11,263,000	—	1.00	2.50	3.50	4.00
2000	100,000	PF65 7.00				

KM# 1004a 50 PENCE
Silver **Ruler:** Elizabeth II **Subject:** Public Library **Obv:** Queen Elizabeth II right **Rev:** Open book above building, CDs in pediment **Edge:** Plain

Date	Mintage	VF20	XF40	MS60	MS63	MS65
2000	7,634	PF65 37.50				

KM# 933 POUND
9.50 g., Nickel-Brass, 22.5 mm. **Ruler:** Elizabeth II **Obv:** Young bust right **Rev:** Shield of Great Britain within the Garter, crowned and supported **Edge Lettering:** DECUS ET TUTAMEN

Date	Mintage	VF20	XF40	MS60	MS63	MS65
1983 933	443,053,510	—	2.50	3.50	5.00	6.00
1983	107,800	PF65 6.00				

KM# 933a POUND
9.50 g., 0.925 Silver 0.2825 oz. ASW, 22.5 mm. **Ruler:** Elizabeth II **Obv:** Young bust right **Rev:** Shield of Great Britain within the Garter, crowned and supported

Date	Mintage	VF20	XF40	MS60	MS63	MS65
1983	50,000	PF65 35.00	PF67 45.00			

Note: Also exists as a Piedfort, P3

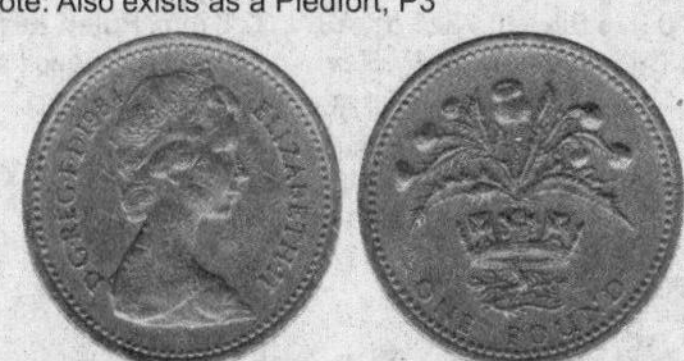

KM# 934 POUND
9.50 g., Nickel-Brass, 22.5 mm. **Ruler:** Elizabeth II **Obv:** Young bust right **Rev:** Scottish thistle **Edge Lettering:** NEMO ME IMPUNE LACESSIT

Date	Mintage	VF20	XF40	MS60	MS63	MS65
1984	146,256,501	—	2.50	3.50	5.00	6.00
1984	106,520	PF65 6.00				

KM# 934a POUND

9.50 g., 0.925 Silver 0.2825 oz. ASW, 22.5 mm. **Ruler:** Elizabeth II **Obv:** Young bust right **Rev:** Scottish thistle

Date	Mintage	VF20	XF40	MS60	MS63	MS65
1984	45,000	PF65 32.00	PF67 42.00			

Note: Also exists as a Piedfort, P4

KM# 941 POUND

9.50 g., Nickel-Brass, 22.5 mm. **Ruler:** Elizabeth II **Obv:** Crowned head right **Rev:** Welsh leek, crown encircles **Edge Lettering:** PLEIDIOL WYF I'M GWLAD

Date	Mintage	VF20	XF40	MS60	MS63	MS65
1985	228,430,749	—	2.50	3.50	5.00	6.00
1985	102,015	PF65 6.00				
1990	97,269,302	—	3.00	4.50	6.00	7.50
1990	79,052	PF65 7.50				

KM# 941a POUND

9.50 g., 0.925 Silver 0.2825 oz. ASW, 22.5 mm. **Ruler:** Elizabeth II **Obv:** Crowned head right **Rev:** Welsh leek, crown encircles

Date	Mintage	VF20	XF40	MS60	MS63	MS65
1985	50,000	PF65 32.00	PF67 42.00			
Note: Also exists as a Piedfort, P5						
1990	Est. 25000	PF65 40.00	PF67 50.00			

KM# 946 POUND

9.50 g., Nickel-Brass, 22.5 mm. **Ruler:** Elizabeth II **Obv:** Crowned head right **Rev:** Northern Ireland - Blooming flax, crown encircles **Edge Lettering:** DECUS ET TUTAMEN

Date	Mintage	VF20	XF40	MS60	MS63	MS65
1986	10,409,501	—	3.00	4.50	6.00	7.50
1986	104,597	PF65 7.50				
1991	38,443,575	—	3.00	4.50	6.00	7.50
1991	55,144	PF65 7.50				

KM# 946a POUND

9.50 g., 0.925 Silver 0.2825 oz. ASW, 22.5 mm. **Ruler:** Elizabeth II **Obv:** Crowned head right **Rev:** Northern Ireland - Blooming flax, crown encircles

Date	Mintage	VF20	XF40	MS60	MS63	MS65
1986	50,000	PF65 32.00	PF67 42.00			
Note: Also exists as a Piedfort, P6						
1991	Est. 25000	PF65 40.00	PF67 50.00			

KM# 948 POUND

9.50 g., Nickel-Brass, 22.5 mm. **Ruler:** Elizabeth II **Obv:** Crowned head right **Rev:** Oak tree, crown encircles **Edge Lettering:** DECUS ET TUTAMEN

Date	Mintage	VF20	XF40	MS60	MS63	MS65
1987	39,298,502	—	3.00	4.50	6.00	7.50
1987	88,659	PF65 7.50				
1992	36,320,487	—	3.00	4.50	6.00	7.50
1992	62,326	PF65 7.50				

KM# 948a POUND

9.50 g., 0.925 Silver 0.2825 oz. ASW, 22.5 mm. **Ruler:** Elizabeth II **Obv:** Crowned head right **Rev:** Oak tree, crown encircles

Date	Mintage	VF20	XF40	MS60	MS63	MS65
1987	50,000	PF65 32.00	PF67 42.00			
Note: Also exists as a Piedfort, P7						
1992	Est. 25000	PF65 40.00	PF67 50.00			

KM# 954 POUND

9.50 g., Nickel-Brass, 22.5 mm. **Ruler:** Elizabeth II **Obv:** Crowned head right **Rev:** Crowned shield of the United Kingdom **Edge Lettering:** DECUS ET TUTAMEN

Date	Mintage	VF20	XF40	MS60	MS63	MS65
1988	7,118,825	—	3.00	4.50	6.00	7.50
1988	79,314	PF65 7.50				

KM# 954a POUND

9.50 g., 0.925 Silver 0.2825 oz. ASW, 22.5 mm. **Ruler:** Elizabeth II **Obv:** Crowned head right **Rev:** Crowned shield of the United Kingdom

Date	Mintage	VF20	XF40	MS60	MS63	MS65
1988	Est. 50000	PF65 35.00	PF67 45.00			

Note: Also exists as a Piedfort, P8

KM# 959 POUND

9.50 g., Nickel-Brass, 22.5 mm. **Ruler:** Elizabeth II **Obv:** Crowned head right **Rev:** Scottish thistle, crown encircles **Edge Lettering:** NEMO ME IMPUNE LACESSIT

Date	Mintage	VF20	XF40	MS60	MS63	MS65
1989	70,580,501	—	3.00	4.50	6.00	7.50
1989	85,704	PF65 7.50				

KM# 959a POUND

9.50 g., 0.925 Silver 0.2825 oz. ASW, 22.5 mm. **Ruler:** Elizabeth II **Obv:** Crowned head right **Rev:** Scottish thistle, crown encircles

Date	Mintage	VF20	XF40	MS60	MS63	MS65
1989	Est. 25000	PF65 40.00	PF67 50.00			

Note: Also exists as a Piedfort, P9

KM# 964 POUND

9.50 g., Nickel-Brass, 22.5 mm. **Ruler:** Elizabeth II **Obv:** Crowned head right **Rev:** Shield of Great Britain with Garter, crowned and supported **Edge Lettering:** DECUS ET TUTAMEN

Date	Mintage	VF20	XF40	MS60	MS63	MS65
1993	114,744,500	—	3.00	4.50	6.00	7.50
1993	66,080	PF65 7.50				

KM# 964a POUND

9.50 g., 0.925 Silver 0.2825 oz. ASW, 22.5 mm. **Ruler:** Elizabeth II **Obv:** Crowned head right **Rev:** Shield of Great Britain within Garter, crowned and supported

Date	Mintage	VF20	XF40	MS60	MS63	MS65
1993	Est. 25000	PF65 40.00	PF67 50.00			

Note: Also exists as a Piedfort, P16

KM# 967 POUND

9.50 g., Nickel-Brass, 22.5 mm. **Ruler:** Elizabeth II **Obv:** Crowned head right **Rev:** Scottish arms; rampant lion left within circle **Edge Lettering:** NEMO ME IMPUNE LACESSIT

Date	Mintage	VF20	XF40	MS60	MS63	MS65
1994	29,752,525	—	3.00	4.50	6.00	7.50
1994	44,649	PF65 7.50				

KM# 967a POUND

9.50 g., 0.925 Silver 0.2825 oz. ASW, 22.5 mm. **Ruler:** Elizabeth II **Obv:** Crowned head right **Rev:** Scottish arms; rampant lion left within circle

Date	Mintage	VF20	XF40	MS60	MS63	MS65
1994	Est. 25000	PF65 40.00	PF67 50.00			

Note: Also exists as a Piedfort, P18

KM# 969 POUND

9.50 g., Nickel-Brass, 22.5 mm. **Ruler:** Elizabeth II **Obv:** Crowned head right **Rev:** Welsh Dragon left **Edge Lettering:** PLEIDIOL WYF I'M GWLAD

Date	Mintage	VF20	XF40	MS60	MS63	MS65
1995 Welsh design	34,503,501	—	5.00	7.00	10.00	12.50
1995 English design	—	—	3.00	4.50	6.00	7.50
1995	60,639	PF65 7.50				

KM# 969a POUND

9.50 g., 0.925 Silver 0.2825 oz. ASW, 22.5 mm. **Ruler:** Elizabeth II **Obv:** Crowned head right **Rev:** Welsh dragon left

Date	Mintage	VF20	XF40	MS60	MS63	MS65
1995	27,000	PF65 40.00	PF67 50.00			

Note: Also exists as a Piedfort, P20

KM# 972 POUND

9.50 g., Nickel-Brass, 22.5 mm. **Ruler:** Elizabeth II **Obv:** Crowned head right **Rev:** Celtic Cross **Edge Lettering:** DECUS ET TUTAMEN

Date	Mintage	VF20	XF40	MS60	MS63	MS65
1996	89,886,000	—	3.00	4.50	6.00	7.50
1996	67,581	PF65 7.50				

KM# 972a POUND

9.50 g., 0.925 Silver 0.2825 oz. ASW, 22.5 mm. **Ruler:** Elizabeth II **Obv:** Crowned head right **Rev:** Celtic cross

Date	Mintage	VF20	XF40	MS60	MS63	MS65
1996	40,000	PF65 35.00	PF67 45.00			

Note: Also exists as a Piedfort, P23

KM# 975 POUND

9.50 g., Nickel-Brass, 22.5 mm. **Ruler:** Elizabeth II **Obv:** Crowned head right **Rev:** Plantagenet lions **Edge Lettering:** DECUS ET TUTAMEN

Date	Mintage	VF20	XF40	MS60	MS63	MS65
1996	—	—	—	—	—	—
Note: Counterfeit date						
1997	57,117,000	—	3.50	5.00	7.50	9.00
1997	80,748	PF65 9.00				

KM# 975a POUND

9.50 g., 0.925 Silver 0.2825 oz. ASW, 22.5 mm. **Ruler:** Elizabeth II **Obv:** Crowned head right **Rev:** Plantagenet lions **Edge Lettering:** DECUS ET TUTAMEN

Date	Mintage	VF20	XF40	MS60	MS63	MS65
1997	30,000	PF65 40.00	PF67 50.00			

Note: Also exists as a Piedfort, P25

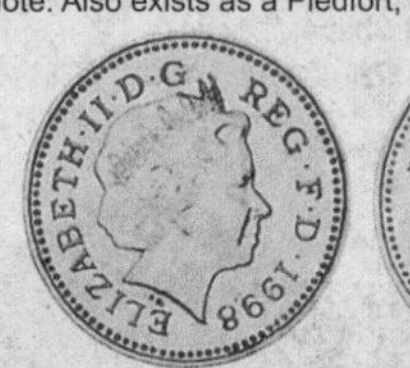

KM# 993 POUND

9.50 g., Nickel-Brass, 22.5 mm. **Ruler:** Elizabeth II **Subject:** United Kingdom **Obv:** Head with tiara right **Rev:** Royal Arms with supporters **Edge:** Reeded and lettered **Edge Lettering:** DECUS ET TUTAMEN

Date	Mintage	VF20	XF40	MS60	MS63	MS65
1998 Sets only	Est. 100000	—	3.50	5.00	7.50	9.00
1998	63,670	PF65 9.00				

KM# 993a POUND

9.50 g., 0.925 Silver 0.2825 oz. ASW, 22.5 mm. **Ruler:** Elizabeth II **Subject:** United Kingdom **Obv:** Head with tiara right **Rev:** Royal Arms with supporters **Edge:** Reeded and lettered **Edge Lettering:** DECUS ET TUTAMEN

Date	Mintage	VF20	XF40	MS60	MS63	MS65
1998	13,863	PF65 45.00	PF67 55.00			

Note: Also exists as a Piedfort, P26

KM# 998 POUND

9.50 g., Nickel-Brass, 22.5 mm. **Ruler:** Elizabeth II **Obv:** Head with tiara right **Rev:** Scottish lion within circle **Edge Lettering:** NEMO ME IMPUNE LACESSTT

Date	Mintage	VF20	XF40	MS60	MS63	MS65
1999 Sets only	—	—	3.50	5.00	7.50	9.00
1999	80,144	PF65 9.00				

KM# 998a POUND

9.50 g., 0.925 Silver 0.2825 oz. ASW, 22.5 mm. **Ruler:** Elizabeth II **Obv:** Head with tiara right **Rev:** Scottish lion within circle

Date	Mintage	VF20	XF40	MS60	MS63	MS65
1999	—	PF65 40.00	PF67 50.00			
1999 Proof, frosted reverse	1,994	PF65 60.00	PF67 70.00			

Note: Also exists as a Piedfort, P31

KM# 1005 POUND

9.50 g., Nickel-Brass, 22.5 mm. **Ruler:** Elizabeth II **Obv:** Head with tiara right **Rev:** Welsh dragon left **Edge:** Reeded and lettered **Edge Lettering:** PLEIDOL WYF I'M GWLAD **Mint:** British Royal Mint

Date	Mintage	VF20	XF40	MS60	MS63	MS65
2000	109,497,000	—	3.00	4.50	6.00	7.50
2000	72,469	PF65 7.50				

KM# 1005a POUND

9.50 g., 0.925 Silver 0.2825 oz. ASW, 22.5 mm. **Ruler:** Elizabeth II **Subject:** Wales **Obv:** Head with tiara right **Rev:** Welsh dragon left **Edge:** Reeded **Edge Lettering:** PLEIDIOL WYF I'M GWLAD **Mint:** British Royal Mint

Date	Mintage	VF20	XF40	MS60	MS63	MS65
2000	15,865	PF65 40.00	PF67 50.00			

Note: Also exists as a Piedfort, P100

KM# 947 2 POUNDS

15.98 g., Nickel-Brass, 28.4 mm. **Ruler:** Elizabeth II **Subject:** Commonwealth Games **Obv:** Crowned head right **Rev:** Thistle on St. Andrew's Cross **Edge Lettering:** XIII COMMONWEALTH GAMES SCOTLAND 1986

Date	Mintage	VF20	XF40	MS60	MS63	MS65
1986	8,212,000	—	4.50	6.50	8.00	10.00
1986	125,000	PF63 10.00	PF65 12.00			

KM# 947a 2 POUNDS

15.98 g., 0.500 Silver 0.2569 oz. ASW, 28.4 mm. **Ruler:** Elizabeth II **Subject:** Commonwealth Games **Obv:** Crowned head right **Rev:** Thistle on St. Andrew's cross

Date	Mintage	VF20	XF40	MS60	MS63	MS65
1986	58,881	—	10.00	12.00	15.00	20.00

KM# 947b 2 POUNDS

15.98 g., 0.925 Silver 0.4752 oz. ASW, 28.4 mm. **Ruler:** Elizabeth II **Subject:** Commonwealth Games **Obv:** Crowned head right **Rev:** Thistle on St. Andrew's Cross

Date	Mintage	VF20	XF40	MS60	MS63	MS65
1986	59,779	PF65 45.00	PF67 55.00			

KM# 947c 2 POUNDS

15.98 g., 0.917 Gold 0.4711 oz. AGW, 28.4 mm. **Ruler:** Elizabeth II **Subject:** Commonwealth Games **Obv:** Crowned head right **Rev:** Thistle on St. Andrew's Cross

Date	Mintage	VF20	XF40	MS60	MS63	MS65
1986	3,277	PF65 750	PF67 775			

KM# 960 2 POUNDS

15.98 g., Nickel-Brass, 28.4 mm. **Ruler:** Elizabeth II **Subject:** Tercentenary - Bill of Rights **Obv:** Crowned head right **Rev:** St. Edward's crown above WM monogram and mace **Mint:** British Royal Mint

Date	Mintage	VF20	XF40	MS60	MS63	MS65
ND-1989	4,432,000	—	4.50	6.00	7.50	9.00
ND-1989	100,000	PF65 11.00				

KM# 960a 2 POUNDS

15.98 g., 0.925 Silver 0.4752 oz. ASW, 28.4 mm. **Ruler:** Elizabeth II **Subject:** Tercentenary - Bill of Rights **Obv:** Crowned head right **Rev:** St. Edward's crowned above sceptre and WM monogram

Date	Mintage	VF20	XF40	MS60	MS63	MS65
ND-1989	25,000	PF65 45.00	PF67 55.00			

Note: Also exists as a Piedfort, P10

KM# 961 2 POUNDS

15.98 g., Nickel-Brass, 28.4 mm. **Ruler:** Elizabeth II **Subject:** Claim of Right, 300th Anniversary **Obv:** Crowned head right **Rev:** Crown of Scotland above WM monogram and mace **Mint:** British Royal Mint

Date	Mintage	VF20	XF40	MS60	MS63	MS65
ND-1989	346,000	—	10.00	12.00	15.00	20.00
ND-1989	100,000	PF65 20.00				

KM# 961a 2 POUNDS

15.98 g., 0.925 Silver 0.4752 oz. ASW, 28.4 mm. **Ruler:** Elizabeth II **Subject:** Claim of Right, 300th Anniversary **Obv:** Crowned head right **Rev:** Crown of Scotland above sceptre and WM monogram

Date	Mintage	VF20	XF40	MS60	MS63	MS65
ND-1989	24,852	PF65 45.00	PF67 55.00			

Note: Also exists as a Piedfort, P11

KM# 968 2 POUNDS

15.98 g., Nickel-Brass, 28.4 mm. **Ruler:** Elizabeth II **Subject:** 300th Anniversary - Bank of England **Obv:** Crowned head right **Rev:** Britiannia seated within oval divides dates, crowned WM monogram above **Edge Lettering:** SIC VOS NON VOBIS

Date	Mintage	VF20	XF40	MS60	MS63	MS65
ND-1994	1,443,000	—	4.50	6.00	7.50	9.00
ND-1994	—	PF65 11.00				

KM# 968a 2 POUNDS

15.98 g., 0.925 Silver 0.4752 oz. ASW, 28.4 mm. **Ruler:** Elizabeth II **Subject:** 300th Anniversary - Bank of England **Obv:** Crowned head right **Rev:** Britiannia seated within oval, Crowned WM monogram above

Date	Mintage	VF20	XF40	MS60	MS63	MS65
ND-1994	—	PF65 45.00	PF67 55.00			

Note: Also exists as a Piedfort, P19

KM# 968b 2 POUNDS

15.98 g., 0.917 Gold 0.4711 oz. AGW, 28.4 mm. **Ruler:** Elizabeth II **Subject:** 300th Anniversary - Bank of England **Obv:** Crowned head right **Rev:** Britiannia seated within oval, Crowned WM monogram above

Date	Mintage	VF20	XF40	MS60	MS63	MS65
ND-1994	Est. 1000	PF65 750	PF67 775			

KM# 1012 2 POUNDS

15.98 g., 0.917 Gold 0.4711 oz. AGW, 28.4 mm. **Ruler:** Elizabeth II **Obv:** Crowned head right **Rev:** Britiannia seated within oval, crowned WM monogram above **Note:** Muled die error.

Date	Mintage	VF20	XF40	MS60	MS63	MS65
ND-1994	—	—	—	—	900	—

KM# 970 2 POUNDS

15.98 g., Nickel-Brass, 28.4 mm. **Ruler:** Elizabeth II **Subject:** 50th Anniversary - End of World War II **Obv:** Crowned head right **Rev:** Large dove with laurel branch **Edge Lettering:** 1945 IN PEACE GOODWILL 1995

Date	Mintage	VF20	XF40	MS60	MS63	MS65
ND-1995	6,057,000	—	4.50	6.00	7.50	9.00
ND-1995	100,000	PF65 11.00				

KM# 970a 2 POUNDS

15.98 g., 0.925 Silver 0.4752 oz. ASW, 28.4 mm. **Ruler:** Elizabeth II **Subject:** 50th Anniversary - End of World War II **Obv:** Crowned head right **Rev:** Dove with laurel branch

Date	Mintage	VF20	XF40	MS60	MS63	MS65
ND-1995	35,751	PF65 45.00	PF67 55.00			

Note: Also exists as a Piedfort, P21

KM# 970b 2 POUNDS

15.98 g., 0.917 Gold 0.4711 oz. AGW, 28.4 mm. **Ruler:** Elizabeth II **Subject:** 50th Anniversary - End of World War II **Obv:** Crowned head right **Rev:** Dove with laurel branch

Date	Mintage	VF20	XF40	MS60	MS63	MS65
ND-1995	2,500	PF65 750	PF67 775			

KM# 971 2 POUNDS

15.98 g., Nickel-Brass, 28.4 mm. **Ruler:** Elizabeth II **Subject:** 50th Anniversary - United Nations **Obv:** Crowned head right **Rev:** Flags and UN Logo **Note:** Mintage included with KM#970.

Date	Mintage	VF20	XF40	MS60	MS63	MS65
ND-1995	Inc. above	—	4.50	6.00	7.50	9.00
ND1995	Inc. above	PF65 11.00				

KM# 971a 2 POUNDS

15.98 g., 0.925 Silver 0.4751 oz. ASW, 28.4 mm. **Ruler:** Elizabeth II **Subject:** 50th Anniversary - United Nations **Obv:** Crowned head right **Rev:** Flags and UN Logo

Date	Mintage	VF20	XF40	MS60	MS63	MS65
ND-1995	Est. 175000	PF65 45.00	PF67 55.00			

Note: Also exists as a Piedfort, P22

KM# 971b 2 POUNDS

15.98 g., 0.917 Gold 0.471 oz. AGW, 28.4 mm. **Ruler:** Elizabeth II **Subject:** 50th Anniversary - United Nations **Obv:** Crowned head right **Rev:** Flags and UN Logo

Date	Mintage	VF20	XF40	MS60	MS63	MS65
ND-1995	17,500	PF65 750	PF67 775			

KM# 973 2 POUNDS

15.98 g., Nickel-Brass, 28.4 mm. **Ruler:** Elizabeth II **Obv:** Crowned head right **Rev:** Soccer ball, date in center **Edge Lettering:** 10th European Championship of Football (Soccer)

Date	Mintage	VF20	XF40	MS60	MS63	MS65
1996	5,141,000	—	4.50	6.00	7.50	9.00
1996	Est. 100000	PF65 11.00				

KM# 973a 2 POUNDS

15.98 g., 0.925 Silver 0.4751 oz. ASW, 28.4 mm. **Ruler:**

Elizabeth II **Obv:** Crowned head right **Rev:** Soccer ball, date at center

Date	Mintage	VF20	XF40	MS60	MS63	MS65
1996	25,163	PF65 45.00	PF67 55.00			

Note: Also exists as a Piefort, P104

KM# 973b 2 POUNDS

15.98 g., 0.9167 Gold 0.4709 oz. AGW, 28.4 mm. **Ruler:** Elizabeth II **Obv:** Crowned head right **Rev:** Soccer ball, date in center

Date	Mintage	VF20	XF40	MS60	MS63	MS65
1996	2,098	PF65 850	PF67 875			

KM# 976 2 POUNDS

12.00 g., Bi-Metallic Copper-Nickel center in Nickel-Brass ring, 28.35 mm. **Ruler:** Elizabeth II **Obv:** Crowned head right **Rev:** Celtic designs within circle **Edge Lettering:** STANDING ON THE SHOULDERS OF GIANTS

Date	Mintage	VF20	XF40	MS60	MS63	MS65
1997	13,735,000	—	4.50	6.00	7.50	9.00
1997	Est. 100000	PF65 11.00				

KM# 976a 2 POUNDS

12.00 g., 0.925 Silver 0.3569 oz. ASW, 28.35 mm. **Ruler:** Elizabeth II **Obv:** Crowned head right **Rev:** Celtic designs within circle **Note:** Gold plated silver ring, silver center.

Date	Mintage	VF20	XF40	MS60	MS63	MS65
1997	29,910	PF65 45.00	PF67 55.00			

Note: Also exists as a Piefort, P27

KM# 976b 2 POUNDS

15.98 g., 0.917 Gold 0.4711 oz. AGW, 28.35 mm. **Ruler:** Elizabeth II **Obv:** Crowned head right **Rev:** Celtic design within circle **Note:** Red gold ring, yellow gold center.

Date	Mintage	VF20	XF40	MS60	MS63	MS65
1997	2,482	PF65 750	PF67 775			

KM# 994 2 POUNDS

12.00 g., Bi-Metallic Copper-Nickel center in Nickel-Brass ring, 28.4 mm. **Ruler:** Elizabeth II **Subject:** Technology **Obv:** Head with tiara right **Rev:** Symbolic depiction in concentric circles of technological development from the Iron Age to the Internet **Edge Lettering:** STANDING ON THE SHOULDERS OF GIANTS

Date	Mintage	VF20	XF40	MS60	MS63	MS65
1998	91,110,375	—	5.00	7.00	9.50	12.00
1998	Est. 100000	PF65 12.00				
1999	33,719,000	—	4.50	6.00	7.50	9.00
1999	—	PF65 11.00				
2000	25,770,000	—	5.00	7.00	9.50	12.00
2000	—	PF65 12.00				

KM# 994a 2 POUNDS

12.00 g., 0.925 Silver 0.3569 oz. ASW, 28.35 mm. **Ruler:** Elizabeth II **Subject:** Technology **Obv:** Head with tiara right **Rev:** Symbolic depiction in concentric circles of technological development from the Iron Age to the Internet **Note:** Gold plated silver ring, silver center.

Date	Mintage	VF20	XF40	MS60	MS63	MS65
1998	19,978	PF65 45.00	PF67 55.00			
Note: Also exists as a Piefort, P30						
2000	15,000	PF65 45.00	PF67 55.00			

KM# 994b 2 POUNDS

12.00 g., 0.925 Silver 0.3569 oz. ASW, 28.35 mm. **Ruler:** Elizabeth II **Subject:** Technology **Obv:** Head with tiara right **Rev:** Symbolic depiction in concentric circles of technological development from the Iron Age to the Internet **Note:** Without gold plating.

Date	Mintage	VF20	XF40	MS60	MS63	MS65
1998	19,978	PF65 45.00	PF67 55.00			

KM# 994c 2 POUNDS

15.98 g., 0.9167 Gold 0.471 oz. AGW, 28.35 mm. **Ruler:** Elizabeth II **Subject:** Technology **Obv:** Head with tiara right **Rev:** Symbolic depiction in concentric circles of technological development from the Iron Age to the Internet

Date	Mintage	VF20	XF40	MS60	MS63	MS65
1998	1,250	PF65 825	PF67 850			

KM# 999 2 POUNDS

12.00 g., Bi-Metallic Copper-Nickel center in Nickel-Brass ring, 28.35 mm. **Ruler:** Elizabeth II **Subject:** Rugby World Cup **Obv:** Head with tiara right **Rev:** 2-tone rugby design **Edge Lettering:** RUGBY WORLD CUP 1999 **Note:** Varieties exist.

Date	Mintage	VF20	XF40	MS60	MS63	MS65
1999	Est. 100000	PF65 12.00				
1999	5,000,000	—	5.00	7.00	9.50	12.00

KM# 999a 2 POUNDS

12.00 g., 0.925 Silver 0.3569 oz. ASW, 28.35 mm. **Ruler:** Elizabeth II **Subject:** Rugby World Cup **Obv:** Head with tiara right **Rev:** 2-tone rugby design **Edge:** Reeded, lettered edge **Note:** Gold plated ring.

Date	Mintage	VF20	XF40	MS60	MS63	MS65
1999	Est. 9665	PF65 50.00	PF67 60.00			

KM# 999b 2 POUNDS

15.98 g., 0.917 Gold 0.4711 oz. AGW, 28.35 mm. **Ruler:** Elizabeth II **Subject:** Rugby World Cup **Obv:** Head with tiara right **Rev:** 2-tone rugby design

Date	Mintage	VF20	XF40	MS60	MS63	MS65
1999	311	PF65 825	PF67 850			

KM# 962 5 POUNDS

28.28 g., Copper-Nickel, 38.61 mm. **Ruler:** Elizabeth II **Subject:** 90th Birthday of Queen Mother **Obv:** Crowned head right **Rev:** Crowned monogram with rose and thistle flanking

Date	Mintage	VF20	XF40	MS60	MS63	MS65
ND-1990	2,761,000	—	—	6.00	10.00	12.00

KM# 962a 5 POUNDS

28.28 g., 0.925 Silver 0.841 oz. ASW, 38.61 mm. **Ruler:** Elizabeth II **Subject:** 90th Birthday of Queen Mother **Obv:** Crowned head right **Rev:** Crowned monogram with rose and thistle flanking

Date	Mintage	VF20	XF40	MS60	MS63	MS65
ND-1990	Est. 150000	PF65 50.00	PF67 60.00			

KM# 962b 5 POUNDS

39.94 g., 0.917 Gold 1.1775 oz. AGW, 38.61 mm. **Ruler:** Elizabeth II **Subject:** 90th Birthday of Queen Mother **Obv:** Crowned head right **Rev:** Crowned monogram with rose and thistle flanking

Date	Mintage	VF20	XF40	MS60	MS63	MS65
ND-1990	Est. 2500	PF65 1,750	PF67 1,850			

KM# 965 5 POUNDS

28.28 g., Copper-Nickel, 38.61 mm. **Ruler:** Elizabeth II **Subject:** 40th Anniversary of Reign **Obv:** Laureate head, right within circle of bugling horsemen **Rev:** Crown within circle

Date	Mintage	VF20	XF40	MS60	MS63	MS65
ND-1993	1,835,000	—	—	5.00	7.00	10.00
ND-1993	Est. 100000	PF65 15.00	PF67 20.00			

KM# 965a 5 POUNDS

28.28 g., 0.925 Silver 0.841 oz. ASW, 38.61 mm. **Ruler:** Elizabeth II **Subject:** 40th Anniversary of Reign **Obv:** Laureate head right within circle of bugling horsemen **Rev:** Crown within circle

Date	Mintage	VF20	XF40	MS60	MS63	MS65
ND-1993	Est. 100000	PF65 50.00	PF67 60.00			

KM# 965b 5 POUNDS

39.94 g., 0.917 Gold 1.1775 oz. AGW, 38.61 mm. **Ruler:** Elizabeth II **Subject:** 40th Anniversary of Reign **Obv:** Laureate head right with circle of bugling horsemen **Rev:** Crown within circle

Date	Mintage	VF20	XF40	MS60	MS63	MS65
ND-1993	Est. 2500	PF65 1,750	PF67 1,850			

KM# 974 5 POUNDS

28.28 g., Copper-Nickel, 38.61 mm. **Ruler:** Elizabeth II **Subject:** 70th Birthday of Queen Elizabeth II **Obv:** Crowned head right **Rev:** Five banners above Windsor Castle **Edge Lettering:** VIVAT REGINA ELIZABETHA

Date	Mintage	VF20	XF40	MS60	MS63	MS65
ND-1996	2,936,000	—	—	6.00	10.00	12.00
ND-1996	—	PF65 15.00	PF67 20.00			

KM# 974a 5 POUNDS

28.28 g., 0.925 Silver 0.841 oz. ASW, 38.61 mm. **Ruler:** Elizabeth II **Subject:** 70th Birthday of Queen Elizabeth II **Obv:** Crowned head right **Rev:** Five banners above Windsor Castle

Date	Mintage	VF20	XF40	MS60	MS63	MS65
ND-1996	Est. 70000	PF65 50.00	PF67 60.00			

KM# 974b 5 POUNDS

39.94 g., 0.917 Gold 1.1775 oz. AGW, 38.61 mm. **Ruler:** Elizabeth II **Subject:** 70th Birthday of Queen Elizabeth II **Obv:** Crowned head right **Rev:** Five banners above Windsor Castle

Date	Mintage	VF20	XF40	MS60	MS63	MS65
ND-1996	Est. 2750	PF65 1,750	PF67 1,850			

KM# 977 5 POUNDS

28.28 g., Copper-Nickel, 38.61 mm. **Ruler:** Elizabeth II **Subject:** Queen Elizabeth II and Prince Philip - Golden Wedding Anniversary **Obv:** Jugate busts right **Rev:** Crown above two shields, anchor below

Date	Mintage	VF20	XF40	MS60	MS63	MS65
ND-1997	1,733,000	—	—	6.00	10.00	12.00
ND-1997	—	PF65 15.00	PF67 20.00			

KM# 977a 5 POUNDS

28.28 g., 0.925 Silver 0.841 oz. ASW, 38.61 mm. **Ruler:** Elizabeth II **Subject:** Queen Elizabeth II and Prince Philip - Golden Wedding Anniversary **Obv:** Jugate busts right **Rev:** Crown above two shields, anchor below

Date	Mintage	VF20	XF40	MS60	MS63	MS65
ND-1997	Est. 70000	PF65 50.00	PF67 60.00			

KM# 977b 5 POUNDS

39.94 g., 0.917 Gold 1.1775 oz. AGW, 38.61 mm. **Ruler:** Elizabeth II **Subject:** Queen Elizabeth II and Prince Philip - Golden Wedding Anniversary **Obv:** Jugate busts right **Rev:** Crown above two shields, anchor below

Date	Mintage	VF20	XF40	MS60	MS63	MS65
ND-1997	Est. 2750	PF65 1,750	PF67 1,850			

KM# 995 5 POUNDS

28.28 g., Copper-Nickel, 38.61 mm. **Ruler:** Elizabeth II **Subject:** 50th Birthday - Prince Charles **Obv:** Head with tiara right **Rev:** Portrait of Prince Charles

Date	Mintage	VF20	XF40	MS60	MS63	MS65
1998	1,407,000	—	—	7.00	12.00	15.00
1998	Est. 100000	PF65 20.00	PF67 25.00			

KM# 995a 5 POUNDS

28.28 g., 0.925 Silver 0.841 oz. ASW, 38.61 mm. **Ruler:** Elizabeth II **Subject:** 50th Birthday - Prince Charles **Obv:** Head right **Rev:** Portrait of Prince Charles

Date	Mintage	VF20	XF40	MS60	MS63	MS65
1998	13,379	PF65 50.00	PF67 60.00			

KM# 995b 5 POUNDS

39.94 g., 0.9167 Gold 1.1771 oz. AGW, 38.61 mm. **Ruler:** Elizabeth II **Subject:** 50th Birthday - Prince Charles **Obv:** Head with tiara right **Rev:** Portrait of Prince Charles

Date	Mintage	VF20	XF40	MS60	MS63	MS65
1998	773	PF65 1,750	PF67 1,850			

KM# 997 5 POUNDS

Copper-Nickel, 38.61 mm. **Ruler:** Elizabeth II **Subject:** In Memory of Diana - Princess of Wales **Obv:** Head with tiara right **Rev:** Head right, dates

Date	Mintage	VF20	XF40	MS60	MS63	MS65
1999	5,000,000	—	—	7.00	12.00	15.00
1999	Est. 100000	PF65 20.00	PF67 25.00			

KM# 997a 5 POUNDS

28.28 g., 0.925 Silver 0.841 oz. ASW, 38.61 mm. **Ruler:** Elizabeth II **Subject:** In Memory of Diana - Princess of Wales **Obv:** Head with tiara right **Rev:** Head right, dates

Date	Mintage	VF20	XF40	MS60	MS63	MS65
1999	Est. 49545	PF65 50.00	PF67 60.00			

KM# 997b 5 POUNDS

39.94 g., 0.917 Gold 1.1775 oz. AGW, 38.61 mm. **Ruler:** Elizabeth II **Subject:** In Memory of Diana - Princess of Wales **Obv:** Head with tiara right **Rev:** Head right, dates

Date	Mintage	VF20	XF40	MS60	MS63	MS65
1999	Est. 7500	PF65 1,750	PF67 1,850			

KM# 1006 5 POUNDS

28.28 g., Copper-Nickel, 38.61 mm. **Ruler:** Elizabeth II **Obv:** Head with tiara right **Rev:** Map with Greenwich Meridian **Edge Lettering:** WHAT'S PAST IS PROLOGUE **Mint:** British Royal Mint

Date	Mintage	VF20	XF40	MS60	MS63	MS65
1999	396,000	—	—	7.00	12.00	15.00
1999	—	PF65 20.00	PF67 25.00			
2000	3,147,010	—	—	7.00	12.00	15.00
2000	Est. 100000	PF65 20.00	PF67 25.00			

Note: Gold overlay on the British Isles

KM# 1006.1 5 POUNDS

28.28 g., Copper-Nickel, 38.61 mm. **Ruler:** Elizabeth II **Obv:** Head with tiara right **Rev:** Map with Greenwich Meridian, London Millennium Dome at 3 o'clock in inner circle **Mint:** Millenium Dome

Date	Mintage	VF20	XF40	MS60	MS63	MS65
2000	—	—	—	—	22.00	28.00
2000 Millennium Dome	—	—	—	—	—	35.00

KM# 1006a 5 POUNDS

28.28 g., 0.925 Silver 0.841 oz. ASW, 38.61 mm. **Ruler:** Elizabeth II **Obv:** Head with tiara right **Rev:** Map with Greenwich Meridian

Date	Mintage	VF20	XF40	MS60	MS63	MS65
1999	75,000	PF65 50.00	PF67 60.00			
2000	—	PF65 50.00	PF67 60.00			

KM# 1006b 5 POUNDS

39.94 g., 0.917 Gold 1.1775 oz. AGW, 38.61 mm. **Ruler:** Elizabeth II **Obv:** Head with tiara right **Rev:** Map with Greenwich Meridian

Date	Mintage	VF20	XF40	MS60	MS63	MS65
1999	2,500	PF65 1,750	PF67 1,850			
2000	—	PF65 1,750	PF67 1,850			

KM# 1006c 5 POUNDS

28.28 g., 0.999 Silver 0.9083 oz. ASW, 38.61 mm. **Ruler:** Elizabeth II **Obv:** Head with tiara right **Rev:** Map with Greenwich Meridian **Note:** With gold-plated British map.

Date	Mintage	VF20	XF40	MS60	MS63	MS65
1999	15,000	PF65 75.00	PF67 85.00			

KM# 1007 5 POUNDS

Copper-Nickel **Ruler:** Elizabeth II **Subject:** 100th Birthday - Queen Elizabeth, The Queen Mother **Obv:** Head with tiara right **Rev:** Head left, signature below **Edge:** Reeded

Date	Mintage	VF20	XF40	MS60	MS63	MS65
2000	3,147,000	—	—	7.00	12.00	15.00

KM# 1007a 5 POUNDS

28.28 g., 0.925 Silver 0.841 oz. ASW, 38.61 mm. **Ruler:** Elizabeth II **Subject:** Queen Mother's Centennial **Obv:** Head with tiara right **Rev:** Head left with signature below **Edge:** Reeded **Mint:** British Royal Mint

Date	Mintage	VF20	XF40	MS60	MS63	MS65
2000	100,000	PF65 50.00	PF67 60.00			

KM# 1007b 5 POUNDS

39.94 g., 0.9167 Gold 1.1771 oz. AGW, 38.61 mm. **Ruler:** Elizabeth II **Subject:** Queen Mother's Centennial **Obv:** Head with tiara right **Rev:** Head left with signature below **Mint:** British Royal Mint

Date	Mintage	VF20	XF40	MS60	MS63	MS65
2000	3,000	PF65 1,750	PF67 1,850			

SOVEREIGN COINAGE

KM# 784 1/2 SOVEREIGN

3.99 g., 0.917 Gold 0.1178 oz. AGW **Ruler:** Victoria **Obv:** Mature draped bust left **Obv. Legend:** VICTORIA • DEI • GRA • BRITT • REGINA • FID • DEF • IND • IMP • **Rev:** St. George slaying the dragon right

Date	Mintage	F12	VF20	XF40	MS60	MS63
1901	2,037,999	—	—	—	150	275

KM# 804 1/2 SOVEREIGN

3.99 g., 0.917 Gold 0.1178 oz. AGW **Ruler:** Edward VII **Obv:** Head right **Rev:** St. George slaying the dragon

Date	Mintage	F12	VF20	XF40	MS60	MS63
1902	4,244,000	—	—	—	150	255
1902	15,000	PF63 325				
1903	2,522,000	—	—	—	150	255
1904	1,717,000	—	—	—	150	255
1905	3,024,000	—	—	—	150	255
1906	4,245,000	—	—	—	150	255
1907	4,233,000	—	—	—	150	255
1908	3,997,000	—	—	—	150	255
1909	4,011,000	—	—	—	150	255
1910	5,024,000	—	—	—	150	255

KM# 819 1/2 SOVEREIGN

3.99 g., 0.917 Gold 0.1178 oz. AGW **Ruler:** George V **Obv:** Head left **Rev:** St. George slaying the dragon

Date	Mintage	F12	VF20	XF40	MS60	MS63
1911	6,104,000	—	—	—	150	255
1911	3,764	PF63 400				
1912	6,224,000	—	—	—	150	255
1913	6,094,000	—	—	—	150	255
1914	7,251,000	—	—	—	150	255
1915	2,043,000	—	—	—	150	255

KM# 858 1/2 SOVEREIGN

3.99 g., 0.917 Gold 0.1178 oz. AGW **Ruler:** George VI **Obv:** Head left **Rev:** St. George slaying the dragon

Date	Mintage	F12	VF20	XF40	MS60	MS63
1937	5,500	PF63 700				
1937 Matte Proof; Unique	—	—	—	—	—	—

KM# 922 1/2 SOVEREIGN

3.99 g., 0.917 Gold 0.1176 oz. AGW **Ruler:** Elizabeth II **Obv:** Young bust right **Rev:** St. George slaying the dragon

Date	Mintage	VF20	XF40	MS60	MS63	MS65
1980	10,000	PF63 157				
1982	23,000	PF63 157				
1982	2,500,000	—	—	—	150	—
1983	22,000	PF63 157				
1984	22,000	PF63 157				

KM# 942 1/2 SOVEREIGN

3.99 g., 0.917 Gold 0.1176 oz. AGW **Ruler:** Elizabeth II **Obv:** Crowned head right **Rev:** St. George slaying the dragon

Date	Mintage	VF20	XF40	MS60	MS63	MS65
1985	25,000	PF63 230				
1986	25,000	PF63 230				
1987	23,000	PF63 230				
1988	Est. 23000	PF63 230				
1990	Est. 20000	PF63 290				
1991	Est. 9000	PF63 290				
1992	7,500	PF63 290				
1993	7,500	PF63 290				
1994	Est. 7500	PF63 260				
1995	4,900	PF63 260				
1996	—	PF63 260				
1997	—	PF63 260				

KM# 955 1/2 SOVEREIGN

3.99 g., 0.917 Gold 0.1176 oz. AGW **Ruler:** Elizabeth II **Subject:** 500th Anniversary of the Gold Sovereign **Obv:** Elizabeth II seated on the Coronation throne **Rev:** Crowned and quartered shield on tudor rose

Date	Mintage	VF20	XF40	MS60	MS63	MS65
ND-1989	Est. 25000	PF63 600				

KM# 1001 1/2 SOVEREIGN

3.99 g., 0.917 Gold 0.1176 oz. AGW **Ruler:** Elizabeth II **Obv:** Head with tiara right **Rev:** St. George slaying the dragon

Date	Mintage	VF20	XF40	MS60	MS63	MS65
1998	—	PF63 157				
1999	—	PF63 157				
2000	146,542	—	—	—	150	—
2000	—	PF63 157				

KM# 785 SOVEREIGN

7.99 g., 0.917 Gold 0.2355 oz. AGW **Ruler:** Victoria **Obv:** Mature draped bust left **Obv. Legend:** VICTORIA • DEI • GRA • BRITT • REGINA • FID • DEF • IND • IMP • **Rev:** St. George slaying the dragon

Date	Mintage	F12	VF20	XF40	MS60	MS63
1901	1,579,000	—	—	300	675	725

KM# 805 SOVEREIGN

7.99 g., 0.917 Gold 0.2355 oz. AGW **Ruler:** Edward VII **Obv:** Head right **Rev:** St. George slaying the dragon

Date	Mintage	F12	VF20	XF40	MS60	MS63
1902	4,738,000	—	—	300	425	—
1902	15,000	PF60 450				
1903	8,889,000	—	—	300	425	—
1904	10,041,000	—	—	300	425	—
1905	5,910,000	—	—	300	425	—
1906	10,467,000	—	—	300	425	—
1907	18,459,000	—	—	300	425	—
1908	11,729,000	—	—	300	425	—
1909	12,157,000	—	—	300	425	—
1910	22,380,000	—	—	300	425	—

KM# 820 SOVEREIGN

7.99 g., 0.917 Gold 0.2355 oz. AGW **Ruler:** George V **Obv:** Head left **Rev:** St. George slaying the dragon

Date	Mintage	F12	VF20	XF40	MS60	MS63
1911	30,044,000	—	—	300	425	—
1911	3,764	PF60 850				
1912	30,318,000	—	—	300	425	—
1913	24,540,000	—	—	300	425	—
1914	11,501,000	—	—	300	425	—
1915	20,295,000	—	—	300	425	—
1916	1,554,000	—	—	300	450	—
1917	1,014,999	3,000	3,750	8,500	12,000	—
1925	4,406,000	—	—	300	425	—

KM# 859 SOVEREIGN

7.99 g., 0.917 Gold 0.2355 oz. AGW **Ruler:** George VI **Obv:** Head left **Rev:** St. George slaying the dragon

Date	Mintage	F12	VF20	XF40	MS60	MS63
1937	5,500	PF60 2,250				
1937 Matte Proof; Unique	—	—	—	—	—	—

KM# 908 SOVEREIGN

7.99 g., 0.917 Gold 0.2355 oz. AGW **Ruler:** Elizabeth II **Obv:** Laureate bust right **Rev:** St. George slaying the dragon

Date	Mintage	F12	VF20	XF40	MS60	MS63
1957	2,072,000	—	—	300	425	—
1957	—	PF60 6,500				
1958	8,700,000	—	—	300	425	—
1958	—	PF60 6,500				
1959	1,358,000	—	—	300	425	—
1959	—	PF60 6,500				
1962	3,000,000	—	—	300	425	—
1962 Proof	—	—	—	—	—	—
1963	7,400,000	—	—	300	425	—
1963	—	PF60 6,750				
1964	3,000,000	—	—	300	425	—
1965	3,800,000	—	—	300	425	—
1966	7,050,000	—	—	300	425	—
1967	5,000,000	—	—	300	425	—
1968	4,203,000	—	—	300	425	—

KM# 919 SOVEREIGN

7.99 g., 0.917 Gold 0.2355 oz. AGW **Ruler:** Elizabeth II **Obv:** Young bust right **Rev:** St. George slaying the dragon

Date	Mintage	F12	VF20	XF40	MS60	MS63
1974	5,003,000	—	—	—	300	—
1976	4,150,000	—	—	—	300	—
1978	6,550,000	—	—	—	300	—
1979	9,100,000	—	—	—	300	—
1979	50,000	PF60 425				
1980	5,100,000	—	—	—	300	—
1980	91,000	PF60 425				
1981	5,000,000	—	—	—	300	—
1981	33,000	PF60 425				
1982	2,950,000	—	—	—	300	—
1982	23,000	PF60 425				
1983	21,000	PF60 425				
1984	20,000	PF60 425				

KM# 943 SOVEREIGN

7.99 g., 0.917 Gold 0.2355 oz. AGW **Ruler:** Elizabeth II **Obv:** Crowned head right **Rev:** St. George slaying the dragon

Date	Mintage	F12	VF20	XF40	MS60	MS63
1985	17,000	PF60 425				
1986	25,000	PF60 425				
1987	22,000	PF60 425				
1988	—	PF60 425				
1990	Est. 20000	PF60 475				
1991	—	PF60 475				
1992	7,500	PF60 475				
1993	7,500	PF60 525				
1994	—	PF60 475				
1995	7,500	PF60 475				
1996	7,500	PF60 475				
1997	7,500	PF60 475				

KM# 956 SOVEREIGN

7.99 g., 0.917 Gold 0.2355 oz. AGW **Ruler:** Elizabeth II **Subject:** 500th Anniversary of the Gold Sovereign **Obv:** Elizabeth II seated on coronation throne **Rev:** Crowned and quartered shield on tudor rose

Date	Mintage	F12	VF20	XF40	MS60	MS63
ND-1989	Est. 28000	PF60 1,250				

KM# 1002 SOVEREIGN

7.99 g., 0.917 Gold 0.2355 oz. AGW **Ruler:** Elizabeth II **Obv:** Head with tiara right **Rev:** St. George slaying the dragon

Date	Mintage	VF20	XF40	MS60	MS63	MS65
1998	10,000	PF63 450				
1999	10,000	PF63 500				
2000	129,069	—	—	—	425	—
2000	10,000	PF63 425				

KM# 806 2 POUNDS

15.98 g., 0.917 Gold 0.471 oz. AGW **Ruler:** Edward VII **Obv:** Head right **Rev:** St. George slaying the dragon

Date	Mintage	F12	VF20	XF40	MS60	MS63
1902	46,000	—	800	1,000	1,200	—
1902	8,066	PF60 1,250				

Note: Proof issues with mint mark S below right rear hoof of horse were struck at Sydney, refer to Australia listings

KM# 821 2 POUNDS

15.98 g., 0.917 Gold 0.471 oz. AGW **Ruler:** George V **Obv:** Head left **Rev:** St. George slaying the dragon

Date	Mintage	F12	VF20	XF40	MS60	MS63
1911	2,812	**PF60** 1,800				

KM# 860 2 POUNDS

15.98 g., 0.917 Gold 0.471 oz. AGW **Ruler:** George VI **Obv:** Head left **Rev:** St. George slaying the dragon

Date	Mintage	F12	VF20	XF40	MS60	MS63
1937	5,500	**PF60** 1,200				
1937 Matte Proof; Unique	—	—	—	—	—	—

KM# 923 2 POUNDS

15.92 g., 0.917 Gold 0.4694 oz. AGW **Ruler:** Elizabeth II **Obv:** Young bust right

Date	Mintage	F12	VF20	XF40	MS60	MS63
1980	10,000	**PF60** 750				
1982	2,500	**PF60** 800				
1983	13,000	**PF60** 750				

KM# 944 2 POUNDS

15.92 g., 0.917 Gold 0.4694 oz. AGW **Ruler:** Elizabeth II **Obv:** Crowned head right **Rev:** St. George slaying the dragon

Date	Mintage	F12	VF20	XF40	MS60	MS63
1985	5,849	**PF60** 750				
1987	14,000	**PF60** 750				
1988	15,000	**PF60** 750				
1990	Est. 12000	**PF60** 750				
1991	Est. 5000	**PF60** 750				
1992	3,000	**PF60** 750				
1993	3,000	**PF60** 750				
1999	—	**PF60** 750				

KM# 957 2 POUNDS

15.98 g., 0.917 Gold 0.4711 oz. AGW **Ruler:** Elizabeth II **Subject:** 500th Anniversary of the Gold Sovereign **Obv:** Elizabeth II seated on Coronation throne **Rev:** Crowned and quartered shield on tudor rose

Date	Mintage	F12	VF20	XF40	MS60	MS63
ND-1989	Est. 17000	**PF60** 800				

KM# 807 5 POUNDS

39.94 g., 0.917 Gold 1.1775 oz. AGW **Ruler:** Edward VII **Obv:** Head right **Rev:** St. George slaying the dragon

Date	Mintage	F12	VF20	XF40	MS60	MS63
1902	Est. 35000	—	1,500	2,400	3,000	—
Note: 27,000 pieces were melted						
1902	8,066	**PF60** 2,750				
Note: Proof issues with mint mark S below right rear hoof of horse were struck at Sydney, refer to Australia listings						

KM# 822 5 POUNDS

39.94 g., 0.917 Gold 1.1775 oz. AGW **Ruler:** George V **Obv:** Head left **Rev:** St. George slaying the dragon

Date	Mintage	F12	VF20	XF40	MS60	MS63
1911	2,812	**PF60** 4,250				

KM# 861 5 POUNDS

39.94 g., 0.917 Gold 1.1775 oz. AGW **Ruler:** George VI **Obv:** Head left **Rev:** St. George slaying the dragon

Date	Mintage	F12	VF20	XF40	MS60	MS63
1937	5,500	**PF60** 2,500				
Note: Impaired and blemished proofs of the 1937 issue are common and trade at much lower values; The value listed here is for blemish-free examples						
1937 Matte Proof; Unique	—	—	—	—	—	—

KM# 924 5 POUNDS

39.94 g., 0.917 Gold 1.1775 oz. AGW **Ruler:** Elizabeth II **Obv:** Young bust right **Rev:** St. George slaying the dragon

Date	Mintage	VF20	XF40	MS60	MS63	MS65
1980	10,000	**PF63** 1,750	**PF65** 1,850			
1981	5,400	**PF63** 1,750	**PF65** 1,850			
1982	2,500	**PF63** 1,750	**PF65** 1,850			
1984	8,000	**PF63** 1,750	**PF65** 1,850			
1984	25,000	—	—	—	1,500	1,650

KM# 945 5 POUNDS

39.94 g., 0.917 Gold 1.1775 oz. AGW **Ruler:** Elizabeth II **Obv:** Crowned head right **Rev:** St. George slaying the dragon

Date	Mintage	VF20	XF40	MS60	MS63	MS65
1985	14,000	—	—	—	1,500	1,650
1985	13,000	**PF63** 1,500	**PF65** 1,650			
1986	7,723	—	—	—	1,750	1,850
1990	1,226	—	—	—	2,000	2,150
1990	Est. 2500	**PF63** 2,000	**PF65** 2,150			
1991	976	—	—	—	2,100	2,250
1991	Est. 1500	**PF63** 2,000	**PF65** 2,150			
1992	797	—	—	—	2,100	2,250
1992	1,250	**PF63** 2,000	**PF65** 2,150			
1993	906	—	—	—	2,100	2,250
1993	—	**PF63** 2,000	**PF65** 2,150			
1994	—	—	—	—	2,000	2,150
1994	Est. 1250	**PF63** 2,100	**PF65** 2,250			
1995	Est. 1000	—	—	—	2,100	2,250
1995	Est. 1250	**PF63** 2,100	**PF65** 2,250			
1996	901	—	—	—	2,100	2,250
1997	802	—	—	—	2,100	2,250

KM# 949 5 POUNDS

39.94 g., 0.917 Gold 1.1775 oz. AGW **Ruler:** Elizabeth II **Obv:** Crowned head right **Rev:** St. George slaying the dragon

Date	Mintage	VF20	XF40	MS60	MS63	MS65
1987	10,000	**PF63** 1,500	**PF65** 1,650			
1988	Est. 10000	**PF63** 1,500	**PF65** 1,650			
1990	—	**PF63** 2,000	**PF65** 2,150			
1991	—	**PF63** 2,000	**PF65** 2,150			

KM# 958 5 POUNDS

39.94 g., 0.917 Gold 1.1775 oz. AGW **Ruler:** Elizabeth II **Subject:** 500th Anniversary of the Gold Sovereign **Obv:** Elizabeth II seated on Coronation throne **Rev:** Crowned and quartered shield on tudor rose

Date	Mintage	VF20	XF40	MS60	MS63	MS65
-1989	10,000	—	—	—	1,750	1,850
-1989	Est. 5000	**PF63** 2,000	**PF65** 2,150			

KM# 1003 5 POUNDS

39.94 g., 0.917 Gold 1.1775 oz. AGW, 36 mm. **Ruler:** Elizabeth II

Obv: Head with tiara right **Rev:** St. George slaying dragon **Edge:** Reeded **Mint:** British Royal Mint

Date	Mintage	VF20	XF40	MS60	MS63	MS65
1998 (u)	825	—	—	—	1,750	1,850
1998	—	PF63 2,100	PF65 2,250			
1999 (u)	970	—	—	—	1,750	1,850
1999	—	PF63 2,000	PF65 2,150			
2000	10,000	—	—	—	1,750	1,850
2000 (u)	994	—	—	—	1,750	1,850
2000	—	PF63 2,100	PF65 2,250			

BULLION COINAGE

Until 1990, .917 Gold was commonly alloyed with copper by the British Royal Mint. Starting in 2013 the bullion coins have been struck at .999 fine.

All proof issues have designers name as P. Nathan. The uncirculated issues use only Nathan.

KM# 978 20 PENCE

3.24 g., 0.958 Silver 0.0998 oz. ASW, 16.5 mm. **Ruler:** Elizabeth II **Obv:** Crowned head right **Rev:** Britannia in chariot **Edge:** Reeded **Mint:** British Royal Mint

Date	Mintage	VF20	XF40	MS60	MS63	MS65
1997	—	PF63 25.00				

KM# 1079 20 PENCE

3.24 g., 0.9584 Silver 0.0998 oz. ASW, 16.5 mm. **Ruler:** Elizabeth II **Obv:** Head with tiara right **Rev:** Britannia standing **Edge:** Reeded **Mint:** British Royal Mint

Date	Mintage	VF20	XF40	MS60	MS63	MS65
1998	—	PF63 25.00				
2000	—	PF63 25.00				

KM# 1082 20 PENCE

3.24 g., 0.9584 Silver 0.0998 oz. ASW, 16.5 mm. **Ruler:** Elizabeth II **Obv:** Head with tiara right **Rev:** Britannia in chariot right **Edge:** Reeded **Mint:** British Royal Mint

Date	Mintage	VF20	XF40	MS60	MS63	MS65
1999	—	PF63 25.00				

KM# 979 50 PENCE

8.11 g., 0.958 Silver 0.2498 oz. ASW, 27.3 mm. **Ruler:** Elizabeth II **Obv:** Crowned head right **Rev:** Britannia in chariot

Date	Mintage	VF20	XF40	MS60	MS63	MS65
1997	Est. 15000	PF63 25.00				

Note: In proof sets only

KM# 1080 50 PENCE

8.11 g., 0.9584 Silver 0.2499 oz. ASW, 22 mm. **Ruler:** Elizabeth II **Obv:** Head with tiara right **Rev:** Britannia standing **Edge:** Reeded **Mint:** British Royal Mint

Date	Mintage	VF20	XF40	MS60	MS63	MS65
1998	—	PF63 35.00				
2000	—	PF63 35.00				

KM# 980 POUND

16.22 g., 0.958 Silver 0.4996 oz. ASW **Ruler:** Elizabeth II **Obv:** Crowned head right **Rev:** Britannia in chariot

Date	Mintage	VF20	XF40	MS60	MS63	MS65
1997	Est. 15000	PF63 40.00				

KM# 1081 POUND

16.22 g., 0.9584 Silver 0.4998 oz. ASW, 27 mm. **Ruler:** Elizabeth II **Obv:** Head with tiara right **Rev:** Britannia standing **Edge:** Reeded **Mint:** British Royal Mint

Date	Mintage	VF20	XF40	MS60	MS63	MS65
1998	—	PF63 50.00				
2000	—	PF63 50.00				

KM# 1084 POUND

16.22 g., 0.9584 Silver 0.4998 oz. ASW, 27 mm. **Ruler:** Elizabeth II **Obv:** Head with tiara right **Rev:** Britannia in chariot right **Edge:** Reeded **Mint:** British Royal Mint

Date	Mintage	VF20	XF40	MS60	MS63	MS65
1999	—	PF63 50.00				

KM# 981 2 POUNDS

32.54 g., 0.958 Silver 1.0022 oz. ASW **Ruler:** Elizabeth II **Obv:** Crowned head right **Rev:** Britannia in chariot

Date	Mintage	VF20	XF40	MS60	MS63	MS65
1997	Est. 35000	PF63 65.00				

KM# 1029 2 POUNDS

32.54 g., 0.958 Silver 1.0022 oz. ASW, 40 mm. **Ruler:** Elizabeth II **Obv:** Head with tiara right **Rev:** Standing Britannia **Edge:** Reeded **Mint:** British Royal Mint

Date	Mintage	VF20	XF40	MS60	MS63	MS65
1998	88,909	—	—	—	35.00	—
1998	—	PF63 65.00				
2000	81,301	—	—	—	37.50	—
2000	—	PF63 65.00				

KM# 1000 2 POUNDS

32.54 g., 0.958 Silver 1.0022 oz. ASW, 40 mm. **Ruler:** Elizabeth II **Obv:** Head with tiara right **Rev:** Britannia in chariot **Edge:** Reeded **Mint:** British Royal Mint

Date	Mintage	VF20	XF40	MS60	MS63	MS65
1999	Est. 100000	PF63 60.00				

KM# 950 10 POUNDS

3.41 g., 0.917 Gold 0.1006 oz. AGW **Ruler:** Elizabeth II **Obv:** Crowned head right **Rev:** Britannia standing **Note:** Copper alloy.

Date	Mintage	VF20	XF40	MS60	MS63	MS65
1987	—	—	—	—	150	—
1987	—	PF63 165				
1988	—	—	—	—	150	—
1988	—	PF63 165				
1989	—	—	—	—	150	—
1989	—	PF63 165				

KM# 950a 10 POUNDS

3.41 g., 0.917 Gold 0.1006 oz. AGW, 16.5 mm. **Ruler:** Elizabeth II **Obv:** Crowned head right **Rev:** Britannia standing **Edge:** Reeded **Mint:** British Royal Mint **Note:** Silver alloy.

Date	Mintage	VF20	XF40	MS60	MS63	MS65
1990	1,571	PF63 170				
1991	—	PF63 170				
1992	1,000	PF63 170				
1993	—	PF63 170				
1994	—	PF63 170				
1995	1,500	PF63 170				
1996	—	PF63 170				

KM# 982 10 POUNDS

3.41 g., 0.9167 Gold 0.1005 oz. AGW **Ruler:** Elizabeth II **Obv:** Crowned head right **Rev:** Britannia in chariot

Date	Mintage	VF20	XF40	MS60	MS63	MS65
1997	11,821	PF63 170				

KM# 1008 10 POUNDS

3.41 g., 0.9167 Gold 0.1005 oz. AGW, 16.5 mm. **Ruler:** Elizabeth II **Obv:** Head with tiara right **Rev:** Britannia standing **Edge:** Reeded **Mint:** British Royal Mint

Date	Mintage	VF20	XF40	MS60	MS63	MS65
1998	—	PF63 170				
1999	1,058	PF63 170				
2000	—	PF63 195				

KM# 951 25 POUNDS

8.51 g., 0.917 Gold 0.251 oz. AGW **Ruler:** Elizabeth II **Obv:** Crowned head right **Rev:** Britannia standing **Note:** Copper alloy.

Date	Mintage	VF20	XF40	MS60	MS63	MS65
1987	—	—	—	—	350	—
1987	—	PF63 410				
1988	—	—	—	—	350	—
1988	Est. 14000	PF63 410				
1989	—	—	—	—	350	—
1989	Est. 4000	PF63 410				

KM# 951a 25 POUNDS

8.51 g., 0.917 Gold 0.251 oz. AGW, 22 mm. **Ruler:** Elizabeth II **Obv:** Crowned head right **Rev:** Britannia standing **Edge:** Reeded **Mint:** British Royal Mint **Note:** Silver alloy.

Date	Mintage	VF20	XF40	MS60	MS63	MS65
1990	Est. 2500	PF63 410				
1991	750	PF63 420				
1992	500	PF63 420				
1993	—	PF63 420				
1994	—	PF63 420				
1995	500	PF63 420				
1996	2,500	PF63 410				

KM# 983 25 POUNDS

8.51 g., 0.9167 Gold 0.2508 oz. AGW **Ruler:** Elizabeth II **Obv:** Crowned head right **Rev:** Britannia in chariot

Date	Mintage	VF20	XF40	MS60	MS63	MS65
1997	Est. 4000	PF63 410				

KM# 1009 25 POUNDS

8.51 g., 0.9167 Gold 0.2508 oz. AGW, 22 mm. **Ruler:** Elizabeth II **Obv:** Head with tiara right **Rev:** Britannia standing **Edge:** Reeded **Mint:** British Royal Mint

Date	Mintage	VF20	XF40	MS60	MS63	MS65
1998	650	PF63 435				
1999	—	—	—	—	385	—
1999	1,000	PF63 435				
2000	—	—	—	—	385	—
2000	Est. 500	PF63 435				

KM# 952 50 POUNDS

17.03 g., 0.917 Gold 0.5019 oz. AGW **Ruler:** Elizabeth II **Obv:** Crowned head right **Rev:** Britannia standing **Note:** Copper alloy.

Date	Mintage	VF20	XF40	MS60	MS63	MS65
1987	—	—	—	—	700	—
1987	—	PF63 670				
1988	—	—	—	—	700	—
1988	—	PF63 670				
1989	—	—	—	—	700	—
1989	—	PF63 670				

KM# 952a 50 POUNDS

17.03 g., 0.917 Gold 0.5019 oz. AGW, 27 mm. **Ruler:** Elizabeth II **Obv:** Crowned head right **Rev:** Britannia standing **Edge:** Reeded **Mint:** British Royal Mint **Note:** Silver alloy.

Date	Mintage	VF20	XF40	MS60	MS63	MS65
1990	—	PF63 670				
1991	—	PF63 670				
1992	500	PF63 670				
1993	—	PF63 700				
1994	—	PF63 700				
1995	500	PF63 670				
1996	—	PF63 700				

KM# 984 50 POUNDS

17.03 g., 0.9167 Gold 0.5019 oz. AGW **Ruler:** Elizabeth II **Obv:** Crowned head right **Rev:** Britannia in chariot

Date	Mintage	VF20	XF40	MS60	MS63	MS65
1997	Est. 1500	PF63 700				

KM# 1010 50 POUNDS

17.03 g., 0.9167 Gold 0.5019 oz. AGW, 27 mm. **Ruler:** Elizabeth II **Obv:** Head with tiara right **Rev:** Britannia standing **Edge:** Reeded **Mint:** British Royal Mint

Date	Mintage	VF20	XF40	MS60	MS63	MS65
1998	—	PF63 670				
1999	—	—	—	—	740	—
1999	—	PF63 670				
2000	—	—	—	—	740	—
2000	750	PF63 670				

KM# 953 100 POUNDS

34.05 g., 0.917 Gold 1.0039 oz. AGW **Ruler:** Elizabeth II **Obv:**

Crowned head right **Rev:** Britannia standing **Note:** Copper alloy.

Date	Mintage	VF20	XF40	MS60	MS63	MS65
1987	—	—	—	—	1,425	—
1987	13,000	PF63 1,350				
1988	—	—	—	—	1,425	—
1988	Est. 8500	PF63 1,350				
1989	—	—	—	—	1,425	—
1989	Est. 2600	PF63 1,350				

KM# 953a 100 POUNDS

34.05 g., 0.917 Gold 1.0039 oz. AGW, 32.7 mm. **Ruler:** Elizabeth II **Obv:** Crowned head right **Rev:** Britannia standing **Edge:** Reeded **Mint:** British Royal Mint **Note:** Silver alloy.

Date	Mintage	VF20	XF40	MS60	MS63	MS65
1990	—	PF63 1,400				
1991	143	PF63 1,400				
1992	500	PF63 1,350				
1993	—	PF63 1,350				
1994	Est. 500	PF63 1,350				
1995	Est. 500	PF63 1,350				
1996	2,500	PF63 1,350				

KM# 985 100 POUNDS

34.05 g., 0.9167 Gold 1.0035 oz. AGW **Ruler:** Elizabeth II **Obv:** Crowned head right **Rev:** Britannia in chariot

Date	Mintage	VF20	XF40	MS60	MS63	MS65
1997	—	—	—	—	1,475	—
1997	164	PF63 1,850				

KM# 1011 100 POUNDS

34.05 g., 0.9167 Gold 1.0035 oz. AGW, 32.7 mm. **Ruler:** Elizabeth II **Obv:** Head with tiara right **Rev:** Britannia standing **Edge:** Reeded **Mint:** British Royal Mint

Date	Mintage	VF20	XF40	MS60	MS63	MS65
1998	—	—	—	—	1,475	—
1998	—	PF63 1,350				
1999	—	—	—	—	1,475	—
1999	—	PF63 1,350				
2000	—	—	—	—	1,475	—
2000	750	PF63 1,400				

TRADE COINAGE

Issued to facilitate British trade in the Orient, the reverse design incorporated the denomination in Chinese characters and Malay script.

This issue was struck at the Bombay (B) and Calcutta (C) Mints in India, except for 1925 and 1930 issues which were struck at London. Through error the mint marks did not appear on some early (1895-1900) issues as indicated.

Britannia Issues

KM# T5 DOLLAR

26.96 g., 0.900 Silver 0.780 oz. ASW, 39 mm. **Obv:** Britannia standing **Rev:** Oriental designs on cross **Note:** The mint mark is incuse and located within the top of the trident held by Britannia.

Date	Mintage	F12	VF20	XF40	MS60	MS63
1901 B	Inc. above	40.00	55.00	70.00	100	—
1901/0 B	25,680,000	45.00	65.00	100	225	—
1901 C	1,514,000	45.00	65.00	110	225	—
1901 B	Inc. above	PF60 800				
1902 B	30,404,000	40.00	55.00	70.00	100	—
1902 C	1,267,000	45.00	65.00	110	225	—
1902 B	Inc. above	PF60 800				
1902 C	Inc. above	PF60 800				
1903/2 B	3,956,000	40.00	55.00	70.00	150	—
1903 B	Inc. above	40.00	55.00	70.00	110	—
1903 B	Inc. above	PF60 800				
1904/898 B	649,000	55.00	85.00	165	300	—
1904/3 B	Inc. above	45.00	55.00	110	250	—
1904/0 B	Inc. above	80.00	125	175	300	—
1904 B	Inc. above	45.00	65.00	110	275	—
1904 B	Inc. above	PF60 700				
1907 B	1,946,000	40.00	55.00	70.00	135	—
1908/3 B	6,871,000	55.00	75.00	120	225	—
1908/7 B	Inc. above	45.00	60.00	90.00	150	—
1908 B	Inc. above	40.00	55.00	70.00	125	—
1908 B	Inc. above	PF60 700				
1909/8 B	5,954,000	45.00	60.00	90.00	165	—
1909 B	Inc. above	40.00	55.00	70.00	125	—
1910/00 B	553,000	45.00	65.00	110	175	—
1910 B	Inc. above	40.00	55.00	70.00	125	—
1911/00 B	—	40.00	55.00	100	175	—
1911 B	37,471,000	40.00	55.00	70.00	125	—
1912 B	5,672,000	40.00	55.00	70.00	125	—
1912 B	Inc. above	PF60 800				
1913/2 B	—	100	150	250	700	—
1913 B	1,567,000	60.00	90.00	175	400	—
1913 B	Inc. above	PF60 800				
1921 B	5	—	—	—	15,000	—
Note: Original mintage 50,211						
1921 B Proof; restrike	—	PF60 4,500				
1925	6,870,000	40.00	65.00	80.00	150	—
1929/1 B	5,100,000	45.00	65.00	80.00	175	—
1929 B	Inc. above	40.00	55.00	70.00	125	—
1929 B	Inc. above	PF60 800				
1930 B	10,400,000	40.00	55.00	70.00	100	—
1930 B	Inc. above	PF60 800				
1930	6,660,000	40.00	55.00	70.00	100	—
1934 B	17,335,000	150	225	350	1,500	—
1934 B	Inc. above	PF60 3,500				
1934 B Proof; restrike	20	PF60 3,000				
1935 B	Est. 25	2,000	2,500	3,500	20,000	—
Note: Original mintage 6,811,995						
1935 B	20	PF60 7,500				
1935 B Proof; restrike	20	PF60 4,000				

KM# T5a DOLLAR

Gold **Obv:** Britannia standing **Rev:** Oriental design on cross

Date	Mintage	F12	VF20	XF40	MS60	MS63
1901 B Proof; restrike	—	PF60 7,500				
1902 B Proof; restrike	—	PF60 7,500				

PIEDFORT

KM#	Date	Mintage	Identification	Mkt Val
P1	1973	—	50 Pence. 0.925. Silver.	1,950
P2	1982	—	20 Pence. 0.925. Silver.	80.00
P3	1983	10,000	Pound. 0.925. Silver. KM#933.	195
P4	1984	15,000	Pound. 0.925. Silver. KM#934.	80.00
P5	1985	15,000	Pound. 0.925. Silver. KM#941.	70.00
P6	1986	15,000	Pound. 0.925. Silver. KM#946.	70.00
P7	1987	15,000	Pound. 0.925. Silver. KM#948.	70.00
P8	1988 (1989)	15,000	Pound. 0.925. Silver. KM#954.	70.00
P9	1989	10,000	Pound. 0.925. Silver. KM#959.	75.00
P10	1989	25,000	2 Pounds. 0.925. Silver. KM#960a.	95.00
P11	1989	10,000	2 Pounds. 0.925. Silver. KM#961a.	95.00
P12	1990	20,000	5 Pence. 0.925. Silver. KM#937c.	39.00
P13	1992	15,000	10 Pence. 0.925. Silver. KM#938b.	80.00
P15	1992	10,993	50 Pence. 0.925. Silver. KM#963a.	110
P16	1993	12,500	Pound. 0.925. Silver. KM#964.	75.00
P17	1994	Est. 10000	50 Pence. 0.925. Silver. KM#966b.	105
P18	1994	11,722	Pound. 0.925. Silver. KM#967.	110
P19	1994	9,569	2 Pounds. 0.925. Silver. KM#968a.	125
P20	1995	8,458	Pound. 0.925. Silver. KM#969.	105
P21	ND1995	10,000	2 Pounds. 0.925. Silver. KM#970a.	110
P22	1995	10,000	2 Pounds. 0.925. Silver. KM#971a.	110
P23	1996	10,000	Pound. 0.925. Silver. KM#972.	90.00
P104	1996	7,634	2 Pounds. 0.925. Silver. KM#937a.	110
P24	1997	—	50 Pence. 0.925. Silver. KM#963.	110
P25	1997	Est. 10000	Pound. 0.925. Silver. KM#975.	110
P26	1998 (1997)	—	Pound. 0.925. Silver. KM#993a.	—
P27	1997	10,000	2 Pounds. 0.925. Silver. KM#976a.	115
P28	1998	—	50 Pence. 0.925. Silver. KM#992a.	110
P29	1998	—	50 Pence. 0.925. Silver. KM#996a.	110
P30	1998	7,646	2 Pounds. 0.925. Silver. KM#994a.	115
P31	1999	9,975	Pound. 0.925. Silver. KM998a.	—
P105	1999	10,000	2 Pounds. 0.925. Silver. KM#999.	—
P39	2000	—	50 Pence. Silver. KM#1004a.	110
P100	2000	9,994	Pound. 0.925. Silver. KM#1005a.	110
P112	2000	14,850	5 Pounds. 0.925. Silver.	150

TRIAL STRIKES

KM#	Date	Mintage	Identification	Mkt Val
TS1	1926	—	3 Pence. Silver. MODEL. Thistle.	1,800
TS2	1926	—	6 Pence. Silver. MODEL.	2,000
TS3	1926	—	Shilling. Silver. MODEL. Lion on crown.	2,000
TS4	1926	—	2 Shilling. Silver. MODEL. Stemmed rose.	2,250
TS5	1926	—	1/2 Crown. Silver. MODEL. Crown over heraldic shield.	4,000
TSA6	1926	—	Crown. Silver. MODEL, Britannia reclining. 2-3 pieces.	10,000
TS6	1926	—	Crown. Silver. Britannia reclining. Blank. (MCMXXVI) Unique.	15,000

Note: A complete set of silver plated copper electro types officially prepared for the designer has been recorded; Market value undetermined.

KM#	Date	Mintage	Identification	Mkt Val
TS6a	1937	—	Farthing. Bronze. Blank. Wren. 1-2 pieces, KM#843.	2,500
TS7	1963	—	1/4 New Penny. Aluminum. Rose. Uniface.	—
TS8	1963	—	1/2 New Penny. Bronze. Winged animal. Uniface.	—
TS9	1963	—	New Penny. Bronze. Uniface.	—
TS10	1963	—	2 New Pence. Bronze. Britannia seated right. Uniface.	—
TS11	1963	—	5 New Pence. Copper-Nickel. Three crowns. Uniface.	—
TS12	1963	—	10 New Pence. Silver. Uniface.	—
TS13	1963	—	20 New Pence. Silver. Uniface.	—
TS14	1963	—	20 New Pence. Silver. Helmeted and supported arms. Uniface.	—

PATTERNS

Including off metal strikes

KM#	Date	Mintage	Identification	Mkt Val
PnA121	1922	Est. 5	Florin. Gold. KM817a.	25,000
PnB121	1923	Est. 2	3 Pence. Nickel. KM#813a.	3,000
PnC121	1923	Est. 20	Shilling. Nickel. KM816a.	1,500
Pn121	1924	—	Shilling. Nickel. KM816a.	1,500
PnD121	1924	1	3 Pence. Gold. KM813a.	15,000
PnE121	1924	3	6 Pence. Gold. KM#815a.1.	15,000
PnF121	1924	Est. 20	Shilling. Nickel. KM816a.	1,500
PnA122	1925	—	3 Pence. Nickel. Modified effigy. KM#831.	2,500
PnB122	1925	Est. 2	3 Pence. Silver. MODEL. Matte proof; KM#831.	2,500
PnC122	1925	Est. 3	6 Pence. Nickel. Modified effigy. KM#832.	2,000
PnD122	1925	Est. 2	6 Pence. Silver. MODEL. Matte proof; KM#832.	2,000
PnE122	1925	Est. 3	Shilling. Nickel. Modified effigy. KM#833.	2,500
PnF122	1925	Est. 2	Shilling. Silver. MODEL. Matte proof; Reverse of KM#833.	2,500
PnG122	1926	Est. 2	1/2 Crown. Silver. MODEL. 1-2 pieces, Matte proof; KM#835.	5,000
PnH122	1926	—	Crown. Silver. MODEL. Matte proof; KM#836.	—
PnI122	1927	—	6 Pence. Nickel. KM#828.	1,500
PnJ122	1927	Est. 2	Florin. Silver. MODEL. Matte proof, KM#834.	2,500
PnJ122A	1927	—	Shilling. Silver. MODEL. Unique. Reverse of KM#833.	3,000
PnK122	1927	—	1/2 Crown. Nickel. Modified effigy. KM830.	—
PnL122	1927	Est. 4	1/2 Crown. Gold. Modified Effigy. KM830.	—
PnM122	1935	—	Crown. Gold. Similar to KM842.	45,000
Pn122	1937	—	Farthing. Bronze. Head left. Wren left. Edward VIII.	—
Pn123	1937	—	1/2 Penny. Bronze. Edward VIII.	30,000
Pn124	1937	—	Penny. Bronze. Head left. Edward VIII.	100,000
Pn125	1937	—	3 Pence. Nickel-Brass. Edward VIII.	30,000
Pn126	1937	—	3 Pence. Nickel-Brass. Head left. Thrift Plant. Edward VIII.	45,000
Pn127	1937	—	6 Pence. 0.500. Silver. Head left. Six joined rings form design. Edward VIII.	25,000
Pn128	1937	—	Shilling. 0.500. Silver. Head left. Scottish Crest. Edward VIII.	37,000
Pn129	1937	—	Florin. 0.500. Silver. Edward VIII.	25,000
Pn130	1937	—	1/2 Crown. 0.500. Silver. Head left. Quartered flag divides crowned monograms. Edward VIII.	75,000
Pn130a	1937	—	1/2 Crown. 0.500. Silver. Head left. Rev Model. Edward III.	15,000
Pn131	1937	—	Crown. 0.500. Silver. Head left. Crowned and quartered shield with supporters. Edward VIII.	150,000
Pn132	1937	6	Sovereign. 0.916. Gold. Head left. St. George slaying the dragon. Edward VIII.	877,500
Pn133	1946	—	6 Pence. Copper-Nickel. KM# 852.	—
PnA133	1946	—	Shilling. Copper-Nickel. KM# 853.	2,000
PnB133	1946	—	2 Shilling. Copper-Nickel. KM# 855.	2,000
PnC133	1946	—	1/2 Crown. Copper-Nickel. KM# 856.	—
PnA134	1950	—	4 Shilling. Copper-Nickel.	10,000
PnA134a	1950	—	Farthing. Copper-Nickel.	1,500
PnB134	1952	—	Shilling. Nickel. KM#876.	—
Pn134	1953	—	Penny. Bronze. Dentilated border.	—
Pn135	1953	—	1/2 Sovereign. 0.916. Gold.	—
PnA135	1953	—	Crown. Copper-Nickel. Matte, KM#894.	—

KM#	Date	Mintage	Identification	Mkt Val
Pn136	1953	—	Sovereign. 0.916. Gold. Y#137.	300,000
Pn137	1953	—	2 Pounds. 0.916. Gold.	—
Pn138	1953	—	5 Pounds. 0.916. Gold.	—
Pn139	1961	—	Cent. Bronze.	—
Pn140	1961	—	2 Cents. Bronze.	—
Pn141	1961	—	5 Cents. Copper-Nickel. Lion on crown.	—
Pn142	1961	—	10 Cents. Copper-Nickel.	—
Pn143	1961	—	20 Cents. Copper-Nickel. Britannia, standing facing.	—
Pn144	1961	—	50 Cents. Silver. Una and lion.	—
Pn145	1963	—	1/2 Penny. Bronze. Decimal.	—
Pn146	1963	—	Penny. Bronze. Decimal.	—

MAUNDY SETS

KM#	Date	Mintage	Identification	Issue Price	Mkt Val
MDS157	1901 (4)	8,976	KM#775-778	—	250
MDS158	1902 (4)	8,976	KM#795-796, 797.1-798	—	220
MDS159	1902 (4)	—	KM#795-796, 797.1-798 Proof	—	250
MDS160	1903 (4)	8,976	KM#795-796; 797.1-798	—	220
MDS161	1904 (4)	8,976	KM#795-796, 797.1-798	—	220
MDS162	1905 (4)	8,976	KM#795-796, 797.2-798	—	220
MDS163	1906 (4)	8,800	KM#795-796, 797.2-798	—	220
MDS164	1907 (4)	8,760	KM#795-796, 797.2-798	—	220
MDS165	1908 (4)	8,760	KM#795-796, 797.2-798	—	220
MDS166	1909 (4)	1,983	KM#795-796, 797.2-798	—	325
MDS167	1910 (4)	1,440	KM#795-796, 797.2-798	—	350
MDS168	1911 (4)	1,768	KM#811-814	—	260
MDS169	1911 (4)	6,007	KM#811-814 Proof	—	300
MDS170	1912 (4)	1,246	KM#811-814	—	260
MDS171	1913 (4)	1,228	KM#811-814	—	260
MDS172	1914 (4)	982	KM#811-814	—	300
MDS173	1915 (4)	1,293	KM#811-814	—	260
MDS174	1916 (4)	1,128	KM#811-814	—	260
MDS175	1917 (4)	1,237	KM#811-814	—	260
MDS176	1918 (4)	1,375	KM#811-814	—	260
MDS177	1919 (4)	1,258	KM#811-814	—	260
MDS178	1920 (4)	1,399	KM#811-814	—	260
MDS179	1921 (4)	1,386	KM#811a-814a	—	260
MDS180	1922 (4)	1,373	KM#811a-814a	—	260
MDS181	1923 (4)	1,430	KM#811a-814a	—	260
MDS182	1924 (4)	1,515	KM#811a-814a	—	260
MDS183	1925 (4)	1,438	KM#811a-814a	—	260
MDS184	1926 (4)	1,504	KM#811a-814a	—	300
MDS185	1927 (4)	1,647	KM#811a-814a	—	260
MDS186	1928 (4)	1,642	KM#827, 839-841	—	250
MDS187	1929 (4)	1,761	KM#827, 839-841	—	260
MDS188	1930 (4)	1,724	KM#827, 839-841	—	260
MDS189	1931 (4)	1,759	KM#827, 839-841	—	260
MDS190	1932 (4)	1,835	KM#827, 839-841	—	260
MDS191	1933 (4)	1,872	KM#827, 839-841	—	260
MDS192	1934 (4)	1,887	KM#827, 839-841	—	260
MDS193	1935 (4)	1,926	KM#827, 839-841	—	260
MDS194	1936 (4)	1,323	KM#827, 839-841	—	275
MDS195	1937 (4)	1,325	KM#846-847, 850-851	—	225
MDS196	1937 (4)	26,000	KM#846-847, 850-851 Proof	—	250
MDS197	1938 (4)	1,275	KM#846-847, 850-851	—	230
MDS198	1939 (4)	1,234	KM#846-847, 850-851	—	230
MDS199	1940 (4)	1,277	KM#846-847, 850-851	—	230
MDS200	1941 (4)	1,253	KM#846-847, 850-851	—	230
MDS201	1942 (4)	1,231	KM#846-847, 850-851	—	230
MDS202	1943 (4)	1,239	KM#846-847, 850-851	—	230
MDS203	1944 (4)	1,259	KM#846-847, 850-851	—	230
MDS204	1945 (4)	1,355	KM#846-847, 850-851	—	230
MDS205	1946 (4)	1,365	KM#846-847, 850-851	—	230
MDS206	1947 (4)	1,375	KM#846a-847a, 850a-851a	—	230
MDS207	1948 (4)	1,385	KM#846a-847a, 850a-851a	—	230
MDS208	1949 (4)	1,395	KM#870-872, 874	—	230
MDS209	1950 (4)	1,405	KM#870-872, 874	—	230
MDS210	1951 (4)	1,468	KM#870-872, 874, also struck in matte proof	—	230
MDS211	1952 (4)	1,012	KM#870-872, 874	—	250
MDS212	1953 (4)	1,025	KM#884-885, 887-888, also struck in gold $30,000	—	950
MDS213	1954 (4)	1,020	KM#898-899, 901-902	—	250
MDS214	1955 (4)	1,036	KM#898-899, 901-902, also struck in matte proof	—	250
MDS215	1956 (4)	1,088	KM#898-899, 901-902	—	250
MDS216	1957 (4)	1,094	KM#898-899, 901-902	—	250
MDS217	1958 (4)	1,100	KM#898-899, 901-902	—	250
MDS218	1959 (4)	1,106	KM#898-899, 901-902	—	250
MDS219	1960 (4)	1,112	KM#898-899, 901-902	—	250
MDS220	1961 (4)	—	KM#898-899, 901-902	—	250
MDS221	1962 (4)	1,125	KM#898-899, 901-902	—	250
MDS222	1963 (4)	1,131	KM#898-899, 901-902	—	250
MDS223	1964 (4)	1,137	KM#898-899, 901-902	—	250
MDS224	1965 (4)	1,143	KM#898-899, 901-902	—	250
MDS225	1966 (4)	1,206	KM#898-899, 901-902	—	250
MDS226	1967 (4)	986	KM#898-899, 901-902	—	275
MDS227	1968 (4)	964	KM#898-899, 901-902	—	275
MDS228	1969 (4)	1,002	KM#898-899, 901-902	—	275
MDS229	1970 (4)	980	KM#898-899, 901-902	—	275
MDS230	1971 (4)	1,018	KM#898-899, 901-902 Tewkesbury Abbey	—	275
MDS231	1972 (4)	1,026	KM#898-899, 901-902 York Minster Abbey	—	275
MDS232	1973 (4)	1,004	KM#898-899, 901-902 Westminster Abbey	—	275
MDS233	1974 (4)	1,042	KM#898-899, 901-902 Salisbury Cathedral	—	275
MDS234	1975 (4)	1,050	KM#898-899, 901-902 Peterborough Cathedral	—	275
MDS235	1976 (4)	1,257	KM#898-899, 901-902 Hereford Cathedral	—	250
MDS236	1977 (4)	1,248	KM#898-899, 901-902 Westminster Abbey	—	250
MDS237	1978 (4)	1,179	KM#898-899, 901-902 Carlisle Cathedral	—	250
MDS238	1979 (4)	1,180	KM#898-899, 901-902 Winchester Cathedral	—	250
MDS239	1980 (4)	1,148	KM#898-899, 901-902 Worcester Cathedral	—	250
MDS240	1981 (4)	1,398	KM#898-899, 901-902 Westminster Abbey	—	250
MDS241	1982 (4)	1,220	KM#898-899, 901-902 St. David's Cathedral	—	250
MDS242	1983 (4)	1,228	KM#898-899, 901-902 Exeter Cathedral	—	250
MDS243	1984 (4)	1,238	KM#898-899, 901-902 Southwell Minster	—	250
MDS244	1985 (4)	1,248	KM#898-899, 901-902 Ripon Cathedral	—	250
MDS245	1986 (4)	1,378	KM#898-899, 901-902 Chichester Cathedral	—	250
MDS246	1987 (4)	1,390	KM#898-899, 901-902 Ely Cathedral	—	250
MDS247	1988 (4)	1,402	KM#898-899, 901-902 Lichfield Cathedral	—	250
MDS248	1989 (4)	1,353	KM#898-899, 901-902 Birmingham Cathedral	—	250
MDS249	1990 (4)	1,523	KM#898-899, 901-902 Newcastle Cathedral	—	250
MDS250	1991 (4)	1,384	KM#898-899, 901-902 Westminster Abbey	—	250
MDS251	1992 (4)	1,424	KM#898-899, 901-902 Chester Cathedral	—	250
MDS252	1993 (4)	1,440	KM#898-899, 901-902 Wells Cathedral	—	250
MDS253	1994 (4)	1,433	KM#898-899, 901-902 Truro Cathedral	—	250
MDS254	1995 (4)	1,466	KM#898-899, 901-902 Coventry Cathedral	—	250
MDS255	1996 (4)	1,629	KM#898-899, 901-902 Norwich Cathedral	—	275
MDS256	1997 (4)	1,786	KM#898-899, 901-902 Birmingham Cathedral	—	275
MDS257	1998 (4)	1,654	KM#898-899, 901-902 Portsmouth Cathedral	—	275
MDS258	1999 (4)	1,676	KM#898-899, 901-902 Bristol Cathedral	—	275
MDS259	2000 (4)	1,686	KM#898-899, 901-902 Lincoln Cathedral	—	275

MINT SETS

KM#	Date	Mintage	Identification	Issue Price	Mkt Val
MS101	1953 (9)	—	KM#881-883, 886, 889-893	1.25	65.00
MS103	1982 (7)	205,000	KM#926-932	6.00	9.50
MSA104	1983 (8)	—	KM#926-7; 916; 929-933	8.75	2,000
MS104	1983 (8)	637,100	KM#926-933	8.75	16.00
MS105	1984 (8)	158,820	KM#926-932, 934	8.75	16.00
MS106	1985 (7)	178,375	KM#935-940.1, 941	8.75	16.00
MS107	1986 (8)	167,224	KM#935-940.1, 946-947	9.75	17.50
MS108	1987 (7)	172,425	KM#935-940.1, 948	9.00	13.50
MS109	1988 (7)	134,067	KM#935-940.1, 954	9.00	15.00
MS110	1989 (7)	77,569	KM#935-940.1, 959	10.00	19.00
MS111	1989 (2)	—	KM#960-961	11.00	17.00
MS112	1990 (7)	102,606	KM#935-936, 937, 936b, 938-940.1, 941	15.00	17.50
MS113	1991 (7)	74,975	KM#935-936, 937b, 938-940.1, 946	15.00	15.00
MS114	1991 (7)	—	KM#935-936, 937b, 938-940.1, 946 Baby Pack	18.50	15.00
MS115	1992 (8)	78,421	KM#935-936, 937b, 938, 938b, 939-940.1, 948, 963	17.50	20.00
MS116	1992 (9)	—	KM#935-936, 937b, 938, 938b, 939-940.1, 948, 963 Baby Pack	22.50	20.00
MS117	1993 (7)	56,945	KM#935a-936a, 937b, 938b, 939-940.1, 964	22.50	20.00
MS118	1994 (8)	177,971	KM#935a, 936a, 937b, 938b, 939, 966-968	22.50	17.50
MS119	1995 (8)	105,647	KM#935a-936a, 937b-938b, 939-940.1, 969-970	—	17.50
MS120	1996 (8)	86,501	KM#935a-936a, 937b-938b, 939-940.1, 972-973	18.50	15.00
MS121	1997 (9)	109,557	KM#935a, 936a, 937b, 938b, 939-940.1, 940.2, 975-976	—	17.50
MS122	1998 (9)	16,192	KM#986-994	25.00	22.50
MS124	1998 (2)	96,149	KM#991-992	15.00	7.50
MS125	1999 (8)	136,492	KM#986a-987a, 988-991, 998-999	20.00	17.50
MS126	2000 (9)	1,686	KM#986-991, 994, 1004, 1005 Wedding Collection	20.00	17.50
MS127	2000 (9)	117,750	KM#986-991, 994, 1004, 1005	25.00	17.50
MS128	2000 (9)	—	M#986-991, 994, 1004, 1005 Baby Gift Set	25.00	17.50

PROOF SETS

KM#	Date	Mintage	Identification	Issue Price	Mkt Val
PS15	1902 (13)	8,066	KM#795-797.1, 798-807	—	5,750
PS16	1902 (11)	7,057	KM#795-797.1, 798-805	—	1,750
PS17	1911 (12)	2,812	KM#811-818.1, 819-822	—	7,200
PS18	1911 (10)	952	KM#811-818.1, 819-820	—	1,900
PS19	1911 (8)	2,241	KM#811-818.1	—	800

KM#	Date	Mintage	Identification	Issue Price	Mkt Val
PSA20	1927 (6)	—	KM#831-836 Matte Proof; Rare	—	25,250
PS20	1927 (6)	15,030	KM#831-836	—	800
PSA21	1937 (15)	—	KM#843-857 Matte Proof; Rare	—	25,000
PS21	1937 (15)	26,402	KM#843-857	—	550
PSA22	1937 (4)	1	KM#858-861 Matte Proof; Unique	—	35,000
PS22	1937 (4)	5,500	KM#858-861	—	6,500
PSA23	1950 (9)	3	KM#867-869, 873, 875-879; Rare, matte proof	—	20,000
PS23	1950 (9)	17,513	KM#867-869, 873, 875-879	2.50	280
PSA24	1951 (10)	3	KM#867-869, 873, 875-880; Rare, matte proof	—	20,000
PS24	1951 (10)	20,000	KM#867-869, 873, 875-880	2.80	300
PSA25	1953 (10)	3	KM#881-883, 886, 889-894; Rare, matte proof	—	22,500
PS25	1953 (10)	40,000	KM#881-883, 886, 889-894	3.50	175
PS26	1970 (8)	750,000	KM#896-897, 900, 903-907 (Issued 1971)	8.75	75.00
PS27	1971 (6)	350,000	KM#911-916 (Issued 1973)	8.85	15.00
PS28	1972 (7)	150,000	KM#911-917 (Issued 1976)	13.00	30.00
PS30	1974 (6)	100,000	KM#911-916 (Issued 1976)	13.00	19.00
PS31	1975 (6)	100,000	KM#911-916 (Issued 1976)	13.00	17.00
PS32	1976 (6)	100,000	KM#911-916	13.00	17.00
PS33	1977 (7)	193,800	KM#911-916, 920	17.00	21.00
PS34	1978 (6)	88,100	KM#911-916	15.00	19.00
PS35	1979 (6)	81,000	KM#911-916	15.00	17.00
PS36	1980 (6)	143,400	KM#911-916	23.00	14.50
PS37	1980 (4)	10,000	KM#919, 922-924	2,650	3,450
PS38	1981 (2)	2,500	KM#919, 925a	—	465
PS39	1981 (6)	—	KM#911-916	26.00	17.00
PS40	1981 (9)	5,000	KM#911-916, 919, 924, 925a	—	2,650
PS41	1982 (7)	—	KM#926-932	21.60	17.50
PS42	1982 (4)	2,500	KM#919, 922-924	—	3,475
PS43	1983 (8)	125,000	KM#926-933	29.95	22.50
PS44	1983 (3)	—	KM#919, 922, 923	775	1,300
PS45	1984 (8)	125,000	KM#926-932, 934	29.95	27.00
PS46	1984 (3)	—	KM#919, 922, 924	1,275	2,575
PS47	1985 (7)	125,000	KM#935-940.1, 941	29.75	25.00
PS48	1985 (4)	12,500	KM#942-945	1,395	3,025
PS49	1986 (8)	125,000	KM#935-940.1, 946-947	29.75	35.00
PS50	1986 (3)	12,500	KM#942-943, 947c	675	1,525
PS51	1987 (7)	125,000	KM#935-940.1, 948	29.75	25.00
PS52	1987 (4)	10,000	KM#950-953	1,595	3,050
PS53	1987 (3)	12,500	KM#942-944	675	1,500
PS54	1987 (2)	12,500	KM#950, 951	325	575
PS55	1988 (7)	125,000	KM#935-940.1, 954	29.75	22.50
PS56	1988 (4)	6,500	KM#950-953	1,595	3,050
PS57	1988 (3)	—	KM#942-944	775	1,500
PS58	1988 (2)	7,500	KM#950-951	340	625
PS59	1989 (9)	100,000	KM#935-940.1, 959-961	34.95	57.00
PS60	1989 (4)	2,500	KM#950-953	1,595	3,050
PS61	1989 (4)	5,000	KM#955-958	1,595	4,900
PS62	1989 (3)	15,000	KM#955-957	775	2,750
PS63	1989 (2)	1,500	KM#950-951	340	625
PS64	1989 (2)	—	KM#960a, 961a	—	90.00
PS65	1989 (2)	—	KM#960, 961	—	30.00
PS66	1990 (8)	100,000	KM#935-937, 937b, 938-940.1, 941 Leatherette Case	35.00	30.00
PS67	1990 (8)	Inc. above	KM#935-937, 937b, 938-940.1, 941 Leather Case	45.00	30.00
PS68	1990 (4)	2,500	KM#942-944, 949	1,595	3,750
PS69	1990 (4)	2,500	KM#950a-953a	1,595	3,150
PS70	1990 (3)	7,500	KM#942-944	775	1,625
PS71	1990 (2)	35,000	KM#937a, 937c	47.50	40.00
PS72	1991 (7)	10,000	KM#935-936, 937b, 938-940.1, 946 Leatherette Case	38.50	30.00
PS73	1991 (7)	10,000	KM#935-936, 937b, 938-940.1, 946 Leather Case	48.50	27.50
PS74	1991 (4)	1,500	KM#942-944, 949	1,750	3,750
PS75	1991 (4)	750	KM#950a-953a	1,750	3,250
PS76	1991 (3)	2,500	KM#942-944	895	1,625
PS77	1992 (9)	100,000	KM#935-936, 937b, 938, 938b, 939-94.1, 948, 963 Leatherette Case	44.50	47.50
PS78	1992 (9)	100,000	KM#935-936, 937b, 938, 938b, 939-940.1, 948, 963 Leather Case	44.50	47.50
PS79	1992 (4)	1,250	KM#942-945	1,750	3,750
PS80	1992 (4)	1,000	KM#938b, 938c, 948a, 963a	122	95.00
PS81	1992 (3)	1,250	KM#942-944	895	1,625
PS82	1992 (2)	—	KM#938a-938c	59.45	46.00
PS83	1993 (8)	100,000	KM#935a-936a, 937b, 938b, 939-940.1, 964-965 Standard Case	50.00	42.50
PS84	1993 (8)	Inc. above	KM#935a-936a, 937b, 938b, 939-940.1, 964-965 Deluxe Case	60.00	43.50
PS85	1993 (4)	500	KM#950a-953a	1,755	3,200
PS86	1993 (4)	1,250	KM#942-945	1,560	3,800
PS87	1993 (3)	1,250	KM#942-944	800	1,650
PS88	1994 (8)	100,000	KM#935a-936a, 937b, 938b, 939, 966-968 Standard Case	45.00	40.00
PS89	1994 (8)	Inc. above	KM#935a-936a, 937b, 938b, 939, 966-968 Deluxe Case	55.00	40.00
PS90	1994 (4)	500	KM#950a-953a	1,499	3,175
PS91	1994 (4)	1,250	KM#942-943, 945, 968c	—	3,950
PS92	1994 (3)	1,250	KM#942-943, 968c	—	1,600
PS93	1995 (8)	42,842	KM#935a-936a, 937b-938b, 939-940.1, 969-970	—	40.00
PS94	1995 (8)	17,797	KM#935a-936a, 937b-938b, 939-940.1, 969-970 Deluxe Case	—	40.00
PS95	1995 (4)	1,250	KM#942-943, 945, 971c	—	3,950
PS96	1995 (4)	500	KM#950a-953a	1,500	3,150
PS97	1995 (3)	1,250	KM#942-943, 945	—	3,100
PS98	1996 (8)	100,000	KM#935a-936a, 937b-938b, 939-940.1, 972-973	44.75	40.00
PS99	1996 (8)	—	KM#935a-936a, 937b-938b, 939-940.1, 972-973 Deluxe Case	56.00	40.00
PS100	1996 (4)	2,500,000	KM#950a-953a	1,600	3,100
PS101	1996 (7)	—	KM#935b, 936b, 937c, 938c, 939a, 940.1a, 972a	—	155
PS102	1997 (10)	70,000	KM#935a, 936a, 937b, 938b, 939, 940.1, 940.2, 975-976, 977a	—	60.00
PS103	1997 (4)	15,000	KM#978-981	145	155
PS104	1997 (4)	1,500	KM#982-985	1,600	3,350
PSA105	1998 (2)	10,000	Piefort versions of KM#992a, 996a	—	160
PS105	1998 (10)	100,000	KM#986,987a, 988-995	55.00	72.00
PS106	1999 (9)	100,000	KM#986a-987a, 988-991, 997-999	50.00	62.00
PS107	1999 (4)	1,000	KM#999a, 1001-1003	1,725	2,700
PS108	1999 (3)	1,250	KM#1001-1003	—	2,650
PS109	1999 (4)	750	KM#950a-953a	1,495	2,050
PS110	1999 (4)	—	KM#1008-1011	1,595	3,150
PS111	2000 (10)	90,000	KM#986-991, 994, 1004-1006 Standard Set	50.00	67.00
PS112	2000 (10)	10,000	KM#986-991, 994, 1004-1006 Deluxe Set	65.00	67.00
PS113	2000 (10)	15,000	KM#986-991, 994, 1004-1006 Executive Set	115	67.00
PS114	2000 (4)	750	KM#1008-1011	1,495	3,250
PSA115	2000 (3)	1,250	KM#994c, 1001, 1002	—	1,325
PS115	2000 (13)	15,000	KM#898, 899, 901, 902, 986b, 987b, 988a, 989a, 990a, 991a, 994a, 1005a, 1006a	—	500
PS157	1998 (4)	—	KM#1029, 1079-1081	—	175
PS158	1999 (4)	—	KM#1000, 1082-1084	—	175
PS159	2000 (4)	—	KM#1029, 1079-1081	—	175

GREECE

The Hellenic (Greek) Republic is situated in southeastern Europe on the southern tip of the Balkan Peninsula. The republic includes many islands, the most important of which are Crete and the Ionian Islands. Greece (including islands) has an area of 50,944 sq. mi. (131,940 sq. km.) and a population of 10.3 million. Capital: Athens. Greece is still largely agricultural. Tobacco, cotton, fruit and wool are exported.

Greece, the Mother of Western civilization, attained the peak of its culture in the 5th century B.C., when it contributed more to government, drama, art and architecture than any other people to this time. Greece fell under Roman domination in the 2nd and 1st centuries B.C., becoming part of the Byzantine Empire until Constantinople fell to the Crusaders in 1202. With the fall of Constantinople to the Turks in 1453, Greece became part of the Ottoman Empire. Independence from Turkey was won with the revolution of 1821-27. In 1833, Greece was established as a monarchy, with sovereignty guaranteed by Britain, France and Russia. After a lengthy power struggle between the monarchist forces and democratic factions, Greece was proclaimed a republic in 1925. The monarchy was restored in 1935 and reconfirmed by a plebiscite in 1946. The Italians invaded Greece via Albania on Oct. 28, 1940 but were driven back well within the Albanian border. Germany began their invasion in April 1941 and quickly overran the entire country and drove off a British Expeditionary force by the end of April. King George II and his new government went into exile. The German-Italian occupation of Greece lasted until Oct. 1944 after which only German troops remained until the end of the occupation. On April 21, 1967, a military junta took control of the government and suspended the constitution. King Constantine II made an unsuccessful attempt against the junta in the fall of 1968 and consequently fled to Italy. The monarchy was formally abolished by plebiscite, Dec. 8, 1974, and Greece was established as the Hellenic Republic, the third republic in Greek history.

RULERS

George I, 1863-1913
Constantine I, 1913-1917, 1920-1922
Alexander I, 1917-1920
George II, 1922-1923, 1935-1947
Paul I, 1947-1964
Constantine II, 1964-1973

MINT MARKS

(a) - Paris, privy marks only
A - Paris
B - Vienna
BB - Strassburg
H - Heaton, Birmingham
K - Bordeaux
KN - King's Norton
(p) - Poissy – Thunderbolt
Anthemion – Greek National Mint, Athens

MONETARY SYSTEM

Commencing 1831

100 Lepta = 1 Drachma

KINGDOM

DECIMAL COINAGE

KM# 62 5 LEPTA

3.00 g., Nickel **Ruler:** George I **Obv:** Crown right of center hole **Rev:** Owl on amphora left of center hole

Date	Mintage	F12	VF20	XF40	MS60	MS63
1912 (a)	25,053,000	0.75	1.00	5.00	25.00	65.00

KM# 63 10 LEPTA

Nickel, 21 mm. **Ruler:** George I **Obv:** Crown right of center hole **Rev:** Owl on amphora left of center hole

Date	Mintage	F12	VF20	XF40	MS60	MS63
1912 (a)	28,973,000	0.75	1.00	5.00	25.00	65.00

KM# 66.1 10 LEPTA

1.52 g., Aluminum **Ruler:** George II **Obv:** Crown above date **Rev:** Olive branch, denomination **Note:** 1.77 - 1.82mm thick.

Date	Mintage	F12	VF20	XF40	MS60	MS63
1922 (p)	120,000,000	0.25	0.50	5.00	20.00	35.00

KM# 66.2 10 LEPTA

1.65 g., Aluminum **Ruler:** Constantine I **Obv:** Crown above date **Rev:** Olive branch, denomination **Note:** 2.2mm thick.

Date	Mintage	F12	VF20	XF40	MS60	MS63
1922 (p)	—	1.00	5.00	12.00	30.00	65.00

KM# 64 20 LEPTA

Nickel **Ruler:** George I **Obv:** Crowned, mantled shield right of center hole **Rev:** Athena standing at left of center hole, olive branch at right

Date	Mintage	F12	VF20	XF40	MS60	MS63
1912 (a)	10,145,000	0.25	1.00	5.00	32.00	70.00

KM# 65 50 LEPTA

Copper-Nickel **Ruler:** Constantine I **Obv:** Crowned, mantled shield right of center hole **Rev:** Olive branch below center hole **Note:** Most of these were melted and only 30 - 40 of each piece are known to exist.

Date	Mintage	F12	VF20	XF40	MS60	MS63
1921 H	1,000,000	—	—	1,500	3,000	6,000
1921 KN	1,524,000	—	—	2,000	5,000	7,500

KM# 60 DRACHMA

5.00 g., 0.835 Silver 0.1342 oz. ASW **Ruler:** George I **Obv:** Head left **Rev:** Mythological figure Thetis with shield of Achilles, seated on sea horse

Date	Mintage	F12	VF20	XF40	MS60	MS63
1910 (a)	4,570,000	5.00	12.00	35.00	90.00	275
1911 (a)	1,881,000	5.00	12.00	45.00	125	450

KM# 61 2 DRACHMAI

10.00 g., 0.835 Silver 0.2685 oz. ASW **Ruler:** George I **Obv:** Head left **Rev:** Mythological figure Thetis with shield of Achilles seated on sea horse

Date	Mintage	F12	VF20	XF40	MS60	MS63
1911 (a)	1,500,000	10.00	20.00	85.00	550	1,100

REPUBLIC

KM# 67 20 LEPTA

1.73 g., Copper-Nickel **Obv:** Denomination above date **Rev:** Athena head left

Date	Mintage	VF20	XF40	MS60	MS63	MS65
1926	20,000,000	0.50	3.00	9.00	18.00	30.00

KM# 68 50 LEPTA

2.89 g., Copper-Nickel **Obv:** Denomination above date **Rev:** Athena head left **Edge:** Reeded

Date	Mintage	VF20	XF40	MS60	MS63	MS65
1926	20,000,000	0.50	3.00	9.00	18.00	30.00
1926B (1930)	20,000,000	0.50	3.00	9.00	18.00	30.00

KM# 69 DRACHMA

5.03 g., Copper-Nickel, 23 mm. **Obv:** Denomination above date **Rev:** Athena head left

Date	Mintage	VF20	XF40	MS60	MS63	MS65
1926B	20,000,000	0.25	3.00	18.00	30.00	70.00
1926	15,000,000	0.25	3.00	12.00	25.00	60.00

KM# 70 2 DRACHMAI

Copper-Nickel, 27 mm. **Obv:** Denomination above date **Rev:** Athena head left

Date	Mintage	VF20	XF40	MS60	MS63	MS65
1926	22,000,000	1.00	4.00	12.00	25.00	55.00

KM# 71.1 5 DRACHMAI

10.00 g., Nickel, 30 mm. **Obv:** Phoenix and flames **Rev:** Denomination within wreath **Note:** LONDON MINT: In second set of berries on left only 1 berry will have a dot on it.

Date	Mintage	VF20	XF40	MS60	MS63	MS65
1930	23,500,000	1.00	4.00	12.00	22.00	50.00
1930	—	PF63 2,500				

KM# 71.2 5 DRACHMAI

10.00 g., Nickel, 30 mm. **Obv:** Phoenix and flames **Rev:** Denomination within wreath **Note:** BRUSSELS MINT: 2 berries will have dots.

Date	Mintage	VF20	XF40	MS60	MS63	MS65
1930	1,500,000	1.00	5.00	30.00	60.00	150

KM# 72 10 DRACHMAI

7.00 g., 0.500 Silver 0.1125 oz. ASW, 25 mm. **Obv:** Grain sprig divides denomination **Rev:** Demeter head left

Date	Mintage	VF20	XF40	MS60	MS63	MS65
1930	7,500,000	5.00	20.00	85.00	175	450
1930	—	PF63 3,500	PF65 5,500			

KM# 73 20 DRACHMAI

11.31 g., 0.500 Silver 0.1818 oz. ASW, 28.43 mm. **Obv:** Prow of ancient ship **Rev:** Poseidon head right

Date	Mintage	VF20	XF40	MS60	MS63	MS65
1930	11,500,000	8.00	16.00	65.00	150	325
1930	—	PF63 3,000	PF65 5,000			

KINGDOM

KM# 77 5 LEPTA

0.85 g., Aluminum, 20.5 mm. **Obv:** Center hole within crowned wreath **Rev:** Grain sprigs left of center hole

Date	Mintage	VF20	XF40	MS60	MS63	MS65
1954	15,000,000	—	—	1.50	2.00	3.00
1971	1,002,000	—	0.25	2.00	4.00	5.50

Note: 1971 dated coins have smaller hole at center

KM# 78 10 LEPTA

1.00 g., Aluminum **Obv:** Center hole within crowned wreath **Rev:** Olives above center hole, double denomination below

Date	Mintage	VF20	XF40	MS60	MS63	MS65
1954	48,000,000	—	—	1.50	3.50	5.00
1959	20,000,000	—	—	1.50	3.50	5.00
1964	12,000,000	—	—	1.50	2.00	3.00
1965 Sets only	—	—	—	—	—	3.00
1965	4,987	PF65 5.00				
1966	20,000,000	—	—	1.50	2.00	3.00
1969	20,000,000	—	—	1.50	2.00	3.00
1971	5,922,000	—	—	1.50	3.50	5.00

Note: Small center hole

KM# 102 10 LEPTA

Aluminum **Obv:** Soldier and Phoenix **Rev:** Trident between two dolphins

Date	Mintage	VF20	XF40	MS60	MS63	MS65
1973	2,742,000	—	—	1.50	2.00	3.00

KM# 79 20 LEPTA

1.20 g., Aluminum, 24 mm. **Obv:** Center hole within crowned wreath **Rev:** Olive branch left of center hole

Date	Mintage	VF20	XF40	MS60	MS63	MS65
1954	24,000,000	—	0.25	1.50	5.00	10.00
1959	20,000,000	—	0.25	1.50	5.00	10.00
1964	8,000,000	—	0.25	1.50	5.00	12.00
1966	15,000,000	—	0.25	1.50	5.00	10.00
1969	20,000,000	—	0.25	1.50	5.00	10.00
1971	4,108,000	—	0.25	1.50	5.00	12.00

Note: Small center hole

KM# 104 20 LEPTA
Aluminum **Obv:** Soldier in front of phoenix, anniversary date below **Rev:** Olive branch, denomination

Date	Mintage	VF20	XF40	MS60	MS63	MS65
1973	2,718,000	—	—	1.50	2.00	3.00

KM# 80 50 LEPTA
2.25 g., Copper-Nickel, 18 mm. **Ruler:** Paul I **Obv:** Head left **Rev:** Crowned arms with supporters **Edge:** Reeded

Date	Mintage	VF20	XF40	MS60	MS63	MS65
1954	37,228,000	—	0.50	7.00	15.00	32.00
1957	5,108,000	1.00	4.00	22.00	55.00	135
1957	—	PF63 1,500		PF65 2,000		
1959	10,160,000	—	3.00	18.00	32.00	65.00
1962	20,500,000	—	0.50	5.00	10.00	20.00
Note: Serrated edge. Plain edge error reported, awaiting confirmation.						
1964	20,000,000	—	0.25	1.50	4.00	8.00
1965 Sets only	—	—	—	—	—	3.00
1965	4,987	PF65 6.00				

KM# 88 50 LEPTA
2.25 g., Copper-Nickel, 18 mm. **Ruler:** Constantine II **Obv:** Head left **Rev:** Crowned arms with supporters **Edge:** Reeded

Date	Mintage	VF20	XF40	MS60	MS63	MS65
1966	30,000,000	—	0.25	1.50	3.50	7.00
1966	—	PF63 1,000		PF65 1,500		
1970	10,160,000	—	0.50	2.00	5.00	10.00

KM# 97.1 50 LEPTA
2.25 g., Copper-Nickel, 18 mm. **Ruler:** Constantine II **Obv:** Small head left **Rev:** Soldier in front of Phoenix **Edge:** Reeded

Date	Mintage	VF20	XF40	MS60	MS63	MS65
1971	10,999,000	—	—	1.50	2.50	5.00
1973	9,342,000	—	—	1.50	2.50	5.00

KM# 97.2 50 LEPTA
2.25 g., Copper-Nickel, 18 mm. **Ruler:** Constantine II **Obv:** Large head left **Rev:** Soldier in front of Phoenix **Edge:** Reeded

Date	Mintage	VF20	XF40	MS60	MS63	MS65
1973	Inc. above	—	—	1.50	2.50	5.00

KM# 81 DRACHMA
3.75 g., Copper-Nickel, 20.8 mm. **Ruler:** Paul I **Obv:** Head left **Rev:** Crowned arms with supporters **Edge:** Reeded

Date	Mintage	VF20	XF40	MS60	MS63	MS65
1954	24,091,000	—	0.50	7.00	15.00	30.00
1957	8,151,000	—	1.00	12.00	25.00	75.00
1957	—	PF63 2,000		PF65 2,500		
1959	10,180,000	—	0.50	12.00	25.00	75.00
1962	20,060,000	—	0.50	3.00	7.00	15.00
1965 Sets only	—	—	—	—	—	3.00
1965	4,987	PF65 6.00				

KM# 89 DRACHMA
3.75 g., Copper-Nickel, 20.8 mm. **Ruler:** Constantine II **Obv:** Head left **Rev:** Crowned arms with supporters **Edge:** Reeded

Date	Mintage	VF20	XF40	MS60	MS63	MS65
1966	20,000,000	—	0.25	1.50	2.50	5.00
1966	—	PF63 1,000		PF65 1,500		
1967	20,000,000	—	0.25	1.50	2.50	5.00
1970	7,001,000	—	0.50	2.00	3.50	7.00
1970	—	PF63 1,000		PF65 1,500		

KM# 98 DRACHMA
3.75 g., Copper-Nickel, 20.8 mm. **Ruler:** Constantine II **Obv:** Head left **Rev:** Soldier in front of Phoenix **Edge:** Reeded

Date	Mintage	VF20	XF40	MS60	MS63	MS65
1971	11,985,000	—	—	1.50	2.50	5.00
1973	8,196,000	—	—	1.50	2.50	5.00

KM# 82 2 DRACHMAI
6.25 g., Copper-Nickel, 22.9 mm. **Ruler:** Paul I **Obv:** Head left **Rev:** Crowned arms with supporters **Edge:** Reeded

Date	Mintage	VF20	XF40	MS60	MS63	MS65
1954	12,609,000	0.25	0.75	8.00	17.00	45.00
1957	10,171,000	1.00	3.00	12.00	28.00	75.00
1957	—	PF63 2,500		PF65 3,000		
1959	5,000,000	1.00	3.00	15.00	45.00	165
1962	10,096,000	—	1.00	5.00	10.00	22.00
1965 Sets only	—	—	—	—	—	3.00
1965	4,987	PF65 6.00				

KM# 90 2 DRACHMAI
6.25 g., Copper-Nickel, 22.9 mm. **Ruler:** Constantine II **Obv:** Head left **Rev:** Crowned arms with supporters **Edge:** Reeded

Date	Mintage	VF20	XF40	MS60	MS63	MS65
1966	10,000,000	—	0.50	2.00	4.00	7.00
1966	—	PF63 1,100		PF65 1,400		
Note: NGSA Auction 12/08 $1105						
1967	10,000,000	—	0.50	2.00	4.00	7.00
1970	7,000,000	—	0.50	2.00	4.00	7.00
1970	—	PF63 1,500		PF65 2,000		

KM# 99 2 DRACHMAI
6.25 g., Copper-Nickel, 22.9 mm. **Ruler:** Constantine II **Obv:** Head left **Rev:** Soldier in front of Phoenix **Edge:** Reeded

Date	Mintage	VF20	XF40	MS60	MS63	MS65
1971	9,998,000	—	0.25	1.50	3.50	7.00
1973	7,972,000	—	0.25	1.50	3.50	7.00

KM# 83 5 DRACHMAI
9.00 g., Copper-Nickel, 27.5 mm. **Ruler:** Paul I **Obv:** Head left **Rev:** Crowned shield with supporters **Edge:** Reeded

Date	Mintage	VF20	XF40	MS60	MS63	MS65
1954	21,000,000	0.50	1.50	7.00	20.00	55.00
1965 Sets only	—	—	—	—	—	3.00
1965	4,987	PF65 7.50				

KM# 91 5 DRACHMAI
9.00 g., Copper-Nickel, 27.5 mm. **Ruler:** Constantine II **Obv:** Head left **Rev:** Crowned arms with supporters **Edge:** Reeded

Date	Mintage	VF20	XF40	MS60	MS63	MS65
1966	12,000,000	0.25	1.00	3.00	5.00	10.00
1966	—	PF63 1,250		PF65 1,500		
1970	5,000,000	0.25	1.50	4.00	6.00	12.00

KM# 100 5 DRACHMAI
9.00 g., Copper-Nickel, 27.5 mm. **Ruler:** Constantine II **Obv:** Head left **Rev:** Soldier in front of Phoenix **Edge:** Reeded

Date	Mintage	VF20	XF40	MS60	MS63	MS65
1971	4,014,000	—	0.50	1.50	3.00	7.00
1973	3,166,000	—	0.50	1.50	3.00	7.00

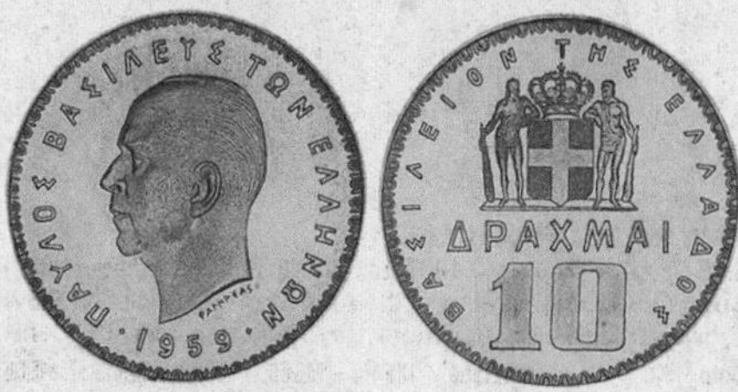

KM# 84 10 DRACHMAI
10.00 g., Nickel, 30 mm. **Ruler:** Paul I **Obv:** Head left **Rev:** Crowned arms with supporters

Date	Mintage	VF20	XF40	MS60	MS63	MS65
1959	20,000,000	—	0.50	7.00	20.00	55.00
1959	—	PF63 2,000		PF65 2,500		
1965 Sets only	—	—	—	—	—	3.00
1965	4,987	PF63 10.00		PF65 15.00		

KM# 96 10 DRACHMAI
10.00 g., Copper-Nickel, 30 mm. **Ruler:** Constantine II **Obv:** Head left **Rev:** Crowned arms with supporters **Edge:** Plain

Date	Mintage	VF20	XF40	MS60	MS63	MS65
1968	40,000,000	—	—	1.50	3.00	7.00

KM# 101 10 DRACHMAI
10.00 g., Copper-Nickel, 30 mm. **Ruler:** Constantine II **Obv:** Head left **Rev:** Soldier in front of Phoenix **Edge:** Reeded

Date	Mintage	VF20	XF40	MS60	MS63	MS65
1971	502,000	—	0.25	2.00	5.00	10.00
1973	541,000	—	0.25	2.00	5.00	10.00

KM# 74 20 DRACHMAI
6.45 g., 0.900 Gold 0.1867 oz. AGW, 22 mm. **Ruler:** George II **Subject:** 5th Anniversary - Restoration of Monarchy **Obv:** Head left **Rev:** Denomination within crowned wreath

Date	Mintage	F12	VF20	XF40	MS60	MS63
ND-1940	200	PF65 18,000				

KM# 85 20 DRACHMAI
7.50 g., 0.835 Silver 0.2013 oz. ASW, 26.2 mm. **Ruler:** Paul I **Obv:** Head left **Rev:** Selene, moon goddess

Date	Mintage	VF20	XF40	MS60	MS63	MS65
1960	20,000,000	—	3.75	5.00	7.00	15.00
1960	—	PF63 1,600	PF65 2,000			
1965	—	—	3.75	5.00	7.00	15.00
1965	4,987	PF63 15.00	PF65 20.00			

KM# 92 20 DRACHMAI
6.45 g., 0.900 Gold 0.1867 oz. AGW **Ruler:** Constantine II **Subject:** Commemorative of the April 21, 1967 revolution **Obv:** Crowned shield with supporters **Rev:** Soldier in front of Phoenix

Date	Mintage	XF40	MS60	MS63	MS65	MS66
ND (1970)	20,000	—	—	300	500	700

KM# 111 20 DRACHMAI
7.54 g., Copper-Nickel, 30 mm. **Ruler:** Constantine II **Obv:** Soldier in front of Phoenix **Rev:** Selene, narrow rim with faint veil or no veil **Edge:** Reeded **Note:** Possible varieties exist; narrow rim with faint veil or no veil / wide rim with heavy veil and broken wave design at rear hoof.

Date	Mintage	VF20	XF40	MS60	MS63	MS65
1973	3,092,000	—	0.50	2.00	3.50	7.00

KM# 111.3 20 DRACHMAI
7.54 g., Copper-Nickel, 30 mm. **Ruler:** Constantine II **Obv:** Soldier in front of Phoenix **Rev:** Selene, wide rim with continuous wave design at rear hoof **Edge:** Reeded

Date	Mintage	VF20	XF40	MS60	MS63	MS65
1973	Inc. above	—	0.50	2.00	3.50	7.00

KM# 86 30 DRACHMAI
18.00 g., 0.835 Silver 0.4832 oz. ASW, 34 mm. **Ruler:** Paul I **Subject:** Centennial - Five Greek Kings **Edge Lettering:** Greek text

Date	Mintage	VF20	XF40	MS60	MS63	MS65
ND-1963	3,000,000	—	9.00	9.00	12.00	15.00

KM# 87 30 DRACHMAI
12.00 g., 0.835 Silver 0.3222 oz. ASW, 30.3 mm. **Ruler:** Constantine II **Subject:** Constantine and Anne-Marie Wedding **Edge Lettering:** Greek text

Date	Mintage	VF20	XF40	MS60	MS63	MS65
1964	1,000,000	—	6.00	7.00	9.00	12.00
Note: Berne: small edge lettering, BØ below epaulette						
1964	1,000,000	—	6.00	7.00	9.00	12.00
Note: Kongsberg: large edge lettering, BØ on top of shoulder						
1964	—	PF63 2,800	PF65 3,500			

KM# 93 50 DRACHMAI
12.50 g., 0.835 Silver 0.3356 oz. ASW **Ruler:** Constantine II **Subject:** April 21, 1967 Revolution **Obv:** Crowned shield with supporters **Rev:** Soldier in front of Phoenix

Date	Mintage	VF20	XF40	MS60	MS63	MS65
1967(1970)	100,000	—	6.25	15.00	30.00	60.00

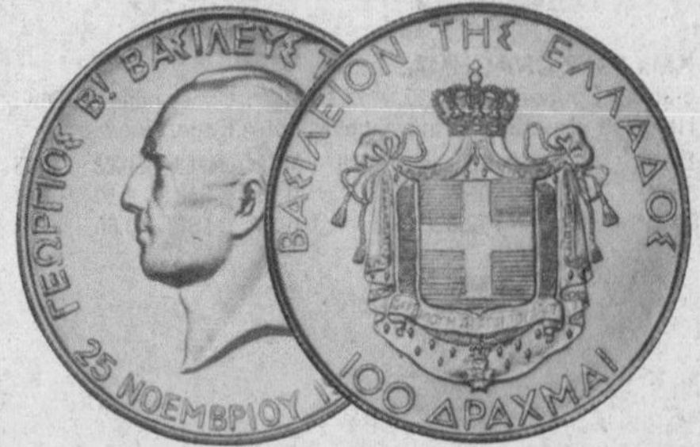

KM# 75 100 DRACHMAI
25.00 g., 0.900 Silver 0.7234 oz. ASW, 38 mm. **Ruler:** George II **Subject:** 5th Anniversary - Restoration of Monarchy **Obv:** Head left **Rev:** Crowned and mantled arms

Date	Mintage	F12	VF20	XF40	MS60	MS63
ND (1940)	500	PF60 2,200	PF63 2,800	PF65 3,500		

Note: These values are for undamaged examples. Many examples are hairlined and worth considerably less.

KM# 76 100 DRACHMAI
32.26 g., 0.900 Gold 0.9334 oz. AGW, 38 mm. **Ruler:** George II **Obv:** Head left **Rev:** Denomination within crowned wreath

Date	Mintage	F12	VF20	XF40	MS60	MS63
ND (1940)	140	PF65 30,000				

KM# 94 100 DRACHMAI
25.00 g., 0.835 Silver 0.6711 oz. ASW, 37 mm. **Ruler:** Constantine II **Subject:** April 21, 1967 Revolution

Date	Mintage	VF20	XF40	MS60	MS63	MS65
ND (1970)	30,000	—	12.50	25.00	45.00	85.00

KM# 95 100 DRACHMAI
32.26 g., 0.900 Gold 0.9334 oz. AGW **Ruler:** Constantine II **Subject:** April 21, 1967 Revolution **Obv:** Crowned arms with supporters **Rev:** Soldier in front of Phoenix

Date	Mintage	XF40	MS60	MS63	MS65	MS66
ND (1970)	10,000	—	—	1,800	2,300	2,600

REPUBLIC

KM# 103 10 LEPTA
1.09 g., Aluminum **Obv:** Phoenix above flame **Rev:** Pair of dolphins flank trident

Date	Mintage	VF20	XF40	MS60	MS63	MS65
1973	15,134,472	—	—	1.00	1.50	2.50

KM# 113 10 LEPTA
Aluminum **Obv:** Arms within wreath **Rev:** Charging bull right

Date	Mintage	VF20	XF40	MS60	MS63	MS65
1976	2,043,000	—	—	1.00	1.50	2.50
1978	791,000	—	0.50	2.25	3.50	5.00
1978	20,000	PF65 2.50				

KM# 105 20 LEPTA
Aluminum **Obv:** Phoenix with date below **Rev:** Olive branch, denomination

Date	Mintage	VF20	XF40	MS60	MS63	MS65
1973	15,265,797	—	0.25	1.00	1.50	2.50

KM# 114 20 LEPTA

Aluminum **Obv:** Arms within wreath **Rev:** Stallion's head left

Date	Mintage	VF20	XF40	MS60	MS63	MS65
1976	2,506,000	—	0.25	1.00	1.50	2.50
1978	803,000	—	1.00	3.00	3.50	5.50
1978	20,000	PF65 2.50				

KM# 106 50 LEPTA

2.50 g., Nickel-Brass, 18 mm. **Obv:** Phoenix and flame **Rev:** Ornamental plume **Edge:** Reeded

Date	Mintage	VF20	XF40	MS60	MS63	MS65
1973	55,231,898	—	—	0.50	0.75	1.00
1973	Inc. above	PF65 500				

KM# 115 50 LEPTA

2.50 g., Nickel-Brass, 18 mm. **Subject:** Markos Botsaris **Obv:** Denomination **Rev:** Bust left **Edge:** Reeded

Date	Mintage	VF20	XF40	MS60	MS63	MS65
1976	51,016,000	—	—	0.25	0.50	0.75
1978	12,010,000	—	—	0.25	0.50	0.75
1978	20,000	PF65 4.00				
1980	6,682,000	—	—	0.25	0.50	0.75
1982	3,365,000	—	—	0.25	0.50	0.75
1984	1,208,000	—	—	0.25	0.50	0.75
1986	—	—	—	0.25	0.50	0.75

KM# 107 DRACHMA

4.00 g., Nickel-Brass, 21 mm. **Obv:** Phoenix and flame **Rev:** Owl left of denomination **Edge:** Reeded

Date	Mintage	VF20	XF40	MS60	MS63	MS65
1973	45,218,431	—	0.25	1.50	2.50	3.50

KM# 116 DRACHMA

4.00 g., Nickel-Brass, 21 mm. **Subject:** Konstantinos Kanaris **Obv:** Full masted ship at sea **Rev:** Bust left **Edge:** Reeded

Date	Mintage	VF20	XF40	MS60	MS63	MS65
1976	102,060,000	—	—	0.25	0.50	0.75
Note: Varieties exist						
1978	21,200,000	—	—	0.25	0.50	0.75
1978	20,000	PF65 4.00				
1980	52,503,000	—	—	0.25	0.50	0.75
1982	54,186,000	—	—	0.25	0.50	0.75
1984	33,665,000	—	—	0.25	0.50	0.75
1986	17,901,000	—	—	0.25	0.50	0.75

KM# 150 DRACHMA

2.75 g., Copper, 18 mm. **Subject:** Lascarina Bouboulina, 1783-1825 **Obv:** Full masted ship at sea **Rev:** Bust left

Date	Mintage	VF20	XF40	MS60	MS63	MS65
1988	36,707,000	—	—	0.25	0.50	0.75
1990	—	—	—	0.25	0.50	0.75
1992	—	—	—	0.25	0.50	0.75
1993 Sets only	—	—	—	—	—	7.50
1993	—	PF65 20.00				
1994	—	—	—	0.25	0.50	0.75
1998	—	—	—	0.25	0.50	0.75
2000	—	—	—	0.25	0.50	0.75
2000	—	PF65 7.50				

KM# 189 DRACHMA

8.50 g., 0.9167 Gold 0.2505 oz. AGW **Obv:** Sailing ship **Rev:** Bouboulina, heroine, bust left

Date	Mintage	VF20	XF40	MS60	MS63	MS65
2000	—	PF63 335	PF65 350			

KM# 108 2 DRACHMAI

6.00 g., Nickel-Brass, 24 mm. **Obv:** Phoenix and flame **Rev:** Owl left of denomination **Edge:** Reeded

Date	Mintage	VF20	XF40	MS60	MS63	MS65
1973	51,163,812	—	0.25	1.50	2.50	3.50

KM# 117 2 DRACHMAI

6.00 g., Nickel-Brass, 24 mm. **Subject:** Georgios Karaiskakis **Obv:** Crossed rifles with branch **Rev:** Bust left **Edge:** Reeded

Date	Mintage	VF20	XF40	MS60	MS63	MS65
1976	92,401,000	—	—	0.25	0.50	0.75
1978	16,772,000	—	—	0.25	0.50	0.75
1978	20,000	PF65 4.00				
1980	45,955,000	—	—	0.25	0.50	0.75

KM# 130 2 DRACHMES

6.00 g., Nickel-Brass, 24 mm. **Subject:** Georgios Karaiskakis **Obv:** Crossed rifles and branch **Rev:** Bust left **Edge:** Reeded

Date	Mintage	VF20	XF40	MS60	MS63	MS65
1982	64,414,000	—	—	0.25	0.50	0.75
1984	37,861,000	—	—	0.25	0.50	0.75
1986	21,019,000	—	—	0.25	0.50	0.75

KM# 151 2 DRACHMES

3.75 g., Copper, 21 mm. **Subject:** Manto Mavrogenous, 1797-1840 - independence hero **Obv:** Ship's wheel, scope and anchor **Rev:** Bust facing looking right

Date	Mintage	VF20	XF40	MS60	MS63	MS65
1988	36,707,000	—	—	0.25	0.50	0.75
1990	—	—	—	0.25	0.50	0.75
1992	—	—	—	0.25	0.50	0.75
1993 Sets only	—	—	—	—	—	7.50
1993	—	PF65 20.00				
1994	—	—	—	0.25	0.50	0.75
1998	—	—	—	0.25	0.50	0.75
2000	—	—	—	0.25	0.50	0.75
2000	—	PF65 7.50				

KM# 109.1 5 DRACHMAI

9.09 g., Copper-Nickel, 25 mm. **Obv:** Phoenix and flame **Rev:** Pegasus rearing right **Note:** Denomination spelling ends with I.

Date	Mintage	VF20	XF40	MS60	MS63	MS65
1973	33,957,473	—	0.25	1.50	2.50	3.50

KM# 109.2 5 DRACHMAI

Copper-Nickel, 25 mm. **Obv:** Phoenix and flame **Rev:** Pegasus rearing right **Note:** Denomination spelling ends with A.

Date	Mintage	VF20	XF40	MS60	MS63	MS65
1973	Inc. above	0.50	1.00	12.00	25.00	50.00

KM# 118 5 DRACHMAI

5.50 g., Copper-Nickel, 22.5 mm. **Subject:** Aristotle **Obv:** Denomination **Rev:** Head left

Date	Mintage	VF20	XF40	MS60	MS63	MS65
1976	85,187,000	—	—	0.25	0.65	1.00
1978	17,404,000	—	—	0.25	0.65	1.00
1978	20,000	PF65 4.00				
1980	33,701,000	—	—	0.25	0.65	1.00

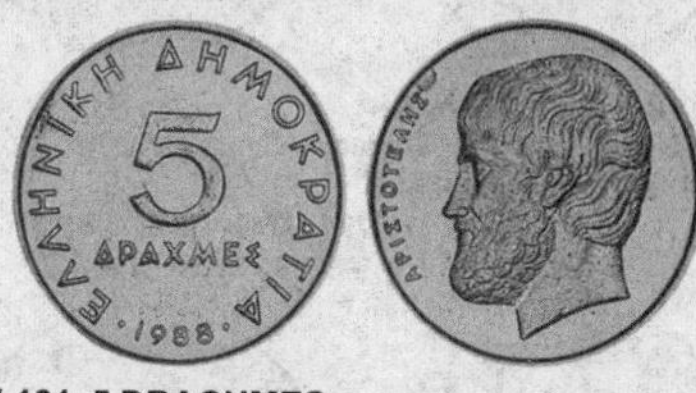

KM# 131 5 DRACHMES

5.50 g., Copper-Nickel, 22.5 mm. **Subject:** Aristotle **Obv:** Denomination **Rev:** Head left **Edge:** Plain

Date	Mintage	VF20	XF40	MS60	MS63	MS65
1982	42,647,000	—	—	0.25	0.65	1.00
1984	29,778,000	—	—	0.25	0.65	1.00
1986	16,730,000	—	—	0.25	0.65	1.00
1988	30,273,000	—	—	0.25	0.50	0.75
1990	—	—	—	0.25	0.50	0.75
1992	—	—	—	0.25	0.50	0.75
1993 Sets only	—	—	—	—	—	7.50
1993	—	PF65 25.00				
1994	—	—	—	0.25	0.50	0.75
1998	—	—	—	0.25	0.50	0.75
2000	—	—	—	0.25	0.50	0.75
2000	—	PF65 5.00				

KM# 110 10 DRACHMAI

7.50 g., Copper-Nickel, 26 mm. **Obv:** Phoenix and flame **Rev:** Pegasus rearing right

Date	Mintage	VF20	XF40	MS60	MS63	MS65
1973	22,599,848	—	0.50	1.50	2.50	3.50

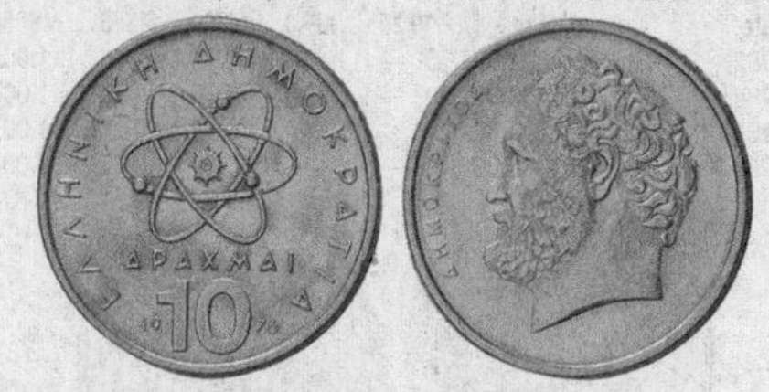

KM# 119 10 DRACHMAI

7.50 g., Copper-Nickel, 26 mm. **Subject:** Democritus **Obv:** Atom design **Rev:** Head left **Edge:** Plain

Date	Mintage	VF20	XF40	MS60	MS63	MS65
1976	76,816,000	—	—	0.25	0.65	1.00
1978	14,637,000	—	—	0.25	0.65	1.00
1978	20,000	PF65 5.00				
1980	28,733,000	—	—	0.25	0.65	1.00

KM# 132 10 DRACHMES
7.50 g., Copper-Nickel, 26 mm. **Subject:** Democritus **Obv:** Atom design **Rev:** Head left

Date	Mintage	VF20	XF40	MS60	MS63	MS65
1982	35,539,000	—	—	0.25	0.50	0.75
1984	23,802,000	—	—	0.25	0.50	0.75
1986	24,441,000	—	—	0.25	0.50	0.75
1988	16,869,000	—	—	0.25	0.50	0.75
1990	—	—	—	0.25	0.50	0.75
1992	—	—	—	0.25	0.50	0.75
1993 Sets only	—	—	—	—	—	10.00
1993	—	PF65 30.00				
1994	—	—	—	0.25	0.50	0.75
1998	—	—	—	0.25	0.50	0.75
2000	—	—	—	0.25	0.50	0.75
2000	—	PF65 6.00				

KM# 112 20 DRACHMAI
Copper-Nickel, 29 mm. **Subject:** Athena **Obv:** Phoenix and flame **Rev:** Helmeted head left

Date	Mintage	VF20	XF40	MS60	MS63	MS65
1973	20,650,087	—	0.25	0.75	1.25	2.00

KM# 120 20 DRACHMAI
11.00 g., Copper-Nickel, 29 mm. **Subject:** Pericles **Obv:** The Parthenon **Rev:** Helmeted head left **Edge Lettering:** In Greek

Date	Mintage	VF20	XF40	MS60	MS63	MS65
1976	53,167,500	—	—	0.50	1.00	1.50
1978	65,353,000	—	—	0.50	1.00	1.50
1978	20,000	PF65 5.00				
1980	17,562,000	—	—	1.50	2.50	3.50

KM# 133 20 DRACHMES
11.00 g., Copper-Nickel, 29 mm. **Subject:** Pericles **Obv:** The Parthenon **Rev:** Helmeted head left **Edge Lettering:** In Greek

Date	Mintage	VF20	XF40	MS60	MS63	MS65
1982	24,299,000	—	—	0.50	0.75	1.00
1984	13,412,000	—	—	0.50	0.75	1.00
1986	10,553,000	—	—	0.50	0.75	1.00
1988	16,196,000	—	—	0.50	0.75	1.00

KM# 154 20 DRACHMES
7.00 g., Aluminum-Bronze, 24.5 mm. **Subject:** Dionysios Solomos, composer of National Anthem **Obv:** Olive branch right of lined field **Rev:** Bust looking right **Edge:** Reeded

Date	Mintage	VF20	XF40	MS60	MS63	MS65
1990 (an)	—	—	—	0.50	0.75	1.00
1992	—	—	—	0.50	0.75	1.00
1993 Sets only	—	—	—	—	—	10.00
1993	—	PF65 40.00				
1994	—	—	—	0.50	0.75	1.00
1998 (an)	—	—	—	0.50	0.75	1.00
2000	—	—	—	0.50	0.75	1.00
2000	—	PF65 10.00				

KM# 124 50 DRACHMAI
12.00 g., Copper-Nickel, 31 mm. **Subject:** Solon the Archon of Athens **Obv:** Denomination above waves and date **Rev:** Head left

Date	Mintage	VF20	XF40	MS60	MS63	MS65
1980 (an)	32,250,999	—	—	1.50	2.50	3.50

KM# 134 50 DRACHMES
12.00 g., Copper-Nickel, 31 mm. **Subject:** Solon the Archon of Athens **Obv:** Denomination above waves and date **Rev:** Head left **Note:** Obv: Denomination in modern Greek

Date	Mintage	VF20	XF40	MS60	MS63	MS65
1982 (an)	18,899,000	—	0.25	0.75	1.25	2.00
1984 (an)	11,411,000	—	0.25	0.75	1.25	2.00

KM# 147 50 DRACHMES
9.00 g., Aluminum-Bronze, 27.5 mm. **Subject:** Homer **Obv:** Ancient sailing boat **Rev:** Head left **Edge:** Reeded

Date	Mintage	VF20	XF40	MS60	MS63	MS65
1986 (an)	12,078,000	—	0.25	0.50	1.00	1.50
1988 (an)	23,589,000	—	0.25	0.50	1.00	1.50
1990 (an)	—	—	—	0.50	1.00	1.50
1992	—	—	—	0.50	1.00	1.50
1993 Sets only	—	—	—	—	—	12.50
1993	—	PF65 35.00				
1994	—	—	—	0.50	1.00	1.50
1998	—	—	—	0.50	1.00	1.50
2000	—	—	—	0.50	1.00	1.50
2000	—	PF65 7.50				

KM# 164 50 DRACHMES
9.00 g., Aluminum-Bronze, 27.5 mm. **Series:** 150th Anniversary of the Constitution **Subject:** Dimitrios Kallergis **Obv:** Bust 3/4 left **Rev:** Center of Parliament Building **Edge:** Reeded

Date	Mintage	VF20	XF40	MS60	MS63	MS65
ND-1994 (an)	7,500,000	—	—	1.00	2.00	3.00

KM# 168 50 DRACHMES
9.00 g., Aluminum-Bronze, 27.5 mm. **Series:** 150th Anniversary of the Constitution **Subject:** Makrygiannis **Obv:** Bust 3/4 left **Rev:** Center of Parliament Building **Edge:** Reeded

Date	Mintage	VF20	XF40	MS60	MS63	MS65
ND-1994 (an)	7,500,000	—	—	1.00	2.00	3.00

KM# 171 50 DRACHMES
9.00 g., Aluminum-Bronze, 27.5 mm. **Subject:** Rigas Feraios **Obv:** Arms within wreath **Rev:** Bust 3/4 right divides dates **Edge:** Reeded

Date	Mintage	VF20	XF40	MS60	MS63	MS65
ND (1998)	—	—	—	1.00	2.00	3.00

KM# 172 50 DRACHMES
9.00 g., Aluminum-Bronze, 27.5 mm. **Subject:** Dionysios Solomos **Obv:** Arms within wreath **Rev:** Bust 3/4 facing divides dates **Edge:** Reeded

Date	Mintage	VF20	XF40	MS60	MS63	MS65
ND (1998)	—	—	—	1.00	2.00	3.00

KM# 121 100 DRACHMAI
13.00 g., 0.650 Silver 0.2717 oz. ASW **Subject:** 50th Anniversary - Bank of Greece **Obv:** Denomination **Rev:** Athena seated right

Date	Mintage	VF20	XF40	MS60	MS63	MS65
1978	25,000	PF63 45.00	PF65 75.00			

KM# 125 100 DRACHMAI
5.78 g., 0.900 Silver 0.1672 oz. ASW **Subject:** Pan-European Games **Obv:** Arms within wreath **Rev:** Ancient olympic broad jump

Date	Mintage	VF20	XF40	MS60	MS63	MS65
1981	150,000	—	—	—	3.00	3.50
1981	150,000	PF63 3.50	PF65 4.00			

KM# 135 100 DRACHMAI
5.78 g., 0.900 Silver 0.1672 oz. ASW **Subject:** Pan-European Games **Obv:** Arms within wreath **Rev:** Olympic high jump

Date	Mintage	VF20	XF40	MS60	MS63	MS65
1982	150,000	—	—	—	3.00	3.50
1982	Inc. above	PF63 3.50	PF65 4.00			

KM# 136 100 DRACHMAI
5.78 g., 0.900 Silver 0.1672 oz. ASW **Subject:** Pan-European

Games **Obv:** Arms within wreath **Rev:** Pole vault

Date	Mintage	VF20	XF40	MS60	MS63	MS65
1982	150,000	—	—	—	3.00	3.50
1982	Inc. above	PF63 3.50	PF65 4.00			

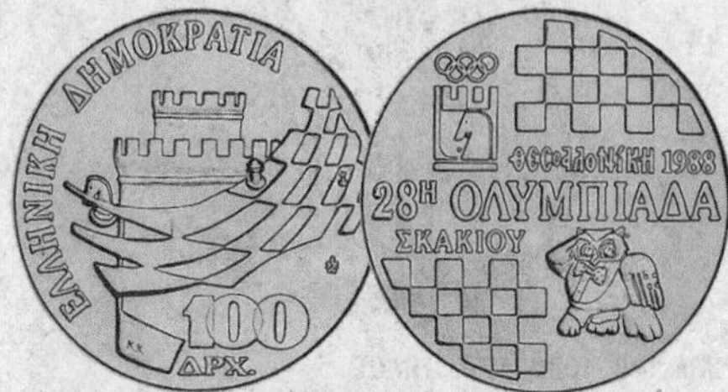

KM# 152 100 DRACHMES
Copper-Nickel **Subject:** 28th Chess Olympics **Obv:** Castle towers and stylized chessboard **Rev:** Legend divides block design, shield at left and owl at right

Date	Mintage	VF20	XF40	MS60	MS63	MS65
1988 (an)	30,000	—	—	3.00	6.00	12.00

KM# 159 100 DRACHMES
10.00 g., Aluminum-Bronze, 29.5 mm. **Subject:** Macedonia - Alexander the Great **Obv:** Radiant design within circle **Rev:** Head right **Edge:** Segmented reeding

Date	Mintage	VF20	XF40	MS60	MS63	MS65
1990	—	—	—	0.50	1.00	1.50
Note: Varieties exist						
1990	—	PF65 1,200				
1992	—	—	—	0.50	1.00	1.50
1993 Sets only	—	—	—	—	—	12.50
1993	—	PF65 50.00				
1994	—	—	—	0.50	1.00	1.50
1998	—	—	—	0.50	1.00	1.50
2000	—	—	—	0.50	1.00	1.50
2000	—	PF65 10.00				

KM# 169 100 DRACHMES
10.00 g., Aluminum-Bronze, 29.5 mm. **Subject:** VI Universal Track Championship Games **Obv:** Ancient city view and track **Rev:** Runner and track **Edge:** Segmented reeding

Date	Mintage	VF20	XF40	MS60	MS63	MS65
1997	5,000,000	—	—	2.00	2.50	3.00

KM# 170 100 DRACHMES
10.00 g., Aluminum-Bronze, 29.5 mm. **Subject:** 13th World Basketball Championships **Obv:** Cup in ball design **Rev:** Four basketball players in action **Edge:** Segmented reeding

Date	Mintage	VF20	XF40	MS60	MS63	MS65
1998	—	—	—	1.50	2.50	3.50

KM# 173 100 DRACHMES
10.00 g., Aluminum-Bronze, 29.5 mm. **Subject:** 45th Annual Greco-Roman Wrestling World Championships **Obv:** Ancient wrestlers above value **Rev:** Modern wrestlers **Edge:** Segmented reeding

Date	Mintage	VF20	XF40	MS60	MS63	MS65
1999	—	—	—	1.00	1.50	2.00

KM# 174 100 DRACHMES
10.00 g., Aluminum-Bronze, 29.5 mm. **Subject:** World Weightlifting Championships **Obv:** Statue of Hercules **Rev:** Weightlifter **Edge:** Segmented reeding

Date	Mintage	VF20	XF40	MS60	MS63	MS65
1999	—	—	—	1.00	1.50	2.00

KM# 126 250 DRACHMAI
14.44 g., 0.900 Silver 0.4178 oz. ASW **Subject:** Pan-European Games **Obv:** Arms within wreath **Rev:** Ancient Olympic javelin throwing

Date	Mintage	VF20	XF40	MS60	MS63	MS65
1981	150,000	—	—	—	7.75	8.50
1981	150,000	PF63 9.00	PF65 9.25			

KM# 137 250 DRACHMAI
14.44 g., 0.900 Silver 0.4178 oz. ASW **Subject:** Pan-European Games **Obv:** Arms within wreath **Rev:** 1896 Olympic discus throwing

Date	Mintage	VF20	XF40	MS60	MS63	MS65
1982	150,000	—	—	—	7.75	8.50
1982	Inc. above	PF63 9.00	PF65 9.25			

KM# 138 250 DRACHMAI
14.44 g., 0.900 Silver 0.4178 oz. ASW **Subject:** Pan-European Games **Obv:** Arms within wreath **Rev:** Shot put

Date	Mintage	VF20	XF40	MS60	MS63	MS65
1982	150,000	—	—	—	7.75	8.50
1982	Inc. above	PF63 9.00	PF65 9.25			

KM# 127 500 DRACHMAI
28.88 g., 0.900 Silver 0.8357 oz. ASW **Subject:** Pan-European Games **Obv:** Arms within wreath **Rev:** Ancient Olympic relay race

Date	Mintage	VF20	XF40	MS60	MS63	MS65
1981	150,000	—	—	—	15.50	17.00
1981	150,000	PF63 18.00	PF65 18.50			

KM# 139 500 DRACHMAI
28.88 g., 0.900 Silver 0.8357 oz. ASW **Subject:** Pan-European Games **Obv:** Arms within wreath **Rev:** 1896 Olympic racers at starting blocks

Date	Mintage	VF20	XF40	MS60	MS63	MS65
1982	150,000	—	—	—	15.50	17.00
1982	Inc. above	PF63 18.00	PF65 18.50			

KM# 140 500 DRACHMAI
28.88 g., 0.900 Silver 0.8357 oz. ASW **Subject:** Pan-European Games **Obv:** Arms within wreath **Rev:** Racers

Date	Mintage	VF20	XF40	MS60	MS63	MS65
1982	150,000	—	—	—	15.50	17.00
1982	Inc. above	PF63 18.00	PF65 18.50			

KM# 122 500 DRACHMES
13.00 g., 0.900 Silver 0.3762 oz. ASW **Subject:** Common Market Membership **Obv:** Inscription above denomination **Rev:** Figure in tree

Date	Mintage	VF20	XF40	MS60	MS63	MS65
ND (1979)	—	—	—	—	—	—
ND (1979)	18,000	PF63 65.00	PF65 100			

KM# 145 500 DRACHMES
18.00 g., 0.900 Silver 0.5208 oz. ASW **Subject:** Olympics **Obv:** Arms within wreath, torch at right **Rev:** Runner with torch

Date	Mintage	VF20	XF40	MS60	MS63	MS65
1984	25,000	—	—	—	10.50	11.50
1984	25,000	PF63 12.00	PF65 13.00			

KM# 153 500 DRACHMES
18.11 g., 0.900 Silver 0.524 oz. ASW **Subject:** 28th Chess Olympics **Obv:** Ancient figures playing chess **Rev:** Legend divides block design, shield at left and owl at right

Date	Mintage	VF20	XF40	MS60	MS63	MS65
1988	3,000	PF63 100	PF65 150			

KM# 157 500 DRACHMES
18.00 g., 0.900 Silver 0.5208 oz. ASW **Subject:** XI Mediterranean Games **Obv:** Design and denomination **Rev:** Fish wearing hat, logo at right

Date	Mintage	VF20	XF40	MS60	MS63	MS65
1991	10,000	PF63 12.50	PF65 14.50			

KM# 160 500 DRACHMES
17.00 g., 0.925 Silver 0.5056 oz. ASW **Subject:** 2500th Anniversary of Democracy **Obv:** Head on old coin right **Rev:** One seated and one standing figure within square

Date	Mintage	VF20	XF40	MS60	MS63	MS65
1993	Est. 30000	PF63 12.50	PF65 15.00			

KM# 162 500 DRACHMES
17.00 g., 0.925 Silver 0.5056 oz. ASW **Subject:** Volleyball Centennial **Rev:** Players in rectangle, date at corners

Date	Mintage	VF20	XF40	MS60	MS63	MS65
1994	1,750	PF63 225	PF65 350			

KM# 175 500 DRACHMES
9.54 g., Copper-Nickel, 28 mm. **Series:** 2004 Olympics **Obv:** Laurel wreath within square, games logo below **Rev:** Arched entry to ancient Olympic stadium **Edge:** Plain

Date	Mintage	VF20	XF40	MS60	MS63	MS65
2000	—	—	—	1.50	2.00	2.50

KM# 176 500 DRACHMES
9.54 g., Copper-Nickel, 28 mm. **Series:** 2004 Olympics **Obv:** Laurel wreath within square, games logo below **Rev:** Runner receiving Olympic torch **Edge:** Plain

Date	Mintage	VF20	XF40	MS60	MS63	MS65
2000	—	—	—	1.50	2.00	2.50

KM# 177 500 DRACHMES
9.54 g., Copper-Nickel, 28 mm. **Series:** 2004 Olympics **Obv:** Laurel wreath within square, games logo below **Rev:** Ancient winner Diagoras being carried **Edge:** Plain

Date	Mintage	VF20	XF40	MS60	MS63	MS65
2000	—	—	—	1.50	2.00	2.50

KM# 178 500 DRACHMES
9.54 g., Copper-Nickel, 28 mm. **Series:** 2004 Olympics **Subject:** President Vikelas and Baron Couberten **Obv:** Laurel wreath within square, games logo below **Rev:** Jugate busts; one left and one facing **Edge:** Plain

Date	Mintage	VF20	XF40	MS60	MS63	MS65
2000	—	—	—	1.50	2.00	2.50

KM# 179 500 DRACHMES
9.54 g., Copper-Nickel, 28 mm. **Series:** 2004 Olympics **Subject:** Spyros Louis, 1896 marathon winner **Obv:** Laurel wreath within square **Rev:** Standing figure **Edge:** Plain

Date	Mintage	VF20	XF40	MS60	MS63	MS65
2000	—	—	—	1.50	2.00	2.50

KM# 180 500 DRACHMES
9.54 g., Copper-Nickel, 28 mm. **Series:** 2004 Olympics **Obv:** Laurel wreath within square, games logo below **Rev:** 1896 Olympic gold medal design **Edge:** Plain

Date	Mintage	VF20	XF40	MS60	MS63	MS65
2000	—	—	—	1.50	2.00	2.50

KM# 148 1000 DRACHMES
23.33 g., 0.925 Silver 0.6938 oz. ASW **Subject:** Decade For Women **Rev:** Statue of women figures with arms raised

Date	Mintage	VF20	XF40	MS60	MS63	MS65
1985	3,660	PF63 75.00	PF65 125	PF67 200		

KM# 155 1000 DRACHMES
18.00 g., 0.900 Silver 0.5208 oz. ASW **Subject:** 50th Anniversary - Italian Invasion of Greece **Obv:** Arms within wreath **Rev:** Soldiers and horse

Date	Mintage	VF20	XF40	MS60	MS63	MS65
1990	7,000	PF63 60.00	PF65 100	PF67 175		

KM# 165 1000 DRACHMES
33.63 g., 0.925 Silver 1.0001 oz. ASW **Subject:** Olympics **Obv:** Track field **Rev:** 4 ancient runners **Edge Lettering:** CITIUS ALTIUS FORTIUS

Date	Mintage	VF20	XF40	MS60	MS63	MS65
1996	100,000	PF63 20.50	PF65 22.00	PF67 25.00		

KM# 166 1000 DRACHMES
33.63 g., 0.925 Silver 1.0001 oz. ASW **Subject:** Olympics **Rev:** 2 ancient wrestlers **Edge Lettering:** CITIUS ALTIUS FORTIUS

Date	Mintage	VF20	XF40	MS60	MS63	MS65
1996	100,000	PF63 20.50	PF65 22.00	PF67 25.00		

KM# 128 2500 DRACHMAI
6.45 g., 0.900 Gold 0.1866 oz. AGW **Series:** Pan-European Games **Subject:** Ancient Olympics, Agon **Obv:** Arms within wreath **Rev:** Winged figure holding rings

Date	Mintage	VF20	XF40	MS60	MS63	MS65
1981	75,000	PF63 250	PF65 260	PF67 285		

KM# 141 2500 DRACHMAI
6.45 g., 0.900 Gold 0.1866 oz. AGW **Series:** Pan-European Games **Subject:** 1896 Olympics, Spiros **Obv:** Arms within wreath **Rev:** Half figure holding wreath

Date	Mintage	VF20	XF40	MS60	MS63	MS65
1982	50,000	PF63 250	PF65 260	PF67 285		

KM# 142 2500 DRACHMAI
6.45 g., 0.900 Gold 0.1866 oz. AGW **Series:** Pan-European Games **Obv:** Arms within wreath **Rev:** Winged statue

Date	Mintage	VF20	XF40	MS60	MS63	MS65
1982	50,000	PF63 250	PF65 260	PF67 285		

KM# 129 5000 DRACHMAI
12.50 g., 0.900 Gold 0.3617 oz. AGW **Series:** Pan-European Games **Subject:** Ancient Olympics, Zeus **Obv:** Arms within wreath **Rev:** Laureate head left

Date	Mintage	VF20	XF40	MS60	MS63	MS65
1981	75,000	PF63 485	PF65 510	PF67 550		

KM# 143 5000 DRACHMAI
12.50 g., 0.900 Gold 0.3617 oz. AGW **Series:** Pan-European Games **Subject:** 1896 Olympics, Pierre de Coubertin **Obv:** Arms within wreath **Rev:** Head 3/4 facing

Date	Mintage	VF20	XF40	MS60	MS63	MS65
1982	50,000	PF63 485	PF65 510	PF67 550		

KM# 144 5000 DRACHMAI
12.50 g., 0.900 Gold 0.3617 oz. AGW **Series:** Pan-European Games **Obv:** Arms within wreath **Rev:** Birds flying

Date	Mintage	VF20	XF40	MS60	MS63	MS65
1982	50,000	PF63 485	PF65 510	PF67 550		

KM# 146 5000 DRACHMES
8.00 g., 0.900 Gold 0.2315 oz. AGW **Subject:** Olympics **Obv:** Arms at left, torch at right **Rev:** Apollo

Date	Mintage	VF20	XF40	MS60	MS63	MS65
1984	15,000	PF63 310	PF65 325	PF67 355		

KM# 123 10000 DRACHMES
20.00 g., 0.900 Gold 0.5787 oz. AGW **Subject:** Common Market Membership **Obv:** Inscription above denomination **Rev:** Seated figure left

Date	Mintage	VF20	XF40	MS60	MS63	MS65
ND (1979)	—	PF63 810	PF65 850	PF67 920		

KM# 149 10000 DRACHMES
7.13 g., 0.900 Gold 0.2063 oz. AGW **Subject:** Decade For Women **Obv:** Arms within wreath **Rev:** Standing figure

Date	Mintage	VF20	XF40	MS60	MS63	MS65
1985	2,835	PF63 275	PF65 290	PF67 315		

KM# 158 10000 DRACHMES
8.00 g., 0.900 Gold 0.2315 oz. AGW **Subject:** XI Mediterranean Games **Obv:** Design, denomination **Rev:** Fish wearing hat, logo at right

Date	Mintage	VF20	XF40	MS60	MS63	MS65
1991	2,000	PF63 325	PF65 340	PF67 370		

KM# 161 10000 DRACHMES
8.50 g., 0.917 Gold 0.2506 oz. AGW **Subject:** 2500th Anniversary of Democracy **Obv:** Statue **Rev:** Head left

Date	Mintage	VF20	XF40	MS60	MS63	MS65
1993	Est. 10000	PF63 335	PF65 350	PF67 385		

KM# 163 10000 DRACHMES
8.50 g., 0.917 Gold 0.2506 oz. AGW **Subject:** Volleyball Centennial **Obv:** Ancient coin divides date

Date	Mintage	VF20	XF40	MS60	MS63	MS65
1994	669	PF63 1,750	PF65 2,250	PF67 2,750		

KM# 156 20000 DRACHMES
8.00 g., 0.900 Gold 0.2315 oz. AGW **Subject:** 50th Anniversary - Italian Invasion of Greece **Rev:** Soldiers and horse

Date	Mintage	VF20	XF40	MS60	MS63	MS65
1990	1,000	PF63 2,250	PF65 2,750	PF67 3,250		

KM# 167 20000 DRACHMES
16.97 g., 0.917 Gold 0.5003 oz. AGW **Subject:** Olympics **Obv:** Track field **Rev:** Ancient javelin throwers **Edge Lettering:** CITIUS ALTIUS FORTIUS

Date	Mintage	VF20	XF40	MS60	MS63	MS65
1996	60,000	PF63 730	PF65 800	PF67 860		

ESSAIS

KM#	Date	Mintage	Identification	Mkt Val
EA23	1911	2	2 Drachmai. Silver. Without mintmark, ESSAI to right of seahorse.	10,250
E23	1911	4	2 Drachmai. Silver. 1868 2 Drachmai. ESSAI to right of denomination.	10,000
E24	1912	—	5 Lepta. Nickel. Crown right of center hole. Owl left of center hole. ESSAI, plain edge, without mintmark.	2,500
E25	1912	—	5 Lepta. Zinc. ESSAI.	3,000
E26	1912	—	10 Lepta. Nickel. Crown right of center hole. Owl left of center hole. ESSAI, plain edge, without mintmark.	3,000
E27	1912	—	10 Lepta. Zinc. ESSAI.	3,000
E28	1912	—	10 Lepta. Nickel. ESSAI, with mintmark.	4,000
E29	1912	—	20 Lepta. Nickel. Crowned arms right of center hole. Center hole divides statue and branch. ESSAI.	3,000
E30	1912	—	20 Lepta. Zinc. ESSAI.	3,200
E31	1913	—	Drachma. Silver. ESSAI.	80,000
E32	1915	—	Drachma. Copper-Nickel. ESSAI.	25,000
Note: NGSA 12/08 $18,000				
E33	1915	—	Drachma. Silver. Head left. Crowned and mantled shield. ESSAI.	75,000
E34	1915	—	Drachma. Gold. ESSAI.	—
E35	1915	—	2 Drachmai. Silver. ESSAI.	100,000
E36	1915	—	2 Drachmai. Gold. ESSAI.	—
E37	1922	—	10 Lepta. Aluminum. Crown above date. Olive branch left of denomination. ESSAI.	2,500
Note: NGSA 12/08 $2,800				

PATTERNS

Including off metal strikes

KM#	Date	Mintage	Identification	Mkt Val
Pn40	1910	—	Drachma. Silver. Value in lower case letters.	8,000
Pn41	1910	—	Drachma. Silver. Without mintmark.	8,000
Pn42	1911	—	2 Drachmai. Silver. Seahorse. Without mintmark.	10,000
PnA44	1922	3	10 Lepta. Nickel. With (IAKOBIAHS) engraver's name.	10,000
PnB44	1922	2	10 Lepta. Aluminum. With (IAKOBIAHS) engraver's name.	10,500
PnC44	1926	—	20 Lepta. Copper-Nickel. Large letters.	5,000
Pn44	1926	—	Drachma. Nickel. Large letters.	5,000
Pn54	1926	—	2 Drachmai. Nickel. Large letters.	3,000
Pn55	1930	—	5 Drachmai. Nickel. With "MODEL" on reverse.	5,000
Pn59	ND (1940)	—	20 Drachmai. Copper. 21mm, KM74.	5,000
Pn60	ND (1940)	—	20 Drachmai. Gold. Without "20", KM74.	50,000
Pn61	ND (1940)	—	100 Drachmai. Copper. KM75.	7,150
Pn62	ND (1940)	—	100 Drachmai. Copper. KM76.	7,150
Pn63	1954	50	50 Lepta. Copper-Nickel. ANAMNKETIKON" above date.	2,500
Pn64	1954	10	50 Lepta. Gold.	6,000
Pn65	1954	—	50 Lepta. Copper-Nickel. hollow cheek" variety, not approved, die use discontinued.	750
Pn66	1954	50	Drachma. Copper-Nickel. ANAMNHETIKON" above date.	3,000
Pn67	1954	10	Drachma. Gold.	6,000
Pn68	1954	—	Drachma. Copper-Nickel. hollow cheek variety, not approved, die use discontinued.	600
Pn69	1954	50	2 Drachmai. Copper-Nickel. ANAMNHETIKON" above date.	3,000
Pn70	1954	10	2 Drachmai. Gold.	6,000
Pn71	1954	—	2 Drachmai. Copper-Nickel. hollow cheek variety, not approved, die use discontinued.	1,500
Pn72	1954	50	5 Drachmai. Copper-Nickel. ANAMNHETIKON" above date.	3,000
Pn73	1954	10	5 Drachmai. Gold.	6,000
PnA74	1954	—	5 Drachmai. Copper-Nickel. hollow cheek variety, not approved, die use discontinued.	50.00
PnB74	1954	—	5 Drachami. Copper-Nickel. No Engravers Name.	2,800
PnA75	1959	—	10 Drachmai. Silver. KM#84.	6,000
Pn75	1959	10	10 Drachmai. Gold.	20,000
Pn77	1960	—	20 Drachmai. Gold.	20,000

Pn78	1963	—	30 Drachmai. Silver. With "ANAMNHETIKON".	7,000
Pn79	1964	—	30 Drachmai. Gold.	15,000
Pn80	1966	—	50 Lepta. Gold.	—

Note: NGSA Auction 12/08 $4,500

PnA81	1966	—	2 Drachmai. Silver.	2,400
PnC81	1966	—	5 Drachami. Silver.	3,000

Note: Rauch Auction 12/10, $3,000

Pn81	1966	—	50 Lepta. Silver.	5,250

Note: Platinum strikes have been reported, but not confirmed

Pn82	1967	—	Drachma. Gold.	6,500

Note: NGSA 12/08 $5,000

Pn83	1967	—	Drachma. Silver.	4,500

Note: Platinum strikes have been reported, but not confirmed. NGSA 12/08 $1,200

Pn84	1967	—	2 Drachmai. Gold.	6,500

Note: NGSA 12/08 $6,000

Pn85	1967	—	2 Drachmai. Silver.	5,250

Note: Platinum strikes have been reported, but not confirmed. NGSA 12/08 $1,400

Pn86	1967	—	5 Drachmai. Gold.	6,500

Note: NGSA Auction 12/08 $10,000

Pn87	1967	—	5 Drachmai. Silver.	8,250

Note: Platinum strikes have been reported, but not confirmed. NGSA Auction 12/08 $1,200

Pn88	1973	—	20 Drachmai. Bronze-Nickel. Low relief and date, without veil.	75.00
Pn89	1976	—	Drachma. Nickel. 4 sails and 2 waves.	2,000
Pn90	1986	4	Drachma. Aluminum.	2,500
Pn91	1986	4	2 Drachmai. Aluminum.	2,500
Pn92	1987	—	Drachma. Copper.	—

Note: Off metal strike resulting from wrong planchet error

Pn93	1987	—	2 Drachmes. Nickel-Brass.	—

Note: Off metal strike resulting from wrong planchet error

PIEDFORT

KM#	Date	Mintage	Identification	Mkt Val
P1	1922	—	10 Lepta. Copper. With ESSAI.	3,000
P3	ND (1940)	2	20 Drachmai. Lead. KM74.	4,000

TRIAL STRIKES

KM#	Date	Mintage	Identification	Mkt Val
TS22	1921	—	5 Lepta. Aluminum. Reverse uniface.	—
TS23	1921	—	5 Lepta. Aluminum. Obverse uniface.	—
TS24	1921	—	50 Lepta. Aluminum. Uniface.	2,000
TS25	1921	—	50 Lepta. Brass. Uniface.	2,500
TS26	1926	—	2 Drachmai. Copper. Uniface.	1,000
TSA27	1926	—	2 Drachmai. Copper.	
TS27	1930	—	5 Drachmai. Copper. Uniface.	1,500
TSA28	1930	—	5 Drachami. Nickel. 'Model' hand engraved on uniface reverse.	10,000

Note: Morten & Eden, 12/2011 Unc. $10,000.

KM#	Date	Mintage	Identification	Mkt Val
TS28	1930	—	20 Drachmai. Brass. Test marks.	500
TS29	1960	—	20 Drachmai. Copper.	5,000
TS30	1969/70	—	10 Lepta. Base Metal. Uniface obverse.	3,500
TS31	ND-1969	—	10 Lepta. Base Metal. Uniface reverse.	3,500
TS32	1969/70	—	10 Lepta. Silver. Uniface obverse.	4,000
TS33	ND-1969	—	10 Lepta. Silver. Uniface reverse.	4,000
TS34	1969/70	—	10 Lepta. Gold. Uniface obverse.	5,000
TS35	ND-1969	—	10 Lepta. Gold. Uniface reverse.	5,000
TS36	1969/4	—	20 Lepta. Base Metal. Uniface obverse.	3,500
TS37	ND-1969	—	20 Lepta. Base Metal. Uniface reverse.	3,500
TS38	1969/4	—	20 Lepta. Aluminum. Uniface obverse.	3,000
TS39	ND1969/4	—	20 Lepta. Silver. Uniface obverse.	4,000
TS40	ND-1969	—	20 Lepta. Silver. Uniface reverse.	4,000
TS41	1969/4	—	20 Lepta. Gold. Uniface obverse.	5,000
TS42	ND-1969	—	20 Lepta. Gold. Uniface reverse.	5,000

MINT SETS

KM#	Date	Mintage	Identification	Issue Price	Mkt Val
MS1	1965 (7)	—	KM78, 80-85	—	25.00
MS2	1978 (8)	50,000	KM#113, 114, 115, 116, 117, 118, 119, 120	—	25.00
MS3	1982 (7)	—	KM115-116, 130-134	—	10.00
MS4	1993 (7)	—	KM#131-132, 147, 150-151, 154, 159	—	225
MS5	2000 (7)	—	KM#131-132, 147, 150-151, 154, 159	—	12.00

PROOF SETS

KM#	Date	Mintage	Identification	Issue Price	Mkt Val
PS1	1965 (7)	4,987	KM78, 80-85	10.25	50.00
PS2	1978 (8)	20,000	KM113-120	—	20.00
PS3	1993 (8)	—	KM131-132, 147, 150-151, 154, 159-160	65.00	300
PS4	1994 (2)	—	KM162, 163	—	3,500
PS5	2000 (7)	—	KM#131-2; 147; 150-1; 154; 159.	—	120

GREENLAND

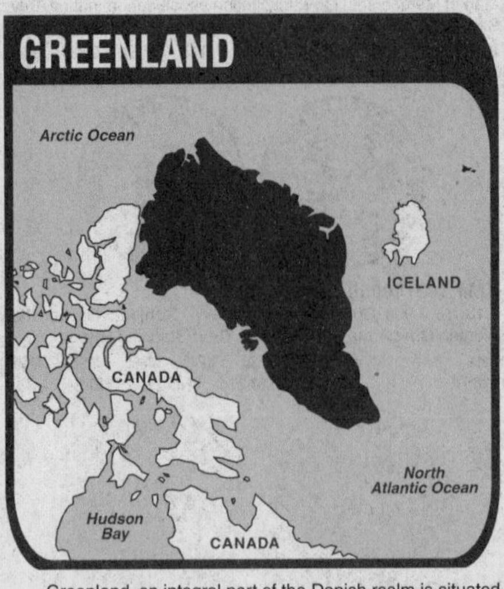

Greenland, an integral part of the Danish realm is situated between the North Atlantic Ocean and the Polar Sea, almost entirely within the Arctic Circle. An island nation, it has an area of 840,000 sq. mi. (2,175,600 sq. km.) and a population of 57,000. Capital: Nuuk (formerly Godthaab). Greenland is the world's only source of natural cryolite, a fluoride of sodium and aluminum important in making aluminum. Fish products and minerals are exported.

Eric the Red discovered Greenland in 982 and established the first settlement in 986. Greenland was a republic until 1261, when the sovereignty of Norway was extended to the island. The original colony was abandoned about 1400 when increasing cold interfered with the breeding of cattle. Successful recolonization was undertaken by Denmark in 1721. In 1921 Denmark extended its claim to include the entire island, and made it a colony of the crown in 1924. The island's colonial status was abolished by amendment to the Danish constitution on June 5, 1953, and Greenland became an integral part of the Kingdom of Denmark. The last Greenlandic coins were withdrawn on July 1, 1967, and since then, Danish coins have been used. Greenland has had home rule since May 1, 1979.

RULERS

Danish

MINT MARKS

Heart (h) Copenhagen (Kobenhavn)

MINTMASTERS' INITIALS

HCN - Hans Christian Nielsen, 1919-1927
C - Alfred Kristian Frederik Christiansen, 1956-1971
GJ - Knud Gunnar Jensen, 1901-1933
S - Harald Salomon, 1933-1968

MONETARY SYSTEM

(Since 1824)

100 Øre = 1 Krone

DANISH COLONY

TOKEN ISSUES - GREENLAND MINING LTD.

Josva (Innatsiaq)

A place in southwest Greenland, where the Grønlandsk Minedrifts Aktieselskab ran a copper mine from 1907-1914 yielding little more than 60 tons of copper, as a minor bonus, over 50 kg of silver and half a kg of gold.

KM# Tn1 10 ØRE

Nickel Plated Zinc **Obv:** Date within legend **Obv. Legend:** GRØNLANDSK MINEDRIFTS-AKTIESELSKAB **Rev:** Crossed hammers over denomination **Note:** Struck at L. Chr. Lauer, Nürnberg, Germany.

Date	Mintage	VG8	F12	VF20	XF40	MS60
1911	5,000	—	10.00	40.00	60.00	90.00

KM# Tn2 25 ØRE

Nickel Plated Zinc **Obv:** Date within legend **Obv. Legend:** GRØNLANDSK MINEDRIFTS-AKTIESELSKAB **Rev:** Crossed hammers over denomination **Note:** Struck at L. Chr. Lauer, Nürnberg, Germany.

Date	Mintage	VG8	F12	VF20	XF40	MS60
1911	5,000	—	10.00	40.00	60.00	90.00

KM# Tn3 100 ØRE

Nickel Plated Zinc **Obv:** Date within legend **Obv. Legend:** GRØNLANDSK MINEDRIFTS-AKTIESELSKAB **Rev:** Crossed hammers over denomination **Note:** Struck at L. Chr. Lauer, Nürnberg, Germany.

Date	Mintage	VG8	F12	VF20	XF40	MS60
1911	5,000	—	10.00	40.00	60.00	90.00

TOKEN ISSUES - IVIGTUT CRYOLITE MINING & TRADING CO.

Series IV, 1922

KM# Tn46 10 ØRE

Copper-Nickel **Obv:** Seated polar bear on helmeted shield, mining tools flank **Obv. Legend:** IVIGTUT KRYOLITHBRUD **Rev:** Denomination at center **Rev. Legend:** KRYOLITH MINE OG HANDELS SELSKABET

Date	Mintage	VG8	F12	VF20	XF40	MS60
1922	10,018	—	8.00	20.00	40.00	75.00

KM# Tn47 50 ØRE

Copper-Nickel **Obv:** Seated polar bear on helmeted shield, mining tools flank **Obv. Legend:** IVIGTUT KRYOLITHBRUD **Rev. Legend:** KRYOLITH MINE OG HANDELS SELSKABET

Date	Mintage	VG8	F12	VF20	XF40	MS60
1922	4,018	—	15.00	35.00	75.00	150

KM# Tn48 2 KRONER

Copper-Nickel **Obv:** Seated polar bear on helmeted shield, mining tools flank **Obv. Legend:** IVIGTUT KRYOLITHBRUD **Rev:** Rosettes flank denomination **Rev. Legend:** KRYOLITH MINE OG HANDELS SELSKABET

Date	Mintage	VG8	F12	VF20	XF40	MS60
1922	4,018	—	15.00	35.00	65.00	125

KM# Tn49 10 KRONER

Copper-Nickel **Obv:** Seated polar bear on shield **Obv. Legend:** IVIGTUT KRYOLITHBRUD **Rev. Legend:** KRYOLITH MINE OG HANDELS SELSKABET **Edge:** Reeded

Date	Mintage	VG8	F12	VF20	XF40	MS60
1922	10,706	—	25.00	40.00	75.00	150

Note: Struck in 1926 using 1922 dies. Many new coins have appeared on the market lately.

KM# Tn49a 10 KRONER

Aluminum-Bronze **Obv:** Polar bear on shield **Edge:** Plain

Date	Mintage	VG8	F12	VF20	XF40	MS60
1922	7,018	—	—	850	1,200	2,200

Note: This token was removed from circulation because it had the same size, weight and color as Denmark's 2 Kroner, issued in 1924.

TOKEN ISSUES - ROYAL GREENLAND TRADE (COMPANY)

(Den Kongelige Grønlandske Handel)

Ammassalik is a municipality in East Greenland with a population of 3100.

KM# Tn25 500 ØRE

Aluminum **Note:** Uniface

Date	Mintage	VG8	F12	VF20	XF40	MS60
ND-1905	200	200	300	450	800	—

DANISH COLONY

MILLED COINAGE

KM# 6 25 ØRE

Copper-Nickel **Obv:** Crowned arms of Denmark **Rev:** Hole at center of polar bear walking, left, denomination above, date below divided by 'GS' **Note:** Center hole added to KM#5.

Date	Mintage	VF20	XF40	MS60	MS63	MS65
1926 (h) HCN GJ	60,000	22.50	60.00	—	—	—

Note: The hole was added 1940/41 in New York to avoid confusion with the 1 Krone coins.

KM# 5 25 ØRE

Copper-Nickel **Obv:** Crowned arms of Denmark **Obv. Legend:** GRØNLANDS STYRELSE **Rev:** Polar bear walking left, denomination above, date below divided by 'GS'

Date	Mintage	VF20	XF40	MS60	MS63	MS65
1926 (h) HCN GJ	310,000	7.00	15.00	25.00	45.00	75.00

KM# 7 50 ØRE

Aluminum-Bronze **Obv:** Crowned arms of Denmark **Obv. Legend:** GRØNLANDS STYRELSE **Rev:** Polar bear walking left, denomination above, date below divided by 'GS'

Date	Mintage	VF20	XF40	MS60	MS63	MS65
1926 (h) HCN GJ	195,837	9.00	18.00	35.00	50.00	85.00

KM# 8 KRONE

Aluminum-Bronze **Obv:** Crowned arms of Denmark **Obv. Legend:** GRØNLANDS STYRELSE **Rev:** Polar bear walking left, denomination above, date below divided by 'GS' **Note:** Exists with or without an incuse dot in the center heart on the obverse

Date	Mintage	VF20	XF40	MS60	MS63	MS65
1926 (h) HCN GJ	286,982	7.00	20.00	40.00	60.00	95.00

KM# 9 5 KRONER

Brass **Obv:** Crowned arms of Denmark **Obv. Legend:** GRØNLANDS STYRELSE **Rev:** Polar bear walking left, denomination above, date below divided by "GS **Note:** Mainly struck for use by American forces in Greenland during WWII, when 5 Kroner was equal to one U.S. dollar.

Date	Mintage	VF20	XF40	MS60	MS63	MS65
1944	100,000	45.00	70.00	120	185	275

Note: Struck at the Philadelphia Mint; without mintmark

DANISH STATE

1953-1979

MILLED COINAGE

KM# 10 KRONE

Aluminum-Bronze, 27.3 mm. **Issuer:** Royal Greenland Trade Company **Obv:** Crowned arms of Denmark and Greenland, date below **Obv. Legend:** DEN KONGELIGE GRØNLANDSKE HANDEL **Rev:** Denomination within floral wreath.

Date	Mintage	VF20	XF40	MS60	MS63	MS65
1957 (h) C S	100,209	7.00	15.00	25.00	45.00	90.00

KM# 10a KRONE

Copper-Nickel, 27.3 mm. **Issuer:** Royal Greenland Trade Company **Obv:** Crowned arms of Denmark and Greenland **Rev:** Denomination within floral wreath

Date	Mintage	VF20	XF40	MS60	MS63	MS65
1960 (h) C S	108,500	6.00	12.00	25.00	45.00	70.00
1964 (h) C S	110,000	6.50	16.00	30.00	50.00	75.00

TRIAL STRIKES

Angmagssalik - Royal Greenland Trade (Company)

KM#	Date	Mintage	Identification	Mkt Val
TS1	ND-1905	—	Øre. Aluminum.	—
	Note: Similar to the zinc-tokens ND (1894)			
TS2	ND-1905	—	5 Øre. Aluminum.	—
	Note: Similar to the zinc-tokens ND (1894)			
TS3	ND-1905	—	10 Øre. Aluminum.	—
	Note: Similar to the zinc-tokens ND (1894)			
TS4	ND-1905	—	25 Øre. Aluminum.	—
	Note: Similar to the zinc-tokens ND (1894)			
TS5	ND-1905	—	50 Øre. Aluminum.	—
	Note: Similar to the zinc-tokens ND (1894)			
TS6	ND-1905	—	100 Øre. Aluminum.	—
	Note: Similar to the zinc-tokens ND (1894)			

THULE-KAP YORK

Trading station founded by Knud Rasmussen in 1910. The money circulated from 1914 to 1937, but they bear the date of the founding year. They were produced by the date of the founding year. They were produced by L. Chr. Lauer, Nürnberg, Germany in 1913.

THULE KAP YORK

TOKEN COINAGE

KM# Tn5.1 5 ØRE

Aluminum **Obv:** Legend, center hole **Obv. Legend:** THULE *KAP YORK* **Rev:** Center hole divides denomination and date of founding of settlement.

Date	Mintage	F12	VF20	XF40	MS60	MS63
1910	5,000	—	3.00	10.00	15.00	25.00

KM# Tn5.2 5 ØRE

Aluminum **Obv:** Legend **Obv. Legend:** THULE *KAP YORK* **Rev:** Denomination above date **Note:** Error - struck without center hole.

Date	Mintage	F12	VF20	XF40	MS60	MS63
1910 Rare	—	—	—	—	—	—

KM# Tn6 25 ØRE

Aluminum **Obv:** Legend, center hole **Obv. Legend:** THULE *KAP YORK* **Rev:** Center hole divides date and denomination

Date	Mintage	F12	VF20	XF40	MS60	MS63
1910	5,000	—	3.00	10.00	15.00	25.00

KM# Tn7 100 ØRE

Aluminum **Obv:** Legend, center hole **Obv. Legend:** THULE *KAP YORK* **Rev:** Center hole divides date and denomination

Date	Mintage	F12	VF20	XF40	MS60	MS63
1910	2,000	3.00	5.00	15.00	35.00	50.00

KM# Tn8 500 ØRE

Aluminum **Obv:** Legend, center hole **Obv. Legend:** THULE *KAP YORK* **Rev:** Center hole divides date and denomination

Date	Mintage	F12	VF20	XF40	MS60	MS63
1910	2,000	3.00	5.00	15.00	35.00	50.00

Note: Tn5-8 were struck at L. Chr. Lauer, Nürnberg, Germany, in 1913

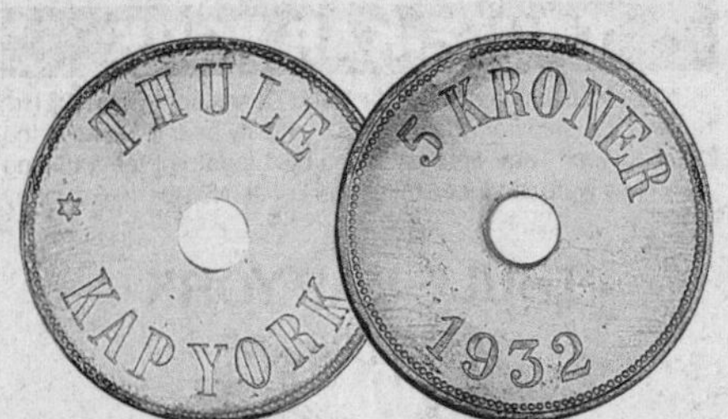

KM# Tn9 5 KRONER
Aluminum **Obv:** Legend, center hole **Obv. Legend:** THULE *KAP YORK* **Rev:** Center hole divides date and denomination

Date	Mintage	F12	VF20	XF40	MS60	MS63
1932	500	15.00	27.50	50.00	100	140

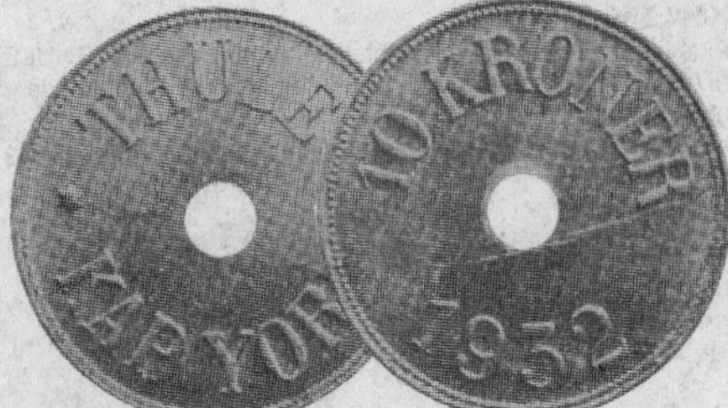

KM# Tn10 10 KRONER
Aluminum **Obv. Legend:** THULE *KAP YORK* **Rev:** Center hole divides date and denomination

Date	Mintage	F12	VF20	XF40	MS60	MS63
1932	500	30.00	50.00	100	225	300

Note: Tn9-10 were struck at H. Th. Neergaard Gravør-og Stempelfabrik, engraving and stamp factory.

GRENADA

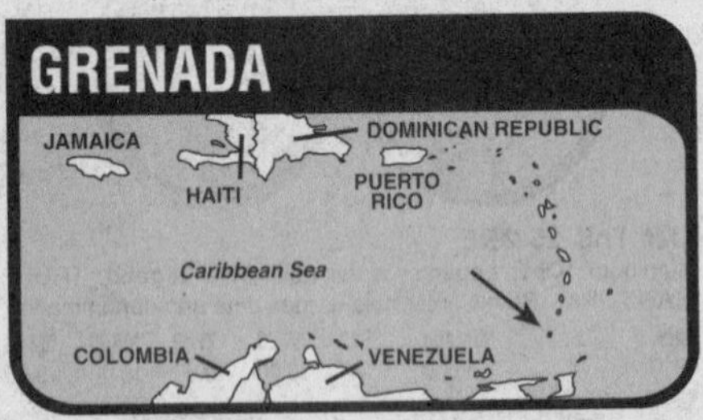

The State of Grenada, located in the Windward Islands of the Caribbean Sea 90 miles (145 km.) north of Trinidad, has(with Carriacou and Petit Martinique) an area of 133 sq. mi. (344 sq. km.) and a population of 94,000. Capital: St.George's. Grenada is the smallest independent nation in the Western Hemisphere. The economy is based on agriculture and tourism. Sugar, coconuts, nutmeg, cocoa and bananas are exported.

Columbus discovered Grenada in 1498 during his third voyage to the Americas. Spain failed to colonize the island, and in 1627 granted it to the British who sold it to the French who colonized it in 1650. Grenada was captured by the British in 1763, retaken by the French in 1779, and finally ceded to the British in 1783. In 1958 Grenada joined the Federation of the West Indies, which was dissolved in 1962. In 1967 it became an internally self-governing British associated state. Full independence was attained on Feb. 4, 1974. Grenada is a member of the Commonwealth of Nations. The prime minister is the Head of Government. Elizabeth II is Head of State as Queen of Grenada.

The early coinage of Grenada consists of cut and countermarked pieces of Spanish or Spanish Colonial Reales, which were valued at 11 Bits. In 1787 8 Reales coins were cut into 11 triangular pieces and countermarked with an incuse G. Later in 1814 large denomination cut pieces were issued being 1/2, 1/3 or 1/6 cuts and countermarked with a TR, incuse G and a number 6, 4, 2, or 1 indicating the value in bitts.

RULERS
British

INDEPENDENT STATE

Commonwealth of Nations

MODERN COINAGE

KM# 15 4 DOLLARS
Copper-Nickel, 38.5 mm. **Series:** F.A.O. **Obv:** Cocoa beans within oval **Rev:** Sugar cane and banana tree branch

Date	Mintage	VF20	XF40	MS60	MS63	MS65
1970	13,000	6.00	10.00	22.00	35.00	45.00
1970	2,000	PF65 55.00				

KM# 16 10 DOLLARS
Copper-Nickel **Subject:** Royal Visit **Obv:** Crowned bust right **Rev:** Arms with supporters within circle

Date	Mintage	VF20	XF40	MS60	MS63	MS65
1985	Est. 100000	—	—	18.00	28.00	40.00

KM# 16a 10 DOLLARS
28.28 g., 0.925 Silver 0.841 oz. ASW **Subject:** Royal Visit **Obv:** Crowned bust right **Rev:** Arms with supporters within circle

Date	Mintage	VF20	XF40	MS60	MS63	MS65
1985	Est. 5000	PF65 120	PF67 145			

KM# 17 100 DOLLARS
129.59 g., 0.925 Silver 3.8539 oz. ASW, 63 mm. **Subject:** Tropical Birds - Grenada Dove **Obv:** Arms within in circle, country name above **Note:** Illustration reduced.

Date	Mintage	VF20	XF40	MS60	MS63	MS65
1988	Est. 10000	PF63 120	PF65 140	PF67 160		

KM# 18 500 DOLLARS
47.54 g., 0.917 Gold 1.4016 oz. AGW **Subject:** Royal Visit **Obv:** Crowned bust right **Rev:** Arms with supporters within circle

Date	Mintage	VF20	XF40	MS60	MS63	MS65
1985	Est. 250	PF65 1,900	PF67 2,000			

GUADELOUPE

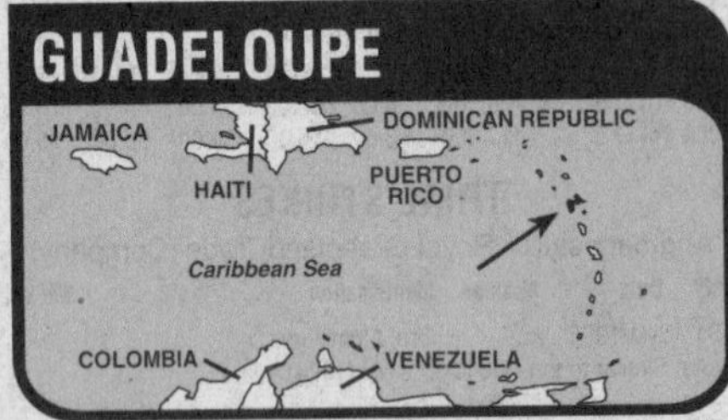

The French Overseas Department of Guadeloupe, located in the Leeward Islands of the West Indies about 300 miles (493 km.) southeast of Puerto Rico, has an area of 687 sq. mi. (1,780 sq. km.) and a population of 306,000. Actually it is two islands separated by a narrow saltwater stream: volcanic Basse-Terre to the west and the flatter limestone formation of Grande-Terre to the east. Capital: Basse-Terre, on the island of that name. The principal industries are agriculture, the distillation of liquors, and tourism. Sugar, bananas, and rum are exported.

Guadeloupe was discovered by Columbus in 1493 and settled in 1635 by two Frenchmen, L'Olive and Duplessis, who took possession in the name of the French Company of the Islands of America. When repeated efforts by private companies to colonize the island failed, it was relinquished to the French crown in 1674, and established as a dependency of Martinique. The British occupied the island on two occasions, 1759-63 and 1810-16, before it passed permanently to France. A colony until 1946 Guadeloupe was then made an overseas territory of the FrenchUnion. In 1958 it voted to become an Overseas Department within the new French Community.

The well-known R.F. in garland oval countermark of the French Government is only legitimate if on a French Colonies 12 deniers 1767 C#4. Two other similar but incuse RF countermarks are on cut pieces in the values of 1 and 4 escalins. Contemporary and modern counterfeits are known of both these types.

RULER
French 1816-

MONETARY SYSTEM
100 Centimes = 1 Franc

FRENCH COLONY

MODERN COINAGE

KM# 45 50 CENTIMES
Copper-Nickel, 22 mm. **Obv:** Armored head left within circle **Rev:** Sugar cane stalk divides date and denomination **Shape:** 18-sided

Date	Mintage	F12	VF20	XF40	MS60	MS63
1903	600,000	35.00	50.00	115	325	600
1921	600,000	25.00	40.00	75.00	185	400

KM# 46 FRANC
Copper-Nickel, 25 mm. **Obv:** Armored head left within circle **Rev:** Sugar cane stalk divides date and denomination **Note:** 20-sided.

Date	Mintage	F12	VF20	XF40	MS60	MS63
1903	700,000	20.00	40.00	90.00	250	550
1921	700,000	15.00	30.00	80.00	200	450

ESSAIS

KM#	Date	Mintage	Identification	Mkt Val
E1	1903	—	50 Centimes. Copper-Nickel.	300
E2	1903	—	50 Centimes. Silver.	600
E3	1903	—	Franc. Copper-Nickel.	350
E4	1903	—	Franc. Silver.	650
E5	19(21) (1921)	—	Franc. Bronze.	225

PIEDFORT

KM#	Date	Mintage	Identification	Mkt Val
P1	1903	—	50 Centimes. Copper-Nickel. Armored head left within circle. Sugar cane stalk divides date and denomination.	600
P2	1903	—	Franc. Copper-Nickel.	650

GUATEMALA

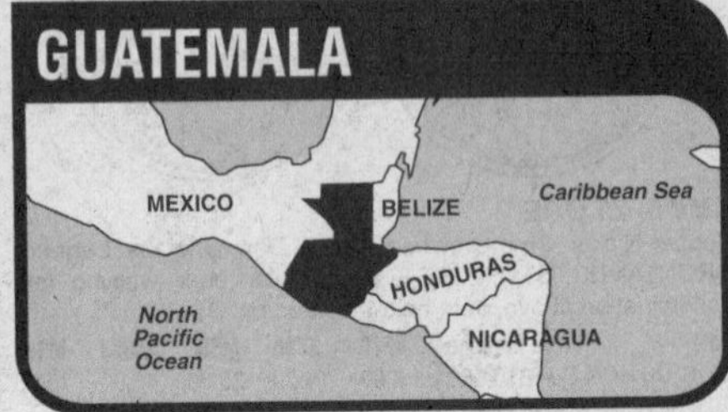

The Republic of Guatemala, the northernmost of the five Central American republics, has an area of 42,042 sq. mi. (108,890 sq. km.) and a population of 10.7 million. Capital: Guatemala City. The economy of Guatemala is heavily dependent on agriculture, however, the country is rich in nickel resources which are being developed. Coffee, cotton and bananas are exported.

Guatemala, once the site of an ancient Mayan civilization, was conquered by Pedro de Alvarado, the resourceful lieutenant of Cortes who undertook the conquest from Mexico. Cruel but strategically skillful, he progressed rapidly along the Pacific coastal lowlands to the highland plain of Quetzaltenango where the decisive battle for Guatemala was fought. After routing the Indian forces, he established the city of Guatemala in 1524. The Spanish Captaincy-General of Guatemala included all Central America but Panama. Guatemala declared its independence of Spain in 1821 and was absorbed into the Mexican empire of Augustin Iturbide (1822-23). From 1823 to 1839 Guatemala was a constituent state of the Central American Republic. Upon dissolution of that confederation, Guatemala proclaimed itself an independent republic. Like El Salvador, Guatemala suffered from internal strife between right-wing, US-backed military government and leftist indigenous peoples from ca. 1954 to ca. 1997.

MINT MARKS
H, (H) - Heaton, Birmingham
(KN) – Birmingham, King's Norton Mint
(L) – London, Royal Mint
(P) – Philadelphia, USA
NG - ??? 1992
(S) – San Francisco, USA

REPUBLIC

STANDARD COINAGE

8 Reales = 1 Peso

KM# 175 1/4 REAL

Copper-Nickel, 13.5 mm. **Obv:** Sun above three mountains **Rev:** Denomination within wreath, 5 stars below **Note:** Medal rotation.

Date	Mintage	F12	VF20	XF40	MS60	MS63
1901 H	5,056,000	0.25	0.45	1.00	2.50	3.50

KM# 176 1/2 REAL (Medio)

Copper-Nickel, 19 mm. **Obv:** Justice seated left **Rev:** Quetzal with scroll and weapons within thick wreath **Note:** Medal rotation.

Date	Mintage	F12	VF20	XF40	MS60	MS63
1901 (H)	6,652,000	0.35	0.65	1.25	3.50	6.00

KM# 177 REAL

Copper-Nickel, 21 mm. **Obv:** Justice seated left **Rev:** National arms, thick wreath **Note:** Medal rotation.

Date	Mintage	F12	VF20	XF40	MS60	MS63
1901 (H)	7,388,000	0.20	0.35	1.20	3.00	5.00
1910 (H)	4,000,000	0.25	0.40	1.25	3.00	5.00
1911 (H)	2,000,000	0.25	0.45	1.35	3.00	5.00
1912 (H)	8,000,000	0.20	0.35	1.00	3.00	5.00

PROVISIONAL COINAGE

1915-1923

KM# 230 12-1/2 CENTAVOS

Copper, 24.5 mm. **Obv:** Word at center divides flower **Rev:** Denomination within circle

Date	Mintage	F12	VF20	XF40	MS60	MS63
1915	6,000,000	1.25	2.00	6.00	15.00	25.00

KM# 231 25 CENTAVOS

Copper, 23 mm. **Obv:** Word at center divides flower **Rev:** Denomination within circle

Date	Mintage	F12	VF20	XF40	MS60	MS63
1915	4,000,000	1.25	2.00	7.00	16.00	25.00

KM# 232.1 50 CENTAVOS

Aluminum-Bronze, 16 mm. **Obv:** Flower design **Rev:** Denomination within circle **Note:** Thin numerals in denomination.

Date	Mintage	F12	VF20	XF40	MS60	MS63
1922	3,803,000	1.25	2.25	8.50	18.00	28.00

KM# 232.2 50 CENTAVOS

Aluminum-Bronze, 16 mm. **Obv:** Flower design **Rev:** Denomination within circle **Note:** Thick numerals in denomination.

Date	Mintage	F12	VF20	XF40	MS60	MS63
1922	Inc. above	1.25	2.25	8.50	18.00	28.00

KM# 233 PESO

Aluminum-Bronze, 20 mm. **Subject:** Miguel Garcia Granados **Obv:** Bust left **Rev:** Denomination

Date	Mintage	F12	VF20	XF40	MS60	MS63
1923	1,477,000	1.50	3.00	10.00	28.00	45.00

KM# 234 5 PESOS

Aluminum-Bronze, 25 mm. **Subject:** Justo Rufino Barrios **Obv:** Bust right **Rev:** Denomination

Date	Mintage	F12	VF20	XF40	MS60	MS63
1923	440,000	3.00	8.00	27.00	45.00	90.00

KM# 234a 5 PESOS

Copper, 25 mm. **Subject:** Justo Rufino Barrios **Obv:** Bust right **Rev:** Denomination

Date	Mintage	F12	VF20	XF40	MS60	MS63
1923	Inc. above	3.00	5.00	25.00	45.00	90.00

REFORM COINAGE

100 Centavos = 1 Quetzal

KM# 248.1 1/2 CENTAVO (Medio)

Brass, 17 mm. **Obv:** National arms **Rev:** Denomination

Date	Mintage	F12	VF20	XF40	MS60	MS63
1932 (L)	6,000,000	0.15	0.50	2.00	3.00	5.00
1932 (L)	—	PF63 200				

KM# 248.2 1/2 CENTAVO (Medio)

Brass, 11 mm. **Obv:** National arms **Rev:** Denomination, center dot

Date	Mintage	F12	VF20	XF40	MS60	MS63
1946	640,000	0.75	1.75	3.75	10.00	15.00

KM# 237 CENTAVO (Un)

Copper **Obv:** Incuse legend on scroll **Rev:** Denomination

Date	Mintage	F12	VF20	XF40	MS60	MS63
1925	357,000	3.00	5.00	15.00	32.00	50.00

KM# 237a CENTAVO (Un)

Bronze **Obv:** National arms **Rev:** Denomination

Date	Mintage	F12	VF20	XF40	MS60	MS63
1925	Inc. above	3.00	5.00	15.00	32.00	50.00

KM# 247 CENTAVO (Un)

Copper **Obv:** National arms **Rev:** Denomination

Date	Mintage	F12	VF20	XF40	MS60	MS63
1929 (L)	500,000	2.00	3.00	8.00	15.00	25.00
1929 (L)	—	PF63 250				

KM# 249 CENTAVO (Un)

Brass, 20.3 mm. **Obv:** National arms **Rev:** Denomination

Date	Mintage	F12	VF20	XF40	MS60	MS63
1932 (L)	3,000,000	0.40	1.00	3.00	10.00	15.00
1932 (L)	—	PF63 250				
1933 (L)	1,500,000	0.40	1.00	3.00	10.00	15.00
1933 (L)	—	PF63 250				
1934 (L)	1,000,000	0.40	1.00	3.00	10.00	15.00
1934 (L)	—	PF63 250				
1936 (L)	1,500,000	0.40	1.00	3.00	10.00	15.00
1936 (L)	—	PF63 250				
1938/7 (L)	1,000,000	0.40	1.00	3.00	10.00	15.00
1938 (L)	Inc. above	0.40	1.00	3.00	10.00	15.00
1938 (L)	—	PF63 250				
1939 (L)	1,500,000	0.40	1.00	3.00	10.00	15.00
1939 (L)	—	PF63 250				
1946	539,000	—	0.25	0.75	4.00	7.00
1947	1,121,000	—	0.15	0.35	3.00	6.00
1948	1,651,000	—	0.15	0.35	3.00	6.00
1949	1,022,000	—	0.15	0.35	3.00	6.00

KM# 251 CENTAVO (Un)

3.00 g., Brass, 20 mm. **Obv:** Bird with shield above date **Rev:** Branch right of denomination

Date	Mintage	F12	VF20	XF40	MS60	MS63
1943 (P)	450,000	1.00	3.00	10.00	20.00	35.00
1944 (S)	2,049,999	0.50	1.25	2.50	8.00	15.00

KM# 254 CENTAVO (Un)

Brass, 22 mm. **Subject:** Fray Bartolome de las Casas **Obv:** National arms **Rev:** Bust left

Date	Mintage	F12	VF20	XF40	MS60	MS63
1949	1,091,000	—	0.15	0.25	3.00	5.00
1950	3,663,000	—	0.15	0.25	2.00	3.00
1951	3,586,000	—	0.15	3.00	15.00	25.00
1952	1,445,000	—	0.15	3.00	12.00	20.00
1953	2,214,000	—	0.15	0.25	3.00	5.00
1954	1,455,000	—	0.15	0.25	2.00	5.00

KM# 259 CENTAVO (Un)

2.94 g., Nickel-Brass, 21 mm. **Subject:** Fray Bartolome de las Casas **Obv:** National arms **Rev:** Larger bust left

Date	Mintage	F12	VF20	XF40	MS60	MS63
1954 (KN)	10,000,000	—	—	0.25	1.50	3.00
1957 (KN)	1,600,000	—	0.15	0.25	1.00	2.00
1958 (KN)	2,000,000	—	0.15	0.25	1.00	2.00

KM# 260 CENTAVO (Un)

2.99 g., Brass, 21 mm. **Subject:** Fray Bartolome de las Casas **Obv:** National arms **Rev:** Bust left **Note:** Larger obverse lettering

Date	Mintage	VF20	XF40	MS60	MS63	MS65
1958	10,001,000	—	0.15	1.00	1.50	—
1961	1,826,000	—	0.15	0.75	1.00	2.00
1963	4,926,000	—	0.15	0.75	1.00	2.00
1964	4,280,000	—	0.15	0.75	1.00	2.00

KM# 265 CENTAVO (Un)

2.45 g., Brass, 19 mm. **Subject:** Fray Bartolome de las Casas **Obv:** National arms **Rev:** Bust left **Note:** Size reduced. Varieties in size and style of date exist.

Date	Mintage	VF20	XF40	MS60	MS63	MS65
1965	3,845,000	—	0.15	0.75	1.00	1.50

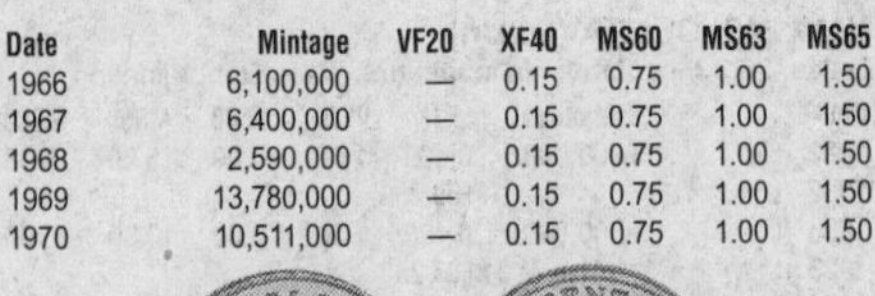

Date	Mintage	VF20	XF40	MS60	MS63	MS65
1966	6,100,000	—	0.15	0.75	1.00	1.50
1967	6,400,000	—	0.15	0.75	1.00	1.50
1968	2,590,000	—	0.15	0.75	1.00	1.50
1969	13,780,000	—	0.15	0.75	1.00	1.50
1970	10,511,000	—	0.15	0.75	1.00	1.50

KM# 273 CENTAVO (Un)

2.44 g., Brass **Subject:** Fray Bartolome de las Casas **Obv:** National arms **Rev:** Bust left **Note:** Smaller date and lettering.

Date	Mintage	VF20	XF40	MS60	MS63	MS65
1972	11,500,000	—	0.15	0.25	0.35	0.50
1973	12,000,000	—	0.15	0.25	0.35	0.50

KM# 275.1 CENTAVO (Un)

2.47 g., Brass, 19.1 mm. **Subject:** Fray Bartolome de las Casas **Obv:** National arms **Rev:** Bust left, larger head **Note:** Larger date and lettering; no dots left and right of date.

Date	Mintage	VF20	XF40	MS60	MS63	MS65
1974	10,000,000	—	0.15	0.25	0.35	0.50
1975	15,000,000	—	0.15	0.25	0.35	0.50
1976	15,230,000	—	0.15	0.25	0.30	0.45
1977	30,000,000	—	0.15	0.25	0.30	0.45
1978	30,000,000	—	0.15	0.25	0.30	0.45
1979	30,000,000	—	0.15	0.25	0.30	0.45

KM# 275.2 CENTAVO (Un)

2.55 g., Brass, 18 mm. **Obv:** National arms **Rev:** Bust left, smaller head **Note:** Smaller legend and date. Dots left and right of date

Date	Mintage	VF20	XF40	MS60	MS63	MS65
1979	Inc. above	—	0.15	0.25	0.30	0.45
1980	20,000,000	—	0.15	0.25	0.30	0.45
1984	20,000,000	—	0.15	0.25	0.30	0.45

KM# 275.4 CENTAVO (Un)

Brass **Obv:** National arms, legend on scroll in relief **Rev:** Bust left **Note:** Varieties exist.

Date	Mintage	VF20	XF40	MS60	MS63	MS65
1981	30,000,000	—	0.15	0.25	0.30	0.45
1982	30,000,000	—	0.15	0.25	0.30	0.45

KM# 275.3 CENTAVO (Un)

2.56 g., Brass, 18.97 mm. **Rev:** Fray Bartolome de las Casas, smaller head **Edge:** Plain **Note:** Smaller legend and date. Dots left and right of date.

Date	Mintage	VF20	XF40	MS60	MS63	MS65
1985	—	—	0.15	0.25	0.30	0.45
1986	—	—	0.15	0.25	0.30	0.45
1987	50,000,000	—	0.15	0.25	0.30	0.45
1988	51,400,000	—	0.15	0.25	0.30	0.45
1989	—	—	0.15	0.25	0.30	0.45
1990	—	—	0.15	0.25	0.30	0.45
1991	—	—	0.15	0.25	0.30	0.45
1992	—	—	0.15	0.25	0.30	0.45

KM# 275.5 CENTAVO (Un)

2.55 g., Brass **Subject:** Fray Bartolome de las Casas **Obv:** National arms **Rev:** Head left, modified portrait

Date	Mintage	VF20	XF40	MS60	MS63	MS65
1993	—	—	0.15	0.25	0.30	0.45
1994	—	—	0.15	0.25	0.30	0.45
1995	—	—	0.15	0.25	0.30	0.45

KM# 282 CENTAVO (Un)

0.80 g., Aluminum, 19 mm. **Subject:** Fray Bartolome de las Casas **Obv:** National arms **Rev:** Bust left **Edge:** Plain **Note:** 7-sided interior field

Date	Mintage	VF20	XF40	MS60	MS63	MS65
1999	—	—	0.15	0.25	0.30	0.45

KM# 250 2 CENTAVOS (Dos)

Brass, 25.5 mm. **Obv:** National arms **Rev:** Denomination

Date	Mintage	F12	VF20	XF40	MS60	MS63
1932 (L)	3,000,000	0.50	1.25	10.00	20.00	35.00
1932 (L)	—	PF63 300				

KM# 252 2 CENTAVOS (Dos)

6.00 g., Brass, 25.5 mm. **Obv:** Bird with shield above date **Rev:** Branch right of denomination

Date	Mintage	F12	VF20	XF40	MS60	MS63
1943 (P)	150,000	2.00	3.00	10.00	35.00	75.00
1944 (S)	1,100,000	0.60	2.00	5.00	20.00	35.00

KM# 238.1 5 CENTAVOS

1.67 g., 0.720 Silver 0.0386 oz. ASW, 15.5 mm. **Obv:** National arms **Rev:** Bird on pillar, engraver's initials 'JAC' below "Centavos"

Date	Mintage	F12	VF20	XF40	MS60	MS63
1925	573,000	2.00	5.00	15.00	30.00	50.00
1944	1,026,000	0.70	1.50	5.00	15.00	20.00
1945	4,026,000	0.70	1.50	5.00	10.00	15.00
1947	1,834,000	0.70	1.50	5.00	10.00	15.00
1948	1,103,000	0.70	1.50	5.00	10.00	15.00
1949	551,000	0.70	1.50	9.00	20.00	35.00

KM# 238.1a 5 CENTAVOS

2.50 g., 0.900 Gold 0.0723 oz. AGW **Obv:** National arms **Rev:** Bird on pillar

Date	Mintage	F12	VF20	XF40	MS60	MS63
1925	8	—	—	1,850	2,500	—

KM# 238.2 5 CENTAVOS

1.67 g., 0.720 Silver 0.0386 oz. ASW, 15.5 mm. **Obv:** National arms, short-tailed quetzal **Rev:** Bird on pillar, without engraver's initials

Date	Mintage	F12	VF20	XF40	MS60	MS63
1928 (L)	1,000,000	0.70	1.50	10.00	30.00	50.00
1928 (L)	—	PF63 400				
1929 (L)	1,000,000	0.70	1.50	5.00	10.00	15.00
1929 (L)	—	PF63 375				
1932 (L)	2,000,000	0.70	1.50	5.00	10.00	15.00
1932 (L)	—	PF63 375				
1933 (L)	600,000	0.70	1.50	5.00	15.00	25.00
1933 (L)	—	PF63 375				
1934 (L)	1,200,000	0.70	1.50	5.00	10.00	15.00
1934 (L)	—	PF63 375				
1937 (L)	400,000	0.70	1.50	5.00	10.00	15.00
1937 (L)	—	PF63 375				
1938 (L)	300,000	0.70	1.50	5.00	15.00	25.00
1938 (L)	—	PF63 375				
1943 (P)	900,000	0.70	1.50	5.00	10.00	15.00

KM# 255 5 CENTAVOS

1.67 g., 0.720 Silver 0.0386 oz. ASW, 15.5 mm. **Obv:** National arms **Rev:** Kapok tree **Note:** Varieties exist with and without dashes.

Date	Mintage	F12	VF20	XF40	MS60	MS63
1949	305,000	0.70	1.50	5.00	20.00	35.00

KM# 257.1 5 CENTAVOS

1.67 g., 0.720 Silver 0.0386 oz. ASW, 15.5 mm. **Obv:** National arms **Rev:** Kapok tree

Date	Mintage	F12	VF20	XF40	MS60	MS63
1950	453,000	0.70	1.00	3.00	10.00	15.00
1951	1,032,000	0.70	1.00	2.00	7.00	12.00
1952	913,000	0.70	1.00	2.00	7.00	12.00
1953	447,000	0.70	1.00	2.00	7.00	12.00
1954	520,000	0.70	1.00	3.00	7.00	12.00
1955	2,061,999	0.70	1.00	1.50	3.00	5.00
1956	1,301,000	0.70	1.00	1.50	3.00	5.00
1957	2,941,000	0.70	1.00	1.50	3.00	5.00

KM# 257.1a 5 CENTAVOS

2.73 g., 0.620 Gold 0.0544 oz. AGW **Obv:** National arms **Rev:** Kapok tree **Note:** Distributed among delegates.

Date	Mintage	F12	VF20	XF40	MS60	MS63
1953	25	—	—	—	550	—

KM# 257.2 5 CENTAVOS

1.67 g., 0.720 Silver 0.0386 oz. ASW, 15.5 mm. **Obv:** National arms **Rev:** Kapok tree **Note:** Small crude date and large crude dates.

Date	Mintage	F12	VF20	XF40	MS60	MS63
1958 Small date	3,025,000	0.70	1.00	1.50	2.50	4.00
1958 Large date	Inc. above	0.70	1.00	1.50	3.00	5.00
1959	232,000	0.70	1.00	1.50	2.50	4.00

KM# 257.3 5 CENTAVOS

1.67 g., 0.720 Silver 0.0386 oz. ASW, 15.5 mm. **Obv:** National arm, short-tailed quetzal **Obv. Legend:** Kapok tree

Date	Mintage	F12	VF20	XF40	MS60	MS63
1958 Small date	—	0.70	1.00	1.50	2.50	4.00
1958 Large date	—	0.70	1.00	1.50	2.50	4.00

KM# 261 5 CENTAVOS

1.67 g., 0.720 Silver 0.0386 oz. ASW, 15.5 mm. **Obv:** National arms **Rev:** Kapok tree, level ground

Date	Mintage	VF20	XF40	MS60	MS63	MS65
1960	4,770,000	0.70	1.00	1.50	1.75	2.50
1961	6,756,000	0.70	1.00	1.50	1.75	2.50
1964	1,529,000	0.70	1.00	1.50	1.75	2.50

KM# 266.1 5 CENTAVOS

1.60 g., Copper-Nickel, 16 mm. **Obv:** National arms **Rev:** Kapok tree **Edge:** Reeded **Note:** Coins dated 1965 are smaller with curved tails in the "9" & "6", while dates for 1967-1970 have straight tails in the "9" & "6".

Date	Mintage	VF20	XF40	MS60	MS63	MS65
1965 Small date	1,642,000	0.15	0.50	1.50	1.75	3.00
1967 Large date	2,800,000	—	0.15	0.35	0.45	0.60
1968 Large date	4,030,000	—	0.15	0.35	0.45	0.60
1969 Large date	7,210,000	—	0.15	0.35	0.45	0.60
1970 Large date	8,121,000	—	0.15	0.35	0.45	0.60

KM# 266.2 5 CENTAVOS

Copper-Nickel, 16 mm. **Obv:** National arms, dashes before and after legend **Rev:** Kapok tree **Note:** Coins dates 1966 are smaller with curved tails in the "9" & "6".

Date	Mintage	VF20	XF40	MS60	MS63	MS65
1966 Small date	3,600,000	—	0.15	0.35	0.45	0.60

KM# 270 5 CENTAVOS

1.60 g., Copper-Nickel, 16 mm. **Obv:** Legend on scroll incuse, small shield and quetzal **Rev:** Kapok tree **Edge:** Reeded

Date	Mintage	VF20	XF40	MS60	MS63	MS65
1971	8,270,000	—	0.15	0.35	0.45	0.60
1974	10,575,000	—	0.15	0.35	0.45	0.60
1975	10,000,000	—	0.15	0.35	0.45	0.60
1976	6,000,000	—	0.15	0.35	0.45	0.60
1977	20,000,000	—	0.15	0.35	0.45	0.60

KM# 276.1 5 CENTAVOS

1.60 g., Copper-Nickel, 16 mm. **Obv:** National arms, large shield and quetzal **Rev:** Kapok tree **Edge:** Reeded

Date	Mintage	VF20	XF40	MS60	MS63	MS65
1977	Inc. above	—	0.15	0.35	0.45	0.60
1978	15,000,000	—	0.15	0.30	0.40	0.50
1979	12,000,000	—	0.15	0.30	0.40	0.50

KM# 276.2 5 CENTAVOS

1.60 g., Copper-Nickel, 16 mm. **Obv:** Legend on scroll in relief **Rev:** Kapok tree **Edge:** Reeded

Date	Mintage	VF20	XF40	MS60	MS63	MS65
1980	8,000,000	—	0.15	0.30	0.40	0.50

KM# 276.3 5 CENTAVOS

1.60 g., Copper-Nickel, 16 mm. **Obv:** National arms **Rev:** Kapok tee modified **Edge:** Reeded

Date	Mintage	VF20	XF40	MS60	MS63	MS65
1981	8,000,000	—	0.15	0.30	0.40	0.50
1985	—	—	0.15	0.30	0.40	0.50

KM# 276.4 5 CENTAVOS

1.60 g., Copper-Nickel, 16 mm. **Obv:** National arms, legend on scroll incuse **Obv. Legend:** REPUBLICA DE GUATEMALA • 1986 • **Rev:** Kapok tree smaller, less ground below **Edge:** Reeded **Note:** Varieties exist.

Date	Mintage	VF20	XF40	MS60	MS63	MS65
1985	—	—	0.15	0.30	0.40	0.50
1986 Large date	—	—	0.15	0.30	0.40	0.50
1986 Small date	—	—	—	—	—	—
1987	25,000,000	—	0.15	0.30	0.40	0.50
1988	21,800,000	—	0.15	0.30	0.40	0.50
1989	—	—	0.15	0.30	0.40	0.50
1990	—	—	0.15	0.30	0.40	0.50
1991	—	—	0.15	0.30	0.40	0.50
1992	—	—	0.15	0.30	0.40	0.50
1993	—	—	0.15	0.30	0.40	0.50
1994	—	—	0.15	0.30	0.40	0.50
1996	—	—	0.15	0.30	0.40	0.50
1998	—	—	0.15	0.30	0.40	0.50

KM# 276.5 5 CENTAVOS

1.60 g., Copper-Nickel, 16 mm. **Obv:** National arms, smaller lettering **Rev:** Kapok tree **Edge:** Reeded

Date	Mintage	VF20	XF40	MS60	MS63	MS65
1995	—	—	0.15	0.30	0.40	0.50

KM# 276.6 5 CENTAVOS

1.60 g., Copper-Nickel, 16 mm. **Obv:** National arms, smaller sized emblem, no dots by date **Obv. Legend:** REPUBLICA DE GUATEMALA 1997 **Rev:** Kapok tree center, value at right, ground below **Edge:** Reeded **Note:** Varieties exist.

Date	Mintage	VF20	XF40	MS60	MS63	MS65
1997	—	—	0.15	0.30	0.40	0.50
1998	—	—	0.15	0.30	0.40	0.50
2000	—	—	0.15	0.30	0.40	0.50

KM# 239.1 10 CENTAVOS

3.33 g., 0.720 Silver 0.0772 oz. ASW **Obv:** National arms **Rev:** Bird on engraved pillar, engraver's initials below "CENTAVOS" **Note:** Varieties exist.

Date	Mintage	F12	VF20	XF40	MS60	MS63
1925	573,000	1.40	5.00	15.00	30.00	45.00
1944	155,000	1.40	3.00	9.00	15.00	25.00
1945	1,499,000	1.40	2.00	3.00	5.00	10.00
1947	471,000	1.40	2.00	3.00	10.00	15.00
1948	324,000	1.40	2.00	3.00	7.00	10.00
1949	145,000	1.40	2.00	5.00	10.00	15.00

KM# 239.1a 10 CENTAVOS

5.00 g., 0.900 Gold 0.1447 oz. AGW **Obv:** National arms **Rev:** Long-tailed quetzal on pillar

Date	Mintage	F12	VF20	XF40	MS60	MS63
1925	8	—	—	—	3,000	—

KM# 239.2 10 CENTAVOS

3.33 g., 0.720 Silver 0.0772 oz. ASW, 20 mm. **Obv:** National arms, short-tailed quetzal **Rev:** Bird on engraved pillar, without engraver's initials **Edge:** Reeded

Date	Mintage	F12	VF20	XF40	MS60	MS63
1928 (L)	500,000	1.40	2.00	6.00	25.00	35.00
1928 (L)	—	PF63 375				
1929 (L)	500,000	1.40	2.00	6.00	25.00	35.00
1929 (L)	—	PF63 375				
1932 (L)	500,000	1.40	2.00	6.00	15.00	25.00
1932 (L)	—	PF63 375				
1933 (L)	650,000	1.40	2.00	6.00	15.00	25.00
1933 (L)	—	PF63 375				
1934 (L)	300,000	1.40	2.00	6.00	15.00	25.00
1934 (L)	—	PF63 375				
1936 (L)	200,000	1.40	2.00	6.00	15.00	25.00
1936 (L)	—	PF63 375				
1938 (L)	150,000	1.40	2.00	4.00	10.00	15.00
1938 (L)	—	PF63 375				
1943 (P)	600,000	1.40	2.00	4.00	8.00	10.00

KM# 239.3 10 CENTAVOS

3.33 g., 0.720 Silver 0.0772 oz. ASW **Obv:** National arms **Rev:** Quetzal on pillar, with engraver's initials **Note:** Mintage included above, in KM#239.1. Varieties exist.

Date	Mintage	F12	VF20	XF40	MS60	MS63
1947	—	1.40	2.00	4.00	8.00	10.00

KM# 256.1 10 CENTAVOS

3.33 g., 0.720 Silver 0.0772 oz. ASW **Obv:** National arms **Rev:** Small monolith

Date	Mintage	VF20	XF40	MS60	MS63	MS65
1949	281,000	2.00	4.00	9.00	12.00	15.00
1950	550,000	2.00	4.00	7.00	9.00	12.00
1951	263,000	2.00	4.00	9.00	12.00	15.00
1952	307,000	2.00	4.00	7.00	9.00	12.00
1953	388,000	2.00	4.00	7.00	9.00	12.00
1955	896,000	2.00	4.00	7.00	9.00	12.00
1956	501,000	2.00	4.00	9.00	12.00	15.00
1958	1,528,000	2.00	4.00	7.00	9.00	12.00

KM# 256.2 10 CENTAVOS

3.33 g., 0.720 Silver 0.0772 oz. ASW **Obv:** National arms **Rev:** Larger monolith

Date	Mintage	VF20	XF40	MS60	MS63	MS65
1957	1,123,000	2.00	3.00	5.00	6.00	8.00
1958	Inc. above	2.00	3.00	5.00	6.00	8.00
1958	Inc. above	5.00	7.00	20.00	30.00	50.00

Note: Medallic die alignment

KM# 256.3 10 CENTAVOS

3.33 g., 0.720 Silver 0.0772 oz. ASW **Obv:** National arms **Rev:** Small monolith

Date	Mintage	VF20	XF40	MS60	MS63	MS65
1958	Inc. above	2.00	3.00	5.00	6.00	8.00
1959	Inc. above	5.00	7.00	20.00	30.00	50.00
Note: Medallic die alignment						
1959	461,000	2.00	3.00	5.00	6.00	8.00

KM# 262 10 CENTAVOS

3.33 g., 0.720 Silver 0.0772 oz. ASW **Obv:** National arms **Rev:** Monolith

Date	Mintage	VF20	XF40	MS60	MS63	MS65
1960	1,743,000	2.00	3.00	5.00	6.00	8.00
1961	2,647,000	2.00	3.00	5.00	6.00	8.00
1964	965,000	2.00	3.00	5.00	6.00	8.00

KM# 267 10 CENTAVOS

2.85 g., Copper-Nickel, 21 mm. **Obv:** National arms **Rev:** Monolith **Note:** Varieties of curved and straight "9" in date exist.

Date	Mintage	VF20	XF40	MS60	MS63	MS65
1965	2,227,000	0.15	0.25	0.50	0.75	1.00
1966	1,550,000	0.15	0.25	0.50	0.75	1.00
1967	3,120,000	0.15	0.25	0.50	0.75	1.00
1968	3,220,000	0.15	0.25	0.50	0.75	1.00
1969	3,530,000	0.15	0.25	0.50	0.75	1.00
1970	4,153,000	0.15	0.25	0.50	0.75	1.00

KM# 271.1 10 CENTAVOS

Copper-Nickel, 21 mm. **Obv:** National arms, small wreath **Rev:** Monolith

Date	Mintage	VF20	XF40	MS60	MS63	MS65
1971	4,580,000	0.15	0.25	0.50	0.75	1.00

KM# 271.2 10 CENTAVOS

Copper-Nickel, 21 mm. **Obv:** National arms, large wreath **Rev:** Monolith

Date	Mintage	VF20	XF40	MS60	MS63	MS65
1971	Inc. above	0.15	0.25	0.50	0.75	1.00
1973	—	0.15	0.25	0.50	0.75	1.00

KM# 274 10 CENTAVOS

3.17 g., Copper-Nickel, 21 mm. **Obv:** National arms **Rev:** Monolith

Date	Mintage	VF20	XF40	MS60	MS63	MS65
1974	3,500,000	0.15	0.25	0.50	0.75	1.00
1975 Dots flank date	6,000,000	0.15	0.25	0.50	0.75	1.00

KM# 277.1 10 CENTAVOS

Copper-Nickel, 21 mm. **Obv:** National arms **Rev:** Monolith **Note:** Wide rim toothed border.

Date	Mintage	VF20	XF40	MS60	MS63	MS65
1976	2,000,000	0.15	0.25	0.50	0.75	1.00
1977	5,000,000	0.15	0.25	0.50	0.75	1.00

KM# 277.2 10 CENTAVOS

3.12 g., Copper-Nickel, 21 mm. **Obv:** National arms **Rev:** Monolith **Note:** Round beads instead of toothed border.

Date	Mintage	VF20	XF40	MS60	MS63	MS65
1978	8,500,000	0.15	0.25	0.50	0.75	1.00
1979	11,000,000	0.15	0.25	0.50	0.75	1.00

KM# 277.3 10 CENTAVOS

Copper-Nickel, 21 mm. **Obv:** Legend on scroll in relief, quetzal in silhouette **Rev:** Monolith, front view

Date	Mintage	VF20	XF40	MS60	MS63	MS65
1980	5,000,000	0.15	0.25	0.50	0.75	1.00
1981	4,000,000	0.15	0.25	0.50	0.75	1.00

KM# 277.4 10 CENTAVOS

3.14 g., Copper-Nickel, 21 mm. **Obv:** Quetzal is solid **Rev:** Monolith, larger

Date	Mintage	VF20	XF40	MS60	MS63	MS65
1983	20,000,000	0.15	0.25	0.50	0.75	1.00
1986	—	0.15	0.25	0.50	0.75	1.00

KM# 277.5 10 CENTAVOS

3.20 g., Copper-Nickel, 21 mm. **Obv:** National arms **Rev:** Monolith, larger **Note:** Varieties exist with fine and coarse characters.

Date	Mintage	VF20	XF40	MS60	MS63	MS65
1986	—	0.15	0.25	0.50	0.75	1.00
1987	17,000,000	0.15	0.25	0.50	0.75	1.00
1988	13,250,000	0.15	0.25	0.50	0.75	1.00
1989	—	0.15	0.25	0.50	0.75	1.00
1990	—	0.15	0.25	0.50	0.75	1.00
1991	—	0.15	0.25	0.50	0.75	1.00
1992	—	0.15	0.25	0.50	0.75	1.00
1993	—	0.15	0.25	0.50	0.75	1.00
1994	—	0.15	0.25	0.50	0.75	1.00

KM# 277.6 10 CENTAVOS

3.20 g., Copper-Nickel, 21 mm. **Obv:** National arms, small letters in legend **Obv. Legend:** REPUBLICA DE GUATEMALA **Rev:** Monolith **Rev. Legend:** MONOLITO DE QUIRIGUA **Edge:** Reeded **Note:** Varieties exist.

Date	Mintage	VF20	XF40	MS60	MS63	MS65
1995	—	0.15	0.25	0.50	0.75	1.00
1996	—	0.15	0.25	0.50	0.75	1.00
1997	—	0.15	0.25	0.50	0.75	1.00
1998	—	0.15	0.25	0.50	0.75	1.00
2000	—	0.15	0.25	0.50	0.75	1.00

KM# 240.1 1/4 QUETZAL

8.33 g., 0.720 Silver 0.1929 oz. ASW, 27 mm. **Obv:** National arms **Rev:** Quetzal on pillar **Edge:** Lettered

Date	Mintage	F12	VF20	XF40	MS60	MS63
1925 (P)	1,160,000	7.00	12.00	30.00	60.00	85.00

KM# 240.2 1/4 QUETZAL

8.33 g., 0.720 Silver 0.1929 oz. ASW, 27 mm. **Obv:** National arms, without NOBLES below scroll **Rev:** Quetzal atop engraved pillar

Date	Mintage	F12	VF20	XF40	MS60	MS63
1925 (P)	Inc. above	20.00	35.00	150	225	450

KM# 240a 1/4 QUETZAL

0.900 Gold **Obv:** National arms **Rev:** Quetzal on pillar

Date	Mintage	F12	VF20	XF40	MS60	MS63
1925 (P) Rare	8	—	—	—	—	—

KM# 243.1 1/4 QUETZAL

8.33 g., 0.720 Silver 0.1929 oz. ASW, 27 mm. **Obv:** National arms **Rev:** Quetzal on pillar, larger design **Edge Lettering:** REPUBLICA DE GUATEMALA AMERICA CENTRAL

Date	Mintage	F12	VF20	XF40	MS60	MS63
1926 (L)	2,000,000	3.50	8.00	17.00	45.00	75.00
1926 (L)	—	PF63 450				
1928 (L)	400,000	3.50	7.00	14.00	45.00	80.00
1928 (L)	—	PF63 450				
1929 (L)	400,000	3.50	7.00	14.00	35.00	65.00
1929 (L)	—	PF63 450				

KM# 243.2 1/4 QUETZAL

8.33 g., 0.720 Silver 0.1929 oz. ASW, 27 mm. **Obv:** National arms **Rev:** Quetzal atop engraved pillar **Edge:** Reeded

Date	Mintage	F12	VF20	XF40	MS60	MS63
1946	203,000	3.50	7.00	16.00	25.00	35.00
1947	134,000	3.50	9.00	14.00	22.50	35.00
1948	129,000	3.50	9.00	14.00	22.50	35.00
1949/8	25,000	7.00	12.00	20.00	35.00	46.00
1949	Inc. above	7.00	15.00	35.00	50.00	100

KM# 253 25 CENTAVOS

8.33 g., 0.720 Silver 0.1929 oz. ASW, 27 mm. **Obv:** Quetzal and map of the state **Rev:** Government buildings

Date	Mintage	VF20	XF40	MS60	MS63	MS65
1943 (P)	900,000	3.50	10.00	22.00	35.00	65.00

Note: 150,000 of total mintage struck in 1943, remainder struck in 1944

KM# 258 25 CENTAVOS

8.33 g., 0.720 Silver 0.1929 oz. ASW, 27 mm. **Obv:** National arms **Rev:** Head left **Note:** Denticulated rims.

Date	Mintage	VF20	XF40	MS60	MS63	MS65
1950	81,000	7.00	10.00	20.00	30.00	50.00
1951	11,000	15.00	25.00	35.00	50.00	100
1952	112,000	3.50	7.00	12.00	17.00	30.00
1954	246,000	3.50	7.00	10.00	14.00	20.00
1955	409,000	3.50	7.00	10.00	14.00	20.00
1956	342,000	3.50	7.00	10.00	14.00	20.00
1957	257,000	3.50	7.00	9.00	12.00	16.00
1958	394,000	3.50	7.00	9.00	12.00	16.00
1959/8	277,000	3.50	7.00	9.00	12.00	16.00
1959	Inc. above	3.50	7.00	10.00	14.00	22.50

KM# 263 25 CENTAVOS

8.33 g., 0.720 Silver 0.1929 oz. ASW, 27 mm. **Obv:** National arms **Rev:** Head left

Date	Mintage	VF20	XF40	MS60	MS63	MS65
1960	560,000	3.50	5.00	7.00	8.00	12.00
1960	Inc. above	25.00	35.00	85.00	100	150
Note: Planchet size and weight vary in 1960 type as well as density of reeding; Medallic die alignment						
1961	750,000	3.50	5.00	7.00	8.00	12.00
1962	—	3.50	5.00	7.00	8.00	12.00
1963	1,100,000	3.50	5.00	7.00	8.00	12.00
1964	299,000	3.50	5.00	7.00	8.00	12.00

KM# 268 25 CENTAVOS

8.00 g., Copper-Nickel, 27 mm. **Obv:** National arms **Rev:** Head left **Edge Lettering:** REPUBLICA DE GUATEMALA C. A.

Date	Mintage	VF20	XF40	MS60	MS63	MS65
1965	1,178,000	0.25	0.40	0.90	1.50	2.00
1966	910,000	0.25	0.40	0.90	1.50	2.00

KM# 269 25 CENTAVOS

8.00 g., Copper-Nickel, 27 mm. **Obv:** National arms **Rev:** Head left, modified design **Edge Lettering:** REPUBLICA DE GUATEMALA C. A.

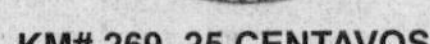

Date	Mintage	VF20	XF40	MS60	MS63	MS65
1967 Small date	1,140,000	0.25	0.40	0.90	1.50	2.00
1968 Medium date	1,540,000	0.25	0.40	0.90	1.50	2.00
1969 Large date	2,069,000	0.25	0.40	0.90	1.50	2.00
1970 Large date	2,501,000	0.25	0.40	0.90	1.50	2.00

KM# 272 25 CENTAVOS

8.00 g., Copper-Nickel, 27 mm. **Obv:** Smaller arms, legend on scroll incuse **Rev:** Head left

Date	Mintage	VF20	XF40	MS60	MS63	MS65
1971	2,850,000	0.25	0.35	0.70	1.00	1.50
1975	1,592,000	0.25	0.35	0.70	1.00	1.50
1976	2,000,000	0.25	0.35	0.70	1.00	1.50

KM# 278.1 25 CENTAVOS
8.00 g., Copper-Nickel, 27 mm. **Obv:** National arms **Rev:** Large head left

Date	Mintage	VF20	XF40	MS60	MS63	MS65
1977	2,000,000	0.25	0.35	0.65	1.00	1.50
1978	4,400,000	0.25	0.35	0.65	1.00	1.50
1979	5,400,000	0.25	0.35	0.65	1.00	1.50

KM# 278.2 25 CENTAVOS
8.00 g., Copper-Nickel, 27 mm. **Obv:** National arms, legend on scroll in relief **Rev:** Small head left **Note:** Wide rim

Date	Mintage	VF20	XF40	MS60	MS63	MS65
1981	1,600,000	0.25	0.35	0.70	1.00	1.50

KM# 278.4 25 CENTAVOS
8.00 g., Copper-Nickel, 27 mm. **Obv:** National arms, quetzal is solid **Rev:** Head left **Note:** Narrow rim.

Date	Mintage	VF20	XF40	MS60	MS63	MS65
1982	2,000,000	0.25	0.35	0.70	1.00	1.50

KM# 278.3 25 CENTAVOS
8.00 g., Copper-Nickel, 27 mm. **Obv:** National arms, legend on scroll incuse **Rev:** Small head left

Date	Mintage	VF20	XF40	MS60	MS63	MS65
1984	2,000,000	0.25	0.35	0.70	1.00	1.50

KM# 278.5 25 CENTAVOS
8.00 g., Copper-Nickel, 27 mm. **Obv:** National arms **Rev:** Large head left **Edge Lettering:** REPUBLICA DE GUATEMALA C. A. **Note:** Varieties exist in number of wing feathers and details on head.

Date	Mintage	VF20	XF40	MS60	MS63	MS65
1985	—	0.25	0.35	0.60	0.85	1.00
1986	—	0.25	0.35	0.60	0.85	1.00
1987	13,316,000	0.25	0.35	0.60	0.85	1.00
1988	6,600,000	0.25	0.35	0.60	0.85	1.00
1989	—	0.25	0.35	0.60	0.85	1.00
1990	—	0.25	0.35	0.60	0.85	1.00
1991	—	0.25	0.35	0.60	0.85	1.00
1992	—	0.25	0.35	0.60	0.85	1.00
1993	—	0.25	0.35	0.60	0.85	1.00
1994	—	0.25	0.35	0.60	0.85	1.00
1995	—	0.25	0.35	0.60	0.85	1.00

KM# 278.6 25 CENTAVOS
8.00 g., Copper-Nickel, 27 mm. **Obv:** Smaller design with wider rims **Rev:** Head left, smaller design with wider rims **Edge Lettering:** REPUBLICA DE GUATEMALA CA **Note:** Varieties exist.

Date	Mintage	VF20	XF40	MS60	MS63	MS65
1996	—	0.25	0.35	0.60	0.85	1.00
1997	—	0.25	0.35	0.60	0.85	1.00
1998	—	0.25	0.35	0.60	0.85	1.00
2000	—	0.25	0.35	0.60	0.85	1.00

KM# 264 50 CENTAVOS
12.00 g., 0.720 Silver 0.2778 oz. ASW, 30.95 mm. **Obv:** National arms **Rev:** Whitenun orchid (lycaste skinneri var. alba) **Rev. Legend:** MONJA BLANCA FLOR NACIONAL **Edge:** Reeded

Date	Mintage	VF20	XF40	MS60	MS63	MS65
1962	1,983,000	—	5.25	10.00	12.00	14.00
1963/2	350,000	—	5.25	12.00	15.00	20.00
1963	Inc. above	—	5.25	10.00	12.00	14.00

KM# 283 50 CENTAVOS
5.50 g., Nickel-Brass, 26.5 mm. **Obv:** National arms **Rev:** Whitenun orchid (lycaste skinneri var. alba orchidaceae) **Edge:** Reeded

Date	Mintage	VF20	XF40	MS60	MS63	MS65
1998	—	—	0.50	1.00	1.25	1.50

KM# 241.1 1/2 QUETZAL
16.67 g., 0.720 Silver 0.3858 oz. ASW, 34 mm. **Obv:** National arms **Rev:** Quetzal on engraved pillar

Date	Mintage	F12	VF20	XF40	MS60	MS63
1925 (P)	400,000	20.00	35.00	75.00	225	350

KM# 241.2 1/2 QUETZAL
16.67 g., 0.720 Silver 0.3858 oz. ASW, 34 mm. **Obv:** Without NOBLES below scroll **Rev:** Quetzal on pillar

Date	Mintage	F12	VF20	XF40	MS60	MS63
1925 (P)	Inc. above	50.00	100	225	450	600

KM# 242 QUETZAL
33.33 g., 0.720 Silver 0.7716 oz. ASW **Obv:** National arms **Rev:** Quetzal on engraved pillar

Date	Mintage	F12	VF20	XF40	MS60	MS63
1925 (P)	Est. 10000	475	675	1,150	1,750	3,000

Note: 7,000 pieces were withdrawn and remelted in 1927 and 1928. Of those remaining, an additonal unknown quantity was melted in 1932, leaving somewhat less than 3000 survivors of this type.

KM# 279 QUETZAL
27.00 g., 0.925 Silver 0.803 oz. ASW **Subject:** Carlos Merida **Obv:** National arms **Rev:** Heads facing and right

Date	Mintage	VF20	XF40	MS60	MS63	MS65
1992 NG	—	PF63 35.00	PF65 45.00	PF67 60.00		

KM# 280 QUETZAL
27.00 g., 0.925 Silver 0.803 oz. ASW **Subject:** Environmental Protection **Rev:** Horned Guan

Date	Mintage	VF20	XF40	MS60	MS63	MS65
1994	20,000	PF63 30.00	PF65 40.00	PF67 55.00		

KM# 281 QUETZAL
27.00 g., 0.925 Silver 0.803 oz. ASW **Subject:** 50th Anniversary - National Bank of Guatemala **Obv:** Coin designs around national emblem **Rev:** Pre-Columbian artisans

Date	Mintage	VF20	XF40	MS60	MS63	MS65
1996	—	PF63 40.00	PF65 55.00	PF67 70.00		

KM# 284 QUETZAL
11.00 g., Nickel-Brass, 29 mm. **Obv:** National arms **Obv. Legend:** REPUBLIC DE GUATEMALA **Rev:** PAZ above stylized dove **Rev. Legend:** Paz Firme y Duradera 29 de Diciembre de 1996 **Edge:** Reeded

Date	Mintage	VF20	XF40	MS60	MS63	MS65
1999 Thin letters	—	—	0.25	1.00	1.50	2.00
2000 Small letters	—	—	0.25	1.00	1.50	2.00

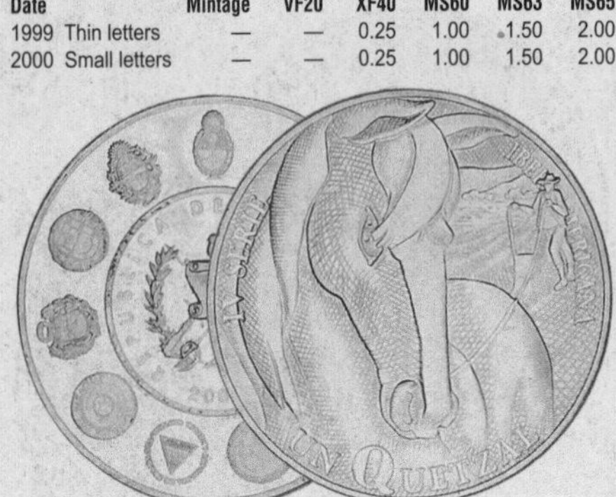

KM# 286 QUETZAL
27.00 g., 0.925 Silver 0.803 oz. ASW, 40 mm. **Subject:** Ibero-America Series **Obv:** National arms in circle of arms **Rev:** Horse pulling a walk-behind plow **Edge:** Reeded

Date	Mintage	VF20	XF40	MS60	MS63	MS65
2000	—	PF63 55.00	PF65 75.00	PF67 90.00		

KM# 244 5 QUETZALES
8.36 g., 0.900 Gold 0.2419 oz. AGW **Obv:** National arms **Rev:** Quetzal atop engraved pillar

Date	Mintage	VF20	XF40	MS60	MS63	MS65
1926 (P)	48,000	—	310	385	625	775

KM# 245 10 QUETZALES
16.72 g., 0.900 Gold 0.4838 oz. AGW **Obv:** National arms **Rev:** Quetzal atop engraved pillar

Date	Mintage	VF20	XF40	MS60	MS63	MS65
1926 (P)	18,000	—	620	770	1,150	1,400

KM# 246 20 QUETZALES
33.44 g., 0.900 Gold 0.9675 oz. AGW **Obv:** National arms **Rev:** Quetzal atop engraved pillar

Date	Mintage	VF20	XF40	MS60	MS63	MS65
1926 (P)	49,000	—	1,250	1,550	2,300	2,700

TRIAL STRIKES

KM#	Date	Mintage	Identification	Mkt Val
TS1	1945	—	10 Centavos. Copper-Nickel.	150
TS2	1955	—	25 Centavos. Silver. as KM#258, struck galvano.	95.00

PATTERNS

Including off metal strikes

KM#	Date	Mintage	Identification	Mkt Val
Pn36	ND1920	—	2 Pesos. Porcelain. QUATEMALA / *PESOS* / large 2 in center. Arms of Quatemala within triangle; coffee tree leaf to each side; below: Meissen mint mark (crossed swords) separates two stars. Made at state porcelain works, Meissen, Germany.	2,000
Pn37	1921	—	Peso. Copper-Nickel. Plain. MONEDA NACIONAL NIQUEL.	—
Pn38	1922	—	5 Pesos. Silver. 3/4 facing bust of Barrios.	—
Pn39	1922	—	5 Pesos. Aluminum-Brass. 3/4 facing bust of Barrios.	—
Pn40	1923	—	5 Pesos. Gold. KM234.	—
Pn41	1949	20	Centavo. Brass. Large bust.	475
Pn42	1949	20	5 Centavos. 0.720. Silver.	500
Pn43	1949	20	10 Centavos. 0.720. Silver.	550
Pn44	1949	20	25 Centavos. 0.720. Silver.	600
Pn45	1960	—	25 Centavos. Aluminum. Plain. KM#263.	—
Pn46	1995	100	Quetzal. Tri-Metallic. National arms. Humming bird flying above lake. Reeded.	100
Pn47	1995	100	50 Quetzales. Tri-Metallic. National arms. Parrot on branch, buildings in back. Reeded.	100

GUERNSEY

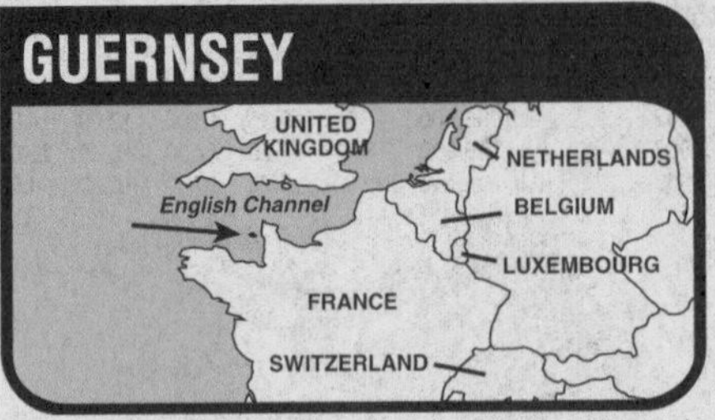

The Bailiwick of Guernsey, a British crown dependency located in the English Channel 30 miles (48 km.) west of Normandy, France, has an area of 30 sq. mi. (194 sq. km.) (including the isles of Alderney, Jethou, Herm, Brechou, and Sark), and a population of 54,000. Capital: St. Peter Port. Agriculture and cattle breeding are the main occupations.

Militant monks from the duchy of Normandy established the first permanent settlements on Guernsey prior to the Norman invasion of England, but the prevalence of prehistoric monuments suggests an earlier occupancy. The island, the only part of the duchy of Normandy belonging to the British crown, has been a possession of Britain since the Norman Conquest of 1066. During the Anglo-French wars, the harbors of Guernsey were employed in the building and out-fitting of ships for the English privateers preying on French shipping. Guernsey is administered by its own laws and customs. Unless the island is mentioned specifically, acts passed by the British Parliament are not applicable to Guernsey. During World War II, German troops occupied the island from June 30, 1940 till May 9,1945.

RULER
British

MINT MARK
H - Heaton, Birmingham

MONETARY SYSTEM
8 Doubles = 1 Penny
12 Pence = 1 Shilling
5 Shillings = 1 Crown
20 Shillings = 1 Pound

1 Stem

3 Stems

BRITISH DEPENDENCY

STANDARD COINAGE

KM# 10 DOUBLE
Bronze **Obv:** National arms **Rev:** Value, date

Date	Mintage	F12	VF20	XF40	MS60	MS63
1902 H	84,000	0.25	0.60	2.50	6.00	12.00
1902 H	—	PF63 250				
1903 H	112,000	0.25	0.50	2.25	5.00	10.00
1911 H	45,000	0.50	1.50	4.00	12.00	20.00

KM# 11 DOUBLE
Bronze **Obv:** Arms **Rev:** Denomination above date

Date	Mintage	F12	VF20	XF40	MS60	MS63
1911 H	90,000	0.30	1.20	3.00	10.00	20.00

Date	Mintage	F12	VF20	XF40	MS60	MS63
1914 H	45,000	1.50	3.00	6.00	12.00	25.00
1929 H	79,000	0.30	0.85	2.50	5.50	15.00
1933 H	96,000	0.30	0.85	2.50	5.50	15.00
1938 H	96,000	0.30	0.85	2.50	5.50	15.00

KM# 9 2 DOUBLES
3.62 g., Bronze, 22 mm. **Obv:** National arms **Rev:** Value, date

Date	Mintage	F12	VF20	XF40	MS60	MS63
1902 H	18,000	2.50	5.00	10.00	20.00	30.00
1902 H	—	PF63 400				
1903 H	18,000	3.50	7.00	15.00	25.00	40.00
1906 H	18,000	3.50	7.00	15.00	25.00	40.00
1908 H	18,000	3.50	7.00	15.00	25.00	40.00
1911 H	29,000	2.50	5.00	10.00	20.00	35.00

KM# 12 2 DOUBLES
Bronze Plated Copper **Obv:** Arms **Rev:** Denomination above date

Date	Mintage	F12	VF20	XF40	MS60	MS63
1914 H	29,000	4.50	9.00	18.00	28.00	45.00
1914 H	—	PF63 125				
1917 H	15,000	10.00	20.00	35.00	75.00	145
1918 H	57,000	1.25	2.50	9.00	15.00	25.00
1920 H	57,000	1.25	2.50	9.00	15.00	25.00
1929 H	79,000	0.35	1.25	6.00	10.00	25.00

KM# 5 4 DOUBLES
4.84 g., Bronze, 26.10 mm. **Obv:** National arms **Rev:** Value, date **Note:** Varieties exist.

Date	Mintage	F12	VF20	XF40	MS60	MS63
1902 H	105,000	1.50	3.00	5.00	15.00	25.00
1902 H	—	PF63 250				
1903 H	52,000	1.50	3.00	9.00	20.00	35.00
1906 H	52,000	1.50	3.00	9.00	20.00	35.00
1908 H	26,000	3.00	7.50	15.00	25.00	40.00
1910 H	52,000	1.50	3.00	9.00	20.00	35.00
1910 H	—	PF63 250				
1911 H	52,000	2.25	4.50	13.50	25.00	40.00

KM# 13 4 DOUBLES
4.76 g., Bronze **Obv:** Arms **Rev:** Denomination above date

Date	Mintage	F12	VF20	XF40	MS60	MS63
1914 H	209,000	0.75	1.50	4.50	15.00	30.00
1918 H	157,000	0.75	1.50	6.00	20.00	35.00
1920 H	157,000	0.45	1.25	4.50	15.00	30.00
1945 H	96,000	0.45	1.25	4.50	10.00	25.00
1949 H	19,000	1.50	3.00	12.00	22.00	35.00

KM# 15 4 DOUBLES
4.82 g., Bronze **Ruler:** Elizabeth II **Obv:** Arms **Rev:** Guernsey lily

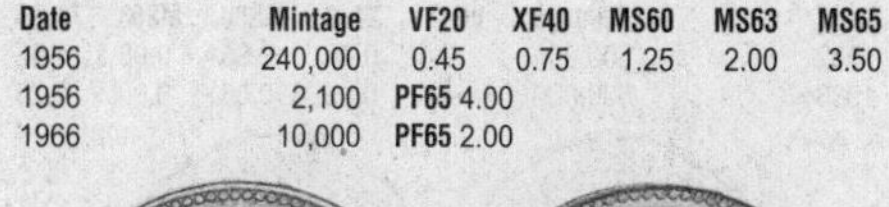

Date	Mintage	VF20	XF40	MS60	MS63	MS65
1956	240,000	0.45	0.75	1.25	2.00	3.50
1956	2,100	PF65 4.00				
1966	10,000	PF65 2.00				

KM# 7 8 DOUBLES

9.60 g., Bronze, 31.6 mm. **Obv:** National arms within 3/4 wreath **Rev:** Value, date within wreath

Date	Mintage	F12	VF20	XF40	MS60	MS63
1902 H	235,000	2.50	5.00	12.00	30.00	50.00
1902 H	—	PF63 250				
1903 H	118,000	1.00	4.00	11.00	28.00	50.00
1910 H	91,000	1.25	4.00	12.50	35.00	60.00
1910 H	—	PF63 250				
1911 H	78,000	6.00	17.00	30.00	50.00	85.00

KM# 14 8 DOUBLES

9.70 g., Bronze, 31.7 mm. **Obv:** Arms within wreath **Rev:** Denomination and date within wreath

Date	Mintage	F12	VF20	XF40	MS60	MS63
1914 H	157,000	1.00	3.00	8.00	15.00	30.00
1914 H	—	PF63 150				
1918 H	157,000	1.50	4.00	11.00	20.00	35.00
1920 H	157,000	1.00	2.00	6.00	12.00	25.00
1920 H	—	PF63 150				
1934 H	124,000	1.00	2.00	6.00	12.00	25.00
1934 H	500	PF63 175				
1938 H	120,000	0.50	1.50	4.00	9.00	20.00
1938 H	—	PF63 250				
1945 H	192,000	0.40	0.85	2.50	5.50	12.50
1947 H	240,000	0.30	0.60	2.25	5.00	12.00
1949 H	230,000	0.30	0.60	2.25	5.00	12.00

KM# 16 8 DOUBLES

9.70 g., Bronze, 31 mm. **Ruler:** Elizabeth II **Obv:** Arms **Rev:** Three-flowered lily

Date	Mintage	VF20	XF40	MS60	MS63	MS65
1956	500,000	—	0.50	0.75	1.25	2.50
1956	2,100	PF65 4.00				
1959	500,000	—	0.50	0.75	1.25	2.50
1959 Proof	—	—	—	—	—	—
1966	10,000	PF65 3.50				

KM# 17 3 PENCE

Copper-Nickel, 21 mm. **Ruler:** Elizabeth II **Obv:** Arms **Rev:** Guernsey cow (bos primigenius taurus) right **Shape:** Scalloped **Note:** Thin flan.

Date	Mintage	VF20	XF40	MS60	MS63	MS65
1956	500,000	—	0.50	0.75	1.50	2.00
1956	2,100	PF65 4.00				

KM# 18 3 PENCE

Copper-Nickel, 21 mm. **Ruler:** Elizabeth II **Obv:** Arms **Rev:** Guernsey cow (bos primigenius taurus) right **Shape:** Scalloped **Note:** Thick flan.

Date	Mintage	VF20	XF40	MS60	MS63	MS65
1959	500,000	—	0.50	0.75	1.50	2.50
1959	—	PF65 150				
1966	10,000	PF65 2.00				

KM# 19 10 SHILLING

Copper-Nickel **Ruler:** Elizabeth II **Series:** 900th Anniversary - Norman Conquest **Subject:** William I **Obv:** Young bust right **Rev:** Crowned bust left **Shape:** 4-sided

Date	Mintage	VF20	XF40	MS60	MS63	MS65
1966	300,000	1.00	1.25	1.75	3.00	6.50
1966	10,000	PF65 3.50				

DECIMAL COINAGE

KM# 20 1/2 NEW PENNY

1.78 g., Bronze, 17.14 mm. **Ruler:** Elizabeth II **Obv:** Arms **Rev:** Denomination and date

Date	Mintage	VF20	XF40	MS60	MS63	MS65
1971	2,066,000	—	0.15	0.30	0.50	0.75
1971	10,000	PF65 1.00				

KM# 33 1/2 PENNY

1.78 g., Bronze, 17.14 mm. **Ruler:** Elizabeth II **Obv:** Arms **Rev:** Denomination and date

Date	Mintage	VF20	XF40	MS60	MS63	MS65
1979	20,000	PF65 1.00				

KM# 21 NEW PENNY

3.56 g., Bronze, 20.32 mm. **Ruler:** Elizabeth II **Obv:** Arms **Rev:** Gannet in flight

Date	Mintage	VF20	XF40	MS60	MS63	MS65
1971	1,922,000	—	0.15	0.25	0.45	1.00
1971	10,000	PF65 1.00				

KM# 27 PENNY

3.56 g., Bronze, 20.32 mm. **Ruler:** Elizabeth II **Obv:** Arms **Rev:** Gannet in flight

Date	Mintage	VF20	XF40	MS60	MS63	MS65
1977	640,000	—	0.15	0.25	0.45	1.00
1979	2,400,000	—	0.15	0.25	0.45	1.00
1979	20,000	PF65 1.00				
1981	10,000	PF65 2.00				

KM# 40 PENNY

3.56 g., Bronze, 20.32 mm. **Ruler:** Elizabeth II **Obv:** Crowned head right, small arms at left **Rev:** Edible crab **Edge:** Plain

Date	Mintage	VF20	XF40	MS60	MS63	MS65
1985	60,000	—	0.15	0.25	0.50	1.00
1985	2,500	PF65 2.00				
1986	1,010,000	—	0.15	0.25	0.50	1.00
1986	2,500	PF65 2.00				
1987	5,000	—	0.15	0.25	0.50	1.00
1987	—	PF65 2.00				
1988	500,000	—	0.15	0.25	0.50	1.00
1988	2,500	PF65 2.00				
1989	1,000,000	—	0.15	0.25	0.50	1.00
1989	—	PF65 2.00				
1990	5,000	—	0.15	0.25	0.50	1.00
1990	700	PF65 4.00				

KM# 40a PENNY

3.56 g., Copper Plated Steel, 20.32 mm. **Ruler:** Elizabeth II **Obv:** Crowned head right, small arms at left **Rev:** Chancre crab

Date	Mintage	VF20	XF40	MS60	MS63	MS65
1992 In sets only	—	—	—	0.20	0.35	1.00
1992	—	PF65 5.00				
1994	750,000	—	—	0.20	0.35	1.00
1997	2,000,000	—	—	0.20	0.35	1.00
1997	—	PF65 5.00				

KM# 89 PENNY

3.56 g., Copper Plated Steel, 20.32 mm. **Ruler:** Elizabeth II **Obv:** Head with tiara right **Rev:** Edible crab **Edge:** Plain

Date	Mintage	VF20	XF40	MS60	MS63	MS65
1998	—	—	—	0.25	0.50	0.75

KM# 22 2 NEW PENCE

7.12 g., Bronze, 25.91 mm. **Ruler:** Elizabeth II **Obv:** Arms **Rev:** Windmill from Sark

Date	Mintage	VF20	XF40	MS60	MS63	MS65
1971	1,680,000	—	0.15	0.20	0.35	0.50
1971	10,000	PF65 1.00				

KM# 28 2 PENCE

7.12 g., Bronze, 25.91 mm. **Ruler:** Elizabeth II **Obv:** Arms **Rev:** Windmill from Sark

Date	Mintage	VF20	XF40	MS60	MS63	MS65
1977	700,000	—	0.15	0.25	0.45	0.65
1979	2,400,000	—	0.15	0.25	0.45	0.65
1979	20,000	PF65 1.00				
1981	10,000	PF65 2.00				

KM# 41 2 PENCE

7.12 g., Bronze, 25.91 mm. **Ruler:** Elizabeth II **Obv:** Crowned head right, small arms at left **Rev:** Guernsey cows **Edge:** Plain

Date	Mintage	VF20	XF40	MS60	MS63	MS65
1985	60,000	—	0.20	0.75	1.25	2.00
1985	2,500	PF65 2.00				
1986	510,000	—	0.20	0.75	1.25	2.00
1986	2,500	PF65 2.00				
1987	5,000	—	0.20	0.75	1.25	2.00
1987	2,500	PF65 2.00				
1988	500,000	—	0.20	0.75	1.25	2.00
1988	2,500	PF65 2.00				
1989	500,000	—	0.20	0.75	1.25	2.00
1989	2,500	PF65 2.00				
1990	380,000	—	0.20	0.75	1.25	2.00
1990	700	PF65 4.00				
1997	—	—	0.20	0.75	1.25	2.00

KM# 41a 2 PENCE

7.12 g., Copper Plated Steel, 25.91 mm. **Ruler:** Elizabeth II **Obv:** Crowned head right, small arms at left **Rev:** Guernsey cows **Edge:** Plain

Date	Mintage	VF20	XF40	MS60	MS63	MS65
1992 Sets only	—	—	—	0.30	0.50	1.00
1992	—	PF65 5.00				
1996	500,000	—	—	0.30	0.50	1.00
1997 In sets only	—	—	—	0.30	0.50	1.00
1997	—	PF65 5.00				

KM# 96 2 PENCE

7,12 g., Copper Plated Steel, 25.91 mm. **Ruler:** Elizabeth II **Obv:** Head with tiara, shield at left **Rev:** Guernsey cows **Edge:** Plain

Date	Mintage	VF20	XF40	MS60	MS63	MS65
1999	600,000	—	—	0.50	0.75	1.25

KM# 23 5 NEW PENCE

5.65 g., Copper-Nickel, 23.6 mm. **Ruler:** Elizabeth II **Obv:** Arms **Rev:** Guernsey lily **Edge:** Reeded

Date	Mintage	VF20	XF40	MS60	MS63	MS65
1968	800,000	—	0.25	0.35	0.45	0.65
1971	10,000	PF65 1.00				

KM# 29 5 PENCE

5.65 g., Copper-Nickel, 23.6 mm. **Ruler:** Elizabeth II **Obv:** Arms **Rev:** Guernsey lily **Edge:** Reeded

Date	Mintage	VF20	XF40	MS60	MS63	MS65
1977	250,000	—	0.20	0.35	0.45	0.65
1979	200,000	—	0.20	0.35	0.45	0.65
1979	20,000	PF65 2.00				
1981	10,000	PF65 3.00				
1982	200,000	—	0.20	0.35	0.45	0.65

KM# 42.1.1 5 PENCE

5.65 g., Copper-Nickel, 23.6 mm. **Ruler:** Elizabeth II **Obv:** Crowned head right, small arms at left **Rev:** Sailboats **Edge:** Reeded

Date	Mintage	VF20	XF40	MS60	MS63	MS65
1985	35,000	—	0.20	0.35	0.45	0.65
1985	2,500	PF65 2.50				
1986	100,000	—	0.20	0.35	0.45	0.65
1986	2,500	PF65 2.50				
1987	300,000	—	0.20	0.35	0.45	0.65
1987	—	PF65 2.50				
1988	405,000	—	0.20	0.35	0.45	0.65
1988	2,500	PF65 2.50				
1989	5,000	—	0.20	0.35	0.50	0.75
1989	—	PF65 2.50				
1990 In sets only	Est. 2520	—	—	0.40	0.60	0.85
1990	700	PF65 5.00				

KM# 42.2.2 5 PENCE

3.25 g., Copper-Nickel, 18 mm. **Ruler:** Elizabeth II **Obv:** Crowned head right, small arms at left **Rev:** Sailboats **Edge:** Reeded **Note:** Reduced size

Date	Mintage	VF20	XF40	MS60	MS63	MS65
1990	2,400,000	—	0.20	0.35	0.45	0.65
1990	700	PF65 5.00				
1992	1,300,000	—	—	0.35	0.50	0.75
1992	—	PF65 6.00				
1997	—	—	—	0.35	0.50	0.75
1997	—	PF65 5.00				

KM# 97 5 PENCE

3.25 g., Copper-Nickel, 18 mm. **Ruler:** Elizabeth II **Obv:** Head with tiara right **Rev:** Sailboat **Edge:** Reeded

Date	Mintage	VF20	XF40	MS60	MS63	MS65
1999	1,700,000	—	—	0.35	0.45	0.65

KM# 24 10 NEW PENCE

11.31 g., Copper-Nickel, 28.52 mm. **Ruler:** Elizabeth II **Obv:** Arms **Rev:** Guernsey cow **Edge:** Reeded

Date	Mintage	VF20	XF40	MS60	MS63	MS65
1968	600,000	0.20	0.40	0.75	1.50	2.50
1970	300,000	0.20	0.40	0.75	1.50	2.50
1971	10,000	PF65 2.00				

KM# 30 10 PENCE

11.31 g., Copper-Nickel, 28.52 mm. **Ruler:** Elizabeth II **Obv:** Arms **Rev:** Guernsey cow **Edge:** Reeded

Date	Mintage	VF20	XF40	MS60	MS63	MS65
1977	480,000	—	0.25	0.50	1.00	2.00
1979	659,000	—	0.25	0.50	1.00	2.00
1979	20,000	PF65 2.00				
1981	10,000	PF65 3.00				
1982	200,000	—	0.35	0.65	1.25	2.00
1984	400,000	—	0.25	0.50	1.00	2.00

KM# 43.1.1 10 PENCE

11.31 g., Copper-Nickel, 28.52 mm. **Ruler:** Elizabeth II **Obv:** Crowned head right, small arms at left **Rev:** Tomato plant **Edge:** Reeded

Date	Mintage	VF20	XF40	MS60	MS63	MS65
1985	110,000	—	0.25	0.40	0.60	0.85
1985	2,500	PF65 2.50				
1986	300,000	—	0.25	0.40	0.60	0.85
1986	2,500	PF65 10.00				
1987	250,000	—	0.25	0.40	0.60	0.85
1987	—	PF65 2.50				
1988	300,000	—	0.25	0.40	0.60	0.85
1988	2,500	PF65 2.50				
1989	200,000	—	0.25	0.40	0.60	0.85
1989	—	PF65 2.50				
1990	3,500	—	0.25	0.40	0.60	0.85
1990	700	PF65 5.00				

KM# 43.2.2 10 PENCE

6.50 g., Copper-Nickel, 24.5 mm. **Ruler:** Elizabeth II **Obv:** Crowned head right, small arms at left **Rev:** Tomato plant **Edge:** Reeded **Note:** Reduced size.

Date	Mintage	VF20	XF40	MS60	MS63	MS65
1992	3,500,000	—	—	0.40	0.60	0.85
1992	—	PF65 6.00				
1997 In sets only	—	—	—	0.40	0.60	0.85
1997	—	PF65 6.00				

KM# 38 20 PENCE

5.00 g., Copper-Nickel, 21.4 mm. **Ruler:** Elizabeth II **Obv:** Arms **Rev:** Guernsey milk can **Shape:** 7-sided

Date	Mintage	VF20	XF40	MS60	MS63	MS65
1982	500,000	—	0.45	0.65	0.90	1.25
1983	500,000	—	0.45	0.65	0.90	1.25

KM# 44 20 PENCE

5.00 g., Copper-Nickel, 21.4 mm. **Ruler:** Elizabeth II **Obv:** Crowned head right, small arms at left **Rev:** Island map within cogwheel **Shape:** 7-sided

Date	Mintage	VF20	XF40	MS60	MS63	MS65
1985	35,000	—	0.45	0.60	0.85	1.20
1985	2,500	PF65 3.00				
1986	10,000	—	0.45	0.60	0.85	1.20
1986	2,500	PF65 3.00				
1987	5,000	—	0.45	0.60	0.85	1.20
1987	—	PF65 3.00				
1988	5,000	—	0.45	0.60	0.85	1.20
1988	2,500	PF65 3.00				
1989	93,000	—	0.45	0.60	0.85	1.20
1989	—	PF65 3.00				
1990	113,000	—	0.45	0.60	0.85	1.20
1990	700	PF65 6.00				
1992	800,000	—	—	0.75	1.00	1.50
1992	—	PF65 7.00				
1997	—	—	—	0.75	1.00	1.50
1997	—	PF65 3.00				

KM# 90 20 PENCE

5.00 g., Copper-Nickel, 21.4 mm. **Ruler:** Elizabeth II **Obv:** Head with tiara right, small arms at left **Rev:** Island map within cogwheel **Shape:** 7-sided

Date	Mintage	VF20	XF40	MS60	MS63	MS65
1999	800,000	—	—	0.65	0.90	1.25
1999	—	PF65 3.00				

KM# 26 25 PENCE

28.28 g., Copper-Nickel, 38.61 mm. **Ruler:** Elizabeth II **Subject:** 25th Wedding Anniversary - Elizabeth and Philip **Obv:** Arms **Rev:** Standing cupid right

Date	Mintage	VF20	XF40	MS60	MS63	MS65
1972	56,000	—	1.50	3.00	4.50	6.00

KM# 26a 25 PENCE

28.28 g., 0.925 Silver 0.8409 oz. ASW, 38.5 mm. **Ruler:** Elizabeth II **Subject:** 25th Wedding Anniversary - Elizabeth and Philip **Obv:** Arms **Rev:** Standing cupid right

Date	Mintage	VF20	XF40	MS60	MS63	MS65
1972	15,000	PF63 17.00		PF65 19.50		PF67 24.00

KM# 31 25 PENCE
28.28 g., Copper-Nickel, 38.61 mm. **Ruler:** Elizabeth II **Subject:** Queen's Silver Jubilee **Obv:** Young bust right **Rev:** Scene from above

Date	Mintage	VF20	XF40	MS60	MS63	MS65
ND-1977	207,000	—	1.25	2.25	3.50	4.00

KM# 31a 25 PENCE
28.28 g., 0.925 Silver 0.8409 oz. ASW, 38.5 mm. **Ruler:** Elizabeth II **Subject:** Queen's Silver Jubilee **Obv:** Young bust right **Rev:** Scene from above

Date	Mintage	VF20	XF40	MS60	MS63	MS65
ND-1977	25,000	PF63 17.00	PF65 19.50	PF67 24.00		

KM# 32 25 PENCE
28.28 g., Copper-Nickel, 38.61 mm. **Ruler:** Elizabeth II **Subject:** Royal Visit **Obv:** Young bust right **Rev:** Arms

Date	Mintage	VF20	XF40	MS60	MS63	MS65
1978	105,000	—	1.25	2.50	3.75	4.50

KM# 32a 25 PENCE
28.28 g., 0.925 Silver 0.8409 oz. ASW, 38.5 mm. **Ruler:** Elizabeth II **Subject:** Royal Visit **Obv:** Young bust right **Rev:** Arms

Date	Mintage	VF20	XF40	MS60	MS63	MS65
1978	25,000	PF63 17.00	PF65 19.50	PF67 24.00		

KM# 35 25 PENCE
28.28 g., Copper-Nickel, 38.61 mm. **Ruler:** Elizabeth II **Subject:** Queen Mother's 80th Birthday **Obv:** Young bust right **Rev:** Bust left

Date	Mintage	VF20	XF40	MS60	MS63	MS65
ND-1980	150,000	—	1.25	2.50	3.75	4.50

KM# 35a 25 PENCE
28.28 g., 0.925 Silver 0.8409 oz. ASW, 38.5 mm. **Ruler:** Elizabeth II **Subject:** Queen Mother's 80th Birthday **Obv:** Young bust right **Rev:** Bust left

Date	Mintage	VF20	XF40	MS60	MS63	MS65
ND-1980	25,000	PF63 17.00	PF65 19.50	PF67 24.00		

KM# 36 25 PENCE
28.28 g., Copper-Nickel, 38.61 mm. **Ruler:** Elizabeth II **Subject:** Wedding of Prince Charles and Lady Diana **Obv:** Young bust right **Rev:** Arms divided by royal couple

Date	Mintage	VF20	XF40	MS60	MS63	MS65
1981	114,000	—	1.50	2.75	4.00	5.00

KM# 36a 25 PENCE
28.28 g., 0.925 Silver 0.8409 oz. ASW, 38.5 mm. **Ruler:** Elizabeth II **Subject:** Wedding of Prince Charles and Lady Diana **Obv:** Young bust right **Rev:** Royal couple divide arms

Date	Mintage	VF20	XF40	MS60	MS63	MS65
1981	12,000	PF63 17.00	PF65 19.50	PF67 24.00		

KM# 25 50 NEW PENCE
13.50 g., Copper-Nickel, 30 mm. **Ruler:** Elizabeth II **Obv:** Arms **Rev:** Ducal cap of the Duke of Normandy **Shape:** 7-sided

Date	Mintage	VF20	XF40	MS60	MS63	MS65
1969	200,000	1.00	1.50	2.50	3.50	4.00
1970	200,000	1.00	1.50	2.50	3.50	4.00
1971	10,000	PF65 4.00				

KM# 34 50 PENCE
13.50 g., Copper-Nickel, 30 mm. **Ruler:** Elizabeth II **Obv:** Arms **Rev:** Ducal cap of the Duke of Normandy **Shape:** 7-sided

Date	Mintage	VF20	XF40	MS60	MS63	MS65
1979	20,000	PF65 4.50				
1981	200,000	—	0.90	1.45	2.25	3.00
1981	10,000	PF65 5.50				
1982	150,000	—	0.90	1.45	2.25	3.00
1983	200,000	—	0.90	1.45	2.25	3.00
1984	200,000	—	0.90	1.45	2.25	3.00

KM# 45.1.1 50 PENCE
13.50 g., Copper-Nickel, 30 mm. **Ruler:** Elizabeth II **Obv:** Crowned head right, small shield at left **Rev:** Freesia flowers **Shape:** 7-sided

Date	Mintage	VF20	XF40	MS60	MS63	MS65
1985	35,000	—	0.90	1.45	2.25	3.00
1985	2,500	PF65 4.00				
1986	10,000	—	0.90	1.45	2.25	3.00
1986	2,500	PF65 10.00				
1987	5,000	—	0.90	1.45	2.25	3.00
1987	—	PF65 10.00				
1988	6,000	—	0.90	1.45	2.25	3.00
1988	2,500	PF65 4.50				
1989	55,000	—	0.90	1.45	2.25	3.00
1989	—	PF65 4.50				
1990	80,000	—	0.90	1.45	2.25	3.00
1990	700	PF65 7.50				
1992	65,000	—	—	2.00	3.00	3.50
1992	—	PF63 7.50	PF65 10.00			
1997	—	PF65 7.50				

Note: In sets only

KM# 45.2.2 50 PENCE
8.00 g., Copper-Nickel, 27.3 mm. **Ruler:** Elizabeth II **Obv:** Crowned head right, small shield at left **Rev:** Freesia flowers **Shape:** 7-sided

Date	Mintage	VF20	XF40	MS60	MS63	MS65
1997	1,000,000	—	—	1.75	2.75	3.25
1997	—	PF65 8.50				

KM# 105 50 PENCE
8.00 g., Copper-Nickel, 27.3 mm. **Ruler:** Elizabeth II **Subject:** 60th Anniversary - Battle of Britain **Obv:** Head with tiara right **Rev:** Pilot and fighter plane **Edge:** Plain **Shape:** 7-sided

Date	Mintage	VF20	XF40	MS60	MS63	MS65
2000	10,000	—	—	2.00	3.00	3.50

KM# 105a 50 PENCE
8.10 g., 0.925 Silver 0.2409 oz. ASW, 27.3 mm. **Ruler:** Elizabeth II **Obv:** Head with tiara right **Rev:** Pilot and fighter plane **Shape:** 7-sided

Date	Mintage	VF20	XF40	MS60	MS63	MS65
2000	15,000	PF65 25.00				

KM# 105b 50 PENCE
15.50 g., 0.917 Gold 0.457 oz. AGW, 27.3 mm. **Ruler:** Elizabeth II **Obv:** Head with tiara right **Rev:** Pilot and fighter plane **Edge:** Plain **Shape:** 7-sided

Date	Mintage	VF20	XF40	MS60	MS63	MS65
2000	1,500	PF65 750				

KM# 37 POUND
7.90 g., Nickel-Brass, 22 mm. **Ruler:** Elizabeth II **Obv:** Arms **Rev:** Guernsey lily

Date	Mintage	VF20	XF40	MS60	MS63	MS65
1981	200,000	1.80	2.00	3.50	4.50	5.00
1981	10,000	PF65 5.00				

KM# 37a POUND
8.00 g., 0.917 Gold 0.2359 oz. AGW, 22 mm. **Ruler:** Elizabeth II **Obv:** Arms **Rev:** Guernsey lily

Date	Mintage	VF20	XF40	MS60	MS63	MS65
1981	4,500	PF65 375				

KM# 39 POUND
9.50 g., Nickel-Brass, 22.5 mm. **Ruler:** Elizabeth II **Obv:** Arms **Rev:** H.M.S. Crescent

Date	Mintage	VF20	XF40	MS60	MS63	MS65
1983	269,000	1.80	2.00	3.50	4.50	5.00

KM# 46 POUND
9.50 g., Nickel-Brass, 22.5 mm. **Ruler:** Elizabeth II **Obv:** Crowned head right, small shield at left **Rev:** Design divides denomination

Date	Mintage	VF20	XF40	MS60	MS63	MS65
1985	35,000	—	1.75	2.50	3.50	4.00
1985	2,500	PF65 6.50				
1986	10,000	—	1.75	2.50	3.50	4.00
1986	2,500	PF65 6.50				
1987	5,000	—	1.75	2.50	3.50	4.00
1987	—	PF65 6.50				
1988	5,000	—	1.75	2.50	3.50	4.00
1988	2,500	PF65 6.50				
1989	5,000	—	1.75	2.50	3.50	4.00
1989	—	PF65 6.50				
1990	—	—	1.75	2.50	3.50	4.00
1990	700	PF65 10.00				
1992 In sets only	—	—	—	3.50	5.00	5.50
1992	—	PF65 12.50				
1997 In sets only	—	—	—	3.50	5.00	5.50
1997	—	PF65 12.50				

KM# 77 POUND
9.50 g., 0.925 Silver 0.2825 oz. ASW, 22.5 mm. **Ruler:** Elizabeth II **Subject:** Queen Elizabeth the Queen Mother **Rev:** Bust facing, flowers flank

Date	Mintage	VF20	XF40	MS60	MS63	MS65
1995	—	PF65 15.00				

KM# 78 POUND
9.50 g., 0.925 Silver 0.2825 oz. ASW, 22.5 mm. **Ruler:** Elizabeth II **Subject:** 70th Birthday of Queen Elizabeth II **Obv:** Crowned head right **Rev:** Elizabeth II at left, arms above fortress at right

Date	Mintage	VF20	XF40	MS60	MS63	MS65
1996	—	PF65 15.00				

KM# 70 POUND
9.50 g., 0.925 Silver 0.2825 oz. ASW, 22.5 mm. **Ruler:** Elizabeth II **Subject:** Golden Wedding Anniversary **Obv:** Crowned head right **Rev:** Queen Elizabeth II and Prince Philip, monogrammed shield, Westminster Abbey

Date	Mintage	VF20	XF40	MS60	MS63	MS65
1997	Est. 50000	PF65 15.00				

KM# 73 POUND
9.50 g., 0.925 Silver 0.2825 oz. ASW, 22.5 mm. **Ruler:** Elizabeth II **Series:** Castle **Subject:** Tower of London

Date	Mintage	VF20	XF40	MS60	MS63	MS65
1997	15,000	PF65 18.00				

KM# 84 POUND
9.50 g., 0.925 Silver 0.2825 oz. ASW, 22.5 mm. **Ruler:** Elizabeth II **Subject:** 80th Anniversary - Royal Air Force **Obv:** Head with tiara right **Rev:** Three Spitfires and RAF Benevolent Fund Crest

Date	Mintage	VF20	XF40	MS60	MS63	MS65
1998	—	PF65 25.00				

KM# 95 POUND
9.50 g., 0.925 Silver 0.2825 oz. ASW, 22.5 mm. **Ruler:** Elizabeth II **Subject:** Prince Edward's Wedding **Obv:** Queen's portrait **Rev:** Portraits of Edward and Sophie **Edge:** Reeded

Date	Mintage	VF20	XF40	MS60	MS63	MS65
1999	—	PF65 15.00				

KM# 109 POUND
9.50 g., 0.925 Silver 0.2825 oz. ASW, 22.5 mm. **Ruler:** Elizabeth II **Subject:** Winston Churchill **Obv:** Queen's portrait **Rev:** Churchill's portrait **Edge:** Reeded

Date	Mintage	VF20	XF40	MS60	MS63	MS65
1999	30,000	PF65 12.00				

KM# 120 POUND
9.50 g., 0.925 Silver 0.2825 oz. ASW, 22.4 mm. **Ruler:** Elizabeth II **Subject:** Queen Mother **Obv:** Head with tiara right **Rev:** Bust 3/4 right **Edge:** Reeded

Date	Mintage	VF20	XF40	MS60	MS63	MS65
1999	—	PF65 20.00				

KM# 87 POUND
9.50 g., 0.925 Silver Gilt 0.2825 oz., 22.5 mm. **Ruler:** Elizabeth II **Subject:** Year 2000 **Obv:** Head with tiara right **Rev:** Hands holding planet Earth, **Note:** Millennium insert for 5 pounds, KM#86.

Date	Mintage	VF20	XF40	MS60	MS63	MS65
2000	Est. 50000	PF65 25.00				

KM# 99 POUND
9.50 g., 0.925 Silver 0.2825 oz. ASW, 22.5 mm. **Ruler:** Elizabeth II **Subject:** Queen Mother's 100th Birthday **Obv:** Head with tiara right **Rev:** Head facing, flowers and age at right **Edge:** Reeded

Date	Mintage	VF20	XF40	MS60	MS63	MS65
2000	50,000	PF65 12.00				

KM# 47 2 POUNDS
28.28 g., Copper-Nickel, 38.61 mm. **Ruler:** Elizabeth II **Subject:** 40th Anniversary - Liberation from Germany **Obv:** Crowned head right, small arms at left **Rev:** Pair of doves sharing laurel branch

Date	Mintage	VF20	XF40	MS60	MS63	MS65
ND-1985	75,000	—	—	3.50	5.50	7.00
ND-1985	2,500	PF65 10.00	PF67 12.00			

KM# 47a 2 POUNDS
28.28 g., 0.925 Silver 0.841 oz. ASW, 38.61 mm. **Ruler:** Elizabeth II **Subject:** 40th Anniversary - Liberation from Germany **Obv:** Crowned head right, small arms at left **Rev:** Pair of doves sharing laurel branch

Date	Mintage	VF20	XF40	MS60	MS63	MS65
ND (1985)	2,500	PF63 22.00	PF65 25.00	PF67 28.00		

KM# 48 2 POUNDS
28.28 g., Copper-Nickel, 38.61 mm. **Ruler:** Elizabeth II **Subject:** Commonwealth Games **Rev:** Eight shields of athletes surround arms

Date	Mintage	VF20	XF40	MS60	MS63	MS65
1986	18,000	—	—	4.00	6.00	7.00
1986	—	PF65 10.00	PF67 12.00			

KM# 48a 2 POUNDS
28.28 g., 0.500 Silver 0.4546 oz. ASW, 38.61 mm. **Ruler:** Elizabeth II **Subject:** Commonwealth Games **Rev:** Eight shields of athletes surround arms

Date	Mintage	VF20	XF40	MS60	MS63	MS65
1986	Est. 50000	—	—	10.00	12.00	15.00

KM# 48b 2 POUNDS
28.28 g., 0.925 Silver 0.841 oz. ASW, 38.61 mm. **Ruler:** Elizabeth II **Subject:** Commonwealth Games **Rev:** Eight shields of athletes surround arms

Date	Mintage	VF20	XF40	MS60	MS63	MS65
1986	Est. 20000	PF63 16.00	PF65 18.00	PF67 22.00		

KM# 49 2 POUNDS
28.28 g., Copper-Nickel, 38.61 mm. **Ruler:** Elizabeth II **Subject:** 900th Anniversary - Death of William the Conqueror **Obv:** Crowned head right, small arms at left **Rev:** Crowned bust left

Date	Mintage	VF20	XF40	MS60	MS63	MS65
ND-1987	18,000	—	—	5.00	6.50	7.50
ND-1987	Est. 2500	PF65 10.00	PF67 12.00			

KM# 49a 2 POUNDS
28.28 g., 0.925 Silver 0.841 oz. ASW, 38.5 mm. **Ruler:** Elizabeth II **Subject:** 900th Anniversary - Death of William the Conqueror **Obv:** Crowned head right, small arms at left **Rev:** Crowned bust left

Date	Mintage	VF20	XF40	MS60	MS63	MS65
ND-1987	2,500	PF63 22.00	PF65 25.00	PF67 28.00		

KM# 49b 2 POUNDS
47.54 g., 0.917 Gold 1.4016 oz. AGW, 38.5 mm. **Ruler:** Elizabeth II **Subject:** 900th Anniversary - Death of William the Conqueror **Obv:** Crowned head right, small arms at left **Rev:** Crowned bust left

Date	Mintage	VF20	XF40	MS60	MS63	MS65
ND-1987	90	PF65 2,000	PF67 2,250			

KM# 50 2 POUNDS
28.28 g., Copper-Nickel, 38.61 mm. **Ruler:** Elizabeth II **Subject:** William II, 1087-1100 **Obv:** Crowned head right, small arms at left **Rev:** Bust facing

Date	Mintage	VF20	XF40	MS60	MS63	MS65
1988	7,500	—	—	5.00	6.50	7.50
1988	2,500	PF65 10.00	PF67 12.00			

KM# 50a 2 POUNDS
28.28 g., 0.925 Silver 0.841 oz. ASW, 38.5 mm. **Ruler:** Elizabeth II **Subject:** William II, 1087-1100 **Obv:** Crowned head right, small arms at left **Rev:** Bust facing

Date	Mintage	VF20	XF40	MS60	MS63	MS65
1988	2,500	PF63 22.00	PF65 25.00	PF67 28.00		

KM# 51 2 POUNDS
28.28 g., Copper-Nickel, 38.61 mm. **Ruler:** Elizabeth II **Subject:** Henry I, 1100-1135 **Obv:** Crowned head right, small arms at left **Rev:** Crowned bust right

Date	Mintage	VF20	XF40	MS60	MS63	MS65
1989	10,000	—	—	5.00	6.50	7.50
1989	Est. 2500	PF65 10.00	PF67 12.00			

KM# 51a 2 POUNDS
28.28 g., 0.925 Silver 0.841 oz. ASW, 38.61 mm. **Ruler:** Elizabeth II **Subject:** Henry I, 1100-1135 **Obv:** Crowned head right, small arms at left **Rev:** Crowned bust right

Date	Mintage	VF20	XF40	MS60	MS63	MS65
1989	Est. 2500	PF63 25.00	PF65 28.00	PF67 32.00		

KM# 52 2 POUNDS
28.28 g., Copper-Nickel, 38.61 mm. **Ruler:** Elizabeth II **Subject:** Royal Visit **Obv:** Crowned bust right **Rev:** Royal Yacht "Britannia"

Date	Mintage	VF20	XF40	MS60	MS63	MS65
1989	5,000	—	—	5.00	7.00	9.00

KM# 52a 2 POUNDS
28.28 g., 0.925 Silver 0.841 oz. ASW, 38.61 mm. **Ruler:** Elizabeth II **Subject:** Royal Visit **Obv:** Crowned bust right **Rev:** Royal yacht, "Britannia"

Date	Mintage	VF20	XF40	MS60	MS63	MS65
1989	5,000	PF63 27.00	PF65 30.00	PF67 35.00		

KM# 53 2 POUNDS
28.28 g., Copper-Nickel, 38.61 mm. **Ruler:** Elizabeth II **Subject:** 90th Birthday of Queen Mother **Obv:** Crowned bust right **Rev:** Crowned monogram flanked by flowers

Date	Mintage	VF20	XF40	MS60	MS63	MS65
ND-1990	9,000	—	—	5.00	7.00	8.00

KM# 53a 2 POUNDS
28.28 g., 0.925 Silver 0.841 oz. ASW, 38.61 mm. **Ruler:** Elizabeth II **Subject:** 90th Birthday of Queen Mother **Obv:** Crowned bust right **Rev:** Crowned monogram flanked by flowers

Date	Mintage	VF20	XF40	MS60	MS63	MS65
ND-1990	1,302	PF63 35.00	PF65 40.00	PF67 45.00		

KM# 54 2 POUNDS
28.28 g., Copper-Nickel, 38.61 mm. **Ruler:** Elizabeth II **Subject:** Henry II, 1154-1189 **Obv:** Crowned head right, small arms at left **Rev:** Crowned bust half left

Date	Mintage	VF20	XF40	MS60	MS63	MS65
1991	1,200	—	—	4.50	6.50	7.50

KM# 54a 2 POUNDS
28.28 g., 0.925 Silver 0.841 oz. ASW, 38.61 mm. **Ruler:** Elizabeth II **Subject:** Henry II, 1154-1189 **Obv:** Crowned head right, small arms at left **Rev:** Crowned half left

Date	Mintage	VF20	XF40	MS60	MS63	MS65
1991	Est. 2500	PF63 35.00	PF65 40.00	PF67 45.00		

KM# 55 2 POUNDS
28.28 g., Copper-Nickel, 38.61 mm. **Ruler:** Elizabeth II **Subject:** 40th Anniversary of Coronation **Obv:** Crowned bust right **Rev:** Crowned, ribbon monogram with date on field of vines and flowers

Date	Mintage	VF20	XF40	MS60	MS63	MS65
ND-1993	13,000	—	—	4.50	6.50	7.50

KM# 55a 2 POUNDS
28.28 g., 0.925 Silver 0.841 oz. ASW, 38.61 mm. **Ruler:** Elizabeth II **Subject:** 40th Anniversary of Coronation **Obv:** Crowned bust right **Rev:** Crowned, ribbon monogram with date on field of vines and flowers

Date	Mintage	VF20	XF40	MS60	MS63	MS65
ND-1993	Est. 10000	PF63 20.00	PF65 22.00	PF67 27.00		

KM# 56 2 POUNDS
28.28 g., Copper-Nickel, 38.61 mm. **Ruler:** Elizabeth II **Subject:** 50th Anniversary - Normandy Landing **Obv:** Crowned head right, small arms at left **Rev:** Cameo portrait above invasion scene

Date	Mintage	VF20	XF40	MS60	MS63	MS65
ND-1994	49,000	—	—	3.00	5.00	7.00

KM# 56a 2 POUNDS
28.28 g., 0.925 Silver 0.841 oz. ASW, 38.61 mm. **Ruler:** Elizabeth II **Subject:** 50th Anniversary - Normandy Landing **Obv:** Crowned head right, small arms at left **Rev:** Cameo portrait above invasion scene

Date	Mintage	VF20	XF40	MS60	MS63	MS65
ND-1994	Est. 10000	PF63 20.00	PF65 22.00	PF67 27.00		

KM# 61 2 POUNDS
Copper-Nickel, 38.5 mm. **Ruler:** Elizabeth II **Subject:** 50th Anniversary of Liberation **Obv:** Crowned head right, small arms at left **Rev:** Soldiers and ship

Date	Mintage	VF20	XF40	MS60	MS63	MS65
ND-1995	42,000	—	—	3.00	5.00	7.00

KM# 61a 2 POUNDS
28.28 g., 0.925 Silver 0.841 oz. ASW, 38.5 mm. **Ruler:** Elizabeth II **Subject:** 50th Anniversary of Liberation **Obv:** Crowned head right, small arms at left **Rev:** Soldiers and ship

Date	Mintage	VF20	XF40	MS60	MS63	MS65
ND-1995	7,000	PF63 25.00	PF65 27.00	PF67 30.00		

KM# 61b 2 POUNDS
56.56 g., 0.925 Silver 1.6821 oz. ASW, 38.5 mm. **Ruler:** Elizabeth II **Subject:** 50th Anniversary of Liberation **Obv:** Crowned head right, small arms at left **Rev:** Soldiers and ship

Date	Mintage	VF20	XF40	MS60	MS63	MS65
ND-1995	800	PF65 100	PF67 120			

KM# 80 2 POUNDS
Copper-Nickel, 38.5 mm. **Ruler:** Elizabeth II **Subject:** WWF Conserving Nature **Obv:** Crowned head right **Rev:** Emperor Moth

Date	Mintage	VF20	XF40	MS60	MS63	MS65
1997	—	—	—	5.00	7.00	9.00

KM# 80a 2 POUNDS
28.28 g., 0.925 Silver 0.841 oz. ASW, 38.5 mm. **Ruler:** Elizabeth II **Subject:** WWF Conserving Nature **Obv:** Crowned head right **Rev:** Emperor moth

Date	Mintage	VF20	XF40	MS60	MS63	MS65
1997	Est. 15000	PF63 22.00	PF65 25.00	PF67 28.00		

KM# 88 2 POUNDS
12.00 g., Bi-Metallic Copper-Nickel center in Nickel-Brass ring, 28.4 mm. **Ruler:** Elizabeth II **Obv:** Crowned head right **Rev:** Latent image arms on cross design **Edge:** BAILIWICK OF GUERNSEY

Date	Mintage	VF20	XF40	MS60	MS63	MS65
1997	—	—	—	4.00	6.00	8.00
1997	—	PF65 10.00	PF67 12.00			

KM# 81 2 POUNDS
28.28 g., Copper-Nickel, 38.61 mm. **Ruler:** Elizabeth II **Subject:** WWF Conserving Nature **Obv:** Crowned head right **Rev:** Brimstone butterfly

Date	Mintage	VF20	XF40	MS60	MS63	MS65
1998	—	—	—	5.00	7.00	9.00

KM# 83 2 POUNDS
12.00 g., Bi-Metallic Copper-Nickel center in Nickel-Brass ring, 28.4 mm. **Ruler:** Elizabeth II **Obv:** Head with tiara right **Rev:** Latent image arms on cross **Edge:** BAILIWICK OF GUERNSEY

Date	Mintage	VF20	XF40	MS60	MS63	MS65
1998	Est. 150000	—	—	4.00	6.00	8.00

KM# 66 5 POUNDS
28.28 g., Copper-Nickel, 38.61 mm. **Ruler:** Elizabeth II **Subject:** Queen Elizabeth the Queen Mother **Obv:** Crowned head right **Rev:** Bust facing, flowers flank

Date	Mintage	VF20	XF40	MS60	MS63	MS65
1995	56,000	—	—	5.00	7.00	9.00

KM# 66a 5 POUNDS
28.28 g., 0.925 Silver 0.841 oz. ASW, 38.61 mm. **Ruler:** Elizabeth II **Subject:** Queen Elizabeth The Queen Mother **Obv:** Crowned head right **Rev:** Bust facing, flowers flank

Date	Mintage	VF20	XF40	MS60	MS63	MS65
1995	Est. 40000	PF63 22.00	PF65 25.00	PF67 28.00		

KM# 67 5 POUNDS
7.81 g., 0.999 Gold 0.2508 oz. AGW **Ruler:** Elizabeth II **Obv:** Crowned head right **Rev:** Queen Mother

Date	Mintage	VF20	XF40	MS60	MS63	MS65
1995	Est. 2500	PF65 375	PF67 425			

KM# 68 5 POUNDS
28.28 g., Copper-Nickel, 38.61 mm. **Ruler:** Elizabeth II **Subject:** European Football **Rev:** Soccer ball and European map

Date	Mintage	VF20	XF40	MS60	MS63	MS65
1996	—	—	—	6.00	8.00	10.00

KM# 68a 5 POUNDS
28.28 g., 0.925 Silver 0.841 oz. ASW, 38.5 mm. **Ruler:** Elizabeth II **Subject:** European Football **Rev:** Soccer ball and European map

Date	Mintage	VF20	XF40	MS60	MS63	MS65
1996	—	PF63 35.00	PF65 42.00	PF67 50.00		

KM# 79 5 POUNDS
28.28 g., Copper-Nickel, 38.61 mm. **Ruler:** Elizabeth II **Subject:** 70th Birthday of Queen Elizabeth II **Obv:** Crowned head right **Rev:** Bust at left looking right, ship and arms at right

Date	Mintage	VF20	XF40	MS60	MS63	MS65
1996	—	—	—	6.00	8.00	10.00

KM# 79a 5 POUNDS
28.28 g., 0.925 Silver 0.841 oz. ASW, 38.5 mm. **Ruler:** Elizabeth II **Subject:** 70th Birthday of Queen Elizabeth II **Obv:** Crowned head right **Rev:** Bust at left looking right, arms and ship at right

Date	Mintage	VF20	XF40	MS60	MS63	MS65
1996	—	PF63 22.00	PF65 25.00	PF67 28.00		

KM# 71 5 POUNDS
28.28 g., Copper-Nickel, 38.61 mm. **Ruler:** Elizabeth II **Subject:** Queen Elizabeth II's Golden Wedding Anniversary **Obv:** Crowned head right **Rev:** Queen Elizabeth II and Prince Philip, monogrammed shield and Westminster Abbey

Date	Mintage	VF20	XF40	MS60	MS63	MS65
1997	22,000	—	—	6.00	8.00	10.00

KM# 71a 5 POUNDS
28.28 g., 0.925 Silver 0.841 oz. ASW, 38.61 mm. **Ruler:** Elizabeth II **Subject:** Queen Elizabeth II's Golden Wedding Anniversary **Obv:** Crowned head right **Rev:** Queen Elizabeth II and Prince Philip, monogrammed shield and Westminster Abbey

Date	Mintage	VF20	XF40	MS60	MS63	MS65
1997	Est. 20000	PF63 35.00	PF65 42.00	PF67 50.00		

KM# 74 5 POUNDS
28.28 g., Copper-Nickel, 38.61 mm. **Ruler:** Elizabeth II **Subject:** Castle Cornet **Obv:** Crowned head right **Rev:** Castle

Date	Mintage	VF20	XF40	MS60	MS63	MS65
1997	—	—	—	6.00	8.00	10.00

KM# 74a 5 POUNDS
28.28 g., 0.925 Silver 0.841 oz. ASW, 38.61 mm. **Ruler:** Elizabeth II **Subject:** Castle Cornet **Obv:** Crowned head right **Rev:** Castle

Date	Mintage	VF20	XF40	MS60	MS63	MS65
1997	Est. 10000	PF63 35.00	PF65 42.00	PF67 50.00		

KM# 75 5 POUNDS
28.28 g., 0.925 Silver 0.841 oz. ASW, 38.5 mm. **Ruler:** Elizabeth II **Subject:** Castle Caernarfon **Obv:** Crowned head right **Rev:** Castle

Date	Mintage	VF20	XF40	MS60	MS63	MS65
1997	Est. 10000	PF63 35.00	PF65 42.00	PF67 50.00		

KM# 76 5 POUNDS
28.28 g., 0.925 Silver 0.841 oz. ASW, 38.5 mm. **Ruler:** Elizabeth II **Subject:** Castle Leeds **Obv:** Crowned head right **Rev:** Castle

Date	Mintage	VF20	XF40	MS60	MS63	MS65
1997	Est. 10000	PF63 35.00	PF65 42.00	PF67 50.00		

KM# 98 5 POUNDS
1.20 g., 0.9167 Gold 0.0354 oz. AGW, 9 mm. **Ruler:** Elizabeth II **Subject:** Queen's 50th Wedding Anniversary **Rev:** Royal couple, shield and church **Edge:** Reeded

Date	Mintage	VF20	XF40	MS60	MS63	MS65
1997	—	PF65 55.00	PF67 65.00			

KM# 82 5 POUNDS
28.28 g., Copper-Nickel, 38.61 mm. **Ruler:** Elizabeth II **Subject:** 80th Anniversary of the Royal Air Force **Obv:** Head with tiara right **Rev:** Three Spitfires and an oval crest

Date	Mintage	VF20	XF40	MS60	MS63	MS65
1998	—	—	—	7.50	10.00	12.00

KM# 82a 5 POUNDS
28.28 g., 0.925 Silver 0.841 oz. ASW, 38.61 mm. **Ruler:** Elizabeth II **Subject:** 80th Anniversary of the Royal Air Force **Obv:** Head with tiara right **Rev:** Three Spitfires and an oval crest

Date	Mintage	VF20	XF40	MS60	MS63	MS65
1998	15,000	PF63 25.00	PF65 32.00	PF67 40.00		

KM# 115 5 POUNDS
1.24 g., 0.999 Gold 0.0398 oz. AGW, 13.92 mm. **Ruler:** Elizabeth II **Subject:** Queen Mother, 98th Birthday

Date	Mintage	VF20	XF40	MS60	MS63	MS65
1998	—	—	—	—	—	100

KM# 86 5 POUNDS
28.28 g., 0.925 Silver 0.841 oz. ASW, 38.5 mm. **Ruler:** Elizabeth II **Subject:** Millennium 2000 **Obv:** Head with tiara right below center hole **Rev:** Rising sun design surrounds center hole

Date	Mintage	VF20	XF40	MS60	MS63	MS65
1999	—	PF63 22.00	PF65 25.00	PF67 28.00		

KM# 91 5 POUNDS
Bi-Metallic Brass center in Copper-Nickel ring, 38.5 mm. **Ruler:** Elizabeth II **Subject:** Millennium 2000 **Obv:** Head with tiara right at center and below **Rev:** Hands holding planet earth in center, rising sun design surrounds

Date	Mintage	VF20	XF40	MS60	MS63	MS65
1999	22,000	—	—	9.50	12.50	15.50

KM# 92 5 POUNDS
28.28 g., Copper-Nickel, 38.61 mm. **Ruler:** Elizabeth II **Subject:** Prince Edward's Marriage **Obv:** Head with tiara right **Rev:** Conjoined heads of Edward and Sophie left **Edge:** Reeded

Date	Mintage	VF20	XF40	MS60	MS63	MS65
1999	19,000	—	—	7.50	9.50	12.50

KM# 92a 5 POUNDS
28.28 g., 0.925 Silver 0.841 oz. ASW, 38.61 mm. **Ruler:** Elizabeth II **Subject:** Prince Edward's Marriage **Obv:** Head with tiara right **Rev:** Conjoined heads left of Edward and Sophie left

Date	Mintage	VF20	XF40	MS60	MS63	MS65
1999	—	PF63 22.00	PF65 25.00	PF67 28.00		

KM# 93 5 POUNDS
28.28 g., Copper-Nickel, 38.61 mm. **Ruler:** Elizabeth II **Subject:** Queen Mother **Obv:** Head with tiara right **Rev:** Bust 3/4 right

Date	Mintage	VF20	XF40	MS60	MS63	MS65
1999	5,000	—	—	—	11.00	14.00

KM# 94 5 POUNDS
28.28 g., Copper-Nickel, 38.61 mm. **Ruler:** Elizabeth II **Subject:** Winston Churchill **Obv:** Head with tiara right **Rev:** Head right **Edge:** Reeded

Date	Mintage	VF20	XF40	MS60	MS63	MS65
1999	5,000	—	—	—	11.00	14.00

KM# 94a 5 POUNDS
28.28 g., 0.925 Silver 0.841 oz. ASW, 38.5 mm. **Ruler:** Elizabeth II **Obv:** Head with tiara right **Rev:** Head right **Rev. Inscription:** Winston Spencer Churchill

Date	Mintage	VF20	XF40	MS60	MS63	MS65
1999	—	PF63 22.00	PF65 25.00	PF67 28.00		

KM# 94b 5 POUNDS
47.54 g., 0.9166 Gold 1.401 oz. AGW, 38.5 mm. **Ruler:** Elizabeth II **Subject:** Winston Churchill **Obv:** Head with tiara right **Rev:** Head right **Edge:** Reeded

Date	Mintage	VF20	XF40	MS60	MS63	MS65
1999	125,000	PF65 2,000	PF67 2,250			

KM# 134 5 POUNDS
1.24 g., 0.999 Gold 0.040 oz. AGW, 13.9 mm. **Ruler:** Elizabeth II **Subject:** Queen Mother **Obv:** Head with tiara right **Rev:** Queen Mother's portrait **Edge:** Reeded

Date	Mintage	VF20	XF40	MS60	MS63	MS65
1999	20,000	—	—	—	—	80.00

KM# 100 5 POUNDS
28.28 g., Copper-Nickel, 38.6 mm. **Ruler:** Elizabeth II **Obv:** Head with tiara right **Rev:** Queen Mother's portrait **Edge:** Reeded

Date	Mintage	VF20	XF40	MS60	MS63	MS65
2000	2,000	—	—	—	7.50	9.00

KM# 100a 5 POUNDS
28.28 g., 0.925 Silver 0.841 oz. ASW, 38.6 mm. **Ruler:** Elizabeth II **Subject:** Queen Mother's 100th Birthday **Obv:** Head with tiara right with gold-plated "100" **Rev:** Queen Mother's portrait **Edge:** Reeded

Date	Mintage	VF20	XF40	MS60	MS63	MS65
2000	20,000	PF63 22.00	PF65 25.00	PF67 28.00		

KM# 101 5 POUNDS
1.13 g., 0.917 Gold 0.0333 oz. AGW, 13.9 mm. **Ruler:** Elizabeth II **Subject:** Queen Mother's 100th Birthday **Obv:** Head with tiara right **Rev:** Queen Mother's portrait **Edge:** Reeded

Date	Mintage	VF20	XF40	MS60	MS63	MS65
2000	20,000	PF65 60.00	PF67 70.00			

KM# 102 5 POUNDS
28.28 g., Copper-Nickel, 38.61 mm. **Ruler:** Elizabeth II **Subject:** Century of Monarchy **Obv:** Head with tiara right **Rev:** Portraits of past five sovereigns **Edge:** Reeded

Date	Mintage	VF20	XF40	MS60	MS63	MS65
2000	10,246	—	—	—	7.50	9.00

KM# 102a 5 POUNDS
28.28 g., 0.925 Silver 0.841 oz. ASW, 38.61 mm. **Ruler:** Elizabeth II **Subject:** Century of Monarchy **Obv:** Head with tiara right **Rev:** Portraits of past five sovereigns **Edge:** Reeded

Date	Mintage	VF20	XF40	MS60	MS63	MS65
2000	10,000	PF63 22.00	PF65 25.00	PF67 28.00		

KM# 102b 5 POUNDS
39.94 g., 0.9166 Gold 1.177 oz. AGW, 38.61 mm. **Ruler:** Elizabeth II **Subject:** Century of Monarchy **Obv:** Head with tiara right **Rev:** Portraits of past five sovereigns **Edge:** Reeded

Date	Mintage	VF20	XF40	MS60	MS63	MS65
2000 Proof	200	—	—	—	—	—

KM# 120b 5 POUNDS
39.94 g., 0.917 Gold 1.1775 oz. AGW, 38.61 mm. **Ruler:** Elizabeth II **Subject:** 20th Century Monarchy **Obv:** Head with tiara right **Rev:** Portraits of past five sovereigns **Edge:** Reeded

Date	Mintage	VF20	XF40	MS60	MS63	MS65
2000	200	PF65 2,100	PF67 2,300			

KM# 57 10 POUNDS
3.13 g., 0.999 Gold 0.1005 oz. AGW **Ruler:** Elizabeth II **Subject:** 50th Anniversary - Normandy Invasion **Rev:** Soldiers and tank

Date	Mintage	VF20	XF40	MS60	MS63	MS65
ND-1994	—	PF65 160	PF67 175			

KM# 62 10 POUNDS
3.13 g., 0.999 Gold 0.1005 oz. AGW **Ruler:** Elizabeth II **Subject:** 50th Anniversary of Liberation **Rev:** Uniformed figure giving speech

Date	Mintage	VF20	XF40	MS60	MS63	MS65
ND-1995	Est. 500	PF65 160	PF67 175			

KM# 157 10 POUNDS
163.20 g., 0.925 Silver 4.8535 oz. ASW with Gold insert, 64.9 mm. **Ruler:** Elizabeth II **Subject:** Queen's Golden Wedding Anniversary **Obv:** Crowned head right **Rev:** Elizabeth and Philip, gold insert shield and cathedral **Edge:** Reeded **Note:** Illustration reduced.

Date	Mintage	VF20	XF40	MS60	MS63	MS65
1997	—	PF65 150	PF67 200			

KM# 171 10 POUNDS
155.52 g., 0.925 Silver 4.625 oz. ASW, 65 mm. **Ruler:** Elizabeth II **Subject:** Queen Mother Elizabeth **Edge:** Reeded

Date	Mintage	VF20	XF40	MS60	MS63	MS65
1998	—	PF65 95.00	PF67 125			

KM# 104 10 POUNDS
141.75 g., 0.999 Silver 4.5528 oz. ASW, 65 mm. **Ruler:** Elizabeth II **Subject:** Century of Monarchy **Obv:** Head with tiara right **Rev:** Portraits of past five sovereigns **Edge:** Reeded

Date	Mintage	VF20	XF40	MS60	MS63	MS65
2000	950	PF65 100	PF67 135			

KM# 138 10 POUNDS
13.66 g., 0.999 Gold 0.4387 oz. AGW, 19.35 mm. **Ruler:** Elizabeth II **Subject:** Millennium **Obv:** Head with tiara right **Rev:** Hands holding planet **Edge:** Reeded

Date	Mintage	VF20	XF40	MS60	MS63	MS65
2000	7,500	—	—	—	—	750

KM# 58 25 POUNDS
7.81 g., 0.999 Gold 0.2508 oz. AGW **Ruler:** Elizabeth II **Subject:** 50th Anniversary - Normandy Invasion **Rev:** Uniformed figure standing at right, invasion scene in background

Date	Mintage	VF20	XF40	MS60	MS63	MS65
ND-1994	Est. 500	—	—	—	—	440
ND-1994	Est. 500	PF65 420	PF67 450			

KM# 63 25 POUNDS
7.81 g., 0.999 Gold 0.2508 oz. AGW **Ruler:** Elizabeth II **Subject:** 50th Anniversary of Liberation **Obv:** Crowned head right, small arms at left **Rev:** Supply worker and ship

Date	Mintage	VF20	XF40	MS60	MS63	MS65
ND-1995	Est. 500	PF65 420	PF67 450			

KM# 69 25 POUNDS
7.81 g., 0.999 Gold 0.2508 oz. AGW **Ruler:** Elizabeth II **Subject:** European Football **Rev:** Soccer ball and European map

Date	Mintage	VF20	XF40	MS60	MS63	MS65
1996	1,500	PF65 400	PF67 440			

KM# 113 25 POUNDS
7.81 g., 0.999 Gold 0.251 oz. AGW, 22 mm. **Ruler:** Elizabeth II **Subject:** Elizabeth II, 70th Birthday **Obv:** Crowned head right **Rev:** Bust at left, fortress at right

Date	Mintage	VF20	XF40	MS60	MS63	MS65
1996	Est. 2500	PF65 425	PF67 500			

KM# 72 25 POUNDS
7.81 g., 0.999 Gold 0.2508 oz. AGW **Ruler:** Elizabeth II **Subject:** Queen Elizabeth II's Golden Wedding Anniversary **Obv:** Crowned head right **Rev:** Queen Elizabeth II and Prince Philip, monogrammed shield and Westminster Abbey

Date	Mintage	VF20	XF40	MS60	MS63	MS65
1997	Est. 5000	PF65 420	PF67 450			

KM# 85 25 POUNDS
7.81 g., 0.999 Gold 0.2508 oz. AGW **Ruler:** Elizabeth II **Subject:** 80th Anniversary - Royal Air Force **Obv:** Head with tiara right **Rev:** Three Spitfires and RAF Benevolent Fund Crest

Date	Mintage	VF20	XF40	MS60	MS63	MS65
1998	Est. 2500	PF65 400	PF67 435			

KM# 132 25 POUNDS
7.81 g., 0.999 Gold 0.2508 oz. AGW, 22 mm. **Ruler:** Elizabeth II **Subject:** Winston Churchill **Obv:** Head with tiara right **Rev:** Head right **Edge:** Reeded

Date	Mintage	VF20	XF40	MS60	MS63	MS65
1999	2,500	PF65 400	PF67 435			

KM# 135 25 POUNDS
7.81 g., 0.999 Gold 0.2508 oz. AGW, 22 mm. **Ruler:** Elizabeth II **Subject:** Queen Mother **Obv:** Head with tiara right **Rev:** Queen Mother's portrait **Edge:** Reeded

Date	Mintage	VF20	XF40	MS60	MS63	MS65
1999	5,000	PF65 400	PF67 435			

KM# 137 25 POUNDS
7.81 g., 0.999 Gold 0.2508 oz. AGW, 22 mm. **Ruler:** Elizabeth II **Subject:** Prince Edward's Marriage **Obv:** Head with tiara right **Rev:** Jugate heads left of Edward and Sophie left **Edge:** Reeded

Date	Mintage	VF20	XF40	MS60	MS63	MS65
1999	5,000	PF65 400	PF67 435			

KM# 103 25 POUNDS
7.81 g., 0.917 Gold 0.2303 oz. AGW, 22 mm. **Ruler:** Elizabeth II **Subject:** Queen Mother's 100th Birthday **Obv:** Head with tiara right **Rev:** Queen Mother's portrait **Edge:** Reeded

Date	Mintage	VF20	XF40	MS60	MS63	MS65
2000	5,000	PF65 375	PF67 400			

KM# 59 50 POUNDS
15.61 g., 0.999 Gold 0.5014 oz. AGW **Ruler:** Elizabeth II **Subject:** 50th Anniversary - Normandy Invasion **Rev:** Paratroopers

Date	Mintage	VF20	XF40	MS60	MS63	MS65
ND-1994	—	PF65 750	PF67 800			

KM# 64 50 POUNDS
15.61 g., 0.999 Gold 0.5014 oz. AGW **Ruler:** Elizabeth II **Subject:** 50th Anniversary of Liberation **Rev:** Uniformed figure signing document, ship in background

Date	Mintage	VF20	XF40	MS60	MS63	MS65
ND-1995	—	PF65 750	PF67 800			

KM# 118 50 POUNDS
15.61 g., 0.999 Gold 0.5013 oz. AGW, 26.5 mm. **Ruler:** Elizabeth II **Subject:** Queen Mother, 98th Birthday

Date	Mintage	VF20	XF40	MS60	MS63	MS65
1998	—	PF65 1,000	PF67 1,100			

KM# 136 50 POUNDS
15.55 g., 0.999 Gold 0.4995 oz. AGW, 27 mm. **Ruler:** Elizabeth II **Subject:** Queen Mother **Obv:** Head with tiara right **Rev:** Queen Mother's portrait **Edge:** Reeded

Date	Mintage	VF20	XF40	MS60	MS63	MS65
1999	1,250	PF65 725	PF67 775			

KM# 60 100 POUNDS
31.21 g., 0.999 Gold 1.0024 oz. AGW **Ruler:** Elizabeth II **Subject:** 50th Anniversary - Normandy Invasion **Obv:** Crowned head right, small arms at left **Rev:** Cameo portrait of Winston Churchill above invasion scene

Date	Mintage	VF20	XF40	MS60	MS63	MS65
ND-1994	Est. 500	PF65 1,600	PF67 1,700			

KM# 65 100 POUNDS
31.21 g., 0.999 Gold 1.0024 oz. AGW **Ruler:** Elizabeth II **Subject:** 50th Anniversary of Liberation **Rev:** Soldiers and ship

Date	Mintage	VF20	XF40	MS60	MS63	MS65
ND-1995	—	PF65 1,600	PF67 1,700			

PIEDFORT

KM#	Date	Mintage	Identification	Mkt Val
P1	1981	500	Pound. KM#37a.	275
P2	2000	10,000	50 Pence. 0.925. Silver. KM#105a.	75.00

MINT SETS

KM#	Date	Mintage	Identification	Issue Price	Mkt Val
MS1	1985 (8)	10,000	KM40-41, 42.1, 43-47	8.75	19.00
MS2	1985 (7)	—	KM40-41, 42.1, 43-46	—	12.00
MS3	1986 (7)	5,000	KM40-46	8.75	12.00
MS4	1987 (7)	7,500	KM40-46	11.00	12.00
MS5	1988 (7)	5,000	KM40-46	13.00	12.00
MS6	1989 (7)	5,000	KM40-46	17.00	12.00
MS7	1990 (8)	2,520	KM40-41, 42.1-42.2, 43-46	16.00	13.00
MS8	1992 (4)	1,500	KM40-41, 42.2, 43-46	22.50	25.00
MS9	1997 (9)	—	KM 40a, 41a, 42.2, 43.2, 44, 45.2, 46, 88	—	30.00

PROOF SETS

KM#	Date	Mintage	Identification	Issue Price	Mkt Val
PS3	1902H (3)	—	KM5, 7-8, 10	—	800
PS4	1910H (2)	—	KM5, 7	—	500
PS5	1956 (3)	1,050	KM15-17 double set	—	24.00
PS6	1966 (4)	10,000	KM15-16, 18, 19	—	11.00
PS7	1971 (6)	10,000	KM20-25	16.00	10.00
PS8	1979 (6)	4,963	KM27-30, 33-34	25.00	11.50
PS9	1981 (6)	10,000	KM27-30, 34, 37	29.00	21.00
PS10	1985 (8)	2,500	KM40-47	29.75	80.00
PS11	1986 (8)	2,500	KM40-46, 48	35.00	37.50
PS12	1987 (8)	2,500	KM40-46, 49	33.00	33.00
PS13	1988 (8)	2,500	KM40-46, 50	45.00	33.00
PS14	1989 (8)	2,500	KM40-46, 51	45.00	33.00
PS15	1990 (8)	700	KM40-41, 42.1-42.2, 43-46	46.00	47.50
PS16	1992 (7)	500	KM40-41, 42.2, 43.2, 44-46	52.50	55.00
PS17	1994 (4)	500	KM57-60	1,595	2,750
PS18	ND (1995) (4)	500	KM62-65	1,600	2,750
PS19	1996 (2)	1,500	KM68a, 69	—	430
PS20	1997 (3)	—	KM70, 71a, 72	—	475
PS21	1997 (4)	—	KM73, 74a, 75-76	181	220
PS22	1997 (9)	—	KM#40a, 41a, 42.2, 43.2, 44, 45.1, 45.2, 46, 88	—	65.00

GUINEA

The Republic of Guinea, situated on the Atlantic Coast of Africa between Sierra Leone and Guinea-Bissau, has an area of 94,964 sq. mi. (245,860 sq. km.) and a population of 6.4 million. Capital: Conakry. Although Guinea contains one-third of the world's reserves of bauxite and significant deposits of iron ore, gold and diamonds, the economy is still dependent on agriculture, aluminum, bananas, copra and coffee are exported.

The coast of Guinea was known to Portuguese navigators of the 15th century but was seldom visited by European traders of the 16th-18th centuries because of its dangerous coastal waters. French penetration of the area began in the mid-19th century with the entering into of protectorate treaties with several of the coastal chiefs. After a long struggle with Guinea's native leader Samory Toure, France secured the area and until 1890 administered it as a part of Senegal. In 1895 the colony (Guinee Francais) became an autonomous part of the federation of French West Africa. The inhabitants were extended French citizenship in 1946 when the colony became an overseas territory of the French Union. Guinea became an independent republic on Oct. 2, 1958, when it declined to enter the new French Community.

MONETARY SYSTEM
100 Centimes = 1 Franc

REPUBLIC

DECIMAL COINAGE

KM# 4 FRANC
Copper-Nickel **Obv:** Head of Ahmed Sekou Toure left **Rev:** Feathers flank denomination within wreath

Date	Mintage	F12	VF20	XF40	MS60	MS63
1962	—	1.25	2.00	3.50	7.00	15.00
1962	—	PF63 50.00				

KM# 1 5 FRANCS
Aluminum-Bronze **Obv:** Head of Ahmed Sekou Toure right **Rev:** Palm trees flank denomination

Date	Mintage	F12	VF20	XF40	MS60	MS63
1959	—	2.75	4.75	12.00	22.50	50.00

KM# 5 5 FRANCS
Copper-Nickel, 20 mm. **Obv:** Head right **Rev:** Denomination within wreath, coconuts below **Note:** Mules with two obverses exist.

Date	Mintage	F12	VF20	XF40	MS60	MS63
1962	—	1.25	2.00	3.00	6.50	12.50
1962	—	PF63 70.00				

KM# 2 10 FRANCS
Aluminum-Bronze **Obv:** Head of Ahmed Sekou Toure left **Rev:** Denomination above spray

Date	Mintage	F12	VF20	XF40	MS60	MS63
1959	—	5.00	20.00	50.00	90.00	150

KM# 6 10 FRANCS
Copper-Nickel, 22 mm. **Obv:** Head of Ahmed Sekou Toure left **Rev:** Denomination within wreath

Date	Mintage	F12	VF20	XF40	MS60	MS63
1962	—	1.75	2.75	6.00	12.00	25.00
1962	—	PF63 85.00				

KM# 3 25 FRANCS
Aluminum-Bronze **Obv:** Head of Ahmed Sekou Toure right **Rev:** Palm trees flank denomination

Date	Mintage	F12	VF20	XF40	MS60	MS63
1959	—	10.00	50.00	110	200	275

KM# 7 25 FRANCS
Copper-Nickel **Obv:** Head of Ahmed Sekou Toure right **Rev:** Denomination within wreath

Date	Mintage	F12	VF20	XF40	MS60	MS63
1962	—	2.50	4.00	7.50	15.00	30.00
1962	—	PF63 120				

KM# 8 50 FRANCS
Copper-Nickel **Obv:** Head of Ahmed Sekou Toure left **Rev:** Denomination within wreath **Note:** Not released into circulation.

Date	Mintage	VF20	XF40	MS60	MS63	MS65
1969	4,000	—	20.00	35.00	55.00	95.00

KM# 9 100 FRANCS
5.65 g., 0.999 Silver 0.1815 oz. ASW **Series:** 10th Anniversary of Independence **Subject:** Martin Luther King **Obv:** Head right **Rev:** National arms and "1000" in an oval c/m at 4 oclock

Date	Mintage	VF20	XF40	MS60	MS63	MS65
1969	9,700	PF65 7.00	PF67 10.00			
1970	Inc. above	PF65 12.00	PF67 15.00			

KM# 9.1 100 FRANCS
5.65 g., 0.999 Silver 0.1815 oz. ASW, 21 mm. **Subject:** Martin Luther King **Obv:** Head right **Rev:** National arms "1000" in oval c/m at 4 oclock and "1 AR" in oval c/m at 8 oclock **Edge:** Reeded

Date	Mintage	VF20	XF40	MS60	MS63	MS65
1970	—	PF65 9.00	PF67 12.00			

KM# 9.2 100 FRANCS
5.65 g., 0.999 Silver 0.1815 oz. ASW, 21 mm. **Subject:** Martin Luther King **Obv:** Head right **Rev:** National arms and "999.9" in oval c/m at 4 oclock **Edge:** Reeded

Date	Mintage	VF20	XF40	MS60	MS63	MS65
1970	—	PF65 9.00	PF67 12.00			

KM# 41 100 FRANCS
Copper-Nickel **Obv:** Head of Ahmed Sekou Toure right **Rev:** Denomination within wreath **Note:** Not released into circulation.

Date	Mintage	VF20	XF40	MS60	MS63	MS65
1971	2,585,000	—	15.00	25.00	55.00	95.00

KM# 10 200 FRANCS
11.70 g., 0.999 Silver 0.3758 oz. ASW **Series:** 10th Anniversary of Independence **Subject:** John and Robert Kennedy **Obv:** Conjoined heads right **Rev:** National arms

Date	Mintage	VF20	XF40	MS60	MS63	MS65
1969	10,000	PF65 15.00	PF67 25.00			
1970	Inc. above	PF65 26.00	PF67 37.00			

KM# 11 200 FRANCS
11.70 g., 0.999 Silver 0.3758 oz. ASW **Series:** 10th Anniversary of Independence **Subject:** Almamy Samory Toure **Obv:** Bust facing divides dates **Rev:** National arms

Date	Mintage	VF20	XF40	MS60	MS63	MS65
1969	6,100	PF65 20.00	PF67 30.00			
1970	Inc. above	PF65 32.00	PF67 45.00			

KM# 12 250 FRANCS
14.53 g., 0.999 Silver 0.4667 oz. ASW, 36 mm. **Series:** 10th Anniversary of Independence **Subject:** Lunar Landing **Obv:** Earth and Moon and orbital paths, astronaut and lunar module **Rev:** National arms

Date	Mintage	VF20	XF40	MS60	MS63	MS65
1969	26,000	PF65 17.50	PF67 27.50			
1970	Inc. above	PF65 28.50	PF67 40.00			

KM# 13 250 FRANCS
14.53 g., 0.999 Silver 0.4667 oz. ASW, 36 mm. **Series:** 10th Anniversary of Independence **Subject:** Alpha Yaya Diallo **Obv:** Bust with spear facing **Rev:** National arms

Date	Mintage	VF20	XF40	MS60	MS63	MS65
1969	6,100	PF65 30.00	PF67 40.00			
1970	Inc. above	PF65 45.00	PF67 55.00			

KM# 14 250 FRANCS
14.53 g., 0.999 Silver 0.4667 oz. ASW, 36 mm. **Series:** 10th Anniversary of Independence **Subject:** Apollo XIII **Obv:** Three charging horses symbolize the spacecraft's path from Earth to Moon; Sun in background. **Rev:** National arms

Date	Mintage	VF20	XF40	MS60	MS63	MS65
1969	4,450	PF65 27.50	PF67 37.50			
1970	Inc. above	PF65 27.50	PF67 37.50			

KM# 21 250 FRANCS
14.53 g., 0.999 Silver 0.4667 oz. ASW **Series:** 10th Anniversary of Independence **Subject:** Spacecraft Soyuz **Obv:** Spacecraft in flight **Rev:** National arms

Date	Mintage	VF20	XF40	MS60	MS63	MS65
1970	3,500	PF65 32.00	PF67 42.00			

KM# 15 500 FRANCS
29.08 g., 0.999 Silver 0.934 oz. ASW, 42 mm. **Series:** 10th Anniversary of Independence **Subject:** Munich Olympics **Obv:** Medals of the Olympics in Helsinki 1952; Melbourne 1956; Rome 1968; Tokyo 1964; Mexico City 1968 **Rev:** National arms

Date	Mintage	VF20	XF40	MS60	MS63	MS65
1969	7,200	PF65 35.00	PF67 45.00			
1970	1,900	PF65 65.00	PF67 80.00			

KM# 16 500 FRANCS
29.08 g., 0.999 Silver 0.934 oz. ASW, 42 mm. **Series:** 10th Anniversary of Independence **Subject:** Oiseaux Dancers **Obv:** Dancers and hut **Rev:** National arms

Date	Mintage	VF20	XF40	MS60	MS63	MS65
1969	7,150	PF65 40.00	PF67 50.00			
1970	—	PF65 70.00	PF67 85.00			

KM# 22 500 FRANCS
29.08 g., 0.999 Silver 0.934 oz. ASW, 42 mm. **Series:** 10th Anniversary of Independence **Subject:** Ikhnaton **Obv:** Head 3/4 facing **Rev:** National arms

Date	Mintage	VF20	XF40	MS60	MS63	MS65
1970	4,180	PF65 31.50	PF67 35.50			

KM# 23 500 FRANCS
29.08 g., 0.999 Silver 0.934 oz. ASW, 42 mm. **Series:** 10th Anniversary of Independence **Subject:** Chephren **Obv:** Head with parrot right **Rev:** National arms

Date	Mintage	VF20	XF40	MS60	MS63	MS65
1970	4,600	PF65 31.50	PF67 35.50			

KM# 24 500 FRANCS
29.08 g., 0.999 Silver 0.934 oz. ASW, 42 mm. **Series:** 10th Anniversary of Independence **Subject:** Cleopatra **Obv:** Head left **Rev:** National arms

Date	Mintage	VF20	XF40	MS60	MS63	MS65
1970	5,250	PF65 33.50	PF67 38.50			

KM# 25 500 FRANCS
29.08 g., 0.999 Silver 0.934 oz. ASW, 42 mm. **Series:** 10th Anniversary of Independence **Subject:** Nefertiti, 1372-1350BC **Obv:** Head left **Rev:** National arms

Date	Mintage	VF20	XF40	MS60	MS63	MS65
1970	4,610	PF65 33.50	PF67 38.50			

KM# 26 500 FRANCS
29.08 g., 0.999 Silver 0.934 oz. ASW, 42 mm. **Series:** 10th Anniversary of Independence **Subject:** Ramses III **Obv:** Head right **Rev:** National arms

Date	Mintage	VF20	XF40	MS60	MS63	MS65
1970	4,330	PF65 33.50	PF67 38.50			

KM# 27 500 FRANCS
29.08 g., 0.999 Silver 0.934 oz. ASW, 42 mm. **Series:** 10th Anniversary of Independence **Subject:** Tutankhamen **Obv:** Bust facing **Rev:** National arms

Date	Mintage	VF20	XF40	MS60	MS63	MS65
1970	4,280	PF65 36.50	PF67 41.50			

KM# 28 500 FRANCS
29.08 g., 0.999 Silver 0.934 oz. ASW, 42 mm. **Series:** 10th Anniversary of Independence **Subject:** Queen Teyi, mother of Pharoah Amenophis IV (Ichnation), reigned 1352-1336BC **Obv:** Head right **Rev:** National arms

Date	Mintage	VF20	XF40	MS60	MS63	MS65
1970	4,120	PF65 31.50	PF67 35.50			

KM# 29 500 FRANCS
29.08 g., 0.999 Silver 0.934 oz. ASW, 42 mm. **Series:** 10th Anniversary of Independence **Subject:** Gamal Abdel Nasser **Obv:** Head right **Rev:** National arms

Date	Mintage	VF20	XF40	MS60	MS63	MS65
1970	950	PF65 145	PF67 165			

KM# 17 1000 FRANCS
4.00 g., 0.900 Gold 0.1157 oz. AGW **Series:** 10th Anniversary of Independence **Subject:** John and Robert Kennedy **Obv:** Jugate heads right **Rev:** National arms

Date	Mintage	VF20	XF40	MS60	MS63	MS65
1969	6,600	PF65 175	PF67 200			
1970	Inc. above	PF65 175	PF67 200			

KM# 18 2000 FRANCS
8.00 g., 0.900 Gold 0.2315 oz. AGW **Series:** 10th Anniversary of Independence **Subject:** Lunar Landing **Obv:** Planets bound together, space shuttle and astronaut **Rev:** National arms

Date	Mintage	VF20	XF40	MS60	MS63	MS65
1969	15,000	PF65 320	PF67 370			

KM# 30 2000 FRANCS
8.00 g., 0.900 Gold 0.2315 oz. AGW **Series:** 10th Anniversary of Independence **Subject:** Apollo XIII **Obv:** Radiant planet back of three charging horses **Rev:** National arms

Date	Mintage	VF20	XF40	MS60	MS63	MS65
1970	1,775	PF65 335	PF67 385			

KM# 31 2000 FRANCS
8.00 g., 0.900 Gold 0.2315 oz. AGW **Series:** 10th Anniversary of Independence **Subject:** Spacecraft Soyuz **Obv:** Spacecraft in flight **Rev:** National arms

Date	Mintage	VF20	XF40	MS60	MS63	MS65
1970	2,840	PF65 325	PF67 375			

KM# 32 5000 FRANCS
20.00 g., 0.900 Gold 0.5787 oz. AGW **Series:** 10th Anniversary of Independence **Subject:** Munich Olympics **Obv:** Medals of the Olympics in Helsinki 1952; Melbourne 1956; Rome 1968; Tokyo 1964; Mexico City 1968 **Rev:** National arms

Date	Mintage	VF20	XF40	MS60	MS63	MS65
1969	2,740	PF65 900	PF67 1,000			
1970	500	PF65 1,000	PF67 1,150			

KM# 19 5000 FRANCS
20.00 g., 0.900 Gold 0.5787 oz. AGW **Series:** 10th Anniversary of Independence **Subject:** Gamel Abdel Nasser **Obv:** Head right **Rev:** National arms

Date	Mintage	VF20	XF40	MS60	MS63	MS65
1970	4,000	PF65 650	PF67 1,100			

KM# 33 5000 FRANCS
20.00 g., 0.900 Gold 0.5787 oz. AGW **Series:** 10th Anniversary of Independence **Subject:** Ikhnaton **Obv:** Head 3/4 facing **Rev:** National arms

Date	Mintage	VF20	XF40	MS60	MS63	MS65
1970	685	PF65 925	PF67 975			

KM# 34 5000 FRANCS
20.00 g., 0.900 Gold 0.5787 oz. AGW **Series:** 10th Anniversary of Independence **Subject:** Chephren **Obv:** Head with parrot right **Rev:** National arms

Date	Mintage	VF20	XF40	MS60	MS63	MS65
1970	675	PF65 925	PF67 975			

KM# 35 5000 FRANCS
20.00 g., 0.900 Gold 0.5787 oz. AGW **Series:** 10th Anniversary of Independence **Subject:** Cleopatra **Obv:** Head left **Rev:** National arms

Date	Mintage	VF20	XF40	MS60	MS63	MS65
1970	789	PF65 900	PF67 950			

KM# 36 5000 FRANCS
20.00 g., 0.900 Gold 0.5787 oz. AGW **Series:** 10th Anniversary of Independence **Subject:** Queen Nefertiti, 1372-1350BC **Obv:** Head left **Rev:** National arms

Date	Mintage	VF20	XF40	MS60	MS63	MS65
1970	774	PF65 900	PF67 950			

KM# 37 5000 FRANCS
20.00 g., 0.900 Gold 0.5787 oz. AGW **Series:** 10th Anniversary of Independence **Subject:** Ramses III **Obv:** Head right **Rev:** National arms

Date	Mintage	VF20	XF40	MS60	MS63	MS65
1970	695	PF65 925	PF67 975			

KM# 38 5000 FRANCS
20.00 g., 0.900 Gold 0.5787 oz. AGW **Series:** 10th Anniversary of Independence **Subject:** Tutankhamen **Obv:** Bust facing **Rev:** National arms

Date	Mintage	VF20	XF40	MS60	MS63	MS65
1970	675	PF65 925	PF67 975			

KM# 39 5000 FRANCS
20.00 g., 0.900 Gold 0.5787 oz. AGW **Series:** 10th Anniversary of Independence **Subject:** Queen Teyi, mother of Pharoah Amenophis IV (Ichnaton), reigned 1352-1336BC **Obv:** Head right **Rev:** National arms

Date	Mintage	VF20	XF40	MS60	MS63	MS65
1970	685	PF65 925	PF67 975			

KM# 20 10000 FRANCS
40.00 g., 0.900 Gold 1.1574 oz. AGW **Series:** 10th Anniversary of Independence **Subject:** Ahmed Sekou Toure **Obv:** Head left **Rev:** National arms

Date	Mintage	VF20	XF40	MS60	MS63	MS65
1969	2,300	PF65 1,650	PF67 1,850			
1970	—	PF65 1,700	PF67 1,950			

DECIMAL COINAGE

100 Cauris = 1 Syli

KM# 42 50 CAURIS
Aluminum **Obv:** Cowrie shell **Rev:** Denomination within wreath **Note:** Nkrumah

Date	Mintage	VF20	XF40	MS60	MS63	MS65
1971	—	2.00	3.00	4.00	6.00	8.00

KM# 43 SYLI
Aluminum **Obv:** Bust facing **Rev:** Denomination within wreath

Date	Mintage	VF20	XF40	MS60	MS63	MS65
1971	—	3.00	5.00	7.00	11.00	13.50

KM# 44 2 SYLIS
Aluminum **Obv:** Head left **Rev:** Denomination within wreath

Date	Mintage	VF20	XF40	MS60	MS63	MS65
1971	—	2.00	3.00	5.00	8.00	10.00

KM# 45 5 SYLIS
2.27 g., Aluminum **Obv:** Head left **Rev:** Denomination within wreath

Date	Mintage	VF20	XF40	MS60	MS63	MS65
1971	—	2.25	4.50	6.00	10.00	12.50

KM# 46 500 SYLI
40.00 g., 0.925 Silver 1.1896 oz. ASW **Subject:** Miriam Makeba, South African singer in exile **Obv:** Bust right divides people at lower right and left **Rev:** National arms

Date	Mintage	VF20	XF40	MS60	MS63	MS65
1977	500	—	—	—	125	175
1977	500	PF63 200	PF65 250			

KM# 47 500 SYLI
40.00 g., 0.925 Silver 1.1896 oz. ASW **Subject:** Patrice Lumumba **Obv:** Bust facing **Rev:** National arms

Date	Mintage	VF20	XF40	MS60	MS63	MS65
1977	250	—	—	—	175	250
1977	150	PF63 225	PF65 275			

KM# 48 1000 SYLI
2.93 g., 0.900 Gold 0.0848 oz. AGW **Subject:** Miriam Makeba, South African singer in exile **Obv:** Bust right divides people at lower right and left **Rev:** National arms

Date	Mintage	VF20	XF40	MS60	MS63	MS65
1977	300	—	—	—	—	165
1977	250	PF65 185				

KM# 49 1000 SYLI
2.93 g., 0.900 Gold 0.0848 oz. AGW **Subject:** Nkrumah **Obv:** Bust right **Rev:** National arms

Date	Mintage	VF20	XF40	MS60	MS63	MS65
1977	150	—	—	—	—	185
1977	150	PF65 195				

KM# 50 2000 SYLI
5.87 g., 0.900 Gold 0.1699 oz. AGW **Subject:** Mao Tse Tung **Obv:** Bust facing **Rev:** National arms

Date	Mintage	VF20	XF40	MS60	MS63	MS65
1977	200	—	—	—	—	325
1977	200	PF65 350				

KM# 51 2000 SYLI
5.87 g., 0.900 Gold 0.1699 oz. AGW **Subject:** Ahmen Sekou Toure **Obv:** Bust left **Rev:** National arms

Date	Mintage	VF20	XF40	MS60	MS63	MS65
1977	100	—	—	—	—	340
1977	50	PF65 385				

REFORM COINAGE

KM# 56 FRANC
1.44 g., Brass Clad Steel, 15.50 mm. **Obv:** Shield with rifle and sword crossed on branch held by bird above **Rev:** Palm branch right of denomination **Edge:** Plain

Date	Mintage	VF20	XF40	MS60	MS63	MS65
1985	—	0.20	0.35	0.60	1.00	1.25

KM# 53 5 FRANCS
2.00 g., Brass Clad Steel, 17.5 mm. **Obv:** Shield with rifle and sword crossed on branch held by bird above **Rev:** Palm branch right of denomination

Date	Mintage	VF20	XF40	MS60	MS63	MS65
1985	—	0.20	0.35	0.60	1.00	1.25

KM# 52 10 FRANCS
2.95 g., Brass Clad Steel, 20.4 mm. **Obv:** Shield with rifle and sword crossed on branch held by bird above **Rev:** Palm branch right of denomination

Date	Mintage	VF20	XF40	MS60	MS63	MS65
1985	—	0.35	0.60	0.80	1.25	1.50

KM# 60 25 FRANCS
4.95 g., Brass, 22.5 mm. **Obv:** Shield with rifle and sword crossed on branch held by bird above **Rev:** Palm branch right of denomination

Date	Mintage	VF20	XF40	MS60	MS63	MS65
1987	—	0.35	0.75	1.00	1.75	2.00

KM# 63 50 FRANCS
Copper-Nickel **Obv:** Without sword and rifle **Rev:** Leaves right of denomination

Date	Mintage	VF20	XF40	MS60	MS63	MS65
1994	—	0.60	1.25	2.00	2.75	3.00

KM# 57 100 FRANCS
16.00 g., 0.999 Silver 0.5139 oz. ASW **Subject:** 1992 Olympics **Obv:** Shield with rifle and sword crossed on branch held by bird above **Rev:** Discus thrower, lady with parasol and shield at left

Date	Mintage	VF20	XF40	MS60	MS63	MS65
1988 Matte	Est. 5000	—	—	—	20.00	35.00

KM# 58 200 FRANCS
16.00 g., 0.999 Silver 0.5139 oz. ASW **Subject:** 1992 Olympics **Obv:** Shield with rifle and sword crossed on branch held by bird above **Rev:** Basketball players, lady with parasol and shield at left

Date	Mintage	VF20	XF40	MS60	MS63	MS65
1988 Matte	Est. 5000	—	—	—	22.00	40.00

KM# 59 300 FRANCS
16.00 g., 0.999 Silver 0.5139 oz. ASW **Subject:** 1992 Olympics **Obv:** Shield with rifle and sword crossed on branch held by bird above **Rev:** Stadium, lady with parasol and shield above

Date	Mintage	VF20	XF40	MS60	MS63	MS65
1988 Matte	Est. 5000	—	—	—	25.00	45.00

KM# 61 10000 FRANCS
25.00 g., 0.999 Silver 0.803 oz. ASW **Subject:** 30th Anniversary of Currency **Obv:** Shield with rifle and sword crossed on branch held by bird above **Rev:** Palm branch and denomination

Date	Mintage	VF20	XF40	MS60	MS63	MS65
ND-1990	1,000	PF63 75.00	PF65 95.00	PF67 120		

KM# 62 10000 FRANCS
15.98 g., 0.917 Gold 0.471 oz. AGW **Subject:** 30th Anniversary of Currency **Obv:** Arms with dates on each side **Rev:** Palm branches and denomination

Date	Mintage	VF20	XF40	MS60	MS63	MS65
1990	Est. 200	PF65 850	PF67 900			

KM# 64 20000 FRANCS
31.47 g., 0.925 Silver 0.9359 oz. ASW **Subject:** 35th Anniversary of Guinea Franc **Obv:** Without sword and rifle **Rev:** Woman planting palm tree

Date	Mintage	VF20	XF40	MS60	MS63	MS65
ND-1995	Est. 5000	PF63 35.00	PF65 50.00	PF67 70.00		

TRIAL STRIKES

KM#	Date	Mintage	Identification	Mkt Val
TS1	ND-1969	—	100 Francs. KM#9.	55.00
TS2	ND-1969	—	200 Francs. KM#11.	55.00
TS3	ND-1969	—	250 Francs. KM#13.	60.00
TS4	ND-1969	—	500 Francs. KM#16.	70.00
TS5	ND-1969	—	1000 Francs. Goldine. Jugate heads right.	110

MINT SETS

KM#	Date	Mintage	Identification	Issue Price	Mkt Val
MS1	1977 (6)	—	KM46-51	—	1,050
MS2	1988 (3)	5,000	KM57-59	150	260

PROOF SETS

KM#	Date	Mintage	Identification	Issue Price	Mkt Val
PS1	1969 (7)	5,000	KM#9-13, 15-16	62.50	175
PS2	1969 (8)	—	KM9, 11, 13, 16-18, 20, 32	—	4,000
PS3	1969 (4)	—	KM#17-20	—	3,850
PS4	1969 (4)	4,000	KM#17, 18, 20, 32	223	3,850
PS7	1970 (3)	900	KM12, 14, 21	30.00	120
PS8	1970 (7)	300	KM#9-13, 15-16	62.50	375
PS9	1970 (7)	750	KM#22-28	201	315
PS10	1970 (7)	—	KM#33-39	440	8,000
PS11	1970 (10)	—	KM#9-16, 21, 29	220	575
PS12	1970 (14)	—	KM#22-28, 33-39	1,650	8,350

GUINEA-BISSAU

The Republic of Guinea-Bissau, formerly Portuguese Guinea, an overseas province on the west coast of Africa between Senegal and Guinea, has an area of 13,948 sq. mi. (36,120 sq. km.) and a population of 1.1 million. Capital: Bissau. The country has undeveloped deposits of oil and bauxite. Peanuts, oil-palm kernels and hides are exported.

Portuguese Guinea was discovered by Portuguese navigator, Nuno Tristao, in 1446. Trading rights in the area were granted to Cape Verde islanders but few prominent posts were established before 1851, and they were principally coastal installations. The chief export of this colony's early period was slaves for South America, a practice that adversely affected trade with the native people and retarded subjection of the interior. Territorial disputes with France delayed final demarcation of the colony's frontiers until 1905.

The African Party for the Independence of Guinea-Bissau was founded in 1956, and several years later began a guerrilla warfare that grew in effectiveness until 1974,when the rebels controlled most of the colony. Portugal's costly overseas wars in her African territories resulted in a military coup in Portugal in April 1974, which appreciably brightened the prospects for freedom for Guinea-Bissau. In August 1974, the Lisbon government signed an agreement granting independence to Portuguese Guinea effective Sept. 10, 1974. The new republic took the name of Guinea-Bissau.

RULER
Portuguese until 1974

PORTUGUESE GUINEA

DECIMAL COINAGE

KM# 1 5 CENTAVOS
Bronze **Obv:** Denomination above date **Rev:** Liberty head left

Date	Mintage	VF20	XF40	MS60	MS63	MS65
1933	100,000	25.00	45.00	85.00	150	200

KM# 2 10 CENTAVOS
Bronze **Obv:** Denomination above date **Rev:** Liberty head left

Date	Mintage	VF20	XF40	MS60	MS63	MS65
1933	250,000	28.00	85.00	500	1,000	—

KM# 12 10 CENTAVOS
Aluminum **Obv:** Denomination above date **Rev:** Divided shield with crowned towers and small shields above on lined circle

Date	Mintage	VF20	XF40	MS60	MS63	MS65
1973	100,000	3.00	6.00	12.00	25.00	32.00

KM# 3 20 CENTAVOS
Bronze **Obv:** Denomination above date **Rev:** Liberty head left

Date	Mintage	VF20	XF40	MS60	MS63	MS65
1933	350,000	7.50	15.00	45.00	75.00	150

KM# 13 20 CENTAVOS
Bronze **Obv:** Denomination above date **Rev:** Crowned towers and small shields above divided shield on lined circle

Date	Mintage	VF20	XF40	MS60	MS63	MS65
1973	100,000	3.00	6.00	15.00	30.00	42.00

KM# 4 50 CENTAVOS
Nickel-Bronze **Obv:** Laureate head right **Rev:** Shield on lined circle within wreath

Date	Mintage	VF20	XF40	MS60	MS63	MS65
1933	600,000	35.00	85.00	175	450	750

KM# 6 50 CENTAVOS
Bronze, 23 mm. **Subject:** 500th Anniversary of Discovery **Obv:** Denomination within circle, dates below **Rev:** Crowned towers above divided shield on lined circle

Date	Mintage	VF20	XF40	MS60	MS63	MS65
ND-1946	2,000,000	2.00	4.00	10.00	15.00	28.00

KM# 8 50 CENTAVOS
Bronze **Obv:** Denomination **Rev:** Towers above divided shield on lined circle

Date	Mintage	VF20	XF40	MS60	MS63	MS65
1952	10,000,000	0.50	1.00	2.00	5.00	8.00

KM# 5 ESCUDO
Nickel-Bronze **Obv:** Laureate head right **Rev:** Shield on lined circle within wreath

Date	Mintage	VF20	XF40	MS60	MS63	MS65
1933	800,000	15.00	65.00	125	450	750

KM# 7 ESCUDO
Bronze, 27 mm. **Subject:** 500th Anniversary of Discovery **Obv:** Denomination within circle **Rev:** Crowned towers and small shields above divided shield on lined circle

Date	Mintage	VF20	XF40	MS60	MS63	MS65
ND-1946	2,000,000	2.00	3.00	6.00	12.00	25.00

KM# 14 ESCUDO
Bronze **Obv:** Denomination **Rev:** Crowned towers and small shields above divided shield on lined circle

Date	Mintage	VF20	XF40	MS60	MS63	MS65
1973	250,000	5.00	7.00	15.00	25.00	45.00

KM# 9 2-1/2 ESCUDOS
3.41 g., Copper-Nickel **Obv:** Shield on lined circle at center of cross **Rev:** Crowned towers and small shields above divided shield on lined circle

Date	Mintage	VF20	XF40	MS60	MS63	MS65
1952	3,010,000	1.00	2.00	4.00	8.00	12.00

KM# 15 5 ESCUDOS
Copper-Nickel **Obv:** Shield on lined circle at center of cross **Rev:** Crowned towers and small shields above divided shield on lined circle

Date	Mintage	VF20	XF40	MS60	MS63	MS65
1973	800,000	2.50	5.00	10.00	20.00	30.00

KM# 10 10 ESCUDOS
5.00 g., 0.720 Silver 0.1157 oz. ASW **Obv:** Shield on lined circle at center of cross **Rev:** Crowned towers and small shields above divided shield on lined circle

Date	Mintage	VF20	XF40	MS60	MS63	MS65
1952	1,200,000	12.00	30.00	75.00	120	185

KM# 16 10 ESCUDOS
Copper-Nickel **Obv:** Shield on lined circle at center of cross **Rev:** Crowned towers and small shields above divided shield on lined circle

Date	Mintage	VF20	XF40	MS60	MS63	MS65
1973	1,700,000	4.00	6.00	12.00	25.00	45.00

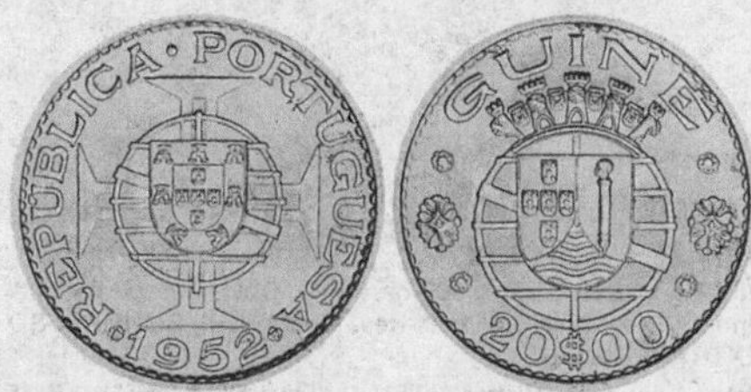

KM# 11 20 ESCUDOS
10.00 g., 0.720 Silver 0.2315 oz. ASW **Obv:** Shield on lined circle at center of cross, date below **Rev:** Crowned towers and small shields above divided shield on lined circle

Date	Mintage	VF20	XF40	MS60	MS63	MS65
1952	750,000	7.00	12.00	25.00	45.00	85.00

REPUBLIC

KM# 17 50 CENTAVOS
2.20 g., Aluminum **Series:** F.A.O. **Obv:** National arms **Rev:** Palm tree left of denomination

Date	Mintage	VF20	XF40	MS60	MS63	MS65
1977	6,000,000	2.00	3.00	4.00	5.00	7.00

KM# 17a 50 CENTAVOS
6.00 g., Aluminum-Bronze, 25 mm. **Obv:** National arms **Rev:** Palm tree left of denomination **Note:** Struck on KM#19 planchet.

Date	Mintage	VF20	XF40	MS60	MS63	MS65
1977	—	—	—	—	—	—

KM# 18 PESO
4.02 g., Aluminum-Bronze **Series:** F.A.O. **Obv:** National arms **Rev:** Denomination below legume plant

Date	Mintage	VF20	XF40	MS60	MS63	MS65
1977	7,000,000	2.25	3.50	5.00	6.00	8.00

KM# 19 2-1/2 PESOS
6.04 g., Aluminum-Bronze **Series:** F.A.O. **Obv:** National arms **Rev:** Tree divides denomination

Date	Mintage	VF20	XF40	MS60	MS63	MS65
1977	4,000,000	2.25	4.50	6.00	7.00	9.00

KM# 20 5 PESOS
8.00 g., Copper-Nickel **Series:** F.A.O. **Obv:** National arms **Rev:** Denomination above peanut plant

Date	Mintage	VF20	XF40	MS60	MS63	MS65
1977	6,000,000	2.50	5.00	7.00	9.00	11.00

KM# 21 20 PESOS
12.65 g., Copper-Nickel **Series:** F.A.O. **Obv:** National arms **Rev:** Plants left of denomination

Date	Mintage	VF20	XF40	MS60	MS63	MS65
1977	2,500,000	4.00	6.00	8.00	10.00	12.00

KM# 28 2000 PESOS
Nickel Plated Steel **Subject:** Olympics **Obv:** National arms **Rev:** Handball player, stylized date in background

Date	Mintage	VF20	XF40	MS60	MS63	MS65
1991	5,000	—	—	—	6.00	9.00

KM# 38 2000 PESOS
Nickel Plated Steel, 32 mm. **Subject:** 50th Anniversary - FAO **Obv:** National arms **Rev:** Pineapple harvest

Date	Mintage	VF20	XF40	MS60	MS63	MS65
ND-1995	—	—	—	—	6.00	9.00

KM# 27 10000 PESOS
16.00 g., 0.999 Silver 0.5139 oz. ASW **Subject:** Nuno Tristao - Discovery of Guinea-Bissau **Obv:** National arms **Rev:** Ships landing

Date	Mintage	VF20	XF40	MS60	MS63	MS65
1991	—	PF63 15.00	PF65 25.00	PF67 35.00		

KM# 29 10000 PESOS
11.97 g., 0.999 Silver 0.3845 oz. ASW **Obv:** National arms **Rev:** Soccer player

Date	Mintage	VF20	XF40	MS60	MS63	MS65
1991	—	—	—	—	20.00	30.00

KM# 30 10000 PESOS
19.67 g., 0.999 Silver 0.6318 oz. ASW **Subject:** XXV Olympics **Obv:** National arms **Rev:** Floor exercise, date below

Date	Mintage	VF20	XF40	MS60	MS63	MS65
1992	Est. 10000	PF63 17.00	PF65 27.00	PF67 37.00		

KM# 39 10000 PESOS
20.00 g., 0.999 Silver 0.6424 oz. ASW **Subject:** European Soccer '94

Date	Mintage	VF20	XF40	MS60	MS63	MS65
1992	—	PF63 22.00	PF65 35.00	PF67 50.00		

KM# 31 10000 PESOS
15.00 g., 0.999 Silver 0.4818 oz. ASW **Obv:** National arms **Rev:** Elephant standing on Africa

Date	Mintage	VF20	XF40	MS60	MS63	MS65
1993	—	PF65 22.00	PF67 25.00			

KM# 32 10000 PESOS
15.00 g., 0.999 Silver 0.4818 oz. ASW **Subject:** Prehistoric Life **Obv:** National arms **Rev:** Stegosaurus

Date	Mintage	VF20	XF40	MS60	MS63	MS65
1993	—	PF63 17.00	PF65 27.00	PF67 37.00		

KM# 35 10000 PESOS
16.10 g., 0.999 Silver 0.5171 oz. ASW **Subject:** Prehistoric Life **Obv:** National arms **Rev:** Vulcanodon

Date	Mintage	VF20	XF40	MS60	MS63	MS65
1994	—	PF63 22.00	PF65 35.00	PF67 50.00		

KM# 25 20000 PESOS
25.00 g., 0.999 Silver 0.803 oz. ASW **Obv:** Stylized national arms **Rev:** Bust 3/4 right **Rev. Legend:** II CONGRESSO EXTRAORDINARIO

Date	Mintage	VF20	XF40	MS60	MS63	MS65
ND-1990	2,000	—	—	45.00	55.00	75.00

KM# 26 20000 PESOS
25.00 g., 0.999 Silver 0.803 oz. ASW **Subject:** 10th Anniversary - L. Cabral Deposed **Obv:** National arms **Rev:** Figure giving speech, soldiers in background

Date	Mintage	VF20	XF40	MS60	MS63	MS65
1990	—	PF63 28.00	PF65 38.00	PF67 55.00		

KM# 33 20000 PESOS
20.00 g., 0.999 Silver 0.6424 oz. ASW **Subject:** Defense of Nature **Obv:** National arms **Rev:** Elephant

Date	Mintage	VF20	XF40	MS60	MS63	MS65
1993	—	PF63 22.00	PF65 35.00	PF67 50.00		

KM# 34 20000 PESOS
20.10 g., 0.999 Silver 0.6456 oz. ASW **Obv:** National arms **Rev:** Sailing ship - Passat

Date	Mintage	VF20	XF40	MS60	MS63	MS65
1993	100	—	—	—	275	300
1993	—	PF63 22.00	PF65 35.00	PF67 50.00		

KM# 41 20000 PESOS
25.00 g., 0.999 Silver 0.803 oz. ASW **Subject:** 50 Years - FAO **Obv:** National arms, value below **Rev:** Woman with basket of pineapples lower right, FAO emblem at left, 2 farm workers above

Date	Mintage	VF20	XF40	MS60	MS63	MS65
1995 Proof	—	—	—	—	—	—

KM# 42 20000 PESOS
Silver, 38 mm. **Subject:** FAO **Obv:** Arms **Rev:** Two men working field, female with basket **Edge:** Reeded

Date	Mintage	VF20	XF40	MS60	MS63	MS65
1995	Est. 2200	PF63 35.00	PF65 50.00	PF67 65.00		

KM# 36 50000 PESOS
31.47 g., 0.925 Silver 0.9359 oz. ASW **Obv:** National arms **Rev:** Female hippopotamus and calf

Date	Mintage	VF20	XF40	MS60	MS63	MS65
1996	Est. 15000	PF63 22.00	PF65 35.00		PF67 50.00	

KM# 37 50000 PESOS
31.47 g., 0.925 Silver 0.9359 oz. ASW **Obv:** National arms **Rev:** Sailing ship - Alvise Da Cadamosto

Date	Mintage	VF20	XF40	MS60	MS63	MS65
1996	Est. 10000	PF63 22.00	PF65 35.00		PF67 50.00	

PATTERNS

KM#	Date	Mintage	Identification	Mkt Val
Pn1	1977	—	2-1/2 Pesos. Aluminum. KM#19.	—

PROVAS

Standard metals; stamped

KM#	Date	Mintage	Identification	Mkt Val
Pr1	1933	—	5 Centavos. Bronze. KM#1.	65.00
Pr2	1933	—	10 Centavos. Bronze. KM#2.	65.00
Pr3	1933	—	20 Centavos. Bronze. KM#3.	65.00
Pr4	1933	—	50 Centavos. Nickel-Bronze. KM#4.	75.00
Pr5	1933	—	Escudo. Nickel-Bronze. KM#5.	80.00
Pr6	1946	—	50 Centavos. Bronze. KM#6.	45.00
Pr7	1946	—	Escudo. Bronze. KM#7.	45.00
Pr8	1952	—	50 Centavos. Bronze. KM#8.	45.00
Pr9	1952	—	2-1/2 Escudos. Copper-Nickel. KM#9.	50.00
Pr10	1952	—	10 Escudos. Silver. KM#10.	80.00
Pr11	1952	—	20 Escudos. Silver. KM#11.	85.00
Pr12	1973	—	Escudo. Bronze. KM#14.	50.00
Pr13	1973	—	10 Escudos. Copper-Nickel. KM#16.	55.00

The Cooperative Republic of Guyana, is situated on the northeast coast of South America, has an area of 83,000 sq. mi. (214,970 sq. km.) and a population of 729,000. Capital: Georgetown. The economy is basically agrarian. Sugar, rice and bauxite are exported.

The original area of Essequibo and Demerary, which included present-day Suriname, French Guiana, and parts of Brazil and Venezuela was sighted by Columbus in 1498. The first European settlement was made late in the 16th century by the Dutch, however, the region was claimed for the British by Sir Walter Raleigh during the reign of Elizabeth I. For the next 150 years, possession alternated between the Dutch and the British, with a short interval of French control. The British exercised de facto control after 1796 over the Dutch colonies of Essequibo, Demerary and Berbice. They were not ceded to them by the Dutch until 1814. From 1803 to 1831, Essequibo and Demerary were administered separately from Berbice. The three colonies were united in the British Crown Colony of British Guiana in 1831. British Guiana won internal self-government in 1952 and full independence, under the traditional name of Guyana, on May 26,1966. Guyana became a republic on Feb. 23, 1970. It is a member of the Commonwealth of Nations. The president is the Chief of State. The prime minister is the Head of Government. Guyana is a member of the Caribbean Community and Common Market (CARICOM).

RULER
British, until 1966

***NOTE**: From 1975-1985 the Franklin Mint produced coinage in up to 3 different qualities. Qualities of issue are designated in ( ) after each date and are defined as follows:
(M) MATTE - Normal circulation strike or a dull finish produced by sandblasting special uncirculated (polish finish) or proof quality dies.
(U) SPECIAL UNCIRCULATED - Polished or proof-like in appearance without any frosted features.
(P) PROOF - The highest quality obtainable having mirror-like fields and frosted features.

REPUBLIC

DECIMAL COINAGE

KM# 31 CENT
1.53 g., Nickel-Brass, 15.99 mm. **Obv:** Denomination within circle **Rev:** Stylized lotus flower **Edge:** Plain

Date	Mintage	VF20	XF40	MS60	MS63	MS65
1967	6,000,000	—	0.10	0.15	0.25	0.35
1967	5,100	PF65 2.00				
1969	4,000,000	—	0.10	0.15	0.25	0.35
1970	6,000,000	—	0.10	0.15	0.25	0.35
1971	4,000,000	—	0.10	0.15	0.25	0.35
1972	4,000,000	—	0.10	0.15	0.25	0.35
1973	4,000,000	—	0.10	0.15	0.25	0.35
1974	11,000,000	—	0.10	0.15	0.20	0.30
1975	—	—	0.10	0.15	0.25	0.35
1976	—	—	0.10	0.15	0.25	0.35
1977	16,000,000	—	0.10	0.15	0.20	0.30
1978	10,450,000	—	0.10	0.15	0.20	0.30
1979	—	—	0.10	0.15	0.20	0.30
1980	12,000,000	—	0.10	0.15	0.20	0.30
1981	10,000,000	—	0.10	0.15	0.20	0.30
1982	8,000,000	—	0.10	0.15	0.20	0.30
1983	12,000,000	—	0.10	0.15	0.20	0.30
1985	8,000,000	—	0.10	0.15	0.20	0.30
1987	6,000,000	—	0.10	0.15	0.20	0.30
1988	80,000	—	0.15	0.25	0.50	0.75
1989	—	—	0.10	0.15	0.20	0.30
1991	—	—	0.10	0.15	0.20	0.30
1992	—	—	0.10	0.15	0.20	0.30

KM# 37 CENT
Nickel-Brass, 16 mm. **Subject:** 10th Anniversary of Independence **Obv:** Helmeted and supported arms **Rev:** Manatee

Date	Mintage	VF20	XF40	MS60	MS63	MS65
1976 FM (M)	15,000	—	0.15	0.35	1.00	4.00
1976 FM (U)	50	—	—	—	—	—
1976 FM (P)	28,000	PF65 3.00				
1977 FM (M)	—	—	1.50	2.00	3.00	4.50
1977 FM (U)	15,000	—	0.20	0.50	1.00	3.00
1977 FM (P)	7,215	PF65 3.00				
1978 FM (M)	—	—	1.50	2.00	3.00	4.50
1978 FM (U)	15,000	—	0.20	0.50	1.00	3.00
1978 FM (P)	5,044	PF65 3.00				
1979 FM (U)	15,000	—	0.20	0.50	1.00	3.00
1979 FM (P)	3,547	PF65 3.00				
1980 FM (U)	30,000	—	0.20	0.50	1.00	3.00
1980 FM (P)	2,763	PF65 3.00				

KM# 32 5 CENTS
Nickel-Brass, 19.5 mm. **Obv:** Denomination within circle **Rev:** Stylized lotus flower **Note:** Varieties exist.

Date	Mintage	VF20	XF40	MS60	MS63	MS65
1967	4,600,000	—	0.10	0.20	0.30	0.50
1967	5,100	PF65 2.00				
1972	1,200,000	—	0.10	0.20	0.35	0.50
1974	3,000,000	—	0.10	0.20	0.35	0.50
1975	—	—	0.10	0.20	0.35	0.50
1976	—	—	0.10	0.20	0.35	0.50
1977	1,500,000	—	0.10	0.20	0.35	0.50
1978	2,000	—	1.25	2.00	4.00	6.00
1979	—	—	0.30	0.50	1.00	1.50
1980	1,000,000	—	0.10	0.20	0.35	0.50
1981	1,000,000	—	0.10	0.20	0.35	0.50
1982	2,000,000	—	0.10	0.20	0.30	0.50
1985	3,000,000	—	0.10	0.20	0.30	0.50
1986	4,000,000	—	0.10	0.20	0.30	0.50
1987	3,000,000	—	0.10	0.20	0.30	0.50
1988	2,000,000	—	0.10	0.20	0.30	0.50
1989	—	—	0.10	0.20	0.30	0.50
1990	—	—	0.10	0.20	0.30	0.50
1991	—	—	0.10	0.20	0.30	0.50
1992	—	—	0.10	0.20	0.30	0.50

KM# 38 5 CENTS
Nickel-Brass, 19.5 mm. **Subject:** 10th Anniversary of Independence **Obv:** Helmeted and supported arms **Rev:** Jaguar (panthera onca)

Date	Mintage	VF20	XF40	MS60	MS63	MS65
1976 FM (M)	15,000	—	0.20	0.50	1.75	5.00
1976 FM (U)	50	—	—	—	—	—
1976 FM (P)	28,000	PF65 2.00				
1977 FM (M)	—	—	1.50	2.00	3.00	5.00
1977 FM (U)	15,000	—	0.20	0.50	1.75	5.00
1977 FM (P)	7,215	PF65 2.00				
1978 FM (M)	—	—	2.50	3.50	5.00	6.50
1978 FM (U)	15,000	—	0.50	1.00	2.00	5.00
1978 FM (P)	5,044	PF65 2.00				
1979 FM (U)	15,000	—	0.50	1.00	2.00	5.00
1979 FM (P)	3,547	PF65 2.25				
1980 FM (U)	30,000	—	0.50	1.00	2.00	5.00
1980 FM (P)	2,763	PF65 2.50				

KM# 33 10 CENTS
2.75 g., Copper-Nickel, 18 mm. **Obv:** Denomination within circle **Rev:** Helmeted and supported arms **Edge:** Reeded

Date	Mintage	VF20	XF40	MS60	MS63	MS65
1967	4,000,000	0.10	0.20	0.25	0.35	0.50
1967	5,100	PF65 2.50				
1973	1,500,000	0.10	0.20	0.25	0.40	0.60
1974	1,700,000	0.10	0.20	0.25	0.40	0.60
1976	—	0.10	0.20	0.25	0.40	0.60
1977	4,000,000	0.10	0.20	0.25	0.40	0.60
1978	2,010,000	0.10	0.20	0.25	0.40	0.60
1979	—	0.10	0.20	0.25	0.40	0.60
1980	1,000,000	0.10	0.20	0.25	0.40	0.60
1981	1,000,000	0.10	0.20	0.25	0.40	0.60
1982	2,000,000	0.10	0.20	0.25	0.35	0.50
1985	3,000,000	0.10	0.20	0.25	0.35	0.50
1986	4,000,000	0.10	0.20	0.25	0.35	0.50
1987	3,000,000	0.10	0.20	0.25	0.35	0.50
1988	2,000,000	0.10	0.20	0.25	0.35	0.50
1989	—	0.10	0.20	0.25	0.35	0.50
1990	—	0.10	0.20	0.25	0.35	0.50
1991	—	0.10	0.20	0.25	0.35	0.50
1992	—	0.10	0.20	0.25	0.35	0.50

KM# 39 10 CENTS
Copper-Nickel, 18 mm. **Subject:** 10th Anniversary of Independence **Obv:** Helmeted and supported arms **Rev:** Squirrel Monkey

Date	Mintage	VF20	XF40	MS60	MS63	MS65
1976	2,006,000	—	0.25	0.75	1.50	3.00
1976 FM (M)	10,000	—	1.00	1.50	2.50	5.00
1976 FM (U)	50	—	—	—	—	—
1976 FM (P)	28,000	PF65 3.00				
1977	1,500,000	—	0.25	0.75	1.50	3.00
1977 FM (M)	—	—	4.00	6.00	8.00	10.00
1977 FM (U)	10,000	—	0.25	0.75	1.50	3.00
1977 FM (P)	7,215	PF65 3.00				
1978 FM (M)	—	—	4.00	6.00	8.00	10.00

Date	Mintage	VF20	XF40	MS60	MS63	MS65
1978 FM (U)	10,000	—	0.25	0.75	1.50	3.00
1978 FM (P)	5,044	PF65 3.00				
1979 FM (U)	10,000	—	0.25	0.75	1.50	3.00
1979 FM (P)	3,547	PF65 3.00				
1980 FM (U)	20,000	—	0.25	0.75	1.50	3.00
1980 FM (P)	2,763	PF65 4.00				

KM# 34 25 CENTS

4.29 g., Copper-Nickel, 20.42 mm. **Obv:** Denomination within circle **Rev:** Helmeted and supported arms **Edge:** Plain

Date	Mintage	VF20	XF40	MS60	MS63	MS65
1967	3,500,000	0.15	0.25	0.45	0.60	0.75
1967	5,100	PF65 2.50				
1972	1,000,000	0.15	0.25	0.50	0.65	0.85
1974	4,000,000	0.15	0.25	0.50	0.65	0.85
1975	—	0.15	0.25	0.50	0.65	0.85
1976	—	0.15	0.25	0.50	0.65	0.85
1977	4,000,000	0.15	0.25	0.50	0.65	0.85
1978	2,006,000	0.15	0.25	0.50	0.65	0.85
1981	1,000,000	0.15	0.25	0.50	0.65	0.85
1982	1,500,000	0.15	0.25	0.50	0.65	0.85
1984	1,000,000	0.15	0.25	0.50	0.65	0.85
1985	2,000,000	0.15	0.25	0.45	0.60	0.75
1986	4,000,000	0.15	0.25	0.45	0.60	0.75
1987	3,000,000	0.15	0.25	0.45	0.60	0.75
1988	4,000,000	0.15	0.25	0.45	0.60	0.75
1989	—	0.15	0.25	0.45	0.60	0.75
1990	—	0.15	0.25	0.45	0.60	0.75
1991	—	0.15	0.25	0.45	0.60	0.75
1992	—	0.15	0.25	0.45	0.60	0.75

KM# 40 25 CENTS

Copper-Nickel, 21.5 mm. **Subject:** 10th Anniversary of Independence **Obv:** Helmeted and supported arms **Rev:** Harpy Eagle

Date	Mintage	VF20	XF40	MS60	MS63	MS65
1976 FM (M)	4,000	—	0.30	1.25	2.50	3.50
1976 FM (U)	50	—	—	—	—	—
1976 FM (P)	28,000	PF65 3.00				
1977	2,000,000	0.15	0.25	1.00	2.00	3.50
1977 FM (M)	—	—	5.00	7.00	10.00	12.00
1977 FM (U)	4,000	—	2.00	3.00	4.00	5.00
1977 FM (P)	7,215	PF65 3.00				
1978 FM (M)	—	—	3.00	6.00	10.00	12.00
1978 FM (U)	4,000	—	1.00	2.00	4.00	5.00
1978 FM (P)	5,044	PF65 3.50				
1979 FM (U)	4,000	—	1.00	2.00	4.00	5.00
1979 FM (P)	3,547	PF65 3.50				
1980 FM (U)	8,437	—	1.00	2.00	4.00	5.00
1980 FM (P)	2,763	PF65 4.50				

KM# 35 50 CENTS

Copper-Nickel, 26 mm. **Obv:** Denomination within circle **Rev:** Helmeted and supported arms

Date	Mintage	VF20	XF40	MS60	MS63	MS65
1967	1,000,000	0.25	0.35	0.50	0.75	1.25
1967	5,100	PF65 3.50				

KM# 41 50 CENTS

Copper-Nickel, 25 mm. **Subject:** 10th Anniversary of Independence **Obv:** Helmeted and supported arms **Rev:** Hoatzin

Date	Mintage	VF20	XF40	MS60	MS63	MS65
1976 FM (M)	2,000	—	0.40	1.00	3.00	6.00
1976 FM (U)	50	—	—	—	—	—
1976 FM (P)	28,000	PF65 4.00				
1977 FM (M)	—	—	10.00	15.00	20.00	22.50
1977 FM (U)	2,000	—	0.40	1.00	3.00	6.00
1977 FM (P)	7,215	PF65 4.00				
1978 FM (M)	—	—	10.00	15.00	20.00	22.50
1978 FM (U)	2,000	—	0.40	1.00	3.00	6.00
1978 FM (P)	5,044	PF65 4.50				
1979 FM (U)	2,000	—	0.40	1.00	3.00	6.00
1979 FM (P)	3,547	PF65 4.50				
1980 FM (U)	4,437	—	0.40	1.00	2.50	5.00
1980 FM (P)	2,763	PF65 5.50				

KM# 36 DOLLAR

Copper-Nickel, 35.5 mm. **Series:** F.A.O. **Obv:** Bulls head left of denomination **Rev:** Head left **Note:** Cuffy, slave who organized a revolt on 23 Feb. 1763, which was the first step towards independence.

Date	Mintage	VF20	XF40	MS60	MS63	MS65
1970	500,000	—	1.50	3.00	5.00	6.00
1970	5,000	PF65 8.00				

KM# 42 DOLLAR

Copper-Nickel, 35.5 mm. **Series:** F.A.O. **Subject:** 10th Anniversary of Independence **Obv:** Helmeted and supported arms **Rev:** Common Caiman

Date	Mintage	VF20	XF40	MS60	MS63	MS65
1976 FM (M)	600	—	1.00	3.00	6.00	7.00
1976 FM (U)	50	—	—	—	—	—
1976 FM (P)	28,000	PF65 7.00				
1977 FM (M)	—	—	12.50	17.00	28.00	32.50
1977 FM (U)	500	—	1.00	3.00	6.00	7.00
1977 FM (P)	7,215	PF65 7.50				
1978 FM (M)	—	—	12.50	17.00	28.00	32.50
1978 FM (U)	500	—	1.00	3.00	6.00	7.00
1978 FM (P)	5,044	PF65 8.00				
1979 FM (U)	500	—	1.00	3.00	6.00	7.00
1979 FM (P)	3,547	PF65 8.00				
1980 FM (U)	1,437	—	1.00	3.00	6.00	7.00
1980 FM (P)	2,763	PF65 8.50				

KM# 50 DOLLAR

2.40 g., Copper Plated Steel, 17 mm. **Obv:** Helmeted and supported arms **Rev:** Hand gathering rice **Edge:** Reeded

Date	Mintage	VF20	XF40	MS60	MS63	MS65
1996	—	—	—	0.35	0.50	0.65

KM# 43 5 DOLLARS

Copper-Nickel **Subject:** 10th Anniversary of Independence **Obv:** Helmeted and supported arms **Rev:** Head at right facing

Date	Mintage	VF20	XF40	MS60	MS63	MS65
1976 FM (M)	400	—	—	7.50	15.00	17.50
1976 FM (U)	150	—	—	8.00	17.50	20.00
1977 FM (M)	—	—	—	15.00	45.00	50.00
1977 FM (U)	100	—	—	20.00	25.00	27.50
1978 FM (M)	—	—	—	30.00	45.00	50.00
1978 FM (U)	100	—	—	12.50	25.00	27.50
1979 FM (U)	100	—	—	12.50	25.00	27.50
1980 FM (U)	200	—	—	12.50	15.00	17.50

KM# 43a 5 DOLLARS

37.30 g., 0.500 Silver 0.5996 oz. ASW **Obv:** Helmeted and supported arms **Rev:** Head at right facing

Date	Mintage	VF20	XF40	MS60	MS63	MS65
1976 FM (P)	18,000	PF63 19.00	PF65 20.50			
1977 FM (P)	5,685	PF63 20.00	PF65 21.50			
1978 FM (P)	3,825	PF63 21.00	PF65 22.50			
1979 FM (P)	2,665	PF63 23.00	PF65 24.50			
1980 FM (P)	2,763	PF63 23.00	PF65 24.50			

KM# 51 5 DOLLARS

3.78 g., Copper Plated Steel, 20.5 mm. **Obv:** Helmeted and supported arms **Rev:** Sugar cane **Edge:** Reeded

Date	Mintage	VF20	XF40	MS60	MS63	MS65
1996	—	—	—	0.35	0.75	1.00

KM# 44 10 DOLLARS

Copper-Nickel **Subject:** 10th Anniversary of Independence **Obv:** Helmeted and supported arms **Rev:** Head at left looking right

Date	Mintage	VF20	XF40	MS60	MS63	MS65
1976 FM (M)	300	—	—	15.00	30.00	40.00
1976 FM (U)	300	—	—	15.00	30.00	40.00
1977 FM (M)	—	—	—	40.00	80.00	100
1977 FM (U)	100	—	—	25.00	50.00	60.00
1978 FM (M)	—	—	—	40.00	80.00	90.00
1978 FM (U)	100	—	—	25.00	50.00	60.00
1979 FM (U)	100	—	—	25.00	50.00	60.00
1980 FM (U)	200	—	—	25.00	40.00	50.00

KM# 44a 10 DOLLARS

43.23 g., 0.925 Silver 1.2856 oz. ASW **Subject:** 10th Anniversary of Independence **Obv:** Helmeted and supported arms **Rev:** Head at left looking right

Date	Mintage	VF20	XF40	MS60	MS63	MS65
1976 FM (P)	18,000	PF63 34.50	PF65 37.00			
1977 FM (P)	5,685	PF63 35.50	PF65 38.00			
1978 FM (P)	3,825	PF63 36.50	PF65 39.00			
1979 FM (P)	2,665	PF63 38.50	PF65 41.00			
1980 FM (P)	2,763	PF63 38.50	PF65 41.00			

KM# 52 10 DOLLARS
5.00 g., Nickel Plated Steel, 23 mm. **Obv:** Helmeted and supported arms **Rev:** Gold mining scene **Edge:** Reeded **Shape:** 7-sided **Note:** Slightly different die for each date.

Date	Mintage	VF20	XF40	MS60	MS63	MS65
1996	—	—	—	0.75	1.25	1.50

KM# 45 50 DOLLARS
48.30 g., 0.925 Silver 1.4364 oz. ASW **Subject:** 10th Anniversary of Independence **Rev:** Enmoe Martyrs

Date	Mintage	VF20	XF40	MS60	MS63	MS65
1976 FM (U)	100	—	—	65.00	110	125
1976 FM (P)	1,001	PF65 120	PF67 140			

KM# 48 50 DOLLARS
28.28 g., 0.925 Silver 0.841 oz. ASW **Subject:** Royal Visit **Rev:** Small portraits of royals above people welcoming the royal ship

Date	Mintage	VF20	XF40	MS60	MS63	MS65
1994	—	PF65 50.00	PF67 65.00			

KM# 46 100 DOLLARS
5.74 g., 0.500 Gold 0.0923 oz. AGW **Subject:** 10th Anniversary of Independence **Obv:** Helmeted and supported arms **Rev:** Arawak Indian

Date	Mintage	VF20	XF40	MS60	MS63	MS65
1976 FM (U)	100	—	—	165	185	200
1976 FM (P)	21,000	PF65 170	PF67 185			

KM# 47 100 DOLLARS
5.58 g., 0.500 Gold 0.0897 oz. AGW **Obv:** Helmeted and supported arms **Rev:** Legendary Golden Man

Date	Mintage	VF20	XF40	MS60	MS63	MS65
1977 FM (U)	100	—	—	160	180	195
1977 FM (P)	7,635	PF65 165	PF67 180			

KM# 49 500 DOLLARS
47.54 g., 0.917 Gold 1.4016 oz. AGW **Subject:** Royal Visit **Obv:** Small portraits left of royals above people welcoming the royal ship

Date	Mintage	VF20	XF40	MS60	MS63	MS65
1994	100	PF63 2,150	PF65 2,350	PF67 2,600		

KM# 53 2000 DOLLARS
28.28 g., 0.925 Silver 0.841 oz. ASW, 38.6 mm. **Subject:** Millennium **Obv:** Helmeted and supported arms **Rev:** World globe and radiant sun within circle **Edge:** Plain **Shape:** 12-sided

Date	Mintage	VF20	XF40	MS60	MS63	MS65
ND-1999	Est. 30000	PF63 25.00	PF65 30.00	PF67 35.00		

KM# 53a 2000 DOLLARS
28.50 g., Copper-Nickel, 38.6 mm. **Subject:** Millennium **Obv:** National arms **Rev:** World globe and radiant sun **Edge:** Plain **Shape:** 12-sided

Date	Mintage	VF20	XF40	MS60	MS63	MS65
ND-1999	—	—	—	—	8.00	12.00

PATTERNS

Including off metal strikes

KM#	Date	Mintage	Identification	Mkt Val
Pn1	1967	—	5 Cents. Silver. KM#32.	—

MINT SETS

KM#	Date	Mintage	Identification	Issue Price	Mkt Val
MS1	1977 (8)	—	KM#37-44	—	150
MS2	1978 (8)	—	KM#37-44	—	85.00

PROOF SETS

KM#	Date	Mintage	Identification	Issue Price	Mkt Val
PS1	1967 (5)	5,100	KM#31-35	10.50	12.50
PS2	1976 (8)	17,536	KM#37-42, 43a, 44a	45.00	55.00
PS3	1976 (6)	10,302	KM#37-42	15.00	16.00
PS4	1977 (8)	5,685	KM#37-42, 43a, 44a	45.00	55.00
PS5	1977 (6)	1,530	KM#37-42	15.00	16.00
PS6	1978 (8)	3,825	KM#37-42, 43a, 44a	47.50	65.00
PS7	1978 (6)	1,219	KM#37-42	16.00	18.00
PS8	1979 (8)	2,665	KM#37-42, 43a, 44a	47.50	75.00
PS9	1979 (6)	882	KM#37-42	16.00	30.00
PS10	1980 (8)	1,900	KM#37-42, 43a, 44a	100	85.00
PS11	1980 (6)	863	KM#37-42	19.00	30.00

HAITI

The Republic of Haiti, which occupies the western one-third of the island of Hispaniola in the Caribbean Sea between Puerto Rico and Cuba, has an area of 10,714 sq. mi. (27,750 sq. km.) and a population of 6.5 million. Capital: Port-au-Prince. The economy is based on agriculture; but light manufacturing and tourism are increasingly important. Coffee, bauxite, sugar, essential oils and handicrafts are exported.

Columbus discovered Hispaniola in 1492. Spain colonized the island, making Santo Domingo the base for exploration of the Western Hemisphere. The area that is now Haiti was ceded to France by Spain in 1697. Slaves brought from Africa to work the coffee and sugar cane plantations made it one of the richest colonies of the French Empire. A slave revolt in the 1790's led to the establishment of the Republic of Haiti in1804, making it the oldest Black republic in the world and the second oldest republic (after the United States) in the Western Hemisphere.

The French language is used on Haitian coins although it is spoken by only about 10% of the populace. A form of Creole is the language of the Haitians.

MINT MARKS

A - Paris
(a) - Paris, privy marks only
HEATON - Birmingham
R - Rome
(w) = Waterbury (Connecticut, USA) (Scoville Mfg. Co.)
(p) – Philadelphia (U.S.A. mint)

MONETARY SYSTEM

100 Centimes = 1 Gourde

REPUBLIC

1863 -

DECIMAL COINAGE

KM# 52 5 CENTIMES
Copper-Nickel **Obv:** National arms **Rev:** Denomination above date **Note:** Struck at the Scovill Mfg. Co., Waterbury, Connecticut; design incorporates Paris privy and mint director's marks.

Date	Mintage	F12	VF20	XF40	MS60	MS63
1904 (w)	—	3.00	10.00	25.00	60.00	75.00
1904 (w)	—	PF63 150				

KM# 53 5 CENTIMES
Copper-Nickel **Obv:** President Pierre Nord Alexis left **Rev:** National arms

Date	Mintage	F12	VF20	XF40	MS60	MS63
1904 (w)	2,000,000	1.00	5.00	15.00	35.00	75.00
1904 (w)	—	PF63 175				
1905 (w)	20,000,000	0.75	3.00	10.00	25.00	45.00
1905 (w)	—	PF63 300				

KM# 57 5 CENTIMES
Copper-Nickel **Obv:** President Dumarsais Estime left **Rev:** National arms

Date	Mintage	VF20	XF40	MS60	MS63	MS65
1949 (p)	10,000,000	0.75	2.00	6.00	10.00	25.00

KM# 59 5 CENTIMES
Copper-Nickel-Zinc **Obv:** President Paul Eugene Magloire left

Date	Mintage	VF20	XF40	MS60	MS63	MS65
1953 (p)	3,000,000	0.35	0.65	1.00	1.50	2.50

KM# 62 5 CENTIMES
Copper-Nickel-Zinc, 20 mm. **Obv:** President Francois Duvalier left **Rev:** National arms

Date	Mintage	VF20	XF40	MS60	MS63	MS65
1958 (p)	15,000,000	—	0.10	0.25	3.00	5.00
1970	5,000,000	—	0.10	0.20	0.35	0.50

KM# 119 5 CENTIMES
2.70 g., Copper-Nickel, 20 mm. **Series:** F.A.O. **Obv:** President Jean-Claude Duvalier left **Rev:** National arms

Date	Mintage	VF20	XF40	MS60	MS63	MS65
1975	16,000,000	—	0.10	0.20	0.35	0.50

KM# 145 5 CENTIMES
Copper-Nickel **Series:** F.A.O. **Obv:** Head right, small logo at left **Rev:** Woman and child **Note:** Denomination as 0.05 Gourdes.

Date	Mintage	VF20	XF40	MS60	MS63	MS65
1981 R	15,000	0.10	0.25	0.75	1.00	1.50

KM# 154 5 CENTIMES
3.10 g., Copper-Nickel-Zinc, 19.9 mm. **Subject:** Charlemagne Peralte, national hero **Obv:** Bust facing **Rev:** National arms

Date	Mintage	VF20	XF40	MS60	MS63	MS65
1986	—	—	—	0.25	0.35	0.50

KM# 154a 5 CENTIMES
3.10 g., Nickel Plated Steel, 20 mm. **Subject:** Charlemagne Peralte, national hero **Obv:** Bust facing **Rev:** National arms

Date	Mintage	VF20	XF40	MS60	MS63	MS65
1995	—	—	—	0.25	0.35	0.50
1997	—	—	—	0.25	0.35	0.50

KM# 54 10 CENTIMES
Copper-Nickel **Obv:** President Pierre Nord Alexis left **Rev:** National arms

Date	Mintage	F12	VF20	XF40	MS60	MS63
1906 (w)	10,000,000	1.00	3.00	7.00	20.00	40.00
1906 (w)	—	PF63 200				

KM# 58 10 CENTIMES
3.78 g., Copper-Nickel, 22.70 mm. **Obv:** President Dumarsais Estime left **Rev:** National arms

Date	Mintage	VF20	XF40	MS60	MS63	MS65
1949 (p)	5,000,000	2.00	6.00	12.00	15.00	20.00

KM# 60 10 CENTIMES
Copper-Nickel-Zinc **Obv:** President Paul Eugene Magloire left **Rev:** National arms

Date	Mintage	VF20	XF40	MS60	MS63	MS65
1953 (p)	1,500,000	0.25	1.00	3.00	5.00	9.00

KM# 63 10 CENTIMES
Copper-Nickel-Zinc, 22.5 mm. **Obv:** President Francois Duvalier left **Rev:** National arms

Date	Mintage	VF20	XF40	MS60	MS63	MS65
1958 (p)	7,500,000	0.10	0.15	0.35	0.50	0.75
1970	2,500,000	—	0.10	0.20	0.40	0.60

KM# 120 10 CENTIMES
Copper-Nickel, 23 mm. **Series:** F.A.O. **Obv:** President Jean-Claude Duvalier left **Rev:** National arms

Date	Mintage	VF20	XF40	MS60	MS63	MS65
1975	12,000,000	—	0.10	0.20	0.40	0.60
1983	2,000,000	—	0.10	0.30	0.50	0.75

KM# 146 10 CENTIMES
Copper-Nickel **Series:** F.A.O. **Obv:** Head right, small logo at left **Rev:** Sun above farmer in field on tractor **Note:** Denomination as 0.10 Gourdes.

Date	Mintage	VF20	XF40	MS60	MS63	MS65
1981 R	15,000	0.10	0.35	0.50	1.00	1.25

KM# 55 20 CENTIMES
Copper-Nickel, 26.5 mm. **Obv:** President Pierre Nord Alexis left **Rev:** National arms **Edge:** Plain

Date	Mintage	F12	VF20	XF40	MS60	MS63
1907 (w)	5,000,000	2.00	6.00	15.00	35.00	55.00
1907 (w)	—	PF63 250				
1908 (w)	—	—	—	—	—	—

Note: Requires Confirmation

KM# 61 20 CENTIMES
Copper-Nickel-Zinc, 26.5 mm. **Obv:** President Paul Eugene Magliore left **Rev:** National arms

Date	Mintage	VF20	XF40	MS60	MS63	MS65
1956 (p)	2,500,000	1.00	2.00	3.00	5.00	6.50

KM# 77 20 CENTIMES
Nickel-Silver **Obv:** President Francois Duvalier left **Rev:** National arms

Date	Mintage	VF20	XF40	MS60	MS63	MS65
1970	1,000,000	0.25	0.35	0.50	0.85	1.00

KM# 100 20 CENTIMES
Copper-Nickel, 26 mm. **Series:** F.A.O. **Obv:** President Jean-Claude Duvalier left **Rev:** National arms

Date	Mintage	VF20	XF40	MS60	MS63	MS65
1972	1,500,000	0.10	0.25	0.60	1.00	1.25
1975	4,000,000	0.10	0.20	0.50	0.85	1.00
1983	1,500,000	0.10	0.20	0.50	0.85	1.00

KM# 147 20 CENTIMES
Copper-Nickel, 26.2 mm. **Series:** F.A.O. **Obv:** Head right, small logo at left **Rev:** Harvesters **Note:** Denomination as 0.20 Gourdes.

Date	Mintage	VF20	XF40	MS60	MS63	MS65
1981 R	15,000	0.25	0.50	0.75	1.25	1.50

KM# 152 20 CENTIMES
7.54 g., Copper-Nickel, 26.15 mm. **Subject:** Charlemagne Peralte, national hero **Obv:** Bust facing **Rev:** National arms **Edge:** Plain **Note:** No accent marks on obverse legend.

Date	Mintage	VF20	XF40	MS60	MS63	MS65
1986	2,500,000	0.10	0.20	0.35	0.65	0.95
1989	—	0.10	0.20	0.35	0.65	0.95
1991	—	0.10	0.20	0.35	0.65	0.95

KM# 152a 20 CENTIMES
Nickel Plated Steel, 26.2 mm. **Subject:** Charlemagne Peralte, national hero **Obv:** Bust facing **Rev:** National arms **Note:** Accent marks on E and Is in obverse legend.

Date	Mintage	VF20	XF40	MS60	MS63	MS65
1995	—	—	—	0.45	0.75	1.00
2000	—	—	—	0.45	0.75	1.00

KM# 56 50 CENTIMES
10.00 g., Copper-Nickel, 29 mm. **Obv:** President Pierre Nord Alexis left **Rev:** National arms

Date	Mintage	F12	VF20	XF40	MS60	MS63
1907 (w)	2,000,000	1.00	5.50	15.00	45.00	65.00
1907 (w)	—	PF63 250				
1908 (w)	800,000	1.25	10.00	30.00	55.00	75.00
1908 (w)	—	PF63 300				

KM# 101 50 CENTIMES
10.00 g., Copper-Nickel, 29 mm. **Series:** F.A.O. **Obv:** President Jean-Claude Duvalier left **Rev:** National arms

Date	Mintage	VF20	XF40	MS60	MS63	MS65
1972	600,000	0.35	0.75	1.25	2.00	3.00

KM# 101a 50 CENTIMES
10.00 g., Copper-Nickel-Zinc, 29 mm. **Obv:** Head left **Rev:** National arms **Note:** Varieties exist.

Date	Mintage	VF20	XF40	MS60	MS63	MS65
1975	1,200,000	0.10	0.20	0.60	1.00	1.50
1979	2,000,000	0.10	0.20	0.60	1.00	1.50
1983	1,000,000	0.10	0.20	0.60	1.00	1.50
1985	—	—	—	0.45	0.75	1.00

KM# 148 50 CENTIMES
10.00 g., Copper-Nickel, 29 mm. **Series:** F.A.O. **Obv:** Head right, small logo at left **Rev:** Plants **Note:** Denomination as 0.50 Gourdes.

Date	Mintage	VF20	XF40	MS60	MS63	MS65
1981 R	15,000	0.35	1.00	1.50	2.50	4.50

KM# 153 50 CENTIMES
10.00 g., Copper-Nickel, 29 mm. **Subject:** Charlemagne Peralte, national hero **Obv:** Bust facing **Rev:** National arms **Edge:** Plain **Note:** No accent marks on obverse legend.

Date	Mintage	VF20	XF40	MS60	MS63	MS65
1986	2,000,000	0.10	0.25	0.60	1.00	1.50
1989	—	0.10	0.25	0.60	1.00	1.50
1991	—	0.10	0.25	0.60	1.00	1.50

KM# 153a 50 CENTIMES
Nickel Plated Steel, 29 mm. **Subject:** Charlemagne Peralte, national hero **Obv:** Bust facing **Rev:** National arms **Note:** Accent marks on obverse legend.

Date	Mintage	VF20	XF40	MS60	MS63	MS65
1995	—	0.10	0.25	0.75	1.25	1.50
1999	—	0.10	0.25	0.75	1.25	1.50

KM# 155 GOURDE
6.30 g., Brass Plated Steel, 23 mm. **Obv:** Citadelle de Roi Christophe **Shape:** 7-sided

Date	Mintage	VF20	XF40	MS60	MS63	MS65
1995	—	—	—	1.00	1.75	2.00
2000	—	—	—	1.00	1.75	2.00

KM# 64.1 5 GOURDES
23.52 g., 0.999 Silver 0.7554 oz. ASW **Series:** 10th Anniversary of Revolution **Subject:** Columbus Discovers America **Obv:** Three ships and map **Rev:** National arms

Date	Mintage	VF20	XF40	MS60	MS63	MS65
1967 IC	4,650	**PF63** 18.00	**PF65** 22.00	**PF67** 25.00		
1968 IC	5,750	**PF63** 18.00	**PF65** 22.00	**PF67** 25.00		
1969 IC	1,175	**PF63** 22.00	**PF65** 27.00	**PF67** 32.00		
1970 IC	2,060	**PF63** 22.00	**PF65** 27.00	**PF67** 32.00		

KM# 64.2 5 GOURDES
23.52 g., 0.999 Silver 0.7554 oz. ASW **Series:** 10th Anniversary of the Revolution **Subject:** Columbus Discovers America **Obv:** Three ships and map **Rev:** Additional "1 AR" countermark at 8 o'clock

Date	Mintage	VF20	XF40	MS60	MS63	MS65
1970	—	**PF63** 20.00	**PF65** 25.00	**PF67** 30.00		

KM# 78 5 GOURDES
23.52 g., 0.999 Silver 0.7554 oz. ASW **Rev:** Haitienne paradise

Date	Mintage	VF20	XF40	MS60	MS63	MS65
1971 IC	1,585	**PF65** 60.00	**PF67** 70.00			

KM# 156 5 GOURDES
9.20 g., Brass Plated Steel, 28 mm. **Obv:** Four portraits in circle of Haitian statesmen top: Gen. Tonsaint Louverture, Left: Henri Christophe, Right: Jean Jacques Dessalines, Bottom: Alexandre Petion, date below **Rev:** National arms **Shape:** 7-sided

Date	Mintage	VF20	XF40	MS60	MS63	MS65
1995	—	—	—	—	2.25	3.00
1998	—	—	—	—	2.25	3.00

KM# 65.1 10 GOURDES
47.05 g., 0.999 Silver 1.5112 oz. ASW, 40 mm. **Series:** 10th Anniversary of Revolution **Subject:** General Toussaint L'Overture **Obv:** Figure on rearing horse left **Rev:** National arms

Date	Mintage	VF20	XF40	MS60	MS63	MS65
1967 IC	6,750	**PF63** 30.00	**PF65** 35.00	**PF67** 40.00		
1968 IC	5,725	**PF63** 30.00	**PF65** 35.00	**PF67** 40.00		
1969 IC	1,100	**PF63** 40.00	**PF65** 50.00	**PF67** 60.00		
1970 IC	1,500	**PF63** 40.00	**PF65** 50.00	**PF67** 60.00		

KM# 65.2 10 GOURDES
47.05 g., 0.999 Silver 1.5112 oz. ASW, 40 mm. **Series:** 10th Anniversary of the Revolution **Subject:** General Toussaint L'Overture **Obv:** Figure on rearing horse left **Rev:** National arms **Note:** Rev; Additional "1 AR" countermark left of the initials "IC"

Date	Mintage	VF20	XF40	MS60	MS63	MS65
1970 IC	—	**PF63** 35.00	**PF65** 45.00	**PF67** 55.00		

KM# 79 10 GOURDES
47.05 g., 0.999 Silver 1.5112 oz. ASW, 40 mm. **Obv:** Seminole Chief - Osceola facing **Rev:** National arms

Date	Mintage	VF20	XF40	MS60	MS63	MS65
1971 IC	3,535	**PF63** 35.00	**PF65** 42.00	**PF67** 47.00		

KM# 80 10 GOURDES
47.05 g., 0.999 Silver 1.5112 oz. ASW, 40 mm. **Obv:** Sioux Chief - Sitting Bull **Rev:** National arms

Date	Mintage	VF20	XF40	MS60	MS63	MS65
1971 IC	3,185	**PF63** 35.00	**PF65** 42.00	**PF67** 47.00		

KM# 81 10 GOURDES
47.05 g., 0.999 Silver 1.5112 oz. ASW, 40 mm. **Obv:** Fox Chief - Playing Fox **Rev:** National arms

Date	Mintage	VF20	XF40	MS60	MS63	MS65
1971 IC	3,035	**PF63** 35.00	**PF65** 42.00	**PF67** 47.00		

KM# 82 10 GOURDES
47.05 g., 0.999 Silver 1.5112 oz. ASW, 40 mm. **Obv:** Chiricahua Chief - Geronimo **Rev:** National arms

Date	Mintage	VF20	XF40	MS60	MS63	MS65
1971 IC	3,285	PF63 35.00	PF65 42.00	PF67 47.00		

KM# 83 10 GOURDES
47.05 g., 0.999 Silver 1.5112 oz. ASW, 40 mm. **Obv:** Seminole Chief - Billy Bowlegs **Rev:** National arms

Date	Mintage	VF20	XF40	MS60	MS63	MS65
1971 IC	3,735	PF63 35.00	PF65 42.00	PF67 47.00		

KM# 84 10 GOURDES
47.05 g., 0.999 Silver 1.5112 oz. ASW, 40 mm. **Obv:** Nez Perce Chief - Joseph **Rev:** National arms

Date	Mintage	VF20	XF40	MS60	MS63	MS65
1971 IC	3,235	PF63 35.00	PF65 42.00	PF67 47.00		

KM# 85 10 GOURDES
47.05 g., 0.999 Silver 1.5112 oz. ASW, 40 mm. **Obv:** Yankton Sioux Chief - War Eagle **Rev:** National arms

Date	Mintage	VF20	XF40	MS60	MS63	MS65
1971 IC	3,135	PF63 35.00	PF65 42.00	PF67 47.00		

KM# 86 10 GOURDES
47.05 g., 0.999 Silver 1.5112 oz. ASW, 40 mm. **Obv:** Oglala Sioux Chief - Red Cloud **Rev:** National arms

Date	Mintage	VF20	XF40	MS60	MS63	MS65
1971 IC	3,235	PF63 35.00	PF65 42.00	PF67 47.00		

KM# 87 10 GOURDES
47.05 g., 0.999 Silver 1.5112 oz. ASW, 40 mm. **Obv:** Cherokee Chief - Stalking Turkey **Rev:** National arms

Date	Mintage	VF20	XF40	MS60	MS63	MS65
1971 IC	3,185	PF63 35.00	PF65 42.00	PF67 47.00		

KM# 66 20 GOURDES
3.95 g., 0.900 Gold 0.1143 oz. AGW **Series:** 10th Anniversary of Revolution **Obv:** Native left with knife in left hand **Rev:** National arms **Note:** Mackandal

Date	Mintage	VF20	XF40	MS60	MS63	MS65
1967 IC	10,351	PF65 200	PF67 225			
1968 IC	—	PF65 200	PF67 225			
1969 IC	—	PF65 200	PF67 225			
1970 IC	—	PF65 200	PF67 225			

KM# 67.1 25 GOURDES
117.60 g., 0.999 Silver 3.7771 oz. ASW, 60 mm. **Subject:** 10th Anniversary of Revolution **Obv:** Art objects **Rev:** National arms

Date	Mintage	VF20	XF40	MS60	MS63	MS65
1967 IC	—	PF63 80.00	PF65 100	PF67 115		
1968 IC	—	PF63 80.00	PF65 100	PF67 115		
1969 IC	1,115	PF63 90.00	PF65 110	PF67 120		
1970 IC	1,000	PF63 90.00	PF65 110	PF67 120		

KM# 67.2 25 GOURDES
117.60 g., 0.999 Silver 3.7771 oz. ASW, 60 mm. **Obv:** Art objects **Rev:** National arms with additional "1 AR" countermark at 8 o'clock

Date	Mintage	VF20	XF40	MS60	MS63	MS65
1970	—	PF63 80.00	PF65 100	PF67 115		

KM# 88 25 GOURDES
117.60 g., 0.999 Silver 3.7771 oz. ASW, 60 mm. **Obv:** International airport **Rev:** National arms

Date	Mintage	VF20	XF40	MS60	MS63	MS65
1971 IC	1,935	PF63 85.00	PF65 110	PF67 120		

KM# 102 25 GOURDES
8.38 g., 0.925 Silver 0.2491 oz. ASW **Obv:** Christopher Columbus bust 3/4 facing left **Rev:** National arms

Date	Mintage	VF20	XF40	MS60	MS63	MS65
1973	6,100	—	—	—	6.00	9.00
1973	5,470	PF65 15.00				
1974	—	PF65 20.00				

KM# 103 25 GOURDES
8.38 g., 0.925 Silver 0.2491 oz. ASW **Subject:** World Soccer Championship Games **Obv:** Games logo **Rev:** National arms

Date	Mintage	VF20	XF40	MS60	MS63	MS65
1973	57,000	—	—	—	6.00	9.00
1973	6,430	PF65 15.00				
1974	—	PF65 20.00				

KM# 112.1 25 GOURDES
8.38 g., 0.925 Silver 0.2491 oz. ASW **Series:** United States Bicentennial **Obv:** Soldiers with cannon **Rev:** National arms

Date	Mintage	VF20	XF40	MS60	MS63	MS65
1974	25,000	—	—	—	6.00	9.00
1974	600	PF65 25.00				
1975	—	PF65 35.00				
1976	10,000	PF65 12.00				

KM# 112.2 25 GOURDES
8.38 g., 0.925 Silver 0.2491 oz. ASW **Obv:** Soldiers with cannon, error; without country name at top **Rev:** National arms

Date	Mintage	VF20	XF40	MS60	MS63	MS65
1974	Inc. above	—	—	—	20.00	35.00

KM# 121 25 GOURDES
8.38 g., 0.925 Silver 0.2491 oz. ASW **Series:** International Women's Year **Obv:** Women with raised arms, inscription **Rev:** National arms

Date	Mintage	VF20	XF40	MS60	MS63	MS65
1975	7,180	—	—	—	15.00	20.00
1975	1,440	PF65 40.00	PF67 50.00			

KM# 72 30 GOURDES
9.11 g., 0.585 Gold 0.1713 oz. AGW **Series:** 10th Anniversary of Revolution **Obv:** Citadel of Saint Christopher **Rev:** National arms

Date	Mintage	VF20	XF40	MS60	MS63	MS65
1969 IC	1,185	PF65 275	PF67 300			
1970 IC	Inc. above	PF65 275	PF67 300			

KM# 73 40 GOURDES
12.15 g., 0.585 Gold 0.2285 oz. AGW **Series:** 10th Anniversary of Revolution **Subject:** J.J. Dessalines **Obv:** Uniformed bust facing divides dates **Rev:** National arms

Date	Mintage	VF20	XF40	MS60	MS63	MS65
1969	1,005	PF65 350	PF67 375			
1970	Inc. above	PF65 350	PF67 375			

KM# 68 50 GOURDES
9.87 g., 0.900 Gold 0.2856 oz. AGW **Series:** 10th Anniversary of Revolution **Obv:** Dancer **Rev:** National arms

Date	Mintage	VF20	XF40	MS60	MS63	MS65
1967 IC	8,681	PF65 450	PF67 475			
1968 IC	—	PF65 450	PF67 475			
1969 IC	—	PF65 450	PF67 475			
1970 IC	—	PF65 450	PF67 475			

KM# 89 50 GOURDES
9.87 g., 0.900 Gold 0.2856 oz. AGW **Series:** 10th Anniversary of Revolution **Obv:** Soldiers **Rev:** National arms **Note:** Heros de Vertieres

Date	Mintage	VF20	XF40	MS60	MS63	MS65
1971 IC	485	PF65 470	PF67 490			

KM# 104.1 50 GOURDES
16.75 g., 0.925 Silver 0.4981 oz. ASW **Obv:** Woman on the beach **Rev:** National arms, fineness mark left of value

Date	Mintage	VF20	XF40	MS60	MS63	MS65
1973	8,685	—	—	—	15.00	17.00
1973	5,973	PF65 25.00				
1974	—	PF65 40.00				

KM# 104.2 50 GOURDES
16.45 g., 0.925 Silver 0.4892 oz. ASW, 37.9 mm. **Obv:** Woman on beach **Rev:** National arms, fineness stamp right of value **Edge:** Reeded

Date	Mintage	VF20	XF40	MS60	MS63	MS65
1973	—	PF65 35.00				

KM# 105 50 GOURDES
16.75 g., 0.925 Silver 0.4981 oz. ASW **Obv:** Woman and child **Rev:** National arms

Date	Mintage	VF20	XF40	MS60	MS63	MS65
1973	7,300	—	—	—	13.00	15.00
1973	5,853	PF65 17.00				
1974	—	—	—	—	27.00	32.00
1974	—	PF65 37.00				

KM# 106 50 GOURDES
16.75 g., 0.925 Silver 0.4981 oz. ASW **Series:** World Soccer Championship Games **Obv:** Games logo **Rev:** National arms

Date	Mintage	VF20	XF40	MS60	MS63	MS65
1973	12,000	PF65 15.00				

KM# 113.1 50 GOURDES
16.75 g., 0.925 Silver 0.4981 oz. ASW **Series:** 1976 Montreal Olympiad **Obv:** Half-figure with torch above Olympic flame flanked by athletes **Rev:** National arms **Note:** Prev. KM#113.

Date	Mintage	VF20	XF40	MS60	MS63	MS65
1974	21,000	—	—	—	12.00	15.00
1974	2,358	PF65 20.00				
1975	—	PF65 25.00				
1976	—	—	—	—	—	—
1976 Thin 6; Proof	8,000	PF65 20.00				
1976 Thick 6; Proof	Inc. above	PF65 27.00				

KM# 113.2 50 GOURDES
16.75 g., 0.925 Silver 0.4981 oz. ASW **Series:** 1976 Montreal Olympiad **Obv:** Half-figure with torch above Olympic flame, athletes flank **Rev:** National arms, smaller 4 in date **Note:** Prev. KM#114.

Date	Mintage	VF20	XF40	MS60	MS63	MS65
1974	—	—	—	—	17.00	20.00
1974	—	PF65 27.00				

KM# 123 50 GOURDES
16.75 g., 0.925 Silver 0.4981 oz. ASW, 38.14 mm. **Subject:** Holy Year **Obv:** Pope Paul and Praying hands above St. Peter's Square **Rev:** National arms **Edge:** Reeded

Date	Mintage	VF20	XF40	MS60	MS63	MS65
1974	—	—	—	—	12.00	15.00
1974	960	PF65 22.00				
1975	—	—	—	—	32.00	37.00
1975	—	PF65 37.00				
1976	6,000	PF65 25.00				

KM# 127 50 GOURDES
21.30 g., 0.925 Silver 0.6334 oz. ASW **Series:** World Soccer Championship Games **Obv:** Soccer ball with date at center **Rev:** National arms

Date	Mintage	VF20	XF40	MS60	MS63	MS65
1977	11,000	—	—	—	18.00	22.00
1977	9,000	PF65 27.00				

KM# 128 50 GOURDES
21.30 g., 0.925 Silver 0.6334 oz. ASW **Subject:** Human Rights **Obv:** Kneeling figure with broken chains **Rev:** National arms

Date	Mintage	VF20	XF40	MS60	MS63	MS65
1977	545	PF65 45.00				
1977	800	—	—	—	32.00	35.00

KM# 129 50 GOURDES
21.30 g., 0.925 Silver 0.6334 oz. ASW **Series:** 1980 Moscow Olympics **Obv:** Olympic flame above date, athletes flank **Rev:** National arms

Date	Mintage	VF20	XF40	MS60	MS63	MS65
1977	3,720	PF65 35.00				
1977	3,969	—	—	—	27.00	30.00
1978	Est. 350	PF65 225				

KM# 130.1 50 GOURDES
21.30 g., 0.925 Silver 0.6334 oz. ASW **Series:** 20th Anniversary of European Market **Obv:** Map of Europe on globe design **Rev:** National arms

Date	Mintage	VF20	XF40	MS60	MS63	MS65
1977	421	—	—	30.00	65.00	70.00
1977	364	PF65 80.00				
1978	—	—	—	30.00	65.00	70.00

KM# 130.2 50 GOURDES
21.30 g., 0.925 Silver 0.6334 oz. ASW **Obv:** Map of Europe on globe design, entire area within circle frosted **Rev:** National arms

Date	Mintage	VF20	XF40	MS60	MS63	MS65
1978	—	PF65 90.00				
1978	—	—	—	25.00	50.00	60.00

KM# 131 50 GOURDES
21.30 g., 0.925 Silver 0.6334 oz. ASW **Obv:** 1959 World Queen of Sugar Cane (Claudinette Fouchard) left **Rev:** National arms

Date	Mintage	VF20	XF40	MS60	MS63	MS65
1977	602	PF65 45.00				
1977	321	—	—	20.00	35.00	40.00

KM# 149 50 GOURDES
20.00 g., 0.925 Silver 0.5948 oz. ASW **Series:** F.A.O. **Obv:** Head left **Rev:** Plants

Date	Mintage	VF20	XF40	MS60	MS63	MS65
1981 R	Est. 14000	—	—	—	12.00	15.00
1981 R	—	PF63 14.00	PF65 16.00			

KM# 150 50 GOURDES
20.00 g., 0.925 Silver 0.5948 oz. ASW **Subject:** Holy Year **Obv:** National arms **Rev:** Buildings

Date	Mintage	VF20	XF40	MS60	MS63	MS65
1983 R	1,000	PF65 80.00	PF67 100			

KM# 74 60 GOURDES
18.22 g., 0.585 Gold 0.3427 oz. AGW **Series:** 10th Anniversary of the Revolution **Obv:** Alexandre Petion **Rev:** National arms

Date	Mintage	VF20	XF40	MS60	MS63	MS65
1969 IC	935	PF65 575	PF67 600			
1970 IC	Inc. above	PF65 675	PF67 700			

KM# 69 100 GOURDES
19.75 g., 0.900 Gold 0.5715 oz. AGW **Series:** 10th Anniversary of the Revolution **Subject:** Marie Jeanne **Obv:** Half-figure left with knife in right hand **Rev:** National arms

Date	Mintage	VF20	XF40	MS60	MS63	MS65
1967 IC	—	PF65 925	PF67 975			
1968 IC	—	PF65 1,150	PF67 1,300			
1969 IC	—	PF65 950	PF67 1,000			
1970 IC	—	PF65 950	PF67 1,000			

KM# 90 100 GOURDES
19.75 g., 0.900 Gold 0.5715 oz. AGW **Obv:** Seminole Tribal Chief - Osceola **Rev:** National arms

Date	Mintage	VF20	XF40	MS60	MS63	MS65
1971 IC	435	PF65 1,100	PF67 1,250			

KM# 91 100 GOURDES
19.75 g., 0.900 Gold 0.5715 oz. AGW **Obv:** Sioux Chief - Sitting Bull **Rev:** National arms

Date	Mintage	VF20	XF40	MS60	MS63	MS65
1971 IC	475	PF65 1,100	PF67 1,250			

KM# 92 100 GOURDES
19.75 g., 0.900 Gold 0.5715 oz. AGW **Obv:** Fox Chief - Playing Fox **Rev:** National arms

Date	Mintage	VF20	XF40	MS60	MS63	MS65
1971 IC	425	PF65 1,100	PF67 1,250			

KM# 93 100 GOURDES
19.75 g., 0.900 Gold 0.5715 oz. AGW **Obv:** Chiricahua Chief - Geronimo **Rev:** National arms

Date	Mintage	VF20	XF40	MS60	MS63	MS65
1971 IC	520	PF65 1,100	PF67 1,250			

KM# 94 100 GOURDES
19.75 g., 0.900 Gold 0.5715 oz. AGW **Obv:** Seminole Chief - Billy Bowlegs **Rev:** National arms

Date	Mintage	VF20	XF40	MS60	MS63	MS65
1971 IC	425	PF65 1,100	PF67 1,250			

KM# 95 100 GOURDES
19.75 g., 0.900 Gold 0.5715 oz. AGW **Obv:** Nez Perce Chief Joseph portrait **Rev:** National arms

Date	Mintage	VF20	XF40	MS60	MS63	MS65
1971 IC	455	PF65 1,100	PF67 1,250			

KM# 96 100 GOURDES
19.75 g., 0.900 Gold 0.5715 oz. AGW **Obv:** Yankton Sioux Chief - War Eagle **Rev:** National arms

Date	Mintage	VF20	XF40	MS60	MS63	MS65
1971 IC	455	PF65 1,100	PF67 1,250			

KM# 97 100 GOURDES
19.75 g., 0.900 Gold 0.5715 oz. AGW **Obv:** Oglala Sioux Chief - Red Cloud **Rev:** National arms

Date	Mintage	VF20	XF40	MS60	MS63	MS65
1971 IC	455	PF65 1,100	PF67 1,250			

KM# 98 100 GOURDES
19.75 g., 0.900 Gold 0.5715 oz. AGW **Obv:** Cherokee Chief - Stalking Turkey **Rev:** National arms

Date	Mintage	VF20	XF40	MS60	MS63	MS65
1971 IC	425	PF65 1,100	PF67 1,250			

KM# 107 100 GOURDES
1.45 g., 0.900 Gold 0.042 oz. AGW **Subject:** Christopher Columbus **Obv:** Bust facing **Rev:** National arms

Date	Mintage	VF20	XF40	MS60	MS63	MS65
1973	3,233	—	—	—	—	70.00
1973	915	PF65 75.00	PF67 95.00			

KM# 132 100 GOURDES
43.00 g., 0.925 Silver 1.2788 oz. ASW **Subject:** Presidents Sadat and Begin **Obv:** Profiles facing each other, Dove of Peace above **Rev:** National arms

Date	Mintage	VF20	XF40	MS60	MS63	MS65
1977	550	—	—	—	65.00	70.00
1977	500	PF65 90.00	PF67 100			

KM# 133 100 GOURDES
43.00 g., 0.925 Silver 1.2788 oz. ASW **Subject:** 20th Anniversary of European Market **Obv:** Ships wheel and sailboat **Rev:** National arms

Date	Mintage	VF20	XF40	MS60	MS63	MS65
1977	321	—	—	—	95.00	100
1977	214	PF65 120	PF67 135			

KM# 134 100 GOURDES
43.00 g., 0.925 Silver 1.2788 oz. ASW **Subject:** 50th Anniversary of Lindbergh's New York to Paris Flight **Obv:** Portrait of Lindbergh in flier's cap above "Spirit of St. Louis" **Rev:** National arms

Date	Mintage	VF20	XF40	MS60	MS63	MS65
1977	321	—	—	—	90.00	95.00
1977	214	PF65 135	PF67 150			

KM# 135 100 GOURDES
43.00 g., 0.925 Silver 1.2788 oz. ASW **Obv:** Statue of Liberty **Rev:** National arms

Date	Mintage	VF20	XF40	MS60	MS63	MS65
1977	321	—	—	—	90.00	95.00
1977	214	PF65 135	PF67 150			

KM# 158 100 GOURDES
40.00 g., 0.925 Silver 1.1896 oz. ASW **Subject:** 10th Anniversary of the Presidency of Jean Claude Duvalier **Obv:** Head right without FAO **Rev:** Woman and child

Date	Mintage	VF20	XF40	MS60	MS63	MS65
1981 R	—	PF67 180				

KM# 159 100 GOURDES
40.00 g., 0.925 Silver 1.1896 oz. ASW **Subject:** 10th Anniversary of the Presidency of Jean Claude Duvalier **Obv:** Head right without FAO **Rev:** Infants on open book

Date	Mintage	VF20	XF40	MS60	MS63	MS65
1981 R	—	PF67 180				

KM# 160 100 GOURDES
40.00 g., 0.925 Silver 1.1896 oz. ASW **Subject:** 10th Anniversary of the Presidency of Jean Claude Duvalier **Obv:** Head right without FAO **Rev:** Nude woman and man

Date	Mintage	VF20	XF40	MS60	MS63	MS65
1981 R	—	PF67 195				

KM# 70 200 GOURDES
39.49 g., 0.900 Gold 1.1427 oz. AGW **Subject:** Revolt of Santo Domingo **Obv:** Native running with weapons **Rev:** National arms

Date	Mintage	VF20	XF40	MS60	MS63	MS65
1967 IC	Est. 4199	PF65 1,800	PF67 1,900			
1968 IC	—	PF65 2,800	PF67 2,900			
1969 IC	—	PF65 1,800	PF67 1,900			
1970 IC	—	PF65 1,800	PF67 1,900			

KM# 99 200 GOURDES
39.49 g., 0.900 Gold 1.1427 oz. AGW **Obv:** Revolutionist from Santo Domingo **Rev:** National arms

Date	Mintage	XF40	MS60	MS63	MS65	MS66
1971 IC	235	PF65 2,000	PF67 2,250	PF69 2,700		

KM# 108 200 GOURDES
2.91 g., 0.900 Gold 0.0842 oz. AGW **Series:** World Soccer Championship Games **Obv:** Games logo **Rev:** National arms

Date	Mintage	VF20	XF40	MS60	MS63	MS65
1973	5,167	—	—	—	—	150
1973	915	PF65 170	PF67 190			

KM# 115 200 GOURDES
2.91 g., 0.900 Gold 0.0842 oz. AGW **Subject:** Holy Year **Obv:** Pope Paul and Praying hands above St. Peter's Square **Rev:** National arms, fineness stamped on hexagonal mound

Date	Mintage	VF20	XF40	MS60	MS63	MS65
1974	4,965	—	—	—	—	155
1974	660	PF65 175	PF67 195			

KM# 124 200 GOURDES
2.91 g., 0.900 Gold 0.0842 oz. AGW **Subject:** Holy Year **Obv:** Pope Paul and Praying hands above St. Peter's Square **Rev:** National arms, fineness stamped on oval mound

Date	Mintage	VF20	XF40	MS60	MS63	MS65
1975	—	PF65 160	PF67 175			

KM# 125 200 GOURDES
2.91 g., 0.900 Gold 0.0842 oz. AGW **Series:** International Women's Year **Obv:** Two women with arms upraised **Rev:** National arms

Date	Mintage	VF20	XF40	MS60	MS63	MS65
1975	2,260	—	—	—	—	155
1975	840	PF65 175	PF67 195			

KM# 75 250 GOURDES
75.95 g., 0.585 Gold 1.4285 oz. AGW **Series:** 10th Anniversary of Revolution **Obv:** King H. Christophe **Rev:** National arms

Date	Mintage	XF40	MS60	MS63	MS65	MS66
1969 IC	470	PF67 2,000	PF69 2,500			
1970 IC	—	PF67 2,200	PF69 2,700			

KM# 136 250 GOURDES
4.25 g., 0.900 Gold 0.123 oz. AGW **Subject:** Human Rights **Obv:** Kneeling figure with broken chains **Rev:** National arms

Date	Mintage	VF20	XF40	MS60	MS63	MS65
1977	282	—	—	—	—	225
1977	288	PF65 235	PF67 255			

KM# 137 250 GOURDES
4.25 g., 0.900 Gold 0.123 oz. AGW **Subject:** Presidents Sadat and Begin **Obv:** Profiles facing each other, Dove of Peace above **Rev:** National arms

Date	Mintage	VF20	XF40	MS60	MS63	MS65
1977	270	—	—	—	—	220
1977	520	PF65 230	PF67 250			

KM# 138 250 GOURDES
4.25 g., 0.900 Gold 0.123 oz. AGW **Subject:** 20th Anniversary of European Market **Obv:** Ships wheel and sailboat **Rev:** National arms

Date	Mintage	VF20	XF40	MS60	MS63	MS65
1977	107	—	—	—	—	240
1977	107	PF65 250	PF67 270			

KM# 139 250 GOURDES
4.25 g., 0.900 Gold 0.123 oz. AGW **Subject:** 50th Anniversary of Lindbergh's New York to Paris Flight **Obv:** Portrait of Lindbergh in flier's cap above "Spirit of St. Louis" **Rev:** National arms

Date	Mintage	VF20	XF40	MS60	MS63	MS65
1977	107	—	—	—	—	260
1977	107	PF65 270	PF67 290			

KM# 76 500 GOURDES
151.90 g., 0.585 Gold 2.857 oz. AGW, 68 mm. **Series:** 10th Anniversary of Revolution **Obv:** Haitian native art **Rev:** National arms **Note:** Illustration reduced.

Date	Mintage	XF40	MS60	MS63	MS65	MS66
1969 IC	435	PF65 4,250	PF67 4,550	PF69 4,850		
1970 IC	—	PF65 4,500	PF67 4,800	PF69 5,100		

KM# 109 500 GOURDES
7.28 g., 0.900 Gold 0.2107 oz. AGW **Obv:** Woman with shell right **Rev:** National arms

Date	Mintage	VF20	XF40	MS60	MS63	MS65
1973	2,380	—	—	—	—	365
1973	915	PF65 375	PF67 395			

KM# 110 500 GOURDES
7.28 g., 0.900 Gold 0.2107 oz. AGW **Obv:** Woman with child **Rev:** National arms

Date	Mintage	VF20	XF40	MS60	MS63	MS65
1973	2,265	—	—	—	—	365
1973	915	PF65 375	PF67 395			

KM# 116 500 GOURDES
6.50 g., 0.900 Gold 0.1881 oz. AGW **Obv:** Battle scene **Rev:** National arms

Date	Mintage	VF20	XF40	MS60	MS63	MS65
1974	—	PF65 335	PF67 355			

KM# 117 500 GOURDES
6.50 g., 0.900 Gold 0.1881 oz. AGW **Series:** 1976 Montreal & Insbruck Olympics **Obv:** Half-figure with torch above Olympic flame, athletes flank **Rev:** National arms, fineness stamped on hexagonal mound

Date	Mintage	VF20	XF40	MS60	MS63	MS65
1974	3,489	—	—	—	—	325
1974	1,140	PF65 335	PF67 355			

KM# 126 500 GOURDES
6.50 g., 0.900 Gold 0.1881 oz. AGW **Series:** 1976 Montreal & Insbruck Olympics **Obv:** Half-figure with torch above Olympic

flame, athletes flank **Rev:** National arms, fineness stamped on oval mound

Date	Mintage	XF40	MS60	MS63	MS65	MS66
1975	120	—	—	—	450	500

KM# 140 500 GOURDES
8.50 g., 0.900 Gold 0.246 oz. AGW **Series:** World Soccer Championship Games **Obv:** Soccer ball with date in center **Rev:** National arms

Date	Mintage	XF40	MS60	MS63	MS65	MS66
1977	450	—	—	—	425	450
1977	200	PF65 450	PF67 475			

KM# 141 500 GOURDES
8.50 g., 0.900 Gold 0.246 oz. AGW **Series:** 1980 Moscow Olympics **Rev:** National arms

Date	Mintage	XF40	MS60	MS63	MS65	MS66
1977	695	—	—	—	425	450
1977	504	PF65 435	PF67 455			
1978	Est. 350	PF67 475				

KM# 142 500 GOURDES
8.50 g., 0.900 Gold 0.246 oz. AGW **Subject:** 20th Anniversary of European Common Market **Obv:** Map of Europe **Rev:** National arms

Date	Mintage	XF40	MS60	MS63	MS65	MS66
1977	207	—	—	—	425	450
1977	257	PF65 450	PF67 475			
1978	—	—	—	—	460	470
1978	150	PF67 480				

KM# 143 500 GOURDES
8.50 g., 0.900 Gold 0.246 oz. AGW **Subject:** Economic Connections **Rev:** National arms

Date	Mintage	XF40	MS60	MS63	MS65	MS66
1977	107	—	—	—	465	475
1977	107	PF67 485				

KM# 144 500 GOURDES
8.50 g., 0.900 Gold 0.246 oz. AGW **Obv:** Jean-Claude Duvalier **Rev:** National arms

Date	Mintage	XF40	MS60	MS63	MS65	MS66
1977	107	—	—	—	465	475
1977	328	PF67 485				

KM# 161 500 GOURDES
7.00 g., 0.900 Gold 0.2025 oz. AGW **Subject:** 10th Anniversary of the Presidency of Jean Claude Duvalier **Obv:** Head right without FAO **Rev:** Sun above farmer on tractor in field

Date	Mintage	VF20	XF40	MS60	MS63	MS65
1981 R	—	PF67 750				

KM# 162 500 GOURDES
7.00 g., 0.900 Gold 0.2025 oz. AGW **Subject:** 10th Anniversary of the Presidency of Jean Claude Duvalier **Obv:** Head right without FAO **Rev:** Plants

Date	Mintage	VF20	XF40	MS60	MS63	MS65
1981 R	—	PF67 750				

KM# 163 500 GOURDES
7.00 g., 0.900 Gold 0.2025 oz. AGW **Subject:** 10th Anniversary of the Presidency of Jean Claude Duvalier **Obv:** Head right without FAO **Rev:** Harvesters

Date	Mintage	VF20	XF40	MS60	MS63	MS65
1981 R	—	PF67 750				

KM# 151 500 GOURDES
10.50 g., 0.900 Gold 0.3038 oz. AGW **Subject:** Papal Visit **Obv:** National arms **Rev:** Bust left above people

Date	Mintage	VF20	XF40	MS60	MS63	MS65
1983 R	1,000	PF65 500	PF67 550			

KM# 165 500 GOURDES
28.28 g., 0.925 Silver 0.841 oz. ASW, 38.5 mm. **Subject:** Millennium **Obv:** Multicolor and gold-plated national arms **Rev:** Dove and partially gold-plated sun rays **Edge:** Reeded

Date	Mintage	VF20	XF40	MS60	MS63	MS65
ND(1999)	—	PF65 85.00				

KM# 71 1000 GOURDES
197.48 g., 0.900 Gold 5.7142 oz. AGW **Series:** 10th Anniversary of Revolution **Obv:** Dr. Francois Duvalier **Rev:** National arms

Date	Mintage	VF20	XF40	MS60	MS63	MS65
1967 IC	Est. 2950	PF65 8,500	PF67 9,000			
1968 IC	—	PF65 10,000	PF67 11,000			
1969 IC	—	PF65 9,000	PF67 9,500			
1970 IC	—	PF65 9,000	PF67 9,500			

KM# 111 1000 GOURDES
13.00 g., 0.900 Gold 0.3762 oz. AGW **Obv:** President Jean Claude Duvalier left **Rev:** National arms

Date	Mintage	VF20	XF40	MS60	MS63	MS65
1973	—	—	—	—	—	725
1973	915	PF65 750	PF67 775			

KM# 118.1 1000 GOURDES
13.00 g., 0.900 Gold 0.3762 oz. AGW **Series:** United States Bicentennial **Obv:** Battle scene **Rev:** National arms

Date	Mintage	VF20	XF40	MS60	MS63	MS65
1974	3,040	—	—	—	—	650
1974	480	PF65 700	PF67 750			
1975	—	PF65 800	PF67 850			

KM# 118.2 1000 GOURDES
13.00 g., 0.900 Gold 0.3762 oz. AGW **Obv:** Error; without country name at top **Rev:** National arms

Date	Mintage	VF20	XF40	MS60	MS63	MS65
1974	—	—	—	—	850	900

KM# 164 1000 GOURDES
14.00 g., 0.900 Gold 0.4051 oz. AGW **Subject:** 10th Anniversary of the Presidency of Jean Claude Duvalier **Obv:** Head right without FAO **Rev:** Three nudes and flag

Date	Mintage	VF20	XF40	MS60	MS63	MS65
1981 R	—	PF67 1,350				

PATTERNS

Including off metal strikes

KM#	Date	Mintage	Identification	Mkt Val
Pn87	1974	—	25 Gourdes. 0.925. Silver. KM#112.	—

TRIAL STRIKES

KM#	Date	Mintage	Identification	Mkt Val
TS1	ND-1971	—	100 Gourdes. Bronze Gilt. Bust in headdress facing. Blank. KM#93.	300

MINT SETS

KM#	Date	Mintage	Identification	Issue Price	Mkt Val
MS1	1973 (8)	8,000	KM#102, 104-105, 107-111	490	1,800
MS2	1973 (8)	—	KM#102, 104.1, 105, 107-111	60.00	1,800
MS3	1974 (2)	—	KM#115, 123	—	185
MS4	1975 (2)	—	KM#121, 125	50.25	195
MS5	1974 (2)	—	KM#113, 117	—	365
MS6	1995 (5)	—	KM#152a-154a, 155, 156	—	10.00

PROOF SETS

KM#	Date	Mintage	Identification	Issue Price	Mkt Val
PSA1	1967 (8)	—	KM#64.1, 65.1, 66, 67.1, 68-71	—	14,000
PS1	1967 (5)	2,525	KM#66, 68-71	722	13,750
PS2	1967 (3)	4,650	KM#64.1, 65.1, 67.1	47.00	225
PS3	1968 (5)	475	KM#66, 68-71	823	18,000
PS4	1968 (3)	5,725	KM#64.1, 65.1, 67.1	53.50	225

KM#	Date	Mintage	Identification	Issue Price	Mkt Val
PS5	1969 (5)	435	KM#72-76	475	8,850
PS6	1969 (5)	140	KM#66, 68-71	823	14,300
PS7	1969 (3)	1,100	KM#64.1, 65.1, 67.1	53.50	250
PS8	1970 (5)	—	KM#66, 68-71	823	14,300
PSA9	1970 (3)	1,000	KM#64.1, 65.1, 67.1	53.50	255
PS9	1970 (3)	—	KM#64.2, 65.2, 67.2	—	290
PSA10	1970-71 (5)	—	KM#64.1, 65.1, 67.1, 78, 88	265	475
PS10	1971 (9)	—	KM#79-87	135	495
PSA11	1971 (18)	—	KM#79-87, 90-98	—	9,950
PS11	1971 (9)	—	KM#90-98	—	9,450
PS12	1973 (8)	1,250	KM#102, 103, 104.1, 105, 107-109, 111	830	1,525
PS13	1973 (4)	3,500	KM#102, 103, 104.1, 105	60.00	90.00
PS14	1974 (4)	—	KM#102, 103, 104.1, 105	—	150
PS15	1975 (2)	—	KM#121, 125	67.25	220
PS17	1976 (3)	—	KM#112.1, 113.1, 123 Although the insert information card in #PS17 state B.U., this issue is considered to be of proof quality.	—	75.00
PS18	1978 (2)	350	KM#129, 141	—	700
PS19	1978 (2)	—	KM#130.2, 142	—	560
PS20	1981R (7)	10	KM#158-164	—	4,150

HEJAZ

Hejaz, a province of Saudi Arabia and a former vilayet of the Ottoman Empire, occupies an 800-mile long (1,287km.) coastal strip between Nejd and the Red Sea. The province was a Turkish dependency until freed in World War I. Husain Ibn Ali, Amir of Mecca, opposed the Turkish control and, with the aid of Lawrence of Arabia, wrested much of Hejaz from the Turks and in 1916 assumed the title of King of Hejaz. Abd Al-Aziz Bin Sa'ud, of Nejd conquered Hejaz in 1925, and in 1926 combined it and Nejd into a single kingdom.

TITLES

الحجاز

Hal-Hejaz

RULERS

al Husain Ibn Ali, AH1334-42/1916-24AD
Abd Al-Aziz Bin Sa'ud, AH1343-1373/1925-1953AD

MONETARY SYSTEM

40 Para = 1 Piastre (Ghirsh)
20 Piastres = 1 Riyal
100 Piastres = 1 Dinar

KINGDOM

COUNTERMARKED COINAGE

Following the defeat of the Ottomans in 1916, Turkish 10, 20 and 40 Para coins of Muhammed V and 40 Para coins of Muhammed VI were countermarked al-Hejaz in Arabic. The countermark was applied to the obverse side effacing the Ottoman Sultan's toughra, and thus refuting Turkish rule in Hejaz.

Countermarks on the reverse are rare errors. The 10 Para of Muhammed V and 10 and 20 Para (billon) of Abdul Mejid and Mahmud II exist with a smaller, 6-millimeter countermark. These are probably unofficial. Other host coins are considered controversial.

Minor Coins

KM# 2 10 PARA

Nickel **Obv:** Reshat **Countermark:** Hejaz **Note:** Large countermark on Turkey 10 Para, KM#760. Accession date: 1327.

CM Date	Host Date	G4	VG8	F12	VF20	XF40
ND(1327)	1327//2-7 Rare	—	—	—	—	—

KM# 3 20 PARA

Nickel **Countermark:** Hejaz **Note:** Countermark on Turkey 20 Para, KM#761. Accession date: 1327.

CM Date	Host Date	G4	VG8	F12	VF20	XF40
ND(1327)	1327//2	5.00	9.00	20.00	40.00	—
ND(1327)	1327//3	4.00	7.00	15.00	30.00	—
ND(1327)	1327//4	3.00	6.00	12.00	25.00	—
ND(1327)	1327//5	3.00	6.00	12.00	25.00	—
ND(1327)	1327//6	3.00	6.00	12.00	25.00	—
ND(1327)	1327//x p.y. obliterated	2.00	5.00	10.00	20.00	—

KM# 4 40 PARA

Nickel **Obv:** El Ghazi **Countermark:** Hejaz **Note:** Countermark on Turkey 40 Para, KM#766. Accession date: 1327.

CM Date	Host Date	G4	VG8	F12	VF20	XF40
ND(1327)	1327//3	6.00	10.00	20.00	40.00	—
ND(1327)	1327//4	3.00	6.00	12.00	25.00	—
ND(1327)	1327//5	3.00	6.00	12.00	25.00	—
ND(1327)	1327//x p.y. obliterated	2.00	5.00	10.00	20.00	—

KM# 5 40 PARA

Copper-Nickel **Countermark:** Hejaz **Note:** Countermark on Turkey 40 Para, KM#779. Accession date: 1327.

CM Date	Host Date	G4	VG8	F12	VF20	XF40
ND(1327)	1327//8	4.00	6.00	12.00	25.00	—
ND(1327)	1327//9	20.00	30.00	75.00	150	—
ND(1327)	1327//x p.y. obliterated	3.00	6.00	10.00	20.00	—

KM# 6 40 PARA

Copper-Nickel **Countermark:** Hejaz **Note:** Countermark on Turkey 40 Para, KM#828. Accession date: 1336.

CM Date	Host Date	G4	VG8	F12	VF20	XF40
ND(1327)	1336//4	50.00	75.00	150	450	—
ND(1327)	1336//x	40.00	50.00	100	275	—

COUNTERMARKED COINAGE

Silver coins of various sizes were also countermarked al-Hejaz. The most common host coins include the Maria Theresa Thaler of Austria, and 5, 10, and 20 Kurush or Qirsh of Turkey and Egypt. The countermark occurs in various sizes and styles of script. These countermarks may have been applied by local silversmiths to discourage re-exportation of the badly needed hard currency and silver of known fineness.

Some crown-sized examples exist with both the al-Hejaz and Nejd countermarks. The authenticity of the silver countermarked coins has long been discussed, and it is likely that most were privately produced. Other host coins are considered controversial.

Silver Coins

KM# 10 5 PIASTRES

Silver **Countermark:** Hejaz **Note:** Countermark on Turkey 5 Kurush, KM#750. Accession date: 1327.

CM Date	Host Date	G4	VG8	F12	VF20	XF40
(1916-20)	(AH1327//1-7)	100	125	200	400	—

KM# 11 5 PIASTRES

Silver **Countermark:** Hejaz **Note:** Countermark on Turkey 5 Kurush, KM#771. Accession date: 1327.

CM Date	Host Date	G4	VG8	F12	VF20	XF40
(1916-20)	(AH1327//7-9)	100	125	200	400	—

KM# 12 5 PIASTRES

Silver **Countermark:** Hejaz **Note:** Countermark on Egypt 5 Qirsh, KM#308. Accession date: 1327.

CM Date	Host Date	G4	VG8	F12	VF20	XF40
(1916-20)	(AH1327//2H-4H 6H)	100	125	200	400	—

KM# 13 10 PIASTRES

Silver **Countermark:** Hejaz **Note:** Countermark on Turkey 10 Kurush, KM#751. Accession date: 1327.

CM Date	Host Date	G4	VG8	F12	VF20	XF40
(1916-20)	(AH1327//1-7)	125	200	300	500	—

KM# 14 10 PIASTRES

Silver **Countermark:** Hejaz **Note:** Countermark on Turkey 10 Kurush, KM#772. Accession date: 1327.

CM Date	Host Date	G4	VG8	F12	VF20	XF40
(1916-20)	(AH1327//7-10)	125	200	300	500	—

KM# 15 10 PIASTRES

Silver **Countermark:** Hejaz **Note:** Countermark on Egypt 10 Qirsh, KM#309. Accession date: 1327.

CM Date	Host Date	G4	VG8	F12	VF20	XF40
(1916-20)	(AH1327//2H-4H 6H)	125	200	300	500	—

KM# 16 20 PIASTRES

Silver **Countermark:** Hejaz **Note:** Countermark on Egypt 20 Qirsh, KM#310. Accession date: 1327.

CM Date	Host Date	G4	VG8	F12	VF20	XF40
(1916-20)	(AH1327//2H-4H 6H)	125	200	300	500	—

KM# 17 20 PIASTRES

24.06 g., Silver, 37 mm. **Countermark:** Hejaz **Note:** Countermark on Turkey 20 Kurush, KM#780. Accession date: 1327.

CM Date	Host Date	G4	VG8	F12	VF20	XF40
(1916-20)	(AH1327//8-10)	125	200	300	500	—

KM# 18 20 PIASTRES

28.06 g., Silver, 41 mm. **Countermark:** Hejaz **Note:** Countermark on Austria Maria Theresa Thaler, KM#T1. Accession date: 1327.

CM Date	Host Date	G4	VG8	F12	VF20	XF40
ND(1916-20)	1780	75.00	125	175	300	—

FIRST REGULAR COINAGE

All the regular coins of Hejaz bear the accessional date AH1334 of Al-Husain Ibn Ali, plus the regnal year. Many of the bronze coins occur with a light silver wash mostly on thicker specimens. A variety of planchet thicknesses exist.

KM# 21 1/8 PIASTRE

Bronze, 12-13 mm. **Note:** Reeded and plain edge varieties exist. Size varies.

Date	Mintage	G4	VG8	F12	VF20	XF40
AH1334//5	—	—	250	400	550	850

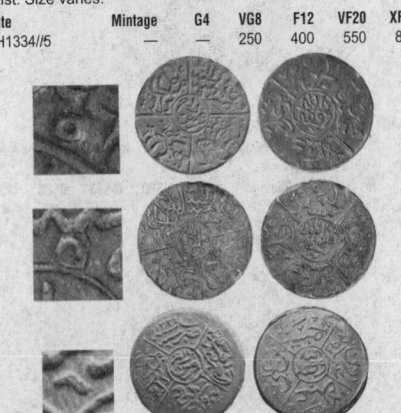

KM# 22 1/4 PIASTRE

1.14 g., Bronze, 16 mm. **Note:** Reeded and plain edge varieties exist.

Date	Mintage	G4	VG8	F12	VF20	XF40
AH1334//5	—	—	20.00	30.00	45.00	65.00
AH1334//6/5	—	—	200	400	600	1,200
AH1334//6	—	—	500	1,000	2,500	4,500

KM# 23 1/2 PIASTRE
Bronze, 18-19 mm. **Note:** Reeded and plain edge varieties exist. Size varies.

Date	Mintage	G4	VG8	F12	VF20	XF40
AH1334//5	—	—	22.00	32.00	47.00	75.00

KM# 24 PIASTRE
Bronze, 21-22 mm. **Edge:** Reeded **Note:** Size varies.

Date	Mintage	G4	VG8	F12	VF20	XF40
AH1334//5	—	—	10.00	20.00	50.00	100
AH1334//6/5	—	—	150	250	400	750

SECOND REGULAR COINAGE

KM# 25 1/4 PIASTRE
Bronze, 17 mm. **Edge:** Plain

Date	Mintage	G4	VG8	F12	VF20	XF40
AH1334//8	—	—	15.00	25.00	40.00	75.00

KM# 26 1/2 PIASTRE
3.14 g., Bronze, 19 mm. **Note:** Similar to 1/4 Piastre, KM#25. Most known specimens were overstruck as "Hejaz & Nejd" KM#1.

Date	Mintage	G4	VG8	F12	VF20	XF40
AH1334//8 Rare; four known	—	—	—	—	—	—

KM# 27 PIASTRE
Bronze, 21 mm. **Edge:** Plain

Date	Mintage	G4	VG8	F12	VF20	XF40
AH1334//8	—	—	100	200	325	550

KM# 28 5 PIASTRES
6.10 g., 0.917 Silver 0.1798 oz. ASW, 24 mm.

Date	Mintage	G4	VG8	F12	VF20	XF40
AH1334//8	—	—	50.00	125	250	500

KM# 29 10 PIASTRES
12.05 g., 0.917 Silver 0.3553 oz. ASW, 28 mm.

Date	Mintage	G4	VG8	F12	VF20	XF40
AH1334//8	—	—	300	500	850	1,750

KM# 30 20 PIASTRES (1 Riyal)
24.10 g., 0.917 Silver 0.7105 oz. ASW, 37 mm.

Date	Mintage	G4	VG8	F12	VF20	XF40
AH1334//8	—	—	40.00	75.00	150	300
AH1334//9	—	—	125	250	500	1,000

Note: Many of the AH1334//9 coins were struck using extremely rusted dies. Value on these strikes in VF is $200

KM# 31 DINAR HASHIMI
7.22 g., Gold, 22 mm.

Date	Mintage	VG8	F12	VF20	XF40	MS60
AH1334//8	—	—	350	550	1,250	1,550

KM# 32 DINAR HASHIMI
Gold **Obv:** As KM 31 but with legend : "King of all Arab Lands"

Date	Mintage	F12	VF20	XF40	MS60	MS63
AH1334//8 Rare	—	—	—	—	—	—

Note: Note: Baldwin's Auction 83, 9-13, good XF realized approximately $19,250.

PATTERNS

Including off metal strikes

KM#	Date	Mintage	Identification	Mkt Val
PnA1	AH1340/1 (1921)	—	10 Piastres. Bronze. Struck at the Heaton Mint..	—
Pn1	AH1340//1 (1921)	—	20 Piastres. Bronze. Struck at the Heaton Mint (not to be confused with the modern copies listed in Unusual World Coins; struck in various metals, including bronze, nickel and silver)..	75,000

HONDURAS

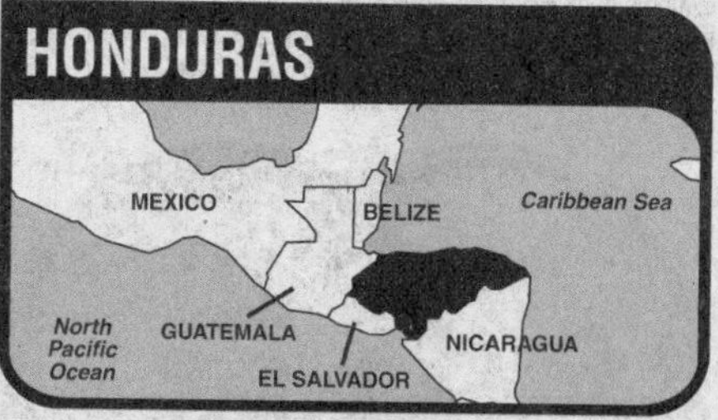

The Republic of Honduras, situated in Central America alongside El Salvador, between Nicaragua and Guatemala, has an area of 43,277sq. mi. (112,090 sq. km.) and a population of 5.6 million. Capital: Tegucigalpa. Agriculture, mining (gold and silver), and logging are the major economic activities, with increasing tourism and emerging petroleum resource discoveries. Precious metals, bananas, timber and coffee are exported.

After declaring its independence from Spain on September 15, 1821, Honduras fell under the Mexican empire of Augustin de Iturbide, and then joined the Central American Republic (1823-39). Upon the effective dissolution of that federation (ca. 1840), Honduras reclaimed its independence as a self-standing republic. Honduras forces played a major part in permanently ending the threat of William Walker to establish a slave holding empire in Central America based on his self engineered elections to the Presidency of Nicaragua. Thrice expelled from Central America, Walker was shot by a Honduran firing squad in 1860. 1876 to 1933 saw a period of instability and for some months were under U.S. Marine Corp military occupation. From 1933 to 1940 General Tiburcio Carias Andino was dictator president of the Republic. Since 1990 democratic practices have become more consistent.

MINT MARKS
T.G. - Yoro
T.L. – Comayagua

MONETARY SYSTEM
100 Centavos = 1 Lempira

REPUBLIC

DECIMAL COINAGE

100 Centavos = 1 Peso

KM# 46 CENTAVO
4.50 g., Bronze, 20 mm. **Obv:** Arms within circle **Rev:** Value, date within wreath **Edge:** Plain, reeded, and plain and reeded **Note:** Varieties exist.

Date	Mintage	VG8	F12	VF20	XF40	MS60
1901/0	98,000	6.50	20.00	42.50	80.00	—
1901	Inc. above	6.50	20.00	42.50	80.00	—
1902 large 0	—	5.00	15.00	27.50	60.00	300
1902 small 0	—	5.00	15.00	27.50	60.00	300
1903/2/1/0	—	50.00	100	200	400	—
Note: 5 known						
1904	—	6.50	20.00	40.00	80.00	—
1907/4	234,000	6.50	20.00	35.00	60.00	—
1907	Inc. above	6.50	20.00	35.00	80.00	—

KM# 59 CENTAVO
4.50 g., Bronze, 20 mm. **Obv:** Arms within circle **Rev:** Value within circle, date below **Note:** Varieties exist.

Date	Mintage	VG8	F12	VF20	XF40	MS60
1907 large UN	—	0.80	2.00	4.00	10.00	25.00
Note: Mintage included in KM#46						
1907 small UN	—	0.80	2.00	4.00	10.00	25.00
Note: Mintage included in KM#46						
1908/7	263,000	9.00	16.50	40.00	100	—
1908	—	9.00	16.50	40.00	100	—

KM# 61 CENTAVO
4.50 g., Bronze, 20 mm. **Obv:** Arms within circle and wreath **Rev:** Value within circle **Note:** The 1890, 1891 and 1908 dates are found with a die-cutting error or broken die that reads REPLBLICA. Other differences exist.

Date	Mintage	VG8	F12	VF20	XF40	MS60
1908	—	6.50	15.00	40.00	100	—

KM# 65 CENTAVO
2.12 g., Bronze **Obv:** Towers front pyramid within circle **Rev:** Denomination and date within wreath **Note:** Obverse and reverse are altered dies of KM45, 1/2 centavo (1881-1891). Numerous reverse varieties exist.

Date	Mintage	VG8	F12	VF20	XF40	MS60
1910/1884	—	10.00	20.00	35.00	70.00	—
1910/5	410,000	10.00	20.00	35.00	70.00	—
1910 large 0	410,000	10.00	20.00	35.00	70.00	—
1911/811	62,000	6.00	15.00	30.00	60.00	—
1911/885	Inc. above	6.00	15.00	30.00	60.00	—
1911/886	Inc. above	6.00	15.00	30.00	60.00	—
1911 CENTAVO	Inc. above	6.00	15.00	30.00	60.00	—
1911 CENTAVOS	Inc. above	100	165	280	450	750

KM# 66 CENTAVO
2.12 g., Bronze **Obv:** Towers front pyramid within circle, obverse of 5 centavos, KM48 (1884-1902) **Rev:** Altered KM#45, 1/2 centavo.

Date	Mintage	VG8	F12	VF20	XF40	MS60
1910	Inc. above	10.00	25.00	50.00	125	500
1610 error, inverted 9	Inc. above	65.00	125	225	350	—

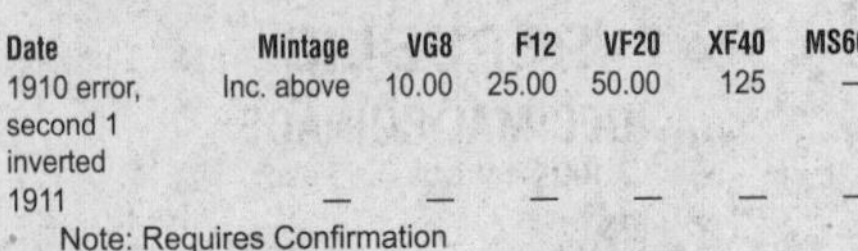

Date	Mintage	VG8	F12	VF20	XF40	MS60
1910 error, second 1 inverted	Inc. above	10.00	25.00	50.00	125	—
1911	—	—	—	—	—	—

Note: Requires Confirmation

KM# 67 CENTAVO

2.12 g., Bronze **Obv:** Towers front pyramid within inner circle, wreath surrounds outer circle, obverse of 5 centavos, KM48 (1884-1902) **Rev:** Denomination within wreath, altered dies of KM48

Date	Mintage	VG8	F12	VF20	XF40	MS60
1910	Inc. above	6.50	10.00	20.00	60.00	175
1911	—	—	—	—	—	—

Note: Requires Confirmation

KM# 68 CENTAVO

2.12 g., Bronze **Obv:** Towers front pyramid within inner circle, obverse of 1/2 centavo KM45 (1881-1891) **Rev:** Denomination within wreath, altered reverse of die of 5 centavos KM48 (1884-1902)

Date	Mintage	VG8	F12	VF20	XF40	MS60
1910	Inc. above	40.00	80.00	150	350	—

KM# 70 CENTAVO

2.12 g., Bronze **Obv:** Towers front pyramid within circle **Rev:** Denomination and date within wreath, CENTAVO omitted

Date	Mintage	VG8	F12	VF20	XF40	MS60
1919	168,000	1.50	4.00	10.00	35.00	—
1920	30,000	3.00	6.00	15.00	45.00	—

KM# 64 2 CENTAVOS

4.25 g., Bronze, 20 mm. **Obv:** Towers front pyramid within circle, obverse of KM46, 1 centavo (1881-1907) **Rev:** Denomination within thick circle, altered reverse of KM49, 10 centavos (1884-1900)

Date	Mintage	VG8	F12	VF20	XF40	MS60
1907 Rare	Inc. below	—	—	—	—	—
1908/7	Inc. below	50.00	100	300	600	—
1908	Inc. below	50.00	100	300	600	—

KM# 69 2 CENTAVOS

Bronze, 20 mm. **Obv:** Towers front pyramid within circle, obverse of KM46, 1 centavo (1881-1907) **Rev:** Denomination and date within wreath **Note:** Reverse dies often very crudely recut of KM46, especially 1910 and 1911. Some coins of 1910 appear to be struck over earlier 1 or 2 Centavos, probably 1907 or 1908. 1912 and 1913 reverse appear newly made.

Date	Mintage	VG8	F12	VF20	XF40	MS60
1910	435,000	1.25	4.00	10.00	20.00	45.00
1911	68,000	6.50	18.50	40.00	85.00	—
1912 CENTAVOS	88,000	1.00	4.50	15.00	35.00	—
1912 CENTAVO	Inc. above	3.00	6.00	20.00	50.00	—
1913	258,000	1.00	2.50	10.00	25.00	—

KM# 71 2 CENTAVOS

4.25 g., Bronze, 20 mm. **Obv:** Towers front pyramid within circle **Rev:** Denomination and date within wreath, CENTAVOS omitted **Note:** Varieties exist.

Date	Mintage	VG8	F12	VF20	XF40	MS60
1919	117,000	2.50	9.00	20.00	55.00	—
1920	283,000	0.65	2.75	15.00	40.00	125
1920 Dot divides date	Inc. above	5.00	10.00	20.00	60.00	—

KM# 48 5 CENTAVOS

1.25 g., 0.835 Silver 0.0336 oz. ASW, 16 mm. **Obv:** Arms within circle and wreath **Rev:** Value within wreath

Date	Mintage	VG8	F12	VF20	XF40	MS60
1902	—	50.00	100	175	300	650

KM# 50a 25 CENTAVOS

6.25 g., 0.835 Silver 0.1678 oz. ASW, 24 mm. **Obv:** Flags sourround arms within circle **Rev:** Standing Liberty **Note:** Varieties exist.

Date	Mintage	VG8	F12	VF20	XF40	MS60
1901/801	54,000	6.00	8.00	16.00	45.00	—
1901/11	Inc. above	8.00	15.00	30.00	60.00	—
1901/0	—	9.00	16.00	35.00	65.00	350
1901 Large first 1	Inc. above	5.50	7.00	10.00	20.00	—
1902/801	—	10.00	17.50	25.00	60.00	350
1902/802	—	10.00	17.50	25.00	60.00	—
1902/812	—	10.00	17.50	25.00	60.00	—
1902/891	—	10.00	17.50	25.00	60.00	350
1902/1 F	—	6.00	7.00	20.00	60.00	350
1902 F	—	6.00	8.00	20.00	60.00	350
1904	—	15.00	35.00	75.00	200	600
1907/4	14,000	20.00	40.00	100	250	—
1907	Inc. above	20.00	40.00	100	250	—
1912 .835/.900	7,168	15.00	30.00	75.00	200	—
1913/0	52,000	15.00	30.00	90.00	200	—
1913/2	Inc. above	—	—	—	—	—
1913	Inc. above	15.00	30.00	90.00	200	—

KM# 51 50 CENTAVOS

12.50 g., 0.900 Silver 0.3617 oz. ASW, 30.5 mm. **Obv:** Flags sourround arms within circle **Rev:** Standing Liberty

Date	Mintage	VG8	F12	VF20	XF40	MS60
1910	602	600	1,000	2,000	—	—

KM# 51a 50 CENTAVOS

12.50 g., Silver, 30.5 mm. **Obv:** Towers front pyramid within inner circle, crowned and flagged decorative mantle behind **Rev:** Seated Liberty figure with flag and tablet, Neptunes symbols flank **Note:** Fineness can be .835 or .900.

Date	Mintage	VG8	F12	VF20	XF40	MS60
1908/897	447	35.00	65.00	150	300	600
1908	Inc. above	30.00	55.00	130	250	550

KM# 52 PESO

25.00 g., 0.900 Silver 0.7234 oz. ASW, 38 mm. **Obv:** Flags sourround arms within circle **Rev:** Standing Liberty **Note:** Overdates and recut dies are prevalent.

Date	Mintage	VG8	F12	VF20	XF40	MS60
1902	—	27.50	50.00	80.00	150	350
1903 flat-top 3	—	27.50	45.00	70.00	150	300
1903 round-top 3	—	30.00	55.00	100	200	400
1904	20,000	30.00	55.00	100	200	400
1914	—	200	500	900	1,500	2,500

KM# 56 PESO

1.61 g., 0.900 Gold 0.0466 oz. AGW **Obv:** Arms within circle, bouquets flanking, banner and stars above **Rev:** Liberty head left

Date	Mintage	F12	VF20	XF40	MS60	MS63
1901	—	150	300	600	1,150	—
1902	—	140	300	500	1,000	—
1907	—	140	250	450	900	—
1914/882	—	275	450	750	1,500	—
1914/03	—	275	450	750	1,500	—
1919	—	150	300	550	1,100	—
1920	—	150	300	550	1,100	—
1922	—	140	250	450	900	—
ND (1922-25)	—	140	250	500	—	—

Note: These are marriage pieces.

KM# 53 5 PESOS

8.06 g., 0.900 Gold 0.2334 oz. AGW **Obv:** Arms within inner circle, bouquets flank outer circle **Rev:** Liberty head left

Date	Mintage	F12	VF20	XF40	MS60	MS63
1902	—	700	1,250	2,500	4,000	—
1908/888	—	600	1,000	2,000	3,000	—
1913	1,200	700	1,250	2,500	5,000	—

KM# 57 20 PESOS

32.26 g., 0.900 Gold 0.9334 oz. AGW **Obv:** Arms within inner circle, bouquets flank outer circle **Rev:** Liberty head left

Date	Mintage	F12	VF20	XF40	MS60	MS63
1908/888	—	—	20,000	30,000	—	—
1908/897 Rare	—	—	—	—	—	—

Note: Stack's Hammel sale 9-82 VF 1908/897 realized $12,000. Ponterio & Associates NYINC. sale 12-86 choice XF realized $30,800. Superior Casterline sale 5-89 choice XF realized $28,600.

Date	Mintage	F12	VF20	XF40	MS60	MS63
1908 Rare	—	—	—	—	—	—

REFORM COINAGE

KM# 77.1 CENTAVO

2.00 g., Bronze, 16 mm. **Obv:** National arms **Rev:** Denomination within circle, wreath surrounds **Note:** Thick planchet.

Date	Mintage	VF20	XF40	MS60	MS63	MS65
1935 (P)	2,000,000	1.00	2.00	6.00	10.00	15.00
1939 (P)	2,000,000	0.75	1.50	4.00	8.00	12.00
1949 (P)	4,000,000	0.50	0.75	2.00	3.00	5.00

KM# 77.2 CENTAVO

1.50 g., Bronze, 16 mm. **Obv:** National arms **Rev:** Denomination within circle, wreath surrounds **Note:** Thin planchet.

Date	Mintage	VF20	XF40	MS60	MS63	MS65
1954	3,500,000	0.15	0.50	1.25	1.50	3.00
1956	2,000,000	0.15	0.50	0.85	1.00	1.50
1957/6	28,000,000	—	—	—	—	—
1957	Inc. above	0.10	0.15	0.30	0.50	0.75

KM# 77a CENTAVO

1.35 g., Copper Plated Steel, 16 mm. **Obv:** National arms, without clouds behind pyramids **Rev:** Denomination within circle, wreath surrounds **Edge:** Plain

Date	Mintage	VF20	XF40	MS60	MS63	MS65
1974	—	0.10	0.15	0.25	0.35	0.50
1985	25,000,000	0.10	0.15	0.25	0.35	0.50
1992	60,000,000	0.10	0.15	0.25	0.35	0.50

Note: Struck with fixed dated dies from 1993-1999

KM# 77b CENTAVO

1.35 g., Copper Plated Steel, 16 mm. **Obv:** National arms, clouds behind pyramids **Rev:** Denomination within circle, wreath surrounds **Edge:** Plain

Date	Mintage	VF20	XF40	MS60	MS63	MS65
1988	50,000,000	0.10	0.15	0.25	0.35	0.50

KM# 78 2 CENTAVOS

3.00 g., Bronze, 21 mm. **Obv:** National arms **Rev:** Denomination within circle, wreath surrounds **Edge:** Plain

Date	Mintage	VF20	XF40	MS60	MS63	MS65
1939 (P)	2,000,000	0.50	1.00	2.00	5.00	10.00
1949 (P)	3,000,000	0.50	0.75	1.50	3.00	6.00
1954 (P)	2,000,000	0.25	0.50	1.50	3.00	6.00
1956	20,000,000	0.10	0.25	0.50	1.00	1.50

KM# 78a 2 CENTAVOS

2.70 g., Copper Clad Steel, 21 mm. **Obv:** National arms **Rev:** Denomination within circle, wreath surrounds **Edge:** Plain

Date	Mintage	VF20	XF40	MS60	MS63	MS65
1974	—	0.10	0.15	0.25	0.35	0.50

KM# 72.1 5 CENTAVOS

5.00 g., Copper-Nickel, 21 mm. **Obv:** National arms **Rev:** Denomination within circle, wreath surrounds **Edge:** Plain **Note:** Dentilated border.

Date	Mintage	VF20	XF40	MS60	MS63	MS65
1931 (P)	2,000,000	1.00	5.00	10.00	15.00	30.00
1932 (P)	1,000,000	0.75	4.00	12.00	20.00	40.00
1949 (P)	2,000,000	0.50	3.00	7.00	10.00	15.00
1956 (P)	10,070,000	0.15	0.25	0.40	0.60	1.00
1972	5,000,000	0.10	0.15	0.25	0.35	0.50

KM# 72.2 5 CENTAVOS

5.00 g., Copper-Nickel, 21 mm. **Obv:** National arms **Rev:** Denomination within circle, wreath surrounds **Edge:** Plain **Note:** Beaded border.

Date	Mintage	VF20	XF40	MS60	MS63	MS65
1954	1,400,000	0.25	0.75	1.50	2.00	3.00
1980	20,000,000	0.10	0.50	1.00	1.50	2.00

KM# 72.2a 5 CENTAVOS

3.20 g., Brass, 21 mm. **Obv:** National arms, without clouds behind pyramids **Rev:** Denomination within circle, wreath surrounds **Edge:** Plain

Date	Mintage	VF20	XF40	MS60	MS63	MS65
1975	20,000,000	0.10	0.15	0.35	0.50	0.75
1989	—	0.10	0.15	0.35	0.50	0.75

KM# 72.3 5 CENTAVOS

3.20 g., Brass, 21 mm. **Obv:** National arms, with clouds behind pyramids **Rev:** Denomination within circle, wreath surrounds **Edge:** Plain

Date	Mintage	VF20	XF40	MS60	MS63	MS65
1993	—	0.10	0.15	0.35	0.50	0.75
1994	—	0.10	0.15	0.35	0.50	0.75

KM# 72.4 5 CENTAVOS

3.20 g., Brass, 21 mm. **Obv:** National arms **Rev:** Value in circle within sprays **Edge:** Plain

Date	Mintage	VF20	XF40	MS60	MS63	MS65
1995	—	—	0.10	0.25	0.35	0.50
1998	—	—	0.10	0.25	0.35	0.50
1999	—	—	0.10	0.25	0.35	0.50

KM# 76.1 10 CENTAVOS

7.00 g., Copper-Nickel, 26 mm. **Obv:** National arms **Rev:** Denomination within circle, wreath surrounds **Note:** Dentilated border.

Date	Mintage	VF20	XF40	MS60	MS63	MS65
1932 (P)	1,500,000	1.00	3.00	15.00	25.00	50.00
1951 (P)	1,000,000	1.00	2.00	7.00	12.00	20.00
1956 (P)	7,560,000	0.25	0.35	0.75	1.00	3.00

KM# 76.2 10 CENTAVOS

7.00 g., Copper-Nickel, 26 mm. **Obv:** National arms **Rev:** Denomination within circle, wreath surrounds **Note:** Beaded border.

Date	Mintage	VF20	XF40	MS60	MS63	MS65
1954	1,200,000	0.25	0.75	3.00	7.00	15.00
1967	—	0.25	0.35	1.00	2.00	3.00
1980	15,000,000	0.25	0.35	1.00	2.00	3.00
1993	—	0.25	0.35	1.00	2.00	3.00

KM# 76.1a 10 CENTAVOS

6.00 g., Brass, 26 mm. **Obv:** Large letters and national arms **Rev:** Denomination within circle, wreath surrounds **Edge:** Plain

Date	Mintage	VF20	XF40	MS60	MS63	MS65
1976	10,000,000	0.15	0.25	0.60	0.75	1.00
1989	—	0.15	0.25	0.60	0.75	1.00

KM# 76.2a 10 CENTAVOS

6.00 g., Brass, 26 mm. **Obv:** Small letters and national arms, with clouds behind pyramids **Rev:** Denomination within circle, wreath surrounds **Edge:** Plain **Note:** Beaded border.

Date	Mintage	VF20	XF40	MS60	MS63	MS65
1993	—	0.10	0.20	0.35	0.45	0.75
1994	—	0.10	0.20	0.35	0.45	0.75
1995	—	0.10	0.20	0.35	0.45	0.75
1995 Small date	—	0.10	0.20	0.35	0.45	0.75

KM# 76.3 10 CENTAVOS

6.00 g., Brass, 26 mm. **Obv:** National arms, without clouds behind pyramid **Rev:** Denomination within circle, wreath surrounds **Edge:** Plain

Date	Mintage	VF20	XF40	MS60	MS63	MS65
1995	—	—	0.20	0.35	0.45	0.65
1995 Small date	—	—	—	—	—	—
1998	—	—	0.20	0.35	0.45	0.65
1999	—	—	0.20	0.35	0.45	0.65

KM# 73 20 CENTAVOS

2.50 g., 0.900 Silver 0.0723 oz. ASW, 18 mm. **Obv:** National arms **Rev:** Chief Lempira left within circle

Date	Mintage	VF20	XF40	MS60	MS63	MS65
1931 (P)	1,000,000	3.50	6.00	25.00	50.00	75.00
1932 (P)	750,000	3.50	9.00	35.00	60.00	85.00
1951 (P)	1,500,000	3.50	6.00	11.00	15.00	20.00
1952 (P)	2,500,000	3.50	6.00	10.00	15.00	20.00
1958 (P)	2,000,000	3.50	5.00	9.00	12.00	17.00

KM# 79 20 CENTAVOS

2.27 g., Copper-Nickel, 18 mm. **Obv:** National arms **Rev:** Chief Lempira left within circle **Edge:** Reeded

Date	Mintage	VF20	XF40	MS60	MS63	MS65
1967	12,000,000	0.10	0.35	0.75	1.00	1.50

KM# 81 20 CENTAVOS

2.27 g., Copper-Nickel, 18 mm. **Obv:** National arms, date below **Rev:** Chief Lempira left within circle **Edge:** Reeded **Note:** Different style lettering.

Date	Mintage	VF20	XF40	MS60	MS63	MS65
1973	15,000,000	0.10	0.20	0.40	0.60	1.00

KM# 83 20 CENTAVOS

2.27 g., Copper-Nickel, 18 mm. **Obv:** National arms **Rev:** Chief Lempira head left within circle **Edge:** Reeded

Date	Mintage	VF20	XF40	MS60	MS63	MS65
1978	30,000,000	0.10	0.20	0.40	0.60	1.00
1990	—	0.10	0.20	0.40	0.60	1.00

KM# 83a.1 20 CENTAVOS

2.00 g., Nickel Plated Steel, 18 mm. **Obv:** Small arms and legend, with clouds behind pyramid **Rev:** Chief Lempira head left within circle **Edge:** Reeded

Date	Mintage	VF20	XF40	MS60	MS63	MS65
1991	—	0.10	0.20	0.40	0.60	1.00
1993	—	0.10	0.20	0.40	0.60	1.00
1994	—	0.10	0.20	0.40	0.60	1.00

KM# 83a.2 20 CENTAVOS

2.00 g., Nickel Plated Steel, 18 mm. **Obv:** National arms, without clouds **Rev:** Chief Lempira head left within circle **Edge:** Reeded

Date	Mintage	VF20	XF40	MS60	MS63	MS65
1995	—	0.10	0.20	0.40	0.60	1.00
1996	—	0.10	0.20	0.40	0.60	1.00
1999	—	0.10	0.20	0.40	0.60	1.00

KM# 74 50 CENTAVOS
6.25 g., 0.900 Silver 0.1808 oz. ASW, 24 mm. **Obv:** National arms **Rev:** Chiefs head left within circle **Edge:** Reeded

Date	Mintage	VF20	XF40	MS60	MS63	MS65
1931 (P)	500,000	8.00	15.00	45.00	75.00	100
1932 (P)	1,100,000	8.00	15.00	40.00	55.00	80.00
1937 (P)	1,000,000	8.00	15.00	40.00	55.00	80.00
1951 (P)	500,000	8.00	15.00	35.00	50.00	75.00

KM# 80 50 CENTAVOS
5.67 g., Copper-Nickel, 24 mm. **Obv:** National arms **Rev:** Chief Lempira left within circle **Edge:** Reeded

Date	Mintage	VF20	XF40	MS60	MS63	MS65
1967	4,800,000	0.25	0.35	0.65	1.00	1.50

KM# 82 50 CENTAVOS
5.67 g., Copper-Nickel, 24 mm. **Series:** F.A.O. **Obv:** National arms **Rev:** Chief Lempira left within circle **Edge:** Reeded

Date	Mintage	VF20	XF40	MS60	MS63	MS65
1973	4,400,000	0.25	0.35	0.65	1.00	1.50

KM# 84 50 CENTAVOS
5.67 g., Copper-Nickel, 24 mm. **Obv:** National arms, with clouds behind pyramid **Rev:** Head left within circle **Edge:** Reeded

Date	Mintage	VF20	XF40	MS60	MS63	MS65
1978	12,000,000	0.25	0.35	0.65	1.00	1.50
1990	—	0.25	0.35	0.65	1.00	1.50

KM# 84a.1 50 CENTAVOS
5.00 g., Nickel Plated Steel, 24 mm. **Obv:** National arms **Rev:** Chief Lempira head left within circle **Edge:** Reeded

Date	Mintage	VF20	XF40	MS60	MS63	MS65
1991	—	0.25	0.35	0.65	1.00	1.50
1994	—	0.25	0.35	0.65	1.00	1.50

KM# 88 50 CENTAVOS
5.00 g., Nickel Plated Steel, 24 mm. **Subject:** 50th Anniversary F.A.O. **Obv:** National arms **Rev:** Head left within circle, logo below **Edge:** Reeded

Date	Mintage	VF20	XF40	MS60	MS63	MS65
1994	2,000,000	0.25	0.35	0.65	1.00	1.50

KM# 84a.2 50 CENTAVOS
5.00 g., Nickel Plated Steel, 24 mm. **Obv:** National arms above date **Rev:** Chief Lempira head left within circle **Edge:** Reeded

Date	Mintage	VF20	XF40	MS60	MS63	MS65
1995	—	0.15	0.35	0.65	1.00	1.50
1996	—	0.15	0.35	0.65	1.00	1.50
1999	—	0.15	0.35	0.65	1.00	1.50

KM# 75 LEMPIRA
12.50 g., 0.900 Silver 0.3617 oz. ASW, 31 mm. **Obv:** National arms **Rev:** Chiefs head left within circle

Date	Mintage	VF20	XF40	MS60	MS63	MS65
1931 (P)	550,000	6.75	20.00	60.00	125	175
1932 (P)	1,000,000	6.75	20.00	50.00	100	150
1933 (P)	400,000	6.75	15.00	35.00	100	150
1934 (P)	600,000	6.75	15.00	30.00	100	150
1935 (P)	1,000,000	6.75	15.00	30.00	90.00	135
1937 (P)	4,000,000	6.75	15.00	25.00	75.00	100

KM# 89 LEMPIRA
33.63 g., 0.925 Silver 1.000 oz. ASW, 38 mm. **Subject:** Central Bank's 50th Anniversary **Obv:** National arms within beaded circle **Rev:** Bank building within beaded circle, wreath surrounds **Edge:** Plain

Date	Mintage	XF40	MS60	MS63	MS65	MS66
ND-2000	3,000	PF65 50.00	PF67 60.00			

KM# 90 LEMPIRA
7.78 g., 0.999 Gold 0.2497 oz. AGW, 24 mm. **Subject:** Central Bank's 50th Anniversary **Obv:** National arms within beaded circle **Rev:** Bank building within beaded circle, wreath surrounds **Edge:** Reeded

Date	Mintage	XF40	MS60	MS63	MS65	MS66
ND-2000	1,200	PF67 400	PF69 450			

KM# 85 100 LEMPIRAS
27.00 g., 0.925 Silver 0.803 oz. ASW **Subject:** 500th Anniversary - Discovery of America **Obv:** National arms in inner circle, legend at top, date below **Rev:** Ship approaching curved wall

Date	Mintage	XF40	MS60	MS63	MS65	MS66
1992	5,000	PF65 37.00	PF67 50.00			

KM# 86 200 LEMPIRAS
6.50 g., 0.900 Gold 0.1881 oz. AGW, 20 mm. **Subject:** Bicentenary of Birth - Gen. Francisco Morazan **Obv:** Emblem within legend **Rev:** Head left

Date	Mintage	XF40	MS60	MS63	MS65	MS66
1992	1,500	PF67 275	PF69 300			

KM# 87 500 LEMPIRAS
12.50 g., 0.900 Gold 0.3617 oz. AGW, 26 mm. **Subject:** Bicentenary of Birth - Gen. Francisco Morazan

Date	Mintage	XF40	MS60	MS63	MS65	MS66
1992	1,500	PF67 550	PF69 600			

PATTERNS

Including off metal strikes

KM#	Date	Mintage	Identification	Mkt Val
Pn22	1909	—	Centavo. Copper.	200
Pn23	1919	—	Peso. Copper. KM#56.	150

HONG KONG

Hong Kong, a former British colony, reverted to control of the People's Republic of China on July 1, 1997 as a Special Administrative Region. It is situated at the mouth of the Canton or Pearl River 90 miles (145 km.) southeast of Canton, has an area of 403 sq. mi. (1,040 sq. km.) and an estimated population of 6.3 million. Capital: Victoria. The free port of Hong Kong, the commercial center of the Far East, is a trans-shipment point for goods destined for China and the countries of the Pacific Rim. Light manufacturing and tourism are important components of the economy.

Long a haven for fishermen-pirates and opium smugglers, the island of Hong Kong was ceded to Britain at the conclusion of the first Opium War, 1839-1842. The acquisition of a 'barren rock' was ridiculed by London and English merchants operating in the Far East. The Kowloon Peninsula and Stonecutter's Island were ceded in 1860, and the so-called New Territories, comprising most of the mainland of the colony, were leased to Britain for 99 years in 1898.

The legends on Hong Kong coinage are bilingual: English and Chinese. The rare 1941 cent was dispatched to Hong Kong in several shipments. One fell into Japanese hands, while another was melted down by the British and a third was sunk during enemy action.

RULER
British 1842-1997

MINT MARKS
H - Heaton
KN - King's Norton

MONETARY SYSTEM
10 Mils (Wen, Ch'ien) = 1 Cent (Hsien)
10 Cents = 1 Chiao
100 Cents = 10 Chiao = 1 Dollar (Yuan)

BRITISH COLONY

DECIMAL COINAGE

KM# 4.3 CENT

7.50 g., Bronze, 27.6 mm. **Ruler:** Victoria **Obv:** Crowned bust left **Rev:** Chinese value within beaded circle

Date	Mintage	F12	VF20	XF40	MS60	MS63
1901	5,000,000	2.50	5.50	16.00	85.00	150
1901 H	10,000,000	2.50	5.50	16.00	75.00	135

KM# 11 CENT

7.50 g., Bronze, 27.7 mm. **Ruler:** Edward VII **Obv:** Crowned bust right **Rev:** English around central Chinese legend

Date	Mintage	F12	VF20	XF40	MS60	MS63
1902	5,000,000	2.50	4.50	10.00	85.00	150
1903	5,000,000	2.50	4.50	10.00	85.00	150
1904 H	10,000,000	1.75	3.50	10.00	65.00	120
1905	2,500,000	3.75	7.50	15.00	120	200
1905 H	12,500,000	2.50	4.50	10.00	85.00	150

KM# 16 CENT

7.50 g., Bronze, 27.6 mm. **Ruler:** George V **Obv:** Crowned bust left **Rev:** English around central Chinese legend

Date	Mintage	F12	VF20	XF40	MS60	MS63
1919 H	2,500,000	2.00	4.00	10.00	65.00	100
1923	2,500,000	1.50	3.00	7.50	50.00	80.00
1924	5,000,000	1.25	2.50	4.50	35.00	60.00
1925	2,500,000	1.25	2.50	4.50	35.00	60.00
1926	2,500,000	1.25	2.50	4.50	35.00	60.00
1926	—	**PF63** 350				

KM# 17 CENT

3.95 g., Bronze, 22 mm. **Ruler:** George V **Obv:** Crowned bust left **Rev:** English around central Chinese legend

Date	Mintage	F12	VF20	XF40	MS60	MS63
1931	5,000,000	0.75	1.00	2.00	8.00	15.00
1931	—	**PF63** 250				
1933	6,500,000	0.75	1.00	2.00	8.00	10.00
1933	—	**PF63** 250				
1934	5,000,000	0.75	1.00	2.00	8.00	10.00
1934	—	**PF63** 250				

KM# 24 CENT

Bronze **Ruler:** George VI **Obv:** Crowned head left **Rev:** English around central Chinese legend

Date	Mintage	F12	VF20	XF40	MS60	MS63
1941	5,000,000	1,500	2,500	4,500	9,000	—
1941	—	**PF63** 12,000				

KM# 5 5 CENTS

1.36 g., 0.800 Silver 0.0349 oz. ASW, 15.53 mm. **Ruler:** Victoria **Obv:** Crowned head left **Rev:** Chinese value within beaded circle **Note:** Coins dated 1866-1868 struck at the Hong Kong Mint; coins without mintmarks dated 1872-1901, were struck at the British Royal Mint.

Date	Mintage	F12	VF20	XF40	MS60	MS63
1901	10,000,000	2.00	3.00	5.00	25.00	60.00

KM# 12 5 CENTS

1.36 g., 0.800 Silver 0.0349 oz. ASW, 15.2 mm. **Ruler:** Edward VII **Obv:** Crowned bust right **Rev:** English around central Chinese legend

Date	Mintage	F12	VF20	XF40	MS60	MS63
1903	6,000,000	2.00	3.00	4.00	20.00	35.00
1903	—	**PF63** 225				
1904	8,000,000	2.00	3.00	4.00	20.00	35.00
1904	—	**PF63** 200				
1905	1,000,000	2.50	3.50	6.50	25.00	45.00
1905 H	7,000,000	2.00	3.00	4.00	20.00	35.00

KM# 18 5 CENTS

1.36 g., 0.800 Silver 0.0349 oz. ASW, 15.2 mm. **Ruler:** George V **Obv:** Crowned bust left **Rev:** English around central Chinese legend

Date	Mintage	F12	VF20	XF40	MS60	MS63
1932	3,000,000	1.75	2.00	4.00	10.00	15.00
1932	—	**PF63** 165				
1933	2,000,000	1.75	2.00	4.50	13.00	18.00
1933	—	**PF63** 165				

KM# 18a 5 CENTS

Copper-Nickel, 15.2 mm. **Ruler:** George V **Obv:** Crowned bust left **Rev:** English around central Chinese legend

Date	Mintage	VF20	XF40	MS60	MS63	MS65
1935	1,000,000	2.50	5.00	10.00	15.00	30.00
1935	—	**PF63** 115				

KM# 20 5 CENTS

2.60 g., Nickel, 16.5 mm. **Ruler:** George VI **Obv:** Crowned head left **Rev:** English around central Chinese legend **Edge:** Reeded with security

Date	Mintage	F12	VF20	XF40	MS60	MS63
1937	3,000,000	0.75	1.25	2.25	5.00	10.00
1937	—	**PF63** 85.00				

KM# 22 5 CENTS

2.60 g., Nickel, 16.5 mm. **Ruler:** George VI **Obv:** Crowned head left **Rev:** English around central Chinese legend **Edge:** Reeded with security

Date	Mintage	F12	VF20	XF40	MS60	MS63
1938	3,000,000	0.50	1.00	2.00	5.00	10.00
1938	—	**PF63** 125				
1939 H	3,090,000	0.50	1.00	2.00	5.00	10.00
1939 H	—	**PF63** 125				
1939 KN	4,710,000	0.50	1.00	2.00	5.00	10.00
1941 H	777,000	350	750	1,000	2,000	3,200
1941 KN	1,075,000	150	300	600	900	1,250

KM# 26 5 CENTS

2.50 g., Nickel-Brass, 16.5 mm. **Ruler:** George VI **Obv:** Crowned head left **Rev:** English around central Chinese legend **Edge:** Reeded with security

Date	Mintage	F12	VF20	XF40	MS60	MS63
1949	15,000,000	0.25	0.50	1.25	3.00	8.00
1949	—	**PF63** 125				
1950	20,400,000	0.25	0.50	1.25	3.00	8.00
1950	—	**PF63** 125				

KM# 29.1 5 CENTS

2.50 g., Nickel-Brass, 16.5 mm. **Ruler:** Elizabeth II **Obv:** Crowned head right **Rev:** English around central Chinese legend **Edge:** Reeded and security

Date	Mintage	F12	VF20	XF40	MS60	MS63
1958 H	5,000,000	—	0.25	0.75	1.00	4.50
1960	5,000,000	—	0.15	0.50	1.00	4.00
1960	—	**PF63** 65.00				
1963	7,000,000	—	0.15	0.50	1.00	4.00
1963	—	**PF63** 65.00				
1964 H	—	50.00	85.00	150	450	750
1965	18,000,000	—	0.10	0.40	0.75	2.50
1967	10,000,000	—	0.10	0.40	0.75	2.50

KM# 29.2 5 CENTS

2.50 g., Nickel-Brass, 16.5 mm. **Ruler:** Elizabeth II **Obv:** Crowned head right **Rev:** English around central Chinese legend **Edge:** Reeded **Note:** Error.

Date	Mintage	F12	VF20	XF40	MS60	MS63
1958 H	Inc. above	2.50	5.00	9.00	20.00	—
1960	Inc. above	2.50	5.00	9.00	20.00	—

KM# 29.3 5 CENTS

2.50 g., Nickel-Brass, 16.5 mm. **Ruler:** Elizabeth II **Obv:** Crowned head right **Rev:** English around central Chinese legend **Edge:** Reeded

Date	Mintage	F12	VF20	XF40	MS60	MS63
1971 KN	14,000,000	—	—	0.25	1.00	1.50
1971 H	6,000,000	—	—	0.25	1.00	1.50
1972 H	14,000,000	—	—	0.25	1.00	1.50
1977	6,000,000	—	—	0.25	0.50	1.00
1978	10,000,000	—	—	0.25	0.50	1.00
1979	4,000,000	—	—	0.25	0.50	1.00
1980 Not issued	50,000,000	—	—	—	—	—

KM# 61 5 CENTS

2.50 g., Nickel-Brass, 16.5 mm. **Ruler:** Elizabeth II **Obv:** Crowned head right **Rev:** English around central Chinese legend

Date	Mintage	VF20	XF40	MS60	MS63	MS65
1988	50,000	—	—	3.00	10.00	15.00
1988	25,000	**PF65** 5.00				

KM# 6.3 10 CENTS

2.72 g., 0.800 Silver 0.0698 oz. ASW, 17.84 mm. **Ruler:** Victoria **Obv:** Crowned bust left with 11 pearls on right arch of crown **Rev:** Chinese value within beaded circle **Note:** Coins dated 1866-1868 struck at the Hong Kong Mint; coins without mintmarks dated 1869-1901, struck at the British Royal Mint.

Date	Mintage	F12	VF20	XF40	MS60	MS63
1901	25,000,000	2.50	3.50	6.00	20.00	30.00

KM# 13 10 CENTS

2.72 g., 0.800 Silver 0.0698 oz. ASW **Ruler:** Edward VII **Obv:** Crowned bust right **Rev:** English around central Chinese legend

Date	Mintage	F12	VF20	XF40	MS60	MS63
1902	18,000,000	2.50	3.50	6.00	20.00	35.00
1902	—	**PF63** 200				
1903	25,000,000	2.50	3.50	6.00	20.00	35.00
1903	—	**PF63** 200				
1904	30,000,000	2.50	3.50	6.00	20.00	35.00
1904	—	**PF63** 165				
1905	33,487,000	225	400	600	1,000	2,000
1905	—	**PF63** 2,500				

KM# 19 10 CENTS

Copper-Nickel, 20.5 mm. **Ruler:** George V **Obv:** Crowned bust left **Rev:** English around central Chinese legend

Date	Mintage	F12	VF20	XF40	MS60	MS63
1935	10,000,000	0.50	1.00	3.50	5.00	12.00
1935	—	PF63 75.00				
1936	5,000,000	0.50	1.00	3.50	5.00	12.00
1936	—	PF63 75.00				

KM# 21 10 CENTS

4.50 g., Nickel, 20.5 mm. **Ruler:** George VI **Obv:** Crowned head left **Rev:** English around central Chinese legend **Edge:** Reeded with security

Date	Mintage	F12	VF20	XF40	MS60	MS63
1937	17,500,000	0.50	0.80	1.50	2.50	5.00
1937	—	PF63 85.00				

KM# 23 10 CENTS

4.50 g., Nickel, 20.5 mm. **Ruler:** George VI **Obv:** Crowned head left **Rev:** English around central Chinese legend **Edge:** Reeded with security

Date	Mintage	F12	VF20	XF40	MS60	MS63
1938	7,500,000	0.65	1.00	2.25	5.00	8.00
1938	—	PF63 85.00				
1939 H	5,000,000	0.65	1.00	2.25	5.00	8.00
1939 KN	5,000,000	0.65	1.00	2.25	5.00	8.00
1939 KN	—	PF63 85.00				

KM# 25 10 CENTS

4.46 g., Nickel-Brass, 20.5 mm. **Ruler:** George VI **Obv:** Crowned head left **Rev:** English around central Chinese legend **Edge:** Reeded and security

Date	Mintage	F12	VF20	XF40	MS60	MS63
1948	30,000,000	0.25	0.50	1.25	5.00	8.00
1948	—	PF63 65.00				
1949	35,000,000	0.25	0.50	1.25	5.00	8.00
1949	—	PF63 65.00				
1950	20,000,000	0.25	0.50	1.25	5.00	8.00
1950	—	PF63 65.00				
1951	5,000,000	0.50	1.00	3.00	10.00	15.00
1951	—	PF63 85.00				

KM# 25a 10 CENTS

4.46 g., Nickel-Brass, 20.5 mm. **Ruler:** George VI **Obv:** Crowned head left **Rev:** English around central Chinese legend **Edge:** Reeded **Note:** Error.

Date	Mintage	VF20	XF40	MS60	MS63	MS65
1950	Inc. above	6.50	12.50	25.00	—	—

KM# 28.1 10 CENTS

4.46 g., Nickel-Brass, 20.5 mm. **Ruler:** Elizabeth II **Obv:** Crowned head right **Rev:** English around central Chinese legend **Edge:** Reeded with security

Date	Mintage	F12	VF20	XF40	MS60	MS63
1955	10,000,000	0.15	0.25	0.50	4.00	8.00
1955	—	PF63 50.00				
1956	3,110,000	0.25	0.50	1.25	4.00	8.00
1956	—	PF63 50.00				
1956 H	4,488,000	0.15	0.25	1.00	5.00	10.00
1956 KN	2,500,000	0.25	0.50	2.00	10.00	18.00
1957 H	5,250,000	0.15	0.25	0.50	3.00	10.00
1957 KN	2,800,000	0.15	0.25	1.00	7.50	15.00
1958 H	—	0.20	0.35	0.75	5.00	12.00
1958 KN	10,000,000	0.15	0.25	0.50	3.00	10.00
1959 H	20,000,000	0.10	0.15	0.25	2.00	6.00
1960	12,500,000	0.10	0.15	0.25	2.00	6.00
1960	—	PF63 50.00				
1960 H	10,000,000	0.10	0.15	0.25	2.00	6.00
1961	20,000,000	0.10	0.15	0.25	1.00	4.00
1961	—	PF63 50.00				
1961 H	5,000,000	0.15	0.25	0.50	1.50	5.00
1961 KN	5,000,000	0.15	0.25	0.50	1.50	5.00
1963	27,000,000	0.10	0.15	0.25	1.00	4.00
1963	—	PF63 50.00				
1963 H	3,000,000	0.20	0.30	0.50	1.00	4.00
1963 KN	Inc. above	0.10	0.15	0.25	0.75	3.50
1964	9,000,000	0.10	0.15	0.25	0.50	2.00
1964 H	21,000,000	0.10	0.15	0.25	0.50	2.00
1965	40,000,000	0.10	0.15	0.25	0.50	2.00
1965 H	8,000,000	0.10	0.15	0.25	0.50	2.00
1965 KN	Inc. above	0.10	0.15	0.25	0.50	2.00
1967	10,000,000	0.10	0.15	0.25	0.50	2.00
1968 H	15,000,000	0.10	0.15	0.25	0.50	2.00

KM# 28.2 10 CENTS

4.46 g., Nickel-Brass, 20.5 mm. **Ruler:** Elizabeth II **Obv:** Crowned head right **Rev:** English around central Chinese legend **Edge:** Reeded **Note:** Error.

Date	Mintage	F12	VF20	XF40	MS60	MS63
1956	Inc. above	2.25	4.50	8.50	25.00	—
1963	—	2.25	4.50	8.50	25.00	—

KM# 28.3 10 CENTS

4.46 g., Nickel-Brass, 20.5 mm. **Ruler:** Elizabeth II **Obv:** Crowned head right **Rev:** English around central Chinese legend **Edge:** Reeded

Date	Mintage	F12	VF20	XF40	MS60	MS63
1971 H	22,000,000	—	0.10	0.15	0.65	1.00
1972 KN	20,000,000	—	0.10	0.15	0.65	1.00
1973	2,250,000	0.15	0.25	0.65	3.50	5.00
1974	4,600,000	—	0.10	0.15	0.65	1.00
1975	44,840,000	—	0.10	0.15	0.65	1.00
1978	57,500,000	—	0.10	0.15	0.65	1.00
1979	101,500,000	—	0.10	0.15	0.65	1.00
1980	24,000,000	—	7.00	15.00	35.00	50.00

Note: Few pieces were released for circulation in 1980, but large numbers have found their way onto the market in subsequent years. About 3,500 are known to exist.

KM# 49 10 CENTS

2.00 g., Nickel-Brass, 17.5 mm. **Ruler:** Elizabeth II **Obv:** Young bust right **Rev:** Denomination

Date	Mintage	VF20	XF40	MS60	MS63	MS65
1982	—	—	0.10	0.25	0.35	0.75
1983	110,016,000	—	0.10	0.25	0.35	0.75
1984	30,016,000	—	0.10	0.25	0.35	0.75

KM# 55 10 CENTS

2.00 g., Nickel-Brass, 17.5 mm. **Ruler:** Elizabeth II **Obv:** Crowned head right **Rev:** Denomination

Date	Mintage	VF20	XF40	MS60	MS63	MS65
1985	34,016,000	—	0.10	0.25	0.35	0.75
1986	40,000,000	—	0.10	0.25	0.35	0.75
1987	—	—	0.10	0.25	0.35	0.75
1988	30,000,000	—	0.10	0.25	0.35	0.75
1988	20,000	PF65 5.00				
1989	40,000,000	—	0.10	0.25	0.35	0.75
1990	—	—	0.10	0.25	0.35	0.75
1991	—	—	0.10	0.25	0.35	0.75
1992	24,000,000	—	0.10	0.25	0.35	0.75

KM# 66 10 CENTS

1.82 g., Brass Plated Steel, 17.5 mm. **Ruler:** Elizabeth II **Obv:** Bauhinia flower **Rev:** Denomination **Edge:** Plain

Date	Mintage	VF20	XF40	MS60	MS63	MS65
1993	—	—	0.10	0.25	0.35	0.50
1993	—	PF65 2.50				
1994	—	—	0.10	0.25	0.35	0.50
1995	—	—	0.10	0.25	0.35	0.50
1996	—	—	0.10	0.25	0.35	0.50
1997	—	—	0.10	0.25	0.35	0.50
1998	—	—	0.10	0.25	0.35	0.50

KM# 14 20 CENTS

5.43 g., 0.800 Silver 0.1397 oz. ASW, 23 mm. **Ruler:** Edward VII **Obv:** Crowned bust right **Rev:** English around central Chinese legend

Date	Mintage	F12	VF20	XF40	MS60	MS63
1902	250,000	20.00	40.00	110	300	500
1902	—	PF63 1,200				
1904	250,000	20.00	40.00	120	450	600
1905	750,000	300	600	1,000	2,000	3,500
1905	—	PF63 7,000				

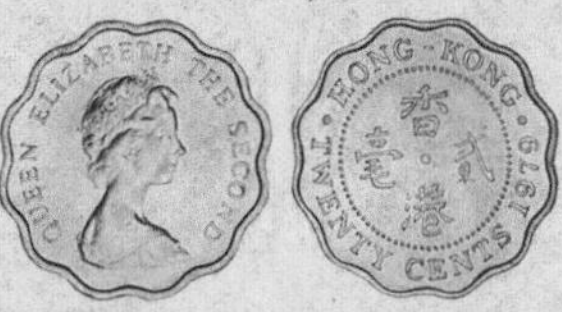

KM# 36 20 CENTS

2.60 g., Nickel-Brass, 19 mm. **Ruler:** Elizabeth II **Obv:** Young bust right **Rev:** English around central Chinese legend **Edge:** Scalloped **Shape:** Scalloped

Date	Mintage	VF20	XF40	MS60	MS63	MS65
1975	71,000,000	0.10	0.20	0.35	0.50	1.00
1976	42,000,000	0.10	0.20	0.35	0.50	1.00
1977	Inc. above	0.10	0.20	0.35	0.50	1.00
1978	86,000,000	0.10	0.20	0.35	0.50	1.00
1979	94,500,000	0.10	0.20	0.35	0.50	1.00
1980	65,000,000	0.10	0.20	0.35	0.50	1.00
1982	30,000,000	0.10	0.20	0.35	0.50	1.00
1983	15,000,000	0.10	0.20	0.35	0.50	1.00

KM# 59 20 CENTS

2.60 g., Nickel-Brass, 19 mm. **Ruler:** Elizabeth II **Obv:** Crowned head right **Rev:** English around central Chinese legend **Edge:** Scalloped **Shape:** Scalloped

Date	Mintage	VF20	XF40	MS60	MS63	MS65
1985	10,000,000	0.10	0.20	0.25	0.35	0.50
1988	Est. 40000	0.10	0.20	0.25	0.35	0.50
1988	Est. 20000	PF65 5.00				
1989	17,000,000	0.10	0.20	0.25	0.35	0.50
1990	—	0.10	0.20	0.25	0.35	0.50
1991	131,000,000	0.10	0.20	0.25	0.35	0.50

KM# 67 20 CENTS

2.60 g., Nickel-Brass, 19 mm. **Ruler:** Elizabeth II **Obv:** Bauhinia flower **Rev:** Denomination **Edge:** Scalloped **Shape:** Scalloped

Date	Mintage	VF20	XF40	MS60	MS63	MS65
1993	—	0.10	0.20	0.30	0.40	0.75
1993	—	PF65 2.50				
1994	—	0.10	0.20	0.30	0.40	0.75
1995	—	0.10	0.20	0.30	0.40	0.75
1997	—	0.10	0.20	0.30	0.40	0.75
1998	—	0.10	0.20	0.30	0.40	0.75

KM# 15 50 CENTS

13.58 g., 0.800 Silver 0.3492 oz. ASW, 31 mm.

Ruler: Edward VII **Obv:** Crowned bust right **Rev:** English and Chinese legend, denomination at center

Date	Mintage	F12	VF20	XF40	MS60	MS63
1902	100,000	30.00	40.00	65.00	250	400
1902	—	PF63 650				
1904	100,000	30.00	40.00	65.00	250	400
1904	—	PF63 650				
1905	300,000	25.00	35.00	60.00	185	350
1905	—	PF63 650				

KM# 27.1 50 CENTS

5.85 g., Copper-Nickel, 23.5 mm. **Ruler:** George VI **Obv:** Crowned head left **Rev:** English around central Chinese legend **Edge:** Reeded and security

Date	Mintage	F12	VF20	XF40	MS60	MS63
1951	15,000,000	1.00	2.00	3.50	7.00	15.00
1951	—	PF63 250				

KM# 27.2 50 CENTS

5.85 g., Copper-Nickel, 23.5 mm. **Ruler:** George VI **Obv:** Crowned head left **Rev:** English around central Chinese legend **Edge:** Reeded **Note:** Error.

Date	Mintage	F12	VF20	XF40	MS60	MS63
1951	Inc. above	3.00	5.00	10.00	22.00	—

KM# 30.1 50 CENTS

5.85 g., Copper-Nickel, 23.5 mm. **Ruler:** Elizabeth II **Obv:** Crowned head right **Rev:** English around central Chinese legend **Edge:** Reeded and security

Date	Mintage	F12	VF20	XF40	MS60	MS63
1958 H	4,000,000	—	0.50	1.25	4.50	8.00
1960	4,000,000	—	0.40	1.00	4.00	7.50
1960	—	PF63 100				
1961	6,000,000	—	0.40	1.00	3.50	7.50
1961	—	PF63 100				
1963 H	10,000,000	—	0.40	1.00	3.50	7.50
1964	5,000,000	—	0.40	1.00	3.50	7.50
1965 KN	8,000,000	—	0.40	1.00	3.00	7.00
1966	5,000,000	—	0.40	1.00	3.50	7.50
1967	12,000,000	—	0.40	1.00	3.00	7.00
1968 H	12,000,000	—	0.40	1.00	3.00	7.00
1970 H	4,600,000	—	0.40	1.00	3.00	7.00

KM# 30.2 50 CENTS

Copper-Nickel, 23.5 mm. **Ruler:** Elizabeth II **Obv:** Crowned head right **Rev:** English around central Chinese legend **Edge:** Reeded **Note:** Error.

Date	Mintage	F12	VF20	XF40	MS60	MS63
1958 H	Inc. above	2.00	4.00	8.00	20.00	—

KM# 34 50 CENTS

5.00 g., Copper-Nickel, 23.5 mm. **Ruler:** Elizabeth II **Obv:** Crowned head right **Rev:** English around central Chinese legend **Edge:** Reeded

Date	Mintage	F12	VF20	XF40	MS60	MS63
1971 KN	—	—	0.20	0.40	1.50	3.00
1972	30,000,000	—	0.20	0.40	1.50	3.00
1973	36,800,000	—	0.20	0.40	1.50	3.00
1974	6,000,000	—	0.20	0.40	1.50	3.00
1975	8,000,000	—	0.20	0.40	1.50	3.00

KM# 41 50 CENTS

5.00 g., Nickel-Brass, 22.5 mm. **Ruler:** Elizabeth II **Obv:** Young bust right **Rev:** English around central Chinese legend **Edge:** Reeded

Date	Mintage	VF20	XF40	MS60	MS63	MS65
1977	60,001,000	0.20	0.30	0.50	0.80	1.25
1978	70,000,000	0.20	0.30	0.50	0.80	1.25
1979	60,640,000	0.20	0.30	0.50	0.80	1.25
1980	120,000,000	0.20	0.30	0.50	0.80	1.25

KM# 62 50 CENTS

4.90 g., Nickel-Brass, 22.5 mm. **Ruler:** Elizabeth II **Obv:** Crowned head right **Rev:** English around central Chinese legend

Date	Mintage	VF20	XF40	MS60	MS63	MS65
1988	50,000	—	2.00	4.00	7.00	15.00
1988	25,000	PF65 10.00				
1990	27,000	0.20	0.30	0.50	0.80	1.25

KM# 68 50 CENTS

5.00 g., Brass Plated Steel, 22.5 mm. **Ruler:** Elizabeth II **Obv:** Bauhinia flower **Rev:** Denomination **Edge:** Reeded

Date	Mintage	VF20	XF40	MS60	MS63	MS65
1993	—	0.20	0.30	0.50	0.80	1.25
1993	—	PF65 5.50				
1994	—	0.20	0.30	0.50	0.80	1.25
1995	—	0.20	0.30	0.50	0.80	1.25
1997	—	0.20	0.30	0.50	0.80	1.25
1998	—	0.20	0.30	0.50	0.80	1.25

KM# 31.1 DOLLAR

11.31 g., Copper-Nickel, 29.8 mm. **Ruler:** Elizabeth II **Obv:** Crowned head right **Rev:** Upright crowned 3/4 lion with orb left **Edge:** Security **Note:** Mint mark is below "LL" of "DOLLAR".

Date	Mintage	F12	VF20	XF40	MS60	MS63
1960 H	40,000,000	—	0.60	1.75	5.50	9.00
1960 H	—	PF63 3,350				
1960 KN	40,000,000	—	0.60	1.75	5.50	9.00
1970 H	15,000,000	—	0.60	1.25	4.50	8.00

KM# 31.2 DOLLAR

11.31 g., Copper-Nickel, 29.8 mm. **Ruler:** Elizabeth II **Obv:** Crowned head right **Rev:** Upright crowned 3/4 lion with orb left **Edge:** Reeded **Note:** Error. Mint mark is below "LL" of "DOLLAR"

Date	Mintage	F12	VF20	XF40	MS60	MS63
1960 H	Inc. above	4.00	7.00	15.00	30.00	—

KM# 35 DOLLAR

11.31 g., Copper-Nickel, 29.8 mm. **Ruler:** Elizabeth II **Obv:** Crowned head right **Rev:** Upright crowned 3/4 lion with orb left **Edge:** Reeded

Date	Mintage	F12	VF20	XF40	MS60	MS63
1971 H	8,000,000	—	0.60	1.25	4.50	8.00
1972	20,000,000	—	0.60	1.25	3.50	7.00
1973	8,125,000	—	0.60	1.25	4.50	8.00
1974	26,000,000	—	0.60	1.25	3.50	7.00
1975	22,500,000	—	0.60	1.25	3.50	7.00

KM# 43 DOLLAR

7.10 g., Copper-Nickel, 25.5 mm. **Ruler:** Elizabeth II **Obv:** Young bust right **Rev:** Upright crowned 3/4 lion with orb left **Edge:** Reeded

Date	Mintage	VF20	XF40	MS60	MS63	MS65
1978	120,000,000	0.40	0.70	1.00	1.50	2.50
1979	104,908,000	0.40	0.70	1.00	1.50	2.50
1980	100,000,000	0.40	0.70	1.00	1.50	2.50

KM# 63 DOLLAR

7.10 g., Copper-Nickel, 25.5 mm. **Ruler:** Elizabeth II **Obv:** Crowned head right **Rev:** Upright crowned 3/4 lion with orb left

Date	Mintage	VF20	XF40	MS60	MS63	MS65
1987	—	0.30	0.50	0.60	1.00	1.50
1988	20,000,000	0.30	0.50	0.60	1.00	1.50
1988	20,000	PF65 20.00				
1989	20,000,000	0.30	0.50	0.60	1.00	1.50
1990	—	0.30	0.50	0.60	1.00	1.50
1991	—	0.30	0.50	0.60	1.00	1.50
1992	25,000,000	0.30	0.50	0.60	1.00	1.50

KM# 69 DOLLAR

7.10 g., Nickel Plated Steel, 25.5 mm. **Ruler:** Elizabeth II **Obv:** Bauhinia flower **Rev:** Denomination, large numeral

Date	Mintage	VF20	XF40	MS60	MS63	MS65
1993	—	0.30	0.50	0.60	1.00	1.50
1993	—	PF65 10.00				

KM# 69a DOLLAR

7.10 g., Copper-Nickel, 25.5 mm. **Ruler:** Elizabeth II **Obv:** Bauhinia flower **Rev:** Denomination, large numeral

Date	Mintage	VF20	XF40	MS60	MS63	MS65
1994	—	0.30	0.50	0.60	1.00	1.50
1995	—	0.30	0.50	0.60	1.00	1.50
1996	—	0.30	0.50	0.60	1.00	1.50
1997	—	0.30	0.50	0.60	1.00	1.50
1998	—	0.30	0.50	0.60	1.00	1.50

KM# 37 2 DOLLARS

8.40 g., Copper-Nickel, 28 mm. **Ruler:** Elizabeth II **Obv:** Young bust right **Rev:** Upright crowned 3/4 lion with orb left **Edge:** Scalloped **Shape:** Scalloped

Date	Mintage	VF20	XF40	MS60	MS63	MS65
1975	60,000,000	0.45	0.85	1.20	2.00	5.00
1978	504,000	0.45	1.00	5.00	10.00	20.00
1979	9,032,000	0.45	0.85	1.25	2.00	5.00
1980	30,000,000	0.45	0.85	1.25	2.00	5.00
1981	30,000,000	0.45	0.85	1.25	2.00	5.00
1982	30,000,000	0.45	0.85	1.25	2.00	5.00
1983	7,002,000	0.45	0.85	1.25	2.00	5.00
1984	22,002,000	0.45	0.85	1.25	2.00	5.00

KM# 60 2 DOLLARS
8.40 g., Copper-Nickel, 28 mm. **Ruler:** Elizabeth II **Obv:** Crowned head right **Rev:** Upright crowned 3/4 lion with orb left **Edge:** Scalloped **Shape:** Scalloped

Date	Mintage	VF20	XF40	MS60	MS63	MS65
1985	10,002,000	0.45	0.65	0.75	1.25	2.00
1986	15,000,000	0.45	0.65	0.75	1.25	2.00
1987	—	0.45	2.00	5.00	10.00	—
1988	5,000,000	0.45	0.65	0.75	1.25	2.00
1988	20,000	PF65 35.00				
1989	33,000,000	0.45	0.65	0.75	1.25	2.00
1990	—	0.45	0.65	0.75	1.25	2.00
1992	4,370,000	0.45	2.00	5.00	10.00	—

KM# 64 2 DOLLARS
8.40 g., Copper-Nickel, 28 mm. **Ruler:** Elizabeth II **Obv:** Bauhinia flower **Rev:** Denomination, large numeral **Edge:** Scalloped **Shape:** Scalloped

Date	Mintage	VF20	XF40	MS60	MS63	MS65
1993	—	0.45	0.65	0.75	1.25	2.00
1993	—	PF65 12.50				
1994	—	0.45	0.65	0.75	1.25	2.00
1995	—	0.45	0.65	0.75	1.25	2.00
1997	—	0.45	0.65	0.75	1.25	2.00
1998	—	0.45	0.65	0.75	1.25	2.00

KM# 39 5 DOLLARS
10.85 g., Copper-Nickel, 30.8 mm. **Ruler:** Elizabeth II **Obv:** Young bust right **Rev:** Upright crowned 3/4 lion with orb left **Shape:** 10-sided

Date	Mintage	VF20	XF40	MS60	MS63	MS65
1976	30,000,000	1.00	2.00	3.00	5.00	10.00
1978	10,000,000	1.00	2.00	3.00	7.50	15.00
1979	12,000,000	1.00	2.00	3.00	6.00	12.00

KM# 46 5 DOLLARS
13.40 g., Copper-Nickel, 27 mm. **Ruler:** Elizabeth II **Obv:** Young bust right **Rev:** Denomination, large numeral

Date	Mintage	VF20	XF40	MS60	MS63	MS65
1980	40,000,000	1.00	1.50	3.00	6.00	7.50
1981	20,000,000	1.00	1.50	3.00	6.00	7.50
1982	10,000,000	1.00	1.50	3.00	6.00	7.50
1983	4,000,000	1.00	1.50	4.00	8.00	10.00
1984	4,500,000	1.00	1.50	4.00	8.00	10.00

KM# 56 5 DOLLARS
13.40 g., Copper-Nickel, 27 mm. **Ruler:** Elizabeth II **Obv:** Crowned head right **Rev:** Denomination, large numeral

Date	Mintage	VF20	XF40	MS60	MS63	MS65
1985	6,000,000	0.75	1.25	1.75	3.50	7.50
1986	8,000,000	0.75	1.25	1.75	3.50	7.50
1987	—	0.75	1.25	1.75	3.50	7.50
1988	16,000,000	0.75	1.25	1.75	3.50	7.50
1988	25,000	PF65 45.00				
1989	37,000,000	0.75	1.25	1.75	3.50	7.50

KM# 65 5 DOLLARS
13.40 g., Copper-Nickel, 27 mm. **Ruler:** Elizabeth II **Obv:** Bauhinia flower **Rev:** Denomination, large numeral **Edge Lettering:** in Chinese: HONG KONG FIVE DOLLARS

Date	Mintage	VF20	XF40	MS60	MS63	MS65
1993	—	0.75	1.25	1.50	2.50	3.50
1993	—	PF65 20.00				
1995	—	0.75	1.25	1.50	2.50	3.50
1997	—	0.75	1.25	1.50	2.50	3.50
1998	—	0.75	1.25	1.50	2.50	3.50

KM# 70 10 DOLLARS
Bi-Metallic Nickel-Brass center in Copper-Nickel ring, 24 mm. **Ruler:** Elizabeth II **Obv:** Bauhinia flower **Rev:** Numerals 10 and denomination in Chinese and English

Date	Mintage	VF20	XF40	MS60	MS63	MS65
1993	—	2.50	3.50	4.50	7.50	10.00
1993	Est. 30000	PF65 20.00				
1994	—	1.50	2.50	3.50	5.00	7.50
1995	—	1.50	2.50	3.50	5.00	7.50

KM# 70a 10 DOLLARS
18.30 g., 0.917 Gold 0.5395 oz. AGW, 24 mm. **Ruler:** Elizabeth II **Obv:** Bauhinia flower **Rev:** Numerals 10 and denomination in Chinese and English

Date	Mintage	VF20	XF40	MS60	MS63	MS65
1994	20,000	—	—	—	760	890

KM# 38 1000 DOLLARS
15.97 g., 0.917 Gold 0.4708 oz. AGW **Ruler:** Elizabeth II **Subject:** Visit of Queen Elizabeth **Obv:** Young bust right **Rev:** Arms with supporters

Date	Mintage	XF40	MS60	MS63	MS65	MS66
1975	15,000	—	—	—	—	650
1975	5,005	PF67 1,250	PF69 1,400			

KM# 40 1000 DOLLARS
15.97 g., 0.917 Gold 0.4708 oz. AGW **Ruler:** Elizabeth II **Subject:** Year of the Dragon **Obv:** Young bust right **Rev:** Dragon left

Date	Mintage	XF40	MS60	MS63	MS65	MS66
1976	20,000	—	—	—	—	650
1976	6,911	PF67 1,350	PF69 1,500			

KM# 42 1000 DOLLARS
15.97 g., 0.917 Gold 0.4708 oz. AGW **Ruler:** Elizabeth II **Subject:** Year of the Snake **Obv:** Young bust right **Rev:** Snake

Date	Mintage	XF40	MS60	MS63	MS65	MS66
1977	20,000	—	—	—	—	700
1977	10,000	PF67 800	PF69 875			

KM# 44 1000 DOLLARS
15.97 g., 0.917 Gold 0.4708 oz. AGW **Ruler:** Elizabeth II **Subject:** Year of the Horse **Obv:** Young bust right **Rev:** Horse left

Date	Mintage	XF40	MS60	MS63	MS65	MS66
1978	20,000	—	—	—	—	700
1978	10,000	PF67 750	PF69 825			

KM# 45 1000 DOLLARS
15.97 g., 0.917 Gold 0.4708 oz. AGW **Ruler:** Elizabeth II **Subject:** Year of the Goat **Obv:** Young bust right **Rev:** Ram left

Date	Mintage	XF40	MS60	MS63	MS65	MS66
1979	30,000	—	—	—	—	700
1979	15,000	PF67 800	PF69 875			

KM# 47 1000 DOLLARS
15.97 g., 0.917 Gold 0.4708 oz. AGW **Ruler:** Elizabeth II **Subject:** Year of the Monkey **Obv:** Young bust right **Rev:** Monkey seated right

Date	Mintage	XF40	MS60	MS63	MS65	MS66
1980	31,000	—	—	—	—	650
1980	18,000	PF67 700	PF69 775			

KM# 48 1000 DOLLARS
15.97 g., 0.917 Gold 0.4708 oz. AGW **Ruler:** Elizabeth II **Subject:** Year of the Cockerel **Obv:** Young bust right **Rev:** Rooster right

Date	Mintage	XF40	MS60	MS63	MS65	MS66
1981	33,000	—	—	—	—	700
1981	22,000	PF67 750	PF69 825			

KM# 50 1000 DOLLARS
15.97 g., 0.917 Gold 0.4708 oz. AGW **Ruler:** Elizabeth II **Subject:** Year of the Dog **Obv:** Young bust right **Rev:** Dog right

Date	Mintage	XF40	MS60	MS63	MS65	MS66
1982	33,000	—	—	—	—	700
1982	22,000	PF67 750	PF69 825			

KM# 51 1000 DOLLARS
15.97 g., 0.917 Gold 0.4708 oz. AGW **Ruler:** Elizabeth II **Subject:** Year of the Pig **Obv:** Young bust right **Rev:** Pig right

Date	Mintage	XF40	MS60	MS63	MS65	MS66
1983	33,000	—	—	—	—	750
1983	22,000	PF67 800	PF69 875			

KM# 52 1000 DOLLARS
15.97 g., 0.917 Gold 0.4708 oz. AGW **Ruler:** Elizabeth II **Subject:** Year of the Rat **Obv:** Young bust right **Rev:** Rat left

Date	Mintage	XF40	MS60	MS63	MS65	MS66
1984	20,000	—	—	—	—	700
1984	10,000	PF67 800	PF69 900			

KM# 53 1000 DOLLARS
15.97 g., 0.917 Gold 0.4708 oz. AGW **Ruler:** Elizabeth II **Subject:** Year of the Ox **Obv:** Young bust right **Rev:** Ox left

Date	Mintage	XF40	MS60	MS63	MS65	MS66
1985	30,000	—	—	—	—	700
1985	10,000	PF67 800	PF69 900			

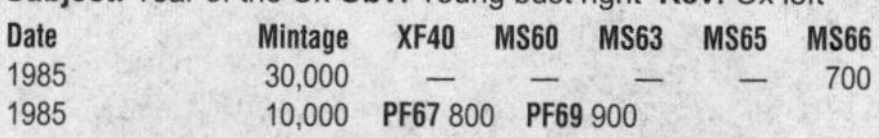

KM# 54 1000 DOLLARS
15.97 g., 0.917 Gold 0.4708 oz. AGW **Ruler:** Elizabeth II **Subject:** Year of the Tiger **Obv:** Young bust right **Rev:** Tiger

Date	Mintage	XF40	MS60	MS63	MS65	MS66
1986	20,000	—	—	—	—	700
1986	10,000	PF67 750	PF69 850			

KM# 57 1000 DOLLARS
15.97 g., 0.917 Gold 0.4708 oz. AGW **Ruler:** Elizabeth II **Subject:** Royal visit of Queen Elizabeth II **Obv:** Crowned head right **Rev:** Arms with supporters

Date	Mintage	XF40	MS60	MS63	MS65	MS66
1986	20,000	—	—	—	—	700
1986	12,000	PF67 800	PF69 900			

KM# 58 1000 DOLLARS
15.97 g., 0.917 Gold 0.4708 oz. AGW **Ruler:** Elizabeth II **Subject:** Year of the Rabbit **Obv:** Young bust right **Rev:** Rabbit left

Date	Mintage	XF40	MS60	MS63	MS65	MS66
1987	20,000	—	—	—	—	700
1987	12,000	PF67 800	PF69 900			

SPECIAL ADMINISTRATION REGION (S.A.R.)

KM# 72 10 CENTS
Brass Plated Steel, 17.55 mm. **Obv:** Bauhinia flower **Rev:** Sailing junk

Date	Mintage	VF20	XF40	MS60	MS63	MS65
1997	—	0.10	0.15	0.30	0.45	0.60
1997	97,000	PF65 1.50				

KM# 73 20 CENTS
Nickel-Brass, 19 mm. **Obv:** Bauhinia flower **Rev:** Butterfly kites

Date	Mintage	VF20	XF40	MS60	MS63	MS65
1997	—	0.10	0.20	0.40	0.60	0.75
1997	97,000	PF65 1.50				

KM# 74 50 CENTS
Brass Plated Steel, 22.5 mm. **Obv:** Bauhinia flower **Rev:** Ox left divides date

Date	Mintage	VF20	XF40	MS60	MS63	MS65
1997	—	0.20	0.30	0.80	1.25	1.50
1997	97,000	PF65 2.50				

KM# 75 DOLLAR
7.10 g., Copper-Nickel, 25.5 mm. **Obv:** Bauhinia flower **Rev:** Chinese unicorn divides date

Date	Mintage	VF20	XF40	MS60	MS63	MS65
1997	—	0.30	0.50	1.00	1.25	1.50
1997	97,000	PF65 3.00				

KM# 76 2 DOLLARS
8.40 g., Copper-Nickel, 28 mm. **Obv:** Bauhinia flower **Rev:** He He brothers (symbol of harmony) divide date **Shape:** Scalloped

Date	Mintage	VF20	XF40	MS60	MS63	MS65
1997	—	0.45	0.65	1.25	1.50	1.75
1997	97,000	PF65 4.00				

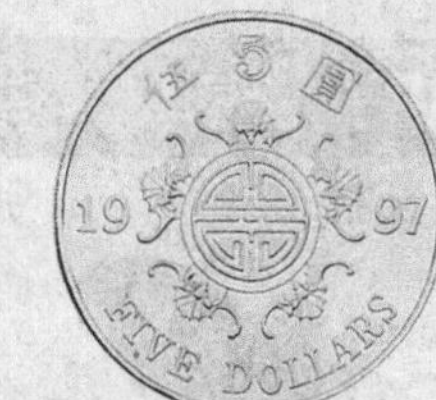

KM# 77 5 DOLLARS
13.40 g., Copper-Nickel, 27 mm. **Obv:** Bauhinia flower **Rev:** Shou character (Good Luck signs) divides date **Edge Lettering:** in Chinese: HONG KONG FIVE DOLLARS

Date	Mintage	VF20	XF40	MS60	MS63	MS65
1997	—	0.75	1.25	2.25	2.50	3.00
1997	97,000	PF65 7.50				

KM# 78 10 DOLLARS
Bi-Metallic Nickel-Brass center in Copper-Nickel ring, 24 mm. **Obv:** Bauhinia flower **Rev:** Suspension bridge (Symbol of transition)

Date	Mintage	VF20	XF40	MS60	MS63	MS65
1997	—	1.75	3.50	5.00	6.00	7.50
1997	97,000	PF65 10.00				

KM# 71 1000 DOLLARS
15.97 g., 0.917 Gold 0.4708 oz. AGW **Subject:** Return of Hong Kong to China **Obv:** Bauhinia flower **Rev:** Skyline view

Date	Mintage	XF40	MS60	MS63	MS65	MS66
1997	97,000	PF67 900	PF69 950			

KM# 79 1000 DOLLARS
15.97 g., 0.917 Gold 0.4708 oz. AGW **Subject:** Hong Kong International Airport **Obv:** Bauhinia flower **Rev:** Stylized airplane lifting off from runway

Date	Mintage	XF40	MS60	MS63	MS65	MS66
1998	15,000	PF67 1,000	PF69 1,100			

MINT SETS

KM#	Date	Mintage	Identification	Issue Price	Mkt Val
MS1	1988 (7)	50,000	KM55-56, 59-63	13.00	32.50
MS2	1993 (7)	—	KM64-70	20.00	20.00
MS3	1997 (7)	—	KM72-78	30.00	15.00

PROOF SETS

KM#	Date	Mintage	Identification	Issue Price	Mkt Val
PS5	1988 (7)	25,000	KM55-56, 59-63	39.75	125
PS6	1993 (7)	30,000	KM64-70	50.00	75.00
PS7	1997 (7)	97,000	KM72-78	—	30.00

The Republic of Hungary, located in central Europe, has an area of 35,929 sq. mi. (93,030 sq. km.) and a population of 10.7 million. Capital: Budapest. The economy is based on agriculture, bauxite and a rapidly expanding industrial sector. Machinery, chemicals, iron and steel, and fruits and vegetables are exported.

The ancient kingdom of Hungary, founded by the Magyars in the 9th century, achieved its greatest extension in the mid-14th century when its dominions touched the Baltic, Black and Mediterranean Seas. After suffering repeated Turkish invasions, Hungary accepted Habsburg rule to escape Turkish occupation, regaining independence in 1867 with the Emperor of Austria as king of a dual Austro-Hungarian monarchy.

After World War I, Hungary lost 2/3 of its territory and 1/2 of its population and underwent a period of drastic political revision. The short-lived republic of 1918 was followed by a chaotic interval of communist rule, 1919, and the restoration of the monarchy in 1920 with Admiral Horthy as regent of the kingdom. Although a German ally in World War II, Hungary was occupied by German troops who imposed a pro-Nazi dictatorship, 1944. Soviet armies drove out the Germans in 1945 and assisted the communist minority in seizing power. A revised constitution published on Aug. 20, 1949, established Hungary as a People's Republic' of the Soviet type. On October 23, 1989, Hungary was pro-claimed the Republic of Hungary.

RULERS

Franz Joseph I, 1848-1916
Karl I, 1916-1918

MINT MARKS

B, K, KB - Kremnitz (Kormoczbanya)
BP - Budapest

MONETARY SYSTEM

1892-1925

100 Filler = 1 Korona

1926-1945

100 Filler = 1 Pengo

Commencing 1946

100 Filler = 1 Forint

NOTE: Many coins of Hungary through 1948, especially 1925-1945, have been restruck in recent times. These may be identified by a rosette in the vicinity of the mintmark. Restrike mintages for KM#440-449, 451-458, 468-469,475-477, 480-483, 494, 496-498 are usually about 1000 pieces, later date mintages are not known.

KINGDOM

REFORM COINAGE

100 Filler = 1 Korona

KM# 480 FILLÉR

Bronze **Ruler:** Franz Joseph I **Obv:** Crown above date **Rev:** Value within wreath **Mint:** Kormoczbanya

Date	Mintage	F12	VF20	XF40	MS60	MS63
1901 KB	5,994,000	4.00	13.00	30.00	45.00	65.00
1902 KB	16,299,000	0.20	2.00	5.00	7.00	12.00
1903 KB	2,291,000	12.00	30.00	55.00	85.00	155
1906 KB	61,000	65.00	160	350	500	750
1914 KB	—	65.00	125	185	285	450
1914 KB	—	PF63 350				

KM# 481 2 FILLÉR

3.28 g., Bronze **Ruler:** Franz Joseph I **Obv:** Crown above date **Rev:** Value within wreath **Mint:** Kormoczbanya

Date	Mintage	F12	VF20	XF40	MS60	MS63
1901 KB	25,805,000	0.50	1.00	2.50	5.00	10.00
1902 KB	6,937,000	5.50	12.00	25.00	40.00	60.00
1903 KB	4,052,000	12.00	20.00	40.00	65.00	130
1904 KB	4,203,000	6.00	12.00	25.00	45.00	70.00
1905 KB	9,335,000	0.70	1.75	3.00	5.00	10.00
1906 KB	3,140,000	1.75	2.50	5.00	10.00	20.00
1907 KB	9,943,000	5.50	9.00	12.00	20.00	40.00
1908 KB	16,486,000	0.50	1.00	2.50	5.00	10.00
1909 KB	19,075,000	0.50	1.00	2.50	5.00	10.00
1910 KB	5,338,000	4.50	7.50	10.00	15.00	30.00
1910 KB Proof, restrike with rosette	—	PF65 10.00				
1914 KB	4,106,000	0.50	1.00	2.00	3.00	5.00
1915 KB	1,296,360	1.50	2.00	3.00	5.00	7.00

KM# 497 2 FILLÉR

Iron **Ruler:** Karl I **Obv:** Crown of St. Stephen **Rev:** Denomination above sprays **Note:** Varieties in planchet thickness exist for 1917.

Date	Mintage	F12	VF20	XF40	MS60	MS63
1916	—	6.00	10.00	25.00	50.00	—
1917	—	1.00	2.50	7.00	25.00	—
1918	—	2.00	4.50	9.00	25.00	—

KM# 482 10 FILLÉR

3.00 g., Nickel **Ruler:** Franz Joseph I **Obv:** Crown above date **Rev:** Value within wreath **Edge:** Reeded **Mint:** Kormoczbanya **Note:** Edge varieties exist.

Date	Mintage	F12	VF20	XF40	MS60	MS63
1906 KB	56,000	75.00	350	550	850	—
1908 KB	6,819,000	0.25	0.50	1.50	3.00	5.00
1909 KB	17,204,000	0.30	0.60	1.75	3.50	5.00
1914 KB Rare	—	—	—	—	—	—

KM# 494 10 FILLÉR

Copper-Nickel-Zinc **Ruler:** Franz Joseph I **Obv:** Crown of St. Stephen **Rev:** Denomination above sprays **Note:** Varieties exist.

Date	Mintage	VF20	XF40	MS60	MS63	MS65
1914	4,400,000	—	650	—	—	—
1915	Inc. above	0.60	1.50	3.00	5.00	7.50
1915	Inc. above	PF65 4.00				
Note: Restrike with rosette						
1916	Inc. above	1.25	2.00	3.50	5.50	8.00

KM# 496 10 FILLÉR

Iron **Ruler:** Karl I **Obv:** Crown of St. Stephen **Rev:** Denomination above sprays **Note:** Varieties exist.

Date	Mintage	F12	VF20	XF40	MS60	MS63
1915	11,500,000	9.00	20.00	80.00	140	—
1916 Rare	Inc. above	—	—	—	—	—
1918	Inc. above	15.00	30.00	55.00	85.00	—
1918 Proof, restrike	—	PF65 18.00				
1920	3,275,000	4.50	19.00	50.00	85.00	—
1920 Proof, restrike	—	PF65 18.00				

KM# 483 20 FILLÉR

4.00 g., Nickel, 21 mm. **Ruler:** Franz Joseph I **Obv:** Crown above date **Rev:** Value within wreath **Edge:** Reeded **Mint:** Kormoczbanya **Note:** Edge varieties exist.

Date	Mintage	F12	VF20	XF40	MS60	MS63
1906 KB	67,000	300	1,300	—	—	—
1907 KB	1,248,000	3.00	6.00	20.00	30.00	50.00
1908 KB	10,770,000	0.75	3.00	5.00	8.00	15.00
1914 KB	5,387,000	3.75	5.50	7.00	10.00	12.00
1914 KB Restrike; proof	—	PF65 12.50				

KM# 498 20 FILLÉR

3.25 g., Iron **Obv:** Crown of St. Stephen **Rev:** Denomination within wreath **Edge:** Reeded **Note:** Edge varieties exist.

Date	Mintage	F12	VF20	XF40	MS60	MS63
1914	18,826,000	18.00	32.50	45.00	70.00	—
1916	Inc. above	0.50	4.00	10.00	20.00	—
1917	Inc. above	0.75	4.00	12.00	20.00	—
1918	Inc. above	0.75	4.00	12.00	20.00	—
1918 Proof, restrike	—	PF65 6.00				
1920	12,000,000	2.50	5.00	15.00	30.00	—
1921	Inc. above	18.00	32.50	60.00	90.00	—
1921 Proof, restrike	—	PF65 12.00				
1922 Rare	—	—	—	—	—	—
1922 Proof, restrike	—	PF65 12.00				

KM# 498a 20 FILLÉR

Brass **Obv:** Crown of St. Stephen **Rev:** Denomination above sprays

Date	Mintage	VF20	XF40	MS60	MS63	MS65
1922 Proolike	400	—	—	—	175	—
1922 Proof, restrike	—	PF65 30.00				

KM# 484 KORONA

5.00 g., 0.835 Silver 0.1342 oz. ASW **Ruler:** Franz Joseph I **Obv:** Laureate head, right **Rev:** Crown, value within wreath **Mint:** Kormoczbanya **Note:** Obverse varieties exist.

Date	Mintage	F12	VF20	XF40	MS60	MS63
1906 KB	24,000	175	350	600	900	—

KM# 492 KORONA

5.00 g., 0.835 Silver 0.1342 oz. ASW **Ruler:** Franz Joseph I **Obv:** Laureate head right **Obv. Legend:** Crown of St. Stephen within wreath

Date	Mintage	VF20	XF40	MS60	MS63	MS65
1912	4,004,000	6.00	9.00	12.00	15.00	18.00
1913	5,214	150	250	350	500	—
1914	5,886,000	3.50	5.00	7.00	10.00	12.00
1915	3,934,000	3.50	5.00	6.00	8.00	10.00
1916	—	6.00	9.00	12.00	15.00	20.00

KM# 493 2 KORONA

10.00 g., 0.835 Silver 0.2685 oz. ASW **Ruler:** Franz Joseph I **Obv:** Laureate head right **Rev:** Crown of St. Stephen supported by two angels, spray below **Mint:** Kormoczbanya

Date	Mintage	VF20	XF40	MS60	MS63	MS65
1912 KB	4,000,000	7.00	9.00	12.00	15.00	20.00
1913 KB	3,000,000	7.00	9.00	12.00	15.00	20.00
1914 KB	500,000	20.00	30.00	50.00	75.00	100

KM# 488 5 KORONA
24.00 g., 0.900 Silver 0.6945 oz. ASW, 36 mm. **Ruler:** Franz Joseph I **Obv:** Laureate head, right **Rev:** Angels holding crown above value and date within sprigs **Mint:** Kormoczbanya

Date	Mintage	VF20	XF40	MS60	MS63	MS65
1906 KB	1,263	1,000	3,500	—	—	—
1907 KB	500,000	30.00	45.00	60.00	90.00	150
1908 KB	1,742,000	27.00	35.00	45.00	75.00	125
1909 KB	1,299,000	30.00	45.00	60.00	90.00	150
1909 KB U.P. Proof, restrike	—	PF65 35.00				

KM# 489 5 KORONA
24.00 g., 0.900 Silver 0.6945 oz. ASW, 36 mm. **Ruler:** Franz Joseph I **Subject:** 40th Anniversary - Coronation of Franz Josef **Obv:** Laureate head right **Rev:** Coronation scene **Edge Lettering:** BIZALMAM AZ OSI ERÈNYBEN

Date	Mintage	VF20	XF40	MS60	MS63	MS65
1907	300,000	28.00	40.00	55.00	75.00	110
1907 Proof, restrike	—	PF65 30.00				
1907 U.P. Proof, restrike	—	PF65 30.00				

KM# 485 10 KORONA
3.39 g., 0.900 Gold 0.098 oz. AGW **Ruler:** Franz Joseph I **Obv:** Emperor standing **Rev:** Crowned shield with angel supporters **Mint:** Kormoczbanya

Date	Mintage	VF20	XF40	MS60	MS63	MS65
1901 KB	230,000	—	125	175	185	200
1902 KB	243,000	—	125	175	185	200
1903 KB	228,000	—	125	175	185	200
1904 KB	1,531,000	—	125	175	185	200
1905 KB	869,000	—	125	175	185	200
1906 KB	748,000	—	125	175	185	200
1907 KB	752,000	—	125	175	185	200
1908 KB	509,000	—	125	175	185	200
1909 KB	574,000	—	125	175	185	200
1910 KB	1,362,000	—	125	175	185	200
1911 KB	1,828,000	—	125	175	185	200
1912 KB	739,000	125	175	180	220	—
1913 KB	137,000	125	175	220	300	—
1914 KB	115,000	125	200	450	550	—
1915 KB	54,000	2,750	4,000	6,500	—	—

KM# 486 20 KORONA
6.78 g., 0.900 Gold 0.196 oz. AGW **Ruler:** Franz Joseph I **Obv:** Emperor standing **Rev:** Crowned shield with angel supporters **Mint:** Kormoczbanya

Date	Mintage	VF20	XF40	MS60	MS63	MS65
1901 KB	510,000	—	250	325	350	375
1901 KB	510,000	—	250	325	350	375
1902 KB	523,000	—	250	325	350	375
1903 KB	505,000	—	250	325	350	375
1904 KB	572,000	—	250	325	350	375
1905 KB	526,000	—	250	325	350	375
1906 KB	353,000	—	250	325	350	375
1907 KB	194,000	—	250	325	350	375
1908 KB	138,000	—	250	325	350	375
1909 KB	459,000	—	250	325	350	375
1910 KB	85,000	—	325	375	450	—
1911 KB	63,000	—	250	325	350	375
1912 KB	211,000	—	250	325	350	375
1913 KB	320,000	—	325	350	375	—
1914 KB	176,000	—	250	325	350	375
1915 KB	690,000	—	325	350	375	—

KM# 495 20 KORONA
6.78 g., 0.900 Gold 0.196 oz. AGW **Ruler:** Franz Joseph I **Obv:** Emperor standing **Rev:** Crowned shield (Bosnian arms added) with angel supporters

Date	Mintage	VF20	XF40	MS60	MS63	MS65
1914	—	—	325	365	400	—
1915	—	—	—	—	—	—
1916	—	350	475	650	700	—

KM# 500 20 KORONA
6.78 g., 0.900 Gold 0.196 oz. AGW **Ruler:** Karl I **Obv. Legend:** KAROLY.

Date	Mintage	VF20	XF40	MS60	MS63	MS65
1918 Rare	—	—	—	—	—	—

KM# 490 100 KORONA
33.88 g., 0.900 Gold 0.9802 oz. AGW, 36 mm. **Ruler:** Franz Joseph I **Subject:** 40th Anniversary - Coronation of Franz Josef **Obv:** Laureate head right **Rev:** Coronation scene **Edge Lettering:** BIZALMAM AZ ÖSI ERÈNYBEN **Mint:** Kormoczbanya

Date	Mintage	VF20	XF40	MS60	MS63	MS65
1907 KB	10,897	1,350	1,850	3,250	5,000	—
1907 KB U.P. Restrike	—	—	—	1,900	—	—

KM# 491 100 KORONA
33.88 g., 0.900 Gold 0.9802 oz. AGW **Ruler:** Franz Joseph I **Obv:** Emperor standing **Rev:** Crowned shield with angel supporters

Date	Mintage	VF20	XF40	MS60	MS63	MS65
1907	1,088	—	1,800	3,200	5,000	—
1907 U.P. Restrike	—	—	—	—	1,700	—
1908	4,038	—	1,650	2,850	3,800	—
1908 U.P Restrike	—	—	—	—	1,700	—

REGENCY COINAGE

1926 - 1945

KM# 505 FILLÉR
1.68 g., Bronze **Obv:** Crown of St. Stephen **Rev:** Denomination **Mint:** Budapest

Date	Mintage	VF20	XF40	MS60	MS63	MS65
1926 BP	6,471,000	1.00	2.00	3.00	4.00	7.00
1927 BP	16,529,000	0.20	0.50	2.00	3.00	7.00
1928 BP	7,000,000	0.50	1.00	2.50	3.75	7.00
1929 BP	418,000	10.00	20.00	25.00	35.00	50.00
1930 BP	3,734,000	0.60	1.50	3.00	5.00	7.00
1931 BP	10,849,000	0.20	0.60	2.00	3.00	7.00
1932 BP	5,000,000	0.50	1.00	2.50	4.00	7.00
1932 BP Proof, restrike	—	PF65 3.75				
1933 BP	5,000,000	0.50	1.00	2.50	4.00	7.00
1934 BP	3,111,000	0.60	1.20	2.75	4.50	7.00
1935 BP	6,889,000	0.50	1.00	2.50	4.00	7.00
1936 BP	10,000,000	0.20	0.60	1.00	2.50	5.00
1938 BP	10,575,000	0.20	0.60	1.00	2.50	5.00
1939 BP	10,425,000	0.20	0.60	1.00	2.50	5.00

KM# 506 2 FILLÉR
3.23 g., Bronze **Obv:** Crown of St. Stephen **Rev:** Denomination **Mint:** Budapest

Date	Mintage	VF20	XF40	MS60	MS63	MS65
1926 BP	17,777,000	0.20	0.40	0.75	2.00	5.00
1927 BP	44,836,000	0.20	0.40	0.75	2.00	5.00
1928 BP	11,448,000	0.20	0.40	0.75	2.00	5.00
1929 BP	8,995,000	0.25	0.50	1.00	2.50	5.00
1930 BP	6,943,000	0.25	0.50	1.00	2.50	5.00
1931 BP	826,000	0.90	2.50	3.50	6.50	9.00
1932 BP	4,174,000	8.00	15.00	20.00	28.00	45.00
1933 BP	501,000	6.00	10.00	15.00	20.00	35.00
1934 BP	9,499,000	0.20	0.40	0.75	2.00	5.00
1935 BP	10,000,000	0.20	0.40	0.75	2.00	5.00
1936 BP	2,049,000	0.30	0.75	2.25	4.00	6.00
1937 BP	7,951,000	0.25	0.50	0.75	2.00	5.00
1938 BP	14,125,000	0.20	0.40	0.65	1.50	3.00
1939 BP	16,875,000	0.20	0.40	0.65	1.50	3.00
1940 BP	7,000,000	0.25	0.50	0.65	1.50	3.00

KM# 518.1 2 FILLÉR
Steel **Obv:** Crown of St. Stephen **Rev:** Denomination

Date	Mintage	F12	VF20	XF40	MS60	MS63
1940	64,500,000	1.00	2.00	5.00	12.00	—

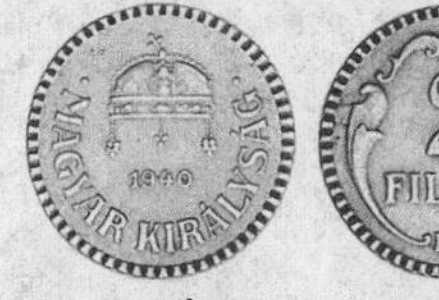

KM# 518.2 2 FILLÉR
3.30 g., Steel **Obv:** Crown of St. Stephen **Rev:** Denomination

Date	Mintage	F12	VF20	XF40	MS60	MS63
1940	78,000,000	0.50	1.00	2.00	4.50	—
1941	12,000,000	30.00	65.00	125	220	—
1942	13,000,000	0.50	1.00	2.00	4.50	—
1942 Proof, restrike	—	PF65 6.50				

KM# 519 2 FILLÉR
Zinc, 17 mm. **Obv:** Crown of St. Stephen **Rev:** Denomination **Note:** Variations in planchets exist.

Date	Mintage	F12	VF20	XF40	MS60	MS63
1943	37,000,000	0.10	0.20	0.70	3.00	—
1943 Proof, restrike	—	PF65 6.50				
1944	55,159,000	0.10	0.20	0.70	1.25	2.50

KM# 507 10 FILLÉR
3.01 g., Copper-Nickel, 19 mm. **Obv:** Crown of St. Stephen within small circle on radiant background **Rev:** Denomination **Mint:** Budapest

Date	Mintage	VF20	XF40	MS60	MS63	MS65
1926 BP	20,001,000	1.50	3.00	5.00	10.00	15.00

Date	Mintage	VF20	XF40	MS60	MS63	MS65
1927 BP	12,255,000	1.50	3.00	4.00	7.00	10.00
1935 BP	4,740,000	1.00	2.00	3.00	4.50	7.50
1936 BP	3,005,000	1.00	2.00	3.00	4.50	7.50
1938 BP	6,700,000	1.00	2.00	3.00	4.50	7.50
1939 BP	4,460,000	5.00	10.00	15.00	20.00	35.00
1940 BP	960,000	25.00	40.00	55.00	85.00	100

KM# 501a 10 FILLÉR

3.08 g., Steel **Obv:** Crown of St. Stephen within small circle on radiant background **Rev:** Denomination

Date	Mintage	VF20	XF40	MS60	MS63	MS65
1940	45,927,000	0.20	0.80	1.50	3.50	7.50
1941	24,963,000	0.20	0.80	1.50	3.50	7.50
1942	44,110,000	0.20	0.80	1.50	3.50	7.50

KM# 508 20 FILLÉR

Copper-Nickel **Obv:** Crown of St. Stephen within small circle on radiant background **Rev:** Denomination **Mint:** Budapest

Date	Mintage	VF20	XF40	MS60	MS63	MS65
1926 BP	25,000,000	3.50	5.00	10.00	15.00	25.00
1927 BP	830,000	25.00	40.00	60.00	110	125
1938 BP	20,150,000	0.25	0.50	1.25	2.50	5.00
1939 BP	2,020,000	8.00	12.00	20.00	35.00	50.00
1940 BP	2,470,000	7.00	12.00	16.00	30.00	50.00

KM# 520 20 FILLÉR

3.56 g., Steel, 21 mm. **Obv:** Crown of St. Stephen above center hole **Rev:** Center hole divides denomination

Date	Mintage	VF20	XF40	MS60	MS63	MS65
1941	75,007,000	0.20	0.90	2.00	4.00	7.50
1943	7,500,000	0.20	0.90	2.00	4.00	7.50
1944	25,000,000	0.20	0.90	2.00	4.00	7.50
1944 Proof, restrike	—	PF65 7.00				

KM# 509 50 FILLÉR

Copper-Nickel **Obv:** Crown of St. Stephen **Rev:** Denomination **Mint:** Budapest

Date	Mintage	VF20	XF40	MS60	MS63	MS65
1926 BP	14,921,000	1.25	2.00	3.50	6.00	10.00
1938 BP	20,079,000	0.40	0.75	1.50	3.00	5.00
1939 BP	2,770,000	15.00	25.00	30.00	55.00	85.00
1939 BP Proof, restrike	—	PF65 20.00				
1940 BP	6,230,000	7.50	15.00	20.00	35.00	50.00

KM# 510 PENGÖ

5.00 g., 0.640 Silver 0.1029 oz. ASW, 23 mm. **Obv:** Crowned shield within branches **Rev:** Denomination within wreath **Mint:** Budapest

Date	Mintage	VF20	XF40	MS60	MS63	MS65
1926 BP	15,000,000	4.00	7.00	10.00	25.00	40.00
1927 BP	18,000,000	4.00	6.00	10.00	15.00	25.00
1937 BP	4,000,000	1.90	4.00	6.00	8.00	15.00
1938 BP	5,000,000	1.90	4.00	6.00	8.00	15.00
1939 BP	13,000,000	1.90	4.00	5.00	6.00	12.00

KM# 521 PENGÖ

1.50 g., Aluminum **Obv:** Crowned shield **Rev:** Denomination and date divide wreath

Date	Mintage	VF20	XF40	MS60	MS63	MS65
1941	80,000,000	0.20	0.45	0.65	1.00	3.00
1942	19,000,000	0.20	0.45	0.65	1.00	3.00
1943	2,000,000	4.00	7.00	10.00	16.00	25.00
1944	16,000,000	0.20	0.45	0.65	1.00	3.00

KM# 511 2 PENGÖ

10.00 g., 0.640 Silver 0.2058 oz. ASW, 27 mm. **Obv:** Angels flank crowned shield above spray **Rev:** Hungarian Madonna **Mint:** Budapest

Date	Mintage	VF20	XF40	MS60	MS63	MS65
1929 BP	5,000,000	9.00	10.00	12.00	15.00	20.00
1931 BP	110,000	30.00	45.00	65.00	115	—
1932 BP	602,000	9.00	12.00	14.00	18.00	25.00
1933 BP	1,051,000	9.00	10.00	12.00	15.00	20.00
1935 BP	50,000	80.00	150	250	325	—
1936 BP	711,000	10.00	12.00	15.00	20.00	35.00
1937 BP	1,500,000	8.00	9.00	12.00	14.00	20.00
1938 BP	6,417,000	8.00	10.00	13.00	15.00	20.00
1939 BP	2,103,000	8.00	10.00	13.00	15.00	20.00

KM# 513 2 PENGÖ

10.00 g., 0.640 Silver 0.2058 oz. ASW, 27 mm. **Subject:** Tercentenary - Founding of Pazmany University **Obv:** Crowned, ornate shield **Rev:** Cardinal Peter Pazmany with two others

Date	Mintage	VF20	XF40	MS60	MS63	MS65
1935 BP	50,000	9.00	12.00	14.00	18.00	25.00
1935 BP	—	PF65 28.00				

Note: Restrike not marked

KM# 514 2 PENGÖ

10.00 g., 0.640 Silver 0.2058 oz. ASW, 27 mm. **Subject:** Bicentennial - Death of Rakoczi, Prince of Hungary and Transylvania **Obv:** Ornaments surround crowned shield **Rev:** Bust right

Date	Mintage	VF20	XF40	MS60	MS63	MS65
1935	100,000	8.00	9.00	10.00	13.00	18.00
1935	—	PF65 22.00				

Note: Restrike not marked

KM# 515 2 PENGÖ

10.00 g., 0.640 Silver 0.2058 oz. ASW, 27 mm. **Subject:** 50th Anniversary - Death of Franz von Liszt **Obv:** Crowned shield within wreath **Rev:** Head right

Date	Mintage	VF20	XF40	MS60	MS63	MS65
1936 BP	200,000	3.75	9.00	10.00	12.00	16.00
1936 BP	—	PF65 20.00				

Note: Restrike not marked

KM# 522.1 2 PENGÖ

2.80 g., Aluminum, 27 mm. **Obv:** Crowned shield within circle **Rev:** Denomination within circle, wreath surrounds

Date	Mintage	VF20	XF40	MS60	MS63	MS65
1941	24,000,000	0.30	0.50	0.75	1.25	2.00
1942	8,000,000	0.30	0.50	0.75	1.25	2.00
1943	10,000,000	0.30	0.50	0.75	1.25	2.00

KM# 522.2 2 PENGÖ

Aluminum, 27 mm. **Obv:** Crowned shield within circle **Rev:** Denomination within circle, wreath surrounds, base of 2 is wavy

Date	Mintage	VF20	XF40	MS60	MS63	MS65
1941	40,000	20.00	30.00	40.00	50.00	75.00
1941 Restrike, rose	—	—	—	—	—	—

KM# 512.1 5 PENGÖ

25.00 g., 0.640 Silver 0.5144 oz. ASW, 36 mm. **Subject:** 10th Anniversary - Regency of Admiral Horthy **Obv:** Bust right **Rev:** Crowned shield with standing angel supporters **Edge:** Raised, sharp reeding **Mint:** Budapest

Date	Mintage	VF20	XF40	MS60	MS63	MS65
1930 BP	3,650,000	9.50	13.00	16.00	20.00	27.50

KM# 512.2 5 PENGÖ

25.33 g., 0.640 Silver 0.5212 oz. ASW, 36 mm. **Subject:** 10th Anniversary - Regency of Admiral Horthy **Obv:** Bust right **Rev:** Crowned shield with standing angel supporters

Date	Mintage	VF20	XF40	MS60	MS63	MS65
1930 Proof, restrike	—	PF65 25.00				

KM# 516 5 PENGÖ

25.00 g., 0.640 Silver 0.5144 oz. ASW, 36 mm. **Subject:** 900th Anniversary - Death of St. Stephan **Obv:** Sword and scepter between crown and shield **Rev:** Crowned bust right

Date	Mintage	VF20	XF40	MS60	MS63	MS65
1938	600,000	9.50	15.00	18.00	22.50	30.00
1938 Proof, restrike not marked	—	PF65 35.00				

KM# 517 5 PENGÖ
25.00 g., 0.640 Silver 0.5144 oz. ASW, 36 mm. **Subject:** Admiral Miklos Horthy **Obv:** Uniformed bust left **Rev:** Crowned shield with standing angel supporters **Edge:** Smooth, ornamented

Date	Mintage	VF20	XF40	MS60	MS63	MS65
1938	60	—	—	—	1,000	—
1939	408,000	9.50	15.00	18.00	22.50	30.00

KM# 523 5 PENGÖ
Aluminum, 36 mm. **Subject:** 75th Birthday of Admiral Horthy **Obv:** Uniformed bust left **Rev:** Crowned shield with standing angel supporters

Date	Mintage	VF20	XF40	MS60	MS63	MS65
1943	2,000,000	1.00	1.50	2.00	3.50	5.00
1943 Proof, restrike	—	PF65 6.00				

PROVISIONAL GOVERNMENT

1944-1946

DECIMAL COINAGE

KM# 525 5 PENGÖ
Aluminum **Obv:** Parliament Building **Rev:** Crowned shield flanked by grain, fruit and leaves **Mint:** Budapest

Date	Mintage	VF20	XF40	MS60	MS63	MS65
1945 BP	5,002,000	1.00	2.00	3.00	5.00	6.00
1945 BP PROBAVERET Proof, restrike	—	PF65 17.50				

FIRST REPUBLIC

1946-1949

KM# 529 2 FILLÉR
3.00 g., Brass, 17 mm. **Obv:** Arms of the Republic **Obv. Legend:** MAGYAR ÁLLAMI VÁLTÓPÉNZ **Rev:** Grain stalk divides denomination **Mint:** Budapest

Date	Mintage	VF20	XF40	MS60	MS63	MS65
1946 BP	13,665,000	0.50	0.75	1.00	1.50	3.00
1947 BP	23,865,000	0.50	0.75	1.00	1.50	3.00
1947 BP Proof, restrike	—	PF65 6.50				

KM# 535 5 FILLÉR
0.60 g., Aluminum, 17 mm. **Obv:** Head left **Obv. Legend:** MAGYAR KÖZTÁRSASÁG **Rev:** Denomination within wreath **Mint:** Budapest

Date	Mintage	VF20	XF40	MS60	MS63	MS65
1948 BP	24,000,000	0.60	1.00	2.00	3.50	6.00
1951 BP	15,000,000	0.50	0.75	1.75	3.00	5.00

KM# 530 10 FILLÉR
3.00 g., Aluminum-Bronze, 19.1 mm. **Obv:** Dove with branch **Obv. Legend:** MAGYAR ÁLLAMI VÁLTÓPÉNZ **Rev:** Denomination **Edge:** Reeded **Mint:** Budapest

Date	Mintage	VF20	XF40	MS60	MS63	MS65
1946 BP	23,565,000	0.30	0.50	0.75	1.00	1.50
1947 BP	29,580,000	0.30	0.50	0.75	1.00	1.50
1947 BP Proof, restrike	—	PF65 7.50				
1948 BP	4,885,000	2.00	3.00	4.00	6.00	9.00
1950 BP	8,000,000	1.00	2.00	3.50	5.00	7.50

KM# 530a 10 FILLÉR
1.00 g., Aluminum **Obv:** Dove with branch **Rev:** Denomination

Date	Mintage	VF20	XF40	MS60	MS63	MS65
1950	—	20.00	30.00	40.00	50.00	75.00

KM# 531 20 FILLÉR
4.00 g., Aluminum-Bronze, 21 mm. **Obv:** Three wheat ears divide date **Obv. Legend:** MAGYAR ÁLLAMI VÁLTÓPÉNZ **Rev:** Denomination **Edge:** Reeded **Mint:** Budapest

Date	Mintage	VF20	XF40	MS60	MS63	MS65
1946 BP	16,560,000	0.50	0.75	1.00	1.50	3.00
1946 BP Proof, restrike	—	PF65 8.00				
1947 BP	18,260,000	0.50	0.75	1.00	2.00	4.00
1948 BP	5,180,000	4.00	7.00	10.00	12.00	15.00
1950 BP	6,000,000	2.00	4.00	7.00	10.00	12.00

KM# 536 50 FILLÉR
1.40 g., Aluminum, 22 mm. **Obv:** Blacksmith sitting on anvil **Obv. Legend:** MAGYAR KÖZTÁRSASÁG **Rev:** Denomination within wreath **Edge:** Plain **Mint:** Budapest

Date	Mintage	VF20	XF40	MS60	MS63	MS65
1948 BP	15,000,000	—	—	55.00	85.00	145
1948 BP Proof, restrike	—	PF65 25.00				

KM# 532 FORINT
1.50 g., Aluminum, 23.7 mm. **Obv:** Arms of the Republic **Rev:** Denomination flanked by leaves **Edge:** Reeded **Mint:** Budapest

Date	Mintage	VF20	XF40	MS60	MS63	MS65
1946 BP	38,900,000	2.00	3.00	5.00	10.00	15.00
1947 BP	2,600,000	7.00	10.00	15.00	25.00	35.00
1949 BP	17,000,000	5.00	7.00	10.00	20.00	30.00

KM# 533 2 FORINT
2.80 g., Aluminum, 28 mm. **Obv:** Shield within wreath, star at top **Rev:** Denomination, large numeral **Edge:** Reeded **Mint:** Budapest

Date	Mintage	VF20	XF40	MS60	MS63	MS65
1946 BP	10,000,000	5.00	7.00	10.00	20.00	30.00
1947 BP	3,500,000	6.00	8.00	15.00	30.00	40.00

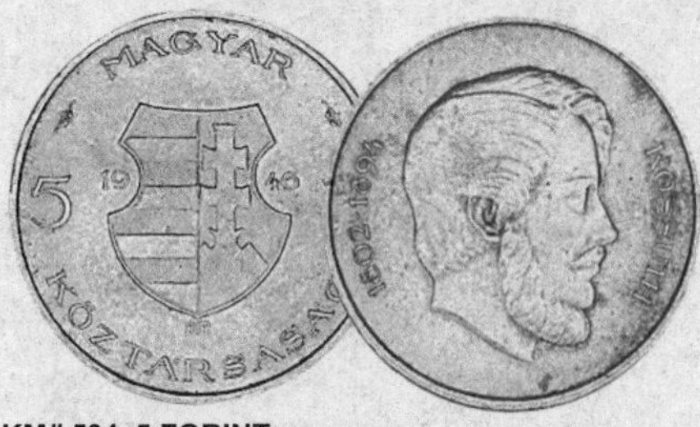

KM# 534 5 FORINT
20.00 g., 0.835 Silver 0.5369 oz. ASW **Subject:** Lajos Kossuth **Obv:** Arms of the Republic **Rev:** Head right **Edge Lettering:** MUNKA A NEMZETI **Mint:** Budapest **Note:** Thick planchet.

Date	Mintage	VF20	XF40	MS60	MS63	MS65
1946 BP	39,802	10.00	20.00	22.50	32.00	45.00

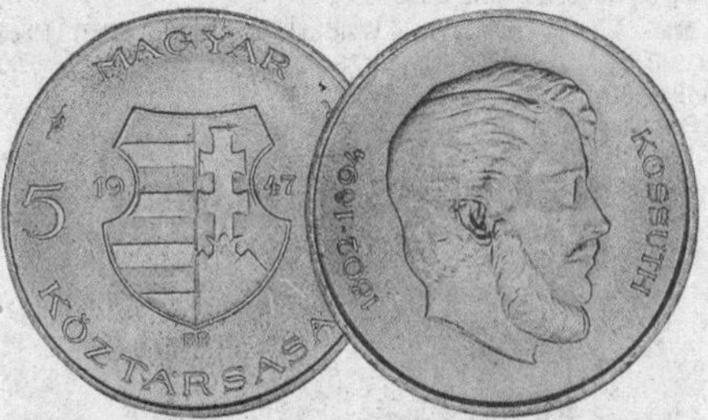

KM# 534a 5 FORINT
12.00 g., 0.500 Silver 0.1929 oz. ASW, 32 mm. **Subject:** Lajos Kossuth **Obv:** Arms of the Republic **Rev:** Head right **Note:** 1.7mm thin planchet.

Date	Mintage	VF20	XF40	MS60	MS63	MS65
1947	10,004,252	—	3.50	6.00	9.00	13.00
1947 Proof, restrike	—	PF65 10.00				

Note: The coins of this type dated 1966 and 1967 are included in the Proof Sets.

KM# 537 5 FORINT
12.00 g., 0.500 Silver 0.1929 oz. ASW, 32 mm. **Subject:** Centenary of 1848 Revolution - Sandor Petofi **Obv:** Denomination above date **Rev:** Head left

Date	Mintage	VF20	XF40	MS60	MS63	MS65
1948	100,000	3.50	8.00	10.00	16.00	22.00
1948 Proof, restrike	—	PF65 10.00				

KM# 538 10 FORINT
20.00 g., 0.500 Silver 0.3215 oz. ASW, 36 mm. **Subject:** Centenary of 1848 Revolution **Obv:** Denomination **Rev:** Istvan Szechenyi **Mint:** Budapest

Date	Mintage	VF20	XF40	MS60	MS63	MS65
1948 BP	100,000	6.00	13.00	15.00	20.00	25.00
1948 BP	—	PF65 15.00				

Proof, restrike

KM# 539 20 FORINT
28.00 g., 0.500 Silver 0.4501 oz. ASW, 40 mm. **Subject:** Centenary of 1848 Revolution **Obv:** Arms of the Republic **Rev:** Mihaly Tancsics **Mint:** Budapest

Date	Mintage	VF20	XF40	MS60	MS63	MS65
1948 BP	50,000	18.00	22.00	25.00	35.00	45.00
1948 BP	—	PF65 20.00				

Proof, restrike

PEOPLES REPUBLIC

1949-1989

KM# 546 2 FILLÉR
0.65 g., Aluminum, 18 mm. **Obv:** Legend and wreath surround center hole **Rev:** Center hole divides denomination within wreath **Edge:** Plain **Mint:** Budapest

Date	Mintage	VF20	XF40	MS60	MS63	MS65
1950 BP	24,990,000	—	—	0.10	0.20	0.50
1952 BP	5,600,000	—	—	0.10	0.30	1.00
1953 BP	9,400,000	—	—	0.10	0.20	0.50
1954 BP	10,000,000	—	—	0.10	0.20	0.50
1955 BP	6,029,000	—	—	0.10	0.25	0.75
1956 BP	4,000,000	—	—	0.15	0.30	1.00
1957 BP	5,000,000	—	—	0.10	0.25	0.50
1960 BP	3,000,000	—	0.10	0.15	0.30	0.60
1961 BP	2,000,000	—	0.20	0.40	0.60	1.00
1962 BP	3,000,000	—	0.10	0.15	0.30	0.60
1963 BP	2,082,000	—	0.10	0.20	0.35	0.70
1965 BP	540,000	—	—	4.00	8.00	16.00
1971 BP	1,041,000	—	0.10	0.15	0.30	0.60
1972 BP	1,000,000	—	0.10	0.15	0.30	0.60
1973 BP	2,820,000	—	0.10	0.15	0.30	0.60
1974 BP	50,000	—	—	0.40	0.80	1.50
1975 BP	50,000	—	—	0.40	0.80	1.50
1976 BP	50,000	—	—	0.40	0.80	1.50
1977 BP	60,000	—	—	0.40	0.80	1.50
1978 BP	50,000	—	—	0.40	0.80	1.50
1979 BP	30,000	—	—	0.75	1.25	2.50
1980 BP	30,000	—	—	0.75	1.25	2.50
1981 BP	30,000	—	—	0.75	1.25	2.50
1982 BP	30,000	—	—	0.75	1.25	2.50
1983 BP	30,000	—	—	0.75	1.25	2.50
1984 BP	30,000	—	—	0.75	1.25	2.50
1985 BP	30,000	—	—	0.75	1.25	2.50
1986 BP	30,000	—	—	0.75	1.25	2.50
1987 BP	30,000	—	—	0.75	1.25	2.50
1988 BP	30,000	—	—	0.75	1.25	2.50
1989 BP	30,000	—	—	0.75	1.25	2.50

KM# 546a 2 FILLÉR
0.65 g., Copper-Nickel, 17 mm. **Obv:** Legend and wreath surround center hole **Rev:** Center hole divides denomination within wreath

Date	Mintage	VF20	XF40	MS60	MS63	MS65
1966	5,000	PF65 4.00				
1967	5,000	PF65 4.00				

KM# 549 5 FILLÉR
0.60 g., Aluminum, 17 mm. **Obv:** Head left **Rev:** Denomination within wreath **Mint:** Budapest

Date	Mintage	VF20	XF40	MS60	MS63	MS65
1953 BP	10,000,000	—	0.10	0.15	0.30	0.50
1955 BP	6,005,000	—	0.15	0.20	0.50	1.00
1956 BP	6,012,000	—	0.15	0.20	0.50	1.00
1957 BP	5,000,000	—	0.20	0.30	0.60	1.20
1959 BP	8,000,000	—	0.15	0.20	0.50	1.00
1960 BP	7,000,000	—	0.15	0.20	0.50	1.00
1961 BP	4,410,000	—	0.20	0.30	0.60	1.20
1962 BP	5,590,000	—	0.20	0.30	0.60	1.20
1963 BP	4,020,000	—	0.20	0.30	0.60	1.20
1964 BP	3,600,000	—	0.20	0.30	0.60	1.20
1965 BP	6,000,000	—	0.20	0.30	0.60	1.20
1970 BP	3,900,000	—	—	2.50	5.00	10.00
1971 BP	100,000	—	—	0.25	0.50	1.00
1972 BP	50,000	—	—	0.25	0.50	1.00
1973 BP	105,000	—	—	0.25	0.50	1.00
1974 BP	60,000	—	—	0.25	0.50	1.00
1975 BP	60,000	—	—	0.25	0.50	1.00
1976 BP	50,000	—	—	0.25	0.50	1.00
1977 BP	60,000	—	—	0.25	0.50	1.00
1978 BP	50,000	—	—	0.25	0.50	1.00
1979 BP	30,000	—	—	0.50	1.00	2.00
1980 BP	30,000	—	—	0.50	1.00	2.00
1981 BP	30,000	—	—	0.50	1.00	2.00
1982 BP	30,000	—	—	0.50	1.00	2.00
1983 BP	30,000	—	—	0.50	1.00	2.00
1984 BP	30,000	—	—	0.50	1.00	2.00
1985 BP	30,000	—	—	0.50	1.00	2.00
1986 BP	30,000	—	—	0.50	1.00	2.00
1987 BP	30,000	—	—	0.50	1.00	2.00
1988 BP	30,000	—	—	0.50	1.00	2.00
1989 BP	30,000	—	—	0.50	1.00	2.00

KM# 549a 5 FILLÉR
Copper-Nickel, 17 mm. **Obv:** Head left **Rev:** Denomination within wreath

Date	Mintage	VF20	XF40	MS60	MS63	MS65
1966	5,000	PF65 5.00				
1967	5,000	PF65 5.00				

KM# 547 10 FILLÉR
0.85 g., Aluminum, 19.1 mm. **Obv:** Dove with branch **Rev:** Denomination **Edge:** Reeded **Mint:** Budapest

Date	Mintage	VF20	XF40	MS60	MS63	MS65
1950 BP	5,040,000	—	10.00	20.00	30.00	50.00
1951 BP	80,950,000	—	1.50	3.00	5.00	10.00
1955 BP	10,019,000	—	2.00	4.00	7.00	15.00
1957 BP	13,000,000	—	2.00	4.00	7.00	15.00
1958 BP	12,015,000	—	2.00	4.00	7.00	15.00
1959 BP	15,000,000	—	2.00	4.00	7.00	15.00
1960 BP	5,000,000	—	2.50	5.00	8.00	17.00
1961 BP	13,000,000	—	2.00	4.00	7.00	15.00
1962 BP	4,000,000	—	2.50	5.00	9.00	18.00
1963 BP	8,000,000	—	2.50	5.00	8.00	17.00
1964 BP	17,008,000	—	2.00	4.00	7.00	15.00
1965 BP	21,880,000	—	2.00	4.00	7.00	15.00
1966 BP	8,120,000	—	2.50	5.00	8.00	17.00

KM# 547a 10 FILLÉR
Copper-Nickel **Obv:** Dove with branch **Rev:** Denomination

Date	Mintage	VF20	XF40	MS60	MS63	MS65
1966	5,000	PF65 6.00				
1967	5,000	PF65 6.00				

KM# 572 10 FILLÉR
0.60 g., Aluminum, 18.5 mm. **Obv:** Dove with branch **Rev:** Denomination **Mint:** Budapest **Note:** Reduced size.

Date	Mintage	VF20	XF40	MS60	MS63	MS65
1967 BP	5,000	—	5.00	10.00	20.00	45.00
1968 BP	16,000,000	—	0.50	1.00	2.50	5.00
1969 BP	50,760,000	—	0.50	1.00	2.50	5.00
1970 BP	28,470,000	—	0.50	1.00	2.50	5.00
1971 BP	28,800,000	—	—	0.50	1.25	2.50
1972 BP	17,220,000	—	—	0.50	1.25	2.50
1973 BP	33,720,000	—	—	0.50	1.25	2.50

Date	Mintage	VF20	XF40	MS60	MS63	MS65
1974 BP	24,930,000	—	—	0.50	1.25	2.50
1975 BP	30,000,000	—	—	0.50	1.25	2.50
1976 BP	20,025,000	—	—	0.50	1.25	2.50
1977 BP	30,075,000	—	—	0.50	1.25	2.50
1978 BP	36,005,000	—	—	0.40	1.00	2.00
1979 BP	36,060,000	—	—	0.40	1.00	2.00
1980 BP	36,010,000	—	—	0.40	1.00	2.00
1981 BP	36,000,000	—	—	0.40	1.00	2.00
1982 BP	45,015,000	—	—	0.30	0.75	1.50
1983 BP	45,030,000	—	—	0.30	0.75	1.50
1984 BP	42,075,000	—	—	0.30	0.75	1.50
1985 BP	40,035,000	—	—	0.30	0.75	1.50
1986 BP	48,075,000	—	—	0.30	0.75	1.50
1987 BP	45,000,000	—	—	0.30	0.75	1.50
1988 BP	48,015,000	—	—	0.30	0.75	1.50
1989 BP	55,515,000	—	—	0.25	0.65	1.50

KM# 550 20 FILLÉR
1.25 g., Aluminum, 21 mm. **Obv:** Three wheat ears divide date **Rev:** Lines divide denomination **Mint:** Budapest

Date	Mintage	VF20	XF40	MS60	MS63	MS65
1953 BP	45,000,000	—	1.00	2.00	4.00	8.00
1955 BP	10,023,000	—	1.25	2.50	5.00	10.00
1957 BP	5,000,000	—	1.75	3.50	7.00	15.00
1958 BP	10,000,000	—	1.25	2.50	5.00	10.00
1959 BP	13,000,000	—	1.25	2.50	5.00	10.00
1961 BP	9,000,000	—	1.25	2.50	5.00	10.00
1963 BP	7,000,000	—	1.50	3.00	6.00	12.00
1964 BP	10,400,000	—	1.25	2.50	5.00	10.00
1965 BP	15,000,000	—	1.25	2.50	5.00	10.00
1966 BP	5,000,000	—	1.50	3.00	6.50	12.50

KM# 550a 20 FILLÉR
Copper-Nickel **Obv:** Three wheat ears divide date **Rev:** Lines divide denomination

Date	Mintage	VF20	XF40	MS60	MS63	MS65
1966	5,000	PF65 8.00				
1967	5,000	PF65 8.00				

KM# 573 20 FILLÉR
0.90 g., Aluminum, 20.4 mm. **Obv:** Three wheat ears divide date **Rev:** Lines divide denomination **Edge:** Reeded **Mint:** Budapest **Note:** Reduced size.

Date	Mintage	VF20	XF40	MS60	MS63	MS65
1967 BP	10,000,000	—	0.25	0.75	2.50	6.00
1968 BP	56,500,000	—	0.10	0.40	1.25	3.00
1969 BP	28,550,000	—	0.15	0.45	1.50	4.00
1970 BP	19,960,000	—	0.20	0.60	2.00	5.00
1971 BP	31,090,000	—	0.10	0.20	0.75	2.00
7971 BP Error	11,000	—	3.50	7.50	15.00	30.00
1972 BP	21,070,000	—	0.15	0.30	0.75	1.50
1973 BP	22,970,000	—	0.15	0.30	0.75	1.50
1974 BP	35,010,000	—	0.15	0.30	0.75	1.50
1975 BP	30,010,000	—	0.15	0.30	0.75	1.50
1976 BP	30,010,000	—	0.15	0.30	0.75	1.50
1977 BP	30,050,000	—	0.15	0.30	0.75	1.50
1978 BP	30,140,000	—	0.15	0.30	0.75	1.50
1979 BP	32,010,000	—	0.15	0.30	0.75	1.50
1980 BP	45,010,000	—	0.10	0.20	0.50	1.00
1981 BP	34,030,000	—	0.10	0.20	0.50	1.00
1982 BP	35,010,000	—	0.10	0.20	0.50	1.00
1983 BP	43,210,000	—	0.10	0.20	0.50	1.00
1984 BP	42,270,000	—	0.10	0.20	0.50	1.00
1985 BP	40,440,000	—	0.10	0.20	0.50	1.00
1986 BP	48,000,000	—	0.10	0.20	0.50	1.00
1987 BP	55,000,000	—	0.10	0.20	0.50	1.00
1988 BP	48,010,000	—	0.10	0.20	0.50	1.00
1989 BP	64,660,000	—	—	0.10	0.20	0.50

KM# 627 20 FILLÉR
0.90 g., Aluminum, 20.4 mm. **Series:** F.A.O. **Obv:** Three wheat ears above banner **Rev:** Lines divide denomination **Mint:** Budapest

Date	Mintage	VF20	XF40	MS60	MS63	MS65
1983 BP	50,000	—	—	0.50	1.00	2.50

KM# 551 50 FILLÉR

1.40 g., Aluminum, 22 mm. **Obv:** Blacksmith seated on anvil **Rev:** Denomination within wreath **Mint:** Budapest

Date	Mintage	VF20	XF40	MS60	MS63	MS65
1953 BP	10,017,000	—	1.50	3.00	6.00	12.00
1965 BP	3,005,000	—	1.25	2.50	5.00	10.00
1966 BP	1,500,000	—	1.75	3.50	7.00	15.00

KM# 551a 50 FILLÉR

Copper-Nickel **Obv:** Blacksmith seated on anvil **Rev:** Denomination within wreath

Date	Mintage	VF20	XF40	MS60	MS63	MS65
1966	5,000	PF65 10.00				
1967	5,000	PF65 10.00				

KM# 574 50 FILLÉR

1.20 g., Aluminum, 21.5 mm. **Subject:** Elizabeth Bridge in Budapest **Obv:** Bridge **Rev:** Denomination above date **Mint:** Budapest

Date	Mintage	VF20	XF40	MS60	MS63	MS65
1967 BP	20,000,000	—	0.50	1.00	2.00	4.00
1968 BP	13,861,000	—	0.60	1.25	2.50	5.00
1969 BP	10,085,000	—	0.60	1.25	2.50	5.00
1971 BP	50,000	—	0.30	0.60	1.25	2.50
1972 BP	470,000	—	0.20	0.50	1.00	2.00
1973 BP	7,600,000	—	0.20	0.50	1.00	2.00
1974 BP	5,000,000	—	0.20	0.50	1.00	2.00
1975 BP	10,160,000	—	0.10	0.30	0.75	1.50
1976 BP	15,130,000	—	0.10	0.30	0.75	1.50
1977 BP	10,050,000	—	0.10	0.30	0.75	1.50
1978 BP	10,110,000	—	0.10	0.30	0.75	1.50
1979 BP	10,070,000	—	0.10	0.30	0.75	1.50
1980 BP	15,000,000	—	0.10	0.30	0.75	1.50
1981 BP	10,030,000	—	0.10	0.30	0.75	1.50
1982 BP	10,000,000	—	0.10	0.30	0.75	1.50
1983 BP	10,070,000	—	0.10	0.30	0.75	1.50
1984 BP	14,060,000	—	0.10	0.30	0.75	1.50
1985 BP	12,020,000	—	0.10	0.30	0.75	1.50
1986 BP	17,140,000	—	0.10	0.30	0.75	1.50
1987 BP	23,000,000	—	—	0.10	0.50	1.00
1988 BP	18,050,000	—	—	0.10	0.50	1.00
1989 BP	18,200,000	—	—	0.10	0.50	1.00

KM# 545 FORINT

1.50 g., Aluminum, 23.7 mm. **Obv:** Wreath surrounds wheat ear and hammer on radiant background below star **Rev:** Leaves flank denomination **Mint:** Budapest

Date	Mintage	VF20	XF40	MS60	MS63	MS65
1949 BP	19,440,000	—	1.50	3.00	6.00	12.00
1950 BP	39,060,000	—	2.25	4.50	9.00	18.00
1952 BP	63,018,000	—	2.00	4.00	8.00	16.00

KM# 555 FORINT

1.50 g., Aluminum, 23.7 mm. **Obv:** Star above shield within wreath **Rev:** Leaves flank denomination **Edge:** Reeded

Date	Mintage	VF20	XF40	MS60	MS63	MS65
1957	7,500,000	—	2.00	4.00	8.00	16.00
1958	5,070,000	—	1.50	3.00	6.00	12.00
1960	5,000,000	—	1.25	2.50	5.00	10.00
1961	5,000,000	—	1.25	2.50	5.00	10.00
1963	3,000,000	—	1.50	3.00	6.50	12.50
1964	6,080,000	—	1.00	2.00	4.00	8.00
1965	9,810,000	—	1.00	2.00	4.00	8.00
1966	5,680,000	—	1.75	3.50	7.50	15.00

KM# 555a FORINT

5.85 g., 0.835 Silver 0.157 oz. ASW, 22.8 mm. **Obv:** Star above shield within wreath **Rev:** Leaves flank denomination

Date	Mintage	VF20	XF40	MS60	MS63	MS65
1966	5,000	PF65 12.50				
1967	5,000	PF65 12.50				

KM# 575 FORINT

1.40 g., Aluminum, 22.8 mm. **Obv:** Star above shield within wreath **Rev:** Leaves flank denomination **Edge:** Reeded

Date	Mintage	VF20	XF40	MS60	MS63	MS65
1967	60,000,000	—	0.65	1.25	2.50	5.00
1968	53,230,000	—	0.65	1.25	2.50	6.00
1969	27,664,000	—	1.00	2.00	4.00	8.00
1970	11,290,000	—	1.00	2.00	4.00	10.00
1971	100,000	—	0.10	0.20	0.50	1.00
1972	110,000	—	0.25	0.50	1.00	2.00
1973	1,990,000	—	0.10	0.20	0.50	1.00
1974	4,990,000	—	0.10	0.20	0.50	1.00
1975	10,000,000	—	0.10	0.20	0.40	0.80
1976	15,000,000	—	0.10	0.20	0.40	0.80
1977	10,050,000	—	0.10	0.20	0.40	0.80
1978	50,000	—	0.20	0.40	0.85	1.75
1979	10,070,000	—	0.10	0.20	0.35	0.70
1980	20,040,000	—	0.10	0.20	0.35	0.70
1981	25,040,000	—	0.10	0.20	0.35	0.70
1982	10,000,000	—	0.10	0.20	0.35	0.70
1983	20,140,000	—	0.10	0.20	0.35	0.70
1984	6,010,000	—	0.15	0.30	0.60	1.20
1985	30,000	—	0.25	0.50	1.00	2.00
1986	30,000	—	0.25	0.50	1.00	2.00
1987	13,000,000	—	0.10	0.20	0.50	1.00
1988	20,080,000	—	0.10	0.20	0.35	0.75
1989	115,920,000	—	—	0.15	0.30	0.60

KM# 548 2 FORINT

5.00 g., Copper-Nickel, 25 mm. **Obv:** Wreath surrounds hammer and wheat ear on radiant background with star above **Rev:** Denomination within 3/4 wreath **Mint:** Budapest

Date	Mintage	VF20	XF40	MS60	MS63	MS65
1950 BP	18,500,000	—	1.75	3.50	7.00	15.00
1951 BP	4,000,000	—	2.00	4.00	8.00	16.00
1952 BP	4,530,000	—	2.00	4.00	8.00	16.00

KM# 556 2 FORINT

5.00 g., Copper-Nickel, 25 mm. **Obv:** Star above shield within wreath **Rev:** Denomination within 3/4 wreath **Edge:** Flora vines

Date	Mintage	VF20	XF40	MS60	MS63	MS65
1957	5,000,000	—	1.50	3.00	6.00	12.50
1958	1,033,000	—	1.75	3.50	7.00	15.00
1960	4,000,000	—	1.50	3.00	6.00	12.50
1961	690,000	—	2.00	4.00	8.00	16.00
1962	1,190,000	—	1.50	3.00	6.00	12.50

KM# 556a 2 FORINT

5.00 g., Copper-Nickel-Zinc, 25 mm. **Obv:** Star above shield within wreath **Rev:** Denomination within 3/4 wreath

Date	Mintage	VF20	XF40	MS60	MS63	MS65
1962	1,210,000	—	1.25	2.50	5.00	10.00
1963	3,100,000	—	1.25	2.50	5.00	10.00
1964	3,250,000	—	1.25	2.50	5.00	10.00
1965	4,395,000	—	1.25	2.50	5.00	10.00
1966	6,630,000	—	1.25	2.50	5.00	10.00

KM# 556b 2 FORINT

6.12 g., 0.835 Silver 0.1643 oz. ASW **Obv:** Star above shield within wreath **Rev:** Denomination within 3/4 wreath

Date	Mintage	VF20	XF40	MS60	MS63	MS65
1966	5,000	PF65 15.00				
1967	5,000	PF65 15.00				

KM# 591 2 FORINT

4.44 g., Brass, 22.4 mm. **Obv:** National arms **Rev:** Denomination divides date

Date	Mintage	VF20	XF40	MS60	MS63	MS65
1970	49,195,000	—	0.50	1.00	2.00	4.00
1971	10,830,000	—	0.10	0.50	1.00	2.00
1972	10,015,000	—	0.10	0.50	1.00	2.00
1973	820,000	—	1.00	2.00	4.00	8.00
1974	10,000,000	—	0.25	0.75	1.50	3.00
1975	20,030,000	—	0.25	0.75	1.50	3.00
1976	15,000,000	—	0.25	0.75	1.50	3.00
1977	10,115,000	—	0.25	0.75	1.50	3.00
1978	12,000,000	—	0.25	0.75	1.50	3.00
1979	10,127,000	—	0.25	0.75	1.50	3.00
1980	12,005,000	—	0.25	0.75	1.50	3.00
1981	10,010,000	—	0.25	0.75	1.50	3.00
1982	10,005,000	—	0.25	0.75	1.50	3.00
1983	20,160,000	—	0.25	0.75	1.50	3.00
1984	5,000,000	—	0.75	1.50	3.00	6.00
1985	10,675,000	—	0.25	0.75	1.50	3.00
1986	30,000	—	1.50	3.00	6.00	12.00
1987	5,030,000	—	0.50	1.00	2.00	4.00
1988	5,035,000	—	0.50	1.00	2.00	4.00
1989	79,223,000	—	0.10	0.25	0.50	1.00

KM# 576 5 FORINT

7.21 g., Copper-Nickel, 27 mm. **Subject:** Lajos Kossuth **Obv:** Star above shield within wreath **Rev:** Head right **Mint:** Budapest

Date	Mintage	VF20	XF40	MS60	MS63	MS65
1967 BP	20,000,000	—	0.50	1.00	2.50	5.00
1968 BP	29,000	—	5.00	10.00	20.00	35.00

KM# 594 5 FORINT

5.73 g., Nickel, 24.3 mm. **Obv:** Head right **Rev:** Small shield above denomination **Edge:** Reeded

Date	Mintage	VF20	XF40	MS60	MS63	MS65
1971	20,004,000	—	0.20	0.35	0.75	1.50
1972	5,000,000	—	0.25	0.50	1.00	2.00
1973	100,000	—	0.35	0.75	1.50	3.00
1974	50,000	—	0.35	0.75	1.50	3.00
1975	50,000	—	0.35	0.75	1.50	3.00
1976	5,090,000	—	0.25	0.50	1.00	2.00
1977	50,000	—	0.35	0.75	1.50	3.00
1978	6,000,000	—	0.25	0.50	1.00	2.00
1979	10,000,000	—	0.25	0.50	1.00	2.00
1980	6,002,000	—	0.25	0.50	1.00	2.00
1981	5,002,000	—	0.25	0.50	1.00	2.00
1982	936,000	—	0.30	0.60	1.25	2.50

KM# 628 5 FORINT
Nickel **Series:** F.A.O. **Obv:** Flower holds logo within circle **Rev:** Small shield above denomination

Date	Mintage	VF20	XF40	MS60	MS63	MS65
1983	50,000	—	—	1.00	2.00	3.50

KM# 635 5 FORINT
5.00 g., Copper-Nickel, 23.4 mm. **Subject:** Lajos Kossuth **Obv:** Head right **Rev:** Small shield above denomination **Edge:** Reeded

Date	Mintage	VF20	XF40	MS60	MS63	MS65
1983	15,240,000	—	0.15	0.25	0.50	1.00
1984	25,018,000	—	0.15	0.25	0.50	1.00
1985	25,286,000	—	0.15	0.25	0.50	1.00
1986	1,030,000	—	0.20	0.35	0.75	1.50
1987	30,000	—	0.30	0.60	1.25	2.50
1988	4,050,000	—	0.20	0.35	0.75	1.50
1989	39,014,000	—	0.15	0.25	0.50	1.00

KM# 552 10 FORINT
12.50 g., 0.800 Silver 0.3215 oz. ASW, 30 mm. **Subject:** 10th Anniversary of Forint **Obv:** National Museum in Budapest **Rev:** Leaves back of denomination, small shield above **Mint:** Budapest

Date	Mintage	VF20	XF40	MS60	MS63	MS65
1956 BP	22,000	—	6.00	8.00	12.00	20.00

KM# 595 10 FORINT
8.83 g., Nickel, 28 mm. **Obv:** Strobl Monument **Rev:** Small shield below denomination

Date	Mintage	VF20	XF40	MS60	MS63	MS65
1971	24,998,000	0.35	0.75	1.50	3.00	4.50
1972	25,078,000	0.35	0.75	1.50	3.00	4.50
1973	78,000	0.60	1.25	2.50	5.00	7.50
1974	50,000	0.60	1.25	2.50	5.00	7.50
1975	50,000	0.60	1.25	2.50	5.00	7.50
1976	3,568,000	0.50	1.00	2.00	4.00	5.50
1977	4,618,000	0.50	1.00	2.00	4.00	5.50
1978	50,000	0.60	1.25	2.50	5.00	7.50
1979	5,000,000	0.50	1.00	2.00	4.00	5.50
1980	2,550,000	0.50	1.00	2.00	4.00	5.50
1982	30,000	0.60	1.25	2.50	5.00	7.50

KM# 620 10 FORINT
8.83 g., Nickel, 28 mm. **Series:** F.A.O. **Obv:** Strobl Monument **Rev:** Small shield below denomination

Date	Mintage	VF20	XF40	MS60	MS63	MS65
1981	60,000	—	—	2.50	5.00	7.50

KM# 629 10 FORINT
8.83 g., Nickel, 28 mm. **Series:** F.A.O. **Obv:** Logo at right of figure with large jar and bowl **Rev:** Small shield below denomination

Date	Mintage	VF20	XF40	MS60	MS63	MS65
1983	50,000	—	—	2.50	5.00	—

KM# 636 10 FORINT
6.01 g., Aluminum-Bronze, 25 mm. **Obv:** Strobl Monument **Rev:** Small shield below denomination **Note:** Circulation coinage.

Date	Mintage	VF20	XF40	MS60	MS63	MS65
1983	11,004,000	0.25	0.50	1.00	2.00	3.00
1984	7,578,000	0.25	0.50	1.00	2.00	3.00
1985	27,648,000	0.25	0.50	1.00	2.00	3.00
1986	15,006,000	0.25	0.50	1.00	2.00	3.00
1987	10,000,000	0.25	0.50	1.00	2.00	3.00
1988	5,000,000	0.25	0.50	1.00	2.00	3.00
1989	37,094,000	0.25	0.50	1.00	2.00	3.00

KM# 553 20 FORINT
17.50 g., 0.800 Silver 0.4501 oz. ASW, 32 mm. **Subject:** 10th Anniversary of Forint **Obv:** Szechenyi suspension bridge in Budapest **Rev:** Shield on ornamental background **Mint:** Budapest

Date	Mintage	VF20	XF40	MS60	MS63	MS65
1956 BP	22,000	—	8.25	12.00	16.00	22.00

KM# 630 20 FORINT
7.06 g., Copper-Nickel, 26.8 mm. **Subject:** György Dózsa **Obv:** Head looking left **Rev:** Small shield above denomination **Edge:** Reeded

Date	Mintage	VF20	XF40	MS60	MS63	MS65
1982	13,404,000	0.25	0.50	0.80	1.60	2.00
1983	18,006,000	0.25	0.50	0.80	1.60	2.00
1984	31,016,000	0.25	0.50	0.80	1.60	2.00
1985	20,122,000	0.25	0.50	0.80	1.60	2.00
1986	6,000,000	0.35	0.65	1.25	2.25	3.00
1987	30,000	0.40	0.75	1.50	3.00	5.00
1988	30,000	0.40	0.75	1.50	3.00	5.00
1989	31,890,000	0.25	0.50	0.80	1.60	2.00

KM# 637 20 FORINT
Copper-Nickel **Subject:** Forestry for Development **Obv:** Leaf within globe above denomination **Rev:** Stylized tree within patterned archway

Date	Mintage	VF20	XF40	MS60	MS63	MS65
1984	15,000	—	—	—	2.00	3.00
1984	5,000	PF65 7.00				

KM# 653 20 FORINT
Copper-Nickel **Series:** F.A.O. **Obv:** Logos with dates within box above stylized denomination **Rev:** Wheat ear divides fish and leaf, lined background

Date	Mintage	VF20	XF40	MS60	MS63	MS65
1985	25,000	—	—	—	2.00	4.00

KM# 554 25 FORINT (Huszonot)
20.00 g., 0.800 Silver 0.5144 oz. ASW, 34 mm. **Subject:** 10th Anniversary Forint **Obv:** Parliament Building in Budapest **Rev:** Leaves within cogwheel, arms above **Mint:** Budapest

Date	Mintage	VF20	XF40	MS60	MS63	MS65
1956 BP	22,000	—	9.50	18.00	23.00	28.00

KM# 557 25 FORINT (Huszonot)
17.50 g., 0.750 Silver 0.422 oz. ASW **Subject:** 150th Anniversary - Birth of Liszt, Musician **Obv:** Harp **Rev:** Head right

Date	Mintage	VF20	XF40	MS60	MS63	MS65
1961	15,000	PF65 15.00				

KM# 558 25 FORINT (Huszonot)
17.50 g., 0.750 Silver 0.422 oz. ASW **Subject:** 80th Anniversary - Birth of Bartok, Composer **Obv:** Small harp above denomination **Rev:** Head left

Date	Mintage	VF20	XF40	MS60	MS63	MS65
1961	15,000	PF65 16.00				

KM# 567 25 FORINT (Huszonot)
12.00 g., 0.640 Silver 0.2469 oz. ASW **Subject:** 40th Anniversary - Death of Zrinyi **Obv:** Monument **Rev:** Head 3/4 right

Date	Mintage	VF20	XF40	MS60	MS63	MS65
1966	11,000	**PF65** 18.00				

KM# 577 25 FORINT (Huszonot)
12.00 g., 0.750 Silver 0.2894 oz. ASW, 32 mm. **Subject:** 85th Birthday of Kodaly, Composer **Obv:** Peacock above denomination **Rev:** Bust 3/4 left **Edge:** Diamonds and flourishes

Date	Mintage	VF20	XF40	MS60	MS63	MS65
1967	15,000	—	—	—	12.00	14.00
1967	—	**PF65** 15.00				

KM# 559 50 FORINT (Otven)
20.00 g., 0.750 Silver 0.4823 oz. ASW **Subject:** 150th Anniversary - Birth of Liszt, Musician **Obv:** Harp below denomination **Rev:** Head right **Mint:** Budapest

Date	Mintage	VF20	XF40	MS60	MS63	MS65
1961 BP	15,000	**PF65** 18.00				

KM# 560 50 FORINT (Otven)
3.84 g., 0.986 Gold 0.1217 oz. AGW **Subject:** 150th Anniversary - Birth of Liszt, Musician **Obv:** Harp below denomination **Rev:** Head right

Date	Mintage	VF20	XF40	MS60	MS63	MS65
1961	2,503	**PF63** 185	**PF65** 200			

KM# 561 50 FORINT (Otven)
20.00 g., 0.750 Silver 0.4823 oz. ASW **Subject:** 80th Anniversary - Birth of Bartok, Composer **Obv:** Small harp above denomination **Rev:** Head left

Date	Mintage	VF20	XF40	MS60	MS63	MS65
1961	15,000	**PF65** 28.00				

KM# 562 50 FORINT (Otven)
3.84 g., 0.986 Gold 0.1217 oz. AGW **Subject:** 80th Anniversary - Birth of Bartok, Composer **Obv:** Small harp above denomination **Rev:** Head left

Date	Mintage	VF20	XF40	MS60	MS63	MS65
1961	2,503	**PF63** 185	**PF65** 200			

KM# 568 50 FORINT (Otven)
20.00 g., 0.640 Silver 0.4115 oz. ASW **Subject:** 400th Anniversary - Death of Zrinyi **Obv:** Monument **Rev:** Head 3/4 right **Mint:** Budapest

Date	Mintage	VF20	XF40	MS60	MS63	MS65
1966 BP	11,000	**PF65** 22.00				

KM# 578 50 FORINT (Otven)
20.00 g., 0.750 Silver 0.4823 oz. ASW **Subject:** 85th Birthday of Kodaly, Composer **Obv:** Peacock above denomination **Rev:** Bust 3/4 left

Date	Mintage	VF20	XF40	MS60	MS63	MS65
1967	15,000	—	—	—	15.00	17.00

KM# 582 50 FORINT (Otven)
20.00 g., 0.640 Silver 0.4115 oz. ASW **Subject:** 150th Anniversary - Birth of Semmelweis **Obv:** Head right **Rev:** Star above shield on radiant background, wreath surrounds

Date	Mintage	VF20	XF40	MS60	MS63	MS65
1968	20,250	—	—	—	13.00	15.00
1968	4,750	**PF65** 18.00				

KM# 583 50 FORINT (Otven)
4.21 g., 0.900 Gold 0.1217 oz. AGW **Subject:** 150th Anniversary - Birth of Semmelweis **Obv:** Head right **Rev:** Star above shield within wreath

Date	Mintage	VF20	XF40	MS60	MS63	MS65
1968	25,000	**PF63** 175	**PF65** 190			

KM# 589 50 FORINT (Otven)
16.00 g., 0.640 Silver 0.3292 oz. ASW, 34 mm. **Subject:** 50th Anniversary - Republic of Councils **Obv:** Small arms above denomination **Rev:** Half figure with arms spread

Date	Mintage	VF20	XF40	MS60	MS63	MS65
1969	12,000	—	—	—	10.00	11.50
1969	3,000	**PF65** 15.00				

KM# 592 50 FORINT (Otven)
16.00 g., 0.640 Silver 0.3292 oz. ASW, 34 mm. **Subject:** 25th Anniversary of Liberation **Obv:** Strobl monument **Rev:** Small shield below denomination

Date	Mintage	VF20	XF40	MS60	MS63	MS65
1970	20,000	—	—	—	10.00	11.50
1970	5,000	**PF65** 14.00				

KM# 596 50 FORINT (Otven)
16.00 g., 0.640 Silver 0.3292 oz. ASW, 34 mm. **Subject:** 1000th Anniversary - Birth of St. Stephen **Obv:** Denomination below coin of Stephen **Rev:** St. Stephen on horseback

Date	Mintage	VF20	XF40	MS60	MS63	MS65
1972	24,000	—	—	—	10.00	11.50
1972	6,000	**PF65** 14.00				

KM# 599 50 FORINT (Otven)
16.00 g., 0.640 Silver 0.3292 oz. ASW, 34 mm. **Subject:** 150th Anniversary - Birth of Sandor Petofi, Poet **Obv:** Ribbon above denomination **Rev:** Bust 3/4 facing, upper right

Date	Mintage	VF20	XF40	MS60	MS63	MS65
1973	24,000	—	—	—	10.00	11.50
1973	6,000	**PF65** 15.00				

KM# 601 50 FORINT (Otven)
16.00 g., 0.640 Silver 0.3292 oz. ASW, 34 mm. **Subject:** 50th Anniversary of National Bank **Obv:** Small shield left of denomination **Rev:** Bank building

Date	Mintage	VF20	XF40	MS60	MS63	MS65
1974	24,000	—	—	—	10.00	11.50
1974	6,000	**PF65** 14.00				

KM# 663 50 FORINT (Otven)
Copper-Nickel **Subject:** 25th Anniversary of World Wildlife Foundation **Obv:** Star above shield within wreath **Rev:** Red-footed Falcon

Date	Mintage	VF20	XF40	MS60	MS63	MS65
1988	45,000	—	—	—	4.50	7.00

KM# 563 100 FORINT (Szaz)
7.68 g., 0.986 Gold 0.2433 oz. AGW **Subject:** 150th Anniversary - Birth of Liszt, Musician **Obv:** Head right **Rev:** Harp below denomination **Mint:** Budapest

Date	Mintage	VF20	XF40	MS60	MS63	MS65
1961 BP	2,500	PF63 375	PF65 400			

KM# 564 100 FORINT (Szaz)
7.68 g., 0.986 Gold 0.2433 oz. AGW **Subject:** 80th Anniversary - Birth of Bartok, Composer **Obv:** Head left **Rev:** Small harp above denomination

Date	Mintage	VF20	XF40	MS60	MS63	MS65
1961	2,500	PF63 375	PF65 400			

KM# 569 100 FORINT (Szaz)
8.41 g., 0.900 Gold 0.2433 oz. AGW **Subject:** 400th Anniversary - Death of Zrinyi **Obv:** Monument **Rev:** Head 3/4 right

Date	Mintage	VF20	XF40	MS60	MS63	MS65
1966	3,300	PF63 375	PF65 400			

KM# 579 100 FORINT (Szaz)
28.00 g., 0.750 Silver 0.6752 oz. ASW **Subject:** 85th Birthday of Kodaly, Composer **Obv:** Peacock above denomination **Rev:** Bust 3/4 left **Mint:** Budapest

Date	Mintage	VF20	XF40	MS60	MS63	MS65
1967 BP	10,000	—	—	—	25.00	28.00

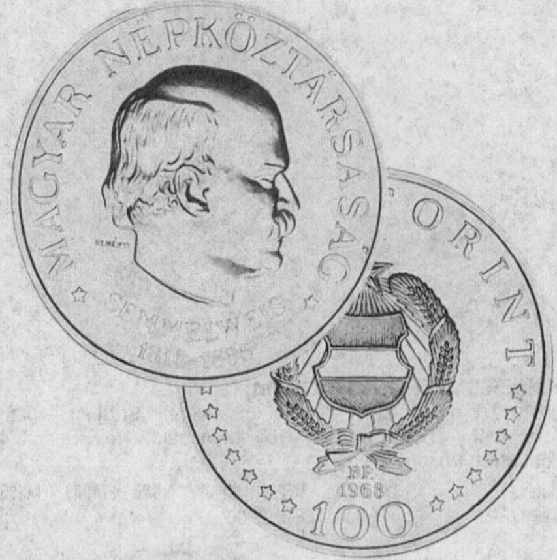

KM# 584 100 FORINT (Szaz)
28.00 g., 0.640 Silver 0.5761 oz. ASW **Subject:** 150th Anniversary - Birth of Semmelweis **Obv:** Head right **Rev:** Star above shield within wreath

Date	Mintage	VF20	XF40	MS60	MS63	MS65
1968	20,250	—	—	—	20.00	22.00
1968	4,750	PF65 28.00				

KM# 585 100 FORINT (Szaz)
8.41 g., 0.900 Gold 0.2433 oz. AGW **Subject:** 150th Anniversary - Birth of Semmelweis **Obv:** Head right **Rev:** Star above shield within wreath

Date	Mintage	VF20	XF40	MS60	MS63	MS65
1968	23,000	PF63 365	PF65 385			

KM# 590 100 FORINT (Szaz)
22.00 g., 0.640 Silver 0.4527 oz. ASW **Subject:** 50th Anniversary - Republic of Councils **Obv:** Denomination below small arms flanked by clovers **Rev:** Half figure with arms spread

Date	Mintage	VF20	XF40	MS60	MS63	MS65
1969	12,000	—	—	—	14.00	16.00
1969	3,000	PF65 20.00				

KM# 593 100 FORINT (Szaz)
22.00 g., 0.640 Silver 0.4527 oz. ASW **Subject:** 25th Anniversary of Liberation **Obv:** Strobl monument **Rev:** Star above shield within wreath

Date	Mintage	VF20	XF40	MS60	MS63	MS65
1970	20,000	—	—	—	14.00	16.00
1970	5,000	PF65 18.00				

KM# 597 100 FORINT (Szaz)
22.00 g., 0.640 Silver 0.4527 oz. ASW **Subject:** 1000th Anniversary - Birth of St. Stephen **Obv:** St. Stephen's monogram **Rev:** Crowned bust facing

Date	Mintage	VF20	XF40	MS60	MS63	MS65
1972	24,000	—	—	—	14.00	16.00
1972	6,000	PF65 18.00				

KM# 598 100 FORINT (Szaz)
22.00 g., 0.640 Silver 0.4527 oz. ASW **Subject:** Buda and Pest Union Centennial **Obv:** Star above shield within wreath **Rev:** Design depicting union, roman numerals below

Date	Mintage	VF20	XF40	MS60	MS63	MS65
1972	25,000	—	—	—	14.00	16.00

KM# 600 100 FORINT (Szaz)
22.00 g., 0.640 Silver 0.4527 oz. ASW **Subject:** 150th Anniversary - Birth of Sandor Petofi, Poet **Obv:** Star above shield within wreath divides date **Rev:** Head 3/4 facing below inscription

Date	Mintage	VF20	XF40	MS60	MS63	MS65
1973	24,000	—	—	—	14.00	16.00
1973	6,000	PF65 18.00				

KM# 602 100 FORINT (Szaz)
22.00 g., 0.640 Silver 0.4527 oz. ASW **Subject:** 25th Anniversary of KGST **Obv:** Star above shield within wreath **Rev:** Coins of Hungary, Russia, Romania, East Germany, Mongolia, Poland, Cuba, Czechslovakia and Bulgaria

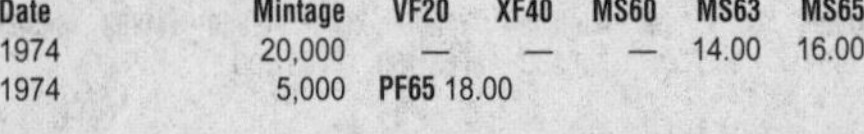

Date	Mintage	VF20	XF40	MS60	MS63	MS65
1974	20,000	—	—	—	14.00	16.00
1974	5,000	PF65 18.00				

KM# 603 100 FORINT (Szaz)
22.00 g., 0.640 Silver 0.4527 oz. ASW **Subject:** 50th Anniversary of National Bank **Obv:** Small shield at upper left **Rev:** Depictions of symbols of various professions

Date	Mintage	VF20	XF40	MS60	MS63	MS65
1974	24,000	—	—	—	14.00	16.00
1974	6,000	PF65 18.00				

KM# 617 100 FORINT (Szaz)
Nickel, 32 mm. **Subject:** 1st Soviet-Hungarian Space Flight **Obv:** Star above shield within wreath **Rev:** Astronauts above globe, shuttle lower right

Date	Mintage	VF20	XF40	MS60	MS63	MS65
1980	180,000	—	—	—	2.00	4.00
1980	20,000	PF65 6.00				

KM# 621 100 FORINT (Szaz)
Nickel, 32 mm. **Subject:** World Food Day **Obv:** Grain stalks **Rev:** Kneeling figure

Date	Mintage	VF20	XF40	MS60	MS63	MS65
1981	80,000	—	—	—	2.00	4.00
1981	20,000	PF65 6.00				

KM# 622 100 FORINT (Szaz)
Copper-Nickel-Zinc, 32 mm. **Subject:** 1300th Anniversary of Bulgarian Statehood **Obv:** Star above shield within wreath, grain stalks flank **Rev:** Sword handle and feather divide heads of Sàndor Petofi and Khristro Botev

Date	Mintage	VF20	XF40	MS60	MS63	MS65
1981	50,000	PF65 6.00				

KM# 626 100 FORINT (Szaz)
Copper-Nickel, 38.5 mm. **Subject:** World Football Championship **Obv:** Star above shield within wreath **Rev:** Soccer players

Date	Mintage	VF20	XF40	MS60	MS63	MS65
1982	150,000	—	—	—	2.00	4.00

KM# 631 100 FORINT (Szaz)
Copper-Nickel, 38.5 mm. **Series:** F.A.O. **Obv:** Denomination and date right of logo on lined background **Rev:** Small hearts below stylized design

Date	Mintage	VF20	XF40	MS60	MS63	MS65
1983	50,000	—	—	—	2.50	3.50
1983	10,000	PF65 5.50				

KM# 632 100 FORINT (Szaz)
Copper-Nickel-Zinc, 32 mm. **Subject:** 200th Anniversary - Birth of Simon Bolivar **Obv:** Andean Condor **Rev:** Grain sprigs form collar below head 3/4 left, map at left

Date	Mintage	VF20	XF40	MS60	MS63	MS65
1983	20,000	—	—	—	4.50	5.50
1983	10,000	PF65 7.50				

KM# 633 100 FORINT (Szaz)
Copper-Nickel-Zinc, 32 mm. **Subject:** Count Istvàn Szèchenyi **Obv:** Small shield above denomination **Rev:** Bust at left, three shields at right

Date	Mintage	VF20	XF40	MS60	MS63	MS65
1983	30,000	—	—	—	4.00	5.00
1983	20,000	PF65 7.00				

KM# 634 100 FORINT (Szaz)
Copper-Nickel-Zinc, 32 mm. **Subject:** 100th Anniversary - Birth of Bèla Czobel, Painter **Obv:** Denomination within wreath **Rev:** Head 3/4 facing

Date	Mintage	VF20	XF40	MS60	MS63	MS65
1983	20,000	—	—	—	4.00	5.00
1983	10,000	PF65 7.00				

KM# 638 100 FORINT (Szaz)
Copper-Nickel-Zinc **Subject:** 200th Anniversary - Birth of Sàndor Kórósicsoma **Obv:** Design divides date and denomination **Rev:** Half figure and dates left

Date	Mintage	VF20	XF40	MS60	MS63	MS65
1984	20,000	—	—	—	4.00	5.00
1984	10,000	PF65 7.00				

KM# 639 100 FORINT (Szaz)
Copper-Nickel-Zinc, 32 mm. **Subject:** Forestry for Development **Obv:** Tree at center of globe **Rev:** Stumps and seedlings

Date	Mintage	VF20	XF40	MS60	MS63	MS65
1984	15,000	—	—	—	4.00	5.00
1984	5,000	PF65 7.00				

KM# 644 100 FORINT (Szaz)
Copper-Nickel-Zinc, 32 mm. **Subject:** Wildlife Preservation **Obv:** Dates within side circles, divided by artistic denomination and legend within box **Rev:** Pond Turtle within square

Date	Mintage	VF20	XF40	MS60	MS63	MS65
1985	20,000	—	—	—	7.00	9.00

KM# 645 100 FORINT (Szaz)
Copper-Nickel-Zinc, 32 mm. **Subject:** Wildlife Preservation

Obv: Dates within side circles, divided by artistic denomination and legend within box **Rev:** European Otter

Date	Mintage	VF20	XF40	MS60	MS63	MS65
1985	20,000	—	—	—	7.00	9.00

KM# 646 100 FORINT (Szaz)
Copper-Nickel-Zinc, 32 mm. **Subject:** Wildlife Preservation **Obv:** Dates within side circles, divided by artistic denomination and legend within box **Rev:** Wildcat

Date	Mintage	VF20	XF40	MS60	MS63	MS65
1985	20,000	—	—	—	7.00	9.00

KM# 647 100 FORINT (Szaz)
Copper-Nickel-Zinc, 38.5 mm. **Subject:** World Football **Obv:** Soccer ball and globe form zeros of denomination **Rev:** Map of Mexico

Date	Mintage	VF20	XF40	MS60	MS63	MS65
1985	30,000	—	—	—	5.00	7.00

KM# 648 100 FORINT (Szaz)
Copper-Nickel-Zinc, 38.5 mm. **Subject:** World Football **Obv:** Soccer ball and globe form zeros of denomination **Rev:** Native Mexican artifacts

Date	Mintage	VF20	XF40	MS60	MS63	MS65
1985	30,000	—	—	—	5.00	7.00

KM# 651 100 FORINT (Szaz)
12.00 g., Copper-Nickel-Zinc, 32 mm. **Subject:** Budapest Cultural Forum **Obv:** Denomination **Rev:** Inscription within window, plant on sill **Edge:** Reeded

Date	Mintage	VF20	XF40	MS60	MS63	MS65
1985	40,000	—	—	—	3.00	4.00

KM# 654 100 FORINT (Szaz)
Copper-Nickel-Zinc, 32 mm. **Series:** F.A.O. **Obv:** Logo and dates within box above denomination **Rev:** Grain sprigs divide fish in water and tree

Date	Mintage	VF20	XF40	MS60	MS63	MS65
1985	20,000	—	—	—	4.00	5.00
1985	5,000	PF65 6.00				

KM# 655 100 FORINT (Szaz)
Copper-Nickel-Zinc, 32 mm. **Subject:** 200th Anniversary - Birth of Andras Fay **Obv:** Denomination and date above legend, fly below **Rev:** Bust at right looking left **Note:** See also KM#678 for similar design.

Date	Mintage	VF20	XF40	MS60	MS63	MS65
1986	42,000	—	—	—	3.00	4.00
1986	8,000	PF65 6.00				

KM# 664 100 FORINT (Szaz)
Copper-Nickel, 38.5 mm. **Subject:** 1990 World Cup Soccer **Obv:** Denomination **Rev:** Soccer players

Date	Mintage	VF20	XF40	MS60	MS63	MS65
1988	23,000	—	—	—	7.00	9.00

KM# 665 100 FORINT (Szaz)
Copper-Nickel-Zinc, 38.5 mm. **Subject:** Europe Football Championship **Obv:** Flag and maps on globes make up denomination numerals **Rev:** Soccer player and net within television screen

Date	Mintage	VF20	XF40	MS60	MS63	MS65
1988	20,000	—	—	—	7.00	9.00

KM# 668 100 FORINT (Szaz)
Copper-Nickel, 38.5 mm. **Subject:** 1990 World Cup Soccer **Obv:** Denomination **Rev:** Players with pennants shaking hands

Date	Mintage	VF20	XF40	MS60	MS63	MS65
1989	23,000	—	—	—	7.00	9.00

KM# 586 200 FORINT (Ketszaz)
16.82 g., 0.900 Gold 0.4867 oz. AGW, 34 mm. **Subject:** 150th Anniversary - Birth of Ignac Semmelweis **Obv:** Head right **Rev:** Star above shield within wreath **Mint:** Budapest

Date	Mintage	VF20	XF40	MS60	MS63	MS65
1968 BP	13,500	PF63 700	PF65 775			

KM# 604 200 FORINT (Ketszaz)
28.00 g., 0.640 Silver 0.5761 oz. ASW, 37 mm. **Subject:** 30th Anniversary of Liberation **Obv:** Small shield divides date, denomination below **Rev:** Dove above legend and bridge **Mint:** Budapest

Date	Mintage	VF20	XF40	MS60	MS63	MS65
1975 BP	20,000	—	—	—	15.00	17.00
1975 BP	10,000	PF65 20.00				

KM# 605 200 FORINT (Ketszaz)
28.00 g., 0.640 Silver 0.5761 oz. ASW, 37 mm. **Subject:** 150th Anniversary - Academy of Science **Obv:** Denomination, legend **Rev:** Legend on building at center divides dates

Date	Mintage	VF20	XF40	MS60	MS63	MS65
1975	20,000	—	—	—	15.00	17.00
1975	10,000	PF65 20.00				

KM# 606 200 FORINT (Ketszaz)
28.00 g., 0.640 Silver 0.5761 oz. ASW **Subject:** 300th Anniversary - Birth of Ferencz Rakoczi II **Obv:** Shield within wreath divides denomination and date **Rev:** Figure on horseback and soldiers

Date	Mintage	VF20	XF40	MS60	MS63	MS65
1976	25,000	—	—	—	15.00	17.00
1976	5,000	PF65 20.00				

KM# 607 200 FORINT (Ketszaz)
28.00 g., 0.640 Silver 0.5761 oz. ASW **Obv:** Quartered design with arms and denomination opposite each other **Rev:** Mihaly Munkacsy, painter

Date	Mintage	VF20	XF40	MS60	MS63	MS65
1976	25,000	—	—	—	15.00	17.00
1976	5,000	PF65 20.00				

KM# 608 200 FORINT (Ketszaz)
28.00 g., 0.640 Silver 0.5761 oz. ASW **Obv:** Quartered design with arms and denomination opposite each other **Rev:** Pal Szinyei Merse, painter

Date	Mintage	VF20	XF40	MS60	MS63	MS65
1976	25,000	—	—	—	15.00	17.00
1976	5,000	PF65 20.00				

KM# 609 200 FORINT (Ketszaz)
28.00 g., 0.640 Silver 0.5761 oz. ASW **Obv:** Quartered design with arms and denomination opposite each other **Rev:** Gyula Derkovits, painter

Date	Mintage	VF20	XF40	MS60	MS63	MS65
1976	25,000	—	—	—	15.00	17.00
1976	5,000	PF65 20.00				

KM# 610 200 FORINT (Ketszaz)
28.00 g., 0.640 Silver 0.5761 oz. ASW **Obv:** Quartered design with arms and denomination opposite each other **Rev:** Adam Manyoki, painter

Date	Mintage	VF20	XF40	MS60	MS63	MS65
1977	25,000	—	—	—	15.00	17.00
1977	5,000	PF65 20.00				

KM# 611 200 FORINT (Ketszaz)
28.00 g., 0.640 Silver 0.5761 oz. ASW **Obv:** Quartered design with arms and denomination opposite each other **Rev:** Tivadar CS. Kosztka, painter

Date	Mintage	VF20	XF40	MS60	MS63	MS65
1977	25,000	—	—	—	15.00	17.00
1977	5,000	PF65 20.00				

KM# 612 200 FORINT (Ketszaz)
28.00 g., 0.640 Silver 0.5761 oz. ASW **Obv:** Quartered design with arms and denomination opposite each other **Rev:** Jozsef Rippl-Ronai, painter

Date	Mintage	VF20	XF40	MS60	MS63	MS65
1977	25,000	—	—	—	15.00	17.00
1977	5,000	PF65 20.00				

KM# 613 200 FORINT (Ketszaz)
28.00 g., 0.640 Silver 0.5761 oz. ASW **Subject:** 175th Anniversary of National Museum **Obv:** Denomination within building, date below **Rev:** Stylized bird with condors flanking

Date	Mintage	VF20	XF40	MS60	MS63	MS65
1977	25,000	—	—	—	15.00	17.00
1977	5,000	PF65 20.00				

KM# 614 200 FORINT (Ketszaz)
28.00 g., 0.640 Silver 0.5761 oz. ASW **Subject:** First Hungarian Gold Forint **Obv:** Artistic fleur design **Rev:** Figure and shield within design

Date	Mintage	VF20	XF40	MS60	MS63	MS65
1978	25,000	—	—	—	15.00	17.00
1978	5,000	PF65 20.00				

KM# 615 200 FORINT (Ketszaz)
28.00 g., 0.640 Silver 0.5761 oz. ASW, 37 mm. **Subject:** International Year of the Child **Obv:** Logo **Rev:** Depictions of childrens artwork

Date	Mintage	VF20	XF40	MS60	MS63	MS65
1979	9,000	—	—	—	15.00	17.00
1979	21,000	PF65 20.00				

KM# 616 200 FORINT (Ketszaz)
22.00 g., 0.640 Silver 0.4527 oz. ASW, 37 mm. **Subject:** 350th Anniversary - Death of Gabor Bethlen **Obv:** Crowned shield at center, legend within circle surrounds **Rev:** Half-figure at left looking right

Date	Mintage	VF20	XF40	MS60	MS63	MS65
1979	15,000	—	—	—	14.00	16.00
1979	5,000	PF65 20.00				

KM# 618 200 FORINT (Ketszaz)
16.00 g., 0.640 Silver 0.3292 oz. ASW, 36 mm. **Series:** XIII Winter Olympics - Lake Placid **Obv:** Two figure skaters and denomination **Rev:** Olympic logo

Date	Mintage	VF20	XF40	MS60	MS63	MS65
1980	15,000	PF65 10.00				

KM# 643 200 FORINT (Ketszaz)
16.00 g., 0.640 Silver 0.3292 oz. ASW **Subject:** Wildlife Preservation **Obv:** Dates within side circles, divided by artistic denomination and legend within box **Rev:** Otter within square

Date	Mintage	VF20	XF40	MS60	MS63	MS65
1985	13,000	—	—	—	13.00	15.00
1985	2,000	PF65 20.00				

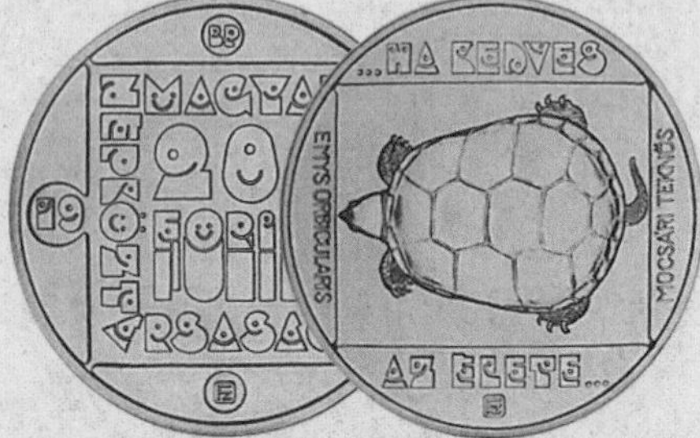

KM# 649 200 FORINT (Ketszaz)
16.00 g., 0.640 Silver 0.3292 oz. ASW **Subject:** Wildlife Preservation **Obv:** Date within side circles divided by artistic denomination and legend within box **Rev:** Pond turtle within square

Date	Mintage	VF20	XF40	MS60	MS63	MS65
1985	13,000	—	—	—	13.00	15.00
1985	2,000	PF65 20.00				

KM# 650 200 FORINT (Ketszaz)
16.00 g., 0.640 Silver 0.3292 oz. ASW **Subject:** Wildlife Preservation **Obv:** Date within side circles, divided by artistic denomination and legend within box **Rev:** Wildcat within square

Date	Mintage	VF20	XF40	MS60	MS63	MS65
1985	13,000	—	—	—	17.00	20.00
1985	2,000	PF65 22.00				

KM# 565 500 FORINT (Otszaz)
38.38 g., 0.986 Gold 1.2167 oz. AGW, 40 mm. **Subject:** 150th Anniversary - Birth of Ferenc Liszt **Obv:** Harp below denomination **Rev:** Head right **Mint:** Budapest

Date	Mintage	VF20	XF40	MS60	MS63	MS65
1961 BP	2,503	PF63 1,650	PF65 1,700			

KM# 566 500 FORINT (Otszaz)
38.38 g., 0.986 Gold 1.2167 oz. AGW, 40 mm. **Subject:** 80th Anniversary - Birth of Bela Bartok, Composer **Obv:** Small harp above denomination **Rev:** Head left

Date	Mintage	VF20	XF40	MS60	MS63	MS65
1961	2,503	PF63 1,650	PF65 1,700			

KM# 570 500 FORINT (Otszaz)
42.05 g., 0.900 Gold 1.2168 oz. AGW, 40 mm. **Subject:** 400th Anniversary - Death of Miklos Zrinyi **Obv:** Monument **Rev:** Head right

Date	Mintage	VF20	XF40	MS60	MS63	MS65
1966	1,100	PF63 1,750	PF65 1,800			

KM# 580 500 FORINT (Otszaz)
42.05 g., 0.900 Gold 1.2168 oz. AGW, 40 mm. **Subject:** 85th Birthday of Zoltan Kodaly, Composer **Obv:** Peacock above denomination **Rev:** Bust 3/4 left

Date	Mintage	VF20	XF40	MS60	MS63	MS65
1967	1,000	PF63 1,750	PF65 1,800			

KM# 587 500 FORINT (Otszaz)
42.05 g., 0.900 Gold 1.2168 oz. AGW, 46 mm. **Subject:** 150th Anniversary - Birth of Ignacz Semmelweis **Obv:** Head right **Rev:** Star above shield within wreath

Date	Mintage	VF20	XF40	MS60	MS63	MS65
1968	9,000	PF63 1,600	PF65 1,650			

KM# 619 500 FORINT (Otszaz)
39.00 g., 0.640 Silver 0.8025 oz. ASW, 46 mm. **Series:** XIII Winter Olympics - Lake Placid **Obv:** Two figure skaters **Rev:** Olympic logo **Mint:** Budapest

Date	Mintage	VF20	XF40	MS60	MS63	MS65
1980 BP	12,500	PF65 50.00				

KM# 623 500 FORINT (Otszaz)
25.00 g., 0.640 Silver 0.5144 oz. ASW **Subject:** Centennial - Birth of Bela Bartok, Composer **Obv:** Musical score, statue and denomination **Rev:** Head left, map in background

Date	Mintage	VF20	XF40	MS60	MS63	MS65
1981	12,500	—	—	—	16.50	18.00
1981	12,500	PF65 20.00				

KM# 624 500 FORINT (Otszaz)
28.00 g., 0.640 Silver 0.5761 oz. ASW **Subject:** World Football Championship **Obv:** Soccer player **Rev:** Soccer field, soccer ball on shield at lower left

Date	Mintage	VF20	XF40	MS60	MS63	MS65
1981	6,000	—	—	—	20.00	23.00
1981	40,000	PF65 18.00				

KM# 625 500 FORINT (Otszaz)
28.00 g., 0.640 Silver 0.5761 oz. ASW **Subject:** World Football Championship **Obv:** Soccer ball on shield within lined design **Rev:** Soccer players

Date	Mintage	VF20	XF40	MS60	MS63	MS65
1981	6,000	—	—	—	20.00	23.00
1981	40,000	PF65 18.00				

KM# 640 500 FORINT (Otszaz)
28.00 g., 0.640 Silver 0.5761 oz. ASW **Subject:** Decade for Women **Obv:** Ankh on shaded stylized dove **Rev:** Kneeling woman

Date	Mintage	VF20	XF40	MS60	MS63	MS65
1984	8,000	—	—	—	18.00	20.00
1984	20,000	PF65 23.00				

KM# 641 500 FORINT (Otszaz)
28.00 g., 0.640 Silver 0.5761 oz. ASW **Series:** Winter Olympics - Sarajevo **Obv:** Olympic flame, snowflakes and denomination **Rev:** Cross-country skiers

Date	Mintage	VF20	XF40	MS60	MS63	MS65
1984	8,000	—	—	—	18.00	20.00
1984	12,000	PF65 22.00				

KM# 642 500 FORINT (Otszaz)
28.00 g., 0.640 Silver 0.5761 oz. ASW **Subject:** Los Angeles Olympics **Obv:** Denomination, torch at left **Rev:** Gymnast

Date	Mintage	VF20	XF40	MS60	MS63	MS65
1984	8,000	—	—	—	18.00	20.00
1984	12,000	PF65 22.00				

KM# 652 500 FORINT (Otszaz)
28.00 g., 0.640 Silver 0.5761 oz. ASW **Subject:** Budapest Cultural Forum **Obv:** Denomination **Rev:** Bird, right of shield within ornamental design, legend within column below

Date	Mintage	VF20	XF40	MS60	MS63	MS65
1985	15,000	—	—	—	18.00	20.00
1985	10,000	PF65 22.00				

KM# 656 500 FORINT (Otszaz)
28.00 g., 0.640 Silver 0.5761 oz. ASW **Subject:** World Football Championship **Obv:** Soccer ball and globe make up zeros of denomination **Rev:** Football players

Date	Mintage	VF20	XF40	MS60	MS63	MS65
1986	8,000	—	—	—	18.00	20.00
1986	17,000	PF65 18.00				

KM# 657 500 FORINT (Otszaz)
28.00 g., 0.640 Silver 0.5761 oz. ASW **Subject:** World Football Championship **Obv:** Denomination **Rev:** Stadium

Date	Mintage	VF20	XF40	MS60	MS63	MS65
1986	8,000	—	—	—	20.00	23.00
1986	17,000	PF65 20.00				

KM# 658 500 FORINT (Otszaz)
28.00 g., 0.900 Silver 0.8102 oz. ASW **Subject:** 300th Anniversary - Repossession of Buda from the Turks **Obv:** Sword crosses top of denomination **Rev:** Village scene

Date	Mintage	VF20	XF40	MS60	MS63	MS65
1986	20,000	—	—	—	26.00	28.00
1986	10,000	PF65 30.00				

KM# 659 500 FORINT (Otszaz)
28.00 g., 0.900 Silver 0.8102 oz. ASW **Series:** Winter Olympics - Calgary 1988 **Obv:** Snowflake designs on flames **Rev:** Speed skater

Date	Mintage	VF20	XF40	MS60	MS63	MS65
1986	15,000	—	—	—	26.00	28.00
1986	15,000	PF65 30.00				

KM# 660 500 FORINT (Otszaz)
28.00 g., 0.900 Silver 0.8102 oz. ASW **Subject:** Seoul Olympics **Obv:** Denomination **Rev:** Wrestlers

Date	Mintage	VF20	XF40	MS60	MS63	MS65
1987	15,000	—	—	—	26.00	28.00
1987	15,000	PF65 30.00				

KM# 661 500 FORINT (Otszaz)
28.00 g., 0.900 Silver 0.8102 oz. ASW **Subject:** World Wildlife Fund **Obv:** Denomination **Rev:** Montagu's Harrier

Date	Mintage	VF20	XF40	MS60	MS63	MS65
1988	10,000	—	—	—	28.00	30.00
1988	25,000	PF65 32.00				

KM# 662 500 FORINT (Otszaz)
28.00 g., 0.900 Silver 0.8102 oz. ASW **Subject:** 950th Anniversary - Death of St. Stephan **Obv:** Ancient coin designs above denomination **Rev:** Figure of King Stephen at left and Queen Gisela of Bavaria at right

Date	Mintage	VF20	XF40	MS60	MS63	MS65
1988	5,000	—	—	—	36.00	40.00
1988	15,000	PF65 28.00				

KM# 666 500 FORINT (Otszaz)
28.00 g., 0.900 Silver 0.8102 oz. ASW **Subject:** Europe Football Championship **Obv:** Stenciled denomination **Rev:** Soccer player behind net

Date	Mintage	VF20	XF40	MS60	MS63	MS65
1988	8,000	—	—	—	26.00	28.00
1988	12,000	PF65 26.00				

KM# 667 500 FORINT (Otszaz)
28.00 g., 0.900 Silver 0.8102 oz. ASW **Subject:** World Football Championship **Obv:** Denomination **Rev:** Soccer players

Date	Mintage	VF20	XF40	MS60	MS63	MS65
1988	7,000	—	—	—	26.00	28.00
1988	14,500	PF65 26.00				

KM# 669 500 FORINT (Otszaz)
28.00 g., 0.900 Silver 0.8102 oz. ASW **Subject:** World Football Championship **Obv:** Denomination **Rev:** Two players

Date	Mintage	VF20	XF40	MS60	MS63	MS65
1989	7,000	—	—	—	26.00	28.00
1989	14,500	PF65 26.00				

KM# 670 500 FORINT (Otszaz)
28.00 g., 0.900 Silver 0.8102 oz. ASW **Subject:** Save the Children Fund **Obv:** Denomination below figure and lined design **Rev:** Seedling within outline of child

Date	Mintage	VF20	XF40	MS60	MS63	MS65
1989	10,000	—	—	—	28.00	30.00
1989	20,000	PF65 32.00				

KM# 671 500 FORINT (Otszaz)
28.00 g., 0.900 Silver 0.8102 oz. ASW **Series:** 1992 Barcelona Olympics **Obv:** Denomination within lined design **Rev:** Torch bearer lighting the flame

Date	Mintage	VF20	XF40	MS60	MS63	MS65
1989	15,000	—	—	—	28.00	30.00
1989	15,000	PF65 32.00				

KM# 571 1000 FORINT (Ezer)
84.10 g., 0.900 Gold 2.4336 oz. AGW **Subject:** 400th Anniversary - Death of Miklos Zrinyi **Obv:** Monument **Rev:** Head 3/4 right **Mint:** Budapest

Date	Mintage	VF20	XF40	MS60	MS63	MS65
1966	330	PF65 7,000				

KM# 581 1000 FORINT (Ezer)
84.10 g., 0.900 Gold 2.4336 oz. AGW **Subject:** 85th Birthday of Zoltan Kodaly, Composer **Obv:** Peacock above denomination **Rev:** Bust 3/4 left

Date	Mintage	VF20	XF40	MS60	MS63	MS65
1967	500	PF63 4,000	PF65 4,500			

KM# 588 1000 FORINT (Ezer)
84.10 g., 0.900 Gold 2.4336 oz. AGW **Subject:** 150th Anniversary - Birth of Ignacz Semmelweis **Rev:** Star above shield within wreath

Date	Mintage	VF20	XF40	MS60	MS63	MS65
1968	7,000	PF63 3,500	PF65 4,000			

TRANSITIONAL COINAGE

KM# 736 FORINT
Aluminum **Obv:** Star above shield within wreath **Rev:** Leaves flank denomination **Note:** Communist design type with New Republic legends

Date	Mintage	VF20	XF40	MS60	MS63	MS65
1990	10,000	—	—	10.00	15.00	20.00

KM# 737 2 FORINT
Brass **Obv:** Star above shield within wreath **Rev:** Large denomination divides date **Note:** Communist design type with New Republic legends

Date	Mintage	VF20	XF40	MS60	MS63	MS65
1990	10,000	—	—	10.00	15.00	20.00

KM# 738 5 FORINT
Copper-Nickel **Subject:** Lajos Kossuth **Obv. Inscription:** Head right **Rev:** Small shield divides date above denomination **Note:** Communist design with New Republic legends

Date	Mintage	VF20	XF40	MS60	MS63	MS65
1990	10,000	—	—	10.00	15.00	20.00

KM# 739 10 FORINT
Aluminum-Bronze **Obv:** Strobl Monument **Rev:** Small shield below denomination

Date	Mintage	VF20	XF40	MS60	MS63	MS65
1990	10,000	—	—	12.00	17.00	22.00

KM# 740 20 FORINT
Copper-Nickel **Subject:** György Dózsa **Obv:** Head looking left **Rev:** Grain sprigs flank denomination, small shield above

Date	Mintage	VF20	XF40	MS60	MS63	MS65
1990	10,000	—	—	14.00	20.00	25.00

SECOND REPUBLIC

1989-present

DECIMAL COINAGE

KM# 673 2 FILLÉR
0.65 g., Aluminum, 18 mm. **Obv:** Wreath surrounds center hole **Rev:** Center hole divides denomination within wreath **Mint:** Budapest

Date	Mintage	VF20	XF40	MS60	MS63	MS65
1990 BP	10,000	—	—	0.50	1.00	2.00
1991 BP	10,000	—	—	0.75	1.50	3.00
1992 BP	30,000	—	—	0.75	1.50	3.00

KM# 674 5 FILLÉR
0.60 g., Aluminum, 17 mm. **Obv:** Head left **Rev:** Denomination within wreath **Mint:** Budapest

Date	Mintage	VF20	XF40	MS60	MS63	MS65
1990 BP	10,000	—	—	0.50	1.00	2.00
1991 BP	10,000	—	—	0.75	1.50	3.00
1992 BP	30,000	—	—	0.75	1.50	3.00

KM# 675 10 FILLÉR
0.60 g., Aluminum, 18.5 mm. **Obv:** Dove with branch **Rev:** Denomination **Mint:** Budapest

Date	Mintage	VF20	XF40	MS60	MS63	MS65
1990 BP	46,515,000	0.15	0.20	0.30	0.50	0.75
1991 BP	2,370,000	0.30	0.40	0.50	0.75	1.00
1992 BP	15,828,000	0.25	0.30	0.45	0.65	0.85
1993 BP	30,000	—	—	0.30	0.50	0.75
1994 BP	30,000	—	—	0.30	0.50	0.75
1995 BP	30,000	—	—	0.30	0.50	0.75
1996 BP	20,000	—	—	0.30	0.50	0.75
1996	—	PF65 1.50				

KM# 676 20 FILLÉR
0.90 g., Aluminum, 20.4 mm. **Obv:** Three wheat ears divide date **Rev:** Lines divide denomination **Edge:** Reeded **Mint:** Budapest

Date	Mintage	VF20	XF40	MS60	MS63	MS65
1990 BP	59,360,000	0.15	0.20	0.30	0.50	0.75
1991 BP	20,210,000	0.25	0.30	0.45	0.65	0.85
1992 BP	30,000	—	—	0.35	0.60	0.85
1993 BP	30,000	—	—	0.35	0.60	0.85
1994 BP	30,000	—	—	0.35	0.60	0.85
1995 BP	30,000	—	—	0.35	0.60	0.85
1996 BP	20,000	—	—	0.50	0.75	1.00
1996	—	PF65 2.00				

KM# 677 50 FILLÉR
1.20 g., Aluminum, 21.5 mm. **Obv:** Erzsebet Bridge **Rev:** Denomination **Edge:** Plain **Mint:** Budapest

Date	Mintage	VF20	XF40	MS60	MS63	MS65
1990 BP	20,550,000	0.10	0.20	0.25	0.35	0.50
1991 BP	31,250,000	—	0.10	0.20	0.30	0.50
1992 BP	440,000	—	—	0.50	0.75	1.00
1993 BP	30,000	—	—	0.50	0.75	1.25
1994 BP	30,000	—	—	0.50	0.75	1.25
1995 BP	30,000	—	—	0.50	0.75	1.25
1996 BP	20,000	—	—	0.75	1.00	1.50
1996	—	PF65 2.00				
1997 BP	10,000	—	—	1.00	1.50	2.00
1998 BP	10,000	—	—	1.00	1.50	2.00
1999 BP	10,000	—	—	1.00	1.50	2.00

KM# 692 FORINT
2.05 g., Nickel-Brass, 16.5 mm. **Obv:** Crowned shield **Rev:** Denomination **Mint:** Budapest

Date	Mintage	VF20	XF40	MS60	MS63	MS65
1992 BP	23,890,100	—	0.10	0.25	0.35	0.50
1992 BP	1,000	PF65 6.00				
1993 BP	75,100,000	—	0.10	0.25	0.35	0.50
1993 BP	30,000	PF65 1.00				
1994 BP	66,605,005	—	0.10	0.25	0.35	0.50
1994 BP	15,000	PF65 1.20				
1995 BP	50,535,000	—	0.10	0.25	0.35	0.50
1995 BP	15,000	PF65 1.20				
1996 BP	66,307,005	—	0.10	0.25	0.35	0.50
1996 BP	3,000	PF65 1.40				
1997 BP	75,007,000	—	0.10	0.25	0.35	0.50
1997 BP	3,000	PF65 3.75				
1998 BP	50,007,000	—	0.10	0.25	0.35	0.50
1998 BP	—	PF65 3.75				
1999 BP	75,007,000	—	0.10	0.25	0.35	0.50
1999 BP	—	PF65 3.75				
2000 BP	75,007,000	—	0.10	0.25	0.35	0.50
2000 BP	—	PF65 3.75				

KM# 693 2 FORINT
3.10 g., Copper-Nickel, 19.2 mm. **Obv:** Native flower: Colchicum Hungaricum **Rev:** Denomination **Edge:** Reeded

Date	Mintage	VF20	XF40	MS60	MS63	MS65
1992 BP	10,380,100	0.10	0.25	0.35	0.50	0.75
1992 BP	1,000	PF65 6.00				
1993 BP	82,915,000	0.10	0.25	0.35	0.50	0.75
1993 BP	30,000	PF65 1.50				
1994 BP	68,370,005	0.10	0.25	0.35	0.50	0.75
1994 BP	15,000	PF65 1.75				
1995 BP	60,945,000	0.10	0.25	0.35	0.50	0.75
1995 BP	15,000	PF65 1.75				
1996 BP	50,010,000	0.10	0.25	0.35	0.50	0.75
1996 BP	10,000	PF65 1.95				
1997 BP	70,007,000	0.10	0.20	0.35	0.50	0.75
1997 BP	3,000	PF65 4.25				
1998 BP	20,007,000	—	—	0.35	0.50	0.75
1998 BP	—	PF65 4.25				
1999 BP	50,007,000	—	—	0.35	0.50	0.75
1999 BP	—	PF65 4.25				
2000 BP	55,007,000	—	—	0.20	0.35	0.65
2000 BP	—	PF65 4.25				

KM# 694 5 FORINT
4.20 g., Nickel-Brass, 21.2 mm. **Obv:** Great White Egret **Rev:** Denomination **Mint:** Budapest

Date	Mintage	VF20	XF40	MS60	MS63	MS65
1992 BP	1,145,300	0.30	0.50	0.75	1.25	1.50
1992 BP	1,000	PF65 7.00				
1993 BP	37,180,000	0.25	0.45	0.65	1.00	1.25
1993 BP	30,000	PF65 2.00				
1994 BP	53,615,000	0.20	0.30	0.50	0.75	1.00
1994 BP	15,000	PF65 2.50				
1995 BP	24,670,000	0.30	0.40	0.60	1.00	1.25
1995 BP	15,000	PF65 2.50				
1996 BP	6,010,005	0.50	0.65	1.00	1.25	1.50
1996 BP	10,000	PF65 3.00				
1997 BP	20,007,000	0.30	0.40	0.60	1.00	1.25
1997 BP	—	PF65 5.00				
1998 BP	7,000	0.30	0.40	0.60	1.00	1.25
1998 BP	—	PF65 5.00				
1999 BP	25,007,000	0.30	0.40	0.60	1.00	1.25
1999 BP	—	PF65 5.00				
2000 BP	30,007,000	0.25	0.35	0.50	0.75	1.00
2000 BP	—	PF65 5.00				

KM# 695 10 FORINT
6.10 g., Copper-Nickel, 24.8 mm. **Obv:** Crowned shield **Rev:** Denomination **Edge:** Segmented reeding

Date	Mintage	VF20	XF40	MS60	MS63	MS65
1992 BP	2,000	—	—	—	4.00	6.00
1992 BP	1,000	PF65 8.00				
1993 BP	35,565,000	0.25	0.45	0.65	1.00	1.50
1993 BP	30,000	PF65 2.50				
1994 BP	69,077,505	0.15	0.35	0.50	0.85	1.50
1994 BP	15,000	PF65 3.00				
1995 BP	40,910,000	0.25	0.45	0.65	1.00	1.50
1995 BP	15,000	PF65 3.00				
1996 BP	10,020,005	0.30	0.50	0.70	1.00	1.50
1996 BP	10,000	PF65 3.50				
1997 BP	8,007,000	0.35	0.55	0.75	1.25	1.75
1997 BP	3,000	PF65 5.50				
1998 BP Sets only	7,000	—	—	—	—	2.50
1998 BP	—	PF65 5.50				
1999 BP Sets only	7,000	—	—	—	—	2.50
1999 BP	—	PF65 5.50				
2000 BP Sets only	7,000	—	—	—	—	2.50
2000 BP	—	PF65 5.50				

KM# 696 20 FORINT
6.90 g., Nickel-Brass, 26.3 mm. **Obv:** Hungarian Iris **Rev:** Denomination **Edge:** Reeded **Mint:** Budapest

Date	Mintage	VF20	XF40	MS60	MS63	MS65
1992 BP	2,000	—	—	—	5.00	7.00
1992 BP	1,000	PF65 9.00				
1993 BP	42,965,000	0.30	0.60	0.75	1.25	1.75
1993 BP	30,000	PF65 3.50				
1994 BP	68,965,005	0.25	0.50	0.65	1.00	1.50

Date	Mintage	VF20	XF40	MS60	MS63	MS65
1994 BP	15,000	PF65 4.00				
1995 BP	53,395,000	0.25	0.50	0.65	1.00	1.50
1995 BP	15,000	PF65 4.00				
1996 BP	6,010,000	0.35	0.70	1.00	1.50	2.00
1996 BP	10,000	PF65 4.00				
1997 BP	7,000	—	—	—	4.00	5.00
1997 BP	3,000	PF65 6.00				
1998 BP	7,000	—	—	—	2.00	3.00
1998 BP	—	PF65 6.00				
1999 BP	7,000	—	—	—	2.00	3.00
1999 BP	3,000	PF65 6.00				
2000 BP	7,000	—	—	—	2.00	3.00
2000 BP	3,000	PF65 6.00				

KM# 697 50 FORINT

7.60 g., Copper-Nickel, 27.5 mm. **Obv:** Saker falcon **Rev:** Denomination **Mint:** Budapest

Date	Mintage	VF20	XF40	MS60	MS63	MS65
1992 BP	2,000	—	—	3.00	5.00	10.00
1992 BP	1,000	PF65 12.00				
1993 BP	860,500	0.65	1.25	1.75	2.50	3.50
1993 BP	30,000	PF65 5.00				
1994 BP	8,397,005	0.45	0.75	1.00	1.25	2.00
1994 BP	15,000	PF65 5.00				
1995 BP	36,985,000	0.25	0.50	1.00	1.25	2.00
1995 BP	15,000	PF65 5.00				
1996 BP	7,010,000	0.50	1.00	1.25	1.75	2.50
1996 BP	10,000	PF65 5.00				
1997 BP	12,007,000	—	—	1.00	1.25	2.00
1997 BP	3,000	PF65 6.50				
1998 BP	7,000	—	—	—	4.00	5.00
1998 BP	—	PF65 6.50				
1999 BP	7,000	—	—	—	4.00	5.00
1999 BP	—	PF65 6.50				
2000 BP	7,000	—	—	—	4.00	5.00
2000 BP	—	PF65 6.50				

KM# 734 75 FORINT

31.46 g., 0.925 Silver 0.9356 oz. ASW, 38.6 mm. **Subject:** 75th Anniversary - Hungarian National Bank **Obv:** Crowned shield above denomination **Rev:** Goddess Juno **Edge:** Reeded

Date	Mintage	VF20	XF40	MS60	MS63	MS65
1999 BP	3,000	—	—	—	35.00	40.00
1999 BP	4,500	PF65 45.00				

KM# 698 100 FORINT

9.40 g., Nickel-Brass, 29.2 mm. **Obv:** Crowned shield **Rev:** Denomination **Mint:** Budapest

Date	Mintage	VF20	XF40	MS60	MS63	MS65
1992 BP	2,000	—	—	5.00	8.00	12.00
1992 BP	1,000	PF65 15.00				
1993 BP	924,500	—	—	1.00	1.50	3.00
1993 BP	30,000	PF65 6.00				
1994 BP	7,861,005	—	—	1.00	1.25	2.50
1994 BP	15,000	PF65 6.00				
1995 BP	27,485,000	—	—	1.00	1.25	2.50
1995 BP	15,000	PF65 6.00				
1996 BP	6,210,000	—	—	1.00	1.25	2.50
1996 BP	10,000	PF65 6.00				
1997 BP	7,000	—	—	—	—	5.00

Date	Mintage	VF20	XF40	MS60	MS63	MS65
1997 BP	3,000	PF65 8.00				
1998 BP	7,000	—	—	—	—	5.00
1998 BP	—	PF65 8.00				

KM# 721 100 FORINT

8.00 g., Bi-Metallic Brass Plated Steel center in Stainless Steel ring, 23.8 mm. **Obv:** Crowned shield **Rev:** Denomination **Edge:** Reeded **Mint:** Budapest

Date	Mintage	VF20	XF40	MS60	MS63	MS65
1996 BP	4,219,005	—	—	1.50	2.50	4.00
1996 BP	1,000	PF65 12.00				
1997 BP	60,007,000	—	—	1.50	2.50	4.00
1997 BP	3,000	PF65 8.00				
1998 BP	60,007,000	—	—	1.50	2.50	4.00
1998 BP	3,000	PF65 8.00				
1999 BP	7,000	—	—	—	—	4.00
1999 BP	3,000	PF65 8.00				
2000 BP	7,000	—	—	—	—	5.00
2000 BP	3,000	PF65 8.00				

KM# 678 100 FORINT (Szaz)

12.00 g., Copper-Nickel-Zinc, 32 mm. **Subject:** Andreas Fay - 150th Anniversary of Savings Bank **Obv:** Fly below legend, denomination and date above **Rev:** Bust 3/4 left **Edge:** Reeded **Mint:** Budapest **Note:** See also #655 for similar type

Date	Mintage	VF20	XF40	MS60	MS63	MS65
1990 BP	20,000	—	—	—	2.00	4.00
1990 BP	10,000	PF65 6.00				

KM# 700 100 FORINT (Szaz)

12.00 g., Copper-Nickel **Subject:** S.O.S. Gyermekfalu, Children's Village **Obv:** Children and flower within box divide date above denomination **Rev:** Mother protecting child

Date	Mintage	VF20	XF40	MS60	MS63	MS65
1990 BP	50,000	PF65 7.00				

KM# 701 100 FORINT (Szaz)

12.00 g., Copper-Nickel **Subject:** Hungarian Theatre **Obv:** Denomination divides date within wreath **Rev:** Theatre scene

Date	Mintage	VF20	XF40	MS60	MS63	MS65
1990 BP	5,000	—	—	—	—	7.00
1990 BP	5,000	PF65 9.00				

KM# 682 100 FORINT (Szaz)

12.00 g., Copper-Nickel-Zinc **Subject:** Papal Visit **Obv:** Arms of the Republic **Rev:** Pope John Paul II

Date	Mintage	VF20	XF40	MS60	MS63	MS65
1991 BP	30,000	—	—	—	2.00	3.00
1991 BP	30,000	PF65 5.00				

KM# 726 100 FORINT (Szaz)

9.40 g., Bronze **Subject:** Revolution of 1848 **Obv:** Hungarian Order of Military Merit (1848-1849) II Class **Rev:** Revolutionary ribbon badge above poetry verse

Date	Mintage	VF20	XF40	MS60	MS63	MS65
1998 BP	15,000	—	—	—	3.00	5.00
1998 BP	15,000	PF65 7.00				

KM# 688 200 FORINT

10.00 g., 0.500 Silver 0.1608 oz. ASW **Obv:** Crowned shield below globe **Rev:** White storks **Mint:** Budapest

Date	Mintage	VF20	XF40	MS60	MS63	MS65
1992 BP	20,000	—	—	—	7.00	9.00
1992 BP	80,000	PF65 12.00				

KM# 689 200 FORINT

12.00 g., 0.500 Silver 0.1929 oz. ASW **Obv:** Erzsebet Bridge, crowned shield divides date above **Rev:** National Bank

Date	Mintage	VF20	XF40	MS60	MS63	MS65
1992 BP	3,514,023	—	—	—	4.00	6.00
1992 BP	29,998	PF65 8.00				
1993 BP	2,540,993	—	—	—	4.00	6.00
1993 BP	30,000	PF65 8.00				

KM# 707 200 FORINT

12.00 g., 0.500 Silver 0.1929 oz. ASW **Obv:** Erzsebet Bridge **Rev:** Ferenc Deak

Date	Mintage	VF20	XF40	MS60	MS63	MS65
1994 BP	5,000,000	—	—	—	4.00	6.00
1994 BP	15,000	PF65 8.00				
1995 BP	85,000	—	—	—	—	7.00
1995 BP	15,000	PF65 9.00				
1997 BP	7,000	—	—	—	—	8.00
1997 BP	3,000	PF65 10.00				
1998 BP	7,000	—	—	—	—	8.00
1998 BP	—	PF65 10.00				

KM# 745 200 FORINT

9.56 g., Brass **Subject:** Millennium **Obv:** Crowned shield above denomination **Rev:** Rodin's "The Thinker" statue and solar system **Edge:** Plain **Mint:** Budapest

Date	Mintage	VF20	XF40	MS60	MS63	MS65
2000 BP	15,000	—	—	—	3.00	5.00
2000 BP	10,000	PF65 7.00				

KM# 672 500 FORINT (Otszaz)

28.00 g., 0.900 Silver 0.8102 oz. ASW **Series:** Albertville Olympics 1992 **Obv:** Denomination, date below **Rev:** Hockey players **Mint:** Budapest

Date	Mintage	VF20	XF40	MS60	MS63	MS65
1989 BP	15,000	—	—	—	26.00	28.00
1989 BP	15,000	PF65 30.00				

KM# 679 500 FORINT (Otszaz)

28.00 g., 0.900 Silver 0.8102 oz. ASW **Obv:** King Mathias on horse left **Rev:** Busts of King Mathias and Queen Beatrix facing each other

Date	Mintage	VF20	XF40	MS60	MS63	MS65
1990 BP	15,000	PF65 32.00				
1990 BP	15,000	PF65 32.00				

KM# 680 500 FORINT (Otszaz)

28.00 g., 0.900 Silver 0.8102 oz. ASW **Obv:** Denomination, legend and date within decorative outline **Rev:** Two capital cities of King Mathias

Date	Mintage	VF20	XF40	MS60	MS63	MS65
1990 BP	15,000	—	—	—	28.00	30.00
1990 BP	15,000	PF65 32.00				

KM# 699 500 FORINT (Otszaz)

28.00 g., 0.900 Silver 0.8102 oz. ASW **Subject:** 200th Anniversary - Birth of Ferenc Kolcsey **Obv:** Crowned arms and denomination **Rev:** Ferenc Kölcsey

Date	Mintage	VF20	XF40	MS60	MS63	MS65
1990 BP	10,000	—	—	—	35.00	38.00
1990 BP	5,000	PF65 42.00				

KM# 683 500 FORINT (Otszaz)

28.00 g., 0.900 Silver 0.8102 oz. ASW **Subject:** Papal Visit **Obv:** Arms of the Republic **Rev:** Pope John Paul II

Date	Mintage	VF20	XF40	MS60	MS63	MS65
1991 BP	10,000	—	—	—	26.00	28.00
1991 BP	20,000	PF65 30.00				

KM# 685 500 FORINT (Otszaz)

28.00 g., 0.900 Silver 0.8102 oz. ASW **Subject:** 200th Anniversary - Birth of Count Szechenyi **Obv:** Locomotive and value **Rev:** Istvan Szechenyi

Date	Mintage	VF20	XF40	MS60	MS63	MS65
1991 BP	15,000	—	—	—	26.00	28.00
1991 BP	15,000	PF65 32.00				

KM# 686 500 FORINT (Otszaz)

28.00 g., 0.900 Silver 0.8102 oz. ASW **Obv:** Denomination **Rev:** Anjou Liliom **Rev. Legend:** Karoly Robert Emlekere

Date	Mintage	VF20	XF40	MS60	MS63	MS65
1992 BP	10,000	—	—	—	26.00	30.00
1992 BP	20,000	PF65 32.00				

KM# 687 500 FORINT (Otszaz)

28.00 g., 0.900 Silver 0.8102 oz. ASW **Subject:** Canonization of King Ladislaus **Obv:** Ladislaus Denar (obv. and rev.) and denomination **Rev:** King Ladislaus

Date	Mintage	VF20	XF40	MS60	MS63	MS65
1992 BP	10,000	—	—	—	26.00	28.00
1992 BP	20,000	PF65 32.00				

KM# 690 500 FORINT (Otszaz)

31.46 g., 0.925 Silver 0.9356 oz. ASW **Obv:** Crowned shield and denomination **Rev:** Telstar I satellite above globe

Date	Mintage	VF20	XF40	MS60	MS63	MS65
1992 BP	Est. 5000	—	—	—	28.00	30.00
1992 BP	Est. 15000	PF65 32.00				

KM# 702 500 FORINT (Otszaz)

31.46 g., 0.925 Silver 0.9356 oz. ASW **Obv:** Denomination above crowned arms **Rev:** Old Danube Ship "Arpad"

Date	Mintage	VF20	XF40	MS60	MS63	MS65
1993 BP	10,000	—	—	—	28.00	30.00
1993 BP	15,000	PF65 32.00				

KM# 704 500 FORINT (Otszaz)

31.46 g., 0.925 Silver 0.9356 oz. ASW **Obv:** Crowned arms divide date above denomination **Rev:** European Currency Union

Date	Mintage	VF20	XF40	MS60	MS63	MS65
1993 BP	10,000	—	—	—	28.00	30.00
1993 BP	30,000	PF65 32.00				

KM# 705 500 FORINT (Otszaz)
31.46 g., 0.925 Silver 0.9356 oz. ASW **Subject:** Expo '96 **Obv:** Logo above denomination **Rev:** Ship sailing on sea of letters

Date	Mintage	VF20	XF40	MS60	MS63	MS65
1993 BP	20,000	—	—	—	28.00	30.00
1993 BP	80,000	PF65 32.00				

KM# 708 500 FORINT (Otszaz)
31.46 g., 0.925 Silver 0.9356 oz. ASW **Obv:** Denomination above crowned arms **Rev:** Old Danube Ship "Carolina"

Date	Mintage	VF20	XF40	MS60	MS63	MS65
1994 BP	10,000	—	—	—	28.00	30.00
1994 BP	15,000	PF65 32.00				

KM# 709 500 FORINT (Otszaz)
31.46 g., 0.925 Silver 0.9356 oz. ASW **Subject:** Death of Lajos Kossuth **Obv:** Denomination within shield outline **Rev:** Bust 3/4 right

Date	Mintage	VF20	XF40	MS60	MS63	MS65
1994 BP	10,000	—	—	—	30.00	32.00
1994 BP	10,000	PF65 35.00				

KM# 710 500 FORINT (Otszaz)
31.46 g., 0.925 Silver 0.9356 oz. ASW **Subject:** International European Union **Obv:** Crowned arms divide date above denomination **Rev:** St. Istvan and Halaszbastya

Date	Mintage	VF20	XF40	MS60	MS63	MS65
1994 BP	10,000	—	—	—	30.00	32.00
1994 BP	30,000	PF65 35.00				

KM# 723 750 FORINT
10.00 g., 0.500 Silver 0.1608 oz. ASW **Subject:** Soccer **Obv:** Denomination in goal **Rev:** Ball in net above the Eiffel Tower

Date	Mintage	VF20	XF40	MS60	MS63	MS65
1997 BP	3,000	—	—	—	23.00	28.00
1997 BP	17,000	PF65 20.00				

KM# 725 750 FORINT
10.00 g., 0.500 Silver 0.1608 oz. ASW **Subject:** 125th Anniversary - Budapest **Obv:** Lanc Bridge **Rev:** City map and arms

Date	Mintage	VF20	XF40	MS60	MS63	MS65
1998 BP	3,000	—	—	—	26.00	30.00
1998 BP	12,000	PF65 20.00				

KM# 706 1000 FORINT
31.46 g., 0.925 Silver 0.9356 oz. ASW **Subject:** World Cup Soccer **Obv:** Small crowned arms above denomination **Rev:** Goalie **Mint:** Budapest

Date	Mintage	VF20	XF40	MS60	MS63	MS65
1993 BP	10,000	—	—	—	30.00	32.00
1993 BP	15,000	PF65 35.00				

KM# 712 1000 FORINT
31.46 g., 0.925 Silver 0.9356 oz. ASW **Series:** Atlanta Olympics **Obv:** Olympic flame in bowl above denomination **Rev:** Swimmers

Date	Mintage	VF20	XF40	MS60	MS63	MS65
1994 BP	10,000	—	—	—	28.00	30.00
1994 BP	40,000	PF65 32.00				

KM# 713 1000 FORINT
31.46 g., 0.925 Silver 0.9356 oz. ASW **Subject:** Protect Our World **Obv:** Stylized bird right below denomination **Rev:** Globe in trunk

Date	Mintage	VF20	XF40	MS60	MS63	MS65
1994 BP	10,000	—	—	—	28.00	30.00
1994 BP	10,000	PF65 32.00				

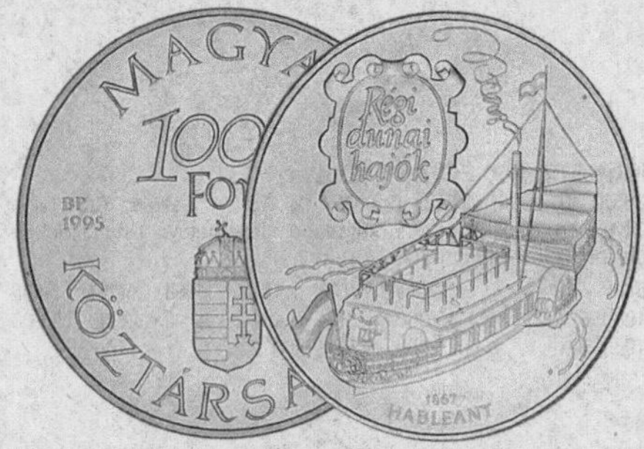

KM# 714 1000 FORINT
31.46 g., 0.925 Silver 0.9356 oz. ASW **Obv:** Crowned shield below denomination **Rev:** Old Danube Ship "Hableany"

Date	Mintage	VF20	XF40	MS60	MS63	MS65
1995 BP	10,000	—	—	—	28.00	30.00
1995 BP	20,000	PF65 32.00				

KM# 715 1000 FORINT
31.46 g., 0.925 Silver 0.9356 oz. ASW **Obv:** Abbot's seal impression and value **Rev:** Pannonhalma ruins

Date	Mintage	VF20	XF40	MS60	MS63	MS65
1995 BP	10,000	—	—	—	28.00	30.00
1995 BP	10,000	PF65 32.00				

KM# 716 1000 FORINT
31.46 g., 0.925 Silver 0.9356 oz. ASW **Series:** Atlanta Olympics **Obv:** Denomination **Rev:** Fencing match

Date	Mintage	VF20	XF40	MS60	MS63	MS65
1995 BP	5,000	—	—	—	30.00	32.00
1995 BP	25,000	PF65 35.00				

KM# 720 1000 FORINT
31.46 g., 0.925 Silver 0.9356 oz. ASW **Subject:** European Union **Obv:** Crowned arms divide date **Rev:** Hungarian Parliament building, "ecu"

Date	Mintage	VF20	XF40	MS60	MS63	MS65
1995 BP	5,000	—	—	—	33.00	38.00
1995 BP	18,000	PF65 35.00				

KM# 717 2000 FORINT
31.46 g., 0.925 Silver 0.9356 oz. ASW **Subject:** 50th Anniversary Forint Rebirth **Obv:** Anjou Lilium below fold of material, crowned arms above **Rev:** 13 coin designs

Date	Mintage	VF20	XF40	MS60	MS63	MS65
1996 BP	5,000	—	—	—	35.00	40.00
1996 BP	5,000	PF65 45.00				

KM# 718 2000 FORINT
31.46 g., 0.925 Silver 0.9356 oz. ASW **Subject:** 1100th Anniversary of Hungarian Nationhood **Obv:** Date and denomination below shield of designs **Rev:** Three equestrian archers above old shield

Date	Mintage	VF20	XF40	MS60	MS63	MS65
1996 BP	10,000	—	—	—	35.00	40.00
1996 BP	10,000	PF65 45.00				

KM# 722 2000 FORINT
31.46 g., 0.925 Silver 0.9356 oz. ASW **Obv:** Lake Balaton view above denomination **Rev:** Steam ships "Helka" and "Kelen"

Date	Mintage	VF20	XF40	MS60	MS63	MS65
1997 BP	5,000	—	—	—	37.00	42.00
1997 BP	15,000	PF65 35.00				

KM# 724 2000 FORINT
31.10 g., 0.925 Silver 0.925 oz. ASW **Subject:** European Union **Obv:** Crowned shield divides date above denomination **Rev:** Royal Palace of Budapest

Date	Mintage	VF20	XF40	MS60	MS63	MS65
1997 BP	3,000	—	—	—	40.00	45.00
1997 BP	27,000	PF65 35.00				

KM# 727 2000 FORINT
31.46 g., 0.925 Silver 0.9356 oz. ASW **Subject:** Revolution of 1848 **Obv:** Hungarian Order of Military Merit (1848-1849) I Class **Rev:** Hungarian military flag over European map

Date	Mintage	VF20	XF40	MS60	MS63	MS65
1998 BP	5,000	—	—	—	37.00	42.00
1998 BP	10,000	PF65 35.00				

KM# 729 2000 FORINT
31.46 g., 0.925 Silver 0.9356 oz. ASW **Subject:** UNICEF - For the Children of the World **Obv:** UNICEF logo above denomination **Rev:** Child's drawing of a princess

Date	Mintage	VF20	XF40	MS60	MS63	MS65
1998 BP	28,000	PF65 45.00				

KM# 730 2000 FORINT
31.46 g., 0.925 Silver 0.9356 oz. ASW **Subject:** World Wildlife Fund **Obv:** World Wildlife Fund logo above arms **Rev:** Fork-tailed barn swallows

Date	Mintage	VF20	XF40	MS60	MS63	MS65
1998 BP	18,000	PF65 40.00				

KM# 731 2000 FORINT
31.46 g., 0.925 Silver 0.9356 oz. ASW **Obv:** Sailboats on Lake Balaton **Rev:** The "Phoenix" under full sail

Date	Mintage	VF20	XF40	MS60	MS63	MS65
1998 BP	5,000	—	—	—	37.50	40.00
1998 BP	10,000	PF65 32.50				

KM# 732 2000 FORINT
31.46 g., 0.925 Silver 0.9356 oz. ASW, 38.6 mm. **Subject:** 150th Birthday - Lorand Eotvos **Obv:** Denomination **Rev:** Framed portrait at right, scientific instrument on fancy table edge at left **Edge:** Reeded

Date	Mintage	VF20	XF40	MS60	MS63	MS65
1998 BP	3,000	—	—	—	40.00	45.00
1998 BP	3,000	PF65 48.00				

KM# 733 2000 FORINT
31.46 g., 0.925 Silver 0.9356 oz. ASW, 38.6 mm. **Subject:** European Union **Obv:** National arms **Rev:** Monuments, Euro logo **Edge:** Reeded

Date	Mintage	VF20	XF40	MS60	MS63	MS65
1998 BP	3,000	—	—	—	42.00	46.00
1998 BP	12,000	PF65 52.00				

KM# 743 2000 FORINT
20.00 g., 0.925 Silver 0.5948 oz. ASW, 33.17 mm. **Subject:** Millennium **Obv:** Crowned shield divides date, denomination below **Rev:** Rodin's "The Thinker" and solar system **Edge:** Plain **Shape:** 7-sided **Mint:** Budapest

Date	Mintage	VF20	XF40	MS60	MS63	MS65
1999 BP	5,000	—	—	—	20.00	30.00
1999 BP	15,000	PF65 27.00				

KM# 744 2000 FORINT
19.98 g., 0.925 Silver 0.5942 oz. ASW, 33.91 mm. **Subject:** Olympics **Obv:** Crowned shield above denomination **Rev:** Hammer throw **Edge:** Reeded

Date	Mintage	VF20	XF40	MS60	MS63	MS65
1999 BP	4,000	—	—	—	17.00	25.00
1999 BP	14,000	PF65 27.50				

KM# 747 2000 FORINT

15.72 g., 0.925 Silver 0.4676 oz. ASW **Obv:** Denomination and date **Rev:** Angel in wreath **Rev. Inscription:** Koll./ Sàrospatak/ • 1531 • **Edge:** Reeded and plain section **Shape:** Half circle **Mint:** Budapest **Note:** 19.3 x 38.4

Date	Mintage	VF20	XF40	MS60	MS63	MS65
2000 BP	3,000	—	—	—	15.00	20.00
2000 BP	—	PF65 22.50				

KM# 748 2000 FORINT

15.72 g., 0.925 Silver 0.4676 oz. ASW **Obv:** Country name, denomination and date **Rev:** Seal and dates **Rev. Inscription:** Lorántffy / Zsuzsanna / 1600 - / 1660 **Shape:** Half circle **Mint:** Budapest

Date	Mintage	VF20	XF40	MS60	MS63	MS65
2000 BP	3,000	—	—	—	15.00	20.00
2000 BP	—	PF65 22.50				

KM# 735 3000 FORINT

31.46 g., 0.925 Silver 0.9356 oz. ASW, 38.6 mm. **Subject:** European Union **Obv:** Crowned arms above denomination **Rev:** Statue and Euro logo **Edge:** Reeded

Date	Mintage	VF20	XF40	MS60	MS63	MS65
1999 BP	3,000	—	—	—	35.00	40.00
1999 BP	17,000	PF65 40.00				

KM# 741 3000 FORINT

31.46 g., 0.925 Silver 0.9356 oz. ASW **Subject:** Hungarian Millennium **Obv:** Crown above denomination within circle, date below **Rev:** Round window design **Edge:** Plain **Mint:** Budapest **Note:** Gold-plated center.

Date	Mintage	VF20	XF40	MS60	MS63	MS65
1999 BP	5,000	—	—	—	40.00	45.00
1999 BP	—	PF65 50.00				

KM# 746 3000 FORINT

31.46 g., 0.925 Silver 0.9356 oz. ASW, 38.55 mm. **Obv:** Denomination **Rev:** Beaver **Edge:** Reeded **Mint:** Budapest

Date	Mintage	VF20	XF40	MS60	MS63	MS65
2000 BP	3,000	—	—	—	40.00	45.00
2000 BP	—	PF65 50.00				

KM# 749 3000 FORINT

31.46 g., 0.925 Silver 0.9356 oz. ASW **Subject:** Hologram inventor - Denes Gabor **Obv:** Hologram initials in center **Rev:** Bust right **Edge:** Reeded **Mint:** Budapest

Date	Mintage	VF20	XF40	MS60	MS63	MS65
2000 BP	3,000	—	—	—	40.00	45.00
2000 BP	—	PF65 50.00				

KM# 750 3000 FORINT

31.46 g., 0.925 Silver 0.9356 oz. ASW, 38.57 mm. **Subject:** 125th Anniversary - Franz Liszt Music Academy **Obv:** Half-length Franz Liszt right **Rev:** Academy entrance **Edge:** Reeded **Mint:** Budapest

Date	Mintage	VF20	XF40	MS60	MS63	MS65
2000 BP	3,000	—	—	—	40.00	45.00
2000 BP	—	PF65 50.00				

KM# 681 5000 FORINT

6.98 g., 0.986 Gold 0.2213 oz. AGW **Subject:** 500th Anniversary - Death of Mathias I **Obv:** Hunyadi coat of arms **Rev:** Seated King Mathias with scepter and orb **Mint:** Budapest

Date	Mintage	VF20	XF40	MS60	MS63	MS65
1990 BP	10,000	PF65 400				

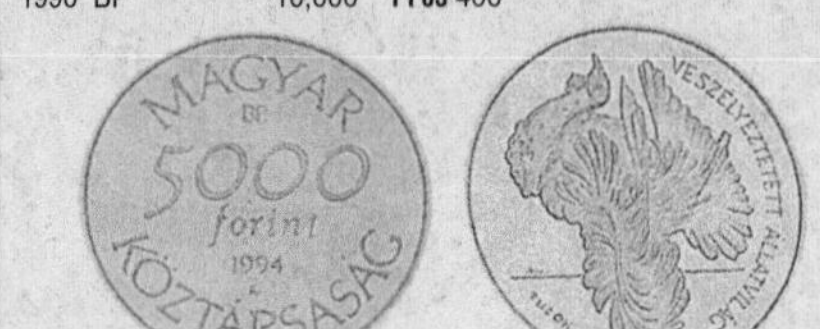

KM# 711 5000 FORINT

7.77 g., 0.584 Gold 0.1459 oz. AGW **Obv:** Denomination and date **Rev:** Great Bustard Bird

Date	Mintage	VF20	XF40	MS60	MS63	MS65
1994 BP	5,000	PF65 250				

KM# 684 10000 FORINT (Tizezer)

6.98 g., 0.986 Gold 0.2213 oz. AGW **Subject:** Papal Visit **Obv:** Crowned shield within beaded circle **Rev:** Madonna and child **Mint:** Budapest

Date	Mintage	VF20	XF40	MS60	MS63	MS65
1991 BP	10,000	PF65 375				

KM# 691 10000 FORINT (Tizezer)

6.98 g., 0.986 Gold 0.2213 oz. AGW **Subject:** 650th Anniversary - Death of King Karoly Robert **Obv:** Denomination **Rev:** Crowned head 3/4 right

Date	Mintage	VF20	XF40	MS60	MS63	MS65
1992 BP	10,000	PF65 375				

KM# 703 10000 FORINT (Tizezer)

6.98.g., 0.986 Gold 0.2213 oz. AGW **Subject:** Centennial - Death of Ferenc Erkel **Obv:** Denomination and date **Rev:** Bust 3/4 left

Date	Mintage	VF20	XF40	MS60	MS63	MS65
1993 BP	5,000	PF65 375				

KM# 719 20000 FORINT

6.98 g., 0.986 Gold 0.2213 oz. AGW **Subject:** 1100th Anniversary of Hungarian Nationhood **Obv:** Denomination and date above designs at bottom **Rev:** Two equestrian archers right

Date	Mintage	VF20	XF40	MS60	MS63	MS65
1996 BP	5,000	PF65 375				

KM# 728 20000 FORINT

6.98 g., 0.986 Gold 0.2213 oz. AGW **Subject:** Revolution of 1848 **Obv:** Hungarian Order of Military Merit III Class **Rev:** Portrait of Lajos Batthyany

Date	Mintage	VF20	XF40	MS60	MS63	MS65
1998 BP	5,000	PF65 375				

KM# 742 20000 FORINT

6.98 g., 0.986 Gold 0.2213 oz. AGW **Subject:** Hungarian State Millennium **Obv:** Portrait of St. Michael the Archangel **Rev:** Crown of St. Stephen **Edge:** Plain **Mint:** Budapest

Date	Mintage	VF20	XF40	MS60	MS63	MS65
1999 BP	3,000	PF65 395				

PATTERNS

Including off metal strikes

KM#	Date	Mintage	Identification	Mkt Val
Pn126	1910	—	2 Korona. Lead. KM#493.	—
Pn127	1913	—	2 Korona. Aluminum. KM#493.	—
Pn128	1914	—	Fillér. Steel. KM#480.	—
Pn129	1914	—	10 Fillér. Silver. KM#482.	800
Pn130	1914	—	2 Korona. Aluminum. KM#493.	—
Pn131	1915	—	2 Fillér. New Silver. KM#481.	130
Pn132	1915	—	10 Fillér. Nickel. KM#494.	—
Pn133	1915	—	10 Fillér. Nickel. KM#496.	—
Pn134	1915	—	20 Fillér. Iron. KM#498.	250
Pn135	1915	—	20 Fillér. Iron. Circle around crown.	—

KM#	Date	Mintage	Identification	Mkt Val
Pn136	1915	—	20 Fillér. Silver. KM#483.	1,000
Pn137	1915	—	1/2 Korona. Silver. Franz Joseph I bust right. Value in wreath.	1,000
Pn138	1916	—	2 Heller. Lead. One side.	—
Pn139	1916	—	2 Fillér. Iron. KM#481.	350
Pn140	1916	—	2 Fillér. Iron. 2 in square.	—
Pn141	1916	—	2 Fillér. Iron. Circle around crown.	—
Pn142	ND(1916)	—	2 Fillér. Lead. Ornaments around 2, without legend.	—
Pn143	1916KB	—	10 Fillér. Iron. KM#496.	—
Pn144	1916	—	20 Fillér. Lead. KM#498.	—
Pn145	1917	—	20 Fillér. Zinc.	—
Pn146	1917	—	2 Fillér. Steel. With rosette.	—
Pn147	1917	—	10 Fillér. Iron. Crown above sceptor and sword. Value between wheat.	—
Pn148	1917	—	10 Fillér. Zinc.	—
Pn149	1917	—	10 Fillér. New Silver.	—
Pn150	1918	—	2 Fillér. Aluminum. KM#497.	—
Pn151	1918	—	50 Fillér. Iron. Large crown.	—
Pn152	1918	—	50 Fillér. Lead.	—
Pn153	ND (1919) BP	—	10 Korona. Silver.	—
Pn154	ND (1919) BP	3	10 Korona. Bronze.	—
Pn155	1922	—	20 Fillér. Bronze.	—
Pn156	1922	—	20 Fillér. New Silver.	—
Pn157	1922	—	20 Fillér. Nickel.	—
Pn158	1922	—	5 Korona. Aluminum.	—
Pn159	1922	—	5 Korona. Brass.	—
Pn160	1926	—	10 Fillér. Lead. KM#507.	—
Pn161	1927	—	10 Pengö. Brass. Fr#100.	—
Pn162	1927	—	10 Pengö. Gold.	—
Pn163	1927	—	20 Pengö. Brass. Denomination in grape-wheat ear wreath. Fr#99.	—
Pn164	1927	—	20 Pengö. Brass. Denomination in wreath. Fr#99.	—
Pn165	1927	—	20 Pengö. Gold. Denomination in grape-wheat ear wreath.	—
Pn166	1927	—	20 Pengö. Gold. Denomination in laurel wreath.	2,800
Pn167	1928BP	—	10 Pengö. Gold. Fr#100.	2,800
Pn168	1928	—	20 Pengö. Brass. Smaller arms. Fr#99a.	—
Pn169	1928BP	—	20 Pengö. Gold. Fr#99.	2,800
Pn170	1929	—	5 Pengö. Lead.	—
Pn171	1929	—	5 Pengö. Silver.	—
Pn172	1929BP	—	20 Pengö. Gold. Fr#99a.	2,800
Pn173	1930	—	5 Pengö. Y#44.	—
Pn174	1935	—	2 Fillér. Nickel. KM#506.	—
Pn175	1935BP	—	2 Pengö.	—
Pn176	1938	—	50 Fillér. Aluminum. KM#509.	—
Pn177	1939	—	Fillér. Aluminum. KM#505.	—
Pn178	1940	—	Fillér. Iron. KM#505.	—
Pn179	1940	—	10 Fillér. Lead. KM#507.	—
Pn180	1941	—	50 Fillér. Iron. KM#509.	—
Pn181	1943	—	2 Fillér. Aluminum. KM#519.	—

PIEDFORT

KM#	Date	Mintage	Identification	Mkt Val
P22	1979	2,500	200 Forint. Silver. KM#615.	110
P23	1979	2,500	200 Forint. Silver. KM#616.	70.00
P24	1980	3,000	100 Forint. Nickel. KM#617.	60.00
P25	1980	3,000	200 Forint. Silver. KM#618.	50.00
P26	1980	1,500	500 Forint. Silver. KM#619.	150

PROBA

KM#	Date	Mintage	Identification	Mkt Val
Pr1	1986	—	500 Forint. Silver. KM#656. Soccer players.	350
Pr2	1986	—	500 Forint. Silver. KM#657. Stadium.	350
Pr3	1988	—	100 Forint. Copper-Nickel. KM#664. Soccer players.	—
Pr4	1988	—	100 Forint. Copper-Nickel. KM#665. Soccer goalie in net.	—
Pr5	1989	—	100 Forint. Copper-Nickel. KM#668. Soccer players shaking hands.	—

TRIAL STRIKES

KM#	Date	Mintage	Identification	Mkt Val
TS39	1907	—	100 Korona. Bronze. KM#491.	—
TS40	1907	—	100 Korona. Bronze. KM#490. Without legend.	—
TS41	1910	—	2 Korona. Lead. KM#493.	—
TS42	1913	—	2 Korona. Aluminum. KM#493.	—
TS43	1914KB	—	Fillér. Iron. KM#480.	—
TS44	1914KB	—	2 Fillér. Nickel. KM#481.	—
TS45	1914KB	—	10 Fillér. Brass. KM#482.	—
TS46	1914	—	10 Fillér. Silver Plated Copper-Nickel-Zinc.	—
TS47	1914KB	—	10 Fillér. Silver. KM#482.	—
TS48	1914KB	—	20 Fillér. Iron. KM#483.	—
TS49	1914	—	2 Korona. Aluminum. KM#493.	—
TS50	1914	—	2 Korona. Bronze. KM#486.	—
TS51	1915KB	—	2 Fillér. Iron. KM#481.	—
TS52	1915KB	—	10 Fillér. Nickel. KM#496.	—
TS53	1915KB	—	20 Fillér. Silver. KM#483.	1,250
TS54	1916	—	20 Fillér. Lead. KM#498.	—
TS55	1916KB	—	1/2 Korona. Silver.	1,250
TS56	1917KB	—	10 Fillér. Lead.	—
TS57	1917KB	—	10 Fillér. Zinc.	—
TS58	1917KB	—	10 Fillér. Copper-Nickel-Zinc.	—
TS59	1918KB	—	50 Fillér. Lead.	—
TS60	1918	—	20 Korona. Lead. KM#486.	—
TS61	1920	—	10 Fillér. Copper-Nickel-Zinc. KM#496.	—
TS62	1922	—	20 Fillér. Nickel. KM#498.	—
TS63	1922	—	20 Fillér. Bronze. KM#498.	—
TS64	1922	—	20 Fillér. Brass. KM#498.	—
TS65	1922	—	20 Fillér. Copper-Nickel-Zinc. KM#498.	—
TS66	1930	—	5 Pengö. Lead. Obverse only, KM#512.	—
TS67	1930	—	5 Pengö. Lead. Reverse only, KM#512.	—
TS68	1935	—	2 Fillér. Nickel. KM#506.	—
TS69	1935	—	2 Pengö. Lead. Reverse only, KM#514.	—
TS70	1936	—	2 Pengö. Lead. Obverse only, KM#515.	—
TS71	1938	—	5 Pengö. Brass. KM#517.	—
TS72	1938	—	5 Pengö. Brass. KM#516.	—
TS73	1938	—	5 Pengö. Lead. Obverse only, KM#516.	—
TS74	1938	—	5 Pengö. Lead. Reverse only, KM#516.	—
TS75	1939	—	Fillér. Aluminum. KM#505.	—
TS76	1939	—	50 Fillér. Aluminum. KM#509.	—
TS77	1941	—	50 Fillér. Iron. KM#509.	—
TS78	1943	—	2 Fillér. Aluminum. KM#519.	—
TS79	1943	—	5 Pengö. Brass. KM#523.	—

MINT SETS

KM#	Date	Mintage	Identification	Issue Price	Mkt Val
MS-A1	1956 (3)	—	KM#552, 553, 554	—	70.00
MS1	1971 (9)	—	KM#546, 549, 572-575, 591, 594, 595	—	15.00
MS2	1972 (9)	—	KM#546, 549, 572-575, 591, 594, 595	—	15.00
MS3	1973 (9)	—	KM#546, 549, 572-575, 591, 594, 595	—	20.00
MS4	1974 (9)	—	KM#546, 549, 572-575, 591, 594, 595	—	16.00
MS5	1975 (9)	—	KM#546, 549, 572-575, 591, 594, 595	—	15.00
MS6	1976 (9)	—	KM#546, 549, 572-575, 591, 594, 595	—	15.00
MSA7	1977 (3)	—	KM#610-612	—	60.00
MS7	1977 (9)	—	KM#546, 549, 572-575, 591, 594, 595	—	15.00
MS8	1978 (9)	—	KM#546, 549, 572-575, 591, 594, 595	—	15.00
MS9	1979 (9)	—	KM#546, 549, 572-575, 591, 594, 595	—	15.00
MS10	1980 (9)	—	KM#546, 549, 572-575, 591, 594, 595	—	15.00
MS11	1981 (9)	—	KM#546, 549, 572-575, 591, 594, 620	—	15.00
MS12	1982 (9)	—	KM#546, 549, 572-575, 591, 594, 595	—	15.00
MSA13	1983 (3)	—	KM#627, 628, 629	—	12.50
MS13	1983 (10)	—	KM#546, 549, 572-575, 591, 630, 635, 636	—	13.00
MS14	1984 (10)	—	KM#546, 549, 572-575, 591, 630, 635, 636	—	16.00
MS15	1985 (10)	—	KM#546, 549, 572-575, 591, 630, 635, 636	—	14.00
MS16	1986 (10)	—	KM#546, 549, 572-575, 591, 630, 635, 636	—	24.00
MS17	1987 (10)	—	KM#546, 549, 572-575, 591, 630, 635, 636	—	16.00
MS18	1988 (10)	—	KM#546, 549, 572-575, 591, 630, 635, 636	—	15.00
MS19	1989 (10)	—	KM#546, 549, 572-575, 591, 630, 635, 636	—	10.00
MS20	1990 (5)	—	KM673-677	—	8.00
MS21	1991 (5)	—	KM673-677	—	8.00
MSA22	1992 (5)	—	KM673-677	—	10.00
MS22	1992 (8)	—	KM689, 692-698	—	35.00
MS23	1993 (11)	—	KM675-677, 689, 692-698	—	15.00
MS24	1994 (11)	—	KM675-677, 692-698, 707	—	15.00
MS26	1995 (11)	—	KM675-677, 692-698, 707	17.50	15.00
MS27	1996 (10)	—	KM675-677, 692-698	—	12.00
MS28	1997 (11)	7,000	KM677, 692-698, 707, 721	18.50	25.00
MS29	1998 (11)	—	KM677, 692-698, 707, 721, 726	22.50	35.00
MS30	1999 (8)	—	KM677, 692-697, 721	—	18.00
MS31	2000 (8)	—	KM692-697, 721, 745	—	18.00

PROOF SETS

KM#	Date	Mintage	Identification	Issue Price	Mkt Val
PSA1	1948 (3)	—	KM537-539	70.00	80.00
PS1	1961 (6)	2,500	KM560, 562-566	—	5,750
PS2	1961 (4)	—	KM557-559, 561	—	65.00
PS3	1966 (8)	2,000	KM546a, 547a, 549a-551a, 555a, 556b, X15	15.00	65.00
PS4	1966 (3)	330	KM569-571	430	7,150
PS5	1966 (2)	11,000	KM567, 568	7.50	35.00
PS6	1967 (8)	5,000	KM546a, 547a, 549a-551a, 555a, 556b, X15	15.00	65.00
PS7	1967 (2)	500	KM580, 581	—	5,675
PS8	1968 (5)	7,000	KM583, 585-588	—	8,200
PS9	1968 (2)	4,750	KM582, 584	35.00	45.00
PS10	1969 (2)	3,000	KM589, 590	35.00	35.00
PS11	1970 (2)	4,000	KM592, 593	25.00	30.00
PS12	1972 (2)	6,000	KM596, 597	25.00	30.00
PS13	1973 (2)	6,000	KM599, 600	—	32.00
PS14	1974 (2)	—	KM601, 603	—	32.00
PS15	1976 (3)	5,000	KM607-609	—	55.00
PS16	1977 (3)	—	KM610-612	—	55.00
PS17	1992 (8)	1,000	KM689, 692-698	—	55.00
PS18	1993 (8)	—	KM689, 692-698	—	25.00
PSA19	1993/4 (2)	—	KM704, 710	—	75.00
PS19	1994 (8)	—	KM692-698, 707	—	25.00
PS20	1995 (8)	—	KM692-698, 707	24.50	25.00
PS21	1996 (10)	—	KM#675-677, 692-698	—	25.00
PS22	1997 (9)	3,000	KM692-698, 707, 721	29.50	50.00
PS23	1998 (10)	—	KM#692-698, 707, 721, 726	—	60.00
PS24	1998 (3)	5,000	KM726-728	267	375
PS25	1999 (7)	—	KM692-697, 721	—	35.00
PS26	1999 (2)	—	KM741, 742	239	400
PS27	2000 (8)	—	KM692-697, 721, 745	—	40.00

SPECIMEN SETS (SS)

KM#	Date	Mintage	Identification	Issue Price	Mkt Val
SS1	1977 (9)	—	KM546, 549, 572-575, 591, 594-595	—	15.00
SS2	1978 (9)	—	KM546, 549, 572-575, 591, 594-595	—	15.00
SS3	1979 (9)	—	KM546, 549, 572-575, 591, 594-595	—	15.00
SS4	1981 (9)	—	KM546, 549, 572-575, 591, 594, 620	—	15.00
SS5	1989 (10)	—	KM546, 549, 572-575, 591, 630, 635, 636	—	12.00

ICELAND

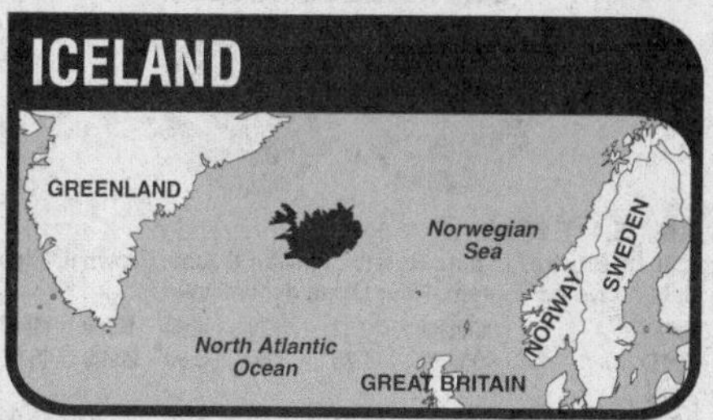

The Republic of Iceland, an island of recent volcanic origin in the North Atlantic east of Greenland and immediately south of the Arctic Circle, has an area of 39,768sq. mi. (103,000 sq. km.) and a population of just over 300,000. Capital: Reykjavik. Fishing is the chief industry and accounts for a little less than 60 percent of the exports.

Iceland was settled by Norwegians in the 9th century and established as an independent republic in 930. The Icelandic assembly called the Althingi', also established in 930, is the oldest parliament in the world. Iceland came under Norwegian sovereignty in 1262, and passed to Denmark when Norway and Denmark were united under the Danish crown in 1380. In 1918 it was established as a virtually independent kingdom in union with Denmark. On June 17, 1944, while Denmark was still under occupation by troops of the Third Reich, Iceland was established by plebiscite as an independent republic.

RULER

Christian X, 1912-1944

MINT MARK

Heart (h) - Copenhagen

MINTMASTERS' INITIALS

HCN - Hans Christian Nielsen, 1919-1927 (for Iceland, 1922-1926)

N - Niels Peter Nielsen, 1927-1955 (for Iceland, 1929-1940)

MONEYERS' INITIALS

GJ - Knud Gunnar Jensen, 1901-1933

MONETARY SYSTEM

100 Aurar = 1 Krona

KINGDOM

TOKEN COINAGE

N. Chr. Gram.; Thingeyri

KM# Tn3 10 ORE

Bronze **Issuer:** N. Chr. Gram. **Note:** Similar to 25 Ore, KM#Tn4.

Date	Mintage	VG8	F12	VF20	XF40	MS60
ND-1902 Rare	—	—	—	—	—	—

KM# Tn4 25 ORE

Bronze **Issuer:** N. Chr. Gram.

Date	Mintage	VG8	F12	VF20	XF40	MS60
ND-1902 Rare	—	—	—	—	—	—

KM# Tn23 50 ORE

Bronze **Issuer:** N. Chr. Gram. **Note:** Similar to 25 Ore, KM#Tn4.

Date	Mintage	VG8	F12	VF20	XF40	MS60
ND-1902 Rare	—	—	—	—	—	—

TOKEN COINAGE

P.J. Thorsteinsson; Bildudal

KM# Tn12 10 AURAR

1.70 g., Brass **Issuer:** P.J. Thorsteinsson **Note:** Similar to 100 Aurar, KM#Tn21. Struck by L. Chr. Lauer of Nurnberg.

Date	Mintage	VG8	F12	VF20	XF40	MS60
ND-1901	—	12.50	27.00	65.00	175	—

KM# Tn15 25 AURAR

1.70 g., Brass **Issuer:** P.J. Thorsteinsson **Note:** Similar to 100 Aurar, KM#Tn21. Struck by L. Chr. Lauer of Nurnberg.

Date	Mintage	VG8	F12	VF20	XF40	MS60
ND-1901	—	6.50	13.00	27.50	80.00	—

KM# Tn18 50 AURAR

2.20 g., Brass **Issuer:** P.J. Thorsteinsson **Note:** Similar to 100 Aurar, KM#Tn21. Struck by L. Chr. Lauer of Nurnberg.

Date	Mintage	VG8	F12	VF20	XF40	MS60
ND-1901	—	6.50	13.00	27.50	70.00	—

KM# Tn21 100 AURAR

1.10 g., Aluminum **Issuer:** P.J. Thorsteinsson **Note:** Struck by L. Chr. Lauer of Nurnberg.

Date	Mintage	VG8	F12	VF20	XF40	MS60
ND-1901 Rare	—	—	—	—	—	—

KM# Tn22 500 AURAR

1.10 g., Aluminum **Issuer:** P.J. Thorsteinsson **Note:** Similar to 100 Aurar, KM#Tn21. Struck by L. Chr. Lauer of Nurnberg.

Date	Mintage	VG8	F12	VF20	XF40	MS60
ND-1901	—	7.50	16.00	35.00	87.50	—

DECIMAL COINAGE

KM# 5.1 EYRIR

1.50 g., Bronze, 15 mm. **Ruler:** Christian X **Obv:** Crown divides date above monogram **Rev:** Large denomination

Date	Mintage	F12	VF20	XF40	MS60	MS63
1926 (h) HCN-GJ	405,000	1.75	3.50	8.00	20.00	45.00
1931 (h) N-GJ	462,000	1.25	2.80	6.75	20.00	45.00
1937 (h) N-GJ Wide date	211,000	2.25	4.75	9.00	30.00	50.00
1937 (h) N-GJ Narrow date	Inc. above	2.25	4.50	8.50	30.00	50.00
1938 (h) N-GJ	279,000	1.25	2.50	4.50	10.00	20.00
1939 (h) N-GJ Large 3	305,000	1.25	2.50	3.75	10.00	20.00
1939 (h) N-GJ Small 3	Inc. above	1.25	2.50	3.75	10.00	20.00

KM# 5.2 EYRIR

1.50 g., Bronze, 15 mm. **Ruler:** Christian X **Obv:** Crown divides date above monogram **Rev:** Large denomination, ornaments flank

Date	Mintage	F12	VF20	XF40	MS60	MS63
1940	1,000,000	0.35	0.60	1.15	2.75	5.00
1940	—	PF63 250				
1942	2,000,000	0.25	0.45	0.85	2.25	5.00

KM# 6.1 2 AURAR

3.00 g., Bronze **Ruler:** Christian X **Obv:** Crown divides date above monogram **Rev:** Large denomination, ornaments flank **Note:** Varieties exist in the appearance of the numeral 8 in 1938 dated coins. As the die slowly deteriorated, "globs" were added to the upper loop and later to the lower loop.

Date	Mintage	F12	VF20	XF40	MS60	MS63
1926 (h) HCN-GJ	498,000	1.00	3.00	5.00	20.00	45.00
1931 (h) N-GJ	446,000	1.00	3.00	5.00	20.00	45.00
1938 (h) N-GJ	206,000	5.00	10.00	15.00	35.00	60.00
1940 (h) N-GJ	257,000	3.00	5.00	10.00	20.00	45.00

KM# 6.2 2 AURAR

3.00 g., Bronze **Ruler:** Christian X **Obv:** Crown divides date above monogram **Rev:** Large denomination, ornaments flank

Date	Mintage	F12	VF20	XF40	MS60	MS63
1940	1,000,000	0.50	0.85	1.75	3.50	5.00
1940	—	PF63 300				
1942	2,000,000	0.25	0.75	1.35	2.50	4.00

KM# 7.1 5 AURAR

6.00 g., Bronze **Ruler:** Christian X **Obv:** Crown divides date above monogram **Rev:** Large denomination, ornaments flank

Date	Mintage	F12	VF20	XF40	MS60	MS63
1926 (h) HCN-GJ	355,000	5.00	9.00	15.00	35.00	75.00
1931 (h) N-GJ	311,000	5.00	9.00	15.00	35.00	75.00

KM# 7.2 5 AURAR

6.00 g., Bronze **Ruler:** Christian X **Obv:** Crown divides date above monogram **Rev:** Large denomination, ornaments flank

Date	Mintage	F12	VF20	XF40	MS60	MS63
1940	1,000,000	0.75	2.50	2.75	5.50	7.00
1940	—	PF63 300				
1942	2,000,000	0.40	1.00	1.75	3.50	5.00

KM# 1.1 10 AURAR

1.50 g., Copper-Nickel **Ruler:** Christian X **Obv:** Ornaments flank denomination **Rev:** Crowned arms divide monogram **Edge:** Reeded

Date	Mintage	F12	VF20	XF40	MS60	MS63
1922 (h) HCN GJ	300,000	1.00	3.00	5.00	20.00	35.00
1923 (h) HCN GJ	302,000	1.00	3.00	5.00	20.00	35.00
1925 (h) HCN GJ	321,000	5.00	15.00	25.00	45.00	75.00
1929 (h) N-GJ	176,000	10.00	20.00	30.00	50.00	85.00
1933 (h) N-GJ	157,000	10.00	20.00	30.00	50.00	85.00
1936 (h) N-GJ	213,000	1.00	3.00	5.00	20.00	35.00
1939/6 (h) N-GJ	208,000	1.00	3.00	5.00	20.00	35.00
1939 (h) N-GJ	Inc. above	1.00	3.00	5.00	20.00	35.00

KM# 1.2 10 AURAR

1.50 g., Copper-Nickel **Ruler:** Christian X **Obv:** Ornaments flank denomination **Rev:** Crowned arms divide monogram **Edge:** Reeded

Date	Mintage	F12	VF20	XF40	MS60	MS63
1940	1,500,000	0.40	0.85	1.75	5.00	7.50
1940	—	PF63 250				

KM# 1a 10 AURAR

1.30 g., Zinc **Ruler:** Christian X **Obv:** Ornaments flank denomination **Rev:** Crowned arms divide monogram **Edge:** Reeded

Date	Mintage	F12	VF20	XF40	MS60	MS63
1942	2,000,000	1.65	3.25	6.50	20.00	35.00
1942 Prooflike	—	—	—	—	—	150

KM# 2.1 25 AURAR

2.40 g., Copper-Nickel, 16 mm. **Ruler:** Christian X **Obv:** Ornaments flank denomination **Rev:** Crowned arms divide monogram **Edge:** Reeded

Date	Mintage	F12	VF20	XF40	MS60	MS63
1922 (h) HCN GJ	300,000	1.15	2.85	4.50	20.00	45.00
1923 (h) HCN GJ	304,000	1.15	2.85	4.50	20.00	45.00
1925 (h) HCN GJ	207,000	2.75	5.00	10.00	30.00	60.00
1933 (h) N-GJ	104,000	10.00	15.00	20.00	40.00	75.00
1937 (h) N-GJ Near 7	201,000	3.35	5.50	10.00	20.00	45.00
1937 (h) N-GJ Far 7	Inc. above	3.35	5.50	10.00	20.00	45.00

KM# 2.2 25 AURAR

2.40 g., Copper-Nickel, 16 mm. **Ruler:** Christian X **Obv:** Ornaments flank denomination **Rev:** Crowned arms divide monogram **Edge:** Reeded

Date	Mintage	F12	VF20	XF40	MS60	MS63
1940	1,500,000	0.30	0.75	1.25	3.00	5.00
1940	—	PF63 270				

KM# 2a 25 AURAR

2.00 g., Zinc, 16 mm. **Ruler:** Christian X **Obv:** Ornaments flank denomination **Rev:** Crowned arms divide monogram **Edge:** Reeded

Date	Mintage	F12	VF20	XF40	MS60	MS63
1942	2,000,000	1.25	3.50	6.00	20.00	35.00
1942 Prooflike	—	—	—	—	—	150

KM# 3.1 KRÓNA

4.75 g., Aluminum-Bronze **Ruler:** Christian X **Obv:** Ornaments flank denomination **Rev:** Crowned shield divide monogram, strikemark flanking bottom of shield **Edge:** Reeded

Date	Mintage	F12	VF20	XF40	MS60	MS63
1925 (h) HCN GJ	252,000	3.50	7.00	30.00	100	225
1929 (h) N-GJ	154,000	5.75	11.00	35.00	125	250
1940 (h) N-GJ	209,000	1.75	2.85	5.50	16.00	20.00

KM# 3.2 KRÓNA

4.74 g., Aluminum-Bronze, 22.3 mm. **Ruler:** Christian X **Obv:** Ornaments flank denomination **Rev:** Crowned arms divide monogram, no strikemark flanking bottom of shield **Edge:** Reeded

Date	Mintage	F12	VF20	XF40	MS60	MS63
1940	715,000	1.25	2.25	4.85	11.00	15.00
1940 Proof; rare	—	—	—	—	—	—

KM# 4.1 2 KRÓNUR

9.50 g., Aluminum-Bronze, 28 mm. **Ruler:** Christian X **Obv:** Ornaments flank denomination **Rev:** Crowned arms divide monogram **Edge:** Reeded

Date	Mintage	F12	VF20	XF40	MS60	MS63
1925 (h) HCN GJ	126,000	8.00	14.00	45.00	150	275
1929 (h) N-GJ	77,000	10.50	25.00	80.00	175	300

KM# 4.2 2 KRÓNUR

9.50 g., Aluminum-Bronze, 28 mm. **Ruler:** Christian X **Obv:** Ornaments flank denomination **Rev:** Crowned arms divide monogram **Edge:** Reeded

Date	Mintage	F12	VF20	XF40	MS60	MS63
1940	546,000	0.85	1.65	4.00	11.50	15.00
1940 Proof; rare	—	—	—	—	—	—

REPUBLIC

KM# 8 EYRIR

1.62 g., Bronze, 15.10 mm. **Obv:** Leaves flank denomination **Rev:** Arms within wreath **Note:** Values for the 1953-59 proof issues are for impaired proofs. Brilliant proofs may bring 3 to 4 times these figures.

Date	Mintage	F12	VF20	XF40	MS60	MS63
1946	4,000,000	0.15	0.20	0.60	1.25	2.50
1946	—	PF63 300				
1953	4,000,000	0.15	0.20	0.60	1.00	2.00
1953	—	PF63 75.00				
1956	2,000,000	0.10	0.15	0.60	1.00	2.00
1956	—	PF63 75.00				
1957	2,000,000	0.10	0.15	0.60	1.00	2.00
1957	—	PF63 80.00				
1958	2,000,000	0.15	0.20	0.45	0.85	1.00
1958	—	PF63 80.00				
1959	1,600,000	0.15	0.20	0.45	0.85	1.00
1959	—	PF63 80.00				
1966	1,000,000	0.15	0.20	0.45	0.85	1.00
1966	15,000	PF63 4.25				

KM# 9 5 AURAR

6.06 g., Bronze **Obv:** Leaves flank denomination **Rev:** Arms within wreath **Note:** Values for the 1958-63 proof issues are for impaired proofs. Brilliant proofs may bring 3 to 4 times these figures.

Date	Mintage	F12	VF20	XF40	MS60	MS63
1946	4,000,000	0.15	0.30	0.60	1.35	2.00
1946	—	PF63 450				
1958	400,000	0.55	2.25	3.75	5.50	7.50
1958	—	PF63 115				
1959	600,000	0.60	2.25	3.25	4.75	6.00
1959	—	PF63 110				
1960	1,200,000	0.20	0.45	1.20	5.00	15.00
1960	—	PF63 115				
1961	1,200,000	0.20	0.45	2.25	2.00	4.50
1961	—	PF63 105				
1963	1,200,000	0.15	0.35	0.85	1.75	3.50
1963	—	PF63 125				
1965	800,000	0.15	0.25	0.60	1.50	2.50
1966	1,000,000	0.10	0.25	0.60	1.50	2.50
1966	15,000	PF63 3.45				

KM# 10 10 AURAR

1.50 g., Copper-Nickel, 15 mm. **Obv:** Leaves flank denomination **Rev:** Arms within wreath **Edge:** Reeded **Note:** Values for the 1953-63 proof issues are for impaired proofs. Brilliant proofs may bring 3 to 4 times these figures.

Date	Mintage	F12	VF20	XF40	MS60	MS63
1946	4,000,000	—	0.15	0.30	0.70	1.00
1946	—	PF63 450				
1953	4,000,000	—	0.15	0.30	0.60	1.00
1953	—	PF63 75.00				
1957	1,200,000	0.30	0.85	2.40	5.50	1.00
1957	—	PF63 75.00				
1958	500,000	0.30	0.55	1.25	3.50	5.00
1958	—	PF63 80.00				
1959	3,000,000	0.30	0.60	1.75	4.50	6.00
1959	—	PF63 80.00				
1960	1,000,000	0.15	0.30	0.55	1.25	2.00
1960	—	PF63 80.00				
1961	2,000,000	—	—	0.15	0.25	1.00
1961	—	PF63 80.00				
1962	3,000,000	—	—	0.15	0.25	1.00
1962	—	PF63 80.00				
1963	4,000,000	—	—	0.15	0.25	1.00
1963	—	PF63 275				
1965	2,000,000	—	—	0.15	0.25	1.00
1966	4,000,000	—	—	0.15	0.25	1.00
1967	2,000,000	—	—	0.15	0.25	1.00
1969	3,200,000	—	—	0.15	0.25	1.00
Note: Coarse edge reeding						
1969	Inc. above	—	—	0.15	0.25	1.00
Note: Fine edge reeding						

KM# 10a 10 AURAR

0.48 g., Aluminum, 14.64 mm. **Obv:** Leaves flank denomination **Rev:** Arms within wreath **Edge:** Reeded

Date	Mintage	F12	VF20	XF40	MS60	MS63
1970	4,800,000	—	—	0.15	0.25	0.50
1971	11,200,000	—	—	0.15	0.25	0.50
1973	4,800,000	—	—	0.15	0.20	0.50
1974	4,800,000	—	—	0.15	0.20	0.50
1974	15,000	PF65 3.75				

KM# 11 25 AURAR

2.40 g., Copper-Nickel, 16 mm. **Obv:** Leaves flank denomination **Rev:** Arms within wreath **Edge:** Reeded **Note:** Values for the 1951-63 proof issues are for impaired proofs. Brilliant proofs may bring 3 to 4 times these figures.

Date	Mintage	F12	VF20	XF40	MS60	MS63
1946	2,000,000	0.15	0.20	0.40	1.40	2.00
1946	—	PF63 475				
1951	2,000,000	0.15	0.20	0.45	0.85	1.00
1951	—	PF63 95.00				
1954	2,000,000	0.15	0.20	0.40	0.85	1.00
1954	—	PF63 90.00				
1957	1,000,000	0.25	0.75	2.00	4.00	6.50
1957	—	PF63 82.50				
1958	500,000	0.25	0.50	1.00	1.25	2.00
1958	—	PF63 90.00				
1959	2,000,000	0.25	0.65	1.75	4.00	6.50
1959	—	PF63 65.00				
1960	1,000,000	—	—	0.15	0.35	1.00
1960	—	PF63 65.00				
1961	1,200,000	—	—	0.15	0.35	1.00
1961	—	PF63 65.00				
1962	2,000,000	—	—	0.15	0.35	1.00
1962	—	PF63 90.00				
1963	3,000,000	—	—	0.15	0.40	1.00
1963	—	PF63 82.50				
1965	4,000,000	—	—	0.15	0.30	1.00
1966	2,000,000	—	—	0.15	0.30	1.00
1967	3,000,000	—	—	0.15	0.30	1.00
1967	15,000	PF63 3.25				

KM# 17 50 AURAR

2.40 g., Nickel-Brass, 19.04 mm. **Obv:** Leaves flank denomination **Rev:** Arms within wreath **Edge:** Reeded

Date	Mintage	VF20	XF40	MS60	MS63	MS65
1969	2,000,000	—	0.15	0.60	1.25	—
1970	2,000,000	—	0.15	0.60	1.25	—
1971	2,000,000	—	0.15	0.60	1.25	—
1973	1,000,000	—	0.15	0.60	1.25	—
1974	2,000,000	—	0.15	0.60	1.25	—
1974	15,000	PF65 3.25				

KM# 12 KRÓNA

4.75 g., Aluminum-Bronze, 22.3 mm. **Obv:** Leaves flank denomination **Rev:** Arms with supporters **Edge:** Reeded

Date	Mintage	F12	VF20	XF40	MS60	MS63
1946	2,175,000	—	0.15	0.60	1.75	3.50
1946	—	PF63 500				

KM# 12a KRÓNA

4.75 g., Nickel-Brass, 22.3 mm. **Obv:** Denomination, leaves flank **Rev:** Shield with supporters, date below **Edge:** Reeded **Note:** Values for the 1957-63 proof issues are for impaired proofs. Brilliant proofs may bring 3 to 4 times these figures.

Date	Mintage	F12	VF20	XF40	MS60	MS63
1957	1,000,000	0.15	0.30	0.50	2.00	3.50
1957	—	PF65 120				
1959	500,000	0.15	0.20	0.75	2.00	3.50
1959	—	PF65 120				
1961	500,000	0.15	0.20	0.75	2.00	3.50
1961	—	PF65 120				
1962	1,000,000	0.15	0.15	0.20	0.60	1.00
1962	—	PF65 120				
1963	1,500,000	—	0.10	0.15	0.50	1.00
1963	—	PF65 120				
1965	2,000,000	—	—	0.15	0.50	1.00
1966	2,000,000	—	—	0.15	0.50	1.00
1969	2,000,000	—	—	0.15	0.25	1.00
1970	3,000,000	—	—	0.15	0.25	1.00
1971	2,500,000	—	—	0.15	0.25	1.00
1973	2,500,000	—	—	0.15	0.50	1.00
Note: Large round-knob 3						
1973	3,500,000	—	—	0.15	0.25	1.00
Note: Thin, square-end 3						
1974	5,000,000	—	—	0.15	0.25	1.00
1975	10,500,000	—	—	0.15	0.25	1.00
1975	15,000	PF65 4.25				

KM# 23 KRÓNA

0.57 g., Aluminum, 16.01 mm. **Obv:** Leaves flank denomination **Rev:** Arms with supporters **Edge:** Reeded

Date	Mintage	VF20	XF40	MS60	MS63	MS65
1976	10,000,000	—	0.10	0.20	0.30	1.00
1977	10,000,000	—	0.10	0.20	0.30	1.00
1978	13,000,000	—	0.10	0.20	0.30	1.00
1980	7,225,000	—	0.10	0.20	0.30	1.00
1980	15,000	PF65 3.25				

KM# 13 2 KRÓNUR

9.50 g., Aluminum-Bronze, 28 mm. **Obv:** Leaves flank denomination **Rev:** Arms with supporters **Edge:** Reeded

Date	Mintage	F12	VF20	XF40	MS60	MS63
1946	1,086,000	0.20	0.40	0.80	3.50	7.50
1946	—	PF63 525				

KM# 13a.1 2 KRÓNUR
9.50 g., Nickel-Brass, 28 mm. **Obv:** Leaves flank denomination **Rev:** Arms with supporters **Edge:** Reeded **Note:** Values for the 1958-63 proof issues are for impaired proofs. Brilliant proofs may bring 3 to 4 times these figures.

Date	Mintage	F12	VF20	XF40	MS60	MS63
1958	500,000	0.20	0.50	1.00	3.00	5.00
1958	—	PF63 135				
1962	500,000	0.20	0.50	1.00	3.00	5.00
1962	—	PF63 130				
1963	750,000	0.15	0.30	0.60	2.00	3.50
1963	—	PF63 130				
1966	1,000,000	0.10	0.20	0.40	1.50	2.50
1966	15,000	PF63 3.25				

KM# 13a.2 2 KRÓNUR
11.50 g., Nickel-Brass, 28 mm. **Obv:** Leaves flank denomination **Rev:** Arms with supporters **Edge:** Reeded **Note:** Thick planchet.

Date	Mintage	F12	VF20	XF40	MS60	MS63
1966	300	—	—	425	500	750

KM# 18 5 KRÓNUR
4.00 g., Copper-Nickel **Obv:** Leaves flank denomination **Rev:** Arms with supporters

Date	Mintage	VF20	XF40	MS60	MS63	MS65
1969	2,000,000	0.20	0.35	0.55	1.00	—
1970	1,000,000	0.20	0.35	0.55	1.00	—
1971	500,000	0.25	0.60	1.25	2.00	—
1973	1,100,000	0.15	0.25	0.45	1.00	—
1974	1,200,000	0.15	0.20	0.30	1.00	—
1975	1,500,000	0.15	0.20	0.30	1.00	—
1976	500,000	0.15	0.25	0.45	1.00	—
1977	1,000,000	0.15	0.20	0.30	1.00	—
1978	4,672,000	0.15	0.20	0.30	1.00	—
1980	2,400,000	0.15	0.20	0.30	1.00	—
1980	15,000	PF65 4.00				

KM# 15 10 KRÓNUR
6.52 g., Copper-Nickel, 25 mm. **Obv:** Leaves flank denomination **Rev:** Arms with supporters

Date	Mintage	VF20	XF40	MS60	MS63	MS65
1967	1,000,000	0.30	0.60	1.00	1.75	3.00
1969	500,000	0.40	1.00	1.50	3.00	5.00
1970	1,500,000	0.20	0.40	0.75	1.25	2.50
1971	1,500,000	0.20	0.40	0.75	1.25	2.50
1973	1,500,000	0.20	0.40	0.75	1.25	2.50
1974	2,000,000	0.20	0.30	0.40	0.65	1.00
1975	2,500,000	0.20	0.30	0.40	0.65	1.00
1976	2,500,000	0.20	0.30	0.40	0.65	1.00
1977	2,000,000	0.20	0.30	0.40	0.65	1.00
1978	10,500,000	0.20	0.30	0.40	0.65	1.00
1980	4,600,000	0.20	0.30	0.40	0.65	1.00
1980	15,000	PF65 3.25				

KM# 16 50 KRÓNUR
12.50 g., Nickel, 30 mm. **Subject:** 50th Anniversary of Sovereignty **Obv:** Denomination **Rev:** Parliament Building in Reikjavik

Date	Mintage	VF20	XF40	MS60	MS63	MS65
1968	100,000	2.75	4.50	7.50	12.00	—

KM# 19 50 KRÓNUR
12.38 g., Copper-Nickel, 30 mm. **Obv:** Denomination **Rev:** Parliament Building in Reykjavic

Date	Mintage	VF20	XF40	MS60	MS63	MS65
1970	800,000	0.60	1.25	1.50	2.25	5.00
1971	500,000	0.60	1.25	1.75	2.75	5.00
1973	50,000	1.75	2.75	3.25	4.50	7.50
1974	200,000	0.75	1.25	1.50	2.25	5.00
1975	500,000	0.45	0.85	1.25	1.75	3.50
1976	500,000	0.45	0.85	1.25	1.75	3.50
1977	200,000	0.45	0.85	1.25	1.75	3.50
1978	2,040,000	0.45	0.60	1.00	1.25	2.50
1980	1,500,000	0.45	0.60	1.00	1.25	2.50
1980	15,000	PF65 3.50				

KM# 14 500 KRÓNUR
8.96 g., 0.900 Gold 0.2593 oz. AGW **Subject:** Jon Sigurdsson Sesquicentennial **Obv:** Arms with supporters **Rev:** Head right

Date	Mintage	VF20	XF40	MS60	MS63	MS65
ND-1961	10,000	—	—	—	450	500
ND-1961	—	PF65 950				

KM# 20 500 KRÓNUR
20.00 g., 0.925 Silver 0.5948 oz. ASW **Subject:** 1100th Anniversary - 1st Settlement **Obv:** Quartered design of eagle, dragon, bull and giant **Rev:** Female and cow

Date	Mintage	VF20	XF40	MS60	MS63	MS65
ND-1974	70,000	—	—	—	13.00	15.00
ND-1974	Est. 58000	PF65 18.00				

Note: 17,000 proof coins were remelted

KM# 21 1000 KRÓNUR
30.00 g., 0.925 Silver 0.8922 oz. ASW **Subject:** 1100th Anniversary - 1st Settlement **Obv:** Quartered design of eagle, dragon, bull and giant **Rev:** Two Vikings and fire

Date	Mintage	VF20	XF40	MS60	MS63	MS65
ND-1974	70,000	—	—	—	20.00	24.50
ND-1974	—	PF65 27.50				

Note: 17,000 proof coins were remelted

KM# 22 10000 KRÓNUR
15.50 g., 0.900 Gold 0.4485 oz. AGW **Subject:** 1100th Anniversary - 1st Settlement **Obv:** Quartered design of eagle, dragon, bull, giant **Rev:** Ingulfur Arnason getting ready to throw his home posts on the beach

Date	Mintage	VF20	XF40	MS60	MS63	MS65
ND-1974	12,000	—	—	—	600	630
ND-1974	8,000	PF65 690				

REFORM COINAGE

100 Old Kronur = 1 New Krona

KM# 24 5 AURAR
1.50 g., Bronze, 14.58 mm. **Obv:** Eagle with upraised wing **Rev:** Denomination on Skate **Edge:** Plain

Date	Mintage	VF20	XF40	MS60	MS63	MS65
1981	15,000,000	—	—	—	0.45	1.25
1981	15,000	PF65 3.50				

KM# 25 10 AURAR
2.00 g., Bronze, 16.95 mm. **Obv:** Bulls head facing **Rev:** Flying squid **Edge:** Plain

Date	Mintage	VF20	XF40	MS60	MS63	MS65
1981	50,000,000	—	—	—	0.55	1.20
1981	15,000	PF65 5.50				

KM# 26 50 AURAR
3.00 g., Bronze, 20 mm. **Obv:** Dragon's head right **Rev:** Northern shrimp

Date	Mintage	VF20	XF40	MS60	MS63	MS65
1981	10,000,000	—	0.15	0.25	0.65	1.25
1981	15,000	PF65 6.50				

KM# 26a 50 AURAR
2.66 g., Bronze Coated Steel, 20 mm. **Obv:** Dragons head right **Rev:** Northern shrimp

Date	Mintage	VF20	XF40	MS60	MS63	MS65
1986	2,144,000	—	—	0.20	0.60	1.20

KM# 27 KRÓNA
4.50 g., Copper-Nickel, 21.5 mm. **Obv:** Giant facing **Rev:** Cod **Edge:** Reeded

Date	Mintage	VF20	XF40	MS60	MS63	MS65
1981	18,000,000	—	0.20	0.40	0.85	1.75
1981	15,000	PF65 8.50				

Date	Mintage	VF20	XF40	MS60	MS63	MS65
1984	7,000,000	—	0.20	0.40	0.85	1.65
1987	7,500,000	—	0.20	0.40	0.85	1.65

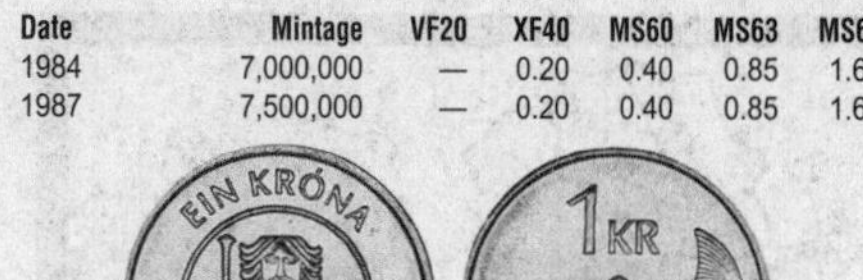

KM# 27a KRÓNA

4.00 g., Nickel Plated Steel, 21.5 mm. **Obv:** Giant facing **Rev:** Cod **Edge:** Reeded

Date	Mintage	VF20	XF40	MS60	MS63	MS65
1989	5,000,000	—	—	0.40	0.85	1.70
1991	5,180,000	—	—	0.40	0.85	1.70
1992	5,000,000	—	—	0.40	0.85	1.70
1994	5,000,000	—	—	0.40	0.85	1.70
1996	6,000,000	—	—	0.40	0.85	1.70
1999	10,000,000	—	—	0.40	0.85	1.70
2000	10,000	—	—	1.00	1.60	2.25

KM# 28 5 KRÓNUR

6.50 g., Copper-Nickel, 24.5 mm. **Obv:** Quartered design of Eagle, dragon, bull and giant **Rev:** Two dolphins leaping left **Edge:** Reeded

Date	Mintage	VF20	XF40	MS60	MS63	MS65
1981	4,350,000	—	0.30	1.00	1.60	2.75
1981	15,000	PF65 10.00				
1984	1,000,000	—	0.30	1.00	1.60	2.75
1987	3,000,000	—	0.30	1.00	1.60	2.75
1992	2,000,000	—	0.30	1.00	1.60	2.75

KM# 28a 5 KRÓNUR

5.60 g., Nickel Plated Steel, 24.5 mm. **Obv:** Quartered design of Eagle, dragon, bull and giant **Rev:** Two dolphins leaping left **Edge:** Reeded

Date	Mintage	VF20	XF40	MS60	MS63	MS65
1996	1,500,000	—	—	1.00	1.60	2.25
1999	2,000,000	—	—	1.00	1.60	2.25
2000	10,000	—	—	1.25	2.25	3.25

KM# 29.1 10 KRÓNUR

8.00 g., Copper-Nickel, 27.5 mm. **Obv:** Quartered design of Eagle, dragon, bull and giant **Rev:** Four capelins left **Edge:** Reeded

Date	Mintage	VF20	XF40	MS60	MS63	MS65
1984	10,000,000	—	0.40	0.75	1.85	3.25
1987	7,500,000	—	0.40	0.75	1.85	3.25
1994	2,500,000	—	0.40	0.75	1.85	3.25

KM# 29.2 10 KRÓNUR

8.00 g., Copper-Nickel, 24.5 mm. **Obv:** Quartered design of Eagle, dragon, bull and giant **Rev:** Four capelins left **Edge:** Reeded **Note:** Struck on flan of Indian Rupee in error.

Date	Mintage	VF20	XF40	MS60	MS63	MS65
1984	Inc. above	—	125	185	275	—

KM# 29.1a 10 KRÓNUR

7.00 g., Nickel Plated Steel, 27.5 mm. **Obv:** Quartered design of Eagle, dragon, bull and giant **Rev:** Four capelins left **Edge:** Reeded

Date	Mintage	VF20	XF40	MS60	MS63	MS65
1996	4,000,000	—	—	0.75	1.80	2.75
2000	10,000	—	—	1.50	2.75	4.00

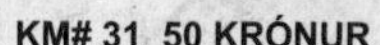

KM# 31 50 KRÓNUR

8.25 g., Nickel-Brass, 23 mm. **Obv:** Quartered design of eagle, dragon, bull and giant **Rev:** Crab **Edge:** Reeded

Date	Mintage	VF20	XF40	MS60	MS63	MS65
1987	4,000,000	—	—	1.50	3.50	5.00
1992	2,000,000	—	—	1.50	3.50	5.00
2000	10,000	—	—	3.50	5.25	7.50

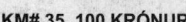

KM# 35 100 KRÓNUR

8.50 g., Nickel-Brass, 25.5 mm. **Obv:** Quartered design of Eagle, dragon, bull and giant **Rev:** Lumpfish left **Edge:** Reeded

Date	Mintage	VF20	XF40	MS60	MS63	MS65
1995	6,000,000	—	—	2.50	4.50	7.50
2000	10,000	—	—	5.00	7.00	12.00

KM# 30 500 KRÓNUR

20.00 g., 0.500 Silver 0.3215 oz. ASW, 35 mm. **Subject:** 100th Anniversary of Icelandic Banknotes **Obv:** Fishing vessel **Rev:** Seated figure with sword and shield

Date	Mintage	VF20	XF40	MS60	MS63	MS65
ND-1986	15,000	—	—	15.00	25.00	45.00

KM# 30a 500 KRÓNUR

20.00 g., 0.925 Silver 0.5948 oz. ASW, 35 mm. **Subject:** 100th Anniversary of Icelandic Banknotes **Obv:** Fishing vessel **Rev:** Seated figure with sword and shield

Date	Mintage	VF20	XF40	MS60	MS63	MS65
ND-1986	5,000	PF65 60.00	PF67 70.00			

KM# 32 1000 KRÓNUR

30.00 g., 0.925 Silver 0.8922 oz. ASW **Subject:** 50th Anniversary of Icelandic Republic - Sveinn Bjornsson **Obv:** Arms with supporters **Rev:** Head left **Note:** In sets only.

Date	Mintage	VF20	XF40	MS60	MS63	MS65
ND-1994	6,000	—	—	30.00	40.00	55.00
ND-1994	3,000	PF65 110	PF67 125			

KM# 33 1000 KRÓNUR

30.00 g., 0.925 Silver 0.8922 oz. ASW **Subject:** Asgeir Asgeirsson **Obv:** Arms with supporters **Rev:** Head left **Note:** In sets only.

Date	Mintage	VF20	XF40	MS60	MS63	MS65
ND-1994	6,000	—	—	30.00	40.00	55.00
ND-1994	3,000	PF65 110	PF67 125			

KM# 34 1000 KRÓNUR

30.00 g., 0.925 Silver 0.8922 oz. ASW **Subject:** Kristjan Eldjarn **Obv:** Arms with supporters **Rev:** Head left **Note:** In sets only.

Date	Mintage	VF20	XF40	MS60	MS63	MS65
ND-1994	6,000	—	—	30.00	40.00	55.00
ND-1994	3,000	PF65 110	PF67 125			

KM# 37 1000 KRÓNUR

26.73 g., 0.900 Silver 0.7734 oz. ASW **Subject:** Leif Ericsson Millennium **Note:** Struck in the U.S. at the Philadelphia Mint.

Date	Mintage	VF20	XF40	MS60	MS63	MS65
ND-2000	150,000	PF65 35.00	PF67 50.00			

KM# 36 10000 KRÓNUR

8.65 g., 0.900 Gold 0.2503 oz. AGW **Subject:** 1000 Years of Christianity **Obv:** Arms with supporters **Rev:** Old crosier top

Date	Mintage	VF20	XF40	MS60	MS63	MS65
ND-2000	3,000	PF65 385	PF67 425			

MINT SETS

KM#	Date	Mintage	Identification	Issue Price	Mkt Val
MS1	1930 (3)	10,000	KM#M1-M3	—	500
MS2	1970 (6)	—	KM#10a, 12a, 15, 17-19	—	10.00
MS3	1971 (6)	—	KM#10a, 12a, 15, 17-19	—	10.00
MS4	1973 (6)	—	KM#10a, 12a (knob 3), 15, 17-19	3.25	10.00
MS5	1974 (6)	—	KM#10a, 12a, 15, 17-19	3.25	10.00
MS6	1974 (2)	70,000	KM#20-21	40.00	45.00
MS7	1975 (4)	—	KM#12a, 15, 18-19	—	6.00
MS8	1976 (4)	—	KM#15, 18-19, 23	—	6.00
MS9	1977 (4)	—	KM#15, 18-19, 23	—	6.00
MS10	1978 (4)	—	KM#15, 18-19, 23	—	6.00
MS11	1980 (4)	—	KM#15, 18-19, 23	—	6.00
MS12	1981 (5)	—	KM#24-28	—	8.00
MS14	1994 (3)	6,000	KM#32-34	110	250
MS15	2000 (5)	10,000	KM#27a, 28a, 29.1a, 31, 35	—	35.00

PROOF SETS

KM#	Date	Mintage	Identification	Issue Price	Mkt Val
PS1	1974 (3)	8,000	KM#20-22	272	900
PS2	1974 (2)	58,000	KM#20-21	38.00	55.00
PS3	1966-1980 (11)	15,000	1966: KM#8-9, 13a.1; 1967: KM#11; 1974: KM#10a, 17; 1975: KM#12a; 1980: KM#15, 18-19, 23	40.50	40.00
PS4	1981 (5)	15,000	KM#24-28	32.00	37.50
PS5	1994 (3)	3,000	KM#32-34	155	385
PS6	2000 (2)	150,000	KM#37 and US Ericson Dollar	68.00	70.00

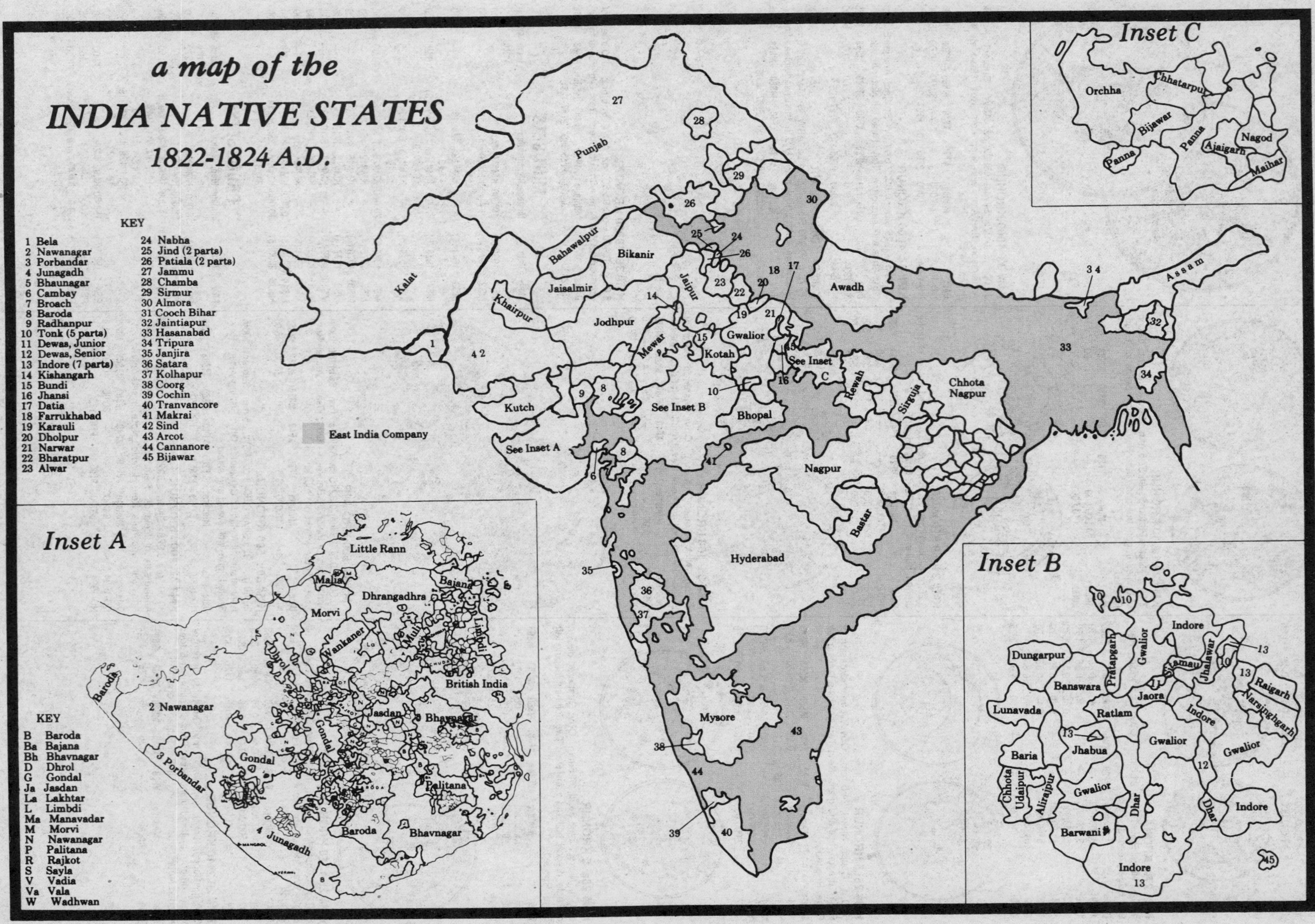

a map of the INDIA NATIVE STATES 1822-1824 A.D.

KEY

1 Bela
2 Nawanagar
3 Porbandar
4 Junagadh
5 Bhaunagar
6 Cambay
7 Broach
8 Baroda
9 Radhanpur
10 Tonk (5 parts)
11 Dewas, Junior
12 Dewas, Senior
13 Indore (7 parts)
14 Kishangarh
15 Bundi
16 Jhansi
17 Datia
18 Farrukhabad
19 Karauli
20 Dholpur
21 Narwar
22 Bharatpur
23 Alwar
24 Nabha
25 Jind (2 parts)
26 Patiala (2 parts)
27 Jammu
28 Chamba
29 Sirmur
30 Almora
31 Cooch Bihar
32 Jaintiapur
33 Hasanabad
34 Tripura
35 Janjira
36 Satara
37 Kolhapur
38 Coorg
39 Cochin
40 Tranvancore
41 Makrai
42 Sind
43 Arcot
44 Cannanore
45 Bijawar

East India Company

Inset A

KEY

B Baroda
Ba Bajana
Bh Bhavnagar
D Dhrol
G Gondal
Ja Jasdan
La Lakhtar
L Limbdi
Ma Manavadar
M Morvi
N Nawanagar
P Palitana
R Rajkot
S Sayla
V Vadia
Va Vala
W Wadhwan

Inset B

Inset C

MONETARY SYSTEMS

In each state, local rates of exchange prevailed. There was no fixed rate between copper, silver or gold coin, but the rates varied in accordance with the values of the metal and by the edict of the local authority.

Within the subcontinent, different regions used distinctive coinage standards. In North India and the Deccan, the silver rupee (11.6 g) and gold mohur (11.0 g) predominated. In Gujarat, the silver kori (4.7 g) and gold kori (6.4 g) were the main currency. In South India the silver fanam (0.7-1.0 g) and gold hun or Pagoda (3.4 g) were current. Copper coins in all parts of India were produced to a myriad of local metrologies with seemingly endless varieties.

NAZARANA ISSUES

Throughout the Indian Princely States listings are Nazarana designations for special full flan strikings of copper, silver and some gold coinage. The purpose of these issues was for presentation to the local monarch to gain favor. For example if one had an audience with one's ruler he would exchange goods, currency notes or the cruder struck circulating coinage for Nazarana pieces which he would present to the ruler as a gift. The borderline between true Nazarana pieces and well struck regular issues is often indistinct. The Nazaranas sometimes circulated alongside the cruder "dump" issues.

PRICING

As the demand for Indian Princely coinage develops, and more dealers handle the material, sale records and price lists enable a firmer basis for pricing most series. For scarcer types adequate sale records are often not available, and prices must be regarded as tentative. Inasmuch as date collectors of Princely States series are few, dates known to be scarce are usually worth little more than common ones. Coins of a dated type, which do not show the full date on their flans should be valued at about 70 per cent of the prices indicated.

DATING

Coins are dated in several eras. Arabic and Devanagari numerals are used in conjunction with the Hejira era (AH), the Vikrama Samvat (VS), Saka Samvat (Saka), Fasli era(FE) Mauludi era (AM), and Malabar era (ME), as well as the Christian era (AD).

GRADING

Copper coins are rarely found in high grade, as they were the workhorse of coinage circulation, and were everywhere used for day-to-day transactions. Moreover, they were carelessly struck and even when 'new', can often only be distinguished from VF coins with difficulty, if at all.

Silver coins were often hoarded and not infrequently, turn up in nearly as-struck condition. The silver coins of Hyderabad (dump coins) are common in high grades, and the rupees of some states are scarcer 'used' than 'new'. Great caution must be exercised in determining the value or scarcity of high grade dump coins.

Dump gold was rarely circulated, and usually occurs in high grades, or is found made into jewelry.

BAHAWALPUR

The Amirs of Bahawalpur established their independence from Afghan control towards the close of the 18th century. In the 1830's the state's independence under British suzerainty became guaranteed by treaty. With the creation of Pakistan in 1947 Bahawalpur, with an area of almost 17,500 square miles, became its premier Princely State. Bahawalpur State, named after its capital, stretched for almost three hundred miles along the left bank of the Sutlej, Panjnad and Indus rivers.

For earlier issues in the names of the Durrani rulers, see Afghanistan.

RULERS

Amirs

Alhaj Muhammad Bahawal Khan V, AH1317-1325/1899-1907AD

Sir Sadiq Muhammad Khan V, AH1325-1365/1907-1947AD

MINT

Bahawalpur

PRINCELY STATE

Alhaj Muhammad Bahawal Khan V

AH1317-1325 / 1899-1907AD

HAMMERED COINAGE

Bahawalpur

Y# 6 PAISA

Copper **Obv:** Legend in Persian **Obv. Legend:** Muhammad Bahawal ... **Mint:** Bahawalpur **Note:** For anonymous Paisas struck during the years of his reign, see Y#2.1, 2.2.

Date	Mintage	G4	VG8	F12	VF20	XF40
AH1324	—	—	5.00	10.00	15.00	25.00
AH1325	—	—	5.00	10.00	15.00	25.00

Anonymous

(Alhaj Muhammad Bahawal Khan V) 1899-1907

ANONYMOUS HAMMERED COINAGE

Y# 2.1 PAISA

Copper **Obv:** Star above cresent, flanked by sprigs **Rev:** Inscription divides date above **Shape:** Irregular or square **Mint:** Bahawalpur

Date	Mintage	G4	VG8	F12	VF20	XF40
AH1321	—	—	10.00	18.00	25.00	30.00
AH1325	—	—	10.00	18.00	25.00	30.00

Y# 2.2 PAISA

Copper **Shape:** Irregular or square **Mint:** Bahawalpur **Note:** Contemporary ND imitations exist.

Date	Mintage	G4	VG8	F12	VF20	XF40
ND(ca. 1909)	—	—	5.00	8.00	15.00	25.00

Y# 2.2a PAISA

Brass **Shape:** Irregular or square **Mint:** Bahawalpur **Note:** These may be modern counterfeits.

Date	Mintage	G4	VG8	F12	VF20	XF40
ND(ca.1909)	—	—	5.00	8.00	15.00	25.00

Sir Sadiq Muhammad Khan V

AH1325-1365 / 1907-1947AD

HAMMERED COINAGE

Y# 7.1 PAISA

Copper **Obv:** Legend in Persian **Obv. Legend:** Sadiq Muhammad ... **Mint:** Bahawalpur

Date	Mintage	G4	VG8	F12	VF20	XF40
AH1326	—	—	10.00	15.00	22.00	30.00
AH1327	—	—	10.00	15.00	22.00	30.00
AH1328	—	—	10.00	15.00	22.00	30.00

Y# 7.2 PAISA

Copper **Obv:** Legend in Persian **Obv. Legend:** Sadiq Muhammad ... **Rev:** Without date **Mint:** Bahawalpur

Date	Mintage	G4	VG8	F12	VF20	XF40
ND(ca. 1910)	—	—	10.00	15.00	22.00	30.00

Y# 7.3 PAISA

Copper **Obv:** Legend in Persian **Obv. Legend:** Sadiq Muhammad ... **Rev:** Without date or star **Mint:** Bahawalpur

Date	Mintage	G4	VG8	F12	VF20	XF40
ND(ca. 1910)	—	—	10.00	20.00	30.00	40.00

Y# 8 PAISA

Copper **Obv:** Toughra **Mint:** Bahawalpur

Date	Mintage	G4	VG8	F12	VF20	XF40
AH1342	—	—	3.00	7.00	12.00	15.00
AH1343	—	—	3.00	7.00	12.00	15.00

MILLED COINAGE

Y# 12 1/2 PICE

Copper **Obv:** Bust of Muhammad Bahawal Khan V left **Rev:** Toughra **Mint:** Bahawalpur

Date	Mintage	F12	VF20	XF40	MS60	MS63
AH1359	—	1.00	3.00	5.00	15.00	—
AH1359	—	PF60 500				

Y# 9 PAISA (1/4 Anna)

Copper or Bronze **Obv:** Toughra **Rev:** Three branches in square **Mint:** Bahawalpur

Date	Mintage	VG8	F12	VF20	XF40	MS60
AH1343	—	25.00	40.00	60.00	80.00	—

Y# 9a PAISA (1/4 Anna)

Brass **Obv:** Toughra **Rev:** Three branches in square **Mint:** Bahawalpur

Date	Mintage	VG8	F12	VF20	XF40	MS60
AH1343	—	25.00	40.00	60.00	80.00	—

Y# 13 1/4 ANNA (Paisa)

Copper **Obv:** Bust of Muhammad Bahawal Khan V left **Rev:** Toughra **Mint:** Bahawalpur

Date	Mintage	F12	VF20	XF40	MS60	MS63
AH1359	—	1.00	3.00	5.00	15.00	—
AH1359	—	PF60 500				

Y# 14 RUPEE

6.50 g., Silver **Obv:** Toughra **Mint:** Bahawalpur **Note:** Experts believe this issue is a modern concoction.

Date	Mintage	VF20	XF40	MS60	MS63	MS65
AH1343	—	—	30.00	60.00	90.00	125

Note: Varieties exist, both thick and thin

BARODA

Maratha state located in western India. The ruling line was descended from Damaji, a Maratha soldier, who received the title of "Distinguished Swordsman" in 1721 (hence the scimitar on most Baroda coins). The Baroda title "Gaikwara" comes from "gaikwar" or cow herd, Damaji's father's occupation.

The Maratha rulers of Baroda, the Gaekwar family rose to prominence in the mid-18th century by carving out for themselves a dominion from territories, which were previously under the control of the Poona Marathas, and to a lesser extent, of the Raja of Jodhpur. Chronic internal disputes regarding the succession to the masnad culminated in the intervention of British troops in support of one candidate, Anand Rao Gaekwar, in 1800. Then, in 1802, an agreement with the East India Company released the Baroda princes from their fear of domination by the Maratha Peshwa of Poona but subordinated them to Company interests. Nevertheless, for almost the next century and a half Baroda maintained a good relationship with the British and continued as a major Princely State right up to 1947, when it acceded to the Indian Union.

RULERS

Gaekwars

Sayaji Rao III, AH1292-1357/VS1932-1995/1875-1938AD

Pratap Singh, VS1995-2008/1938-1951AD

PRINCELY STATE

Sayaji Rao III

AH1292-1357 / VS1932-95 / 1875-1938AD

MILLED COINAGE

Baroda

Y# 37 1/6 MOHUR

Gold, 14.5 mm. **Obv:** Crowned bust, right **Rev:** Inscription, scimitar, date within wreath **Mint:** Baroda **Note:** 1.04-1.18 grams.

Date	Mintage	VG8	F12	VF20	XF40	MS60
VS1959	—	—	750	1,100	1,500	—

Y# 38 1/3 MOHUR

Gold, 16 mm. **Obv:** Bust of Sayaji Rao III right **Mint:** Baroda **Note:** Weight varies: 2.07-2.39 grams.

Date	Mintage	VG8	F12	VF20	XF40	MS60
VS1959 (1902)	—	1,000	1,500	2,250	3,000	—

Y# 39 MOHUR

Gold, 21 mm. **Obv:** Crowned bust, right **Rev:** Inscription, scimitar, date within wreath **Mint:** Baroda **Note:** Weight varies: 6.20-6.40 grams.

Date	Mintage	VG8	F12	VF20	XF40	MS60
VS1959 (1902)	—	1,500	1,750	2,000	2,500	3,000

BHAUNAGAR

State located in northwest India on the west shore of the Gulf of Cambay.

The Thakurs of Bhaunagar, as the rulers were titled, were Gohel Rajputs. They traced their control of the area back to the 13th century. Under the umbrella of British paramountcy, the Thakurs of Bhaunagar were regarded as relatively enlightened rulers. The State was absorbed into Saurashtra in February 1948.

Anonymous Types: Bearing the distinguishing Nagari legend *Bahadur* in addition to the Mughal legends.

MONETARY SYSTEM

2 Trambiyo = 1 Dokda

1-1/2 Dokda = 1 Dhingla

PRINCELY STATE

Thakurs of Bhaunagar

Gohel Rajputs

ANONYMOUS HAMMERED COINAGE

KM# 1 DOKDA

Copper **Mint:** (no Mint Information)

Date	Mintage	G4	VG8	F12	VF20	XF40
VS2004(1947)	—	30.00	40.00	50.00	80.00	100

BUNDI

State in Rajputana in northwest India.

Bundi was founded in 1342 by a Chauhan Rajput, Rao Dewa (Deoraj). Until the Maratha defeat early in the 19th century, Bundi was greatly harassed by the forces of Holkar and Sindhia. In 1818 it came under British protection and control and remained so until 1947. In 1948 the State was absorbed into Rajasthan.

RULERS

Raghubir Singh VS1946-1984/1889-1927AD

Ishwari Singh VS1984-2004/1927-1947AD

MINT

PERSO-ARABIC DEVANAGARI

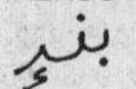
बुन्दी

Bundi

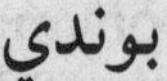

Mintname: Bundi

PRINCELY STATE

Edward VII

1901-1910AD

HAMMERED COINAGE

Regal Style

Y# A12 1/2 PAISA

Copper **Obv:** Katar **Obv. Legend:** EDWARD VII EMPEROR **Note:** Weight varies: 4.70-5.10 grams.

Date	Mintage	G4	VG8	F12	VF20	XF40
NDVS1963 (1906)	—	—	2.00	4.00	7.00	10.00
VS1965 (1908)	—	—	2.00	4.00	7.00	10.00
VS1966 (1909)	—	—	2.00	4.00	7.00	10.00
VS1967 (1910)	—	—	2.00	4.00	7.00	10.00
VS1973 (1916)	—	—	2.00	4.00	7.00	10.00
VS1974 (1917)	—	—	2.00	4.00	7.00	10.00
VS1976 (1918)	—	—	2.00	4.00	7.00	10.00

Y# B11 1/4 RUPEE

Silver **Obv:** Seated figure holding katar **Obv. Legend:** EMPEROR-EDWARD VII **Note:** Weight varies: 2.65-2.70 grams.

Date	Mintage	G4	VG8	F12	VF20	XF40
VS1958	—	—	30.00	45.00	60.00	75.00
VS1959	—	—	30.00	45.00	60.00	75.00
VS1961	—	—	30.00	45.00	60.00	75.00
VS1962	—	—	30.00	45.00	60.00	75.00

Y# 12 1/4 RUPEE

Silver **Obv:** Katar **Obv. Legend:** EDWARD VII EMPEROR **Note:** Weight varies: 2.65-2.70 grams.

Date	Mintage	G4	VG8	F12	VF20	XF40
VS1963	—	—	30.00	40.00	50.00	60.00
VS1964	—	—	30.00	40.00	50.00	60.00
VS1965	—	—	30.00	40.00	50.00	60.00
VS1966	—	—	30.00	40.00	50.00	60.00

Y# A11 1/2 RUPEE

Silver, 16-18 mm. **Obv:** Seated figure holding katar **Obv. Legend:** EMPEROR-EDWARD VII **Note:** Weight varies: 5.30-5.40 grams.

Date	Mintage	G4	VG8	F12	VF20	XF40
VS1958	—	—	50.00	100	200	300

Y# 13 1/2 RUPEE

Silver, 16-18 mm. **Obv:** Katar **Obv. Legend:** EDWARD VII EMPEROR **Note:** Weight varies: 5.30-5.40 grams.

Date	Mintage	G4	VG8	F12	VF20	XF40
VS1963	—	—	30.00	40.00	50.00	60.00
VS1964	—	—	30.00	40.00	50.00	60.00
VS1965	—	—	30.00	40.00	50.00	60.00
VS1966	—	—	30.00	40.00	50.00	60.00

Y# 11 RUPEE

Silver, 21-25 mm. **Obv:** Seated figure holding katar **Obv. Legend:** EMPEROR-EDWARD VII **Note:** Weight varies: 10.60-10.70 grams. Size varies.

Date	Mintage	G4	VG8	F12	VF20	XF40
VS1958	—	—	30.00	40.00	50.00	60.00
VS1959	—	—	30.00	40.00	50.00	60.00
VS1960	—	—	30.00	40.00	50.00	60.00
VS1961	—	—	30.00	40.00	50.00	60.00
VS1962	—	—	30.00	40.00	50.00	60.00
VS1963	—	—	30.00	40.00	50.00	60.00

Y# 14 RUPEE

Silver, 18-21 mm. **Obv:** Katar **Obv. Legend:** EDWARD VII EMPEROR **Note:** Weight varies: 10.60-10.70 grams. Size varies.

Date	Mintage	G4	VG8	F12	VF20	XF40
VS1963	—	—	20.00	30.00	40.00	50.00
VS1964	—	—	20.00	30.00	40.00	50.00
VS1965	—	—	20.00	30.00	40.00	50.00
VS1966	—	—	20.00	30.00	40.00	50.00
VS1967	—	—	20.00	30.00	40.00	50.00
VS1968	—	—	20.00	30.00	40.00	50.00
VS1969	—	—	20.00	30.00	40.00	50.00

Y# 11a NAZARANA RUPEE

Silver **Obv:** Seated figure holding katar **Obv. Legend:** EMPEROR-EDWARD VII **Shape:** Broad, square flan **Note:** Weight varies: 10.60-10.70 grams.

Date	Mintage	G4	VG8	F12	VF20	XF40
VS1962	—	—	300	400	500	600

Y# 14a NAZARANA RUPEE

Silver **Obv:** Katar **Obv. Legend:** EDWARD VII EMPEROR **Note:** Weight varies: 10.60-10.70 grams. Struck on square flan.

Date	Mintage	G4	VG8	F12	VF20	XF40
VS1965	—	—	200	300	450	600
VS1966	—	—	200	300	450	600
VS1967	—	—	200	300	450	600
VS1968	—	—	200	300	450	600
VS1969	—	—	200	300	450	600
VS1970	—	—	200	300	450	600

George V

1910-1936AD

Y# 15.1 1/2 PAISA

Copper **Obv:** Katar **Obv. Legend:** EMPEROR-GEORGE V **Shape:** Rectangular or square **Note:** Weight varies: 5.00-5.35 grams.

Date	Mintage	G4	VG8	F12	VF20	XF40
VS1973	—	—	2.00	4.00	7.00	10.00
VS1974	—	—	2.00	4.00	7.00	10.00
VS1976	—	—	2.00	4.00	7.00	10.00
VS1977	—	—	2.00	4.00	7.00	10.00

Y# 15.2 1/2 PAISA

Copper **Obv:** Katar **Obv. Legend:** GEORGE V EMPEROR

Shape: Rectangular or square **Note:** Weight varies: 5.00-5.35 grams. Size varies.

Date	Mintage	G4	VG8	F12	VF20	XF40
VS1980	—	—	2.00	4.00	7.00	10.00
VS1981	—	—	2.00	4.00	7.00	10.00
VS1982	—	—	2.00	4.00	7.00	10.00
VS1983	—	—	2.00	4.00	7.00	10.00
VS1984	—	—	2.00	4.00	7.00	10.00
VS1986	—	—	2.00	4.00	7.00	10.00
VS1987	—	—	2.00	4.00	7.00	10.00
VS1988	—	—	2.00	4.00	7.00	10.00
VS1990	—	—	2.00	4.00	7.00	10.00
VS1991	—	—	2.00	4.00	7.00	10.00
VS1992	—	—	2.00	4.00	7.00	10.00

Y# 16.1 1/4 RUPEE
Silver **Obv:** Katar **Obv. Legend:** EMPEROR-GEORGE V **Note:** Weight varies: 2.60-2.70 grams.

Date	Mintage	G4	VG8	F12	VF20	XF40
VS1972	—	—	10.00	20.00	35.00	50.00
VS1973	—	—	10.00	20.00	35.00	50.00
VS1974	—	—	10.00	20.00	35.00	50.00

Y# 16.2 1/4 RUPEE
Silver **Obv:** Katar **Obv. Legend:** GEORGE V EMPEROR **Note:** Weight varies: 2.60-2.70 grams.

Date	Mintage	G4	VG8	F12	VF20	XF40
VS1980	—	—	10.00	20.00	35.00	50.00
VS1981	—	—	10.00	20.00	35.00	50.00
VS1982	—	—	10.00	20.00	35.00	50.00

Y# A19 1/4 RUPEE
Silver, 13 mm. **Obv:** Date 1925 at center **Obv. Legend:** EMPEROR GEORGE V **Note:** Weight varies: 2.60-2.70 grams.

Date	Mintage	G4	VG8	F12	VF20	XF40
VS1915	—	—	10.00	20.00	35.00	50.00

Y# 17.1 1/2 RUPEE
Silver **Note:** Weight varies: 5.30-5.40 grams.

Date	Mintage	G4	VG8	F12	VF20	XF40
VS1972	—	—	25.00	35.00	45.00	60.00
VS1973	—	—	25.00	35.00	45.00	60.00
VS1974	—	—	25.00	35.00	45.00	60.00
VS1979	—	—	25.00	35.00	45.00	60.00

Y# 17.2 1/2 RUPEE
Silver **Obv:** Legend arranged differently **Note:** Weight varies: 5.30-5.40 grams.

Date	Mintage	G4	VG8	F12	VF20	XF40
VS1979	—	—	25.00	35.00	45.00	60.00
VS1980	—	—	25.00	35.00	45.00	60.00
VS1981	—	—	25.00	35.00	45.00	60.00
VS1982	—	—	25.00	35.00	45.00	60.00
VS1983	—	—	25.00	35.00	45.00	60.00
VS1984	—	—	25.00	35.00	45.00	60.00

Y# 19 1/2 RUPEE
Silver **Obv:** Date 1925 at center **Obv. Legend:** EMPEROR GEORGE V **Note:** Weight varies: 5.30-5.40 grams.

Date	Mintage	G4	VG8	F12	VF20	XF40
VS1915	—	—	100	150	200	300

Y# 18.1 RUPEE
Silver **Obv:** Katar **Obv. Legend:** EMPEROR GEORGE V **Note:** Weight varies: 10.60-10.70 grams.

Date	Mintage	G4	VG8	F12	VF20	XF40
VS1972	—	—	20.00	30.00	40.00	60.00
VS1973	—	—	20.00	30.00	40.00	60.00
VS1974	—	—	20.00	30.00	40.00	60.00
VS1975	—	—	20.00	30.00	40.00	60.00
VS1979	—	—	20.00	30.00	40.00	60.00

Y# 18.2 RUPEE
Silver **Obv:** Katar **Obv. Legend:** GEORGE V EMPEROR **Note:** Weight varies: 10.60-10.70 grams.

Date	Mintage	G4	VG8	F12	VF20	XF40
VS1979	—	—	20.00	30.00	40.00	60.00
VS1980	—	—	20.00	30.00	40.00	60.00
VS1981	—	—	20.00	30.00	40.00	60.00
VS1982	—	—	20.00	30.00	40.00	60.00
VS1983	—	—	20.00	30.00	40.00	60.00
VS1984	—	—	20.00	30.00	40.00	60.00
VS1985	—	—	20.00	30.00	40.00	60.00
VS1987	—	—	20.00	30.00	40.00	60.00
VS1989	—	—	20.00	30.00	40.00	60.00

Y# 20 RUPEE
Silver **Obv:** Date "1925" at center **Obv. Legend:** EMPEROR GEORGE V **Note:** Weight varies: 10.60-10.70 grams.

Date	Mintage	G4	VG8	F12	VF20	XF40
VS1915	—	—	200	300	400	500

Y# 18a.1 NAZARANA RUPEE
Silver **Obv:** Katar **Obv. Legend:** EMPEROR GEORGE V **Shape:** Square **Note:** Weight varies: 10.55-10.80 grams.

Date	Mintage	G4	VG8	F12	VF20	XF40
VS1965	—	—	200	300	450	600
VS1971	—	—	200	300	450	600
VS1974	—	—	200	300	450	600
VS1975	—	—	200	300	450	600
VS1977	—	—	200	300	450	600

Y# 18a.2 NAZARANA RUPEE
Silver **Obv:** Katar **Obv. Legend:** GEORGE V **Shape:** Square **Note:** Weight varies: 10.55-10.80 grams.

Date	Mintage	G4	VG8	F12	VF20	XF40
VS1979	—	100	200	300	400	500
VS1980	—	100	200	300	400	500
VS1981	—	100	200	300	400	500
VS1983	—	100	200	300	400	500
VS1984	—	100	200	300	400	500
VS1987	—	100	200	300	400	500

Y# 20a NAZARANA RUPEE
Silver **Obv:** Date "1925" at center **Obv. Legend:** EMPEROR GEORGE V **Shape:** Square **Note:** Weight varies: 10.55-10.80 grams.

Date	Mintage	G4	VG8	F12	VF20	XF40
VS1915	—	—	200	300	400	500

CAMBAY

Khanbayat
Normal 0 0 1 69 397 3 1 487 11.1539

Although of very ancient origins as a port, located at the head of the Gulf of Cambay in West India, Cambay did not come into existence as a separate state until about 1730 after the breakdown of Mughal authority in Delhi. The nawabs of Cambay traced their ancestry to Momin Khan II, the last of the Muslim governors of Gujerat. The State came under British control after two decades of Maratha rule.

RULER
Ja'far Ali Khan, AH1297-1333/VS1937-1972/1880-1915AD

MINT
Mint: Khanbayat

PRINCELY STATE

Jafar Ali Khan

1880-1915AD

ANONYMOUS HAMMERED COINAGE

Y# 5 1/2 PAISA
Copper **Obv:** Persian inscription **Obv. Inscription:** Cambay **Rev:** Denomination in words **Note:** Varieties in countermark exist.

Date	Mintage	G4	VG8	F12	VF20	XF40
VS1963(1906)	—	10.00	15.00	20.00	25.00	30.00
VS1964(1907)	—	10.00	15.00	20.00	25.00	30.00

Y# 5a 1/2 PAISA
Copper **Obv:** Persian inscription **Obv. Inscription:** Cambay **Rev:** Denomination in numerals

Date	Mintage	G4	VG8	F12	VF20	XF40
VS1964(1907)	—	—	2.00	7.00	14.00	20.00
VS1965(1908)	—	—	2.00	7.00	14.00	20.00
VS1966(1909)	—	—	2.00	7.00	14.00	20.00

Y# 6 PAISA
Copper **Obv:** Persian inscription **Obv. Inscription:** Cambay **Note:** Varieties exist.

Date	Mintage	G4	VG8	F12	VF20	XF40
VS1962(1905)	—	2.00	4.00	5.00	6.00	10.00
VS1963(1906)	—	2.00	4.00	5.00	6.00	10.00
VS1964(1907)	—	2.00	4.00	5.00	6.00	10.00
VS1965(1908)	—	2.00	4.00	5.00	6.00	10.00
VS1966(1909)	—	2.00	4.00	5.00	6.00	10.00
VS1967 (1910)	—	2.00	4.00	5.00	6.00	10.00
VS1968(1911)	—	2.00	4.00	5.00	6.00	10.00
VS1970(1913)	—	2.00	4.00	5.00	6.00	10.00

HAMMERED COINAGE

Y# 10 RUPEE
Silver, 19-20 mm. **Obv:** Inscription **Obv. Inscription:** Ja'afar Ali Khan **Rev:** Mint name **Mint:** Cambay **Note:** Weight varies, 10.70-11.60 grams. Size varies.

Date	Mintage	G4	VG8	F12	VF20	XF40
AH1319//23	—	60.00	80.00	100	125	175

COUNTERMARKED COINAGE

Y# 2 1/4 PAISA
Copper **Shape:** Round flan **Countermark:** Persian "Shah" **Note:** Varieties in countermark exist.

CM Date	Host Date	G4	VG8	F12	VF20	XF40
ND		—	3.00	8.00	10.00	12.00

Y# 3 1/2 PAISA

Copper **Shape:** Round and square flans **Countermark:** Persian "Shah" **Note:** Varieties in countermark exist.

CM Date	Host Date	G4	VG8	F12	VF20	XF40
ND		—	3.00	8.00	10.00	12.00

DATIA

State located in north-central India, governed by Maharajas.

Datia was founded in 1735 by Bhagwan Das, son of Narsingh Dev of the Orchha royal house. In 1804 the State concluded its first treaty with the East India Company and thereafter came under British protection and control.

RULERS

Bhawani Singh, AH1274-1325/1857-1907AD
Govind Singh, AH1325-1368/1907-1948AD

MINT

Dalipnagar

Gaja Shahi Series

Struck for more than 100 years, with the AH date on the obverse and the regnal year on the reverse bearing little relationship to each other. These are close copies of Orchha C#24-32 and can only be distinguished by the symbols, which are always different from those of Orchha, except for the Gaja (mace):

Gaja always on reverse

On obverse (Datia Mint Symbol)

On reverse

BRITISH PROTECTORATE

HAMMERED COINAGE

Gaja Shahi Series

C# 36 1/4 RUPEE

Silver **Obv:** Inscription, date **Rev:** Inscription, mint mark **Mint:** (no Mint Information) **Note:** Weight varies: 2.68-2.90 grams.

Date	Mintage	G4	VG8	F12	VF20	XF40
AHxxxx//36 (1900-01)	—	—	50.00	75.00	110	150

Bhawani Singh

AH1274-1325 / 1857-1907AD

C# 22 1/2 PAISA

6.00 g., Copper **Obv:** Inscription **Rev:** Inscription **Mint:** (no Mint Information) **Note:** Weight varies 6.00-6.50 grams. Posthumous regnal years of Muhammad Akbar II.

Date	Mintage	G4	VG8	F12	VF20	XF40
AH1320(1902)	—	5.00	7.00	11.00	15.00	20.00

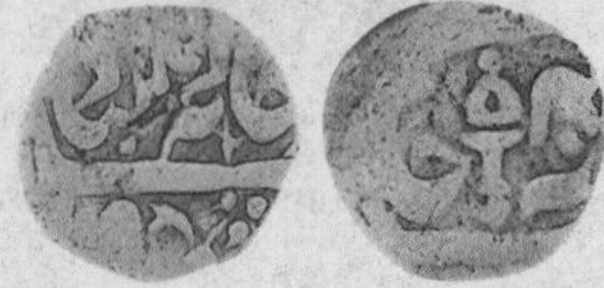

C# 23 PAISA

Copper **Obv:** Inscription **Rev:** Inscription, mint mark **Shape:** Round or square **Mint:** (no Mint Information) **Note:** Weight varies 12 - 13 grams. Regular and posthumous regnal years of Muhammad Akbar II.

Date	Mintage	G4	VG8	F12	VF20	XF40
AH1320 /46 (sic)	—	5.00	7.00	11.00	15.00	20.00

DEWAS

A Maratha state located in west-central India. The raja, the brother of the raja of Dewas Senior Branch had a palace in Dewas City. They descended from two brothers, Tukoji and Jiwaji who were given Dewas City in 1726 by Peshwa Baji Rao as a reward for army services.

Largely due to its geographical location Dewas suffered much at the hands of the armies of Holkar and Sindhia,and from Pindari incursions. In 1818 the State came under British protection.

LOCAL RULER

Vikrama Simha Rao, 1937-1948AD

BRITISH PROTECTORATE

Senior Branch

Narayan Rao

HAMMERED COINAGE

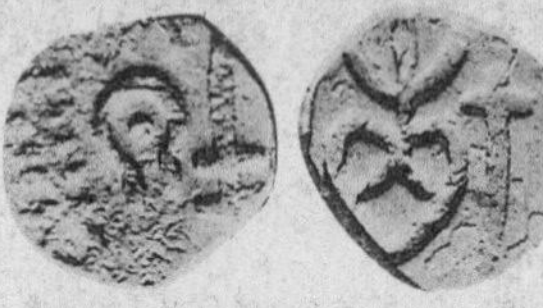

Allote

KM# 10 PAISA

Copper **Rev:** Heart, cross **Mint:** Allote **Note:** Weight varies 10.50-12.77 grams; varieties exist; struck at the Allote Mint.

Date	Mintage	G4	VG8	F12	VF20	XF40
ND(c.185)	—	10.00	15.00	25.00	40.00	60.00

Vikrama Simha Rao

VS1994-2005 / 1937-1948AD

MILLED COINAGE

Regal Style

KM# 13 PAISA

Copper **Obv:** Bust of Vikrama Simha Rao right **Rev:** Arms **Mint:** Allote

Date	Mintage	VG8	F12	VF20	XF40	MS60
2001/1944	—	—	500	750	1,100	1,500
2000/1944	—	—	500	750	1,100	1,500

DUNGARPUR

A district in northwest India which became part of Rajasthan in 1948.

The maharawals of Dungarpur were descended from the Mewar chieftains of the 12th century. In 1527 the upper Mahi basin was bifurcated to form the Princely States of Dungarpur and Banswara. Thereafter Dungarpur came successively under Mughal and Maratha control until in 1818 it came under British protection.

RULERS

Bijey Singh, VS1955-1975/1898-1918AD
Lakshman Singh, VS1975-2005/1918-1948AD

INSCRIPTION

Rajya Dungarpur

BRITISH PROTECTORATE

Lakshman Singh

VS1975-2005 / 1918-1948AD

HAMMERED COINAGE

KM# 9 NAZARANA MOHUR

11.00 g., Gold **Obv:** Sword and "jhar" to right **Rev. Inscription:** Rajya/Dungarpur **Mint:** (no Mint Information)

Date	Mintage	G4	VG8	F12	VF20	XF40
VS1996 (1939)	—	—	5,000	6,000	7,000	8,000

WW II EMERGENCY COINAGE

KM# 7 PAISA

Copper **Rev:** 2 bars above 'P' in "Paisa" **Mint:** (no Mint Information)

Date	Mintage	G4	VG8	F12	VF20	XF40
VS2001(1944)	—	20.00	40.00	60.00	80.00	100

KM# 8 PAISA

Copper **Rev:** One bar above 'P' in "Paisa" **Mint:** (no Mint Information)

Date	Mintage	G4	VG8	F12	VF20	XF40
VS2001(1944)	—	20.00	40.00	60.00	80.00	100

GWALIOR

Sindhia

State located in central India. Capital originally was Ujjain (= Daru-l-fath), but was later transferred to Gwalior in 1810. The Gwalior ruling family, the Sindhias, were descendants of the Maratha chief Ranoji Sindhia (d.1750). His youngest son, Mahadji Sindhia (d.1794) was anxious to establish his independence from the overlordship of the Peshwas of Poona. Unable to achieve this alone, it was the Peshwa's crushing defeat by Ahmad Shah Durrani at Panipat in 1761, which helped realize his ambitions. Largely in the interests of sustaining this autonomy, but partly as a result of a defeat at East India Company hands in 1781, Mahadji concluded an alliance with the British in 1782. In 1785, he reinstalled the fallen Mughal Emperor, Shah Alam, on the throne at Dehli. Very early in the 19th century, Gwalior's relationship with the British began to deteriorate, a situation which culminated in the Anglo-Maratha War of 1803. Gwalior's forces under Daulat Rao were defeated. In consequence, and by the terms of the peace treaty which followed, his territory was truncated. In 1818, Gwalior suffered a further loss of land at British hands. In the years that ensued, as the East India Company's possessions became transformed into empire and as the Pax Britannica swept across the subcontinent, the Sindhia family's relationship with their British overlords steadily improved.

RULERS

Madho Rao, VS1943-1982/1886-1925AD
Jivaji Rao, VS1982-2005/1925-1948AD

MINT

Gwalior Fort

KINGDOM

Madho Rao

VS1943-1982 / 1886-1925AD

MILLED COINAGE

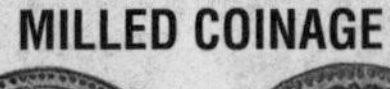

Gwalior Fort

KM# 164 1/2 PICE

Copper, 20 mm. **Obv:** Cobra above crossed spear and trident **Mint:** Gwalior Fort

Date	Mintage	G4	VG8	F12	VF20	XF40
VS1958	—	1.00	2.00	4.00	7.00	10.00

KM# 169 1/4 ANNA
Copper **Obv:** Cobra above crossed spear and trident

Date	Mintage	VG8	F12	VF20	XF40	MS60
VS1958	—	1.00	2.00	5.00	7.00	10.00

KM# 170 1/4 ANNA
6.60 g., Copper **Obv:** Bust of Madho Rao right **Rev:** Arms **Note:** Thick planchet, 2.2mm.

Date	Mintage	VG8	F12	VF20	XF40	MS60
VS1970	—	1.00	2.00	5.00	7.00	10.00

KM# 171 1/4 ANNA
5.10 g., Copper **Obv:** Bust of Madho Rao right **Rev:** Arms **Note:** Thin planchet, 1.6mm.

Date	Mintage	VG8	F12	VF20	XF40	MS60
VS1970	—	1.00	2.00	5.00	7.00	10.00
VS1974	—	1.00	2.00	5.00	7.00	10.00

KM# 172 1/4 ANNA
Copper **Obv:** Bust of Madho Rao right, continuous legend around portrait **Rev:** Arms

Date	Mintage	VG8	F12	VF20	XF40	MS60
VS1974	—	1.00	2.00	5.00	7.00	10.00

KM# 175 1/3 MOHUR
3.45 g., Gold **Obv:** Bust of Madho Rao right **Rev:** Arms

Date	Mintage	VG8	F12	VF20	XF40	MS60
VS1959	—	2,000	3,000	4,000	5,000	—

Jivaji Rao
VS1985-2005 / 1925-1948AD

KM# 176.1 1/4 ANNA
Copper **Obv:** Fine style bust of Jivaji Rao left **Rev:** Arms **Note:** Thick planchet. 4.65-5.15 grams.

Date	Mintage	VG8	F12	VF20	XF40	MS60
VS1986	—	—	0.75	1.50	3.00	6.00

KM# 176.2 1/4 ANNA
Copper **Obv:** Crude style "pug-nose" bust of Jivaji Rao left **Rev:** Arms

Date	Mintage	VG8	F12	VF20	XF40	MS60
VS1986	—	—	0.75	1.50	3.00	6.00

KM# 177 1/4 ANNA
Copper **Obv:** Crude style bust of Jivaji Rao left **Rev:** Arms **Note:** Thin planchet. 3.00-3.15 grams.

Date	Mintage	VG8	F12	VF20	XF40	MS60
VS1986	—	—	0.75	1.50	3.00	6.00
VS1999	—	—	0.75	1.50	3.00	6.00

KM# 178.1 1/4 ANNA
Copper **Obv:** Facing coiled cobras below bust of Jivaji Rao left **Rev:** Arms, without inscription on side

Date	Mintage	VG8	F12	VF20	XF40	MS60
VS1999	—	—	0.75	1.50	3.00	6.00

KM# 178.2 1/4 ANNA
Copper **Obv:** Without facing coiled cobras below bust of Jivaji Rao left **Rev:** Arms

Date	Mintage	VG8	F12	VF20	XF40	MS60
VS1999	—	—	0.75	1.50	3.00	6.00

KM# 179 1/2 ANNA
Brass **Obv:** Bust of Jivaji Rao left **Rev:** Arms

Date	Mintage	VG8	F12	VF20	XF40	MS60
VS1999	—	—	0.75	1.50	3.00	6.00
VS1999	—	PF63 500				

PATTERNS
Including off metal strikes

KM#	Date	Mintage	Identification	Mkt Val
Pn1	VS1977(1920)	—	4 Anna. Silver.	—

HYDERABAD

Haidarabad

Hyderabad State, the largest Indian State and the last remnant of Mughal suzeraintv in South or Central India, traced its foundation to Nizam-ul Mulk, the Mughal viceroy in the Deccan. From about 1724 the first nizam, as the rulers of Hyderabad came to be called, took advantage of Mughal decline in the North to assert an all but ceremonial independence of the emperor. The East India Company defeated Hyderabad's natural enemies, the Muslim rulers of Mysore and the Marathas, with the help of troops furnished under alliances between them and the Nizam. This formed the beginning of a relationship, which persisted for a century and a half until India's Independence. Hyderabad was the premier Princely State, with a population (in 1935) of fourteen and a half million. It was not absorbed into the Indian Union until 1948. Hyderabad City is located beside Golkonda, the citadel of the Qutb Shahi sultans until they were overthrown by Aurangzeb in 1687. A beautifully located city on the bank of the Musi river, the mint epithet was appropriately Farkhanda Bunyad, "of happy foundation".

Hyderabad exercised authority over a number of feudatories or samasthans. Some of these, such as Gadwal and Shorapur, paid tribute to both the Nizam and the Marathas. These feudatories were generally in the hands of local rajas whose ancestry predated the establishment of Hyderabad State. There were also many mints in the State, both private and government. There was little or no standardization of the purity of silver coinage until the 20th century. At least one banker, Pestonji Meherji by name, was distinguished by minting his own coins.

RULERS
Mir Mahbub Ali Khan II, AH1285-1329/1869-1911AD
Mir Usman Ali Khan, AH1329-1367/1911-1948AD

MINTS

فرخنده بنیاد حیدراباد

Haidarabad
Mint name: Farkhanda Bunyad Haidarabad

NIZAMATE
Mir Mahbub Ali Khan II
AH1285-1329 / 1869-1911AD
HAMMERED COINAGE

Haidarabad (Farkhanda Bunyad)

Y# 13 1/16 RUPEE
0.70 g., 0.818 Silver 0.0184 oz. ASW **Obv:** Persian letter "M" for Mahbub above "k" of "Mulk" **Obv. Inscription:** Asaf Jah, Nizam al-Mulk **Mint:** Haidarabad (Farkhanda Bunyad)

Date	Mintage	G4	VG8	F12	VF20	XF40
AH1321//37	—	—	150	200	250	300

Y# 14 1/8 RUPEE
1.40 g., 0.818 Silver 0.0367 oz. ASW **Obv:** Persian letter "M" for Mahbub above "k" of "Mulk" **Obv. Inscription:** Asaf Jah, Nizam al-Mulk **Mint:** Haidarabad (Farkhanda Bunyad)

Date	Mintage	G4	VG8	F12	VF20	XF40
AH1318	—	—	15.00	20.00	30.00	40.00
AH1321//37	—	—	15.00	20.00	30.00	40.00

Y# 15 1/4 RUPEE
2.79 g., 0.818 Silver 0.0735 oz. ASW **Obv:** Persian letter "M" for Mahbub above "k" of "Mulk" **Obv. Inscription:** Asaf Jah, Nizam al-Mulk **Mint:** Haidarabad (Farkhanda Bunyad)

Date	Mintage	G4	VG8	F12	VF20	XF40
AH1307//24 (sic)	—	—	15.00	20.00	30.00	40.00
AH1321//37	—	—	15.00	20.00	30.00	40.00

Y# 17 RUPEE
11.18 g., 0.818 Silver 0.294 oz. ASW **Obv:** Persian letter "M" for Mahbub above "k" of "Mulk" **Obv. Inscription:** Asaf Jah, Nizam al-Mulk **Mint:** Haidarabad (Farkhanda Bunyad)

Date	Mintage	G4	VG8	F12	VF20	XF40
AH1318//34	—	—	20.00	25.00	30.00	40.00

Y# 18 1/16 ASHRAFI
0.70 g., 0.910 Gold 0.0204 oz. AGW **Obv:** Persian letter "M" for Mahbub above "k" of "Mulk" **Obv. Inscription:** Asaf Jah, Nizam al-Mulk **Mint:** Haidarabad (Farkhanda Bunyad)

Date	Mintage	VG8	F12	VF20	XF40	MS60
AH1321//37	—	300	400	500	600	—

Y# 19 1/8 ASHRAFI
1.40 g., 0.910 Gold 0.0409 oz. AGW **Obv:** Persian letter "M" for Mahbub above "k" of "Mulk" **Obv. Inscription:** Asaf Jah, Nizam al-Mulk **Mint:** Haidarabad (Farkhanda Bunyad)

Date	Mintage	VG8	F12	VF20	XF40	MS60
AH1318	—	350	500	600	700	—
AH1320	—	350	500	600	700	—
AH1321	—	350	500	600	700	—

Y# 20 1/4 ASHRAFI
2.79 g., 0.910 Gold 0.0817 oz. AGW **Obv:** Persian letter "M" for Mahbub above "k" of "Mulk" **Obv. Inscription:** Asaf Jah, Nizam al-Mulk **Mint:** Haidarabad (Farkhanda Bunyad)

Date	Mintage	VG8	F12	VF20	XF40	MS60
AH1318//35 (sic)	—	450	600	700	800	—
AH1319//35	—	450	600	700	800	—

Y# 21 1/2 ASHRAFI
5.59 g., 0.910 Gold 0.1635 oz. AGW **Obv:** Persian letter "M" for Mahbub above "k" of "Mulk" **Obv. Inscription:** Asaf Jah, Nizam al-Mulk **Mint:** Haidarabad (Farkhanda Bunyad)

Date	Mintage	VG8	F12	VF20	XF40	MS60
AH1320	—	650	900	1,000	1,200	—
AH1321	—	650	900	1,000	1,200	—

Y# 22 ASHRAFI
11.18 g., 0.910 Gold 0.327 oz. AGW **Obv:** Persian letter "M" for Mahbub above "k" of "Mulk" **Obv. Inscription:** Asaf Jah, Nizam al-Mulk **Mint:** Haidarabad (Farkhanda Bunyad)

Date	Mintage	VG8	F12	VF20	XF40	MS60
AH1318	—	650	800	900	1,000	—
AH1319	—	650	800	900	1,000	—
AH1320	—	650	800	900	1,000	—
AH1321	—	650	800	900	1,000	—

MILLED COINAGE

Provisional Series

Y# 29 2 ANNAS
1.40 g., 0.818 Silver 0.0367 oz. ASW **Obv:** Persian letter "M" for Mahbub above "k" of "Mulk" **Obv. Inscription:** "Asaf Jah, Nizam al-Mulk", (Founder of the Nizami line) **Mint:** Haidarabad (Farkhanda Bunyad)

Date	Mintage	VG8	F12	VF20	XF40	MS60
AH1318//35 (sic)	—	50.00	80.00	100	125	—

Y# 30 4 ANNAS
2.79 g., 0.818 Silver 0.0735 oz. ASW **Obv:** Persian letter "M" for Mahbub above "k" of "Mulk" **Obv. Inscription:** Asaf Jah, Nizam al-Mulk **Mint:** Haidarabad (Farkhanda Bunyad)

Date	Mintage	VG8	F12	VF20	XF40	MS60
AH1318//32 (sic)	—	150	200	250	300	—
AH1318//34	—	150	200	250	300	—
AH1318//35 (sic)	—	150	200	250	300	—

Y# 31 8 ANNAS
5.59 g., 0.818 Silver 0.147 oz. ASW **Obv:** Persian letter "M" for Mahbub above "k" of "Mulk" **Obv. Inscription:** Asaf Jah, Nizam al-Mulk **Mint:** Haidarabad (Farkhanda Bunyad)

Date	Mintage	VG8	F12	VF20	XF40	MS60
AH1318//34	—	175	250	300	350	400
AH1318//34	—	175	250	300	350	400

Y# 32 RUPEE
11.18 g., 0.818 Silver 0.294 oz. ASW **Obv:** Inscription with Persian letter "M" for Mahbub above "k" of "Mulk" **Obv. Inscription:** Asaf Jah, Nizam al-Mulk **Mint:** Haidarabad (Farkhanda Bunyad)

Date	Mintage	G4	VG8	F12	VF20	XF40
AH1318//34	—	—	28.00	40.00	45.00	50.00

MILLED COINAGE

Standard Series

Year 25

Note: The AH date exists with two different regnal years in many cases.

Type I

Type II

The early renditions of the name of Asaf Jah in Type I included an accent bar at lower right. This was removed for Type II during the production year of AH 1328. Numerals for 92 appear above similar to earlier coinage not to be confused with regnal years or date.

Y# 34 PAI
Copper **Obv:** Toughra **Mint:** Haidarabad (Farkhanda Bunyad)

Date	Mintage	VG8	F12	VF20	XF40	MS60
AH1326//42	—	—	1.00	2.00	3.00	5.00
AH1327//42	—	—	1.00	2.00	3.00	5.00

Y# 35 2 PAI
Copper **Obv:** Toughra **Mint:** Haidarabad (Farkhanda Bunyad)

Date	Mintage	VG8	F12	VF20	XF40	MS60
AH1322//37	—	—	0.20	0.50	1.00	2.00
AH1322//38	—	—	0.20	0.50	1.00	2.00
AH1322//39 (sic)	—	—	0.20	0.50	1.00	2.00
AH1323//38	—	—	0.20	0.50	1.00	2.00
AH1323//39	—	—	0.20	0.50	1.00	2.00
AH1323//40 (sic)	—	—	0.20	0.50	1.00	2.00
AH1323//41(sic)	—	—	0.20	0.50	1.00	2.00
AH1324//39	—	—	0.20	0.50	1.00	2.00
AH1324//40	—	—	0.20	0.50	1.00	2.00
AH1324//41 (sic)	—	—	0.20	0.50	1.00	2.00
AH1325//40	—	—	0.20	0.50	1.00	2.00
AH1325//41	—	—	0.20	0.50	1.00	2.00
AH1328//42	—	—	0.20	0.50	1.00	2.00
AH1329//43 (sic)	—	—	0.20	0.50	1.00	2.00
AH1329//44	—	—	0.20	0.50	1.00	2.00
AH1329//45 (sic)	—	—	0.20	0.50	1.00	2.00

Y# 36 1/2 ANNA
Copper **Obv:** Toughra **Mint:** Haidarabad (Farkhanda Bunyad)

Date	Mintage	VG8	F12	VF20	XF40	MS60
AH1324//38 (sic)	—	1.00	2.00	3.00	5.00	7.00
AH1324//40	—	1.00	2.00	3.00	5.00	7.00
AH1325//40	—	1.00	2.00	3.00	5.00	7.00
AH1325//41 (sic)	—	1.00	2.00	3.00	5.00	7.00

Date	Mintage	VG8	F12	VF20	XF40	MS60
AH1324//41	—	1.00	2.00	3.00	5.00	7.00
AH1326//41	—	1.00	2.00	3.00	5.00	7.00
AH1329//44	—	1.00	2.00	3.00	5.00	7.00

Y# 37 2 ANNAS
1.39 g., 0.818 Silver 0.0366 oz. ASW, 15 mm. **Obv:** Char Minar gateway **Mint:** Haidarabad (Farkhanda Bunyad)

Date	Mintage	VG8	F12	VF20	XF40	MS60
AH1323//34	—	—	30.00	35.00	40.00	50.00
Note: R.Y. '34' error for '39'						
AH1323//39	—	—	30.00	35.00	40.00	50.00

Y# 38.1 4 ANNAS
2.79 g., 0.818 Silver 0.0735 oz. ASW, 20 mm. **Obv:** Char Minar gateway, signature variety Type I between minarets **Mint:** Haidarabad (Farkhanda Bunyad)

Date	Mintage	VG8	F12	VF20	XF40	MS60
AH1323//39	—	—	20.00	25.00	30.00	40.00
AH1326//43 (sic)	—	—	20.00	25.00	30.00	40.00

Y# 38.2 4 ANNAS
2.79 g., 0.818 Silver 0.0735 oz. ASW, 20 mm. **Obv:** Char Minar gateway, signature variety Type I between minarets **Mint:** Haidarabad (Farkhanda Bunyad) **Note:** Struck with dies of 1/2 Ashrafi.

Date	Mintage	VG8	F12	VF20	XF40	MS60
AH1324//40 Rare	—	—	—	—	—	—

Y# 38.3 4 ANNAS
2.79 g., 0.818 Silver 0.0735 oz. ASW, 20 mm. **Obv:** Char Minar gateway, signature variety Type II between minarets **Mint:** Haidarabad (Farkhanda Bunyad)

Date	Mintage	VG8	F12	VF20	XF40	MS60
AH1328//43	—	—	20.00	25.00	30.00	40.00
AH1329//44	—	—	20.00	25.00	30.00	40.00

Y# 39.1 8 ANNAS
5.59 g., 0.818 Silver 0.147 oz. ASW, 24 mm. **Obv:** Char Minar gateway, signature variety Type I **Mint:** Haidarabad (Farkhanda Bunyad)

Date	Mintage	VG8	F12	VF20	XF40	MS60
AH1322//38	—	—	300	400	600	800

Y# 39.2 8 ANNAS
5.59 g., 0.818 Silver 0.147 oz. ASW, 24 mm. **Obv:** Char Minar gateway, signature variety Type II between minarets **Mint:** Haidarabad (Farkhanda Bunyad)

Date	Mintage	VG8	F12	VF20	XF40	MS60
AH1328//43	—	—	100	125	150	200
AH1329//44	—	—	100	125	150	200

Y# 40.1 RUPEE
11.18 g., 0.818 Silver 0.294 oz. ASW, 30 mm. **Obv:** Char Minar gateway, signature variety Type I between minarets **Mint:** Haidarabad (Farkhanda Bunyad)

Date	Mintage	VG8	F12	VF20	XF40	MS60
AH1319//35	—	—	15.00	20.00	25.00	30.00

Date	Mintage	VG8	F12	VF20	XF40	MS60
AH1320//35	—	—	400	450	500	600
AH1321//37	—	—	15.00	20.00	25.00	30.00
AH1322//38 (sic)	—	—	15.00	20.00	25.00	30.00
AH1321//38	—	—	15.00	20.00	25.00	30.00
AH1323//39 (sic)	—	—	15.00	20.00	25.00	30.00
AH1322//39	—	—	15.00	20.00	25.00	30.00
AH1324//40	—	—	15.00	20.00	25.00	30.00
AH1323//40	—	—	40.00	60.00	90.00	120
AH1325//41	—	—	15.00	20.00	25.00	30.00
AH1326//41	—	—	15.00	20.00	25.00	30.00

Y# 40.2 RUPEE

11.18 g., 0.818 Silver 0.294 oz. ASW, 30 mm. **Obv:** Char Minar gateway, signature variety Type II between minarets **Mint:** Haidarabad (Farkhanda Bunyad)

Date	Mintage	VG8	F12	VF20	XF40	MS60
AH1328//43	—	—	15.00	20.00	25.00	30.00
AH1329//44	—	—	15.00	20.00	25.00	30.00

Y# 41.1 1/8 ASHRAFI

1.39 g., 0.910 Gold 0.0408 oz. AGW **Obv:** Char Minar gateway, signature variety Type I between minarets **Mint:** Haidarabad (Farkhanda Bunyad)

Date	Mintage	VG8	F12	VF20	XF40	MS60
AH1325//41	—	—	500	700	850	1,000

Y# 41.2 1/8 ASHRAFI

1.39 g., 0.910 Gold 0.0408 oz. AGW **Obv:** Char Minar gateway, signature variety Type II between minarets **Mint:** Haidarabad (Farkhanda Bunyad)

Date	Mintage	VG8	F12	VF20	XF40	MS60
AH1329//44	—	—	500	700	850	1,000

Y# 42.1 1/4 ASHRAFI

2.79 g., 0.910 Gold 0.0817 oz. AGW **Obv:** Char Minar gateway, signature variety Type I between minarets **Mint:** Haidarabad (Farkhanda Bunyad)

Date	Mintage	VG8	F12	VF20	XF40	MS60
AH1325//41	—	—	700	1,000	1,100	1,200

Y# 42.2 1/4 ASHRAFI

2.79 g., 0.910 Gold 0.0817 oz. AGW **Obv:** Char Minar gateway, signature variety Type II between minarets **Mint:** Haidarabad (Farkhanda Bunyad)

Date	Mintage	VG8	F12	VF20	XF40	MS60
AH1327//42	—	—	700	1,000	1,100	1,200
AH1328//43	—	—	700	1,000	1,100	1,200
AH1329//44	—	—	700	1,000	1,100	1,200

Y# 43.1 1/2 ASHRAFI

5.59 g., 0.910 Gold 0.1635 oz. AGW **Obv:** Char Minar gateway, signature variety Type I between minarets **Mint:** Haidarabad (Farkhanda Bunyad)

Date	Mintage	VG8	F12	VF20	XF40	MS60
AH1325//41	—	—	1,500	2,200	2,500	3,000
AH1326//41	—	—	1,500	2,200	2,500	3,000

Y# 43.2 1/2 ASHRAFI

5.59 g., 0.910 Gold 0.1635 oz. AGW **Obv:** Char Minar gateway, signature variety Type II between minarets **Mint:** Haidarabad (Farkhanda Bunyad)

Date	Mintage	VG8	F12	VF20	XF40	MS60
AH1328//43	—	—	1,500	2,200	2,500	3,000
AH1329//44	—	—	1,500	2,200	2,500	3,000

Y# 44.1 ASHRAFI

11.18 g., 0.910 Gold 0.327 oz. AGW **Obv:** Char Minar gateway, signature variety Type I between minarets **Mint:** Haidarabad (Farkhanda Bunyad)

Date	Mintage	VG8	F12	VF20	XF40	MS60
AH1325//41	—	—	2,500	3,500	4,000	4,500

Y# 44.2 ASHRAFI

11.18 g., 0.910 Gold 0.327 oz. AGW **Obv:** Char Minar gateway, signature variety Type II between minarets **Mint:** Haidarabad (Farkhanda Bunyad)

Date	Mintage	VG8	F12	VF20	XF40	MS60
AH1328//43	—	—	2,500	3,500	4,000	4,500
AH1329//44	—	—	2,500	3,500	4,000	4,500

Mir Usman Ali Khan

AH1329-1367 / 1911-1948AD

MILLED COINAGE

First Series

Y# 45 PAI

Bronze **Obv:** Toughra **Mint:** Haidarabad (Farkhanda Bunyad)

Date	Mintage	VG8	F12	VF20	XF40	MS60
AH1338	—	—	0.20	0.50	1.00	3.00
AH1344//15	—	—	0.20	0.50	1.00	3.00
AH1349//20	—	—	0.20	0.50	1.00	3.00
AH1352//23	—	—	0.20	0.50	1.00	3.00
AH1353//23 (sic)	—	—	0.20	0.50	1.00	3.00
AH1352//24	—	—	0.20	0.50	1.00	3.00
AH1353//24	—	—	0.20	0.50	1.00	3.00

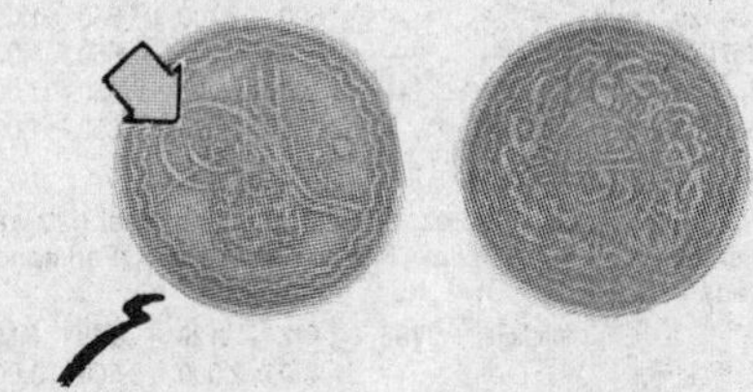

Y# 46 2 PAI

Bronze **Obv:** Short "Ain" in toughra **Mint:** Haidarabad (Farkhanda Bunyad) **Note:** See also 1 Rupee, Y#53 and Y#53a.

Date	Mintage	VG8	F12	VF20	XF40	MS60
AH1329//1	—	4.00	6.00	10.00	15.00	30.00
AH1330//1	—	4.00	6.00	10.00	15.00	30.00

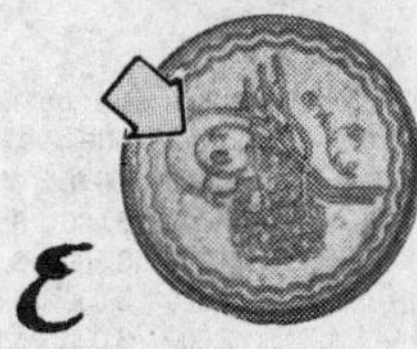
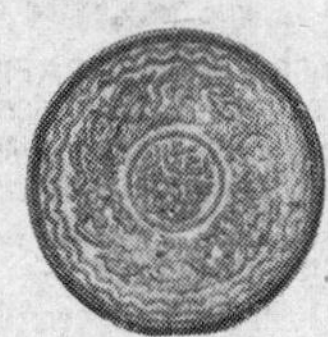

Y# 46a 2 PAI

3.90 g., Bronze **Obv:** Full "Ain" in toughra **Mint:** Haidarabad (Farkhanda Bunyad)

Date	Mintage	VG8	F12	VF20	XF40	MS60
AH1330//1	—	—	0.20	0.50	1.00	2.00
AH1330//2	—	—	0.20	0.50	1.00	2.00
AH1331//2	—	—	0.20	0.50	1.00	2.00
AH1331//3	—	—	0.20	0.50	1.00	2.00
AH1332//3	—	—	0.20	0.50	1.00	2.00
AH1333//3 (sic)	—	—	0.20	0.50	1.00	2.00
AH1332//4	—	—	0.20	0.50	1.00	2.00
AH1333//4	—	—	0.20	0.50	1.00	2.00
AH1334//3 (sic)	—	—	0.20	0.50	1.00	2.00
AH1333//5	—	—	0.20	0.50	1.00	2.00
AH1335//6	—	—	0.20	0.50	1.00	2.00
AH1336//7	—	—	0.20	0.50	1.00	2.00
AH1335//7	—	—	0.20	0.50	1.00	2.00
AH1337//7	—	—	0.20	0.50	1.00	2.00
AH1336//8	—	—	0.20	0.50	1.00	2.00
AH1337//8	—	—	0.20	0.50	1.00	2.00
AH1338//8	—	—	0.20	0.50	1.00	2.00
AH1338//9	—	—	0.20	0.50	1.00	2.00
AH1339//10	—	—	0.20	0.50	1.00	2.00
AH1338//11 (sic)	—	—	0.20	0.50	1.00	2.00
AH1339//11	—	—	0.20	0.50	1.00	2.00
AH1342//13	—	—	0.20	0.50	1.00	2.00
AH1342//14	—	—	0.20	0.50	1.00	2.00
AH1343//14	—	—	0.20	0.50	1.00	2.00
AH1343//15	—	—	0.20	0.50	1.00	2.00
AH1344//15	—	—	0.20	0.50	1.00	2.00
AH1344//16	—	—	0.20	0.50	1.00	2.00
AH1345//16	—	—	0.20	0.50	1.00	2.00
AH1347//18	—	—	0.20	0.50	1.00	2.00
AH1347//19	—	—	0.20	0.50	1.00	2.00
AH1348//19	—	—	0.20	0.50	1.00	2.00
AH1348//20	—	—	0.20	0.50	1.00	2.00
AH1349//20	—	—	0.20	0.50	1.00	2.00

Y# 47 1/2 ANNA

Bronze **Obv:** Toughra **Mint:** Haidarabad (Farkhanda Bunyad)

Date	Mintage	VG8	F12	VF20	XF40	MS60
AH1332//2 (sic)	—	—	0.40	1.00	2.00	5.00
AH1332//3	—	—	0.40	1.00	2.00	5.00
AH1334//4 (sic)	—	—	0.40	1.00	2.00	5.00
AH1344//15	—	—	0.40	1.00	2.00	5.00
AH1348//20	—	—	0.40	1.00	2.00	5.00

Y# 48 ANNA

Copper-Nickel **Obv:** Toughra **Mint:** Haidarabad (Farkhanda Bunyad) **Note:** Round flan.

Date	Mintage	VG8	F12	VF20	XF40	MS60
AH1338	—	—	0.20	0.50	1.00	2.00
AH1339	—	—	0.20	0.50	1.00	2.00
AH1340	—	—	0.20	0.50	1.00	2.00
AH1341	—	—	0.20	0.50	1.00	2.00
AH1344	—	—	0.20	0.50	1.00	2.00
AH1347	—	—	0.20	0.50	1.00	2.00
AH1348	—	—	0.20	0.50	1.00	2.00
AH1349	—	—	0.20	0.50	1.00	2.00
AH1351	—	—	0.20	0.50	1.00	2.00
AH1352	—	—	0.20	0.50	1.00	2.00
AH1353	—	—	0.20	0.50	1.00	2.00
AH1354	—	—	0.20	0.50	1.00	2.00

Y# 49 ANNA

Copper-Nickel **Obv:** Toughra **Mint:** Haidarabad (Farkhanda Bunyad) **Note:** Square flan.

Date	Mintage	VG8	F12	VF20	XF40	MS60
AH1356	—	—	0.20	0.50	1.00	2.00
AH1357	—	—	0.20	0.50	1.00	2.00
AH1358	—	—	0.20	0.50	1.00	2.00
AH1359	—	—	0.20	0.50	1.00	2.00
AH1360	—	—	0.20	0.50	1.00	2.00
AH1361	—	—	0.20	0.50	1.00	2.00

Y# 50 2 ANNAS

1.40 g., 0.818 Silver 0.0367 oz. ASW **Obv:** Char Minar gateway **Mint:** Haidarabad (Farkhanda Bunyad)

Date	Mintage	VG8	F12	VF20	XF40	MS60
AH1335//6	—	12.00	15.00	18.00	22.00	25.00
AH1337//9	—	12.00	15.00	18.00	22.00	25.00
AH1338//10	—	12.00	15.00	18.00	22.00	25.00
AH1340//11	—	12.00	15.00	18.00	22.00	25.00
AH1342//13	—	12.00	15.00	18.00	22.00	25.00
AH1341//13	—	12.00	15.00	18.00	22.00	25.00
AH1341//14 (sic)	—	12.00	15.00	18.00	22.00	25.00
AH1343//14	—	12.00	15.00	18.00	22.00	25.00
AH1343//15	—	12.00	15.00	18.00	22.00	25.00
AH1347//18	—	12.00	15.00	18.00	22.00	25.00
AH1348//19	—	12.00	15.00	18.00	22.00	25.00
AH1351//22	—	12.00	15.00	18.00	22.00	25.00
AH1355//26	—	12.00	15.00	18.00	22.00	25.00

Y# 51 4 ANNAS

2.79 g., 0.818 Silver 0.0735 oz. ASW **Obv:** Char Minar gateway **Mint:** Haidarabad (Farkhanda Bunyad)

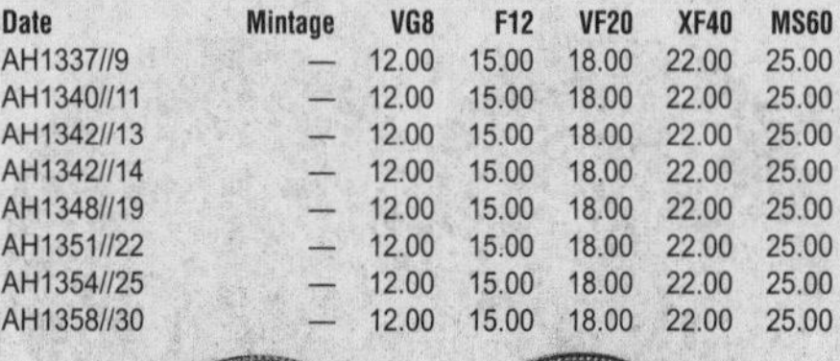

Date	Mintage	VG8	F12	VF20	XF40	MS60
AH1337//9	—	12.00	15.00	18.00	22.00	25.00
AH1340//11	—	12.00	15.00	18.00	22.00	25.00
AH1342//13	—	12.00	15.00	18.00	22.00	25.00
AH1342//14	—	12.00	15.00	18.00	22.00	25.00
AH1348//19	—	12.00	15.00	18.00	22.00	25.00
AH1351//22	—	12.00	15.00	18.00	22.00	25.00
AH1354//25	—	12.00	15.00	18.00	22.00	25.00
AH1358//30	—	12.00	15.00	18.00	22.00	25.00

Y# 52 8 ANNAS

5.59 g., 0.818 Silver 0.147 oz. ASW **Obv:** Char Minar gateway **Mint:** Haidarabad (Farkhanda Bunyad)

Date	Mintage	VG8	F12	VF20	XF40	MS60
AH1337//9	—	—	60.00	80.00	100	120
AH1342//13	—	—	60.00	80.00	100	120
AH1343//13 (sic)	—	—	60.00	80.00	100	120
AH1354//25	—	—	60.00	80.00	100	120

Y# 53 RUPEE

11.18 g., 0.818 Silver 0.294 oz. ASW **Obv:** Char Minar gateway with short initials "Ain" in doorway **Mint:** Haidarabad (Farkhanda Bunyad)

Date	Mintage	VG8	F12	VF20	XF40	MS60
AH1330//1	—	—	—	15.00	20.00	25.00

Y# 53a RUPEE

11.18 g., 0.818 Silver 0.294 oz. ASW **Obv:** Char Minar gateway with full "Ain" in doorway **Mint:** Haidarabad (Farkhanda Bunyad)

Date	Mintage	VG8	F12	VF20	XF40	MS60
AH1330//1	—	—	12.00	15.00	20.00	25.00
AH1330//2	—	—	12.00	15.00	20.00	25.00
AH1331//2	—	—	12.00	15.00	20.00	25.00
AH1331//3	—	—	12.00	15.00	20.00	25.00
AH1332//3	—	—	12.00	15.00	20.00	25.00
AH1334//6	—	—	12.00	15.00	20.00	25.00
AH1335//6	—	—	12.00	15.00	20.00	25.00
AH1335//7	—	—	12.00	15.00	20.00	25.00
AH1336//7	—	—	12.00	15.00	20.00	25.00
AH1337//7	—	—	35.00	50.00	75.00	100
AH1337//8	—	—	12.00	15.00	20.00	25.00
AH1337//9	—	—	35.00	50.00	75.00	100
AH1338//9	—	—	12.00	15.00	20.00	25.00
AH1339//9 (sic)	—	—	700	1,000	1,250	150
AH1340//11	—	—	65.00	100	125	150
AH1341//12	—	—	12.00	15.00	20.00	25.00
AH1342//13	—	—	12.00	15.00	20.00	25.00
AH1343//14	—	—	12.00	15.00	20.00	25.00

Y# 54.1 1/8 ASHRAFI

1.39 g., 0.910 Gold 0.0408 oz. AGW **Obv:** Char Minar gateway with short "Ain" in doorway **Mint:** Haidarabad (Farkhanda Bunyad)

Date	Mintage	VG8	F12	VF20	XF40	MS60
AH1329//1 Rare	—	—	—	—	—	—

Y# 54.2 1/8 ASHRAFI

1.39 g., 0.910 Gold 0.0408 oz. AGW **Obv:** Char Minar gateway with full "Ain" in doorway **Mint:** Haidarabad (Farkhanda Bunyad)

Date	Mintage	VG8	F12	VF20	XF40	MS60
AH1337//8	—	—	200	300	400	500
AH1340//11	—	—	200	300	400	500
AH1343//14	—	—	200	300	400	500
AH1344//15	—	—	200	300	400	500
AH1353//24	—	—	200	300	400	500
AH1354//25	—	—	200	300	400	500
AH1356//27	—	—	200	300	400	500
AH1360//31	—	—	200	300	400	500
AH1366//37	—	—	200	300	400	500
AH1368//39	—	—	200	300	400	500

Y# 55 1/4 ASHRAFI

2.79 g., 0.910 Gold 0.0817 oz. AGW **Obv:** Char Minar gateway **Mint:** Haidarabad (Farkhanda Bunyad)

Date	Mintage	VG8	F12	VF20	XF40	MS60
AH1337//8	—	—	500	700	850	1,000
AH1342//13	—	—	500	700	850	1,000
AH1342//14	—	—	500	700	850	1,000
AH1349//20	—	—	500	700	850	1,000
AH1353//23 (sic)	—	—	500	700	850	1,000
AH1354//25	—	—	500	700	850	1,000
AH1357//29	—	—	500	700	850	1,000
AH1360//31	—	—	500	700	850	1,000
AH1367//38	—	—	500	700	850	1,000

Y# 56.1 1/2 ASHRAFI

5.59 g., 0.910 Gold 0.1635 oz. AGW **Obv:** Char Minar gateway with short "Ain" in doorway **Mint:** Haidarabad (Farkhanda Bunyad)

Date	Mintage	VG8	F12	VF20	XF40	MS60
AH1329//1	—	—	1,400	2,000	2,500	3,000

Y# 56.2 1/2 ASHRAFI

5.59 g., 0.910 Gold 0.1635 oz. AGW **Obv:** Char Minar gateway with full "Ain" in doorway **Mint:** Haidarabad (Farkhanda Bunyad)

Date	Mintage	VG8	F12	VF20	XF40	MS60
AH1337//8	—	—	1,700	2,500	3,000	3,500
AH1341//12	—	—	1,700	2,500	3,000	3,500
AH1343//14	—	—	1,700	2,500	3,000	3,500
AH1342//14	—	—	1,700	2,500	3,000	3,500
AH1344//14 (sic)	—	—	1,700	2,500	3,000	3,500
AH1345//16	—	—	1,700	2,500	3,000	3,500
AH1349//20	—	—	1,700	2,500	3,000	3,500
AH1354//25	—	—	1,700	2,500	3,000	3,500
AH1357//29	—	—	1,700	2,500	3,000	3,500
AH1366//37	—	—	1,700	2,500	3,000	3,500
AH1367//38	—	—	1,700	2,500	3,000	3,500

Y# 57 ASHRAFI

11.18 g., 0.910 Gold 0.327 oz. AGW **Obv:** Char Minar gateway with short initial "Ain" in doorway **Mint:** Haidarabad (Farkhanda Bunyad)

Date	Mintage	VG8	F12	VF20	XF40	MS60
AH1330//1	—	—	1,700	2,500	3,000	3,500
AH1329//1	—	—	1,700	2,500	3,000	3,500

Y# 57a ASHRAFI

11.18 g., 0.910 Gold 0.327 oz. AGW **Obv:** Char Minar gateway with full initial "Ain" in doorway **Mint:** Haidarabad (Farkhanda Bunyad)

Date	Mintage	VG8	F12	VF20	XF40	MS60
AH1331//3	—	—	1,700	2,500	3,000	3,500
AH1332//4	—	—	1,700	2,500	3,000	3,500
AH1333//4	—	—	1,700	2,500	3,000	3,500
AH1337//8	—	—	1,700	2,500	3,000	3,500
AH1338//9	—	—	1,700	2,500	3,000	3,500
AH1337//9	—	—	1,700	2,500	3,000	3,500
AH1340//11	—	—	1,700	2,500	3,000	3,500
AH1343//14	—	—	1,700	2,500	3,000	3,500
AH1342//14	—	—	1,700	2,500	3,000	3,500
AH1344//15	—	—	1,700	2,500	3,000	3,500
AH1348//19	—	—	1,700	2,500	3,000	3,500
AH1349//20	—	—	1,700	2,500	3,000	3,500
AH1354//25	—	—	1,700	2,500	3,000	3,500
AH1358//30	—	—	1,700	2,500	3,000	3,500
AH1360//31	—	—	1,700	2,500	3,000	3,500
AH1362//34	—	—	1,700	2,500	3,000	3,500
AH1364//35	—	—	1,700	2,500	3,000	3,500

MILLED COINAGE

Second Series

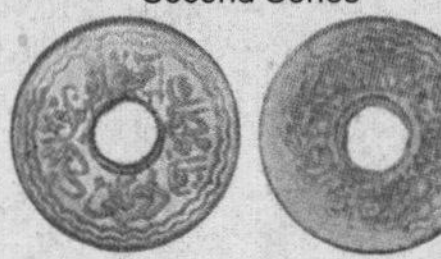

Y# 58 2 PAI

Bronze **Mint:** Haidarabad (Farkhanda Bunyad)

Date	Mintage	VG8	F12	VF20	XF40	MS60
AH1362//33	—	—	—	0.35	0.50	1.00
AH1363//34	—	—	—	0.35	0.50	1.00
AH1363//35	—	—	—	0.25	0.50	1.00
AH1364//35	—	—	—	0.25	0.50	1.00
AH1365//36	—	—	—	0.25	0.50	1.00
AH1366//37	—	—	—	0.25	0.50	1.00
AH1368//39	—	—	—	0.25	0.50	1.00

Y# 59 ANNA

Bronze **Obv:** Toughra **Mint:** Haidarabad (Farkhanda Bunyad) **Note:** Square flan.

Date	Mintage	VG8	F12	VF20	XF40	MS60
AH1361	—	—	0.25	0.50	0.75	1.50
AH1362	—	—	0.25	0.50	0.75	1.50
AH1364	—	—	0.25	0.50	0.75	1.50
AH1365	—	—	0.25	0.50	0.75	1.50
AH1366	—	—	0.25	0.50	0.75	1.50
AH1368	—	—	0.25	0.50	0.75	1.50

Y# 60 2 ANNAS

1.40 g., 0.818 Silver 0.0367 oz. ASW, 15 mm. **Mint:** Haidarabad (Farkhanda Bunyad)

Date	Mintage	VG8	F12	VF20	XF40	MS60
AH1362//33	—	—	4.00	5.00	6.00	8.00

Y# 64 2 ANNAS

1.50 g., Nickel, 15.2 mm. **Mint:** Haidarabad (Farkhanda Bunyad)

Date	Mintage	VG8	F12	VF20	XF40	MS60
AH1366//37	—	—	—	6.00	7.00	8.00
AH1368//39	—	—	—	6.00	7.00	8.00

Y# 61 4 ANNAS

2.79 g., 0.818 Silver 0.0735 oz. ASW, 20 mm. **Mint:** Haidarabad (Farkhanda Bunyad)

Date	Mintage	VG8	F12	VF20	XF40	MS60
AH1362//33	—	—	—	4.00	6.00	8.00
AH1362//34	—	—	—	4.00	6.00	8.00
AH1364//33 (sic)	—	—	—	4.00	6.00	8.00
AH1364//35	—	—	—	4.00	6.00	8.00
AH1364//36	—	—	—	4.00	6.00	8.00
AH1365//36	—	—	—	4.00	6.00	8.00

Y# 65 4 ANNAS
2.80 g., Nickel, 20 mm. **Mint:** Haidarabad (Farkhanda Bunyad)

Date	Mintage	VG8	F12	VF20	XF40	MS60
AH1366//37	—	—	0.25	0.50	0.75	1.50
AH1368//39	—	—	0.25	0.50	0.75	1.50

Y# 62 8 ANNAS
5.59 g., 0.818 Silver 0.147 oz. ASW, 24 mm. **Mint:** Haidarabad (Farkhanda Bunyad)

Date	Mintage	VG8	F12	VF20	XF40	MS60
AH1363//34	—	—	35.00	50.00	60.00	75.00

Y# 66 8 ANNAS
5.50 g., Nickel, 23.8 mm. **Mint:** Haidarabad (Farkhanda Bunyad)

Date	Mintage	VG8	F12	VF20	XF40	MS60
AH1366//37	—	—	—	18.00	22.00	80.00

Y# 63 RUPEE
11.18 g., 0.818 Silver 0.294 oz. ASW, 30 mm. **Mint:** Haidarabad (Farkhanda Bunyad)

Date	Mintage	VG8	F12	VF20	XF40	MS60
AH1361//32	—	—	14.00	18.00	20.00	24.00
AH1361//31	—	—	14.00	18.00	20.00	24.00
AH1362//34	—	—	14.00	18.00	20.00	24.00
AH1364//35	—	—	14.00	18.00	20.00	24.00
AH1364//36	—	—	14.00	18.00	20.00	24.00
AH1365//36	—	—	14.00	18.00	20.00	24.00

Y# 67 ASHRAFI
11.18 g., 0.910 Gold 0.327 oz. AGW **Mint:** Haidarabad (Farkhanda Bunyad)

Date	Mintage	VG8	F12	VF20	XF40	MS60
AH1368//39 Rare	—	—	—	—	—	—

PATTERNS

Including off metal strikes

KM#	Date	Mintage	Identification	Mkt Val
Pn13	AH1362/33 (1943)	—	2 Annas. Copper. Copper, Y#60.	5,000
Pn14	AH1366/37 (1946)	—	2 Pai. Bronze. Small, thin flan, larger hole, Y#58.	5,000
Pn10	AH1319//35 (1901)	—	Rupee. Silver. Y#53a.	5,000
Pn11	AH1324//40 (1906)	—	1/2 Ashrafi. Silver. Y#43.	5,000
Pn12	AH1324//40 (1906)	—	Ashrafi. Silver. Y#44.	5,000

INDORE

The Holkars were one of the three dominant Maratha powers (with the Peshwas and Sindhias), with major landholdings in Central India.

Indore State originated in 1728 with a grant of land north of the Narbada river by the Maratha Peshwa of Poona to Malhar Rao Holkar, a cavalry commander in his service. After Holkar's death (ca.1765) his daughter-in-law, Ahalya Bai, assumed the position of Queen Regent.Together with Tukoji Rao she effectively ruled the State until her death thirty years later. But it was left to Tukoji's son, Jaswant Rao, to challenge the dominance of the Poona Marathas in the Maratha Confederacy, eventually defeating the Peshwa's army in 1802. But at this point the fortunes of the Holkars suffered a serious reverse. Although Jaswant Rao had initially defeated a small British force under Col. William Monson, he was badly beaten by a contingent under Lord Lake. As a result Holkar was forced to cede a considerable portion of his territory and from this time until India's independence in 1947, the residual State of Indore was obliged to accept British protection.

For more detailed data on the Indore series, see *A Study of Holkar State Coinage*, by P.K.Sethi, S.K. Bhatt and R. Holkar (1976).

HOLKAR RULERS
Shivaji Rao, VS1943-1960/FE1296-1313/1886-1903AD
Tukoji Rao III, VS1960-1983/1903-1926AD
Yashwant Rao II, VS1983-2005/1926-1948AD

HONORIFIC TITLE
Bahadur

MINTS

اندور or इंदोर

Indore

BRITISH PROTECTORATE

Shivaji Rao

VS1943-1960 / FE1296-1313 / 1886-1903AD

MILLED COINAGE

Indore

KM# 33.3 1/4 ANNA
Copper, 27 mm. **Obv:** Continuous legend around reclining bull **Obv. Legend:** Shivaji Rao...Bahadur **Rev:** "Indore" above denomination and date **Mint:** Indore **Note:** Floral border varieties exist. Weight varies 6.026-6.674 grams.

Date	Mintage	G4	VG8	F12	VF20	XF40
VS1958(1901)	—	—	2.00	4.00	7.00	10.00
VS1959(1902)	—	—	2.00	4.00	7.00	10.00

KM# 35.3 1/2 ANNA
Copper, 31 mm. **Obv:** Continuous legend around reclining bull **Obv. Legend:** Shivaji Rao **Rev:** "Indore" above denomination and date **Mint:** Indore

Date	Mintage	G4	VG8	F12	VF20	XF40
VS1958(1901)	—	3.00	6.00	9.00	15.00	20.00
VS1959(1902)	—	3.00	6.00	9.00	15.00	20.00

MILLED COINAGE

This series was introduced in 1898 to counteract counterfeiting of the second series which had begun to proliferate as a result of a sharp fall in the price of silver. Idle minting machines were reactivated for this purpose, but the series was short-lived.

Third Series

KM# 47.2 RUPEE
11.20 g., Silver **Obv:** Bust facing; continuous legend **Rev:** Arms **Mint:** Indore

Date	Mintage	VG8	F12	VF20	XF40	MS60
VS1958	—	—	800	1,000	1,300	2,000

Yashwant Rao II

VS1983-2005 / 1926-1948AD

MILLED COINAGE

Fourth Series

KM# 49 1/4 ANNA
Copper **Obv:** Bust facing 3/4 right **Mint:** Indore

Date	Mintage	F12	VF20	XF40	MS60	MS63
1992 - 1935	—	2.00	5.00	10.00	25.00	50.00

KM# 50 1/2 ANNA
Copper **Obv:** Bust facing **Mint:** Indore

Date	Mintage	F12	VF20	XF40	MS60	MS63
1992 - 1935	—	7.00	10.00	15.00	35.00	75.00

JAIPUR

Tradition has it that the region of Jaipur, located in norTradition has it that the region of Jaipur, located in northwest India, once belonged to an ancient Kachwaha Rajput dynasty which claimed descent from Kush, one of the sons of Rama, King of Ayodhya. But the Princely State of Jaipur originated in the 12th century. Comparatively small in size, the State remained largely unnoticed until after the 16th century when the Jaipur royal house became famous for its military skills and thereafter supplied the Mughals with some of their more distinguished generals. The city of Jaipur was founded about 1728 by Maharaja Jai Singh II who was well known for his knowledge of mathematics and astronomy. The late 18th and early 19th centuries were difficult times for Jaipur. They were marked by internal rivalry, exacerbated by Maratha or Pindari incursions. In 1818 this culminated with a treaty whereby Jaipur came under British protection and oversight.

RULERS
Madho Singh II, AH1298-1341/1880-1922AD
Man Singh II, AH1341-1369/1922-1949AD

MINT NAMES

Coins were struck at two mints, which bear the following characteristic marks on the reverse:
Sawai Jaipur
Sawai Madhopur

JAIPUR MINT

In the names of Queen Victoria

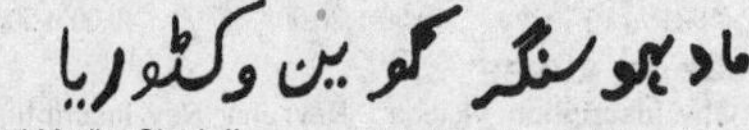

And Madho Singh II

Years 1-43/1880-1922AD

NOTE: Queen Victoria's name was retained on Madho Singh II's coinage until 1922AD. No coins were struck with Edward VII's name by Madho Singh II

PRINCELY STATE

Madho Singh II

AH1298-1341 / 1880-1922AD

HAMMERED COINAGE

To distinguish coins between Ram Singh and his son/successor Madho Singh II, note that the coins of Ram Singh have a small slanting cross or dagger between the Ram and Singh symbols, whereas the coins of Singh II do not.

Regal Style

Sawai Jaipur

KM# 130 PAISA

Copper **Obv:** Inscription: Queen Victoria... **Rev:** Jhar, inscription **Rev. Inscription:** Madho Singh II **Mint:** Sawai Jaipur **Note:** Weight varies 6.15-6.30g.

Date	Mintage	G4	VG8	F12	VF20	XF40
ND//22 (1901)	—	2.00	4.00	6.00	8.00	10.00
ND//23 (1902)	—	2.00	4.00	6.00	8.00	10.00
ND//24 (1903)	—	2.00	4.00	6.00	8.00	10.00
ND//25 (1904)	—	2.00	4.00	6.00	8.00	10.00
ND//25 (1904)	—	2.00	4.00	6.00	8.00	10.00
ND//27 (1906)	—	2.00	4.00	6.00	8.00	10.00
ND//28 (1907)	—	2.00	4.00	6.00	8.00	10.00
ND//29 (1908)	—	2.00	4.00	6.00	8.00	10.00
ND//37 (1916)	—	2.00	4.00	6.00	8.00	10.00
ND//38 (1917)	—	2.00	4.00	6.00	8.00	10.00
ND//39 (1918)	—	2.00	4.00	6.00	8.00	10.00
ND//41 (1920)	—	2.00	4.00	6.00	8.00	10.00

KM# 135 1/16 RUPEE

Silver **Obv. Inscription:** Victoria... **Rev:** Jhar **Rev. Inscription:** Madho Singh II **Mint:** Sawai Jaipur **Note:** Weight varies 0.67-0.72g.

Date	Mintage	G4	VG8	F12	VF20	XF40
ND//33 (1912)	—	10.00	20.00	30.00	40.00	50.00

KM# 137 1/8 RUPEE

Silver **Obv. Inscription:** Victoria... **Rev:** Jhar **Rev. Inscription:** Madho Singh II **Mint:** Sawai Jaipur **Note:** Weight varies 1.34-1.45g.

Date	Mintage	G4	VG8	F12	VF20	XF40
ND//22 (1901)	—	10.00	20.00	30.00	40.00	50.00
ND//23 (1902)	—	10.00	20.00	30.00	40.00	50.00
ND//26 (1905)	—	10.00	20.00	30.00	40.00	50.00
ND//27 (1906)	—	10.00	20.00	30.00	40.00	50.00
ND//28 (1907)	—	10.00	20.00	30.00	40.00	50.00
ND//29 (1908)	—	10.00	20.00	30.00	40.00	50.00
ND//41 (1920)	—	10.00	20.00	30.00	40.00	50.00
ND//42 (1921)	—	10.00	20.00	30.00	40.00	50.00

KM# 139 1/4 RUPEE

Silver **Obv. Inscription:** Victoria... **Rev:** Jhar **Rev. Inscription:** Madho Singh II **Mint:** Sawai Jaipur **Note:** Weight varies 2.68-2.90g.

Date	Mintage	G4	VG8	F12	VF20	XF40
ND//22 (1901)	—	10.00	20.00	30.00	40.00	50.00
ND//23 (1902)	—	10.00	20.00	30.00	40.00	50.00
ND//24 (1903)	—	10.00	20.00	30.00	40.00	50.00
ND//26 (1905)	—	10.00	20.00	30.00	40.00	50.00
ND//27 (1906)	—	10.00	20.00	30.00	40.00	50.00
ND//28 (1907)	—	10.00	20.00	30.00	40.00	50.00
ND//29 (1908)	—	10.00	20.00	30.00	40.00	50.00
ND//30 (1909)	—	10.00	20.00	30.00	40.00	50.00
ND//34 (1913)	—	10.00	20.00	30.00	40.00	50.00
ND//37 (1916)	—	10.00	20.00	30.00	40.00	50.00
ND//38 (1917)	—	10.00	20.00	30.00	40.00	50.00
ND//42 (1921)	—	10.00	20.00	30.00	40.00	50.00

KM# 142 1/2 RUPEE

Silver **Obv. Inscription:** Victoria... **Rev:** Jhar **Rev. Inscription:** Madho Singh II **Mint:** Sawai Jaipur **Note:** Weight varies 5.35-5.80g.

Date	Mintage	G4	VG8	F12	VF20	XF40
ND//22 (1901)	—	10.00	20.00	30.00	40.00	50.00
ND//23 (1902)	—	10.00	20.00	30.00	40.00	50.00
ND//25 (1904)	—	10.00	20.00	30.00	40.00	50.00
ND//26 (1905)	—	10.00	20.00	30.00	40.00	50.00
ND//27 (1906)	—	10.00	20.00	30.00	40.00	50.00
ND//28 (1907)	—	10.00	20.00	30.00	40.00	50.00
ND//29 (1908)	—	10.00	20.00	30.00	40.00	50.00
ND//30 (1909)	—	10.00	20.00	30.00	40.00	50.00
ND//34 (1913)	—	10.00	20.00	30.00	40.00	50.00
ND//37 (1916)	—	10.00	20.00	30.00	40.00	50.00

KM# 145 RUPEE

Silver **Obv. Inscription:** Victoria... **Rev:** Jhar **Rev. Inscription:** Madho Singh II **Mint:** Sawai Jaipur **Note:** Weight varies 10.70-11.60g.

Date	Mintage	G4	VG8	F12	VF20	XF40
ND//23 (1902)	—	—	20.00	30.00	40.00	50.00
ND//24 (1903)	—	—	20.00	30.00	40.00	50.00
ND//25 (1904)	—	—	20.00	30.00	40.00	50.00
ND//26 (1905)	—	—	20.00	30.00	40.00	50.00
ND//27 (1906)	—	—	20.00	30.00	40.00	50.00
ND//29 (1908)	—	—	20.00	30.00	40.00	50.00
ND//30 (1909)	—	—	20.00	30.00	40.00	50.00
ND//31 (1910)	—	—	20.00	30.00	40.00	50.00
ND//33 (1912)	—	—	20.00	30.00	40.00	50.00
ND//37 (1916)	—	—	20.00	30.00	40.00	50.00
191(8)//39	—	—	20.00	30.00	40.00	50.00
ND//40 (1919)	—	—	20.00	30.00	40.00	50.00
ND//42 (1921)	—	—	20.00	30.00	40.00	50.00
ND//43(1922)	—	—	20.00	30.00	40.00	50.00

KM# 150 MOHUR

Gold **Obv. Inscription:** Victoria.... **Rev:** Jhar **Rev. Inscription:** Madho Singh II **Mint:** Sawai Jaipur **Note:** Weight varies 10.70-11.40 g.

Date	Mintage	G4	VG8	F12	VF20	XF40
ND//25 (1904)	—	—	—	800	900	1,000
ND//32 (1911)	—	—	—	800	900	1,000
ND//37 (1916)	—	—	—	800	900	1,000
ND//40 (1919)	—	—	—	800	900	1,000
ND//41 (1920)	—	—	—	800	900	1,000

MILLED COINAGE

KM# 132 NAZARANA NEW PAISA

Copper, 32-36 mm. **Obv. Inscription:** Victoria... **Rev:** Jhar **Rev. Inscription:** Madho Singh II **Mint:** Sawai Jaipur **Note:** Size varies. Well-centered issues on thin planchets may be restrikes.

Date	Mintage	G4	VG8	F12	VF20	XF40
1901//22	—	—	—	20.00	35.00	50.00
1902//23	—	—	—	20.00	35.00	50.00
1903//24	—	—	—	20.00	35.00	50.00
1904//25	—	—	—	20.00	35.00	50.00
1905//26	—	—	—	20.00	35.00	50.00
1906//27	—	—	—	20.00	35.00	50.00
1907//28	—	—	—	20.00	35.00	50.00
1908//29	—	—	—	20.00	35.00	50.00
1909//30	—	—	—	20.00	35.00	50.00
1910//31	—	—	—	20.00	35.00	50.00
1911//32	—	—	—	20.00	35.00	50.00
1912//33	—	—	—	20.00	35.00	50.00
1913//34	—	—	—	20.00	35.00	50.00
1914//35	—	—	—	20.00	35.00	50.00
1915//36	—	—	—	20.00	35.00	50.00
1916//37	—	—	—	20.00	35.00	50.00
1917//38	—	—	—	20.00	35.00	50.00

KM# 147 NAZARANA RUPEE

Silver **Obv. Inscription:** Victoria... **Rev:** Jhar **Rev. Inscription:** Madho Singh II **Mint:** Sawai Jaipur **Note:** Size varies 36-37mm.

Date	Mintage	G4	VG8	F12	VF20	XF40
1901//22	—	—	—	100	150	200
1903//24	—	—	—	100	150	200
1904//25	—	—	—	100	150	200
1906//27	—	—	—	100	150	200
1908//29	—	—	—	100	150	200
1909//30	—	—	—	100	150	200
1910//31	—	—	—	100	150	200
1911//32	—	—	—	100	150	200
1912//33	—	—	—	100	150	200
1913//34	—	—	—	100	150	200
1914/35	—	—	—	100	150	200
1915/36	—	—	—	100	150	200
1916//37	—	—	—	100	150	200
1917/38	—	—	—	100	150	200
1918/39	—	—	—	100	150	200
1919/40	—	—	—	100	150	200
1920//41	—	—	—	100	150	200
1921//42	—	—	—	100	150	200

Man Singh II

AH1341-1369 / 1922-1949AD

HAMMERED COINAGE

To distinguish coins between Ram Singh and his son/ successor Madho Singh II, note that the coins of Ram Singh have a small slanting cross or dagger between the Ram and Singh symbols, whereas the coins of Singh II do not.

Regal Style

KM# 175 1/2 PAISA

Copper, 21-23 mm. **Obv. Inscription:** George VI... **Rev:** Jhar **Rev. Inscription:** Man Singh (II)... **Mint:** Sawai Jaipur **Note:** Size varies.

Date	Mintage	G4	VG8	F12	VF20	XF40
ND//21 (1942)	—	1.00	2.00	4.00	8.00	12.00
ND//22(1943)	—	1.00	2.00	4.00	8.00	12.00

KM# 158 RUPEE

10.70 g., Silver **Obv. Inscription:** George V... **Rev:** Jhar **Rev. Inscription:** Man Singh II... **Mint:** Sawai Jaipur

Date	Mintage	G4	VG8	F12	VF20	XF40
1922//1	—	—	20.00	30.00	40.00	50.00

KM# 163 MOHUR

Gold **Obv. Inscription:** George V... **Rev:** Jhar **Rev. Inscription:** Man Singh II... **Mint:** Sawai Jaipur **Note:** Weight varies 10.70-11.40 g.

Date	Mintage	G4	VG8	F12	VF20	XF40
ND//2 (1923)	—	—	—	800	900	1,000
1(924)//3	—	—	—	800	900	1,000
1925//4	—	—	—	800	900	1,000
19(28)//7	—	—	—	800	900	1,000

KM# 200 MOHUR

Gold **Obv. Inscription:** George (VI)... **Rev. Inscription:** Man Singh (II)... **Mint:** Sawai Jaipur **Note:** Weight varies 10.70-11.40 g.

Date	Mintage	G4	VG8	F12	VF20	XF40
ND//20 (1941)	—	—	—	800	900	1,000
ND//22 (1943)	—	—	—	800	900	1,000
ND//23 (1944)	—	—	—	800	900	1,000
ND//26 (1947)	—	—	—	800	900	1,000
ND//27 (1948)	—	—	—	800	900	1,000
1949//28	—	—	—	800	900	1,000

MILLED COINAGE

KM# 185 ANNA

Brass **Obv:** Jhar **Mint:** Sawai Jaipur

Date	Mintage	G4	VG8	F12	VF20	XF40
1943	—	—	1.00	3.00	5.00	8.00
Note: Large and small denomination variety						
1944/3	—	—	1.00	3.00	5.00	8.00
1944	—	—	1.00	3.00	5.00	8.00

KM# 186 ANNA

5.17 g., Brass **Obv:** Jhar **Mint:** Sawai Jaipur **Note:** Thick planchet; weight varies.

Date	Mintage	G4	VG8	F12	VF20	XF40
1943	—	—	1.00	3.00	5.00	8.00

KM# 187 ANNA
2.78 g., Brass **Obv:** Jhar **Mint:** Sawai Jaipur **Note:** Thin planchet.

Date	Mintage	G4	VG8	F12	VF20	XF40
1943	—	—	1.00	3.00	5.00	8.00

KM# 188 ANNA
Brass **Obv:** Bust of Man Singh II right **Rev:** Jhar **Mint:** Sawai Jaipur

Date	Mintage	G4	VG8	F12	VF20	XF40
1944	—	—	5.00	6.00	8.00	10.00
1944 Proof; Restrike	—	PF65 1,000				

KM# 190 2 ANNA
Brass **Rev:** Jhar **Mint:** Sawai Jaipur **Note:** Square flan.

Date	Mintage	G4	VG8	F12	VF20	XF40
1942//21	—	10.00	20.00	30.00	40.00	50.00

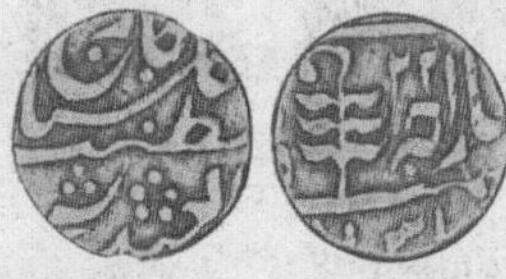

KM# 176 1/2 PAISA
Copper, 21-23 mm. **Obv:** George VI **Rev:** Jhar **Rev. Inscription:** Man Singh (II)... **Mint:** Sawai Jaipur **Note:** Crude struck in collar. Size varies.

Date	Mintage	G4	VG8	F12	VF20	XF40
ND//22 (1943)	—	1.00	2.00	3.00	4.00	5.00
ND//23 (1944)	—	1.00	2.00	3.00	4.00	5.00

KM# 155 NAZARANA PAISA
Copper **Obv. Inscription:** George V... **Rev:** Jhar **Rev. Inscription:** Man Singh II... **Mint:** Sawai Jaipur

Date	Mintage	G4	VG8	F12	VF20	XF40
1922//1	—	20.00	30.00	40.00	50.00	60.00
1923//2	—	20.00	30.00	40.00	50.00	60.00
1924//3	—	20.00	30.00	40.00	50.00	60.00
1924//4	—	20.00	30.00	40.00	50.00	60.00
1925//4	—	20.00	30.00	40.00	50.00	60.00
1926//5	—	20.00	30.00	40.00	50.00	60.00
1927//5	—	20.00	30.00	40.00	50.00	60.00
1927//6	—	20.00	30.00	40.00	50.00	60.00
1928//7	—	20.00	30.00	40.00	50.00	60.00
1929//8	—	20.00	30.00	40.00	50.00	60.00
1930//9	—	20.00	30.00	40.00	50.00	60.00
1931//10	—	20.00	30.00	40.00	50.00	60.00
1932//11	—	20.00	30.00	40.00	50.00	60.00
1933//12	—	20.00	30.00	40.00	50.00	60.00
1934//13	—	20.00	30.00	40.00	50.00	60.00
1935//14	—	20.00	30.00	40.00	50.00	60.00

KM# 167 NAZARANA PAISA
6.44 g., Copper **Obv. Inscription:** Edward (VIII)... **Rev:** Jhar **Rev. Inscription:** Man Singh (II)... **Mint:** Sawai Jaipur

Date	Mintage	G4	VG8	F12	VF20	XF40
1936//15	—	—	75.00	150	225	300

KM# 180 NAZARANA PAISA
Copper **Obv. Inscription:** George VI... **Rev:** Jhar **Rev. Inscription:** Man Singh (II)... **Mint:** Sawai Jaipur

Date	Mintage	G4	VG8	F12	VF20	XF40
1937//16	—	—	30.00	40.00	50.00	60.00
1938//17	—	—	30.00	40.00	50.00	60.00
1939//18	—	—	30.00	40.00	50.00	60.00
1940//19	—	—	30.00	40.00	50.00	60.00
1941//19	—	—	30.00	40.00	50.00	60.00
1941//20	—	—	30.00	40.00	50.00	60.00
1942//21	—	—	30.00	40.00	50.00	60.00
1943//22	—	—	30.00	40.00	50.00	60.00
1944//23	—	—	30.00	40.00	50.00	60.00
1945//24	—	—	30.00	40.00	50.00	60.00
1946//25	—	—	30.00	40.00	50.00	60.00
1947//27	—	—	30.00	40.00	50.00	60.00
1947//26	—	—	30.00	40.00	50.00	60.00
1948//27	—	—	30.00	40.00	50.00	60.00
1949//28	—	—	30.00	40.00	50.00	60.00

KM# 159 NAZARANA RUPEE
10.70 g., Silver **Obv. Inscription:** George V... **Rev:** Jhar **Rev. Inscription:** Man Singh II... **Mint:** Sawai Jaipur

Date	Mintage	G4	VG8	F12	VF20	XF40
1924//3	—	—	50.00	110	145	220
1928//7	—	—	50.00	110	145	220
1932//11	—	—	50.00	110	145	220

KM# 196 NAZARANA RUPEE
Silver, 37-38 mm. **Obv. Inscription:** George (VI)... **Rev. Inscription:** Man Singh (II).... **Mint:** Sawai Jaipur

Date	Mintage	G4	VG8	F12	VF20	XF40
1938//20	—	—	50.00	100	150	200
1939//18	—	—	50.00	100	150	200
1941//20	—	—	50.00	100	150	200
1943//22	—	—	50.00	100	150	200
1945//24	—	—	50.00	100	150	200
1948//27	—	—	50.00	100	150	200
1949//28	—	—	50.00	100	150	200

KM# A196 NAZARANA RUPEE
Silver, 30 mm. **Obv. Inscription:** George (V)... **Rev. Inscription:** Man Singh (II)...

Date	Mintage	G4	VG8	F12	VF20	XF40
1941//20	—	—	125	250	350	600

JODHPUR

Jodhpur, also known as Marwar, located in northwest India, was the largest Princely State in the Rajputana Agency. Its population in 1941 exceeded two and a half million. The "Maharajadhirajas" ("Great Kings of Kings") of Jodhpur were Rathor Rajputs who claimed an extremely ancient ancestry from Rama, king of Ayodhya. With the collapse of the Rathor rulers of Kanauj in 1194 the family entered Marwar where they laid the foundation of the new state. The city of Jodhpur was built by Rao Jodha in 1459, and the city and the state were named after him. In 1561 the Mughal Emperor Akbar invaded Jodhpur, forcing its submission. In 1679 Emperor Aurangzeb sacked the city, an experience which stimulated the Rajput royal house to forge a new unity among themselves in order to extricate themselves from Mughal hegemony. Internal dissension once again asserted itself and Rajput unity, which had both benefited from and accelerated Mughal decline, fell apart before the Marathas. In 1818 Jodhpur came under British protection and control and after Indian independence in 1947 the State was merged into Rajasthan. Jodhpur is best known for its particular style of riding breeches (jodpurs) which became very popular in the West in the late 19th century.

RULERS
Sardar Singh, VS1952-1968/1895-1911AD
Sumer Singh, VS1968-1975/1911-1918AD
Umaid Singh, VS1975-2004/1918-1947AD
Hanwant Singh, as Titular Ruler, VS2004-2009/1947-1949AD

MINTS

جودھپور

Jodhpur

جودپور

Jodpur

دارالمنصور

Dar-al-Mansur

Issues of Edward VII and George V and Sardar Singh and Sumer Singh

म

Jodhpur (KM#91-95, 98-100, 109, 113-115)
Jodhpur (KM#120)

Issues of George V and Sumer Singh

द

Jodhpur (KM#111-112)

Issues of George V and Umaid Singh

Jodhpur (KM#128 & 129)

श्री

Jodhpur (KM#129)

Issues of Edward VIII and Umaid Singh

Jodhpur all

Issues of George VI and Umaid Singh

Jodhpur (KM#141-143)

Jodhpur (KM#144-147, 150-151)

Issues of George VI and Hanwant Singh

Jodhpur all

The Daroga's marks generally consist of a symbol or a single Nagari letter, sometimes inverted, and even lying on its side. Some letters are found on more than one series, so that the mark is not a positive identification, but taken together with the city mark and the style of the coin, will provide a correct attribution.

JODHPUR MINT

Operative between 1761AD (AH1175) and 1945AD (VS2002). There are a number of mules of late Jodhpur types struck in 1945 and later for collectors.

KINGDOM

Sardar Singh

VS1952-1968 / 1895-1911AD

HAMMERED COINAGE

Jodhpur

KM# 91.1 1/4 ANNA
10.50 g., Copper, 18 mm. **Obv. Inscription:** Edward (VII)... **Rev:** Inscription; date at top **Rev. Inscription:** Sardar Singh... **Mint:** Jodhpur **Note:** Other blundered dates may exist. Y#20.

Date	Mintage	G4	VG8	F12	VF20	XF40
1901	—	1.00	2.00	3.00	4.00	6.00
1902	—	1.00	2.00	3.00	4.00	6.00

Date	Mintage	G4	VG8	F12	VF20	XF40
1903	—	1.00	2.00	3.00	4.00	6.00
1904	—	1.00	2.00	3.00	4.00	6.00
1905	—	1.00	2.00	3.00	4.00	6.00
1906	—	1.00	2.00	3.00	4.00	6.00
1609 Error	—	1.00	2.00	3.00	4.00	6.00
1907	—	1.00	2.00	3.00	4.00	6.00
1908	—	1.00	2.00	3.00	4.00	6.00
1909	—	1.00	2.00	3.00	4.00	6.00
1910	—	1.00	2.00	3.00	4.00	6.00
1290(1910) Error	—	—	—	—	—	—
1291(1910) Error	—	—	—	—	—	—
1292(1910) Error	—	—	—	—	—	—
1967(1910) Error	—	—	—	—	—	—
2091(1910) Error	—	—	—	—	—	—
5201(1910) Error	—	—	—	—	—	—
5291(1910) Error	—	—	—	—	—	—
0291(1910) Error	—	—	—	—	—	—
0292 (1910) Error	—	—	—	—	—	—
192 (1910) Error	—	—	—	—	—	—
0192 (1910) Error	—	—	—	—	—	—
1091 (1910) Error	—	—	—	—	—	—
0196 (1910) Error	—	—	—	—	—	—
1291 (1910) Retrograde 9	—	—	—	—	—	—
1067 (1910) Error	—	—	—	—	—	—
1291 (1910) 2 engraved over 1	—	—	—	—	—	—

KM# 91.2 1/4 ANNA

10.50 g., Copper, 16 mm. **Obv. Inscription:** Edward (VII)... **Rev:** Inscription; date at bottom **Rev. Inscription:** Sardar Singh... **Mint:** Jodhpur **Note:** Y#20.

Date	Mintage	G4	VG8	F12	VF20	XF40
1906	—	—	—	—	—	—

KM# 92.1 1/2 ANNA

Copper **Obv. Inscription:** Edward (VII)... **Rev. Inscription:** Sardar Singh... **Mint:** Jodhpur **Note:** 20.00-21.00 grams. Y#21.

Date	Mintage	G4	VG8	F12	VF20	XF40
1906	—	2.00	3.00	8.00	12.00	20.00
1908	—	2.00	3.00	8.00	12.00	20.00

KM# 92.2 1/2 ANNA

Copper **Obv. Inscription:** Edward (VII)... **Rev:** Legend without Bahadur **Rev. Inscription:** Sardar Singh... **Mint:** Jodhpur **Note:** Y#21.

Date	Mintage	G4	VG8	F12	VF20	XF40
1906	—	2.00	3.00	8.00	12.00	20.00
1908	—	2.00	3.00	8.00	12.00	20.00

KM# 93 1/8 RUPEE

1.40 g., Silver **Obv. Inscription:** Edward (VII)... **Rev. Inscription:** Sardar Singh... **Mint:** Jodhpur

Date	Mintage	G4	VG8	F12	VF20	XF40
ND-1908	—	—	50.00	75.00	100	150

KM# 94 1/4 RUPEE

2.80 g., Silver, 19 mm. **Obv. Inscription:** Edward (VII)... **Rev. Inscription:** Sardar Singh... **Mint:** Jodhpur **Note:** Y#22.

Date	Mintage	G4	VG8	F12	VF20	XF40
VS1965	—	—	50.00	100	150	200

KM# 95 1/2 RUPEE

5.60 g., Silver, 13 mm. **Obv. Inscription:** Edward (VII)... **Rev. Inscription:** Sardar Singh... **Mint:** Jodhpur

Date	Mintage	G4	VG8	F12	VF20	XF40
1906	—	—	200	300	400	500
ND-1908	—	—	200	300	400	500

KM# 98 1/4 MOHUR

2.80 g., Gold **Obv. Inscription:** Edward (VII)... **Rev. Inscription:** Sardar Singh... **Mint:** Jodhpur **Note:** Y#23.

Date	Mintage	G4	VG8	F12	VF20	XF40
ND-1906	—	—	300	400	500	700

KM# 99 1/2 MOHUR

5.50 g., Gold, 18 mm. **Obv. Inscription:** Edward (VII)... **Rev. Inscription:** Sardar Singh... **Mint:** Jodhpur **Note:** Y#24.

Date	Mintage	G4	VG8	F12	VF20	XF40
ND-1906	—	—	500	600	800	1,000

KM# 100.1 MOHUR

11.00 g., Gold, 20 mm. **Obv:** Ma. **Obv. Inscription:** Edward (VII)... **Rev. Inscription:** Sardar Singh... **Mint:** Jodhpur **Note:** Y#25.

Date	Mintage	G4	VG8	F12	VF20	XF40
1906	—	—	800	1,000	1,250	1,500

KM# 100.2 MOHUR

11.00 g., Gold, 20 mm. **Obv:** Sa. **Obv. Inscription:** Edward (VII)... **Rev. Inscription:** Sardar Singh... **Mint:** Jodhpur **Note:** Y#25.

Date	Mintage	G4	VG8	F12	VF20	XF40
1906	—	—	800	1,000	1,250	1,500

Sumar Singh

KM# 110 1/4 ANNA

10.50 g., Copper, 16-18 mm. **Obv. Inscription:** George V, "Emperor"... **Rev. Inscription:** Sumar Singh... **Mint:** Jodhpur **Note:** Y#27. Size varies.

Date	Mintage	G4	VG8	F12	VF20	XF40
1914	—	3.00	5.00	10.00	15.00	20.00

KM# 111 1/4 ANNA

10.50 g., Copper, 16-18 mm. **Obv. Inscription:** George V, "Shah"... **Rev. Inscription:** Sumar Singh... **Mint:** Jodhpur **Note:** Y#27. Size varies.

Date	Mintage	G4	VG8	F12	VF20	XF40
1914	—	—	—	—	—	—

KM# 112.1 1/2 ANNA

21.00 g., Copper, 25 mm. **Obv. Inscription:** George V, "Emperor"... **Rev. Inscription:** Sumar Singh... **Mint:** Jodhpur **Note:** Y#28.

Date	Mintage	G4	VG8	F12	VF20	XF40
1914	—	3.00	5.00	10.00	15.00	20.00

KM# 112.2 1/2 ANNA

21.00 g., Copper, 25 mm. **Obv. Inscription:** George V, "Shah"... **Rev. Inscription:** Sumar Singh... **Mint:** Jodhpur **Note:** Y#28.

Date	Mintage	G4	VG8	F12	VF20	XF40
1914	—	3.00	5.00	10.00	15.00	20.00

KM# 113 1/8 RUPEE

1.40 g., Silver, 13 mm. **Obv. Inscription:** George V, "Shah"... **Rev. Inscription:** Sumar Singh... **Mint:** Jodhpur **Note:** Y#29.

Date	Mintage	G4	VG8	F12	VF20	XF40
ND(1911-18)	—	—	100	200	350	500

KM# 114 1/4 RUPEE

2.80 g., Silver, 14 mm. **Mint:** Jodhpur **Note:** Y#30.

Date	Mintage	G4	VG8	F12	VF20	XF40
ND(1911-18)	—	—	100	200	350	500

KM# 115 1/2 RUPEE

5.60 g., Silver, 18 mm. **Mint:** Jodhpur **Note:** Y#31.

Date	Mintage	G4	VG8	F12	VF20	XF40
ND(1911-18)	—	—	100	200	350	500

KM# 116 RUPEE

11.20 g., Silver, 21 mm. **Mint:** Jodhpur **Note:** Y#32.

Date	Mintage	G4	VG8	F12	VF20	XF40
ND(1911-18)	—	—	100	200	350	500

KM# 119 1/2 MOHUR

5.50 g., Gold, 19 mm. **Obv. Inscription:** Ha **Mint:** Jodhpur **Note:** Y#26.

Date	Mintage	G4	VG8	F12	VF20	XF40
ND(1911-18)	—	—	500	600	750	1,000

KM# 120.1 MOHUR

11.00 g., Gold, 18 mm. **Obv:** Ma. **Mint:** Jodhpur **Note:** Y#33.

Date	Mintage	G4	VG8	F12	VF20	XF40
ND(1911-18)	—	—	800	1,000	1,250	1,500

KM# 120.2 MOHUR

11.00 g., Gold, 18 mm. **Obv. Inscription:** Ha **Mint:** Jodhpur **Note:** Y#33.

Date	Mintage	G4	VG8	F12	VF20	XF40
ND(1911-18)	—	—	800	1,000	1,250	1,500

Umaid Singh

KM# 131 1/4 ANNA

10.50 g., Copper **Obv:** Without Persian "8" left of Daroga's mark **Obv. Inscription:** Edward (VIII)... **Rev. Inscription:** Umaid Singh... **Mint:** Jodhpur **Note:** Y#39.

Date	Mintage	G4	VG8	F12	VF20	XF40
1936	—	—	1.00	2.00	3.00	5.00

KM# 132 1/4 ANNA

10.50 g., Copper **Obv:** Large Persian "8" left of Daroga's mark **Obv. Inscription:** Edward (VIII)... **Rev. Inscription:** Umaid Singh... **Mint:** Jodhpur **Note:** Varieties include 2 dots replacing the Persian "8" in the inscription and are quite common.

Date	Mintage	G4	VG8	F12	VF20	XF40
1936	—	—	1.00	2.00	3.00	5.00

Note: Blundered legend varieties also exist

KM# 133 1/4 ANNA

10.50 g., Copper **Obv:** Small Persian "8" left of Daroga's mark **Obv. Inscription:** Edward (VIII)... **Rev. Inscription:** Umaid Singh... **Mint:** Jodhpur **Note:** Varieties include 2 dots replacing the Persian "8" in the inscription and are quite common.

Date	Mintage	G4	VG8	F12	VF20	XF40
1936	—	—	1.00	2.00	3.00	5.00

KM# 141 1/4 ANNA

Copper **Obv. Inscription:** George (VI)... **Rev:** Inscription; date at top **Rev. Inscription:** Umaid Singh... **Mint:** Jodhpur **Note:** Thick, 10.50-10.70 grams. Y#40.

Date	Mintage	G4	VG8	F12	VF20	XF40
1937	—	—	1.00	2.00	3.00	5.00
1938	—	—	1.00	2.00	3.00	5.00
1939	—	—	1.00	2.00	3.00	5.00

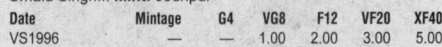

KM# 142 1/4 ANNA

Copper **Obv. Inscription:** George (VI)... **Rev. Inscription:** Umaid Singh... **Mint:** Jodhpur

Date	Mintage	G4	VG8	F12	VF20	XF40
VS1996	—	—	1.00	2.00	3.00	5.00

KM# 143 1/4 ANNA
Copper, 19-20 mm. **Obv. Inscription:** George (VI)... **Rev. Inscription:** Umaid Singh... **Mint:** Jodhpur **Note:** Size varies.

Date	Mintage	G4	VG8	F12	VF20	XF40
ND (1939)	—	—	1.00	2.00	3.00	5.00

KM# 124 1/4 RUPEE
3.10 g., Silver **Obv. Inscription:** George (V)... **Rev. Inscription:** Umaid Singh... **Mint:** Jodhpur **Note:** Y#35.

Date	Mintage	G4	VG8	F12	VF20	XF40
ND(1918-35)	—	—	100	150	225	300

KM# 125 1/2 RUPEE
Silver **Obv. Inscription:** George (V)... **Rev. Inscription:** Umaid Singh... **Shape:** Round **Mint:** Jodhpur

Date	Mintage	G4	VG8	F12	VF20	XF40
ND(1918-35)	—	—	100	150	225	300

KM# 125a 1/2 RUPEE
Silver **Obv. Inscription:** George (V)... **Rev. Inscription:** Umaid Singh... **Mint:** Jodhpur **Note:** Square flan.

Date	Mintage	G4	VG8	F12	VF20	XF40
ND(1918-35)	—	—	100	150	225	300

KM# 126 RUPEE
Silver **Obv. Inscription:** George (V)... **Rev. Inscription:** Umaid Singh... **Mint:** Jodhpur

Date	Mintage	G4	VG8	F12	VF20	XF40
ND(1918-35)	—	—	100	200	350	500

KM# 127.1 1/4 MOHUR
2.70 g., Gold, 16 mm. **Obv:** OM **Obv. Inscription:** George (V)... **Rev. Inscription:** Umaid Singh... **Mint:** Jodhpur **Note:** Y#36.

Date	Mintage	G4	VG8	F12	VF20	XF40
ND(1918-35)	—	—	—	300	500	700

KM# 127.2 1/4 MOHUR
2.70 g., Gold, 16 mm. **Obv:** Shri **Obv. Inscription:** George (V)... **Rev. Inscription:** Umaid Singh... **Mint:** Jodhpur **Note:** Y#36.

Date	Mintage	G4	VG8	F12	VF20	XF40
ND(1918-35)	—	—	—	300	500	700

KM# 128 1/2 MOHUR
5.50 g., Gold, 18 mm. **Obv. Inscription:** George (V)... **Rev. Inscription:** Umaid Singh... **Mint:** Jodhpur **Note:** Y#37.

Date	Mintage	G4	VG8	F12	VF20	XF40
ND(1918-35)	—	—	—	500	750	1,000

KM# 129 MOHUR
11.00 g., Gold, 18-20 mm. **Obv:** Om **Obv. Inscription:** George (V)... **Rev. Inscription:** Umaid Singh... **Mint:** Jodhpur **Note:** Y#38. Size varies.

Date	Mintage	G4	VG8	F12	VF20	XF40
19x8	—	—	—	800	1,100	1,500

KM# 130 MOHUR
11.00 g., Gold, 18-20 mm. **Obv:** Shri **Obv. Inscription:** George (V)... **Rev. Inscription:** Umaid Singh... **Mint:** Jodhpur **Note:** Y#38. Size varies.

Date	Mintage	G4	VG8	F12	VF20	XF40
ND(1918-35)	—	—	—	800	1,100	1,500

KM# 140 MOHUR
11.01 g., Gold **Obv. Inscription:** Edward VIII **Mint:** Jodhpur

Date	Mintage	G4	VG8	F12	VF20	XF40
1936	—	—	—	800	1,100	1,500

KM# 150 MOHUR
11.00 g., Gold, 18 mm. **Obv:** Large legend, Persian "6" after "George" **Obv. Inscription:** George (VI)... **Rev:** Large legend, Persian "6" after "George" **Rev. Inscription:** Umaid Singh... **Mint:** Jodhpur **Note:** Y#42.

Date	Mintage	G4	VG8	F12	VF20	XF40
VS1997 (1940)	—	—	—	800	1,100	1,500
ND-1943	—	—	—	800	1,100	1,500

KM# 151.1 MOHUR
11.02 g., Gold **Obv:** Small legend, without Persian "6" **Obv. Inscription:** George (VI)... **Rev:** Small legend, without Persian "6" **Rev. Inscription:** Umaid Singh... **Mint:** Jodhpur

Date	Mintage	G4	VG8	F12	VF20	XF40
VS1999	—	—	—	800	1,100	1,500
ND-1942	—	—	—	800	1,100	1,500
VS2000	—	—	—	800	1,100	1,500

KM# 151.2 MOHUR
11.02 g., Gold **Obv:** With Persian "6" below Daroga's mark **Obv. Inscription:** George (VI)... **Rev. Inscription:** Umaid Singh ... **Mint:** Jodhpur **Note:** Varieties exist.

Date	Mintage	G4	VG8	F12	VF20	XF40
VS2001 (1944)	—	—	—	800	1,100	1,500

MILLED COINAGE

KM# 144 1/4 ANNA
3.00 g., Copper **Obv:** Without Persian "6" below Daroga's mark **Obv. Inscription:** George (VI)... **Rev. Inscription:** Umaid Singh... **Mint:** Jodhpur **Note:** Thin flan. Y#41.

Date	Mintage	G4	VG8	F12	VF20	XF40
ND (1943)	—	1.00	2.00	3.00	4.00	—
Date off flan						
VS2000	—	1.00	2.00	3.00	4.00	—

KM# 147 1/4 ANNA
2.60 g., Copper **Obv:** Cock with wings raised facing left, legend around **Obv. Inscription:** George (VI)... **Rev:** Date and "Rajya Marwar" **Rev. Inscription:** Umaid Singh... **Mint:** Jodhpur

Date	Mintage	G4	VG8	F12	VF20	XF40
VS2000 Rare	—	—	—	—	—	—

KM# 145 1/4 ANNA
2.60 g., Copper **Obv:** Persian "6" below Daroga's mark **Obv. Inscription:** George (VI)... **Rev. Inscription:** Umaid Singh... **Mint:** Jodhpur **Note:** Varieties exist.

Date	Mintage	G4	VG8	F12	VF20	XF40
VS2001	—	1.00	2.00	3.00	4.00	—
VS2002	—	1.00	2.00	3.00	4.00	—

KM# 146 1/4 ANNA
2.60 g., Copper **Obv:** Persian 2 (error for 6) below Daroga's mark **Obv. Inscription:** George (VI)... **Rev. Inscription:** Umaid Singh... **Mint:** Jodhpur

Date	Mintage	G4	VG8	F12	VF20	XF40
VS2002	—	2.00	4.00	6.00	8.00	13.00

Hanwant Singh
as Titular Ruler
HAMMERED COINAGE

KM# 152 1/4 ANNA
4.20 g., Copper **Obv. Inscription:** George (VI)... **Rev. Inscription:** Hanwant Singh... **Mint:** Jodhpur **Note:** Y#43.

Date	Mintage	G4	VG8	F12	VF20	XF40
VS-2004	—	5.00	7.00	10.00	25.00	50.00

KM# 158 1/4 MOHUR
2.70 g., Gold **Obv. Inscription:** George (VI)... **Rev. Inscription:** Hanwant Singh... **Mint:** Jodhpur

Date	Mintage	G4	VG8	F12	VF20	XF40
VS-2004	—	—	—	500	750	1,000

KM# 160 MOHUR
11.00 g., Gold **Obv. Inscription:** George (VI)... **Rev. Inscription:** Hanwant Singh... **Mint:** Jodhpur

Date	Mintage	G4	VG8	F12	VF20	XF40
VS-2004	—	—	—	800	900	1,100

JUNAGADH

A state located in the Kathiawar peninsula of Western India was originally a petty Rajput kingdom until conquered by the Sultan of Ahmadabad in 1472. It became a Mughal dependency under the Emperor Akbar, administered by the Ahmadabad Subah. In 1735, when the empire began to disintegrate, a Mughal officer and military adventurer, Sher Khan Babi, expelled the Mughal governor and asserted his independence. From that time until Indian independence his descendents ruled the state as nawabs. In 1947 the Nawab of Junagadh tried to accede to the new nation of Pakistan but the Hindu majority in the state objected and Junagadh was absorbed by the Republic of India.

Junagadh first entered into treaty relations with the British in 1807 and maintained a close and friendly association with the Raj. In 1924 this relationship was formalized when Junagadh was placed under an Agent to the Governor General in the western India States. In 1935 the state comprised 3,337 square miles with a population of 545,152, four-fifths of whom were Hindus.

RULERS

Rasul Muhammad Khan, AH1309-1329/VS1948-1968/1891-1911AD

Mahabat Khan III, AH1329-1368/VS1968-2005/1911-1948AD

KINGDOM

Rasul Muhammad Khan
AH1309-1329 / VS1948-1968 / 1891-1911AD
MILLED COINAGE

Junagadh

KM# 43 DOKDO
Copper **Obv. Inscription:** Perso-Arabic "Ek paisa Junagadh Riiyaasat (government)" **Rev. Inscription:** Devanagari-Shri Sorath Sarkaar **Mint:** Junagadh

Date	Mintage	G4	VG8	F12	VF20	XF40
AH1325/VS1963	—	—	0.50	1.00	1.50	2.00

KM# 44.1 DOKDO
Copper **Obv. Inscription:** Perso-Arabic Ek paisa Junagadh Riiyaasat (government) **Rev:** Inscription; date without rosettes **Rev. Inscription:** Devanagari-Shri Sorath Sarkaar **Mint:** Junagadh

Date	Mintage	G4	VG8	F12	VF20	XF40
VS1963(1906)	—	—	0.50	1.00	1.50	2.00
VS1964(1907)	—	—	0.50	1.00	1.50	2.00

KM# 44.2 DOKDO
Copper **Obv. Inscription:** Perso-Arabic Ek paisa Junagadh Riiyaasat (government) **Rev:** Inscription; date with annulets **Rev. Inscription:** Devanagari-Shri Sorath Sarkaar **Mint:** Junagadh

Date	Mintage	G4	VG8	F12	VF20	XF40
VS1964	—	—	0.50	1.00	1.50	2.00

KM# 44.3 DOKDO
Copper **Obv. Inscription:** Perso-Arabic Ek paisa Junagadh Riiyaasat (government) **Rev:** Inscription; date between solid stars **Rev. Inscription:** Devanagari-Shri Sorath Sarkaar **Mint:** Junagadh

Date	Mintage	G4	VG8	F12	VF20	XF40
VS1964	—	—	0.50	1.00	1.50	2.00

KM# 44.4 DOKDO
Copper **Obv. Inscription:** Perso-Arabic Ek paisa Junagadh Riiyaasat (government) **Rev:** Date with outlined stars **Rev. Inscription:** Devanagari-Shri Sorath Sarkaar **Mint:** Junagadh

Date	Mintage	G4	VG8	F12	VF20	XF40
VS1964	—	—	0.50	1.00	1.50	2.00

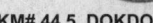

KM# 44.5 DOKDO
Copper **Obv. Inscription:** Perso-Arabic Ek paisa Junagadh Riiyaasat (government) **Rev:** Inscription; solid star only to left of date **Rev. Inscription:** Devanagari-Shri Sorath Sarkaar **Mint:** Junagadh **Note:** Prev. KM#44.3a.

Date	Mintage	G4	VG8	F12	VF20	XF40
VS1964	—	—	0.50	1.00	1.50	2.00

KM# 45.1 DOKDO
3.93 g., Copper **Obv. Inscription:** Perso-Arabic Ek paisa Junagadh Riiyaasat (government) **Rev:** Date between rosettes **Rev. Inscription:** Devanagari-Shri Sorath Sarkaar **Mint:** Junagadh

Date	Mintage	G4	VG8	F12	VF20	XF40
VS1964(1907)	—	—	0.50	1.00	2.00	—
VS1965(1908)	—	—	0.50	1.00	2.00	—
VS1966(1909)	—	—	0.50	1.00	2.00	—
VS1967(1910)	—	—	0.50	1.00	2.00	—

KM# 45.2 DOKDO
Copper **Obv. Inscription:** Perso-Arabic Ek paisa Junagadh Riiyaasat (government) **Rev:** Date divided by space in legend **Rev. Inscription:** Devanagari-Shri Sorath Sarkaar **Mint:** Junagadh

Date	Mintage	G4	VG8	F12	VF20	XF40
VS1966(1909)	—	—	0.50	1.00	2.00	—

KM# 45.3 DOKDO
Copper **Obv. Inscription:** Perso-Arabic Ek paisa Junagadh Riiyaasat (government) **Rev:** Date at top in legend **Rev. Inscription:** Devanagari-Shri Sorath Sarkaar **Mint:** Junagadh

Date	Mintage	G4	VG8	F12	VF20	XF40
VS1966(1909)	—	—	1.00	2.00	5.00	—

KM# 46.1 DOKDO
Copper **Obv. Inscription:** Perso-Arabic Ek paisa Junagadh Riiyaasat (government) **Rev. Inscription:** Devanagari-Shri Sorath Sarkaar **Mint:** Junagadh

Date	Mintage	G4	VG8	F12	VF20	XF40
ND(1909)	—	—	1.00	2.00	5.00	—

KM# 46.2 DOKDO
Copper **Obv. Inscription:** Perso-Arabic Ek paisa Junagadh Riiyaasat (government) **Rev:** Stars between inscriptions **Rev. Inscription:** Devanagari-Shri Sorath Sarkaar **Mint:** Junagadh

Date	Mintage	G4	VG8	F12	VF20	XF40
ND(1909)	—	—	1.00	2.00	5.00	—

KM# 48 2 DOKDA
Copper **Obv. Inscription:** Perso-Arabic Ek paisa Junagadh Riiyaasat (government) **Rev. Inscription:** Devanagari-Shri Sorath Sarkaar **Mint:** Junagadh

Date	Mintage	G4	VG8	F12	VF20	XF40
VS1964(1907)	—	—	7.00	15.00	25.00	—

KM# 52 KORI
4.60 g., Silver, 15 mm. **Mint:** Junagadh

Date	Mintage	VG8	F12	VF20	XF40	MS60
VS1966	—	—	34.50	46.25	70.00	—

KM# 58 GOLD KORI
Gold **Obv:** Perso-Arabic inscription **Obv. Inscription:** Nawab Bahadur Muhammad Khanji **Rev:** Date, mint name **Mint:** Junagadh **Note:** Weight varies: 4.02-4.77 grams.

Date	Mintage	VG8	F12	VF20	XF40	MS60
AH1325/VS1963	—	—	—	2,000	3,000	5,000

KM# 60 MOHUR
11.54 g., Gold **Obv:** Perso-Arabic inscription **Obv. Inscription:** Nawab Bahadur Muhammad Khanji **Rev:** Date, mint name **Mint:** Junagadh

Date	Mintage	VG8	F12	VF20	XF40	MS60
AH1325/VS1963	—	—	—	2,000	3,000	5,000

KM# 61 MOHUR
11.54 g., Gold **Obv:** "Shri Divan" in Devanagari below **Mint:** Junagadh

Date	Mintage	G4	VG8	F12	VF20	XF40
AH1325(1907) Rare	—	—	—	—	—	—

Mahabat Khan III

AH1329-1368 / VS1968-2005 / 1911-1948AD

KM# 63 DOKDO
Copper

Date	Mintage	G4	VG8	F12	VF20	XF40
VS1985(1928)	—	—	50.00	100	150	200
VS1990(1933)	—	—	50.00	100	150	200

KARAULI

State located in Rajputana, northwest India.

Karauli was established in the 11th century by Jadon Rajputs, of the same stock as the royal house of Jaisalmir. They are thought to have migrated to Rajasthan from the Mathura region some years earlier. The state passed successively under Mughal and Maratha suzerainty before coming under British authority in 1817.

The Maharajas of Karauli first struck coins in the reign of Manak Pal.

RULERS
Bhanwar Pal, 1886-1927

MINT
Karauli

KINGDOM, BRITISH PROTECTORATE

HAMMERED COINAGE

Regal Style

KM# 18 NAZRANA MOHUR
10.80 g., Silver **Obv. Inscription:** Shah Alam II **Note:** All known pieces are the part of the nacles, the hook is removed

Date	Mintage	G4	VG8	F12	VF20	XF40
AH1196//26	—	—	—	—	—	—

KISHANGARH

The maharajas of Kishangarh, a small state in northwest India, in the vicinity of Ajmer, belonged to the Rathor Rajputs. The town of Kishangarh, which gave its name to the state, was founded in 1611 and was itself named after Kishen Singh, the first ruler. The maharajas succeeded in reaching terms with Akbar in the late 16th century, and again in 1818 with the British. In 1949 the state was merged into Rajasthan.

RULERS
Sardul Singh, VS1936-1957/1879-1900AD
Madan Singh, VS1957-1983/1900-1926AD
Yaghyanarayan Singh, VS1983-1995/1926-1938AD
Sumer Singh, VS1995-2000/1938-1949AD

MINT

Kishangarh

MINT MARK

Symbol on reverse: Jhar

KINGDOM

HAMMERED COINAGE

1900-1926

Regal Style

Y# B3 1/4 RUPEE
2.70 g., Silver **Obv. Inscription:** Edward (VII)... **Rev:** Jhar **Rev. Inscription:** Madan Singh...

Date	Mintage	G4	VG8	F12	VF20	XF40
ND//24 (sic)	—	—	50.00	75.00	100	125

Y# 3 1/2 RUPEE
5.40 g., Silver **Obv. Inscription:** Edward (VII)... **Rev:** Jhar **Rev. Inscription:** Madan Singh...

Date	Mintage	G4	VG8	F12	VF20	XF40
1902//24	—	—	40.00	60.00	80.00	100

Y# C3 RUPEE
10.80 g., Silver **Obv. Inscription:** Empress Victoria... **Rev:** Jhar **Rev. Inscription:** Madan Singh...

Date	Mintage	G4	VG8	F12	VF20	XF40
ND(1900-01)	—	—	—	—	—	—

Y# D3 MOHUR
10.90 g., Gold **Obv. Inscription:** Empress Victoria... **Rev:** Jhar **Rev. Inscription:** Madan Singh...

Date	Mintage	G4	VG8	F12	VF20	XF40
ND(1900-01)	—	—	—	800	1,100	1,500

HAMMERED COINAGE

1926-1938

Y# 4 1/4 RUPEE
2.70 g., Silver **Obv. Inscription:** George (V)... **Rev:** Jhar **Rev. Inscription:** Yaghyanarayan...

Date	Mintage	G4	VG8	F12	VF20	XF40
ND//24 (sic) (1926-38)	—	—	50.00	80.00	125	150

Y# 5 1/2 RUPEE
5.40 g., Silver **Obv. Inscription:** George (V)... **Rev:** Jhar **Rev. Inscription:** Yaghyanarayan...

Date	Mintage	G4	VG8	F12	VF20	XF40
ND//24 (sic) (1926-38)	—	—	40.00	50.00	60.00	80.00

Y# 6 RUPEE
10.80 g., Silver **Obv. Inscription:** George (V)... **Rev:** Jhar **Rev. Inscription:** Yaghyanarayan...

Date	Mintage	G4	VG8	F12	VF20	XF40
ND//24 (sic) (1926-38)	—	—	40.00	50.00	60.00	80.00

Y# 6a NAZARANA RUPEE
Silver **Obv. Inscription:** George (V)... **Rev:** Jhar **Rev. Inscription:** Yaghyanarayan... **Note:** Weight varies: 10.70-10.80 grams.

Date	Mintage	G4	VG8	F12	VF20	XF40
ND(1926-38)	—	—	200	300	400	600

Y# 7 1/2 MOHUR
Gold, 18 mm. **Obv. Inscription:** George (V)... **Rev:** Jhar **Rev. Inscription:** Yaghyanarayan... **Note:** Approximately 5.50 grams.

Date	Mintage	G4	VG8	F12	VF20	XF40
ND//24 (sic) (1926-38)	—	—	500	600	700	800

Y# 8 MOHUR
Gold, 19 mm. **Obv. Inscription:** George (V)... **Rev:** Jhar **Rev. Inscription:** Yaghyanarayan... **Note:** Approximately 11.00 grams.

Date	Mintage	G4	VG8	F12	VF20	XF40
ND//24 (sic) (1926-38)	—	—	800	900	1,000	1,200

ANONYMOUS HAMMERED COINAGE

First Series

Y# 9 1/8 RUPEE
1.35 g., Silver, 12 mm. **Obv. Inscription:** Nagari "Chadi" (silver) **Rev:** Jhar

Date	Mintage	G4	VG8	F12	VF20	XF40
ND//24 (sic) (ca.1902-38)	—	—	50.00	75.00	125	200

Y# 10 1/4 RUPEE
2.70 g., Silver, 15 mm. **Obv. Inscription:** Nagari "Chadi" (silver) **Rev:** Jhar

Date	Mintage	G4	VG8	F12	VF20	XF40
ND//24 (sic) (ca.1902-38)	—	—	50.00	60.00	75.00	100

Y# 11 1/2 RUPEE
5.40 g., Silver, 17-18 mm. **Obv. Inscription:** Nagari "Chadi" (silver) **Rev:** Jhar **Note:** Size varies.

Date	Mintage	VG8	F12	VF20	XF40	MS60
ND(ca.1902-38)	—	50.00	60.00	75.00	100	—

Y# A11 1/2 RUPEE
(No Composition) **Obv:** As #Y11. **Obv. Inscription:** Nagari "Chadi" (Silver) **Rev:** As #Y5. **Rev. Inscription:** Maharajah Yaghyanarayan... **Note:** Mule.

Date	Mintage	VG8	F12	VF20	XF40	MS60
ND(1902-38) Rare	—	—	—	—	—	—

KM# 12.1 RUPEE
Silver, 20-24 mm. **Obv. Inscription:** Nagari "Chadi" (silver) **Rev:** Jhar **Note:** Weight varies: 10.85-11.05 grams. Small flan, thick.

Date	Mintage	G4	VG8	F12	VF20	XF40
ND//24 (sic) (ca.1902-38)	—	—	30.00	50.00	70.00	100

KM# 12.2 RUPEE
Silver, 20-24 mm. **Obv. Inscription:** Nagari "Chadi" (silver) **Rev:** Jhar **Note:** Weight varies: 10.85-11.05 g. Large flan, thin.

Date	Mintage	G4	VG8	F12	VF20	XF40
ND//24 (sic) (ca.1902-38)	—	—	30.00	50.00	70.00	100

ANONYMOUS HAMMERED COINAGE

Denominations in Nagari, Persian and 'merchants numerals' in Annas on obverse.

Second Series

Y# 13 2 ANNAS
1.32 g., Silver, 11 mm. **Rev:** Jhar

Date	Mintage	G4	VG8	F12	VF20	XF40
ND//24 (sic) (ca.1902-38)	—	—	100	150	225	300

Y# 14 4 ANNAS
2.62 g., Silver, 12-13 mm. **Rev:** Jhar **Note:** Size varies.

Date	Mintage	G4	VG8	F12	VF20	XF40
ND//24 (sic) (ca.1902-38)	—	—	100	150	225	300

Y# 15 8 ANNAS
5.35 g., Silver, 16 mm. **Rev:** Jhar

Date	Mintage	G4	VG8	F12	VF20	XF40
ND//24 (sic) (ca.1902-38)	—	—	100	150	225	300

KOTAH

Kotah State, located in northwest India was subdivided out of Bundi early in the 17th century when it was given to a younger son of the Bundi raja by the Mughal emperor. The ruler, or maharao, was a Chauhan Rajput. During the years of Maratha ascendancy Kotah fell on hard times, especially from the depredations of Holkar. In 1817 the State came under treaty with the British.

RULERS
Ram Singh II, VS1885-1923/1828-1866AD
Chattar Singh, VS1923-1946/1866-1889AD
Umed Singh II, VS1946-1992/1889-1935AD

MINT

نندگانو

Mintname: *Nandgaon*

نندگانو عرف کوته

Kotah urf Nandgaon
or *Nandgaon urf Kotah* on earliest issues.

MINT MARKS

1. 2. 3. 4. 5.

Mint mark #1 appears beneath #4 on most Kotah coins, and serves to distinguish coins of Kotah from similar issues of Bundi in the pre-Victoria period.

C#28 has mint mark #2 on obv., #1, 3 and 4 on rev. All later issues have #1 on obv., #1, 5 and 4 on rev.

BRITISH PROTECTORATE

HAMMERED COINAGE

Regal Style

Y# 6 RUPEE
11.20 g., Silver, 18-20 mm. **Obv. Inscription:** Badshah Zaman Inglistan... (Victoria) **Note:** Size varies.

Date	Mintage	G4	VG8	F12	VF20	XF40
ND//44 (1901)	—	20.00	30.00	40.00	50.00	60.00

Y# 6a NAZARANA RUPEE
11.20 g., Silver, 26-30 mm. **Obv. Inscription:** Badshah Zaman Inglistan... (Victoria) **Note:** Size varies.

Date	Mintage	G4	VG8	F12	VF20	XF40
ND//44 (1901)	—	300	350	400	450	500

Y# 8 MOHUR
10.70 g., Gold, 18 mm. **Obv. Inscription:** Badshah Zaman Inglistan... (Victoria)

Date	Mintage	VG8	F12	VF20	XF40	MS60
ND//44 (1901)	—	800	1,000	1,250	1,500	—

KUTCH

State located in northwest India, consisting of a peninsula north of the Gulf of Kutch.

The rulers of Kutch were Jareja Rajputs who, coming from Tatta in Sind, conquered Kutch in the 14th or 15th centuries. The capital city of Bhuj is thought to date from the mid-16th century. In 1617, after Akbar's conquest of Gujerat and the fall of the Gujerat sultans, the Kutch ruler, Rao Bharmal I (1586-1632) visited Jahangir and established a relationship which was sufficiently warm as to leave Kutch virtually independent throughout the Mughal period. Early in the 19th century internal disorder and the existence of rival claimants to the throne resulted in British intrusion into the state's affairs. Rao Bharmalji II was deposed in favor of Rao Desalji II who proved much more amenable to the Government of India's wishes. He and his successors continued to rule in a manner considered by the British to be most enlightened and, as a result, Maharao Khengarji III was created a Knight Grand Commander of the Indian Empire. In view of its geographical isolation Kutch came under the direct control of the Central Government at India's independence.

First coinage was struck in 1617AD.

RULERS
Khengarji III, VS1932-1999/1875-1942AD

M(a)-ha-ra-o Sri Khen-ga-r-ji

मा हा रा उ खें गा र जी

Ma-ha-ra-o Khen-ga-r-ji

मा हा राजा।धिराज।मिरजा महाराओ श्री

Ma-ha-ra-ja Dhi-ra-j Mi-r-ja M(a)-ha-ra-o Sri

खेंगारजी बहादुर कछभुज

Khen-ga-r-ji B(a)-ha-du-r K(a)-chh-bhu-j

मिरजामहाराओश्री खेंगारजी

Mi-r-jan M(a)-ha-ra-o Sri Khen-ga-r-ji

महाराओश्री खेंगारजी

M(a)-ha-ra-o Sri Khen-ga-r-ji

महाराजाधिराजमिरजा महाराउ

M(a)-ha-ra-ja Dhi-ra-j Mi-r-jan M(a)-ha-ra-o

श्री खेंगारजीबहादुर

Sri-Khen-ga-r-ji B(a)-ha-du-r

श्री खेंगारजीसवाई बहादुर

Sri Khen-ga-r-ji Sa-va-i B(a)-ha-du-r

महाराउश्री खेंगारजी कच्छभुज

M(a)-ha-ra-o Sri Khen-ga-r-ji K(a)-chchh-bhu-j
Vijayarajji, VS1999-2004/1942-1947AD

विजयराजजी

Vi-j(a)-y(a)-ra-j-ji

महाराओश्री विजयराजजी

M(a)-ha-ra-o Sri Vi-j(a)-y(a)-ra-j-ji K(a)-chchh 2000
Madanasinhji, VS2004-- /1947-1948AD

मदनसिंहजी

M(a)-d(a)-n(a)-sin-h-ji
Pragmalji III & Maharani Pritidevi, VS2048-/1991AD-

MINT

Bhuj	भुज (Devanagari)	بهج (Persian)

KINGDOM

Khengarji III

VS1932-98 / 1875-1942AD

MILLED COINAGE

Regal Issues - Second Series

Y# 35.1 KORI
4.70 g., 0.610 Silver 0.0922 oz. ASW **Obv. Inscription:** Victoria, Empress of India **Rev:** Open crescent

Date	Mintage	G4	VG8	F12	VF20	XF40
1901//VS1957	—	15.00	16.00	18.00	20.00	25.00

Y# 37.6 5 KORI
13.87 g., 0.937 Silver 0.4178 oz. ASW **Obv. Inscription:** Victoria, Empress of India

Date	Mintage	G4	VG8	F12	VF20	XF40
1901//VS1957	—	30.00	32.00	35.00	38.00	40.00

MILLED COINAGE

Regal Issues - Third Series

Y# 38 TRAMBIYO
4.00 g., Copper, 16 mm. **Obv. Legend:** Edward VII...

Date	Mintage	G4	VG8	F12	VF20	XF40
1908/VS1965	—	1.00	2.00	3.00	4.00	5.00
1909/VS1965	—	1.00	2.00	3.00	4.00	5.00
1909/VS1966	—	1.00	2.00	3.00	4.00	5.00
1910/VS1966	—	1.00	2.00	3.00	4.00	5.00

Y# 39 DOKDO
8.00 g., Copper, 20.5 mm. **Obv. Legend:** Edward VII...

Date	Mintage	G4	VG8	F12	VF20	XF40
1909/VS1965	—	1.00	2.00	3.00	4.00	5.00
1909/VS1966	—	1.00	2.00	3.00	4.00	5.00

Y# 40 1-1/2 DOKDA
12.00 g., Copper, 23 mm. **Obv. Legend:** Edward VII...

Date	Mintage	G4	VG8	F12	VF20	XF40
1909/VS1965	—	30.00	60.00	100	115	150

Y# 41 3 DOKDA
24.00 g., Copper **Obv. Legend:** Edward VII...

Date	Mintage	G4	VG8	F12	VF20	XF40
1909/VS1965	—	200	225	250	275	300

Y# 45 5 KORI
13.87 g., 0.937 Silver 0.4178 oz. ASW **Obv. Legend:** Edward VII...

Date	Mintage	G4	VG8	F12	VF20	XF40
1902/VS1959	—	2,000	2,200	2,400	2,800	3,000
1903/VS1960	—	2,000	2,200	2,400	2,800	3,000
1904/VS1961	—	2,000	2,200	2,400	2,800	3,000
1905/VS1962	—	2,000	2,200	2,400	2,800	3,000
1906/VS1963	—	2,000	2,200	2,400	2,800	3,000
1907VS1964	—	2,000	2,200	2,400	2,800	3,000
1908/VS1965	—	2,000	2,200	2,400	2,800	3,000
1909/VS1966	—	2,000	2,200	2,400	2,800	3,000

MILLED COINAGE

Regal Issues - Fourth Series

Y# 46 TRAMBIYO
4.00 g., Copper, 16 mm. **Obv. Inscription:** George V...

Date	Mintage	G4	VG8	F12	VF20	XF40
1919/VS1976	—	1.00	1.50	1.75	2.00	2.50
1920/VS1976	—	1.00	1.50	1.75	2.00	2.50
1920/VS1977	—	1.00	1.50	1.75	2.00	2.50

Y# 54 TRAMBIYO
4.00 g., Copper, 16 mm. **Obv. Inscription:** George V...

Date	Mintage	G4	VG8	F12	VF20	XF40
1928/VS1984	—	1.00	1.25	1.50	2.00	3.00
1928/VS1985	—	1.00	1.25	1.50	2.00	3.00

Y# 47 DOKDO
8.00 g., Copper, 21 mm. **Obv. Inscription:** George V...

Date	Mintage	G4	VG8	F12	VF20	XF40
1920/VS1976	—	1.00	1.25	1.50	2.00	3.00
1920/VS1977	—	1.00	1.25	1.50	2.00	3.00

Y# 55 DOKDO
8.00 g., Copper, 21 mm. **Obv. Inscription:** George V...

Date	Mintage	G4	VG8	F12	VF20	XF40
1922/VS1982 (sic)	—	1.00	1.25	1.75	2.50	5.00
1928/VS1984	—	1.00	1.25	1.75	2.50	5.00
1929/VS1985	—	1.00	1.25	1.75	2.50	5.00

Y# 48 1-1/2 DOKDA
12.00 g., Copper, 23.5 mm. **Obv. Inscription:** George V...

Date	Mintage	G4	VG8	F12	VF20	XF40
1926/VS1982	—	1.00	1.25	1.75	2.50	5.00

Y# 56 1-1/2 DOKDA
12.00 g., Copper, 23 mm. **Obv. Inscription:** George V...

Date	Mintage	G4	VG8	F12	VF20	XF40
1928/VS1985	—	1.00	1.25	1.75	2.50	5.00
1929/VS1985	—	1.00	1.25	1.75	2.50	5.00
1929/VS1986	—	1.00	1.25	1.75	2.50	5.00
1931/VS1987	—	1.00	1.25	1.75	2.50	5.00
1931/VS1988	—	1.00	1.25	1.75	2.50	5.00
1932/VS1988	—	1.00	1.25	1.75	2.50	5.00
1932/VS1989	—	1.00	1.25	1.75	2.50	5.00

Y# 49 3 DOKDA
24.00 g., Copper, 33 mm. **Obv. Inscription:** George V...

Date	Mintage	G4	VG8	F12	VF20	XF40
1926/VS1982	—	3.00	4.00	5.00	6.00	8.00

Y# 57 3 DOKDA
24.00 g., Copper, 33 mm. **Obv. Inscription:** George V...

Date	Mintage	G4	VG8	F12	VF20	XF40
1928/VS1985	—	2.00	3.00	4.00	5.00	7.00
1929/VS1985	—	2.00	3.00	4.00	5.00	7.00
1929/VS1986	—	2.00	3.00	4.00	5.00	7.00
1930/VS1987	—	2.00	3.00	4.00	5.00	7.00
1931/VS1987	—	2.00	3.00	4.00	5.00	7.00
1934/VS1990	—	2.00	3.00	4.00	5.00	7.00
1934/VS1991	—	2.00	3.00	4.00	5.00	7.00
1935/VS1992	—	2.00	3.00	4.00	5.00	7.00

Y# 58 1/2 KORI

2.35 g., 0.601 Silver 0.0454 oz. ASW, 14 mm. **Obv. Inscription:** George V...

Date	Mintage	G4	VG8	F12	VF20	XF40
1928/VS1985	—	12.00	15.00	18.00	20.00	25.00

Y# 51 KORI

4.70 g., 0.601 Silver 0.0908 oz. ASW **Obv. Inscription:** George V...

Date	Mintage	VG8	F12	VF20	XF40	MS60
1913/VS1970	—	6.00	8.00	10.00	12.00	15.00
1923/VS1979	—	6.00	8.00	10.00	12.00	15.00
1923/VS1980	—	6.00	8.00	10.00	12.00	15.00
1927/VS1984	—	6.00	8.00	10.00	12.00	15.00

Y# 59 KORI

4.70 g., 0.601 Silver 0.0908 oz. ASW, 17 mm. **Obv. Legend:** George V...

Date	Mintage	VG8	F12	VF20	XF40	MS60
1928/VS1985	—	5.00	6.00	7.00	8.00	11.50
1929/VS1985	—	5.00	6.00	7.00	8.00	11.50
1931/VS1987	—	5.00	6.00	7.00	8.00	11.50
1931/VS1988	—	5.00	6.00	7.00	8.00	11.50
1932/VS1988	—	5.00	6.00	7.00	8.00	11.50
1932/VS1989	—	5.00	6.00	7.00	8.00	11.50
1933/VS1989	—	5.00	6.00	7.00	8.00	11.50
1933/VS1990	—	5.00	6.00	7.00	8.00	11.50
1934/VS1990	—	5.00	6.00	7.00	8.00	11.50
1934/VS1991	—	5.00	6.00	7.00	8.00	11.50
1935/VS1991	—	5.00	6.00	7.00	8.00	11.50
1935/VS1992	—	5.00	6.00	7.00	8.00	11.50
1936/VS1992	—	5.00	6.00	7.00	8.00	11.50

Y# 52 2-1/2 KORI

6.94 g., 0.937 Silver 0.2089 oz. ASW **Obv. Inscription:** George V...

Date	Mintage	VG8	F12	VF20	XF40	MS60
1916/VS1973	—	25.00	26.00	27.00	28.00	30.00
1917/VS1973	—	25.00	26.00	27.00	28.00	30.00
1917/VS1974	—	25.00	26.00	27.00	28.00	30.00
1918/VS1974	—	25.00	26.00	27.00	28.00	30.00
1919/VS1975	—	25.00	26.00	27.00	28.00	30.00
1922/VS1978	—	25.00	26.00	27.00	28.00	30.00
1922/VS1979	—	25.00	26.00	27.00	28.00	30.00
1924/VS1981	—	25.00	26.00	27.00	28.00	30.00
1926/VS1983	—	25.00	26.00	27.00	28.00	30.00

Y# 52a 2-1/2 KORI

6.94 g., 0.937 Silver 0.2089 oz. ASW **Obv. Inscription:** George V... **Rev:** Smaller legend

Date	Mintage	VG8	F12	VF20	XF40	MS60
1927/VS1984	—	25.00	26.00	27.00	28.00	30.00
1928/VS1985	—	25.00	26.00	27.00	28.00	30.00
1930/VS1986	—	25.00	26.00	27.00	28.00	30.00
1930/VS1987	—	25.00	26.00	27.00	28.00	30.00
1932/VS1988	—	25.00	26.00	27.00	28.00	30.00
1932/VS1989	—	25.00	26.00	27.00	28.00	30.00
1933/VS1989	—	25.00	26.00	27.00	28.00	30.00
1933/VS1990	—	25.00	26.00	27.00	28.00	30.00
1934/VS1990	—	25.00	26.00	27.00	28.00	30.00
1934/VS1991	—	25.00	26.00	27.00	28.00	30.00
1935/VS1991	—	25.00	26.00	27.00	28.00	30.00
1935/VS1992	—	25.00	26.00	27.00	28.00	30.00

Y# 53 5 KORI

13.87 g., 0.937 Silver 0.4178 oz. ASW, 32 mm. **Obv. Inscription:** George V... **Note:** 5 Kori coins were issued with reeded edges until 1928AD, which is when the security edge was introduced. Due to counterfeiting, the government recalled pieces and added lettering as a mark of authentication.

Date	Mintage	VG8	F12	VF20	XF40	MS60
1913/VS1970	—	25.00	26.00	27.00	28.00	30.00
1915/VS1972	—	25.00	26.00	27.00	28.00	30.00
1916/VS1973	—	25.00	26.00	27.00	28.00	30.00
1916/VS1975 (Sic)	—	25.00	26.00	27.00	28.00	30.00
1917/VS1973	—	25.00	26.00	27.00	28.00	30.00
1917/VS1974	—	25.00	26.00	27.00	28.00	30.00
1918/VS1974	—	25.00	26.00	27.00	28.00	30.00
1918/VS1975	—	25.00	26.00	27.00	28.00	30.00
1919/VS1975	—	25.00	26.00	27.00	28.00	30.00
1919/VS1976	—	25.00	26.00	27.00	28.00	30.00
1920/VS1977	—	25.00	26.00	27.00	28.00	30.00
1921/VS1977	—	25.00	26.00	27.00	28.00	30.00
1921/VS1978	—	25.00	26.00	27.00	28.00	30.00
1922/VS1974 (Sic)	—	25.00	26.00	27.00	28.00	30.00
1922/VS1978	—	25.00	26.00	27.00	28.00	30.00
1922/VS1979	—	25.00	26.00	27.00	28.00	30.00
1922/VS1982 (Sic)	—	25.00	26.00	27.00	28.00	30.00
1923/VS1979	—	25.00	26.00	27.00	28.00	30.00
1924/VS1978 (Sic)	—	25.00	26.00	27.00	28.00	30.00
1924/VS1980	—	25.00	26.00	27.00	28.00	30.00
1924/VS1981	—	25.00	26.00	27.00	28.00	30.00
1925/VS1982	—	25.00	26.00	27.00	28.00	30.00
1926/VS1978 (Sic)	—	25.00	26.00	27.00	28.00	30.00
1926/VS1982	—	25.00	26.00	27.00	28.00	30.00
1926/VS1893	—	25.00	26.00	27.00	28.00	30.00
1927/VS1984	—	25.00	26.00	27.00	28.00	30.00
1927/VS1984 Proof-Rare	—	—	—	—	—	—

Y# 53a 5 KORI

13.87 g., 0.937 Silver 0.4178 oz. ASW **Obv:** Smaller legend **Obv. Inscription:** George V... **Rev:** Smaller legend

Date	Mintage	VG8	F12	VF20	XF40	MS60
1928/VS1985	—	25.00	26.00	28.00	30.00	35.00
1929/VS1986	—	25.00	26.00	28.00	30.00	35.00
1930/VS1986	—	25.00	26.00	28.00	30.00	35.00
1930/VS1987	—	25.00	26.00	28.00	30.00	35.00
1931/VS1987	—	25.00	26.00	28.00	30.00	35.00
1931/VS1988	—	25.00	26.00	28.00	30.00	35.00
1932/VS1988	—	25.00	26.00	28.00	30.00	35.00
1932/VS1989	—	25.00	26.00	28.00	30.00	35.00
1933/VS1989	—	25.00	26.00	28.00	30.00	35.00
1933/VS1990	—	25.00	26.00	28.00	30.00	35.00
1934/VS1990	—	25.00	26.00	28.00	30.00	35.00
1934/VS1991	—	25.00	26.00	28.00	30.00	35.00
1935/VS1991	—	25.00	26.00	28.00	30.00	35.00
1935/VS1992	—	25.00	26.00	28.00	30.00	35.00
1936/VS1992	—	25.00	26.00	28.00	30.00	35.00

MILLED COINAGE

Regal Issues - Fifth Series

Y# 63 3 DOKDA

24.00 g., Copper **Obv. Legend:** Edward VIII...

Date	Mintage	G4	VG8	F12	VF20	XF40
1936/VS1993	—	3.00	4.00	5.00	8.00	10.00

Y# 65 KORI

4.70 g., 0.601 Silver 0.0908 oz. ASW **Obv. Legend:** Edward VIII...

Date	Mintage	VG8	F12	VF20	XF40	MS60
1936/VS1992	—	30.00	32.00	35.00	38.00	40.00
1936/VS1993	—	30.00	32.00	35.00	38.00	40.00

Y# 66 2-1/2 KORI

6.94 g., 0.937 Silver 0.2089 oz. ASW **Obv. Inscription:** Edward VIII...

Date	Mintage	VG8	F12	VF20	XF40	MS60
1936/VS1992	—	30.00	32.00	35.00	38.00	40.00
1936/VS1993	—	30.00	32.00	35.00	38.00	40.00

Y# 67 5 KORI

13.87 g., 0.937 Silver 0.4178 oz. ASW **Obv. Inscription:** Edward VIII...

Date	Mintage	VG8	F12	VF20	XF40	MS60
1936/VS1992	—	30.00	32.00	35.00	38.00	40.00
1936/VS1993	—	30.00	32.00	35.00	38.00	40.00

MILLED COINAGE

Regal Issues - Sixth Series

Y# 71 3 DOKDA

24.00 g., Copper **Obv. Legend:** George VI

Date	Mintage	VG8	F12	VF20	XF40	MS60
1937/VS1993	—	20.00	22.00	25.00	28.00	30.00

Y# 73 KORI

4.70 g., 0.601 Silver 0.0908 oz. ASW **Obv. Legend:** George VI

Date	Mintage	VG8	F12	VF20	XF40	MS60
1937/VS1993	—	6.00	7.00	8.00	9.00	10.00
1937/VS1994	—	6.00	7.00	8.00	9.00	10.00
1938/VS1995	—	6.00	7.00	8.00	9.00	10.00
1939/VS1995	—	6.00	7.00	8.00	9.00	10.00
1939/VS1996	—	6.00	7.00	8.00	9.00	10.00
1940/VS1996	—	6.00	7.00	8.00	9.00	10.00

Y# 74 2-1/2 KORI

6.94 g., 0.937 Silver 0.2089 oz. ASW **Obv. Inscription:** George VI

Date	Mintage	VG8	F12	VF20	XF40	MS60
1937/VS1993	—	25.00	28.00	30.00	32.00	35.00

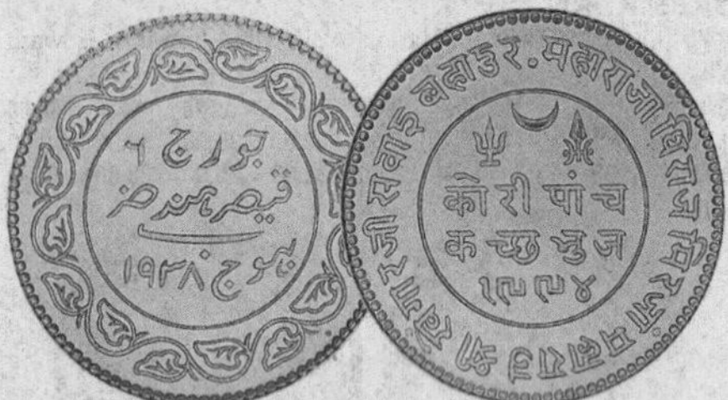

Y# 75 5 KORI

13.87 g., 0.937 Silver 0.4178 oz. ASW **Obv. Inscription:** George VI

Date	Mintage	VG8	F12	VF20	XF40	MS60
1936/VS1993	—	25.00	28.00	30.00	32.00	35.00
1937/VS1993	—	25.00	28.00	30.00	32.00	35.00
1937/VS1994	—	25.00	28.00	30.00	32.00	35.00
1938/VS1994	—	25.00	28.00	30.00	32.00	35.00
1938/VS1995	—	25.00	28.00	30.00	32.00	35.00
1941/VS1997	—	25.00	28.00	30.00	32.00	35.00
1941/VS1998	—	25.00	28.00	30.00	32.00	35.00

Vijayarajji

VS1998-2004 / 1942-1947AD

Y# 76 TRAMBIYO

Copper **Obv. Legend:** George VI

Date	Mintage	VG8	F12	VF20	XF40	MS60
1943/VS2000	—	3.00	4.00	5.00	6.00	10.00
1944/VS2000	—	3.00	4.00	5.00	6.00	10.00

Y# 77 DHINGLO (1/16 Kori = 1-1/2 Dokda)

4.11 g., Copper, 21 mm. **Obv. Legend:** George VI

Date	Mintage	VG8	F12	VF20	XF40	MS60
1943/VS2000	—	2.00	3.00	4.00	5.00	6.00
1944/VS2000	—	2.00	3.00	4.00	5.00	6.00
1947/VS2004	—	2.00	3.00	4.00	5.00	6.00
1948/VS2004	—	2.00	3.00	4.00	5.00	6.00

Y# 78 DHABU (1/8 Kori = 3 Dokda)

Copper, 23 mm. **Obv. Legend:** George VI

Date	Mintage	VG8	F12	VF20	XF40	MS60
1943/VS1999	—	2.00	3.00	4.00	5.00	6.00
1943/VS2000	—	2.00	3.00	4.00	5.00	6.00
1944/VS2000	—	2.00	3.00	4.00	5.00	6.00
1947/VS2004	—	2.00	3.00	4.00	5.00	6.00

Y# 79 PAYALO (1/4 Kori)

Copper, 27 mm. **Obv. Legend:** George VI

Date	Mintage	VG8	F12	VF20	XF40	MS60
1943/VS1999	—	3.00	4.00	5.00	6.00	10.00
1943/VS2000	—	3.00	4.00	5.00	6.00	10.00
1944/VS2000	—	3.00	4.00	5.00	6.00	10.00
1944/VS2001	—	3.00	4.00	5.00	6.00	10.00
1945/VS2001	—	3.00	4.00	5.00	6.00	10.00
1945/VS2002	—	3.00	4.00	5.00	6.00	10.00
1946/VS2002	—	3.00	4.00	5.00	6.00	10.00
1946/VS2003	—	3.00	4.00	5.00	6.00	10.00
1947/VS2003	—	3.00	4.00	5.00	6.00	10.00

Y# 80 ADHIO (1/2 Kori)

Copper, 36 mm. **Obv. Legend:** George VI

Date	Mintage	VG8	F12	VF20	XF40	MS60
1943/VS1999	—	15.00	16.00	18.00	20.00	50.00
1943/VS2000	—	15.00	16.00	18.00	20.00	50.00
1944/VS2001	—	15.00	16.00	18.00	20.00	50.00
1945/VS2001	—	15.00	16.00	18.00	20.00	50.00
1945/VS2002	—	15.00	16.00	18.00	20.00	50.00
1946/VS2002	—	15.00	16.00	18.00	20.00	50.00

Y# 81 KORI

4.70 g., 0.601 Silver 0.0908 oz. ASW **Obv. Legend:** George VI

Date	Mintage	VG8	F12	VF20	XF40	MS60
1942/VS1999	—	5.00	5.50	6.00	6.50	7.00
1943/VS1999	—	5.00	5.50	6.00	6.50	7.00
1943/VS2000	—	5.00	5.50	6.00	6.50	7.00
1944/VS2000	—	5.00	5.50	6.00	6.50	7.00
1944/VS2001	—	5.00	5.50	6.00	6.50	7.00

Y# A81 KORI

4.66 g., Silver **Obv. Legend:** George VI **Note:** Similar to Y#51.

Date	Mintage	VG8	F12	VF20	XF40	MS60
1942/VS1998 Rare	—	—	—	—	—	—

Y# 82 5 KORI

13.87 g., 0.937 Silver 0.4178 oz. ASW **Obv. Inscription:** George VI

Date	Mintage	VG8	F12	VF20	XF40	MS60
1942/VS1998	—	25.00	28.00	30.00	32.00	35.00
1942/VS1999	—	25.00	28.00	30.00	32.00	35.00
1943/VS1998 Requires Confirmation	—	—	—	—	—	—

Y# 82A 10 KORI

17.39 g., Silver **Obv. Inscription:** George VI

Date	Mintage	VG8	F12	VF20	XF40	MS60
1943/VS1999 Rare	—	—	—	—	—	—

Madanasinghji

VS2004-2005 / 1947-1948AD

Y# 83 DHABU (1/8 Kori)

Copper **Subject:** Victory for Indian Independence

Date	Mintage	VG8	F12	VF20	XF40	MS60
VS2004	—	4.00	5.00	6.00	8.00	25.00

Y# 84 KORI

4.70 g., 0.601 Silver 0.0908 oz. ASW **Subject:** Victory for Indian Independence

Date	Mintage	VG8	F12	VF20	XF40	MS60
VS2004	—	20.00	22.00	25.00	28.00	30.00

Y# 85 5 KORI

13.87 g., 0.937 Silver 0.4178 oz. ASW **Subject:** Victory for Indian Independence

Date	Mintage	VG8	F12	VF20	XF40	MS60
VS2004	—	1,000	1,250	1,350	1,500	1,800

LUNAVADA

This small state in the Panch Mahal district of western India was ruled by Solanki Rajputs who claimed descent from Sidraj Jaisingh, the ruler of Anhalwara Patan and Gujerat. The rulers, or maharanas, traced their sovereignty to the early decades of the 15th century. At different times the State was feudatory to either Baroda or Sindhia.

PRINCELY STATE

Wakhat Singhji

VS1924-1986/1867-1929AD

HAMMERED COINAGE

KM# A12 1/2 PAISA

Copper **Obv:** Chamber **Rev:** Persian legend shape **Mint:** (no Mint Information)

Date	Mintage	G4	VG8	F12	VF20	XF40
ND (1911)	—	—	10.00	20.00	35.00	50.00

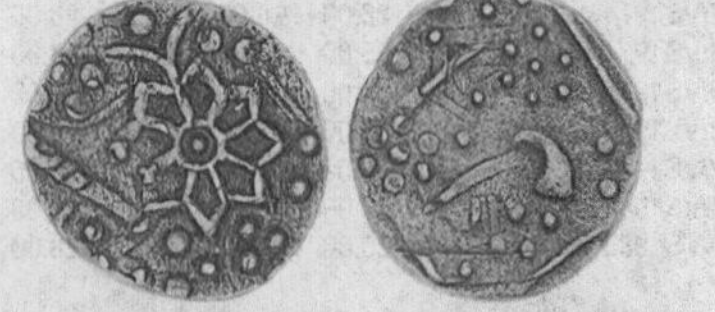

KM# 12 PAISA

Copper **Obv:** Lotus Blossom **Rev:** Persian legend **Shape:** Round **Mint:** (no Mint Information) **Note:** Weight varies: 6.50-8.30 grams.

Date	Mintage	G4	VG8	F12	VF20	XF40
VS1968(1911)	—	—	10.00	20.00	35.00	50.00
ND(ca.1911)	—	—	10.00	20.00	35.00	50.00

KM# A33.16 PAISA

10.20 g., Copper **Obv:** Muhammad Akbar II **Rev:** Rayed sun, mint mark **Mint:** Baroda **Note:** Size varies: 18 - 24mm

Date	Mintage	G4	VG8	F12	VF20	XF40
AH1247//27	—	40.00	60.00	80.00	125	150
AH124x//23	—	40.00	60.00	80.00	125	150

MAKRAI

The rajas of Makrai belong to a very ancient Gond family whose title, Raja Hatiyarai, had been conferred upon them by the emperors of Delhi. This small state of some forty-five villages struggled with varying degrees of success against the Poona Peshwa, Sindhia and the Pindaris before passing under British protection in the 19th century.

RULER
Raja Bharat Shah, 1886-1920AD

BRITISH PROTECTORATE

HAMMERED COINAGE

KM# 1 PAISA
Copper **Ruler:** Raja Bharat Shah **Obv:** Katar **Rev. Legend:** SHRI/MAK/RAI **Rev. Inscription:** Hindi **Note:** Weight varies: 9.00-11.00 grams.

Date	Mintage	G4	VG8	F12	VF20	XF40
ND(1886-1920)	—	—	5.00	8.00	15.00	25.00

KM# 2 PAISA
Copper **Ruler:** Raja Bharat Shah **Obv:** Katar **Rev. Legend:** SHRI/MAK/RAI **Rev. Inscription:** Hindi **Shape:** Square **Note:** Weight varies: 9.00-11.00 grams.

Date	Mintage	G4	VG8	F12	VF20	XF40
ND(1886-1920)	—	—	5.00	8.00	15.00	25.00

MALER KOTLA

State located in the Punjab in northwest India, founded by the Maler Kotla family who were Sherwani Afghans who had travelled to India from Kabul in 1467 as officials of the Delhi emperors.

Coins are rupees of Ahmad Shah Durrani, and except for the last ruler, contain the chief's initial on the reverse. The chiefs were called Ra'is until 1821, Nawabs thereafter.

For similar issues see Jind, Nabha and Patiala.

RULERS
Ibrahim Ali Khan, AH1288-1326/1871-1908AD
Ahmad ali Khan, AH1326/1908AD

PRINCELY STATE

Ibrahim Ali Khan

AH1288-1326 / 1871-1908AD

HAMMERED COINAGE

Y# 4 1/4 RUPEE
Silver **Note:** 2.68-2.90 grams.

Date	Mintage	G4	VG8	F12	VF20	XF40
ND(1871-1908)	—	—	100	150	225	300

Y# 5 1/2 RUPEE
Silver, 16 mm. **Note:** 5.35-5.80 grams.

Date	Mintage	G4	VG8	F12	VF20	XF40
ND(1871-1908)	—	—	100	150	225	300

Y# 6 RUPEE
Silver **Note:** 10-70.11.60 grams.

Date	Mintage	G4	VG8	F12	VF20	XF40
ND(1871-1908)	—	—	20.00	30.00	40.00	60.00

Ahmad Ali Khan

AH1326- / 1908- AD

Y# 7 1/2 PAISA
Copper **Obv:** Persian inscription **Obv. Inscription:** Ahmad Ali Khan ...

Date	Mintage	G4	VG8	F12	VF20	XF40
AH1326	—	—	10.00	20.00	35.00	50.00

Y# 8 PAISA
Copper **Obv:** Persian inscription **Obv. Inscription:** Ahmad Ali Khan ...

Date	Mintage	G4	VG8	F12	VF20	XF40
AH1326	—	—	20.00	40.00	70.00	100

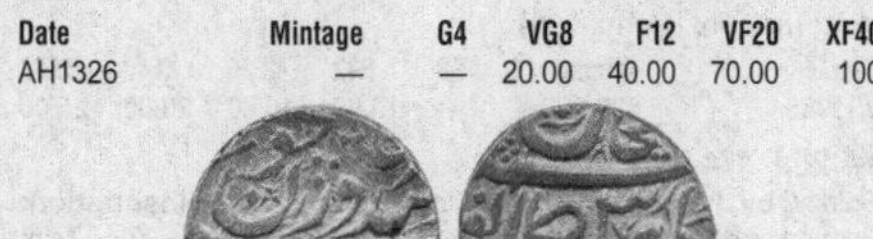

Y# 9 RUPEE
Silver **Obv:** Persian inscription **Obv. Inscription:** Ahmad Ali Khan ... **Note:** Weight varies: 10.70-11.60 grams.

Date	Mintage	G4	VG8	F12	VF20	XF40
ND(1908-09)	—	—	25.00	30.00	40.00	60.00

Y# A9 RUPEE
10.77 g., Silver, 18.5 mm. **Obv. Inscription:** Persian "Ahmad Ali Kahn"... **Rev. Inscription:** "Nawab" to left of "S" in "Julus" **Edge:** Plain

Date	Mintage	F12	VF20	XF40	MS60	MS63
ND (1908)	—	—	—	—	—	—

Y# 10 NAZARANA 2 RUPEE
22.00 g., Silver **Obv:** Persian inscription **Obv. Inscription:** Ahmad Ali Khan ...

Date	Mintage	G4	VG8	F12	VF20	XF40
AH1326 Rare	—	—	—	—	—	—

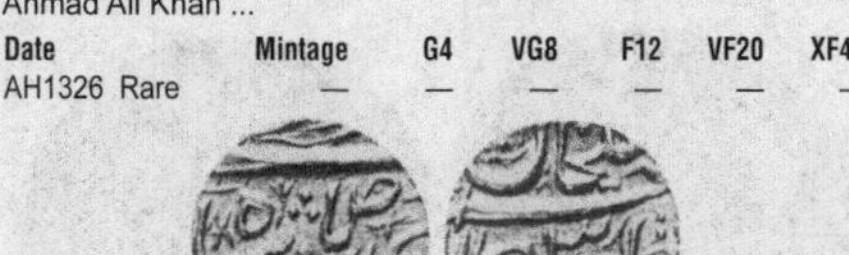

Y# 11 1/2 MOHUR
5.94 g., Gold **Obv:** Persian inscription **Obv. Inscription:** Ahmad Ali Khan ...

Date	Mintage	F12	VF20	XF40	MS60	MS63
AH1326	—	—	—	—	—	—

MEWAR

State located in Rajputana, northwest India. Capital:Udaipur.

The rulers of Mewar were universally regarded as the highest ranking Rajput house in India. The maharana of Mewar was looked upon as the representative of Rama, the ancient king of Ayodhya - and the family who were Sesodia Rajputs of the Gehlot clan, traced its descent through Rama to Kanak Sen who ruled in the 2nd century. The clan is believed to have migrated to Chitor from Gujarat sometime in the 8th century.

None of the indigenous rulers of India resisted the Muslim invasions into India with greater tenacity than the Rajputs of Mewar. It was their proud boast that they had never permitted a daughter to go into the Mughal harem. Three times the fortress and town of Chitor had fallen to Muslim invaders, to Alauddin Khilji (1303), to Bahadur Shah of Gujarat (1534) and to Akbar (1568). Each time Chitor gradually recovered but the last was the most traumatic experience of all. Rather than to submit to the Mughal onslaught, the women burned themselves on funeral pyres in a fearful rite called jauhar, and the men fell on the swords of the invaders.

After the sacking of Chitor the rana, Udai Singh, retired to the Aravali hills where he founded Udaipur, the capital after 1570. Udai Singh's son, Partab, refused to submit to the Mughal and recovered most of the territory lost in 1568. In the early 19th century Mewar suffered much at the hands of Marathas - Holkar, Sindhia and the Pindaris - until, in 1818, the State came under British supervision. In April 1948 Mewar was merged into Rajasthan and the maharana became governor Maharaj pramukh of the new province.

RULERS
Fatteh Singh, VS1941-1986/1884-1929AD
Bhupal Singh, VS1987-2005/1930-1948AD

MINTS

بهيلوارا
Bhilwara

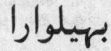

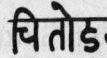

चितोड़
Chitor

चित्रकूट
Chitarkot

उदयपुर
Udaipur

NOTE: All Mewar coinage is struck without ruler's name, and is largely undated. Certain types were generally struck over several reigns.

BRITISH PROTECTORATE

HAMMERED COINAGE

Y# 7.1 1/16 RUPEE
0.65 g., Silver **Series:** Swarupshahi **Obv. Inscription:** Chitarkot/Udaipur **Rev. Inscription:** Dosti Lundhun - Friendship With London **Shape:** Round **Mint:** Udaipur

Date	Mintage	G4	VG8	F12	VF20	XF40
ND(1858-1920)	—	5.00	10.00	15.00	20.00	25.00

Y# 7.2 1/16 RUPEE
0.65 g., Silver, 8-10 mm. **Obv. Inscription:** Chitarkot/Udaipur **Rev. Inscription:** Dosti Lundhun - Friendship With London **Shape:** Irregular **Mint:** Udaipur

Date	Mintage	G4	VG8	F12	VF20	XF40
ND(1858-1920)	—	5.00	10.00	15.00	20.00	25.00

Y# B12 1/8 MOHUR
1.35 g., Gold **Series:** Swarupshahi **Obv. Inscription:** Chitarkot/Udaipur **Mint:** Udaipur

Date	Mintage	VG8	F12	VF20	XF40	MS60
ND(1858-1920)	—	400	450	500	600	—

Y# A12 1/4 MOHUR
Gold **Series:** Swarupshahi **Obv. Inscription:** Chitarkot/Udaipur **Mint:** Udaipur **Note:** Weight varies: 2.70-2.75 grams.

Date	Mintage	VG8	F12	VF20	XF40	MS60
ND(1858-1920)	—	500	550	600	700	—

Y# C12 1/2 MOHUR
5.40 g., Gold **Series:** Swarupshahi **Obv. Inscription:** Chitarkot/Udaipur **Mint:** Udaipur

Date	Mintage	VG8	F12	VF20	XF40	MS60
ND(1858-1920)	—	—	800	1,000	1,200	—

Y# 12 MOHUR
10.95 g., Gold, 23-24 mm. **Series:** Swarupshahi **Obv. Inscription:** Chitarkot/Udaipur **Mint:** Udaipur **Note:** Size varies.

Date	Mintage	VG8	F12	VF20	XF40	MS60
ND(1858-1920)	—	800	1,000	1,200	1,500	—

Fatteh Singh

VS1941-1986 / 1884-1929AD

MILLED COINAGE

VS1985 ie. 1928AD, but actually struck at the Alipore Mint in Calcutta between 1931-1932AD, the Y#22 rupee in 1931, the rest in 1932

Y# 13 PIE
2.50 g., Copper, 16 mm. **Obv:** Inscription and date **Obv. Inscription:** Chitor, date **Rev. Inscription:** Udaipur **Mint:** Udaipur

Date	Mintage	G4	VG8	F12	VF20	XF40
VS1975(1918)	—	20.00	40.00	60.00	80.00	100

Y# 14 PIE
2.10 g., Copper **Obv:** Inscription and date **Obv. Inscription:** Chitor, date **Rev. Inscription:** Udaipur **Mint:** Udaipur

Date	Mintage	G4	VG8	F12	VF20	XF40
VS1978(1921)	—	20.00	40.00	60.00	80.00	100

Y# 18 1/16 RUPEE
0.95 g., Silver, 12 mm. **Obv. Inscription:** Chitarkot / Udaipur **Rev. Inscription:** Dosti Lundhun (Friendship with London) **Mint:** (no Mint Information)

Date	Mintage	VG8	F12	VF20	XF40	MS60
VS1985	3,262,000	—	8.00	10.00	12.00	15.00

Y# 18a 1/16 RUPEE
Gold **Obv. Inscription:** Chitarkot / Udaipur **Rev. Inscription:** Dosti Lundhun (Friendship with London) **Mint:** (no Mint Information)

Date	Mintage	VG8	F12	VF20	XF40	MS60
VS1985 Proof	—	—	—	—	—	—

Y# 19 1/8 RUPEE
1.36 g., Silver, 15 mm. **Obv. Inscription:** Chitarkot/Udaipur **Rev. Inscription:** Dosti Lundhun (Friendship with London) **Mint:** (no Mint Information)

Date	Mintage	VG8	F12	VF20	XF40	MS60
VS1985	800,000	—	10.00	15.00	20.00	25.00

Y# 19a 1/8 RUPEE
Gold **Obv. Inscription:** Chitarkot / Udaipur **Rev. Inscription:** Dosti Lundhun (Friendship with London) **Mint:** (no Mint Information)

Date	Mintage	VG8	F12	VF20	XF40	MS60
VS1985	—	PF60 800				

Y# 20 1/4 RUPEE
2.72 g., Silver, 19 mm. **Obv. Inscription:** Chitarkot/Udaipur **Rev. Inscription:** Dosti Lundhun (Friendship with London) **Mint:** (no Mint Information)

Date	Mintage	VG8	F12	VF20	XF40	MS60
VS1985	839,000	—	10.00	15.00	20.00	25.00

Y# 20a 1/4 RUPEE
Gold **Obv. Inscription:** Chitarkot / Udaipur **Rev. Inscription:** Dosti Lundhun (Friendship with London) **Mint:** (no Mint Information)

Date	Mintage	VG8	F12	VF20	XF40	MS60
VS1985	—	PF60 800				

Y# 21 1/2 RUPEE
5.46 g., Silver, 24 mm. **Obv. Inscription:** Chitarkot/Udaipur **Rev. Inscription:** Dosti Lundhun (Friendship with London) **Mint:** (no Mint Information)

Date	Mintage	VG8	F12	VF20	XF40	MS60
VS1985	648,000	—	15.00	20.00	25.00	45.00

Y# 21a 1/2 RUPEE
Gold, 24 mm. **Obv. Inscription:** Chitarkot/Udaipur **Rev. Inscription:** Dosti Lundhun (Friendship with London) **Mint:** (no Mint Information) **Note:** Weight varies: 5.35-5.70 grams.

Date	Mintage	VG8	F12	VF20	XF40	MS60
VS1985	—	PF60 4,000				

Y# 22.1 RUPEE
10.86 g., Silver, 30 mm. **Obv. Inscription:** Thin characters, Chitarkot/Udaipur **Rev. Inscription:** Dosti Lundhun (Friendship with London) **Mint:** (no Mint Information)

Date	Mintage	VG8	F12	VF20	XF40	MS60
VS1985	14,906,000	—	10.00	15.00	25.00	35.00

Y# 22.2 RUPEE
10.86 g., Silver, 30 mm. **Obv. Inscription:** Thick characters, Chitarkot/Udaipur **Rev. Inscription:** Dosti Lundhun (Friendship with London) **Mint:** (no Mint Information)

Date	Mintage	VG8	F12	VF20	XF40	MS60
VS1985	Inc. above	—	10.00	15.00	25.00	35.00

Y# 22a RUPEE
Gold, 30 mm. **Obv. Inscription:** Chitarkot/Udaipur **Rev. Inscription:** Dosti Lundhun (Friendship with London) **Mint:** (no Mint Information)

Date	Mintage	VG8	F12	VF20	XF40	MS60
VS1985	—	PF60 5,000				

Bhupal Singh

VS1987-2005 / 1930-1948AD

HAMMERED COINAGE

Umarda Local Issues

Y# 24 1/2 PAISA
Copper **Mint:** (no Mint Information) **Note:** Varieties exist.

Date	Mintage	G4	VG8	F12	VF20	XF40
ND(1938-1941)	—	2.00	3.00	4.00	7.00	10.00

MILLED COINAGE

VS1985 ie. 1928AD, but actually struck at the Alipore Mint in Calcutta between 1931-1932AD, the Y#22 rupee in 1931, the rest in 1932

Y# 15 1/4 ANNA
2.20 g., Copper **Obv. Inscription:** Chitarkot/Udaipur **Mint:** (no Mint Information)

Date	Mintage	VG8	F12	VF20	XF40	MS60
VS1999 (1942)	—	3.00	4.00	6.00	8.00	—

Y# 16.1 1/2 ANNA
3.50 g., Copper **Obv:** Large character inscription **Obv. Inscription:** Chitarkot/Udaipur **Mint:** (no Mint Information)

Date	Mintage	VG8	F12	VF20	XF40	MS60
VS1999 (1942)	—	3.00	4.00	7.00	10.00	—

Y# 16.2 1/2 ANNA
3.50 g., Copper **Obv:** Small characters inscription **Obv. Inscription:** Chitarkot/Udaipur **Mint:** (no Mint Information)

Date	Mintage	VG8	F12	VF20	XF40	MS60
VS1999 (1942)	—	—	—	—	—	—

Y# 16.3 1/2 ANNA
Copper **Obv. Inscription:** Chitarkot / Udaipur **Mint:** (no Mint Information) **Note:** Octagonal flan.

Date	Mintage	VG8	F12	VF20	XF40	MS60
VS1999 (1942)	—	3.00	4.00	7.00	10.00	—

Y# 17 ANNA
4.30 g., Copper **Obv. Inscription:** Chitarkot/Udaipur **Mint:** (no Mint Information) **Note:** Variations with 3 or 4 brushes exist.

Date	Mintage	VG8	F12	VF20	XF40	MS60
VS2000	—	3.00	4.00	6.00	8.00	—

PATTERNS

Including off metal strikes

KM#	Date	Mintage	Identification	Mkt Val
Pn1	VS1985(1928)	—	1/16 Rupee. Silver. Rare	—
Pn2	VS1985 (1928)	—	1/16 Rupee. Gold. Y18a. Rare.	—
Pn3	VS1985(1928)	—	1/8 Rupee. Silver. Rare.	—
Pn4	VS1985 (1928)	—	1/8 Rupee. Gold. Y19a. Rare.	—

Pn5	VS1985(1928)	—	1/4 Rupee. Silver.	1,000
Pn6	VS1985(1928)	—	1/4 Rupee. Gold. KM20a.	2,000
Pn7	VS1985(1928)	—	1/2 Rupee. Silver.	2,000
Pn8	VS1985 (1928)	—	1/2 Rupee. Gold. Y21a.	3,000
Pn9	VS1985 (1928)	—	Rupee. Silver. Y22a.	2,000
Pn10	VS1985 (1928)	—	Rupee. Gold.	4,000

PATIALA

State located in the Punjab in northwest India. In the mid-18th century the Raja was given his title and mint right by Ahmad Shah Durrani of Afghanistan, whose coin he copied.
The rulers became Maharajas in 1810AD. The maharaja of Patiala was also recognized as the leader of the Phulkean tribe. Unlike others, Patiala's Sikh rulers had never hesitated to seek British assistance at those times when they felt threatened by their co-religionist neighbors. In 1857, Patiala's forces were immediately made available on the side of the British.

RULERS
Bhupindar Singh, VS1958-1994/1900-1937AD
Yadvindar Singh, VS1994-2005/1937-1948AD

PRINCELY STATE

HAMMERED COINAGE

KM# A20.1 MOHUR
Gold **Obv:** Name of Ahmed Shah Durrani, letter **Rev:** Suaad is Seen **Note:** Weight 10.8 to 11.6

Date	Mintage	G4	VG8	F12	VF20	XF40
NDXXXX//XX	—	—	—	1,200	1,400	1,600

KM# A20.3 MOHUR
Gold **Obv:** Name of Ahmed Shah Durrani, letter **Rev:** Suaad is Seen **Note:** Weight 10.8 to 11.6

Date	Mintage	G4	VG8	F12	VF20	XF40
NDXXXX//XX	—	—	—	1,200	1,400	1,600

Bhupindar Singh

VS1958-1994 / 1900-1937AD

KM# 28 RUPEE
Silver **Obv:** Persian inscription **Obv. Inscription:** Guru Govind Singh **Rev:** Dagger at left **Note:** Weight varies: 11.10-11.20 grams. Prev. Y#A3.

Date	Mintage	VG8	F12	VF20	XF40	MS60
VS1958	—	2,000	2,500	3,000	3,500	—

Y# 14 1/6 MOHUR
1.75 g., Gold **Obv:** Persian inscription **Obv. Inscription:** Ahmad Shah Durrani **Rev:** Dagger at left

Date	Mintage	VG8	F12	VF20	XF40	MS60
VS(19)58	—	—	500	700	1,000	—
VS(19)90	—	—	500	700	1,000	—

KM# 15 1/3 MOHUR
3.50 g., Gold **Obv:** Persian inscription **Obv. Inscription:** Ahmad Shah Durrani **Rev:** Dagger at left

Date	Mintage	VG8	F12	VF20	XF40	MS60
VS(19)58	—	—	500	700	1,000	—

Y# 16 2/3 MOHUR
7.00 g., Gold **Obv:** Persian inscription **Obv. Inscription:** Ahmad Shah Durrani **Rev:** Dagger at left

Date	Mintage	VG8	F12	VF20	XF40	MS60
VS(19)58	—	—	600	800	1,100	—

Y# 17 MOHUR
10.50 g., Gold **Obv:** Persian inscription **Obv. Inscription:** Ahmad Shah Durrani **Rev:** Dagger at left

Date	Mintage	VG8	F12	VF20	XF40	MS60
VS(19)58	—	—	800	1,000	1,200	—

Yadvindar Singh

VS1994-2005 / 1937-1948AD

KM# 27 1/4 RUPEE
Silver **Obv:** Persian inscription **Obv. Inscription:** Guru Govind Singh **Rev:** Bayoneted rifle at left **Note:** Weight varies: 11.10-11.20 grams. Prev. Y#A1.

Date	Mintage	VG8	F12	VF20	XF40	MS60
VS1994 Rare	—	—	—	—	—	—

KM# 29 1/6 MOHUR
1.75 g., Gold **Obv:** Persian inscription **Obv. Inscription:** Ahmad Shah Durrani **Rev:** Bayoneted rifle at left **Note:** Prev. Y#19.

Date	Mintage	VG8	F12	VF20	XF40	MS60
VS(19)94	—	—	400	600	800	1,000

KM# 30 1/3 MOHUR
3.50 g., Gold **Obv:** Persian inscription **Obv. Inscription:** Ahmad Shah Durrani **Rev:** Bayoneted rifle at left **Note:** Prev. KM#20.

Date	Mintage	VG8	F12	VF20	XF40	MS60
VS(19)94	—	—	400	600	800	1,000

KM# 31 2/3 MOHUR
7.00 g., Gold **Obv:** Persian inscription **Obv. Inscription:** Ahmad Shah Durrani **Rev:** Bayoneted rifle at left **Note:** Prev. Y#21.

Date	Mintage	VG8	F12	VF20	XF40	MS60
VS(19)94	—	—	600	700	850	1,100

PUDUKKOTTAI

PRINCELY STATE

MILLED COINAGE

KM# 6 AMMAN CASH
1.25 g., Copper, 12 mm. **Ruler:** Martanda Bhairana **Obv:** Seated Goddess Brihadamba facing **Note:** Prev. Y#1. Later struck at Calcutta.

Date	Mintage	VG8	F12	VF20	XF40	MS60
ND(1886-1947)	5,000,000	1.00	2.00	3.00	5.00	8.00

RAMPURA

This tiny estate of four and a half square miles was held by Chauda Rajputs in the old Gujerat States Agency Area. It was feudatory to Lunavada and the estate was controlled by a thakur or latterly by four shareholders.

PRINCELY STATE

HAMMERED COINAGE

The following listings may be from Lunavada or from Rampur. They are often found overstruck on coins of Lunavada, and over other states, including Sailana.

KM# 1 1/2 PAISA
Copper **Obv:** Open hand in square **Rev. Legend:** RAMPAR **Note:** Weight varies: 3-4g.

Date	Mintage	G4	VG8	F12	VF20	XF40
ND(1880-1920)	—	5.00	9.00	14.00	20.00	—

KM# 2 1/2 PAISA
Copper **Obv:** Sunbursts **Rev. Legend:** RAMPAR **Note:** Weight varies: 3-4g.

Date	Mintage	G4	VG8	F12	VF20	XF40
ND(1880-1920)	—	5.00	10.00	15.00	20.00	25.00

KM# 3 PAISA
Copper **Obv:** Sunbursts **Rev. Legend:** RAMPAR **Shape:** Square **Note:** Weight varies: 1.90-4.30g.

Date	Mintage	G4	VG8	F12	VF20	XF40
ND(1880-1920)	—	5.00	10.00	15.00	20.00	25.00

KM# 4 PAISA
Copper **Obv:** Spears **Rev:** Spears **Shape:** Square **Note:** Weight varies: 1.90-4.30g.

Date	Mintage	G4	VG8	F12	VF20	XF40
ND(1880-1920)	—	5.00	10.00	15.00	20.00	25.00

KM# 5 PAISA
8.50 g., Copper **Obv:** Spears **Rev. Legend:** RAMPAR **Shape:** Round or square

Date	Mintage	G4	VG8	F12	VF20	XF40
ND(1880-1920)	—	5.00	10.00	15.00	20.00	25.00

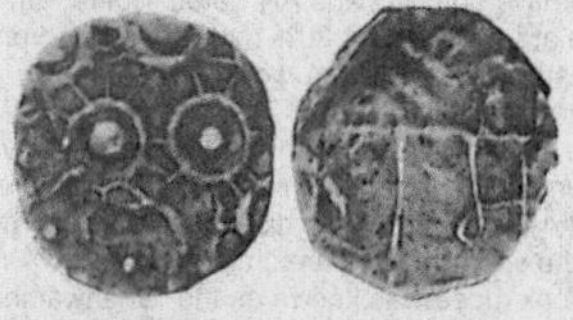

KM# 6.1 PAISA
Copper **Obv:** Sunbursts **Rev. Legend:** RAMPAR **Shape:** Round

Date	Mintage	G4	VG8	F12	VF20	XF40
ND(1880-1920)	—	5.00	10.00	15.00	20.00	25.00

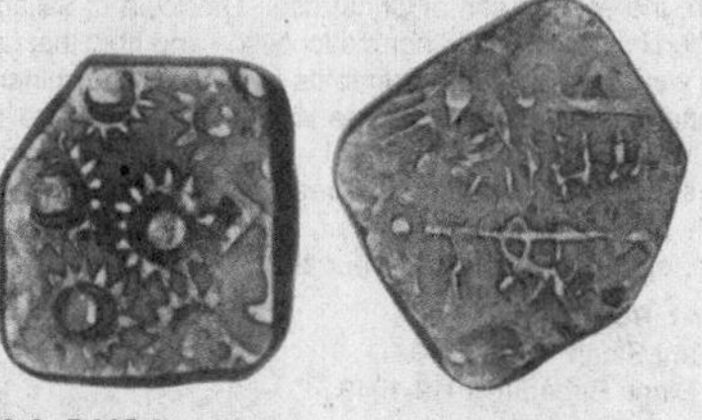

KM# 6.2 PAISA
Copper **Obv:** Solar symbols with serrated rays **Rev. Legend:** RAMPURA

Date	Mintage	G4	VG8	F12	VF20	XF40
ND(1880-1920)	—	5.00	10.00	15.00	20.00	25.00

KM# 7 PAISA
Copper **Obv:** Solar symbol **Rev. Legend:** RAMPAR **Shape:** Square **Note:** Weight varies: 7.50-8.30g.

Date	Mintage	G4	VG8	F12	VF20	XF40
ND(1880-1920)	—	10.00	15.00	20.00	25.00	30.00

KM# 8 PAISA
Copper **Obv:** Spears **Rev:** Persian legend

Date	Mintage	G4	VG8	F12	VF20	XF40
ND(1880-1920)	—	5.00	10.00	15.00	20.00	25.00

KM# 9 PAISA
Copper **Obv:** Open hands **Rev. Legend:** RAMPUR **Shape:** Square

Date	Mintage	G4	VG8	F12	VF20	XF40
ND(1880-1920)	—	5.00	10.00	15.00	20.00	25.00

KM# 12 PIE
2.30 g., Copper

Date	Mintage	G4	VG8	F12	VF20	XF40
ND(1880-1920)	—	10.00	15.00	20.00	25.00	30.00

RATLAM

State located northwest of Indore in Madhya Pradesh.
The rajas of Ratlam were Rathor Rajputs, descendants of the younger branch of the Jodhpur ruling family. Ratlam became the premier Rajput state in western Malwa. The founder, Ratan Singh, received the territory as a grant from Shah Jahan in 1631. Before Maratha collapse some 15% of the state's annual revenue went to Sindhia as tribute. Under British protection it was supervised by the Central India Agency and in 1948 Ratlam became a district of Madhya Bharat.

RULER
Ranjit Singh, VS1921-1950/1864-1893AD

MINT
Ratlam

NOTE: For 1 Paisa previously listed here refer to Banswara-IPS.

BRITISH PROTECTORATE

MILLED COINAGE

KM# 25 PAISA
Copper Weight varies: 2.50-3.30g. **Ruler:** Ranjit Singh **Obv:** Hanuman walking left **Note:** Thin, crude restrike of KM#24.

Date	Mintage	G4	VG8	F12	VF20	XF40
VS1947(1890)	—	—	3.00	6.00	10.00	15.00

Note: Restruck ca.1942-1945AD

SAILANA

This small state in west-central India, of slightly over one hundred square miles had once been part of Ratlam, but about 1709 it asserted its independence under the leadership of Pratab Singh, the second son of Chhatrasal. The town of Sailana was founded in 1730 by Jai Singh's successor, and from that date the state was named after it. Due to its small size and vulnerability, Sailana was obliged to become tributary to Sindhia to ensure its survival. In 1819 this payment was limited to one-third of the state's revenues. Later, under agreements of 1840 and 1860, the tribute went to the British for the support of British Indian troops in the region. Barmawal was feudatory to Sailana.

LOCAL RULERS

Jaswant Singh, 1895-1919AD
Dilip Singh Bahadur, 1919-1948

PRINCELY STATE

Jaswant Singh

1890-1919AD

MILLED COINAGE

Regal Series

KM# 15 1/4 ANNA

Copper **Obv:** Bust of King Edward VII right **Mint:** (no Mint Information)

Date	Mintage	F12	VF20	XF40	MS60	MS63
1908	224,000	25.00	50.00	75.00	250	—
1908	—	PF63 1,500				

KM# 16 1/4 ANNA

Copper **Obv:** Crowned bust of King George V left **Mint:** (no Mint Information)

Date	Mintage	VF20	XF40	MS60	MS63	MS65
1912	224,000	25.00	50.00	150	225	—
1912	—	PF63 1,500				

SUNTH

Located 15 miles east of Lunawada with an area of 394 sq. miles, (1,020 sq. km.). This state was ruled by a Maharana who was a member of the Pramara Rajput clan. The state capital was Rampur.

RULERS

Jarawar Singhji, 1896-?

KINGDOM

HAMMERED COINAGE

KM# 1 1/2 PAISA

Copper **Obv:** Open hand in square **Rev. Legend:** Rampura **Note:** Weight varies: 3.00-4.00 grams.

Date	Mintage	G4	VG8	F12	VF20	XF40
ND(1870-1920)	—	3.00	9.00	14.00	20.00	—

KM# 2 1/2 PAISA

Copper **Obv:** Sunbursts **Rev. Legend:** Rampura **Note:** Weight varies: 3.00-4.00 grams.

Date	Mintage	G4	VG8	F12	VF20	XF40
ND(1870-1920)	—	5.00	12.00	18.00	27.50	—

KM# 3 PAISA

Copper **Obv:** Sunbursts **Rev. Legend:** Rampura **Shape:** Rectangular or square **Note:** Weight varies: 1.90-4.30 grams.

Date	Mintage	G4	VG8	F12	VF20	XF40
ND(1870-1920)	—	1.75	4.00	7.00	11.00	—

KM# 4 PAISA

Copper **Obv:** Spears **Rev:** Spears **Shape:** Rectangular or square **Note:** Weight varies: 1.90-4.30 grams. Attribution uncertain.

Date	Mintage	G4	VG8	F12	VF20	XF40
ND(1870-1920)	—	4.00	6.00	8.00	10.00	—

KM# 5 PAISA

8.50 g., Copper **Obv:** Spears **Rev. Legend:** Rampura **Shape:** Round, rectangular, or square

Date	Mintage	G4	VG8	F12	VF20	XF40
ND(1870-1920)	—	1.75	4.00	7.00	11.00	—

KM# 6.1 PAISA

Copper **Obv:** Sunbursts **Rev. Legend:** Rampura

Date	Mintage	G4	VG8	F12	VF20	XF40
ND(1870-1920)	—	1.75	4.00	7.00	11.00	—

KM# 6.2 PAISA

Copper **Obv:** Sunburst with serrated rays **Rev. Legend:** Rampura **Shape:** Odd, rectangular, or square

Date	Mintage	G4	VG8	F12	VF20	XF40
ND(1870-1920)	—	2.75	6.00	9.00	15.00	—

KM# 7 PAISA

Copper **Obv:** Solar symbol **Rev. Legend:** Rampura **Shape:** Odd or square **Note:** Weight varies: 7.50-8.30 grams.

Date	Mintage	G4	VG8	F12	VF20	XF40
ND(1870-1920)	—	5.00	8.00	12.00	19.00	—

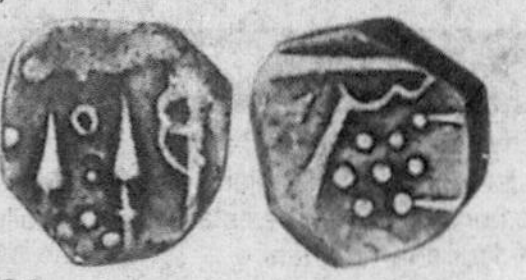

KM# 8 PAISA

Copper **Obv:** Spears **Rev:** Persian legend **Shape:** Odd **Note:** Attribution uncertain.

Date	Mintage	G4	VG8	F12	VF20	XF40
ND(1870-1920)	—	4.00	6.00	8.00	10.00	—

KM# 9 PAISA

Copper **Obv:** Open hands **Rev:** Rampur **Shape:** Rectangular or square

Date	Mintage	G4	VG8	F12	VF20	XF40
ND(1870-1920)	—	2.75	6.00	9.00	15.00	—

TONK

Tunk

State located partially in Rajputana and in central India. Tonk was founded in 1806 by Amir Khan (d. 1834), the Pathan Pindari leader who received the territory from Holkar. Amir Khan caused great havoc in Central India by his lightning raids into neighboring states. In 1817 he was forced into submission by the East India Company and remained under British control until India's independence. In March 1948 Tonk was incorporated into Rajasthan.

RULERS

Muhammad Ibrahim Ali Khan, AH1284-1349/ 1868-1930AD
Muhammad Sa'adat Ali Khan, AH1349-1368/ 1930-1949AD

MINT MARKS

سرونج

Sironj

تونك

Tonk

Flower (on all)

Leaf (several forms)

Beginning with the reign of Muhammad Ibrahim Ali Khan, most coins have both AD and AH dates. Coins with both dates fully legible are worth about 20% more than listed prices. Coins with one date fully legible are worth prices shown. Coins with both dates off are of little value.

There are many minor and major variations of type, varying with location of date, orientation of leaf, arrangement of legend. Although these fall into easily distinguished patterns, they are strictly for the specialist and are omitted here.

The Tonk rupee was known as the "Chanwarshahi".

BRITISH PROTECTORATE

Muhammad Ibrahim Ali Khan

AH1284-1349 / 1868-1930AD

HAMMERED COINAGE

Regal Series

Tonk

Y# 18 1/4 RUPEE

Silver **Obv. Inscription:** Muhammad Ibrahim Ali Khan **Rev. Inscription:** Victoria, Empress **Mint:** Tonk **Note:** Weight varies: 2.68-2.90 grams. Size varies: 14-15mm.

Date	Mintage	G4	VG8	F12	VF20	XF40
AH1318	—	40.00	50.00	60.00	80.00	100

HAMMERED COINAGE

Y# A24 1/2 PAISA

5.40 g., Copper **Obv. Inscription:** George V... **Rev. Inscription:** Muhammad Ibrahim Ali Khan... **Mint:** Tonk

Date	Mintage	G4	VG8	F12	VF20	XF40
AH13(46)//1928	—	—	7.00	15.00	25.00	—

Y# 24.1 PAISA

7.30 g., Copper **Obv. Inscription:** George V... **Rev. Inscription:** Muhammad Ibrahim Ali Khan... **Mint:** Tonk

Date	Mintage	G4	VG8	F12	VF20	XF40
AH1329//1911	—	—	0.50	1.00	3.00	—
AH1329(sic)//1329	—	—	0.50	1.00	3.00	—
1911(sic)	—	—	0.50	1.00	3.00	—
AH1330//1911	—	—	0.50	1.00	3.00	—

Y# 24.2 PAISA

5.00 g., Copper **Obv. Inscription:** George V... **Rev. Inscription:** Muhammad Ibrahim Ali Khan... **Mint:** Tonk **Note:** Reduced weight.

Date	Mintage	G4	VG8	F12	VF20	XF40
AH1335//1917	—	—	0.50	1.00	3.00	—
AH(13)38//1924	—	—	0.50	1.00	3.00	—
AH1342//1924	—	—	0.50	1.00	3.00	—
AH1344//1925	—	—	0.50	1.00	3.00	—
AH1344//1926	—	—	0.50	1.00	3.00	—
AH1345//1927	—	—	0.50	1.00	3.00	—
AH134x//1928	—	—	0.50	1.00	3.00	—

Y# A25.1 1/4 ANNA

8.30 g., Copper **Obv. Inscription:** George V... **Rev. Inscription:** Muhammad Ibrahim Ali Khan... **Mint:** Tonk

Date	Mintage	G4	VG8	F12	VF20	XF40
AH1335//1917	—	—	1.50	3.00	5.00	—
AH1336//1917	—	—	1.50	3.00	5.00	—

Y# A25.2 1/4 ANNA

5.40 g., Copper **Obv. Inscription:** George V... **Rev. Inscription:** Muhammad Ibrahim Ali Khan... **Mint:** Tonk **Note:** Reduced weight.

Date	Mintage	G4	VG8	F12	VF20	XF40
AH1336//1917	—	—	1.50	3.00	5.00	—

Y# 25 1/8 RUPEE

Silver **Obv. Inscription:** George V... **Rev. Inscription:** Muhammad Ibrahim Ali Khan... **Mint:** Tonk **Note:** Weight varies: 1.34-1.45 grams.

Date	Mintage	G4	VG8	F12	VF20	XF40
AH1340//1922	—	—	25.00	50.00	100	150
AH-//1927	—	—	25.00	50.00	100	150
AH1346//1928	—	—	25.00	50.00	100	150

Y# 26 1/4 RUPEE
Silver **Obv. Inscription:** George V... **Rev. Inscription:** Muhammad Ibrahim Ali Khan... **Mint:** Tonk **Note:** Weight varies: 2.68-2.90 grams.

Date	Mintage	G4	VG8	F12	VF20	XF40
AH1346//1928	—	—	25.00	50.00	100	150

Y# 27 1/2 RUPEE
Silver **Obv. Inscription:** George V... **Rev. Inscription:** Muhammad Ibrahim Ali Khan... **Mint:** Tonk **Note:** Weight varies: 5.35-5.80 grams.

Date	Mintage	G4	VG8	F12	VF20	XF40
AH1346//1928	—	—	25.00	50.00	75.00	100

Y# 28 RUPEE
Silver **Obv. Inscription:** George V... **Rev. Inscription:** Muhammad Ibrahim Ali Khan... **Mint:** Tonk **Note:** Weight varies: 10.70-11.60 grams.

Date	Mintage	G4	VG8	F12	VF20	XF40
AH1329//1911	—	—	20.00	25.00	30.00	35.00
AH1330//1912	—	—	20.00	25.00	30.00	35.00
AH1341//1923	—	—	20.00	25.00	30.00	35.00
AH1342//1923	—	—	20.00	25.00	30.00	35.00
AH1342//1924	—	—	20.00	25.00	30.00	35.00
AH1343//1924	—	—	20.00	25.00	30.00	35.00
AH1343//1925	—	—	20.00	25.00	30.00	35.00
AH1344//1925	—	—	20.00	25.00	30.00	35.00
AH1344//1926	—	—	20.00	25.00	30.00	35.00
AH1345//1926	—	—	20.00	25.00	30.00	35.00
AH1346//1926	—	—	20.00	25.00	30.00	35.00
AH1346//1927	—	—	20.00	25.00	30.00	35.00
AH1347//1928	—	—	20.00	25.00	30.00	35.00
AH1348//1928	—	—	20.00	25.00	30.00	35.00
AH1348//1929	—	—	20.00	25.00	30.00	35.00
AH134x//1930	—	—	20.00	25.00	30.00	35.00

Muhammad Sa'adat Ali Khan

AH1349-1368 / 1930-1949AD

Y# 30 1/8 RUPEE
Silver **Obv. Inscription:** George V... **Rev. Inscription:** Muhammad Sa'adat Ali Khan... **Mint:** Tonk **Note:** Weight varies: 1.34-1.45 grams.

Date	Mintage	G4	VG8	F12	VF20	XF40
AH1351//1932	—	—	20.00	40.00	60.00	80.00
AH1352//1933	—	—	20.00	40.00	60.00	80.00
AH1353//1934	—	—	20.00	40.00	60.00	80.00

MILLED COINAGE

KM# 29 PICE (Paisa)
Copper, 26 mm. **Obv:** Arms **Rev:** Leaf

Date	Mintage	F12	VF20	XF40	MS60	MS63
AH1350//1932	640,000	—	0.50	1.00	2.00	3.00

KM# 29a PICE (Paisa)
Copper, 21 mm. **Obv:** Arms **Rev:** Leaf

Date	Mintage	F12	VF20	XF40	MS60	MS63
AH1350//1932	640,000	—	0.50	1.00	2.00	3.00

TRAVANCORE

State located in extreme southwest India. A mint was established in ME965/1789-1790AD.

The region of Travancore had a lengthy history before being annexed by the Vijayanagar kingdom. With Vijayanagar's defeat at the battle of Talikota in 1565, Travancore passed under Muslim control until the late 18th century, when it merged as a state in its own right under Raja Martanda Varma. At this time the raja allied himself with British interests as a protection against the Muslim dynasty of Mysore. In 1795 the raja of Travancore officially accepted a subsidiary alliance with the East India Company, and remained within the orbit of British influence from then until India's independence.

RULERS
Rama Varma VI, ME1062-1101/1885-1924AD
Bala Rama Varma II, ME1101-1126/1924-1949AD

DATING
ME dates are of the Malabar Era. Add 824 or 825 to the ME date for the AD date. (i.e., ME1112 plus 824-825 =1936-1937AD).

KINGDOM

Ayilyam Tirunal Rama Varma

ME 1035-1055 / 1860-1880 AD

HAMMERED COINAGE

KM# 21 CHUCKRAM
Silver **Rev:** Without dot at center, over leaf spray

Date	Mintage	G4	VG8	F12	VF20	XF40
ND(1860-1901)	—	—	2.00	3.00	4.00	6.00

Rama Varma VI

ME1062-1101 / 1885-1924AD

MILLED COINAGE

KM# 40 CASH
0.65 g., Copper **Obv. Legend:** CASH 1

Date	Mintage	F12	VF20	XF40	MS60	MS63
ND-1901	—	—	300	350	400	—

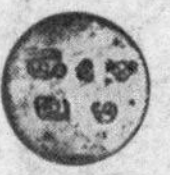

KM# 46 CASH
0.65 g., Copper **Obv:** Sankha (conch shell) in 8-pointed star **Note:** Thick

Date	Mintage	F12	VF20	XF40	MS60	MS63
ND(1901-10)	—	—	—	0.25	0.50	1.00

Note: Refer to Bala Rama Varma II listings for thin variety, KM#57

KM# 41 4 CASH
Copper **Obv:** RV monogram **Obv. Legend:** CASH FOUR **Rev:** Sankha (conch shell) in sprays

Date	Mintage	F12	VF20	XF40	MS60	MS63
ND(1901-10)	—	1.50	3.00	5.00	15.00	25.00

KM# 47 4 CASH
Copper **Obv:** RV monogram **Obv. Legend:** FOUR CASH **Rev:** Sankha (conch shell) in sprays

Date	Mintage	F12	VF20	XF40	MS60	MS63
ND(1906-35)	—	1.00	2.00	3.00	5.00	15.00
ND(1906-35)	—	PF63 200				

KM# 42 8 CASH
Copper **Obv:** RV monogram **Obv. Legend:** CASH EIGHT **Rev:** Sankha (conch shell) in sprays

Date	Mintage	F12	VF20	XF40	MS60	MS63
ND(1901-10)	—	2.00	3.00	8.00	25.00	35.00

KM# 48 8 CASH
Copper **Obv:** RV monogram **Obv. Legend:** EIGHT CASH **Rev:** Sankha (conch shell) in sprays

Date	Mintage	F12	VF20	XF40	MS60	MS63
ND(1906-35)	—	—	0.50	1.00	5.00	10.00
ND(1906-35)	—	PF63 75.00				

KM# 43 CHUCKRAM
Copper **Obv:** RV monogram **Obv. Legend:** CHUCKRAM ONE **Rev:** Sankha (conch shell) in sprays

Date	Mintage	F12	VF20	XF40	MS60	MS63
ND(1901-10)	—	4.00	7.00	15.00	25.00	40.00

KM# 49 CHUCKRAM
Copper **Obv:** RV monogram **Obv. Legend:** ONE CHUCKRAM **Rev:** Sankha (conch shell) in sprays

Date	Mintage	F12	VF20	XF40	MS60	MS63
ND(1906-35)	—	1.00	2.00	5.00	15.00	25.00

KM# 44 2 CHUCKRAMS
Silver, 10 mm. **Obv:** RV monogram **Obv. Legend:** CHS. 2 **Rev:** Sankha (conch shell) in sprays

Date	Mintage	F12	VF20	XF40	MS60	MS63
ND-1901	—	—	—	—	300	—

KM# 50 2 CHUCKRAMS
Silver **Obv:** RV monogram **Obv. Legend:** 2 CHS. **Rev:** Sankha (conch shell) in sprays

Date	Mintage	F12	VF20	XF40	MS60	MS63
ND(1906-28)	—	—	—	—	300	—

KM# 54 FANAM
Silver **Obv:** RV monogram **Obv. Legend:** ONE FANAM **Rev:** Sankha (conch shell) in sprays **Edge:** Plain

Date	Mintage	F12	VF20	XF40	MS60	MS63
ND-1901	—	—	—	—	100	—

KM# 45 FANAM
Silver **Obv:** RV monogram **Obv. Legend:** FANAM ONE **Rev:** Sankha (conch shell) in sprays **Edge:** Plain

Date	Mintage	F12	VF20	XF40	MS60	MS63
ND-1911	—	4.00	7.00	14.00	35.00	—

KM# 51 FANAM
0.950 Silver **Rev:** Sankha (conch shell) in sprays

Date	Mintage	F12	VF20	XF40	MS60	MS63
ME1087(1911-12)	1,100,000	—	2.00	3.00	7.00	16.00
ME1096 (1920-21)	350,000	—	2.00	3.00	7.00	16.00
ME1099 (1923-24)	350,000	—	2.00	3.00	7.00	16.00
ME1100 (1924-25)	700,000	—	2.00	3.00	7.00	16.00
ME1103 (1927-28)	700,000	—	2.00	3.00	7.00	16.00
ME1106 (1930-31)	—	—	2.00	3.00	7.00	16.00

KM# 55 FANAM

Silver **Obv:** RV monogram **Obv. Legend:** FANAM ONE **Rev:** Sankha (conch shell) in sprays **Edge:** Reeded

Date	Mintage	F12	VF20	XF40	MS60	MS63
ND-1911	—	2.00	5.00	8.00	15.00	35.00

KM# 52 1/4 RUPEE

2.72 g., 0.950 Silver 0.0831 oz. ASW **Obv. Legend:** RAMA VURMA-TRAVENCORE **Rev:** Sankha (conch shell) in sprays

Date	Mintage	F12	VF20	XF40	MS60	MS63
ME1082 (1906-07)	—	25.00	50.00	75.00	125	150
ME1083 (1907-08)	—	25.00	50.00	75.00	125	150
ME1085 (1909-10)	—	25.00	50.00	75.00	125	150
ME1086 (1910-11)	—	25.00	50.00	75.00	125	150
ME1087 (1911-12)	400,000	25.00	50.00	75.00	125	150
ME1096 (1920-21)	—	25.00	50.00	75.00	125	150
ME1099 (1923-24)	—	25.00	50.00	75.00	125	150
ME1100 (1924-25)	—	25.00	50.00	75.00	125	150
ME1103 (1927-28)	200,000	25.00	50.00	75.00	125	150
ME1106 (1930-31)	200,000	25.00	50.00	75.00	125	150

KM# 53 1/2 RUPEE

5.44 g., 0.950 Silver 0.1662 oz. ASW **Rev:** Legend shorter on bottom

Date	Mintage	F12	VF20	XF40	MS60	MS63
ME1084 (1908-09)	—	10.00	20.00	30.00	50.00	75.00
ME1085 (1909-10)	—	10.00	20.00	30.00	50.00	75.00
ME1086 (1910-11)	—	10.00	20.00	30.00	50.00	75.00
ME1087 (1911-12)	300,000	10.00	20.00	30.00	50.00	75.00
ME1103 (1927-28)	100,000	10.00	20.00	30.00	50.00	75.00
ME1106 (1930-31)	100,000	10.00	20.00	30.00	50.00	75.00
ME1106 (1930-31) Proof; Rare	—	**PF63** 1,000				
ME1107 (1931-32)	800,000	10.00	20.00	30.00	50.00	75.00

Regent Maharani Sethu Lakshmi Bayi

ME1101-1107 / 1924-1931 AD

HAMMERED COINAGE

KM# D56 FANAM ONE

1.50 g., Silver, 15 mm. **Obv:** RV monogram **Obv. Legend:** FANAM ONE, Malayalam "Panam Onnu" **Rev:** Sankh (conch shell) in wreath

Date	Mintage	VG8	F12	VF20	XF40	MS60
ME1100 (1924-25)	—	10.00	20.00	30.00	40.00	50.00
ME1103 (1927-28)	—	10.00	20.00	30.00	40.00	50.00
ME1106 (1930-31)	—	10.00	20.00	30.00	40.00	50.00

KM# A56 4 CASH

Copper, 18 mm. **Obv:** RV monogram **Obv. Legend:** FOUR CASH, Malayalam "Nalu Kasu" **Rev:** Sankh (conch shell) in wreath

Date	Mintage	F12	VF20	XF40	MS60	MS63
ND(1924-31)	—	—	—	—	—	—

KM# B56 8 CASH

4.87 g., Copper, 22 mm. **Obv:** RV monogram **Obv. Legend:** EIGHT CASH, Malayalam "Ettu Kasu" **Rev:** Sankh (conch shell) in wreath

Date	Mintage	F12	VF20	XF40	MS60	MS63
ND(1924-31)	—	—	—	—	—	—

KM# C56 CHUCKRAM

Copper, 26 mm. **Obv:** RV monogram **Obv. Legend:** ONE CHUKRAM, Malayalam "Oru Chakram" **Rev:** Sankh (conch shell) in wreath

Date	Mintage	F12	VF20	XF40	MS60	MS63
ND(1924-31)	—	—	—	—	—	—

KM# G56 2 CHUCKRAMS

0.75 g., Silver, 10 mm. **Obv:** RV monogram **Obv. Legend:** 2 CHS, Malayalam legend "2 chuckram" **Rev:** Sankh

Date	Mintage	F12	VF20	XF40	MS60	MS63
ND(1924-31)	—	—	—	—	—	—

KM# E56 1/4 RUPEE

2.54 g., Silver, 20 mm. **Obv. Legend:** RAMA VURMA TRAVANCORE, 1/4 Rupee (date) **Rev:** Sankh (conch shell) in wreath **Rev. Legend:** Malayalam "Thiruvathamkur Kal Roopa"

Date	Mintage	F12	VF20	XF40	MS60	MS63
ME1100 (1924-25)	—	20.00	30.00	40.00	50.00	—
ME1103 (1927-28)	—	20.00	30.00	40.00	50.00	—
ME1106 (1930-31)	—	20.00	30.00	40.00	50.00	—

Bala Rama Varma II

ME1101-1126 / 1924-1949AD

MILLED COINAGE

KM# 57 CASH

0.48 g., Copper **Obv:** Sankha (conch shell) in 8-pointed star **Rev:** Malayalam "Oru Kasu" (one cash) **Note:** Thin .8mm planchet.

Date	Mintage	F12	VF20	XF40	MS60	MS63
ND(1928-49)	—	1.00	3.00	5.00	7.00	10.00
Note: Refer to Rama Varma VI listings for thick variety, KM#46						
ND(1928-49)	—	**PF63** 300				

KM# 58 4 CASH

1.94 g., Bronze, 17.5 mm. **Obv:** RV monogram **Rev:** Sankha (conch shell) in sprays **Edge:** Plain

Date	Mintage	F12	VF20	XF40	MS60	MS63
ND(1938-49)	—	1.00	3.00	5.00	9.00	12.00
ND(1938-49) Proof, Rare	—	**PF63** 300				

KM# 59 8 CASH

Bronze **Obv:** BRV monogram **Rev:** Sankha (conch shell) in sprays

Date	Mintage	F12	VF20	XF40	MS60	MS63
ND(1938-49)	—	1.00	3.00	5.00	9.00	15.00
ND(1938-49)	—	**PF63** 300				

KM# 60 CHUCKRAM

Bronze **Obv:** Bust of Bala Rama Barma II right **Rev:** Sankha (conch shell) in sprays

Date	Mintage	F12	VF20	XF40	MS60	MS63
ME1114(1938-39)	—	3.00	5.00	9.00	15.00	25.00
ND(1939-40)	—	3.00	5.00	9.00	15.00	25.00
ND(1939-40)	—	**PF63** 400				

KM# 60a CHUCKRAM

Gold **Obv:** Bust of Bala Rama Barma II right **Rev:** Sankha (conch shell) in sprays

Date	Mintage	F12	VF20	XF40	MS60	MS63
ND(1939-40) Prooflike; restrike	—	**PF63** 8,000				

KM# 61 FANAM

0.95 g., Silver **Obv. Legend:** BALA RAMA VARMA-TRAVENCORE **Rev:** Sankha (conch shell) in sprays

Date	Mintage	F12	VF20	XF40	MS60	MS63
ME1112(1936-37)	350,000	1.00	3.00	5.00	15.00	35.00

KM# 65 FANAM

1.51 g., 0.500 Silver 0.0243 oz. ASW **Obv. Legend:** BALA RAMA VARMA-TRAVANCORE **Rev:** Sankha (conch shell) in sprays

Date	Mintage	F12	VF20	XF40	MS60	MS63
ME1116(1940-41)	2,096,000	1.00	3.00	5.00	15.00	35.00
ME1118(1942-43)	4,157,000	1.00	3.00	5.00	15.00	35.00
ME1121(1945-46)	1,925,000	1.00	3.00	5.00	15.00	35.00

KM# 62 1/4 RUPEE

0.95 g., Silver **Obv. Legend:** BALA RAMA VARMA-TRAVANCORE

Date	Mintage	F12	VF20	XF40	MS60	MS63
ME1112(1936-37)	200,000	5.00	10.00	20.00	35.00	75.00

KM# 66 1/4 RUPEE

2.66 g., 0.500 Silver 0.0428 oz. ASW **Obv. Legend:** BALA RAMA VARMA-TRAVANCORE

Date	Mintage	F12	VF20	XF40	MS60	MS63
ME1116(1940-41)	126,000	10.00	15.00	20.00	35.00	50.00
ME1116(1940-41)	—	**PF63** 600				
ME1118(1942-43)	—	10.00	15.00	20.00	35.00	50.00

KM# 63 1/2 RUPEE

0.95 g., Silver **Obv. Legend:** BALA RAMA VARMA-TRAVENCORE

Date	Mintage	F12	VF20	XF40	MS60	MS63
ME1112(1936-37)	200,000	15.00	30.00	50.00	100	150

KM# 64 1/2 CHITRA RUPEE

Silver **Obv. Legend:** BALA RAMA VARMA-TRAVENCORE **Edge:** Reeded

Date	Mintage	F12	VF20	XF40	MS60	MS63
ME1114 (1938-39)	—	15.00	30.00	50.00	75.00	100

KM# 67 1/2 CHITRA RUPEE

5.31 g., 0.500 Silver 0.0854 oz. ASW **Obv. Legend:** BALA RAMA VARMA-TRAVENCORE **Edge:** Security

Date	Mintage	F12	VF20	XF40	MS60	MS63
ME1116(1940-41)	1,600,000	15.00	25.00	35.00	60.00	85.00
ME1118/6(1942-43)	1,111,000	15.00	25.00	35.00	60.00	85.00
ME1118(1942-43)	Inc. above	15.00	25.00	35.00	60.00	85.00
ME1118(1942-43)	—	**PF63** 500				
ME1121(1945-46)	200,000	15.00	25.00	35.00	60.00	85.00

PATTERNS

Including off metal strikes

KM#	Date	Mintage	Identification	Mkt Val
Pn3	ME1086(1910)	—	1/4 Rupee. Bronze. KM#52.	100

Vasco da Gama, the Portuguese explorer, first visited India in 1498. Portugal seized control of a number of islands and small enclaves on the west coast of India, and for the next hundred years enjoyed a monopoly on trade. With the arrjval of powerful Dutch and English fleets in the first half of the 17th century, Portuguese power in the area declined until virtually all of India that remained under Portuguese control were the west coast enclaves of Goa, Damao and Diu. They were forcibly annexed by India in 1962.

RULER

Portuguese, until 1961

DENOMINATION

The denomination of most copper coins appears in numerals on the reverse, though 30 Reis is often given as "1/2 T," and 60 Reis as "T" (T = Tanga). The silver coins have the denomination in words, usually on the obverse until 1850, then on the reverse.

MONETARY SYSTEM

960 Reis = 16 Tanga = 1 Rupia

PORTUGUESE ADMINISTRATION

Kingdom of Portugal

MILLED COINAGE

KM# 13 1/12 TANGA

Bronze **Obv:** Head of Carlos I right **Rev:** Crowned shield **Note:** Roman numeral dating.

Date	Mintage	F12	VF20	XF40	MS60	MS63
1901	960,000	15.00	30.00	60.00	120	175
1901 Prooflike	—	—	—	—	—	1,800
1903	960,000	15.00	30.00	60.00	120	175

KM# 14 1/8 TANGA

Bronze, 21 mm. **Obv:** Head of Carlos I right **Rev:** Crowned shield **Note:** Roman numeral dating

Date	Mintage	F12	VF20	XF40	MS60	MS63
1901	960,000	15.00	25.00	60.00	110	175
1901 Prooflike	—	—	—	—	—	1,550
1903	960,000	15.00	25.00	60.00	110	175

KM# 15 1/4 TANGA (15 Reis)

Bronze **Obv:** Head of Carlos I right **Rev:** Crowned shield **Note:** Roman numeral dating.

Date	Mintage	F12	VF20	XF40	MS60	MS63
1901	800,000	15.00	25.00	60.00	110	175
1901 Prooflike	—	—	—	—	1,300	—
1903	800,000	10.00	20.00	50.00	100	150

KM# 16 1/2 TANGA (30 Reis)

Bronze **Obv:** Head of Carlos I right **Note:** Roman numeral dating.

Date	Mintage	F12	VF20	XF40	MS60	MS63
1901	800,000	10.00	20.00	50.00	100	150
1901 Prooflike	—	—	—	—	950	—
1903	800,000	10.00	20.00	50.00	100	150

KM# 17 RUPIA

11.66 g., 0.917 Silver 0.3438 oz. ASW **Obv:** Head of Carlos I right **Rev:** Crowned shield within wreath

Date	Mintage	F12	VF20	XF40	MS60	MS63
1903	200,000	10.00	20.00	50.00	100	150
1904	100,000	15.00	25.00	60.00	110	175

PORTUGUESE ADMINISTRATION

Republic of Portugal

KM# 19 TANGA (60 Reis)

Bronze **Obv:** Divided shield **Rev:** Five shields on shield

Date	Mintage	VF20	XF40	MS60	MS63	MS65
1934	100,000	25.00	50.00	150	350	—

KM# 24 TANGA (60 Reis)

Bronze, 25 mm. **Obv:** Denomination **Rev:** Tiny towers and shields above divided shield on lined circle

Date	Mintage	VF20	XF40	MS60	MS63	MS65
1947	1,000,000	5.00	10.00	20.00	40.00	75.00

KM# 28 TANGA (60 Reis)

Bronze, 20 mm. **Obv:** Denomination **Rev:** Tiny towers and shields above divided shield on lined circle

Date	Mintage	VF20	XF40	MS60	MS63	MS65
1952	9,600,000	5.00	10.00	20.00	30.00	50.00

KM# 20 2 TANGAS

Copper-Nickel

Date	Mintage	VF20	XF40	MS60	MS63	MS65
1934	150,000	25.00	50.00	125	300	—

KM# 21 4 TANGAS

Copper-Nickel **Obv:** Divided shield **Rev:** Five shields on shield

Date	Mintage	VF20	XF40	MS60	MS63	MS65
1934	100,000	35.00	75.00	150	350	—

KM# 25 1/4 RUPIA

Copper-Nickel **Obv:** Denomination **Rev:** Tiny towers and shields above divided shield on lined circle

Date	Mintage	VF20	XF40	MS60	MS63	MS65
1947	800,000	7.00	12.00	25.00	40.00	75.00
1952	4,000,000	3.00	5.00	10.00	15.00	35.00

KM# 23 1/2 RUPIA
6.00 g., 0.917 Silver 0.1769 oz. ASW, 25 mm. **Obv:** Shield on lined circle at center of Maltese Cross **Rev:** Divided shield

Date	Mintage	VF20	XF40	MS60	MS63	MS65
1936	100,000	3.00	5.00	10.00	12.00	20.00

KM# 26 1/2 RUPIA
Copper-Nickel **Obv:** Denomination **Rev:** Tiny towers and shields above divided shield on lined circle

Date	Mintage	VF20	XF40	MS60	MS63	MS65
1947	600,000	10.00	20.00	35.00	50.00	100
1952	2,000,000	3.00	5.00	10.00	15.00	35.00

KM# 18 RUPIA
11.66 g., 0.917 Silver 0.3438 oz. ASW **Obv:** Liberty head left **Rev:** Denomination within wreath

Date	Mintage	F12	VF20	XF40	MS60	MS63
1912/1	300,000	12.00	25.00	45.00	150	375
1912/1 Proof	—	—	—	—	—	1,750
1912	Inc. above	12.00	25.00	45.00	150	375

KM# 22 RUPIA
12.00 g., 0.917 Silver 0.3538 oz. ASW **Obv:** Shield on lined circle at center of Maltese Cross **Rev:** Divided shield

Date	Mintage	VF20	XF40	MS60	MS63	MS65
1935	300,000	6.50	9.00	12.00	15.00	25.00

KM# 27 RUPIA
12.00 g., 0.500 Silver 0.1929 oz. ASW **Obv:** Shield on lined circle at center of Maltese Cross **Rev:** Tiny towers and shields above divided shield on lined circle

Date	Mintage	VF20	XF40	MS60	MS63	MS65
1947	900,000	12.00	25.00	50.00	75.00	125

KM# 29 RUPIA
Copper-Nickel **Obv:** Shield on lined circle at center of Maltese cross **Rev:** Tiny towers and shields above divided shield on lined circle

Date	Mintage	VF20	XF40	MS60	MS63	MS65
1952	1,000,000	7.00	12.00	25.00	40.00	60.00

DECIMAL COINAGE

100 Centavos = 1 Escudo

KM# 30 10 CENTAVOS
2.00 g., Bronze, 18 mm. **Obv:** Denomination **Rev:** Tiny towers and shields above divided shield on lined circle

Date	Mintage	VF20	XF40	MS60	MS63	MS65
1958	5,000,000	2.00	4.00	7.00	12.00	25.00
1959	Inc. above	2.00	4.00	7.00	12.00	25.00
1961	1,000,000	2.00	4.00	7.00	12.00	25.00

KM# 31 30 CENTAVOS
Bronze **Obv:** Denomination **Rev:** Tiny towers and shields above divided shield on lined circle

Date	Mintage	VF20	XF40	MS60	MS63	MS65
1958	5,000,000	2.00	4.00	7.00	12.00	25.00
1959	Inc. above	2.00	4.00	7.00	12.00	25.00

KM# 32 60 CENTAVOS
Copper-Nickel **Obv:** Shield on lined circle at center of Maltese Cross **Rev:** Tiny towers and shields above divided shield on lined circle

Date	Mintage	VF20	XF40	MS60	MS63	MS65
1958	5,000,000	2.00	4.00	7.00	12.00	25.00
1959	Inc. above	2.00	4.00	7.00	12.00	25.00

KM# 33 ESCUDO
Copper-Nickel **Obv:** Shield on lined circle at center of Maltese Cross **Rev:** Tiny towers and shields above divided shield on lined circle

Date	Mintage	VF20	XF40	MS60	MS63	MS65
1958	6,000,000	2.00	4.00	7.00	12.00	25.00
1959	Inc. above	2.00	4.00	7.00	12.00	25.00

KM# 34 3 ESCUDOS
Copper-Nickel **Obv:** Shield on lined circle at center of Maltese Cross **Rev:** Tiny towers and shields above divided shield on lined circle

Date	Mintage	VF20	XF40	MS60	MS63	MS65
1958	5,000,000	3.00	5.00	9.00	15.00	30.00
1959	Inc. above	3.00	5.00	9.00	15.00	30.00

KM# 35 6 ESCUDOS
Copper-Nickel **Obv:** Shield on lined circle at center of Maltese Cross **Rev:** Tiny towers and shields above divided shield on lined circle

Date	Mintage	VF20	XF40	MS60	MS63	MS65
1959	4,000,000	3.00	5.00	9.00	15.00	30.00

PATTERNS

Including off metal strikes

KM#	Date	Mintage	Identification	Mkt Val
Pn28	1901	—	1/2 Tanga. Aluminum. KM#13.	1,250
Pn29	1901	—	1/8 Tanga. Aluminum. KM#14.	1,100
Pn30	1901	—	1/4 Tanga. Aluminum. KM#15.	1,100
Pn31	1911	—	Rupia. Silver. KM#18.	2,200
Pn32	1911	—	Rupia. Copper. KM#18.	1,250

PROVAS

Standard metals unless otherwise noted; Stamped

KM#	Date	Mintage	Identification	Mkt Val
Pr1	1934	—	Tanga. Bronze. KM#19.	650
Pr2	1934	—	2 Tangas. Copper-Nickel. KM#20.	650
Pr3	1934	—	4 Tangas. Copper-Nickel. KM#21.	1,250
Pr4	1935	—	Rupia. Silver. KM#22.	625
Pr5	1936	—	1/2 Rupia. Silver. KM#23.	625
Pr6	1947	—	1/4 Rupia. Copper-Nickel. KM#25.	575
Pr7	1947	—	1/2 Rupia. Copper-Nickel. KM#26.	575
Pr8	1947	—	Tanga. Bronze. KM#24.	575
Pr9	1947	—	Rupia. Silver. KM#27.	650
Pr10	1952	—	1/4 Rupia. Copper-Nickel. KM#25.	650
Pr11	1952	—	1/2 Rupia. Copper-Nickel. KM#26.	500
Pr12	1952	—	Tanga. Bronze. KM#28.	500
Pr13	1952	—	Rupia. Copper-Nickel. KM#29.	725
Pr14	1954	—	Rupia. Copper-Nickel. KM#29.	1,200
Pr15	1958	—	10 Centavos. Bronze. KM#30.	525
Pr16	1958	—	30 Centavos. Bronze. KM#31.	525
Pr17	1958	—	60 Centavos. Copper-Nickel. KM#32.	525
Pr18	1958	—	Escudo. Copper-Nickel. KM#33.	550
Pr19	1958	—	3 Escudos. Copper-Nickel. KM#34.	550
Pr20	1959	—	10 Centavos. Bronze. KM#30.	525
Pr21	1959	—	30 Centavos. Bronze. KM#31.	525
Pr22	1959	—	60 Centavos. Copper-Nickel. KM#32.	525
Pr23	1959	—	Escudo. Copper-Nickel. KM#33.	525
Pr24	1959	—	3 Escudos. Copper-Nickel. KM#34.	525
Pr25	1959	—	6 Escudos. Copper-Nickel. KM#35.	525
Pr26	1961	—	10 Centavos. Bronze. KM#30.	525
Pr27	1961	—	10 Centavos. Nickel-Brass. Incuse N; KM#30.	525

INDIA - BRITISH

COLONIAL COINAGE

This section lists the coins of British India from the reign of William IV (1835) to the reign of George VI (1947). The issues are divided into two main parts:

Coins struck under the authority of the East India Company (E.I.C.) from 1835 until the trading monopoly of the E.I.C. was abolished in 1853. From August 2, 1858, the property and powers of the Company were transferred to the British Crown. From November 1, 1858 to November 1, 1862, the coins continued to bear the design and inscription of the Company.

Coins struck under the authority of the Crown (Regal issues) from 1862 until 1947.

The first regal issues bear the date 1862 and were struck with the date 1862 unchanged until 1874. From then onward all coins bear the year date.

The copper coins dated 1862 have been tentatively attributed by their size to the mint of issue. The silver coins dated 1862 have been attributed to various years of issue by their characteristic marks according to mint records.

In 1877 Queen Victoria was proclaimed Empress of India and the title of the obverse legend was changed accordingly.

For a detailed account of the work of the various mints and the numerous die varieties the general collector and specialist should refer to *The Coins of the British Commonwealth of Nations*, to the end of the reign of King George VI – 1952, Part 4, India, Vol. 1 and 2, by F. Pridmore, Spink, 1980.

RULER

British until 1947

MINT MARKS

The coins of British India were struck at the following mints, indicated in the catalogue by either capital letters after the date when the actual letter appears on the coins or small letters in () designating the mint of issue. Plain dates indicate Royal Mint strikes.

B – Mumbai (Bombay), 1835-1947, (dot on coin)
C or CM – Calcutta, 1835-1947, (no mint mark on coin)
I – Mumbai (Bombay), 1918-1919
L – Lahore, 1943-1945
P – Pretoria, South Africa, 1943-1944

In 1947 British rule came to an end and India was divided into two self-governing countries, India and Pakistan. In 1971 Bangladash seceded from Pakistan. All are now independent republics and although they are still members of the British Commonwealth of Nations, their coinages do not belong to the British India series.

MONETARY SYSTEM

3 Pies = 1 Pice (Paisa)
4 Pice = 1 Anna
16 Annas = 1 Rupee
15 Rupees = 1 Mohur

The transition from the coins of the Moslem monetary system began with the silver pattern Rupees of William IV, 1834, issued by the East India Company, with the value on the reverse, given in English, Bengali, Persian and Nagari characters. This coinage was struck for several years, as dated, except for the currency, Rupee, which was struck from 1835-1840, all dated 1835.

The portrait coins issued by the East India Company for Victoria show two different head designs on the obverse, which are called Type I and Type II. The coins with Type I head have a continuous obverse legend and were struck from 1840 to 1851. The coins with the Type II head have a divided obverse legend and were struck from 1850 (Calcutta) until 1862. The date on the coins remained unchanged: The Rupee, 1/2 Rupee and 1/4 Rupee are dated 1840. Noticeable differences in the ribbon designs of the English vs. Indian obverses exist.

Type I coins have on the reverse a dot after the date those of Type II have no dot, except for some rare 1/4 Rupees and 2 Annas. The latter are mules, struck from reverse dies of the preceding issue.

KING GEORGE VI: First and Second Heads

While King George VI's First Head is engraved in somewhat higher relief than his second head on all denominations from the 1/12 Anna to the Rupee, an easier way of distinguishing between the two types is that on the First Head the two *fleurs-de-lis* on the royal crown are larger and extend upward to touch the beaded crest at the top of the crown, while the two *fleurs-de-lis* on the crown of the Second Head are smaller and extend upward to touch only the line on the crown below the beaded crest.

ENGRAVERS' INITIALS

The following initials appear on the obverse on the truncation:

S incuse (Type I).
WW raised or incuse (Type II).
WWS or SWW (Type II).
WWB raised (Type II).

Proof and Prooflike restrikes

Original proofs are similar to early English Specimen strikes with wire edges and matte finish busts, arms, etc. Restrikes of most of the coins minted from the period 1835 were regularly supplied until this practice was discontinued on July 1, 1970.

Early proof restrikes are found with slight hairlines from polishing of the old dies. Bust, field, arms, etc. are of even smoothness.

Modern proof-like (P/L) restrikes usually have many hairlines from excessive polishing of the old dies and have a glassy, varnished or proof-like appearance. Many are common while some are quite scarce including some unusual mulings. These listings are indicated by **P/L; Restrike** after the date and mint mark, for example; "1907(s) P/L; Restrike".

DISTINGUISHING FEATURES

Pice

NOTE: There are three types of the crown, which is on the obverse at the top. These are shown below and are designated as (RC) Round Crown, (HC) High Crown, and (FC) Flat Crown. Calcutta Mint issues have no mint mark. The issues from the other mints have the mint mark below the date as follows: Lahore, raised "L"; Pretoria, small round dot; Mumbai (Bombay), diamond dot or "large" round dot. On the Mumbai (Bombay) issues dated 1944 the mint mark appears to be a large dot over a diamond.

Round Crown (RC)

High Crown (HC)

Flat Crown (FC)

½ Anna

The Calcutta Mint continued to issue this denomination with the dot before and after INDIA in 1946 and 1947. Mumbai (Bombay) also struck in 1946 and 1947, the 1946 issue denoted by a small dot in the center of the dashes before and after the date on the reverse (as well as a dot before and after INDIA, like Calcutta); the characteristics of the 1947 Bombay issue have not been determined but are thought also to resemble the 1946 issue. This denomination is also reported to have been struck in a quantity of 50,829,000 pieces in 1946 at the new Lahore Mint but no way of distinguishing this issue has been found. The proof issue in 1946 was struck by Mumbai (Bombay), not Calcutta. Source: Pridmore.

¼ Rupee

BUST A - Front of dress has 4 panels. The bottom panel has 3 leaves at left and a small flower at upper right.

BUST B - Front of dress has 3-1/2 panels. The bottom incomplete panel has only 3 leaf tops.

REVERSE I - Large top flower; 2 large petals above the base of the top flower are long and curved downward.

REVERSE II - Small top flower; 2 large petals above the base of the top flower are short and horizontal.

First Head
Small head, high relief, small denticles

Second Head
Small head, low relief, large denticles

Second Head
Large head, low relief, small denticles

From 1942 to 1945 the reverse designs of the silver coins change slightly every year. However, a distinct reverse variety occurs on Rupees and 1/4 Rupees dated 1943-44 and on the half Rupee dated 1944, all struck at Mumbai (Bombay). This variety may be distinguished from the other coins by the design of the center bottom flower as illustrated, and is designated as Reverse B.

On the normal common varieties dated 1943-44 the three "scalloped circles" are not connected to each other and the bead in the center is not attached to the nearest circle.

Obv: First head, reeded edge

Calcutta Mint issues have no mint mark. Mumbai (Bombay) coins have a small bead below the lotus flower at the bottom on the reverse, except those dated 1943-1944 with reverse B which has a diamond. Lahore Mint issues have a small "L" in the same position. The nickel coins have a diamond below the date on the reverse.

Rupee
Obverse Dies

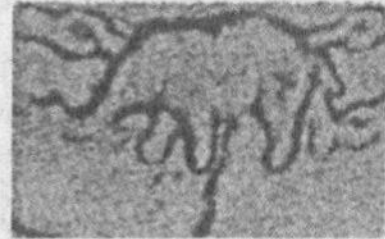

Type I

Type II

Type I - Obv. die w/elephant with pig-like feet and short tail. Nicknamed "pig rupee."

Type II - Obv. die w/redesigned elephant with outlined ear, heavy feet and long tail.

The Rupees, dated 1911, were rejected by the public because the elephant, on the Order of the Indian Empire shown on the King's robe, was thought to resemble a pig, an animal considered unclean by most Indians. Out of a total of 9.4 million pieces struck at both mints, only 700,000 were issued, and many of these were withdrawn and melted with un-issued pieces. The issues dated 1912 and later have a re-designed elephant.

COLONY

MILLED COINAGE

Regal Style

KM# 483 1/12 ANNA (1 Pie)

2.07 g., Copper, 17.5 mm. **Ruler:** Victoria **Obv:** Crowned bust left **Obv. Legend:** VICTORIA EMPRESS **Rev:** Value and date within beaded circle and wreath

Date	Mintage	F12	VF20	XF40	MS60	MS63
1901 (c)	21,345,000	1.25	5.00	10.00	30.00	—
1901 (c)	—	PF63 800				
1901 (c) P/L; Restrike	—	—	—	—	—	600

KM# 483c 1/12 ANNA (1 Pie)

Gold **Ruler:** Victoria **Obv:** Crowned bust left **Rev:** Value and date within beaded circle and wreath **Note:** All dates of this type are prooflike restrikes.

Date	Mintage	F12	VF20	XF40	MS60	MS63
1901 (c)	—	—	—	—	—	3,000

KM# 483b 1/12 ANNA (1 Pie)

Silver **Ruler:** Victoria **Obv:** Crowned bust left **Rev:** Value and date within beaded circle and wreath

Date	Mintage	F12	VF20	XF40	MS60	MS63
1901 (c) P/L; Restrike	—	—	—	—	—	1,000

KM# 497 1/12 ANNA (1 Pie)

Copper, 17.5 mm. **Ruler:** Edward VII **Obv:** Head right **Obv. Legend:** EDWARD VII KING & EMPEROR **Rev:** Date and denomination within circle, wreath surrounds **Note:** Thick planchet.

Date	Mintage	F12	VF20	XF40	MS60	MS63
1903 (c)	7,883,000	0.60	3.00	10.00	25.00	—
1903 (c)	—	PF63 1,000				
1903 (c) P/L; Restrike	—	—	—	—	—	700

Date	Mintage	F12	VF20	XF40	MS60	MS63
1904 (c)	16,506,000	0.60	3.00	10.00	25.00	—
1904 (c)	—	PF63 1,000				
1904 (c) P/L; Restrike	—	—	—	—	—	700
1905 (c)	13,060,000	0.60	3.00	10.00	25.00	—
1905 (c) P/L; Restrike	—	—	—	—	—	700
1906 (c)	9,072,000	0.60	3.00	10.00	25.00	—
1906 (c)	—	PF63 1,000				
1906 (c) P/L; Restrike	—	—	—	—	—	700

KM# 497a 1/12 ANNA (1 Pie)

Silver **Ruler:** Edward VII **Obv:** Head right **Rev:** Date and denomination within circle, wreath surrounds

Date	Mintage	F12	VF20	XF40	MS60	MS63
1904 (c) P/L; Restrike	—	—	—	—	—	600
1905 (c) P/L; Restrike	—	—	—	—	—	600

KM# 498 1/12 ANNA (1 Pie)

Bronze, 17.5 mm. **Ruler:** Edward VII **Obv:** Head right **Obv. Legend:** EDWARD VII KING & EMPEROR **Rev:** Date and denomination within circle, wreath surrounds **Note:** Thin planchet.

Date	Mintage	F12	VF20	XF40	MS60	MS63
1906	2,184,000	0.60	3.00	10.00	25.00	—
1906	—	PF63 1,000				
1907	20,985,000	0.60	3.00	10.00	25.00	—
1907	—	PF63 1,000				
1907 (c) P/L; Restrike	—	—	—	—	—	800
1908	22,036,000	0.60	3.00	10.00	25.00	—
1908	—	PF63 1,000				
1908 (c) P/L; Restrike	—	—	—	—	—	800
1909	12,316,000	0.60	3.00	10.00	25.00	—
1909 (c) P/L; Restrike	—	—	—	—	—	1,000
1910	23,520,000	0.60	3.00	10.00	25.00	—
1910 (c) P/L; Restrike	—	—	—	—	—	1,000

KM# 498a 1/12 ANNA (1 Pie)

Aluminum, 17.5 mm. **Ruler:** Edward VII **Obv:** Head right **Rev:** Date and denomination within circle, wreath surrounds

Date	Mintage	F12	VF20	XF40	MS60	MS63
1909	—	PF63 1,500				

KM# 509 1/12 ANNA (1 Pie)

1.60 g., Bronze, 17.4 mm. **Ruler:** George V **Obv:** Crowned bust left **Obv. Legend:** GEORGE V KING EMPEROR **Rev:** Date and denomination within circle, wreath surrounds

Date	Mintage	F12	VF20	XF40	MS60	MS63
1912 (c)	25,938,000	0.60	1.50	4.00	10.00	—
1912 (c)	—	PF63 1,000				
1912 (c) P/L; Restrike	—	—	—	—	—	600
1913 (c)	16,149,000	0.60	1.50	4.00	10.00	—
1913 (c)	—	PF63 1,000				
1913 (c) P/L; Restrike	—	—	—	—	—	600
1914 (c)	19,814,000	0.60	1.50	4.00	10.00	—
1914 (c)	—	PF63 1,000				
1914 (c) P/L; Restrike	—	—	—	—	—	600
1915 (c)	20,563,000	0.60	1.50	4.00	10.00	—
1915 (c)	—	PF63 1,000				
1915 (c) P/L; Restrike	—	—	—	—	—	600
1916 (c)	14,438,000	0.60	1.50	4.00	10.00	—
1916 (c)	—	PF63 1,000				
1916 (c) P/L; Restrike	—	—	—	—	—	600
1917 (c)	35,174,000	0.60	1.50	4.00	10.00	—
1917 (c)	—	PF63 1,000				
1917 (c) P/L; Restrike	—	—	—	—	—	600
1918 (c)	24,192,000	0.60	1.50	4.00	10.00	—
1918 (c)	—	PF63 1,000				
1918 (c) P/L; Restrike	—	—	—	—	—	600
1919 (c)	17,472,000	0.60	1.50	4.00	10.00	—
1919 (c)	—	PF63 1,000				
1919 (c) P/L; Restrike	—	—	—	—	—	6,000
1920 (c)	39,878,000	0.60	1.50	4.00	10.00	—
1920 (c)	—	PF63 1,000				
1920 (c) P/L; Restrike	—	—	—	—	—	600
1921 (c)	19,334,000	0.60	1.50	4.00	10.00	—
1921 (c) P/L; Restrike	—	—	—	—	—	1,000
1921 (c)	—	PF63 1,000				
1923 (c)	8,429,000	0.60	1.50	4.00	10.00	—
1923 (c)	—	PF63 1,000				
1923 (b)	8,717,000	0.60	1.50	4.00	10.00	—
1923 (b)	—	PF63 1,000				
1923 (b) P/L; Restrike	—	—	—	—	—	600
1924 (c)	7,200,000	0.60	1.50	4.00	10.00	—
1924 (c)	—	PF63 1,000				
1924 (b)	9,869,000	0.60	1.50	4.00	10.00	—
1924 (b)	—	PF63 1,000				
1924 (b) P/L; Restrike	—	—	—	—	—	600
1925 (c)	5,818,000	0.60	1.50	4.00	10.00	—
1925 (c)	—	PF63 1,000				
1925 (b)	6,415,000	0.60	1.50	4.00	10.00	—
1925 (b)	—	PF63 1,000				
1925 (b) P/L; Restrike	—	—	—	—	—	600
1926 (c)	4,147,000	0.60	1.50	4.00	10.00	—
1926 (c)	—	PF63 1,000				
1926 (b)	15,464,000	0.60	1.50	4.00	10.00	—
1926 (b)	—	PF63 1,000				
1926 (b) P/L; Restrike	—	—	—	—	—	600
1927 (c)	6,662,000	0.60	1.50	4.00	10.00	—
1927 (c)	—	PF63 1,000				
1927 (b)	6,788,000	0.60	1.50	4.00	10.00	—
1927 (b)	—	PF63 1,000				
1927 (b) P/L; Restrike	—	—	—	—	—	600
1928 (c)	8,064,000	0.60	1.50	4.00	10.00	—
1928 (c)	—	PF63 1,000				
1928 (b)	6,135,000	0.60	1.50	4.00	10.00	—
1928 (b)	—	PF63 1,000				
1928 (b) P/L; Restrike	—	—	—	—	—	600
1929 (c)	15,130,000	0.60	1.50	4.00	10.00	—
1929 (c)	—	PF63 1,000				
1929 (c) P/L; Restrike	—	—	—	—	—	600
1930 (c)	13,498,000	0.60	1.50	4.00	10.00	—
1930 (c)	—	PF63 1,000				
1930 (c) P/L; Restrike	—	—	—	—	—	600
1931 (c)	18,278,000	0.60	1.50	4.00	10.00	—
1931 (c)	—	PF63 1,000				
1931 (c) P/L; Restrike	—	—	—	—	—	600
1932 (c)	23,213,000	0.60	1.50	4.00	10.00	—
1932 (c)	—	PF63 1,000				
1932 (c) P/L; Restrike	—	—	—	—	—	600
1933 (c)	16,896,000	0.60	1.50	4.00	10.00	—
1933 (c)	—	PF63 1,000				
1933 (c) P/L; Restrike	—	—	—	—	—	600
1934 (c)	17,146,000	0.60	1.50	4.00	10.00	—
1934 (c)	—	PF63 1,000				
1934 (c) P/L; Restrike	—	—	—	—	—	600
1935 (c)	19,142,000	0.60	1.50	4.00	10.00	—
1935 (c)	—	PF63 1,000				
1935 (c) P/L; Restrike	—	—	—	—	—	600
1936 (c)	23,213,000	0.60	1.50	4.00	10.00	—
1936 (b)	12,887,000	0.60	1.50	4.00	10.00	—
1936 (b) P/L; Restrike	—	—	—	—	—	600

KM# 526 1/12 ANNA (1 Pie)

Bronze, 17.5 mm. **Ruler:** George VI **Obv:** Crowned head left **Obv. Legend:** GEORGE VI KING EMPEROR **Rev:** Date and denomination within circle, wreath surrounds **Note:** First head.

Date	Mintage	F12	VF20	XF40	MS60	MS63
1938 (c)	—	PF63 1,000				
1939 (b)	17,407,000	0.60	1.50	4.00	10.00	—
1939 (c)	3,571,000	0.60	1.50	4.00	10.00	—

KM# 527 1/12 ANNA (1 Pie)

Bronze, 17.5 mm. **Ruler:** George VI **Obv:** Crowned head left **Obv. Legend:** GEORGE VI KING EMPEROR **Rev:** Date and denomination within circle, wreath surrounds **Note:** Second head.

Date	Mintage	F12	VF20	XF40	MS60	MS63
1938 (c) P/L; Restrike	—	—	—	—	—	—
1939 (c)	5,245,000	0.60	1.00	2.00	4.00	—
1939 (c)	—	PF63 700				
1939 (b)	31,306,000	0.60	1.00	2.00	4.00	—
1939 (b)	—	PF63 700				
1939 (b) P/L; Restrike	—	—	—	—	—	700
1941 (b)	6,137,000	0.60	1.00	2.00	4.00	—
1942 (b)	6,124,000	3.00	5.00	8.00	10.00	—
1942 (b)	—	PF63 700				
1942 (b) P/L; Restrike	—	—	—	—	—	500

KM# 484 1/2 PICE

Copper **Ruler:** Victoria **Obv:** Crowned bust left **Obv. Legend:** VICTORIA EMPRESS **Rev:** Value and date within beaded circle and wreath

Date	Mintage	F12	VF20	XF40	MS60	MS63
1901	16,057,000	4.00	10.00	20.00	40.00	—
1901	—	PF63 1,800				
1901 (c) P/L; Restrike	—	—	—	—	—	1,200

KM# 484c 1/2 PICE

Gold **Ruler:** Victoria **Obv:** Crowned bust left **Rev:** Value and date within beaded circle and wreath **Note:** All dates of this type are prooflike restrikes.

Date	Mintage	F12	VF20	XF40	MS60	MS63
1901 (c)	—	—	—	—	—	4,000

KM# 484b 1/2 PICE

Silver **Ruler:** Victoria **Obv:** Crowned bust left **Rev:** Value and date within beaded circle and wreath

Date	Mintage	F12	VF20	XF40	MS60	MS63
1901 (c) P/L; Restrike	—	—	—	—	—	2,500

KM# 499 1/2 PICE

Copper **Ruler:** Edward VII **Obv:** Head right **Obv. Legend:** EDWARD VII KING & EMPEROR **Rev:** Date and denomination within circle, wreath surrounds

Date	Mintage	F12	VF20	XF40	MS60	MS63
1903	5,376,000	1.00	3.00	10.00	30.00	—
1903	—	PF63 1,200				
1903 (c) P/L; Restrike	—	—	—	—	—	700
1904	8,464,000	1.00	3.00	10.00	30.00	—
1904	—	PF63 1,200				
1904 (c) P/L; Restrike	—	—	—	—	—	700
1905	8,922,000	1.00	3.00	10.00	30.00	—
1905 (c) P/L; Restrike	—	—	—	—	—	1,200
1906	6,346,000	1.00	3.00	10.00	30.00	—
1906	—	PF63 1,200				
1906 (c) P/L; Restrike	—	—	—	—	—	700

KM# 500 1/2 PICE

Bronze **Ruler:** Edward VII **Obv. Legend:** EDWARD VII KING & EMPEROR **Note:** Thinner planchets.

Date	Mintage	F12	VF20	XF40	MS60	MS63
1904	—	PF63 1,200				
1906	5,860,000	1.00	3.00	10.00	30.00	—
1906	—	PF63 1,200				
1907	8,060,000	1.00	3.00	10.00	30.00	—
1907	—	PF63 1,200				
1907 (c) P/L; Restrike	—	—	—	—	—	700
1908	10,035,000	1.00	3.00	10.00	30.00	—
1908	—	PF63 1,200				
1908 (c) P/L; Restrike	—	—	—	—	—	700
1909	8,493,000	1.00	3.00	10.00	30.00	—
1909 (c) P/L; Restrike	—	—	—	—	—	700
1910	17,408,000	1.00	3.00	10.00	30.00	—

KM# 500a 1/2 PICE

Aluminum **Ruler:** Edward VII

Date	Mintage	F12	VF20	XF40	MS60	MS63
1909	—	PF63 2,000				

KM# 500b 1/2 PICE

Nickel **Ruler:** Edward VII

Date	Mintage	F12	VF20	XF40	MS60	MS63
1904	—	PF63 2,000				

KM# 500c 1/2 PICE

Silver **Ruler:** Edward VII

Date	Mintage	F12	VF20	XF40	MS60	MS63
1903 (c) P/L; Restrike	—	—	—	—	—	2,000
1904 (c) P/L; Restrike	—	—	—	—	—	2,000
1905 (c) P/L; Restrike	—	—	—	—	—	2,000

KM# A510 1/2 PICE

Nickel **Ruler:** George V **Obv:** Crowned bust left **Obv. Legend:** George V King Emperor **Rev:** Date and denomination within circle, wreath surrounds **Note:** All Restrike PL

Date	Mintage	F12	VF20	XF40	MS60	MS63
1912	—	—	—	—	—	500
1913	—	—	—	—	—	500
1914	—	—	—	—	—	500
1915	—	—	—	—	—	500
1916	—	—	—	—	—	500
1917	—	—	—	—	—	500
1918	—	—	—	—	—	500
1919	—	—	—	—	—	500
1920	—	—	—	—	—	500
1921	—	—	—	—	—	500
1922	—	—	—	—	—	500
1923	—	—	—	—	—	500
1924	—	—	—	—	—	500
1925	—	—	—	—	—	500
1926	—	—	—	—	—	500
1927	—	—	—	—	—	500
1928	—	—	—	—	—	500
1929	—	—	—	—	—	500
1930	—	—	—	—	—	500
1931	—	—	—	—	—	500
1932	—	—	—	—	—	500
1933	—	—	—	—	—	500
1934	—	—	—	—	—	500
1935	—	—	—	—	—	500
1936	—	—	—	—	—	500

KM# 510 1/2 PICE

Bronze **Ruler:** George V **Obv:** Crowned bust left **Obv. Legend:** GEORGE V KING EMPEROR **Rev:** Date and denomination within circle, wreath surrounds

Date	Mintage	F12	VF20	XF40	MS60	MS63
1912	12,911,000	1.00	3.00	5.00	12.00	—
1912	—	PF63 800				
1912 (c) P/L; Restrike	—	—	—	—	—	500
1913	10,897,000	1.00	3.00	5.00	12.00	—
1913	—	PF63 800				
1913 (c) P/L; Restrike	—	—	—	—	—	500
1914	4,877,000	1.00	3.00	5.00	12.00	—
1914	—	PF63 800				
1914 (c) P/L; Restrike	—	—	—	—	—	500
1915	9,830,000	1.00	3.00	5.00	12.00	—
1915	—	PF63 800				
1915 (c) P/L; Restrike	—	—	—	—	—	500
1916	5,734,000	1.00	3.00	5.00	12.00	—
1916	—	PF63 800				
1916 (c) P/L; Restrike	—	—	—	—	—	500
1917	15,296,000	1.00	3.00	5.00	12.00	—
1917	—	PF63 800				
1917 (c) P/L; Restrike	—	—	—	—	—	500
1918	6,244,000	1.00	3.00	5.00	12.00	—
1918	—	PF63 800				
1918 (c) P/L; Restrike	—	—	—	—	—	500
1919	11,162,000	1.00	3.00	5.00	12.00	—
1919	—	PF63 800				
1919 (c) P/L; Restrike	—	—	—	—	—	500
1920	4,493,000	1.00	3.00	5.00	12.00	—
1920	—	PF63 800				
1920 (c) P/L; Restrike	—	—	—	—	—	500
1921	6,234,000	1.00	3.00	5.00	12.00	—
1921	—	PF63 800				
1921 (c) P/L; Restrike	—	—	—	—	—	500
1922	6,336,000	1.00	3.00	5.00	12.00	—
1922	—	PF63 800				
1922 (c) P/L; Restrike	—	—	—	—	—	500
1923	7,411,000	1.00	3.00	5.00	12.00	—
1923	—	PF63 800				
1923 (c) P/L; Restrike	—	—	—	—	—	500
1924	9,523,000	1.00	3.00	5.00	12.00	—
1924	—	PF63 800				
1924 (c) P/L; Restrike	—	—	—	—	—	500
1925	3,981,000	1.00	3.00	5.00	12.00	—
1925	—	PF63 800				
1925 (c) P/L; Restrike	—	—	—	—	—	500
1926	7,885,000	1.00	3.00	5.00	12.00	—
1926	—	PF63 800				
1926 (c) P/L; Restrike	—	—	—	—	—	500
1927	5,888,000	1.00	3.00	5.00	12.00	—
1927	—	PF63 800				
1927 (c) P/L; Restrike	—	—	—	—	—	500
1928	5,456,000	1.00	3.00	5.00	12.00	—
1928	—	PF63 800				
1928 (c) P/L; Restrike	—	—	—	—	—	500
1929	7,654,000	1.00	3.00	5.00	12.00	—
1929	—	PF63 800				
1929 (c) P/L; Restrike	—	—	—	—	—	500
1930	7,181,000	1.00	3.00	5.00	12.00	—
1930	—	PF63 800				
1930 (c) P/L; Restrike	—	—	—	—	—	500
1931	8,794,000	1.00	3.00	5.00	12.00	—
1931	—	PF63 800				
1931 (c) P/L; Restrike	—	—	—	—	—	500
1932	5,440,000	1.00	3.00	5.00	12.00	—
1932	—	PF63 800				
1932 (c) P/L; Restrike	—	—	—	—	—	500
1933	9,242,000	1.00	3.00	5.00	12.00	—
1933	—	PF63 800				
1933 (c) P/L; Restrike	—	—	—	—	—	500
1934	8,947,000	1.00	3.00	5.00	12.00	—
1934	—	PF63 800				
1934 (c) P/L; Restrike	—	—	—	—	—	500
1935	15,501,000	1.00	3.00	5.00	12.00	—
1935	—	PF63 800				
1935 (c) P/L; Restrike	—	—	—	—	—	500
1936	26,726,000	1.00	3.00	5.00	12.00	—
1936 (c) P/L; Restrike	—	—	—	—	—	500

KM# 528 1/2 PICE

Bronze **Ruler:** George VI **Obv:** First head; high relief **Obv. Legend:** GEORGE VI KING EMPEROR **Rev:** Date and denomination within circle, wreath surrounds **Note:** Calcutta Mint issues have no mint mark. Mumbai (Bombay) Mint issues have a small dot below the date.

Date	Mintage	F12	VF20	XF40	MS60	MS63
1938 (c)	—	400	500	700	1,000	—
1938 (c)	—	PF63 1,500				
1938 (c) P/L; Restrike	—	—	—	—	—	1,200
1939 (c)	17,357,000	1.00	2.00	5.00	8.00	—
1939 (c)	—	PF63 1,000				
1939 (b)	9,343,000	1.00	2.00	5.00	8.00	—
1939 (b)	—	PF63 1,000				
1939 (b) P/L; Restrike	—	—	—	—	—	—
1940 (c)	23,770,000	1.00	2.00	5.00	8.00	—
1940 (c)	—	PF63 1,000				
1940 (c) P/L; Restrike	—	—	—	—	—	—

KM# 529 1/2 PICE

Bronze **Ruler:** George VI **Obv:** Second head; low relief **Obv. Legend:** GEORGE VI KING EMPEROR **Rev:** Date and denomination within circle, wreath surrounds

Date	Mintage	F12	VF20	XF40	MS60	MS63
1942	—	PF63 1,000				
1942 (b) P/L; Restrike	—	—	—	—	—	600

PICE

NOTE: There are three types of the crown, which is on the obverse at the top. These are shown below and are designated as (RC) Round Crown, (HC) High Crown, and (FC) Flat Crown. Calcutta Mint issues have no mint mark. The issues from the other mints have the mint mark below the date as following: Lahore, raised "L"; Pretoria, small round dot; Bombay, diamond dot or "large" round dot. On the Bombay issues dated 1944 the mint mark appears to be a large dot over a diamond.

Round Crown (RC)

High Crown (HC) Flat Crown (FC)

KM# 532 PICE

Bronze **Ruler:** George VI **Obv:** Small date, small legends

Date	Mintage	F12	VF20	XF40	MS60	MS63
1943 (RC) diamond	164,659	0.30	0.50	1.00	3.50	—

KM# 533 PICE

2.00 g., Bronze, 21.32 mm. **Ruler:** George VI **Obv:** Center hole, large date, large legends **Rev:** Wreath surrounds center hole

Date	Mintage	F12	VF20	XF40	MS60	MS63
1943 (b) (HC) large dot	—	0.20	0.40	0.80	1.50	—
1943 (p) (HC) small dot	98,997,000	0.20	0.40	0.80	1.50	—
1944 (c) (HC) Rare	—	—	—	—	—	—
1944 (c) (HC)	—	PF63 400				
1944 (b) (HC) large dot	195,354,000	0.20	0.40	0.80	1.50	—
1944 (b) (HC) diamond	—	0.20	0.50	0.90	2.50	—
1944 (b) (FC) large dot	—	0.20	0.50	0.90	2.50	—

Date	Mintage	F12	VF20	XF40	MS60	MS63
1944 (b) P/L; Restrike	—	—	—	—	—	300
1944 (p) (HC) small dot	141,003,000	0.20	0.50	0.90	2.50	—
1944 L (HC)	29,802,000	0.20	0.50	1.00	4.00	—
1945 (c) (FC)	156,322,000	0.20	0.40	0.80	1.50	—
1945 (b) (FC) diamond	237,197,000	0.20	0.40	0.80	1.50	—
1945 (b) (FC) large dot	Inc. above	0.20	0.40	0.80	1.50	—
1945 (b) P/L; Restrike	—	—	—	—	—	300
1945 L (FC)	238,825,000	0.20	0.40	0.80	1.50	—
1947 (c) (HC)	153,702,000	0.20	0.40	0.80	1.50	—
1947 (b) (HC) diamond	43,654,000	0.20	0.50	1.00	4.00	—
1947 (b)	—	PF63 400				
1947 P/L; Restrike	—	—	—	—	—	300

KM# 486 1/4 ANNA

6.40 g., Copper **Ruler:** Victoria **Obv:** Crowned bust left **Obv. Legend:** VICTORIA EMPRESS **Rev:** Value and date within beaded circle and wreath

Date	Mintage	F12	VF20	XF40	MS60	MS63
1901 (c)	136,091,000	2.00	5.00	20.00	60.00	—
1901 (c)	—	PF63 1,000				
1901 (c) P/L; Restrike	—	—	—	—	—	600

KM# 486b 1/4 ANNA

Silver **Ruler:** Victoria **Obv:** Crowned bust left **Rev:** Value and date within beaded circle and wreath

Date	Mintage	F12	VF20	XF40	MS60	MS63
1901 (c) P/L; Restrike	—	—	—	—	—	2,000

KM# 486c 1/4 ANNA

Gold **Ruler:** Victoria **Obv:** Crowned bust left **Rev:** Value and date within beaded circle and wreath **Note:** All dates of this type are Prooflike Restrikes.

Date	Mintage	F12	VF20	XF40	MS60	MS63
1901 (c) P/L; Restrike	—	—	—	—	—	4,000

KM# 501 1/4 ANNA

6.48 g., Copper **Ruler:** Edward VII **Obv. Legend:** EDWARD VII KING & EMPEROR

Date	Mintage	F12	VF20	XF40	MS60	MS63
1903	105,974,000	0.60	3.00	10.00	60.00	—
1903	—	PF63 1,000				
1903 (c) P/L; Restrike	—	—	—	—	—	750
1904	104,595,000	0.60	3.00	10.00	60.00	—
1904	—	PF63 1,000				
1904 (c) P/L; Restrike	—	—	—	—	—	750
1905	130,058,000	0.60	3.00	10.00	60.00	—
1905	—	PF63 1,000				
1905 (c) P/L; Restrike	—	—	—	—	—	750
1906	47,229,000	0.60	3.00	10.00	60.00	—
1906	—	PF63 1,000				

KM# 501b 1/4 ANNA

Silver **Ruler:** Edward VII **Obv. Legend:** EDWARD VII KING & EMPEROR

Date	Mintage	F12	VF20	XF40	MS60	MS63
1903 (c) P/L; Restrike	—	—	—	—	—	1,750
1904 (c) P/L; Restrike	—	—	—	—	—	1,750
1905 (c) P/L; Restrike	—	—	—	—	—	1,750

KM# 501a 1/4 ANNA

Nickel **Ruler:** Edward VII **Obv. Legend:** EDWARD VII KING & EMPEROR

Date	Mintage	F12	VF20	XF40	MS60	MS63
1906	—	PF63 1,500				

KM# 502 1/4 ANNA

4.83 g., Bronze, 25.3 mm. **Ruler:** Edward VII **Obv:** Head right **Obv. Legend:** EDWARD VII KING & EMPEROR **Rev:** Date and denomination within circle, wreath surrounds **Note:** Thinner planchet.

Date	Mintage	F12	VF20	XF40	MS60	MS63
1906	115,786,000	0.60	3.00	10.00	50.00	—
1906	—	PF63 1,200				
1907	234,682,000	0.60	3.00	10.00	50.00	—
1907	—	PF63 1,200				
1907 (c) P/L; Restrike	—	—	—	—	—	700
1908	58,066,000	0.60	3.00	10.00	50.00	—
1908	—	PF63 1,200				
1908 (c) P/L; Restrike	—	—	—	—	—	700
1909	29,966,000	2.00	5.00	50.00	200	—
1909	—	PF63 1,200				
1909 (c) P/L; Restrike	—	—	—	—	—	700
1910	47,265,000	0.60	3.00	10.00	50.00	—
1910 (c) P/L; Restrike	—	—	—	—	—	1,200

KM# 502a 1/4 ANNA

Aluminum **Ruler:** Edward VII **Obv:** Head right **Obv. Legend:** EDWARD VII KING & EMPEROR **Rev:** Date and denomination within circle, wreath surrounds

Date	Mintage	VG8	F12	VF20	XF40	MS60
1908	—	PF63 2,000				

KM# 511 1/4 ANNA

Bronze **Ruler:** George V **Obv:** Type I **Obv. Legend:** GEORGE V KING EMPEROR **Note:** Calcutta Mint issues have no mint mark. Mumbai (Bombay) Mint issues have a small dot below the date. The pieces dated 1911, like the other coins with that date, show the "Pig" elephant.

Date	Mintage	F12	VF20	XF40	MS60	MS63
1911	55,918,000	15.00	30.00	100	250	—
1911	—	PF63 1,300				
1911 (c) P/L; Restrike	—	—	—	—	—	700

KM# 512 1/4 ANNA

4.72 g., Bronze, 25.4 mm. **Ruler:** George V **Obv:** Crowned bust left, type II **Obv. Legend:** GEORGE V KING EMPEROR **Rev:** Date and denomination within circle, wreath surrounds

Date	Mintage	F12	VF20	XF40	MS60	MS63
1912 (c)	107,456,000	0.50	1.00	2.00	5.00	—
1912 (c)	—	PF63 1,000				
1912 (c) P/L; Restrike	—	—	—	—	—	600
1913 (c)	82,061,000	0.50	1.00	2.00	5.00	—
1913 (c)	—	PF63 1,000				
1913 (c) P/L; Restrike	—	—	—	—	—	600
1914 (c)	40,576,000	0.50	1.00	2.00	5.00	—
1914 (c)	—	PF63 1,000				
1914 (c) P/L; Restrike	—	—	—	—	—	600
1916 (c)	1,632,000	15.00	30.00	100	300	—
1916 (c)	—	PF63 1,000				
1917 (c)	69,370,000	0.50	1.00	2.00	5.00	—
1917 (c)	—	PF63 1,000				
1917 (c) P/L; Restrike	—	—	—	—	—	600
1918 (c)	84,045,000	0.50	1.00	2.00	5.00	—
1918 (c)	—	PF63 1,000				
1918 (c) P/L; Restrike	—	—	—	—	—	600
1919 (c)	212,467,000	0.50	1.00	2.00	5.00	—
1919 (c)	—	PF63 1,000				
1919 (c) P/L; Restrike	—	—	—	—	—	600
1920 (c)	96,019,000	0.50	1.00	2.00	5.00	—
1920 (c)	—	PF63 1,000				
1920 (c) P/L; Restrike	—	—	—	—	—	600
1921 (c)	—	PF63 2,000				
1924 (b)	16,322,000	0.50	1.00	2.00	5.00	—
1924 (b)	—	PF63 1,000				
1925 (c)	14,598,000	0.50	1.00	2.00	5.00	—
1925 (b)	14,588,000	0.50	1.00	2.00	5.00	—
1925 (b)	—	PF63 1,000				
1926 (c)	17,389,000	0.50	1.00	2.00	5.00	—
1926 (c)	—	PF63 1,000				
1926 (b)	16,073,000	0.50	1.00	2.00	5.00	—
1926 (b)	—	PF63 1,000				
1926 (b) P/L; Restrike	—	—	—	—	—	600
1927 (c)	6,925,000	0.50	1.00	2.00	5.00	—
1927 (c)	—	PF63 1,000				
1927 (b)	12,440,000	0.50	1.00	2.00	5.00	—
1927 (b)	—	PF63 1,000				
1927 (b) P/L; Restrike	—	—	—	—	—	600
1928 (c)	257,779,000	0.50	1.00	2.00	5.00	—
1928 (c)	—	PF63 1,000				
1928 (b)	10,057,000	0.50	1.00	2.00	5.00	—
1928 (b)	—	PF63 1,000				
1928 (b) P/L; Restrike	—	—	—	—	—	600
1929 (c)	61,542,000	0.50	1.00	2.00	5.00	—
1929 (c)	—	PF63 1,000				
1929 (c) P/L; Restrike	—	—	—	—	—	600
1930 (c)	40,698,000	0.50	1.00	2.00	5.00	—
1930 (c)	—	PF63 1,000				
1930 (b)	9,646,000	0.50	1.00	2.00	5.00	—
1930 (b)	—	PF63 1,000				
1930 (b) P/L; Restrike	—	—	—	—	—	600
1931 (c)	6,835,000	0.50	1.00	2.00	5.00	—
1931 (c)	—	PF63 1,000				
1931 (c) P/L; Restrike	—	—	—	—	—	600
1933 (c)	40,230,000	0.50	1.00	2.00	5.00	—
1933 (c)	—	PF63 1,000				
1933 (c) P/L; Restrike	—	—	—	—	—	600
1934 (c)	80,506,000	0.50	1.00	2.00	5.00	—
1934 (c)	—	PF63 1,000				
1934 (c) P/L; Restrike	—	—	—	—	—	600
1935 (c)	92,595,000	0.50	1.00	2.00	5.00	—
1935 (c)	—	PF63 1,000				
1935 (c) P/L; Restrike	—	—	—	—	—	600
1936 (c)	227,501,000	0.50	1.00	2.00	5.00	—
1936 (b)	61,926,000	0.50	1.00	2.00	5.00	—
1936 (b)	—	PF63 1,000				
1936 (b) P/L; Restrike	—	—	—	—	—	600

KM# 530 1/4 ANNA

4.86 g., Bronze **Ruler:** George VI **Obv:** First head; high relief **Obv. Legend:** GEORGE VI KING EMPEROR **Rev:** Date and denomination within circle, wreath surrounds

Date	Mintage	F12	VF20	XF40	MS60	MS63
1938 (c)	33,792,000	0.50	1.00	2.00	5.00	—
1938 (c)	—	PF63 1,000				
1938 (b)	16,796,000	0.50	1.00	2.00	5.00	—
1938 (b) P/L; Restrike	—	—	—	—	—	1,000
1939 (c)	78,279,000	0.50	1.00	2.00	5.00	—
1939 (c)	—	PF63 1,000				
1939 (b)	60,171,000	0.50	1.00	2.00	5.00	—
1939 (b)	—	PF63 1,000				
1939 (b) P/L; Restrike	—	—	—	—	—	550
1940 (b)	116,721,000	0.50	1.00	2.00	5.00	—

KM# 530.1 1/4 ANNA

4.86 g., Bronze **Ruler:** George VI **Obv:** Second head; low relief **Obv. Legend:** George VI King Emperor **Rev:** Date and denomination within circle, wreath surrounds **Note:** 2nd head

Date	Mintage	F12	VF20	XF40	MS60	MS63
1939 B	—	20.00	30.00	50.00	80.00	—
1939 C	—	20.00	30.00	50.00	80.00	—

KM# 531 1/4 ANNA

4.60 g., Bronze, 25.33 mm. **Ruler:** George VI **Obv:** Second head; low relief **Obv. Legend:** GEORGE VI KING EMPEROR **Rev:** Denomination and date within wreath

Date	Mintage	F12	VF20	XF40	MS60	MS63
1940 (c)	140,410,000	0.40	0.60	1.25	4.00	—
1940 (c)	—	PF63 1,000				
1940 (b)	—	0.40	0.60	1.25	4.00	—

Note: Mintage included in KM#530

Date	Mintage	F12	VF20	XF40	MS60	MS63
1940 (b) P/L; Restrike	—	—	—	—	—	550
1941 (c)	121,107,000	0.40	0.60	1.25	4.00	—
1941 (b)	1,446,000	30.00	50.00	100	150	—
1941 (b) P/L; Restrike	—	—	—	—	—	550
1942 (c)	34,298,000	0.40	0.60	1.25	4.00	—
1942 (b)	8,768,000	0.40	0.60	1.25	4.00	—
1942 (b) P/L; Restrike	—	—	—	—	—	550

KM# 503 1/2 ANNA

Copper **Ruler:** Edward VII **Obv:** Head of Edward VII **Rev:** Value and date within beaded circle and wreath

Date	Mintage	F12	VF20	XF40	MS60	MS63
1904	—	**PF63** 6,000				

KM# 534 1/2 ANNA

Copper-Nickel **Ruler:** George VI **Obv:** Crowned head left **Obv. Legend:** GEORGE VI KING EMPEROR **Rev:** Denomination and date within decorative outline **Rev. Legend:** • INDIA • **Shape:** 4-sided

Date	Mintage	F12	VF20	XF40	MS60	MS63
1940 (c)	—	**PF63** 15,000				
1940 (c) P/L; Restrike	—	—	—	—	—	5,000

KM# 534a 1/2 ANNA

Gold **Ruler:** George VI **Obv:** Crowned head left **Rev:** Denomination and date within decorative outline

Date	Mintage	F12	VF20	XF40	MS60	MS63
1940 (c)	—	—	—	—	10,000	—

Note: Prooflike; Restrike

KM# 534b.1 1/2 ANNA

2.92 g., Nickel-Brass **Ruler:** George VI **Obv:** Crowned head left, second head **Obv. Legend:** GEORGE VI KING EMPEROR **Rev:** Denomination and date within decorative outline **Rev. Legend:** INDIA (without dots) **Note:** Bombay Mint issues dated 1942-1945 are without a dot before and after India.

Date	Mintage	F12	VF20	XF40	MS60	MS63
1942	7,945,000	0.50	1.00	2.50	5.00	—
1942 (b) P/L; Restrike	—	—	—	—	—	500
1943 (b) P/L; Restrike	—	—	—	—	—	500
1944 (b) P/L; Restrike	—	—	—	—	—	500
1945 (b) P/L; Restrike	—	—	—	—	—	500

KM# 534b.2 1/2 ANNA

2.87 g., Nickel-Brass, 17.3 mm. **Ruler:** George VI **Obv:** Crowned head left **Rev:** Denomination and date within decorative outline **Rev. Legend:** • INDIA •

Date	Mintage	F12	VF20	XF40	MS60	MS63
1942	159,000,000	15.00	25.00	35.00	50.00	—
1942	—	**PF63** 1,000				
1943	437,760,000	0.50	1.00	2.50	5.00	—
1943	—	**PF63** 1,000				
1944	514,800,000	0.50	1.00	2.50	5.00	—
1944	—	**PF63** 1,000				
1945	215,732,000	0.50	1.00	2.50	5.00	—
1945	—	**PF63** 1,000				

The Calcutta Mint continued to issue this denomination with the dot before and after INDIA in 1946 and 1947. Bombay also struck in 1946 and 1947, the 1946 issue denoted by a small dot in the center of the dashes before and after the date on the reverse (as well as a dot before and after INDIA, like Calcutta); the characteristics of the 1947 Bombay issue have not been determined but are thought also to resemble the 1946 issue. This denomination is also reported to have been struck in a quantity of 50,829,000 pieces in 1946 at the new Lahore Mint but no way of distinguishing this issue has been found. The proof issue in 1946 was struck by Bombay, not Calcutta. Source: Pridmore.

KM# 535.1 1/2 ANNA

2.87 g., Copper-Nickel **Ruler:** George VI **Obv:** Crowned head left **Rev:** Denomination and date within decorative outline **Shape:** 4-sided

Date	Mintage	F12	VF20	XF40	MS60	MS63
1946	48,744,000	0.50	1.00	2.50	5.00	—
1946	—	**PF63** 800				
1946 (b) P/L; Restrike	—	—	—	—	—	500
1947 (b)	—	50.00	100	200	500	—
1947 (b) P/L; Restrike	—	—	—	—	—	500

KM# 535.2 1/2 ANNA

2.90 g., Copper-Nickel **Ruler:** George VI **Obv:** Crowned head left **Rev:** Denomination and date within decorative outline **Shape:** 4-sided

Date	Mintage	F12	VF20	XF40	MS60	MS63
1946	75,159,000	0.50	1.00	2.50	5.00	—
1947	126,392,000	0.50	1.00	2.50	5.00	—
1947	—	**PF63** 1,200				
1947 (c) P/L; Restrike	—	—	—	—	—	500

KM# 535.3 1/2 ANNA

2.90 g., Copper-Nickel **Ruler:** George VI **Obv:** Crowned head left **Rev:** Denomination and date within decorative outline **Shape:** 4-sided

Date	Mintage	F12	VF20	XF40	MS60	MS63
1946 L	—	—	—	—	1,000	—
1947 L	—	—	—	—	400	—

KM# 504 ANNA

Copper-Nickel **Ruler:** Edward VII **Obv:** Crowned bust right **Obv. Legend:** EDWARD VII KING & EMPEROR **Rev:** Denomination and date within decorative outline **Shape:** Scalloped **Note:** Struck only at the Mumbai (Bombay) Mint. Small incuse "B" mint mark in the space below the cross pattee of the crown on the obverse.

Date	Mintage	F12	VF20	XF40	MS60	MS63
1906 B	200,000	**PF63** 5,000				
1907 B	37,256,000	15.00	30.00	100	200	—
1907 B	—	**PF63** 1,000				
1908 B	22,536,000	15.00	30.00	100	200	—
1908 B	—	**PF63** 1,000				
1909 B	24,800,000	15.00	30.00	100	200	—
1909 B	—	**PF63** 1,000				
1910 B	40,200,000	15.00	30.00	100	200	—
1910 B	—	**PF63** 1,000				

KM# 513 ANNA

3.80 g., Copper-Nickel, 21 mm. **Ruler:** George V **Obv:** Crowned bust left **Obv. Legend:** GEORGE V KING EMPEROR **Rev:** Denomination and date within decorative outline **Shape:** Scalloped **Note:** Until 1920, all were struck at the Mumbai (Bombay) Mint without mint mark. From 1923 on, the Mumbai (Bombay) Mint issues have a small, raised bead or dot below the date. Calcutta Mint issues have no mint mark.

Date	Mintage	F12	VF20	XF40	MS60	MS63
1911 (C)	—	**PF63** 2,000				
1912 (b)	39,400,000	1.00	3.00	8.00	60.00	—
1912	—	**PF63** 1,200				
1913 (b)	39,776,000	2.00	6.00	12.00	100	—
1913	—	**PF63** 1,200				
1914 (b)	48,000,000	2.00	6.00	12.00	100	—
1914	—	**PF63** 1,200				
1915 (b)	7,670,000	40.00	75.00	200	400	—
1915	—	**PF63** 3,000				
1916 (b)	39,087,000	1.00	3.00	5.00	20.00	—
1917 (b)	58,067,000	1.00	3.00	5.00	20.00	—
1917	—	**PF63** 1,200				
1918 (b)	80,692,000	1.00	3.00	5.00	20.00	—
1918 (b)	—	**PF63** 1,200				
1919 (b)	122,795,000	1.00	3.00	5.00	20.00	—
1919 (b)	—	**PF63** 1,200				
1919 (c)	—	**PF63** 1,200				
1920 (b)	9,264,000	1.00	3.00	5.00	20.00	—
1920 (b)	—	**PF63** 1,200				
1923 (b)	7,125,000	1.00	3.00	8.00	60.00	—
1923 (b)	—	**PF63** 1,200				
1924 (c)	16,640,000	1.00	3.00	8.00	60.00	—
1924 (c)	—	**PF63** 1,200				
1924 (b)	17,285,000	1.00	3.00	8.00	60.00	—
1924 (b)	—	**PF63** 1,200				
1924 (b) P/L; Restrike	—	—	—	—	—	500
1925 (c)	22,388,000	1.00	3.00	8.00	60.00	—
1925 (c)	—	**PF63** 1,200				
1925 (b)	11,763,000	1.00	3.00	8.00	60.00	—
1925 (b)	—	**PF63** 1,200				
1925 (b) P/L; Restrike	—	—	—	—	—	500
1926 (c)	13,440,000	1.00	3.00	8.00	60.00	—
1926 (c)	—	**PF63** 1,200				
1926 (b)	8,088,000	1.00	3.00	8.00	60.00	—
1926 (b)	—	**PF63** 1,200				
1926 (b) P/L; Restrike	—	—	—	—	—	500
1927 (c)	6,296,000	1.00	3.00	8.00	60.00	—
1927 (c)	—	**PF63** 1,200				
1927 (b)	12,953,000	1.00	3.00	8.00	60.00	—
1927 (b)	—	**PF63** 1,200				
1927 (b) P/L; Restrike	—	—	—	—	—	500
1928 (c)	29,568,000	1.00	3.00	8.00	60.00	—
1928 (c)	—	**PF63** 1,200				
1928 (b)	4,832,000	1.00	3.00	8.00	60.00	—
1928 (b)	—	**PF63** 1,200				
1928 (b) P/L; Restrike	—	—	—	—	—	500
1929 (c)	42,200,000	1.00	3.00	8.00	60.00	—
1929 (c)	—	**PF63** 1,200				
1929 (c) P/L; Restrike	—	—	—	—	—	500
1930 (c)	22,816,000	1.00	3.00	8.00	60.00	—
1930 (c)	—	**PF63** 1,200				
1930 (c) P/L; Restrike	—	—	—	—	—	500
1933 (c)	17,432,000	1.00	3.00	8.00	60.00	—
1933 (c)	—	**PF63** 1,200				
1933 (c) P/L; Restrike	—	—	—	—	—	500
1934 (c)	34,216,000	1.00	3.00	5.00	20.00	—
1934 (c)	—	**PF63** 1,200				
1934 (c) P/L; Restrike	—	—	—	—	—	500
1935 (c)	12,952,000	1.00	3.00	5.00	20.00	—
1935 (c)	—	**PF63** 1,200				
1935 (b)	41,112,000	1.00	3.00	5.00	20.00	—
1935 (b)	—	**PF63** 1,200				
1935 (b) P/L; Restrike	—	—	—	—	—	500
1936 (b)	107,136,000	1.00	3.00	5.00	20.00	—
1936 (b)	—	**PF63** 1,200				

KM# 536 ANNA

3.70 g., Copper-Nickel **Ruler:** George VI **Obv:** First head, high relief **Obv. Legend:** GEORGE VI KING EMPEROR **Rev:** Denomination and date within decorative outline **Shape:** Scalloped **Note:** Calcutta Mint issues have no mint mark. Bombay Mint issues have a small dot below the date.

Date	Mintage	VG8	F12	VF20	XF40	MS60
1938 (c)	7,128,000	—	10.00	25.00	50.00	125
1938 (c)	—	PF63 1,500				
1938 (b)	3,126,000	—	10.00	25.00	50.00	125
1938 (b) P/L; Restrike	—	—	—	—	—	—
1939 (c)	18,192,000	—	1.00	1.25	2.00	3.00
1939 (b)	36,157,000	—	1.00	1.25	2.00	3.00
1939 (b) P/L; Restrike	—	—	—	—	—	—
1940 (c)	60,945,000	—	4.00	10.00	20.00	40.00
1940 (c) P/L; Restrike	—	—	—	—	—	—
1940 (b)	—	—	4.00	10.00	20.00	40.00

KM# 537 ANNA

Copper-Nickel **Ruler:** George VI **Obv:** Second head, low relief, large crown **Obv. Legend:** GEORGE VI KING EMPEROR **Rev:** Large denomination and date within decorative outline **Shape:** Scalloped

Date	Mintage	VG8	F12	VF20	XF40	MS60
1939 B	—	—	40.00	60.00	75.00	120
1940 (c)	76,392,000	—	1.00	1.25	2.00	3.00
1940 (c) P/L; Restrike	—	—	—	—	—	—
1940 (b)	144,712,000	—	1.00	1.25	2.00	3.00
1940 (b) P/L; Restrike	—	—	—	—	—	—
1941 (c)	62,480,000	—	1.00	1.25	2.00	3.00
1941 (b)	40,170,000	—	1.00	1.25	2.00	3.00
1941 (b) P/L; Restrike	—	—	—	—	—	—

KM# 537a ANNA

3.89 g., Nickel-Brass, 20.50 mm. **Ruler:** George VI **Obv:** Second head, low relief, large crown **Obv. Legend:** GEORGE VI KING EMPEROR **Rev:** Large denomination and date within decorative outline **Shape:** Scalloped

Date	Mintage	VG8	F12	VF20	XF40	MS60
1942 (c)	194,056,000	—	1.00	1.25	2.00	3.00
1942 (c)	—	PF63 1,000				
1942 (b)	103,240,000	—	1.00	1.25	2.00	3.00
1942 (b) P/L; Restrike	—	—	—	—	—	—
1943 (c)	352,256,000	—	1.00	1.25	2.00	3.00
1943 (c)	—	PF63 1,000				
1943 (b)	134,500,000	—	1.00	1.25	2.00	3.00
1943 (b) P/L; Restrike	—	—	—	—	—	—
1944 (c)	457,608,000	—	1.00	1.25	2.00	3.00
1944 (c)	—	PF63 1,000				
1944 (b)	175,208,000	—	1.00	1.25	2.00	3.00
1944 (b) P/L; Restrike	—	—	—	—	—	—
1945 (c)	278,360,000	—	1.00	1.25	2.00	3.00
1945 (b)	61,228,000	—	1.00	1.25	2.00	3.00

KM# 539 ANNA

Nickel-Brass, 21 mm. **Ruler:** George VI **Obv:** Second head, low relief, small crown **Obv. Legend:** GEORGE VI KING EMPEROR **Rev:** Denomination and date within decorative outline **Shape:** Scalloped

Date	Mintage	VG8	F12	VF20	XF40	MS60
1945 (c)	278,360,000	—	1.00	1.25	2.00	3.00
1945 (c)	—	PF63 1,000				
1945 (b)	61,228,000	—	1.00	1.25	2.00	3.00
1945 (b) P/L; Restrike	—	—	—	—	—	—

KM# 538 ANNA

3.87 g., Copper-Nickel **Ruler:** George VI **Obv:** Second head, low relief, small crown **Obv. Legend:** GEORGE VI KING EMPEROR **Rev:** Denomination and date within decorative outline **Shape:** Scalloped

Date	Mintage	F12	VF20	XF40	MS60	MS63
1946 (c)	100,820,000	1.00	1.25	2.00	3.00	—
1946 (b)	82,052,000	1.00	1.25	2.00	3.00	—
1946 (b)	—	PF63 1,000				
1946 (b) P/L; Restrike	—	—	—	—	—	250
1947 (c)	148,656,000	1.00	1.25	2.00	3.00	—
1947 (c)	—	PF63 1,000				
1947 (b)	50,096,000	1.00	1.25	2.00	3.00	—
1947 (b)	—	PF63 1,000				

KM# 488 2 ANNAS

1.46 g., 0.917 Silver 0.043 oz. ASW **Ruler:** Victoria **Obv:** Crowned bust left **Obv. Legend:** VICTORIA EMPRESS **Rev:** Value and date within wreath

Date	Mintage	F12	VF20	XF40	MS60	MS63
1901 C Incuse	8,944,000	10.00	20.00	40.00	60.00	—
Note: Type B Bust, Type II Reverse						
1901 C	—	PF63 1,200				
1901 B Incuse	—	10.00	20.00	40.00	60.00	—
Note: Type B Bust, Type I Reverse						
1901 B Incuse	1,706,000	40.00	60.00	80.00	100	—
Note: Type B Bust, Type II Reverse						
1901 B	—	PF63 1,200				
1901 B P/L; Restrike	—	—	—	—	—	800
1901 B Raised	—	10.00	20.00	40.00	60.00	—
Note: Type B Bust, Type I Reverse						
1901 B Raised	Inc. above	40.00	60.00	80.00	100	—
Note: Type B Bust, Type II Reverse						

KM# 505 2 ANNAS

1.46 g., 0.917 Silver 0.043 oz. ASW **Ruler:** Edward VII **Obv:** Head right **Obv. Legend:** EDWARD VII KING AND EMPEROR **Rev:** Crown above denomination, sprays flank

Date	Mintage	F12	VF20	XF40	MS60	MS63
1903 (c)	4,434,000	8.00	12.00	18.00	30.00	—
1903 (c)	—	PF63 1,200				
1903 (c) P/L; Restrike	—	—	—	—	—	600
1904 (c)	14,632,000	8.00	12.00	18.00	30.00	—
1904 (c)	—	PF63 1,200				
1904 (c) P/L; Restrike	—	—	—	—	—	600
1905 (c)	19,303,000	8.00	12.00	18.00	30.00	—
1905 (c) P/L; Restrike	—	—	—	—	—	1,200
1906 (c)	13,031,000	8.00	12.00	18.00	30.00	—
1906 (c) P/L; Restrike	—	—	—	—	—	1,200
1907 (c)	22,145,000	8.00	12.00	18.00	30.00	—
1907 (c)	—	PF63 1,200				
1908 (c)	21,600,000	8.00	12.00	18.00	30.00	—
1908 (c)	—	PF63 1,200				
1908 (c) P/L; Restrike	—	—	—	—	—	300
1909 (b) Beed in floral design in right stem	—	140	275	400	600	—
1909 (c)	6,769,000	120	225	350	500	—
1909 (c)	—	PF63 2,000				
1909 (c) P/L; Restrike	—	—	—	—	—	1,500
1910 (c)	1,604,000	10.00	15.00	20.00	40.00	—
1910 (c)	—	PF63 1,200				
1910 (c) P/L; Restrike	—	—	—	—	—	300

KM# 505a 2 ANNAS

Gold **Ruler:** Edward VII **Obv:** Head right **Obv. Legend:** EDWARD VII KING AND EMPEROR **Rev:** Crown above denomination, sprays flank **Note:** All dates of this type are prooflike restrikes.

Date	Mintage	F12	VF20	XF40	MS60	MS63
1904 (c)	—	—	—	—	4,000	—
1906 (c)	—	—	—	—	4,000	—
1910 (c)	—	—	—	—	4,000	—

KM# 514 2 ANNAS

1.46 g., 0.917 Silver 0.043 oz. ASW **Ruler:** George V **Obv:** Crowned bust left, type I **Obv. Legend:** GEORGE V KING EMPEROR **Rev:** Denomination within wreath

Date	Mintage	F12	VF20	XF40	MS60	MS63
1911 (c)	16,760,000	100	150	200	300	—
1911 (c)	—	PF63 2,000				
1911 (c) P/L; Restrike	—	—	—	—	—	1,000

KM# 515 2 ANNAS

1.46 g., 0.917 Silver 0.043 oz. ASW **Ruler:** George V **Obv:** Crowned bust left, type II (Elephant Type) **Obv. Legend:** GEORGE V KING EMPEROR **Rev:** Denomination within wreath

Date	Mintage	F12	VF20	XF40	MS60	MS63
1912 (c)	7,724,000	8.00	12.00	15.00	20.00	—
1912 (c)	—	PF63 1,500				
1912 (b)	2,462,000	8.00	12.00	15.00	20.00	—
1912 (b)	—	PF63 1,500				
1912 (b) P/L; Restrike	—	—	—	—	—	1,000
1913 (c)	13,959,000	8.00	12.00	15.00	20.00	—
1913 (c)	—	PF63 1,500				
1913 (b)	5,461,000	8.00	12.00	15.00	20.00	—
1913 (b)	—	PF63 1,500				
1913 (b) P/L; Restrike	—	—	—	—	—	1,000
1914 (c)	13,622,000	8.00	12.00	15.00	20.00	—
1914 (c)	—	PF63 1,500				
1914 (b)	8,579,000	8.00	12.00	15.00	20.00	—
1914 (b) P/L; Restrike	—	—	—	—	—	1,500
1915 (c)	5,892,000	16.00	30.00	50.00	100	—
1915 (c)	—	PF63 1,700				
1915 (b)	5,943,000	8.00	12.00	15.00	20.00	—
1915 (b) P/L; Restrike	—	—	—	—	—	1,500
1916 (c)	197,878,000	8.00	12.00	15.00	20.00	—
1916 (c)	—	PF63 1,500				
1916 (c) P/L; Restrike	—	—	—	—	—	1,000
1917 (c)	25,560,000	8.00	12.00	15.00	20.00	—
1917 (c)	—	PF63 1,500				
1917 (c) P/L; Restrike	—	—	—	—	—	1,000

KM# 516 2 ANNAS

5.62 g., Copper-Nickel **Ruler:** George V **Obv:** Crowned bust left within circle **Obv. Legend:** GEORGE V KING EMPEROR **Rev:** Large denomination within square **Shape:** 4-sided **Note:** Calcutta Mint issues have no mint mark. Bombay Mint issues have a small raised dot on the reverse at the bottom near the rim.

Date	Mintage	F12	VF20	XF40	MS60	MS63
1918 (c)	53,412,000	3.00	5.00	10.00	20.00	—
1918 (c)	—	PF63 1,200				
1918 (b)	9,191,000	3.00	5.00	10.00	20.00	—
1918 (b)	—	PF63 1,200				
1918 (b) P/L; Restrike	—	—	—	—	—	1,000
1919 (c)	89,040,000	3.00	5.00	10.00	20.00	—
1919 (c)	—	PF63 1,200				
1919 (c) P/L; Restrike	—	—	—	—	—	1,000
1920 (b)	—	PF63 2,200				
1920 (c)	13,520,000	3.00	5.00	10.00	20.00	—

Date	Mintage	F12	VF20	XF40	MS60	MS63
1920 (c)	—	PF63 2,200				
1921 (c) P/L; Restrike	—	—	—	—	—	1,000
1923 (c)	7,656,000	3.00	5.00	10.00	20.00	—
1923 (c)	—	PF63 1,200				
1923 (b)	6,431,000	3.00	5.00	10.00	20.00	—
1923 (b)	—	PF63 1,200				
1923 (b) P/L; Restrike	—	—	—	—	—	650
1924 (c)	8,384,000	3.00	5.00	10.00	20.00	—
1924 (c)	—	PF63 1,200				
1924 (b)	4,818,000	4.00	10.00	25.00	80.00	—
1924 (b)	—	PF63 1,200				
1924 (b) P/L; Restrike	—	—	—	—	—	600
1925 (c)	10,848,000	3.00	5.00	10.00	20.00	—
1925 (c)	—	PF63 1,200				
1925 (b)	8,348,000	3.00	5.00	10.00	20.00	—
1925 (b)	—	PF63 1,200				
1925 (b) P/L; Restrike	—	—	—	—	—	650
1926 (c)	8,352,000	3.00	5.00	10.00	20.00	—
1926 (c)	—	PF63 1,200				
1926 (b)	2,927,000	4.00	10.00	25.00	80.00	—
1926 (b)	—	PF63 1,200				
1926 (b) P/L; Restrike	—	—	—	—	—	600
1927 (c)	—	PF63 1,200				
1927 (c)	6,424,000	3.00	5.00	10.00	20.00	—
1927 (b)	4,835,000	4.00	10.00	25.00	80.00	—
1927 (b)	—	PF63 1,200				
1927 (b) P/L; Restrike	—	—	—	—	—	650
1928 (c)	7,352,000	3.00	5.00	10.00	20.00	—
1928 (c)	—	PF63 1,200				
1928 (b)	4,876,000	4.00	10.00	25.00	80.00	—
1928 (b)	—	PF63 1,200				
1928 (b) P/L; Restrike	—	—	—	—	—	650
1929 (c)	13,408,000	3.00	5.00	10.00	20.00	—
1929 (c)	—	PF63 1,200				
1929 (c) P/L; Restrike	—	—	—	—	—	650
1930 (c)	8,888,000	3.00	5.00	10.00	20.00	—
1930 (c)	—	PF63 1,200				
1930 (c) P/L; Restrike	—	—	—	—	—	650
1930 (b)	—	3.00	5.00	10.00	20.00	—
1933 (c)	4,300,000	4.00	10.00	25.00	80.00	—
1933 (c)	—	PF63 1,200				
1933 (c) P/L; Restrike	—	—	—	—	—	650
1934 (c)	7,016,000	20.00	40.00	75.00	200	—
1934 (c)	—	PF63 1,200				
1934 (c) P/L; Restrike	—	—	—	—	—	650
1935 (c)	12,344,000	3.00	5.00	10.00	20.00	—
1935 (b)	21,017,000	3.00	5.00	10.00	20.00	—
1935 (b)	—	PF63 1,200				
1935 (b) P/L; Restrike	—	—	—	—	—	650
1936 (b)	36,295,000	3.00	5.00	10.00	20.00	—
1936 (b)	—	PF63 1,200				

KM# 540 2 ANNAS

Copper-Nickel, 25 mm. **Ruler:** George VI **Obv:** First head, high relief **Obv. Legend:** GEORGE VI KING EMPEROR **Rev:** Denomination and date within decorative outlines **Shape:** Square **Note:** Calcutta Mint issues have no mint mark. Mumbai (Bombay) Mint issues have a small dot before and after the date.

Date	Mintage	F12	VF20	XF40	MS60	MS63
1939 (c)	4,148,000	2.00	4.00	8.00	10.00	—
1939 (b)	3,392,000	2.00	4.00	8.00	10.00	—
1940 (b)	—	150	225	350	500	—
1940 (c)	—	150	225	350	500	—

KM# 541 2 ANNAS

5.84 g., Copper-Nickel, 25 mm. **Ruler:** George VI **Obv:** Second head, low relief, large crown **Obv. Legend:** GEORGE VI KING EMPEROR **Rev:** Denomination and date within decorative outlines **Shape:** 4-sided

Date	Mintage	F12	VF20	XF40	MS60	MS63
1939 (c)	Inc. above	10.00	15.00	20.00	40.00	—
1939 (c)	—	PF63 1,200				
1939 (b)	Inc. above	10.00	15.00	20.00	40.00	—
1939 (b)	—	PF63 1,200				
1939 (b) P/L; Restrike	—	—	—	—	—	600
1940 (c)	37,636,000	2.00	4.00	6.00	10.00	—
1940 (c)	—	PF63 1,200				
1940 (b)	50,599,000	2.00	4.00	6.00	10.00	—
1940 (b) P/L; Restrike	—	—	—	—	—	600
1941 (c)	63,456,000	2.00	4.00	6.00	10.00	—
1941 (b)	10,760,000	2.00	4.00	6.00	10.00	—
1941 (b)	—	PF63 1,200				
1941 (b) P/L; Restrike	—	—	—	—	—	600

KM# 541a 2 ANNAS

5.74 g., Nickel-Brass, 25 mm. **Ruler:** George VI **Obv:** Second head, low relief, large crown **Obv. Legend:** GEORGE VI KING EMPEROR **Rev:** Denomination and date within decorative outlines **Shape:** 4-sided

Date	Mintage	F12	VF20	XF40	MS60	MS63
1942 (b) Small 4	133,000,000	0.40	1.00	2.00	6.00	—
1942 (b) Large 4	Inc. above	0.40	1.00	2.00	6.00	—
1943 (C)	—	0.40	1.00	2.00	6.00	—
1943 (b)	343,680,000	0.40	1.00	2.00	6.00	—
1944 (b) Small 4	219,700,000	0.40	1.00	2.00	6.00	—
1944 (b) Large 4	Inc. above	40.00	60.00	100	200	—
1944 (C) Large 4	—	200	300	400	600	—
Note: On 1944 Calcutta issues, No mark in the four quatrefoil angles.						
1944 L	6,352,000	40.00	60.00	100	200	—
Note: On 1944 Lahore issues, a tiny L replaces the decorative stroke in the four quatrefoil angles.						

KM# 543 2 ANNAS

Nickel-Brass **Ruler:** George VI **Obv:** Second head, low relief, large crown **Obv. Legend:** GEORGE VI KING EMPEROR **Rev:** Small "2" **Shape:** Square

Date	Mintage	F12	VF20	XF40	MS60	MS63
1945 (c)	24,260,000	0.20	0.90	1.50	20.00	—
1945 (c)	—	PF63 1,200				
1945 (b)	136,688,000	0.40	1.00	2.00	6.00	—
1945 (b) P/L; Restrike	—	—	—	—	—	675

KM# 542 2 ANNAS

5.90 g., Copper-Nickel **Ruler:** George VI **Obv:** Second head, low relief, small crown **Obv. Legend:** GEORGE VI KING EMPEROR **Rev:** Denomination and date within decorative outlines **Shape:** Square

Date	Mintage	F12	VF20	XF40	MS60	MS63
1946 (c)	67,267,000	0.40	1.00	2.00	6.00	—
1946 (b)	52,500,000	0.40	1.00	2.00	6.00	—
1946 (b)	—	PF63 1,200				
1946 (b) P/L; Restrike	—	—	—	—	—	850
1946 (l)	25,480,000	0.20	0.40	0.60	2.75	—
Note: Without "L" mintmark but with small diamond-shaped mark left of "l" on reverse						
1947 (c)	57,428,000	0.40	1.00	2.00	6.00	—
1947 (b)	38,908,000	0.40	1.00	2.00	6.00	—
1947 (b)	—	PF63 1,200				
1947 (b) P/L; Restrike	—	—	—	—	—	650

KM# 519 4 ANNAS

6.50 g., Copper-Nickel **Ruler:** George V **Obv:** Crowned bust left within circle **Obv. Legend:** GEORGE V KING EMPEROR • INDIA • **Rev:** Denomination within square **Shape:** Scalloped **Note:** Calcutta Mint issues have no mint mark. Bombay Mint issues have a small raised dot on the reverse at the bottom near the rim.

Date	Mintage	F12	VF20	XF40	MS60	MS63
1919 (c)	18,632,000	10.00	25.00	75.00	140	—
1919 (c)	—	PF63 1,500				
1919 (b)	7,672,000	10.00	25.00	75.00	140	—
1919 P/L; Restrike	—	—	—	—	—	1,000
1920 (c)	18,191,000	10.00	25.00	75.00	140	—
1920 (c)	—	PF63 1,500				
1920 (b)	1,666,000	10.00	25.00	75.00	140	—
1920 (b)	—	PF63 1,500				
1920 (b) P/L; Restrike	—	—	—	—	—	850
1921 (c)	—	100	200	400	600	—
1921 (c)	—	PF63 1,500				
1921 (c) P/L; Restrike	—	—	—	—	—	1,200
1921 (b)	1,219,000	60.00	80.00	125	200	—
1921 (b)	—	PF63 1,500				

KM# 520 8 ANNAS

Copper-Nickel **Ruler:** George V **Obv:** Crowned bust left **Obv. Legend:** GEORGE V KING EMPEROR **Rev:** Denomination and date within scallop, square surrounds **Note:** Calcutta Mint issues have no mint mark. Mumbai (Bombay) Mint issues have a small raised dot on the reverse at the bottom near the rim.

Date	Mintage	F12	VF20	XF40	MS60	MS63
1919 (c)	2,980,000	40.00	50.00	70.00	200	—
1919 (c)	—	PF63 2,000				
1919 (b)	1,400,000	40.00	50.00	70.00	200	—
1919 (b) P/L; Restrike	—	—	—	—	—	1,200
1920 (c)	—	PF63 3,000				
1920 (c) P/L; Restrike	—	—	—	—	—	2,000
1920 (b)	1,000,000	800	1,000	1,200	1,500	—
1920 (b)	—	PF63 2,000				
1920 (b) P/L; Restrike	—	—	—	—	—	1,500

KM# 490 1/4 RUPEE

2.92 g., 0.917 Silver 0.0861 oz. ASW **Ruler:** Victoria **Obv:** Crowned bust left **Obv. Legend:** VICTORIA EMPRESS **Rev:** Value and date within wreath **Note:** Mule.

Date	Mintage	F12	VF20	XF40	MS60	MS63
1901 C Incuse	4,476,000	30.00	40.00	50.00	60.00	—
Note: Type C Bust, Type II Reverse						
1901 C	—	PF63 2,500				
1901 C P/L; Restrike	—	—	—	—	—	1,500

KM# 506 1/4 RUPEE

2.92 g., 0.917 Silver 0.0861 oz. ASW **Ruler:** Edward VII **Obv:** Head right **Obv. Legend:** EDWARD VII KING AND EMPEROR **Rev:** Crown above denomination, sprays flank

Date	Mintage	F12	VF20	XF40	MS60	MS63
1903 (c)	7,060,000	10.00	20.00	30.00	60.00	—
1903 (c)	—	PF63 2,000				

Date	Mintage	F12	VF20	XF40	MS60	MS63
1903 (c) P/L; Restrike	—	—	—	—	—	1,000
1904 (c)	10,026,000	10.00	20.00	30.00	60.00	—
1904 (c)	—	PF63 2,000				
1904 (c) P/L; Restrike	—	—	—	—	—	1,000
1905 (c)	6,300,000	10.00	20.00	30.00	60.00	—
1905 (c)	—	PF63 2,000				
1905 (c) P/L; Restrike	—	—	—	—	—	1,000
1906 (c)	10,672,000	10.00	20.00	30.00	60.00	—
1906 (c) P/L; Restrike	—	—	—	—	—	2,000
1907 (c)	11,464,000	10.00	20.00	30.00	60.00	—
1907 (c)	—	PF63 2,000				
1907 (c) P/L; Restrike	—	—	—	—	—	1,000
1908 (c)	7,084,000	10.00	20.00	30.00	60.00	—
1908 (c)	—	PF63 2,000				
1908 (c) P/L; Restrike	—	—	—	—	—	1,000
1909 (c)	—	PF63 2,000				
1909 (c) P/L; Restrike	—	—	—	—	—	1,000
1910 (b)	—	40.00	50.00	60.00	80.00	—
1910 (c)	8,024,000	10.00	20.00	30.00	60.00	—
1910 (c)	—	PF63 2,000				
1910 (c) P/L; Restrike	—	—	—	—	—	1,000

KM# 506a 1/4 RUPEE

Gold **Ruler:** Edward VII **Obv:** Head right **Rev:** Crown above denomination, sprays flank

Date	Mintage	F12	VF20	XF40	MS60	MS63
1910 (c) P/L; Restrike	—	—	—	—	—	10,000

KM# 517 1/4 RUPEE

2.92 g., 0.917 Silver 0.0861 oz. ASW **Ruler:** George V **Obv:** Type I **Obv. Legend:** GEORGE V KING EMPEROR

Date	Mintage	F12	VF20	XF40	MS60	MS63
1911 (c)	2,245,000	200	400	600	1,000	—
1911 (c)	—	PF63 2,000				
1911 (c) P/L; Restrike	—	—	—	—	—	1,500

KM# 518 1/4 RUPEE

2.92 g., 0.917 Silver 0.0861 oz. ASW **Ruler:** George V **Obv:** Crowned bust left, type II **Obv. Legend:** GEORGE V KING EMPEROR **Rev:** Denomination and date within circle, wreath surrounds

Date	Mintage	F12	VF20	XF40	MS60	MS63
1912 (c)	9,587,000	15.00	20.00	30.00	40.00	—
1912 (c)	—	PF63 1,350				
1912 (b)	2,200,000	15.00	20.00	30.00	40.00	—
1912 (b)	—	PF63 1,350				
1912 (b) P/L; Restrike	—	—	—	—	—	800
1913 (c)	12,686,000	15.00	20.00	30.00	40.00	—
1913 (c)	—	PF63 1,350				
1913 (b)	2,276,000	15.00	20.00	30.00	40.00	—
1913 (b)	—	PF63 1,350				
1913 (b) P/L; Restrike	—	—	—	—	—	800
1914 (c)	1,423,000	15.00	20.00	30.00	40.00	—
1914 (c)	—	PF63 1,350				
1914 (b)	7,949,000	15.00	20.00	30.00	40.00	—
1914 (b) P/L; Restrike	—	—	—	—	—	1,350
1915 (c)	851,000	40.00	100	200	400	—
1915 (c)	—	PF63 2,500				
1915 (b)	2,096,000	40.00	100	200	400	—
1915 (c) P/L; Restrike	—	—	—	—	—	—
1915 (b) P/L; Restrike	—	—	—	—	—	2,500
1916 (c)	13,178,000	15.00	20.00	30.00	40.00	—
1916 (c)	—	PF63 1,350				
1916 (c) P/L; Restrike	—	—	—	—	—	800
1917 (c)	21,072,000	15.00	20.00	30.00	40.00	—
1917 (c)	—	PF63 1,350				
1917 (c) P/L; Restrike	—	—	—	—	—	800
1918 (c)	50,575,000	15.00	20.00	30.00	40.00	—
1918 (c)	—	PF63 1,350				
1919 (b)	—	15.00	20.00	30.00	40.00	—
1919 (c)	26,135,000	15.00	20.00	30.00	40.00	—
1919 (c)	—	PF63 1,350				
1920 (b)	—	15.00	20.00	30.00	40.00	—
1925 (b)	4,007,000	15.00	20.00	30.00	40.00	—
1925 (b)	—	PF63 1,350				
1925 (b) P/L; Restrike	—	—	—	—	—	800
1926 (c)	8,169,000	15.00	20.00	30.00	40.00	—
1926 (c)	—	PF63 1,350				
1926 (c) P/L; Restrike	—	—	—	—	—	800
1928 (b)	4,023,000	15.00	20.00	30.00	40.00	—
1928 (b)	—	PF63 1,350				
1929 (c)	4,013,000	15.00	20.00	30.00	40.00	—
1929 (c)	—	PF63 1,350				
1929 (c) P/L; Restrike	—	—	—	—	—	800
1930 (c)	3,222,000	15.00	20.00	30.00	40.00	—
1930 (c)	—	PF63 1,350				
1930 (c) P/L; Restrike	—	—	—	—	—	800
1934 (c)	3,946,000	15.00	20.00	30.00	40.00	—
1936 (c)	25,744,000	8.00	12.00	15.00	20.00	—
1936 (b)	9,864,000	8.00	12.00	15.00	20.00	—
1936 (b) P/L; Restrike	—	—	—	—	—	700

First Head

Second Head (small) Second Head (large)

From 1942 to 1945 the reverse designs of the silver coins change slightly every year. However, a distinct reverse variety occurs on Rupees and 1/4 Rupees dated 1943-44 and on the half Rupee dated 1944, all struck at Bombay. This variety may be distinguished from the other coins by the design of the center bottom flower as illustrated, and is designated as Reverse B.

On the normal common varieties dated 1943-44 the three "scalloped circles" are not connected to each other and the bead in the center is not attached to the nearest circle.

Obv: First head, reeded edge.

NOTE: Calcutta Mint issues have no mint mark. Bombay coins have a small bead below the lotus flower at the bottom on the reverse, except those dated 1943-1944 with reverse B which have a diamond. Lahore Mint issues have a small "L" in the same position. The nickel coins have a diamond below the date on the reverse.

KM# 544 1/4 RUPEE

2.92 g., 0.917 Silver 0.0861 oz. ASW **Ruler:** George VI **Obv:** Crowned head left **Obv. Legend:** GEORGE VI KING EMPEROR **Rev:** Denomination and date within circle, wreath surrounds

Date	Mintage	F12	VF20	XF40	MS60	MS63
1938 (c)	—	PF63 1,500				
1938 (c) P/L; Restrike	—	—	—	—	—	1,000
1939 (c)	3,072,000	12.00	15.00	17.00	20.00	—
1939 (c)	—	PF63 850				
1939 (b)	6,770,000	12.00	15.00	17.00	20.00	—
1939 (b) P/L; Restrike	—	—	—	—	—	—
1939 Mature Head	—	1,000	1,500	2,000	3,000	—

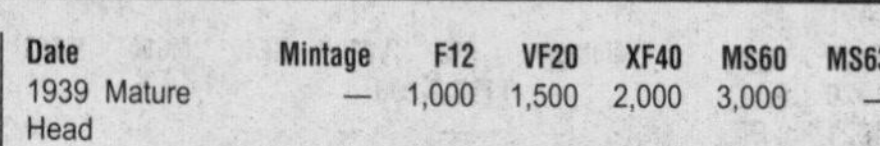

KM# 544a 1/4 RUPEE

2.92 g., 0.500 Silver 0.0469 oz. ASW **Ruler:** George VI **Obv:** Crowned head left **Obv. Legend:** GEORGE VI KING EMPEROR **Rev:** Denomination and date within circle, wreath surrounds

Date	Mintage	F12	VF20	XF40	MS60	MS63
1940 (b)	24,635,000	15.00	20.00	30.00	40.00	—

KM# 545 1/4 RUPEE

2.92 g., 0.500 Silver 0.0469 oz. ASW **Ruler:** George VI **Obv:** Large second head, small rim decoration **Obv. Legend:** GEORGE VI KING EMPEROR **Rev:** Denomination and date within circle, wreath surrounds **Edge:** Reeded

Date	Mintage	VG8	F12	VF20	XF40	MS60
1940 (c)	68,675,000	—	6.00	8.00	10.00	12.00
1940 (c)	—	PF63 1,500				
1940 (b)	28,947,000	—	6.00	8.00	10.00	12.00

KM# 546 1/4 RUPEE

2.92 g., 0.500 Silver 0.0469 oz. ASW **Ruler:** George VI **Obv:** Small second head, large rim decoration **Obv. Legend:** GEORGE VI KING EMPEROR **Rev:** Denomination and date within circle, wreath surrounds **Edge:** Reeded

Date	Mintage	F12	VF20	XF40	MS60	MS63
1942 (c)	88,096,000	6.00	8.00	10.00	12.00	—
1943 (c)	90,994,000	6.00	8.00	10.00	12.00	—

KM# 547 1/4 RUPEE

2.90 g., 0.500 Silver 0.0466 oz. ASW, 19 mm. **Ruler:** George VI **Obv:** Small second head, large rim decoration **Obv. Legend:** GEORGE VI KING EMPEROR **Rev:** Denomination and date within circle, wreath surrounds **Edge:** Security

Date	Mintage	F12	VF20	XF40	MS60	MS63
1943 B	95,200,000	6.00	8.00	10.00	12.00	—
1943 B	—	PF63 1,500				
1943 B Reverse B	Inc. above	6.00	8.00	10.00	12.00	—
1943 L	23,700,000	6.00	8.00	10.00	12.00	—
1944 B	170,504,000	6.00	8.00	10.00	12.00	—
1944 B Reverse B	Inc. above	6.00	8.00	10.00	12.00	—
1944 L	86,400,000	6.00	8.00	10.00	12.00	—
1945 (b) Small 5	181,648,000	6.00	8.00	10.00	12.00	—
1945 (b) Large 5	Inc. above	30.00	50.00	70.00	80.00	—
1945 L Small 5	29,751,000	6.00	8.00	10.00	12.00	—
1945 L Large 5	Inc. above	200	400	600	800	—

KM# 548 1/4 RUPEE

2.90 g., Nickel **Ruler:** George VI **Obv:** Crowned head left **Obv. Legend:** GEORGE VI KING EMPEROR **Rev:** Indian tiger (panthera tigris) **Edge:** Reeded

Date	Mintage	F12	VF20	XF40	MS60	MS63
1946 (b)	83,600,000	0.40	0.80	1.20	2.00	4.00
1947 (b)	109,948,000	0.40	0.80	1.20	2.00	4.00
1947 (b)	—	PF63 200				

KM# 507 1/2 RUPEE

5.83 g., 0.917 Silver 0.1719 oz. ASW **Ruler:** Edward VII **Obv:** Head right **Obv. Legend:** EDWARD VII KING AND EMPEROR **Rev:** Crown above denomination, sprays flank **Note:** Calcutta Mint issues have no mint mark. Mumbai (Bombay) Mint issues have a small incuse "B" in the space below the cross pattee of the crown on the reverse.

Date	Mintage	F12	VF20	XF40	MS60	MS63
1904 (c)	—	PF63 3,000				
1904 (c) P/L; Restrike	—	—	—	—	—	2,000
1905 (c)	823,000	100	150	200	300	—
1905 (c) P/L; Restrike	—	—	—	—	—	2,500
1906 (c)	3,036,000	30.00	40.00	60.00	200	—
1906 B	400,000	60.00	80.00	100	300	—
1906 B P/L; Restrike	—	—	—	—	—	1,500
1907 (c)	2,786,000	30.00	40.00	60.00	200	—
1907 (c)	—	PF63 2,000				
1907 B	1,856,000	30.00	40.00	60.00	200	—
1907 B	—	PF63 2,000				
1907 B P/L; Restrike	—	—	—	—	—	1,500
1908 (c)	1,577,000	30.00	40.00	60.00	200	—
1908 (c)	—	PF63 2,000				
1908 (c) P/L; Restrike	—	—	—	—	—	475
1909 (c)	1,569,000	80.00	100	150	500	—
1909 (c)	—	PF63 2,000				
1909 (c) P/L; Restrike	—	—	—	—	—	2,000
1909 B	—	PF63 3,000				
1909 B P/L; Restrike	—	—	—	—	—	2,000
1910 (c)	3,413,000	30.00	40.00	60.00	200	—
1910 (c)	—	PF63 2,000				
1910 B	809,000	30.00	40.00	60.00	200	—
1910 B	—	PF63 2,000				
1910 B P/L; Restrike	—	—	—	—	—	1,500

KM# 521 1/2 RUPEE

5.83 g., 0.917 Silver 0.1719 oz. ASW **Ruler:** George V **Obv:** Crowned bust left, type I **Obv. Legend:** GEORGE V KING EMPEROR **Rev:** Denomination and date within circle, wreath surrounds **Note:** Calcutta Mint issues have no mint mark. The half Rupee dated 1911 like the Rupee and all the other issues of that year has the "Pig" elephant. It was struck only at the Calcutta Mint.

Date	Mintage	F12	VF20	XF40	MS60	MS63
1911 (c)	2,293,000	3,500	4,500	6,000	10,000	—
1911 (c)	—	PF63 10,000				
1911 (c) P/L; Restrike	—	—	—	—	—	8,000

KM# 522 1/2 RUPEE

5.83 g., 0.917 Silver 0.1719 oz. ASW **Ruler:** George V **Obv:** Crowned bust left, type II **Obv. Legend:** GEORGE V KING EMPEROR **Rev:** Denomination and date within circle, wreath surrounds

Date	Mintage	F12	VF20	XF40	MS60	MS63
1912 (c)	3,390,000	15.00	20.00	30.00	50.00	—
1912 (c)	—	PF63 2,000				
1912 (b)	1,505,000	15.00	20.00	30.00	50.00	—
1912 (b)	—	PF63 2,000				
1912 (b) P/L; Restrike	—	—	—	—	—	1,500
1913 (c)	2,723,000	15.00	20.00	30.00	50.00	—
1913 (c)	—	PF63 2,000				
1913 (b)	1,825,000	30.00	50.00	80.00	100	—
1913 (b)	—	PF63 2,000				
1913 (b) P/L; Restrike	—	—	—	—	—	1,500
1914 (c)	1,400,000	15.00	20.00	30.00	50.00	—
1914 (c)	—	PF63 2,000				
1914 (b)	903,000	15.00	20.00	30.00	50.00	—
1914 (b) P/L; Restrike	—	—	—	—	—	2,000
1915 (c)	2,804,000	50.00	100	200	500	—
1915 (c)	—	PF63 2,200				
1915 (c) P/L; Restrike	—	—	—	—	—	1,800
1916 (c)	3,644,000	15.00	20.00	30.00	50.00	—
1916 (c)	—	PF63 2,000				
1916 (b)	5,880,000	15.00	20.00	30.00	50.00	—
1917 (c)	—	PF63 2,000				
1917 (b)	8,822,000	15.00	20.00	30.00	50.00	—
1917 (b)	—	PF63 2,000				
1918 (c) P/L; Restrike	—	—	—	—	—	1,500
1918 (b) P/L; Restrike	—	—	—	—	—	1,500
1918 (b)	10,325,000	15.00	20.00	30.00	50.00	—
1919 (b)	8,958,000	15.00	20.00	30.00	50.00	—
1919 (b)	—	PF63 2,000				
1919 (b) P/L; Restrike	—	—	—	—	—	400
1919 (c) P/L; Restrike	—	—	—	—	—	400
1921 (c)	5,804,000	15.00	20.00	30.00	50.00	—
1921 (c)	—	PF63 2,000				
1921 (c) P/L; Restrike	—	—	—	—	—	400
1922 (c)	5,551,000	15.00	20.00	30.00	50.00	—
1922 (c)	—	PF63 2,000				
1922 (b)	1,037,000	15.00	20.00	30.00	50.00	—
1922 (b)	—	PF63 2,000				
1922 (b) P/L; Restrike	—	—	—	—	—	1,500
1923 (c)	3,925,000	15.00	20.00	30.00	50.00	—
1923 (c) P/L; Restrike	—	—	—	—	—	2,000
1923 (b)	2,076,000	15.00	20.00	30.00	50.00	—
1923 (b)	—	PF63 2,000				
1923 (b) P/L; Restrike	—	—	—	—	—	1,500
1924 (c)	4,007,000	15.00	20.00	30.00	50.00	—
1924 (c)	—	PF63 2,000				
1924 (b)	2,664,000	15.00	20.00	30.00	50.00	—
1924 (b)	—	PF63 2,000				
1924 (b) P/L; Restrike	—	—	—	—	—	1,500
1925 (c)	4,119,000	15.00	20.00	30.00	50.00	—
1925 (c)	—	PF63 2,000				
1925 (b)	1,627,000	15.00	20.00	30.00	50.00	—
1925 (b)	—	PF63 2,000				
1925 (b) P/L; Restrike	—	—	—	—	—	1,500
1926 (c)	4,027,000	15.00	20.00	30.00	50.00	—
1926 (c)	—	PF63 2,000				
1926 (b)	2,011,000	15.00	20.00	30.00	50.00	—
1926 (b)	—	PF63 2,000				
1926 (b) P/L; Restrike	—	—	—	—	—	1,500
1927 (c)	2,032,000	15.00	20.00	30.00	50.00	—
1927 (c)	—	PF63 2,000				
1927 (c) P/L; Restrike	—	—	—	—	—	1,500
1928 (b)	2,466,000	15.00	20.00	30.00	50.00	—
1928 (b)	—	PF63 2,000				
1929 (c)	4,050,000	15.00	20.00	30.00	50.00	—
1929 (c)	—	PF63 2,000				
1929 (c) P/L; Restrike	—	—	—	—	—	1,500
1930 (c)	2,036,000	15.00	20.00	30.00	50.00	—
1930 (c)	—	PF63 2,000				
1930 (c) P/L; Restrike	—	—	—	—	—	1,500
1933/2 (c)	4,056,000	15.00	20.00	30.00	50.00	—
1933 (c)	Inc. above	15.00	20.00	30.00	50.00	—
1933 (c)	—	PF63 2,000				
1933 (c) P/L; Restrike	—	—	—	—	—	1,500
1934 (c)	4,056,000	15.00	20.00	30.00	50.00	—
1934 (c)	—	PF63 2,000				
1934 (c) P/L; Restrike	—	—	—	—	—	1,500
1936 (c)	16,919,000	15.00	20.00	30.00	50.00	—
1936 (b)	6,693,000	15.00	20.00	30.00	50.00	—
1936 (b) P/L; Restrike	—	—	—	—	—	2,000

KM# A549 1/2 RUPEE

Copper-Nickel **Ruler:** George VI **Obv:** Crowned head left **Obv. Legend:** GEORGE VI KING EMPEROR **Rev:** Denomination and date within circle, wreath surrounds **Note:** Mule.

Date	Mintage	F12	VF20	XF40	MS60	MS63
1938 (c) P/L; Restrike	—	—	—	—	—	2,500

KM# 549 1/2 RUPEE

5.83 g., 0.917 Silver 0.1719 oz. ASW **Ruler:** George VI **Obv:** Crowned head left, first head **Obv. Legend:** GEORGE VI KING EMPEROR **Rev:** Denomination and date within circle, wreath surrounds **Edge:** Reeded

Date	Mintage	F12	VF20	XF40	MS60	MS63
1938 (c)	—	PF63 2,500				
1938 (b)	2,200,000	25.00	30.00	35.00	40.00	—
1938 (b) P/L; Restrike	—	—	—	—	—	1,500
1939 (c)	3,300,000	14.00	16.00	20.00	25.00	—
1939 (c)	—	PF63 1,500				
1939 (b)	10,096,000	14.00	16.00	20.00	25.00	—
1939 (b)	—	PF63 1,500				
1939 (b) P/L; Restrike	—	—	—	—	—	1,200

KM# 550 1/2 RUPEE

5.83 g., 0.917 Silver 0.1719 oz. ASW **Ruler:** George VI **Obv:** Large second head, small rim decoration **Obv. Legend:** GEORGE VI KING EMPEROR **Rev:** Denomination and date within circle, wreath surrounds **Edge:** Reeded

Date	Mintage	VG8	F12	VF20	XF40	MS60
1939 (c)	Inc. above	—	30.00	40.00	50.00	60.00
1939 (b)	Inc. above	—	200	300	500	700

KM# 550a 1/2 RUPEE

5.83 g., 0.500 Silver 0.0937 oz. ASW **Ruler:** George VI **Obv:** Large second head, small rim decoration **Obv. Legend:** GEORGE VI KING EMPEROR **Rev:** Denomination and date within circle, wreath surrounds

Date	Mintage	F12	VF20	XF40	MS60	MS63
1940 (c)	32,898,000	7.00	9.00	12.00	20.00	—
1940 (c)	—	PF63 1,500				
1940 (b)	17,811,000	7.00	9.00	12.00	20.00	—
1940 (b) P/L; Restrike	—	—	—	—	—	1,200

KM# 551 1/2 RUPEE

5.83 g., 0.500 Silver 0.0937 oz. ASW **Ruler:** George VI **Obv:** Large second head, small rim decoration **Obv. Legend:** GEORGE VI KING EMPEROR **Rev:** Denomination and date within circle, wreath surrounds **Edge:** Security

Date	Mintage	VG8	F12	VF20	XF40	MS60
1941 (b)	26,100,000	—	7.00	9.00	12.00	20.00
1942 (b)	61,600,000	—	20.00	30.00	40.00	60.00

NOTE: Example of large 5 in date 1945.

KM# 552 1/2 RUPEE

5.84 g., 0.500 Silver 0.0939 oz. ASW, 24.1 mm. **Ruler:** George VI **Obv:** Small second head, large rim decoration **Obv. Legend:** GEORGE VI KING EMPEROR **Rev:** Denomination and inner circle smaller **Edge:** Security

Date	Mintage	F12	VF20	XF40	MS60	MS63
1942 (b)	Inc. above	7.00	9.00	12.00	20.00	—
1943 (b) Dot	90,400,000	7.00	9.00	12.00	20.00	—
1943 (b)	—	PF63 2,000				
1943 (b) Diamond	—	100	150	200	300	—
1943 L	9,000,000	7.00	9.00	12.00	20.00	—
1943 L	—	PF63 2,000				
1944 (b) Dot	46,200,000	7.00	9.00	12.00	20.00	—
1944 (b) Diamond	Inc. above	7.00	9.00	12.00	20.00	—
1944 L	79,100,000	7.00	9.00	12.00	20.00	—
1944 L	—	PF63 2,000				
1945 L Large 5	—	200	300	450	600	—
1945 (b) Small 5	32,722,000	7.00	9.00	12.00	20.00	—
1945 (b) Large 5	—	300	400	500	700	—
1945 L Small 5	—	7.00	9.00	12.00	20.00	—
1945 L	—	PF63 2,000				
1945 L Large dot	Inc. above	7.00	9.00	12.00	20.00	—

KM# 553 1/2 RUPEE

5.80 g., Nickel **Ruler:** George VI **Obv:** Crowned head left **Obv. Legend:** GEORGE VI KING EMPEROR **Rev:** Indian tiger (panthera tigris) **Edge:** Reeded

Date	Mintage	F12	VF20	XF40	MS60	MS63
1946 (b)	47,500,000	1.00	2.00	3.00	10.00	15.00
1947 (b)	62,724,000	1.00	2.00	3.00	10.00	15.00
1947 (b)	—	PF63 1,000				

KM# 473.1 RUPEE

11.66 g., 0.917 Silver 0.3438 oz. ASW, 30.78 mm. **Ruler:** Victoria **Obv:** Crowned bust left **Obv. Legend:** VICTORIA QUEEN **Rev:** Value and date within wreath **Edge:** Reeded

Date	Mintage	F12	VF20	XF40	MS60	MS63
1962 (b)	—	300	400	500	800	—

Note: Type B Bust, Type II Reverse, 0/6

KM# 492 RUPEE

11.66 g., 0.917 Silver 0.3438 oz. ASW, 30.79 mm. **Ruler:** Victoria **Obv:** Crowned bust left **Obv. Legend:** VICTORIA EMPRESS **Rev:** Value and date within wreath **Edge:** Reeded

Date	Mintage	F12	VF20	XF40	MS60	MS63
1901 C C/I, "C" incuse	72,017,000	24.00	36.00	40.00	60.00	—
1901 C C/I, "C" incuse	—	200	300	400	500	—
1901 C	—	PF63 3,000				
1901 B A/I, "B" incuse	130,258,000	24.00	36.00	40.00	60.00	—
1901 B	—	PF63 3,000				
1901 B P/L; Restrike	—	—	—	—	—	1,700
1901 B C/I, "B" incuse	Inc. above	24.00	36.00	40.00	60.00	—

KM# 508 RUPEE

11.66 g., 0.917 Silver 0.3438 oz. ASW **Ruler:** Edward VII **Obv:** Head right **Obv. Legend:** EDWARD VII KING & EMPEROR **Rev:** Crown above denomination, sprays flank **Note:** Calcutta Mint issues have no mint mark. Mumbai (Bombay) Mint issues have a small incuse "B" in the space below the cross pattee of the crown on the reverse.

Date	Mintage	F12	VF20	XF40	MS60	MS63
1903 (C)	—	80.00	140	200	300	—
Note: 3dots instead of 5 Dotes in Persial Legend						
1903 (C)	—	100	200	300	400	—
Note: 4dots instead of 5 Dotes in Presian legend						
1903 (c)	49,403,000	24.00	30.00	40.00	100	—
1903 (c)	—	PF63 3,000				
1903 B In relief, Raised	52,969	50.00	70.00	100	200	—
1903 B	—	PF63 3,000				
1903 B Incuse	Inc. above	24.00	30.00	40.00	100	—
1903 B P/L; Restrike	—	—	—	—	—	1,500
1904 (c)	58,339,000	24.00	30.00	40.00	100	—
1904 (c)	—	PF63 3,000				
1904 B	101,949,000	24.00	30.00	40.00	100	—
1904 B	—	PF63 3,000				
1904 B P/L; Restrike	—	—	—	—	—	1,500
1905 (c)	51,258,000	24.00	30.00	40.00	100	—
1905 (c)	—	PF63 3,000				
1905 B	76,202,000	24.00	30.00	40.00	100	—
1905 B	—	PF63 3,000				
1905 B P/L; Restrike	—	—	—	—	—	1,500
1906 (c)	104,797,000	24.00	30.00	40.00	100	—
1906 B	158,953,000	24.00	30.00	40.00	100	—
1906 B	—	PF63 3,000				
1906 B P/L; Restrike	—	—	—	—	—	1,500
1907 (c)	81,338,000	24.00	30.00	40.00	100	—
1907 (c)	—	PF63 3,000				
1907 B	170,912,000	24.00	30.00	40.00	100	—
1907 B	—	PF63 3,000				
1907 B P/L; Restrike	—	—	—	—	—	1,500
1908 (c)	20,218,000	24.00	30.00	40.00	100	—
1908 (c)	—	PF63 3,000				
1908 B	10,715,000	24.00	30.00	40.00	100	—
1908 B	—	PF63 3,000				
1908 B P/L; Restrike	—	—	—	—	—	1,500
1909 (c)	12,759,000	24.00	30.00	40.00	150	—
1909 (c)	—	PF63 3,000				
1909 B	9,539,000	24.00	30.00	40.00	150	—
1909 B	—	PF63 3,000				
1909 B P/L; Restrike	—	—	—	—	—	1,500
1910 (c)	12,627,000	24.00	30.00	40.00	150	—
1910 (c)	—	PF63 3,000				
1910 B	10,885,000	24.00	30.00	40.00	150	—
1910 B	—	PF63 3,000				
1910 B P/L; Restrike	—	—	—	—	—	1,500

NOTE: Calcutta Mint issues have no mint mark. Bombay Mint issues have a small raised bead or dot in the space below the lotus flower at the bottom of the reverse.

Obverse Dies

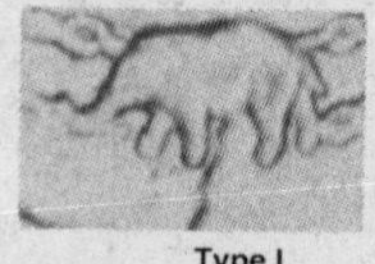

Type I

Type II

Type I - Obv. die w/elephant with pig-like feet and short tail. Nicknamed "pig rupee".

Type II - Obv. die w/redesigned elephant with outlined ear, heavy feet and long tail.

The Rupees dated 1911 were rejected by the public because the elephant, on the Order of the Indian Empire shown on the King's robe, was thought to resemble a pig, an animal considered unclean by most Indians. Out of a total of 9.4 million pieces struck at both mints, only 700,000 were issued, and many of these were withdrawn and melted with unissued pieces. The issues dated 1912 and later have a re-designed elephant.

KM# 523 RUPEE

11.66 g., 0.917 Silver 0.3438 oz. ASW **Ruler:** George V **Obv:** Type I **Obv. Legend:** GEORGE V KING EMPEROR

Date	Mintage	F12	VF20	XF40	MS60	MS63
1911 (c)	4,300,000	60.00	80.00	100	150	—
1911 (c) Proof	—	—	—	—	—	—
1911 (b)	5,143,000	60.00	80.00	100	150	—
1911 (b) P/L; Restrike	—	—	—	—	—	3,000

KM# 524 RUPEE

11.66 g., 0.917 Silver 0.3438 oz. ASW **Ruler:** George V **Obv:** Crowned bust left, type II **Obv. Legend:** GEORGE V KING EMPEROR **Rev:** Denomination and date within circle, wreath surrounds

Date	Mintage	F12	VF20	XF40	MS60	MS63
1912 (c)	45,122,000	24.00	30.00	35.00	40.00	—
1912 (c)	—	PF63 3,000				
1912 (b)	79,067,000	24.00	30.00	35.00	40.00	—
1912 (b)	—	PF63 3,000				
1912 B P/L; Restrike	—	—	—	—	—	1,500
1913 (c)	75,800,000	24.00	30.00	35.00	40.00	—
1913 (c)	—	PF63 3,000				
1913 (b)	87,466,000	24.00	30.00	35.00	40.00	—
1913 (b)	—	PF63 3,000				
1913 (b) P/L; Restrike	—	—	—	—	—	1,500
1914 (c)	33,100,000	24.00	30.00	35.00	40.00	—
1914 (c)	—	PF63 3,000				
1914 (b)	15,270,000	24.00	30.00	35.00	40.00	—
1914 (b)	—	PF63 3,000				
1914 (b) P/L; Restrike	—	—	—	—	—	1,500
1915 (c)	9,900,000	30.00	40.00	50.00	100	—
1915 (c)	—	PF63 3,000				
1915 (b)	5,372,000	30.00	40.00	50.00	100	—
1915 (b)	—	PF63 3,000				
1915 (b) P/L; Restrike	—	—	—	—	—	1,500
1916 (c)	115,000,000	24.00	30.00	35.00	40.00	—
1916 (c)	—	PF63 3,000				
1916 (b)	97,900,000	24.00	30.00	35.00	40.00	—
1916 (b)	—	PF65 500				
1916 (b) P/L; Restrike	—	—	—	—	—	1,500
1917 (c)	114,974,000	24.00	30.00	35.00	40.00	—
1917 (c)	—	PF63 3,000				
1917 (b)	151,583,000	24.00	30.00	35.00	40.00	—
1917 (b)	—	PF63 3,000				
1917 (b) P/L; Restrike	—	—	—	—	—	1,500
1918 (c)	205,420,000	24.00	30.00	35.00	40.00	—
1918 (c)	—	PF63 3,000				
1918 (b)	210,550,000	24.00	30.00	35.00	40.00	—
1918 (b)	—	PF63 3,000				
1918 (b) P/L; Restrike	—	—	—	—	—	1,500
1919 (c)	211,206,000	24.00	30.00	35.00	40.00	—
1919 (c)	—	PF63 3,000				
1919 (b)	226,706,000	24.00	30.00	35.00	40.00	—
1919 (b)	—	PF63 3,000				
1919 (b) P/L; Restrike	—	—	—	—	—	1,500
1920 (c)	50,500,000	24.00	30.00	35.00	40.00	—
1920 (c)	—	PF63 3,000				
1920 (b)	55,937,000	24.00	30.00	35.00	40.00	—
1920 (b)	—	PF63 3,000				
1921 (b)	5,115,000	60.00	90.00	125	150	—
1921 (b)	—	PF63 3,000				
1922 (b)	2,051,000	60.00	90.00	125	150	—
1922 (b)	—	PF63 3,000				
1935 (c)	—	PF63 3,000				
1935 (c) P/L; Restrike	—	—	—	—	—	1,500
1936 (c)	—	PF63 3,000				

KM# 554 RUPEE

11.66 g., 0.917 Silver 0.3438 oz. ASW **Ruler:** George VI **Obv:** Crowned head left, first head **Obv. Legend:** GEORGE VI KING EMPEROR **Rev:** Denomination and date within circle, wreath surrounds **Edge:** Reeded

Date	Mintage	F12	VF20	XF40	MS60	MS63
1938 (c)	—	PF63 3,000				
1939 (c)	—	PF63 25,000				

KM# 555 RUPEE

11.66 g., 0.917 Silver 0.3438 oz. ASW **Ruler:** George VI **Obv:** Second head, small rim decoration **Obv. Legend:** GEORGE VI KING EMPEROR **Rev:** Denomination and date within circle, wreath surrounds **Edge:** Reeded

Date	Mintage	F12	VF20	XF40	MS60	MS63
1938 (b) Without dot	7,352,000	125	175	200	300	—
1938 (b) Dot	Inc. above	125	175	200	300	—
1938 (b) P/L; Restrike	—	—	—	—	—	2,000
1939 (b) Dot	2,450,000	8,000	1,000	12,000	15,000	—

KM# A556 RUPEE

Copper-Nickel **Ruler:** George VI **Obv:** Small second head, large rim decoration **Obv. Legend:** GEORGE VI KING EMPEROR **Rev:** Denomination and date within circle, wreath surrounds **Note:** Mule.

Date	Mintage	F12	VF20	XF40	MS60	MS63
1938 (c) P/L; Restrike	—	—	—	—	5,000	—

KM# 556 RUPEE

11.66 g., 0.500 Silver 0.1874 oz. ASW **Ruler:** George VI **Obv:** Crowned head left **Obv. Legend:** GEORGE VI KING EMPEROR **Rev:** Denomination and date within circle, wreath surrounds **Edge:** Security

Date	Mintage	F12	VF20	XF40	MS60	MS63
1939 (b)	—	—	—	—	140,000	—
1940 (b)	153,120,000	10.00	13.00	18.00	25.00	—
1941 (b)	111,480,000	10.00	13.00	18.00	25.00	—
1943 (b)	—	60.00	80.00	125	200	—
Note: 1943(b) mintage included with KM#557.1.						
1943 (b) Reverse B	—	200	300	400	600	—

KM# 557.1 RUPEE

11.66 g., 0.500 Silver 0.1874 oz. ASW, 30.5 mm. **Ruler:** George VI **Obv:** Small second head, large rim decoration **Obv. Legend:** GEORGE VI KING EMPEROR **Rev:** Denomination and date within circle, wreath surrounds **Edge:** Security

Date	Mintage	F12	VF20	XF40	MS60	MS63
1942 (b) Without dot	7,352,000	10.00	13.00	18.00	25.00	—
1943 (b)	65,995,000	20.00	30.00	50.00	80.00	—
1943 (b) Reverse B	Inc. above	20.00	30.00	50.00	80.00	—
1944 (b) Reverse B	146,206,000	10.00	13.00	18.00	25.00	—
1944 (b)	Inc. above	10.00	13.00	18.00	25.00	—
1944 L Small L	91,400,000	10.00	13.00	18.00	25.00	—
1944 L Large L	Inc. above	10.00	13.00	18.00	25.00	—
1944 L Reverse B	—	1,000	1,500	2,000	2,500	—
1945 (b) Small 5	142,666,000	10.00	13.00	18.00	25.00	—
1945 (b) Large 5	Inc. above	500	650	800	1,000	—
1945 (b) Proof	—	—	—	—	—	3,000
1945 L Small 5	118,126,000	10.00	13.00	18.00	25.00	—
1945 L Large 5	—	700	800	900	1,100	—

KM# 557a RUPEE

Copper-Nickel, 30.5 mm. **Ruler:** George VI **Obv:** Crowned head left **Obv. Legend:** GEORGE VI KING EMPEROR **Rev:** Denomination and date within circle, wreath surrounds

Date	Mintage	F12	VF20	XF40	MS60	MS63
1943 (b) P/L; Restrike	—	—	—	—	—	2,500

KM# 557.2 RUPEE

11.66 g., 0.917 Silver 0.3438 oz. ASW **Ruler:** George VI **Obv:** Crowned head left **Rev:** Denomination and date within circle, wreath surrounds **Note:** Reeded edge (error). Prev. KM#558.

Date	Mintage	F12	VF20	XF40	MS60	MS63
1944 (b)	—	400	600	800	1,200	—
1945 (b)	—	400	600	800	1,200	—

KM# 559 RUPEE

Nickel **Ruler:** George VI **Obv:** Crowned head left **Rev:** Indian tiger (panthera tigris) **Edge:** Security

Date	Mintage	F12	VF20	XF40	MS60	MS63
1947 (b)	118,028,000	2.00	3.00	6.00	10.00	—
1947 B	—	PF63 1,500				
Note: Mumbai (Bombay) issue has diamond mark below date						
1947 (l)	41,911,000	3.00	5.00	8.00	25.00	—
Note: Lahore issue without privy mark						

KM# 525 15 RUPEES

7.99 g., 0.917 Gold 0.2355 oz. AGW **Ruler:** George V **Obv:** Crowned bust left **Obv. Legend:** GEORGE V KING EMPEROR **Rev:** Denomination and date within circle, wreath surrounds **Note:** This issue is equal in weight and fineness to the British sovereign.

Date	Mintage	F12	VF20	XF40	MS60	MS63
1918 (b)	2,110,000	2,500	3,000	3,500	4,000	—
1918 (b)	12	PF63 6,000				
1918 (b) P/L; Restrike	—	—	—	—	—	5,000

TRADE COINAGE

The Mansfield Commission of 1868 allowed for the admission of British and Australian sovereigns (see Australian section; sovereigns with shield reverse were struck for export to India) as payment for sums due.

The fifth branch of the Royal Mint was established in a section of the Mumbai (Bombay) Mint as of December 21, 1917. This was a war-time measure, its purpose being to strike into sovereigns the gold blanks supplied by the Mumbai and other Indian mints. The Mumbai sovereigns bear the mint mark 'I' and were struck from August 15, 1918, to April 22, 1919. The branch mint was closed in May 1919.

KM# A525 SOVEREIGN

7.99 g., 0.917 Gold 0.2355 oz. AGW **Ruler:** George V **Obv:** Head left **Rev:** St. George slaying the dragon **Note:** Mint mark "I".

Date	Mintage	F12	VF20	XF40	MS60	MS63
1918	1,295,000	300	345	360	375	—
1918 Proof	—	—	—	—	—	—
1918 P/L; Restrike	—	—	—	—	—	2,000

PATTERNS

Including off metal strikes

KM#	Date	Mintage	Identification	Mkt Val
Pn66	1901(c)	—	Rupee. Silver. Prid.#1045.	3,000
Pn67	1901(c)	—	Rupee. Silver. Prid.#1046.	4,000
PnA68	1903(c)	—	Rupee. Gold. Proof, Rare.	—
Pn68	1903(c)	—	1/4 Rupee. Silver. With "718" countermark. Prid.#1074.	—
Pn69	1903(c)	—	Anna. Nickel. Prid.#1053.	6,000
Pn70	1904(c)	—	1/4 Anna. Copper. Prid.#1051.	8,500
Pn71	1904(c)	—	Anna. Copper-Nickel. Prid.#1054.	5,000
Pn72	1904(c)	—	Anna. Tin. Prid.#1055.	6,000
Pn73	1904(c)	—	Anna. Copper-Nickel. Prid.#1056.	4,000
Pn74	1904(c)	—	Anna. Copper-Nickel. Prid.#1058.	5,000
Pn75	1904(c)	—	Anna. Copper-Nickel. Prid.#1059.	5,000
Pn76	1904(c)	—	Anna. Copper-Nickel. Prid.#1060.	5,000
Pn77	1904(c)	—	Anna. White Metal. Prid.#1061.	5,000
Pn78	1904(c)	—	Anna. Copper-Nickel. Prid.#1062.	5,000
Pn79	1904(c)	—	Anna. Copper-Nickel. Prid.#1063.	5,000
PnA80	1904(c)	—	1/4 Rupee. Copper. as Prid.#1075.	5,000
Pn80	1904(c)	—	1/4 Rupee. Nickel. Prid.#1075.	5,000
Pn80a	1904C	—	1/4 Rupee. Bronze. Edward VII. Denomination. Scalloped.	8,000
Pn81	1905(c)	—	Anna. Copper-Nickel. Prid.#924.	—
Pn82	1905(c)	—	Anna. White Metal. Prid.#1057.	5,000
Pn83	1905(c)	—	Anna.	5,000
Pn84	1905(c)	—	Anna. White Metal. Low relief bust; Prid.#1066.	5,000
Pn85	1905(c)	—	Anna. White Metal. High relief bust; Prid.#1067.	5,000
Pn86	1905(c)	—	Anna. Copper. High relief bust; Prid.#1069.	5,000
Pn87	1905(c)	—	Anna. Silver. High relief bust; Prid.#1068.	5,000
Pn88	1905(c)	—	Anna. White Metal. Without dot border. Prid.#1070A.	5,000
Pn89	1905	—	Anna. Copper-Nickel.	—
Pn90	1905(c)	—	Anna. Silver. Without dot border. Prid.#1070B.	5,000
Pn91	1906(c)	—	Anna. White Metal. Raised bar. Prid.#1064.	5,000
Pn92	1906(c)	—	Anna. White Metal. Double raised bar. Prid.#1065.	5,000
Pn93	1906(c)	—	Anna. Copper-Nickel. Scalloped planchet; Prid.#1071.	5,000
Pn94	1906(c)	—	Rupee. Copper-Nickel. SPECIMEN" divided by crown. Lettered. Prid.#1047.	—
Pn95	1907(b)	—	Rupee. Silver. Prid.#1048.	—
Pn96	1908	—	1/2 Anna. Copper-Nickel.	5,000
Pn97	1908(c)	—	1/2 Anna. White Metal. Prid.#1073.	7,500
Pn98	1909	—	1/2 Pice. Aluminum.	5,000
Pn99	1910(c)	—	Rupee. Silver. Prid.#1049.	9,000
Pn100	1910(c)	—	Rupee. Gold. Prid.#1050.	9,000
Pn101	ND (1910) (c)	—	2 Annas. Tin. Prid.#1052.	9,000
Pn102	1917(c)	—	2 Annas. Copper-Nickel. Round; Prid.#1078.	9,000

KM#	Date	Mintage	Identification	Mkt Val
Pn103	1917(c)	—	2 Annas. Copper-Nickel. Square; Prid.#1079.	9,000
Pn104	1918(c)	—	4 Annas. Copper-Nickel. Round with center hole; Prid.#1076.	9,000
Pn105	1919(c)	—	2 Annas. Copper-Nickel. Eight-lobed planchet; Prid.#1087.	9,000
Pn106	1919(c)	—	4 Annas. Copper-Nickel. Triangle; Prid.#1077.	9,000
Pn107	1921(c)	—	Anna. Copper-Nickel. Prid.#1080.	4,000
Pn108	1921(c)	—	Anna. Copper. Prid.#1081.	4,000
Pn109	1921(c)	—	Anna. Gold. Prid.#1082.	10,000
Pn110	1929(c)	—	Anna. Copper-Nickel. Prid.#1083.	2,500
Pn111	1929(c)	—	Anna. Copper-Nickel. Wide border; Prid.#1084.	8,500
Pn112	1937(c)	—	2 Annas. Copper-Nickel. Prid.#1093.	8,500
Pn113	1937(c)	—	2 Annas. Copper-Nickel. Serrated circular border. Prid.#1094.	8,500
Pn114	1938(b)	—	1/4 Anna. Bronze. Head of George V.	—
Pn115	1938(c)	—	1/2 Anna. Nickel. Prid.#1095.	7,500
Pn116	1938(b)	—	Rupee. Silver. Head of George V.	—
Pn117	1941(c)	—	Dollar. Silver. Prid.#1088A.	—
Pn118	1941(c)	—	Dollar. Silver. Fine milled.	8,000
Pn119	1941(b)	—	Dollar. Silver. S" in "RUPEES" 1/2 to left of large "1"; Prid.#1088B.	—
Pn120	1941(c)	—	Dollar. Silver. Prid.#1089.	—
Pn121	1943(c)	—	Pice. Bronze. Prid.#1091.	6,500
Pn122	1945(c)	—	Pie. Bronze. Prid.#1092.	—
Pn123	1946(c)	—	Pie. Bronze. Tiger left. Prid.#1090.	—
PnA13	1949	—	Rupee. Silver. KM#458.9.	5,000
PnB13	1949	—	1/8 Rupee. Silver. KM#465.5.	5,000
PnC13	1949	—	1/4 Rupee. Silver. KM#454.6.	5,000
PnD13	1949	—	1/8 Rupee. Silver. KM#460.5.	5,000

PROOF SETS

KM#	Date	Mintage	Identification	Issue Price	Mkt Val
PS3	1904 (5)	—	KM#497, 499, 503, Pn70(2)	—	5,600
PS4	1904 (3)	—	KM#497, 499, 501(bronze) with "1" countermark on reverse	—	3,000
PS5	1911(c) (4)	—	KM#514, 517, 521, 523	—	4,800
PS6	1919(c) (4)	—	KM#513, 516, 519-520 (2 each - V.I.P.)	—	4,400
PS7	1938(c) (5)	—	KM#527-528, 530, 536, 544, 555	—	1,200
PS8	1947(b) (7)	—	KM#533, 535, 538, 542, 548, 553, 559	—	3,000

INDIA - REPUBLIC

The Republic of India, a subcontinent jutting southward from the mainland of Asia, has an area of 1,269,346 sq. mi. (3,287,590 sq. km.) and a population of over 1.1 billion, second only to that of the People's Republic of China. Capital: New Delhi. India's economy is based on agriculture and industrial activity. Engineering goods, cotton apparel and fabrics, handicrafts, tea, iron and steel are exported.

The Indian Mutiny (called the first War of Independence by Indian Nationalists) of 1857-58, begun by Indian troops in the service of the British East India Company, revealed the intensity of the growing resentment against British domination. The widespread rebellion against British rule was unsuccessful, but resulted in the transfer of government from the company to the British crown, and was a source of inspiration, to later Indian nationalists. Agitation for representation in the government continued.

Following World War I, in which India sent six million troops to fight at the side of the Allies, Indian nationalism intensified under the banner of the Indian National Congress and the leadership of Mohandas Karamchand Gandhi, who called for non-violent revolt against British authority. The Government of India Act of 1935 proposed a federal status linking the British Indian provinces with the many princely states; in addition, provincial legislatures were to be created. The federal status was never implemented, but the legislatures were created after the election of 1937, with the National Congress winning majorities in most of the provinces.

When Britain declared war on Germany in Sept. 1939, the Viceroy declared India also to be at war with a common enemy. The Congress, however, demanded independence as a condition for cooperation; Britain refused. But as the Japanese advanced into Asia, Britain offered to transfer to Indians power over all but military affairs during the war, and set forth a plan for postwar independence. Congress was willing to accept the wartime transfer of power, but both Congress and the Muslim League rejected Britain's plan for independence; Congress because it did not sufficiently safeguard Indian unity, the Muslims (who wanted a separate Muslim state) because of fears of what would happen to Muslims within a united India.

Early in 1947, Prime Minister Clement Attlee announced that Britain would leave India "by a date not later than June 1948," even though the Hindus and Muslims could not agree among themselves on a plan for self-government. The National Congress, aware that the Muslim League would revolt rather than accept an all-India government, reluctantly agreed to the formation of a separate Muslim state. The Muslim-majority provinces of the North West Frontier, Sindh and West Punjab in the west, and East Bengal in the east were separated from India to form the Muslim state of Pakistan, which became independent on Aug. 14, 1947. India became independent on the following day. Because British India coins dated 1947 were struck until 1950, they can be considered the first coins of Independent India. India became a republic on Jan. 26, 1950.

The Republic of India is a member of the Commonwealth of Nations. The president is the Chief of State. The prime minister is the Head of Government.

MINT MARKS

(Mint marks usually appear directly below the date.)

B - Mumbai (Bombay), proof issues only (1969 until 1995)
(B) - Mumbai (Bombay), diamond
C – Ottawa (1985 25 Paise; 1988 10, 25 & 50 Paise)
(C) – Kolkata (Calcutta) no mint mark
H - Birmingham (1985 Rupee only)
(H) - Hyderabad, star (1963)
(Hd) - Hyderabad, diamond split vertically (1953-1960)
(Hy) - Hyderabad, incuse dot in diamond (1960-1968)
(K) - Kremnica, Slovakia, MK in circle
(L) – British Royal Mint, Llantrisant (1985 rupee only), diamond below first date digit(Ld) – British Royal Mint Llantrisant, tower, looks like a bridge
M - Mumbai (Bombay), proof only starting 1996
(M) - Mexico City, M beneath O
(N) - Noida, dot
(P) - Pretoria, M in oval
(R) – Moscow, MMD in oval
(T) - Taegu (Korea), star below first or last date (1997 and 98 2 Rupees only)From 1950 through 1964 the Republic of India proof coins carry the regular diamond mint mark and can be distinguished from circulation issues only by their proof-like finish. From 1969 proofs carry the capital "B" mint mark. Some Bombay issues after 1969 have a "proof-like" appearance although bearing the diamond mint mark of circulation issues. Beginning in 1972 proofs of the larger denominations - 10, 20 and 100 rupees -were partly frosted on their main features, including numerals. From 1975 all proofs were similarly frosted, from the 1 paisa to 100 rupees. Proof-like issues are often erroneously offered as proofs.

MONETARY SYSTEM

(Until 1957)

4 Pice = 1 Anna
16 Annas = 1 Rupee

In addition to the denomination, the value as fraction of the Rupee is added in words above the denomination numeral for educational purposes on all 1, 2,5, 10, 25, and 50 Naya Paisa on the first 1, 2, 5, 10, 25, and 50 Paisa types (i.e. Naya Paisa – 1/100 Rupee).

REPUBLIC

STANDARD COINAGE

KM# 1.1 PICE

Bronze **Obv:** Asoka lion pedestal **Rev:** Horse (equus caballus equidae) **Note:** 1.6mm thick, 0.3mm edge rim.

Date	Mintage	VF20	XF40	MS60	MS63	MS65
1950 (B)	32,080,000	2.00	3.00	5.00	6.00	—

KM# 1.2 PICE

Bronze **Obv:** Asoka lion pedestal **Rev:** Horse left **Note:** 1.6mm thick, 1.0mm edge rim.

Date	Mintage	VF20	XF40	MS60	MS63	MS65
1950 (B)	Inc. above	4.00	6.00	8.00	10.00	—
1950 (B)	—	PF63 100				
1950 C	14,000,000	2.00	3.00	4.50	6.00	—

KM# 1.3 PICE

Bronze **Obv:** Asoka lion pedestal **Rev:** Horse left **Note:** 1.2mm thick, 0.8mm edge rim.

Date	Mintage	VF20	XF40	MS60	MS63	MS65
1951 (B)	104,626,000	1.00	2.00	3.00	5.00	—
1951 (C)	127,300,000	1.00	2.00	3.00	5.00	—

KM# 1.4 PICE

2.95 g., Bronze, 21 mm. **Obv:** Asoka lion pedestal **Rev:** Horse left **Note:** Larger date, 2mm thick, 0.8mm edge rim.

Date	Mintage	VF20	XF40	MS60	MS63	MS65
1952 (B)	213,830,000	4.00	5.00	6.00	10.00	—
1953 (Hd)	Inc. above	200	400	600	800	—
1953 (B)	242,358,000	4.00	5.00	6.00	10.00	—
1953 (C)	111,000,000	4.00	5.00	6.00	10.00	—

Date	Mintage	VF20	XF40	MS60	MS63	MS65
1954 (B)	136,758,000	1.00	2.00	3.00	5.00	—
1954 (C)	52,600,000	1.00	2.00	3.00	5.00	—
1954 (Hd)	Inc. above	20.00	40.00	60.00	100	—
1954 (B)	Inc. above	PF63 300				
1955 (B)	24,423,000	6.00	10.00	20.00	2.50	—
1955 (Hd)	Inc. above	20.00	50.00	100	180	—

KM# 2.1 1/2 ANNA

2.89 g., Copper-Nickel **Obv:** Asoka lion pedestal **Rev:** Zebu **Shape:** 4-sided

Date	Mintage	VF20	XF40	MS60	MS63	MS65
1950 (B)	26,076,000	6.00	8.00	10.00	25.00	—
1950 (B)	—	PF63 250				
1950 (C)	3,100,000	10.00	30.00	50.00	100	—

KM# 2.2 1/2 ANNA

2.85 g., Copper-Nickel **Obv:** Asoka lion pedestal **Rev:** Zebu, larger date **Shape:** Square

Date	Mintage	VF20	XF40	MS60	MS63	MS65
1954 (B)	14,000,000	4.00	6.00	8.00	15.00	—
1954 (B)	—	PF63 250				
1954 (C)	20,800,000	4.00	6.00	8.00	15.00	—
1955 (B)	22,488,000	6.00	8.00	10.00	25.00	—

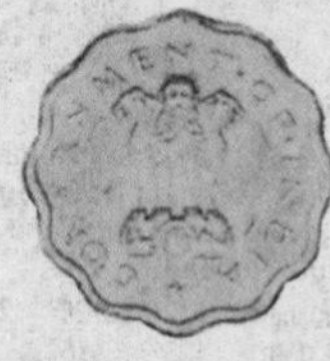

KM# 3.1 ANNA

Copper-Nickel **Obv:** Asoka lion pedestal **Rev:** Zebu **Shape:** Scalloped **Note:** A similar shaped Independence commemorative token issued in 1947, bearing a map of India, circulated to some degree as an Anna coin.

Date	Mintage	VF20	XF40	MS60	MS63	MS65
1950 (B)	9,944,000	6.00	10.00	16.00	30.00	—
1950 (B)	—	PF63 150				

KM# 3.2 ANNA

Copper-Nickel **Obv:** Asoka lion pedestal **Rev:** Zebu, larger date, first Hindi letter varieties **Shape:** Scalloped

Date	Mintage	VF20	XF40	MS60	MS63	MS65
1954 (B)	20,388,000	6.00	10.00	16.00	30.00	—
1954 (B)	—	PF63 300				

KM# 4.1 2 ANNAS

5.78 g., Copper-Nickel **Obv:** Asoka lion pedestal **Rev:** Zebu **Note:** A similar shaped Independence commemorative token issued in 1947, bearing a map of India, circulated to some degree as a 2 Anna coin. (Refer to 5th edition of Unusual World Coins, X#104.)

Date	Mintage	VF20	XF40	MS60	MS63	MS65
1950 (B)	7,536,000	16.00	30.00	40.00	80.00	—
1950 (B)	—	PF63 250				

KM# 4.2 2 ANNAS

Copper-Nickel **Obv:** Asoka lion pedestal **Rev:** Zebu **Note:** Larger date.

Date	Mintage	VF20	XF40	MS60	MS63	MS65
1954 (B)	10,548,000	16.00	30.00	40.00	80.00	—
1954 (B)	—	PF63 400				
1955 (B)	—	500	900	1,600	3,000	—

KM# 5.1 1/4 RUPEE

2.50 g., Nickel, 19 mm. **Obv:** Asoka lion pedestal **Rev:** Grain sprigs flank denomination **Edge:** Reeded **Note:** Large lion.

Date	Mintage	VF20	XF40	MS60	MS63	MS65
1950 (B)	7,650,000	1.00	2.50	4.00	10.00	—
1950 (B)	—	PF63 225				
1950 (C)	7,800,000	2.00	5.00	10.00	25.00	—
1951 (B)	41,439,000	1.00	2.50	4.00	10.00	—
1951 (C)	13,500,000	1.00	2.50	4.00	10.00	—

KM# 5.2 1/4 RUPEE

2.50 g., Nickel, 19 mm. **Obv:** Asoka lion pedestal **Rev:** Grain sprigs flank denomination **Edge:** Reeded **Note:** Larger date, large lion.

Date	Mintage	VF20	XF40	MS60	MS63	MS65
1954 (C)	58,300,000	4.00	6.00	10.00	20.00	—
1954 (B)	Inc. above	PF63 325				
1955 (B)	57,936,000	1.00	2.50	4.00	10.00	—

KM# 5.3 1/4 RUPEE

2.50 g., Nickel, 19 mm. **Obv:** Asoka lion pedestal **Rev:** Grain sprigs flank denomination **Edge:** Reeded **Note:** Small lion.

Date	Mintage	VF20	XF40	MS60	MS63	MS65
1954 (C)	Inc. above	1.00	2.50	4.00	10.00	—
1955 (C)	28,900,000	1.00	2.50	4.00	10.00	—
1956 (C)	22,000,000	2.00	4.00	6.00	15.00	—

KM# 6.1 1/2 RUPEE

5.00 g., Nickel **Obv:** Asoka lion pedestal **Rev:** Grain sprigs flank denomination **Note:** Large lion.

Date	Mintage	VF20	XF40	MS60	MS63	MS65
1950 (B)	12,352,000	2.00	4.00	6.00	15.00	—
1950 (B)	—	PF63 250				
1950 (C)	1,100,000	6.00	14.00	20.00	50.00	—
1951 (B)	9,239,000	2.00	4.00	6.00	15.00	—

KM# 6.2 1/2 RUPEE

5.00 g., Nickel **Obv:** Asoka lion pedestal **Rev:** Grain sprigs flank denomination **Note:** Larger date, large lion.

Date	Mintage	VF20	XF40	MS60	MS63	MS65
1954 (C)	36,300,000	2.00	4.00	6.00	15.00	—
1954 (B)	—	PF63 460				
1955 (B)	18,977,000	6.00	18.00	30.00	30.00	—

KM# 6.3 1/2 RUPEE

5.00 g., Nickel **Obv:** Asoka lion pedestal within circle, dots missing between words **Rev:** Grain sprigs flank denomination

Date	Mintage	VF20	XF40	MS60	MS63	MS65
1956 (C)	24,900,000	2.00	4.00	6.00	15.00	—

KM# 7.1 RUPEE

10.00 g., Nickel **Obv:** Asoka lion pedestal **Rev:** Grain sprigs flank denomination, thick numeral

Date	Mintage	VF20	XF40	MS60	MS63	MS65
1950 (B)	19,412,000	6.00	15.00	20.00	40.00	—
1950 (B)	—	PF63 275				

KM# 7.2 RUPEE

10.00 g., Nickel **Obv:** Asoka lion pedestal **Rev:** Thick numeral, first Hindi letter varieties, larger date

Date	Mintage	VF20	XF40	MS60	MS63	MS65
1954 (B)	Inc. above	20.00	35.00	50.00	100	—
1954 (B)	—	PF63 475				

DECIMAL COINAGE

100 Naye Paise = 1 Rupee (1957-63);
100 Paise = 1 Rupee (1964-)

NOTE: The Paisa was at first called Naya Paisa (= New Paisa), so that people would distinguish from the old non-decimal Paisa (or Pice, equal to 1/64 Rupee).

After 7 years, the word new was dropped, and the coin was simply called a Paisa.

NOTE: Many of the Paisa standard types come with three obverse varieties.

1957-1989

TYPE 1: Side lions toothless with 2 to 3 fur rows, short squat D in INDIA.

1967-1994

TYPE 2: Asoka lion pedestal more imposing. Side lions with 3 or 4 fur rows, more elegant D in INDIA. The shape of the D in INDIA is the easiest way to distinguish this obverse.

1979-

TYPE 3: Similar to Type I but 2 teeth, 4 to 5 fur rows, smaller lion head.

NOTE: Paisa standard pieces with mint mark B, 1969 to date, were struck only in proof.

NOTE: Indian mintage figures are not divided by mint, and often include dates other than the year in which struck. They should be regarded with reserve.

KM# 8 NAYA PAISA

1.50 g., Bronze, 16.04 mm. **Obv:** Asoka lion pedestal **Rev:** Denomination and date

Date	Mintage	VF20	XF40	MS60	MS63	MS65
1957 (B)	618,630,000	0.60	1.00	2.00	4.00	—
1957 (C)	Inc. above	1.00	2.00	3.00	6.00	—
1957 (Hd)	Inc. above	1.00	2.00	3.00	6.00	—
1958 (B)	468,630,000	0.60	1.00	2.00	4.00	—
1958 (Hd)	Inc. above	0.60	1.00	2.00	4.00	—
1959 (B)	351,120,000	0.60	1.00	2.00	4.00	—
1959 (C)	Inc. above	1.00	2.00	3.00	6.00	—
1959 (Hd)	Inc. above	0.60	1.00	2.00	4.00	—
1960 (B)	357,940,000	0.60	1.00	2.00	4.00	—
1960 (B)	—	PF63 80.00				
1960 (C)	Inc. above	2.00	4.00	6.00	15.00	—
1960 (Hd)	Inc. above	2.00	4.00	6.00	15.00	—
1961 (B)	573,170,000	0.60	1.00	2.00	4.00	—
1961 (B)	—	PF63 10.00				
1961 (C)	Inc. above	0.60	1.00	2.00	4.00	—
1961 (Hy)	Inc. above	2.00	4.00	6.00	15.00	—
1962 (B)	—	PF63 25.00				

Note: 1962(B) has only been found in some of the 1962 uncirculated mint sets; varieties of the split diamond have been reported.

KM# 8 NAYA PAISA

1.51 g., Nickel-Brass, 16 mm. **Obv:** Asoka lion pedestal **Rev:** Denomination and date

Date	Mintage	VF20	XF40	MS60	MS63	MS65
1962 (B)	235,103,000	0.60	1.00	2.00	4.00	—
1962 (B)	—	PF63 20.00				
1962 (C)	Inc. above	0.60	1.00	2.00	4.00	—
1962 (Hy)	Inc. above	0.60	1.00	2.00	4.00	—
1963 (B)	343,313,000	0.60	1.00	2.00	4.00	—
1963 (B)	—	PF63 20.00				
1963 (C)	Inc. above	0.60	1.00	2.00	4.00	—
1963 (H)	Inc. above	0.60	1.00	2.00	4.00	—

KM# 9 PAISA

1.48 g., Nickel-Brass **Obv:** Asoka lion pedestal **Rev:** Denomination and date **Note:** Type I.

Date	Mintage	VF20	XF40	MS60	MS63	MS65
1964 (B)	539,068,000	0.60	1.00	2.00	4.00	—
1964 (C)	Inc. above	0.60	1.00	2.00	4.00	—
1964 (H)	Inc. above	0.60	1.00	2.00	4.00	—

KM# 9 PAISA

Bronze **Obv:** Asoka lion pedestal **Rev:** Denomination and date **Note:** Included in mintage of KM#9. Type 1.

Date	Mintage	VF20	XF40	MS60	MS63	MS65
1964 (H)	Inc. above	1.00	1.50	3.00	6.00	—

KM# 10.1 PAISA

0.75 g., Aluminum, 14.67x14.67 mm. **Obv:** Asoka lion pedestal **Rev:** Denomination and date **Edge:** Plain **Shape:** Square **Note:** Type 1.

Date	Mintage	VF20	XF40	MS60	MS63	MS65
1965 (B)	223,480,000	1.00	2.00	3.00	5.00	—
1965 (Hy)	Inc. above	1.00	2.00	3.00	5.00	—
1966 (B)	404,200,000	1.00	2.00	3.00	5.00	—
1966 (C)	Inc. above	1.00	2.00	3.00	5.00	—
1966 (Hy)	Inc. above	1.00	2.00	3.00	5.00	—
1967 (B)	450,433,000	1.00	2.00	3.00	5.00	—
1967 (C)	Inc. above	1.00	2.00	3.00	5.00	—
1967 (Hy)	Inc. above	1.00	2.00	3.00	5.00	—
1968 (B)	302,720,000	1.00	2.00	3.00	5.00	—
1968 (C)	Inc. above	1.00	2.00	3.00	5.00	—
1968 (Hy)	Inc. above	1.00	2.00	3.00	5.00	—
1969 (B)	125,930,000	4.00	6.00	8.00	20.00	—
1969 B	9,147	PF63 20.00				
1969 (H)	Inc. above	6.00	8.00	10.00	30.00	—
1970 (B)	15,800,000	6.00	8.00	10.00	30.00	—

Date	Mintage	VF20	XF40	MS60	MS63	MS65
Note: 1970(B) is found only in the uncirculated sets. It has a mirror-like surface.						
1970 B	3,046	PF63 8.00				
1971 B	4,375	PF63 8.00				
1971 (H)	112,100,000	0.60	1.00	2.00	4.00	—
1972 (B)	62,090,000	0.60	1.00	2.00	4.00	—
1972 B	7,895	PF63 10.00				
1972 (H)	Inc. above	0.60	1.00	2.00	4.00	—
1973 B	7,562	PF63 8.00				
1974 B	—	PF63 8.00				
1975 B	—	PF63 8.00				
1976 B	—	PF63 8.00				
1977 B	—	PF63 8.00				
1978 B	—	PF63 8.00				
1979 B	—	PF63 8.00				
1980 B	—	PF63 8.00				
1981 B	—	PF63 8.00				

KM# 10.2 PAISA

Aluminum **Obv:** Asoka lion pedestal **Rev:** Denomination and date **Shape:** 4-sided **Note:** Type 2.

Date	Mintage	VF20	XF40	MS60	MS63	MS65
1969 (C)	Inc. above	4.00	5.00	6.00	10.00	—
1970 (C)	Inc. above	2.00	3.00	4.00	7.00	—

KM# 11 2 NAYE PAISE

2.95 g., Copper-Nickel **Obv:** Asoka lion pedestal **Rev:** Denomination and date **Shape:** Scalloped

Date	Mintage	VF20	XF40	MS60	MS63	MS65
1957 (B)	406,230,000	0.60	1.20	2.00	4.00	—
1957 (C)	Inc. above	0.60	1.20	2.00	4.00	—
1958 (B)	245,660,000	0.60	1.20	2.00	4.00	—
1958 (C)	Inc. above	0.60	1.20	2.00	4.00	—
1959 (B)	171,445,000	0.60	1.20	2.00	4.00	—
1959 (C)	Inc. above	0.60	1.20	2.00	4.00	—
1960 (B)	121,820,000	1.00	2.00	4.00	8.00	—
1960 (B)	—	PF63 50.00				
1960 (C)	Inc. above	0.60	1.20	2.00	4.00	—
1961 (B)	190,610,000	0.60	1.20	2.00	4.00	—
1961 (B)	—	PF63 50.00				
1961 (C)	Inc. above	0.60	1.20	2.00	4.00	—
1962 (B)	318,181,000	0.60	1.20	2.00	4.00	—
1962 (B)	—	PF63 50.00				
1962 (C)	Inc. above	0.60	1.20	2.00	4.00	—
1963 (B)	372,380,000	0.60	1.20	2.00	4.00	—
1963 (B)	—	PF63 50.00				
1963 (C)	Inc. above	0.60	1.20	2.00	4.00	—

KM# 12 2 PAISE

Copper-Nickel **Obv:** Asoka lion pedestal **Rev:** Denomination and date **Shape:** Scalloped **Note:** Type 1.

Date	Mintage	VF20	XF40	MS60	MS63	MS65
1964 (B)	323,504,000	0.60	1.20	2.00	4.00	—
1964 (C)	Inc. above	0.60	1.20	2.00	4.00	—

KM# 13.1 2 PAISE

1.02 g., Aluminum **Obv:** Asoka lion pedestal **Rev:** Denomination and date, 10mm "2 **Shape:** Scalloped **Note:** Type 1.

Date	Mintage	VF20	XF40	MS60	MS63	MS65
1965 (B)	175,770,000	0.60	1.20	2.00	4.00	—
1965 (C)	Inc. above	1.00	2.00	3.00	6.00	—
1966 (B)	386,795,000	0.60	1.20	2.00	4.00	—
1966 (C)	Inc. above	0.60	1.20	2.00	4.00	—
1967 (B)	454,593,000	0.60	1.20	2.00	4.00	—

KM# 13.2 2 PAISE

Aluminum **Obv:** Asoka lion pedestal **Rev:** Denomination and date, 10-1/2mm "2" **Note:** Type 1.

Date	Mintage	VF20	XF40	MS60	MS63	MS65
1967 (C)	Inc. above	4.00	5.00	6.00	10.00	—

KM# 13.3 2 PAISE

Aluminum **Obv:** Asoka lion pedestal **Rev:** Denomination and date, 10mm "2 **Note:** Type 2.

Date	Mintage	VF20	XF40	MS60	MS63	MS65
1967 (B)	—	20.00	30.00	40.00	65.00	—

KM# 13.4 2 PAISE

Aluminum **Obv:** Asoka lion pedestal **Rev:** Denomination and date, 11mm "2" **Note:** Type 1.

Date	Mintage	VF20	XF40	MS60	MS63	MS65
1968 (C)	—	10.00	25.00	40.00	75.00	—
1977 (B)	—	0.60	1.20	2.00	4.00	—
1978 (B)	—	0.60	1.20	2.00	4.00	—

KM# 13.5 2 PAISE

1.00 g., Aluminum **Obv:** Asoka lion pedestal **Rev:** Denomination and date, 11mm "2" **Shape:** Scalloped **Note:** Type 2.

Date	Mintage	VF20	XF40	MS60	MS63	MS65
1968 (B)	305,205,000	0.60	1.20	2.00	4.00	—
1968 (C)	Inc. above	0.60	1.20	2.00	4.00	—
1969 (B)	5,335,000	16.00	30.00	50.00	75.00	—
1969 B	9,147	PF63 100				
1970 (B)	—	6.00	8.00	10.00	15.00	—
Note: 1970(B) is found only in the uncirculated sets of that year; It has a mirror-like surface.						
1970 B	3,046	PF63 10.00				
1970 (C)	79,100,000	PF63 4.00				
1971 (C)	207,900,000	0.60	1.20	2.00	4.00	—
1971 B	4,375	PF63 10.00				

KM# 13.6 2 PAISE

1.00 g., Aluminum, 19.84 mm. **Obv:** Asoka lion pedestal **Rev:** Denomination and small date **Edge:** Plain scalloped **Note:** Varieties of date size exist. Type 2.

Date	Mintage	VF20	XF40	MS60	MS63	MS65
1972 B	7,895	PF63 8.00				
1972 (C)	261,270,000	0.60	1.20	2.00	4.00	—
1972 (H)	Inc. above	0.60	1.20	2.00	4.00	—
1973 B	7,562	PF63 8.00				
1973 (C)	—	0.60	1.20	2.00	4.00	—
1973 (H)	—	0.60	1.20	2.00	4.00	—
1974 B	—	PF63 8.00				
1974 (C)	—	0.60	1.20	2.00	4.00	—
1974 (H)	—	0.60	1.20	2.00	4.00	—
1975 B	—	PF63 8.00				
1975 (C)	184,500,000	4.00	7.00	10.00	20.00	—
1975 (H)	Inc. above	0.60	1.20	2.00	4.00	—
1976 (B)	68,140,000	0.60	1.20	2.00	4.00	—
1976 B	—	PF63 8.00				
1976 (H)	—	0.60	1.20	2.00	4.00	—
1977 (B)	251,955,000	0.60	1.20	2.00	4.00	—
1977 B	—	PF63 8.00				
1977 (H)	Inc. above	0.60	1.20	2.00	4.00	—
1978 B	—	PF63 8.00				
1978 (H)	144,010,000	0.60	1.20	2.00	4.00	—
1979 B	—	PF63 8.00				
1979 (H)	—	6.00	12.00	20.00	40.00	—

KM# 14.1 3 PAISE

1.23 g., Aluminum, 19.5 mm. **Obv:** Asoka lion pedestal **Rev:** Denomination and date **Shape:** 6-sided **Note:** Type 1.

Date	Mintage	VF20	XF40	MS60	MS63	MS65
1964 (B)	138,890,000	0.60	1.20	2.00	4.00	—
1964 (C)	Inc. above	0.60	1.20	2.00	4.00	—
1965 (B)	459,825,000	0.60	1.20	2.00	4.00	—
1965 (C)	Inc. above	0.60	1.20	2.00	4.00	—
1966 (B)	390,440,000	0.60	1.20	2.00	4.00	—
1966 (C)	Inc. above	0.60	1.20	2.00	4.00	—
1966 (Hy)	Inc. above	1.00	2.00	4.00	6.00	—
1967 (B)	167,018,000	0.60	1.20	2.00	4.00	—
1967 (C)	Inc. above	0.60	1.20	2.00	4.00	—
1967 (H)	Inc. above	1.00	2.00	4.00	6.00	—
1968 (B)	—	6.00	8.00	10.00	20.00	—
1968 (H)	—	10.00	35.00	50.00	100	—

KM# 14.2 3 PAISE

1.23 g., Aluminum **Obv:** Asoka lion pedestal **Rev:** Denomination and date **Shape:** 6-sided **Note:** Type 2.

Date	Mintage	VF20	XF40	MS60	MS63	MS65
1967 (C)	—	10.00	35.00	50.00	100	—
1967 (H)	Inc. above	10.00	35.00	50.00	100	—
1968 (B)	246,390,000	0.60	1.20	2.00	4.00	—
1968 (C)	Inc. above	0.60	1.20	2.00	4.00	—
1968 (H)	Inc. above	0.60	1.20	2.00	4.00	—
1969 (B)	—	0.60	1.20	2.00	4.00	—
1969 B	9,147	PF63 25.00				
1969 (C)	7,025,000	1.00	2.00	4.00	8.00	—
1969 (H)	Inc. above	4.00	7.00	10.00	15.00	—
1970 (B)	—	—	—	5.00	—	—
Note: 1970(B) is found only in the uncirculated sets of that year; It has a mirror-like surface.						
1970 B	3,046	PF63 5.00				
1970 (C)	15,300,000	0.60	1.20	2.00	4.00	—
1971 B	4,375	PF63 5.00				
1971 (C)	203,100,000	0.60	1.20	2.00	4.00	—
1971 (H)	Inc. above	0.60	1.20	2.00	4.00	—

KM# 15 3 PAISE

Aluminum **Obv:** Asoka lion pedestal **Rev:** Denomination and date **Shape:** 6-sided **Note:** Type 2.

Date	Mintage	VF20	XF40	MS60	MS63	MS65
1972 B	7,895	PF63 10.00				
1973 B	7,562	PF63 10.00				
1974 B	—	PF63 10.00				
1975 B	—	PF63 10.00				
1976 B	—	PF63 10.00				
1977 B	—	PF63 10.00				
1978 B	—	PF63 10.00				
1979 B	—	PF63 10.00				

KM# 16 5 NAYE PAISE

4.05 g., Copper-Nickel, 22 mm. **Obv:** Asoka lion pedestal **Rev:** Denomination and date **Shape:** Rounded square

Date	Mintage	VF20	XF40	MS60	MS63	MS65
1957 (B)	227,210,000	0.60	1.20	2.00	4.00	—
1957 (C)	Inc. above	0.60	1.20	2.00	4.00	—
1958 (B)	214,320,000	0.60	1.20	2.00	4.00	—
1958 (C)	Inc. above	0.60	1.20	2.00	4.00	—
1959 (B)	137,105,000	0.60	1.20	2.00	4.00	—
1959 (C)	Inc. above	2.00	4.00	6.00	18.00	—
1960 (B)	93,345,000	0.60	1.20	2.00	4.00	—
1960 (B)	—	PF63 50.00				
1960 (C)	Inc. above	2.00	3.00	4.00	6.00	—
1960 (Hy)	Inc. above	6.00	10.00	50.00	—	—
1961 (B)	197,620,000	0.60	1.20	2.00	4.00	—
1961 (B)	—	PF63 50.00				
1961 (C)	Inc. above	0.60	1.20	2.00	4.00	—
1961 (Hy)	Inc. above	4.00	6.00	10.00	16.00	—
1962 (B)	224,277,000	0.60	1.20	2.00	4.00	—
1962 (B)	—	PF63 50.00				
1962 (C)	Inc. above	0.60	1.20	2.00	4.00	—
1962 (Hy)	Inc. above	4.00	6.00	10.00	16.00	—
1963 (B)	332,600,000	0.60	1.20	2.00	4.00	—
1963 (B)	—	PF63 50.00				
1963 (C)	Inc. above	0.60	1.20	2.00	4.00	—
1963 (H)	Inc. above	4.00	6.00	10.00	16.00	—

KM# 17 5 PAISE

4.05 g., Copper-Nickel **Obv:** Asoka lion pedestal **Rev:** Denomination and date **Shape:** Rounded square **Note:** Type 1.

Date	Mintage	VF20	XF40	MS60	MS63	MS65
1964 (B)	156,000,000	0.60	1.20	2.00	4.00	—
1964 (C)	Inc. above	0.60	1.20	2.00	4.00	—
1964 (H)	Inc. above	10.00	15.00	20.00	50.00	—
1965 (B)	203,855,000	0.60	1.20	2.00	4.00	—
1965 (C)	Inc. above	0.60	1.20	2.00	4.00	—
1965 (H)	Inc. above	10.00	15.00	20.00	50.00	—
1966 (B)	101,395,000	6.00	8.00	10.00	20.00	—
1966 (C)	Inc. above	6.00	8.00	10.00	20.00	—

KM# 18.1 5 PAISE

Aluminum **Obv:** Asoka lion pedestal **Rev:** Denomination and date, 6mm "5" **Shape:** 4-sided **Note:** Type 1.

Date	Mintage	VF20	XF40	MS60	MS63	MS65
1967 (B)	608,533,000	2.00	4.00	6.00	9.00	—
1967 (C)	—	0.60	1.20	2.00	4.00	—

KM# 18.2 5 PAISE

Aluminum **Obv:** Asoka lion pedestal **Rev:** Denomination and date, 7mm "5". **Note:** Type 1.

Date	Mintage	VF20	XF40	MS60	MS63	MS65
1967 (B)	Inc. above	2.00	4.00	6.00	9.00	—
1967 (C)	Inc. above	0.60	1.20	2.00	4.00	—
1967 (H)	Inc. above	0.60	1.20	2.00	4.00	—
1968 (B)	—	10.00	25.00	40.00	75.00	—
1968 (C)	—	10.00	25.00	40.00	75.00	—
1968 (H)	666,750,000	10.00	25.00	50.00	75.00	—
1971 (H)	499,200,000	0.60	1.20	2.00	4.00	—

KM# 18.3 5 PAISE

1.50 g., Aluminum **Obv:** Asoka lion pedestal **Rev:** Denomination and date, 7mm "5" **Note:** Type 2.

Date	Mintage	VF20	XF40	MS60	MS63	MS65
1967 (H)	—	10.00	25.00	40.00	75.00	—
1968 (B)	—	0.60	1.20	2.00	4.00	—
Note: Mintage included in KM18.2						
1968 (C)	—	0.60	1.20	2.00	4.00	—
Note: Mintage included in KM18.2						
1968 (H)	—	0.60	1.20	2.00	4.00	—
Note: Mintage included in KM18.2						
1969 (B)	3,740,000	20.00	35.00	50.00	100	—
1969 B	9,147	PF63 75.00				
1970 (B)	39,900,000	8.00	15.00	20.00	35.00	—
1970 B	3,046	PF63 40.00				
1970 (C)	Inc. above	6.00	8.00	10.00	18.00	—
1970 (H)	Inc. above	6.00	8.00	10.00	18.00	—
1971 (B)	—	0.60	1.20	2.00	4.00	—
Note: Included with 1971(H) of KM18.2						
1971 B	4,375	PF63 10.00				
1971 (C)	Inc. above	0.60	1.20	2.00	4.00	—
1971 (H)	—	0.60	1.20	2.00	4.00	—

KM# 18.4 5 PAISE

Aluminum **Obv:** Asoka lion pedestal **Rev:** Larger 11mm "5", date **Note:** Type 1.

Date	Mintage	VF20	XF40	MS60	MS63	MS65
1972 (H)	512,430,000	6.00	8.00	10.00	15.00	—

KM# 18.6 5 PAISE

1.53 g., Aluminum, 20 mm. **Obv:** Asoka lion pedestal **Rev:** Denomination and date **Shape:** Rounded-off square **Note:** Type 2.

Date	Mintage	VF20	XF40	MS60	MS63	MS65
1972 (B)	—	0.60	1.20	2.00	4.00	—
Note: Mintage included in KM18.4						
1972 (C)	—	0.60	1.20	2.00	4.00	—
Note: Mintage included in KM18.4						
1972 (H)	—	10.00	15.00	20.00	35.00	—
1972 B	7,895	PF63 8.00				
1973 (B)	—	0.60	1.20	2.00	4.00	—
1973 B	7,562	PF63 8.00				
1973 (C)	—	0.60	1.20	2.00	4.00	—
1973 (H)	—	0.60	1.20	2.00	4.00	—
1974 B	—	PF63 8.00				
1974 (B)	—	0.60	1.20	2.00	—	—
1974 (C)	—	0.60	1.20	2.00	—	—
1974 (H)	—	0.60	1.20	2.00	—	—
1975 (B)	—	0.60	1.20	2.00	—	—
1975 B	—	PF63 8.00				
1975 (C)	289,080,000	0.60	1.20	2.00	4.00	—
1975 (H)	Inc. above	0.60	1.20	2.00	4.00	—
1976 (B)	53,205,000	0.60	1.20	2.00	4.00	—
1976 (C)	—	0.60	1.20	2.00	4.00	—
1976 (H)	—	0.60	1.20	2.00	4.00	—
1977 (B)	257,899,999	0.60	1.20	2.00	4.00	—
1977 (C)	Inc. above	0.60	1.20	2.00	4.00	—
1977 (H)	Inc. above	0.60	1.20	2.00	4.00	—
1978 B	—	0.60	1.20	2.00	4.00	—
1978 (C)	—	0.60	1.20	2.00	4.00	—
1978 (H)	—	0.60	1.20	2.00	4.00	—
1979 (B)	—	0.60	1.20	2.00	4.00	—
1979 (C)	—	0.60	1.20	2.00	4.00	—
1979 (H)	—	0.60	1.20	2.00	4.00	—
1980 (B)	21,440,000	0.60	1.20	2.00	4.00	—
1980 B	—	PF63 8.00				
1980 (C)	Inc. above	10.00	30.00	50.00	75.00	—
1980 (H)	Inc. above	0.60	1.20	2.00	4.00	—
1981 B	—	PF63 8.00				
1981 (C)	4,365,000	0.60	1.20	2.00	4.00	—
1981 (H)	Inc. above	0.60	1.20	2.00	4.00	—
Note: Due to faulty dies, 1981(H) often resembles the non-existent 1981(B).						
1982 B	3,499,000	PF63 8.00				
1982 (C)	Inc. above	0.60	1.20	2.00	4.00	—
1982 (H)	Inc. above	0.60	1.20	2.00	4.00	—
1983 (C)	3,110,000	0.60	1.20	2.00	4.00	—
1983 (H)	Inc. above	0.60	1.20	2.00	4.00	—
1984 (C)	—	0.60	1.20	2.00	4.00	—
1984 (H)	Inc. above	0.60	1.20	2.00	4.00	—

KM# 18.5 5 PAISE

Aluminum **Obv:** Asoka lion pedestal **Rev:** Larger 11mm "5", date **Note:** Type 1. Varieties in Hindi style exist.

Date	Mintage	VF20	XF40	MS60	MS63	MS65
1973 (H)	—	10.00	15.00	20.00	35.00	—
1977 (B)	—	10.00	15.00	20.00	35.00	—
1978 (B)	—	6.00	8.00	10.00	18.00	—

KM# 19 5 PAISE

1.51 g., Aluminum, 22 mm. **Series:** F.A.O. **Subject:** Food and Work For All **Obv:** Asoka lion pedestal **Rev:** Figure on tractor, utility pole and buildings in background **Edge:** Plain **Shape:** Square **Note:** 18.95mm x 18.95mm.

Date	Mintage	VF20	XF40	MS60	MS63	MS65
1976 (B)	34,680,000	1.00	2.00	3.00	5.00	—
1976 B	—	PF63 8.00				
1976 (C)	60,040,000	1.00	2.00	3.00	5.00	—
1976 (H)	60,290,000	1.00	2.00	3.00	5.00	—

KM# 20 5 PAISE

1.50 g., Aluminum **Series:** F.A.O. **Subject:** Save For Development **Obv:** Asoka lion pedestal **Rev:** Symbols and date **Shape:** Square

Date	Mintage	VF20	XF40	MS60	MS63	MS65
1977 (B)	20,100,000	1.00	2.00	3.00	—	—
1977 B	2,224	PF63 8.00				
1977 (C)	40,470,000	1.00	2.00	3.00	—	—
1977 (H)	20,380,000	1.00	2.00	3.00	—	—

KM# 21 5 PAISE

Aluminum **Series:** F.A.O. **Subject:** Food and Shelter For All **Obv:** Asoka lion pedestal **Rev:** Building, grain sprig and road within circle **Shape:** Square

Date	Mintage	VF20	XF40	MS60	MS63	MS65
1978 (B)	28,440,000	1.00	2.00	3.00	5.00	—
1978 B	—	PF63 8.00				
1978 (C)	30,870,000	1.00	2.00	3.00	5.00	—
1978 (H)	21,100,000	1.00	2.00	3.00	5.00	—

KM# 22 5 PAISE

1.52 g., Aluminum **Series:** International Year of the Child **Obv:** Asoka lion pedestal **Rev:** Logo within circle, wreath surrounds **Shape:** Square

Date	Mintage	VF20	XF40	MS60	MS63	MS65
1979 (B)	39,860,000	1.00	2.00	3.00	5.00	—
1979 B	—	PF63 8.00				
1979 (C)	80,370,000	1.00	2.00	3.00	5.00	—
1979 (H)	1,100,000	1.00	2.00	3.00	5.00	—

KM# 23 5 PAISE

1.52 g., Aluminum **Obv:** Satymave Jayate Below Ashoka Lion Pedestal **Rev:** Denomination and date

Date	Mintage	VF20	XF40	MS60	MS63	MS65
1984 (C)	—	40.00	70.00	100	175	—

KM# 23 5 PAISE

1.03 g., Aluminum, 22x22 mm. **Obv:** Asoka lion pedestal **Rev:** Denomination and date **Edge:** Plain **Shape:** Square **Note:** Weight reduced.

Date	Mintage	VF20	XF40	MS60	MS63	MS65
1985 (B)	54,860,000	10.00	15.00	20.00	35.00	—
1985 (C)	Inc. above	20.00	25.00	30.00	50.00	—
1985 (H)	Inc. above	0.60	1.20	2.00	4.00	—
1986 (C)	—	0.60	1.20	2.00	4.00	—
1986 (H)	—	0.60	1.20	2.00	4.00	—
1987 (C)	—	0.60	1.20	2.00	4.00	—
1987 (H)	—	0.60	1.20	2.00	4.00	—
1988 (C)	—	0.60	1.20	2.00	4.00	—
1988 (H)	—	0.60	1.20	2.00	4.00	—
1989 (C)	—	0.60	1.20	2.00	4.00	—
1989 (H)	—	0.60	1.20	2.00	4.00	—
1990 (B)	—	4.00	7.00	10.00	16.00	—
1990 (C)	—	0.60	1.20	2.00	4.00	—
1990 (H)	—	0.60	1.20	2.00	4.00	—
1991 (C)	—	0.60	1.20	2.00	4.00	—
1991 (H)	—	0.60	1.20	2.00	4.00	—
1992 (B)	—	4.00	7.00	10.00	16.00	—
1992 (H)	—	0.60	1.20	2.00	4.00	—
1993 (C)	—	6.00	8.00	10.00	16.00	—
1993 (H)	—	0.60	1.20	2.00	4.00	—
1994 (H)	—	0.60	1.20	2.00	4.00	—

KM# 24.1 10 NAYE PAISE

4.85 g., Copper-Nickel, 23 mm. **Obv:** Asoka lion pedestal **Rev:** Denomination and date, 6.5mm "10" **Shape:** Scalloped

Date	Mintage	VF20	XF40	MS60	MS63	MS65
1957 (B)	139,655,000	1.00	1.50	2.00	3.00	—
1957 (C)	Inc. above	1.00	1.50	2.00	3.00	—

KM# 24.2 10 NAYE PAISE

5.00 g., Copper-Nickel, 23 mm. **Obv:** Asoka lion pedestal **Rev:** Denomination and date, 7mm "10"

Date	Mintage	VF20	XF40	MS60	MS63	MS65
1958 (B)	123,160,000	1.00	1.50	2.00	3.00	—
1958 (C)	Inc. above	1.00	1.50	2.00	3.00	—
1959 (B)	148,570,000	1.00	1.50	2.00	3.00	—
1959 (C)	Inc. above	1.00	1.50	2.00	3.00	—
1960 (B)	52,335,000	2.00	3.00	4.00	7.00	—
1960 (B)	—	PF63 40.00				
1961 (B)	172,545,000	1.00	1.50	2.00	3.00	—
1961 (B)	—	PF63 9.00				
1961 (C)	Inc. above	1.00	1.50	2.00	3.00	—
1961 (Hy)	Inc. above	4.00	6.00	8.00	17.00	—
1962 (B)	172,777,000	1.00	1.50	2.00	3.00	—
1962 (B)	—	PF63 8.00				
1962 (C)	Inc. above	1.00	1.50	2.00	3.00	—
1962 (Hy)	Inc. above	4.00	5.00	6.00	10.00	—
1963 (B)	182,834,000	1.00	1.50	2.00	3.00	—
1963 (B)	—	PF63 8.00				
1963 (C)	Inc. above	1.00	1.50	2.00	3.00	—
1963 (H)	Inc. above	4.00	6.00	10.00	17.00	—

KM# 25 10 PAISE

Copper-Nickel, 23 mm. **Obv:** Asoka lion pedestal **Rev:** Denomination and date, 6.5mm "10" **Shape:** Scalloped **Note:** Type 1.

Date	Mintage	VF20	XF40	MS60	MS63	MS65
1964 (B) Open 4	84,112,000	1.00	1.50	2.00	3.00	—
1964 (B) Closed 4	Inc. above	6.00	8.00	10.00	16.00	—
1964 (C)	Inc. above	2.00	3.00	4.00	7.00	—
1964 (H)	Inc. above	4.00	5.00	6.00	10.00	—
1965 (B)	253,430,000	1.00	1.50	2.00	3.00	—
1965 (C)	Inc. above	1.00	1.50	2.00	3.00	—
1965 (Hy) Dot in Diamond	Inc. above	10.00	20.00	30.00	50.00	—
1965 (H) Star MM	Inc. above	2.00	3.00	4.00	7.00	—
1966 (B)	326,990,000	1.00	1.50	2.00	3.00	—
1966 (C)	Inc. above	1.00	1.50	2.00	3.00	—
1966 (Hy)	Inc. above	1.00	1.50	2.00	3.00	—
1967 (B)	59,443,000	2.00	3.00	4.00	7.00	—
1967 (C)	Inc. above	2.00	3.00	4.00	7.00	—
1967 (H)	Inc. above	3.00	5.00	7.00	12.00	—

KM# 26.1 10 PAISE

4.24 g., Nickel-Brass, 23 mm. **Obv:** Asoka lion pedestal **Rev:** Denomination and date **Note:** Type 1.

Date	Mintage	VF20	XF40	MS60	MS63	MS65
1968 (H)	55,940,000	10.00	25.00	40.00	60.00	—

KM# 26.2 10 PAISE

4.24 g., Nickel-Brass, 23 mm. **Obv:** Asoka lion pedestal **Rev:** 6.5mm "10", date **Shape:** Scalloped **Note:** Type 2. Mintage included in KM26.1. Some, not all, have die damage in 9 of 1968.

Date	Mintage	VF20	XF40	MS60	MS63	MS65
1968 (B)	—	1.00	1.50	2.00	3.00	—
1968 (C)	—	1.00	1.50	2.00	3.00	—
1968 (H)	—	1.00	1.50	2.00	3.00	—

KM# 26.3 10 PAISE

4.18 g., Nickel-Brass, 23 mm. **Obv:** Asoka lion pedestal **Rev:** Denomination and date, 7mm "10" **Shape:** Scalloped **Note:** Type 2.

Date	Mintage	VF20	XF40	MS60	MS63	MS65
1969 (B)	65,405,000	1.00	1.50	2.00	—	—
1969 B	9,147	PF63 15.00				
1969 (C)	Inc. above	1.00	1.50	2.00	—	—
1969 (H)	Inc. above	1.00	1.50	2.00	—	—
1970 (B)	48,400,000	1.00	1.50	2.00	—	—
1970 B	3,046	PF63 8.00				
1970 (C)	Inc. above	1.00	1.50	2.00	—	—
1971 (B)	88,800,000	1.00	1.50	2.00	—	—
1971 B	4,375	PF63 8.00				

KM# 27.1 10 PAISE

2.30 g., Aluminum, 26 mm. **Obv:** Asoka lion pedestal within beaded circle, wreath surrounds **Rev:** Denomination and date within beaded circle, wreath surrounds, 9mm "10 **Shape:** Scalloped **Note:** Type 2.

Date	Mintage	VF20	XF40	MS60	MS63	MS65
1971 (B)	146,100,000	1.00	1.50	2.00	3.00	—
1971 (C)	Inc. above	1.00	1.50	2.00	3.00	—
1971 (H)	Inc. above	1.00	1.50	2.00	3.00	—
1972 (B)	735,090,000	1.00	1.50	2.00	3.00	—
1972 B	7,895	PF63 8.00				
1972 (C)	Inc. above	1.00	1.50	2.00	3.00	—
1973 (B)	—	1.00	1.50	2.00	3.00	—
1973 B	7,567	PF63 8.00				
1973 (C)	—	1.00	1.50	2.00	3.00	—
1973 (H)	—	4.00	6.00	10.00	16.00	—
1974 (B)	—	1.00	1.50	2.00	3.00	—
1974 (C)	—	1.00	1.50	2.00	3.00	—
1974 (H)	—	10.00	15.00	20.00	28.00	—
1975 (B)	—	2.00	3.00	4.00	6.00	—
1975 (C)	298,830,000	2.00	3.00	4.00	6.00	—
1976 (C)	Inc. above	4.00	5.00	6.00	10.00	—
1977 (B)	25,288,000	6.00	7.00	8.00	12.00	—
1977 (C)	Inc. above	6.00	7.00	8.00	12.00	—
1978 (B)	48,215,000	1.00	1.50	2.00	3.00	—
1978 (C)	Inc. above	1.00	1.50	2.00	3.00	—
1978 (H)	Inc. above	1.00	1.50	2.00	3.00	—

KM# 27.2 10 PAISE

Aluminum, 26 mm. **Obv:** Asoka lion pedestal within beaded circle, wreath surrounds **Rev:** Denomination and date within beaded circle, wreath surrounds, 8mm "10" **Shape:** Scalloped **Note:** Type 2.

Date	Mintage	VF20	XF40	MS60	MS63	MS65
1979 (B)	—	2.00	3.00	4.00	7.00	—
1979 (H)	—	2.00	3.00	4.00	7.00	—
1980 (C)	—	40.00	60.00	100	150	—

KM# 27.3 10 PAISE

2.31 g., Aluminum, 26 mm. **Obv:** Asoka lion pedestal within beaded circle, wreath surrounds **Rev:** Denomination and date within beaded circle, wreath surrounds **Note:** Type 3.

Date	Mintage	VF20	XF40	MS60	MS63	MS65
1980 (B)	—	1.00	1.50	2.00	3.00	—
1980 (C)	—	1.00	1.50	2.00	3.00	—
1980 (H)	—	1.00	1.50	2.00	3.00	—
1981 (B)	—	1.00	1.50	2.00	3.00	—
1981 (C)	—	1.00	1.50	2.00	3.00	—
1982 (C)	—	1.00	1.50	2.00	3.00	—
1982 (H)	—	1.00	1.50	2.00	3.00	—

KM# 28 10 PAISE

2.29 g., Aluminum, 26 mm. **Series:** F.A.O. **Obv:** Asoka lion pedestal **Rev:** Family above date within triangle, grain sprigs flank **Shape:** Scalloped

Date	Mintage	VF20	XF40	MS60	MS63	MS65
1974 (B)	146,070,000	1.00	1.50	2.00	3.00	—
1974 B	—	PF63 10.00				
1974 (C)	168,500,000	1.00	1.50	2.00	3.00	—
1974 (H)	10,010,000	10.00	15.00	20.00	30.00	—

KM# 29 10 PAISE

2.29 g., Aluminum, 26 mm. **Series:** F.A.O. **Subject:** Women's Year **Obv:** Asoka lion pedestal **Rev:** Bust at left looking right, grain sprig at right **Shape:** Scalloped **Note:** Mint mark is below wheat stalk.

Date	Mintage	VF20	XF40	MS60	MS63	MS65
1975 (B)	69,160,000	1.50	2.00	3.00	—	—
1975 B	—	PF63 8.00				
1975 (C)	84,820,000	1.50	2.00	3.00	—	—

KM# 30 10 PAISE

2.29 g., Aluminum, 26 mm. **Series:** F.A.O. **Subject:** Food and Work For All **Obv:** Asoka lion pedestal **Rev:** Figure on tractor, utility pole and buildings in background **Shape:** Scalloped

Date	Mintage	VF20	XF40	MS60	MS63	MS65
1976 (B)	36,040,000	2.00	3.00	4.00	6.00	—
1976 B	—	PF63 11.00				
1976 (C)	26,180,000	2.00	3.00	4.00	6.00	—

KM# 31 10 PAISE

2.29 g., Aluminum, 26 mm. **Series:** F.A.O. **Subject:** Save For Development **Obv:** Asoka lion pedestal **Rev:** Symbols and date **Shape:** Scalloped

Date	Mintage	VF20	XF40	MS60	MS63	MS65
1977 (B)	17,040,000	2.00	3.00	4.00	6.00	—
1977 B	2,224	PF63 8.00				
1977 (C)	8,020,000	2.00	3.00	4.00	6.00	—

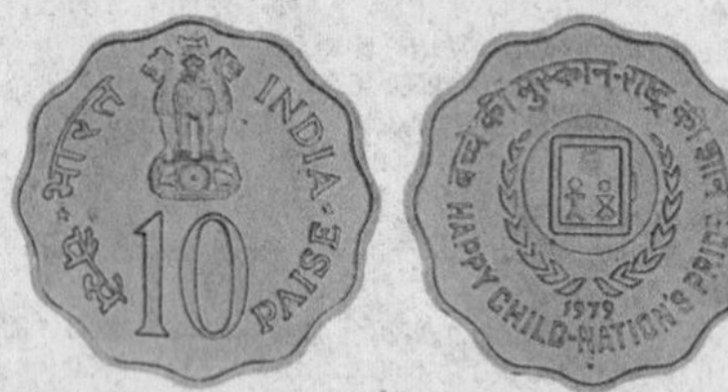

KM# 32 10 PAISE

2.29 g., Aluminum, 26 mm. **Series:** F.A.O. **Subject:** Food and Shelter For All **Obv:** Asoka lion pedestal **Rev:** Building, grain sprig and road within circle **Shape:** Scalloped

Date	Mintage	VF20	XF40	MS60	MS63	MS65
1978 (B)	24,470,000	1.00	1.50	2.00	—	—
1978 B	—	PF63 8.00				
1978 (C)	26,160,000	1.00	1.50	2.00	—	—
1978 (H)	12,100,000	1.00	1.50	2.00	—	—

KM# 33 10 PAISE

2.29 g., Aluminum, 26 mm. **Series:** International Year of the Child **Obv:** Asoka lion pedestal **Rev:** Logo on square within circle, wreath surrounds **Shape:** Scalloped

Date	Mintage	VF20	XF40	MS60	MS63	MS65
1979 (B)	39,270,000	1.00	1.50	2.00	—	—
1979 B	—	PF63 8.00				
1979 (C)	61,700,000	1.00	1.50	2.00	—	—
1979 (H)	2,250,000	1.00	1.50	2.00	—	—

KM# 34 10 PAISE

2.29 g., Aluminum, 26 mm. **Obv:** Asoka lion pedestal, denomination below **Rev:** Emblem on square, within circle, wreath surrounds, date below **Note:** Mule.

Date	Mintage	VF20	XF40	MS60	MS63	MS65
1979 (B)	—	40.00	65.00	100	175	—

KM# 35 10 PAISE

2.29 g., Aluminum, 26 mm. **Subject:** Rural Women's Advancement **Obv:** Asoka lion pedestal **Rev:** Woman grinding wheat within circle **Shape:** Scalloped

Date	Mintage	VF20	XF40	MS60	MS63	MS65
1980 (B)	38,080,000	1.00	1.50	2.00	—	—
1980 B	—	**PF63** 8.00				
1980 (C)	42,830,000	1.00	1.50	2.00	—	—
1980 (H)	11,070,000	1.00	1.50	2.00	—	—

KM# 36 10 PAISE

2.30 g., Aluminum, 26 mm. **Subject:** World Food Day **Obv:** Asoka lion pedestal **Rev:** Man and woman, man carrying sheaf **Shape:** Scalloped

Date	Mintage	VF20	XF40	MS60	MS63	MS65
1981 (B)	83,280,000	1.00	1.50	2.00	—	—
1981 B	—	**PF63** 8.00				
1981 (C)	33,930,000	1.00	1.50	2.00	—	—

KM# 37 10 PAISE

2.29 g., Aluminum, 26 mm. **Subject:** IX Asian Games **Obv:** Asoka lion pedestal **Rev:** Sun above symbol **Shape:** Scalloped

Date	Mintage	VF20	XF40	MS60	MS63	MS65
1982 (B)	—	1.00	1.50	2.00	3.00	—
1982 B	—	**PF63** 8.00				
1982 (C)	30,560,000	1.00	1.50	2.00	3.00	—
1982 (H)	17,080,000	1.00	1.50	2.00	3.00	—

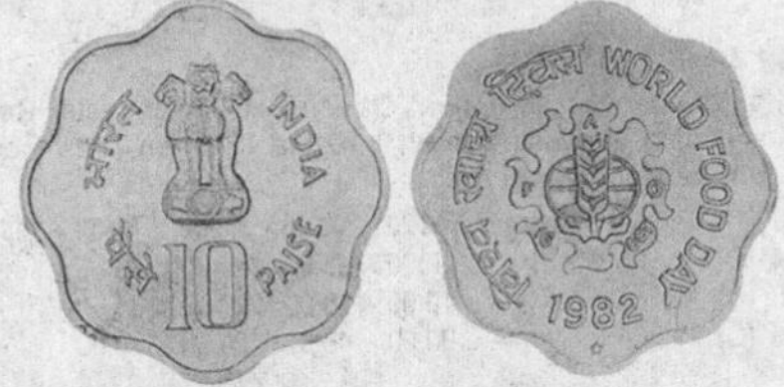

KM# 38 10 PAISE

2.29 g., Aluminum, 23 mm. **Subject:** World Food Day **Obv:** Asoka lion pedestal **Rev:** Grain sprig within stylized sun design **Shape:** Scalloped

Date	Mintage	VF20	XF40	MS60	MS63	MS65
1982 (C)	2,970,000	5.00	6.00	10.00	17.00	—
1982 (H)	11,690,000	4.00	6.00	6.00	10.00	—

KM# 39 10 PAISE

2.30 g., Aluminum, 26 mm. **Obv:** Asoka lion pedestal **Rev:** Denomination and date **Shape:** Scalloped

Date	Mintage	VF20	XF40	MS60	MS63	MS65
1983 (B)	—	1.00	1.50	2.00	3.00	—
1983 (C)	—	1.00	1.50	2.00	3.00	—
1983 (H)	—	1.00	1.50	2.00	3.00	—
1984 (B)	112,050,000	1.00	1.50	2.00	3.00	—
1984 (C)	Inc. above	1.00	1.50	2.00	3.00	—
1984 (H)	Inc. above	1.00	1.50	2.00	3.00	—
1985 (B)	184,655,000	1.00	1.50	2.00	3.00	—
1985 (C)	Inc. above	1.00	1.50	2.00	3.00	—
1985 (H)	Inc. above	2.00	3.00	4.00	6.00	—
1986 (B)	298,525,000	1.00	1.50	2.00	3.00	—
1986 (C)	Inc. above	1.00	1.50	2.00	3.00	—
1986 (H)	Inc. above	1.00	1.50	2.00	3.00	—
1987 (C)	299,460,000	1.00	1.50	2.00	3.00	—
1987 (H)	Inc. above	1.00	1.50	2.00	3.00	—
1988 (B)	264,510,000	1.00	1.50	2.00	3.00	—
1988 (C)	Inc. above	1.00	1.50	2.00	3.00	—
1988 (H)	Inc. above	2.00	3.00	4.00	6.00	—
1989 (B)	—	1.00	1.50	2.00	3.00	—
1989 (C)	—	1.00	1.50	2.00	3.00	—
1989 (H)	—	1.00	1.50	2.00	3.00	—
1990 (B)	—	2.00	3.00	4.00	6.00	—
1991 (B)	—	1.00	1.50	2.00	3.00	—
1991 (C)	—	1.00	1.50	2.00	3.00	—
1991 (H)	—	1.00	1.50	2.00	3.00	—
1993 (C)	—	2.00	3.00	4.00	6.00	—

KM# 40.1 10 PAISE

2.00 g., Stainless Steel, 16 mm. **Obv:** Asoka lion pedestal **Obv. Legend:** BHARAT **Rev:** Denomination and date

Date	Mintage	VF20	XF40	MS60	MS63	MS65
1988 C	183,040,000	4.00	6.00	10.00	15.00	—
1988 (B)	4,040,000	0.60	1.00	1.50	2.00	—
1988 (C)	Inc. above	0.60	1.00	1.50	2.00	—
1988 (H)	Inc. above	1.00	1.50	2.00	3.00	—
1988 (N)	—	0.60	1.00	1.50	2.00	—
1989 (B)	—	0.60	1.00	1.50	2.00	—
1989 (C)	—	0.60	1.00	1.50	2.00	—
1989 (H)	—	0.60	1.00	1.50	2.00	—
1989 (N)	—	0.60	1.00	1.50	2.00	—
1990 (B)	—	0.60	1.00	1.50	2.00	—
1990 (C)	—	0.60	1.00	1.50	2.00	—
1990 (H)	—	0.60	1.00	1.50	2.00	—
1990 (N)	—	0.60	1.00	1.50	2.00	—
Small mm						
1990 (N)	—	0.60	1.00	1.50	2.00	—
Large mm						
1991 (C)	—	0.60	1.00	1.50	2.00	—
1991 (H)	—	0.60	1.00	1.50	2.00	—
1991 (N)	—	0.60	1.00	1.50	2.00	—
1992 (N)	—	0.60	1.00	1.50	2.00	—
1993 (H)	—	2.00	3.00	4.00	6.00	—
1996 (B)	—	0.60	1.00	1.50	2.00	—
1996 (C)	—	0.60	1.00	1.50	2.00	—
1996 (N)	—	0.60	1.00	1.50	2.00	—
1997 (B)	—	0.60	1.00	1.50	2.00	—
1997 (C)	—	2.00	3.00	4.00	6.00	—
1997 (H)	—	0.60	1.00	1.50	2.00	—
1998 (B)	—	1.00	1.50	2.00	3.00	—
1998 (C)	—	1.00	1.50	2.00	3.00	—

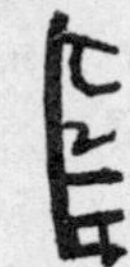

KM# 40.2 10 PAISE

2.03 g., Stainless Steel, 15.95 mm. **Obv:** Error: MARAT for BHARAT **Rev:** Denomination and date **Edge:** Plain

Date	Mintage	VF20	XF40	MS60	MS63	MS65
1988 C	—	3.00	5.00	7.00	10.00	—
1989 C	—	3.50	5.50	8.00	11.00	—

KM# 41 20 PAISE

Nickel-Brass **Obv:** Asoka lion pedestal **Rev:** Lotus blossom **Note:** Varieties of high and low date exist.

Date	Mintage	VF20	XF40	MS60	MS63	MS65
1968 (B)	10,585,000	1.00	1.50	2.00	3.00	—
1968 (C)	Inc. above	2.00	4.00	6.00	8.00	—
1969 (B)	197,940,000	2.00	3.00	4.00	6.00	—
1969 (C)	—	1.00	1.50	2.00	3.00	—
1970 (B)	Inc. above	1.00	1.50	2.00	3.00	—
1970 (C)	Inc. above	1.00	1.50	2.00	3.00	—
1970 (H)	Inc. above	1.00	1.50	2.00	3.00	—
1971 (B)	124,200,000	1.00	1.50	2.00	3.00	—

KM# 42.1 20 PAISE

4.45 g., Aluminum-Bronze **Subject:** Centennial - Birth of Mahatma Gandhi **Obv:** Asoka lion pedestal **Obv. Legend:** .7-.9 from rims **Rev:** Head left

Date	Mintage	VF20	XF40	MS60	MS63	MS65
ND-1969 (B)	45,010	1.00	2.00	3.00	—	—
ND-1969 B	9,147	**PF63** 20.00				
ND-1969 (C)	45,070,000	1.00	2.00	3.00	—	—
ND-1969 (H)	3,000,000	1.00	3.00	4.00	—	—

KM# 42.2 20 PAISE

4.45 g., Aluminum-Bronze **Obv:** Asoka lion pedestal **Obv. Legend:** 1.2mm from rim **Rev:** Head left

Date	Mintage	VF20	XF40	MS60	MS63	MS65
ND-1969 (B)	—	4.00	5.00	6.00	8.00	—
ND-1969 (C)	—	6.00	8.00	10.00	12.00	—

KM# 42.3 20 PAISE

4.45 g., Aluminum-Bronze **Obv:** Asoka lion pedestal **Rev:** Head left **Note:** Eyes, mustache recut, legends 1.2mm from rim.

Date	Mintage	VF20	XF40	MS60	MS63	MS65
ND-1969 (B)	—	1.00	2.00	3.00	5.00	—

Note: The KM 42 subtypes were struck during 1969 and 1970

KM# 43.1 20 PAISE

4.45 g., Aluminum-Bronze **Series:** F.A.O. **Subject:** Food For All **Obv:** Asoka lion pedestal **Rev:** Sun above floating lotus **Note:** Wide rims.

Date	Mintage	VF20	XF40	MS60	MS63	MS65
1970 (B)	5,160,000	2.00	4.00	6.00	8.00	—
1970 B	3,046	**PF63** 20.00				
1970 (C)	5,010,000	2.00	4.00	6.00	8.00	—

KM# 43.2 20 PAISE

4.45 g., Aluminum-Bronze **Obv:** Asoka lion pedestal **Rev:** Sun above floating lotus **Note:** Narrow rims.

Date	Mintage	VF20	XF40	MS60	MS63	MS65
1971 B	4,375	**PF63** 20.00				

KM# 44 20 PAISE

2.15 g., Aluminum, 26 mm. **Obv:** Asoka lion pedestal **Rev:** Denomination and date within decorative wreath **Shape:** 6-sided

Date	Mintage	VF20	XF40	MS60	MS63	MS65
1982 (B)	—	1.00	2.00	3.00	5.00	—
1982 (H)	—	2.00	3.00	4.00	6.00	—
1982 (H)	—	1.00	2.00	3.00	5.00	—
Without mm						
1983 (C)	28,505,000	1.00	2.00	3.00	5.00	—
1983 (H)	Inc. above	1.00	2.00	3.00	5.00	—
1984 (B)	—	1.00	2.00	3.00	5.00	—
1984 (C)	Inc. above	1.00	2.00	3.00	5.00	—
1984 (H)	Inc. above	1.00	2.00	3.00	5.00	—
1985 (B)	84,495,000	1.00	2.00	3.00	5.00	—
1985 (C)	Inc. above	1.00	2.00	3.00	5.00	—
1985 (H)	Inc. above	1.00	2.00	3.00	5.00	—
1986 (B)	155,610,000	1.00	2.00	3.00	5.00	—
1986 (C)	Inc. above	1.00	2.00	3.00	5.00	—
1986 (H)	Inc. above	1.00	2.00	3.00	5.00	—
1987 (C)	—	1.00	2.00	3.00	5.00	—
1987 (H)	153,073,000	1.00	2.00	3.00	5.00	—
1988 (B)	125,048,000	1.00	2.00	3.00	5.00	—

Date	Mintage	VF20	XF40	MS60	MS63	MS65
1988 (C)	Inc. above	1.00	2.00	3.00	5.00	—
1988 (H)	Inc. above	1.00	2.00	3.00	5.00	—
1989 (C)	—	1.00	2.00	3.00	5.00	—
1989 (H)	—	1.00	2.00	3.00	5.00	—
1990 (C)	—	1.00	2.00	3.00	5.00	—
1990 (H)	—	1.00	2.00	3.00	5.00	—
1991 (C)	—	1.00	2.00	3.00	5.00	—
1991 (H)	—	1.00	2.00	3.00	5.00	—
1992 (H)	—	2.00	3.00	4.00	5.00	—
1994 (H)	—	2.00	3.00	4.00	5.00	—
1996 (H)	—	10.00	15.00	20.00	25.00	—
1997 (H)	—	10.00	20.00	40.00	60.00	—

KM# 45 20 PAISE

Aluminum **Series:** F.A.O. **Obv:** Asoka lion pedestal **Rev:** Grain sprig within stylized sun design **Shape:** 6-sided

Date	Mintage	VF20	XF40	MS60	MS63	MS65
1982 (C)	—	4.00	15.00	20.00	30.00	—
1982 (H)	—	2.00	6.00	10.00	15.00	—

KM# 46 20 PAISE

2.15 g., Aluminum, 26 mm. **Series:** F.A.O. **Subject:** Fisheries **Obv:** Asoka lion pedestal **Rev:** People with fishing nets **Shape:** 6-sided

Date	Mintage	VF20	XF40	MS60	MS63	MS65
1983 (C)	—	5.00	6.00	7.50	10.00	—
Note: Mintage included in KM44						
1983 (H)	—	5.00	6.00	7.50	10.00	—
Note: Mintage included in KM44						

KM# 47.1 25 NAYE PAISE

2.42 g., Nickel, 19 mm. **Obv:** Asoka lion pedestal **Rev:** Denomination and date

Date	Mintage	VF20	XF40	MS60	MS63	MS65
1957 (B)	5,640,000	3.00	4.00	7.00	—	—
1957 (C)	Inc. above	3.00	4.00	7.00	—	—
1959 (B)	43,080,000	2.00	3.00	4.50	—	—
1959 (C)	Inc. above	2.00	3.00	4.50	—	—
1960 (B)	115,320,000	1.50	2.00	4.00	—	—
1960 (B)	—	PF63 45.00				
1960 (C)	Inc. above	1.50	2.00	4.00	—	—

KM# 47.2 25 NAYE PAISE

2.50 g., Nickel, 19 mm. **Obv:** Asoka lion pedestal **Rev:** Denomination and date, large 25

Date	Mintage	VF20	XF40	MS60	MS63	MS65
1961 (B)	109,008,000	1.00	1.50	2.00	—	—
1961 (B)	—	PF63 8.00				
1961 (C)	Inc. above	1.00	1.50	2.00	—	—
1962 (B)	79,242,000	1.00	1.50	2.00	—	—
1962 (B)	—	PF63 8.00				
1962 (C)	Inc. above	1.00	1.50	2.00	—	—
1963 (B)	101,565,000	1.00	1.50	2.00	—	—
1963 (B)	—	PF63 8.00				
1963 (C)	Inc. above	1.00	1.50	2.00	—	—

KM# 48.1 25 PAISE

2.55 g., Nickel, 19 mm. **Obv:** Asoka lion pedestal **Rev:** Denomination and date **Note:** Type 1.

Date	Mintage	VF20	XF40	MS60	MS63	MS65
1964 (B)	85,321,000	1.00	1.50	2.00	4.00	—
1964 (C)	Inc. above	1.00	1.50	2.00	4.00	—

KM# 48.2 25 PAISE

2.55 g., Nickel, 19 mm. **Obv:** Asoka lion pedestal **Rev:** Smaller date and denomination **Note:** Type 1.

Date	Mintage	VF20	XF40	MS60	MS63	MS65
1965 (B)	143,662,000	1.00	1.50	2.00	4.00	—
1965 (C)	Inc. above	1.00	1.50	2.00	4.00	—
1966 (B)	59,040,000	1.00	1.50	2.00	4.00	—
1966 (C)	Inc. above	1.00	1.50	2.00	4.00	—
1967 (B)	30,027,000	6.00	10.00	20.00	35.00	—

KM# 48.3 25 PAISE

2.55 g., Nickel, 19 mm. **Obv:** Asoka lion pedestal **Rev:** Denomination and date **Note:** Type 2. Mintage included in KM48.2.

Date	Mintage	VF20	XF40	MS60	MS63	MS65
1967 (C)	—	2.00	3.00	4.00	7.00	—
1968 (C)	—	4.00	6.00	10.00	15.00	—

KM# 49.1 25 PAISE

2.50 g., Copper-Nickel, 19 mm. **Obv:** Asoka lion pedestal **Rev:** Denomination and date **Note:** Type 1, but lion with whiskers and faces and wheel redesigned. 1984-86 have edges rounded (local blanks) or flat (Korean blanks).

Date	Mintage	VF20	XF40	MS60	MS63	MS65
1972 (B)	367,640,000	1.00	1.50	2.00	4.00	—
1972 B	7,895	PF63 8.00				
1972 (H)	Inc. above	2.00	3.00	4.00	7.00	—
1973 (B)	—	1.00	1.50	2.00	4.00	—
1973 B	7,567	PF63 8.00				
1973 (H)	—	1.00	1.50	2.00	4.00	—
1974 (B)	—	1.00	1.50	2.00	4.00	—
1974 B	—	PF63 8.00				
1974 (H)	—	1.00	1.50	2.00	4.00	—
1975 (B)	559,980,000	1.00	1.50	2.00	4.00	—
1975 B	—	PF63 8.00				
1975 (H)	Inc. above	10.00	20.00	30.00	50.00	—
1976 (B)	30,016,000	1.00	1.50	2.00	4.00	—
1976 B	Inc. above	PF63 8.00				
1976 (H)	Inc. above	1.00	1.50	2.00	4.00	—
1977 (B)	270,520,000	1.00	1.50	2.00	4.00	—
1977 B	Inc. above	PF63 8.00				
1977 (C)	Inc. above	1.00	1.50	2.00	4.00	—
1977 (H)	Inc. above	1.00	1.50	2.00	4.00	—
1978 B	—	PF63 8.00				
1978 (C)	131,632,000	1.00	1.50	2.00	4.00	—
1978 (H)	—	1.00	1.50	2.00	4.00	—
1979 (C)	—	2.00	3.00	4.00	7.00	—
1979 (H)	—	2.00	3.00	4.00	7.00	—
1980 (C)	6,175,000	2.00	3.00	4.00	7.00	—
1980 (B)	—	400	700	1,000	—	—
1980 (H)	Inc. above	1.00	1.50	2.00	4.00	—
1981 (B)	11,048,000	1.00	1.50	2.00	4.00	—
1981 (C)	Inc. above	10.00	20.00	30.00	50.00	—
1981 (H)	Inc. above	1.00	1.50	2.00	4.00	—
1982 (B)	—	10.00	20.00	30.00	50.00	—
1982 (C)	38,288,000	10.00	20.00	30.00	50.00	—
1983 (C)	137,488,000	1.00	1.50	2.00	4.00	—
1984 (B)	98,740,000	1.00	1.50	2.00	4.00	—
1984 (C)	Inc. above	1.00	1.50	2.00	4.00	—
1984 (H)	—	30.00	40.00	60.00	100	—
1985 (B)	113,872,000	10.00	15.00	20.00	30.00	—
1985 C	Inc. above	1.00	1.50	2.00	4.00	—
1985 (C)	Inc. above	1.00	1.50	2.00	4.00	—
1985 (H)	Inc. above	1.00	1.50	2.00	4.00	—
1986 (B)	362,624,000	1.00	1.50	2.00	4.00	—
1986 (C)	Inc. above	1.00	1.50	2.00	4.00	—
1986 (H)	Inc. above	1.00	1.50	2.00	4.00	—
1987 (C)	341,160,000	1.00	1.50	2.00	4.00	—
1987 (H)	Inc. above	1.00	1.50	2.00	4.00	—
1988 (H)	303,252,000	1.00	1.50	2.00	4.00	—

KM# 49.2 25 PAISE

2.50 g., Copper-Nickel, 19 mm. **Obv:** Asoka lion pedestal **Rev:** Denomination and date **Note:** Type 2, 9mm between lions' nose tips, 15mm across field.

Date	Mintage	VF20	XF40	MS60	MS63	MS65
1972 (C)	—	1.00	1.50	2.00	4.00	—
1977 (B)	—	1.00	1.50	2.00	4.00	—
Note: Mintage included in KM49.1						
1977 B	—	PF63 12.00				
Note: Mintage included in KM49.1						
1978 (B)	—	10.00	20.00	50.00	75.00	—
Note: Mintage included in KM49.1						
1979 B	—	PF63 12.00				

KM# 49.3 25 PAISE

2.40 g., Copper-Nickel, 19 mm. **Obv:** Asoka lion pedestal **Rev:** Denomination and date **Note:** Type 2, 10mm between lion nosetips, 16-16.3mm across field. Bull has three legs.

Date	Mintage	VF20	XF40	MS60	MS63	MS65
1972 (C)	—	10.00	15.00	20.00	30.00	—
Note: Mintage included in KM49.1						
1973 (C)	—	2.00	3.00	4.00	7.00	—
1974 (C)	—	2.00	3.00	4.00	7.00	—

KM# 49.7 25 PAISE

2.50 g., Copper-Nickel, 19 mm. **Obv:** KM#48.2. **Rev:** KM#49.1. **Edge:** Reeded **Note:** Mule. Type 1, lion without whiskers.

Date	Mintage	VF20	XF40	MS60	MS63	MS65
1972 (B)	—	20.00	30.00	50.00	75.00	—

KM# 49.4 25 PAISE

2.50 g., Copper-Nickel, 19 mm. **Obv:** Asoka lion pedestal **Rev:** Denomination and date **Note:** Type 1, central lion with bull and horse re-engraved.

Date	Mintage	VF20	XF40	MS60	MS63	MS65
1974 (B)	—	20.00	30.00	40.00	60.00	—
1975 (B)	—	30.00	40.00	60.00	90.00	—
1975 (H)	—	20.00	30.00	40.00	60.00	—
1976 (H)	—	40.00	50.00	70.00	100	—
1977 (B)	—	20.00	25.00	30.00	45.00	—
1978 (B)	—	10.00	15.00	20.00	40.00	—
1979 (B)	—	20.00	25.00	30.00	45.00	—
1981 (B)	—	30.00	40.00	50.00	75.00	—

KM# 49.6 25 PAISE

2.61 g., Copper-Nickel, 19 mm. **Obv:** Asoka lion pedestal **Rev:** Denomination and date **Note:** 9-1/2mm between lions' nose tips. Bull has four legs. Type 2.

Date	Mintage	VF20	XF40	MS60	MS63	MS65
1974 (C)	—	10.00	15.00	20.00	35.00	—
1975 (C)	—	10.00	15.00	20.00	35.00	—
1976 (C)	—	30.00	40.00	50.00	70.00	—

KM# 49.5 25 PAISE

2.50 g., Copper-Nickel, 19 mm. **Obv:** Asoka lion pedestal **Rev:** Denomination and date **Note:** Type 3.

Date	Mintage	VF20	XF40	MS60	MS63	MS65
1986 (B)	—	1.00	1.50	2.00	4.00	—
1986 (C)	—	1.00	1.50	2.00	4.00	—
1986 (H)	—	1.00	1.50	2.00	4.00	—
1987 (B)	—	1.00	1.50	2.00	4.00	—
1987 (C)	—	1.00	1.50	2.00	4.00	—
1987 (C) Long 7	—	1.00	1.50	2.00	4.00	—
1988 (B)	—	1.00	1.50	2.00	4.00	—
1988 (C) 8's 1.3mm tall	—	1.00	1.50	2.00	4.00	—
1988 (C) 8's 1.8mm tall	—	4.00	6.00	10.00	15.00	—
1988 (H)	—	1.00	1.50	2.00	4.00	—
1989 (B)	—	1.00	1.50	2.00	4.00	—
1989 (C)	—	6.00	8.00	10.00	13.00	—
1989 (H)	—	40.00	65.00	100	150	—
1990 (B)	—	4.00	7.00	10.00	15.00	—
1990 (C)	—	4.00	7.00	10.00	15.00	—

KM# 50 25 PAISE
Copper-Nickel, 19 mm. **Subject:** Rural Women's Advancement **Obv:** Asoka lion pedestal **Rev:** Woman grinding wheat

Date	Mintage	VF20	XF40	MS60	MS63	MS65
1980 (B)	15,050,000	5.00	6.00	7.00	9.00	—
1980 B	—	PF63 8.00				
1980 (C)	8,520,000	5.00	6.00	7.00	9.00	—
1980 (H)	10,380,000	4.00	5.00	7.00	9.00	—

KM# 51 25 PAISE
Copper-Nickel, 19 mm. **Subject:** World Food Day **Obv:** Asoka lion pedestal **Rev:** Man and woman, man carrying sheaf

Date	Mintage	VF20	XF40	MS60	MS63	MS65
1981 (B)	2,170,000	5.00	7.00	8.00	12.00	—
1981 B	—	PF63 10.00				
1981 (C)	4,500,000	6.00	8.00	10.00	15.00	—
1981 (H)	9,340,000	5.00	6.00	8.00	12.00	—

KM# 52 25 PAISE
Copper-Nickel, 19 mm. **Subject:** IX Asian Games **Obv:** Asoka lion pedestal **Rev:** Sun above symbol

Date	Mintage	VF20	XF40	MS60	MS63	MS65
1982 (B)	12,000,000	4.00	5.00	6.00	10.00	—
1982 B	—	PF63 10.00				
1982 (C)	12,000,000	4.00	5.00	6.00	10.00	—
1982 (H) 3 Pointed Star	330,000	4.00	6.00	10.00	13.00	—
1982 (H) 5 Pointed Star	330,000	40.00	65.00	100	125	—

KM# 53 25 PAISE
2.50 g., Copper-Nickel, 19 mm. **Subject:** Forestry **Obv:** Asoka lion pedestal **Rev:** Central tree divides squatting figure and stag **Edge:** Rounded

Date	Mintage	VF20	XF40	MS60	MS63	MS65
1985 (B)	—	10.00	15.00	20.00	25.00	—

Note: Mintage included in KM49.1. 1985 (B) have rounded or flat edge

Date	Mintage	VF20	XF40	MS60	MS63	MS65
1985 (C)	—	8.00	10.00	15.00	20.00	—
1985 (H)	—	8.00	10.00	15.00	20.00	—

Note: Mintage included in KM49.1

KM# 54 25 PAISE
2.82 g., Stainless Steel, 19 mm. **Obv:** Small Lion capitol of Ashoka Pillar above value **Rev:** Rhinoceros left **Edge:** Plain **Note:** Varieties of date size exist.

Date	Mintage	VF20	XF40	MS60	MS63	MS65
1988 C	305,280,000	2.00	3.00	4.00	7.00	—
1988 (B)	—	1.00	3.00	4.00	7.00	—
1988 (C)	18,920,000	4.00	6.00	10.00	15.00	—
1988 (H)	—	4.00	6.00	10.00	15.00	—
1988 (N)	Inc. above	1.00	3.00	4.00	7.00	—
1989 (B)	—	1.00	3.00	4.00	7.00	—
1989 (C) fine grass below rhino	—	1.00	3.00	4.00	7.00	—
1989 (C) bold grass below rhino	—	1.00	3.00	4.00	7.00	—
1989 (H)	—	2.00	3.00	4.00	7.00	—
1989 (N)	—	1.00	3.00	4.00	7.00	—
1990 (B)	—	1.00	3.00	4.00	7.00	—
1990 (C)	—	1.00	3.00	4.00	7.00	—
1990 (H)	—	1.00	3.00	4.00	7.00	—
1990 (N) Small mm	—	1.00	3.00	4.00	7.00	—
1991 (B)	—	1.00	3.00	4.00	7.00	—
1991 (C)	—	1.00	3.00	4.00	7.00	—
1991 (H)	—	1.00	3.00	4.00	7.00	—
1991 (N)	—	1.00	3.00	4.00	7.00	—
1992 (B)	—	1.00	3.00	4.00	7.00	—
1992 (C)	—	10.00	15.00	20.00	30.00	—
1992 (H)	—	10.00	15.00	20.00	30.00	—
1992 (N)	—	1.00	3.00	4.00	7.00	—
1993 (B)	—	2.00	3.00	4.00	7.00	—
1993 (C)	—	4.00	7.00	10.00	15.00	—
1993 (H)	—	60.00	100	160	225	—
1993 (N)	—	1.00	3.00	4.00	7.00	—
1994 (B)	—	1.00	3.00	4.00	7.00	—
1994 (C)	—	1.00	3.00	4.00	7.00	—
1994 (H)	—	1.00	3.00	4.00	7.00	—
1994 (N)	—	1.00	3.00	4.00	7.00	—
1995 (B)	—	1.00	3.00	4.00	7.00	—
1995 (C)	—	1.00	3.00	4.00	7.00	—
1995 (H)	—	1.00	3.00	4.00	7.00	—
1995 (N)	—	1.00	3.00	4.00	7.00	—
1996 (B)	—	1.00	3.00	4.00	7.00	—
1996 (C)	—	1.00	3.00	4.00	7.00	—
1996 (H)	—	1.00	3.00	4.00	7.00	—
1996 (N)	—	1.00	3.00	4.00	7.00	—
1997 (B)	—	1.00	3.00	4.00	7.00	—
1997 (C)	—	10.00	15.00	20.00	30.00	—
1997 (H)	—	10.00	15.00	20.00	30.00	—
1997 (N)	—	1.00	3.00	4.00	7.00	—
1998 (B)	—	1.00	3.00	4.00	7.00	—
1998 (C)	—	1.00	3.00	4.00	7.00	—
1998 (H)	—	1.00	3.00	4.00	7.00	—
1998 (N)	—	1.00	3.00	4.00	7.00	—
1999 (B)	—	1.00	3.00	4.00	7.00	—
1999 (C)	—	1.00	3.00	4.00	7.00	—
1999 (H)	—	1.00	3.00	4.00	7.00	—
1999 (N)	—	1.00	3.00	4.00	7.00	—
2000 (B)	—	1.00	3.00	4.00	7.00	—
2000 (C)	—	1.00	3.00	4.00	7.00	—
2000 (H)	—	1.00	3.00	4.00	7.00	—
2000 (N)	—	1.00	3.00	4.00	7.00	—

KM# 55 50 NAYE PAISE
5.00 g., Nickel, 24 mm. **Obv:** Asoka lion pedestal **Rev:** Denomination and date

Date	Mintage	VF20	XF40	MS60	MS63	MS65
1957 (B)	—	600	900	1,200	1,500	—
1959 (B)	—	400	700	1,000	1,300	—
1960 (B)	11,224,000	4.00	5.00	6.00	10.00	—
1960 (B)	—	PF63 200				
1960 (C)	Inc. above	4.00	5.00	6.00	10.00	—
1961 (B)	45,992,000	1.00	3.00	4.00	7.00	—
1961 (B)	—	PF63 25.00				
1961 (C)	Inc. above	1.00	3.00	4.00	7.00	—
1962 (B)	64,227,999	1.00	3.00	4.00	7.00	—
1962 (B)	—	PF63 25.00				
1962 (C)	Inc. above	1.00	3.00	4.00	7.00	—
1963 (B)	58,168,000	1.00	3.00	4.00	7.00	—
1963 (B)	—	PF63 25.00				
1963 (C)	Inc. above	4.00	7.00	10.00	15.00	—

KM# 56 50 PAISE
5.00 g., Nickel, 24 mm. **Subject:** Death of Jawaharlal Nehru **Obv:** Asoka lion pedestal **Rev:** Head left **Rev. Legend:** English **Note:** Struck from 1964 until 1967.

Date	Mintage	VF20	XF40	MS60	MS63	MS65
ND-1964 (B)	21,900,000	4.00	5.00	6.00	10.00	—
ND-1964 B	—	PF63 200				
ND-1964 B Proof, packaged	—	PF63 500				
ND-1964 (C)	7,160,000	4.00	7.00	10.00	15.00	—

KM# 57 50 PAISE
5.00 g., Nickel, 24 mm. **Subject:** Death of Jawaharlal Nehru **Obv:** Asoka lion pedestal **Rev:** Head left **Rev. Legend:** Hindi **Note:** Struck from 1964 until 1967.

Date	Mintage	VF20	XF40	MS60	MS63	MS65
ND-1964 (B)	36,190,000	1.00	3.00	4.00	7.00	—
ND-1964 (C)	28,350,000	1.00	3.00	4.00	7.00	—

KM# 58.1 50 PAISE
5.00 g., Nickel, 24 mm. **Obv:** Asoka lion pedestal **Rev:** 7mm "50", date **Note:** Type 1.

Date	Mintage	VF20	XF40	MS60	MS63	MS65
1964 (C)	23,361,000	4.00	5.00	6.00	10.00	—
1967 (B)	19,267,000	1.00	3.00	4.00	7.00	—

Note: Varieties of 1967(B) reverse edges exist, half teeth and the scarce full teeth

KM# 58.2 50 PAISE
5.00 g., Nickel, 24 mm. **Obv:** Asoka lion pedestal **Rev:** 6.5mm "50", date **Note:** Type 2.

Date	Mintage	VF20	XF40	MS60	MS63	MS65
1967 (C)	—	2.00	3.00	4.00	6.00	—
1968 (B)	28,076,000	2.00	3.00	4.00	6.00	—

Note: A scarce 1968(B) variety exists with crude obverse, no whiskers, thick horsetail

Date	Mintage	VF20	XF40	MS60	MS63	MS65
1968 (C)	Inc. above	2.00	3.00	4.00	6.00	—
1969 (B)	59,388,000	2.00	3.00	4.00	6.00	—
1969 (C)	Inc. above	2.00	3.00	4.00	6.00	—
1970 (B)	Inc. above	2.00	3.00	4.00	6.00	—
1970 (C)	Inc. above	2.00	3.00	4.00	6.00	—
1971 (C)	57,900,000	2.00	3.00	4.00	6.00	—

KM# 59 50 PAISE
5.00 g., Nickel, 24 mm. **Subject:** Centennial - Birth of Mahatma Gandhi **Obv:** Asoka lion pedestal **Rev:** Head left **Note:** Struck during 1969 and 1970.

Date	Mintage	VF20	XF40	MS60	MS63	MS65
ND-1969 (B)	10,260,000	2.00	3.00	4.00	6.00	—
ND-1969 B	9,147	PF63 30.00				
ND-1969 (C)	12,100,000	2.00	3.00	4.00	6.00	—

KM# 58.3 50 PAISE
5.00 g., Nickel, 24 mm. **Obv:** Asoka lion pedestal **Rev:** 6.5mm "50", date **Note:** Type 1.

Date	Mintage	VF20	XF40	MS60	MS63	MS65
1970 (B)	—	20.00	30.00	40.00	60.00	—

Note: Mintage included with 1969

Date	Mintage	VF20	XF40	MS60	MS63	MS65
1970 B	3,046	PF63 30.00				
1971 B	4,375	PF63 40.00				

KM# 60 50 PAISE
5.00 g., Copper-Nickel, 24 mm. **Subject:** 25th Anniversary of Independence **Obv:** Asoka lion pedestal **Rev:** Figures with flag, building in background

Date	Mintage	VF20	XF40	MS60	MS63	MS65
ND-1972 (B)	43,800,000	4.00	5.00	6.00	8.00	—
ND-1972 B	7,895	PF63 30.00				
ND-1972 (C)	40,080,000	2.00	3.00	4.00	6.00	—

KM# 61 50 PAISE

5.00 g., Copper-Nickel, 24 mm. **Obv:** Asoka lion pedestal **Rev:** Denomination above date, lettering spaced out **Note:** Type 2. Wide and narrow security edge varieties exist.

Date	Mintage	VF20	XF40	MS60	MS63	MS65
1972 (B)	—	2.00	3.00	4.00	6.00	—
1972 (C)	—	2.00	3.00	4.00	6.00	—
1973 (B)	—	2.00	3.00	4.00	6.00	—
1973 (C)	—	4.00	7.00	10.00	15.00	—

KM# 62 50 PAISE

5.00 g., Copper-Nickel, 24 mm. **Series:** F.A.O. **Subject:** Grow More Food **Obv:** Asoka lion pedestal **Rev:** Inscription on shield within grain sprigs

Date	Mintage	VF20	XF40	MS60	MS63	MS65
1973 (B)	28,720,000	2.00	3.00	4.00	6.00	—
1973 B	11,000	PF63 30.00				
1973 (C)	40,100,000	2.00	3.00	4.00	6.00	—

KM# 63 50 PAISE

5.00 g., Copper-Nickel, 24 mm. **Obv:** Asoka lion pedestal **Rev:** Denomination above date, lettering close **Note:** Type 2.

Date	Mintage	VF20	XF40	MS60	MS63	MS65
1974 (B)	—	2.00	3.00	4.00	6.00	—
1974 B	—	PF63 30.00				
1974 (C)	—	2.00	3.00	4.00	6.00	—
1975 (B)	225,880,000	2.00	3.00	4.00	6.00	—
1975 B	—	PF63 30.00				
1975 (C)	Inc. above	2.00	3.00	4.00	6.00	—
1975 (H)	—	4.00	5.00	6.00	9.00	—
1976 (B)	99,564,000	2.00	3.00	4.00	6.00	—
1976 B	Inc. above	PF63 30.00				
1976 (C)	Inc. above	2.00	3.00	4.00	6.00	—
1976 (H)	Inc. above	4.00	5.00	6.00	9.00	—
1977 (B)	97,272,000	2.00	3.00	4.00	6.00	—
1977 B	Inc. above	PF63 30.00				
1977 (C)	Inc. above	4.00	5.00	6.00	9.00	—
1977 (H)	Inc. above	4.00	5.00	6.00	9.00	—
1978 (B)	—	30.00	40.00	60.00	90.00	—
1978 B	25,648,000	PF63 30.00				
1978 (C)	—	2.00	3.00	4.00	6.00	—
1979 B	—	PF63 30.00				
1980 (B)	—	2.00	3.00	4.00	6.00	—
1980 B	—	PF63 30.00				
1980 (C)	—	10.00	25.00	40.00	60.00	—
1981 B	—	PF63 30.00				
1983 (C)	62,634,000	10.00	25.00	40.00	60.00	—

KM# 64 50 PAISE

5.00 g., Copper-Nickel, 24 mm. **Subject:** National Integration **Obv:** Asoka lion pedestal **Rev:** Flag on map

Date	Mintage	VF20	XF40	MS60	MS63	MS65
1982 (B)	9,804,000	2.00	3.00	4.00	6.00	—
1982 B	—	PF63 30.00				
1982 (C)	Inc. above	10.00	40.00	60.00	100	—

KM# 65 50 PAISE

5.09 g., Copper-Nickel, 24 mm. **Obv:** Asoka lion pedestal, ornaments surround **Rev:** Denomination and date, ornaments surround **Note:** Type 3.

Date	Mintage	VF20	XF40	MS60	MS63	MS65
1984 (B)	61,548,000	2.00	3.00	4.00	6.00	—
1984 (C)	Inc. above	2.00	3.00	4.00	6.00	—
1984 (H)	—	2.00	3.00	4.00	6.00	—
1985 (B)	210,964,000	2.00	3.00	4.00	6.00	—
1985 (C)	Inc. above	2.00	3.00	4.00	6.00	—
1985 (H)	Inc. above	2.00	3.00	4.00	6.00	—
1985 (T)	Inc. above	2.00	3.00	4.00	6.00	—
1986 (B)	—	60.00	100	160	250	—
1986 (C)	117,576,000	4.00	7.00	10.00	15.00	—
1987 (B)	—	2.00	3.00	4.00	6.00	—
1987 (C)	145,140,000	2.00	3.00	4.00	6.00	—
1987 (H)	Inc. above	2.00	3.00	4.00	6.00	—
1988 (B)	149,092,000	2.00	3.00	4.00	6.00	—
1988 (C)	Inc. above	2.00	3.00	4.00	6.00	—
1988 (H)	Inc. above	4.00	5.00	6.00	9.00	—
1988 (N)	—	200	300	500	750	—
1989 (B)	—	2.00	3.00	4.00	6.00	—
1989 (C)	—	2.00	3.00	4.00	6.00	—
1989 (H)	—	20.00	40.00	60.00	75.00	—
1990 (B)	—	6.00	8.00	10.00	15.00	—

KM# 66 50 PAISE

5.00 g., Copper-Nickel, 24 mm. **Subject:** Golden Jubilee of Reserve Bank of India **Obv:** Asoka lion pedestal **Rev:** Lion beneath trees

Date	Mintage	VF20	XF40	MS60	MS63	MS65
ND-1985 (B)	—	4.00	5.00	6.00	10.00	—
Note: Mintage included in KM65						
ND-1985 B	—	PF63 30.00				
Note: Mintage included in KM#65						
ND-1985 (C)	—	4.00	7.00	10.00	15.00	—
ND-1985 (H)	—	4.00	5.00	6.00	10.00	—
Note: Mintage included in KM65						

KM# 67.1 50 PAISE

5.00 g., Copper-Nickel, 24 mm. **Subject:** Death of Indira Gandhi - statesperson, 1917-1984 **Obv:** Asoka lion pedestal **Rev:** Head right

Date	Mintage	VF20	XF40	MS60	MS63	MS65
ND-1985 (B)	—	4.00	5.00	6.00	—	—
Note: Mintage included in KM65						
ND-1985 B	—	PF63 30.00				
Note: Mintage included in KM65						
ND-1985 (C)	—	4.00	5.00	6.00	—	—
Note: Mintage included in KM65						
ND-1985 (H)	—	4.00	5.00	6.00	—	—
Note: Mintage included in KM65						

KM# 67.2 50 PAISE

5.00 g., Copper-Nickel, 24 mm. **Subject:** Death of Indira Gandhi, 1917-1984 statesperson **Obv:** Asoka lion pedestal **Rev:** Head right **Note:** Mule.

Date	Mintage	VF20	XF40	MS60	MS63	MS65
ND-1985 (C)	—	4.00	10.00	20.00	50.00	—

KM# 68.1 50 PAISE

5.00 g., Copper-Nickel, 24 mm. **Series:** F.A.O. **Subject:** Fisheries **Obv:** Asoka lion pedestal **Rev:** People with fishing nets

Date	Mintage	VF20	XF40	MS60	MS63	MS65
1986 (B)	—	5.00	8.50	10.00	—	—
Note: Mintage included in KM65						
1986 B	—	PF63 0.30				
Note: Mintage included in KM65						
1986 (C)	—	5.00	8.50	10.00	15.00	—
1986 (H)	—	5.00	8.50	10.00	15.00	—
Note: Mintage included in KM65						

KM# 68.2 50 PAISE

5.00 g., Copper-Nickel, 24 mm. **Obv:** Asoka lion pedestal **Rev:** People with fishing nets **Note:** Mule.

Date	Mintage	VF20	XF40	MS60	MS63	MS65
1986 (C)	—	20.00	40.00	60.00	75.00	—

KM# 69 50 PAISE

3.80 g., Stainless Steel, 22 mm. **Subject:** Parliament Building in New Delhi **Obv:** Denomination **Rev:** Building

Date	Mintage	VF20	XF40	MS60	MS63	MS65
1988 (B)	—	1.00	1.50	2.00	4.00	—
1988 C	272,160,000	1.00	1.50	2.00	4.00	—
1988 (C)	2,195,000	4.00	7.00	10.00	15.00	—
1988 (H)	Inc. above	4.00	7.00	10.00	15.00	—
1988 (N)	—	1.00	1.50	2.00	4.00	—
1989 (B)	—	1.00	1.50	2.00	4.00	—
1989 (C)	—	4.00	5.00	6.00	9.00	—
1989 (H)	—	4.00	5.00	6.00	9.00	—
1989 (N)	—	1.00	1.50	2.00	4.00	—
1990 (B)	—	1.00	1.50	2.00	4.00	—
1990 (C)	—	1.00	1.50	2.00	4.00	—
1990 (H)	—	1.00	1.50	2.00	4.00	—
1990 (N)	—	1.00	1.50	2.00	4.00	—
Note: Small (.35mm) mint mark						
1990 (N)	—	1.00	1.50	2.00	4.00	—
Note: Large (.75mm) mint mark						
1991 (B)	—	1.00	1.50	2.00	4.00	—
1991 (C)	—	1.00	1.50	2.00	4.00	—
1991 (H)	—	1.00	1.50	2.00	4.00	—
1991 (N)	—	1.00	1.50	2.00	4.00	—
1992 (B)	—	1.00	1.50	2.00	4.00	—
1992 (C)	—	1.00	1.50	2.00	4.00	—
1992 (H)	—	1.00	1.50	2.00	4.00	—
1992 (N)	—	1.00	1.50	2.00	4.00	—
1992	—	10.00	23.00	40.00	60.00	—
1993 (C)	—	4.00	7.00	10.00	15.00	—
1993 (N)	—	1.00	1.50	2.00	4.00	—
1994 (B)	—	1.00	1.50	2.00	4.00	—
1994 (C)	—	1.00	1.50	2.00	4.00	—
1994 (H)	—	1.00	1.50	2.00	4.00	—
1994 (N)	—	1.00	1.50	2.00	4.00	—
1995 (B)	—	1.00	1.50	2.00	4.00	—
1995 (C)	—	1.00	1.50	2.00	4.00	—
1995 (H)	—	1.00	1.50	2.00	4.00	—
1995 (N)	—	1.00	1.50	2.00	4.00	—
1996 (B)	—	1.00	1.50	2.00	4.00	—
1996 (C)	—	1.00	1.50	2.00	4.00	—
1996 (H)	—	1.00	1.50	2.00	4.00	—
1996 (N)	—	1.00	1.50	2.00	4.00	—
1997 (B)	—	1.00	1.50	2.00	4.00	—
1997 (C)	—	6.00	8.00	10.00	15.00	—
1997 (H)	—	6.00	8.00	10.00	15.00	—
1997 (N)	—	1.00	1.50	2.00	4.00	—
1998 (B)	—	1.00	1.50	2.00	4.00	—
1998 (C)	—	1.00	1.50	2.00	4.00	—
1998 (H)	—	1.00	1.50	2.00	4.00	—
1998 (N)	—	1.00	1.50	2.00	4.00	—
1999 (B)	—	1.00	1.50	2.00	4.00	—
1999 (C)	—	1.00	1.50	2.00	4.00	—
1999 (H)	—	1.00	1.50	2.00	4.00	—
2000 (B)	—	1.00	1.50	2.00	4.00	—
2000 (C)	—	1.00	1.50	2.00	4.00	—
2000 (H)	—	1.00	1.50	2.00	4.00	—

KM# 70 50 PAISE

Stainless Steel **Subject:** 50th Anniversary of Independence **Obv:** Small Asoka lion pedestal above denomination **Rev:** Line of people

Date	Mintage	VF20	XF40	MS60	MS63	MS65
1997 (B)	—	4.00	5.00	6.00	10.00	—
1997 (C)	—	4.00	6.00	8.00	10.00	—
1997 (H)	—	4.00	6.00	8.00	10.00	—

Date	Mintage	VF20	XF40	MS60	MS63	MS65
1997	—	2.00	3.00	4.00	7.00	—
1997 (N)	—	PF63 30.00				

KM# 75.1 RUPEE

10.00 g., Nickel, 28 mm. **Obv:** Asoka lion pedestal **Rev:** Denomination and date, grain ears flank **Note:** Type 1.

Date	Mintage	VF20	XF40	MS60	MS63	MS65
1962 (C)	3,689,000	2.00	6.00	10.00	15.00	—
1962 (B)	—	PF63 4,000				

KM# 75.2 RUPEE

10.00 g., Nickel, 28 mm. **Obv:** Asoka lion pedestal **Rev:** Smaller date and denomination **Note:** Type 1.

Date	Mintage	VF20	XF40	MS60	MS63	MS65
1970 (B)	Inc. above	60.00	100	160	200	—
1970 B	3,046	PF63 100				
1971 B	4,375	PF63 100				
1972 B	7,895	PF63 100				
1973 B	7,567	PF63 100				
1974 B	—	PF63 100				

KM# 76 RUPEE

10.00 g., Nickel, 27 mm. **Subject:** Death of Jawaharlal Nehru **Obv:** Small Asoka lion pedestal **Rev:** Head left **Note:** Type II. Struck from 1964 until 1967.

Date	Mintage	VF20	XF40	MS60	MS63	MS65
ND-1964 (B)	10,010,000	2.00	6.00	10.00	15.00	—
ND-1964 B	—	PF63 200				
ND-1964 (C)	10,020,000	2.00	6.00	10.00	15.00	—

KM# 77 RUPEE

10.00 g., Nickel, 28 mm. **Subject:** Centennial - Birth of Mahatma Gandhi **Obv:** Asoka lion pedestal **Rev:** Head left **Note:** Struck during 1969 and 1970.

Date	Mintage	VF20	XF40	MS60	MS63	MS65
ND-1969 (B)	5,180,000	1.00	6.00	10.00	15.00	—
ND-1969 B	9,147	PF63 30.00				
ND-1969 (C)	6,690,000	1.00	6.00	10.00	15.00	—

KM# 78.1 RUPEE

8.00 g., Copper-Nickel, 28 mm. **Obv:** Asoka lion pedestal **Rev:** Denomination and date, grain ears flank **Note:** Type 1.

Date	Mintage	VF20	XF40	MS60	MS63	MS65
1975 (B)	98,850,000	1.00	1.50	2.00	4.00	—
1975 B	—	PF63 30.00				
1975 (C)	—	10.00	17.00	30.00	40.00	—
1976 (B)	161,895,000	1.00	1.50	2.00	4.00	—
1976 B	Inc. above	PF63 30.00				
1977 (B)	177,105,000	1.00	1.50	2.00	4.00	—
1977 B	Inc. above	PF63 30.00				
1978 (B)	127,348,000	1.00	1.50	2.00	4.00	—
1978 B	Inc. above	PF63 30.00				
1978 (C)	Inc. above	1.00	1.50	2.00	4.00	—
1979 (B)	—	1.00	1.50	2.00	4.00	—
1979 (C)	—	20.00	25.00	40.00	50.00	—

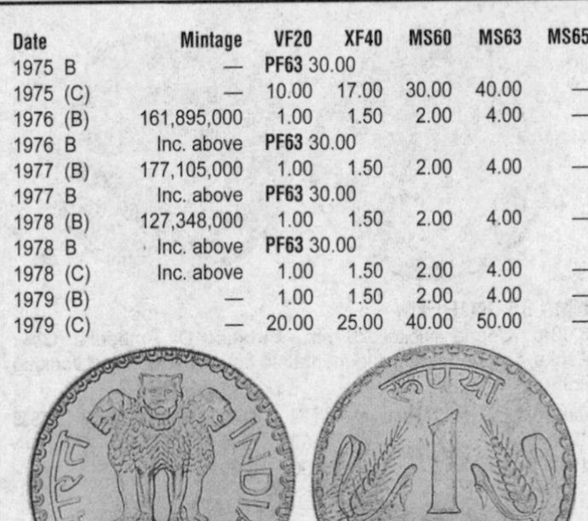

KM# 78.2 RUPEE

8.00 g., Copper-Nickel, 28 mm. **Obv:** Asoka lion pedestal **Rev:** Denomination and date, grain ears flank **Note:** Type 2.

Date	Mintage	VF20	XF40	MS60	MS63	MS65
1975 (C)	—	1.00	1.50	2.00	4.00	—
Note: Mintage included in KM78.1						
1976 (C)	—	1.00	1.50	2.00	4.00	—
Note: Mintage included in KM78.1						

KM# 78.3 RUPEE

8.00 g., Copper-Nickel, 28 mm. **Obv:** Asoka lion pedestal **Rev:** Denomination and date, grain ears flank **Note:** Type 3. Border varieties of long vs. short teeth on 1981 reverse and 1982 obverse. Wide and narrow security edge varieties exist.

Date	Mintage	VF20	XF40	MS60	MS63	MS65
1979 (B)	—	1.00	1.50	2.00	4.00	—
1979 B	—	PF63 30.00				
1979 (C)	—	1.00	1.50	2.00	4.00	—
1980 (B)	84,768,000	1.00	1.50	2.00	4.00	—
1980 B	—	PF63 30.00				
1980 (C)	Inc. above	1.00	1.50	2.00	4.00	—
1981 (B)	82,458,000	1.00	1.50	2.00	4.00	—
1981 B	—	PF63 30.00				
1981 (C)	Inc. above	1.00	1.50	2.00	4.00	—
1982 (B)	116,811,000	2.00	3.00	4.00	7.00	—

KM# 79.1 RUPEE

6.00 g., Copper-Nickel, 26 mm. **Obv:** Asoka lion pedestal within seven sided beaded outline **Rev:** Denomination and date, grain ears flank, seven-sided outline surrounds **Edge:** Security **Note:** Type 3. Lions' hair and ears on 1984(B)-1989(B) issues vary from others.

Date	Mintage	VF20	XF40	MS60	MS63	MS65
1982 (B)	—	300	400	800	1,000	—
1983 (B)	32,490,000	1.00	1.50	2.00	4.00	—
1983 (C)	Inc. above	1.00	1.50	2.00	4.00	—
1984 (C)	Inc. above	1.00	1.50	2.00	4.00	—
1984 (B)	152,378,000	1.00	1.50	2.00	4.00	—
1984 (H)	Inc. above	4.00	5.00	6.00	8.00	—
1985 (B)	444,516,000	1.00	1.50	2.00	4.00	—
1985 (C)	Inc. above	1.00	1.50	2.00	4.00	—
1985 H	Inc. above	1.00	1.50	2.00	4.00	—
1985 (L)	Inc. above	1.00	1.50	2.00	4.00	—
1986 (C)	Inc. above	1.00	1.50	2.00	4.00	—
1986 (B)	1,396,074,000	1.00	1.50	2.00	4.00	—
1986 (H)	Inc. above	4.00	7.00	10.00	15.00	—
1987 (B)	685,502,000	1.00	1.50	2.00	4.00	—
1987 (H)	Inc. above	1.00	1.50	2.00	4.00	—
1988 (B)	240,447,000	1.00	1.50	2.00	4.00	—
1988 (C)	Inc. above	1.00	1.50	2.00	4.00	—
1988 (H)	Inc. above	1.00	1.50	2.00	4.00	—
1988 (N)	—	10.00	15.00	20.00	30.00	—
1989 (B)	—	1.00	1.50	2.00	4.00	—
1989 (C)	—	1.00	1.50	2.00	4.00	—
1989 (H)	—	1.00	1.50	2.00	4.00	—
1989 (N)	—	4.00	7.00	10.00	15.00	—
1990 (C)	—	10.00	15.00	20.00	30.00	—
1990 (H)	—	1.00	1.50	2.00	4.00	—

KM# 80 RUPEE

6.00 g., Copper-Nickel, 26 mm. **Subject:** Youth Year **Obv:** Small asoka lion pedestal above denomination **Rev:** Three outlined profiles between dove and laurel branch **Edge:** Security

Date	Mintage	VF20	XF40	MS60	MS63	MS65
1985 (B)	—	7.00	10.00	12.00	15.00	—
Note: Mintage included in KM79.1						
1985 (C)	—	8.00	10.00	12.00	15.00	—
Note: Mintage included in KM79.1						
1985 (C)	—	PF63 40.00				
Note: Mintage included in KM79.1						

KM# 81 RUPEE

6.00 g., Copper-Nickel, 26 mm. **Series:** F.A.O. **Obv:** Asoka lion pedestal **Rev:** Two figures working in field

Date	Mintage	VF20	XF40	MS60	MS63	MS65
1987 (B)	234,223,000	3.00	4.00	5.00	6.00	—
1987 B	—	PF63 60.00				
1987 (C)	Inc. above	4.00	20.00	40.00	60.00	—
1987 (H)	191,120,000	10.00	7.00	10.00	40.00	—

KM# 79.2 RUPEE

6.00 g., Copper-Nickel, 26 mm. **Obv:** Horse on pedestal different, more detailed, 7-sided beaded outline surrounds **Rev:** Denomination and date, grain ears flank, within 7-sided beaded outline **Note:** Type 3.

Date	Mintage	VF20	XF40	MS60	MS63	MS65
1988 (B)	—	1.50	2.25	4.00	—	—
1989	—	1.50	2.25	4.00	—	—
1990	—	1.50	2.25	4.00	—	—

KM# 79.3 RUPEE

6.00 g., Copper-Nickel, 26 mm. **Obv:** Lions' chest hairs restyled, 7-sided beaded outline surrounds **Rev:** Denomination and date, grain ears flank, 7-sided beaded outline surrounds **Note:** Type 3.

Date	Mintage	VF20	XF40	MS60	MS63	MS65
1988 (B)	—	1.00	1.50	2.00	4.00	—
1989 (B)	—	1.00	1.50	2.00	4.00	—
1990 (B)	—	1.00	1.50	2.00	4.00	—

KM# 79.4 RUPEE

6.00 g., Copper-Nickel, 26 mm. **Obv:** Asoka lion pedestal, within 7-sided beaded outline, similar to 79.1 **Rev:** Denomination and date, grain ears flank, 7-sided beaded outline surrounds **Edge:** Milled **Note:** Traces of security edge and/or mostly smooth edges are encountered, especially for 1989. 1989-1991(C) is a variety with bulging eyes on side lions and irregular straight hair on central lion.

Date	Mintage	VF20	XF40	MS60	MS63	MS65
1988 (C)	—	10.00	20.00	40.00	—	—
1989 (B)	—	20.00	30.00	60.00	—	—
1989 (C)	—	10.00	20.00	40.00	—	—
1989 (H)	—	20.00	30.00	60.00	—	—
1990 (C)	—	1.00	1.50	4.00	—	—
1990 (H)	—	1.00	1.50	4.00	—	—
1991 (C)	—	1.00	1.50	4.00	—	—

KM# 82 RUPEE

6.00 g., Copper-Nickel, 26 mm. **Series:** F.A.O. **Subject:** Rainfed farming **Obv:** Asoka lion pedestal **Rev:** Figure with flowers, rain cloud in background

Date	Mintage	VF20	XF40	MS60	MS63	MS65
1988 (B)	—	5.00	6.00	7.00	9.00	—
Note: Mintage included in KM79.1						
1988 (C)	—	4.00	5.00	6.00	9.00	—

KM# 83.1 RUPEE

6.00 g., Copper-Nickel, 26 mm. **Subject:** 100th Anniversary of Nehru's Birth **Obv:** Asoka lion pedestal **Rev:** Head right

Date	Mintage	VF20	XF40	MS60	MS63	MS65
1989 (B)	—	3.00	4.00	5.00	6.00	—
1989 B	—	PF63 100				
1989 (C)	—	2.00	3.00	4.00	6.00	—
1989 (H)	—	2.00	3.00	4.00	6.00	—
1989 (N)	—	2.00	3.00	4.00	6.00	—

KM# 83.2 RUPEE

Copper-Nickel, 26 mm. **Obv:** Asoka lion pedestal, similar to KM#90. **Rev:** Small Head, Long rim teath

Date	Mintage	VF20	XF40	MS60	MS63	MS65
1989 (B)	—	20.00	30.00	40.00	60.00	—

KM# 84 RUPEE

6.00 g., Copper-Nickel, 26 mm. **Series:** F.A.O. **Subject:** Food and Environment **Obv:** Asoka lion pedestal **Rev:** Sun above wheat stalks

Date	Mintage	VF20	XF40	MS60	MS63	MS65
1989 (B)	—	4.00	6.00	10.00	15.00	—
1989 (H)	—	6.00	10.00	15.00	20.00	—
1989 (N)	—	10.00	20.00	30.00	50.00	—

KM# 79.5 RUPEE

6.00 g., Copper-Nickel, 26 mm. **Obv:** Lions' chest hairs restyled, 7-sided beaded outline surrounds **Rev:** Denomination and date, grain ears flank, 7-sided beaded outline surrounds **Note:** Type 3.

Date	Mintage	VF20	XF40	MS60	MS63	MS65
1990 (B)	—	1.00	1.50	2.00	4.00	—
1990 (C)	—	4.00	7.00	10.00	15.00	—
1991 (B)	—	1.00	1.50	2.00	4.00	—
1991 (H)	—	1.00	1.50	2.00	4.00	—

KM# A85 RUPEE

6.00 g., Copper-Nickel, 26 mm. **Subject:** Dr. Ambedkar **Obv:** Asoka lion pedestal, denomination below **Rev:** Bust looking right

Date	Mintage	VF20	XF40	MS60	MS63	MS65
1990 (B)	—	200	400	600	—	—

KM# 85 RUPEE

6.00 g., Copper-Nickel, 26 mm. **Subject:** Dr. Ambedkar **Obv:** Asoka lion pedestal, denomination below **Rev:** Bust looking right

Date	Mintage	VF20	XF40	MS60	MS63	MS65
1990 (B)	—	4.00	5.00	7.00	—	—
1990 (H)	—	2.00	3.00	4.00	—	—

KM# 86 RUPEE

6.00 g., Copper-Nickel, 26 mm. **Subject:** 15th Anniversary of I.C.D.S. **Obv:** Asoka lion pedestal, denomination below **Rev:** Seated figure holding child, radiant design surrounds **Edge:** Narrow and wide reeded **Note:** Varieties exist.

Date	Mintage	VF20	XF40	MS60	MS63	MS65
ND-1990 (B)	—	4.00	6.00	8.00	—	—
ND-1990 (H)	—	4.00	7.00	10.00	—	—

KM# 87.1 RUPEE

6.00 g., Copper-Nickel, 26 mm. **Subject:** SAARC Year - Care for the Girl Child **Obv:** Asoka lion pedestal **Rev:** Girl cutout below sun, symbol at left **Edge:** Security

Date	Mintage	VF20	XF40	MS60	MS63	MS65
1990 (B)	—	6.00	9.00	10.00	—	—

KM# 87.2 RUPEE

6.00 g., Copper-Nickel, 26 mm. **Subject:** SAARC Year - Care for the Girl Child **Obv:** Asoka lion pedestal, denomination below **Rev:** Girl cutout below sun, symbol at left **Edge:** Milled **Note:** Edge varieties exist.

Date	Mintage	VF20	XF40	MS60	MS63	MS65
1990 (B)	—	4.00	5.00	6.00	—	—
1990 (H)	—	4.00	5.00	6.00	—	—

KM# 88.1 RUPEE

6.00 g., Copper-Nickel, 26 mm. **Series:** F.A.O. **Obv:** Asoka lion pedestal, denomination below **Rev:** Farming scene **Edge:** Reeded

Date	Mintage	VF20	XF40	MS60	MS63	MS65
1990 (C)	—	9.00	10.00	20.00	—	—
Note: 1990(C) is seldom well struck						
1990 (H)	—	9.00	10.00	12.00	—	—

KM# 88.2 RUPEE

6.00 g., Copper-Nickel, 26 mm. **Series:** F.A.O. **Obv:** Asoka lion pedestal **Rev:** Farming scene **Edge:** Plain

Date	Mintage	VF20	XF40	MS60	MS63	MS65
1990 (H)	—	20.00	30.00	50.00	—	—

KM# 89 RUPEE

6.00 g., Copper-Nickel, 26 mm. **Subject:** Rajiv Gandhi **Obv:** Asoka lion pedestal, denomination below **Rev:** Head looking left **Note:** Edge varieties exist.

Date	Mintage	VF20	XF40	MS60	MS63	MS65
ND-1991 (B)	—	5.00	6.00	7.00	—	—
Note: The Mumbai (Bombay) mint mark occasionally resembles the Noida mintmark						
ND-1991 (H)	—	5.00	6.00	7.00	—	—

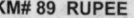

KM# 90 RUPEE

6.00 g., Copper-Nickel, 26 mm. **Subject:** Commonwealth Parliamentary Conference **Obv:** Asoka lion pedestal, denomination below **Rev:** Building **Note:** Variety of breast with flat details exist (worn dies).

Date	Mintage	VF20	XF40	MS60	MS63	MS65
1991 (B)	—	—	—	—	—	—
1991 B	—	PF63 100				

KM# 91 RUPEE

6.00 g., Copper-Nickel, 26 mm. **Subject:** Tourism Year **Obv:** Asoka lion pedestal above denomination **Rev:** Stylized peacock

Date	Mintage	VF20	XF40	MS60	MS63	MS65
1991 (B)	—	5.00	6.00	7.00	—	—
1991 B	—	PF63 100				
1991 (H)	—	2.00	3.00	4.00	—	—

KM# 92.1 RUPEE

4.85 g., Stainless Steel, 25 mm. **Obv:** Asoka lion pedestal **Rev:** Denomination and date, grain ears flank **Edge:** Milled **Note:** Edge sometimes faint, mintmark varieties exist.

Date	Mintage	VF20	XF40	MS60	MS63	MS65
1992 (B)	—	0.25	1.00	1.50	—	—
1992 (H)	—	0.25	1.00	1.50	—	—
1993 (N)	—	0.25	1.00	1.50	—	—
1993 (B)	—	0.25	1.00	1.50	—	—
Note: Two mintmark shapes exist						
1993 (C)	—	0.25	1.00	1.50	—	—
1993 (H)	—	0.25	1.00	1.50	—	—
1994 (N)	—	0.25	1.00	1.50	—	—
1994 (B)	—	0.25	1.00	1.50	—	—
Note: Two mintmark shapes exist						
1994 (C)	—	0.25	1.00	1.50	—	—
1994 (H)	—	0.25	1.00	1.50	—	—
1995 (N)	—	0.25	1.00	1.50	—	—
1995 (B)	—	0.25	1.00	1.50	—	—
1995 (C)	—	0.25	1.00	1.50	—	—
1995 (H)	—	0.25	1.00	1.50	—	—
1996 (H)	—	4.00	5.00	6.00	—	—

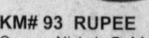

KM# 93 RUPEE

Copper-Nickel **Subject:** Quit India **Obv:** Asoka lion pedestal, denomination below **Rev:** Monument **Edge:** Milled

Date	Mintage	VF20	XF40	MS60	MS63	MS65
ND-1992 (B)	—	2.00	3.00	4.00	—	—
ND-1992 (B)	—	PF63 10.00				
ND-1992 (C)	—	4.00	3.00	6.00	—	—
ND-1992 (H)	—	2.00	3.00	4.00	—	—

KM# 94 RUPEE

Copper-Nickel **Series:** World Food Day **Obv:** Asoka lion pedestal, denomination below **Rev:** Food items left of grain stalks **Edge:** Milled

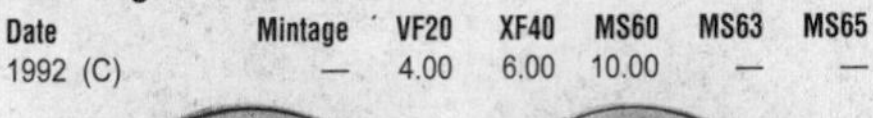

Date	Mintage	VF20	XF40	MS60	MS63	MS65
1992 (C)	—	4.00	6.00	10.00	—	—

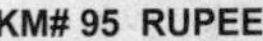

KM# 95 RUPEE

Copper-Nickel **Subject:** Inter Parliamentary Union Conference **Obv:** Asoka lion pedestal, denomination below **Rev:** Small building and date within wreath below curved building

Date	Mintage	VF20	XF40	MS60	MS63	MS65
1993 (B)	—	2.00	4.00	6.00	—	—

KM# 96.1 RUPEE

Stainless Steel **Subject:** International Year of the Family **Obv:** Asoka lion pedestal, denomination below **Rev:** Family group forms circular design at center **Edge:** Reeded

Date	Mintage	VF20	XF40	MS60	MS63	MS65
1994 (B)	—	7.00	10.00	12.00	—	—

KM# 96.2 RUPEE

Stainless Steel **Subject:** International Year of the Family **Obv:** Arms **Rev:** Family inside inner circle **Edge:** Plain

Date	Mintage	VF20	XF40	MS60	MS63	MS65
1994 (B)	—	10.00	25.00	50.00	—	—

KM# 92.2 RUPEE

4.90 g., Stainless Steel, 25 mm. **Obv:** Lion capitol of Ashoka Pillar **Rev:** Denomination and date, grain ears flank **Edge:** Plain **Note:** Mint mark varieties exist.

Date	Mintage	VF20	XF40	MS60	MS63	MS65
1995 (B)	—	4.00	5.00	6.00	—	—
1995 (H)	—	4.00	5.00	6.00	—	—
1996 (B)	—	0.50	1.00	1.50	—	—
1996 (C)	—	0.50	1.00	1.50	—	—
1996 (H)	—	0.50	1.00	1.50	—	—
1996 (N)	—	0.50	1.00	1.50	—	—
1997 (B)	—	0.50	1.00	1.50	—	—
1997 (C)	—	0.50	1.00	1.50	—	—
1997 (H)	—	2.00	4.00	6.00	—	—
1997 (M)	—	0.50	1.00	1.50	—	—
1997 (N)	—	0.50	1.00	1.50	—	—
1998 (B)	—	0.50	1.00	1.50	—	—
1998 (C)	—	0.50	1.00	1.50	—	—
1998 (H)	—	0.50	1.00	1.50	—	—
1998 (K)	—	0.50	1.00	1.50	—	—
1998 (N)	—	0.50	1.00	1.50	—	—
1998 (P)	—	0.50	1.00	1.50	—	—
1999 (B)	—	0.50	1.00	1.50	—	—
1999 (K)	—	0.50	1.00	1.50	—	—
1999 (P)	—	0.50	1.00	1.50	—	—
1999 (C)	—	0.50	1.00	1.50	—	—
1999 (H)	—	0.50	1.00	1.50	—	—
2000 (B)	—	0.50	1.00	1.50	—	—
2000 (K)	—	0.50	1.00	1.50	—	—
2000 (C)	—	0.50	1.00	1.50	—	—
2000 (H)	—	0.50	1.00	1.50	—	—

KM# 97.1 RUPEE

Stainless Steel **Subject:** Eighth World Tamil Conference **Obv:** Asoka lion pedestal, denomination below **Rev:** St. Thiruvalluvar **Edge:** Milled

Date	Mintage	VF20	XF40	MS60	MS63	MS65
1995 (B)	—	2.00	5.00	6.00	—	—
1995 (H)	—	2.00	5.00	6.00	—	—

KM# 97.2 RUPEE

Stainless Steel **Subject:** Eighth World Tamil Conference **Obv:** Asoka lion pedestal, denomination below **Rev:** St. Thiruvalluvar **Edge:** Plain

Date	Mintage	VF20	XF40	MS60	MS63	MS65
1995 (H)	—	10.00	15.00	20.00	—	—

KM# 98 RUPEE

Stainless Steel **Obv:** Asoka lion pedestal, denomination below **Rev:** Cellular jail, Port Blair **Note:** Varieties exist.

Date	Mintage	VF20	XF40	MS60	MS63	MS65
1997 (C)	—	PF63 10.00				
1997 (B)	—	7.00	10.00	15.00	—	—
1997 (C)	—	2.00	3.00	4.00	—	—
1997 (H)	—	2.00	3.00	4.00	—	—
1997 (N)	—	2.00	3.00	4.00	—	—

KM# 295.1 RUPEE

4.85 g., Stainless Steel **Subject:** St. Dnyaneshwar **Obv:** Asoka lion pedestal, denomination below **Rev:** Seated figure **Note:** Asoka column 13.2mm tall.

Date	Mintage	VF20	XF40	MS60	MS63	MS65
1999 (B)	—	10.00	15.00	20.00	—	—
1999 (C)	—	2.00	3.00	4.00	—	—
1999 (C)	—	PF63 40.00				

KM# 295.2 RUPEE

4.85 g., Stainless Steel **Subject:** St. Dnyaneshwar **Obv:** Asoka lion pedestal, denomination below **Rev:** Seated figure **Note:** Asoka column 13.8mm tall.

Date	Mintage	VF20	XF40	MS60	MS63	MS65
1999 (B)	—	2.00	3.00	4.00	—	—

KM# 295.3 RUPEE

4.85 g., Stainless Steel **Subject:** St. Dnyaneshwar **Obv:** Asoka lion pedestal, denominaton below **Rev:** Seated figure **Note:** Asoka column 14.5mm tall.

Date	Mintage	VF20	XF40	MS60	MS63	MS65
1999	—	4.00	7.00	10.00	—	—

2 RUPEES

2 Rupee Obverses

Type A. Asoka column 15mm tall. 5 fur rows on right lion. No lion whiskers.

Type B. Asoka column 14mm tall. 3 fur rows on right lion. 5 lion whiskers.

Type C. Asoka column 13mm tall. 4 fur rows on right lion.

Type D. Asoka column 13mm tall. 4 fur rows. Recut chest on central lion.

Type E. Asoka column 13mm tall. No fur rows on right lion. 2 whiskers on central lion

NOTE: Obverses C and D include both 4.5 x 5mm and 5 x 5.5mm numeral 2 varieties.

KM# 120 2 RUPEES

Copper-Nickel, 28 mm. **Subject:** IX Asian Games **Obv:** Asoka lion pedestal, denomination below **Rev:** Sun above logo **Note:** Incomplete security edge known.

Date	Mintage	VF20	XF40	MS60	MS63	MS65
1982 (B)	12,720,000	1.00	1.50	2.00	—	—
1982 B	Inc. above	PF63 40.00				
1982 (C)	Inc. above	1.00	1.50	2.00	—	—

KM# 121.1 2 RUPEES

7.95 g., Copper-Nickel, 28 mm. **Subject:** National Integration **Rev:** Flag on map **Note:** Security edge, small date.

Date	Mintage	VF20	XF40	MS60	MS63	MS65
1982 (B)	—	1.00	1.50	2.00	—	—
Note: Mintage included in KM120						
1982 B	—	PF63 40.00				
1982 (C)	—	1.00	1.50	2.00	—	—
Note: Mintage included in KM120						

KM# 122 2 RUPEES

Copper-Nickel **Subject:** Golden Jubilee of Reserve Bank of India **Obv:** Asoka lion pedestal, denomination below **Rev:** Lion in front of tree

Date	Mintage	VF20	XF40	MS60	MS63	MS65
ND-1985 (B)	—	PF63 60.00				
Note: Sets only						

KM# 121.2 2 RUPEES

8.02 g., Copper-Nickel, 28 mm. **Subject:** National Integration **Rev:** Flag on map **Note:** Incomplete security edges known, large date.

Date	Mintage	VF20	XF40	MS60	MS63	MS65
1990 (B)	—	1.00	1.50	2.00	—	—
1990 (C)	—	1.00	1.50	2.00	—	—
1990 (C) Plain edge	—	10.00	15.00	20.00	—	—
1990 (H)	—	2.00	3.00	4.00	—	—
1990 (H) Milled edge	—	10.00	17.00	30.00	—	—

KM# 123 2 RUPEES

Copper-Nickel **Subject:** Tourism Year **Obv:** Asoka lion pedestal above denomination **Rev:** Stylized design

Date	Mintage	VF20	XF40	MS60	MS63	MS65
1991 (B)	—	PF63 60.00				
Note: Sets only.						

KM# 121.3 2 RUPEES

6.00 g., Copper-Nickel, 26 mm. **Subject:** National Integration **Obv:** Type A Lion capitol of Ashoka Pillar **Rev:** Flag on map **Edge:** Plain **Shape:** 11-sided **Note:** Reduced size, non magnetic.

Date	Mintage	VF20	XF40	MS60	MS63	MS65
1992 (B)	—	8.00	14.00	20.00	—	—
1992 (C)	—	4.00	7.00	10.00	—	—
1992 (H)	—	4.00	7.00	10.00	—	—
1993 (C)	—	1.00	1.50	2.00	—	—
1993 (H)	—	1.00	1.50	2.00	—	—
1994 (C)	—	1.00	1.50	2.00	—	—
1994 (H)	—	1.00	1.50	2.00	—	—
1995 (B)	—	10.00	15.00	30.00	—	—
1995 (C)	—	1.00	1.50	2.00	—	—
1995 (H)	—	1.00	1.50	2.00	—	—
1996 (C)	—	1.00	1.50	2.00	—	—
1996 (H)	—	1.00	1.50	2.00	—	—
1997 (C)	—	1.00	1.50	2.00	—	—
1997 (H)	—	1.00	1.50	2.00	—	—
1998 (C)	—	1.00	1.50	2.00	—	—
1999 (C)	—	1.00	1.50	2.00	—	—
2000 (C)	—	1.00	1.50	2.00	—	—
2000 (R)	—	1.00	1.50	2.00	—	—

KM# 121.4 2 RUPEES

6.00 g., Copper-Nickel, 26 mm. **Subject:** National Integration **Obv:** Type B **Rev:** Flag on map **Edge:** Plain

Date	Mintage	VF20	XF40	MS60	MS63	MS65
1992 (B)	—	0.60	0.80	1.20	—	—
1993 (B)	—	0.60	0.80	1.20	—	—
1994 (B)	—	0.60	0.80	1.20	—	—
1994 (H)	—	10.00	15.00	20.00	—	—
1994 (N)	—	4.00	7.00	10.00	—	—
1995 (B)	—	0.60	0.80	1.50	—	—
1995 (H)	—	12.00	17.00	24.00	—	—
1995 (N)	—	0.60	0.80	1.20	—	—
1996 (B)	—	6.00	8.00	10.00	—	—
1996 (N)	—	0.50	0.80	1.20	—	—
1997 (B)	—	0.60	0.80	1.20	—	—
1998 (N)	—	0.60	0.80	1.20	—	—
1999 (N)	—	0.60	0.80	1.20	—	—

KM# 323 2 RUPEES

5.75 g., Copper-Nickel, 26.4 mm. **Subject:** National Land Conservation **Obv:** Asoka lion pedestal above denomination **Rev:** Tree above wavy lines **Edge:** Plain **Shape:** 11-sided **Note:** Minted in 1993, but never released in circulation or sets.

Date	Mintage	VF20	XF40	MS60	MS63	MS65
1992	—	2,000	3,000	4,000	—	—

KM# 124.1 2 RUPEES

Copper-Nickel **Subject:** Small Family Happy Family **Obv:** Type B **Rev:** Family scene

Date	Mintage	VF20	XF40	MS60	MS63	MS65
1993 (B)	—	1.50	3.50	7.00	—	—

KM# 124.2 2 RUPEES

Copper-Nickel **Subject:** Small Family Happy Family **Obv:** Type A **Rev:** Family scene

Date	Mintage	VF20	XF40	MS60	MS63	MS65
1993 (H)	—	1.00	3.00	6.00	—	—

KM# 125.1 2 RUPEES

Copper-Nickel **Series:** World Food Day **Subject:** Bio Diversity **Obv:** Type B **Rev:** Mountains, trees and fish

Date	Mintage	VF20	XF40	MS60	MS63	MS65
1993 (B)	—	1.00	3.50	7.00	—	—

KM# 125.2 2 RUPEES

Copper-Nickel **Subject:** Bio Diversity **Obv:** Type A **Rev:** Mountains, trees and fish

Date	Mintage	VF20	XF40	MS60	MS63	MS65
1993 (H)	—	2.00	6.00	10.00	—	—

KM# 126.1 2 RUPEES

Copper-Nickel **Series:** F.A.O. **Subject:** Water For Life **Obv:** Type A **Rev:** Large teardrop above water

Date	Mintage	VF20	XF40	MS60	MS63	MS65
1994 (B)	—	4.00	6.00	7.00	—	—
1994 (C)	—	1.00	5.00	10.00	—	—
1994 (H)	—	1.00	5.00	10.00	—	—

KM# 126.2 2 RUPEES

Copper-Nickel **Subject:** Water for Life **Obv:** Type B **Rev:** Large teardrop above water

Date	Mintage	VF20	XF40	MS60	MS63	MS65
1994 (B)	—	10.00	24.00	40.00	—	—

KM# 121.5 2 RUPEES

6.06 g., Copper-Nickel, 26 mm. **Subject:** National Integration **Obv:** Type C Lion capitol of Ashoka Pillar **Rev:** Flag on map **Edge:** Plain **Note:** 11-sided

Date	Mintage	VF20	XF40	MS60	MS63	MS65
1995 (B)	—	6.00	8.00	12.00	—	—
1996 (B)	—	0.60	0.80	1.20	—	—
1996 (H)	—	0.60	0.80	1.20	—	—
1997 (B)	—	0.60	0.80	1.20	—	—
1997 (H)	—	0.60	0.80	1.20	—	—
1997 (T)	—	0.60	0.80	1.20	—	—
1998 (B)	—	0.60	0.80	1.20	—	—
1998 (C)	—	10.00	20.00	30.00	—	—
1998 (H)	—	0.60	0.80	1.20	—	—
1998 (P)	—	0.60	0.80	1.20	—	—
1998 (T)	—	0.60	0.80	1.20	—	—
1999 (B)	—	0.60	0.80	1.20	—	—
1999 (C)	—	10.00	13.00	20.00	—	—
1999 (H)	—	0.60	0.80	1.20	—	—
1999 (Ld)	—	0.60	0.80	1.20	—	—
2000 (H)	—	0.60	0.80	1.20	—	—
2000 (R)	—	0.60	0.80	1.20	—	—
2000 (B)	—	0.60	0.80	1.20	—	—

KM# 127.1 2 RUPEES

Copper-Nickel **Subject:** Globalizing Indian Agriculture - Agriexpo 95 **Obv:** Type A **Rev:** Steer head within wreath of two stalks of wheat

Date	Mintage	VF20	XF40	MS60	MS63	MS65
1995 (B)	—	7.00	9.00	10.00	—	—
1995 (C)	—	7.00	9.00	12.00	—	—

KM# 127.2 2 RUPEES

Copper-Nickel **Subject:** Globalizing Indian Agriculture - Agriexpo 55 **Obv:** Type B **Rev:** Steer head within wreath of two stalks of wheat

Date	Mintage	VF20	XF40	MS60	MS63	MS65
1995 (B)	—	10.00	25.00	40.00	—	—

KM# 127.3 2 RUPEES

Copper-Nickel **Obv:** Type C **Rev:** Steer head within wreath of two stalks of wheat

Date	Mintage	VF20	XF40	MS60	MS63	MS65
1995 (B)	—	10.00	30.00	60.00	—	—

KM# 128.1 2 RUPEES

Copper-Nickel **Subject:** Eighth World Tamil Conference **Obv:** Type C, Asoka column 13mm tall **Rev:** St. Thiruvalluvar

Date	Mintage	VF20	XF40	MS60	MS63	MS65
1995 (B)	—	1.00	1.50	2.00	—	—

KM# 128.2 2 RUPEES

Copper-Nickel **Subject:** 8th World Tamil Conference **Obv:** Type B **Rev:** St. Thiruvalluvar

Date	Mintage	VF20	XF40	MS60	MS63	MS65
1995 (B)	—	30.00	60.00	100	—	—

KM# 129.1 2 RUPEES

Copper-Nickel **Subject:** Sardar Vallabhbhai Patel **Obv:** Type A **Rev:** Bust right

Date	Mintage	VF20	XF40	MS60	MS63	MS65
1996 (C)	—	10.00	30.00	60.00	—	—

KM# 129.2 2 RUPEES

Copper-Nickel **Subject:** Sardar Vallabhbhai Patel **Obv:** Type B **Rev:** Bust right

Date	Mintage	VF20	XF40	MS60	MS63	MS65
1996 (N)	—	2.00	3.00	4.00	—	—

KM# 129.3 2 RUPEES

Copper-Nickel **Subject:** Sardar Vallabhbhai Patel **Obv:** Type C **Rev:** Bust right

Date	Mintage	VF20	XF40	MS60	MS63	MS65
1996 (B)	—	1.50	2.50	3.50	—	—
1996 (C)	—	2.00	3.00	4.00	—	—
1996 (H)	—	1.00	1.50	2.00	—	—
1996 M	—	PF63 40.00				

KM# 129.4 2 RUPEES

Copper-Nickel **Subject:** Sardar Vallabhbhai Patel **Obv:** Type D **Rev:** Bust right

Date	Mintage	VF20	XF40	MS60	MS63	MS65
1996 (B)	—	1.00	1.50	2.00	—	—
1996 (C)	—	4.00	7.00	10.00	—	—

KM# 129.5 2 RUPEES

Copper-Nickel **Subject:** Sardar Vallabhbhai Patel **Obv:** Type E **Rev:** Bust right

Date	Mintage	VF20	XF40	MS60	MS63	MS65
1996 (B)	—	40.00	60.00	100	—	—
1996 (B) Broken Die	—	20.00	30.00	40.00	—	—

KM# 130.3 2 RUPEES
6.00 g., Copper-Nickel **Subject:** Subhas Chandra Bose **Obv:** Type C **Rev:** Bust left

Date	Mintage	VF20	XF40	MS60	MS63	MS65
1996 (C)	—	60.00	125	200	—	—

KM# 130.1 2 RUPEES
6.00 g., Copper-Nickel **Subject:** Subhas Chandra Bose **Obv:** Type C **Rev:** Bust left

Date	Mintage	VF20	XF40	MS60	MS63	MS65
1997 (B)	—	1.00	1.50	2.00	—	—
1997 (C)	—	1.00	1.50	2.00	—	—
1997 (C)	—	PF63 40.00				
1997 (H)	—	2.00	3.00	4.00	—	—

KM# 130.2 2 RUPEES
6.00 g., Copper-Nickel **Subject:** Subhas Chandra Bose **Obv:** Type B **Rev:** Bust left

Date	Mintage	VF20	XF40	MS60	MS63	MS65
1997 (N)	—	1.00	1.50	2.00	—	—

KM# 121.3a 2 RUPEES
Nickel magnetic **Obv:** Type A **Edge:** Plain **Shape:** 11-sided

Date	Mintage	VF20	XF40	MS60	MS63	MS65
1998 (C)	—	10.00	25.00	40.00	—	—

KM# 121.6 2 RUPEES
Copper-Nickel, 26 mm. **Subject:** National Integration **Obv:** Type D **Rev:** Flag on map **Edge:** Plain **Shape:** 11-sided

Date	Mintage	VF20	XF40	MS60	MS63	MS65
1998 (B)	—	0.40	0.80	1.20	—	—
1998 (H)	—	0.40	0.80	1.20	—	—
1999 (B)	—	0.40	0.80	1.20	—	—
2000 (B)	—	0.40	0.80	1.20	—	—

KM# 131.1 2 RUPEES
6.00 g., Copper-Nickel **Subject:** Sri Aurobindo **Obv:** Type C **Rev:** Head 3/4 facing

Date	Mintage	VF20	XF40	MS60	MS63	MS65
1998 (B)	—	1.00	2.50	3.50	—	—
1998 (C)	—	2.00	3.00	4.00	—	—
1998 M	—	PF63 40.00				

KM# 131.2 2 RUPEES
Copper-Nickel **Subject:** Sri Aurobindo **Obv:** Type D **Rev:** Head 3/4 facing

Date	Mintage	VF20	XF40	MS60	MS63	MS65
1998 (C)	—	1.00	1.50	2.00	—	—
1998 (B)	—	1.00	1.50	2.00	—	—
1998 (N)	—	1.00	1.50	2.00	—	—

KM# 131.3 2 RUPEES
Copper-Nickel **Subject:** Sri Aurobindo **Obv:** Type A **Rev:** Bust facing

Date	Mintage	VF20	XF40	MS60	MS63	MS65
1998 (C)	—	40.00	60.00	100	—	—

KM# 296.1 2 RUPEES
6.00 g., Copper-Nickel **Subject:** Deshbandhu Chittaranjan Das **Obv:** Type A **Rev:** Head facing

Date	Mintage	VF20	XF40	MS60	MS63	MS65
1998 (C)	—	10.00	25.00	60.00	—	—

KM# 296.2 2 RUPEES
Copper-Nickel **Subject:** Deshbandhu Chittaranjan Das **Obv:** Type B **Rev:** Head facing **Note:** The dot mint mark exists in large and small sizes.

Date	Mintage	VF20	XF40	MS60	MS63	MS65
1998 (N)	—	4.00	7.00	10.00	—	—

KM# 296.3 2 RUPEES
Copper-Nickel **Subject:** Deshbandhu Chittaranjan Das **Obv:** Type C **Rev:** Head facing **Note:** 7mm, edge flat.

Date	Mintage	VF20	XF40	MS60	MS63	MS65
1998 (C)	—	10.00	15.00	20.00	—	—
1998 (C)	—	PF63 40.00				

KM# 296.4 2 RUPEES
6.00 g., Copper-Nickel **Subject:** Deshbandhu Chittaranjan Das **Obv:** Type C **Rev:** Head facing **Note:** 5-6mm, edge flat.

Date	Mintage	VF20	XF40	MS60	MS63	MS65
1998 (C)	—	14.00	20.00	30.00	—	—

KM# 296.5 2 RUPEES
6.00 g., Copper-Nickel **Subject:** Deshbandhu Chittaranjan Das **Obv:** Type C **Rev:** Head facing **Note:** 3-5mm, edge flat.

Date	Mintage	VF20	XF40	MS60	MS63	MS65
1998	—	1.00	1.50	2.00	—	—
1998 (C)	—	400	500	600	—	—

KM# 296.6 2 RUPEES
Copper-Nickel **Subject:** Deshbandhu Chittaranjan Das **Obv:** Type D **Rev:** Head facing **Note:** 3-5mm, edge flat.

Date	Mintage	VF20	XF40	MS60	MS63	MS65
1998 (C)	—	3.00	6.00	9.00	—	—

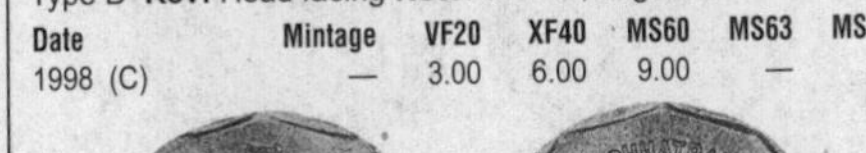

KM# 290 2 RUPEES
6.00 g., Copper-Nickel **Subject:** Chhatrapati Shivaji **Obv:** Type C **Rev:** Turbaned bust right

Date	Mintage	VF20	XF40	MS60	MS63	MS65
1999 (B)	—	1.00	2.50	4.00	—	—
1999 (C)	—	2.00	4.00	6.00	—	—
1999 (H)	—	4.00	7.00	10.00	—	—
1999 M	—	PF63 40.00				
1999 (N)	—	1.00	1.50	2.00	—	—

KM# 291 2 RUPEES
6.00 g., Copper-Nickel **Subject:** Supreme Court: 50 Years **Obv:** Type C **Rev:** Wheel above asoka lion pedestal **Edge:** Plain

Date	Mintage	VF20	XF40	MS60	MS63	MS65
2000 (B)	—	1.00	2.50	4.00	—	—
2000 (C)	—	1.00	1.50	2.00	—	—
2000 (C)	—	PF63 10.00				
2000 (N)	—	1.00	1.50	2.00	—	—

KM# 150 5 RUPEES
Copper-Nickel **Subject:** Death of Indira Gandi - statesperson, 1917-1984 **Obv:** Asoka lion pedestal, denomination below **Rev:** Bust right

Date	Mintage	VF20	XF40	MS60	MS63	MS65
ND-1985 (B)	59,288,000	2.00	6.00	8.00	—	—
ND-1985 B	Inc. above	PF63 60.00				
ND-1985 (H)	Inc. above	6.00	8.00	10.00	—	—

KM# 151 5 RUPEES
Copper-Nickel **Subject:** 100th Anniversary - Nehru's Birth **Obv:** Asoka lion pedestal, denomination below **Rev:** Head right

Date	Mintage	VF20	XF40	MS60	MS63	MS65
1989 (B)	—	2.00	4.00	6.00	—	—
Note: Large head. Short rim teeth.						
1989 (B)	—	10.00	30.00	60.00	—	—
Note: Small head. Long rim teeth.						
1989	—	PF63 60.00				
1989 (H)	—	10.00	15.00	20.00	—	—

KM# 152 5 RUPEES
Copper-Nickel **Subject:** Commonwealth Parliamentary Conference **Obv:** Asoka lion pedestal, denomination below **Rev:** Building

Date	Mintage	VF20	XF40	MS60	MS63	MS65
1991 B	—	PF63 60.00				

KM# 153 5 RUPEES
Copper-Nickel **Subject:** Tourism Year **Obv:** Asoka lion pedestal, denomination below **Rev:** Stylized design

Date	Mintage	VF20	XF40	MS60	MS63	MS65
1991 B	—	PF63 60.00				
1991 B Proof, packaged	—	PF63 200				

KM# 154.1 5 RUPEES
9.30 g., Copper-Nickel, 23.4 mm. **Obv:** Lion capitol of Ashoka Pillar. Type I **Rev:** Denomination flanked by flowers **Edge:** Security **Note:** (C) - Calcutta mint has issued 2 distinctly different security edge varieties every year 1992-2003 with large dots and thick center line, w/small dots and narrow center line.

Date	Mintage	VF20	XF40	MS60	MS63	MS65
1992 (B)	—	1.00	1.50	2.00	—	—
1992 (C)	—	1.00	1.50	2.00	—	—
1992 (H)	—	1.00	1.50	2.00	—	—
1993 (B)	—	1.00	1.50	2.00	—	—
1993 (C)	—	1.00	1.50	2.00	—	—
1994 (B)	—	1.00	1.50	2.00	—	—
1994 (C)	—	1.00	1.50	2.00	—	—
1994 (H)	—	1.00	1.50	2.00	—	—
1995 (B)	—	1.00	1.50	2.00	—	—
1995 (C)	—	1.00	1.50	2.00	—	—
1995 (H)	—	1.00	1.50	2.00	—	—
1995 (N)	—	1.00	1.50	2.00	—	—
1996 (B)	—	1.00	1.50	2.00	—	—
1996 (C)	—	1.00	1.50	2.00	—	—
1996 (H)	—	1.00	1.50	2.00	—	—
1996 (N)	—	1.00	1.50	2.00	—	—
1997 (B)	—	1.00	1.50	2.00	—	—
1997 (C)	—	1.00	1.50	2.00	—	—
1997 (H)	—	1.00	1.50	2.00	—	—
1997 (N)	—	1.00	1.50	2.00	—	—
1998 (B)	—	1.00	1.50	2.00	—	—
1998 (C)	—	1.00	1.50	2.00	—	—
1998 (H)	—	1.00	1.50	2.00	—	—
1998 (N)	—	1.00	1.50	2.00	—	—
1999 (B)	—	10.00	20.00	40.00	—	—
1999 (C)	—	1.00	1.50	2.00	—	—
1999 (H)	—	1.00	1.50	2.00	—	—
1999 (N)	—	1.00	1.50	2.00	—	—
1999 (R)	—	1.00	1.50	2.00	—	—
2000 (C)	—	1.00	1.50	2.00	—	—
2000 (H)	—	1.00	1.50	2.00	—	—
2000 (N)	—	1.00	1.50	2.00	—	—
2000 (R)	—	1.00	1.50	2.00	—	—

KM# 154.2 5 RUPEES
8.91 g., Copper-Nickel, 23 mm. **Obv:** Lion capitol of Ashoka

Pillar **Rev:** Denomination flanked by flowers **Edge:** Reeded

Date	Mintage	VF20	XF40	MS60	MS63	MS65
1992 (C)	—	10.00	19.00	20.00	—	—
1992 (H)	—	10.00	19.00	20.00	—	—
1993 (B)	—	10.00	19.00	20.00	—	—
1993 (C)	—	10.00	19.00	20.00	—	—
1994 (B)	—	10.00	19.00	20.00	—	—
1994 (C)	—	10.00	19.00	20.00	—	—
1994 (H)	—	10.00	19.00	20.00	—	—
1995 (B)	—	10.00	19.00	20.00	—	—
1995 (C)	—	10.00	19.00	20.00	—	—
1995 (H)	—	10.00	19.00	20.00	—	—
1996 (B)	—	10.00	19.00	20.00	—	—
1996 (C)	—	10.00	19.00	20.00	—	—
1996 (H)	—	10.00	19.00	20.00	—	—
1997 (B)	—	10.00	19.00	20.00	—	—
1997 (C)	—	10.00	19.00	20.00	—	—
1998 (C)	—	10.00	19.00	20.00	—	—
1998 (B)	—	10.00	19.00	20.00	—	—
1998 (H)	—	10.00	19.00	20.00	—	—
1999 (B)	—	10.00	19.00	20.00	—	—
1999 (C)	—	10.00	19.00	20.00	—	—
1999 (H)	—	10.00	19.00	20.00	—	—
2000 (C)	—	10.00	19.00	20.00	—	—
2000 (B)	—	10.00	19.00	20.00	—	—
2000 (H)	—	10.00	19.00	20.00	—	—

KM# 155.1 5 RUPEES
Copper-Nickel, 23 mm. **Subject:** World of Work "ILO" **Obv:** Asoka lion pedestal, denomination below **Rev:** With logo of Internation Labour Origintion **Edge:** Security

Date	Mintage	VF20	XF40	MS60	MS63	MS65
ND-1994 (B)	—	5.00	8.00	10.00	—	—
ND-1994 B	—	PF63 50.00				
ND-1994 (H)	—	5.00	8.00	10.00	—	—

KM# 155.2 5 RUPEES
Copper-Nickel, 23 mm. **Subject:** World of Work **Obv:** Asoka lion pedestal, denomination below **Rev:** Denomination within broken dentil circle, wreath surrounds **Edge:** Milled

Date	Mintage	VF20	XF40	MS60	MS63	MS65
1994 (B)	—	10.00	18.00	30.00	—	—
1994 (H)	—	10.00	18.00	30.00	—	—
1995 (N)	—	10.00	18.00	30.00	—	—

KM# 156.1 5 RUPEES
Copper-Nickel, 23 mm. **Series:** 50 Years - United Nations **Obv:** Asoka lion pedestal, denomination below **Rev:** Date above UN logo **Edge:** Security or plain **Note:** Tall and short letters

Date	Mintage	VF20	XF40	MS60	MS63	MS65
1995 (B)	—	7.00	8.00	10.00	—	—
1995 (N)	—	2.00	5.00	9.00	—	—

KM# 156.2 5 RUPEES
Copper-Nickel, 23 mm. **Subject:** 50 Years United Nations **Obv:** Asoka lion pedestal similar to 2 Rupees, KM#121.3 **Rev:** Date above UN logo

Date	Mintage	VF20	XF40	MS60	MS63	MS65
1995 (B)	—	10.00	30.00	50.00	—	—

KM# 157 5 RUPEES
Copper-Nickel, 23 mm. **Series:** 50th Anniversary - F.A.O. **Obv:** Asoka lion pedestal, denomination below **Rev:** Hand clutching stalks of wheat **Edge:** Milled or security

Date	Mintage	VF20	XF40	MS60	MS63	MS65
1995 (B)	—	3.00	6.00	10.00	—	—
1995 (H)	—	2.00	5.00	9.00	—	—
1995 (N)	—	2.00	5.00	9.00	—	—

KM# 158 5 RUPEES
Copper-Nickel, 23 mm. **Subject:** Eighth World Tamil Conference **Obv:** Asoka lion pedestal, denomination below **Rev:** St. Thiruvalluvar **Edge:** Milled or security

Date	Mintage	VF20	XF40	MS60	MS63	MS65
1995 (B)	—	2.00	5.00	10.00	—	—
1995 (N)	—	10.00	20.00	23.00	—	—

KM# 159 5 RUPEES
Copper-Nickel, 23 mm. **Subject:** Mother's Health is Child's Health **Edge:** Milled or security

Date	Mintage	VF20	XF40	MS60	MS63	MS65
1996 (B)	—	3.00	6.00	10.00	—	—
1996 (H)	—	3.00	6.00	10.00	—	—
1996 (N)	—	3.00	6.00	10.00	—	—

KM# 160 5 RUPEES
9.00 g., Copper-Nickel, 23 mm. **Subject:** 2nd International Crop Science Conference **Obv:** Asoka lion pedestal, denomination below **Rev:** Plants on globe, spray below, braid above **Edge:** Security **Note:** This conference was never held.

Date	Mintage	VF20	XF40	MS60	MS63	MS65
1996 (C)	11,000	100	150	225	—	—
1996 (C) Restrike	—	—	—	225	—	—

Note: In set of 2 coins.

KM# 154.3 5 RUPEES
Copper-Nickel, 23 mm. **Obv:** Asoka lion pedestal **Rev:** Denomination flanked by flowers **Edge:** Plain

Date	Mintage	VF20	XF40	MS60	MS63	MS65
1998 (H)	—	10.00	20.00	30.00	—	—
1999 (H)	—	10.00	20.00	30.00	—	—

KM# 154.4 5 RUPEES
9.30 g., Copper-Nickel, 23.4 mm. **Obv:** Lion capitol of Ashoka Pillar, Type II, Small Lion **Rev:** Denomination flanked by flowers **Edge:** Security

Date	Mintage	VF20	XF40	MS60	MS63	MS65
1998 (B)	—	2.00	6.00	10.00	—	—
1999 (B)	—	1.00	1.50	2.00	—	—
2000 (B)	—	1.00	1.50	2.00	—	—

KM# 185 10 RUPEES
15.00 g., 0.800 Silver 0.3858 oz. ASW, 34 mm. **Subject:** Centennial - Mahatma Gandhi's Birth **Obv:** Asoka lion pedestal, denomination below **Rev:** Head left **Note:** Struck during 1969 and 1970.

Date	Mintage	VF20	XF40	MS60	MS63	MS65
ND-1969 (B)	3,160,000	—	30.00	40.00	45.00	—
ND-1969 B	9,147	PF65 50.00				
ND-1969 (C)	100,000	—	40.00	50.00	70.00	—

KM# 186 10 RUPEES
15.00 g., 0.800 Silver 0.3858 oz. ASW, 34 mm. **Series:** F.A.O. **Obv:** Asoka lion pedestal **Rev:** Floating lotus flower below sun

Date	Mintage	VF20	XF40	MS60	MS63	MS65
1970 (B)	300,000	—	—	70.00	90.00	—
1970 B	3,046	PF65 150				
1970 Proof, packaged	—	PF65 325				
1970 (C)	100,000	—	—	70.00	90.00	—
1971 (B)	—	—	—	70.00	90.00	—
1971 B	1,594	PF65 150				

KM# 187.1 10 RUPEES
22.50 g., 0.500 Silver 0.3617 oz. ASW, 39 mm. **Subject:** 25th Anniversary of Independence **Obv:** Asoka lion pedestal **Rev:** Figures holding flag, building in background **Note:** Inner flag circle complete.

Date	Mintage	VF20	XF40	MS60	MS63	MS65
ND-1972 (B)	1,000,000	—	—	30.00	40.00	—
ND-1972 B	7,895	PF65 60.00				
ND-1972 B Proof, packaged	—	PF65 175				

KM# 187.2 10 RUPEES
22.50 g., 0.500 Silver 0.3617 oz. ASW, 39 mm. **Subject:** 25th Anniversary of Independence **Obv:** Aslka lion pedestal **Rev:** Figures holding flag, building in background **Note:** Rim thinner, inner flag circle missing on Calcutta issues.

Date	Mintage	VF20	XF40	MS60	MS63	MS65
ND-1972 (C)	—	—	—	30.00	40.00	—
ND-1972 (C)	—	PF65 60.00				

KM# 188 10 RUPEES
22.50 g., 0.500 Silver 0.3617 oz. ASW, 39 mm. **Series:** F.A.O. **Obv:** Asoka lion pedestal **Rev:** Inscription on shield within grain stalks

Date	Mintage	VF20	XF40	MS60	MS63	MS65
1973 (B)	64,000	—	—	38.00	45.00	—
1973 B	15,000	PF65 70.00				

KM# 189 10 RUPEES

Copper-Nickel, 39 mm. **Series:** F.A.O. **Obv:** Asoka lion pedestal **Rev:** Family within triangle, grain ears flank

Date	Mintage	VF20	XF40	MS60	MS63	MS65
1974 (B)	65,000	—	—	30.00	40.00	—
1974 B	12,000	PF65 60.00				

KM# 190 10 RUPEES

Copper-Nickel, 39 mm. **Series:** F.A.O. **Subject:** Women's Year **Obv:** Asoka lion pedestal **Rev:** Bust at left looking right, grain ear at right

Date	Mintage	VF20	XF40	MS60	MS63	MS65
1975 (B)	49,000	—	—	30.00	40.00	—
1975 B	2,531	PF65 60.00				

KM# 191 10 RUPEES

Copper-Nickel **Series:** F.A.O. **Subject:** Food and Work For All **Obv:** Asoka lion pedestal **Rev:** Figure on tractor, utility pole and buildings in background

Date	Mintage	VF20	XF40	MS60	MS63	MS65
1976 (B)	49,000	—	—	30.00	40.00	—
1976 B	3,400	PF65 60.00				

KM# 192 10 RUPEES

Copper-Nickel **Series:** F.A.O. **Subject:** Save For Development **Obv:** Asoka lion pedestal **Rev:** Symbols of development

Date	Mintage	VF20	XF40	MS60	MS63	MS65
1977 (B)	20,000	—	—	30.00	40.00	—
1977 B	5,969	PF65 60.00				

KM# 193 10 RUPEES

Copper-Nickel **Series:** F.A.O. **Subject:** Food and Shelter For All **Obv:** Asoka lion pedestal **Rev:** Grain sprig, house and road within circle

Date	Mintage	VF20	XF40	MS60	MS63	MS65
1978 (B)	25,000	—	—	30.00	40.00	—
1978 B	—	PF65 60.00				

KM# 194 10 RUPEES

Copper-Nickel **Series:** International Year of the Child **Obv:** Asoka lion pedestal, denomination below **Rev:** Logo on square within circle, wreath surrounds

Date	Mintage	VF20	XF40	MS60	MS63	MS65
1979 (B)	—	—	—	45.00	60.00	—
1979 B	—	PF65 80.00				

KM# 195 10 RUPEES

Copper-Nickel **Subject:** Rural Women's Advancement **Obv:** Asoka lion pedestal, denomination below **Rev:** Woman grinding wheat

Date	Mintage	VF20	XF40	MS60	MS63	MS65
1980 (B)	—	—	—	45.00	60.00	—
1980 B	—	PF65 80.00				

KM# 196 10 RUPEES

Copper-Nickel **Series:** World Food Day **Obv:** Asoka lion pedestal **Rev:** Man and woman, man carrying sheaf

Date	Mintage	VF20	XF40	MS60	MS63	MS65
1981 (B)	—	—	—	45.00	60.00	—
1981 B	—	PF65 80.00				

KM# 197 10 RUPEES

Copper-Nickel **Subject:** IX Asian Games

Date	Mintage	VF20	XF40	MS60	MS63	MS65
1982 (B)	—	—	—	45.00	60.00	—
1982 B	—	PF65 80.00				

KM# 198 10 RUPEES

Copper-Nickel **Subject:** National Integration **Obv:** Asoka lion pedestal **Rev:** Flag on map

Date	Mintage	VF20	XF40	MS60	MS63	MS65
1982 (B)	—	—	—	45.00	60.00	—
1982 B	—	PF65 80.00				

KM# 199 10 RUPEES

Copper-Nickel **Subject:** Golden Jubilee - Reserve Bank of India **Obv:** Asoka lion pedestal **Rev:** Lion in front of tree

Date	Mintage	VF20	XF40	MS60	MS63	MS65
ND-1985 (B)	—	—	—	50.00	70.00	—
ND-1985 B	—	PF65 120				

Note: Sets only

KM# 200 10 RUPEES

Copper-Nickel **Subject:** International Youth Year **Obv:** Small asoka pedestal above denomination **Rev:** Three outlined profiles between dove and laurel branch

Date	Mintage	VF20	XF40	MS60	MS63	MS65
1985 (C)	—	—	—	50.00	70.00	—
1985 (C)	—	PF65 90.00				
1985 (C) Proof, packaged	—	PF65 250				

KM# 201 10 RUPEES

Copper-Nickel **Subject:** Commonwealth Parliamentary Conference **Obv:** Asoka lion pedestal above denomination **Rev:** Building

Date	Mintage	VF20	XF40	MS60	MS63	MS65
1991 (B) Prooflike	—	—	—	50.00	70.00	—
1991 B	—	PF65 90.00				

KM# 202 10 RUPEES

Copper-Nickel **Subject:** India **Obv:** Asoka lion pedestal above denomination **Rev:** Monument

Date	Mintage	VF20	XF40	MS60	MS63	MS65
1992 B	—	—	—	50.00	70.00	—
1992 B	—	PF65 90.00				

KM# 203 10 RUPEES

Copper-Nickel **Subject:** 100th Anniversary - Birth of Patel **Obv:** Type A **Rev:** Head right

Date	Mintage	VF20	XF40	MS60	MS63	MS65
1996 (B)	—	—	—	50.00	70.00	—
1996 M	—	PF65 90.00				

KM# 204 10 RUPEES

12.50 g., Copper-Nickel, 31 mm. **Subject:** Subhas Chandra Bose **Obv:** Type C **Rev:** Bust left

Date	Mintage	VF20	XF40	MS60	MS63	MS65
1997 (C)	—	—	—	50.00	80.00	—
1997 (C)	—	PF65 90.00				

KM# 205 10 RUPEES

12.50 g., Copper-Nickel, 31 mm. **Subject:** Sri Aurobindo **Obv:** Type C **Rev:** Head 3/4 facing **Edge:** Reeded

Date	Mintage	VF20	XF40	MS60	MS63	MS65
1998 (B)	—	—	—	120	150	—
1998 M	—	PF65 225				

KM# 297 10 RUPEES

12.50 g., Copper-Nickel, 31 mm. **Subject:** Deshbandhu Chittaranjan Das **Obv:** Asoka lion pedestal above denomination **Rev:** Bust facing **Edge:** Reeded

Date	Mintage	VF20	XF40	MS60	MS63	MS65
1998 (C)	—	—	—	60.00	80.00	—
1998 (C)	—	PF65 120				

KM# 240 20 RUPEES

30.00 g., 0.500 Silver 0.4823 oz. ASW, 44 mm. **Series:** F.A.O. **Obv:** Asoka lion pedestal, denomination below **Rev:** Inscription on shield, grain stalks flank

Date	Mintage	VF20	XF40	MS60	MS63	MS65
1973 (B)	64,000	—	—	80.00	100	—
1973 B	12,000	PF65 150				

KM# 241 20 RUPEES

23.00 g., Copper-Nickel, 39 mm. **Subject:** Death of Indira Gandhi - statesperson, 1917-1984 **Rev:** Head right **Edge:** Reeded

Date	Mintage	VF20	XF40	MS60	MS63	MS65
ND-1985 (B)	—	—	—	100	125	—
ND-1985 B	—	PF65 200				

KM# 242 20 RUPEES

Copper-Nickel **Series:** F.A.O. **Subject:** Fisheries **Obv:** Asoka lion pedestal, denomination below **Rev:** People with fishing nets

Date	Mintage	VF20	XF40	MS60	MS63	MS65
1986 (B)	—	—	—	100	125	—
1986 B	—	PF65 200				

KM# 243 20 RUPEES

Copper-Nickel **Series:** F.A.O. **Subject:** Small Farmers **Obv:** Asoka lion pedestal, denomination below **Rev:** Farmers planting

Date	Mintage	VF20	XF40	MS60	MS63	MS65
1987 (B)	—	—	—	100	125	—
1987 B	—	PF65 200				

KM# 244 20 RUPEES

Copper-Nickel **Subject:** 100th Anniversary of Nehru's Birth **Obv:** Asoka lion pedestal, denomination below **Rev:** Head right

Date	Mintage	VF20	XF40	MS60	MS63	MS65
1989 (B)	—	—	—	100	125	—
1989 B	—	PF65 200				

KM# 255 50 RUPEES

34.70 g., 0.500 Silver 0.5578 oz. ASW, 44 mm. **Series:** F.A.O. **Obv:** Asoka lion pedestal, denomination below **Rev:** Family within triangle, grain ears flank

Date	Mintage	VF20	XF40	MS60	MS63	MS65
1974 (B)	82,000	—	—	100	125	—
1974 B	13,000	PF65 200				

KM# 256 50 RUPEES

34.70 g., 0.500 Silver 0.5578 oz. ASW, 44 mm. **Series:** F.A.O. **Subject:** Women's Year **Obv:** Asoka lion pedestal, denomination below **Rev:** Bust at left looking right, grain sprig at right

Date	Mintage	VF20	XF40	MS60	MS63	MS65
1975 (B)	65,000	—	—	100	125	—
1975 B	2,691	PF65 200				

KM# 257 50 RUPEES

34.70 g., 0.500 Silver 0.5578 oz. ASW **Series:** F.A.O. **Subject:** Food and Work For All **Obv:** Asoka lion pedestal, denomination below **Rev:** Figure on tractor, utility pole and buildings in background

Date	Mintage	VF20	XF40	MS60	MS63	MS65
1976 (B)	42,000	—	—	100	125	—
1976 B	3,385	PF65 200				

KM# 258 50 RUPEES

34.70 g., 0.500 Silver 0.5578 oz. ASW **Series:** F.A.O. **Subject:** Save For Development **Obv:** Asoka lion pedestal, denomination below **Rev:** Symbols of development

Date	Mintage	VF20	XF40	MS60	MS63	MS65
1977 (B)	26,000	—	—	100	125	—
1977 B	2,544	PF65 200				

KM# 259 50 RUPEES

34.70 g., 0.500 Silver 0.5578 oz. ASW **Series:** F.A.O. **Subject:** Food and Shelter For All **Obv:** Asoka lion pedestal, denomination below **Rev:** Grain stalk, house and road within circle

Date	Mintage	VF20	XF40	MS60	MS63	MS65
1978 (B)	25,000	—	—	100	125	—
1978 B	—	PF65 200				

KM# 260 50 RUPEES
34.70 g., 0.500 Silver 0.5578 oz. ASW **Series:** International Year of the Child **Obv:** Asoka lion pedestal, denomination below **Rev:** Emblem on square within circle, wreath surrounds

Date	Mintage	VF20	XF40	MS60	MS63	MS65
1979 (B)	—	—	—	50.00	60.00	—
1979 (B) Packaged	—	—	—	—	80.00	—
1979 B	—	PF65 80.00				

KM# 261 50 RUPEES
Copper-Nickel **Subject:** India **Obv:** Asoka lion pedestal, denomination below **Rev:** Monument

Date	Mintage	VF20	XF40	MS60	MS63	MS65
1992 (B)	—	—	—	50.00	60.00	—
1992 (B)	—	PF65 80.00				

KM# 262 50 RUPEES
30.00 g., Copper-Nickel, 39 mm. **Subject:** International Labor Organization, 75th Anniversary **Obv:** Asoka lion pedestal, denomination below **Rev:** Denomination within broken dentil circle, wreath surrounds **Edge:** Reeded

Date	Mintage	VF20	XF40	MS60	MS63	MS65
ND-1994	—	—	—	140	160	—
ND-1994	—	PF65 250				

KM# 263 50 RUPEES
30.00 g., Copper-Nickel, 39 mm. **Subject:** Patel, 100th Anniversary of Birth **Obv:** Type A **Rev:** Head right **Edge:** Reeded

Date	Mintage	VF20	XF40	MS60	MS63	MS65
1996 (B)	—	—	—	100	125	—
1996 M	—	PF65 200				

KM# 264 50 RUPEES
30.00 g., Copper-Nickel, 39 mm. **Subject:** Subhas Chandra Bose **Obv:** Type C **Rev:** Bust left

Date	Mintage	VF20	XF40	MS60	MS63	MS65
1997 (C)	—	—	—	100	125	—
1997 (C)	—	PF65 200				

KM# 265 50 RUPEES
22.50 g., 0.500 Silver 0.3617 oz. ASW **Subject:** 50th Anniversary of Independence **Obv:** Small Asoka lion pedestal above large denomination **Rev:** Line of people

Date	Mintage	VF20	XF40	MS60	MS63	MS65
1997 (B)	—	—	—	100	125	—
1997 M	—	PF65 200				

KM# 266 50 RUPEES
30.00 g., Copper-Nickel, 39 mm. **Subject:** Sri Aurobindo **Obv:** Type C **Rev:** Head 3/4 facing

Date	Mintage	VF20	XF40	MS60	MS63	MS65
1998 (B)	—	—	—	100	125	—
1998 M	—	PF65 200				

KM# 298 50 RUPEES
30.00 g., Copper-Nickel, 39 mm. **Subject:** Deshbandhu Chittaranjan Das **Obv:** Type C **Rev:** Bust facing **Edge:** Reeded

Date	Mintage	VF20	XF40	MS60	MS63	MS65
1998 (C)	—	—	—	100	125	—
1998 (C)	—	PF65 200				

KM# 300 50 RUPEES
30.00 g., Copper-Nickel, 39 mm. **Subject:** Chhatrapati Shivaji **Obv:** Asoka lion pedestal above denomination **Rev:** Turbaned bust right **Edge:** Reeded

Date	Mintage	VF20	XF40	MS60	MS63	MS65
1999 (B)	—	—	—	120	150	—
1999 M	—	PF65 225				
1999 M Proof, packaged	—	PF65 280				

KM# 293 50 RUPEES
22.50 g., 0.500 Silver 0.3617 oz. ASW, 39 mm. **Subject:** Supreme Court - 50 Years **Obv:** Type C **Rev:** Wheel above asoka lion pedestal **Edge:** Reeded

Date	Mintage	VF20	XF40	MS60	MS63	MS65
2000 (C)	—	—	—	200	240	—
2000 (C)	—	PF65 350				

KM# 275 100 RUPEES
35.00 g., 0.500 Silver 0.5626 oz. ASW **Subject:** Rural Women's Advancement **Obv:** Asoka lion pedestal above denomination **Rev:** Woman grinding wheat

Date	Mintage	VF20	XF40	MS60	MS63	MS65
1980 (B)	21,000	—	—	100	120	—
1980 B	5,811	PF65 200				
1980 B Proof, packaged	—	PF65 200				

KM# 276 100 RUPEES
35.00 g., 0.500 Silver 0.5626 oz. ASW **Series:** World Food Day

Date	Mintage	VF20	XF40	MS60	MS63	MS65
1981 (B)	22,000	—	—	100	120	—
1981 B	2,950	PF65 200				
1981 B Proof, packaged	—	PF65 475				

KM# 277 100 RUPEES
29.16 g., 0.925 Silver 0.8672 oz. ASW **Series:** International Year of the Child **Obv:** Asoka lion pedestal, denomination below **Rev:** Native musicians and dancer

Date	Mintage	VF20	XF40	MS60	MS63	MS65
1981 B	—	—	—	700	900	—
1981 B	—	PF65 1,200				

KM# 278 100 RUPEES
35.00 g., 0.500 Silver 0.5626 oz. ASW **Subject:** IX Asian Games

Date	Mintage	VF20	XF40	MS60	MS63	MS65
1982 (B)	—	—	—	50.00	60.00	—
1982 B	—	PF65 80.00				
1982 B Proof, packaged	—	PF65 275				

KM# 279 100 RUPEES
35.00 g., 0.500 Silver 0.5626 oz. ASW **Subject:** National Integration **Obv:** Asoka lion pedestal above denomination **Rev:** Flag on map

Date	Mintage	VF20	XF40	MS60	MS63	MS65
1982 (B)	—	—	—	100	120	—
1982 B	—	PF65 150				
1982 B Proof, package	—	PF65 375				

KM# 280 100 RUPEES
35.00 g., 0.500 Silver 0.5626 oz. ASW **Subject:** Golden Jubilee - Reserve Bank of India

Date	Mintage	VF20	XF40	MS60	MS63	MS65
1985 (B)	—	—	—	80.00	100	—
1985 B	—	PF65 150				
1985 B Proof, packaged	—	PF65 480				

KM# 281 100 RUPEES
35.00 g., 0.500 Silver 0.5626 oz. ASW **Subject:** Death of Indira Gandhi - statesperson, 1917-1984 **Obv:** Asoka lion pedestal above denomination **Rev:** Bust right

Date	Mintage	VF20	XF40	MS60	MS63	MS65
ND-1985 (B)	—	—	—	160	180	—
ND-1985 B	—	PF65 250				
ND-1985 B Proof, packaged	—	PF65 400				

KM# 282 100 RUPEES
35.00 g., 0.500 Silver 0.5626 oz. ASW **Subject:** Youth Year **Obv:** Small Asoka lion pedestal, denomination below **Rev:** Three outlined profiles between dove and laurel branch

Date	Mintage	VF20	XF40	MS60	MS63	MS65
1985 (C)	16,000	—	—	42.00	50.00	—
1985 (C)	6,267	PF65 70.00				
1985 (C) Proof, packaged	—	PF65 300				

KM# 283 100 RUPEES
35.00 g., 0.500 Silver 0.5626 oz. ASW **Series:** F.A.O. **Subject:** Fisheries **Obv:** Asoka lion pedestal, denomination below **Rev:** People with fishing nets

Date	Mintage	VF20	XF40	MS60	MS63	MS65
1986 (B)	—	—	—	160	180	—
1986 B	—	PF65 250				
1986 B Proof, packaged	—	PF65 410				

KM# 284 100 RUPEES

35.00 g., 0.500 Silver 0.5626 oz. ASW **Series:** F.A.O. **Subject:** Small Farmers **Obv:** Asoka lion pedestal, denomination below **Rev:** Farmers planting

Date	Mintage	VF20	XF40	MS60	MS63	MS65
1987 (B)	—	—	—	42.00	50.00	—
1987 B	—	PF65 70.00				
1987 B Proof, packaged	—	PF65 550				

KM# 285 100 RUPEES

35.00 g., 0.500 Silver 0.5626 oz. ASW **Subject:** 100th Anniversary of Nehru's Birth **Obv:** Asoka lion pedestal, denomination below **Rev:** Head right

Date	Mintage	VF20	XF40	MS60	MS63	MS65
1989 (B)	—	—	—	160	180	—
1989 B	—	PF65 250				
1989 B Proof, packaged	—	PF65 300				

KM# 286 100 RUPEES

35.00 g., 0.500 Silver 0.5626 oz. ASW **Subject:** Quit India Moment, 50th Anniversary **Obv:** Asoka lion pedestal, denomination below **Rev:** Monument

Date	Mintage	VF20	XF40	MS60	MS63	MS65
1992 (B)	—	—	—	160	180	—
1992 (B)	—	PF65 250				
1992 (B) Proof, packaged	—	PF65 500				

KM# 287 100 RUPEES

35.00 g., 0.500 Silver 0.5626 oz. ASW, 44 mm. **Subject:** International Labor Organization, 75th Anniversary **Obv:** Asoka lion pedestal, denomination below **Rev:** Denomination within broken dentil circle, wreath surrounds **Edge:** Reeded

Date	Mintage	VF20	XF40	MS60	MS63	MS65
ND-1994 (B)	—	—	—	220	250	—
ND-1994 B	—	PF65 350				
ND-1994 B Proof, packaged	—	PF65 475				

KM# 288 100 RUPEES

35.00 g., 0.500 Silver 0.5626 oz. ASW **Subject:** 100th Anniversary - Birth of Patel **Obv:** Type A **Rev:** Head right

Date	Mintage	VF20	XF40	MS60	MS63	MS65
1996 (B)	—	—	—	120	150	—
1996 B	—	PF65 225				
1996 B Proof, packaged	—	PF65 250				

KM# 289 100 RUPEES

35.00 g., 0.500 Silver 0.5626 oz. ASW, 44 mm. **Subject:** Subhas Chandra Bose **Obv:** Type C **Rev:** Bust left

Date	Mintage	VF20	XF40	MS60	MS63	MS65
1997 (C)	—	—	—	150	180	—
1997 (C)	—	PF65 250				
1997 (C) Proof, packaged	—	PF65 400				

KM# 292 100 RUPEES

35.00 g., 0.500 Silver 0.5626 oz. ASW, 44 mm. **Subject:** Sri Aurobindo **Obv:** Type C **Rev:** Head 3/4 facing **Edge:** Reeded

Date	Mintage	VF20	XF40	MS60	MS63	MS65
1998 (B)	—	—	—	160	180	—
1998 M	—	PF65 250				
1998 M Proof, packaged	—	PF65 600				

KM# 299 100 RUPEES

35.00 g., 0.500 Silver 0.5626 oz. ASW, 44 mm. **Subject:** Deshbandhu Chittaranjan Das **Obv:** Asoka lion pedestal, denomination below **Rev:** Bust facing **Edge:** Reeded

Date	Mintage	VF20	XF40	MS60	MS63	MS65
1998 (C)	—	—	—	160	180	—
1998 (C)	—	PF65 250				
1998 (C) Proof, packaged	—	PF65 525				

KM# 301 100 RUPEES

35.00 g., 0.500 Silver 0.5626 oz. ASW, 44 mm. **Subject:** Chhatrapati Shivaji **Obv:** Asoka lion pedestal, denomination below **Rev:** Turbaned bust right **Edge:** Reeded

Date	Mintage	VF20	XF40	MS60	MS63	MS65
1999 (B)	—	—	—	160	180	—
1999 M	—	PF65 250				
1999 M Proof, packaged	—	PF65 300				

KM# 302 100 RUPEES

35.00 g., 0.500 Silver 0.5626 oz. ASW, 44 mm. **Subject:** St. Dnyanneshwar **Obv:** Asoka lion pedestal, denomination below **Rev:** Seated figure **Edge:** Reeded

Date	Mintage	VF20	XF40	MS60	MS63	MS65
1999 (C)	—	—	—	300	375	—
1999 (C)	—	PF65 500				

PATTERNS

Including off metal strikes

KM#	Date	Mintage	Identification	Mkt Val
Pn1	1946(B)	—	1/4 Rupee. Nickel. KM#548.	—
Pn2	1946(B)	—	1/2 Rupee. Nickel. KM#553.	—
Pn3	1946(B)	—	Rupee. Nickel. KM#559.	—
Pn4	1947(B)	—	1/4 Rupee. Copper-Nickel.	—
Pn5	1947(B)	—	1/2 Rupee. Copper-Nickel.	—
Pn6	1947(B)	—	Rupee. Copper-Nickel.	—
Pn7	1947(B)	—	Rupee. Nickel. Set of Pn1-3.	—
Pn8	1949	—	Pice. Bronze.	8,000
Pn9	1949	—	Anna. Copper-Nickel.	8,500
Pn10	1949	—	2 Annas. Copper-Nickel. Profile peacock left.	9,500
Pn11	1949	—	2 Annas. Copper-Nickel. Facing displayed peacock.	9,500
PnA12	1949	—	2 Annas. Brass. Proof.	8,500
Pn12	1949	—	1/4 Rupee. Nickel.	10,000
Pn13	1949	—	1/2 Rupee. Nickel. Worker with finished background.	11,000
Pn14	1949	—	1/2 Rupee. Nickel. Worker with plain background.	11,000
Pn15	1949	—	Rupee. Nickel. Standing figure.	12,500
Pn16	1949	—	Rupee. Nickel. Similar to Pn9.	12,500
Pn17	1964(C)	—	Paisa. Copper. Half thickness and weight.	—
Pn18	1992(C)	—	2 Rupees.	—

PIEDFORT

KM#	Date	Mintage	Identification	Mkt Val
P1	1981	—	100 Rupees. Silver. KM#277.	400
P2	1981	—	100 Rupees. Silver. KM#277.	2,250

MINT SETS

KM#	Date	Mintage	Identification	Issue Price	Mkt Val
MS1	1950(B) (7)	—	KM#1.2, 2.1, 3.1, 4.1, 5.1, 6.1, 7.1 Rupia & Anna series.	—	1,350
MS2	1954(B) (7)	—	KM1.4, 2.2, 3.2, 4.2, 5.2, 6.2, 7.2. Rupia & Anna series.	—	2,000
MS3	1962(B) (6)	—	KM#8a, 11, 16, 24.2, 47.2, 55	1.50	2,000
MS3A	1962(B) (7)	—	KM#8a, 11, 16, 24.2, 47.2, 55, 75.1(C)	3.60	2,250
MS4	ND(1964) (B) (2)	—	KM#56, 76	1.00	270
MS5	1965 (3)	—	KM#8a, 11,16, 24.2, 47.2, 55, 56, 76, Nehru and regular issues.	—	270
MS6	1967(B) (8)	—	KM#10.1, 13.1, 14.1, 18.1, 25, 48.2, 58.1, 75.1 (1962 dated Rupee)	1.00	90.00
MS11	ND(1969) (B) (4)	25,281	KM#42.1, 59, 77, 185 Blue plastic case Gandhi.	2.50	75.00
MS12	1970(B) (8)	—	KM#10.1, 13.5, 14.2, 18.3, 26.3, 41, 58.2, 75.2 Brown vinyl case	1.00	72.00

KM#	Date	Mintage	Identification	Issue Price	Mkt Val
MS13	1970(B) (2)	22,999	KM#43.1, 186 F.A.O. 25th Anniversary.	2.00	100
MS14	1971(B) (2)	9,987	KM#43.2, 186 F.A.O. 25th Anniversary.	—	225
MS15	1972(B) (2)	—	KM#60, 187a Independence, 25th Anniversary.	2.00	84.00
MS16	1973(B) (2)	48,670	KM#188, 240 Grow more food.	—	90.00
MS17	1974(B) (2)	50,219	KM#189, 255 Planned Families.	10.00	80.00
MS18	1975(B) (2)	40,279	KM#190, 256 Equality, Development, Peace.	12.00	100
MS19	1976(B) (2)	25,105	KM#191, 257 Food & Work for all.	12.00	95.00
MS20	1977(B) (2)	17,071	KM#192, 258 Save for Development.	12.00	100
MS21	1978(B) (2)	15,041	KM#193, 259 Food & Shelter for all.	10.00	100
MS22	1979(B) (2)	—	KM#194, 260 Children, Nation's pride.	—	100
MS23	1980(B) (2)	—	KM#195, 275 Rural Women's Advancement.	—	100
MS24	1981(B) (2)	—	KM#196, 276 World Food Day.	—	100
MS25	1982(B) (2)	—	KM#197, 278 IX Asian Games.	—	100
MS27	1985(B) (2)	—	KM#199, 280 Reserve Bank of India.	48.00	150
MS28	ND(1985) (C) (2)	—	KM#200, 282 International youth year.	—	165
MS29	ND(1985) (B) (2)	—	KM#241, 281 Indira Gandhi.	43.00	150
MS30	1986 (2)	—	KM#242, 283 Fisheries.	45.00	150
MS31	1987(B) (2)	—	KM#243, 284 Small farmers	45.00	270
MS32	1989(B) (2)	—	KM#244, 285 Nehru Centennial.	40.00	135
MS33	1988 (2)	—	KM#83, 151, 224, 285 Nehru.	—	150
MS34	1990 (0)	—	KM#88.1 Food for Future.	—	30.00
MS35	1991(B) (2)	—	KM#152, 201 Commonwealth Parliamentary Conference.	—	100
MS36	1991(B) (3)	—	KM#90, 152, 201 Commonwealth Parliamentary Conference.	—	100
MS37	1991(B) (2)	—	KM#123, 153 Tourism.	—	100
MS38	1991(B) (3)	—	KM#91, 123, 153 Tourism.	—	100
MS39	1992 (1)	—	KM#89. Rajiv Gandhi.	—	35.00
MS41	1992(B) (4)	—	KM#92.1, 202, 261, 286 Quit India Moment.	—	285
MS42	1994 (2)	—	KM#262, 287 I.L.O.	—	285
MS43	1994(B) (3)	—	KM#155, 262, 287 ILO.	—	295
MS44	1996 (2)	—	KM#160 (2) International Crop Conference, velvet box.	—	100
MS45	1996(M) (2)	—	KM#263, 288 Sardar Vallabh Bhai Patel.	65.00	145
MS46	1996(M) (3)	—	KM#203, 263, 288 Sardar Vallabh Bhai Patel.	—	175
MS47	1997 (2)	—	KM#70, 265 Independence, 50th Anniversary.	—	75.00
MS49	1997 (2)	—	KM#264, 289. Netaji Subhash Chandra Bose.	—	160
MS50	1997(C) (3)	—	KM#204, 264, 289 Netaji Subhash Chandra Bose.	—	185
MS51	1997 (2)	—	KM398 (2) Cellular Jail, Port Blair.	—	45.00
MS52	1998 (2)	—	KM#266, 290. Sri Aurbindo, All life is yoga	—	225
MS53	1998(B) (4)	—	KM#131.1, 205, 266, 292 Sri Aurbindo, All life is yoga.	—	150
MS54	1998 (2)	—	KM#298, 299. Deshbandhu Chittranjan Das.	—	195
MS55	1998(C) (3)	—	KM#297, 298, 299 Deshbandhu Chittranjan Das	—	240
MS56	1999(B) (3)	—	KM#290, 300, 301 Chhatrapati Shivaji	—	165
MS57	2000(B) (2)	—	KM#291, 293 Supreme Court.	—	165
MS58	2000 (2)	—	KM#295.1 (2) Saint Dnyaneshwar, pouch.	—	30.00
MS59	1999(C) (2)	—	KM#295, 302 Saint Dnyaneshwar.	—	250

PROOF SETS

KM#	Date	Mintage	Identification	Issue Price	Mkt Val
PSA1	1949 (8)	—	KM#Pn8-15.	—	—
PS1	1950(B) (7)	—	KM#1.2, 2.1, 3.1, 4, 5.1, 6.1, 7.1 Rupia & Anna series	8.40	1,500
PS2	1954(B) (7)	—	KM#1.3, 2.2, 3.2, 4, 5.1, 6.1, 7.2 Rupia & Anna series	8.40	2,500
PS3	1960(B) (6)	—	KM#8, 11, 16, 24.2, 47.1, 55 Naya Paisa series	7.00	2,500
PS4	1961(B) (6)	—	KM#8, 11, 16, 24.2, 47.2, 55 Naya Paisa series	7.00	2,800
PS5	ND(1964) (B) (2)	—	KM#56, 76 Jawaharlal Nehru	5.00	375
PS6	1963(B) (7)	—	KM#8a, 11, 16, 24.2, 47.2, 55, 75.1 Naya Paisa series (card).	7.00	1,800
PS7	1969B (9)	9,097	KM#10.1, 13.5, 14.2, 18.3, 26.3, 42.1, 59, 77, 185 Gandhi, 100th Anniversary	15.25	150
PS8	1970B (9)	2,900	KM#10.1, 13.5, 14.2, 18.3, 26.3, 43.1, 58.3, 75.2, 186 F.A.O. 25th Anniversary	15.25	200
PS9	1971B (9)	4,161	KM#10.1, 13.5, 14.2, 18.3, 26.3, 43.2, 58.3, 75.2, 186 F.A.O. 25th Anniversary	15.25	300
PS10	1972B (9)	7,701	KM#10.1, 13.6, 15, 18.6, 27.1, 49.1, 60, 75.2, 187 Independence, frosted.	15.25	200
PS11	1973B (2)	2,408	KM#188, 240 F.A.O. Grow more food.	17.50	135
PS12	1973B (10)	3,326	KM#10.1, 13.6, 15, 18.6, 27.1, 49.1, 62, 75.2, 188, 240 F.A.O., Grow More Food.	15.25	150
PS13	1973B (10)	7,563	KM#10.1, 13.6 15, 18.6, 27.1, 49.1, 62, 75.2 188, 240 F.A.O. Grow more food.	26.00	100
PS14	1974B (2)	1,712	KM#189, 255 F.A.O. planned families.	7.50	120
PS15	1974B (10)	9,138	KM#10.1, 13.6, 15, 18.6, 28, 49.1, 63, 75.2, 189, 255 F.A.O. planned families.	29.00	165
PS16	1975B (2)	160	KM#190, 256 F.A.O. Equality, development, peace.	22.00	240
PS17	1975B (8)	2,370	KM#10.1, 13.6, 15, 18.6, 29, 49.1, 63, 78.1 F.A.O. Equality, development, peace.	35.00	195
PS18	1976B (2)	190	KM#191, 257 F.A.O. Food & work for all.	22.00	245
PS19	1976B (10)	3,209	KM#10.1, 13.6, 15, 19, 30, 49.1, 63, 78.1, 191, 257 F.A.O. Food & work for all.	35.00	195
PS20	1977B (2)	—	KM#192, 258 F.A.O. Safe for development.	—	225
PS21	1977B (10)	2,222	KM#10.1, 13.6, 15, 20, 31, 63, 78.1, 192, 258 F.A.O. Safe for development.	35.00	195
PS21A	1978B (2)	—	KM#193, 259 F.A.O. Food & shelter for all.	—	60.00
PS22	1978B (10)	1,390	KM#10.1, 13.6, 15, 21, 32, 49.1, 63, 78.1, 193, 259 F.A.O. Food & shelter for all.	35.00	285
PS23	1979B (2)	—	KM#194, 260 International year of the child.	—	125
PS24	1979B (10)	—	KM#10.1, 13.6, 15, 22, 33, 49.2, 63, 78.3, 194, 260 International year of the child.	—	165
PS25	1980B (2)	—	KM#195, 275 Rural women's advancement.	—	130
PS26	1980B (4)	—	KM#35, 50, 195, 275 Rural women's advancement.	—	165
PS27	1981B (2)	—	KM#196, 276 World food day.	—	190
PS28	1981 (6)	—	KM#36, 51, 196, 276 F.A.O. World food day.	—	240
PS29	1982B (2)	—	KM#197, 278 IX Asian Games.	38.00	125
PS30	1982B (4)	—	KM#52, 120, 197, 278 IX Asian Games	48.00	165
PS31	1982B (2)	—	KM#198, 279 National intergration	—	165
PS32	1982B (4)	—	KM#64, 121.1, 198, 279 National intergration	—	180
PS33	ND(1985) B (2)	—	KM#241, 281 Indira Gandhi.	48.00	200
PS34	ND(1985) B (4)	—	KM#67.1, 150, 241, 281 Indira Gandhi.	88.00	245
PS35	1985(C) (3)	—	KM#80, 200, 282 Youth year.	—	270
PS36	1987 (3)	—	KM#80, 200, 280 Youth Year. restrike.	—	240
PS37	1985B (2)	—	KM#199, 280 Reserve Bank of India	58.00	250
PS38	1985B (4)	—	KM#66, 122, 199, 280 Reserve Bank of India	98.00	270
PS39	1986B (2)	—	KM#242, 283 F.A.O. Fisheries.	50.00	195
PS40	1986B (3)	—	KM#68.1, 242, 283 F.A.O. Fisheries.	70.00	240
PS41	1987B (2)	—	KM#243, 284 F.A.O. Small farmers.	60.00	345
PS42	1987B (3)	—	KM#81, 243, 284 F.A.O. small farmers.	65.00	360
PS43	1989B (2)	—	KM#244, 285 Nehru Centennial.	65.00	55.00
PS44	1989B (4)	—	KM#83.1, 151, 244, 285 Nehru Centennial.	90.00	100
PS45	1988 (4)	—	KM#83.1, 151, 244, 285 Nehru Centennial, with stand.	—	300
PS46	1991 (2)	—	KM#152, 201 Commonwealth Parliamentary Conference.	—	135
PS47	1991(B) (3)	—	KM#90, 152, 201	—	140
PS48	1991 (2)	—	KM#123, 153 Tourism Year.	—	135
PS49	1991(B) (3)	—	KM#91, 123, 153	—	140
PS50	1996M (4)	—	KM#129, 203, 263, 288	110	200
PS52	1993 (2)	—	KM#261, 286 Quit India Moment.	—	300
PS53	1992 (4)	—	KM#93, 202, 261, 286 Quit India Moment.	—	345
PS54	ND(1994) (2)	—	KM#262, 287	18.05	300
PS55	ND(1994) (3)	—	KM#155, 262, 287	18.75	360
PS56	1996M (2)	—	KM#263, 288	100	180
PS58	1997M (2)	—	KM#70, 265	75.00	120
PS59	1997 (2)	—	KM#264, 289 Netaji Subhash Chandra Bose.	—	270
PS60	1997(C) (4)	—	KM#130.1, 204, 264, 289	—	300
PS61	1997 (2)	—	KM#98 (2) Cellular Jail.	—	75.00
PS62	1998 (2)	—	KM#266, 290 Sri Aurbindo, All life is yoga	—	375
PS63	1998M (4)	—	KM#131.1, 205, 266, 290	—	390
PS64	1998 (2)	—	KM#298, 299 Deshbandhu Chittranjan Das.	—	285
PS65	1998(C) (4)	—	KM#296.3, 298, 299, 297	—	300
PS66	1999 (3)	—	KM#290, 300, 301 Chhatrapati Shivaji.	—	200
PS67	2000 (2)	—	KM#291, 293 Supreme Court.	—	240
PS68	1999 (2)	—	KM#295.1, 302 Saint Dayaneshwar.	—	390

SPECIAL SETS

KM#	Date	Mintage	Identification	Issue Price	Mkt Val
MS40	1993 (2)	—	KM#261, 286. Quit India Moment.	—	270

INDONESIA

The Republic of Indonesia, the world's largest archipelago, extends for more than 3,000 miles (4,827 km.) along the equator from the mainland of southeast Asia to Australia. The 17,508 islands comprising the archipelago have a combined area of 788,425 sq. mi. (1,919,440 sq.km.) and a population of 205 million, including East Timor. On August 30, 1999, the Timorese majority voted for independence. The Inter FET (International Forces for East Timor) is now in charge of controlling the chaotic situation. Capitol: Jakarta. Petroleum, timber, rubber, and coffee are exported.

Had Columbus succeeded in reaching the fabled Spice Islands, he would have found advanced civilizations a millennium old, and temples still ranking among the finest examples of ancient art. During the opening centuries of the Christian era, the islands were influenced by Hindu priests and traders who spread their culture and religion. Moslem invasions began in the 13th century, fragmenting the island kingdoms into small states which were unable to resist Western colonial infiltration. Portuguese traders established posts in the 16th century, but they were soon outnumbered by the Dutch who arrived in 1596 and gradually asserted control over the islands comprising present-day Indonesia. Dutch dominance, interrupted by British incursions during the Napoleonic Wars, established the Netherlands East Indies as one of the richest colonial possessions in the world.

The Indonesian independence movement, which began between the two world wars, was encouraged by the Japanese during their 3 1/2-year occupation during World War II. Indonesia proclaimed its independence on Aug. 17,1945, three days after the surrender of Japan and full sovereignty. On Dec. 27, 1949, after four years of guerilla warfare including two large-scale campaigns by the Dutch in an effort to reassert control, complete independence was established. Rebellions in Bandung and on the Molluccan Islands occurred in 1950. During the reign of President Mohammad Achmad Sukarno (1950-67) the new Republic not only held together but started to develop. West Irian, formerly Netherlands New Guinea, came under the administration of Indonesia on May 1, 1963. In 1965, the army staged an anti-communist coup in which thousands perished.

On November 28, 1975, the Portuguese Province of Timor, an overseas province occupying the eastern half of the East Indian island of Timor, attained independence as the People's Democratic Republic of East Timor. On December 5, 1975, the government of the People's Democratic Republic was seized by a guerrilla faction sympathetic to the Indonesian territorial claim to East Timor which ousted the constitutional government and replaced it with the Provisional Government of East Timor. On July 17, 1976, the Provisional Government enacted a law that dissolved the free republic and made East Timor the 27th province of Indonesia.

The VOC (United East India Company) struck coins and emergency issues for the Indonesian Archipelago and for the islands at various mints in the Netherlands and the islands. In 1798 the VOC was subsumed by the Dutch government, which issued VOC type transitional and regal types during the Batavian Republic and the Kingdom of the Netherlands until independence. The British issued a coinage during the various occupations by the British East Indian Company, 1811-24. Modern coinage issued by the Republic of Indonesia includes separate series for West Irian and for the Riau Archipelago, an area of small islands between Singapore and Sumatra.

MONETARY SYSTEM

100 Sen = 1 Rupiah

REPUBLIC

STANDARD COINAGE

KM# 7 SEN

0.75 g., Aluminum, 18 mm. **Obv:** Rice stalk surrounds center hole **Rev:** Malay-Arabic text around center hole

Date	Mintage	VF20	XF40	MS60	MS63	MS65
1952 (u)	100,000	0.20	0.40	0.85	1.25	1.65

KM# 5 5 SEN

1.30 g., Aluminum, 22 mm. **Obv:** Rice stalk surrounds center hole **Rev:** Malay-Arabic text around center hole

Date	Mintage	F12	VF20	XF40	MS60	MS63
1951	—	—	0.10	0.25	0.60	0.75
1954	—	—	0.10	0.25	0.60	0.75

KM# 6 10 SEN

1.72 g., Aluminum, 23 mm. **Obv:** Denomination within scalloped design, ornaments flank date below **Rev:** National emblem **Edge:** Reeded

Date	Mintage	F12	VF20	XF40	MS60	MS63
1951	—	—	0.10	0.20	0.35	0.45
1954	50,000,000	—	0.10	0.20	0.35	0.50

KM# 12 10 SEN

Aluminum, 23 mm. **Obv:** Denomination within scalloped design, ornaments flank date below **Rev:** National emblem **Edge:** Reeded

Date	Mintage	VF20	XF40	MS60	MS63	MS65
1957	50,224,000	0.20	0.40	0.75	1.00	1.25

KM# 8 25 SEN

2.20 g., Aluminum, 26 mm. **Obv:** Denomination within scalloped design, ornaments flank date below **Rev:** National emblem

Date	Mintage	VF20	XF40	MS60	MS63	MS65
1952	200,000,000	0.10	0.20	0.25	0.35	0.50

KM# 11 25 SEN

Aluminum **Obv:** Denomination within scalloped design, ornaments flank date below **Rev:** National emblem

Date	Mintage	VF20	XF40	MS60	MS63	MS65
1955	25,767,000	0.10	0.20	0.35	0.45	0.65
1957	99,752,926	0.10	0.20	0.35	0.45	0.60

KM# 9 50 SEN

3.30 g., Copper-Nickel, 20 mm. **Obv:** Denomination within scalloped design, ornaments flank date below **Rev:** Prince Diponegoro facing left

Date	Mintage	VF20	XF40	MS60	MS63	MS65
1952	100,000,000	0.10	0.20	0.35	0.45	0.60

KM# 10.1 50 SEN

3.24 g., Copper-Nickel **Obv:** Denomination within scalloped design, ornaments flank date below **Rev:** Prince Diponegoro facing left

Date	Mintage	VF20	XF40	MS60	MS63	MS65
1954	1,290,000	1.00	2.25	5.00	6.50	—
1955	15,000,000	0.10	0.20	0.35	0.50	0.75

KM# 10.2 50 SEN

3.00 g., Copper-Nickel, 29 mm. **Obv:** Denomination within scalloped design, ornaments flank date below **Rev:** Different head, larger lettering

Date	Mintage	VF20	XF40	MS60	MS63	MS65
1957	26,267,313	0.10	0.20	0.35	0.45	0.65

KM# 13 50 SEN

Aluminum **Obv:** Denomination within inner circle, ornaments flank date below **Rev:** National emblem

Date	Mintage	VF20	XF40	MS60	MS63	MS65
1958	33,740,000	0.10	0.20	0.40	0.50	0.75

KM# 14 50 SEN

3.02 g., Aluminum, 29 mm. **Obv:** Denomination within inner circle, ornaments flank date below **Rev:** National emblem, modified eagle

Date	Mintage	VF20	XF40	MS60	MS63	MS65
1959	100,009,000	0.10	0.20	0.35	0.50	0.75
1961	150,000,000	0.10	0.20	0.35	0.50	0.75

KM# 20 RUPIAH

1.44 g., Aluminum, 22 mm. **Rev:** Fantail flycatcher **Edge:** Plain

Date	Mintage	VF20	XF40	MS60	MS63	MS65
1970	136,010,000	—	0.15	0.30	0.50	0.75

KM# 21 2 RUPIAH

2.30 g., Aluminum, 26 mm. **Obv:** Stars flank date below denomination **Rev:** Rice and cotton stalks

Date	Mintage	VF20	XF40	MS60	MS63	MS65
1970	139,230,000	—	0.10	0.20	0.30	0.50

KM# 22 5 RUPIAH

2.80 g., Aluminum, 28 mm. **Obv:** Stars flank date below denomination **Rev:** Black drongo

Date	Mintage	VF20	XF40	MS60	MS63	MS65
1970	448,000,000	0.15	0.25	0.45	0.75	1.00

KM# 37 5 RUPIAH

3.00 g., Aluminum, 28.6 mm. **Subject:** Family Planning Program **Obv:** Stars flank date below denomination **Rev:** The ideal family within rice and cotton stalk wreath

Date	Mintage	VF20	XF40	MS60	MS63	MS65
1974	447,910,000	0.10	0.15	0.25	0.30	0.40

KM# 43 5 RUPIAH

1.40 g., Aluminum, 23 mm. **Subject:** Family Planning Program **Obv:** Stars flank date below denomination, inner circle surrounds **Rev:** The ideal family within rice and cotton stalk wreath, inner circle surrounds

Date	Mintage	VF20	XF40	MS60	MS63	MS65
1979	413,200,000	0.10	0.15	0.25	0.30	0.40
1995	6,420,000	0.20	0.30	0.60	0.75	1.00
1996	—	0.20	0.30	0.60	0.75	1.00

KM# 33 10 RUPIAH

1.77 g., Copper-Nickel, 15.6 mm. **Series:** F.A.O. **Rev:** Rice and cotton stalks

Date	Mintage	VF20	XF40	MS60	MS63	MS65
1971	286,360,000	0.10	0.25	0.50	0.60	0.80

KM# 38 10 RUPIAH

4.00 g., Brass Clad Steel, 22 mm. **Subject:** National Saving Program **Obv:** Stars flank date below denomination **Rev:** Legends around winged piggy bank

Date	Mintage	VF20	XF40	MS60	MS63	MS65
1974	222,910,000	0.10	0.25	0.75	1.00	1.25

KM# 44 10 RUPIAH

1.90 g., Aluminum, 25 mm. **Series:** F.A.O. **Obv:** Stars flank date below denomination **Rev:** Legends around winged piggy bank

Date	Mintage	VF20	XF40	MS60	MS63	MS65
1979	285,670,000	0.10	0.20	0.40	0.50	0.70

KM# 34 25 RUPIAH

3.50 g., Copper-Nickel, 28 mm. **Obv:** Stars flank date below denomination **Rev:** Victoria crowned pigeon **Edge:** Reeded

Date	Mintage	VF20	XF40	MS60	MS63	MS65
1971	1,221,610,000	0.10	0.25	0.75	1.00	1.25

KM# 55 25 RUPIAH

1.25 g., Aluminum, 18.01 mm. **Obv:** National emblem **Rev:** Nutmeg plant **Edge:** Plain

Date	Mintage	VF20	XF40	MS60	MS63	MS65
1991	30,000,000	—	0.40	0.75	1.00	1.25
1992	64,000,000	—	0.40	0.75	1.00	1.25
1993	20,000,000	—	0.40	0.75	1.00	1.25
1994	250,000,000	—	0.25	0.50	0.60	0.80
1995	184,480,000	—	0.25	0.50	0.60	0.80
1995	—	PF65 250				
1996	—	—	0.25	0.50	0.60	0.80

KM# 35 50 RUPIAH

6.00 g., Copper-Nickel, 24 mm. **Obv:** Stars flank date below denomination **Rev:** Greater Bird of Paradise

Date	Mintage	VF20	XF40	MS60	MS63	MS65
1971	1,035,435,000	0.25	0.80	1.00	1.25	1.50

KM# 52 50 RUPIAH

3.20 g., Aluminum-Bronze, 19.94 mm. **Obv:** National emblem **Rev:** Komodo dragon lizard **Edge:** Reeded

Date	Mintage	VF20	XF40	MS60	MS63	MS65
1991	67,000,000	0.10	0.30	0.75	1.00	1.75
1992	70,000,000	0.10	0.30	0.75	1.00	1.75
1993	120,000,000	0.10	0.30	0.75	1.00	1.50
1994	300,000,000	0.10	0.30	0.75	1.00	1.50
1995	591,880,000	0.10	0.30	0.75	1.00	1.50
1995	—	PF65 250				
1996	—	0.10	0.30	0.75	1.00	1.50
1997	150,000	0.10	0.30	0.75	1.00	1.50
1998	150,000	0.10	0.30	0.75	1.00	1.50

KM# 60 50 RUPIAH

1.35 g., Aluminum, 19.95 mm. **Obv:** National emblem **Rev:** Black-naped Oriole **Edge:** Plain

Date	Mintage	VF20	XF40	MS60	MS63	MS65
1999	—	—	—	0.40	0.60	0.80

KM# 36 100 RUPIAH

9.75 g., Copper-Nickel, 28.54 mm. **Obv:** Stars flank date below denomination **Rev:** Minangkabau house

Date	Mintage	VF20	XF40	MS60	MS63	MS65
1973	252,868,000	0.35	0.75	1.50	2.00	3.00

KM# 42 100 RUPIAH

7.00 g., Copper-Nickel, 28.5 mm. **Subject:** Forestry for prosperity **Obv:** Minangkabu house **Rev:** Legendary tree of life

Date	Mintage	VF20	XF40	MS60	MS63	MS65
1978	907,773,000	0.25	0.50	1.00	1.50	2.00

KM# 53 100 RUPIAH

4.15 g., Aluminum-Bronze, 22 mm. **Subject:** Buffalo racing **Obv:** National emblem **Rev:** Buffalo racers **Edge:** Reeded

Date	Mintage	VF20	XF40	MS60	MS63	MS65
1991	94,000,000	0.20	0.40	0.75	1.00	1.50
1992	120,000,000	0.15	0.30	0.60	0.75	1.00
1993	300,000,000	0.15	0.30	0.60	0.75	1.00
1994	550,000,000	0.15	0.30	0.60	0.75	1.00
1995	798,100,000	0.15	0.30	0.60	0.75	1.00
1995	—	PF65 250				
1996	41,000,000	0.20	0.40	0.75	1.00	1.50
1997	150,000,000	0.15	0.30	0.65	0.80	1.25
1998	59,000,000	0.20	0.40	0.75	1.00	1.50

KM# 61 100 RUPIAH

1.79 g., Aluminum, 23 mm. **Obv:** National emblem **Rev:** Palm Cockatoo **Edge:** Plain

Date	Mintage	VF20	XF40	MS60	MS63	MS65
1999	—	—	—	0.75	1.25	2.00
2000	—	—	—	0.75	1.25	2.00

KM# 23 200 RUPIAH

8.00 g., 0.999 Silver 0.2569 oz. ASW **Subject:** 25th anniversary of independence **Obv:** Great Bird of Paradise (paradisea apoda- Paradisaeidae) **Rev:** National emblem

Date	Mintage	VF20	XF40	MS60	MS63	MS65
1970	—	PF63 15.00	PF65 20.00			

KM# 24 250 RUPIAH

10.00 g., 0.999 Silver 0.3212 oz. ASW **Subject:** 25th anniversary of independence **Obv:** Manjusri statue from Temple of Tumpang **Rev:** National emblem

Date	Mintage	VF20	XF40	MS60	MS63	MS65
1970	—	PF63 15.00	PF65 18.00			

KM# 25 500 RUPIAH

20.00 g., 0.999 Silver 0.6424 oz. ASW, 40 mm. **Subject:** 25th Anniversary of Independence **Obv:** Wayang dancer **Rev:** National emblem

Date	Mintage	VF20	XF40	MS60	MS63	MS65
1970	—	PF63 20.00	PF65 27.00			

KM# 54 500 RUPIAH
5.30 g., Aluminum-Bronze, 23.95 mm. **Obv:** National emblem **Rev:** Jasmine **Edge:** Plain

Date	Mintage	VF20	XF40	MS60	MS63	MS65
1991	71,000,000	—	1.25	2.25	2.50	3.00
1992	100,000,000	—	1.25	2.25	2.50	3.00
1993	—	—	1.25	2.25	2.50	3.00
1994	—	—	1.25	2.25	2.50	3.00
1995	—	PF65 350				

KM# 59 500 RUPIAH
5.35 g., Aluminum-Bronze, 24 mm. **Obv:** National emblem **Rev:** Jasmine above denomination

Date	Mintage	VF20	XF40	MS60	MS63	MS65
1997	—	—	—	2.00	2.25	2.50
1999	—	—	—	2.00	2.25	2.50
2000	—	—	—	2.00	2.25	2.50

KM# 26 750 RUPIAH
30.00 g., 0.999 Silver 0.9636 oz. ASW, 45 mm. **Subject:** 25th Anniversary of Independence **Obv:** Garuda bird **Rev:** National emblem

Date	Mintage	VF20	XF40	MS60	MS63	MS65
1970	—	PF63 30.00	PF65 40.00			

KM# 27 1000 RUPIAH
40.00 g., 0.999 Silver 1.2847 oz. ASW, 55 mm. **Subject:** 25th Anniversary of Independence - Gen. Sudirman **Obv:** Bust 3/4 facing **Rev:** National emblem

Date	Mintage	VF20	XF40	MS60	MS63	MS65
1970	—	PF63 50.00	PF65 70.00			

KM# 56 1000 RUPIAH
8.61 g., Bi-Metallic Brass center in Copper-Nickel ring, 26.25 mm. **Obv:** National emblem within inner circle **Rev:** Palm tree within inner circle

Date	Mintage	VF20	XF40	MS60	MS63	MS65
1993	5,000,000	—	—	4.00	5.00	6.00
1994	6,000,000	—	—	3.00	4.00	5.00
1995	19,900,000	—	—	3.00	4.00	5.00
1995	—	PF65 300				
1996	—	—	—	3.00	4.00	5.00
1997	—	—	—	3.00	4.00	5.00
2000	—	—	—	3.00	4.00	5.00

KM# 28 2000 RUPIAH
4.93 g., 0.900 Gold 0.1427 oz. AGW **Subject:** 25th Anniversary of Independence **Obv:** Great Bird of Paradise **Rev:** National emblem

Date	Mintage	VF20	XF40	MS60	MS63	MS65
1970	—	PF63 250	PF65 300			

KM# 39 2000 RUPIAH
25.65 g., 0.500 Silver 0.4123 oz. ASW, 38.6 mm. **Subject:** Conservation series **Obv:** National emblem **Rev:** Javan tiger (panthera tigris-felidae)

Date	Mintage	VF20	XF40	MS60	MS63	MS65
1974	43,000	—	—	12.00	15.00	20.00

KM# 39a 2000 RUPIAH
28.28 g., 0.925 Silver 0.841 oz. ASW, 38.6 mm. **Subject:** Conservation series **Obv:** National emblem **Rev:** Javan tiger (panthera tigris-felidae)

Date	Mintage	VF20	XF40	MS60	MS63	MS65
1974	18,000	PF63 20.00	PF65 22.00			

KM# 29 5000 RUPIAH
12.34 g., 0.900 Gold 0.3571 oz. AGW **Subject:** 25th Anniversary of Independence **Obv:** Manjusri statue from Temple of Tumpang **Rev:** National emblem

Date	Mintage	VF20	XF40	MS60	MS63	MS65
1970	—	PF63 600	PF65 650			

KM# 40 5000 RUPIAH
32.00 g., 0.500 Silver 0.5144 oz. ASW, 42 mm. **Series:** Conservation **Obv:** National emblem **Rev:** Orang Utan (pongo pygmaeus Pongidae)

Date	Mintage	VF20	XF40	MS60	MS63	MS65
1974	43,000	—	—	15.00	18.00	22.00

KM# 40a 5000 RUPIAH
35.00 g., 0.925 Silver 1.0409 oz. ASW, 42 mm. **Series:** Conservation **Obv:** National emblem **Rev:** Orangutan

Date	Mintage	VF20	XF40	MS60	MS63	MS65
1974	17,000	PF63 25.00	PF65 30.00			

KM# 30 10000 RUPIAH
24.68 g., 0.900 Gold 0.7141 oz. AGW **Subject:** 25th Anniversary of Independence **Obv:** Wayang dancer **Rev:** National emblem

Date	Mintage	VF20	XF40	MS60	MS63	MS65
1970	1,440	PF63 1,200	PF65 1,300			

KM# 45 10000 RUPIAH
19.44 g., 0.925 Silver 0.5781 oz. ASW **Subject:** Wildlife **Obv:** National emblem **Rev:** Babi rusa (wild pig)

Date	Mintage	VF20	XF40	MS60	MS63	MS65
1987	—	PF63 22.00	PF65 28.00			

KM# 50 10000 RUPIAH
19.44 g., 0.925 Silver 0.5781 oz. ASW **Series:** Save the Child **Obv:** National emblem **Rev:** Playing badminton

Date	Mintage	VF20	XF40	MS60	MS63	MS65
1990	—	PF63 40.00	PF65 50.00			

KM# 62 10000 RUPIAH
28.28 g., 0.925 Silver 0.841 oz. ASW, 38.61 mm. **Obv:** National emblem; UNICEF logo at left **Rev:** Two girl scouts planting a tree **Edge:** Milled **Note:** Struck at Hungarian Mint.

Date	Mintage	VF20	XF40	MS60	MS63	MS65
1999	—	PF63 35.00	PF65 45.00			

KM# 31 20000 RUPIAH
49.37 g., 0.900 Gold 1.4286 oz. AGW **Subject:** 25th Anniversary of Independence **Obv:** Garuda bird **Rev:** National emblem

Date	Mintage	VF20	XF40	MS60	MS63	MS65
1970	1,285	PF63 2,400	PF65 2,800			

KM# 32 25000 RUPIAH
61.71 g., 0.900 Gold 1.7856 oz. AGW **Subject:** 25th Anniversary of Independence - Gen. Sudirman **Obv:** Bust facing **Rev:** National Emblem

Date	Mintage	VF20	XF40	MS60	MS63	MS65
1970	—	PF63 3,000	PF65 3,250			

KM# 41 100000 RUPIAH
33.44 g., 0.900 Gold 0.9675 oz. AGW **Series:** Conservation **Obv:** National emblem **Rev:** Komodo dragon lizard (varanus komodensis)

Date	Mintage	VF20	XF40	MS60	MS63	MS65
1974	5,333	—	—	1,500	1,550	1,650
1974	1,369	PF63 1,800	PF65 1,900			

KM# 47 125000 RUPIAH
8.00 g., 0.958 Gold 0.2464 oz. AGW **Subject:** Museum of Struggle '45 **Obv:** National emblem **Rev:** Museum

Date	Mintage	VF20	XF40	MS60	MS63	MS65
1990	16,000	PF63 400	PF65 425			

KM# 63 150000 RUPIAH
6.22 g., 0.999 Gold 0.1998 oz. AGW, 22 mm. **Subject:** UNICEF - For the Children of the World **Obv:** National emblem; UNICEF logo at left **Rev:** Young boy riding a horse **Edge:** Milled.

Date	Mintage	VF20	XF40	MS60	MS63	MS65
1999	—	PF63 325	PF65 375			

KM# 46 200000 RUPIAH
10.00 g., 0.917 Gold 0.2948 oz. AGW **Subject:** Wildlife **Obv:** National emblem **Rev:** Javan rhinoceros right

Date	Mintage	VF20	XF40	MS60	MS63	MS65
1987	—	PF63 475	PF65 525			

KM# 51 200000 RUPIAH
10.00 g., 0.917 Gold 0.2948 oz. AGW **Series:** Save the Children **Obv:** National emblem **Rev:** Balinese dancer

Date	Mintage	VF20	XF40	MS60	MS63	MS65
1990	—	PF63 475	PF65 525			

KM# 48 250000 RUPIAH
17.00 g., 0.958 Gold 0.5236 oz. AGW **Subject:** 45 years - Indonesian Independence **Obv:** National emblem **Rev:** Map, dates and denomination below

Date	Mintage	VF20	XF40	MS60	MS63	MS65
1990	16,000	PF63 850	PF65 925			

KM# 57 300000 RUPIAH
17.00 g., 0.9583 Gold 0.5238 oz. AGW **Subject:** 50th Anniversary of Independence **Obv:** National emblem **Rev:** Presidential talk show

Date	Mintage	VF20	XF40	MS60	MS63	MS65
1995	3,000	PF63 875	PF65 975			

KM# 49 750000 RUPIAH
45.00 g., 0.958 Gold 1.386 oz. AGW **Subject:** 45 Years - Arms of Generation 1945 **Obv:** National emblem **Rev:** National emblem within wreath of rice and cotton stalks

Date	Mintage	VF20	XF40	MS60	MS63	MS65
1990	16,000	PF63 2,250	PF65 2,550			

KM# 58 850000 RUPIAH
50.00 g., 0.9583 Gold 1.5405 oz. AGW **Subject:** 50th Anniversary of Independence - President Soeharto **Obv:** National emblem **Rev:** Bust facing

Date	Mintage	VF20	XF40	MS60	MS63	MS65
1995	3,000	PF63 2,600	PF65 3,000			

PATTERNS

Including off metal strikes

KM#	Date	Mintage	Identification	Mkt Val
Pn1	1951	—	25 Sen. Aluminum.	450
Pn2	1955	—	50 Sen. Raised SPECIMEN.	500
Pn3	1963	—	2-1/2 Rupiah. Aluminum.	290
PnA4	1965	—	50 Sen. Aluminum. Sukarno. Arms.	290
Pn4	1970	—	Rupiah. Bronze. KM20.	250
Pn5	1970	—	2 Rupiah. Copper. KM21.	250
Pn6	1970	—	2 Rupiah. Bronze. KM20.	250
Pn7	1970	—	25 Rupiah. Bronze.	—
Pn8	1973	—	100 Rupiah. Aluminum.	400
PnA9	1974	—	10 Rupiah. Brass Plated Steel. Prambanan Temple at left.	—
Pn9	1979	—	10 Rupiah. Copper-Nickel.	—
Pn10	1990	—	125000 Rupiah. Gold. Gold-plated base metal. KM#47.	—
Pn11	1990	—	250000 Rupiah. Gold. Gold-plated base metal. KM#48.	—
Pn12	1990	—	750000 Rupiah. Gold. Gold-plated base metal. KM#49.	—
Pn13	1991	—	500 Rupiah. Copper-Nickel.	—
Pn14	1992	—	500 Rupiah. Bronze.	—
Pn15	1993	—	50 Rupiah. Copper-Nickel.	—
Pn16	1993	—	100 Rupiah. Copper-Nickel.	—
Pn17	1998	—	500 Rupiah. Aluminum. Octagonal. KM#54.	—
Pn18	1998	—	100 Rupiah. Aluminum. KM#53.	—

PIEDFORT

KM#	Date	Mintage	Identification	Mkt Val
P1	1970	—	5 Rupiah. Bronze.	—

MINT SETS

KM#	Date	Mintage	Identification	Issue Price	Mkt Val
MS1	Mixed dates (14)	—	KM5-6 (1951, 1954), 7-9 (1952), 10.1 (1955), 10.2 (1957), 11 (1955, 1957), 12 (1957), 14 (1961)	—	18.00
MS2	Mixed dates (9)	—	KM20-21 (1970), 33-35 (1971), 36 (1973), 37-38 (1974), 42 (1978)	2.40	12.00
MS3	1970 (3)	—	KM20-22	—	2.25
MS4	1971 (3)	—	KM33-35	—	3.25

PROOF SETS

KM#	Date	Mintage	Identification	Issue Price	Mkt Val
PS1	1970 (10)	970	KM23-32	490	8,250
PS2	1970 (5)	4,250	KM23-27	50.00	175
PS3	1974 (2)	30,000	KM39a, 40a	50.00	50.00
PS4	1990 (3)	15,750	KM47-49	755	3,950
PS5	1990 (2)	—	KM50, 51	—	600
PS6	1995 (2)	3,000	KM57, 58	2,975	3,800

IRIAN BARAT

(West Irian, Irian Jaya, Netherlands New Guinea)

A province of Indonesia comprising the western half of the island of New Guinea. A special set of coins dated 1962 were issued in 1964, were recalled December 31, 1971, and are no longer legal tender.

INDONESIAN PROVINCE

STANDARD COINAGE

No inscription on edge

KM# 5 SEN

Aluminum **Subject:** Mohammed Ahmad Sukarno **Obv:** Head left **Rev:** Denomination within wreath of cotton and rice stalks **Edge:** Plain

Date	Mintage	F12	VF20	XF40	MS60	MS63
1962	—	0.15	0.25	0.50	1.00	2.00

KM# 6 5 SEN

Aluminum **Subject:** Mohammed Ahmad Sukarno **Obv:** Head left **Rev:** Denomination within wreath of cotton and rice stalks **Edge:** Plain

Date	Mintage	F12	VF20	XF40	MS60	MS63
1962	—	0.20	0.30	0.65	1.25	2.50

KM# 7 10 SEN

Aluminum **Subject:** Mohammed Ahmad Sukarno **Obv:** Head left **Rev:** Denomination within rice and cotton stalks **Edge:** Plain

Date	Mintage	F12	VF20	XF40	MS60	MS63
1962	—	0.20	0.30	0.65	1.25	2.50

KM# 8.1 25 SEN

Aluminum **Subject:** Mohammed Ahmad Sukarno **Obv:** Head left **Rev:** Denomination within wreath of cotton and rice stalks **Edge:** Reeded

Date	Mintage	F12	VF20	XF40	MS60	MS63
1962	—	—	—	—	—	—

KM# 8.2 25 SEN

Aluminum **Obv:** Head left **Rev:** Denomination within wreath of cotton and rice stalks

Date	Mintage	F12	VF20	XF40	MS60	MS63
1962	—	0.35	0.75	1.50	2.50	4.00

KM# 9 50 SEN

Aluminum, 29 mm. **Subject:** Mohammed Ahmad Sukarno **Obv:** Head left **Rev:** Denomination within wreath of cotton and rice stalks **Edge:** Reeded

Date	Mintage	F12	VF20	XF40	MS60	MS63
1962	—	0.40	0.85	1.60	3.00	5.00

PATTERNS

Including off metal strikes

KM#	Date	Mintage	Identification	Mkt Val
Pn1	1962	—	50 Sen. Aluminum. Double reverse as KM#9.	125
Pn2	1963	—	2-1/2 Rupiah.	100
Pn3	1965	—	25 Sen. Aluminum. Plain. KM#8.2.	100
Pn4	1965	—	50 Sen. Aluminum. Reeded. KM#9.	100
Pn5	1965	—	50 Sen. Aluminum. Plain. KM#9.	100
Pn6	1965//1962 (1965)	—	50 Sen. Aluminum. As KM#9.	150

RIAU ARCHIPELAGO

A group of 3,214 islands off the tip of the Malay Peninsula. Coins were issued near the end of 1963 (although dated 1962) and recalled as worthless on Sept. 30, 1964. They were legal tender from Oct. 15, 1963 to July 1, 1964.

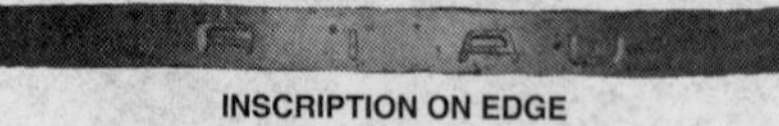

INSCRIPTION ON EDGE
KEPULAUAN RIAU

INDONESIAN PROVINCE

STANDARD COINAGE

Inscription on edge: "Kepulauan Riau"

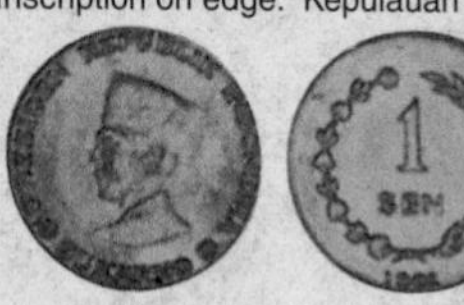

KM# 5 SEN

Aluminum **Obv:** Head left **Rev:** Denomination within wreath of cotton and rice stalks

Date	Mintage	F12	VF20	XF40	MS60	MS63
1962	—	0.25	0.35	0.75	1.25	2.25

KM# 6 5 SEN

Aluminum **Obv:** Head left **Rev:** Denomination within wreath of cotton and rice stalks

Date	Mintage	F12	VF20	XF40	MS60	MS63
1962	—	0.20	0.30	0.60	1.50	2.50

KM# 7 10 SEN

Aluminum **Subject:** Mohammed Ahmad Sukarno **Obv:** Head left **Rev:** Denomination within wreath of cotton and rice stalks

Date	Mintage	F12	VF20	XF40	MS60	MS63
1962	—	0.25	0.35	0.70	1.75	3.00

KM# 8.1 25 SEN

Aluminum **Obv:** Head left **Rev:** Denomination within wreath of cotton and rice stalks

Date	Mintage	F12	VF20	XF40	MS60	MS63
1962	—	—	—	—	—	—

KM# 8.2 25 SEN

Aluminum **Subject:** Mohammed Ahmad Sukarno **Obv:** Head left **Rev:** Denomination within wreath of cotton and rice stalks

Date	Mintage	F12	VF20	XF40	MS60	MS63
1962	—	0.40	0.85	1.60	2.75	4.50

KM# 9 50 SEN

Aluminum, 29 mm. **Subject:** Mohammed Ahmad Sukarno **Obv:** Bust left **Rev:** Denomination within wreath of cotton and rice stalks

Date	Mintage	F12	VF20	XF40	MS60	MS63
1962	—	0.50	1.00	2.00	3.50	5.50

IRAN

The Islamic Republic of Iran, located between the Caspian Sea and the Persian Gulf in southwestern Asia, has an area of 636,296 sq. mi. (1,648,000 sq. km.) and a population of 59.7 million. Capital: Tehran. Although predominantly an agricultural state, Iran depends heavily on oil for foreign exchange. Crude oil, carpets and agricultural products are exported.

Iran (historically known as Persia until 1931AD) is one of the world's most ancient and resilient nations. Strategically astride the lower land gate to Asia, it has been conqueror and conquered, sovereign nation and vassal state, ever emerging from its periods of glory or travail with its culture and political individuality intact. Iran (Persia) was a powerful empire under Cyrus the Great (600-529 B.C.), its borders extending from the Indus to the Nile. It has also been conquered by the predatory empires of antique and recent times - Assyrian, Medean, Macedonian, Seljuq, Turk, Mongol - and more recently been coveted by Russia, the Third Reich and Great Britain. Revolts against the absolute power of the Persian shahs resulted in the establishment of a constitutional monarchy in 1906.

With 4,000 troops, Reza Khan marched on the capital arriving in Tehran in the early morning of Feb. 22,1921. The government was taken over with hardly a shot and Zia ad-Din was set up as premier, but the real power was with Reza Khan, although he was officially only the minister of war. In 1923, Reza Khan appointed himself prime minister and summoned the "majlis." Who eventually gave him military powers and he became independent of the shah's authority. In 1925 Reza Khan Pahlavi was elected Shah of Persia. A few weeks later his eldest son, Shahpur Mohammed Reza was appointed Crown Prince and was crowned on April 25, 1926.

On March 22, 1935 the Kingdom of Persia became the Kingdom of Iran. In 1979 the monarchy was toppled and an Islamic Republic proclaimed.

TITLE

دار الخلافة

Dar al-Khilafat

RULERS

Qajar Dynasty

مظفرالدین

Muzaffar al-Din Shah, AH1313-1324/1896-1907AD

محمد علی

Muhammad Ali Shah, AH1324-1327/1907-1909AD

سلطان احمد

Sultan Ahmad Shah, AH1327-1344/1909-1925AD

Pahlavi Dynasty

رضا

Reza Shah, as prime minister, SH1302-1304/ 1923-1925AD as Shah, SH1304-1320/1925-1941AD

محمد رضا

Mohammad Reza Pahlavi, Shah SH1320-1358/ 1941-1979AD

جمهوری اسلامی ایران

Islamic Republic, SH1358-/1979-AD

MINT NAME

طهران

Tehran

تفلیس

Tiflis

MINT MARKS

H - Heaton (Birmingham)
L - Leningrad (St. Petersburg)

COIN DATING

Iranian coins were dated according to the Moslem lunar calendar until March 21, 1925 (AD), when dating was switched to a new calendar based on the solar year, indicated by the notation SH. The monarchial calendar system was adopted in 1976 = MS2535 and was abandoned in 1978 = MS2537. The previously used solar year calendar was restored at that time.

MONETARY SYSTEM

1825-1931
(AH1241-1344, SH1304-09)

50 Dinars = 1 Shahi
20 Shahis = 1 Kran (Qiran)
10 Krans = 1 Toman

NOTE: From AD1830-34 (AH1245-50) the gold Toman was known as a 'Keshwarsetan.'

1932-Date (SH1310-Date)

5 Dinars = 1 Shahi
20 Shahis = 1 Rial (100 Dinars)
10 Rials = 1 Toman

NOTE: The Toman ceased to be an official unit in 1932, but continues to be applied in popular usage. Thus, '135 Rials' is always expressed as '13 Toman, 5 Rials'. The term 'Rial' is often used in conversation, as well as either Kran' or Ezar' (short for Hazar = 1000) is used.

NOTE: The Law of 18 March 1930 fixed the gold Pahlavi at 20 Rials. No gold coins were struck. The Law of 13 March1932 divided the Pahlavi into 100 Rials, instead of 20. The Rial's weight was reduced from 0.3661 grams of pure gold to 0.0732. Since 1937 gold has been allowed to float and the Pahlavi is quoted daily in Rials in the marketplaces.

KINGDOM

NOTE: Other mints also produced local Falus, for which examples were not available to illustrate. Still other mints operated only or largely at earlier dates. These include Damavand, Damghan, Darabjird, Fa'Farafad, Kangan, Ra', Semnan, Tus, Tuy and others.

SILVER AND GOLD COINAGE

The precious metal monetary system of Qajar Persia prior to the reforms of 1878 was the direct descendant of the Mongol system introduced by Ghazan Mahmud in 1297AD, and was the last example of a medieval islamic coinage. It is not a modern system, and cannot be understood as such. It is not possible to list types, dates, and mints as for other countries, both because of the nature of the coinage, and because very little research has been done on the series. The following comments should help elucidate its nature.

STANDARDS: The weight of the primary silver and gold coins was set by law and was expressed in terms of the Mesqal (about 4.61 g) and the Nokhod (24 Nokhod = 1 Mesqal). The primary silver coin was the Rupee from AH1211-1212, the Riyal from AH1212-1241, and the Gheran from AH1241-1344. The standard gold coin was the Toman. Currently the price of gold is quoted in Mesqals.

DENOMINATIONS: In addition to the primary denominations, noted in the last paragraph, fractional pieces were coined, valued at one-eighth, one-fourth, and one-half the primary denomination, usually in much smaller quantities. These were ordinarily struck from the same dies as the larger pieces, sometimes on broad, thin flans, sometimes on thick, dumpy flans. On the smaller coins, the denomination can best be determined only by weighing the coin. The denomination is almost never expressed on the coin!

OVERSIZE COINS: Occasionally, multiples of the primary denominations were produced, usually on special occasions for presentation by the Shah to his favorites. These 'coins' did not circulate (except as bullion), and were usually worn as ornaments. They were the 'NCLT's' of their day.

ARRANGEMENT

The following listings are arranged first by ruler, with various standards explained. Then, the coins are listed by denomination within each reign. For each denomination, one or more pieces, when available, are illustrated, with the mint and date noted beneath each photo. For each type, a date range is given, but this range indicates the years during which the particular type was current, and does not imply that every year of the interval is known on actual coins. Because dates were carelessly engraved, and old dies were used until they wore out or broke, we occasionally find coins of a particular type dated before or after the indicated interval. Such coins command no premium. No attempt has been made to determine which mints actually exist for which types.

KRAN STANDARD

AH1293-1344, SH1304-1309, 1876-1931AD
50 Dinars = 1 Shahi
1000 Dinars = 20 Shahis = 1 Kran (Qiron)
10 Krans = 1 Toman

Special Gold Issue

AH1337/1918-1919AD
1 Ashrafi (= 1 Toman)
SH1305-1309/1927-1931AD

Toman replaced by Pahlavi (light standard). Relationship of Pahlavi to Kran not known.

SHAHI SEFID
(White Shahi)

Called the White (i.e. silver) Shahi to distinguish it from the Black or Copper Shahi, the Shahi Sefid was actually worth 3 Shahis (150 Dinars) or 3 1/8 Shahis (156 ¼ Dinars). It was used primarily for distribution on New Year's Day (now RUZ) as good-luck gifts. Since 1926 special privately struck tokens, having no monetary value, have been used instead of coins. The Shahi Sefid was broader, but much thinner than the ¼ Kran (Rob'l), worth 250 Dinars.

MILLED GOLD COINAGE: Modern imitations exist of many types, particularly the small 1/5, 1/2, and 1 Toman coins. These are usually underweight (or rarely overweight), and are sold in the bazaars at a small premium over bullion. They are usually crude and probably not intended to deceive collectors, but some are sold for jewelry and some are dated outside the reign of the ruler whose name or portrait they bear. A few deceptive counterfeits are known of the large 10 Toman pieces.

KINGDOM

Muzaffar al-Din Shah
AH1313-1324 / 1896-1907AD

MILLED COINAGE

Tehran

KM# 961 50 DINARS

Copper-Nickel **Obv:** Legend within beaded circle with crown on top **Rev:** Radiant lion holding sword within wreath

Date	Mintage	F12	VF20	XF40	MS60	MS63
AH1318	10,000,000	0.75	1.50	2.50	4.00	8.00
AH1319	12,000,000	1.00	2.50	4.00	7.00	10.00
AH1321	10,000,000	0.75	1.50	2.50	4.00	8.00
AH1326	8,000,000	4.00	7.00	12.00	20.00	30.00
AH1332	6,000,000	1.00	1.75	3.00	5.00	12.50
AH1337	7,000,000	1.50	3.50	5.00	8.00	12.00

KM# 965 SHAHI SEFID (White Shahi)

0.80 g., 0.900 Silver 0.0231 oz. ASW **Obv:** Legend and value within circle and wreath **Obv. Legend:** Muzaffar al-Din Shah **Rev:** Crown above lion and sun within wreath

Date	Mintage	F12	VF20	XF40	MS60	MS63
ND (1895)	—	8.00	20.00	40.00	80.00	—

Note: Some undated issues show traces of an old date (usually AH1301 or AH1303) below wreath on reverse; these are worth slightly more than other undated issues

Date	Mintage	F12	VF20	XF40	MS60	MS63
AH1318	—	15.00	30.00	60.00	120	—
AH1319	—	15.00	30.00	60.00	120	—
AH1039	—	25.00	50.00	100	200	—
Note: Error for 1319						
AH1320	150,000	15.00	30.00	60.00	120	—

KM# 966 SHAHI SEFID (White Shahi)

0.80 g., 0.900 Silver 0.0231 oz. ASW **Obv:** Legend within circle and wreath **Rev:** Radiant lion holding sword within crowned wreath

Date	Mintage	F12	VF20	XF40	MS60	MS63
ND (1901)	—	50.00	80.00	165	300	—
AH1319 Rare	—	—	—	—	—	—

Note: A number of varieties and mulings of KM#965 and KM#966 with other denominations, especially 1/4 Krans and 500 Dinar pieces, are reported; these command a premium over others of the same types; a total of 58,000 pieces were reported struck in AH1322, 1323 and 1324, but none are known with those dates; the specimens were either struck from old dies or were undated types.

KM# 967 SHAHI SEFID (White Shahi)

0.80 g., 0.900 Silver 0.0231 oz. ASW **Obv:** Legend within center circle of wreath **Obv. Legend:** Muzaffar al-Din Shah **Rev:** Legend within center circle of wreath **Rev. Legend:** Sahib al-Zaman **Note:** Thick and thin lettering varieties exist.

Date	Mintage	F12	VF20	XF40	MS60	MS63
ND (1903)	—	50.00	85.00	165	300	—

KM# 962 100 DINARS (2 Shahi)

4.40 g., Copper-Nickel **Obv:** Legend within beaded circle and crowned wreath **Rev:** Radiant lion holding sword within crowned wreath

Date	Mintage	F12	VF20	XF40	MS60	MS63
AH1318	10,000,000	2.50	4.00	6.00	10.00	20.00
AH1319	9,000,000	2.50	4.00	6.00	10.00	20.00
AH1321/19	5,000,000	6.00	12.00	18.00	30.00	50.00
AH1321	Inc. above	0.75	1.50	2.50	4.00	8.00
AH1326	6,000,000	1.50	2.50	4.00	6.00	15.00
AH1332	5,000,000	1.00	2.00	3.00	5.00	12.50
AH1337	6,500,000	2.00	4.00	6.00	10.00	18.00

KM# 968 1/4 KRAN (Robi = 5 Shahis)

1.15 g., 0.900 Silver 0.0333 oz. ASW **Obv:** Legend and value within circle and wreath **Obv. Legend:** Muzaffar al-din Shah **Rev:** Crown above lion and sun within wreath **Note:** 300 specimens reportedly struck in AH1322, but none known to exist.

Date	Mintage	F12	VF20	XF40	MS60	MS63
AH1318	—	25.00	50.00	85.00	165	—
AH1319	—	20.00	35.00	65.00	130	—

KM# 969 500 DINARS (10 Shahis = 1/2 Kran)

2.30 g., 0.900 Silver 0.0666 oz. ASW **Obv:** Legend and value within circle and wreath **Obv. Legend:** "Muzaffar al-din", 500 Dinars **Rev:** Crown above lion and sun within wreath **Note:** Some reverse dies were previously used under Nasir al-Din and show traces of old date beneath wreath on reverse.

Date	Mintage	F12	VF20	XF40	MS60	MS63
ND (1895)	—	10.00	20.00	35.00	70.00	—

Date	Mintage	F12	VF20	XF40	MS60	MS63
AH1318	—	30.00	50.00	125	250	—
AH1319	—	20.00	40.00	100	200	—
AH1322	—	20.00	30.00	50.00	100	—

KM# 977 500 DINARS (10 Shahis = 1/2 Kran)
2.30 g., 0.900 Silver 0.0666 oz. ASW **Obv:** Uniformed bust 1/4 right **Rev:** Radiant lion holding sword within crowned wreath

Date	Mintage	F12	VF20	XF40	MS60	MS63
AH1323	130,000	20.00	35.00	80.00	160	—

1000 DINARS: یکهزار دینار

1 KRAN: یکقران

KM# 972 1000 DINARS (Kran, Qiran)
4.61 g., 0.900 Silver 0.1332 oz. ASW **Obv:** Legend and value within circle and wreath **Rev:** Crown above lion and sun within wreath

Date	Mintage	F12	VF20	XF40	MS60	MS63
AH1318	—	100	175	250	350	—
AH1319	—	150	225	350	500	—
AH1322	—	100	175	250	350	—

KM# 978 1000 DINARS (Kran, Qiran)
4.61 g., 0.900 Silver 0.1332 oz. ASW **Obv:** Uniformed bust 1/4 right **Rev:** Radiant lion holding sword within crowned wreath

Date	Mintage	F12	VF20	XF40	MS60	MS63
AH1323	125,000	20.00	30.00	65.00	125	—

KM# 974 2000 DINARS (2 Kran)
9.21 g., 0.900 Silver 0.2665 oz. ASW **Obv:** Legend and value within wreath, star above **Rev:** Crown above lion and sun within wreath **Note:** Blundered dates exist.

Date	Mintage	F12	VF20	XF40	MS60	MS63
AH1318	—	10.00	20.00	35.00	90.00	—
AH1319	—	12.00	25.00	42.00	110	—
AH1320	13,959,000	12.00	25.00	42.00	90.00	—

KM# 975 2000 DINARS (2 Kran)
9.21 g., 0.900 Silver 0.2665 oz. ASW **Obv:** Legend within circle and wreath **Rev:** Radiant lion holding sword within crowned wreath **Rev. Legend:** 2 Krans

Date	Mintage	F12	VF20	XF40	MS60	MS63
AH1320	Inc. above	15.00	25.00	48.00	120	—
AH1321	18,108,000	18.00	27.50	55.00	120	—
Note: In blundered form as 13201						
AH1322	8,640,000	10.00	18.00	36.00	95.00	—

KM# 979 2000 DINARS (2 Kran)
9.21 g., 0.900 Silver 0.2665 oz. ASW **Obv:** Uniformed bust 1/4 right within wreath **Rev:** Radiant lion holding sword within crowned wreath

Date	Mintage	F12	VF20	XF40	MS60	MS63
AH1323	—	17.00	33.00	65.00	130	—
Note: Mintage inluded in AH1323 above						
AH'13'	—	65.00	110	220	450	—
Note: 23 of 1323 filled in or never punched						
AH13233	—	49.50	95.00	210	425	—
Note: Error						

KM# 976 5000 DINARS (5 Kran)
23.03 g., 0.900 Silver 0.6662 oz. ASW **Obv:** Legend within crowned wreath **Obv. Legend:** Muzaffar al-din Shah **Rev:** Radiant lion holding sword within crowned wreath **Note:** Dav.#288.

Date	Mintage	F12	VF20	XF40	MS60	MS63
AH1320	250,000	25.00	30.00	50.00	125	—
Note: Actual mintage must be considerably greater						

KM# 980 5000 DINARS (5 Kran)
23.03 g., 0.900 Silver 0.6662 oz. ASW, 36 mm. **Subject:** Royal Birthday **Obv:** Uniformed bust 1/4 right within wreath **Rev:** Radiant lion holding sword within crowned wreath **Note:** Dav.#287.

Date	Mintage	F12	VF20	XF40	MS60	MS63
AH1322	—	350	750	1,500	5,000	—

KM# 981 5000 DINARS (5 Kran)
23.03 g., 0.900 Silver 0.6662 oz. ASW, 36 mm. **Obv:** Uniformed bust 1/4 right within wreath **Rev:** Radiant lion holding sword within crowned wreath **Note:** Dav.#289. Without additional inscription flanking head

Date	Mintage	F12	VF20	XF40	MS60	MS63
AH1324	3,040	1,000	2,000	4,000	7,500	—

KM# 922 2000 DINARS (1/5 Toman)
0.65 g., 0.900 Gold 0.0189 oz. AGW **Rev:** Legend and value within circle and wreath **Note:** Mule. Reverse: KM#923, reverse: KM#991.

Date	Mintage	VG8	F12	VF20	XF40	MS60
AH1295 (sic)	—	200	350	700	1,500	—

KM# 986 2000 DINARS (1/5 Toman)
0.65 g., 0.900 Gold 0.0189 oz. AGW **Obv. Legend:** Mazaffar-al-Din Shah **Rev:** Crown above lion and sun within wreath

Date	Mintage	F12	VF20	XF40	MS60	MS63
AH9301 Error for 1319	—	200	350	700	1,500	—

KM# 991 2000 DINARS (1/5 Toman)
0.57 g., 0.900 Gold 0.0166 oz. AGW **Obv:** Uniformed bust left **Rev:** Legend and value within circle and wreath

Date	Mintage	F12	VF20	XF40	MS60	MS63
AH1319	—	200	300	600	1,250	—

KM# 992 2000 DINARS (1/5 Toman)
0.57 g., 0.900 Gold 0.0166 oz. AGW **Obv:** Date and denomination added

Date	Mintage	F12	VF20	XF40	MS60	MS63
AH1319	—	50.00	100	175	350	—
AH1322	—	50.00	100	175	350	—
AH1323	—	50.00	100	175	350	—
AH1324	—	50.00	100	175	350	—

KM# 994.1 5000 DINARS (1/2 Toman)
1.44 g., 0.900 Gold 0.0416 oz. AGW **Obv:** Uniformed bust 3/4 right **Rev:** Legend and value within cirlce and wreath **Note:** Prev. KM#994.

Date	Mintage	F12	VF20	XF40	MS60	MS63
AH1318	—	70.00	100	200	350	—
AH1319	—	70.00	100	200	350	—
AH1320	—	70.00	100	200	350	—
AH1321	—	70.00	100	200	350	—
AH1322	—	70.00	100	200	350	—
AH1324	—	70.00	100	200	350	—

KM# 994.2 5000 DINARS (1/2 Toman)
1.44 g., 0.900 Gold 0.0416 oz. AGW **Obv:** Bust with headdress 3/4 right divides date **Rev:** Legend within circle and wreath

Date	Mintage	F12	VF20	XF40	MS60	MS63
AH1323	—	75.00	110	220	375	—

KM# 995 TOMAN
2.87 g., 0.900 Gold 0.0832 oz. AGW, 19 mm. **Obv:** Uniformed bust 3/4 right, accession date, AH1314 above left **Rev:** Legend and value within circle and wreath

Date	Mintage	F12	VF20	XF40	MS60	MS63
AH1318	—	160	220	275	450	—
AH1319	—	145	160	195	370	—
AH1321	—	150	180	295	520	—

KM# 996 2 TOMAN
5.75 g., 0.900 Gold 0.1663 oz. AGW, 19 mm. **Obv:** Uniformed bust 3/4 left, date at left **Rev:** Legend within circle and wreath **Rev. Legend:** Muzaffer al-Din Shah

Date	Mintage	F12	VF20	XF40	MS60	MS63
AH1322	—	300	650	2,000	4,000	—

KM# 997 2 TOMAN
5.75 g., 0.900 Gold 0.1663 oz. AGW, 19 mm. **Subject:** Royal Birthday **Obv:** Uniformed bust 3/4 left divides legend **Rev:** Legend within circle and wreath **Rev. Legend:** Muzaffer al-Din Shah

Date	Mintage	F12	VF20	XF40	MS60	MS63
AH1322	—	300	500	1,000	1,500	—

Muhammad Ali Shah
AH1324-1327 / 1907-1909AD

Tehran

KM# 1006 SHAHI SEFID (White Shahi)
0.07 g., 0.900 Silver 0.002 oz. ASW, 17 mm. **Obv:** Legend within circle and wreath **Obv. Legend:** Muhammad Ali Shah **Rev:** Radiant lion holding sword within crowned wreath

Date	Mintage	F12	VF20	XF40	MS60	MS63
AH1325	—	30.00	60.00	110	200	—
AH1326	—	25.00	40.00	90.00	180	—
AH1327	—	20.00	40.00	80.00	160	—

KM# 1007 SHAHI SEFID (White Shahi)
0.07 g., 0.900 Silver 0.002 oz. ASW **Obv:** Legend within circle and wreath **Obv. Legend:** Sahib al-Zaman **Rev:** Radiant lion holding sword within crowned wreath

Date	Mintage	F12	VF20	XF40	MS60	MS63
AH1326	—	60.00	125	175	325	—

KM# 1008 SHAHI SEFID (White Shahi)
0.07 g., 0.900 Silver 0.002 oz. ASW **Obv:** Legend within circle and wreath **Rev:** Radiant lion holding sword within crowned wreath

Date	Mintage	F12	VF20	XF40	MS60	MS63
ND (1909)	—	50.00	80.00	150	300	—

KM# 1009 1/4 KRAN (Robi = 5 Shahis)
1.15 g., 0.900 Silver 0.0333 oz. ASW, 15 mm. **Obv:** Legend within circle and wreath **Obv. Legend:** Muhammad Ali Shah **Rev:** Radiant lion holding sword within crowned wreath

Date	Mintage	F12	VF20	XF40	MS60	MS63
AH1325	—	30.00	50.00	100	200	—
AH1326	—	15.00	27.50	40.00	80.00	—
AH1327	—	10.00	20.00	35.00	70.00	—

KM# 1010 500 DINARS (10 Shahis = 1/2 Kran)
2.30 g., 0.900 Silver 0.0666 oz. ASW, 18 mm. **Obv:** Legend within circle and wreath **Obv. Legend:** Muhammad Ali Shah **Rev:** Radiant lion holding sword within crowned wreath

Date	Mintage	F12	VF20	XF40	MS60	MS63
AH1325	218,000	40.00	75.00	160	300	—
AH1335 Error for 1325	—	50.00	85.00	175	325	—
AH1326	218,000	25.00	50.00	110	225	—
AH1336 Error for 1326	Inc. above	35.00	60.00	125	250	—

KM# 1014 500 DINARS (10 Shahis = 1/2 Kran)
2.30 g., 0.900 Silver 0.0666 oz. ASW **Obv:** Uniformed bust 3/4 left within wreath, date **Rev:** Crown above lion and sun within wreath, date

Date	Mintage	F12	VF20	XF40	MS60	MS63
AH1325	—	125	175	320	500	—
AH1326	—	100	150	240	400	—

KM# 1013 500 DINARS (10 Shahis = 1/2 Kran)
2.30 g., 0.900 Silver 0.0666 oz. ASW **Obv:** Uniformed bust 1/4 left within sprigs **Rev:** Radiant lion holding sword within crowned wreath

Date	Mintage	F12	VF20	XF40	MS60	MS63
AH1326	—	40.00	85.00	150	300	—
Note: Mintage included in KM#1010						
AH1327	—	40.00	85.00	150	300	—

KM# 1011 1000 DINARS (Kran, Qiran)
4.61 g., 0.900 Silver 0.1332 oz. ASW, 23 mm. **Obv:** Legend within circle and crowned wreath **Obv. Legend:** Muhammad Ali Shah **Rev:** Radiant lion holding sword within crowned wreath

Date	Mintage	F12	VF20	XF40	MS60	MS63
AH1325	289,000	150	300	600	800	—
AH1326	289,000	150	300	600	800	—

KM# 1015 1000 DINARS (Kran, Qiran)
4.61 g., 0.900 Silver 0.1332 oz. ASW **Obv:** Uniformed bust 3/4 left within wreath, date below **Rev:** Radiant lion holding sword within crowned wreath

Date	Mintage	F12	VF20	XF40	MS60	MS63
AH1326	—	55.00	90.00	270	675	—
Note: Mintage included in KM#1011						
AH1327/6	—	50.00	75.00	225	625	—
AH1327	—	50.00	75.00	225	625	—

KM# 1016 1000 DINARS (Kran, Qiran)
4.61 g., 0.900 Silver 0.1332 oz. ASW **Obv:** Uniformed bust 3/4 left within wreath, date **Rev:** Radiant lion holding sword within crowned wreath, date

Date	Mintage	F12	VF20	XF40	MS60	MS63
AH1326	—	125	200	350	500	—
Note: Mintage included in KM#1011						

KM# 1012 2000 DINARS (2 Kran)
9.21 g., 0.900 Silver 0.2665 oz. ASW, 28 mm. **Obv:** Legend within circle and crowned wreath **Obv. Legend:** Muhammad Ali Shah **Rev:** Radiant lion holding sword within crowned wreath

Date	Mintage	F12	VF20	XF40	MS60	MS63
AH1325	3,076,000	15.00	25.00	50.00	100	—
AH1326	3,069,000	10.00	12.50	25.00	50.00	—
AH1327	—	10.00	12.50	25.00	50.00	—

KM# 1017 2000 DINARS (2 Kran)
9.21 g., 0.900 Silver 0.2665 oz. ASW **Obv:** Uniformed bust 3/4 left within wreath, date below **Rev:** Radiant lion holding sword within crowned wreath

Date	Mintage	F12	VF20	XF40	MS60	MS63
AH1326	—	750	1,500	3,000	7,500	—
Note: Mintage included in KM#1012						

KM# 1018 5000 DINARS (5 Kran)
23.03 g., 0.900 Silver 0.6662 oz. ASW **Obv:** Uniformed bust 3/4 left within wreath **Rev:** Crown above lion and sun within wreath **Note:** Dav.#290.

Date	Mintage	F12	VF20	XF40	MS60	MS63
AH1327	—	600	1,250	2,500	7,500	—
Note: Obverse always weakly struck with little detail in head and face						

KM# 1024 2000 DINARS (1/5 Toman)
0.57 g., 0.900 Gold 0.0166 oz. AGW **Obv:** Uniformed bust 3/4 left within wreath **Rev:** Legend in wreath

Date	Mintage	F12	VF20	XF40	MS60	MS63
AH1326	—	75.00	150	300	600	—
AH1327	—	75.00	150	300	600	—

KM# 1021 5000 DINARS (1/2 Toman)
1.44 g., 0.900 Gold 0.0416 oz. AGW, 17 mm. **Obv:** Legend within circle and wreath **Obv. Legend:** Muhammad Ali Shah **Rev:** Radiant lion holding sword within crowned wreath

Date	Mintage	F12	VF20	XF40	MS60	MS63
AH1324	—	80.00	125	250	500	—
AH1325	—	90.00	150	350	750	—

KM# 1025 5000 DINARS (1/2 Toman)
1.44 g., 0.900 Gold 0.0416 oz. AGW, 17 mm. **Obv:** Uniformed bust 3/4 left divides date **Rev:** Legend within circle and wreath **Rev. Legend:** Muhammad Ali Shah

Date	Mintage	F12	VF20	XF40	MS60	MS63
AH1326	—	80.00	125	250	500	—
AH1362 Error for 1326	—	80.00	125	250	500	—
AH1327	—	80.00	125	250	500	—

KM# 1022 TOMAN
2.87 g., 0.900 Gold 0.0832 oz. AGW, 19 mm. **Obv:** Legend within circle and wreath **Obv. Legend:** Muhammad Ali Shah **Rev:** Radiant lion holding sword within crowned wreath

Date	Mintage	F12	VF20	XF40	MS60	MS63
AH1324	—	150	300	750	1,500	—

KM# 1026 TOMAN
2.87 g., 0.900 Gold 0.0832 oz. AGW **Obv:** Uniformed bust 3/4 left divides date **Rev:** Legend within circle and closed wreath **Rev. Legend:** Muhammad Ali Shah

Date	Mintage	F12	VF20	XF40	MS60	MS63
AH1327	—	150	300	650	1,250	—

MILLED COINAGE

Silver Kran Standard

Tehran

KM# 891 SHAHI SEFID (White Shahi)
Copper-Nickel Clad Brass **Obv. Legend:** "Nasir al-Din" (KM#889) **Rev. Legend:** "Shahib al-zaman" (obverse of KM#1007) **Note:** Mule using old obverse die.

Date	Mintage	F12	VF20	XF40	MS60	MS63
ND (1908)	—	50.00	75.00	125	250	—

Sultan Ahmad Shah

AH1327-1344 / 1909-1925AD

MILLED COINAGE

KM# 1031 SHAHI SEFID (White Shahi)
0.07 g., 0.900 Silver 0.002 oz. ASW **Obv:** Legend within circle and wreath **Obv. Legend:** Ahmad Shah **Rev:** Radiant lion holding sword within crowned wreath

Date	Mintage	F12	VF20	XF40	MS60	MS63
AH1328	—	5.00	10.00	20.00	40.00	—
AH1329	—	6.00	12.00	25.00	50.00	—
AH1330	189,000	4.00	10.00	20.00	40.00	—

KM# 1032 SHAHI SEFID (White Shahi)
0.07 g., 0.900 Silver 0.002 oz. ASW **Obv:** Legend within circle and wreath **Rev:** Radiant lion holding sword within crowned wreath

Date	Mintage	F12	VF20	XF40	MS60	MS63
AH1332	10,000	30.00	50.00	85.00	150	—

KM# 1033 SHAHI SEFID (White Shahi)
0.07 g., 0.900 Silver 0.002 oz. ASW **Obv:** Legend within circle and wreath **Obv. Legend:** Ahmad Shah **Rev:** Legend within circle and wreath **Rev. Legend:** Sahib-al-Zaman

Date	Mintage	F12	VF20	XF40	MS60	MS63
ND (1913)	—	60.00	125	200	400	—

KM# 1049 SHAHI SEFID (White Shahi)
0.07 g., 0.900 Silver 0.002 oz. ASW **Obv:** Legend within circle and wreath **Rev:** Radiant lion holding sword within crowned wreath **Rev. Legend:** Sahib-al-Zaman

Date	Mintage	F12	VF20	XF40	MS60	MS63
ND (1913)	—	10.00	20.00	40.00	75.00	—
AH1332	—	10.00	18.00	35.00	80.00	—
Note: Included in KM#1032						
AH1333	—	10.00	20.00	40.00	80.00	—
Note: Included in KM#1047						
AH1337	—	10.00	20.00	40.00	80.00	—
Note: Included in KM#1047						
AH1341	3,000	15.00	25.00	50.00	100	—
AH1342	—	15.00	25.00	50.00	100	—
Note: Included in KM#1047						

KM# 1047 SHAHI SEFID (White Shahi)
0.07 g., 0.900 Silver 0.002 oz. ASW **Obv:** Legend within circle and wreath, date below **Rev:** Radiant lion holding sword within crowned wreath **Note:** Varieties exist.

Date	Mintage	F12	VF20	XF40	MS60	MS63
AH1333	78,000	5.00	10.00	20.00	40.00	—
AH1334	6,000	12.00	20.00	40.00	80.00	—
AH1335	73,000	8.00	15.00	30.00	60.00	—
AH1335//1337	Inc. above	40.00	80.00	165	250	—
AH1337	76,000	8.00	15.00	30.00	60.00	—
AH1337//1337	—	40.00	75.00	150	280	—
AH1339	10,000	12.00	20.00	40.00	80.00	—
AH1342	20,000	12.00	20.00	40.00	80.00	—

KM# 1048 SHAHI SEFID (White Shahi)
0.07 g., 0.900 Silver 0.002 oz. ASW **Obv:** Legend within circle and wreath **Rev:** Legend within circle and wreath, date below **Rev. Legend:** Sahib-al-Zaman

Date	Mintage	F12	VF20	XF40	MS60	MS63
AH1335	—	50.00	80.00	150	300	—
Note: Mintage included in KM#1047 of AH1335						

KM# 1050 SHAHI SEFID (White Shahi)
0.69 g., 0.900 Silver 0.020 oz. ASW **Obv:** Legend within circle and wreath, dated AH1339 **Rev:** Radiant lion with sword within crowned wreath with AH1341 between lion's legs, AH1327 below wreath

Date	Mintage	F12	VF20	XF40	MS60	MS63
AH1339//1341 & 1327	—	50.00	80.00	150	300	—

Note: Numerous silver Nouruz tokens, some with dates SH1328-1346, are available in Tehran for a fraction of the price of true Shahis

KM# 1035 1/4 KRAN (Robi = 5 Shahis)
1.15 g., 0.900 Silver 0.0333 oz. ASW, 15 mm. **Obv:** Legend within circle and wreath **Obv. Legend:** Ahmad Shah **Rev:** Radiant lion holding sword within crowned wreath

Date	Mintage	F12	VF20	XF40	MS60	MS63
AH1327	—	5.00	10.00	20.00	40.00	—
AH1328	—	4.00	7.50	15.00	30.00	—
AH1329	130,000	12.50	20.00	40.00	80.00	—
AH1330	156,000	4.00	7.50	15.00	30.00	—
AH1331	30,000	—	—	—	—	—
Note: Requires Confirmation.						
AH1313 Error for 1331	Inc. above	—	—	—	—	—
Note: Requires Confirmation.						

KM# 1052 1/4 KRAN (Robi = 5 Shahis)
1.15 g., 0.900 Silver 0.0333 oz. ASW **Obv:** Legend within circle and wreath, date below **Obv. Legend:** Ahmad Shah **Rev:** Radiant lion holding sword within crowned wreath **Note:** Mule.

Date	Mintage	F12	VF20	XF40	MS60	MS63
ND (1909)	—	45.00	65.00	125	200	—
AH1327	—	65.00	135	185	300	—

KM# 1051 1/4 KRAN (Robi = 5 Shahis)
1.15 g., 0.900 Silver 0.0333 oz. ASW **Obv:** Legend within circle and wreath **Obv. Legend:** Ahmad Shah **Rev:** Radiant lion holding sword within crowned wreath

Date	Mintage	F12	VF20	XF40	MS60	MS63
AH1332	252,000	5.00	10.00	20.00	40.00	—
AH1333	Inc. above	6.00	12.00	25.00	50.00	—
AH1334	70,000	10.00	20.00	50.00	100	—
AH1335	260,000	4.00	8.00	15.00	30.00	—
AH1336	160,000	4.00	8.00	15.00	30.00	—
AH1337	80,000	6.00	12.00	25.00	50.00	—
AH1339	28,000	9.00	15.00	30.00	60.00	—
AH1341	22,000	12.00	20.00	40.00	80.00	—
AH1342	110,000	6.00	12.00	25.00	50.00	—
AH1343	186,000	4.00	8.00	15.00	30.00	—

KM# 1053 1/4 KRAN (Robi = 5 Shahis)
1.15 g., 0.900 Silver 0.0333 oz. ASW **Obv:** Legend within circle and wreath **Rev:** Radiant lion holding sword within crowned wreath

Date	Mintage	F12	VF20	XF40	MS60	MS63
AH1334	—	35.00	75.00	150	250	—
Note: Mintage included with KM#1051						

KM# 1036 500 DINARS (10 Shahis = 1/2 Kran)
2.30 g., 0.900 Silver 0.0666 oz. ASW, 18 mm. **Obv:** Legend within circle and wreath **Obv. Legend:** Ahmad Shah **Rev:** Radiant lion holding sword within crowned wreath

Date	Mintage	F12	VF20	XF40	MS60	MS63
AH1327	—	8.00	15.00	30.00	50.00	—
AH1328	—	5.00	12.50	20.00	40.00	—
AH1329	44,000	10.00	20.00	40.00	80.00	—
AH1330	627,000	8.00	15.00	30.00	50.00	—

KM# 1054 500 DINARS (10 Shahis = 1/2 Kran)
2.30 g., 0.900 Silver 0.0666 oz. ASW **Obv:** Uniformed bust 1/4 left within wreath, date below **Rev:** Radiant lion holding sword within crowned wreath

Date	Mintage	F12	VF20	XF40	MS60	MS63
AH1331	—	8.00	15.00	30.00	50.00	—
Note: Mintage included in AH1330 above						
AH1332	560,000	8.00	15.00	30.00	50.00	—
AH1333	292,000	5.00	10.00	15.00	30.00	—
AH1334	65,000	5.00	10.00	15.00	30.00	—
AH1335	150,000	8.00	15.00	30.00	60.00	—
AH1336	240,000	4.00	8.00	20.00	40.00	—
AH1339	—	17.50	25.00	40.00	80.00	—
AH1343	160,000	6.00	10.00	25.00	50.00	—
Note: 10,000 reported struck in AH1337 probably dated AH1336						

KM# 1055 500 DINARS (10 Shahis = 1/2 Kran)
2.30 g., 0.900 Silver 0.0666 oz. ASW **Obv:** Uniformed bust 1/4 left within wreath, date below **Rev:** Radiant lion holding sword within crowned wreath **Note:** Dated on both sides

Date	Mintage	F12	VF20	XF40	MS60	MS63
AH1332	—	60.00	150	350	750	—
Note: Mintage included in KM#1054						

KM# 1037 1000 DINARS (Kran, Qiran)
4.61 g., 0.900 Silver 0.1332 oz. ASW **Obv:** Legend within circle and wreath **Rev:** Radiant lion holding sword within crowned wreath **Note:** Mule.

Date	Mintage	F12	VF20	XF40	MS60	MS63
AH1336	—	500	1,000	2,000	5,000	—

KM# 1038 1000 DINARS (Kran, Qiran)
4.61 g., 0.900 Silver 0.1332 oz. ASW, 23 mm. **Obv:** Legend within circle and wreath **Obv. Legend:** Sultan Ahmad Shah **Rev:** Radiant lion holding sword within crowned wreath

Date	Mintage	F12	VF20	XF40	MS60	MS63
AH1327	—	8.50	15.00	30.00	60.00	—
AH1328	—	7.50	12.50	25.00	50.00	—
AH1329	3,000,000	7.50	12.50	25.00	50.00	—
AH1330	—	7.50	12.50	25.00	50.00	—

KM# 1056 1000 DINARS (Kran, Qiran)
4.61 g., 0.900 Silver 0.1332 oz. ASW **Obv:** Uniformed bust 1/4 left within wreath, date below **Rev:** Radiant lion holding sword within crowned wreath

Date	Mintage	F12	VF20	XF40	MS60	MS63
AH1331	1,310,000	7.00	10.00	27.50	42.00	—
AH1332	1,891,000	5.00	7.00	15.00	32.00	—
AH1333	2,179,000	10.00	14.00	27.50	42.00	—
AH1334	1,273,000	5.00	7.00	15.00	27.50	—
AH1335	2,162,000	5.00	7.00	15.00	27.50	—
AH1336	1,412,000	6.00	8.00	17.00	32.00	—
AH1337	3,330,000	5.00	7.00	15.00	27.50	—
AH1339	35,000	12.50	25.00	55.00	95.00	—
AH1330 Error for 1340	—	30.00	65.00	125	175	—
AH1340	28,000	15.00	30.00	60.00	100	—
AH1341	170,000	8.00	15.00	35.00	60.00	—
AH1342	255,000	5.00	8.00	22.50	32.00	—
AH1343	1,345,000	5.00	8.00	22.50	32.00	—
AH1344	2,978,000	6.00	8.00	22.50	37.00	—

KM# 1059 1000 DINARS (Kran, Qiran)
4.61 g., 0.900 Silver 0.1332 oz. ASW, 23 mm. **Subject:** 10th Year of Reign **Obv:** Uniformed bust 1/4 left within wreath, date below **Rev:** Radiant lion holding sword within crowned wreath

Date	Mintage	F12	VF20	XF40	MS60	MS63
AH1337	975,000	35.00	75.00	125	250	—

KM# 1040 2000 DINARS (2 Kran)
9.21 g., 0.900 Silver 0.2665 oz. ASW, 28 mm. **Obv:** Legend within circle and crowned wreath **Obv. Legend:** Ahmad Shah **Rev:** Radiant lion holding sword within crowned wreath

Date	Mintage	F12	VF20	XF40	MS60	MS63
AH1327	—	11.00	17.00	40.00	60.00	—
Note: Mintage included in KM#1328						
AH1328	30,000,000	10.00	12.00	30.00	50.00	—
AH1329	29,250,000	10.00	12.00	30.00	50.00	—

KM# 1041 2000 DINARS (2 Kran)
9.21 g., 0.900 Silver 0.2665 oz. ASW **Obv:** Legend within circle and crowned wreath **Rev:** Radiant lion holding sword within crowned wreath

Date	Mintage	F12	VF20	XF40	MS60	MS63
AH1330	2,901,000	11.00	17.00	40.00	70.00	—

KM# 1043 2000 DINARS (2 Kran)
9.21 g., 0.900 Silver 0.2665 oz. ASW **Obv:** Legend within circle and crowned wreath **Obv. Legend:** Ahmad Shah **Rev:** Radiant lion holding sword within crowned wreath

Date	Mintage	F12	VF20	XF40	MS60	MS63
AH1330	—	11.00	17.00	40.00	70.00	—
Note: Mintage included in KM#1041						
AH1331	13,412,000	11.00	17.00	40.00	70.00	—

KM# 1057 2000 DINARS (2 Kran)
9.21 g., 0.900 Silver 0.2665 oz. ASW **Obv:** Uniformed bust 1/4 left within wreath, date below **Rev:** Radiant lion holding sword within crowned wreath

Date	Mintage	F12	VF20	XF40	MS60	MS63
AH1331	—	9.00	17.00	40.00	70.00	—
Note: Mintage included in KM#1043						
AH1332	12,926,000	9.00	12.00	28.00	48.00	—
AH1333	Inc. above	9.00	12.00	28.00	48.00	—
AH1334	4,299,000	9.00	12.00	28.00	48.00	—
AH1335	9,777,000	9.00	12.00	28.00	48.00	—
AH1336	5,401,000	9.00	12.00	28.00	48.00	—
AH1337	2,951,000	9.00	12.00	28.00	48.00	—
AH1339	1,085,000	9.00	17.00	40.00	70.00	—
AH1330 Error for 1340	—	50.00	100	160	260	—
Note: Mintage included in KM#1043						

Date	Mintage	F12	VF20	XF40	MS60	MS63
AH1340	254,000	13.00	20.00	45.00	85.00	—
AH1341	4,460,000	9.00	12.00	28.00	48.00	—
AH1342	2,245,000	9.00	12.00	35.00	55.00	—
AH1343	5,205,000	9.00	12.00	35.00	55.00	—
AH1344/34	12,354	10.00	16.00	40.00	75.00	—
AH1344	Inc. above	9.00	14.00	35.00	55.00	—

KM# 1060 2000 DINARS (2 Kran)
9.21 g., 0.900 Silver 0.2665 oz. ASW, 28 mm. **Subject:** 10th Anniversary of Reign **Obv:** Uniformed bust 1/4 left within wreath **Rev:** Radiant lion with sword within crowned wreath

Date	Mintage	F12	VF20	XF40	MS60	MS63
AH1337	3,503,000	60.00	100	150	300	—

KM# 1058 5000 DINARS (5 Kran)
23.03 g., 0.900 Silver 0.6662 oz. ASW **Obv:** Uniformed bust 1/4 left within wreath, date below **Rev:** Radiant lion holding sword within crowned wreath **Note:** Dav.#291.

Date	Mintage	F12	VF20	XF40	MS60	MS63
AH1331	—	150	300	600	1,500	—
AH1332	3,000,000	25.00	35.00	55.00	175	—
AH1333	667,000	25.00	35.00	60.00	185	—
AH1334	443,000	25.00	35.00	60.00	185	—
AH1335	1,884,000	25.00	35.00	60.00	185	—
AH1337	165,000	30.00	45.00	80.00	225	—
AH1339	90,000	40.00	55.00	95.00	260	—
AH1340	303,000	30.00	45.00	80.00	225	—
AH1341	757,000	25.00	35.00	60.00	185	—
AH1342/32	546,000	25.00	35.00	60.00	185	—
AH1342	Inc. above	25.00	35.00	60.00	185	—
AH1343/33	935,000	25.00	35.00	60.00	185	—
AH1343	Inc. above	25.00	35.00	60.00	185	—
AH1344/34	2,284,000	25.00	35.00	55.00	175	—
AH1344	Inc. above	30.00	40.00	65.00	195	—

Note: Beware of altered date AH1331 specimens. 9,000 reported minted in AH1336, probably dated earlier

KM# 1066 2000 DINARS (1/5 Toman)
0.57 g., 0.900 Gold 0.0166 oz. AGW, 14 mm. **Obv:** Legend within circle and wreath **Obv. Legend:** Ahmad Shah **Rev:** Radiant lion holding sword within crowned wreath

Date	Mintage	F12	VF20	XF40	MS60	MS63
AH1328	—	100	175	250	500	—
AH1329	—	125	200	350	750	—
AH1330	—	100	175	250	500	—

KM# 1070 2000 DINARS (1/5 Toman)
0.57 g., 0.900 Gold 0.0166 oz. AGW, 14 mm. **Obv:** Uniformed bust 1/4 left divides date **Rev:** Legend within circle and wreath **Rev. Legend:** Ahmad Shah

Date	Mintage	F12	VF20	XF40	MS60	MS63
AH1332	—	22.00	45.00	95.00	165	—
AH1333	—	22.00	45.00	75.00	140	—
AH1334	—	22.00	45.00	75.00	140	—
AH1335	—	22.00	45.00	75.00	140	—
AH1337	—	2.00	45.00	75.00	140	—
AH1339	—	35.00	45.00	95.00	165	—
AH1340	—	22.00	38.50	75.00	140	—
AH1341	—	22.00	38.50	75.00	140	—
AH1342	—	22.00	38.50	75.00	140	—
AH1343/33	—	22.00	38.50	75.00	140	—
AH1343	—	22.00	38.50	75.00	140	—

KM# 1067 5000 DINARS (1/2 Toman)
1.44 g., 0.900 Gold 0.0416 oz. AGW **Obv:** Legend within circle and wreath **Obv. Legend:** Ahmad Shah **Rev:** Radiant lion holding sword within crowned wreath

Date	Mintage	F12	VF20	XF40	MS60	MS63
AH1328	—	75.00	125	200	350	—
AH1329	—	75.00	125	200	350	—
AH1330	—	75.00	125	200	350	—

KM# 1071 5000 DINARS (1/2 Toman)
1.44 g., 0.900 Gold 0.0416 oz. AGW, 17 mm. **Obv:** Uniformed bust 1/4 left divides date **Rev:** Legend within circle and wreath **Rev. Legend:** Ahmad Shah

Date	Mintage	F12	VF20	XF40	MS60	MS63
AH1331	—	75.00	125	250	500	—
AH1332	—	55.00	75.00	120	150	—
AH1333	—	55.00	75.00	120	150	—
AH1334	—	55.00	75.00	120	150	—
AH1335	—	55.00	75.00	120	150	—
AH1336	—	55.00	75.00	120	150	—
AH1337	—	55.00	75.00	120	150	—
AH1339	—	75.00	90.00	150	250	—
AH1340	—	55.00	75.00	120	150	—
AH1341	—	55.00	75.00	120	150	—
AH1342	—	55.00	75.00	120	150	—
AH1343/33	—	55.00	75.00	120	150	—
AH1343	—	55.00	75.00	120	150	—

KM# 1072 5000 DINARS (1/2 Toman)
1.44 g., 0.900 Gold 0.0416 oz. AGW **Obv:** Bust with headdress 1/4 left within sprigs **Rev. Legend:** Sahib al-Zaman

Date	Mintage	F12	VF20	XF40	MS60	MS63
AH1339	—	125	250	500	1,000	—
AH1340	—	125	250	500	1,000	—

KM# 1068 TOMAN
2.87 g., 0.900 Gold 0.0832 oz. AGW, 19 mm. **Obv. Legend:** "Ahmad Shah", AH1328-1332 **Rev:** Lion and sun

Date	Mintage	F12	VF20	XF40	MS60	MS63
AH1329 Rare	—	—	—	—	—	—
Note: Only two examples are known						

KM# 1073 TOMAN
2.87 g., 0.900 Gold 0.0832 oz. AGW, 19 mm. **Obv:** Bust with headdress 1/4 left **Rev:** Ahmad Shah Pattern 2 Toman **Note:** The reverse die used was of an unadopted pattern.

Date	Mintage	F12	VF20	XF40	MS60	MS63
AH1331	—	450	750	1,200	2,000	—
AH1332	—	300	600	900	1,500	—
AH1333	—	350	650	1,000	1,750	—

KM# 1074 TOMAN
2.87 g., 0.900 Gold 0.0832 oz. AGW, 19 mm. **Obv:** Uniformed bust 1/4 left divides date **Rev:** Legend within circle and wreath **Rev. Legend:** Ahmad Shah

Date	Mintage	F12	VF20	XF40	MS60	MS63
AH1332	—	110	170	250	500	—
AH1333	—	110	170	250	500	—
AH1334	—	110	150	175	300	—
AH1335	—	110	150	175	300	—
AH1337	—	110	160	175	300	—
AH1339	—	110	170	250	400	—
AH1340	—	150	170	250	400	—
AH1341	—	110	150	175	300	—
AH1342	—	110	150	175	300	—
AH1343	—	110	150	175	300	—

KM# 1075 5 TOMAN
14.37 g., 0.900 Gold 0.4159 oz. AGW, 30 mm. **Obv:** Legend

within beaded circle and wreath **Obv. Legend:** Ahmad Shah **Rev:** Radiant lion holding sword within wreath

Date	Mintage	F12	VF20	XF40	MS60	MS63
AH1332/1	—	1,000	1,800	3,000	5,000	—
AH1334/2/1	—	850	1,500	2,500	4,000	—

Note: A number of gold medals of 5 Toman weight were struck between 1297 and 1326; These bear a couplet which clearly indicates that they are medals awarded by the Shah for bravery

KM# 1076 10 TOMAN
28.74 g., 0.900 Gold 0.8317 oz. AGW, 37 mm. **Obv:** Uniformed bust 1/4 left within wreath, date below **Obv. Legend:** Ahmad Shah **Rev:** Legend within circle and wreath

Date	Mintage	F12	VF20	XF40	MS60	MS63
AH1331	—	2,500	4,500	7,500	12,500	—
AH1334 Rare	—	—	—	—	—	—
AH1337//1334	—	—	—	7,500	12,500	—

Note: The date on the AH1334 reverse die was not changed for use as the reverse to the 1337 issue

KM# 1077 10 TOMAN
28.74 g., 0.900 Gold 0.8317 oz. AGW **Obv:** Uniformed bust 1/4 left within wreath, date **Rev:** Radiant lion holding sword within wreath

Date	Mintage	F12	VF20	XF40	MS60	MS63
AH1337	—	1,850	3,500	6,000	10,000	—

KM# 1080 ASHRAFI
Gold **Obv:** Bust of Ahmad Shah **Rev:** Lion and sun within crowned wreath

Date	Mintage	F12	VF20	XF40	MS60	MS63
AH1337	—	—	775	1,450	2,400	—

KM# A1081 2 ASHRAFI
Gold **Obv:** Uniformed bust 1/4 left within wreath **Rev:** Crown above lion and sun within wreath

Date	Mintage	F12	VF20	XF40	MS60	MS63
AH1337	—	—	900	1,800	3,000	—

KM# 1081 5 ASHRAFI
Gold **Obv:** Uniformed bust 1/4 left within wreath **Rev:** Lion and sun within crowned wreath

Date	Mintage	F12	VF20	XF40	MS60	MS63
AH1337	—	—	1,750	3,000	5,000	—

KM# 1082 10 ASHRAFI
Gold **Obv:** Uniformed bust 1/4 left within wreath **Rev:** Lion and sun within crowned wreath

Date	Mintage	F12	VF20	XF40	MS60	MS63
AH1337	—	1,150	2,250	4,500	7,500	—

CLANDESTINE COINAGE

KM# 1039 1000 DINARS (Kran, Qiran)
Silver **Obv:** Legend within beaded circle and wreath **Rev:** Radiant lion holding sword within crowned wreath

Date	Mintage	F12	VF20	XF40	MS60	MS63
AH1330 (sic)	—	18.00	30.00	50.00	75.00	—
AH1330 (sic) Proof, rare	—	—	—	—	—	—

Note: KM#1039 differs from KM#1038 in that it is about 1 millimeter broader and has a much thicker rim and more clearly defined denticles. Struck in Germany, without Iranian authorization, for circulation in western Iran during World War I. Also, the lion lacks the triangular face and fierce expression of KM#1038 and the point of the Talwar (scimitar) does not touch the sunburst as it does on Tehran issues.

KM# 1042 2000 DINARS (2 Kran)
Silver **Rev:** Lion's face has friendly expression

Date	Mintage	F12	VF20	XF40	MS60	MS63
AH1330 (sic)	—	15.00	25.00	50.00	75.00	—

Note: See general note for KM#1039

Reza Shah
AH1344-1360 / 1925-1941AD

MILLED COINAGE

Tehran

KM# 1091 50 DINARS
19.00 g., Copper-Nickel, 19 mm. **Obv:** Legend within circle and crowned wreath **Rev:** Radiant lion holding sword within crowned wreath, date **Edge:** Plain

Date	Mintage	F12	VF20	XF40	MS60	MS63
SH1305	11,000,000	2.50	5.00	10.00	20.00	—
SH1307	2,500,000	2.50	5.00	10.00	20.00	—

KM# 1092 100 DINARS (2 Shahi)
4.50 g., Copper-Nickel, 21 mm. **Obv:** Legend within circle and crowned wreath **Rev:** Radiant lion holding sword within crowned wreath, 1305 **Edge:** Plain

Date	Mintage	F12	VF20	XF40	MS60	MS63
SH1305	4,500,000	2.50	5.00	10.00	20.00	—
SH1307	3,750,000	2.50	5.00	10.00	20.00	—

Tehran

KM# 1093 1/4 KRAN (Robi = 5 Shahis)
1.15 g., 0.900 Silver 0.0333 oz. ASW **Obv:** Legend within circle and wreath **Rev:** Crown above lion and sun within wreath **Note:** 8,000 reported struck in SH1305, but that year not yet found and presumed not to exist.

Date	Mintage	F12	VF20	XF40	MS60	MS63
SH1304	Est. 24000	20.00	50.00	85.00	160	—

Note: For similar looking coins dated SH1315, see 1/4 Rial, KM#1127.

KM# 1094 500 DINARS (10 Shahis = 1/2 Kran)
2.30 g., 0.900 Silver 0.0666 oz. ASW **Obv:** Legend within circle and wreath **Rev:** Radiant lion holding sword within crowned wreath

Date	Mintage	F12	VF20	XF40	MS60	MS63
SH1304 Rare	—	—	—	—	—	—

KM# 1098 500 DINARS (10 Shahis = 1/2 Kran)
2.30 g., 0.900 Silver 0.0666 oz. ASW **Obv:** Legend within wreath **Obv. Legend:** Reza Shah **Rev:** Lion and sun within wreath

Date	Mintage	F12	VF20	XF40	MS60	MS63
SH1305	10,000	150	250	500	750	—

KM# 1102 500 DINARS (10 Shahis = 1/2 Kran)
2.30 g., 0.900 Silver 0.0666 oz. ASW **Obv:** Uniformed bust 3/4 right within wreath divides date **Rev:** Radiant lion holding sword within crowned wreath

Date	Mintage	F12	VF20	XF40	MS60	MS63
SH1306	5,000	75.00	175	300	600	—
SH1307	46,000	10.00	15.00	30.00	60.00	—
SH1308	464,000	10.00	15.00	30.00	60.00	—

Note: Some of the coins reported in SH1308 were dated 1307

KM# 1095 1000 DINARS (Kran, Qiran)
4.61 g., 0.900 Silver 0.1332 oz. ASW **Obv:** Legend within circle and wreath **Rev:** Radiant lion holding sword within crowned wreath

Date	Mintage	F12	VF20	XF40	MS60	MS63
SH1304	2,573,000	10.00	20.00	30.00	50.00	—
SH1305	2,265,000	10.00	20.00	30.00	50.00	—

KM# 1099 1000 DINARS (Kran, Qiran)
4.61 g., 0.900 Silver 0.1332 oz. ASW **Obv:** Legend within circle and wreath **Obv. Legend:** Reza Shah **Rev:** Radiant lion holding sword within crowned wreath

Date	Mintage	F12	VF20	XF40	MS60	MS63
SH1305	—	10.00	20.00	30.00	50.00	—
Note: Mintage included in KM#1095						
SH1306/5	3,130,000	6.00	10.00	18.00	30.00	—
SH1306	Inc. above	10.00	20.00	30.00	50.00	—

KM# 1103 1000 DINARS (Kran, Qiran)
4.61 g., 0.900 Silver 0.1332 oz. ASW, 23.5 mm. **Obv:** Uniformed bust 3/4 right within wreath divides date of Ascession in SH1304 **Rev:** Lion and sun within crowned wreath

Date	Mintage	F12	VF20	XF40	MS60	MS63
SH1306	—	10.00	20.00	30.00	60.00	—
Note: Mintage included in KM#1099						
SH1307	4,300,000	10.00	20.00	30.00	50.00	—
SH1308	603,000	10.00	20.00	30.00	50.00	—

KM# 1104 2000 DINARS (2 Kran)
9.21 g., 0.900 Silver 0.2665 oz. ASW **Obv:** Uniformed bust 3/4 right within wreath divides date of Ascession in SH1304 **Rev:** Radiant lion holding sword within crowned wreath

Date	Mintage	F12	VF20	XF40	MS60	MS63
SH1306	—	10.00	12.00	25.00	50.00	—
Note: Mintage included in KM#1100						
SH1306 H	11,714,000	10.00	12.00	25.00	50.00	—
SH1306 H	—	PF60 375				
SH1306 L	7,500,000	10.00	12.00	25.00	50.00	—
SH1307	11,146,000	10.00	12.00	25.00	50.00	—
SH1308	1,611,000	10.00	12.00	25.00	50.00	—

Tehran

KM# 1096 2000 DINARS (2 Kran)
9.21 g., 0.900 Silver 0.2665 oz. ASW **Obv:** Legend within circle and wreath **Rev:** Date below lion

Date	Mintage	F12	VF20	XF40	MS60	MS63
SH1304	11,920,000	15.00	30.00	50.00	75.00	—
SH1305	9,785,000	15.00	30.00	50.00	75.00	—

KM# 1100 2000 DINARS (2 Kran)
9.21 g., 0.900 Silver 0.2665 oz. ASW, 27 mm. **Obv:** Legend within circle and wreath **Obv. Legend:** Reza Shah **Rev:** Radiant lion holding sword within crowned wreath

Date	Mintage	F12	VF20	XF40	MS60	MS63
SH1305	—	15.00	30.00	50.00	75.00	—
SH1306	9,380,000	10.00	12.00	20.00	40.00	—

KM# 1105 2000 DINARS (2 Kran)
9.21 g., 0.900 Silver 0.2665 oz. ASW **Obv:** Uniformed bust 3/4 right within wreath **Rev:** Crown above lion and sun within wreath **Note:** Mule.

Date	Mintage	F12	VF20	XF40	MS60	MS63
SH1306	—	—	—	50.00	100	—

KM# 1097 5000 DINARS (5 Kran)
23.03 g., 0.900 Silver 0.6662 oz. ASW **Obv:** Legend within crowned wreath **Rev:** Radiant lion holding sword within wreath **Note:** Dav.#292.

Date	Mintage	F12	VF20	XF40	MS60	MS63
SH1304	500,000	25.00	40.00	75.00	150	—
SH1305	1,363,000	25.00	40.00	75.00	150	—

KM# 1101 5000 DINARS (5 Kran)
23.03 g., 0.900 Silver 0.6662 oz. ASW **Obv:** Legend within crowned wreath **Obv. Legend:** Reza Shah **Rev:** Radiant lion holding sword within wreath **Note:** Dav.#293.

Date	Mintage	F12	VF20	XF40	MS60	MS63
SH1305	—	35.00	70.00	100	150	—
Note: Mintage included in KM#1097						
SH1306	3,186,000	35.00	70.00	100	150	—

KM# 1106 5000 DINARS (5 Kran)
23.03 g., 0.900 Silver 0.6662 oz. ASW **Obv:** Uniformed bust 3/4 right within divides date of Ascession in SH1304 **Rev:** Crown above lion and sun within wreath **Note:** Dav.#294. Mint marks located as on 2000 Dinars, KM#1104.

Date	Mintage	F12	VF20	XF40	MS60	MS63
SH1306	—	24.00	28.00	50.00	100	—
Note: Mintage including in KM#1101						
SH1306	—	PF60 400				

Date	Mintage	F12	VF20	XF40	MS60	MS63
SH1306 H	4,711,000	24.00	28.00	50.00	100	—
SH1306 L	3,000,000	24.00	28.00	50.00	100	—
SH1307	3,928,000	25.00	35.00	75.00	150	—
SH1308	584,000	25.00	35.00	75.00	150	—

KM# 1107 5000 DINARS (5 Kran)
23.03 g., 0.900 Silver 0.6662 oz. ASW **Obv:** Uniformed bust 3/4 right within wreath **Rev:** Crown above lion and sun within wreath **Note:** Reverse of KM#1058, different crown above lion.

Date	Mintage	F12	VF20	XF40	MS60	MS63
SH1306	—	—	200	350	—	—

KM# 1108 TOMAN
2.87 g., Gold, 19 mm. **Subject:** Reza's First New Year Celebration **Obv:** Reza type legend **Rev:** Radiant lion holding sword within crowned wreath

Date	Mintage	F12	VF20	XF40	MS60	MS63
SH1305	—	240	350	600	900	—

KM# 1111 PAHLAVI
1.92 g., Gold **Obv:** Legend within crowned wreath **Rev:** Radiant lion holding sword within crowned wreath

Date	Mintage	F12	VF20	XF40	MS60	MS63
SH1305	5,000	150	300	475	725	—

KM# 1114 PAHLAVI
1.92 g., Gold **Obv:** Uniformed bust right above sprays **Rev:** Value and legend within beaded circle and crowned wreath

Date	Mintage	F12	VF20	XF40	MS60	MS63
SH1306	21,000	—	150	200	400	500
SH1307	5,000	—	150	200	400	500
SH1308	989	—	—	—	—	—
Note: None known.						

KM# 1112 2 PAHLAVI
3.84 g., Gold **Obv:** Legend within crowned wreath **Rev:** Radiant lion holding sword within crowned wreath

Date	Mintage	F12	VF20	XF40	MS60	MS63
SH1305	1,134	325	650	1,200	2,100	—

KM# 1115 2 PAHLAVI
3.84 g., Gold **Obv:** Uniformed bust right above sprays **Rev:** Value and legend within beaded circle and crowned wreath

Date	Mintage	F12	VF20	XF40	MS60	MS63
SH1306	2,494	—	175	325	550	—
SH1307	7,000	—	175	325	550	—
SH1308	789	—	210	425	725	—

KM# 1113 5 PAHLAVI
9.59 g., Gold **Obv:** Legend within crowned wreath **Rev:** Radiant lion holding sword within crowned wreath

Date	Mintage	F12	VF20	XF40	MS60	MS63
SH1305	271	600	1,200	2,000	3,500	—

KM# 1116 5 PAHLAVI
9.59 g., Gold **Obv:** Uniformed bust right above sprays **Rev:** Legend and value within beaded circle and crowned wreath

Date	Mintage	F12	VF20	XF40	MS60	MS63
SH1306	909	650	1,150	2,250	4,000	—
SH1307	785	650	1,150	2,250	4,000	—
SH1308	121	800	1,350	2,750	4,500	—

REFORM COINAGE

KM# 1126.1 2-1/2 ABBASI (10 Shahi)
4.45 g., Copper, 24.5 mm. **Obv:** Radiant lion holding sword within crowned wreath **Rev:** Legend within beaded heart shaped circle within designed crowned wreath **Edge:** Plain

Date	Mintage	F12	VF20	XF40	MS60	MS63
SH1314	Inc. below	5.00	10.00	15.00	35.00	75.00

KM# 1126.2 2-1/2 ABBASI (10 Shahi)
4.45 g., Copper, 24.5 mm. **Obv:** Radiant lion holding sword within crowned wreath **Rev:** Legend within beaded heart-shaped circle within designed crowned wreath **Edge:** Reeded

Date	Mintage	F12	VF20	XF40	MS60	MS63
SH1314 Large date	Inc. above	5.00	10.00	15.00	35.00	50.00
SH1314 Small date	20,000,000	5.00	10.00	15.00	35.00	50.00

KM# 1121 DINAR
1.70 g., Bronze, 16 mm. **Obv:** Radiant lion holding sword within crowned wreath **Rev:** Value within large flowered wreath **Edge:** Plain

Date	Mintage	F12	VF20	XF40	MS60	MS63
SH1310	10,000,000	15.00	30.00	50.00	75.00	175

KM# 1122 2 DINARS
1.80 g., Bronze, 26.5 mm. **Obv:** Radiant lion holding sword within crowned wreath **Rev:** Value within large flowered wreath **Edge:** Plain

Date	Mintage	F12	VF20	XF40	MS60	MS63
SH1310	5,000,000	15.00	30.00	50.00	75.00	175

KM# 1123 5 DINARS
1.95 g., Copper-Nickel, 18.5 mm. **Obv:** Radiant lion holding sword within crowned wreath **Rev:** Value within beaded circle and designed crowned wreath **Edge:** Plain

Date	Mintage	F12	VF20	XF40	MS60	MS63
SH1310	3,750,000	15.00	30.00	60.00	175	350

KM# 1123a 5 DINARS
2.15 g., Copper, 18.2 mm. **Obv:** Radiant lion holding sword within crowned wreath **Rev:** Value within beaded circle and crowned designed wreath **Edge:** Plain

Date	Mintage	F12	VF20	XF40	MS60	MS63
SH1314	480,000	200	400	750	—	—

KM# 1138 5 DINARS

Aluminum-Bronze, 16 mm. **Obv:** Radiant lion holding sword within crowned wreath **Rev:** Value within large flowered wreath

Date	Mintage	F12	VF20	XF40	MS60	MS63
SH1315	5,665,000	—	1.00	2.50	5.00	10.00
SH1316	Inc. above	—	0.40	0.75	1.50	5.00
SH1317	13,025,000	—	0.40	0.75	1.50	5.00
SH1318	—	—	0.40	0.75	1.50	5.00
SH1319	—	—	0.40	0.75	1.50	5.00
SH1320	—	—	0.40	0.75	1.50	4.00
SH1321	—	—	0.40	0.75	1.50	5.00

KM# 1124 10 DINARS

3.80 g., Copper-Nickel, 21 mm. **Obv:** Radiant lion holding sword within crowned wreath **Rev:** Value within beaded circle and crowned designed wreath **Edge:** Plain **Note:** Struck at Berlin.

Date	Mintage	F12	VF20	XF40	MS60	MS63
SH1310	3,750,000	15.00	30.00	60.00	150	325

KM# 1139 10 DINARS

2.65 g., Aluminum-Bronze, 18 mm. **Obv:** Radiant lion holding sword within crowned wreath **Rev:** Value within wreath

Date	Mintage	F12	VF20	XF40	MS60	MS63
SH1315	6,195,000	—	1.50	3.00	7.50	15.00
SH1316	Inc. above	—	0.80	1.50	4.00	10.00
SH1317	17,120,000	—	0.40	0.80	2.00	6.00
SH1318	—	—	0.40	0.80	2.00	6.00
SH1319	—	—	0.40	0.80	2.00	6.00
SH1320	—	—	0.40	0.80	2.00	6.00
SH1321	—	—	0.45	1.00	2.50	7.00

Tehran

KM# 1124a 10 DINARS

3.20 g., Copper, 21 mm. **Obv:** Radiant lion holding sword within crowned wreath **Rev:** Value within beaded circle and crowned designed wreath **Edge:** Plain **Note:** Struck at Tehran.

Date	Mintage	F12	VF20	XF40	MS60	MS63
SH1314	11,350,000	7.00	15.00	50.00	120	250

KM# 1125 25 DINARS

4.85 g., Copper-Nickel, 24 mm. **Obv:** Radiant lion holding sword within crowned wreath **Rev:** Value within beaded circle and crowned designed wreath **Edge:** Plain

Date	Mintage	F12	VF20	XF40	MS60	MS63
SH1310	750,000	20.00	40.00	100	200	375

KM# 1125a 25 DINARS

4.20 g., Copper, 24.2 mm. **Obv:** Radiant lion holding sword within crowned wreath **Rev:** Value within beaded circle and crowned designed wreath **Edge:** Plain

Date	Mintage	F12	VF20	XF40	MS60	MS63
SH1314	1,152,000	15.00	30.00	75.00	150	500

KM# 1142 50 DINARS

3.47 g., Aluminum-Bronze, 20 mm. **Obv:** Radiant lion holding sword within crowned wreath **Rev:** Value within wreath

Date	Mintage	F12	VF20	XF40	MS60	MS63
SH1315	15,968,000	—	1.50	3.50	7.50	20.00
SH1316	34,200,000	—	1.25	2.50	6.00	18.00
SH1317	17,314,000	—	0.60	1.50	4.00	15.00
SH1318	—	—	0.60	1.50	4.00	15.00
SH1319	—	—	1.50	2.50	6.00	18.00
SH1320	—	—	0.75	1.50	3.00	10.00
SH1321/0	—	—	0.75	1.50	3.00	15.00
SH1322/10	—	—	0.75	1.50	3.00	15.00
SH1322/12	—	—	0.75	1.50	3.00	10.00
SH1322/0	—	—	0.75	1.50	3.00	10.00
SH1322/1	—	—	0.75	1.50	3.00	10.00
SH1331	8,162,000	—	3.50	4.50	10.00	25.00
SH1332	22,892,000	—	2.00	3.00	5.00	10.00

KM# 1142a 50 DINARS

Copper **Obv:** Radiant lion holding sword within crowned wreath **Rev:** Value within wreath

Date	Mintage	F12	VF20	XF40	MS60	MS63
SH1322	—	—	1.00	3.00	7.00	12.00
SH1322/0	—	—	1.50	4.00	9.00	15.00

KM# 1127 1/4 RIAL

1.25 g., 0.828 Silver 0.0333 oz. ASW **Obv:** Value within circle and wreath **Rev:** Radiant lion holding sword within crowned wreath

Date	Mintage	F12	VF20	XF40	MS60	MS63
SH1315	600,000	—	1.00	2.00	3.00	5.00

Note: The second "1" is often short, so that the date looks like 1305

KM# 1128 1/2 RIAL

2.50 g., 0.828 Silver 0.0666 oz. ASW, 18 mm. **Obv:** Value within crowned wreath **Obv. Legend:** Reza Shah **Rev:** Radiant lion holding sword within crowned wreath **Note:** All 1/2 Rials dated SH1311-1315 are recut dies, usually from SH1310.

Date	Mintage	F12	VF20	XF40	MS60	MS63
SH1310	2,000,000	—	2.00	3.00	5.00	7.50
SH1311	—	—	50.00	100	150	200
SH1312	—	—	2.00	3.00	5.00	7.50
SH1313	1,945,000	—	2.00	3.00	5.00	7.50
SH1314	100,000	—	2.00	3.00	5.00	7.50
SH1315	800,000	—	3.00	5.00	7.50	10.00

KM# 1129 RIAL

5.00 g., 0.828 Silver 0.1331 oz. ASW, 22.5 mm. **Obv:** Value within crowned wreath **Rev:** Radiant lion holding sword within crowned wreath

Date	Mintage	F12	VF20	XF40	MS60	MS63
SH1310	2,190,000	—	5.00	10.00	25.00	35.00
AH1311	10,256,000	—	5.00	10.00	25.00	45.00
AH1312	25,768,000	—	5.00	10.00	25.00	45.00
AH1313	6,670,000	—	5.00	10.00	25.00	45.00

KM# 1130 2 RIALS

10.00 g., 0.828 Silver 0.2662 oz. ASW, 26 mm. **Obv:** Value within crowned wreath **Obv. Legend:** Reza Shah **Rev:** Radiant lion holding sword within crowned wreath **Note:** All coins dated SH1311-13 cut or punched over SH1310.

Date	Mintage	F12	VF20	XF40	MS60	MS63
SH1310	6,145,000	—	5.00	10.00	25.00	35.00
SH1311	8,838,000	—	5.00	10.00	25.00	45.00
SH1312	19,175,000	—	5.00	10.00	25.00	45.00
SH1313	4,015,000	—	5.00	10.00	25.00	45.00

KM# 1131 5 RIALS

25.00 g., 0.828 Silver 0.6655 oz. ASW, 37 mm. **Obv:** Value within crowned wreath **Obv. Legend:** Reza Shah **Rev:** Radiant lion holding sword within crowned wreath **Note:** Most coins dated SH1311-13 are cut or punched over SH1310.

Date	Mintage	F12	VF20	XF40	MS60	MS63
SH1310	5,471,000	—	15.00	20.00	35.00	75.00
SH1311	4,527,000	—	15.00	20.00	35.00	75.00
SH1312/0	5,502,000	—	15.00	20.00	35.00	75.00
SH1312	Inc. above	—	15.00	20.00	35.00	75.00
SH1313	1,208,000	—	15.00	20.00	35.00	75.00

KM# 1132 1/2 PAHLAVI

4.07 g., 0.900 Gold 0.1177 oz. AGW **Obv:** Uniformed bust left **Rev:** Radiant lion holding sword within crowned wreath

Date	Mintage	F12	VF20	XF40	MS60	MS63
SH1310	696	—	195	435	550	1,150
SH1311	286	—	195	450	600	1,200
SH1312	892	—	195	425	500	1,050
SH1313	531	—	195	450	600	1,200
SH1314	—	—	195	450	600	1,200
SH1315	1,042	—	195	435	550	1,150

KM# 1133 PAHLAVI

8.14 g., 0.900 Gold 0.2354 oz. AGW **Obv:** Uniformed bust left **Rev:** Radiant lion holding sword within crowned wreath

Date	Mintage	F12	VF20	XF40	MS60	MS63
SH1310	304	—	1,500	3,000	4,000	5,000

Muhammad Reza Pahlavi Shah

SH1320-1358 / 1941-1979AD

KM# 1140 25 DINARS

Aluminum-Bronze, 19 mm. **Obv:** Radiant lion holding sword within crowned wreath **Rev:** Value within wreath

Date	Mintage	VF20	XF40	MS60	MS63	MS65
SH1326	—	20.00	30.00	60.00	125	—
SH1327	—	25.00	50.00	100	150	—
SH1329	—	25.00	50.00	100	150	—

KM# 1141 25 DINARS

Aluminum-Bronze **Obv:** Value within wreath **Rev:** Radiant lion holding sword within crowned wreath **Note:** Mule

Date	Mintage	VF20	XF40	MS60	MS63	MS65
SH1329	—	500	750	1,000	1,500	—

KM# 1156 50 DINARS

2.91 g., Aluminum-Bronze, 18 mm. **Obv:** Radiant lion holding sword within crowned wreath **Rev:** Value within wreath **Note:** Reduced thickness = 1mm; wide and narrow rim varieties exist for some dates.

Date	Mintage	VF20	XF40	MS60	MS63	MS65
SH1332	—	25.00	30.00	40.00	50.00	—
SH1333	4,036,000	0.75	1.50	2.50	8.00	—
SH1334	1,370,000	0.75	1.50	4.00	10.00	—
SH1335	926,000	0.75	1.50	2.50	8.00	—
SH1336	—	0.75	1.25	2.00	8.00	—
Note: Mint reports record 126,500 in SH1337 and 20,000 in SH1338; these were probably dated SH1336						
SH1342	800,000	0.60	1.00	1.75	6.00	—
SH1343	1,400,000	0.60	1.00	1.75	6.00	—
SH1344	1,600,000	0.35	0.65	1.25	5.00	—
SH1345	1,690,000	0.35	0.65	1.25	5.00	—
SH1346	—	0.20	0.25	0.50	2.00	—
Note: Mintage report seems excessive for this and all SH1346 coinage						
SH1347	2,000,000	0.20	0.25	0.50	2.00	—
SH1348	1,500,000	0.20	0.25	0.50	2.00	—
SH1349	360,000	2.00	3.00	4.50	12.50	—
SH1350	—	0.30	0.50	0.75	2.00	—
SH1351	—	0.30	0.50	0.75	2.00	—
SH1353	60,000	0.30	0.50	0.75	2.00	—
SH1354	16,000	0.75	1.25	2.00	5.00	—

KM# 1156a 50 DINARS

Brass Plated Steel, 18 mm. **Obv:** Radiant lion holding sword within crowned wreath **Rev:** Value within wreath

Date	Mintage	VF20	XF40	MS60	MS63	MS65
MS2535	27,000	5.00	10.00	20.00	30.00	—
MS2536	—	5.00	10.00	20.00	30.00	—
MS2537	—	5.00	10.00	20.00	30.00	—
SH1357	—	5.00	10.00	20.00	30.00	—
SH1358	—	7.00	12.00	25.00	40.00	—

KM# 1143 RIAL

1.60 g., 0.600 Silver 0.0309 oz. ASW, 18 mm. **Obv:** Value within crowned wreath **Obv. Legend:** Muhammad Reza Shah Pahlavi **Rev:** Radiant lion holding sword within crowned wreath

Date	Mintage	VF20	XF40	MS60	MS63	MS65
SH1322	—	0.65	1.25	1.50	2.50	6.00
SH1323/3	—	—	—	—	—	—
SH1323	—	0.65	1.25	1.50	2.50	6.00
SH1324/3	—	—	—	—	—	—
SH1324	—	0.65	1.25	1.50	2.50	6.00
SH1424 Error for 1324	—	—	—	—	—	—
SH1325	—	0.65	1.25	2.00	2.50	6.00
SH1326	567,000	22.00	42.00	50.00	65.00	125
SH1327	5,795,000	1.00	2.00	3.00	5.00	10.00
SH1328	1,565,000	1.00	2.00	3.00	5.00	10.00
SH1329	144,000	32.00	65.00	125	190	250
SH1330	—	1.25	2.50	4.00	6.00	19.00

KM# 1157 RIAL

Copper-Nickel, 18.5 mm. **Obv:** Value within wreath **Obv. Legend:** Muhammad Reza Shah Pahlavi **Rev:** Radiant lion holding sword within crowned wreath

Date	Mintage	VF20	XF40	MS60	MS63	MS65
SH(13)31	4,735,000	0.50	1.00	2.00	5.00	7.50
SH(13)32	—	1.00	2.00	5.00	7.50	10.00
SH(13)33	16,405,000	0.30	0.60	1.00	2.00	5.00
SH(13)34	8,980,000	0.30	0.60	1.00	2.00	5.00
SH(13)35	8,910,000	0.25	0.50	1.00	1.00	5.00
SH(13)36	4,450,000	0.50	1.00	2.00	5.00	7.50

KM# 1171 RIAL

2.00 g., Copper-Nickel **Obv:** Value within crowned wreath **Obv. Legend:** Muhammad Reza Pahlavi **Rev:** Radiant lion holding sword within crowned wreath

Date	Mintage	VF20	XF40	MS60	MS63	MS65
SH1337	8,005,000	0.25	0.50	1.00	1.50	3.50

KM# 1171a RIAL

1.75 g., Copper-Nickel, 18.3 mm. **Obv:** Value within crowned wreath **Rev:** Radiant lion holding sword within crowned wreath **Note:** Date varieties exist.

Date	Mintage	VF20	XF40	MS60	MS63	MS65
SH1338	14,940,000	—	0.10	0.20	0.40	1.50
SH1339	8,400,000	—	0.25	0.50	1.00	2.00
SH1340	8,490,000	—	0.25	0.50	1.00	2.00
SH1341	8,680,000	—	0.25	0.50	1.00	2.00
SH1342	13,332,000	—	0.10	0.20	0.40	1.50
SH1343	14,746,000	—	0.10	0.15	0.25	1.50
SH1344	12,050,000	—	0.10	0.20	0.50	1.50
SH1345	13,786,000	—	0.10	0.15	0.20	1.50
SH1346	155,321,000	—	0.10	0.15	0.20	1.50
SH1347	20,664,000	—	0.10	0.15	0.25	1.50
SH1348	22,960,000	—	0.10	0.15	0.20	1.50
SH1349	19,918,000	—	0.10	0.15	0.20	1.50
SH1350	24,248,000	—	0.10	0.20	0.65	1.75
SH1351/0	21,825,000	—	0.10	0.25	0.40	1.50
SH1351	Inc. above	—	0.10	0.15	0.20	1.50
SH1352	31,449,000	—	0.10	0.15	0.20	1.50
SH1353 Large date	33,700,000	—	0.10	0.20	0.25	1.50
SH1353 Small date	Inc. above	—	0.10	0.15	0.20	1.50
SH1354	—	—	1.00	1.50	2.50	5.00
MS2536	—	—	1.00	1.50	2.50	5.00

KM# 1183 RIAL

1.76 g., Copper-Nickel, 18.5 mm. **Series:** F.A.O. **Obv:** Head left divides date **Obv. Legend:** Muhammad Reza Shah Pahlavi **Rev:** Crown above lion and sun within wreath

Date	Mintage	VF20	XF40	MS60	MS63	MS65
SH1350	2,770,000	—	0.50	1.00	1.50	3.50
SH1351	8,605,000	—	0.50	1.00	1.50	3.50
SH1353	2,000,000	—	0.50	1.00	1.50	3.50
SH1354	1,000,000	—	0.50	1.00	1.50	3.50

KM# 1205 RIAL

1.74 g., Copper-Nickel, 18.3 mm. **Subject:** 50th Anniversary of Pahlavi Rule **Obv:** Value within crowned wreath **Rev:** Radiant lion holding sword within crowned wreath

Date	Mintage	VF20	XF40	MS60	MS63	MS65
MS2535	61,945,000	—	0.50	1.00	1.50	3.50

KM# 1172 RIAL

1.77 g., Copper-Nickel, 18.3 mm. **Obv:** Value within crowned wreath, "Aryamehr" added to legend **Rev:** Radiant lion holding sword within crowned wreath

Date	Mintage	VF20	XF40	MS60	MS63	MS65
MS2536	71,150,000	—	0.50	1.00	1.50	3.50
MS2537	—	—	0.50	1.00	1.50	3.50
MS2537/6537 Error 2/6	—	—	0.50	1.00	1.50	3.50
SH1357/6	—	—	0.50	1.00	1.50	3.50
SH1357	—	—	0.50	1.00	1.50	3.50

KM# 1144 2 RIALS

3.20 g., 0.600 Silver 0.0617 oz. ASW, 22 mm. **Obv:** Value within crowned wreath **Obv. Legend:** Muhammad Reza Shah Pahlavi **Rev:** Radiant lion holding sword within crowned wreath

Date	Mintage	VF20	XF40	MS60	MS63	MS65
SH1322	—	—	2.25	3.00	4.00	7.50
SH1323/2	—	2.50	5.00	7.50	10.00	35.00
SH1323	—	—	2.25	3.00	4.00	7.50
SH1324	—	—	3.00	5.00	7.50	10.00
SH1325	—	2.25	5.00	12.00	17.00	30.00
SH1326	187,000	2.25	5.00	12.00	25.00	45.00
SH1327	3,140,000	—	2.25	3.00	5.00	7.50
SH1328	1,198,000	—	2.25	3.00	5.00	7.50
SH1329	—	35.00	75.00	150	250	375
SH1330	—	—	3.00	5.00	10.00	15.00

KM# 1158 2 RIALS

Copper-Nickel, 22.5 mm. **Obv:** Value above sprigs **Obv. Legend:** Muhammad Reza Shah Pahlavi **Rev:** Crown above radiant lion holding sword within wreath

Date	Mintage	VF20	XF40	MS60	MS63	MS65
SH1331	5,335,000	—	0.50	1.00	3.00	7.50
SH1332	6,870,000	—	0.50	1.00	3.00	5.00
SH1333	13,668,000	—	0.50	1.00	3.00	5.00
SH1334	7,185,000	—	0.50	1.00	3.00	5.00
SH1335	2,400,000	—	0.50	1.00	3.00	5.00
SH1336	325,000	5.00	10.00	25.00	35.00	75.00

KM# 1173 2 RIALS

3.00 g., Copper-Nickel, 22.3 mm. **Obv:** Value within crowned wreath **Obv. Legend:** Muhammad Reza Pahlavi **Rev:** Radiant lion holding sword within crowned wreath

Date	Mintage	VF20	XF40	MS60	MS63	MS65
SH1338	17,610,000	—	0.10	0.25	1.00	1.50
SH1339	8,575,000	—	0.10	0.25	1.00	1.50
SH1340	5,668,000	—	0.10	0.25	1.00	1.50
SH1341	5,820,000	—	0.10	0.25	1.00	1.50
SH1342	8,570,000	—	0.10	0.25	1.00	1.50
SH1343	11,250,000	—	0.10	0.25	1.00	1.50
SH1344	5,155,000	—	0.10	0.25	1.00	1.50
SH1345	2,267,000	—	0.15	0.30	1.25	1.75
SH1346	92,792,000	—	—	0.10	1.00	1.50
SH1347	10,300,000	—	—	0.10	1.00	1.50
SH1348	9,319,000	—	0.20	0.45	1.50	2.00
SH1349	9,895,000	—	0.20	0.40	1.25	1.75
SH1350	9,545,000	—	0.15	0.35	1.00	1.50
SH1351	13,305,000	—	0.15	0.35	1.00	1.50
SH1352	15,910,000	—	—	0.10	1.00	1.50
SH1353	28,477,000	—	—	0.10	1.00	1.50
SH1354/3	—	—	0.20	0.40	1.25	1.75
SH1354	41,700,000	—	—	0.10	1.00	1.50
MS2536	54,725,000	—	—	0.10	1.00	1.50

KM# 1206 2 RIALS

3.01 g., Copper-Nickel, 22.5 mm. **Subject:** 50th Anniversary of Pahlavi Rule **Obv:** Value within crowned wreath **Rev:** Radiant lion holding sword within crowned wreath

Date	Mintage	VF20	XF40	MS60	MS63	MS65
MS2535	59,568,000	—	0.75	1.50	2.50	5.00

KM# 1174 2 RIALS

3.04 g., Copper-Nickel **Obv:** Value within crowned wreath **Obv. Legend:** "Muhammad Reza Pahlavi", "Aryamehr" added **Rev:** Radiant lion holding sword within crowned wreath

Date	Mintage	VF20	XF40	MS60	MS63	MS65
MS2536	Inc. above	—	0.50	1.00	1.50	2.50
MS2537	—	—	0.50	1.00	1.50	2.50
SH1357	—	—	1.00	2.00	3.00	5.00

KM# 1145 5 RIALS

8.00 g., 0.600 Silver 0.1543 oz. ASW, 26 mm. **Obv:** Value within crowned wreath **Obv. Legend:** Muhammad Reza Shah Pahlavi **Rev:** Radiant lion holding sword within crowned wreath

Date	Mintage	VF20	XF40	MS60	MS63	MS65
SH1322	—	—	2.75	3.75	5.75	8.25
SH1323	—	—	2.75	3.75	5.75	8.25
SH1324	—	—	2.75	3.75	5.75	8.25
SH1325	—	—	2.75	3.75	5.75	8.25
SH1326	61,000	—	6.00	12.00	25.00	50.00
SH1327	836,000	—	5.00	10.00	15.00	35.00
SH1328	282,000	—	5.00	10.00	20.00	45.00
SH1329	—	25.00	50.00	100	150	225

KM# 1159 5 RIALS

6.70 g., Copper-Nickel, 26 mm. **Obv:** Value above sprigs, date below **Obv. Legend:** Muhammad Reza Shah Pahlavi **Rev:** Crown above radiant lion holding sword within wreath

Date	Mintage	VF20	XF40	MS60	MS63	MS65
SH1331	3,660,000	—	1.50	3.00	5.00	10.00
SH1332	16,350,000	—	1.00	1.50	3.00	5.00
SH1333	6,582,000	—	1.00	1.50	3.00	5.00
SH1334	300,000	—	3.00	7.50	10.00	25.00
SH1336	1,410,000	—	3.00	7.50	10.00	25.00

KM# 1175 5 RIALS

7.00 g., Copper-Nickel, 25.5 mm. **Obv:** Value within crowned wreath **Obv. Legend:** Muhammad Reza Shah Pahlavi **Rev:** Radiant lion holding sword within crowned wreath

Date	Mintage	VF20	XF40	MS60	MS63	MS65
SH1337	3,660,000	—	1.00	2.50	5.00	7.50
SH1338	10,467,000	—	0.50	2.50	5.00	7.50

KM# 1175a 5 RIALS

5.00 g., Copper-Nickel, 25.6 mm. **Obv:** Value within crowned wreath **Rev:** Radiant lion holding sword within crowned wreath

Date	Mintage	VF20	XF40	MS60	MS63	MS65
SH1338	Inc. above	—	0.25	0.40	1.00	1.50
SH1339	3,980,000	—	0.25	0.40	1.00	1.50
SH1340	3,814,000	—	0.25	0.40	1.00	1.50
SH1341	2,332,000	—	0.25	0.40	1.00	1.50
SH1342	7,838,000	—	0.25	0.40	1.00	1.50
SH1343	9,484,000	—	0.25	0.40	1.00	1.50
SH1344	3,468,000	—	0.25	0.40	1.00	1.50
SH1345	6,092,000	—	0.25	0.40	1.00	1.50
SH1346/36	74,781,000	—	0.25	0.40	1.00	1.50
SH1346	Inc. above	—	0.25	0.40	1.00	1.50

KM# 1176 5 RIALS

4.60 g., Copper-Nickel, 24.8 mm. **Obv:** Value and legend within crowned wreath, "Aryamehr" added to legend **Rev:** Radiant lion holding sword within crowned wreath

Date	Mintage	VF20	XF40	MS60	MS63	MS65
SH1347	7,745,000	—	0.50	0.85	1.50	3.00
SH1348	9,193,000	—	0.50	0.75	1.25	2.50
SH1349	7,300,000	—	0.50	0.75	1.25	2.50
SH1350	10,160,000	—	0.35	0.75	1.25	2.50
SH1351	20,582,000	—	0.25	0.75	1.25	2.50
SH1352	23,590,000	—	0.25	0.75	1.25	2.50
SH1353	28,367,000	—	0.25	0.75	1.25	2.50
SH1353 Large date	Inc. above	—	0.25	0.75	1.25	2.50
SH1354	27,294,000	—	0.25	0.75	1.25	2.50
MS2536	47,906,000	—	0.20	0.50	1.25	2.50
MS2537	—	—	0.35	0.65	1.25	2.50
SH1357	—	—	0.50	1.50	3.00	5.00

KM# 1207 5 RIALS

4.54 g., Copper-Nickel, 24.8 mm. **Subject:** 50th Anniversary of Pahlavi Rule

Date	Mintage	VF20	XF40	MS60	MS63	MS65
MS2535	37,144,000	—	0.50	1.00	1.50	3.00

KM# 1146 10 RIALS

16.00 g., 0.600 Silver 0.3086 oz. ASW, 32 mm. **Obv:** Value and legend within crowned wreath **Obv. Legend:** Muhammad Reza Shah Pahlavi **Rev:** Radiant lion holding sword within crowned wreath **Note:** Counterfeits are known dated SH1322.

Date	Mintage	VF20	XF40	MS60	MS63	MS65
SH1323/2	—	—	—	7.50	12.00	20.00
SH1323	—	—	—	5.75	8.75	15.00
SH1324	—	—	—	5.75	8.75	18.00
SH1325	—	—	—	5.75	8.75	20.00
SH1326	—	—	7.50	12.00	25.00	75.00

KM# 1177 10 RIALS

12.00 g., Copper-Nickel, 31.12 mm. **Obv:** Crown above value and legend within wreath **Obv. Legend:** Muhammad Reza Shah Pahlavi **Rev:** Crown above lion and sun within wreath

Date	Mintage	VF20	XF40	MS60	MS63	MS65
SH1333	—	—	—	—	—	—
SH1335	6,225,000	—	0.50	1.00	3.00	5.00
SH1336	4,415,000	—	1.00	3.00	5.00	7.50
SH1337	715,000	—	1.00	3.00	5.00	7.50
SH1338	1,210,000	—	0.50	1.00	3.00	5.00
SH1339	2,775,000	—	0.50	1.00	3.00	5.00
SH1340	3,660,000	—	0.50	1.00	3.00	5.00
SH1341	744,000	—	3.00	10.00	15.00	25.00
SH1343	6,874,000	—	0.50	1.00	3.00	5.00

KM# 1177a 10 RIALS

9.00 g., Copper-Nickel, 31 mm. **Obv:** Crown above value and legend wtihin wreath **Rev:** Crown above radiant lion holding sword within wreath **Note:** Thin flan.

Date	Mintage	VF20	XF40	MS60	MS63	MS65
SH1341	—	—	0.35	1.00	1.50	2.50
Note: Mintage included in KM#1177						
SH1342	3,763,000	—	0.35	1.00	1.50	2.50
SH1343	—	—	0.35	0.75	1.50	2.50
Note: Mintage included in KM#1177						
SH1344	1,627,000	—	0.35	0.75	1.50	2.50

KM# 1178 10 RIALS

7.00 g., Copper-Nickel, 28 mm. **Obv:** Head left, legend above, date below **Obv. Legend:** Muhammad Reza Shah Pahlavi **Rev:** Crown above radiant lion holding sword within wreath

Date	Mintage	VF20	XF40	MS60	MS63	MS65
SH1345	1,699,000	—	0.50	0.60	1.20	2.75
SH1346	38,897,000	—	0.40	0.50	1.00	2.50
SH1347	8,220,000	—	0.40	0.65	1.25	3.00
SH1348	7,156,000	—	0.40	0.50	1.00	2.50
SH1349	7,397,000	—	0.40	0.50	1.00	2.50
SH1350	8,972,000	—	0.40	0.50	1.00	2.50
SH1351	9,912,000	—	0.40	0.50	1.00	2.50
SH1352	28,776,000	—	0.50	0.75	1.50	3.50

KM# 1182 10 RIALS

Copper-Nickel **Series:** F.A.O. **Obv:** Head left, legend above **Rev:** Crown above radiant lion holding sword within wreath, dates and F.A.O.

Date	Mintage	VF20	XF40	MS60	MS63	MS65
SH1348	150,000	—	0.50	1.00	1.50	3.00

KM# 1179 10 RIALS

7.00 g., Copper-Nickel, 28 mm. **Obv:** Head left, legend above, date below **Rev:** Crown above lion, sun and numeral value within wreath

Date	Mintage	VF20	XF40	MS60	MS63	MS65
SH1352	Inc. above	—	0.30	0.60	1.00	1.50
SH1353	22,234,000	—	0.30	0.60	1.00	1.50
SH1354	23,482,000	—	0.30	0.60	1.00	1.50
MS2536	24,324,000	—	0.30	0.60	1.00	1.50
MS2537	—	—	0.30	0.60	1.00	1.50
SH1357	—	—	1.50	3.00	5.00	7.50

KM# 1208 10 RIALS

Copper-Nickel **Subject:** 50th Anniversary of Pahlavi Rule **Obv:** Head left, legend above, date below **Rev:** Crown above lion, sun and numeral value within wreath

Date	Mintage	VF20	XF40	MS60	MS63	MS65
MS2535	29,859,000	—	0.50	1.00	1.50	2.50

KM# 1180 20 RIALS

Copper-Nickel **Obv:** Head left, legend above, date below **Obv. Legend:** Muhammad Reza Shah Pahlavi **Rev:** Crown above lion, sun and written value within wreath

Date	Mintage	VF20	XF40	MS60	MS63	MS65
SH1350	2,349,000	—	0.25	0.75	1.00	1.50
SH1351	11,416,000	—	0.25	0.75	1.00	1.50
SH1352	7,172,000	—	0.25	0.75	1.00	1.50

KM# 1181 20 RIALS

Copper-Nickel, 30 mm. **Obv:** Head left, legend above, date below **Rev:** Crown above lion, sun and numeral value within wreath **Note:** Varieties exist in date size.

Date	Mintage	VF20	XF40	MS60	MS63	MS65
SH1352	—	—	0.25	0.75	1.00	2.00
Note: Mintage included in KM#1180						
SH1353	12,601,000	—	0.25	0.75	1.00	2.00
SH1354	16,246,000	—	0.25	0.75	1.00	2.00
MS2536	—	—	0.40	0.75	1.00	2.00
MS2537	—	—	0.50	0.75	1.00	2.00
SH1357	—	—	1.00	3.00	5.00	7.50

KM# 1196 20 RIALS

Copper-Nickel **Subject:** 7th Asian Games **Obv:** Head left, legend above **Rev:** Star design within entwined circles and written words

Date	Mintage	VF20	XF40	MS60	MS63	MS65
SH1353	Inc. above	—	1.50	3.00	5.00	7.50

KM# 1209 20 RIALS

7.00 g., Copper-Nickel, 28 mm. **Subject:** 50th Anniversary of Pahlavi Rule **Obv:** Head left, legend above, date below **Rev:** Crown above lion, sun and numeral value within wreath

Date	Mintage	VF20	XF40	MS60	MS63	MS65
MS2535	—	—	1.50	3.00	5.00	7.50

KM# 1211 20 RIALS

8.92 g., Copper-Nickel, 31.2 mm. **Series:** F.A.O. **Obv:** Head left, legend above **Rev:** Crown above lion, sun and numeral value within wreath

Date	Mintage	VF20	XF40	MS60	MS63	MS65
MS2535-1976	10,000,000	—	0.50	1.50	3.00	5.00
MS2536-1977	23,370,000	—	0.50	1.50	3.00	5.00

KM# 1214 20 RIALS

Copper-Nickel **Subject:** 50th Anniversary of Bank Melli **Obv:** Head left, legend above and below **Rev:** Head left, legend above and below

Date	Mintage	VF20	XF40	MS60	MS63	MS65
SH1357	—	—	3.00	5.00	7.50	10.00

KM# 1215 20 RIALS

Copper-Nickel **Series:** F.A.O. **Obv:** Head left, legend above **Rev:** Crown above lion, sun, numeral value, dates and F.A.O. within wreath

Date	Mintage	VF20	XF40	MS60	MS63	MS65
SH1357-1978	5,000,000	—	0.50	1.50	3.00	5.00

KM# 1184 25 RIALS

7.50 g., 0.999 Silver 0.2409 oz. ASW **Subject:** 2500th Anniversary of Persian Empire **Obv:** Small crown over lion and sun above value within circle of crowns **Rev:** Conjoined column heads **Note:** Column head from Artaxerxes' Palace in Susa. With "1 AR" and 1000 assayer's marks

Date	Mintage	VF20	XF40	MS60	MS63	MS65
SH1350-1971	18,000	PF63 15.00	PF65 25.00			

KM# 1185 50 RIALS

15.00 g., 0.999 Silver 0.4818 oz. ASW **Subject:** 2500th Anniversary of Persian Empire **Obv:** Small crown over lion and sun above value and dates within circle of crowns **Rev:** Winged griffin with ram antlers **Note:** With "1 AR" and 1000 assayer's marks

Date	Mintage	VF20	XF40	MS60	MS63	MS65
SH1350-1971	18,000	PF63 20.00	PF65 35.00			

KM# 1186 75 RIALS

22.50 g., 0.999 Silver 0.7227 oz. ASW, 34 mm. **Subject:** 2500th Anniversary of Persian Empire **Obv:** Small crown above radiant lion holding sword above value and dates within circle of crowns **Rev:** Arms above Stone of Cyrus II and inscription, wreath of crowns surrounds **Note:** With "1 AR" and 1000 assayer's marks

Date	Mintage	VF20	XF40	MS60	MS63	MS65
SH1350-1971	18,000	PF63 30.00	PF65 50.00			

KM# 1187.1 100 RIALS

30.00 g., 0.999 Silver 0.9636 oz. ASW, 38 mm. **Subject:** 2500th Anniversary of Persian Empire **Obv:** Small crown over lion and sun, value and date below **Rev:** Polished field below pillared palace

Date	Mintage	VF20	XF40	MS60	MS63	MS65
SH1350-1971	18,000	PF63 50.00	PF65 75.00			

KM# 1187.2 100 RIALS

30.00 g., 0.999 Silver 0.9636 oz. ASW, 38 mm. **Obv:** Small crown over lion and sun above value and dates within circle of crowns **Rev:** Frosted field below pillared palace **Note:** Countermarked with "1 AR" and "1000" on reverse.

Date	Mintage	VF20	XF40	MS60	MS63	MS65
SH1350-1971	Inc. above	PF63 50.00	PF65 75.00			

KM# 1188 200 RIALS

60.00 g., 0.999 Silver 1.9271 oz. ASW, 50 mm. **Subject:** 2500th Anniversary of Persian Empire **Obv:** Conjoined busts left **Rev:** Small crown over lion and sun above value and dates within circle of crowns **Note:** Countermarked with "1 AR" and "1000" on reverse.

Date	Mintage	VF20	XF40	MS60	MS63	MS65
SH1350-1971	23,000	PF63 90.00	PF65 125			

KM# 1189 500 RIALS

6.51 g., 0.900 Gold 0.1884 oz. AGW **Subject:** 2500th Anniversary of Persian Empire **Obv:** Small crown over lion and sun above value and dates within circle of crowns **Rev:** Walking griffin with ram antlers

Date	Mintage	VF20	XF40	MS60	MS63	MS65
SH1350-1971	11,000	PF63 300	PF65 350			

KM# 1190 750 RIALS
9.77 g., 0.900 Gold 0.2827 oz. AGW **Subject:** 2500th Anniversary of Persian Empire **Obv:** Small crown above lion and sun, value and date below **Rev:** Arms above Stone of Cyrus II and inscription within wreath of crowns

Date	Mintage	VF20	XF40	MS60	MS63	MS65
SH1350-1971	10,000	PF63 450	PF65 525			

KM# 1191.1 1000 RIALS
13.03 g., 0.900 Gold 0.377 oz. AGW **Subject:** 2500th Anniversary of Persian Empire **Obv:** Small crown over lion and sun above value and dates within circle of crowns **Rev:** Polished fields below pillared palace

Date	Mintage	VF20	XF40	MS60	MS63	MS65
SH1350-1971	10,000	PF63 575	PF65 675			

KM# 1191.2 1000 RIALS
13.03 g., 0.900 Gold 0.377 oz. AGW **Subject:** 2500th Anniversary of Persian Empire **Obv:** Small crown over lion and sun above value and dates within circle of crowns **Rev:** Polished fields below pillared palace

Date	Mintage	VF20	XF40	MS60	MS63	MS65
SH1350-1971	Inc. above	PF63 575	PF65 675			

KM# 1192 2000 RIALS
26.06 g., 0.900 Gold 0.7541 oz. AGW **Subject:** 2500th Anniversary of Persian Empire **Obv:** Conjoined busts left **Rev:** Small crown over lion and sun above value and dates within circle of crowns

Date	Mintage	VF20	XF40	MS60	MS63	MS65
SH1350-1971	9,805	PF63 1,150	PF65 1,300			

KM# 1160 1/4 PAHLAVI
2.03 g., 0.900 Gold 0.0589 oz. AGW, 14 mm. **Obv:** Head left, legend above, date below **Rev:** Crown over lion and sun above value within wreath

Date	Mintage	VF20	XF40	MS60	MS63	MS65
SH1332	41,000	—	75.00	110	155	190
SH1333	7,000	—	110	90.00	175	240
SH1334	—	—	—	75.00	100	115
SH1335	41,000	—	75.00	110	210	190
SH1336	—	—	75.00	115	210	400

KM# 1160a 1/4 PAHLAVI
2.03 g., 0.900 Gold 0.0589 oz. AGW, 16 mm. **Obv:** Head left, legend above, date below **Rev:** Crown above lion holding sword within wreath **Note:** Thinner and broader.

Date	Mintage	VF20	XF40	MS60	MS63	MS65
SH1336	7,000	—	—	110	175	350
SH1337	33,000	—	—	—	75.00	110
SH1338	136,000	—	—	—	75.00	110
SH1339	156,000	—	—	—	75.00	110
SH1340	60,000	—	—	—	75.00	110
SH1342	80,000	—	—	—	75.00	110
SH1344	30,000	—	—	110	130	175
SH1345	40,000	—	—	—	75.00	110
SH1346	30,000	—	—	—	75.00	110
SH1347	60,000	—	—	—	75.00	110
SH1348	60,000	—	—	—	75.00	110
SH1349	80,000	—	—	—	75.00	110
SH1350	80,000	—	—	—	75.00	110
SH1351	103,000	—	—	—	75.00	110
SH1352	—	—	—	—	75.00	110

KM# 1198 1/4 PAHLAVI
2.03 g., 0.900 Gold 0.0589 oz. AGW **Obv:** Head left, legend above, date below, "Aryamehr" added to legend **Rev:** Crown above lion and sun within wreath

Date	Mintage	VF20	XF40	MS60	MS63	MS65
SH1353	—	—	—	—	75.00	110
SH1354	106,000	—	—	—	75.00	110
SH1355	186,000	—	—	—	75.00	110
MS2536	—	—	—	—	75.00	110
MS2537	—	—	—	—	75.00	110
SH1358	—	—	75.00	110	175	350

KM# 1147 1/2 PAHLAVI
4.07 g., 0.900 Gold 0.1177 oz. AGW **Obv:** Legend **Obv. Legend:** Muhammad Reza Shah **Rev:** Crown above radiant lion holding sword within wreath

Date	Mintage	VF20	XF40	MS60	MS63	MS65
SH1320	—	—	250	425	750	1,250
SH1321	—	—	—	750	1,250	2,000
SH1322	—	—	—	—	150	225
SH1323	76,000	—	—	—	150	225

KM# 1149 1/2 PAHLAVI
4.07 g., 0.900 Gold 0.1177 oz. AGW **Obv:** High relief head left, legend above and date below **Rev:** Crown above radiant lion holding sword within wreath

Date	Mintage	VF20	XF40	MS60	MS63	MS65
SH1324	—	—	—	150	225	250
SH1325	—	—	—	150	225	250
SH1326	36,000	—	—	150	225	250
SH1327	36,000	—	—	150	225	250
SH1328	—	—	—	150	225	250
SH1329	75	—	—	300	500	750
SH1330	98,000	—	—	225	325	500

KM# 1161 1/2 PAHLAVI
4.07 g., 0.900 Gold 0.1177 oz. AGW **Obv:** Low relief head left, legend above with date below **Rev:** Crown above radiant lion holding sword within wreath

Date	Mintage	VF20	XF40	MS60	MS63	MS65
SH1330	—	—	—	150	225	250
Note: Mintage included in KM#1149						
SH1332	—	—	—	375	750	1,250
SH1333	—	—	150	250	300	350
SH1334	—	—	150	250	300	350
SH1335	—	—	—	—	150	225
SH1336	132,000	—	—	—	150	225
SH1337	102,000	—	—	—	150	225
SH1338	140,000	—	—	—	150	225
SH1339	142,000	—	—	—	150	225
SH1340	439,000	—	—	—	150	225
SH1342	40,000	—	—	—	150	225
SH1344	30,000	—	—	150	250	250
SH1345	40,000	—	—	—	150	225
SH1346	40,000	—	—	—	150	225
SH1347	50,000	—	—	—	150	225
SH1348	40,000	—	—	—	150	225
SH1349	80,000	—	—	—	150	225
SH1350	80,000	—	—	—	150	225
SH1351	103,000	—	—	—	150	225
SH1352	67,000	—	—	—	150	225
SH1353	—	—	—	—	150	225

KM# 1199 1/2 PAHLAVI
4.07 g., 0.900 Gold 0.1177 oz. AGW **Obv:** Head left, legend above and date below, "Aryamehr" added to legend **Rev:** Crown above radiant lion holding sword within wreath

Date	Mintage	VF20	XF40	MS60	MS63	MS65
SH1354	37,000	—	—	—	150	225
SH1355	153,000	—	—	—	150	225
MS2536	—	—	—	—	150	225
MS2537	—	—	—	—	150	225
SH1358	—	—	150	225	275	400

KM# 1148 PAHLAVI
8.14 g., 0.900 Gold 0.2354 oz. AGW **Obv:** Legend and date **Obv. Legend:** Muhammad Reza Shah **Rev:** Crown above radiant lion holding sword within wreath

Date	Mintage	VF20	XF40	MS60	MS63	MS65
SH1320	—	—	—	—	2,000	3,000
SH1321	—	—	—	—	2,500	3,500
SH1322	—	—	—	—	300	450
SH1323	311,000	—	—	—	300	450
SH1324	—	—	—	—	300	450

KM# 1150 PAHLAVI
8.14 g., 0.900 Gold 0.2354 oz. AGW **Obv:** High relief head left, legend above and date below **Rev:** Crown above radiant lion holding sword within wreath

Date	Mintage	VF20	XF40	MS60	MS63	MS65
SH1324	—	—	—	—	300	450
SH1325	—	—	—	—	300	450
SH1326	151,000	—	—	—	300	450
SH1327	20,000	—	—	—	300	450
SH1328	4,000	—	—	300	450	500
SH1329	4,000	—	—	475	550	800
SH1330	48,000	—	—	450	500	600

KM# 1162 PAHLAVI
8.14 g., 0.900 Gold 0.2354 oz. AGW **Obv:** Low relief head left, legend above and date below **Rev:** Crown above radiant lion holding sword within wreath

Date	Mintage	VF20	XF40	MS60	MS63	MS65
SH1330	—	—	—	—	300	450
SH1331	—	—	450	500	650	1,000
SH1332	—	—	450	600	1,000	1,750
SH1333	—	—	300	450	460	475
SH1334	—	—	300	450	460	475
SH1335	—	—	—	—	300	450
SH1336	453,000	—	—	—	300	450
SH1337	665,000	—	—	—	300	450
SH1338	776,000	—	—	—	300	450
SH1339	847,000	—	—	—	300	450
SH1340	528,000	—	—	—	300	450
SH1342	20,000	—	—	—	300	450
SH1344	—	—	—	300	460	475
SH1345	20,000	—	—	—	300	450
SH1346	30,000	—	—	—	300	450
SH1347	40,000	—	—	—	300	450
SH1348	70,000	—	—	—	300	450

Date	Mintage	VF20	XF40	MS60	MS63	MS65
SH1349	70,000	—	—	—	300	450
SH1350	60,000	—	—	—	300	450
SH1351	100,000	—	—	—	300	450
SH1352	320,000	—	—	—	300	450
SH1353	—	—	—	—	300	450

KM# 1200 PAHLAVI

8.14 g., 0.900 Gold 0.2354 oz. AGW **Obv:** Head left, legend above, date below, "Aryamehr" added to legend **Rev:** Crown above radiant lion holding sword within wreath

Date	Mintage	VF20	XF40	MS60	MS63	MS65
SH1354	21,000	—	—	—	300	450
SH1355	203,000	—	—	—	300	450
MS2536	—	—	—	—	300	450
MS2537	—	—	—	—	300	450
SH1358	—	—	300	450	475	550

KM# A1163 2-1/2 PAHLAVI

20.34 g., 0.900 Gold 0.5886 oz. AGW **Obv:** Head left, legend above **Rev:** Inscription and date

Date	Mintage	VF20	XF40	MS60	MS63	MS65
SH1338	—	—	—	750	1,100	1,200

KM# 1163 2-1/2 PAHLAVI

20.34 g., 0.900 Gold 0.5886 oz. AGW **Obv:** Head left, legend above **Rev:** Crown above lion, sun and value within wreath

Date	Mintage	VF20	XF40	MS60	MS63	MS65
SH1339	1,682	—	—	—	750	1,100
SH1340	2,788	—	—	—	750	1,100
SH1342	30	—	—	—	2,000	5,000
SH1348	3,000	—	—	—	750	1,100
SH1350	2,000	—	—	—	750	1,100
SH1351	2,500	—	—	—	750	1,100
SH1352	3,000	—	—	—	750	1,100
SH1353	—	—	—	—	750	1,100

KM# 1201 2-1/2 PAHLAVI

20.34 g., 0.900 Gold 0.5886 oz. AGW, 30 mm. **Obv:** Head left, legend above, date below, "Aryamehr" added to legend **Rev:** Crown above radiant lion holding sword within wreath **Edge:** Reeded

Date	Mintage	VF20	XF40	MS60	MS63	MS65
SH1354	18,000	—	—	750	1,100	1,300
SH1355	16,000	—	—	750	1,100	1,300
MS2536	—	—	—	750	1,100	1,300
MS2537	—	—	—	750	1,100	1,300
SH1358 Rare	—	—	—	—	—	—

KM# 1164 5 PAHLAVI

40.68 g., 0.900 Gold 1.1771 oz. AGW **Obv:** Head left, legend above **Rev:** Crown above lion and sun within wreath

Date	Mintage	VF20	XF40	MS60	MS63	MS65
SH1339	2,225	—	—	—	1,500	2,250
SH1340	2,430	—	—	—	1,500	2,250
SH1342	20	—	—	—	5,000	10,000
SH1348	2,000	—	—	—	1,500	2,250
SH1350	2,000	—	—	—	1,500	2,250
SH1351	2,500	—	—	—	1,500	2,250
SH1352	2,100	—	—	—	1,500	2,250
SH1353	—	—	—	—	1,500	2,250

KM# 1202 5 PAHLAVI

40.68 g., 0.900 Gold 1.1771 oz. AGW **Obv:** Head left, legend above, date below, "Aryamehr" added to legend **Rev:** Crown above radiant lion holding sword within wreath

Date	Mintage	VF20	XF40	MS60	MS63	MS65
SH1354	10,000	—	—	—	1,500	2,250
SH1355	17,000	—	—	—	1,500	2,250
MS2536	—	—	—	—	1,500	2,250
MS2537	—	—	—	—	1,500	2,250
SH1358	—	—	1,500	2,100	2,300	2,500

KM# 1210 10 PAHLAVI

81.36 g., 0.900 Gold 2.3542 oz. AGW **Subject:** 50th Anniversary of Pahlavi Rule **Obv:** Conjoined busts left **Rev:** Crown, inscription and date at center circle of circle wreaths

Date	Mintage	VF20	XF40	MS60	MS63	MS65
MS2535	—	—	—	—	3,000	4,500

KM# 1212 10 PAHLAVI

81.36 g., 0.900 Gold 2.3542 oz. AGW **Subject:** Centenary of Reza Shah's Birth **Obv:** Conjoined busts left **Rev:** Crown above inscription and date within wreath

Date	Mintage	VF20	XF40	MS60	MS63	MS65
MS2536	—	—	—	—	3,000	4,500

KM# 1213 10 PAHLAVI

81.36 g., 0.900 Gold 2.3542 oz. AGW **Obv:** Head left, legend above, date below, "Aryamehr" added to legend **Rev:** Crown above radiant lion holding sword within wreath

Date	Mintage	VF20	XF40	MS60	MS63	MS65
MS2537	—	—	—	—	3,000	4,500
SH1358	—	—	—	—	4,750	5,500

ISLAMIC REPUBLIC

MILLED COINAGE

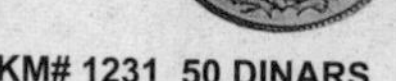

KM# 1231 50 DINARS

Brass Clad Steel **Obv:** Radiant lion holding sword within wreath **Rev:** Value within flowered wreath

Date	Mintage	VF20	XF40	MS60	MS63	MS65
SH1358	—	—	3.00	10.00	15.00	25.00

KM# 1232 RIAL

1.80 g., Copper-Nickel **Obv:** Inscription within wreath **Rev:** Value and date within wreath

Date	Mintage	VF20	XF40	MS60	MS63	MS65
SH1358	—	—	—	0.25	0.75	1.75
SH1359	—	—	—	0.25	0.75	1.75
SH1360	—	—	—	0.25	0.75	1.75
SH1361	—	—	—	0.25	0.75	1.75
SH1362	—	—	—	0.25	0.75	1.75
SH1363	—	—	—	0.25	0.75	1.75
SH1364	—	—	—	0.25	0.75	1.75
SH1365	—	—	—	0.15	0.65	1.25
SH1366	—	—	—	0.15	0.65	1.25
SH1367	—	—	—	0.15	0.65	1.25

KM# 1245 RIAL

Brass Clad Steel, 20 mm. **Subject:** World Jerusalem Day **Obv:** Value flanked by tulips **Rev:** Mosque above date

Date	Mintage	VF20	XF40	MS60	MS63	MS65
SH1359	—	—	—	0.50	0.75	1.00

KM# 1263 RIAL

Brass **Obv:** Value and date divides inscription and flower sprig within beaded circle **Rev:** Mountain within beaded circle

Date	Mintage	VF20	XF40	MS60	MS63	MS65
SH1371	—	—	—	3.00	5.00	7.50
SH1372	—	—	—	3.00	5.00	7.50
SH1373	—	—	—	3.00	5.00	7.50
SH1374	—	—	—	3.00	5.00	7.50

KM# 1233 2 RIALS

3.00 g., Copper-Nickel, 22.4 mm. **Obv:** Inscription within tulip wreath **Rev:** Value and date within wreath

Date	Mintage	VF20	XF40	MS60	MS63	MS65
SH1358	—	—	—	0.60	1.25	2.00
SH1359	—	—	—	0.50	1.25	2.00
SH1360	—	—	—	0.50	1.25	2.00
SH1361	—	—	—	0.50	1.00	2.00
SH1362	—	—	—	0.35	0.75	2.00
SH1363	—	—	—	0.50	1.00	2.00
SH1364	—	—	—	0.35	0.75	1.50
SH1365	—	—	—	0.25	0.75	1.50
SH1366	—	—	—	0.25	0.75	1.50
SH1367	—	—	—	0.25	0.75	1.50

KM# 1234 5 RIALS

5.00 g., Copper-Nickel, 25 mm. **Obv:** Inscription within tulip wreath **Rev:** Value and date within wreath **Note:** Date varieties exist.

Date	Mintage	VF20	XF40	MS60	MS63	MS65
SH1358	—	—	—	0.75	1.00	1.50
SH1359	—	—	—	0.75	1.00	1.50
SH1360	—	—	—	0.75	1.00	1.50
SH1361	—	—	—	0.75	1.00	1.50
SH1362	—	—	—	0.75	1.00	1.50
SH1363	—	—	—	0.75	1.00	1.50
SH1364	—	—	—	0.75	1.00	1.50
SH1365	—	—	—	0.75	1.00	1.50
SH1366	—	—	—	0.75	1.00	1.50
SH1367	—	—	—	0.75	1.00	1.50
SH1368	—	—	—	0.75	1.00	1.50

KM# 1258 5 RIALS

2.00 g., Brass, 19.5 mm. **Obv:** Value and date divides inscription and flower sprig within beaded circle **Rev:** Tomb within beaded circle

Date	Mintage	VF20	XF40	MS60	MS63	MS65
SH1371	—	—	—	0.50	0.75	1.25
SH1372	—	—	—	0.50	0.75	1.25
SH1373	—	—	—	0.50	0.75	1.25
AH1374	—	—	—	0.50	0.75	1.25
SH1375	—	—	—	0.50	0.75	1.25
SH1376	—	—	—	0.50	0.75	1.25
SH1378	—	—	—	0.50	0.75	1.25

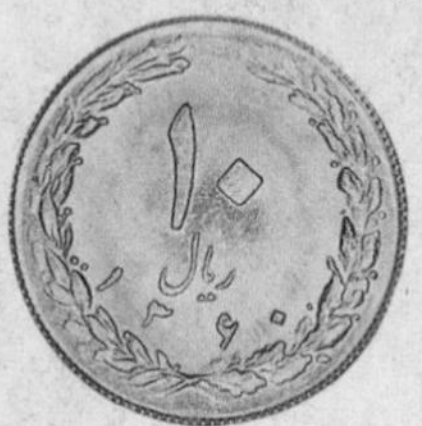

KM# 1235.1 10 RIALS

Copper-Nickel, 28 mm. **Obv:** Inscription and value within tulip wreath **Rev:** Value and date within wreath

Date	Mintage	VF20	XF40	MS60	MS63	MS65
SH1358	—	—	—	0.50	1.00	1.50
SH1358 Large date	—	—	—	0.50	1.00	1.50
SH1359	—	—	—	0.50	1.00	1.50
SH1360	—	—	—	0.50	1.00	1.50
SH1361	—	—	—	0.50	1.00	1.50

KM# 1243 10 RIALS

Copper-Nickel, 28 mm. **Subject:** 1st Anniversary of Revolution **Obv:** Value and inscription within wreath **Rev:** Tulips in center of inscription, dates and value

Date	Mintage	VF20	XF40	MS60	MS63	MS65
SH1358	—	—	—	1.50	3.00	5.00

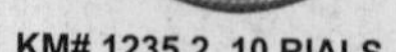

KM# 1235.2 10 RIALS

Copper-Nickel, 28 mm. **Obv:** Inscription and value within tulip

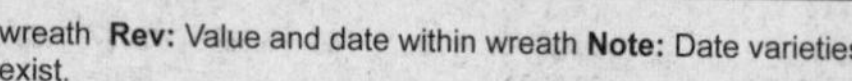

wreath **Rev:** Value and date within wreath **Note:** Date varieties exist.

Date	Mintage	VF20	XF40	MS60	MS63	MS65
SH1361	—	—	—	0.75	1.25	1.50
SH1362	—	—	—	0.75	1.25	1.50
SH1363	—	—	—	1.00	3.00	5.00
SH1364	—	—	—	0.75	1.25	1.50
SH1365	—	—	—	0.75	1.25	1.50
SH1366	—	—	—	0.75	1.25	1.50
SH1366 Small date	—	—	—	0.75	1.25	1.50
SH1367	—	—	—	0.75	1.25	1.50

KM# 1249 10 RIALS

6.97 g., Copper-Nickel, 28 mm. **Subject:** Moslem Unity **Obv:** Capitol building flanked by dates **Rev:** Kaaba at Mecca, date with value below **Edge:** Reeded

Date	Mintage	VF20	XF40	MS60	MS63	MS65
SH1361-AH1402	—	—	—	1.50	3.00	5.00

KM# 1253 10 RIALS

3.02 g., Copper-Nickel, 21.2 mm. **Subject:** World Jerusalem Day **Obv:** Dome of the Rock in Jerusalem divides date **Rev:** Kaaba at Mecca divides date with value below **Edge:** Plain

Date	Mintage	VF20	XF40	MS60	MS63	MS65
SH1368	—	—	—	0.50	1.00	1.50

Note: Also dated AH1409 and AD1989

KM# 1259 10 RIALS

3.00 g., Aluminum-Bronze, 21.2 mm. **Subject:** Tomb of Ferdousi **Obv:** Value and date divides inscription and flower sprig within beaded circle **Rev:** Tomb within beaded circle

Date	Mintage	VF20	XF40	MS60	MS63	MS65
SH1371	—	—	—	0.50	1.00	1.50
SH1372	—	—	—	0.50	1.00	1.50
SH1373	—	—	—	0.50	1.00	1.50
SH1374	—	—	—	0.50	1.00	1.50
SH1375	—	—	—	0.50	1.00	1.50
SH1376	—	—	—	0.50	1.00	1.50

KM# 1236 20 RIALS

9.01 g., Copper-Nickel, 31 mm. **Obv:** Inscription within tulip wreath **Rev:** Value and date within wreath **Note:** Date varieties exist.

Date	Mintage	VF20	XF40	MS60	MS63	MS65
SH1358	—	—	—	1.00	1.50	2.50
SH1359	—	—	—	1.00	1.50	2.50
SH1360	—	—	—	1.00	1.50	2.50
SH1361	—	—	—	1.00	1.50	2.50
SH1362	—	—	—	1.00	1.50	2.50
SH1363	—	—	—	1.00	1.50	2.50
SH1364	—	—	—	1.00	1.50	2.50
SH1365	—	—	—	1.00	1.50	2.50
SH1366	—	—	—	1.00	1.50	2.50
SH1367	—	—	—	1.00	1.50	2.50

KM# 1244 20 RIALS

Copper-Nickel, 31 mm. **Subject:** 1400th Anniversary of Mohammed's Flight **Obv:** Value and inscription within wreath **Rev:** Inscription within banner on top of world globe under radiant sun

Date	Mintage	VF20	XF40	MS60	MS63	MS65
SH1358-AH1400	—	—	—	1.50	3.00	5.00

KM# 1246 20 RIALS

Copper-Nickel, 31 mm. **Subject:** 2nd Anniversary of Islamic Revolution **Obv:** Value flanked by tulips and inscription with date below **Rev:** Legend

Date	Mintage	VF20	XF40	MS60	MS63	MS65
SH1359	—	—	—	1.50	3.00	5.00

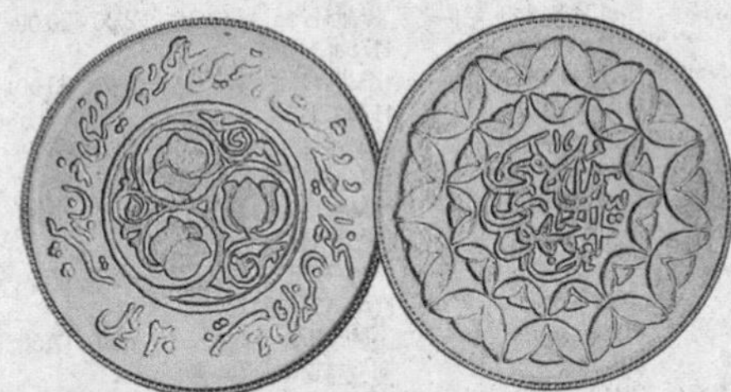

KM# 1247 20 RIALS

Copper-Nickel, 31 mm. **Subject:** 3rd Anniversary of Islamic Revolution **Obv:** Artistic tulip design within circle **Rev:** Inscription within artistic design

Date	Mintage	VF20	XF40	MS60	MS63	MS65
SH1360	—	—	—	1.50	3.00	5.00

KM# 1251 20 RIALS

Copper-Nickel, 31 mm. **Subject:** Islamic Banking Week **Obv:** Inscription within tulip wreath **Rev:** Building within 1/2 wreath and gear design

Date	Mintage	VF20	XF40	MS60	MS63	MS65
SH1367	—	—	—	1.50	3.00	5.00

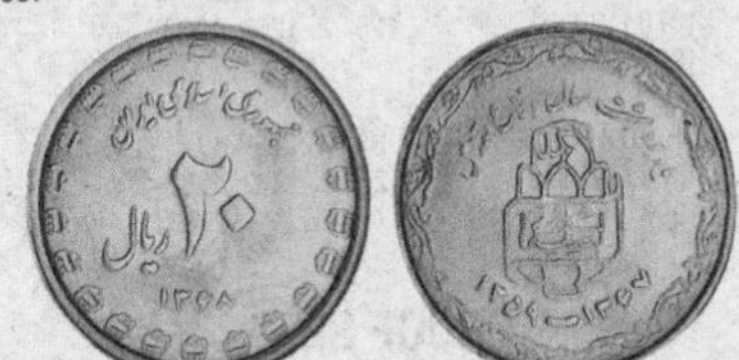

KM# 1254.1 20 RIALS

Copper-Nickel, 24 mm. **Subject:** 8 Years of Sacred Defense **Obv:** Value and date within circle of 22 small ornaments **Rev:** Shield divides dates and inscription within wreath **Note:** 1.48 mm thick.

Date	Mintage	VF20	XF40	MS60	MS63	MS65
SH1368	—	—	—	1.50	3.00	5.00

KM# 1254.2 20 RIALS

4.64 g., Copper-Nickel, 24 mm. **Obv:** Value, date and inscription within circle of 20 small ornaments **Rev:** Shield divides inscription and dates within wreath **Note:** 1.46 mm thick.

Date	Mintage	VF20	XF40	MS60	MS63	MS65
SH1368	—	—	—	1.50	3.00	5.00

KM# 1254.3 20 RIALS

Copper-Nickel, 24 mm. **Obv:** Inscription, value and date within circle of 20 small ornaments **Rev:** Shield divides inscription and dates within wreath

Date	Mintage	VF20	XF40	MS60	MS63	MS65
SH1368	—	—	—	1.50	3.00	5.00

KM# 1237.1 50 RIALS

Aluminum-Bronze, 26 mm. **Subject:** Oil and Agriculture **Obv:** Value at upper left of towers within 1/2 gear and oat sprigs **Rev:** Map labels in relief **Edge:** Lettered in Arabic **Note:** Two varieties of edge lettering exist.

Date	Mintage	VF20	XF40	MS60	MS63	MS65
SH1359	—	—	—	0.75	1.50	3.00
SH1360	—	—	—	0.75	1.50	3.00
SH1361	—	—	—	0.75	1.50	3.00
SH1362	—	—	—	0.75	1.50	3.00
SH1364	—	—	—	0.75	1.50	3.00
SH1365	—	—	—	0.75	1.50	3.00

KM# 1237.2 50 RIALS

Aluminum-Bronze, 26 mm. **Obv:** Value at upper left of towers within 1/2 gear and oat sprigs **Rev:** Map labels incuse **Edge:** Lettered in Farsi **Edge Lettering:** banke markazi jomhoriye eslami iran

Date	Mintage	VF20	XF40	MS60	MS63	MS65
SH1366	—	—	—	1.50	3.00	5.00
SH1367	—	—	—	1.50	3.00	5.00
SH1368	—	—	—	2.50	5.00	7.50

KM# 1252 50 RIALS

Copper-Nickel **Subject:** 10th Anniversary of Revolution **Obv:** Value at upper left of towers within 1/2 gear and oat sprigs **Rev:** Flower-like design above inscription and date within designed border

Date	Mintage	VF20	XF40	MS60	MS63	MS65
SH1367	—	—	—	1.50	3.00	5.00

KM# 1237.1a 50 RIALS

7.00 g., Copper-Nickel, 26.4 mm. **Obv:** Value at upper left of towers within 1/2 gear and oat sprigs **Rev:** Map in relief **Edge:** Lettered in Arabic

Date	Mintage	VF20	XF40	MS60	MS63	MS65
SH1368	—	—	—	1.00	1.50	3.00
SH1369	—	—	—	1.00	1.50	3.00
SH1370	—	—	—	1.00	1.50	3.00

KM# 1260 50 RIALS

Copper-Nickel, 26 mm. **Subject:** Shrine of Hazrat Masumah **Obv:** Value and date **Rev:** Shrine within beaded circle **Edge:** Reeded

Date	Mintage	VF20	XF40	MS60	MS63	MS65
SH1371	—	—	—	1.00	1.50	2.50
SH1372	—	—	—	1.00	1.50	2.50
SH1373	—	—	—	1.00	1.50	2.50
SH1374	—	—	—	1.00	1.50	2.50
SH1375	—	—	—	1.00	1.50	2.50
SH1376	—	—	—	1.00	1.50	2.50
SH1377	—	—	—	1.00	1.50	2.50
SH1378	—	—	—	1.00	1.50	2.50
SH1379	—	—	—	1.00	1.50	2.50

KM# 1261.1 100 RIALS

8.78 g., Copper-Nickel **Subject:** Shrine of Imam Reza **Obv:** Value and date divides inscription and flower sprig within beaded border **Rev:** Shrine within designed border **Note:** Thin denomination and numerals

Date	Mintage	VF20	XF40	MS60	MS63	MS65
SH1371	—	—	—	1.00	1.50	2.50

KM# 1261.2 100 RIALS

Copper-Nickel, 29 mm. **Obv:** Value and date **Rev:** Shrine within designed border **Note:** Thick denomination and numerals

Date	Mintage	VF20	XF40	MS60	MS63	MS65
SH1372	—	—	—	1.00	1.50	2.50
SH1373	—	—	—	1.00	1.50	2.50
SH1374	—	—	—	1.00	1.50	2.50
SH1375	—	—	—	1.00	1.50	2.50
SH1376	—	—	—	1.00	1.50	2.50
SH1377	—	—	—	1.00	1.50	2.50
SH1378	—	—	—	1.00	1.50	2.50
SH1379	—	—	—	1.00	1.50	2.50

KM# 1262 250 RIALS

10.70 g., Bi-Metallic Copper-Nickel center in Brass ring, 28.3 mm. **Obv:** Value within circle, inscription and date divide wreath **Rev:** Stylized flower within circle and wreath

Date	Mintage	VF20	XF40	MS60	MS63	MS65
SH1372	—	—	—	1.50	2.50	5.00
SH1371	—	—	—	1.50	2.50	5.00
SH1373	—	—	—	1.50	2.50	5.00
SH1374	—	—	—	1.50	2.50	5.00
SH1375	—	—	—	1.50	2.50	5.00
SH1376	—	—	—	1.50	2.50	5.00
SH1377	—	—	—	1.50	2.50	5.00
SH1378	—	—	—	1.50	2.50	5.00
SH1379	—	—	—	1.50	2.50	5.00

BULLION COINAGE

Issued by the National Bank of Iran

KM# 1238 1/4 AZADI

2.03 g., 0.900 Gold 0.0589 oz. AGW **Obv:** Mosque within circle **Obv. Legend:** 1st Spring of Freedom **Rev:** Artistic design within hexagon and designed border

Date	Mintage	VF20	XF40	MS60	MS63	MS65
SH1358	—	—	—	—	86.00	102

KM# 1265 1/4 AZADI

2.03 g., 0.900 Gold 0.0589 oz. AGW **Obv. Legend:** Spring of Freedom

Date	Mintage	VF20	XF40	MS60	MS63	MS65
SH1366	—	—	—	—	86.00	102
SH1368	—	—	—	—	86.00	102
SH1369	—	—	—	—	86.00	102
SH1370	—	—	—	—	86.00	102

KM# 1239 1/2 AZADI

4.07 g., 0.900 Gold 0.1177 oz. AGW **Obv:** Mosque within circle **Obv. Legend:** 1st Spring of Freedom **Rev:** Artistic design within hexagon and designed border

Date	Mintage	VF20	XF40	MS60	MS63	MS65
SH1358	—	—	—	—	172	202

KM# 1250.1 1/2 AZADI

4.07 g., 0.900 Gold 0.1177 oz. AGW **Obv:** Legend shortened **Obv. Legend:** Spring of Freedom

Date	Mintage	VF20	XF40	MS60	MS63	MS65
SH1363	—	—	—	—	172	202

KM# 1250.2 1/2 AZADI

4.07 g., 0.900 Gold 0.1177 oz. AGW **Obv:** Legend larger **Obv. Legend:** Spring of Freedom

Date	Mintage	VF20	XF40	MS60	MS63	MS65
SH1366	—	—	—	—	172	202
SH1368	—	—	—	—	172	202
SH1370	—	—	—	—	172	202

KM# 1240 AZADI

8.14 g., 0.900 Gold 0.2354 oz. AGW **Obv:** Mosque within circle **Obv. Legend:** 1st Spring of Freedom **Rev:** Artistic design within hexagon and designed border

Date	Mintage	VF20	XF40	MS60	MS63	MS65
SH1358	—	—	—	—	345	405

KM# 1248.1 AZADI

8.14 g., 0.900 Gold 0.2354 oz. AGW **Obv:** Mosque within circle **Obv. Legend:** Spring of Freedom **Rev:** Artistic design within hexagon and designed border **Note:** Legend shortened

Date	Mintage	VF20	XF40	MS60	MS63	MS65
SH1363	—	—	—	—	345	405

KM# 1248.2 AZADI

8.14 g., 0.900 Gold 0.2354 oz. AGW **Obv:** Mosque within circle **Obv. Legend:** Spring of Freedom **Rev:** Artistic design within hexagon and designed border **Note:** Larger legend

Date	Mintage	VF20	XF40	MS60	MS63	MS65
SH1364	—	—	—	—	345	405
SH1365	—	—	—	—	345	405
SH1366	—	—	—	—	345	405
SH1367	—	—	—	—	345	405
SH1368	—	—	—	—	345	405
SH1369	—	—	—	—	345	405
SH1370	—	—	—	—	345	405

KM# 1264 AZADI

8.14 g., 0.900 Gold 0.2354 oz. AGW **Subject:** Central Bank of Islamic Republic of Iran **Obv:** Bank within circle **Rev:** Head 3/4 right above date

Date	Mintage	VF20	XF40	MS60	MS63	MS65
SH1370	—	—	—	—	345	405
SH1373	—	—	—	—	345	405
SH1374	—	—	—	—	345	405
SH1375	—	—	—	—	345	405

Tehran

KM# A1264 AZADI

8.14 g., 0.900 Gold 0.2354 oz. AGW, 23.7 mm. **Obv:** Mosque within circle **Rev:** Head left above date **Edge:** Reeded

Date	Mintage	VF20	XF40	MS60	MS63	MS65
SH1370	—	—	—	—	345	405

KM# 1241 2-1/2 AZADI

20.34 g., 0.900 Gold 0.5886 oz. AGW **Obv:** Mosque within circle **Obv. Legend:** 1st Spring of Freedom **Rev:** Artistic design within hexagon within designed border

Date	Mintage	VF20	XF40	MS60	MS63	MS65
SH1358	6	—	—	—	—	1,800

Note: A mintage of 6 pieces is reported, but more exist

KM# 1242 5 AZADI

40.68 g., 0.900 Gold 1.1771 oz. AGW **Obv:** Mosque within circle **Obv. Legend:** 1st Spring of Freedom **Rev:** Artistic design within hexagon within designed border

Date	Mintage	VF20	XF40	MS60	MS63	MS65
SH1358	—	—	—	—	—	2,700

PATTERNS

Including off metal strikes

KM#	Date	Mintage	Identification	Mkt Val
Pn27	AH1319 (1901)	—	250 Dinars. Silver. Plain. Mouzaffer profile.	1,500
Pn28	AH1319 (1901)	—	500 Dinars. Silver. Plain.	1,500
Pn30	AH1319 (1901)	—	2000 Dinars. Silver. Plain.	2,000
Pn31	AH1319 (1901)	—	5000 Dinars. Silver. Plain.	5,000
Pn32	AH1319 (1901)	—	1/4 Toman.	400
Pn26	AH1319 (1901)H	—	1/4 Kran.	—
Pn29	AH1319 (1901)	—	1000 Dinars. Silver. Plain.	1,500
Pn33	AH1326 (1908)	—	2000 Dinars. Gold. KM#1024.	1,250
Pn33a	AH1326 (1908)	—	2000 Dinars. Gold. Mule. Obv. KM#1024, Rev. KM#1070.	3,150
Pn34	AH1326 (1908)	—	5000 Dinars. Gold. Legend in open wreath. KM#1025.	1,900
Pn34a	AH1326 (1908)	—	5000 Dinars. Gold. Mule. Obv. KM#1025, Rev. KM#1071.	3,750
Pn35	AH1326 (1908)	—	Toman. Gold. Legend in open wreath. KM#1026.	525
Pn36	AH1326 (1908)	—	2 Ashrafi. Legend in open wreath.	3,150
PnA37	AH1330 (1911)	—	2000 Dinars. Nickel. Struck at Berlin.	—
Pn37	AH1331 (1912)	—	Toman. Bronze Gilt.	1,250
Pn38	AH1331 (1912)	—	2 Toman. Bronze Gilt. Portrait of Ahmed Shah.	1,250
Pn40a	AH1331 (1912)	—	2000 Dinars. Gold. Mule. Obv. KM#1071, Rev. KM#1025.	3,750
Pn39	AH1332 (1913)	—	5 Krans. Silver. Plain.	1,250
Pn40	AH1332 (1913)	—	2000 Dinars. Gold.	—
Pn41	AH1337 (1918)	—	2 Toman. Gold. KM#1080; "2 Ashrafi.	—
Pn42	AH1337 (1918)	—	2000 Dinars. Gold.	4,500
Pn43	AH1337 (1918)	—	2000 Dinars. Gold.	4,400
Pn44	AH1337 (1918)	—	5 Toman. Gold. KM#1081; "5 Ashrafi.	4,400
Pn45	AH1337 (1918)	—	10 Toman. Gold. KM#1082.	—
Pn46	SH1305 (1926)	—	2000 Dinars. Silver. Reeded.	8,100
Pn47	SH1305 (1926)	—	5000 Dinars. Silver. Reeded.	12,000
Pn25	AH1318 (1900)	—	5 Krans. Silver. Struck at Paris Mint.	2,000
Pn49	SH1354 (1974)	—	2-1/2 Pahlavi. 0.916. Silver. KM#1201.	95.00
Pn48	MS2537 (1978)	—	10 Pahlavi. Silver. Reeded. KM#1213.	—
Pn50	MS2537 (1978)	—	5 Pahlavi. 0.9167. Silver. KM#1202.	150

MINT SETS

KM#	Date	Mintage	Identification	Issue Price	Mkt Val
MS1	SH1342 (1963) (4)	—	KM#1171a, 1173, 1175a, 1177a	2.00	20.00
MS2	SH1342-1343 (1963-64) (4)	—	KM#1171a, 1173, 1175a, 1177a	2.00	20.00
MS4	SH1343-44 (1964-65) (4)	—	KM#1171a, 1173, 1175a, 1177	2.00	20.00
MS5	SH1344 (1965) (4)	—	KM#1171a, 1173, 1175a, 1177a	2.00	20.00
MS6	SH1344-45 (1965-66) (4)	—	KM#1171a, 1173, 1175a, 1177a	2.00	20.00
MS7	SH1348 (1969) (5)	—	KM#1156, 1171a, 1173, 1176, 1178	2.00	17.50
MS8	SH1350 (1971) (5)	—	KM#1156, 1171a, 1173, 1176, 1178	2.00	17.50
MS9	SH1353 (1974) (6)	—	KM#1156, 1171a, 1173, 1176, 1179, 1181	2.00	20.00
MS10	SH1354 (1975) (6)	—	KM#1156, 1171a, 1173, 1176, 1179, 1181	2.00	32.50
MS11	MS2535 (1976) (6)	—	KM#1156a, 1205-1209	2.50	85.00
MS12	MS2536 (1977) (6)	—	KM#1156a, 1172-1173, 1176, 1179, 1181	2.50	55.00
MS13	SH1358 (1989) (8)	—	KM#1243-1244 dated 1358; 1246 dated 1359; 1247 dated 1360; 1252 dated 1367; 1253.1, 1253.2, 1254.1 dated 1368	—	100
MS14	SH1366 (1989) (7)	—	KM#1232-1234, 1236 dated 1366; 1235.2, 1237.2 dated 1367; 1237.1a dated 1368	—	60.00
MS15	SH1371 (1993) (5)	—	KM#1258-1262	—	60.00
MS16	SH1372, 1375, 1378 (1993, 1996, 1999) (6)	—	KM#1258-1260, 1261.2, 1262, 1263	—	100
MS17	SH1373, 1375, 1378 (1994, 1996, 1999) (6)	—	KM#1258-1260, 1261.2, 1262, 1263	—	100

PROOF SETS

KM#	Date	Mintage	Identification	Issue Price	Mkt Val
PS1	SH1306 (1927) (2)	20	KM#1104, 1106	—	1,700
PS2	SH1350 (1971) (9)	9,805	KM#1184-1192	261	3,100
PS3	SH1350 (1971) (5)	18,100	KM#1184-1188	59.50	300

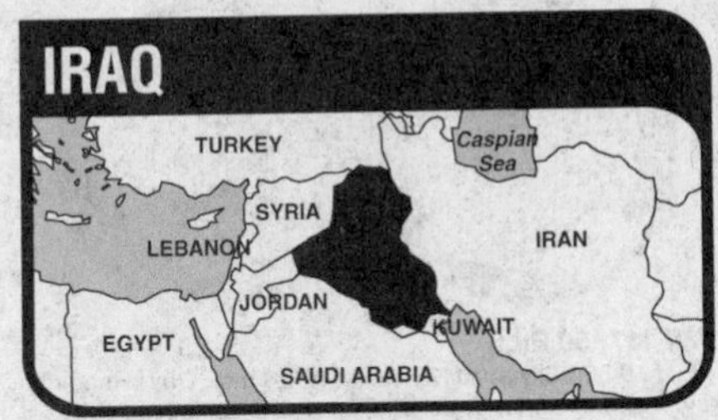

The Republic of Iraq, historically known as Mesopotamia, is located in the Near East and is bordered by Kuwait, Iran, Turkey, Syria, Jordan and Saudi Arabia. It has an area of 167,925 sq. mi. (434,920 sq. km.) and a population of 19 million. Capital: Baghdad. The economy of Iraq is based on agriculture and petroleum. Crude oil accounted for 94 percent of the exports before the war with Iran began in 1980.

Mesopotamia was the site of a number of flourishing civilizations of antiquity - Sumeria, Assyria, Babylonia, Parthia, Persia and the Biblical cities of Ur, Ninevehand and Babylon. Desired because of its favored location, which embraced the fertile alluvial plains of the Tigris and Euphrates Rivers, Mesopotamia - 'land between the rivers'- was conquered by Cyrus the Great of Persia, Alexander of Macedonia and by Arabs who made the legendary city of Baghdad the capital of the ruling caliphate. Suleiman the Magnificent conquered Mesopotamia for Turkey in 1534, and it formed part of the Ottoman Empire until 1623, and from 1638 to 1917. Great Britain, given a League of Nations mandate over the territory in 1920, recognized Iraq as a kingdom in 1922. Iraq became an independent constitutional monarchy presided over by the Hashemite family, direct descendants of the prophet Mohammed, in 1932. In 1958, the army-led revolution of July 14 overthrew the monarchy and proclaimed a republic.

NOTE: The 'I' mintmark on 1938 and 1943 issues appears on the obverse near the point of the bust. Some of the issues of 1938 have a dot to denote a composition change from nickel to copper-nickel.

RULERS
Ottoman, until 1917
British, 1921-1922
Faisal I, 1921-1933
Ghazi I, 1933-1939
Faisal II, Regency, 1939-1953
As King, 1953-1958

MINT MARK
I – Bombay

MONETARY SYSTEM

Falus, Fulus Fals, Fils Falsan

50 Fils = 1 Dirham
200 Fils = 1 Riyal
1000 Fils = 1 Dinar (Pound)

TITLES

العراق

Al-Iraq

المملكة العراقية

Al-Mamlaka(t) al-Iraqiya(t)

الجمهورية العرقية

Al-Jumhuriya(t) al-Iraqiya(t)

KINGDOM OF IRAQ

Faisal I
1921-1933AD

DECIMAL COINAGE

KM# 95 FILS
2.50 g., Bronze, 19.5 mm. **Obv:** Head right **Rev:** Value in center circle flanked by dates

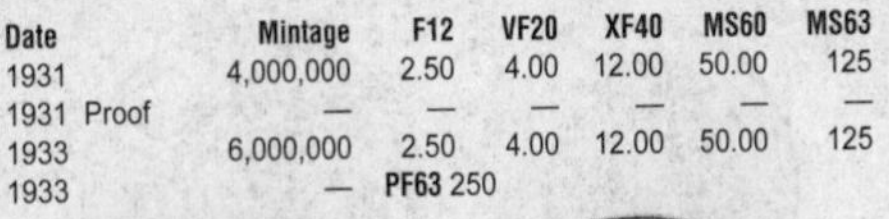

Date	Mintage	F12	VF20	XF40	MS60	MS63
1931	4,000,000	2.50	4.00	12.00	50.00	125
1931 Proof	—	—	—	—	—	—
1933	6,000,000	2.50	4.00	12.00	50.00	125
1933	—	PF63 250				

KM# 96 2 FILS
5.00 g., Bronze, 24 mm. **Obv:** Head right **Rev:** Value in center circle flanked by dates

Date	Mintage	F12	VF20	XF40	MS60	MS63
1931	2,500,000	3.00	5.00	15.00	75.00	150
1931	—	PF63 1,350	PF65 1,650			
1933	1,000,000	3.00	5.00	15.00	75.00	150
1933 Proof	—	—	—	—	—	—

KM# 97 4 FILS
4.00 g., Nickel, 21 mm. **Obv:** Head right **Rev:** Value in center circle flanked by dates **Shape:** Scalloped

Date	Mintage	F12	VF20	XF40	MS60	MS63
1931	4,500,000	1.50	4.00	25.00	100	150
1931 Proof	—	—	—	—	—	—
1933	6,500,000	1.50	4.00	25.00	100	150
1933 Proof	—	—	—	—	—	—

KM# 98 10 FILS
6.75 g., Nickel, 25 mm. **Obv:** Head right **Rev:** Value within center circle flanked by dates **Shape:** Scalloped

Date	Mintage	F12	VF20	XF40	MS60	MS63
1931	2,400,000	2.00	5.00	35.00	125	200
1931 Proof	—	—	—	—	—	—
1933	2,200,000	2.00	5.00	35.00	125	200
1933 Proof	—	—	—	—	—	—

KM# 99 20 FILS
3.60 g., 0.500 Silver 0.0579 oz. ASW, 20.5 mm. **Obv:** Head right **Rev:** Value in center circle flanked by dates

Date	Mintage	F12	VF20	XF40	MS60	MS63
1931	1,500,000	20.00	50.00	150	350	600
1931 Proof	—	—	—	—	—	—
1933	1,100,000	20.00	50.00	150	350	600
1933 Proof	—	—	—	—	—	—
1933 (error) 1252	Inc. above	600	750	950	1,750	2,800

KM# 100 50 FILS
9.00 g., 0.500 Silver 0.1447 oz. ASW, 26.5 mm. **Obv:** Head right **Rev:** Value in center circle flanked by dates

Date	Mintage	F12	VF20	XF40	MS60	MS63
1931	8,800,000	25.00	60.00	175	500	750
1931 Proof	—	—	—	—	—	—
1933	800,000	40.00	100	250	750	1,250
1933 Proof	—	—	—	—	—	—

KM# 101 RIYAL (200 Fils)
20.00 g., 0.500 Silver 0.3215 oz. ASW, 34 mm. **Obv:** Head right **Rev:** Value in center circle flanked by dates **Note:** Dav. #255.

Date	Mintage	F12	VF20	XF40	MS60	MS63
1932	500,000	35.00	90.00	250	750	1,250
1932	Est. 20	PF63 3,000				

Ghazi I
1933-1939AD

KM# 102 FILS
2.50 g., Bronze, 19.5 mm. **Obv:** Head left **Rev:** Value in center circle flanked by dates **Note:** Struck at Royal and Bombay Mint.

Date	Mintage	F12	VF20	XF40	MS60	MS63
1936	3,000,000	2.50	5.00	25.00	65.00	120
1936	—	PF63 350	PF65 700			
1938	36,000,000	0.50	0.75	3.00	8.00	25.00
1938 Proof	—	—	—	—	—	—
1938 I	3,000,000	2.00	5.00	10.00	40.00	65.00

KM# 105 4 FILS
4.00 g., Nickel, 21 mm. **Obv:** Head left **Rev:** Value within center circle flanked by dates **Shape:** Scalloped

Date	Mintage	F12	VF20	XF40	MS60	MS63
1938	1,000,000	4.00	10.00	25.00	95.00	160
1938 Proof	—	—	—	—	—	—
1939	1,000,000	6.00	15.00	40.00	150	280
1939 Proof	—	—	—	—	—	—

KM# 105a 4 FILS
4.00 g., Copper-Nickel, 21 mm. **Obv:** Head left **Rev:** Value within center circle flanked by dates **Shape:** Scalloped **Note:** Struck at Royal and Bombay Mint.

Date	Mintage	F12	VF20	XF40	MS60	MS63
1938	2,750,000	2.00	5.00	10.00	65.00	110
1938 Proof	—	—	—	—	—	—
1938 I	2,500,000	2.00	5.00	10.00	40.00	65.00

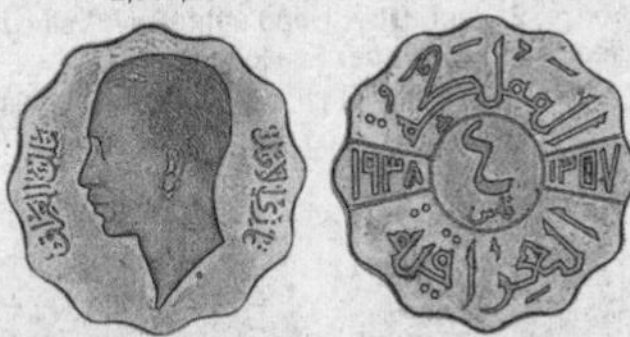

KM# 105b 4 FILS
4.00 g., Bronze, 21 mm. **Obv:** Head left **Rev:** Value in center circle flanked by dates **Shape:** Scalloped

Date	Mintage	F12	VF20	XF40	MS60	MS63
1938	8,000,000	2.00	4.00	10.00	45.00	85.00
1938 Proof	—	—	—	—	—	—

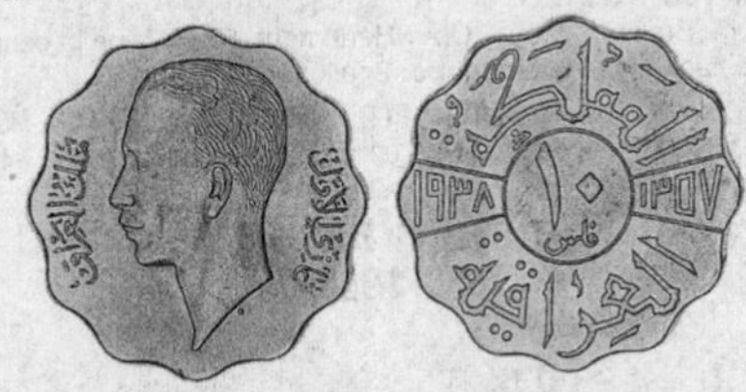

KM# 103 10 FILS
6.75 g., Nickel, 25 mm. **Obv:** Head left **Rev:** Value in center circle flanked by dates **Shape:** Scalloped

Date	Mintage	F12	VF20	XF40	MS60	MS63
1937	400,000	8.00	25.00	50.00	200	375
1937	—	PF63 400				
1938	600,000	5.00	15.00	35.00	150	250
1938 Proof	—	—	—	—	—	—

KM# 103a 10 FILS
6.75 g., Copper-Nickel, 25 mm. **Obv:** Head left **Rev:** Value within center circle flanked by dates **Shape:** Scalloped **Note:** Struck at Royal and Bombay Mint.

Date	Mintage	F12	VF20	XF40	MS60	MS63
1938 Proof	—	—	—	—	—	—

Date	Mintage	F12	VF20	XF40	MS60	MS63
1938 I	1,500,000	2.00	5.00	15.00	50.00	90.00
1938	1,100,000	2.00	5.00	15.00	50.00	90.00

KM# 103b 10 FILS

6.75 g., Bronze, 25 mm. **Obv:** Head left **Rev:** Value within center circle flanked by dates **Shape:** Scalloped

Date	Mintage	F12	VF20	XF40	MS60	MS63
1938 Proof	—	—	—	—	—	—
1938	8,250,000	1.00	3.00	10.00	40.00	72.00

KM# 106 20 FILS

3.60 g., 0.500 Silver 0.0579 oz. ASW, 20.5 mm. **Obv:** Head left **Rev:** Value in center circle flanked by dates

Date	Mintage	F12	VF20	XF40	MS60	MS63
1938	1,200,000	3.00	5.00	15.00	75.00	120
1938 I	1,350,000	3.00	6.00	18.00	85.00	135

KM# 104 50 FILS

9.00 g., 0.500 Silver 0.1447 oz. ASW, 26.5 mm. **Obv:** Head left **Rev:** Value in center circle flanked by dates **Note:** Struck at Royal and Bombay Mint.

Date	Mintage	F12	VF20	XF40	MS60	MS63
1937	1,200,000	10.00	25.00	65.00	240	400
1937 Proof	—	—	—	—	—	—
1938	5,300,000	5.00	12.00	20.00	75.00	120
1938 Proof	—	—	—	—	—	—
1938 I	7,500,000	5.00	12.00	20.00	75.00	120

Faisal II as Regent
1939-1953AD

KM# 107 4 FILS

4.00 g., Bronze, 21 mm. **Obv:** Head right **Rev:** Value in center circle flanked by dates **Shape:** Scalloped

Date	Mintage	F12	VF20	XF40	MS60	MS63
1943 I	1,500,000	6.00	20.00	40.00	90.00	200

KM# 108 10 FILS

6.75 g., Bronze, 25 mm. **Obv:** Head right **Rev:** Value in center circle flanked by dates **Shape:** Scalloped

Date	Mintage	F12	VF20	XF40	MS60	MS63
1943 #NAM	1,500,000	15.00	30.00	75.00	225	450

Faisal II as King
1953-1958AD

KM# 109 FILS

Bronze **Obv:** Head right **Rev:** Value in center circle flanked by dates

Date	Mintage	F12	VF20	XF40	MS60	MS63
1953	41,000,000	0.25	0.50	1.00	5.00	8.00
1953	200	PF63 300				

KM# 110 2 FILS

Bronze **Obv:** Head right **Rev:** Value in center circle flanked by dates

Date	Mintage	F12	VF20	XF40	MS60	MS63
1953	500,000	25.00	50.00	75.00	125	175
1953	200	PF63 300				

KM# 111 4 FILS

4.00 g., Copper-Nickel, 21 mm. **Obv:** Head right **Rev:** Value in center circle flanked by dates **Shape:** Scalloped

Date	Mintage	F12	VF20	XF40	MS60	MS63
1953	20,750,000	0.50	1.00	3.00	8.00	15.00
1953	200	PF63 400				

KM# 112 10 FILS

6.75 g., Copper-Nickel, 25 mm. **Obv:** Head right **Rev:** Value in center circle flanked by dates **Shape:** Scalloped

Date	Mintage	F12	VF20	XF40	MS60	MS63
1953	11,400,000	0.50	1.00	3.00	10.00	15.00
1953	200	PF63 400				

KM# 113 20 FILS

3.60 g., 0.500 Silver 0.0579 oz. ASW, 20.5 mm. **Obv:** Head right **Rev:** Value in center circle flanked by dates

Date	Mintage	F12	VF20	XF40	MS60	MS63
1953	250,000	45.00	75.00	100	225	300
1953	200	PF63 500				

KM# 116 20 FILS

2.80 g., 0.500 Silver 0.045 oz. ASW, 19 mm. **Obv:** Head right **Rev:** Value in center circle, date above sprigs, legend above

Date	Mintage	F12	VF20	XF40	MS60	MS63
1955	4,000,000	3.00	7.00	12.00	30.00	—
1955	—	PF63 500				

KM# 114 50 FILS

9.00 g., 0.500 Silver 0.1447 oz. ASW, 26.5 mm. **Obv:** Head right **Rev:** Value in center circle flanked by dates

Date	Mintage	F12	VF20	XF40	MS60	MS63
1953	560,000	50.00	125	200	350	400
1953	200	PF63 750				

KM# 117 50 FILS

7.00 g., 0.500 Silver 0.1125 oz. ASW, 26 mm. **Obv:** Head right **Rev:** Value in center circle, date above sprigs, legend above

Date	Mintage	F12	VF20	XF40	MS60	MS63
1955	12,000,000	3.00	7.00	12.00	20.00	30.00
1955	—	PF63 500				

KM# 115 100 FILS

10.00 g., 0.900 Silver 0.2894 oz. ASW, 29 mm. **Obv:** Head right **Rev:** Value in center circle flanked by dates

Date	Mintage	F12	VF20	XF40	MS60	MS63
1953	1,200,000	15.00	25.00	65.00	150	200
1953	200	PF63 600				

KM# 118 100 FILS

10.00 g., 0.500 Silver 0.1608 oz. ASW, 29 mm. **Obv:** Head right **Rev:** Value in center circle flanked by dates

Date	Mintage	F12	VF20	XF40	MS60	MS63
1955	1,000,000	—	2,000	2,500	3,500	5,000
1955	—	PF63 6,000				

REPUBLIC

KM# 119 FILS

2.50 g., Bronze, 19 mm. **Obv:** Value in center circle, dates above sprig, legend above **Rev:** Oat sprig within center circle of star design **Shape:** 10-sided

Date	Mintage	VF20	XF40	MS60	MS63	MS65
1959	72,000,000	0.25	0.50	0.75	1.00	—
1959	400	PF63 60.00	PF65 120			

KM# 120 5 FILS

5.00 g., Copper-Nickel, 22 mm. **Obv:** Value in center circle above dates and sprigs, legend above **Rev:** Oat sprig within center circle of star design **Shape:** Scalloped

Date	Mintage	VF20	XF40	MS60	MS63	MS65
1959	30,000,000	0.25	0.50	0.75	1.00	—
1959	400	PF63 60.00	PF65 120			

KM# 125 5 FILS

5.00 g., Copper-Nickel, 22 mm. **Obv:** Value in center circle above oat sprigs, legend above **Rev:** Palm trees divide dates **Shape:** Scalloped

Date	Mintage	VF20	XF40	MS60	MS63	MS65
1967	17,000,000	0.15	0.25	0.40	0.50	0.75
1971	15,000,000	0.15	0.25	0.40	0.50	0.75

KM# 125a 5 FILS

5.04 g., Stainless Steel, 22 mm. **Obv:** Value in center circle above oat sprigs, legend above **Rev:** Palm trees divide dates

Date	Mintage	VF20	XF40	MS60	MS63	MS65
1971	2,000,000	0.20	0.30	0.60	0.75	1.00
1974	15,000,000	0.10	0.15	0.30	0.35	0.50
1975	94,800,000	0.10	0.15	0.30	0.35	0.50
1981	29,840,000	0.10	0.15	0.30	0.35	0.50

Note: Non-magnetic

KM# 141 5 FILS

Stainless Steel **Series:** F.A.O. **Obv:** Value in center circle divides legend **Rev:** Palm trees divide date **Shape:** Scalloped

Date	Mintage	VF20	XF40	MS60	MS63	MS65
1975	2,000,000	0.10	0.15	0.35	0.50	0.75

KM# 159 5 FILS

Stainless Steel **Subject:** Babylon-Ruins **Obv:** Value in center circle divides legend **Rev:** Dates above ruins **Shape:** Scalloped

Date	Mintage	VF20	XF40	MS60	MS63	MS65
1982	—	0.10	0.15	0.35	0.50	0.75

KM# 159a 5 FILS

Copper-Nickel **Subject:** Babylon-Ruins **Obv:** Value in center circle divides legend **Rev:** Dates above ruins

Date	Mintage	VF20	XF40	MS60	MS63	MS65
1982	—	PF65 3.00				

KM# 121 10 FILS

6.75 g., Copper-Nickel, 26 mm. **Obv:** Value in center circle above dates and sprigs, legend above **Rev:** Oat sprig within center circle of star-like design **Shape:** Scalloped

Date	Mintage	VF20	XF40	MS60	MS63	MS65
1959	24,000,000	0.35	0.65	1.00	1.25	—
1959	400	PF63 60.00	PF65 120			

KM# 126 10 FILS

6.81 g., Copper-Nickel, 26 mm. **Obv:** Value in center circle above oat sprigs, legend above **Rev:** Palm trees divide dates **Shape:** Scalloped

Date	Mintage	VF20	XF40	MS60	MS63	MS65
1967	13,400,000	0.20	0.30	0.80	1.00	1.25
1971	12,000,000	0.20	0.30	0.80	1.00	1.25

KM# 126a 10 FILS

5.80 g., Stainless Steel, 26 mm. **Obv:** Value in center circle above sprigs, legend above **Rev:** Palm trees divide dates

Date	Mintage	VF20	XF40	MS60	MS63	MS65
1971	1,550,000	0.25	0.35	0.85	1.00	1.25
1974	12,000,000	0.20	0.30	0.75	1.00	1.25
1975	52,456,000	0.20	0.30	0.75	1.00	1.25
1979	13,800,000	0.20	0.30	0.75	1.00	1.25
1981	63,736,000	0.20	0.30	0.75	1.00	1.25

Note: Non-magnetic

KM# 142 10 FILS

5.80 g., Stainless Steel, 26 mm. **Series:** F.A.O. **Obv:** Value within circle divides legend **Rev:** Palm trees divide dates **Shape:** Scalloped

Date	Mintage	VF20	XF40	MS60	MS63	MS65
1975	1,000,000	0.15	0.25	0.60	0.75	1.00

KM# 160 10 FILS

Stainless Steel, 26 mm. **Obv:** Value within circle divides legends **Rev:** Dates above ruins **Rev. Legend:** Babylon - Ishtar Gate **Shape:** Scalloped

Date	Mintage	VF20	XF40	MS60	MS63	MS65
1982	—	—	—	0.60	0.75	1.00

KM# 160a 10 FILS

Copper-Nickel **Obv:** Value within circle divides legends **Rev:** Dates above ruins **Rev. Legend:** Babylon - Ishtar Gate **Shape:** Scalloped

Date	Mintage	VF20	XF40	MS60	MS63	MS65
1982	—	PF63 3.00				

KM# 122 25 FILS

2.80 g., 0.500 Silver 0.045 oz. ASW, 20 mm. **Obv:** Value within circle above dates and sprigs, legend above **Rev:** Oat sprig within center circle of star-like design

Date	Mintage	VF20	XF40	MS60	MS63	MS65
1959	400	PF63 100	PF65 200			
1959	12,000,000	1.00	3.00	5.00	7.50	—

KM# 127 25 FILS

2.80 g., Copper-Nickel, 20 mm. **Obv:** Value in center circle above sprigs, legend above **Rev:** Palm trees divide dates

Date	Mintage	VF20	XF40	MS60	MS63	MS65
1969	6,000,000	0.20	0.30	0.75	1.00	1.25
1970	6,000,000	0.20	0.30	0.75	1.00	1.25
1972	12,000,000	0.20	0.30	0.75	1.00	1.25
1975	48,000,000	0.20	0.30	0.75	1.00	1.25
1981	60,000,000	0.20	0.30	0.75	1.00	1.25

KM# 161 25 FILS

2.80 g., Copper-Nickel, 20 mm. **Obv:** Value in center circle divides legend **Rev:** Dates above lion

Date	Mintage	VF20	XF40	MS60	MS63	MS65
1982	—	—	—	0.35	0.50	1.25
1982	—	PF65 4.00				

KM# 123 50 FILS

5.00 g., 0.500 Silver 0.0804 oz. ASW, 23 mm. **Obv:** Value in center circle above dates and sprigs, legend above **Rev:** Oat sprig within center circle of star-like design

Date	Mintage	VF20	XF40	MS60	MS63	MS65
1959	24,000,000	3.00	5.00	7.50	10.00	—
1959	400	PF63 160	PF65 320			

KM# 128 50 FILS

5.54 g., Copper-Nickel, 23 mm. **Obv:** Value within circle above sprigs, legend above **Rev:** Palm trees divide dates

Date	Mintage	VF20	XF40	MS60	MS63	MS65
1969	12,000,000	0.25	0.35	0.80	1.00	1.25
1970	12,000,000	0.25	0.35	0.80	1.00	1.25
1972	12,000,000	0.25	0.35	0.80	1.00	1.25
1975	36,000,000	0.25	0.35	0.80	1.00	1.25
1979	1,500,000	0.25	0.35	0.80	1.00	1.25
1980	23,520,000	0.25	0.35	0.80	1.00	1.25
1981	138,995,000	0.25	0.35	0.80	1.00	1.25
1990	—	0.25	0.35	0.80	1.00	1.25

KM# 162 50 FILS

Copper-Nickel, 23 mm. **Obv:** Value in center circle divides legend **Rev:** Horse right

Date	Mintage	VF20	XF40	MS60	MS63	MS65
1982	—	0.25	0.50	0.85	1.00	1.25
1982	—	PF65 6.00				

KM# 124 100 FILS

10.00 g., 0.500 Silver 0.1608 oz. ASW, 29 mm. **Obv:** Value within circle above dates and sprigs, legend above **Rev:** Oat sprig within center circle of star-like design

Date	Mintage	VF20	XF40	MS60	MS63	MS65
1959	6,000,000	5.00	9.00	15.00	18.00	—
1959	400	PF63 350	PF65 700			

KM# 129 100 FILS

10.95 g., Copper-Nickel, 29.2 mm. **Obv:** Value within circle above sprigs, legend above **Rev:** Palm trees divide dates

Date	Mintage	VF20	XF40	MS60	MS63	MS65
1970	6,000,000	0.35	0.50	0.85	1.00	1.50
1972	6,000,000	0.35	0.50	0.85	1.00	1.50
1975	12,000,000	0.35	0.50	0.85	1.00	1.50
1979	1,000,000	0.35	0.75	1.75	2.00	3.00

KM# 130 250 FILS

Nickel, 33 mm. **Series:** F.A.O. **Subject:** Agrarian Reform Day **Obv:** Value within circle above sprigs, legend above **Rev:** Palm trees divide dates

Date	Mintage	VF20	XF40	MS60	MS63	MS65
1970	500,000	—	1.50	4.00	5.00	7.50
1970	1,000	PF65 15.00				

Note: Varieties exist with edge inscription w/FAO-250-repeated three times in relief

KM# 131 250 FILS

15.15 g., Nickel, 33 mm. **Subject:** 1st Anniversary Peace with Kurds **Obv:** Value within circle above dates and sprigs, legend above **Rev:** Value, design and dove within circle, outer circle consists of 1/2 gear and 1/2 sprigs

Date	Mintage	VF20	XF40	MS60	MS63	MS65
1971	1,000	PF65 15.00				
1971	500,000	—	1.50	4.00	5.00	7.50

KM# 135 250 FILS
14.90 g., Nickel, 33 mm. **Subject:** Silver Jublilee of Al Baath Party **Obv:** Value within circle above dates, legend above and below **Rev:** Palm trees divide dates

Date	Mintage	VF20	XF40	MS60	MS63	MS65
1972	250,000	—	1.50	4.00	5.00	7.50

KM# 136 250 FILS
14.90 g., Nickel, 33 mm. **Subject:** 25th Anniversary of Central Bank **Obv:** Value within circle above dates, legend above and below **Rev:** Palm trees divide dates

Date	Mintage	VF20	XF40	MS60	MS63	MS65
1972	250,000	—	1.50	4.00	5.00	7.50

KM# 138 250 FILS
Nickel, 33 mm. **Subject:** Oil Nationalization **Obv:** Value within circle above dates, legend above and below **Rev:** Torch divides oil rig tower and pump, flanked by dates

Date	Mintage	VF20	XF40	MS60	MS63	MS65
1973	5,000	PF65 12.00				
1973	260,000	—	1.50	4.00	5.00	7.50

KM# 144 250 FILS
Nickel, 33 mm. **Subject:** International Year of the Child **Obv:** Value within circle divides legends and emblems **Rev:** Child's laureate head right within circle

Date	Mintage	VF20	XF40	MS60	MS63	MS65
1979	10,000	PF65 8.00				

KM# 146 250 FILS
Copper-Nickel **Subject:** 1st Anniversary of Hussein as President

Obv: Value within center circle flanked by dates,legend above and below **Rev:** Bust 1/4 left

Date	Mintage	VF20	XF40	MS60	MS63	MS65
1980	—	1.00	2.00	4.00	7.00	12.00

KM# 147 250 FILS
10.40 g., Copper-Nickel, 29.8 mm. **Obv:** Value within circle above sprigs, legend above **Rev:** Palm trees divide dates **Shape:** Octagon

Date	Mintage	VF20	XF40	MS60	MS63	MS65
1980	—	—	1.00	2.50	3.00	5.00
1981	25,568,000	—	1.00	2.50	3.00	5.00
1990	—	—	1.00	2.50	3.00	5.00

KM# 152 250 FILS
10.10 g., Copper-Nickel, 30 mm. **Subject:** World Food Day **Obv:** F.A.O logo below value flanked by designs, legend above and below **Rev:** Design within circle divides dates **Shape:** Octagon

Date	Mintage	VF20	XF40	MS60	MS63	MS65
1981	46,432,000	—	1.00	2.50	3.00	5.00

KM# 155 250 FILS
10.20 g., Copper-Nickel, 30 mm. **Subject:** Nonaligned Nations Baghdad Conference **Obv:** Value within circle, legend above and below **Rev:** Stylized tree divides dates above legend **Shape:** Octagon

Date	Mintage	VF20	XF40	MS60	MS63	MS65
1982	—	—	1.00	2.50	3.00	5.00

KM# 163 250 FILS
10.30 g., Copper-Nickel, 30 mm. **Obv:** Value within circle, legend above and below **Rev:** Monument flanked by dates **Shape:** Octagon

Date	Mintage	VF20	XF40	MS60	MS63	MS65
1982	—	—	1.00	2.50	3.00	5.00
1982	—	PF65 8.00				

KM# 132 500 FILS
Nickel, 36 mm. **Subject:** 50th Anniversary of Iraqi Army **Obv:** Value in circle flanked by designs , legend above and below **Rev:** Conjoined armored busts divide dates

Date	Mintage	VF20	XF40	MS60	MS63	MS65
1971	100,000	—	2.50	5.50	7.00	10.00
1971	5,000	PF65 15.00				

KM# 139 500 FILS
Nickel, 36 mm. **Subject:** Oil Nationalization **Obv:** Value within circle, date below, legend above and below **Rev:** Oil rig divides dates

Date	Mintage	VF20	XF40	MS60	MS63	MS65
1973	260,000	—	2.50	5.50	7.00	10.00
1973	5,000	PF65 17.50				

KM# 165 500 FILS
9.08 g., Nickel, 30.1 mm. **Obv:** Value within circle above sprigs, "500 Fals" **Rev:** Palm trees divide dates **Shape:** Square

Date	Mintage	VF20	XF40	MS60	MS63	MS65
1982	—	—	1.50	3.00	5.00	7.00

KM# 165a 500 FILS
8.98 g., Nickel, 30.1 mm. **Obv:** Value within circle above sprigs, "500 Falsan" **Rev:** Palm trees divide dates **Shape:** Square **Note:** Reduced weight.

Date	Mintage	VF20	XF40	MS60	MS63	MS65
1982	—	15.00	25.00	50.00	85.00	—

KM# 168 500 FILS
9.08 g., Nickel, 30 mm. **Obv:** Value within circle divides legend, "500 Fals" **Rev:** Lion of Babylon flanked by dates **Shape:** Square

Date	Mintage	VF20	XF40	MS60	MS63	MS65
1982	—	—	1.25	2.50	4.00	6.00
1982	—	PF65 12.50				

KM# 168a 500 FILS
9.08 g., Nickel **Obv:** Value within circle divides legend, "500 Falsan" **Rev:** Lion of Babylon flanked by dates **Shape:** Square

Date	Mintage	VF20	XF40	MS60	MS63	MS65
1982	—	10.00	20.00	50.00	75.00	—

KM# 133 DINAR
31.00 g., 0.900 Silver 0.897 oz. ASW, 40 mm. **Subject:** 50th Anniversary of Iraqi Army **Obv:** Value within circle flanked by designs, legend above and below **Rev:** Conjoined armored busts divide dates

Date	Mintage	VF20	XF40	MS60	MS63	MS65
1971	14,500	—	—	25.00	30.00	35.00
1971	5,500	PF63 40.00	PF65 50.00			

KM# 137 DINAR
31.00 g., 0.500 Silver 0.4983 oz. ASW, 40 mm. **Subject:** 25th Anniversary of Central Bank **Obv:** Value within circle flanked by designs, legend above and below **Rev:** Palm trees divide dates

Date	Mintage	VF20	XF40	MS60	MS63	MS65
1972	50,000	—	—	12.00	15.00	20.00
1972	—	PF63 28.00	PF65 38.00			

KM# 140 DINAR
31.00 g., 0.500 Silver 0.4983 oz. ASW, 40 mm. **Subject:** Oil Nationalization **Obv:** Value within circle flanked by designs, legend above and below **Rev:** Half radiant sun divides dates above long ship

Date	Mintage	VF20	XF40	MS60	MS63	MS65
1973	60,000	—	—	12.00	15.00	20.00
1973	5,000	PF63 30.00	PF65 40.00			

KM# 143 DINAR
31.00 g., 0.900 Silver 0.897 oz. ASW, 40 mm. **Subject:** Inauguaration of Tharthat-Euphrates Canal **Obv:** Value within circle flanked by designs, legend above and below **Rev:** Dam with inscription above and dates below

Date	Mintage	VF20	XF40	MS60	MS63	MS65
1977	7,000	PF63 40.00	PF65 50.00			

KM# 145 DINAR
31.00 g., 0.900 Silver 0.897 oz. ASW, 40 mm. **Subject:** International Year of the Child **Obv:** Value within circle flanked by designs, legend above and below **Rev:** Child's laureate head right within circle

Date	Mintage	VF20	XF40	MS60	MS63	MS65
1979	5,000	PF63 45.00	PF65 55.00			

KM# 148 DINAR
30.53 g., 0.900 Silver 0.8834 oz. ASW **Subject:** 15th Century of Hegira **Obv:** Value and dates within circle with legend around border **Rev:** Stylized value within Mosque

Date	Mintage	VF20	XF40	MS60	MS63	MS65
1980	25,000	PF63 40.00	PF65 50.00			

KM# 149 DINAR
Nickel **Subject:** Battle of Qadissyiat **Obv:** Value within circle flanked by dates, legends and map **Rev:** Bust 1/4 left in front of battle scene **Shape:** 10-sided

Date	Mintage	VF20	XF40	MS60	MS63	MS65
1980	—	—	5.00	10.00	20.00	—
1980	—	PF63 30.00	PF65 40.00			

KM# 153 DINAR
Nickel **Subject:** 50th Anniversary of Iraq Air Force **Obv:** Value within circle with legend above and dates and legend below **Rev:** Bust left divides dates, planes above with banner, sprigs below **Shape:** 10-sided

Date	Mintage	VF20	XF40	MS60	MS63	MS65
1981	—	—	5.00	15.00	25.00	35.00

KM# 170 DINAR
Nickel **Subject:** Circulation Coinage **Obv:** Value within circle above sprigs, legend above **Rev:** Palm trees divide dates **Shape:** 10-sided

Date	Mintage	VF20	XF40	MS60	MS63	MS65
1981	—	—	1.00	2.50	4.00	—

KM# 156 DINAR
13.20 g., Nickel, 32.8 mm. **Subject:** Nonaligned Nations Baghdad Conference **Obv:** Value within circle with legend above and below **Rev:** Stylized tree divides dates within legend **Shape:** 10-sided

Date	Mintage	VF20	XF40	MS60	MS63	MS65
1982	—	—	1.50	4.00	7.00	—

KM# 164 DINAR
13.20 g., Nickel, 32.7 mm. **Obv:** Value within circle divides legend **Rev:** Tower of Babylon flanked by dates **Shape:** 10-sided

Date	Mintage	VF20	XF40	MS60	MS63	MS65
1982	—	—	1.50	4.00	7.00	—
1982	—	PF65 12.50				

KM# 134 5 DINARS
13.57 g., 0.917 Gold 0.4001 oz. AGW **Subject:** 50th Anniversary of Iraqi Army **Obv:** Value within circle flanked by designs with legend above and below **Rev:** Conjoined armored busts divide dates

Date	Mintage	VF20	XF40	MS60	MS63	MS65
1971	20,000	—	—	510	650	750
1971	—	PF63 850	PF65 1,000			

KM# 171 5 DINARS
Bronze, 28 mm. **Obv:** Denomination and legend **Rev:** Two swords arched above palm tree

Date	Mintage	VF20	XF40	MS60	MS63	MS65
1990	—	—	—	350	500	600

Note: Not released to circulation

KM# 172 10 DINARS
Bronze **Obv:** Denomination and legend **Rev:** Two swords arched above palm tree

Date	Mintage	VF20	XF40	MS60	MS63	MS65
1990	—	—	—	250	300	450

Note: Not released to circulation

KM# 166 50 DINARS
13.70 g., 0.917 Gold 0.4039 oz. AGW **Subject:** International Year of the Child **Obv:** Value within circle flanked designs with legend above and below **Rev:** Child's laureate head right within circle

Date	Mintage	VF20	XF40	MS60	MS63	MS65
1979	10,000	PF63 850	PF65 1,000	PF67 1,500		
1979 Impaired Proof	Inc. above	PF60 570				

KM# 150 50 DINARS
13.00 g., 0.917 Gold 0.3833 oz. AGW **Subject:** 15th Century of Hegira **Obv:** Value and inscription within center circle of legend **Rev:** Stylized value within Mosque

Date	Mintage	VF20	XF40	MS60	MS63	MS65
1980	13,000	PF63 750	PF65 850			
1980 Impaired Proof	Inc. above	PF60 540				

KM# 173 50 DINARS
16.97 g., 0.917 Gold 0.5002 oz. AGW **Subject:** 1st Anniversary of Hussein as President

Date	Mintage	VF20	XF40	MS60	MS63	MS65
1980	—	PF63 900	PF65 1,000			

KM# 157 50 DINARS
13.70 g., 0.917 Gold 0.4039 oz. AGW **Subject:** Nonaligned Nations Baghdad Conference

Date	Mintage	VF20	XF40	MS60	MS63	MS65
1982	10,000	PF63 800	PF65 950			

KM# 167 100 DINARS
26.00 g., 0.917 Gold 0.7665 oz. AGW **Subject:** International Year of the Child **Obv:** Value within circle flanked by designs, legend above and below **Rev:** Child's laureate head right within circle

Date	Mintage	VF20	XF40	MS60	MS63	MS65
1979	10,000	PF63 1,450	PF65 1,600			
1979 Impaired Proof	Inc. above	PF60 1075				

KM# 151 100 DINARS
26.00 g., 0.917 Gold 0.7665 oz. AGW **Subject:** 15th Century of Hegira **Obv:** Inscription and value within center circle of legend **Rev:** Stylized value within Mosque

Date	Mintage	VF20	XF40	MS60	MS63	MS65
1980	14,000	PF63 1,450	PF65 1,600			
1980 Impaired Proof	Inc. above	PF60 1,075				

KM# 174 100 DINARS
33.93 g., 0.917 Gold 1.0003 oz. AGW **Subject:** 1st Anniversary of Hussein as President

Date	Mintage	VF20	XF40	MS60	MS63	MS65
1980	—	PF63 1,950	PF65 2,250			

KM# 158 100 DINARS
26.06 g., 0.917 Gold 0.7683 oz. AGW **Subject:** Nonaligned Nations Baghdad Conference **Obv:** Value within circle with legend above and below **Rev:** Stylized tree divides dates

Date	Mintage	VF20	XF40	MS60	MS63	MS65
1982	10,000	PF63 1,450	PF65 1,600			

PATTERNS

Including off metal strikes

KM#	Date	Mintage	Identification	Mkt Val
Pn1	1935	—	20 Fils. Silver. KM106.	—
Pn2	1935	—	50 Fils. Silver. KM104.	—
Pn3	1936	—	2 Fils. Bronze. KM96.	—
Pn4	1936	—	4 Fils. Nickel. KM105.	—
Pn5	1936	—	10 Fils. Nickel. KM103.	—
Pn6	1936	—	20 Fils. Silver. KM106.	—
Pn7	1936	—	50 Fils. Silver. KM104.	—
Pn8	AH139x // 197x (1976)	—	10 Fils. Nickel.	—

PROOF SETS

KM#	Date	Mintage	Identification	Issue Price	Mkt Val
PS1	1953 (7)	200	KM109-115	—	3,000
PS2	1955 (3)	—	KM116-118	—	6,000
PS3	1959 (6)	400	KM119-124	—	1,500
PS4	1959 (7)	—	KM119-124, plus medallic crown (X1)	—	1,750
PS5	1973 (3)	5,000	KM138-140	—	125
PS6	1982 (7)	—	KM159a, 160a, 161-164, 168	—	75.00

IRELAND REPUBLIC

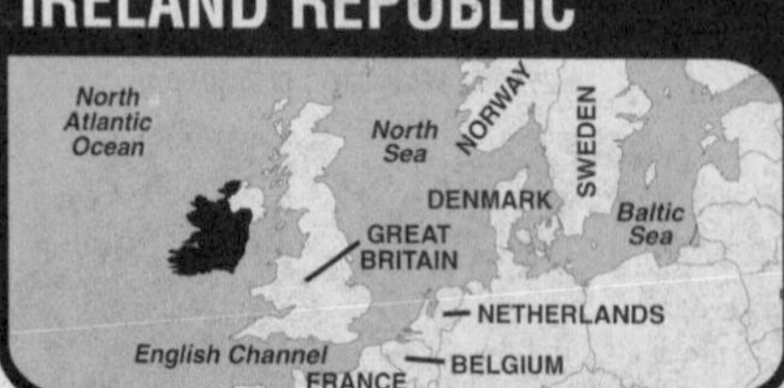

The Republic of Ireland, which occupies five-sixths of the island of Ireland located in the Atlantic Ocean west of Great Britain, has an area of 27,136 sq. mi. (70,280 sq. km.) and a population of 4.3 million. Capital: Dublin. Agriculture and dairy farming are the principal industries. Meat, livestock, dairy products and textiles are exported.

A race of tall, red-haired Celts from Gaul arrived in Ireland about 400 B.C., assimilated the native Erainn and Picts, and established a Gaelic civilization. After the arrival of St. Patrick in 432AD, Ireland evolved into a center of Latin learning, which sent missionaries to Europe and possibly North America. In 1154, Pope Adrian IV gave all of Ireland to English King Henry II to administer as a Papal fief. Because of the enactment of anti-Catholic laws and the awarding of vast tracts of Irish land to Protestant absentee landowners, English control did not become reasonably absolute until 1800 when England and Ireland became the 'United Kingdom of Great Britain and Ireland'. Religious freedom was restored to the Irish in 1829, but agitation for political autonomy continued until the Irish Free State was established as a dominion on Dec. 6, 1921 until 1937 when it became Éire. Ireland proclaimed itself a republic on April 18, 1949. The government, however, does not use the term 'Republic of Ireland,' which tacitly acknowledges the partitioning of the island into Ireland and Northern Ireland, but refers to the country simply as 'Ireland.'

RULER
British, until 1921

MONETARY SYSTEM

(1928-1971)
4 Farthings = 1 Penny 12 Pence = 1 Shilling 2 Shillings = 1 Florin 20 Shillings = 1 Pound

IRISH FREE STATE

STERLING COINAGE

KM# 1 FARTHING
2.83 g., Bronze, 20.3 mm. **Obv:** Irish harp divides date **Obv. Legend:** SAORSTAT EIREANN **Rev:** Woodcock below value **Edge:** Plain

Date	Mintage	F12	VF20	XF40	MS60	MS63
1928	300,000	0.50	1.50	4.50	10.00	15.00
1928	6,001	PF63 15.00				
1930	288,000	0.75	1.50	4.50	15.00	25.00
1930 Proof; Rare	—	—	—	—	—	—
1931	192,000	1.00	3.00	7.50	25.00	35.00
1931 Proof; Rare	—	—	—	—	—	—
1932	192,000	1.00	3.00	7.50	25.00	35.00
1932 Proof; Rare	—	—	—	—	—	—
1933	480,000	0.75	1.50	4.00	15.00	25.00
1933 Proof; Rare	—	—	—	—	—	—
1935	192,000	1.00	3.00	7.50	25.00	35.00
1935 Proof; Rare	—	—	—	—	—	—
1936	192,000	1.00	3.00	7.50	25.00	35.00
1936 Proof; Rare	—	—	—	—	—	—
1937	480,000	0.50	1.50	3.00	15.00	25.00
1937 Proof; Rare	—	—	—	—	—	—

KM# 2 1/2 PENNY
5.67 g., Bronze, 25.5 mm. **Obv:** Irish harp divides date **Obv. Legend:** SAORSTAT EIREANN **Rev:** Sow with piglets below value **Edge:** Plain

Date	Mintage	F12	VF20	XF40	MS60	MS63
1928	2,880,000	0.75	2.00	5.00	15.00	35.00
1928	6,001	PF63 15.00				
1933	720,000	5.00	9.00	35.00	150	275
1933 Proof; Rare	—	—	—	—	—	—
1935	960,000	2.00	6.00	20.00	100	200
1935 Proof; Rare	—	—	—	—	—	—
1937	960,000	1.00	3.00	9.00	20.00	35.00
1937 Proof; Rare	—	—	—	—	—	—

KM# 3 PENNY
9.45 g., Bronze, 30.9 mm. **Obv:** Irish harp divides date **Obv. Legend:** SAORSTAT EIREANN **Rev:** Hen with chicks **Edge:** Plain

Date	Mintage	F12	VF20	XF40	MS60	MS63
1928	9,000,000	0.50	1.00	4.00	15.00	30.00
1928	6,001	PF63 18.50				
1931	2,400,000	1.00	2.00	7.50	35.00	50.00
1931	—	PF63 1,500				

Date	Mintage	F12	VF20	XF40	MS60	MS63
1933	1,680,000	1.00	2.50	9.00	75.00	125
1933 Proof; Rare	—	—	—	—	—	—
1935	5,472,000	0.50	1.00	5.00	20.00	35.00
1935 Proof; Rare	—	—	—	—	—	—
1937	5,400,000	0.50	1.00	7.50	50.00	75.00
1937	—	**PF63** 1,250				

KM# 4 3 PENCE
3.24 g., Nickel, 17.6 mm. **Obv:** Irish harp divides date **Obv. Legend:** SAORSTAT EIREANN **Rev:** Hare **Edge:** Plain

Date	Mintage	F12	VF20	XF40	MS60	MS63
1928	1,500,000	0.50	1.00	3.50	10.00	25.00
1928	6,001	**PF63** 20.00				
1933	320,000	3.00	5.00	35.00	175	275
1933 Proof; Rare	—	—	—	—	—	—
1934	800,000	1.00	2.00	12.50	45.00	75.00
1934 Proof; Rare	—	—	—	—	—	—
1935	240,000	3.00	5.00	20.00	100	150
1935 Proof; Rare	—	—	—	—	—	—

KM# 5 6 PENCE
4.54 g., Nickel, 20.8 mm. **Obv:** Irish harp divides date **Obv. Legend:** SAORSTAT EIREANN **Rev:** Irish Wolfhound **Edge:** Plain

Date	Mintage	F12	VF20	XF40	MS60	MS63
1928	3,201,000	0.50	1.00	5.00	17.50	35.00
1928	6,001	**PF63** 25.00				
1934	600,000	1.00	2.00	18.00	75.00	15.00
1934 Proof; Rare	—	—	—	—	—	—
1935	520,000	1.00	3.00	30.00	150	275
1935 Proof; Rare	—	—	—	—	—	—

KM# 6 SHILLING
5.66 g., 0.750 Silver 0.1364 oz. ASW, 23.6 mm. **Obv:** Irish harp divides date **Obv. Legend:** SAORSTAT EIREANN **Rev:** Bull and value **Edge:** Reeded

Date	Mintage	F12	VF20	XF40	MS60	MS63
1928	2,700,000	5.00	7.00	12.00	25.00	45.00
1928	6,001	**PF63** 32.00				
1930	460,000	8.00	15.00	35.00	150	275
1930	—	**PF63** 1,400				
1931	400,000	6.00	10.00	35.00	100	175
1931 Proof; Rare	—	—	—	—	—	—
1933	300,000	7.00	12.00	40.00	125	225
1933 Proof; Rare	—	—	—	—	—	—
1935	400,000	5.00	9.00	15.00	45.00	75.00
1935 Proof; Rare	—	—	—	—	—	—
1937	100,000	14.00	30.00	200	575	1,000
1937 Proof; Rare	—	—	—	—	—	—

KM# 7 FLORIN
11.31 g., 0.750 Silver 0.2727 oz. ASW, 28.5 mm. **Obv:** Irish harp divides date **Obv. Legend:** SAORSTAT EIREANN **Rev:** Salmon and value **Edge:** Reeded

Date	Mintage	F12	VF20	XF40	MS60	MS63
1928	2,025,000	7.50	12.00	20.00	35.00	90.00
1928	6,001	**PF63** 50.00				
1930	330,000	7.50	15.00	35.00	150	350
1930 Proof; Rare	—	—	—	—	—	—
1931	200,000	7.50	20.00	50.00	200	450
1931 Proof; Rare	—	—	—	—	—	—
1933	300,000	7.50	15.00	50.00	200	450
1933 Proof; Rare	—	—	—	—	—	—

Date	Mintage	F12	VF20	XF40	MS60	MS63
1934	—	**PF63** 3,150				
1934	150,000	7.50	30.00	75.00	300	500
1935	390,000	7.50	15.00	35.00	100	300
1935 Proof; Rare	—	—	—	—	—	—
1937	150,000	7.50	20.00	75.00	250	500
1937 Proof; Rare	—	—	—	—	—	—

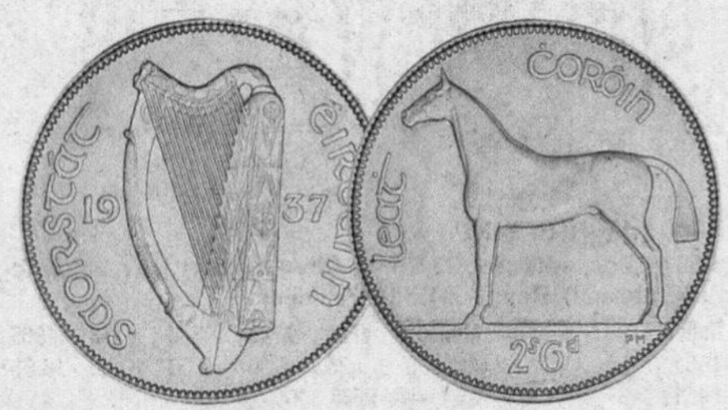

KM# 8 1/2 CROWN
14.14 g., 0.750 Silver 0.3409 oz. ASW, 32.3 mm. **Obv:** Irish harp divides date **Obv. Legend:** SAORSTAT EIREANN **Rev:** Horse and value **Edge:** Reeded **Note:** Close O and I in COROIN. 8 tufts in horse's tail, with 156 beads.

Date	Mintage	F12	VF20	XF40	MS60	MS63
1928	2,160,000	10.00	15.00	25.00	50.00	125
1928	6,001	**PF63** 65.00				
1930	352,000	12.00	20.00	75.00	175	400
1930 Proof; Rare	—	—	—	—	—	—
1931	160,000	12.00	20.00	100	300	675
1931 Proof; Rare	—	—	—	—	—	—
1933	336,000	12.00	20.00	90.00	200	500
1933 Proof; Rare	—	—	—	—	—	—
1934	480,000	12.00	20.00	45.00	125	200
1934 Proof; Rare	—	—	—	—	—	—
1937	40,000	35.00	75.00	450	1,000	2,000
1937 Proof; Rare	—	—	—	—	—	—

REPUBLIC

KM# 9 FARTHING
2.83 g., Bronze, 20.3 mm. **Obv:** Irish harp **Obv. Legend:** EIRE (Ireland) **Rev:** Woodcock below value **Edge:** Plain

Date	Mintage	VF20	XF40	MS60	MS63	MS65
1939	786,000	0.50	1.00	5.00	15.00	35.00
1939	—	**PF63** 815				
1940	192,000	1.00	3.00	8.00	20.00	45.00
1940 Proof; Rare	—	—	—	—	—	—
1941	480,000	0.50	0.75	2.00	6.50	15.00
1941 Proof; Rare	—	—	—	—	—	—
1943	480,000	0.50	0.75	2.00	6.50	15.00
1944	480,000	0.75	1.25	3.00	10.00	25.00
1946	480,000	0.50	0.75	2.00	6.00	12.50
1946 Proof; Rare	—	—	—	—	—	—
1949	192,000	0.75	3.00	6.00	18.00	35.00
1949	—	**PF63** 300				
1953	192,000	0.25	0.50	1.25	3.00	7.50
1953	—	**PF63** 300				
1959	192,000	0.25	0.50	1.25	3.00	7.50
1959 Proof; Rare	—	—	—	—	—	—
1966	96,000	0.35	0.75	1.50	3.50	5.00

KM# 10 1/2 PENNY
5.67 g., Bronze, 25.5 mm. **Obv:** Irish harp **Obv. Legend:** EIRE (Ireland) **Rev:** Sow with piglets below value **Edge:** Plain

Date	Mintage	VF20	XF40	MS60	MS63	MS65
1939	240,000	5.00	20.00	50.00	75.00	175
1939	—	**PF63** 1,000				
1940	1,680,000	3.00	10.00	25.00	60.00	125
1940 Proof; Rare	—	—	—	—	—	—
1941	2,400,000	0.25	1.50	7.50	12.00	25.00
1941 Proof; Rare	—	—	—	—	—	—
1942	6,931,000	0.10	0.25	1.50	5.00	10.00
1943	2,669,000	0.25	1.50	7.50	15.00	30.00
1946	720,000	1.00	2.50	15.00	35.00	50.00
1946 Proof; Rare	—	—	—	—	—	—
1949	1,344,000	0.10	0.25	1.00	5.00	7.50
1949 Proof; Rare	—	—	—	—	—	—
1953	2,400,000	0.10	0.15	1.00	3.00	5.00
1953	—	**PF63** 400				

Date	Mintage	VF20	XF40	MS60	MS63	MS65
1964	2,160,000	0.10	0.15	1.00	1.50	3.00
1964 Proof; Rare	—	—	—	—	—	—
1965	1,440,000	0.10	0.15	1.00	1.50	3.00
1966	1,680,000	0.10	0.15	1.00	1.50	3.00
1967	1,200,000	0.10	0.15	1.00	1.50	3.00

KM# 11 PENNY
9.45 g., Bronze, 30.9 mm. **Obv:** Irish harp **Obv. Legend:** EIRE (Ireland) **Rev:** Hen with chicks **Edge:** Plain **Note:** Varieties exist.

Date	Mintage	VF20	XF40	MS60	MS63	MS65
1940	312,000	5.00	25.00	175	400	—
1940 Proof; Rare	—	—	—	—	—	—
1941	4,680,000	0.25	1.50	12.00	25.00	35.00
1941 Proof; Rare	—	—	—	—	—	—
1942	17,520,000	0.25	1.50	5.00	10.00	20.00
1942 Proof; Rare	—	—	—	—	—	—
1943	3,360,000	0.75	1.50	10.00	20.00	30.00
1946	4,800,000	0.25	1.50	5.00	15.00	25.00
1946 Proof; Rare	—	—	—	—	—	—
1948	4,800,000	0.25	1.50	3.00	5.00	7.50
1948 Proof; Rare	—	—	—	—	—	—
1949	4,080,000	0.25	1.50	3.00	5.00	7.50
1949	—	**PF63** 600				
1950	2,400,000	0.25	0.50	1.50	7.50	10.00
1950	—	**PF63** 600				
1952	2,400,000	0.25	0.50	1.00	3.00	5.00
1952 Proof; Rare	—	—	—	—	—	—
1962	1,200,000	0.75	1.00	1.50	5.00	7.50
1962	—	**PF63** 175				
1963	—	**PF63** 175				
1963	9,600,000	—	0.25	0.50	0.75	1.50
1964	6,000,000	—	0.25	0.50	0.75	1.50
1964 Proof; Rare	—	—	—	—	—	—
1965	11,160,000	—	0.25	0.50	0.75	1.50
1966	6,000,000	—	0.25	0.50	0.75	1.50
1967	2,400,000	—	0.25	0.50	0.75	1.50
1968	21,000,000	—	0.25	0.50	0.75	1.50
1968	—	**PF63** 350				

KM# 12 3 PENCE
3.24 g., Nickel, 17.6 mm. **Obv:** Irish harp **Obv. Legend:** EIRE (Ireland) **Rev:** Hare **Edge:** Plain

Date	Mintage	VF20	XF40	MS60	MS63	MS65
1939	64,000	5.00	10.00	35.00	250	375
1939	—	**PF63** 1,725				
1940	720,000	1.50	3.00	12.50	35.00	75.00
1940 Proof; Rare	—	—	—	—	—	—

KM# 12a 3 PENCE
3.24 g., Copper-Nickel, 18 mm. **Obv:** Irish harp **Obv. Legend:** EIRE (Ireland) **Rev:** Hare **Edge:** Plain

Date	Mintage	VF20	XF40	MS60	MS63	MS65
1942	—	**PF63** 750				
1942	4,000,000	1.00	3.00	12.00	18.00	30.00
1943 Proof; Rare	—	—	—	—	—	—
1943	1,360,000	2.00	5.00	25.00	45.00	75.00
1946	800,000	2.00	5.00	15.00	25.00	45.00
1946	—	**PF63** 200				
1948	1,600,000	4.00	10.00	40.00	75.00	120
1948 Proof; Rare	—	—	—	—	—	—
1949	—	**PF63** 200				
1949	1,200,000	0.25	1.50	7.50	15.00	25.00
1950	—	**PF63** 400				
1950	1,600,000	0.25	1.50	7.50	12.00	15.00
1953	1,600,000	0.25	1.50	5.00	7.50	10.00
1953 Proof; Rare	—	—	—	—	—	—
1956	1,200,000	0.25	1.00	3.00	8.00	15.00
1956 Proof; Rare	—	—	—	—	—	—
1961	2,400,000	0.15	0.50	1.50	3.00	5.00
1961 Proof; Rare	—	—	—	—	—	—
1962	3,200,000	0.15	0.50	1.50	3.00	5.00

Date	Mintage	VF20	XF40	MS60	MS63	MS65
1962 Proof; Rare	—	—	—	—	—	—
1963	4,000,000	0.15	0.50	1.50	3.00	5.00
1963 Proof; Rare	—	—	—	—	—	—
1964	4,000,000	0.15	0.50	1.00	1.50	3.00
1965	3,600,000	0.15	0.50	1.00	1.50	3.00
1966	4,000,000	0.15	0.50	1.00	1.50	3.00
1967	2,400,000	0.15	0.50	1.00	1.50	3.00
1968	4,000,000	0.15	0.50	1.00	1.50	3.00
1968 Proof; Rare	—	—	—	—	—	—

KM# 13 6 PENCE

4.54 g., Nickel, 20.8 mm. **Obv:** Irish harp **Obv. Legend:** EIRE (Ireland) **Rev:** Irish Wolfhound **Edge:** Plain

Date	Mintage	VF20	XF40	MS60	MS63	MS65
1939	876,000	0.75	2.00	8.00	25.00	50.00
1939	—	**PF63** 1,300				
1940	1,120,000	0.75	2.00	6.00	20.00	45.00
1940 Proof; Rare	—	—	—	—	—	—

KM# 13a 6 PENCE

4.54 g., Copper-Nickel, 20.8 mm. **Obv:** Irish harp **Obv. Legend:** EIRE (Ireland) **Rev:** Irish Wolfhound **Edge:** Plain

Date	Mintage	VF20	XF40	MS60	MS63	MS65
1942	1,320,000	1.00	5.00	20.00	35.00	50.00
1942 Proof; Rare	—	—	—	—	—	—
1945	400,000	5.00	20.00	90.00	200	350
1945 Proof; Rare	—	—	—	—	—	—
1946	720,000	5.00	20.00	120	250	500
1946 Proof; Rare	—	—	—	—	—	—
1947	800,000	5.00	10.00	35.00	50.00	80.00
1947 Proof; Rare	—	—	—	—	—	—
1948	800,000	1.50	5.00	15.00	35.00	50.00
1948 Proof; Rare	—	—	—	—	—	—
1949	600,000	1.50	5.00	15.00	35.00	50.00
1949 Proof; Rare	—	—	—	—	—	—
1950	800,000	1.00	5.00	15.00	35.00	50.00
1950 Proof; Rare	—	—	—	—	—	—
1952	800,000	1.00	3.00	5.00	12.00	25.00
1952	—	**PF63** 175				
1953	800,000	1.00	3.00	5.00	12.00	25.00
1953 Proof; Rare	—	—	—	—	—	—
1955	600,000	1.00	3.00	5.00	12.00	25.00
1955 Proof; Rare	—	—	—	—	—	—
1956	600,000	1.00	3.00	5.00	12.00	25.00
1956 Proof; Rare	—	—	—	—	—	—
1958	600,000	1.00	3.00	12.00	30.00	45.00
1958	—	**PF63** 350				
1959	2,000,000	0.25	1.00	5.00	12.00	25.00
1959 Proof; Rare	—	—	—	—	—	—
1960	2,020,000	0.25	1.00	3.00	7.50	20.00
1960 Proof; Rare	—	—	—	—	—	—
1961	3,000,000	0.25	0.75	1.50	3.00	5.00
1961 Proof; Rare	—	—	—	—	—	—
1962	4,000,000	0.25	1.00	10.00	25.00	35.00
1962 Proof; Rare	—	—	—	—	—	—
1963	4,000,000	0.15	0.25	1.00	3.00	5.00
1963 Proof; Rare	—	—	—	—	—	—
1964	6,000,000	0.15	0.25	1.00	3.00	5.00
1966	2,000,000	0.15	0.25	1.00	3.00	5.00
1967	4,000,000	0.15	0.25	1.00	3.00	5.00
1968	8,000,000	0.15	0.25	1.00	3.00	5.00
1969	2,000,000	0.15	0.25	1.00	3.00	5.00

KM# 14 SHILLING

5.66 g., 0.750 Silver 0.1364 oz. ASW, 23.6 mm. **Obv:** Irish harp **Obv. Legend:** EIRE (Ireland) **Rev:** Bull and value **Edge:** Reeded

Date	Mintage	VF20	XF40	MS60	MS63	MS65
1939	1,140,000	3.00	5.00	25.00	35.00	75.00
1939	—	**PF63** 1,050				
1940	580,000	3.00	5.00	20.00	35.00	75.00
1940 Proof; Rare	—	—	—	—	—	—
1941	300,000	3.00	5.00	25.00	40.00	80.00

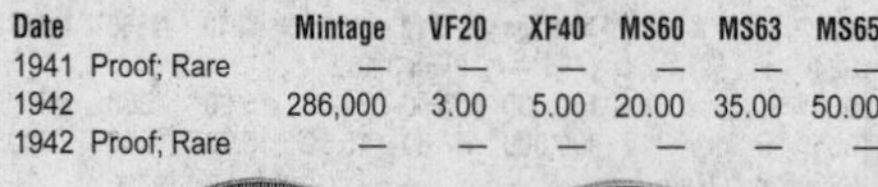

Date	Mintage	VF20	XF40	MS60	MS63	MS65
1941 Proof; Rare	—	—	—	—	—	—
1942	286,000	3.00	5.00	20.00	35.00	50.00
1942 Proof; Rare	—	—	—	—	—	—

KM# 14a SHILLING

5.66 g., Copper-Nickel, 23.6 mm. **Obv:** Irish harp **Obv. Legend:** EIRE (Ireland) **Rev:** Bull **Edge:** Reeded

Date	Mintage	VF20	XF40	MS60	MS63	MS65
1951	2,000,000	0.25	1.00	5.00	10.00	18.00
1951	—	**PF63** 500				
1954	3,000,000	0.25	1.00	5.00	10.00	18.00
1954 Proof; Rare	—	—	—	—	—	—
1955	1,000,000	0.25	1.00	5.00	10.00	18.00
1955 Proof; Rare	—	—	—	—	—	—
1959	2,000,000	0.25	1.00	10.00	20.00	35.00
1959 Proof; Rare	—	—	—	—	—	—
1962	4,000,000	0.25	1.00	3.00	7.50	10.00
1962 Proof; Rare	—	—	—	—	—	—
1963	4,000,000	0.25	1.00	3.00	5.00	7.50
1963 Proof; Rare	—	—	—	—	—	—
1964	4,000,000	0.25	1.00	3.00	5.00	7.50
1966	3,000,000	0.25	1.00	3.00	5.00	7.50
1968	4,000,000	0.25	1.00	3.00	5.00	7.50

KM# 15 FLORIN

11.31 g., 0.750 Silver 0.2727 oz. ASW, 28.5 mm. **Obv:** Irish harp **Obv. Legend:** EIRE (Ireland) **Rev:** Salmon and value **Edge:** Reeded

Date	Mintage	VF20	XF40	MS60	MS63	MS65
1939	1,080,000	7.50	12.00	35.00	60.00	90.00
1939	—	**PF63** 1,050				
1940	670,000	7.50	12.00	35.00	60.00	90.00
1940 Proof; Rare	—	—	—	—	—	—
1941	—	**PF63** 925				
1941	400,000	7.50	12.00	35.00	60.00	90.00
1942	109,000	7.50	12.00	35.00	50.00	75.00
1943	—	8,000	12,500	—	—	—

Note: Approximately 35 known

KM# 15a FLORIN

11.31 g., Copper-Nickel, 28.5 mm. **Obv:** Irish harp **Obv. Legend:** EIRE (Ireland) **Rev:** Salmon **Edge:** Reeded

Date	Mintage	VF20	XF40	MS60	MS63	MS65
1951	1,000,000	1.00	2.00	7.50	12.00	20.00
1951	—	**PF63** 600				
1954	1,000,000	1.00	2.00	7.50	12.00	20.00
1954	—	**PF63** 900				
1955	1,000,000	1.00	2.00	7.50	12.00	20.00
1955	—	**PF63** 900				
1959	2,000,000	0.50	1.00	5.00	9.00	15.00
1959 Proof; Rare	—	—	—	—	—	—
1961	2,000,000	0.50	1.00	10.00	15.00	25.00
1961 Proof; Rare	—	—	—	—	—	—
1962	2,400,000	0.50	1.00	3.00	9.00	15.00
1962 Proof; Rare	—	—	—	—	—	—
1963	3,000,000	0.25	1.00	3.00	4.00	15.00
1963 Proof; Rare	—	—	—	—	—	—
1964	4,000,000	0.25	1.00	3.00	5.00	7.50
1965	2,000,000	0.25	1.00	3.00	5.00	7.50
1966	3,625,000	0.25	1.00	3.00	5.00	7.50
1968	1,000,000	0.25	1.00	3.00	5.00	7.50
1969	—	0.25	1.00	3.00	5.00	7.50

KM# 16 1/2 CROWN

14.14 g., 0.750 Silver 0.3409 oz. ASW, 32.3 mm. **Obv:** Irish harp **Obv. Legend:** EIRE (Ireland) **Rev:** Horse and value **Edge:** Reeded **Note:** Normal spacing between O and I in COROIN, 7 tufts in horse's tail, with 151 beads in border.

Date	Mintage	VF20	XF40	MS60	MS63	MS65
1939	888,000	7.50	15.00	30.00	50.00	125
1939	—	**PF63** 1,050				
1940	752,000	7.50	15.00	35.00	65.00	150
1940 Proof; Rare	—	—	—	—	—	—
1941	320,000	7.50	15.00	45.00	85.00	175
1941 Proof; Rare	—	—	—	—	—	—
1942	286,000	7.50	12.00	30.00	50.00	90.00
1943	Est. 1000	300	525	1,650	4,250	—

Note: Approximately 500 known

KM# 16a 1/2 CROWN

14.16 g., Copper-Nickel, 32.3 mm. **Obv:** Irish harp **Obv. Legend:** EIRE (Ireland) **Rev:** Horse **Edge:** Reeded **Note:** Normal spacing between O and I on "COROIN", 7 tufts in horse's tail, with 151 beads in border.

Date	Mintage	VF20	XF40	MS60	MS63	MS65
1951	800,000	3.00	5.00	15.00	25.00	35.00
1951	—	**PF63** 600				
1954	400,000	3.00	5.00	20.00	30.00	45.00
1954	—	**PF63** 500				
1955	1,080,000	1.00	2.00	10.00	15.00	25.00
1955	—	**PF63** 1,000				
1959	1,600,000	1.00	1.75	7.50	10.00	15.00
1959 Proof; Rare	—	—	—	—	—	—
1961	1,600,000	1.00	1.75	7.50	10.00	15.00
1961 Proof; Rare	—	—	—	—	—	—
1962	3,200,000	0.50	1.00	5.00	7.50	10.00
1962 Proof; Rare	—	—	—	—	—	—
1963	2,400,000	0.50	1.00	5.00	7.50	10.00
1963 Proof; Rare	—	—	—	—	—	—
1964	3,200,000	0.50	1.00	2.00	5.00	7.50
1966	700,000	0.75	1.50	3.00	6.00	9.00
1967	2,000,000	0.50	1.00	2.00	5.00	7.50

Note: 1967 exists struck with a polished reverse die; Estimated value is $15.00 in Uncirculated

KM# 17 1/2 CROWN

Copper-Nickel **Obv:** Irish harp **Rev:** Horse **Note:** Mule. Distinguishing characteristics: 2s6d the d is open, PM the P is not under the hoof.

Date	Mintage	VF20	XF40	MS60	MS63	MS65
1961	Inc. above	8.00	25.00	100	750	—

KM# 18 10 SHILLING

18.14 g., 0.8333 Silver 0.486 oz. ASW, 30.5 mm. **Subject:** 50th Anniversary - Irish Uprising of Easter, 1916 **Obv:** Bust right **Obv. Legend:** EIRE 1966 **Rev:** Monument **Edge Lettering:** EIRI AMAC NA CASCA 1916 (both normal and inverted)

Date	Mintage	VF20	XF40	MS60	MS63	MS65
1966	Est. 2000000	—	12.00	15.00	18.00	25.00

Note: Approximately 1,270,000 melted down

Date	Mintage		
1966	20,000	**PF63** 25.00	**PF65** 35.00

DECIMAL COINAGE

100 Pence = 1 Pound (Punt)

KM# 19 1/2 PENNY

1.78 g., Bronze, 17.1 mm. **Obv:** Irish harp **Rev:** Stylized bird and value **Edge:** Plain

Date	Mintage	VF20	XF40	MS60	MS63	MS65
1971	100,500,000	—	0.10	0.25	0.35	0.50
1971	50,000	**PF65** 1.00				
1975	10,500,000	—	0.10	0.25	0.35	0.50
1976	5,464,000	—	0.10	0.25	0.35	0.50
1978	20,302,000	—	—	0.25	0.35	0.50
1980	20,616,000	—	—	0.25	0.35	0.50
1982	9,660,000	—	0.10	0.25	0.35	0.50
1985	2,784,000	—	—	—	2,000	3,000
1986	Est. 12250	—	—	—	—	—

Note: This mintage figure represents a surplus of coins minted for Polished Standard Specimen Sets (Proof Sets) later released into circulation. The entire surplus was presumably remelted due to demonitization of this denomination Jan. 1, 1987.

Date	Mintage	VF20	XF40	MS60	MS63	MS65
1986	6,750	**PF65** 150				

KM# 20 PENNY

3.56 g., Bronze, 20.3 mm. **Obv:** Irish harp **Rev:** Stylized bird and value **Edge:** Plain

Date	Mintage	VF20	XF40	MS60	MS63	MS65
1971	100,500,000	—	0.10	0.30	0.45	0.75
1971	50,000	**PF65** 1.25				
1974	10,000,000	—	0.10	0.35	0.50	0.75
1975	10,000,000	—	0.10	0.35	0.50	0.75
1976	38,164,000	—	0.10	0.30	0.45	0.75
1978	25,746,000	—	0.10	0.30	0.45	0.75
1979	21,766,000	—	0.10	0.30	0.45	0.75
1980	86,712,000	—	0.10	0.30	0.45	0.75
1982	54,189,000	—	0.10	0.30	0.45	0.75
1985	19,242,000	—	0.10	0.30	0.45	0.75
1986	36,584,000	—	0.10	0.30	0.45	0.75
1986	6,750	**PF65** 1.25				
1988	56,772,000	—	0.10	0.30	0.45	0.75

KM# 20a PENNY

3.56 g., Copper Plated Steel, 20.3 mm. **Obv:** Irish harp **Rev:** Styilized bird and value **Edge:** Plain

Date	Mintage	VF20	XF40	MS60	MS63	MS65
1988	Inc. above	—	—	—	—	—
1990	65,099,000	—	0.10	0.15	0.25	0.50
1992	25,643,000	—	0.10	0.15	0.25	0.50
1993	10,000,000	—	0.10	0.15	0.25	0.50
1994	45,800,000	—	0.10	0.15	0.25	0.50
1995	70,836,000	—	0.10	0.15	0.25	0.50
1996	190,092,000	—	0.10	0.15	0.25	0.50
1998	40,744,000	—	0.10	0.15	0.25	0.50
2000	133,760,000	—	0.10	0.15	0.25	0.50

KM# 21 2 PENCE

7.12 g., Bronze, 25.9 mm. **Obv:** Irish harp **Rev:** Stylized bird and value **Edge:** Plain

Date	Mintage	VF20	XF40	MS60	MS63	MS65
1971	75,500,000	—	—	1.00	1.20	1.50
1971	50,000	**PF65** 2.00				
1975	20,010,000	—	0.10	0.40	0.60	0.75
1976	5,414,000	—	0.10	0.50	0.70	0.85
1978	12,000,000	—	0.10	0.40	0.60	0.75
1979	32,373,000	—	0.10	0.40	0.60	0.75
1980	59,828,000	—	0.10	0.40	0.60	0.75
1982	30,435,000	—	0.10	0.40	0.60	0.75
1985	14,469,000	—	0.10	0.40	0.60	0.75
1986	23,865,000	—	0.10	0.40	0.60	0.75
1986	6,750	**PF65** 1.50				
1988	35,868,000	—	0.10	0.40	0.60	0.75

KM# 21a 2 PENCE

7.12 g., Copper Plated Steel, 25.9 mm. **Obv:** Irish harp **Rev:** Stylized bird **Edge:** Plain

Date	Mintage	VF20	XF40	MS60	MS63	MS65
1988	Inc. above	—	—	—	—	—
1990	34,284,000	—	0.10	0.25	0.35	0.50
1992	10,215,000	—	0.10	0.25	0.35	0.50
1995	55,459,000	—	0.10	0.25	0.35	0.50
1996	69,342,000	—	0.10	0.25	0.35	0.50
1998	33,688,000	—	0.10	0.25	0.35	0.50
2000	66,960,000	—	0.10	0.25	0.35	0.50

KM# 22 5 PENCE

5.66 g., Copper-Nickel, 23.6 mm. **Obv:** Irish harp **Rev:** Bull right **Edge:** Reeded

Date	Mintage	VF20	XF40	MS60	MS63	MS65
1969	5,000,000	0.10	0.15	0.75	1.00	1.25
1970	10,000,000	—	0.10	0.75	1.00	1.25
1971	8,000,000	—	0.10	0.75	1.00	1.25
1971	50,000	**PF65** 2.00				
1974	7,000,000	—	0.10	0.75	1.00	1.25
1975	10,000,000	—	0.10	0.75	1.00	1.25
1976	20,616,000	—	0.10	0.75	1.00	1.25
1978	28,536,000	—	0.10	0.75	1.00	1.25
1980	22,190,000	—	0.10	0.75	1.00	1.25
1982	24,404,000	—	0.10	0.75	1.00	1.25
1985	4,202,000	—	0.10	0.75	1.00	1.25
1986	15,298,000	0.10	0.15	0.75	1.00	1.25
1986	6,750	**PF65** 2.00				
1990	7,547,000	—	0.10	0.75	1.00	1.25

KM# 28 5 PENCE

3.25 g., Copper-Nickel, 18.5 mm. **Obv:** Irish harp **Rev:** Bull left **Edge:** Reeded **Note:** Reduced size: 18.5mm. Varieties exist.

Date	Mintage	VF20	XF40	MS60	MS63	MS65
1992	74,526,000	—	0.10	0.35	0.50	0.75
1993	89,109,000	—	0.10	0.35	0.50	0.75
1994	31,058,000	—	0.10	0.35	0.50	0.75
1995	14,667,000	—	0.10	0.35	0.50	0.75
1996	158,546,000	—	0.10	0.35	0.50	0.75
1998	63,247,000	—	0.10	0.35	0.50	0.75
2000	58,000,000	—	0.10	0.35	0.50	0.75

KM# 23 10 PENCE

11.32 g., Copper-Nickel, 28.5 mm. **Obv:** Irish harp **Rev:** Salmon right **Edge:** Reeded

Date	Mintage	VF20	XF40	MS60	MS63	MS65
1969	27,000,000	—	0.40	1.25	1.50	2.00
1971	4,000,000	—	0.40	1.25	1.50	2.00
1971	50,000	**PF65** 2.50				
1973	2,500,000	—	0.40	1.50	1.75	2.50
1974	7,500,000	—	0.35	1.25	1.50	2.00
1975	15,000,000	—	0.35	1.25	1.50	2.00
1976	9,433,000	—	0.35	1.25	1.50	2.00
1978	30,905,000	—	0.25	1.00	1.25	1.75
1980	44,605,000	—	0.25	1.00	1.25	1.75
1982	7,374,000	—	0.25	1.00	1.25	1.75
1985	4,099,999	—	0.25	1.25	1.50	2.00
1986	Est. 4250	2.00	5.00	12.50	17.50	—

Note: This mintage figure represents a surplus of coins minted for Polished Standard Specimen Sets (Proof Sets), later released into circulation.

Date	Mintage	VF20	XF40	MS60	MS63	MS65
1986	6,750	**PF65** 16.50				

KM# 29 10 PENCE

5.45 g., Copper-Nickel, 22 mm. **Obv:** Irish harp **Rev:** Salmon left **Edge:** Reeded **Note:** Reduced size.

Date	Mintage	VF20	XF40	MS60	MS63	MS65
1993	80,061,000	—	0.25	0.50	0.75	1.25
1994	58,510,000	—	0.25	0.50	0.75	1.25
1995	15,781,000	—	0.25	0.50	0.75	1.25
1996	18,402,000	—	0.25	0.50	0.75	1.25
1997	10,033,000	—	0.25	0.50	0.75	1.25
1998	10,000,000	—	0.25	0.50	0.75	1.25
1999	24,500,000	—	0.25	0.50	0.75	1.25
2000	45,679,000	—	0.25	0.50	0.75	1.25

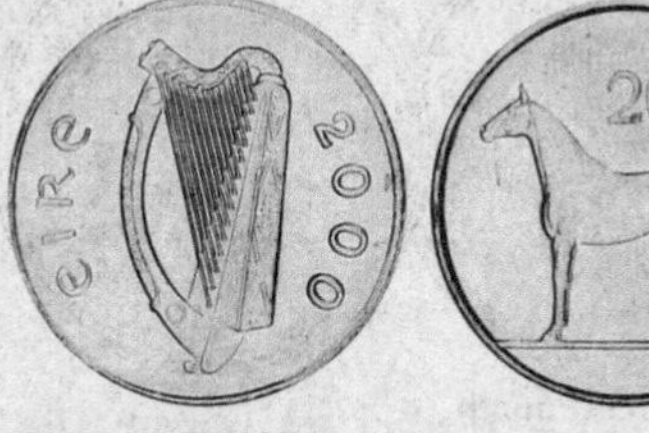

KM# 25 20 PENCE

8.47 g., Nickel-Bronze, 27.1 mm. **Obv:** Irish harp **Rev:** Horse **Edge:** Segmented reeding

Date	Mintage	VF20	XF40	MS60	MS63	MS65
1986	6,750	**PF65** 3.50				
1986	50,430,000	—	0.50	1.50	2.50	4.00
1988	20,661,000	—	0.50	1.50	2.50	4.00
1992	14,761,000	—	0.50	1.50	2.50	4.00
1994	11,086,000	—	0.50	1.50	2.50	4.00
1995	18,160,000	—	0.50	1.50	2.50	4.00
1996	29,291,000	—	0.50	1.50	2.50	4.00
1998	25,024,000	—	0.50	1.50	2.50	4.00
1999	11,000,000	—	0.50	1.50	2.50	4.00
2000	28,500,000	—	0.50	1.50	2.50	4.00

KM# 24 50 PENCE

13.30 g., Copper-Nickel, 30 mm. **Obv:** Harp **Rev:** Woodcock **Edge:** Plain **Shape:** 7 curved sides

Date	Mintage	VF20	XF40	MS60	MS63	MS65
1970	9,000,000	—	1.50	3.00	4.00	5.00
1971	600,000	1.00	2.00	4.00	6.00	8.00
1971	50,000	**PF65** 3.50				
1974	1,000,000	1.00	2.00	5.00	7.00	9.00
1975	2,000,000	—	1.50	3.00	4.00	5.00
1976	3,000,000	—	1.25	2.00	3.00	4.00
1977	4,800,000	—	1.25	2.00	3.00	4.00
1978	4,500,000	—	1.25	2.00	3.00	4.00
1979	4,000,000	—	1.25	2.00	3.00	4.00
1981	6,000,000	—	1.00	1.50	2.50	3.50
1982	2,000,000	—	1.25	2.00	3.00	4.00
1983	7,000,000	—	1.00	1.50	2.50	3.50
1986	3,250	3.00	6.00	15.00	20.00	—

Note: This circulation mintage figure represents a surplus of coins minted for Polished Standard Specimen Sets (Proof Sets), later released into circulation

Date	Mintage	VF20	XF40	MS60	MS63	MS65
1986	6,750	**PF65** 18.50				
1988	Est. 7000500	—	1.00	2.00	2.75	3.50
1996	6,000,000	—	1.00	2.00	2.75	3.50
1997	6,000,000	—	1.00	2.00	2.75	3.50
1998	13,825,000	—	1.00	2.00	2.75	3.50
1999	7,000,000	—	1.00	2.00	2.75	3.50
2000	15,600,000	—	1.00	2.00	2.75	3.50

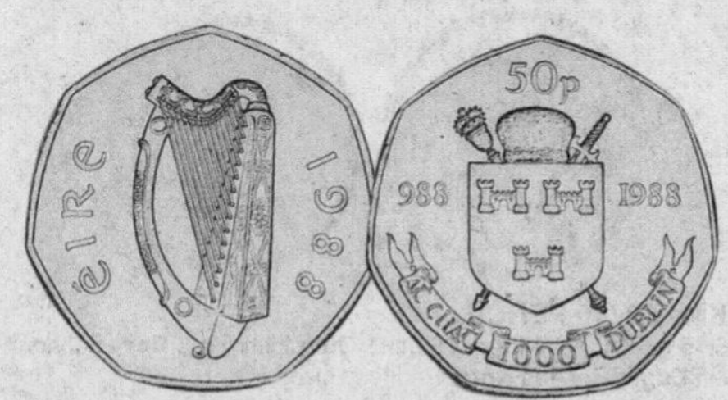

KM# 26 50 PENCE
13.50 g., Copper-Nickel, 30 mm. **Subject:** Dublin Millennium **Obv:** Irish harp **Rev:** Shield above banner with value above

Date	Mintage	VF20	XF40	MS60	MS63	MS65
1988	5,000,000	—	1.00	2.50	3.00	4.00
1988	50,000	PF65 15.00				

KM# 27 PUNT (Pound)
10.00 g., Copper-Nickel, 31.1 mm. **Obv:** Irish harp **Rev:** Irish Red Deer left **Note:** The normal KM27 was milled and engrailed. Examples with plain edge, or partial engrailing command a premium of approximately four times the values listed here.

Date	Mintage	VF20	XF40	MS60	MS63	MS65
1990	62,292,000	1.75	2.25	3.50	5.00	7.00
1990	42,000	PF63 12.00	PF65 15.00			
1994	14,925,000	1.75	2.25	4.00	6.00	8.00
1995	10,215,000	1.75	2.25	4.00	6.00	8.00
1996	9,230,000	1.75	2.25	4.00	6.00	8.00
1998	22,955,000	1.75	2.25	4.00	6.00	8.00
1999	10,000,000	1.75	2.25	4.00	6.00	8.00
2000	31,913,000	1.75	2.25	4.00	6.00	8.00

KM# 30 PUNT (Pound)
28.28 g., 0.925 Silver 0.841 oz. ASW, 38.6 mm. **Subject:** 50th Anniversary - United Nations **Obv:** Irish harp above dates **Rev:** Dove holding banner with dates to left of U.N. logo and numeral 50 **Rev. Inscription:** NATIONS UNITED FOR PEACE **Edge:** Milled

Date	Mintage	VF20	XF40	MS60	MS63	MS65
ND-1995	—	PF63 35.00	PF65 50.00			

KM# 31 PUNT (Pound)
10.00 g., Copper-Nickel **Subject:** Millennium **Obv:** Irish harp **Rev:** Cross within stylized ancient ship **Edge:** Milled and engrailed

Date	Mintage	VF20	XF40	MS60	MS63	MS65
2000	5,000,000	—	1.50	2.00	2.50	3.75

PATTERNS

Including off metal strikes

KM#	Date	Mintage	Identification	Mkt Val
Pn1	1938	—	Penny. Bronze. KM11.	—
Note: One in National Museum of Ireland and one in private hands				
Pn2	1938	—	1/2 Crown. 0.750. Silver. KM16. Unique.	—
Note: In National Museum of Ireland				
Pn3	1985	—	20 Pence. Nickel-Bronze. KM#25.	9,000

PROVAS

Publio Morbiducci Series

KM#	Date	Mintage	Identification	Mkt Val
Pr1	1927	—	Farthing.	—
Pr2	1927	—	1/2 Penny.	—
Pr3	1927	—	Penny. Silver Plated Bronze. Irish harp. Hen with chicks.	9,000
Pr4	1927	4	3 Pence. Nickel. Irish harp. Hare.	8,000
Pr5	1927	4	6 Pence. Nickel. Irish harp. Irish wolfhound.	8,000
Pr6	1927	5	Shilling. Silver. Irish harp. Bull with head down.	8,000
Pr7	1927	4	Florin. Silver. Irish harp. Fish.	9,500
Pr8	1927	5	1/2 Crown. Silver. Irish harp. Rearing horse.	12,000
Pr9	1927	—	1/2 Crown. Copper. Irish harp. Rearing horse.	—

Note: This series exists in other than standard metals

PIEDFORT

KM#	Date	Mintage	Identification	Mkt Val
P1	2000	Est. 95000	Punt. Silver. Stylized ancient ship. as KM#31.	45.00

MINT SETS

KM#	Date	Mintage	Identification	Issue Price	Mkt Val
MS1	1928 (8)	—	KM#1-8	—	210
MS2	1966 (8)	96,000	KM9-11, 12a-16a	—	35.00
MS3	1969-1971 (6)	—	KM19-21(1971), 22 (1970), 23(1969), 24(1970), mixed dates	—	10.00
MS4	1971 (6)	—	KM19-24	1.50	12.00
MS4A	1975 (6)	—	KM19-24	—	—
MS5	1978 (6)	—	KM19-24	—	8.00
MS6	1982 (6)	—	KM19-24	—	7.00
MS7	1996 (7)	—	KM20a-21a, 24-25, 27-29	—	15.00
MS8	1998 (7)	—	KM20a-21a, 25-25, 27-29	—	15.00
MS9	2000 (7)	—	KM20a-21a, 24-25, 28-29, 31	—	15.00

PROOF SETS

KM#	Date	Mintage	Identification	Issue Price	Mkt Val
PS1	1928 (8)	6,001	KM1-8	—	400
PS2	1966 (2)	1,000	KM18. One of each: normal and inverted edge lettering	—	90.00
PS3	1971 (6)	50,000	KM19-24	4.40	12.00
PS4	1986 (7)	6,750	KM19-25	—	40.00

ISLE OF MAN

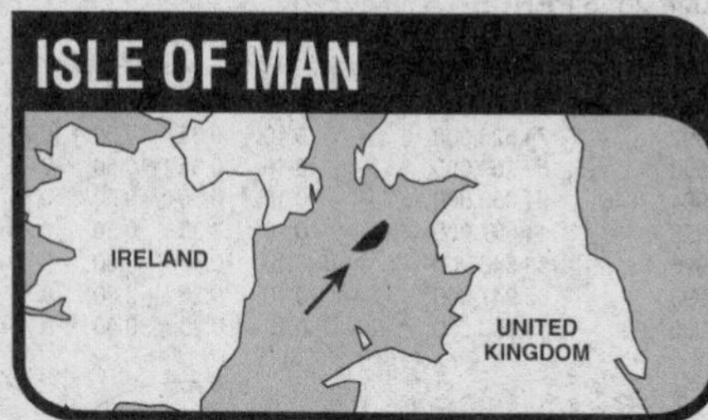

The Isle of Man, a dependency of the British Crown located in the Irish Sea equidistant from Ireland, Scotland and England, has an area of 227 sq. mi. (588 sq. km.) and a population of 68,000. Capital: Douglas. Agriculture, dairy farming, fishing and tourism are the chief industries.

The prevalence of prehistoric artifacts and monuments on the island give evidence that it's mild, almost sub-tropical climate was enjoyed by mankind before the dawn of history. Vikings came to the Isle of Man during the 9th century and remained until ejected by the Scottish in 1266. The island came under the protection of the British Crown in 1288, and in 1406 was granted, in perpetuity, to the earls of Derby, from whom it was inherited, 1736, by the Duke of Atholl. The British Crown purchased the rights and title in 1765; the remaining privileges of the Atholl family were transferred to the crown in 1829. The Isle of Man is ruled by its own legislative council and the House of Keys, the oldest, continuous legislative assembly in the world. Acts of Parliament passed in London do not affect the island unless it is specifically mentioned.

MINT MARK
PM - Pobjoy Mint

PRIVY MARKS
(a) - Big Apple - 1988
(at) - Angel Blowing Trumpet – 1997

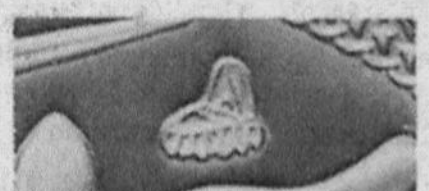

(b) - Baby crib - 1982
(ba) - Basel bugle - 1990
(bb) - Big Ben - 1987-1988
(br) - Brooklyn Bridge - 1989
(bs) - Teddy Bear in stocking - 1996
(c) - Chicago water tower CICF - 1990-1991
(cc) - Christmas cracker - 1991
(d) - St. Paul's Cathedral - 1989
(f) - FUN logo - 1988
(fl) - Fleur de Lis - 1990
(fr) - Frauenkirche - Munich Numismata - 1990-1991
(fw) - Fairy w/magic wand - 1999
(h) - Horse - Hong Kong Int. - 1990
(lc) - Lion crowned - 1989
(m) - Queen Mother's portrait - 1980
(ma) - Maple leaf - CNA - 1990
(mt) - Mistletoe - Christmas - 1987, 1989
(ns) - North Star - 1994
(p) - Carrier pigeon - Basel - 1988-1989
(pi) - Pine tree - 1986
(pt) - Partridge in a pear tree - 1988
(py) - Poppy - 1995
(s) - Bridge - SINPEX - 1987
(sb) - Soccer ball - 1982
(sc) - Santa Claus - 1995
(sg) - Sleigh - Christmas - 1990
(SL) - St. Louis Arch - 1987
(ss) - Sailing ship - Sydney – 1988
(st) – Statue of Liberty - 1987
(t) - Stylized triskelion - 1979
(tb) - Tower Bridge - 1990
(ti) - TICC logo - Tokyo - 1990
(v) - Viking ship - 1980
(vw) - Viking ship in wreath - 1986
(w) - Stylized triskelion - 1985
(x) - Snowman - 1998

PRIVY LETTERS
A - ANA - 1985-1992
C - Coinex, London - 1985-1989
D.M.I.H.E. - Ideal Home Exhibit, London, 1980
D.M.I.H.E.N. - Ideal Home Exhibit, Manchester, 1980
F - FUN - 1987
H - Hong Kong Expo - 1985
L - Long Beach - 1985-1987
T - Torex, Toronto - 1986
U - Uncirculated - 1988, 1990, 1994, 1995
X - Ameripex - 1986

BRITISH DEPENDENCY

DECIMAL COINAGE

100 Pence = 1 Pound

KM# 19 1/2 NEW PENNY
1.78 g., Bronze, 17.14 mm. **Ruler:** Elizabeth II **Obv:** Young bust right **Rev:** Flowered weed

Date	Mintage	VF20	XF40	MS60	MS63	MS65
1971	495,000	—	0.15	0.25	0.35	0.75
1971	10,000	PF65 1.50				
1972	1,000	—	—	—	18.00	20.00
1973	1,000	—	—	—	18.00	20.00
1974	1,000	—	—	—	18.00	20.00
1975	825,000	—	0.15	0.20	0.30	0.65

KM# 19a 1/2 NEW PENNY
2.10 g., 0.925 Silver 0.0625 oz. ASW, 17.14 mm. **Ruler:** Elizabeth II **Obv:** Young bust right **Rev:** Flowered weed

Date	Mintage	VF20	XF40	MS60	MS63	MS65
1975	20,000	—	—	—	2.50	3.00

KM# 19b 1/2 NEW PENNY
4.00 g., 0.950 Platinum 0.1222 oz. APW, 17.14 mm. **Ruler:** Elizabeth II **Obv:** Young bust right **Rev:** Flowered weed

Date	Mintage	VF20	XF40	MS60	MS63	MS65
1975	600	PF65 230				

KM# 32 1/2 PENNY
1.78 g., Bronze, 17.14 mm. **Ruler:** Elizabeth II **Obv:** Young bust right **Rev:** Atlantic herring

Date	Mintage	VF20	XF40	MS60	MS63	MS65
1976	600,000	—	0.20	0.30	0.45	1.00
1978	—	—	0.20	0.30	0.45	1.00
1978	—	PF65 1.25				
1979 AA(t)	—	—	0.20	0.30	0.45	1.00
1979 AB(t)	—	—	0.20	0.30	0.45	1.00

KM# 32a 1/2 PENNY

2.10 g., 0.925 Silver 0.0625 oz. ASW, 17.14 mm. **Ruler:** Elizabeth II **Obv:** Young bust right **Rev:** Atlantic herring

Date	Mintage	VF20	XF40	MS60	MS63	MS65
1976	20,000	—	—	—	2.25	2.75
1978	10,000	—	—	—	2.25	2.75
1979 (t)	10,000	PF65 3.00				

KM# 32b 1/2 PENNY

4.00 g., 0.950 Platinum 0.1222 oz. APW, 17.14 mm. **Ruler:** Elizabeth II **Obv:** Young bust right **Rev:** Atlantic herring

Date	Mintage	VF20	XF40	MS60	MS63	MS65
1976	600	PF65 250				
1978	600	PF65 250				
1979 (t)	500	PF65 250				

KM# 40 1/2 PENNY

1.78 g., Bronze, 17.14 mm. **Ruler:** Elizabeth II **Series:** F.A.O. **Obv:** Young bust right **Rev:** Atlantic herring

Date	Mintage	VF20	XF40	MS60	MS63	MS65
1977	700,000	—	0.20	0.30	0.45	1.00
Note: 1977 PM on both sides						
1977	Inc. above	—	—	—	5.00	6.00
Note: 1977 PM on obverse only						

KM# 40a 1/2 PENNY

2.10 g., 0.925 Silver 0.0625 oz. ASW, 17.14 mm. **Ruler:** Elizabeth II **Obv:** Young bust right **Rev:** Atlantic herring

Date	Mintage	VF20	XF40	MS60	MS63	MS65
1977	10,000	PF65 4.00				

KM# 58 1/2 PENNY

1.78 g., Bronze, 17.14 mm. **Ruler:** Elizabeth II **Obv:** Young bust right **Rev:** Atlantic herring within net

Date	Mintage	VF20	XF40	MS60	MS63	MS65
1980 AA	—	—	0.15	0.25	0.35	0.75
1980 AB	—	—	0.15	0.25	0.35	0.75
1980 PM DD	—	PF65 1.00				
1981 AA	—	—	0.15	0.25	0.35	0.75
1981 DD	—	PF65 1.00				
1982 AA	—	—	0.15	0.25	0.35	0.75
1982 (b)	—	—	0.15	0.25	0.35	0.75
1982 (b)	25,000	PF65 1.00				
1983 AA	—	—	0.15	0.25	0.35	0.75

KM# 58a 1/2 PENNY

2.10 g., 0.500 Silver 0.0338 oz. ASW, 17.14 mm. **Ruler:** Elizabeth II **Obv:** Young bust right **Rev:** Atlantic herring within net

Date	Mintage	VF20	XF40	MS60	MS63	MS65
1980	10,000	PF65 4.00				

KM# 58b 1/2 PENNY

2.10 g., 0.925 Silver 0.0625 oz. ASW, 17.14 mm. **Ruler:** Elizabeth II **Obv:** Young bust right **Rev:** Atlantic herring within net

Date	Mintage	VF20	XF40	MS60	MS63	MS65
1982	10,000	PF65 4.00				
1983	5,000	PF65 5.00				

KM# 58c 1/2 PENNY

3.55 g., 0.917 Gold 0.1047 oz. AGW, 17.14 mm. **Ruler:** Elizabeth II **Obv:** Young bust right **Rev:** Atlantic herring within net

Date	Mintage	VF20	XF40	MS60	MS63	MS65
1980	—	PF65 190				
1982 (b)	500	PF65 190				
1983	—	PF65 190				

KM# 58d 1/2 PENNY

4.00 g., 0.950 Platinum 0.1222 oz. APW, 17.14 mm. **Ruler:** Elizabeth II **Obv:** Young bust right **Rev:** Atlantic herring within net

Date	Mintage	VF20	XF40	MS60	MS63	MS65
1980	500	PF65 250				
1982 (b)	500	PF65 250				
1983	—	PF65 250				

KM# 72.1 1/2 PENNY

1.78 g., Bronze, 17.14 mm. **Ruler:** Elizabeth II **Series:** F.A.O. **Obv:** Young bust right **Rev:** Atlantic herring, F.A.O. above

Date	Mintage	VF20	XF40	MS60	MS63	MS65
1981	—	—	—	0.35	0.50	1.00

KM# 72.2 1/2 PENNY

1.78 g., Bronze, 17.14 mm. **Ruler:** Elizabeth II **Subject:** World Food Day **Obv:** Young bust right **Rev:** Atlantic herring, 16-10-81 above

Date	Mintage	VF20	XF40	MS60	MS63	MS65
1981	10,000	2.00	5.00	7.00	10.00	12.50

KM# 111 1/2 PENNY

1.78 g., Bronze, 17.14 mm. **Ruler:** Elizabeth II **Subject:** Quincentenary of the College of Arms **Obv:** Young bust right **Rev:** Fuchsia blossom on garnished and scrolled shield

Date	Mintage	VF20	XF40	MS60	MS63	MS65
1984 AA	—	—	—	—	0.15	0.25

KM# 111a 1/2 PENNY

2.10 g., 0.925 Silver 0.0625 oz. ASW, 17.14 mm. **Ruler:** Elizabeth II **Obv:** Young bust right **Rev:** Fuchsia blossom on garnished and scrolled shield

Date	Mintage	VF20	XF40	MS60	MS63	MS65
1984	—	PF65 5.00				

KM# 111b 1/2 PENNY

3.55 g., 0.917 Gold 0.1047 oz. AGW, 17.14 mm. **Ruler:** Elizabeth II **Obv:** Young bust right **Rev:** Fuchsia blossom on garnished and scrolled shield

Date	Mintage	VF20	XF40	MS60	MS63	MS65
1984	150	PF65 190				

KM# 142 1/2 PENNY

1.78 g., Bronze, 17.14 mm. **Ruler:** Elizabeth II **Obv:** Crowned head right **Rev:** Fuchsia blossom on garnished and scrolled shield

Date	Mintage	VF20	XF40	MS60	MS63	MS65
1985 AA(w)	—	—	—	—	0.15	0.25
1985	50,000	PF65 2.00				

KM# 142a 1/2 PENNY

2.10 g., 0.925 Silver 0.0625 oz. ASW, 17.14 mm. **Ruler:** Elizabeth II **Obv:** Crowned head right **Rev:** Fuchsia blossom on garnished and scrolled shield

Date	Mintage	VF20	XF40	MS60	MS63	MS65
1985	10,000	PF65 4.00				

KM# 142b 1/2 PENNY

3.55 g., 0.917 Gold 0.1047 oz. AGW, 17.14 mm. **Ruler:** Elizabeth II **Obv:** Crowned head right **Rev:** Fuchsia blossom on garnished and scrolled shield

Date	Mintage	VF20	XF40	MS60	MS63	MS65
1985	300	PF65 190				

KM# 142c 1/2 PENNY

4.00 g., 0.950 Platinum 0.1222 oz. APW, 17.14 mm. **Ruler:** Elizabeth II **Obv:** Crowned head right **Rev:** Fuchsia blossom on garnished and scrolled shield

Date	Mintage	VF20	XF40	MS60	MS63	MS65
1985	200	PF65 250				

KM# 20 NEW PENNY

3.56 g., Bronze, 20.32 mm. **Ruler:** Elizabeth II **Obv:** Young bust right **Rev:** Celtic cross

Date	Mintage	VF20	XF40	MS60	MS63	MS65
1971	100,000	—	0.10	0.25	0.35	0.65
1971	10,000	PF65 2.00				
1972	1,000	—	—	—	18.00	20.00
1973	1,000	—	—	—	18.00	20.00
1974	1,000	—	—	—	18.00	20.00
1975	855,000	—	0.10	0.15	0.25	0.50

KM# 20a NEW PENNY

4.20 g., 0.925 Silver 0.1249 oz. ASW, 20.32 mm. **Ruler:** Elizabeth II **Obv:** Young bust right **Rev:** Celtic cross

Date	Mintage	VF20	XF40	MS60	MS63	MS65
1975	20,000	—	—	—	5.00	6.50

KM# 20b NEW PENNY

8.00 g., 0.950 Platinum 0.2443 oz. APW, 20.32 mm. **Ruler:** Elizabeth II **Obv:** Young bust right **Rev:** Celtic cross

Date	Mintage	VF20	XF40	MS60	MS63	MS65
1975	600	PF65 500				

KM# 33 PENNY

3.56 g., Bronze, 20.3 mm. **Ruler:** Elizabeth II **Obv:** Young bust right **Rev:** Loaghtyn sheep

Date	Mintage	VF20	XF40	MS60	MS63	MS65
1976	900,000	—	0.25	0.35	0.75	1.25
1977	1,000,000	—	0.25	0.35	0.75	1.25
1978	—	—	0.25	0.35	0.75	1.25
1978	—	PF65 1.50				
1979 AA(t)	—	—	0.25	0.35	0.75	1.25
1979 AB(t)	—	—	0.25	0.35	0.75	1.25
1979 AC(t)	—	—	0.25	0.35	0.75	1.25
1979 AD(t)	—	—	0.25	0.35	0.75	1.25
1979 AE(t)	—	—	0.25	0.35	0.75	1.25

KM# 33a PENNY

4.20 g., 0.925 Silver 0.1249 oz. ASW, 20.32 mm. **Ruler:** Elizabeth II **Obv:** Young bust right **Rev:** Loaghtyn sheep

Date	Mintage	VF20	XF40	MS60	MS63	MS65
1976	20,000	—	—	—	5.00	6.00
1977	10,000	PF65 6.00				
1978	10,000	—	—	—	5.00	6.00
1979 (t)	10,000	PF65 6.00				

KM# 33b PENNY

8.00 g., 0.950 Platinum 0.2443 oz. APW, 20.32 mm. **Ruler:** Elizabeth II **Obv:** Young bust right **Rev:** Loaghtyn sheep

Date	Mintage	VF20	XF40	MS60	MS63	MS65
1976	600	PF65 500				
1978	600	PF65 500				
1979 (t)	500	PF65 500				

KM# 59 PENNY

3.56 g., Bronze, 20.32 mm. **Ruler:** Elizabeth II **Obv:** Young bust right **Rev:** Manx cat

Date	Mintage	VF20	XF40	MS60	MS63	MS65
1980 AA	—	—	0.25	0.75	1.50	3.00
1980 AB	—	—	0.25	0.75	1.50	3.00
1980 AC	—	—	0.25	0.75	1.50	3.00
1980 AD	—	—	0.25	0.75	1.50	3.00
1980 PM DD	—	PF65 2.75				
1981 AA	—	—	0.25	0.75	1.50	3.00
1981 DD	—	PF65 2.75				
1982 AA	—	—	0.25	0.75	1.50	3.00
1982 (b)	—	—	0.25	0.75	1.50	3.00
1982 (b)	25,000	PF65 2.75				
1983 AA	—	—	0.25	0.75	1.50	3.00
1983 AC	—	—	0.25	0.75	1.50	3.00
1983 AB	—	—	0.25	0.75	1.50	3.00

KM# 59a PENNY

4.20 g., 0.500 Silver 0.0675 oz. ASW, 20.32 mm. **Ruler:** Elizabeth II **Obv:** Young bust right **Rev:** Manx cat

Date	Mintage	VF20	XF40	MS60	MS63	MS65
1980	10,000	PF65 6.00				

KM# 59b PENNY

4.20 g., 0.925 Silver 0.1249 oz. ASW, 20.32 mm. **Ruler:** Elizabeth II **Obv:** Young bust right **Rev:** Manx cat

Date	Mintage	VF20	XF40	MS60	MS63	MS65
1981	—	PF65 7.00				
1982 (b)	10,000	PF65 7.00				
1983	5,000	PF65 7.00				

KM# 59c PENNY

7.10 g., 0.917 Gold 0.2093 oz. AGW, 20.32 mm. **Ruler:** Elizabeth II **Obv:** Young bust right **Rev:** Manx cat

Date	Mintage	VF20	XF40	MS60	MS63	MS65
1980	300	PF65 400				
1982 (b)	500	PF65 400				
1983	—	PF65 400				

KM# 59d PENNY

8.00 g., 0.950 Platinum 0.2443 oz. APW, 20.32 mm. **Ruler:** Elizabeth II **Obv:** Young bust right **Rev:** Manx cat

Date	Mintage	VF20	XF40	MS60	MS63	MS65
1980	500	PF65 500				
1982 (b)	500	PF65 500				
1983	—	PF65 500				

KM# 112 PENNY
3.56 g., Bronze, 20.32 mm. **Ruler:** Elizabeth II **Subject:** Quincentenary of the College of Arms **Obv:** Young bust right **Rev:** Shag bird on tilting shield

Date	Mintage	VF20	XF40	MS60	MS63	MS65
1984 AA	—	—	0.25	0.35	0.50	1.50

KM# 112a PENNY
4.20 g., 0.925 Silver 0.1249 oz. ASW, 20.32 mm. **Ruler:** Elizabeth II **Obv:** Young bust right **Rev:** Shag bird on tilting shield

Date	Mintage	VF20	XF40	MS60	MS63	MS65
1984	—	PF65 6.00				

KM# 112b PENNY
7.10 g., 0.917 Gold 0.2093 oz. AGW, 20.32 mm. **Ruler:** Elizabeth II **Obv:** Young bust right **Rev:** Shag bird on tilting shield

Date	Mintage	VF20	XF40	MS60	MS63	MS65
1984	150	PF65 380				

KM# 143 PENNY
3.56 g., Bronze, 20.32 mm. **Ruler:** Elizabeth II **Obv:** Crowned head right **Rev:** Shag bird on tilting shield

Date	Mintage	VF20	XF40	MS60	MS63	MS65
1985 AA(w)	—	—	0.10	0.25	0.50	1.50
1985	50,000	PF65 2.00				
1986 AA	—	—	0.10	0.25	0.50	1.50
1987 AA	—	—	0.10	0.25	0.50	1.50
1987 AB	—	—	0.10	0.25	0.50	1.50
1987 AC	—	—	0.10	0.25	0.50	1.50

KM# 143a PENNY
4.20 g., 0.925 Silver 0.1249 oz. ASW, 20.32 mm. **Ruler:** Elizabeth II **Obv:** Crowned head right **Rev:** Shag bird on tilting shield

Date	Mintage	VF20	XF40	MS60	MS63	MS65
1985	10,000	PF65 5.00				

KM# 143b PENNY
7.10 g., 0.917 Gold 0.2093 oz. AGW, 20.32 mm. **Ruler:** Elizabeth II **Obv:** Crowned head right **Rev:** Shag bird on tilting shield

Date	Mintage	VF20	XF40	MS60	MS63	MS65
1985	300	PF65 380				

KM# 143c PENNY
8.00 g., 0.950 Platinum 0.2443 oz. APW, 20.32 mm. **Ruler:** Elizabeth II **Obv:** Crowned head right **Rev:** Shag bird on tilting shield

Date	Mintage	VF20	XF40	MS60	MS63	MS65
1985	200	PF65 500				

KM# 207 PENNY
3.56 g., Bronze, 20.32 mm. **Ruler:** Elizabeth II **Obv:** Crowned head right **Rev:** Precision lathe superimposed on a cog wheel

Date	Mintage	VF20	XF40	MS60	MS63	MS65
1988 AA	—	—	—	0.15	0.20	0.35
1988 AB	—	—	0.10	0.20	0.30	0.50
1988 AC	—	—	0.10	0.20	0.30	0.50
1988 AD	—	—	0.10	0.20	0.30	0.50
1989 AA	—	—	—	0.15	0.20	0.35
1989 AB	—	—	0.10	0.20	0.30	0.50
1989 AC	—	—	0.10	0.20	0.30	0.50
1989 AD	—	—	0.10	0.20	0.30	0.50
1989 AE	—	—	0.10	0.20	0.30	0.50
1990 AA	—	—	—	0.15	0.20	0.35
1991 AA	—	—	—	0.15	0.20	0.35
1991 AB	—	—	—	0.15	0.20	0.35
1991 AC	—	—	—	0.15	0.20	0.35
1991 AD	—	—	—	0.15	0.20	0.35
1991 AE	—	—	—	0.15	0.20	0.35
1992 AA	—	—	—	0.15	0.20	0.35
1993 AA	—	—	—	0.15	0.20	0.35
1994 AA	—	—	—	0.15	0.20	0.35
1995 AA	—	—	—	0.15	0.20	0.35

KM# 588 PENNY
3.56 g., Copper Plated Steel, 20.32 mm. **Ruler:** Elizabeth II **Subject:** Sports **Obv:** Crowned head right **Rev:** Rugby ball within 3/4 square and wreath

Date	Mintage	VF20	XF40	MS60	MS63	MS65
1996 AA	—	—	—	0.15	0.20	0.35
1997 AA	—	—	—	0.15	0.20	0.35
1998 AA	—	—	—	0.15	0.20	0.35

KM# 588a PENNY
4.20 g., 0.925 Silver 0.1249 oz. ASW, 20.32 mm. **Ruler:** Elizabeth II **Subject:** Sports **Obv:** Crowned head right **Rev:** Rugby ball within 3/4 square and wreath

Date	Mintage	VF20	XF40	MS60	MS63	MS65
1996	—	PF65 10.00				

KM# 823.1 PENNY
3.56 g., Copper Plated Steel, 20.32 mm. **Ruler:** Elizabeth II **Obv:** Head with tiara right **Rev:** Rugby ball within 3/4 square and wreath

Date	Mintage	VF20	XF40	MS60	MS63	MS65
1998 AA	—	—	—	0.15	0.20	0.35

KM# 823.2 PENNY
3.56 g., Copper Plated Steel, 20.32 mm. **Ruler:** Elizabeth II **Obv:** Head with tiara right with small triskeles dividing legend **Rev:** Rugby ball within 3/4 square and wreath

Date	Mintage	VF20	XF40	MS60	MS63	MS65
1998 PM AA	—	—	—	0.15	0.20	0.35
1999 PM AA	—	—	—	0.15	0.20	0.35
1999 PM AB	—	—	—	0.15	0.20	0.35
1999 PM BA	—	—	—	0.15	0.20	0.35

KM# 1036 PENNY
3.56 g., Copper Plated Steel, 20.32 mm. **Ruler:** Elizabeth II **Obv:** Head with tiara right with small triskeles dividing legend **Rev:** Ruins **Edge:** Plain

Date	Mintage	VF20	XF40	MS60	MS63	MS65
2000 PMM AA	—	—	—	0.15	0.25	0.45

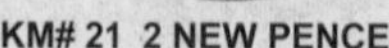

KM# 21 2 NEW PENCE
7.12 g., Bronze, 25.91 mm. **Ruler:** Elizabeth II **Obv:** Young bust right **Rev:** Falcons

Date	Mintage	VF20	XF40	MS60	MS63	MS65
1971	100,000	—	0.25	0.50	1.00	2.00
1971	10,000	PF65 2.50				
1972	1,000	—	—	—	18.00	20.00
1973	1,000	—	—	—	18.00	20.00
1974	1,000	—	—	—	18.00	20.00
1975	725,000	—	0.25	0.50	1.00	1.50

KM# 21a 2 NEW PENCE
8.40 g., 0.925 Silver 0.2498 oz. ASW, 25.91 mm. **Ruler:** Elizabeth II **Obv:** Young bust right **Rev:** Falcons

Date	Mintage	VF20	XF40	MS60	MS63	MS65
1975	20,000	—	—	—	8.50	9.50

KM# 21b 2 NEW PENCE
16.00 g., 0.950 Platinum 0.4887 oz. APW, 25.91 mm. **Ruler:** Elizabeth II **Obv:** Young bust right **Rev:** Falcons

Date	Mintage	VF20	XF40	MS60	MS63	MS65
1975	600	PF65 1,000				

KM# 34 2 PENCE
7.12 g., Bronze, 25.91 mm. **Ruler:** Elizabeth II **Obv:** Young bust right **Rev:** Bird in flight over map

Date	Mintage	VF20	XF40	MS60	MS63	MS65
1976	800,000	—	0.20	0.30	0.50	1.00
1977	1,000,000	—	0.20	0.30	0.50	1.00
1978	—	—	—	0.30	0.50	1.00
1978	—	PF65 1.25				
1979 AA(t)	10,000	—	0.20	0.30	0.50	1.00
1979 AB(t)	—	—	0.20	0.30	0.50	1.00
1979 AC(t)	—	—	0.20	0.30	0.50	1.00
1979 AD(t)	—	—	0.20	0.30	0.50	1.00
1979 AE(t)	—	—	0.20	0.30	0.50	1.00
1979 AF(t)	—	—	0.20	0.30	0.50	1.00
1979 AG(t)	—	—	0.20	0.30	0.50	1.00
1979 AH(t)	—	—	0.20	0.30	0.50	1.00

KM# 34a 2 PENCE
8.40 g., 0.925 Silver 0.2498 oz. ASW, 25.91 mm. **Ruler:** Elizabeth II **Obv:** Young bust right **Rev:** Bird in flight over map

Date	Mintage	VF20	XF40	MS60	MS63	MS65
1976	20,000	—	—	—	8.50	9.00
1977	10,000	PF65 9.50				
1978	10,000	—	—	—	8.50	9.00
1979 (t)	10,000	PF65 9.50				

KM# 34b 2 PENCE
16.00 g., 0.950 Platinum 0.4887 oz. APW, 25.91 mm. **Ruler:** Elizabeth II **Obv:** Young bust right **Rev:** Bird in flight over map

Date	Mintage	VF20	XF40	MS60	MS63	MS65
1976	600	PF65 950				
1977	600	PF65 950				
1978	—	PF65 950				
1979 (t)	500	PF65 950				

KM# 60 2 PENCE
7.12 g., Bronze, 25.91 mm. **Ruler:** Elizabeth II **Obv:** Young bust right **Rev:** Red Billed Chough bird in center of design

Date	Mintage	VF20	XF40	MS60	MS63	MS65
1980 AA	—	—	0.25	0.35	0.70	1.50
1980 AB	—	—	0.25	0.35	0.70	1.50
1980 AC	—	—	0.25	0.35	0.70	1.50
1980 AD	—	—	0.25	0.35	0.70	1.50
1980 PM DD	—	PF65 1.75				
1981 AA	—	—	0.25	0.35	0.70	1.50
1981 AB	—	—	0.25	0.35	0.70	1.50
1981 DD	—	PF65 1.75				
1982 AA	—	—	0.25	0.35	0.70	1.50
1982 (b)	—	—	0.25	0.35	0.70	1.50
1982 (b)	25,000	PF65 1.75				
1983 AA	—	—	0.25	0.35	0.70	1.50
1983 AB	—	—	0.25	0.35	0.70	1.50
1983 AC	—	—	0.25	0.35	0.70	1.50
1983 AD	—	—	0.25	0.35	0.70	1.50
1983 AE	—	—	0.25	0.35	0.70	1.50

KM# 60a 2 PENCE
8.40 g., 0.500 Silver 0.135 oz. ASW, 25.91 mm. **Ruler:** Elizabeth II **Obv:** Young bust right **Rev:** Bird in center of design

Date	Mintage	VF20	XF40	MS60	MS63	MS65
1980	10,000	PF65 8.50				

KM# 60b 2 PENCE
8.40 g., 0.925 Silver 0.2498 oz. ASW, 25.91 mm. **Ruler:** Elizabeth II **Obv:** Young bust right **Rev:** Bird in center of design

Date	Mintage	VF20	XF40	MS60	MS63	MS65
1981	—	PF65 10.00				
1982 (b)	10,000	PF65 8.50				
1983	5,000	PF65 9.00				

KM# 60c 2 PENCE
14.20 g., 0.917 Gold 0.4186 oz. AGW, 25.91 mm. **Ruler:** Elizabeth II **Obv:** Young bust right **Rev:** Bird in center of design

Date	Mintage	VF20	XF40	MS60	MS63	MS65
1980	300	PF65 750				
1982 (b)	500	PF65 750				
1983	—	PF65 750				

KM# 60d 2 PENCE
16.00 g., 0.950 Platinum 0.4887 oz. APW, 25.91 mm. **Ruler:** Elizabeth II **Obv:** Young bust right **Rev:** Bird in center of design

Date	Mintage	VF20	XF40	MS60	MS63	MS65
1980	500	PF65 950				
1982 (b)	500	PF65 950				
1983	—	PF65 950				

KM# 113 2 PENCE
7.12 g., Bronze, 25.91 mm. **Ruler:** Elizabeth II **Subject:** Quincentenary of the College of Arms **Obv:** Young bust right **Rev:** Falcon on ornamented shield

Date	Mintage	VF20	XF40	MS60	MS63	MS65
1984 AA	—	—	0.20	0.50	1.00	3.00

KM# 113a 2 PENCE
8.40 g., 0.925 Silver 0.2498 oz. ASW, 25.91 mm. **Ruler:** Elizabeth II **Obv:** Young bust right **Rev:** Falcon on ornamented shield

Date	Mintage	VF20	XF40	MS60	MS63	MS65
1984	—	PF65 10.00				

KM# 113b 2 PENCE
14.20 g., 0.917 Gold 0.4186 oz. AGW, 25.91 mm. **Ruler:** Elizabeth II **Obv:** Young bust right **Rev:** Falcon on ornamented shield

Date	Mintage	VF20	XF40	MS60	MS63	MS65
1984	150	PF65 750				

KM# 144 2 PENCE
7.12 g., Bronze, 25.91 mm. **Ruler:** Elizabeth II **Obv:** Crowned head right **Rev:** Falcon on ornamented shield

Date	Mintage	VF20	XF40	MS60	MS63	MS65
1985 AA(w)	—	—	0.20	0.60	1.25	3.00
1985 AB(w)	—	—	0.20	0.60	1.25	3.00
1985	50,000	PF65 3.00				
1986 AA	—	—	0.20	0.60	1.25	3.00
1986 AB	—	—	0.20	0.60	1.25	3.00
1986 AC	—	—	0.20	0.60	1.25	3.00
1986 AD	—	—	0.20	0.60	1.25	3.00
1987 AA	—	—	0.20	0.60	1.25	3.00
1987 AB	—	—	0.20	0.60	1.25	3.00
1987 AC	—	—	0.20	0.60	1.25	3.00
1987 AD	—	—	0.20	0.60	1.25	3.00

KM# 144a 2 PENCE
8.40 g., 0.925 Silver 0.2498 oz. ASW, 25.91 mm. **Ruler:** Elizabeth II **Obv:** Crowned head right **Rev:** Falcon on ornamented shield

Date	Mintage	VF20	XF40	MS60	MS63	MS65
1985	10,000	PF65 12.50				

KM# 144b 2 PENCE
14.20 g., 0.917 Gold 0.4186 oz. AGW, 25.91 mm. **Ruler:** Elizabeth II **Obv:** Crowned head right **Rev:** Falcon on ornamented shield

Date	Mintage	VF20	XF40	MS60	MS63	MS65
1985	300	PF65 750				

KM# 144c 2 PENCE
16.00 g., 0.950 Platinum 0.4887 oz. APW, 25.91 mm. **Ruler:** Elizabeth II **Obv:** Crowned head right **Rev:** Falcon on ornamented shield

Date	Mintage	VF20	XF40	MS60	MS63	MS65
1985	200	PF65 950				

KM# 208 2 PENCE
7.12 g., Bronze, 25.91 mm. **Ruler:** Elizabeth II **Obv:** Crowned head right **Rev:** Assorted designs within celtic cross within circle

Date	Mintage	VF20	XF40	MS60	MS63	MS65
1988 AA	—	—	—	0.20	0.30	0.50
1988 AB	—	—	0.10	0.20	0.30	0.50
1988 AC	—	—	0.10	0.20	0.30	0.50
1988 AD	—	—	0.10	0.20	0.30	0.50
1989 AA	—	—	—	0.20	0.30	0.50
1989 AB	—	—	0.10	0.20	0.30	0.50
1989 AC	—	—	0.10	0.20	0.30	0.50
1989 AD	—	—	0.10	0.20	0.30	0.50
1989 AE	—	—	0.10	0.20	0.30	0.50
1990 AA	—	—	—	0.20	0.30	0.50
1991 AA	—	—	—	0.20	0.30	0.50
1992 AA	—	—	—	0.20	0.30	0.50
1993 AA	—	—	—	0.20	0.30	0.50
1994 AA	—	—	—	0.20	0.30	0.50
1995 AA	—	—	—	0.20	0.30	0.50
1995 Proof	—	—	—	—	—	—

KM# 589 2 PENCE
7.12 g., Copper Plated Steel, 25.91 mm. **Ruler:** Elizabeth II **Subject:** Sports **Obv:** Crowned head right **Rev:** Bicyclists within sprigs

Date	Mintage	VF20	XF40	MS60	MS63	MS65
1996 AA	—	—	—	0.15	0.25	0.50
1997 AA	—	—	—	0.15	0.25	0.50

KM# 901.1 2 PENCE
7.12 g., Copper Plated Steel, 25.91 mm. **Ruler:** Elizabeth II **Obv:** Head with tiara right **Rev:** Two bicyclists within sprigs

Date	Mintage	VF20	XF40	MS60	MS63	MS65
1998 AA	—	—	—	0.15	0.25	0.50
1999	—	—	—	0.15	0.25	0.50

KM# 901.2 2 PENCE
7.12 g., Copper Plated Steel, 25.91 mm. **Ruler:** Elizabeth II **Obv:** Head with tiara right with small triskeles dividing legend **Rev:** Two bicyclists within sprigs

Date	Mintage	VF20	XF40	MS60	MS63	MS65
1998 PM AA	—	—	—	0.15	0.25	0.50
1999 PM AA	—	—	—	0.15	0.25	0.50

KM# 1037 2 PENCE
7.12 g., Copper Plated Steel, 25.9 mm. **Ruler:** Elizabeth II **Obv:** Head with tiara right **Rev:** Sailboat **Edge:** Plain

Date	Mintage	VF20	XF40	MS60	MS63	MS65
2000 PM AA	—	—	—	0.20	0.40	0.60

KM# 22 5 NEW PENCE
5.65 g., Copper-Nickel, 23.59 mm. **Ruler:** Elizabeth II **Obv:** Young bust right **Rev:** Towers on hill

Date	Mintage	VF20	XF40	MS60	MS63	MS65
1971	100,000	—	0.10	0.25	0.50	1.00
1971	10,000	PF65 2.50				
1972	1,000	—	—	—	20.00	22.50
1973	1,000	—	—	—	20.00	22.50
1974	1,000	—	—	—	20.00	22.50
1975	1,400,000	—	0.10	0.15	0.25	0.50

KM# 22a 5 NEW PENCE
6.50 g., 0.925 Silver 0.1933 oz. ASW, 23.59 mm. **Ruler:** Elizabeth II **Obv:** Young bust right **Rev:** Towers on hill

Date	Mintage	VF20	XF40	MS60	MS63	MS65
1975	20,000	—	—	—	7.00	8.00

KM# 22b 5 NEW PENCE
12.50 g., 0.950 Platinum 0.3818 oz. APW, 23.59 mm. **Ruler:** Elizabeth II **Obv:** Young bust right **Rev:** Towers on hill

Date	Mintage	VF20	XF40	MS60	MS63	MS65
1975	600	PF65 800				

KM# 35.1 5 PENCE
5.65 g., Copper-Nickel, 23.59 mm. **Ruler:** Elizabeth II **Obv:** Young bust right **Rev:** Laxey wheel **Note:** Lady Isabella; Mint mark: PM on obverse and reverse.

Date	Mintage	VF20	XF40	MS60	MS63	MS65
1976	800,000	—	0.10	0.30	0.60	0.85
1977	—	—	0.10	0.30	0.60	0.85
1978	—	—	0.10	0.30	0.60	0.85
1978	—	PF65 1.50				
1979 AA(t)	—	—	0.10	0.30	0.60	0.85
1979 AB(t)	—	—	0.10	0.30	0.60	0.85

KM# 35.2 5 PENCE
5.65 g., Copper-Nickel, 23.59 mm. **Ruler:** Elizabeth II **Obv:** Young bust right **Rev:** Laxey wheel **Note:** Mint mark: PM on obverse only.

Date	Mintage	VF20	XF40	MS60	MS63	MS65
1976	Inc. above	—	0.15	0.35	0.75	1.25

KM# 35a.1 5 PENCE
6.50 g., 0.925 Silver 0.1933 oz. ASW, 23.59 mm. **Ruler:** Elizabeth II **Obv:** Young bust right **Rev:** Laxey wheel

Date	Mintage	VF20	XF40	MS60	MS63	MS65
1976	20,000	—	—	—	7.00	8.00
1977	10,000	PF65 9.00				
1978	10,000	—	—	—	7.00	8.00
1979(t) AA	10,000	PF65 9.00				

KM# 35b.1 5 PENCE
12.50 g., 0.950 Platinum 0.3818 oz. APW, 23.59 mm. **Ruler:** Elizabeth II **Obv:** Young bust right **Rev:** Laxey wheel

Date	Mintage	VF20	XF40	MS60	MS63	MS65
1976	600	PF65 800				
1978	600	PF65 800				
1979	500	PF65 800				

KM# 61 5 PENCE
5.65 g., Copper-Nickel, 23.59 mm. **Ruler:** Elizabeth II **Obv:** Young bust right **Rev:** Stylized Loagthyn sheep

Date	Mintage	VF20	XF40	MS60	MS63	MS65
1980 AB	—	—	0.15	0.35	0.75	1.25
1980 AC	—	—	0.15	0.35	0.75	1.25
1980 AA	—	—	0.15	0.35	0.75	1.25
1980 PM DD	—	PF65 1.50				
1981 AA	—	—	0.15	0.35	0.75	1.25
1981 DD	—	PF65 1.50				
1982 (b)	—	—	0.15	0.35	0.75	1.25
1982 AA	—	—	0.15	0.35	0.75	1.25
1982 (b)	25,000	PF65 1.50				
1983 AA	—	—	0.15	0.35	0.75	1.25

KM# 61a 5 PENCE
6.50 g., 0.500 Silver 0.1045 oz. ASW, 23.59 mm. **Ruler:** Elizabeth II **Obv:** Young bust right **Rev:** Stylized Loagthyn sheep

Date	Mintage	VF20	XF40	MS60	MS63	MS65
1980	10,000	PF65 6.75				

KM# 61b 5 PENCE
6.50 g., 0.925 Silver 0.1933 oz. ASW, 23.59 mm. **Ruler:** Elizabeth II **Obv:** Young bust right **Rev:** Stylized Loagthyn sheep

Date	Mintage	VF20	XF40	MS60	MS63	MS65
1981	—	PF65 7.00				
1982	10,000	PF65 7.00				
1983	5,000	PF65 7.00				

KM# 61c 5 PENCE

11.00 g., 0.917 Gold 0.3243 oz. AGW, 23.59 mm. **Ruler:** Elizabeth II **Obv:** Young bust right **Rev:** Stylized Loagthyn sheep

Date	Mintage	VF20	XF40	MS60	MS63	MS65
1980	300	PF65 600				
1982 (b)	500	PF65 600				
1983	—	PF65 600				

KM# 61d 5 PENCE

12.50 g., 0.950 Platinum 0.3818 oz. APW, 23.59 mm. **Ruler:** Elizabeth II **Obv:** Young bust right **Rev:** Stylized Loagthyn sheep

Date	Mintage	VF20	XF40	MS60	MS63	MS65
1980	500	PF65 750				
1982	500	PF65 750				
1983	—	PF65 750				

KM# 114 5 PENCE

5.65 g., Copper-Nickel, 23.59 mm. **Ruler:** Elizabeth II **Subject:** Quincentenary of the College of Arms **Obv:** Young bust right **Rev:** Cushag within design

Date	Mintage	VF20	XF40	MS60	MS63	MS65
1984 AA	—	—	0.10	0.25	0.50	0.75

KM# 114a 5 PENCE

6.50 g., 0.925 Silver 0.1933 oz. ASW, 23.59 mm. **Ruler:** Elizabeth II **Obv:** Young bust right **Rev:** Cushag within design

Date	Mintage	VF20	XF40	MS60	MS63	MS65
1984	—	PF65 8.00				

KM# 114b 5 PENCE

11.00 g., 0.917 Gold 0.3243 oz. AGW, 23.59 mm. **Ruler:** Elizabeth II **Obv:** Young bust right **Rev:** Cushag within design

Date	Mintage	VF20	XF40	MS60	MS63	MS65
1984	150	PF65 600				

KM# 145 5 PENCE

5.65 g., Copper-Nickel, 23.59 mm. **Ruler:** Elizabeth II **Obv:** Crowned head right **Rev:** Cushag within design

Date	Mintage	VF20	XF40	MS60	MS63	MS65
1985 AA(w)	—	—	0.10	0.25	0.50	0.75
1985	50,000	PF65 3.00				
1986 AA	—	—	0.10	0.25	0.50	0.75
1986 AB	—	—	0.10	0.25	0.50	0.75
1986 AC	—	—	0.10	0.25	0.50	0.75
1986 AD	—	—	0.10	0.25	0.50	0.75
1987 AA	—	—	0.10	0.25	0.50	0.75

KM# 145a 5 PENCE

6.50 g., 0.925 Silver 0.1933 oz. ASW, 23.59 mm. **Ruler:** Elizabeth II **Obv:** Crowned head right **Rev:** Cushag within design

Date	Mintage	VF20	XF40	MS60	MS63	MS65
1985	10,000	PF65 9.00				

KM# 145b 5 PENCE

11.00 g., 0.917 Gold 0.3243 oz. AGW, 23.59 mm. **Ruler:** Elizabeth II **Obv:** Crowned head right **Rev:** Cushag within design

Date	Mintage	VF20	XF40	MS60	MS63	MS65
1985	300	PF65 600				

KM# 145c 5 PENCE

12.50 g., 0.950 Platinum 0.3818 oz. APW, 23.59 mm. **Ruler:** Elizabeth II **Obv:** Crowned head right **Rev:** Cushag within design

Date	Mintage	VF20	XF40	MS60	MS63	MS65
1985	200	PF65 750				

KM# 209.1 5 PENCE

5.65 g., Copper-Nickel, 23.59 mm. **Ruler:** Elizabeth II **Obv:** Crowned head right **Rev:** Windsurfing

Date	Mintage	VF20	XF40	MS60	MS63	MS65
1988 AA	—	—	—	0.30	0.60	0.85
1989 AA	—	—	—	0.30	0.60	0.85
1990	—	—	—	0.30	0.60	0.85

KM# 209.2 5 PENCE

3.25 g., Copper-Nickel, 18 mm. **Ruler:** Elizabeth II **Obv:** Crowned head right **Rev:** Windsurfing **Edge:** Reeded **Note:** Reduced size.

Date	Mintage	VF20	XF40	MS60	MS63	MS65
1990 AA	—	—	—	0.30	0.60	0.85
1990 AB	—	—	—	0.30	0.60	0.85
1991 AA	—	—	—	0.30	0.60	0.85
1991 AB	—	—	—	0.30	0.60	0.85
1992 AA	—	—	—	0.30	0.60	0.85
1993 AA	—	—	—	0.30	0.60	0.85

KM# 392 5 PENCE

3.25 g., Copper-Nickel, 18 mm. **Ruler:** Elizabeth II **Obv:** Crowned head right **Rev:** Golf clubs and ball **Edge:** Reeded

Date	Mintage	VF20	XF40	MS60	MS63	MS65
1994 AA	—	—	—	0.30	0.60	0.85
1995 AA	—	—	—	0.30	0.60	0.85

KM# 392a 5 PENCE

3.25 g., 0.925 Silver 0.0967 oz. ASW, 18 mm. **Ruler:** Elizabeth II **Obv:** Crowned head right **Rev:** Golf clubs and ball

Date	Mintage	VF20	XF40	MS60	MS63	MS65
1994	Est. 25000	PF65 10.00				

KM# 392b 5 PENCE

3.25 g., 0.917 Gold 0.0958 oz. AGW, 18 mm. **Ruler:** Elizabeth II **Obv:** Crowned head right **Rev:** Golf clubs and ball

Date	Mintage	VF20	XF40	MS60	MS63	MS65
1994	10,000	PF65 175				

KM# 392c 5 PENCE

3.25 g., 0.950 Platinum 0.0993 oz. APW, 18 mm. **Ruler:** Elizabeth II **Obv:** Crowned head right **Rev:** Golf clubs and ball

Date	Mintage	VF20	XF40	MS60	MS63	MS65
1994	3,500	PF65 200				

KM# 590 5 PENCE

3.25 g., Copper-Nickel, 18 mm. **Ruler:** Elizabeth II **Subject:** Sports **Obv:** Crowned head right **Rev:** Golpher within sprigs **Edge:** Reeded

Date	Mintage	VF20	XF40	MS60	MS63	MS65
1996 AA	—	—	—	0.25	0.50	0.75
1997 AA	—	—	—	0.25	0.50	0.75

KM# 590a 5 PENCE

3.25 g., 0.925 Silver 0.0967 oz. ASW, 18 mm. **Ruler:** Elizabeth II **Subject:** Sports **Obv:** Crowned head right **Rev:** Golfer within sprigs

Date	Mintage	VF20	XF40	MS60	MS63	MS65
1996	—	PF65 10.00				

KM# 902.1 5 PENCE

3.25 g., Copper-Nickel, 18 mm. **Ruler:** Elizabeth II **Obv:** Head with tiara right **Rev:** Golfer within sprigs **Edge:** Reeded

Date	Mintage	VF20	XF40	MS60	MS63	MS65
1998 AA	—	—	—	0.25	0.50	0.75

KM# 902.2 5 PENCE

3.25 g., Copper-Nickel, 18 mm. **Ruler:** Elizabeth II **Obv:** Head with tiara right with small triskeles dividing legend **Rev:** Golfer within sprigs **Edge:** Reeded

Date	Mintage	VF20	XF40	MS60	MS63	MS65
1998 PM AA	—	—	—	0.25	0.50	0.75
1999 PM AA	—	—	—	0.25	0.50	0.75
Note: Mintmark AA exists in two positions.						
1999 PM AB	—	—	—	0.25	0.50	0.75

KM# 1038 5 PENCE

3.25 g., Copper-Nickel, 18 mm. **Ruler:** Elizabeth II **Obv:** Head with tiara right **Rev:** Gaut's Cross **Edge:** Reeded

Date	Mintage	VF20	XF40	MS60	MS63	MS65
2000 AA	—	—	—	0.35	0.75	1.00
2000 PMM AA	—	—	—	0.35	0.75	1.00
2000 AB	—	—	—	0.35	0.75	1.00
2000 PMM AC	—	—	—	0.35	0.75	1.00

KM# 23 10 NEW PENCE

11.50 g., Copper-Nickel, 28.5 mm. **Ruler:** Elizabeth II **Obv:** Young bust right **Rev:** Triskeles

Date	Mintage	VF20	XF40	MS60	MS63	MS65
1971	100,000	—	0.20	0.30	0.50	1.00
1971	10,000	PF65 3.50				
1972	1,000	—	—	—	20.00	22.50
1973	1,000	—	—	—	20.00	22.50
1974	1,000	—	—	—	20.00	22.50
1975	1,500,000	—	0.20	0.30	0.40	0.75

KM# 23a 10 NEW PENCE

13.00 g., 0.925 Silver 0.3866 oz. ASW, 28.5 mm. **Ruler:** Elizabeth II **Obv:** Young bust right **Rev:** Triskeles

Date	Mintage	VF20	XF40	MS60	MS63	MS65
1975	20,000	—	—	—	7.25	14.00

KM# 23b 10 NEW PENCE

25.00 g., 0.950 Platinum 0.7636 oz. APW, 28.5 mm. **Ruler:** Elizabeth II **Obv:** Young bust right **Rev:** Triskeles

Date	Mintage	VF20	XF40	MS60	MS63	MS65
1975	600	PF65 1,500				

KM# 36.1 10 PENCE

11.31 g., Copper-Nickel, 28.5 mm. **Ruler:** Elizabeth II **Obv:** Young bust right **Rev:** Triskeles on map **Edge:** Reeded **Note:** PM mintmark on both sides.

Date	Mintage	VF20	XF40	MS60	MS63	MS65
1976 PM	2,800,000	—	0.20	0.40	0.80	1.00
1977 PM	—	—	0.20	0.40	0.80	1.00
1978 PM	—	—	0.20	0.40	0.80	1.00
1978 PM	—	PF65 2.00				
1979(t) PM AA	—	—	0.20	0.40	0.80	1.00
1979(t) PM AB	—	—	0.20	0.40	0.80	1.00

KM# 36.2 10 PENCE

11.31 g., Copper-Nickel, 28.5 mm. **Ruler:** Elizabeth II **Obv:** Young bust right **Rev:** Triskeles on map **Edge:** Reeded **Note:** Mintmark: PM on obverse only.

Date	Mintage	VF20	XF40	MS60	MS63	MS65
1976 PM	Inc. above	—	0.20	0.50	1.00	1.25
1977 PM	—	—	0.20	0.50	1.00	1.25

KM# 36a.1 10 PENCE

13.00 g., 0.925 Silver 0.3866 oz. ASW, 28.5 mm. **Ruler:** Elizabeth II **Obv:** Young bust right **Rev:** Triskeles on map

Date	Mintage	VF20	XF40	MS60	MS63	MS65
1976	20,000	—	—	—	7.25	14.00
1977	10,000	PF65 15.00				
1978	10,000	—	—	—	7.25	14.00
1979 (t)	10,000	PF65 15.00				

KM# 36b.1 10 PENCE

25.00 g., 0.950 Platinum 0.7636 oz. APW, 28.5 mm. **Ruler:** Elizabeth II **Obv:** Young bust right **Rev:** Triskeles on map

Date	Mintage	VF20	XF40	MS60	MS63	MS65
1976	600	PF65 1,500				
1978	600	PF65 1,500				
1979 (t)	500	PF65 1,500				

KM# 62 10 PENCE
11.31 g., Copper-Nickel, 28.5 mm. **Ruler:** Elizabeth II **Obv:** Young bust right **Rev:** Falcon within design **Edge:** Reeded

Date	Mintage	VF20	XF40	MS60	MS63	MS65
1980 PM AA	—	—	0.25	0.50	1.00	2.00
1980 PM AB	—	—	0.25	0.50	1.00	2.00
1980 PM DD	—	PF65 2.50				
1981 PM AA	—	—	0.25	0.50	1.00	2.00
1981 PM DD	—	PF65 2.50				
1982 PM AA	—	—	0.25	0.50	1.00	2.00
1982 PM AB	—	—	0.25	0.50	1.00	2.00
1982 PM AB(b)	—	—	0.25	0.50	1.00	2.00
1982 PM AC	—	—	0.25	0.50	1.00	2.00
1982 PM AD	—	—	0.25	0.50	1.00	2.00
1982 PM (b)	25,000	PF65 2.50				
1983 PM AA	—	—	0.25	0.50	1.00	2.00
1983 PM AB	—	—	0.25	0.50	1.00	2.00
1983 PM AC	—	—	0.25	0.50	1.00	2.00
1983 PM AD	—	—	0.25	0.50	1.00	2.00

KM# 62a 10 PENCE
13.00 g., 0.500 Silver 0.209 oz. ASW, 28.5 mm. **Ruler:** Elizabeth II **Obv:** Young bust right **Rev:** Falcon within design

Date	Mintage	VF20	XF40	MS60	MS63	MS65
1980	10,000	PF65 14.00				

KM# 62b 10 PENCE
13.00 g., 0.925 Silver 0.3866 oz. ASW, 28.5 mm. **Ruler:** Elizabeth II **Obv:** Young bust right **Rev:** Falcon within design

Date	Mintage	VF20	XF40	MS60	MS63	MS65
1981	—	PF65 14.00				
1982	10,000	PF65 14.00				
1983	5,000	PF65 14.00				

KM# 62c 10 PENCE
22.00 g., 0.917 Gold 0.6486 oz. AGW, 28.5 mm. **Ruler:** Elizabeth II **Obv:** Young bust right **Rev:** Falcon within design

Date	Mintage	VF20	XF40	MS60	MS63	MS65
1980	300	PF65 1,150				
1982 (b)	500	PF65 1,150				
1983	—	PF65 1,150				

KM# 62d 10 PENCE
25.00 g., 0.950 Platinum 0.7636 oz. APW, 28.5 mm. **Ruler:** Elizabeth II **Obv:** Young bust right **Rev:** Falcon within design

Date	Mintage	VF20	XF40	MS60	MS63	MS65
1980	500	PF65 1,500				
1982 (b)	500	PF65 1,500				
1983	—	PF65 1,500				

KM# 115 10 PENCE
11.31 g., Copper-Nickel, 28.5 mm. **Ruler:** Elizabeth II **Subject:** Quincentenary of the College of Arms **Obv:** Young bust right **Rev:** Loagthyn ram within shield **Edge:** Reeded

Date	Mintage	VF20	XF40	MS60	MS63	MS65
1984 PM AA	—	—	0.25	0.50	1.00	1.25
1984 PM AB	—	—	0.25	0.50	1.00	1.25
1984 PM AC	—	—	0.25	0.50	1.00	1.25
1984 PM AD	—	—	0.25	0.50	1.00	1.25
1984 PM AE	—	—	0.25	0.50	1.00	1.25
1984 PM AF	—	—	0.25	0.50	1.00	1.25
1984 PM AG	—	—	0.25	0.50	1.00	1.25

KM# 115a 10 PENCE
0.925 Silver, 28.5 mm. **Ruler:** Elizabeth II **Obv:** Young bust right **Rev:** Loagthyn ram within shield

Date	Mintage	VF20	XF40	MS60	MS63	MS65
1984	—	PF65 14.00				

KM# 115b 10 PENCE
22.00 g., 0.917 Gold 0.6486 oz. AGW, 28.5 mm. **Ruler:** Elizabeth II **Obv:** Young bust right **Rev:** Loagthyn ram within shield

Date	Mintage	VF20	XF40	MS60	MS63	MS65
1984	150	PF65 1,150				

KM# 146 10 PENCE
11.31 g., Copper-Nickel, 28.5 mm. **Ruler:** Elizabeth II **Obv:** Crowned head right **Rev:** Loagthyn ram within designed shield **Edge:** Reeded

Date	Mintage	VF20	XF40	MS60	MS63	MS65
1985 PM AA(w)	—	—	0.20	0.40	0.80	1.00
1985 PM AB(w)	—	—	0.20	0.40	0.80	1.00
1985 PM	50,000	PF65 3.00				
1986 PM AA	—	—	0.20	0.40	0.80	1.00
1987 PM AA	—	—	0.20	0.40	0.80	1.00

KM# 146a 10 PENCE
13.00 g., 0.925 Silver 0.3866 oz. ASW, 28.5 mm. **Ruler:** Elizabeth II **Obv:** Crowned head right **Rev:** Loagthyn ram within designed shield

Date	Mintage	VF20	XF40	MS60	MS63	MS65
1985	10,000	PF65 18.00				

KM# 146b 10 PENCE
22.00 g., 0.917 Gold 0.6486 oz. AGW, 28.5 mm. **Ruler:** Elizabeth II **Obv:** Crowned head right **Rev:** Loagthyn ram within designed shield

Date	Mintage	VF20	XF40	MS60	MS63	MS65
1985	300	PF65 1,150				

KM# 146c 10 PENCE
25.00 g., 0.950 Platinum 0.7636 oz. APW, 28.5 mm. **Ruler:** Elizabeth II **Obv:** Crowned head right **Rev:** Loagthyn ram within designed shield

Date	Mintage	VF20	XF40	MS60	MS63	MS65
1985	200	PF65 1,500				

KM# 210 10 PENCE
11.31 g., Copper-Nickel, 28.5 mm. **Ruler:** Elizabeth II **Obv:** Crowned head right **Rev:** Island and portcullis on globe **Edge:** Reeded

Date	Mintage	VF20	XF40	MS60	MS63	MS65
1988 PM AA	—	—	—	0.35	0.75	1.00
1989 PM AA	—	—	—	0.35	0.75	1.00
1990 PM AA	—	—	—	0.35	0.75	1.00
1991 PM AA	—	—	—	0.35	0.75	1.00
1991 PM AB	—	—	—	0.35	0.75	1.00
1991 PM AC	—	—	—	0.35	0.75	1.00
1992 PM AA	—	—	—	0.35	0.75	1.00

KM# 337 10 PENCE
6.50 g., Copper-Nickel, 24.5 mm. **Ruler:** Elizabeth II **Obv:** Crowned head right **Rev:** Triskeles and value **Edge:** Reeded **Note:** Varieties exist.

Date	Mintage	VF20	XF40	MS60	MS63	MS65
1992 PM AA	—	—	—	0.35	0.75	1.00
1992 PM AB	—	—	—	0.35	0.75	1.00
1992 PM AC	—	—	—	0.35	0.75	1.00
1992 PM AD	—	—	—	0.35	0.75	1.00
1992 PM AE	—	—	—	0.50	1.00	1.25
1993 PM AA	—	—	—	0.35	0.75	1.00
1994 PM AA	—	—	—	0.35	0.75	1.00
1995 PM AD	—	—	—	0.35	0.75	1.00
1995 PM AA	—	—	—	0.35	0.75	1.00

KM# 337a 10 PENCE
8.05 g., 0.925 Silver 0.2393 oz. ASW, 24.5 mm. **Ruler:** Elizabeth II **Obv:** Crowned head right **Rev:** Triskeles and value

Date	Mintage	VF20	XF40	MS60	MS63	MS65
1992 PM D	—	PF65 13.50				

KM# 337b 10 PENCE
13.62 g., 0.917 Gold 0.4014 oz. AGW, 24.5 mm. **Ruler:** Elizabeth II **Obv:** Crowned head right **Rev:** Triskeles and value

Date	Mintage	VF20	XF40	MS60	MS63	MS65
1992	—	PF65 730				

KM# 337c 10 PENCE
15.47 g., 0.950 Platinum 0.4726 oz. APW, 24.5 mm. **Ruler:** Elizabeth II **Obv:** Crowned head right **Rev:** Triskeles and value

Date	Mintage	VF20	XF40	MS60	MS63	MS65
1992	—	PF65 900				

KM# 591 10 PENCE
6.50 g., Copper-Nickel, 24.5 mm. **Ruler:** Elizabeth II **Subject:** Sports **Obv:** Crowned head right **Rev:** Sailboat divides wreath **Edge:** Reeded

Date	Mintage	VF20	XF40	MS60	MS63	MS65
1996 PM AA	—	—	—	0.50	1.00	1.50
1997 PM AA	—	—	—	0.50	1.00	1.50

KM# 591a 10 PENCE
8.05 g., 0.925 Silver 0.2393 oz. ASW, 24.5 mm. **Ruler:** Elizabeth II **Subject:** Sports **Obv:** Crowned head right **Rev:** Sailboat divides wreath

Date	Mintage	VF20	XF40	MS60	MS63	MS65
1996	—	PF65 22.50				

KM# 903.1 10 PENCE
6.50 g., Copper-Nickel, 24.5 mm. **Ruler:** Elizabeth II **Obv:** Head with tiara right **Rev:** Sailboat divides wreath **Edge:** Reeded

Date	Mintage	VF20	XF40	MS60	MS63	MS65
1998 PM AA	—	—	—	0.50	1.00	1.50

KM# 903.2 10 PENCE
6.50 g., Copper-Nickel, 24.5 mm. **Ruler:** Elizabeth II **Obv:** Head with tiara right with small triskeles dividing legend **Rev:** Sailboat divides wreath **Edge:** Reeded

Date	Mintage	VF20	XF40	MS60	MS63	MS65
1998 PM AA	—	—	—	0.50	1.00	1.50
1999 PM AA	—	—	—	0.50	1.00	1.50

KM# 1039 10 PENCE
6.50 g., Copper-Nickel, 24.5 mm. **Ruler:** Elizabeth II **Obv:** Head with tiara right **Rev:** Cathedral **Edge:** Reeded

Date	Mintage	VF20	XF40	MS60	MS63	MS65
2000 PM AA	—	—	—	0.50	1.00	1.50

KM# 90 20 PENCE
5.00 g., Copper-Nickel, 21.4 mm. **Ruler:** Elizabeth II **Subject:** Medieval Norse History **Obv:** Young bust right **Rev:** Ship within small circle within artistic design with viking helmet above **Shape:** 7-sided

Date	Mintage	VF20	XF40	MS60	MS63	MS65
1982 AA	30,000	—	0.35	0.50	1.00	1.50
1982 AB	—	—	0.35	0.50	1.00	1.50
1982 AB(b)	—	—	0.35	0.50	1.00	1.50
1982 AC	—	—	0.35	0.50	1.00	1.50
1982 AD	—	—	0.35	0.50	1.00	1.50
1982 (b)	25,000	PF65 6.00				
1982 BB	—	PF65 1.50				
1982 BC	—	PF65 1.50				
1983 AA	—	—	0.35	0.50	1.00	1.50

KM# 90a 20 PENCE
6.00 g., 0.925 Silver 0.1784 oz. ASW, 21.4 mm. **Ruler:** Elizabeth II **Subject:** Medieval Norse History **Obv:** Young bust right **Rev:** Ship within small circle of design with Viking helmet above **Shape:** 7-sided

Date	Mintage	VF20	XF40	MS60	MS63	MS65
1982	15,000	PF65 10.00				
1982 (b)	10,000	PF65 10.00				
1983	5,000	PF65 15.00				

KM# 90b 20 PENCE
10.00 g., 0.917 Gold 0.2948 oz. AGW, 21.4 mm. **Ruler:** Elizabeth II **Subject:** Medieval Norse History **Obv:** Young bust right **Rev:** Ship within small circle of design with Viking helmet above **Shape:** 7-sided

Date	Mintage	VF20	XF40	MS60	MS63	MS65
1982	1,500	PF65 525				
1982 (b)	500	PF65 525				
1983	—	PF65 525				

KM# 90c 20 PENCE
11.30 g., 0.950 Platinum 0.3451 oz. APW, 21.4 mm. **Ruler:** Elizabeth II **Subject:** Medieval Norse History **Obv:** Young bust right **Rev:** Ship within small circle of design with Viking helmet above **Shape:** 7-sided

Date	Mintage	VF20	XF40	MS60	MS63	MS65
1982	250	PF65 700				
1982 (b)	500	PF65 700				
1983	—	PF65 700				

KM# 116 20 PENCE
5.00 g., Copper-Nickel, 21.4 mm. **Ruler:** Elizabeth II **Subject:** Quincentenary of the College of Arms **Obv:** Young bust right **Rev:** Atlantic herring within designed shield **Shape:** 7-sided

Date	Mintage	VF20	XF40	MS60	MS63	MS65
1984 AA	—	—	0.35	0.50	1.00	1.50

KM# 116a 20 PENCE
0.925 Silver, 21.4 mm. **Ruler:** Elizabeth II **Subject:** Quincentenary of the College of Arms **Obv:** Young bust right **Rev:** Atlantic herring within designed shield **Shape:** 7-sided

Date	Mintage	VF20	XF40	MS60	MS63	MS65
1984	—	PF65 20.00				

KM# 116b 20 PENCE
5.00 g., 0.917 Gold 0.1474 oz. AGW, 21.4 mm. **Ruler:** Elizabeth II **Subject:** Quincentenary of the College of Arms **Obv:** Young bust right **Rev:** Atlantic herring within designed shield **Shape:** 7-sided

Date	Mintage	VF20	XF40	MS60	MS63	MS65
1984	150	PF65 275				

KM# 147 20 PENCE
5.00 g., Copper-Nickel, 21.4 mm. **Ruler:** Elizabeth II **Obv:** Crowned head right **Rev:** Atlantic herring within designed shield **Shape:** 7-sided

Date	Mintage	VF20	XF40	MS60	MS63	MS65
1985(w) AA	—	—	0.35	0.50	1.00	1.50
1985	50,000	PF65 3.00				
1986 AA	—	—	0.35	0.50	1.00	1.50
1986 AB	—	—	0.35	0.50	1.00	1.50
1986 AC	—	—	0.35	0.50	1.00	1.50
1987 AA	—	—	0.35	0.50	1.00	1.50

KM# 147a 20 PENCE
5.00 g., 0.925 Silver 0.1487 oz. ASW, 21.4 mm. **Ruler:** Elizabeth II **Obv:** Crowned head right **Rev:** Atlantic herring within designed shield **Shape:** 7-sided

Date	Mintage	VF20	XF40	MS60	MS63	MS65
1985	10,000	PF65 9.00				

KM# 147b 20 PENCE
5.00 g., 0.917 Gold 0.1474 oz. AGW, 21.4 mm. **Ruler:** Elizabeth II **Obv:** Crowned head right **Rev:** Atlantic herring within designed shield **Shape:** 7-sided

Date	Mintage	VF20	XF40	MS60	MS63	MS65
1985	300	PF65 275				

KM# 147c 20 PENCE
5.00 g., 0.950 Platinum 0.1527 oz. APW, 21.4 mm. **Ruler:** Elizabeth II **Obv:** Crowned head right **Rev:** Atlantic herring within designed shield **Shape:** 7-sided

Date	Mintage	VF20	XF40	MS60	MS63	MS65
1985	200	PF65 325				

KM# 211 20 PENCE
5.00 g., Copper-Nickel, 21.4 mm. **Ruler:** Elizabeth II **Obv:** Crowned head right **Rev:** Combine within sprigs **Shape:** 7-sided

Date	Mintage	VF20	XF40	MS60	MS63	MS65
1988 AA	—	—	—	0.50	1.00	1.50
1989 AA	—	—	—	0.50	1.00	1.50
1990 AA	—	—	—	0.50	1.00	1.50
1991 AA	—	—	—	0.50	1.00	1.50
1992 AA	—	—	—	0.50	1.00	1.50

KM# 391 20 PENCE
5.00 g., Copper-Nickel, 21.4 mm. **Ruler:** Elizabeth II **Obv:** Crowned head right **Rev:** Combine within sprigs **Shape:** 7-sided **Note:** Obverse and reverse design revised with border.

Date	Mintage	VF20	XF40	MS60	MS63	MS65
1993 AA	—	—	—	0.50	1.00	1.50
1994 AA	—	—	—	0.50	1.00	1.50
1995 AA	—	—	—	0.50	1.00	1.50

KM# 592 20 PENCE
5.00 g., Copper-Nickel, 21.4 mm. **Ruler:** Elizabeth II **Subject:** Sports **Obv:** Crowned head right **Rev:** Race cars within sprigs **Shape:** 7-sided

Date	Mintage	VF20	XF40	MS60	MS63	MS65
1996 AA	—	—	—	0.60	1.25	1.75
1997 AA	—	—	—	0.60	1.25	1.75

KM# 904.1 20 PENCE
5.00 g., Copper-Nickel, 21.4 mm. **Ruler:** Elizabeth II **Obv:** Head with tiara right with small triskeles dividing legend **Obv. Legend:** ELIZABETH II - ISLE OF MAN **Rev:** Rally cars above sprigs **Shape:** 7-sided **Note:** Prev. KM#904.

Date	Mintage	VF20	XF40	MS60	MS63	MS65
1998 PM AA	—	—	—	0.60	1.25	1.75

KM# 904.2 20 PENCE
5.00 g., Copper-Nickel, 21.4 mm. **Ruler:** Elizabeth II **Obv:** Head with tiara right with small triskeles dividing legend **Obv. Legend:** ISLE OF MAN - ELIZABETH II **Rev:** Rally cars above sprigs **Shape:** 7-sided

Date	Mintage	VF20	XF40	MS60	MS63	MS65
1999 PM AA	—	—	—	0.60	1.25	1.75

KM# 1040 20 PENCE
5.00 g., Copper-Nickel, 21.4 mm. **Ruler:** Elizabeth II **Subject:** Rushen Abbey **Obv:** Head with tiara right **Rev:** Monk writing **Edge:** Plain **Shape:** 7-sided

Date	Mintage	VF20	XF40	MS60	MS63	MS65
2000 AA	—	—	—	0.75	1.50	2.00

KM# 25 25 PENCE
28.28 g., Copper-Nickel, 38.61 mm. **Ruler:** Elizabeth II **Subject:** 25th Wedding Anniversary **Obv:** Young bust right **Rev:** Tilted shields divide date within rope wreath **Note:** Struck at the Royal Canadian Mint.

Date	Mintage	VF20	XF40	MS60	MS63	MS65
1972	70,000	—	—	—	4.50	5.00

KM# 25a 25 PENCE
28.28 g., 0.925 Silver 0.841 oz. ASW, 38.5 mm. **Ruler:** Elizabeth II **Obv:** Young bust right **Rev:** Tilted shields divide dates within rope wreath **Note:** Struck at the Royal Canadian Mint.

Date	Mintage	VF20	XF40	MS60	MS63	MS65
1972	15,000	PF65 30.00				

KM# 31 25 PENCE
28.28 g., Copper-Nickel, 38.61 mm. **Ruler:** Elizabeth II **Obv:** Young bust right **Rev:** Manx cat

Date	Mintage	VF20	XF40	MS60	MS63	MS65
1975	35,000	—	—	—	10.00	12.00

KM# 31a 25 PENCE
28.28 g., 0.925 Silver 0.841 oz. ASW, 38.5 mm. **Ruler:** Elizabeth II **Obv:** Young bust right **Rev:** Manx cat

Date	Mintage	VF20	XF40	MS60	MS63	MS65
1975	—	—	—	—	—	50.00
1975	30,000	PF65 55.00				

KM# 24 50 NEW PENCE
13.50 g., Copper-Nickel, 30 mm. **Ruler:** Elizabeth II **Obv:** Young bust right **Rev:** Sailing Viking ship **Shape:** 7-sided

Date	Mintage	VF20	XF40	MS60	MS63	MS65
1971	100,000	—	—	1.00	5.00	7.50
1971	10,000	PF65 8.00				
1972	1,000	—	—	—	25.00	30.00
1973	1,000	—	—	—	25.00	30.00
1974	1,000	—	—	—	25.00	30.00
1975	227,000	—	—	1.00	5.00	7.50

KM# 24a 50 NEW PENCE
15.50 g., 0.925 Silver 0.461 oz. ASW, 30 mm. **Ruler:** Elizabeth II **Obv:** Young bust right **Rev:** Sailing Viking ship **Shape:** 7-sided

Date	Mintage	VF20	XF40	MS60	MS63	MS65
1975	20,000	—	—	—	8.50	17.00

KM# 24b 50 NEW PENCE
30.40 g., 0.950 Platinum 0.9285 oz. APW, 30 mm. **Ruler:** Elizabeth II **Obv:** Young bust right **Rev:** Sailing Viking ship **Shape:** 7-sided

Date	Mintage	VF20	XF40	MS60	MS63	MS65
1975	600	PF65 1,750				

KM# 39 50 PENCE

13.50 g., Copper-Nickel, 30 mm. **Ruler:** Elizabeth II **Obv:** Young bust right **Rev:** Sailing Viking ship **Shape:** 7-sided

Date	Mintage	VF20	XF40	MS60	MS63	MS65
1976	250,000	—	—	0.75	2.00	3.00
1977	50,000	—	—	0.75	2.50	3.50
1978	25,000	—	—	0.75	2.50	3.50
1978	—	PF65 4.50				
1979 AA(t)	—	—	—	0.75	3.00	4.00

KM# 39a 50 PENCE

15.50 g., 0.925 Silver 0.461 oz. ASW, 30 mm. **Ruler:** Elizabeth II **Obv:** Young bust right **Rev:** Sailing Viking ship **Shape:** 7-sided

Date	Mintage	VF20	XF40	MS60	MS63	MS65
1976	20,000	—	—	—	16.00	17.00
1977	10,000	PF65 16.00				
1978	10,000	—	—	—	16.00	17.00
1979 (t)	10,000	PF65 16.00				

KM# 39b 50 PENCE

30.40 g., 0.950 Platinum 0.9285 oz. APW, 30 mm. **Ruler:** Elizabeth II **Obv:** Young bust right **Rev:** Sailing Viking ship **Shape:** 7-sided

Date	Mintage	VF20	XF40	MS60	MS63	MS65
1976	600	PF65 1,650				
1978	600	PF65 1,650				
1979 (t)	500	PF65 1,650				

KM# 51.1 50 PENCE

13.50 g., Copper-Nickel, 30 mm. **Ruler:** Elizabeth II **Subject:** Manx Day of Tynwald, July 5 **Obv:** Young bust right **Rev:** Viking ship **Edge:** Upright with obverse on top **Edge Lettering:** H.M Q.E-II ROYAL VISIT I.O.M. JULY 1979 **Shape:** 7-sided

Date	Mintage	VF20	XF40	MS60	MS63	MS65
1979 AA	50,000	—	—	—	4.50	5.00
1979 AB	—	—	—	—	4.50	5.00

KM# 51.2 50 PENCE

13.50 g., Copper-Nickel, 30 mm. **Ruler:** Elizabeth II **Obv:** Young bust right **Rev:** Viking ship **Edge:** Lettering upright with reverse on top **Shape:** 7-sided

Date	Mintage	VF20	XF40	MS60	MS63	MS65
1979 AA	—	—	—	—	4.50	5.00
1979 AB	—	—	—	—	4.50	5.00

KM# 51.3 50 PENCE

13.50 g., Copper-Nickel, 30 mm. **Ruler:** Elizabeth II **Obv:** Young bust right **Rev:** Viking ship **Note:** Inscription not centered in flat sections.

Date	Mintage	VF20	XF40	MS60	MS63	MS65
1979 AA	—	—	—	—	4.50	5.00
1979 AB	—	—	—	—	4.50	5.00

KM# 51a 50 PENCE

15.50 g., 0.925 Silver 0.461 oz. ASW, 30 mm. **Ruler:** Elizabeth II **Obv:** Young bust right **Rev:** Viking ship **Shape:** 7-sided

Date	Mintage	VF20	XF40	MS60	MS63	MS65
1979	10,000	—	—	—	9.00	16.00
1979 D	5,000	PF65 18.00				
1979 E	—	PF65 18.00				
1979 D	5,000	PF65 18.00				

KM# 51b 50 PENCE

30.40 g., 0.950 Platinum 0.9285 oz. APW, 30 mm. **Ruler:** Elizabeth II **Subject:** Manx Millennium of Tynwald **Obv:** Young bust right **Rev:** Viking ship **Edge:** H.M.Q.E. II ROYAL VISIT I.O.M. JULY 5, 1979

Date	Mintage	VF20	XF40	MS60	MS63	MS65
1979	500	PF65 1,650				

KM# 53 50 PENCE

13.50 g., Copper-Nickel, 30 mm. **Ruler:** Elizabeth II **Obv:** Young bust right **Rev:** Odin's Raven, Point of Ayre lighthouse **Note:** Same as KM#51.1 with no edge lettering.

Date	Mintage	VF20	XF40	MS60	MS63	MS65
1979 AA	—	—	—	—	3.00	4.00
1979 AB	—	—	—	—	3.00	4.00

KM# 53a 50 PENCE

15.50 g., 0.925 Silver 0.461 oz. ASW, 30 mm. **Ruler:** Elizabeth II **Obv:** Young bust right **Rev:** Odin's Raven, Point of Ayre lighhouse

Date	Mintage	VF20	XF40	MS60	MS63	MS65
1979	—	—	—	—	9.00	16.00
1979	—	PF65 18.00				

KM# 57 50 PENCE

15.50 g., 0.925 Silver 0.461 oz. ASW, 30 mm. **Ruler:** Elizabeth II **Obv:** Young bust right **Rev:** Christmas scene with stage coach **Note:** Mule: obverse KM#69 and reverse KM#71.

Date	Mintage	VF20	XF40	MS60	MS63	MS65
1980	—	—	—	—	—	—

KM# 57a 50 PENCE

13.50 g., Copper-Nickel, 30 mm. **Ruler:** Elizabeth II **Subject:** Christmas **Obv:** Young bust right **Rev:** Christmas scene with stagecoach **Shape:** 7-sided **Note:** Mule: obverse KM#69 and reverse KM#71.

Date	Mintage	VF20	XF40	MS60	MS63	MS65
1980	—	—	—	—	45.00	50.00

KM# 69 50 PENCE

13.50 g., Copper-Nickel, 30 mm. **Ruler:** Elizabeth II **Obv:** Young bust right **Obv. Legend:** ELIZABETH THE SECOND **Edge Lettering:** ODINS RAVEN VIKING EXHIBN NEW YORK 1980 **Note:** Same as KM#51.1, different edge lettering.

Date	Mintage	VF20	XF40	MS60	MS63	MS65
1980 AA Prooflike	20,000	—	—	—	4.00	5.00
1980 PM AB Prooflike	Inc. above	—	—	—	4.00	5.00
1980 PM AC Prooflike	Inc. above	—	—	—	4.00	5.00

KM# 69a 50 PENCE

15.50 g., 0.925 Silver 0.461 oz. ASW, 30 mm. **Ruler:** Elizabeth II **Obv:** Young bust right **Obv. Legend:** ELIZABETH THE SECOND

Date	Mintage	VF20	XF40	MS60	MS63	MS65
1980	—	—	—	—	16.00	18.00
1980	5,000	PF65 20.00				

KM# 69b 50 PENCE

26.00 g., 0.917 Gold 0.7665 oz. AGW, 30 mm. **Ruler:** Elizabeth II **Obv:** Young bust right **Obv. Legend:** ELIZABETH THE SECOND **Edge Lettering:** ODINS RAVEN VIKING EXHIBN NEW YORK 1980

Date	Mintage	VF20	XF40	MS60	MS63	MS65
1980	250	—	—	—	—	1,250

KM# 69c 50 PENCE

30.40 g., 0.950 Platinum 0.9285 oz. APW, 30 mm. **Ruler:** Elizabeth II **Obv:** Young bust right **Obv. Legend:** ELIZABETH THE SECOND

Date	Mintage	VF20	XF40	MS60	MS63	MS65
1980	50	PF65 1,600				

KM# 70.1 50 PENCE

13.50 g., Copper-Nickel, 30 mm. **Ruler:** Elizabeth II **Obv:** Young bust right **Rev:** Viking longship within design **Shape:** 7-sided

Date	Mintage	VF20	XF40	MS60	MS63	MS65
1980 AA	10,000	—	—	1.00	4.00	6.00
1980 AB	—	—	—	1.00	4.00	6.00
1980 PM DD	—	PF65 8.00				

KM# 70a 50 PENCE

15.50 g., 0.500 Silver 0.2492 oz. ASW, 30 mm. **Ruler:** Elizabeth II **Obv:** Young bust right **Rev:** Viking longship within design **Shape:** 7-sided

Date	Mintage	VF20	XF40	MS60	MS63	MS65
1980	10,000	PF65 10.00				
1982 (b)	10,000	PF65 15.00				

KM# 70c 50 PENCE

26.00 g., 0.917 Gold 0.7665 oz. AGW, 30 mm. **Ruler:** Elizabeth II **Obv:** Young bust right **Rev:** Viking longship within design **Shape:** 7-sided

Date	Mintage	VF20	XF40	MS60	MS63	MS65
1980	300	PF65 1,250				
1982 (b)	500	PF65 1,250				
1983	—	PF65 1,250				

KM# 70d 50 PENCE

30.40 g., 0.950 Platinum 0.9285 oz. APW, 30 mm. **Ruler:** Elizabeth II **Obv:** Young bust right **Rev:** Viking longship within design **Shape:** 7-sided

Date	Mintage	VF20	XF40	MS60	MS63	MS65
1980	500	PF65 1,650				
1982 (b)	500	PF65 1,650				
1983	—	PF65 1,650				

KM# 71 50 PENCE

13.50 g., Copper-Nickel, 30 mm. **Ruler:** Elizabeth II **Subject:** Christmas 1980 **Obv:** Young bust right **Rev:** Carriage pulled by horses, ship in background **Shape:** 7-sided

Date	Mintage	VF20	XF40	MS60	MS63	MS65
1980 AA	30,000	—	—	—	7.00	10.00
1980 AB	—	—	—	—	7.00	10.00
1980 AC	—	—	—	—	7.00	10.00
1980 AD	—	—	—	—	7.00	10.00
1980 PM BC	—	—	—	—	7.00	10.00

Note: Pobjoy called this item a "Diamond finish".

KM# 71a 50 PENCE

15.50 g., 0.925 Silver 0.461 oz. ASW, 30 mm. **Ruler:** Elizabeth II **Obv:** Young bust right **Rev:** Carriage pulled by horses, ship in background **Shape:** 7-sided

Date	Mintage	VF20	XF40	MS60	MS63	MS65
1980 D	5,000	PF65 20.00				

KM# 71b 50 PENCE

26.00 g., 0.917 Gold 0.7665 oz. AGW, 30 mm. **Ruler:** Elizabeth II **Subject:** Christmas 1980 **Obv:** Young bust right **Rev:** Carriage pulled by horses, ship in background **Shape:** 7-sided

Date	Mintage	VF20	XF40	MS60	MS63	MS65
1980	250	PF65 1,300				

KM# 71c 50 PENCE

30.40 g., 0.950 Platinum 0.9285 oz. APW, 30 mm. **Ruler:** Elizabeth II **Obv:** Young bust right **Rev:** Carriage pulled by horses, ship in background **Shape:** 7-sided

Date	Mintage	VF20	XF40	MS60	MS63	MS65
1980	50	PF65 1,650				

KM# 70.2 50 PENCE

13.50 g., Copper-Nickel **Ruler:** Elizabeth II **Obv:** Young bust right **Rev:** Viking longship within design **Shape:** 7-sided

Date	Mintage	VF20	XF40	MS60	MS63	MS65
1981 AA	—	—	—	1.00	4.00	6.00
1982 (b)	—	—	—	1.00	4.00	6.00
1982 (b)	Est. 25000	PF65 8.00				
1982 AC	—	—	—	1.00	4.00	6.00
1983 AA	—	—	—	1.00	4.00	6.00
1983 AB	—	—	—	1.00	4.00	6.00
1984 AA	—	—	—	1.00	4.00	6.00

KM# 70b 50 PENCE

15.50 g., 0.925 Silver 0.461 oz. ASW, 30 mm. **Ruler:** Elizabeth II **Obv:** Young bust right **Rev:** Viking longship within design **Shape:** 7-sided

Date	Mintage	VF20	XF40	MS60	MS63	MS65
1981	—	PF65 18.50				
1983	5,000	PF65 18.50				

KM# 83 50 PENCE

13.50 g., Copper-Nickel, 30 mm. **Ruler:** Elizabeth II **Subject:** Tourist Trophy Motorcycle Races **Obv:** Young bust right **Rev:** Motorcyclist within sprigs **Shape:** 7-sided

Date	Mintage	VF20	XF40	MS60	MS63	MS65
1981 AA	30,000	—	—	—	3.00	4.00
1981 AB	Inc. above	—	—	—	3.00	4.00
1981 PM BB Proof	—	—	—	—	—	—

KM# 83a 50 PENCE

15.50 g., 0.925 Silver 0.461 oz. ASW, 30 mm. **Ruler:** Elizabeth II **Subject:** Tourist Trophy Motorcycle Races **Obv:** Young bust right **Rev:** Motorcyclist within sprigs **Shape:** 7-sided

Date	Mintage	VF20	XF40	MS60	MS63	MS65
1981 PM D	5,000	PF65 20.00				

KM# 83b 50 PENCE

26.00 g., 0.917 Gold 0.7665 oz. AGW, 30 mm. **Ruler:** Elizabeth II **Subject:** Tourist Trophy Motorcycle Races **Obv:** Young bust right **Rev:** Motorcyclist within sprigs **Shape:** 7-sided

Date	Mintage	VF20	XF40	MS60	MS63	MS65
1981	250	PF65 1,300				

KM# 83c 50 PENCE
30.40 g., 0.950 Platinum 0.9285 oz. APW, 30 mm. **Ruler:** Elizabeth II **Subject:** Tourist Trophy Motorcycle Races **Obv:** Young bust right **Rev:** Motorcyclist within sprigs **Shape:** 7-sided

Date	Mintage	VF20	XF40	MS60	MS63	MS65
1981	50	PF65 1,650				

KM# 84 50 PENCE
13.50 g., Copper-Nickel, 30 mm. **Ruler:** Elizabeth II **Subject:** Christmas 1981 **Obv:** Young bust right **Rev:** Boat, standing figures and value **Shape:** 7-sided

Date	Mintage	VF20	XF40	MS60	MS63	MS65
1981 AA	30,000	—	—	—	7.00	10.00
1981 AB	Inc. above	—	—	—	7.00	10.00
1981 PM BB	30,000	PF65 12.00				
1981 PM BC	Inc. above	PF65 12.00				

KM# 84a 50 PENCE
15.50 g., 0.925 Silver 0.461 oz. ASW, 30 mm. **Ruler:** Elizabeth II **Subject:** Christmas 1981 **Obv:** Young bust right **Rev:** Boat, standing figures and value **Shape:** 7-sided

Date	Mintage	VF20	XF40	MS60	MS63	MS65
1981 PM D	5,000	PF65 20.00				

KM# 84b 50 PENCE
26.00 g., 0.917 Gold 0.7665 oz. AGW, 30 mm. **Ruler:** Elizabeth II **Subject:** Christmas 1981 **Obv:** Young bust right **Rev:** Boat, standing figures and value **Shape:** 7-sided

Date	Mintage	VF20	XF40	MS60	MS63	MS65
1981	250	PF65 1,300				

KM# 84c 50 PENCE
30.40 g., 0.950 Platinum 0.9285 oz. APW, 30 mm. **Ruler:** Elizabeth II **Subject:** Christmas 1981 **Obv:** Young bust right **Rev:** Boat, standing figures and value **Shape:** 7-sided

Date	Mintage	VF20	XF40	MS60	MS63	MS65
1981	—	PF65 1,650				

KM# 101 50 PENCE
13.50 g., Copper-Nickel, 30 mm. **Ruler:** Elizabeth II **Subject:** Tourist Trophy Motorcycle Races **Obv:** Young bust right **Rev:** Motorcyclist within sprigs **Shape:** 7-sided

Date	Mintage	VF20	XF40	MS60	MS63	MS65
1982 AA	30,000	—	—	—	3.00	4.00
1982	—	PF65 7.50				

KM# 101a 50 PENCE
15.50 g., 0.925 Silver 0.461 oz. ASW, 30 mm. **Ruler:** Elizabeth II **Subject:** Tourist Trophy Motorcycle Races **Obv:** Young bust right **Rev:** Motorcyclist within sprigs **Shape:** 7-sided

Date	Mintage	VF20	XF40	MS60	MS63	MS65
1982	5,000	PF65 20.00				

KM# 101b 50 PENCE
26.00 g., 0.917 Gold 0.7665 oz. AGW, 30 mm. **Ruler:** Elizabeth II **Subject:** Tourist Trophy Motorcycle Races **Obv:** Young bust right **Rev:** Motorcyclist within sprigs **Shape:** 7-sided

Date	Mintage	VF20	XF40	MS60	MS63	MS65
1982	250	PF65 1,300				

KM# 101c 50 PENCE
30.40 g., 0.950 Platinum 0.9285 oz. APW, 30 mm. **Ruler:** Elizabeth II **Subject:** Tourist Trophy Motorcycle Races **Obv:** Young bust right **Rev:** Motorcyclist within sprigs **Shape:** 7-sided

Date	Mintage	VF20	XF40	MS60	MS63	MS65
1982	50	PF65 1,650				

KM# 102 50 PENCE
13.50 g., Copper-Nickel, 30 mm. **Ruler:** Elizabeth II **Subject:** Christmas 1982 **Obv:** Young bust right **Rev:** Carolers around tree **Shape:** 7-sided

Date	Mintage	VF20	XF40	MS60	MS63	MS65
1982 AA	30,000	—	—	—	7.00	10.00
1982 AB	Inc. above	—	—	—	7.00	10.00
1982 PM BB	30,000	PF65 12.00				

KM# 102a 50 PENCE
15.50 g., 0.925 Silver 0.461 oz. ASW, 30 mm. **Ruler:** Elizabeth II **Subject:** Christmas 1982 **Obv:** Young bust right **Rev:** Carolers around tree **Shape:** 7-sided

Date	Mintage	VF20	XF40	MS60	MS63	MS65
1982 PM D	5,000	PF65 20.00				

KM# 102b 50 PENCE
26.00 g., 0.917 Gold 0.7665 oz. AGW, 30 mm. **Ruler:** Elizabeth II **Subject:** Christmas 1982 **Obv:** Young bust right **Rev:** Carolers around tree **Shape:** 7-sided

Date	Mintage	VF20	XF40	MS60	MS63	MS65
1982	250	PF65 1,300				

KM# 102c 50 PENCE
30.40 g., 0.950 Platinum 0.9285 oz. APW, 30 mm. **Ruler:** Elizabeth II **Subject:** Christmas 1982 **Obv:** Young bust right **Rev:** Carolers around tree **Shape:** 7-sided

Date	Mintage	VF20	XF40	MS60	MS63	MS65
1982	50	PF65 1,650				

KM# 107 50 PENCE
13.50 g., Copper-Nickel, 30 mm. **Ruler:** Elizabeth II **Subject:** Christmas 1983 **Obv:** Young bust right **Rev:** Ford Model T driving left **Shape:** 7-sided

Date	Mintage	VF20	XF40	MS60	MS63	MS65
1983 AA	—	—	—	—	7.00	10.00
1983 AB	—	—	—	—	7.00	10.00
1983 AC	30,000	—	—	—	7.00	10.00
1983 AA/C	—	—	—	—	7.00	10.00
1983 AD	—	—	—	—	7.00	10.00
1983 BB	—	PF65 12.00				

KM# 107a 50 PENCE
15.50 g., 0.925 Silver 0.461 oz. ASW, 30 mm. **Ruler:** Elizabeth II **Series:** Christmas 1983 **Obv:** Young bust right **Rev:** Ford Model T driving left **Shape:** 7-sided

Date	Mintage	VF20	XF40	MS60	MS63	MS65
1983	5,000	PF65 20.00				

KM# 107b 50 PENCE
26.00 g., 0.917 Gold 0.7665 oz. AGW, 30 mm. **Ruler:** Elizabeth II **Subject:** Christmas 1983 **Obv:** Young bust right **Rev:** Ford Model T driving left **Shape:** 7-sided

Date	Mintage	VF20	XF40	MS60	MS63	MS65
1983	250	PF65 1,300				

KM# 107c 50 PENCE
30.40 g., 0.950 Platinum 0.9285 oz. APW, 30 mm. **Ruler:** Elizabeth II **Subject:** Christmas 1983 **Obv:** Young bust right **Rev:** Ford Model T driving left **Shape:** 7-sided

Date	Mintage	VF20	XF40	MS60	MS63	MS65
1983	50	PF65 1,650				

KM# 108 50 PENCE
13.50 g., Copper-Nickel, 30 mm. **Ruler:** Elizabeth II **Subject:** Tourist Trophy Motorcycle Races **Obv:** Young bust right **Rev:** Motorcyclist within sprigs **Shape:** 7-sided

Date	Mintage	VF20	XF40	MS60	MS63	MS65
1983 AA	30,000	—	—	—	5.00	6.00
1983 AB	Inc. above	—	—	—	5.00	6.00
1983 AC	Inc. above	—	—	—	5.00	6.00
1983 AD	Inc. above	—	—	—	5.00	6.00

KM# 108a 50 PENCE
15.50 g., 0.925 Silver 0.461 oz. ASW, 30 mm. **Ruler:** Elizabeth II **Obv:** Young bust right **Rev:** Motorcyclist within sprigs **Edge Lettering:** Tourist Trophy Motorcycle Races **Shape:** 7-sided

Date	Mintage	VF20	XF40	MS60	MS63	MS65
1983	5,000	PF65 20.00				

KM# 108b 50 PENCE
26.00 g., 0.917 Gold 0.7665 oz. AGW, 30 mm. **Ruler:** Elizabeth II **Subject:** Tourist Trophy Motorcycle Races **Obv:** Young bust right **Rev:** Motorcyclist within sprigs **Shape:** 7-sided

Date	Mintage	VF20	XF40	MS60	MS63	MS65
1983	250	PF65 1,300				

KM# 108c 50 PENCE
30.40 g., 0.950 Platinum 0.9285 oz. APW, 30 mm. **Ruler:** Elizabeth II **Subject:** Tourist Trophy Motorcycle Races **Obv:** Young bust right **Rev:** Motorcyclist within sprigs **Shape:** 7-sided

Date	Mintage	VF20	XF40	MS60	MS63	MS65
1983	50	PF65 1,650				

KM# 125 50 PENCE
13.50 g., Copper-Nickel, 30 mm. **Ruler:** Elizabeth II **Subject:** Quincentenary of the College of Arms **Obv:** Young bust right **Rev:** Viking longship on shield **Shape:** 7-sided

Date	Mintage	VF20	XF40	MS60	MS63	MS65
1984 AA	—	—	—	—	5.00	6.00
1984 AB	—	—	—	—	5.00	6.00

KM# 125a 50 PENCE
15.50 g., 0.925 Silver 0.461 oz. ASW, 30 mm. **Ruler:** Elizabeth II **Subject:** Quincentenary of the College of Arms **Obv:** Young bust right **Rev:** Viking longship on shield **Shape:** 7-sided

Date	Mintage	VF20	XF40	MS60	MS63	MS65
1984	—	PF65 20.00				

KM# 125b 50 PENCE
26.00 g., 0.917 Gold 0.7665 oz. AGW, 30 mm. **Ruler:** Elizabeth II **Subject:** Quincentenary of the College of Arms **Obv:** Young bust right **Rev:** Viking longship on shield **Shape:** 7-sided

Date	Mintage	VF20	XF40	MS60	MS63	MS65
1984	150	PF65 1,300				

KM# 126 50 PENCE
13.50 g., Copper-Nickel, 30 mm. **Ruler:** Elizabeth II **Subject:** Tourist Trophy Motorcycle Races **Obv:** Young bust right **Rev:** Motorcyclists within sprigs **Shape:** 7-sided

Date	Mintage	VF20	XF40	MS60	MS63	MS65
1984 AA	30,000	—	—	—	5.00	6.00

KM# 126a 50 PENCE
15.50 g., 0.925 Silver 0.461 oz. ASW, 30 mm. **Ruler:** Elizabeth II **Subject:** Tourist Trophy Motorcyle Races **Obv:** Young bust right **Rev:** Motorcyclists within sprigs **Shape:** 7-sided

Date	Mintage	VF20	XF40	MS60	MS63	MS65
1984	5,000	PF65 20.00				

KM# 126b 50 PENCE
26.00 g., 0.917 Gold 0.7665 oz. AGW, 30 mm. **Ruler:** Elizabeth II **Subject:** Tourist Trophy Motorcycle Races **Obv:** Young bust right **Rev:** Motorcyclists within sprigs **Shape:** 7-sided

Date	Mintage	VF20	XF40	MS60	MS63	MS65
1984	250	PF65 1,300				

KM# 126c 50 PENCE
30.40 g., 0.950 Platinum 0.9285 oz. APW, 30 mm. **Ruler:** Elizabeth II **Subject:** Tourist Trophy Motorcycle Races **Obv:** Young bust right **Rev:** Motorcyclists within sprigs **Shape:** 7-sided

Date	Mintage	VF20	XF40	MS60	MS63	MS65
1984	50	PF65 1,650				

KM# 127 50 PENCE
13.50 g., Copper-Nickel, 30 mm. **Ruler:** Elizabeth II **Subject:** Christmas 1984 **Obv:** Young bust right **Rev:** Train and standing figures **Shape:** 7-sided

Date	Mintage	VF20	XF40	MS60	MS63	MS65
1984 AA	—	—	—	—	7.00	10.00
1984 AB	—	—	—	—	7.00	10.00
1984 AC	—	—	—	—	7.00	10.00
1984 AD	—	—	—	—	7.00	10.00
1984 BB	30,000	PF65 12.00				

KM# 127a 50 PENCE

15.50 g., 0.925 Silver 0.461 oz. ASW, 30 mm. **Ruler:** Elizabeth II **Subject:** Christmas 1984 **Obv:** Young bust right **Rev:** Train and standing figures **Shape:** 7-sided

Date	Mintage	VF20	XF40	MS60	MS63	MS65
1984	—	PF65 25.00				

KM# 127b 50 PENCE

26.00 g., 0.917 Gold 0.7665 oz. AGW, 30 mm. **Ruler:** Elizabeth II **Subject:** Christmas 1984 **Obv:** Young bust right **Rev:** Train and standing figures **Shape:** 7-sided

Date	Mintage	VF20	XF40	MS60	MS63	MS65
1984	250	PF65 1,300				

KM# 127c 50 PENCE

30.40 g., 0.950 Platinum 0.9285 oz. APW **Ruler:** Elizabeth II **Subject:** Christmas 1984 **Obv:** Young bust right **Rev:** Train and standing figures **Shape:** 7-sided

Date	Mintage	VF20	XF40	MS60	MS63	MS65
1984	—	PF65 1,650				

KM# 148 50 PENCE

13.50 g., Copper-Nickel, 30 mm. **Ruler:** Elizabeth II **Obv:** Crowned head right **Rev:** Viking longship on shield **Shape:** 7-sided

Date	Mintage	VF20	XF40	MS60	MS63	MS65
1985(w) AA	—	—	—	—	5.00	6.00
1985(w) AB	—	—	—	—	5.00	6.00
1985 (w)	50,000	PF65 8.00				
1986 AA	—	—	—	—	5.00	6.00
1986 AB	—	—	—	—	5.00	6.00
1987 AA	—	—	—	—	5.00	6.00

KM# 148a 50 PENCE

15.50 g., 0.925 Silver 0.461 oz. ASW, 30 mm. **Ruler:** Elizabeth II **Obv:** Crowned head right **Rev:** Viking longship on shield **Shape:** 7-sided

Date	Mintage	VF20	XF40	MS60	MS63	MS65
1985	Est. 10000	PF65 20.00				

KM# 148b 50 PENCE

26.00 g., 0.917 Gold 0.7665 oz. AGW, 30 mm. **Ruler:** Elizabeth II **Obv:** Crowned head right **Rev:** Viking longship on shield **Shape:** 7-sided

Date	Mintage	VF20	XF40	MS60	MS63	MS65
1985	Est. 300	PF65 1,300				

KM# 148c 50 PENCE

30.40 g., 0.950 Platinum 0.9285 oz. APW, 30 mm. **Ruler:** Elizabeth II **Obv:** Crowned head right **Rev:** Viking longship on shield **Shape:** 7-sided

Date	Mintage	VF20	XF40	MS60	MS63	MS65
1985	Est. 200	PF65 1,650				

KM# 158 50 PENCE

13.50 g., Copper-Nickel, 30 mm. **Ruler:** Elizabeth II **Subject:** Christmas 1985, commemorates first Christmas air mail of 1935 **Obv:** Crowned head right **Rev:** Airplanes **Shape:** 7-sided

Date	Mintage	VF20	XF40	MS60	MS63	MS65
1985 AA	—	—	—	—	7.00	10.00
1985 AB	—	—	—	—	7.00	10.00
1985 BB	—	—	—	—	7.00	10.00
1985	—	PF65 12.00				

KM# 158a 50 PENCE

15.50 g., 0.925 Silver 0.461 oz. ASW, 30 mm. **Ruler:** Elizabeth II **Subject:** Christmas 1985 **Obv:** Crowned head right **Rev:** Airplanes **Shape:** 7-sided

Date	Mintage	VF20	XF40	MS60	MS63	MS65
1985	5,000	PF65 20.00				

KM# 158b 50 PENCE

26.00 g., 0.917 Gold 0.7665 oz. AGW, 30 mm. **Ruler:** Elizabeth II **Subject:** Christmas 1985 **Obv:** Crowned head right **Rev:** Airplanes **Shape:** 7-sided

Date	Mintage	VF20	XF40	MS60	MS63	MS65
1985	—	PF65 1,300				

KM# 158c 50 PENCE

30.40 g., 0.950 Platinum 0.9285 oz. APW, 30 mm. **Ruler:** Elizabeth II **Subject:** Christmas 1985 **Obv:** Crowned head right **Rev:** Airplanes **Shape:** 7-sided

Date	Mintage	VF20	XF40	MS60	MS63	MS65
1985	—	PF65 1,650				

KM# 172 50 PENCE

13.50 g., Copper-Nickel, 30 mm. **Ruler:** Elizabeth II **Subject:** Christmas 1986 **Obv:** Crowned head right **Rev:** Horse-drawn tram **Shape:** 7-sided

Date	Mintage	VF20	XF40	MS60	MS63	MS65
1986 AA	—	—	—	—	7.00	10.00
1986 AB	—	—	—	—	7.00	10.00
1986	—	PF65 12.00				

KM# 172a 50 PENCE

15.50 g., 0.925 Silver 0.461 oz. ASW, 30 mm. **Ruler:** Elizabeth II **Subject:** Christmas 1986 **Obv:** Crowned head right **Rev:** Horse-drawn tram **Shape:** 7-sided

Date	Mintage	VF20	XF40	MS60	MS63	MS65
1986	Est. 5000	PF65 20.00				

KM# 172b 50 PENCE

26.00 g., 0.917 Gold 0.7665 oz. AGW, 30 mm. **Ruler:** Elizabeth II **Subject:** Christmas 1986 **Obv:** Crowned head right **Rev:** Horse-drawn tram **Shape:** 7-sided

Date	Mintage	VF20	XF40	MS60	MS63	MS65
1986	—	PF65 1,300				

KM# 190 50 PENCE

13.50 g., Copper-Nickel, 30 mm. **Ruler:** Elizabeth II **Subject:** Christmas 1987 **Obv:** Crowned head right **Rev:** Bus and standing figures **Shape:** 7-sided

Date	Mintage	VF20	XF40	MS60	MS63	MS65
1987 AA	Est. 30000	—	—	—	7.00	10.00
1987 D	—	—	—	—	7.00	10.00
1987	—	PF65 12.00				

KM# 190a 50 PENCE

15.50 g., 0.925 Silver 0.461 oz. ASW, 30 mm. **Ruler:** Elizabeth II **Subject:** Christmas 1987 **Obv:** Crowned head right **Rev:** Bus and standing figures **Shape:** 7-sided

Date	Mintage	VF20	XF40	MS60	MS63	MS65
1987	Est. 5000	PF65 20.00				

KM# 190b 50 PENCE

26.00 g., 0.917 Gold 0.7665 oz. AGW, 30 mm. **Ruler:** Elizabeth II **Subject:** Christmas 1987 **Obv:** Crowned head right **Rev:** Bus and standing figures **Shape:** 7-sided

Date	Mintage	VF20	XF40	MS60	MS63	MS65
1987	Est. 250	PF65 1,300				

KM# 190c 50 PENCE

30.40 g., 0.950 Platinum 0.9285 oz. APW, 30 mm. **Ruler:** Elizabeth II **Subject:** Christmas 1987 **Obv:** Crowned head right **Rev:** Bus and standing figures **Shape:** 7-sided

Date	Mintage	VF20	XF40	MS60	MS63	MS65
1987	Est. 50	PF65 1,650				

KM# 212 50 PENCE

13.50 g., Copper-Nickel, 30 mm. **Ruler:** Elizabeth II **Obv:** Crowned head right **Rev:** Computer **Shape:** 7-sided

Date	Mintage	VF20	XF40	MS60	MS63	MS65
1988 AA	—	—	—	—	5.00	6.00
1989 AA	—	—	—	—	5.00	6.00

Date	Mintage	VF20	XF40	MS60	MS63	MS65
1990 AA	—	—	—	—	5.00	6.00
1991 AA	—	—	—	—	5.00	6.00
1992 AA	—	—	—	—	5.00	6.00
1993 AA	—	—	—	—	5.00	6.00
1994 AA	—	—	—	—	5.00	6.00
1995 AA	—	—	—	—	5.00	6.00
1997 AA	—	—	—	—	5.00	6.00

KM# 244 50 PENCE

13.50 g., Copper-Nickel, 30 mm. **Ruler:** Elizabeth II **Subject:** Christmas 1988 **Obv:** Crowned head right **Rev:** Motorbike and sidecar **Shape:** 7-sided

Date	Mintage	VF20	XF40	MS60	MS63	MS65
1988 AA	—	—	—	—	7.00	10.00
1988 BA	—	—	—	—	7.00	10.00
1988 BB	—	PF65 12.00				

KM# 244a 50 PENCE

15.50 g., 0.925 Silver 0.461 oz. ASW, 30 mm. **Ruler:** Elizabeth II **Subject:** Christmas 1988 **Obv:** Crowned head right **Rev:** Motorbike and sidecar **Shape:** 7-sided

Date	Mintage	VF20	XF40	MS60	MS63	MS65
1988	—	PF65 20.00				

KM# 244b 50 PENCE

26.00 g., 0.917 Gold 0.7665 oz. AGW, 30 mm. **Ruler:** Elizabeth II **Subject:** Christmas 1988 **Obv:** Crowned head right **Rev:** Motorbike and sidecar **Shape:** 7-sided

Date	Mintage	VF20	XF40	MS60	MS63	MS65
1988	—	PF65 1,300				

KM# 244c 50 PENCE

30.40 g., 0.950 Platinum 0.9285 oz. APW, 30 mm. **Ruler:** Elizabeth II **Subject:** Christmas 1988 **Obv:** Crowned head right **Rev:** Motorbike and sidecar **Shape:** 7-sided

Date	Mintage	VF20	XF40	MS60	MS63	MS65
1988	—	PF65 1,650				

KM# 259 50 PENCE

13.50 g., Copper-Nickel, 30 mm. **Ruler:** Elizabeth II **Subject:** Christmas 1989 **Obv:** Crowned head right **Rev:** Electric trolley car **Shape:** 7-sided

Date	Mintage	VF20	XF40	MS60	MS63	MS65
1989 AA	—	—	—	—	7.00	10.00
1989 BB	—	PF65 12.00				

KM# 259a 50 PENCE

15.50 g., 0.925 Silver 0.461 oz. ASW, 30 mm. **Ruler:** Elizabeth II **Subject:** Christmas 1989 **Obv:** Crowned head right **Rev:** Electric trolly car **Shape:** 7-sided

Date	Mintage	VF20	XF40	MS60	MS63	MS65
1989	—	PF65 40.00				

KM# 259b 50 PENCE

26.00 g., 0.917 Gold 0.7665 oz. AGW, 30 mm. **Ruler:** Elizabeth II **Subject:** Christmas 1989 **Obv:** Crowned head right **Rev:** Electric trolley car **Shape:** 7-sided

Date	Mintage	VF20	XF40	MS60	MS63	MS65
1989	—	PF65 1,300				

KM# 259c 50 PENCE

30.40 g., 0.950 Platinum 0.9285 oz. APW, 30 mm. **Ruler:** Elizabeth II **Subject:** Christmas 1989 **Obv:** Crowned head right **Rev:** Electric trolley car **Shape:** 7-sided

Date	Mintage	VF20	XF40	MS60	MS63	MS65
1989	—	PF65 1,650				

KM# 282 50 PENCE
13.50 g., Copper-Nickel, 30 mm. **Ruler:** Elizabeth II **Subject:** Christmas 1990 **Obv:** Crowned head right **Rev:** Ship and standing figures **Shape:** 7-sided

Date	Mintage	VF20	XF40	MS60	MS63	MS65
1990 AA	—	—	—	—	7.00	10.00
1990 AB	—	—	—	—	7.00	10.00
1990	30,000	PF65 12.00				

KM# 282a 50 PENCE
15.50 g., 0.925 Silver 0.461 oz. ASW, 30 mm. **Ruler:** Elizabeth II **Subject:** Christmas 1990 **Obv:** Crowned head right **Rev:** Ship and standing figures **Shape:** 7-sided

Date	Mintage	VF20	XF40	MS60	MS63	MS65
1990	5,000	PF65 40.00				

KM# 282b 50 PENCE
26.00 g., 0.917 Gold 0.7665 oz. AGW, 30 mm. **Ruler:** Elizabeth II **Subject:** Christmas 1990 **Obv:** Crowned head right **Rev:** Ship and standing figures **Shape:** 7-sided

Date	Mintage	VF20	XF40	MS60	MS63	MS65
1990	250	PF65 1,300				

KM# 282c 50 PENCE
30.40 g., 0.950 Platinum 0.9285 oz. APW, 30 mm. **Ruler:** Elizabeth II **Subject:** Christmas 1990 **Obv:** Crowned head right **Rev:** Ship and standing figures **Shape:** 7-sided

Date	Mintage	VF20	XF40	MS60	MS63	MS65
1990	50	PF65 1,650				

KM# 303 50 PENCE
13.50 g., Copper-Nickel, 30 mm. **Ruler:** Elizabeth II **Subject:** Christmas 1991 **Obv:** Crowned head right **Rev:** Nativity scene **Shape:** 7-sided

Date	Mintage	VF20	XF40	MS60	MS63	MS65
1991 AA	—	—	—	—	7.00	10.00
1991	30,000	PF65 12.00				

KM# 303a 50 PENCE
15.50 g., 0.925 Silver 0.461 oz. ASW, 30 mm. **Ruler:** Elizabeth II **Subject:** Christmas 1991 **Obv:** Crowned head right **Rev:** Nativity scene **Shape:** 7-sided

Date	Mintage	VF20	XF40	MS60	MS63	MS65
1991	5,000	PF65 40.00				

KM# 303b 50 PENCE
26.00 g., 0.917 Gold 0.7665 oz. AGW, 30 mm. **Ruler:** Elizabeth II **Subject:** Christmas 1991 **Obv:** Crowned head right **Rev:** Nativity scene **Shape:** 7-sided

Date	Mintage	VF20	XF40	MS60	MS63	MS65
1991	250	PF65 1,300				

KM# 303c 50 PENCE
30.40 g., 0.950 Platinum 0.9285 oz. APW, 30 mm. **Ruler:** Elizabeth II **Subject:** Christmas 1991 **Obv:** Crowned head right **Rev:** Nativity scene **Shape:** 7-sided

Date	Mintage	VF20	XF40	MS60	MS63	MS65
1991	50	PF65 1,650				

KM# 335 50 PENCE
13.50 g., Copper-Nickel, 30 mm. **Ruler:** Elizabeth II **Subject:** Christmas 1992 **Obv:** Crowned head right **Rev:** Newspaper boy hawking the Manx Mercury **Shape:** 7-sided

Date	Mintage	VF20	XF40	MS60	MS63	MS65
1992 AA	—	—	—	—	7.00	10.00
1992	—	PF65 12.00				

KM# 335a 50 PENCE
15.50 g., 0.925 Silver 0.461 oz. ASW, 30 mm. **Ruler:** Elizabeth II **Subject:** Christmas 1992 **Obv:** Crowned head right **Rev:** Newspaper boy hawking the Manx Mercury **Shape:** 7-sided

Date	Mintage	VF20	XF40	MS60	MS63	MS65
1992	5,000	PF65 40.00				

KM# 335b 50 PENCE
26.00 g., 0.917 Gold 0.7665 oz. AGW, 30 mm. **Ruler:** Elizabeth II **Subject:** Christmas 1992 **Obv:** Crowned head right **Rev:** Newspaper boy hawking the Manx Mercury **Shape:** 7-sided

Date	Mintage	VF20	XF40	MS60	MS63	MS65
1992	—	PF65 1,300				

KM# 335c 50 PENCE
30.40 g., 0.950 Platinum 0.9285 oz. APW, 30 mm. **Ruler:** Elizabeth II **Subject:** Christmas 1992 **Obv:** Crowned head right **Rev:** Newspaper boy hawking the Manx Mercury **Shape:** 7-sided

Date	Mintage	VF20	XF40	MS60	MS63	MS65
1992	—	PF65 1,650				

KM# 356 50 PENCE
13.50 g., Copper-Nickel, 30 mm. **Ruler:** Elizabeth II **Subject:** Christmas 1993 **Obv:** Crowned head right **Rev:** Framed nativity scene **Shape:** 7-sided

Date	Mintage	VF20	XF40	MS60	MS63	MS65
1993 AA	—	—	—	—	7.00	10.00
1993 D	—	—	—	—	7.00	10.00
1993	30,000	PF65 12.00				

KM# 356a 50 PENCE
15.50 g., 0.925 Silver 0.461 oz. ASW, 30 mm. **Ruler:** Elizabeth II **Subject:** Christmas 1993 **Obv:** Crowned head right **Rev:** Framed nativity scene **Shape:** 7-sided

Date	Mintage	VF20	XF40	MS60	MS63	MS65
1993	Est. 5000	PF65 40.00				

KM# 356b 50 PENCE
26.00 g., 0.917 Gold 0.7665 oz. AGW, 30 mm. **Ruler:** Elizabeth II **Subject:** Christmas 1993 **Obv:** Crowned head right **Rev:** Framed nativity scene **Shape:** 7-sided

Date	Mintage	VF20	XF40	MS60	MS63	MS65
1993	Est. 250	PF65 1,300				

KM# 356c 50 PENCE
30.40 g., 0.950 Platinum 0.9285 oz. APW, 30 mm. **Ruler:** Elizabeth II **Subject:** Christmas 1993 **Obv:** Crowned head right **Rev:** Framed nativity scene **Shape:** 7-sided

Date	Mintage	VF20	XF40	MS60	MS63	MS65
1993	Est. 50	PF65 1,650				

KM# 425 50 PENCE
13.50 g., Copper-Nickel, 30 mm. **Ruler:** Elizabeth II **Subject:** Christmas 1994 **Obv:** Crowned head right **Rev:** Two young boys with pole **Edge:** Smooth **Shape:** 7-sided

Date	Mintage	VF20	XF40	MS60	MS63	MS65
1994 AA	—	—	—	—	7.00	10.00
1994	—	—	—	—	7.00	10.00

KM# 425a 50 PENCE
15.50 g., 0.925 Silver 0.461 oz. ASW, 30 mm. **Ruler:** Elizabeth II **Subject:** Christmas 1994 **Obv:** Crowned head right **Rev:** Two young boys with pole **Shape:** 7-sided

Date	Mintage	VF20	XF40	MS60	MS63	MS65
1994	—	PF65 40.00				

KM# 456 50 PENCE
13.50 g., Copper-Nickel, 30 mm. **Ruler:** Elizabeth II **Subject:** Legislative Building Centenary **Obv:** Crowned head right **Rev:** Building **Edge:** Smooth **Shape:** 7-sided

Date	Mintage	VF20	XF40	MS60	MS63	MS65
1994 AA	—	—	—	—	3.00	5.00

KM# 456a 50 PENCE
15.50 g., 0.925 Silver 0.461 oz. ASW, 30 mm. **Ruler:** Elizabeth II **Subject:** Legislative Building Centenary **Obv:** Crowned head right **Rev:** Building **Shape:** 7-sided

Date	Mintage	VF20	XF40	MS60	MS63	MS65
1994	—	PF65 40.00				

KM# 521 50 PENCE
13.50 g., Copper-Nickel, 30 mm. **Ruler:** Elizabeth II **Subject:** Christmas 1995 **Obv:** Crowned head right **Rev:** Sledding scene **Edge:** Smooth **Shape:** 7-sided

Date	Mintage	VF20	XF40	MS60	MS63	MS65
1995 AA	Est. 30000	—	—	—	7.00	10.00

KM# 521a 50 PENCE
15.50 g., 0.925 Silver 0.461 oz. ASW, 30 mm. **Ruler:** Elizabeth II **Subject:** Christmas 1995 **Obv:** Crowned head right **Rev:** Sledding scene **Shape:** 7-sided

Date	Mintage	VF20	XF40	MS60	MS63	MS65
1995	Est. 5000	PF65 40.00				

KM# 521b 50 PENCE
26.00 g., 0.917 Gold 0.7665 oz. AGW, 30 mm. **Ruler:** Elizabeth II **Subject:** Christmas 1995 **Obv:** Crowned head right **Rev:** Sledding scene **Shape:** 7-sided

Date	Mintage	VF20	XF40	MS60	MS63	MS65
1995	Est. 250	PF65 1,300				

KM# 593 50 PENCE
13.50 g., Copper-Nickel, 30 mm. **Ruler:** Elizabeth II **Subject:** Sports **Obv:** Crowned head right **Rev:** Motorcyclists **Edge:** Smooth

Date	Mintage	VF20	XF40	MS60	MS63	MS65
1996 AA	—	—	—	—	3.00	4.00
1997 AA	—	—	—	—	3.00	4.00

KM# 694 50 PENCE
13.50 g., Copper-Nickel, 30 mm. **Ruler:** Elizabeth II **Subject:** Christmas 1996 **Obv:** Crowned head right **Rev:** Children throwing snowballs in front of church **Edge:** Smooth **Shape:** 7-sided

Date	Mintage	VF20	XF40	MS60	MS63	MS65
1996 AA	Est. 30000	—	—	—	7.00	10.00

KM# 694a 50 PENCE

15.50 g., 0.925 Silver 0.461 oz. ASW, 30 mm. **Ruler:** Elizabeth II **Subject:** Christmas 1996 **Obv:** Crowned head right **Rev:** Children throwing snowballs in front of church **Shape:** 7-sided

Date	Mintage	VF20	XF40	MS60	MS63	MS65
1996	Est. 5000	PF65 40.00				

KM# 694b 50 PENCE

26.00 g., 0.917 Gold 0.7665 oz. AGW, 30 mm. **Ruler:** Elizabeth II **Subject:** Christmas 1996 **Obv:** Crowned head right **Rev:** Children throwing snowballs in front of church **Shape:** 7-sided

Date	Mintage	VF20	XF40	MS60	MS63	MS65
1996	Est. 250	PF65 1,300				

KM# 794 50 PENCE

8.00 g., Copper-Nickel, 27.3 mm. **Ruler:** Elizabeth II **Subject:** Christmas 1997 **Obv:** Crowned head right **Rev:** Cameo at lower left of figures on book **Edge:** Smooth **Shape:** 7-sided

Date	Mintage	VF20	XF40	MS60	MS63	MS65
1997	—	—	—	—	7.00	10.00

KM# 794a 50 PENCE

8.00 g., 0.925 Silver 0.2379 oz. ASW, 27.3 mm. **Ruler:** Elizabeth II **Subject:** Christmas 1987 **Obv:** Crowned head right **Rev:** Cameo at lower left of figures on book **Shape:** 7-sided

Date	Mintage	VF20	XF40	MS60	MS63	MS65
1997	Est. 5000	PF65 40.00				

KM# 794b 50 PENCE

8.00 g., 0.916 Gold 0.2356 oz. AGW, 27.3 mm. **Ruler:** Elizabeth II **Subject:** Christmas 1997 **Obv:** Crowned head right **Rev:** Cameo to lower left of figures on book **Shape:** 7-sided

Date	Mintage	VF20	XF40	MS60	MS63	MS65
1997	250	PF65 425				

KM# 806 50 PENCE

8.00 g., Copper-Nickel, 27.3 mm. **Ruler:** Elizabeth II **Obv:** Crowned head right **Rev:** Two motorcycle racers **Edge:** Plain **Shape:** 7-sided

Date	Mintage	VF20	XF40	MS60	MS63	MS65
1997 PM AA	—	—	—	—	3.00	4.00

KM# 806a 50 PENCE

8.00 g., 0.925 Silver 0.2379 oz. ASW, 27.3 mm. **Ruler:** Elizabeth II **Obv:** Crowned head right **Rev:** Two motorcycle racers **Edge:** Plain **Shape:** 7-sided

Date	Mintage	VF20	XF40	MS60	MS63	MS65
1997 PM	5,000	PF65 35.00				

KM# 806b 50 PENCE

8.00 g., 0.9999 Gold 0.2572 oz. AGW, 27.3 mm. **Ruler:** Elizabeth II **Obv:** Crowned head right **Rev:** Two motorcycle racers **Edge:** Plain **Shape:** 7-sided

Date	Mintage	VF20	XF40	MS60	MS63	MS65
1997 PM	250	PF65 450				

KM# 905 50 PENCE

8.00 g., Copper-Nickel, 27.3 mm. **Ruler:** Elizabeth II **Obv:** Head with tiara right **Rev:** Motorcyclists **Edge:** Smooth **Shape:** 7-sided

Date	Mintage	VF20	XF40	MS60	MS63	MS65
1998 PM AA	—	—	—	—	3.00	4.00
1999 PM AA	—	—	—	—	3.00	4.00

Note: Lettering varieties exist.

KM# 905a 50 PENCE

8.00 g., 0.925 Silver 0.2379 oz. ASW, 27.3 mm. **Ruler:** Elizabeth II **Obv:** Head with tiara right **Rev:** Two motorcycle racers **Shape:** 7-sided

Date	Mintage	VF20	XF40	MS60	MS63	MS65
1998 PM	5,000	PF65 35.00				

KM# 905b 50 PENCE

8.00 g., 0.9999 Gold 0.2572 oz. AGW, 27.3 mm. **Ruler:** Elizabeth II **Obv:** Head with tiara right **Rev:** Two motorcycle racers **Shape:** 7-sided

Date	Mintage	VF20	XF40	MS60	MS63	MS65
1998 PM	—	PF65 450				

KM# 908 50 PENCE

Copper-Nickel, 27.3 mm. **Ruler:** Elizabeth II **Subject:** Christmas 1998 **Obv:** Head with tiara right **Rev:** Kitchen scene **Edge:** Smooth **Shape:** 7-sided

Date	Mintage	VF20	XF40	MS60	MS63	MS65
1998 PM	Est. 30000	—	—	—	7.00	10.00

KM# 908a 50 PENCE

8.00 g., 0.925 Silver 0.2379 oz. ASW, 27.3 mm. **Ruler:** Elizabeth II **Subject:** Christmas 1998 **Obv:** Head with tiara right **Rev:** Kitchen scene **Shape:** 7-sided

Date	Mintage	VF20	XF40	MS60	MS63	MS65
1998	5,000	PF65 35.00				

KM# 908b 50 PENCE

8.00 g., 0.9167 Gold 0.2358 oz. AGW, 27.3 mm. **Ruler:** Elizabeth II **Subject:** Christmas 1998 **Obv:** Head with tiara right **Rev:** Kitchen scene **Shape:** 7-sided

Date	Mintage	VF20	XF40	MS60	MS63	MS65
1998	250	PF65 400				

KM# 993 50 PENCE

Copper-Nickel, 27.3 mm. **Ruler:** Elizabeth II **Obv:** Head with tiara right **Rev:** Motorcyclist within sprigs **Edge:** Smooth **Shape:** 7-sided

Date	Mintage	VF20	XF40	MS60	MS63	MS65
1999 PM AA	—	—	—	—	3.00	4.00

KM# 993a 50 PENCE

8.00 g., 0.925 Silver 0.2379 oz. ASW, 27.3 mm. **Ruler:** Elizabeth II **Obv:** Head with tiara right **Rev:** Motorcyclist within sprigs **Shape:** 7-sided

Date	Mintage	VF20	XF40	MS60	MS63	MS65
1999	Est. 5000	PF65 35.00				

KM# 993b 50 PENCE

8.00 g., 0.916 Gold 0.2356 oz. AGW, 27.3 mm. **Ruler:** Elizabeth II **Obv:** Head with tiara right **Rev:** Motorcyclist within sprigs **Shape:** 7-sided

Date	Mintage	VF20	XF40	MS60	MS63	MS65
1999	Est. 250	PF65 400				

KM# 1011 50 PENCE

8.00 g., Copper-Nickel, 27.3 mm. **Ruler:** Elizabeth II **Subject:** Christmas 1999 **Obv:** Head with tiara right **Rev:** Tree decorating scene **Edge:** Smooth **Shape:** 7-sided

Date	Mintage	VF20	XF40	MS60	MS63	MS65
1999 AA	Est. 30000	—	—	—	7.00	10.00

KM# 1011a 50 PENCE

8.00 g., 0.925 Silver 0.2379 oz. ASW, 27.3 mm. **Ruler:** Elizabeth II **Subject:** Christmas 1999 **Obv:** Head with tiara right **Rev:** Tree decorating scene **Shape:** 7-sided

Date	Mintage	VF20	XF40	MS60	MS63	MS65
1999	Est. 5000	PF65 35.00				

KM# 1011b 50 PENCE

8.00 g., 0.916 Gold 0.2356 oz. AGW, 27.3 mm. **Ruler:** Elizabeth II **Subject:** Christmas 1999 **Obv:** Head with tiara right **Rev:** Tree decorating scene **Shape:** 7-sided

Date	Mintage	VF20	XF40	MS60	MS63	MS65
1999	Est. 250	PF65 400				

KM# 1041 50 PENCE

8.00 g., Copper-Nickel, 27.3 mm. **Ruler:** Elizabeth II **Obv:** Head with tiara right **Rev:** Stylized crucifix **Edge:** Plain **Shape:** 7-sided

Date	Mintage	VF20	XF40	MS60	MS63	MS65
2000 PM AA	—	—	—	—	2.25	2.75

KM# 1050 50 PENCE

8.00 g., Copper-Nickel, 27.3 mm. **Ruler:** Elizabeth II **Obv:** Head with tiara right **Rev:** Seated figure at desk **Edge:** Plain **Shape:** 7-sided

Date	Mintage	VF20	XF40	MS60	MS63	MS65
2000 BB	30,000	—	—	—	7.00	10.00

KM# 1050a 50 PENCE

8.00 g., 0.925 Silver 0.2379 oz. ASW, 27.3 mm. **Ruler:** Elizabeth II **Obv:** Head with tiara right **Rev:** Seated figure at desk **Edge:** Plain **Shape:** 7-sided

Date	Mintage	VF20	XF40	MS60	MS63	MS65
2000	5,000	PF65 35.00				

KM# 1050b 50 PENCE

8.00 g., 0.916 Gold 0.2356 oz. AGW, 27.3 mm. **Ruler:** Elizabeth II **Obv:** Head with tiara right **Rev:** Seated figure at desk **Edge:** Plain **Shape:** 7-sided

Date	Mintage	VF20	XF40	MS60	MS63	MS65
2000	250	PF65 400				

KM# 15 1/2 SOVEREIGN (1/2 Pound)

3.99 g., 0.917 Gold 0.1178 oz. AGW **Ruler:** Elizabeth II **Subject:** 200th Anniversary of Acquisition **Obv:** Crowned bust right **Rev:** Triskeles on shield within rope wreath

Date	Mintage	VF20	XF40	MS60	MS63	MS65
1965	1,500	—	—	—	172	187

KM# 15a 1/2 SOVEREIGN (1/2 Pound)

4.00 g., 0.980 Gold 0.126 oz. AGW **Ruler:** Elizabeth II **Subject:** 200th Anniversary of Acquisition **Obv:** Crowned bust right **Rev:** Triskeles on shield within rope wreath

Date	Mintage	VF20	XF40	MS60	MS63	MS65
1965	1,000	PF65 210				

KM# 26 1/2 SOVEREIGN (1/2 Pound)

3.98 g., 0.917 Gold 0.1174 oz. AGW **Ruler:** Elizabeth II **Obv:** Young bust right **Rev:** Armored equestrian

Date	Mintage	VF20	XF40	MS60	MS63	MS65
1973 A	14,000	—	—	—	172	187
1973	1,250	PF65 195				
1974 A	6,566	—	—	—	172	187
1974 B	Inc. above	—	—	—	172	187
1974	2,500	PF65 195				
1975 A	1,956	—	—	—	172	187
1975 B	Inc. above	—	—	—	172	187
1975	—	PF65 195				
1976 A	2,558	—	—	—	172	187
1976 B	Inc. above	—	—	—	172	187
1976	—	PF65 195				
1977 A	—	—	—	—	172	187
1977 B	—	—	—	—	172	187
1977	1,250	PF65 195				
1978	1,250	PF65 195				
1979 (t) A	8,000	—	—	—	172	187
1979 (t) B	Inc. above	—	—	—	172	187
1979 (t)	30,000	PF65 195				
1980 A	—	—	—	—	—	—
1980 B	—	—	—	—	—	—
1980 (m)	7,500	PF65 195				
1980 (v)	—	PF65 195				

Date	Mintage	VF20	XF40	MS60	MS63	MS65
1982 (b)	40,000	—	—	—	172	187
1982 (b)	30,000	PF65 195				

KM# 85 1/2 SOVEREIGN (1/2 Pound)

3.98 g., 0.917 Gold 0.1174 oz. AGW **Ruler:** Elizabeth II **Subject:** Wedding of Prince Charles and Lady Diana **Obv:** Young bust right **Rev:** Portraits of Royal Couple, joined shields

Date	Mintage	VF20	XF40	MS60	MS63	MS65
1981	30,000	PF65 195				

KM# 260 1/2 SOVEREIGN (1/2 Pound)

3.98 g., 0.917 Gold 0.1174 oz. AGW **Ruler:** Elizabeth II **Obv:** Young bust right **Rev:** Four crowned shields

Date	Mintage	VF20	XF40	MS60	MS63	MS65
1984	20	PF65 195				
1984	20	—	—	—	172	187

KM# 264 1/2 SOVEREIGN (1/2 Pound)

3.98 g., 0.917 Gold 0.1174 oz. AGW **Ruler:** Elizabeth II **Obv:** Crowned head right **Rev:** Four crowned shields

Date	Mintage	VF20	XF40	MS60	MS63	MS65
1988	5,879	PF65 195				

KM# 16 SOVEREIGN (Pound)

7.99 g., 0.917 Gold 0.2355 oz. AGW **Ruler:** Elizabeth II **Subject:** 200th Anniversary of Acquisition **Obv:** Crowned bust right **Rev:** Triskeles on shield within rope wreath

Date	Mintage	VF20	XF40	MS60	MS63	MS65
1965	2,000	—	—	—	345	375

KM# 16a SOVEREIGN (Pound)

8.00 g., 0.980 Gold 0.2521 oz. AGW **Ruler:** Elizabeth II **Subject:** 200th Anniversary of Acquisition **Obv:** Crowned bust right **Rev:** Triskeles on shield within rope wreath

Date	Mintage	VF20	XF40	MS60	MS63	MS65
1965	1,000	PF65 420				

KM# 27 SOVEREIGN (Pound)

7.96 g., 0.917 Gold 0.2348 oz. AGW **Ruler:** Elizabeth II **Obv:** Young bust right **Rev:** Armored equestrian

Date	Mintage	VF20	XF40	MS60	MS63	MS65
1973 A	40,000	—	—	—	—	360
1973 B	Inc. above	—	—	—	—	360
1973 C	Inc. above	—	—	—	—	360
1973	1,250	PF65 375				
1974 A	8,604	—	—	—	—	360
1974 B	Inc. above	—	—	—	—	360
1974 C	Inc. above	—	—	—	—	360
1974	2,500	PF65 375				
1975 A	956	—	—	—	—	360
1975 B	Inc. above	—	—	—	—	360
1975 C	Inc. above	—	—	—	—	360
1975	—	PF65 375				
1976 A	1,238	—	—	—	—	360
1976 B	Inc. above	—	—	—	—	360
1976 C	Inc. above	—	—	—	—	360
1976	—	PF65 375				
1977 A	—	—	—	—	—	360
1977 B	—	—	—	—	—	360
1977 C	—	—	—	—	—	360
1977	1,250	PF65 375				
1978	1,250	PF65 375				
1979 B	—	—	—	—	—	360
1979 C	—	—	—	—	—	360
1979 AA (t)	10,000	—	—	—	—	360
1979 D (t)	—	—	—	—	—	360
1979 (t)	30,000	PF65 375				
1980 D (m)	5,000	PF65 375				
1980 (v)	—	PF65 375				
1982 (b)	40,000	PF65 375				
1982 (b)	30,000	—	—	—	—	360

KM# 44a SOVEREIGN (Pound)

4.60 g., 0.925 Silver 0.1368 oz. ASW **Ruler:** Elizabeth II **Obv:** Young bust right **Rev:** Triskeles flanked by designs **Edge:** Smooth, reeded alternating edge

Date	Mintage	VF20	XF40	MS60	MS63	MS65
1978 PM D	100,000	PF65 8.00				
1978 PM E	Inc. above	PF65 8.00				
1979 PM D(t)	75,000	PF65 15.00				
1979 PM E(t)	Inc. above	PF65 15.00				
1980 PM	75,000	PF65 8.00				
1981 PM	—	PF65 8.00				
1982 PM (b)	1,000	PF65 35.00				

KM# 44b SOVEREIGN (Pound)

9.00 g., 0.950 Platinum 0.2749 oz. APW **Ruler:** Elizabeth II **Obv:** Young bust right **Rev:** Triskeles flanked by designs

Date	Mintage	VF20	XF40	MS60	MS63	MS65
1978	1,000	PF65 425				
1979	—	PF65 425				
1980	1,000	PF65 425				
1982 (b)	100	PF65 500				

KM# 44c SOVEREIGN (Pound)

7.96 g., 0.917 Gold 0.2348 oz. AGW **Ruler:** Elizabeth II **Obv:** Young bust right **Rev:** Triskeles flanked by designs

Date	Mintage	VF20	XF40	MS60	MS63	MS65
1980	5,000	PF65 375				
1980 T.T.	300	PF65 375				
1982 (b)	250	—	—	—	—	360
1982 (b)	750	PF65 375				

KM# 44d SOVEREIGN (Pound)

4.60 g., 0.500 Silver 0.0739 oz. ASW **Ruler:** Elizabeth II **Obv:** Young bust right **Rev:** Triskeles flanked by designs

Date	Mintage	VF20	XF40	MS60	MS63	MS65
1980	10,000	PF65 15.00				

KM# 86 SOVEREIGN (Pound)

7.96 g., 0.917 Gold 0.2348 oz. AGW **Ruler:** Elizabeth II **Subject:** Wedding of Prince Charles and Lady Diana **Obv:** Young bust right **Rev:** Portraits of Royal Couple, joined shields

Date	Mintage	VF20	XF40	MS60	MS63	MS65
1981	40,000	PF65 375				

KM# 261 SOVEREIGN (Pound)

7.96 g., 0.917 Gold 0.2348 oz. AGW, 22.5 mm. **Ruler:** Elizabeth II **Obv:** Young bust right **Rev:** Four crowned shields

Date	Mintage	VF20	XF40	MS60	MS63	MS65
1984	20	—	—	—	345	375
1984	20	PF65 390				

KM# 135 SOVEREIGN (Pound)

4.60 g., 0.925 Silver 0.1368 oz. ASW, 22.5 mm. **Ruler:** Elizabeth II **Obv:** Young bust right **Rev:** Shield **Edge:** Reeded, smooth alternating edge

Date	Mintage	VF20	XF40	MS60	MS63	MS65
1985 D	—	—	—	—	12.00	14.00
1985 D	Est. 5000	PF65 22.50				

KM# 135b SOVEREIGN (Pound)

7.96 g., 0.917 Gold 0.2348 oz. AGW, 22.5 mm. **Ruler:** Elizabeth II **Obv:** Young bust right **Rev:** Shield

Date	Mintage	VF20	XF40	MS60	MS63	MS65
1985	Est. 150	PF65 375				

KM# 135c SOVEREIGN (Pound)

9.00 g., 0.950 Platinum 0.2749 oz. APW, 22.5 mm. **Ruler:** Elizabeth II **Obv:** Young bust right **Rev:** Shield

Date	Mintage	VF20	XF40	MS60	MS63	MS65
1985	—	PF65 475				

KM# 265 SOVEREIGN (Pound)

7.96 g., 0.917 Gold 0.2348 oz. AGW, 22.5 mm. **Ruler:** Elizabeth II **Obv:** Crowned head right **Rev:** Four crowned shields

Date	Mintage	VF20	XF40	MS60	MS63	MS65
1988	5,876	—	—	—	—	360
1988	1,600	PF65 375				

KM# 44 POUND

Virenium **Ruler:** Elizabeth II **Obv:** Young bust right **Rev:** Triskeles flanked by designs

Date	Mintage	VF20	XF40	MS60	MS63	MS65
1978 AA	—	—	—	—	3.00	3.50
1978 AB	—	—	—	—	3.00	3.50
1978 AC	—	—	—	—	2.50	3.00
1978 AD	3,780	—	—	—	7.50	8.50
1978 BB Proof	150,000	—	—	—	—	—
1978 BC	Inc. above	PF65 3.50				
1979 AA(t)	—	—	—	—	2.50	3.00
1979 AB(t)	—	—	—	—	2.50	3.00
1979 AC(t)	—	—	—	—	2.50	3.00
1979 BB(t)	—	PF65 3.50				
1979 (t) Crossed oars	—	—	—	—	2.50	3.00
1980 AA DMIHE	30,000	—	—	—	2.50	3.00
1980 AA DMIHEN	—	—	—	—	2.50	3.00
1980 AA TT	—	—	—	—	2.50	3.00
1980 AB DMIHE	—	—	—	—	2.50	3.00
1980 AB DHIHEN	—	—	—	—	2.50	3.00
1980 AB TT	—	—	—	—	5.50	6.50
1980 AC DMIHE	100,000	—	—	—	2.50	3.00
1980 PM BB	5,000	PF65 10.00				
1980 AA	—	—	—	—	2.50	3.00
1980 AB	—	—	—	—	2.50	3.00
1980 AC	—	—	—	—	2.50	3.00
1981 PM BB	26,000	PF65 10.00				
1981 AA	—	—	—	—	2.50	3.00
1982 PM (b)	—	PF65 10.00				

KM# 109 POUND

9.50 g., Nickel-Brass, 22.5 mm. **Ruler:** Elizabeth II **Obv:** Young bust right **Rev:** City view with ships within circle

Date	Mintage	VF20	XF40	MS60	MS63	MS65
1983 AA	—	—	—	—	3.50	4.00
1983 AB	—	—	—	—	3.50	4.00

KM# 109a POUND

4.60 g., 0.925 Silver 0.1368 oz. ASW, 22.5 mm. **Ruler:** Elizabeth II **Obv:** Young bust right **Rev:** City view with ships within cricle **Edge:** Reeded, smooth alternating edge

Date	Mintage	VF20	XF40	MS60	MS63	MS65
1983 D	—	PF65 20.00				

KM# 109b POUND

9.50 g., 0.374 Gold 0.1142 oz. AGW, 22.5 mm. **Ruler:** Elizabeth II **Obv:** Young bust right **Rev:** City view with ships within circle

Date	Mintage	VF20	XF40	MS60	MS63	MS65
1983	—	PF65 195				

KM# 109c POUND

7.96 g., 0.917 Gold 0.2348 oz. AGW, 22.5 mm. **Ruler:** Elizabeth II **Obv:** Young bust right **Rev:** City view with ships within circle

Date	Mintage	VF20	XF40	MS60	MS63	MS65
1983	—	PF65 400				

KM# 109d POUND

9.00 g., 0.950 Platinum 0.2749 oz. APW, 22.5 mm. **Ruler:** Elizabeth II **Obv:** Young bust right **Rev:** City view with ships within circle

Date	Mintage	VF20	XF40	MS60	MS63	MS65
1983	—	PF65 525				

KM# 128 POUND

9.50 g., Nickel-Brass, 22.5 mm. **Ruler:** Elizabeth II **Obv:** Young bust right **Rev:** Crown flanked by designs above city view within shield **Edge:** Segmented reeding

Date	Mintage	VF20	XF40	MS60	MS63	MS65
1984 D	—	—	—	—	4.00	4.50
1984 AA	—	—	—	—	4.00	4.50

KM# 128a POUND

4.60 g., 0.925 Silver 0.1368 oz. ASW, 22.5 mm. **Ruler:** Elizabeth II **Obv:** Young bust right **Rev:** Crown flanked by designs above city view within shield **Edge:** Reeded, smooth alternating edge

Date	Mintage	VF20	XF40	MS60	MS63	MS65
1984	—	—	—	—	12.00	14.00
1984 D	—	PF65 22.50				

KM# 128b POUND
9.50 g., 0.374 Gold 0.1142 oz. AGW, 22.5 mm. **Ruler:** Elizabeth II **Obv:** Young bust right **Rev:** Crown flanked by designs above city view within shield

Date	Mintage	VF20	XF40	MS60	MS63	MS65
1984	4,950	PF65 195				

KM# 128c POUND
7.96 g., 0.917 Gold 0.2348 oz. AGW, 22.5 mm. **Ruler:** Elizabeth II **Obv:** Young bust right **Rev:** Crown flanked by designs above city view within shield

Date	Mintage	VF20	XF40	MS60	MS63	MS65
1984	950	PF65 400				

KM# 128d POUND
9.00 g., 0.950 Platinum 0.2749 oz. APW, 22.5 mm. **Ruler:** Elizabeth II **Obv:** Young bust right **Rev:** Crown flanked by designs above city view within shield

Date	Mintage	VF20	XF40	MS60	MS63	MS65
1984	—	PF65 525				

KM# 151 POUND
9.50 g., Nickel-Brass, 22.5 mm. **Ruler:** Elizabeth II **Obv:** Crowned head right **Rev:** Shield **Edge:** Segmented reeding

Date	Mintage	VF20	XF40	MS60	MS63	MS65
1985 AA	25,000	PF65 6.00				
1985 AA	—	—	—	—	3.50	4.00
1985 AA(w)	—	—	—	—	3.50	4.00
1985 AA	25,000	PF65 6.00				

KM# 151a POUND
4.60 g., 0.925 Silver 0.1368 oz. ASW, 22.5 mm. **Ruler:** Elizabeth II **Obv:** Crowned head right **Rev:** Shield

Date	Mintage	VF20	XF40	MS60	MS63	MS65
1985	—	PF65 35.00				

KM# 136 POUND
4.60 g., 0.925 Silver 0.1368 oz. ASW, 22.5 mm. **Ruler:** Elizabeth II **Obv:** Crowned head right **Rev:** Shield

Date	Mintage	VF20	XF40	MS60	MS63	MS65
1986 AA	—	—	—	—	12.00	14.00
1986 D	—	PF65 25.00				

KM# 136b POUND
7.96 g., 0.917 Gold 0.2348 oz. AGW, 22.5 mm. **Ruler:** Elizabeth II **Obv:** Crowned head right **Rev:** Shield

Date	Mintage	VF20	XF40	MS60	MS63	MS65
1986	—	PF65 395				

KM# 136c POUND
9.00 g., 0.950 Platinum 0.2749 oz. APW, 22.5 mm. **Ruler:** Elizabeth II **Obv:** Crowned head right **Rev:** Shield

Date	Mintage	VF20	XF40	MS60	MS63	MS65
1986	—	PF65 525				

KM# 175 POUND
9.50 g., Nickel-Brass, 22.5 mm. **Ruler:** Elizabeth II **Obv:** Crowned head right **Rev:** Shield

Date	Mintage	VF20	XF40	MS60	MS63	MS65
1986	—	—	—	—	3.50	4.00
1986	25,000	PF65 6.00				

KM# 182 POUND
9.50 g., Nickel-Brass, 22.5 mm. **Ruler:** Elizabeth II **Obv:** Crowned head right **Rev:** Rearing armored equestrian within circle **Edge:** Segmented reeding

Date	Mintage	VF20	XF40	MS60	MS63	MS65
1987 AA	—	—	—	—	3.50	4.00

KM# 213 POUND
9.50 g., Nickel-Brass, 22.5 mm. **Ruler:** Elizabeth II **Obv:** Crowned head right **Rev:** Cordless phone divides satellite and receiving station **Edge:** Segmented reeding

Date	Mintage	VF20	XF40	MS60	MS63	MS65
1988 AA	—	—	—	—	2.50	3.00
1988 BB	—	—	—	—	2.50	3.00
1988 D	—	—	—	—	2.50	3.00
1989 AA	—	—	—	—	2.50	3.00
1990 AA	—	—	—	—	2.50	3.00
1991 AA	—	—	—	—	2.50	3.00
1992 AB	—	—	—	—	2.50	3.00
1993 AA	—	—	—	—	2.50	3.00
1994 AA	—	—	—	—	2.50	3.00
1995 AA	—	—	—	—	2.50	3.00

KM# 213a POUND
4.60 g., 0.925 Silver 0.1368 oz. ASW, 22.5 mm. **Ruler:** Elizabeth II **Obv:** Crowned head right **Rev:** Cordless phone divides satelite and receiving station

Date	Mintage	VF20	XF40	MS60	MS63	MS65
1988	—	PF65 12.00				
1989	—	PF65 12.00				
1990	—	PF65 12.00				
1991	—	PF65 12.00				
1992	—	PF65 12.00				

KM# 594 POUND
9.50 g., Nickel-Brass, 22.5 mm. **Ruler:** Elizabeth II **Subject:** Sports **Obv:** Crowned head right **Rev:** Cricket equipment

Date	Mintage	VF20	XF40	MS60	MS63	MS65
1996 AA	—	—	—	—	4.00	4.50
1997 AA	—	—	—	—	4.00	4.50

KM# 594a POUND
4.60 g., 0.925 Silver 0.1368 oz. ASW, 22.5 mm. **Ruler:** Elizabeth II **Subject:** Sports **Obv:** Crowned head right **Rev:** Cricket equipment

Date	Mintage	VF20	XF40	MS60	MS63	MS65
1996	—	PF65 25.00				

KM# 655 POUND
9.50 g., Nickel-Brass, 22.5 mm. **Ruler:** Elizabeth II **Subject:** Douglas Centenary **Obv:** Crowned head right **Rev:** City arms

Date	Mintage	VF20	XF40	MS60	MS63	MS65
1996 AA	—	—	—	—	4.00	4.50

KM# 655a POUND
9.50 g., 0.925 Silver 0.2825 oz. ASW, 22.5 mm. **Ruler:** Elizabeth II **Subject:** Douglas Centenary **Obv:** Crowned head right **Rev:** City arms

Date	Mintage	VF20	XF40	MS60	MS63	MS65
1996	25,000	PF65 16.00				

KM# 655b POUND
9.50 g., 0.916 Gold 0.2798 oz. AGW, 22.5 mm. **Ruler:** Elizabeth II **Subject:** Douglas Centenary **Obv:** Crowned head right **Rev:** City arms

Date	Mintage	VF20	XF40	MS60	MS63	MS65
1996	Est. 10000	PF65 475				

KM# 906.1 POUND
9.50 g., Nickel-Brass, 22.5 mm. **Ruler:** Elizabeth II **Obv:** Head with tiara right **Rev:** Cricket equipment flanked by sprigs

Date	Mintage	VF20	XF40	MS60	MS63	MS65
1998 AA	—	—	—	—	4.00	4.50

KM# 906.2 POUND
9.50 g., Nickel-Brass, 22.5 mm. **Ruler:** Elizabeth II **Obv:** Head with tiara right with small triskeles dividing legend **Rev:** Cricket equipment

Date	Mintage	VF20	XF40	MS60	MS63	MS65
1998 PM AA	—	—	—	—	4.00	4.50
1999 PM AA	—	—	—	—	4.00	4.50

KM# 1042 POUND
9.50 g., Nickel-Brass, 22.5 mm. **Ruler:** Elizabeth II **Subject:** Millennium Bells **Obv:** Head with tiara right **Rev:** Triskeles and three bells **Edge:** Segmented reeding

Date	Mintage	VF20	XF40	MS60	MS63	MS65
2000 PM AA	—	—	—	—	4.00	5.00

KM# 28 2 POUNDS
15.93 g., 0.917 Gold 0.4695 oz. AGW **Ruler:** Elizabeth II **Obv:** Young bust right **Rev:** Armored equestrian

Date	Mintage	VF20	XF40	MS60	MS63	MS65
1973 A	3,612	—	—	—	—	750
1973	1,250	PF65 780				
1974 A	1,257	—	—	—	—	750
1974 B	Inc. above	—	—	—	—	750
1974	2,500	PF65 780				
1975 A	456	—	—	—	—	750
1975 B	Inc. above	—	—	—	—	750
1975	—	PF65 780				
1976 A	578	—	—	—	—	750
1976 B	Inc. above	—	—	—	—	750
1976	—	PF65 780				
1977 A	—	—	—	—	—	750
1977 B	Inc. above	—	—	—	—	750
1977	1,250	PF65 780				
1978	1,250	PF65 780				
1979 (t) A	2,000	—	—	—	—	750
1979 (t) B	Inc. above	—	—	—	—	750
1979 (t)	30,000	PF65 780				
1980 (m)	2,000	PF65 780				
1982 (b)	15,000	—	—	—	—	750
1982 (b)	5,000	PF65 780				

KM# 87 2 POUNDS
15.93 g., 0.917 Gold 0.4695 oz. AGW **Ruler:** Elizabeth II **Subject:** Wedding of Prince Charles and Lady Diana **Obv:** Young bust right **Rev:** Portraits of Royal Couple, joined shields

Date	Mintage	VF20	XF40	MS60	MS63	MS65
1981	5,000	PF65 780				

KM# 129 2 POUNDS
Virenium **Ruler:** Elizabeth II **Obv:** Young bust right **Rev:** Tower of Refuge and Manx Shearwater in flight

Date	Mintage	VF20	XF40	MS60	MS63	MS65
1984 PM	—	—	—	—	—	—

Note: Requires Confirmation

KM# 129a 2 POUNDS
Silver **Ruler:** Elizabeth II **Obv:** Young bust right **Rev:** Tower of Refuge and Manx Shearwater in flight

Date	Mintage	VF20	XF40	MS60	MS63	MS65
1984 PM	—	—	—	—	—	—

Note: Requires Confirmation

KM# 262 2 POUNDS
15.92 g., 0.917 Gold 0.4694 oz. AGW **Ruler:** Elizabeth II **Obv:** Young bust right **Rev:** Four crowned shields

Date	Mintage	VF20	XF40	MS60	MS63	MS65
1984	20	—	—	—	—	750
1984	20	PF65 780				

KM# 149 2 POUNDS
Virenium **Ruler:** Elizabeth II **Obv:** Crowned head right **Rev:** Tower of Refuge and Manx Shearwater in flight

Date	Mintage	VF20	XF40	MS60	MS63	MS65
1985	—	—	—	—	—	—

Note: Requires Confirmation

KM# 149a 2 POUNDS
Silver **Ruler:** Elizabeth II **Obv:** Crowned head right **Rev:** Tower of Refuge and Manx Shearwater in flight

Date	Mintage	VF20	XF40	MS60	MS63	MS65
1985	—	—	—	—	—	—

Note: Requires Confirmation

KM# 167 2 POUNDS
Virenium **Ruler:** Elizabeth II **Obv:** Crowned head right **Rev:** Bird above Tower of Refuge

Date	Mintage	VF20	XF40	MS60	MS63	MS65
1986	—	PF65 10.00				
1986 (vw)	—	—	—	—	7.50	8.50
1987 AA	—	—	—	—	7.50	8.50

KM# 214 2 POUNDS
Virenium **Ruler:** Elizabeth II **Obv:** Crowned head right **Rev:** BAC 146-100 jet

Date	Mintage	VF20	XF40	MS60	MS63	MS65
1988 D	—	—	—	—	7.50	8.50
1988 AA	—	—	—	—	7.50	8.50
1989	—	—	—	—	7.50	8.50
1990 AA	—	—	—	—	7.50	8.50
1991 AA	—	—	—	—	7.50	8.50
1992 AA	—	—	—	—	7.50	8.50
1993 AA	—	—	—	—	7.50	8.50

KM# 257 2 POUNDS
Virenium **Ruler:** Elizabeth II **Obv:** Crowned head right **Rev:** Blimp

Date	Mintage	VF20	XF40	MS60	MS63	MS65
1989 AA Rare						

Note: Most recalled by government; Few actually issued.

KM# 257a 2 POUNDS
9.30 g., 0.925 Silver 0.2766 oz. ASW **Ruler:** Elizabeth II **Obv:** Crowned head right **Rev:** Blimp

Date	Mintage	VF20	XF40	MS60	MS63	MS65
1989	—	—	—	—	—	—

Note: Requires Confirmation

KM# 257b 2 POUNDS
15.94 g., 0.917 Gold 0.4699 oz. AGW **Ruler:** Elizabeth II **Obv:** Crowned head right **Rev:** Blimp

Date	Mintage	VF20	XF40	MS60	MS63	MS65
1989	—	—	—	—	—	—

Note: Requires Confirmation

KM# 257c 2 POUNDS
18.00 g., 0.950 Platinum 0.5498 oz. APW **Ruler:** Elizabeth II **Obv:** Crowned head right **Rev:** Blimp **Note:** Requires Confirmation; most recalled by government; few actually issued

Date	Mintage	VF20	XF40	MS60	MS63	MS65
1989	—	—	—	—	—	—

Note: Requires Confirmation

KM# 344 2 POUNDS
Virenium **Ruler:** Elizabeth II **Subject:** World Champion - Nigel Mansell **Obv:** Crowned head right **Rev:** Racecars

Date	Mintage	VF20	XF40	MS60	MS63	MS65
(1993) No die letters	—	—	—	—	8.00	10.00
1993 AA	—	—	—	—	6.50	9.00

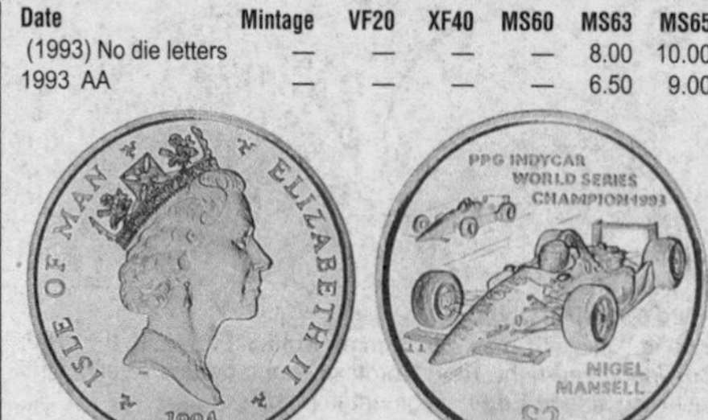

KM# 398 2 POUNDS
Virenium **Ruler:** Elizabeth II **Subject:** Indycar World Series Champion - Nigel Mansell **Obv:** Crowned head right **Rev:** Racecars

Date	Mintage	VF20	XF40	MS60	MS63	MS65
1994 AA	—	—	—	—	8.00	10.00

KM# 465 2 POUNDS
Virenium **Ruler:** Elizabeth II **Subject:** 50th Anniversary - VE and VJ Day **Obv:** Crowned head right **Rev:** Lion head within crowned circular design within flowered wreath

Date	Mintage	VF20	XF40	MS60	MS63	MS65
1995	—	—	—	—	7.00	8.00

KM# 595 2 POUNDS
Virenium **Ruler:** Elizabeth II **Subject:** Sports **Obv:** Crowned head right **Rev:** Racecars within sprigs **Edge:** Reeded, smooth alternating edge

Date	Mintage	VF20	XF40	MS60	MS63	MS65
1996 AA	—	—	—	—	7.50	8.50
1997 AA	—	—	—	—	7.50	8.50

KM# 844 2 POUNDS
12.00 g., Bi-Metallic Copper-Nickel center in Nickel-Brass ring, 28.4 mm. **Ruler:** Elizabeth II **Obv:** Crowned head right within beaded circle **Rev:** Race cars within beaded circle and sprigs **Edge:** Reeded

Date	Mintage	VF20	XF40	MS60	MS63	MS65
1997 AA	—	—	—	—	8.00	9.00

KM# 858 2 POUNDS
12.00 g., Bi-Metallic Copper-Nickel center in Nickel-Brass ring, 28.4 mm. **Ruler:** Elizabeth II **Obv:** Head with tiara right within beaded circle **Rev:** Three race cars **Edge:** Reeded

Date	Mintage	VF20	XF40	MS60	MS63	MS65
1998 AA	—	—	—	—	8.00	9.00
1999 AA	—	—	—	—	8.00	9.00

KM# 1043 2 POUNDS
12.00 g., Bi-Metallic Copper-Nickel center in Nickel-Brass ring, 28.4 mm. **Ruler:** Elizabeth II **Subject:** Thorwald's Cross **Obv:** Head with tiara right within beaded circle **Rev:** Ancient drawing within circle **Edge:** Reeded

Date	Mintage	VF20	XF40	MS60	MS63	MS65
2000 PM AA	—	—	—	—	6.50	7.50

KM# 17 5 POUNDS
39.94 g., 0.917 Gold 1.1775 oz. AGW **Ruler:** Elizabeth II **Subject:** 200th Anniversary of Acquisition **Obv:** Crowned bust right **Rev:** Triskeles on shield within rope wreath

Date	Mintage	VF20	XF40	MS60	MS63	MS65
1965	500	—	—	—	—	1,725

KM# 17a 5 POUNDS
39.95 g., 0.980 Gold 1.2587 oz. AGW **Ruler:** Elizabeth II **Subject:** 200th Anniversary of Acquisition **Obv:** Crowned bust right **Rev:** Triskeles on shield within rope wreath

Date	Mintage	VF20	XF40	MS60	MS63	MS65
1965	1,000	PF65 1,925				

KM# 29 5 POUNDS
39.81 g., 0.917 Gold 1.1738 oz. AGW **Ruler:** Elizabeth II **Obv:** Young bust right **Rev:** Rearing armored equestrian

Date	Mintage	VF20	XF40	MS60	MS63	MS65
1973 A	3,035	—	—	—	—	1,725
1973 B	Inc. above	—	—	—	—	1,725
1973 C	Inc. above	—	—	—	—	1,725
1973 D	Inc. above	—	—	—	—	1,725
1973 E	Inc. above	—	—	—	—	1,725
1973	1,250	PF65 1,800				
1974 A	481	—	—	—	—	1,725
1974 B	Inc. above	—	—	—	—	1,725
1974	2,500	PF65 1,800				
1975 A	306	—	—	—	—	1,725
1975 B	Inc. above	—	—	—	—	1,725
1975	—	PF65 1,800				
1976 A	370	—	—	—	—	1,725
1976 B	Inc. above	—	—	—	—	1,725
1976	—	PF65 1,800				
1977 A	—	—	—	—	—	1,725
1977 B	Inc. above	—	—	—	—	1,725
1977	1,250	PF65 1,800				
1978	1,250	PF65 1,800				
1979 (t) A	1,000	—	—	—	—	1,725
1979 (t) B	Inc. above	—	—	—	—	1,725
1979 (t)	1,000	PF65 1,800				
1980 (m)	250	—	—	—	—	1,725
1982 (b)	500	PF65 1,800				
1982 (b)	10,000	—	—	—	—	1,725

KM# 29a 5 POUNDS

23.84 g., 0.980 Silver 0.7511 oz. ASW, 36.1 mm. **Ruler:** Elizabeth II **Obv:** Young bust right **Rev:** Rearing armored equestrian **Edge:** Reeded **Note:** Subject is a possible pattern.

Date	Mintage	VF20	XF40	MS60	MS63	MS65
1980(m) PM	—	PF65 45.00				

KM# 88 5 POUNDS

Virenium, 36.5 mm. **Ruler:** Elizabeth II **Obv:** Young bust right **Rev:** Triskeles on map **Edge:** Reeded, smooth alternating edge

Date	Mintage	VF20	XF40	MS60	MS63	MS65
1981 AA	—	—	—	—	10.00	12.50
1981 AB	—	—	—	—	10.00	12.50
1981 AC	—	—	—	—	10.00	12.50
1981 AD	—	—	—	—	10.00	12.50
1981 PM BB	30,000	PF65 14.00				
1982	—	PF65 14.00				
1982 (b)	—	PF65 14.00				
1983 AA	—	—	—	—	20.00	22.00
1984 AA	—	—	—	—	20.00	22.00
1984 AB	—	—	—	—	20.00	22.00
1984 AC	—	—	—	—	10.00	12.50

KM# 88a 5 POUNDS

23.50 g., 0.925 Silver 0.6989 oz. ASW, 36.5 mm. **Ruler:** Elizabeth II **Obv:** Young bust right **Rev:** Triskeles on map

Date	Mintage	VF20	XF40	MS60	MS63	MS65
1981	500	PF65 45.00				
1982 (b)	1,000	PF65 35.00				
1983	5,000	PF65 25.00				

KM# 88b 5 POUNDS

39.90 g., 0.917 Gold 1.1763 oz. AGW, 36.5 mm. **Ruler:** Elizabeth II **Obv:** Young bust right **Rev:** Triskeles on map

Date	Mintage	VF20	XF40	MS60	MS63	MS65
1981	1,000	PF65 1,800				
1982 (b)	250	PF65 1,800				
1982 (b)	750	PF65 1,800				
1983	—	PF65 1,800				

KM# 88c 5 POUNDS

45.50 g., 0.950 Platinum 1.3897 oz. APW, 36.5 mm. **Ruler:** Elizabeth II **Obv:** Young bust right **Rev:** Triskeles on map

Date	Mintage	VF20	XF40	MS60	MS63	MS65
1981	500	PF65 1,900				
1982 (b)	100	PF65 1,900				
1983	—	PF65 1,900				

KM# 89 5 POUNDS

39.81 g., 0.917 Gold 1.1738 oz. AGW **Ruler:** Elizabeth II **Subject:** Wedding of Prince Charles and Lady Diana **Obv:** Young bust right **Rev:** Portraits of Royal Couple, joined shields

Date	Mintage	VF20	XF40	MS60	MS63	MS65
1981	1,000	PF65 1,800				

KM# 134 5 POUNDS

Virenium, 36.5 mm. **Ruler:** Elizabeth II **Subject:** Quincentenery of the College of Arms **Obv:** Young bust right **Rev:** Mounted knight in armor with sword facing right within circle

Date	Mintage	VF20	XF40	MS60	MS63	MS65
1984 AA	—	—	—	—	10.00	12.50
1984 BB	—	—	—	—	10.00	12.50

KM# 134a 5 POUNDS

23.50 g., 0.925 Silver 0.6989 oz. ASW, 36.5 mm. **Ruler:** Elizabeth II **Subject:** Quincentenery of the College of Arms **Obv:** Young bust right **Rev:** Mounted knight in armor with sword, facing right within circle

Date	Mintage	VF20	XF40	MS60	MS63	MS65
1984	—	PF65 45.00				

KM# 134b 5 POUNDS

39.90 g., 0.917 Gold 1.1763 oz. AGW, 36.5 mm. **Ruler:** Elizabeth II **Subject:** Quincentenery of the College of Arms **Obv:** Young bust right **Rev:** Mounted knight in armor with sword, facing right within circle

Date	Mintage	VF20	XF40	MS60	MS63	MS65
1984	150	PF65 1,800				

KM# 134c 5 POUNDS

45.50 g., 0.950 Platinum 1.3897 oz. APW, 36.5 mm. **Ruler:** Elizabeth II **Subject:** Quincentenery of the College of Arms **Obv:** Young bust right **Rev:** Mounted knight in armor with sword facing right within circle

Date	Mintage	VF20	XF40	MS60	MS63	MS65
1984	—	PF65 1,900				

KM# 263 5 POUNDS

39.83 g., 0.917 Gold 1.1743 oz. AGW **Ruler:** Elizabeth II **Obv:** Young bust right **Rev:** Four crowned shields

Date	Mintage	VF20	XF40	MS60	MS63	MS65
1984	20	—	—	—	—	1,800
1984	20	PF65 1,875				

KM# 150 5 POUNDS

Virenium, 36.5 mm. **Ruler:** Elizabeth II **Obv:** Crowned head right **Rev:** Similar to KM#134 with additional sports privy mark **Edge:** Reeded, smooth alternating edge

Date	Mintage	VF20	XF40	MS60	MS63	MS65
1985 AA(w)	—	—	—	—	10.00	12.50
1985	25,000	PF65 12.50				
1986 AA	—	—	—	—	10.00	12.50
1987 AA	—	—	—	—	10.00	12.50

KM# 150a 5 POUNDS

23.50 g., 0.925 Silver 0.6989 oz. ASW, 36.5 mm. **Ruler:** Elizabeth II **Obv:** Crowned head right **Rev:** Mounted knight in armor with sword facing right within circle

Date	Mintage	VF20	XF40	MS60	MS63	MS65
1985	Est. 5000	PF65 45.00				

KM# 150b 5 POUNDS

39.90 g., 0.917 Gold 1.1763 oz. AGW, 36.5 mm. **Ruler:** Elizabeth II **Obv:** Crowned head right **Rev:** Mounted knight in armor with sword facing right within circle

Date	Mintage	VF20	XF40	MS60	MS63	MS65
1985	Est. 150	PF65 1,800				

KM# 150c 5 POUNDS

45.50 g., 0.950 Platinum 1.3897 oz. APW, 36.5 mm. **Ruler:** Elizabeth II **Obv:** Crowned head right **Rev:** Mounted knight in armor with sword facing right within circle

Date	Mintage	VF20	XF40	MS60	MS63	MS65
1985	Est. 100	PF65 1,900				

KM# 215 5 POUNDS

Virenium, 36.5 mm. **Ruler:** Elizabeth II **Obv:** Crowned head right **Rev:** Boat below triskeles within circle **Edge:** Smooth, reeded alternating edge

Date	Mintage	VF20	XF40	MS60	MS63	MS65
1988 AA	—	—	—	—	10.00	12.50
1989 AA	—	—	—	—	10.00	12.50
1990 AA	—	—	—	—	10.00	12.50
1991 AA	—	—	—	—	10.00	12.50
1992 AA	—	—	—	—	10.00	12.50
1993 AA	—	—	—	—	10.00	12.50

KM# 336 5 POUNDS

Virenium, 36.5 mm. **Ruler:** Elizabeth II **Subject:** World Champion - Nigel Mansell **Obv:** Crowned head right **Rev:** Racecars **Edge:** Reeded, smooth alternating edge

Date	Mintage	VF20	XF40	MS60	MS63	MS65
1993 AA	—	—	—	—	12.50	16.50

KM# 399 5 POUNDS

Virenium, 36.5 mm. **Ruler:** Elizabeth II **Subject:** Indycar World Series Champion - Nigel Mansell **Obv:** Crowned head right **Rev:** Two racecars

Date	Mintage	VF20	XF40	MS60	MS63	MS65
1994 AA	—	—	—	—	15.00	18.50

KM# 466 5 POUNDS

Virenium, 36.5 mm. **Ruler:** Elizabeth II **Subject:** 50th Anniversary - End of World War II **Obv:** Crowned head right **Rev:** Bust facing giving peace sign

Date	Mintage	VF20	XF40	MS60	MS63	MS65
1995 AA	—	—	—	—	14.50	17.50

KM# 466a 5 POUNDS

23.50 g., 0.925 Silver 0.6989 oz. ASW, 36.5 mm. **Ruler:** Elizabeth II **Subject:** 50th Anniversary - End of World War II **Obv:** Crowned head right **Rev:** Bust facing giving peace sign

Date	Mintage	VF20	XF40	MS60	MS63	MS65
1995	—	PF65 45.00				

KM# 466b 5 POUNDS

39.83 g., 0.917 Gold 1.1743 oz. AGW, 36.5 mm. **Ruler:** Elizabeth II **Subject:** 50th Anniversary - End of World War II **Obv:** Crowned head right **Rev:** Bust facing giving peace sign

Date	Mintage	VF20	XF40	MS60	MS63	MS65
1995	Est. 850	PF65 1,800				

KM# 587 5 POUNDS

Virenium, 36.5 mm. **Ruler:** Elizabeth II **Subject:** European Soccer Championships **Obv:** Crowned head right **Rev:** Soccer players

Date	Mintage	VF20	XF40	MS60	MS63	MS65
1996 AA	—	—	—	—	14.50	17.50

KM# 587a 5 POUNDS

23.50 g., 0.925 Silver 0.6989 oz. ASW, 36.5 mm. **Ruler:** Elizabeth II **Subject:** European Soccer Championships **Obv:** Crowned head right **Rev:** Soccer players

Date	Mintage	VF20	XF40	MS60	MS63	MS65
1996	Est. 5000	PF65 45.00				

KM# 587b 5 POUNDS

39.83 g., 0.916 Gold 1.173 oz. AGW, 36.5 mm. **Ruler:** Elizabeth II **Subject:** European Soccer Championships **Obv:** Crowned head right **Rev:** Soccer players

Date	Mintage	VF20	XF40	MS60	MS63	MS65
1996	Est. 850	PF65 1,800				

KM# 769 5 POUNDS

Virenium, 36.5 mm. **Ruler:** Elizabeth II **Subject:** 50th Anniversary - Queen Elizabeth and Prince Philip **Obv:** Crowned head right **Rev:** Current portrait of Queen Elizabeth and Prince Philip **Edge:** Reeded, smooth alternating edge

Date	Mintage	VF20	XF40	MS60	MS63	MS65
1997 AA	—	—	—	—	14.50	17.50

KM# 769a 5 POUNDS

23.50 g., 0.925 Silver 0.6989 oz. ASW, 36.5 mm. **Ruler:** Elizabeth II **Subject:** 50th Anniversary - Queen Elizabeth and Prince Philip **Obv:** Crowned head right **Rev:** Current portrait of Queen Elizabeth and Prince Philip

Date	Mintage	VF20	XF40	MS60	MS63	MS65
1997	—	PF65 45.00				

KM# 769b 5 POUNDS

39.83 g., 0.9167 Gold 1.1739 oz. AGW, 36.5 mm. **Ruler:** Elizabeth II **Subject:** 50th Anniversary - Queen Elizabeth and Prince Philip **Obv:** Crowned head right **Rev:** Current portrait of Queen Elizabeth and Prince Philip

Date	Mintage	VF20	XF40	MS60	MS63	MS65
1997	Est. 850	PF65 1,800				

KM# 912 5 POUNDS

Virenium, 36.5 mm. **Ruler:** Elizabeth II **Subject:** 50th Birthday - Prince Charles **Obv:** Head with tiara right **Rev:** Portrait of Prince Charles **Edge:** Reeded, smooth alternating edge

Date	Mintage	VF20	XF40	MS60	MS63	MS65
1998 AA	—	—	—	—	15.50	17.50

KM# 912a 5 POUNDS

23.50 g., 0.925 Silver 0.6989 oz. ASW, 36.5 mm. **Ruler:** Elizabeth II **Subject:** 50th Birthday - Prince Charles **Obv:** Head with tiara right **Rev:** Portrait of Prince Charles

Date	Mintage	VF20	XF40	MS60	MS63	MS65
1998	—	PF65 50.00				

KM# 912b 5 POUNDS

39.83 g., 0.9167 Gold 1.1739 oz. AGW, 36.5 mm. **Ruler:** Elizabeth II **Subject:** 50th Birthday - Prince Charles **Obv:** Head with tiara right **Rev:** Portrait of Prince Charles

Date	Mintage	VF20	XF40	MS60	MS63	MS65
1998	Est. 850	PF65 1,800				

KM# 991 5 POUNDS

Virenium, 36.5 mm. **Ruler:** Elizabeth II **Subject:** Soccer **Obv:** Head with tiara right **Rev:** Soccer players flanked by sprigs **Edge:** Reeded, smooth alternating edge

Date	Mintage	VF20	XF40	MS60	MS63	MS65
1998 AA	—	—	—	—	16.50	18.00
1999 AA	—	—	—	—	16.50	18.00

KM# 943 5 POUNDS

Virenium, 36.5 mm. **Ruler:** Elizabeth II **Subject:** 175th Anniversary of the RN LI **Obv:** Head with tiara right **Rev:** Lifeboat with flag

Date	Mintage	VF20	XF40	MS60	MS63	MS65
1999	—	—	—	—	15.50	17.50

KM# 943a 5 POUNDS

23.50 g., 0.925 Silver 0.6989 oz. ASW, 36.5 mm. **Ruler:** Elizabeth II **Subject:** 175th Anniversary of the RN LI **Obv:** Head with tiara right **Rev:** Lifeboat with flag

Date	Mintage	VF20	XF40	MS60	MS63	MS65
1999	Est. 10000	PF65 50.00				

KM# 943b 5 POUNDS

39.83 g., 0.9167 Gold 1.1739 oz. AGW, 36.5 mm. **Ruler:** Elizabeth II **Subject:** 175th Anniversary of the RN LI **Obv:** Head with tiara right **Rev:** Lifeboat with flag

Date	Mintage	VF20	XF40	MS60	MS63	MS65
1999	850	PF65 1,800				

KM# 1044 5 POUNDS

20.10 g., Virenium, 36.5 mm. **Ruler:** Elizabeth II **Subject:** St. Patrick's Hymn **Obv:** Head with tiara right **Rev:** Stylized cross design **Edge:** Segmented reeding

Date	Mintage	VF20	XF40	MS60	MS63	MS65
2000 PM AA	—	—	—	—	15.00	16.50

KM# 345 10 POUNDS

10.00 g., 0.925 Silver 0.2974 oz. ASW **Ruler:** Elizabeth II **Subject:** Indycar World Series Champion - Nigel Mansell **Obv:** Crowned head right **Rev:** Racecar

Date	Mintage	VF20	XF40	MS60	MS63	MS65
1993	Est. 20000	PF65 35.00				

KM# 400 10 POUNDS

10.00 g., 0.925 Silver 0.2974 oz. ASW **Ruler:** Elizabeth II **Subject:** Indycar World Series Champion - Nigel Mansell **Obv:** Crowned head right **Rev:** Two racecars

Date	Mintage	VF20	XF40	MS60	MS63	MS65
1994	Est. 20000	PF65 35.00				

KM# 1510 12 1/2 POUNDS

1.99 g., 0.9167 Gold 0.0587 oz. AGW, 14 mm. **Ruler:** Elizabeth II **Subject:** Nigel Mansell Formula 1 Champion **Obv:** Crowned head right **Rev:** Two racecars within wreath

Date	Mintage	VF20	XF40	MS60	MS63	MS65
ND (1993)	Est. 500	PF65 150				

KM# 346 25 POUNDS

28.28 g., 0.925 Silver 0.841 oz. ASW **Ruler:** Elizabeth II **Subject:** World Champion - Nigel Mansell **Obv:** Crowned bust right **Rev:** Two racecars

Date	Mintage	VF20	XF40	MS60	MS63	MS65
1993	Est. 15000	PF65 50.00				

KM# 1511 25 POUNDS

3.99 g., 0.9167 Gold 0.1176 oz. AGW, 19.3 mm. **Ruler:** Elizabeth II **Subject:** Nigel Mansell Formula 1 Champion **Obv:** Crowned head right **Rev:** Two race cars within wreath

Date	Mintage	VF20	XF40	MS60	MS63	MS65
ND (1993)	Est. 500	PF65 250				

KM# 347 50 POUNDS

6.22 g., 0.999 Gold 0.1998 oz. AGW **Ruler:** Elizabeth II **Subject:** World Champion - Nigel Mansell **Obv:** Crowned bust right **Rev:** Two racecars

Date	Mintage	VF20	XF40	MS60	MS63	MS65
1993	Est. 5000	PF65 375				

KM# 1512 50 POUNDS

7.98 g., 0.9167 Gold 0.2352 oz. AGW, 22.05 mm. **Ruler:** Elizabeth II **Subject:** Nigel Mansell Formula 1 Champion **Obv:** Crowned head right **Rev:** Two race cars within wreath

Date	Mintage	VF20	XF40	MS60	MS63	MS65
ND (1993)	Est. 500	PF65 500				

KM# 401 50 POUNDS

6.22 g., 0.999 Gold 0.1998 oz. AGW **Ruler:** Elizabeth II **Subject:** Indycar World Series Champion - Nigel Mansell **Obv:** Crowned bust right **Rev:** Two racecars

Date	Mintage	VF20	XF40	MS60	MS63	MS65
1994	Est. 5000	PF65 375				

KM# 1513 100 POUNDS

15.98 g., 0.9167 Gold 0.471 oz. AGW, 28.4 mm. **Ruler:** Elizabeth II **Subject:** Nigel Mansell Formula 1 Champion **Obv:** Crowned head right **Rev:** Two race cars within wreath

Date	Mintage	VF20	XF40	MS60	MS63	MS65
ND (1993)	Est. 500	PF65 1,000				

KM# 1514 250 POUNDS

39.94 g., 0.9167 Gold 1.1771 oz. AGW, 36.02 mm. **Ruler:** Elizabeth II **Subject:** Nigel Mansell Formula 1 Champion **Obv:** Crowned head right **Rev:** Two race cars within wreath

Date	Mintage	VF20	XF40	MS60	MS63	MS65
ND (1993)	Est. 500	PF65 1,750				

KM# 1503a 1/5 CROWN

6.22 g., 0.999 Platinum 0.1998 oz. APW, 22 mm. **Ruler:** Elizabeth II **Subject:** Winston Churchill, 25th Anniversary of Death **Obv:** Crowned bust right **Rev:** Churchill in robes of Garter

Date	Mintage	VF20	XF40	MS60	MS63	MS65
1990	Est. 100	PF65 350				

CROWN SERIES

(M) MATTE - Normal circulation strike

(U) SPECIAL UNCIRCULATED - Polished or prooflike in appearance, slightly frosted features.

(P) PROOF - The highest quality obtainable having mirror-like fields and frosted features.

KM# 235 1/25 CROWN

1.24 g., 0.999 Gold 0.040 oz. AGW, 13.9 mm. **Ruler:** Elizabeth II **Obv:** Crowned bust right **Rev:** Manx cat

Date	Mintage	VF20	XF40	MS60	MS63	MS65
1988	5,000	PF65 74.00				
1988	40,000	—	—	—	—	69.00

KM# 252 1/25 CROWN

1.24 g., 0.999 Gold 0.040 oz. AGW, 13.9 mm. **Ruler:** Elizabeth II **Obv:** Crowned bust right **Rev:** Persian cat

Date	Mintage	VF20	XF40	MS60	MS63	MS65
1989	—	—	—	—	—	69.00
1989	—	PF65 74.00				

KM# 467 1/25 CROWN

1.24 g., 0.9995 Platinum 0.040 oz. APW, 13.9 mm. **Ruler:** Elizabeth II **Obv:** Crowned bust right **Rev:** Persian cat

Date	Mintage	VF20	XF40	MS60	MS63	MS65
1989	—	—	—	—	—	59.00
1989	—	PF65 64.00				

KM# 277 1/25 CROWN

1.24 g., 0.999 Gold 0.040 oz. AGW, 13.9 mm. **Ruler:** Elizabeth II **Obv:** Crowned bust right **Rev:** Alley cat

Date	Mintage	VF20	XF40	MS60	MS63	MS65
1990	—	PF65 74.00				
1990	—	—	—	—	—	69.00

KM# 1502.5 1/25 CROWN

6.22 g., 0.999 Platinum 0.1998 oz. APW, 22 mm. **Ruler:** Elizabeth II **Subject:** Winston Churchill, 25th Anniversary of Death **Obv:** Crowned bust right **Rev:** Churchill with cigar

Date	Mintage	VF20	XF40	MS60	MS63	MS65
1990	Est. 100	PF65 300				

KM# 294 1/25 CROWN

1.24 g., 0.999 Gold 0.040 oz. AGW, 13.9 mm. **Ruler:** Elizabeth II **Obv:** Crowned bust right **Rev:** Norwegian cat

Date	Mintage	VF20	XF40	MS60	MS63	MS65
1991	—	PF65 74.00				
1991	—	—	—	—	—	69.00

KM# 322 1/25 CROWN

1.24 g., 0.999 Gold 0.040 oz. AGW, 13.9 mm. **Ruler:** Elizabeth II **Subject:** America's Cup **Obv:** Crowned bust right **Rev:** Cameo of "Star of India" above two modern sailboats

Date	Mintage	VF20	XF40	MS60	MS63	MS65
1992 Prooflike	50,000	—	—	—	—	64.00

KM# 328 1/25 CROWN

1.24 g., 0.999 Gold 0.040 oz. AGW, 13.9 mm. **Ruler:** Elizabeth II **Obv:** Crowned bust right **Rev:** Siamese cat

Date	Mintage	VF20	XF40	MS60	MS63	MS65
1992	—	—	—	—	—	69.00
1992	—	PF65 74.00				

KM# 338 1/25 CROWN

1.24 g., 0.999 Gold 0.040 oz. AGW, 13.9 mm. **Ruler:** Elizabeth II **Subject:** Year of the Cockerel **Obv:** Crowned bust right **Rev:** Cockerel within circle

Date	Mintage	VF20	XF40	MS60	MS63	MS65
1993	—	PF65 64.00				

KM# 349 1/25 CROWN

1.24 g., 0.999 Gold 0.040 oz. AGW, 13.9 mm. **Ruler:** Elizabeth II **Obv:** Crowned bust right **Rev:** Maine Coon cat

Date	Mintage	VF20	XF40	MS60	MS63	MS65
1993	—	—	—	—	—	69.00
1993	—	PF65 74.00				

KM# 376 1/25 CROWN

1.24 g., 0.999 Gold 0.040 oz. AGW, 13.9 mm. **Ruler:** Elizabeth II **Obv:** Crowned bust right **Rev:** Japanese Bobtail cat

Date	Mintage	VF20	XF40	MS60	MS63	MS65
1994	—	—	—	—	—	69.00
1994	—	PF65 74.00				

KM# 402 1/25 CROWN

1.24 g., 0.999 Gold 0.040 oz. AGW, 13.9 mm. **Ruler:** Elizabeth II **Obv:** Crowned bust right **Rev:** Pekingese

Date	Mintage	VF20	XF40	MS60	MS63	MS65
1994	Est. 25000	PF65 64.00				

KM# 473 1/25 CROWN

1.24 g., 0.9995 Platinum 0.040 oz. APW, 13.9 mm. **Ruler:** Elizabeth II **Obv:** Crowned bust right **Rev:** Japanese Bobtail cat

Date	Mintage	VF20	XF40	MS60	MS63	MS65
1994	—	—	—	—	—	59.00
1994	—	PF65 64.00				

KM# 442 1/25 CROWN

1.24 g., 0.999 Gold 0.040 oz. AGW, 13.9 mm. **Ruler:** Elizabeth II **Obv:** Crowned bust right **Rev:** Turkish cat

Date	Mintage	VF20	XF40	MS60	MS63	MS65
1995 U	—	—	—	—	—	69.00
1995	—	PF65 74.00				

KM# 449 1/25 CROWN

1.24 g., 0.999 Gold 0.040 oz. AGW, 13.9 mm. **Ruler:** Elizabeth II **Subject:** Year of the Pig **Obv:** Crowned bust right **Rev:** Sow with piglets

Date	Mintage	VF20	XF40	MS60	MS63	MS65
1995	Est. 25000	PF65 64.00				

KM# 478 1/25 CROWN

1.24 g., 0.9995 Platinum 0.040 oz. APW, 13.9 mm. **Ruler:** Elizabeth II **Obv:** Crowned bust right **Rev:** Turkish cat

Date	Mintage	VF20	XF40	MS60	MS63	MS65
1995	—	—	—	—	—	59.00
1995	—	PF65 64.00				

KM# 597 1/25 CROWN

1.24 g., 0.999 Gold 0.040 oz. AGW, 13.9 mm. **Ruler:** Elizabeth II **Series:** Flower Fairies **Obv:** Crowned bust right **Rev:** Orchis

Date	Mintage	VF20	XF40	MS60	MS63	MS65
1996	—	PF65 64.00				

KM# 598 1/25 CROWN

1.24 g., 0.999 Gold 0.040 oz. AGW, 13.9 mm. **Ruler:** Elizabeth II **Series:** Flower Fairies **Obv:** Crowned bust right **Rev:** Rose

Date	Mintage	VF20	XF40	MS60	MS63	MS65
1996	Est. 25000	PF65 64.00				

KM# 599 1/25 CROWN

1.24 g., 0.999 Gold 0.040 oz. AGW, 13.9 mm. **Ruler:** Elizabeth II **Series:** Flower Fairies **Obv:** Crowned bust right **Rev:** Fuchsia

Date	Mintage	VF20	XF40	MS60	MS63	MS65
1996	—	PF65 64.00				

KM# 600 1/25 CROWN

1.24 g., 0.999 Gold 0.040 oz. AGW, 13.9 mm. **Ruler:** Elizabeth II **Series:** Flower Fairies **Obv:** Crowned bust right **Rev:** Pinks

Date	Mintage	VF20	XF40	MS60	MS63	MS65
1996	Est. 25000	PF65 64.00				

KM# 613 1/25 CROWN

1.24 g., 0.999 Gold 0.040 oz. AGW, 13.9 mm. **Ruler:** Elizabeth II **Obv:** Crowned bust right **Rev:** Burmese cat **Note:** #621a.

Date	Mintage	VF20	XF40	MS60	MS63	MS65
1996 U	—	—	—	—	—	69.00
1996	—	PF65 74.00				

KM# 614 1/25 CROWN

1.24 g., 0.9995 Platinum 0.040 oz. APW, 13.9 mm. **Ruler:** Elizabeth II **Obv:** Crowned bust right **Rev:** Burmese cat

Date	Mintage	VF20	XF40	MS60	MS63	MS65
1996	—	—	—	—	—	59.00
1996	—	PF65 64.00				

KM# 728 1/25 CROWN

1.24 g., 0.999 Gold 0.040 oz. AGW, 13.9 mm. **Ruler:** Elizabeth II **Subject:** Year of the Rat **Obv:** Crowned bust right **Rev:** Rat

Date	Mintage	VF20	XF40	MS60	MS63	MS65
1996 Proof	—	—	—	—	—	—

Note: Entire series purchased by one buyer; Mintage, disposition, and market value unknown

KM# 721 1/25 CROWN

1.24 g., 0.999 Gold 0.040 oz. AGW, 13.9 mm. **Ruler:** Elizabeth II **Subject:** Year of the Ox **Obv:** Crowned bust right **Rev:** Ox laying down

Date	Mintage	VF20	XF40	MS60	MS63	MS65
1997	Est. 20000	PF65 64.00				

KM# 735 1/25 CROWN

1.24 g., 0.999 Gold 0.040 oz. AGW, 13.9 mm. **Ruler:** Elizabeth II **Series:** Flower Fairies **Obv:** Crowned bust right **Rev:** Candytuft

Date	Mintage	VF20	XF40	MS60	MS63	MS65
1997	Est. 25000	PF65 64.00				

KM# 735a 1/25 CROWN

1.25 g., 0.995 Platinum 0.040 oz. APW, 13.9 mm. **Ruler:** Elizabeth II **Series:** Flower Fairies **Obv:** Crowned bust right **Rev:** Candytuft

Date	Mintage	VF20	XF40	MS60	MS63	MS65
1997	Est. 7500	PF65 64.00				

KM# 736 1/25 CROWN

1.24 g., 0.9999 Gold 0.040 oz. AGW, 13.9 mm. **Ruler:** Elizabeth II **Series:** Flower Fairies **Obv:** Crowned bust right **Rev:** Snowdrop

Date	Mintage	VF20	XF40	MS60	MS63	MS65
1997	Est. 25000	PF65 64.00				

KM# 736a 1/25 CROWN

1.25 g., 0.995 Platinum 0.040 oz. APW, 13.9 mm. **Ruler:** Elizabeth II **Series:** Flower Fairies **Obv:** Crowned bust right **Rev:** Snowdrop

Date	Mintage	VF20	XF40	MS60	MS63	MS65
1997	Est. 7500	PF65 64.00				

KM# 737 1/25 CROWN

1.24 g., 0.9999 Gold 0.040 oz. AGW, 13.9 mm. **Ruler:** Elizabeth II **Series:** Flower Fairies **Obv:** Crowned bust right **Rev:** Tulip

Date	Mintage	VF20	XF40	MS60	MS63	MS65
1997	Est. 25000	PF65 64.00				

KM# 737a 1/25 CROWN

1.25 g., 0.995 Platinum 0.040 oz. APW, 13.9 mm. **Ruler:** Elizabeth II **Series:** Flower Fairies **Obv:** Crowned bust right **Rev:** Tulip

Date	Mintage	VF20	XF40	MS60	MS63	MS65
1997	Est. 7500	PF65 64.00				

KM# 738 1/25 CROWN

1.24 g., 0.9999 Gold 0.040 oz. AGW, 13.9 mm. **Ruler:** Elizabeth II **Series:** Flower Fairies **Obv:** Crowned bust right **Rev:** Jasmine

Date	Mintage	VF20	XF40	MS60	MS63	MS65
1997	Est. 25000	PF65 64.00				

KM# 738a 1/25 CROWN

1.25 g., 0.995 Platinum 0.040 oz. APW, 13.9 mm. **Ruler:** Elizabeth II **Series:** Flower Fairies **Obv:** Crowned bust right **Rev:** Jasmine

Date	Mintage	VF20	XF40	MS60	MS63	MS65
1997	Est. 7500	PF65 64.00				

KM# 770 1/25 CROWN

1.24 g., 0.9999 Gold 0.040 oz. AGW, 13.9 mm. **Ruler:** Elizabeth II **Obv:** Crowned bust right **Rev:** Long-haired Smoke cat

Date	Mintage	VF20	XF40	MS60	MS63	MS65
1997	—	—	—	—	—	69.00
1997	—	PF65 74.00				

KM# 770a 1/25 CROWN

1.24 g., 0.9999 Platinum 0.040 oz. APW, 13.9 mm. **Ruler:** Elizabeth II **Obv:** Crowned bust right **Rev:** Long-haired Smoke cat

Date	Mintage	VF20	XF40	MS60	MS63	MS65
1997	—	—	—	—	—	59.00
1997	—	PF65 64.00				

KM# 789 1/25 CROWN

1.24 g., 0.9999 Gold 0.040 oz. AGW, 13.9 mm. **Ruler:** Elizabeth II **Subject:** History of the Cat **Obv:** Crowned bust right **Rev:** Cat stalking a spider

Date	Mintage	VF20	XF40	MS60	MS63	MS65
1997	Est. 25000	PF65 74.00				

KM# 812 1/25 CROWN

1.24 g., 0.9999 Gold 0.040 oz. AGW, 13.9 mm. **Ruler:** Elizabeth II **Subject:** Year of the Tiger **Obv:** Crowned bust right **Rev:** Tiger

Date	Mintage	VF20	XF40	MS60	MS63	MS65
1998	Est. 20000	PF65 64.00				

KM# 828 1/25 CROWN

1.24 g., 0.9999 Gold 0.040 oz. AGW, 13.9 mm. **Ruler:** Elizabeth II **Series:** Flower Fairies **Obv:** Crowned bust right **Rev:** Fairy standing, lavender

Date	Mintage	VF20	XF40	MS60	MS63	MS65
1998	Est. 25000	PF65 64.00				

KM# 828a 1/25 CROWN

1.24 g., 0.9995 Platinum 0.040 oz. APW, 13.9 mm. **Ruler:** Elizabeth II **Series:** Flower Fairies **Obv:** Crowned bust right **Rev:** Fairy standing, lavender

Date	Mintage	VF20	XF40	MS60	MS63	MS65
1998	Est. 7500	PF65 64.00				

KM# 829 1/25 CROWN

1.24 g., 0.9999 Gold 0.040 oz. AGW, 13.9 mm. **Ruler:** Elizabeth II **Series:** Flower Fairies **Obv:** Crowned bust right **Rev:** Two fairies, sweet pea

Date	Mintage	VF20	XF40	MS60	MS63	MS65
1998	Est. 25000	PF65 64.00				

KM# 829a 1/25 CROWN

1.24 g., 0.9995 Platinum 0.040 oz. APW, 13.9 mm. **Ruler:** Elizabeth II **Series:** Flower Fairies **Obv:** Crowned bust right **Rev:** Two fairies, sweet pea

Date	Mintage	VF20	XF40	MS60	MS63	MS65
1998	Est. 7500	PF65 64.00				

KM# 830 1/25 CROWN

1.24 g., 0.9999 Gold 0.040 oz. AGW, 13.9 mm. **Ruler:** Elizabeth II **Series:** Flower Fairies **Obv:** Crowned bust right **Rev:** Two fairies, sweet pea

Date	Mintage	VF20	XF40	MS60	MS63	MS65
1998	—	PF65 64.00				

KM# 830a 1/25 CROWN

1.24 g., 0.9995 Platinum 0.040 oz. APW, 13.9 mm. **Ruler:** Elizabeth II **Series:** Flower Fairies **Obv:** Crowned bust right **Rev:** Two fairies, sweet pea

Date	Mintage	VF20	XF40	MS60	MS63	MS65
1998	Est. 30000	PF65 64.00				

KM# 831 1/25 CROWN

1.24 g., 0.9999 Gold 0.040 oz. AGW, 13.9 mm. **Ruler:** Elizabeth II **Series:** Flower Fairies **Obv:** Crowned bust right **Rev:** Fairy standing, daffodil

Date	Mintage	VF20	XF40	MS60	MS63	MS65
1998	—	PF65 64.00				

KM# 831a 1/25 CROWN
1.24 g., 0.9995 Platinum 0.040 oz. APW, 13.9 mm. **Ruler:** Elizabeth II **Series:** Flower Fairies **Obv:** Crowned bust right **Rev:** Fairy standing, daffodil

Date	Mintage	VF20	XF40	MS60	MS63	MS65
1998	Est. 7500	PF65 64.00				

KM# 853 1/25 CROWN
1.24 g., 0.9999 Gold 0.040 oz. AGW, 13.9 mm. **Ruler:** Elizabeth II **Obv:** Crowned bust right **Rev:** Birman cat

Date	Mintage	VF20	XF40	MS60	MS63	MS65
1998 U	—	—	—	—	—	69.00
1998	1,000	PF65 74.00				

KM# 853a 1/25 CROWN
1.24 g., 0.9995 Platinum 0.040 oz. APW, 13.9 mm. **Ruler:** Elizabeth II **Obv:** Crowned bust right **Rev:** Birman cat

Date	Mintage	VF20	XF40	MS60	MS63	MS65
1998	—	PF65 64.00				

KM# 859 1/25 CROWN
1.24 g., 0.9999 Gold 0.040 oz. AGW, 13.9 mm. **Ruler:** Elizabeth II **Subject:** History of the Cat **Obv:** Crowned bust right **Rev:** Egyptian Mau cat with earring

Date	Mintage	VF20	XF40	MS60	MS63	MS65
1998	Est. 25000	PF65 74.00				

KM# 948 1/25 CROWN
1.24 g., 0.9999 Gold 0.040 oz. AGW, 13.9 mm. **Ruler:** Elizabeth II **Subject:** Year of the Rabbit **Obv:** Crowned bust right **Rev:** Two rabbits

Date	Mintage	VF20	XF40	MS60	MS63	MS65
1999	Est. 20000	PF65 64.00				

KM# 958 1/25 CROWN
1.24 g., 0.9999 Gold 0.040 oz. AGW, 13.9 mm. **Ruler:** Elizabeth II **Obv:** Crowned bust right **Rev:** British Blue cat

Date	Mintage	VF20	XF40	MS60	MS63	MS65
1999	—	—	—	—	—	69.00
1999	—	PF65 74.00				
1999 U Y2K	20,000	—	—	—	—	69.00

KM# 958a 1/25 CROWN
1.24 g., 0.9995 Platinum 0.040 oz. APW, 13.9 mm. **Ruler:** Elizabeth II **Obv:** Crowned bust right **Rev:** British Blue cat

Date	Mintage	VF20	XF40	MS60	MS63	MS65
1999	—	PF65 64.00				

KM# 1012 1/25 CROWN
1.24 g., 0.9999 Gold 0.040 oz. AGW, 13.9 mm. **Ruler:** Elizabeth II **Subject:** Year of the Dragon **Obv:** Crowned bust right **Rev:** Dragon, Chinese characters

Date	Mintage	VF20	XF40	MS60	MS63	MS65
2000	Est. 20000	PF65 64.00				

KM# 1052 1/25 CROWN
1.24 g., 0.9999 Gold 0.0399 oz. AGW, 13.92 mm. **Ruler:** Elizabeth II **Obv:** Crowned bust right **Rev:** Scottish fold kitten **Edge:** Reeded

Date	Mintage	VF20	XF40	MS60	MS63	MS65
2000	—	—	—	—	—	64.00
2000	—	PF65 64.00				

KM# 1052a 1/25 CROWN
1.24 g., 0.9995 Platinum 0.040 oz. APW, 13.9 mm. **Ruler:** Elizabeth II **Obv:** Crowned bust right **Rev:** Scottish fold kitten

Date	Mintage	VF20	XF40	MS60	MS63	MS65
2000	—	—	—	—	—	59.00

KM# 236 1/10 CROWN
3.11 g., 0.999 Gold 0.0999 oz. AGW **Ruler:** Elizabeth II **Obv:** Crowned bust right **Rev:** Manx cat

Date	Mintage	VF20	XF40	MS60	MS63	MS65
1988	12,000	—	—	—	—	172
1988	5,000	PF65 177				

KM# 253 1/10 CROWN
3.11 g., 0.999 Gold 0.0999 oz. AGW, 17.95 mm. **Ruler:** Elizabeth II **Obv:** Crowned bust right **Rev:** Persian cat

Date	Mintage	VF20	XF40	MS60	MS63	MS65
1989	—	—	—	—	—	172
1989	—	PF65 177				

KM# 253a 1/10 CROWN
3.11 g., 0.9995 Platinum 0.0999 oz. APW, 17.95 mm. **Ruler:** Elizabeth II **Obv:** Crowned bust right **Rev:** Persian cat **Note:** Prev. KM#468.

Date	Mintage	VF20	XF40	MS60	MS63	MS65
1989	—	—	—	—	—	147
1989	—	PF65 152				

KM# 278 1/10 CROWN
3.11 g., 0.999 Gold 0.0999 oz. AGW, 17.95 mm. **Ruler:** Elizabeth II **Obv:** Crowned bust right **Rev:** Alley cat

Date	Mintage	VF20	XF40	MS60	MS63	MS65
1990	—	—	—	—	—	172
1990	—	PF65 177				

KM# 1427 1/10 CROWN
3.11 g., 0.999 Gold 0.0999 oz. AGW, 17.95 mm. **Ruler:** Elizabeth II **Rev:** Penny Black, Great Britain's first postage stamp

Date	Mintage	VF20	XF40	MS60	MS63	MS65
1990 PM	—	PF65 177				

KM# 295 1/10 CROWN
3.11 g., 0.999 Gold 0.0999 oz. AGW, 17.95 mm. **Ruler:** Elizabeth II **Obv:** Crowned bust right **Rev:** Norwegian cat

Date	Mintage	VF20	XF40	MS60	MS63	MS65
1991	—	—	—	—	—	172
1991	—	PF65 177				

KM# 323 1/10 CROWN
3.11 g., 0.999 Gold 0.0999 oz. AGW, 17.95 mm. **Ruler:** Elizabeth II **Subject:** America's Cup **Obv:** Crowned bust right **Rev:** Cameo of "Star of India" above modern sailboat, Sidney Opera House and Harbor Bridge.

Date	Mintage	VF20	XF40	MS60	MS63	MS65
1992 Prooflike	25,000	—	—	—	—	160

KM# 323a 1/10 CROWN
3.11 g., 0.9995 Platinum 0.0999 oz. APW, 17.95 mm. **Ruler:** Elizabeth II **Subject:** America's Cup **Obv:** Crowned bust right **Rev:** Sailboat

Date	Mintage	VF20	XF40	MS60	MS63	MS65
1992 Prooflike	5,000	—	—	—	—	147

KM# 329 1/10 CROWN
3.11 g., 0.999 Gold 0.0999 oz. AGW, 17.95 mm. **Ruler:** Elizabeth II **Obv:** Crowned bust right **Rev:** Siamese cat

Date	Mintage	VF20	XF40	MS60	MS63	MS65
1992	—	—	—	—	—	172
1992	—	PF65 177				

KM# 339 1/10 CROWN
3.11 g., 0.999 Gold 0.0999 oz. AGW, 17.95 mm. **Ruler:** Elizabeth II **Subject:** Year of the Cockerel **Obv:** Crowned bust right **Rev:** Cockerel in inner circle

Date	Mintage	VF20	XF40	MS60	MS63	MS65
1993	Est. 20000	PF65 165				

KM# 350 1/10 CROWN
3.11 g., 0.999 Gold 0.0999 oz. AGW, 17.95 mm. **Ruler:** Elizabeth II **Obv:** Crowned bust right **Rev:** Maine Coon cat

Date	Mintage	VF20	XF40	MS60	MS63	MS65
1993	—	—	—	—	—	172
1993	—	PF65 177				

KM# 377 1/10 CROWN
3.11 g., 0.999 Gold 0.0999 oz. AGW, 17.95 mm. **Ruler:** Elizabeth II **Obv:** Crowned bust right **Rev:** Japanese Bobtail cat

Date	Mintage	VF20	XF40	MS60	MS63	MS65
1994	—	—	—	—	—	172
1994	—	PF65 177				

KM# 377a 1/10 CROWN
3.11 g., 0.9995 Platinum 0.0999 oz. APW, 17.95 mm. **Ruler:** Elizabeth II **Obv:** Crowned bust right **Rev:** Japanese Bobtail cat **Note:** Prev. KM#474.

Date	Mintage	VF20	XF40	MS60	MS63	MS65
1994	—	—	—	—	—	147
1994	—	PF65 152				

KM# 403 1/10 CROWN
3.11 g., 0.999 Gold 0.0999 oz. AGW, 17.95 mm. **Ruler:** Elizabeth II **Obv:** Crowned bust right **Rev:** Pekingese dog

Date	Mintage	VF20	XF40	MS60	MS63	MS65
1994	20,000	PF65 172				

KM# 443 1/10 CROWN
3.11 g., 0.999 Gold 0.0999 oz. AGW, 17.95 mm. **Ruler:** Elizabeth II **Obv:** Crowned bust right **Rev:** Turkish cat

Date	Mintage	VF20	XF40	MS60	MS63	MS65
1995	—	—	—	—	—	172
1995	—	PF65 177				

KM# 443a 1/10 CROWN
3.11 g., 0.9995 Platinum 0.0999 oz. APW, 17.95 mm. **Ruler:** Elizabeth II **Obv:** Crowned bust right **Rev:** Turkish cat **Note:** Prev. KM#479.

Date	Mintage	VF20	XF40	MS60	MS63	MS65
1995	—	—	—	—	—	147
1995	—	PF65 152				

KM# 450 1/10 CROWN
3.11 g., 0.999 Gold 0.0999 oz. AGW, 17.95 mm. **Ruler:** Elizabeth II **Subject:** Year of the Pig **Obv:** Crowned bust right **Rev:** Sow with piglets

Date	Mintage	VF20	XF40	MS60	MS63	MS65
1995	Est. 20000	PF65 182				

KM# 601 1/10 CROWN
3.11 g., 0.999 Gold 0.0999 oz. AGW, 17.95 mm. **Ruler:** Elizabeth II **Series:** Flower Fairies **Obv:** Crowned bust right **Rev:** Orchis

Date	Mintage	VF20	XF40	MS60	MS63	MS65
1996	Est. 20000	PF65 177				

KM# 602 1/10 CROWN
3.11 g., 0.999 Gold 0.0999 oz. AGW, 17.95 mm. **Ruler:** Elizabeth II **Series:** Flower Fairies **Obv:** Crowned bust right **Rev:** Rose

Date	Mintage	VF20	XF40	MS60	MS63	MS65
1996	Est. 20000	PF65 177				

KM# 603 1/10 CROWN
3.11 g., 0.999 Gold 0.0999 oz. AGW, 17.95 mm. **Ruler:** Elizabeth II **Series:** Flower Fairies **Obv:** Crowned bust right **Rev:** Fuchsia

Date	Mintage	VF20	XF40	MS60	MS63	MS65
1996	Est. 20000	PF65 177				

KM# 604 1/10 CROWN
3.11 g., 0.999 Gold 0.0999 oz. AGW, 17.95 mm. **Ruler:** Elizabeth II **Obv:** Crowned bust right **Rev:** Pinks

Date	Mintage	VF20	XF40	MS60	MS63	MS65
1996	—	PF65 177				

KM# 615 1/10 CROWN
3.11 g., 0.999 Gold 0.0999 oz. AGW, 17.95 mm. **Ruler:** Elizabeth II **Obv:** Crowned bust right **Rev:** Burmese cat

Date	Mintage	VF20	XF40	MS60	MS63	MS65
1996	—	—	—	—	—	177
1996	—	PF65 177				

KM# 615a 1/10 CROWN
3.11 g., 0.9995 Platinum 0.0999 oz. APW, 17.95 mm. **Ruler:** Elizabeth II **Obv:** Crowned bust right **Rev:** Burmese cat **Note:** Prev. KM#616.

Date	Mintage	VF20	XF40	MS60	MS63	MS65
1996	—	—	—	—	—	147
1996	—	PF65 152				

KM# 729 1/10 CROWN
3.11 g., 0.999 Gold 0.0999 oz. AGW, 17.95 mm. **Ruler:** Elizabeth II **Subject:** Year of the Rat **Obv:** Crowned bust right **Rev:** Rat

Date	Mintage	VF20	XF40	MS60	MS63	MS65
1996 Proof	—	—	—	—	—	—

Note: Entire series purchased by one buyer. Mintage, disposition and market value unknown

KM# 722 1/10 CROWN
3.11 g., 0.999 Gold 0.0999 oz. AGW, 17.95 mm. **Ruler:** Elizabeth II **Subject:** Year of the Ox **Obv:** Crowned bust right **Rev:** Ox laying down

Date	Mintage	VF20	XF40	MS60	MS63	MS65
1997	Est. 15000	PF65 177				

KM# 743 1/10 CROWN
3.11 g., 0.999 Gold 0.0999 oz. AGW, 17.95 mm. **Ruler:** Elizabeth II **Series:** Flower Fairies **Obv:** Crowned bust right **Rev:** Candytuft

Date	Mintage	VF20	XF40	MS60	MS63	MS65
1997	Est. 20000	PF65 177				

KM# 743a 1/10 CROWN
3.13 g., 0.995 Platinum 0.100 oz. APW, 17.95 mm. **Ruler:** Elizabeth II **Series:** Flower Fairies **Obv:** Crowned bust right **Rev:** Candytuft

Date	Mintage	VF20	XF40	MS60	MS63	MS65
1997	Est. 5000	PF65 152				

KM# 744 1/10 CROWN
3.11 g., 0.9999 Gold 0.100 oz. AGW, 17.95 mm. **Ruler:** Elizabeth II **Obv:** Crowned bust right **Rev:** Snowdrop

Date	Mintage	VF20	XF40	MS60	MS63	MS65
1997	Est. 20000	PF65 177				

KM# 744a 1/10 CROWN
3.13 g., 0.995 Platinum 0.100 oz. APW, 17.95 mm. **Ruler:** Elizabeth II **Series:** Flower Fairies **Obv:** Crowned bust right **Rev:** Snowdrop

Date	Mintage	VF20	XF40	MS60	MS63	MS65
1997	Est. 5000	PF65 152				

KM# 745 1/10 CROWN
3.11 g., 0.9999 Gold 0.100 oz. AGW, 17.95 mm. **Ruler:** Elizabeth II **Series:** Flower Fairies **Obv:** Crowned bust right **Rev:** Tulip

Date	Mintage	VF20	XF40	MS60	MS63	MS65
1997	Est. 20000	PF65 172				

KM# 745a 1/10 CROWN
3.13 g., 0.995 Platinum 0.100 oz. APW, 17.95 mm. **Ruler:** Elizabeth II **Series:** Flower Fairies **Obv:** Crowned bust right **Rev:** Tulip

Date	Mintage	VF20	XF40	MS60	MS63	MS65
1997	Est. 5000	PF65 152				

KM# 746 1/10 CROWN
3.11 g., 0.9999 Gold 0.100 oz. AGW, 17.95 mm. **Ruler:** Elizabeth II **Series:** Flower Fairies **Obv:** Crowned bust right **Rev:** Jasmine

Date	Mintage	VF20	XF40	MS60	MS63	MS65
1997	Est. 20000	PF65 172				

KM# 746a 1/10 CROWN
3.13 g., 0.995 Platinum 0.100 oz. APW, 17.95 mm. **Ruler:** Elizabeth II **Series:** Flower Fairies **Obv:** Crowned bust right **Rev:** Jasmine

Date	Mintage	VF20	XF40	MS60	MS63	MS65
1997	Est. 5000	PF65 152				

KM# 771 1/10 CROWN
3.11 g., 0.9999 Gold 0.100 oz. AGW, 17.95 mm. **Ruler:** Elizabeth II **Obv:** Crowned bust right **Rev:** Long-haired Smoke cat

Date	Mintage	VF20	XF40	MS60	MS63	MS65
1997	—	—	—	—	—	177
1997	—	PF65 177				

KM# 771a 1/10 CROWN
3.11 g., 0.9995 Platinum 0.0999 oz. APW, 17.95 mm. **Ruler:** Elizabeth II **Obv:** Crowned bust right **Rev:** Long-haired Smoke cat

Date	Mintage	VF20	XF40	MS60	MS63	MS65
1997	—	—	—	—	—	147
1997	—	PF65 152				

KM# 790 1/10 CROWN
3.11 g., 0.9999 Gold 0.100 oz. AGW, 17.95 mm. **Ruler:** Elizabeth II **Subject:** History of the Cat **Obv:** Crowned bust right **Rev:** Cat stalking a spider

Date	Mintage	VF20	XF40	MS60	MS63	MS65
1997	Est. 20000	PF65 177				

KM# 813 1/10 CROWN
3.11 g., 0.9999 Gold 0.100 oz. AGW, 17.95 mm. **Ruler:** Elizabeth II **Subject:** Year of the Tiger **Obv:** Crowned bust right **Rev:** Tiger

Date	Mintage	VF20	XF40	MS60	MS63	MS65
1998	Est. 15000	PF65 172				

KM# 832 1/10 CROWN
3.11 g., 0.9999 Gold 0.100 oz. AGW, 17.95 mm. **Ruler:** Elizabeth II **Series:** Flower Fairies **Obv:** Crowned bust right **Rev:** Standing fairy, lavender

Date	Mintage	VF20	XF40	MS60	MS63	MS65
1998	Est. 20000	PF65 172				

KM# 832a 1/10 CROWN
3.11 g., 0.9995 Platinum 0.0999 oz. APW, 17.95 mm. **Ruler:** Elizabeth II **Series:** Flower Fairies **Obv:** Crowned bust right **Rev:** Standing fairy, lavender

Date	Mintage	VF20	XF40	MS60	MS63	MS65
1998	Est. 5000	PF65 152				

KM# 833 1/10 CROWN
3.11 g., 0.9999 Gold 0.100 oz. AGW, 17.95 mm. **Ruler:** Elizabeth II **Series:** Flower Fairies **Obv:** Crowned bust right **Rev:** Two fairies, sweet pea

Date	Mintage	VF20	XF40	MS60	MS63	MS65
1998	Est. 20000	PF65 172				

KM# 833a 1/10 CROWN
3.11 g., 0.9995 Platinum 0.0999 oz. APW, 17.95 mm. **Ruler:** Elizabeth II **Series:** Flower Fairies **Obv:** Crowned bust right **Rev:** Two fairies, sweet pea

Date	Mintage	VF20	XF40	MS60	MS63	MS65
1998	Est. 5000	PF65 152				

KM# 834 1/10 CROWN
3.11 g., 0.9999 Gold 0.100 oz. AGW, 17.95 mm. **Ruler:** Elizabeth II **Obv:** Crowned bust right **Rev:** Fairy looking into flower, White Bindweed

Date	Mintage	VF20	XF40	MS60	MS63	MS65
1998	—	PF65 172				

KM# 834a 1/10 CROWN
3.11 g., 0.9995 Platinum 0.0999 oz. APW, 17.95 mm. **Ruler:** Elizabeth II **Series:** Flower Fairies **Obv:** Crowned bust right **Rev:** Fairy looking into flower, White Bindweed

Date	Mintage	VF20	XF40	MS60	MS63	MS65
1998	Est. 5000	PF65 152				

KM# 835 1/10 CROWN
3.11 g., 0.9999 Gold 0.100 oz. AGW, 17.95 mm. **Ruler:** Elizabeth II **Series:** Flower Fairies **Obv:** Crowned bust right **Rev:** Fairy standing with flower, daffodil

Date	Mintage	VF20	XF40	MS60	MS63	MS65
1998	Est. 20000	PF65 172				

KM# 835a 1/10 CROWN
3.11 g., 0.9995 Platinum 0.0999 oz. APW, 17.95 mm. **Ruler:** Elizabeth II **Obv:** Crowned bust right **Rev:** Fairy standing with flower, daffodil **Rev. Legend:** Flower Fairies

Date	Mintage	VF20	XF40	MS60	MS63	MS65
1998	Est. 5000	PF65 152				

KM# 854 1/10 CROWN
3.11 g., 0.9999 Gold 0.100 oz. AGW, 17.95 mm. **Ruler:** Elizabeth II **Obv:** Crowned bust right **Rev:** Birman cat

Date	Mintage	VF20	XF40	MS60	MS63	MS65
1998	—	—	—	—	—	177
1998	1,000	PF65 177				

KM# 854a 1/10 CROWN
3.11 g., 0.9995 Platinum 0.0999 oz. APW, 17.95 mm. **Ruler:** Elizabeth II **Obv:** Crowned bust right **Rev:** Birman cat

Date	Mintage	VF20	XF40	MS60	MS63	MS65
1998	—	PF65 152				

KM# 860 1/10 CROWN
3.11 g., 0.9999 Gold 0.100 oz. AGW, 17.95 mm. **Ruler:** Elizabeth II **Subject:** History of the Cat **Obv:** Crowned bust right **Rev:** Egyptian Mau cat with earring

Date	Mintage	VF20	XF40	MS60	MS63	MS65
1998	Est. 20000	PF65 177				

KM# 949 1/10 CROWN
3.11 g., 0.9999 Gold 0.100 oz. AGW, 17.95 mm. **Ruler:** Elizabeth II **Subject:** Year of the Rabbit **Obv:** Crowned bust right **Rev:** Two rabbits

Date	Mintage	VF20	XF40	MS60	MS63	MS65
1999	—	PF65 172				

KM# 960 1/10 CROWN
3.11 g., 0.9999 Gold 0.100 oz. AGW, 17.95 mm. **Ruler:** Elizabeth II **Obv:** Crowned bust right **Rev:** British Blue cat cleaning its paw

Date	Mintage	VF20	XF40	MS60	MS63	MS65
1999	—	—	—	—	—	177
1999	—	PF65 177				
1999 U Y2K	10,000	—	—	—	—	177

KM# 960a 1/10 CROWN
3.11 g., 0.9995 Platinum 0.100 oz. APW, 17.95 mm. **Ruler:** Elizabeth II **Obv:** Crowned bust right **Rev:** British Blue cat cleaning its paw

Date	Mintage	VF20	XF40	MS60	MS63	MS65
1999	—	PF65 152				

KM# 1013 1/10 CROWN
3.11 g., 0.9999 Gold 0.100 oz. AGW, 17.95 mm. **Ruler:** Elizabeth II **Subject:** Year of the Dragon **Obv:** Crowned bust right **Rev:** Dragon, Chinese characters

Date	Mintage	VF20	XF40	MS60	MS63	MS65
2000	Est. 15000	PF65 172				

KM# 1053 1/10 CROWN
3.11 g., 0.9999 Gold 0.100 oz. AGW, 17.95 mm. **Ruler:** Elizabeth II **Obv:** Crowned bust right **Rev:** Scottish kitten playing with the world **Edge:** Reeded

Date	Mintage	VF20	XF40	MS60	MS63	MS65
2000	—	—	—	—	—	172
2000	—	PF65 172				

KM# 1053a 1/10 CROWN
3.11 g., 0.9995 Platinum 0.100 oz. APW, 17.95 mm. **Ruler:** Elizabeth II **Obv:** Crowned bust right **Rev:** Scottish kitten playing with the world

Date	Mintage	VF20	XF40	MS60	MS63	MS65
2000	—	—	—	—	—	147

KM# 237 1/5 CROWN
6.22 g., 0.999 Gold 0.1998 oz. AGW, 22 mm. **Ruler:** Elizabeth II **Obv:** Crowned bust right **Rev:** Manx cat

Date	Mintage	VF20	XF40	MS60	MS63	MS65
1988	6,750	—	—	—	—	320
1988	5,000	PF65 325				

KM# 254 1/5 CROWN
6.22 g., 0.999 Gold 0.1998 oz. AGW, 22 mm. **Ruler:** Elizabeth II **Obv:** Crowned bust right **Rev:** Persian cat

Date	Mintage	VF20	XF40	MS60	MS63	MS65
1989	—	—	—	—	—	320
1989	—	PF65 325				

KM# 254a 1/5 CROWN
6.22 g., 0.999 Platinum 0.1998 oz. APW, 22 mm. **Ruler:** Elizabeth II **Obv:** Crowned bust right **Rev:** Persian cat **Note:** Prev. KM#469.

Date	Mintage	VF20	XF40	MS60	MS63	MS65
1989	—	—	—	—	—	285
1989	—	PF65 290				

KM# 274 1/5 CROWN
6.22 g., 0.999 Gold 0.1998 oz. AGW, 22 mm. **Ruler:** Elizabeth II **Obv:** Crowned bust right **Rev:** Cameo head facing within circle

Date	Mintage	VF20	XF40	MS60	MS63	MS65
1989	Est. 5000	PF65 320				

KM# 268 1/5 CROWN
6.22 g., 0.999 Gold 0.1998 oz. AGW, 22 mm. **Ruler:** Elizabeth II **Subject:** 150th Anniversary of "Penny Black" Stamp **Obv:** Crowned bust right **Rev:** Penny Black Stamp

Date	Mintage	VF20	XF40	MS60	MS63	MS65
1990	Est. 5000	PF65 320				

KM# 279.1 1/5 CROWN
6.22 g., 0.999 Gold 0.1998 oz. AGW, 22 mm. **Ruler:** Elizabeth II **Obv:** Crowned bust right **Rev:** Alley cat

Date	Mintage	VF20	XF40	MS60	MS63	MS65
1990	—	—	—	—	—	320
1990	—	PF65 325				

KM# 279.1a 1/5 CROWN
6.22 g., 0.999 Platinum 0.1998 oz. APW, 22 mm. **Ruler:** Elizabeth II **Obv:** Crowned bust right **Rev:** Alley cat **Note:** Prev. KM#472.

Date	Mintage	VF20	XF40	MS60	MS63	MS65
1990	—	—	—	—	—	285
1990	—	PF65 290				

KM# 279.2 1/5 CROWN
6.22 g., 0.999 Gold 0.1998 oz. AGW, 22 mm. **Ruler:** Elizabeth II **Obv:** Crowned bust right **Rev:** Alley cat **Note:** Error.(Rev) Dies claiming platinum metal content

Date	Mintage	VF20	XF40	MS60	MS63	MS65
1990	467	—	—	—	—	345

KM# 306 1/5 CROWN
6.22 g., 0.999 Gold 0.1998 oz. AGW, 22 mm. **Ruler:** Elizabeth II **Obv:** Crowned bust right **Rev:** Queen Mother with two daughters

Date	Mintage	VF20	XF40	MS60	MS63	MS65
1990	—	PF65 320				

KM# 306a 1/5 CROWN
6.22 g., 0.999 Platinum 0.1998 oz. APW, 22 mm. **Ruler:** Elizabeth II **Obv:** Crowned bust right **Rev:** Queen Mother with two daughters

Date	Mintage	VF20	XF40	MS60	MS63	MS65
1990	—	PF65 290				

KM# 819 1/5 CROWN
6.22 g., 0.999 Gold 0.1998 oz. AGW, 22 mm. **Ruler:** Elizabeth II **Subject:** Soccer **Obv:** Crowned bust right **Rev:** Milano

Date	Mintage	VF20	XF40	MS60	MS63	MS65
1990	Est. 500	PF65 320				

KM# 819a 1/5 CROWN
6.22 g., 0.999 Platinum 0.1998 oz. APW, 22 mm. **Ruler:** Elizabeth II **Subject:** Soccer **Obv:** Crowned bust right **Rev:** Milano

Date	Mintage	VF20	XF40	MS60	MS63	MS65
1990	Est. 250	PF65 290				

KM# 820 1/5 CROWN
6.22 g., 0.999 Gold 0.1998 oz. AGW, 22 mm. **Ruler:** Elizabeth II **Subject:** Soccer **Obv:** Crowned bust right **Rev:** Torino

Date	Mintage	VF20	XF40	MS60	MS63	MS65
1990	—	PF65 320				

KM# 820a 1/5 CROWN
6.22 g., 0.999 Platinum 0.1998 oz. APW, 22 mm. **Ruler:** Elizabeth II **Subject:** Soccer **Obv:** Crowned bust right **Rev:** Torino

Date	Mintage	VF20	XF40	MS60	MS63	MS65
1990	Est. 250	PF65 290				

KM# 821 1/5 CROWN
6.22 g., 0.999 Gold 0.1998 oz. AGW, 22 mm. **Ruler:** Elizabeth II **Subject:** Soccer **Obv:** Crowned bust right **Rev:** Bologna

Date	Mintage	VF20	XF40	MS60	MS63	MS65
1990	—	PF65 320				

KM# 821a 1/5 CROWN
6.22 g., 0.999 Platinum 0.1998 oz. APW, 22 mm. **Ruler:** Elizabeth II **Subject:** Soccer **Obv:** Crowned bust right **Rev:** Bologna

Date	Mintage	VF20	XF40	MS60	MS63	MS65
1990	Est. 250	PF65 290				

KM# 822 1/5 CROWN
6.22 g., 0.999 Gold 0.1998 oz. AGW, 22 mm. **Ruler:** Elizabeth II **Subject:** Soccer **Obv:** Crowned bust right **Rev:** Palermo

Date	Mintage	VF20	XF40	MS60	MS63	MS65
1990	Est. 500	PF65 320				

KM# 822a 1/5 CROWN
6.22 g., 0.999 Platinum 0.1998 oz. APW, 22 mm. **Ruler:** Elizabeth II **Subject:** Soccer **Obv:** Crowned bust right **Rev:** Palermo

Date	Mintage	VF20	XF40	MS60	MS63	MS65
1990	—	PF65 290				

KM# 1502 1/5 CROWN
6.22 g., 0.999 Gold 0.1998 oz. AGW, 22 mm. **Ruler:** Elizabeth II **Subject:** Winston Churchill, 25th Anniversary of Death **Obv:** Crowned bust right **Rev:** Churchill with cigar

Date	Mintage	VF20	XF40	MS60	MS63	MS65
1990	Est. 500	PF65 320				

KM# 1503 1/5 CROWN
6.22 g., 0.999 Gold 0.1998 oz. AGW, 22 mm. **Ruler:** Elizabeth II **Subject:** Winston Churchill, 25th Anniversary of Death **Obv:** Crowned bust right **Rev:** Churchill in robes of the Garter

Date	Mintage	VF20	XF40	MS60	MS63	MS65
1990	Est. 500	PF65 320				

KM# 290 1/5 CROWN
6.22 g., 0.999 Gold 0.1998 oz. AGW, 22 mm. **Ruler:** Elizabeth II **Subject:** 100th Anniversary - American Numismatic Association **Obv:** Crowned bust right **Rev:** Assorted famous world coins

Date	Mintage	VF20	XF40	MS60	MS63	MS65
1991	100	PF65 320				

KM# 296 1/5 CROWN
6.22 g., 0.999 Gold 0.1998 oz. AGW, 22 mm. **Ruler:** Elizabeth II **Obv:** Crowned bust right **Rev:** Norwegian cat

Date	Mintage	VF20	XF40	MS60	MS63	MS65
1991	—	—	—	—	—	320
1991	—	PF65 325				

KM# 302 1/5 CROWN
6.22 g., 0.999 Gold 0.1998 oz. AGW, 22 mm. **Ruler:** Elizabeth II **Subject:** America's Cup **Obv:** Crowned bust right **Rev:** Cameo above two modern sailboats

Date	Mintage	VF20	XF40	MS60	MS63	MS65
1991	—	PF65 320				

KM# 1504 1/5 CROWN
6.22 g., 0.999 Gold 0.1998 oz. AGW, 22 mm. **Ruler:** Elizabeth II **Subject:** Charles and Diana, 10th Wedding anniversary **Obv:** Crowned bust right **Rev:** Prince Charles

Date	Mintage	VF20	XF40	MS60	MS63	MS65
1991	—	PF65 320				

KM# 1505 1/5 CROWN
6.22 g., 0.999 Gold 0.1998 oz. AGW, 22 mm. **Ruler:** Elizabeth II **Subject:** Charles and Diana, 10th Wedding anniversary **Obv:** Crowned bust right **Rev:** Princess Diana

Date	Mintage	VF20	XF40	MS60	MS63	MS65
1991	—	PF65 320				

KM# 324 1/5 CROWN
6.22 g., 0.999 Gold 0.1998 oz. AGW, 22 mm. **Ruler:** Elizabeth II **Subject:** America's Cup **Obv:** Crowned bust right **Rev:** Cameo above modern sailboat, Sidney Opera House and the Harbor bridge.

Date	Mintage	VF20	XF40	MS60	MS63	MS65
1992 Prooflike	10,000	—	—	—	—	305

KM# 330 1/5 CROWN
6.22 g., 0.999 Gold 0.1998 oz. AGW, 22 mm. **Ruler:** Elizabeth II **Obv:** Crowned bust right **Rev:** Siamese cat

Date	Mintage	VF20	XF40	MS60	MS63	MS65
1992	—	—	—	—	—	320
1992	—	PF65 325				

KM# 1506 1/5 CROWN
6.22 g., 0.999 Gold 0.1998 oz. AGW, 22 mm. **Ruler:** Elizabeth II **Obv:** Crowned bust right **Rev:** Locomotive Jupiter

Date	Mintage	VF20	XF40	MS60	MS63	MS65
1992	—	PF65 320				

KM# 1507 1/5 CROWN
6.22 g., 0.999 Gold 0.1998 oz. AGW, 22 mm. **Ruler:** Elizabeth II **Obv:** Crowned bust right **Rev:** Locomotive 119

Date	Mintage	VF20	XF40	MS60	MS63	MS65
1992	—	PF65 320				

KM# 1508 1/5 CROWN
6.22 g., 0.999 Gold 0.1998 oz. AGW, 22 mm. **Ruler:** Elizabeth II **Obv:** Crowned bust right **Rev:** Meeting of Central Pacific and Union Pacific at Promontory Summit, Utah

Date	Mintage	VF20	XF40	MS60	MS63	MS65
1992	—	PF65 320				

KM# 340 1/5 CROWN
6.22 g., 0.999 Gold 0.1998 oz. AGW, 22 mm. **Ruler:** Elizabeth II **Subject:** Year of the Cockerel **Obv:** Crowned bust right within circle **Rev:** Cockerel within circle

Date	Mintage	VF20	XF40	MS60	MS63	MS65
1993	Est. 10000	PF65 320				

KM# 351 1/5 CROWN
6.22 g., 0.999 Gold 0.1998 oz. AGW, 22 mm. **Ruler:** Elizabeth II **Obv:** Crowned bust right **Rev:** Maine Coon cat

Date	Mintage	VF20	XF40	MS60	MS63	MS65
1993	—	—	—	—	—	320
1993	—	PF65 325				

KM# 1515 1/5 CROWN
6.22 g., 0.999 Gold 0.1998 oz. AGW, 22 mm. **Ruler:** Elizabeth II **Obv:** Crowned bust right **Rev:** Iguana dinosaur

Date	Mintage	VF20	XF40	MS60	MS63	MS65
1993	Est. 5000	PF65 320				

KM# 1516 1/5 CROWN
6.22 g., 0.999 Gold 0.1998 oz. AGW, 22 mm. **Ruler:** Elizabeth II **Obv:** Crowned bust right **Rev:** Diplodocus Dinosaur

Date	Mintage	VF20	XF40	MS60	MS63	MS65
1993	Est. 5000	PF65 320				

KM# 365 1/5 CROWN
6.22 g., 0.999 Gold 0.1998 oz. AGW, 22 mm. **Ruler:** Elizabeth II **Subject:** World Cup Soccer - Type I **Obv:** Crowned bust right **Rev:** Player in foreground kicking ball

Date	Mintage	VF20	XF40	MS60	MS63	MS65
1994	Est. 5000	PF65 320				

KM# 367 1/5 CROWN
6.22 g., 0.999 Gold 0.1998 oz. AGW, 22 mm. **Ruler:** Elizabeth II **Subject:** World Cup Soccer - Type II **Obv:** Crowned bust right **Rev:** Three players

Date	Mintage	VF20	XF40	MS60	MS63	MS65
1994	Est. 5000	PF65 320				

KM# 369 1/5 CROWN
6.22 g., 0.999 Gold 0.1998 oz. AGW, 22 mm. **Ruler:** Elizabeth II **Subject:** World Cup Soccer - Type III **Obv:** Crowned bust right **Rev:** Soccer players

Date	Mintage	VF20	XF40	MS60	MS63	MS65
1994	—	PF65 320				

KM# 371 1/5 CROWN
6.22 g., 0.999 Gold 0.1998 oz. AGW, 22 mm. **Ruler:** Elizabeth II **Subject:** World Cup Soccer - Type IV **Obv:** Crowned bust right **Rev:** Soccer players

Date	Mintage	VF20	XF40	MS60	MS63	MS65
1994	Est. 5000	PF65 320				

KM# 373 1/5 CROWN
6.22 g., 0.999 Gold 0.1998 oz. AGW, 22 mm. **Ruler:** Elizabeth II **Subject:** World Cup Soccer - Type V **Obv:** Crowned bust right **Rev:** Goalie catching ball in hand

Date	Mintage	VF20	XF40	MS60	MS63	MS65
1994	—	PF65 325				

KM# 375 1/5 CROWN
6.22 g., 0.999 Gold 0.1998 oz. AGW, 22 mm. **Ruler:** Elizabeth II **Subject:** World Cup Soccer - Type VI **Obv:** Crowned bust right **Rev:** Soccer players

Date	Mintage	VF20	XF40	MS60	MS63	MS65
1994	—	PF65 320				

KM# 378 1/5 CROWN
6.22 g., 0.999 Gold 0.1998 oz. AGW, 22 mm. **Ruler:** Elizabeth II **Obv:** Crowned bust right **Rev:** Japanese Bobtail cat

Date	Mintage	VF20	XF40	MS60	MS63	MS65
1994	—	—	—	—	—	320
1994	—	PF65 325				

KM# 378a 1/5 CROWN
6.22 g., 0.999 Platinum 0.1998 oz. APW, 22 mm. **Ruler:** Elizabeth II **Obv:** Crowned bust right **Rev:** Japanese Bobtail cat **Note:** Prev. KM#475.

Date	Mintage	VF20	XF40	MS60	MS63	MS65
1994	—	—	—	—	—	285
1994	—	PF65 290				

KM# 383 1/5 CROWN
6.22 g., 0.999 Gold 0.1998 oz. AGW, 22 mm. **Ruler:** Elizabeth II **Series:** Preserve Planet Earth **Obv:** Crowned bust right **Rev:** Woolly mammoth

Date	Mintage	VF20	XF40	MS60	MS63	MS65
1994	Est. 5000	PF65 320				

KM# 388 1/5 CROWN
6.22 g., 0.999 Gold 0.1998 oz. AGW, 22 mm. **Ruler:** Elizabeth II **Series:** Preserve Planet Earth **Obv:** Crowned bust right **Rev:** Kangaroos

Date	Mintage	VF20	XF40	MS60	MS63	MS65
1994	5,000	PF65 320				

KM# 389 1/5 CROWN
6.22 g., 0.999 Gold 0.1998 oz. AGW, 22 mm. **Ruler:** Elizabeth II **Series:** Preserve Planet Earth **Obv:** Crowned bust right **Rev:** Seals

Date	Mintage	VF20	XF40	MS60	MS63	MS65
1994	5,000	PF65 320				

KM# 390 1/5 CROWN

6.22 g., 0.999 Gold 0.1998 oz. AGW, 22 mm. **Ruler:** Elizabeth II **Series:** Preserve Planet Earth **Obv:** Crowned bust right **Rev:** Deer

Date	Mintage	VF20	XF40	MS60	MS63	MS65
1994	5,000	PF65 320				

KM# 404 1/5 CROWN

6.22 g., 0.999 Gold 0.1998 oz. AGW, 22 mm. **Ruler:** Elizabeth II **Obv:** Crowned bust right **Rev:** Pekingese

Date	Mintage	VF20	XF40	MS60	MS63	MS65
1994	10,000	PF65 320				

KM# 409 1/5 CROWN

6.22 g., 0.999 Gold 0.1998 oz. AGW, 22 mm. **Ruler:** Elizabeth II **Series:** Man in Flight **Obv:** Crowned bust right **Rev:** Manned glider

Date	Mintage	VF20	XF40	MS60	MS63	MS65
1994	Est. 5000	PF65 320				

KM# 410 1/5 CROWN

6.22 g., 0.999 Gold 0.1998 oz. AGW, 22 mm. **Ruler:** Elizabeth II **Series:** Man in Flight **Obv:** Crowned bust right **Rev:** Dirigible, Ferdinand von Zeppelin

Date	Mintage	VF20	XF40	MS60	MS63	MS65
1994	Est. 5000	PF65 320				

KM# 411 1/5 CROWN

6.22 g., 0.999 Gold 0.1998 oz. AGW, 22 mm. **Ruler:** Elizabeth II **Series:** Man in Flight **Obv:** Crowned bust right **Rev:** Bust of Louis Bleriot behind plane flying across channel

Date	Mintage	VF20	XF40	MS60	MS63	MS65
1994	Est. 5000	PF65 320				

KM# 412 1/5 CROWN

6.22 g., 0.999 Gold 0.1998 oz. AGW, 22 mm. **Ruler:** Elizabeth II **Series:** Man in Flight **Obv:** Crowned bust right **Rev:** Plane in flight above ocean

Date	Mintage	VF20	XF40	MS60	MS63	MS65
1994	Est. 5000	PF65 320				

KM# 413 1/5 CROWN

6.22 g., 0.999 Gold 0.1998 oz. AGW, 22 mm. **Ruler:** Elizabeth II **Series:** Man in Flight **Subject:** First England to Australia Flight **Obv:** Crowned bust right **Rev:** Biplane flying

Date	Mintage	VF20	XF40	MS60	MS63	MS65
1994	Est. 5000	PF65 320				

KM# 414 1/5 CROWN

6.22 g., 0.999 Gold 0.1998 oz. AGW, 22 mm. **Ruler:** Elizabeth II **Series:** Man in Flight **Subject:** 60th Anniversary of Airmail **Obv:** Crowned bust right **Rev:** Plane flying left above inscription

Date	Mintage	VF20	XF40	MS60	MS63	MS65
1994	Est. 5000	PF65 320				

KM# 415 1/5 CROWN

6.22 g., 0.999 Gold 0.1998 oz. AGW, 22 mm. **Ruler:** Elizabeth II **Series:** Man in Flight **Subject:** 50th Anniversary of International Civil Aviation Organization **Obv:** Crowned bust right **Rev:** Trademark of ICAO

Date	Mintage	VF20	XF40	MS60	MS63	MS65
1994	Est. 5000	PF65 320				

KM# 416 1/5 CROWN

6.22 g., 0.999 Gold 0.1998 oz. AGW, 22 mm. **Ruler:** Elizabeth II **Series:** Man in Flight **Subject:** First Concorde Flight **Obv:** Crowned bust right **Rev:** Concorde waiting at airport

Date	Mintage	VF20	XF40	MS60	MS63	MS65
1994	Est. 5000	PF65 320				

KM# 1519 1/5 CROWN

6.22 g., 0.999 Gold 0.1998 oz. AGW, 22 mm. **Ruler:** Elizabeth II **Subject:** Normandy Anniversary **Obv:** Crowned bust right **Rev:** Troop ship

Date	Mintage	VF20	XF40	MS60	MS63	MS65
1994	—	PF65 320				

KM# 1520 1/5 CROWN

6.22 g., 0.999 Gold 0.1998 oz. AGW, 22 mm. **Ruler:** Elizabeth II **Subject:** Normandy Anniversary **Obv:** Crowned bust right **Rev:** American soldier beach landing

Date	Mintage	VF20	XF40	MS60	MS63	MS65
1994	—	PF65 320				

KM# 1521 1/5 CROWN

6.22 g., 0.999 Gold 0.1998 oz. AGW, 22 mm. **Ruler:** Elizabeth II **Subject:** Normandy Anniversary **Obv:** Crowned bust right **Rev:** Soldier dug in on the beach

Date	Mintage	VF20	XF40	MS60	MS63	MS65
1994	—	PF65 320				

KM# 1522 1/5 CROWN

6.22 g., 0.999 Gold 0.1998 oz. AGW, 22 mm. **Ruler:** Elizabeth II **Subject:** Normandy Anniversary **Obv:** Crowned bust right **Rev:** German machine gun position

Date	Mintage	VF20	XF40	MS60	MS63	MS65
1994	—	PF65 320				

KM# 1523 1/5 CROWN

6.22 g., 0.999 Gold 0.1998 oz. AGW, 22 mm. **Ruler:** Elizabeth II **Subject:** Normandy Anniversary **Obv:** Crowned bust right **Rev:** British beach landing

Date	Mintage	VF20	XF40	MS60	MS63	MS65
1994	—	PF65 320				

KM# 1524 1/5 CROWN

6.22 g., 0.999 Gold 0.1998 oz. AGW, 22 mm. **Ruler:** Elizabeth II **Subject:** Normandy Anniversary **Obv:** Crowned bust right **Rev:** General Eisenhower

Date	Mintage	VF20	XF40	MS60	MS63	MS65
1994	—	PF65 320				

KM# 1525 1/5 CROWN

6.22 g., 0.999 Gold 0.1998 oz. AGW, 22 mm. **Ruler:** Elizabeth II **Subject:** Normandy Anniversary **Obv:** Crowned bust right **Rev:** General Omar Bradley

Date	Mintage	VF20	XF40	MS60	MS63	MS65
1994	—	PF65 320				

KM# 1526 1/5 CROWN

6.22 g., 0.999 Gold 0.1998 oz. AGW, 22 mm. **Ruler:** Elizabeth II **Subject:** Normandy Anniversary **Obv:** Crowned bust right **Rev:** General Montgomery

Date	Mintage	VF20	XF40	MS60	MS63	MS65
1994	—	PF65 320				

KM# 426 1/5 CROWN

6.22 g., 0.999 Gold 0.1998 oz. AGW, 22 mm. **Ruler:** Elizabeth II **Series:** Man in Flight **Obv:** Crowned bust right **Rev:** Icarus' wings melting

Date	Mintage	VF20	XF40	MS60	MS63	MS65
1995	—	PF65 320				

KM# 427 1/5 CROWN

6.22 g., 0.999 Gold 0.1998 oz. AGW, 22 mm. **Ruler:** Elizabeth II **Series:** Man in Flight **Obv:** Crowned bust right **Rev:** Leonardo Da Vinci and aircraft design

Date	Mintage	VF20	XF40	MS60	MS63	MS65
1995	Est. 5000	PF65 320				

KM# 428 1/5 CROWN

6.22 g., 0.999 Gold 0.1998 oz. AGW, 22 mm. **Ruler:** Elizabeth II **Series:** Man in Flight **Obv:** Crowned bust right **Rev:** Balloon in flight

Date	Mintage	VF20	XF40	MS60	MS63	MS65
1995	—	PF65 320				

KM# 429 1/5 CROWN

6.22 g., 0.999 Gold 0.1998 oz. AGW, 22 mm. **Ruler:** Elizabeth II **Series:** Man in Flight **Obv:** Crowned bust right **Rev:** Airplane in flight

Date	Mintage	VF20	XF40	MS60	MS63	MS65
1995	—	PF65 320				

KM# 430 1/5 CROWN

6.22 g., 0.999 Gold 0.1998 oz. AGW, 22 mm. **Ruler:** Elizabeth II **Series:** Man in Flight **Subject:** 1st Flight Tokyo to Paris by Abe and Kawachi **Obv:** Crowned bust right **Rev:** Busts above airplane

Date	Mintage	VF20	XF40	MS60	MS63	MS65
1995	Est. 5000	PF65 320				

KM# 431 1/5 CROWN

6.22 g., 0.999 Gold 0.1998 oz. AGW, 22 mm. **Ruler:** Elizabeth II **Series:** Man in Flight **Subject:** FW109, First Diesel Powered Aircraft **Obv:** Crowned bust right **Rev:** Grounded airplane

Date	Mintage	VF20	XF40	MS60	MS63	MS65
1995	Est. 5000	PF65 320				

KM# 432 1/5 CROWN

6.22 g., 0.999 Gold 0.1998 oz. AGW, 22 mm. **Ruler:** Elizabeth II **Series:** Man in Flight **Subject:** ME262, First Jet Aircraft **Obv:** Crowned bust right **Rev:** Jet flying into clouds

Date	Mintage	VF20	XF40	MS60	MS63	MS65
1995	Est. 5000	PF65 320				

KM# 433 1/5 CROWN

6.22 g., 0.999 Gold 0.1998 oz. AGW, 22 mm. **Ruler:** Elizabeth II **Series:** Man in Flight **Subject:** 25th Anniversary of Boeing 747 **Obv:** Crowned bust right **Rev:** Jumbo jet in flight

Date	Mintage	VF20	XF40	MS60	MS63	MS65
1995	Est. 5000	PF65 320				

KM# 444 1/5 CROWN

6.22 g., 0.999 Gold 0.1998 oz. AGW, 22 mm. **Ruler:** Elizabeth II **Obv:** Crowned bust right **Rev:** Turkish cat

Date	Mintage	VF20	XF40	MS60	MS63	MS65
1995	—	—	—	—	—	320
1995	—	PF65 325				

KM# 444a 1/5 CROWN

6.22 g., 0.999 Platinum 0.1998 oz. APW, 22 mm. **Ruler:** Elizabeth II **Obv:** Crowned bust right **Rev:** Turkish cat **Note:** Prev. KM#480.

Date	Mintage	VF20	XF40	MS60	MS63	MS65
1995	—	—	—	—	—	285
1995	—	PF65 290				

KM# 451 1/5 CROWN

6.22 g., 0.999 Gold 0.1998 oz. AGW, 22 mm. **Ruler:** Elizabeth II **Subject:** Year of the Pig **Obv:** Crowned bust right **Rev:** Sow and piglets

Date	Mintage	VF20	XF40	MS60	MS63	MS65
1995	Est. 10000	PF65 320				

KM# 457 1/5 CROWN

6.22 g., 0.999 Gold 0.1998 oz. AGW, 22 mm. **Ruler:** Elizabeth II **Subject:** 95th Birthday of Queen Mother **Obv:** Crowned bust right **Rev:** Bust of Queen Mother

Date	Mintage	VF20	XF40	MS60	MS63	MS65
1995	Est. 5000	PF65 320				

KM# 459 1/5 CROWN

6.22 g., 0.999 Gold 0.1998 oz. AGW, 22 mm. **Ruler:** Elizabeth II **Series:** Preserve Planet Earth **Obv:** Crowned bust right **Rev:** Otter

Date	Mintage	VF20	XF40	MS60	MS63	MS65
1995	—	PF65 320				

KM# 460 1/5 CROWN

6.22 g., 0.999 Gold 0.1998 oz. AGW, 22 mm. **Ruler:** Elizabeth II **Series:** Preserve Planet Earth **Obv:** Crowned bust right **Rev:** Egret Birds

Date	Mintage	VF20	XF40	MS60	MS63	MS65
1995	Est. 5000	PF65 320				

KM# 483 1/5 CROWN

6.22 g., 0.999 Gold 0.1998 oz. AGW, 22 mm. **Ruler:** Elizabeth II **Series:** Aircraft of World War II **Obv:** Crowned bust right **Rev:** Hawker Hurricane

Date	Mintage	VF20	XF40	MS60	MS63	MS65
1995	Est. 5000	PF65 320				

KM# 484 1/5 CROWN

6.22 g., 0.999 Gold 0.1998 oz. AGW, 22 mm. **Ruler:** Elizabeth II **Series:** Aircraft of World War II **Obv:** Crowned bust right **Rev:** P-51 Mustang

Date	Mintage	VF20	XF40	MS60	MS63	MS65
1995	Est. 5000	PF65 320				

KM# 485 1/5 CROWN

6.22 g., 0.999 Gold 0.1998 oz. AGW, 22 mm. **Ruler:** Elizabeth II **Series:** Aircraft of World War II **Obv:** Crowned bust right **Rev:** Letrov S328

Date	Mintage	VF20	XF40	MS60	MS63	MS65
1995	Est. 5000	PF65 320				

KM# 486 1/5 CROWN

6.22 g., 0.999 Gold 0.1998 oz. AGW, 22 mm. **Ruler:** Elizabeth II **Series:** Aircraft of World War II **Obv:** Crowned bust right **Rev:** Messerschmitt ME262

Date	Mintage	VF20	XF40	MS60	MS63	MS65
1995	Est. 5000	PF65 320				

KM# 487 1/5 CROWN

6.22 g., 0.999 Gold 0.1998 oz. AGW, 22 mm. **Ruler:** Elizabeth II **Series:** Aircraft of World War II **Obv:** Crowned bust right **Rev:** JU87 Stuka

Date	Mintage	VF20	XF40	MS60	MS63	MS65
1995	Est. 5000	PF65 320				

KM# 488 1/5 CROWN

6.22 g., 0.999 Gold 0.1998 oz. AGW, 22 mm. **Ruler:** Elizabeth II **Series:** Aircraft of World War II **Obv:** Crowned bust right **Rev:** MIG 3

Date	Mintage	VF20	XF40	MS60	MS63	MS65
1995	Est. 5000	PF65 320				

KM# 489 1/5 CROWN

6.22 g., 0.999 Gold 0.1998 oz. AGW, 22 mm. **Ruler:** Elizabeth II **Series:** Aircraft of World War II **Obv:** Crowned bust right **Rev:** Nakajima Ki-49 Donryu

Date	Mintage	VF20	XF40	MS60	MS63	MS65
1995	Est. 5000	PF65 320				

KM# 490 1/5 CROWN

6.22 g., 0.999 Gold 0.1998 oz. AGW, 22 mm. **Ruler:** Elizabeth II **Series:** Aircraft of World War II **Obv:** Crowned bust right **Rev:** Vickers Wellington

Date	Mintage	VF20	XF40	MS60	MS63	MS65
1995	Est. 5000	PF65 320				

KM# 491 1/5 CROWN

6.22 g., 0.999 Gold 0.1998 oz. AGW, 22 mm. **Ruler:** Elizabeth II **Series:** Aircraft of World War II **Obv:** Crowned bust right **Rev:** Spitfire

Date	Mintage	VF20	XF40	MS60	MS63	MS65
1995	—	PF65 320				

KM# 492 1/5 CROWN

6.22 g., 0.999 Gold 0.1998 oz. AGW, 22 mm. **Ruler:** Elizabeth II **Series:** Aircraft of World War II **Obv:** Crowned bust right **Rev:** Fokker G. 1a

Date	Mintage	VF20	XF40	MS60	MS63	MS65
1995	Est. 5000	PF65 320				

KM# 493 1/5 CROWN

6.22 g., 0.999 Gold 0.1998 oz. AGW, 22 mm. **Ruler:** Elizabeth II **Series:** Aircraft of World War II **Obv:** Crowned bust right **Rev:** Commonwealth Boomerang CA-13

Date	Mintage	VF20	XF40	MS60	MS63	MS65
1995	—	PF65 320				

KM# 494 1/5 CROWN

6.22 g., 0.999 Gold 0.1998 oz. AGW, 22 mm. **Ruler:** Elizabeth II **Series:** Aircraft of World War II **Obv:** Crowned bust right **Rev:** Briston Blenheim 142M

Date	Mintage	VF20	XF40	MS60	MS63	MS65
1995	Est. 5000	PF65 320				

KM# 495 1/5 CROWN

6.22 g., 0.999 Gold 0.1998 oz. AGW, 22 mm. **Ruler:** Elizabeth II **Series:** Aircraft of World War II **Obv:** Crowned bust right **Rev:** Mitsubishi Zero

Date	Mintage	VF20	XF40	MS60	MS63	MS65
1995	Est. 5000	PF65 320				

KM# 496 1/5 CROWN
6.22 g., 0.999 Gold 0.1998 oz. AGW, 22 mm. **Ruler:** Elizabeth II **Series:** Aircraft of World War II **Obv:** Crowned bust right **Rev:** Heinkel HE111

Date	Mintage	VF20	XF40	MS60	MS63	MS65
1995	Est. 5000	PF65 320				

KM# 497 1/5 CROWN
6.22 g., 0.999 Gold 0.1998 oz. AGW, 22 mm. **Ruler:** Elizabeth II **Series:** Aircraft of World War II **Obv:** Crowned bust right **Rev:** Boulton Paul P82 Defiant

Date	Mintage	VF20	XF40	MS60	MS63	MS65
1995	Est. 5000	PF65 320				

KM# 498 1/5 CROWN
6.22 g., 0.999 Gold 0.1998 oz. AGW, 22 mm. **Ruler:** Elizabeth II **Series:** Aircraft of World War II **Obv:** Crowned bust right **Rev:** Boeing B289 - Enola Gay

Date	Mintage	VF20	XF40	MS60	MS63	MS65
1995	Est. 5000	PF65 320				

KM# 499 1/5 CROWN
6.22 g., 0.999 Gold 0.1998 oz. AGW, 22 mm. **Ruler:** Elizabeth II **Series:** Aircraft of World War II **Obv:** Crowned bust right **Rev:** Douglas DC-3 (C47)

Date	Mintage	VF20	XF40	MS60	MS63	MS65
1995	—	PF65 320				

KM# 500 1/5 CROWN
6.22 g., 0.999 Gold 0.1998 oz. AGW, 22 mm. **Ruler:** Elizabeth II **Series:** Aircraft of World War II **Obv:** Crowned bust right **Rev:** Fairey Swordfish

Date	Mintage	VF20	XF40	MS60	MS63	MS65
1995	Est. 5000	PF65 320				

KM# 501 1/5 CROWN
6.22 g., 0.999 Gold 0.1998 oz. AGW, 22 mm. **Ruler:** Elizabeth II **Series:** Aircraft of World War II **Obv:** Crowned bust right **Rev:** Curtiss P40

Date	Mintage	VF20	XF40	MS60	MS63	MS65
1995	Est. 5000	PF65 320				

KM# 523 1/5 CROWN
6.22 g., 0.999 Gold 0.1998 oz. AGW, 22 mm. **Ruler:** Elizabeth II **Subject:** America's Cup **Obv:** Crowned bust right **Rev:** Boats

Date	Mintage	VF20	XF40	MS60	MS63	MS65
1995	Est. 5000	PF65 320				

KM# 525 1/5 CROWN
6.22 g., 0.9999 Gold 0.200 oz. AGW, 22 mm. **Ruler:** Elizabeth II **Series:** Inventions of the Modern World **Obv:** Crowned bust right **Rev:** Cameo of Tsai Lun, paper and tree

Date	Mintage	VF20	XF40	MS60	MS63	MS65
1995	Est. 5000	PF65 320				

KM# 527 1/5 CROWN
6.22 g., 0.9999 Gold 0.200 oz. AGW, 22 mm. **Ruler:** Elizabeth II **Series:** Inventions of the Modern World **Obv:** Crowned bust right **Rev:** Cameo of Chang Heng and Seismograph

Date	Mintage	VF20	XF40	MS60	MS63	MS65
1995	Est. 5000	PF65 320				

KM# 529 1/5 CROWN
6.22 g., 0.9999 Gold 0.200 oz. AGW, 22 mm. **Ruler:** Elizabeth II **Series:** Inventions of the Modern World **Obv:** Crowned bust right **Rev:** Cameo of Tsu Chung Chih and compass cart

Date	Mintage	VF20	XF40	MS60	MS63	MS65
1995	—	PF65 320				

KM# 531 1/5 CROWN
6.22 g., 0.9999 Gold 0.200 oz. AGW, 22 mm. **Ruler:** Elizabeth II **Series:** Inventions of the Modern World **Obv:** Crowned bust right **Rev:** Cameo bust facing and movable type

Date	Mintage	VF20	XF40	MS60	MS63	MS65
1995	Est. 5000	PF65 320				

KM# 533 1/5 CROWN
6.22 g., 0.9999 Gold 0.200 oz. AGW, 22 mm. **Ruler:** Elizabeth II **Series:** Inventions of the Modern World **Obv:** Crowned bust right **Rev:** Cameo of Charles Babbage and first computer

Date	Mintage	VF20	XF40	MS60	MS63	MS65
1995	—	PF65 320				

KM# 535 1/5 CROWN
6.22 g., 0.9999 Gold 0.200 oz. AGW, 22 mm. **Ruler:** Elizabeth II **Series:** Inventions of the Modern World **Obv:** Crowned bust right **Rev:** Cameo of Fox Talbot, photography

Date	Mintage	VF20	XF40	MS60	MS63	MS65
1995	—	PF65 320				

KM# 537 1/5 CROWN
6.22 g., 0.9999 Gold 0.200 oz. AGW, 22 mm. **Ruler:** Elizabeth II **Series:** Inventions of the Modern World **Obv:** Crowned bust right **Rev:** Cameo of Rudolf Diesel, diesel engine

Date	Mintage	VF20	XF40	MS60	MS63	MS65
1995	—	PF65 320				

KM# 539 1/5 CROWN
6.22 g., 0.9999 Gold 0.200 oz. AGW, 22 mm. **Ruler:** Elizabeth II **Series:** Inventions of the Modern World **Obv:** Crowned bust right **Rev:** Cameo of Wilhelm K. Roentgen and x-ray of hand

Date	Mintage	VF20	XF40	MS60	MS63	MS65
1995	Est. 5000	PF65 320				

KM# 541 1/5 CROWN
6.22 g., 0.9999 Gold 0.200 oz. AGW, 22 mm. **Ruler:** Elizabeth II **Series:** Inventions of the Modern World **Obv:** Crowned bust right **Rev:** Cameo bust facing and radio equipment

Date	Mintage	VF20	XF40	MS60	MS63	MS65
1995	Est. 5000	PF65 320				

KM# 543 1/5 CROWN
6.22 g., 0.9999 Gold 0.200 oz. AGW, 22 mm. **Ruler:** Elizabeth II **Series:** Inventions of the Modern World **Obv:** Crowned bust right **Rev:** Cameo of John L. Baird and television equipment

Date	Mintage	VF20	XF40	MS60	MS63	MS65
1995	Est. 5000	PF65 320				

KM# 545 1/5 CROWN
6.22 g., 0.9999 Gold 0.200 oz. AGW, 22 mm. **Ruler:** Elizabeth II **Series:** Inventions of the Modern World **Obv:** Crowned bust right **Rev:** Cameo of Alexander Fleming and microscope

Date	Mintage	VF20	XF40	MS60	MS63	MS65
1995	—	PF65 320				

KM# 547 1/5 CROWN
6.22 g., 0.9999 Gold 0.200 oz. AGW, 22 mm. **Ruler:** Elizabeth II **Series:** Inventions of the Modern World **Obv:** Crowned bust right **Rev:** Cameo of Lazlo Biro and ballpoint pen

Date	Mintage	VF20	XF40	MS60	MS63	MS65
1995	Est. 5000	PF65 320				

KM# 549 1/5 CROWN
6.22 g., 0.9999 Gold 0.200 oz. AGW, 22 mm. **Ruler:** Elizabeth II **Series:** Inventions of the Modern World **Obv:** Crowned bust right **Rev:** Cameo of Wernher von Braun and rocket

Date	Mintage	VF20	XF40	MS60	MS63	MS65
1996	Est. 5000	PF65 320				

KM# 550 1/5 CROWN
6.22 g., 0.9999 Gold 0.200 oz. AGW, 22 mm. **Ruler:** Elizabeth II **Series:** Inventions of the Modern World **Obv:** Crowned bust right **Rev:** Cameo of Thomas Edison, electricity

Date	Mintage	VF20	XF40	MS60	MS63	MS65
1996	Est. 5000	PF65 320				

KM# 551 1/5 CROWN
6.22 g., 0.9999 Gold 0.200 oz. AGW, 22 mm. **Ruler:** Elizabeth II **Series:** Inventions of the Modern World **Obv:** Crowned bust right **Rev:** Compass

Date	Mintage	VF20	XF40	MS60	MS63	MS65
1996	Est. 5000	PF65 320				

KM# 552 1/5 CROWN
6.22 g., 0.9999 Gold 0.200 oz. AGW, 22 mm. **Ruler:** Elizabeth II **Series:** Inventions of the Modern World **Obv:** Crowned bust right **Rev:** Cameo of Michael Faraday, electricity

Date	Mintage	VF20	XF40	MS60	MS63	MS65
1996	Est. 5000	PF65 320				

KM# 553 1/5 CROWN
6.22 g., 0.9999 Gold 0.200 oz. AGW, 22 mm. **Ruler:** Elizabeth II **Series:** Inventions of the Modern World **Obv:** Crowned bust right **Rev:** Cameo of Emile Berliner and gramophone

Date	Mintage	VF20	XF40	MS60	MS63	MS65
1996	Est. 5000	PF65 320				

KM# 554 1/5 CROWN
6.22 g., 0.9999 Gold 0.200 oz. AGW, 22 mm. **Ruler:** Elizabeth II **Series:** Inventions of the Modern World **Obv:** Crowned bust right **Rev:** Cameo of Alexander Graham Bell, voice transmission

Date	Mintage	VF20	XF40	MS60	MS63	MS65
1996	Est. 5000	PF65 320				

KM# 561 1/5 CROWN
6.22 g., 0.9999 Gold 0.200 oz. AGW, 22 mm. **Ruler:** Elizabeth II **Series:** 1996 Summer Olympics - Atlanta **Obv:** Crowned bust right **Rev:** Hurdler

Date	Mintage	VF20	XF40	MS60	MS63	MS65
1996	Est. 5000	PF65 320				

KM# 562 1/5 CROWN
6.22 g., 0.9999 Gold 0.200 oz. AGW, 22 mm. **Ruler:** Elizabeth II **Series:** 1996 Summer Olympics - Atlanta **Obv:** Crowned bust right **Rev:** Runners

Date	Mintage	VF20	XF40	MS60	MS63	MS65
1996	Est. 5000	PF65 320				

KM# 563 1/5 CROWN
6.22 g., 0.9999 Gold 0.200 oz. AGW, 22 mm. **Ruler:** Elizabeth II **Series:** 1996 Summer Olympics - Atlanta **Obv:** Crowned bust right **Rev:** Sailing

Date	Mintage	VF20	XF40	MS60	MS63	MS65
1996	Est. 5000	PF65 320				

KM# 564 1/5 CROWN
6.22 g., 0.9999 Gold 0.200 oz. AGW, 22 mm. **Ruler:** Elizabeth II **Series:** 1996 Summer Olympics - Atlanta **Obv:** Crowned bust right **Rev:** Swimmers

Date	Mintage	VF20	XF40	MS60	MS63	MS65
1996	Est. 5000	PF65 320				

KM# 565 1/5 CROWN
6.22 g., 0.9999 Gold 0.200 oz. AGW, 22 mm. **Ruler:** Elizabeth II **Series:** 1996 Summer Olympics - Atlanta **Obv:** Crowned bust right **Rev:** Equestrian

Date	Mintage	VF20	XF40	MS60	MS63	MS65
1996	Est. 5000	PF65 320				

KM# 566 1/5 CROWN
6.22 g., 0.9999 Gold 0.200 oz. AGW, 22 mm. **Ruler:** Elizabeth II **Series:** 1996 Summer Olympics - Atlanta **Obv:** Crowned bust right **Rev:** Cyclists and Nike

Date	Mintage	VF20	XF40	MS60	MS63	MS65
1996	Est. 5000	PF65 320				

KM# 573 1/5 CROWN
6.22 g., 0.999 Gold 0.1998 oz. AGW, 22 mm. **Ruler:** Elizabeth II **Series:** Bicentennial of Robert Burns **Obv:** Crowned bust right **Rev:** Seated

Date	Mintage	VF20	XF40	MS60	MS63	MS65
1996	Est. 5000	PF65 320				

KM# 574 1/5 CROWN
6.22 g., 0.999 Gold 0.1998 oz. AGW, 22 mm. **Ruler:** Elizabeth II **Series:** Bicentennial of Robert Burns **Obv:** Crowned bust right **Rev:** Pirate ships

Date	Mintage	VF20	XF40	MS60	MS63	MS65
1996	Est. 5000	PF65 320				

KM# 575 1/5 CROWN
6.22 g., 0.999 Gold 0.1998 oz. AGW, 22 mm. **Ruler:** Elizabeth II **Series:** Bicentennial of Robert Burns **Obv:** Crowned bust right **Rev:** Auld Lang Syne

Date	Mintage	VF20	XF40	MS60	MS63	MS65
1996	Est. 5000	PF65 320				

KM# 576 1/5 CROWN
6.22 g., 0.999 Gold 0.1998 oz. AGW, 22 mm. **Ruler:** Elizabeth II **Series:** Bicentennial of Robert Burns **Obv:** Crowned bust right **Rev:** Edinburgh Castle

Date	Mintage	VF20	XF40	MS60	MS63	MS65
1996	Est. 5000	PF65 320				

KM# 581 1/5 CROWN
6.22 g., 0.999 Gold 0.1998 oz. AGW, 22 mm. **Ruler:** Elizabeth II **Subject:** Queen's Birthday **Obv:** Crowned bust right **Rev:** Flowers

Date	Mintage	VF20	XF40	MS60	MS63	MS65
1996	Est. 5000	PF65 320				

KM# 583 1/5 CROWN
6.22 g., 0.999 Gold 0.1998 oz. AGW, 22 mm. **Ruler:** Elizabeth II **Subject:** Preserve Planet Earth **Obv:** Crowned bust right **Rev:** Whale

Date	Mintage	VF20	XF40	MS60	MS63	MS65
1996	Est. 5000	PF65 320				

KM# 584 1/5 CROWN
6.22 g., 0.999 Gold 0.1998 oz. AGW, 22 mm. **Ruler:** Elizabeth II **Subject:** Preserve Planet Earth **Obv:** Crowned bust right **Rev:** Razorbill feeding chick

Date	Mintage	VF20	XF40	MS60	MS63	MS65
1996	Est. 5000	PF65 320				

KM# 605 1/5 CROWN
6.22 g., 0.999 Gold 0.1998 oz. AGW, 22 mm. **Ruler:** Elizabeth II **Series:** Flower Fairies **Obv:** Crowned bust right **Rev:** Orchis

Date	Mintage	VF20	XF40	MS60	MS63	MS65
1996	Est. 5000	PF65 320				

KM# 606 1/5 CROWN
6.22 g., 0.999 Gold 0.1998 oz. AGW, 22 mm. **Ruler:** Elizabeth II **Series:** Flower Fairies **Obv:** Crowned bust right **Rev:** Rose

Date	Mintage	VF20	XF40	MS60	MS63	MS65
1996	Est. 5000	PF65 320				

KM# 607 1/5 CROWN
6.22 g., 0.999 Gold 0.1998 oz. AGW, 22 mm. **Ruler:** Elizabeth II **Series:** Flower Fairies **Obv:** Crowned bust right **Rev:** Fuchsia

Date	Mintage	VF20	XF40	MS60	MS63	MS65
1996	Est. 5000	PF65 320				

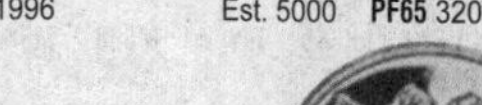

KM# 608 1/5 CROWN
6.22 g., 0.999 Gold 0.1998 oz. AGW, 22 mm. **Ruler:** Elizabeth II **Series:** Flower Fairies **Obv:** Crowned bust right **Rev:** Pinks

Date	Mintage	VF20	XF40	MS60	MS63	MS65
1996	—	PF65 320				

KM# 617 1/5 CROWN
6.22 g., 0.999 Gold 0.1998 oz. AGW, 22 mm. **Ruler:** Elizabeth II **Obv:** Crowned bust right **Rev:** Burmese cat

Date	Mintage	VF20	XF40	MS60	MS63	MS65
1996	—	—	—	—	—	320
1996	—	PF65 325				

KM# 617a 1/5 CROWN
6.22 g., 0.999 Platinum 0.1998 oz. APW, 22 mm. **Ruler:** Elizabeth II **Obv:** Crowned bust right **Rev:** Burmese cat **Note:** Prev. KM#618.

Date	Mintage	VF20	XF40	MS60	MS63	MS65
1996	—	—	—	—	—	285
1996	—	PF65 290				

KM# 625 1/5 CROWN
6.22 g., 0.999 Gold 0.1998 oz. AGW, 22 mm. **Ruler:** Elizabeth II **Obv:** Crowned bust right **Rev:** Portrait of Ferdinand Magellan, map and ship

Date	Mintage	VF20	XF40	MS60	MS63	MS65
1996	Est. 5000	PF65 320				

KM# 628 1/5 CROWN
6.22 g., 0.999 Gold 0.1998 oz. AGW, 22 mm. **Ruler:** Elizabeth II **Obv:** Crowned bust right **Rev:** Portrait of Sir Francis Drake, map and ship

Date	Mintage	VF20	XF40	MS60	MS63	MS65
1996	Est. 5000	PF65 320				

KM# 631 1/5 CROWN
6.22 g., 0.999 Gold 0.1998 oz. AGW, 22 mm. **Ruler:** Elizabeth II **Series:** European Football Championship **Obv:** Crowned bust right **Rev:** Romania vs Bulgaria

Date	Mintage	VF20	XF40	MS60	MS63	MS65
1996	Est. 5000	PF65 320				

KM# 634 1/5 CROWN
6.22 g., 0.999 Gold 0.1998 oz. AGW, 22 mm. **Ruler:** Elizabeth II **Series:** European Football Championship **Obv:** Crowned bust right **Rev:** Czech Republic vs Italy

Date	Mintage	VF20	XF40	MS60	MS63	MS65
1996	Est. 5000	PF65 320				

KM# 637 1/5 CROWN
6.22 g., 0.999 Gold 0.1998 oz. AGW, 22 mm. **Ruler:** Elizabeth II **Series:** European Football Championship **Obv:** Crowned bust right **Rev:** Germany vs Russia

Date	Mintage	VF20	XF40	MS60	MS63	MS65
1996	Est. 5000	PF65 320				

KM# 640 1/5 CROWN
6.22 g., 0.999 Gold 0.1998 oz. AGW, 22 mm. **Ruler:** Elizabeth II **Series:** European Football Championship **Obv:** Crowned bust right **Rev:** Spain vs France

Date	Mintage	VF20	XF40	MS60	MS63	MS65
1996	—	PF65 320				

KM# 643 1/5 CROWN
6.22 g., 0.999 Gold 0.1998 oz. AGW, 22 mm. **Ruler:** Elizabeth II **Series:** European Football Championship **Obv:** Crowned bust right **Rev:** Turkey vs Croatia

Date	Mintage	VF20	XF40	MS60	MS63	MS65
1996	Est. 5000	PF65 320				

KM# 646 1/5 CROWN
6.22 g., 0.999 Gold 0.1998 oz. AGW, 22 mm. **Ruler:** Elizabeth II **Series:** European Football Championship **Obv:** Crowned bust right **Rev:** Denmark vs Portugal

Date	Mintage	VF20	XF40	MS60	MS63	MS65
1996	Est. 5000	PF65 320				

KM# 649 1/5 CROWN
6.22 g., 0.999 Gold 0.1998 oz. AGW, 22 mm. **Ruler:** Elizabeth II **Series:** European Football Championship **Obv:** Crowned bust right **Rev:** Scotland vs England

Date	Mintage	VF20	XF40	MS60	MS63	MS65
1996	Est. 5000	PF65 320				

KM# 652 1/5 CROWN
6.22 g., 0.999 Gold 0.1998 oz. AGW, 22 mm. **Ruler:** Elizabeth II **Series:** European Football Championship **Obv:** Crowned bust right **Rev:** Holland vs Switzerland

Date	Mintage	VF20	XF40	MS60	MS63	MS65
1996	Est. 5000	PF65 320				

KM# 656 1/5 CROWN
6.22 g., 0.999 Gold 0.1998 oz. AGW, 22 mm. **Ruler:** Elizabeth II **Series:** European Football Championship **Obv:** Crowned bust right **Rev:** Winner, Germany

Date	Mintage	VF20	XF40	MS60	MS63	MS65
1996	Est. 5000	PF65 320				

KM# 659 1/5 CROWN
6.22 g., 0.999 Gold 0.1998 oz. AGW, 22 mm. **Ruler:** Elizabeth II **Series:** Legend of King Arthur **Obv:** Crowned bust right **Rev:** King Arthur with sword, orb

Date	Mintage	VF20	XF40	MS60	MS63	MS65
1996	Est. 5000	PF65 320				

KM# 659a 1/5 CROWN
6.22 g., 0.999 Platinum 0.1998 oz. APW, 22 mm. **Ruler:** Elizabeth II **Series:** Legend of King Arthur **Obv:** Crowned bust right **Rev:** King Arthur with sword, orb **Note:** Prev. KM#664.

Date	Mintage	VF20	XF40	MS60	MS63	MS65
1996	Est. 5000	PF65 290				

KM# 660 1/5 CROWN
6.22 g., 0.999 Gold 0.1998 oz. AGW, 22 mm. **Ruler:** Elizabeth II **Series:** Legend of King Arthur **Obv:** Crowned bust right **Rev:** 3/4-length figure of Queen Guinevere coming through archway

Date	Mintage	VF20	XF40	MS60	MS63	MS65
1996	Est. 5000	PF65 320				

KM# 660a 1/5 CROWN
6.22 g., 0.999 Platinum 0.1998 oz. APW, 22 mm. **Ruler:** Elizabeth II **Series:** Legend of King Arthur **Obv:** Crowned bust right **Rev:** Queen Guinevere **Note:** Prev. KM#665.

Date	Mintage	VF20	XF40	MS60	MS63	MS65
1996	—	PF65 290				

KM# 661 1/5 CROWN
6.22 g., 0.999 Gold 0.1998 oz. AGW, 22 mm. **Ruler:** Elizabeth II **Series:** Legend of King Arthur **Obv:** Crowned bust right **Rev:** Sir Lancelot

Date	Mintage	VF20	XF40	MS60	MS63	MS65
1996	—	PF65 320				

KM# 661a 1/5 CROWN
6.22 g., 0.999 Platinum 0.1998 oz. APW, 22 mm. **Ruler:** Elizabeth II **Series:** Legend of King Arthur **Obv:** Crowned bust right **Rev:** Sir Lancelot **Note:** Prev. KM#666.

Date	Mintage	VF20	XF40	MS60	MS63	MS65
1996	—	PF65 290				

KM# 662 1/5 CROWN
6.22 g., 0.999 Gold 0.1998 oz. AGW, 22 mm. **Ruler:** Elizabeth II **Series:** Legend of King Arthur **Obv:** Crowned bust right **Rev:** Merlin

Date	Mintage	VF20	XF40	MS60	MS63	MS65
1996	—	PF65 320				

KM# 662a 1/5 CROWN
6.22 g., 0.999 Platinum 0.1998 oz. APW, 22 mm. **Ruler:** Elizabeth II **Series:** Legend of King Arthur **Obv:** Crowned bust right **Rev:** Merlin **Note:** Prev. KM#667.

Date	Mintage	VF20	XF40	MS60	MS63	MS65
1996	—	PF65 290				

KM# 663 1/5 CROWN
6.22 g., 0.999 Gold 0.1998 oz. AGW, 22 mm. **Ruler:** Elizabeth II **Series:** Legend of King Arthur **Obv:** Crowned bust right **Rev:** Camelot Castle within circle

Date	Mintage	VF20	XF40	MS60	MS63	MS65
1996	Est. 5000	PF65 320				

KM# 663a 1/5 CROWN
6.22 g., 0.999 Platinum 0.1998 oz. APW, 22 mm. **Ruler:** Elizabeth II **Series:** Legend of King Arthur **Obv:** Crowned bust right **Rev:** Camelot Castle **Note:** Prev. KM#668.

Date	Mintage	VF20	XF40	MS60	MS63	MS65
1996	Est. 5000	PF65 290				

KM# 730 1/5 CROWN
6.22 g., 0.999 Gold 0.1998 oz. AGW, 22 mm. **Ruler:** Elizabeth II **Subject:** Year of the Rat **Obv:** Crowned bust right **Rev:** Rat

Date	Mintage	VF20	XF40	MS60	MS63	MS65
1996 Proof	—	—	—	—	—	—

Note: Entire series purchased by one buyer. Mintage, disposition and market value unknown

KM# 723 1/5 CROWN
6.22 g., 0.999 Gold 0.1998 oz. AGW, 22 mm. **Ruler:** Elizabeth II **Subject:** Year of the Ox **Obv:** Crowned bust right **Rev:** Ox laying down

Date	Mintage	VF20	XF40	MS60	MS63	MS65
1997	Est. 12000	PF65 320				

KM# 751 1/5 CROWN
6.22 g., 0.999 Gold 0.1998 oz. AGW, 22 mm. **Ruler:** Elizabeth II **Series:** Flower Fairies **Obv:** Crowned bust right **Rev:** Candytuft

Date	Mintage	VF20	XF40	MS60	MS63	MS65
1997	Est. 5000	PF65 320				

KM# 751a 1/5 CROWN
6.25 g., 0.995 Platinum 0.200 oz. APW, 22 mm. **Ruler:** Elizabeth II **Series:** Flower Fairies **Obv:** Crowned bust right **Rev:** Candytuft

Date	Mintage	VF20	XF40	MS60	MS63	MS65
1997	—	PF65 290				

KM# 752 1/5 CROWN
6.22 g., 0.9999 Gold 0.200 oz. AGW, 22 mm. **Ruler:** Elizabeth II **Series:** Flower Fairies **Obv:** Crowned bust right **Rev:** Snowdrop

Date	Mintage	VF20	XF40	MS60	MS63	MS65
1997	Est. 5000	PF65 320				

KM# 752a 1/5 CROWN
6.25 g., 0.995 Platinum 0.200 oz. APW, 22 mm. **Ruler:** Elizabeth II **Series:** Flower Fairies **Obv:** Crowned bust right **Rev:** Snowdrop

Date	Mintage	VF20	XF40	MS60	MS63	MS65
1997	—	PF65 290				

KM# 753 1/5 CROWN
6.22 g., 0.9999 Gold 0.200 oz. AGW, 22 mm. **Ruler:** Elizabeth II **Series:** Flower Fairies **Obv:** Crowned bust right **Rev:** Tulip

Date	Mintage	VF20	XF40	MS60	MS63	MS65
1997	—	PF65 320				

KM# 753a 1/5 CROWN
6.25 g., 0.995 Platinum 0.200 oz. APW, 22 mm. **Ruler:** Elizabeth II **Series:** Flower Fairies **Obv:** Crowned bust right **Rev:** Tulip

Date	Mintage	VF20	XF40	MS60	MS63	MS65
1997	—	PF65 290				

KM# 754 1/5 CROWN
6.22 g., 0.9999 Gold 0.200 oz. AGW, 22 mm. **Ruler:** Elizabeth II **Series:** Flower Fairies **Obv:** Crowned bust right **Rev:** Jasmine

Date	Mintage	VF20	XF40	MS60	MS63	MS65
1997	Est. 5000	PF65 320				

KM# 754a 1/5 CROWN
6.25 g., 0.995 Platinum 0.200 oz. APW, 22 mm. **Ruler:** Elizabeth II **Series:** Flower Fairies **Obv:** Crowned bust right **Rev:** Jasmine

Date	Mintage	VF20	XF40	MS60	MS63	MS65
1997	Est. 2500	PF65 290				

KM# 763 1/5 CROWN
6.22 g., 0.9999 Gold 0.200 oz. AGW, 22 mm. **Ruler:** Elizabeth II **Subject:** Leif Eriksson 999-1001 **Obv:** Crowned bust right **Rev:** Portrait and Viking ship with map sail

Date	Mintage	VF20	XF40	MS60	MS63	MS65
1997	Est. 5000	PF65 320				

KM# 766 1/5 CROWN
6.22 g., 0.9999 Gold 0.200 oz. AGW, 22 mm. **Ruler:** Elizabeth II **Subject:** Fridtjof Nansen 1861-1930 **Obv:** Crowned bust right **Rev:** Portrait, map and ship "The Fram"

Date	Mintage	VF20	XF40	MS60	MS63	MS65
1997	Est. 5000	PF65 320				

KM# 772 1/5 CROWN
6.22 g., 0.9999 Gold 0.200 oz. AGW, 22 mm. **Ruler:** Elizabeth II **Obv:** Crowned bust right **Rev:** Long-haired Smoke cat

Date	Mintage	VF20	XF40	MS60	MS63	MS65
1997	—	—	—	—	—	320
1997	—	PF65 325				

KM# 772a 1/5 CROWN
6.22 g., 0.9999 Platinum 0.200 oz. APW, 22 mm. **Ruler:** Elizabeth II **Obv:** Crowned bust right **Rev:** Long-haired Smoke cat

Date	Mintage	VF20	XF40	MS60	MS63	MS65
1997	—	PF65 290				

KM# 776 1/5 CROWN

6.22 g., 0.9999 Gold 0.200 oz. AGW, 22 mm. **Ruler:** Elizabeth II **Subject:** History of the Cat **Obv:** Crowned bust right **Rev:** Cat stalking a spider

Date	Mintage	VF20	XF40	MS60	MS63	MS65
1997	Est. 7500	**PF65** 320				

KM# 781 1/5 CROWN

6.22 g., 0.9999 Gold 0.200 oz. AGW, 22 mm. **Ruler:** Elizabeth II **Subject:** 90th Anniversary of the TT - 1907 **Obv:** Crowned bust right **Rev:** 1907 winner Charlie Collier

Date	Mintage	VF20	XF40	MS60	MS63	MS65
1997	Est. 5000	**PF65** 320				

KM# 783 1/5 CROWN

6.22 g., 0.9999 Gold 0.200 oz. AGW, 22 mm. **Ruler:** Elizabeth II **Subject:** 90th Anniversary of the TT - 1907 **Obv:** Crowned bust right **Rev:** 1937 winner Omobono Tenni

Date	Mintage	VF20	XF40	MS60	MS63	MS65
1997	—	**PF65** 320				

KM# 785 1/5 CROWN

6.22 g., 0.9999 Gold 0.200 oz. AGW, 22 mm. **Ruler:** Elizabeth II **Subject:** 90th Anniversary of the TT - 1907 **Obv:** Crowned bust right **Rev:** 1957 winner Bob McIntyre

Date	Mintage	VF20	XF40	MS60	MS63	MS65
1997	Est. 5000	**PF65** 320				

KM# 787 1/5 CROWN

6.22 g., 0.9999 Gold 0.200 oz. AGW, 22 mm. **Ruler:** Elizabeth II **Subject:** 90th Anniversary of the TT - 1907 **Obv:** Crowned bust right **Rev:** 1967 winner Mike Hailwood

Date	Mintage	VF20	XF40	MS60	MS63	MS65
1997	Est. 5000	**PF65** 320				

KM# 792 1/5 CROWN

6.22 g., 0.9999 Gold 0.200 oz. AGW, 22 mm. **Ruler:** Elizabeth II **Subject:** Golden Wedding Anniversary of Queen Elizabeth II and Prince Philip **Obv:** Crowned bust right **Rev:** Wedding portrait

Date	Mintage	VF20	XF40	MS60	MS63	MS65
1997	Est. 3500	**PF65** 320				

KM# 798 1/5 CROWN

6.22 g., 0.9999 Gold 0.200 oz. AGW, 22 mm. **Ruler:** Elizabeth II **Series:** Year 2000 **Subject:** Birth of Christ **Obv:** Crowned bust right **Rev:** Madonna and child with angels

Date	Mintage	VF20	XF40	MS60	MS63	MS65
1997	Est. 2000	**PF65** 320				

KM# 800 1/5 CROWN

6.22 g., 0.9999 Gold 0.200 oz. AGW, 22 mm. **Ruler:** Elizabeth II **Series:** Year 2000 **Subject:** Fall of the Roman Empire 476 **Obv:** Crowned bust right **Rev:** Barbarian defeating Roman soldier

Date	Mintage	VF20	XF40	MS60	MS63	MS65
1997	—	**PF65** 320				

KM# 802 1/5 CROWN

6.22 g., 0.9999 Gold 0.200 oz. AGW, 22 mm. **Ruler:** Elizabeth II **Series:** Year 2000 **Subject:** Flight of Mohammed 622 **Obv:** Crowned bust right **Rev:** Arabs and camels at an oasis

Date	Mintage	VF20	XF40	MS60	MS63	MS65
1997	—	**PF65** 320				

KM# 804 1/5 CROWN

6.22 g., 0.9999 Gold 0.200 oz. AGW, 22 mm. **Ruler:** Elizabeth II **Series:** Year 2000 **Subject:** Norman Conquest 1066 **Obv:** Crowned bust right **Rev:** William the Conqueror rallying his troops

Date	Mintage	VF20	XF40	MS60	MS63	MS65
1997	Est. 2000	**PF65** 320				

KM# 807 1/5 CROWN

6.22 g., 0.9999 Gold 0.200 oz. AGW, 22 mm. **Ruler:** Elizabeth II **Series:** World Cup Soccer **Obv:** Crowned bust right **Rev:** Standing figures shaking hands within circle

Date	Mintage	VF20	XF40	MS60	MS63	MS65
1998	Est. 5000	**PF65** 320				

KM# 814 1/5 CROWN

6.22 g., 0.9999 Gold 0.200 oz. AGW, 22 mm. **Ruler:** Elizabeth II **Series:** Year of the Tiger **Obv:** Crowned bust right **Rev:** Tiger

Date	Mintage	VF20	XF40	MS60	MS63	MS65
1998	Est. 12000	**PF65** 320				

KM# 824 1/5 CROWN

6.22 g., 0.9999 Gold 0.200 oz. AGW, 22 mm. **Ruler:** Elizabeth II **Obv:** Crowned bust right **Rev:** Portrait of Marco Polo, caravan and palace

Date	Mintage	VF20	XF40	MS60	MS63	MS65
1998	Est. 5000	**PF65** 320				

KM# 826 1/5 CROWN

6.22 g., 0.9999 Gold 0.200 oz. AGW, 22 mm. **Ruler:** Elizabeth II **Obv:** Crowned bust right **Rev:** Bust with headdress facing, ship and African map

Date	Mintage	VF20	XF40	MS60	MS63	MS65
1998	Est. 5000	**PF65** 320				

KM# 836 1/5 CROWN

6.22 g., 0.9999 Gold 0.200 oz. AGW, 22 mm. **Ruler:** Elizabeth II **Series:** Flower Fairies **Obv:** Crowned bust right **Rev:** Fairy standing, lavender

Date	Mintage	VF20	XF40	MS60	MS63	MS65
1998	Est. 5000	**PF65** 320				

KM# 836a 1/5 CROWN

6.22 g., 0.9999 Platinum 0.200 oz. APW, 22 mm. **Ruler:** Elizabeth II **Series:** Flower Fairies **Obv:** Crowned bust right **Rev:** Fairy standing, lavender

Date	Mintage	VF20	XF40	MS60	MS63	MS65
1998	Est. 2500	**PF65** 290				

KM# 837 1/5 CROWN

6.22 g., 0.9999 Gold 0.200 oz. AGW, 22 mm. **Ruler:** Elizabeth II **Series:** Flower Fairies **Obv:** Crowned bust right **Rev:** Two fairies, sweet pea

Date	Mintage	VF20	XF40	MS60	MS63	MS65
1998	—	**PF65** 320				

KM# 837a 1/5 CROWN

6.22 g., 0.9999 Platinum 0.200 oz. APW, 22 mm. **Ruler:** Elizabeth II **Series:** Flower Fairies **Obv:** Crowned bust right **Rev:** Two fairies, sweet pea

Date	Mintage	VF20	XF40	MS60	MS63	MS65
1998	Est. 2500	**PF65** 290				

KM# 838 1/5 CROWN

6.22 g., 0.9999 Gold 0.200 oz. AGW, 22 mm. **Ruler:** Elizabeth II **Series:** Flower Fairies **Obv:** Crowned bust right **Rev:** Fairy looking into flower, White Bindweed

Date	Mintage	VF20	XF40	MS60	MS63	MS65
1998	—	**PF65** 320				

KM# 838a 1/5 CROWN

6.22 g., 0.9999 Platinum 0.200 oz. APW, 22 mm. **Ruler:** Elizabeth II **Series:** Flower Fairies **Obv:** Crowned bust right **Rev:** Fairy looking into flower, White Bindweed

Date	Mintage	VF20	XF40	MS60	MS63	MS65
1998	Est. 2500	**PF65** 290				

KM# 839 1/5 CROWN

6.22 g., 0.9999 Gold 0.200 oz. AGW, 22 mm. **Ruler:** Elizabeth II **Series:** Flower Fairies **Obv:** Crowned bust right **Rev:** Fairy standing, daffodil

Date	Mintage	VF20	XF40	MS60	MS63	MS65
1998	Est. 5000	**PF65** 320				

KM# 839a 1/5 CROWN

6.22 g., 0.9999 Platinum 0.200 oz. APW, 22 mm. **Ruler:** Elizabeth II **Series:** Flower Fairies **Obv:** Crowned bust right **Rev:** Fairy standing, daffodil

Date	Mintage	VF20	XF40	MS60	MS63	MS65
1998	Est. 2500	**PF65** 290				

KM# 845 1/5 CROWN

6.22 g., 0.9999 Gold 0.200 oz. AGW, 22 mm. **Ruler:** Elizabeth II **Series:** Winter Olympics - Nagano **Obv:** Crowned bust right **Rev:** Ski jumper

Date	Mintage	VF20	XF40	MS60	MS63	MS65
1998	Est. 5000	**PF65** 320				

KM# 846 1/5 CROWN

6.22 g., 0.9999 Gold 0.200 oz. AGW, 22 mm. **Ruler:** Elizabeth II **Series:** Winter Olympics - Nagano **Obv:** Crowned bust right **Rev:** Slalom skier

Date	Mintage	VF20	XF40	MS60	MS63	MS65
1998	—	**PF65** 320				

KM# 847 1/5 CROWN

6.22 g., 0.9999 Gold 0.200 oz. AGW, 22 mm. **Ruler:** Elizabeth II **Series:** Winter Olympics - Nagano **Obv:** Crowned bust right **Rev:** Figure skaters below flames

Date	Mintage	VF20	XF40	MS60	MS63	MS65
1998	Est. 5000	**PF65** 320				

KM# 848 1/5 CROWN

6.22 g., 0.9999 Gold 0.200 oz. AGW, 22 mm. **Ruler:** Elizabeth II **Series:** Winter Olympics - Nagano **Obv:** Crowned bust right **Rev:** Figure skater, speed skater and skier

Date	Mintage	VF20	XF40	MS60	MS63	MS65
1998	Est. 5000	**PF65** 320				

KM# 855 1/5 CROWN

6.22 g., 0.9999 Gold 0.200 oz. AGW, 22 mm. **Ruler:** Elizabeth II **Obv:** Crowned bust right **Rev:** Birman cat

Date	Mintage	VF20	XF40	MS60	MS63	MS65
1998	1,000	**PF65** 325				

KM# 855a 1/5 CROWN

6.22 g., 0.9995 Platinum 0.1999 oz. APW, 22 mm. **Ruler:** Elizabeth II **Obv:** Crowned bust right **Rev:** Birman cat

Date	Mintage	VF20	XF40	MS60	MS63	MS65
1998	—	**PF65** 290				

KM# 861 1/5 CROWN

6.22 g., 0.9999 Gold 0.200 oz. AGW, 22 mm. **Ruler:** Elizabeth II **Series:** History of the Cat **Obv:** Crowned bust right **Rev:** Egyptian Mau cat with earring

Date	Mintage	VF20	XF40	MS60	MS63	MS65
1998	Est. 7500	**PF65** 325				

KM# 871 1/5 CROWN

6.22 g., 0.9999 Gold 0.200 oz. AGW, 22 mm. **Ruler:** Elizabeth II **Subject:** 125th Anniversary of the Steam Railway **Obv:** Crowned bust right **Rev:** "The General" locomotive

Date	Mintage	VF20	XF40	MS60	MS63	MS65
1998	Est. 5000	**PF65** 320				

KM# 873 1/5 CROWN

6.22 g., 0.9999 Gold 0.200 oz. AGW, 22 mm. **Ruler:** Elizabeth II **Subject:** 125th Anniversary of the Steam Railway **Obv:** Crowned bust right **Rev:** "The Rocket" locomotive and portrait

Date	Mintage	VF20	XF40	MS60	MS63	MS65
1998	Est. 5000	**PF65** 320				

KM# 875 1/5 CROWN

6.22 g., 0.9999 Gold 0.200 oz. AGW, 22 mm. **Ruler:** Elizabeth II **Subject:** 125th Anniversary of the Steam Railway **Obv:** Crowned bust right **Rev:** Orient Express parlor car, interior view

Date	Mintage	VF20	XF40	MS60	MS63	MS65
1998	Est. 5000	**PF65** 320				

KM# 877 1/5 CROWN

6.22 g., 0.9999 Gold 0.200 oz. AGW, 22 mm. **Ruler:** Elizabeth II **Subject:** 125th Anniversary of the Steam Railway **Obv:** Crowned bust right **Rev:** Mount Pilatus Railway

Date	Mintage	VF20	XF40	MS60	MS63	MS65
1998	Est. 5000	**PF65** 320				

KM# 879 1/5 CROWN

6.22 g., 0.9999 Gold 0.200 oz. AGW, 22 mm. **Ruler:** Elizabeth II **Subject:** 125th Anniversary of the Steam Railway **Obv:** Crowned bust right **Rev:** Locomotive No. 1 "Sutherland"

Date	Mintage	VF20	XF40	MS60	MS63	MS65
1998	—	**PF65** 320				

KM# 881 1/5 CROWN
6.22 g., 0.9999 Gold 0.200 oz. AGW, 22 mm. **Ruler:** Elizabeth II **Subject:** 125th Anniversary of the Steam Railway **Obv:** Crowned bust right **Rev:** The "Flying Scotsman" locomotive

Date	Mintage	VF20	XF40	MS60	MS63	MS65
1998	Est. 5000	PF65 320				

KM# 883 1/5 CROWN
6.22 g., 0.9999 Gold 0.200 oz. AGW, 22 mm. **Ruler:** Elizabeth II **Subject:** 125th Anniversary of the Steam Railway **Obv:** Crowned bust right **Rev:** A Mallard class locomotive

Date	Mintage	VF20	XF40	MS60	MS63	MS65
1998	Est. 5000	PF65 320				

KM# 885 1/5 CROWN
6.22 g., 0.9999 Gold 0.200 oz. AGW, 22 mm. **Ruler:** Elizabeth II **Subject:** 125th Anniversary of the Steam Railway **Obv:** Crowned bust right **Rev:** A Big Boy class locomotive

Date	Mintage	VF20	XF40	MS60	MS63	MS65
1998	Est. 5000	PF65 320				

KM# 887 1/5 CROWN
6.22 g., 0.9999 Gold 0.200 oz. AGW, 22 mm. **Ruler:** Elizabeth II **Series:** Year 2000 **Obv:** Crowned bust right **Rev:** American Independence 1776

Date	Mintage	VF20	XF40	MS60	MS63	MS65
1998	Est. 2000	PF65 320				

KM# 889 1/5 CROWN
6.22 g., 0.9999 Gold 0.200 oz. AGW, 22 mm. **Ruler:** Elizabeth II **Series:** Year 2000 **Obv:** Crowned bust right **Rev:** French Revolution 1789

Date	Mintage	VF20	XF40	MS60	MS63	MS65
1998	Est. 2000	PF65 320				

KM# 891 1/5 CROWN
6.22 g., 0.9999 Gold 0.200 oz. AGW, 22 mm. **Ruler:** Elizabeth II **Series:** Year 2000 **Obv:** Crowned bust right **Rev:** Reformation of the Church 1517

Date	Mintage	VF20	XF40	MS60	MS63	MS65
1998	Est. 2000	PF65 320				

KM# 893 1/5 CROWN
6.22 g., 0.9999 Gold 0.200 oz. AGW, 22 mm. **Ruler:** Elizabeth II **Series:** Year 2000 **Obv:** Crowned bust right **Rev:** 400th Anniversary of the Renaissance

Date	Mintage	VF20	XF40	MS60	MS63	MS65
1998	Est. 2000	PF65 320				

KM# 895 1/5 CROWN
6.22 g., 0.9999 Gold 0.200 oz. AGW, 22 mm. **Ruler:** Elizabeth II **Subject:** Year of the Ocean **Obv:** Crowned bust right **Rev:** Ocean wave and sea gull

Date	Mintage	VF20	XF40	MS60	MS63	MS65
1998	Est. 5000	PF65 320				

KM# 913 1/5 CROWN
6.22 g., 0.9999 Gold 0.200 oz. AGW, 22 mm. **Ruler:** Elizabeth II **Subject:** Battle of Waterloo 1815 **Obv:** Crowned bust right **Rev:** Duke of Wellington on horseback

Date	Mintage	VF20	XF40	MS60	MS63	MS65
1999	Est. 2000	PF65 320				

KM# 915 1/5 CROWN
6.22 g., 0.9999 Gold 0.200 oz. AGW, 22 mm. **Ruler:** Elizabeth II **Subject:** U.S. Civil War **Obv:** Crowned bust right **Rev:** Cameos of General Lee and Grant, flags, sword and drum

Date	Mintage	VF20	XF40	MS60	MS63	MS65
1999	Est. 2000	PF65 320				

KM# 917 1/5 CROWN
6.22 g., 0.9999 Gold 0.200 oz. AGW, 22 mm. **Ruler:** Elizabeth II **Subject:** Bolshevik Revolution 1917 **Obv:** Crowned bust right **Rev:** V. I. Lenin above the Aurora

Date	Mintage	VF20	XF40	MS60	MS63	MS65
1999	Est. 2000	PF65 320				

KM# 919 1/5 CROWN
6.22 g., 0.9999 Gold 0.200 oz. AGW, 22 mm. **Ruler:** Elizabeth II **Subject:** Armistice Day 1918 **Obv:** Crowned bust right **Rev:** Biplane above tank

Date	Mintage	VF20	XF40	MS60	MS63	MS65
1999	Est. 2000	PF65 320				

KM# 921 1/5 CROWN
6.22 g., 0.9999 Gold 0.200 oz. AGW, 22 mm. **Ruler:** Elizabeth II **Series:** Summer Olympics - Sydney **Obv:** Crowned bust right **Rev:** Three javelin throwers

Date	Mintage	VF20	XF40	MS60	MS63	MS65
1999	Est. 5000	PF65 320				

KM# 923 1/5 CROWN
6.22 g., 0.9999 Gold 0.200 oz. AGW, 22 mm. **Ruler:** Elizabeth II **Series:** Summer Olympics - Sydney **Obv:** Crowned bust right **Rev:** Female diver

Date	Mintage	VF20	XF40	MS60	MS63	MS65
1999	Est. 5000	PF65 320				

KM# 925 1/5 CROWN
6.22 g., 0.9999 Gold 0.200 oz. AGW, 22 mm. **Ruler:** Elizabeth II **Series:** Summer Olympics - Sydney **Obv:** Crowned bust right **Rev:** Sailboat, Sydney Opera House and Harbor Bridge

Date	Mintage	VF20	XF40	MS60	MS63	MS65
1999	Est. 5000	PF65 320				

KM# 927 1/5 CROWN
6.22 g., 0.9999 Gold 0.200 oz. AGW, 22 mm. **Ruler:** Elizabeth II **Series:** Summer Olympics - Sydney **Obv:** Crowned bust right **Rev:** Two runners

Date	Mintage	VF20	XF40	MS60	MS63	MS65
1999	Est. 5000	PF65 320				

KM# 929 1/5 CROWN
6.22 g., 0.9999 Gold 0.200 oz. AGW, 22 mm. **Ruler:** Elizabeth II **Series:** Summer Olympics - Sydney **Obv:** Crowned bust right **Rev:** Two hurdlers

Date	Mintage	VF20	XF40	MS60	MS63	MS65
1999	Est. 5000	PF65 320				

KM# 931 1/5 CROWN
6.22 g., 0.9999 Gold 0.200 oz. AGW, 22 mm. **Ruler:** Elizabeth II **Series:** World Cup Rugby 1999 **Obv:** Crowned bust right **Rev:** Bust of William Webb Ellis

Date	Mintage	VF20	XF40	MS60	MS63	MS65
1999	Est. 5000	PF65 320				

KM# 933 1/5 CROWN
6.22 g., 0.9999 Gold 0.200 oz. AGW, 22 mm. **Ruler:** Elizabeth II **Series:** World Cup Rugby 1999 **Obv:** Crowned bust right **Rev:** Rugby scrum

Date	Mintage	VF20	XF40	MS60	MS63	MS65
1999	Est. 5000	PF65 320				

KM# 935 1/5 CROWN
6.22 g., 0.9999 Gold 0.200 oz. AGW, 22 mm. **Ruler:** Elizabeth II **Series:** World Cup Rugby 1999 **Obv:** Crowned bust right **Rev:** Player running for catch

Date	Mintage	VF20	XF40	MS60	MS63	MS65
1999	Est. 5000	PF65 325				

KM# 937 1/5 CROWN
6.22 g., 0.9999 Gold 0.200 oz. AGW, 22 mm. **Ruler:** Elizabeth II **Series:** World Cup Rugby 1999 **Obv:** Crowned bust right **Rev:** Goal kick

Date	Mintage	VF20	XF40	MS60	MS63	MS65
1999	Est. 5000	PF65 320				

KM# 939 1/5 CROWN
6.22 g., 0.9999 Gold 0.200 oz. AGW, 22 mm. **Ruler:** Elizabeth II **Series:** World Cup Rugby 1999 **Obv:** Crowned bust right **Rev:** Tackled ball carrier

Date	Mintage	VF20	XF40	MS60	MS63	MS65
1999	Est. 5000	PF65 320				

KM# 941 1/5 CROWN
6.22 g., 0.9999 Gold 0.200 oz. AGW, 22 mm. **Ruler:** Elizabeth II **Series:** World Cup Rugby 1999 **Obv:** Crowned bust right **Rev:** Player leaping for catch

Date	Mintage	VF20	XF40	MS60	MS63	MS65
1999	Est. 5000	PF65 325				

KM# 950 1/5 CROWN
6.22 g., 0.9999 Gold 0.200 oz. AGW, 22 mm. **Ruler:** Elizabeth II **Series:** Year of the Rabbit **Obv:** Crowned bust right **Rev:** Two rabbits

Date	Mintage	VF20	XF40	MS60	MS63	MS65
1999	Est. 12000	PF65 320				

KM# 954 1/5 CROWN
6.22 g., 0.9999 Gold 0.200 oz. AGW, 22 mm. **Ruler:** Elizabeth II **Obv:** Crowned bust right **Rev:** Portrait Sir Walter Raleigh, ship and dates

Date	Mintage	VF20	XF40	MS60	MS63	MS65
1999	Est. 5000	PF65 320				

KM# 956 1/5 CROWN
6.22 g., 0.9999 Gold 0.200 oz. AGW, 22 mm. **Ruler:** Elizabeth II **Obv:** Crowned bust right **Rev:** Portrait Robert Falcon Scott and compass

Date	Mintage	VF20	XF40	MS60	MS63	MS65
1999	Est. 5000	PF65 320				

KM# 962 1/5 CROWN
6.22 g., 0.9999 Gold 0.200 oz. AGW, 22 mm. **Ruler:** Elizabeth II **Subject:** British Blue Cat **Obv:** Crowned bust right **Rev:** Cat cleaning paw

Date	Mintage	VF20	XF40	MS60	MS63	MS65
1999	—	—	—	—	—	325
1999	—	PF65 330				
1999 U Y2K	Est. 5000	—	—	—	—	325

KM# 962a 1/5 CROWN
6.22 g., 0.9995 Platinum 0.1999 oz. APW, 22 mm. **Ruler:** Elizabeth II **Subject:** British Blue Cat **Obv:** Crowned bust right **Rev:** Cat cleaning paw

Date	Mintage	VF20	XF40	MS60	MS63	MS65
1999	—	PF65 290				

KM# 975 1/5 CROWN
6.22 g., 0.9999 Gold 0.200 oz. AGW, 22 mm. **Ruler:** Elizabeth II **Series:** The Life and Times of the Queen Mother **Obv:** Crowned bust right **Rev:** Child in chair

Date	Mintage	VF20	XF40	MS60	MS63	MS65
1999	Est. 5000	PF65 320				

KM# 977 1/5 CROWN
6.22 g., 0.9999 Gold 0.200 oz. AGW, 22 mm. **Ruler:** Elizabeth II **Series:** The Life and Times of the Queen Mother **Obv:** Crowned bust right **Rev:** Engagement portrait

Date	Mintage	VF20	XF40	MS60	MS63	MS65
1999	Est. 5000	PF65 320				

KM# 979 1/5 CROWN
6.22 g., 0.9999 Gold 0.200 oz. AGW, 22 mm. **Ruler:** Elizabeth II **Series:** The Life and Times of the Queen Mother **Obv:** Crowned bust right **Rev:** Honeymoon departure

Date	Mintage	VF20	XF40	MS60	MS63	MS65
1999	Est. 5000	PF65 320				

KM# 994 1/5 CROWN
6.22 g., 0.9999 Gold 0.200 oz. AGW, 22 mm. **Ruler:** Elizabeth II **Subject:** The Wedding of HRH Prince Edward **Obv:** Crowned bust right **Rev:** Portrait of Prince Edward

Date	Mintage	VF20	XF40	MS60	MS63	MS65
1999	Est. 5000	PF65 320				

KM# 995 1/5 CROWN
6.22 g., 0.9999 Gold 0.200 oz. AGW, 22 mm. **Ruler:** Elizabeth II **Subject:** The Wedding of HRH Prince Edward **Obv:** Crowned bust right **Rev:** Head of Prince Edward

Date	Mintage	VF20	XF40	MS60	MS63	MS65
1999	—	PF65 320				

KM# 997 1/5 CROWN
6.22 g., 0.9999 Gold 0.200 oz. AGW, 22 mm. **Ruler:** Elizabeth II **Subject:** The Wedding of HRH Prince Edward **Obv:** Crowned bust right **Rev:** Head of Sophie Rhys-Jones

Date	Mintage	VF20	XF40	MS60	MS63	MS65
1999	Est. 5000	PF65 320				

KM# 999 1/5 CROWN
6.22 g., 0.9999 Gold 0.200 oz. AGW, 22 mm. **Ruler:** Elizabeth II **Subject:** 30th Anniversary of First Man on the Moon **Obv:** Crowned bust right **Rev:** Apollo XI, two moon walkers, date

Date	Mintage	VF20	XF40	MS60	MS63	MS65
1999	Est. 2000	PF65 320				

KM# 1001 1/5 CROWN
6.22 g., 0.9999 Gold 0.200 oz. AGW, 22 mm. **Ruler:** Elizabeth II **Subject:** 30th Anniversary of First Man on the Moon **Obv:** Crowned bust right **Rev:** Mariner IX, 1971, spacecraft orbiting Mars

Date	Mintage	VF20	XF40	MS60	MS63	MS65
1999	Est. 2000	PF65 320				

KM# 1003 1/5 CROWN
6.22 g., 0.9999 Gold 0.200 oz. AGW, 22 mm. **Ruler:** Elizabeth II **Subject:** 30th Anniversary of First Man on the Moon **Obv:** Crowned bust right **Rev:** Apollo-Soyuz link-up

Date	Mintage	VF20	XF40	MS60	MS63	MS65
1999	Est. 2000	PF65 320				

KM# 1005 1/5 CROWN
6.22 g., 0.9999 Gold 0.200 oz. AGW, 22 mm. **Ruler:** Elizabeth II **Subject:** 30th Anniversary of First Man on the Moon **Obv:** Crowned bust right **Rev:** Viking Mars Lander, 1978

Date	Mintage	VF20	XF40	MS60	MS63	MS65
1999	Est. 2000	PF65 320				

KM# 1007 1/5 CROWN
6.22 g., 0.9999 Gold 0.200 oz. AGW, 22 mm. **Ruler:** Elizabeth II **Subject:** 30th Anniversary of First Man on the Moon **Obv:** Crowned bust right **Rev:** Shuttle Columbia, 1981

Date	Mintage	VF20	XF40	MS60	MS63	MS65
1999	Est. 2000	PF65 320				

KM# 1009 1/5 CROWN
6.22 g., 0.9999 Gold 0.200 oz. AGW, 22 mm. **Ruler:** Elizabeth II **Subject:** 30th Anniversary of First Man on the Moon **Obv:** Crowned bust right **Rev:** Mars Pathfinder, 1997

Date	Mintage	VF20	XF40	MS60	MS63	MS65
1999	—	PF65 320				

KM# 984 1/5 CROWN
6.22 g., 0.9999 Gold 0.200 oz. AGW, 22 mm. **Ruler:** Elizabeth II **Subject:** Founding of the UN - Millennium **Obv:** Crowned bust right **Rev:** UN Building, logo

Date	Mintage	VF20	XF40	MS60	MS63	MS65
2000	Est. 2000	PF65 320				

KM# 984a 1/5 CROWN
28.28 g., 0.925 Silver 0.841 oz. ASW **Ruler:** Elizabeth II **Subject:** Founding of the UN 1945 **Obv:** Crowned bust right **Rev:** UN building and logo

Date	Mintage	VF20	XF40	MS60	MS63	MS65
2000	—	PF65 26.00				

KM# 985 1/5 CROWN
6.22 g., 0.9999 Gold 0.200 oz. AGW, 22 mm. **Ruler:** Elizabeth II **Subject:** First Man on the Moon - Millennium **Obv:** Crowned bust right **Rev:** Landing scene, date

Date	Mintage	VF20	XF40	MS60	MS63	MS65
2000	—	PF65 320				

KM# 987 1/5 CROWN
6.22 g., 0.9999 Gold 0.200 oz. AGW, 22 mm. **Ruler:** Elizabeth II **Subject:** Fall of the Berlin Wall - Millennium **Obv:** Crowned bust right **Rev:** Crowds surrounding wall

Date	Mintage	VF20	XF40	MS60	MS63	MS65
2000	Est. 2000	PF65 320				

KM# 989 1/5 CROWN
6.22 g., 0.9999 Gold 0.200 oz. AGW, 22 mm. **Ruler:** Elizabeth II **Subject:** Millennium 2000 - The Future **Obv:** Crowned bust right **Rev:** International space station

Date	Mintage	VF20	XF40	MS60	MS63	MS65
2000	Est. 2000	PF65 320				

KM# 1014 1/5 CROWN
6.22 g., 0.9999 Gold 0.200 oz. AGW, 22 mm. **Ruler:** Elizabeth II **Subject:** Year of the Dragon **Obv:** Crowned bust right **Rev:** Dragon, Chinese characters

Date	Mintage	VF20	XF40	MS60	MS63	MS65
2000	Est. 12000	PF65 320				

KM# 1020 1/5 CROWN
6.22 g., 0.9999 Gold 0.200 oz. AGW, 22 mm. **Ruler:** Elizabeth II **Obv:** Crowned bust right **Rev:** Armored portrait of Francisco Pizarro, map and ship **Edge:** Reeded

Date	Mintage	VF20	XF40	MS60	MS63	MS65
2000	—	PF65 320				

KM# 1022 1/5 CROWN
6.22 g., 0.9999 Gold 0.200 oz. AGW, 22 mm. **Ruler:** Elizabeth II **Obv:** Crowned bust right **Rev:** Portrait, ship on ice and map, Willem Barents

Date	Mintage	VF20	XF40	MS60	MS63	MS65
2000	—	PF65 320				

KM# 1024 1/5 CROWN
6.22 g., 0.9999 Gold 0.200 oz. AGW, 22 mm. **Ruler:** Elizabeth II **Series:** Queen Mother **Obv:** Crowned bust right **Rev:** 1931 family scene **Edge:** Reeded

Date	Mintage	VF20	XF40	MS60	MS63	MS65
2000	5,000	PF65 320				

KM# 1026 1/5 CROWN
6.22 g., 0.9999 Gold 0.200 oz. AGW, 22 mm. **Ruler:** Elizabeth II **Series:** Queen Mother **Obv:** Crowned bust right **Rev:** 1937 Coronation scene

Date	Mintage	VF20	XF40	MS60	MS63	MS65
2000	—	PF65 320				

KM# 1028 1/5 CROWN
6.22 g., 0.9999 Gold 0.200 oz. AGW, 22 mm. **Ruler:** Elizabeth II **Series:** Queen Mother **Obv:** Crowned bust right **Rev:** 1945 Victory Visit scene

Date	Mintage	VF20	XF40	MS60	MS63	MS65
2000	—	PF65 320				

KM# 1030 1/5 CROWN
6.22 g., 0.9999 Gold 0.200 oz. AGW, 22 mm. **Ruler:** Elizabeth II **Series:** Queen Mother **Obv:** Crowned bust right **Rev:** 1963 Royal Visit scene

Date	Mintage	VF20	XF40	MS60	MS63	MS65
2000	175	PF65 320				

KM# 1032 1/5 CROWN
6.22 g., 0.999 Gold 0.1998 oz. AGW, 22 mm. **Ruler:** Elizabeth II **Subject:** Battle of Britain **Obv:** Crowned bust right **Rev:** Aerial battle scene **Edge:** Reeded

Date	Mintage	VF20	XF40	MS60	MS63	MS65
2000	—	PF65 320				

KM# 1034 1/5 CROWN
6.22 g., 0.999 Gold 0.1998 oz. AGW, 22 mm. **Ruler:** Elizabeth II **Subject:** Global Challenge Yacht Race **Obv:** Crowned bust right **Rev:** Partial view of ship and map

Date	Mintage	VF20	XF40	MS60	MS63	MS65
2000	—	PF65 320				

KM# 1046 1/5 CROWN
6.22 g., 0.9999 Gold 0.200 oz. AGW, 22 mm. **Ruler:** Elizabeth II **Obv:** Crowned bust right **Rev:** Prince William's portrait **Edge:** Reeded

Date	Mintage	VF20	XF40	MS60	MS63	MS65
2000	5,000	PF65 320				

KM# 1048 1/5 CROWN
6.22 g., 0.9999 Gold 0.200 oz. AGW, 22 mm. **Ruler:** Elizabeth II **Obv:** Crowned bust right **Rev:** Bust with hat facing

Date	Mintage	VF20	XF40	MS60	MS63	MS65
2000	2,000	PF65 320				

KM# 1054 1/5 CROWN
6.22 g., 0.9999 Gold 0.200 oz. AGW, 22 mm. **Ruler:** Elizabeth II **Obv:** Crowned bust right **Rev:** Scottish kitten **Edge:** Reeded

Date	Mintage	VF20	XF40	MS60	MS63	MS65
2000	—	—	—	—	—	320
2000	—	PF65 320				

KM# 1054a 1/5 CROWN
6.22 g., 0.9995 Platinum 0.1999 oz. APW, 22 mm. **Ruler:** Elizabeth II **Obv:** Crowned bust right **Rev:** Scottish kitten

Date	Mintage	VF20	XF40	MS60	MS63	MS65
2000	—	—	—	—	—	290

KM# 669 1/4 CROWN
0.999 Bi-Metallic Gold center in Platinum ring **Ruler:** Elizabeth II **Series:** Legend of King Arthur **Obv:** Crowned bust right **Rev:** King Arthur with sword and orb

Date	Mintage	VF20	XF40	MS60	MS63	MS65
1996	—	PF65 450				

KM# 669a 1/4 CROWN
3.89 g., 0.995 Platinum 0.1244 oz. APW **Ruler:** Elizabeth II **Series:** Legend of King Arthur **Obv:** Crowned bust right **Rev:** King Arthur with sword and orb **Note:** Prev. KM#674.

Date	Mintage	VF20	XF40	MS60	MS63	MS65
1996	Est. 5000	PF65 187				

KM# 670 1/4 CROWN
0.999 Bi-Metallic Gold center in Platinum ring **Ruler:** Elizabeth II **Series:** Legend of King Arthur **Obv:** Crowned bust right **Rev:** Queen Guinevere

Date	Mintage	VF20	XF40	MS60	MS63	MS65
1996	Est. 5000	PF65 450				

KM# 670a 1/4 CROWN
3.89 g., 0.995 Platinum 0.1244 oz. APW **Ruler:** Elizabeth II **Series:** Legend of King Arthur **Obv:** Crowned bust right **Rev:** Queen Guinevere **Note:** Prev. KM#675.

Date	Mintage	VF20	XF40	MS60	MS63	MS65
1996	Est. 5000	PF65 187				

KM# 671 1/4 CROWN
0.999 Bi-Metallic Gold center in Platinum ring **Ruler:** Elizabeth II **Series:** Legend of King Arthur **Obv:** Crowned bust right **Rev:** Sir Lancelot

Date	Mintage	VF20	XF40	MS60	MS63	MS65
1996	Est. 5000	PF65 450				

KM# 671a 1/4 CROWN
3.89 g., 0.995 Platinum 0.1244 oz. APW **Ruler:** Elizabeth II **Series:** Legend of King Arthur **Obv:** Crowned bust right **Rev:** Sir Lancelot **Note:** Prev. KM#676.

Date	Mintage	VF20	XF40	MS60	MS63	MS65
1996	Est. 5000	PF65 187				

KM# 672 1/4 CROWN
0.999 Bi-Metallic Gold center in Platinum ring **Ruler:** Elizabeth II **Series:** Legend of King Arthur **Obv:** Crowned bust right **Rev:** Merlin

Date	Mintage	VF20	XF40	MS60	MS63	MS65
1996	Est. 5000	PF65 450				

KM# 672a 1/4 CROWN
3.89 g., 0.995 Platinum 0.1244 oz. APW **Ruler:** Elizabeth II **Series:** Legend of King Arthur **Obv:** Crowned bust right **Rev:** Merlin **Note:** Prev. KM#677.

Date	Mintage	VF20	XF40	MS60	MS63	MS65
1996	—	PF65 187				

KM# 673 1/4 CROWN
0.999 Bi-Metallic Gold center in Platinum ring **Ruler:** Elizabeth II **Series:** Legend of King Arthur **Obv:** Crowned bust right **Rev:** Camelot Castle

Date	Mintage	VF20	XF40	MS60	MS63	MS65
1996	Est. 5000	PF65 450				

KM# 673a 1/4 CROWN
3.89 g., 0.995 Platinum 0.1244 oz. APW **Ruler:** Elizabeth II **Series:** Legend of King Arthur **Obv:** Crowned bust right within circle **Rev:** Castle within circle **Note:** Prev. KM#678.

Date	Mintage	VF20	XF40	MS60	MS63	MS65
1996	—	PF65 187				

KM# 187 1/2 CROWN
15.55 g., 0.999 Gold 0.4994 oz. AGW **Ruler:** Elizabeth II **Subject:** U.S. Constitution **Obv:** Crowned bust right within circle **Rev:** Statue of Liberty at center of Presidential busts within circle

Date	Mintage	VF20	XF40	MS60	MS63	MS65
1987	12,000	PF65 730				

KM# 187a 1/2 CROWN
15.55 g., 0.999 Platinum 0.4994 oz. APW **Ruler:** Elizabeth II **Subject:** U.S. Constitution **Obv:** Crowned bust right **Rev:** Busts of American presidents, Statue of Liberty at center

Date	Mintage	VF20	XF40	MS60	MS63	MS65
1987	250	PF65 650				

KM# 238 1/2 CROWN
15.55 g., 0.999 Gold 0.4994 oz. AGW **Ruler:** Elizabeth II **Obv:** Crowned bust right **Rev:** Manx cat

Date	Mintage	VF20	XF40	MS60	MS63	MS65
1988	6,375	—	—	—	—	730
1988	5,000	PF65 740				

KM# 286 1/2 CROWN
16.40 g., 0.948 Gold 0.4999 oz. AGW **Ruler:** Elizabeth II **Subject:** Australian Bicentennial **Obv:** Crowned bust right within circle **Rev:** Cockatoo on branch within circle

Date	Mintage	VF20	XF40	MS60	MS63	MS65
1988	Est. 7500	PF65 730				

KM# 286a 1/2 CROWN
15.55 g., 0.999 Platinum 0.4994 oz. APW **Ruler:** Elizabeth II **Subject:** Australian Bicentennial **Obv:** Crowned bust right **Rev:** Cockatoo **Note:** Prev. KM#359.

Date	Mintage	VF20	XF40	MS60	MS63	MS65
1988	—	PF65 660				

KM# 287 1/2 CROWN
16.40 g., 0.948 Gold 0.4999 oz. AGW **Ruler:** Elizabeth II **Subject:** Australian Bicentennial **Obv:** Crowned bust right **Rev:** Koala bear

Date	Mintage	VF20	XF40	MS60	MS63	MS65
1988	Est. 7500	PF65 730				

KM# 287a 1/2 CROWN
15.55 g., 0.999 Platinum 0.4994 oz. APW **Ruler:** Elizabeth II **Subject:** Australian Bicentennial **Obv:** Crowned bust right **Rev:** Koala bear **Note:** Prev. KM#360.

Date	Mintage	VF20	XF40	MS60	MS63	MS65
1988	—	PF65 660				

KM# 288 1/2 CROWN
16.40 g., 0.948 Gold 0.4999 oz. AGW **Ruler:** Elizabeth II **Subject:** Australian Bicentennial **Obv:** Crowned bust right **Rev:** Duckbill platypus

Date	Mintage	VF20	XF40	MS60	MS63	MS65
1988	—	PF65 730				

KM# 288a 1/2 CROWN
15.55 g., 0.999 Platinum 0.4994 oz. APW **Ruler:** Elizabeth II **Subject:** Australian Bicentennial **Obv:** Crowned bust right **Rev:** Duckbill platypus **Note:** Prev. KM#361.

Date	Mintage	VF20	XF40	MS60	MS63	MS65
1988	—	PF65 660				

KM# 289 1/2 CROWN
16.40 g., 0.948 Gold 0.4999 oz. AGW **Ruler:** Elizabeth II **Subject:** Australian Bicentennial **Obv:** Crowned bust right within circle **Rev:** Kangaroo within circle

Date	Mintage	VF20	XF40	MS60	MS63	MS65
1988	Est. 7500	PF65 730				

KM# 289a 1/2 CROWN
15.55 g., 0.999 Platinum 0.4994 oz. APW **Ruler:** Elizabeth II **Subject:** Australian Bicentennial **Obv:** Crowned bust right **Rev:** Kangaroo **Note:** Prev. KM#362.

Date	Mintage	VF20	XF40	MS60	MS63	MS65
1988	—	PF65 660				

KM# 363 1/2 CROWN
15.55 g., 0.999 Platinum 0.4994 oz. APW **Ruler:** Elizabeth II **Subject:** Australian Bicentennial **Obv:** Crowned bust right **Rev:** Dingo Dog

Date	Mintage	VF20	XF40	MS60	MS63	MS65
1988	—	PF65 660				

KM# 255 1/2 CROWN
16.40 g., 0.948 Gold 0.4999 oz. AGW **Ruler:** Elizabeth II **Obv:** Crowned bust right **Rev:** Persian cat

Date	Mintage	VF20	XF40	MS60	MS63	MS65
1989	—	—	—	—	—	730
1989	—	PF65 740				

KM# 255a 1/2 CROWN
15.55 g., 0.999 Platinum 0.4994 oz. APW **Ruler:** Elizabeth II **Obv:** Crowned bust right **Rev:** Persian cat **Note:** Prev. KM#470.

Date	Mintage	VF20	XF40	MS60	MS63	MS65
1989	—	—	—	—	—	660
1989	—	PF65 670				

KM# 280 1/2 CROWN
16.40 g., 0.948 Gold 0.4999 oz. AGW **Ruler:** Elizabeth II **Obv:** Crowned bust right **Rev:** Alley cat

Date	Mintage	VF20	XF40	MS60	MS63	MS65
1990	—	—	—	—	—	740
1990	—	PF65 740				

KM# 1265 1/2 CROWN
15.55 g., 0.999 Gold 0.4994 oz. AGW, 30 mm. **Ruler:** Elizabeth II **Obv:** Crowned bust right **Rev:** Stamp design in black center **Edge:** Reeded

Date	Mintage	VF20	XF40	MS60	MS63	MS65
1990 PM	—	—	—	—	—	730

KM# 297 1/2 CROWN
15.55 g., 0.999 Gold 0.4994 oz. AGW **Ruler:** Elizabeth II **Obv:** Crowned bust right **Rev:** Norwegian cat

Date	Mintage	VF20	XF40	MS60	MS63	MS65
1991	—	—	—	—	—	740
1991	—	PF65 740				

KM# 325 1/2 CROWN
15.55 g., 0.999 Gold 0.4994 oz. AGW **Ruler:** Elizabeth II **Subject:** America's Cup **Obv:** Crowned bust right **Rev:** Cameo of "Star of India" above two modern sailboats

Date	Mintage	VF20	XF40	MS60	MS63	MS65
1992 Prooflike	2,000	—	—	—	—	730

KM# 331 1/2 CROWN
15.55 g., 0.999 Gold 0.4994 oz. AGW **Ruler:** Elizabeth II **Obv:** Crowned bust right **Rev:** Siamese cat

Date	Mintage	VF20	XF40	MS60	MS63	MS65
1992	—	—	—	—	—	740
1992	—	PF65 740				

KM# 341 1/2 CROWN
15.55 g., 0.999 Gold 0.4994 oz. AGW **Ruler:** Elizabeth II **Subject:** Year of the Rooster **Obv:** Crowned bust right **Rev:** Cockerel within circle

Date	Mintage	VF20	XF40	MS60	MS63	MS65
1993	Est. 5000	PF65 730				

KM# 352 1/2 CROWN
15.55 g., 0.999 Gold 0.4994 oz. AGW **Ruler:** Elizabeth II **Obv:** Crowned bust right **Rev:** Maine coon cat

Date	Mintage	VF20	XF40	MS60	MS63	MS65
1993	—	—	—	—	—	740
1993	—	PF65 740				

KM# 379 1/2 CROWN
15.55 g., 0.999 Gold 0.4994 oz. AGW **Ruler:** Elizabeth II **Obv:** Crowned bust right **Rev:** Japanese bobtail cat

Date	Mintage	VF20	XF40	MS60	MS63	MS65
1994	—	—	—	—	—	740
1994	—	PF65 740				

KM# 379a 1/2 CROWN
15.55 g., 0.999 Platinum 0.4994 oz. APW **Ruler:** Elizabeth II **Obv:** Crowned bust right **Rev:** Japanese bobtail cat **Note:** Prev. KM#476.

Date	Mintage	VF20	XF40	MS60	MS63	MS65
1994	—	—	—	—	—	660
1994	—	PF65 670				

KM# 405 1/2 CROWN
15.55 g., 0.999 Gold 0.4994 oz. AGW **Ruler:** Elizabeth II **Obv:** Crowned bust right **Rev:** Pekingese dog

Date	Mintage	VF20	XF40	MS60	MS63	MS65
1994	5,000	PF65 730				

KM# 1527 1/2 CROWN
15.55 g., 0.999 Gold 0.4994 oz. AGW **Ruler:** Elizabeth II **Subject:** Normandy Anniversary

Date	Mintage	VF20	XF40	MS60	MS63	MS65
1994	—	PF65 730				

KM# 445 1/2 CROWN
15.55 g., 0.999 Gold 0.4994 oz. AGW **Ruler:** Elizabeth II **Obv:** Crowned bust right **Rev:** Turkish cat looking back

Date	Mintage	VF20	XF40	MS60	MS63	MS65
1995 U	—	—	—	—	—	740
1995	—	PF65 740				

KM# 445a 1/2 CROWN
15.55 g., 0.999 Platinum 0.4994 oz. APW **Ruler:** Elizabeth II **Obv:** Crowned bust right **Rev:** Turkish cat **Note:** Prev. KM#481.

Date	Mintage	VF20	XF40	MS60	MS63	MS65
1995	—	—	—	—	—	610
1995	—	PF65 610				

KM# 452 1/2 CROWN
15.55 g., 0.999 Gold 0.4994 oz. AGW **Ruler:** Elizabeth II **Subject:** Year of the Pig **Obv:** Crowned bust right **Rev:** Sow with piglets

Date	Mintage	VF20	XF40	MS60	MS63	MS65
1995	Est. 5000	PF65 740				

KM# 619 1/2 CROWN
15.55 g., 0.999 Gold 0.4994 oz. AGW **Ruler:** Elizabeth II **Obv:** Crowned bust right **Rev:** Burmese cat

Date	Mintage	VF20	XF40	MS60	MS63	MS65
1996 U	—	—	—	—	—	740
1996	—	PF65 740				

KM# 619a 1/2 CROWN
15.55 g., 0.999 Platinum 0.4994 oz. APW **Ruler:** Elizabeth II **Obv:** Crowned bust right **Rev:** Burmese cat

Date	Mintage	VF20	XF40	MS60	MS63	MS65
1996 U	—	—	—	—	—	610
1996	—	PF65 610				

KM# 724 1/2 CROWN
15.55 g., 0.9999 Gold 0.4999 oz. AGW **Ruler:** Elizabeth II **Subject:** Year of the Ox **Obv:** Crowned bust right **Rev:** Ox laying down

Date	Mintage	VF20	XF40	MS60	MS63	MS65
1996	Est. 6000	PF65 740				

KM# 731 1/2 CROWN
15.55 g., 0.9999 Gold 0.4999 oz. AGW **Ruler:** Elizabeth II **Subject:** Year of the Rat **Obv:** Crowned bust right **Rev:** Rat

Date	Mintage	VF20	XF40	MS60	MS63	MS65
1996	—	PF65 740				

KM# 764 1/2 CROWN
15.55 g., 0.9999 Gold 0.4999 oz. AGW **Ruler:** Elizabeth II **Obv:** Crowned bust right **Rev:** Portrait of Leif Eriksson and Viking ship with map sail

Date	Mintage	VF20	XF40	MS60	MS63	MS65
1997	Est. 2500	PF65 740				

KM# 764a 1/2 CROWN
15.55 g., 0.9999 Silver 0.4999 oz. ASW **Ruler:** Elizabeth II **Obv:** Crowned bust right **Rev:** Portrait of Leif Eriksson and Viking ship with map sail

Date	Mintage	VF20	XF40	MS60	MS63	MS65
1997	—	PF65 35.00				

KM# 767 1/2 CROWN
15.55 g., 0.9999 Gold 0.4999 oz. AGW **Ruler:** Elizabeth II **Obv:** Crowned bust right **Rev:** Portrait of Fridtjof Nansen, map and ship "The Fram"

Date	Mintage	VF20	XF40	MS60	MS63	MS65
1997	Est. 2500	PF65 740				

KM# 767a 1/2 CROWN
15.55 g., 0.999 Silver 0.4994 oz. ASW **Ruler:** Elizabeth II **Obv:** Crowned bust right **Rev:** Portrait of Fridtjof Nansen, map and ship "The Fram"

Date	Mintage	VF20	XF40	MS60	MS63	MS65
1997	—	PF65 35.00				

KM# 773 1/2 CROWN

15.55 g., 0.9999 Gold 0.4999 oz. AGW **Ruler:** Elizabeth II **Obv:** Crowned bust right **Rev:** Long-haired Smoke cat

Date	Mintage	VF20	XF40	MS60	MS63	MS65
1997	—	—	—	—	—	740
1997	—	PF65 740				

KM# 791 1/2 CROWN

15.55 g., 0.9999 Gold 0.4999 oz. AGW **Ruler:** Elizabeth II **Subject:** History of the Cat **Obv:** Crowned bust right **Rev:** Cat stalking a spider

Date	Mintage	VF20	XF40	MS60	MS63	MS65
1997	Est. 2500	PF65 740				

KM# 815 1/2 CROWN

15.50 g., 0.9999 Gold 0.4983 oz. AGW **Ruler:** Elizabeth II **Subject:** Year of the Tiger **Obv:** Crowned bust right **Rev:** Tiger

Date	Mintage	VF20	XF40	MS60	MS63	MS65
1998	Est. 6000	PF65 740				

KM# 856 1/2 CROWN

15.55 g., 0.9999 Gold 0.4999 oz. AGW **Ruler:** Elizabeth II **Obv:** Crowned bust right **Rev:** Birman cat

Date	Mintage	VF20	XF40	MS60	MS63	MS65
1998	—	—	—	—	—	740
1998	1,000	PF65 740				

KM# 856a 1/2 CROWN

15.55 g., 0.9995 Platinum 0.4997 oz. APW **Ruler:** Elizabeth II **Obv:** Crowned bust right **Rev:** Birman cat

Date	Mintage	VF20	XF40	MS60	MS63	MS65
1998	—	—	—	—	—	—

Note: Requires Confirmation

KM# 862 1/2 CROWN

15.55 g., 0.9999 Gold 0.4999 oz. AGW **Ruler:** Elizabeth II **Subject:** History of the Cat **Obv:** Crowned bust right **Rev:** Egyptain Mau cat with earring

Date	Mintage	VF20	XF40	MS60	MS63	MS65
1998	—	PF65 740				

KM# 951 1/2 CROWN

15.55 g., 0.9999 Gold 0.4999 oz. AGW **Ruler:** Elizabeth II **Subject:** Year of the Rabbit **Obv:** Crowned bust right **Rev:** Two rabbits

Date	Mintage	VF20	XF40	MS60	MS63	MS65
1999	Est. 6000	PF65 740				

KM# 964 1/2 CROWN

15.55 g., 0.9999 Gold 0.4999 oz. AGW **Ruler:** Elizabeth II **Subject:** British Blue cat **Obv:** Crowned bust right **Rev:** Cat cleaning paw

Date	Mintage	VF20	XF40	MS60	MS63	MS65
1999	—	—	—	—	—	740
1999	—	PF65 740				

KM# 964a 1/2 CROWN

15.55 g., 0.9995 Platinum 0.4998 oz. APW **Ruler:** Elizabeth II **Subject:** British Blue cat **Obv:** Crowned bust right **Rev:** Cat cleaning paw

Date	Mintage	VF20	XF40	MS60	MS63	MS65
1999	—	—	—	—	—	—

Note: Requires Confirmation

KM# 1015 1/2 CROWN

15.55 g., 0.9999 Gold 0.4999 oz. AGW **Ruler:** Elizabeth II **Subject:** Year of the Dragon **Obv:** Head with tiara right **Rev:** Dragon, Chinese characters

Date	Mintage	VF20	XF40	MS60	MS63	MS65
2000	Est. 6000	PF65 740				

KM# 1055 1/2 CROWN

15.55 g., 0.9999 Gold 0.4999 oz. AGW, 30 mm. **Ruler:** Elizabeth II **Subject:** Scottish Fold Kitten **Obv:** Crowned bust right **Rev:** Kitten playing with world **Edge:** Reeded

Date	Mintage	VF20	XF40	MS60	MS63	MS65
2000	—	—	—	—	—	740
2000	—	PF65 740				

KM# 1055a 1/2 CROWN

6.22 g., 0.9995 Platinum 0.1999 oz. APW **Ruler:** Elizabeth II **Subject:** Scottish Fold Kitten **Obv:** Crowned bust right **Rev:** Kitten playing with world

Date	Mintage	VF20	XF40	MS60	MS63	MS65
2000	—	—	—	—	—	260

KM# 1084 1/2 CROWN

9.00 g., 0.999 Bi-Metallic 0.2891 oz. Titanium center in Gold ring, 32.25 mm. **Ruler:** Elizabeth II **Subject:** Greenwich Meridian Time Clock **Obv:** Head with tiara right within beaded circle **Rev:** Greenwich meridian line on map clock face **Edge:** Reeded

Date	Mintage	VF20	XF40	MS60	MS63	MS65
2000	10,000	PF65 300				

KM# 1263 1/2 CROWN

15.04 g., Titanium, 38.5 mm. **Ruler:** Elizabeth II **Obv:** Crowned bust right **Rev:** Space station and shuttle **Edge:** Reeded

Date	Mintage	VF20	XF40	MS60	MS63	MS65
2000 PM Matte	—	—	—	—	—	75.00

KM# 18 CROWN

Copper-Nickel, 38.5 mm. **Ruler:** Elizabeth II **Obv:** Young bust right **Rev:** Manx cat **Edge:** Reeded

Date	Mintage	VF20	XF40	MS60	MS63	MS65
1970	150,000	—	—	—	10.00	14.00

KM# 18a CROWN

28.28 g., 0.925 Silver 0.841 oz. ASW, 38.5 mm. **Ruler:** Elizabeth II **Obv:** Young bust right **Rev:** Manx cat

Date	Mintage	VF20	XF40	MS60	MS63	MS65
1970	11,000	PF65 70.00				

KM# 30 CROWN

Copper-Nickel, 38.5 mm. **Ruler:** Elizabeth II **Subject:** Centenary - Birth of Winston Churchill **Obv:** Young bust right **Rev:** Bust of Winston Churchill facing **Edge:** Reeded **Note:** Most of this issue are doubled die.

Date	Mintage	VF20	XF40	MS60	MS63	MS65
1974	45,000	—	—	—	5.00	6.00

KM# 30a CROWN

28.28 g., 0.925 Silver 0.841 oz. ASW **Ruler:** Elizabeth II **Obv:** Young bust right **Rev:** Bust of Winston Churchill facing **Edge:** Reeded

Date	Mintage	VF20	XF40	MS60	MS63	MS65
1974	—	—	—	—	16.00	22.00
1974	30,000	PF65 24.00				

KM# 37 CROWN

Copper-Nickel, 38.5 mm. **Ruler:** Elizabeth II **Subject:** Bicentenary of American Independence **Obv:** Young bust right **Rev:** Bust of George Washington left **Edge:** Reeded **Note:** Doubled die strike exists.

Date	Mintage	VF20	XF40	MS60	MS63	MS65
1976	50,000	—	—	—	6.00	7.00

KM# 37a CROWN

28.28 g., 0.925 Silver 0.841 oz. ASW, 38.5 mm. **Ruler:** Elizabeth II **Subject:** Bicentenary of American Independence **Obv:** Young bust right **Rev:** Bust of George Washington left

Date	Mintage	VF20	XF40	MS60	MS63	MS65
1976	—	—	—	—	16.00	22.00
1976	30,000	PF65 24.00				

KM# 38 CROWN

Copper-Nickel, 38.5 mm. **Ruler:** Elizabeth II **Obv:** Young bust right **Rev:** Horse-drawn tram **Edge:** Reeded **Note:** Doubled die strike exists.

Date	Mintage	VF20	XF40	MS60	MS63	MS65
1976	50,000	—	—	—	7.50	10.00

KM# 38a CROWN

28.28 g., 0.925 Silver 0.841 oz. ASW, 38.5 mm. **Ruler:** Elizabeth II **Obv:** Young bust right **Rev:** Horse-drawn tram

Date	Mintage	VF20	XF40	MS60	MS63	MS65
1976	—	—	—	—	16.00	22.00
1976	30,000	PF65 24.00				

KM# 41 CROWN

Copper-Nickel, 38.5 mm. **Ruler:** Elizabeth II **Subject:** Silver Jubilee **Obv:** Young bust right **Rev:** Triskeles in center of crowns **Edge:** Reeded

Date	Mintage	VF20	XF40	MS60	MS63	MS65
ND-1977	—	—	—	—	4.50	6.00
ND-1977	—	PF65 15.00				

KM# 41a CROWN

28.28 g., 0.925 Silver 0.841 oz. ASW, 38.5 mm. **Ruler:** Elizabeth II **Subject:** Silver Jubilee **Obv:** Crowned bust right **Rev:** Triskeles in center of crowns **Edge:** Reeded

Date	Mintage	VF20	XF40	MS60	MS63	MS65
ND-1977	—	—	—	—	16.00	22.00
ND-1977	—	PF65 24.00				

KM# 42 CROWN

Copper-Nickel, 38.5 mm. **Ruler:** Elizabeth II **Subject:** Queen's Jubilee Appeal **Obv:** Young bust right **Rev:** Triskeles on shield and crown divide wreath with monogram at center **Edge:** Reeded

Date	Mintage	VF20	XF40	MS60	MS63	MS65
1977	—	—	—	—	6.00	7.00

Note: Wide and narrow rims exist

KM# 42a CROWN

28.28 g., 0.925 Silver 0.841 oz. ASW, 38.5 mm. **Ruler:** Elizabeth II **Subject:** Queen's Jubilee Appeal **Obv:** Young bust right **Rev:** Triskeles on shield and crown divide wreath with monogram at center

Date	Mintage	VF20	XF40	MS60	MS63	MS65
1977	70,000	—	—	—	16.00	22.00
1977	30,000	PF65 24.00				

KM# 43 CROWN

Copper-Nickel, 38.5 mm. **Ruler:** Elizabeth II **Subject:** 25th Anniversary of Coronation **Obv:** Young bust right **Rev:** Falcons **Edge:** Reeded **Note:** For mule of Isle of Man obverse with Ascension Island KM#1 reverse, refer to Ascension Island listings.

Date	Mintage	VF20	XF40	MS60	MS63	MS65
1978	—	—	—	—	10.00	15.00
1978	—	PF65 17.50				

KM# 43a CROWN

28.28 g., 0.925 Silver 0.841 oz. ASW, 38.5 mm. **Ruler:** Elizabeth II **Subject:** 25th Anniversary of Coronation **Obv:** Young bust right **Rev:** Falcons

Date	Mintage	VF20	XF40	MS60	MS63	MS65
1978	70,000	—	—	—	16.00	22.00
1978	30,000	PF65 24.00				

KM# 45 CROWN

28.47 g., Copper-Nickel, 38.47 mm. **Ruler:** Elizabeth II **Subject:** 300th Anniversary of Manx Coinage **Obv:** Head with tiara right **Rev:** Triskeles coin at center of 8 assorted coins **Edge:** Reeded

Date	Mintage	VF20	XF40	MS60	MS63	MS65
1979 PM	—	—	—	—	8.00	9.00
1979 PM	—	PF65 10.00				

KM# 45a CROWN

28.28 g., 0.925 Silver 0.841 oz. ASW, 38.47 mm. **Ruler:** Elizabeth II **Subject:** 300th Anniversary of Manx Coinage **Obv:** Head with tiara right **Rev:** Triskeles coin at center of 8 assorted coins **Edge:** Reeded

Date	Mintage	VF20	XF40	MS60	MS63	MS65
1979 PM	70,000	—	—	—	16.00	22.00
1979 PM	30,000	PF65 24.00				

KM# 46 CROWN

Copper-Nickel, 38.5 mm. **Ruler:** Elizabeth II **Subject:** Millennium of Tynwald **Obv:** Young bust right **Rev:** Viking longship, Godred Crovan **Edge:** Reeded

Date	Mintage	VF20	XF40	MS60	MS63	MS65
1979	100,000	—	—	—	3.50	4.50

KM# 46a CROWN

28.28 g., 0.925 Silver 0.841 oz. ASW, 38.5 mm. **Ruler:** Elizabeth II **Subject:** Millennium of Tynwald **Obv:** Young bust right **Rev:** Viking longship, Godred Cravan

Date	Mintage	VF20	XF40	MS60	MS63	MS65
1979	25,000	—	—	—	16.00	22.00
1979	10,000	PF65 24.00				

KM# 46b CROWN

43.00 g., 0.917 Gold 1.2677 oz. AGW, 38.5 mm. **Ruler:** Elizabeth II **Subject:** Millennium of Tynwald **Obv:** Young bust right **Rev:** Viking longship

Date	Mintage	VF20	XF40	MS60	MS63	MS65
1979	300	PF65 1,850				

KM# 46c CROWN

52.00 g., 0.950 Platinum 1.5882 oz. APW, 38.5 mm. **Ruler:** Elizabeth II **Subject:** Millennium of Tynwald **Obv:** Young bust right **Rev:** Viking longship

Date	Mintage	VF20	XF40	MS60	MS63	MS65
1979	100	PF65 2,000				

KM# 47 CROWN

Copper-Nickel, 38.5 mm. **Ruler:** Elizabeth II **Subject:** Millennium of Tynwald **Obv:** Young bust right **Rev:** English cog, Castle Rushen **Edge:** Reeded

Date	Mintage	VF20	XF40	MS60	MS63	MS65
1979	100,000	—	—	—	6.50	7.50
1979 CB	—	—	—	—	6.50	7.50

KM# 47a CROWN

28.28 g., 0.925 Silver 0.841 oz. ASW, 38.5 mm. **Ruler:** Elizabeth II **Subject:** Millennium of Tynwald **Obv:** Young bust right **Rev:** English cog, Castle Rushen

Date	Mintage	VF20	XF40	MS60	MS63	MS65
1979	25,000	—	—	—	16.00	22.00
1979	10,000	PF65 24.00				

KM# 47b CROWN

43.00 g., 0.917 Gold 1.2677 oz. AGW, 38.5 mm. **Ruler:** Elizabeth II **Subject:** Millennium of Tynwald **Obv:** Young bust right **Rev:** English cog, Castle Rushen

Date	Mintage	VF20	XF40	MS60	MS63	MS65
1979	300	PF65 1,850				

KM# 47c CROWN

52.00 g., 0.950 Platinum 1.5882 oz. APW, 38.5 mm. **Ruler:** Elizabeth II **Subject:** Millennium of Tynwald **Obv:** Young bust right **Rev:** English cog, Castle Rushen

Date	Mintage	VF20	XF40	MS60	MS63	MS65
1979	100	PF65 2,000				

KM# 48 CROWN

Copper-Nickel, 38.5 mm. **Ruler:** Elizabeth II **Subject:** Millennium of Tynwald **Obv:** Young bust right **Rev:** Ship **Edge:** Reeded

Date	Mintage	VF20	XF40	MS60	MS63	MS65
1979	100,000	—	—	—	8.00	9.00

KM# 48a CROWN

28.28 g., 0.925 Silver 0.841 oz. ASW, 38.5 mm. **Ruler:** Elizabeth II **Subject:** Millennium of Tynwald **Obv:** Young bust right **Rev:** Ship

Date	Mintage	VF20	XF40	MS60	MS63	MS65
1979	25,000	—	—	—	16.00	22.00
1979	10,000	PF65 24.00				

KM# 48b CROWN

43.00 g., 0.917 Gold 1.2677 oz. AGW, 38.5 mm. **Ruler:** Elizabeth II **Subject:** Millennium of Tynwald **Obv:** Young bust right **Rev:** Ship

Date	Mintage	VF20	XF40	MS60	MS63	MS65
1979	300	PF65 1,850				

KM# 48c CROWN

52.00 g., 0.950 Platinum 1.5882 oz. APW, 38.5 mm. **Ruler:** Elizabeth II **Subject:** Millennium of Tynwald **Obv:** Young bust right **Rev:** Ship

Date	Mintage	VF20	XF40	MS60	MS63	MS65
1979	100	PF65 2,000				

KM# 49 CROWN

28.28 g., Copper-Nickel, 38.5 mm. **Ruler:** Elizabeth II **Subject:** Millennium of Tynwald **Obv:** Young bust right **Rev:** Standing figure and ship **Edge:** Reeded

Date	Mintage	VF20	XF40	MS60	MS63	MS65
1979	100,000	—	—	—	8.00	9.00

KM# 49a CROWN

28.28 g., 0.925 Silver 0.841 oz. ASW, 38.5 mm. **Ruler:** Elizabeth II **Subject:** Millennium of Tynwald **Obv:** Young bust right **Rev:** Standing figure and ship

Date	Mintage	VF20	XF40	MS60	MS63	MS65
1979	10,000	PF65 24.00				
1979	25,000	—	—	—	16.00	22.00

KM# 49b CROWN

43.00 g., 0.917 Gold 1.2677 oz. AGW, 38.5 mm. **Ruler:** Elizabeth II **Subject:** Millennium of Tynwald **Obv:** Young bust right **Rev:** Standing figure and ship

Date	Mintage	VF20	XF40	MS60	MS63	MS65
1979	300	PF65 1,850				

KM# 49c CROWN

52.00 g., 0.950 Platinum 1.5882 oz. APW, 38.5 mm. **Ruler:** Elizabeth II **Subject:** Millennium of Tynwald **Obv:** Young bust right **Rev:** Standing figure and ship

Date	Mintage	VF20	XF40	MS60	MS63	MS65
1979	100	PF65 2,000				

KM# 50 CROWN

28.28 g., Copper-Nickel, 38.5 mm. **Ruler:** Elizabeth II **Subject:** Millennium of Tynwald **Obv:** Young bust right **Rev:** Lifeboat and Sir William Hillory portrait **Edge:** Reeded

Date	Mintage	VF20	XF40	MS60	MS63	MS65
1979	100,000	—	—	—	8.00	9.00

KM# 50a CROWN

28.28 g., 0.925 Silver 0.841 oz. ASW, 38.5 mm. **Ruler:** Elizabeth II **Subject:** Millennium of Tynwald **Obv:** Young bust right **Rev:** Lifeboat and Sir William Hillory portrait

Date	Mintage	VF20	XF40	MS60	MS63	MS65
1979	25,000	—	—	—	16.00	22.00
1979	10,000	PF65 24.00				

KM# 50b CROWN

43.00 g., 0.917 Gold 1.2677 oz. AGW, 38.5 mm. **Ruler:** Elizabeth II **Subject:** Millennium of Tynwald **Obv:** Young bust right **Rev:** Lifeboat and Sir William Hillory portrait

Date	Mintage	VF20	XF40	MS60	MS63	MS65
1979	300	PF65 1,850				

KM# 50c CROWN

52.00 g., 0.950 Platinum 1.5882 oz. APW, 38.5 mm. **Ruler:** Elizabeth II **Subject:** Millennium of Tynwald **Obv:** Young bust right **Rev:** Lifeboat and Sir William Hillory portrait

Date	Mintage	VF20	XF40	MS60	MS63	MS65
1979	100	PF65 2,000				

KM# 63 CROWN

Copper-Nickel, 38.5 mm. **Ruler:** Elizabeth II **Subject:** Derby Bicentennial **Obv:** Young bust right **Rev:** Men racing horses **Edge:** Reeded

Date	Mintage	VF20	XF40	MS60	MS63	MS65
1980	100,000	—	—	—	6.00	10.00

KM# 63a CROWN

28.28 g., 0.925 Silver 0.841 oz. ASW, 38.5 mm. **Ruler:** Elizabeth II **Subject:** Derby Bicentennial **Obv:** Young bust right **Rev:** Men racing horses

Date	Mintage	VF20	XF40	MS60	MS63	MS65
1980	35,000	—	—	—	16.00	22.00
1980	20,000	PF65 24.00				

KM# 63b CROWN

43.00 g., 0.917 Gold 1.2677 oz. AGW, 38.5 mm. **Ruler:** Elizabeth II **Subject:** Derby Bicentennial **Obv:** Young bust right **Rev:** Men racing horses

Date	Mintage	VF20	XF40	MS60	MS63	MS65
1980	—	PF65 1,850				

KM# 63c CROWN

52.00 g., 0.950 Platinum 1.5882 oz. APW, 38.5 mm. **Ruler:** Elizabeth II **Subject:** Derby Bicentennial **Obv:** Young bust right **Rev:** Men racing horses

Date	Mintage	VF20	XF40	MS60	MS63	MS65
1980	500	PF65 2,000				

KM# 64 CROWN

Copper-Nickel, 38.5 mm. **Ruler:** Elizabeth II **Subject:** 1980 Winter Olympics - Lake Placid **Obv:** Young bust right **Rev:** Triskeles at center of assorted olympic figures **Edge:** Reeded

Date	Mintage	VF20	XF40	MS60	MS63	MS65
1980	—	—	—	—	—	—
Note: With dot between Olympics and Lake						
1980	100,000	—	—	—	3.00	4.00
Note: Without dot						
1980 Prooflike	—	—	—	—	7.50	9.00

KM# 64a CROWN

28.28 g., 0.925 Silver 0.841 oz. ASW, 38.5 mm. **Ruler:** Elizabeth II **Subject:** 1980 Winter Olympics - Lake Placid **Obv:** Young bust right **Rev:** Triskeles at center of assorted olympic figures

Date	Mintage	VF20	XF40	MS60	MS63	MS65
1980 Matte	—	—	—	—	26.00	28.00
1980	10,000	PF65 32.00				

KM# 64b CROWN

39.80 g., 0.917 Gold 1.1734 oz. AGW, 38.5 mm. **Ruler:** Elizabeth II **Subject:** 1980 Winter Olympics - Lake Placid **Obv:** Young bust right **Rev:** Triskeles at center of assorted olympic figures

Date	Mintage	VF20	XF40	MS60	MS63	MS65
1980	1,500	—	—	—	—	1,850
Note: With dot between Olympics and Lake						
1980	500	PF65 1,850				

KM# 64c CROWN

52.00 g., 0.950 Platinum 1.5882 oz. APW, 38.5 mm. **Ruler:** Elizabeth II **Subject:** 1980 Winter Olympics - Lake Placid **Obv:** Young bust right **Rev:** Triskeles at center of assorted olympic figures

Date	Mintage	VF20	XF40	MS60	MS63	MS65
1980	100	PF65 2,000				
Note: With dot between Olympics and Lake						

KM# 65 CROWN

Copper-Nickel, 38.5 mm. **Ruler:** Elizabeth II **Subject:** 1980 Summer Olympics - Moscow **Obv:** Young bust right **Rev:** Triskeles at center of assorted olympic figures

Date	Mintage	VF20	XF40	MS60	MS63	MS65
1980	—	—	—	—	3.50	4.00
Note: Without dot between Olympiad and Moscow; without dots to right and left of One Crown						
1980	—	—	—	—	3.50	4.00
Note: Without dot between Olympiad and Moscow; with dots to right and left of One Crown						
1980	30,000	—	—	—	3.50	4.00
Note: With dot between Olympiad and Moscow; with dots to right and left of One Crown						
1980 Prooflike	—	—	—	—	7.50	9.00

KM# 65a CROWN

28.28 g., 0.925 Silver 0.841 oz. ASW, 38.5 mm. **Ruler:** Elizabeth II **Subject:** 1980 Summer Olympics - Moscow **Obv:** Young bust right **Rev:** Triskeles at center of assorted olympic figures

Date	Mintage	VF20	XF40	MS60	MS63	MS65
1980	—	—	—	—	16.00	22.00
Note: Without dot between Olympiad and Moscow; without dots to right and left of One Crown						
1980	—	—	—	—	16.00	22.00
Note: Without dot between Olympiad and Moscow; with dots to right and left of One Crown						
1980	—	—	—	—	16.00	22.00
Note: With dot between Olympiad and Moscow; with dots to right and left of One Crown						
1980	10,000	PF65 24.00				

KM# 65b CROWN

39.80 g., 0.917 Gold 1.1734 oz. AGW, 38.5 mm. **Ruler:** Elizabeth II **Subject:** 1980 Summer Olympics - Moscow **Obv:** Young bust right **Rev:** Triskeles at center of assorted olympic figures

Date	Mintage	VF20	XF40	MS60	MS63	MS65
1980	1,500	—	—	—	—	1,850
Note: With dot between Olympiad and Moscow; with dots to right and left of One Crown						

KM# 65c CROWN

52.00 g., 0.950 Platinum 1.5882 oz. APW, 38.5 mm. **Ruler:** Elizabeth II **Subject:** 1980 Summer Olympics - Moscow **Obv:** Young bust right **Rev:** Triskeles at center of assorted olympic figures

Date	Mintage	VF20	XF40	MS60	MS63	MS65
1980	100	PF65 2,000				
Note: With dot between Olympiad and Moscow; with dots to right and left of One Crown						

KM# 66 CROWN

Copper-Nickel, 38.5 mm. **Ruler:** Elizabeth II **Subject:** 1980 Summer Olympics - Moscow **Obv:** Young bust right **Rev:** Triskeles at center of assorted olympic figures **Edge:** Reeded

Date	Mintage	VF20	XF40	MS60	MS63	MS65
1980	30,000	—	—	—	6.00	7.00
1980 Prooflike	—	—	—	—	7.50	9.00

KM# 66a CROWN

28.28 g., 0.925 Silver 0.841 oz. ASW, 38.5 mm. **Ruler:** Elizabeth II **Subject:** 1980 Summer Olympics - Moscow **Obv:** Young bust right **Rev:** Triskeles at center of assorted olympic figures

Date	Mintage	VF20	XF40	MS60	MS63	MS65
1980 Matte	—	—	—	—	16.00	22.00
1980	10,000	PF65 24.00				

KM# 66b CROWN

39.80 g., 0.917 Gold 1.1734 oz. AGW, 38.5 mm. **Ruler:** Elizabeth II **Subject:** 1980 Summer Olympics - Moscow **Obv:** Young bust right **Rev:** Triskeles at center of assorted olympic figures

Date	Mintage	VF20	XF40	MS60	MS63	MS65
1980	1,500	—	—	—	—	1,850

KM# 66c CROWN

52.00 g., 0.950 Platinum 1.5882 oz. APW, 38.5 mm. **Ruler:** Elizabeth II **Subject:** 1980 Summer Olympics - Moscow **Obv:** Young bust right **Rev:** Triskeles at center of assorted olympic figures

Date	Mintage	VF20	XF40	MS60	MS63	MS65
1980	100	PF65 2,000				

KM# 67 CROWN

Copper-Lead Alloy, 38.5 mm. **Ruler:** Elizabeth II **Subject:** 1980 Summer Olympics - Moscow **Obv:** Young bust right **Rev:** Triskeles at center of assorted olympic figures **Edge:** Reeded

Date	Mintage	VF20	XF40	MS60	MS63	MS65
1980	30,000	—	—	—	6.00	7.00
1980 Proof like	—	—	—	—	7.50	9.00

KM# 67a CROWN

28.28 g., 0.925 Silver 0.841 oz. ASW, 38.5 mm. **Ruler:** Elizabeth II **Subject:** 1980 Summer Olympics - Moscow **Obv:** Young bust right **Rev:** Triskeles at center of assorted olympic figures

Date	Mintage	VF20	XF40	MS60	MS63	MS65
1980 Matte	—	—	—	—	16.00	22.00
1980	10,000	PF65 24.00				

KM# 67b CROWN
39.80 g., 0.917 Gold 1.1734 oz. AGW, 38.5 mm. **Ruler:** Elizabeth II **Subject:** 1980 Summer Olympics - Moscow **Obv:** Young bust right **Rev:** Triskeles at center of assorted olympic figures

Date	Mintage	VF20	XF40	MS60	MS63	MS65
1980	1,500	—	—	—	—	1,850

KM# 67c CROWN
52.00 g., 0.950 Platinum 1.5882 oz. APW, 38.5 mm. **Ruler:** Elizabeth II **Subject:** 1980 Summer Olympics - Moscow **Obv:** Young bust right **Rev:** Triskeles at center of assorted olympic figures

Date	Mintage	VF20	XF40	MS60	MS63	MS65
1980	100	PF65 2,000				

KM# 68 CROWN
Copper-Nickel, 38.5 mm. **Ruler:** Elizabeth II **Subject:** 80th Birthday of Queen Mother **Obv:** Young bust right **Rev:** Crowned head facing divides dates **Edge:** Reeded

Date	Mintage	VF20	XF40	MS60	MS63	MS65
1980	100,000	—	—	—	5.00	6.00

KM# 68a CROWN
28.28 g., 0.500 Silver 0.4546 oz. ASW, 38.5 mm. **Ruler:** Elizabeth II **Subject:** 80th Birthday of Queen Mother **Obv:** Young bust right **Rev:** Crowned head facing divides dates

Date	Mintage	VF20	XF40	MS60	MS63	MS65
1980	50,000	—	—	—	16.00	17.50

KM# 68b CROWN
28.28 g., 0.925 Silver 0.841 oz. ASW, 38.5 mm. **Ruler:** Elizabeth II **Subject:** 80th Birthday of Queen Mother **Obv:** Young bust right **Rev:** Crowned head facing divides dates

Date	Mintage	VF20	XF40	MS60	MS63	MS65
1980	30,000	PF65 32.50				

KM# 68c CROWN
5.00 g., 0.374 Gold 0.0601 oz. AGW **Ruler:** Elizabeth II **Subject:** 80th Birthday of Queen Mother **Obv:** Young bust right **Rev:** Crowned head of Queen Mother facing, divides dates

Date	Mintage	VF20	XF40	MS60	MS63	MS65
1980	50,000	—	—	—	—	120

KM# 68d CROWN
7.96 g., 0.917 Gold 0.2347 oz. AGW, 38.5 mm. **Ruler:** Elizabeth II **Subject:** 80th Birthday of Queen Mother **Obv:** Young bust right **Rev:** Crowned head of Queen Mother facing, divides dates

Date	Mintage	VF20	XF40	MS60	MS63	MS65
1980	1,000	—	—	—	—	400

KM# 73 CROWN
Copper-Nickel, 38.5 mm. **Ruler:** Elizabeth II **Subject:** Duke of Edinburgh Award Scheme **Obv:** Young bust right **Rev:** Bust facing **Edge:** Reeded

Date	Mintage	VF20	XF40	MS60	MS63	MS65
1981	50,000	—	—	—	2.50	3.50

KM# 73a CROWN
28.28 g., 0.925 Silver 0.841 oz. ASW, 38.5 mm. **Ruler:** Elizabeth II **Subject:** Duke of Edinburgh Award Scheme **Obv:** Young bust right **Rev:** Bust facing

Date	Mintage	VF20	XF40	MS60	MS63	MS65
1981	20,000	—	—	—	16.00	22.00
1981	15,000	PF65 24.00				

KM# 73b CROWN
5.10 g., 0.374 Gold 0.0613 oz. AGW **Ruler:** Elizabeth II **Subject:** Duke of Edinburgh Award Scheme **Obv:** Young bust right **Rev:** Bust facing

Date	Mintage	VF20	XF40	MS60	MS63	MS65
1981	10,000	PF65 125				

KM# 73c CROWN
7.96 g., 0.917 Gold 0.2347 oz. AGW **Ruler:** Elizabeth II **Subject:** Duke of Edinburgh Award Scheme **Obv:** Young bust right **Rev:** Bust facing

Date	Mintage	VF20	XF40	MS60	MS63	MS65
1981	1,000	PF65 400				

KM# 73d CROWN
52.00 g., 0.950 Platinum 1.5882 oz. APW, 38.5 mm. **Ruler:** Elizabeth II **Subject:** Duke of Edinburgh Award Scheme **Obv:** Young bust right **Rev:** Bust facing

Date	Mintage	VF20	XF40	MS60	MS63	MS65
1981	100	PF65 2,000				

KM# 74 CROWN
Copper-Nickel, 38.5 mm. **Ruler:** Elizabeth II **Subject:** Duke of Edinburgh Award Scheme **Obv:** Young bust right **Rev:** Monogram within crowned belt within sprigs **Edge:** Reeded

Date	Mintage	VF20	XF40	MS60	MS63	MS65
1981	50,000	—	—	—	6.00	7.00

KM# 74a CROWN
28.28 g., 0.925 Silver 0.841 oz. ASW, 38.5 mm. **Ruler:** Elizabeth II **Subject:** Duke of Edinburgh Award Scheme **Obv:** Young bust right **Rev:** Monogram within crowned belt within sprigs

Date	Mintage	VF20	XF40	MS60	MS63	MS65
1981	20,000	—	—	—	16.00	22.00
1981	15,000	PF65 24.00				

KM# 74b CROWN
5.10 g., 0.374 Gold 0.0613 oz. AGW **Ruler:** Elizabeth II **Subject:** Duke of Edinburgh Award Scheme **Obv:** Young bust right **Rev:** Monogram within crowned garter within sprigs

Date	Mintage	VF20	XF40	MS60	MS63	MS65
1981	10,000	PF65 125				

KM# 74c CROWN
7.96 g., 0.917 Gold 0.2347 oz. AGW **Ruler:** Elizabeth II **Subject:** Duke of Edinburgh Award Scheme **Obv:** Young bust right **Rev:** Monogram within crowned garter within sprigs

Date	Mintage	VF20	XF40	MS60	MS63	MS65
1981	1,000	PF65 400				

KM# 74d CROWN
52.00 g., 0.950 Platinum 1.5882 oz. APW, 38.5 mm. **Ruler:** Elizabeth II **Subject:** Duke of Edinburgh Award Scheme **Obv:** Young bust right **Rev:** Monogram within crowned garter within sprigs

Date	Mintage	VF20	XF40	MS60	MS63	MS65
1981	100	PF65 2,000				

KM# 75 CROWN
Copper-Nickel, 38.5 mm. **Ruler:** Elizabeth II **Subject:** Duke of Edinburgh Award Scheme **Obv:** Young bust right **Rev:** Nursing, hiking, swimming **Edge:** Reeded

Date	Mintage	VF20	XF40	MS60	MS63	MS65
1981	50,000	—	—	—	6.00	7.00

KM# 75a CROWN
28.28 g., 0.925 Silver 0.841 oz. ASW, 38.5 mm. **Ruler:** Elizabeth II **Subject:** Duke of Edinburgh Award Scheme **Obv:** Young bust right **Rev:** Nursing, hiking, swimming

Date	Mintage	VF20	XF40	MS60	MS63	MS65
1981	20,000	—	—	—	16.00	22.00
1981	15,000	PF65 24.00				

KM# 75b CROWN
5.10 g., 0.374 Gold 0.0613 oz. AGW **Ruler:** Elizabeth II **Subject:** Duke of Edinburgh Award Scheme **Obv:** Young bust right **Rev:** Nursing, hiking, swimming

Date	Mintage	VF20	XF40	MS60	MS63	MS65
1981	10,000	PF65 120				

KM# 75c CROWN
7.96 g., 0.917 Gold 0.2347 oz. AGW **Ruler:** Elizabeth II **Subject:** Duke of Edinburgh Award Scheme **Obv:** Young bust right **Rev:** Nursing, hiking, swimming

Date	Mintage	VF20	XF40	MS60	MS63	MS65
1981	1,000	PF65 400				

KM# 75d CROWN
52.00 g., 0.950 Platinum 1.5882 oz. APW, 38.5 mm. **Ruler:** Elizabeth II **Subject:** Duke of Edinburgh Award Scheme **Obv:** Young bust right **Rev:** Nursing, hiking, swimming

Date	Mintage	VF20	XF40	MS60	MS63	MS65
1981	100	PF65 2,000				

KM# 76 CROWN
Copper-Nickel, 38.5 mm. **Ruler:** Elizabeth II **Subject:** Duke of Edinburgh Award Scheme **Obv:** Young bust right **Rev:** Rock climbing, sailing, motorcycling **Edge:** Reeded

Date	Mintage	VF20	XF40	MS60	MS63	MS65
1981	50,000	—	—	—	6.00	7.00

KM# 76a CROWN
28.28 g., 0.925 Silver 0.841 oz. ASW, 38.5 mm. **Ruler:** Elizabeth II **Subject:** Duke of Edinburgh Award Scheme **Obv:** Young bust right **Rev:** Rock climbing, sailing, motorcycling

Date	Mintage	VF20	XF40	MS60	MS63	MS65
1981	20,000	—	—	—	16.00	22.00
1981	15,000	PF65 24.00				

KM# 76b CROWN
5.10 g., 0.374 Gold 0.0613 oz. AGW **Ruler:** Elizabeth II **Subject:** Duke of Edinburgh Award Scheme **Obv:** Young bust right **Rev:** Rock climbing, sailing, motorcycling

Date	Mintage	VF20	XF40	MS60	MS63	MS65
1981	10,000	PF65 120				

KM# 76c CROWN
7.96 g., 0.917 Gold 0.2347 oz. AGW **Ruler:** Elizabeth II **Subject:** Duke of Edinburgh Award Scheme **Obv:** Young bust right **Rev:** Rock climbing, sailing, motorcycling

Date	Mintage	VF20	XF40	MS60	MS63	MS65
1981	1,000	PF65 400				

KM# 76d CROWN
52.00 g., 0.950 Platinum 1.5882 oz. APW, 38.5 mm. **Ruler:** Elizabeth II **Subject:** Duke of Edinburgh Award Scheme **Obv:** Young bust right **Rev:** Rock climbing, sailing, motorcycling

Date	Mintage	VF20	XF40	MS60	MS63	MS65
1981	100	PF65 2,000				

KM# 77 CROWN
Copper-Nickel, 38.5 mm. **Ruler:** Elizabeth II **Subject:** International Year of Disabled **Obv:** Young bust right **Rev:** Braille and bust 1/4 left **Edge:** Reeded

Date	Mintage	VF20	XF40	MS60	MS63	MS65
1981	50,000	—	—	—	2.50	3.50
1981 Prooflike	—	—	—	—	5.00	6.00

KM# 77a CROWN
28.28 g., 0.925 Silver 0.841 oz. ASW, 38.5 mm. **Ruler:** Elizabeth II **Subject:** International Year of Disabled **Obv:** Young bust right **Rev:** Braille and bust 1/4 left

Date	Mintage	VF20	XF40	MS60	MS63	MS65
1981	20,000	—	—	—	16.00	22.00
1981	15,000	PF65 24.00				

KM# 77b CROWN

5.10 g., 0.374 Gold 0.0613 oz. AGW **Ruler:** Elizabeth II **Subject:** International Year of Disabled **Obv:** Young bust right **Rev:** Braille and bust 1/4 left

Date	Mintage	VF20	XF40	MS60	MS63	MS65
1981	10,000	PF65 120				

KM# 77c CROWN

7.96 g., 0.917 Gold 0.2347 oz. AGW **Ruler:** Elizabeth II **Subject:** International Year of Disabled **Obv:** Young bust right **Rev:** Braille and bust 1/4 left

Date	Mintage	VF20	XF40	MS60	MS63	MS65
1981	1,000	PF65 400				

KM# 77d CROWN

52.00 g., 0.950 Platinum 1.5882 oz. APW, 38.5 mm. **Ruler:** Elizabeth II **Subject:** International Year of Disabled **Obv:** Young bust right **Rev:** Braille and bust 1/4 left

Date	Mintage	VF20	XF40	MS60	MS63	MS65
1981	100	PF65 2,000				

KM# 78 CROWN

Copper-Nickel, 38.5 mm. **Ruler:** Elizabeth II **Subject:** International Year of Disabled **Obv:** Young bust right **Rev:** Beethoven, violin and music score **Edge:** Reeded

Date	Mintage	VF20	XF40	MS60	MS63	MS65
1981	50,000	—	—	—	8.00	9.00
1981 Prooflike	—	—	—	—	10.00	12.00

KM# 78a CROWN

28.28 g., 0.925 Silver 0.841 oz. ASW, 38.5 mm. **Ruler:** Elizabeth II **Subject:** International Year of Disabled **Obv:** Young bust right **Rev:** Beethoven, violin and music score

Date	Mintage	VF20	XF40	MS60	MS63	MS65
1981	20,000	—	—	—	16.00	22.00
1981	15,000	PF65 24.00				

KM# 78b CROWN

5.10 g., 0.374 Gold 0.0613 oz. AGW **Ruler:** Elizabeth II **Subject:** International Year of Disabled **Obv:** Young bust right **Rev:** Beethoven, violin and music score

Date	Mintage	VF20	XF40	MS60	MS63	MS65
1981	10,000	PF65 120				

KM# 78c CROWN

7.96 g., 0.917 Gold 0.2347 oz. AGW **Ruler:** Elizabeth II **Subject:** International Year of Disabled **Obv:** Young bust right **Rev:** Beethoven, violin and music score

Date	Mintage	VF20	XF40	MS60	MS63	MS65
1981	1,000	PF65 400				

KM# 78d CROWN

52.00 g., 0.950 Platinum 1.5882 oz. APW, 38.5 mm. **Ruler:** Elizabeth II **Subject:** International Year of Disabled **Obv:** Young bust right **Rev:** Beethoven, violin and music score

Date	Mintage	VF20	XF40	MS60	MS63	MS65
1981	100	PF65 2,000				

KM# 79 CROWN

Copper-Nickel, 38.5 mm. **Ruler:** Elizabeth II **Subject:** International Year of Disabled **Obv:** Young bust right **Rev:** Bust facing **Edge:** Reeded

Date	Mintage	VF20	XF40	MS60	MS63	MS65
1981	50,000	—	—	—	8.00	9.00
1981 Prooflike	—	—	—	—	9.00	10.00

KM# 79a CROWN

28.28 g., 0.925 Silver 0.841 oz. ASW, 38.5 mm. **Ruler:** Elizabeth II **Subject:** International Year of Disabled **Obv:** Young bust right **Rev:** Bust facing

Date	Mintage	VF20	XF40	MS60	MS63	MS65
1981	20,000	—	—	—	16.00	22.00
1981	15,000	PF65 24.00				

KM# 79b CROWN

5.10 g., 0.374 Gold 0.0613 oz. AGW **Ruler:** Elizabeth II **Subject:** International Year of Disabled **Obv:** Young bust right **Rev:** Bust facing

Date	Mintage	VF20	XF40	MS60	MS63	MS65
1981	10,000	PF65 120				

KM# 79c CROWN

7.96 g., 0.917 Gold 0.2347 oz. AGW **Ruler:** Elizabeth II **Subject:** International Year of Disabled **Obv:** Young bust right **Rev:** Bust facing

Date	Mintage	VF20	XF40	MS60	MS63	MS65
1981	1,000	PF65 400				

KM# 79d CROWN

52.00 g., 0.950 Platinum 1.5882 oz. APW, 38.5 mm. **Ruler:** Elizabeth II **Subject:** International Year of Disabled **Obv:** Young bust right **Rev:** Bust facing

Date	Mintage	VF20	XF40	MS60	MS63	MS65
1981	100	PF65 2,000				

KM# 80 CROWN

Copper-Nickel, 38.5 mm. **Ruler:** Elizabeth II **Subject:** International Year of Disabled **Obv:** Young bust right **Rev:** Sir Francis Chichester (1901-1972) bust 1/4 left and sailboat **Edge:** Reeded

Date	Mintage	VF20	XF40	MS60	MS63	MS65
1981	50,000	—	—	—	8.00	9.00
1981 Prooflike	—	—	—	—	9.00	10.00

KM# 80a CROWN

28.28 g., 0.925 Silver 0.841 oz. ASW, 38.5 mm. **Ruler:** Elizabeth II **Subject:** International Year of Disabled **Obv:** Young bust right **Rev:** Uniformed bust 1/4 left and sailboat

Date	Mintage	VF20	XF40	MS60	MS63	MS65
1981	20,000	—	—	—	16.00	22.00
1981	15,000	PF65 24.00				

KM# 80b CROWN

5.10 g., 0.374 Gold 0.0613 oz. AGW **Ruler:** Elizabeth II **Subject:** International Year of Disabled **Obv:** Young bust right **Rev:** Uniformed bust 1/4 left and sailboat

Date	Mintage	VF20	XF40	MS60	MS63	MS65
1981	10,000	PF65 120				

KM# 80c CROWN

7.96 g., 0.917 Gold 0.2347 oz. AGW **Ruler:** Elizabeth II **Subject:** International Year of Disabled **Obv:** Young bust right **Rev:** Uniformed bust 1/4 left and sailboat

Date	Mintage	VF20	XF40	MS60	MS63	MS65
1981	1,000	PF65 400				

KM# 80d CROWN

52.00 g., 0.950 Platinum 1.5882 oz. APW, 38.5 mm. **Ruler:** Elizabeth II **Subject:** International Year of Disabled **Obv:** Young bust right **Rev:** Uniformed bust 1/4 left and sailboat

Date	Mintage	VF20	XF40	MS60	MS63	MS65
1981	100	PF65 2,000				

KM# 81 CROWN

Copper-Nickel, 38.5 mm. **Ruler:** Elizabeth II **Subject:** Wedding of Prince Charles and Lady Diana **Obv:** Young bust right **Rev:** Crown above shields

Date	Mintage	VF20	XF40	MS60	MS63	MS65
1981	50,000	—	—	—	6.00	7.00

KM# 81a CROWN

28.28 g., 0.925 Silver 0.841 oz. ASW, 38.5 mm. **Ruler:** Elizabeth II **Subject:** Wedding of Prince Charles and Lady Diana **Obv:** Young bust right **Rev:** Crown above shields

Date	Mintage	VF20	XF40	MS60	MS63	MS65
1981	20,000	—	—	—	16.00	22.00
1981	15,000	PF65 24.00				

KM# 81b CROWN

5.10 g., 0.374 Gold 0.0613 oz. AGW **Ruler:** Elizabeth II **Subject:** Wedding of Prince Charles and Lady Diana **Obv:** Young bust right **Rev:** Crown above shields **Edge:** Reeded

Date	Mintage	VF20	XF40	MS60	MS63	MS65
1981	10,000	PF65 120				

KM# 81c CROWN

7.96 g., 0.917 Gold 0.2347 oz. AGW **Ruler:** Elizabeth II **Subject:** Wedding of Prince Charles and Lady Diana **Obv:** Young bust right **Rev:** Crown above shields

Date	Mintage	VF20	XF40	MS60	MS63	MS65
1981	1,000	PF65 400				

KM# 81d CROWN

52.00 g., 0.950 Platinum 1.5882 oz. APW, 38.5 mm. **Ruler:** Elizabeth II **Subject:** Wedding of Prince Charles and Lady Diana **Obv:** Young bust right **Rev:** Crown above shields

Date	Mintage	VF20	XF40	MS60	MS63	MS65
1981	100	PF65 2,000				

KM# 82 CROWN

Copper-Nickel, 38.5 mm. **Ruler:** Elizabeth II **Subject:** Wedding of Prince Charles and Lady Diana **Obv:** Young bust right **Rev:** Conjoined heads right **Edge:** Reeded

Date	Mintage	VF20	XF40	MS60	MS63	MS65
1981	50,000	—	—	—	6.00	7.00

KM# 82a CROWN

28.28 g., 0.925 Silver 0.841 oz. ASW, 38.5 mm. **Ruler:** Elizabeth II **Subject:** Wedding of Prince Charles and Lady Diana **Obv:** Young bust right **Rev:** Conjoined heads right

Date	Mintage	VF20	XF40	MS60	MS63	MS65
1981	20,000	—	—	—	16.00	22.00
1981	15,000	PF65 24.00				

KM# 82b CROWN

5.10 g., 0.374 Gold 0.0613 oz. AGW **Ruler:** Elizabeth II **Subject:** Wedding of Prince Charles and Lady Diana **Obv:** Young bust right **Rev:** Conjoined heads right

Date	Mintage	VF20	XF40	MS60	MS63	MS65
1981	10,000	PF65 120				

KM# 82c CROWN

7.96 g., 0.917 Gold 0.2347 oz. AGW **Ruler:** Elizabeth II **Subject:** Wedding of Prince Charles and Lady Diana **Obv:** Young bust right **Rev:** Conjoined heads right

Date	Mintage	VF20	XF40	MS60	MS63	MS65
1981	1,000	PF65 400				

KM# 82d CROWN

52.00 g., 0.950 Platinum 1.5882 oz. APW, 38.5 mm. **Ruler:** Elizabeth II **Subject:** Wedding of Prince Charles and Lady Diana **Obv:** Young bust right **Rev:** Conjoined heads right

Date	Mintage	VF20	XF40	MS60	MS63	MS65
1981	—	PF65 2,000				

KM# 91 CROWN

Copper-Nickel, 38.5 mm. **Ruler:** Elizabeth II **Series:** XII World Cup - Spain **Obv:** Young bust right **Rev:** Half figure holding World Cup trophy within map

Date	Mintage	VF20	XF40	MS60	MS63	MS65
1982	50,000	—	—	—	3.50	4.50

KM# 91a CROWN

28.28 g., 0.925 Silver 0.841 oz. ASW, 38.5 mm. **Ruler:** Elizabeth II **Series:** XII World Cup - Spain **Obv:** Young bust right **Rev:** Half figure holding World Cup trophy within map

Date	Mintage	VF20	XF40	MS60	MS63	MS65
1982	20,000	—	—	—	16.00	22.00
1982	15,000	PF65 24.00				

KM# 91b CROWN

5.10 g., 0.374 Gold 0.0613 oz. AGW **Ruler:** Elizabeth II **Series:** XII World Cup - Spain **Obv:** Young bust right **Rev:** Half figure holding World Cup trophy within map

Date	Mintage	VF20	XF40	MS60	MS63	MS65
1982	40,000	PF65 120				

KM# 91c CROWN
7.96 g., 0.917 Gold 0.2347 oz. AGW **Ruler:** Elizabeth II **Series:** XII World Cup - Spain **Obv:** Young bust right **Rev:** Half figure holding World Cup trophy within map

Date	Mintage	VF20	XF40	MS60	MS63	MS65
1982	4,000	PF65 400				

KM# 91d CROWN
52.00 g., 0.950 Platinum 1.5882 oz. APW, 38.5 mm. **Ruler:** Elizabeth II **Series:** XII World Cup - Spain **Obv:** Young bust right **Rev:** Half figure holding World Cup trophy within map

Date	Mintage	VF20	XF40	MS60	MS63	MS65
1982	100	PF65 2,000				

KM# 92 CROWN
Copper-Nickel, 38.5 mm. **Ruler:** Elizabeth II **Series:** XII World Cup - Spain **Obv:** Young bust right **Rev:** Triskeles at center of assorted shields

Date	Mintage	VF20	XF40	MS60	MS63	MS65
1982	50,000	—	—	—	3.50	4.50

KM# 92a CROWN
28.28 g., 0.925 Silver 0.841 oz. ASW, 38.5 mm. **Ruler:** Elizabeth II **Series:** XII World Cup - Spain **Obv:** Young bust right **Rev:** Triskeles at center of assorted shields

Date	Mintage	VF20	XF40	MS60	MS63	MS65
1982	20,000	—	—	—	16.00	22.00
1982	15,000	PF65 24.00				

KM# 92b CROWN
5.10 g., 0.374 Gold 0.0613 oz. AGW **Ruler:** Elizabeth II **Series:** XII World Cup - Spain **Obv:** Young bust right **Rev:** Triskeles at center of assorted shields

Date	Mintage	VF20	XF40	MS60	MS63	MS65
1982	40,000	PF65 120				

KM# 92c CROWN
7.96 g., 0.917 Gold 0.2347 oz. AGW **Ruler:** Elizabeth II **Series:** XII World Cup - Spain **Obv:** Young bust right **Rev:** Triskeles at center of assorted shields

Date	Mintage	VF20	XF40	MS60	MS63	MS65
1982	4,000	PF65 400				

KM# 92d CROWN
52.00 g., 0.950 Platinum 1.5882 oz. APW, 38.5 mm. **Ruler:** Elizabeth II **Series:** XII World Cup - Spain **Obv:** Young bust right **Rev:** Triskeles at center of assorted shields

Date	Mintage	VF20	XF40	MS60	MS63	MS65
1982	100	PF65 2,000				

KM# 93 CROWN
Copper-Nickel, 38.5 mm. **Ruler:** Elizabeth II **Series:** XII World Cup - Spain **Obv:** Young bust right **Rev:** Soccer scenes

Date	Mintage	VF20	XF40	MS60	MS63	MS65
1982	50,000	—	—	—	8.00	9.00
1982 (sb)	—	—	—	—	9.00	10.00

KM# 93a CROWN
28.28 g., 0.925 Silver 0.841 oz. ASW, 38.5 mm. **Ruler:** Elizabeth II **Series:** XII World Cup - Spain **Obv:** Young bust right **Rev:** Soccer scenes

Date	Mintage	VF20	XF40	MS60	MS63	MS65
1982	20,000	—	—	—	16.00	22.00
1982	15,000	PF65 24.00				

KM# 93b CROWN
5.10 g., 0.374 Gold 0.0613 oz. AGW **Ruler:** Elizabeth II **Series:** XII World Cup - Spain **Obv:** Young bust right **Rev:** Soccer scenes

Date	Mintage	VF20	XF40	MS60	MS63	MS65
1982	40,000	PF65 120				

KM# 93c CROWN
7.96 g., 0.917 Gold 0.2347 oz. AGW **Ruler:** Elizabeth II **Series:** XII World Cup - Spain **Obv:** Young bust right **Rev:** Soccer scenes

Date	Mintage	VF20	XF40	MS60	MS63	MS65
1982	4,000	PF65 400				

KM# 93d CROWN
52.00 g., 0.950 Platinum 1.5882 oz. APW, 38.5 mm. **Ruler:** Elizabeth II **Series:** XII World Cup - Spain **Obv:** Young bust right **Rev:** Soccer scenes

Date	Mintage	VF20	XF40	MS60	MS63	MS65
1982	100	PF65 2,000				

KM# 94 CROWN
Copper-Nickel, 38.5 mm. **Ruler:** Elizabeth II **Series:** XII World Cup - Spain **Obv:** Young bust right **Rev:** Soccer scenes

Date	Mintage	VF20	XF40	MS60	MS63	MS65
1982	50,000	—	—	—	8.00	9.00

KM# 94a CROWN
28.28 g., 0.925 Silver 0.841 oz. ASW, 38.5 mm. **Ruler:** Elizabeth II **Series:** XII World Cup - Spain **Obv:** Young bust right **Rev:** Soccer scenes

Date	Mintage	VF20	XF40	MS60	MS63	MS65
1982	20,000	—	—	—	16.00	22.00
1982	15,000	PF65 24.00				

KM# 94b CROWN
5.10 g., 0.374 Gold 0.0613 oz. AGW **Ruler:** Elizabeth II **Series:** XII World Cup - Spain **Obv:** Young bust right **Rev:** Soccer scenes

Date	Mintage	VF20	XF40	MS60	MS63	MS65
1982	40,000	PF65 120				

KM# 94c CROWN
7.96 g., 0.917 Gold 0.2347 oz. AGW **Ruler:** Elizabeth II **Series:** XII World Cup - Spain **Obv:** Young bust right **Rev:** Soccer scenes

Date	Mintage	VF20	XF40	MS60	MS63	MS65
1982	4,000	PF65 400				

KM# 94d CROWN
52.00 g., 0.950 Platinum 1.5882 oz. APW, 38.5 mm. **Ruler:** Elizabeth II **Series:** XII World Cup - Spain **Obv:** Young bust right **Rev:** Soccer scenes

Date	Mintage	VF20	XF40	MS60	MS63	MS65
1982	100	PF65 2,000				

KM# 95 CROWN
Copper-Nickel, 38.5 mm. **Ruler:** Elizabeth II **Series:** XII World Cup - Spain **Obv:** Young bust right **Rev:** Assorted shields

Date	Mintage	VF20	XF40	MS60	MS63	MS65
1982	—	—	—	—	3.50	4.50

KM# 95a CROWN
28.28 g., 0.925 Silver 0.841 oz. ASW, 38.5 mm. **Ruler:** Elizabeth II **Series:** XII World Cup - Spain **Obv:** Young bust right **Rev:** Assorted shields

Date	Mintage	VF20	XF40	MS60	MS63	MS65
1982	—	PF65 24.00				

KM# 95b CROWN
5.10 g., 0.374 Gold 0.0613 oz. AGW **Ruler:** Elizabeth II **Series:** XII World Cup - Spain **Obv:** Young bust right **Rev:** Assorted shields

Date	Mintage	VF20	XF40	MS60	MS63	MS65
1982	3,000	PF65 120				

KM# 95c CROWN
7.96 g., 0.917 Gold 0.2347 oz. AGW **Ruler:** Elizabeth II **Series:** XII World Cup - Spain **Obv:** Young bust right **Rev:** Assorted shields

Date	Mintage	VF20	XF40	MS60	MS63	MS65
1982	—	PF65 400				

KM# 95d CROWN
52.00 g., 0.950 Platinum 1.5882 oz. APW, 38.5 mm. **Ruler:** Elizabeth II **Series:** XII World Cup - Spain **Obv:** Young bust right **Rev:** Assorted shields

Date	Mintage	VF20	XF40	MS60	MS63	MS65
1982	—	PF65 2,000				

KM# 96 CROWN
Copper-Nickel, 38.5 mm. **Ruler:** Elizabeth II **Series:** Maritime Heritage **Obv:** Young bust right **Rev:** Mayflower and cameo

Date	Mintage	VF20	XF40	MS60	MS63	MS65
1982	Est. 50000	—	—	—	9.00	10.00
1982 Prooflike	Inc. above	—	—	—	10.00	12.00

KM# 96a CROWN
28.28 g., 0.925 Silver 0.841 oz. ASW, 38.5 mm. **Ruler:** Elizabeth II **Series:** Maritime Heritage **Obv:** Young bust right **Rev:** Ship and cameo

Date	Mintage	VF20	XF40	MS60	MS63	MS65
1982	15,000	—	—	—	16.00	22.00
1982	10,000	PF65 24.00				

KM# 96b CROWN
5.10 g., 0.374 Gold 0.0613 oz. AGW **Ruler:** Elizabeth II **Series:** Maritime Heritage **Obv:** Crowned bust right **Rev:** Ship and cameo

Date	Mintage	VF20	XF40	MS60	MS63	MS65
1982	22,000	PF65 120				

KM# 96c CROWN
7.96 g., 0.917 Gold 0.2347 oz. AGW **Ruler:** Elizabeth II **Series:** Maritime Heritage **Obv:** Young bust right **Rev:** Ship and cameo

Date	Mintage	VF20	XF40	MS60	MS63	MS65
1982	2,000	PF65 400				

KM# 96d CROWN
52.00 g., 0.950 Platinum 1.5882 oz. APW, 38.5 mm. **Ruler:** Elizabeth II **Series:** Maritime Heritage **Obv:** Young bust right **Rev:** Ship and cameo

Date	Mintage	VF20	XF40	MS60	MS63	MS65
1982	50	PF65 2,000				

KM# 97 CROWN
Copper-Nickel, 38.5 mm. **Ruler:** Elizabeth II **Series:** Maritime Heritage **Obv:** Young bust right **Rev:** HMS Bounty and cameo of Fletcher Christian

Date	Mintage	VF20	XF40	MS60	MS63	MS65
1982	Est. 50000	—	—	—	3.00	4.00
1982 Prooflike	Inc. above	—	—	—	5.00	7.00

KM# 97a CROWN
28.28 g., 0.925 Silver 0.841 oz. ASW, 38.5 mm. **Ruler:** Elizabeth II **Series:** Maritime Heritage **Obv:** Young bust right **Rev:** Ship and cameo

Date	Mintage	VF20	XF40	MS60	MS63	MS65
1982	15,000	—	—	—	16.00	22.00
1982	10,000	PF65 24.00				

KM# 97b CROWN
5.10 g., 0.374 Gold 0.0613 oz. AGW **Ruler:** Elizabeth II **Series:** Maritime Heritage **Obv:** Young bust right **Rev:** Ship and cameo

Date	Mintage	VF20	XF40	MS60	MS63	MS65
1982	22,000	PF65 120				

KM# 97c CROWN
7.96 g., 0.917 Gold 0.2347 oz. AGW **Ruler:** Elizabeth II **Series:** Maritime Heritage **Obv:** Young bust right **Rev:** Ship and cameo

Date	Mintage	VF20	XF40	MS60	MS63	MS65
1982	2,000	PF65 400				

KM# 97d CROWN
52.00 g., 0.950 Platinum 1.5882 oz. APW, 38.5 mm. **Ruler:** Elizabeth II **Series:** Maritime Heritage **Obv:** Young bust right **Rev:** Ship and cameo

Date	Mintage	VF20	XF40	MS60	MS63	MS65
1982	50	PF65 2,000				

KM# 98 CROWN
Copper-Nickel, 38.5 mm. **Ruler:** Elizabeth II **Series:** Maritime Heritage **Obv:** Young bust right **Rev:** HMS Victory and cameo of Admiral Nelson

Date	Mintage	VF20	XF40	MS60	MS63	MS65
1982	Est. 50000	—	—	—	8.00	9.00
1982 Prooflike	Inc. above	—	—	—	9.00	10.00

KM# 98a CROWN
28.28 g., 0.925 Silver 0.841 oz. ASW, 38.5 mm. **Ruler:** Elizabeth II **Series:** Maritime Heritage **Obv:** young bust right **Rev:** Ship and cameo

Date	Mintage	VF20	XF40	MS60	MS63	MS65
1982	15,000	—	—	—	16.00	22.00
1982	10,000	PF65 24.00				

KM# 98b CROWN
5.10 g., 0.374 Gold 0.0613 oz. AGW **Ruler:** Elizabeth II **Series:** Maritime Heritage **Obv:** Young bust right **Rev:** Ship and cameo

Date	Mintage	VF20	XF40	MS60	MS63	MS65
1982	22,000	PF65 120				

KM# 98c CROWN
7.96 g., 0.917 Gold 0.2347 oz. AGW **Ruler:** Elizabeth II **Series:** Maritime Heritage **Obv:** Young bust right **Rev:** Ship and cameo

Date	Mintage	VF20	XF40	MS60	MS63	MS65
1982	2,000	PF65 400				

KM# 98d CROWN
52.00 g., 0.950 Platinum 1.5882 oz. APW, 38.5 mm. **Ruler:** Elizabeth II **Series:** Maritime Heritage **Obv:** Young bust right **Rev:** Ship and cameo

Date	Mintage	VF20	XF40	MS60	MS63	MS65
1982	50	PF65 2,000				

KM# 99 CROWN
Copper-Nickel, 38.5 mm. **Ruler:** Elizabeth II **Series:** Maritime Heritage **Obv:** Young bust right **Rev:** Ship and cameo

Date	Mintage	VF20	XF40	MS60	MS63	MS65
1982	Est. 50000	—	—	—	3.00	4.00
1982 Prooflike	Inc. above	—	—	—	5.00	7.00

KM# 99a CROWN
28.28 g., 0.925 Silver 0.841 oz. ASW, 38.5 mm. **Ruler:** Elizabeth II **Series:** Maritime Heritage **Obv:** Young bust right **Rev:** Ship and cameo

Date	Mintage	VF20	XF40	MS60	MS63	MS65
1982	15,000	—	—	—	16.00	22.00
1982	10,000	PF65 24.00				

KM# 99b CROWN
5.10 g., 0.374 Gold 0.0613 oz. AGW **Ruler:** Elizabeth II **Series:** Maritime Heritage **Obv:** Young bust right **Rev:** Ship and cameo

Date	Mintage	VF20	XF40	MS60	MS63	MS65
1982	22,000	PF65 120				

KM# 99c CROWN
7.96 g., 0.917 Gold 0.2347 oz. AGW **Ruler:** Elizabeth II **Series:** Maritime Heritage **Obv:** Young bust right **Rev:** Ship and cameo

Date	Mintage	VF20	XF40	MS60	MS63	MS65
1982	2,000	PF65 400				

KM# 99d CROWN
52.00 g., 0.950 Platinum 1.5882 oz. APW, 38.5 mm. **Ruler:** Elizabeth II **Series:** Maritime Heritage **Obv:** Young bust right **Rev:** Ship and cameo

Date	Mintage	VF20	XF40	MS60	MS63	MS65
1982	50	PF65 2,000				

KM# 103 CROWN
Copper-Nickel, 38.5 mm. **Ruler:** Elizabeth II **Series:** Manned Flight **Obv:** Young bust right **Rev:** Hot air balloon

Date	Mintage	VF20	XF40	MS60	MS63	MS65
1983	50,000	—	—	—	8.00	10.00
1983 DMIHE	—	—	—	—	15.00	17.00

KM# 103a CROWN
28.28 g., 0.925 Silver 0.841 oz. ASW, 38.5 mm. **Ruler:** Elizabeth II **Series:** Manned Flight **Obv:** Young bust right **Rev:** Hot air balloon

Date	Mintage	VF20	XF40	MS60	MS63	MS65
1983	15,000	—	—	—	16.00	22.00
1983	11,000	PF65 24.00				

KM# 103b CROWN
5.10 g., 0.374 Gold 0.0613 oz. AGW **Ruler:** Elizabeth II **Series:** Manned Flight **Obv:** Young bust right **Rev:** Hot air balloon

Date	Mintage	VF20	XF40	MS60	MS63	MS65
1983	5,500	PF65 125				

KM# 103c CROWN
7.96 g., 0.917 Gold 0.2347 oz. AGW **Ruler:** Elizabeth II **Series:** Manned Flight **Obv:** Young bust right **Rev:** Hot air balloon

Date	Mintage	VF20	XF40	MS60	MS63	MS65
1983	500	PF65 400				

KM# 103d CROWN
52.00 g., 0.950 Platinum 1.5882 oz. APW, 38.5 mm. **Ruler:** Elizabeth II **Series:** Manned Flight **Obv:** Young bust right **Rev:** Hot air balloon

Date	Mintage	VF20	XF40	MS60	MS63	MS65
1983	50	PF65 2,000				

KM# 104 CROWN
Copper-Nickel, 38.5 mm. **Ruler:** Elizabeth II **Series:** Manned Flight **Obv:** Young bust right **Rev:** Biplane

Date	Mintage	VF20	XF40	MS60	MS63	MS65
1983	50,000	—	—	—	8.00	10.00
1983 DMIHE	—	—	—	—	15.00	17.00

KM# 104a CROWN
28.28 g., 0.925 Silver 0.841 oz. ASW, 38.5 mm. **Ruler:** Elizabeth II **Series:** Manned Flight **Obv:** Young bust right **Rev:** Biplane

Date	Mintage	VF20	XF40	MS60	MS63	MS65
1983	15,000	—	—	—	16.00	22.00
1983	11,000	PF65 24.00				

KM# 104b CROWN
5.10 g., 0.374 Gold 0.0613 oz. AGW **Ruler:** Elizabeth II **Series:** Manned Flight **Obv:** Young bust right **Rev:** Biplane

Date	Mintage	VF20	XF40	MS60	MS63	MS65
1983	5,500	PF65 125				

KM# 104c CROWN
7.96 g., 0.917 Gold 0.2347 oz. AGW **Ruler:** Elizabeth II **Series:** Manned Flight **Obv:** Young bust right **Rev:** Biplane

Date	Mintage	VF20	XF40	MS60	MS63	MS65
1983	500	PF65 400				

KM# 104d CROWN
52.00 g., 0.950 Platinum 1.5882 oz. APW, 38.5 mm. **Ruler:** Elizabeth II **Series:** Manned Flight **Obv:** Young bust right **Rev:** Biplane

Date	Mintage	VF20	XF40	MS60	MS63	MS65
1983	50	PF65 2,000				

KM# 105 CROWN
Copper-Nickel, 38.5 mm. **Ruler:** Elizabeth II **Series:** Manned Flight **Obv:** Young bust right **Rev:** Jet

Date	Mintage	VF20	XF40	MS60	MS63	MS65
1983	50,000	—	—	—	8.00	10.00
1983 DMIHE	—	—	—	—	15.00	17.00

KM# 105a CROWN
28.28 g., 0.925 Silver 0.841 oz. ASW, 38.5 mm. **Ruler:** Elizabeth II **Series:** Manned Flight **Obv:** Young bust right **Rev:** Jet

Date	Mintage	VF20	XF40	MS60	MS63	MS65
1983	15,000	—	—	—	16.00	22.00
1983	11,000	PF65 24.00				

KM# 105b CROWN
5.10 g., 0.374 Gold 0.0613 oz. AGW **Ruler:** Elizabeth II **Series:** Manned Flight **Obv:** Young bust right **Rev:** Jet

Date	Mintage	VF20	XF40	MS60	MS63	MS65
1983	5,500	PF65 125				

KM# 105c CROWN
7.96 g., 0.917 Gold 0.2347 oz. AGW **Ruler:** Elizabeth II **Series:** Manned Flight **Obv:** Young bust right **Rev:** Jet

Date	Mintage	VF20	XF40	MS60	MS63	MS65
1983	500	PF65 400				

KM# 105d CROWN
52.00 g., 0.950 Platinum 1.5882 oz. APW, 38.5 mm. **Ruler:** Elizabeth II **Series:** Manned Flight **Obv:** Young bust right **Rev:** Jet

Date	Mintage	VF20	XF40	MS60	MS63	MS65
1983	50	PF65 2,000				

KM# 106 CROWN
Copper-Nickel, 38.5 mm. **Ruler:** Elizabeth II **Series:** Manned Flight **Obv:** Young bust right **Rev:** Space Shuttle

Date	Mintage	VF20	XF40	MS60	MS63	MS65
1983	50,000	—	—	—	8.00	10.00
1983 DMIHE	—	—	—	—	15.00	17.00

KM# 106a CROWN
28.28 g., 0.925 Silver 0.841 oz. ASW, 38.5 mm. **Ruler:** Elizabeth II **Series:** Manned Flight **Obv:** Young bust right **Rev:** Space shuttle

Date	Mintage	VF20	XF40	MS60	MS63	MS65
1983	15,000	—	—	—	16.00	22.00
1983	11,000	PF65 24.00				

KM# 106b CROWN
5.10 g., 0.374 Gold 0.0613 oz. AGW **Ruler:** Elizabeth II **Series:** Manned Flight **Obv:** Young bust right **Rev:** Space shuttle

Date	Mintage	VF20	XF40	MS60	MS63	MS65
1983	5,500	PF65 125				

KM# 106c CROWN
7.96 g., 0.917 Gold 0.2347 oz. AGW **Ruler:** Elizabeth II **Series:** Manned Flight **Obv:** Young bust right **Rev:** Space shuttle

Date	Mintage	VF20	XF40	MS60	MS63	MS65
1983	500	PF65 400				

KM# 106d CROWN
52.00 g., 0.950 Platinum 1.5882 oz. APW, 38.5 mm. **Ruler:** Elizabeth II **Series:** Manned Flight **Obv:** Young bust right **Rev:** Space Shuttle

Date	Mintage	VF20	XF40	MS60	MS63	MS65
1983	50	PF65 2,200				

KM# 117 CROWN
Copper-Nickel, 38.5 mm. **Ruler:** Elizabeth II **Series:** 1984 Winter Olympics - Sarajevo **Obv:** Young bust right **Rev:** Figure skaters

Date	Mintage	VF20	XF40	MS60	MS63	MS65
1984	50,000	—	—	—	8.00	9.00
1984	—	PF65 10.00				

KM# 117a CROWN
28.28 g., 0.925 Silver 0.841 oz. ASW, 38.5 mm. **Ruler:** Elizabeth II **Series:** 1984 Winter Olympics - Sarajevo **Obv:** Young bust right **Rev:** Figure Skaters

Date	Mintage	VF20	XF40	MS60	MS63	MS65
1984	15,000	PF65 24.00				

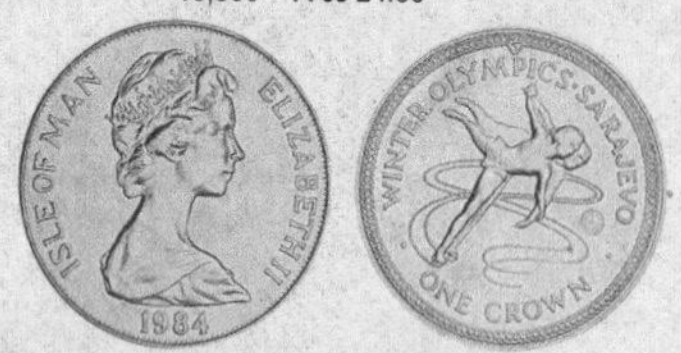

KM# 117b CROWN
5.10 g., 0.374 Gold 0.0613 oz. AGW **Ruler:** Elizabeth II **Series:** 1984 Winter Olympics - Sarajevo **Obv:** Young bust right **Rev:** Figure skaters

Date	Mintage	VF20	XF40	MS60	MS63	MS65
1984	10,000	PF65 125				

KM# 117c CROWN
7.96 g., 0.917 Gold 0.2347 oz. AGW **Ruler:** Elizabeth II **Series:** 1984 Winter Olympics - Sarajevo **Obv:** Young bust right **Rev:** Figure skaters

Date	Mintage	VF20	XF40	MS60	MS63	MS65
1984	1,000	PF65 400				

KM# 117d CROWN
52.00 g., 0.950 Platinum 1.5882 oz. APW, 38.5 mm. **Ruler:** Elizabeth II **Series:** 1984 Winter Olympics - Sarajevo **Obv:** Young bust right **Rev:** Figure skaters

Date	Mintage	VF20	XF40	MS60	MS63	MS65
1984	100	PF65 2,000				

KM# 117e CROWN
Silver Clad Copper-Nickel, 38.5 mm. **Ruler:** Elizabeth II **Series:** 1984 Winter Olympics - Sarajevo **Obv:** Young bust right **Rev:** Figure skaters

Date	Mintage	VF20	XF40	MS60	MS63	MS65
1984	20,000	—	—	—	18.00	20.00

KM# 118 CROWN
Copper-Nickel, 38.5 mm. **Ruler:** Elizabeth II **Series:** 1984 Olympics - Los Angeles **Obv:** Young bust right **Rev:** Runners

Date	Mintage	VF20	XF40	MS60	MS63	MS65
1984	50,000	—	—	—	6.00	7.00
1984	—	PF65 8.50				

KM# 118a CROWN
28.28 g., 0.925 Silver 0.841 oz. ASW, 38.5 mm. **Ruler:** Elizabeth II **Series:** 1984 Olympics - Los Angeles **Obv:** Young bust right **Rev:** Runners

Date	Mintage	VF20	XF40	MS60	MS63	MS65
1984	15,000	PF65 24.00				

KM# 118b CROWN
5.10 g., 0.374 Gold 0.0613 oz. AGW **Ruler:** Elizabeth II **Series:** 1984 Olympics - Los Angeles **Obv:** Young bust right **Rev:** Runners

Date	Mintage	VF20	XF40	MS60	MS63	MS65
1984	10,000	PF65 125				

KM# 118c CROWN
7.96 g., 0.917 Gold 0.2347 oz. AGW **Ruler:** Elizabeth II **Series:** 1984 Olympics - Los Angeles **Obv:** Young bust right **Rev:** Runners

Date	Mintage	VF20	XF40	MS60	MS63	MS65
1984	1,000	PF65 400				

KM# 118d CROWN
52.00 g., 0.950 Platinum 1.5882 oz. APW, 38.5 mm. **Ruler:** Elizabeth II **Series:** 1984 Olympics - Los Angeles **Obv:** Young bust right **Rev:** Runners

Date	Mintage	VF20	XF40	MS60	MS63	MS65
1984	100	PF65 2,000				

KM# 118e CROWN
Silver Clad Copper-Nickel, 38.5 mm. **Ruler:** Elizabeth II **Series:** 1984 Olympics - Los Angeles **Obv:** Young bust right **Rev:** Runners

Date	Mintage	VF20	XF40	MS60	MS63	MS65
1984	20,000	—	—	—	18.00	20.00

KM# 119 CROWN
Copper-Nickel, 38.5 mm. **Series:** 1984 Olympics - Los Angeles **Obv:** Young bust right **Rev:** Gymnastics

Date	Mintage	VF20	XF40	MS60	MS63	MS65
1984	50,000	—	—	—	3.50	5.00
1984	—	PF65 8.50				

KM# 119a CROWN
28.28 g., 0.925 Silver 0.841 oz. ASW, 38.5 mm. **Ruler:** Elizabeth II **Series:** 1984 Olympics - Los Angeles **Obv:** Young bust right **Rev:** Gymnastics

Date	Mintage	VF20	XF40	MS60	MS63	MS65
1984	15,000	PF65 24.00				

KM# 119b CROWN
5.10 g., 0.374 Gold 0.0613 oz. AGW **Ruler:** Elizabeth II **Series:** 1984 Olympics - Los Angeles **Obv:** Young bust right **Rev:** Gymnastics

Date	Mintage	VF20	XF40	MS60	MS63	MS65
1984	10,000	PF65 125				

KM# 119c CROWN
7.96 g., 0.917 Gold 0.2347 oz. AGW **Ruler:** Elizabeth II **Series:** 1984 Olympics - Los Angeles **Obv:** Young bust right **Rev:** Gymnastics

Date	Mintage	VF20	XF40	MS60	MS63	MS65
1984	1,000	PF65 400				

KM# 119d CROWN
52.00 g., 0.950 Platinum 1.5882 oz. APW, 38.5 mm. **Ruler:** Elizabeth II **Series:** 1984 Olympics - Los Angeles **Obv:** Young bust right **Rev:** Gymnastics

Date	Mintage	VF20	XF40	MS60	MS63	MS65
1984	100	PF65 2,000				

KM# 119e CROWN
Silver Clad Copper-Nickel, 38.5 mm. **Ruler:** Elizabeth II **Series:** 1984 Olympics - Los Angeles **Obv:** Young bust right **Rev:** Gymnastics

Date	Mintage	VF20	XF40	MS60	MS63	MS65
1984	20,000	—	—	—	18.00	20.00

KM# 120 CROWN
Copper-Nickel, 38.5 mm. **Ruler:** Elizabeth II **Series:** 1984 Olympics - Los Angeles **Obv:** Young bust right **Rev:** Equestrian

Date	Mintage	VF20	XF40	MS60	MS63	MS65
1984	50,000	—	—	—	6.00	7.00
1984	—	PF65 8.50				

KM# 120a CROWN
28.28 g., 0.925 Silver 0.841 oz. ASW, 38.5 mm. **Ruler:** Elizabeth II **Series:** 1984 Olympics - Los Angeles **Obv:** Young bust right **Rev:** Equestrian

Date	Mintage	VF20	XF40	MS60	MS63	MS65
1984	15,000	PF65 24.00				

KM# 120b CROWN
5.10 g., 0.374 Gold 0.0613 oz. AGW **Ruler:** Elizabeth II **Series:** 1984 Olympics - Los Angeles **Obv:** Young bust right **Rev:** Equestrian

Date	Mintage	VF20	XF40	MS60	MS63	MS65
1984	10,000	PF65 125				

KM# 120c CROWN
7.96 g., 0.917 Gold 0.2347 oz. AGW **Ruler:** Elizabeth II **Series:** 1984 Olympics - Los Angeles **Obv:** Young bust right **Rev:** Equestrian

Date	Mintage	VF20	XF40	MS60	MS63	MS65
1984	1,000	PF65 400				

KM# 120d CROWN
52.00 g., 0.950 Platinum 1.5882 oz. APW, 38.5 mm. **Ruler:** Elizabeth II **Series:** 1984 Olympics - Los Angeles **Obv:** Young bust right **Rev:** Equestrian

Date	Mintage	VF20	XF40	MS60	MS63	MS65
1984	100	PF65 2,000				

KM# 120e CROWN
Silver Clad Copper-Nickel, 38.5 mm. **Ruler:** Elizabeth II **Series:** 1984 Olympics - Los Angeles **Obv:** Young bust right **Rev:** Equestrian

Date	Mintage	VF20	XF40	MS60	MS63	MS65
1984	20,000	—	—	—	18.00	20.00

KM# 121 CROWN
Copper-Nickel, 38.5 mm. **Ruler:** Elizabeth II **Subject:** Quincentenary **Obv:** Young bust right **Rev:** Arms with supporters

Date	Mintage	VF20	XF40	MS60	MS63	MS65
1984	—	—	—	—	6.00	7.00
1984 Prooflike	—	—	—	—	—	8.50

KM# 121a CROWN
28.28 g., 0.925 Silver 0.841 oz. ASW, 38.5 mm. **Ruler:** Elizabeth II **Subject:** Quincentenary **Obv:** Young bust right **Rev:** Arms with supporters

Date	Mintage	VF20	XF40	MS60	MS63	MS65
1984	—	—	—	—	18.00	20.00
1984	—	PF65 24.00				

KM# 121b CROWN
5.10 g., 0.374 Gold 0.0613 oz. AGW **Ruler:** Elizabeth II **Subject:** Quincentenary **Obv:** Young bust right **Rev:** Arms with supporters

Date	Mintage	VF20	XF40	MS60	MS63	MS65
1984	10,000	PF65 125				

KM# 121c CROWN
7.96 g., 0.917 Gold 0.2347 oz. AGW **Ruler:** Elizabeth II **Subject:** Quincentenary **Obv:** Young bust right **Rev:** Arms with supporters

Date	Mintage	VF20	XF40	MS60	MS63	MS65
1984	1,000	PF65 400				

KM# 121d CROWN
52.00 g., 0.950 Platinum 1.5882 oz. APW, 38.5 mm. **Ruler:** Elizabeth II **Subject:** Quincentenary **Obv:** Young bust right **Rev:** Arms with supporters

Date	Mintage	VF20	XF40	MS60	MS63	MS65
1984	—	PF65 2,000				

KM# 122 CROWN
Copper-Nickel, 38.5 mm. **Ruler:** Elizabeth II **Subject:** Quincentenary **Obv:** Young bust right **Rev:** Lion above shields

Date	Mintage	VF20	XF40	MS60	MS63	MS65
1984	—	—	—	—	6.00	7.00
1984 Prooflike	—	—	—	—	—	8.50

KM# 122a CROWN
28.28 g., 0.925 Silver 0.841 oz. ASW, 38.5 mm. **Ruler:** Elizabeth II **Subject:** Quincentenary **Obv:** Young bust right **Rev:** Lion above shields

Date	Mintage	VF20	XF40	MS60	MS63	MS65
1984	—	—	—	—	18.00	20.00
1984	—	PF65 24.00				

KM# 122b CROWN
5.10 g., 0.374 Gold 0.0613 oz. AGW **Ruler:** Elizabeth II **Subject:** Quincentenary **Obv:** Young bust right **Rev:** Lion above shields

Date	Mintage	VF20	XF40	MS60	MS63	MS65
1984	10,000	PF65 125				

KM# 122c CROWN
7.96 g., 0.917 Gold 0.2347 oz. AGW **Ruler:** Elizabeth II **Subject:** Quincentenary **Obv:** Young bust right **Rev:** Lion above shields

Date	Mintage	VF20	XF40	MS60	MS63	MS65
1984	1,000	PF65 400				

KM# 122d CROWN
52.00 g., 0.950 Platinum 1.5882 oz. APW, 38.5 mm. **Ruler:** Elizabeth II **Subject:** Quincentenary **Obv:** Young bust right **Rev:** Lion above shields

Date	Mintage	VF20	XF40	MS60	MS63	MS65
1984	—	PF65 2,000				

KM# 123 CROWN
Copper-Nickel, 38.5 mm. **Ruler:** Elizabeth II **Subject:** Quincentenary of the College of Arms **Obv:** Young bust right **Rev:** Eagle and ducal hat above shields **Edge:** Reeded

Date	Mintage	VF20	XF40	MS60	MS63	MS65
1984	—	—	—	—	6.00	7.00
1984 Prooflike	—	—	—	—	—	8.50

KM# 123a CROWN
28.28 g., 0.925 Silver 0.841 oz. ASW, 38.5 mm. **Ruler:** Elizabeth II **Subject:** Quincentenary **Obv:** Young bust right **Rev:** Bird above shields

Date	Mintage	VF20	XF40	MS60	MS63	MS65
1984	—	—	—	—	18.00	20.00
1984	—	PF65 24.00				

KM# 123b CROWN
5.10 g., 0.374 Gold 0.0613 oz. AGW **Ruler:** Elizabeth II **Subject:** Quincentenary **Obv:** Young bust right **Rev:** Bird above shields

Date	Mintage	VF20	XF40	MS60	MS63	MS65
1984	10,000	PF65 125				

KM# 123c CROWN
7.96 g., 0.917 Gold 0.2347 oz. AGW **Ruler:** Elizabeth II **Subject:** Quincentenary **Obv:** Young bust right **Rev:** Bird above shields

Date	Mintage	VF20	XF40	MS60	MS63	MS65
1984	1,000	PF65 400				

KM# 123d CROWN
52.00 g., 0.950 Platinum 1.5882 oz. APW, 38.5 mm. **Ruler:** Elizabeth II **Subject:** Quincentenary **Obv:** Young bust right **Rev:** Bird above shields

Date	Mintage	VF20	XF40	MS60	MS63	MS65
1984	—	PF65 2,000				

KM# 124 CROWN
Copper-Nickel, 38.5 mm. **Ruler:** Elizabeth II **Subject:** Quincentenary **Obv:** Young bust right **Rev:** Arms with supporters

Date	Mintage	VF20	XF40	MS60	MS63	MS65
1984	—	—	—	—	6.00	7.00
1984 Prooflike	—	—	—	—	—	8.50

KM# 124a CROWN

28.28 g., 0.925 Silver 0.841 oz. ASW, 38.5 mm. **Ruler:** Elizabeth II **Subject:** Quincentenary **Obv:** Young bust right **Rev:** Arms with supporters

Date	Mintage	VF20	XF40	MS60	MS63	MS65
1984	—	—	—	—	18.00	20.00
1984	—	PF65 24.00				

KM# 124b CROWN

5.10 g., 0.374 Gold 0.0613 oz. AGW **Ruler:** Elizabeth II **Subject:** Quincentenary of the College of Arms **Obv:** Crowned bust right **Rev:** 3 helmets above arms with supporters

Date	Mintage	VF20	XF40	MS60	MS63	MS65
1984	10,000	PF65 125				

KM# 124c CROWN

7.96 g., 0.917 Gold 0.2347 oz. AGW **Ruler:** Elizabeth II **Subject:** Quincentenary **Obv:** Young bust right **Rev:** Arms with supporters

Date	Mintage	VF20	XF40	MS60	MS63	MS65
1984	1,000	PF65 400				

KM# 124d CROWN

52.00 g., 0.950 Platinum 1.5882 oz. APW, 38.5 mm. **Ruler:** Elizabeth II **Subject:** Quincentenary **Obv:** Young bust right **Rev:** Arms with supporters

Date	Mintage	VF20	XF40	MS60	MS63	MS65
1984	—	PF65 2,000				

KM# 130 CROWN

Copper-Nickel, 38.5 mm. **Ruler:** Elizabeth II **Subject:** 30th Commonwealth Parliamentary Conference **Obv:** Young bust right **Rev:** Conjoined heads right within circle **Rev. Legend:** Celtic uncial script

Date	Mintage	VF20	XF40	MS60	MS63	MS65
1984	—	—	—	—	3.00	4.00

KM# 130a CROWN

28.28 g., 0.925 Silver 0.841 oz. ASW, 38.5 mm. **Ruler:** Elizabeth II **Subject:** 30th Commonwealth Parliamentary Conference **Obv:** Young bust right **Rev:** Conjoined heads right within circle **Rev. Legend:** Celtic uncial script

Date	Mintage	VF20	XF40	MS60	MS63	MS65
1984	—	—	—	—	18.00	20.00
1984	—	PF65 24.00				

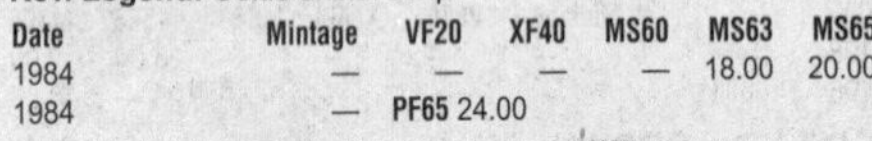

KM# 130b CROWN

5.10 g., 0.374 Gold 0.0613 oz. AGW **Ruler:** Elizabeth II **Subject:** 30th Commonwealth Parliamentary Conference **Obv:** Young bust right **Rev:** Conjoined heads right within circle **Rev. Legend:** Celtic uncial script

Date	Mintage	VF20	XF40	MS60	MS63	MS65
1984	10,000	PF65 125				

KM# 130c CROWN

7.96 g., 0.917 Gold 0.2347 oz. AGW **Ruler:** Elizabeth II **Subject:** 30th Commonwealth Parliamentary Conference **Obv:** Young bust right **Rev:** Conjoined heads right within circle **Rev. Legend:** Celtic uncial script

Date	Mintage	VF20	XF40	MS60	MS63	MS65
1984	1,000	PF65 400				

KM# 130d CROWN

52.00 g., 0.950 Platinum 1.5882 oz. APW, 38.5 mm. **Ruler:** Elizabeth II **Subject:** 30th Commonwealth Parliamentary Conference **Obv:** Young bust right **Rev:** Conjoined heads right within circle **Rev. Legend:** Celtic uncial script

Date	Mintage	VF20	XF40	MS60	MS63	MS65
1984	—	PF65 2,000				

KM# 131 CROWN

Copper-Nickel, 38.5 mm. **Ruler:** Elizabeth II **Subject:** 30th Commonwealth Parliamentary Conference **Obv:** Young bust right **Rev:** Throne, shield and sword **Rev. Legend:** Celtic uncial script

Date	Mintage	VF20	XF40	MS60	MS63	MS65
1984	—	—	—	—	3.00	4.00

KM# 131a CROWN

28.28 g., 0.925 Silver 0.841 oz. ASW, 38.5 mm. **Ruler:** Elizabeth II **Subject:** 30th Commonwealth Parliamentary Conference **Obv:** Young bust right **Rev:** Throne, sword and shield **Rev. Legend:** Celtic uncial script

Date	Mintage	VF20	XF40	MS60	MS63	MS65
1984	—	—	—	—	18.00	20.00
1984	—	PF65 24.00				

KM# 131b CROWN

5.10 g., 0.374 Gold 0.0613 oz. AGW **Ruler:** Elizabeth II **Subject:** 30th Commonwealth Parliamentary Conference **Obv:** Young bust right **Rev:** Throne, sword and shield **Rev. Legend:** Celtic uncial script

Date	Mintage	VF20	XF40	MS60	MS63	MS65
1984	10,000	PF65 125				

KM# 131c CROWN

7.96 g., 0.917 Gold 0.2347 oz. AGW **Ruler:** Elizabeth II **Subject:** 30th Commonwealth Parliamentary Conference **Obv:** Young bust right **Rev:** Throne, sword and shield **Rev. Legend:** Celtic uncial script

Date	Mintage	VF20	XF40	MS60	MS63	MS65
1984	1,000	PF65 400				

KM# 131d CROWN

52.00 g., 0.950 Platinum 1.5882 oz. APW, 38.5 mm. **Ruler:** Elizabeth II **Subject:** 30th Commonwealth Parliamentary Conference **Obv:** Young bust right **Rev:** Throne, shield and sword **Rev. Legend:** Celtic uncial script

Date	Mintage	VF20	XF40	MS60	MS63	MS65
1984	—	PF65 2,000				

KM# 132 CROWN

Copper-Nickel, 38.5 mm. **Ruler:** Elizabeth II **Subject:** 30th Commonwealth Parliamentary Conference **Obv:** Young bust right **Rev:** Crowned head facing within circle **Rev. Legend:** Celtic uncial script

Date	Mintage	VF20	XF40	MS60	MS63	MS65
1984	—	—	—	—	3.00	4.00

KM# 132a CROWN

28.28 g., 0.925 Silver 0.841 oz. ASW, 38.5 mm. **Ruler:** Elizabeth II **Subject:** 30th Commonwealth Parliamentary Conference **Obv:** Young bust right **Rev:** Crowned head facing within circle **Rev. Legend:** Celtic uncial script

Date	Mintage	VF20	XF40	MS60	MS63	MS65
1984	—	—	—	—	16.00	22.00
1984	—	PF65 24.00				

KM# 132b CROWN

5.10 g., 0.374 Gold 0.0613 oz. AGW **Ruler:** Elizabeth II **Subject:** 30th Commonwealth Parliamentary Conference **Obv:** Young bust right **Rev:** crowned head facing within circle **Rev. Legend:** Celtic uncial script

Date	Mintage	VF20	XF40	MS60	MS63	MS65
1984	10,000	PF65 125				

KM# 132c CROWN

7.96 g., 0.917 Gold 0.2347 oz. AGW **Ruler:** Elizabeth II **Subject:** 30th Commonwealth Parliamentary Conference **Obv:** Young bust right **Rev:** Crowned head facing within circle **Rev. Legend:** Celtic uncial script

Date	Mintage	VF20	XF40	MS60	MS63	MS65
1984	1,000	PF65 400				

KM# 132d CROWN

52.00 g., 0.950 Platinum 1.5882 oz. APW, 38.5 mm. **Ruler:** Elizabeth II **Subject:** 30th Commonwealth Parliamentary Conference **Obv:** Young bust right **Rev:** Crowned head facing within circle **Rev. Legend:** Celtic uncial script

Date	Mintage	VF20	XF40	MS60	MS63	MS65
1984	—	PF65 2,000				

KM# 133 CROWN

Copper-Nickel, 38.5 mm. **Ruler:** Elizabeth II **Subject:** 30th Commonwealth Parliamentary Conference **Obv:** Young bust right **Rev:** Conference tent **Rev. Legend:** Celtic uncial script

Date	Mintage	VF20	XF40	MS60	MS63	MS65
1984	—	—	—	—	3.00	4.00

KM# 133a CROWN

28.28 g., 0.925 Silver 0.841 oz. ASW, 38.5 mm. **Ruler:** Elizabeth II **Subject:** 30th Commonwealth Parliamentary Conference **Obv:** Young bust right **Rev:** Conference tent **Rev. Legend:** Celtic uncial script

Date	Mintage	VF20	XF40	MS60	MS63	MS65
1984	—	—	—	—	16.00	22.00
1984	—	PF65 24.00				

KM# 133b CROWN

5.10 g., 0.374 Gold 0.0613 oz. AGW **Ruler:** Elizabeth II **Subject:** 30th Commonwealth Parliamentary Conference **Obv:** Young bust right **Rev:** Conference tent within circle **Rev. Legend:** Celtic uncial script

Date	Mintage	VF20	XF40	MS60	MS63	MS65
1984	10,000	PF65 125				

KM# 133c CROWN

7.96 g., 0.917 Gold 0.2347 oz. AGW **Ruler:** Elizabeth II **Subject:** 30th Commonwealth Parliamentary Conference **Obv:** Young bust right **Rev:** Conference tent **Rev. Legend:** Celtic uncial script

Date	Mintage	VF20	XF40	MS60	MS63	MS65
1984	1,000	PF65 400				

KM# 133d CROWN

52.00 g., 0.950 Platinum 1.5882 oz. APW, 38.5 mm. **Ruler:** Elizabeth II **Subject:** 30th Commonwealth Parliamentary Conference **Obv:** Young bust right **Rev:** Conference tent **Rev. Legend:** Celtic uncial script

Date	Mintage	VF20	XF40	MS60	MS63	MS65
1984	—	PF65 2,000				

KM# 216 CROWN

Copper-Nickel, 38.5 mm. **Ruler:** Elizabeth II **Obv:** Crowned bust right **Rev:** Child half figure facing

Date	Mintage	VF20	XF40	MS60	MS63	MS65
1985	Est. 50000	—	—	—	2.50	3.50

KM# 216a CROWN

Silver Clad Copper-Nickel, 38.5 mm. **Ruler:** Elizabeth II **Obv:** Crowned bust right **Rev:** Child half figure facing

Date	Mintage	VF20	XF40	MS60	MS63	MS65
1985	—	PF65 10.00				

KM# 216b CROWN

28.28 g., 0.925 Silver 0.841 oz. ASW, 38.5 mm. **Ruler:** Elizabeth II **Obv:** Crowned bust right **Rev:** Child half figure facing

Date	Mintage	VF20	XF40	MS60	MS63	MS65
1985	Est. 15000	PF65 24.00				

KM# 216c CROWN

5.10 g., 0.374 Gold 0.0613 oz. AGW **Ruler:** Elizabeth II **Obv:** Crowned bust right **Rev:** Child half figure facing

Date	Mintage	VF20	XF40	MS60	MS63	MS65
1985	Est. 10000	PF65 125				

KM# 216d CROWN
7.96 g., 0.917 Gold 0.2347 oz. AGW **Ruler:** Elizabeth II **Obv:** Crowned bust right **Rev:** Child half figure facing

Date	Mintage	VF20	XF40	MS60	MS63	MS65
1985	Est. 1000	PF65 400				

KM# 216e CROWN
52.00 g., 0.950 Platinum 1.5882 oz. APW, 38.5 mm. **Ruler:** Elizabeth II **Obv:** Crowned bust right **Rev:** Child half figure facing

Date	Mintage	VF20	XF40	MS60	MS63	MS65
1985	Est. 100	PF65 2,000				

KM# 217 CROWN
Copper-Nickel, 38.5 mm. **Ruler:** Elizabeth II **Obv:** Crowned bust right **Rev:** Conjoined busts facing

Date	Mintage	VF20	XF40	MS60	MS63	MS65
1985	Est. 50000	—	—	—	2.50	3.50

KM# 217a CROWN
Silver Clad Copper-Nickel, 38.5 mm. **Ruler:** Elizabeth II **Obv:** Crowned bust right **Rev:** Conjoined busts facing

Date	Mintage	VF20	XF40	MS60	MS63	MS65
1985	Est. 20000	PF65 10.00				

KM# 217b CROWN
28.28 g., 0.925 Silver 0.841 oz. ASW **Ruler:** Elizabeth II **Obv:** Crowned bust right **Rev:** Conjoined busts facing

Date	Mintage	VF20	XF40	MS60	MS63	MS65
1985	Est. 15000	PF65 24.00				

KM# 217c CROWN
5.10 g., 0.374 Gold 0.0613 oz. AGW **Ruler:** Elizabeth II **Obv:** Crowned bust right **Rev:** Conjoined busts facing

Date	Mintage	VF20	XF40	MS60	MS63	MS65
1985	Est. 10000	PF65 125				

KM# 217d CROWN
7.96 g., 0.917 Gold 0.2347 oz. AGW **Ruler:** Elizabeth II **Obv:** Crowned bust right **Rev:** Conjoined busts facing

Date	Mintage	VF20	XF40	MS60	MS63	MS65
1985	Est. 1000	PF65 400				

KM# 217e CROWN
52.00 g., 0.950 Platinum 1.5882 oz. APW, 38.5 mm. **Ruler:** Elizabeth II **Obv:** Crowned bust right **Rev:** Conjoined busts facing

Date	Mintage	VF20	XF40	MS60	MS63	MS65
1985	Est. 100	PF65 2,000				

KM# 218 CROWN
Copper-Nickel, 38.5 mm. **Ruler:** Elizabeth II **Obv:** Crowned bust right **Rev:** Royal Wedding couple

Date	Mintage	VF20	XF40	MS60	MS63	MS65
1985	—	—	—	—	2.50	3.50

KM# 218a CROWN
Silver Clad Copper-Nickel, 38.5 mm. **Ruler:** Elizabeth II **Obv:** Crowned bust right **Rev:** 3/4 length figures of Royal couple facing

Date	Mintage	VF20	XF40	MS60	MS63	MS65
1985	Est. 20000	PF65 10.00				

KM# 218b CROWN
28.28 g., 0.925 Silver 0.841 oz. ASW, 38.5 mm. **Ruler:** Elizabeth II **Obv:** Crowned bust right **Rev:** 3/4 length figures of Royal couple facing

Date	Mintage	VF20	XF40	MS60	MS63	MS65
1985	Est. 15000	PF65 24.00				

KM# 218c CROWN
5.10 g., 0.374 Gold 0.0613 oz. AGW **Ruler:** Elizabeth II **Obv:** Crowned bust right **Rev:** 3/4 length figures of Royal couple facing

Date	Mintage	VF20	XF40	MS60	MS63	MS65
1985	Est. 10000	PF65 125				

KM# 218d CROWN
7.96 g., 0.917 Gold 0.2347 oz. AGW **Ruler:** Elizabeth II **Obv:** Crowned bust right **Rev:** 3/4 length figures of Royal couple facing

Date	Mintage	VF20	XF40	MS60	MS63	MS65
1985	Est. 1000	PF65 400				

KM# 218e CROWN
52.00 g., 0.950 Platinum 1.5882 oz. APW, 38.5 mm. **Ruler:** Elizabeth II **Obv:** Crowned bust right **Rev:** 3/4 length figures of Royal couple facing

Date	Mintage	VF20	XF40	MS60	MS63	MS65
1985	Est. 100	PF65 2,000				

KM# 219 CROWN
Copper-Nickel, 38.5 mm. **Ruler:** Elizabeth II **Obv:** Crowned bust right **Rev:** Queen Mother and Princess Elizabeth

Date	Mintage	VF20	XF40	MS60	MS63	MS65
1985	—	—	—	—	2.50	3.50

KM# 219a CROWN
Silver Clad Copper-Nickel, 38.5 mm. **Ruler:** Elizabeth II **Obv:** Crowned bust right **Rev:** Queen Mother and Princess Elizabeth

Date	Mintage	VF20	XF40	MS60	MS63	MS65
1985	Est. 20000	PF65 10.00				

KM# 219b CROWN
28.28 g., 0.925 Silver 0.841 oz. ASW, 38.5 mm. **Ruler:** Elizabeth II **Obv:** Crowned bust right **Rev:** Queen Mother and Princess Elizabeth

Date	Mintage	VF20	XF40	MS60	MS63	MS65
1985	Est. 15000	PF65 24.00				

KM# 219c CROWN
5.10 g., 0.374 Gold 0.0613 oz. AGW **Ruler:** Elizabeth II **Obv:** Crowned bust right **Rev:** Queen Mother and Princess Elizabeth

Date	Mintage	VF20	XF40	MS60	MS63	MS65
1985	Est. 10000	PF65 125				

KM# 219d CROWN
7.96 g., 0.917 Gold 0.2347 oz. AGW **Ruler:** Elizabeth II **Obv:** Crowned bust right **Rev:** Queen Mother and Princess Elizabeth

Date	Mintage	VF20	XF40	MS60	MS63	MS65
1985	Est. 1000	PF65 400				

KM# 219e CROWN
52.00 g., 0.950 Platinum 1.5882 oz. APW, 38.5 mm. **Ruler:** Elizabeth II **Obv:** Crowned bust right **Rev:** Queen Mother and Princess Elizabeth

Date	Mintage	VF20	XF40	MS60	MS63	MS65
1985	Est. 100	PF65 2,000				

KM# 220 CROWN
Copper-Nickel, 38.5 mm. **Ruler:** Elizabeth II **Obv:** Crowned bust right **Rev:** Adult and two children facing

Date	Mintage	VF20	XF40	MS60	MS63	MS65
1985	Est. 50000	—	—	—	2.50	3.50
1990	—	—	—	—	2.50	3.50
1990 PM	—	PF65 10.00				

KM# 220a CROWN
Silver Clad Copper-Nickel, 38.5 mm. **Ruler:** Elizabeth II **Obv:** Crowned bust right **Rev:** Adult and two children facing

Date	Mintage	VF20	XF40	MS60	MS63	MS65
1985	Est. 20000	PF65 15.00				
1990 PM	—					

KM# 220b CROWN
28.28 g., 0.925 Silver 0.841 oz. ASW, 38.5 mm. **Ruler:** Elizabeth II **Obv:** Crowned bust right **Rev:** Adult and two children facing

Date	Mintage	VF20	XF40	MS60	MS63	MS65
1985	Est. 15000	PF65 24.00				
1990	—	PF65 24.00				

KM# 220c CROWN
5.10 g., 0.374 Gold 0.0613 oz. AGW **Ruler:** Elizabeth II **Obv:** Crowned bust right **Rev:** Adult and two children facing

Date	Mintage	VF20	XF40	MS60	MS63	MS65
1985	Est. 10000	PF65 125				

KM# 220d CROWN
7.96 g., 0.917 Gold 0.2347 oz. AGW **Ruler:** Elizabeth II **Obv:** Crowned bust right **Rev:** Adult and two children facing

Date	Mintage	VF20	XF40	MS60	MS63	MS65
1985	Est. 1000	PF65 400				

KM# 220e CROWN
52.00 g., 0.950 Platinum 1.5882 oz. APW, 38.5 mm. **Ruler:** Elizabeth II **Obv:** Crowned bust right **Rev:** Adult and two children facing

Date	Mintage	VF20	XF40	MS60	MS63	MS65
1985	Est. 100	PF65 2,000				

KM# 221 CROWN
Copper-Nickel, 38.5 mm. **Ruler:** Elizabeth II **Subject:** 85th Birthday of Queen Mother **Obv:** Crowned bust right **Rev:** Queen Mother

Date	Mintage	VF20	XF40	MS60	MS63	MS65
1985	Est. 50000	—	—	—	2.50	3.50

KM# 221a CROWN
Silver Clad Copper-Nickel, 38.5 mm. **Ruler:** Elizabeth II **Subject:** 85th Birthday of Queen Mother **Obv:** Crowned bust right **Rev:** Queen Mother

Date	Mintage	VF20	XF40	MS60	MS63	MS65
1985	Est. 20000	PF65 10.00				

KM# 221b CROWN
28.28 g., 0.925 Silver 0.841 oz. ASW, 38.5 mm. **Ruler:** Elizabeth II **Subject:** 85th Birthday of Queen Mother **Obv:** Crowned bust right **Rev:** Queen Mother

Date	Mintage	VF20	XF40	MS60	MS63	MS65
1985	Est. 15000	PF65 24.00				

KM# 221c CROWN
5.10 g., 0.374 Gold 0.0613 oz. AGW **Ruler:** Elizabeth II **Subject:** 85th Birthday of Queen Mother **Obv:** Crowned bust right **Rev:** Queen Mother

Date	Mintage	VF20	XF40	MS60	MS63	MS65
1985	Est. 10000	PF65 125				

KM# 221d CROWN
7.96 g., 0.917 Gold 0.2347 oz. AGW **Ruler:** Elizabeth II **Subject:** 85th Birthday of Queen Mother **Obv:** Crowned bust right **Rev:** Queen Mother

Date	Mintage	VF20	XF40	MS60	MS63	MS65
1985	Est. 1000	PF65 400				

KM# 221e CROWN
52.00 g., 0.950 Platinum 1.5882 oz. APW, 38.5 mm. **Ruler:** Elizabeth II **Subject:** 85th Birthday of Queen Mother **Obv:** Crowned bust right **Rev:** Queen Mother

Date	Mintage	VF20	XF40	MS60	MS63	MS65
1985	Est. 100	PF65 2,000				

KM# 160 CROWN
Copper-Nickel, 38.5 mm. **Ruler:** Elizabeth II **Series:** World Cup Soccer - Mexico **Obv:** Crowned bust right **Rev:** Map and soccer players within circle **Edge:** Reeded

Date	Mintage	VF20	XF40	MS60	MS63	MS65
1986	—	—	—	—	2.50	3.50

KM# 160a CROWN
Silver Clad Copper-Nickel, 38.5 mm. **Ruler:** Elizabeth II **Series:** World Cup Soccer - Mexico **Obv:** Crowned bust right **Rev:** Map and soccer players within circle

Date	Mintage	VF20	XF40	MS60	MS63	MS65
1986	Est. 20000	PF65 10.00				

KM# 160b CROWN
28.28 g., 0.925 Silver 0.841 oz. ASW, 38.5 mm. **Ruler:** Elizabeth II **Series:** World Cup Soccer - Mexico **Obv:** Crowned bust right **Rev:** Map and soccer players within circle

Date	Mintage	VF20	XF40	MS60	MS63	MS65
1986	Est. 15000	PF65 24.00				

KM# 160c CROWN
5.10 g., 0.374 Gold 0.0613 oz. AGW **Ruler:** Elizabeth II **Series:** World Cup Soccer - Mexico **Obv:** Crowned bust right **Rev:** Map and soccer players within circle

Date	Mintage	VF20	XF40	MS60	MS63	MS65
1986	Est. 10000	PF65 125				

KM# 160d CROWN
7.96 g., 0.917 Gold 0.2347 oz. AGW **Ruler:** Elizabeth II **Series:** World Cup Soccer - Mexico **Obv:** Crowned bust right **Rev:** Map and soccer players within circle

Date	Mintage	VF20	XF40	MS60	MS63	MS65
1986	Est. 1000	PF65 400				

KM# 160e CROWN
52.00 g., 0.950 Platinum 1.5882 oz. APW, 38.5 mm. **Ruler:** Elizabeth II **Series:** World Cup Soccer - Mexico **Obv:** Crowned bust right **Rev:** Map and soccer players within circle

Date	Mintage	VF20	XF40	MS60	MS63	MS65
1986	Est. 200	PF65 2,000				

KM# 161 CROWN
Copper-Nickel, 38.5 mm. **Ruler:** Elizabeth II **Series:** World Cup Soccer - Mexico **Obv:** Crowned bust right **Rev:** Soccer players within circle

Date	Mintage	VF20	XF40	MS60	MS63	MS65
1986	—	—	—	—	2.50	3.50

KM# 161a CROWN
Silver Clad Copper-Nickel, 38.5 mm. **Ruler:** Elizabeth II **Series:** World Cup Soccer - Mexico **Obv:** Crowned bust right **Rev:** Soccer players within circle

Date	Mintage	VF20	XF40	MS60	MS63	MS65
1986	Est. 20000	PF65 10.00				

KM# 161b CROWN
28.28 g., 0.925 Silver 0.841 oz. ASW, 38.5 mm. **Ruler:** Elizabeth II **Series:** World Cup Soccer - Mexico **Obv:** Crowned bust right **Rev:** Soccer players within circle

Date	Mintage	VF20	XF40	MS60	MS63	MS65
1986	Est. 15000	PF65 24.00				

KM# 161c CROWN
5.10 g., 0.374 Gold 0.0613 oz. AGW **Ruler:** Elizabeth II **Series:** World Cup Soccer - Mexico **Obv:** Crowned bust right **Rev:** Soccer players within circle

Date	Mintage	VF20	XF40	MS60	MS63	MS65
1986	Est. 10000	PF65 125				

KM# 161d CROWN
7.96 g., 0.917 Gold 0.2347 oz. AGW **Ruler:** Elizabeth II **Series:** World Cup Soccer - Mexico **Obv:** Crowned bust right **Rev:** Soccer players within circle

Date	Mintage	VF20	XF40	MS60	MS63	MS65
1986	Est. 1000	PF65 400				

KM# 161e CROWN
52.00 g., 0.950 Platinum 1.5882 oz. APW, 38.5 mm. **Ruler:** Elizabeth II **Series:** World Cup Soccer - Mexico **Obv:** Crowned bust right **Rev:** Soccer players within circle

Date	Mintage	VF20	XF40	MS60	MS63	MS65
1986	Est. 200	PF65 2,000				

KM# 162 CROWN
Copper-Nickel, 38.5 mm. **Ruler:** Elizabeth II **Series:** World Cup Soccer - Mexico **Obv:** Crowned bust right **Rev:** Soccer players within circle **Edge:** Reeded

Date	Mintage	VF20	XF40	MS60	MS63	MS65
1986	—	—	—	—	2.50	3.50

KM# 162a CROWN
Silver Clad Copper-Nickel, 38.5 mm. **Ruler:** Elizabeth II **Series:** World Cup Soccer - Mexico **Obv:** Crowned bust right **Rev:** Soccer players within circle

Date	Mintage	VF20	XF40	MS60	MS63	MS65
1986	Est. 20000	PF65 10.00				

KM# 162b CROWN
28.28 g., 0.925 Silver 0.841 oz. ASW, 38.5 mm. **Ruler:** Elizabeth II **Series:** World Cup Soccer - Mexico **Obv:** Crowned bust right **Rev:** Soccer players within circle

Date	Mintage	VF20	XF40	MS60	MS63	MS65
1986	Est. 15000	PF65 24.00				

KM# 162c CROWN
5.10 g., 0.374 Gold 0.0613 oz. AGW **Ruler:** Elizabeth II **Series:** World Cup Soccer - Mexico **Obv:** Crowned bust right **Rev:** Soccer players within circle

Date	Mintage	VF20	XF40	MS60	MS63	MS65
1986	Est. 10000	PF65 125				

KM# 162d CROWN
7.96 g., 0.917 Gold 0.2347 oz. AGW **Ruler:** Elizabeth II **Series:** World Cup Soccer - Mexico **Obv:** Crowned bust right **Rev:** Soccer players within circle

Date	Mintage	VF20	XF40	MS60	MS63	MS65
1986	Est. 1000	PF65 400				

KM# 162e CROWN
52.00 g., 0.950 Platinum 1.5882 oz. APW, 38.5 mm. **Ruler:** Elizabeth II **Series:** World Cup Soccer - Mexico **Obv:** Crowned bust right **Rev:** Soccer players within circle

Date	Mintage	VF20	XF40	MS60	MS63	MS65
1986	Est. 200	PF65 2,000				

KM# 163 CROWN
Copper-Nickel, 38.5 mm. **Ruler:** Elizabeth II **Series:** World Cup Soccer - Mexico **Obv:** Crowned bust right **Rev:** Net and soccer players within circle **Edge:** Reeded

Date	Mintage	VF20	XF40	MS60	MS63	MS65
1986	Est. 50000	—	—	—	2.50	3.50

KM# 163a CROWN
Silver Clad Copper-Nickel **Ruler:** Elizabeth II **Series:** World Cup Soccer - Mexico **Obv:** Crowned bust right **Rev:** Net and soccer players within circle

Date	Mintage	VF20	XF40	MS60	MS63	MS65
1986	—	PF65 10.00				

KM# 163b CROWN
28.28 g., 0.925 Silver 0.841 oz. ASW, 38.5 mm. **Ruler:** Elizabeth II **Series:** World Cup Soccer - Mexico **Obv:** Crowned bust right **Rev:** Net and soccer players within circle

Date	Mintage	VF20	XF40	MS60	MS63	MS65
1986	Est. 15000	PF65 24.00				

KM# 163c CROWN
5.10 g., 0.374 Gold 0.0613 oz. AGW **Ruler:** Elizabeth II **Series:** World Cup Soccer - Mexico **Obv:** Crowned bust right **Rev:** Net and soccer players within circle

Date	Mintage	VF20	XF40	MS60	MS63	MS65
1986	Est. 10000	PF65 125				

KM# 163d CROWN
7.96 g., 0.917 Gold 0.2347 oz. AGW **Ruler:** Elizabeth II **Series:** World Cup Soccer - Mexico **Obv:** Crowned bust right **Rev:** Net and soccer players within circle

Date	Mintage	VF20	XF40	MS60	MS63	MS65
1986	Est. 1000	PF65 400				

KM# 163e CROWN
52.00 g., 0.950 Platinum 1.5882 oz. APW, 38.5 mm. **Ruler:** Elizabeth II **Series:** World Cup Soccer - Mexico **Obv:** Crowned bust right **Rev:** Net and soccer players within circle

Date	Mintage	VF20	XF40	MS60	MS63	MS65
1986	Est. 200	PF65 2,000				

KM# 164 CROWN
Copper-Nickel, 38.5 mm. **Ruler:** Elizabeth II **Series:** World Cup Soccer - Mexico **Obv:** Crowned bust right **Rev:** Globe **Edge:** Reeded

Date	Mintage	VF20	XF40	MS60	MS63	MS65
1986	Est. 50000	—	—	—	2.50	3.50

KM# 164a CROWN
Silver Clad Copper-Nickel, 38.5 mm. **Ruler:** Elizabeth II **Series:** World Cup Soccer - Mexico **Obv:** Crowned bust right **Rev:** Globe

Date	Mintage	VF20	XF40	MS60	MS63	MS65
1986	—	PF65 10.00				
1989	—	—	—	—	80.00	—

KM# 164b CROWN
28.28 g., 0.925 Silver 0.841 oz. ASW, 38.5 mm. **Ruler:** Elizabeth II **Series:** World Cup Soccer - Mexico **Obv:** Crowned bust right **Rev:** Globe

Date	Mintage	VF20	XF40	MS60	MS63	MS65
1986	Est. 15000	PF65 24.00				

KM# 164c CROWN
5.10 g., 0.374 Gold 0.0613 oz. AGW **Ruler:** Elizabeth II **Series:** World Cup Soccer - Mexico **Obv:** Crowned bust right **Rev:** Globe

Date	Mintage	VF20	XF40	MS60	MS63	MS65
1986	Est. 10000	PF65 125				

KM# 164d CROWN
7.96 g., 0.917 Gold 0.2347 oz. AGW **Ruler:** Elizabeth II **Series:** World Cup Soccer - Mexico **Obv:** Crowned bust right **Rev:** Globe

Date	Mintage	VF20	XF40	MS60	MS63	MS65
1986	Est. 1000	PF65 400				

KM# 164e CROWN
52.00 g., 0.950 Platinum 1.5882 oz. APW, 38.5 mm. **Ruler:** Elizabeth II **Series:** World Cup Soccer - Mexico **Obv:** Crowned bust right **Rev:** Globe

Date	Mintage	VF20	XF40	MS60	MS63	MS65
1986	Est. 200	PF65 2,000				

KM# 165 CROWN
Copper-Nickel, 38.5 mm. **Ruler:** Elizabeth II **Series:** World Cup Soccer - Mexico **Obv:** Crowned bust right **Rev:** Flags within circle **Edge:** Reeded

Date	Mintage	VF20	XF40	MS60	MS63	MS65
1986	Est. 50000	—	—	—	2.50	3.50

KM# 165a CROWN
Silver Clad Copper-Nickel, 38.5 mm. **Ruler:** Elizabeth II **Series:** World Cup Soccer - Mexico **Obv:** Crowned bust right **Rev:** Flags within circle

Date	Mintage	VF20	XF40	MS60	MS63	MS65
1986	Est. 20000	PF65 10.00				
1989	—	—	—	—	80.00	—

KM# 165b CROWN
28.28 g., 0.925 Silver 0.841 oz. ASW, 38.5 mm. **Ruler:** Elizabeth II **Series:** World Cup Soccer - Mexico **Obv:** Crowned bust right **Rev:** Flags within circle

Date	Mintage	VF20	XF40	MS60	MS63	MS65
1986	Est. 15000	PF65 24.00				

KM# 165c CROWN
5.10 g., 0.374 Gold 0.0613 oz. AGW **Ruler:** Elizabeth II **Series:** World Cup Soccer - Mexico **Obv:** Crowned bust right **Rev:** Flags within circle

Date	Mintage	VF20	XF40	MS60	MS63	MS65
1986	Est. 10000	PF65 125				

KM# 165d CROWN

7.96 g., 0.917 Gold 0.2347 oz. AGW **Ruler:** Elizabeth II **Series:** World Cup Soccer - Mexico **Obv:** Crowned bust right **Rev:** Flags within circle

Date	Mintage	VF20	XF40	MS60	MS63	MS65
1986	Est. 1000	PF65 400				

KM# 165e CROWN

52.00 g., 0.950 Platinum 1.5882 oz. APW, 38.5 mm. **Ruler:** Elizabeth II **Series:** World Cup Soccer - Mexico **Obv:** Crowned bust right **Rev:** Flags within circle

Date	Mintage	VF20	XF40	MS60	MS63	MS65
1986	Est. 200	PF65 2,000				

KM# 173 CROWN

Copper-Nickel, 38.5 mm. **Ruler:** Elizabeth II **Subject:** Prince Andrew's Wedding **Obv:** Crowned bust right **Rev:** Conjoined heads left **Edge:** Reeded

Date	Mintage	VF20	XF40	MS60	MS63	MS65
1986	—	—	—	—	4.00	5.00
1986	—	PF65 8.00				

KM# 173a CROWN

Silver Clad Copper-Nickel, 38.5 mm. **Ruler:** Elizabeth II **Subject:** Prince Andrew's Wedding **Obv:** Crowned bust right **Rev:** Conjoined heads left

Date	Mintage	VF20	XF40	MS60	MS63	MS65
1986	Est. 20000	PF65 12.00				

KM# 173b CROWN

28.28 g., 0.925 Silver 0.841 oz. ASW, 38.5 mm. **Ruler:** Elizabeth II **Subject:** Prince Andrew's Wedding **Obv:** Crowned bust right **Rev:** Conjoined heads left

Date	Mintage	VF20	XF40	MS60	MS63	MS65
1986	Est. 20000	—	—	—	16.00	22.00
1986	Est. 15000	PF65 24.00				

KM# 173c CROWN

5.10 g., 0.374 Gold 0.0613 oz. AGW **Ruler:** Elizabeth II **Subject:** Prince Andrew's Wedding **Obv:** Crowned bust right **Rev:** Conjoined heads left

Date	Mintage	VF20	XF40	MS60	MS63	MS65
1986	Est. 10000	PF65 125				

KM# 173d CROWN

7.96 g., 0.917 Gold 0.2347 oz. AGW **Ruler:** Elizabeth II **Subject:** Prince Andrew's Wedding **Obv:** Crowned bust right **Rev:** Conjoined heads left

Date	Mintage	VF20	XF40	MS60	MS63	MS65
1986	Est. 1000	PF65 400				

KM# 173e CROWN

52.00 g., 0.950 Platinum 1.5882 oz. APW, 38.5 mm. **Ruler:** Elizabeth II **Subject:** Prince Andrew's Wedding **Obv:** Crowned bust right **Rev:** Conjoined heads left

Date	Mintage	VF20	XF40	MS60	MS63	MS65
1986	Est. 100	PF65 2,000				

KM# 174 CROWN

Copper-Nickel, 38.5 mm. **Ruler:** Elizabeth II **Subject:** Prince Andrew's Wedding **Obv:** Crowned bust right **Rev:** Two sets of arms **Edge:** Reeded

Date	Mintage	VF20	XF40	MS60	MS63	MS65
1986	Est. 50000	—	—	—	4.00	5.00
1986	—	PF65 8.00				

KM# 174a CROWN

Silver Clad Copper-Nickel, 38.5 mm. **Ruler:** Elizabeth II **Subject:** Prince Andrew's Wedding **Obv:** Crowned bust right **Rev:** Two sets of arms

Date	Mintage	VF20	XF40	MS60	MS63	MS65
1986	Est. 20000	PF65 12.00				

KM# 174b CROWN

28.28 g., 0.925 Silver 0.841 oz. ASW, 38.5 mm. **Ruler:** Elizabeth II **Subject:** Prince Andrew's Wedding **Obv:** Crowned bust right **Rev:** Two sets of arms

Date	Mintage	VF20	XF40	MS60	MS63	MS65
1986	Est. 20000	—	—	—	16.00	22.00
1986	Est. 15000	PF65 24.00				

KM# 174c CROWN

5.10 g., 0.374 Gold 0.0613 oz. AGW **Ruler:** Elizabeth II **Subject:** Prince Andrew's Wedding **Obv:** Crowned bust right **Rev:** Two sets of arms

Date	Mintage	VF20	XF40	MS60	MS63	MS65
1986	Est. 10000	PF65 125				

KM# 174d CROWN

7.96 g., 0.917 Gold 0.2347 oz. AGW **Ruler:** Elizabeth II **Subject:** Prince Andrew's Wedding **Obv:** Crowned bust right **Rev:** Two sets of arms

Date	Mintage	VF20	XF40	MS60	MS63	MS65
1986	Est. 1000	PF65 400				

KM# 174e CROWN

52.00 g., 0.950 Platinum 1.5882 oz. APW, 38.5 mm. **Ruler:** Elizabeth II **Subject:** Prince Andrew's Wedding **Obv:** Crowned bust right **Rev:** Two sets of arms

Date	Mintage	VF20	XF40	MS60	MS63	MS65
1986	Est. 100	PF65 2,000				

KM# 176 CROWN

Copper-Nickel, 38.5 mm. **Ruler:** Elizabeth II **Subject:** United States Constitution **Obv:** Crowned bust right **Rev:** Statue of Liberty divides dates within circle of Presidential busts **Edge:** Reeded

Date	Mintage	VF20	XF40	MS60	MS63	MS65
1987	—	—	—	—	5.00	6.00

KM# 176a CROWN

31.10 g., 0.999 Palladium 0.9989 oz. APW, 38.5 mm. **Ruler:** Elizabeth II **Subject:** United States Constitution Bicentennial **Obv:** Crowned bust right **Rev:** Statue of Liberty divides dates within circle of Presidential busts

Date	Mintage	VF20	XF40	MS60	MS63	MS65
1987	—	PF65 825				

KM# 176b CROWN

31.10 g., 0.995 Platinum 0.9949 oz. APW, 38.5 mm. **Ruler:** Elizabeth II **Subject:** United States Constitution Bicentennial **Obv:** Crowned bust right **Rev:** Statue of Liberty divides dates within circle of Presidential busts

Date	Mintage	VF20	XF40	MS60	MS63	MS65
1987	Est. 1000	PF65 1,650				

KM# 179 CROWN

Copper-Nickel, 38.5 mm. **Ruler:** Elizabeth II **Series:** Americ'a Cup **Obv:** Crowned bust right within circle **Rev:** Sailboats and map within circle **Edge:** Reeded

Date	Mintage	VF20	XF40	MS60	MS63	MS65
1987	50,000	—	—	—	10.00	11.50

KM# 179a CROWN

28.28 g., Silver Clad Copper-Nickel, 38.5 mm. **Ruler:** Elizabeth II **Obv:** Crowned bust right within circle **Rev:** Sailboats and map within circle **Edge:** Reeded

Date	Mintage	VF20	XF40	MS60	MS63	MS65
1987 PM	20,000	PF65 7.00				

KM# 179b CROWN

28.28 g., 0.925 Silver 0.841 oz. ASW, 38.5 mm. **Ruler:** Elizabeth II **Series:** America's Cup **Obv:** Crowned bust right within circle **Rev:** Sailboats and map within circle

Date	Mintage	VF20	XF40	MS60	MS63	MS65
1987	Est. 20000	—	—	—	16.00	22.00
1987	Est. 15000	PF65 45.00				

KM# 179c CROWN

31.10 g., 0.999 Palladium 0.999 oz. APW **Ruler:** Elizabeth II **Series:** America's Cup **Obv:** Crowned bust right within circle **Rev:** Sailboats and map within circle

Date	Mintage	VF20	XF40	MS60	MS63	MS65
1987	1,000	PF65 825				

KM# 183 CROWN

Copper-Nickel, 38.5 mm. **Ruler:** Elizabeth II **Series:** America's Cup **Obv:** Crowned bust right **Rev:** Sailboats and cup **Edge:** Reeded

Date	Mintage	VF20	XF40	MS60	MS63	MS65
1987	50,000	—	—	—	10.00	11.50

KM# 183b CROWN

28.28 g., 0.925 Silver 0.841 oz. ASW, 38.5 mm. **Ruler:** Elizabeth II **Series:** America's Cup **Obv:** Crowned bust right **Rev:** Sailboats and cup

Date	Mintage	VF20	XF40	MS60	MS63	MS65
1987	Est. 20000	—	—	—	16.00	22.00
1987	Est. 15000	PF65 45.00				

KM# 183c CROWN

31.10 g., 0.999 Palladium 0.999 oz. APW **Ruler:** Elizabeth II **Series:** America's Cup **Obv:** Crowned bust right **Rev:** Sailboats and cup

Date	Mintage	VF20	XF40	MS60	MS63	MS65
1987	1,000	PF65 825				

KM# 184 CROWN

Copper-Nickel, 38.5 mm. **Ruler:** Elizabeth II **Series:** America's Cup **Obv:** Crowned bust right **Rev:** Statue of Liberty and sailboats **Edge:** Reeded

Date	Mintage	VF20	XF40	MS60	MS63	MS65
1987	50,000	—	—	—	10.00	11.50

KM# 184b CROWN

28.28 g., 0.925 Silver 0.841 oz. ASW, 38.5 mm. **Ruler:** Elizabeth II **Series:** Americ'a Cup **Obv:** Crowned bust right **Rev:** Statue of Liberty and sailboats

Date	Mintage	VF20	XF40	MS60	MS63	MS65
1987	Est. 20000	—	—	—	16.00	22.00
1987	Est. 15000	PF65 45.00				

KM# 184c CROWN

31.10 g., 0.999 Palladium 0.999 oz. APW **Ruler:** Elizabeth II **Series:** America's Cup **Obv:** Crowned bust right **Rev:** Statue of Liberty and sailboats

Date	Mintage	VF20	XF40	MS60	MS63	MS65
1987	1,000	PF65 825				

KM# 185 CROWN

Copper-Nickel, 38.5 mm. **Ruler:** Elizabeth II **Series:** America's Cup **Obv:** Crowned bust right **Rev:** Bust of George Steers and sailboat **Edge:** Reeded

Date	Mintage	VF20	XF40	MS60	MS63	MS65
1987	50,000	—	—	—	10.00	11.50

KM# 185b CROWN

28.28 g., 0.925 Silver 0.841 oz. ASW, 38.5 mm. **Ruler:** Elizabeth II **Series:** America's Cup **Obv:** Crowned bust right **Rev:** Bust of George Steers and sailboat

Date	Mintage	VF20	XF40	MS60	MS63	MS65
1987	Est. 20000	—	—	—	16.00	22.00
1987	Est. 15000	PF65 45.00				

KM# 185c CROWN

31.10 g., 0.999 Palladium 0.999 oz. APW **Ruler:** Elizabeth II **Series:** America's Cup **Obv:** Crowned bust right **Rev:** Bust of George Steers and sailboat

Date	Mintage	VF20	XF40	MS60	MS63	MS65
1987	1,000	PF65 825				

KM# 186 CROWN

Copper-Nickel, 38.5 mm. **Ruler:** Elizabeth II **Series:** America's Cup **Obv:** Crowned bust right **Rev:** Bust of Sir Thomas Lipton and sailboat **Edge:** Reeded

Date	Mintage	VF20	XF40	MS60	MS63	MS65
1987	50,000	—	—	—	10.00	11.50

KM# 186b CROWN

28.28 g., 0.925 Silver 0.841 oz. ASW, 38.5 mm. **Ruler:** Elizabeth II **Series:** America's Cup **Obv:** Crowned bust right **Rev:** Bust of Sir Thomas Lipton and sailboat

Date	Mintage	VF20	XF40	MS60	MS63	MS65
1987	Est. 20000	—	—	—	18.00	20.00
1987	Est. 15000	PF65 45.00				

KM# 186c CROWN

31.10 g., 0.999 Palladium 0.999 oz. APW **Ruler:** Elizabeth II **Series:** America's Cup **Obv:** Crowned bust right **Rev:** Bust of Sir Thomas Lipton and sailboat

Date	Mintage	VF20	XF40	MS60	MS63	MS65
1987	1,000	PF65 825				

KM# 222 CROWN

Copper-Nickel, 38.5 mm. **Ruler:** Elizabeth II **Subject:** Australian Bicentennial **Obv:** Crowned bust right **Rev:** Cockatoo on branch within circle

Date	Mintage	VF20	XF40	MS60	MS63	MS65
1988	—	—	—	—	10.00	17.50
1988	500	PF65 30.00				

KM# 222a CROWN

31.10 g., 0.999 Silver 0.9989 oz. ASW, 38.5 mm. **Ruler:** Elizabeth II **Subject:** Australian Bicentennial **Obv:** Crowned bust right **Rev:** Cockatoo on branch within circle

Date	Mintage	VF20	XF40	MS60	MS63	MS65
1988	—	PF65 175				

KM# 223 CROWN

Copper-Nickel, 38.5 mm. **Ruler:** Elizabeth II **Subject:** Australian Bicentennial **Obv:** Crowned bust right **Rev:** Koala bear in tree within circle

Date	Mintage	VF20	XF40	MS60	MS63	MS65
1988	—	—	—	—	10.00	17.50
1988	500	PF65 30.00				

KM# 223a CROWN

31.10 g., 0.999 Silver 0.9989 oz. ASW, 38.5 mm. **Ruler:** Elizabeth II **Subject:** Australian Bicentennial **Obv:** Crowned bust right **Rev:** Koala bear in tree within circle

Date	Mintage	VF20	XF40	MS60	MS63	MS65
1988	—	PF65 175				

KM# 224 CROWN

Copper-Nickel, 38.5 mm. **Ruler:** Elizabeth II **Subject:** Australian Bicentennial **Obv:** Crowned bust right **Rev:** Duckbill platypus below two men and tent, all within circle

Date	Mintage	VF20	XF40	MS60	MS63	MS65
1988	—	—	—	—	12.00	17.50
1988	500	PF65 30.00				

KM# 224a CROWN

31.10 g., 0.999 Silver 0.9989 oz. ASW, 38.5 mm. **Ruler:** Elizabeth II **Subject:** Australian Bicentennial **Obv:** Crowned bust right **Rev:** Duckbill platypus below two men and tent all within circle

Date	Mintage	VF20	XF40	MS60	MS63	MS65
1988	—	PF65 175				

KM# 225 CROWN

Copper-Nickel, 38.5 mm. **Ruler:** Elizabeth II **Subject:** Australian Bicentennial **Obv:** Crowned bust right **Rev:** Kangaroo within circle

Date	Mintage	VF20	XF40	MS60	MS63	MS65
1988	—	—	—	—	12.00	17.50
1988	500	PF65 30.00				

KM# 225a CROWN

31.10 g., 0.9999 Silver 0.9998 oz. ASW, 38.5 mm. **Ruler:** Elizabeth II **Subject:** Australian Bicentennial **Obv:** Crowned bust right **Rev:** Kangaroo within circle

Date	Mintage	VF20	XF40	MS60	MS63	MS65
1988	—	PF65 175				

KM# 226 CROWN

Copper-Nickel, 38.5 mm. **Ruler:** Elizabeth II **Subject:** Australian Bicentennial **Obv:** Crowned bust right **Rev:** Dingo and train within circle

Date	Mintage	VF20	XF40	MS60	MS63	MS65
1988	—	—	—	—	12.50	17.50

KM# 226a CROWN

31.10 g., 0.9999 Silver 0.9998 oz. ASW, 38.5 mm. **Ruler:** Elizabeth II **Subject:** Australian Bicentennial **Obv:** Crowned bust right **Rev:** Dingo and train within circle

Date	Mintage	VF20	XF40	MS60	MS63	MS65
1988	—	PF65 175				

KM# 227 CROWN

Copper-Nickel, 38.5 mm. **Ruler:** Elizabeth II **Subject:** Australian Bicentennial **Obv:** Crowned bust right **Rev:** Tasmanian devil and map within circle

Date	Mintage	VF20	XF40	MS60	MS63	MS65
1988	—	—	—	—	12.00	17.50

KM# 227a CROWN

31.10 g., 0.9999 Silver 0.9998 oz. ASW, 38.5 mm. **Ruler:** Elizabeth II **Subject:** Australian Bicentennial **Obv:** Crowned bust right **Rev:** Tasmanian devil and map within circle

Date	Mintage	VF20	XF40	MS60	MS63	MS65
1988	—	PF65 175				

KM# 228 CROWN

Copper-Nickel, 38.5 mm. **Ruler:** Elizabeth II **Series:** Steam Navigation **Obv:** Crowned bust right **Rev:** Patrick Miller's Number One

Date	Mintage	VF20	XF40	MS60	MS63	MS65
1988	—	—	—	—	8.00	10.00

KM# 229 CROWN

Copper-Nickel, 38.5 mm. **Ruler:** Elizabeth II **Series:** Steam Navigation **Obv:** Crowned bust right **Rev:** Sirius within circle

Date	Mintage	VF20	XF40	MS60	MS63	MS65
1988	—	—	—	—	8.00	10.00

KM# 230 CROWN

Copper-Nickel, 38.5 mm. **Ruler:** Elizabeth II **Series:** Steam Navigation **Obv:** Crowned bust right **Rev:** Chaperon within circle

Date	Mintage	VF20	XF40	MS60	MS63	MS65
1988	—	—	—	—	8.00	10.00

KM# 231 CROWN

Copper-Nickel, 38.5 mm. **Ruler:** Elizabeth II **Series:** Steam Navigation **Obv:** Crowned bust right **Rev:** Mauretania within circle

Date	Mintage	VF20	XF40	MS60	MS63	MS65
1988	—	—	—	—	8.00	10.00

KM# 232 CROWN

Copper-Nickel, 38.5 mm. **Ruler:** Elizabeth II **Series:** Steam Navigation **Obv:** Crowned bust right **Rev:** Queen Mary within circle

Date	Mintage	VF20	XF40	MS60	MS63	MS65
1988	—	—	—	—	8.00	10.00

KM# 233 CROWN

Copper-Nickel, 38.5 mm. **Ruler:** Elizabeth II **Series:** Steam Navigation **Obv:** Crowned bust right **Rev:** Steamship divides circle

Date	Mintage	VF20	XF40	MS60	MS63	MS65
1988	—	—	—	—	8.00	10.00

KM# 245 CROWN

Copper-Nickel, 38.5 mm. **Ruler:** Elizabeth II **Obv:** Crowned bust right **Rev:** Manx cat

Date	Mintage	VF20	XF40	MS60	MS63	MS65
1988	—	—	—	—	12.00	16.00
1988	250	PF65 30.00				

KM# 245a CROWN

31.10 g., 0.999 Silver 0.9989 oz. ASW, 38.5 mm. **Ruler:** Elizabeth II **Subject:** Cat - Manx **Obv:** Crowned bust right **Rev:** Manx cat **Note:** Prev. KM#234.

Date	Mintage	VF20	XF40	MS60	MS63	MS65
1988	15,000	PF65 70.00				

KM# 245b CROWN

31.10 g., 0.999 Gold 0.9989 oz. AGW **Ruler:** Elizabeth II **Subject:** Cat - Manx **Obv:** Crowned bust right **Rev:** Manx cat **Note:** Prev. KM#239.

Date	Mintage	VF20	XF40	MS60	MS63	MS65
1988 U	4,300	—	—	—	—	1,700
1988	5,000	PF65 1,725				

KM# 240 CROWN

Copper-Nickel, 38.5 mm. **Ruler:** Elizabeth II **Series:** Bicentenary of the Mutiny on the Bounty **Obv:** Crowned bust right **Rev:** Standing figures facing within circle

Date	Mintage	VF20	XF40	MS60	MS63	MS65
1989	—	—	—	—	3.25	4.50
1989 Prooflike	—	—	—	—	—	15.00
1989	—	PF65 18.50				

KM# 240a CROWN

28.28 g., 0.925 Silver 0.841 oz. ASW, 38.5 mm. **Ruler:** Elizabeth II **Series:** Mutiny on the Bounty **Obv:** Crowned bust right **Rev:** Standing figures facing within circle

Date	Mintage	VF20	XF40	MS60	MS63	MS65
1989	—	PF65 45.00				

KM# 241 CROWN

Copper-Nickel, 38.5 mm. **Ruler:** Elizabeth II **Series:** Mutiny on the Bounty **Obv:** Crowned bust right **Rev:** H.M.S. Bounty

Date	Mintage	VF20	XF40	MS60	MS63	MS65
1989	—	—	—	—	7.50	9.00
1989 Prooflike	—	—	—	—	—	15.00
1989	—	PF65 18.50				

KM# 241a CROWN

28.28 g., 0.925 Silver 0.841 oz. ASW, 38.5 mm. **Ruler:** Elizabeth II **Series:** Mutiny on the Bounty **Obv:** Crowned bust right **Rev:** H.M.S. Bounty

Date	Mintage	VF20	XF40	MS60	MS63	MS65
1989	—	PF65 45.00				

KM# 242 CROWN

Copper-Nickel, 38.5 mm. **Ruler:** Elizabeth II **Series:** Mutiny on the Bounty **Obv:** Crowned bust right **Rev:** Captain Bligh and crew set afloat

Date	Mintage	VF20	XF40	MS60	MS63	MS65
1989	—	—	—	—	7.50	9.00
1989 Prooflike	—	—	—	—	—	15.00
1989	—	PF65 18.50				

KM# 242a CROWN

28.28 g., 0.925 Silver 0.841 oz. ASW, 38.5 mm. **Ruler:** Elizabeth II **Series:** Mutiny on the Bounty **Obv:** Crowned bust right **Rev:** Captain Bligh and crew set afloat

Date	Mintage	VF20	XF40	MS60	MS63	MS65
1989	—	PF65 45.00				

KM# 243 CROWN

Copper-Nickel, 38.5 mm. **Ruler:** Elizabeth II **Series:** Muntiny on the Bounty **Obv:** Crowned bust right **Rev:** Pitcairn Island

Date	Mintage	VF20	XF40	MS60	MS63	MS65
1989	—	—	—	—	7.50	9.00
1989 Prooflike	—	—	—	—	—	15.00
1989	—	PF65 18.50				

KM# 243a CROWN

28.28 g., 0.925 Silver 0.841 oz. ASW, 38.5 mm. **Ruler:** Elizabeth II **Series:** Mutiny on the Bounty **Obv:** Crowned bust right **Rev:** Pitcairn Island

Date	Mintage	VF20	XF40	MS60	MS63	MS65
1989	—	PF65 45.00				

KM# 246 CROWN

Copper-Nickel, 38.5 mm. **Ruler:** Elizabeth II **Obv:** Crowned bust right **Rev:** Washington crossing the Delaware

Date	Mintage	VF20	XF40	MS60	MS63	MS65
1989	—	—	—	—	2.75	3.50
1989	—	PF65 9.00				

KM# 246a CROWN

28.28 g., 0.925 Silver 0.841 oz. ASW, 38.5 mm. **Ruler:** Elizabeth II **Obv:** Crowned bust right **Rev:** Washington crossing the Delaware

Date	Mintage	VF20	XF40	MS60	MS63	MS65
1989	—	PF65 24.00				

KM# 247 CROWN

Copper-Nickel, 38.5 mm. **Ruler:** Elizabeth II **Subject:** George Washington Inauguration **Obv:** Crowned bust right **Rev:** Head of George Washington **Edge:** Reeded

Date	Mintage	VF20	XF40	MS60	MS63	MS65
1989	—	—	—	—	2.75	3.50
1989	—	PF65 9.00				

KM# 247a CROWN

28.28 g., 0.925 Silver 0.841 oz. ASW, 38.5 mm. **Ruler:** Elizabeth II **Subject:** George Washington Inauguration **Obv:** Crowned bust right **Rev:** Head of George Washington

Date	Mintage	VF20	XF40	MS60	MS63	MS65
1989	—	PF65 24.00				

KM# 248 CROWN

Copper-Nickel, 38.5 mm. **Ruler:** Elizabeth II **Subject:** George Washington Inauguration **Obv:** Crowned bust right **Rev:** Cameo within eagle **Edge:** Reeded

Date	Mintage	VF20	XF40	MS60	MS63	MS65
1989	—	—	—	—	7.00	8.00
1989	—	PF65 9.00				

KM# 248a CROWN

28.28 g., 0.925 Silver 0.841 oz. ASW, 38.5 mm. **Ruler:** Elizabeth II **Subject:** George Washington Inauguration **Obv:** Crowned bust right **Rev:** Cameo within eagle

Date	Mintage	VF20	XF40	MS60	MS63	MS65
1989	—	PF65 24.00				

KM# 249 CROWN

Copper-Nickel, 38.5 mm. **Ruler:** Elizabeth II **Subject:** George Washington Inauguration **Obv:** Crowned bust right **Rev:** George Washington taking oath **Edge:** Reeded

Date	Mintage	VF20	XF40	MS60	MS63	MS65
1989	—	—	—	5.00	6.00	8.00
1989	—	PF65 9.00				

KM# 249a CROWN

28.28 g., 0.925 Silver 0.841 oz. ASW, 38.5 mm. **Ruler:** Elizabeth II **Subject:** George Washington Inauguration **Obv:** Crowned bust right **Rev:** George Washington taking oath

Date	Mintage	VF20	XF40	MS60	MS63	MS65
1989	—	PF65 24.00				

KM# 250 CROWN

Copper-Nickel, 38.5 mm. **Ruler:** Elizabeth II **Obv:** Crowned bust right **Rev:** Persian cat **Edge:** Reeded

Date	Mintage	VF20	XF40	MS60	MS63	MS65
1989	250	PF65 35.00				
1989	—	—	—	—	12.00	16.00

KM# 250a CROWN

31.10 g., 0.999 Silver 0.9989 oz. ASW, 38.5 mm. **Ruler:** Elizabeth II **Obv:** Crowned bust right **Rev:** Persian cat **Note:** Prev. KM#251.

Date	Mintage	VF20	XF40	MS60	MS63	MS65
1989	—	PF65 75.00				

KM# 250b CROWN

31.10 g., 0.999 Gold 0.9989 oz. AGW **Ruler:** Elizabeth II **Obv:** Crowned bust right **Rev:** Persian cat **Note:** Prev. KM#256.

Date	Mintage	VF20	XF40	MS60	MS63	MS65
1989	—	—	—	—	—	1,700
1989	—	PF65 1,725				

KM# 250c CROWN

31.10 g., 0.9995 Platinum 0.9995 oz. APW **Ruler:** Elizabeth II **Obv:** Crowned bust right **Rev:** Persian cat **Note:** Prev. KM#471.

Date	Mintage	VF20	XF40	MS60	MS63	MS65
1989	—	—	—	—	—	1,725
1989	—	PF65 1,750				

KM# 273 CROWN

Copper-Nickel, 38.5 mm. **Ruler:** Elizabeth II **Subject:** Royal Visit **Obv:** Crowned bust right **Rev:** Three scenes from ship **Edge:** Reeded

Date	Mintage	VF20	XF40	MS60	MS63	MS65
1989	Est. 50000	—	—	—	8.00	9.00

KM# 273a CROWN

31.10 g., 0.999 Silver 0.9989 oz. ASW, 38.5 mm. **Ruler:** Elizabeth II **Subject:** Royal Visit **Obv:** Crowned bust right **Rev:** Three scenes from ship

Date	Mintage	VF20	XF40	MS60	MS63	MS65
1989	Est. 20000	PF65 40.00				

KM# 273b CROWN

31.10 g., 0.999 Gold 0.9989 oz. AGW **Ruler:** Elizabeth II **Subject:** Royal Visit **Obv:** Crowned bust right **Rev:** Three scenes from ship

Date	Mintage	VF20	XF40	MS60	MS63	MS65
1989	Est. 7500	PF65 1,725				

KM# 267 CROWN

Copper-Nickel, 38.5 mm. **Ruler:** Elizabeth II **Subject:** 150th Anniversary of "Penny Black" Stamp **Obv:** Crowned bust right **Rev:** Crowned head left within stamp **Note:** Struck in "pearl black" Copper-Nickel.

Date	Mintage	VF20	XF40	MS60	MS63	MS65
1990	—	—	—	—	12.50	13.50
1990	50,000	PF65 16.50				

KM# 267a CROWN

28.28 g., 0.925 Silver 0.841 oz. ASW, 38.5 mm. **Ruler:** Elizabeth II **Subject:** 150th Anniversary of "Penny Black" Stamp **Obv:** Crowned bust right **Rev:** Crowned head left within stamp **Edge:** Reeded

Date	Mintage	VF20	XF40	MS60	MS63	MS65
1990	30,000	PF65 35.00				

KM# 267b CROWN

31.10 g., 0.999 Gold 0.9989 oz. AGW **Ruler:** Elizabeth II **Subject:** 150th Anniversary of "Penny Black" Stamp **Obv:** Crowned bust right **Rev:** Crowned head of Queen Victoria left within stamp

Date	Mintage	VF20	XF40	MS60	MS63	MS65
1990	Est. 1000	PF65 1,750				

KM# 267c CROWN

52.00 g., 0.950 Platinum 1.5882 oz. APW, 38.5 mm. **Ruler:** Elizabeth II **Subject:** 150th Anniversary of "Penny Black" Stamp **Obv:** Crowned bust right **Rev:** Crowned head left within stamp

Date	Mintage	VF20	XF40	MS60	MS63	MS65
1990	Est. 50	PF65 2,200				

KM# 269 CROWN

Copper-Nickel, 38.5 mm. **Ruler:** Elizabeth II **Series:** World Cup - Italy **Obv:** Crowned bust right **Rev:** Soccer players and shield **Edge:** Reeded

Date	Mintage	VF20	XF40	MS60	MS63	MS65
1990	—	—	—	—	3.25	4.50

KM# 269a CROWN

28.28 g., 0.925 Silver 0.841 oz. ASW, 38.5 mm. **Ruler:** Elizabeth II **Series:** World Cup - Italy **Obv:** Crowned bust right **Rev:** Soccer players and shield

Date	Mintage	VF20	XF40	MS60	MS63	MS65
1990	—	PF65 24.00				

KM# 269b CROWN

6.22 g., 0.999 Gold 0.1998 oz. AGW **Ruler:** Elizabeth II **Series:** World Cup - Italy **Obv:** Crowned bust right **Rev:** Soccer players and shield

Date	Mintage	VF20	XF40	MS60	MS63	MS65
1990	Est. 500	PF65 345				

KM# 269c CROWN

6.22 g., 0.999 Platinum 0.1999 oz. APW **Ruler:** Elizabeth II **Series:** World Cup - Italy **Obv:** Crowned bust right **Rev:** Soccer players and shield

Date	Mintage	VF20	XF40	MS60	MS63	MS65
1990	Est. 100	PF65 375				

KM# 270 CROWN

Copper-Nickel, 38.5 mm. **Ruler:** Elizabeth II **Series:** World Cup - Italy **Obv:** Crowned bust right **Rev:** Soccer player in center of three shields

Date	Mintage	VF20	XF40	MS60	MS63	MS65
1990	—	—	—	—	6.00	7.00

KM# 270a CROWN

28.28 g., 0.925 Silver 0.841 oz. ASW, 38.5 mm. **Ruler:** Elizabeth II **Series:** World Cup - Italy **Obv:** Crowned bust right **Rev:** Soccer player in center of three shields

Date	Mintage	VF20	XF40	MS60	MS63	MS65
1990	Est. 30000	PF65 24.00				

KM# 270b CROWN

6.22 g., 0.999 Gold 0.1998 oz. AGW **Ruler:** Elizabeth II **Series:** World Cup - Italy **Obv:** Crowned bust right **Rev:** Soccer player in center of three shields

Date	Mintage	VF20	XF40	MS60	MS63	MS65
1990	Est. 500	PF65 345				

KM# 270c CROWN

6.22 g., 0.999 Platinum 0.1999 oz. APW **Ruler:** Elizabeth II **Series:** World Cup - Italy **Obv:** Crowned bust right **Rev:** Soccer player in center of three shields

Date	Mintage	VF20	XF40	MS60	MS63	MS65
1990	Est. 100	PF65 375				

KM# 271 CROWN

Copper-Nickel, 38.5 mm. **Ruler:** Elizabeth II **Series:** World Cup - Italy **Obv:** Crowned bust right **Rev:** Three shields flanked by emblems with soccer ball below **Edge:** Reeded

Date	Mintage	VF20	XF40	MS60	MS63	MS65
1990	—	—	—	—	6.00	7.00

KM# 271a CROWN

28.28 g., 0.925 Silver 0.841 oz. ASW, 38.5 mm. **Ruler:** Elizabeth II **Series:** World Cup - Italy **Obv:** Crowned bust right **Rev:** Three shields flanked by emblems with soccer ball below

Date	Mintage	VF20	XF40	MS60	MS63	MS65
1990	Est. 30000	PF65 24.00				

KM# 271b CROWN

6.22 g., 0.999 Gold 0.1998 oz. AGW **Ruler:** Elizabeth II **Series:** World Cup - Italy **Obv:** Crowned bust right **Rev:** Three shields flanked by emblems with soccer ball below

Date	Mintage	VF20	XF40	MS60	MS63	MS65
1990	Est. 500	PF65 345				

KM# 271c CROWN

6.22 g., 0.999 Platinum 0.1999 oz. APW **Ruler:** Elizabeth II **Series:** World Cup - Italy **Obv:** Crowned bust right **Rev:** Three shields flanked by emblems with soccer ball below

Date	Mintage	VF20	XF40	MS60	MS63	MS65
1990	Est. 100	PF65 375				

KM# 272 CROWN

Copper-Nickel, 38.5 mm. **Ruler:** Elizabeth II **Series:** World Cup - Italy **Obv:** Crowned bust right **Rev:** Three shields flanked by soccer players **Edge:** Reeded

Date	Mintage	VF20	XF40	MS60	MS63	MS65
1990	—	—	—	—	6.00	7.00

KM# 272a CROWN

28.28 g., 0.925 Silver 0.841 oz. ASW, 38.5 mm. **Ruler:** Elizabeth II **Series:** World Cup - Italy **Obv:** Crowned bust right **Rev:** Three shields flanked by soccer players

Date	Mintage	VF20	XF40	MS60	MS63	MS65
1990	Est. 30000	PF65 24.00				

KM# 272b CROWN

6.22 g., 0.999 Gold 0.1998 oz. AGW **Ruler:** Elizabeth II **Series:** World Cup - Italy **Obv:** Crowned bust right **Rev:** Three shields flanked by soccer players

Date	Mintage	VF20	XF40	MS60	MS63	MS65
1990	—	PF65 345				

KM# 272c CROWN

6.22 g., 0.999 Platinum 0.1999 oz. APW **Ruler:** Elizabeth II **Series:** World Cup - Italy **Obv:** Crowned bust right **Rev:** Three shields flanked by soccer players

Date	Mintage	VF20	XF40	MS60	MS63	MS65
1990	Est. 100	PF65 375				

KM# 275 CROWN

Copper-Nickel, 38.5 mm. **Ruler:** Elizabeth II **Obv:** Crowned bust right **Rev:** Alley cat

Date	Mintage	VF20	XF40	MS60	MS63	MS65
1990	—	—	—	—	12.00	16.00
1990	250	PF65 35.00				

KM# 275a CROWN

31.10 g., 0.999 Silver 0.9989 oz. ASW, 38.5 mm. **Ruler:** Elizabeth II **Obv:** Crowned bust right **Rev:** Alley cat **Note:** Prev. KM#276.

Date	Mintage	VF20	XF40	MS60	MS63	MS65
1990	—	PF65 80.00				

KM# 275b CROWN

31.10 g., 0.999 Gold 0.9989 oz. AGW **Ruler:** Elizabeth II **Obv:** Crowned bust right **Rev:** Alley cat **Note:** Prev. KM#281.

Date	Mintage	VF20	XF40	MS60	MS63	MS65
1990	—	—	—	—	—	1,700
1990	—	PF65 1,725				

KM# 283 CROWN

Copper-Nickel, 38.5 mm. **Ruler:** Elizabeth II **Obv:** Crowned bust right **Rev:** Winston Churchill bust right with hat and cigar **Edge:** Reeded

Date	Mintage	VF20	XF40	MS60	MS63	MS65
1990	—	—	—	—	3.25	4.50

KM# 283a CROWN

28.28 g., 0.925 Silver 0.841 oz. ASW, 38.5 mm. **Ruler:** Elizabeth II **Obv:** Crowned bust right **Rev:** Winston Churchill bust right with hat and cigar

Date	Mintage	VF20	XF40	MS60	MS63	MS65
1990	Est. 25000	PF65 50.00				

KM# 283b CROWN

6.22 g., 0.999 Gold 0.1999 oz. AGW **Ruler:** Elizabeth II **Obv:** Crowned bust right **Rev:** Winston Churchill bust right with hat and cigar

Date	Mintage	VF20	XF40	MS60	MS63	MS65
1990	Est. 500	PF65 345				

KM# 283c CROWN
6.22 g., 0.999 Platinum 0.1999 oz. APW **Ruler:** Elizabeth II **Obv:** Crowned bust right **Rev:** Winston Churchill bust right with hat and cigar

Date	Mintage	VF20	XF40	MS60	MS63	MS65
1990	Est. 100	PF65 375				

KM# 284 CROWN
Copper-Nickel, 38.5 mm. **Ruler:** Elizabeth II **Obv:** Crowned bust right **Rev:** Winston Churchill bust left **Edge:** Reeded

Date	Mintage	VF20	XF40	MS60	MS63	MS65
1990	—	—	—	—	3.25	4.50

KM# 284a CROWN
28.28 g., 0.925 Silver 0.841 oz. ASW, 38.5 mm. **Ruler:** Elizabeth II **Obv:** Crowned bust right **Rev:** Winston Churchill bust left

Date	Mintage	VF20	XF40	MS60	MS63	MS65
1990	Est. 25000	PF65 50.00				

KM# 284b CROWN
6.22 g., 0.999 Gold 0.1999 oz. AGW **Ruler:** Elizabeth II **Obv:** Crowned bust right **Rev:** Winston Churchill bust left

Date	Mintage	VF20	XF40	MS60	MS63	MS65
1990	Est. 500	PF65 345				

KM# 284c CROWN
6.22 g., 0.999 Platinum 0.1999 oz. APW **Ruler:** Elizabeth II **Obv:** Crowned bust right **Rev:** Winston Churchill bust left

Date	Mintage	VF20	XF40	MS60	MS63	MS65
1990	Est. 100	PF65 375				

KM# 307 CROWN
28.28 g., Copper-Nickel, 38.6 mm. **Ruler:** Elizabeth II **Obv:** Crowned bust right **Rev:** Adult and two children facing **Edge:** Reeded

Date	Mintage	VF20	XF40	MS60	MS63	MS65
1990 PM	—	—	—	—	10.00	12.00

KM# 307a CROWN
28.28 g., 0.925 Silver 0.841 oz. ASW, 38.6 mm. **Ruler:** Elizabeth II **Obv:** Crowned bust right **Rev:** Adult and two children facing

Date	Mintage	VF20	XF40	MS60	MS63	MS65
1990 PM	—	PF65 50.00				

KM# 291 CROWN
Copper-Nickel, 38.5 mm. **Ruler:** Elizabeth II **Subject:** 100th Anniversary - American Numismatic Association **Obv:** Crowned bust right **Rev:** Cat within circle of assorted coins **Edge:** Reeded

Date	Mintage	VF20	XF40	MS60	MS63	MS65
1991	—	—	—	—	4.50	6.50

KM# 291a CROWN
28.28 g., 0.925 Silver 0.841 oz. ASW, 38.5 mm. **Ruler:** Elizabeth II **Subject:** 100th Anniversary - American Numismatic Association **Obv:** Crowned bust right **Rev:** Cat within circle of assorted coins

Date	Mintage	VF20	XF40	MS60	MS63	MS65
1991	—	PF65 45.00				

KM# 292 CROWN
Copper-Nickel, 38.5 mm. **Ruler:** Elizabeth II **Obv:** Crowned bust right **Rev:** Norwegian cat **Edge:** Reeded

Date	Mintage	VF20	XF40	MS60	MS63	MS65
1991	—	—	—	—	12.00	26.00
1991 Proof	25	—	—	—	—	—

KM# 292a CROWN
31.10 g., 0.999 Silver 0.9989 oz. ASW, 38.5 mm. **Ruler:** Elizabeth II **Obv:** Crowned bust right **Rev:** Norwegian cat **Note:** Prev. KM#293.

Date	Mintage	VF20	XF40	MS60	MS63	MS65
1991	50,000	PF65 70.00				

KM# 292b CROWN
31.10 g., 0.999 Gold 0.9989 oz. AGW **Ruler:** Elizabeth II **Obv:** Crowned bust right **Rev:** Norwegian cat **Note:** Prev. KM#298.

Date	Mintage	VF20	XF40	MS60	MS63	MS65
1991	—	—	—	—	—	1,700
1991	—	PF65 1,725				

KM# 304 CROWN
Copper-Nickel, 38.5 mm. **Ruler:** Elizabeth II **Subject:** 10th Wedding Anniversary **Obv:** Crowned bust right **Rev:** Head of Prince Charles

Date	Mintage	VF20	XF40	MS60	MS63	MS65
1991	—	—	—	—	4.00	6.00

KM# 304a CROWN
28.28 g., 0.925 Silver 0.841 oz. ASW, 38.5 mm. **Ruler:** Elizabeth II **Subject:** 10th Wedding Anniversary **Obv:** Crowned bust right **Rev:** Head of Prince Charles

Date	Mintage	VF20	XF40	MS60	MS63	MS65
1991	—	PF65 42.00				

KM# 304b CROWN
6.22 g., 0.999 Gold 0.1998 oz. AGW **Ruler:** Elizabeth II **Subject:** 10th Wedding Anniversary **Obv:** Crowned bust right **Rev:** Head of Prince Charles

Date	Mintage	VF20	XF40	MS60	MS63	MS65
1991	—	PF65 345				

KM# 305 CROWN
Copper-Nickel, 38.5 mm. **Ruler:** Elizabeth II **Subject:** 10th Wedding Anniversary **Obv:** Crowned bust right **Rev:** Head of Princess Diana

Date	Mintage	VF20	XF40	MS60	MS63	MS65
1991	—	—	—	—	4.00	6.00

KM# 305a CROWN
28.28 g., 0.925 Silver 0.841 oz. ASW, 38.5 mm. **Ruler:** Elizabeth II **Subject:** 10th Wedding Anniversary **Obv:** Crowned bust right **Rev:** Head of Princess Diana

Date	Mintage	VF20	XF40	MS60	MS63	MS65
1991	—	PF65 42.00				

KM# 305b CROWN
6.22 g., 0.999 Gold 0.1998 oz. AGW **Ruler:** Elizabeth II **Subject:** 10th Wedding Anniversary **Obv:** Crowned bust right **Rev:** Head of Princess Diana 1/2 left

Date	Mintage	VF20	XF40	MS60	MS63	MS65
1991	—	PF65 345				

KM# 320 CROWN
28.28 g., Copper-Nickel, 38.6 mm. **Ruler:** Elizabeth II **Subject:** America's Cup **Obv:** Crowned bust right **Rev:** Cameo of sailboats with no roman numerals in legend **Edge:** Reeded **Note:** Officially "sales samples" about 25 pieces were sold or presented to distributors

Date	Mintage	VF20	XF40	MS60	MS63	MS65
1991 PM	100	—	—	—	35.00	40.00

KM# 320a CROWN
28.28 g., 0.925 Silver 0.841 oz. ASW, 38.6 mm. **Ruler:** Elizabeth II **Subject:** America's Cup - San Diego **Obv:** Crowned bust right **Rev:** Cameo of sailboats **Rev. Legend:** AMERICA'S CUP CHALLENGE

Date	Mintage	VF20	XF40	MS60	MS63	MS65
1991	15	PF65 475				

KM# 326a CROWN
28.28 g., 0.925 Silver 0.841 oz. ASW, 38.5 mm. **Ruler:** Elizabeth II **Subject:** America's Cup - San Diego **Obv:** Crowned bust right **Rev:** Cameo above sailboats

Date	Mintage	VF20	XF40	MS60	MS63	MS65
1992 Proof	25,000	—	—	—	60.00	65.00

KM# 310 CROWN

Copper-Nickel, 38.5 mm. **Ruler:** Elizabeth II **Series:** Discovery of America **Obv:** Crowned bust right **Rev:** Head with hat facing and train engine within circle

Date	Mintage	VF20	XF40	MS60	MS63	MS65
1992	—	—	—	—	3.75	4.50
1992	—	PF65 12.00				

KM# 310a CROWN

28.28 g., 0.925 Silver 0.841 oz. ASW, 38.5 mm. **Ruler:** Elizabeth II **Series:** Discovery of America **Obv:** Crowned bust right **Rev:** Head with hat facing and train engine within circle

Date	Mintage	VF20	XF40	MS60	MS63	MS65
1992	—	PF65 45.00				

KM# 311 CROWN

Copper-Nickel, 38.5 mm. **Ruler:** Elizabeth II **Series:** Discovery of America **Obv:** Crowned bust right **Rev:** Head facing and train engine within circle

Date	Mintage	VF20	XF40	MS60	MS63	MS65
1992	—	—	—	—	3.75	4.50
1992	—	PF65 12.00				

KM# 311a CROWN

28.28 g., 0.925 Silver 0.841 oz. ASW, 38.5 mm. **Ruler:** Elizabeth II **Series:** Discovery of America **Obv:** Crowned bust right **Rev:** Head facing and train engine within circle

Date	Mintage	VF20	XF40	MS60	MS63	MS65
1992	—	PF65 45.00				

KM# 312 CROWN

Copper-Nickel, 38.5 mm. **Ruler:** Elizabeth II **Series:** Discovery of America **Obv:** Crowned bust right **Rev:** Group of standing figures within circle

Date	Mintage	VF20	XF40	MS60	MS63	MS65
1992	—	PF65 10.00				
1992	—	—	—	—	3.75	4.50

KM# 312a CROWN

28.28 g., 0.925 Silver 0.841 oz. ASW, 38.5 mm. **Ruler:** Elizabeth II **Series:** Discovery of America **Obv:** Crowned bust right **Rev:** Group of standing figures within circle

Date	Mintage	VF20	XF40	MS60	MS63	MS65
1992	—	PF65 45.00				

KM# 313 CROWN

Copper-Nickel, 38.5 mm. **Ruler:** Elizabeth II **Series:** Discovery of America **Obv:** Crowned bust right **Rev:** Triskeles on shield above crossed flags within circle

Date	Mintage	VF20	XF40	MS60	MS63	MS65
1992	—	PF65 10.00				
1992	—	—	—	—	8.00	9.00

KM# 313a CROWN

28.28 g., 0.925 Silver 0.841 oz. ASW, 38.5 mm. **Ruler:** Elizabeth II **Series:** Discovery of America **Obv:** Bust of Queen Elizabeth II right **Rev:** Triskeles on shield above crossed flags within circle

Date	Mintage	VF20	XF40	MS60	MS63	MS65
1992	—	PF65 32.00				

KM# 326 CROWN

Copper-Nickel, 38.5 mm. **Ruler:** Elizabeth II **Subject:** America's Cup - San Diego **Obv:** Crowned bust right **Rev:** Cameo above sailboats **Rev. Legend:** AMERICA'S CUP • SAN DIEGO • 1992

Date	Mintage	VF20	XF40	MS60	MS63	MS65
1992	—	—	—	—	4.75	6.00
1992	—	PF65 12.50				

KM# 326b CROWN

31.03 g., 0.999 Gold 0.9966 oz. AGW **Ruler:** Elizabeth II **Subject:** America's Cup - San Diego **Obv:** Crowned bust right **Rev:** Cameo above sailboats

Date	Mintage	VF20	XF40	MS60	MS63	MS65
1992	—	PF65 1,725				

KM# 332 CROWN

Copper-Nickel, 38.5 mm. **Ruler:** Elizabeth II **Obv:** Crowned bust right **Rev:** Seated Siamese cat

Date	Mintage	VF20	XF40	MS60	MS63	MS65
1992	—	—	—	—	12.00	16.00

KM# 332a CROWN

31.10 g., 0.999 Silver 0.9989 oz. ASW, 38.5 mm. **Ruler:** Elizabeth II **Obv:** Crowned bust right **Rev:** Seated Siamese cat right **Note:** Prev. KM#333.

Date	Mintage	VF20	XF40	MS60	MS63	MS65
1992	50,000	PF65 70.00				

KM# 332b CROWN

31.10 g., 0.999 Gold 0.9989 oz. AGW **Ruler:** Elizabeth II **Obv:** Crowned bust right **Rev:** Seated Siamese cat **Note:** Prev. KM#334.

Date	Mintage	VF20	XF40	MS60	MS63	MS65
1992	—	—	—	—	—	1,700
1992	—	PF65 1,725				

KM# 342 CROWN

31.10 g., 0.999 Gold 0.9989 oz. AGW **Ruler:** Elizabeth II **Subject:** Year of the Cockerel **Obv:** Crowned bust right **Rev:** Cockerel within circle

Date	Mintage	VF20	XF40	MS60	MS63	MS65
1993	Est. 2500	PF65 1,725				

KM# 353 CROWN

Copper-Nickel, 38.5 mm. **Ruler:** Elizabeth II **Obv:** Crowned bust right **Rev:** Maine coon cat

Date	Mintage	VF20	XF40	MS60	MS63	MS65
1993	—	—	—	—	12.00	16.00

KM# 353a CROWN

31.10 g., 0.999 Silver 0.9989 oz. ASW, 38.5 mm. **Ruler:** Elizabeth II **Obv:** Crowned bust right **Rev:** Maine coon cat **Note:** Prev. KM#354.

Date	Mintage	VF20	XF40	MS60	MS63	MS65
1993	50,000	PF65 80.00				

KM# 353b CROWN

31.10 g., 0.999 Gold 0.9989 oz. AGW **Ruler:** Elizabeth II **Obv:** Crowned bust right **Rev:** Maine coon cat **Note:** Prev. KM#355.

Date	Mintage	VF20	XF40	MS60	MS63	MS65
1993	—	—	—	—	—	1,700
1993	—	PF65 1,725				

KM# 357 CROWN
Copper-Nickel, 38.5 mm. **Ruler:** Elizabeth II **Series:** Preserve Planet Earth **Obv:** Crowned bust right **Rev:** Dinosaur

Date	Mintage	VF20	XF40	MS60	MS63	MS65
1993	—	—	—	—	10.00	14.00

KM# 357a CROWN
Silver, 38.5 mm. **Ruler:** Elizabeth II **Series:** Preserve Planet Earth **Obv:** Crowned bust right **Rev:** Dinosaur

Date	Mintage	VF20	XF40	MS60	MS63	MS65
1993	—	—	—	—	—	—

KM# 358 CROWN
Copper-Nickel, 38.5 mm. **Ruler:** Elizabeth II **Series:** Preserve Planet Earth **Obv:** Crowned bust right **Rev:** Diplodocus

Date	Mintage	VF20	XF40	MS60	MS63	MS65
1993	—	—	—	—	9.00	14.00

KM# 364 CROWN
Copper-Nickel, 38.5 mm. **Ruler:** Elizabeth II **Series:** World Cup Soccer - U.S.A. **Obv:** Crowned bust right **Rev:** Two players

Date	Mintage	VF20	XF40	MS60	MS63	MS65
1994	—	—	—	—	6.00	7.00

KM# 364a CROWN
28.28 g., 0.925 Silver 0.841 oz. ASW, 38.5 mm. **Ruler:** Elizabeth II **Series:** World Cup Soccer - U.S.A. **Obv:** Crowned bust right **Rev:** Two players

Date	Mintage	VF20	XF40	MS60	MS63	MS65
1994	Est. 30000	PF65 28.50				

KM# 366 CROWN
Copper-Nickel, 38.5 mm. **Ruler:** Elizabeth II **Series:** World Cup Soccer - U.S.A. **Obv:** Crowned bust right **Rev:** Three players

Date	Mintage	VF20	XF40	MS60	MS63	MS65
1994	—	—	—	—	6.00	7.00

KM# 366a CROWN
28.28 g., 0.925 Silver 0.841 oz. ASW, 38.5 mm. **Ruler:** Elizabeth II **Series:** World Cup Soccer - U.S.A. **Obv:** Crowned bust right **Rev:** Three players

Date	Mintage	VF20	XF40	MS60	MS63	MS65
1994	Est. 30000	PF65 28.50				

KM# 368 CROWN
Copper-Nickel, 38.5 mm. **Ruler:** Elizabeth II **Series:** World Cup Soccer - U.S.A. **Obv:** Crowned bust right **Rev:** Soccer players

Date	Mintage	VF20	XF40	MS60	MS63	MS65
1994	—	—	—	—	6.00	7.00

KM# 368a CROWN
28.28 g., 0.925 Silver 0.841 oz. ASW, 38.5 mm. **Ruler:** Elizabeth II **Series:** World Cup Soccer - U.S.A. **Obv:** Crowned bust right **Rev:** Soccer players

Date	Mintage	VF20	XF40	MS60	MS63	MS65
1994	Est. 30000	PF65 28.50				

KM# 370 CROWN
Copper-Nickel, 38.5 mm. **Ruler:** Elizabeth II **Series:** World Cup Soccer - U.S.A. **Obv:** Crowned bust right **Rev:** Soccer players

Date	Mintage	VF20	XF40	MS60	MS63	MS65
1994	—	—	—	—	6.00	7.00

KM# 370a CROWN
28.28 g., 0.925 Silver 0.841 oz. ASW, 38.5 mm. **Ruler:** Elizabeth II **Series:** World Cup Soccer - U.S.A. **Obv:** Crowned bust right **Rev:** Soccer players

Date	Mintage	VF20	XF40	MS60	MS63	MS65
1994	Est. 30000	PF65 28.50				

KM# 372 CROWN
Copper-Nickel, 38.5 mm. **Ruler:** Elizabeth II **Series:** World Cup Soccer - U.S.A. **Obv:** Crowned bust right **Rev:** Soccer players

Date	Mintage	VF20	XF40	MS60	MS63	MS65
1994	—	—	—	—	8.00	9.00

KM# 372a CROWN
28.28 g., 0.925 Silver 0.841 oz. ASW, 38.5 mm. **Ruler:** Elizabeth II **Series:** World Cup Soccer - U.S.A. **Obv:** Crowned bust right **Rev:** Soccer players

Date	Mintage	VF20	XF40	MS60	MS63	MS65
1994	Est. 30000	PF65 28.50				

KM# 374 CROWN
Copper-Nickel, 38.5 mm. **Ruler:** Elizabeth II **Series:** World Cup Soccer - U.S.A. **Obv:** Crowned bust right **Rev:** Soccer players

Date	Mintage	VF20	XF40	MS60	MS63	MS65
1994	—	—	—	—	6.00	7.00

KM# 374a CROWN
28.28 g., 0.925 Silver 0.841 oz. ASW, 38.5 mm. **Ruler:** Elizabeth II **Series:** World Cup Soccer - U.S.A. **Obv:** Crowned bust right **Rev:** Soccer players

Date	Mintage	VF20	XF40	MS60	MS63	MS65
1994	Est. 30000	PF65 28.50				

KM# 380 CROWN
Copper-Nickel, 38.5 mm. **Ruler:** Elizabeth II **Obv:** Crowned bust right **Rev:** Japanese bobtail cat

Date	Mintage	VF20	XF40	MS60	MS63	MS65
1994	—	—	—	—	12.00	16.00

KM# 380a CROWN
31.10 g., 0.999 Silver 0.9989 oz. ASW, 38.5 mm. **Ruler:** Elizabeth II **Obv:** Crowned bust right **Rev:** Japanese bobtail cat **Note:** Prev. KM#381.

Date	Mintage	VF20	XF40	MS60	MS63	MS65
1994	—	PF65 70.00				

KM# 380b CROWN
31.10 g., 0.999 Gold 0.9989 oz. AGW **Ruler:** Elizabeth II **Obv:** Crowned bust right **Rev:** Japanese bobtail cat **Note:** Prev. KM#382.

Date	Mintage	VF20	XF40	MS60	MS63	MS65
1994	—	—	—	—	—	1,700
1994	—	PF65 1,725				

KM# 380c CROWN
31.10 g., 0.9995 Platinum 0.9995 oz. APW **Ruler:** Elizabeth II **Obv:** Crowned bust right **Rev:** Japanese bobtail cat **Note:** Prev. KM#477.

Date	Mintage	VF20	XF40	MS60	MS63	MS65
1994	—	—	—	—	—	1,800
1994	—	PF65 1,900				

KM# 384 CROWN
Copper-Nickel, 38.5 mm. **Ruler:** Elizabeth II **Series:** Preserve Planet Earth **Obv:** Crowned bust right **Rev:** Woolly mammoth

Date	Mintage	VF20	XF40	MS60	MS63	MS65
1994	—	—	—	—	10.00	17.50

KM# 384a CROWN
28.28 g., 0.925 Silver 0.841 oz. ASW, 38.5 mm. **Ruler:** Elizabeth II **Series:** Preserve Planet Earth **Obv:** Crowned bust right **Rev:** Woolly mammoth

Date	Mintage	VF20	XF40	MS60	MS63	MS65
1994	Est. 30000	PF65 40.00				

KM# 385 CROWN
Copper-Nickel, 38.5 mm. **Ruler:** Elizabeth II **Series:** Preserve Planet Earth **Obv:** Crowned bust right **Rev:** Kangaroos

Date	Mintage	VF20	XF40	MS60	MS63	MS65
1994	—	—	—	—	9.00	14.00

KM# 385a CROWN
28.28 g., 0.925 Silver 0.841 oz. ASW, 38.5 mm. **Ruler:** Elizabeth II **Series:** Preserve Planet Earth **Obv:** Crowned bust right **Rev:** Kangaroos

Date	Mintage	VF20	XF40	MS60	MS63	MS65
1994	Est. 30000	PF65 28.50				

KM# 386 CROWN
Copper-Nickel, 38.5 mm. **Ruler:** Elizabeth II **Series:** Preserve Planet Earth **Obv:** Crowned bust right **Rev:** Seals

Date	Mintage	VF20	XF40	MS60	MS63	MS65
1994	—	—	—	—	9.00	14.00

KM# 386a CROWN
28.28 g., 0.925 Silver 0.841 oz. ASW, 38.5 mm. **Ruler:** Elizabeth II **Series:** Preserve Planet Earth **Obv:** Crowned bust right **Rev:** Seals

Date	Mintage	VF20	XF40	MS60	MS63	MS65
1994	—	PF65 28.50				

KM# 387 CROWN
Copper-Nickel, 38.5 mm. **Ruler:** Elizabeth II **Series:** Preserve Planet Earth **Obv:** Crowned bust right **Rev:** Deer

Date	Mintage	VF20	XF40	MS60	MS63	MS65
1994	—	—	—	—	9.00	14.00

KM# 387a CROWN
28.28 g., 0.925 Silver 0.841 oz. ASW, 38.5 mm. **Ruler:** Elizabeth II **Series:** Preserve Planet Earth **Obv:** Crowned bust right **Rev:** Deer

Date	Mintage	VF20	XF40	MS60	MS63	MS65
1994	—	PF65 28.50				

KM# 406 CROWN
Copper-Nickel, 38.5 mm. **Ruler:** Elizabeth II **Subject:** Year of the Dog **Obv:** Crowned bust right **Rev:** Shih Tzu within circle

Date	Mintage	VF20	XF40	MS60	MS63	MS65
1994	—	—	—	—	10.00	16.00

KM# 407 CROWN
31.10 g., 0.999 Silver 0.9989 oz. ASW, 38.5 mm. **Ruler:** Elizabeth II **Subject:** Year of the Dog **Obv:** Crowned bust right **Rev:** Pekingese within circle

Date	Mintage	VF20	XF40	MS60	MS63	MS65
1994	—	PF65 45.00				

KM# 408 CROWN
31.10 g., 0.999 Gold 0.9989 oz. AGW **Ruler:** Elizabeth II **Subject:** Year of the Dog **Obv:** Crowned bust right **Rev:** Pekingese within circle

Date	Mintage	VF20	XF40	MS60	MS63	MS65
1994	Est. 5000	PF65 1,725				

KM# 417 CROWN
Copper-Nickel, 38.5 mm. **Ruler:** Elizabeth II **Series:** Man in Flight **Obv:** Crowned bust right **Rev:** Otto Lilienthal

Date	Mintage	VF20	XF40	MS60	MS63	MS65
1994	—	—	—	—	7.00	8.00

KM# 417a CROWN
28.28 g., 0.925 Silver 0.841 oz. ASW, 38.5 mm. **Ruler:** Elizabeth II **Series:** Man in Flight **Obv:** Crowned bust right **Rev:** Otto Lilienthal

Date	Mintage	VF20	XF40	MS60	MS63	MS65
1994	—	PF65 40.00				

KM# 418 CROWN
Copper-Nickel, 38.5 mm. **Ruler:** Elizabeth II **Series:** Man in Flight **Obv:** Crowned bust right **Rev:** Ferdinand von Zeppelin

Date	Mintage	VF20	XF40	MS60	MS63	MS65
1994	—	—	—	—	11.00	13.50

KM# 419 CROWN
Copper-Nickel, 38.5 mm. **Ruler:** Elizabeth II **Series:** Man in Flight **Obv:** Crowned bust right **Rev:** Louis Bleriot

Date	Mintage	VF20	XF40	MS60	MS63	MS65
1994	—	—	—	—	8.00	9.00

KM# 419a CROWN
28.28 g., 0.925 Silver 0.841 oz. ASW, 38.5 mm. **Ruler:** Elizabeth II **Series:** Man in Flight **Subject:** First Channel Crossing - 1909 **Obv:** Crowned bust right **Rev:** Louis Bleriot

Date	Mintage	VF20	XF40	MS60	MS63	MS65
1994	—	PF65 40.00				

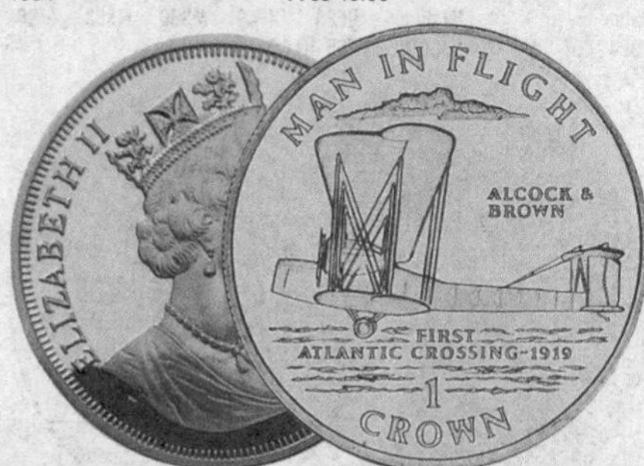

KM# 420 CROWN
Copper-Nickel, 38.5 mm. **Ruler:** Elizabeth II **Series:** Man in Flight **Subject:** First Atlantic Crossing - 1919 **Obv:** Crowned bust right **Rev:** Alcock and Brown

Date	Mintage	VF20	XF40	MS60	MS63	MS65
1994	—	—	—	—	10.00	12.00

KM# 420a CROWN
28.28 g., 0.925 Silver 0.841 oz. ASW, 38.5 mm. **Ruler:** Elizabeth II **Series:** Man in Flight **Subject:** First Atlantic Crossing - 1919 **Obv:** Crowned bust right **Rev:** Alcock and Brown

Date	Mintage	VF20	XF40	MS60	MS63	MS65
1994	Est. 30000	PF65 40.00				

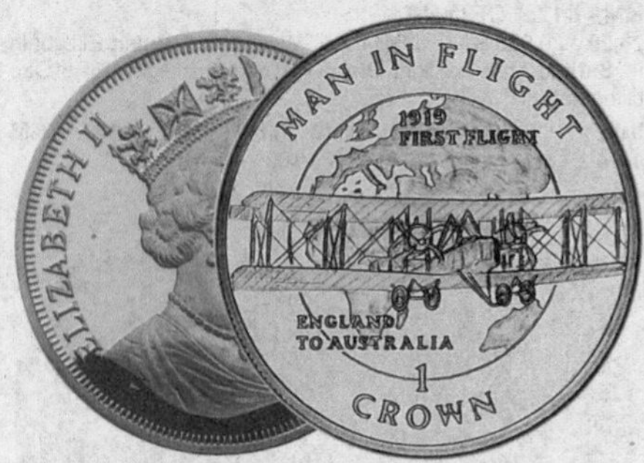

KM# 421 CROWN

Copper-Nickel, 38.5 mm. **Ruler:** Elizabeth II **Series:** Man in Flight **Subject:** First England to Australia flight **Obv:** Crowned bust right **Rev:** Biplane

Date	Mintage	VF20	XF40	MS60	MS63	MS65
1994	—	—	—	—	8.00	9.50

KM# 421a CROWN

28.28 g., 0.925 Silver 0.841 oz. ASW, 38.5 mm. **Ruler:** Elizabeth II **Series:** Man in Flight **Subject:** First England to Australia flight **Obv:** Crowned bust right **Rev:** Biplane

Date	Mintage	VF20	XF40	MS60	MS63	MS65
1994	Est. 30000	PF65 40.00				

KM# 422 CROWN

Copper-Nickel, 38.5 mm. **Ruler:** Elizabeth II **Series:** Man in Flight **Subject:** 60th Anniversary of Airmail **Obv:** Crowned bust right **Rev:** Airplane

Date	Mintage	VF20	XF40	MS60	MS63	MS65
1994	—	—	—	—	8.00	9.50

KM# 422a CROWN

28.28 g., 0.925 Silver 0.841 oz. ASW, 38.5 mm. **Ruler:** Elizabeth II **Series:** Man in Flight **Subject:** 60th Anniversary of Airmail **Obv:** Crowned bust right **Rev:** Airplane

Date	Mintage	VF20	XF40	MS60	MS63	MS65
1994	Est. 30000	PF65 40.00				

KM# 423 CROWN

Copper-Nickel, 38.5 mm. **Ruler:** Elizabeth II **Series:** Man in Flight **Subject:** 50th Anniversary of International Civil Aviation Organization **Obv:** Crowned bust right **Rev:** Emblem

Date	Mintage	VF20	XF40	MS60	MS63	MS65
1994	—	—	—	—	8.00	9.50

KM# 423a CROWN

28.28 g., 0.925 Silver 0.841 oz. ASW, 38.5 mm. **Ruler:** Elizabeth II **Series:** Man in Flight **Subject:** 50th Anniversary of International Civil Aviation Organization **Obv:** Crowned bust right **Rev:** Emblem

Date	Mintage	VF20	XF40	MS60	MS63	MS65
1994	Est. 30000	PF65 40.00				

KM# 424 CROWN

Copper-Nickel, 38.5 mm. **Ruler:** Elizabeth II **Series:** Man in Flight **Subject:** 25th Anniversary of First Concorde Flight **Obv:** Crowned bust right **Rev:** Concorde

Date	Mintage	VF20	XF40	MS60	MS63	MS65
1994	—	—	—	—	8.00	9.50

KM# 424a CROWN

28.28 g., 0.925 Silver 0.841 oz. ASW, 38.5 mm. **Ruler:** Elizabeth II **Series:** Man in Flight **Subject:** 25th Anniversary of First Concorde Flight **Obv:** Crowned bust right **Rev:** Concorde

Date	Mintage	VF20	XF40	MS60	MS63	MS65
1994	Est. 30000	PF65 40.00				

KM# 695 CROWN

Copper-Nickel, 38.5 mm. **Ruler:** Elizabeth II **Series:** Normandy Invasion **Obv:** Crowned bust right **Rev:** Troop ship and landing craft

Date	Mintage	VF20	XF40	MS60	MS63	MS65
1994	—	—	—	—	6.50	7.50

KM# 695a CROWN

28.28 g., 0.925 Silver 0.841 oz. ASW, 38.5 mm. **Ruler:** Elizabeth II **Series:** Normandy Invasion **Obv:** Crowned bust right **Rev:** Troop ship and landing craft

Date	Mintage	VF20	XF40	MS60	MS63	MS65
1994	Est. 30000	PF65 23.00				

KM# 696 CROWN

Copper-Nickel, 38.5 mm. **Ruler:** Elizabeth II **Series:** Normandy Invasion **Obv:** Crowned bust right **Rev:** American troops landing

Date	Mintage	VF20	XF40	MS60	MS63	MS65
1994	—	—	—	—	6.50	7.50

KM# 696a CROWN

28.28 g., 0.925 Silver 0.841 oz. ASW, 38.5 mm. **Ruler:** Elizabeth II **Series:** Normandy Invasion **Obv:** Crowned bust right **Rev:** American troops landing

Date	Mintage	VF20	XF40	MS60	MS63	MS65
1994	—	PF65 23.00				

KM# 696b CROWN

6.22 g., 0.9999 Gold 0.200 oz. AGW **Ruler:** Elizabeth II **Series:** Normandy Invasion **Obv:** Crowned bust right **Rev:** American troops landing **Note:** Prev. KM#704.

Date	Mintage	VF20	XF40	MS60	MS63	MS65
1994	Est. 5000	PF65 315				

KM# 697 CROWN

Copper-Nickel, 38.5 mm. **Ruler:** Elizabeth II **Series:** Normandy Invasion **Obv:** Crowned bust right **Rev:** American soldier behind rock

Date	Mintage	VF20	XF40	MS60	MS63	MS65
1994	—	—	—	—	6.50	7.50

KM# 697a CROWN

28.28 g., 0.925 Silver 0.841 oz. ASW, 38.5 mm. **Ruler:** Elizabeth II **Series:** Normandy Invasion **Obv:** Crowned bust right **Rev:** American soldier behind rock

Date	Mintage	VF20	XF40	MS60	MS63	MS65
1994	Est. 30000	PF65 23.00				

KM# 697b CROWN

6.22 g., 0.9999 Gold 0.200 oz. AGW **Ruler:** Elizabeth II **Series:** Normandy Invasion **Obv:** Crowned bust right **Rev:** American soldier behind rock **Note:** Prev. KM#705.

Date	Mintage	VF20	XF40	MS60	MS63	MS65
1994	—	PF65 315				

KM# 698 CROWN

Copper-Nickel, 38.5 mm. **Ruler:** Elizabeth II **Series:** Normandy Invasion **Obv:** Crowned bust right **Rev:** German machine gun nest

Date	Mintage	VF20	XF40	MS60	MS63	MS65
1994	—	—	—	—	6.50	7.50

KM# 698a CROWN

28.28 g., 0.925 Silver 0.841 oz. ASW, 38.5 mm. **Ruler:** Elizabeth II **Series:** Normandy Invasion **Obv:** Crowned bust right **Rev:** German machine gun nest

Date	Mintage	VF20	XF40	MS60	MS63	MS65
1994	Est. 30000	PF65 23.00				

KM# 698b CROWN

6.22 g., 0.9999 Gold 0.200 oz. AGW **Ruler:** Elizabeth II **Series:** Normandy Invasion **Obv:** Crowned bust right **Rev:** German machine gun nest **Note:** Prev. KM#706.

Date	Mintage	VF20	XF40	MS60	MS63	MS65
1994	—	PF65 315				

KM# 699 CROWN

Copper-Nickel, 38.5 mm. **Ruler:** Elizabeth II **Series:** Normandy Invasion **Obv:** Crowned bust right **Rev:** British troops landing

Date	Mintage	VF20	XF40	MS60	MS63	MS65
1994	—	—	—	—	6.50	7.50

KM# 699a CROWN
28.28 g., 0.925 Silver 0.841 oz. ASW, 38.5 mm. **Ruler:** Elizabeth II **Series:** Normandy Invasion **Obv:** Crowned bust right **Rev:** British troops landing

Date	Mintage	VF20	XF40	MS60	MS63	MS65
1994	Est. 30000	PF65 23.00				

KM# 699b CROWN
6.22 g., 0.9999 Gold 0.200 oz. AGW **Ruler:** Elizabeth II **Series:** Normandy Invasion **Obv:** Crowned bust right **Rev:** Troop ship and landing craft **Note:** Prev. KM#703.

Date	Mintage	VF20	XF40	MS60	MS63	MS65
1994	Est. 5000	PF65 315				

KM# 700 CROWN
Copper-Nickel, 38.5 mm. **Ruler:** Elizabeth II **Series:** Normandy Invasion **Obv:** Crowned bust right **Rev:** General Eisenhower left

Date	Mintage	VF20	XF40	MS60	MS63	MS65
1994	—	—	—	—	6.50	7.50

KM# 700a CROWN
28.28 g., 0.925 Silver 0.841 oz. ASW, 38.5 mm. **Ruler:** Elizabeth II **Series:** Normandy Invasion **Obv:** Crowned bust right **Rev:** General Eisenhower left

Date	Mintage	VF20	XF40	MS60	MS63	MS65
1994	Est. 30000	PF65 23.00				

KM# 700b CROWN
6.22 g., 0.9999 Gold 0.200 oz. AGW **Ruler:** Elizabeth II **Series:** Normandy Invasion **Obv:** Crowned bust right **Rev:** General Eisenhower left **Note:** Prev. KM#708.

Date	Mintage	VF20	XF40	MS60	MS63	MS65
1994	Est. 5000	PF65 315				

KM# 701 CROWN
Copper-Nickel, 38.5 mm. **Ruler:** Elizabeth II **Series:** Normandy Invasion **Obv:** Crowned bust right **Rev:** General Omar Bradley looking right

Date	Mintage	VF20	XF40	MS60	MS63	MS65
1994	—	—	—	—	6.50	7.50

KM# 701a CROWN
28.28 g., 0.925 Silver 0.841 oz. ASW, 38.5 mm. **Ruler:** Elizabeth II **Series:** Normandy Invasion **Obv:** Crowned bust right **Rev:** General Omar Bradley looking right

Date	Mintage	VF20	XF40	MS60	MS63	MS65
1994	Est. 30000	PF65 23.00				

KM# 701b CROWN
6.22 g., 0.9999 Gold 0.200 oz. AGW **Ruler:** Elizabeth II **Series:** Normandy Invasion **Obv:** Crowned bust right **Rev:** General Omar Bradley right **Note:** Prev. KM#709.

Date	Mintage	VF20	XF40	MS60	MS63	MS65
1994	Est. 5000	PF65 315				

KM# 702 CROWN
Copper-Nickel, 38.5 mm. **Ruler:** Elizabeth II **Series:** Normandy Invasion **Obv:** Crowned bust right **Rev:** General Montgomery left

Date	Mintage	VF20	XF40	MS60	MS63	MS65
1994	—	—	—	—	6.50	7.50

KM# 702a CROWN
28.28 g., 0.925 Silver 0.841 oz. ASW, 38.5 mm. **Ruler:** Elizabeth II **Series:** Normandy Invasion **Obv:** Crowned bust right **Rev:** General Montgomery left

Date	Mintage	VF20	XF40	MS60	MS63	MS65
1994	Est. 30000	PF65 23.00				

KM# 702b CROWN
6.22 g., 0.9999 Gold 0.200 oz. AGW **Ruler:** Elizabeth II **Series:** Normandy Invasion **Obv:** Crowned bust right **Rev:** General Montgomery left **Note:** Prev. KM#710.

Date	Mintage	VF20	XF40	MS60	MS63	MS65
1994	Est. 5000	PF65 315				

KM# 707 CROWN
6.22 g., 0.9999 Gold 0.200 oz. AGW **Ruler:** Elizabeth II **Series:** Normandy Invasion **Obv:** Crowned bust right **Rev:** British troops landing

Date	Mintage	VF20	XF40	MS60	MS63	MS65
1994	Est. 5000	PF65 315				

KM# 434 CROWN
Copper-Nickel, 38.5 mm. **Ruler:** Elizabeth II **Series:** Man in Flight **Obv:** Crowned bust right **Rev:** Icarus' wings melting

Date	Mintage	VF20	XF40	MS60	MS63	MS65
1995	—	PF65 7.50				

KM# 434a CROWN
28.28 g., 0.925 Silver 0.841 oz. ASW, 38.5 mm. **Ruler:** Elizabeth II **Series:** Man in Flight **Obv:** Crowned bust right **Rev:** Icarus' wings melting

Date	Mintage	VF20	XF40	MS60	MS63	MS65
1995	Est. 30000	PF65 40.00				

KM# 435 CROWN
Copper-Nickel, 38.5 mm. **Ruler:** Elizabeth II **Series:** Man in Flight **Obv:** Crowned bust right **Rev:** Leonardo Da Vinci and aircraft design

Date	Mintage	VF20	XF40	MS60	MS63	MS65
1995	—	PF65 7.50				

KM# 435a CROWN
28.28 g., 0.925 Silver 0.841 oz. ASW, 38.5 mm. **Ruler:** Elizabeth II **Series:** Man in Flight **Obv:** Crowned bust right **Rev:** Leonardo da Vinci and aircraft design

Date	Mintage	VF20	XF40	MS60	MS63	MS65
1995	—	PF65 40.00				

KM# 436 CROWN
Copper-Nickel, 38.5 mm. **Ruler:** Elizabeth II **Series:** Man in Flight **Obv:** Crowned bust right **Rev:** Montgolfier Brothers' balloon

Date	Mintage	VF20	XF40	MS60	MS63	MS65
1995	—	PF65 7.50				

KM# 436a CROWN
28.28 g., 0.925 Silver 0.841 oz. ASW, 38.5 mm. **Ruler:** Elizabeth II **Series:** Man in Flight **Obv:** Crowned bust right **Rev:** Montgolfier Brothers' balloon

Date	Mintage	VF20	XF40	MS60	MS63	MS65
1995	Est. 30000	PF65 40.00				

KM# 437 CROWN
Copper-Nickel, 38.5 mm. **Ruler:** Elizabeth II **Series:** Man in Flight **Obv:** Crowned bust right **Rev:** Wright Brothers' airplane

Date	Mintage	VF20	XF40	MS60	MS63	MS65
1995	—	—	—	—	7.00	9.00

KM# 437a CROWN
28.28 g., 0.925 Silver 0.841 oz. ASW, 38.5 mm. **Ruler:** Elizabeth II **Series:** Man in Flight **Obv:** Crowned bust right **Rev:** Wright brothers' airplane

Date	Mintage	VF20	XF40	MS60	MS63	MS65
1995	Est. 30000	PF65 40.00				

KM# 438 CROWN
Copper-Nickel, 38.5 mm. **Ruler:** Elizabeth II **Series:** Man in Flight **Subject:** First Flight Toyko to Paris **Obv:** Crowned bust right **Rev:** Heads of Abe and Kawachi over airplane

Date	Mintage	VF20	XF40	MS60	MS63	MS65
1995	—	PF65 6.50				

KM# 438a CROWN
28.28 g., 0.925 Silver 0.841 oz. ASW, 38.5 mm. **Ruler:** Elizabeth II **Series:** Man in Flight **Subject:** First Flight Tokyo to Paris **Obv:** Crowned bust right **Rev:** Heads of Abe and Kawachi above plane

Date	Mintage	VF20	XF40	MS60	MS63	MS65
1995	Est. 30000	PF65 42.50				

KM# 439.1 CROWN
Copper-Nickel, 38.5 mm. **Ruler:** Elizabeth II **Series:** Man in Flight **Obv:** Crowned bust right **Rev:** FW190, first diesel powered aircraft

Date	Mintage	VF20	XF40	MS60	MS63	MS65
1995	500	PF63 12.50	PF65 18.00			

KM# 439.1a CROWN
28.28 g., 0.925 Silver 0.841 oz. ASW, 38.5 mm. **Ruler:** Elizabeth II **Series:** Man in Flight **Obv:** Crowned bust right **Rev:** First diesel powered aircraft

Date	Mintage	VF20	XF40	MS60	MS63	MS65
1995	Est. 30000	PF65 42.50				

KM# 439.2 CROWN
Copper-Nickel, 38.5 mm. **Ruler:** Elizabeth II **Series:** Man in Flight **Obv:** Crowned bust right **Rev:** FW190 BMW injection aero engine

Date	Mintage	VF20	XF40	MS60	MS63	MS65
1995	—	—	—	—	6.50	7.50

KM# 440.1 CROWN
Copper-Nickel, 38.5 mm. **Ruler:** Elizabeth II **Series:** Man in Flight **Obv:** Crowned bust right **Rev:** ME262, first jet aircraft 1941

Date	Mintage	VF20	XF40	MS60	MS63	MS65
1995	500	PF65 12.50				

KM# 440.1a CROWN
28.28 g., 0.925 Silver 0.841 oz. ASW, 38.5 mm. **Ruler:** Elizabeth II **Series:** Man in Flight **Obv:** Crowned bust right **Rev:** ME262, first jet aircraft 1941

Date	Mintage	VF20	XF40	MS60	MS63	MS65
1995	Est. 30000	PF65 42.50				

KM# 440.2 CROWN
Copper-Nickel, 38.5 mm. **Ruler:** Elizabeth II **Series:** Man in Flight **Obv:** Crowned bust right **Rev:** Jet powered aircraft 1942

Date	Mintage	VF20	XF40	MS60	MS63	MS65
1995	—	—	—	—	6.50	7.50

KM# 441 CROWN
Copper-Nickel, 38.5 mm. **Ruler:** Elizabeth II **Series:** Man in Flight **Subject:** 25th Anniversary of Boeing 747 **Obv:** Crowned bust right **Rev:** Boeing 747

Date	Mintage	VF20	XF40	MS60	MS63	MS65
1995	—	PF65 7.50				

KM# 441a CROWN
28.28 g., 0.925 Silver 0.841 oz. ASW, 38.5 mm. **Ruler:** Elizabeth II **Series:** Man in Flight **Subject:** 25th Anniversary of Boeing 747 **Obv:** Crowned bust right **Rev:** Boeing 747

Date	Mintage	VF20	XF40	MS60	MS63	MS65
1995	Est. 30000	PF65 42.50				

KM# 446 CROWN
Copper-Nickel, 38.5 mm. **Ruler:** Elizabeth II **Obv:** Crowned bust right **Rev:** Turkish cat

Date	Mintage	VF20	XF40	MS60	MS63	MS65
1995	—	—	—	—	12.00	16.00

KM# 446a CROWN
31.10 g., 0.999 Silver 0.9989 oz. ASW, 38.5 mm. **Ruler:** Elizabeth II **Obv:** Crowned bust right **Rev:** Turkish cat **Note:** Prev. KM#447.

Date	Mintage	VF20	XF40	MS60	MS63	MS65
1995	—	PF65 75.00				

KM# 446b CROWN
31.10 g., 0.999 Gold 0.9989 oz. AGW **Ruler:** Elizabeth II **Obv:** Crowned bust right **Rev:** Turkish cat **Note:** Prev. KM#448.

Date	Mintage	VF20	XF40	MS60	MS63	MS65
1995 U	—	—	—	—	—	1,700
1995	—	PF65 1,725				

KM# 446c CROWN
31.10 g., 0.9995 Platinum 0.9995 oz. APW **Ruler:** Elizabeth II **Obv:** Crowned bust right **Rev:** Turkish cat **Note:** Prev. KM#482.

Date	Mintage	VF20	XF40	MS60	MS63	MS65
1995	—	—	—	—	—	1,800
1995	—	PF65 1,900				

KM# 453 CROWN
Copper-Nickel, 38.5 mm. **Ruler:** Elizabeth II **Subject:** Year of the Pig **Obv:** Crowned bust right **Rev:** Sow with piglets

Date	Mintage	VF20	XF40	MS60	MS63	MS65
1995	—	—	—	—	10.00	15.00

KM# 453a CROWN
31.10 g., 0.999 Silver 0.999 oz. ASW, 38.5 mm. **Ruler:** Elizabeth II **Subject:** Year of the Pig **Obv:** Crowned bust right **Rev:** Sow with piglets **Note:** Prev. KM#454.

Date	Mintage	VF20	XF40	MS60	MS63	MS65
1995	—	PF65 45.00				

KM# 453b CROWN
31.10 g., 0.999 Gold 0.999 oz. AGW **Ruler:** Elizabeth II **Subject:** Year of the Pig **Obv:** Crowned bust right **Rev:** Sow with piglets **Note:** Prev. KM#455.

Date	Mintage	VF20	XF40	MS60	MS63	MS65
1995	Est. 2500	PF65 1,725				

KM# 458 CROWN
Copper-Nickel, 38.5 mm. **Ruler:** Elizabeth II **Subject:** 95th Birthday of Queen Mother **Obv:** Crowned bust right **Rev:** Crowned bust facing

Date	Mintage	VF20	XF40	MS60	MS63	MS65
1995	—	—	—	—	6.00	7.00

KM# 458a CROWN
28.28 g., 0.925 Silver 0.841 oz. ASW, 38.5 mm. **Ruler:** Elizabeth II **Subject:** 95th Birthday of Queen Mother **Obv:** Crowned bust right **Rev:** Crowned bust facing

Date	Mintage	VF20	XF40	MS60	MS63	MS65
1995	Est. 30000	PF65 37.50				

KM# 461 CROWN
Copper-Nickel, 38.5 mm. **Ruler:** Elizabeth II **Series:** Preserve Planet Earth **Obv:** Crowned bust right **Rev:** European otter

Date	Mintage	VF20	XF40	MS60	MS63	MS65
1995	—	—	—	—	12.00	15.00

KM# 461a CROWN
28.28 g., 0.925 Silver 0.841 oz. ASW, 38.5 mm. **Ruler:** Elizabeth II **Series:** Preserve Planet Earth **Obv:** Crowned bust right **Rev:** European otter

Date	Mintage	VF20	XF40	MS60	MS63	MS65
1995	Est. 30000	PF65 45.00				

KM# 462 CROWN
Copper-Nickel, 38.5 mm. **Ruler:** Elizabeth II **Series:** Preserve Planet Earth **Obv:** Crowned bust right **Rev:** Egrets

Date	Mintage	VF20	XF40	MS60	MS63	MS65
1995	—	—	—	—	11.00	15.00

KM# 462a CROWN
28.28 g., 0.925 Silver 0.841 oz. ASW, 38.5 mm. **Ruler:** Elizabeth II **Series:** Preserve Planet Earth **Obv:** Crowned bust right **Rev:** Egrets

Date	Mintage	VF20	XF40	MS60	MS63	MS65
1995	Est. 30000	PF65 45.00				

KM# 502 CROWN
Copper-Nickel, 38.5 mm. **Ruler:** Elizabeth II **Series:** Aircraft of World War II **Obv:** Crowned bust right **Rev:** Airplanes

Date	Mintage	VF20	XF40	MS60	MS63	MS65
1995	—	—	—	—	5.50	7.50

KM# 502a CROWN
28.28 g., 0.925 Silver 0.841 oz. ASW, 38.5 mm. **Ruler:** Elizabeth II **Series:** Aircraft of World War II **Obv:** Crowned bust right **Rev:** Airplanes

Date	Mintage	VF20	XF40	MS60	MS63	MS65
1995	Est. 30000	PF65 25.50				

KM# 503 CROWN
Copper-Nickel, 38.5 mm. **Ruler:** Elizabeth II **Series:** Aircraft of World War II **Obv:** Crowned bust right **Rev:** P-51 Mustang

Date	Mintage	VF20	XF40	MS60	MS63	MS65
1995	—	—	—	—	5.50	7.50

KM# 503a CROWN
28.28 g., 0.925 Silver 0.841 oz. ASW, 38.5 mm. **Ruler:** Elizabeth II **Series:** Aircraft of World War II **Obv:** Crowned bust right **Rev:** P-51 Mustang

Date	Mintage	VF20	XF40	MS60	MS63	MS65
1995	—	PF65 25.50				

KM# 504 CROWN
Copper-Nickel, 38.5 mm. **Ruler:** Elizabeth II **Series:** Aircraft of World War II **Obv:** Crowned bust right **Rev:** Letov 5328 **Edge:** Reeded

Date	Mintage	VF20	XF40	MS60	MS63	MS65
1995	—	—	—	—	5.50	7.50

KM# 504a CROWN
28.28 g., 0.925 Silver 0.841 oz. ASW, 38.5 mm. **Ruler:** Elizabeth II **Series:** Aircraft of World War II **Obv:** Crowned bust right **Rev:** Letov 5328

Date	Mintage	VF20	XF40	MS60	MS63	MS65
1995	—	PF65 25.50				

KM# 505 CROWN
Copper-Nickel, 38.5 mm. **Ruler:** Elizabeth II **Series:** Aircraft of World War II **Obv:** Crowned bust right **Rev:** Messerschmitt ME262 **Edge:** Reeded

Date	Mintage	VF20	XF40	MS60	MS63	MS65
1995	—	—	—	—	5.50	7.50

KM# 505a CROWN
28.28 g., 0.925 Silver 0.841 oz. ASW, 38.5 mm. **Ruler:** Elizabeth II **Series:** Aircraft of World War II **Obv:** Crowned bust right **Rev:** Messerschmitt ME262

Date	Mintage	VF20	XF40	MS60	MS63	MS65
1995	Est. 30000	PF65 25.50				

KM# 506 CROWN
Copper-Nickel, 38.5 mm. **Ruler:** Elizabeth II **Series:** Aircraft of World War II **Obv:** Crowned bust right **Rev:** JU87 Stuka **Edge:** Reeded

Date	Mintage	VF20	XF40	MS60	MS63	MS65
1995	—	—	—	—	5.50	7.50

KM# 506a CROWN
28.28 g., 0.925 Silver 0.841 oz. ASW, 38.5 mm. **Ruler:** Elizabeth II **Series:** Aircraft of World War II **Obv:** Crowned bust right **Rev:** JU87 Stuka

Date	Mintage	VF20	XF40	MS60	MS63	MS65
1995	—	PF65 25.50				

KM# 507 CROWN
Copper-Nickel, 38.5 mm. **Ruler:** Elizabeth II **Series:** Aircraft of World War II **Obv:** Crowned bust right **Rev:** MIG 3 **Edge:** Reeded

Date	Mintage	VF20	XF40	MS60	MS63	MS65
1995	—	—	—	—	5.50	7.50

KM# 507a CROWN
28.28 g., 0.925 Silver 0.841 oz. ASW, 38.5 mm. **Ruler:** Elizabeth II **Series:** Aircraft of World War II **Obv:** Crowned bust right **Rev:** MIG 3

Date	Mintage	VF20	XF40	MS60	MS63	MS65
1995	Est. 30000	PF65 25.50				

KM# 508 CROWN
Copper-Nickel, 38.5 mm. **Ruler:** Elizabeth II **Series:** Aircraft of World War II **Obv:** Crowned bust right **Rev:** Nakajima KI-49 Donryu **Edge:** Reeded

Date	Mintage	VF20	XF40	MS60	MS63	MS65
1995	—	—	—	—	5.50	7.50

KM# 508a CROWN
28.28 g., 0.925 Silver 0.841 oz. ASW, 38.5 mm. **Ruler:** Elizabeth II **Series:** Aircraft of World War II **Obv:** Crowned bust right **Rev:** Nakajima KI-49 Donryu

Date	Mintage	VF20	XF40	MS60	MS63	MS65
1995	—	PF65 25.50				

KM# 509 CROWN
Copper-Nickel, 38.5 mm. **Ruler:** Elizabeth II **Series:** Aircraft of World War II **Obv:** Crowned bust right **Rev:** Vickers Wellington **Edge:** Reeded

Date	Mintage	VF20	XF40	MS60	MS63	MS65
1995	—	—	—	—	5.50	7.50

KM# 509a CROWN
28.28 g., 0.925 Silver 0.841 oz. ASW, 38.5 mm. **Ruler:** Elizabeth II **Series:** Aircraft of World War II **Obv:** Crowned bust right **Rev:** Vickers Wellington

Date	Mintage	VF20	XF40	MS60	MS63	MS65
1995	—	PF65 25.50				

KM# 510 CROWN

Copper-Nickel, 38.5 mm. **Ruler:** Elizabeth II **Series:** Aircraft of World War II **Obv:** Crowned bust right **Rev:** Supermarine Spitfire **Edge:** Reeded

Date	Mintage	VF20	XF40	MS60	MS63	MS65
1995 (py)	—	—	—	—	6.00	8.00
1995	—	—	—	—	6.00	8.00

KM# 510a CROWN

28.28 g., 0.925 Silver 0.841 oz. ASW, 38.5 mm. **Ruler:** Elizabeth II **Series:** Aircraft of World War II **Obv:** Crowned bust right **Rev:** Supermarine Spitfire

Date	Mintage	VF20	XF40	MS60	MS63	MS65
1995	Est. 30000	PF65 25.50				

KM# 511 CROWN

Copper-Nickel, 38.5 mm. **Ruler:** Elizabeth II **Series:** Aircraft of World War II **Obv:** Crowned bust right **Rev:** Fokker G.1a **Edge:** Reeded

Date	Mintage	VF20	XF40	MS60	MS63	MS65
1995	—	—	—	—	5.50	7.50

KM# 511a CROWN

28.28 g., 0.925 Silver 0.841 oz. ASW, 38.5 mm. **Ruler:** Elizabeth II **Series:** Aircraft of World War II **Obv:** Crowned bust right **Rev:** Fokker G.1a

Date	Mintage	VF20	XF40	MS60	MS63	MS65
1995	Est. 30000	PF65 25.50				

KM# 512 CROWN

Copper-Nickel, 38.5 mm. **Ruler:** Elizabeth II **Series:** Aircraft of World War II **Obv:** Crowned bust right **Rev:** Commonwealth Boomerang CA-13 **Edge:** Reeded

Date	Mintage	VF20	XF40	MS60	MS63	MS65
1995	—	—	—	—	5.50	7.50

KM# 512a CROWN

28.28 g., 0.925 Silver 0.841 oz. ASW, 38.5 mm. **Ruler:** Elizabeth II **Series:** Aircraft of World War II **Obv:** Crowned bust right **Rev:** Boomerang CA-13

Date	Mintage	VF20	XF40	MS60	MS63	MS65
1995	Est. 30000	PF65 25.50				

KM# 513 CROWN

Copper-Nickel, 38.5 mm. **Ruler:** Elizabeth II **Series:** Aircraft of World War II **Obv:** Crowned bust right **Rev:** Bristol Blenheim 142 **Edge:** Reeded

Date	Mintage	VF20	XF40	MS60	MS63	MS65
1995	—	—	—	—	5.50	7.50

KM# 513a CROWN

28.28 g., 0.925 Silver 0.841 oz. ASW, 38.5 mm. **Ruler:** Elizabeth II **Series:** Aircraft of World War II **Obv:** Crowned bust right **Rev:** Bristol Blenheim 142

Date	Mintage	VF20	XF40	MS60	MS63	MS65
1995	Est. 30000	PF65 25.50				

KM# 514 CROWN

Copper-Nickel, 38.5 mm. **Ruler:** Elizabeth II **Series:** Aircraft of World War II **Obv:** Crowned bust right **Rev:** Mitsubishi Zero **Edge:** Reeded

Date	Mintage	VF20	XF40	MS60	MS63	MS65
1995	—	—	—	—	5.50	7.50

KM# 514a CROWN

28.28 g., 0.925 Silver 0.841 oz. ASW, 38.5 mm. **Ruler:** Elizabeth II **Series:** Aircraft of World War II **Obv:** Crowned bust right **Rev:** Mitsubishi Zero

Date	Mintage	VF20	XF40	MS60	MS63	MS65
1995	Est. 30000	PF65 25.50				

KM# 515 CROWN

Copper-Nickel, 38.5 mm. **Ruler:** Elizabeth II **Series:** Aircraft of World War II **Obv:** Crowned bust right **Rev:** Heinkel HE 111 **Edge:** Reeded

Date	Mintage	VF20	XF40	MS60	MS63	MS65
1995	—	—	—	—	5.50	7.50

KM# 515a CROWN

28.28 g., 0.925 Silver 0.841 oz. ASW, 38.5 mm. **Ruler:** Elizabeth II **Series:** Aircraft of World War II **Obv:** Crowned bust right **Rev:** Heinkel HE 111

Date	Mintage	VF20	XF40	MS60	MS63	MS65
1995	Est. 30000	PF65 25.50				

KM# 516 CROWN

Copper-Nickel, 38.5 mm. **Ruler:** Elizabeth II **Series:** Aircraft of World War II **Obv:** Crowned bust right **Rev:** Boulton Paul P.82 Defiant **Edge:** Reeded

Date	Mintage	VF20	XF40	MS60	MS63	MS65
1995	—	—	—	—	5.50	7.50

KM# 516a CROWN

28.28 g., 0.925 Silver 0.841 oz. ASW, 38.5 mm. **Ruler:** Elizabeth II **Series:** Aircraft of World War II **Obv:** Crowned bust right **Rev:** Boulton Paul P.82 Defiant

Date	Mintage	VF20	XF40	MS60	MS63	MS65
1995	Est. 30000	PF65 25.50				

KM# 517 CROWN

Copper-Nickel, 38.5 mm. **Ruler:** Elizabeth II **Series:** Aircraft of World War II **Obv:** Crowned bust right **Rev:** Boeing B-29 Enola Gay **Edge:** Reeded

Date	Mintage	VF20	XF40	MS60	MS63	MS65
1995	—	—	—	—	5.50	7.50

KM# 517a CROWN

28.28 g., 0.925 Silver 0.841 oz. ASW, 38.5 mm. **Ruler:** Elizabeth II **Series:** Aircraft of World War II **Obv:** Crowned bust right **Rev:** Boeing B-29 Enola Gay

Date	Mintage	VF20	XF40	MS60	MS63	MS65
1995	Est. 30000	PF65 25.50				

KM# 518 CROWN

Copper-Nickel, 38.5 mm. **Ruler:** Elizabeth II **Series:** Aircraft of World War II **Obv:** Crowned bust right **Rev:** Douglas DC-3 (C-47) Dakota **Edge:** Reeded

Date	Mintage	VF20	XF40	MS60	MS63	MS65
1995	—	—	—	—	5.50	7.50

KM# 518a CROWN

28.28 g., 0.925 Silver 0.841 oz. ASW, 38.5 mm. **Ruler:** Elizabeth II **Series:** Aircraft of World War II **Obv:** Crowned bust right **Rev:** Douglas DC-3 (C-47) Dakota

Date	Mintage	VF20	XF40	MS60	MS63	MS65
1995	Est. 30000	PF65 25.50				

KM# 519 CROWN
Copper-Nickel, 38.5 mm. **Ruler:** Elizabeth II **Series:** Aircraft of World War II **Obv:** Crowned bust right **Rev:** Fairey Swordfish **Edge:** Reeded

Date	Mintage	VF20	XF40	MS60	MS63	MS65
1995	—	—	—	—	5.50	7.50

KM# 519a CROWN
28.28 g., 0.925 Silver 0.841 oz. ASW, 38.5 mm. **Ruler:** Elizabeth II **Series:** Aircraft of World War II **Obv:** Crowned bust right **Rev:** Fairey Swordfish

Date	Mintage	VF20	XF40	MS60	MS63	MS65
1995	Est. 30000	PF65 25.50				

KM# 520 CROWN
Copper-Nickel, 38.5 mm. **Ruler:** Elizabeth II **Series:** Aircraft of WWII **Obv:** Crowned bust right **Rev:** Curtiss P-40 Tomahawk **Edge:** Reeded

Date	Mintage	VF20	XF40	MS60	MS63	MS65
1995	—	—	—	—	5.50	7.50

KM# 520a CROWN
28.28 g., 0.925 Silver 0.841 oz. ASW, 38.5 mm. **Ruler:** Elizabeth II **Series:** Aircraft of WWII **Obv:** Crowned bust right **Rev:** Curtiss P-40 Tomahawk

Date	Mintage	VF20	XF40	MS60	MS63	MS65
1995	—	PF65 25.50				

KM# 524 CROWN
Copper-Nickel, 38.5 mm. **Ruler:** Elizabeth II **Series:** America's Cup **Obv:** Crowned bust right **Rev:** Sailboats **Edge:** Reeded

Date	Mintage	VF20	XF40	MS60	MS63	MS65
1995	—	—	—	—	5.00	6.50

KM# 524a CROWN
28.28 g., 0.925 Silver 0.841 oz. ASW, 38.5 mm. **Ruler:** Elizabeth II **Series:** America's Cup **Obv:** Crowned bust right **Rev:** Sailboats

Date	Mintage	VF20	XF40	MS60	MS63	MS65
1995	Est. 30000	PF65 50.00				

KM# 526 CROWN
Copper-Nickel, 38.5 mm. **Ruler:** Elizabeth II **Series:** Inventions of the Modern World **Obv:** Crowned bust right **Rev:** Cameo Tsai Lun, paper and tree **Edge:** Reeded

Date	Mintage	VF20	XF40	MS60	MS63	MS65
1995	—	—	—	—	6.00	8.00

KM# 526a CROWN
28.28 g., 0.925 Silver 0.841 oz. ASW, 38.5 mm. **Ruler:** Elizabeth II **Series:** Inventions of the Modern World **Obv:** Crowned bust right **Rev:** Cameo of Tsai Lun, paper and tree

Date	Mintage	VF20	XF40	MS60	MS63	MS65
1995	Est. 30000	PF65 29.50				

KM# 528 CROWN
Copper-Nickel, 38.5 mm. **Ruler:** Elizabeth II **Series:** Inventions of the Modern World **Obv:** Crowned bust right **Rev:** Cameo of Chang Heng and seismograph **Edge:** Reeded

Date	Mintage	VF20	XF40	MS60	MS63	MS65
1995	—	—	—	—	5.00	6.50

KM# 528a CROWN
28.28 g., 0.925 Silver 0.841 oz. ASW, 38.5 mm. **Ruler:** Elizabeth II **Series:** Inventions of the Modern World **Obv:** Crowned bust right **Rev:** Cameo of Chang Heng and seismograph

Date	Mintage	VF20	XF40	MS60	MS63	MS65
1995	—	PF65 29.50				

KM# 530 CROWN
Copper-Nickel, 38.5 mm. **Ruler:** Elizabeth II **Series:** Inventions of the Modern World **Obv:** Crowned bust right **Rev:** Cameo of Tsu Chung Chih and compass cart **Edge:** Reeded

Date	Mintage	VF20	XF40	MS60	MS63	MS65
1995	—	—	—	—	8.00	10.00

KM# 530a CROWN
28.28 g., 0.925 Silver 0.841 oz. ASW, 38.5 mm. **Ruler:** Elizabeth II **Series:** Inventions of the Modern World **Obv:** Crowned bust right **Rev:** Cameo of Tsu Chung Chih and compass car

Date	Mintage	VF20	XF40	MS60	MS63	MS65
1995	Est. 30000	PF65 29.50				

KM# 532 CROWN
Copper-Nickel, 38.5 mm. **Ruler:** Elizabeth II **Series:** Inventions of the Modern World **Obv:** Crowned bust right **Rev:** Cameo of Pi Sheng and movable type **Edge:** Reeded

Date	Mintage	VF20	XF40	MS60	MS63	MS65
1995	—	—	—	—	5.00	6.50

KM# 532a CROWN
28.28 g., 0.925 Silver 0.841 oz. ASW, 38.5 mm. **Ruler:** Elizabeth II **Series:** Inventions of the Modern World **Obv:** Crowned bust right **Rev:** Cameo of Pi Sheng and movable type

Date	Mintage	VF20	XF40	MS60	MS63	MS65
1995	Est. 30000	PF65 29.50				

KM# 534 CROWN
Copper-Nickel, 38.5 mm. **Ruler:** Elizabeth II **Series:** Inventions of the Modern World **Obv:** Crowned bust right **Rev:** Cameo of Charles Babbage and first computer **Edge:** Reeded

Date	Mintage	VF20	XF40	MS60	MS63	MS65
1995	—	—	—	—	6.00	8.00

KM# 534a CROWN
28.28 g., 0.925 Silver 0.841 oz. ASW, 38.5 mm. **Ruler:** Elizabeth II **Series:** Inventions of the Modern World **Obv:** Crowned bust right **Rev:** Cameo of Charles Babbage and first computer

Date	Mintage	VF20	XF40	MS60	MS63	MS65
1995	Est. 30000	PF65 29.50				

KM# 536 CROWN
Copper-Nickel, 38.5 mm. **Ruler:** Elizabeth II **Series:** Inventions of the Modern World **Obv:** Crowned bust right **Rev:** Cameo of Fox Talbot, photography **Edge:** Reeded

Date	Mintage	VF20	XF40	MS60	MS63	MS65
1995	—	—	—	—	8.00	10.00

KM# 536a CROWN
28.28 g., 0.925 Silver 0.841 oz. ASW, 38.5 mm. **Ruler:** Elizabeth II **Series:** Inventions of the Modern World **Obv:** Crowned bust right **Rev:** Cameo of Fox Talbot, photography

Date	Mintage	VF20	XF40	MS60	MS63	MS65
1995	Est. 30000	PF65 29.50				

KM# 538 CROWN

Copper-Nickel, 38.5 mm. **Ruler:** Elizabeth II **Series:** Inventions of the Modern World **Obv:** Crowned bust right **Rev:** Cameo Rudolf Diesel and engine

Date	Mintage	VF20	XF40	MS60	MS63	MS65
1995	—	—	—	—	5.00	6.50

KM# 538a CROWN

28.28 g., 0.925 Silver 0.841 oz. ASW, 38.5 mm. **Ruler:** Elizabeth II **Series:** Inventions of the Modern World **Obv:** Crowned bust right **Rev:** Cameo of Rudolf Diesel and engine

Date	Mintage	VF20	XF40	MS60	MS63	MS65
1995	Est. 30000	PF65 29.50				

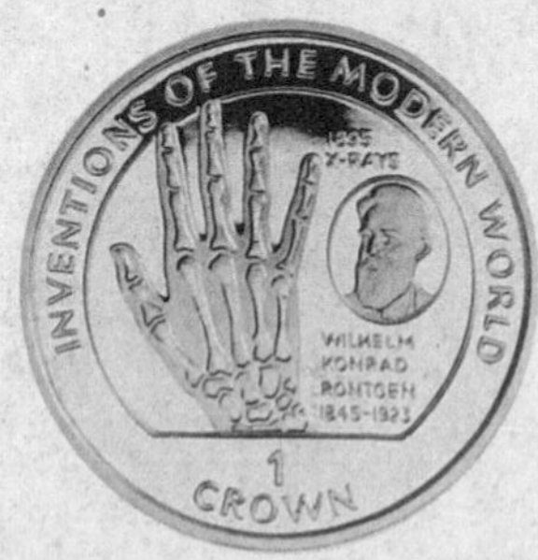

KM# 540 CROWN

Copper-Nickel, 38.5 mm. **Ruler:** Elizabeth II **Series:** Inventions of the Modern World **Obv:** Crowned bust right **Rev:** Cameo of Wilhelm K. Roentgern, xray **Edge:** Reeded

Date	Mintage	VF20	XF40	MS60	MS63	MS65
1995	—	—	—	—	5.00	6.50

KM# 540a CROWN

28.28 g., 0.925 Silver 0.841 oz. ASW, 38.5 mm. **Ruler:** Elizabeth II **Series:** Inventions of the Modern World **Obv:** Crowned bust right **Rev:** Cameo of Wilhelm K. Roentgen, xray

Date	Mintage	VF20	XF40	MS60	MS63	MS65
1995	Est. 30000	PF65 29.50				

KM# 542 CROWN

Copper-Nickel, 38.5 mm. **Ruler:** Elizabeth II **Series:** Inventions of the Modern World **Obv:** Crowned bust right **Rev:** Cameo of Guglielmo Marconi, radio equipment **Edge:** Reeded

Date	Mintage	VF20	XF40	MS60	MS63	MS65
1995	—	—	—	—	5.00	6.50

KM# 542a CROWN

28.28 g., 0.925 Silver 0.841 oz. ASW, 38.5 mm. **Ruler:** Elizabeth II **Series:** Inventions of the Modern World **Obv:** Crowned bust right **Rev:** Cameo of Guglielmo Marconi and radio equipment

Date	Mintage	VF20	XF40	MS60	MS63	MS65
1995	—	PF65 29.50				

KM# 544 CROWN

Copper-Nickel, 38.5 mm. **Ruler:** Elizabeth II **Series:** Inventions of the Modern World **Obv:** Crowned bust right **Rev:** Cameo L. Baird and television equipment **Edge:** Reeded

Date	Mintage	VF20	XF40	MS60	MS63	MS65
1995	—	—	—	—	5.00	6.50

KM# 544a CROWN

28.28 g., 0.925 Silver 0.841 oz. ASW, 38.5 mm. **Ruler:** Elizabeth II **Series:** Inventions of the Modern World **Obv:** Crowned bust right **Rev:** Cameo of John L. Baird and television equipment

Date	Mintage	VF20	XF40	MS60	MS63	MS65
1995	Est. 30000	PF65 29.50				

KM# 546 CROWN

Copper-Nickel, 38.5 mm. **Ruler:** Elizabeth II **Series:** Inventions of the Modern World **Obv:** Crowned bust right **Rev:** Cameo of Alexander Fleming and microscope **Edge:** Reeded

Date	Mintage	VF20	XF40	MS60	MS63	MS65
1995	—	—	—	—	5.00	6.50

KM# 546a CROWN

28.28 g., 0.925 Silver 0.841 oz. ASW, 38.5 mm. **Ruler:** Elizabeth II **Series:** Inventions of the Modern World **Obv:** Crowned bust right **Rev:** Cameo of Alexander Fleming and microscope

Date	Mintage	VF20	XF40	MS60	MS63	MS65
1995	—	PF65 29.50				

KM# 548 CROWN

Copper-Nickel, 38.5 mm. **Ruler:** Elizabeth II **Series:** Inventions of the Modern World **Obv:** Crowned bust right **Rev:** Cameo of Lazlo Biro, ball-point pen **Edge:** Reeded

Date	Mintage	VF20	XF40	MS60	MS63	MS65
1995	—	—	—	—	5.00	6.50

KM# 548a CROWN

28.28 g., 0.925 Silver 0.841 oz. ASW, 38.5 mm. **Ruler:** Elizabeth II **Series:** Inventions of the Modern World **Obv:** Crowned bust right **Rev:** Cameo of Lazlo Biro, ball-point pen

Date	Mintage	VF20	XF40	MS60	MS63	MS65
1995	Est. 30000	PF65 29.50				

KM# 555 CROWN

Copper-Nickel, 38.5 mm. **Ruler:** Elizabeth II **Series:** Inventions of the Modern World **Obv:** Crowned bust right **Rev:** Cameo of Wernher von Braun and rocket **Edge:** Reeded

Date	Mintage	VF20	XF40	MS60	MS63	MS65
1996	—	—	—	—	5.00	6.50

KM# 555a CROWN

28.28 g., 0.925 Silver 0.841 oz. ASW, 38.5 mm. **Ruler:** Elizabeth II **Series:** Inventions of the Modern World **Obv:** Crowned bust right **Rev:** Cameo of Wernher von Braun and rocket

Date	Mintage	VF20	XF40	MS60	MS63	MS65
1996	Est. 30000	PF65 29.50				

KM# 556 CROWN

Copper-Nickel, 38.5 mm. **Ruler:** Elizabeth II **Series:** Inventions of the Modern World **Obv:** Crowned bust right **Rev:** Cameo of Thomas Edison, electricity **Edge:** Reeded

Date	Mintage	VF20	XF40	MS60	MS63	MS65
1996	—	—	—	—	8.00	10.00

KM# 556a CROWN

28.28 g., 0.925 Silver 0.841 oz. ASW, 38.5 mm. **Ruler:** Elizabeth II **Series:** Inventions of the Modern World **Obv:** Crowned bust right **Rev:** Cameo of Thomas Edison, electricity

Date	Mintage	VF20	XF40	MS60	MS63	MS65
1996	—	PF65 29.50				

KM# 557 CROWN

Copper-Nickel, 38.5 mm. **Ruler:** Elizabeth II **Series:** Inventions of the Modern World **Obv:** Crowned bust right **Rev:** Compass

Date	Mintage	VF20	XF40	MS60	MS63	MS65
1996	—	—	—	—	6.00	8.00

KM# 557a CROWN

28.28 g., 0.925 Silver 0.841 oz. ASW, 38.5 mm. **Ruler:** Elizabeth II **Series:** Inventions of the Modern World **Obv:** Crowned bust right **Rev:** Compass

Date	Mintage	VF20	XF40	MS60	MS63	MS65
1996	—	PF65 29.50				

KM# 558.1 CROWN

Copper-Nickel, 38.5 mm. **Ruler:** Elizabeth II **Series:** Inventions of the Modern World **Obv:** Crowned bust right **Rev:** Cameo of Michael Faraday, electricity **Edge:** Reeded

Date	Mintage	VF20	XF40	MS60	MS63	MS65
1996	—	—	—	—	5.00	6.50

KM# 558.2 CROWN

Copper-Nickel, 38.5 mm. **Ruler:** Elizabeth II **Series:** Inventions of the Modern World **Obv:** Crowned bust right **Rev:** Cameo of Michael Faraday, electricity; legend error **Rev. Legend:** EXRERIMENTAL **Edge:** Reeded

Date	Mintage	VF20	XF40	MS60	MS63	MS65
1996	—	—	—	—	11.50	12.50

KM# 558.2a CROWN

28.28 g., 0.925 Silver 0.841 oz. ASW, 38.5 mm. **Ruler:** Elizabeth II **Series:** Inventions of the Modern World **Obv:** Crowned bust right **Rev:** Cameo of Michael Faraday, electricity; legend error **Rev. Legend:** EXRERIMENTAL

Date	Mintage	VF20	XF40	MS60	MS63	MS65
1996	Est. 30000	PF65 29.50				

KM# 559 CROWN

Copper-Nickel, 38.5 mm. **Ruler:** Elizabeth II **Series:** Inventions of the Modern World **Obv:** Crowned bust right **Rev:** Emile Berliner, gramophone **Edge:** Reeded

Date	Mintage	VF20	XF40	MS60	MS63	MS65
1996	—	—	—	—	5.00	6.50

KM# 559a CROWN

28.28 g., 0.925 Silver 0.841 oz. ASW, 38.5 mm. **Ruler:** Elizabeth II **Series:** Inventions of the Modern World **Obv:** Crowned bust right **Rev:** Cameo of Emile Berliner and gramophone

Date	Mintage	VF20	XF40	MS60	MS63	MS65
1996	—	PF65 29.50				

KM# 560 CROWN

Copper-Nickel, 38.5 mm. **Ruler:** Elizabeth II **Series:** Inventions of the Modern World **Obv:** Crowned bust right **Rev:** Cameo of Alexander Graham Bell, voice transmission **Edge:** Reeded

Date	Mintage	VF20	XF40	MS60	MS63	MS65
1996	—	—	—	—	8.00	10.00

KM# 560a CROWN

28.28 g., 0.925 Silver 0.841 oz. ASW, 38.5 mm. **Ruler:** Elizabeth II **Series:** Inventions of the Modern World **Obv:** Crowned bust right **Rev:** Cameo of Alexander Graham Bell, voice transmission

Date	Mintage	VF20	XF40	MS60	MS63	MS65
1996	30,000	PF65 29.50				

KM# 567 CROWN

Copper-Nickel, 38.5 mm. **Ruler:** Elizabeth II **Series:** 1996 Summer Olympics - Atlanta **Obv:** Crowned bust right **Rev:** Hurdler within sprigs

Date	Mintage	VF20	XF40	MS60	MS63	MS65
1996	—	—	—	—	6.00	8.00

KM# 567a CROWN

28.28 g., 0.925 Silver 0.841 oz. ASW, 38.5 mm. **Ruler:** Elizabeth II **Series:** 1996 Summer Olympics - Atlanta **Obv:** Crowned bust right **Rev:** Hurdler within sprigs

Date	Mintage	VF20	XF40	MS60	MS63	MS65
1996	—	PF65 25.50				

KM# 568 CROWN

Copper-Nickel, 38.5 mm. **Ruler:** Elizabeth II **Series:** 1996 Summer Olympics - Atlanta **Obv:** Crowned bust right **Rev:** Runners

Date	Mintage	VF20	XF40	MS60	MS63	MS65
1996	—	—	—	—	6.00	8.00

KM# 568a CROWN

28.28 g., 0.925 Silver 0.841 oz. ASW, 38.5 mm. **Ruler:** Elizabeth II **Series:** 1996 Summer Olympics - Atlanta **Obv:** Crowned bust right **Rev:** Runners

Date	Mintage	VF20	XF40	MS60	MS63	MS65
1996	Est. 30000	PF65 25.50				

KM# 569 CROWN

Copper-Nickel, 38.5 mm. **Ruler:** Elizabeth II **Series:** 1996 Summer Olympics - Atlanta **Obv:** Crowned bust right **Rev:** Sailing

Date	Mintage	VF20	XF40	MS60	MS63	MS65
1996	—	—	—	—	6.00	8.00

KM# 569a CROWN

28.28 g., 0.925 Silver 0.841 oz. ASW, 38.5 mm. **Ruler:** Elizabeth II **Series:** 1996 Summer Olympics - Atlanta **Obv:** Crowned bust right **Rev:** Sailing

Date	Mintage	VF20	XF40	MS60	MS63	MS65
1996	Est. 30000	PF65 25.50				

KM# 570 CROWN

Copper-Nickel, 38.5 mm. **Ruler:** Elizabeth II **Series:** 1996 Summer Olympics - Atlanta **Obv:** Crowned bust right **Rev:** Swimming

Date	Mintage	VF20	XF40	MS60	MS63	MS65
1996	—	—	—	—	6.00	8.00

KM# 570a CROWN

28.28 g., 0.925 Silver 0.841 oz. ASW, 38.5 mm. **Ruler:** Elizabeth II **Series:** 1996 Summer Olympics - Atlanta **Obv:** Crowned bust right **Rev:** Swimming

Date	Mintage	VF20	XF40	MS60	MS63	MS65
1996	Est. 30000	PF65 25.50				

KM# 571 CROWN

Copper-Nickel, 38.5 mm. **Ruler:** Elizabeth II **Series:** 1996 Summer Olympics - Atlanta **Obv:** Crowned bust right **Rev:** Equestrian within wreath

Date	Mintage	VF20	XF40	MS60	MS63	MS65
1996	—	—	—	—	6.00	8.00

KM# 571a CROWN

28.28 g., 0.925 Silver 0.841 oz. ASW, 38.5 mm. **Ruler:** Elizabeth II **Series:** 1996 Summer Olympics - Atlanta **Obv:** Crowned bust right **Rev:** Equestrian within wreath

Date	Mintage	VF20	XF40	MS60	MS63	MS65
1996	Est. 30000	PF65 25.50				

KM# 572 CROWN

Copper-Nickel, 38.5 mm. **Ruler:** Elizabeth II **Series:** 1996 Summer Olympics - Atlanta **Obv:** Crowned bust right **Rev:** Cyclists and Nike

Date	Mintage	VF20	XF40	MS60	MS63	MS65
1996	—	—	—	—	6.00	8.00

KM# 572a CROWN

28.28 g., 0.925 Silver 0.841 oz. ASW, 38.5 mm. **Ruler:** Elizabeth II **Series:** 1996 Summer Olympics - Atlanta **Obv:** Crowned bust right **Rev:** Cyclists and Nike

Date	Mintage	VF20	XF40	MS60	MS63	MS65
1996	Est. 30000	PF65 25.50				

KM# 577 CROWN

Copper-Nickel, 38.5 mm. **Ruler:** Elizabeth II **Series:** Bicentenary of Robert Burns **Obv:** Crowned bust right **Rev:** Seated figure facing right within circle **Edge:** Reeded

Date	Mintage	VF20	XF40	MS60	MS63	MS65
1996	—	—	—	—	8.00	10.00

KM# 577a CROWN

28.28 g., 0.925 Silver 0.841 oz. ASW, 38.5 mm. **Ruler:** Elizabeth II **Series:** Bicentenary of Robert Burns **Obv:** Crowned bust right **Rev:** Seated figure facing right within circle

Date	Mintage	VF20	XF40	MS60	MS63	MS65
1996	Est. 30000	**PF65** 45.00				

KM# 578 CROWN

Copper-Nickel, 38.5 mm. **Ruler:** Elizabeth II **Series:** Bicentenary of Robert Burns **Obv:** Crowned bust right **Rev:** Pirate ship **Edge:** Reeded

Date	Mintage	VF20	XF40	MS60	MS63	MS65
1996	—	—	—	—	5.00	6.50

KM# 578a CROWN

28.28 g., 0.925 Silver 0.841 oz. ASW, 38.5 mm. **Ruler:** Elizabeth II **Series:** Bicentenary of Robert Burns **Obv:** Crowned bust right **Rev:** Pirate ship

Date	Mintage	VF20	XF40	MS60	MS63	MS65
1996	Est. 30000	**PF65** 45.00				

KM# 579 CROWN

Copper-Nickel, 38.5 mm. **Ruler:** Elizabeth II **Series:** Bicentenary of Robert Burns **Obv:** Crowned bust right **Rev:** Auld Lang Syne

Date	Mintage	VF20	XF40	MS60	MS63	MS65
1996	—	—	—	—	5.00	6.50

KM# 579a CROWN

28.28 g., 0.925 Silver 0.841 oz. ASW, 38.5 mm. **Ruler:** Elizabeth II **Series:** Bicentenary of Robert Burns **Obv:** Crowned bust right **Rev:** Auld Lang Syne

Date	Mintage	VF20	XF40	MS60	MS63	MS65
1996	Est. 30000	**PF65** 45.00				

KM# 580 CROWN

Copper-Nickel, 38.5 mm. **Ruler:** Elizabeth II **Series:** Bicentenary of Robert Burns **Obv:** Crowned bust right **Rev:** Edinburgh Castle

Date	Mintage	VF20	XF40	MS60	MS63	MS65
1996	—	—	—	—	8.00	10.00

KM# 580a CROWN

28.28 g., 0.925 Silver 0.841 oz. ASW, 38.5 mm. **Ruler:** Elizabeth II **Series:** Bicentenary of Robert Burns **Obv:** Crowned bust right **Rev:** Edinburgh Castle

Date	Mintage	VF20	XF40	MS60	MS63	MS65
1996	Est. 30000	**PF65** 45.00				

KM# 582 CROWN

28.28 g., Copper-Nickel, 38.5 mm. **Ruler:** Elizabeth II **Subject:** 70th Birthday of Queen Elizabeth II **Obv:** Crowned bust right **Rev:** Monogram and numeral 70 flanked by flower sprigs

Date	Mintage	VF20	XF40	MS60	MS63	MS65
1996	—	—	—	—	6.00	8.00

KM# 582a CROWN

28.28 g., 0.925 Silver 0.841 oz. ASW, 38.5 mm. **Ruler:** Elizabeth II **Subject:** 70th Birthday of Queen Elizabeth II **Obv:** Crowned bust right **Rev:** Monogram and numeral 70 flanked by flower sprigs

Date	Mintage	VF20	XF40	MS60	MS63	MS65
1996	Est. 30000	**PF65** 42.50				

KM# 585 CROWN

Copper-Nickel, 38.5 mm. **Ruler:** Elizabeth II **Series:** Preserve Planet Earth **Obv:** Crowned bust right **Rev:** Killer whale

Date	Mintage	VF20	XF40	MS60	MS63	MS65
1996	—	—	—	—	12.00	15.00

KM# 585a CROWN

28.28 g., 0.925 Silver 0.841 oz. ASW, 38.5 mm. **Ruler:** Elizabeth II **Series:** Preserve Planet Earth **Obv:** Crowned bust right **Rev:** Killer whale

Date	Mintage	VF20	XF40	MS60	MS63	MS65
1996	Est. 30000	**PF65** 28.50				

KM# 586 CROWN

Copper-Nickel, 38.5 mm. **Ruler:** Elizabeth II **Series:** Preserve Planet Earth **Obv:** Crowned bust right **Rev:** Razorbill feeding chick

Date	Mintage	VF20	XF40	MS60	MS63	MS65
1996	—	—	—	—	12.00	14.00

KM# 586a CROWN

28.28 g., 0.925 Silver 0.841 oz. ASW, 38.5 mm. **Ruler:** Elizabeth II **Series:** Preserve Planet Earth **Obv:** Crowned bust right **Rev:** Razorbill feeding chick

Date	Mintage	VF20	XF40	MS60	MS63	MS65
1996	Est. 30000	**PF65** 28.50				

KM# 609 CROWN

Copper-Nickel, 38.5 mm. **Ruler:** Elizabeth II **Series:** Flower Fairies **Obv:** Crowned bust right **Rev:** Orchis

Date	Mintage	VF20	XF40	MS60	MS63	MS65
1996	—	—	—	—	5.00	6.50

KM# 609a CROWN

28.28 g., 0.925 Silver 0.841 oz. ASW, 38.5 mm. **Ruler:** Elizabeth II **Series:** Flower Fairies **Obv:** Crowned bust right **Rev:** Orchis

Date	Mintage	VF20	XF40	MS60	MS63	MS65
1996	Est. 30000	**PF65** 42.50				

KM# 610 CROWN

Copper-Nickel, 38.5 mm. **Ruler:** Elizabeth II **Series:** Flower Fairies **Obv:** Crowned bust right **Rev:** Rose

Date	Mintage	VF20	XF40	MS60	MS63	MS65
1996	—	—	—	—	8.00	10.00

KM# 610a CROWN

28.28 g., 0.925 Silver 0.841 oz. ASW, 38.5 mm. **Ruler:** Elizabeth II **Series:** Flower Fairies **Obv:** Crowned bust right **Rev:** Rose

Date	Mintage	VF20	XF40	MS60	MS63	MS65
1996	—	**PF65** 42.50				

KM# 611 CROWN

Copper-Nickel, 38.5 mm. **Ruler:** Elizabeth II **Series:** Flower Fairies **Obv:** Crowned bust right **Rev:** Fuchsia

Date	Mintage	VF20	XF40	MS60	MS63	MS65
1996	—	—	—	—	5.00	6.50

KM# 611a CROWN

28.28 g., 0.925 Silver 0.841 oz. ASW, 38.5 mm. **Ruler:** Elizabeth II **Series:** Flower Fairies **Obv:** Crowned bust right **Rev:** Fuchsia

Date	Mintage	VF20	XF40	MS60	MS63	MS65
1996	Est. 30000	PF65 42.50				

KM# 612 CROWN

Copper-Nickel, 38.5 mm. **Ruler:** Elizabeth II **Series:** Flower Fairies **Obv:** Crowned bust right **Rev:** Pinks

Date	Mintage	VF20	XF40	MS60	MS63	MS65
1996	—	—	—	—	5.00	6.50

KM# 612a CROWN

28.28 g., 0.925 Silver 0.841 oz. ASW, 38.5 mm. **Ruler:** Elizabeth II **Series:** Flower Fairies **Obv:** Crowned bust right **Rev:** Pinks

Date	Mintage	VF20	XF40	MS60	MS63	MS65
1996	Est. 30000	PF65 42.50				

KM# 621 CROWN

Copper-Nickel, 38.5 mm. **Ruler:** Elizabeth II **Obv:** Crowned bust right **Rev:** Burmese cat

Date	Mintage	VF20	XF40	MS60	MS63	MS65
1996	—	—	—	—	12.50	17.50

KM# 621a CROWN

31.10 g., 0.999 Silver 0.999 oz. ASW, 38.5 mm. **Ruler:** Elizabeth II **Obv:** Crowned bust right **Rev:** Burmese cat

Date	Mintage	VF20	XF40	MS60	MS63	MS65
1996	Est. 50000	PF65 80.00				

KM# 621b CROWN

31.10 g., 0.999 Gold 0.9989 oz. AGW **Ruler:** Elizabeth II **Obv:** Crowned bust right **Rev:** Burmese cat

Date	Mintage	VF20	XF40	MS60	MS63	MS65
1996 U	—	—	—	—	—	1,700
1996	—	PF65 1,725				

KM# 621c CROWN

31.10 g., 0.9995 Platinum 0.9995 oz. APW **Ruler:** Elizabeth II **Obv:** Crowned bust right **Rev:** Burmese cat **Note:** Prev. KM#624.

Date	Mintage	VF20	XF40	MS60	MS63	MS65
1996	—	—	—	—	—	1,800
1996	—	PF65 1,900				

KM# 626 CROWN

Copper-Nickel, 38.5 mm. **Ruler:** Elizabeth II **Obv:** Crowned bust right **Rev:** Bust within map and ship

Date	Mintage	VF20	XF40	MS60	MS63	MS65
1996	—	—	—	—	7.50	10.00

KM# 626a CROWN

28.28 g., 0.925 Silver 0.841 oz. ASW, 38.5 mm. **Ruler:** Elizabeth II **Obv:** Crowned bust right **Rev:** Bust within map and ship

Date	Mintage	VF20	XF40	MS60	MS63	MS65
1996	Est. 30000	PF65 42.50				

KM# 629 CROWN

Copper-Nickel, 38.5 mm. **Ruler:** Elizabeth II **Obv:** Crowned bust right **Rev:** Bust, map and ship

Date	Mintage	VF20	XF40	MS60	MS63	MS65
1996	—	—	—	—	7.00	9.00

KM# 629a CROWN

28.28 g., 0.925 Silver 0.841 oz. ASW, 38.5 mm. **Ruler:** Elizabeth II **Obv:** Crowned bust right **Rev:** Bust, map and ship

Date	Mintage	VF20	XF40	MS60	MS63	MS65
1996	Est. 30000	PF65 42.50				

KM# 632 CROWN

Copper-Nickel, 38.5 mm. **Ruler:** Elizabeth II **Series:** European Football Championship **Obv:** Crowned bust right **Rev:** Football player flanked by emblems within broken circle

Date	Mintage	VF20	XF40	MS60	MS63	MS65
1996	—	—	—	—	7.00	9.00

KM# 632a CROWN

28.28 g., 0.925 Silver 0.841 oz. ASW, 38.5 mm. **Ruler:** Elizabeth II **Series:** European Football Championship **Obv:** Crowned bust right **Rev:** Football player flanked by emblems within broken circle

Date	Mintage	VF20	XF40	MS60	MS63	MS65
1996	Est. 30000	PF65 45.00				

KM# 635 CROWN

Copper-Nickel, 38.5 mm. **Ruler:** Elizabeth II **Series:** European Football Championship **Obv:** Crowned bust right **Rev:** Czech Republic vs Itay

Date	Mintage	VF20	XF40	MS60	MS63	MS65
1996	—	—	—	—	7.00	9.00

KM# 635a CROWN

28.28 g., 0.925 Silver 0.841 oz. ASW, 38.5 mm. **Ruler:** Elizabeth II **Series:** European Football Championship **Obv:** Crowned bust right **Rev:** Czech Republic vs Italy

Date	Mintage	VF20	XF40	MS60	MS63	MS65
1996	Est. 30000	PF65 45.00				

KM# 638 CROWN

Copper-Nickel, 38.5 mm. **Ruler:** Elizabeth II **Series:** European Football Championship **Obv:** Crowned bust right **Rev:** Germany vs Russia

Date	Mintage	VF20	XF40	MS60	MS63	MS65
1996	—	—	—	—	7.00	9.00

KM# 638a CROWN

28.28 g., 0.925 Silver 0.841 oz. ASW, 38.5 mm. **Ruler:** Elizabeth II **Series:** European Football Championship **Obv:** Crowned bust right **Rev:** Germany vs Russia

Date	Mintage	VF20	XF40	MS60	MS63	MS65
1996	Est. 30000	PF65 45.00				

KM# 641 CROWN

Copper-Nickel, 38.5 mm. **Ruler:** Elizabeth II **Series:** European Football Championship **Obv:** Crowned bust right **Rev:** Spain vs France

Date	Mintage	VF20	XF40	MS60	MS63	MS65
1996	—	—	—	—	7.00	9.00

KM# 641a CROWN

28.28 g., 0.925 Silver 0.841 oz. ASW, 38.5 mm. **Ruler:** Elizabeth II **Series:** European Football Championship **Obv:** Crowned bust right **Rev:** Spain vs France

Date	Mintage	VF20	XF40	MS60	MS63	MS65
1996	Est. 30000	PF65 45.00				

KM# 644 CROWN
Copper-Nickel, 38.5 mm. **Ruler:** Elizabeth II **Series:** European Football Championship **Obv:** Crowned bust right **Rev:** Turkey vs Croatia

Date	Mintage	VF20	XF40	MS60	MS63	MS65
1996	—	—	—	—	7.00	9.00

KM# 644a CROWN
28.28 g., 0.925 Silver 0.841 oz. ASW, 38.5 mm. **Ruler:** Elizabeth II **Series:** European Football Championship **Obv:** Crowned bust right **Rev:** Turkey vs Croatia

Date	Mintage	VF20	XF40	MS60	MS63	MS65
1996	Est. 30000	PF65 45.00				

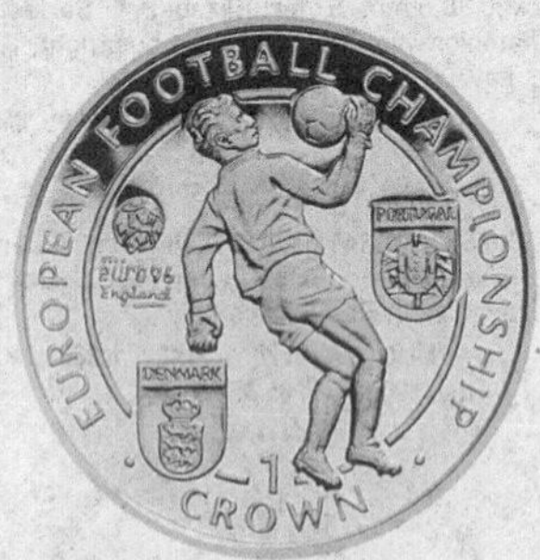

KM# 647 CROWN
Copper-Nickel, 38.5 mm. **Ruler:** Elizabeth II **Series:** European Football Championship **Obv:** Crowned bust right **Rev:** Denmark vs Portugal

Date	Mintage	VF20	XF40	MS60	MS63	MS65
1996	—	—	—	—	6.00	8.00

KM# 647a CROWN
28.28 g., 0.925 Silver 0.841 oz. ASW, 38.5 mm. **Ruler:** Elizabeth II **Series:** European Football Championship **Obv:** Crowned bust right **Rev:** Denmark vs Portugal

Date	Mintage	VF20	XF40	MS60	MS63	MS65
1996	Est. 30000	PF65 45.00				

KM# 650 CROWN
Copper-Nickel, 38.5 mm. **Ruler:** Elizabeth II **Series:** European Football Championship **Obv:** Crowned bust right **Rev:** Scotland vs England

Date	Mintage	VF20	XF40	MS60	MS63	MS65
1996	—	—	—	—	7.00	9.00

KM# 650a CROWN
28.28 g., 0.925 Silver 0.841 oz. ASW, 38.5 mm. **Ruler:** Elizabeth II **Series:** European Football Championship **Obv:** Crowned bust right **Rev:** Scotland vs England

Date	Mintage	VF20	XF40	MS60	MS63	MS65
1996	Est. 30000	PF65 45.00				

KM# 653 CROWN
Copper-Nickel, 38.5 mm. **Ruler:** Elizabeth II **Series:** European Football Championship **Obv:** Crowned bust right **Rev:** Holland vs Switzerland

Date	Mintage	VF20	XF40	MS60	MS63	MS65
1996	—	—	—	—	7.00	9.00

KM# 653a CROWN
28.28 g., 0.925 Silver 0.841 oz. ASW, 38.5 mm. **Ruler:** Elizabeth II **Series:** European Football Championship **Obv:** Crowned bust right **Rev:** Holland vs Switzerland

Date	Mintage	VF20	XF40	MS60	MS63	MS65
1996	Est. 30000	PF65 45.00				

KM# 657 CROWN
Copper-Nickel, 38.5 mm. **Ruler:** Elizabeth II **Series:** European Football Championship **Obv:** Crowned bust right **Rev:** German shield, winner

Date	Mintage	VF20	XF40	MS60	MS63	MS65
1996	—	—	—	—	7.00	9.00

KM# 657a CROWN
28.28 g., 0.925 Silver 0.841 oz. ASW, 38.5 mm. **Ruler:** Elizabeth II **Series:** European Football Championship **Obv:** Crowned bust right **Rev:** German shield, winner

Date	Mintage	VF20	XF40	MS60	MS63	MS65
1996	Est. 30000	PF65 45.00				

KM# 679 CROWN
Copper-Nickel, 38.5 mm. **Ruler:** Elizabeth II **Series:** Legend of King Arthur **Obv:** Crowned bust right **Rev:** King Arthur with sword and orb

Date	Mintage	VF20	XF40	MS60	MS63	MS65
1996	Est. 30000	—	—	—	10.00	12.00

KM# 679a CROWN
28.28 g., 0.925 Silver 0.841 oz. ASW, 38.5 mm. **Ruler:** Elizabeth II **Series:** Legend of King Arthur **Obv:** Crowned bust right **Rev:** King Arthur with sword and orb

Date	Mintage	VF20	XF40	MS60	MS63	MS65
1996	Est. 30000	PF65 23.00				

KM# 680 CROWN
Copper-Nickel, 38.5 mm. **Ruler:** Elizabeth II **Series:** Legend of King Arthur **Obv:** Crowned bust right **Rev:** Crowned Queen Guinevere facing walking through archway

Date	Mintage	VF20	XF40	MS60	MS63	MS65
1996	—	—	—	—	10.00	12.50

KM# 680a CROWN
28.28 g., 0.925 Silver 0.841 oz. ASW, 38.5 mm. **Ruler:** Elizabeth II **Series:** Legend of King Arthur **Obv:** Crowned bust right **Rev:** Crowned Queen Guinevere facing walking through archway

Date	Mintage	VF20	XF40	MS60	MS63	MS65
1996	—	PF65 23.00				

KM# 681 CROWN
Copper-Nickel, 38.5 mm. **Ruler:** Elizabeth II **Series:** Legend of King Arthur **Obv:** Crowned bust right **Rev:** Sir Lancelot on horse right within inner circle

Date	Mintage	VF20	XF40	MS60	MS63	MS65
1996	—	—	—	—	10.00	12.50

KM# 681a CROWN
28.28 g., 0.925 Silver 0.841 oz. ASW, 38.5 mm. **Ruler:** Elizabeth II **Series:** Legend of King Arthur **Obv:** Crowned bust right **Rev:** Sir Lancelot on horse right within inner circle

Date	Mintage	VF20	XF40	MS60	MS63	MS65
1996	Est. 30000	PF65 23.00				

KM# 682 CROWN
Copper-Nickel, 38.5 mm. **Ruler:** Elizabeth II **Series:** Legend of King Arthur **Obv:** Crowned bust right **Rev:** Merlin

Date	Mintage	VF20	XF40	MS60	MS63	MS65
1996	—	—	—	—	10.00	12.50

KM# 682a CROWN
28.28 g., 0.925 Silver 0.841 oz. ASW, 38.5 mm. **Ruler:** Elizabeth II **Series:** Legend of King Arthur **Obv:** Crowned bust right **Rev:** Merlin

Date	Mintage	VF20	XF40	MS60	MS63	MS65
1996	—	PF65 23.00				

KM# 683 CROWN

Copper-Nickel, 38.5 mm. **Ruler:** Elizabeth II **Series:** Legend of King Arthur **Obv:** Crowned bust right **Rev:** Camelot Castle

Date	Mintage	VF20	XF40	MS60	MS63	MS65
1996	—	—	—	—	10.00	12.50

KM# 683a CROWN

28.28 g., 0.925 Silver 0.841 oz. ASW, 38.5 mm. **Ruler:** Elizabeth II **Series:** Legend of King Arthur **Obv:** Crowned bust right **Rev:** Camelot Castle

Date	Mintage	VF20	XF40	MS60	MS63	MS65
1996	Est. 30000	PF65 25.00				

KM# 732 CROWN

Copper-Nickel, 38.5 mm. **Ruler:** Elizabeth II **Subject:** Year of the Rat **Obv:** Crowned bust right within circle **Rev:** Rat within circle

Date	Mintage	VF20	XF40	MS60	MS63	MS65
1996	—	—	—	—	12.00	15.00

KM# 732a CROWN

28.28 g., 0.925 Silver 0.841 oz. ASW, 38.5 mm. **Ruler:** Elizabeth II **Subject:** Year of the Rat **Obv:** Crowned bust right within circle **Rev:** Rat within circle

Date	Mintage	VF20	XF40	MS60	MS63	MS65
1996 Proof	—	—	—	—	—	—

Note: Entire silver issue purchased by one buyer. Mintage, disposition and market value unknown

KM# 732b CROWN

31.10 g., 0.9999 Gold 0.9999 oz. AGW **Ruler:** Elizabeth II **Subject:** Year of the Rat **Obv:** Crowned bust right **Rev:** Rat **Note:** Prev. KM#733.

Date	Mintage	VF20	XF40	MS60	MS63	MS65
1996 Proof	—	—	—	—	—	—

Note: Entire gold issue purchased by one buyer. Mintage, disposition and market value unknown

KM# 725 CROWN

Copper-Nickel, 38.5 mm. **Ruler:** Elizabeth II **Subject:** Year of the Ox **Obv:** Crowned bust right **Rev:** Ox laying down

Date	Mintage	VF20	XF40	MS60	MS63	MS65
1997	—	—	—	—	10.00	14.00

KM# 725a CROWN

28.28 g., 0.925 Silver 0.841 oz. ASW, 38.5 mm. **Ruler:** Elizabeth II **Subject:** Year of the Ox **Obv:** Crowned bust right **Rev:** Ox laying down

Date	Mintage	VF20	XF40	MS60	MS63	MS65
1997	Est. 30000	PF65 37.50				

KM# 725b CROWN

31.10 g., 0.9999 Gold 0.9999 oz. AGW **Ruler:** Elizabeth II **Subject:** Year of the Ox **Obv:** Crowned bust right **Rev:** Ox laying down **Note:** Prev. KM#726.

Date	Mintage	VF20	XF40	MS60	MS63	MS65
1997	Est. 2000	PF65 1,825				

KM# 759 CROWN

Copper-Nickel, 38.5 mm. **Ruler:** Elizabeth II **Series:** Flower Fairies **Obv:** Crowned bust right **Rev:** Fairy sitting on flowers - Candytuft

Date	Mintage	VF20	XF40	MS60	MS63	MS65
1997	—	—	—	—	8.00	10.00

KM# 759a CROWN

28.28 g., 0.925 Silver 0.841 oz. ASW, 38.5 mm. **Ruler:** Elizabeth II **Series:** Flower Fairies **Obv:** Crowned bust right **Rev:** Fairy sitting on flowers - Candytuft

Date	Mintage	VF20	XF40	MS60	MS63	MS65
1997	Est. 30000	PF65 42.50				

KM# 760 CROWN

Copper-Nickel, 38.5 mm. **Ruler:** Elizabeth II **Series:** Flower Fairies **Obv:** Crowned bust right **Rev:** Snowdrop

Date	Mintage	VF20	XF40	MS60	MS63	MS65
1997	—	—	—	—	8.00	10.00

KM# 760a CROWN

28.28 g., 0.925 Silver 0.841 oz. ASW, 38.5 mm. **Ruler:** Elizabeth II **Series:** Flower Fairies **Obv:** Crowned bust right **Rev:** Snowdrop

Date	Mintage	VF20	XF40	MS60	MS63	MS65
1997	Est. 30000	PF65 42.50				

KM# 761 CROWN

Copper-Nickel, 38.5 mm. **Ruler:** Elizabeth II **Series:** Flower Fairies **Obv:** Crowned bust right **Rev:** Tulip

Date	Mintage	VF20	XF40	MS60	MS63	MS65
1997	—	—	—	—	8.00	10.00

KM# 761a CROWN

28.28 g., 0.925 Silver 0.841 oz. ASW, 38.5 mm. **Ruler:** Elizabeth II **Series:** Flower Fairies **Obv:** Crowned bust right **Rev:** Tulip

Date	Mintage	VF20	XF40	MS60	MS63	MS65
1997	Est. 30000	PF65 42.50				

KM# 762 CROWN

Copper-Nickel, 38.5 mm. **Ruler:** Elizabeth II **Series:** Flower Fairies **Obv:** Crowned bust right **Rev:** Jasmine

Date	Mintage	VF20	XF40	MS60	MS63	MS65
1997	—	—	—	—	8.00	10.00

KM# 762a CROWN

28.28 g., 0.925 Silver 0.841 oz. ASW, 38.5 mm. **Ruler:** Elizabeth II **Series:** Flower Fairies **Obv:** Crowned bust right **Rev:** Jasmine

Date	Mintage	VF20	XF40	MS60	MS63	MS65
1997	Est. 30000	PF65 42.50				

KM# 765 CROWN

Copper-Nickel, 38.5 mm. **Ruler:** Elizabeth II **Obv:** Crowned bust right **Rev:** Leif Eriksson 999-1001, viking ship with map sail

Date	Mintage	VF20	XF40	MS60	MS63	MS65
1997	—	—	—	—	8.00	10.00

KM# 765a CROWN

28.28 g., 0.925 Silver 0.841 oz. ASW, 38.5 mm. **Ruler:** Elizabeth II **Obv:** Crowned bust right **Rev:** Leif Eriksson 999-1001, viking ship with map sail

Date	Mintage	VF20	XF40	MS60	MS63	MS65
1997	Est. 30000	PF65 45.00				

KM# 768 CROWN

Copper-Nickel, 38.5 mm. **Ruler:** Elizabeth II **Obv:** Crowned bust right **Rev:** Bust of Fridtjof Nansen, map and his ship "The Fram"

Date	Mintage	VF20	XF40	MS60	MS63	MS65
1997	—	—	—	—	8.00	10.00

KM# 768a CROWN

28.28 g., 0.925 Silver 0.841 oz. ASW, 38.5 mm. **Ruler:** Elizabeth II **Obv:** Crowned bust right **Rev:** Bust of Fridtjof Nansen, map and his ship "The Fram"

Date	Mintage	VF20	XF40	MS60	MS63	MS65
1997	Est. 30000	PF65 45.00				

KM# 774 CROWN

Copper-Nickel, 38.5 mm. **Ruler:** Elizabeth II **Obv:** Crowned bust right **Rev:** Long-haired Smoke cat

Date	Mintage	VF20	XF40	MS60	MS63	MS65
1997	—	—	—	—	12.00	16.00
1997	—	PF65 28.00				

KM# 774a CROWN

31.10 g., 0.9999 Silver 0.9999 oz. ASW, 38.5 mm. **Ruler:** Elizabeth II **Obv:** Crowned bust right **Rev:** Long-haired Smoke cat

Date	Mintage	VF20	XF40	MS60	MS63	MS65
1997	Est. 50000	PF65 80.00				

KM# 774b CROWN

31.10 g., 0.9999 Gold 0.9999 oz. AGW **Ruler:** Elizabeth II **Obv:** Crowned bust right **Rev:** Long-haired Smoke cat

Date	Mintage	VF20	XF40	MS60	MS63	MS65
1997	—	—	—	—	—	1,700
1997	—	PF65 1,725				

KM# 777 CROWN

28.28 g., 0.925 Silver 0.841 oz. ASW, 38.5 mm. **Ruler:** Elizabeth II **Series:** History of the Cat **Obv:** Crowned bust right **Rev:** Ancestry of Felidae, evolution of the cat

Date	Mintage	VF20	XF40	MS60	MS63	MS65
1997	Est. 10000	PF65 60.00				

KM# 778 CROWN

28.28 g., 0.925 Silver 0.841 oz. ASW, 38.5 mm. **Ruler:** Elizabeth II **Series:** History of the Cat **Obv:** Crowned bust right **Rev:** Snarling cat

Date	Mintage	VF20	XF40	MS60	MS63	MS65
1997	Est. 10000	PF65 60.00				

KM# 779 CROWN

28.28 g., 0.925 Silver 0.841 oz. ASW, 38.5 mm. **Ruler:** Elizabeth II **Series:** History of the Cat **Obv:** Crowned bust right **Rev:** Cat walking left

Date	Mintage	VF20	XF40	MS60	MS63	MS65
1997	Est. 10000	PF65 60.00				

KM# 780 CROWN

28.28 g., 0.925 Silver 0.841 oz. ASW, 38.5 mm. **Ruler:** Elizabeth II **Series:** History of the Cat **Obv:** Crowned bust right **Rev:** Ancient Egyptian Goddess Bast and artifacts

Date	Mintage	VF20	XF40	MS60	MS63	MS65
1997	Est. 10000	PF65 47.50				

KM# 782 CROWN

Copper-Nickel, 38.5 mm. **Ruler:** Elizabeth II **Subject:** 90th Anniversary of the TT **Obv:** Crowned bust right **Rev:** Motorcyclist flanked by emblems above sprigs

Date	Mintage	VF20	XF40	MS60	MS63	MS65
1997	—	—	—	—	8.00	10.00

KM# 782a CROWN

28.28 g., 0.925 Silver 0.841 oz. ASW, 38.5 mm. **Ruler:** Elizabeth II **Subject:** 90th Anniversary of the TT **Obv:** Crowned bust right **Rev:** Motorcyclist flanked by emblems above sprigs

Date	Mintage	VF20	XF40	MS60	MS63	MS65
1997	Est. 30000	PF65 45.00				

KM# 784 CROWN

Copper-Nickel, 38.5 mm. **Ruler:** Elizabeth II **Subject:** 90th Anniversary of the TT **Obv:** Crowned bust right **Rev:** 1937 winner Omobono Tenni

Date	Mintage	VF20	XF40	MS60	MS63	MS65
1997	—	—	—	—	9.50	11.50

KM# 784a CROWN

28.28 g., 0.925 Silver 0.841 oz. ASW, 38.5 mm. **Ruler:** Elizabeth II **Subject:** 90th Anniversary of the TT **Obv:** Crowned bust right **Rev:** 1937 winner Omobono Tenni

Date	Mintage	VF20	XF40	MS60	MS63	MS65
1997	Est. 30000	PF65 45.00				

KM# 786 CROWN

Copper-Nickel, 38.5 mm. **Ruler:** Elizabeth II **Subject:** 90th Anniversary of the TT **Obv:** Crowned bust right **Rev:** 1957 winner Bob McIntyre

Date	Mintage	VF20	XF40	MS60	MS63	MS65
1997	—	—	—	—	9.50	11.50

KM# 786a CROWN

28.28 g., 0.925 Silver 0.841 oz. ASW, 38.5 mm. **Ruler:** Elizabeth II **Subject:** 90th Anniversary of the TT **Obv:** Crowned bust right **Rev:** 1957 winner Bob McIntyre

Date	Mintage	VF20	XF40	MS60	MS63	MS65
1997	Est. 30000	PF65 45.00				

KM# 788 CROWN

Copper-Nickel, 38.5 mm. **Ruler:** Elizabeth II **Subject:** 90th Anniversary of the TT **Obv:** Crowned bust right **Rev:** 1967 winner Mike Hailwood

Date	Mintage	VF20	XF40	MS60	MS63	MS65
1997	—	—	—	—	9.50	11.50

KM# 788a CROWN

28.28 g., 0.925 Silver 0.841 oz. ASW, 38.5 mm. **Ruler:** Elizabeth II **Subject:** 90th Anniversary of the TT **Obv:** Crowned bust right **Rev:** 1967 winner Mike Hailwood

Date	Mintage	VF20	XF40	MS60	MS63	MS65
1997	Est. 30000	PF65 45.00				

KM# 793 CROWN

Copper-Nickel, 38.5 mm. **Ruler:** Elizabeth II **Subject:** 50th Wedding Anniversary of Queen Elizabeth II and Prince Philip **Obv:** Crowned bust right **Rev:** Conjoined 3/4 length figures facing

Date	Mintage	VF20	XF40	MS60	MS63	MS65
1997	—	—	—	—	8.00	10.00

KM# 793a CROWN
28.28 g., 0.925 Gold Clad Silver 0.841 oz., 38.5 mm. **Ruler:** Elizabeth II **Subject:** 50th Wedding Anniversary of Queen Elizabeth II and Prince Philip **Obv:** Crowned bust right **Rev:** Conjoined 3/4 length figures facing

Date	Mintage	VF20	XF40	MS60	MS63	MS65
1997	Est. 10000	PF65 45.00				

KM# 799 CROWN
Copper-Nickel, 38.5 mm. **Ruler:** Elizabeth II **Series:** Year 2000 **Subject:** Birth of Christ **Obv:** Crowned bust right **Rev:** Madonna and child with angels

Date	Mintage	VF20	XF40	MS60	MS63	MS65
1997	—	—	—	—	7.50	9.50

KM# 799a CROWN
28.28 g., 0.925 Silver 0.841 oz. ASW, 38.5 mm. **Ruler:** Elizabeth II **Series:** Year 2000 **Subject:** Birth of Christ **Obv:** Crowned bust right **Rev:** Madonna and child with angels

Date	Mintage	VF20	XF40	MS60	MS63	MS65
1997	Est. 10000	PF65 50.00				

KM# 801 CROWN
Copper-Nickel, 38.5 mm. **Ruler:** Elizabeth II **Series:** Year 2000 **Subject:** Fall of the Roman Empire 476 **Obv:** Crowned bust right **Rev:** Barbarian defeating soldier

Date	Mintage	VF20	XF40	MS60	MS63	MS65
1997	—	—	—	—	7.50	9.50

KM# 801a CROWN
28.28 g., 0.925 Silver 0.841 oz. ASW, 38.5 mm. **Ruler:** Elizabeth II **Series:** Year 2000 **Subject:** Fall of the Roman Empire 476 **Obv:** Crowned bust right **Rev:** Barbarian defeating soldier

Date	Mintage	VF20	XF40	MS60	MS63	MS65
1997	Est. 10000	PF65 50.00				

KM# 803 CROWN
Copper-Nickel, 38.5 mm. **Ruler:** Elizabeth II **Series:** Year 2000 **Subject:** Flight of Mohammed 622 **Obv:** Crowned bust right **Rev:** Arabs and camels at oasis

Date	Mintage	VF20	XF40	MS60	MS63	MS65
1997	—	—	—	—	7.50	12.00

KM# 803a CROWN
28.28 g., 0.925 Silver 0.841 oz. ASW, 38.5 mm. **Ruler:** Elizabeth II **Series:** Year 2000 **Subject:** Flight of Mohammed 622 **Obv:** Crowned bust right **Rev:** Arabs and camels at oasis

Date	Mintage	VF20	XF40	MS60	MS63	MS65
1997	Est. 10000	PF65 47.50				

KM# 805 CROWN
Copper-Nickel, 38.5 mm. **Ruler:** Elizabeth II **Series:** Year 2000 **Subject:** Norman Conquest 1066 **Obv:** Crowned bust right **Rev:** William the Conqueror rallying his troops

Date	Mintage	VF20	XF40	MS60	MS63	MS65
1997	—	—	—	—	7.50	9.50

KM# 805a CROWN
28.28 g., 0.925 Silver 0.841 oz. ASW, 38.5 mm. **Ruler:** Elizabeth II **Series:** Year 2000 **Subject:** Norman Conquest 1066 **Obv:** Crowned bust right **Rev:** Armored equestrian rallying his troops

Date	Mintage	VF20	XF40	MS60	MS63	MS65
1997	Est. 10000	PF65 50.00				

KM# 808 CROWN
Copper-Nickel, 38.5 mm. **Ruler:** Elizabeth II **Series:** World Cup Soccer **Obv:** Crowned bust right **Rev:** Soccer players within ball

Date	Mintage	VF20	XF40	MS60	MS63	MS65
1998	—	—	—	—	7.50	9.50

KM# 808a CROWN
28.28 g., 0.925 Silver 0.841 oz. ASW, 38.5 mm. **Ruler:** Elizabeth II **Series:** World Cup Soccer **Obv:** Crowned bust right **Rev:** Soccer players within ball

Date	Mintage	VF20	XF40	MS60	MS63	MS65
1998	Est. 30000	PF65 47.50				

KM# 809 CROWN
Copper-Nickel, 38.5 mm. **Ruler:** Elizabeth II **Series:** World Cup Soccer **Obv:** Crowned bust right **Rev:** Soccer players

Date	Mintage	VF20	XF40	MS60	MS63	MS65
1998	—	—	—	—	7.50	9.50

KM# 809a CROWN
28.28 g., 0.925 Silver 0.841 oz. ASW, 38.5 mm. **Ruler:** Elizabeth II **Series:** World Cup Soccer **Obv:** Crowned bust right **Rev:** Soccer players

Date	Mintage	VF20	XF40	MS60	MS63	MS65
1998	Est. 30000	PF65 47.50				

KM# 810 CROWN
Copper-Nickel, 38.5 mm. **Ruler:** Elizabeth II **Series:** World Cup Soccer **Obv:** Crowned bust right **Rev:** Soccer players

Date	Mintage	VF20	XF40	MS60	MS63	MS65
1998	—	—	—	—	7.50	9.50

KM# 810a CROWN
28.28 g., 0.925 Silver 0.841 oz. ASW, 38.5 mm. **Ruler:** Elizabeth II **Series:** World Cup Soccer **Obv:** Crowned bust right **Rev:** Soccer players

Date	Mintage	VF20	XF40	MS60	MS63	MS65
1998	Est. 30000	PF65 47.50				

KM# 811 CROWN
Copper-Nickel, 38.5 mm. **Ruler:** Elizabeth II **Series:** World Cup Soccer **Obv:** Crowned bust right **Rev:** Soccer players

Date	Mintage	VF20	XF40	MS60	MS63	MS65
1998	—	—	—	—	7.50	9.50

KM# 811a CROWN
28.28 g., 0.925 Silver 0.841 oz. ASW, 38.5 mm. **Ruler:** Elizabeth II **Series:** World Cup Soccer **Obv:** Crowned bust right **Rev:** Soccer players

Date	Mintage	VF20	XF40	MS60	MS63	MS65
1998	Est. 30000	PF65 47.50				

KM# 816 CROWN
Copper-Nickel, 38.5 mm. **Ruler:** Elizabeth II **Subject:** Year of the Tiger **Obv:** Crowned bust right within circle **Rev:** Tiger within circle

Date	Mintage	VF20	XF40	MS60	MS63	MS65
1998	—	—	—	—	12.00	15.00

KM# 816a CROWN
28.28 g., 0.925 Silver 0.841 oz. ASW, 38.5 mm. **Ruler:** Elizabeth II **Subject:** Year of the Tiger **Obv:** Crowned bust right within circle **Rev:** Tiger within circle

Date	Mintage	VF20	XF40	MS60	MS63	MS65
1998	—	PF65 50.00				

KM# 817 CROWN
31.10 g., 0.9999 Gold 0.9999 oz. AGW **Ruler:** Elizabeth II **Subject:** Year of the Tiger **Obv:** Crowned bust right **Rev:** Tiger

Date	Mintage	VF20	XF40	MS60	MS63	MS65
1998	Est. 2000	PF65 1,800				

KM# 825 CROWN

Copper-Nickel, 38.5 mm. **Ruler:** Elizabeth II **Subject:** Marco Polo **Obv:** Crowned bust right **Rev:** Bust right, caravan and palace

Date	Mintage	VF20	XF40	MS60	MS63	MS65
1998	—	—	—	—	8.00	10.00

KM# 825a CROWN

28.28 g., 0.925 Silver 0.841 oz. ASW, 38.5 mm. **Ruler:** Elizabeth II **Subject:** Marco Polo **Obv:** Crowned bust right **Rev:** Bust right, caravan and palace

Date	Mintage	VF20	XF40	MS60	MS63	MS65
1998	Est. 30000	PF65 47.50				

KM# 827 CROWN

Copper-Nickel, 38.5 mm. **Ruler:** Elizabeth II **Series:** Great Explorers **Subject:** Vasco da Gama **Obv:** Crowned bust right **Rev:** Bust, ship and African map

Date	Mintage	VF20	XF40	MS60	MS63	MS65
1998	—	—	—	—	8.00	10.00

KM# 827a CROWN

28.28 g., 0.925 Silver 0.841 oz. ASW, 38.5 mm. **Ruler:** Elizabeth II **Obv:** Crowned bust right **Rev:** Bust, ship and African map

Date	Mintage	VF20	XF40	MS60	MS63	MS65
1998	Est. 30000	PF65 47.50				

KM# 840 CROWN

Copper-Nickel, 38.5 mm. **Ruler:** Elizabeth II **Series:** Flower Fairies **Obv:** Crowned bust right **Rev:** Standing fairy - Lavender

Date	Mintage	VF20	XF40	MS60	MS63	MS65
1998	—	—	—	—	8.00	10.00

KM# 840a CROWN

28.28 g., 0.925 Silver 0.841 oz. ASW, 38.5 mm. **Ruler:** Elizabeth II **Series:** Flower Fairies **Obv:** Crowned bust right **Rev:** Standing fairy - Lavender

Date	Mintage	VF20	XF40	MS60	MS63	MS65
1998	Est. 30000	PF65 47.50				

KM# 841 CROWN

Copper-Nickel, 38.5 mm. **Ruler:** Elizabeth II **Series:** Flower Fairies **Obv:** Crowned bust right **Rev:** Sweet pea, two fairies

Date	Mintage	VF20	XF40	MS60	MS63	MS65
1998	—	—	—	—	7.50	9.50

KM# 841a CROWN

28.28 g., 0.925 Silver 0.841 oz. ASW, 38.5 mm. **Ruler:** Elizabeth II **Series:** Flower Fairies **Obv:** Crowned bust right **Rev:** Sweet pea, two fairies

Date	Mintage	VF20	XF40	MS60	MS63	MS65
1998	Est. 30000	PF65 47.50				

KM# 842 CROWN

Copper-Nickel, 38.5 mm. **Ruler:** Elizabeth II **Series:** Flower Fairies **Obv:** Crowned bust right **Rev:** Fairy looking into flower - White Bindweed

Date	Mintage	VF20	XF40	MS60	MS63	MS65
1998	—	—	—	—	7.50	9.50

KM# 842a CROWN

28.28 g., 0.925 Silver 0.841 oz. ASW, 38.5 mm. **Ruler:** Elizabeth II **Series:** Flower Fairies **Obv:** Crowned bust right **Rev:** Fairy looking into flower - White Bindweed

Date	Mintage	VF20	XF40	MS60	MS63	MS65
1998	—	PF65 47.50				

KM# 843 CROWN

Copper-Nickel, 38.5 mm. **Ruler:** Elizabeth II **Series:** Flower Fairies **Obv:** Crowned bust right **Rev:** Fairy standing with flower - Daffodil

Date	Mintage	VF20	XF40	MS60	MS63	MS65
1998	—	—	—	—	8.00	10.00

KM# 843a CROWN

28.28 g., 0.925 Silver 0.841 oz. ASW, 38.5 mm. **Ruler:** Elizabeth II **Series:** Flower Fairies **Obv:** Crowned bust right **Rev:** Fairy standing with flower - Daffodil

Date	Mintage	VF20	XF40	MS60	MS63	MS65
1998	Est. 20000	PF65 47.50				

KM# 849 CROWN

Copper-Nickel, 38.5 mm. **Ruler:** Elizabeth II **Series:** Winter Olympics - Nagano **Obv:** Crowned bust right **Rev:** Bobsled

Date	Mintage	VF20	XF40	MS60	MS63	MS65
1998	—	—	—	—	7.50	9.50

KM# 849a CROWN

28.28 g., 0.925 Silver 0.841 oz. ASW, 38.5 mm. **Ruler:** Elizabeth II **Series:** Winter Olympics - Nagano **Obv:** Crowned bust right **Rev:** Bobsled

Date	Mintage	VF20	XF40	MS60	MS63	MS65
1998	Est. 30000	PF65 47.50				

KM# 850 CROWN

Copper-Nickel, 38.5 mm. **Ruler:** Elizabeth II **Series:** Winter Olympics - Nagano **Obv:** Crowned bust right **Rev:** Cross-country skier

Date	Mintage	VF20	XF40	MS60	MS63	MS65
1998	—	—	—	—	7.50	9.50

KM# 850a CROWN

28.28 g., 0.925 Silver 0.841 oz. ASW, 38.5 mm. **Ruler:** Elizabeth II **Series:** Winter Olympics - Nagano **Obv:** Crowned bust right **Rev:** Cross-country skier

Date	Mintage	VF20	XF40	MS60	MS63	MS65
1998	—	PF65 47.50				

KM# 851 CROWN

Copper-Nickel, 38.5 mm. **Ruler:** Elizabeth II **Series:** Winter Olympics - Nagano **Obv:** Crowned bust right **Rev:** Two hockey players

Date	Mintage	VF20	XF40	MS60	MS63	MS65
1998	—	—	—	—	7.50	9.50

KM# 851a CROWN

28.28 g., 0.925 Silver 0.841 oz. ASW, 38.5 mm. **Ruler:** Elizabeth II **Series:** Winter Olympics - Nagano **Obv:** Crowned bust right **Rev:** Two hockey players

Date	Mintage	VF20	XF40	MS60	MS63	MS65
1998	—	PF65 47.50				

KM# 852 CROWN

Copper-Nickel, 38.5 mm. **Ruler:** Elizabeth II **Series:** Winter Olympics - Nagano **Obv:** Crowned bust right **Rev:** Two speed skaters

Date	Mintage	VF20	XF40	MS60	MS63	MS65
1998	—	—	—	—	7.50	9.50

KM# 852a CROWN

28.28 g., 0.925 Silver 0.841 oz. ASW, 38.5 mm. **Ruler:** Elizabeth II **Series:** Winter Olympics - Nagano **Obv:** Crowned bust right **Rev:** Two speed skaters

Date	Mintage	VF20	XF40	MS60	MS63	MS65
1998	—	PF65 47.50				

KM# 857 CROWN

Copper-Nickel, 38.5 mm. **Ruler:** Elizabeth II **Obv:** Crowned bust right **Rev:** Birman cat

Date	Mintage	VF20	XF40	MS60	MS63	MS65
1998	—	—	—	—	12.00	16.00
1998	—	PF65 28.00				

KM# 857a CROWN

31.10 g., 0.9999 Silver 0.9999 oz. ASW, 38.5 mm. **Ruler:** Elizabeth II **Obv:** Crowned bust right **Rev:** Birman cat

Date	Mintage	VF20	XF40	MS60	MS63	MS65
1998	—	PF65 80.00				

KM# 857b CROWN

31.10 g., 0.9999 Gold 0.9999 oz. AGW **Ruler:** Elizabeth II **Obv:** Crowned bust right **Rev:** Birman cat

Date	Mintage	VF20	XF40	MS60	MS63	MS65
1998	—	—	—	—	—	1,700
1998	1,000	PF65 1,725				

KM# 872 CROWN

28.40 g., Copper-Nickel, 38.52 mm. **Ruler:** Elizabeth II **Subject:** 125th Anniversary of the Steam Railway **Obv:** Crowned bust right **Rev:** American steam locomotive "The General" **Edge:** Reeded

Date	Mintage	VF20	XF40	MS60	MS63	MS65
1998 PM	—	—	—	—	12.00	15.00

KM# 872a CROWN

28.28 g., 0.925 Silver 0.841 oz. ASW, 38.52 mm. **Ruler:** Elizabeth II **Subject:** 125th Anniversary of the Steam Railway **Obv:** Crowned bust right **Rev:** American steam locomotive "The General" **Edge:** Reeded

Date	Mintage	VF20	XF40	MS60	MS63	MS65
1998 PM	Est. 30000	PF65 47.50				

KM# 874 CROWN

28.40 g., Copper-Nickel, 38.52 mm. **Ruler:** Elizabeth II **Subject:** 125th Anniversary of the Steam Railway **Obv:** Crowned bust right **Rev:** English steam locomotive "The Rocket" below bust of George Stephenson **Edge:** Reeded

Date	Mintage	VF20	XF40	MS60	MS63	MS65
1998 PM	—	—	—	—	10.00	12.00

KM# 874a CROWN

28.28 g., 0.925 Silver 0.841 oz. ASW, 38.52 mm. **Ruler:** Elizabeth II **Subject:** 125th Anniversary of the Steam Railway **Obv:** Crowned bust right **Rev:** English steam locomotive "The Rocket" below bust of George Stephenson **Edge:** Reeded

Date	Mintage	VF20	XF40	MS60	MS63	MS65
1998 PM	Est. 30000	PF65 47.50				

KM# 876 CROWN

Copper-Nickel, 38.5 mm. **Ruler:** Elizabeth II **Subject:** 125th Anniversary of the Steam Railway **Obv:** Crowned bust right **Rev:** View within parlor car

Date	Mintage	VF20	XF40	MS60	MS63	MS65
1998	—	—	—	—	10.00	12.00

KM# 876a CROWN

28.28 g., 0.925 Silver 0.841 oz. ASW, 38.5 mm. **Ruler:** Elizabeth II **Subject:** 125th Anniversary of the Steam Railway **Obv:** Crowned bust right **Rev:** View within parlor car

Date	Mintage	VF20	XF40	MS60	MS63	MS65
1998	Est. 30000	PF65 47.50				

KM# 878 CROWN

28.40 g., Copper-Nickel, 38.52 mm. **Ruler:** Elizabeth II **Subject:** 125th Anniversary of the Steam Railway **Obv:** Crowned bust right **Rev:** Mount Pilatus Railway **Edge:** Reeded

Date	Mintage	VF20	XF40	MS60	MS63	MS65
1998 PM	—	—	—	—	10.00	12.00

KM# 878a CROWN

28.28 g., 0.925 Silver 0.841 oz. ASW, 38.52 mm. **Ruler:** Elizabeth II **Subject:** 125th Anniversary of the Steam Railway **Obv:** Crowned bust right **Rev:** Mount Pilatus Railway **Edge:** Reeded

Date	Mintage	VF20	XF40	MS60	MS63	MS65
1998 PM	Est. 30000	PF65 47.50				

KM# 880 CROWN

28.40 g., Copper-Nickel, 38.52 mm. **Ruler:** Elizabeth II **Subject:** 125th Anniversary of the Steam Railway **Obv:** Crowned bust right **Rev:** English steam locomotive "No. 1 Sutherland" **Edge:** Reeded

Date	Mintage	VF20	XF40	MS60	MS63	MS65
1998 PM	—	—	—	—	10.00	12.00

KM# 880a CROWN

28.28 g., 0.925 Silver 0.841 oz. ASW, 38.52 mm. **Ruler:** Elizabeth II **Subject:** 125th Anniversary of the Steam Railway **Obv:** Crowned bust right **Rev:** English steam locomotive "No. 1 Sutherland" **Edge:** Reeded

Date	Mintage	VF20	XF40	MS60	MS63	MS65
1998 PM	Est. 30000	PF65 47.50				

KM# 882 CROWN

Copper-Nickel, 38.5 mm. **Ruler:** Elizabeth II **Subject:** 125th Anniversary of the Steam Railway **Obv:** Crowned bust right **Rev:** "Flying Scotsman" locomotive

Date	Mintage	VF20	XF40	MS60	MS63	MS65
1998	—	—	—	—	10.00	12.00

KM# 882a CROWN

28.28 g., 0.925 Silver 0.841 oz. ASW, 38.5 mm. **Ruler:** Elizabeth II **Subject:** 125th Anniversary of the Steam Railway **Obv:** Crowned bust right **Rev:** "Flying Scotsman" locomotive

Date	Mintage	VF20	XF40	MS60	MS63	MS65
1998	Est. 30000	PF65 47.50				

KM# 884 CROWN

Copper-Nickel, 38.6 mm. **Ruler:** Elizabeth II **Subject:** 125th Anniversary of the Steam Railway **Obv:** Crowned bust right **Rev:** "The Mallard" locomotive

Date	Mintage	VF20	XF40	MS60	MS63	MS65
1998	—	—	—	—	10.00	12.00

KM# 884a CROWN

28.28 g., 0.925 Silver 0.841 oz. ASW, 38.5 mm. **Ruler:** Elizabeth II **Subject:** 125th Anniversary of the Steam Railway **Obv:** Crowned bust right **Rev:** "The Mallard" locomotive

Date	Mintage	VF20	XF40	MS60	MS63	MS65
1998	Est. 30000	PF65 47.50				

KM# 886 CROWN

Copper-Nickel, 38.5 mm. **Ruler:** Elizabeth II **Subject:** 125th Anniversary of the Steam Railway **Obv:** Crowned bust right **Rev:** "The Big Boy" locomotive

Date	Mintage	VF20	XF40	MS60	MS63	MS65
1998	—	—	—	—	10.00	12.00

KM# 886a CROWN

28.28 g., 0.925 Silver 0.841 oz. ASW, 38.5 mm. **Ruler:** Elizabeth II **Subject:** 125th Anniversary of the Steam Railway **Obv:** Bust of Queen Elizabeth II right **Rev:** "The Big Boy" locomotive

Date	Mintage	VF20	XF40	MS60	MS63	MS65
1998	Est. 30000	PF65 47.50				

KM# 888 CROWN

Copper-Nickel, 38.5 mm. **Ruler:** Elizabeth II **Series:** Year 2000 **Obv:** Crowned bust right **Rev:** Group of standing figures

Date	Mintage	VF20	XF40	MS60	MS63	MS65
1998	—	—	—	—	10.00	12.00

KM# 888a CROWN

28.28 g., 0.925 Silver 0.841 oz. ASW, 38.5 mm. **Ruler:** Elizabeth II **Series:** Year 2000 **Obv:** Crowned bust right **Rev:** Group of standing figures

Date	Mintage	VF20	XF40	MS60	MS63	MS65
1998	—	PF65 32.50				

KM# 890 CROWN

Copper-Nickel, 38.5 mm. **Ruler:** Elizabeth II **Series:** Year 2000 **Obv:** Crowned bust right **Rev:** French Revolution 1789

Date	Mintage	VF20	XF40	MS60	MS63	MS65
1998	—	—	—	—	7.50	9.50

KM# 890a CROWN

28.28 g., 0.925 Silver 0.841 oz. ASW, 38.5 mm. **Ruler:** Elizabeth II **Series:** Year 2000 **Obv:** Crowned bust right **Rev:** French Revolution 1789

Date	Mintage	VF20	XF40	MS60	MS63	MS65
1998	Est. 30000	PF65 32.50				

KM# 892 CROWN

Copper-Nickel, 38.5 mm. **Ruler:** Elizabeth II **Series:** Year 2000 **Obv:** Crowned bust right **Rev:** Reformation of the Church 1517

Date	Mintage	VF20	XF40	MS60	MS63	MS65
1998	—	—	—	—	7.50	9.50

KM# 892a CROWN

28.28 g., 0.925 Silver 0.841 oz. ASW, 38.5 mm. **Ruler:** Elizabeth II **Series:** Year 2000 **Obv:** Crowned bust right **Rev:** Reformation of the Church 1517

Date	Mintage	VF20	XF40	MS60	MS63	MS65
1998	Est. 30000	PF65 32.50				

KM# 894 CROWN

Copper-Nickel, 38.5 mm. **Ruler:** Elizabeth II **Series:** Year 2000 **Obv:** Crowned bust right **Rev:** 400th Anniversary of the Renaissance

Date	Mintage	VF20	XF40	MS60	MS63	MS65
1998	—	—	—	—	7.50	9.50

KM# 894a CROWN

28.28 g., 0.925 Silver 0.841 oz. ASW, 38.5 mm. **Ruler:** Elizabeth II **Series:** Year 2000 **Obv:** Crowned bust right **Rev:** 400th Anniversary of the Renaissance

Date	Mintage	VF20	XF40	MS60	MS63	MS65
1998	Est. 30000	PF65 32.50				

KM# 896 CROWN

Copper-Nickel, 38.5 mm. **Ruler:** Elizabeth II **Series:** Year of the Ocean **Obv:** Crowned bust right **Rev:** Basking shark

Date	Mintage	VF20	XF40	MS60	MS63	MS65
1998	—	—	—	—	12.50	17.50

KM# 896a CROWN

28.28 g., 0.925 Silver 0.841 oz. ASW, 38.5 mm. **Ruler:** Elizabeth II **Series:** Year of the Ocean **Obv:** Crowned bust right **Rev:** Basking shark

Date	Mintage	VF20	XF40	MS60	MS63	MS65
1998	—	PF65 47.50				

KM# 897 CROWN

Copper-Nickel, 38.5 mm. **Ruler:** Elizabeth II **Series:** Year of the Ocean **Obv:** Crowned bust right **Rev:** Humpback whale

Date	Mintage	VF20	XF40	MS60	MS63	MS65
1998	—	—	—	—	12.50	15.00

KM# 897a CROWN

28.28 g., 0.925 Silver 0.841 oz. ASW, 38.5 mm. **Ruler:** Elizabeth II **Series:** Year of the Ocean **Obv:** Crowned bust right **Rev:** Humpback whale

Date	Mintage	VF20	XF40	MS60	MS63	MS65
1998	Est. 30000	PF65 47.50				

KM# 898 CROWN

Copper-Nickel, 38.5 mm. **Ruler:** Elizabeth II **Series:** Year of the Ocean **Obv:** Crowned bust right **Rev:** Penguins and seals

Date	Mintage	VF20	XF40	MS60	MS63	MS65
1998	—	—	—	—	12.00	18.00

KM# 898a CROWN

28.28 g., 0.925 Silver 0.841 oz. ASW, 38.5 mm. **Ruler:** Elizabeth II **Series:** Year of the Ocean **Obv:** Crowned bust right **Rev:** Penguins and seals

Date	Mintage	VF20	XF40	MS60	MS63	MS65
1998	Est. 30000	PF65 45.00				

KM# 899 CROWN

Copper-Nickel, 38.5 mm. **Ruler:** Elizabeth II **Series:** Year of the Ocean **Obv:** Crowned bust right **Rev:** Sailboats

Date	Mintage	VF20	XF40	MS60	MS63	MS65
1998	—	—	—	—	10.00	12.00

KM# 899a CROWN

28.28 g., 0.925 Silver 0.841 oz. ASW, 38.5 mm. **Ruler:** Elizabeth II **Series:** Year of the Ocean **Obv:** Crowned bust right **Rev:** Sailboats

Date	Mintage	VF20	XF40	MS60	MS63	MS65
1998	Est. 30000	PF65 47.50				

KM# 914 CROWN

Copper-Nickel, 38.5 mm. **Ruler:** Elizabeth II **Subject:** Battle of Waterloo 1815 **Obv:** Crowned bust right **Rev:** Napoleon on horse half left

Date	Mintage	VF20	XF40	MS60	MS63	MS65
1999	—	—	—	—	8.00	10.00

KM# 914a CROWN

28.28 g., 0.925 Silver 0.841 oz. ASW, 38.5 mm. **Ruler:** Elizabeth II **Subject:** Battle of Waterloo 1815 **Obv:** Crowned bust right **Rev:** Napoleon on horse half left

Date	Mintage	VF20	XF40	MS60	MS63	MS65
1999	Est. 10000	PF65 50.00				

KM# 916 CROWN

Copper-Nickel, 38.5 mm. **Ruler:** Elizabeth II **Subject:** American Civil War 1865 **Obv:** Crowned bust right **Rev:** Cameos, swords, flag and drum

Date	Mintage	VF20	XF40	MS60	MS63	MS65
1999	—	—	—	—	9.50	11.50

KM# 916a CROWN

28.28 g., 0.925 Silver 0.841 oz. ASW, 38.5 mm. **Ruler:** Elizabeth II **Subject:** American Civil War 1865 **Obv:** Crowned bust right **Rev:** Cameos, swords, flag and drum

Date	Mintage	VF20	XF40	MS60	MS63	MS65
1999	Est. 10000	PF65 50.00				

KM# 918 CROWN

Copper-Nickel, 38.5 mm. **Ruler:** Elizabeth II **Subject:** Russian Revolution 1917 **Obv:** Crowned bust right **Rev:** Lenin above the Aurora

Date	Mintage	VF20	XF40	MS60	MS63	MS65
1999	—	—	—	—	7.50	9.50

KM# 918a CROWN

28.28 g., 0.925 Silver 0.841 oz. ASW, 38.5 mm. **Ruler:** Elizabeth II **Subject:** Russian Revolution 1917 **Obv:** Crowned bust right **Rev:** Lenin above the Aurora

Date	Mintage	VF20	XF40	MS60	MS63	MS65
1999	Est. 10000	PF65 50.00				

KM# 920 CROWN

Copper-Nickel, 38.5 mm. **Ruler:** Elizabeth II **Subject:** World War I Armistice Day 1918 **Obv:** Crowned bust right **Rev:** Biplane above tank **Edge:** Reeded

Date	Mintage	VF20	XF40	MS60	MS63	MS65
1999	—	—	—	—	7.50	9.50

KM# 920a CROWN

28.28 g., 0.925 Silver 0.841 oz. ASW, 38.5 mm. **Ruler:** Elizabeth II **Subject:** World War I Armistice Day 1918 **Obv:** Crowned bust right **Rev:** Biplane above tank

Date	Mintage	VF20	XF40	MS60	MS63	MS65
1999	Est. 10000	PF65 50.00				

KM# 922 CROWN

Copper-Nickel, 38.5 mm. **Ruler:** Elizabeth II **Series:** Summer Olympics - Sydney **Obv:** Crowned bust right **Rev:** Javelin throwers **Edge:** Reeded

Date	Mintage	VF20	XF40	MS60	MS63	MS65
1999	—	—	—	—	7.50	9.50

KM# 922a CROWN

28.28 g., 0.925 Silver 0.841 oz. ASW, 38.5 mm. **Ruler:** Elizabeth II **Series:** Summer Olympics - Sydney **Obv:** Crowned bust right **Rev:** Javelin throwers

Date	Mintage	VF20	XF40	MS60	MS63	MS65
1999	Est. 10000	PF65 55.00				

KM# 924 CROWN

Copper-Nickel, 38.5 mm. **Ruler:** Elizabeth II **Series:** Summer Olympics - Sydney **Obv:** Crowned bust right **Rev:** Diver divides map **Edge:** Reeded

Date	Mintage	VF20	XF40	MS60	MS63	MS65
1999	—	—	—	—	7.50	9.50

KM# 924a CROWN

28.28 g., 0.925 Silver 0.841 oz. ASW, 38.5 mm. **Ruler:** Elizabeth II **Series:** Summer Olympics - Sydney **Obv:** Crowned bust right **Rev:** Diver divides map

Date	Mintage	VF20	XF40	MS60	MS63	MS65
1999	Est. 10000	PF65 55.00				

KM# 926 CROWN

Copper-Nickel, 38.5 mm. **Ruler:** Elizabeth II **Series:** Summer Olympics - Sydney **Obv:** Crowned bust right **Rev:** Sailboat and Sydney Opera House **Edge:** Reeded

Date	Mintage	VF20	XF40	MS60	MS63	MS65
1999	—	—	—	—	7.50	9.50

KM# 926a CROWN

28.28 g., 0.925 Silver 0.841 oz. ASW, 38.5 mm. **Ruler:** Elizabeth II **Series:** Summer Olympics - Sydney **Obv:** Crowned bust right **Rev:** Sailboat and Sydney Opera House

Date	Mintage	VF20	XF40	MS60	MS63	MS65
1999	Est. 10000	PF65 55.00				

KM# 928 CROWN

Copper-Nickel, 38.5 mm. **Ruler:** Elizabeth II **Series:** Summer Olympics - Sydney **Obv:** Crowned bust right **Rev:** Runners and torch **Edge:** Reeded

Date	Mintage	VF20	XF40	MS60	MS63	MS65
1999	—	—	—	—	7.50	9.50

KM# 928a CROWN

28.28 g., 0.925 Silver 0.841 oz. ASW, 38.5 mm. **Ruler:** Elizabeth II **Series:** Summer Olympics - Sydney **Obv:** Crowned bust right **Rev:** Runners and torch

Date	Mintage	VF20	XF40	MS60	MS63	MS65
1999	Est. 10000	PF65 55.00				

KM# 930 CROWN

Copper-Nickel, 38.5 mm. **Ruler:** Elizabeth II **Series:** Summer Olympics - Sydney **Obv:** Crowned bust right **Rev:** Hurdlers and Sydney Opera House **Edge:** Reeded

Date	Mintage	VF20	XF40	MS60	MS63	MS65
1999	—	—	—	—	7.50	9.50

KM# 930a CROWN

28.28 g., 0.925 Silver 0.841 oz. ASW, 38.5 mm. **Ruler:** Elizabeth II **Series:** Summer Olympics - Sydney **Obv:** Crowned bust right **Rev:** Hurdlers and Sydney Opera House

Date	Mintage	VF20	XF40	MS60	MS63	MS65
1999	Est. 10000	PF65 55.00				

KM# 932 CROWN

Copper-Nickel, 38.5 mm. **Ruler:** Elizabeth II **Series:** World Cup Rugby 1999 **Obv:** Crowned bust right **Rev:** Bust 1/4 right flanked by players **Edge:** Reeded

Date	Mintage	VF20	XF40	MS60	MS63	MS65
1999	—	—	—	—	8.00	10.00

KM# 932a CROWN

28.28 g., 0.925 Silver 0.841 oz. ASW, 38.5 mm. **Ruler:** Elizabeth II **Series:** World Cup Rugby 1999 **Obv:** Crowned bust right **Rev:** Bust 1/4 right flanked by players

Date	Mintage	VF20	XF40	MS60	MS63	MS65
1999	Est. 10000	PF65 50.00				

KM# 934 CROWN

Copper-Nickel, 38.5 mm. **Ruler:** Elizabeth II **Series:** World Cup Rugby 1999 **Obv:** Crowned bust right **Rev:** Rugby scrum **Edge:** Reeded

Date	Mintage	VF20	XF40	MS60	MS63	MS65
1999	—	—	—	—	8.00	10.00

KM# 934a CROWN

28.28 g., 0.925 Silver 0.841 oz. ASW, 38.5 mm. **Ruler:** Elizabeth II **Series:** World Cup Rugby 1999 **Obv:** Crowned bust right **Rev:** Rugby scrum

Date	Mintage	VF20	XF40	MS60	MS63	MS65
1999	Est. 10000	PF65 50.00				

KM# 936 CROWN

Copper-Nickel, 38.5 mm. **Ruler:** Elizabeth II **Series:** World Cup Rugby 1999 **Obv:** Crowned bust right **Rev:** Player catching ball **Edge:** Reeded

Date	Mintage	VF20	XF40	MS60	MS63	MS65
1999	—	—	—	—	10.00	12.00

KM# 936a CROWN

28.28 g., 0.925 Silver 0.841 oz. ASW, 38.5 mm. **Ruler:** Elizabeth II **Series:** World Cup Rugby 1999 **Obv:** Crowned bust right **Rev:** Player catching ball

Date	Mintage	VF20	XF40	MS60	MS63	MS65
1999	Est. 10000	PF65 55.00				

KM# 938 CROWN

Copper-Nickel, 38.5 mm. **Ruler:** Elizabeth II **Series:** World Cup Rugby 1999 **Obv:** Crowned bust right **Rev:** Goal kick **Edge:** Reeded

Date	Mintage	VF20	XF40	MS60	MS63	MS65
1999	—	—	—	—	8.00	10.00

KM# 938a CROWN

28.28 g., 0.925 Silver 0.841 oz. ASW, 38.5 mm. **Ruler:** Elizabeth II **Series:** World Cup Rugby 1999 **Obv:** Crowned bust right **Rev:** Goal kick

Date	Mintage	VF20	XF40	MS60	MS63	MS65
1999	Est. 10000	PF65 50.00				

KM# 940 CROWN

Copper-Nickel, 38.5 mm. **Ruler:** Elizabeth II **Series:** World Cup Rugby 1999 **Obv:** Crowned bust right **Rev:** Ball runner being tackled **Edge:** Reeded

Date	Mintage	VF20	XF40	MS60	MS63	MS65
1999	—	—	—	—	8.00	10.00

KM# 940a CROWN

28.28 g., 0.925 Silver 0.841 oz. ASW, 38.5 mm. **Ruler:** Elizabeth II **Series:** World Cup Rugby 1999 **Obv:** Crowned bust right **Rev:** Ball runner being tackled

Date	Mintage	VF20	XF40	MS60	MS63	MS65
1999	Est. 10000	PF65 50.00				

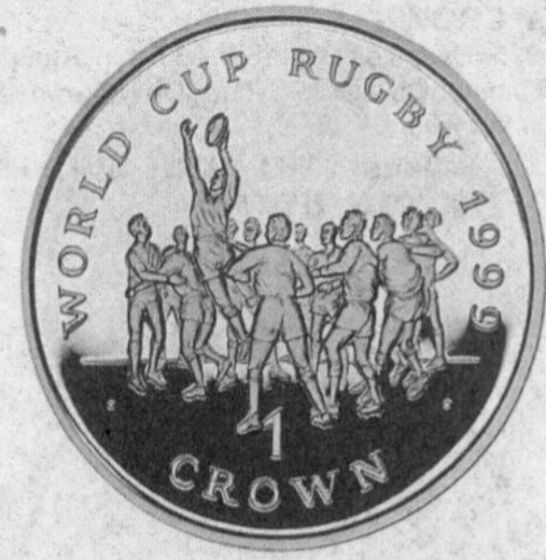

KM# 942 CROWN

Copper-Nickel, 38.5 mm. **Ruler:** Elizabeth II **Series:** World Cup Rugby 1999 **Obv:** Crowned bust right **Rev:** Player jumping for catch **Edge:** Reeded

Date	Mintage	VF20	XF40	MS60	MS63	MS65
1999	—	—	—	—	10.00	12.00

KM# 942a CROWN

28.28 g., 0.925 Silver 0.841 oz. ASW, 38.5 mm. **Ruler:** Elizabeth II **Series:** World Cup Rugby 1999 **Obv:** Crowned bust right **Rev:** Player jumping for catch

Date	Mintage	VF20	XF40	MS60	MS63	MS65
1999	Est. 10000	PF65 55.00				

KM# 952 CROWN

Copper-Nickel, 38.5 mm. **Ruler:** Elizabeth II **Subject:** Year of the Rabbit **Obv:** Crowned bust right **Rev:** Rabbits **Edge:** Reeded

Date	Mintage	VF20	XF40	MS60	MS63	MS65
1999	—	—	—	—	12.00	15.00

KM# 952a CROWN

28.28 g., 0.925 Silver 0.841 oz. ASW, 38.5 mm. **Ruler:** Elizabeth II **Subject:** Year of the Rabbit **Obv:** Crowned bust right **Rev:** Rabbits

Date	Mintage	VF20	XF40	MS60	MS63	MS65
1999	Est. 10000	PF65 47.50				

KM# 952b CROWN

31.10 g., 0.9999 Gold 0.9999 oz. AGW **Ruler:** Elizabeth II **Subject:** Year of the Rabbit **Obv:** Crowned bust right **Rev:** Rabbits

Date	Mintage	VF20	XF40	MS60	MS63	MS65
1999	Est. 2000	PF65 1,700				

KM# 955 CROWN

Copper-Nickel, 38.5 mm. **Ruler:** Elizabeth II **Subject:** Sir Walter Raleigh **Obv:** Crowned bust right **Rev:** Bust with hat, map of America and ship **Edge:** Reeded

Date	Mintage	VF20	XF40	MS60	MS63	MS65
1999	—	—	—	—	8.00	10.00

KM# 955a CROWN

28.28 g., 0.925 Silver 0.841 oz. ASW, 38.5 mm. **Ruler:** Elizabeth II **Subject:** Sir Walter Raleigh **Obv:** Crowned bust right **Rev:** Bust with hat, map of America and ship

Date	Mintage	VF20	XF40	MS60	MS63	MS65
1999	Est. 10000	PF65 50.00				

KM# 957 CROWN

Copper-Nickel, 38.5 mm. **Ruler:** Elizabeth II **Obv:** Crowned bust right **Rev:** Compass, bust of Robert Falcon Scott and men pulling sled **Edge:** Reeded

Date	Mintage	VF20	XF40	MS60	MS63	MS65
1999	—	—	—	—	8.00	10.00

KM# 957a CROWN

28.28 g., 0.925 Silver 0.841 oz. ASW, 38.5 mm. **Ruler:** Elizabeth II **Obv:** Crowned bust right **Rev:** Compass, bust of Robert Falcon Scott and men pulling sled

Date	Mintage	VF20	XF40	MS60	MS63	MS65
1999	Est. 10000	PF65 50.00				

KM# 966 CROWN

Copper-Nickel, 38.5 mm. **Ruler:** Elizabeth II **Obv:** Crowned bust right **Rev:** British Blue cat cleaning its paws **Edge:** Reeded

Date	Mintage	VF20	XF40	MS60	MS63	MS65
1999	—	—	—	—	9.00	15.00

KM# 966a CROWN

31.10 g., 0.999 Silver 0.999 oz. ASW, 38.5 mm. **Ruler:** Elizabeth II **Obv:** Crowned bust right **Rev:** British Blue cat cleaning its paws **Note:** Prev. KM#967.

Date	Mintage	VF20	XF40	MS60	MS63	MS65
1999	—	PF65 42.50				

KM# 966b CROWN

31.10 g., 0.999 Gold 0.999 oz. AGW **Ruler:** Elizabeth II **Obv:** Crowned bust right **Rev:** British Blue cat cleaning its paws **Note:** Prev. KM#968

Date	Mintage	VF20	XF40	MS60	MS63	MS65
1999	—	—	—	—	—	1,700
1999	—	PF65 1,725				

KM# 976 CROWN

Copper-Nickel, 38.5 mm. **Ruler:** Elizabeth II **Series:** The Life and Times of the Queen Mother **Obv:** Crowned bust right **Rev:** Seated child facing **Edge:** Reeded

Date	Mintage	VF20	XF40	MS60	MS63	MS65
1999	—	—	—	—	7.50	9.50

KM# 976a CROWN

28.28 g., 0.925 Silver 0.841 oz. ASW, 38.5 mm. **Ruler:** Elizabeth II **Series:** The Life and Times of the Queen Mother **Obv:** Crowned bust right **Rev:** Seated child facing

Date	Mintage	VF20	XF40	MS60	MS63	MS65
1999	Est. 10000	PF65 50.00				

KM# 978 CROWN

Copper-Nickel, 38.5 mm. **Ruler:** Elizabeth II **Series:** The Life and Times of the Queen Mother **Obv:** Crowned bust right **Rev:** Royal engagement portrait **Edge:** Reeded

Date	Mintage	VF20	XF40	MS60	MS63	MS65
1999	—	—	—	—	7.50	9.50

KM# 978a CROWN

28.28 g., 0.925 Silver 0.841 oz. ASW, 38.5 mm. **Ruler:** Elizabeth II **Series:** The Life and Times of the Queen Mother **Obv:** Crowned bust right **Rev:** Royal engagement portrait

Date	Mintage	VF20	XF40	MS60	MS63	MS65
1999	Est. 10000	PF65 50.00				

KM# 980 CROWN

Copper-Nickel, 38.5 mm. **Ruler:** Elizabeth II **Series:** The Life and Times of the Queen Mother **Obv:** Crowned bust right **Rev:** Wedding portrait **Edge:** Reeded

Date	Mintage	VF20	XF40	MS60	MS63	MS65
1999	—	—	—	—	7.50	9.50

KM# 980a CROWN

28.28 g., 0.925 Silver 0.841 oz. ASW **Ruler:** Elizabeth II **Series:** The Life and Times of the Queen Mother **Obv:** Crowned bust right **Rev:** Wedding portrait

Date	Mintage	VF20	XF40	MS60	MS63	MS65
1999	Est. 10000	PF65 50.00				

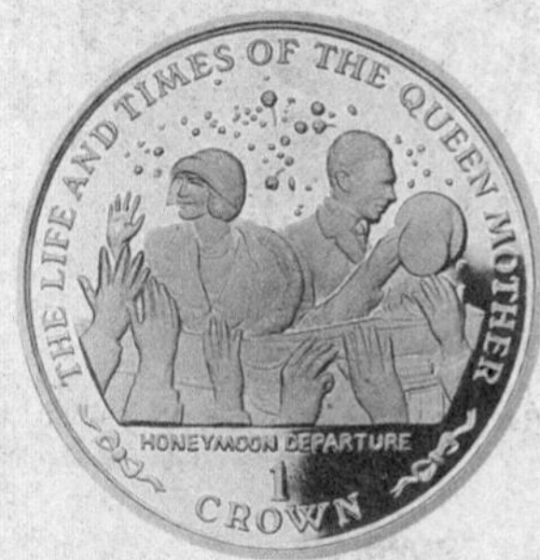

KM# 982 CROWN

Copper-Nickel, 38.5 mm. **Ruler:** Elizabeth II **Subject:** The Life and Times of the Queen Mother **Obv:** Crowned bust right **Rev:** Honeymoon departure **Edge:** Reeded

Date	Mintage	VF20	XF40	MS60	MS63	MS65
1999	—	—	—	—	7.50	9.50

KM# 982a CROWN

28.28 g., 0.925 Silver 0.841 oz. ASW, 38.5 mm. **Ruler:** Elizabeth II **Series:** The Life and Times of the Queen Mother **Obv:** Crowned bust right **Rev:** Honeymoon departure

Date	Mintage	VF20	XF40	MS60	MS63	MS65
1999	Est. 10000	PF65 50.00				

KM# A984 CROWN

Copper-Nickel, 38.5 mm. **Ruler:** Elizabeth II **Subject:** Founding of the UN 1945 **Obv:** Crowned bust right **Rev:** UN Building and logo

Date	Mintage	VF20	XF40	MS60	MS63	MS65
2000	—	—	—	—	8.00	10.00

KM# 988 CROWN

Copper-Nickel, 38.5 mm. **Ruler:** Elizabeth II **Subject:** Fall of Berlin Wall 1989 **Obv:** Crowned bust right **Rev:** Crowds around wall **Edge:** Reeded

Date	Mintage	VF20	XF40	MS60	MS63	MS65
2000	—	—	—	—	7.50	9.50

KM# 988a CROWN

28.28 g., 0.925 Silver 0.841 oz. ASW, 38.5 mm. **Ruler:** Elizabeth II **Subject:** Fall of Berlin Wall 1989 **Obv:** Crowned bust right **Rev:** Crowds around wall

Date	Mintage	VF20	XF40	MS60	MS63	MS65
2000	Est. 10000	PF65 50.00				

KM# 990 CROWN

Copper-Nickel, 38.5 mm. **Ruler:** Elizabeth II **Subject:** Millennium 2000 - The Future **Obv:** Crowned bust right **Rev:** International Space Station **Edge:** Reeded

Date	Mintage	VF20	XF40	MS60	MS63	MS65
2000	—	—	—	—	7.50	9.50

KM# 990a CROWN

28.28 g., 0.925 Silver 0.841 oz. ASW, 38.5 mm. **Ruler:** Elizabeth II **Subject:** Millennium 2000 - The Future **Obv:** Crowned bust right **Rev:** International Space Station

Date	Mintage	VF20	XF40	MS60	MS63	MS65
2000	Est. 10000	PF65 50.00				

KM# 996 CROWN

Copper-Nickel, 38.5 mm. **Ruler:** Elizabeth II **Subject:** The Wedding of HRH Prince Edward and Sophie Rhys-Jones **Obv:** Crowned bust right **Rev:** Head right

Date	Mintage	VF20	XF40	MS60	MS63	MS65
1999	—	—	—	—	7.50	9.50

KM# 996a CROWN

28.28 g., 0.925 Silver 0.841 oz. ASW, 38.5 mm. **Ruler:** Elizabeth II **Subject:** The Wedding of HRH Prince Edward and Sophie Rhys-Jones **Obv:** Crowned bust right **Rev:** Head right

Date	Mintage	VF20	XF40	MS60	MS63	MS65
1999	Est. 10000	PF65 55.00				

KM# 998 CROWN

Copper-Nickel, 38.5 mm. **Ruler:** Elizabeth II **Subject:** The Wedding of HRH Prince Edward and Sophie Rhys-Jones **Obv:** Crowned bust right **Rev:** Head left

Date	Mintage	VF20	XF40	MS60	MS63	MS65
1999	—	—	—	—	7.50	9.50

KM# 998a CROWN

28.28 g., 0.925 Silver 0.841 oz. ASW, 38.5 mm. **Ruler:** Elizabeth II **Subject:** The Wedding of HRH Prince Edward and Sophie Rhys-Jones **Obv:** Crowned bust right **Rev:** Head left

Date	Mintage	VF20	XF40	MS60	MS63	MS65
1999	Est. 10000	PF65 55.00				

KM# 1000 CROWN

Copper-Nickel, 38.5 mm. **Ruler:** Elizabeth II **Subject:** 30th Anniversary of First Man on the Moon **Obv:** Crowned bust right **Rev:** Apollo XI and moon walkers

Date	Mintage	VF20	XF40	MS60	MS63	MS65
1999	—	—	—	—	7.50	9.50

KM# 1000a CROWN

28.28 g., 0.925 Silver 0.841 oz. ASW, 38.5 mm. **Ruler:** Elizabeth II **Subject:** 30th Anniversary of First Man on the Moon **Obv:** Crowned bust right **Rev:** Apollo XI and two moon walkers

Date	Mintage	VF20	XF40	MS60	MS63	MS65
1999	Est. 10000	PF65 50.00				

KM# 1002 CROWN

Copper-Nickel, 38.5 mm. **Ruler:** Elizabeth II **Subject:** 30th Anniversary of First Man on the Moon **Obv:** Crowned bust right **Rev:** Mariner IX, 1971 and orbiting Mars

Date	Mintage	VF20	XF40	MS60	MS63	MS65
1999	—	—	—	—	7.50	9.50

KM# 1002a CROWN
28.28 g., 0.925 Silver 0.841 oz. ASW, 38.5 mm. **Ruler:** Elizabeth II **Subject:** 30th Anniversary of First Man on the Moon **Obv:** Crowned bust right **Rev:** Mariner IX orbiting Mars

Date	Mintage	VF20	XF40	MS60	MS63	MS65
1999	Est. 10000	PF65 50.00				

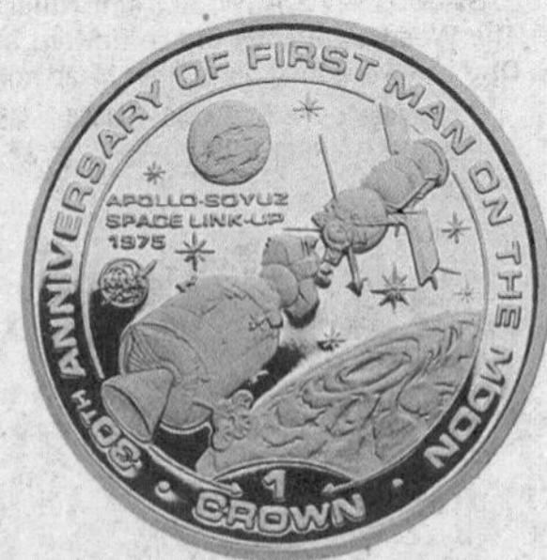

KM# 1004 CROWN
Copper-Nickel, 38.5 mm. **Ruler:** Elizabeth II **Subject:** 30th Anniversary of First Man on the Moon **Obv:** Crowned bust right **Rev:** Apollo-Soyuz link-up, 1975

Date	Mintage	VF20	XF40	MS60	MS63	MS65
1999	—	—	—	—	7.50	9.50

KM# 1004a CROWN
28.28 g., 0.925 Silver 0.841 oz. ASW, 38.5 mm. **Ruler:** Elizabeth II **Subject:** 30th Anniversary of First Man on the Moon **Obv:** Crowned bust right **Rev:** Apollo-Soyuz link-up, 1975

Date	Mintage	VF20	XF40	MS60	MS63	MS65
1999	Est. 10000	PF65 50.00				

KM# 1006 CROWN
Copper-Nickel, 38.5 mm. **Ruler:** Elizabeth II **Subject:** 30th Anniversary of First Man on the Moon **Obv:** Crowned bust right **Rev:** Viking Mars Lander, 1978

Date	Mintage	VF20	XF40	MS60	MS63	MS65
1999	—	—	—	—	7.50	9.50

KM# 1006a CROWN
28.28 g., 0.925 Silver 0.841 oz. ASW, 38.5 mm. **Ruler:** Elizabeth II **Subject:** 30th Anniversary of First Man on the Moon **Obv:** Crowned bust right **Rev:** Viking Mars lander, 1978

Date	Mintage	VF20	XF40	MS60	MS63	MS65
1999	Est. 10000	PF65 50.00				

KM# 1008 CROWN
Copper-Nickel, 38.5 mm. **Ruler:** Elizabeth II **Subject:** 30th Anniversary of First Man on the Moon **Obv:** Crowned bust right **Rev:** Shuttle orbiter Columbia, 1981

Date	Mintage	VF20	XF40	MS60	MS63	MS65
1999	—	—	—	—	8.00	10.00

KM# 1008a CROWN
28.28 g., 0.925 Silver 0.841 oz. ASW, 38.5 mm. **Ruler:** Elizabeth II **Subject:** 30th Anniversary of First Man on the Moon **Obv:** Crowned bust right **Rev:** Shuttle orbiter Columbia, 1981

Date	Mintage	VF20	XF40	MS60	MS63	MS65
1999	Est. 10000	PF65 50.00				

KM# 1010 CROWN
Copper-Nickel, 38.5 mm. **Ruler:** Elizabeth II **Subject:** 30th Anniversary of First Man on the Moon **Obv:** Crowned bust right **Rev:** Mars Pathfinder, 1997

Date	Mintage	VF20	XF40	MS60	MS63	MS65
1999	—	—	—	—	12.00	14.00

KM# 1010a CROWN
28.28 g., 0.925 Silver 0.841 oz. ASW, 38.5 mm. **Ruler:** Elizabeth II **Subject:** 30th Anniversary of First Man on the Moon **Obv:** Crowned bust right **Rev:** Mars Pathfinder, 1997

Date	Mintage	VF20	XF40	MS60	MS63	MS65
1999	Est. 10000	PF65 50.00				

KM# 986 CROWN
Copper-Nickel, 38.5 mm. **Ruler:** Elizabeth II **Subject:** First Man on the Moon **Obv:** Crowned bust right **Rev:** Astronauts on moon and flag

Date	Mintage	VF20	XF40	MS60	MS63	MS65
2000	—	—	—	—	7.50	9.50

KM# 986a CROWN
28.28 g., 0.925 Silver 0.841 oz. ASW, 38.5 mm. **Ruler:** Elizabeth II **Subject:** First Man on the Moon **Obv:** Crowned bust right **Rev:** Astronauts on moon and flag

Date	Mintage	VF20	XF40	MS60	MS63	MS65
2000	Est. 10000	PF65 50.00				

KM# 1016 CROWN
Copper-Nickel, 38.5 mm. **Ruler:** Elizabeth II **Subject:** Year of the Dragon **Obv:** Crowned bust right **Rev:** Dragon

Date	Mintage	VF20	XF40	MS60	MS63	MS65
2000	—	—	—	—	12.00	15.00

KM# 1016a CROWN
28.28 g., 0.925 Silver 0.841 oz. ASW, 38.5 mm. **Ruler:** Elizabeth II **Subject:** Year of the Dragon **Obv:** Crowned bust right **Rev:** Dragon

Date	Mintage	VF20	XF40	MS60	MS63	MS65
2000	Est. 30000	PF65 47.50				

KM# 1016b CROWN
31.10 g., 0.9999 Gold 0.9999 oz. AGW, 32.7 mm. **Ruler:** Elizabeth II **Subject:** Year of the Dragon **Obv:** Crowned bust right **Rev:** Dragon **Note:** Prev. KM#1017.

Date	Mintage	VF20	XF40	MS60	MS63	MS65
2000	Est. 2000	PF65 1,725				

KM# 1019 CROWN
28.28 g., Copper-Nickel, 38.6 mm. **Ruler:** Elizabeth II **Subject:** Millennium **Obv:** Crowned bust right **Rev:** Stylized monogram **Edge:** Reeded

Date	Mintage	VF20	XF40	MS60	MS63	MS65
2000	—	—	—	—	8.00	10.00

KM# 1019a CROWN
28.28 g., 0.925 Silver 0.841 oz. ASW, 38.6 mm. **Ruler:** Elizabeth II **Subject:** Millennium **Obv:** Crowned bust right **Rev:** Stylized monogram **Edge:** Reeded

Date	Mintage	VF20	XF40	MS60	MS63	MS65
2000	10,000	PF65 47.50				

KM# 1021 CROWN
28.28 g., Copper-Nickel, 38.6 mm. **Ruler:** Elizabeth II **Obv:** Crowned bust right **Rev:** Armored 1/2 bust, map and ship

Date	Mintage	VF20	XF40	MS60	MS63	MS65
2000	—	—	—	—	8.00	10.00

KM# 1021a CROWN
28.28 g., 0.925 Silver 0.841 oz. ASW, 38.6 mm. **Ruler:** Elizabeth II **Obv:** Crowned bust right **Rev:** Armored 1/2 bust, map and ship

Date	Mintage	VF20	XF40	MS60	MS63	MS65
2000	10,000	PF65 47.50				

KM# 1023 CROWN
Copper-Nickel, 38.5 mm. **Ruler:** Elizabeth II **Obv:** Crowned bust right **Rev:** Portrait of Willem Barents, ship on ice, map

Date	Mintage	VF20	XF40	MS60	MS63	MS65
2000	—	—	—	—	8.00	10.00

KM# 1023a CROWN
28.28 g., 0.925 Silver 0.841 oz. ASW, 38.5 mm. **Ruler:** Elizabeth II **Obv:** Crowned bust right **Rev:** Portrait of Willem Barents, ship on ice, map

Date	Mintage	VF20	XF40	MS60	MS63	MS65
2000	10,000	PF65 47.50				

KM# 1025 CROWN
28.28 g., Copper-Nickel, 38.5 mm. **Ruler:** Elizabeth II **Series:** Queen Mother **Obv:** Crowned bust right **Rev:** 1931 family scene **Edge:** Reeded

Date	Mintage	VF20	XF40	MS60	MS63	MS65
2000	—	—	—	—	10.00	12.00

KM# 1025a CROWN
28.28 g., 0.925 Silver 0.841 oz. ASW, 38.5 mm. **Ruler:** Elizabeth II **Series:** Queen Mother **Obv:** Crowned bust right **Rev:** 1931 family scene **Edge:** Reeded

Date	Mintage	VF20	XF40	MS60	MS63	MS65
2000	—	PF65 47.50				

KM# 1027 CROWN
Copper-Nickel, 38.5 mm. **Ruler:** Elizabeth II **Obv:** Crowned bust right **Rev:** 1937 Coronation scene

Date	Mintage	VF20	XF40	MS60	MS63	MS65
2000	—	—	—	—	10.00	12.00

KM# 1027a CROWN
28.28 g., 0.925 Silver 0.841 oz. ASW, 38.5 mm. **Ruler:** Elizabeth II **Obv:** Crowned bust right **Rev:** Coronation scene

Date	Mintage	VF20	XF40	MS60	MS63	MS65
2000	10,000	PF65 47.50				

KM# 1029 CROWN
Copper-Nickel, 38.5 mm. **Ruler:** Elizabeth II **Obv:** Crowned bust right **Rev:** 1945 Victory Visit

Date	Mintage	VF20	XF40	MS60	MS63	MS65
2000	—	—	—	—	10.00	12.00

KM# 1029a CROWN
28.28 g., 0.925 Silver 0.841 oz. ASW, 38.5 mm. **Ruler:** Elizabeth II **Obv:** Crowned bust right **Rev:** 1945 Victory Visit

Date	Mintage	VF20	XF40	MS60	MS63	MS65
2000	10,000	PF65 47.50				

KM# 1029b CROWN
28.65 g., 0.925 Silver Gilt 0.852 oz., 38.5 mm. **Ruler:** Elizabeth II **Subject:** Queen Mother **Obv:** Crowned bust right **Rev:** 1945 Royal visit to Isle of Man **Edge:** Reeded

Date	Mintage	VF20	XF40	MS60	MS63	MS65
2000 PM	—	PF65 50.00				

KM# 1031 CROWN
Copper-Nickel, 38.5 mm. **Ruler:** Elizabeth II **Obv:** Crowned bust right **Rev:** Queen Mother, coach, and man

Date	Mintage	VF20	XF40	MS60	MS63	MS65
2000	—	—	—	—	10.00	12.00

KM# 1031a CROWN
28.28 g., 0.925 Silver 0.841 oz. ASW, 38.5 mm. **Ruler:** Elizabeth II **Obv:** Crowned bust right **Rev:** Queen Mother, coach, and man

Date	Mintage	VF20	XF40	MS60	MS63	MS65
2000	10,000	PF65 47.50				

KM# 1031b CROWN
28.65 g., 0.925 Silver Gilt 0.852 oz., 38.6 mm. **Ruler:** Elizabeth II **Subject:** Queen Mother **Obv:** Crowned bust right **Rev:** 1963 Visit to Isle of Man **Edge:** Reeded

Date	Mintage	VF20	XF40	MS60	MS63	MS65
2000 PM	—	PF65 50.00				

KM# 1033 CROWN
28.28 g., Copper-Nickel, 38.5 mm. **Ruler:** Elizabeth II **Subject:** Battle of Britain **Obv:** Crowned bust right **Rev:** Aerial battle scene

Date	Mintage	VF20	XF40	MS60	MS63	MS65
2000	—	—	—	—	10.00	12.00

KM# 1033a CROWN
28.28 g., 0.925 Silver 0.841 oz. ASW, 38.5 mm. **Ruler:** Elizabeth II **Subject:** Battle of Britain **Obv:** Crowned bust right **Rev:** Aerial battle scene

Date	Mintage	VF20	XF40	MS60	MS63	MS65
2000	10,000	PF65 47.50				

KM# 1035 CROWN
Copper-Nickel, 38.5 mm. **Ruler:** Elizabeth II **Subject:** Global Challenge Yacht Race **Obv:** Crowned bust right **Rev:** Partial ship and map

Date	Mintage	VF20	XF40	MS60	MS63	MS65
2000	—	—	—	—	10.00	12.00

KM# 1035a CROWN
28.28 g., 0.925 Silver 0.841 oz. ASW, 38.5 mm. **Ruler:** Elizabeth II **Subject:** Global Challenge Yacht Race **Obv:** Crowned bust right **Rev:** Partial ship and map

Date	Mintage	VF20	XF40	MS60	MS63	MS65
2000	10,000	PF65 47.50				

KM# 1047 CROWN
28.28 g., Copper-Nickel, 38.5 mm. **Ruler:** Elizabeth II **Obv:** Crowned bust right **Rev:** Head 3/4 right **Edge:** Reeded

Date	Mintage	VF20	XF40	MS60	MS63	MS65
2000	—	—	—	—	7.50	9.50

KM# 1047a CROWN
28.28 g., 0.925 Silver 0.841 oz. ASW, 38.5 mm. **Ruler:** Elizabeth II **Obv:** Crowned bust right **Rev:** Head 3/4 right **Edge:** Reeded

Date	Mintage	VF20	XF40	MS60	MS63	MS65
2000	10,000	PF65 50.00				

KM# 1049 CROWN
Copper-Nickel, 38.5 mm. **Ruler:** Elizabeth II **Obv:** Crowned bust right **Rev:** Queen Mother's portrait

Date	Mintage	VF20	XF40	MS60	MS63	MS65
2000	—	—	—	—	10.00	12.00

KM# 1049a CROWN
28.28 g., 0.925 Silver 0.841 oz. ASW, 38.5 mm. **Ruler:** Elizabeth II **Obv:** Crowned bust right **Rev:** Queen Mother's portrait

Date	Mintage	VF20	XF40	MS60	MS63	MS65
2000	10,000	PF65 47.50				

KM# 1051 CROWN
28.28 g., 0.925 Silver 0.841 oz. ASW, 38.6 mm. **Ruler:** Elizabeth II **Subject:** Millennium-Meridian **Obv:** Crowned bust right **Rev:** Observatory clock face with an embedded brass strip **Edge:** Reeded

Date	Mintage	VF20	XF40	MS60	MS63	MS65
2000	10,000	PF65 47.50				

KM# 1056 CROWN
Copper-Nickel, 38.6 mm. **Ruler:** Elizabeth II **Subject:** Scottish Fold Kitten **Obv:** Crowned bust right **Rev:** Kitten playing with world **Edge:** Reeded

Date	Mintage	VF20	XF40	MS60	MS63	MS65
2000	—	—	—	—	11.00	14.00

KM# 1056a CROWN
31.10 g., 0.9999 Silver 0.9999 oz. ASW, 38.6 mm. **Ruler:** Elizabeth II **Subject:** Scottish Fold Kitten **Obv:** Crowned bust right **Rev:** Kitten playing with world **Edge:** Reeded

Date	Mintage	VF20	XF40	MS60	MS63	MS65
2000	50,000	PF65 70.00				

KM# 1056b CROWN
31.10 g., 0.9999 Gold 0.9999 oz. AGW, 32.7 mm. **Ruler:** Elizabeth II **Subject:** Scottish Fold Kitten **Obv:** Crowned bust right **Rev:** Kitten playing with world **Edge:** Reeded **Note:** Prev. KM#1057

Date	Mintage	VF20	XF40	MS60	MS63	MS65
2000	—	—	—	—	—	1,700
2000	—	PF63 1,725	PF65 1,750			

KM# 1264 CROWN
28.28 g., Copper-Nickel, 38.5 mm. **Ruler:** Elizabeth II **Obv:** Crowned bust right **Rev:** Space station and shuttle **Edge:** Reeded

Date	Mintage	VF20	XF40	MS60	MS63	MS65
2000 PM	—	—	—	—	15.00	17.00

KM# 1264a CROWN
28.28 g., 0.925 Silver 0.841 oz. ASW, 38.5 mm. **Ruler:** Elizabeth II **Obv:** Crowned bust right **Rev:** Space station and shuttle **Edge:** Reeded

Date	Mintage	VF20	XF40	MS60	MS63	MS65
2000 PM	—	PF65 50.00				

KM# 1267 CROWN
28.28 g., 0.925 Silver 0.841 oz. ASW, 38.7 mm. **Ruler:** Elizabeth II **Subject:** Fall of the Berlin Wall - 1989 **Obv:** Crowned bust right **Rev:** Brandenburg Gate behind crowd holding pennant with slogan, Love and Peace in West & East **Edge:** Reeded

Date	Mintage	VF20	XF40	MS60	MS63	MS65
2000	—	—	—	—	30.00	32.50

KM# 1500 2 CROWNS
62.20 g., 0.999 Gold 1.9978 oz. AGW, 40 mm. **Ruler:** Elizabeth II **Obv:** Crowned bust right **Rev:** Penny black stamp, pearl black patina

Date	Mintage	F12	VF20	XF40	MS60	MS63
1990	Est. 200	PF65 4,000				

KM# 177 5 CROWN

155.55 g., 0.999 Silver 4.996 oz. ASW, 65 mm. **Ruler:** Elizabeth II **Subject:** Bicentennial of U.S. Constitution **Obv:** Crowned bust right **Rev:** Statue of Liberty divides dates within circle of assorted Presidential busts **Note:** Illustration reduced.

Date	Mintage	VF20	XF40	MS60	MS63	MS65
1987	9,000	PF63 150	PF65 175			

KM# 180 5 CROWN

155.55 g., 0.999 Silver 4.996 oz. ASW, 65 mm. **Ruler:** Elizabeth II **Series:** America's Cup **Obv:** Crowned bust right **Rev:** Sailboats and trophy **Note:** Illustration reduced.

Date	Mintage	VF20	XF40	MS60	MS63	MS65
1987	6,000	PF63 150	PF65 175			

KM# 299 5 CROWN

155.55 g., 0.999 Silver 4.996 oz. ASW, 65 mm. **Ruler:** Elizabeth II **Series:** America's Cup **Obv:** Crowned bust right **Rev:** Sailboats and Statue of Liberty **Note:** Illustration reduced.

Date	Mintage	VF20	XF40	MS60	MS63	MS65
1987	200	PF63 150	PF65 175			

KM# 308 5 CROWN

155.55 g., 0.999 Silver 4.996 oz. ASW, 65 mm. **Ruler:** Elizabeth II **Series:** America's Cup **Obv:** Crowned bust right **Rev:** Sailboats and map **Note:** Illustration reduced.

Date	Mintage	VF20	XF40	MS60	MS63	MS65
1987	—	PF63 150	PF65 175			

KM# 206 5 CROWN

155.55 g., 0.999 Silver 4.996 oz. ASW, 65 mm. **Ruler:** Elizabeth II **Subject:** Steam Navigation **Obv:** Crowned bust right **Rev:** Ship **Note:** Illustration reduced.

Date	Mintage	VF20	XF40	MS60	MS63	MS65
1988	—	—	—	125	150	175

KM# 285 5 CROWN

155.55 g., 0.999 Silver 4.996 oz. ASW, 65 mm. **Ruler:** Elizabeth II **Subject:** Australian Bicentennial **Obv:** Crowned bust right **Rev:** Kangaroo **Note:** Illustration reduced.

Date	Mintage	VF20	XF40	MS60	MS63	MS65
1988	—	PF63 150	PF65 175			

KM# 1501 5 CROWN

155.50 g., 0.999 Gold 4.9944 oz. AGW, 50 mm. **Ruler:** Elizabeth II **Obv:** Crowned bust right **Rev:** Penny Black stamp with pearl black patina

Date	Mintage	VF20	XF40	MS60	MS63	MS65
1990	Est. 99	PF65 8,500				

KM# 321 5 CROWN

155.55 g., 0.999 Silver 4.996 oz. ASW, 65 mm. **Ruler:** Elizabeth II **Series:** America's Cup **Obv:** Crowned bust right **Rev:** Cameo above two modern sailboats **Note:** Officially a "sales sample" about 10 pieces were sold or presented to distributors

Date	Mintage	VF20	XF40	MS60	MS63	MS65
1991 Proof	Est. 15	—	—	—	—	—

KM# 327 5 CROWN

155.55 g., 0.999 Silver 4.996 oz. ASW, 65 mm. **Ruler:** Elizabeth II **Series:** America's Cup **Obv:** Crowned bust right **Rev:** Cameo above two modern sailboats

Date	Mintage	VF20	XF40	MS60	MS63	MS65
1992	—	—	—	125	150	175

KM# 348 5 CROWN

155.55 g., 0.999 Silver 4.996 oz. ASW, 65 mm. **Ruler:** Elizabeth II **Obv:** Crowned bust right **Rev:** Siamese cat

Date	Mintage	VF20	XF40	MS60	MS63	MS65
1992	—	PF63 200	PF65 225			

KM# 689 5 CROWN

155.52 g., 0.999 Silver 4.995 oz. ASW, 65 mm. **Ruler:** Elizabeth II **Series:** Legend of King Arthur **Obv:** Crowned bust right **Rev:** King Arthur with sword and orb **Note:** Illustration reduced.

Date	Mintage	VF20	XF40	MS60	MS63	MS65
1996	—	PF63 150	PF65 175			

KM# 690 5 CROWN
155.52 g., 0.999 Silver 4.995 oz. ASW, 65 mm. **Ruler:** Elizabeth II **Series:** Legend of King Arthur **Obv:** Crowned bust right **Rev:** Queen Guinevere **Note:** Illustration reduced.

Date	Mintage	VF20	XF40	MS60	MS63	MS65
1996	Est. 999	PF63 150	PF65 175			

KM# 691 5 CROWN
155.52 g., 0.999 Silver 4.995 oz. ASW, 65 mm. **Ruler:** Elizabeth II **Series:** Legend of King Arthur **Obv:** Crowned bust right **Rev:** Sir Lancelot **Note:** Illustration reduced.

Date	Mintage	VF20	XF40	MS60	MS63	MS65
1996	Est. 999	PF63 150	PF65 175			

KM# 692 5 CROWN
155.52 g., 0.999 Silver 4.995 oz. ASW, 65 mm. **Ruler:** Elizabeth II **Series:** Legend of King Arthur **Obv:** Crowned bust right **Rev:** Merlin **Note:** Illustration reduced.

Date	Mintage	VF20	XF40	MS60	MS63	MS65
1996	Est. 999	PF63 150	PF65 170			

KM# 693 5 CROWN
155.52 g., 0.999 Silver 4.995 oz. ASW, 65 mm. **Ruler:** Elizabeth II **Series:** Legend of King Arthur **Obv:** Crowned bust right **Rev:** Camelot Castle

Date	Mintage	VF20	XF40	MS60	MS63	MS65
1996	Est. 999	PF63 150	PF65 175			

KM# 734 5 CROWN
155.52 g., 0.9999 Gold 4.9995 oz. AGW **Ruler:** Elizabeth II **Subject:** Year of the Rat **Obv:** Crowned bust right **Rev:** Rat

Date	Mintage	VF20	XF40	MS60	MS63	MS65
1996 Proof	—	—	—	—	—	—

Note: Entire series purchased by one buyer. Mintage, disposition, and market value unknown

KM# 727 5 CROWN
155.52 g., 0.9999 Gold 4.9995 oz. AGW **Ruler:** Elizabeth II **Subject:** Year of the Ox **Obv:** Crowned bust right **Rev:** Ox laying down

Date	Mintage	VF20	XF40	MS60	MS63	MS65
1997	Est. 250	PF63 8,000	PF65 9,000			

KM# 818 5 CROWN
155.52 g., 0.9999 Gold 4.9995 oz. AGW **Ruler:** Elizabeth II **Subject:** Year of the Tiger **Obv:** Crowned bust right **Rev:** Tiger

Date	Mintage	VF20	XF40	MS60	MS63	MS65
1998	Est. 250	PF63 8,000	PF65 9,000			

KM# 953 5 CROWN
155.52 g., 0.9999 Gold 4.9995 oz. AGW **Ruler:** Elizabeth II **Subject:** Year of the Rabbit **Obv:** Crowned bust right **Rev:** Two rabbits

Date	Mintage	VF20	XF40	MS60	MS63	MS65
1999	Est. 250	PF63 8,000	PF65 9,000			

KM# 1018 5 CROWN
155.52 g., 0.9999 Gold 4.9995 oz. AGW **Ruler:** Elizabeth II **Subject:** Year of the Dragon **Obv:** Crowned bust right **Rev:** Dragon

Date	Mintage	VF20	XF40	MS60	MS63	MS65
2000	Est. 250	PF63 8,000	PF65 9,000			

KM# 181 10 CROWN
311.04 g., 0.999 Silver 9.990 oz. ASW, 75 mm. **Ruler:** Elizabeth II **Series:** America's Cup **Obv:** Crowned bust right **Rev:** Sailboats and Statue of Liberty **Note:** Similar to 5 Crown, KM#299.

Date	Mintage	VF20	XF40	MS60	MS63	MS65
1987	2,000	PF63 300	PF65 350			

KM# 188 10 CROWN
311.04 g., 0.999 Silver 9.990 oz. ASW, 75 mm. **Ruler:** Elizabeth II **Subject:** Bicentenary of America's Constitution **Obv:** Crowned bust right **Rev:** Statue of Liberty within circle of assorted Presidential busts **Note:** Similar to 5 Crowns, KM#177.

Date	Mintage	VF20	XF40	MS60	MS63	MS65
1987	6,000	PF63 275	PF65 325			

KM# 300 10 CROWN
311.04 g., 0.999 Silver 9.990 oz. ASW, 75 mm. **Ruler:** Elizabeth II **Series:** America's Cup **Obv:** Crowned bust right **Rev:** Sailboats and trophy **Note:** Similar to 5 Crowns, KM#180.

Date	Mintage	VF20	XF40	MS60	MS63	MS65
1987	69	PF63 325	PF65 375			

KM# 309 10 CROWN
311.04 g., 0.999 Silver 9.990 oz. ASW, 75 mm. **Ruler:** Elizabeth II **Series:** America's Cup **Obv:** Crowned bust right **Rev:** Sailboats and map **Note:** Similar to 5 Crowns, KM#308.

Date	Mintage	VF20	XF40	MS60	MS63	MS65
1987	—	PF63 300	PF65 350			

KM# 258 10 CROWN
311.04 g., 0.999 Silver 9.990 oz. ASW, 75 mm. **Ruler:** Elizabeth II **Subject:** Australian Bicentennial **Obv:** Crowned bust right **Rev:** Koala **Note:** Illustration reduced.

Date	Mintage	VF20	XF40	MS60	MS63	MS65
1988	Est. 13000	PF63 275	PF65 325			

KM# 992 10 CROWN
311.04 g., 0.999 Silver 9.990 oz. ASW, 75 mm. **Ruler:** Elizabeth II **Obv:** Crowned bust right **Rev:** Siamese cat **Note:** Similar to 5 Crowns, KM#348.

Date	Mintage	VF20	XF40	MS60	MS63	MS65
1992	—	PF63 325	PF65 375			

KM# 775 10 CROWN
311.03 g., 0.925 Silver 9.2499 oz. ASW, 75 mm. **Ruler:** Elizabeth II **Subject:** 10th Anniversary of the Manx Cat **Obv:** Crowned bust right **Rev:** Cat in center of assorted cat coins **Note:** Illustration reduced.

Date	Mintage	VF20	XF40	MS60	MS63	MS65
1997	Est. 1997	PF63 350	PF65 425			

SILVER BULLION COINAGE

Angel Series

KM# 522 ANGEL
31.10 g., 0.9999 Silver 0.9999 oz. ASW, 38.5 mm. **Ruler:** Elizabeth II **Obv:** Crowned bust right **Rev:** Archangel Michael slaying dragon right

Date	Mintage	VF20	XF40	MS60	MS63	MS65
1995	—	PF65 40.00				

KM# 1326 5 ANGEL
155.52 g., 0.9999 Silver 4.9994 oz. ASW **Ruler:** Elizabeth II **Obv:** Crowned bust right **Rev:** Archangel Michael slaying dragon

Date	Mintage	VF20	XF40	MS60	MS63	MS65
1995 PM	—	PF63 160	PF65 180			

SILVER BULLION COINAGE

Nobel Series

KM# 1518 NOBLE
31.11 g., 0.999 Silver 0.999 oz. ASW **Ruler:** Elizabeth II **Obv:** Crowned bust right **Rev:** Viking ship

Date	Mintage	VF20	XF40	MS60	MS63	MS65
1994	—	PF65 60.00				

GOLD BULLION COINAGE

Angel Issues

KM# 166 1/20 ANGEL
1.70 g., 0.917 Gold 0.050 oz. AGW **Ruler:** Elizabeth II **Obv:** Crowned bust right **Rev:** Archangel Michael slaying dragon

Date	Mintage	VF20	XF40	MS60	MS63	MS65
1986 (pi)	5,000	PF65 90.00				
1986	—	—	—	—	—	85.00
1987	—	—	—	—	—	85.00
1987	—	PF65 90.00				

KM# 193 1/20 ANGEL
1.70 g., 0.917 Gold 0.050 oz. AGW **Ruler:** Elizabeth II **Obv:** Crowned bust right **Rev:** Archangel Michael slaying dragon

Date	Mintage	VF20	XF40	MS60	MS63	MS65
1988	—	—	—	—	—	85.00
1988 (pi)	—	PF65 90.00				
1989 (h)	Est. 5000	PF65 90.00				
1989 (mt)	3,000	PF65 90.00				
1990 (sg)	Est. 3000	PF65 90.00				
1991 (cc)	1,000	PF65 90.00				
1992 (cb)	1,000	PF65 90.00				
1993	Est. 1000	PF65 90.00				

KM# 393 1/20 ANGEL
1.56 g., 0.9999 Gold 0.050 oz. AGW, 18 mm. **Ruler:** Elizabeth II **Obv:** Crowned bust right **Rev:** Archangel Michael slaying dragon right

Date	Mintage	VF20	XF40	MS60	MS63	MS65
1994	—	—	—	—	—	85.00
1994	—	PF65 90.00				
1994 (ns)	Est. 1000	PF65 95.00				
1995	—	—	—	—	—	85.00
1995	—	PF65 90.00				
1995 (sc) Proof	Est. 1000	—	—	—	—	—
Note: Privy mark: Santa						
1996	—	—	—	—	—	85.00
1996	—	PF65 90.00				
1996 (bs)	Est. 1000	PF65 95.00				
Note: Privy mark: Teddy bear						
1997	—	—	—	—	—	85.00
1997	—	PF65 90.00				
1997 (at)	Est. 1000	PF65 95.00				
Note: Privy mark: Angel						
1998	—	—	—	—	—	85.00
1998	—	PF65 90.00				
1998 (x)	Est. 1000	PF65 95.00				
Note: Privy mark: Snowman						
1999	—	—	—	—	—	85.00
1999	—	PF65 90.00				
1999 (fw)	Est. 1000	PF65 95.00				
Note: Privy mark: Fairy						
2000	—	—	—	—	—	85.00
2000	—	PF65 90.00				
2000 (ch)	Est. 1000	PF65 95.00				
Note: Privy mark: Candle						

KM# 138 1/10 ANGEL
3.39 g., 0.917 Gold 0.0999 oz. AGW **Ruler:** Elizabeth II **Obv:** Crowned bust right **Rev:** Archangel Michael slaying dragon

Date	Mintage	VF20	XF40	MS60	MS63	MS65
1984	5,000	PF65 175				

KM# 140 1/10 ANGEL
3.39 g., 0.917 Gold 0.0999 oz. AGW **Ruler:** Elizabeth II **Obv:** Crowned bust right **Rev:** Archangel Michael slaying dragon left

Date	Mintage	VF20	XF40	MS60	MS63	MS65
1985	8,000	—	—	—	—	165
1985	3,000	PF65 175				
1986	—	PF65 175				
1986	—	—	—	—	—	165
1987	—	—	—	—	—	165
1987	—	PF65 175				

KM# 159 1/10 ANGEL
3.39 g., 0.917 Gold 0.0999 oz. AGW **Ruler:** Elizabeth II **Obv:** Crowned bust right **Rev:** Archangel Michael slaying dragon left

Date	Mintage	VF20	XF40	MS60	MS63	MS65
1985 A	1,000	—	—	—	—	165
1985 L	1,000	—	—	—	—	165
1985 C	1,000	—	—	—	—	165
1985 H	1,000	—	—	—	—	165
1985	5,000	—	—	—	—	165
1986 A	1,000	—	—	—	—	165
1986 X	1,000	—	—	—	—	165
1986 T	1,000	—	—	—	—	165
1987 A	1,000	—	—	—	—	165
1987 L	1,000	—	—	—	—	165
1987 F	1,000	PF65 175				
1987 (mt)	3,000	PF65 175				
1988 A	1,000	PF65 175				

KM# 194 1/10 ANGEL
3.39 g., 0.917 Gold 0.0999 oz. AGW **Ruler:** Elizabeth II **Obv:** Crowned bust right **Rev:** Archangel Michael slaying dragon

Date	Mintage	VF20	XF40	MS60	MS63	MS65
1988	—	—	—	—	—	165
1989 A	250	PF65 175				
1990 A	1,000	PF65 175				
1991 A	400	PF65 175				
Note: 299 pieces have been melted						
1992 A	100	—	—	—	—	165

KM# 394 1/10 ANGEL
3.11 g., 0.9999 Gold 0.100 oz. AGW, 23 mm. **Ruler:** Elizabeth II **Obv:** Crowned bust right **Rev:** Archangel Michael

Date	Mintage	VF20	XF40	MS60	MS63	MS65
1994	—	PF65 175				
1995	—	—	—	—	—	165
1995	—	PF65 175				
1996	—	—	—	—	—	165
1996	—	PF65 175				
1997	—	—	—	—	—	165
1997	—	PF65 175				
1998	—	PF65 175				
1998	—	—	—	—	—	165
1999	—	PF65 175				
1999	—	—	—	—	—	165
2000	—	PF65 175				
2000	—	—	—	—	—	165

KM# 152.1 1/4 ANGEL
8.48 g., 0.917 Gold 0.2501 oz. AGW **Ruler:** Elizabeth II **Obv:** Crowned bust right **Rev:** Archangel Michael slaying dragon left

Date	Mintage	VF20	XF40	MS60	MS63	MS65
1985	2,117	—	—	—	—	400
1985	51	PF65 440				
1986 L	1,000	—	—	—	—	400
1986	—	PF65 440				

KM# 152.2 1/4 ANGEL
8.48 g., 0.917 Gold 0.2501 oz. AGW **Ruler:** Elizabeth II **Obv:** Crowned bust right **Rev:** Archangel Michael slaying dragon

Date	Mintage	VF20	XF40	MS60	MS63	MS65
1987	—	—	—	—	—	400
1987 (s)	1,000	PF65 440				
1987 (bb)	1,000	PF65 440				
1987 (SL)	568	PF65 440				
1987	—	PF65 440				

KM# 195 1/4 ANGEL
8.48 g., 0.917 Gold 0.2501 oz. AGW **Ruler:** Elizabeth II **Obv:** Crowned bust right **Rev:** Archangel Michael slaying dragon left

Date	Mintage	VF20	XF40	MS60	MS63	MS65
1988 (p)	1,000	PF65 440				
1988 (f)	1,000	PF65 440				
1988	—	—	—	—	—	400
1988 (ss)	1,000	PF65 440				
1989 (hk)	1,000	PF65 440				
1989 (y)	—	—	—	—	—	400
1989 (p)	500	PF65 440				
1989 C (d)	1,000	PF65 440				
1990 (ba)	1,000	PF65 440				
Note: 513 pieces melted						
1990 (c)	250	PF65 440				
1990 (ma)	200	PF65 440				
Note: 40 pieces melted						
1990 (h)	1,000	PF65 440				
1990 (tb)	1,000	—	—	—	—	400
Note: 10 pieces melted						
1990 (fl)	1,000	—	—	—	—	400
Note: 9 pieces melted						
1991 (c)	200	PF65 420				
Note: 57 pieces melted						
1991 (fr)	500	PF65 420				
1993	—	PF65 420				

KM# 395 1/4 ANGEL
7.78 g., 0.9999 Gold 0.250 oz. AGW **Ruler:** Elizabeth II **Obv:** Crowned bust right **Rev:** Archangel Michael slaying dragon

Date	Mintage	VF20	XF40	MS60	MS63	MS65
1994	—	PF65 420				
1995	—	—	—	—	—	400
1995	—	PF65 420				
1996	—	PF65 420				
1996	—	—	—	—	—	400
1997	—	PF65 420				
1997	—	—	—	—	—	400
1998	—	PF65 420				
1998	—	—	—	—	—	400
1999	—	—	—	—	—	400
1999	—	PF65 420				
2000	—	—	—	—	—	400
2000	—	PF65 420				

KM# 155 1/2 ANGEL
16.94 g., 0.917 Gold 0.4994 oz. AGW **Ruler:** Elizabeth II **Obv:** Crowned bust right **Rev:** Archangel Michael slaying dragon left

Date	Mintage	VF20	XF40	MS60	MS63	MS65
1985	51	PF65 875				
1985	1,776	—	—	—	—	775
1986	3,000	PF65 795				
1986	—	—	—	—	—	775
1987	—	PF65 795				
1987	—	—	—	—	—	775

KM# 196 1/2 ANGEL
16.94 g., 0.917 Gold 0.4994 oz. AGW **Ruler:** Elizabeth II **Obv:** Crowned bust right **Rev:** Archangel Michael slaying dragon

Date	Mintage	VF20	XF40	MS60	MS63	MS65
1988	—	—	—	—	—	775

KM# 396 1/2 ANGEL
15.55 g., 0.9999 Gold 0.4999 oz. AGW **Ruler:** Elizabeth II **Obv:** Crowned bust right **Rev:** Archangel Michael slaying dragon

Date	Mintage	VF20	XF40	MS60	MS63	MS65
1994	—	—	—	—	—	775
1994	—	PF65 795				
1995	—	PF65 795				
1995	—	—	—	—	—	775
1996	—	—	—	—	—	775
1996	—	PF65 795				
1997	—	—	—	—	—	775
1997	—	PF65 795				
1998	—	—	—	—	—	775
1998	—	PF65 795				
1999	—	—	—	—	—	775
1999	—	PF65 795				

KM# 139 ANGEL
33.93 g., 0.917 Gold 1.0003 oz. AGW **Ruler:** Elizabeth II **Obv:** Young bust right **Rev:** Archangel Michael slaying dragon left

Date	Mintage	VF20	XF40	MS60	MS63	MS65
1984	—	—	—	—	—	1,475
1984	3,000	PF65 1,500				

KM# 141 ANGEL
33.93 g., 0.917 Gold 1.0003 oz. AGW **Ruler:** Elizabeth II **Obv:** Crowned bust right **Rev:** Archangel Michael slaying dragon left

Date	Mintage	VF20	XF40	MS60	MS63	MS65
1985	28,000	—	—	—	—	1,475
1985 Prooflike	—	—	—	—	—	1,475
1985	3,000	PF65 1,500				
1986	—	—	—	—	—	1,475
1986	—	PF65 1,500				
1987	—	—	—	—	—	1,475
1987	—	PF65 1,500				

KM# 191 ANGEL
33.93 g., 0.917 Gold 1.0003 oz. AGW **Ruler:** Elizabeth II **Subject:** Hong Kong Coin Show **Obv:** Crowned bust right **Rev:** Archangel Michael slaying dragon left

Date	Mintage	VF20	XF40	MS60	MS63	MS65
1987	—	—	—	—	—	1,475
1987	1,000	PF65 1,500				

KM# 197 ANGEL
33.93 g., 0.917 Gold 1.0003 oz. AGW **Ruler:** Elizabeth II **Obv:** Crowned bust right **Rev:** Archangel Michael slaying dragon left

Date	Mintage	VF20	XF40	MS60	MS63	MS65
1988	—	—	—	—	—	1,475
1988 (ss)	1,000	PF65 1,500				

KM# 397 ANGEL
31.10 g., 0.9999 Gold 0.9999 oz. AGW **Ruler:** Elizabeth II **Obv:** Crowned bust right **Rev:** Archangel Michael slaying dragon right

Date	Mintage	VF20	XF40	MS60	MS63	MS65
1994	—	—	—	—	—	1,475
1994	—	PF65 1,500				
1995	—	—	—	—	—	1,475
1995	—	PF65 1,500				
1996	—	PF65 1,500				
1996	—	—	—	—	—	1,475
1997	—	PF65 1,500				
1997	—	—	—	—	—	1,475
1998	—	PF65 1,500				
1998	—	—	—	—	—	1,475
1999	—	—	—	—	—	1,475
1999	—	PF65 1,500				
2000	—	—	—	—	—	1,475
2000	—	PF65 1,500				

KM# 156 5 ANGEL
169.67 g., 0.917 Gold 5.0022 oz. AGW **Ruler:** Elizabeth II **Obv:** Crowned bust right **Rev:** Archangel Michael slaying dragon left

Date	Mintage	VF20	XF40	MS60	MS63	MS65
1985	104	—	—	—	—	7,600
1985	90	PF65 7,650				
1986	89	—	—	—	—	7,600
1986	250	PF65 7,650				
1987	150	—	—	—	—	7,600
1987	27	PF65 7,650				

KM# 198 5 ANGEL
169.67 g., 0.917 Gold 5.0022 oz. AGW **Ruler:** Elizabeth II **Obv:** Crowned bust right **Rev:** Archangel Michael slaying dragon

Date	Mintage	VF20	XF40	MS60	MS63	MS65
1988	250	—	—	—	—	7,600

KM# 1517 5 ANGEL
155.50 g., 0.999 Gold 4.9944 oz. AGW **Ruler:** Elizabeth II **Obv:** Crowned bust right **Rev:** St. Michael slaying dragon

Date	Mintage	VF20	XF40	MS60	MS63	MS65
1994	Est. 94	PF65 7,650				

KM# 157 10 ANGEL
339.34 g., 0.917 Gold 10.0043 oz. AGW **Ruler:** Elizabeth II **Obv:** Crowned bust right **Rev:** Archangel Michael slaying dragon left **Note:** Similar to 5 Angel, KM#156.

Date	Mintage	VF20	XF40	MS60	MS63	MS65
1985	79	—	—	—	—	16,000
1985	68	PF65 16,500				
1986	47	—	—	—	—	16,000
1986	250	PF65 16,500				
1987	30	PF65 16,500				
1987	150	—	—	—	—	16,000

KM# 199 10 ANGEL
339.34 g., 0.917 Gold 10.0043 oz. AGW **Ruler:** Elizabeth II **Obv:** Crowned bust right **Rev:** Archangel Michael slaying dragon

Date	Mintage	VF20	XF40	MS60	MS63	MS65
1988	250	PF65 16,500				

KM# 189 15 ANGEL
508.96 g., 0.917 Gold 15.0052 oz. AGW **Ruler:** Elizabeth II **Obv:** Crowned bust right **Rev:** Archangel Michael slaying dragon

Date	Mintage	VF20	XF40	MS60	MS63	MS65
1987	150	—	—	—	—	25,000
1987	18	PF65 26,000				

KM# 200 15 ANGEL
508.96 g., 0.917 Gold 15.0052 oz. AGW **Ruler:** Elizabeth II **Obv:** Crowned bust right **Rev:** Archangel Michael slaying dragon left **Note:** Similar to 5 Angel, KM#156.

Date	Mintage	VF20	XF40	MS60	MS63	MS65
1988	—	PF65 26,000				

KM# 201 20 ANGEL
678.67 g., 0.917 Gold 20.0088 oz. AGW, 75.2 mm. **Ruler:** Elizabeth II **Obv:** Crowned bust right **Rev:** Archangel Michael slaying dragon left **Note:** Similar to 5 Angel, KM#156.

Date	Mintage	VF20	XF40	MS60	MS63	MS65
1988	250	—	—	—	—	32,500
1988	100	PF65 35,000				

KM# 201a 20 ANGEL
Silver Gilt **Ruler:** Elizabeth II **Obv:** Crowned bust right **Rev:** Archangel Michael slaying dragon left

Date	Mintage	VF20	XF40	MS60	MS63	MS65
1988	—	—	—	—	—	—

KM# 301 25 ANGEL
848.28 g., 0.917 Gold 25.009 oz. AGW **Ruler:** Elizabeth II **Obv:** Crowned bust right **Rev:** Archangel Michael slaying dragon

Date	Mintage	VF20	XF40	MS60	MS63	MS65
1989	—	—	—	—	—	42,500

GOLD BULLION COINAGE

Sovereign Issues

KM# 969 1/5 SOVEREIGN
1.00 g., 0.9999 Gold 0.0321 oz. AGW **Ruler:** Elizabeth II **Obv:** Head with tiara right **Rev:** Triskeles **Shape:** Rectangular

Date	Mintage	VF20	XF40	MS60	MS63	MS65
1999	—	—	—	—	57.00	—

KM# 970 1/2 SOVEREIGN
2.50 g., 0.9999 Gold 0.0804 oz. AGW **Ruler:** Elizabeth II **Obv:** Head with tiara right **Rev:** Triskeles **Shape:** Rectangular

Date	Mintage	VF20	XF40	MS60	MS63	MS65
1999	—	—	—	—	132	—

KM# 971 3/4 SOVEREIGN
3.50 g., 0.9999 Gold 0.1125 oz. AGW **Ruler:** Elizabeth II **Obv:** Head with tiara right **Rev:** Triskeles **Shape:** Rectangular

Date	Mintage	VF20	XF40	MS60	MS63	MS65
1999	—	—	—	—	180	—

KM# 972 SOVEREIGN
5.00 g., 0.9999 Gold 0.1607 oz. AGW **Ruler:** Elizabeth II **Obv:** Head with tiara right **Rev:** Triskeles **Shape:** Rectangular

Date	Mintage	VF20	XF40	MS60	MS63	MS65
1999	—	—	—	—	245	—

KM# 973 2 SOVEREIGNS
10.00 g., 0.9999 Gold 0.3215 oz. AGW **Ruler:** Elizabeth II **Obv:** Head with tiara right **Rev:** Triskeles **Shape:** Rectangular

Date	Mintage	VF20	XF40	MS60	MS63	MS65
1999	—	—	—	—	450	—

KM# 974 5 SOVEREIGNS
31.10 g., 0.9999 Gold 0.9999 oz. AGW **Ruler:** Elizabeth II **Obv:** Head with tiara right **Rev:** Triskeles **Shape:** Rectangular

Date	Mintage	VF20	XF40	MS60	MS63	MS65
1999	—	—	—	—	1,350	—

GOLD BULLION COINAGE

Platina Issues

KM# 944 1/25 PLATINA
1.24 g., 0.750 Gold 0.030 oz. AGW (white) **Ruler:** Elizabeth II **Obv:** Crowned bust right **Rev:** Crowned arms

Date	Mintage	VF20	XF40	MS60	MS63	MS65
1999	Est. 10000	PF65 60.00				

KM# 945 1/10 PLATINA
3.11 g., 0.750 Gold 0.075 oz. AGW (white) **Ruler:** Elizabeth II **Obv:** Crowned bust right **Rev:** Crowned arms

Date	Mintage	VF20	XF40	MS60	MS63	MS65
1999	Est. 7500	PF65 125				

KM# 946 1/5 PLATINA
6.22 g., 0.750 Gold 0.150 oz. AGW (White) **Ruler:** Elizabeth II **Obv:** Crowned bust right **Rev:** Crowned arms flanked by falcons

Date	Mintage	VF20	XF40	MS60	MS63	MS65
1999	Est. 5000	PF65 250				

KM# 947 1/2 PLATINA
15.55 g., 0.750 Gold 0.375 oz. AGW (White) **Ruler:** Elizabeth II **Obv:** Crowned bust right **Rev:** Crowned arms

Date	Mintage	VF20	XF40	MS60	MS63	MS65
1999	—	PF65 625				

BI-METALLIC BULLION COINAGE

KM# 1065 1/4 ANGEL
Bi-Metallic .124 AGW Gold center in .124 APW Platinum ring., 22 mm. **Ruler:** Elizabeth II **Obv:** Crowned bust right **Rev:** Archangel Michael slaying dragon **Edge:** Reeded

Date	Mintage	VF20	XF40	MS60	MS63	MS65
1995	—	PF65 500				

KM# 1066 1/4 NOBLE
Bi-Metallic Platinum center in Gold ring, 22 mm. **Ruler:** Elizabeth II **Obv:** Crowned bust right **Rev:** Viking ship **Edge:** Reeded

Date	Mintage	VF20	XF40	MS60	MS63	MS65
1995	—	PF65 675				

PLATINUM BULLION COINAGE

Noble Series

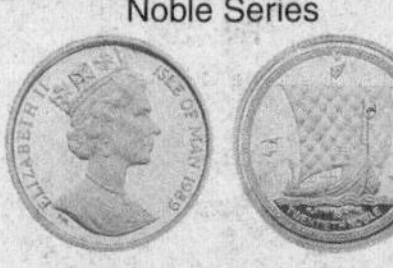

KM# 266 1/20 NOBLE
1.56 g., 0.9995 Platinum 0.050 oz. APW **Ruler:** Elizabeth II **Obv:** Crowned bust right **Rev:** Viking ship

Date	Mintage	VF20	XF40	MS60	MS63	MS65
1989	10,000	PF65 110				
1992	—	—	—	—	—	90.00

KM# 137 1/10 NOBLE
3.11 g., 0.9995 Platinum 0.0999 oz. APW **Ruler:** Elizabeth II **Obv:** Young bust right **Rev:** Viking ship

Date	Mintage	VF20	XF40	MS60	MS63	MS65
1984	—	—	—	—	—	180
1984	5,000	PF65 190				

KM# 153 1/10 NOBLE
3.11 g., 0.9995 Platinum 0.0999 oz. APW **Ruler:** Elizabeth II **Obv:** Crowned head right **Rev:** Viking ship

Date	Mintage	VF20	XF40	MS60	MS63	MS65
1985	5,000	PF65 190				
1985	99,000	—	—	—	—	180
1986	5,000	PF65 190				
1986	—	—	—	—	—	180
1987	5,000	PF65 190				
1987	—	—	—	—	—	180

KM# 202 1/10 NOBLE
3.11 g., 0.9995 Platinum 0.0999 oz. APW **Ruler:** Elizabeth II **Obv:** Crowned bust right **Rev:** Viking ship with hologram sail

Date	Mintage	VF20	XF40	MS60	MS63	MS65
1988	5,000	—	—	—	—	180
1989	5,000	—	—	—	—	180

KM# 168 1/4 NOBLE
7.78 g., 0.9995 Platinum 0.2499 oz. APW **Ruler:** Elizabeth II **Obv:** Crowned bust right **Rev:** Viking ship

Date	Mintage	VF20	XF40	MS60	MS63	MS65
1986	2,015	PF65 425				
1987	3,250	PF65 425				
1987 PM	750	PF65 425				

KM# 203 1/4 NOBLE
7.78 g., 0.9995 Platinum 0.2499 oz. APW **Ruler:** Elizabeth II **Obv:** Crowned bust right **Rev:** Viking ship

Date	Mintage	VF20	XF40	MS60	MS63	MS65
1988 (bb)	1,000	PF65 425				
1988	—	—	—	—	—	400
1988 (p)	1,000	PF65 425				
1988 (a)	100	—	—	—	—	400

Date	Mintage	VF20	XF40	MS60	MS63	MS65
1989 (br)	250	PF65 450				
1989 (p)	500	PF65 450				
1990 (ba)	1,000	PF65 425				
1990 (ti)	Est. 1000	PF65 425				

KM# 717 1/4 NOBLE
7.78 g., 0.9995 Platinum 0.2499 oz. APW **Ruler:** Elizabeth II **Obv:** Crowned bust right **Rev:** Ship with hologram sail

Date	Mintage	VF20	XF40	MS60	MS63	MS65
1996	Est. 10000	PF65 425				

KM# 169 1/2 NOBLE
15.55 g., 0.9995 Platinum 0.4997 oz. APW **Ruler:** Elizabeth II **Obv:** Crowned bust right **Rev:** Ship with hologram sail

Date	Mintage	VF20	XF40	MS60	MS63	MS65
1986	2,015	PF65 900				
1987	3,000	PF65 875				

KM# 204 1/2 NOBLE
15.55 g., 0.9995 Platinum 0.4997 oz. APW **Ruler:** Elizabeth II **Obv:** Crowned bust right **Rev:** Viking ship

Date	Mintage	VF20	XF40	MS60	MS63	MS65
1988	3,000	PF65 875				
1989	3,000	PF65 875				
1994 PM	250	PF65 925				

Note: The 1994 date was issued as a 2-piece set with a rhodium-plated silver medal marking the 10th anniversary of the platinum noble series

KM# 110 NOBLE
31.10 g., 0.9995 Platinum 0.9995 oz. APW **Ruler:** Elizabeth II **Obv:** Young bust right **Rev:** Viking ship

Date	Mintage	VF20	XF40	MS60	MS63	MS65
1983	1,700	—	—	—	—	1,700
1983	94	PF65 1,800				
1984	2,000	PF65 1,750				
1984	—	—	—	—	—	1,700

KM# 154 NOBLE
31.10 g., 0.9995 Platinum 0.9995 oz. APW **Ruler:** Elizabeth II **Obv:** Crowned bust right **Rev:** Viking ship

Date	Mintage	VF20	XF40	MS60	MS63	MS65
1985	3,000	PF65 1,750				
1985	—	—	—	—	—	1,700
1986	3,000	PF65 1,750				
1986	—	—	—	—	—	1,700
1987	—	—	—	—	—	1,700
1987	3,000	PF65 1,750				

KM# 205 NOBLE
31.10 g., 0.9995 Platinum 0.9995 oz. APW **Ruler:** Elizabeth II **Obv:** Crowned bust right **Rev:** Viking ship

Date	Mintage	VF20	XF40	MS60	MS63	MS65
1988	3,000	PF65 1,750				
1989	3,000	PF65 1,750				

KM# 170 5 NOBLE
155.51 g., 0.9995 Platinum 4.9974 oz. APW **Ruler:** Elizabeth II **Obv:** Crowned head right **Rev:** Viking ship

Date	Mintage	VF20	XF40	MS60	MS63	MS65
1986	15	PF65 7,500				
1987	11	PF65 7,500				

KM# 1498 5 NOBLE
155.51 g., 0.999 Platinum 4.9948 oz. APW **Ruler:** Elizabeth II **Obv:** Crowned bust right **Rev:** Viking ship

Date	Mintage	VF20	XF40	MS60	MS63	MS65
1988	—	PF65 7,500				

KM# 171 10 NOBLE
311.03 g., 0.9995 Platinum 9.9948 oz. APW, 63 mm. **Ruler:** Elizabeth II **Obv:** Crowned head right **Rev:** Viking ship

Date	Mintage	VF20	XF40	MS60	MS63	MS65
1986	15	PF65 16,500				
1987	11	PF65 16,500				

KM# 1499 10 NOBLE
311.00 g., 0.999 Platinum 9.9889 oz. APW **Ruler:** Elizabeth II **Obv:** Crowned bust right **Rev:** Viking ship

Date	Mintage	VF20	XF40	MS60	MS63	MS65
1988	—	PF65 16,500				

TRADE COINAGE

Ecu Series

KM# 711 15 ECUS
10.00 g., 0.925 Silver 0.2974 oz. ASW, 30 mm. **Ruler:** Elizabeth II **Obv:** Crowned bust right **Rev:** Manx cat within shield and wings **Edge:** Reeded

Date	Mintage	VF20	XF40	MS60	MS63	MS65
1994 PM	—	PF65 45.00				

KM# 714 15 ECUS
10.00 g., 0.925 Silver 0.2974 oz. ASW, 30 mm. **Ruler:** Elizabeth II **Subject:** 50th Anniversary of United Nations **Obv:** Crowned bust right **Rev:** Blacksmith **Edge:** Reeded

Date	Mintage	VF20	XF40	MS60	MS63	MS65
1995 PM	—	PF65 42.50				

KM# 712 25 ECUS
19.20 g., 0.925 Silver 0.571 oz. ASW **Ruler:** Elizabeth II **Subject:** 50th Anniversary of United Nations **Obv:** Crowned bust right **Rev:** Viking boat on helmeted shield

Date	Mintage	VF20	XF40	MS60	MS63	MS65
1994	Est. 15000	—	—	—	52.50	55.00

KM# 715 25 ECUS
19.20 g., 0.925 Silver 0.571 oz. ASW **Ruler:** Elizabeth II **Subject:** 50th Anniversary of United Nations **Obv:** Crowned bust right **Rev:** Ram's head within shield

Date	Mintage	VF20	XF40	MS60	MS63	MS65
1995	Est. 15000	PF65 55.00				

KM# 713 75 ECUS
6.22 g., 0.999 Gold 0.1998 oz. AGW **Ruler:** Elizabeth II **Obv:** Crowned bust right **Rev:** Triskeles on crowned shield

Date	Mintage	VF20	XF40	MS60	MS63	MS65
1994	Est. 2000	—	—	—	—	320

KM# 716 75 ECUS

6.22 g., 0.999 Gold 0.1998 oz. AGW **Ruler:** Elizabeth II **Obv:** Crowned bust right **Rev:** Falcons on shield

Date	Mintage	VF20	XF40	MS60	MS63	MS65
1995	Est. 2000	PF65 325				

TRADE COINAGE

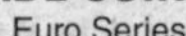

Euro Series

KM# 718 10 EURO

10.00 g., 0.925 Silver 0.2974 oz. ASW **Ruler:** Elizabeth II **Subject:** Spain - 10 years Membership E.C. **Obv:** Crowned bust right **Rev:** Head facing below standing figures within circle

Date	Mintage	VF20	XF40	MS60	MS63	MS65
1996	Est. 30000	PF65 40.00				

KM# 795 10 EURO

10.00 g., 0.925 Silver 0.2974 oz. ASW **Ruler:** Elizabeth II **Subject:** 200th Anniversary - Birth of Franza Schubert **Obv:** Crowned bust right **Rev:** Head below piano recital scene

Date	Mintage	VF20	XF40	MS60	MS63	MS65
1997	Est. 30000	PF65 40.00				

KM# 796 10 EURO

10.00 g., 0.925 Silver 0.2974 oz. ASW Ruler: Elizabeth II **Subject:** Netherlands as President of the EU **Obv:** Crowned bust right **Rev:** Head below organ player

Date	Mintage	VF20	XF40	MS60	MS63	MS65
1997 PM	—	PF65 40.00				

KM# 909 10 EURO

10.00 g., 0.925 Silver 0.2974 oz. ASW **Ruler:** Elizabeth II **Subject:** 125th Anniversary of the Isle of Man Railway **Obv:** Crowned bust right **Rev:** Old steam train

Date	Mintage	VF20	XF40	MS60	MS63	MS65
1998	Est. 30000	PF65 40.00				

KM# 910 10 EURO

10.00 g., 0.925 Silver 0.2974 oz. ASW, 30 mm. **Ruler:** Elizabeth II **Subject:** Myths and Legends - Manannan **Obv:** Crowned bust right **Rev:** Equestrian **Edge:** Reeded

Date	Mintage	VF20	XF40	MS60	MS63	MS65
1998 PM	Est. 30000	PF65 40.00				

KM# 719 15 EURO

19.20 g., 0.925 Silver 0.571 oz. ASW **Ruler:** Elizabeth II **Subject:** First Performance - La Boheme **Obv:** Crowned bust right **Rev:** Head below standing figures

Date	Mintage	VF20	XF40	MS60	MS63	MS65
1996	Est. 15000	PF65 75.00				

KM# 720 50 EURO

6.22 g., 0.9999 Gold 0.200 oz. AGW **Ruler:** Elizabeth II **Subject:** 125th Anniversary of Aida-Verdi **Obv:** Crowned bust right **Rev:** Head below standing figures

Date	Mintage	VF20	XF40	MS60	MS63	MS65
1996	Est. 2000	PF65 325				

KM# 797 50 EURO

6.22 g., 0.9999 Gold 0.200 oz. AGW **Ruler:** Elizabeth II **Obv:** Crowned bust right **Rev:** Head below harp player

Date	Mintage	VF20	XF40	MS60	MS63	MS65
1997	Est. 2000	PF65 325				

KM# 911 50 EURO

6.22 g., 0.9999 Gold 0.200 oz. AGW **Ruler:** Elizabeth II **Subject:** St. George **Obv:** Crowned bust right **Rev:** Rider spearing dragon as captive damsel watches

Date	Mintage	VF20	XF40	MS60	MS63	MS65
1998	Est. 2000	PF65 325				

WW I P.O.W. TOKEN COINAGE

KM# Tn22 6 PENCE

Brass **Obv:** PEEL **Rev:** 6d in sprays

Date	Mintage	F12	VF20	XF40	MS60	MS63
ND (1915)	—	75.00	135	—	—	—

WW II P.O.W TOKEN COINAGE

KM# Tn23 1/2 PENNY

Brass

Date	Mintage	F12	VF20	XF40	MS60	MS63
ND (1941)	2,000	17.50	35.00	75.00	170	—

KM# Tn24 PENNY

Brass

Date	Mintage	F12	VF20	XF40	MS60	MS63
ND (1941)	20,000	6.00	15.00	35.00	90:00	—

KM# Tn25 6 PENCE

Brass

Date	Mintage	F12	VF20	XF40	MS60	MS63
ND (1941)	2,500	12.00	28.00	60.00	145	—

PATTERNS

Including off metal strikes

KM#	Date	Mintage	Identification	Mkt Val
Pn20	1987	30	1/2 Crown. Silver.	500
Pn21	1989	Est. 50	Crown. Copper-Nickel. Black finish, first penny postage stamp.	—
Pn23	1992	—	5 Pounds. Virenium. Nigell Mansell, KM336.	—

PIEDFORT

KM#	Date	Mintage	Identification	Mkt Val
P4	1983	4,950	Pound. Silver. KM109.	65.00
P5	1983	4,950	Pound. Silver. KM127.	65.00
P6	1983	4,950	Pound. Silver. KM130.	75.00
P7	1983	4,950	Pound. Silver. KM131.	75.00
P8	1984	1,000	Pound. 0.374. Gold.	350
P9	1984	250	Pound. 0.917. Gold.	700
P10	1985	4,950	Pound. Silver.	75.00
P11	1985	950	Pound. 0.374. Gold.	200
P12	1985	250	Pound. 0.917. Gold.	700
P13	1985	50	Pound. Platinum.	1,500

MINT SETS

KM#	Date	Mintage	Identification	Issue Price	Mkt Val
MS1	1965 (3)	1,500	KM15-17	—	2,750
MS2	1971 (6)	50,000	KM19-24	3.00	13.00
MS3	1973 (4)	2,500	KM26-29	760	3,575
MS4	1974 (4)	250	KM26-29	—	3,575
MS5	1975 (6)	20,000	KM19-24	—	12.50
MS6	1975 (6)	20,000	KM19a-24a	56.50	60.00
MS7	1975 (4)	200	KM26-29	—	3,575
MS8	1976 (6)	20,000	KM32-34, 35.1,36.2, 39	—	9.00
MS9	1976 (6)	20,000	KM32a-34a, 35.1a-36.1a, 39a	—	57.50
MS10	1976 (4)	—	KM26-29	—	3,575
MS11	1977 (6)	50,000	KM33-34, 35.1-36.1, 39-40	—	9.00
MS12	1977 (4)	180	KM26-29	—	3,575
MS13	1978 (6)	10,000	KM32a-34a, 35.1a-36.1a, 39a	—	57.50
MS14	1978 (6)	—	KM32-34, 35.1-36.1, 39	—	9.00
MS15	1979 (6)	—	KM32-34, 35.1-36.1, 39	—	9.50
MS16	1979 (4)	—	KM26-29	—	3,575
MS17	1980 (6)	30,000	KM58-62, 70.1	—	17.50
MS18	1981 (6)	—	KM58-62, 70.1	—	17.50
MS20	1983 (9)	—	KM58-62, 70.1, 88, 90, 109	—	45.00
MS21	1983 (6)	—	KM58-62, 70.1	—	17.50

KM#	Date	Mintage	Identification	Issue Price	Mkt Val
MS22	1989 (9)	—	KM207-208, 209.1, 210-215	—	35.00
MS23	1990 (9)	—	KM207-208, 209.1, 210-215	25.00	35.00
MS24	1992 (9)	—	KM207-208, 209.2, 210-215	25.00	35.00
MS25	1994 (9)	—	KM207-208, 212-213, 337, 391-392, 398-399	25.00	42.50
MS26	1995 (9)	—	KM207-208, 212-213, 337, 391-392, 465-466	—	40.00
MS27	1996 (9)	—	KM587-595	—	40.00
MS28	1997 (5)	5,000	KM770-773, 774b	—	3,350
MS29	1985 (9)	—	KM142-148, 150-151, plus rectangular medal	—	32.50

PROOF SETS

KM#	Date	Mintage	Identification	Issue Price	Mkt Val
PS1	1965 (3)	1,000	KM15a-17a	—	2,900
PS2	1971 (6)	10,000	KM19-24	20.00	20.00
PS3	1973 (4)	1,250	KM26-29	950	3,650
PS4	1974 (4)	2,500	KM26-29	900	3,650
PS5	1975 (6)	600	KM19b-24b	1,175	6,000
PS6	1975 (4)	—	KM26-29	—	3,650
PS7	1976 (6)	600	KM32b-34b, 35.1b-36.1b, 39b	—	6,050
PS8	1976 (4)	—	KM26-29	—	3,650
PS9	1977 (6)	10,000	KM33a-34a, 35.1a-36.1a, 39a, 40a	—	60.00
PS10	1977 (4)	1,250	KM26-29	—	3,650
PS11	1978 (7)	—	KM32-34, 35.1-36.1, 39, 44	—	15.50
PS12	1978 (7)	600	KM32b-34b, 35.1b-36.1b, 39b, 44b	—	6,700
PS13	1979 (7)	10,000	KM32a-34a, 35.1a-36.1a, 39a, 44a	110	75.00
PS14	1979 (7)	500	KM32b-34b, 35.1b, 36.1b, 39b, 44b	2,765	6,700
PS15	1979 (4)	1,000	KM26-29	—	3,650
PSA16	1980 (7)	—	KM44, 58-62, 70	—	27.50
PS16	1980 (7)	10,000	KM44d, 58a-62a, 70a	—	65.00
PS17	1980 (7)	—	KM44c, 58c-62c, 70c	—	5,000
PS18	1980 (7)	300	KM44b, 58d-62d, 70d	—	6,700
PSA19	1981 (7)	—	KM44a, 59b-62b, 70b, 88a,	—	110
PSB19	1982 (9)	—	KM44, 58, 59, 60, 61, 62, 70, 90, 88	—	50.00
PS19	1982 (9)	1,000	KM44a, 58b-62b, 70a, 88a, 90a	—	135
PS20	1982 (8)	250	KM44c, 58b-62b, 88b, 90b	—	3,150
PS21	1982 (8)	100	KM44b, 58c-62c, 88c, 90c	—	6,975
PSA22	1982 (8)	—	KM44a, 59b-62b, 70a, 88a, 90a	—	130
PS22	1982 (7)	25,000	KM58-62, 70, 90	—	22.50
PS23	1982 (7)	9,000	KM58b-62b, 70a, 90a	—	65.00
PS24	1982 (7)	250	KM58c-62c, 70c, 90b	—	5,100
PS25	1982 (7)	400	KM58d-62d, 70d, 90c	—	6,750
PS26	1983 (7)	—	KM58d-62d, 90a, 109a	—	4,250
PS27	1983 (7)	—	KM58b-62b, 90b, 109b	—	600
PS28	1983 (7)	—	KM58c-62c, 90c, 109c	—	4,250
PSA29	1983 (9)	—	KM59b-62b, 70b, 88a, 90a, 109a	—	120
PS29	1985 (9)	25,000	KM142-148, 150-151	36.00	42.50
PS30	1985 (9)	5,000	KM135, 142a-148a, 150a	120	150
PS32	1985 (9)	100	KM135c, 142c-148c, 150c	3,600	9,175
PS33	1985 (7)	25,000	KM142-148	20.00	24.00
PS34	1985 (7)	5,000	KM142a-148a	72.00	75.00
PS35	1985 (7)	150	KM142b-148b	2,160	4,750
PS36	1985 (7)	100	KM142c-148c	2,400	6,000
PS37	1985 (6)	51	KM140-141, 152.1, 155-157	—	29,650
PS38	1986 (7)	17	KM140-141, 152.1, 155-157, 166	—	29,750
PS39	1986 (6)	15	KM153-154, 168-171	—	32,150
PS40	1986 (4)	2,000	KM153-154, 168-169	1,950	3,650
PS41	1986 (5)	2,500	KM140-141, 152.1, 155, 166	—	3,400
PS42	1987 (4)	—	KM176a, 177, 187-188	—	2,250
PS44	1987 (5)	—	KM140-141, 152.2, 155, 166	—	3,300
PS45	1987 (4)	3,000	KM140-141, 152.2, 155	—	3,200
PS46	1987 (6)	11	KM153-154, 168-169, 170-171	—	32,100
PS47	1987 (4)	2,500	KM153-154, 168-169	—	3,600
PS48	1988 (5)	611	KM235-239	—	3,400
PS49	1988 (4)	500	KM222-225	—	120
PS50	1988 (4)	7,500	KM286-289 Medal	—	3,600
PS53	1989 (4)	—	KM#240-243	—	75.00
PS54	1994 (1)	250	KM#204 plus Rhodium-plated Silver 31 g medal 10th Anniversary of the Platinum Noble Coin Series	—	1,150
PS55	1996 (5)	500	KM613, 615, 617, 619, 621b	—	3,375
PS56	1998 (5)	1,000	KM853-856, 857b	—	3,375
PS57	1999 (5)	1,000	KM958, 960, 962, 964, 968	1,300	3,350
PS58	2000 (5)	1,000	KM1052-1055, 1057	1,300	3,300

PROOF-LIKE SETS (PL)

KM#	Date	Mintage	Identification	Issue Price	Mkt Val
PL1	1980 (4)	—	KM64-67	—	37.50
PL2	1981 (4)	—	KM77-80	—	38.00
PL3	1982 (4)	50,000	KM96-99	—	37.50
PL4	1984 (4)	—	KM121-124	—	35.00
PL5	1986 (2)	—	KM173-174	—	16.00
PL6	1989 (6)	50,000	KM240-243	—	60.00

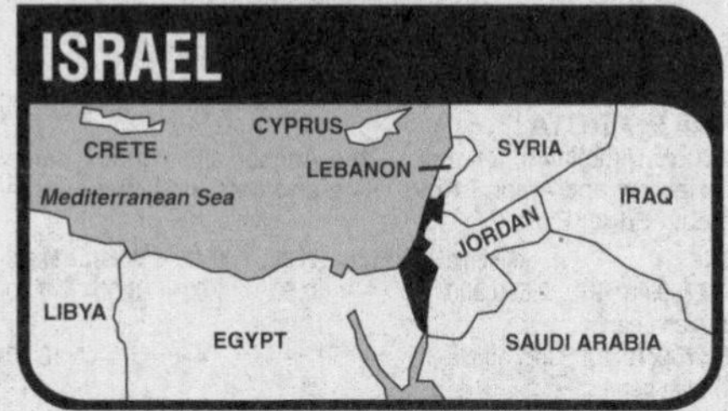

The state of Israel, a Middle Eastern republic at the eastern end of the Mediterranean Sea, bounded by Lebanon on the north, Syria on the northeast, Jordan on the east, and Egypt on the southwest, has an area of 9,000 sq. mi. (20,770 sq. km.) and a population of 6 million. Capital: Jerusalem. Finished diamonds, chemicals, citrus, textiles, minerals, electronic and transportation equipment are exported.

HEBREW COIN DATING

Israeli coins are dated according to the Jewish year (JE) with the commemorative coins also dated according to the Christian year (AD). The JE New Year falls in September or early October. In the case of dual-dated coins, with some exceptions, the JE date is 3,760 years greater than the AD date. Thus, for example, JE5735 is equivalent to AD1975. Exceptions are almost all of the Hanukka (Festival of Lights) commemorative coins because Hanukka falls early in the JE year and late in the AD year (late November or December) and certain other commemorative coins issued early in the JE year. In the case of the dual-dated Hanukka coins (other than the JE5720 coin) and certain others, the difference is 3,761 years. However, for ease of reference, except in the case of such dual-dated coins, the AD date given is always 3,760 years greater than the JE date (including the Hanukka coins bearing only a JE date). In the case of sets of Hanukka coins, however, where the packaging gives an AD date that differs from the JE date by 3,761 years, the AD date on the packaging is also given in brackets.

Israel's coins carry Hebrew dating formed from a combination of the 22 consonant letters of the Hebrew alphabet and read from right to left. The Jewish calendar dates back more than 5700 years; but five millenniums are assumed in the dating of coins (until 1981). Thus, the year 5735 (1975AD) appears as 735, with the first two characters from the right indicating the number of years in hundreds; tav (400), plus shin (300). The next is lamedh (30), followed by a separation mark which has the appearance of double quotation marks, then heh (5).

The separation mark - generally similar to a single quotation mark through 5718 (1958 AD), and like a double quotation mark thereafter - serves the purpose of indicating that the letters form a number, not a word, and on some issues can be confused with the character yodh (10), which in a stylized rendering can appear similar, although slightly larger and thicker. The separation mark does not appear in either form on a few commemorative issues.

The Star of David is not a mintmark. It appears only on some coins sold by the Israel Government Coins and Medals Corporation Ltd., which is owned by the Israel government, and is a division of the Prime Minister's office and sole distributor to collectors. The Star of David was first used in 1971 on the science coin to signify that it was minted in Jerusalem, but was later used by different mint facilities.

AD DATE		JEWISH ERA
1948	תש״ח	5708
1949	תש״ט	5709
1952	תשי״ב	5712
1954	תשי״ד	5714
1955	תשט״ו	5715
1957	תשי״ז	5717
1958	תשי״ח	5718
1959	תשי״ט	5719
1960	תש״ך	5720
1960	תשך	5720
1961	תשכ״א	5721
1962	תשכ״ב	5722
1963	תשכ״ג	5723
1964	תשכ״ד	5724
1965	תשכ״ה	5725
1966	תשכ״ו	5726
1967	תשכ״ז	5727
1968	תשכ״ח	5728
1969	תשכ״ט	5729
1970	תש״ל	5730
1971	תשל״א	5731
1972	תשל״ב	5732
1973	תשל״ג	5733
1974	תשל״ד	5734
1975	תשל״ה	5735
1976	תשל״ו	5736
1977	תשל״ז	5737
1978	תשל״ח	5738
1979	תשל״ט	5739
1980	תש״ם	5740
1981	תשמ״א	5741
1981	התשמ״א	5741
1982	התשמ״ב	5742
1983	התשמ״ג	5743
1984	התשמ״ד	5744
1985	התשמ״ה	5745
1986	התשמ״ו	5746
1987	התשמ״ז	5747
1988	התשמ״ח	5748
1989	התשמ״ט	5749
1990	התש״ן	5750
1991	התשנ״א	5751
1992	התשנ״ב	5752

1993	התשנ״ג	5753
1994	התשנ״ד	5754
1995	התשנ״ה	5755
1996	התשנ״ו	5756
1997	התשנ״ז	5757
1998	התשנ״ח	5758
1999	התשנ״ט	5759
2000	התש״ס	5760

MINT COIN FINISHES

(M) MATTE - Normal circulation strike or a dull finish produced by sandblasting special uncirculated (polish finish) or proof quality dies.

(U) SPECIAL UNCIRCULATED - Polished or prooflike in appearance without any frosted features.

(P) PROOF - The highest quality obtainable having mirror-like fields and frosted features.

MINT MARKS

(a) -	Athens
(b) -	Berne (Swiss mint)
(bp) -	Budapest
(c) -	Canberra (Royal Australian mint)
(d) -	Munich
(dg) -	Daejeon (Korea; KOMSCO)
(f) -	Stuttgart
H, (ht) -	Heaton (Birmingham)
(h) -	Kongsberg (Norway)
(hn) -	Holon (location of machine shop in which Israel's first coins were minted)
(i) -	Imperial Chemical Industries (Great Britain)
(ig) -	Israel Government Coins and Medals Corp.
(j) -	Jerusalem
(k) -	Kretschmer (private mint in Jerusalem)
(ld)	Tower Mint, England
(m) -	Madrid
(o) -	Ottawa
(p) -	Paris
(r) -	Rome
(s) -	San Francisco
(sa) -	Pretoria (South African mint)
(sg) -	Singapore
(sl) -	Seoul
(so) -	Santiago
(t) -	Tel Aviv
(u) -	Utrecht (Netherlands)
(v) -	Vantaa (Finland)
(va) -	Vienna
(w) -	Warsaw
(wg) -	Winnipeg

MONETARY SYSTEM

1000 Mils = 1 Pound

NOTE: All proof commemoratives with the exception of the 1 and 5 Lirot issues of 1985 are distinguished from the uncirculated editions by the presence of the Hebrew letter "mem".

REPUBLIC

MIL COINAGE

KM# 8 25 MILS

Aluminum, 30 mm. **Obv:** Grape cluster and country name in Hebrew and Arabic **Rev:** Value within wreath **Edge:** Plain **Note:** Released April 6, 1949.

Date	Mintage	F12	VF20	XF40	MS60	MS63
JE5708 (1948) (hn)	42,650	35.00	60.00	200	800	1,000
JE5709 (1949) (j) closed link	650,000	5.00	8.00	20.00	50.00	—
JE5709 (1949) (hn) open link	Inc. above	15.00	25.00	60.00	150	—

REFORM COINAGE

The 1949 Pruta coins, except for the 100 and 500 Pruta values, occur with and without a small pearl under the bar connecting the wreath on the reverse. Only the 50 and 100 Pruta coins were issued in 5709. All later coins were struck with frozen dates.

1000 Pruta (Prutot) = 1 Lira

KM# 9 PRUTA

1.30 g., Aluminum, 21 mm. **Obv:** Anchor and country name in Hebrew and Arabic **Rev:** Value and date in Hebrew within wreath **Edge:** Plain

Date	Mintage	F12	VF20	XF40	MS60	MS63
JE5709 (1949) (i) With pearl	2,660,000	—	0.50	1.00	3.00	5.00
JE5709(1949) (i) With pearl, Proof like	Inc. above	—	—	—	—	10.00
JE5709 (1949) (ht) Without pearl	2,500,000	1.00	2.00	5.00	8.00	12.50
JE5709 (1949) (i)	20,000	PF63 600				

KM# 10 5 PRUTA

3.20 g., Bronze, 20 mm. **Obv:** 4-stringed lyre and country name in Hebrew and Arabic **Rev:** Value and date in Hebrew within wreath **Edge:** Plain

Date	Mintage	F12	VF20	XF40	MS60	MS63
JE5709 (1949) (i) With pearl	5,020,000	—	1.00	2.00	4.00	6.00
JE5709 (1949) (i)	25,000	PF63 600				
JE5709 (1949) (ht) Without pearl	5,000,000	1.00	3.00	5.00	10.00	15.00

KM# 11 10 PRUTA

6.10 g., Bronze, 27 mm. **Obv:** Amphora and country name in Hebrew and Arabic **Rev:** Value within wreath and date in Hebrew **Edge:** Plain

Date	Mintage	F12	VF20	XF40	MS60	MS63
JE5709 (1949) (i) With pearl	7,428,000	—	1.00	3.00	15.00	20.00
JE5709 (1949) (i)	20,000	PF63 1,000				
JE5709 (1949) (ht) Without pearl	7,500,000	—	0.50	1.00	2.00	3.00

KM# 17 10 PRUTA

1.60 g., Aluminum, 24.5 mm. **Obv:** Ceremonial pitcher flanked by sprigs and country name in Hebrew and Arabic **Rev:** Value and date in Hebrew within wreath **Shape:** Scalloped

Date	Mintage	F12	VF20	XF40	MS60	MS63
JE5712 (1952) (i)	26,042,000	—	0.35	0.75	1.00	2.00

KM# 20 10 PRUTOT

1.60 g., Aluminum, 24.5 mm. **Obv:** Ceremonial pitcher flanked by sprigs and country name in Hebrew and Arabic **Rev:** Value and date in Hebrew within wreath **Edge:** Plain

Date	Mintage	F12	VF20	XF40	MS60	MS63
JE5717 (1957) (t)	1,000,000	—	0.35	0.75	1.00	2.00

KM# 20a 10 PRUTOT

1.60 g., Copper Plated Aluminum, 24.5 mm. **Obv:** Ceremonial pitcher flanked by sprigs and country name in Hebrew and Arabic **Rev:** Value and date in Hebrew within wreath **Edge:** Plain

Date	Mintage	F12	VF20	XF40	MS60	MS63
JE5717 (1957) (t)	1,088,000	—	0.35	0.75	1.00	2.00

KM# 12 25 PRUTA

2.80 g., Copper-Nickel, 19.5 mm. **Obv:** Grape cluster and country name in Hebrew and Arabic **Rev:** Value and date in Hebrew within wreath **Edge:** Reeded

Date	Mintage	F12	VF20	XF40	MS60	MS63
JE5709 (1949) (i) With pearl	10,500,000	—	0.50	0.75	1.00	3.00
JE5709 (1949) (ht) Without pearl	2,500,000	—	1.50	3.00	10.00	15.00
JE5709 (1949) (i)	20,000	PF63 1,000				

KM# 12a 25 PRUTA

2.50 g., Nickel Clad Steel, 19.5 mm. **Obv:** Grape cluster and country name in Hebrew and Arabic **Rev:** Value and date in Hebrew within wreath

Date	Mintage	F12	VF20	XF40	MS60	MS63
JE5714 (1954) (t)	3,697,347	—	0.50	1.00	1.50	3.00

KM# 13.1 50 PRUTA

5.60 g., Copper-Nickel, 23.5 mm. **Obv:** Grape leaves and country name in Hebrew and Arabic **Rev:** Value and date in Hebrew within wreath **Edge:** Reeded

Date	Mintage	F12	VF20	XF40	MS60	MS63
JE5709 (1949) (i) With pearl	6,020,000	—	3.00	5.00	15.00	22.00
JE5709 (1949) (i)	20,000	PF63 1,000				
JE5709 (1949) (ht) Without pearl	6,000,000	—	0.75	1.25	2.00	3.50
JE5714 (1954) (t)	250,000	2.00	5.00	12.00	25.00	35.00

KM# 13.2 50 PRUTA

5.60 g., Copper-Nickel, 23.5 mm. **Obv:** Grape leaves and country name in Hebrew and Arabic **Rev:** Value and date in Hebrew within wreath **Edge:** Plain

Date	Mintage	F12	VF20	XF40	MS60	MS63
JE5714 (1954) (t)	4,500,000	—	0.50	1.00	1.50	3.00

KM# 13.2a 50 PRUTA

5.00 g., Nickel Clad Steel, 23.6 mm. **Obv:** Grape leaves and country name in Hebrew and Arabic **Rev:** Value and date in Hebrew within wreath **Edge:** Plain

Date	Mintage	F12	VF20	XF40	MS60	MS63
JE5714 (1954) (t)	17,773,633	—	0.50	1.00	1.50	3.00

KM# 14 100 PRUTA

11.30 g., Copper-Nickel, 28.5 mm. **Obv:** Date palm and country name in Hebrew and Arabic **Rev:** Value and date in Hebrew within wreath **Edge:** Reeded

Date	Mintage	F12	VF20	XF40	MS60	MS63
JE5709 (1949)	6,042,000	—	0.75	1.25	2.00	3.50
Note: 3,042,000 minted at (i) and 3,000,000 minted at (ht).						
JE5709 (1949) (i)	20,000	PF63 1,000				
JE5715 (1955) (t)	5,867,674	—	0.75	1.25	2.00	3.50

KM# 18 100 PRUTA

7.30 g., Nickel Clad Steel, 25.6 mm. **Obv:** Date palm and country name in Hebrew and Arabic **Rev:** Value and date in Hebrew within wreath **Note:** Reduced size, die manufactured in Bern.

Date	Mintage	F12	VF20	XF40	MS60	MS63
JE5714 (1954) (t)	700,000	—	1.00	1.50	2.50	4.00

KM# 18.1 100 PRUTA

7.50 g., Copper-Nickel, 25.6 mm. **Obv:** Date palm and country name in Hebrew and Arabic **Rev:** Value and date in Hebrew within wreath, wreath close to rim **Note:** Dies manufactured in Bern; coin non-magnetic, probably an error minted in Tel Aviv but possibly a trial coin minted in Bern.

Date	Mintage	F12	VF20	XF40	MS60	MS63
JE5714 (1954) (t)	Est. 500	120	150	350	750	1,000

KM# 19 100 PRUTA

7.30 g., Nickel Clad Steel, 25.6 mm. **Obv:** Date palm and country name in Hebrew and Arabic **Rev:** Value and date in Hebrew within wreath **Note:** Reduced size, greater space between wreath and rim.

Date	Mintage	F12	VF20	XF40	MS60	MS63
JE5714 (1954) (t)	20,000	75.00	125	300	1,000	—

KM# 19.1 100 PRUTA

7.50 g., Copper-Nickel, 25.6 mm. **Obv:** Date palm and country name in Hebrew and Arabic **Rev:** Value and date in Hebrew within wreath, wreath close to rim **Note:** Dies manufactured in Ultrecht; coin non-magnetic, probably an error minted in Tel Aviv but possibly a trial coin minted in Utrecht

Date	Mintage	F12	VF20	XF40	MS60	MS63
JE5714 (1954) (t)	Est. 20	750	1,000	1,500	2,500	—

KM# 15 250 PRUTA

14.10 g., Copper-Nickel, 32.2 mm. **Obv:** Oat sprigs and country name in Hebrew and Arabic **Rev:** Value and date in Hebrew within wreath **Edge:** Reeded

Date	Mintage	F12	VF20	XF40	MS60	MS63
JE5709 (1949) (i) With pearl	1,496,000	—	2.50	4.00	9.00	15.00
JE5709 (1949) (ht) Without pearl	524,000	—	1.00	2.00	5.00	7.50

KM# 15a 250 PRUTA

14.40 g., 0.500 Silver 0.2315 oz. ASW, 32.2 mm. **Obv:** Oat sprigs and country name in Hebrew and Arabic **Rev:** Value and date in Hebrew within wreath

Date	Mintage	F12	VF20	XF40	MS60	MS63
JE5709 (1949) H	44,125	—	7.50	10.00	15.00	25.00
Note: Not placed into circulation						

KM# 16 500 PRUTA

25.00 g., 0.500 Silver 0.4019 oz. ASW, 37.1 mm. **Obv:** Pomegranates and country name in Hebrew and Arabic **Rev:** Value and date in Hebrew within wreath **Edge:** Reeded **Note:** Dav. #257.

Date	Mintage	F12	VF20	XF40	MS60	MS63
JE5709 (1949) (ht)	33,812	—	15.00	16.50	25.00	35.00
Note: Not placed into circulation						

REFORM COINAGE

100 Agorot = 1 Lira; January 1, 1960-1980

KM# 24.1 AGORA

1.03 g., Aluminum, 20 mm. **Obv:** Country name in Arabic and Hebrew to left and below oat sprigs **Rev:** Value and date in Hebrew **Shape:** Scalloped

Date	Mintage	F12	VF20	XF40	MS60	MS63
JE5720 (1960) (i)	12,768,000	—	—	4.00	8.00	20.00
Note: Letter "Lamed" in Israel with serif						
JE5720 (1960) (i)	Inc. above		—	10.00	20.00	100
Note: Letter "Lamed" in Israel without lower serif						
JE5720 (1960) (i)	300	—	100	200	350	800
Note: Large date						
JE5721 (1961) (i)	19,262,000	—	—	0.50	2.00	5.00
JE5721 (1961) (i)	Inc. above	—	—	5.00	15.00	100
Note: Thick date						
JE5721 (1961) (i)	Inc. above	—	—	5.00	15.00	100
Note: Wide date						
JE5722 (1962)	14,500,000	—	—	0.10	0.40	1.00
Note: Large date, 10,600,000 struck by (b) and 3,900,000 by (t)						
JE5722 (1962)	Inc. above	—	—	5.00	10.00	20.00
Note: Small date, small serifs						
JE5723 (1963) (b)	6,000,000	—	—	0.10	0.40	0.75
JE5723 (1963) (t)	8,804,000	—	—	0.10	0.40	0.75
Note: Medal alignment						
JE5723 (1963) (t)	—	—	—	2.00	4.00	9.00
Note: Coin alignment						
JE5724 (1964) (t)	22,604,241	—	—	—	—	0.75
JE5724 (1964) (b)	4,950,000	—	—	—	—	0.75
JE5725 (1965) (b)	10,024,000	—	—	—	—	0.25
JE5725 (1965) (t)	10,707,625	—	—	—	—	0.25
JE5726 (1966) (b)	1,680,000	—	—	—	—	0.25
JE5726 (1966) (t)	8,482,502	—	—	—	—	0.25
JE5727 (1967) (j)	6,782,271	—	—	—	—	0.25
JE5728 (1968) (j)	20,899,000	—	—	—	—	0.25
JE5729 (1969) (j)	22,120,000	—	—	—	—	0.25
JE5730 (1970) (j)	17,748,000	—	—	—	—	0.25
JE5731 (1971) (j)	10,290,000	—	—	—	—	0.25
JE5732 (1972) (j)	24,512,000	—	—	—	—	0.25
JE5733 (1973) (j)	20,496,000	—	—	—	—	0.25
JE5734 (1974) (j) Matte	8,080,000	—	—	—	—	0.75
JE5734 (1974) (o) Prooflike	34,000,000	—	—	—	—	0.25
JE5735 (1975) (j)	1,574,000	—	—	—	—	0.30
JE5736 (1976) (j)	4,512,000	—	—	—	—	0.25
JE5737 (1977) (j)	9,680,000	—	—	—	—	0.25
JE5738 (1978) (j)	8,864,000	—	—	—	—	0.25
JE5739 (1979) (j)	4,048,763	—	—	—	—	0.25
JE5740 (1980) (j)	2,599,634	—	—	—	—	1.00

KM# 24.2 AGORA

1.03 g., Aluminum, 20 mm. **Obv:** Country name in Arabic and Hebrew to left and below oat sprigs, star of David in field **Rev:** Value and date in Hebrew **Edge:** Plain **Shape:** Scalloped

Date	Mintage	F12	VF20	XF40	MS60	MS63
JE5731 (1971) (j) Sets only	125,921	—	—	—	—	0.75
JE5732 (1972) (j) Sets only	68,513	—	—	—	—	0.75
JE5734 (1974) (j) Sets only	92,868	—	—	—	—	0.75
JE5735 (1975) (j) Sets only	61,686	—	—	—	—	1.00
JE5736 (1976) (j) Sets only	64,654	—	—	—	—	0.75
JE5737 (1977) (j) Sets only	37,208	—	—	—	—	1.00
JE5738 (1978) (j) Sets only	57,072	—	—	—	—	0.75
JE5739 (1979) (j) Sets only	31,590	—	—	—	—	1.00

KM# 63 AGORA

1.03 g., Aluminum, 20 mm. **Series:** Independence Day **Subject:** Declaration of Independence; Israel's 25th Anniversary **Obv:** Text to left and below oat sprigs **Rev:** Value **Shape:** Scalloped **Note:** Struck for sets only.

Date	Mintage	F12	VF20	XF40	MS60	MS63
JE5733 (1973) (j) Sets only	98,107	—	—	—	—	0.75

KM# 96 AGORA

Nickel, 20 mm. **Subject:** 25th Anniversary of Bank of Israel **Obv:** Text to left and below oat sprigs **Rev:** Value **Shape:** Scalloped **Note:** Struck for sets only

Date	Mintage	F12	VF20	XF40	MS60	MS63
JE5740 (1980) (b) Sets only	35,000	—	—	—	—	2.00

KM# 25 5 AGOROT

2.30 g., Aluminum-Bronze, 17.5 mm. **Obv:** Pomegranates **Rev:** Value **Edge:** Plain

Date	Mintage	F12	VF20	XF40	MS60	MS63
JE5720 (1960) (t)	8,019,000	—	—	4.00	8.00	20.00
JE5721 (1961)	15,090,000	—	—	0.25	0.50	1.50
Note: Sharp, flat date; 5,012,000 struck by (b) and 10,078,000 by (t)						
JE5721 (1961) (i)	5,000,000	—	—	10.00	20.00	50.00
Note: High date with serifs						
JE5722 (1962) (t) Large date	11,198,000	—	—	0.25	0.50	1.00
JE5722 (1962) (t) Small date	Inc. above	—	—	5.00	10.00	25.00
JE5723 (1963) (t)	1,429,000	—	—	0.25	0.50	1.25
JE5724 (1964) (t)	21,451	—	8.00	20.00	90.00	400

Date	Mintage	F12	VF20	XF40	MS60	MS63
JE5725 (1965) (t)	201,281	—	—	—	0.25	0.50
JE5726 (1966) (t)	290,866	—	—	—	0.25	0.50
JE5727 (1967) (j)	2,195,114	—	—	—	0.15	0.40
JE5728 (1968) (j)	4,020,000	—	—	—	0.15	0.40
JE5729 (1969) (j)	2,200,103	—	—	—	0.15	0.40
JE5730 (1970) (j)	4,004,000	—	—	—	0.15	0.40
JE5731 (1971) (j)	14,010,000	—	—	—	0.10	0.25
JE5732 (1972) (j)	9,005,000	—	—	—	0.10	0.25
JE5733 (1973) (o)	16,340,000	—	—	—	0.10	0.25
JE5733 (1973) (j)	9,380,000	—	—	—	0.10	0.25
JE5734 (1974) (j)	10,470,000	—	—	—	0.10	0.25
JE5735 (1975) (j)	10,232,000	—	—	—	0.10	0.25

KM# 25a 5 AGOROT

2.30 g., Aluminum-Bronze, 17.5 mm. **Obv:** Pomegranates, Star of David in field **Rev:** Value **Edge:** Plain

Date	Mintage	F12	VF20	XF40	MS60	MS63
JE5731 (1971) (j) Sets only	125,921	—	—	—	—	0.75
JE5732 (1972) (j) Sets only	68,513	—	—	—	—	0.75

KM# 25b 5 AGOROT

0.77 g., Aluminum, 17.5 mm. **Obv:** Pomegranates **Rev:** Value **Edge:** Plain

Date	Mintage	F12	VF20	XF40	MS60	MS63
JE5736 (1976) (j)	13,156,000	—	—	—	0.10	0.50
JE5737 (1977) (j) Matte	16,800,000	—	—	—	0.10	0.50
JE5737 (1977) (wg) Prooflike	15,000,010	—	—	—	—	0.50
JE5738 (1978) (j) Matte	21,480,000	—	—	—	0.10	0.50
JE5738 (1978) (wg) Prooflike	38,716,000	—	—	—	—	0.50
JE5739 (1979) (j)	12,835,709	—	—	—	0.10	0.50

KM# 25c 5 AGOROT

Copper-Nickel, 17.5 mm. **Obv:** Pomegranates **Rev:** Value **Edge:** Plain

Date	Mintage	F12	VF20	XF40	MS60	MS63
JE5734 (1974) (j) Sets only	92,868	—	—	—	—	0.75
JE5735 (1975) (j) Sets only	61,686	—	—	—	—	1.00
JE5736 (1976) (j) Sets only	64,654	—	—	—	—	0.75
JE5737 (1977) (j) Sets only	37,208	—	—	—	—	1.00
JE5738 (1978) (j) Sets only	57,072	—	—	—	—	0.75
JE5739 (1979) (j) Sets only	31,590	—	—	—	—	1.00

KM# 64 5 AGOROT

Copper-Nickel, 17.5 mm. **Series:** Independence Day **Subject:** Declaration of Independence; Israel's 25th Anniversary **Obv:** Pomegranates **Rev:** Value **Edge:** Plain **Note:** In sets only.

Date	Mintage	F12	VF20	XF40	MS60	MS63
JE5733 (1973) (j) Sets only	98,107	—	—	—	—	0.75

KM# 97 5 AGOROT

Nickel, 17.5 mm. **Subject:** 25th Anniversary of Bank of Israel **Obv:** Pomegranates **Rev:** Value **Edge:** Plain **Note:** Struck for sets only.

Date	Mintage	F12	VF20	XF40	MS60	MS63
JE5740 (1980) (b) Sets only	35,000	—	—	—	—	2.00

KM# 26 10 AGOROT

4.30 g., Aluminum-Bronze, 21.5 mm. **Obv:** Date palm **Rev:** Value **Edge:** Plain

Date	Mintage	F12	VF20	XF40	MS60	MS63
JE5720 (1960) (t)	14,397,000	—	—	0.50	1.00	10.00
JE5721 (1961)	Inc. above	—	5.00	25.00	60.00	325
Note: Fatha in Arabic legend: "Israel"						
JE5721 (1961)	12,821,000	—	—	0.50	1.00	7.00
Note: 95,000 struck by (b) 5,000,000 by (i) and 7,726,000 by (j)						
JE5722 (1962) (t) Large date, thick letters	8,845,000	—	—	0.25	0.50	1.00
JE5722 (1962) (t) Small date, thin letters	Inc. above	—	—	5.00	10.00	20.00
JE5723 (1963) (t)	3,931,000	—	—	0.25	0.50	1.00
JE5724 (1964) (t) Large date	3,612,000	—	—	0.25	0.50	1.00
Note: Hebrew letter "shin" is rounded						
JE5724 (1964) (t) Small date	Inc. above	—	3.00	8.00	15.00	40.00
Note: Hebrew letter "shin" is straight and sharp						
JE5725 (1965) (t)	200,561	—	—	—	0.25	0.50
JE5726 (1966) (t)	7,276,610	—	—	—	0.15	0.30
JE5727 (1967) (j)	6,426,438	—	—	—	0.15	0.30
JE5728 (1968) (j)	4,825,000	—	—	—	0.15	0.30
JE5729 (1969) (j)	6,810,000	—	—	—	0.15	0.30
JE5730 (1970) (j)	6,131,000	—	—	—	0.15	0.30
JE5731 (1971) (j)	6,810,000	—	—	—	0.15	0.30
JE5732 (1972) (j)	1,260,000	—	—	—	0.20	0.30
JE5732 (1972) (b)	18,393,112	—	—	—	0.15	0.30
JE5733 (1973) (j)	5,625,000	—	—	—	0.15	0.30
JE5733 (1973) (o)	10,580,000	—	—	—	0.15	0.30
JE5734 (1974) (j)	3,880,000	—	—	—	0.15	0.30
JE5734 (1974) (o)	18,160,000	—	—	—	0.10	0.25
JE5735 (1975) (j)	25,135,000	—	—	—	0.10	0.25
JE5736 (1976) (j)	34,870,000	—	—	—	0.10	0.25
JE5736 (1976) (o)	20,000,000	—	—	—	0.10	0.25
JE5737 (1977) (j)	27,885,863	—	—	—	0.10	0.25

KM# 26a 10 AGOROT

5.00 g., Aluminum-Bronze, 21.5 mm. **Obv:** Date palm with star of David in field **Rev:** Value **Edge:** Plain

Date	Mintage	F12	VF20	XF40	MS60	MS63
JE5731 (1971) (j) Sets only	125,921	—	—	—	—	0.75
JE5732 (1972) (j) Sets only	68,513	—	—	—	—	0.75

KM# 26b 10 AGOROT

1.61 g., Aluminum, 21.5 mm. **Series:** Independence Day **Subject:** 60th Anniversary of Yad Vashem; Israel's 65th Anniversary **Obv:** Date palm **Rev:** Value **Edge:** Plain

Date	Mintage	F12	VF20	XF40	MS60	MS63
JE5737 (1977) (wg) Prooflike	30,000,010	—	—	—	0.10	0.25
JE5738 (1978) (j) Matte	24,050,000	—	—	—	0.10	0.25
JE5738 (1978) (wg) Prooflike	104,335,750	—	—	—	0.10	0.25
JE5739 (1979) (j)	22,201,469	—	—	—	0.10	0.25
JE5740 (1980) (j)	4,752,333	—	—	—	0.15	0.50

Note: Most of the 5740 dated coins were melted down before being issued.

KM# 26c 10 AGOROT

Copper-Nickel, 21.5 mm. **Obv:** Date palm with star of David in field **Rev:** Value **Edge:** Plain **Note:** In sets only.

Date	Mintage	F12	VF20	XF40	MS60	MS63
JE5734 (1974) (j) Sets only	92,868	—	—	—	—	0.75
JE5735 (1975) (j) Sets only	61,686	—	—	—	—	1.00
JE5736 (1976) (j) Sets only	64,654	—	—	—	—	0.75
JE5737 (1977) (j) Sets only	37,208	—	—	—	—	1.00
JE5738 (1978) (j) Sets only	57,072	—	—	—	—	0.75
JE5739 (1979) (j) Sets only	31,590	—	—	—	—	1.00

KM# 65 10 AGOROT

Copper-Nickel, 21.5 mm. **Series:** Independence Day **Subject:** Declaration of Independence; Israel's 25th Anniversary **Obv:** Date palm **Rev:** Value **Edge:** Plain **Note:** In sets only.

Date	Mintage	F12	VF20	XF40	MS60	MS63
JE5733 (1973) (j) Sets only	98,107	—	—	—	—	0.75

KM# 98 10 AGOROT

Nickel, 21.5 mm. **Subject:** 25th Anniversary of Bank of Israel **Obv:** Date palm **Rev:** Value **Edge:** Plain **Note:** Struck for sets only.

Date	Mintage	F12	VF20	XF40	MS60	MS63
JE5740 (1980) (b) Sets only	35,000	—	—	—	—	2.00

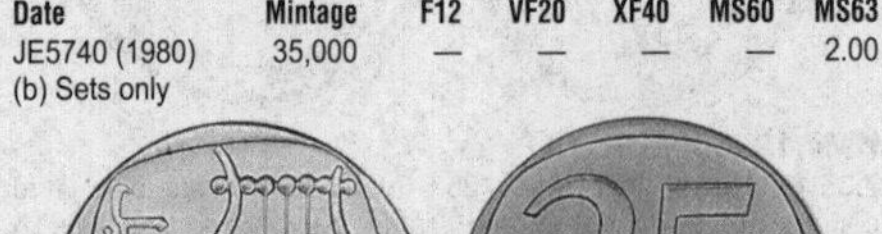

KM# 27 25 AGOROT

6.50 g., Aluminum-Bronze, 25.5 mm. **Obv:** Three-string lyre **Rev:** Value **Edge:** Plain

Date	Mintage	F12	VF20	XF40	MS60	MS63
JE5720 (1960) (b)	40,000	—	—	0.25	0.50	3.00
JE5720 (1960) (t)	4,351,000	—	—	0.25	0.50	3.00
JE5721 (1961) (b)	2,010,000	—	—	0.15	0.25	1.00
JE5721 (1961) (t)	2,994,000	—	—	0.15	0.25	1.00
JE5721 (1961) (u)	5,000	—	—	0.15	0.25	1.00
JE5722 (1962) (t)	882,000	—	—	0.20	0.40	1.50
JE5723 (1963) (t)	194,000	—	—	0.50	1.00	4.00
JE5724 (1964)	—	—	—	—	—	—
Note: Five trial pieces only						
JE5725 (1965) (t)	186,544	—	—	0.50	1.00	2.00
JE5726 (1966) (t)	320,000	—	—	—	0.25	0.50
JE5727 (1967) (j)	325,041	—	—	—	0.25	0.50
JE5728 (1968) (j)	445,000	—	—	—	0.25	0.50

Date	Mintage	F12	VF20	XF40	MS60	MS63
JE5729 (1969) (j)	432,004	—	—	—	0.25	0.50
JE5730 (1970) (j)	417,000	—	—	—	0.25	0.50
JE5731 (1971) (j)	500,030	—	—	—	0.25	0.50
JE5732 (1972) (j)	1,883,000	—	—	—	0.20	0.40
JE5733 (1973) (j)	3,770,000	—	—	—	0.20	0.40
JE5734 (1974) (j)	2,320,000	—	—	—	0.20	0.40
JE5735 (1975) (j)	3,968,000	—	—	—	0.20	0.40
JE5736 (1976) (j)	3,901,000	—	—	—	0.20	0.40
JE5737 (1977) (j)	1,832,000	—	—	—	0.20	0.40
JE5738 (1978) (j)	12,200,000	—	—	—	0.15	0.40
JE5739 (1979) (j)	10,842,140	—	—	—	0.15	0.40

KM# 27a 25 AGOROT

6.50 g., Aluminum-Bronze, 25.5 mm. **Obv:** Three stringed lyre with star of David in field **Rev:** Value **Edge:** Plain

Date	Mintage	F12	VF20	XF40	MS60	MS63
JE5731 (1971) (j) Sets only	125,921	—	—	—	—	0.75
JE5732 (1972) (j) Sets only	68,513	—	—	—	—	0.75

KM# 27b 25 AGOROT

Copper-Nickel, 25.5 mm. **Obv:** Three stringed lyre with star of David in field **Rev:** Value **Edge:** Plain **Note:** Struck for sets only.

Date	Mintage	F12	VF20	XF40	MS60	MS63
JE5734 (1974) (j) Sets only	92,868	—	—	—	—	0.75
JE5735 (1975) (j) Sets only	61,686	—	—	—	—	1.00
JE5736 (1976) (j) Sets only	64,654	—	—	—	—	0.75
JE5737 (1977) (j) Sets only	37,208	—	—	—	—	1.00
JE5738 (1978) (j) Sets only	57,072	—	—	—	—	0.75
JE5739 (1979) (j) Sets only	31,590	—	—	—	—	1.00

KM# 66 25 AGOROT

Copper-Nickel, 25.5 mm. **Series:** Independence Day **Subject:** Declaration of Independence; Israel's 25th Anniversary **Obv:** Three-string lyre **Rev:** Value **Note:** Struck for sets only.

Date	Mintage	F12	VF20	XF40	MS60	MS63
JE5733 (1973) (j) Sets only	98,107	—	—	—	—	0.75

KM# 99 25 AGOROT

Nickel, 25.5 mm. **Subject:** 25th Anniversary of Bank of Israel **Obv:** Three-string lyre **Rev:** Value **Note:** Struck for sets only.

Date	Mintage	F12	VF20	XF40	MS60	MS63
JE5740 (1980) (b) Sets only	35,000	—	—	—	—	2.00

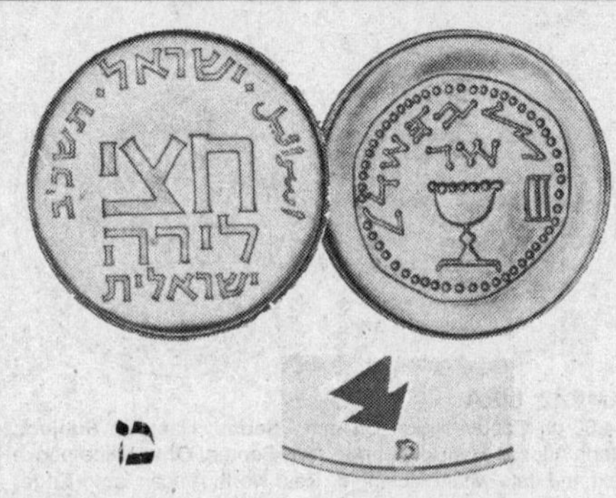

KM# 31 1/2 LIRA

Copper-Nickel, 30 mm. **Subject:** Feast of Purim **Obv:** Inscription **Rev:** Chalice within beaded circle **Edge:** Plain

Date	Mintage	F12	VF20	XF40	MS60	MS63
JE5721 (1961) (u)	19,939	—	—	—	—	5.00
JE5721 (1961) (u)	4,901	PF63 10.00				
JE5722 (1962) (u)	19,890	—	—	—	—	6.00
JE5722 (1962) (u)	9,894	PF63 9.00				

KM# 36.1 1/2 LIRA

6.80 g., Copper-Nickel, 24.5 mm. **Obv:** Menorah flanked by sprigs **Rev:** Value **Edge:** Reeded

Date	Mintage	F12	VF20	XF40	MS60	MS63
JE5723 (1963) (t) Large animals	5,593,000	—	—	0.50	2.00	5.00
JE5723 (1963) (b) Small animals	14,000	—	—	3.00	15.00	30.00
JE5724 (1964) (t)	3,761,890	—	—	0.25	0.75	2.00
JE5725 (1965) (t)	1,551,167	—	—	0.15	0.25	1.00
JE5726 (1966) (t)	2,139,000	—	—	0.15	0.25	0.60
JE5727 (1967) (j)	1,941,579	—	—	0.15	0.25	0.60
JE5728 (1968) (j)	1,183,000	—	—	0.15	0.25	0.75
JE5729 (1969) (j)	450,000	—	—	0.20	0.50	1.00
JE5730 (1970) (j)	1,001,023	—	—	0.15	0.25	0.75
JE5731 (1971) (j)	500,008	—	—	0.20	0.50	1.00
JE5732 (1972) (j)	421,000	—	—	0.20	0.50	1.00
JE5733 (1973) (b)	3,115,000	—	—	0.15	0.25	0.60
JE5733 (1973) (j)	110,000	—	—	0.15	0.25	0.60
JE5734 (1974) (j)	4,275,015	—	—	0.15	0.25	0.60
JE5735 (1975) (c)	5,000,010	—	—	0.15	0.25	0.60
JE5735 (1975) (j)	6,066,000	—	—	0.15	0.25	0.60
JE5736 (1976) (j)	4,959,000	—	—	0.15	0.25	0.60
JE5737 (1977) (j)	4,983,010	—	—	0.15	0.25	0.60
JE5738 (1978) (j)	14,325,000	—	—	0.10	0.15	0.50
JE5739 (1979) (j)	21,391,170	—	—	0.10	0.15	0.50

KM# 36.2 1/2 LIRA

6.80 g., Copper-Nickel, 24.5 mm. **Obv:** Menorah with star of David in field flanked by sprigs **Rev:** Value **Edge:** Reeded **Note:** Struck for sets only.

Date	Mintage	F12	VF20	XF40	MS60	MS63
JE5731 (1971) (j) Sets only	125,921	—	—	—	—	1.00
JE5732 (1972) (j) Sets only	68,513	—	—	—	—	1.00
JE5734 (1974) (j) Sets only	92,868	—	—	—	—	1.00
JE5735(1975) (j) Sets only	61,686	—	—	—	—	1.00
JE5736 (1976) (j) Sets only	64,654	—	—	—	—	1.00
JE5737 (1977) (j) Sets only	37,208	—	—	—	—	1.25
JE5738 (1978) (j) Sets only	57,072	—	—	—	—	1.00
JE5739 (1979) (j) Sets only	31,590	—	—	—	—	1.25

KM# 67 1/2 LIRA

6.80 g., Copper-Nickel, 24.5 mm. **Series:** Independence Day **Subject:** Declaration of Independence; Israel's 25th Anniversary **Obv:** Menorah flanked by sprigs **Rev:** Value **Edge:** Reeded **Note:** Struck for sets only.

Date	Mintage	F12	VF20	XF40	MS60	MS63
JE5733 (1973) (j) Sets only	98,107	—	—	—	—	1.50

KM# 100 1/2 LIRA

Nickel, 24.5 mm. **Subject:** 25th Anniversary of Bank of Israel **Obv:** Menorah flanked by sprigs **Rev:** Value **Edge:** Reeded **Note:** Struck for sets only.

Date	Mintage	F12	VF20	XF40	MS60	MS63
JE5740 (1980) (b) Sets only	35,000	—	—	—	—	3.00

KM# 22 LIRA

14.00 g., Copper-Nickel, 32 mm. **Series:** Hanukka **Subject:** Law Is Light **Obv:** Value to upper right of text and date **Rev:** Menorah flanked by stars with text below **Edge:** Smooth

Date	Mintage	F12	VF20	XF40	MS60	MS63
JE5719-1958 (b)	149,594	—	—	—	—	2.00
JE5719-1958 (b)	—	PF63 20.00				

KM# 28 LIRA

14.00 g., Copper-Nickel, 32 mm. **Series:** Hanukka **Subject:** 50th Anniversary of Deganya, Oldest Kibbutz, founded in 1909 **Obv:** Text at upper left of desert scene **Rev:** Text at upper and lower left of value **Edge:** Plain

Date	Mintage	F12	VF20	XF40	MS60	MS63
JE5720-1960 (u)	49,455	—	—	—	—	3.00
JE5720-1960 (u)	4,702	PF63 20.00				

KM# 32 LIRA
14.00 g., Copper-Nickel, 32 mm. **Series:** Hanukka **Subject:** Henrietta Szold **Obv:** Block-like design **Rev:** Seated hooded figure holding lamb **Edge:** Smooth

Date	Mintage	F12	VF20	XF40	MS60	MS63
JE5721-1960 (u)	16,781	—	—	—	—	14.00
JE5721-1960 (u)	3,000	**PF63** 85.00				

KM# 34 LIRA
14.00 g., Copper-Nickel, 32 mm. **Series:** Hanukka **Subject:** Macabbean Hero **Obv:** Large torch flanked by text with small value at upper right **Rev:** Rearing elephant **Edge:** Plain

Date	Mintage	F12	VF20	XF40	MS60	MS63
JE5722-1961 (u)	18,801	—	—	—	5.00	7.00
JE5722-1961 (u)	9,324	**PF63** 8.00				

KM# 38 LIRA
14.00 g., Copper-Nickel, 32 mm. **Series:** Hanukka **Subject:** Italian Hanukka Lamp, 17th Century **Obv:** Italian lamp **Rev:** Value above text and date **Edge:** Plain

Date	Mintage	F12	VF20	XF40	MS60	MS63
JE5723-1962 (b)	9,560	—	—	—	11.00	13.00
JE5723-1962 (b)	5,941	**PF63** 25.00				

KM# 37 LIRA
9.00 g., Copper-Nickel, 27.5 mm. **Obv:** Menorah flanked by sprigs **Rev:** Value **Edge:** Reeded

Date	Mintage	F12	VF20	XF40	MS60	MS63
JE5723 (1963) Large animals	4,212,000	—	—	0.50	1.50	3.00
JE5723 (1963) Small animals	Inc. above	—	—	1.00	10.00	30.00
JE5724 (1964)	—	—	—	—	—	—
Note: Only ten trial pieces struck						
JE5725 (1965) (t)	166,053	—	—	0.40	0.75	1.50
JE5726 (1966) (t)	290,000	—	—	0.40	0.75	1.50
JE5727 (1967) (j)	180,066	—	—	0.40	0.75	1.50

KM# 42 LIRA
14.00 g., Copper-Nickel, 32 mm. **Series:** Hanukka **Subject:** North Aftrican Hanukka Lamp, 18th Century **Obv:** Value above text and date within rectangle **Rev:** North African lamp **Edge:** Plain

Date	Mintage	F12	VF20	XF40	MS60	MS63
JE5724-1963 (u)	9,928	—	—	—	10.00	12.00
JE5724-1963 (u)	5,412	**PF63** 25.00				

KM# 47.1 LIRA
9.00 g., Copper-Nickel, 27.5 mm. **Obv:** Pomegranates **Rev:** Value flanked by stars above text **Edge:** Segmented reeding

Date	Mintage	F12	VF20	XF40	MS60	MS63
JE5727 (1967) (j)	3,830,388	—	—	0.15	0.30	1.00
JE5728 (1968) (j)	3,932,061	—	—	0.15	0.30	1.00
JE5729 (1969) (j)	12,484,016	—	—	0.15	0.25	0.75
JE5730 (1970) (j)	4,793,663	—	—	0.15	0.30	0.75
JE5731 (1971) (j)	2,993,000	—	—	0.15	0.30	0.75
JE5732 (1972) (j)	2,485,041	—	—	0.15	0.30	0.75
JE5733 (1973) (b)	10,115,000	—	—	0.15	0.25	0.75
JE5733 (1973) (j)	150,000	—	—	0.15	0.25	0.75
JE5734 (1974) (j)	2,287,000	—	—	0.15	0.25	0.75
JE5734 (1974) (o)	4,000,000	—	—	0.15	0.25	0.75
JE5735 (1975) (c)	6,000,000	—	—	0.15	0.25	0.75
JE5735 (1975) (j)	7,225,000	—	—	0.15	0.25	0.75
JE5736 (1976) (j)	4,268,000	—	—	0.15	0.30	1.00
JE5737 (1977) (j)	11,129,000	—	—	0.10	0.25	0.75
JE5738 (1978) (wg)	36,391,000	—	—	0.10	0.25	0.75
JE5738 (1978) (j)	25,361,000	—	—	0.10	0.25	0.75
JE5739 (1979) (j)	10,615,464	—	—	0.10	0.25	0.75
JE5739 (1979) (o)	24,200,000	—	—	0.10	0.25	0.75
JE5740 (1980) (j)	10,840,424	—	—	0.25	0.40	1.00

Note: Most of the 5740 dated coins were melted down before being issued.

KM# 47.2 LIRA
9.00 g., Copper-Nickel, 27.5 mm. **Obv:** Pomegranates with star of David in field **Rev:** Value flanked by stars above text **Edge:** Segmented reeding **Note:** Struck for sets only.

Date	Mintage	F12	VF20	XF40	MS60	MS63
JE5731 (1971) (j) Sets only	125,921	—	—	—	—	1.00
JE5732 (1972) (j) Sets only	68,513	—	—	—	—	1.00
JE5734 (1974) (j) Sets only	92,868	—	—	—	—	1.00
JE5735 (1975) (j) Sets only	61,686	—	—	—	—	1.00
JE5736 (1976) (j) Sets only	64,654	—	—	—	—	1.00
JE5737 (1977) (j) Sets only	37,208	—	—	—	—	1.50
JE5738 (1978) (j) Sets only	57,072	—	—	—	—	1.00
JE5739 (1979) (j) Sets only	31,590	—	—	—	—	1.50

KM# 68 LIRA
9.00 g., Copper-Nickel, 27.5 mm. **Series:** Independence Day **Subject:** Declaration of Independence; Israel's 25th Anniversary **Obv:** Pomegranates with star of David in field **Rev:** Value flanked by stars above text **Edge:** Segmented reeding **Note:** Struck for sets only.

Date	Mintage	F12	VF20	XF40	MS60	MS63
JE5733 (1973) (j) Sets only	98,107	—	—	—	—	1.00

KM# 101 LIRA
9.00 g., Nickel, 27.5 mm. **Subject:** 25th Anniversary of Bank of Israel **Obv:** Pomegranates with star of David in field **Rev:** Value flanked by stars above text **Edge:** Segmented reeding

Date	Mintage	F12	VF20	XF40	MS60	MS63
JE5740 (1980) (b) Sets only	35,000	—	—	—	—	4.00

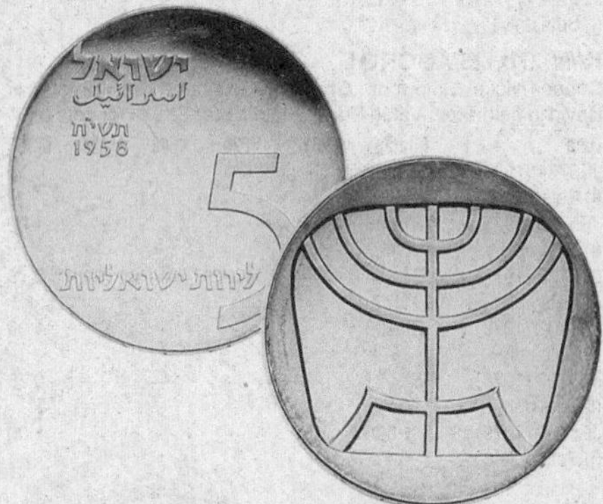

KM# 21 5 LIROT
25.00 g., 0.900 Silver 0.7234 oz. ASW, 34 mm. **Series:** Independence Day **Subject:** Menorah; Israel's 10th Anniversary **Obv:** Large value at lower right of text **Rev:** Menorah **Edge:** Hebrew lettering **Note:** Dav. #258.

Date	Mintage	VF20	XF40	MS60	MS63	MS65
JE5718-1958 (u)	97,860	—	—	25.00	28.00	32.00
JE5718-1958 (u) Frosted Proof	2,000	**PF65** 220				

KM# 23 5 LIROT
25.00 g., 0.900 Silver 0.7234 oz. ASW, 34 mm. **Series:** Independence Day **Subject:** Ingathering of the Exiles; Israel's 11th Anniversary **Obv:** Value at lower right of text **Rev:** Ingathering of exiles **Edge:** Hebrew lettering **Note:** Dav. #259.

Date	Mintage	VF20	XF40	MS60	MS63	MS65
JE5719-1959 (b)	27,016	—	—	25.00	28.00	32.00
JE5719-1959 (b)	4,682	**PF65** 42.00				

KM# 29 5 LIROT
25.00 g., 0.900 Silver 0.7234 oz. ASW, 34 mm. **Series:** Independence Day **Subject:** 100th Anniversary of Birth of Theodore Herzl; Israel's 12th Anniversary **Obv:** Value at lower right of text **Rev:** Head left within square at upper right **Edge:** Hebrew lettering **Note:** Dav. #29.

Date	Mintage	VF20	XF40	MS60	MS63	MS65
JE5720-1960 (b)	34,281	—	—	25.00	28.00	32.00
JE5720-1960 (b)	4,827	PF65 42.00				

KM# 33 5 LIROT
25.00 g., 0.900 Silver 0.7234 oz. ASW, 34 mm. **Series:** Independence Day **Subject:** Bar Mitzvah; Israel's 13th Anniversary **Obv:** Olive branch with 10 leaves and 3 olives **Rev:** Ark of the law with 6 torah **Edge:** Hebrew lettering **Note:** Dav. #261.

Date	Mintage	VF20	XF40	MS60	MS63	MS65
JE5721-1961 (u)	19,363	—	—	28.00	32.00	35.00
JE5721-1961 (u)	4,455	PF65 55.00				

KM# 35 5 LIROT
25.00 g., 0.900 Silver 0.7234 oz. ASW, 34 mm. **Series:** Independence Day **Subject:** Israel Shall Blossom; Israel's 14th Anniversary **Rev:** Negev Industrialization **Edge:** Hebrew lettering **Note:** Dav. #262.

Date	Mintage	VF20	XF40	MS60	MS63	MS65
JE5722-1962 (u)	10,380	—	—	28.00	28.00	35.00
JE5722-1962 (u)	4,960	PF65 45.00				

KM# 39 5 LIROT
25.00 g., 0.900 Silver 0.7234 oz. ASW, 34 mm. **Series:** Independence Day **Subject:** Seafaring; Israel's 15th Anniversary **Obv:** Value and star within upright design **Rev:** Longship **Edge:** Hebrew lettering **Note:** Dav. #263.

Date	Mintage	VF20	XF40	MS60	MS63	MS65
JE5723-1963 (r)	5,960	—	—	180	190	200
JE5723-1963 (r)	4,495	PF65 210				

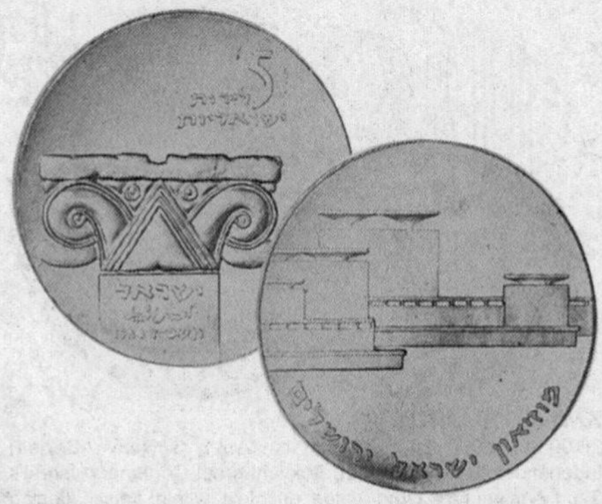

KM# 43 5 LIROT
25.00 g., 0.900 Silver 0.7234 oz. ASW, 34 mm. **Series:** Independence Day **Subject:** Israel Museum; Israel's 16th Anniversary **Obv:** Israel Museum **Rev:** Ionic style column with value at upper right **Edge:** Hebrew lettering **Note:** Dav. #264.

Date	Mintage	VF20	XF40	MS60	MS63	MS65
JE5724-1964 (r)	10,967	—	—	34.00	37.00	40.00
JE5724-1964 (r)	4,421	PF65 40.00				

KM# 45 5 LIROT
25.00 g., 0.900 Silver 0.7234 oz. ASW, 34 mm. **Series:** Independence Day **Subject:** Knesset; Israel's 17th Anniversary **Rev:** Knesset Building **Edge:** Hebrew lettering **Note:** Dav. #265.

Date	Mintage	VF20	XF40	MS60	MS63	MS65
JE5725-1965 (r)	25,147	—	—	25.00	28.00	32.00
JE5725-1965 (r)	7,537	PF65 40.00				

KM# 46 5 LIROT
25.00 g., 0.900 Silver 0.7234 oz. ASW, 34 mm. **Series:** Independence Day **Subject:** People of Israel Live On; Israel's 18th Anniversary **Rev:** Abstract design **Edge:** Hebrew lettering **Note:** Dav. #266.

Date	Mintage	VF20	XF40	MS60	MS63	MS65
JE5726-1966 (u)	32,356	—	—	25.00	28.00	32.00
JE5726-1966 (u)	10,368	PF65 40.00				

KM# 48 5 LIROT
25.00 g., 0.900 Silver 0.7234 oz. ASW, 34 mm. **Series:** Independence Day **Subject:** Port of Eilat; Israel's 19th Anniversary **Obv:** Large stylized value **Rev:** Port of Eilat **Edge:** Hebrew lettering **Note:** Dav. #267.

Date	Mintage	VF20	XF40	MS60	MS63	MS65
JE5727-1967 (u)	30,158	—	—	25.00	28.00	32.00
JE5727-1967 (u)	7,680	PF65 40.00				
JE5727-1967 (u) Frosted Proof	Inc. above	PF65 70.00				

KM# 69.1 5 LIROT
20.00 g., 0.750 Silver 0.4823 oz. ASW, 34 mm. **Series:** Hanukka **Subject:** Russian Hanukka Lamp, 18th Century **Obv:** Menorah flanked by sprigs to left of value with text around top half **Rev:** Russian lamp **Edge:** Plain

Date	Mintage	VF20	XF40	MS60	MS63	MS65
JE5733-1972 (j)	74,506	—	—	14.00	16.00	17.00

KM# 69.2 5 LIROT
20.00 g., 0.750 Silver 0.4823 oz. ASW, 34 mm. **Series:** Hanukka **Subject:** Russian Hanukka Lamp, 18th Century **Obv:** Menorah flanked by sprigs to left of value with text around top half **Rev:** Russian lamp **Edge:** Reeded

Date	Mintage	VF20	XF40	MS60	MS63	MS65
JE5733-1972 (j)	22,336	PF65 18.00				

KM# 75.1 5 LIROT
20.00 g., 0.500 Silver 0.3215 oz. ASW, 34 mm. **Series:** Hanukka **Subject:** Babylonian (Iraqi) Hanukka Lamp, 20th Century **Rev:** Babylonian lamp **Edge:** Plain

Date	Mintage	VF20	XF40	MS60	MS63	MS65
JE5734-1973 (j)	94,686	—	—	12.00	13.50	15.00

KM# 75.2 5 LIROT
20.00 g., 0.500 Silver 0.3215 oz. ASW, 34 mm. **Series:** Hanukka **Subject:** Babylonian (Iraqi) Hanukka Lamp, 20th Century **Rev:** Babylonian lamp **Edge:** Reeded

Date	Mintage	VF20	XF40	MS60	MS63	MS65
JE5734-1973 (j)	44,860	PF65 16.00				

KM# 90 5 LIROT
11.20 g., Copper-Nickel, 30 mm. **Obv:** Roaring lion left with menorah above **Rev:** Value flanked by stars **Edge:** Smooth

Date	Mintage	VF20	XF40	MS60	MS63	MS65
JE5738 (1978) (j)	8,350,000	0.40	1.00	3.00	5.00	—
JE5739 (1979) (j)	5,646,428	0.40	1.00	2.50	4.00	—
JE5739 (1979) (c)	32,000,000	0.40	1.00	2.50	4.00	—

KM# 90a 5 LIROT
11.20 g., Copper-Nickel, 30 mm. **Obv:** Roaring lion left with star of David in field **Rev:** Value flanked by stars **Edge:** Smooth **Note:** Struck for sets only.

Date	Mintage	VF20	XF40	MS60	MS63	MS65
JE5739 (1979)	31,590	—	—	3.00	5.00	—

(j) Sets only

KM# 102 5 LIROT
Nickel, 30 mm. **Subject:** 25th Anniversary of Bank of Israel **Obv:** Roaring lion left with menorah above **Rev:** Value flanked by stars **Edge:** Smooth **Note:** Struck for sets only.

Date	Mintage	VF20	XF40	MS60	MS63	MS65
JE5740 (1980)	35,000	—	—	3.00	7.00	—
(b) Sets only						

KM# 49 10 LIROT
26.00 g., 0.900 Silver 0.7523 oz. ASW, 37 mm. **Subject:** Six Day War Victory **Obv:** Artistic star-like design with a sprig wrapped around the sword with text below **Rev:** Wailing Wall with text around bottom **Edge:** "28 Iyar-2 Sivan 5727" and small stars **Note:** Dav. #268.

Date	Mintage	VF20	XF40	MS60	MS63	MS65
JE5727-1967 (b)	234,461	—	—	25.00	28.00	32.00

KM# 49a 10 LIROT
26.00 g., 0.935 Silver 0.7816 oz. ASW, 37 mm. **Subject:** Six Day War Victory **Obv:** Artistic star-like design with sprig wrapped around sword with text below **Rev:** Wailing Wall with text below **Edge:** 28 Iyar-2 Sivan 5727 and three small diamonds **Note:** Dav. #268.

Date	Mintage	VF20	XF40	MS60	MS63	MS65
JE5727-1967 (k)	50,380	PF65 40.00				

KM# 51 10 LIROT
26.00 g., 0.935 Silver 0.7816 oz. ASW, 37 mm. **Series:** Independence Day **Subject:** Reunification of Jerusalem; Israel's 20th Anniversary **Obv:** Building with pillars with text and dates below **Rev:** City view to right of menorah flanked by sprigs **Edge:** Hebrew lettering **Edge Lettering:** Hebrew **Note:** Dav. #269.

Date	Mintage	VF20	XF40	MS60	MS63	MS65
JE5728-1968 (b)	49,996	—	—	25.00	28.00	32.00
JE5728-1968 (b)	20,494	PF65 45.00				

KM# 53 10 LIROT
26.00 g., 0.900 Silver 0.7523 oz. ASW, 37 mm. **Series:** Independence Day **Subject:** Peace and Unknown Soldier; Israel's 21st Anniversary **Obv:** Pyramid of block letters **Rev:** Shalom **Edge:** Hebrew lettering

Date	Mintage	VF20	XF40	MS60	MS63	MS65
JE5729-1969 (s)	39,884	—	—	25.00	28.00	32.00
JE5729-1969 (s)	19,838	PF65 40.00				
JE5729-1969 (k)	20,185	—	—	33.00	37.00	40.00

Note: Hebrew letter KOF below helmet

KM# 55 10 LIROT
26.00 g., 0.900 Silver 0.7523 oz. ASW, 37 mm. **Series:** Independence Day **Subject:** Mikveh Israel Centenary; Israel's 22nd Anniversary **Obv:** Value and text within artistic design **Rev:** Mikveh Israel Centenary **Edge:** Hebrew lettering **Edge Lettering:** Hebrew

Date	Mintage	VF20	XF40	MS60	MS63	MS65
JE5730-1970 (k)	47,509	—	—	25.00	28.00	32.00
JE5730-1970 (b)	22,434	PF65 35.00				

KM# 56.1 10 LIROT
26.00 g., 0.900 Silver 0.7523 oz. ASW, 37 mm. **Subject:** Pidyon Haben **Obv:** Menorah flanked by sprigs at upper left of text **Rev:** Text among the letter M flanked by diamonds **Edge:** Plain

Date	Mintage	VF20	XF40	MS60	MS63	MS65
JE5730-1970 (j)	48,847	—	—	22.00	25.00	32.00

KM# 56.2 10 LIROT
26.00 g., 0.900 Silver 0.7523 oz. ASW, 37 mm. **Subject:** Pidyon Haben **Obv:** Menorah flanked by sprigs to upper left of text **Rev:** Text within letter M flanked by diamonds **Edge:** Reeded

Date	Mintage	VF20	XF40	MS60	MS63	MS65
JE5730-1970 (s)	14,719	PF65 35.00				

KM# 57.1 10 LIROT
26.00 g., 0.900 Silver 0.7523 oz. ASW, 37 mm. **Subject:** Pidyon Haben **Obv:** Menorah flanked by sprigs to upper left of text **Rev:** Text within letter M flanked by diamonds **Edge:** Plain

Date	Mintage	VF20	XF40	MS60	MS63	MS65
JE5731-1971 (j)	30,144	—	—	25.00	28.00	32.00

KM# 57.2 10 LIROT
26.00 g., 0.900 Silver 0.7523 oz. ASW, 37 mm. **Subject:** Pidyon Haben **Obv:** Menorah flanked by sprigs to upper left of text **Rev:** Text within letter M flanked by diamonds **Edge:** Reeded

Date	Mintage	VF20	XF40	MS60	MS63	MS65
JE5731-1971 (s)	13,897	PF65 35.00				

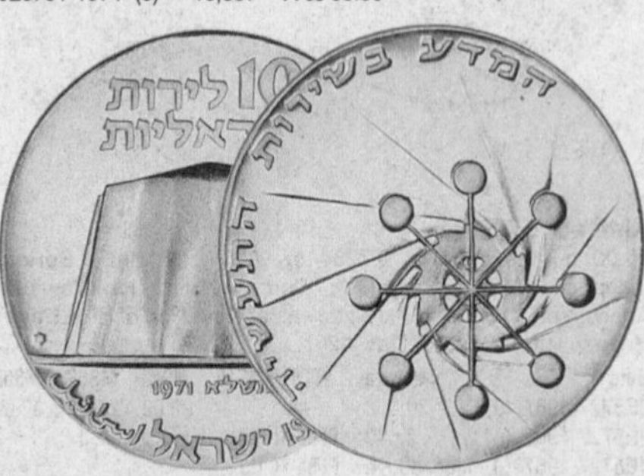

KM# 58 10 LIROT
26.00 g., 0.900 Silver 0.7523 oz. ASW, 37 mm. **Series:** Independence Day **Subject:** Science in the Service of Industry; Israel's 23rd Anniversary **Obv:** Stylized atomic reactor **Rev:** Molecule, cog wheel **Edge:** Hebrew lettering

Date	Mintage	VF20	XF40	MS60	MS63	MS65
JE5731-1971 (u)	29,943	—	—	25.00	28.00	32.00
Without star						
JE5731-1971 (j)	22,697	—	—	25.00	28.00	32.00
With star						
JE5731-1971 (u)	17,481	PF65 40.00				

KM# 59.1 10 LIROT
26.00 g., 0.900 Silver 0.7523 oz. ASW, 37 mm. **Subject:** Let My People Go **Obv:** Menorah flanked by sprigs to upper left of text and date **Rev:** Text within rectangle **Edge:** Plain

Date	Mintage	VF20	XF40	MS60	MS63	MS65
JE5731-1971 (j)	73,444	—	—	25.00	28.00	32.00
JE5731-1971 (j)	20,132	PF65 38.00				

KM# 59.2 10 LIROT
26.00 g., 0.900 Silver 0.7523 oz. ASW, 37 mm. **Subject:** Let My People Go **Obv:** Menorah flanked by sprigs to upper left of text and date **Rev:** Text within rectangle **Edge:** Plain **Note:** Bern die, open "mem".

Date	Mintage	VF20	XF40	MS60	MS63	MS65
JE5731-1971 (j)	80	PF65 700				

KM# 61.1 10 LIROT
26.00 g., 0.900 Silver 0.7523 oz. ASW, 37 mm. **Subject:** Pidyon Haben **Obv:** Menorah flanked by sprigs below value and text **Rev:** Text within the letter M flanked by diamonds **Edge:** Plain

Date	Mintage	VF20	XF40	MS60	MS63	MS65
JE5732-1972	29,744	—	—	25.00	28.00	32.00
(j) With star						
JE5732-1972	14,944	—	—	25.00	28.00	32.00
(j) Without star						

KM# 61.2 10 LIROT
26.00 g., 0.900 Silver 0.7523 oz. ASW, 37 mm. **Subject:** Pidyon Haben **Obv:** Menorah flanked by sprigs below value and text **Rev:** Text within letter M flanked by diamonds **Edge:** Reeded

Date	Mintage	VF20	XF40	MS60	MS63	MS65
JE5732-1972 (j)	12,443	PF65 35.00				

KM# 62 10 LIROT
26.00 g., 0.900 Silver 0.7523 oz. ASW, 37 mm. **Series:** Independence Day **Subject:** Israeli Aviation; Israel's 24th Anniversary **Obv:** Value as the 1 being a rocket **Rev:** Flying jet **Edge:** Lettered

Date	Mintage	VF20	XF40	MS60	MS63	MS65
JE5732-1972 (j)	49,832	—	—	25.00	28.00	32.00
JE5732-1972 (j)	14,989	PF65 40.00				

KM# 70.1 10 LIROT
26.00 g., 0.900 Silver 0.7523 oz. ASW, 37 mm. **Subject:** Pidyon Haben **Obv:** Menorah flanked by sprigs above text **Rev:** Artistic design within oblong circle **Edge:** Plain

Date	Mintage	VF20	XF40	MS60	MS63	MS65
JE5733-1973 (j)	100,676	—	—	25.00	27.00	30.00

KM# 70.2 10 LIROT
26.00 g., 0.900 Silver 0.7523 oz. ASW, 37 mm. **Subject:** Pidyon Haben **Obv:** Menorah flanked by sprigs above text **Rev:** Artistic designs within oblong circle **Edge:** Reeded

Date	Mintage	VF20	XF40	MS60	MS63	MS65
JE5733-1973 (j)	14,837	PF65 35.00				

KM# 71 10 LIROT
26.00 g., 0.900 Silver 0.7523 oz. ASW, 37 mm. **Series:** Independence Day **Subject:** Declaration of Independence; Israel's 25th Anniversary **Obv:** Menorah flanked by sprigs above text **Rev:** Text on scroll **Edge:** Lettered

Date	Mintage	VF20	XF40	MS60	MS63	MS65
JE5733-1973 (j)	123,953	—	—	25.00	27.00	30.00
JE5733-1973 (j)	41,484	PF65 35.00				

KM# 76.1 10 LIROT
26.00 g., 0.900 Silver 0.7523 oz. ASW, 37 mm. **Subject:** Pidyon Haben **Obv:** Value above menorah flanked by sprigs **Rev:** Artistic design within oblong circle **Edge:** Plain

Date	Mintage	VF20	XF40	MS60	MS63	MS65
JE5734-1974 (j)	108,547	—	—	25.00	27.00	30.00

KM# 76.2 10 LIROT
26.00 g., 0.900 Silver 0.7523 oz. ASW, 37 mm. **Subject:** Pidyon Haben **Obv:** Value above menorah flanked by sprigs **Rev:** Artistic designs within oblong circle **Edge:** Reeded

Date	Mintage	VF20	XF40	MS60	MS63	MS65
JE5734-1974 (j)	44,348	PF65 35.00				

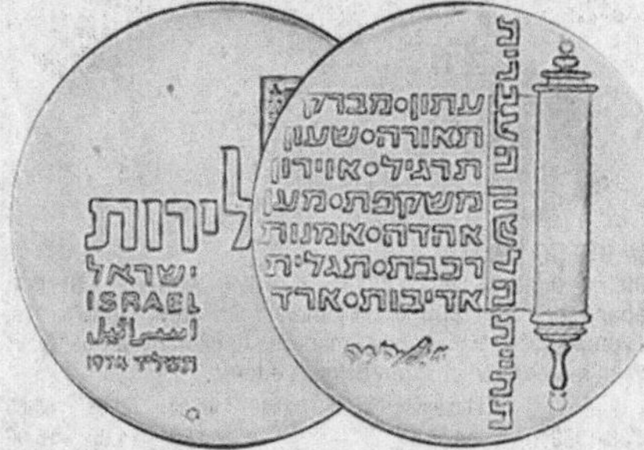

KM# 77 10 LIROT
26.00 g., 0.900 Silver 0.7523 oz. ASW, 37 mm. **Series:** Independence Day **Subject:** Revival of the Hebrew Language; Israel's 26th Anniversary **Obv:** Value at upper right of text **Rev:** Text to left of upright design **Edge:** Lettered

Date	Mintage	VF20	XF40	MS60	MS63	MS65
JE5734-1974 (j)	127,195	—	—	25.00	27.00	30.00
JE5734-1974 (j)	49,657	PF65 35.00				

KM# 78.1 10 LIROT
20.00 g., 0.500 Silver 0.3215 oz. ASW, 34 mm. **Series:** Hanukka **Subject:** Damascus (Syrian) Hanukka Lamp, 18th Century **Obv:** Value and date above text **Rev:** Damascus lamp **Edge:** Plain

Date	Mintage	VF20	XF40	MS60	MS63	MS65
JE5735-1974 (j)	74,112	—	—	12.00	13.00	15.00

KM# 78.2 10 LIROT
20.00 g., 0.500 Silver 0.3215 oz. ASW, 34 mm. **Series:** Hanukka **Subject:** Damascus (Syrian) Hanukka Lamp , 18th Century **Obv:** Value and date above text **Rev:** Damascus lamp **Edge:** Reeded

Date	Mintage	VF20	XF40	MS60	MS63	MS65
JE5735-1974 (j)	58,642	PF65 16.00				

KM# 84.1 10 LIROT
20.00 g., 0.500 Silver 0.3215 oz. ASW, 34 mm. **Series:** Hanukka **Subject:** Dutch Hanukka Lamp, 18th Century **Obv:** Value above text with date below **Rev:** Holland lamp **Edge:** Plain

Date	Mintage	VF20	XF40	MS60	MS63	MS65
JE5736-1975 (j)	44,215	—	—	12.00	13.00	15.00

KM# 84.2 10 LIROT
20.00 g., 0.500 Silver 0.3215 oz. ASW, 34 mm. **Series:** Hanukka **Subject:** Dutch Hanukka Lamp, 18th Century **Obv:** Value above text with date below **Rev:** Holland lamp **Edge:** Reeded

Date	Mintage	VF20	XF40	MS60	MS63	MS65
JE5736-1975 (j)	33,537	PF65 16.00				

KM# 87.1 10 LIROT
20.00 g., 0.500 Silver 0.3215 oz. ASW, 34 mm. **Series:** Hanukka **Subject:** Early American Hanukka Lamp **Obv:** Value within square **Rev:** U.S. lamp **Edge:** Plain

Date	Mintage	VF20	XF40	MS60	MS63	MS65
JE5737-1976 (j)	24,844	—	—	13.00	15.00	17.00

KM# 87.2 10 LIROT
20.00 g., 0.500 Silver 0.3215 oz. ASW, 34 mm. **Series:** Hanukka **Subject:** Early American Hanukka Lamp **Obv:** Value within square **Rev:** U.S. lamp **Edge:** Reeded

Date	Mintage	VF20	XF40	MS60	MS63	MS65
JE5737-1976 (j)	19,989	PF65 20.00				

KM# 91.1 10 LIROT
15.00 g., Copper-Nickel, 34 mm. **Series:** Hanukka **Subject:** Jerusalem Hanukka Lamp, 20th Century **Obv:** Text to left and below value **Rev:** Jerusalem lamp **Edge:** Plain

Date	Mintage	VF20	XF40	MS60	MS63	MS65
JE5738-1977 (j)	46,106	—	—	2.00	3.00	—

KM# 91.2 10 LIROT
15.00 g., Copper-Nickel, 34 mm. **Series:** Hanukka **Subject:** Jerusalem Hanukka Lamp, 20th Century **Obv:** Text to left and below value **Rev:** Jerusalem lamp **Edge:** Reeded **Note:** Open style "mem".

Date	Mintage	VF20	XF40	MS60	MS63	MS65
JE5738-1977 (j)	29,516	PF65 6.00				

KM# 91.3 10 LIROT
15.00 g., Copper-Nickel, 34 mm. **Series:** Hanukka **Subject:** Jerusalem Hanukka Lamp, 20th Century **Obv:** Text to left and below value **Rev:** Jerusalem lamp **Edge:** Reeded **Note:** Closed style "mem".

Date	Mintage	VF20	XF40	MS60	MS63	MS65
JE5738-1977 (j) Inc. above		PF65 8.00				

KM# 30 20 LIROT
7.99 g., 0.917 Gold 0.2355 oz. AGW, 22 mm. **Series:** Independence Day **Subject:** 100th Anniversary of Birth of Theodore Herzl; Israel's 12th Anniversary **Obv:** Menorah flanked by sprigs within beaded circle **Rev:** Head left within rectangle **Edge:** Reeded

Date	Mintage	VF20	XF40	MS60	MS63	MS65
JE5720-1960 (b)	10,460	—	—	—	400	425

KM# 79.1 25 LIROT
26.00 g., 0.935 Silver 0.7816 oz. ASW, 37 mm. **Subject:** 1st Anniversary of Death of David Ben-Gurion **Obv:** Menorah flanked by sprigs **Rev:** Head left within rectangle **Edge:** Plain

Date	Mintage	VF20	XF40	MS60	MS63	MS65
JE5735-1974 (j)	99,291	—	—	25.00	28.00	32.00

KM# 79.2 25 LIROT
26.00 g., 0.935 Silver 0.7816 oz. ASW, 37 mm. **Subject:** 1st Anniversary of Death of David Ben-Gurion **Obv:** Menorah flanked by sprigs **Rev:** Head left within rectangle **Edge:** Reeded

Date	Mintage	VF20	XF40	MS60	MS63	MS65
JE5735-1974 (b)	64,153	PF65 35.00				

KM# 80.1 25 LIROT
26.00 g., 0.900 Silver 0.7523 oz. ASW, 37 mm. **Series:** Pidyon Haben **Subject:** Pidyon Haben **Obv:** Menorah flanked by sprigs

above value **Rev:** Artistic designs within oblong circle **Edge:** Plain

Date	Mintage	VF20	XF40	MS60	MS63	MS65
JE5735-1975 (j)	62,187	—	—	25.00	28.00	32.00

KM# 80.2 25 LIROT

26.00 g., 0.900 Silver 0.7523 oz. ASW, 37 mm. **Series:** Pidyon Haben **Subject:** Pidyon Haben **Obv:** Menorah flanked by sprigs above value **Rev:** Artistic designs within oblong circle **Edge:** Reeded

Date	Mintage	VF20	XF40	MS60	MS63	MS65
JE5735-1975 (j)	49,192	PF65 35.00				

KM# 81 25 LIROT

30.00 g., 0.800 Silver 0.7716 oz. ASW, 40 mm. **Series:** Independence Day **Subject:** 25th Anniversary of Israel Bond Program; Israel's 27th Anniversary **Obv:** Large value above menorah flanked by sprigs **Rev:** Artistic design **Edge:** Lettered

Date	Mintage	VF20	XF40	MS60	MS63	MS65
JE5735-1975 (j)	49,140	—	—	25.00	28.00	35.00
JE5735-1975 (j)	39,847	PF65 40.00				

KM# 85 25 LIROT

26.00 g., 0.900 Silver 0.7523 oz. ASW, 37 mm. **Series:** Independence Day **Subject:** Strength to Israel; Israel's 28th Anniversary **Obv:** Value menorah flanked by sprigs **Rev:** Block-like text with star to upper left **Edge:** Lettered

Date	Mintage	VF20	XF40	MS60	MS63	MS65
JE5736-1976 (j)	37,813	—	—	25.00	28.00	32.00
JE5736-1976 (j)	27,471	PF65 40.00				

KM# 86.1 25 LIROT

30.00 g., 0.800 Silver 0.7716 oz. ASW, 40 mm. **Series:** Pidyon Haben **Subject:** Pidyon Haben **Obv:** Menorah flanked by sprigs at upper left above text **Rev:** Artistic star-like design **Edge:** Plain

Date	Mintage	VF20	XF40	MS60	MS63	MS65
JE5736-1976 (j)	37,345	—	—	25.00	28.00	32.00

KM# 86.2 25 LIROT

30.00 g., 0.800 Silver 0.7716 oz. ASW, 40 mm. **Series:** Pidyon Haben **Subject:** Pidyon Haben **Obv:** Menorah flanked by sprigs to upper left above text **Rev:** Artistic star-like design **Edge:** Reeded

Date	Mintage	VF20	XF40	MS60	MS63	MS65
JE5736-1976 (j)	29,430	PF65 40.00				

KM# 88 25 LIROT

20.00 g., 0.500 Silver 0.3215 oz. ASW, 34 mm. **Series:** Independence Day **Subject:** Brotherhood in Jerusalem; Israel's 29th Anniversary **Obv:** Large value above menorah flanked by sprigs **Rev:** Stylized bird below castle **Edge:** Lettered

Date	Mintage	VF20	XF40	MS60	MS63	MS65
JE5737-1977 (j)	36,976	—	—	12.00	13.00	15.00
JE5737-1977 (j)	26,735	PF65 18.00				

KM# 89.1 25 LIROT

26.00 g., 0.900 Silver 0.7523 oz. ASW, 37 mm. **Series:** Pidyon Haben **Subject:** Pidyon Haben **Obv:** Value above menorah flanked by sprigs **Rev:** Artistic star-like design **Edge:** Plain

Date	Mintage	VF20	XF40	MS60	MS63	MS65
JE5737-1977 (j)	32,089	—	—	25.00	28.00	32.00

KM# 89.2 25 LIROT

26.00 g., 0.900 Silver 0.7523 oz. ASW, 37 mm. **Series:** Pidyon Haben **Subject:** Pidyon Haben **Obv:** Value above menorah flanked by sprigs **Rev:** Artistic star-like design **Edge:** Reeded

Date	Mintage	VF20	XF40	MS60	MS63	MS65
JE5737-1977 (j)	18,541	PF65 40.00				

KM# 94.1 25 LIROT

15.00 g., Copper-Nickel, 34 mm. **Series:** Hanukka **Subject:** French Hanukka Lamp, 14th Century **Obv:** Value above text **Rev:** French lamp **Edge:** Plain

Date	Mintage	VF20	XF40	MS60	MS63	MS65
JE5739-1978 (j)	36,200	—	—	2.75	3.00	4.00

KM# 94.2 25 LIROT

15.00 g., Copper-Nickel, 34 mm. **Series:** Hanukka **Subject:** French Hanukka Lamp, 14th Century **Rev:** French lamp **Edge:** Reeded

Date	Mintage	VF20	XF40	MS60	MS63	MS65
JE5739-1978 (j)	22,300	PF65 5.00				

KM# 40 50 LIROT

13.34 g., 0.917 Gold 0.3933 oz. AGW, 27 mm. **Subject:** 10th Anniversary of Death of Chaim Weizmann **Obv:** Menorah flanked by sprigs within circle **Rev:** Bust left within rectangle **Edge:** Reeded

Date	Mintage	VF20	XF40	MS60	MS63	MS65
JE5723-1962 (b)	6,185	PF65 700				
Note: With "mem"						
JE5723-1962 (b)	10	PF65 2,000				
Note: Without "mem"						

KM# 44 50 LIROT

13.34 g., 0.917 Gold 0.3933 oz. AGW, 27 mm. **Subject:** 10th Anniversary of Bank of Israel **Obv:** Menorah flanked by sprigs **Rev:** Artistic design to upper right of text **Edge:** Reeded

Date	Mintage	VF20	XF40	MS60	MS63	MS65
JE5725-1964 (b)	5,975	—	—	640	660	675
JE5725-1964 (b)	1,502	PF65 2,350				
Note: Includes 702 used officially by the Bank of Israel						

KM# 72 50 LIROT

7.00 g., 0.900 Gold 0.2025 oz. AGW, 22 mm. **Series:** Independence Day **Subject:** Declaration of Independence; Israel's 25th Anniversary **Obv:** Menorah flanked by sprigs above text **Rev:** Text on scroll **Edge:** Reeded

Date	Mintage	VF20	XF40	MS60	MS63	MS65
JE5733-1973 (b)	27,724	PF65 375				

KM# 92.1 50 LIROT

20.00 g., 0.500 Silver 0.3215 oz. ASW, 34 mm. **Series:** Independence Day **Subject:** People United with its Land; Israel's 30th Anniversary **Obv:** Menorah flanked by sprigs above value **Rev:** Text within tree **Edge:** Lettered

Date	Mintage	VF20	XF40	MS60	MS63	MS65
JE5738-1978 (j)	40,402	—	—	12.00	13.00	15.00

KM# 92.2 50 LIROT

20.00 g., 0.500 Silver 0.3215 oz. ASW, 34 mm. **Series:** Independence Day **Subject:** People United with its Land; Israel's 30th Anniversary **Obv:** Menorah flanked by sprigs above value **Rev:** Text within tree **Edge:** Reeded

Date	Mintage	VF20	XF40	MS60	MS63	MS65
JE5738-1978 (b)	21,806	PF65 18.00				

KM# 95 50 LIROT

20.00 g., 0.500 Silver 0.3215 oz. ASW, 34 mm. **Series:** Independence Day **Subject:** Mother of Children; Israel's 31st Anniversary **Obv:** Value above menorah flanked by sprigs **Rev:** Stylized mother and children **Edge:** Lettered

Date	Mintage	VF20	XF40	MS60	MS63	MS65
JE5739-1979 (j)	24,108	—	—	13.00	14.00	16.00
JE5739-1979 (o)	16,102	PF65 20.00				

KM# 41 100 LIROT
26.68 g., 0.917 Gold 0.7866 oz. AGW, 33 mm. **Series:** 10th Anniversary - Death of Weizmann **Subject:** 10th Anniversary of Death of Chaim Weizmann **Obv:** Menorah flanked by sprigs within circle **Rev:** Head left within rectangle **Edge:** Reeded

Date	Mintage	VF20	XF40	MS60	MS63	MS65
JE5723-1962 (b)	6,186	PF65 1,350				
Note: With "mem"						
JE5723-1962 (b)	10	PF65 2,500				
Note: Without "mem"						

KM# 50 100 LIROT
26.68 g., 0.917 Gold 0.7866 oz. AGW, 33 mm. **Series:** Six Day War Victory **Subject:** Six Day War Victory **Obv:** Leafy sprig around sword within artistic star-like design **Rev:** Western Wall, Temple of Solomon **Edge:** Hebrew lettering

Date	Mintage	VF20	XF40	MS60	MS63	MS65
JE5727-1967 (b)	9,004	PF65 1,500				

KM# 52 100 LIROT
25.00 g., 0.800 Gold 0.643 oz. AGW, 33 mm. **Series:** Independence Day **Subject:** Reunification of Jerusalem; Israel's 20th Anniversary **Obv:** Building pillars, text and value **Rev:** Menorah flanked by sprigs to upper left of city view **Edge:** Plain

Date	Mintage	VF20	XF40	MS60	MS63	MS65
JE5728-1968 (b)	12,490	PF65 1,100				

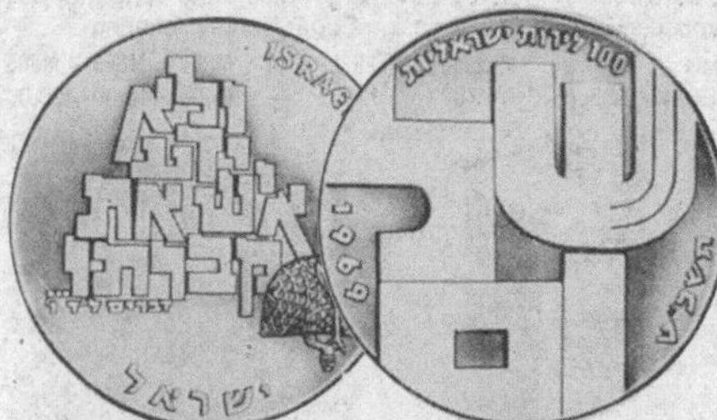

KM# 54 100 LIROT
25.00 g., 0.800 Gold 0.643 oz. AGW, 33 mm. **Series:** Independence Day **Subject:** Peace and Unknown Soldier; Israel's 21st Anniversary **Obv:** Block-like letters within triangular design **Rev:** Shalom **Edge:** Plain

Date	Mintage	VF20	XF40	MS60	MS63	MS65
JE5729-1969 (u)	12,500	PF65 1,100				

KM# 60 100 LIROT
22.00 g., 0.900 Gold 0.6366 oz. AGW, 30 mm. **Series:** Let My People Go **Subject:** Let My People Go **Obv:** Menorah flanked by sprigs to upper left of text **Rev:** Text within rectangle to right of moon within lines **Edge:** Reeded

Date	Mintage	VF20	XF40	MS60	MS63	MS65
JE5731-1971 (b)	9,956	PF65 1,100				

KM# 73 100 LIROT
13.50 g., 0.900 Gold 0.3906 oz. AGW, 27 mm. **Series:** Independence Day **Subject:** Declaration of Independence; Israel's 25th Anniversary **Obv:** Text on scroll **Rev:** Menorah flanked by sprigs above text **Edge:** Reeded

Date	Mintage	VF20	XF40	MS60	MS63	MS65
JE5733-1973 (b)	27,472	PF65 700				

KM# 103.1 100 LIROT
20.00 g., 0.500 Silver 0.3215 oz. ASW, 34 mm. **Series:** Hanukka **Subject:** Egyptian Hanukka Lamp, 19th Century **Obv:** Value **Rev:** Egyptian lamp within star design **Edge:** Plain

Date	Mintage	VF20	XF40	MS60	MS63	MS65
JE5740-1979 (b)	31,588	—	—	14.00	15.00	16.00

KM# 103.2 100 LIROT
20.00 g., 0.500 Silver 0.3215 oz. ASW, 34 mm. **Series:** Hanukka **Subject:** Egyptian Hanukka Lamp, 19th Century **Obv:** Value **Rev:** Egyptian lamp **Edge:** Reeded

Date	Mintage	VF20	XF40	MS60	MS63	MS65
JE5740-1979 (b)	19,019	PF65 18.00				

KM# 74 200 LIROT
27.00 g., 0.900 Gold 0.7813 oz. AGW, 33 mm. **Series:** Independence Day **Subject:** Declaration of Independence; Israel's 25th Anniversary **Obv:** Menorah flanked by sprigs above text **Rev:** Text on scroll **Edge:** Reeded

Date	Mintage	VF20	XF40	MS60	MS63	MS65
JE5733-1973 (b)	17,889	PF65 1,350				

KM# 104 200 LIROT
26.00 g., 0.900 Silver 0.7523 oz. ASW, 37 mm. **Series:** Independence Day **Subject:** Israel-Egypt Peace Treaty; Israel's 32nd Anniversary **Obv:** Menorah flanked by sprigs to upper right of text and value **Rev:** Sprig divides text **Edge:** Lettered

Date	Mintage	VF20	XF40	MS60	MS63	MS65
JE5740-1980 (b)	20,197	—	—	28.00	30.00	33.00
JE5740-1980 (b)	12,911	PF65 40.00				

KM# 82 500 LIROT
28.00 g., 0.900 Gold 0.8102 oz. AGW, 35 mm. **Series:** 1st Anniversary - Death of David Ben Gurion **Subject:** 1st Anniversary of Death of David Ben-Gurion **Obv:** Menorah flanked by sprigs **Rev:** Head left within rectangle **Edge:** Reeded

Date	Mintage	VF20	XF40	MS60	MS63	MS65
JE5735-1974 (b)	47,528	PF65 1,350				

KM# 83 500 LIROT
20.00 g., 0.900 Gold 0.5787 oz. AGW, 30 mm. **Series:** Independence Day **Subject:** 25th Anniversary of Israel Bond Program; Israel's 27th Anniversary **Obv:** Large value above menorah flanked by sprigs **Rev:** Artistic design **Edge:** Reeded

Date	Mintage	VF20	XF40	MS60	MS63	MS65
JE5735-1975 (u)	31,693	PF65 1,000				

KM# 93 1000 LIROT
12.00 g., 0.900 Gold 0.3472 oz. AGW, 25 mm. **Series:** Independence Day **Subject:** People United with its Land; Israel's 30th Anniversary **Obv:** Text and value above menorah flanked by sprigs **Rev:** Text within tree **Edge:** Reeded

Date	Mintage	VF20	XF40	MS60	MS63	MS65
JE5738-1978 (b)	12,043	PF65 575				

KM# 105 5000 LIROT
17.28 g., 0.900 Gold 0.500 oz. AGW, 30 mm. **Series:** Independence Day **Subject:** Israel-Egypt Peace Treaty; Israel's 32nd Anniversary **Obv:** Menorah flanked by sprigs above text and value **Rev:** Sprig divides text **Edge:** Reeded

Date	Mintage	VF20	XF40	MS60	MS63	MS65
JE5740-1980 (o)	6,382	PF65 900				

REFORM COINAGE

10 (old) Agorot = 1 New Agora;
100 New Agorot = 1 Sheqel; February 24, 1980-1985

KM# 106 NEW AGORA
0.60 g., Aluminum, 15 mm. **Obv:** Date palm **Rev:** Value **Edge:** Plain

Date	Mintage	VF20	XF40	MS60	MS63	MS65
JE5740 (1980) (wg)	200,000,000	—	—	—	0.20	—
Note: 90 million coins were reportedly melted down						
JE5741 (1981) (wg)	1,000,000	—	—	0.20	1.00	—
JE5742 (1982) (f)	1,000,000	—	—	0.20	1.00	—

KM# 107 5 NEW AGOROT
0.90 g., Aluminum, 18.5 mm. **Obv:** Menorah flanked by sprigs **Rev:** Value **Edge:** Reeded

Date	Mintage	VF20	XF40	MS60	MS63	MS65
JE5740 (1980) (wg)	69,532,000	—	—	—	0.25	—
JE5741 (1981) (wg)	1,000,000	—	—	0.20	1.00	—
JE5742 (1982) (f)	5,000,000	—	—	—	0.25	—

KM# 108 10 NEW AGOROT
2.10 g., Nickel-Bronze, 16 mm. **Obv:** Pomegranate **Rev:** Value **Edge:** Reeded

Date	Mintage	VF20	XF40	MS60	MS63	MS65
JE5740 (1980) (wg)	167,932,000	—	—	—	0.20	—
Note: 70.2 million coins were reportedly melted down						
JE5741 (1981)	241,100,000	—	—	—	0.20	—
Note: 123,000,000 were minted at (f); 90,000,000 at (p) and 28,160,000 at (j).						
JE5742 (1982) (f)	23,000,000	—	—	—	0.20	—
JE5743 (1983) (j)	2,500,000	—	—	0.15	0.50	—
JE5744 (1984) (j)	500,000	—	—	0.25	1.00	—

KM# 109 1/2 SHEQEL
3.00 g., Copper-Nickel, 20 mm. **Obv:** Roaring lion left **Rev:** Value flanked by stars **Edge:** Reeded

Date	Mintage	VF20	XF40	MS60	MS63	MS65
JE5740 (1980) (b)	52,308,000	—	0.50	1.00	1.25	—
JE5741 (1981)	53,272,000	—	0.50	1.00	1.25	—
Note: 37,976,000 minted at (j) and 15,296,000 minted at (p).						
JE5742 (1982) (j)	18,808,484	—	0.50	1.00	1.25	—
JE5743 (1983) (j)	250,000	—	0.50	1.00	1.25	—
JE5744 (1984) (j)	250,000	—	0.50	1.00	1.25	—

KM# 121 1/2 SHEQEL
7.20 g., 0.850 Silver 0.1968 oz. ASW, 23 mm. **Series:** Holyland Sites **Subject:** Qumran Caves **Obv:** Value **Edge:** Plain **Shape:** 12-sided

Date	Mintage	VF20	XF40	MS60	MS63	MS65
JE5743-1982 (p)	15,151	—	—	11.00	12.00	—

KM# 126 1/2 SHEQEL
7.20 g., 0.850 Silver 0.1968 oz. ASW, 23 mm. **Series:** Holyland Sites **Subject:** Herodian Ruins **Obv:** Value **Rev:** Herodion Ruins **Edge:** Plain **Shape:** 12-sided

Date	Mintage	VF20	XF40	MS60	MS63	MS65
JE5744-1983 (d)	11,044	—	—	10.00	11.00	—

KM# 140 1/2 SHEQEL
7.20 g., 0.850 Silver 0.1968 oz. ASW, 23 mm. **Series:** Holyland Sites **Subject:** Kidron Valley **Obv:** Value **Rev:** Kidron Valley **Edge:** Plain **Shape:** 12-sided

Date	Mintage	VF20	XF40	MS60	MS63	MS65
JE5745-1984 (p)	7,538	—	—	12.00	13.00	—

KM# 152 1/2 SHEQEL
7.20 g., 0.850 Silver 0.1968 oz. ASW, 23 mm. **Series:** Holyland Sites **Subject:** Capernaum **Obv:** Value **Rev:** Capernaum **Edge:** Plain **Shape:** 12-sided

Date	Mintage	VF20	XF40	MS60	MS63	MS65
JE5746-1985 (p)	6,010	—	—	13.00	15.00	—

KM# 110.1 SHEQEL
14.40 g., 0.850 Silver 0.3935 oz. ASW, 30 mm. **Series:** Hanukka **Subject:** Corfu (Greek) Hanukka Lamp, 19th Century **Obv:** Value **Rev:** Corfu lamp **Edge:** Plain

Date	Mintage	VF20	XF40	MS60	MS63	MS65
JE5741-1980 (o)	23,753	—	—	13.00	15.00	—

KM# 110.2 SHEQEL
14.40 g., 0.850 Silver 0.3935 oz. ASW, 30 mm. **Series:** Hanukka **Subject:** Corfu (Greek) Hanukka Lamp, 19th Century **Rev:** Corfu lamp **Edge:** Reeded

Date	Mintage	VF20	XF40	MS60	MS63	MS65
JE5741-1980 (o)	15,428	PF65 18.00				

KM# 111 SHEQEL
5.00 g., Copper-Nickel, 23 mm. **Obv:** Value **Rev:** Chalice **Edge:** Segmented reeding

Date	Mintage	VF20	XF40	MS60	MS63	MS65
JE5741 (1981)	154,540,000	—	—	0.30	0.50	—
Note: 99,000,000 minted at (p); 39,970,000 minted at (j) and 15,570,000 minted at (b).						
JE5742 (1982) (p)	15,850,000	—	—	0.30	0.50	—
JE5743 (1983) (j)	26,360,200	—	—	0.30	0.50	—
JE5744 (1984)	32,205,000	—	—	0.30	0.50	—
Note: 30,000,000 minted at (wg) and 2,205,000 minted at (j).						
JE5745 (1985) (j)	500,000	—	—	1.00	2.00	—

KM# 116.1 SHEQEL
14.40 g., 0.850 Silver 0.3935 oz. ASW, 30 mm. **Series:** Hanukka **Subject:** Polish Hanukka Lamp, 19th Century **Obv:** Value at left of menorah flanked by sprigs **Rev:** Polish lamp **Edge:** Plain

Date	Mintage	VF20	XF40	MS60	MS63	MS65
JE5742 -1981 (p)	16,115	—	—	15.00	16.00	18.00

KM# 116.2 SHEQEL
14.40 g., 0.850 Silver 0.3935 oz. ASW, 30 mm. **Series:** Hanukka **Subject:** Polish Hanukka Lamp, 19th Century **Rev:** Polish lamp **Edge:** Reeded

Date	Mintage	VF20	XF40	MS60	MS63	MS65
JE5742 -1981 (f)	11,186	PF65 20.00				

KM# 122 SHEQEL
14.40 g., 0.850 Silver 0.3935 oz. ASW, 30 mm. **Series:** Holyland Sites **Subject:** Qumran Caves **Obv:** Value **Rev:** Qumran caves **Edge:** Reeded

Date	Mintage	VF20	XF40	MS60	MS63	MS65
JE5743-1982 (d)	9,000	PF65 22.00				

KM# 123 SHEQEL
14.40 g., 0.850 Silver 0.3935 oz. ASW, 30 mm. **Series:** Hanukka **Subject:** Yemenite Hanukka Lamp **Obv:** Value below menorah flanked by sprigs **Rev:** Yemen lamp **Edge:** Plain

Date	Mintage	VF20	XF40	MS60	MS63	MS65
JE5743-1982 (p)	14,475	—	—	16.00	18.00	20.00

KM# 127 SHEQEL
14.40 g., 0.850 Silver 0.3935 oz. ASW, 30 mm. **Series:** Independence Day **Subject:** Valor, Israel Defense Forces; Israel's 35th Anniversary **Obv:** Large value **Rev:** Sprig wrapped around sword within star design **Edge:** Hebrew lettering

Date	Mintage	VF20	XF40	MS60	MS63	MS65
JE5743-1983 (f)	14,782	—	—	16.00	18.00	20.00

KM# 128 SHEQEL
14.40 g., 0.850 Silver 0.3935 oz. ASW, 30 mm. **Series:** Holyland Sites **Subject:** Herodion Ruins **Obv:** Value **Rev:** Herodion Ruins **Edge:** Reeded **Shape:** 12-sided

Date	Mintage	VF20	XF40	MS60	MS63	MS65
JE5744-1983 (d)	10,372	PF65 25.00				

KM# 129 SHEQEL

14.40 g., 0.850 Silver 0.3935 oz. ASW, 30 mm. **Series:** Hanukka **Subject:** Prague Hanukka Lamp, 18th Century **Obv:** Value **Rev:** Prague lamp **Edge:** Plain

Date	Mintage	VF20	XF40	MS60	MS63	MS65
JE5744-1983 (p)	12,777	—	—	16.00	18.00	20.00

KM# 135 SHEQEL

14.40 g., 0.850 Silver 0.3935 oz. ASW, 30 mm. **Series:** Independence Day **Subject:** Brotherhood; Israel's 36th Anniversary **Obv:** Value below menorah flanked by sprigs **Rev:** Kinsmen **Edge:** Hebrew lettering

Date	Mintage	VF20	XF40	MS60	MS63	MS65
JE5744-1984 (p)	9,476	—	—	18.00	20.00	22.00

KM# 141 SHEQEL

14.40 g., 0.850 Silver 0.3935 oz. ASW, 30 mm. **Series:** Holyland Sites **Subject:** Kidron Valley **Obv:** Value **Rev:** Kidron Valley **Edge:** Reeded **Shape:** 12-sided

Date	Mintage	VF20	XF40	MS60	MS63	MS65
JE5745-1984 (f)	6,798	PF65 28.00				

KM# 144 SHEQEL

14.40 g., 0.850 Silver 0.3935 oz. ASW, 30 mm. **Series:** Hanukka **Subject:** Theresienstadt Concentration Camp Hanukka Lamp **Obv:** Vertical lined value **Rev:** Theresienstadt lamp **Edge:** Plain

Date	Mintage	VF20	XF40	MS60	MS63	MS65
JE5745-1984 (p)	11,004	—	—	18.00	20.00	22.00

KM# 148 SHEQEL

14.40 g., 0.850 Silver 0.3935 oz. ASW, 30 mm. **Series:** Independence Day **Subject:** Scientific Achievements is Israel; Israel's 37th Anniversary **Obv:** Value **Rev:** Scientific Achievement **Edge:** Hebrew lettering

Date	Mintage	VF20	XF40	MS60	MS63	MS65
JE5745-1985 (p)	8,520	—	—	18.00	20.00	22.00

KM# 153 SHEQEL

14.40 g., 0.850 Silver 0.3935 oz. ASW, 30 mm. **Series:** Holyland Sites **Subject:** Capernaum **Obv:** Value **Rev:** Capernaum **Edge:** Reeded **Shape:** 12-sided

Date	Mintage	VF20	XF40	MS60	MS63	MS65
JE5746-1985 (f)	6,010	PF65 28.00				

KM# 155 SHEQEL

14.40 g., 0.850 Silver 0.3935 oz. ASW, 30 mm. **Series:** Ship of Oniyahu **Subject:** Ship of Oniyahu **Obv:** Value **Rev:** Ancient ship **Edge:** Plain

Date	Mintage	VF20	XF40	MS60	MS63	MS65
JE5745-1985 (f) Prooflike	12,951	—	—	18.00	20.00	22.00

KM# 161 SHEQEL

14.40 g., 0.850 Silver 0.3935 oz. ASW, 30 mm. **Series:** Hanukka **Subject:** German Hanukka Lamp, 16th Century **Obv:** Value **Rev:** Ashkenaz lamp **Edge:** Plain

Date	Mintage	VF20	XF40	MS60	MS63	MS65
JE5745-1985 (p)	9,460	—	—	16.00	18.00	20.00

KM# 112 2 SHEQALIM

28.80 g., 0.850 Silver 0.787 oz. ASW, 37 mm. **Series:** Independence Day **Subject:** People of the Book; Israel's 33rh Anniversary **Obv:** Large stylized value **Rev:** Stylized design within book **Edge:** Lettered

Date	Mintage	VF20	XF40	MS60	MS63	MS65
JE5741-1981 (o)	16,316	—	—	30.00	32.00	35.00
JE5741-1981 (o)	11,317	PF65 40.00				

KM# 117 2 SHEQALIM

28.80 g., 0.850 Silver 0.787 oz. ASW, 37 mm. **Series:** Independence Day **Subject:** Baron Edmond de Rothschild; Israel's 34th Anniversary **Obv:** Menorah flanked by sprigs above text **Rev:** Head facing **Edge:** Lettered

Date	Mintage	VF20	XF40	MS60	MS63	MS65
JE5742-1982 (p)	13,272	—	—	30.00	32.00	35.00
JE5742-1982 (f)	9,506	PF65 40.00				

KM# 124 2 SHEQALIM

28.80 g., 0.850 Silver 0.787 oz. ASW, 37 mm. **Series:** Hanukka **Subject:** Yemenite Hanukka Lamp **Obv:** Menorah flanked by sprigs above text and dates **Rev:** Yemen lamp **Edge:** Reeded

Date	Mintage	VF20	XF40	MS60	MS63	MS65
JE5743-1982 (f)	8,996	PF65 38.00				

KM# 130 2 SHEQALIM

28.80 g., 0.850 Silver 0.787 oz. ASW, 37 mm. **Series:** Independence Day **Subject:** Valor, Israel Defense Forces; Israel's 35th Anniversary **Obv:** State emblem and value **Rev:** Sprig wrapped around sword within star design **Edge:** Hebrew lettering

Date	Mintage	VF20	XF40	MS60	MS63	MS65
JE5743-1983 (f)	9,999	PF65 35.00				

KM# 131 2 SHEQALIM

28.80 g., 0.850 Silver 0.787 oz. ASW, 37 mm. **Series:** Hanukka **Subject:** Prague Hanukka Lamp, 18th Century **Obv:** Value above menorah flanked by sprigs **Rev:** Prague lamp **Edge:** Reeded

Date	Mintage	VF20	XF40	MS60	MS63	MS65
JE5744-1983 (b)	10,894	PF65 38.00				

KM# 136 2 SHEQALIM

28.80 g., 0.850 Silver 0.787 oz. ASW, 37 mm. **Series:** Independence Day **Subject:** Brotherhood; Israel's 36th Anniversary **Obv:** Menorah flanked by sprigs **Rev:** Kinsmen **Edge:** Hebrew lettering

Date	Mintage	VF20	XF40	MS60	MS63	MS65
JE5744-1984 (f)	8,551	PF65 45.00				

KM# 145 2 SHEQALIM

28.80 g., 0.850 Silver 0.787 oz. ASW, 37 mm. **Series:** Hanukka **Subject:** Theresienstadt Concentration Camp Hanukka Lamp **Obv:** Value to right of menorah flanked by sprigs **Rev:** Theresianstadt lamp **Edge:** Reeded

Date	Mintage	VF20	XF40	MS60	MS63	MS65
JE5745-1984 (b)	10,011	PF65 38.00				

KM# 149 2 SHEQALIM
28.80 g., 0.850 Silver 0.787 oz. ASW, 37 mm. **Series:** Independence Day **Subject:** Scientific Achievements is Israel; Israel's 37th Anniversary **Obv:** Menorah flanked by sprigs above text within circular designs **Rev:** Scientific achievement **Edge:** Hebrew lettering

Date	Mintage	VF20	XF40	MS60	MS63	MS65
JE5745-1985 (f)	8,330	PF65 40.00				

KM# 162 2 SHEQALIM
28.80 g., 0.850 Silver 0.787 oz. ASW, 37 mm. **Series:** Hanukka **Subject:** German Hanukka Lamp, 16th Century **Obv:** Value, partial feather and menorah flanked by sprigs **Rev:** Ashkenaz lamp **Edge:** Reeded

Date	Mintage	VF20	XF40	MS60	MS63	MS65
JE5746-1985 (b)	9,225	PF65 38.00				

KM# 118 5 SHEQALIM
6.10 g., Aluminum-Bronze, 24 mm. **Obv:** Cornucopia **Rev:** Value flanked by stars **Edge:** Reeded

Date	Mintage	VF20	XF40	MS60	MS63	MS65
JE5742 (1982)	30,000,000	—	—	0.50	0.75	—
Note: 18,000,000 minted at (so); 12,000,000 minted at (p).						
JE5743 (1983) (j)	994,000	—	—	1.00	2.00	—
JE5744 (1984)	17,389,000	—	—	0.50	0.75	—
Note: 9,000,000 minted at (so); 8,389,400 minted at (j).						
JE5745 (1985) (j)	250,005	—	—	1.00	2.50	—

KM# 125 5 SHEQALIM
8.64 g., 0.250 Gold 0.0694 oz. AGW, 22 mm. **Series:** Holyland Sites **Subject:** Qumran Caves **Rev:** Qumran Caves **Edge:** Reeded **Shape:** 12-sided

Date	Mintage	VF20	XF40	MS60	MS63	MS65
JE5743-1982 (d)	4,927	PF65 425				

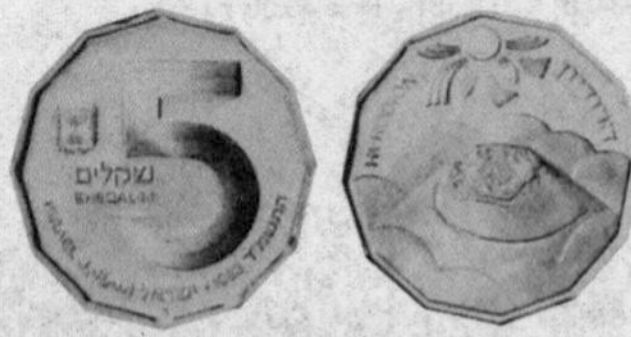

KM# 132 5 SHEQALIM
8.64 g., 0.250 Gold 0.0694 oz. AGW, 22 mm. **Series:** Holyland Sites **Subject:** Herodion Ruins **Obv:** Value **Rev:** Herodion Ruins **Edge:** Reeded **Shape:** 12-sided

Date	Mintage	VF20	XF40	MS60	MS63	MS65
JE5744-1983 (d)	4,346	PF65 425				

KM# 142 5 SHEQALIM
8.64 g., 0.250 Gold 0.0694 oz. AGW, 22 mm. **Series:** Holyland Sites **Subject:** Kidron Valley **Obv:** Value **Rev:** Kidron Valley **Edge:** Reeded **Shape:** 12-sided

Date	Mintage	VF20	XF40	MS60	MS63	MS65
JE5745 -1984 (b)	2,601	PF65 450				

KM# 154 5 SHEQALIM
8.64 g., 0.250 Gold 0.0694 oz. AGW, 22 mm. **Series:** Holyland Sites **Subject:** Capernaum **Obv:** Value **Rev:** Capernaum **Edge:** Reeded **Shape:** 12-sided

Date	Mintage	VF20	XF40	MS60	MS63	MS65
JE5746-1985 (b)	2,633	PF65 425				

KM# 113 10 SHEQALIM
17.28 g., 0.900 Gold 0.500 oz. AGW, 30 mm. **Series:** Independence Day **Subject:** People of the Book; Israel's 33rd Anniversary **Obv:** Large stylized value **Rev:** Stylized design within book **Edge:** Reeded

Date	Mintage	VF20	XF40	MS60	MS63	MS65
JE5741-1981 (o)	5,634	PF65 900				

KM# 119 10 SHEQALIM
8.00 g., Copper-Nickel, 26 mm. **Obv:** Ancient Galley **Rev:** Value flanked by stars **Edge:** Plain

Date	Mintage	VF20	XF40	MS60	MS63	MS65
JE5742 (1982)	36,084,123	—	—	0.75	1.25	—
Note: 18,000,000 minted at (f) and 18,084,123 at (j).						
JE5743 (1983) (j)	17,850,750	—	—	0.75	1.25	—
JE5744 (1984) (j)	31,950,200	—	—	0.75	1.25	—
JE5745 (1985)	25,864,436	—	—	0.50	0.75	—
Note: 15,864,436 struck by (j) and 10,000,000 by (f).						

KM# 120 10 SHEQALIM
17.28 g., 0.900 Gold 0.500 oz. AGW, 30 mm. **Series:** Independence Day **Subject:** Baron Edmond de Rothschild; Israel's 34th Anniversary **Obv:** Menorah flanked by sprigs above text **Rev:** Head of de Rothschild facing **Edge:** Reeded

Date	Mintage	VF20	XF40	MS60	MS63	MS65
JE5742-1982 (o)	4,875	PF65 950				

KM# 133 10 SHEQALIM
17.28 g., 0.900 Gold 0.500 oz. AGW, 30 mm. **Series:** Independence Day **Subject:** Valor, Israel Defense Forces; Israel's 35th Anniversary **Obv:** Menorah flanked by sprigs within stylized value **Rev:** Sprig wrapped around sword within star design **Edge:** Reeded

Date	Mintage	VF20	XF40	MS60	MS63	MS65
JE5743-1983 (b)	3,814	PF65 900				

KM# 134 10 SHEQALIM
8.00 g., Copper-Nickel, 26 mm. **Series:** Hanukka **Subject:** Hanukka **Obv:** Ancient Galley **Rev:** Value flanked by stars **Edge:** Plain

Date	Mintage	VF20	XF40	MS60	MS63	MS65
JE5744 (1984) (j)	2,000,000	—	—	1.00	2.00	—

KM# 137 10 SHEQALIM
8.00 g., Copper-Nickel, 26 mm. **Subject:** Theodore Herzl **Obv:** Head of Theodore Herzl left **Rev:** Value flanked by stars **Edge:** Plain

Date	Mintage	VF20	XF40	MS60	MS63	MS65
JE5744 (1984) (b)	2,002,500	—	—	1.00	2.00	—

KM# 138 10 SHEQALIM
17.28 g., 0.900 Gold 0.500 oz. AGW, 30 mm. **Series:** Independence Day **Subject:** Brotherhood; Israel's 36th Anniversary **Obv:** Menorah flanked by sprigs **Rev:** Kinsmen **Edge:** Reeded

Date	Mintage	VF20	XF40	MS60	MS63	MS65
JE5744-1984 (o)	3,798	PF65 900				

KM# 150 10 SHEQALIM
17.28 g., 0.900 Gold 0.500 oz. AGW, 30 mm. **Series:** Independence Day **Subject:** Scientific Achievements is Israel; Israel's 37th Anniversary **Obv:** Menorah, text and value within circular designs **Rev:** Scientific achievement **Edge:** Reeded

Date	Mintage	VF20	XF40	MS60	MS63	MS65
JE5745-1985 (o)	3,240	PF65 900				

KM# 114.1 25 SHEQEL
26.00 g., 0.900 Silver 0.7523 oz. ASW, 37 mm. **Series:** 100th Anniversary - Birth of Zeev Jabotinsky **Subject:** 100th Anniversary of Birth of Ze'ev Jabotinsky **Obv:** State arms above value **Rev:** Head 3/4 left **Edge:** Plain

Date	Mintage	VF20	XF40	MS60	MS63	MS65
JE5741-1980 (o)	14,469	—	—	32.00	35.00	—

KM# 114.2 25 SHEQEL
26.00 g., 0.900 Silver 0.7523 oz. ASW, 37 mm. **Series:** 100th Anniversary - Birth of Zeev Jabotinsky **Subject:** 100th Anniversary of Birth of Ze'ev Jabotinsky **Obv:** State arms above value **Rev:** Head left **Edge:** Reeded

Date	Mintage	VF20	XF40	MS60	MS63	MS65
JE5741-1980 (o)	12,236	PF65 40.00				

KM# 139 50 SHEQALIM
9.00 g., Aluminum-Bronze, 28 mm. **Obv:** Ancient coin **Rev:** Value flanked by stars **Edge:** Reeded

Date	Mintage	VF20	XF40	MS60	MS63	MS65
JE5744 (1984) (j)	13,993,658	—	—	0.50	1.00	—
JE5745 (1985) (j)	1,000,100	—	—	1.00	2.00	—

KM# 147 50 SHEQALIM
9.00 g., Aluminum-Bronze,, 28 mm. **Obv:** Head of David Ben-Gurion left **Rev:** Value flanked by stars **Edge:** Reeded

Date	Mintage	VF20	XF40	MS60	MS63	MS65
JE5745 (1985) (p)	1,000,000	—	—	1.00	2.00	—

KM# 143 100 SHEQALIM
10.80 g., Copper-Nickel, 29 mm. **Obv:** Menorah **Rev:** Value **Edge:** Wide reeding

Date	Mintage	VF20	XF40	MS60	MS63	MS65
JE5744 (1984) (j)	15,028,433	—	—	0.75	1.50	—
JE5744 (1984) (c)	15,000,000	—	—	0.75	1.50	—
JE5745 (1985) (j)	19,637,806	—	—	0.75	1.50	—

KM# 146 100 SHEQALIM
10.80 g., Copper-Nickel, 29 mm. **Series:** Hanukka **Subject:** Hanukka **Obv:** Menorah **Rev:** Value **Edge:** Wide reeding

Date	Mintage	VF20	XF40	MS60	MS63	MS65
JE5745 (1985) (j)	2,000,000	—	—	1.00	2.00	—

KM# 151 100 SHEQALIM
10.80 g., Copper-Nickel, 29 mm. **Obv:** Head of Ze'ev Jabotinsky 1/4 left **Rev:** Value **Edge:** Wide reeding

Date	Mintage	VF20	XF40	MS60	MS63	MS65
JE5745 (1985) (p)	2,000,000	—	—	1.00	2.00	—

KM# 115 500 SHEQEL
17.28 g., 0.900 Gold 0.500 oz. AGW, 30 mm. **Series:** 100th Anniversary - Birth of Zeev Jabotinsky **Subject:** 100th Anniversary of Birth of Ze'ev Jabotinsky **Obv:** Menorah flanked by sprigs above value **Edge:** Reeded

Date	Mintage	VF20	XF40	MS60	MS63	MS65
JE5741-1980 (o)	7,471	PF65 1,000				

REFORM COINAGE

100 Agorot = 1 New Sheqel
1,000 Sheqalim = 1 New Sheqel; September 4, 1985-present

KM# 156 AGORA
2.00 g., Aluminum-Bronze, 17 mm. **Obv:** Ancient ship **Rev:** Value within lined square **Edge:** Plain

Date	Mintage	VF20	XF40	MS60	MS63	MS65
JE5745 (1985)	58,144,000	—	—	—	—	0.50
Note: 40,000,000 struck by (p) and 18,144,000 by (f).						
JE5746 (1986)	95,272,000	—	—	—	—	0.50
Note: 50,112,000 struck by (p); 30,856,000 by (f) and 14,304,000 by (j).						
JE5747 (1987) (j)	1,080,000	—	—	—	—	0.50
JE5748 (1988) (j)	15,768,000	—	—	—	—	0.50
JE5749 (1989) (j)	10,801,000	—	—	—	—	0.50
JE5750 (1990) (j)	4,968,000	—	—	—	—	0.50
JE5751 (1991) (j)	12,000	—	—	—	2.00	3.00
Note: Sets only, probably 5,254 melted.						

KM# 171 AGORA
2.00 g., Aluminum-Bronze, 17 mm. **Series:** Hanukka **Subject:** Hanukka **Obv:** Ancient ship **Rev:** Value within lined square **Edge:** Plain

Date	Mintage	VF20	XF40	MS60	MS63	MS65
JE5747 (1987) (p)	1,004,000	—	—	—	0.20	0.75
JE5748 (1988) (j)	540,000	—	—	—	0.25	1.00
JE5749 (1989) (j)	504,000	—	—	—	0.25	1.00
JE5750 (1990) (j)	2,160,000	—	—	—	0.15	0.75
JE5751 (1991) (j)	432,000	—	—	—	0.25	1.00

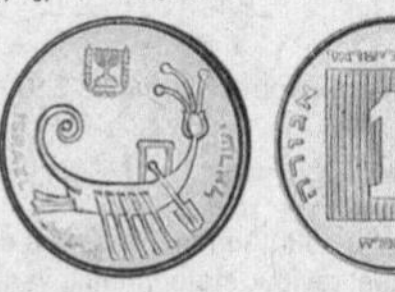

KM# 193 AGORA
2.00 g., Aluminum-Bronze, 17 mm. **Series:** Independence Day **Subject:** Israel's 40th Anniversary **Obv:** Ancient ship **Rev:** Value within lined square **Edge:** Plain

Date	Mintage	VF20	XF40	MS60	MS63	MS65
JE5748 (1988) (j)	504,000	—	—	—	0.25	1.00

KM# 157 5 AGOROT
3.00 g., Aluminum-Bronze, 19.5 mm. **Obv:** Ancient coin **Rev:** Value within lined square **Edge:** Plain

Date	Mintage	VF20	XF40	MS60	MS63	MS65
JE5745 (1985) (p)	25,000,000	—	—	—	0.10	0.20
JE5745 (1985) (f)	9,504,000	—	—	—	0.10	0.20
JE5746 (1986) (j)	6,912,050	—	—	—	0.10	0.20
JE5746 (1986) (f)	5,472,000	—	—	—	0.10	0.20
JE5747 (1987) (j)	14,257,298	—	—	—	0.10	0.20
JE5748 (1988) (j)	9,360,000	—	—	—	0.10	0.20
JE5749 (1989) (j)	4,896,000	—	—	—	0.10	0.20
JE5750 (1990) (j)	576,000	—	—	—	0.25	1.00
JE5751 (1991) (j)	4,464,000	—	—	—	0.10	0.20
JE5752 (1992) (j)	7,664,000	—	—	—	0.10	0.20
JE5752 (1992) (so)	18,432,000	—	—	—	0.10	0.20
Note: A coin-alignment error exists. Value $100 in Unc, $50 in XF.						
JE5754 (1994) (a)	5,952,000	—	—	—	0.10	0.15
JE5754 (1994) (h)	6,144,000	—	—	—	0.10	0.15
JE5755 (1995) (so)	6,144,000	—	—	—	0.10	0.15
JE5756 (1996) (sg)	6,144,000	—	—	—	0.10	0.15
JE5757 (1997) (so)	6,144,000	—	—	—	0.10	0.15
JE5758 (1998) (so)	12,288,000	—	—	—	0.10	0.15
Note: A coin-alignment error exists. Value $100 in Unc, $50 in XF.						
JE5759 (1999) (so)	6,144,000	—	—	—	0.10	0.15
JE5760 (2000) (so)	12,288,000	—	—	—	0.10	0.15
Note: A coin-alignment error exists. Value $100 in Unc, $50 in XF.						

KM# 172 5 AGOROT
3.00 g., Aluminum-Bronze, 19.5 mm. **Series:** Hanukka **Subject:** Hanukka **Obv:** Ancient coin **Rev:** Value within lined square **Edge:** Plain **Note:** JE5754-5768 coins contain the Star of David mint mark; the JE5747-5753 coins do not.

Date	Mintage	VF20	XF40	MS60	MS63	MS65
JE5747 (1987) (p)	1,004,000	—	—	—	0.10	0.30
JE5748 (1988) (j)	536,000	—	—	—	0.25	1.00
JE5749 (1989) (j)	504,000	—	—	—	0.25	1.00
JE5750 (1990) (j)	2,016,000	—	—	—	0.10	0.30
JE5751 (1991) (j)	1,488,000	—	—	—	0.10	0.30
JE5752 (1992) (j)	960,000	—	—	—	0.10	0.30
JE5753 (1993) (j)	960,000	—	—	—	0.10	0.30
JE5754 (1994) (u) Sets only	12,000	—	—	—	—	2.00
JE5755 (1995) (u) Sets only	10,000	—	—	—	—	2.00
JE5756 (1996) (u) Sets only	7,500	—	—	—	—	2.00
JE5757 (1997) (u) Sets only	7,500	—	—	—	—	2.00
JE5758 (1998) (u) Sets only	10,000	—	—	—	—	2.00
JE5759 (1999) (u) Sets only	6,000	—	—	—	—	2.50
JE5760 (2000) (u) Sets only	5,000	—	—	—	—	2.50

KM# 194 5 AGOROT
3.00 g., Aluminum-Bronze, 19.5 mm. **Series:** Independence Day **Subject:** Israel's 40th Anniversary **Obv:** Ancient coin **Rev:** Value within lined square **Edge:** Plain

Date	Mintage	VF20	XF40	MS60	MS63	MS65
JE5748 (1988) (j)	504,000	—	—	—	0.35	1.00

KM# 158 10 AGOROT
4.00 g., Aluminum-Bronze, 22 mm. **Obv:** Menorah **Rev:** Value within lined square **Edge:** Plain

Date	Mintage	VF20	XF40	MS60	MS63	MS65
JE5745 (1985) (f)	45,000,000	—	—	—	0.15	0.25
JE5746 (1986) (j)	20,934,048	—	—	—	0.15	0.25
JE5746 (1986) (b)	71,820,000	—	—	—	0.15	0.25

Date	Mintage	VF20	XF40	MS60	MS63	MS65
JE5747 (1987) (j)	19,351,382	—	—	—	0.15	0.25
JE5748 (1988) (j)	8,640,298	—	—	—	0.15	0.25
JE5749 (1989) (j)	420,000	—	—	0.40	0.60	1.00
JE5750 (1990) (j)	2,376,000	—	—	—	0.20	0.50
JE5751 (1991) (j)	11,905,000	—	—	—	0.15	0.25

Note: Exist with 6mm or 7mm long date; thick or thin letters; and 7mm or 7.5mm value 10

Date	Mintage	VF20	XF40	MS60	MS63	MS65
JE5751 (1991) (so)	30,240,000	—	—	—	0.15	0.25
JE5751 (1991) (f)	17,280,000	—	—	—	0.15	0.25
JE5752 (1992) (j)	1,728,000	—	—	—	0.15	0.25
JE5753 (1993) (so)	25,920,000	—	—	—	0.15	0.25
JE5754 (1994) (u)	30,096,000	—	—	—	0.15	0.25
JE5754 (1994) (f)	21,600,000	—	—	—	0.15	0.25
JE5755 (1995) (h)	17,280,000	—	—	—	0.15	0.25
JE5756 (1996) (so)	43,200,000	—	—	—	0.15	0.25
JE5757 (1997) (h)	21,600,000	—	—	—	0.15	0.25

Note: The Hebrew letter "heh" in the date (first letter) is open.

Date	Mintage	VF20	XF40	MS60	MS63	MS65
JE5757 (1997) (u)	21,600,000	—	—	—	0.15	0.25

Note: The Hebrew letter "heh" in the date (first letter) is closed.

Date	Mintage	VF20	XF40	MS60	MS63	MS65
JE5758 (1998) (so)	60,480,000	—	—	—	0.15	0.25

Note: A coin-alignment error exists. Value $100 in Unc, $50 in XF.

Date	Mintage	VF20	XF40	MS60	MS63	MS65
JE5759 (1999) (a)	21,600,000	—	—	—	0.15	0.25
JE5759 (1999) (dj)	4,601,000	—	—	—	0.15	0.25
JE5759 (1999) (w)	2,000	—	—	—	0.15	0.25
JE5760 (2000) (so)	82,944,000	—	—	—	0.15	0.25

KM# 173 10 AGOROT

4.00 g., Aluminum-Bronze, 22 mm. **Series:** Hanukka **Subject:** Hanukka **Obv:** Menorah **Rev:** Value within lined square **Edge:** Plain **Note:** JE5754-5770 have the Star of David mint mark, JE5747-5753 coins do not.

Date	Mintage	VF20	XF40	MS60	MS63	MS65
JE5747 (1987) (p)	1,004,000	—	—	—	0.25	0.40
JE5748 (1988) (j)	834,000	—	—	—	0.25	0.40
JE5749 (1989) (j)	798,000	—	—	—	0.25	0.40
JE5750 (1990) (j)	2,052,000	—	—	—	0.25	0.40
JE5751 (1991) (j)	1,488,000	—	—	—	0.25	0.40
JE5752 (1992) (j)	1,404,000	—	—	—	0.25	0.40
JE5753 (1993) (j)	1,404,000	—	—	—	0.25	0.40
JE5754 (1994) (u) Sets only	12,000	—	—	—	—	2.00
JE5755 (1995) (u) Sets only	10,000	—	—	—	—	2.00
JE5756 (1996) (u) Sets only	7,500	—	—	—	—	2.00
JE5757 (1997) (u) Sets only	7,500	—	—	—	—	2.00
JE5758 (1998) (u) Sets only	10,000	—	—	—	—	2.00
JE5759 (1999) (u) Sets only	6,000	—	—	—	—	2.50
JE5760 (2000) (u) Sets only	5,000	—	—	—	—	3.00

KM# 195 10 AGOROT

4.00 g., Aluminum-Bronze, 22 mm. **Series:** Independence Day **Subject:** Israel's 40th Anniversary **Obv:** Menorah **Rev:** Value within lined square **Edge:** Plain

Date	Mintage	VF20	XF40	MS60	MS63	MS65
JE5748 (1988) (j)	504,000	—	—	—	0.40	1.00

KM# 159 1/2 NEW SHEQEL

6.50 g., Aluminum-Bronze, 26 mm. **Obv:** Value **Rev:** Lyre **Edge:** Plain

Date	Mintage	VF20	XF40	MS60	MS63	MS65
JE5745 (1985) (f)	4,032,000	—	—	—	0.50	0.75
JE5745 (1985) (j)	1,296,000	—	—	—	0.50	0.75
JE5745 (1985) (p)	15,000,000	—	—	—	0.50	0.75

Note: Exist with thick E and trimmed thin E, but which mint(s) produced which coin is not known

Date	Mintage	VF20	XF40	MS60	MS63	MS65
JE5746 (1986) (j)	4,392,000	—	—	—	0.50	0.75
JE5747 (1987) (j)	144,000	—	—	0.75	1.50	2.50
JE5748 (1988) (j)	20,000	—	1.00	2.00	3.00	5.00

Note: Most in sets but a few were placed into circulation.

Date	Mintage	VF20	XF40	MS60	MS63	MS65
JE5749 (1989) (j)	756,000	—	—	—	0.50	1.00
JE5750 (1990) (j)	648,000	—	—	—	0.50	1.00
JE5751 (1991) (j)	288,000	—	—	—	0.75	1.50
JE5752 (1992) (f)	2,688,000	—	—	—	0.50	0.75
JE5752 (1992) (j)	828,000	—	—	—	0.50	0.75
JE5752 (1992) (so)	10,752,000	—	—	—	0.50	0.75
JE5753 (1993) (c)	2,496,000	—	—	—	0.50	0.75
JE5753 (1993) (f)	2,688,000	—	—	—	0.50	0.75
JE5755 (1995) (a)	5,376,000	—	—	—	0.50	0.75
JE5755 (1995) (so)	5,376,000	—	—	—	0.50	0.75
JE5757 (1997) (so)	5,376,000	—	—	—	0.50	0.75
JE5758 (1998) (u)	5,376,000	—	—	—	0.50	0.75
JE5759 (1999) (so)	8,064,000	—	—	—	0.50	0.75

Note: A coin-alignment error exists. Value $100 in Unc, $50 in XF.

Date	Mintage	VF20	XF40	MS60	MS63	MS65
JE5760 (2000) (so)	2,880,000	—	—	—	—	—

Note: Reported in the 2000 Annual Review, a correction in the 2002 Annual review, stated that it was in error.

KM# 167 1/2 NEW SHEQEL

6.50 g., Aluminum-Bronze, 26 mm. **Subject:** Baron Edmond de Rothschild **Obv:** Value **Rev:** Bust of Edmond de Rothschild facing within names of settlements funded **Edge:** Plain

Date	Mintage	VF20	XF40	MS60	MS63	MS65
JE5746 (1986) (u)	2,000,000	—	—	—	1.00	3.00

KM# 168 1/2 NEW SHEQEL

7.20 g., 0.850 Silver 0.1968 oz. ASW, 23 mm. **Series:** Holyland Sites **Subject:** Akko **Obv:** Value **Rev:** Akko **Edge:** Plain **Shape:** 12-sided

Date	Mintage	VF20	XF40	MS60	MS63	MS65
JE5747-1986 (u)	6,224	—	—	—	11.00	—

KM# 174 1/2 NEW SHEQEL

6.50 g., Aluminum-Bronze, 26 mm. **Series:** Hanukka **Subject:** Hanukka **Obv:** Value **Rev:** Lyre **Edge:** Plain **Note:** Coins dated JE5754-5770 have the Star of David mint mark; the coins dated JE5747-5753 do not.

Date	Mintage	VF20	XF40	MS60	MS63	MS65
JE5747 (1987) (p)	1,004,000	—	—	—	0.35	0.85
JE5748 (1988) (j)	532,000	—	—	—	0.50	1.00
JE5749 (1989) (j)	504,000	—	—	—	0.50	1.00
JE5750 (1990) (j)	2,016,000	—	—	—	0.35	0.85
JE5751 (1991) (j)	960,000	—	—	—	0.40	0.90
JE5752 (1992) (j)	288,000	—	—	—	0.75	1.50
JE5753 (1993) (j)	304,000	—	—	—	0.75	1.50
JE5754 (1994) (u) Sets only	12,000	—	—	—	—	2.00
JE5755 (1995) (u) Sets only	10,000	—	—	—	—	2.00
JE5756 (1996) (u) Sets only	7,500	—	—	—	—	2.00
JE5757 (1997) (u) Sets only	7,500	—	—	—	—	2.00
JE5758 (1998) (u) Sets only	10,000	—	—	—	—	2.00
JE5759 (1999) (u) Sets only	6,000	—	—	—	—	2.50
JE5760 (2000) (u) Sets only	5,000	—	—	—	—	3.00

KM# 180 1/2 NEW SHEQEL

7.20 g., 0.850 Silver 0.1968 oz. ASW, 23 mm. **Series:** Holyland Sites **Subject:** Jericho **Rev:** Jericho **Edge:** Plain **Shape:** 12-sided

Date	Mintage	VF20	XF40	MS60	MS63	MS65
JE5748-1987 (p)	7,590	—	—	—	12.00	—

KM# 188 1/2 NEW SHEQEL

7.20 g., 0.850 Silver 0.1968 oz. ASW, 23 mm. **Series:** Holyland Sites **Subject:** Caesarea **Obv:** Value **Rev:** Caesarea **Edge:** Plain **Shape:** 12-sided

Date	Mintage	VF20	XF40	MS60	MS63	MS65
JE5749-1988 (p)	5,865	—	—	—	14.00	—

KM# 196 1/2 NEW SHEQEL
6.50 g., Aluminum-Bronze, 26 mm. **Series:** Independence Day **Subject:** Israel's 40th Anniversary **Obv:** Value **Rev:** Lyre **Edge:** Plain

Date	Mintage	VF20	XF40	MS60	MS63	MS65
JE5748 (1988) (j)	500,000	—	—	0.50	1.00	2.00

KM# 202 1/2 NEW SHEQEL
7.20 g., 0.850 Silver 0.1968 oz. ASW, 23 mm. **Series:** Holyland Sites **Subject:** Jaffa **Obv:** Value **Rev:** Jaffa Harbor **Edge:** Plain **Shape:** 12-sided

Date	Mintage	VF20	XF40	MS60	MS63	MS65
JE5750-1989 (f)	4,940	—	—	—	16.00	—

KM# 209 1/2 NEW SHEQEL
7.20 g., 0.850 Silver 0.1968 oz. ASW, 23 mm. **Series:** Holyland Sites **Subject:** Sea of Galilee **Obv:** Value **Rev:** Sea of Galilee sites map **Edge:** Plain **Shape:** 12-sided

Date	Mintage	VF20	XF40	MS60	MS63	MS65
JE5751-1990 (f)	4,346	—	—	—	18.00	—

KM# 303 1/2 NEW SHEQEL
6.50 g., Aluminum-Bronze, 26 mm. **Series:** Hanukka **Subject:** Theresienstadt Concentration Camp Hanukka Lamp **Obv:** Value **Rev:** Theresienstadt lamp **Note:** Struck for sets only.

Date	Mintage	VF20	XF40	MS60	MS63	MS65
JE5754 (1994)	12,000	—	—	—	6.00	—
(u) Sets only						

KM# 304 1/2 NEW SHEQEL
6.50 g., Aluminum-Bronze, 26 mm. **Series:** Hanukka **Subject:** Early American Hanukka Lamp **Obv:** Value **Rev:** Early American lamp **Note:** Struck for sets only.

Date	Mintage	VF20	XF40	MS60	MS63	MS65
JE5755 (1995)	10,000	—	—	—	7.00	—
(u) Sets only						

KM# 368 1/2 NEW SHEQEL
14.50 g., Aluminum-Bronze, 26 mm. **Series:** Independence Day **Subject:** Environment; Israel's 46th Anniversary **Obv:** Value **Rev:** Globe within flower design **Edge:** Plain **Shape:** 12-sided **Note:** Struck for sets only. Piefort only type, (P78).

Date	Mintage	VF20	XF40	MS60	MS63	MS65
JE5754 (1994)	8,000	—	—	—	10.00	—
(u) Sets only						

Note: Piefort only type (P78)

KM# 305 1/2 NEW SHEQEL
6.50 g., Aluminum-Bronze, 26 mm. **Series:** Hanukka **Subject:** French Hanukka Lamp, 14th Century **Obv:** Value **Rev:** French lamp **Note:** Struck for sets only.

Date	Mintage	VF20	XF40	MS60	MS63	MS65
JE5756 (1996)	7,500	—	—	—	8.00	—
(u) Sets only						

KM# 392 1/2 NEW SHEQEL
14.50 g., Aluminum-Bronze, 26 mm. **Series:** Independence Day **Subject:** Medicine in Israel; Israel's 47th Anniversary **Note:** Struck for sets only. Piefort only type, (P85)

Date	Mintage	VF20	XF40	MS60	MS63	MS65
JE5755 (1995)	10,000	—	—	—	10.00	—
(u) Sets only						

Note: Piefort only type (P85)

KM# 318 1/2 NEW SHEQEL
6.50 g., Aluminum-Bronze, 26 mm. **Series:** Hanukka **Subject:** Russian Hanukka Lamp, 18th Century **Obv:** Value **Rev:** Russian lamp **Note:** Struck for sets only.

Date	Mintage	VF20	XF40	MS60	MS63	MS65
JE5757 (1997)	7,500	—	—	—	8.00	—
(u) Sets only						

KM# 393 1/2 NEW SHEQEL
14.50 g., Aluminum-Bronze, 26 mm. **Series:** Independence Day **Subject:** Jerusalem 3000; Israel's 48th Anniversary **Note:** Struck for sets only. Piefort only type, (P93).

Date	Mintage	VF20	XF40	MS60	MS63	MS65
JE5756 (1996)	8,000	—	—	—	10.00	—
(h) Sets only						

Note: Piefort only type (P93)

KM# 314 1/2 NEW SHEQEL
6.50 g., Aluminum-Bronze, 26 mm. **Series:** Hanukka **Subject:** English Hanukka Lamp, 18th Century **Obv:** Value **Rev:** English lamp **Note:** Struck for sets only.

Date	Mintage	VF20	XF40	MS60	MS63	MS65
JE5758 (1998)	10,000	—	—	—	8.00	—
(u) Sets only						

KM# 394 1/2 NEW SHEQEL
14.50 g., Aluminum-Bronze, 26 mm. **Series:** Independence Day **Subject:** First Zionist Congress Centennial; Israel's 49th Anniversary **Note:** Struck for sets only. Piefort only type, (P101).

Date	Mintage	VF20	XF40	MS60	MS63	MS65
JE5757 (1997)	6,000	—	—	—	12.00	—
(h) Sets only						

Note: Piefort only type (P101)

KM# 331 1/2 NEW SHEQEL
6.50 g., Aluminum-Bronze, 26 mm. **Series:** Hanukka **Subject:** Knesset Menorah **Obv:** Value **Rev:** Menorah **Note:** Struck for sets only.

Date	Mintage	VF20	XF40	MS60	MS63	MS65
JE5759 (1999)	6,000	—	—	—	8.00	—
(u) Sets only						

KM# 395 1/2 NEW SHEQEL
14.50 g., Aluminum-Bronze, 26 mm. **Series:** Independence Day **Subject:** Israel's 50th Anniversary **Note:** Struck for sets only. Piefort only type, (P109).

Date	Mintage	VF20	XF40	MS60	MS63	MS65
JE5758 (1998)	8,000	—	—	—	10.00	—
(h) Sets only						

Note: Piefort only type (P109)

KM# 324 1/2 NEW SHEQEL
14.50 g., Aluminum-Bronze, 26 mm. **Series:** Independence Day **Subject:** High Tech in Israel; Israel's 51st Anniversary **Obv:** Value **Rev:** Stylized mosaic bouquet **Note:** Struck for sets only. Piefort only type, (P117).

Date	Mintage	VF20	XF40	MS60	MS63	MS65
JE5759 (1999)	6,000	—	—	—	12.00	—
(h) Sets only						

Note: Piefort only type (P117)

KM# 332 1/2 NEW SHEQEL
6.50 g., Aluminum-Bronze, 26 mm. **Series:** Hanukka **Subject:** Jerusalem Hanukka Lamp, 20th Century **Obv:** Value **Rev:** Jerusalem Hanukka lamp **Note:** Struck for sets only.

Date	Mintage	VF20	XF40	MS60	MS63	MS65
JE5760 (2000)	7,000	—	—	—	8.00	—
(u) Sets only						

KM# 363 1/2 NEW SHEQEL
14.50 g., Aluminum-Bronze, 26 mm. **Series:** Independence Day **Subject:** Love Thy Neighbor; Israel's 52nd Anniversary **Obv:** Value **Rev:** Arch **Edge:** Plain **Shape:** 12-sided **Note:** Struck for sets only. Piefort only type, (P125).

Date	Mintage	VF20	XF40	MS60	MS63	MS65
JE5760 (2000)	4,000	—	—	—	12.00	—
(h) Sets only						

Note: Piefort only type (P125)

KM# 160 NEW SHEQEL
4.00 g., Copper-Nickel, 18 mm. **Obv:** Value **Rev:** Lily, state emblem and ancient Hebrew inscription **Edge:** Plain

Date	Mintage	VF20	XF40	MS60	MS63	MS65
JE5745 (1985) (b)	29,088,000	—	—	—	0.75	1.50
JE5746 (1986) (f)	8,000,000	—	—	—	0.75	1.50
JE5746 (1986) (j)	12,960,055	—	—	—	0.75	1.50
JE5747 (1987) (j)	216,000	—	—	0.75	1.00	3.00
JE5748 (1988) (j)	6,372,000	—	—	—	0.75	1.50
JE5748 (1988) (u)	14,004,000	—	—	—	0.75	1.50
JE5749 (1989) (j)	8,706,000	—	—	—	0.75	1.50
JE5750 (1990) (j)	756,000	—	—	0.50	0.75	2.00
JE5751 (1991) (j)	1,152,000	—	—	0.50	0.75	1.50
JE5752 (1992) (f)	8,640,000	—	—	—	0.75	1.50
JE5752 (1992) (wg)	1,512,000	—	—	—	0.75	1.50
JE5752 (1992) (o)	17,280,000	—	—	—	0.75	1.50
JE5753 (1993) (f)	8,640,000	—	—	—	0.75	1.50

KM# 163 NEW SHEQEL
4.00 g., Copper-Nickel, 18 mm. **Series:** Hanukka **Subject:** Hanukka **Obv:** Value **Rev:** Lily, state emblem and ancient Hebrew inscription. **Edge:** Plain **Note:** Coins dated JE5754-5769 have the Star of David mint mark; the JE5746-5753 coins do not.

Date	Mintage	VF20	XF40	MS60	MS63	MS65
JE5746 (1986) (b)	1,056,000	—	—	—	0.75	1.50
JE5747 (1987) (p)	1,004,000	—	—	—	0.75	1.50
JE5748 (1988) (j)	534,000	—	—	0.50	0.75	2.00
JE5749 (1989) (j)	504,000	—	—	0.50	0.75	2.00
JE5750 (1990) (j)	2,052,000	—	—	—	0.75	1.50
JE5751 (1991) (f)	1,080,000	—	—	—	0.75	1.50
JE5751 (1991) (j)	24,000	—	—	—	0.75	1.50
JE5752 (1992) (j)	1,044,000	—	—	—	0.75	1.50
JE5753 (1993) (j)	922,000	—	—	—	0.75	1.50

KM# 164 NEW SHEQEL
14.40 g., 0.850 Silver 0.3935 oz. ASW, 30 mm. **Series:** Independence Day **Subject:** Art in Israel, Israel's 38th Anniversary **Obv:** Value, half rainbow and menorah flanked by sprigs **Rev:** Artistic designs **Edge:** Hebrew lettering

Date	Mintage	VF20	XF40	MS60	MS63	MS65
JE5746-1986 (p)	8,010	—	—	—	18.00	20.00

KM# 169 NEW SHEQEL
14.40 g., 0.850 Silver 0.3935 oz. ASW, 30 mm. **Series:** Holyland Sites **Subject:** Akko **Obv:** Value **Rev:** Akko **Edge:** Reeded **Shape:** 12-sided

Date	Mintage	VF20	XF40	MS60	MS63	MS65
JE5747-1986 (f)	6,117	PF65 25.00				

KM# 175 NEW SHEQEL
14.40 g., 0.850 Silver 0.3935 oz. ASW, 30 mm. **Series:** Hanukka **Subject:** Algerian Hanukka Lamp, 19th Century **Obv:** Value **Rev:** Algerian lamp **Edge:** Plain

Date	Mintage	VF20	XF40	MS60	MS63	MS65
JE5747-1986 (f)	8,227	—	—	—	22.00	—

KM# 177 NEW SHEQEL
14.40 g., 0.850 Silver 0.3935 oz. ASW, 30 mm. **Series:** Independence Day **Subject:** 20th Anniversary of United Jerusalem; Israel's 39th Anniversary **Obv:** Menorah flanked by sprigs within rectangle **Rev:** Circular city of Jerusalem to right of numeral two **Edge:** Hebrew lettering

Date	Mintage	VF20	XF40	MS60	MS63	MS65
JE5747-1987 (p)	8,107	—	—	—	18.00	20.00

KM# 181 NEW SHEQEL
14.40 g., 0.850 Silver 0.3935 oz. ASW, 30 mm. **Series:** Holyland Sites **Subject:** Jericho **Obv:** Value **Rev:** Jericho **Edge:** Reeded **Shape:** 12-sided

Date	Mintage	VF20	XF40	MS60	MS63	MS65
JE5748-1987 (f)	8,196	PF65 28.00				

KM# 183 NEW SHEQEL
14.40 g., 0.850 Silver 0.3935 oz. ASW, 30 mm. **Series:** Hanukka **Subject:** English Hanukka Lamp, 18th Century **Obv:** Value, text and menorah flanked by sprigs within design **Rev:** English lamp **Edge:** Plain

Date	Mintage	VF20	XF40	MS60	MS63	MS65
JE5748-1987 (f)	7,810	—	—	—	22.00	—

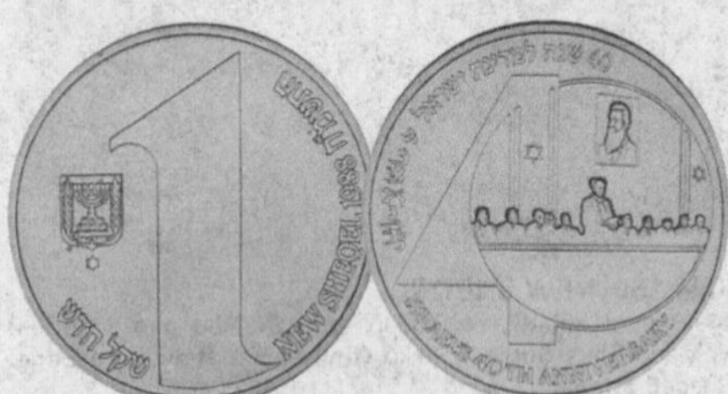

KM# 185 NEW SHEQEL
14.40 g., 0.850 Silver 0.3935 oz. ASW, 30 mm. **Series:** Independence Day **Subject:** Declaration of Independence; Israel's 40th Anniversary **Obv:** Large stylized value **Rev:** Stylized figures of government within large numeral 40 **Edge:** Hebrew lettering

Date	Mintage	VF20	XF40	MS60	MS63	MS65
JE5748-1988 (p)	8,990	—	—	—	18.00	20.00

KM# 189 NEW SHEQEL
14.40 g., 0.850 Silver 0.3935 oz. ASW, 30 mm. **Series:** Holyland Sites **Subject:** Caesarea **Obv:** Value **Rev:** Caesarea **Edge:** Reeded **Shape:** 12-sided

Date	Mintage	VF20	XF40	MS60	MS63	MS65
JE5749-1988 (f)	6,560	PF65 28.00				

KM# 191 NEW SHEQEL
14.40 g., 0.850 Silver 0.3935 oz. ASW, 30 mm. **Series:** Hanukka **Subject:** Tunisian Hanukka Lamp, 19th Century **Obv:** Value and text within design **Rev:** Tunisian lamp **Edge:** Plain

Date	Mintage	VF20	XF40	MS60	MS63	MS65
JE5749-1988 (u)	6,688	—	—	—	20.00	22.00

KM# 197 NEW SHEQEL
4.00 g., Copper-Nickel, 18 mm. **Series:** Independence Day **Subject:** Israel's 40th Anniversary **Obv:** Value **Rev:** Lis **Edge:** Plain

Date	Mintage	VF20	XF40	MS60	MS63	MS65
JE5748 (1988) (j)	504,000	—	—	0.75	1.25	2.00

KM# 198 NEW SHEQEL
4.00 g., Copper-Nickel, 18 mm. **Subject:** Maimonides **Obv:** Value **Rev:** Bust of Maimonides facing **Edge:** Plain

Date	Mintage	VF20	XF40	MS60	MS63	MS65
JE5748 (1988) (d)	1,000,000	—	—	0.75	1.25	2.00

KM# 199 NEW SHEQEL
14.40 g., 0.850 Silver 0.3935 oz. ASW, 30 mm. **Series:** Independence Day **Subject:** Promised Land; Israel's 41st Anniversary **Obv:** Value covers left side of lined area **Rev:** Roe deer standing to right in wooded area **Edge:** Hebrew lettering

Date	Mintage	VF20	XF40	MS60	MS63	MS65
JE5749-1989 (f)	6,249	—	—	—	21.00	—

KM# 203 NEW SHEQEL
14.40 g., 0.850 Silver 0.3935 oz. ASW, 30 mm. **Series:** Holyland Sites **Subject:** Jaffa **Obv:** Value **Rev:** Jaffa Harbor **Edge:** Reeded **Shape:** 12-sided

Date	Mintage	VF20	XF40	MS60	MS63	MS65
JE5750-1989 (f)	4,844	PF65 28.00				

KM# 205 NEW SHEQEL
14.40 g., 0.850 Silver 0.3935 oz. ASW, 30 mm. **Series:** Hanukka **Subject:** Persian Hanukka Lamp, 17th Century **Obv:** Value **Rev:** Persian lamp **Edge:** Plain

Date	Mintage	VF20	XF40	MS60	MS63	MS65
JE5750-1989 (m)	6,171	—	—	—	22.00	25.00

KM# 210 NEW SHEQEL
14.40 g., 0.850 Silver 0.3935 oz. ASW, 30 mm. **Series:** Holyland Sites **Subject:** Sea of Galilee **Obv:** Value **Rev:** Sea of Galilee sites map **Edge:** Reeded **Shape:** 12-sided

Date	Mintage	VF20	XF40	MS60	MS63	MS65
JE5751-1990 (f)	4,735	PF65 30.00				

KM# 212 NEW SHEQEL
14.40 g., 0.850 Silver 0.3935 oz. ASW, 30 mm. **Series:** Independence Day **Subject:** Archaeology; Israel's 42nd Anniversary **Obv:** Linear value **Rev:** Archaeology **Edge:** Hebrew lettering

Date	Mintage	VF20	XF40	MS60	MS63	MS65
JE5750-1990 (f)	5,509	—	—	—	22.00	—

KM# 215 NEW SHEQEL
14.40 g., 0.850 Silver 0.3935 oz. ASW, 30 mm. **Series:** Hanukka **Subject:** Cochin (India) Hanukka Lamp, 19th Century **Obv:** Value, text and menorah flanked by sprigs **Rev:** Cochin lamp **Edge:** Plain

Date	Mintage	VF20	XF40	MS60	MS63	MS65
JE5751-1990 (f)	5,259	—	—	—	24.00	—

KM# 218 NEW SHEQEL
14.40 g., 0.925 Silver 0.4282 oz. ASW, 30 mm. **Series:** Independence Day **Subject:** Immigration; Israel's 43rd Anniversary **Obv:** Value within diagonal lines **Rev:** Plane above stylized standing figures **Edge:** Hebrew lettering

Date	Mintage	VF20	XF40	MS60	MS63	MS65
JE5751-1991 (f)	5,508	—	—	—	21.00	—

KM# 220 NEW SHEQEL
14.40 g., 0.925 Silver 0.4282 oz. ASW, 30 mm. **Series:** Wildlife **Subject:** Dove and Cedar Tree **Obv:** Cedar trees and value **Rev:** Dove and tree trunk **Edge:** Plain

Date	Mintage	VF20	XF40	MS60	MS63	MS65
JE5752-1991 (f)	4,125	—	—	—	30.00	—

KM# 223 NEW SHEQEL
14.40 g., 0.925 Silver 0.4282 oz. ASW, 30 mm. **Series:** Judaica **Subject:** Kiddush Cup **Obv:** Value within diagonal lines to right of cup **Rev:** Kiddush cup flanked by dates within circular design **Edge:** Plain

Date	Mintage	VF20	XF40	MS60	MS63	MS65
JE5752-1991 (f)	4,876	—	—	—	20.00	—

KM# 342 NEW SHEQEL
3.46 g., 0.900 Gold 0.1001 oz. AGW, 18 mm. **Series:** Wildlife **Subject:** Dove and Cedar Tree **Obv:** Cedar trees and value **Rev:** Dove and tree trunk **Edge:** Reeded

Date	Mintage	VF20	XF40	MS60	MS63	MS65
JE5752-1991 (o)	2,515	PF65 200				

KM# 225 NEW SHEQEL
14.40 g., 0.925 Silver 0.4282 oz. ASW, 30 mm. **Series:** Independence Day **Subject:** Law in Israel; Israel's 44th Anniversary **Obv:** Value **Rev:** Balance scale above arch within square **Edge:** Hebrew lettering

Date	Mintage	VF20	XF40	MS60	MS63	MS65
JE5752-1992 (p)	4,047	—	—	—	35.00	—

KM# 231 NEW SHEQEL
14.40 g., 0.925 Silver 0.4282 oz. ASW, 30 mm. **Series:** Wildlife **Subject:** Roe and Lily **Obv:** Value at upper right of lilies **Rev:** Rose and Lily **Edge:** Plain

Date	Mintage	VF20	XF40	MS60	MS63	MS65
JE5753-1992 (f)	4,105	—	—	—	30.00	—

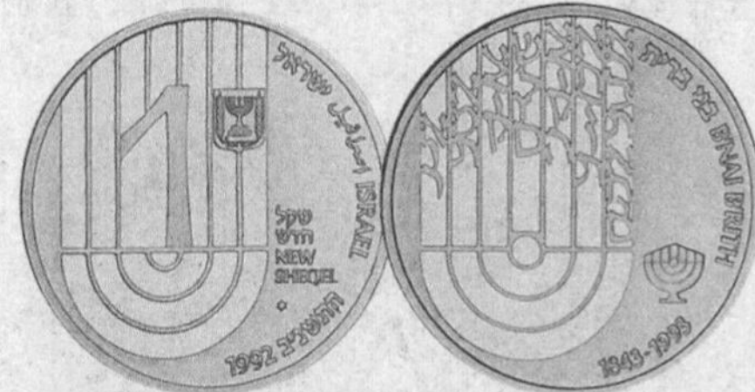

KM# 234 NEW SHEQEL
14.40 g., 0.925 Silver 0.4282 oz. ASW, 30 mm. **Series:** B'nai B'rith - 150th Anniversary. **Subject:** 150th Anniversary of B'nai Brith **Obv:** Value and menorah within stylized design **Rev:** Text within stylized design **Edge:** Plain

Date	Mintage	VF20	XF40	MS60	MS63	MS65
JE5752-1992 (u)	4,034	—	—	—	24.00	—

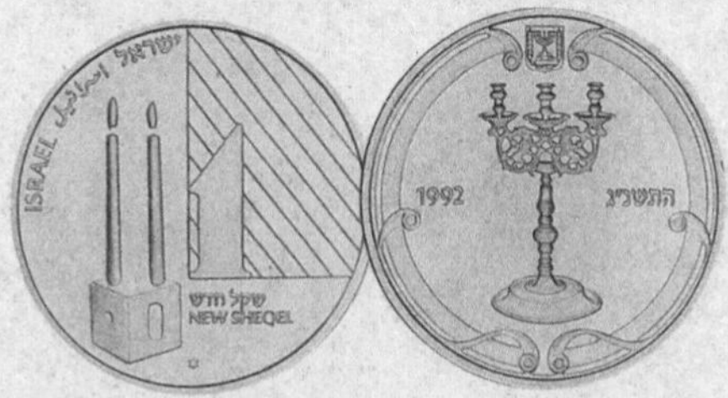

KM# 238 NEW SHEQEL
14.40 g., 0.925 Silver 0.4282 oz. ASW, 30 mm. **Series:** Judaica **Subject:** Sabbath Candlesticks **Obv:** Value within diagonal lines to right of candles on box **Rev:** Shabbat candles **Edge:** Plain

Date	Mintage	VF20	XF40	MS60	MS63	MS65
JE5753-1992 (u)	5,564	—	—	—	20.00	—

KM# 343 NEW SHEQEL
3.46 g., 0.900 Gold 0.1001 oz. AGW, 18 mm. **Series:** Wildlife **Subject:** Roe and Lily **Rev:** Roe and Lily **Edge:** Reeded

Date	Mintage	VF20	XF40	MS60	MS63	MS65
JE5753-1992 (p)	2,000	PF65 200				

KM# 240 NEW SHEQEL
14.40 g., 0.925 Silver 0.4282 oz. ASW, 30 mm. **Series:** Independence Day **Subject:** Tourism; Israel's 45th Anniversary **Obv:** Value, text, dates and menorah flanked by sprigs **Rev:** Tourism attractions **Edge:** Plain

Date	Mintage	VF20	XF40	MS60	MS63	MS65
JE5753-1993 (u) Prooflike	6,985	—	—	—	—	25.00

KM# 243 NEW SHEQEL
14.40 g., 0.925 Silver 0.4282 oz. ASW, 30 mm. **Series:** Wildlife **Subject:** Hart and Apple Tree **Obv:** Value at upper right of apple blossom **Rev:** Buck and young Hart deer standing in grass **Edge:** Plain

Date	Mintage	VF20	XF40	MS60	MS63	MS65
JE5754-1993 (f)	3,761	—	—	—	32.00	—

KM# 244 NEW SHEQEL
3.46 g., 0.900 Gold 0.1001 oz. AGW, 18 mm. **Series:** Wildlife **Subject:** Hart and Apple Tree **Obv:** Value at upper right of apple blossom **Rev:** Buck and young Hart standing in grass **Edge:** Reeded

Date	Mintage	VF20	XF40	MS60	MS63	MS65
JE5754-1993 (u)	1,679	PF65 210				

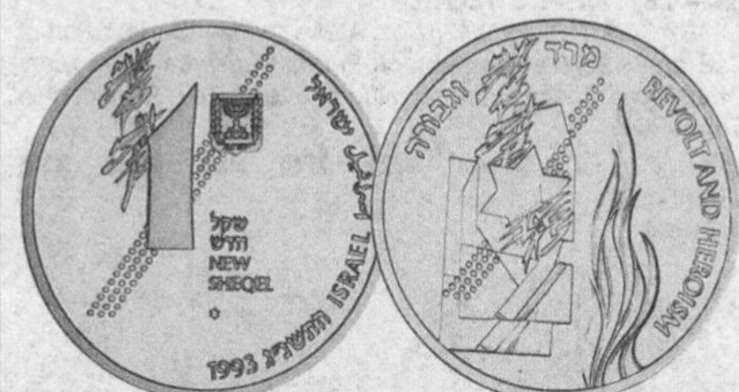

KM# 247 NEW SHEQEL
14.40 g., 0.925 Silver 0.4282 oz. ASW, 30 mm. **Series:** Revolt and Heroism **Subject:** Revolt and Heroism **Obv:** Value and menorah within beaded diagonal line **Rev:** Medal with star within beaded diagonal lines to left of flames **Edge:** Plain

Date	Mintage	VF20	XF40	MS60	MS63	MS65
JE5753-1993 (u)	4,642	—	—	—	27.00	—

KM# 250 NEW SHEQEL
14.40 g., 0.925 Silver 0.4282 oz. ASW, 30 mm. **Series:** Judaica **Subject:** Havdalah Spicebox **Obv:** Torah crown at left of value within lined 1/4 square **Rev:** Havdalah spicebox **Edge:** Plain

Date	Mintage	VF20	XF40	MS60	MS63	MS65
JE5754-1993 (u)	3,288	—	—	—	20.00	—

KM# 160a NEW SHEQEL
3.45 g., Nickel Plated Steel, 17.97 mm. **Obv:** Value **Rev:** Lily, state emblem and ancient Hebrew inscription **Edge:** Plain

Date	Mintage	VF20	XF40	MS60	MS63	MS65
JE5754 (1994) (f)	8,496,000	—	—	—	0.75	1.00
JE5754 (1994) (u)	12,960,000	—	—	—	0.75	1.00
Note: Coin alignment error exists. Value: $100 in Unc, $50 in XF.						
JE5755 (1995) (u)	25,920,000	—	—	—	0.75	1.00
JE5756 (1996) (u)	8,640,000	—	—	—	0.75	1.00
JE5757 (1997) (u)	30,240,000	—	—	—	0.75	1.00
JE5758 (1998) (sa)	4,295,500	—	—	—	0.75	1.00
JE5759 (1999) (u)	17,280,000	—	—	—	0.75	1.00
JE5760 (2000) (wg)	20,738,000	—	—	—	0.75	1.00

KM# 163a NEW SHEQEL
4.00 g., Nickel Plated Steel, 18 mm. **Series:** Hanukka **Subject:** Hanukka **Obv:** Value, small menorah, country name in Hebrew, English and Arabic and inscription "HANUKKA" in Hebrew and English **Rev:** Lily, state emblem, ancient Hebrew inscription and Star of David mintmark **Edge:** Plain **Note:** Non-magnetic.

Date	Mintage	VF20	XF40	MS60	MS63	MS65
JE5754 (1994) (u)	12,000	—	—	—	—	2.50
Note: Sets only						
JE5755 (1995) (u)	10,000	—	—	—	—	2.50
Note: Sets only						
JE5756 (1996) (u)	7,500	—	—	—	—	2.50
Note: Sets only						
JE5757 (1997) (u)	7,500	—	—	—	—	2.50
Note: Sets only						
JE5758 (1998) (u)	10,000	—	—	—	—	2.50
Note: Sets only						
JE5759 (1999) (u)	6,000	—	—	—	—	3.00
Note: Sets only						

KM# 252 NEW SHEQEL
14.40 g., 0.925 Silver 0.4282 oz. ASW, 30 mm. **Series:** Independence Day **Subject:** Environment; Israel's 46th Anniversary **Obv:** Slanted value **Rev:** Globe within flower design **Edge:** Hebrew lettering

Date	Mintage	VF20	XF40	MS60	MS63	MS65
JE5754-1994 (f)	3,490	—	—	—	—	32.00

KM# 256 NEW SHEQEL
14.40 g., 0.925 Silver 0.4282 oz. ASW, 30 mm. **Series:** Biblical Art **Subject:** Binding of Isaac **Rev:** Abraham's willingness to sacrifice Isaac **Edge:** Plain

Date	Mintage	VF20	XF40	MS60	MS63	MS65
JE5755-1994 (f) Prooflike	3,468	—	—	—	—	52.00

KM# 259 NEW SHEQEL

14.40 g., 0.925 Silver 0.4282 oz. ASW, 30 mm. **Series:** Wildlife **Subject:** Leopard and Palm Tree **Obv:** Palm tree to right of value and text **Rev:** Leopard **Edge:** Plain

Date	Mintage	VF20	XF40	MS60	MS63	MS65
JE5755-1994 (u)	3,286	—	—	—	—	35.00

KM# 260 NEW SHEQEL

3.46 g., 0.900 Gold 0.1001 oz. AGW, 18 mm. **Series:** Wildlife **Subject:** Leopard and Palm Tree **Obv:** Palm tree to right of value and text **Rev:** Leopard **Edge:** Reeded

Date	Mintage	VF20	XF40	MS60	MS63	MS65
JE5755-1994 (o)	1,355	PF65 200				

KM# 263 NEW SHEQEL

14.40 g., 0.925 Silver 0.4282 oz. ASW, 30 mm. **Series:** Independence Day **Subject:** Medicine in Israel; Israel's 47th Anniversary **Obv:** Snake on a menorrah **Rev:** Value, text and menorah flanked by sprigs **Edge:** Hebrew lettering

Date	Mintage	VF20	XF40	MS60	MS63	MS65
JE5755-1995	3,468	—	—	—	—	32.00

(f) Prooflike

KM# 267 NEW SHEQEL

14.40 g., 0.925 Silver 0.4282 oz. ASW, 30 mm. **Series:** 50th Anniversary - Defeat of Nazi Germany **Subject:** 50th Anniversary of Defeat of Nazi Germany **Obv:** Value above text **Rev:** V-shape design with state emblems within **Edge:** Plain

Date	Mintage	VF20	XF40	MS60	MS63	MS65
JE5755-1995	3,450	—	—	—	—	45.00

(h) Prooflike

KM# 271 NEW SHEQEL

14.40 g., 0.925 Silver 0.4282 oz. ASW, 30 mm. **Series:** 50th Anniversary of the F.A.O. **Subject:** 50th Anniversary of the F.A.O. **Obv:** Value within wheat sprigs and diagonal lines **Rev:** FAO logo **Edge:** Plain

Date	Mintage	VF20	XF40	MS60	MS63	MS65
JE5755-1995	3,564	—	—	—	—	30.00

(v) Prooflike

KM# 274 NEW SHEQEL

14.40 g., 0.925 Silver 0.4282 oz. ASW, 30 mm. **Series:** Wildlife **Subject:** Fox and Vineyard **Obv:** Value and cluster of grapes **Rev:** Fox **Edge:** Plain

Date	Mintage	VF20	XF40	MS60	MS63	MS65
JE5756-1995	2,438	—	—	—	—	37.00

(v) Prooflike

KM# 275 NEW SHEQEL

3.46 g., 0.900 Gold 0.1001 oz. AGW, 18 mm. **Series:** Wildlife **Subject:** Fox and Vineyard **Obv:** Grapes **Rev:** Fox **Edge:** Reeded

Date	Mintage	VF20	XF40	MS60	MS63	MS65
JE5756-1995 (o)	837	PF65 250				

KM# 278 NEW SHEQEL

14.40 g., 0.925 Silver 0.4282 oz. ASW, 30 mm. **Series:** Peace Treaty with Jordan **Subject:** Peace Treaty with Jordan **Obv:** Text divides value and menorah flanked by sprigs **Rev:** Sprig divides text **Edge:** Plain

Date	Mintage	VF20	XF40	MS60	MS63	MS65
JE5755-1995	3,301	—	—	—	—	32.00

(bp) Prooflike

KM# 281 NEW SHEQEL

14.40 g., 0.925 Silver 0.4282 oz. ASW, 30 mm. **Series:** Biblical Art **Subject:** Solomon's Judgement **Obv:** Value above text **Rev:** Medieval linear design **Edge:** Plain

Date	Mintage	VF20	XF40	MS60	MS63	MS65
JE5755-1995	2,826	—	—	—	—	55.00

(f) Prooflike

KM# 287 NEW SHEQEL

14.40 g., 0.925 Silver 0.4282 oz. ASW, 30 mm. **Series:** Port of Caesarea - 2000 years **Subject:** Port of Caesarea, 2000 Years **Obv:** Anchor to lower left of value and text **Rev:** Ancient ship **Edge:** Plain

Date	Mintage	VF20	XF40	MS60	MS63	MS65
JE5755-1995	2,633	—	—	—	—	28.00

(f) Prooflike

KM# 284 NEW SHEQEL

14.40 g., 0.925 Silver 0.4282 oz. ASW, 30 mm. **Series:** Independence Day **Subject:** Jerusalem 3000 **Obv:** Value flanked by menorah and design above text **Rev:** Inscription at center **Edge:** Plain

Date	Mintage	VF20	XF40	MS60	MS63	MS65
JE5756-1996	4,497	—	—	—	—	40.00

(f) Prooflike

KM# 290 NEW SHEQEL

14.40 g., 0.925 Silver 0.4282 oz. ASW, 30 mm. **Series:** Wildlife **Subject:** Nightingale and Fig Tree **Obv:** Fig leaves and value **Rev:** Nightingale **Edge:** Plain

Date	Mintage	VF20	XF40	MS60	MS63	MS65
JE5757-1996	2,451	—	—	—	—	42.00

(v) Prooflike

KM# 291 NEW SHEQEL

3.46 g., 0.900 Gold 0.1001 oz. AGW, 18 mm. **Series:** Wildlife **Subject:** Nightingale and Fig Tree **Rev:** Nightingale **Edge:** Reeded

Date	Mintage	VF20	XF40	MS60	MS63	MS65
JE5757-1996 (v)	912	PF65 300				

KM# 294 NEW SHEQEL

14.40 g., 0.925 Silver 0.4282 oz. ASW, 30 mm. **Series:** Biblical Art **Subject:** Miriam and the Women **Obv:** Value above design and text **Rev:** Miriam and the women **Edge:** Plain

Date	Mintage	VF20	XF40	MS60	MS63	MS65
JE5757-1996	2,236	—	—	—	—	55.00

(u) Prooflike

KM# 297 NEW SHEQEL

14.40 g., 0.925 Silver 0.4282 oz. ASW, 30 mm. **Subject:** Yitzhak Rabin **Obv:** Menorah above value and text **Rev:** Head of Rabin facing left **Edge:** Plain

Date	Mintage	VF20	XF40	MS60	MS63	MS65
JE5757-1996	5,296	—	—	—	—	38.00

(u) Prooflike

KM# 300 NEW SHEQEL

14.40 g., 0.925 Silver 0.4282 oz. ASW, 30 mm. **Series:** Independence Day **Subject:** First Zionist Congress Centennial; Israel's 49th Anniversary **Obv:** Value flanked by menorah, star design and text **Rev:** Half-figure left leaning on bridge **Edge:** Plain

Date	Mintage	VF20	XF40	MS60	MS63	MS65
JE5757-1997	4,028	—	—	—	—	32.00

(u) Prooflike

KM# 306 NEW SHEQEL
14.40 g., 0.925 Silver 0.4282 oz. ASW, 30 mm. **Series:** Wildlife **Subject:** Lion and Pomegranate **Obv:** Pomegranates, value and text **Rev:** Lion right **Edge:** Plain

Date	Mintage	VF20	XF40	MS60	MS63	MS65
JE5758-1997	2,135	—	—	—	—	36.00
(u) Prooflike						

KM# 307 NEW SHEQEL
3.46 g., 0.900 Gold 0.1001 oz. AGW, 18 mm. **Series:** Wildlife **Subject:** Lion and Pomegranate **Obv:** Pomegranates and value **Rev:** Lion **Edge:** Reeded

Date	Mintage	VF20	XF40	MS60	MS63	MS65
JE5758-1997 (u)	770	PF65 325				

KM# 310 NEW SHEQEL
14.43 g., 0.925 Silver 0.4291 oz. ASW, 30 mm. **Series:** Independence Day **Subject:** Israel's 50th Anniversary **Obv:** Value and menorah above text **Rev:** Flag within stars **Edge:** Plain

Date	Mintage	VF20	XF40	MS60	MS63	MS65
JE5758-1998	9,819	—	—	—	—	40.00
(u) Prooflike						

KM# 316 NEW SHEQEL
14.43 g., 0.925 Silver 0.4291 oz. ASW, 30 mm. **Series:** Biblical Art **Subject:** Noah's Ark **Obv:** Dove, rainbow and value **Rev:** Stylized figure releasing dove **Edge:** Plain

Date	Mintage	VF20	XF40	MS60	MS63	MS65
JE5758-1998	2,198	—	—	—	—	55.00
(u) Prooflike						

KM# 320 NEW SHEQEL
14.43 g., 0.925 Silver 0.4291 oz. ASW, 30 mm. **Series:** Wildlife **Subject:** Stork and Fir Tree **Obv:** Fir trees and value **Rev:** Stork **Edge:** Plain

Date	Mintage	VF20	XF40	MS60	MS63	MS65
JE5759-1998	2,147	—	—	—	—	40.00
(u) Prooflike						

KM# 321 NEW SHEQEL
3.46 g., 0.900 Gold 0.1001 oz. AGW, 18 mm. **Series:** Wildlife **Subject:** Stork and Fir Tree **Obv:** Fir trees and value **Rev:** Stork **Edge:** Reeded

Date	Mintage	VF20	XF40	MS60	MS63	MS65
JE5759-1998 (u)	553	PF65 375				

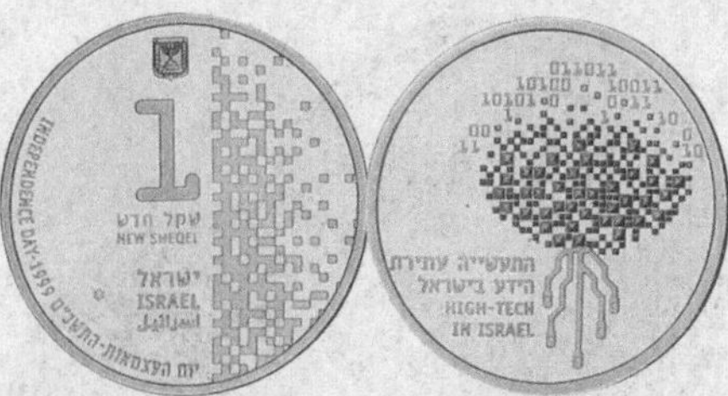

KM# 325 NEW SHEQEL
14.40 g., 0.925 Silver 0.4282 oz. ASW, 30 mm. **Series:** Independence Day **Subject:** High Tech in Israel; Israel's 51st Anniversary **Obv:** Value and mosaic **Rev:** 01 Computer code as bouquet **Edge:** Plain

Date	Mintage	VF20	XF40	MS60	MS63	MS65
JE5759-1999	1,713	—	—	—	—	30.00
(u) Prooflike						

KM# 328 NEW SHEQEL
14.40 g., 0.925 Silver 0.4282 oz. ASW, 30 mm. **Series:** Millennium 2000 **Subject:** Millennium 2000 **Obv:** Value and olive branch **Rev:** Year 2000 motif incorporating dove with olive branch **Edge:** Plain

Date	Mintage	VF20	XF40	MS60	MS63	MS65
JE5759-1999	4,629	—	—	—	—	30.00
(u) Prooflike						

KM# 333 NEW SHEQEL
14.40 g., 0.925 Silver 0.4282 oz. ASW, 30 mm. **Series:** Biblical Art **Subject:** Abraham and the Stars **Obv:** Value, text and menorah to right of stars **Rev:** Abraham looking at the stars **Edge:** Plain

Date	Mintage	VF20	XF40	MS60	MS63	MS65
JE5759-1999	2,146	—	—	—	—	55.00
(o) Prooflike						

KM# 163b NEW SHEQEL
3.50 g., Nickel Bonded Steel, 18 mm. **Series:** Hanukka **Subject:** Hanukka **Obv:** Value, small menorah, country name in Hebrew, English and Arabic and inscription "HANUKKA" in Hebrew and English **Rev:** Lily, state emblem, ancient Hebrew inscription and Star of David mintmark **Edge:** Plain

Date	Mintage	VF20	XF40	MS60	MS63	MS65
JE5760 (2000) (u)	5,000	—	—	—	—	3.50

Note: Sets only

KM# 336 NEW SHEQEL
14.40 g., 0.925 Silver 0.4282 oz. ASW, 30 mm. **Series:** Independence Day **Subject:** Love Thy Neighbor; Israel's 52nd Anniversary **Obv:** Value within dome design **Rev:** Arch above text **Rev. Inscription:** Love Thy Neighbor, As Thyself **Edge:** Plain

Date	Mintage	VF20	XF40	MS60	MS63	MS65
JE5760-2000	2,516	—	—	—	—	30.00
(u) Prooflike						

KM# 339 NEW SHEQEL
14.40 g., 0.925 Silver 0.4282 oz. ASW, 30 mm. **Series:** Biblical Art **Subject:** Joseph and his Brothers **Obv:** Value and text **Rev:** Joseph standing before sheaves of wheat into his brothers **Edge:** Plain

Date	Mintage	VF20	XF40	MS60	MS63	MS65
JE5760-2000	2,249	—	—	—	—	70.00
(u) Prooflike						

KM# 347 NEW SHEQEL
14.40 g., 0.925 Silver 0.4282 oz. ASW, 30 mm. **Series:** Wildlife **Subject:** Wild Goat and Acacia Tree **Obv:** Acacia tree and value **Rev:** Ibex **Edge:** Plain

Date	Mintage	VF20	XF40	MS60	MS63	MS65
JE5761-2000	2,000	—	—	—	—	40.00
(u) Prooflike						

KM# 348 NEW SHEQEL
3.46 g., 0.900 Gold 0.1001 oz. AGW, 18 mm. **Series:** Wildlife **Subject:** Wild Goat and Acacia Tree **Obv:** Acacia tree **Rev:** Ibex **Edge:** Reeded

Date	Mintage	VF20	XF40	MS60	MS63	MS65
JE5761-2000 (u)	700	PF65 300				

KM# 165 2 NEW SHEQALIM
28.80 g., 0.850 Silver 0.787 oz. ASW, 37 mm. **Series:** Independence Day **Subject:** Jerusalem 3000; Israel's 48th Anniversary **Obv:** Value, partial rainbow and menorah **Rev:** Artistic designs **Edge:** Hebrew lettering

Date	Mintage	VF20	XF40	MS60	MS63	MS65
JE5746-1986 (p)	7,344	PF65 40.00				

KM# 176 2 NEW SHEQALIM
28.80 g., 0.850 Silver 0.787 oz. ASW, 37 mm. **Series:** Hanukka **Subject:** Algerian Hanukka Lamp, 19th Century **Obv:** Value and text **Rev:** Algerian lamp **Edge:** Reeded

Date	Mintage	VF20	XF40	MS60	MS63	MS65
JE5747-1986 (f)	8,343	PF65 38.00				

KM# 178 2 NEW SHEQALIM

28.80 g., 0.850 Silver 0.787 oz. ASW, 37 mm. **Series:** Independence Day **Subject:** 20th Anniversary of United Jerusalem; Israel's 39th Anniversary **Obv:** Stylized value **Rev:** Circular city within numeral value **Edge:** Hebrew lettering

Date	Mintage	VF20	XF40	MS60	MS63	MS65
JE5747-1987 (u)	7,788	PF65 40.00				

KM# 184 2 NEW SHEQALIM

28.80 g., 0.850 Silver 0.787 oz. ASW, 37 mm. **Series:** Hanukka **Subject:** English Hanukka Lamp, 18th Century **Obv:** Value above text **Rev:** English lamp **Edge:** Reeded

Date	Mintage	VF20	XF40	MS60	MS63	MS65
JE5748-1987 (d)	8,039	PF65 38.00				

KM# 186 2 NEW SHEQALIM

28.80 g., 0.850 Silver 0.787 oz. ASW, 37 mm. **Series:** Independence Day **Subject:** Declaration of Independence; Israel's 40th Anniversary **Obv:** Menorah flanked by sprigs to to upper left of stylized value **Rev:** Stylized figures of government within large numeral 40 **Edge:** Hebrew lettering

Date	Mintage	VF20	XF40	MS60	MS63	MS65
JE5748-1988 (p)	9,100	PF65 40.00				

KM# 192 2 NEW SHEQALIM

28.80 g., 0.850 Silver 0.787 oz. ASW, 37 mm. **Series:** Hanukka **Subject:** Tunisian Hanukka Lamp, 19th Century **Obv:** Value above text **Rev:** Tunisian lamp **Edge:** Reeded

Date	Mintage	VF20	XF40	MS60	MS63	MS65
JE5749-1988 (u)	7,110	PF65 35.00				

KM# 200 2 NEW SHEQALIM

28.80 g., 0.850 Silver 0.787 oz. ASW, 37 mm. **Series:** Independence Day **Subject:** Promised Land; Israel's 41st Anniversary **Obv:** Value to left within horizontal lines **Rev:** Roe deer facing right among trees **Edge:** Hebrew lettering

Date	Mintage	VF20	XF40	MS60	MS63	MS65
JE5749-1989 (f)	7,062	PF65 40.00				

KM# 206 2 NEW SHEQALIM

28.80 g., 0.850 Silver 0.787 oz. ASW, 37 mm. **Series:** Hanukka **Subject:** Persian Hanukka Lamp, 17th Century **Obv:** Value at upper left above text **Rev:** Persian lamp **Edge:** Reeded

Date	Mintage	VF20	XF40	MS60	MS63	MS65
JE5750-1989 (m)	6,282	PF65 38.00				

KM# 213 2 NEW SHEQALIM

28.80 g., 0.850 Silver 0.787 oz. ASW, 37 mm. **Series:** Independence Day **Subject:** Archaeology; Israel's 42nd Anniversary **Obv:** Linear value to right of menorah flanked by sprigs **Rev:** Archaeology **Edge:** Hebrew lettering

Date	Mintage	VF20	XF40	MS60	MS63	MS65
JE5750-1990 (f)	5,457	PF65 40.00				

KM# 216 2 NEW SHEQALIM

28.80 g., 0.850 Silver 0.787 oz. ASW, 37 mm. **Series:** Hanukka **Subject:** Cochin (India) Hanukka Lamp, 19th Century **Obv:** Value at lower left **Rev:** Cochin lamp **Edge:** Reeded

Date	Mintage	VF20	XF40	MS60	MS63	MS65
JE5751-1990 (f)	5,383	PF65 40.00				

KM# 219 2 NEW SHEQALIM

28.80 g.; 0.925 Silver 0.8565 oz. ASW, 38.7 mm. **Series:** Independence Day **Subject:** Immigration; Israel's 43rd Anniversary **Obv:** Value to left within shaded diagonal lines **Rev:** Plane above stylized standing figures **Edge:** Hebrew lettering

Date	Mintage	VF20	XF40	MS60	MS63	MS65
JE5751-1991 (u)	6,695	PF65 45.00				

KM# 221 2 NEW SHEQALIM

28.80 g., 0.925 Silver 0.8565 oz. ASW, 38.7 mm. **Series:** Wildlife **Subject:** Dove and Cedar Tree **Obv:** Trees and value **Rev:** Stylized dove and tree trunk **Edge:** Reeded

Date	Mintage	VF20	XF40	MS60	MS63	MS65
JE5752-1991 (f)	5,005	PF65 55.00				

KM# 224 2 NEW SHEQALIM

28.80 g., 0.925 Silver 0.8565 oz. ASW, 38.7 mm. **Series:** Judaica **Subject:** Kiddush Cup **Obv:** Value and cup **Rev:** Kiddush cup **Edge:** Reeded

Date	Mintage	VF20	XF40	MS60	MS63	MS65
JE5752-1991 (f)	6,575	PF65 40.00				

KM# 226 2 NEW SHEQALIM
28.80 g., 0.925 Silver 0.8565 oz. ASW, 38.7 mm. **Series:** Independence Day **Subject:** Law in Israel; Israel's 44th Anniversary **Obv:** Value **Rev:** Scales above arched doorway **Edge:** Hebrew lettering

Date	Mintage	VF20	XF40	MS60	MS63	MS65
JE5752-1992 (p)	4,486	PF65 50.00				

KM# 228 2 NEW SHEQALIM
28.80 g., 0.925 Silver 0.8565 oz. ASW, 38.7 mm. **Series:** IX Paralympic Games **Subject:** IX Paralympic Games **Obv:** Value to right of menorah flanked by sprigs **Rev:** Shaded star in center of horizontal lines to right and upper left **Edge:** Reeded

Date	Mintage	VF20	XF40	MS60	MS63	MS65
JE5752-1992 (f)	3,718	PF65 45.00				

KM# 232 2 NEW SHEQALIM
28.80 g., 0.925 Silver 0.8565 oz. ASW, 38.7 mm. **Series:** Wildlife **Subject:** Roe and Lily **Obv:** Value at upper right of lilies **Rev:** Roe deer facing left **Edge:** Reeded

Date	Mintage	VF20	XF40	MS60	MS63	MS65
JE5753-1992 (p)	4,724	PF65 50.00				

KM# 235 2 NEW SHEQALIM
28.80 g., 0.925 Silver 0.8565 oz. ASW, 38.7 mm. **Series:** 150th Anniversary of Binai Brith **Subject:** 150th Anniversary of B'nai Brith **Obv:** Stylized design with value at center **Rev:** Stylized design with inscription **Edge:** Reeded

Date	Mintage	VF20	XF40	MS60	MS63	MS65
JE5752-1992 (f)	4,622	PF65 40.00				

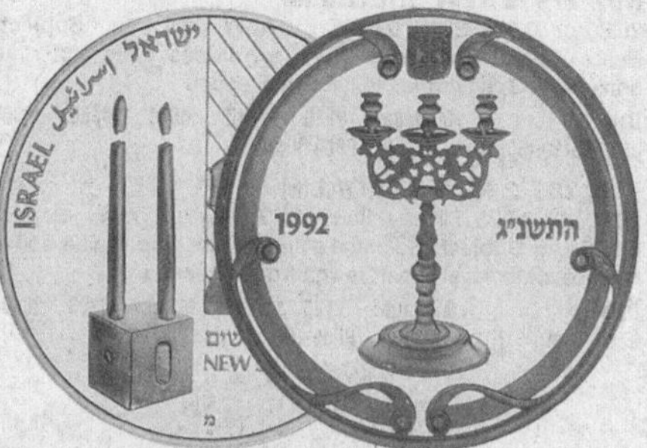

KM# 239 2 NEW SHEQALIM
28.80 g., 0.925 Silver 0.8565 oz. ASW, 38.7 mm. **Series:** Judaica **Subject:** Shabbat Candlesticks **Obv:** Value at center right within diagonal lines, lit candles on box at lower left **Rev:** Shabbat candles **Edge:** Reeded

Date	Mintage	VF20	XF40	MS60	MS63	MS65
JE5753-1992 (p)	4,975	PF65 40.00				

KM# 241 2 NEW SHEQALIM
28.80 g., 0.925 Silver 0.8565 oz. ASW, 38.7 mm. **Series:** Independence Day **Subject:** Tourism; Israel's 45th Anniversary **Obv:** Menorah flanked by sprigs above value and date **Rev:** Tourism objects **Edge:** Hebrew lettering

Date	Mintage	VF20	XF40	MS60	MS63	MS65
JE5753-1993 (u)	4,570	PF65 42.00				

KM# 245 2 NEW SHEQALIM
28.80 g., 0.925 Silver 0.8565 oz. ASW, 38.7 mm. **Series:** Wildlife **Subject:** Hart and Apple Tree **Obv:** Apple tree sprig to lower left of value **Rev:** Buck and young hart deer facing left **Edge:** Reeded

Date	Mintage	VF20	XF40	MS60	MS63	MS65
JE5754-1993 (f)	5,382	PF65 50.00				

KM# 248 2 NEW SHEQALIM
28.80 g., 0.925 Silver 0.8565 oz. ASW, 38.7 mm. **Subject:** Revolt and Heroism **Obv:** Diagonal dotted lines with value to upper left **Rev:** Medal with diagonal dotted lines and star to left of flame **Edge:** Reeded

Date	Mintage	VF20	XF40	MS60	MS63	MS65
JE5753-1993 (u)	4,994	PF65 42.00				

KM# 251 2 NEW SHEQALIM
28.80 g., 0.925 Silver 0.8565 oz. ASW, 38.7 mm. **Series:** Judaica **Subject:** Havdalah Spicebox **Obv:** Torah crown to left of value **Rev:** Havdalah spicebox **Edge:** Reeded

Date	Mintage	VF20	XF40	MS60	MS63	MS65
JE5754-1993 (f)	4,750	PF65 40.00				

KM# 253 2 NEW SHEQALIM
28.80 g., 0.925 Silver 0.8565 oz. ASW, 38.7 mm. **Series:** Independence Day **Subject:** Environment; Israel's 46th Anniversary **Rev:** World globe and flower **Edge:** Hebrew lettering

Date	Mintage	VF20	XF40	MS60	MS63	MS65
JE5754-1994 (f)	4,272	PF65 50.00				

KM# 257 2 NEW SHEQALIM
28.80 g., 0.925 Silver 0.8565 oz. ASW, 38.7 mm. **Series:** Biblical Art **Subject:** Binding of Isaac **Obv:** Value above text to right of menorah flanked by sprigs **Rev:** Stylized figures below angel **Edge:** Reeded

Date	Mintage	VF20	XF40	MS60	MS63	MS65
JE5755-1994 (u)	4,439	PF65 100				

KM# 261 2 NEW SHEQALIM
28.80 g., 0.925 Silver 0.8565 oz. ASW, 38.7 mm. **Series:** Wildlife **Subject:** Leopard and Palm Tree **Obv:** Palm tree **Rev:** Leopard **Edge:** Reeded

Date	Mintage	VF20	XF40	MS60	MS63	MS65
JE5755-1994 (u)	4,283	PF65 55.00				

KM# 264 2 NEW SHEQALIM

28.80 g., 0.925 Silver 0.8565 oz. ASW, 38.7 mm. **Series:** Independence Day **Subject:** Medicine in Israel; Israel's 47th Anniversary **Obv:** Snake on a menorah **Rev:** Value, text and menorah flanked by sprigs **Edge:** Hebrew lettering

Date	Mintage	VF20	XF40	MS60	MS63	MS65
JE5755-1995 (f)	3,698	PF65 50.00				

KM# 268 2 NEW SHEQALIM

28.80 g., 0.925 Silver 0.8565 oz. ASW, 38.7 mm. **Series:** 50th Anniversary - Defeat of Nazi Germany **Subject:** 50th Anniversary of Defeat of Nazi Germany **Obv:** Value above text to right of menorah flanked by sprigs **Rev:** Shaded v-shape with state emblems within **Edge:** Reeded

Date	Mintage	VF20	XF40	MS60	MS63	MS65
JE5755-1995 (h)	5,808	PF65 50.00				

KM# 272 2 NEW SHEQALIM

28.80 g., 0.925 Silver 0.8565 oz. ASW, 38.7 mm. **Subject:** 50th Anniversary of the F.A.O. **Obv:** Barley stalks and value **Rev:** FAO logo and dates **Edge:** Reeded

Date	Mintage	VF20	XF40	MS60	MS63	MS65
JE5755-1995 (v)	3,945	PF65 50.00				

KM# 272a 2 NEW SHEQALIM

32.80 g., 0.925 Silver 0.9755 oz. ASW, 37.8 mm. **Subject:** 50th Anniversary of the F.A.O. **Obv:** Barley stalks, value and country name in Hebrew, English and Arabic, state emblem and legend "Fiftieth Anniversary F.A.O." in Hebrew and English **Rev:** Large F.A.O. logo and legends "1945-1995" and "Deal thy bread to the hungry (Isaiah 58:7)" in English and Hebrew **Edge:** Reeded **Note:** This coin is identical to KM#272 but approximately 4g. heavier and 0.2mm thicker

Date	Mintage	VF20	XF40	MS60	MS63	MS65
JE5755 (1995) (v)	Inc. above	PF65 55.00				

KM# 276 2 NEW SHEQALIM

28.80 g., 0.925 Silver 0.8565 oz. ASW, 38.7 mm. **Series:** Wildlife **Subject:** Fox and Vineyard **Obv:** Value and grape cluster **Rev:** Fox **Edge:** Reeded

Date	Mintage	VF20	XF40	MS60	MS63	MS65
JE5756-1995 (v)	3,436	PF65 60.00				

KM# 279 2 NEW SHEQALIM

28.80 g., 0.925 Silver 0.8565 oz. ASW, 38.7 mm. **Subject:** Peace Treaty with Jordan **Obv:** Text divides value and state arms **Rev:** Sprig divides text **Edge:** Reeded

Date	Mintage	VF20	XF40	MS60	MS63	MS65
JE5755-1995 (o)	3,536	PF65 50.00				

KM# 282 2 NEW SHEQALIM

28.80 g., 0.925 Silver 0.8565 oz. ASW, 38.7 mm. **Series:** Biblical Art **Subject:** Solomon's Judgement **Obv:** Value above text **Rev:** Medieval linear design **Edge:** Reeded

Date	Mintage	VF20	XF40	MS60	MS63	MS65
JE5755-1995 (f)	2,993	PF65 100				

KM# 288 2 NEW SHEQALIM

28.80 g., 0.925 Silver 0.8565 oz. ASW, 38.7 mm. **Series:** Port of Caesarea - 2000 years **Subject:** Port of Caesarea, 2000 years **Rev:** Ancient ship **Edge:** Reeded

Date	Mintage	VF20	XF40	MS60	MS63	MS65
JE5755-1995 (f)	2,560	PF65 45.00				

KM# 292 2 NEW SHEQALIM

28.80 g., 0.925 Silver 0.8565 oz. ASW, 38.7 mm. **Series:** Wildlife **Subject:** Nightingale and Fig Tree **Obv:** Value **Rev:** Nightingale **Edge:** Reeded

Date	Mintage	VF20	XF40	MS60	MS63	MS65
JE5757-1996 (v)	2,500	PF65 60.00				

KM# 295 2 NEW SHEQALIM

28.80 g., 0.925 Silver 0.8565 oz. ASW, 38.7 mm. **Series:** Biblical Art **Subject:** Miriam and the Women **Obv:** Value above text, state arms and star design at left **Rev:** Miriam and the women **Edge:** Reeded

Date	Mintage	VF20	XF40	MS60	MS63	MS65
JE5757-1996 (u)	2,568	PF65 100				

KM# 298 2 NEW SHEQALIM

28.80 g., 0.925 Silver 0.8565 oz. ASW, 38.7 mm. **Subject:** Yitzhak Rabin **Obv:** National arms and denomination **Rev:** Head of Yitzhak Rabin facing left **Edge:** Reeded

Date	Mintage	VF20	XF40	MS60	MS63	MS65
JE5756-1996 (u)	5,293	PF65 55.00				

KM# 301 2 NEW SHEQALIM

28.80 g., 0.925 Silver 0.8565 oz. ASW, 38.7 mm. **Series:** Independence Day **Subject:** First Zionist Congress Centennial; Israel's 49th Anniversary **Obv:** Value **Rev:** Half length figure leaning on rail facing left **Edge:** Reeded

Date	Mintage	VF20	XF40	MS60	MS63	MS65
JE5757-1997 (u)	4,281	PF65 50.00				

KM# 308 2 NEW SHEQALIM

28.80 g., 0.925 Silver 0.8565 oz. ASW, 38.7 mm. **Series:** Wildlife **Subject:** Lion and Pomegranate **Obv:** Lion walking right **Rev:** Pomegranates at upper left of value **Edge:** Reeded

Date	Mintage	VF20	XF40	MS60	MS63	MS65
JE5758-1997 (u)	2,277	PF65 60.00				

KM# 311 2 NEW SHEQALIM

28.80 g., 0.925 Silver 0.8565 oz. ASW, 38.7 mm. **Series:** Independence Day **Subject:** Israel's 50th Anniversary **Obv:** Value to right of menorah flanked by sprigs above text **Rev:** Flag within stars **Edge:** Reeded

Date	Mintage	VF20	XF40	MS60	MS63	MS65
JE5758-1998 (u)	8,279	PF65 50.00				

KM# 317 2 NEW SHEQALIM

28.80 g., 0.925 Silver 0.8565 oz. ASW, 38.7 mm. **Series:** Biblical Art **Subject:** Noah's Ark **Obv:** Dove, rainbow and value **Rev:** Noah releasing dove **Edge:** Reeded

Date	Mintage	VF20	XF40	MS60	MS63	MS65
JE5758-1998 (u)	2,164	PF65 100				

KM# 322 2 NEW SHEQALIM

28.80 g., 0.925 Silver 0.8565 oz. ASW, 38.7 mm. **Series:** Wildlife **Subject:** Stork and Fir Tree **Obv:** Fir tree and value **Rev:** Stork **Edge:** Reeded

Date	Mintage	VF20	XF40	MS60	MS63	MS65
JE5759-1998 (u)	2,500	PF65 55.00				

KM# 326 2 NEW SHEQALIM

28.80 g., 0.925 Silver 0.8565 oz. ASW, 38.7 mm. **Series:** Independence Day **Subject:** High Tech in Israel; Israel's 51st Anniversary **Obv:** Value and 01 computer code **Rev:** 10 computer code as bouquet **Edge:** Reeded

Date	Mintage	VF20	XF40	MS60	MS63	MS65
JE5759-1999 (u)	1,850	PF65 50.00				

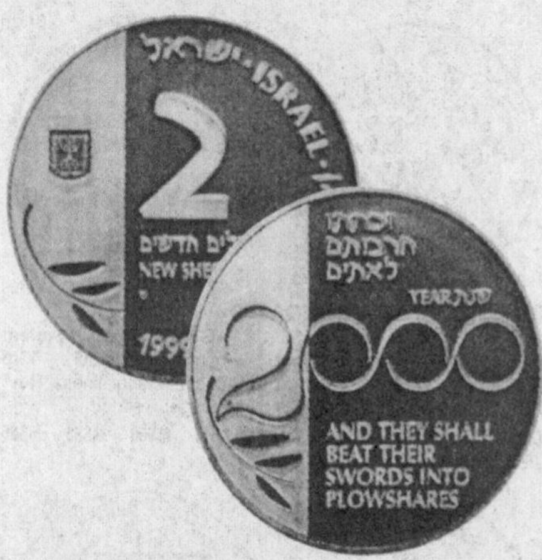

KM# 329 2 NEW SHEQALIM
28.80 g., 0.925 Silver 0.8565 oz. ASW, 38.7 mm. **Series:** Millenium 2000 **Subject:** Millenium 2000 **Obv:** Value and olive branch **Rev:** Year 2000 motif incorporating dove with olive branch **Edge:** Reeded **Edge Lettering:** The Millennium

Date	Mintage	VF20	XF40	MS60	MS63	MS65
JE5759-1999 (u)	4,092	PF65 45.00				

KM# 334 2 NEW SHEQALIM
28.80 g., 0.925 Silver 0.8565 oz. ASW, 38.7 mm. **Series:** Biblical Art **Subject:** Abraham and the Stars **Obv:** Menorah, value and date among stars above text **Rev:** Abraham looking at stars **Edge:** Reeded

Date	Mintage	VF20	XF40	MS60	MS63	MS65
JE5759-1999 (o)	5,843	PF65 100				

KM# 337 2 NEW SHEQALIM
28.80 g., 0.925 Silver 0.8565 oz. ASW, 38.7 mm. **Series:** Independence Day **Subject:** Love Thy Neighbor; Israel's 52nd Anniversary **Obv:** Value **Rev:** Arch above inscription **Rev. Inscription:** Love Thy Neighbor, As Thyself **Edge:** Reeded

Date	Mintage	VF20	XF40	MS60	MS63	MS65
JE5760-2000 (u)	2,258	PF65 50.00				

KM# 340 2 NEW SHEQALIM
28.80 g., 0.925 Silver 0.8565 oz. ASW, 38.7 mm. **Series:** Biblical Art **Subject:** Joseph and his Brothers **Obv:** Denomination **Rev:** Joseph standing before sheaves of wheat into brothers **Edge:** Reeded

Date	Mintage	VF20	XF40	MS60	MS63	MS65
JE5760-2000 (u)	2,100	PF65 100				

KM# 170 5 NEW SHEQALIM
8.63 g., 0.900 Gold 0.2497 oz. AGW, 22 mm. **Series:** Holyland Sites **Subject:** Akko **Rev:** Akko **Edge:** Reeded **Shape:** 12-sided

Date	Mintage	VF20	XF40	MS60	MS63	MS65
JE5747-1986 (b)	2,800	PF65 450				

KM# 182 5 NEW SHEQALIM
8.63 g., 0.900 Gold 0.2497 oz. AGW, 22 mm. **Series:** Holyland Sites **Subject:** Jericho **Obv:** Value **Rev:** Jericho to left of menorah and palm trees **Edge:** Reeded **Shape:** 12-sided

Date	Mintage	VF20	XF40	MS60	MS63	MS65
JE5748-1987 (o)	4,000	PF65 475				

KM# 190 5 NEW SHEQALIM
8.63 g., 0.900 Gold 0.2497 oz. AGW, 22 mm. **Series:** Holyland Sites **Subject:** Caesarea **Obv:** Value **Rev:** Caesarea **Edge:** Reeded **Shape:** 12-sided

Date	Mintage	VF20	XF40	MS60	MS63	MS65
JE5749-1988 (o)	3,454	PF65 475				

KM# 204 5 NEW SHEQALIM
8.63 g., 0.900 Gold 0.2497 oz. AGW, 22 mm. **Series:** Holyland Sites **Subject:** Jaffa **Obv:** Value **Rev:** Jaffa Harbor **Edge:** Reeded **Shape:** 12-sided

Date	Mintage	VF20	XF40	MS60	MS63	MS65
JE5750-1989 (o)	2,402	PF65 475				

KM# 207 5 NEW SHEQALIM
8.20 g., Copper-Nickel, 24 mm. **Obv:** Value **Rev:** Ancient column capitol **Edge:** Plain **Shape:** 12-sided

Date	Mintage	VF20	XF40	MS60	MS63	MS65
JE5750 (1990) (f)	15,000,000	—	—	—	3.00	3.75
JE5751 (1991) (j)	324,000	—	—	3.00	3.50	5.00
JE5752 (1992) (j)	413,000	—	—	3.00	3.50	5.00
JE5754 (1994) (v)	2,016,000	—	—	—	3.00	3.75
JE5755 (1995) (v)	2,160,000	—	—	—	3.00	3.75
JE5757 (1997) (u)	2,160,000	—	—	—	3.00	3.75
JE5757 (1997) (v)	2,160,000	—	—	—	3.00	3.75
JE5758 (1998) (h)	2,160,000	—	—	—	3.00	3.75
JE5759 (1999) (h)	2,160,000	—	—	—	3.00	3.75
JE5759 (1999) (u)	2,160,000	—	—	—	3.00	3.75
Note: Rounded						
JE5760 (2000) (v)	4,464,000	—	—	—	3.00	3.75

KM# 208 5 NEW SHEQALIM
8.20 g., Copper-Nickel, 24 mm. **Subject:** Levi Eshkol **Obv:** Value **Rev:** Bust of Levi Eshlol facing **Edge:** Plain **Shape:** 12-sided

Date	Mintage	VF20	XF40	MS60	MS63	MS65
JE5750 (1990) (f)	1,500,000	—	—	—	3.00	7.00

KM# 211 5 NEW SHEQALIM
8.63 g., 0.900 Gold 0.2497 oz. AGW, 22 mm. **Series:** Holyland Sites **Subject:** Sea of Galilee **Obv:** Value **Rev:** Sea of Galilee map **Edge:** Reeded

Date	Mintage	VF20	XF40	MS60	MS63	MS65
JE5751-1990 (o)	1,935	PF65 475				

KM# 217 5 NEW SHEQALIM
8.20 g., Copper-Nickel, 24 mm. **Obv:** Value, small menorah and inscription Hanukka **Rev:** Ancient column capitol **Edge:** Plain **Shape:** 12-sided **Note:** Coins dated JE5754-5770 have the Star of David mint mark; the JE5751-5753 coins do not.

Date	Mintage	VF20	XF40	MS60	MS63	MS65
JE5751 (1991) (j)	500,000	—	—	—	3.50	4.00
JE5752 (1992) (j)	486,000	—	—	—	3.50	4.00
JE5753 (1993) (j)	500,000	—	—	—	3.50	4.00
JE5754 (1994) (u) Sets only	12,000	—	—	—	—	4.00
JE5755 (1995) (u) Sets only	10,000	—	—	—	—	4.00
JE5756 (1996) (u) Sets only	7,500	—	—	—	—	4.00
JE5758 (1998) (u) Sets only	10,000	—	—	—	—	4.00
JE5757 (1997) (u) Sets only	7,500	—	—	—	—	4.00
JE5759 (1999) (u) Sets only	6,000	—	—	—	—	6.00
JE5760 (2000) (u) Sets only	5,000	—	—	—	—	6.00
JE5761 (2001) (u) Sets only	4,000	—	—	—	—	7.00

KM# 222 5 NEW SHEQALIM
8.63 g., 0.900 Gold 0.2497 oz. AGW, 22 mm. **Series:** Wildlife **Subject:** Dove and Cedar Tree **Obv:** Cedar trees and value **Rev:** Dove and tree trunk within legend **Edge:** Reeded

Date	Mintage	VF20	XF40	MS60	MS63	MS65
JE5752-1991 (o)	2,000	PF65 475				

KM# 229 5 NEW SHEQALIM
8.63 g., 0.900 Gold 0.2497 oz. AGW, 22 mm. **Subject:** IX Paralympic Games **Obv:** Value at center with half horizontal lines at right **Rev:** Shaded star within horizontal lines **Edge:** Reeded

Date	Mintage	VF20	XF40	MS60	MS63	MS65
JE5752-1992 (u)	1,629	PF65 425				

KM# 233 5 NEW SHEQALIM
8.63 g., 0.900 Gold 0.2497 oz. AGW, 22 mm. **Series:** Wildlife **Subject:** Roe and Lily **Obv:** Value at upper right of lily **Rev:** Roe deer facing left **Edge:** Reeded

Date	Mintage	VF20	XF40	MS60	MS63	MS65
JE5753-1992 (p)	2,150	PF65 475				

KM# 236 5 NEW SHEQALIM
8.63 g., 0.900 Gold 0.2497 oz. AGW, 22 mm. **Subject:** 150th Anniversary of B'nai Brith **Obv:** Stylized design with value at upper left **Rev:** Stylized design with inscription **Edge:** Reeded

Date	Mintage	VF20	XF40	MS60	MS63	MS65
JE5753-1992 (u)	2,305	PF65 425				

KM# 237 5 NEW SHEQALIM

8.20 g., Copper-Nickel, 24 mm. **Obv:** Value **Rev:** Bust of Chaim Weizmann facing **Edge:** Plain **Shape:** 12-sided

Date	Mintage	VF20	XF40	MS60	MS63	MS65
JE5753 (1993) (j)	1,500,000	—	—	2.50	3.50	5.50

KM# 246 5 NEW SHEQALIM

8.63 g., 0.900 Gold 0.2497 oz. AGW, 22 mm. **Series:** Wildlife **Subject:** Hart and Apple Tree **Obv:** Value at upper right of apple tree sprig **Rev:** Buck and young hart **Edge:** Reeded

Date	Mintage	VF20	XF40	MS60	MS63	MS65
JE5754-1993 (u)	1,782	PF65 475				

KM# 254 5 NEW SHEQALIM

8.63 g., 0.900 Gold 0.2497 oz. AGW, 22 mm. **Series:** Independence Day **Subject:** Environment; Israel's 46th Anniversary **Obv:** Value **Rev:** World globe within flower **Edge:** Reeded

Date	Mintage	VF20	XF40	MS60	MS63	MS65
JE5754-1994 (sa)	1,407	PF65 425				

KM# 262 5 NEW SHEQALIM

8.63 g., 0.900 Gold 0.2497 oz. AGW, 22 mm. **Series:** Wildlife **Subject:** Leopard and Palm Tree **Obv:** Palm tree and value **Rev:** Leopard **Edge:** Reeded

Date	Mintage	VF20	XF40	MS60	MS63	MS65
JE5755-1994 (o)	1,355	PF65 475				

KM# 265 5 NEW SHEQALIM

8.63 g., 0.900 Gold 0.2497 oz. AGW, 22 mm. **Series:** Independence Day **Subject:** Medicine in Israel; Israel's 47th Anniversary **Obv:** Snake on a menorah **Rev:** Value **Edge:** Reeded

Date	Mintage	VF20	XF40	MS60	MS63	MS65
JE5755-1995 (o)	1,147	PF65 425				

KM# 277 5 NEW SHEQALIM

8.63 g., 0.900 Gold 0.2497 oz. AGW, 22 mm. **Series:** Wildlife **Subject:** Fox and Vineyard **Obv:** Value and grape cluster **Rev:** Fox **Edge:** Reeded

Date	Mintage	VF20	XF40	MS60	MS63	MS65
JE5756-1995 (u)	877	PF65 525				

KM# 293 5 NEW SHEQALIM

8.63 g., 0.900 Gold 0.2497 oz. AGW, 22 mm. **Series:** Wildlife **Subject:** Nightingale and Fig Tree **Obv:** Fig leaves and value **Rev:** Nightingale **Edge:** Reeded

Date	Mintage	VF20	XF40	MS60	MS63	MS65
JE5757-1996 (v)	805	PF65 575				

KM# 309 5 NEW SHEQALIM

8.63 g., 0.900 Gold 0.2497 oz. AGW, 22 mm. **Series:** Wildlife **Subject:** Lion and Pomegranate **Obv:** Pomegranates and value **Rev:** Lion walking right **Edge:** Reeded

Date	Mintage	VF20	XF40	MS60	MS63	MS65
JE5758-1997 (u)	742	PF65 550				

KM# 323 5 NEW SHEQALIM

8.63 g., 0.900 Gold 0.2497 oz. AGW, 22 mm. **Series:** Wildlife **Subject:** Stork and Fir Tree **Obv:** Fir trees and value **Rev:** Stork **Edge:** Reeded

Date	Mintage	VF20	XF40	MS60	MS63	MS65
JE5759-1998 (u)	615	PF65 600				

KM# 350 5 NEW SHEQALIM

8.63 g., 0.900 Gold 0.2497 oz. AGW, 22 mm. **Series:** Wildlife **Subject:** Wild Goat and Acacia Tree **Obv:** Acacia tree **Rev:** Ibex **Edge:** Reeded

Date	Mintage	VF20	XF40	MS60	MS63	MS65
JE5761-2000 (u)	600	PF65 600				

KM# 166 10 NEW SHEQALIM

17.28 g., 0.900 Gold 0.500 oz. AGW, 30 mm. **Series:** Independence Day **Subject:** Art in Israel, Israel's 38th Anniversary **Obv:** Value **Rev:** Stylized designs **Edge:** Reeded

Date	Mintage	VF20	XF40	MS60	MS63	MS65
JE5746-1986 (d)	2,485	PF65 850				

KM# 179 10 NEW SHEQALIM

17.28 g., 0.900 Gold 0.500 oz. AGW, 30 mm. **Series:** Independence Day **Subject:** 20th Anniversary of United Jerusalem; Israel's 39th Anniversary **Edge:** Reeded

Date	Mintage	VF20	XF40	MS60	MS63	MS65
JE5747-1987 (p)	3,200	PF65 850				

KM# 187 10 NEW SHEQALIM

17.28 g., 0.900 Gold 0.500 oz. AGW, 30 mm. **Series:** Independence Day **Subject:** Declaration of Independence; Israel's 40th Anniversary **Obv:** Menorah within stylized value **Rev:** Stylized figures of government within large numeral 40 **Edge:** Reeded

Date	Mintage	VF20	XF40	MS60	MS63	MS65
JE5748-1988 (d)	4,575	PF65 850				

KM# 201 10 NEW SHEQALIM

17.28 g., 0.900 Gold 0.500 oz. AGW, 30 mm. **Series:** Independence Day **Subject:** Promised Land; Israel's 41st Anniversary **Rev:** Gazelle in forest, legend at left **Edge:** Reeded

Date	Mintage	VF20	XF40	MS60	MS63	MS65
JE5749-1989 (o)	2,743	PF65 850				

KM# 214 10 NEW SHEQALIM

17.28 g., 0.900 Gold 0.500 oz. AGW, 30 mm. **Series:** Independence Day **Subject:** Archaeology; Israel's 42nd Anniversary **Obv:** Menorah to left of large linear value **Rev:** Archaeology **Edge:** Reeded

Date	Mintage	VF20	XF40	MS60	MS63	MS65
JE5750-1990 (p)	1,815	PF65 950				

KM# 230 10 NEW SHEQALIM

17.28 g., 0.900 Gold 0.500 oz. AGW, 30 mm. **Series:** Independence Day **Subject:** Immigration; Israel's 43rd Anniversary **Obv:** Value within shaded diagonal lines **Rev:** Plane above stylized standing figures **Edge:** Reeded

Date	Mintage	VF20	XF40	MS60	MS63	MS65
JE5751-1991 (u)	2,236	PF65 850				

KM# 227 10 NEW SHEQALIM

17.28 g., 0.900 Gold 0.500 oz. AGW, 30 mm. **Series:** Independence Day **Subject:** Law in Israel; Israel's 44th Anniversary **Obv:** Value **Rev:** Scales above arched doorway **Edge:** Reeded **Note:** Edge varieties exist.

Date	Mintage	VF20	XF40	MS60	MS63	MS65
JE5752-1992 (p)	1,750	PF65 950				
Note: Narrow spaced edge reeding						
JE5752-1992 (u)	375	PF65 2,000				
Note: Wide spaced edge reeding						

KM# 242 10 NEW SHEQALIM

17.28 g., 0.900 Gold 0.500 oz. AGW, 30 mm. **Series:** Independence Day **Subject:** Tourism; Israel's 45th Anniversary **Obv:** Value **Rev:** Tourism objects **Edge:** Reeded

Date	Mintage	VF20	XF40	MS60	MS63	MS65
JE5753-1993 (u)	1,944	PF65 850				

KM# 249 10 NEW SHEQALIM

17.28 g., 0.900 Gold 0.500 oz. AGW, 30 mm. **Series:** Revolt and Heroism **Subject:** Revolt and Heroism **Obv:** Value within beaded diagonal lines **Rev:** Medal with star within beaded diagonal lines to left of flame **Edge:** Reeded

Date	Mintage	VF20	XF40	MS60	MS63	MS65
JE5753-1993 (u)	1,583	PF65 850				

KM# 255 10 NEW SHEQALIM

17.28 g., 0.900 Gold 0.500 oz. AGW, 30 mm. **Series:** Independence Day **Subject:** Environment; Israel's 46th Anniversary **Obv:** Slanted value **Rev:** World globe within flower **Edge:** Reeded

Date	Mintage	VF20	XF40	MS60	MS63	MS65
JE5754-1994 (sa)	1,482	PF65 850				

KM# 258 10 NEW SHEQALIM

17.28 g., 0.900 Gold 0.500 oz. AGW, 30 mm. **Series:** Biblical Art **Subject:** Binding of Isaac **Rev:** Abraham's willingness to sacrifice Isaac **Edge:** Reeded

Date	Mintage	VF20	XF40	MS60	MS63	MS65
JE5755-1994 (o)	1,209	PF65 1,100				

KM# 266 10 NEW SHEQALIM

17.28 g., 0.900 Gold 0.500 oz. AGW, 30 mm. **Series:** Independence Day **Subject:** Medicine in Israel; Israel's 47th Anniversary **Obv:** Value **Rev:** Snake on a menorah **Edge:** Reeded

Date	Mintage	VF20	XF40	MS60	MS63	MS65
JE5755-1995 (o)	1,230	PF65 850				

KM# 269 10 NEW SHEQALIM

16.96 g., 0.917 Gold 0.500 oz. AGW, 30 mm. **Subject:** 50th Anniversary of Defeat of Nazi Germany **Obv:** Value above text to right of menorah flanked by sprigs **Rev:** Flag and emblems within v-shaped design **Edge:** Reeded

Date	Mintage	VF20	XF40	MS60	MS63	MS65
JE5755-1995 (h)	1,742	PF65 850				

KM# A270 10 NEW SHEQALIM

7.00 g., Bi-Metallic Aureate Bonded Bronze center in Nickel Bonded Steel ring, 23 mm. **Obv:** Value and vertical line in center **Rev:** Palm tree and two baskets **Edge:** Reeded **Note:** Mule obverse of KM#270 and reverse of KM#315

Date	Mintage	VF20	XF40	MS60	MS63	MS65
JE5755 (1995) (u)	—	—	60.00	75.00	125	200

KM# 270 10 NEW SHEQALIM

7.00 g., Bi-Metallic Aureate Bonded Bronze center in Nickel Bonded Steel ring, 23 mm. **Obv:** Value, vertical lines and text within circle **Rev:** Palm tree and baskets within half beaded circle **Edge:** Reeded

Date	Mintage	VF20	XF40	MS60	MS63	MS65
JE5755 (1995) (u)	28,224,000	—	—	—	4.00	5.00

KM# 273 10 NEW SHEQALIM

7.00 g., Bi-Metallic Aureate Bonded Bronze center in Nickel Bonded Steel ring, 23 mm. **Obv:** Value, text and vertical lines within circle **Rev:** Bust of Golda Meir facing at right within vertical lines and circle **Edge:** Reeded

Date	Mintage	VF20	XF40	MS60	MS63	MS65
JE5755 (1995) (u)	1,584,000	—	—	—	4.50	8.00

KM# 280 10 NEW SHEQALIM

16.96 g., 0.917 Gold 0.500 oz. AGW, 30 mm. **Subject:** Peace Treaty with Jordan **Edge:** Reeded

Date	Mintage	VF20	XF40	MS60	MS63	MS65
JE5755-1995 (o)	1,451	PF65 850				

KM# 283 10 NEW SHEQALIM

17.28 g., 0.900 Gold 0.500 oz. AGW, 30 mm. **Series:** Biblical Art **Subject:** Solomon's Judgement **Obv:** Value above text **Rev:** Medieval linear design **Edge:** Reeded

Date	Mintage	VF20	XF40	MS60	MS63	MS65
JE5756-1995 (o)	961	PF65 1,100				

KM# 289 10 NEW SHEQALIM

16.96 g., 0.917 Gold 0.500 oz. AGW, 30 mm. **Subject:** Port of Caesarea, 2000 years **Obv:** Anchor to lower left of value and text **Rev:** Port of Caesarea, ancient ship **Edge:** Reeded

Date	Mintage	VF20	XF40	MS60	MS63	MS65
JE5755-1995 (o)	927	PF65 950				

KM# 285 10 NEW SHEQALIM

16.96 g., 0.917 Gold 0.500 oz. AGW, 30 mm. **Series:** Independence Day **Subject:** Jerusalem 3000; Israel's 48th Anniversary **Obv:** State arms left of large value **Rev:** Inscription at center **Edge:** Reeded

Date	Mintage	VF20	XF40	MS60	MS63	MS65
JE5756-1996 (sa)	1,642	PF65 950				

KM# 296 10 NEW SHEQALIM

17.28 g., 0.900 Gold 0.500 oz. AGW, 30 mm. **Series:** Biblical Art **Subject:** Miriam and the Women **Obv:** Value above text, state arms and star design at left **Rev:** Miriam and the women **Edge:** Reeded

Date	Mintage	VF20	XF40	MS60	MS63	MS65
JE5757-1996 (u)	855	PF65 1,150				

KM# 315 10 NEW SHEQALIM

7.00 g., Bi-Metallic Aureate Bonded Bronze center in Nickel Bonded Steel ring, 23 mm. **Series:** Hanukka **Subject:** Hanukka **Obv:** Value, text and menorah within circle and vertical lines **Rev:** Palm tree and baskets within half beaded circle **Edge:** Reeded

Date	Mintage	VF20	XF40	MS60	MS63	MS65
JE5756 (1996) (u) Sets only	7,500	—	—	—	—	7.00
JE5757 (1997) (u) Sets only	7,500	—	—	—	—	7.00
JE5758 (1998) (u) Sets only	10,000	—	—	—	—	7.00
JE5759 (1999) (u) Sets only	6,000	—	—	—	—	8.00
JE5760 (2000) (u) Sets only	5,000	—	—	—	—	9.00

KM# 302 10 NEW SHEQALIM

16.96 g., 0.917 Gold 0.500 oz. AGW, 30 mm. **Series:** Independence Day **Subject:** First Zionist Congress Centennial; Israel's 49th Anniversary **Obv:** Denomination **Rev:** Portrait of Herzl **Edge:** Reeded

Date	Mintage	VF20	XF40	MS60	MS63	MS65
JE5757-1997 (u)	1,326	PF65 850				

KM# 312 10 NEW SHEQALIM

15.55 g., 0.999 Gold 0.4994 oz. AGW, 30 mm. **Series:** Independence Day **Subject:** Israel's 50th Anniversary **Obv:** Value **Rev:** Flag **Edge:** Reeded

Date	Mintage	VF20	XF40	MS60	MS63	MS65
JE5758-1998 (u)	2,406	PF65 1,050				

KM# 319 10 NEW SHEQALIM

17.28 g., 0.900 Gold 0.500 oz. AGW, 30 mm. **Series:** Biblical Art **Subject:** Noah's Ark **Obv:** Rainbow, dove and value **Rev:** Noah releasing dove from ark **Edge:** Reeded

Date	Mintage	VF20	XF40	MS60	MS63	MS65
JE5758-1998 (u)	744	PF65 1,150				

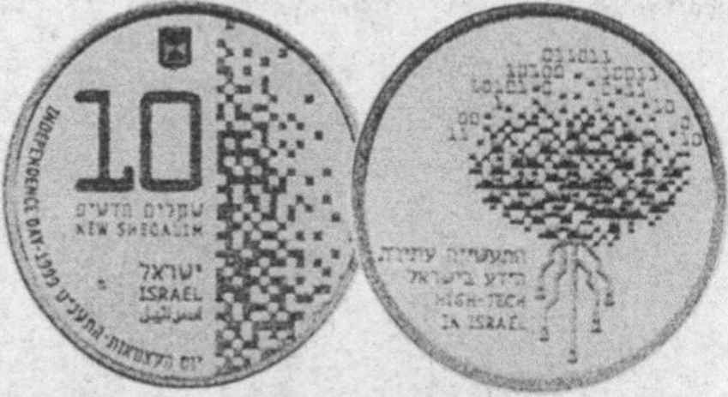

KM# 327 10 NEW SHEQALIM

16.96 g., 0.917 Gold 0.500 oz. AGW, 30 mm. **Series:** Independence Day **Subject:** High Tech in Israel; Israel's 51st Anniversary **Obv:** Value and 01 computer code **Rev:** 01 computer code as bouquet **Edge:** Reeded

Date	Mintage	VF20	XF40	MS60	MS63	MS65
JE5759-1999 (u)	751	PF65 1,100				

KM# 330 10 NEW SHEQALIM

16.96 g., 0.917 Gold 0.500 oz. AGW, 30 mm. **Subject:** Millennium 2000 **Obv:** Value and olive branch **Rev:** Year 2000 motif incorporating dove with olive branch **Edge:** Reeded

Date	Mintage	VF20	XF40	MS60	MS63	MS65
JE5759-1999 (u)	1,859	PF65 1,100				

KM# 335 10 NEW SHEQALIM

17.28 g., 0.900 Gold 0.500 oz. AGW, 30 mm. **Series:** Biblical Art **Subject:** Abraham and the Stars **Obv:** Arms above denomination **Rev:** Abraham gazing at the stars **Edge:** Reeded

Date	Mintage	VF20	XF40	MS60	MS63	MS65
JE5759-1999 (u)	687	PF65 1,150				

KM# 338 10 NEW SHEQALIM

16.96 g., 0.917 Gold 0.500 oz. AGW, 30 mm. **Series:** Independence Day **Subject:** Love Thy Neighbor; Israel's 52nd Anniversary **Obv:** Value **Rev:** Arch above inscription **Rev. Inscription:** Love Thy Neighbor, As Thyself **Edge:** Reeded

Date	Mintage	VF20	XF40	MS60	MS63	MS65
JE5760-2000 (u)	794	PF65 1,125				

KM# 341 10 NEW SHEQALIM

16.96 g., 0.917 Gold 0.500 oz. AGW, 30 mm. **Series:** Biblical Art **Subject:** Joseph and his Brothers **Obv:** Value **Rev:** Joseph standing before sheaves of wheat into his brothers **Edge:** Reeded

Date	Mintage	VF20	XF40	MS60	MS63	MS65
JE5760-2000 (u)	700	PF65 1,150				

KM# 299 20 NEW SHEQALIM
31.10 g., 0.999 Gold 0.999 oz. AGW, 35 mm. **Subject:** Yitzhak Rabin **Obv:** Menorah flanked by sprigs above text, value and date **Rev:** Head of Yitzhak Rabin facing left **Edge:** Reeded

Date	Mintage	VF20	XF40	MS60	MS63	MS65
JE5757-1996 (va)	1,949	PF65 2,200				

KM# 313 20 NEW SHEQALIM
31.10 g., 0.999 Gold 0.999 oz. AGW, 35 mm. **Series:** Independence Day **Subject:** Israel's 50th Anniversary **Obv:** Value **Rev:** Flag **Edge:** Reeded

Date	Mintage	VF20	XF40	MS60	MS63	MS65
JE5758-1998 (u)	2,345	PF65 2,200				

KM# 286 30 NEW SHEQALIM
155.52 g., 0.999 Silver 4.995 oz. ASW, 65 mm. **Series:** Independence Day **Subject:** Jerusalem 3000; Israel's 48th Anniversary **Obv:** State arms left of value **Rev:** Inscription at center **Edge:** Reeded **Note:** Illustration reduced.

Date	Mintage	VF20	XF40	MS60	MS63	MS65
JE5756-1996 (f)	2,929	PF65 275				

PATTERNS

KM#	Date	Mintage	Identification	Mkt Val
Pn1	JE5720 (1960)	2	Agora. 8 fat and wide grains. Large 9.50mm 1 and date.	7,500
Pn2	JE5720 (1960)	4	Agora. 8 thin and narrow grains. Small 9.00mm 1 and large date.	7,500
Pn3	JE5720 (1960)	1	Agora. 8 thin and narrow grains. Large 9.50mm 1 and date.	—
Pn4	JE5720 (1960)	1	Agora. Aluminum. 8 fate and wide grains. Small 9 mm 1. Struck as coin turn.	6,000
Pn5	JE5722 (1962)	3	Lira. Copper-Nickel. As KM#38 but mis-spelling of Hanukka in Hebrew. Letter "Nun" instead of "Kof".	2,500

PIEDFORT

KM#	Date	Mintage	Identification	Mkt Val
P1	JE5741 (1981)	30,217	New Agora. Copper-Nickel. KM#106.	2.00
P2	JE5741 (1981)	30,217	5 New Agorot. Copper-Nickel. KM#107.	2.00
P3	JE5741 (1981)	30,217	10 New Agorot. Bronze. KM#108.	2.50
P4	JE5741 (1981)	30,217	1/2 Sheqel. Copper-Nickel. KM#109.	2.50
P5	JE5741 (1981)	30,217	Sheqel. Copper-Nickel. KM#111.	3.50

Note: P1-5 were struck at the Bern Mint

KM#	Date	Mintage	Identification	Mkt Val
P6	JE5742 (1982)	18,735	New Agora. Copper-Nickel. KM#106.	2.00
P7	JE5742 (1982)	19,735	5 New Agorot. Copper-Nickel. KM#107.	2.00
P8	JE5742 (1982)	18,735	10 New Agorot. Bronze. KM#108.	2.50
P9	JE5742 (1982)	21,735	1/2 Sheqel. Copper-Nickel. KM#109.	2.50
P10	JE5742 (1982)	19,735	Sheqel. Copper-Nickel. KM#111.	3.00
P11	JE5742 (1982)	20,735	5 Sheqalim. Aluminum-Bronze. KM#118.	3.50
P12	JE5743 (1983)	17,177	New Agora. Copper-Nickel. Plain. KM#106.	1.00
P13	JE5743 (1983)	17,177	5 New Agorot. Copper-Nickel. Plain. KM#107.	1.50
P14	JE5743 (1983)	17,177	10 New Agorot. Bronze. KM#108.	1.50
P15	JE5743 (1983)	17,177	1/2 Sheqel. Copper-Nickel. KM#109.	2.00
P16	JE5743 (1983)	17,177	Sheqel. Copper-Nickel. KM#111.	2.00
P17	JE5743 (1983)	17,177	5 Sheqalim. Aluminum-Bronze. KM#118.	2.50
P18	JE5743 (1983)	17,177	10 Sheqalim. Copper-Nickel. KM#119.	3.00
P19	JE5744 (1984)	15,572	Agora. Copper-Nickel. Plain. KM#107.	1.00
P20	JE5744 (1984)	15,572	5 New Agorot. Copper-Nickel. Plain. KM#107.	1.50
P21	JE5744 (1984)	15,572	10 New Agorot. Bronze. KM#108.	1.50
P22	JE5744 (1984)	15,572	1/2 Sheqel. Copper-Nickel. KM#109.	2.00
P23	JE5744 (1984)	15,572	Sheqel. Copper-Nickel. KM#111.	2.00
P24	JE5744 (1984)	15,572	5 Sheqalim. Aluminum-Bronze. KM#118.	2.50
P25	JE5744 (1984)	15,572	10 Sheqalim. Copper-Nickel. KM#119.	3.00

Note: P6-25 were struck at the Rome Mint

KM#	Date	Mintage	Identification	Mkt Val
P26	JE5745 (1985)	14,768	Sheqel. Copper-Nickel. KM#111.	2.00
P27	JE5745 (1985)	14,768	5 Sheqalim. Aluminum-Bronze. KM#118.	2.00
P28	JE5745 (1985)	14,768	10 Sheqalim. Copper-Nickel. KM#119.	2.50
P29	JE5745 (1985)	14,768	50 Sheqalim. Aluminum-Bronze. KM#139.	3.00
P30	JE5745 (1985)	14,768	100 Sheqalim. Copper-Nickel. KM#143.	3.50

Note: P26-30 were struck at the Bern Mint

KM#	Date	Mintage	Identification	Mkt Val
P31	JE5746 (1986)	12,665	Agora. Aluminum-Bronze. KM#156.	2.00
P32	JE5746 (1986)	12,665	5 Agorot. Aluminum-Bronze. KM#157.	3.00
P33	JE5746 (1986)	12,665	10 Agorot. Aluminum-Bronze. KM#158.	4.00
P34	JE5746 (1986)	12,665	1/2 New Sheqel. Aluminum-Bronze. KM#159.	5.00
P35	JE5746 (1986)	12,665	New Sheqel. Copper-Nickel. KM#160.	6.00

Note: P31-35 were struck at the Paris Mint

KM#	Date	Mintage	Identification	Mkt Val
P36	JE5747 (1987)	11,529	Agora. Aluminum-Bronze. KM#156.	2.00
P37	JE5747 (1987)	11,529	5 Agorot. Aluminum-Bronze. KM#157.	3.00
P38	JE5747 (1987)	11,529	10 Agorot. Aluminum-Bronze. KM#158.	4.00
P39	JE5747 (1987)	11,529	1/2 New Sheqel. Aluminum-Bronze. KM#159.	5.00
P40	JE5747 (1987)	11,529	New Sheqel. Copper-Nickel. KM#160.	6.00
PA41	JE5748 (1988)	12,027	Agora. Nickel. KM#193.	2.50
P41	JE5748 (1988)	12,027	5 Agorot. Nickel. KM#194.	3.50
P42	JE5748 (1988)	12,027	10 Agorot. Nickel. KM#195.	4.50
P43	JE5748 (1988)	12,027	1/2 New Sheqel. Nickel. KM#196.	5.50
P44	JE5748 (1988)	12,027	New Sheqel. Nickel. KM#197.	6.00

Note: P36-44 were struck at the Stuttgart Mint

KM#	Date	Mintage	Identification	Mkt Val
P45	JE5749 (1989)	9,622	Agora. Aluminum-Bronze. KM#156.	2.00
P46	JE5749 (1989)	9,622	5 Agorot. Aluminum-Bronze. KM#157.	3.00
P47	JE5749 (1989)	9,622	10 Agorot. Aluminum-Bronze. KM#158.	4.00
P48	JE5749 (1989)	9,622	1/2 New Sheqel. Aluminum-Bronze. KM#159.	5.00
P49	JE5749 (1989)	9,622	New Sheqel. Copper-Nickel. KM#160.	6.00
P50	JE5750 (1990)	7,038	Agora. Aluminum-Bronze. KM#156.	2.00
P51	JE5750 (1990)	7,038	5 Agorot. Bronze. KM#157.	3.00
P52	JE5750 (1990)	7,038	10 Agorot. Aluminum-Bronze. KM#158.	4.00
P53	JE5750 (1990)	7,038	1/2 New Sheqel. Bronze. KM#159.	5.00
P54	JE5750 (1990)	7,038	New Sheqel. Copper-Nickel. KM#160.	5.00
P55	JE5750 (1990)	7,038	5 New Sheqalim. Copper-Nickel. KM#207.	6.00

Note: P45-55 were struck at the Stuttgart mint.

KM#	Date	Mintage	Identification	Mkt Val
P56	JE5751 (1991)	6,617	Agora. Aluminum-Bronze. KM#156.	2.00
P57	JE5751 (1991)	6,617	5 Agorot. Aluminum-Bronze. KM#157.	3.00
P58	JE5751 (1991)	6,617	10 Agorot. Aluminum-Bronze. KM#158.	4.00
P59	JE5751 (1991)	6,617	1/2 New Sheqel. Aluminum-Bronze. KM#159.	5.00
P60	JE5751 (1991)	6,617	New Sheqel. Copper-Nickel. KM#160.	6.00
P61	JE5751 (1991)	6,617	5 New Sheqalim. Copper-Nickel. KM#207.	6.00
P62	JE5752 (1992)	6,339	Agora. Aluminum-Bronze. KM#156.	2.00
P63	JE5752 (1992)	6,339	5 Agorot. Aluminum-Bronze. KM#157.	3.00
P64	JE5752 (1992)	6,339	10 Agorot. Aluminum-Bronze. KM#158.	4.00
P65	JE5752 (1992)	6,339	1/2 New Sheqel. Aluminum-Bronze. KM159.	5.00
P66	JE5752 (1992)	6,339	New Sheqel. Copper-Nickel. KM#160.	6.00
P67	JE5752 (1992)	6,339	5 New Sheqalim. Copper-Nickel. KM#207.	6.00
P68	JE5753 (1993)	7,993	Agora. Aluminum-Bronze. KM#156.	2.00
P69	JE5753 (1993)	7,993	5 Agorot. Aluminum-Bronze. KM#157.	3.00
P70	JE5753 (1993)	7,993	10 Agorot. Aluminum-Bronze. KM#158.	4.00
P71	JE5753 (1993)	7,993	1/2 New Sheqel. Aluminum-Bronze. KM#159.	5.00
P72	JE5753 (1993)	7,993	New Sheqel. Copper-Nickel. KM#160.	6.00
P73	JE5753 (1993)	7,993	5 New Sheqalim. Copper-Nickel. KM#207.	6.00
P74	JE5754 (1994)	8,000	Agora. Aluminum-Bronze. KM#156.	3.00
P75	JE5754 (1994)	8,000	5 Agorot. Aluminum-Bronze. KM#157.	4.00
P76	JE5754 (1994)	8,000	10 Agorot. Aluminum-Bronze. KM#158.	5.00
P77	JE5754 (1994)	8,000	1/2 New Sheqel. Aluminum-Bronze. KM#159.	6.00
P78	JE5754 (1994)	8,000	1/2 New Sheqel. Aluminum-Bronze. Value. Flower. Plain. KM#368.	10.00
P79	JE5754 (1994)	8,000	New Sheqel. Copper-Nickel. KM#160.	7.00
P80	JE5754 (1994)	8,000	5 New Sheqalim. Copper-Nickel. KM#207.	9.00
P81	JE5755 (1995)	10,000	Agora. Aluminum-Bronze. KM#156.	2.00
P82	JE5755 (1995)	10,000	5 Agorot. Aluminum-Bronze. KM#157.	3.00
P83	JE5755 (1995)	10,000	10 Agorot. Aluminum-Bronze. KM#158.	4.00
P84	JE5755 (1995)	10,000	1/2 New Sheqel. Aluminum-Bronze. KM#159.	5.00
P85	JE5755 (1995)	10,000	1/2 New Sheqel. Aluminum-Bronze. Value. Medical symbols. Plain. KM#392.	10.00
P86	JE5755 (1995)	10,000	New Sheqel. Copper-Nickel. KM#160.	6.00
P87	JE5755 (1995)	10,000	5 New Sheqalim. Copper-Nickel. KM207.	8.00
P88	JE5755 (1995)	10,000	10 New Sheqalim. Bi-Metallic. KM#270.	12.00

Note: P56-88 were struck at the Utrecht mint

KM#	Date	Mintage	Identification	Mkt Val
P89	JE5756 (1996)	8,000	Agora. Aluminum-Bronze. KM#156.	2.00
P90	JE5756 (1996)	8,000	5 Agorot. Aluminum-Bronze. KM#157.	3.00
P91	JE5756 (1996)	8,000	10 Agorot. Aluminum-Bronze. KM#158.	4.00
P92	JE5756 (1996)	8,000	1/2 New Sheqel. Aluminum-Bronze. KM#159.	5.00
P93	JE5756 (1996)	8,000	1/2 New Sheqel. Aluminum-Bronze. Value. Hebrew inscription. Plain. KM#393.	10.00
P94	JE5756 (1996)	8,000	New Sheqel. Copper-Nickel. KM#160.	6.00
P95	JE5756 (1996)	8,000	5 New Sheqalim. Copper-Nickel. KM#217.	8.00
P96	JE5756 (1996)	8,000	10 New Sheqalim. Bi-Metallic. KM#270.	12.00
P97	JE5757 (1997)	6,000	Agora. Aluminum-Bronze. KM#156.	2.00
P98	JE5757 (1997)	6,000	5 Agorot. Aluminum-Bronze. KM#157.	3.00
P99	JE5757 (1997)	6,000	10 Agorot. Aluminum-Bronze. KM#158.	4.00
P100	JE5757 (1997)	6,000	1/2 New Sheqel. Aluminum-Bronze. KM#159.	5.00

KM#	Date	Mintage	Identification	Mkt Val
P101	JE5757-(1997)	6,000	1/2 New Sheqel. Aluminum-Bronze. KM#394.	12.00
P102	JE5757 (1997)	6,000	New Sheqel. Copper-Nickel. KM#160.	6.00
P103	JE5757 (1997)	6,000	5 New Sheqalim. Copper-Nickel. KM#207.	8.00
P104	JE5757 (1997)	6,000	10 New Sheqalim. Bi-Metallic. KM#270.	12.00
P105	JE5758 (1998)	8,000	Agora. Aluminum-Bronze. KM#156.	2.00
P106	JE5758 (1998)	8,000	5 Agorot. Aluminum-Bronze. KM#157.	3.00
P107	JE5758 (1998)	8,000	10 Agorot. Aluminum-Bronze. KM#158.	4.00
P108	JE5758 (1998)	8,000	1/2 New Sheqel. Aluminum-Bronze. KM#159.	5.00
P109	JE5758 (1998)	8,000	1/2 New Sheqel. Aluminum-Bronze. Value. Flag and stars. Plain. KM#395.	10.00
P110	JE5758 (1998)	8,000	New Sheqel. Copper-Nickel. KM#160.	6.00
P111	JE5758 (1998)	8,000	5 New Sheqalim. Copper-Nickel. KM#207.	8.00
P112	JE5758 (1998)	8,000	10 New Sheqalim. Bi-Metallic. KM#270.	12.00
P113	JE5759 (1999)	6,000	Agora. Aluminum-Bronze. KM#156.	2.00
P114	JE5759 (1999)	6,000	5 Agorot. Aluminum-Bronze. KM#157.	3.00
P115	JE5759 (1999)	6,000	10 Agorot. Aluminum-Bronze. KM#158.	4.00
P116	JE5759 (1999)	6,000	1/2 New Sheqel. Aluminum-Bronze. KM#159.	5.00
P117	JE5759 (1999)	6,000	1/2 New Sheqel. Aluminum-Bronze. High Tech KM#324.	12.00
P118	JE5759 (1999)	6,000	New Sheqel. Copper-Nickel. KM#160.	6.00
P119	JE5759 (1999)	6,000	5 New Sheqalim. Copper-Nickel. KM#207.	8.00
P120	JE5759 (1999)	6,000	10 New Sheqalim. Bi-Metallic. KM#270.	12.00
P121	JE5760 (2000)	4,000	Agora. Aluminum-Bronze. Plain. KM#156.	2.00
P122	JE5760 (2000)	4,000	5 Agorot. Aluminum-Bronze. Plain. KM#157.	3.00
P123	JE5760 (2000)	4,000	10 Agorot. Aluminum-Bronze. Plain. KM#158.	4.00
P124	JE5760 (2000)	4,000	1/2 New Sheqel. Aluminum-Bronze. Plain. KM#159.	5.00
P125	JE5760 (2000)	4,000	1/2 New Sheqel. Aluminum-Bronze. Plain. KM#363.	12.00
P126	JE5760 (2000)	4,000	New Sheqel. Copper-Nickel. Plain. KM#160.	6.00
P127	JE5760 (2000)	4,000	5 New Sheqalim. Copper-Nickel. Plain. KM#207.	8.00
P128	JE5760 (2000)	4,000		12.00

MINT SETS

KM#	Date	Mintage	Identification	Issue Price	Mkt Val
MS1	JE5709 (1949) (10)	300	KM#8 (closed link), 9-12 (with pearl), 13.1 (with pearl), 14, 15 (without pearl), 15a, 16 in "muffin tin" (two piece plastic case with clear swivel top and light blue bottom - large yellow lettering on case; Hebrew letter on the far left extends to the left of KM#8)	—	150
MS2	JE5709 (1949) (10)	300	KM#8 (closed link), 9-12 (with pearl), 13.1 (with pearl), 14, 15 (without pearl), 15a, 16 in "muffin tin" (two piece plastic case with clear swivel top and light blue bottom), small dark yellow lettering on case, Hebrew letter on the far left is below KM#8 and hick Menora between KM#13.1 and 14)	—	150
MS3	JE5709 (1949) (10)	300	KM#8 (closed link), 9-12 (with pearl), 13.1 (with pearl), 14, 15 (without pearl), 15a, 16 in "muffin tin" (two piece plastic case with clear swivel top and light blue bottom), small pale yellow lettering on case, Hebrew letter on the far left below KM#8 and thin Menora between KM#13.1 and 14)	—	150
MS4	JE5709-5722 (1949-1962) (16) (17)	4,000	KM#9-12, 13.1, 13.2a, 15, 15a, 16, 17, 19, 20, 24.1, 25-27, (various dates) (issued 1962)	18.50	75.00
MS4a	JE5709-5722 (1949-1962) (16)	—	KM#9-12, 13.1, 13.2a, 15, 15a, 16, 17, 19, 20, 24.1, 25-27 (various dates) (bottom line of logo on left inside cover is in Hebrew) (issued 1962)	18.50	75.00
MS5	JE5709-5723 (1949-1963) (18)	20,000	KM#9-12, 13.1, 13.2a, 15, 15a, 16, 17, 19, 20, 24.1, 25-27, 36.1, 37 (various dates) - some circulated and cleaned (case inscribed Israel Coins and Medals company) (issued 1963)	21.50	65.00
MS6	JE5709-5723 (1949-1963) (18)	20,000	KM#9-12, 13.1, 13.2a, 15, 15a, 16, 17, 19, 20, 24.1, 25-27, 36.1, 37 (various dates) - many circulated and cleaned (black case inscribed Israel Government Coins and Medals Corporation (issued 1964)	—	60.00
MS7	JE5709-5723 (1949-1963) (18) (18)	20,000	KM#9-12, 13.1, 13.2a, 15, 15a, 16, 17, 19, 20, 24.1, 25-27, 36.1, 37 (various dates) - many circulated and cleaned (blue case inscribed Israel Government Coins and Medals Corporation) (issued 1964)	—	75.00
MS8	JE5720-5723 (1960-1963) (6) (6)	200	KM#24.1 (medal alignment), 25-27, 36.1, 37 (KM#27 dated JE5720; others dated JE5723) (plain white card with coins individually covered by plastic) (card is stapled or glued), market value is for close to perfect sets	2.60	160
MS9	JE5722-5723 (1962-1963) (6)	200	KM24.1, (medal alignment), 25-27, 36.1, 37 (KM#27 dated JE5722; others dated JE5723) (plain white card with coins individually covered by plastic), card is stapled or glued), market value is for close to perfect sets	2.60	135
MS10	JE5722-5723 (1962-1963) (6)	1,800	KM#24.1 medal alignment), 25-27, 36.1, 37 (KM#27 dated JE5722; others dated JE5723) (plain white card entirely covered by plastic), market value is for close to perfect sets	2.60	150
MS11	JE5722-5723 (1962-1963) (6)	1,800	KM#24.1 (coin alignment; inverted reverse), 25-27, 36.1, 37 (KM#27 dated JE5722; others dated JE5723) (plain white card entirely covered by plastic), market value is for close to perfect sets	2.60	190
MS12	JE5723 (1963) (6)	1,800	KM#24.1 (medal alignment), 25-27, 36.1, 37 (all coins dated JE5723) (plain white card entirely covered by plastic), market value is for close to perfect sets	2.60	100
MS13	JE5723 (1963) (6)	1,800	KM#24.1 (coin alignment; inverted reverse), 25-27, 36.1, 37 (all coins dated JE5723) (plain white card entirely covered by plastic), market value is for close to perfect sets	2.60	175
MS14	JE5723 (1963) (6) (6)	100	KM#24.1 (medal alignment), 25-27, 36.1, 37 (white plastic wallet with holed cardboard inscribed Government Printer Mint of Israel)	—	1,500
MS15	JE5723 (1963) (6) (6)	100	KM#24.1 (medal alignment), 25-27, 36.1, 37 (blue plastic wallet with holed cardboard inscribed Bank of Israel)	—	1,500
MS16	JE5723 (1963) (6)	10,455	KM#24.1,(medal alignment), 25-27, 36.1, 37 (pale blue and white card with map)	2.60	7.00
MS17	JE5723 (1963) (6)	10,455	KM#24.1 (coin alignment; inverted reverse), 25-27, 36.1, 37 (pale blue and white card with map)	2.60	20.00
MS18	JE5725 (1965) (6)	153,424	KM24.1, 25-27, 36.1, 37 (gray and white card)	3.00	3.00
MS19	JE5726 (1966) (6)	114,714	KM24.1, 25-27, 36.1, 37 (orange and white card)	3.00	3.00
MS20	JE5727 (1967) (6)	128,184	KM24.1, 25-27, 36.1, 37 (turquoise card)	3.00	3.00
MS21	JE5728 (1968) (6)	184,552	KM24.1, 25-27, 36.1, 47.1 (blue card)	3.00	3.00
MS22	JE5729 (1969) (6)	158,052	KM24.1, 25-27, 36.1, 47.1 (reddish-brown card)	3.00	3.00
MS23	JE5730 (1970) (6)	64,800	KM24.1, 25-27, 36.1, 47.1 (blue card)	3.00	3.25
MS24	JE5730 (1970) (6)	60,045	KM24.1, 25-27, 36.1, 47.1 (in red wallet with English insert cards)	3.00	3.25
MS25	JE5730 (1970) (6)	60,045	KM#24.1, 25-27, 36.1, 47.1 (red wallet with German insert cards)	—	5.00
MS26	JE5731 (1971) (6)	32,543	KM24.1, 25-27, 36.1, 47.1 (blue wallet with front insert card having black and red printing)	3.00	3.50
MS27	JE5731 (1971) (6) (6)	32,543	KM#24.1, 25-27, 36.1, 47.1 (blue wallet with the front insert card having black and blue printing)	3.00	3.50
MS28	JE5731 (1971) (6)	125,921	KM#24.2, 25a, 26a, 27a, 36.2, 47.2 (pink plastic case)	3.50	3.00
MS29	JE5732 (1972) (6)	21,486	KM24.1, 25-27, 36.1, 47.1 (violet wallet)	3.00	3.50
MS30	JE5732 (1972) (6)	68,513	KM#24.2, 25a, 26a, 27a, 36.2, 47.2 (violet plastic case)	3.50	3.00
MS31	JE5733 (1973) (6)	98,107	KM63-68 (blue plastic case)	3.50	3.25
MS32	JE5734 (1974) (6)	92,868	KM24.2, 25c, 26c, 27b, 36.2, 47.2 (dark brown plastic case)	3.50	3.00
MS33	JE 5735 (1975) (6)	61,686	KM#24.2, 25c, 26c, 27b, 36.2, 47.2 (brown plastic case)	3.50	3.00
MS34	JE5736 (1976) (6)	64,654	KM24.2, 25c, 26c, 27b, 36.2, 47.2 (olive green plastic case)	3.50	3.00
MS35	JE5737 (1977) (6)	37,208	KM#24.2, 25c, 26c, 27b, 36.2, 47.2 (reddish-brown plastic case)	3.50	3.50
MS37	JE5739 (1979) (7)	58,433	KM#24.1, 25b, 26b, 27, 36.1, 47.1, 90 (dark blue wallet with gold lettering and two English insert cards having blue printing)	1.80	3.00

KM#	Date	Mintage	Identification	Issue Price	Mkt Val
MS37a	JE5739 (1979) (7)	Inc. Above	KM#24.1, 25b, 26b, 27, 36.1, 47.1, 90 (dark blue wallet with white lettering and two English insert cards with black lettering).	—	15.00
MS38	JE5739 (1979) (7) (7)	58,433	KM#24.1, 25b, 26b, 27, 36.1, 47.1, 90 (dark blue wallet with gold lettering and one English insert card having black printing)	1.80	6.00
MS39	JE5739 (1979) (7)	58,433	KM#24.1, 25b, 26b, 27, 36.1, 47.1, 90 (dark blue wallet with gold lettering and two Hebrew insert cards having blue printing)	—	3.00
MS40	JE5739 (1979) (7)	58,433	KM#24.1, 25b, 26b, 27, 36.1, 47.1, 90 (dark blue wallet with white lettering and two Hebrew insert cards having black printing)	—	15.00
MS41	JE5739 (1979) (7)	31,590	KM#24.2, 25c, 26c, 27b, 36.2, 47.2, 90a (brown plastic case)	3.75	4.00
MS42	JE5740 (1980) (7)	27,000	KM#24.1, 26b, 47.1, 106-109 (turquoise plastic case)	3.50	7.00
MS43	JE5740 (1980) (7)	31,348	KM96-102 (blue plastic case)	13.00	8.50
MS44	JE5742 (1982) (7)	19,660	KM106-109, 111, 118, 119 (olive green plastic case)	3.50	8.00
MS45	JE5743 (1983) (5)	17,478	KM108, 109, 111, 118, 119 (reddish-brown plasic case)	3.50	4.50
MS46	JE5744 (1984) (9)	13,403	KM#108, 109, 111, 118, 119, 134, 137, 139, 143 (orange-brown plastic case)	4.50	13.00
MS47	JE5744 (1984) (18) (1)	—	KM#137 (white card with blue lettering) (issued 1985)	5.00	15.00
MS47a	JE577 (1984) (18)	—	KM#137 (white card with black lettering) (issued 1985)	—	20.00
MS48	JE5745 (1985) (8)	15,224	KM#111, 118, 119, 139, 143, 146, 147, 151 (purple plastic case)	4.50	9.00
MS49	JE5745 (1985) (5) (1)	—	KM#147 (white card with blue lettering)	2.50	20.00
MS50	JE5745 (1985) (1) (1)	—	KM#151 (white card with blue lettering) (issued 1986)	—	15.00
MS51	JE5745 (1985) (5)	7,760	KM#156-160 (gray plastic case)	10.00	20.00
MS52	JE5746-47 (1986-87) (12) (11)	14,305	KM#156-160, 163, 167 (JE5746), 163, 171-174 (JE5747) plus Hanukka medal (silver and blue plastic case)	9.00	11.00
MS53	JE5747 (1987) (5)	14,000	KM163, 171-174 (plastic case)	—	15.00
MS54	JE5747-5748 (1987-1988) (10)	11,094	KM#156-160 (JE5747), 163, 171-174 (JE5748) (reddish-brown and gold plastic case)	10.00	12.00
MS55	JE5748 (1988) (5) (5)	28,800	KM#163, 171-174 (reddish-brown and gold plastic case; issued 1987)	6.50	8.50
MS56	JE5748 (1988) (6)	15,795	KM156-160, 198 (green plasic case)	7.50	16.00
MS57	JE5748 (1988) (5)	16,649	KM#193-197 plus medal (blue plastic case)	6.50	14.00
MS58	JE5749 (1989) (5)	14,833	KM#163, 171-174 plus Hanukka medal (blue plastic case; issued 1988)	8.00	16.00
MS59	JE5749 (1989) (10)	9,716	KM#156-160, 163, 171-174 (light green plastic case)	7.00	10.00
MS60	JE5750 (1990) (5)	7,562	KM#163, 171-174 (red plastic case; issued 1989)	5.00	14.00
MS61	JE5750 (1990) (6)	5,598	KM#156-160, 207 (dark green plastic case)	8.00	11.00
MS62	JE5751 (1991) (6)	7,929	KM#163, 171-174, 217 (red plastic case; issued 1990)	8.00	12.00
MS63	JE5750-5751 (1990-1991) (7)	6,746	KM#208 (JE5750), 156-160, 207 (JE5751) (green plastic case)	10.00	18.00
MS64	JE5752 (1992) (5)	6,886	KM#163, 172-174, 217 (dark blue plastic case; issued 1991)	8.00	11.00
MS65	JE5752 (1992) (5)	5,998	KM#157-160, 207 (pink plastic case)	8.00	16.00
MS66	JE5744-5753 (1984-1993) (7)	8,000	KM#137, 147, 151, 167, 198, 208, 237 (various dates) (blue folder) Jewish Leaders	14.90	18.00
MS67	JE5753 (1993) (5)	8,000	KM#163, 172-174, 217 (green folder) Hanukka Gelt (issued 1992)	9.50	12.00
MS68	JE5754 (1994) (6)	11,956	KM#163a, 172-174, 217, 303 (folder) Jewish Heroism (issued 1993)	16.00	11.00
MS69	JE5753-5754 (1993-1994) (7)	8,000	KM#158-160 (JE5753), 157, 158, 160a, 207 (JE5754) (folder) Praise Him with the Harp and Lyre	14.50	12.00
MS70	JE5755 (1995) (6)	10,000	KM#163a, 172-174, 217, 304 (folder) American Jewry, The Liberty Connection (issued 1994)	17.00	25.00
MS71	JE5755 (1995) (6)	5,000	KM#157-159, 160a, 207, 270 (folder) Coins of the Holy Land	—	25.00
MS72	JE5756 (1996) (7)	7,500	KM#163a, 172-174, 217, 305, 315 (folder) Zahal, The Peoples, Army (issued 1995)	29.00	35.00
MS73	JE5757 (1997) (7)	7,500	KM#163a, 172-174, 217, 315, 318 (folder) Russian Jewry (issued 1996)	—	33.00
MS74	JE5757 (1997) (7)	7,500	KM#163a, 172-174, 217, 315, 318 (blue and gold laminated card) Russian Jewry (issued 1996)	—	38.00
MS75	JE5757 (1997) (5)	5,000	KM#157-159, 160a, 207 (plastic case) The White Lily	—	32.00
MS76	JE5758 (1998) (7)	10,000	KM#163a, 172-174, 217, 314, 315 (folder) Israel's 50th Anniversary (issued 1997)	—	36.00
MS77	JE5758 (1998) (7)	10,000	KM#163a, 172-174, 217, 314, 315 (plastic case) Israel's 50th Anniversary (issued 1977)	—	38.00
MS78	JE5758 (1998) (5)	5,000	KM#157-159, 160a, 207 (plastic case) Lulav and Etrog	—	30.00
MS79	JE5759 (1999) (7)	6,000	KM#163a, 172-174, 217, 315, 331 (folder) The Menorah (issued 1998)	—	35.00
MS80	JE5758 (1999) (7)	6,000	KM#163a, 172-174, 217, 315, 331 (plastic case) The Menorah (issued 1998)	—	35.00
MS81	JE5759 (1999) (5)	—	KM#157-159, 160a, 207 (plastic case)	—	35.00
MS82	JE5760 (2000) (7)	7,000	KM#163b, 172-174, 217, 315, 332 (folder) Jerusalem 2000 (issued 1999)	32.00	33.00
MS83	JE5760 (2000) (7)	7,000	KM#163b, 172-174, 217, 315, 332 (plasic case) Jerusalem 2000 (issued 1999)	—	35.00
MS84	JE5760 (2000) (4)	3,000	KM#157, 158, 160a, 207 plus ANA medal (plastic case) Israel Salutes the ANA	—	18.00

OFFICIALLY ASSEMBLED HISTORICAL SETS

KM#	Date	Mintage	Identification	Issue Price	Mkt Val
HS1	JE5709-5717 (1949-1957) (6)	5,000	KM#9-11, 12 or 12a, 17, 20a (various dates) - all circulated (light blue and white card) (issued 1962) market value is for close to perfect sets.	—	50.00
HS2	JE5709-5717 (1949-1957) (6)	5,000	KM#9, 12 or 12a, 13.1, 13.2 or 13.2a, 14, 17, 18 (various dates) - all circulated (light blue and white card) (issued 1962) market value is for close to perfect sets	—	40.00
HS3	JE5720-5740 (1960-1980) (7)	5,000	Souvenir from the Lira Period Set - KM#24.1, 25 or 25b, 26 or 26b, 27, 36.1, 47.1, 90 (various dates) (light blue wallet with dark blue lettering) (issued 1981)	—	25.00
HS4	JE5731-5740 (1971-1980) (7)	—	Souvenir from the Lira Period Set - Mint Marked - KM#24.2, 63 or 96, 25a, 25c, 64 or 97, 26a, 26c, 65 or 98, 27a, 27b, 66 or 99, 36.2, 67 or 100, 47.2, 68 or 101, 90a or 102 (various dates) (light blue wallet with white lettering) (issued 1985)	—	9.00
HS5	JE5731-5740 (1971-1980) (7)	—	Souvenir from the Lira Period Set - Mint Marked - KM#24.2, 63 or 96, 25a, 25c, 64 or 97, 26a, 26c, 65 or 98, 27a, 27b, 66 or 99, 36.2, 67 or 100, 47.2, 68 or 101, 90a or 102 (various dates) (9.9 cm x 15.0 cm black wallet with white lettering) (issued 1985)	—	30.00
HS6	JE5731-5740 (1971-1980) (7)	—	Souvenir from the Lira Period Set - Mint Marked - KM#24.2, 63 or 96, 25a, 25c, 64 or 97, 26a, 26c, 65 or 98, 27a, 27b, 66 or 99, 36.2, 67 or 100, 47.2, 68 or 101, 90a or 102 (various dates) (10.9 cm x 15.8 cm black wallet with white lettering) (issued 1985)	—	30.00
HS7	JE5731-5740 (1971-1980) (7)	—	Souvenir from the Lira Period Set - Mint Marked - KM#24.2, 63 or 96, 25a, 25c, 64 or 97, 26a, 26c, 65 or 98, 27a, 27b, 66 or 99, 36.2, 67 or 100, 47.2, 68 or 101, 90a or 102 (various dates) (reddish-brown wallet with white lettering) (issued 1985)	—	40.00
HS8	JE5731-5740 (1971-1980) (6)	—	Souvenir from the Lira Period Set - Mint Marked - KM#24.1, 25a, 25c, 64 or 97, 26a, 26c, 65 or 98, 27a, 27b, 66 or 99, 36.2, 67 or 100, 47.2, 68 or 101, 90a or 102 (various dates) (brown wallet with gold lettering) (issued 1985)	—	35.00
HS9	JE5709-5718 (1949-55) (7)	18,000	The Coin and the Moon Set, KM#9, 10, 12, 13.1, 13.2 or 13.2a, 14, 15, 17 and Palestine KM#1 (various dates) - most circulated, plus medal (folder) (issued 1994)	15.00	15.00
HS10	JE5709-5744 (1949-1984) (9)	26,000	Historical Coin Set - KM#11, 13.1 or 13.2, 14, 27a, 36.2, 47.2, 107-109 (various dates) - some circulated, plus medal (folder) (issued 1994).	15.00	17.00
HS11	JE5709-5740 (1949-1980) (18)	110	KM#9-12, 13.1, 14, 15, 15a, 16-18, 20a, 24.1, 25b, 26b, 27, 36.1, 37 (various dates) - some circulated, plus IL 1/2 and 1 banknotes (beech wood box) (issued 2008)	259	260

KM#	Date	Mintage	Identification	Issue Price	Mkt Val
HS12	JE5740-5745 (1980-1985) (14)	500	KM#106-109, 111, 118, 119, 134, 137, 139, 143, 146, 147, 151 (various dates) (wood box) (issued 2008)	123	125
HS13	5739-5740 (1979-1980) (2)	Est. 999	KM#90 (JE5739) and 107 (JE5740) Western Wall Jerusalem Coin Set (issued 2011)	13.00	13.00
HS14	5739-5740 (1979-1980) (2)	Est. 999	KM#90 (JE5739) and 107 (JE5740) Tower of David Jerusalem Coin Set (issued 2011)	13.00	13.00

PIEFORT PROOF SETS (PPS)

KM#	Date	Mintage	Identification	Issue Price	Mkt Val
PPS1	JE5741 (1981) (b) (5)	30,217	KM#P1-P5 (card in folder)	10.00	7.00
PPS2	JE5742 (1982) (r) (6)	18,735	KM#P6-P11 (card in folder)	11.00	8.00
PPS3	JE5743 (1983) (d) (7)	17,177	KM#P12-P18 (card in folder)	10.00	9.00
PPS4	JE5744 (1984) (b) (7)	15,572	KM#P19-P25 (card in folder)	10.00	8.00
PPS5	JE5745 (1985) (b) (5)	14,768	KM#P26-P30 (card in folder)	10.00	12.00
PPS6	JE5746 (1986) (p) (5)	12,665	KM#P31-P35 (card in folder)	12.00	12.00
PPS7	JE5747 (1987) (f) (5)	11,529	KM#P36-P40 (card in folder)	15.00	10.00
PPS8	JE5748 (1988) (f) (5)	12,027	KM#PA41, P41-P44 (card in box)	15.00	15.00
PPS9	JE5749 (1989) (f) (5)	9,622	KM#P45-P49 (folder)	15.00	13.00
PPS10	JE5750 (1990) (f) (6)	7,038	KM#P50-P55 (folder)	18.00	15.00
PPS11	JE5751 (1991) (u) (6)	6,617	KM#P56-P61 (folder)	15.00	18.00
PPS12	JE5752 (1992) (u) (6)	6,339	KM#P62-P67 (folder)	18.00	19.00
PPS13	JE5753 (1993) (u) (6)	7,993	KM#P68-P73 plus Jerusalem medal (folder)	15.00	16.00
PPS14	JE5754 (1994) (u) (7)	8,000	KM#P74-P80 (folder)	22.50	18.00
PPS15	JE5755 (1995) (u) (8)	10,000	KM#P81-P88 (folder)	33.00	36.00
PPS16	JE5756 (1996) (b) & (u) (8)	8,000	KM#P89-P96 (folder)	33.00	35.00
PPS17	JE5757 (1997) (h) & (u) (8)	6,000	KM#P97-P104 (folder)	—	40.00
PPS18	JE5757 (1997) (h) & (u) (8)	6,000	KM#P97-P104 (plastic case)	—	45.00
PPS19	JE5758 (1998) (h) & (u) (8)	8,000	KM#P105-P112 (folder)	—	40.00
PPS20	JE5758 (1998) (h) & (u) (8)	8,000	KM#P105-P112 (plastic case)	—	40.00
PPS21	JE5759 (1999) (h) & (u) (8)	6,000	KM#P113-P120 (folder)	—	40.00
PPS22	JE5759 (1999) (8)	6,000	KM#P113-P120 (plastic case)	—	40.00
PPS23	JE5760 (2000) (8)	4,000	KM#P121-P128 (folder) (h) & (u)	—	45.00
PPS24	JE5760 (2000) (h) & (u) (8)	4,000	KM#P121-P128 (plastic case)	—	45.00

SPECIAL SELECT SETS

KM#	Date	Mintage	Identification	Issue Price	Mkt Val
SS1	1949 (10)	Est. 300	KM8-13.1 w/pearl, 14, 15 w/pearl, 15 w/o pearl, 16 in two piece heavy plastic case (light blue molded bottom and a clear swivel top)	—	245

ITALIAN SOMALILAND

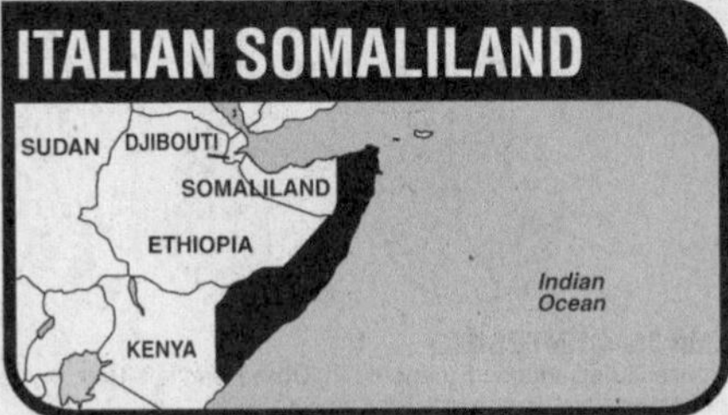

Italian Somaliland, a former Italian Colony in East Africa, extended south from Ras Asir to Kenya. Area: 178,218 sq. miles (461,585 sq. km). Capital: Mogadisho. In 1885, Italy obtained commercial concessions in the area of the sultan of Zanzibar, and in 1905 purchased the coast from Warshek to Brava. The Italians then extended their occupation inward. Cession of the Jubaland Province by Britain in 1924, and seizure of the sultanates of Obbia and Mejertein in 1925-27 brought direct Italian administration over the whole territory. Italian dominance continued until WW II. British troops occupied Italian Somaliland in 1941. Britain administered the colony until 1950 when it became a UN trust territory administered by Italy. On July 1, 1960. Italian Somaliland united with British Somaliland to form the Independent Somali Democratic Republic.

TITLE

الصومال الايطالية

Al-Somal Al-Italiyaniya(t)

MONETARY SYSTEM

100 Bese = 1 Rupia

COLONY

STANDARD COINAGE

KM# 1 BESA

Bronze **Ruler:** Vittorio Emanuele III **Obv:** Uniformed bust left **Rev:** Value and date within circle

Date	Mintage	F12	VF20	XF40	MS60	MS63
1909 R	2,000,000	15.00	30.00	50.00	110	270
1910 R	500,000	15.00	30.00	70.00	145	295
1913 R	200,000	22.50	45.00	120	320	550
1921 R	500,000	18.50	35.00	70.00	145	295

KM# 2 2 BESE

Bronze **Ruler:** Vittorio Emanuele III **Obv:** Uniformed bust left **Rev:** Value and date within circle

Date	Mintage	F12	VF20	XF40	MS60	MS63
1909 R	500,000	18.50	37.50	75.00	170	345
1910 R	250,000	18.50	37.50	75.00	195	395
1913 R	300,000	22.50	45.00	120	250	500
1921 R	600,000	18.50	37.50	75.00	170	345
1923 R	1,500,000	18.50	35.00	75.00	170	345
1924 R	Inc. above	18.50	30.00	60.00	170	345

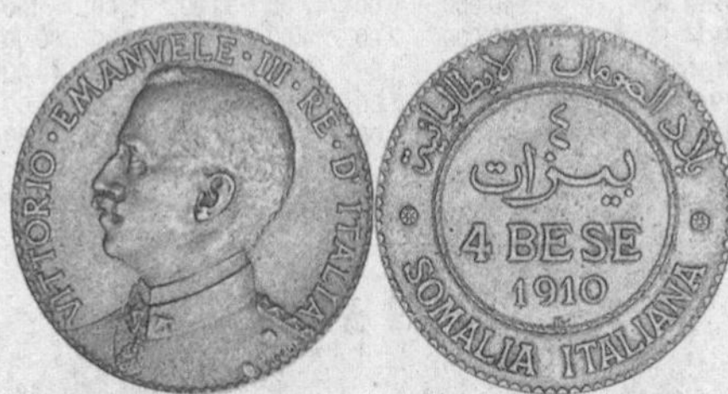

KM# 3 4 BESE

Bronze **Ruler:** Vittorio Emanuele III **Obv:** Uniformed bust left **Rev:** Value and date within circle

Date	Mintage	F12	VF20	XF40	MS60	MS63
1909 R	250,000	27.50	55.00	120	375	800
1910 R	250,000	27.50	55.00	120	375	800
1913 R	50,000	50.00	100	300	550	1,100
1921 R	200,000	30.00	60.00	120	370	800
1923 R	1,000,000	30.00	60.00	120	370	800
1924 R	Inc. above	30.00	75.00	145	430	900

KM# 4 1/4 RUPIA

2.92 g., 0.917 Silver 0.086 oz. ASW **Ruler:** Vittorio Emanuele III **Obv:** Head right **Rev:** Crown above value and date flanked by sprigs

Date	Mintage	F12	VF20	XF40	MS60	MS63
1910 R	400,000	20.00	40.00	95.00	220	400
1913 R	100,000	30.00	55.00	145	320	550

KM# 5 1/2 RUPIA

5.83 g., 0.917 Silver 0.1719 oz. ASW **Ruler:** Vittorio Emanuele III **Obv:** Head right **Rev:** Crown above value and date flanked by sprigs

Date	Mintage	F12	VF20	XF40	MS60	MS63
1910 R	400,000	30.00	60.00	95.00	235	475
1912 R	100,000	35.00	70.00	170	320	600
1913 R	100,000	35.00	70.00	145	295	545
1915 R	50,000	55.00	120	420	725	1,150
1919 R	200,000	30.00	60.00	100	245	500

KM# 6 RUPIA

11.66 g., 0.917 Silver 0.3439 oz. ASW **Ruler:** Vittorio Emanuele III **Obv:** Head right **Rev:** Crown above value and date flanked by sprigs

Date	Mintage	F12	VF20	XF40	MS60	MS63
1910 R	300,000	40.00	60.00	100	240	545
1912 R	600,000	40.00	60.00	100	240	545
1913 R	300,000	40.00	60.00	100	240	500
1914 R	300,000	40.00	60.00	100	240	500
1915 R	250,000	40.00	60.00	100	240	500
1919 R	400,000	40.00	60.00	100	240	500
1920 R	1,300,000	900	1,500	3,400	7,600	—
1921 R	940,000	1,850	3,750	6,000	12,550	—

REFORM COINAGE

100 Centesimi = 1 Lira

KM# 7 5 LIRE

6.00 g., 0.835 Silver 0.1611 oz. ASW **Ruler:** Vittorio Emanuele III **Obv:** Crowned bust right **Rev:** Crowned shield flanked by sprigs divides value with date below

Date	Mintage	VF20	XF40	MS60	MS63	MS65
1925 R	400,000	—	200	375	650	1,000

KM# 8 10 LIRE

12.00 g., 0.835 Silver 0.3222 oz. ASW **Ruler:** Vittorio Emanuele III **Obv:** Crowned bust right **Rev:** Crowned shield flanked by sprigs divides value with date below

Date	Mintage	VF20	XF40	MS60	MS63	MS65
1925 R	100,000	—	250	500	1,000	1,500

PROVAS

KM#	Date	Mintage	Identification	Mkt Val
Pr1	1909R	—	Besa. Bronze.	—
Pr2	1909R	—	2 Bese. Bronze.	1,350
Pr3	1909R	—	4 Bese. Bronze.	1,250
Pr4	1909R	—	4 Bese. Silver.	—
Pr5	1910R	—	4 Bese. Nickel.	—
Pr6	1910R	—	1/4 Rupia. Silver. Head right. Crown above value and date flanked by sprigs.	1,800
Pr7	1910R	—	1/2 Rupia. Silver. Head right. Crown above value, sprigs flank.	3,000
Pr8	1910R	—	Rupia. Silver. Head right. Crown above value and date flanked by sprigs.	3,750
Pr9	1915R	—	1/2 Rupia. Silver. 1 ANNO/DI GUERRA flanks crown.	—
Pr10	1915R	—	Rupia. Silver. 1 ANNO/DI GUERRA flanks crown.	—
Pr11	1925R	—	5 Lire. Silver. PROVA.	1,500
Pr12	1925R	—	5 Lire. Silver. PROVA DI STAMPA.	4,500
Pr13	1925R	—	10 Lire. Silver. PROVA.	3,500
Pr14	1925R	—	10 Lire. Silver. PROVA DI STAMPA.	3,750

TRIAL STRIKES

KM#	Date	Mintage	Identification	Mkt Val
TS1	1909	—	Besa. Pewter.	450
TS2	1909	—	2 Bese. Lead.	—
TS3	1910	—	4 Bese. Pewter.	900

ITALY

The Italian Republic, a 700-mile-long peninsula extending into the heart of the Mediterranean Sea, has an area of 116,304 sq. mi. (301,230 sq. km.) and a population of 60 million. Capital: Rome. The economy centers around agriculture, manufacturing, forestry and fishing. Machinery, textiles, clothing and motor vehicles are exported.

From the fall of Rome until modern times, 'Italy' was little more than a geographical expression. Although nominally included in the Empire of Charlemagne and the Holy Roman Empire, it was in reality divided into a number of independent states and kingdoms presided over by wealthy families, soldiers of fortune or hereditary rulers. The 19th century unification movement fostered by Mazzini, Garibaldi and Cavour attained fruition in 1860-70 with the creation of the Kingdom of Italy and the installation of Victor Emmanuel, king of Sardinia, as king of Italy. Benito Mussolini came to power during the post-World War I period of economic and political unrest, and installed a Fascist dictatorship with a figurehead king as titular Head of State. Mussolini entered Italy into the German-Japanese anti-comitern pact (Tri-Partite Pact) and withdrew from the League of Nations. The war did not go well for Italy and Germany was forced to assist Italy in its failed invasion of Greece. The Allied invasion of Sicily on July 10, 1943 and bombings of Rome brought the Fascist council to a no vote of confidence on July 23, 1943. Mussolini was arrested but soon escaped and set up a government in Salo. Rome fell to the Allied forces in June, 1944 and the country was allowed the status of cobelligerent against Germany. The Germans held northern Italy for another year. Mussolini was eventually captured and executed by partisans.

Following the defeat of the Axis powers, the Italian monarchy was dissolved by plebiscite, and the Italian Republic proclaimed.

RULERS

Vittorio Emanuele III, 1900-1946
Umberto II, 1946
Republic, 1946-

MONETARY SYSTEM

100 Centesimi = 1 Lira

KINGDOM

DECIMAL COINAGE

KM# 35 CENTESIMO

Bronze **Ruler:** Vittorio Emanuele III **Obv:** Head left **Rev:** Value and date within wreath with star above

Date	Mintage	F12	VF20	XF40	MS60	MS63
1902 R	26,000	300	500	1,000	2,500	3,500
1903 R	5,655,000	1.00	2.00	4.00	10.00	30.00
1904/0 R	14,626,000	1.00	2.00	4.00	10.00	30.00
1904 R	Inc. above	1.00	2.00	4.00	10.00	30.00
1905/0 R	8,531,000	3.00	6.00	12.00	30.00	80.00
1905 R	Inc. above	1.00	2.00	5.00	10.00	20.00
1908 R	3,859,000	1.00	3.00	6.00	15.00	30.00

KM# 40 CENTESIMO

Bronze **Ruler:** Vittorio Emanuele III **Obv:** Bust left **Rev:** Female standing on prow

Date	Mintage	F12	VF20	XF40	MS60	MS63
1908 R	57,000	150	300	600	1,800	2,400
1909 R	3,539,000	1.00	2.00	4.00	16.00	40.00
1910 R	3,599,000	1.00	2.00	4.00	18.00	60.00
1911 R	700,000	12.00	22.00	55.00	100	150
1912 R	3,995,000	1.00	2.00	4.00	12.00	40.00
1913 R	3,200,000	1.00	2.00	4.00	12.00	40.00
1914 R	11,585,000	1.00	2.00	4.00	12.00	40.00
1915 R	9,757,000	1.00	2.00	4.00	12.00	40.00
1916 R	9,845,000	1.00	2.00	4.00	12.00	40.00
1917 R	2,400,000	1.00	2.00	4.00	12.00	40.00
1918 R	2,710,000	7.00	15.00	30.00	70.00	150

KM# 38 2 CENTESIMI

Bronze **Ruler:** Vittorio Emanuele III **Obv:** Head left **Rev:** Value and date within wreath

Date	Mintage	F12	VF20	XF40	MS60	MS63
1903 R	5,000,000	1.00	3.00	7.00	20.00	50.00
1905 R	1,260,000	2.00	5.00	20.00	50.00	100
1906 R	3,145,000	1.00	3.00	7.00	20.00	50.00
1907 R	230,000	80.00	150	350	850	1,500
1908 R	1,518,000	2.00	4.00	10.00	50.00	100

KM# 41 2 CENTESIMI

Bronze **Ruler:** Vittorio Emanuele III **Obv:** Bust left **Rev:** Female standing on prow

Date	Mintage	F12	VF20	XF40	MS60	MS63
1908 R	298,000	15.00	25.00	60.00	120	300
1909 R	2,419,000	1.00	2.50	6.00	15.00	40.00
1910 R	590,000	12.00	20.00	55.00	125	250
1911 R	2,777,000	1.00	2.50	6.00	15.00	40.00
1912 R	840,000	5.00	12.00	30.00	75.00	150
1914 R	1,648,000	2.00	4.00	12.00	40.00	80.00
1915 R	4,860,000	1.00	2.50	6.00	15.00	40.00
1916 R	1,540,000	1.00	2.50	6.00	15.00	40.00
1917 R	3,638,000	1.00	2.50	6.00	15.00	40.00

KM# 42 5 CENTESIMI

5.00 g., Bronze, 25 mm. **Ruler:** Vittorio Emanuele III **Obv:** Bust left **Rev:** Female standing on prow

Date	Mintage	F12	VF20	XF40	MS60	MS63
1908 R	824,000	12.00	22.00	45.00	100	220
1909 R	1,734,000	5.00	10.00	20.00	75.00	150
1912 R	743,000	5.00	10.00	30.00	100	200
1913 R Dot after D	1,964,000	2.00	4.00	10.00	50.00	100
1913 R Without dot after D	Inc. above	50.00	100	300	800	1,500
1915 R	1,038,000	5.00	10.00	20.00	75.00	150
1918 R	4,242,000	3.00	7.00	20.00	50.00	100

KM# 59 5 CENTESIMI

3.26 g., Bronze, 19.8 mm. **Ruler:** Vittorio Emanuele III **Obv:** Head left **Rev:** Wheat ear divides value

Date	Mintage	F12	VF20	XF40	MS60	MS63
1919 R	13,208,000	2.00	4.00	10.00	30.00	100
1920 R	33,372,000	—	0.10	0.60	3.00	15.00
1921 R	80,111,000	—	0.10	0.60	3.00	15.00
1922 R	42,914,000	—	0.10	0.60	3.00	15.00
1923 R	29,614,000	—	0.10	0.60	3.00	15.00
1924 R	20,352,000	—	0.10	0.60	3.00	15.00
1925 R	40,460,000	—	0.10	0.60	3.00	15.00
1926 R	21,158,000	—	0.10	0.60	3.00	15.00
1927 R	15,800,000	—	0.10	0.60	3.00	15.00
1928 R	16,090,000	—	0.10	0.60	3.00	15.00
1929 R	29,000,000	—	0.10	0.60	3.00	15.00
1930 R	22,694,000	—	0.10	0.60	3.00	15.00
1931 R	20,000,000	—	0.10	0.60	3.00	15.00
1932 R	11,456,000	—	0.10	0.60	3.00	15.00
1933 R	20,720,000	—	0.10	0.60	3.00	15.00
1934 R	16,000,000	—	0.10	0.60	3.00	15.00
1935 R	11,000,000	—	0.10	0.60	3.00	15.00
1936 R	9,462,000	0.15	0.30	3.00	20.00	60.00
1937 R	972,000	12.00	22.00	55.00	110	220

KM# 73 5 CENTESIMI

3.20 g., Bronze **Ruler:** Vittorio Emanuele III **Obv:** Head right **Rev:** Eagle with wings spread

Date	Mintage	F12	VF20	XF40	MS60	MS63
1936 R Yr. XIV	4,998,000	1.00	2.00	10.00	20.00	40.00
1937 R Yr. XV	7,207,000	1.00	2.00	4.00	7.00	15.00
1938 R Yr. XVI	24,000,000	—	0.10	0.50	2.50	10.00
1939 R Yr. XVII	22,000,000	—	0.10	0.50	2.50	10.00

KM# 73a 5 CENTESIMI

3.00 g., Aluminum-Bronze **Ruler:** Vittorio Emanuele III **Obv:** Head right **Rev:** Eagle with wings spread **Rev. Legend:** G. Romagnoli

Date	Mintage	F12	VF20	XF40	MS60	MS63
1939 R Yr. XVII	10,000,000	—	0.10	0.20	1.00	6.00
1940 R Yr. XVIII	16,340,000	—	0.10	0.20	1.00	6.00
1941 R Yr. XIX	25,200,000	—	0.10	0.20	1.00	6.00
1942 R Yr. XX	13,922,000	—	0.10	0.20	1.00	6.00
1943 R Yr. XXI	372,000	1.50	3.00	6.00	15.00	30.00

KM# 43 10 CENTESIMI

Bronze **Ruler:** Vittorio Emanuele III **Obv:** Bust left **Rev:** Female standing on prow

Date	Mintage	F12	VF20	XF40	MS60	MS63
1908 R Unique	—	—	—	—	—	—

KM# 51 10 CENTESIMI

9.97 g., Bronze, 30.13 mm. **Ruler:** Vittorio Emanuele III **Subject:** 50th Anniversary of the Kingdom **Obv:** Head left **Rev:** Two classical figures standing **Edge:** Plain

Date	Mintage	F12	VF20	XF40	MS60	MS63
1911 R	2,000,000	1.50	3.00	10.00	30.00	70.00

KM# 60 10 CENTESIMI

5.34 g., Bronze, 23 mm. **Ruler:** Vittorio Emanuele III **Obv:** Head left **Rev:** Honey Bee

Date	Mintage	F12	VF20	XF40	MS60	MS63
1919 R	986,000	12.00	25.00	100	300	600
1920 R	37,995,000	—	0.10	0.75	4.00	20.00
1921 R	66,510,000	—	0.10	0.75	4.00	20.00
1922 R	45,217,000	—	0.10	0.75	4.00	20.00
1923 R	31,529,000	—	0.10	0.75	4.00	20.00
1924 R	35,312,000	—	0.10	0.75	4.00	20.00
1925 R	22,370,000	—	0.10	0.75	4.00	20.00
1926 R	25,190,000	—	0.10	0.75	4.00	20.00
1927 R	22,673,000	—	0.10	0.75	4.00	20.00
1928 R	15,680,000	—	0.10	3.00	20.00	60.00
1929 R	15,593,000	—	0.10	0.75	4.00	20.00
1930 R	17,115,000	—	0.10	0.75	4.00	20.00
1931 R	10,750,000	—	0.10	0.75	4.00	20.00
1932 R	5,678,000	—	0.10	5.00	50.00	100
1933 R	10,250,000	—	0.10	0.75	4.00	20.00
1934 R	18,300,000	—	0.10	0.75	4.00	20.00
1935 R	10,500,000	—	0.10	0.75	4.00	20.00
1936 R	8,770,000	—	0.10	3.00	40.00	100
1937 R	5,500,000	—	0.10	3.00	40.00	100

KM# 74 10 CENTESIMI

5.50 g., Copper, 23 mm. **Ruler:** Vittorio Emanuele III **Obv:** Head left **Rev:** Savoy arms on fasces with wheat ear and oak leaf flanking

Date	Mintage	F12	VF20	XF40	MS60	MS63
1936 R Yr. XIV	8,195,000	1.50	3.00	6.00	20.00	50.00
1937 R Yr. XV	7,212,000	—	0.10	0.20	2.00	7.00
1938 R Yr. XVI	18,750,000	—	0.10	0.20	2.00	7.00
1939 R Yr. XVII	24,750,000	—	0.10	0.20	2.00	7.00

KM# 74a 10 CENTESIMI

4.80 g., Aluminum-Bronze, 23 mm. **Ruler:** Vittorio Emanuele III **Obv:** Head right **Rev:** Savoy arms on fasces with wheat ear and oak leaf flanking

Date	Mintage	F12	VF20	XF40	MS60	MS63
1939 R Yr. XVII	26,105,000	—	—	0.10	1.00	4.50
1940 R Yr. XVIII	23,355,000	—	—	0.10	1.00	4.50
1941 R Yr. XIX	27,050,000	—	—	0.10	1.00	4.50
1942 R Yr. XX	18,100,000	—	—	0.10	1.00	4.50
1943 R Yr. XXI	25,400,000	—	—	0.10	1.00	4.50

KM# 44 20 CENTESIMI

4.00 g., Nickel, 21.5 mm. **Ruler:** Vittorio Emanuele III **Obv:** Head left admiring wheat ear **Rev:** Victory in flight with Savoy arms below **Edge:** Reeded

Date	Mintage	VF20	XF40	MS60	MS63	MS65
1908 R	14,315,000	0.50	2.00	15.00	25.00	55.00
1909 R	19,280,000	0.50	2.00	15.00	25.00	55.00
1910 R	21,887,000	0.50	2.00	15.00	25.00	55.00
1911 R	13,671,000	0.50	2.00	15.00	25.00	55.00
1912 R	21,040,000	0.50	2.00	15.00	25.00	55.00
1913 R	20,729,000	0.50	2.00	15.00	25.00	55.00
1914 R	14,308,000	0.50	2.00	15.00	25.00	55.00
1919 R	3,475,000	3.50	10.00	25.00	100	200
1920 R	27,284,000	0.50	2.00	15.00	25.00	55.00
1921 R	50,372,000	0.50	2.00	15.00	25.00	55.00
1922 R	17,134,000	0.50	2.00	15.00	25.00	55.00
1926 R	500	—	—	350	700	—
1927 R	100	—	—	—	1,500	—
1928 R	50	—	—	—	1,500	—
1929 R	50	—	—	—	1,500	—
1930 R	50	—	—	—	1,500	—
1931 R	50	—	—	—	1,500	—
1932 R	50	—	—	—	1,500	—
1933 R	50	—	—	—	1,500	—
1934 R	50	—	—	—	1,500	—
1935 R	50	—	—	—	1,500	—

KM# 58 20 CENTESIMI

4.00 g., Copper-Nickel, 21.5 mm. **Ruler:** Vittorio Emanuele III **Obv:** Crowned Savoy shield flanked by oak and laurel sprigs **Rev:** Value and date within hexagon box **Edge:** Segmented reeding **Note:** Overstruck on KM#28.

Date	Mintage	VF20	XF40	MS60	MS63	MS65
1918 R	43,097,000	0.20	2.00	15.00	45.00	95.00
1919 R	33,432,000	0.20	2.00	15.00	45.00	95.00
1920 R	923,000	7.00	25.00	50.00	100	300

KM# 75 20 CENTESIMI

Nickel, 21.5 mm. **Ruler:** Vittorio Emanuele III **Obv:** Head left **Rev:** Savoy shield within head right

Date	Mintage	VF20	XF40	MS60	MS63	MS65
1936 R Yr. XIV	117,000	40.00	80.00	150	300	500
1937 R Yr. XV	50	—	—	—	2,000	—
1938 R Yr. XVII	20	—	—	—	5,000	—

KM# 75a 20 CENTESIMI

Stainless Steel, 22.5 mm. **Ruler:** Vittorio Emanuele III **Obv:** Head left **Rev:** Savoy shield within head right **Edge:** Plain **Note:** Magnetic.

Date	Mintage	VF20	XF40	MS60	MS63	MS65
1939 R Yr. XVII	10,462,000	0.20	1.00	5.00	15.00	30.00
1940 R Yr. XVIII	35,350,000	0.20	1.00	5.00	15.00	30.00
1942 R Yr. XX	48,500,000	0.20	1.00	5.00	15.00	30.00

KM# 75b 20 CENTESIMI

4.04 g., Stainless Steel, 21.8 mm. **Ruler:** Vittorio Emanuele III **Obv:** Head left **Rev:** Savoy shield within head right **Edge:** Reeded **Note:** Magnetic.

Date	Mintage	VF20	XF40	MS60	MS63	MS65
1939 R Yr. XVII	10,462,000	0.10	0.40	1.00	2.00	4.00
1939 R Yr. XVIII	Inc. above	0.10	0.40	1.00	2.00	4.00
1940 R Yr. XVIII	Inc. above	0.10	0.40	1.00	2.00	4.00
1941 R Yr. XIX	97,300,000	0.10	0.40	1.00	2.00	4.00
1942 R Yr. XX	Inc. above	0.10	0.40	1.00	2.00	4.00
1943 R Yr. XXI	18,453,000	0.10	0.40	1.00	2.00	4.00

KM# 75c 20 CENTESIMI

Stainless Steel, 22.5 mm. **Ruler:** Vittorio Emanuele III **Obv:** Head left **Rev:** Savoy shield within head right **Edge:** Plain **Note:** Non-magnetic.

Date	Mintage	VF20	XF40	MS60	MS63	MS65
1939 R Yr. XVII	Inc. above	2.00	6.00	18.00	50.00	—

KM# 75d 20 CENTESIMI

4.03 g., Stainless Steel, 21.8 mm. **Ruler:** Vittorio Emanuele III **Obv:** Head left **Rev:** Savoy shield within head right **Edge:** Reeded **Note:** Non-magnetic.

Date	Mintage	VF20	XF40	MS60	MS63	MS65
1939 R Yr. XVII	Inc. above	0.10	0.40	1.00	2.00	4.00
1939 R Yr. XVIII	25,300,000	0.10	0.40	1.00	2.00	4.00
1940 R Yr. XVIII	Inc. above	0.10	0.40	1.00	2.00	4.00

KM# 36 25 CENTESIMI

4.00 g., Nickel, 21.5 mm. **Ruler:** Vittorio Emanuele III **Obv:** Crowned eagle with Savoy shield on chest **Rev:** Value above sprigs

Date	Mintage	VF20	XF40	MS60	MS63	MS65
1902 R	7,773,000	30.00	65.00	125	200	400
1903 R	5,895,000	30.00	65.00	125	200	400

KM# 61.1 50 CENTESIMI

6.10 g., Nickel, 24 mm. **Ruler:** Vittorio Emanuele III **Obv:** Head left **Rev:** Four lions pulling cart with seated Aequitas **Edge:** Plain

Date	Mintage	VF20	XF40	MS60	MS63	MS65
1919 R	3,700,000	7.00	15.00	40.00	100	200
1920 R	29,450,000	1.00	5.00	20.00	50.00	100
1921 R	16,849,000	1.00	5.00	20.00	50.00	100
1924 R	599,000	400	800	2,000	4,000	—
1925 R	24,884,000	1.00	5.00	20.00	50.00	100
1926 R	500	—	—	—	600	—
1927 R	100	—	—	—	1,000	—
1928 R	50	—	—	—	2,000	—

KM# 61.2 50 CENTESIMI

6.00 g., Nickel, 24 mm. **Ruler:** Vittorio Emanuele III **Obv:** Head left **Rev:** Four lions pulling cart with seated Aequitas **Edge:** Reeded

Date	Mintage	VF20	XF40	MS60	MS63	MS65
1919 R	Inc. above	20.00	100	800	1,650	3,500
1920 R	Inc. above	20.00	100	1,200	2,500	4,000
1921 R	Inc. above	20.00	100	1,200	2,500	4,000
1924 R	Inc. above	100	300	700	1,500	3,000
1925 R	Inc. above	15.00	30.00	500	1,000	2,000
1929 R	50	—	—	—	2,000	—
1930 R	50	—	—	—	2,000	—
1931 R	50	—	—	—	2,000	—
1932 R	50	—	—	—	2,000	—
1933 R	50	—	—	—	2,000	—
1934 R	50	—	—	—	2,000	—
1935 R	50	—	—	—	2,000	—

KM# 76 50 CENTESIMI

Nickel, 24 mm. **Ruler:** Vittorio Emanuele III **Obv:** Head right **Rev:** Eagle standing right on fasces

Date	Mintage	F12	VF20	XF40	MS60	MS63
1936 R Yr. XIV	118,000	17.00	30.00	75.00	150	350
1937 R Yr. XV	50	—	—	—	—	2,000
1938 R Yr. XVII	20	—	—	—	—	4,000

KM# 76a 50 CENTESIMI

6.13 g., Stainless Steel, 24 mm. **Ruler:** Vittorio Emanuele III **Obv:** Head right **Rev:** Eagle standing right on fasces **Edge:** Reeded **Note:** Non-magnetic.

Date	Mintage	F12	VF20	XF40	MS60	MS63
1939 R Yr. XVII	9,373,000	—	0.10	0.20	5.00	10.00
1939 R Yr. XVIII	10,005,000	—	0.10	0.20	5.00	10.00
1940 R Yr. XVIII	19,005,000	—	0.10	0.20	5.00	10.00

KM# 76b 50 CENTESIMI

6.00 g., Stainless Steel, 24 mm. **Ruler:** Vittorio Emanuele III **Obv:** Head right **Rev:** Eagle standing right on fasces **Edge:** Reeded **Note:** Magnetic.

Date	Mintage	F12	VF20	XF40	MS60	MS63
1939 R Yr. XVII	9,373,000	—	0.10	0.20	1.50	5.00
1939 R Yr. XVIII	Inc. above	—	0.10	0.20	1.50	5.00
1940 R Yr. XVIII	19,005,000	—	0.10	0.20	1.50	5.00
1941 R Yr. XIX	58,100,000	—	0.10	0.20	1.50	5.00
1942 R Yr. XX	26,450,000	—	0.10	0.20	1.50	5.00
1943 R Yr. XXI	3,681,000	12.00	20.00	50.00	90.00	180

KM# 32 LIRA

5.00 g., 0.835 Silver 0.1342 oz. ASW **Ruler:** Vittorio Emanuele III **Obv:** Head right **Rev:** Crowned eagle with savoy shield

Date	Mintage	F12	VF20	XF40	MS60	MS63
1901 R	2,590,000	7.00	12.00	40.00	135	315
1902 R	4,084,000	7.00	12.00	25.00	90.00	275
1905 R	700,000	65.00	120	350	1,250	2,700
1906 R	4,665,000	7.00	12.00	25.00	90.00	275
1907 R	8,472,000	7.00	12.00	18.00	75.00	270

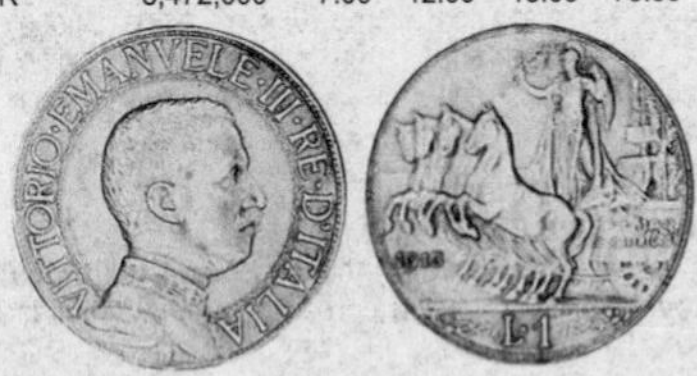

KM# 45 LIRA

5.00 g., 0.835 Silver 0.1342 oz. ASW **Ruler:** Vittorio Emanuele III **Obv:** Bust right **Rev:** Quadriga with standing female figure

Date	Mintage	F12	VF20	XF40	MS60	MS63
1908 R	2,212,000	10.00	20.00	60.00	270	630
1909 R	3,475,000	8.00	15.00	50.00	225	540
1910 R	5,525,000	6.00	10.00	20.00	45.00	180
1912 R	5,865,000	4.00	7.00	10.00	36.00	90.00
1913 R	16,177,000	4.00	7.00	10.00	18.00	45.00

KM# 57 LIRA

5.00 g., 0.835 Silver 0.1342 oz. ASW **Ruler:** Vittorio Emanuele III **Obv:** Bust right **Rev:** Quadriga with standing female figure

Date	Mintage	F12	VF20	XF40	MS60	MS63
1915 R	5,229,000	5.00	8.00	25.00	45.00	110
1916 R	1,835,000	12.00	20.00	40.00	90.00	180
1917 R	9,744,000	4.00	7.00	15.00	27.00	72.00

KM# 62 LIRA

8.00 g., Nickel, 27 mm. **Ruler:** Vittorio Emanuele III **Obv:** Female seated left **Rev:** Crowned Savoy shield and value within wreath **Edge:** Reeded

Date	Mintage	VF20	XF40	MS60	MS63	MS65
1922 R	82,267,000	0.60	2.00	20.00	35.00	100
1923 R	20,175,000	1.00	5.00	45.00	75.00	150
1924 R Closed 2	29,288,000	1.00	5.00	45.00	75.00	150
1926 R	500	—	—	—	500	—
1927 R	100	—	—	—	1,000	—
1928 R	19,996,000	5.00	20.00	100	300	—
1929 R	50	—	—	—	2,000	—
1930 R	50	—	—	—	2,000	—
1931 R	50	—	—	—	2,000	—
1932 R	50	—	—	—	2,000	—
1933 R	50	—	—	—	2,000	—
1934 R	50	—	—	—	2,000	—
1935 R	50	—	—	—	2,000	—

KM# 77 LIRA

8.00 g., Nickel, 27 mm. **Ruler:** Vittorio Emanuele III **Obv:** Head left **Rev:** Eagle with wings open

Date	Mintage	VF20	XF40	MS60	MS63	MS65
1936 R Yr. XIV	119,000	30.00	60.00	100	200	450
1937 R Yr. XV	50	—	—	—	2,000	—
1938 R XVII	20	—	—	—	4,000	—

KM# 77a LIRA

8.10 g., Stainless Steel, 27 mm. **Ruler:** Vittorio Emanuele III **Obv:** Head left **Rev:** Eagle with wings open **Edge:** Reeded **Note:** Non-magnetic.

Date	Mintage	VF20	XF40	MS60	MS63	MS65
1939 R Yr. XVII	10,034,000	0.20	0.60	2.00	5.00	8.00
1939 R Yr. XVIII	15,977,000	0.20	0.60	2.00	5.00	8.00
1940 R Yr. XVIII	25,997,000	0.20	0.60	2.00	5.00	8.00

KM# 77b LIRA

7.90 g., Stainless Steel, 27 mm. **Ruler:** Vittorio Emanuele III **Obv:** Head left **Rev:** Eagle with wings open **Edge:** Reeded **Note:** Magnetic.

Date	Mintage	VF20	XF40	MS60	MS63	MS65
1939 R Yr. XVII	Inc. above	0.20	0.50	1.00	2.50	4.00
1939 R Yr. XVIII	Inc. above	0.20	0.50	1.00	2.50	4.00
1940 R Yr. XVIII	Inc. above	0.20	0.50	1.00	2.50	4.00
1941 R Yr. XIX	8,550,000	0.20	0.50	1.00	2.50	4.00
1942 R Yr. XX	5,700,000	0.20	0.50	1.00	2.50	4.00
1943 R Yr. XXI	11,500,000	5.00	10.00	30.00	50.00	100

KM# 33 2 LIRE

10.00 g., 0.835 Silver 0.2685 oz. ASW **Ruler:** Vittorio Emanuele III **Obv:** Head right **Rev:** Crowned eagle with Savoy shield on chest

Date	Mintage	F12	VF20	XF40	MS60	MS63
1901 R	72,000	350	650	1,250	3,500	7,750
1902 R	549,000	75.00	150	300	900	2,750
1903 R	54,000	1,000	2,000	3,000	9,000	18,000
1904 R	157,000	300	600	1,200	2,700	5,400
1905 R	1,643,000	35.00	75.00	150	360	720
1906 R	970,000	40.00	80.00	160	360	720
1907 R	1,245,000	35.00	75.00	150	360	720

KM# 46 2 LIRE

10.00 g., 0.835 Silver 0.2685 oz. ASW **Ruler:** Vittorio Emanuele III **Obv:** Bust right **Rev:** Quadriga with standing female

Date	Mintage	F12	VF20	XF40	MS60	MS63
1908 R	2,283,000	17.00	30.00	70.00	225	450
1910 R	719,000	60.00	100	200	450	1,800
1911 R	535,000	120	200	500	900	2,550
1912 R	2,166,000	17.00	30.00	100	180	450

KM# 52 2 LIRE

10.00 g., 0.835 Silver 0.2685 oz. ASW, 27 mm. **Ruler:** Vittorio Emanuele III **Subject:** 50th Anniversary of the Kingdom **Obv:** Head left **Rev:** Two classical figures standing

Date	Mintage	F12	VF20	XF40	MS60	MS63
1911 R	1,000,000	17.00	30.00	75.00	135	270

KM# 55 2 LIRE

10.00 g., 0.835 Silver 0.2685 oz. ASW, 27 mm. **Ruler:** Vittorio Emanuele III **Obv:** Bust right **Rev:** Quadriga with standing female

Date	Mintage	F12	VF20	XF40	MS60	MS63
1914 R	10,390,000	6.00	10.00	20.00	37.00	85.00
1915 R	7,948,000	6.00	10.00	20.00	37.00	85.00
1916 R	10,923,000	6.00	10.00	20.00	37.00	85.00
1917 R	6,123,000	8.00	15.00	25.00	70.00	135

KM# 63 2 LIRE

10.07 g., Nickel, 29.1 mm. **Ruler:** Vittorio Emanuele III **Obv:** Bust right **Rev:** Axe head within fasces with value at left

Date	Mintage	VF20	XF40	MS60	MS63	MS65
1923 R	32,260,000	3.00	10.00	25.00	70.00	150
1924 R	45,051,000	3.00	10.00	25.00	70.00	150
1925 R	14,628,000	3.00	20.00	35.00	95.00	200
1926 R	5,101,000	30.00	100	700	1,500	—
1927 R	1,632,000	80.00	400	1,500	3,000	—
1928 R	50	—	—	—	1,500	—
1929 R	50	—	—	—	1,500	—
1930 R	50	—	—	—	1,500	—
1931 R	50	—	—	—	1,500	—
1932 R	50	—	—	—	1,500	—
1933 R	50	—	—	—	1,500	—
1934 R	50	—	—	—	1,500	—
1935 R	50	—	—	—	1,500	—

KM# 78 2 LIRE

Nickel **Ruler:** Vittorio Emanuele III **Obv:** Head right **Rev:** Eagle with open wings standing on fasces within wreath **Edge:** Plain

Date	Mintage	VF20	XF40	MS60	MS63	MS65
1936 R Yr. XIV	120,000	50.00	120	200	400	—
1937 R Yr. XV	50	—	—	—	3,000	—
1939 R Yr. XVII	20	—	—	—	5,000	—

KM# 78a 2 LIRE

Stainless Steel, 29 mm. **Ruler:** Vittorio Emanuele III **Obv:** Head right **Rev:** Eagle with open wings standing on fasces within wreath **Edge:** Reeded **Note:** Non-magnetic.

Date	Mintage	VF20	XF40	MS60	MS63	MS65
1939 R Yr. XVII	2,900,000	0.20	3.00	10.00	15.00	25.00
1939 R Yr. XVIII	4,873,000	0.20	1.00	3.00	8.00	15.00

Date	Mintage	VF20	XF40	MS60	MS63	MS65
1940 R Yr. XVIII	5,742,000	0.20	1.00	3.00	8.00	15.00

KM# 78b 2 LIRE

Stainless Steel, 29 mm. **Ruler:** Vittorio Emanuele III **Obv:** Head right **Rev:** Eagle with open wings standing on fasces within wreath **Edge:** Reeded **Note:** Magnetic.

Date	Mintage	VF20	XF40	MS60	MS63	MS65
1939 R Yr. XVII	Inc. above	0.20	1.00	3.00	8.00	15.00
1939 R Yr. XVIII	Inc. above	2.00	4.00	6.00	25.00	50.00
1940 R Yr. XVIII	Inc. above	0.40	2.00	4.00	10.00	17.00
1941 R Yr. XIX	1,865,000	0.20	1.00	3.00	8.00	15.00
1942 R Yr. XX	2,450,000	60.00	100	250	500	—
1943 R Yr. XXI	600,000	60.00	100	250	500	—

KM# 34 5 LIRE

25.00 g., 0.900 Silver 0.7234 oz. ASW **Ruler:** Vittorio Emanuele III **Obv:** Head right **Rev:** Crowned eagle with Savoy shield on chest

Date	Mintage	VF20	XF40	MS60	MS63	MS65
1901 R	114	—	—	—	60,000	90,000

KM# 53 5 LIRE

25.00 g., 0.900 Silver 0.7234 oz. ASW, 37 mm. **Ruler:** Vittorio Emanuele III **Subject:** 50th Anniversary of the Kingdom **Obv:** Head left **Rev:** Two classical figures standing

Date	Mintage	VF20	XF40	MS60	MS63	MS65
1911 R	60,000	500	750	1,500	2,500	3,500

KM# 56 5 LIRE

25.00 g., 0.900 Silver 0.7234 oz. ASW **Ruler:** Vittorio Emanuele III **Obv:** Head right **Rev:** Quadriga with standing female

Date	Mintage	VF20	XF40	MS60	MS63	MS65
1914 R	273,000	—	5,000	7,500	9,000	12,500

KM# 67.1 5 LIRE

5.00 g., 0.835 Silver 0.1342 oz. ASW, 23 mm. **Ruler:** Vittorio Emanuele III **Obv:** Head left **Rev:** Eagle with open wings standing on fascis **Edge Lettering:** *FERT*

Date	Mintage	VF20	XF40	MS60	MS63	MS65
1926 R	5,405,000	8.00	20.00	30.00	75.00	150
1927 R	92,887,000	4.50	6.50	12.50	25.00	50.00
1928 R	9,908,000	7.00	20.00	30.00	75.00	150
1929 R	33,803,000	4.50	6.50	12.50	25.00	50.00
1930 R	19,525,000	4.50	6.50	12.50	25.00	50.00
1931 R	50	—	—	—	2,500	—
1932 R	50	—	—	—	2,500	—
1933 R	50	—	—	—	2,500	—
1934 R	50	—	—	—	2,500	—
1935 R	50	—	—	—	2,500	—

KM# 67.2 5 LIRE

5.00 g., 0.835 Silver 0.1342 oz. ASW, 23 mm. **Ruler:** Vittorio Emanuele III **Obv:** Head left **Rev:** Eagle with wings open standing on fascis **Edge Lettering:** ** FERT **

Date	Mintage	VF20	XF40	MS60	MS63	MS65
1927 R	Inc. above	4.50	6.50	12.50	25.00	50.00
1928 R	Inc. above	10.00	40.00	200	600	—
1929 R	Inc. above	4.50	6.50	12.50	25.00	50.00

KM# 79 5 LIRE

5.00 g., 0.835 Silver 0.1342 oz. ASW **Ruler:** Vittorio Emanuele III **Obv:** Head left **Rev:** Mother seated with three children

Date	Mintage	F12	VF20	XF40	MS60	MS63
1936 R Yr. XIV	1,016,000	12.00	20.00	40.00	75.00	150
1937 R Yr. XV	100,000	17.00	30.00	60.00	100	250
1938 R Yr. XVIII	20	—	—	—	—	2,500
1939 R Yr. XVIII	20	—	—	—	—	2,500
1940 R Yr. XIX	20	—	—	—	—	2,500
1941 R Yr. XX	20	—	—	—	—	2,500

KM# 47 10 LIRE

3.23 g., 0.900 Gold 0.0933 oz. AGW, 18 mm. **Ruler:** Vittorio Emanuele III

Date	Mintage	VF20	XF40	MS60	MS63	MS65
1910 R Rare	—	—	—	—	—	—
Note: All but one piece melted						
1912 R	6,796	1,250	2,000	3,500	6,500	9,500
1926 R	40	—	—	—	14,000	—
1927 R	30	—	—	—	16,000	—

KM# 68.1 10 LIRE

10.00 g., 0.835 Silver 0.2685 oz. ASW **Ruler:** Vittorio Emanuele III **Obv:** Head left **Rev:** Biga with female **Edge Lettering:** *FERT*

Date	Mintage	F12	VF20	XF40	MS60	MS63
1926 R	1,748,000	60.00	100	250	500	1,000
1927 R	44,801,000	8.00	15.00	35.00	75.00	150
1928 R	6,652,000	30.00	50.00	100	250	500
1929 R	6,800,000	60.00	100	200	850	1,700
1930 R	3,668,000	60.00	100	200	500	1,000
1931 R	50	—	—	—	—	3,000
1932 R	50	—	—	—	—	3,000
1933 R	50	—	—	—	—	3,000
1934 R	50	—	—	—	—	3,000

KM# 68.2 10 LIRE

10.00 g., 0.835 Silver 0.2685 oz. ASW **Ruler:** Vittorio Emanuele III **Obv:** Head left **Rev:** Biga with female **Edge Lettering:** **FERT**

Date	Mintage	F12	VF20	XF40	MS60	MS63
1927 R	Inc. above	6.00	10.00	30.00	80.00	150
1928 R	Inc. above	150	250	400	1,000	2,000
1929 R	Inc. above	30.00	50.00	125	250	500

KM# 80 10 LIRE

10.00 g., 0.835 Silver 0.2685 oz. ASW, 27 mm. **Ruler:** Vittorio Emanuele III **Obv:** Head right **Rev:** Female standing on prow

Date	Mintage	F12	VF20	XF40	MS60	MS63
1936 R Yr. XIV	619,000	15.00	25.00	45.00	90.00	225
1937 R Yr. XV	50	—	—	—	—	3,000
1938 R Yr. XVII	20	—	—	—	—	7,000
1939 R Yr. XVIII	20	—	—	—	—	7,000
1940 R Yr. XIX	20	—	—	—	—	7,000
1941 R Yr. XX	20	—	—	—	—	7,000

KM# 37.1 20 LIRE

6.45 g., 0.900 Gold 0.1867 oz. AGW **Ruler:** Vittorio Emanuele III **Obv:** Head left **Rev:** Crowned eagle with Savoy shield on chest

Date	Mintage	VF20	XF40	MS60	MS63	MS65
1902 R	181	15,000	27,500	42,000	—	—
1903 R	1,800	2,000	3,000	4,000	6,500	—
1905 R	8,715	500	850	1,500	2,500	3,750
1908 R Rare	—	—	—	—	—	—

KM# 37.2 20 LIRE

6.45 g., 0.900 Gold 0.1867 oz. AGW **Ruler:** Vittorio Emanuele III **Obv:** Head left **Rev:** Crowned eagle with Savoy shield on chest **Note:** A small anchor below the neck indicates that the gold in the coin is from Eritrea.

Date	Mintage	VF20	XF40	MS60	MS63	MS65
1902 R	115	13,500	27,000	42,000	—	—

KM# 48 20 LIRE

6.45 g., 0.900 Gold 0.1867 oz. AGW **Ruler:** Vittorio Emanuele III **Obv:** Uniformed bust left **Rev:** Female standing on prow

Date	Mintage	VF20	XF40	MS60	MS63	MS65
1910 R	Est. 33000	—	—	75,000	—	—
Note: Six pieces currently known to exist						
1912 R	59,000	450	750	1,150	1,750	2,750
1926 R	40	—	15,000	30,000	—	—
1927 R	30	—	17,500	40,000	—	—

KM# 64 20 LIRE

6.45 g., 0.900 Gold 0.1867 oz. AGW, 21 mm. **Ruler:** Vittorio Emanuele III **Subject:** 1st Anniversary of Fascist Government **Obv:** Head left **Rev:** Axe head within fasces with value at left

Date	Mintage	VF20	XF40	MS60	MS63	MS65
1923 R	20,000	700	1,000	1,750	2,850	4,000

KM# 69 20 LIRE

15.00 g., 0.800 Silver 0.3858 oz. ASW **Ruler:** Vittorio Emanuele III **Obv:** Head right **Rev:** Standing male with fasces approaching seated Italia

Date	Mintage	F12	VF20	XF40	MS60	MS63
1927 R Yr. V	100	—	—	5,000	8,000	13,000
1927 R Yr. VI	3,518,000	50.00	80.00	175	375	750
1928 R Yr. VI	2,487,000	50.00	80.00	175	375	750

Date	Mintage	F12	VF20	XF40	MS60	MS63
1929 R Yr. VII	50	—	—	—	—	5,000
1930 R Yr. VIII	50	—	—	—	—	5,000
1931 R Yr. IX	50	—	—	—	—	5,000
1932 R Yr. X	50	—	—	—	—	5,000
1933 R Yr. XI	50	—	—	—	—	5,000
1934 R Yr. XII	50	—	—	—	—	5,000

KM# 70 20 LIRE
20.00 g., 0.600 Silver 0.3858 oz. ASW, 35 mm. **Ruler:** Vittorio Emanuele III **Subject:** 10th Anniversary - End of World War I **Obv:** Helmeted head left **Rev:** Fasces, lion's head and axe head **Note:** Similar 20 and 100 Lire pieces were struck in gold. Silver and silvered brass items are modern fantasies.

Date	Mintage	F12	VF20	XF40	MS60	MS63
1928 R Yr. VI	3,536,250	60.00	100	250	650	1,350

KM# 81 20 LIRE
20.00 g., 0.800 Silver 0.5144 oz. ASW **Ruler:** Vittorio Emanuele III **Obv:** Head left **Rev:** Quadriga and seated female

Date	Mintage	VF20	XF40	MS60	MS63	MS65
1936 R Yr. XIV	10,000	450	750	1,250	2,250	5,000
1937 R Yr. XV	50	—	—	—	7,500	—
1938 R Yr. XVII	20	—	—	—	10,000	—
1939 R Yr. XVIII	20	—	—	—	10,000	—
1940 R Yr. XIX	20	—	—	—	10,000	—
1941 R Yr. XX	20	—	—	—	10,000	—

KM# 49 50 LIRE
16.13 g., 0.900 Gold 0.4667 oz. AGW **Ruler:** Vittorio Emanuele III **Obv:** Bust left **Rev:** Female with plow

Date	Mintage	F12	VF20	XF40	MS60	MS63
1910 R Rare	2,096	—	—	—	—	—
1912 R	11,000	1,200	1,750	2,800	4,250	5,500
1926 R	40	—	—	—	42,000	—
1927 R	30	—	—	—	52,000	—

KM# 54 50 LIRE
16.13 g., 0.900 Gold 0.4667 oz. AGW, 28 mm. **Ruler:** Vittorio Emanuele III **Subject:** 50th Anniversary of the Kingdom **Obv:** Head left **Rev:** Standing classical couple

Date	Mintage	VF20	XF40	MS60	MS63	MS65
ND-1911 R	20,000	950	1,450	1,850	2,600	4,500

KM# 71 50 LIRE
4.40 g., 0.900 Gold 0.1273 oz. AGW **Ruler:** Vittorio Emanuele III **Obv:** Head left **Rev:** Man striding right

Date	Mintage	F12	VF20	XF40	MS60	MS63
1931 R Yr. IX	19,750	300	500	600	750	1,250
1931 R Yr. X	12,630	300	500	600	750	1,250
1932 R Yr. X	12,000	300	500	600	750	1,250
1933 R Yr. XI	6,463	500	600	1,000	2,200	3,200

KM# 82 50 LIRE
4.40 g., 0.900 Gold 0.1273 oz. AGW **Ruler:** Vittorio Emanuele III **Obv:** Head left **Rev:** Eagle with wings spread above Savoy shield

Date	Mintage	F12	VF20	XF40	MS60	MS63
1936 R Yr. XIV	790	3,000	5,500	7,500	11,500	20,000

KM# 39 100 LIRE
32.26 g., 0.900 Gold 0.9334 oz. AGW **Ruler:** Vittorio Emanuele III **Obv:** Head left **Rev:** Crowned eagle with Savoy shield on chest

Date	Mintage	F12	VF20	XF40	MS60	MS63
1903 R	966	7,000	11,000	22,000	32,000	50,000
1905 R	1,012	6,500	10,000	18,000	30,000	50,000

KM# 50 100 LIRE
32.26 g., 0.900 Gold 0.9334 oz. AGW **Ruler:** Vittorio Emanuele III **Obv:** Bust left **Rev:** Female with plow

Date	Mintage	VF20	XF40	MS60	MS63	MS65
1910 R Rare	2,013	—	—	—	—	—
1912 R	4,946	4,500	6,500	10,000	18,000	25,500
1926 R	40	18,000	22,000	35,000	50,000	—
1927 R	30	20,000	28,000	45,000	60,000	—

KM# 65 100 LIRE
32.26 g., 0.900 Gold 0.9334 oz. AGW, 35 mm. **Ruler:** Vittorio Emanuele III **Subject:** 1st Anniversary of Fascist Government **Obv:** Head left **Rev:** Axe within fasces with value at left

Date	Mintage	F12	VF20	XF40	MS60	MS63
1923 R Matte finish	20,000	2,250	3,000	4,000	7,000	11,000
1923 R Bright finish, rare	—	—	—	—	—	—

KM# 66 100 LIRE
32.26 g., 0.900 Gold 0.9334 oz. AGW, 35 mm. **Ruler:** Vittorio Emanuele III **Subject:** 25th year of reign, 10th Anniversary - World War I Entry **Obv:** Head left above oak sprigs **Rev:** Heroic male figure kneeling on large rock holding flag and small Victory

Date	Mintage	F12	VF20	XF40	MS60	MS63
1925 R Matte finish	5,000	4,500	6,500	10,000	16,500	—
1925 R Bright finish, rare	—	—	—	—	—	—

KM# 72 100 LIRE
8.80 g., 0.900 Gold 0.2546 oz. AGW **Ruler:** Vittorio Emanuele III **Obv:** Head left **Rev:** Female on prow

Date	Mintage	F12	VF20	XF40	MS60	MS63
1931 R Yr. IX	34,000	400	600	900	1,700	2,500
1931 R Yr. X	Inc. above	400	600	900	1,700	2,500
1932 R Yr. X	9,081	450	650	950	1,800	2,700
1933 R Yr. XI	6,464	500	700	1,250	2,000	3,000

KM# 83 100 LIRE
8.80 g., 0.900 Gold 0.2546 oz. AGW, 25 mm. **Ruler:** Vittorio Emanuele III **Obv:** Head right **Rev:** Male figure striding left

Date	Mintage	F12	VF20	XF40	MS60	MS63
1936 R Yr. XIV	812	4,000	6,000	9,000	14,500	23,000

KM# 84 100 LIRE
5.19 g., 0.900 Gold 0.1502 oz. AGW, 20 mm. **Ruler:** Vittorio Emanuele III **Obv:** Head right **Rev:** Male figure striding left

Date	Mintage	F12	VF20	XF40	MS60	MS63
1937 R Yr. XVI	249	12,500	20,000	35,000	45,000	60,000
1940 R Yr. XVIII, rare	2	—	—	—	—	—

REPUBLIC

KM# 87 LIRA
Aluminum **Obv:** Wheat sprigs within head left **Rev:** Orange sprig

Date	Mintage	VF20	XF40	MS60	MS63	MS65
1946 R	104,000	50.00	90.00	125	200	400
1947 R	12,000	300	450	750	1,200	2,000
1948 R	9,000,000	0.50	2.00	4.00	15.00	35.00
1949 R	13,200,000	0.50	2.00	4.00	15.00	35.00
1950 R	1,942,000	1.00	3.00	7.00	20.00	50.00

KM# 91 LIRA

0.62 g., Aluminum, 17 mm. **Obv:** Balance scales **Rev:** Cornucopia, value and date **Note:** The 1968-1969 and 1982-2001 dates were issued in sets only.

Date	Mintage	VF20	XF40	MS60	MS63	MS65
1951 R	3,680,000	0.10	0.50	2.00	5.00	10.00
1952 R	2,720,000	0.10	0.50	2.00	5.00	10.00
1953 R	2,800,000	0.10	0.50	2.00	5.00	10.00
1954 R	41,040,000	0.10	0.25	0.50	1.00	2.00
1955 R	32,640,000	0.10	0.25	0.50	1.00	2.00
1956 R	1,840,000	3.00	5.00	10.00	18.00	30.00
1957 R	7,440,000	0.10	0.25	0.50	1.00	2.00
1958 R	5,280,000	0.10	0.25	0.50	1.00	2.00
1959 R	1,680,000	0.10	0.25	0.50	1.00	2.00
1968 R	100,000	—	—	—	—	20.00
1969 R	310,000	—	—	—	—	4.00
1970 R	1,011,000	—	—	—	—	2.00
1980 R	1,500,000	—	—	—	—	4.00
1981 R	500,000	—	—	—	—	4.00
1982 R	85,000	—	—	—	—	4.00
1983 R	76,000	—	—	—	—	20.00
1984 R	77,000	—	—	—	—	15.00
1985 R	73,000	—	—	—	—	10.00
1985 R	20,000	PF65 15.00				
1986 R	13,200	—	—	—	—	8.00
1986 R	17,500	PF65 15.00				
1987 R	177,000	—	—	—	—	12.00
1987 R	—	PF65 20.00				
1988 R	51,000	—	—	—	—	25.00
1988 R	9,000	PF65 40.00				
1989 R	51,200	—	—	—	—	15.00
1989 R	9,260	PF65 20.00				
1990 R	52,300	—	—	—	—	15.00
1990 R	9,600	PF65 20.00				
1991 R	56,000	—	—	—	—	8.00
1991 R	11,000	PF65 20.00				
1992 R	52,000	—	—	—	—	15.00
1992 R	9,500	PF65 20.00				
1993 R	50,200	—	—	—	—	15.00
1993 R	8,500	PF65 20.00				
1994 R	44,500	—	—	—	—	25.00
1994 R	8,500	PF65 30.00				
1995 R	44,600	—	—	—	—	40.00
1995 R	7,960	PF65 60.00				
1996 R	45,000	—	—	—	—	15.00
1996 R	8,000	PF65 20.00				
1997 R	43,600	—	—	—	—	40.00
1997 R	8,440	PF65 60.00				
1998 R	55,200	—	—	—	—	10.00
1998 R	9,000	PF65 20.00				
1999 R	51,800	—	—	—	—	10.00
1999 R	8,000	PF65 20.00				
2000 R	61,400	—	—	—	—	10.00
2000 R	9,000	PF65 20.00				

KM# 204 LIRA

14.60 g., 0.835 Silver 0.3919 oz. ASW **Series:** History of the Lira **Subject:** Lira of 1901, KM#32 **Obv:** Head right within circle **Rev:** Crowned eagle with shield on chest within beaded circle **Edge:** Reeded and plain

Date	Mintage	VF20	XF40	MS60	MS63	MS65
1999 R	31,700	—	—	—	—	25.00
1999 R	6,400	PF65 40.00				

KM# 205 LIRA

14.60 g., 0.835 Silver 0.3919 oz. ASW **Series:** History of the Lira **Subject:** Lira of 1915, KM#57 **Obv:** Head right within circle **Rev:** Quadriga with standing female within circle

Date	Mintage	VF20	XF40	MS60	MS63	MS65
1999 R	31,700	—	—	—	—	25.00
1999 R	6,400	PF65 40.00				

KM# 206 LIRA

14.60 g., 0.835 Silver 0.3919 oz. ASW, 34 mm. **Series:** History of the Lira **Subject:** Lira of 1922, KM#62 **Obv:** Seated allegorical figure within circle **Rev:** Crowned shield and value within wreath flanked by small circles **Edge:** Reeded and plain sections

Date	Mintage	VF20	XF40	MS60	MS63	MS65
2000 R	30,000	—	—	—	—	30.00
2000 R	6,300	PF65 50.00				

KM# 207 LIRA

14.60 g., 0.835 Silver 0.3919 oz. ASW, 34 mm. **Series:** History of the Lire **Subject:** Lira of 1936, KM#77 **Obv:** Head left within circle **Rev:** Eagle in front of fasces within circle flanked by sprigs **Edge:** Reeded and plain sections

Date	Mintage	VF20	XF40	MS60	MS63	MS65
2000 R	30,000	—	—	—	—	30.00
2000 R	6,300	PF65 50.00				

KM# 88 2 LIRE

1.75 g., Aluminum, 24.1 mm. **Obv:** Ploughman **Rev:** Wheat ear divides value **Edge:** Plain

Date	Mintage	VF20	XF40	MS60	MS63	MS65
1946 R	123,000	60.00	100	150	275	500
1947 R	12,000	300	600	900	1,350	1,850
1948 R	7,200,000	0.50	2.00	4.00	10.00	30.00
1949 R	1,350,000	10.00	25.00	45.00	85.00	200
1950 R	2,640,000	1.50	3.00	6.00	12.00	30.00

KM# 94 2 LIRE

0.80 g., Aluminum, 18 mm. **Obv:** Honey bee **Rev:** Olive branch and value **Edge:** Reeded **Note:** The 1968-1969 and 1982-2001 dates were issued in sets only.

Date	Mintage	VF20	XF40	MS60	MS63	MS65
1953 R	4,125,000	0.20	0.50	1.00	2.00	5.00
1954 R	22,500,000	0.20	0.50	1.00	2.00	5.00
1955 R	2,750,000	0.20	0.50	1.00	2.00	5.00
1956 R	1,500,000	2.00	4.00	7.00	15.00	32.00
1957 R	6,313,000	0.20	0.50	1.00	2.00	5.00
1958 R	125,000	65.00	125	225	350	600
1959 R	2,000,000	0.20	0.50	1.00	2.00	5.00
1968 R	100,000	—	—	—	—	15.00
1969 R	310,000	—	—	—	—	3.00
1970 R	1,140,000	—	—	—	—	2.50
1980 R	857,000	—	—	—	—	2.00
1981 R	162,000	—	—	—	—	2.00
1982 R	119,000	—	—	—	—	2.00
1983 R	76,000	6.00	12.00	16.00	22.00	40.00
1984 R	77,000	—	—	5.00	8.00	20.00
1985 R	91,220	—	—	—	—	10.00
1985 R	20,000	PF65 15.00				
1986 R	73,200	—	—	—	—	10.00
1986 R	17,500	PF65 15.00				
1987 R	57,500	—	—	—	—	16.00
1987 R	10,000	PF65 20.00				
1988 R	51,050	—	—	—	—	25.00
1988 R	9,000	PF65 30.00				
1989 R	51,200	—	—	—	—	18.00
1989 R	9,260	PF65 22.00				
1990 R	53,300	—	—	—	—	22.00
1990 R	9,600	PF65 25.00				
1991 R	54,000	—	—	—	—	17.00
1991 R	11,000	PF65 22.00				
1992 R	52,000	—	—	—	—	17.00
1992 R	9,500	PF65 22.00				
1993 R	50,200	—	—	—	—	17.00
1993 R	8,500	PF65 20.00				
1994 R	44,500	—	—	—	—	17.00
1994 R	8,500	PF65 22.00				
1995 R	44,588	—	—	—	—	35.00
1995 R	7,960	PF65 60.00				
1996 R	45,000	—	—	—	—	12.00
1996 R	8,000	PF65 22.00				
1997 R	43,600	—	—	—	—	35.00
1997 R	8,660	PF65 50.00				
1998 R	55,200	—	—	—	—	10.00
1998 R	9,000	PF65 15.00				
1999 R	51,800	—	—	—	—	10.00
1999 R	8,500	PF65 15.00				
2000 R	9,000	PF65 20.00				
2000 R	61,500	—	—	—	—	10.00

KM# 89 5 LIRE

2.50 g., Aluminum, 26.7 mm. **Obv:** Female head holding torch facing right **Rev:** Grape cluster **Edge:** Reeded

Date	Mintage	VF20	XF40	MS60	MS63	MS65
1946 R	81,000	200	350	800	1,400	2,000
1947 R	17,000	300	450	950	1,500	2,400
1948 R	25,125,000	0.50	3.00	10.00	30.00	50.00
1949 R	71,100,000	0.30	3.00	10.00	30.00	50.00
1950 R	114,790,000	0.30	3.00	10.00	30.00	50.00

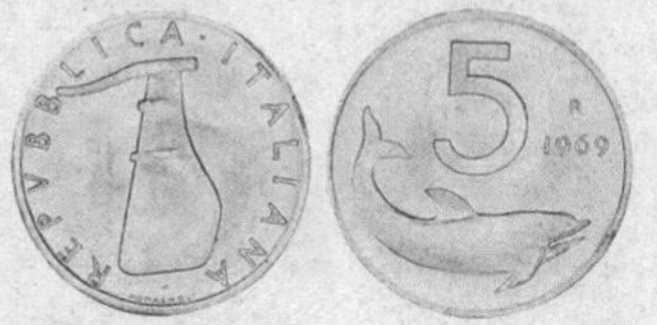

KM# 92 5 LIRE

1.04 g., Aluminum, 20.12 mm. **Obv:** Rudder **Rev:** Dolphin and value **Edge:** Plain

Date	Mintage	VF20	XF40	MS60	MS63	MS65
1951 R	40,260,000	0.10	0.25	1.00	2.50	6.00
1952 R	57,400,000	0.10	0.25	1.00	2.50	6.00
1953 R	196,200,000	0.10	0.25	0.50	1.50	3.00
1954 R	436,400,000	0.10	0.25	0.50	1.50	3.00
1955 R	159,000,000	0.10	0.25	0.50	1.00	2.00
1956 R	400,000	50.00	200	400	750	1,500
1966 R	1,200,000	0.25	0.50	1.50	3.00	6.00
1967 R	10,600,000	0.10	0.25	0.50	0.75	1.50
1968 R	7,500,000	—	—	0.10	0.25	0.75
1969 R	7,910,000	—	—	0.10	0.25	0.75
1969 R Inverted 1 (die break at base of 1)	969,000	5.00	15.00	25.00	40.00	80.00
1970 R	4,200,000	—	—	0.10	0.25	0.75
1971 R	8,600,000	—	—	0.10	0.25	0.75
1972 R	16,400,000	—	—	0.10	0.20	0.50
1973 R	28,800,000	—	—	0.10	0.20	0.50
1974 R	6,600,000	—	—	0.10	0.20	0.50
1975 R	7,000,000	—	—	0.10	0.20	0.50
1976 R	8,800,000	—	—	0.10	0.20	0.50
1977 R	6,700,000	—	—	0.10	0.20	0.50
1978 R	3,600,000	—	—	0.10	0.20	0.50
1979 R	5,000,000	—	—	0.10	0.20	0.50
1980 R	5,000,000	—	—	0.10	0.20	0.50
1981 R	5,000,000	—	—	0.10	0.20	0.50
1982 R	8,700,000	—	—	0.10	0.20	0.50
1983 R	5,000,000	—	—	0.10	0.35	1.00
1984 R	2,100,000	—	—	0.10	0.35	1.00
1985 R	3,000,000	—	—	0.10	0.35	1.00
1985 R	20,000	PF65 10.00				
1986 R	5,000,000	—	—	0.10	0.20	0.50
1986 R	17,500	PF65 10.00				
1987 R	7,000,000	—	—	0.10	0.20	0.50
1987 R	10,000	PF65 10.00				
1988 R	5,000,000	—	—	0.10	0.20	0.50
1988 R	9,000	PF65 10.00				

Date	Mintage	VF20	XF40	MS60	MS63	MS65
1989 R	2,500,000	—	—	0.10	0.20	0.50
Note: Coin rotation						
1989 R	—	2.00	4.00	7.00	10.00	18.00
Note: Medal rotation						
1989 R	9,260	PF65 10.00				
1990 R	2,500,000	—	—	0.10	0.20	0.50
1990 R	9,400	PF65 10.00				
1991 R	2,000,000	—	—	0.10	0.20	0.50
1991 R	11,000	PF65 10.00				
1992 R	1,000,000	—	—	0.10	0.20	0.50
1992 R	8,500	PF65 12.00				
1993 R	1,000,000	—	—	0.10	0.20	0.50
1993 R	9,500	PF65 12.00				
1994 R	1,000,000	—	—	0.10	0.20	0.50
1994 R	8,500	PF65 12.00				
1995 R	3,000,000	—	—	0.10	0.20	0.50
1995 R	7,960	PF65 12.00				
1996 R	2,500,000	—	—	0.10	0.20	0.50
1996 R	8,000	PF65 12.00				
1997 R	1,000,000	—	—	0.10	0.20	0.50
1997 R	8,660	PF65 12.00				
1998 R	1,500,000	—	—	0.10	0.20	0.50
1998 R	9,000	PF65 12.00				
1999 R	51,800	—	—	—	—	32.00
1999 R	8,500	PF65 50.00				
2000 R	61,400	—	—	—	—	18.00
2000 R	10,000	PF65 20.00				

KM# 90 10 LIRE

3.00 g., Aluminum, 29 mm. **Obv:** Pegasus **Rev:** Olive branch divides value

Date	Mintage	VF20	XF40	MS60	MS63	MS65
1946 R	101,000	100	200	350	650	1,000
1947 R	12,000	500	900	1,600	3,000	5,000
1948 R	14,400,000	4.00	10.00	20.00	35.00	65.00
1949 R	49,500,000	0.50	1.00	2.00	5.00	20.00
1950 R	53,311,000	0.50	1.00	2.00	5.00	20.00

KM# 93 10 LIRE

1.60 g., Aluminum, 23.25 mm. **Obv:** Plow **Rev:** Value within wheat ears **Edge:** Plain

Date	Mintage	VF20	XF40	MS60	MS63	MS65
1951 R	96,600,000	0.10	0.50	1.00	3.00	30.00
1952 R	105,150,000	0.10	0.50	1.00	3.00	30.00
1953 R	151,500,000	0.10	0.50	1.00	3.00	30.00
1954 R	95,250,000	0.10	0.50	1.00	3.00	30.00
1955 R	274,950,000	0.10	0.15	0.50	2.00	5.00
1956 R	76,650,000	0.10	0.15	0.50	2.00	5.00
1965 R	1,050,000	1.50	5.00	10.00	20.00	40.00
1966 R	16,500,000	0.10	0.25	0.50	1.00	3.00
1967 R	29,450,000	0.10	0.25	0.50	1.00	3.00
1968 R	32,200,000	—	—	0.10	0.35	0.75
1969 R	23,710,000	—	—	0.10	0.35	0.75
1970 R	14,100,000	—	—	0.10	0.35	0.75
1971 R	23,550,000	—	—	0.10	0.35	0.75
1972 R	61,300,000	—	—	0.10	0.20	0.50
1973 R	145,800,000	—	—	0.10	0.20	0.50
1974 R	85,000,000	—	—	0.10	0.20	0.50
1975 R	76,800,000	—	—	0.10	0.20	0.50
1976 R	82,000,000	—	—	0.10	0.20	0.50
1977 R	80,750,000	—	—	0.10	0.20	0.50
1978 R	43,800,000	—	—	0.10	0.20	0.50
1979 R	98,000,000	—	—	0.10	0.20	0.50
1980 R	89,000,000	—	—	0.10	0.20	0.50
1981 R	91,750,000	—	—	0.10	0.20	0.50
1982 R	44,500,000	—	—	0.10	0.20	0.50
1983 R	15,110,000	—	—	0.50	0.65	1.00
1984 R	11,122,000	—	—	0.50	0.65	1.00
1985 R	15,000,000	—	—	0.10	0.20	0.50
1985 R	20,000	PF65 8.00				
1986 R	16,000,000	—	—	0.10	0.20	0.50
1986 R	17,500	PF65 8.00				
1987 R	13,000,000	—	—	0.10	0.20	0.50
1987 R	10,000	PF65 8.00				
1988 R	13,000,000	—	—	0.10	0.20	0.50
1988 R	9,000	PF65 12.00				
1989 R	16,000,000	—	—	0.10	0.20	0.50
1989 R	9,260	PF65 12.00				

Date	Mintage	VF20	XF40	MS60	MS63	MS65
1990 R	14,000,000	—	—	0.10	0.40	1.00
1990 R	9,400	PF65 12.00				
1991 R	5,000,000	—	—	0.10	0.40	1.00
1991 R	11,000	PF65 8.00				
1992 R	1,000,000	—	—	0.10	0.40	1.00
1992 R	9,500	PF65 10.00				
1993 R	1,000,000	—	—	0.10	0.40	1.00
1993 R	8,500	PF65 10.00				
1994 R	1,000,000	—	—	0.10	0.40	1.00
1994 R	8,500	PF65 10.00				
1995 R	2,500,000	—	—	0.10	0.40	1.00
1995 R	7,960	PF65 12.00				
1996 R	3,500,000	—	—	0.10	0.40	1.00
1996 R	8,000	PF65 12.00				
1997 R	2,000,000	—	—	0.10	0.40	1.00
1997 R	8,440	PF65 12.00				
1998 R	1,500,000	—	—	0.10	0.40	1.00
1998 R	9,000	PF65 12.00				
1999 R	1,500,000	—	—	0.10	0.40	1.00
1999 R	8,500	PF65 12.00				
2000 R	61,400	—	—	—	—	14.00
2000 R	10,000	PF65 18.00				

KM# 97.1 20 LIRE

3.60 g., Aluminum-Bronze, 21.25 mm. **Obv:** Wheat sprigs within head left **Rev:** Oak leaves divide value and date **Edge:** Reeded

Date	Mintage	VF20	XF40	MS60	MS63	MS65
1957 R Serifed 7	Est. 60075000	0.20	0.40	1.00	2.00	10.00
1957 R Plain 7	Inc. above	0.20	0.40	1.00	2.00	10.00
1958 R	80,550,000	0.10	0.40	1.00	2.00	10.00
1959 R	4,005,000	0.50	2.00	5.00	15.00	35.00

KM# 97.2 20 LIRE

3.60 g., Aluminum-Bronze, 21.25 mm. **Obv:** Wheat sprigs within head left **Rev:** Oak leaves divide value and date **Edge:** Plain

Date	Mintage	VF20	XF40	MS60	MS63	MS65
1968 R	100,000	3.00	6.00	12.00	25.00	60.00
1969 R	16,735,000	0.10	0.15	0.25	0.35	0.65
1970 R	31,500,000	0.10	0.15	0.25	0.35	0.65
1971 R	12,375,000	0.10	0.15	0.25	0.35	0.65
1972 R	34,400,000	0.10	0.15	0.25	0.35	0.65
1973 R	20,000,000	0.10	0.15	0.25	0.35	0.65
1974 R	17,000,000	0.10	0.15	0.20	0.35	0.65
1975 R	25,000,000	0.10	0.15	0.20	0.35	0.65
1976 R	17,325,000	0.10	0.15	0.20	0.35	0.65
1977 R	10,000,000	0.10	0.15	0.20	0.35	0.65
1978 R	13,521,000	0.10	0.15	0.20	0.35	0.65
1979 R	40,465,000	0.10	0.15	0.20	0.30	0.50
1980 R	61,795,000	0.10	0.15	0.20	0.30	0.50
1981 R	81,510,000	0.10	0.15	0.20	0.30	0.50
1982 R	34,500,000	0.10	0.15	0.20	0.30	0.50
1983 R	15,110,000	0.10	0.15	0.20	0.30	0.50
1984 R	5,122,000	0.10	0.15	0.75	1.50	3.00
1985 R	15,000,000	0.10	0.15	0.20	0.30	0.50
1985 R	20,000	PF65 8.00				
1986 R	13,000,000	0.10	0.15	0.20	0.30	0.50
1986 R	17,500	PF65 8.00				
1987 R	2,766,000	0.10	0.15	0.75	1.50	3.00
1987 R	10,000	PF65 10.00				
1988 R	13,000,000	0.10	0.15	0.20	0.30	0.50
1988 R	9,000	PF65 12.00				
1989 R	16,000,000	0.10	0.15	0.20	0.30	0.50
1989 R	9,260	PF65 8.00				
1990 R	15,500,000	0.10	0.15	0.20	0.30	0.50
1990 R	9,400	PF65 8.00				
1991 R	13,000,000	0.10	0.15	0.20	0.30	0.50
1991 R	11,000	PF65 8.00				
1992 R	2,500,000	0.10	0.15	0.75	1.50	3.00
1992 R	9,500	PF65 8.00				
1993 R	1,000,000	0.10	0.15	0.25	0.50	1.00
1993 R	8,500	PF65 8.00				
1994 R	1,000,000	0.10	0.15	0.20	0.30	0.50
1994 R	8,500	PF65 8.00				
1995 R	1,000,000	0.10	0.15	0.25	0.50	1.00
1995 R	7,950	PF65 12.00				
1996 R	1,000,000	0.10	0.15	0.25	0.50	1.00
1996 R	8,000	PF65 8.00				
1997 R	1,000,000	0.10	0.15	0.25	0.50	1.00
1997 R	8,440	PF65 12.00				
1998 R	1,000,000	0.10	0.15	0.25	0.50	1.00
1998 R	9,000	PF65 8.00				
1999 R	500,000	0.10	0.15	0.75	1.50	3.00
1999 R	8,500	PF65 12.00				
2000 R	61,400	—	—	—	—	18.00
2000 R	8,960	PF65 25.00				

KM# 95.1 50 LIRE

6.25 g., Stainless Steel, 24.8 mm. **Obv:** Head right **Rev:** Vulcan standing at anvil facing left divides date and value **Edge:** Reeded

Date	Mintage	VF20	XF40	MS60	MS63	MS65
1954 R	17,600,000	1.00	5.00	10.00	25.00	75.00
1955 R	70,500,000	0.50	1.50	3.50	10.00	35.00
1956 R	69,400,000	0.50	1.50	3.50	10.00	35.00
1957 R	8,925,000	4.00	8.00	16.00	35.00	75.00
1958 R	825,000	10.00	25.00	50.00	100	250
1959 R	8,800,000	4.00	8.00	16.00	35.00	75.00
1960 R	2,025,000	5.00	10.00	20.00	40.00	90.00
1961 R	11,100,000	0.50	1.50	3.50	10.00	35.00
1962 R	17,700,000	0.20	0.75	1.50	5.00	15.00
1963 R	31,600,000	0.20	0.50	1.00	2.00	5.00
1964 R	37,900,000	0.20	0.50	1.00	2.00	5.00
1965 R	25,300,000	0.20	0.50	1.00	2.00	5.00
1966 R	27,400,000	0.20	0.50	1.00	2.00	5.00
1967 R	28,000,000	0.20	0.50	1.00	2.00	5.00
1968 R	17,800,000	0.10	0.20	0.50	1.00	2.00
1969 R	23,010,000	0.10	0.20	0.50	1.00	2.00
1970 R	21,411,000	0.10	0.20	0.50	1.00	2.00
1971 R	33,410,000	0.10	0.20	0.50	1.00	2.00
1972 R	39,000,000	0.10	0.20	0.50	1.00	2.00
1973 R	48,700,000	0.10	0.20	0.50	1.00	2.00
1974 R	63,000,000	0.10	0.20	0.35	0.60	1.25
1975 R	87,000,000	0.10	0.15	0.25	0.35	0.75
1976 R	180,600,000	0.10	0.15	0.25	0.35	0.75
1977 R	293,800,000	0.10	0.15	0.25	0.35	0.75
1978 R	416,808,000	0.10	0.15	0.25	0.35	0.75
1979 R	321,086,000	0.10	0.15	0.25	0.35	0.75
1980 R	94,819,000	0.10	0.15	0.25	0.35	0.75
1981 R	139,080,000	0.10	0.15	0.25	0.35	0.75
1982 R	54,500,000	0.10	0.15	0.25	0.35	0.75
1983 R	20,000,000	0.10	0.15	0.25	0.35	0.75
1984 R	10,000,000	0.10	0.15	0.25	0.35	0.75
1985 R	10,000,000	0.10	0.15	0.25	0.35	0.75
1985 R	20,000	PF65 8.00				
1986 R	15,000,000	0.10	0.15	0.25	0.35	0.75
1986 R	17,500	PF65 8.00				
1987 R	14,682,000	0.10	0.15	0.25	0.35	0.75
1987 R	10,000	PF65 8.00				
1988 R	20,000,000	0.10	0.15	0.25	0.35	0.75
1988 R	9,000	PF65 15.00				
1989 R	26,500,000	0.10	0.15	0.25	0.35	0.75
1989 R	9,200	PF65 10.00				

KM# 95.2 50 LIRE

2.73 g., Stainless Steel, 17 mm. **Obv:** Head right **Rev:** Vulcan standing at anvil facing left divides date and value **Edge:** Plain **Note:** Reduced size.

Date	Mintage	VF20	XF40	MS60	MS63	MS65
1990 R	45,500,000	—	0.10	0.20	0.30	0.50
1990 R	9,400	PF65 8.00				
1991 R	60,000,000	—	0.10	0.20	0.30	0.50
1991 R	11,000	PF65 8.00				
1992 R	90,000,000	—	0.10	0.20	0.30	0.50
1992 R	—	PF65 8.00				
1993 R	160,000,000	—	0.10	0.20	0.30	0.50
1993 R	—	PF65 8.00				
1994 R	95,255,000	—	0.10	0.20	0.30	0.50
1994 R	8,500	PF65 8.00				
1995 R	82,000,000	—	0.10	0.20	0.30	0.50
1995 R	7,960	PF65 12.00				

KM# 183 50 LIRE

4.50 g., Copper-Nickel, 19 mm. **Obv:** Turreted head left **Rev:** Large value within wreath of produce

Date	Mintage	VF20	XF40	MS60	MS63	MS65
1996 R	110,000,000	—	0.10	0.20	0.30	0.50
1996 R	8,000	PF65 12.00				
1997 R	10,000,000	—	0.10	0.20	0.40	1.00
1997 R	8,440	PF65 15.00				
1998 R	10,000,000	—	0.10	0.20	0.40	1.00
1998 R	9,000	PF65 12.00				

Date	Mintage	VF20	XF40	MS60	MS63	MS65
1999 R	55,000,000	—	0.10	0.20	0.40	1.00
1999 R	8,500	PF65 12.00				
2000 R	61,400	—	—	—	—	10.00
2000 R	8,960	PF65 15.00				

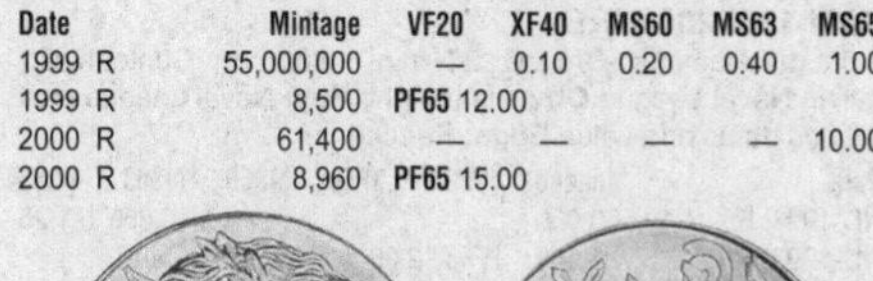

KM# 96.1 100 LIRE

8.00 g., Stainless Steel, 27.8 mm. **Obv:** Laureate head left **Rev:** Standing figure holding olive tree **Edge:** Reeded

Date	Mintage	VF20	XF40	MS60	MS63	MS65
1955 R	8,600,000	1.00	4.00	10.00	25.00	125
1956 R	99,800,000	0.25	1.50	3.00	7.00	25.00
1957 R	90,600,000	0.25	1.50	3.00	7.00	25.00
1958 R	25,640,000	0.25	1.50	3.00	10.00	60.00
1959 R	19,500,000	0.25	1.50	3.00	10.00	60.00
1960 R	20,700,000	0.25	1.50	3.00	10.00	60.00
1961 R	11,860,000	0.25	1.50	3.00	10.00	60.00
1962 R	21,700,000	0.20	0.50	1.50	4.50	20.00
1963 R	33,100,000	0.20	0.50	1.50	3.00	10.00
1964 R	31,300,000	0.20	0.50	1.50	3.00	10.00
1965 R	37,000,000	0.20	0.50	1.50	3.00	10.00
1966 R	52,500,000	0.15	0.25	1.00	3.00	10.00
1967 R	23,700,000	0.15	0.25	1.00	3.00	10.00
1968 R	34,200,000	0.15	0.25	0.50	1.00	2.00
1969 R	27,710,000	0.15	0.25	0.50	1.00	2.00
1970 R	25,011,000	0.15	0.25	0.50	1.00	2.00
1971 R	24,700,000	0.15	0.25	0.50	1.00	2.00
1972 R	31,170,000	0.15	0.25	0.50	1.50	3.00
1973 R	30,780,000	0.15	0.25	0.50	1.50	3.00
1974 R	61,000,000	0.15	0.25	0.35	0.50	0.85
1975 R	106,650,000	0.15	0.25	0.35	0.50	0.85
1976 R	160,020,000	0.15	0.25	0.35	0.50	0.85
1977 R	253,980,000	0.15	0.25	0.35	0.50	0.85
1978 R	343,626,000	0.15	0.25	0.35	0.50	0.85
1979 R	351,583,600	0.15	0.25	0.35	0.50	0.85
1980 R	69,938,500	0.15	0.25	0.35	0.50	0.85
1981 R	122,381,700	0.15	0.25	0.35	0.50	0.85
1982 R	39,500,000	0.15	0.25	0.35	0.50	0.85
1983 R	25,000,000	0.15	0.25	0.35	0.50	0.85
1984 R	10,000,000	0.15	0.25	1.00	1.50	3.00
1985 R	10,000,000	0.15	0.25	1.00	1.50	3.00
1985 R	20,000	PF65 8.00				
1986 R	18,000,000	0.15	0.25	0.50	0.75	1.00
1986 R	17,500	PF65 8.00				
1987 R	25,000,000	0.15	0.25	0.50	0.75	1.00
1987 R	10,000	PF65 8.00				
1988 R	23,000,000	0.15	0.25	0.50	0.75	1.00
1988 R	9,000	PF65 12.00				
1989 R	34,000,000	0.15	0.25	0.50	0.75	1.00
1989 R	9,260	PF65 12.00				

KM# 96.2 100 LIRE

3.25 g., Stainless Steel **Obv:** Laureate head left **Rev:** Standing figure holding olive tree **Edge:** Reeded **Note:** Reduced size. Prev. KM#96a.

Date	Mintage	VF20	XF40	MS60	MS63	MS65
1990 R	9,600	PF65 12.00				
1990 R	60,000,000	—	—	—	0.50	1.00
1991 R	100,000,000	—	—	—	0.50	1.00
1991 R	11,000	PF65 12.00				
1992 R	166,000,000	—	—	—	0.50	1.00
1992 R	9,500	PF65 12.00				

KM# 102 100 LIRE

8.00 g., Stainless Steel, 27.8 mm. **Subject:** 100th Anniversary - Birth of Guglielmo Marconi, Physicist **Obv:** Head facing **Rev:** Early radio-wave receiver flanked by date and value

Date	Mintage	VF20	XF40	MS60	MS63	MS65
ND-1974 R	50,000,000	—	0.25	0.35	0.50	1.00

KM# 106 100 LIRE

8.00 g., Stainless Steel, 27.8 mm. **Series:** F.A.O. **Rev:** Cow nursing calf, value and date

Date	Mintage	VF20	XF40	MS60	MS63	MS65
1979 R	78,340,000	—	0.25	0.35	0.50	1.00

KM# 108 100 LIRE

8.00 g., Stainless Steel, 27.8 mm. **Subject:** Centennial of Livorno Naval Academy **Obv:** Anchor and ship's wheel **Rev:** Building divides dates with flag and value below

Date	Mintage	VF20	XF40	MS60	MS63	MS65
ND-1981 R	39,500,000	—	0.25	0.35	0.50	1.00

KM# 127 100 LIRE

8.00 g., 0.835 Silver 0.2148 oz. ASW, 27.8 mm. **Subject:** 900th Anniversary - University of Bologna **Obv:** Medieval student in thought **Rev:** Towered building

Date	Mintage	VF20	XF40	MS60	MS63	MS65
1988 R	68,000	—	—	—	6.00	8.00
1988 R	13,000	PF65 15.00				

KM# 159 100 LIRE

4.50 g., Copper-Nickel, 22 mm. **Obv:** Turreted head left **Rev:** Large value within circle flanked by sprigs **Edge:** Segmented reeding

Date	Mintage	VF20	XF40	MS60	MS63	MS65
1993 R	211,501,200	—	0.15	0.25	0.35	0.75
1993 R	Inc. above	—	—	—	—	30.00
Small head						
1993 R	8,500	PF65 12.00				
1994 R	180,000,000	—	0.15	0.25	0.35	0.75
1994 R	8,500	PF65 12.00				
1996 R	210,000,000	—	0.15	0.25	0.35	0.75
1996 R	8,000	PF65 12.00				
1997 R	70,000,000	—	0.15	0.25	0.35	0.75
1997 R	8,440	PF65 15.00				
1998 R	120,000,000	—	0.15	0.25	0.35	0.75
1998 R	9,000	PF65 12.00				
1999 R	120,000,000	—	0.15	0.25	0.35	0.75
1999 R	8,500	PF65 12.00				
2000 R	61,400	—	0.15	0.25	0.50	2.50
2000 R	10,000	PF65 12.00				

KM# 171 100 LIRE

4.50 g., 0.835 Silver 0.1208 oz. ASW **Subject:** 100th Anniversary - Bank of Italy **Rev:** Printing press

Date	Mintage	VF20	XF40	MS60	MS63	MS65
ND-1993 R	52,000	—	—	—	3.00	5.00
Sets only						
ND-1993 R	10,000	PF65 8.00				

KM# 180 100 LIRE

4.50 g., Copper-Nickel, 22 mm. **Series:** F.A.O. **Obv:** Turreted head left **Rev:** Logo and value within globe design **Edge:** Segmented reeding

Date	Mintage	VF20	XF40	MS60	MS63	MS65
ND-1995 R	100,000,000	—	0.15	0.25	0.35	0.75
ND-1995 R	7,960	PF65 15.00				

KM# 105 200 LIRE

5.00 g., Aluminum-Bronze, 24 mm. **Obv:** Head right **Rev:** Value within gear **Edge:** Reeded

Date	Mintage	VF20	XF40	MS60	MS63	MS65
1977 R	15,900,000	0.20	0.25	0.35	0.60	1.25
1978 R	461,034,000	0.20	0.25	0.35	0.60	1.25
1979 R	437,325,000	0.20	0.25	0.35	0.60	1.25
1980 R	105,690,000	0.20	0.25	0.35	0.60	1.25
1981 R	72,500,000	0.20	0.25	0.35	0.60	1.25
1982 R	9,500,000	0.20	0.25	0.75	1.50	4.00
1983 R	20,000,000	0.20	0.25	0.75	1.50	3.00
1984 R	10,000,000	0.20	0.25	0.75	1.50	3.00
1985 R	15,000,000	0.20	0.25	0.75	1.50	3.00
1985 R	20,000	PF65 8.00				
1986 R	15,000,000	0.20	0.25	0.75	1.50	3.00
1986 R	17,500	PF65 8.00				
1987 R	26,180,000	0.20	0.25	0.35	0.60	1.25
1987 R	10,000	PF65 8.00				
1988 R	37,000,000	0.20	0.25	0.35	0.60	1.25
1988 R	9,000	PF65 15.00				
1991 R	70,000,000	0.20	0.25	0.35	0.60	1.25
1991 R	11,000	PF65 12.00				
1995 R	170,000,000	0.20	0.25	0.35	0.60	1.25
1995 R	7,960	PF65 25.00				
1998 R	120,000,000	0.20	0.25	0.35	0.60	1.25
1998 R	9,000	PF65 12.00				
2000 R	61,400	—	—	—	—	15.00
2000 R	8,960	PF65 15.00				

KM# 107 200 LIRE

5.00 g., Aluminum-Bronze, 24 mm. **Series:** F.A.O. **Subject:** International Women's Year **Obv:** Bust facing **Rev:** Seated woman with knee bent and child standing at her back facing right **Edge:** Reeded

Date	Mintage	VF20	XF40	MS60	MS63	MS65
1980 R	48,500,000	—	0.20	0.25	0.35	1.50

KM# 109 200 LIRE

5.00 g., Aluminum-Bronze, 24 mm. **Subject:** World Food Day **Obv:** Villa Lubin façade **Rev:** Female advancing left holding cornucopia **Edge:** Reeded

Date	Mintage	VF20	XF40	MS60	MS63	MS65
1981 R	45,207,600	—	0.20	0.25	0.35	1.50

KM# 128 200 LIRE

5.00 g., 0.835 Silver 0.1342 oz. ASW **Subject:** 900th Anniversary - University of Bologna **Obv:** Medieval student in thought **Rev:** Courtyard view within oval rope wreath

Date	Mintage	VF20	XF40	MS60	MS63	MS65
1988 R	68,000	—	—	—	6.00	8.00
1988 R	13,000	**PF65** 12.00				

KM# 130 200 LIRE

5.00 g., Aluminum-Bronze, 24 mm. **Subject:** Taranto Naval Yards **Obv:** Head right **Rev:** Ships and dates **Edge:** Reeded

Date	Mintage	VF20	XF40	MS60	MS63	MS65
ND-1989 R	48,000,000	—	—	—	1.00	2.00
ND-1989 R	9,260	**PF65** 8.00				

KM# 133 200 LIRE

5.00 g., 0.835 Silver 0.1342 oz. ASW **Subject:** Soccer **Obv:** Head left **Rev:** Ball superimposed on world globe within assorted shields bordering

Date	Mintage	VF20	XF40	MS60	MS63	MS65
1989 R	86,000	—	—	—	—	15.00
1989 R	28,000	**PF65** 15.00				

KM# 138 200 LIRE

5.00 g., 0.835 Silver 0.1342 oz. ASW **Subject:** Christopher Columbus **Obv:** Bust 3/4 right within globe design **Rev:** Shield divides date and value above dolphin

Date	Mintage	VF20	XF40	MS60	MS63	MS65
1989 R	75,000	—	—	—	—	15.00
1989 R	25,000	**PF65** 15.00				

KM# 135 200 LIRE

5.00 g., Aluminum-Bronze, 24 mm. **Obv:** Head right **Rev:** State Council building divides dates and value **Edge:** Reeded

Date	Mintage	VF20	XF40	MS60	MS63	MS65
ND-1990 R	64,500,000	—	—	—	1.00	2.00
ND-1990 R	9,600	**PF65** 8.00				

KM# 142 200 LIRE

9.00 g., 0.835 Silver 0.2416 oz. ASW **Subject:** Italian Flora and Fauna **Obv:** Female head left with flora and fauna in hair **Rev:** Wolf divides date and value

Date	Mintage	VF20	XF40	MS60	MS63	MS65
1991 R	57,000	—	—	—	—	20.00
1991 R	10,000	**PF65** 25.00				

KM# 151 200 LIRE

5.00 g., Aluminum-Bronze, 24 mm. **Subject:** Genoa Stamp Exposition **Obv:** Head right **Rev:** Stylized sailing ship **Edge:** Reeded

Date	Mintage	VF20	XF40	MS60	MS63	MS65
1992 R	110,000,000	—	—	—	1.25	2.50
1992 R	9,500	**PF65** 10.00				

KM# 155 200 LIRE

5.00 g., Aluminum-Bronze, 24 mm. **Subject:** 70th Anniversary of Military Aviation **Obv:** Head right **Rev:** Quartered arms within circle **Edge:** Reeded

Date	Mintage	VF20	XF40	MS60	MS63	MS65
1993 R	170,000,000	—	—	—	1.25	2.50
1993 R	8,500	**PF65** 8.00				

KM# 172 200 LIRE

5.00 g., 0.835 Silver 0.1342 oz. ASW **Subject:** 100th Anniversary - Bank of Italy **Obv:** Female head left with headdress **Rev:** Hammered minting scene **Note:** Both uncirculated and proof versions were issued in sets only.

Date	Mintage	VF20	XF40	MS60	MS63	MS65
ND-1993 R	52,000	—	—	—	7.00	10.00
ND-1993 R	10,000	**PF65** 35.00				

KM# 164 200 LIRE

5.00 g., Aluminum-Bronze, 24 mm. **Subject:** 180th Anniversary - Carabinieri **Obv:** Head right **Rev:** Flaming bomb above banner and value **Edge:** Reeded

Date	Mintage	VF20	XF40	MS60	MS63	MS65
ND-1994 R	200,000,000	—	—	—	1.00	2.00
ND-1994 R	8,500	**PF65** 10.00				

KM# 184 200 LIRE

5.00 g., Aluminum-Bronze, 24 mm. **Subject:** Centennial - Customs Service Academy **Obv:** Old and new buildings **Rev:** Shield above value, hat and sword **Edge:** Reeded

Date	Mintage	VF20	XF40	MS60	MS63	MS65
ND-1996 R	8,000	**PF65** 10.00				
ND-1996 R	200,000,000	—	—	—	0.75	1.50

KM# 186 200 LIRE

5.00 g., Aluminum-Bronze, 24 mm. **Subject:** Centennial - Italian Naval League **Obv:** Head right **Rev:** Naval League seal divides dates and value **Edge:** Reeded

Date	Mintage	VF20	XF40	MS60	MS63	MS65
ND-1997 R	40,000,000	—	—	—	0.65	1.25
ND-1997 R	8,440	**PF65** 12.00				

KM# 218 200 LIRE

5.00 g., Aluminum-Bronze, 24 mm. **Subject:** The Carabinieri, Protectors of Art Heritage **Rev:** Flaming bomb and David statue **Edge:** Reeded

Date	Mintage	VF20	XF40	MS60	MS63	MS65
ND-1999 R	105,000,000	—	—	—	0.75	1.50
ND-1999 R	8,500	**PF65** 10.00				

KM# 98 500 LIRE

11.00 g., 0.835 Silver 0.2953 oz. ASW, 29.3 mm. **Obv:** Columbus' ships **Rev:** Bust left within wreath **Edge:** Dates in raised lettering

Date	Mintage	VF20	XF40	MS60	MS63	MS65
1958 R	24,240,000	—	5.50	9.00	14.00	—
1958 R Prooflike	Inc. above	—	—	—	—	30.00
1959 R	19,360,000	—	5.50	9.00	14.00	—
1959 R Prooflike	Inc. above	—	—	—	—	30.00
1960 R	24,080,000	—	5.50	9.00	14.00	—
1960 R Prooflike	Inc. above	—	—	—	—	30.00
1961 R	6,560,000	—	9.00	14.00	22.00	—
1961 R Prooflike	Inc. above	—	—	—	—	45.00
1964 R	4,880,000	—	5.50	12.00	20.00	—
1964 R Prooflike	Inc. above	—	—	—	—	30.00
1965 R	3,120,000	—	5.50	12.00	20.00	—
1965 R Prooflike	Inc. above	—	—	—	—	30.00
1966 R	13,120,000	—	5.50	9.00	14.00	—
Note: Varieties exist						
1966 R Prooflike	Inc. above	—	—	—	—	25.00
1967 R	2,480,000	—	5.50	12.00	20.00	—
1967 R Prooflike	Inc. above	—	—	—	—	25.00
1968 R	100,000	—	—	15.00	25.00	45.00
1968 R	Inc. above	**PF65** 60.00				
1969 R	310,000	—	—	—	12.00	20.00
1969 R	Inc. above	**PF65** 25.00				
1970 R	1,140,000	—	—	—	10.00	15.00
1970 R	Inc. above	**PF65** 20.00				
1980 R	257,270	—	—	—	12.00	20.00
1980 R	Inc. above	**PF65** 25.00				
1981 R	162,794	—	—	—	12.00	20.00
1981 R	Inc. above	**PF65** 25.00				
1982 R	115,000	—	—	—	12.00	20.00
1982 R	Inc. above	**PF65** 25.00				
1983 R	76,000	—	—	—	20.00	40.00
1984 R	77,000	—	—	—	20.00	35.00
1985 R	74,600	—	—	—	20.00	35.00
1985 R	15,000	**PF65** 45.00				
1986 R	73,200	—	—	—	15.00	25.00
1986 R	Inc. above	**PF65** 35.00				
1987 R	57,500	—	—	—	15.00	25.00
1987 R	10,000	**PF65** 55.00				
1988 R	51,050	—	—	—	35.00	60.00
1988 R	10,000	**PF65** 80.00				
1989 R	51,200	—	—	—	25.00	45.00
1989 R	10,000	**PF65** 65.00				
1990 R	52,300	—	—	—	15.00	25.00
1990 R	10,000	**PF65** 45.00				
1991 R	54,000	—	—	—	20.00	35.00
1991 R	11,000	**PF65** 60.00				
1992 R	52,000	—	—	—	15.00	25.00
1992 R	9,500	**PF65** 45.00				
1993 R	50,200	—	—	—	15.00	25.00
1993 R	8,500	**PF65** 55.00				
1994 R	44,500	—	—	—	20.00	35.00
1994 R	8,500	**PF65** 60.00				
1995 R	44,558	—	—	—	20.00	35.00
1995 R	7,960	**PF65** 60.00				
1996 R	45,000	—	—	—	25.00	45.00
1996 R	8,000	**PF65** 70.00				
1997 R	43,600	—	—	—	25.00	45.00
1997 R	8,440	**PF65** 80.00				
1998 R	55,100	—	—	—	15.00	25.00
1998 R	9,000	**PF65** 45.00				
1999 R	51,800	—	—	—	15.00	25.00

Date	Mintage	VF20	XF40	MS60	MS63	MS65
1999 R	8,500	PF65 50.00				
2000 R	61,400	—	—	—	15.00	25.00
2000 R	8,960	PF65 50.00				

KM# 99 500 LIRE
11.00 g., 0.835 Silver 0.2953 oz. ASW, 29.3 mm. **Subject:** Italian Unification Centennial **Obv:** Female seated left **Rev:** Quadriga

Date	Mintage	VF20	XF40	MS60	MS63	MS65
ND-1961 R Prooflike	Inc. above	—	—	—	—	30.00
ND-1961 R	27,120,000	—	5.50	10.00	12.00	—

KM# 100 500 LIRE
11.00 g., 0.835 Silver 0.2953 oz. ASW, 29.3 mm. **Subject:** 700th Anniversary - Birth of Dante Alighieri, Poet **Obv:** Head left **Rev:** Radiant sun above flame, value and date

Date	Mintage	VF20	XF40	MS60	MS63	MS65
1965 R	4,272,000	—	5.50	12.00	15.00	—
1965 R Prooflike	Inc. above	—	—	—	—	20.00

KM# 103 500 LIRE
11.00 g., 0.835 Silver 0.2953 oz. ASW, 29.3 mm. **Subject:** 100th Anniversary - Birth of Guglielmo Marconi, Physicist **Obv:** Bust left **Rev:** Map of Italy with radio tower loops

Date	Mintage	VF20	XF40	MS60	MS63	MS65
ND-1974 R	689,752	—	—	—	12.00	—
ND-1974 R Prooflike	Inc. above	—	—	—	—	15.00

KM# 104 500 LIRE
11.00 g., 0.835 Silver 0.2953 oz. ASW, 29.3 mm. **Subject:** 500th Anniversary - Birth of Michelangelo Buonarroti **Obv:** Bust left **Rev:** Seated statue divides dates with value below

Date	Mintage	VF20	XF40	MS60	MS63	MS65
1975 R	269,000	—	—	—	12.00	—
1975 R Prooflike	Inc. above	—	—	—	—	15.00

KM# 110 500 LIRE
11.00 g., 0.835 Silver 0.2953 oz. ASW, 29.3 mm. **Subject:** 2000th Anniversary - Death of Virgil **Obv:** Head left **Rev:** Tree divides cow, horse and dates with value below

Date	Mintage	VF20	XF40	MS60	MS63	MS65
1981 R -1982	341,000	—	—	—	12.00	—
1981 R (1982) Prooflike	Inc. above	—	—	—	—	15.00

KM# 111 500 LIRE
6.80 g., Bi-Metallic Aluminum-Bronze center in Stainless Steel ring, 25.8 mm. **Obv:** Head left within circle **Rev:** Plaza within circle flanked by sprigs **Edge:** Segmented reeding

Date	Mintage	VF20	XF40	MS60	MS63	MS65
1982 R	162,000	—	0.40	0.60	1.20	2.00
Note: Obverse portrait varieties exist						
1983 R	137,974,000	—	0.40	0.60	1.20	2.00
1984 R	162,000,000	—	0.40	0.60	1.20	2.00
1985 R	162,000,000	—	0.40	0.60	1.20	2.00
1985 R	20,000	PF65 7.00				
1986 R	165,000,000	—	0.40	0.60	1.20	2.00
1986 R	17,500	PF65 7.00				
1987 R	200,000,000	—	0.40	0.60	1.20	2.00
1987 R	10,000	PF65 7.00				
1988 R	142,000,000	—	0.40	0.60	1.20	2.00
1988 R	9,000	PF65 12.00				
1989 R	155,000,000	—	0.40	0.60	1.20	2.00
1989 R	9,250	PF65 7.00				
1990 R	130,000,000	—	0.40	0.60	1.20	2.00
1990 R	9,400	PF65 9.00				
1991 R	140,000,000	—	0.40	0.60	1.20	2.00
1991 R	11,400	PF65 12.00				
1992 R	150,000,000	—	0.40	0.60	1.20	2.00
Note: Obverse portrait varieties exist						
1992 R	9,500	PF65 12.00				
1995 R	110,000,000	—	0.40	0.60	1.20	2.00
1995 R	7,960	PF65 25.00				
2000 R	61,400	—	—	—	—	12.00
2000 R	10,000	PF65 20.00				

KM# 112 500 LIRE
11.00 g., 0.835 Silver 0.2953 oz. ASW, 29.3 mm. **Subject:** 100th Anniversary - Death of Giuseppe Garibaldi **Obv:** Bust right **Rev:** Island map divides value and date

Date	Mintage	VF20	XF40	MS60	MS63	MS65
1982 R -1983	193,000	—	—	—	15.00	—
1982 R (1983) Prooflike	Inc. above	—	—	—	—	20.00

KM# 113 500 LIRE
11.00 g., 0.835 Silver 0.2953 oz. ASW, 29.3 mm. **Obv:** Bust of G. Galiei facing **Rev:** Dog within crowned wreath dividing dates with value below

Date	Mintage	VF20	XF40	MS60	MS63	MS65
ND-1983 R	198,000	—	—	—	15.00	—
ND-1983 R Prooflike	Inc. above	—	—	—	—	20.00

KM# 114 500 LIRE
11.00 g., 0.835 Silver 0.2953 oz. ASW, 29.3 mm. **Subject:** Los Angeles Olympics **Obv:** Head right between dove at left and torch at right **Rev:** Three figures holding up Olympic flame

Date	Mintage	VF20	XF40	MS60	MS63	MS65
1984 R	193,000	—	—	—	15.00	—
1984 R Prooflike	—	—	—	—	—	20.00

KM# 115 500 LIRE
11.00 g., 0.835 Silver 0.2953 oz. ASW, 29.3 mm. **Subject:** First Italian President of Common Market **Obv:** Head left with map, stars and globe within scalp **Rev:** Flags above stylized ancient stadium

Date	Mintage	VF20	XF40	MS60	MS63	MS65
1985 R	103,000	—	—	—	—	20.00
1985 R	29,000	PF65 35.00				

KM# 116 500 LIRE
11.00 g., 0.835 Silver 0.2953 oz. ASW, 29.3 mm. **Obv:** Town's architectural montage **Rev:** Hilltop castle above two hemispheres

Date	Mintage	VF20	XF40	MS60	MS63	MS65
1985 R	126,000	—	—	—	15.00	—
1985 R Prooflike	Inc. above	—	—	—	—	20.00

KM# 117 500 LIRE
11.00 g., 0.835 Silver 0.2953 oz. ASW, 29.3 mm. **Subject:** European Year of Music **Obv:** Muse of music left **Rev:** Pipe organ frontal view

Date	Mintage	VF20	XF40	MS60	MS63	MS65
1985 R	96,000	—	—	—	15.00	—
1985 R Prooflike	Inc. above	—	—	—	—	20.00

KM# 118 500 LIRE
11.00 g., 0.835 Silver 0.2953 oz. ASW, 29.3 mm. **Subject:** Etruscan Culture **Obv:** Standing warrior **Rev:** Two winged horses left

Date	Mintage	VF20	XF40	MS60	MS63	MS65
1985 R	104,000	—	—	—	15.00	—
1985 R Prooflike	Inc. above	—	—	—	—	20.00

KM# 123 500 LIRE
11.00 g., 0.835 Silver 0.2953 oz. ASW, 29.3 mm. **Subject:** 200th Anniversary - Birth of Alessandro Manzoni **Obv:** Bust 3/4 facing **Rev:** Headdress

Date	Mintage	VF20	XF40	MS60	MS63	MS65
1985 R	91,218	—	—	—	—	30.00
1985 R	20,000	PF65 50.00				

KM# 119 500 LIRE
11.00 g., 0.835 Silver 0.2953 oz. ASW, 29.3 mm. **Subject:** Soccer Championship - Mexico **Obv:** Map of Italy and soccer ball **Rev:** Aztec Calendar within soccer ball

Date	Mintage	VF20	XF40	MS60	MS63	MS65
1986 R	91,000	—	—	—	—	20.00
1986 R	21,000	PF65 30.00				

KM# 120 500 LIRE
11.00 g., 0.835 Silver 0.2953 oz. ASW, 29.3 mm. **Subject:** Year of Peace **Obv:** Head right **Rev:** Ancient tree

Date	Mintage	VF20	XF40	MS60	MS63	MS65
1986 R	90,000	—	—	—	—	20.00
1986 R	19,000	PF65 30.00				

KM# 124 500 LIRE
11.00 g., 0.835 Silver 0.2953 oz. ASW, 29.3 mm. **Subject:** 600th Anniversary - Birth of Donatello **Obv:** Head with headdress 1/4 left **Rev:** Standing male statue to left of value and date

Date	Mintage	VF20	XF40	MS60	MS63	MS65
1986 R	73,000	—	—	—	—	35.00
1986 R	17,500	PF65 60.00				

KM# 121 500 LIRE
11.00 g., 0.835 Silver 0.2953 oz. ASW, 29.3 mm. **Subject:** Year of the Family **Obv:** Head left **Rev:** Family scene

Date	Mintage	VF20	XF40	MS60	MS63	MS65
1987 R	85,000	—	—	—	—	20.00
1987 R	20,000	PF65 30.00				

KM# 122 500 LIRE
11.00 g., 0.835 Silver 0.2953 oz. ASW, 29.3 mm. **Subject:** World Athletic Championships **Obv:** Stylized runner left **Rev:** Ancient and modern sprinter, Coliseum in background

Date	Mintage	VF20	XF40	MS60	MS63	MS65
1987 R	80,000	—	—	—	—	20.00
1987 R	20,000	PF65 30.00				

KM# 132 500 LIRE
10.96 g., 0.835 Silver 0.2942 oz. ASW, 29.01 mm. **Subject:** 150th Anniversary Death of Giacomo Leopardi, poet **Obv:** Bust 3/4 left **Obv. Legend:** REPUBBLICA - ITALIANA **Rev:** Female standing 3/4 left at center **Rev. Legend:** ERA IL MAGGIO - ODOROSO **Edge:** Lettered **Edge Lettering:** GIACOMO LEOPARDI 1837-1987

Date	Mintage	VF20	XF40	MS60	MS63	MS65
1987 R	58,000	—	—	—	—	80.00
1987 R	10,000	PF65 120				

KM# 125 500 LIRE
11.00 g., 0.835 Silver 0.2953 oz. ASW, 29.3 mm. **Subject:** Summer Olympics - Seoul **Obv:** Face left with dove and torch **Rev:** Two artistic figures within wreath above rings

Date	Mintage	VF20	XF40	MS60	MS63	MS65
1988 R	70,000	—	—	—	—	20.00
1988 R	13,000	PF65 35.00				

KM# 126 500 LIRE
11.00 g., 0.835 Silver 0.2953 oz. ASW, 29.3 mm. **Subject:** 40th Anniversary of Constitution **Obv:** Turreted head left **Rev:** Oak and laurel sprig within partial text with dates and value below

Date	Mintage	VF20	XF40	MS60	MS63	MS65
ND-1988 R	67,000	—	—	—	—	20.00
ND-1988 R	13,000	PF65 35.00				

KM# 129 500 LIRE
11.00 g., 0.835 Silver 0.2953 oz. ASW, 29.3 mm. **Subject:** 900th Anniversary - University of Bologna **Obv:** Medieval student in thought **Rev:** Emblem

Date	Mintage	VF20	XF40	MS60	MS63	MS65
1988 R	68,000	—	—	—	—	20.00
1988 R	13,000	PF65 35.00				

KM# 144 500 LIRE
11.00 g., 0.835 Silver 0.2953 oz. ASW, 29.3 mm. **Subject:** 100th Anniversary - Death of Giovanni Bosco **Obv:** Bust facing **Rev:** Mother, father and seated child

Date	Mintage	VF20	XF40	MS60	MS63	MS65
1988 R	51,000	—	—	—	—	35.00
1988 R	9,000	PF65 65.00				

KM# 131 500 LIRE
11.00 g., 0.835 Silver 0.2953 oz. ASW, 29.3 mm. **Subject:** Fight Against Cancer **Obv:** Female doctor and DNA **Rev:** Heartbeat, microscope and hand

Date	Mintage	VF20	XF40	MS60	MS63	MS65
1989 R	46,000	—	—	—	—	40.00
1989 R	7,598	PF65 60.00				

KM# 134 500 LIRE
11.00 g., 0.835 Silver 0.2953 oz. ASW, 29.3 mm. **Subject:** Soccer **Obv:** Head left with world cup trophy within hair **Rev:** Map of Italy within world globe

Date	Mintage	VF20	XF40	MS60	MS63	MS65
1989 R	88,000	—	—	—	—	15.00
1989 R	28,000	PF65 25.00				

KM# 139 500 LIRE
11.00 g., 0.835 Silver 0.2953 oz. ASW, 29.3 mm. **Subject:** Christopher Columbus **Obv:** Bust 1/4 right within globe design **Rev:** Ships in dock

Date	Mintage	VF20	XF40	MS60	MS63	MS65
1989 R	75,000	—	—	—	—	20.00
1989 R	25,000	PF65 30.00				

KM# 145 500 LIRE
11.00 g., 0.835 Silver 0.2953 oz. ASW, 29.3 mm. **Subject:** 350th Anniversary - Death of Tommaso Campanella **Obv:** Bust 3/4 right **Rev:** Half sun face at left, half dome at right, text below

Date	Mintage	VF20	XF40	MS60	MS63	MS65
1989 R	51,000	—	—	—	—	40.00
1989 R	9,260	PF65 55.00				

KM# 136 500 LIRE

11.00 g., 0.835 Silver 0.2953 oz. ASW, 29.3 mm. **Subject:** Soccer **Obv:** Head left with world cup trophy within hair **Rev:** Dove within globe and soccer ball

Date	Mintage	VF20	XF40	MS60	MS63	MS65
1990 R	67,500	—	—	—	—	20.00
1990 R	24,500	PF65 25.00				

KM# 137 500 LIRE

11.00 g., 0.835 Silver 0.2953 oz. ASW, 29.3 mm. **Subject:** Italian Presidency of the E.E.C. Council **Obv:** Head left **Rev:** Logo

Date	Mintage	VF20	XF40	MS60	MS63	MS65
1990 R	54,000	—	—	—	—	20.00
1990 R	10,000	PF65 30.00				

KM# 140 500 LIRE

11.00 g., 0.835 Silver 0.2953 oz. ASW, 29.3 mm. **Subject:** Columbus - Discovery of America **Obv:** Head left and new world map **Rev:** Stylized ship within an instrument

Date	Mintage	VF20	XF40	MS60	MS63	MS65
1990 R	75,000	—	—	—	—	20.00
1990 R	25,000	PF65 40.00				

KM# 146 500 LIRE

11.00 g., 0.835 Silver 0.2953 oz. ASW, 29.3 mm. **Subject:** 500th Anniversary - Birth of Tizian **Obv:** Head left **Rev:** Buildings

Date	Mintage	VF20	XF40	MS60	MS63	MS65
1990 R	52,300	—	—	—	—	35.00
1990 R	9,450	PF65 50.00				

KM# 141 500 LIRE

11.00 g., 0.835 Silver 0.2953 oz. ASW **Subject:** 250th Anniversary - Death of Antonio Vivaldi **Obv:** Violinist right, building in background **Rev:** Music score and mountain scene

Date	Mintage	VF20	XF40	MS60	MS63	MS65
ND-1991 R	55,000	—	—	—	—	50.00
ND-1991 R	11,000	PF65 100				

KM# 143 500 LIRE

15.00 g., 0.835 Silver 0.4027 oz. ASW **Subject:** Italian Flora and Fauna **Obv:** Head facing within assorted animals and flowers **Rev:** Man within center of dead and living tree

Date	Mintage	VF20	XF40	MS60	MS63	MS65
1991 R	50,000	—	—	—	—	20.00
1991 R	9,500	PF65 35.00				

KM# 147 500 LIRE

15.00 g., 0.835 Silver 0.4027 oz. ASW **Subject:** 2100th Anniversary of Ponte Milvio **Obv:** Head right with bridge and shield within hair **Rev:** Stone arch bridge

Date	Mintage	VF20	XF40	MS60	MS63	MS65
1991 R	59,000	—	—	—	—	20.00
1991 R	14,000	PF65 30.00				

KM# 148 500 LIRE

11.00 g., 0.835 Silver 0.2953 oz. ASW **Subject:** Discovery of America **Obv:** Radiant head facing **Rev:** Mapped scroll divides compass and date

Date	Mintage	VF20	XF40	MS60	MS63	MS65
1991 R	75,000	—	—	—	—	20.00
1991 R	25,000	PF65 30.00				

KM# 149 500 LIRE

15.00 g., 0.835 Silver 0.4027 oz. ASW **Subject:** 500th Anniversary - Death of Lorenzo de' Medici **Obv:** Bust left **Rev:** Florence tower, books, dates and value

Date	Mintage	VF20	XF40	MS60	MS63	MS65
ND-1992 R	50,000	—	—	—	—	20.00
ND-1992 R	11,000	PF65 30.00				

KM# 150 500 LIRE

11.00 g., 0.835 Silver 0.2953 oz. ASW **Subject:** Christopher Columbus **Obv:** Bust 3/4 facing **Rev:** Landing scene

Date	Mintage	VF20	XF40	MS60	MS63	MS65
1992 R	67,000	—	—	—	—	20.00
1992 R	18,000	PF65 30.00				

KM# 152 500 LIRE

15.00 g., 0.835 Silver 0.4027 oz. ASW **Subject:** 200th Anniversary - Birth of Gioacchino Rossini **Obv:** Bust facing **Rev:** Signature on music staff sheet

Date	Mintage	VF20	XF40	MS60	MS63	MS65
1992 R	45,000	—	—	—	—	30.00
1992 R	9,000	PF65 40.00				

KM# 153 500 LIRE

15.00 g., 0.835 Silver 0.4027 oz. ASW **Subject:** Olympics **Obv:** Laureate head facing and half of oval track **Rev:** Buildings and 3/4 oval track

Date	Mintage	VF20	XF40	MS60	MS63	MS65
1992 R	48,040	—	—	—	—	20.00
1992 R	12,000	PF65 25.00				

KM# 154 500 LIRE

15.00 g., 0.835 Silver 0.4027 oz. ASW **Subject:** Flora and Fauna **Obv:** Head left with bird and flora within hair **Rev:** Square enclosing dolphin, flamingo and other animals

Date	Mintage	VF20	XF40	MS60	MS63	MS65
1992 R	43,000	—	—	—	—	20.00
1992 R	8,500	PF65 35.00				

KM# 161 500 LIRE

11.00 g., 0.835 Silver 0.2953 oz. ASW **Subject:** 500th Anniversary - Death of Piero Della Francesca

Date	Mintage	VF20	XF40	MS60	MS63	MS65
1992 R	52,000	—	—	—	—	50.00
1992 R	9,500	PF65 80.00				

KM# 156 500 LIRE

15.00 g., 0.835 Silver 0.4027 oz. ASW **Subject:** 2000th Anniversary - Death of Horace **Obv:** Column divides date and value **Rev:** Bust left

Date	Mintage	VF20	XF40	MS60	MS63	MS65
1993 R	50,000	—	—	—	—	20.00
1993 R	10,000	PF65 30.00				

KM# 157 500 LIRE

15.00 g., 0.835 Silver 0.4027 oz. ASW **Subject:** Wildlife protection **Obv:** Head facing flanked by flowers **Rev:** Storks and swordfish divide date and value

Date	Mintage	VF20	XF40	MS60	MS63	MS65
1993 R	36,000	—	—	—	—	30.00
1993 R	10,000	PF65 40.00				

KM# 158 500 LIRE

15.00 g., 0.835 Silver 0.4027 oz. ASW **Subject:** 650th Anniversary - University of Pisa **Obv:** Seated figure right with open book **Rev:** Leaning Tower of Pisa to right of building

Date	Mintage	VF20	XF40	MS60	MS63	MS65
1993 R	41,000	—	—	—	—	25.00
1993 R	9,080	PF65 40.00				

KM# 160 500 LIRE

6.80 g., Bi-Metallic Aluminum-Bronze center in Stainless Steel ring, 25.8 mm. **Subject:** Centennial - Bank of Italy **Obv:** Head left within circle **Rev:** Monogram within design divides dates within circle **Edge:** Segmented reeding **Note:** Large and small designer's name, G ROSSI, exist.

Date	Mintage	VF20	XF40	MS60	MS63	MS65
ND-1993 R	Est. 90000000	—	—	1.00	2.00	3.50
ND-1993 R	8,500	PF65 12.00				

KM# 163 500 LIRE

11.00 g., 0.835 Silver 0.2953 oz. ASW **Subject:** 200th Anniversary - Death of Carolo Goldoni

Date	Mintage	VF20	XF40	MS60	MS63	MS65
1993 R	50,000	—	—	—	—	50.00
1993 R	8,500	PF65 90.00				

KM# 173 500 LIRE

11.00 g., 0.835 Silver 0.2953 oz. ASW **Subject:** Centennial - Bank of Italy **Obv:** Head left **Rev:** Statues and building **Note:** Both uncirculated and proof versions were offered in sets only.

Date	Mintage	VF20	XF40	MS60	MS63	MS65
ND-1993 R	52,000	—	—	—	—	15.00
ND-1993 R	10,000	PF65 25.00				

KM# 167 500 LIRE

6.80 g., Bi-Metallic Aluminum-Bronze center in Stainless Steel ring, 25.8 mm. **Subject:** 500th Anniversary - Publication of Mathematical Work by Luca Pacioli **Obv:** Head left within circle **Rev:** Bust facing within circle **Edge:** Segmented reeding

Date	Mintage	VF20	XF40	MS60	MS63	MS65
ND-1994 R	50,000,000	—	—	1.00	2.00	3.50
ND-1994 R	8,500	PF65 12.00				

KM# 181 500 LIRE

6.80 g., Bi-Metallic Aluminum-Bronze center in Stainless Steel ring, 25.8 mm. **Subject:** Istituto Nazionale di Statistica **Obv:** Head left within circle **Rev:** Institute building within circle **Edge:** Segmented reeding

Date	Mintage	VF20	XF40	MS60	MS63	MS65
ND-1996 R	96,755,000	—	—	1.00	2.00	3.50
ND-1996 R	8,000	PF65 12.00				

KM# 187 500 LIRE

6.80 g., Bi-Metallic Aluminum-Bronze center in Stainless Steel ring, 25.8 mm. **Subject:** 50th Anniversary - National Police Code **Obv:** Head left within circle **Rev:** Mythological figure above crowned shield within wreath and circle **Edge:** Segmented reeding

Date	Mintage	VF20	XF40	MS60	MS63	MS65
ND-1997 R	40,000,000	—	—	1.00	2.00	3.50
ND-1997 R	8,440	PF65 12.00				

KM# 193 500 LIRE

6.80 g., Bi-Metallic Aluminum-Bronze center in Stainless Steel ring, 25.8 mm. **Series:** F.A.O. **Subject:** 20 years - IFAD **Obv:** Allegorical portrait **Rev:** Hand and grains **Edge:** Segmented reeding

Date	Mintage	VF20	XF40	MS60	MS63	MS65
ND-1998 R	100,000,000	—	—	1.00	2.00	3.50
ND-1998 R	9,000	PF65 12.00				

KM# 203 500 LIRE

6.80 g., Bi-Metallic Aluminum-Bronze center in Stainless Steel ring, 25.8 mm. **Subject:** European Parliamentary Elections **Obv:** Allegorical portrait **Rev:** Ballot box **Edge:** Segmented reeding

Date	Mintage	VF20	XF40	MS60	MS63	MS65
ND-1999 R	50,000,000	—	—	1.00	2.00	3.50
ND-1999 R	8,500	PF65 12.00				

KM# 101 1000 LIRE

14.60 g., 0.835 Silver 0.3919 oz. ASW, 31.2 mm. **Subject:** Centennial of Rome as Italian capital **Obv:** Concordia veiled bust right **Rev:** Flower-like symbol above value

Date	Mintage	VF20	XF40	MS60	MS63	MS65
ND-1970 R	3,011,000	—	—	—	15.00	20.00
ND-1970 R	—	—	—	—	—	40.00

Prooflike

KM# 165 1000 LIRE

14.60 g., 0.835 Silver 0.3919 oz. ASW **Subject:** 900th Anniversary - St. Mark's Basilica **Obv:** Church façade **Rev:** Figures within boat

Date	Mintage	VF20	XF40	MS60	MS63	MS65
1994 R	41,000	—	—	—	15.00	25.00
1994 R	8,600	PF65 40.00				

KM# 168 1000 LIRE

14.60 g., 0.835 Silver 0.3919 oz. ASW **Subject:** Flora and Fauna Protection **Obv:** Female bust facing with tree as left side of hair **Rev:** Bird, tree and dolphin divides date and value

Date	Mintage	VF20	XF40	MS60	MS63	MS65
1994 R	40,000	—	—	—	12.00	20.00
1994 R	7,700	PF65 50.00				

KM# 169 1000 LIRE

14.60 g., 0.835 Silver 0.3919 oz. ASW **Obv:** Tintoretto in oval **Rev:** Collage of his paintings

Date	Mintage	VF20	XF40	MS60	MS63	MS65
1994 R	45,000	—	—	—	65.00	110
1994 R	8,500	PF65 150				

KM# 185 1000 LIRE

14.60 g., 0.835 Silver 0.3919 oz. ASW **Subject:** Pietro Mascagni **Obv:** Bust right **Rev:** Theater interior view

Date	Mintage	VF20	XF40	MS60	MS63	MS65
1995 R	45,000	—	—	—	120	200
1995 R	—	PF65 280				

KM# 182 1000 LIRE
14.60 g., 0.835 Silver 0.3919 oz. ASW **Subject:** Olympics - Atlanta **Obv:** Female head right with laurel wreath and olympic rings as hair style **Rev:** Torch runner, Statue of Liberty silhouette, stadium track and value

Date	Mintage	VF20	XF40	MS60	MS63	MS65
1996 R	38,000	—	—	—	15.00	25.00
1996 R	7,435	PF65 40.00				

KM# 199 1000 LIRE
14.60 g., 0.835 Silver 0.3919 oz. ASW **Subject:** Montale Commemorative **Note:** Both uncirculated and proof versions were offered in sets only.

Date	Mintage	VF20	XF40	MS60	MS63	MS65
1996 R	45,000	—	—	—	40.00	65.00
1996 R	—	PF65 140				

KM# 190 1000 LIRE
Bi-Metallic Copper-Nickel center in Aluminum-Bronze ring, 27 mm. **Subject:** European Union **Obv:** Allegorical portrait **Rev:** Pernazza **Note:** Mistake on European map.

Date	Mintage	VF20	XF40	MS60	MS63	MS65
1997 R	100,000,000	—	—	1.00	2.00	3.50

KM# 194 1000 LIRE
8.80 g., Bi-Metallic Copper-Nickel center in Aluminum-Bronze ring, 27 mm. **Subject:** European Union **Obv:** Head left within circle **Rev:** Corrected map with United Germany within globe design **Edge:** Segmented reeding

Date	Mintage	VF20	XF40	MS60	MS63	MS65
1997 R	80,000,000	—	—	1.00	2.00	3.50
1997 R	8,440	PF65 15.00				
1998 R	180,000,000	—	—	1.00	2.00	3.50
1998 R	9,000	PF65 15.00				
1999 R	51,800	—	—	—	20.00	30.00
1999 R	8,500	PF65 40.00				
2000 R	61,400	—	—	—	12.00	20.00
2000 R	8,960	PF65 30.00				

KM# 200 1000 LIRE
14.60 g., 0.835 Silver 0.3919 oz. ASW **Subject:** Donizetti Commemorative **Note:** Both uncirculated and proof versions were offered in sets only.

Date	Mintage	VF20	XF40	MS60	MS63	MS65
1997 R	44,000	—	—	—	75.00	125
1997 R	—	PF65 250				

KM# 201 1000 LIRE
14.60 g., 0.835 Silver 0.3919 oz. ASW **Obv:** Bernini bust and St. Peter's Colonnade in background **Rev:** Architectural renderings and sunburst **Note:** Both uncirculated and proof versions were offered in sets only.

Date	Mintage	VF20	XF40	MS60	MS63	MS65
1998 R	55,200	—	—	—	20.00	30.00
1998 R	9,000	PF65 70.00				

KM# 221 1000 LIRE
14.60 g., 0.835 Silver 0.3919 oz. ASW, 31.4 mm. **Subject:** Vittorio Alfieri **Obv:** Bust looking right **Rev:** Rope over book **Edge:** Raised ornamentation

Date	Mintage	VF20	XF40	MS60	MS63	MS65
1999 R	51,800	—	—	—	28.00	45.00
1999 R	8,500	PF65 100				

KM# 235 1000 LIRE
14.60 g., 0.835 Silver 0.3919 oz. ASW, 31.4 mm. **Obv:** Giordano Bruno **Rev:** Three sun faces

Date	Mintage	VF20	XF40	MS60	MS63	MS65
2000 R	51,400	—	—	—	28.00	45.00
2000 R	8,960	PF65 100				

KM# 195 2000 LIRE
16.00 g., 0.835 Silver 0.4295 oz. ASW **Subject:** Christian Millennium **Obv:** Leaves and birds sprouting from globe top **Rev:** Jesus above value

Date	Mintage	VF20	XF40	MS60	MS63	MS65
1998 R	36,300	—	—	—	20.00	30.00
1998 R	—	PF65 50.00				

KM# 196 2000 LIRE
16.00 g., 0.835 Silver 0.4295 oz. ASW **Obv:** Stars and birds circling world globe **Rev:** Creative brain unraveling DNA above value

Date	Mintage	VF20	XF40	MS60	MS63	MS65
1998 R	36,300	—	—	—	20.00	30.00
1998 R	—	PF65 50.00				

KM# 202 2000 LIRE
16.00 g., 0.835 Silver 0.4295 oz. ASW **Subject:** National Museum in Rome **Obv:** Head left on ancient coin **Rev:** Seated gladiator

Date	Mintage	VF20	XF40	MS60	MS63	MS65
1999 R	35,500	—	—	—	12.00	20.00
1999 R	6,700	PF65 40.00				

KM# 170 5000 LIRE
18.00 g., 0.835 Silver 0.4832 oz. ASW **Subject:** University of Pisa **Obv:** Wings surround head facing **Rev:** Building and design at center of circle with small towers between points

Date	Mintage	VF20	XF40	MS60	MS63	MS65
1993 R	42,000	—	—	—	12.00	20.00
1993 R	8,500	PF65 55.00				

KM# 175 5000 LIRE
18.00 g., 0.835 Silver 0.4832 oz. ASW **Subject:** 600th Anniversary - Birth of Pisanello **Obv:** Bust left wearing floppy hat **Rev:** Equestrian right

Date	Mintage	VF20	XF40	MS60	MS63	MS65
1995 R	38,000	—	—	—	20.00	30.00
1995 R	7,800	PF65 50.00				

KM# 178 5000 LIRE
18.00 g., 0.835 Silver 0.4832 oz. ASW **Subject:** Italian Presidency of the European Union **Obv:** Female head left **Rev:** Letter E, flags, stars and assorted designs

Date	Mintage	VF20	XF40	MS60	MS63	MS65
1996 R	38,000	—	—	—	28.00	45.00
1996 R	7,996	PF65 70.00				

KM# 189 5000 LIRE
18.00 g., 0.835 Silver 0.4832 oz. ASW **Subject:** Giovanni Antonio Canal **Obv:** Bust right and Venice city view **Rev:** Harbor full of sailboats

Date	Mintage	VF20	XF40	MS60	MS63	MS65
ND-1997 R	36,000	—	—	—	12.00	20.00
ND-1997 R	7,550	PF65 50.00				

KM# 197 5000 LIRE
18.00 g., 0.835 Silver 0.4832 oz. ASW **Subject:** 1999 **Obv:**

Birds sprouting from globe **Rev:** Saint Francis selling cloth to merchant

Date	Mintage	VF20	XF40	MS60	MS63	MS65
1999 R	37,600	—	—	—	20.00	35.00
1999 R	—	PF65 50.00				

KM# 198 5000 LIRE
18.00 g., 0.835 Silver 0.4832 oz. ASW **Subject:** 1999 **Obv:** Three birds and nine stars encircle world **Rev:** Satellite dish and wheels

Date	Mintage	VF20	XF40	MS60	MS63	MS65
1999 R	37,600	—	—	—	20.00	35.00
1999 R	—	PF65 50.00				

KM# 166 10000 LIRE
22.00 g., 0.835 Silver 0.5906 oz. ASW **Subject:** World Cup Soccer **Obv:** Head right with stars in hair **Rev:** Olive branch, value and banner within globe

Date	Mintage	VF20	XF40	MS60	MS63	MS65
1994 R	43,000	—	—	—	32.00	55.00
1994 R	9,000	PF65 80.00				

KM# 174 10000 LIRE
22.00 g., 0.835 Silver 0.5906 oz. ASW **Subject:** 40th Anniversary - Conference of Messina **Obv:** Europa on bull right **Rev:** Letter E and numeral 5 within globe design and star border

Date	Mintage	VF20	XF40	MS60	MS63	MS65
1995 R	42,000	—	—	—	32.00	55.00
1995 R	8,050	PF65 80.00				

KM# 179 10000 LIRE
22.00 g., 0.835 Silver 0.5906 oz. ASW **Subject:** 50th Anniversary of the Republic **Obv:** Bust right with star in background **Rev:** Man leading horse right

Date	Mintage	VF20	XF40	MS60	MS63	MS65
1996 R	38,000	—	—	—	—	55.00
1996 R	7,900	PF65 80.00				

KM# 188 10000 LIRE
22.00 g., 0.835 Silver 0.5906 oz. ASW **Subject:** 200th Anniversary - Italian Flag **Obv:** Allegorical portrait **Rev:** Woman wearing flag like a cape

Date	Mintage	VF20	XF40	MS60	MS63	MS65
ND-1997 R	36,000	—	—	—	20.00	35.00
ND-1997 R	7,695	PF65 60.00				

KM# 192 10000 LIRE
22.00 g., 0.835 Silver 0.5906 oz. ASW **Subject:** Soccer **Obv:** Head left **Rev:** Stylized soccer design

Date	Mintage	VF20	XF40	MS60	MS63	MS65
1998 R	34,000	—	—	—	20.00	30.00
1998 R	7,000	PF65 50.00				

KM# 208 10000 LIRE
22.00 g., 0.835 Silver 0.5906 oz. ASW, 34 mm. **Obv:** Birds and grass sprouting **Rev:** Standing figure flanked by tall weeds **Edge:** Reeded and plain sections

Date	Mintage	VF20	XF40	MS60	MS63	MS65
2000 R	33,700	—	—	—	20.00	30.00
2000 R	7,000	PF65 50.00				

KM# 209 10000 LIRE
22.00 g., 0.835 Silver 0.5906 oz. ASW, 34 mm. **Obv:** Doves and stars around world globe **Rev:** Da Vinci's wing and airplane design **Edge:** Reeded and plain sections

Date	Mintage	VF20	XF40	MS60	MS63	MS65
2000 R	33,700	—	—	—	20.00	30.00
2000 R	7,000	PF65 50.00				

KM# 176 50000 LIRE
7.50 g., 0.900 Gold 0.217 oz. AGW **Subject:** Bank of Italy **Obv:** Bust left **Rev:** Building and value

Date	Mintage	VF20	XF40	MS60	MS63	MS65
ND-1994 R	22,560	PF65 600				

KM# 223 50000 LIRE
7.50 g., 0.900 Gold 0.217 oz. AGW, 20 mm. **Subject:** 800th Anniversary - Birth of Saint Anthony of Padova **Obv:** Corner view of Basilica **Rev:** Interior view - Chapel, date and value

Date	Mintage	VF20	XF40	MS60	MS63	MS65
1995 R	—	PF65 600				

KM# 225 50000 LIRE
7.50 g., 0.900 Gold 0.217 oz. AGW, 20 mm. **Subject:** 800th Anniversary - Battistero in Parma **Obv:** Battistero **Rev:** Decorations from the Battistero, date and value

Date	Mintage	VF20	XF40	MS60	MS63	MS65
1996 R	—	PF65 600				

KM# 191 50000 LIRE
7.50 g., 0.900 Gold 0.217 oz. AGW **Subject:** 1600th Anniversary - Death of St. Ambrose **Obv:** St. Ambrose Church in Milan **Rev:** Investiture of St. Ambrose

Date	Mintage	VF20	XF40	MS60	MS63	MS65
ND-1997 R	5,750	PF65 600				

KM# 228 50000 LIRE
7.50 g., 0.900 Gold 0.217 oz. AGW, 20 mm. **Subject:** 850th Anniversary - Church of San Giovanni of the Hermits in Palermo **Obv:** Church of San Giovanni **Rev:** Curved arches

Date	Mintage	VF20	XF40	MS60	MS63	MS65
1998 R	—	PF65 600				

KM# 230 50000 LIRE
7.50 g., 0.900 Gold 0.217 oz. AGW, 20 mm. **Subject:** 900th Anniversary - Foundation of the Cathedral in Modena **Obv:** Front of Cathedral **Rev:** Arch with lion, date and denomination

Date	Mintage	VF20	XF40	MS60	MS63	MS65
1999 R	—	PF65 600				

KM# 232 50000 LIRE
7.50 g., 0.900 Gold 0.217 oz. AGW, 20 mm. **Subject:** 500th Anniversary - Birth of Benvenuto Cellini **Obv:** Bust of Cellini **Rev:** Figure, date and denomination

Date	Mintage	VF20	XF40	MS60	MS63	MS65
2000 R	4,375	PF65 600				

KM# 177 100000 LIRE
15.00 g., 0.900 Gold 0.434 oz. AGW **Subject:** Centennial of the Bank of Italy **Obv:** Bust facing **Rev:** Value and building **Note:** 1996 strikes do not exist.

Date	Mintage	VF20	XF40	MS60	MS63	MS65
ND-1994 R	21,196	PF65 1,200				

KM# 222 100000 LIRE
15.00 g., 0.900 Gold 0.434 oz. AGW, 25 mm. **Subject:** 700th Anniversary - Basilica of Santa Croce in Florence **Obv:** Front of the Basilica of Santa Croce **Rev:** Interior view, date and denomination

Date	Mintage	VF20	XF40	MS60	MS63	MS65
1995 R	—	PF65 1,200				

KM# 224 100000 LIRE
15.00 g., 0.900 Gold 0.434 oz. AGW, 25 mm. **Subject:** 600th Anniversary - Foundation of Certosa Di Pavia **Obv:** Exterior angled view **Rev:** Interior view

Date	Mintage	VF20	XF40	MS60	MS63	MS65
1996 R	—	PF65 1,200				

KM# 226 100000 LIRE
15.00 g., 0.900 Gold 0.434 oz. AGW, 25 mm. **Subject:** 800th Anniversary - Dedication of the Basilica Superiore of San Nicola of Bari **Obv:** Exterior view of the Basilica **Rev:** Interior view

Date	Mintage	VF20	XF40	MS60	MS63	MS65
1997 R	—	PF65 1,200				

KM# 227 100000 LIRE
15.00 g., 0.900 Gold 0.434 oz. AGW, 25 mm. **Subject:** 650th Anniversary - Completion of the Tower - Palace of Siena **Obv:** Tower **Rev:** Anniversary dates and denomination

Date	Mintage	VF20	XF40	MS60	MS63	MS65
1998 R	—	PF65 1,200				

KM# 229 100000 LIRE
15.00 g., 0.900 Gold 0.434 oz. AGW, 25 mm. **Subject:** Repair of the Basilica of St. Francis of Assisi **Obv:** Front of Basilica **Rev:** Round seal, date and denomination

Date	Mintage	VF20	XF40	MS60	MS63	MS65
1999 R	—	PF65 1,200				

KM# 231 100000 LIRE

15.00 g., 0.900 Gold 0.434 oz. AGW, 20 mm. **Subject:** 700th Anniversary - First Jubilee of 1300 **Obv:** The Quadrangle **Rev:** Detail of the fresco of Giotto

Date	Mintage	VF20	XF40	MS60	MS63	MS65
2000 R	—	PF65 1,200				

TRIAL STRIKES

KM#	Date	Mintage	Identification	Mkt Val
TS1	1927R	—	20 Lire. Inscription. Seated and standing figures above value. KM69.	2,200
TS2	1927R	—	20 Lire. Faceless head right. KM69.	13,000
TS3	1940	—	5 Lire. Silver. Helmeted bust left. Uniface.	1,500
TS4	1940	—	5 Lire. Silver. Crowned savoy shield with fases and axe within circle. Uniface. Illustration reduced.	1,500

PATTERNS

Including off metal strikes

KM#	Date	Mintage	Identification	Mkt Val
Pn2	1903R	—	10 Centesimi. Bronze.	750
Pn3	1903R	—	2 Lire. Silver Plated Bronze.	—
Pn4	1903	—	5 Lire. Silver.	2,000
PnA5	1903 (M)	—	20 Lire. Gold.	4,000
Pn5	1903R	—	20 Lire. Silver Gilt.	1,800
PnA6	1903 (M)	—	100 Lire. Gold.	9,000
Pn6	1903R	—	100 Lire. Bronze Gilt.	1,250
PnA7	1904	5	Centesimo. Bronze. KM37.	—
PnB7	1904	—	50 Lire. Brass. Head of Vittorio left. Eagle with spread wings facing, head left, crown above.	—
Pn7	1905R	—	20 Centesimi. Bronze.	—
Pn8	1905R	—	20 Centesimi. Nickel.	—
Pn9	1906R	—	20 Lire. Bronze Gilt.	225
Pn10	1907	—	20 Centesimi. Nickel.	1,500
Pn11	1907	—	100 Lire.	—
P4	1908	—	10 Centesimi. Copper.	4,000
PnA12	1908	—	100 Lire. Silver.	5,000
Pn12	1908	—	100 Lire. Bronze.	250
Pn13	1915R	—	10 Centesimi. Nickel. Obv: Helmeted head right. Rev: Grain ear.	—
Pn14	1915R	—	10 Centesimi. Nickel. Obv: Diademed and jeweled head right. Rev: Grain ear.	950
Pn15	1915R	—	10 Centesimi. Nickel. Obv: Diademed and jeweled head right. Rev: Grain ear.	950
Pn16	1915	—	10 Centesimi. Nickel.	—
Pn17	1918	—	5 Centesimi. Ferro-nickel.	450
Pn18	1918	—	5 Centesimi. Ferro-nickel.	2,000
Pn19	1918	—	5 Centesimi. Ferro-nickel.	450
Pn20	1918	—	5 Centesimi. Ferro-nickel.	450
Pn21	1918	—	5 Centesimi. Ferro-nickel.	450
Pn22	1918	—	10 Centesimi. Ferro-nickel.	—
Pn23	1918	—	20 Centesimi. Nickel.	—
Pn24	1918	—	20 Centesimi. Nickel.	—
Pn25	1918	—	20 Centesimi. Nickel.	—
Pn26	1918	—	20 Centesimi. Nickel.	—
Pn27	1918	—	20 Centesimi. Ferro-nickel.	—
PnA28	1918	—	25 Centesimi. Iron. Obv: Turreted and grain-wreathed head of Italia right. Rev: Denomination above ornament, PROVA S.J. below.	450
Pn28	1918	—	25 Centesimi. Bronze.	—
Pn29	1918	—	50 Centesimi.	—
Pn30	1918	—	50 Centesimi. Nickel.	—
Pn31	1919R	—	5 Centesimi. Ferro-nickel.	8,000
Pn32	1919	—	5 Centesimi. Bronze.	—
Pn33	ND-1919	—	10 Centesimi. Bronze.	—
Pn34	1920R	—	Lira. Nickel.	—
Pn35	1920R	—	Lira. Nickel.	—
Pn36	1920R	—	Lira. Nickel.	—
PnA37	1922	—	2 Lire. Nickel.	500
Pn37	1922	—	2 Lire. Nickel.	500
PnA38	1922R	—	2 Lire. Nickel.	500
Pn38	1922R	—	2 Lire. Nickel.	500
Pn39	1926R	—	5 Lire. Silver.	500
Pn40	ND-1927	—	20 Lire. Silver.	500
Pn41	ND-1927	—	20 Lire. Silver.	5,000
Pn42	1950	—	50 Lire. Stainless Steel.	—
Pn43	1950	—	100 Lire. Silver.	—
Pn44	1950	—	100 Lire. Nickel-Silver.	—
Pn45	1950	—	100 Lire. Nickel.	—
Pn46	1951R	—	Lira. Aluminum.	—
Pn47	1951R	—	2 Lire. Aluminum.	—
Pn48	1951R	—	10 Lire. Aluminum.	—
PrB81	1954R	—	50 Lire. Stainless Steel. KM95.1.	1,000
Pn49	1955R	—	20 Lire. Aluminum-Bronze.	—
Pn50	1955R	—	20 Lire. Aluminum-Bronze.	—
Pn51	1956R	—	20 Lire. Aluminum-Bronze. Bottom of neck rounded.	—
Pn52	1956R	1,200	20 Lire. Aluminum-Bronze. Bottom of neck at angle.	—
Pn53	1957R	—	500 Lire. Silver.	—
Pn54	1957R	—	500 Lire. Silver.	—
Pn55	1957R	—	500 Lire. Silver.	—
Pn56	1957R	—	500 Lire. Silver.	—
Pn57	1957R	—	500 Lire. Silver.	—
Pn58	1957R	—	500 Lire. Silver.	—
Pn59	1957R	—	Florino. Bronze Gilt.	—
Pn60	1957R	—	Florino. Bronze Gilt.	—
Pn61	1957R	—	2 Florini. Bronze Gilt.	—
Pn62	1957R	—	2 Florini. Bronze Gilt.	—
Pn63	1970	—	1000 Lire. Silver.	—
Pn64	1970	—	1000 Lire. Silver.	—
Pn65	ND (1970)	—	10000 Lire. Bronze Gilt.	—

PROVAS

PROVA in field;
Standard metals unless otherwise noted

KM#	Date	Mintage	Identification	Mkt Val
Pr1	1903	—	20 Lire. Head right. Standing figures facing.	6,000
Pr2	1903	—	100 Lire. Head right. Standing figures facing.	22,000
Pr3	1906 (M)	—	20 Lire. Head left. Honey bee.	19,000
PrA4	1906	—	20 Lire. Bronze.	—
Pr4	1906 (M)	—	100 Lire. Gold. Head right. Lions pulling man in chariot.	25,000
PrB4	1907R	—	20 Centesimi. Nickel. KM44 Prova R.Z.	1,500
Pr5	1907R	—	20 Lire. KM48.	7,500
PrA6	1907 (M)	—	20 Lire. KM48.	7,500
Pr6	1907 (M)	—	50 Lire. Bust left. Seated figure left.	20,000
Pr7	1907R	—	100 Lire. KM50.	25,000
Pr8	1908R	—	2 Centesimi. Bronze. KM41, PROVA.	1,000
Pr9	1908R	—	5 Centesimi. KM42, PROVA.	1,000
PrA10	1908R	—	Lira. Silver. KM45.	3,000
Pr10	1908R	—	10 Centesimi. Bronze. KM43, PROVA.	12,000
Pr11	1908 (M)	—	100 Lire. Head right. Female striding left divides value and date.	30,000
PrA12	1910R	—	100 Lire. KM50, PROVA.	35,000
PrB12	1911R	—	10 Centesimi. Bronze. KM51.	1,000
Pr12	1911R	—	2 Lire. KM52, PROVA.	7,000
Pr13	1911R	—	5 Lire. KM53, PROVA.	18,000
Pr14	1911R	—	50 Lire. KM54, PROVA horizontally.	15,000
PrB15	1911R	—	50 Lire. Gold. KM54; PROVA CIRC.	15,000
PrB15	1911R	—	50 Lire. Gold. KM54; PROVA CIRC.	15,000
PrA15	1912	—	10 Lire. KM47, PROVA.	8,000
Pr15	1912	—	20 Lire. KM48, PROVA.	25,000
Pr16	1913R	—	5 Lire. (No Composition). KM56. PROVA.	30,000
Pr17	1914	—	2 Lire. KM55, PROVA.	1,200
Pr18	1914R	—	5 Lire. (No Composition). KM56. PROVA.	30,000
Pr19	1914R	—	5 Lire. Copper. KM56.	—
Pr21	1914R	—	5 Lire. Silver. KM56.	30,000
Pr22	1914R	—	5 Lire. KM56.	30,000
PrA25	1915R	—	Lira. Silver. KM57. PROVA.	1,000
PrB26	1915R	—	Lira. Silver. KM57, Di Stampa.	2,500
PrC26	1918R	—	5 Centesimi. Iron-Nickel. KM59.	2,000
PrC26	1918R	—	20 Centesimi. Copper-Nickel. KM58. PROVA.	1,300
Pr23	1919R	—	50 Centesimi. KM61.1, PROVA.	1,800
Pr24	1919R	—	50 Centesimi. KM61.1.	1,500
Pr25	1919R	—	5 Centesimi. (No Composition). KM59. PROVA.	800
Pr26	1919R	—	10 Centesimi. KM60, PROVA DI STAMPA.	1,000
PrA27	1919R	—	10 Centesimi. Bronze. KM60. PROVA.	1,500
Pr27	1921R	—	Lira. Seated figure left. Value and crowned shield within wreath. KM62, PROVA.	3,000
Pr28	1923R	—	2 Lire. KM63, PROVA.	700
Pr29	1923R	—	2 Lire. KM63.	700
Pr30	1923R P. (for Prova)	—	2 Lire. KM63.	700
Pr31	1923R	—	20 Lire. KM64, PROVA.	20,000
Pr32	1923R	—	100 Lire. KM65, PROVA.	11,500
Pr33	1923R P. (for Prova)	—	100 Lire. KM65.	30,000
Pr34	1925R	—	100 Lire. KM66, PROVA.	23,000
Pr35	1926R	—	50 Centesimi. KM61.	—
Pr36	1926R	—	5 Lire. Silver. KM67, PROVA.	3,600
Pr37	1926R	—	5 Lire. Head left. Eagle with wings open standing on fascis. KM67.	3,000
Pr38	1926R	—	5 Lire. KM67.	350
Pr39	1926R	—	10 Lire. PROVA at top. KM68.	20,000
Pr40	1926R	—	10 Lire. PROVA beneath horses. KM68.	3,500
Pr41	1926R	—	10 Lire. KM68.	5,000
Pr42	1926R	—	10 Lire. KM68.	500
Pr43	1927R V	—	5 Lire. PROVA DI STAMPA above eagle. KM67.	2,500
Pr44	1927R V	—	5 Lire. PROVA DI STAMPA at right side of eagle. KM67.	2,500
PrA45	1927R V	—	10 Lire. PROVA beneath horses. KM68.	3,500
PrB45	1927R V	—	10 Lire. PROVA DI STAMPA above. KM68.	16,000
Pr45	1927R V	—	20 Lire. KM69, Unc., circular PROVA.	15,000
Pr46	1927R V	—	20 Lire. KM69.	15,000
Pr49	1928R VI	—	20 Lire. KM70.	6,000
Pr50	1928R VI	—	20 Lire. KM70.	4,500
Pr51	1928R VI	—	20 Lire. KM70.	12,000
Pr52	1928R VI	—	20 Lire. KM70, horizontal PROVA.	18,000
Pr53	1928R V VI	—	20 Lire. Gold. KM70.	150,000
Pr54	1928R VI	—	20 Lire. PROVA behind head. KM69.	16,000
Pr55	1931R IX	—	50 Lire. (No Composition). KM71. PROVA.	12,000
Pr56	1931R IX	—	100 Lire. KM72, PROVA.	12,000
Pr57	1936R XIV	—	5 Centesimi. KM73, PROVA.	650
Pr58	1936R XIV	—	10 Centesimi. KM74, PROVA.	650
Pr59	1936R XIV	—	20 Centesimi. KM75, PROVA.	1,200
Pr60	1936R XIV	—	50 Centesimi. KM76, PROVA.	800
Pr61	1936R XIV	—	Lira. KM77, PROVA.	800
Pr62	1936R XIV	—	2 Lire. Plain. KM78, PROVA.	1,000
Pr63	1936R XIV	—	5 Lire. KM79, PROVA.	2,800
Pr64	1936R XIV	—	10 Lire. KM80, PROVA.	2,000
Pr65	1936R XIV	—	20 Lire. KM81, PROVA.	10,000
Pr66	1936R	—	50 Lire. KM82, PROVA.	15,000
Pr67	1936R	—	100 Lire. KM83, PROVA.	28,000
PrA68	1937 XVI	—	100 Lire. Gold. KM84. PROVA.	45,000
PrB68	1938 XVII	—	Centesimo. Stainless Steel. KM75b.	3,000
PrC68	1938R XVII	—	Lira. Stainless Steel. KM77b.	3,000
Pr68	1939R	—	5 Centesimi. KM73a, PROVA.	700
Pr69	1939R XVII	—	10 Centesimi. KM74a, PROVA.	700
Pr70	1939R XVII	—	20 Centesimi. Nickel-Steel. KM75a, PROVA.	2,000
Pr71	1939R	—	50 Centesimi. Nickel-Steel. KM76a, PROVA.	1,200
Pr72	1939R XVII	—	Lira. Nickel-Steel. KM77a, PROVA.	1,500
Pr73	1939R	—	2 Lire. Nickel-Steel. KM78a, PROVA.	1,800
Pr74	1946R	—	Lira. KM87, P, Unc.	10,000
Pr75	1946R	—	2 Lire. (No Composition). KM88, P, Unc.	10,000
Pr76	1946R	—	5 Lire. KM89, P, Unc.	10,000
Pr77	1946R	—	10 Lire. KM90, P, Unc.	10,000
Pr78	1951R	—	Lira. KM91, PROVA, Unc.	5,000
Pr79	1951R	—	5 Lire. KM92, PROVA, Unc.	5,000
Pr80	1951R	—	10 Lire. KM93, PROVA, Unc.	5,000
Pr81	1953R	—	2 Lire. KM94, PROVA, Unc.	5,000
PrA81	1954R	—	100 Lire. (No Composition). KM96, PROVA.	5,000
PrA82	1956R	—	20 Lire. (No Composition). PROVA, KM97.1, Unc.	18,000
Pr82	1956R	—	20 Lire. P for PROVA, KM97.1, Unc.	3,000
PrA83	1957R	—	500 Lire. KM98, Proof.	20,000
Pr83	1957R	1,004	500 Lire. KM98, Unc., PROVA.	15,000
PrA84	1965R	—	500 Lire. (No Composition). KM100, Proof.	6,000
Pr84	1965R	570	500 Lire. KM100, PROVA, Unc.	5,000
PrA85	1968R	—	20 Lire. KM97.2, Proof.	—
Pr85	1968R	999	20 Lire. KM97.2, Unc., P.	1,300
PrA86	1970R	—	1000 Lire. KM101, Proof.	1,000
Pr86	1970R	2,500	1000 Lire. KM101, PROVA, Unc.	1,500
Pr87	1974R	—	100 Lire. (No Composition). KM102, Unc. Silver.	700
PrA88	1974R	—	100 Lire. Silver. KM102, PROVA, Unc.	600
Pr88	1974R	—	100 Lire. (No Composition). KM102, Silver, Unc.	700
PrA89	1974R	—	100 Lire. Copper-Nickel. KM102, PROVA. Unc.	350
Pr89	1974R	—	100 Lire. Copper-Nickel. KM102, Unc.	500
PrA91	1974R	—	500 Lire. KM103, PROVA, Unc.	1,600
Pr91	1974R	730	500 Lire. KM103, Proof.	—
Pr92	1977R	417	200 Lire. KM105, PROVA, Unc.	2,000
Pr93	1984R	—	50 Lire. Stainless Steel. KM95.2.	1,000

MINT SETS

KM#	Date	Mintage	Identification	Issue Price	Mkt Val
MS1	1968 (8)	100,000	KM91-94, 95.1, 96.1, 97.2, 98	6.50	100
MS2	1969 (8)	310,000	KM91-94, 95.1, 96.1, 97.2, 98	6.50	15.00
MS3	1970 (9)	1,011,000	KM91-94, 95.1, 96.1, 97.2, 98, 101	—	30.00
MS4	1980 (10)	257,272	KM91-94, 95.1, 96.1, 97.2, 98, 105, 107	—	22.50
MS5	1981 (11)	162,794	KM91-4, 95.1, 96.1, 97.2, 98, 105, 108, 109	—	22.50
MS7	1982 (10)	120,000	KM91-96, 97.2, 98, 105, 111	—	30.00
MS9	1983 (10)	76,000	KM91-94, 95.1, 96.1, 97.2, 98, 105, 111	175	75.00
MS11	1984 (10)	77,000	KM91-94, 95.1, 96.1, 97.2, 98, 105, 111	—	45.00
MS13	1985 (10)	5,000	KM91-94, 95.1, 96.1, 97.2, 105, 111, 123	—	37.50
MS14	1985 (11)	75,000	KM91-94, 95.1, 96.1, 97.2, 98, 105, 111, 123	—	52.00
MS17	1986 (11)	73,000	KM91-94, 95.1, 96.1, 97.2, 98, 105, 111, 124	—	52.00
MS18	1987 (11)	58,000	KM91-94, 95.1, 96.1, 97.2, 98, 105, 111, 132	—	85.00
MS19	1988 (11)	51,000	KM91-94, 95.1, 96.1, 97.2, 98, 105, 111, 144	46.00	185
MS21	1988 (3)	68,000	KM127-129	—	45.00
MS22	1989 (11)	51,000	KM91-94, 95.1, 96.1, 97.2, 98, 111, 130, 145	—	75.00
MS23	1989 (2)	88,000	KM133-134	—	30.00
MS24	1989 (2)	75,000	KM138-139	—	30.00
MS25	1990 (11)	52,800	KM91-94, 95.2-97.2, 98, 111, 135, 146	—	52.00
MS26	1991 (11)	64,000	KM91-94, 95a-96a, 97.2, 98, 105, 111, 141	50.00	75.00
MS27	1991 (2)	50,000	KM142-143	—	37.50
MS28	1992 (11)	52,000	KM91-94, 95.2-97.2, 98, 111, 151, 161	50.00	75.00
MS29	1993 (11)	50,000	KM91-94, 95.2, 97.2, 98, 155, 159, 160, 163	—	75.00
MS30	1994 (11)	44,500	KM91-94, 95.2, 97.2, 98, 159, 164, 167, 169	—	115
MS31	ND (1993) (3)	52,100	KM171-173	31.00	48.00
MS32	1995 (11)	44,600	KM91-94, 95.2, 97.2, 98, 105, 111, 180, 185	—	210
MS33	1996 (11)	45,000	KM91-94, 97.2, 98, 159, 181, 183-184, 199	—	75.00
MS34	1997 (10)	43,500	KM91-94, 97.2, 98, 159, 183, 186-187, 196, 200	—	135
MS35	1998 (12)	55,200	KM91-94, 97.2, 98, 105, 159, 183, 193-194, 201	—	45.00
MS36	1998 (2)	34,000	KM195-196	—	68.00
MS37	1999 (12)	51,800	KM#91-94, 97.2, 98, 105, 111, 159, 183, 194, 221	—	75.00
MS38	2000 (12)	50,000	KM#91-94, 97.2, 98, 105, 111, 159, 183, 194, 235	—	85.00

PROOF SETS

KM#	Date	Mintage	Identification	Issue Price	Mkt Val
PS1	1985 (10)	5,000	KM91-94, 95.1, 96.1, 97.2, 105, 111, 123	—	60.00
PS2	1985 (11)	15,000	KM91-94, 95.1, 96.1, 97.2, 98, 105, 111, 123	—	75.00
PS4	1986 (11)	18,000	KM91-94, 95.1, 96.1, 97.2, 98, 105, 111, 124	—	60.00
PS5	1987 (11)	10,000	KM91-94, 95.1, 96.1, 97.2, 98, 105, 111, 132	—	125
PS6	1988 (11)	9,000	KM91-94, 95.1, 96.1, 97.2, 98, 105, 111, 144	100	270
PS7	1988 (3)	12,700	KM127-129	—	75.00
PS8	1989 (11)	9,260	KM91-96, 97.2, 98, 111, 130, 145	—	100
PS9	1990 (11)	9,400	KM91-94, 95.2-97.2, 98, 111, 135, 146	—	80.00
PS10	1989 (2)	25,000	KM133-134	—	37.50
PS11	1989 (2)	25,000	KM138-139	—	37.50
PS12	1991 (11)	11,000	KM91-94, 95.1-97.2, 98, 105, 111, 141	100	100
PS13	1992 (11)	9,500	KM91-94, 95.2-97.2, 98, 111, 151, 161	90.00	125
PS14	1993 (11)	8,500	KM91-94, 95.2, 97.2, 98, 155, 159, 160, 163	—	125
PS15	ND (1993) (3)	10,500	KM171-173	60.00	52.00
PS16	1994 (11)	8,500	KM#91-94, 95.2, 97.2, 98, 159, 164, 167, 169	—	175
PS17	1995 (11)	7,960	KM#91-94, 95.2, 97.2, 98, 105, 111, 180, 185	—	300
PS18	1996 (11)	8,000	KM#91-94, 97.2, 98, 159, 181, 183, 184, 199	—	160
PS19	1997 (12)	8,450	KM#91-94, 97.2, 98, 159, 183, 186, 187, 196, 200	—	260
PS20	1998 (2)	7,000	KM195-196	—	90.00
PS21	1998 (12)	7,000	KM#91-94, 97.2, 98, 105, 159, 183, 193, 194, 201	—	85.00
PS22	1999 (2)	8,700	KM197-198	—	90.00
PS23	1999 (12)	8,500	KM#91-94, 97.2, 98, 105, 111, 159, 183, 194, 221	—	120
PS24	2000 (12)	7,000	KM#91-94, 97.2, 98, 105, 111, 159, 183, 194, 235	—	170

IVORY COAST

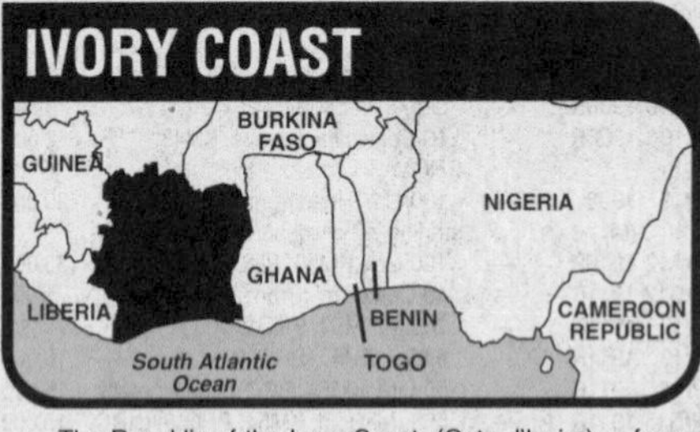

The Republic of the Ivory Coast, (Cote d'Ivoire), a former French Overseas territory located on the south side of the African bulge between Liberia and Ghana, has an area of 124,504 sq. mi. (322,463 sq. km.) and a population of 11.8 million. Capital: Yamoussoukro. The predominantly agricultural economy is one of Africa's most prosperous. Coffee, tropical woods, cocoa, and bananas are exported.

French and Portuguese navigators visited the Ivory Coast in the 15th century. French traders set up establishments in the 19th century, and gradually extended their influence along the coast and inland. The area was organized as a territory in 1893, and from 1904 to 1958 was a constituent unit of the Federation of French West Africa - as a Colony under the Third Republic and an Overseas Territory under the Fourth. In 1958 Ivory Coast became an autonomous republic within the French Community. Independence was attained on Aug. 7, 1960.

REPUBLIC

DECIMAL COINAGE

KM# 1 10 FRANCS
25.00 g., 0.925 Silver 0.7435 oz. ASW, 35 mm. **Obv:** Head right **Rev:** Elephant and value within wreath **Note:** Varieties exist in 2.9mm and 3.5mm planchets.

Date	Mintage	XF40	MS60	MS63	MS65	MS66
1966	—	PF65 65.00	PF67 85.00			

KM# 2 10 FRANCS
3.20 g., 0.900 Gold 0.0926 oz. AGW

Date	Mintage	XF40	MS60	MS63	MS65	MS66
1966	2,000	PF65 150	PF67 180			

KM# 3 25 FRANCS
8.00 g., 0.900 Gold 0.2315 oz. AGW **Obv:** Head right **Rev:** Elephant and value within wreath

Date	Mintage	XF40	MS60	MS63	MS65	MS66
1966	2,000	PF65 375	PF67 450			

KM# 4 50 FRANCS
16.00 g., 0.900 Gold 0.463 oz. AGW **Obv:** Head right **Rev:** Elephant and value within wreath

Date	Mintage	XF40	MS60	MS63	MS65	MS66
1966	2,000	PF65 750	PF67 900			

KM# 5 100 FRANCS
32.00 g., 0.900 Gold 0.9259 oz. AGW **Obv:** Head right **Rev:** Elephant within wreath

Date	Mintage	XF40	MS60	MS63	MS65	MS66
1966	2,000	PF65 1,400	PF67 1,650			

ESSAIS

Standard metals unless otherwise noted

KM#	Date	Mintage	Identification	Mkt Val
E1	1966	—	100 Francs. Silver. KM5.	175

PIEDFORT WITH ESSAI

KM#	Date	Mintage	Identification	Mkt Val
PE1	1966	—	100 Francs. Silver. KM5.	325

PROOF SETS

KM#	Date	Mintage	Identification	Issue Price	Mkt Val
PS1	1966 (4)	2,000	KM#2-5	—	3,250

JAMAICA

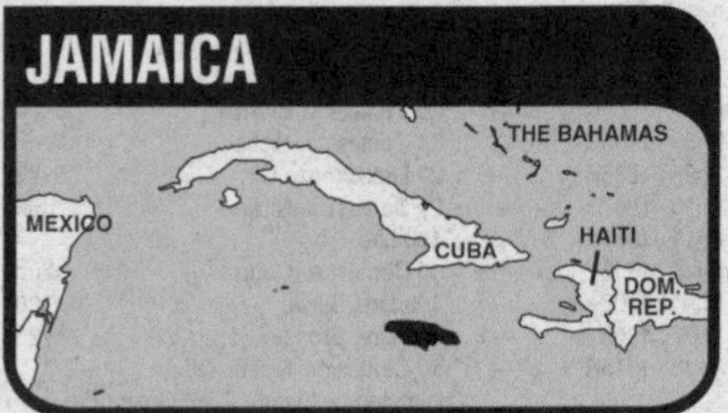

Jamaica is situated in the Caribbean Sea 90 miles south of Cuba, has an area of 4,244 sq. mi. (10,990 sq. km.) and a population of 2.1 million. Capital: Kingston. The economy is founded chiefly on mining, tourism and agriculture. Aluminum, bauxite, sugar, rum and molasses are exported.

Jamaica was discovered by Columbus on May 3, 1494, and settled by Spain in 1509. The island was captured in1655 by a British naval force under the command of Admiral William Penn, sent by Oliver Cromwell and ceded to Britain by the Treaty of Madrid, 1670. For more than 150 years, the Jamaican economy of sugar, slaves and piracy was one of the most prosperous in the new world. Dissension between the property-oriented island legislature and the home government prompted parliament to establish a crown colony government for Jamaica in 1866. From 1958 to 1961 Jamaica was a member of the West Indies Federation, withdrawing when Jamaican voters rejected the association. The colony attained independence on Aug. 6, 1962. Jamaica is a member of the Commonwealth of Nations. Elizabeth II is the Head of State, as Queen of Jamaica.

In 1758, the Jamaican Assembly authorized stamping a certain amount of Spanish milled coinage. Token coinage by merchants aided the island's monetary supply in the early19th century. Sterling coinage was introduced in Jamaica in 1825, with the additional silver three halfpence under William IV and Victoria. Certain issues of three pence of William IV and Victoria were intended for colonial use, including Jamaica, as were the last dates of three pence for George VI.

There was an extensive token and work tally coinage for Jamaica in the late 19th and early 20th centuries.

A decimal standard currency system was adopted on Sept. 8, 1969.

RULER
British, until 1962

MINT MARKS
C - Royal Canadian Mint, Ottawa
H - Heaton
FM - Franklin Mint, U.S.A.**
(fm) - Franklin Mint, U.S.A.*
no mint mark - Royal Mint, London

***NOTE:** During 1970 the Franklin Mint produced matte and proof coins (1 cent-1 dollar) using dies similar to/or Royal Mint without the FM mint mark.

NOTE: From 1975-1985 the Franklin Mint produced coinage in up to 3 different qualities. Qualities of issue are designated in ( ) after each date and are defined as follows:

(M) MATTE - Normal circulation strike or a dull finish produced by sandblasting special uncirculated (polish finish) or proof quality dies.

(U) SPECIAL UNCIRCULATED - Polished or proof-like in appearance without any frosted features.

(P) PROOF - The highest quality obtainable having mirror-like fields and frosted features.

MONETARY SYSTEM
4 Farthings = 1 Penny
12 Pence = 1 Shilling
8 Reales = 6 Shillings, 8 Pence

(Commencing 1969)

100 Cents = 1 Dollar

COMMONWEALTH

REGULAR COINAGE

KM# 18 FARTHING

Copper-Nickel, 20.2 mm. **Ruler:** Edward VII **Obv:** Crowned bust right within beaded circle **Rev:** Arms with horizontal shading within beaded circle

Date	Mintage	VF20	XF40	MS60	MS63	MS65
1902	144,000	10.00	20.00	45.00	55.00	85.00
1903	144,000	10.00	20.00	45.00	55.00	85.00

KM# 21 FARTHING

Copper-Nickel, 20.2 mm. **Ruler:** Edward VII **Obv:** Crowned bust right within beaded circle **Rev:** Arms with vertical shading within beaded circle

Date	Mintage	VF20	XF40	MS60	MS63	MS65
1904	192,000	5.00	12.00	35.00	42.50	65.00
1904	—	**PF63** 350	**PF65** 600			
1905	192,000	5.00	12.00	35.00	42.50	65.00
1906	528,000	3.00	9.00	28.00	35.00	55.00
1907	192,000	5.00	12.00	35.00	42.50	65.00
1909	144,000	6.00	20.00	45.00	50.00	75.00
1910	48,000	15.00	30.00	50.00	65.00	100

KM# 24 FARTHING

Copper-Nickel, 20.2 mm. **Ruler:** George V **Obv:** Crowned bust left within beaded circle **Rev:** Arms within beaded circle

Date	Mintage	VF20	XF40	MS60	MS63	MS65
1914	192,000	5.00	12.00	35.00	42.50	65.00
1916 H	480,000	2.00	6.00	20.00	27.50	40.00
1916 H	—	**PF63** 525	**PF65** 850			
1918 C	208,000	2.00	8.00	25.00	30.00	45.00
1918 C	—	**PF63** 475	**PF65** 750			
1919 C	401,000	2.00	6.00	20.00	27.50	40.00
1926	240,000	2.00	8.00	25.00	30.00	45.00
1928	480,000	2.00	6.00	20.00	25.00	37.50
1928	—	**PF63** 475	**PF65** 750			
1932	480,000	2.00	6.00	20.00	27.50	40.00
1932 Proof	—	—	—	—	—	—
1934	480,000	2.00	6.00	20.00	27.50	40.00
1934 Proof	—	—	—	—	—	—

KM# 27 FARTHING

Nickel-Brass, 20.2 mm. **Ruler:** George VI **Obv:** Crowned head left **Rev:** Arms divide date

Date	Mintage	VF20	XF40	MS60	MS63	MS65
1937	480,000	1.50	5.00	15.00	20.00	30.00
1937	—	**PF63** 375	**PF65** 625			

KM# 30 FARTHING

2.80 g., Nickel-Brass, 20.2 mm. **Ruler:** George VI **Obv:** Crowned head left **Rev:** Arms divide date

Date	Mintage	VF20	XF40	MS60	MS63	MS65
1938	480,000	1.50	5.00	15.00	20.00	30.00
1938 Proof	—	—	—	—	—	—
1942	480,000	1.50	5.00	15.00	20.00	30.00
1945	480,000	1.50	5.00	15.00	20.00	30.00
1945	—	**PF63** 250	**PF65** 425			
1947	192,000	3.00	7.50	20.00	27.50	40.00
1947	—	**PF63** 250	**PF65** 425			

KM# 33 FARTHING

Nickel-Brass, 20.2 mm. **Ruler:** George VI **Obv:** Crowned head left **Obv. Legend:** Without AND EMPEROR OF INDIA in legend **Rev:** Arms divide date

Date	Mintage	VF20	XF40	MS60	MS63	MS65
1950	288,000	0.25	0.80	3.25	15.00	22.50
1950	—	**PF63** 375	**PF65** 625			
1952	288,000	0.25	0.80	3.50	17.50	25.00
1952	—	**PF63** 375	**PF65** 625			

KM# 19 1/2 PENNY

Copper-Nickel **Ruler:** Edward VII **Obv:** Crowned bust right within beaded circle **Rev:** Arms with horizontal shading within beaded circle

Date	Mintage	VF20	XF40	MS60	MS63	MS65
1902	48,000	10.00	20.00	50.00	65.00	100
1903	48,000	10.00	20.00	60.00	75.00	115

KM# 22 1/2 PENNY

Copper-Nickel, 25.3 mm. **Ruler:** Edward VII **Obv:** Crowned bust right within beaded circle **Rev:** Arms with vertical shading within beaded circle

Date	Mintage	VF20	XF40	MS60	MS63	MS65
1904	48,000	5.00	25.00	70.00	85.00	125
1905	48,000	5.00	25.00	70.00	85.00	125
1906	432,000	3.00	7.50	25.00	32.50	50.00
1907	504,000	3.00	7.50	25.00	32.50	50.00
1909	144,000	5.00	10.00	40.00	45.00	70.00
1910	144,000	2.00	10.00	40.00	45.00	70.00

KM# 25 1/2 PENNY

Copper-Nickel **Ruler:** George V **Obv:** Crowned bust left within beaded circle **Rev:** Arms within beaded circle

Date	Mintage	VF20	XF40	MS60	MS63	MS65
1914	96,000	6.00	25.00	75.00	95.00	150
1916 H	192,000	1.50	6.00	20.00	27.50	40.00
1918 C	251,000	1.50	6.00	20.00	27.50	40.00
1918 C	—	**PF63** 400	**PF65** 650			
1919 C	312,000	1.50	7.50	20.00	27.50	40.00
1920	480,000	1.50	7.50	20.00	27.50	40.00
1926	240,000	1.50	7.50	30.00	35.00	55.00
1928	120,000	3.00	10.00	35.00	40.00	60.00
1928	—	**PF63** 400	**PF65** 650			

KM# 28 1/2 PENNY

Nickel-Brass **Ruler:** George VI **Obv:** Crowned head left **Rev:** Arms divide date

Date	Mintage	VF20	XF40	MS60	MS63	MS65
1937	960,000	1.00	3.50	12.00	15.00	22.50
1937	—	**PF63** 375	**PF65** 625			

KM# 31 1/2 PENNY

Nickel-Brass **Ruler:** George VI **Obv:** Crowned head left **Rev:** Arms divide date

Date	Mintage	VF20	XF40	MS60	MS63	MS65
1938	960,000	0.75	3.50	12.00	15.00	22.50
1938	—	**PF63** 375	**PF65** 625			
1940	960,000	0.75	3.50	12.00	15.00	22.50
1940	—	**PF63** 375	**PF65** 625			
1942	960,000	0.75	3.50	12.00	15.00	22.50
1945	960,000	0.75	3.50	12.00	15.00	22.50
1945	—	**PF63** 375	**PF65** 625			
1947	960,000	0.75	3.50	12.00	15.00	22.50
1947	—	**PF63** 450	**PF65** 650			

KM# 34 1/2 PENNY

4.38 g., Nickel-Brass **Ruler:** George VI **Obv:** Crowned head left **Rev:** Arms divide date

Date	Mintage	VF20	XF40	MS60	MS63	MS65
1950	1,440,000	0.20	0.30	3.25	5.00	8.00
1950	—	**PF63** 375	**PF65** 625			
1952	1,200,000	0.20	0.30	3.25	5.00	8.00
1952	—	**PF63** 375	**PF65** 625			

KM# 36 1/2 PENNY

4.60 g., Nickel-Brass, 22.5 mm. **Ruler:** Elizabeth II **Obv:** Crowned bust right **Rev:** Arms divide date

Date	Mintage	VF20	XF40	MS60	MS63	MS65
1955	1,440,000	0.15	0.40	2.00	3.00	5.00
1955	—	**PF63** 325	**PF65** 600			
1957	600,000	2.00	4.00	6.00	9.00	14.00
1957 Proof	—	—	—	—	—	—
1958	960,000	0.20	0.50	2.00	3.00	5.00
1958	—	**PF63** 325	**PF65** 600			
1959	960,000	0.20	0.50	2.00	3.00	5.00
1959 Proof	—	—	—	—	—	—
1961	480,000	0.40	1.00	4.00	5.00	8.00
1961 Proof	—	—	—	—	—	—
1962	960,000	0.15	0.30	1.75	2.50	4.00
1962	—	**PF63** 325	**PF65** 600			
1963	960,000	0.15	0.30	1.75	2.50	4.00
1963	—	**PF63** 325	**PF65** 600			

KM# 38 1/2 PENNY

4.50 g., Nickel-Brass **Ruler:** Elizabeth II **Obv:** Crowned bust right **Rev:** Arms with supporters

Date	Mintage	VF20	XF40	MS60	MS63	MS65
1964	1,440,000	0.15	0.20	0.80	1.00	1.50
1965	1,200,000	0.15	0.20	0.80	1.00	1.50
1966	1,680,000	0.15	0.20	0.80	1.00	1.50

KM# 41 1/2 PENNY

Copper-Nickel-Zinc **Ruler:** Elizabeth II **Subject:** Jamaican Coinage Centennial **Obv:** Crowned bust right **Rev:** Arms with supporters

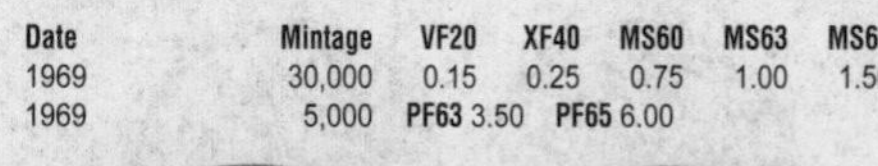

Date	Mintage	VF20	XF40	MS60	MS63	MS65
1969	30,000	0.15	0.25	0.75	1.00	1.50
1969	5,000	**PF63** 3.50	**PF65** 6.00			

KM# 20 PENNY

Copper-Nickel, 30.9 mm. **Ruler:** Edward VII **Obv:** Crowned bust right within beaded circle **Rev:** Arms with horizontal shading within beaded circle

Date	Mintage	F12	VF20	XF40	MS60	MS63
1902	60,000	2.25	6.00	25.00	70.00	90.00
1903	60,000	2.25	6.00	25.00	70.00	90.00

KM# 23 PENNY

8.10 g., Copper-Nickel, 30.9 mm. **Ruler:** Edward VII **Obv:** Crowned bust right within beaded circle **Rev:** Arms with vertical shading within beaded circle

Date	Mintage	VF20	XF40	MS60	MS63	MS65
1904	24,000	20.00	50.00	125	150	225
1904	—	**PF63** 550	**PF65** 850			
1905	48,000	6.50	35.00	70.00	90.00	150
1906	156,000	2.50	12.00	45.00	60.00	100
1907	108,000	2.50	12.00	45.00	60.00	100
1909	144,000	2.50	12.00	45.00	60.00	100
1910	144,000	2.50	12.00	45.00	60.00	100

KM# 26 PENNY

Copper-Nickel, 30.9 mm. **Ruler:** George V **Obv:** Crowned bust left within beaded circle **Rev:** Arms within beaded circle

Date	Mintage	VF20	XF40	MS60	MS63	MS65
1914	24,000	20.00	65.00	175	200	300
1916 H	24,000	20.00	60.00	175	200	300
1918 C	187,000	5.00	15.00	60.00	75.00	125
1918 C	—	**PF63** 450	**PF65** 650			
1919 C	251,000	4.75	12.00	50.00	65.00	100
1920	360,000	2.50	9.50	32.50	40.00	60.00
1926	240,000	2.50	9.50	35.00	40.00	60.00
1928	360,000	2.50	9.50	35.00	40.00	60.00
1928	—	**PF63** 450	**PF65** 650			

KM# 29 PENNY

Nickel-Brass **Ruler:** George VI **Obv:** Crowned head left **Rev:** Arms divide date

Date	Mintage	VF20	XF40	MS60	MS63	MS65
1937	1,200,000	1.75	3.25	12.00	15.00	25.00
1937	—	**PF63** 400	**PF65** 650			

KM# 32 PENNY

Nickel-Brass **Ruler:** George VI **Obv:** Crowned head left **Rev:** Arms divide date

Date	Mintage	VF20	XF40	MS60	MS63	MS65
1938	1,200,000	0.65	3.25	12.00	15.00	22.50
1938	—	**PF63** 400	**PF65** 650			
1940	1,200,000	0.65	3.25	12.00	15.00	22.50
1940	—	**PF63** 400	**PF65** 650			
1942	1,200,000	0.65	3.25	12.00	15.00	22.50
1942	—	**PF63** 400	**PF65** 650			
1945	1,200,000	0.65	3.25	12.00	15.00	22.50
1945	—	**PF63** 400	**PF65** 650			
1947	480,000	7.50	10.00	25.00	35.00	55.00
1947	—	**PF63** 400	**PF65** 650			

KM# 35 PENNY

Nickel-Brass **Ruler:** George VI **Obv:** Crowned head left **Obv. Legend:** Without AND EMPEROR OF INDIA in legend **Rev:** Arms divide date

Date	Mintage	VF20	XF40	MS60	MS63	MS65
1950	600,000	0.35	2.00	10.00	14.00	22.00
1950	—	**PF63** 400	**PF65** 650			
1952	725,000	0.35	2.00	10.00	14.00	22.00
1952	—	**PF63** 400	**PF65** 650			

KM# 37 PENNY

7.60 g., Nickel-Brass, 27 mm. **Ruler:** Elizabeth II **Obv:** Crowned bust right **Rev:** Arms divide date

Date	Mintage	VF20	XF40	MS60	MS63	MS65
1953	1,200,000	0.20	0.50	1.50	2.00	3.00
1953	—	**PF63** 350	**PF65** 650			
1955	960,000	0.25	1.00	4.00	5.00	8.00
1955	—	**PF63** 350	**PF65** 650			
1957	600,000	0.25	1.00	4.00	5.00	8.00
1957 Proof	—	—	—	—	—	—
1958	1,080,000	0.20	0.30	3.00	4.50	7.50
1958	—	**PF63** 325	**PF65** 600			
1959	1,368,000	0.20	0.30	2.50	3.00	5.00
1959 Proof	—	—	—	—	—	—
1960	1,368,000	0.20	0.30	2.50	3.00	5.00
1960 Proof	—	—	—	—	—	—
1961	1,368,000	0.20	0.30	2.50	3.00	5.00
1961 Proof	—	—	—	—	—	—
1962	1,920,000	0.20	0.30	2.50	3.00	5.00
1962	—	**PF63** 325	**PF65** 600			
1963	720,000	4.00	10.00	50.00	65.00	100
1963	—	**PF63** 350	**PF65** 650			

KM# 39 PENNY

7.47 g., Nickel-Brass **Ruler:** Elizabeth II **Obv:** Crowned bust right **Rev:** Arms with supporters

Date	Mintage	VF20	XF40	MS60	MS63	MS65
1964	480,000	0.15	0.50	1.00	1.50	2.50
1965	1,200,000	0.15	0.20	0.35	1.00	1.50
1966	1,200,000	0.15	0.20	0.35	1.00	1.50
1967	2,760,000	0.15	0.20	0.35	1.00	1.50

KM# 42 PENNY

7.30 g., Copper-Nickel-Zinc **Ruler:** Elizabeth II **Subject:** Jamaican Coinage Centennial **Obv:** Crowned bust right **Rev:** Arms with supporters

Date	Mintage	VF20	XF40	MS60	MS63	MS65
1969	30,000	0.15	0.30	0.75	1.25	2.00
1969	5,000	**PF63** 3.50	**PF65** 6.00			

KM# 40 5 SHILLING

Copper-Nickel **Ruler:** Elizabeth II **Subject:** VIII Commonwealth Games **Obv:** Arms with supporters **Rev:** Crown divides date above inscription within chain link wreath

Date	Mintage	VF20	XF40	MS60	MS63	MS65
1966	190,000	2.50	4.00	3.50	5.00	7.00
1966	20,000	**PF65** 10.00				

DECIMAL COINAGE

The Franklin Mint and Royal Mint had both struck 1 Cent through 1 Dollar coinage. In 1970 both mints used similar dies without mintmark. The Royal Mint issues have JAMAICA extending beyond the native headdress feathers. The Franklin Mint issues from 1971-84 have JAMAICA within the headdress feathers.

KM# 45 CENT

4.20 g., Bronze, 20.7 mm. **Ruler:** Elizabeth II **Obv:** Arms with supporters **Rev:** Ackee fruit above value

Date	Mintage	VF20	XF40	MS60	MS63	MS65
1969	30,200,000	—	0.10	0.25	0.35	0.50
1969	19,000	**PF65** 0.50				
1970 (RM) Small date	10,000,000	—	0.10	0.25	0.35	0.50
1970 (fm) (M); Large date	5,000	—	0.10	0.25	0.35	0.50
1970 (fm) (P)	12,000	**PF65** 0.50				
1971 (RM)	5,625,000	—	0.10	0.25	0.35	0.50

KM# 51 CENT

4.20 g., Bronze **Ruler:** Elizabeth II **Obv:** Arms with supporters **Rev:** Ackee fruit above value

Date	Mintage	VF20	XF40	MS60	MS63	MS65
1971 FM (M)	4,834	—	0.10	0.25	0.35	0.50
1971 FM (P)	14,000	**PF65** 0.50				
1972 FM (M)	7,982	—	0.10	0.25	0.35	0.50
1972 FM (P)	17,000	**PF65** 0.50				
1973 FM (M)	29,000	—	0.10	0.25	0.35	0.50
1973 FM (P)	28,000	**PF65** 0.50				
1974 FM (M)	28,000	—	0.10	0.25	0.35	0.50
1974 FM (P)	22,000	**PF65** 0.50				
1975 FM (M)	36,000	—	0.10	0.25	0.35	0.50
1975 FM (U)	4,683	—	—	0.25	0.35	0.50
1975 FM (P)	16,000	**PF65** 0.50				

KM# 52 CENT

4.20 g., Bronze **Ruler:** Elizabeth II **Series:** F.A.O. **Obv:** Arms with supporters **Rev:** Ackee fruit above value

Date	Mintage	VF20	XF40	MS60	MS63	MS65
1971	20,000	—	0.50	0.75	1.00	1.25
1972	5,000,000	—	0.10	0.30	0.75	1.00
1973	5,500,000	—	0.10	0.30	0.75	1.00
1974	3,000,000	—	0.10	0.30	0.75	1.00

KM# 64 CENT

1.22 g., Aluminum, 21.08 mm. **Ruler:** Elizabeth II **Series:** F.A.O. **Obv:** National arms, country named spaced beyond supporters **Obv. Legend:** JAMAICA **Rev:** Ackee fruit above value **Edge:** Plain **Shape:** 12-sided

Date	Mintage	VF20	XF40	MS60	MS63	MS65
1975	15,000,000	—	0.10	0.20	0.35	0.50
1976	16,000,000	—	0.10	0.20	0.35	0.50
1977	—	—	0.10	0.20	0.35	0.50
1978	8,400,000	—	0.10	0.20	0.35	0.50
1980	10,000,000	—	0.10	0.20	0.35	0.50
1981	8,000,000	—	0.10	0.20	0.35	0.50
1982	10,000,000	—	0.10	0.20	0.35	0.50
1983	1,342,000	—	—	0.15	0.25	0.50
1984	8,704,000	—	—	0.15	0.25	0.50
1985	5,112,000	—	—	0.15	0.25	0.50
1985	—	PF65 0.50				
1986	17,534,000	—	—	0.15	0.25	0.50
1987	9,968,000	—	—	0.15	0.25	0.50
1987	—	PF65 0.50				
1988	—	PF65 0.50				
1989	—	PF65 0.50				
1990	—	—	—	0.15	0.25	0.50
1990	—	PF65 0.50				
1991	—	—	—	0.15	0.25	0.50
1991	—	PF65 0.50				
1992	—	PF65 0.50				
1993	—	PF65 0.50				
1995	—	PF65 0.50				
1996	—	—	—	0.15	0.25	0.50
2000	—	—	0.25	0.35	0.50	0.75
2000	—	PF65 1.00				

KM# 68 CENT

1.22 g., Aluminum, 21.08 mm. **Ruler:** Elizabeth II **Obv:** Arms with supporters, country name spaced narrow, within supporters **Rev:** Ackee fruit above value **Shape:** 12-sided

Date	Mintage	VF20	XF40	MS60	MS63	MS65
1976 FM (M)	28,000	—	—	0.15	0.25	0.50
1976 FM (U)	1,802	—	—	0.15	0.25	0.50
1976 FM (P)	24,000	PF65 0.50				
1977 FM (M)	28,000	—	—	0.15	0.20	0.30
1977 FM (U)	597	—	—	1.25	1.50	2.00
1977 FM (P)	10,000	PF65 0.50				
1978 FM (M)	28,000	—	—	0.15	0.20	0.30
1978 FM (U)	1,282	—	—	0.35	0.50	0.75
1978 FM (P)	6,058	PF65 0.60				
1979 FM (M)	28,000	—	—	0.15	0.25	0.50
1979 FM (U)	2,608	—	—	0.35	0.50	0.75
1979 FM (P)	4,049	PF65 0.60				
1980 FM (M)	28,000	—	—	0.15	0.25	0.50
1980 FM (U)	3,668	—	—	0.35	0.50	0.70
1980 FM (P)	2,688	PF65 0.75				
1981 FM (U)	482	—	—	1.25	1.50	2.00
1981 FM (P)	1,577	PF65 0.75				
1982 FM (U)	—	—	—	0.35	0.50	0.70
1982 FM (P)	—	PF65 0.75				
1984 FM (U)	—	—	—	0.35	0.50	0.70
1984 FM (P)	—	PF65 0.75				

KM# 136 CENT

1.22 g., Aluminum, 21.08 mm. **Ruler:** Elizabeth II **Note:** Mule. Two obverses of KM#64.

Date	Mintage	VF20	XF40	MS60	MS63	MS65
1982 FM	—	—	125	150	200	275

KM# 137 CENT

1.22 g., Aluminum, 21.08 mm. **Ruler:** Elizabeth II **Note:** Mule. Two reverses of KM#64.

Date	Mintage	VF20	XF40	MS60	MS63	MS65
1982 FM	—	—	150	175	250	325

KM# 101 CENT

1.22 g., Aluminum, 21.08 mm. **Ruler:** Elizabeth II **Subject:** 21st Anniversary of Independence **Obv:** Arms with supporters **Rev:** Ackee plant (blighia sapida)

Date	Mintage	VF20	XF40	MS60	MS63	MS65
ND-1983 M (U)	—	—	—	0.15	0.35	0.75
ND-1983 FM (P)	—	PF65 0.75				

KM# 46 5 CENTS

2.83 g., Copper-Nickel, 19.4 mm. **Ruler:** Elizabeth II **Obv:** Arms with supporters **Rev:** American crocodile above value **Edge:** Reeded

Date	Mintage	VF20	XF40	MS60	MS63	MS65
1969	12,008,000	—	0.10	0.25	0.50	1.00
1969	30,000	PF65 0.65				
1970 (fm) (M)	5,000	—	0.10	0.25	0.50	1.00
1970 (fm) (P)	12,000	PF65 0.65				
1972	6,000,000	—	0.10	0.25	0.50	0.75
1975	6,010,000	—	0.10	0.25	0.50	0.75
1977	2,400,000	—	0.10	0.25	0.50	0.75
1978	2,000,000	—	0.10	0.25	0.50	0.75
1980	2,272,000	—	0.10	0.25	0.50	0.75
1981	2,001,000	—	0.10	0.25	0.50	0.75
1982	2,000,000	—	0.10	0.25	0.50	0.75
1983	992,000	—	0.45	0.75	1.00	1.50
1984	3,508,000	—	0.10	0.25	0.50	0.75
1985	4,760,000	—	0.10	0.25	0.50	0.75
1985	—	PF65 0.65				
1986	14,504,000	—	0.10	0.25	0.50	0.75
1987	13,166,000	—	0.10	0.25	0.50	0.75
1987	—	PF65 0.65				
1988	9,780,000	—	0.10	0.25	0.50	0.75
1988	—	PF65 0.65				
1989	—	—	0.10	0.25	0.50	0.75
1989	—	PF65 0.65				

KM# 46a 5 CENTS

2.80 g., Nickel Plated Steel, 19.4 mm. **Ruler:** Elizabeth II **Obv:** Arms with supporters **Rev:** American crocodile above value **Edge:** Reeded

Date	Mintage	VF20	XF40	MS60	MS63	MS65
1990	—	PF65 0.65				
1990	—	—	0.10	0.25	0.50	0.75
1991	—	—	0.10	0.25	0.50	0.75
1991	—	PF65 0.65				
1992	—	—	0.10	0.25	0.50	0.75
1992	—	PF65 0.65				
1993	—	—	0.10	0.25	0.50	0.75
1993	—	PF65 0.65				

KM# 53 5 CENTS

2.83 g., Copper-Nickel, 19.4 mm. **Ruler:** Elizabeth II **Obv:** Arms with supporters **Rev:** American crocodile above value **Edge:** Reeded

Date	Mintage	VF20	XF40	MS60	MS63	MS65
1971 FM (M)	4,834	—	0.10	0.35	0.75	1.00
1971 FM (P)	14,000	PF65 0.50				
1972 FM (M)	7,982	—	0.10	0.35	0.75	1.00
1972 FM (P)	17,000	PF65 0.50				
1973 FM (M)	17,000	—	0.10	0.35	0.75	1.00
1973 FM (P)	28,000	PF65 0.50				
1974 FM (M)	16,000	—	0.10	0.35	0.75	1.00
1974 FM (P)	22,000	PF65 0.50				
1975 FM (M)	6,240	—	0.10	0.35	0.75	1.00
1975 FM (U)	4,683	—	—	0.35	0.75	1.00
1975 FM (P)	16,000	PF65 0.50				
1976 FM (M)	5,560	—	0.10	0.35	0.75	1.00
1976 FM (U)	1,802	—	—	0.35	0.75	1.00
1976 FM (P)	24,000	PF65 0.50				
1977 FM (M)	5,560	—	0.10	0.35	0.75	1.00
1977 FM (U)	597	—	—	1.00	1.50	2.00
1977 FM (P)	10,000	PF65 0.50				
1978 FM (M)	5,560	—	0.10	0.35	0.75	1.00
1978 FM (U)	1,282	—	—	0.40	0.85	1.50
1978 FM (P)	6,058	PF65 0.85				
1979 FM (M)	5,560	—	0.10	0.35	0.75	1.50
1979 FM (U)	2,608	—	—	0.40	0.80	1.60
1979 FM (P)	4,049	PF65 0.85				
1980 FM (M)	5,560	—	0.10	0.35	0.75	1.50
1980 FM (U)	3,668	—	—	0.40	0.80	1.60
1980 FM (P)	2,688	PF65 1.00				
1981 FM (U)	482	—	—	1.00	1.50	2.00
1981 FM (P)	1,577	PF65 1.00				
1982 FM (U)	—	—	—	0.40	0.80	1.60
1982 FM (P)	—	PF65 1.00				
1984 FM (U)	—	—	—	0.40	0.80	1.60
1984 FM (P)	—	PF65 1.00				

KM# 102 5 CENTS

2.83 g., Copper-Nickel, 19.4 mm. **Ruler:** Elizabeth II **Subject:** 21st Anniversary of Independence **Obv:** Arms with supporters **Rev:** American crocodile above value **Edge:** Reeded

Date	Mintage	VF20	XF40	MS60	MS63	MS65
ND-1983 FM (U)	—	—	—	0.75	1.25	1.75
ND-1983 FM (P)	—	PF65 1.75				

KM# 47 10 CENTS

5.65 g., Copper-Nickel, 23.6 mm. **Ruler:** Elizabeth II **Obv:** Arms with supporters **Rev:** Butterfly within leafy sprigs above value **Edge:** Reeded

Date	Mintage	VF20	XF40	MS60	MS63	MS65
1969	19,508,000	—	0.10	0.25	0.50	0.75
1969	30,000	PF65 0.75				
1970 (fm) (M)	5,000	—	0.10	0.25	0.50	0.75
1970 (fm) (P)	12,000	PF65 0.75				
1972	6,000,000	—	0.10	0.25	0.50	0.75
1975	10,010,000	—	0.10	0.20	0.40	0.65
1977	8,000,000	—	0.10	0.20	0.40	0.65
1981	8,000,000	—	0.10	0.15	0.30	0.60
1982	8,000,000	—	0.10	0.15	0.30	0.60
1983	2,000,000	—	0.10	0.15	0.30	0.60
1984	5,000,000	—	0.10	0.15	0.30	0.60
1985	8,310,000	—	0.10	0.15	0.30	0.60
1985	—	PF65 0.75				
1986	21,677,000	—	0.10	0.15	0.30	0.60
1987	29,089,000	—	0.10	0.15	0.30	0.60
1987	—	PF65 0.75				
1988	15,660,000	—	0.10	0.15	0.30	0.60
1988	—	PF65 0.75				
1989	—	—	0.10	0.15	0.30	0.60
1989	—	PF65 0.75				

KM# 47a 10 CENTS

5.65 g., Nickel Plated Steel, 23.6 mm. **Ruler:** Elizabeth II **Obv:** Arms with supporters **Rev:** Butterfly within leafy sprigs above value **Edge:** Reeded

Date	Mintage	VF20	XF40	MS60	MS63	MS65
1990	—	—	0.10	0.15	0.30	0.60
1990	—	PF65 0.75				

KM# 54 10 CENTS

5.65 g., Copper-Nickel, 23.6 mm. **Ruler:** Elizabeth II **Obv:** Arms with supporters **Rev:** Butterfly within leafy sprigs above value **Edge:** Reeded

Date	Mintage	VF20	XF40	MS60	MS63	MS65
1971 FM (M)	4,834	—	0.10	0.20	0.35	0.70
1971 FM (P)	14,000	PF65 0.75				
1972 FM (M)	7,982	—	0.10	0.20	0.35	0.70
1972 FM (P)	17,000	PF65 0.75				
1973 FM (M)	15,000	—	0.10	0.20	0.35	0.70
1973 FM (P)	28,000	PF65 0.75				
1974 FM (M)	14,000	—	0.10	0.20	0.35	0.70
1974 FM (P)	22,000	PF65 0.75				
1975 FM (M)	3,120	—	0.10	0.20	0.35	0.75
1975 FM (U)	4,683	—	—	0.20	0.35	0.75
1975 FM (P)	16,000	PF65 0.75				
1976 FM (M)	2,780	—	0.10	0.20	0.35	0.75
1976 FM (U)	1,802	—	—	0.20	0.35	0.75
1976 FM (P)	24,000	PF65 0.75				
1977 FM (M)	2,780	—	0.10	0.25	0.50	0.80
1977 FM (U)	597	—	—	1.00	1.50	2.50
1977 FM (P)	10,000	PF65 0.75				
1978 FM (M)	2,780	—	0.10	0.25	0.50	0.80
1978 FM (U)	4,062	—	—	0.30	0.60	0.85
1978 FM (P)	6,058	PF65 1.00				
1979 FM (M)	2,780	—	0.10	0.25	0.50	0.80
1979 FM (U)	2,608	—	—	0.30	0.60	0.85
1979 FM (P)	4,049	PF65 1.00				
1980 FM (M)	2,780	—	0.10	0.25	0.50	0.80

Date	Mintage	VF20	XF40	MS60	MS63	MS65
1980 FM (U)	3,668	—	—	0.25	0.50	0.80
1980 FM (P)	2,688	PF65 1.50				
1981 FM (U)	482	—	—	1.00	1.50	2.00
1981 FM (P)	1,577	PF65 1.50				
1982 FM (U)	—	—	—	0.25	0.50	0.80
1982 FM (P)	—	PF65 1.50				
1984 FM (U)	—	—	—	0.25	0.50	0.80
1984 FM (P)	—	PF65 1.50				

KM# 103 10 CENTS

5.65 g., Copper-Nickel, 23.6 mm. **Ruler:** Elizabeth II **Subject:** 21st Anniversary of Independence **Obv:** Arms with supporters **Rev:** Butterfly within leafy sprigs above value **Edge:** Reeded

Date	Mintage	VF20	XF40	MS60	MS63	MS65
ND-1983 FM (U)	—	—	—	0.25	0.50	0.80
ND-1983 FM (P)	—	PF65 1.50				

KM# 146.1 10 CENTS

5.68 g., Nickel Plated Steel **Ruler:** Elizabeth II **Subject:** Paul Bogle **Obv:** Arms with supporters **Rev:** Bust facing **Edge:** Reeded

Date	Mintage	VF20	XF40	MS60	MS63	MS65
1991	—	—	—	0.25	0.50	0.80
1991	—	PF65 1.50				
1992	—	—	—	0.25	0.50	0.80
1992	—	PF65 1.50				
1993	—	—	—	0.25	0.50	0.80
1993	—	PF65 1.50				
1994	—	—	—	0.25	0.50	0.80
1994	—	PF65 1.50				

KM# 146.2 10 CENTS

2.40 g., Copper Plated Steel, 17 mm. **Ruler:** Elizabeth II **Series:** National Heroes **Subject:** Paul Bogle **Obv:** National arms **Obv. Legend:** JAMAICA **Rev:** Bust facing **Edge:** Plain **Note:** Reduced size.

Date	Mintage	VF20	XF40	MS60	MS63	MS65
1995	—	—	—	0.15	0.25	0.50
1995	—	PF65 2.00				
1996	—	—	—	0.15	0.25	0.50
2000	—	—	—	0.15	0.25	0.50
2000	—	PF65 2.00				

KM# 48 20 CENTS

11.31 g., Copper-Nickel, 28.5 mm. **Ruler:** Elizabeth II **Obv:** Arms with supporters **Rev:** Mahoe trees above value **Edge:** Reeded

Date	Mintage	VF20	XF40	MS60	MS63	MS65
1969	3,758,000	—	0.25	0.35	0.75	1.00
1969	30,000	PF65 1.00				
1970 (fm) (M)	5,000	—	0.25	0.35	0.75	1.00
1970 (fm) (P)	12,000	PF65 1.00				
1975	10,000	—	0.80	1.25	2.50	3.00
1982	1,000,000	—	0.25	0.35	0.65	1.00
1984	2,000,000	—	0.25	0.35	0.65	1.00
1986	2,530,000	—	0.25	0.35	0.65	1.00
1987	5,545,000	—	0.25	0.35	0.65	1.00
1987	—	PF65 1.00				
1988	5,016,000	—	0.25	0.35	0.65	1.00
1988	—	PF65 1.00				
1989	—	—	0.25	0.35	0.65	1.00
1989	—	PF65 1.00				
1990	—	PF65 1.00				

KM# 55 20 CENTS

11.31 g., Copper-Nickel, 28.5 mm. **Ruler:** Elizabeth II **Obv:** Arms with supporters **Rev:** Mahoe trees above value **Edge:** Reeded

Date	Mintage	VF20	XF40	MS60	MS63	MS65
1971 FM (M)	4,834	—	0.20	0.25	0.50	1.00
1971 FM (P)	14,000	PF65 1.00				
1972 FM (M)	7,982	—	0.20	0.25	0.50	1.00
1972 FM (P)	17,000	PF65 1.00				
1973 FM (M)	13,000	—	0.20	0.25	0.50	1.00
1973 FM (P)	28,000	PF65 1.00				
1974 FM (M)	12,000	—	0.20	0.25	0.50	1.00
1974 FM (P)	22,000	PF65 1.00				
1975 FM (M)	1,560	—	0.20	0.25	0.50	1.00
1975 FM (U)	4,683	—	—	—	0.50	1.00
1975 FM (P)	16,000	PF65 1.00				
1976 FM (M)	1,390	—	0.20	0.25	0.50	1.00
1976 FM (U)	1,802	—	0.20	0.25	0.50	1.00
1976 FM (P)	24,000	PF65 1.00				

KM# 69 20 CENTS

11.31 g., Copper-Nickel, 28.5 mm. **Ruler:** Elizabeth II **Series:** F.A.O. **Obv:** Arms with supporters **Rev:** Mahoe trees above value **Edge:** Reeded

Date	Mintage	VF20	XF40	MS60	MS63	MS65
1976	3,000,000	—	0.20	0.50	1.00	1.50
1981	—	—	0.20	0.50	1.00	1.50
1982	—	—	0.20	0.50	1.00	1.50
Note: Mintage included with KM#48						
1984	—	—	0.20	0.50	1.00	1.50
1987	—	—	0.20	0.50	1.00	1.50

KM# 73 20 CENTS

11.31 g., Copper-Nickel, 28.5 mm. **Ruler:** Elizabeth II **Obv:** Arms with supporters **Rev:** Mahoe trees above value **Edge:** Reeded

Date	Mintage	VF20	XF40	MS60	MS63	MS65
1977 FM (M)	1,390	—	0.25	0.35	0.75	1.25
1977 FM (U)	597	—	—	1.25	2.00	2.50
1977 FM (P)	10,000	PF65 1.00				
1978 FM (M)	1,390	—	0.25	0.35	0.75	1.25
1978 FM (U)	1,282	—	0.25	0.35	0.75	1.25
1978 FM (P)	6,058	PF65 1.50				
1979 FM (M)	1,390	—	0.25	0.35	0.75	1.25
1979 FM (U)	2,608	—	—	0.35	0.75	1.25
1979 FM (P)	4,049	PF65 1.50				
1980 FM (M)	1,390	—	0.25	0.30	0.60	1.00
1980 FM (U)	3,668	—	—	0.30	0.60	1.00
1980 FM (P)	2,688	PF65 2.00				
1981 FM (U)	482	—	—	1.25	2.00	2.50
1981 FM (P)	1,577	PF65 2.00				
1982 FM (U)	—	—	—	0.30	0.60	1.00
1982 FM (P)	—	PF65 2.00				
1984 FM (U)	—	—	—	0.30	0.60	1.00
1984 FM (P)	—	PF65 2.00				

KM# 90 20 CENTS

11.31 g., Copper-Nickel, 28.5 mm. **Ruler:** Elizabeth II **Subject:** World Food Day **Obv:** Arms with supporters **Rev:** Figs within leaves above value **Edge:** Reeded

Date	Mintage	VF20	XF40	MS60	MS63	MS65
1981 FM (M)	—	—	—	0.75	1.50	2.00

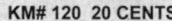

KM# 120 20 CENTS

11.31 g., Copper-Nickel, 28.5 mm. **Ruler:** Elizabeth II **Obv:** Arms with supporters **Rev:** Figs within leaves above value **Edge:** Reeded

Date	Mintage	VF20	XF40	MS60	MS63	MS65
1981	—	—	—	0.30	0.60	1.00
1984	2,000,000	—	—	0.30	0.60	1.00
1985	2,988,000	—	—	0.30	0.60	1.00
1985	—	PF65 2.00				
1986	2,530,000	—	—	0.30	0.60	1.00
1988	—	—	—	0.30	0.60	1.00

KM# 104 20 CENTS

11.31 g., Copper-Nickel, 28.5 mm. **Ruler:** Elizabeth II **Subject:** 21st Anniversary of Independence **Obv:** Arms with supporters **Rev:** Mahoe trees above value **Edge:** Reeded

Date	Mintage	VF20	XF40	MS60	MS63	MS65
ND-1983 FM (U)	—	—	—	0.30	0.60	1.00
ND-1983 FM (P)	—	PF65 2.00				

KM# 49 25 CENTS

14.55 g., Copper-Nickel, 32.3 mm. **Ruler:** Elizabeth II **Obv:** Arms with supporters **Rev:** Streamer-tailed hummingbird above value **Edge:** Reeded

Date	Mintage	VF20	XF40	MS60	MS63	MS65
1969	758,000	—	0.45	0.65	1.25	2.00
1969	30,000	PF65 3.00				
1970 (fm) (M)	5,000	—	0.45	0.65	1.25	2.00
1970 (fm) (P)	12,000	PF65 3.00				
1973	160,000	—	0.45	0.65	1.25	2.00
1975	3,110,000	—	0.45	0.65	1.25	2.00
1982	1,000,000	—	0.45	0.65	1.25	2.00
1984	2,002,000	—	0.45	0.65	1.25	2.00
1985	1,999,000	—	0.45	0.65	1.25	2.00
1985	—	PF65 3.00				
1986	2,635,000	—	0.45	0.65	1.25	2.00
1987	6,006,000	—	0.45	0.65	1.25	2.00
1987	—	PF65 3.00				
1988	3,034,000	—	0.45	0.65	1.25	2.00
1988	—	PF65 3.00				
1989	—	—	0.45	0.65	1.25	2.00
1989	—	PF65 3.00				
1990	—	PF65 3.00				

KM# 56 25 CENTS

14.55 g., Copper-Nickel, 32.3 mm. **Ruler:** Elizabeth II **Obv:** Arms with supporters **Rev:** Streamer-tailed hummingbird above value **Edge:** Reeded

Date	Mintage	VF20	XF40	MS60	MS63	MS65
1971 FM (M)	4,834	—	0.60	0.75	1.50	2.50
1971 FM (P)	14,000	PF65 3.00				
1972 FM (M)	8,382	—	0.60	0.75	1.50	2.50
1972 FM (P)	17,000	PF65 3.00				
1973 FM (M)	13,000	—	0.60	0.75	1.50	2.50
1973 FM (P)	28,000	PF65 3.00				
1974 FM (M)	12,000	—	0.60	0.75	1.50	2.50
1974 FM (P)	22,000	PF65 3.00				
1975 FM (M)	1,503	—	0.60	0.75	1.50	2.50
1975 FM (U)	4,683	—	—	—	1.50	2.50
1975 FM (P)	16,000	PF65 3.00				
1976 FM (M)	1,112	—	0.60	0.75	1.50	2.50
1976 FM (U)	1,802	—	—	—	1.50	2.50
1976 FM (P)	24,000	PF65 3.00				
1977 FM (M)	1,112	—	0.60	0.75	1.50	2.50
1977 FM (U)	597	—	—	—	3.00	4.50
1977 FM (P)	10,000	PF65 3.00				
1978 FM (M)	1,112	—	0.60	0.75	1.50	2.50
1978 FM (U)	1,282	—	0.60	0.75	1.50	2.50
1978 FM (P)	6,058	PF65 3.00				
1979 FM (M)	1,112	—	0.60	0.75	1.50	2.50
1979 FM (U)	2,608	—	0.60	0.75	1.50	2.50
1979 FM (P)	4,049	PF65 3.00				
1980 FM (M)	1,112	—	0.60	0.75	1.50	2.50
1980 FM (U)	3,668	—	0.60	0.75	1.50	2.50
1980 FM (P)	2,688	PF65 3.50				
1981 FM (U)	482	—	—	—	3.00	4.50
1981 FM (P)	1,577	PF65 3.50				
1982 FM (U)	—	—	0.60	0.75	1.50	2.50
1982 FM (P)	—	PF65 3.50				
1984 FM (U)	—	—	0.60	0.75	1.50	2.50
1984 FM (P)	—	PF65 3.50				

KM# 105 25 CENTS

14.55 g., Copper-Nickel, 32.3 mm. **Ruler:** Elizabeth II **Subject:** 21st Anniversary of Independence **Obv:** Arms with supporters **Rev:** Streamer-tailed hummingbird above value **Edge:** Reeded

Date	Mintage	VF20	XF40	MS60	MS63	MS65
ND-1983 FM (U)	—	—	0.60	0.75	1.50	3.00
ND-1983 FM (P)	—	PF65 3.00				

KM# 154 25 CENTS

14.55 g., Copper-Nickel, 32.3 mm. **Ruler:** Elizabeth II **Subject:** 25th Anniversary - Bank of Jamaica **Obv:** Arms with supporters **Rev:** Streamer-tailed hummingbird above value **Edge:** Reeded

Date	Mintage	VF20	XF40	MS60	MS63	MS65
1985	—	—	0.75	1.25	2.50	5.00

KM# 147 25 CENTS

6.00 g., Nickel Plated Steel **Ruler:** Elizabeth II **Subject:** Marcus Garvey **Obv:** Arms with supporters **Rev:** Head 1/4 right **Shape:** 7-sided

Date	Mintage	VF20	XF40	MS60	MS63	MS65
1991	—	—	—	0.50	1.00	1.50
1991	—	PF65 3.00				
1992	—	—	—	0.50	1.00	1.50
1992	—	PF65 3.00				
1993	—	—	—	0.50	1.00	1.50
1993	—	PF65 3.00				
1994	—	—	—	0.50	1.00	1.50

KM# 167 25 CENTS

3.60 g., Copper Plated Steel, 20 mm. **Ruler:** Elizabeth II **Series:** National Heroes **Subject:** Marcus Garvey **Obv:** National arms **Obv. Legend:** JAMAICA **Rev:** Head 1/4 right **Edge:** Plain

Date	Mintage	VF20	XF40	MS60	MS63	MS65
1995	—	—	—	—	0.50	0.75
1995	—	PF65 3.00				
1996	—	—	—	—	0.50	0.75
2000	—	—	—	—	0.50	0.75
2000	—	PF65 3.00				

KM# 65 50 CENTS

12.45 g., Copper-Nickel, 30 mm. **Ruler:** Elizabeth II **Subject:** Marcus Garvey **Obv:** Arms with supporters **Rev:** Head 1/4 right **Shape:** 10-sided

Date	Mintage	VF20	XF40	MS60	MS63	MS65
1975	12,010,000	0.15	0.50	0.75	1.25	1.50
1984	2,000,000	0.15	0.50	0.75	1.25	1.50
1985	2,119,000	0.15	0.50	0.75	1.25	1.50
1985	—	PF65 3.00				
1986	3,404,000	0.15	0.50	0.75	1.25	1.50
1987	5,545,000	0.15	0.50	0.75	1.25	1.50
1988	10,505,000	0.15	0.50	0.75	1.25	1.50
1988	—	PF65 3.00				
1989	—	0.15	0.50	0.75	1.25	1.50
1989	—	PF65 3.00				
1990	—	PF65 3.00				

KM# 70 50 CENTS

12.45 g., Copper-Nickel, 30 mm. **Ruler:** Elizabeth II **Subject:** Marcus Garvey **Obv:** Arms with supporters **Rev:** Head 1/4 right **Shape:** 10-sided

Date	Mintage	VF20	XF40	MS60	MS63	MS65
1976 FM (M)	1,112	—	—	1.00	1.50	2.00
1976 FM (U)	1,802	—	—	1.00	1.50	2.00
1976 FM (P)	24,000	PF65 1.50				
1977 FM (M)	556	—	—	—	3.50	5.00
1977 FM (U)	597	—	—	—	3.50	5.00
1977 FM (P)	10,000	PF65 1.50				
1978 FM (M)	556	—	—	—	3.50	5.00
1978 FM (U)	1,838	—	—	—	2.00	3.00
1978 FM (P)	6,058	PF65 2.50				
1979 FM (M)	556	—	—	—	3.50	5.00
1979 FM (U)	1,282	—	—	—	2.50	3.50
1979 FM (P)	4,049	PF65 3.00				
1980 FM (M)	556	—	—	—	3.50	5.00
1980 FM (U)	3,668	—	—	—	2.00	3.00
1980 FM (P)	2,688	PF65 3.00				
1981 FM (U)	482	—	—	—	3.50	5.00
1981 FM (P)	1,577	PF65 3.00				
1982 FM (U)	—	—	—	—	1.50	3.00
1982 FM (P)	—	PF65 3.00				
1984 FM (U)	—	—	—	—	1.50	3.00
1984 FM (P)	—	PF65 3.00				

KM# 106 50 CENTS

12.45 g., Copper-Nickel, 30 mm. **Ruler:** Elizabeth II **Subject:** 21st Anniversary of Independence - Marcus Garvey **Obv:** Arms with supporters **Rev:** Head 1/4 right **Shape:** 10-sided

Date	Mintage	VF20	XF40	MS60	MS63	MS65
ND-1983 FM (U)	—	—	—	—	1.50	3.00
ND-1983 FM (P)	—	PF65 4.00				

KM# 132 50 CENTS

12.45 g., Copper-Nickel, 30 mm. **Ruler:** Elizabeth II **Subject:** 100th Anniversary - Birth of Marcus Garvey **Obv:** Arms with supporters **Rev:** Head 1/4 right

Date	Mintage	VF20	XF40	MS60	MS63	MS65
1987	500	PF65 10.00				

KM# 50 DOLLAR

29.00 g., Copper-Nickel, 38 mm. **Ruler:** Elizabeth II **Obv:** Arms with supporters, country name spaced wide, beyond supporters **Rev:** Bust right **Edge:** Reeded

Date	Mintage	VF20	XF40	MS60	MS63	MS65
1969	47,000	—	—	1.00	2.00	3.00
1969	30,000	PF65 4.50				
1970 (fm) (M)	5,000	—	—	—	2.50	3.50
1970 (fm) (P)	14,000	PF65 5.00				

KM# 57 DOLLAR

29.00 g., Copper-Nickel, 38 mm. **Ruler:** Elizabeth II **Obv:** Arms with supporters, country name spaced narrow, above supporters **Rev:** Bust right **Edge:** Reeded

Date	Mintage	VF20	XF40	MS60	MS63	MS65
1971 FM	5,024	—	—	—	1.50	2.50
1971 FM (P)	15,000	PF65 4.00				
1972 FM (M)	7,982	—	—	—	1.50	2.50
1972 FM (P)	17,000	PF65 3.00				
1973 FM	10,000	—	—	—	1.50	2.50
1973 FM (P)	28,000	PF65 3.00				
1974 FM (M)	8,961	—	—	—	1.50	2.50
1974 FM (P)	22,000	PF65 3.00				
1975 FM (M)	5,312	—	—	—	2.50	3.50
1975 FM (U)	4,683	—	—	—	2.50	3.50
1975 FM (P)	16,000	PF65 3.00				
1976 FM (M)	284	—	—	—	17.50	20.00
1976 FM (U)	1,802	—	—	—	3.00	5.00
1976 FM (P)	24,000	PF65 2.50				
1977 FM (M)	287	—	—	—	17.50	20.00
1977 FM (U)	597	—	—	—	7.00	10.00
1977 FM (P)	10,000	PF65 4.00				

Date	Mintage	VF20	XF40	MS60	MS63	MS65
1978 FM (U)	1,566	—	—	—	3.00	5.00
1978 FM (P)	6,058	PF65 5.00				
1979 FM (M)	284	—	—	—	17.50	20.00
1979 FM (U)	2,608	—	—	—	3.00	5.00
1979 FM (P)	4,049	PF65 5.00				

KM# 84.1 DOLLAR

Copper-Nickel **Ruler:** Elizabeth II **Obv:** Arms with supporters **Rev:** Bust right

Date	Mintage	VF20	XF40	MS60	MS63	MS65
1980 FM (M)	284	—	—	—	20.00	22.50
1980 FM (U)	3,668	—	—	—	3.00	5.00
1980 FM (P)	2,688	PF65 15.00				
1981 FM (U)	482	—	—	—	10.00	12.50
1981 FM (P)	1,577	PF65 17.50				
1982 FM (U)	—	—	—	—	5.00	7.00
1982 FM (P)	—	PF65 17.50				

KM# 91 DOLLAR

Copper-Nickel **Ruler:** Elizabeth II **Subject:** World Food Day **Obv:** Arms with supporters **Rev:** World globe above produce

Date	Mintage	VF20	XF40	MS60	MS63	MS65
ND-1981 FM (U)	—	—	—	—	5.50	7.50

KM# 96 DOLLAR

Copper-Nickel **Ruler:** Elizabeth II **Subject:** World Championship of Football **Obv:** Arms with supporters **Rev:** Goalie catching attempted score

Date	Mintage	VF20	XF40	MS60	MS63	MS65
1982	—	—	—	—	2.50	4.50

KM# 107 DOLLAR

Copper-Nickel **Ruler:** Elizabeth II **Subject:** 21st Anniversary of Independence **Obv:** Arms with supporters **Rev:** Bust right

Date	Mintage	VF20	XF40	MS60	MS63	MS65
ND-1983 FM (U)	3,710	—	—	6.00	8.00	10.00
ND-1983 FM (P)	609	PF63 25.00	PF65 30.00			

KM# 134 DOLLAR

Copper-Nickel **Ruler:** Elizabeth II **Subject:** 21st Anniversary of Independence **Obv:** Arms with supporters **Rev:** Number 21 divides heads facing above dates and braided rope

Date	Mintage	VF20	XF40	MS60	MS63	MS65
ND-1983 FM (P)	—	PF65 14.00				

KM# 113 DOLLAR

Copper-Nickel **Ruler:** Elizabeth II **Subject:** 100th Anniversary - Birth of Bustamante **Obv:** Arms with supporters **Rev:** Bust 1/4 left

Date	Mintage	VF20	XF40	MS60	MS63	MS65
1984 FM (U)	—	—	—	—	2.00	3.50
1984 FM (P)	268	PF65 25.00				

KM# 84.2 DOLLAR

Copper-Nickel **Ruler:** Elizabeth II **Obv:** Arms with supporters **Rev:** Bust right **Edge:** Reeded

Date	Mintage	VF20	XF40	MS60	MS63	MS65
1985	—	—	—	—	2.00	3.50
1985	—	PF65 7.50				
1987	—	PF65 7.50				
1988	—	PF65 7.50				
1989	—	PF65 7.50				
1990	—	—	—	—	2.00	3.50

KM# 145 DOLLAR

9.00 g., Nickel-Brass, 23.8 mm. **Ruler:** Elizabeth II **Subject:** Sir Alexander Bustamante **Obv:** Arms with supporters **Rev:** Bust facing **Edge:** BANK OF JAMAICA

Date	Mintage	VF20	XF40	MS60	MS63	MS65
1990	—	—	—	—	1.50	2.25
1990	—	PF65 5.00				
1991	—	—	—	—	1.50	2.25
1991	—	PF65 5.00				
1992	—	—	—	—	1.50	2.25
1992	—	PF65 10.00				
1993	—	—	—	—	1.50	2.25
1993	—	PF65 5.00				

KM# 145a DOLLAR

8.00 g., Brass Plated Steel, 24 mm. **Ruler:** Elizabeth II **Subject:** Sir Alexander Bustamante **Obv:** Arms with supporters **Rev:** Bust facing **Edge:** Reeded

Date	Mintage	VF20	XF40	MS60	MS63	MS65
1993	—	—	—	—	1.50	2.25
1993	500	PF65 15.00				
1994	—	—	—	—	1.50	2.25

KM# 164 DOLLAR

2.91 g., Nickel Plated Steel, 18.5 mm. **Ruler:** Elizabeth II **Series:** National Heroes **Subject:** Sir Alexander Bustamante **Obv:** National arms **Obv. Legend:** JAMAICA **Rev:** Bust facing **Edge:** Plain **Shape:** 7-sided

Date	Mintage	VF20	XF40	MS60	MS63	MS65
1994	—	—	—	0.50	0.75	1.25
1995	—	—	—	0.50	0.75	1.25
1995	—	PF65 4.00				
1996	—	—	—	0.50	0.75	1.25
1999	—	—	—	0.50	0.75	1.25
2000	—	—	—	0.50	0.75	1.25
2000	—	PF65 4.00				

KM# 58 5 DOLLARS

42.15 g., 0.925 Silver 1.2535 oz. ASW, 58 mm. **Ruler:** Elizabeth II **Obv:** Arms with supporters **Rev:** Bust facing **Note:** His widow did not like this design, and the following year it was replaced by a left profile.

Date	Mintage	VF20	XF40	MS60	MS63	MS65
1971 FM	4,072	—	—	—	37.00	40.00
1971 FM (P)	13,000	PF63 40.00	PF65 45.00			

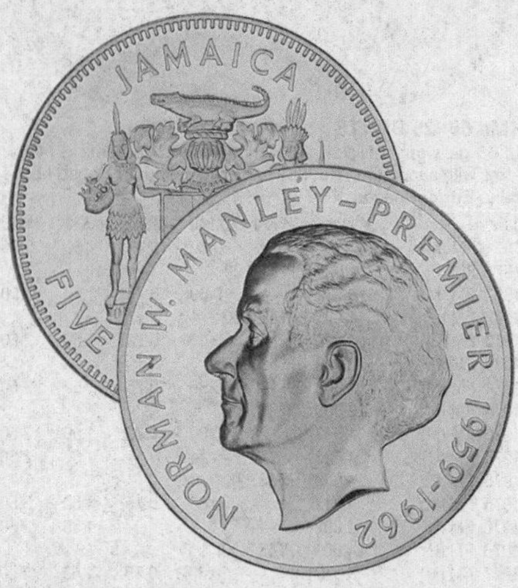

KM# 59 5 DOLLARS

41.48 g., 0.925 Silver 1.2336 oz. ASW, 45 mm. **Ruler:** Elizabeth II **Obv:** Arms with supporters **Rev:** Head left

Date	Mintage	VF20	XF40	MS60	MS63	MS65
1972 FM	3,232	—	—	—	37.00	40.00
1972 FM (P)	21,000	PF63 40.00	PF65 45.00			
1973 FM	6,484	—	—	—	37.00	40.00
1973 FM (P)	36,000	PF63 40.00	PF65 45.00			

KM# 62 5 DOLLARS

Copper-Nickel, 45 mm. **Ruler:** Elizabeth II **Obv:** Arms with supporters **Rev:** Head left

Date	Mintage	VF20	XF40	MS60	MS63	MS65
1974 FM (M)	8,661	—	—	—	5.00	6.50
1975 FM (M)	65	—	—	—	—	—
1975 FM (U)	4,683	—	—	—	6.00	7.50
1976 FM (M)	56	—	—	—	—	—
1976 FM (U)	1,802	—	—	—	7.00	9.00
1977 FM (M)	56	—	—	—	—	—
1977 FM (U)	597	—	—	—	10.00	12.00
1978 FM (U)	1,338	—	—	—	6.00	8.00
1979 FM (M)	56	—	—	—	—	—
1979 FM (U)	2,608	—	—	—	5.00	7.00

KM# 62a 5 DOLLARS

37.60 g., 0.500 Silver 0.6044 oz. ASW, 45 mm. **Ruler:** Elizabeth II **Obv:** Arms with supporters **Rev:** Head left

Date	Mintage	VF20	XF40	MS60	MS63	MS65
1974 FM (P)	22,000	PF65 15.00				
1975 FM (P)	16,000	PF65 17.50				
1976 FM (P)	23,000	PF65 15.00				
1977 FM (P)	10,000	PF65 17.50				
1978 FM (P)	6,058	PF65 20.00				
1979 FM (P)	4,049	PF65 25.00				

KM# 85.1 5 DOLLARS

Copper-Nickel **Ruler:** Elizabeth II **Obv:** Arms with supporters **Rev:** Head left **Note:** Similar to KM#62, but smaller size.

Date	Mintage	VF20	XF40	MS60	MS63	MS65
1980 FM (M)	56	—	—	—	—	—
1980 FM (U)	3,668	—	—	—	12.00	14.00
1981 FM (U)	482	—	—	—	17.00	19.00
1982 FM (U)	—	—	—	—	7.00	9.00
1984 FM (U)	—	—	—	—	7.00	9.00

KM# 85.1a 5 DOLLARS

18.56 g., 0.500 Silver 0.2984 oz. ASW **Ruler:** Elizabeth II **Obv:** Arms with supporters **Rev:** Head left

Date	Mintage	VF20	XF40	MS60	MS63	MS65
1980 FM (P)	2,688	PF65 12.00				
1981 FM (P)	1,577	PF65 15.00				
1982 FM (P)	1,040	PF65 15.00				
1984 FM (P)	268	PF65 42.00				

KM# 108 5 DOLLARS

Copper-Nickel **Ruler:** Elizabeth II **Subject:** 21st Anniversary of Independence **Obv:** Arms with supporters **Rev:** Head left

Date	Mintage	VF20	XF40	MS60	MS63	MS65
1983 FM (U)	—	—	—	—	7.00	9.00

KM# 108a 5 DOLLARS

18.56 g., 0.500 Silver 0.2984 oz. ASW **Ruler:** Elizabeth II **Obv:** Arms with supporters **Rev:** Head left

Date	Mintage	VF20	XF40	MS60	MS63	MS65
1983 FM (P)	—	PF65 17.50				

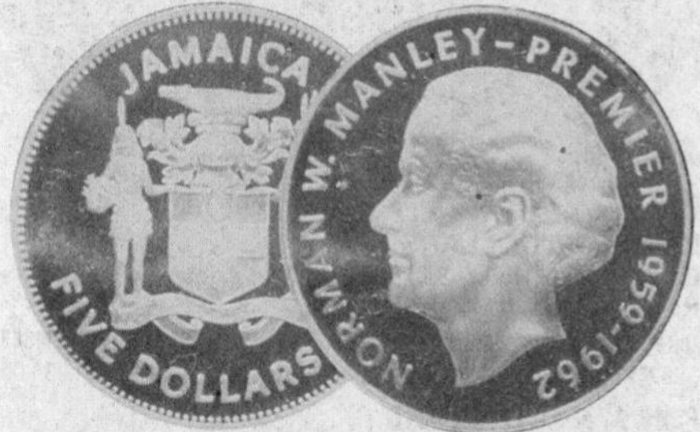

KM# 85.2 5 DOLLARS

18.56 g., 0.500 Silver 0.2984 oz. ASW **Ruler:** Elizabeth II **Obv:** Arms with supporters **Rev:** Head left

Date	Mintage	VF20	XF40	MS60	MS63	MS65
1985	—	—	—	—	12.00	15.00
1985	—	PF65 18.00				
1987	—	PF65 18.00				
1988	—	PF65 18.00				
1989	—	PF65 18.00				
1990	500	PF65 18.00				
1991	—	PF65 18.00				
1992	—	PF65 18.00				
1993	—	PF65 18.00				

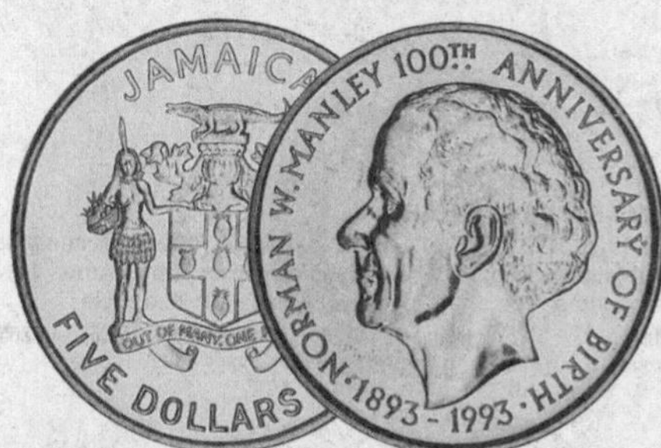

KM# 157 5 DOLLARS

Nickel Plated Steel **Ruler:** Elizabeth II **Subject:** Centennial - Birth of Norman Manley **Obv:** Arms with supporters **Rev:** Head left

Date	Mintage	VF20	XF40	MS60	MS63	MS65
1993	—	—	—	—	2.50	4.00

KM# 157a 5 DOLLARS

18.50 g., 0.500 Silver 0.2974 oz. ASW **Ruler:** Elizabeth II **Subject:** Centennial - Birth of Norman Manley **Obv:** Arms with supporters **Rev:** Head left

Date	Mintage	VF20	XF40	MS60	MS63	MS65
1993	Est. 2000	PF63 25.00	PF65 35.00			

KM# 163 5 DOLLARS

4.30 g., Nickel Plated Steel, 21.5 mm. **Ruler:** Elizabeth II **Series:** National Heroes **Subject:** Norman Manley **Obv:** National arms **Obv. Legend:** JAMAICA **Rev:** Head left **Edge:** Reeded

Date	Mintage	VF20	XF40	MS60	MS63	MS65
1994	—	—	0.75	1.50	2.00	2.50
1995	—	—	0.75	1.50	2.00	2.50
1995	—	PF65 5.00				
1996	—	—	0.75	1.50	2.00	2.50
2000	—	—	0.75	1.50	2.00	2.50
2000	—	PF65 5.00				

KM# 60 10 DOLLARS

49.20 g., 0.925 Silver 1.4632 oz. ASW, 45 mm. **Ruler:** Elizabeth II **Subject:** 10th Anniversary of Independence **Obv:** Arms with supporters **Rev:** Conjoined heads facing each other above map

Date	Mintage	VF20	XF40	MS60	MS63	MS65
ND-1972	42,000	—	—	30.00	40.00	50.00
ND-1972	33,000	PF63 55.00	PF65 70.00			

KM# 63 10 DOLLARS

Copper-Nickel, 45 mm. **Ruler:** Elizabeth II **Subject:** Sir Henry Morgan **Obv:** Arms with supporters **Rev:** Bust 1/4 left

Date	Mintage	VF20	XF40	MS60	MS63	MS65
1974 FM (M)	15,000	—	—	—	6.00	7.50

KM# 63a 10 DOLLARS

42.80 g., 0.925 Silver 1.2728 oz. ASW, 45 mm. **Ruler:** Elizabeth II **Subject:** Sir Henry Morgan **Obv:** Arms with supporters **Rev:** Bust 1/4 left

Date	Mintage	VF20	XF40	MS60	MS63	MS65
1974 FM (P)	42,000	PF63 30.00	PF65 35.00			

KM# 66 10 DOLLARS

Copper-Nickel, 45 mm. **Ruler:** Elizabeth II **Subject:** Christopher Columbus **Obv:** Arms with supporters **Rev:** Bust looking left at right, ship at left

Date	Mintage	VF20	XF40	MS60	MS63	MS65
1975 FM (M)	30	—	—	—	—	—
1975 FM (U)	5,758	—	—	—	10.00	12.00

KM# 66a 10 DOLLARS

42.80 g., 0.925 Silver 1.2728 oz. ASW, 45 mm. **Ruler:** Elizabeth II **Subject:** Christopher Columbus **Obv:** Arms with supporters **Rev:** Bust looking left at right, ship at left

Date	Mintage	VF20	XF40	MS60	MS63	MS65
1975 FM (P)	29,000	PF63 30.00	PF65 35.00			

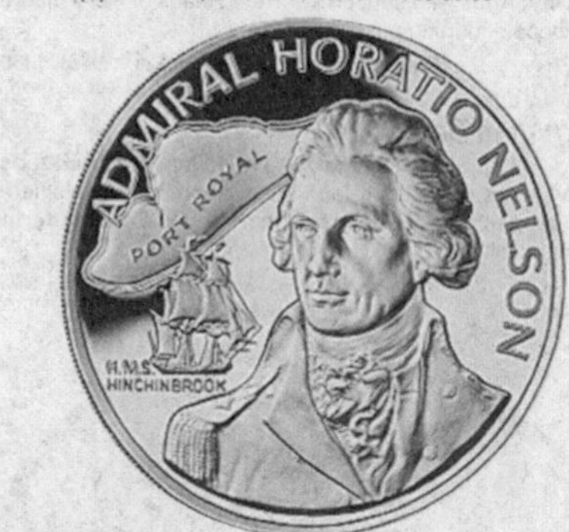

KM# 71 10 DOLLARS

Copper-Nickel, 45 mm. **Ruler:** Elizabeth II **Subject:** Admiral Horatio Nelson **Obv:** Arms with supporters **Rev:** Uniformed bust 1/4 left, map and ship at far left

Date	Mintage	VF20	XF40	MS60	MS63	MS65
1976 FM (M)	27	—	—	—	—	—
1976 FM (U)	2,302	—	—	—	12.00	15.00

KM# 71a 10 DOLLARS

42.80 g., 0.925 Silver 1.2728 oz. ASW, 45 mm. **Ruler:** Elizabeth II **Subject:** Admiral Horation Nelson **Obv:** Arms with supporters **Rev:** Uniformed bust 1/4 left with ship and map at far left

Date	Mintage	VF20	XF40	MS60	MS63	MS65
1976 FM (P)	31,000	PF63 30.00	PF65 35.00			

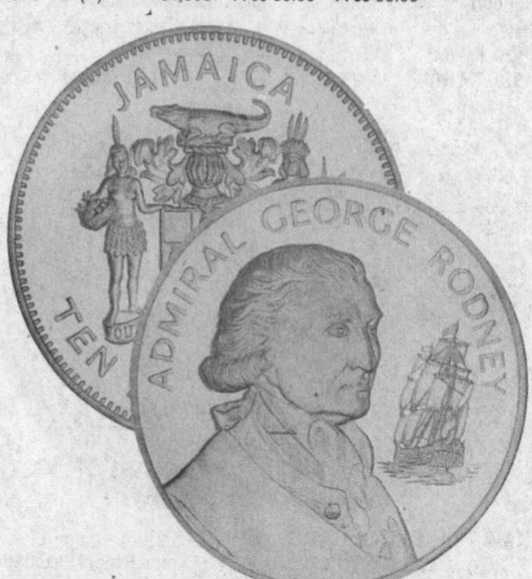

KM# 74 10 DOLLARS

Copper-Nickel, 45 mm. **Ruler:** Elizabeth II **Subject:** Admiral George Rodney **Obv:** Arms with supporters **Rev:** Bust right looking at ship at right

Date	Mintage	VF20	XF40	MS60	MS63	MS65
1977 FM (U)	847	—	—	—	25.00	30.00
1977 FM (M)	27	—	—	—	—	—

KM# 74a 10 DOLLARS
42.80 g., 0.925 Silver 1.2728 oz. ASW, 45 mm. **Ruler:** Elizabeth II **Subject:** Admiral George Rodney **Obv:** Arms with supporters **Rev:** Bust right looking at ship at right

Date	Mintage	VF20	XF40	MS60	MS63	MS65
1977 FM (P)	14,000	PF63 30.00	PF65 35.00			

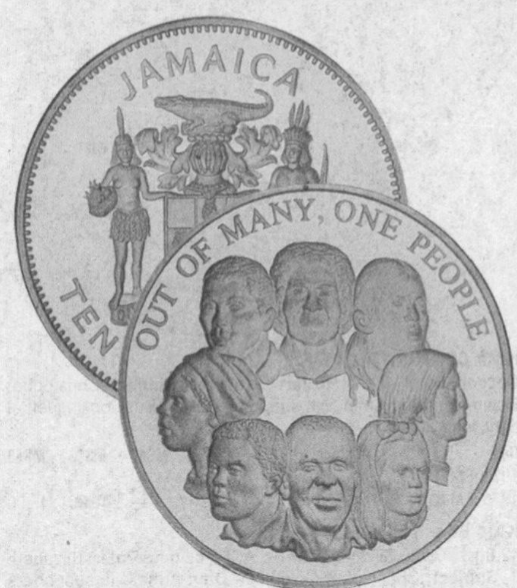

KM# 75 10 DOLLARS
Copper-Nickel, 45 mm. **Ruler:** Elizabeth II **Subject:** Jamaican Unity **Obv:** Arms with supporters **Rev:** Heads of many different ethnic people forming a circle

Date	Mintage	VF20	XF40	MS60	MS63	MS65
1978 FM (U)	1,559	—	—	—	17.00	20.00

KM# 75a 10 DOLLARS
42.80 g., 0.925 Silver 1.2728 oz. ASW, 45 mm. **Ruler:** Elizabeth II **Obv:** Arms with supporters **Rev:** Heads of many different ethnic people forming a circle **Edge:** Reeded **Edge Lettering:** Jamaican Unity

Date	Mintage	VF20	XF40	MS60	MS63	MS65
1978 FM (P)	12,000	PF63 30.00	PF65 35.00			

KM# 79 10 DOLLARS
Copper-Nickel, 45 mm. **Ruler:** Elizabeth II **Obv:** Arms with supporters **Rev:** Butterflies and flowers above date

Date	Mintage	VF20	XF40	MS60	MS63	MS65
1979 FM (M)	27	—	—	—	—	—
1979 FM (U)	2,608	—	—	27.00	35.00	45.00

KM# 79a 10 DOLLARS
42.80 g., 0.925 Silver 1.2728 oz. ASW, 45 mm. **Ruler:** Elizabeth II **Obv:** Arms with supporters **Rev:** Butterflies and flowers above date

Date	Mintage	VF20	XF40	MS60	MS63	MS65
1979 FM (P)	8,308	PF63 40.00	PF65 45.00			

KM# 80 10 DOLLARS
22.45 g., 0.925 Silver 0.6676 oz. ASW **Ruler:** Elizabeth II **Subject:** International Year of the Child **Obv:** Arms with supporters **Rev:** Map back of child playing cricket

Date	Mintage	VF20	XF40	MS60	MS63	MS65
1979	20,000	PF63 14.00	PF65 18.00			

KM# 86 10 DOLLARS
Copper-Nickel **Ruler:** Elizabeth II **Obv:** Arms with supporters **Rev:** Streamer-tailed Hummingbirds

Date	Mintage	VF20	XF40	MS60	MS63	MS65
1980 FM (M)	27	—	—	—	—	—
1980 FM (U)	5,668	—	—	15.00	20.00	25.00

KM# 86a 10 DOLLARS
22.45 g., 0.925 Silver 0.6676 oz. ASW **Ruler:** Elizabeth II **Obv:** Arms with supporters **Rev:** Streamer-tailed Hummingbirds

Date	Mintage	VF20	XF40	MS60	MS63	MS65
1980 FM (P)	5,394	PF63 35.00	PF65 40.00			

KM# 87 10 DOLLARS
30.28 g., 0.500 Silver 0.4868 oz. ASW **Ruler:** Elizabeth II **Subject:** 10th Anniversary of Caribbean Development Bank **Obv:** Arms with supporters **Rev:** Legend around globe, Horn of Plenty and fruit below

Date	Mintage	VF20	XF40	MS60	MS63	MS65
ND-1980 FM (P)	2,327	PF63 25.00	PF65 30.00			

KM# 92 10 DOLLARS
28.28 g., 0.925 Silver 0.841 oz. ASW **Ruler:** Elizabeth II **Subject:** Wedding of Prince Charles and Lady Diana **Obv:** Arms with supporters **Rev:** Conjoined busts right

Date	Mintage	VF20	XF40	MS60	MS63	MS65
1981	40,000	PF63 20.00	PF65 25.00			

KM# 93 10 DOLLARS
Copper-Nickel **Ruler:** Elizabeth II **Obv:** Arms with supporters **Rev:** American Crocodile above date

Date	Mintage	VF20	XF40	MS60	MS63	MS65
1981 FM (U)	804	—	—	30.00	35.00	40.00

KM# 93a 10 DOLLARS
22.45 g., 0.925 Silver 0.6676 oz. ASW **Ruler:** Elizabeth II **Obv:** Arms with supporters **Rev:** American Crocodile above date

Date	Mintage	VF20	XF40	MS60	MS63	MS65
1981 FM (P)	3,216	PF63 35.00	PF65 40.00			

KM# 97 10 DOLLARS
Copper-Nickel **Ruler:** Elizabeth II **Obv:** Arms with supporters **Rev:** Small Indian Mongoose

Date	Mintage	VF20	XF40	MS60	MS63	MS65
1982 FM (U)	—	—	—	25.00	30.00	35.00

KM# 97a 10 DOLLARS
22.45 g., 0.925 Silver 0.6676 oz. ASW **Ruler:** Elizabeth II **Obv:** Arms with supporters **Rev:** Small Indian Mongoose

Date	Mintage	VF20	XF40	MS60	MS63	MS65
1982 FM (P)	1,852	PF63 50.00	PF65 60.00			

KM# 98 10 DOLLARS
22.45 g., 0.925 Silver 0.6676 oz. ASW **Ruler:** Elizabeth II **Subject:** Soccer - World Championships **Obv:** Arms with supporters **Rev:** Standing player with ball divides circle

Date	Mintage	VF20	XF40	MS60	MS63	MS65
1982	9,775	PF63 14.00	PF65 18.00			

KM# 109 10 DOLLARS

Copper-Nickel **Ruler:** Elizabeth II **Subject:** 21st Anniversary of Independence **Obv:** Arms with supporters **Rev:** Numeral 21 divides heads facing above dates and braided rope

Date	Mintage	VF20	XF40	MS60	MS63	MS65
ND-1983 FM (U)	1,320	—	—	—	12.00	15.00

KM# 109a 10 DOLLARS

22.45 g., 0.925 Silver 0.6676 oz. ASW **Ruler:** Elizabeth II **Subject:** 21st Anniversary of Independence **Obv:** Arms with supporters **Rev:** Numeral 21 divides heads facing above dates and braided rope

Date	Mintage	VF20	XF40	MS60	MS63	MS65
ND-1983 FM (P)	1,187	PF63 30.00	PF65 35.00			

KM# 111 10 DOLLARS

22.45 g., 0.925 Silver 0.6676 oz. ASW **Ruler:** Elizabeth II **Subject:** Royal visit **Obv:** Arms with supporters **Rev:** Conjoined busts left

Date	Mintage	VF20	XF40	MS60	MS63	MS65
1983	—	PF63 20.00	PF65 25.00			

KM# 114 10 DOLLARS

Copper-Nickel **Ruler:** Elizabeth II **Obv:** Arms with supporters **Rev:** Blue Marlin breaking water

Date	Mintage	VF20	XF40	MS60	MS63	MS65
1984 FM (U)	—	—	—	20.00	25.00	30.00

KM# 114a 10 DOLLARS

22.45 g., 0.925 Silver 0.6676 oz. ASW **Ruler:** Elizabeth II **Obv:** Arms with supporters **Rev:** Blue Marlin breaking water

Date	Mintage	VF20	XF40	MS60	MS63	MS65
1984 FM (P)	335	PF63 75.00	PF65 85.00			

KM# 115 10 DOLLARS

22.45 g., 0.925 Silver 0.6676 oz. ASW **Ruler:** Elizabeth II **Subject:** Decade for Women **Obv:** Arms with supporters **Rev:** Woman with basket on head, map behind

Date	Mintage	VF20	XF40	MS60	MS63	MS65
1984	1,100	PF63 30.00	PF65 45.00			
1985	610	PF63 55.00	PF65 65.00			

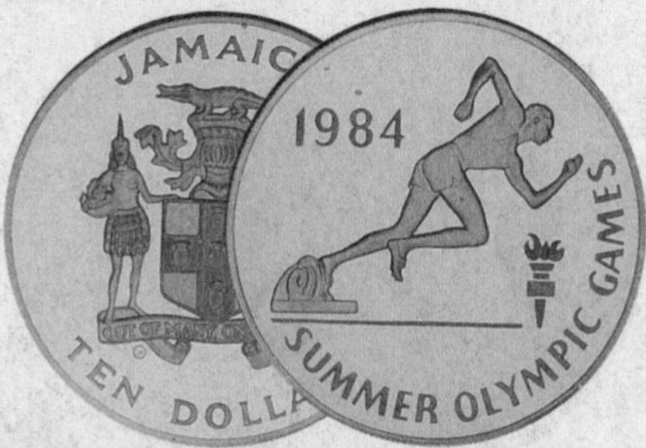

KM# 125 10 DOLLARS

22.45 g., 0.925 Silver 0.6676 oz. ASW **Ruler:** Elizabeth II **Subject:** Summer Olympics **Obv:** Arms with supporters **Rev:** Sprinter

Date	Mintage	VF20	XF40	MS60	MS63	MS65
1984	10,000	PF63 14.00	PF65 18.00			

KM# 123 10 DOLLARS

22.45 g., 0.925 Silver 0.6676 oz. ASW **Ruler:** Elizabeth II **Subject:** Year of Youth **Obv:** Arms with supporters **Rev:** Collage of many youth's heads

Date	Mintage	VF20	XF40	MS60	MS63	MS65
1985	1,000	PF63 35.00	PF65 45.00			

KM# 121 10 DOLLARS

22.45 g., 0.925 Silver 0.6676 oz. ASW **Ruler:** Elizabeth II **Subject:** XIII Commonwealth Games - Edinburgh **Obv:** Arms with supporters **Rev:** Relay runners

Date	Mintage	VF20	XF40	MS60	MS63	MS65
1986	50,000	—	—	—	13.50	18.00

KM# 121a 10 DOLLARS

28.28 g., 0.925 Silver 0.841 oz. ASW **Ruler:** Elizabeth II **Subject:** XIII Commonwealth Games - Edinburgh **Obv:** Arms with supporters **Rev:** Relay runners

Date	Mintage	VF20	XF40	MS60	MS63	MS65
1986	20,000	PF65 24.50				

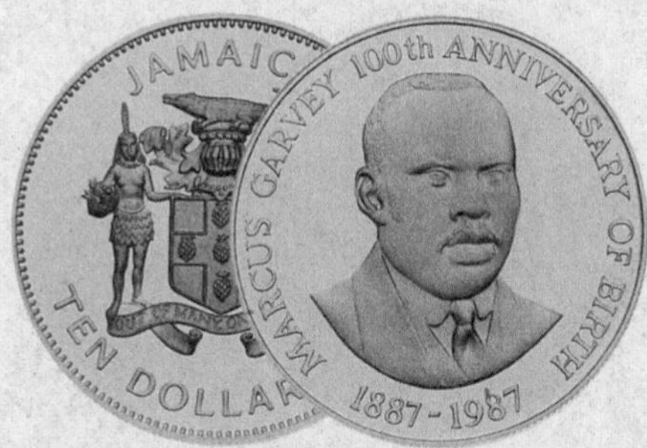

KM# 128 10 DOLLARS

22.45 g., 0.925 Silver 0.6676 oz. ASW **Ruler:** Elizabeth II **Subject:** 100th Anniversary - Birth of Marcus Garvey **Obv:** Arms with supporters **Rev:** Bust 1/4 right

Date	Mintage	VF20	XF40	MS60	MS63	MS65
1987	1,000	PF63 40.00	PF65 50.00			

KM# 133 10 DOLLARS

22.45 g., 0.925 Silver 0.6676 oz. ASW, 38.6 mm. **Ruler:** Elizabeth II **Subject:** 25th Anniversary of Independence **Obv:** Crowned bust right **Rev:** Arms with supporters

Date	Mintage	VF20	XF40	MS60	MS63	MS65
1987	Est. 500	PF63 42.00	PF65 47.00			

KM# 138 10 DOLLARS

Copper-Nickel **Ruler:** Elizabeth II **Subject:** Year of the Worker **Obv:** Arms with supporters **Rev:** Two figures standing on board with shovel and pitch-fork above heads

Date	Mintage	VF20	XF40	MS60	MS63	MS65
1988	—	—	—	—	4.00	6.00

KM# 138a 10 DOLLARS

22.45 g., 0.925 Silver 0.6676 oz. ASW **Ruler:** Elizabeth II **Subject:** Year of the Worker **Obv:** Arms with supporters **Rev:** Two standing figures on board with pitch fork and shovel raised above heads

Date	Mintage	VF20	XF40	MS60	MS63	MS65
1988	Est. 1000	PF63 42.00	PF65 47.00			

KM# 140 10 DOLLARS

Copper-Nickel **Ruler:** Elizabeth II **Subject:** Columbus' Discovery of the New World **Obv:** Arms with supporters **Rev:** Several ships at sea

Date	Mintage	VF20	XF40	MS60	MS63	MS65
1989	—	—	—	—	6.00	8.00

KM# 140a 10 DOLLARS

22.45 g., 0.925 Silver 0.6676 oz. ASW **Ruler:** Elizabeth II **Subject:** Columbus' Discovery of the New World **Obv:** Arms with supporters **Rev:** Several ships at sea

Date	Mintage	VF20	XF40	MS60	MS63	MS65
1989	—	PF63 25.00	PF65 30.00			

KM# 144 10 DOLLARS
Copper-Nickel **Ruler:** Elizabeth II **Subject:** Columbus' Arrival in New World **Obv:** Arms with supporters **Rev:** Bust 1/4 right and ship at far right

Date	Mintage	VF20	XF40	MS60	MS63	MS65
1990	—	—	—	—	4.00	6.00
1990	—	PF65 15.00				

KM# 144a 10 DOLLARS
22.45 g., 0.925 Silver 0.6676 oz. ASW **Ruler:** Elizabeth II **Subject:** Columbus' Arrival in New World **Obv:** Arms with supporters **Rev:** Bust 1/4 right and ship at far right

Date	Mintage	VF20	XF40	MS60	MS63	MS65
1990	Est. 11000	PF65 32.00				

KM# 148 10 DOLLARS
Copper-Nickel **Ruler:** Elizabeth II **Subject:** Arrival in the New World **Obv:** Arms with supporters **Rev:** Columbus' ship - Pinta

Date	Mintage	VF20	XF40	MS60	MS63	MS65
1991	—	—	—	—	4.00	6.00
1991	—	PF65 18.00				

KM# 148a 10 DOLLARS
22.45 g., 0.925 Silver 0.6676 oz. ASW **Ruler:** Elizabeth II **Subject:** Arrival in the New World **Obv:** Arms with supporters **Rev:** Columbus' ship - Pinta

Date	Mintage	VF20	XF40	MS60	MS63	MS65
1991	Est. 5500	PF63 28.00	PF65 32.00			

KM# 152 10 DOLLARS
22.45 g., 0.925 Silver 0.6676 oz. ASW **Ruler:** Elizabeth II **Subject:** 500th Anniversary of Columbus' Arrival **Obv:** Arms with supporters **Rev:** Ship

Date	Mintage	VF20	XF40	MS60	MS63	MS65
1992	5,500	PF63 28.00	PF65 32.00			

KM# 155 10 DOLLARS
22.45 g., 0.925 Silver 0.6676 oz. ASW **Ruler:** Elizabeth II **Subject:** 40th Anniversary - Coronation of Queen Elizabeth II **Obv:** Arms with supporters **Rev:** Crowned bust facing holding scepters

Date	Mintage	VF20	XF40	MS60	MS63	MS65
1993	Est. 5500	PF63 28.00	PF65 32.00			

KM# 161 10 DOLLARS
28.28 g., 0.925 Silver 0.841 oz. ASW **Ruler:** Elizabeth II **Subject:** Royal Visit **Obv:** Arms with supporters **Rev:** Standing sailor beating drum on map of Jamaica to left of ship with cameo above

Date	Mintage	VF20	XF40	MS60	MS63	MS65
1994	—	PF63 28.00	PF65 32.00			

KM# 168 10 DOLLARS
20.00 g., 0.500 Silver 0.3215 oz. ASW **Ruler:** Elizabeth II **Subject:** Ernest Hemingway 1899-1961 **Obv:** Arms with supporters **Rev:** Bust at left looking right, ship at sea at right

Date	Mintage	VF20	XF40	MS60	MS63	MS65
1994	Est. 10000	—	—	—	12.00	18.00

KM# 187 10 DOLLARS
28.30 g., 0.925 Silver 0.8416 oz. ASW, 38.6 mm. **Ruler:** Elizabeth II **Obv:** Arms with supporters **Rev:** Two Black-billed parrots **Edge:** Reeded

Date	Mintage	VF20	XF40	MS60	MS63	MS65
1995	1,000	PF63 65.00	PF65 80.00			

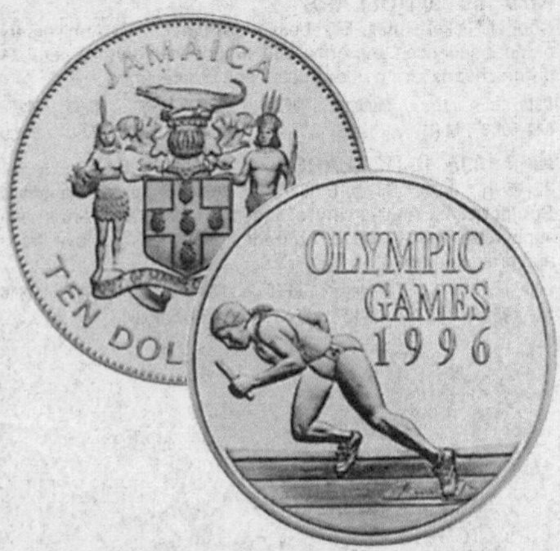

KM# 176 10 DOLLARS
28.28 g., 0.925 Silver 0.841 oz. ASW **Ruler:** Elizabeth II **Subject:** Olympic Games - 1996 **Obv:** Arms with supporters **Rev:** Relay runner left

Date	Mintage	VF20	XF40	MS60	MS63	MS65
1996	Est. 10000	PF63 25.00	PF65 30.00			

KM# 191 10 DOLLARS
28.28 g., 0.925 Silver 0.841 oz. ASW, 38.61 mm. **Ruler:** Elizabeth II **Subject:** Elizabeth II, 70th Birthday

Date	Mintage	VF20	XF40	MS60	MS63	MS65
1996	—	PF63 40.00	PF65 50.00			

KM# 192 10 DOLLARS
28.28 g., 0.925 Silver 0.841 oz. ASW, 38.61 mm. **Ruler:** Elizabeth II **Subject:** Endangered Wildlife **Rev:** Manati

Date	Mintage	VF20	XF40	MS60	MS63	MS65
1997	500	PF63 75.00	PF65 95.00			

KM# 194 10 DOLLARS
28.28 g., 0.925 Silver 0.841 oz. ASW, 38.61 mm. **Ruler:** Elizabeth II **Subject:** 16th World Cup **Rev:** Soccer player and stadium

Date	Mintage	VF20	XF40	MS60	MS63	MS65
1998	500	PF63 75.00	PF65 95.00			

KM# 181 10 DOLLARS
5.94 g., Nickel Plated Steel **Ruler:** Elizabeth II **Series:** National Heroes **Subject:** George William Gordon **Obv:** National arms **Obv. Legend:** JAMAICA / TEN DOLLARS - (date) **Rev:** Bust facing **Edge:** Plain **Shape:** Scalloped **Note:** Diameter varies: 24-24.6.

Date	Mintage	VF20	XF40	MS60	MS63	MS65
1999	—	—	—	—	2.50	3.50
2000	—	—	—	—	2.50	3.50
2000	—	PF65 9.00				

KM# 195 10 DOLLARS
28.28 g., 0.925 Silver 0.841 oz. ASW, 38.61 mm. **Ruler:** Elizabeth II **Subject:** Millenium **Rev:** Family before a rising sun

Date	Mintage	VF20	XF40	MS60	MS63	MS65
1999	500	PF63 75.00	PF65 95.00			

KM# 196 10 DOLLARS
28.28 g., 0.925 Silver 0.841 oz. ASW, 38.61 mm. **Ruler:** Elizabeth II **Subject:** Summer Olympics, Sydney **Rev:** Two Hurdlers

Date	Mintage	VF20	XF40	MS60	MS63	MS65
2000	—	PF63 75.00	PF65 95.00			

KM# 61 20 DOLLARS
15.75 g., 0.500 Gold 0.2532 oz. AGW **Ruler:** Elizabeth II **Subject:** 10th Anniversary of Independence **Obv:** Arms with supporters and dates within rope wreath **Rev:** Map of Jamaica above ships

Date	Mintage	VF20	XF40	MS60	MS63	MS65
ND-1972	30,000	—	—	—	—	405
ND-1972	20,000	PF65 450				

KM# 182 20 DOLLARS
7.80 g., Bi-Metallic Copper-Nickel center in Nickel-Brass ring, 23 mm. **Ruler:** Elizabeth II **Series:** National Heroes **Subject:** Marcus Garvey **Obv:** Value above national arms within circle **Obv. Legend:** JAMAICA **Rev:** Head 1/4 right within circle **Edge:** Segmented reeding

Date	Mintage	VF20	XF40	MS60	MS63	MS65
2000	—	—	—	—	2.50	3.50
2000	—	PF65 7.00				

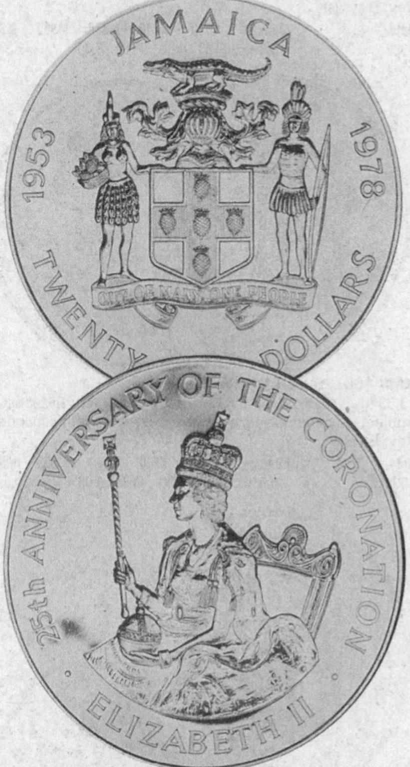

KM# 76 25 DOLLARS
136.08 g., 0.925 Silver 4.0469 oz. ASW **Ruler:** Elizabeth II **Subject:** 25th Anniversary of Coronation **Obv:** Arms with supporters **Rev:** Queen left on throne with crown, sceptre and orb

Date	Mintage	VF20	XF40	MS60	MS63	MS65
ND-1978	11,000	—	—	—	94.00	105
ND-1978	22,000	PF65 100				

KM# 81 25 DOLLARS
136.08 g., 0.925 Silver 4.0469 oz. ASW **Ruler:** Elizabeth II **Subject:** 10th Anniversary - Investiture of Prince Charles **Obv:** Arms with supporters **Rev:** Crowned half figure left in regal dress

Date	Mintage	VF20	XF40	MS60	MS63	MS65
ND-1979	16,000	—	—	—	99.00	110
ND-1979	25,000	PF65 105				

KM# 88 25 DOLLARS
136.08 g., 0.500 Silver 2.1875 oz. ASW **Ruler:** Elizabeth II **Subject:** 1980 Olympics **Obv:** Arms with supporters **Rev:** Circle of heads of previous Gold Medal winners

Date	Mintage	VF20	XF40	MS60	MS63	MS65
1980	—	—	—	50.00	70.00	90.00
1980	6,969	PF63 90.00	PF65 110			

KM# 94 25 DOLLARS
136.08 g., 0.925 Silver 4.0469 oz. ASW **Ruler:** Elizabeth II **Subject:** Wedding of Prince Charles and Lady Diana **Obv:** Crowned bust right **Rev:** Conjoined busts of royal couple

Date	Mintage	VF20	XF40	MS60	MS63	MS65
1981 (T)	6,450	PF63 105	PF65 115			

KM# 99 25 DOLLARS
136.08 g., 0.925 Silver 4.0469 oz. ASW **Ruler:** Elizabeth II **Subject:** World Championship Soccer Games **Obv:** Arms with supporters **Rev:** Player kicking ball to right **Note:** Illustration reduced.

Date	Mintage	VF20	XF40	MS60	MS63	MS65
1982	30,000	PF63 97.00	PF65 107			

KM# 112 25 DOLLARS
136.08 g., 0.925 Silver 4.0469 oz. ASW **Ruler:** Elizabeth II **Subject:** Royal Visit **Obv:** Arms with supporters **Rev:** Conjoined busts left

Date	Mintage	VF20	XF40	MS60	MS63	MS65
1983	—	PF63 93.00	PF65 105			

KM# 116 25 DOLLARS
136.08 g., 0.925 Silver 4.0469 oz. ASW **Ruler:** Elizabeth II **Subject:** Summer Olympics **Obv:** Arms with supporters **Rev:** Sprinter

Date	Mintage	VF20	XF40	MS60	MS63	MS65
1984	3,300	PF63 105	PF65 115			

KM# 126 25 DOLLARS
23.44 g., 0.925 Silver 0.6971 oz. ASW **Ruler:** Elizabeth II **Subject:** Decade For Women **Obv:** Arms with supporters **Rev:**

Map and female with basket of fruit on head facing **Note:** Mule. Denomination error for KM#115.

Date	Mintage	VF20	XF40	MS60	MS63	MS65
1984	—	PF63 100	PF65 125			

KM# 119 25 DOLLARS
136.08 g., 0.925 Silver 4.0469 oz. ASW **Ruler:** Elizabeth II **Subject:** Humpback Whale Protection **Obv:** Arms with supporters **Rev:** Value and map divides humpback whales

Date	Mintage	VF20	XF40	MS60	MS63	MS65
1985	2,600	PF63 105	PF65 115			

KM# 127 25 DOLLARS
23.50 g., 0.925 Silver 0.6989 oz. ASW **Ruler:** Elizabeth II **Subject:** World Championship Soccer - Mexico **Obv:** Arms with supporters **Rev:** Date within globe above two soccer players

Date	Mintage	VF20	XF40	MS60	MS63	MS65
1986	—	—	—	—	30.00	40.00

KM# 130 25 DOLLARS
37.78 g., 0.925 Silver 1.1236 oz. ASW **Ruler:** Elizabeth II **Subject:** 25th Anniversary of Independence **Obv:** Crowned bust right **Rev:** Arms with supporters

Date	Mintage	VF20	XF40	MS60	MS63	MS65
1987	1,900	PF63 35.00	PF65 45.00			

KM# 141 25 DOLLARS
23.33 g., 0.925 Silver 0.6938 oz. ASW **Ruler:** Elizabeth II **Subject:** Olympics **Obv:** Arms with supporters **Rev:** Relay runners

Date	Mintage	VF20	XF40	MS60	MS63	MS65
1988	Est. 15000	PF63 14.00	PF65 18.00			

KM# 142 25 DOLLARS
23.33 g., 0.925 Silver 0.6938 oz. ASW **Ruler:** Elizabeth II **Subject:** World Championship Soccer **Obv:** Arms with supporters **Rev:** Soccer player

Date	Mintage	VF20	XF40	MS60	MS63	MS65
1990	—	PF63 15.00	PF65 20.00			

KM# 150 25 DOLLARS
23.33 g., 0.925 Silver 0.6938 oz. ASW **Ruler:** Elizabeth II **Subject:** Columbus' Jamaican Landfall of 1494 **Obv:** Arms with supporters **Rev:** Bust of Columbus at left, Queen Isabella at right, ship between, Island of Jamaica below

Date	Mintage	VF20	XF40	MS60	MS63	MS65
1991 Matte	650	—	—	—	60.00	75.00
1991	Est. 25000	PF63 18.00	PF65 25.00			

KM# 151 25 DOLLARS
23.33 g., 0.925 Silver 0.6938 oz. ASW **Ruler:** Elizabeth II **Subject:** Discovery of America - Landfall **Obv:** Arms with supporters **Rev:** Bust 1/4 right, ship within globe to right

Date	Mintage	VF20	XF40	MS60	MS63	MS65
1992 Matte	550	—	—	—	60.00	75.00
1992	—	PF63 18.00	PF65 25.00			

KM# 159 25 DOLLARS
23.33 g., 0.925 Silver 0.6938 oz. ASW **Ruler:** Elizabeth II **Subject:** Summer Olympic Games **Obv:** Arms with supporters **Rev:** Bicyclists

Date	Mintage	VF20	XF40	MS60	MS63	MS65
1992	15,000	PF63 14.00	PF65 18.00			

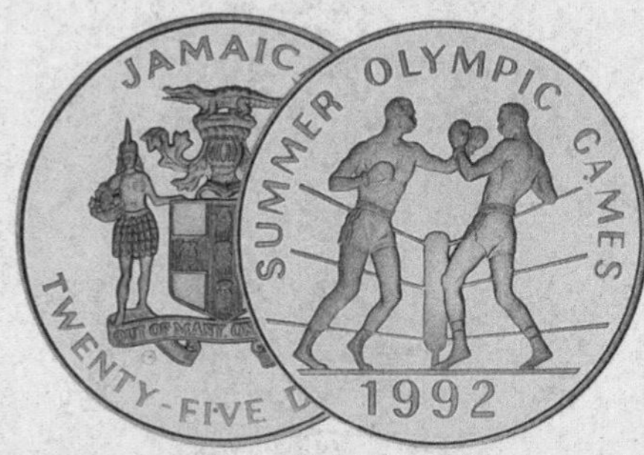

KM# 160 25 DOLLARS
23.33 g., 0.925 Silver 0.6938 oz. ASW **Ruler:** Elizabeth II **Subject:** Summer Olympic Games **Obv:** Arms with supporters **Rev:** Boxers

Date	Mintage	VF20	XF40	MS60	MS63	MS65
1992	15,000	PF63 14.00	PF65 18.00			

KM# 165 25 DOLLARS
28.20 g., 0.925 Silver 0.8387 oz. ASW, 38.57 mm. **Ruler:** Elizabeth II **Subject:** XV World Cup Soccer - USA **Obv:** National arms **Rev:** Soccer player chasing ball, large ball outline in background **Edge:** Reeded

Date	Mintage	VF20	XF40	MS60	MS63	MS65
1994	Est. 10000	PF63 25.00	PF65 35.00			

KM# 169 25 DOLLARS
31.47 g., 0.925 Silver 0.9359 oz. ASW **Ruler:** Elizabeth II **Subject:** Queen Elizabeth's Wedding Anniversary and Queen Mother's Birthday **Obv:** Arms with supporters **Rev:** Queen Mother's wedding portrait

Date	Mintage	VF20	XF40	MS60	MS63	MS65
1994	Est. 20000	PF63 20.00	PF65 25.00			

KM# 166 25 DOLLARS
28.20 g., 0.925 Silver 0.8387 oz. ASW **Ruler:** Elizabeth II **Subject:** 25th Anniversary - Caribbean Development Bank **Obv:** Arms with supporters **Rev:** Map within grid on globe

Date	Mintage	VF20	XF40	MS60	MS63	MS65
1995	Est. 2000	—	—	—	40.00	50.00

KM# 170 25 DOLLARS
28.28 g., 0.925 Silver 0.841 oz. ASW **Ruler:** Elizabeth II **Obv:** Arms with supporters **Rev:** Tycho Brahe at right, world globe at left

Date	Mintage	VF20	XF40	MS60	MS63	MS65
1995	Est. 10000	PF63 22.00	PF65 28.00			

KM# 173 25 DOLLARS
28.28 g., 0.925 Silver 0.841 oz. ASW **Ruler:** Elizabeth II **Subject:** U.N. 50th Anniversary **Obv:** Arms with supporters **Rev:** Embracing children above logo and numeral 50

Date	Mintage	VF20	XF40	MS60	MS63	MS65
ND-1995	Est. 105000	PF63 20.00	PF65 25.00			

KM# 174 25 DOLLARS
28.28 g., 0.925 Silver 0.841 oz. ASW **Ruler:** Elizabeth II **Subject:** Endangered Wildlife **Obv:** Arms with supporters **Rev:** Black-billed Amazon Parrots

Date	Mintage	VF20	XF40	MS60	MS63	MS65
1995	Est. 10000	PF63 25.00	PF65 35.00			

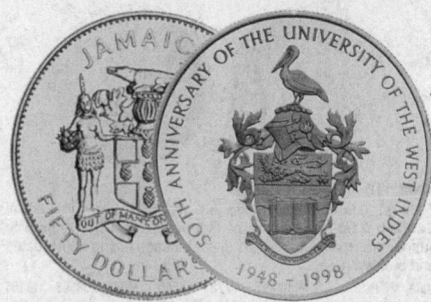

KM# 193 25 DOLLARS
28.28 g., 0.925 Silver 0.841 oz. ASW partially gilt, 38.61 mm. **Ruler:** Elizabeth II **Subject:** Elizabeth II and Prince Philip 50th Wedding Anniversary

Date	Mintage	VF20	XF40	MS60	MS63	MS65
1997	Est. 25000	PF65 55.00				

KM# 177 25 DOLLARS
28.28 g., 0.925 Silver 0.841 oz. ASW **Ruler:** Elizabeth II **Subject:** World Cup Soccer **Obv:** Arms with supporters **Rev:** Soccer player

Date	Mintage	VF20	XF40	MS60	MS63	MS65
1998	Est. 10000	PF63 25.00	PF65 35.00			

KM# 183 25 DOLLARS
28.28 g., 0.925 Silver 0.841 oz. ASW, 38.6 mm. **Ruler:** Elizabeth II **Series:** Olympics **Obv:** Arms with supporters **Rev:** Two women hurdlers **Edge:** Reeded

Date	Mintage	VF20	XF40	MS60	MS63	MS65
2000	5,500	PF63 35.00	PF65 50.00			

KM# 171 50 DOLLARS
28.28 g., 0.925 Silver 0.841 oz. ASW **Ruler:** Elizabeth II **Subject:** 50th Anniversary The Hon Robert Nesta Marley **Obv:** Arms with supporters **Rev:** Head left

Date	Mintage	VF20	XF40	MS60	MS63	MS65
1995	30,000	PF63 25.00	PF65 35.00			

KM# 175 50 DOLLARS
7.78 g., 0.5833 Gold 0.1458 oz. AGW **Ruler:** Elizabeth II **Obv:** Arms with supporters **Rev:** Queen Mother's wedding portrait

Date	Mintage	VF20	XF40	MS60	MS63	MS65
1995	Est. 5000	PF65 235				

KM# 179 50 DOLLARS
28.28 g., 0.925 Silver 0.841 oz. ASW **Ruler:** Elizabeth II **Subject:** 50th Anniversary - University of the West Indies **Obv:** Arms with supporters **Rev:** University arms with pelican standing at top

Date	Mintage	VF20	XF40	MS60	MS63	MS65
1998	20,000	PF65 35.00				

KM# 67 100 DOLLARS
7.83 g., 0.900 Gold 0.2266 oz. AGW **Ruler:** Elizabeth II **Subject:** Christopher Columbus **Obv:** Arms with supporters **Rev:** Bust with hat 3/4 left

Date	Mintage	VF20	XF40	MS60	MS63	MS65
1975 FM (M)	100	—	—	—	425	475
1975 FM (U)	10,000	—	—	—	345	385
1975 FM (P)	21,000	PF63 320	PF65 340			

KM# 72 100 DOLLARS
7.83 g., 0.900 Gold 0.2266 oz. AGW **Ruler:** Elizabeth II **Subject:** Admiral Horatio Nelson **Obv:** Arms with supporters **Rev:** Uniformed bust looking left, ship and map at left

Date	Mintage	VF20	XF40	MS60	MS63	MS65
1976 FM (M)	100	—	—	—	—	425
1976 FM (P)	8,952	PF65 365				

KM# 77 100 DOLLARS
11.34 g., 0.900 Gold 0.3281 oz. AGW **Ruler:** Elizabeth II **Subject:** 25th Anniversary of Coronation of Elizabeth II **Obv:** Arms with supporters **Rev:** Queen on throne with crown, sceptre and orb

Date	Mintage	VF20	XF40	MS60	MS63	MS65
ND-1978	—	—	—	—	—	525
ND-1978	5,835	PF65 510				

KM# 82 100 DOLLARS
11.34 g., 0.900 Gold 0.3281 oz. AGW **Ruler:** Elizabeth II **Subject:** 10th Anniversary - Investiture of Prince Charles **Obv:** Arms with supporters **Rev:** Crowned half figure left in regal dress

Date	Mintage	VF20	XF40	MS60	MS63	MS65
ND-1979	2,891	PF65 530				

KM# 110 100 DOLLARS
7.13 g., 0.900 Gold 0.2063 oz. AGW **Ruler:** Elizabeth II **Subject:** 21st Anniversary of Independence **Obv:** Arms with supporters **Rev:** Number 21 divides heads facing above dates and braided rope

Date	Mintage	VF20	XF40	MS60	MS63	MS65
ND-1983 FM (P)	638	PF63 325	PF65 375			

KM# 117 100 DOLLARS
7.13 g., 0.900 Gold 0.2063 oz. AGW **Ruler:** Elizabeth II **Subject:** 100th Anniversary - Birth of Bustamante **Obv:** Arms with supporters **Rev:** Bust 1/4 left

Date	Mintage	VF20	XF40	MS60	MS63	MS65
1984 FM (P)	531	PF65 375				

KM# 122 100 DOLLARS
136.08 g., 0.925 Silver 4.0469 oz. ASW **Ruler:** Elizabeth II **Subject:** World Championship Soccer - Mexico **Obv:** Arms with supporters **Rev:** Date within globe above two soccer players

Date	Mintage	VF20	XF40	MS60	MS63	MS65
1986	20,000	PF63 102	PF65 115			

KM# 129 100 DOLLARS
11.34 g., 0.900 Gold 0.3281 oz. AGW **Ruler:** Elizabeth II **Subject:** 100th Anniversary - Birth of Marcus Garvey **Obv:** Arms with supporters **Rev:** Portrait of Garvey facing

Date	Mintage	VF20	XF40	MS60	MS63	MS65
1987	500	PF63 525	PF65 600			

KM# 139 100 DOLLARS
136.08 g., 0.925 Silver 4.0469 oz. ASW **Ruler:** Elizabeth II **Obv:** Arms with supporters **Rev:** Streamer-tailed Hummingbird **Note:** Illustration reduced.

Date	Mintage	VF20	XF40	MS60	MS63	MS65
1987	—	PF63 105	PF65 117			

KM# 135 100 DOLLARS
136.08 g., 0.925 Silver 4.0469 oz. ASW **Ruler:** Elizabeth II **Subject:** Summer Olympics - Relay Race **Obv:** Arms with supporters **Rev:** Handoff of baton during relay race

Date	Mintage	VF20	XF40	MS60	MS63	MS65
1988	15,000	PF63 99.00	PF65 110			

KM# 143 100 DOLLARS
136.08 g., 0.925 Silver 4.0469 oz. ASW **Ruler:** Elizabeth II **Subject:** World Championship Soccer **Obv:** Arms with supporters **Rev:** Soccer player

Date	Mintage	VF20	XF40	MS60	MS63	MS65
1990	—	PF63 110	PF65 122			

KM# 149 100 DOLLARS
137.80 g., 0.925 Silver 4.0981 oz. ASW **Ruler:** Elizabeth II **Subject:** Olympics - Boxing **Obv:** Arms with supporters **Rev:** Boxers

Date	Mintage	VF20	XF40	MS60	MS63	MS65
1992	10,000	PF63 100	PF65 112			

KM# 158 100 DOLLARS
11.34 g., 0.900 Gold 0.3281 oz. AGW **Ruler:** Elizabeth II **Subject:** Centennial - Birth of Norman Manley **Obv:** Arms with supporters **Rev:** Head left

Date	Mintage	VF20	XF40	MS60	MS63	MS65
1993	500	PF63 525	PF65 600			

KM# 172 100 DOLLARS
15.98 g., 0.9167 Gold 0.471 oz. AGW, 28.4 mm. **Ruler:** Elizabeth II **Subject:** Robert Marley **Obv:** Arms with supporters **Rev:** Head left

Date	Mintage	VF20	XF40	MS60	MS63	MS65
1995	2,000	PF65 775				

KM# 178 100 DOLLARS
15.98 g., 0.999 Gold 0.5133 oz. AGW **Ruler:** Elizabeth II **Subject:** World Cup Soccer **Obv:** Arms with supporters **Rev:** Soccer player

Date	Mintage	VF20	XF40	MS60	MS63	MS65
1998	—	PF63 825	PF65 875			

KM# 180 100 DOLLARS
15.97 g., 0.9167 Gold 0.4707 oz. AGW **Ruler:** Elizabeth II **Subject:** 50th Anniversary - University of the West Indies **Obv:** Arms with supporters **Rev:** University arms

Date	Mintage	VF20	XF40	MS60	MS63	MS65
1998	1,000	PF65 800				

KM# 188 100 DOLLARS
16.00 g., Gold, 28.3 mm. **Ruler:** Elizabeth II **Obv:** National arms **Obv. Legend:** JAMAICA **Rev:** Small family of four at center, rays above, water below **Rev. Legend:** ONE PEOPLE INTO THE MILLENIUM / 1999 - 2000 **Edge:** Reeded

Date	Mintage	VF20	XF40	MS60	MS63	MS65
2000	—	PF65 900				

KM# 78 250 DOLLARS
43.22 g., 0.900 Gold 1.2506 oz. AGW **Ruler:** Elizabeth II **Subject:** 25th Anniversary of Coronation **Obv:** Arms with supporters **Rev:** Queen seated on throne with crown, sceptre and orb

Date	Mintage	XF40	MS60	MS63	MS65	MS66
ND-1978	3,005	PF65 1,850	PF67 2,150			

KM# 83 250 DOLLARS
43.22 g., 0.900 Gold 1.2506 oz. AGW **Ruler:** Elizabeth II **Subject:** 10th Anniversary - Investiture of Prince Charles **Obv:** Arms with supporters **Rev:** Crowned half figure left in regal dress

Date	Mintage	XF40	MS60	MS63	MS65	MS66
ND-1979	1,650	PF65 1,950	PF67 2,250			

KM# 89 250 DOLLARS
11.34 g., 0.900 Gold 0.3281 oz. AGW **Ruler:** Elizabeth II **Subject:** 1980 Olympics **Obv:** Arms with supporters **Rev:** Heads around outer circle of previous Gold Medal winners

Date	Mintage	VF20	XF40	MS60	MS63	MS65
1980	902	PF63 550	PF65 700			

KM# 95 250 DOLLARS
11.34 g., 0.900 Gold 0.3281 oz. AGW **Ruler:** Elizabeth II **Subject:** Wedding of Prince Charles and Lady Diana **Obv:** Crowned bust right

Date	Mintage	VF20	XF40	MS60	MS63	MS65
1981	1,491	PF63 525	PF65 675			

KM# 100 250 DOLLARS
11.34 g., 0.900 Gold 0.3281 oz. AGW **Ruler:** Elizabeth II **Subject:** World Championship of Football **Obv:** Arms with supporters **Rev:** Goalie catching attempted score

Date	Mintage	VF20	XF40	MS60	MS63	MS65
1982	694	PF63 575	PF65 725			

KM# 124 250 DOLLARS
11.32 g., 0.900 Gold 0.3276 oz. AGW **Ruler:** Elizabeth II **Subject:** Royal Visit **Obv:** Arms with supporters **Rev:** Conjoined heads of royal couple left

Date	Mintage	VF20	XF40	MS60	MS63	MS65
1983	5,000	PF63 550	PF65 600			

KM# 118 250 DOLLARS
11.34 g., 0.900 Gold 0.3281 oz. AGW **Ruler:** Elizabeth II **Subject:** Decade for Women **Obv:** Arms with supporters **Rev:** Woman with basket on head facing, map in background

Date	Mintage	VF20	XF40	MS60	MS63	MS65
1984	559	PF63 650	PF65 800			

KM# 131 250 DOLLARS
16.00 g., 0.900 Gold 0.463 oz. AGW **Ruler:** Elizabeth II **Subject:** 25th Anniversary of Independence **Obv:** Crowned bust right **Rev:** Arms with supporters

Date	Mintage	VF20	XF40	MS60	MS63	MS65
1987	250	PF63 775	PF65 900			

KM# 156 250 DOLLARS
11.34 g., 0.900 Gold 0.3281 oz. AGW **Ruler:** Elizabeth II **Subject:** 40th Anniversary - Coronation of Queen Elizabeth **Obv:** Crowned bust right **Rev:** Arms with supporters

Date	Mintage	VF20	XF40	MS60	MS63	MS65
1993	—	PF63 600	PF65 750			

KM# 153 500 DOLLARS
11.34 g., 0.900 Gold 0.3281 oz. AGW **Ruler:** Elizabeth II **Subject:** Columbus Quincentennial **Obv:** Arms with supporters **Rev:** "500" on ship's sail

Date	Mintage	VF20	XF40	MS60	MS63	MS65
1992	500	PF63 600	PF65 750			

KM# 162 500 DOLLARS
47.54 g., 0.917 Gold 1.4016 oz. AGW **Ruler:** Elizabeth II **Subject:** Royal Visit **Obv:** Arms with supporters **Rev:** Drummer on island map with yacht at right

Date	Mintage	XF40	MS60	MS63	MS65	MS66
1994	100	PF65 2,400	PF67 2,800			

PIEDFORT

KM#	Date	Mintage	Identification	Mkt Val
P1	1979	—	10 Dollars. Silver. KM#80.	975
P2	1983	32	250 Dollars. 0.900. Gold. Design like 10 Dollars, KM#80.	1,750

MINT SETS

KM#	Date	Mintage	Identification	Issue Price	Mkt Val
MS1	1969 (2)	30,000	KM#41-42	0.90	2.25
MS2	1969 (6)	30,000	KM#45-50	—	5.00
MS3	1970 (6)	5,000	KM#45-50	16.00	7.00
MS4	1971 (7)	4,072	KM#51, 53-58	19.50	25.00
MS5	1971 (6)	4,834	KM#51, 53-57	—	5.00
MS6	1972 (7)	2,982	KM#51, 53-57, 59	19.75	40.00
MS7	1972 (6)	4,000	KM#51, 53-57	10.00	5.00
MS8	1973 (7)	6,404	KM#51, 53-57, 59	19.75	40.00
MS9	1973 (6)	3,000	KM#51, 53-57	9.95	5.00
MS10	1974 (8)	8,361	KM#51, 53-57, 59, 63	25.00	35.00
MS11	1975 (8)	4,683	KM#51, 53-57, 62, 66	27.50	30.00
MS12	1976 (9)	1,802	KM#53-57, 62, 68, 70, 71	27.50	45.00
MS13	1977 (9)	597	KM#53-54, 56-57, 62, 68, 70, 73, 74	27.50	75.00
MS14	1978 (9)	1,282	KM#53-54, 56-57, 62, 68, 70, 73, 75	27.50	45.00
MS15	1979 (9)	2,608	KM#53-54, 56-57, 62, 68, 70, 73, 79	27.50	75.00
MS16	1980 (9)	3,668	KM#53-54, 56, 68, 70, 73, 84.1-86	30.00	80.00
MS17	1981 (9)	482	KM#53-54, 56, 68, 70, 73, 84.1, 85.1, 93	31.00	80.00
MS18	1982 (9)	—	KM#53-54, 56, 68, 70, 73, 84.1-85.1, 97	31.00	55.00
MS19	1983 (9)	1,210	KM#101-109	37.00	50.00
MS20	1984 (9)	—	KM#53-54, 56, 68, 70, 73, 85.1, 113-114	37.00	55.00
MS21	2000 (7)	—	KM#64, 146.2, 163, 164, 167, 181-182	25.00	12.00

PROOF SETS

KM#	Date	Mintage	Identification	Issue Price	Mkt Val
PS1	1918C (3)	—	KM#24-26	—	625
PS2	1928 (3)	20	KM#24-26	—	625
PS3	1937 (3)	—	KM#27-29	—	550
PS4	1969 (6)	8,530	KM#45-50	15.00	8.00
PS5	1969 (2)	5,000	KM#41-42	2.70	5.00
PS6	1970 (6)	11,540	KM#45-50	15.00	8.00
PS7	1971 (7)	12,739	KM#51, 53-58	26.50	45.00
PS8	1971 (6)	1,048	KM#51, 53-57	15.00	8.00
PS9	1972 (7)	16,967	KM#51, 53-57, 59	27.50	35.00
PS10	1973 (7)	28,405	KM#51, 53-57, 59	27.50	35.00
PS11	1974 (8)	22,026	KM#51, 53-57, 62a-63a	50.00	45.00
PS12	1975 (8)	15,638	KM#51, 53-57, 62a, 66a	55.00	50.00
PS13	1976 (9)	22,900	KM#53-57, 62a, 68, 70, 71a	55.00	50.00
PS14	1976 (7)	1,503	KM#53-57, 68, 70	22.50	10.00
PS15	1977 (9)	10,054	KM#53-54, 56-57, 62a, 68, 70, 73, 74a	55.00	60.00
PS16	1978 (9)	6,058	KM#53-54, 56-57, 62a, 68, 70, 73, 75a	59.00	60.00
PS17	1979 (9)	4,049	KM#53-54, 56-57, 62a, 68, 70, 73, 79a	59.00	65.00
PS18	1980 (9)	2,688	KM#53-54, 56, 68, 70, 73, 84.1, 85.1a, 86a	90.00	65.00
PS19	1981 (9)	1,577	KM#53-54, 56, 68, 70, 73, 84.1, 85.1a, 93a	92.00	70.00
PS20	1982 (9)	—	KM#53-54, 56, 68, 70, 73, 84.1, 85.1a, 97a	92.00	70.00
PS21	1983 (9)	1,210	KM#101-107, 108a-109a	—	75.00
PS22	1984 (9)	—	KM#53-54, 56, 68, 70, 73, 85.1a, 113, 114a	92.00	125
PS23	1985 (9)	—	KM#46-47, 49, 64-65, 84.2-85.2, 120, 123	—	75.00
PS24	1987 (9)	500	KM#46-49, 64, 84.2, 85.2, 132, 133	90.00	75.00
PS25	1988 (9)	500	KM#46-49, 64-65, 84.2, 85.2, 138a	115	75.00
PS26	1989 (9)	500	KM#46-49, 64-65, 84.2, 85.2, 140a	120	75.00
PS27	1990 (9)	500	KM#46a-47a, 48-49, 64-65, 85.2, 144, 145	125	55.00
PS28	1991 (7)	500	KM#46a, 64, 85.2, 145, 146-148	—	55.00
PS29	1992 (7)	500	KM#46a, 64, 85.2, 145-147, 152	138	65.00
PS30	1993 (7)	500	KM#46a, 64, 85.2, 145a, 146.1, 147, 155	—	70.00
PS31	1995 (6)	—	KM#64, 146.2, 163, 164, 167 and 187	—	75.00
PS32	2000 (8)	500	KM#64, 146.2, 163, 164, 167, 181-183	99.00	80.00

Japan, a constitutional monarchy situated off the east coast of Asia, has an area of 145,809 sq. mi. (377,835 sq. km.) and a population of 123.2 million. Capital: Tokyo. Japan, one of the major industrial nations of the world, exports machinery, motor vehicles, electronics and chemicals.

Japan, founded (so legend holds) in 660 B.C. by a direct descendant of the Sun Goddess, was first brought into contact with the west by a storm-blown Portuguese ship in 1542. European traders and missionaries proceeded to enlarge the contact until the Shogunate, sensing a military threat in the foreign presence, expelled all foreigners and restricted relations with the outside world in the 17th century. After Commodore Perry's U.S. flotilla visited in 1854, Japan rapidly industrialized, abolished the Shogunate and established a parliamentary form of government, and by the end of the 19th century achieved the status of a modern economic and military power. A series of wars with China and Russia, and participation with the allies in World War I, enlarged Japan territorially but brought its interests into conflict with the Far Eastern interests of the United States, Britain and the Netherlands, causing it to align with the Axis Powers for the pursuit of World War II. After its defeat in World War II, General Douglas MacArthur forced Japan to renounce military aggression as a political instrument, and he instituted constitutional democratic self-government. Japan quickly gained a position as an economic world power.

Japanese coinage of concern to this catalog includes those issued for the Ryukyu Islands (also called Liuchu), a chain of islands extending southwest from Japan toward Taiwan (Formosa), before the Japanese government converted the islands into a prefecture under the name Okinawa. Many of the provinces of Japan issued their own definitive coinage under the Shogunate.

RULERS

Emperors

Mutsuhito (Meiji), 1867-1912

明治 or 治明

Years 1-45

Yoshihito (Taisho), 1912-1926

大正 or 正大

Years 1-15

Hirohito (Showa), 1926-1989

昭和 or 和昭

Years 1-64

Akihito (Heisei), 1989-

平成

Years 1 –

NOTE: The personal name of the emperor is followed by the name that he chose for his regnal era.

MONETARY SYSTEM

Commencing 1870

10 Rin = 1 Sen
100 Sen = 1 Yen

MONETARY UNITS

厘

Rin

銭

Sen

Yen

DATING

Year

2

x10

3

Reading right to left, 3x10+2 = 32 year

Meiji

Dai Nippon
Great Japan

EMPIRE

DECIMAL COINAGE

Y# 41 5 RIN

2.10 g., Bronze, 18.8 mm. **Ruler:** Yoshihito **Obv:** Large paulownia crest in center flanked by cherry blossoms **Rev:** Value within circle of flowered wreath

Date	Mintage	F12	VF20	XF40	MS60	MS63
Yr.5(1916)	8,000,000	0.50	1.50	2.75	10.00	25.00
Yr.6(1917)	5,287,584	0.50	1.50	2.75	10.00	27.00
Yr.7(1918)	11,661,877	0.25	0.75	2.00	7.50	20.00
Yr.8(1919)	17,130,539	0.25	0.75	2.00	6.00	13.00

Y# 20 SEN

7.13 g., Bronze, 27.9 mm. **Ruler:** Mutsuhito **Obv:** Sunburst within beaded circle with legend separated by dots around border **Rev:** Value within center of rice wreath

Date	Mintage	F12	VF20	XF40	MS60	MS63
Yr.34(1901)	5,555,155	2.00	4.50	16.00	65.00	195
Yr.35(1902)	4,444,845	5.00	10.00	25.00	145	220
Yr.39(1906)	—	—	—	—	—	—
Note: None struck for circulation						
Yr.42(1909)	—	—	—	—	—	—
Note: None struck for circulation						

Y# 35 SEN

7.13 g., Bronze, 27.8 mm. **Ruler:** Yoshihito **Obv:** Sunburst within beaded circle with legend separated by dots around border **Rev:** Value within center of rice wreath

Date	Mintage	F12	VF20	XF40	MS60	MS63
Yr.2(1913)	15,000,000	1.50	2.25	4.00	32.00	110
Yr.3(1914)	10,000,000	1.50	2.25	4.00	32.00	85.00
Yr.4(1915)	13,000,000	1.50	2.25	4.00	32.00	85.00

Y# 42 SEN

3.75 g., Bronze, 23 mm. **Ruler:** Yoshihito **Obv:** Paulownia crest flanked by cherry blossoms **Rev:** Value within circle of flowered wreath

Date	Mintage	F12	VF20	XF40	MS60	MS63
Yr.5(1916)	19,193,946	0.45	0.75	1.25	30.00	110
Yr.6(1917)	27,183,078	0.25	0.45	0.75	25.00	85.00
Yr.7(1918)	121,794,756	0.25	0.45	0.75	9.50	25.00
Yr.8(1919)	209,959,359	0.15	0.25	0.50	4.50	16.00
Yr.9(1920)	118,829,256	0.15	0.25	0.50	4.50	16.00
Yr.10(1921)	252,440,000	0.15	0.25	0.50	4.50	16.00
Yr.11(1922)	253,210,000	0.15	0.25	0.50	4.50	16.00
Yr.12(1923)	155,500,000	0.15	0.25	0.50	5.50	22.00
Yr.13(1924)	106,250,000	0.15	0.25	0.50	4.50	16.00

Y# 47 SEN

3.75 g., Bronze, 23 mm. **Ruler:** Hirohito **Obv:** Paulownia crest flanked by cherry blossoms with authority on top and date below **Rev:** Value within circle of flowered wreath

Date	Mintage	F12	VF20	XF40	MS60	MS63
Yr.2(1927)	26,500,000	1.25	2.00	2.75	32.00	85.00
Yr.4(1929)	3,000,000	2.75	5.50	12.50	45.00	110
Yr.5(1930)	5,000,000	2.00	3.50	6.00	70.00	275
Yr.6(1931)	25,001,222	0.25	0.45	1.25	12.50	37.00
Yr.7(1932)	35,066,715	0.25	0.45	1.25	9.00	30.00
Yr.8(1933)	38,936,907	0.15	0.25	0.50	2.50	14.00
Yr.9(1934)	100,004,950	0.15	0.25	0.50	2.50	14.00
Yr.10(1935)	200,009,912	0.15	0.25	0.50	1.50	7.00
Yr.11(1936)	109,170,428	0.15	0.25	0.50	1.50	7.00
Yr.12(1937)	133,196,568	0.15	0.25	0.50	1.50	7.00
Yr.13(1938)	87,649,338	0.15	0.25	0.50	1.50	7.00

Y# 55 SEN

3.75 g., Bronze, 23 mm. **Ruler:** Hirohito **Obv:** Bird within clouds flanked by cherry blossoms **Rev:** Value in center of sacred mirror within wave-like wreath

Date	Mintage	F12	VF20	XF40	MS60	MS63
Yr.13(1938)	113,600,000	0.15	0.25	0.50	1.50	4.00

Y# 56 SEN

0.90 g., Aluminum, 17.6 mm. **Ruler:** Hirohito **Obv:** Bird within clouds flanked by cherry blossoms **Rev:** Value in center of sacred mirror within wave-like wreath

Date	Mintage	F12	VF20	XF40	MS60	MS63
Yr.13(1938)	45,502,266	—	0.50	1.50	8.50	17.00
Yr.14(1939)	444,602,146	—	1.25	2.25	12.00	24.00
Type A						
Yr.14(1939)	Inc. above	—	0.25	0.45	1.50	2.00
Type B						
Yr.15(1940)	601,110,015	—	0.25	0.45	1.50	2.00

Y# 59 SEN

0.65 g., Aluminum, 16 mm. **Ruler:** Hirohito **Obv:** Value in center with authority above and date below **Rev:** Chrysanthemum above Mount Fuji with value below

Date	Mintage	F12	VF20	XF40	MS60	MS63
Yr.16(1941)	1,016,620,734	—	0.15	0.25	0.50	1.00
Yr.17(1942)	119,709,832	—	0.15	0.25	0.75	1.00
Yr.18(1943)	1,163,949,434	—	0.15	0.25	0.50	1.00

Y# 59a SEN

0.55 g., Aluminum, 16 mm. **Ruler:** Hirohito **Obv:** Value in center with authority above and date below **Rev:** Chrysanthemum above Mt. Fuji with value below **Note:** Thinner

Date	Mintage	F12	VF20	XF40	MS60	MS63
Yr.18(1943)	627,160,000	—	0.15	0.50	1.00	1.50

Y# 62 SEN

1.30 g., Tin-Zinc, 15 mm. **Ruler:** Hirohito **Obv:** Chrysanthemum flanked by sprigs with value above and below **Rev:** Authority inscribed vertically in center with date below

Date	Mintage	F12	VF20	XF40	MS60	MS63
Yr.19(1944)	1,629,580,000	—	0.15	0.25	0.50	1.00
Yr.20(1945)	Inc. above	—	0.25	0.50	0.75	1.50

KM# 110 SEN

0.80 g., Baked Clay reddish-brown, 15 mm. **Ruler:** Hirohito **Obv:** Stylized cherry blossom surrounded by three characters "Dai Nippon" **Rev:** Mountain with character "one" at upper left

Date	Mintage	F12	VF20	XF40	MS60	MS63
ND-1945	—	16.00	22.50	27.50	35.00	47.00

Note: Circulated unofficially for a few days before the end of WWII in Central Japan; varieties of color exist

Y# 21 5 SEN

4.67 g., Copper-Nickel, 20.6 mm. **Ruler:** Mutsuhito **Obv:** Sunburst within circle, 3 legends separated by dots around border **Rev:** Value within rice wreath

Date	Mintage	F12	VF20	XF40	MS60	MS63
Yr.34(1901)	7,124,824	6.00	12.00	18.50	125	250
Yr.35(1902)	2,448,544	9.00	18.50	30.00	285	375
Yr.36(1903)	372,000	120	200	300	2,500	3,000
Yr.37(1904)	1,628,000	15.00	27.50	60.00	400	1,000
Yr.38(1905)	6,000,000	4.00	8.00	13.50	115	250
Yr.39(1906)	—	—	—	—	—	—

Note: None struck for circulation; Spink-Taisei Hong Kong sale 9-91 BU realized $10,000

Y# 43 5 SEN

4.28 g., Copper-Nickel, 20.6 mm. **Ruler:** Yoshihito **Obv:** Flower-like form of sacred mirror around hole in center flanked by dots **Rev:** Chrysanthemum flanked by value with hole in center and paulownia foliage on bottom 1/2

Date	Mintage	F12	VF20	XF40	MS60	MS63
Yr.6(1917)	6,781,830	6.00	12.00	18.50	50.00	100
Yr.7(1918)	9,131,211	4.00	8.00	15.00	35.00	80.00
Yr.8(1919)	44,980,633	2.50	4.50	9.00	20.00	37.00
Yr.9(1920)	21,906,326	2.50	4.50	9.00	20.00	37.00

Y# 44 5 SEN

2.63 g., Copper-Nickel, 19.1 mm. **Ruler:** Yoshihito **Obv:** Flower-like form of sacred mirror around hole in center flanked by dots **Rev:** Chrysanthemum flanked by value with hole in center and paulownia foliage on bottom 1/2

Date	Mintage	F12	VF20	XF40	MS60	MS63
Yr.9(1920)	100,455,537	0.35	0.65	1.50	15.00	60.00
Yr.10(1921)	133,020,000	0.25	0.45	1.20	5.00	15.00
Yr.11(1922)	163,980,000	0.25	0.45	1.20	5.00	15.00
Yr.12(1923)	80,000,000	0.25	0.45	1.20	5.00	15.00

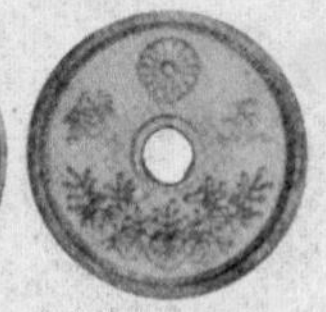

Y# 48 5 SEN

2.63 g., Copper-Nickel, 19.1 mm. **Ruler:** Hirohito **Obv:** Flower-like form of sacred mirror around hole in center flanked by dots **Rev:** Chrysanthemum flanked by value with hole in center and paulownia foliage on bottom 1/2

Date	Mintage	F12	VF20	XF40	MS60	MS63
Yr.7(1932)	8,000,394	0.25	0.45	1.50	7.00	45.00

Y# 53 5 SEN

2.80 g., Nickel, 19 mm. **Ruler:** Hirohito **Obv:** Rings around center hole flanked by cherry blossoms with authority above and date below **Rev:** Bird with wings spread below hole in center with rays of sun on upper 1/2 of border with chrysanthemum flanked by value

Date	Mintage	F12	VF20	XF40	MS60	MS63
Yr.8(1933)	16,150,806	0.45	1.25	2.25	5.50	17.00
Yr.9(1934)	33,851,607	0.45	0.75	1.50	4.50	14.00
Yr.10(1935)	13,680,677	0.75	1.50	2.75	7.50	17.00
Yr.11(1936)	36,321,796	0.45	0.75	1.50	4.50	14.00
Yr.12(1937)	44,402,201	0.45	0.75	1.50	5.50	17.00
Yr.13(1938) 4 known	10,000,000	—	—	—	—	—

Note: Almost entire mintage remelted

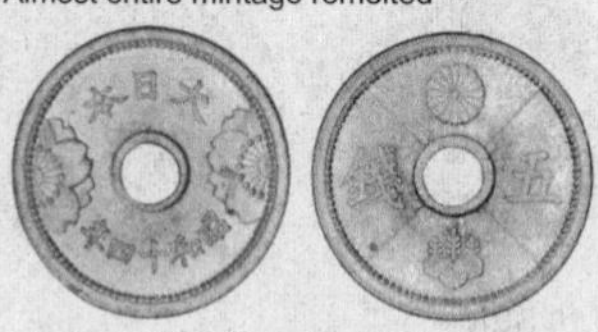

Y# 57 5 SEN

Aluminum-Bronze **Ruler:** Hirohito **Obv:** Hole in center flanked by 1/2 cherry blossoms with authority above and date below **Rev:** Hole in center divides quarters, upper and lower quarter in relief, value at either side

Date	Mintage	F12	VF20	XF40	MS60	MS63
Yr.13(1938)	40,001,977	0.45	0.75	1.25	4.00	11.00
Yr.14(1939)	97,903,873	0.45	0.75	1.25	4.00	11.00
Yr.15(1940)	34,501,716	0.45	0.75	1.25	5.00	12.00

Y# 60 5 SEN

1.20 g., Aluminum, 19 mm. **Ruler:** Hirohito **Obv:** Bird with wings spread with authority on top and date below **Rev:** Chrysanthemum within clouds with value above and below **Note:** Variety I

Date	Mintage	F12	VF20	XF40	MS60	MS63
Yr.15(1940)	410,020,460	—	0.25	0.75	3.00	6.00
Yr.16(1941)	Inc. above	—	0.25	0.50	2.25	4.50

Y# 60a 5 SEN

1.00 g., Aluminum, 19 mm. **Ruler:** Hirohito **Obv:** Bird with wings spread with authority on top and date below **Rev:** Chrysanthemum among clouds with value above and below **Note:** Variety 2

Date	Mintage	F12	VF20	XF40	MS60	MS63
Yr.16(1941)	478,023,877	1.25	2.75	6.00	35.00	55.00
Yr.17(1942)	Inc. above	—	0.25	0.65	1.50	2.00

Y# 60b 5 SEN

0.80 g., Aluminum, 19 mm. **Ruler:** Hirohito **Obv:** Bird with wings spread with authority on top and date below **Rev:** Chrysanthemum within clouds with value above and below **Note:** Variety 3

Date	Mintage	F12	VF20	XF40	MS60	MS63
Yr.18(1943)	276,493,742	—	0.25	0.75	2.00	4.00

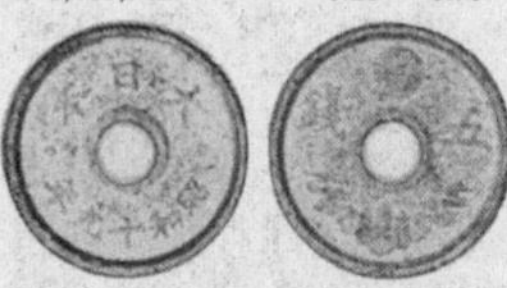

Y# 63 5 SEN

1.95 g., Tin-Zinc, 17 mm. **Ruler:** Hirohito **Obv:** Hole in center flanked by dots with authority on top and date below **Rev:** Chrysanthemum on top flanked by value above hole in center with paulownia crest within cloud-like swirls below

Date	Mintage	F12	VF20	XF40	MS60	MS63
Yr.19(1944)	70,000,000	—	0.25	0.75	2.50	3.00

Y# 65 5 SEN

2.00 g., Tin-Zinc, 17 mm. **Ruler:** Hirohito **Obv:** Large value in center flanked by paulownia crests with authority above and date below **Rev:** Bird with wings spread flanked by value with chrysanthemum above

Date	Mintage	F12	VF20	XF40	MS60	MS63
Yr.20(1945)	180,000,000	—	0.45	1.00	3.50	6.00
Yr.21(1946)	Inc. above	—	0.45	1.00	3.50	4.50

KM# 111 5 SEN

1.30 g., Baked Clay reddish-brown, 18 mm. **Ruler:** Hirohito **Obv:** Heart shapes around symbol in center with authority on top and value below **Rev:** Chrysanthemum above text

Date	Mintage	F12	VF20	XF40	MS60	MS63
Yr.20(1945)	—	250	350	450	650	750

Note: Not issued for circulation; varieties of color exist

明

Y# 23 10 SEN

2.70 g., 0.800 Silver 0.0694 oz. ASW, 17.6 mm. **Ruler:** Mutsuhito **Obv:** Dragon within beaded circle, 3 legends separated by dots around border **Rev:** Value within center of flowered wreath, chrysanthemum above

Date	Mintage	F12	VF20	XF40	MS60	MS63
Yr.34(1901)	797,561	80.00	115	155	925	1,950
Yr.35(1902)	1,204,439	65.00	100	130	900	2,300
Yr.37(1904)	11,106,638	4.00	6.00	9.00	38.00	110
Yr.38(1905)	34,182,194	4.00	6.00	9.00	38.00	110
Yr.39(1906)	4,710,168	4.00	6.00	9.00	38.00	110

Y# 29 10 SEN

2.25 g., 0.720 Silver 0.0521 oz. ASW **Ruler:** Mutsuhito **Obv:** Sunburst within cherry blossom circle with 3 legends separated by dots around border **Rev:** Value within center of flowered wreath with chrysanthemum above

Date	Mintage	F12	VF20	XF40	MS60	MS63
Yr.40(1907)	12,000,000	2.25	4.00	9.00	70.00	400
Yr.41(1908)	12,273,239	2.25	4.00	9.00	65.00	290
Yr.42(1909)	20,279,846	2.00	3.00	4.00	30.00	95.00
Yr.43(1910)	20,339,816	2.00	3.00	4.00	28.00	90.00
Yr.44(1911)	38,729,680	2.00	3.00	4.00	30.00	95.00
Yr.45(1912)	10,755,009	2.00	3.00	4.00	33.00	110

Y# 36.1 10 SEN
2.25 g., 0.720 Silver 0.0521 oz. ASW **Ruler:** Yoshihito **Obv:** Sunburst within cherry blossom circle with 3 legends separated by dots around border **Rev:** Value within flowered wreath with chrysanthemum on top

Date	Mintage	F12	VF20	XF40	MS60	MS63
Yr.1(1912)	10,344,307	2.25	4.00	8.00	70.00	230

Y# 36.2 10 SEN
2.25 g., 0.720 Silver 0.0521 oz. ASW **Ruler:** Yoshihito **Obv:** Sunburst within cherry blossom circle with 3 legends separated by dots around border **Rev:** Value within flowered wreath with chrysanthemum on top

Date	Mintage	F12	VF20	XF40	MS60	MS63
Yr.2(1913)	13,321,466	2.00	2.50	4.00	14.00	38.00
Yr.3(1914)	10,325,327	2.00	2.50	4.00	14.00	38.00
Yr.4(1915)	16,836,225	2.00	2.50	4.00	14.00	38.00
Yr.5(1916)	10,324,179	2.00	2.50	3.00	14.00	38.00
Yr.6(1917)	35,170,906	1.75	2.25	3.00	12.00	25.00

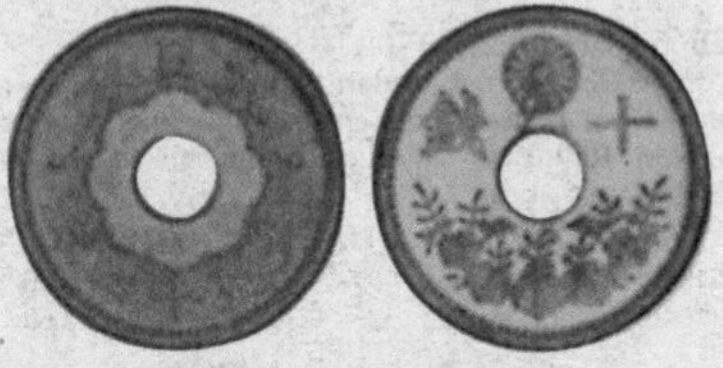

Y# 45 10 SEN
3.75 g., Copper-Nickel, 22.1 mm. **Ruler:** Yoshihito **Obv:** Flower-like form of sacred mirror around hole in center flanked by dots with authority on top and date below **Rev:** Chrysanthemum flanked by value above hole in center with paulownia foliage on bottom 1/2

Date	Mintage	F12	VF20	XF40	MS60	MS63
Yr.9(1920)	4,894,420	0.45	0.75	2.50	25.00	75.00
Yr.10(1921)	61,870,000	0.25	0.50	1.25	5.00	14.00
Yr.11(1922)	159,770,000	0.25	0.50	1.25	5.00	14.00
Yr.12(1923)	190,010,000	0.25	0.50	1.25	4.50	14.00
Yr.14(1925)	54,475,000	0.25	0.50	1.25	5.00	14.00
Yr.15(1926)	58,675,000	0.25	0.50	1.25	5.00	14.00

Y# 49 10 SEN
3.75 g., Copper-Nickel **Ruler:** Hirohito **Obv:** Flower-like form of sacred mirror around hole in center flanked by dots with authority on top and date below **Rev:** Chrysanthemum flanked by value above hole in center with paulownia foliage on bottom 1/2

Date	Mintage	F12	VF20	XF40	MS60	MS63
Yr.2(1927)	36,050,000	0.25	0.45	1.25	6.00	19.00
Yr.3(1928)	41,450,000	0.25	0.45	1.25	5.00	14.00
Yr.4(1929)	10,050,000	0.45	0.75	1.50	25.00	165
Yr.6(1931)	1,850,087	0.60	1.25	2.00	9.00	32.00
Yr.7(1932)	23,151,177	0.25	0.45	1.25	5.00	17.00

Y# 54 10 SEN
4.02 g., Nickel **Ruler:** Hirohito **Obv:** Center hole within 1/3 vertical portion recessed flanked by wave-like pattern with cherry blossoms **Rev:** Hole in center flanked by value and denomination, karakusa sprays are vertical in rectangular display, chrysanthemum on top, paulownia on bottom

Date	Mintage	F12	VF20	XF40	MS60	MS63
Yr.8(1933)	14,570,714	0.45	0.75	1.50	5.50	22.00
Yr.9(1934)	37,351,832	0.25	0.50	1.25	4.75	12.00
Yr.10(1935)	35,586,755	0.30	0.75	1.50	5.00	12.00
Yr.11(1936)	77,948,804	0.25	0.50	1.25	4.75	12.00
Yr.12(1937)	40,001,969	0.30	0.75	1.50	5.50	17.00

Y# 58 10 SEN
4.00 g., Aluminum-Bronze **Ruler:** Hirohito **Obv:** Double petal cherry blossom around center hole flanked by paulownia crest with authority on top and date below **Rev:** Chrysanthemum flanked by value with sun rays on upper 1/2 above hole in center with rolling waves below

Date	Mintage	F12	VF20	XF40	MS60	MS63
Yr.13(1938)	46,999,990	0.35	0.65	1.25	4.75	12.00
Yr.14(1939)	121,500,000	0.25	0.45	1.00	4.50	12.00
Yr.15(1940)	165,000,000	0.65	1.25	2.25	12.00	27.00

Y# 61.1 10 SEN
1.50 g., Aluminum, 22 mm. **Ruler:** Hirohito **Obv:** Double petal cherry blossom flanked by dots with authority on top and date below **Rev:** Chrysanthemum flanked by dots with value above and paulownia foliage below **Edge:** Reeded

Date	Mintage	F12	VF20	XF40	MS60	MS63
Yr.15(1940)	575,600,000	—	0.20	0.35	1.50	3.00
Yr.16(1941)	Inc. above	—	0.20	0.35	1.50	3.00

Y# 61.2 10 SEN
1.20 g., Aluminum, 22 mm. **Ruler:** Hirohito **Obv:** Double petal cherry blossom flanked by dots with authority on top and date below **Rev:** Chrysanthemum flanked by dots with value above and paulownia foliage below **Edge:** Reeded

Date	Mintage	F12	VF20	XF40	MS60	MS63
Yr.16(1941)	944,900,000	0.10	0.35	0.50	2.00	4.00
Yr.17(1942)	Inc. above	—	0.20	0.35	1.50	2.00
Yr.18(1943)	Inc. above	0.75	2.25	3.75	30.00	55.00

Y# 61.3 10 SEN
1.00 g., Aluminum, 22 mm. **Ruler:** Hirohito **Obv:** Double petal cherry blossom flanked by dots with authority on top and date below **Rev:** Chrysanthemum flanked by dots with value above and paulownia foliage below **Edge:** Reeded

Date	Mintage	F12	VF20	XF40	MS60	MS63
Yr.18(1943)	756,000,000	—	0.20	0.35	1.25	2.50

Y# 64 10 SEN
2.40 g., Tin-Zinc, 19 mm. **Ruler:** Hirohito **Obv:** Hole in center flanked by dots, authority on top, date on bottom **Rev:** Chrysanthemum on top flanked by value with paulownia crest within cloud-like swirls below

Date	Mintage	F12	VF20	XF40	MS60	MS63
Yr.19(1944)	450,000,000	—	0.20	0.35	1.25	1.75

Y# 68 10 SEN
1.00 g., Aluminum **Ruler:** Hirohito **Obv:** Large numeral 10 overlaps double petal cherry blossom in center, authority on top, date on bottom **Rev:** Two rice stalks drooping downward, value and denomination at lower left, chrysanthemum at top

Date	Mintage	F12	VF20	XF40	MS60	MS63
Yr.20(1945)	237,590,000	—	0.20	0.35	1.00	1.50
Yr.21(1946)	Inc. above	—	0.20	0.35	1.00	1.50

KM# 112 10 SEN
2.00 g., Baked Clay reddish-brown, 21.9 mm. **Ruler:** Hirohito **Obv:** Paulownia crest flanked by cherry blossoms with authority on top and date below **Rev:** Chrysanthemum in center with value above and below flanked by sprigs

Date	Mintage	F12	VF20	XF40	MS60	MS63
Yr.20(1945)	—	300	500	750	950	1,250

Note: Not issued for circulation; varieties of color exist

明

Y# 24 20 SEN
5.39 g., 0.800 Silver 0.1386 oz. ASW, 23.5 mm. **Ruler:** Mutsuhito **Obv:** Dragon within beaded circle **Rev:** Chrysanthemum divides wreath, value within

Date	Mintage	F12	VF20	XF40	MS60	MS63
Yr.34(1901)	500,000	140	200	325	2,600	3,450
Yr.37(1904)	5,250,000	5.00	10.00	18.00	80.00	175
Yr.38(1905)	8,444,930	5.00	10.00	18.00	70.00	175

Y# 30 20 SEN
4.05 g., 0.800 Silver 0.1042 oz. ASW **Ruler:** Mutsuhito **Obv:** Sunburst within cherry blossom circle with 3 legends separated by dots around border **Rev:** Value and denomination within flowered wreath, chrysanthemum on top

Date	Mintage	F12	VF20	XF40	MS60	MS63
Yr.39(1906)	6,555,070	6.00	12.00	22.50	230	575
Yr.40(1907)	20,000,000	4.00	7.00	14.00	85.00	165
Yr.41(1908)	15,000,000	5.00	7.00	14.00	85.00	165
Yr.42(1909)	8,824,702	4.00	7.00	14.00	85.00	165
Yr.43(1910)	21,175,298	4.00	7.00	14.00	85.00	165
Yr.44(1911)	500,000	50.00	105	230	1,300	3,200

Y# 25 50 SEN
13.48 g., 0.800 Silver 0.3467 oz. ASW, 30.5 mm. **Ruler:** Mutsuhito **Obv:** Dragon within beaded circle with 3 legends separated by dots around border **Rev:** Value within wreath, chrysanthemum above

Date	Mintage	F12	VF20	XF40	MS60	MS63
Yr.34(1901)	1,790,000	14.00	27.50	45.00	225	900
Yr.35(1902)	1,023,280	27.50	48.75	70.00	375	1,350
Yr.36(1903)	1,503,068	17.00	27.50	55.00	255	975
Yr.37(1904)	5,373,652	12.00	14.00	22.50	125	265
Yr.38(1905)	9,566,100	12.00	14.00	22.50	125	265
Type I						
Note: Bottom left stem cut with point on top						
Yr.38 (1905)	Inc. above	13.00	16.00	25.00	150	400
Type II						
Note: Bottom left stem cut with point on bottom						

Y# 31 50 SEN
10.10 g., 0.800 Silver 0.2598 oz. ASW **Ruler:** Mutsuhito **Obv:** Sunburst within cherry blossom circle with 3 legends separated by dots around border **Rev:** Value and denomination within flowered wreath, chrysanthemum on top

Date	Mintage	F12	VF20	XF40	MS60	MS63
Yr.39(1906)	12,478,264	10.00	13.00	22.50	225	600
Yr.40(1907)	24,062,952	9.00	11.00	16.00	75.00	250
Yr.41(1908)	25,470,371	9.00	11.00	16.00	75.00	250

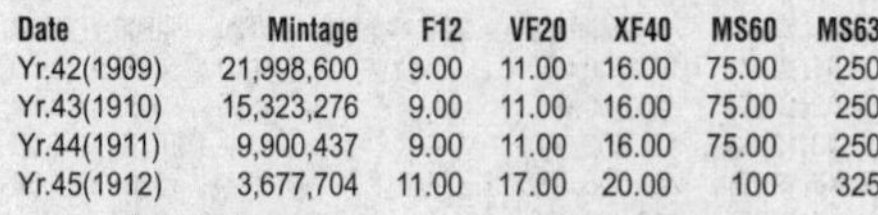

Date	Mintage	F12	VF20	XF40	MS60	MS63
Yr.42(1909)	21,998,600	9.00	11.00	16.00	75.00	250
Yr.43(1910)	15,323,276	9.00	11.00	16.00	75.00	250
Yr.44(1911)	9,900,437	9.00	11.00	16.00	75.00	250
Yr.45(1912)	3,677,704	11.00	17.00	20.00	100	325

Y# 37.1 50 SEN

10.13 g., 0.800 Silver 0.2605 oz. ASW **Ruler:** Yoshihito **Obv:** Sunburst within cherry blossom circle, 3 legends separated by dots around border **Rev:** Value and denomination within flowered wreath, chrysanthemum on top

Date	Mintage	F12	VF20	XF40	MS60	MS63
Yr.1(1912)	1,928,649	12.50	20.00	40.00	160	450

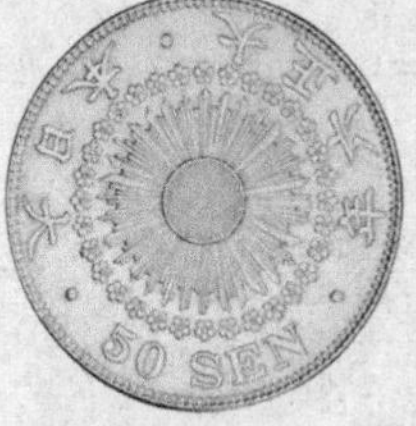

Y# 37.2 50 SEN

10.13 g., 0.800 Silver 0.2605 oz. ASW **Ruler:** Yoshihito **Obv:** Sunburst within cherry blossom circle, 3 legends separated by dots around border **Rev:** Value and denomination within flowered wreath, chrysanthemum on top

Date	Mintage	F12	VF20	XF40	MS60	MS63
Yr.2(1913)	5,910,063	10.00	13.00	23.00	60.00	250
Yr.3(1914)	1,872,331	20.00	35.00	55.00	200	600
Yr.4(1915)	2,011,253	17.50	30.00	50.00	160	450
Yr.5(1916)	8,736,768	9.00	12.00	18.00	35.00	125
Yr.6(1917)	9,963,232	9.00	12.00	18.00	35.00	140

Y# 46 50 SEN

4.95 g., 0.720 Silver 0.1146 oz. ASW, 23.8 mm. **Ruler:** Yoshihito **Obv:** Sunburst in center flanked by cherry blossoms, authority on top, date on bottom, all within sacred mirror **Rev:** Vertical value and denomination flanked by phoenix, paulownia crest flanked by karakusa sprigs, chrysanthemum on top

Date	Mintage	F12	VF20	XF40	MS60	MS63
Yr.11(1922)	76,320,000	2.00	4.25	7.00	28.00	85.00
Yr.12(1923)	185,180,000	2.00	4.25	5.00	20.00	27.00
Yr.13(1924)	78,520,000	2.00	4.25	5.00	20.00	27.00
Yr.14(1925)	47,808,000	2.00	4.25	5.00	22.00	45.00
Yr.15(1926)	32,572,000	2.00	4.25	5.00	25.00	55.00

Y# 50 50 SEN

4.95 g., 0.720 Silver 0.1146 oz. ASW **Ruler:** Hirohito **Obv:** Sunburst in center flanked by cherry blossoms, authority on top, date on bottom, all within sacred mirror **Rev:** Vertical value and denomination flanked by phoenix, paulownia crest flanked by karakusa sprigs, chrysanthemum on top

Date	Mintage	F12	VF20	XF40	MS60	MS63
Yr.3(1928)	38,592,000	—	2.00	5.00	11.00	32.00
Yr.4(1929)	12,568,000	2.00	4.25	7.00	33.00	110
Yr.5(1930)	10,200,000	2.00	4.25	7.00	22.00	70.00
Yr.6(1931)	27,677,501	—	2.00	4.25	10.00	20.00
Yr.7(1932)	24,132,795	—	2.00	4.25	10.00	20.00
Yr.8(1933)	10,001,973	2.00	4.25	9.00	25.00	70.00
Yr.9(1934)	20,003,995	—	2.00	4.25	10.00	20.00
Yr.10(1935)	11,738,334	—	2.00	4.25	10.00	25.00
Yr.11(1936)	44,272,796	—	2.00	4.25	8.00	17.00
Yr.12(1937)	48,000,533	—	2.00	4.25	8.00	17.00
Yr.13(1938)	3,600,717	55.00	85.00	140	275	375

Y# 67 50 SEN

4.50 g., Brass **Ruler:** Hirohito **Obv:** Stalks of wheat and rice flanked by fish, crossed pick and hoe within stalks, authority on top, date on bottom **Rev:** Phoenix among clouds, chrysanthemum on top, value and denomination on bottom **Note:** Varieties exist.

Date	Mintage	F12	VF20	XF40	MS60	MS63
Yr.21(1946)	268,161,000	0.25	0.50	1.00	2.50	3.50
Yr.22(1947)	Inc. above	—	600	900	1,700	2,250

Note: Not released to circulation

Y# 69 50 SEN

2.80 g., Brass **Ruler:** Hirohito **Obv:** Numeral 50 within center circle flanked by dots, authority on top, date on bottom **Rev:** Value and denomination at left of 1/2 cherry blossom wreath, chrysanthemum on top

Date	Mintage	F12	VF20	XF40	MS60	MS63
Yr.22(1947)	849,234,445	0.10	0.20	0.40	0.90	1.25
Yr.23(1948)	Inc. above	0.10	0.20	0.40	0.90	1.25

Y# A25.3 YEN

26.96 g., 0.900 Silver 0.7801 oz. ASW, 38.1 mm. **Ruler:** Mutsuhito **Obv:** Dragon within beaded circle, legends above, written value below **Rev:** Value within wreath, chrysanthemum above **Note:** Reduced size.

Date	Mintage	F12	VF20	XF40	MS60	MS63
Yr.34(1901)	1,256,252	28.00	50.00	95.00	175	350
Yr.35(1902)	668,782	40.00	85.00	150	300	500
Yr.36(1903)	5,131,096	28.00	40.00	70.00	175	300
Yr.37(1904)	6,970,843	28.00	40.00	70.00	175	300
Yr.38(1905)	5,031,503	28.00	40.00	70.00	175	300
Yr.39(1906)	3,471,297	28.00	50.00	95.00	450	550
Yr.41(1908)	334,705	85.00	175	300	600	1,000
Yr.45(1912)	5,000,000	28.00	40.00	60.00	150	250

Y# 38 YEN

26.96 g., 0.900 Silver 0.7801 oz. ASW **Ruler:** Yoshihito **Obv:** Dragon within beaded circle, 3 legends separated by dots around border **Rev:** Value and denomination within flowered wreath, chrysanthemum on top

Date	Mintage	F12	VF20	XF40	MS60	MS63
Yr.3(1914)	11,500,000	28.00	35.00	55.00	125	275

Y# 32 5 YEN

4.17 g., 0.900 Gold 0.1206 oz. AGW, 16.96 mm. **Ruler:** Mutsuhito **Obv:** Sunburst superimposed on sacred mirror, legends around border, value separated by paulownia crests **Rev:** Value within wreath, chrysanthemum above

Date	Mintage	F12	VF20	XF40	MS60	MS63
Yr.36(1903)	21,956	700	800	1,000	1,750	1,950
Yr.44(1911)	59,880	600	700	900	1,500	1,750
Yr.45(1912)	59,880	600	700	800	1,300	1,500

Y# 39 5 YEN

4.17 g., 0.900 Gold 0.1206 oz. AGW **Ruler:** Yoshihito **Obv:** Sunburst within mirror, 3 legends around border, value on bottom **Rev:** Value and denomination within flowered wreath, chrysanthemum on top

Date	Mintage	F12	VF20	XF40	MS60	MS63
Yr.2(1913)	89,820	800	850	950	1,400	1,750
Yr.13(1924)	76,037	550	650	850	1,150	1,450

Y# 51 5 YEN

4.17 g., 0.900 Gold 0.1206 oz. AGW **Ruler:** Hirohito

Date	Mintage	F12	VF20	XF40	MS60	MS63
Yr.5(1930)	852,563	20,000	35,000	50,000	65,000	75,000

Y# 33 10 YEN

8.33 g., 0.900 Gold 0.2411 oz. AGW, 21.21 mm. **Ruler:** Mutsuhito **Obv:** Sunburst superimposed on sacred mirror, legends around border, value separated by paulownia crests **Rev:** Value within wreath, chrysanthemum above

Date	Mintage	VG8	F12	VF20	XF40	MS63
Yr.34(1901)	1,654,682	305	425	475	600	1,000
Yr.35(1902)	3,023,940	305	425	475	600	1,000
Yr.36(1903)	2,902,184	305	425	475	600	1,000
Yr.37(1904)	724,548	500	950	1,100	1,150	2,750
Yr.40(1907)	157,684	305	475	600	725	1,250
Yr.41(1908)	1,160,674	305	425	450	550	925
Yr.42(1909)	2,165,660	305	425	450	550	875
Yr.43(1910)	8,982	6,000	10,000	15,000	22,000	—

Y# 34 20 YEN

16.67 g., 0.900 Gold 0.4823 oz. AGW, 28.78 mm. **Ruler:** Mutsuhito **Obv:** Sunburst superimposed on sacred mirror, legends around border, authority above, date below **Rev:** Value within wreath, chrysanthemum above

Date	Mintage	F12	VF20	XF40	MS60	MS63
Yr.36(1903) Rare	—	—	—	—	—	—
Yr.37(1904)	2,759,470	875	975	1,100	1,700	2,100
Yr.38(1905)	1,045,904	875	975	1,100	1,700	2,100
Yr.39(1906)	1,331,332	875	975	1,100	1,700	2,100
Yr.40(1907)	817,362	1,750	2,050	2,550	3,750	4,950
Yr.41(1908)	458,082	1,800	2,150	2,650	3,750	4,950
Yr.42(1909)	557,882	1,800	2,150	2,650	3,750	4,950
Yr.43(1910)	2,163,644	875	975	1,100	1,700	2,100
Yr.44(1911)	1,470,054	875	975	1,100	1,700	2,100
Yr.45(1912)	1,272,450	875	975	1,150	1,850	2,200

Y# 40.1 20 YEN

16.67 g., 0.900 Gold 0.4823 oz. AGW **Ruler:** Yoshihito **Obv:** Japanese character "first" used in date **Rev:** Value and denomination within wreath, chrysanthemum on top

Date	Mintage	F12	VF20	XF40	MS60	MS63
Yr.1(1912)	177,644	900	1,000	1,150	1,650	2,000

Y# 40.2 20 YEN

16.67 g., 0.900 Gold 0.4823 oz. AGW **Ruler:** Yoshihito **Obv:** Sunburst within mirror, 3 legends separated by cherry blossoms, date on bottom **Rev:** Value and denomination within wreath, chrysanthemum on top

Date	Mintage	F12	VF20	XF40	MS60	MS63
Yr.2(1913)	869,248	850	900	1,000	1,500	1,800
Yr.3(1914)	1,042,890	850	900	1,000	1,500	1,800
Yr.4(1915)	1,509,962	850	900	1,000	1,500	1,800
Yr.5(1916)	2,376,641	850	900	1,000	1,500	1,800
Yr.6(1917)	6,208,885	850	900	1,000	1,450	1,700
Yr.7(1918)	3,118,647	850	900	1,000	1,500	1,800
Yr.8(1919)	1,531,217	850	900	1,000	1,500	1,800
Yr.9(1920)	370,366	850	900	1,200	1,900	2,450

Y# 52 20 YEN

16.67 g., 0.900 Gold 0.4823 oz. AGW **Ruler:** Hirohito **Obv:** Sunburst within mirror, legends separated by cherry blossoms around border **Rev:** Value and denomination within wreath, chrysanthemum on top

Date	Mintage	VG8	F12	VF20	XF40	MS63
Yr.5(1930)	11,055,500	9,000	15,000	25,000	35,000	45,000
Yr.6(1931)	7,526,476	10,000	17,500	27,500	37,500	47,500
Yr.7(1932) Rare		—	—	—	—	—

REFORM COINAGE

Y# 70 YEN

3.20 g., Brass, 19.5 mm. **Ruler:** Hirohito **Obv:** Numeral 1 within circle, flanked by dots, authority on top, date on bottom **Rev:** Value and denomination above 3/4 orange blossom wreath

Date	Mintage	F12	VF20	XF40	MS60	MS63
Yr.23(1948)	451,170,000	—	0.25	0.50	2.00	3.00
Yr.24(1949)	Inc. above	—	0.15	0.35	1.25	2.00
Yr.25(1950)	Inc. above	—	0.15	0.35	1.25	2.00

Y# 74 YEN

1.00 g., Aluminum, 20 mm. **Ruler:** Hirohito **Obv:** Sprouting branch in center, authority on top, value and denomination on bottom **Rev:** Numeral 1 within 2 inner circles, date on bottom

Date	Mintage	VG8	F12	VF20	XF40	MS63
Yr.30(1955)	381,700,000	—	—	—	—	15.00
Yr.31(1956)	500,900,000	—	—	—	—	7.50
Yr.32(1957)	492,000,000	—	—	—	—	7.50
Yr.33(1958)	374,900,000	—	—	—	—	7.50
Yr.34(1959)	208,600,000	—	—	—	—	9.00
Yr.35(1960)	300,000,000	—	—	—	—	5.00
Yr.36(1961)	432,400,000	—	—	—	—	3.00
Yr.37(1962)	572,000,000	—	—	—	—	2.00
Yr.38(1963)	788,700,000	—	—	—	—	2.00
Yr.39(1964)	1,665,100,000	—	—	—	—	2.00
Yr.40(1965)	1,743,256,000	—	—	—	—	1.50
Yr.41(1966)	807,344,000	—	—	—	—	1.50
Yr.42(1967)	220,600,000	—	—	—	—	1.50
Yr.44(1969)	184,700,000	—	—	—	—	1.50
Yr.45(1970)	556,400,000	—	—	—	—	1.00
Yr.46(1971)	904,950,000	—	—	—	—	1.00
Yr.47(1972)	1,274,950,000	—	—	—	—	0.75
Yr.48(1973)	1,470,000,000	—	—	—	—	0.75
Yr.49(1974)	1,750,000,000	—	—	—	—	0.75
Yr.50(1975)	1,656,150,000	—	—	—	—	0.75
Yr.51(1976)	928,850,000	—	—	—	—	0.75
Yr.52(1977)	895,000,000	—	—	—	—	0.50
Yr.53(1978)	864,000,000	—	—	—	—	0.50
Yr.54(1979)	1,015,000,000	—	—	—	—	0.50
Yr.55(1980)	1,145,000,000	—	—	—	—	0.50
Yr.56(1981)	1,206,000,000	—	—	—	—	0.50
Yr.57(1982)	1,017,000,000	—	—	—	—	0.50
Yr.58(1983)	1,086,000,000	—	—	—	—	0.50
Yr.59(1984)	981,850,000	—	—	—	—	0.50
Yr.60(1985)	837,150,000	—	—	—	—	0.50
Yr.61(1986)	417,960,000	—	—	—	—	0.25
Yr.62(1987)	955,545,000	—	—	—	—	0.25
Yr.62(1987)	230,000	PF65 5.00				
Yr.63(1988)	1,268,812,000	—	—	—	—	0.25
Yr.63(1988)	200,000	PF65 3.00				
Yr.64(1989)	116,100,000	—	—	—	—	0.25

Y# 95.1 YEN

1.00 g., Aluminum, 20 mm. **Ruler:** Akihito **Obv:** Sprouting branch in center, authority on top, value and denomination on bottom **Rev:** Numeral 1 within two circles, date on bottom

Date	Mintage	VF20	XF40	MS60	MS63	MS65
Yr.1(1989)	2,366,770,000	—	—	—	0.15	—
Yr.1(1989)	200,000	PF65 3.00				

Y# 95.2 YEN

1.00 g., Aluminum, 20 mm. **Ruler:** Akihito **Obv:** Sprouting branch divides authority and value **Rev:** Value within circles above date **Edge:** Plain

Date	Mintage	VF20	XF40	MS60	MS63	MS65
Yr.2(1990)	2,768,753,000	—	—	—	0.15	—
Yr.2(1990)	200,000	PF65 3.00				
Yr.3(1991)	2,300,900,000	—	—	—	0.15	—
Yr.3(1991)	220,000	PF65 3.00				
Yr.4(1992)	1,298,880,000	—	—	—	0.15	—
Yr.4(1992)	250,000	PF65 3.00				
Yr.5(1993)	1,260,990,000	—	—	—	0.15	—
Yr.5(1993)	250,000	PF65 3.00				
Yr.6(1994)	1,040,540,000	—	—	—	0.15	—
Yr.6(1994)	227,000	PF65 3.00				
Yr.7(1995)	1,041,674,000	—	—	—	0.15	—
Yr.7(1995)	200,000	PF65 4.00				
Yr.8(1996)	942,024,000	—	—	—	0.15	—
Yr.8(1996)	189,000	PF65 4.00				
Yr.9(1997)	782,874,000	—	—	—	0.15	—
Yr.9(1997)	212,000	PF65 3.00				
Yr.10(1998)	452,412,000	—	—	—	0.15	—
Yr.10(1998)	200,000	PF65 4.00				
Yr.11(1999)	66,850,000	—	—	—	0.15	—
Yr.11(1999)	270,000	PF65 3.00				
Yr.12(2000)	11,800,000	—	—	0.50	0.75	—
Yr.12(2000)	226,000	PF65 5.00				

Y# 71 5 YEN

4.00 g., Brass **Ruler:** Hirohito **Obv:** Pigeon within circle with authority on top, date below **Rev:** Building within circle flanked by value and denomination, all within wreath

Date	Mintage	VG8	F12	VF20	XF40	MS63
Yr.23(1948)	74,520,000	—	—	0.50	0.75	12.50
Yr.24(1949)	179,692,000	—	—	0.15	0.40	8.00

Y# 72 5 YEN

3.75 g., Brass, 22 mm. **Ruler:** Hirohito **Obv:** Hole in center flanked by seed leaf, authority on top and date below **Rev:** Gear design around center hole with horizontal lines below, large bending stalk of rice above **Note:** Old script.

Date	Mintage	VG8	F12	VF20	XF40	MS63
Yr.24(1949)	111,896,000	—	—	0.15	0.25	9.00
Yr.25(1950)	181,824,000	—	—	0.15	0.25	6.50
Yr.26(1951)	197,980,000	—	—	0.15	0.25	6.50
Yr.27(1952)	55,000,000	—	—	0.30	0.60	100
Yr.28(1953)	45,000,000	—	—	0.30	0.60	6.50
Yr.32(1957)	10,000,000	—	—	4.00	8.00	40.00
Yr.33(1958)	50,000,000	—	—	0.25	0.50	3.50

Y# 72a 5 YEN

3.75 g., Brass, 22 mm. **Ruler:** Hirohito **Obv:** Hole in center flanked by a seed leaf with authority on top and date below **Rev:** Gear design around center hole with horizontal lines below, large bending stalk of rice above **Note:** New script.

Date	Mintage	VG8	F12	VF20	XF40	MS63
Yr.34(1959)	33,000,000	—	—	0.25	0.50	5.00
Yr.35(1960)	34,800,000	—	—	0.20	0.40	5.00
Yr.36(1961)	61,000,000	—	—	0.15	0.35	4.00
Yr.37(1962)	126,700,000	—	—	0.10	0.30	3.00
Yr.38(1963)	171,800,000	—	—	0.10	0.30	2.50
Yr.39(1964)	379,700,000	—	—	0.10	0.30	2.50
Yr.40(1965)	384,200,000	—	—	0.10	0.30	2.00
Yr.41(1966)	163,100,000	—	—	0.10	0.30	2.00
Yr.42(1967)	26,000,000	—	—	0.25	0.50	2.50
Yr.43(1968)	114,000,000	—	—	—	0.10	1.50
Yr.44(1969)	240,000,000	—	—	—	0.10	1.50
Yr.45(1970)	340,000,000	—	—	—	0.10	1.50
Yr.46(1971)	362,050,000	—	—	—	0.10	1.50
Yr.47(1972)	562,950,000	—	—	—	0.10	0.75
Yr.48(1973)	745,000,000	—	—	—	0.10	0.75
Yr.49(1974)	950,000,000	—	—	—	0.10	0.75
Yr.50(1975)	970,000,000	—	—	—	0.10	0.75
Yr.51(1976)	200,000,000	—	—	—	0.10	0.75
Yr.52(1977)	340,000,000	—	—	—	0.10	0.75
Yr.53(1978)	318,000,000	—	—	—	0.10	0.75
Yr.54(1979)	317,000,000	—	—	—	0.10	0.75
Yr.55(1980)	385,000,000	—	—	—	0.10	0.75
Yr.56(1981)	95,000,000	—	—	—	0.10	1.50
Yr.57(1982)	455,000,000	—	—	—	0.10	0.75
Yr.58(1983)	410,000,000	—	—	—	0.10	0.75
Yr.59(1984)	202,850,000	—	—	—	0.10	0.75
Yr.60(1985)	153,150,000	—	—	—	0.10	1.00
Yr.61(1986)	113,960,000	—	—	—	0.10	1.50
Yr.62(1987)	631,545,000	—	—	—	0.10	0.25
Yr.62(1987)	230,000	PF65 3.50				
Yr.63(1988)	368,920,000	—	—	—	—	0.25
Yr.63(1988)	200,000	PF65 3.50				
Yr.64(1989)	67,332,000	—	—	—	—	0.50

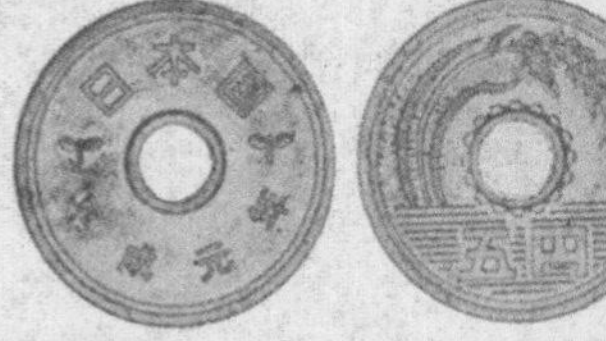

Y# 96.1 5 YEN

3.75 g., Brass, 22 mm. **Ruler:** Akihito **Obv:** Hole in center flanked by a seed leaf with authority on top and date below **Rev:** Gear around center hole with bending rice stalk above value

Date	Mintage	VF20	XF40	MS60	MS63	MS65
Yr.1(1989)	960,460,000	—	—	0.20	0.35	—
Yr.1(1989)	200,000	PF65 3.50				

Y# 96.2 5 YEN

3.75 g., Brass, 22 mm. **Ruler:** Akihito **Obv:** Hole in center flanked by a seed leaf with authority on top and date below **Rev:** Gear design around center hole with bending rice stalk above value in horizontal lines below

Date	Mintage	VF20	XF40	MS60	MS63	MS65
Yr.2(1990)	520,753,000	—	—	0.20	0.35	—
Yr.2(1990)	200,000	PF65 3.50				
Yr.3(1991)	516,900,000	—	—	0.20	0.35	—
Yr.3(1991)	220,000	PF65 3.50				
Yr.4(1992)	300,880,000	—	—	0.20	0.35	—
Yr.4(1992)	250,000	PF65 3.50				
Yr.5(1993)	412,990,000	—	—	0.20	0.35	—
Yr.5(1993)	250,000	PF65 3.50				
Yr.6(1994)	197,540,000	—	—	0.20	0.35	—
Yr.6(1994)	227,000	PF65 3.50				
Yr.7(1995)	351,674,000	—	—	0.20	0.35	—
Yr.7(1995)	200,000	PF65 3.50				
Yr.8(1996)	207,024,000	—	—	0.20	0.35	—
Yr.8(1996)	189,000	PF65 3.50				
Yr.9(1997)	238,874,000	—	—	0.20	0.35	—
Yr.9(1997)	212,000	PF65 3.50				
Yr.10(1998)	172,412,000	—	—	0.20	0.35	—
Yr.10(1998)	200,000	PF65 3.50				
Yr.11(1999)	59,850,000	—	—	0.20	0.35	—
Yr.11(1999)	270,000	PF65 3.50				
Yr.12(2000)	8,804,000	—	—	1.50	2.50	—
Yr.12(2000)	—	PF65 3.50				

Y# 73 10 YEN

4.50 g., Bronze, 23.5 mm. **Ruler:** Hirohito **Obv:** Temple in center with authority on top and value below **Rev:** Value and denomination within wreath **Edge:** Reeded

Date	Mintage	VG8	F12	VF20	XF40	MS63
Yr.26(1951)	101,068,000	—	—	0.20	0.35	150
Yr.27(1952)	486,632,000	—	—	0.20	0.35	40.00
Yr.28(1953)	466,300,000	—	—	0.20	0.35	40.00

Date	Mintage	VG8	F12	VF20	XF40	MS63
Yr.29(1954)	520,900,000	—	—	0.20	0.35	50.00
Yr.30(1955)	123,100,000	—	—	0.20	0.35	50.00
Yr.32(1957)	50,000,000	—	—	0.25	0.65	100
Yr.33(1958)	25,000,000	—	—	0.40	1.00	115

Y# 73a 10 YEN

4.50 g., Bronze, 23.5 mm. **Ruler:** Hirohito **Obv:** Temple in center with authority on top and value below **Rev:** Value and denomination within wreath **Edge:** Plain

Date	Mintage	VG8	F12	VF20	XF40	MS63
Yr.34(1959)	62,400,000	—	—	—	0.20	60.00
Yr.35(1960)	225,900,000	—	—	—	0.20	45.00
Yr.36(1961)	229,900,000	—	—	—	0.20	40.00
Yr.37(1962)	284,200,000	—	—	—	0.20	5.00
Yr.38(1963)	411,300,000	—	—	—	0.20	5.00
Yr.39(1964)	479,200,000	—	—	—	0.20	3.50
Yr.40(1965)	387,600,000	—	—	—	0.20	2.50
Yr.41(1966)	395,900,000	—	—	—	0.20	2.50
Yr.42(1967)	158,900,000	—	—	—	0.20	10.00
Yr.43(1968)	363,600,000	—	—	—	0.20	2.50
Yr.44(1969)	414,800,000	—	—	—	0.20	1.50
Yr.45(1970)	382,700,000	—	—	—	0.20	2.50
Yr.46(1971)	610,050,000	—	—	—	0.20	2.00
Yr.47(1972)	634,950,000	—	—	—	0.20	1.50
Yr.48(1973)	1,345,000,000	—	—	—	0.20	1.00
Yr.49(1974)	1,780,000,000	—	—	—	0.20	1.00
Yr.50(1975)	1,280,260,000	—	—	—	0.20	1.00
Yr.51(1976)	1,369,740,000	—	—	—	0.20	1.00
Yr.52(1977)	1,467,000,000	—	—	—	0.20	1.00
Yr.53(1978)	1,435,000,000	—	—	—	0.20	1.00
Yr.54(1979)	1,207,000,000	—	—	—	0.20	1.00
Yr.55(1980)	1,127,000,000	—	—	—	0.20	0.75
Yr.56(1981)	1,369,000,000	—	—	—	0.20	0.75
Yr.57(1982)	890,000,000	—	—	—	0.20	0.75
Yr.58(1983)	870,000,000	—	—	—	0.20	0.75
Yr.59(1984)	533,850,000	—	—	—	0.20	0.75
Yr.60(1985)	335,150,000	—	—	—	0.20	0.75
Yr.61(1986)	68,960,000	—	—	—	0.25	1.50
Yr.62(1987)	165,545,000	—	—	—	0.20	0.70
Yr.62(1987)	230,000	**PF65** 1.75				
Yr.63(1988)	617,912,000	—	—	—	0.20	0.50
Yr.63(1988)	200,000	**PF65** 1.75				
Yr.64(1989)	74,692,000	—	—	—	0.25	0.75

Y# 97.1 10 YEN

4.50 g., Bronze, 23.5 mm. **Ruler:** Akihito **Obv:** Temple divides authority and value **Rev:** Japanese character "first" in date

Date	Mintage	VF20	XF40	MS60	MS63	MS65
Yr.1(1989)	666,108,000	—	—	0.35	0.45	—
Yr.1(1989)	200,000	**PF65** 1.75				

Y# 97.2 10 YEN

4.50 g., Bronze, 23.5 mm. **Ruler:** Akihito **Obv:** Temple divides authority and value **Rev:** Value within wreath

Date	Mintage	VF20	XF40	MS60	MS63	MS65
Yr.2(1990)	754,753,000	—	—	0.35	0.45	—
Yr.2(1990)	200,000	**PF65** 1.75				
Yr.3(1991)	631,900,000	—	—	0.35	0.45	—
Yr.3(1991)	220,000	**PF65** 1.75				
Yr.4(1992)	537,880,000	—	—	0.35	0.45	—
Yr.4(1992)	250,000	**PF65** 1.75				
Yr.5(1993)	248,990,000	—	—	0.35	0.45	—
Yr.5(1993)	250,000	**PF65** 1.75				
Yr.6(1994)	190,540,000	—	—	0.35	0.45	—
Yr.6(1994)	227,000	**PF65** 1.75				
Yr.7(1995)	248,674,000	—	—	0.35	0.45	—
Yr.7(1995)	200,000	**PF65** 1.75				
Yr.8(1996)	546,024,000	—	—	0.35	0.45	—
Yr.8(1996)	189,000	**PF65** 1.75				
Yr.9(1997)	490,874,000	—	—	0.35	0.45	—
Yr.9(1997)	212,000	**PF65** 1.75				
Yr.10(1998)	410,412,000	—	—	0.35	0.45	—
Yr.10(1998)	200,000	**PF65** 1.75				
Yr.11(1999)	358,850,000	—	—	0.35	0.45	—
Yr.11(1999)	270,000	**PF65** 1.75				
Yr.12(2000)	314,800,000	—	—	0.35	0.45	—
Yr.12(2000)	226,000	**PF65** 1.75				

Y# 75 50 YEN

5.50 g., Nickel, 24 mm. **Ruler:** Hirohito **Obv:** Chrysanthemum blossom, authority on top, value at bottom **Rev:** 50 within center design, regnal era on top, date on bottom **Edge:** Reeded

Date	Mintage	VG8	F12	VF20	XF40	MS63
Yr.30(1955)	63,700,000	—	—	1.00	1.50	15.00
Yr.31(1956)	91,300,000	—	—	1.00	1.25	15.00
Yr.32(1957)	39,000,000	—	—	1.00	1.50	15.00
Yr.33(1958)	18,000,000	—	—	1.25	2.50	25.00

Y# 76 50 YEN

5.00 g., Nickel, 25 mm. **Ruler:** Hirohito **Rev:** Value above hole in center

Date	Mintage	VG8	F12	VF20	XF40	MS63
Yr.34(1959)	23,900,000	—	—	1.00	2.50	12.50
Yr.35(1960)	6,000,000	—	—	12.50	22.50	50.00
Yr.36(1961)	16,000,000	—	—	2.00	4.00	15.00
Yr.37(1962)	50,300,000	—	—	1.00	1.50	5.00
Yr.38(1963)	55,000,000	—	—	1.00	1.50	5.00
Yr.39(1964)	69,200,000	—	—	1.00	1.50	5.00
Yr.40(1965)	189,300,000	—	—	1.00	1.25	2.00
Yr.41(1966)	171,500,000	—	—	1.00	1.25	2.50

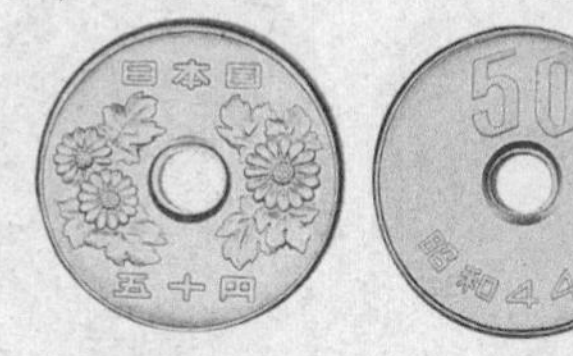

Y# 81 50 YEN

4.00 g., Copper-Nickel, 21 mm. **Ruler:** Hirohito **Obv:** Center hole flanked by chrysanthemums, authority on top and value below **Rev:** Numeral 50 above center hole with date below **Edge:** Reeded

Date	Mintage	VG8	F12	VF20	XF40	MS63
Yr.42(1967)	238,400,000	—	—	—	0.75	7.50
Yr.43(1968)	200,000,000	—	—	—	0.75	5.00
Yr.44(1969)	210,900,000	—	—	—	0.75	5.00
Yr.45(1970)	269,800,000	—	—	—	0.75	5.00
Yr.46(1971)	80,950,000	—	—	—	0.75	5.00
Yr.47(1972)	138,980,000	—	—	—	0.75	4.00
Yr.48(1973)	200,970,000	—	—	—	0.75	4.00
Yr.49(1974)	470,000,000	—	—	—	0.75	2.00
Yr.50(1975)	238,120,000	—	—	—	0.75	1.50
Yr.51(1976)	241,880,000	—	—	—	0.75	1.50
Yr.52(1977)	176,000,000	—	—	—	0.75	4.00
Yr.53(1978)	234,000,000	—	—	—	0.75	1.50
Yr.54(1979)	110,000,000	—	—	—	0.75	2.00
Yr.55(1980)	51,000,000	—	—	—	0.75	2.00
Yr.56(1981)	179,000,000	—	—	—	0.75	1.50
Yr.57(1982)	30,000,000	—	—	—	0.75	2.00
Yr.58(1983)	30,000,000	—	—	—	0.75	2.00
Yr.59(1984)	29,850,000	—	—	—	0.75	2.50
Yr.60(1985)	10,150,000	—	—	—	0.75	4.00
Yr.61(1986)	9,960,000	—	—	—	0.75	2.50
Yr.62(1987)	545,000	—	—	40.00	60.00	85.00
Yr.62(1987)	230,000	**PF65** 2.00				
Yr.63(1988)	108,912,000	—	—	—	0.75	1.50
Yr.63(1988)	200,000	**PF65** 2.00				

Y# 101.1 50 YEN

4.00 g., Copper-Nickel, 21 mm. **Ruler:** Akihito **Obv:** Center hole flanked by chrysanthemums, authority at top and value below **Rev:** Numeral 50 above center hole with date below **Edge:** Reeded

Date	Mintage	VF20	XF40	MS60	MS63	MS65
Yr.1(1989)	244,800,000	—	—	0.75	1.00	—
Yr.1(1989)	200,000	**PF65** 2.00				

Y# 101.2 50 YEN

4.00 g., Copper-Nickel, 21 mm. **Ruler:** Akihito **Obv:** Center hole flanked by chrysanthemums, authority at top and value below **Rev:** Value above hole in center **Edge:** Reeded

Date	Mintage	VF20	XF40	MS60	MS63	MS65
Yr.2(1990)	274,753,000	—	—	0.75	1.00	—
Yr.2(1990)	200,000	**PF65** 2.00				
Yr.3(1991)	208,900,000	—	—	0.75	1.00	—
Yr.3(1991)	220,000	**PF65** 2.00				
Yr.4(1992)	48,880,000	—	—	0.75	1.00	—
Yr.4(1992)	250,000	**PF65** 2.00				
Yr.5(1993)	50,990,000	—	—	0.75	1.00	—
Yr.5(1993)	250,000	**PF65** 2.00				
Yr.6(1994)	65,540,000	—	—	0.75	1.00	—
Yr.6(1994)	227,000	**PF65** 2.00				
Yr.7(1995)	111,674,000	—	—	0.75	1.00	—
Yr.7(1995)	200,000	**PF65** 2.00				
Yr.8(1996)	82,024,000	—	—	0.75	1.00	—
Yr.8(1996)	189,000	**PF65** 2.00				
Yr.9(1997)	149,874,000	—	—	0.75	1.00	—
Yr.9(1997)	212,000	**PF65** 2.00				
Yr.10(1998)	100,412,000	—	—	0.75	1.00	—
Yr.10(1998)	200,000	**PF65** 2.00				
Yr.11(1999)	58,850,000	—	—	0.75	1.00	—
Yr.11(1999)	270,000	**PF65** 2.00				
Yr.12(2000)	6,800,000	—	2.50	5.00	12.00	—
Yr.12(2000)	226,000	**PF65** 3.00				

Y# 77 100 YEN

4.80 g., 0.600 Silver 0.0926 oz. ASW, 22.5 mm. **Ruler:** Hirohito **Obv:** Phoenix

Date	Mintage	F12	VF20	XF40	MS60	MS63
Yr.32(1957)	30,000,000	1.70	3.50	5.00	9.00	12.00
Yr.33(1958)	70,000,000	1.70	3.50	5.00	8.00	10.00

Y# 78 100 YEN

4.80 g., 0.600 Silver 0.0926 oz. ASW, 22.5 mm. **Ruler:** Hirohito **Obv:** Sheaf of rice in center with authority on top and value below **Rev:** Numeral 100 within circle flanked by 1/4 lined wreath with era on top and year below

Date	Mintage	VG8	F12	VF20	XF40	MS63
Yr.34(1959)	110,000,000	—	1.70	3.50	5.00	9.00
Yr.35(1960)	50,000,000	—	1.70	3.50	5.00	12.00
Yr.36(1961)	15,000,000	—	1.70	3.50	5.00	12.00
Yr.38(1963)	45,000,000	—	1.70	3.50	5.00	12.00
Yr.39(1964)	10,000,000	—	1.70	3.50	6.00	12.00
Yr.40(1965)	62,500,000	—	1.70	3.50	5.00	7.00
Yr.41(1966)	97,500,000	—	1.70	3.50	5.00	7.00

Y# 79 100 YEN

4.80 g., 0.600 Silver 0.0926 oz. ASW, 22.5 mm. **Ruler:** Hirohito **Subject:** 1964 Olympic Games **Obv:** Olympic circles on base of flaming torch flanked by authority above and value below **Rev:** Numeral 100 within center circle

Date	Mintage	VG8	F12	VF20	XF40	MS63
Yr.39/1964	80,000,000	—	1.70	3.50	4.50	7.00

Y# 82 100 YEN

4.80 g., Copper-Nickel, 22.5 mm. **Ruler:** Hirohito **Obv:** Cherry blossoms **Rev:** Large numeral 100 in center **Edge:** Reeded

Date	Mintage	VG8	F12	VF20	XF40	MS63
Yr.42(1967)	432,200,000	—	—	—	1.50	7.50
Note: Varieties exist						
Yr.43(1968)	471,000,000	—	—	—	1.50	5.00
Yr.44(1969)	323,700,000	—	—	—	1.50	7.50
Yr.45(1970)	237,100,000	—	—	—	1.50	5.00
Yr.46(1971)	481,050,000	—	—	—	1.50	2.50
Yr.47(1972)	468,950,000	—	—	—	1.50	2.00
Yr.48(1973)	680,000,000	—	—	—	1.50	2.00
Yr.49(1974)	660,000,000	—	—	—	1.50	2.00
Yr.50(1975)	437,160,000	—	—	—	1.50	2.00
Yr.51(1976)	322,840,000	—	—	—	1.50	2.00
Yr.52(1977)	440,000,000	—	—	—	1.50	2.00
Yr.53(1978)	292,000,000	—	—	—	1.50	2.00
Yr.54(1979)	382,000,000	—	—	—	1.50	2.00
Yr.55(1980)	588,000,000	—	—	—	1.50	2.00
Yr.56(1981)	348,000,000	—	—	—	1.50	2.00
Yr.57(1982)	110,000,000	—	—	—	1.50	3.00
Yr.58(1983)	50,000,000	—	—	—	1.50	5.00
Yr.59(1984)	41,850,000	—	—	—	1.50	5.00
Yr.60(1985)	58,150,000	—	—	—	1.50	5.00
Yr.61(1986)	99,960,000	—	—	—	1.50	2.00
Yr.62(1987)	193,545,000	—	—	—	1.50	2.00
Yr.62(1987)	230,000	PF65 10.00				
Yr.63(1988)	362,912,000	—	—	—	1.50	2.00
Yr.63(1988)	200,000	PF65 7.00				

Y# 83 100 YEN

9.00 g., Copper-Nickel, 28 mm. **Ruler:** Hirohito **Subject:** Osaka Expo '70 **Obv:** Mt. Fuji **Rev:** Circles within world globe with value above

Date	Mintage	VG8	F12	VF20	XF40	MS63
Yr.45(1970)	40,000,000	—	—	2.50	3.50	6.00

Y# 84 100 YEN

12.00 g., Copper-Nickel, 30 mm. **Ruler:** Hirohito **Subject:** 1972 Winter Olympic Games - Sapporo **Obv:** Olympic torch with flame flanked by authority and city name **Rev:** Large numeral 100 above olympic circles flanked by flower designs

Date	Mintage	VG8	F12	VF20	XF40	MS63
Yr.47/1972	30,000,000	—	—	3.00	4.50	7.50

Y# 85 100 YEN

4.80 g., Copper-Nickel, 22.5 mm. **Ruler:** Hirohito **Subject:** Okinawa Expo '75 **Obv:** Gate of Shurei **Rev:** Value in center flanked by dolphins with legend above and below

Date	Mintage	VG8	F12	VF20	XF40	MS63
Yr.50(1975)	120,000,000	—	—	1.75	2.50	3.50

Y# 86 100 YEN

12.00 g., Copper-Nickel, 30 mm. **Ruler:** Hirohito **Subject:** 50th Anniversary of Reign **Obv:** Imperial Palace and Niju Bridge **Rev:** Chrysanthemum in center flanked by phoenix with inscription above and below

Date	Mintage	VG8	F12	VF20	XF40	MS63
Yr.51(1976)	70,000,000	—	—	2.50	3.50	6.00

Y# 98.1 100 YEN

4.80 g., Copper-Nickel, 22.5 mm. **Ruler:** Akihito **Obv:** Cherry blossoms **Rev:** Japanese character "first" in date **Edge:** Reeded

Date	Mintage	VF20	XF40	MS60	MS63	MS65
Yr.1(1989)	368,800,000	—	—	1.50	2.00	2.50
Yr.1(1989)	200,000	PF65 7.00				

Y# 98.2 100 YEN

4.80 g., Copper-Nickel, 22.6 mm. **Ruler:** Akihito **Obv:** Cherry blossoms **Rev:** Large numeral 100, date in western numerals **Edge:** Reeded

Date	Mintage	VF20	XF40	MS60	MS63	MS65
Yr.2(1990)	444,753,000	—	—	1.75	2.00	2.50
Yr.2(1990)	200,000	PF65 7.00				
Yr.3(1991)	374,900,000	—	—	1.75	2.00	2.50
Yr.3(1991)	220,000	PF65 6.00				
Yr.4(1992)	210,880,000	—	—	1.75	2.00	2.50
Yr.4(1992)	250,000	PF65 6.00				
Yr.5(1993)	81,990,000	—	—	1.75	2.00	2.50
Yr.5(1993)	250,000	PF65 6.00				
Yr.6(1994)	81,540,000	—	—	1.75	2.00	2.50
Yr.6(1994)	227,000	PF65 6.00				
Yr.7(1995)	92,674,000	—	—	1.75	2.00	2.50
Yr.7(1995)	200,000	PF65 7.00				
Yr.8(1996)	237,024,000	—	—	1.75	2.00	2.50
Yr.8(1996)	189,000	PF65 7.00				
Yr.9(1997)	271,874,000	—	—	1.75	2.00	2.50
Yr.9(1997)	212,000	PF65 7.00				
Yr.10(1998)	252,412,000	—	—	1.75	2.00	2.50
Yr.10(1998)	200,000	PF65 7.00				
Yr.11(1999)	178,850,000	—	—	1.75	2.00	2.50
Yr.11(1999)	270,000	PF65 6.00				
Yr.12(2000)	171,800,000	—	—	1.75	2.00	2.50
Yr.12(2000)	—	PF65 6.00				

Y# 87 500 YEN

7.20 g., Copper-Nickel, 26.5 mm. **Ruler:** Hirohito **Obv:** Pawlownia flower **Rev:** Numeral 500 in center flanked by cherry blossoms **Edge Lettering:** NIPPON 500

Date	Mintage	VG8	F12	VF20	XF40	MS63
Yr.57(1982)	300,000,000	—	—	—	7.00	9.00
Yr.58(1983)	240,000,000	—	—	—	7.00	9.00
Yr.59(1984)	342,850,000	—	—	—	7.00	9.00
Yr.60(1985)	97,150,000	—	—	—	7.00	9.00
Yr.61(1986)	49,960,000	—	—	—	7.00	9.00
Yr.62(1987)	2,545,000	—	—	7.00	9.00	15.00
Yr.62(1987)	230,000	PF65 20.00				
Yr.63(1988)	148,018,000	—	—	—	7.00	9.00
Yr.63(1988)	200,000	PF65 12.00				
Yr.64(1989)	16,042,000	—	—	—	7.00	12.00

Y# 88 500 YEN

13.00 g., Copper-Nickel, 30 mm. **Ruler:** Hirohito **Subject:** 1985 Tsukuba Expo **Obv:** Mt. Tsukuba above cherry blossoms **Rev:** Circles within triangular design above value flanked by cherry blossom **Edge Lettering:** TSUKUBA EXPO '85

Date	Mintage	VG8	F12	VF20	XF40	MS63
Yr.60(1985)	70,000,000	—	—	—	7.50	10.00

Y# 89 500 YEN

13.00 g., Copper-Nickel, 30 mm. **Ruler:** Hirohito **Subject:** 100th Anniversary - Governmental Cabinet System **Obv:** Prime Minister's official residence **Rev:** Large numeral 500 within center square **Edge Lettering:** NAIKAKU 100 NEN

Date	Mintage	VG8	F12	VF20	XF40	MS63
Yr.60(1985)	70,000,000	—	—	—	7.50	10.00

Y# 90 500 YEN

13.00 g., Copper-Nickel, 30 mm. **Ruler:** Hirohito **Subject:** 60 Years of Reign of Hirohito **Obv:** Large chrysanthemum with legends around border **Rev:** Shishinden Palace

Date	Mintage	VG8	F12	VF20	XF40	MS63
Yr.61(1986)	50,000,000	—	—	—	8.00	12.00

Y# 93 500 YEN

13.00 g., Copper-Nickel, 30 mm. **Ruler:** Hirohito **Subject:** Opening of Seikan Tunnel **Obv:** Seikan tunnel flanked by sea gulls **Rev:** Map within ribbon above value

Date	Mintage	VG8	F12	VF20	XF40	MS63
Yr.63(1988)	20,000,000	—	—	—	8.50	12.50

Y# 94 500 YEN

13.00 g., Copper-Nickel, 30 mm. **Ruler:** Hirohito **Subject:** Opening of Seto Bridge **Obv:** Seto Bridge **Rev:** Map within ribbon above value

Date	Mintage	VG8	F12	VF20	XF40	MS63
Yr.63(1988)	20,000,000	—	—	—	8.50	12.50

Y# 99.1 500 YEN

7.20 g., Copper-Nickel, 26.5 mm. **Ruler:** Akihito **Obv:** Pawlownia flower **Rev:** Value flanked by cherry blossoms, Japanese character "first" in date

Date	Mintage	VF20	XF40	MS60	MS63	MS65
Yr.1(1989)	192,652,000	—	7.00	8.00	9.00	—
Yr.1(1989)	200,000	PF65 15.00				

Y# 99.2 500 YEN

7.20 g., Copper-Nickel, 26.5 mm. **Ruler:** Akihito **Obv:** Pawlownia flower **Rev:** Value flanked by cherry blossoms, date in western numerals

Date	Mintage	VF20	XF40	MS60	MS63	MS65
Yr.2(1990)	159,753,000	—	7.00	8.00	9.00	—
Yr.2(1990)	200,000	PF65 25.00				
Yr.3(1991)	169,900,000	—	7.00	8.00	9.00	—
Yr.3(1991)	220,000	PF65 22.00				
Yr.4(1992)	87,880,000	—	7.00	8.00	9.00	—
Yr.4(1992)	250,000	PF65 22.00				
Yr.5(1993)	131,990,000	—	7.00	8.00	9.00	—
Yr.5(1993)	250,000	PF65 22.00				
Yr.6(1994)	105,545,000	—	7.00	8.00	9.00	—
Yr.6(1994)	227,000	PF65 22.00				
Yr.7(1995)	182,669,000	—	7.00	8.00	9.00	—
Yr.7(1995)	200,000	PF65 25.00				
Yr.8(1996)	99,024,000	—	7.00	8.00	9.00	—
Yr.8(1996)	189,000	PF65 25.00				
Yr.9(1997)	172,878,000	—	7.00	8.00	9.00	—
Yr.9(1997)	212,000	PF65 22.00				
Yr.10(1998)	214,408,000	—	7.00	8.00	9.00	—
Yr.10(1998)	200,000	PF65 25.00				
Yr.11(1999)	164,850,000	—	7.00	8.00	9.00	—
Yr.11(1999)	270,000	PF65 22.00				

Y# 102 500 YEN

13.00 g., Copper-Nickel, 30 mm. **Ruler:** Akihito **Subject:** Enthronement of Emperor Akihito **Obv:** Carriage **Rev:** Chrysanthemum crest among leaves above value

Date	Mintage	VF20	XF40	MS60	MS63	MS65
Yr.2(1990)	30,000,000	—	10.00	12.00	13.50	—

Y# 106 500 YEN

13.00 g., Copper-Nickel, 30 mm. **Ruler:** Akihito **Subject:** 20th Anniversary - Reversion of Okinawa **Obv:** Building **Rev:** Value and denomination flanked by upright dragons

Date	Mintage	VF20	XF40	MS60	MS63	MS65
Yr.4(1992)	19,950,000	—	11.00	13.00	15.00	—
Yr.4(1992)	50,000	PF65 25.00				

Y# 107 500 YEN

7.20 g., Copper-Nickel, 26.5 mm. **Ruler:** Akihito **Subject:** Royal wedding of Crown Prince **Obv:** Chrysanthemum flanked by cherry blossom sprigs with legend around border **Rev:** Pair of flying herons

Date	Mintage	VF20	XF40	MS60	MS63	MS65
Yr.5(1993)	29,800,000	—	12.00	14.00	16.00	—
Yr.5(1993)	200,000	PF65 20.00				

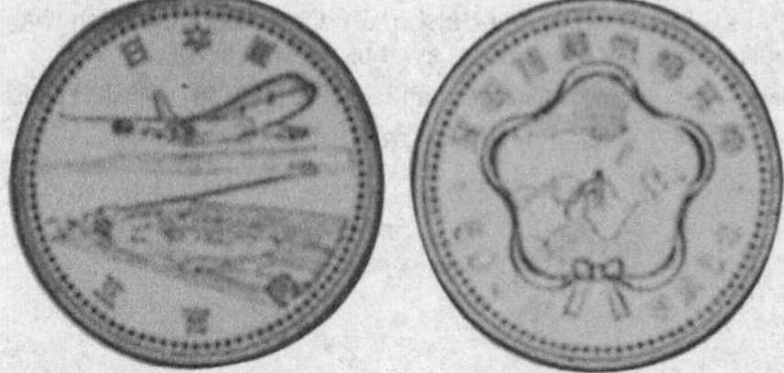

Y# 110 500 YEN

7.20 g., Copper-Nickel, 26.5 mm. **Ruler:** Akihito **Subject:** Opening of Kansai International Airport **Obv:** Flying jet **Rev:** Design within ribbon

Date	Mintage	VF20	XF40	MS60	MS63	MS65
Yr.6(1994)	19,900,000	—	11.00	12.00	14.50	—
Yr.6(1994)	100,000	PF65 40.00				

Y# 111 500 YEN

7.20 g., Copper-Nickel, 26.5 mm. **Ruler:** Akihito **Subject:** 12th Asian Games **Obv:** Stylized runners **Rev:** Artistic design above value

Date	Mintage	VF20	XF40	MS60	MS63	MS65
Yr.6(1994)	9,900,000	—	10.00	12.00	13.50	—
Yr.6(1994)	100,000	PF65 30.00				

Y# 112 500 YEN

7.20 g., Copper-Nickel, 26.5 mm. **Ruler:** Akihito **Subject:** 12th Asian Games **Obv:** Stylized swimmers **Rev:** Artistic design above value

Date	Mintage	VF20	XF40	MS60	MS63	MS65
Yr.6(1994)	9,900,000	—	10.00	12.00	13.50	—
Yr.6(1994)	100,000	PF65 30.00				

Y# 113 500 YEN

7.20 g., Copper-Nickel, 26.5 mm. **Ruler:** Akihito **Subject:** 12th Asian Games **Obv:** Stylized jumper **Rev:** Artistic design above value

Date	Mintage	VF20	XF40	MS60	MS63	MS65
Yr.6(1994)	9,900,000	—	10.00	12.00	13.50	—
Yr.6(1994)	100,000	PF65 30.00				

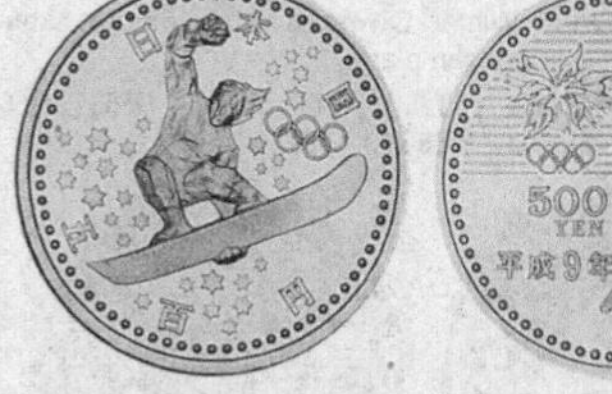

Y# 114 500 YEN

7.20 g., Copper-Nickel, 26.5 mm. **Ruler:** Akihito **Series:** 1998 Nagano Winter Olympics **Obv:** Snowboarder **Rev:** Bird, value and dates

Date	Mintage	VF20	XF40	MS60	MS63	MS65
Yr.9(1997)	19,867,000	—	11.00	13.00	15.00	—
Yr.9(1997)	133,000	PF65 32.00				

Y# 117 500 YEN

7.20 g., Copper-Nickel, 26.5 mm. **Ruler:** Akihito **Series:** 1998 Nagano Winter Olympics **Obv:** Bobsledding **Rev:** Bird, value and dates

Date	Mintage	VF20	XF40	MS60	MS63	MS65
Yr.9(1997)	19,867,000	—	11.00	13.00	15.00	—
Yr.9(1997)	133,000	PF65 32.00				

Y# 118 500 YEN

7.20 g., Copper-Nickel, 26.5 mm. **Ruler:** Akihito **Series:** 1998 Nagano Winter Olympics **Obv:** Acrobat skier **Rev:** Bird, value and dates

Date	Mintage	VF20	XF40	MS60	MS63	MS65
Yr.10(1998)	19,867,000	—	11.00	13.00	15.00	—
Yr.10(1998)	133,000	PF65 32.00				

Y# 123 500 YEN

7.20 g., Copper-Nickel, 26.5 mm. **Ruler:** Akihito **Subject:** 10th Anniversary of Enthronement **Obv:** Mt. Fuji and chrysanthemums **Rev:** Chrysanthemum within wreath

Date	Mintage	VF20	XF40	MS60	MS63	MS65
Yr.11(1999)	14,900,000	—	8.00	9.00	12.00	—
Yr.11(1999)	—	PF65 30.00				

Y# 125 500 YEN

7.00 g., Nickel-Brass, 26.5 mm. **Ruler:** Akihito **Obv:** Pawlownia flower and highlighted legends **Rev:** Value with latent zeros **Edge:** Slanted reeding

Date	Mintage	VF20	XF40	MS60	MS63	MS65
Yr.12(2000)	595,743,000	—	—	7.00	9.00	11.00
Yr.12(2000)	226,000	PF65 20.00				

Y# 80 1000 YEN

20.00 g., 0.925 Silver 0.5948 oz. ASW, 35 mm. **Ruler:** Hirohito **Series:** 1964 Olympic Games **Obv:** Mt. Fuji within sprigs of cherry blossoms **Rev:** Value and olympic circles flanked by cherry blossoms **Note:** Dav. #276

Date	Mintage	VF20	XF40	MS60	MS63	MS65
Yr.39(1964)	15,000,000	—	—	16.00	22.00	32.00

Y# 100 5000 YEN

15.00 g., 0.925 Silver 0.4461 oz. ASW, 30 mm. **Ruler:** Akihito **Subject:** Osaka Garden Exposition **Obv:** Head with flowers in hair left **Rev:** Flower design above value

Date	Mintage	VF20	XF40	MS60	MS63	MS65
Yr.2 (1990)	10,000,000	—	—	45.00	50.00	55.00

Y# 103 5000 YEN

15.00 g., 0.925 Silver 0.4461 oz. ASW, 30 mm. **Ruler:** Akihito

Subject: Centennial of Parliament **Obv:** Parliament building **Rev:** Winged figures flank central figure

Date	Mintage	VF20	XF40	MS60	MS63	MS65
Yr.2(1990)	5,000,000	—	—	42.00	45.00	50.00

Y# 104 5000 YEN

15.00 g., 0.925 Silver 0.4461 oz. ASW, 30 mm. **Ruler:** Akihito **Subject:** Centennial of Judicial System **Obv:** Court room scene **Rev:** Value within center circle and flowered wreath

Date	Mintage	VF20	XF40	MS60	MS63	MS65
Yr.2(1990)	5,000,000	—	—	42.00	45.00	50.00

Y# 108 5000 YEN

15.00 g., 1.000 Silver 0.4823 oz. ASW, 30 mm. **Ruler:** Akihito **Subject:** Royal Wedding of Crown Prince **Obv:** Chrysanthemum flanked by sprigs **Rev:** Pair of flying herons

Date	Mintage	VF20	XF40	MS60	MS63	MS65
Yr.5(1993)	4,800,000	—	—	45.00	50.00	60.00
Yr.5(1993)	200,000	PF65 80.00	PF67 100			

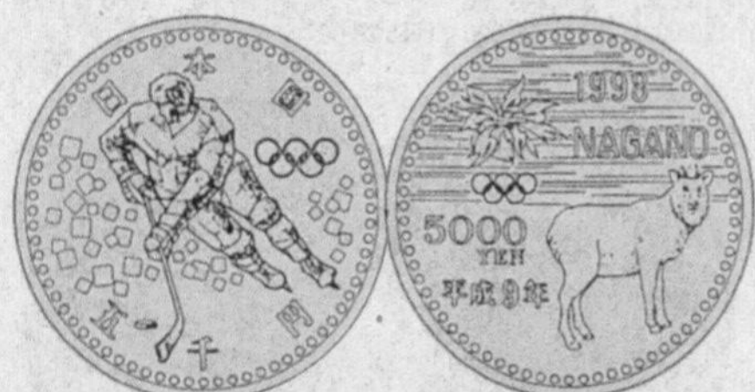

Y# 115 5000 YEN

15.00 g., 0.925 Silver 0.4461 oz. ASW, 30 mm. **Ruler:** Akihito **Series:** 1998 Nagano Winter Olympics **Obv:** Hockey player **Rev:** Value, dates, and Serow

Date	Mintage	VF20	XF40	MS60	MS63	MS65
Yr.9(1997)	4,867,000	—	—	45.00	50.00	60.00
Yr.9(1997)	133,000	PF65 95.00	PF67 115			

Y# 119 5000 YEN

15.00 g., 0.925 Silver 0.4461 oz. ASW, 30 mm. **Ruler:** Akihito **Series:** 1998 Nagano Winter Olympics **Obv:** Biathlon **Rev:** Value, dates, and antelope

Date	Mintage	VF20	XF40	MS60	MS63	MS65
Yr.9(1997)	4,867,000	—	—	45.00	50.00	60.00
Yr.9(1997)	133,000	PF65 95.00	PF67 115			

Y# 120 5000 YEN

15.00 g., 0.925 Silver 0.4461 oz. ASW, 30 mm. **Ruler:** Akihito **Series:** 1998 Nagano Winter Olympics **Obv:** Paralympic skier **Rev:** Value, dates, and antelope

Date	Mintage	VF20	XF40	MS60	MS63	MS65
Yr.10(1998)	4,867,000	—	—	45.00	50.00	60.00
Yr.10(1998)	133,000	PF65 95.00	PF67 115			

Y# 91 10000 YEN

20.00 g., 0.999 Silver 0.6424 oz. ASW, 35 mm. **Ruler:** Hirohito **Subject:** 60 Years - Reign of Hirohito **Obv:** Large chrysanthemum with legends around border **Rev:** Flying birds above center circle with hills and lines below

Date	Mintage	VG8	F12	VF20	XF40	MS63
Yr.61(1986)	10,000,000	—	—	—	—	115

Y# 116 10000 YEN

15.60 g., 1.000 Gold 0.5016 oz. AGW, 26 mm. **Ruler:** Akihito **Series:** 1998 Nagano Winter Olympics **Obv:** Ski jumper **Rev:** Value, dates, and gentian plant

Date	Mintage	VF20	XF40	MS60	MS63	MS65
Yr.9(1997)	55,000	PF65 850	PF67 900			

Y# 121 10000 YEN

15.60 g., 1.000 Gold 0.5016 oz. AGW, 26 mm. **Ruler:** Akihito **Series:** 1998 Nagano Winter Olympics **Obv:** Figure skater **Rev:** Value, dates, and gentian plant

Date	Mintage	VF20	XF40	MS60	MS63	MS65
Yr.9(1997)	55,000	PF65 850	PF67 900			

Y# 122 10000 YEN

15.60 g., 1.000 Gold 0.5016 oz. AGW, 26 mm. **Ruler:** Akihito **Series:** 1998 Nagano Winter Olympics **Obv:** Speed skater **Rev:** Value, dates, and gentian plant

Date	Mintage	VF20	XF40	MS60	MS63	MS65
Yr.10(1998)	55,000	PF65 850	PF67 900			

Y# 124 10000 YEN

20.00 g., 1.000 Gold 0.643 oz. AGW, 28 mm. **Ruler:** Akihito **Subject:** 10th Anniversary of Enthronement **Obv:** Chrysanthemum within wreath **Rev:** Stylized Green Phoenix

Date	Mintage	VF20	XF40	MS60	MS63	MS65
Yr.11(1999)	200,000	PF65 1,100	PF67 1,150			

Y# 109 50000 YEN

18.00 g., 1.000 Gold 0.5787 oz. AGW, 27 mm. **Ruler:** Akihito **Subject:** Royal wedding of Crown Prince **Obv:** Chrysanthemum flanked by cherry blossom sprigs **Rev:** Pair of herons

Date	Mintage	VF20	XF40	MS60	MS63	MS65
Yr.5(1993)	1,900,000	—	—	750	950	1,000
Yr.5(1993)	100,000	PF65 1,100	PF67 1,200			

Y# 92 100000 YEN

20.00 g., 1.000 Gold 0.643 oz. AGW, 30 mm. **Ruler:** Hirohito **Subject:** 60 Years - Reign of Hirohito **Obv:** Large chrysanthemum with legends around border **Rev:** Pair of birds within artistic design

Date	Mintage	VF20	XF40	MS60	MS63	MS65
Yr.61(1986)	10,000,000	—	—	825	1,100	1,200
Yr.62(1987)	875,487	—	—	825	1,125	1,225
Yr.62(1987)	124,513	PF65 1,250	PF67 1,350			

Y# 105 100000 YEN

30.00 g., 1.000 Gold 0.9645 oz. AGW, 33 mm. **Ruler:** Akihito **Subject:** Enthronement of Emperor Akihito **Obv:** Chrysanthemum within wreath **Rev:** Stylized Green Phoenix

Date	Mintage	VF20	XF40	MS60	MS63	MS65
Yr.3(1990)	1,900,000	—	—	1,250	1,600	1,750
Yr.3(1990)	100,000	PF65 1,900	PF67 2,000			

PLATINUM BULLION COINAGE

KM# 20 10 MOMME

1.2056 Platinum APW **Ruler:** Hirohito

Date	Mintage	VG8	F12	VF20	XF40	MS63
1937	1,500	—	—	—	—	2,000

LEPROSARIUM COINAGE

Oshima-Seisho En

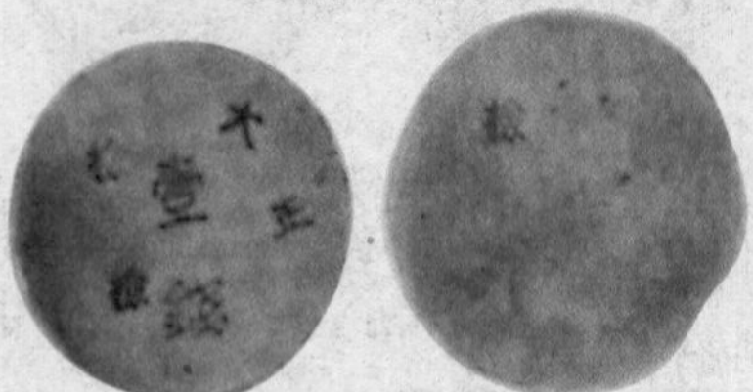

KM# L11 SEN

Brass **Issuer:** Oshima-Seisho En **Obv:** Denomination with mulitple stamps **Rev:** "Ken" symbol = inspection

Date	Mintage	F12	VF20	XF40	MS60	MS63
ND(1912-25) Rare	—	—	—	—	—	—

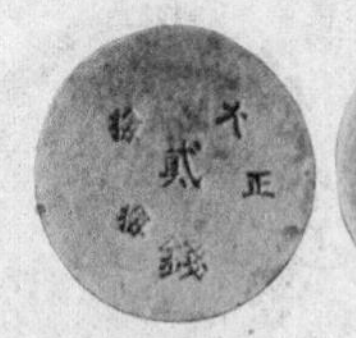
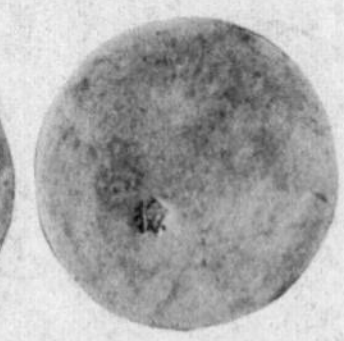

KM# L12 2 SEN
Brass **Issuer:** Oshima-Seisho En

Date	Mintage	F12	VF20	XF40	MS60	MS63
ND(1912-25) Rare	—	—	—	—	—	—

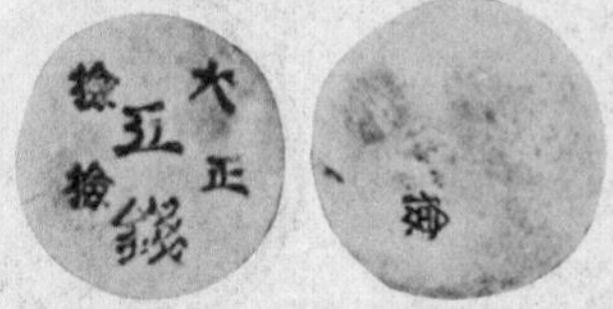

KM# L13 5 SEN
Brass **Issuer:** Oshima-Seisho En

Date	Mintage	F12	VF20	XF40	MS60	MS63
ND(1912-25) Rare	—	—	—	—	—	—

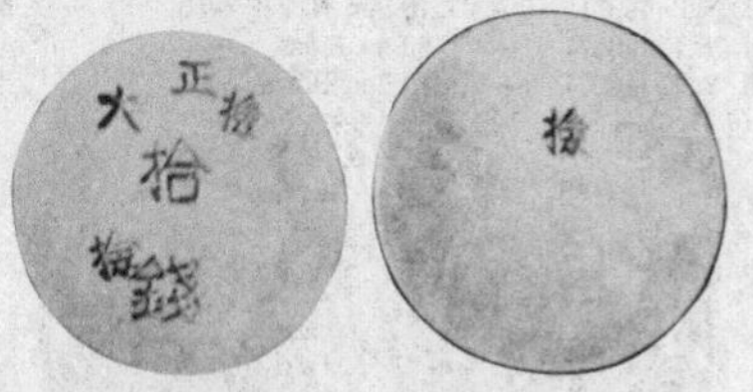

KM# L14 10 SEN
Brass **Issuer:** Oshima-Seisho En

Date	Mintage	F12	VF20	XF40	MS60	MS63
ND(1912-25) Rare	—	—	—	—	—	—

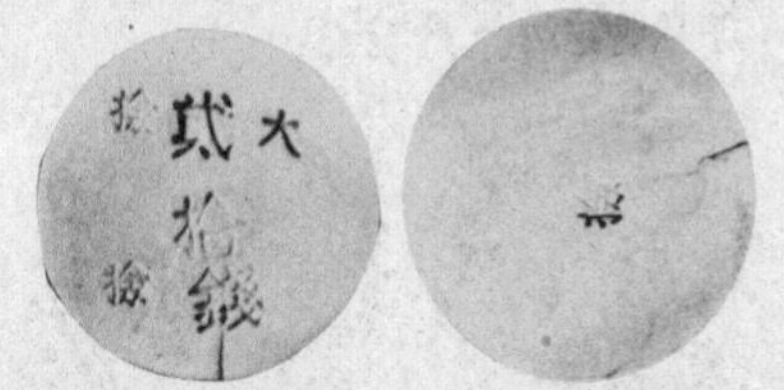

KM# L15 20 SEN
Brass **Issuer:** Oshima-Seisho En

Date	Mintage	F12	VF20	XF40	MS60	MS63
ND(1912-25) Rare	—	—	—	—	—	—

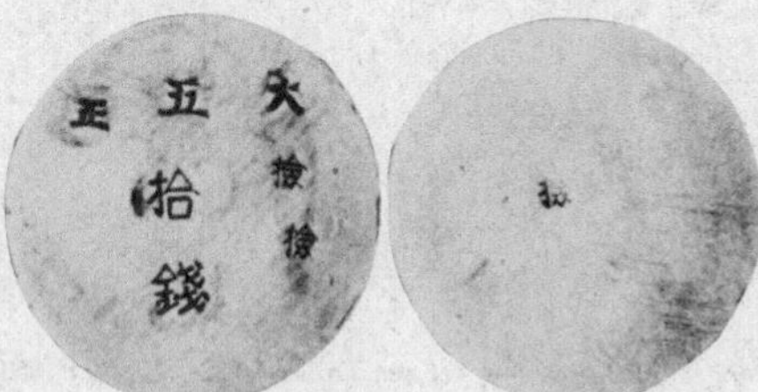

KM# L16 50 SEN
Brass **Issuer:** Oshima-Seisho En

Date	Mintage	F12	VF20	XF40	MS60	MS63
ND(1912-25) Rare	—	—	—	—	—	—

LEPROSARIUM COINAGE

Tama-Zensei En

KM# L20 SEN
Brass lacquered **Issuer:** Tama-Zensei En **Note:** Uniface. Oval with central hole, denomination, rays at border.

Date	Mintage	F12	VF20	XF40	MS60	MS63
ND(1926-28) Rare	—	—	—	—	—	—

KM# L21 5 SEN
Brass lacquered **Issuer:** Tama-Zensei En **Note:** Round with central hole, perpendicular rays fill border from flower.

Date	Mintage	F12	VF20	XF40	MS60	MS63
ND(1926-28) Rare	—	—	—	—	—	—

KM# L22 10 SEN
Brass lacquered **Issuer:** Tama-Zensei En **Note:** Similar to 5 Sen, L21.

Date	Mintage	F12	VF20	XF40	MS60	MS63
ND(1926-28) Rare	—	—	—	—	—	—

KM# L23 50 SEN
Brass lacquered **Issuer:** Tama-Zensei En **Note:** Rectangular with center hole. Sunset with ornate border.

Date	Mintage	F12	VF20	XF40	MS60	MS63
ND(1926-28) Rare	—	—	—	—	—	—

LEPROSARIUM COINAGE

Nagashima-Aisei En

KM# L1 SEN
Brass lacquered **Issuer:** Nagashima-Aisei En **Note:** Uniface. Badge of Aisei En above denomination.

Date	Mintage	F12	VF20	XF40	MS60	MS63
ND(1931-48) Rare	—	—	—	—	—	—

KM# L2 SEN
Aluminum lacquered **Issuer:** Nagashima-Aisei En

Date	Mintage	F12	VF20	XF40	MS60	MS63
ND(1931-48)	—	—	800	1,400	—	—

KM# L3 5 SEN
Brass lacquered **Issuer:** Nagashima-Aisei En

Date	Mintage	F12	VF20	XF40	MS60	MS63
ND(1931-48) Rare	—	—	—	—	—	—

KM# L3a 5 SEN
Aluminum lacquered **Issuer:** Nagashima-Aisei En

Date	Mintage	F12	VF20	XF40	MS60	MS63
ND(1931-48)	—	—	1,350	2,250	—	—

KM# L4 10 SEN
Brass lacquered **Issuer:** Nagashima-Aisei En

Date	Mintage	F12	VF20	XF40	MS60	MS63
ND(1931-48) Rare	—	—	—	—	—	—

KM# L4a 10 SEN
Aluminum lacquered **Issuer:** Nagashima-Aisei En

Date	Mintage	F12	VF20	XF40	MS60	MS63
ND(1931-48)	—	—	1,350	2,250	—	—

KM# L5 50 SEN
Brass lacquered **Issuer:** Nagashima-Aisei En

Date	Mintage	F12	VF20	XF40	MS60	MS63
ND(1931-48)	—	—	1,650	2,750	—	—

KM# L6 YEN
Brass **Issuer:** Nagashima-Aisei En **Rev:** Stylized badge of Aisei En

Date	Mintage	F12	VF20	XF40	MS60	MS63
ND(1931-48)	—	—	2,800	4,500	—	—

OCCUPATION COINAGE

The following issues were struck at the Osaka Mint for use in the Netherlands East Indies. The only inscription found on them is Dai Nippon: Great Japan. The war situation had worsened to the point that shipping the coins became virtually impossible. Consequently, none of these coins were issued in the East Indies and almost the entire issue was lost or were remelted at the mint. Y numbers are for the Netherlands Indies and dates are from the Japanese Shinto dynastic calendar.

Y# A66 SEN
Aluminum **Obv:** Puppet's head **Note:** Prev. NEI Y#22.

Date	Mintage	F12	VF20	XF40	MS60	MS63
NE2603	233,190,000	375	450	525	600	750
NE2604	66,810,000	350	400	500	700	900

Y# B66 5 SEN
Aluminum **Rev:** Stick puppet **Note:** Prev. NEI Y#23.

Date	Mintage	F12	VF20	XF40	MS60	MS63
NE2603	—	6,000	7,500	10,000	—	—

Y# 66 10 SEN
3.50 g., Tin Alloy, 23 mm. **Rev:** Stick puppet **Note:** Prev. NEI Y#24.

Date	Mintage	F12	VF20	XF40	MS60	MS63
NE2603	69,490,000	250	300	350	450	700
NE2604	110,510,000	180	200	300	450	700

PATTERNS

Including off metal strikes

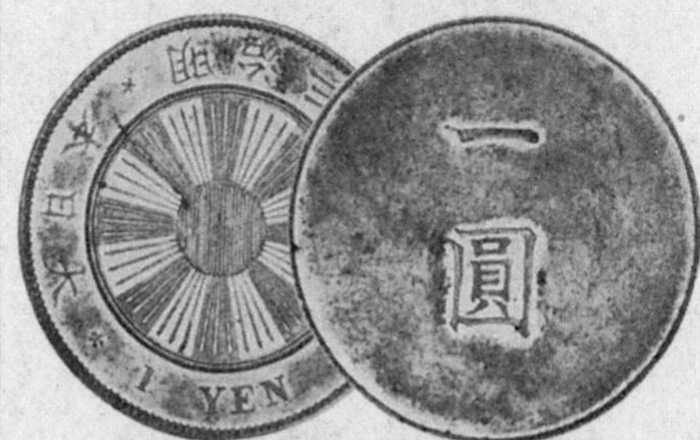

KM#	Date	Mintage	Identification	Mkt Val
Pn31	Yr.34 (1901)	—	Yen. Copper.	—

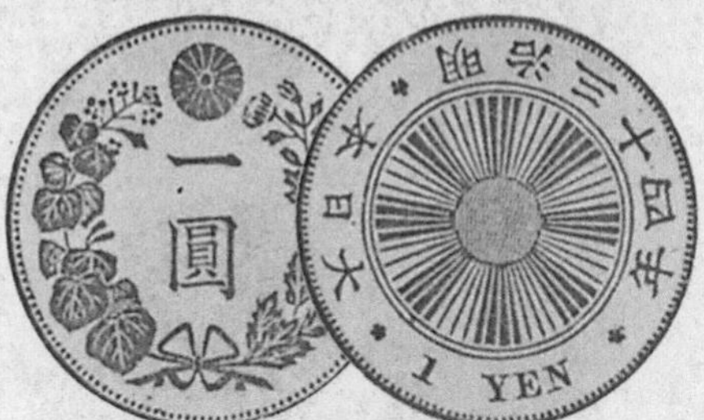

KM#	Date	Mintage	Identification	Mkt Val
Pn32	Yr.34 (1901)	—	Yen. Silver.	—
Pn33	Yr.39 (1906)	—	5 Rin. Copper.	—

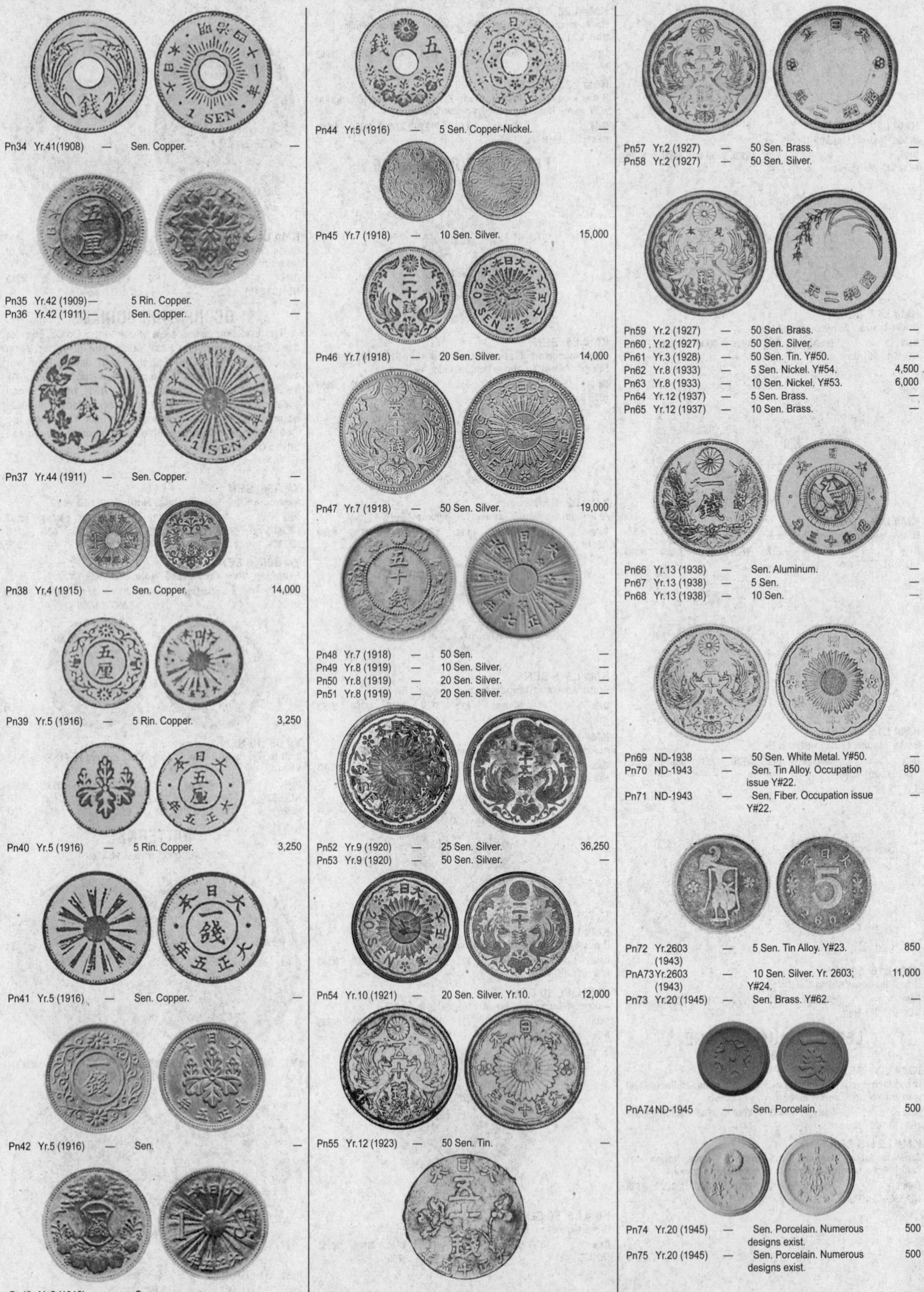

Pn34 Yr.41(1908) — Sen. Copper. —

Pn35 Yr.42 (1909) — 5 Rin. Copper. —
Pn36 Yr.42 (1911) — Sen. Copper. —

Pn37 Yr.44 (1911) — Sen. Copper. —

Pn38 Yr.4 (1915) — Sen. Copper. 14,000

Pn39 Yr.5 (1916) — 5 Rin. Copper. 3,250

Pn40 Yr.5 (1916) — 5 Rin. Copper. 3,250

Pn41 Yr.5 (1916) — Sen. Copper. —

Pn42 Yr.5 (1916) — Sen. —

Pn43 Yr.5 (1916) — Sen. —

Pn44 Yr.5 (1916) — 5 Sen. Copper-Nickel. —

Pn45 Yr.7 (1918) — 10 Sen. Silver. 15,000

Pn46 Yr.7 (1918) — 20 Sen. Silver. 14,000

Pn47 Yr.7 (1918) — 50 Sen. Silver. 19,000

Pn48 Yr.7 (1918) — 50 Sen. —
Pn49 Yr.8 (1919) — 10 Sen. Silver. —
Pn50 Yr.8 (1919) — 20 Sen. Silver. —
Pn51 Yr.8 (1919) — 20 Sen. Silver. —

Pn52 Yr.9 (1920) — 25 Sen. Silver. 36,250
Pn53 Yr.9 (1920) — 50 Sen. Silver. —

Pn54 Yr.10 (1921) — 20 Sen. Silver. Yr.10. 12,000

Pn55 Yr.12 (1923) — 50 Sen. Tin. —

Pn56 Yr.15 (1926) — 50 Sen. Tin. —

Pn57 Yr.2 (1927) — 50 Sen. Brass. —
Pn58 Yr.2 (1927) — 50 Sen. Silver. —

Pn59 Yr.2 (1927) — 50 Sen. Brass. —
Pn60 Yr.2 (1927) — 50 Sen. Silver. —
Pn61 Yr.3 (1928) — 50 Sen. Tin. Y#50. —
Pn62 Yr.8 (1933) — 5 Sen. Nickel. Y#54. 4,500
Pn63 Yr.8 (1933) — 10 Sen. Nickel. Y#53. 6,000
Pn64 Yr.12 (1937) — 5 Sen. Brass. —
Pn65 Yr.12 (1937) — 10 Sen. Brass. —

Pn66 Yr.13 (1938) — Sen. Aluminum. —
Pn67 Yr.13 (1938) — 5 Sen. —
Pn68 Yr.13 (1938) — 10 Sen. —

Pn69 ND-1938 — 50 Sen. White Metal. Y#50. —
Pn70 ND-1943 — Sen. Tin Alloy. Occupation issue Y#22. 850
Pn71 ND-1943 — Sen. Fiber. Occupation issue Y#22. —

Pn72 Yr.2603 (1943) — 5 Sen. Tin Alloy. Y#23. 850
PnA73 Yr.2603 (1943) — 10 Sen. Silver. Yr. 2603; Y#24. 11,000
Pn73 Yr.20 (1945) — Sen. Brass. Y#62. —

PnA74 ND-1945 — Sen. Porcelain. 500

Pn74 Yr.20 (1945) — Sen. Porcelain. Numerous designs exist. 500
Pn75 Yr.20 (1945) — Sen. Porcelain. Numerous designs exist. 500

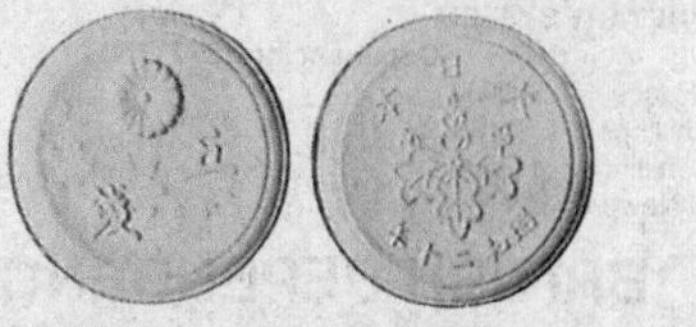

KM#	Date	Mintage	Identification	Mkt Val
Pn76	Yr.20 (1945)	—	5 Sen. Porcelain. Numerous designs exist.	550
Pn77	Yr.20 (1945)	—	5 Sen. Porcelain. Numerous designs exist.	550
Pn78	Yr.20 (1945)	—	10 Sen. Porcelain. Numerous designs exist.	600
Pn79	Yr.20 (1945)	—	10 Sen. Porcelain. Numerous designs exist.	600
Pn80	Yr.21 (1946)	—	10 Sen. Brass. Small size; Y#68.	9,500
Pn81	Yr.25 (1950)	—	Yen. Brass. Y#70.	—
Pn82	Yr.25 (1950)	—	10 Yen. Aluminum. Y#73.	—
Pn83	Yr.25 (1950)	—	10 Yen. Copper-Nickel.	—
Pn84	Yr.26 (1951)	—	5 Yen. Aluminum. Y#72.	—
Pn85	Yr.26 (1951)	—	10 Yen. Copper-Nickel.	—
Pn86	Yr.33 (1958)	—	5 Yen. Brass.	—

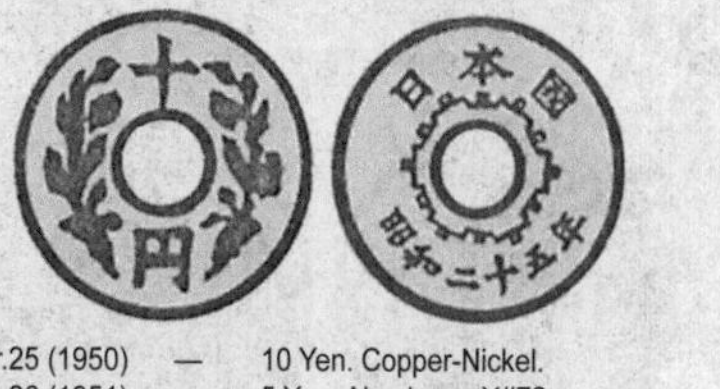

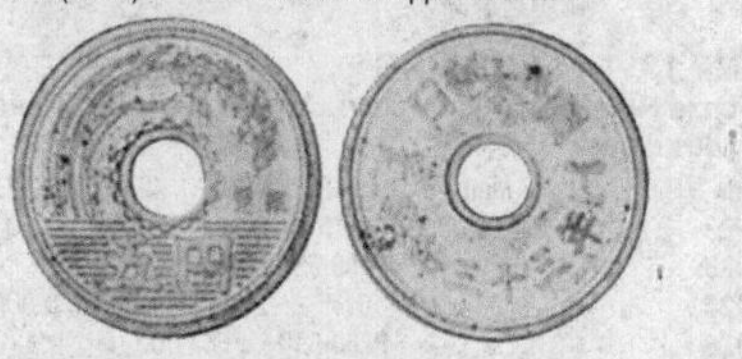

MINT SETS

KM#	Date	Mintage	Identification	Issue Price	Mkt Val
MS1	1969 (5)	6,162	Y#72a, 73a, 74, 81, 82	1.25	750
MS2	1970 (6)	26,000	Y#72a, 73a, 74, 81-83	2.00	70.00
MS3	1971 (5)	14,653	Y#72a, 73a, 74, 81, 82	1.60	100
MS4	1972 (6)	30,000	Y#72a, 73a, 74, 81, 82, 84	2.90	50.00
MS5	1975 (5)	720,000	Y#72a, 73a, 74, 81, 82	2.30	5.00
MS6	1976 (5)	580,000	Y#72a, 73a, 74, 81, 82	2.80	5.00
MS7	1977 (5)	520,000	Y#72a, 73a, 74, 81, 82	3.00	7.50
MS8	1978 (5)	488,000	Y#72a, 73a, 74, 81, 82	3.50	6.00
MS9	1979 (5)	400,000	Y#72a, 73a, 74, 81, 82	3.80	6.00
MS10	1980 (5)	520,000	Y#72a, 73a, 74, 81, 82	3.20	6.00
MS11	1981 (5)	568,000	Y#72a, 73a, 74, 81, 82	4.00	6.00
MS12	1982 (6)	632,000	Y#72a, 73a, 74, 81, 82, 87	6.80	14.00
MS13	1983 (6)	502,000	Y#72a, 73a, 74, 81, 82, 87	6.80	15.00
MS14	1984 (6)	520,000	Y#72a, 73a, 74, 81, 82, 87	7.40	17.00
MS15	1985 (7)	720,000	Y#72a, 73a, 74, 81, 82, 87, 88 Tsukuba Expo box	8.50	30.00
MS16	1985 (7)	100,000	Y#72a, 73a, 74, 81, 82, 87, 88 Tsukuba Expo box, sold on the grounds of the Expo	8.50	115
MS17	1985 (7)	746,000	Y#72a, 73a, 74, 81, 82, 87, 89	10.50	30.00
MS18	1986 (7)	597,000	Y#72a, 73a, 74, 81, 82, 87, 90	15.00	27.00
MS19	1986 (6)	642,000	Y#72a, 73a, 74, 81, 82, 87	9.20	15.00
MSB20	1987 (3)	13,832	Y#90-92 60 years of Reign - Hirohito	1,040	2,000
MS20	1987 (6)	496,463	Y#72a, 73a, 74, 81, 82, 87	12.00	160
MS21	1987 (6)	48,537	Y#72a, 73a, 74, 81, 82, 87 Cherry blossom box	12.00	180
MS22	1988 (6)	605,021	Y#72a, 73a, 74, 81, 82, 87	12.40	12.00
MS23	1988 (6)	41,979	Y#72a, 73a, 74, 81, 82, 87 Cherry blossom box	12.40	27.00
MS24	1988 (2)	400,000	Y#93-94	15.20	22.00
MS25	1989 (6)	647,000	Y#95.1-99.1, 101.1	12.80	27.00
MSA26	1990 (2)	100,000	Y#103, 104 Centenaries of Parliament and the Judicial System	94.00	175
MS26	1990 (6)	600,000	Y95.2-99.2, 101.2	12.00	12.00
MSA27	1991 (2)	100,000	Y#102, 105 Enthronement of Emperor Akihito (coins dated 1990)	850	1,400
MS27	1991 (6)	600,000	Y#95.2-99.2, 101.2	13.00	12.00
MS28	1991 (6)	10,000	Y#95.2-99.2, 101.2 Hiroshima cherry blossom box	13.60	50.00
MS29	1991 (6)	50,000	Y#95.2-99.2, 101.2 Osaka cherry blossom box	13.60	22.00
MS30	1991 (6)	40,000	Y#95.2-99.2, 101.2 120th Anniversary of the Mint box	13.60	18.00
MS31	1992 (7)	700,000	Y#95.2-99.2, 101.2, 106	18.40	28.00
MS32	1992 (6)	20,000	Y#95.2-99.2, 101.2 Hiroshima cherry blossom box	13.60	28.00
MS33	1992 (6)	50,000	Y#95.2-99.2, 101.2 Osaka cherry blossom box	13.60	22.00
MS34	1992 (6)	30,000	Y#95.2-99.2, 101.2 Toyama Expo box	13.60	28.00
MS35	1993 (7)	800,000	Y#95.2-99.2, 101.2, 107	22.50	28.00
MS36	1993 (6)	70,000	Y#95.2-99.2, 101.2 Osaka cherry blossom box	17.10	28.00
MS37	1993 (6)	30,000	Y#95.2-99.2, 101.2 Hiroshima cherry blossom box	17.10	28.00
MS38	1993 (6)	10,000	Y#95.2-99.2, 101.2 Tokyo Coin Expo box	17.10	42.00
MS39	1993 (6)	30,000	Y#95.2-99.2, 101.2 Nagano-Shinano Expo box	17.10	25.00
MS40	1993 (6)	100,000	Y#95.2-99.2, 101.2 Respect for the Aged box	19.80	18.00
MS41	1994 (6)	80,000	Y#95.2-99.2, 101.2 Osaka cherry blossom box	19.00	30.00
MS42	1994 (6)	20,000	Y#95.2-99.2, 101.2 Hiroshima cherry blossom box	19.00	28.00
MS43	1994 (6)	10,000	Y#95.2-99.2, 101.2 5th International Tokyo Coin Convention box	19.00	30.00
MS44	1994 (6)	10,000	Y#95.2-99.2, 101.2 Transfer of the Heian Capital box	19.00	115
MS45	1994 (6)	30,000	Y#95.2-99.2, 101.2 Mie Festival Exposition box	19.00	28.00
MS46	1994 (6)	570,000	Y#95.2-99.2, 101.2 Mint box	18.00	15.00
MS47	1994 (6)	100,000	Y#95.2-99.2, 101.2 Respect for the Aged box	22.00	18.00
MS48	1994 (6)	10,000	Y#95.2-99.2, 101.2 Tokyo Branch Mint Coin Fair box	19.00	27.00
MSA49	1994 (1)	20,000	Y#99.2 Mint visit souvenir folder	9.00	15.00
MS49	1995 (6)	80,000	Y#95.2-99.2, 101.2 Osaka cherry blossom box	19.00	27.00
MS50	1995 (6)	10,000	Y#95.2-99.2, 101.2 Hiroshima cherry blossom box	19.00	30.00
MS51	1995 (6)	10,000	Y#95.2-99.2, 101.2 6th Tokyo International Coin Convention	19.00	30.00
MS52	1995 (6)	10,000	Y#95.2-99.2, 101.2 Romantopia '95 box	19.00	32.00
MS53	1995 (6)	10,000	Y#95.2-99.2, 101.2 Coin and Banknote Fair box	19.00	30.00
MS54	1995 (6)	12,000	Y#95.2-99.2, 101.2 50th Anniversary Hiroshima Branch Mint	19.00	30.00
MS55	1995 (6)	355,000	Y#95.2-99.2, 101.2 Mint production scenes box	18.00	25.00
MS56	1995 (6)	200,000	Y#95.2-99.2, 101.2 Respect for the Aged box	22.00	18.00
MS57	1995 (6)	390,000	Y#95.2-99.2, 101.2 Horyuji Temple folder	19.00	17.00
MS58	1995 (6)	192,500	Y#95.2-99.2, 101.2 Himeji Castle folder	19.00	18.00
MS59	1995 (6)	191,500	Y#95.2-99.2, 101.2 Ancient Kyoto folder	19.00	18.00
MS60	1995 (6)	177,500	Y#95.2-99.2, 101.2 Yakushima folder	19.00	18.00
MS61	1995 (6)	174,500	Y#95.2-99.2, 101.2 Shirakami Mountains folder	19.00	18.00
MS62	1995 (6)	10,000	Y#95.2-99.2, 101.2 Tokyo Mint Fair box	18.00	25.00
MS63	1995 (1)	20,000	Y#99.2 Mint visit souvenir folder	8.50	10.00
MS64	1995 (6)	20,000	Y#95.2-99.2, 101.2 Birthday folder	20.00	25.00
MS65	1996 (6)	80,000	Y#95.2-99.2, 101.2 Osaka cherry blossom box	17.00	30.00
MS66	1996 (6)	10,000	Y#95.2-99.2, 101.2 Hiroshima cherry blossom box	17.00	30.00
MS67	1996 (1)	10,000	Y#99.2 Mint visit souvenir folder	8.00	10.00
MS68	1996 (6)	10,000	Y#95.2-99.2, 101.2 Birthday folder	19.00	32.00
MS69	1996 (6)	10,000	Y#95.2-99.2, 101.2 7th Tokyo International Coin Convention box	17.00	30.00
MS70	1996 (6)	20,000	Y#95.2-99.2, 101.2 Saga World Ceramics Expo box	17.00	28.00
MS71	1996 (6)	8,000	Y#95.2-99.2, 101.2 Okayama Coin, Banknote, and Stamp Exhibition box	17.00	32.00
MS72	1996 (6)	290,000	Y#95.2-99.2, 101.2 Shirakawa district folder	18.00	20.00
MS73	1996 (6)	200,000	Y#95.2-99.2, 101.2 Respect for the Aged box	20.00	25.00
MS74	1996 (6)	100,000	Y#95.2-99.2, 101.2 125th Anniversary Birth of the Yen folder	27.00	60.00
MS75	1996 (6)	321,000	Y#95.2-99.2, 101.2 Aerial view of old and new mint box	16.00	25.00
MS76	1996 (6)	6,000	Y#95.2-99.2, 101.2 Tokyo Branch Mint fair box	17.00	30.00
MS77	1997 (1)	10,000	Y#101.2 Mint visit souvenir folder	8.00	10.00
MS78	1997 (6)	12,000	Y#95.2-99.2, 101.2 Anniversary folder	17.00	30.00
MS79	1997 (6)	80,000	Y#95.2-99.2, 101.2 Osaka cherry blossom box	16.00	30.00
MS80	1997 (6)	10,000	Y#95.2-99.2, 101.2 Hiroshima cherry blossom box	16.00	32.00
MS81	1997 (6)	10,000	Y#95.2-99.2, 101.2 8th Tokyo International Coin Convention box	16.00	30.00
MS82	1997 (6)	10,000	Y#95.2-99.2, 101.2 Tottori '97 Expo box	16.00	32.00
MS83	1997 (6)	7,000	Y#95.2-99.2, 101.2 Yamagata Coin, Note, and Stamp Exhibition box	16.00	32.00
MS84	1997 (6)	331,000	Y#95.2-99.2, 101.2 Mint Bureau box	14.00	18.00
MS85	1997 (6)	250,000	Y#95.2-99.2, 101.2 Respect for the Aged box	15.50	20.00
MS86	1997 (6)	8,000	Y#95.2-99.2, 101.2 Tokyo Mint Fair box	15.00	28.00
MS87	1997 (6)	195,000	Y#95.2-99.2, 101.2 Hiroshima Peace Dome folder	15.50	22.00

KM#	Date	Mintage	Identification	Issue Price	Mkt Val
MS88	1997 (6)	205,000	Y#95.2-99.2, 101.2 Itsukushima Shrine folder	15.50	22.00
MS89	1998 (1)	10,000	Y#99.2 Mint visit souvenir folder	7.00	10.00
MS90	1998 (6)	10,000	Y#95.2-99.2, 101.2 Anniversary folder	16.00	32.00
MS91	1998 (6)	81,000	Y#95.2-99.2, 101.2 Osaka cherry blossom box	14.50	30.00
MS92	1998 (6)	10,000	Y#95.2-99.2, 101.2 Hiroshima cherry blossom box	14.50	30.00
MS93	1998 (6)	13,000	Y#95.2-99.2, 101.2 9th Tokyo International Coin Convention box	14.50	30.00
MS94	1998 (6)	257,000	Y#95.2-99.2, 101.2 Respect for the Aged box	17.00	22.00
MS95	1998 (6)	10,000	Y#95.2-99.2, 101.2 World Cup - Japan vs. Argentina box	17.00	35.00
MS96	1998 (6)	10,000	Y#95.2-99.2, 101.2 World Cup - Japan vs. Croatia box	17.00	35.00
MS97	1998 (6)	10,000	Y#95.2-99.2, 101.2 World Cup - Japan vs. Jamaica box	17.00	35.00
MS98	1998 (6)	336,000	Y#95.2-99.2, 101.2 Mint Bureau box	17.50	22.00
MS99	1998 (6)	6,000	Y#95.2-99.2, 101.2 Tokyo Mint Fair box	18.05	28.00
MS100	1999 (6)	20,000	Y#95.2-99.2, 101.2 Anniversary folder	19.95	32.00
MS101	1999 (1)	20,000	Y#99.2 Mint visit souvenir folder	8.55	10.00
MS102	1999 (6)	6,000	Y#95.2-99.2, 101.2 Kumamoto mint box	18.05	45.00
MS103	1999 (6)	80,000	Y#95.2-99.2, 101.2 Osaka cherry blossom box	18.05	30.00
MS104	1999 (6)	10,000	Y#95.2-99.2, 101.2 Hiroshima cherry blossom box	18.05	32.00
MS105	1999 (6)	10,000	Y#95.2-99.2, 101.2 10th Tokyo International Coin Convention box	18.05	30.00
MS106	1999 (6)	6,000	Y#95.2-99.2, 101.2 Akita exhibit box	18.55	32.00
MS107	1999 (6)	6,000	Y#95.2-99.2, 101.2 Tokyo Mint Fair box	18.55	32.00
MS108	1999 (6)	200,000	Y#95.2-99.2, 101.2 Nara Monasteries folder	18.55	30.00
MS109	1999 (6)	250,000	Y#95.2-99.2, 101.2 Respect for the Aged box	18.55	30.00
MS110	1999 (6)	300,000	Y#95.2-99.2, 101.2 Mint Bureau box	18.55	32.00
MS111	2000 (5)	5,000	Y#95.2-98.2, 101.2 Mint exhibition in Nagoya box	11.00	50.00
MS112	2000 (6)	65,000	Y#95.2-98.2, 101.2, 125 Osaka cherry blossom box	11.00	45.00
MS113	2000 (6)	10,000	Y#95.2-98.2, 101.2, 125 Hiroshima cherry blossom box	11.00	40.00
MS114	2000 (5)	10,000	Y#95.2-98.2, 101.2, 125 400th Anniversary Japanese-Dutch relation at Nagsaki box	11.00	45.00
MS115	2000 (6)	10,000	Y#95.2-98.2, 101.2, 125 11th Tokyo International Coin Convention box	11.00	45.00
MS116	2000 (6)	7,000	Y#95.2-98.2, 101.2, 125 Otaru Coin and Stamp Show box	11.00	30.00
MS117	2000 (6)	4,000	Y#95.2-98.2, 101.2, 125 Tokyo Mint Fair box	11.00	40.00
MS118	2000 (5)	5,600	Y#95.2-99.2, 101.2 Japan Coin Set box	17.00	30.00
MS119	2000 (2)	4,000	Y#96.2, 125 Japan Coins short set	8.50	25.00
MS120	2000 (5)	222,300	Y#95.2-99.2, 101.2 Nikko World Cultural Sites	17.00	30.00
MS121	2000 (5)	340,200	Y#95.2-99.2, 101.2 Mint Bureau box	15.00	25.00
MS122	2000 (6)	4,500	Y#95.2-98.2, 101.2, 125 Anniversary folder	18.00	45.00
MS123	2000 (12)	155,400	Y#95.2-98.2, 101.2, 125 Millennium Respect for the Aged box	19.00	40.00
MS124	2000 (12)	8,000	Y#95.2-98.2, 101.2, 125 Branch mint in Kanazawa box	16.00	40.00

PROOF SETS

KM#	Date	Mintage	Identification	Issue Price	Mkt Val
PS1	1987 (6)	230,000	Y#72a, 73a, 74, 81, 82, 87	37.40	160
PS2	1988 (6)	200,000	Y#72a, 73a, 74, 81, 82, 87	46.50	40.00
PS3	1989 (6)	200,000	Y#95.1-99.1, 101.1	47.90	40.00
PS4	1990 (6)	200,000	Y#95.2-99.2, 101.2	47.90	50.00
PS5	1991 (6)	220,000	Y#95.2-99.2, 101.2	58.75	50.00
PS6	1992 (6)	250,000	Y#95.2-99.2, 101.2	55.65	45.00
PS7	1993 (6)	250,000	Y#95.2-99.2, 101.2	72.00	45.00
PS8	1993 (3)	100,000	Y#107-109 Crown Prince's Wedding	630	1,000
PS9	1993 (2)	100,000	Y#107, 108 Crown Prince's Wedding	100	120
PS10	1994 (6)	227,000	Y#95.2-99.2, 101.2	72.00	35.00
PS11	1994 (3)	100,000	Y#111-113 12th Asian Games	68.00	95.00
PS12	1994 (1)	100,000	Y#110 Kansai Airport	27.00	40.00
PS13	1995 (6)	200,000	Y#95.2-99.2, 101.2	72.00	50.00
PS14	1996 (6)	189,000	Y#95.2-99.2, 101.2	103	60.00
PS15	1997 (3)	33,000	Y#114-116 Nagano Olympics	413	800
PS16	1997 (2)	100,000	Y#114, 115 Nagano Olympics	99.00	150
PS17	1997 (3)	33,000	Y#117, 119, 121 Nagano Olympics	406	800
PS18	1997 (2)	100,000	Y#117, 119 Nagano Olympics	97.00	150
PS19	1997 (6)	1,000	Y#95.2-99.2, 101.2 Japan Expo Tottori '97	59.00	1,200
PS20	1997 (6)	186,000	Y#95.2-99.2, 101.2	56.00	60.00
PS21	1997 (6)	25,000	Y#95.2-99.2, 101.2 Tokyo Bay Aqualine Opening	56.00	100
PS22	1998 (3)	33,000	Y#118, 120, 122 Nagano Olympics	375	800
PS23	1998 (2)	100,000	Y#118, 120 Nagano Olympics	90.00	150
PS24	1998 (6)	30,000	Y#95.2-99.2, 101.2 Akashi Strait Bridge Opening	59.00	80.00
PS25	1998 (6)	170,000	Y#95.2-99.2, 101.2 Mint Bureau box	62.50	55.00
PS26	1999 (6)	80,000	Y#95.2-99.2, 101.2 Old Type Coin series (20 yen medallet)	69.85	95.00
PS27	1999 (6)	50,000	Y#95.2-99.2, 101.2 Coastal Highway	69.85	95.00
PS28	1999 (6)	150,000	Y#95.2-99.2, 101.2 Bureau box	69.85	80.00
PS29	1999 (2)	100,000	Y#123, 124 10th Anniversary of Enthronement	370	1,200
PS30	2000 (6)	100,000	Y#95.2-98.2, 101.2, 125 Old Type Coin Series (1 yen crown medallet)	62.50	75.00
PS31	2000 (6)	126,000	Y#95.2-98.2, 101.2, 125 Mint Bureau Box	62.50	75.00

JERSEY

The Bailiwick of Jersey, a British Crown dependency located in the English Channel 12 miles (19 km.) west of Normandy, France, has an area of 45 sq. mi. (117 sq. km.) and a population of 74,000. Capital: St. Helier. The economy is based on agriculture and cattle breeding – the importation of cattle is prohibited to protect the purity of the island's world-famous strain of milch cows.

Jersey was occupied by Neanderthal man by 100,000 B.C., and by Iberians of 2000 B.C. who left their chamber tombs in the island's granite cliffs. Roman legions almost certainly visited the island although they left no evidence of settlement. The country folk of Jersey still speak an archaic form of Norman-French, lingering evidence of the Norman annexation of the island in 933 A.D. Jersey was annexed to England in 1206, 140 years after the Norman Conquest. The dependency is administered by its own laws and customs; laws enacted by the British Parliament do not apply to Jersey unless it is specifically mentioned. During World War II, German troops occupied the island from July1, 1940 until May 9, 1945.

Coins of pre-Roman Gaul and of Rome have been found in abundance on Jersey.

RULER

British

MINT MARK

H - Heaton, Birmingham

MONETARY SYSTEM

Commencing 1877

12 Pence = 1 Shilling
5 Shillings = 1 Crown
20 Shillings = 1 Pound
100 New Pence = 1 Pound

BRITISH DEPENDENCY

STANDARD COINAGE

KM# 9 1/24 SHILLING

Bronze **Ruler:** Edward VII **Obv:** Crowned bust right **Rev:** Pointed shield divides date

Date	Mintage	F12	VF20	XF40	MS60	MS63
1909	120,000	1.00	2.50	11.50	40.00	60.00

KM# 11 1/24 SHILLING

Bronze **Ruler:** George V **Obv:** Crowned bust left **Rev:** Pointed shield divides date

Date	Mintage	F12	VF20	XF40	MS60	MS63
1911	72,000	1.00	2.50	11.50	40.00	60.00
1913	72,000	1.00	2.50	11.50	28.00	45.00
1923	72,000	1.00	2.50	11.50	28.00	45.00

KM# 13 1/24 SHILLING

Bronze **Ruler:** George V **Obv:** Crowned bust left **Rev:** Shield divides date

Date	Mintage	F12	VF20	XF40	MS60	MS63
1923	72,000	0.75	3.00	5.50	22.50	35.00
1923	—	**PF60** 550	**PF63** 800			
1926	120,000	0.75	2.50	4.50	20.00	32.00
1926	—	**PF60** 550	**PF63** 800			

KM# 15 1/24 SHILLING

Bronze **Ruler:** George V **Obv:** Crowned bust left **Rev:** Shield divides date

Date	Mintage	F12	VF20	XF40	MS60	MS63
1931	72,000	0.50	1.00	3.00	15.00	25.00
1931	—	**PF60** 250	**PF63** 400	**PF65** 600		
1933	72,000	0.50	1.00	3.00	15.00	25.00
1933	—	**PF60** 250	**PF63** 400	**PF65** 600		
1935	72,000	0.50	1.00	3.00	15.00	25.00
1935	—	**PF60** 250	**PF63** 400	**PF65** 600		

KM# 17 1/24 SHILLING

Bronze **Ruler:** George VI **Obv:** Crowned head left **Rev:** Shield divides date

Date	Mintage	F12	VF20	XF40	MS60	MS63
1937	72,000	0.50	1.00	3.00	15.00	25.00
1937	—	**PF60** 175	**PF63** 275	**PF65** 450		

KM# 33 10 NEW PENCE
11.30 g., Copper-Nickel, 28.5 mm. **Ruler:** Elizabeth II **Obv:** Young bust right **Rev:** Shield above written value

Date	Mintage	VF20	XF40	MS60	MS63	MS65
1968	1,500,000	0.20	0.35	0.50	0.80	1.50
1975	1,022,000	0.20	0.30	0.50	0.80	1.50
1980	1,000,000	0.20	0.30	0.50	0.80	1.50
1980	10,000	PF65 5.50				

KM# 49 10 PENCE
11.30 g., Copper-Nickel, 28.5 mm. **Ruler:** Elizabeth II **Obv:** Young bust right **Rev:** Shield divides date

Date	Mintage	VF20	XF40	MS60	MS63	MS65
1981	50,000	—	0.30	0.50	0.85	1.75
1981	15,000	PF65 2.25				

KM# 57.1 10 PENCE
11.30 g., Copper-Nickel, 28.5 mm. **Ruler:** Elizabeth II **Obv:** Young bust right **Rev:** La Houque Bie, Faldouet, St. Martin

Date	Mintage	VF20	XF40	MS60	MS63	MS65
1983	30,000	—	0.30	0.50	1.00	2.00
1984	100,000	—	0.30	0.50	1.00	2.00
1985	100,000	—	0.30	0.50	1.00	2.00
1986	400,000	—	0.30	0.50	1.00	2.00
1987	800,000	—	0.30	0.50	1.00	2.00
1988	650,000	—	0.30	0.50	1.00	2.00
1989	700,000	—	0.30	0.50	1.00	2.00
1990	850,000	—	0.30	0.50	1.00	2.00

KM# 57.1a 10 PENCE
13.20 g., 0.925 Silver 0.3926 oz. ASW, 28.5 mm. **Ruler:** Elizabeth II **Obv:** Young bust right **Rev:** La Houque Bie, Faldouet, St. Martin

Date	Mintage	VF20	XF40	MS60	MS63	MS65
1983	5,000	PF65 15.00				

KM# 57.2 10 PENCE
Copper-Nickel, 24.5 mm. **Ruler:** Elizabeth II **Obv:** Young bust right **Rev:** La Houque Bie, Faldouet, St. Martin **Note:** Reduced size.

Date	Mintage	VF20	XF40	MS60	MS63	MS65
1992	7,000,000	—	0.30	0.50	1.00	2.00
1997	5,500	—	—	—	—	2.00
Note: Sets only						
1998	—	—	—	0.50	1.00	2.00

KM# 53 20 PENCE
5.00 g., Copper-Nickel, 21.4 mm. **Ruler:** Elizabeth II **Subject:** 100th Anniversary of Lighthouse at Corbiere **Obv:** Young bust right **Rev:** Date below lighthouse **Shape:** 7-sided

Date	Mintage	VF20	XF40	MS60	MS63	MS65
1982	200,000	—	0.50	1.00	1.50	2.00

KM# 53a 20 PENCE
5.83 g., 0.925 Silver 0.1734 oz. ASW, 21.4 mm. **Ruler:** Elizabeth II **Subject:** 100th Anniversary of Lighthouse at Corbiere **Obv:** Young bust right **Rev:** Date below lighthouse **Shape:** 7-sided

Date	Mintage	VF20	XF40	MS60	MS63	MS65
1982	1,500	PF65 12.00				

KM# 66 20 PENCE
5.00 g., Copper-Nickel, 21.4 mm. **Ruler:** Elizabeth II **Subject:** 100th Anniversary of Lighthouse at Corbiere **Obv:** Young bust right **Rev:** Written value below lighthouse **Shape:** 7-sided

Date	Mintage	VF20	XF40	MS60	MS63	MS65
1983	400,000	—	0.50	1.00	1.50	2.00
1984	250,000	—	0.50	1.00	1.50	2.00
1986	100,000	—	0.50	1.00	1.50	2.00
1987	100,000	—	0.50	1.00	1.50	2.00
1989	100,000	—	0.50	1.00	1.50	2.00
1990	150,000	—	0.50	1.00	1.50	2.00
1992	—	—	—	—	—	2.00
Note: Sets only						
1994	200,000	—	0.50	1.00	1.50	2.00
1996	250,000	—	0.50	1.00	1.50	2.00
1997	600,000	—	0.50	1.00	1.50	2.00

KM# 66a 20 PENCE
5.83 g., 0.925 Silver 0.1734 oz. ASW, 21.4 mm. **Ruler:** Elizabeth II **Subject:** 100th Anniversary of Lighthouse at Corbiere **Obv:** Young bust right **Rev:** Written value below lighthouse **Shape:** 7-sided

Date	Mintage	VF20	XF40	MS60	MS63	MS65
1983	5,000	PF65 12.00				

KM# 107 20 PENCE
5.00 g., Copper-Nickel, 21.4 mm. **Ruler:** Elizabeth II **Obv:** Head with tiara right

Date	Mintage	VF20	XF40	MS60	MS63	MS65
1998	900,000	—	0.50	0.75	1.25	2.00

KM# 44 25 PENCE
28.28 g., Copper-Nickel, 38.61 mm. **Ruler:** Elizabeth II **Subject:** Queen's Silver Jubilee **Obv:** Young bust right **Rev:** Mont Orgueil Castle and Gorey Harbour **Edge:** Reeded

Date	Mintage	VF20	XF40	MS60	MS63	MS65
ND(1977)	262,000	—	—	1.50	2.50	3.50

KM# 44a 25 PENCE
28.28 g., 0.925 Silver 0.841 oz. ASW **Ruler:** Elizabeth II **Subject:** Queen's Silver Jubilee **Obv:** Young bust right **Rev:** Mont Orgueil and sailboats

Date	Mintage	VF20	XF40	MS60	MS63	MS65
ND(1977)	25,000	PF65 28.00				

KM# 34 50 NEW PENCE
13.50 g., Copper-Nickel, 30 mm. **Ruler:** Elizabeth II **Obv:** Young bust right **Rev:** Shield above written value **Shape:** 7-sided

Date	Mintage	VF20	XF40	MS60	MS63	MS65
1969	480,000	—	—	1.00	1.50	2.50
1980	100,000	—	—	1.00	1.50	2.50
1980	10,000	PF65 9.00				

KM# 35 50 PENCE
5.42 g., 0.925 Silver 0.1612 oz. ASW **Ruler:** Elizabeth II **Subject:** 25th Wedding Anniversary **Obv:** Young bust right **Rev:** Mace divides map

Date	Mintage	VF20	XF40	MS60	MS63	MS65
1972	24,000	—	—	4.00	6.00	8.00
1972	1,500	PF65 15.00				

KM# 50 50 PENCE
13.50 g., Copper-Nickel, 30 mm. **Ruler:** Elizabeth II **Obv:** Young bust right **Rev:** Shield divides date **Shape:** 7-sided

Date	Mintage	VF20	XF40	MS60	MS63	MS65
1981	50,000	—	0.75	1.00	1.50	2.50
1981	15,000	PF65 3.00				

KM# 58.1 50 PENCE
13.50 g., Copper-Nickel, 30 mm. **Ruler:** Elizabeth II **Obv:** Young bust right **Rev:** Grosnez Castle **Shape:** 7-sided

Date	Mintage	VF20	XF40	MS60	MS63	MS65
1983	50,000	—	0.75	1.00	1.50	2.50
1984	50,000	—	0.75	1.00	1.50	2.50
1986	30,000	—	0.75	1.00	1.50	2.50
1987	150,000	—	0.75	1.00	1.50	2.50
1988	130,000	—	0.75	1.00	1.50	2.50
1989	180,000	—	0.75	1.00	1.50	2.50
1990	370,000	—	0.75	1.00	1.50	2.50
1992	—	—	—	—	—	2.50
Note: Sets only						
1994	200,000	—	0.75	1.00	1.50	2.50
1997	5,500	—	—	—	—	2.50
Note: Sets only						

KM# 58.1a 50 PENCE
15.50 g., 0.925 Silver 0.461 oz. ASW, 30 mm. **Ruler:** Elizabeth II **Obv:** Young bust right **Rev:** Grosnez Castle **Shape:** 7-sided

Date	Mintage	VF20	XF40	MS60	MS63	MS65
1983	5,000	PF63 18.00	PF65 22.00			

KM# 58.2 50 PENCE
Copper-Nickel, 27.3 mm. **Ruler:** Elizabeth II **Obv:** Young bust right **Rev:** Grosnez Castle **Shape:** 7-sided **Note:** Small size.

Date	Mintage	VF20	XF40	MS60	MS63	MS65
1997	1,500,000	—	—	—	2.50	3.50

KM# 63 50 PENCE
13.50 g., Copper-Nickel, 30 mm. **Ruler:** Elizabeth II **Subject:** 40th Anniversary - Liberation of 1945 **Obv:** Crowned bust right **Rev:** Crossed flags divides dates above chain links with value below **Shape:** 7-sided

Date	Mintage	VF20	XF40	MS60	MS63	MS65
1985	1,000,000	—	—	1.25	2.50	3.50

KM# 108 50 PENCE
8.00 g., Copper-Nickel, 27.3 mm. **Ruler:** Elizabeth II **Obv:** Crowned bust right **Rev:** Gothic gate arch **Edge:** Plain **Shape:** 7-sided

Date	Mintage	VF20	XF40	MS60	MS63	MS65
1998	2,000,000	—	0.75	1.00	2.00	3.00

KM# 36 POUND
10.84 g., 0.925 Silver 0.3224 oz. ASW **Ruler:** Elizabeth II **Subject:** 25th Wedding Anniversary **Obv:** Young bust right **Rev:** Lillies

Date	Mintage	VF20	XF40	MS60	MS63	MS65
1972	24,000	—	—	8.00	10.00	12.00
1972	1,500	PF63 15.00	PF65 20.00			

KM# 51 POUND
9.00 g., Copper-Nickel **Ruler:** Elizabeth II **Subject:** Bicentennial - Battle of Jersey **Obv:** Young bust right **Rev:** Badge of the Royal Jersey Militia **Shape:** 4-sided

Date	Mintage	VF20	XF40	MS60	MS63	MS65
ND-1981	200,000	—	—	—	2.50	3.50
ND-1981	15,000	PF65 6.00				

KM# 51a POUND
10.45 g., 0.925 Silver 0.3108 oz. ASW **Ruler:** Elizabeth II **Subject:** Bicentennial - Battle of Jersey **Obv:** Young bust right **Rev:** Crowned shaded pointed shield within X design divides dates **Shape:** Square

Date	Mintage	VF20	XF40	MS60	MS63	MS65
ND-1981	10,000	PF65 12.00				

KM# 51b POUND
17.55 g., 0.917 Gold 0.5174 oz. AGW **Ruler:** Elizabeth II **Subject:** Bicentennial - Battle of Jersey **Obv:** Young bust right **Rev:** Crowned shaded pointed shield within X design divides dates **Shape:** Square

Date	Mintage	VF20	XF40	MS60	MS63	MS65
ND-1981	5,000	PF63 800	PF65 950	PF67 1,000		

KM# 59 POUND
9.50 g., Nickel-Brass, 22.5 mm. **Ruler:** Elizabeth II **Obv:** Young bust right **Rev:** Shield above written value **Edge Lettering:** CAESAREA INSULA

Date	Mintage	VF20	XF40	MS60	MS63	MS65
1983	100,000	—	—	—	2.50	3.50

KM# 59a POUND
11.68 g., 0.925 Silver 0.3474 oz. ASW, 22.5 mm. **Ruler:** Elizabeth II **Obv:** Young bust right **Rev:** Shield above written value

Date	Mintage	VF20	XF40	MS60	MS63	MS65
1983	2,500	PF63 12.00	PF65 18.00			

KM# 59b POUND
19.65 g., 0.917 Gold 0.5793 oz. AGW, 22.5 mm. **Ruler:** Elizabeth II **Obv:** Young bust right **Rev:** Shield above written value

Date	Mintage	VF20	XF40	MS60	MS63	MS65
1983	250	PF63 775	PF65 825	PF67 900		

Note: 497 pieces were remelted

KM# 60 POUND
9.50 g., Nickel-Brass, 22.5 mm. **Ruler:** Elizabeth II **Obv:** Young bust right **Rev:** Shield above written value **Edge Lettering:** CAESAREA INSULA

Date	Mintage	VF20	XF40	MS60	MS63	MS65
1984	20,000	—	—	—	2.50	3.50

KM# 60a POUND
11.68 g., 0.925 Silver 0.3474 oz. ASW, 22.5 mm. **Ruler:** Elizabeth II **Obv:** Young bust right **Rev:** Shield above written value

Date	Mintage	VF20	XF40	MS60	MS63	MS65
1984	2,500	PF63 12.00	PF65 18.00			

KM# 60b POUND
19.65 g., 0.917 Gold 0.5793 oz. AGW, 22.5 mm. **Ruler:** Elizabeth II **Obv:** Young bust right **Rev:** Shield above written value

Date	Mintage	VF20	XF40	MS60	MS63	MS65
1984	250	PF63 775	PF65 850	PF67 900		

KM# 61 POUND
9.50 g., Nickel-Brass, 22.5 mm. **Ruler:** Elizabeth II **Obv:** Young bust right **Rev:** Shield above written value **Edge Lettering:** CAESAREA INSULA

Date	Mintage	VF20	XF40	MS60	MS63	MS65
1984	20,000	—	—	—	2.50	3.50

KM# 61a POUND
11.68 g., 0.925 Silver 0.3474 oz. ASW, 22.5 mm. **Ruler:** Elizabeth II **Obv:** Young bust right **Rev:** Shield above written value

Date	Mintage	VF20	XF40	MS60	MS63	MS65
1984	2,500	PF63 12.00	PF65 18.00			

KM# 61b POUND
19.65 g., 0.917 Gold 0.5793 oz. AGW, 22.5 mm. **Ruler:** Elizabeth II **Obv:** Young bust right **Rev:** Shield above written value

Date	Mintage	VF20	XF40	MS60	MS63	MS65
1984	250	PF63 775	PF65 850	PF67 900		

KM# 62 POUND
9.50 g., Nickel-Brass, 22.5 mm. **Ruler:** Elizabeth II **Obv:** Young bust right **Rev:** Shield above written value **Edge Lettering:** CAESAREA INSULA

Date	Mintage	VF20	XF40	MS60	MS63	MS65
1985	25,000	—	—	—	2.50	3.50

KM# 62a POUND
11.68 g., 0.925 Silver 0.3474 oz. ASW, 22.5 mm. **Ruler:** Elizabeth II **Obv:** Young bust right **Rev:** Shield above written value

Date	Mintage	VF20	XF40	MS60	MS63	MS65
1985	2,500	PF63 12.00	PF65 18.00			

KM# 62b POUND
19.65 g., 0.917 Gold 0.5793 oz. AGW, 22.5 mm. **Ruler:** Elizabeth II **Obv:** Young bust right **Rev:** Shield above written value

Date	Mintage	VF20	XF40	MS60	MS63	MS65
1985	124	PF63 875	PF65 1,000	PF67 1,050		

KM# 65 POUND
9.50 g., Nickel-Brass, 22.5 mm. **Ruler:** Elizabeth II **Obv:** Young bust right **Rev:** Shield above written value **Edge Lettering:** CAESAREA INSULA

Date	Mintage	VF20	XF40	MS60	MS63	MS65
1985	10,000	—	—	—	2.50	3.50

KM# 65a POUND
11.68 g., 0.925 Silver 0.3474 oz. ASW, 22.5 mm. **Ruler:** Elizabeth II **Obv:** Young bust right **Rev:** Shield above written value

Date	Mintage	VF20	XF40	MS60	MS63	MS65
1985	2,500	PF63 12.00	PF65 18.00			

KM# 65b POUND
19.65 g., 0.917 Gold 0.5793 oz. AGW, 22.5 mm. **Ruler:** Elizabeth II **Obv:** Young bust right **Rev:** Shield above written value

Date	Mintage	VF20	XF40	MS60	MS63	MS65
1985	108	PF63 875	PF65 1,000	PF67 1,050		

KM# 68 POUND
9.50 g., Nickel-Brass, 22.5 mm. **Ruler:** Elizabeth II **Obv:** Young bust right **Rev:** Shield above written value **Edge Lettering:** CAESAREA INSULA

Date	Mintage	VF20	XF40	MS60	MS63	MS65
1986	10,000	—	—	—	2.50	3.50

KM# 68a POUND
11.68 g., 0.925 Silver 0.3474 oz. ASW, 22.5 mm. **Ruler:** Elizabeth II **Obv:** Young bust right **Rev:** Shield above written value

Date	Mintage	VF20	XF40	MS60	MS63	MS65
1986	2,500	PF63 12.00	PF65 18.00			

KM# 68b POUND
19.65 g., 0.917 Gold 0.5793 oz. AGW, 22.5 mm. **Ruler:** Elizabeth II **Obv:** Young bust right **Rev:** Shield above written value

Date	Mintage	VF20	XF40	MS60	MS63	MS65
1986	250	PF63 775	PF65 850	PF67 900		

KM# 69 POUND
9.50 g., Nickel-Brass, 22.5 mm. **Ruler:** Elizabeth II **Obv:** Young bust right **Rev:** Shield above written value **Edge Lettering:** CAESAREA INSULA

Date	Mintage	VF20	XF40	MS60	MS63	MS65
1986	10,000	—	—	—	2.50	3.50

KM# 69a POUND
11.68 g., 0.925 Silver 0.3474 oz. ASW, 22.5 mm. **Ruler:** Elizabeth II **Obv:** Young bust right **Rev:** Shield above written value

Date	Mintage	VF20	XF40	MS60	MS63	MS65
1986	2,500	PF63 12.00	PF65 18.00			

KM# 69b POUND
19.65 g., 0.917 Gold 0.5793 oz. AGW, 22.5 mm. **Ruler:** Elizabeth II **Obv:** Young bust right **Rev:** Shield above written value

Date	Mintage	VF20	XF40	MS60	MS63	MS65
1986	250	PF63 775	PF65 850	PF67 900		

KM# 71 POUND
9.50 g., Nickel-Brass, 22.5 mm. **Ruler:** Elizabeth II **Obv:** Young bust right **Rev:** Shield above written value **Edge Lettering:** CAESAREA INSULA

Date	Mintage	VF20	XF40	MS60	MS63	MS65
1987	10,000	—	—	—	2.50	3.50

KM# 71a POUND

11.68 g., 0.925 Silver 0.3474 oz. ASW, 22.5 mm. **Ruler:** Elizabeth II **Obv:** Young bust right **Rev:** Shield above written value

Date	Mintage	VF20	XF40	MS60	MS63	MS65
1987	2,500	PF63 12.00	PF65 18.00			

KM# 71b POUND

19.65 g., 0.917 Gold 0.5793 oz. AGW, 22.5 mm. **Ruler:** Elizabeth II **Obv:** Young bust right **Rev:** Shield above written value

Date	Mintage	VF20	XF40	MS60	MS63	MS65
1987	250	PF63 775	PF65 850	PF67 900		

KM# 72 POUND

9.50 g., Nickel-Brass, 22.5 mm. **Ruler:** Elizabeth II **Obv:** Young bust right **Rev:** Shield above written value **Edge Lettering:** CAESAREA INSULA

Date	Mintage	VF20	XF40	MS60	MS63	MS65
1987	10,000	—	—	—	2.50	3.50

KM# 72a POUND

11.68 g., 0.925 Silver 0.3474 oz. ASW, 22.5 mm. **Ruler:** Elizabeth II **Obv:** Young bust right **Rev:** Shield above written value

Date	Mintage	VF20	XF40	MS60	MS63	MS65
1987	2,500	PF63 12.00	PF65 18.00			

KM# 72b POUND

19.65 g., 0.917 Gold 0.5793 oz. AGW, 22.5 mm. **Ruler:** Elizabeth II **Obv:** Young bust right **Rev:** Shield above written value

Date	Mintage	VF20	XF40	MS60	MS63	MS65
1987	250	PF63 775	PF65 850	PF67 900		

KM# 73 POUND

9.50 g., Nickel-Brass, 22.5 mm. **Ruler:** Elizabeth II **Obv:** Young bust right **Rev:** Shield above written value **Edge Lettering:** CAESAREA INSULA

Date	Mintage	VF20	XF40	MS60	MS63	MS65
1988	10,000	—	—	—	2.75	4.00

KM# 73a POUND

11.68 g., 0.925 Silver 0.3474 oz. ASW, 22.5 mm. **Ruler:** Elizabeth II **Obv:** Young bust right **Rev:** Shield above written value

Date	Mintage	VF20	XF40	MS60	MS63	MS65
1988	2,500	PF63 12.00	PF65 18.00			

KM# 73b POUND

19.65 g., 0.917 Gold 0.5793 oz. AGW, 22.5 mm. **Ruler:** Elizabeth II **Obv:** Young bust right **Rev:** Shield above written value

Date	Mintage	VF20	XF40	MS60	MS63	MS65
1988	250	PF63 775	PF65 850	PF67 900		

KM# 74 POUND

9.50 g., Nickel-Brass, 22.5 mm. **Ruler:** Elizabeth II **Obv:** Young bust right **Rev:** Shield above written value **Edge Lettering:** CAESAREA INSULA

Date	Mintage	VF20	XF40	MS60	MS63	MS65
1988	10,000	—	—	—	2.50	3.50

KM# 74a POUND

11.68 g., 0.925 Silver 0.3474 oz. ASW, 22.5 mm. **Ruler:** Elizabeth II **Obv:** Young bust right **Rev:** Shield above written value

Date	Mintage	VF20	XF40	MS60	MS63	MS65
1988	2,500	PF63 12.00	PF65 18.00			

KM# 74b POUND

19.65 g., 0.917 Gold 0.5793 oz. AGW, 22.5 mm. **Ruler:** Elizabeth II **Obv:** Young bust right **Rev:** Shield above written value

Date	Mintage	VF20	XF40	MS60	MS63	MS65
1988	250	PF63 775	PF65 850	PF67 900		

KM# 75 POUND

9.50 g., Nickel-Brass, 22.5 mm. **Ruler:** Elizabeth II **Obv:** Young bust right **Rev:** Shield above written value **Edge Lettering:** CAESAREA INSULA

Date	Mintage	VF20	XF40	MS60	MS63	MS65
1989	25,000	—	—	—	2.50	3.50

KM# 75a POUND

11.68 g., 0.925 Silver 0.3474 oz. ASW, 22.5 mm. **Ruler:** Elizabeth II **Obv:** Young bust right **Rev:** Shield above written value

Date	Mintage	VF20	XF40	MS60	MS63	MS65
1989	2,500	PF63 12.00	PF65 18.00			

KM# 75b POUND

19.65 g., 0.917 Gold 0.5793 oz. AGW, 22.5 mm. **Ruler:** Elizabeth II **Obv:** Young bust right **Rev:** Shield above written value

Date	Mintage	VF20	XF40	MS60	MS63	MS65
1989	250	PF63 775	PF65 850	PF67 900		

KM# 84 POUND

9.50 g., Nickel-Brass, 22.5 mm. **Ruler:** Elizabeth II **Obv:** Young bust right **Rev:** Schooner, The Tickler **Edge Lettering:** CAESAREA INSULA

Date	Mintage	VF20	XF40	MS60	MS63	MS65
1991	15,000	—	—	—	2.50	3.50

KM# 84a POUND

11.68 g., 0.925 Silver 0.3474 oz. ASW, 22.5 mm. **Ruler:** Elizabeth II **Obv:** Young bust right **Rev:** Schooner, The Tickler

Date	Mintage	VF20	XF40	MS60	MS63	MS65
1991	3,000	PF63 12.00	PF65 18.00			

KM# 84b POUND

19.65 g., 0.917 Gold 0.5793 oz. AGW, 22.5 mm. **Ruler:** Elizabeth II **Obv:** Young bust right **Rev:** Schooner, The Tickler

Date	Mintage	VF20	XF40	MS60	MS63	MS65
1991	250	PF63 775	PF65 850	PF67 900		

KM# 85 POUND

9.50 g., Nickel-Brass, 22.5 mm. **Ruler:** Elizabeth II **Obv:** Young bust right **Rev:** Sailing ship, Percy Douglas **Edge Lettering:** CAESAREA INSULA

Date	Mintage	VF20	XF40	MS60	MS63	MS65
1991	20,000	—	—	—	2.50	3.50

KM# 85a POUND

11.68 g., 0.925 Silver 0.3474 oz. ASW, 22.5 mm. **Ruler:** Elizabeth II **Obv:** Young bust right **Rev:** Sailing ship, Percy Douglas

Date	Mintage	VF20	XF40	MS60	MS63	MS65
1991	3,000	PF63 12.00	PF65 18.00			

KM# 85b POUND

19.65 g., 0.917 Gold 0.5793 oz. AGW, 22.5 mm. **Ruler:** Elizabeth II **Obv:** Young bust right **Rev:** Sailing ship, Percy Douglas

Date	Mintage	VF20	XF40	MS60	MS63	MS65
1991	250	PF63 775	PF65 850	PF67 900		

KM# 86 POUND

9.50 g., Nickel-Brass, 22.5 mm. **Ruler:** Elizabeth II **Obv:** Young bust right **Rev:** Brig, Hebe

Date	Mintage	VF20	XF40	MS60	MS63	MS65
1992	2,000	—	—	—	2.50	3.50

KM# 86a POUND

11.68 g., 0.925 Silver 0.3474 oz. ASW, 22.5 mm. **Ruler:** Elizabeth II **Obv:** Young bust right **Rev:** Sailing ship, Hebe

Date	Mintage	VF20	XF40	MS60	MS63	MS65
1992	Est. 3000	PF63 12.00	PF65 18.00			

KM# 86b POUND

19.65 g., 0.917 Gold 0.5793 oz. AGW, 22.5 mm. **Ruler:** Elizabeth II **Obv:** Young bust right **Rev:** Sailing ship, Hebe

Date	Mintage	VF20	XF40	MS60	MS63	MS65
1992	250	PF63 775	PF65 850	PF67 900		

KM# 87 POUND

9.50 g., Nickel-Brass, 22.5 mm. **Ruler:** Elizabeth II **Obv:** Young bust right **Rev:** Bailiwick seal

Date	Mintage	VF20	XF40	MS60	MS63	MS65
1992	20,000	—	—	—	2.50	3.50

KM# 87a POUND

11.68 g., 0.925 Silver 0.3474 oz. ASW, 22.5 mm. **Ruler:** Elizabeth II **Obv:** Young bust right **Rev:** Ornamented shield

Date	Mintage	VF20	XF40	MS60	MS63	MS65
1992	3,000	PF63 12.00	PF65 18.00			

KM# 87b POUND

19.65 g., 0.917 Gold 0.5793 oz. AGW, 22.5 mm. **Ruler:** Elizabeth II **Obv:** Young bust right **Rev:** Ornamented shield

Date	Mintage	VF20	XF40	MS60	MS63	MS65
1992	250	PF63 775	PF65 850	PF67 900		

KM# 88 POUND

9.50 g., Nickel-Brass, 22.5 mm. **Ruler:** Elizabeth II **Obv:** Young bust right **Rev:** Barque, Gemini

Date	Mintage	VF20	XF40	MS60	MS63	MS65
1993	—	—	—	—	2.50	3.50

KM# 88a POUND

11.68 g., 0.925 Silver 0.3474 oz. ASW, 22.5 mm. **Ruler:** Elizabeth II **Obv:** Young bust right **Rev:** Sailing ship, Gemini

Date	Mintage	VF20	XF40	MS60	MS63	MS65
1993	3,000	PF63 12.00	PF65 18.00			

KM# 88b POUND

19.65 g., 0.917 Gold 0.5793 oz. AGW, 22.5 mm. **Ruler:** Elizabeth II **Obv:** Young bust right **Rev:** Sailing ship, Gemini

Date	Mintage	VF20	XF40	MS60	MS63	MS65
1993	250	PF63 775	PF65 850	PF67 900		

KM# 90 POUND

9.50 g., Nickel-Brass, 22.5 mm. **Ruler:** Elizabeth II **Obv:** Young bust right **Rev:** Brigantine, Century

Date	Mintage	VF20	XF40	MS60	MS63	MS65
1993	—	—	—	—	2.50	3.50

KM# 90a POUND

11.68 g., 0.925 Silver 0.3474 oz. ASW, 22.5 mm. **Ruler:** Elizabeth II **Obv:** Young bust right **Rev:** Brigantine, Century

Date	Mintage	VF20	XF40	MS60	MS63	MS65
1993	Est. 3000	PF63 12.00	PF65 18.00			

KM# 90b POUND

19.65 g., 0.917 Gold 0.5793 oz. AGW, 22.5 mm. **Ruler:** Elizabeth II **Obv:** Young bust right **Rev:** Sailing ship, Century

Date	Mintage	VF20	XF40	MS60	MS63	MS65
1993	250	PF63 775	PF65 850	PF67 900		

KM# 91 POUND

9.50 g., Nickel-Brass, 22.5 mm. **Ruler:** Elizabeth II **Obv:** Young bust right **Rev:** Topsail Schooner, Resolute

Date	Mintage	VF20	XF40	MS60	MS63	MS65
1994	60,000	—	—	—	2.50	3.50
1997	101,000	—	—	—	2.50	3.50

KM# 91a POUND

11.68 g., 0.925 Silver 0.3474 oz. ASW, 22.5 mm. **Ruler:** Elizabeth II **Obv:** Young bust right **Rev:** Schooner, Resolute

Date	Mintage	VF20	XF40	MS60	MS63	MS65
1994	3,000	PF63 12.00	PF65 18.00			

KM# 91b POUND

19.65 g., 0.917 Gold 0.5793 oz. AGW, 22.5 mm. **Ruler:** Elizabeth II **Obv:** Young bust right **Rev:** Schooner, Resolute

Date	Mintage	VF20	XF40	MS60	MS63	MS65
1994	250	PF63 775	PF65 850	PF67 900		

KM# 101 POUND

9.50 g., Nickel-Brass, 22.5 mm. **Ruler:** Elizabeth II **Obv:** Head with tiara right **Rev:** Schooner, Resolute **Edge Lettering:** CAESAREA INSULA

Date	Mintage	VF20	XF40	MS60	MS63	MS65
1998	174,000	—	—	—	2.50	3.50

KM# 110 SOVEREIGN

7.98 g., 0.9167 Gold 0.2352 oz. AGW, 22.5 mm. **Ruler:** Elizabeth II **Subject:** William I - Duke of Normandy **Obv:** Crowned bust right **Rev:** William seated on throne

Date	Mintage	VF20	XF40	MS60	MS63	MS65
2000	Est. 2000	—	—	350	400	—
2000	Est. 2000	PF63 400	PF65 450			

KM# 37 2 POUNDS

21.68 g., 0.925 Silver 0.6448 oz. ASW, 36 mm. **Ruler:** Elizabeth II **Subject:** 25th Wedding Anniversary **Obv:** Crowned bust right **Rev:** Sailing ship "Alexandria"

Date	Mintage	VF20	XF40	MS60	MS63	MS65
1972	24,000	—	—	15.00	18.00	22.00
1972	1,500	PF63 35.00	PF65 45.00			

KM# 52 2 POUNDS

Copper-Nickel, 38.5 mm. **Ruler:** Elizabeth II **Subject:** Wedding of Prince Charles and Lady Diana **Obv:** Crowned bust right **Rev:** Conjoined busts right

Date	Mintage	VF20	XF40	MS60	MS63	MS65
ND-1981	150,000	—	—	—	4.00	6.00

KM# 52a 2 POUNDS

28.28 g., 0.925 Silver 0.841 oz. ASW, 38.5 mm. **Ruler:** Elizabeth II **Subject:** Wedding of Prince Charles and Lady Diana **Obv:** Crowned bust right **Rev:** Conjoined busts right

Date	Mintage	VF20	XF40	MS60	MS63	MS65
ND-1981	35,000	PF65 30.00				

KM# 52b 2 POUNDS

15.98 g., 0.917 Gold 0.4711 oz. AGW, 38.5 mm. **Ruler:** Elizabeth II **Subject:** Wedding of Prince Charles and Lady Diana **Obv:** Crowned bust right **Rev:** Conjoined busts right

Date	Mintage	VF20	XF40	MS60	MS63	MS65
ND-1981	1,500	PF65 800				

KM# 64 2 POUNDS

Copper-Nickel, 38.5 mm. **Ruler:** Elizabeth II **Subject:** 40th Anniversary of Liberation of 1945 **Obv:** Crowned bust right **Rev:** H.M.S. Beagle, destroyer **Edge Lettering:** OUR DEAR CHANNEL ISLANDS WILL ALSO BE FREED TODAY

Date	Mintage	VF20	XF40	MS60	MS63	MS65
1985	20,000	—	—	—	4.00	6.00

KM# 64a 2 POUNDS

28.28 g., 0.925 Silver 0.841 oz. ASW, 38.5 mm. **Ruler:** Elizabeth II **Subject:** 40th Anniversary of Liberation of 1945 **Obv:** Crowned bust right **Rev:** H.M.S. Beagle, destroyer

Date	Mintage	VF20	XF40	MS60	MS63	MS65
1985	2,500	PF65 35.00				

KM# 64b 2 POUNDS

47.54 g., 0.917 Gold 1.4016 oz. AGW, 38.5 mm. **Ruler:** Elizabeth II **Subject:** 40th Anniversary of Liberation of 1945 **Obv:** Crowned bust right **Rev:** H.M.S. Beagle, destroyer

Date	Mintage	VF20	XF40	MS60	MS63	MS65
1985	40	PF65 2,200				

KM# 67.1 2 POUNDS

Copper-Nickel, 38.5 mm. **Ruler:** Elizabeth II **Subject:** XIII Commonwealth Games - Edinburgh **Obv:** Crowned bust right **Rev:** Two sprinters **Edge Lettering:** XIII COMMONWEALTH GAMES

Date	Mintage	VF20	XF40	MS60	MS63	MS65
1986	50,000	—	—	—	4.00	6.00

KM# 67.1a 2 POUNDS

28.28 g., 0.500 Silver 0.4546 oz. ASW, 38.5 mm. **Ruler:** Elizabeth II **Subject:** XIII Commonwealth Games - Edinburgh **Obv:** Crowned bust right **Rev:** Two sprinters

Date	Mintage	VF20	XF40	MS60	MS63	MS65
1986	20,000	—	—	—	12.00	16.00

KM# 67.1b 2 POUNDS

28.28 g., 0.925 Silver 0.841 oz. ASW, 38.5 mm. **Ruler:** Elizabeth II **Subject:** XIII Commonwealth Games - Edinburgh **Obv:** Crowned bust right **Rev:** Two sprinters

Date	Mintage	VF20	XF40	MS60	MS63	MS65
1986	20,000	PF65 40.00				

KM# 67.2 2 POUNDS

Copper-Nickel, 38.5 mm. **Ruler:** Elizabeth II **Subject:** XIII Commonwealth Games - Edinburgh **Obv:** Crowned bust right **Rev:** Two sprinters **Note:** Without edge lettering.

Date	Mintage	VF20	XF40	MS60	MS63	MS65
1986	5,000	—	—	—	5.00	7.00

KM# 70 2 POUNDS

Copper-Nickel, 38.5 mm. **Ruler:** Elizabeth II **Subject:** World Wildlife Fund **Obv:** Crowned bust right **Rev:** Pigeons

Date	Mintage	VF20	XF40	MS60	MS63	MS65
1987	23,000	—	—	—	7.00	9.00

KM# 70a 2 POUNDS

28.28 g., 0.925 Silver 0.841 oz. ASW, 38.5 mm. **Ruler:** Elizabeth II **Subject:** World Wildlife Fund **Obv:** Crowned bust right **Rev:** Pigeons

Date	Mintage	VF20	XF40	MS60	MS63	MS65
1987	25,000	PF65 30.00				

KM# 76 2 POUNDS

Copper-Nickel, 38.5 mm. **Ruler:** Elizabeth II **Subject:** Royal Visit **Obv:** Crowned bust right **Rev:** Royal Mace divides map

Date	Mintage	VF20	XF40	MS60	MS63	MS65
1989	10,000	—	—	—	4.00	6.00

KM# 76a 2 POUNDS

28.30 g., 0.925 Silver 0.8416 oz. ASW, 38.5 mm. **Ruler:** Elizabeth II **Subject:** Royal Visit **Obv:** Crowned bust right **Rev:** Royal Mace divides map

Date	Mintage	VF20	XF40	MS60	MS63	MS65
1989	3,000	PF65 32.00				

KM# 77 2 POUNDS

28.30 g., 0.925 Silver 0.8416 oz. ASW, 38.5 mm. **Ruler:** Elizabeth II **Subject:** 50th Anniversary - The Battle of Britain **Obv:** Crowned bust right **Rev:** Spitfire divides map

Date	Mintage	VF20	XF40	MS60	MS63	MS65
ND-1990	Est. 10000	PF65 35.00				

KM# 83 2 POUNDS

Copper-Nickel, 38.5 mm. **Ruler:** Elizabeth II **Subject:** 90th Birthday of Queen Mother **Obv:** Crowned bust right **Rev:** Crowned double "E" monogram

Date	Mintage	VF20	XF40	MS60	MS63	MS65
ND-1990	10,000	—	—	—	5.00	7.00

KM# 83a 2 POUNDS

28.35 g., 0.925 Silver 0.8431 oz. ASW, 38.5 mm. **Ruler:** Elizabeth II **Subject:** 90th Birthday of Queen Mother **Obv:** Crowned bust right **Rev:** Crowned double "E" monogram

Date	Mintage	VF20	XF40	MS60	MS63	MS65
ND-1990	3,000	PF65 50.00				

KM# 83b 2 POUNDS

15.98 g., 0.917 Gold 0.4711 oz. AGW **Ruler:** Elizabeth II **Subject:** 90th Birthday of Queen Mother **Obv:** Crowned bust right **Rev:** Crowned double "E" monogram

Date	Mintage	VF20	XF40	MS60	MS63	MS65
ND-1990	90	PF65 900				

KM# 89 2 POUNDS

Copper-Nickel, 38.5 mm. **Ruler:** Elizabeth II **Subject:** 40th Anniversary - Coronation of Queen Elizabeth II **Obv:** Crowned bust right **Rev:** Crown, royal mace and shield

Date	Mintage	VF20	XF40	MS60	MS63	MS65
ND-1993	12,000	—	—	—	4.00	6.00

KM# 89a 2 POUNDS

28.28 g., 0.925 Silver 0.841 oz. ASW, 38.5 mm. **Ruler:** Elizabeth II **Subject:** 40th Anniversary - Coronation of Queen Elizabeth II **Obv:** Crowned bust right **Rev:** Crown, royal mace and shield

Date	Mintage	VF20	XF40	MS60	MS63	MS65
ND-1993	Est. 10000	PF65 50.00				

KM# 89b 2 POUNDS

15.98 g., 0.9167 Gold 0.471 oz. AGW **Ruler:** Elizabeth II **Subject:** 40th Anniversary - Coronation of Queen Elizabeth II **Obv:** Crowned bust right **Rev:** Crown, royal mace and shield

Date	Mintage	VF20	XF40	MS60	MS63	MS65
ND-1993	Est. 500	PF65 850				

KM# 92 2 POUNDS

Copper-Nickel, 38.5 mm. **Ruler:** Elizabeth II **Subject:** 50th Anniversary of Liberation **Obv:** Crowned bust right **Rev:** Bird with sprig within letter V above dates within ribbon

Date	Mintage	VF20	XF40	MS60	MS63	MS65
1995	42,000	—	—	—	6.00	8.00

Note: Also released in special wallet with 1 Pound commemorative banknote (6,000). Market value: $20.00

KM# 92a 2 POUNDS

28.28 g., 0.925 Silver 0.841 oz. ASW, 38.5 mm. **Ruler:** Elizabeth II **Subject:** 50th Anniversary of Liberation **Obv:** Crowned bust right **Rev:** Bird with sprig within letter V above dates within ribbon

Date	Mintage	VF20	XF40	MS60	MS63	MS65
1995	7,000	PF65 50.00				

KM# 97 2 POUNDS

Copper-Nickel, 38.5 mm. **Ruler:** Elizabeth II **Subject:** Queen Elizabeth's 70th Birthday **Obv:** Crowned bust right **Rev:** Lillies

Date	Mintage	VF20	XF40	MS60	MS63	MS65
1996	—	—	—	—	5.00	7.00

KM# 97a 2 POUNDS

28.38 g., 0.925 Silver 0.844 oz. ASW, 38.5 mm. **Ruler:** Elizabeth II **Subject:** Queen Elizabeth's 70th Birthday **Obv:** Crowned bust right **Rev:** Lillies

Date	Mintage	VF20	XF40	MS60	MS63	MS65
1996	—	—	—	—	—	42.00

KM# 99 2 POUNDS

12.00 g., Bi-Metallic Copper-Nickel center in Nickel-Brass ring, 28.35 mm. **Ruler:** Elizabeth II **Obv:** Crowned bust right **Rev:** Value within center circle of assorted shields

Date	Mintage	VF20	XF40	MS60	MS63	MS65
1997 Sets only	5,500	—	—	—	6.00	8.00

KM# 99a 2 POUNDS

Bi-Metallic Silver center in Gold-plated Silver ring, 28.35 mm. **Ruler:** Elizabeth II **Obv:** Crowned bust right **Rev:** Value within center circle of assorted shields

Date	Mintage	VF20	XF40	MS60	MS63	MS65
1997	500	PF65 95.00				

KM# 102 2 POUNDS

12.00 g., Bi-Metallic Copper-Nickel center in Nickel-Brass ring, 28.4 mm. **Ruler:** Elizabeth II **Obv:** Head with tiara right **Rev:** Latent image value within circle of assorted shields **Edge Lettering:** CAESAREA INSULA

Date	Mintage	VF20	XF40	MS60	MS63	MS65
1998	720,000	—	—	—	7.00	9.00

KM# 38 2 POUNDS 50 PENCE

27.10 g., 0.925 Silver 0.8059 oz. ASW, 40 mm. **Ruler:** Elizabeth II **Subject:** 25th Wedding Anniversary **Obv:** Young bust right **Rev:** European Lobster

Date	Mintage	VF20	XF40	MS60	MS63	MS65
1972	24,000	—	—	—	25.00	30.00
1972	1,500	PF65 40.00				

KM# 39 5 POUNDS

2.62 g., 0.917 Gold 0.0772 oz. AGW **Ruler:** Elizabeth II **Subject:** 25th Wedding Anniversary **Obv:** Young bust right **Rev:** Garden shrew

Date	Mintage	VF20	XF40	MS60	MS63	MS65
1972	8,500	—	—	—	—	145
1972	1,500	PF65 160				

KM# 78 5 POUNDS

155.56 g., 0.999 Silver 4.9964 oz. ASW, 65 mm. **Ruler:** Elizabeth II **Subject:** 50th Anniversary - The Battle of Britain **Obv:** Crowned bust right **Rev:** Spitfire divides map **Note:** Illustration reduced.

Date	Mintage	VF20	XF40	MS60	MS63	MS65
ND-1990	—	PF63 145	PF65 175			

KM# 100 5 POUNDS

Copper-Nickel **Ruler:** Elizabeth II **Subject:** Queen's Golden Wedding Anniversary **Obv:** Crowned bust right **Rev:** Conjoined busts of royal couple and coat of arms

Date	Mintage	VF20	XF40	MS60	MS63	MS65
1997	6,000	—	—	—	12.00	14.00

KM# 100a 5 POUNDS

28.28 g., 0.925 Silver 0.841 oz. ASW **Ruler:** Elizabeth II **Subject:** Queen's Golden Wedding Anniversary **Obv:** Crowned bust right **Rev:** Conjoined busts of royal couple and gold-plated coat of arms

Date	Mintage	VF20	XF40	MS60	MS63	MS65
1997	Est. 30000	PF65 35.00				

KM# 109 5 POUNDS

28.28 g., 0.925 Silver 0.841 oz. ASW **Ruler:** Elizabeth II **Subject:** Millennium **Obv:** Head with tiara right **Rev:** Gold-plated island map on globe

Date	Mintage	VF20	XF40	MS60	MS63	MS65
2000	32,000	PF65 35.00				

KM# 40 10 POUNDS

4.64 g., 0.917 Gold 0.1368 oz. AGW **Ruler:** Elizabeth II **Subject:** 25th Wedding Anniversary **Obv:** Young bust right **Rev:** Gold torque, excavated 1899 in St. Helier, Jersey.

Date	Mintage	XF40	MS60	MS63	MS65	MS66
1972	8,500	—	—	—	225	250
1972	1,500	PF65 275	PF67 325			

KM# 79 10 POUNDS

3.13 g., 0.999 Gold 0.1005 oz. AGW **Ruler:** Elizabeth II **Subject:** 50th Anniversary - The Battle of Britain **Obv:** Crowned bust right **Rev:** Crowned air force badge divides dates

Date	Mintage	VF20	XF40	MS60	MS63	MS65
ND (1990)	Est. 500	PF65 195				

KM# 93 10 POUNDS

3.13 g., 0.999 Gold 0.1005 oz. AGW **Ruler:** Elizabeth II **Subject:** 50th Anniversary of Liberation **Obv:** Crowned bust right **Rev:** Red Cross bringing supplies to Jersey immediately following liberation

Date	Mintage	VF20	XF40	MS60	MS63	MS65
1995	500	PF63 220	PF65 250			

KM# 41 20 POUNDS
9.26 g., 0.917 Gold 0.273 oz. AGW **Ruler:** Elizabeth II **Subject:** 25th Wedding Anniversary **Obv:** Young bust right **Rev:** Ormer shell

Date	Mintage	XF40	MS60	MS63	MS65	MS66
1972	8,500	—	—	—	450	475
1972	1,500	PF65 500	PF67 550			

KM# 42 25 POUNDS
11.90 g., 0.917 Gold 0.3508 oz. AGW **Ruler:** Elizabeth II **Subject:** 25th Wedding Anniversary **Obv:** Young bust right **Rev:** Arms of Queen Elizabeth I

Date	Mintage	XF40	MS60	MS63	MS65	MS66
1972	8,500	—	—	—	550	575
1972	1,500	PF65 600	PF67 650			

KM# 80 25 POUNDS
7.81 g., 0.999 Gold 0.2508 oz. AGW **Ruler:** Elizabeth II **Subject:** 50th Anniversary - The Battle of Britain **Obv:** Crowned bust right **Rev:** Spitfire

Date	Mintage	VF20	XF40	MS60	MS63	MS65
1990	Est. 500	PF65 450				

KM# 94 25 POUNDS
7.81 g., 0.999 Gold 0.2508 oz. AGW **Ruler:** Elizabeth II **Subject:** 50th Anniversary of Liberation **Obv:** Crowned bust right **Rev:** Family encircled around flags with written value below

Date	Mintage	VF20	XF40	MS60	MS63	MS65
1995	500	PF63 450	PF65 525			

KM# 43 50 POUNDS
22.63 g., 0.917 Gold 0.6672 oz. AGW **Ruler:** Elizabeth II **Subject:** 25th Wedding Anniversary **Obv:** Young bust right **Rev:** Shield above written value

Date	Mintage	XF40	MS60	MS63	MS65	MS66
1972	8,500	—	—	—	1,000	1,050
1972	1,500	PF65 1,100	PF67 1,150			

KM# 81 50 POUNDS
15.61 g., 0.999 Gold 0.5014 oz. AGW **Ruler:** Elizabeth II **Subject:** 50th Anniversary - Battle of Britain **Obv:** Crowned bust right **Rev:** Crowned air force badge divides dates

Date	Mintage	VF20	XF40	MS60	MS63	MS65
ND (1990)	Est. 500	PF63 850				

KM# 95 50 POUNDS
15.61 g., 0.999 Gold 0.5014 oz. AGW **Ruler:** Elizabeth II **Subject:** 50th Anniversary of Liberation **Obv:** Crowned bust right **Rev:** Letter V divides dates above figures facing each other with flags

Date	Mintage	VF20	XF40	MS60	MS63	MS65
1995	500	PF63 850	PF65 950			

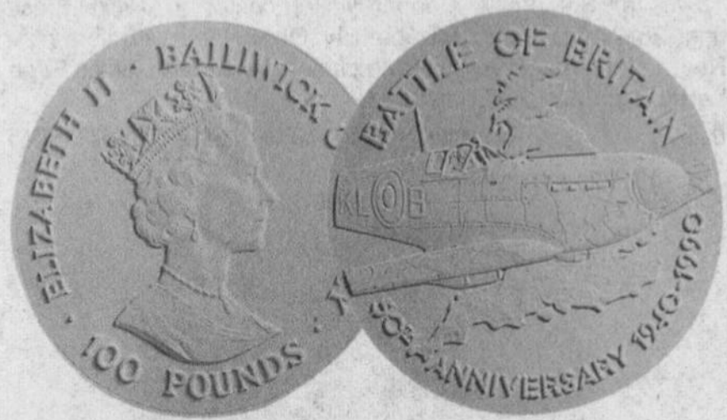

KM# 82 100 POUNDS
31.21 g., 0.999 Gold 1.0024 oz. AGW **Ruler:** Elizabeth II **Subject:** 50th Anniversary - The Battle of Britain **Obv:** Crowned bust right **Rev:** Spitfire

Date	Mintage	VF20	XF40	MS60	MS63	MS65
ND (1990)	Est. 500	PF63 1,650	PF65 1,850			

KM# 96 100 POUNDS
31.21 g., 0.999 Gold 1.0024 oz. AGW **Ruler:** Elizabeth II **Subject:** 50th Anniversary of Liberation **Obv:** Crowned bust right **Rev:** Small shield within map with bird above within diagonal lines into map

Date	Mintage	VF20	XF40	MS60	MS63	MS65
1995	500	PF63 1,600	PF65 1,850			

PIEDFORT

KM#	Date	Mintage	Identification	Mkt Val
P1	1982	1,500	20 Pence. Silver. Date. KM53a.	45.00
P2	1995	Est. 1000	2 Pounds. 0.925. Silver. KM92a.	90.00

MINT SETS

KM#	Date	Mintage	Identification	Issue Price	Mkt Val
MS1	1972 (9)	8,500	KM35-43	348	2,250
MS2	1972 (4)	15,000	KM35-38	24.00	75.00
MS3	1983 (7)	25,000	KM54, 55, 56.1, 57.1, 58.1, 59, 66	—	9.00
MS4	1987 (7)	—	KM54-55, 56.1, 57.1, 58.1, 66, 71	—	8.00
MS5	1992 (7)	6,000	KM54,55b, 56.2, 57.2, 58.1, 66, 86	22.50	22.50
MS6	1997 (8)	5,500	KM#54b 55b, 56.2, 57.2, 58.2, 66, 91, 99	—	28.00

PROOF SETS

KM#	Date	Mintage	Identification	Issue Price	Mkt Val
PS1	1957 (4)	1,050	KM21-22 two each	—	30.00
PSA2	1960 (2)	Inc. above	KM22, 24 two each	—	160
PS2	1960 (2)	2,100	KM22- 23 two each	—	25.00
PS3	1964 (4)	10,000	KM21, 25 two each	—	8.00
PS4	1966 (4)	15,000	KM26-27 two each	—	8.00
PS5	1966 (1)	15,000	KM28 two pieces	—	15.00
PS6	1972 (9)	1,500	KM35-43	648	2,400
PS7	1980 (6)	10,000	KM29-34	—	25.00
PS8	1981 (7)	15,000	KM45-51	31.00	20.00
PS9	1983 (7)	5,000	KM54a-55a, 56.1a-57.1a, 58a-59a, 66a	—	105
PS10	1990 (4)	500	KM79-82	1,595	2,800
PS11	1995 (4)	500	KM93-96	1,600	2,775

JORDAN

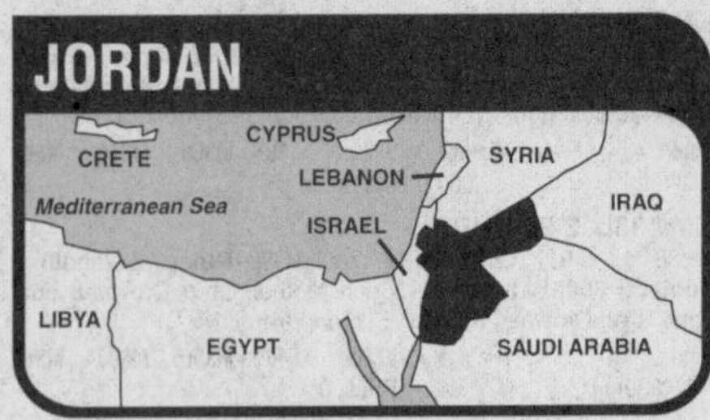

The Hashemite Kingdom of Jordan, a constitutional monarchy in southwest Asia, has an area of 37,738 sq. mi.(91,880 sq. km.) and a population of 3.5 million. Capital: Amman. Agriculture and tourism comprise Jordan's economic base. Chief exports are phosphates, tomatoes and oranges.

Jordan is the Edom and Moab of the time of Moses. It became part of the Roman province of Arabia in 106 A.D., was conquered by the Arabs in 633-36, and was part of the Ottoman Empire from the 16th century until World War I. At that time, the regions presently known as Jordan and Israel were mandated to Great Britain by the League of Nations as Transjordan and Palestine. In 1922 Transjordan was established as the semi-autonomous Emirate of Transjordan, ruled by the Hashemite Prince Abdullah but still nominally a part of the British mandate. The mandate over Transjordan was terminated in 1946, the country becoming the independent Hashemite Kingdom of Transjordan. The kingdom was renamed the Hashemite Kingdom of Jordan in 1950.

Several 1964 and 1965 issues were limited to respective quantities of 3,000 and 5,000 examples struck to make up sets for sale to collectors.

TITLES

المملكة الاردنية الهاشمية

el-Mamlaka(t) el-Urduniya(t) el-Hashemiya(t)

RULERS
Abdullah Ibn Al-Hussein, 1946-1951
Talal Ibn Abdullah, 1951-1952
Hussein Ibn Talal, 1952-1999
Abdullah Ibn Al-Hussein, 1999-

MONETARY SYSTEM
100 Fils = 1 Dirham
1000 Fils = 10 Dirhams = 1 Dinar
Commencing 1992
100 Piastres = 1 Dinar

KINGDOM

DECIMAL COINAGE

KM# 1 FIL
3.00 g., Bronze, 18 mm. **Ruler:** Abdullah **Obv:** Value and date within crowned circle within sprigs **Rev:** Value within circle above date **Edge:** Plain

Date	Mintage	VF20	XF40	MS60	MS63	MS65
AH1368//1949	350,000	10.00	20.00	25.00	30.00	50.00
AH1368//1949	25	PF60 500	PF63 750	PF65 1,000		

Note: "FIL" is an error for "FILS," the correct Arabic singular

KM# 2 FILS
3.00 g., Bronze, 18 mm. **Ruler:** Abdullah **Obv:** Value and date within crowned circle within sprigs **Rev:** Value within circle above date **Edge:** Plain

Date	Mintage	VF20	XF40	MS60	MS63	MS65
AH1368//1949	Inc. above	7.50	15.00	20.00	25.00	45.00
AH1368//1949	25	PF60 500	PF63 750	PF65 1,000		

KM# 8 FILS
3.00 g., Bronze, 18 mm. **Ruler:** Hussein **Obv:** Value and date within crowned circle within sprigs **Rev:** Value within circle above date **Edge:** Plain

Date	Mintage	VF20	XF40	MS60	MS63	MS65
AH1374//1955	200,000	5.00	10.00	15.00	20.00	45.00

Date	Mintage	VF20	XF40	MS60	MS63	MS65
AH1374//1955	—	PF60 750	PF63 1,000	PF65 1,250		
AH1379//1960	150,000	7.00	15.00	25.00	30.00	50.00
AH1380//1960	—	PF60 1,000	PF63 1,250	PF65 1,500		
AH1382//1963	200,000	1.00	3.00	7.50	10.00	15.00
AH1382//1963	—	PF60 750	PF63 1,000	PF65 1,250		
AH1383//1964	3,000	—	—	7.50	13.00	20.00
Note: Sets only						
AH1385//1965	5,000	—	—	7.50	13.00	20.00
Note: Sets only						
AH1385//1965	10,000	PF60 10.00	PF63 15.00	PF65 20.00		

KM# 14 FILS
3.00 g., Bronze, 18 mm. **Ruler:** Hussein **Obv:** Head right **Rev:** Value and date within circle flanked by sprigs **Edge:** Plain

Date	Mintage	VF20	XF40	MS60	MS63	MS65
AH1387-1968	60,000	2.50	3.50	7.50	10.00	15.00

KM# 35 FILS
3.00 g., Bronze, 18 mm. **Ruler:** Hussein **Obv:** Head right **Rev:** Value and date within circle flanked by sprigs **Edge:** Plain

Date	Mintage	VF20	XF40	MS60	MS63	MS65
AH1398-1978	20,000	PF60 5.00	PF63 7.50	PF65 10.00		
AH1404-1984	100,000	1.00	2.50	5.00	7.50	10.00
AH1406-1985	—	—	—	5.00	7.50	10.00
Note: Sets only						
AH1406-1985	5,000	PF60 7.50	PF63 10.00	PF65 12.50		

KM# 3 5 FILS (1/2 Qirsh)
4.50 g., Bronze, 21 mm. **Ruler:** Abdullah **Obv:** Value and date within crowned circle within sprigs **Rev:** Value within circle above date **Edge:** Plain

Date	Mintage	VF20	XF40	MS60	MS63	MS65
AH1368//1949	3,300,000	2.00	5.00	10.00	15.00	30.00
AH1368//1949	25	PF60 500	PF63 750	PF65 1,000		

KM# 9 5 FILS (1/2 Qirsh)
4.50 g., Bronze, 21 mm. **Ruler:** Hussein **Obv:** Value and date within crowned circle within sprigs **Rev:** Value within circle above date **Edge:** Plain

Date	Mintage	VF20	XF40	MS60	MS63	MS65
AH1374-1955	3,500,000	3.00	8.00	15.00	25.00	40.00
AH1374-1955	—	PF60 750	PF63 1,000	PF65 1,250		
AH1379-1960	540,000	5.00	10.00	20.00	30.00	50.00
AH1379-1960	—	PF60 1,000	PF63 1,250	PF65 1,500		
AH1382-1962	250,000	1.50	3.00	10.00	15.00	20.00
AH1382-1962	—	PF60 250	PF63 450	PF65 750		
AH1383-1964	3,000	—	—	5.00	7.50	10.00
Note: Sets only						
AH1384-1964	2,500,000	1.50	3.00	10.00	15.00	20.00
AH1385-1965	5,000	—	—	5.00	7.50	10.00
Note: Sets only						
AH1385-1965	10,000	PF60 10.00	PF63 15.00	PF65 20.00		
AH1387-1967	2,000,000	1.50	3.00	10.00	15.00	20.00

KM# 15 5 FILS (1/2 Qirsh)
4.50 g., Bronze, 21 mm. **Ruler:** Hussein **Obv:** Head right **Rev:** Value and date within circle flanked by sprigs **Edge:** Plain

Date	Mintage	VF20	XF40	MS60	MS63	MS65
AH1387//1968	800,000	1.50	3.00	10.00	15.00	20.00
AH1390//1970	1,400,000	1.50	3.00	10.00	15.00	20.00
AH1392//1972	400,000	4.00	7.50	15.00	25.00	40.00
AH1394//1974	2,000,000	0.75	1.00	3.00	5.00	10.00
AH1395//1975	9,000,000	0.50	0.75	1.00	2.50	4.00

KM# 36 5 FILS (1/2 Qirsh)
4.50 g., Bronze, 21 mm. **Ruler:** Hussein **Obv:** Head right **Rev:** Value and date within circle flanked by sprigs **Edge:** Plain

Date	Mintage	VF20	XF40	MS60	MS63	MS65
AH1398-1978	60,200,000	0.35	0.50	0.75	1.50	3.00
AH1398-1978	20,000	PF60 5.00	PF63 7.50	PF65 10.00		
AH1406-1985	—	—	—	5.00	7.50	10.00
Note: Sets only						
AH1406-1985	5,000	PF60 7.00	PF63 8.50	PF65 10.00		

KM# 60 1/2 QIRSH (1/2 Piastre)
4.01 g., Copper Plated Steel, 21 mm. **Ruler:** Hussein **Obv:** Bust left **Rev:** Value at left within lines with date above and written value at lower right **Edge:** Plain

Date	Mintage	VF20	XF40	MS60	MS63	MS65
AH1416-1996	—	0.35	0.50	0.75	1.00	1.50
AH1416-1996	—	PF60 7.00	PF63 8.50	PF65 10.00		

KM# 4 10 FILS (Qirsh, Piastre)
5.90 g., Bronze, 25 mm. **Ruler:** Abdullah **Obv:** Value and date within crowned circle within sprigs **Rev:** Value within circle above date and star **Edge:** Plain

Date	Mintage	VF20	XF40	MS60	MS63	MS65
AH1368//1949	2,700,000	2.50	6.00	12.00	17.00	35.00
AH1368//1949	25	PF60 500	PF63 750	PF65 1,000		

KM# 10 10 FILS (Qirsh, Piastre)
5.90 g., Bronze, 25 mm. **Ruler:** Hussein **Obv:** Value and date within crowned circle within sprigs **Rev:** Value within circle above date and star **Edge:** Plain

Date	Mintage	VF20	XF40	MS60	MS63	MS65
AH1374//1955	1,500,000	4.00	9.00	18.00	30.00	45.00
AH1374//1955	—	PF60 750	PF63 1,000	PF65 1,250		
AH1379//1960	60,000	7.50	12.00	25.00	35.00	75.00
AH1379//1960	—	PF60 1,000	PF63 1,250	PF65 1,500		
AH1382//1962	2,300,000	2.50	3.50	7.00	15.00	20.00
AH1382//1962	—	PF60 250	PF63 450	PF65 750		
AH1383//1964	1,253,000	2.00	3.50	5.00	7.50	10.00
AH1385//1965	1,003,000	2.00	3.50	5.00	7.50	10.00
AH1385//1965	10,000	PF60 10.00	PF63 15.00	PF65 20.00		
AH1387//1967	1,000,000	2.00	5.00	15.00	20.00	30.00

KM# 16 10 FILS (Qirsh, Piastre)
5.90 g., Bronze, 25 mm. **Ruler:** Hussein **Obv:** Head right **Rev:** Value and date within circle flanked by sprigs

Date	Mintage	VF20	XF40	MS60	MS63	MS65
AH1387-1968	500,000	2.00	5.00	15.00	20.00	30.00
AH1390-1970	1,000,000	2.00	5.00	15.00	20.00	30.00
AH1392-1972	600,000	4.00	7.50	15.00	25.00	40.00
AH1394-1974	1,000,000	0.75	1.00	3.00	5.00	10.00
AH1395-1975	5,000,000	0.50	0.75	1.00	2.50	4.00

KM# 37 10 FILS (Qirsh, Piastre)
5.90 g., Bronze, 25 mm. **Ruler:** Hussein **Obv:** Head right **Rev:** Value and date within circle flanked by sprigs **Edge:** Plain

Date	Mintage	VF20	XF40	MS60	MS63	MS65
AH1398-1978	30,000,000	0.50	0.75	2.00	4.00	6.00
AH1398-1978	20,000	PF60 5.00	PF63 7.50	PF65 10.00		
AH1404-1984	10,000,000	0.50	0.75	1.00	2.00	3.00
AH1406-1985	—	—	—	5.00	7.50	10.00
Note: Sets only						
AH1406-1985	5,000	PF60 7.00	PF63 8.50	PF65 10.00		
AH1409-1989	8,000,000	0.50	0.75	1.00	2.00	3.00

KM# 56 QIRSH (Piastre)
5.50 g., Copper Plated Steel, 25 mm. **Ruler:** Hussein **Obv:** Head left **Rev:** Value to left within lines below date with written value at lower right **Edge:** Plain

Date	Mintage	VF20	XF40	MS60	MS63	MS65
AH1414-1994	—	0.35	0.45	0.75	1.00	1.25
AH1416-1996	—	0.35	0.45	0.75	1.00	1.25
AH1416-1996	—	PF60 7.00	PF63 8.50	PF65 10.00		

KM# 78.1 QIRSH (Piastre)
5.47 g., Copper Plated Steel, 25 mm. **Ruler:** Abdullah II **Obv:** King Abdullah II **Rev:** Christian date left, Islamic date right **Edge:** Plain

Date	Mintage	VF20	XF40	MS60	MS63	MS65
AH1421-2000	—	0.35	0.45	0.75	1.00	1.25

KM# 78.2 QIRSH (Piastre)
5.47 g., Copper Plated Steel, 24.9 mm. **Ruler:** Abdullah **Obv:** King Abdullah II **Rev:** Islamic date left, Christian date right **Edge:** Plain

Date	Mintage	VF20	XF40	MS60	MS63	MS65
AH1421-2000	—	3.00	5.00	7.50	8.50	10.00
Note: Gregorian and Hijra dates are flipped.						

KM# 5 20 FILS
Copper-Nickel **Ruler:** Abdullah **Obv:** Value and date within crowned circle within sprigs **Rev:** Value within circle above date and star **Edge:** Milled

Date	Mintage	VF20	XF40	MS60	MS63	MS65
AH1368//1949	1,570,000	2.00	5.00	10.00	20.00	30.00
AH1368//1949	25	PF60 500	PF63 750	PF65 1,000		

KM# 13 20 FILS
Copper-Nickel, 19.8 mm. **Ruler:** Hussein **Obv:** Value and date within crowned circle within sprigs **Rev:** Value within circle above date and star **Edge:** Milled

Date	Mintage	VF20	XF40	MS60	MS63	MS65
AH1383//1964	3,000	—	—	5.00	7.50	10.00
Note: Sets only						
AH1385//1965	5,000	—	—	5.00	7.50	10.00
Note: Sets only						
AH1385//1965	10,000	PF60 10.00	PF63 15.00	PF65 20.00		

KM# 17 25 FILS (1/4 Dirham)
4.76 g., Copper-Nickel, 22 mm. **Ruler:** Hussein **Obv:** Head right **Rev:** Value and date within circle flanked by sprigs **Edge:** Milled

Date	Mintage	VF20	XF40	MS60	MS63	MS65
AH1387-1968	200,000	2.50	5.00	10.00	15.00	25.00
AH1390-1970	240,000	2.00	3.50	7.50	15.00	22.50
AH1394-1974	800,000	0.50	1.50	5.00	12.50	20.00
AH1395-1975	2,000,000	0.30	1.00	5.00	12.50	20.00
AH1397-1977	1,600,000	0.30	0.50	1.00	1.50	2.50

KM# 38 25 FILS (1/4 Dirham)
4.75 g., Copper-Nickel, 22 mm. **Ruler:** Hussein **Obv:** Head right **Rev:** Value and date within circle flanked by sprigs **Edge:** Milled

Date	Mintage	VF20	XF40	MS60	MS63	MS65
AH1398-1978	20,000	PF60 5.00	PF63 7.50	PF65 10.00		
AH1401-1981	2,000,000	0.50	0.75	2.00	2.50	4.00
AH1404-1984	4,000,000	0.30	0.50	1.50	2.00	3.50
AH1406-1985	—	—	—	5.00	7.50	10.00
Note: Sets only						
AH1406-1985	5,000	PF60 7.00	PF63 8.50	PF65 10.00		
AH1411-1991	5,000,000	0.30	0.50	1.00	1.50	2.50

KM# 53 2-1/2 PIASTRES
Stainless Steel **Ruler:** Hussein **Obv:** Bust left **Rev:** Value at left within lines below date with written value to lower right **Edge:** Milled

Date	Mintage	VF20	XF40	MS60	MS63	MS65
AH1412-1992	—	0.35	0.50	0.75	1.50	1.75
AH1416-1996	—	0.35	0.50	0.75	1.50	1.75
AH1416-1996	—	PF60 7.00	PF63 8.50	PF65 10.00		

KM# 6 50 FILS (1/2 Dirham)
7.50 g., Copper-Nickel, 26 mm. **Ruler:** Abdullah II **Obv:** Value and date within crowned circle within sprigs **Rev:** Value within circle above date and star **Edge:** Milled

Date	Mintage	VF20	XF40	MS60	MS63	MS65
AH1368//1949	2,500,000	5.00	10.00	20.00	30.00	40.00
AH1368//1949	25	PF60 500	PF63 750	PF65 1,000		

KM# 11 50 FILS (1/2 Dirham)
7.50 g., Copper-Nickel, 26 mm. **Ruler:** Hussein **Obv:** Value and date within crowned circle within sprigs **Rev:** Value within circle above date and star **Edge:** Milled

Date	Mintage	VF20	XF40	MS60	MS63	MS65
AH1374//1955	2,500,000	3.00	10.00	25.00	35.00	45.00
AH1374//1955	—	PF60 750	PF63 1,000	PF65 1,250		
AH1382//1962	750,000	2.00	3.50	5.00	10.00	15.00
AH1382//1962	—	PF60 1,000	PF63 1,250	PF65 1,500		
AH1383//1964	1,003,000	2.00	3.50	5.00	7.50	10.00
AH1385//1965	1,505,000	2.00	3.50	5.00	7.50	10.00
AH1385//1965	10,000	PF60 10.00	PF63 15.00	PF65 20.00		

KM# 18 50 FILS (1/2 Dirham)
7.50 g., Copper-Nickel, 26 mm. **Ruler:** Hussein **Obv:** Head right **Rev:** Value and date within circle flanked by sprigs **Edge:** Milled

Date	Mintage	VF20	XF40	MS60	MS63	MS65
AH1387-1968	400,000	2.00	3.00	5.00	10.00	15.00
AH1390-1970	1,000,000	1.50	2.00	4.00	9.00	14.00
AH1394-1974	1,000,000	1.50	2.00	4.00	9.00	14.00
AH1395-1975	2,000,000	1.00	1.00	3.00	5.00	10.00
AH1397-1977	6,000,000	0.75	1.00	2.50	4.00	7.00

KM# 39 50 FILS (1/2 Dirham)
7.50 g., Copper-Nickel, 26 mm. **Ruler:** Hussein **Obv:** Bust right **Rev:** Legend within wreath **Edge:** Milled

Date	Mintage	VF20	XF40	MS60	MS63	MS65
AH1398-1978	6,168,000	0.75	1.00	2.50	4.00	7.00
AH1398-1978	20,000	PF60 5.00	PF63 7.50	PF65 10.00		
AH1401-1981	5,000,000	0.50	1.00	2.00	2.50	3.50
AH1404-1984	10,000,000	0.50	1.00	2.00	2.50	3.50
AH1406-1985	—	—	—	5.00	7.50	10.00
Note: Sets only						
AH1406-1985	5,000	PF60 7.00	PF63 8.50	PF65 10.00		
AH1409-1989	6,000,000	0.50	1.00	2.00	2.50	3.50
AH1411-1991	10,000,000	0.50	1.00	2.00	2.50	3.50

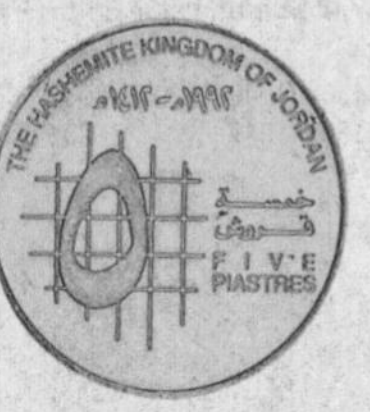

KM# 54 5 PIASTRES
Nickel Plated Steel **Ruler:** Hussein **Obv:** Bust left **Rev:** Value at left within lines below date with written value at lower right **Edge:** Milled

Date	Mintage	VF20	XF40	MS60	MS63	MS65
AH1412-1992	—	0.50	1.00	3.00	4.00	4.50
AH1414-1993	—	0.50	1.00	2.00	2.50	3.50
AH1416-1996	—	0.50	1.00	2.00	2.50	3.50
AH1416-1996	—	PF60 7.00	PF63 8.50	PF65 10.00		
AH1418-1998	—	0.50	1.00	2.00	2.50	2.75

KM# 73 5 PIASTRES
5.00 g., Nickel Plated Steel, 25.8 mm. **Ruler:** Abdullah II **Obv:** Bust right **Rev:** Value to left within lines below date with written value at lower right **Edge:** Milled

Date	Mintage	VF20	XF40	MS60	MS63	MS65
AH1421-2000	—	0.50	0.70	1.50	2.00	2.50

KM# 7 100 FILS (Dirham)
12.00 g., Copper-Nickel, 30 mm. **Ruler:** Abdullah **Obv:** Value and date within crowned circle within sprigs **Rev:** Value within circle above date and star **Edge:** Milled

Date	Mintage	VF20	XF40	MS60	MS63	MS65
AH1368//1949	2,000,000	3.50	5.00	25.00	45.00	75.00
AH1368//1949	25	PF60 500	PF63 750	PF65 1,000		

KM# 12 100 FILS (Dirham)
12.00 g., Copper-Nickel, 30 mm. **Ruler:** Hussein **Obv:** Value and date within crowned circle within sprigs **Rev:** Value within circle above date and star **Edge:** Milled

Date	Mintage	VF20	XF40	MS60	MS63	MS65
AH1374//1955	500,000	5.00	7.50	35.00	65.00	95.00
AH1374//1955	—	PF60 750	PF63 1,000	PF65 1,250		
AH1382//1962	600,000	2.50	3.50	10.00	15.00	25.00
AH1382//1962	—	PF60 1,000	PF63 1,250	PF65 1,500		
AH1383//1964	3,000	—	—	5.00	7.50	10.00
Note: Sets only						
AH1385//1965	405,000	2.00	3.00	5.00	7.50	10.00
AH1385//1965	10,000	PF60 10.00	PF63 15.00	PF65 20.00		

KM# 19 100 FILS (Dirham)
12.00 g., Copper-Nickel, 30 mm. **Ruler:** Hussein **Obv:** Head right **Rev:** Value and date within circle flanked by sprigs **Edge:** Milled

Date	Mintage	VF20	XF40	MS60	MS63	MS65
AH1387-1968	175,000	2.00	3.50	5.00	10.00	15.00
AH1395-1975	2,500,000	1.00	2.00	3.00	5.00	10.00
AH1397-1977	2,000,000	1.00	2.00	3.00	5.00	10.00

KM# 40 100 FILS (Dirham)
12.00 g., Copper-Nickel, 30 mm. **Ruler:** Hussein **Obv:** Head right **Rev:** Value and date within circle flanked by sprigs **Edge:** Milled

Date	Mintage	VF20	XF40	MS60	MS63	MS65
AH1398-1978	3,000,000	2.00	3.50	5.00	10.00	15.00
AH1398-1978	20,000	PF60 5.00	PF63 7.50	PF65 10.00		
AH1401-1981	4,000,000	0.75	1.75	2.50	5.00	7.50
AH1404-1984	5,000,000	0.50	1.50	2.00	2.75	5.50
AH1406-1985	—	—	—	5.00	7.50	10.00
Note: Sets only						
AH1406-1985	5,000	PF60 7.00	PF63 8.50	PF65 10.00		
AH1409-1989	4,000,000	0.50	1.00	1.50	2.50	5.00
AH1411-1991	6,000,000	0.50	1.00	1.50	2.50	5.00

KM# 55 10 PIASTRES

Nickel Plated Steel **Ruler:** Hussein **Obv:** Bust left **Rev:** Value at left within lines below date with written value at lower right **Edge:** Milled

Date	Mintage	VF20	XF40	MS60	MS63	MS65
AH1412-1992	—	0.50	0.75	3.00	4.00	5.00
AH1414-1993	—	0.50	0.75	2.00	2.75	3.50
AH1416-1996	—	0.50	0.75	2.00	2.75	3.50
AH1416-1996	—	PF60 7.00	PF63 8.50	PF65 10.00		

KM# 74 10 PIASTRES

8.00 g., Nickel Plated Steel, 28 mm. **Ruler:** Abdullah II **Obv:** Bust right **Rev:** Value at left within lines below date with written value at lower right **Edge:** Milled

Date	Mintage	VF20	XF40	MS60	MS63	MS65
AH1421-2000	—	0.35	0.50	1.00	1.50	3.00

KM# 20 1/4 DINAR

17.00 g., Copper-Nickel, 34 mm. **Ruler:** Hussein **Series:** F.A.O. **Obv:** Head right **Rev:** Date below olive tree within circled wreath with F.A.O. logo below **Edge:** Milled

Date	Mintage	VF20	XF40	MS60	MS63	MS65
AH1389-1969	60,000	2.00	3.00	4.00	5.00	7.00

KM# 28 1/4 DINAR

17.00 g., Copper-Nickel, 34 mm. **Ruler:** Hussein **Obv:** Head right **Rev:** Date below olive tree within circled wreath **Edge:** Milled

Date	Mintage	VF20	XF40	MS60	MS63	MS65
AH1390-1970	500,000	1.00	1.50	5.00	10.00	15.00
AH1394-1974	400,000	1.00	1.50	5.00	10.00	15.00
AH1395-1975	100,000	2.00	3.00	7.00	15.00	20.00

KM# 29 1/4 DINAR

19.04 g., 0.925 Silver 0.5662 oz. ASW, 34 mm. **Ruler:** Hussein **Subject:** 10th Anniversary - Central Bank of Jordan **Obv:** Head right **Rev:** Olive tree within circled wreath with value and dates around wreath **Edge:** Milled

Date	Mintage	VF20	XF40	MS60	MS63	MS65
AH1394-1974	550	PF60 250	PF63 350	PF65 500		

KM# 29a 1/4 DINAR

33.19 g., 0.917 Gold 0.9785 oz. AGW, 34 mm. **Ruler:** Hussein **Subject:** 10th Anniversary - Central Bank of Jordan **Obv:** Head right **Rev:** Tree within circlular wreath with dates and value around wreath **Edge:** Milled

Date	Mintage	VF20	XF40	MS60	MS63	MS65
AH1394-1974	100	PF60 2,000	PF63 2,500	PF65 2,750		

KM# 30 1/4 DINAR

17.00 g., Copper-Nickel, 34 mm. **Ruler:** Hussein **Subject:** 25th Anniversary of Reign **Obv:** Head facing 1/4 right within small circle flanked by sprigs, all within design with crown on top and date below **Rev:** The Treasury of Petra above dates **Edge:** Reeded

Date	Mintage	VF20	XF40	MS60	MS63	MS65
AH1397-1977	200,000	1.00	2.00	4.00	5.00	6.00

KM# 41 1/4 DINAR

17.00 g., Copper-Nickel, 34 mm. **Ruler:** Hussein **Obv:** Head right **Rev:** Date below olive tree within circled wreath

Date	Mintage	VF20	XF40	MS60	MS63	MS65
AH1398-1978	200,000	1.00	2.00	4.00	5.00	6.00
AH1398-1978	20,000	PF60 7.00	PF63 8.50	PF65 10.00		
AH1401-1981	800,000	0.75	1.50	3.00	4.00	5.00
AH1406-1985	—	—	—	5.00	7.50	10.00
Note: Sets only						
AH1406-1985	5,000	PF60 7.00	PF63 8.50	PF65 10.00		

KM# 61 1/4 DINAR

7.30 g., Nickel-Brass, 26.5 mm. **Ruler:** Hussein **Obv:** Bust left **Rev:** Value in circle within artistic design **Edge:** Plain **Shape:** 7-sided

Date	Mintage	VF20	XF40	MS60	MS63	MS65
AH1416-1996	—	PF60 7.00	PF63 8.50	PF65 10.00		
AH1416-1996	—	1.00	1.50	3.00	4.00	5.00
AH1417-1997	—	1.00	1.50	3.00	4.00	5.00

KM# 21 1/2 DINAR

20.00 g., 0.999 Silver 0.6424 oz. ASW, 35 mm. **Ruler:** Hussein **Rev:** Al Harraneh Palace above value **Edge:** Milled

Date	Mintage	VF20	XF40	MS60	MS63	MS65
AH1389//1969	6,100	PF60 45.00	PF63 60.00	PF65 70.00		

KM# 42 1/2 DINAR

Copper-Nickel **Ruler:** Hussein **Subject:** 1400th Anniversary of Hijra (Mohammed's Pilgrimage) **Obv:** Bust facing 1/4 right **Rev:** Capitol building and sun within circle at right, sprig to left within larger circle **Edge:** Plain **Shape:** 7-sided

Date	Mintage	VF20	XF40	MS60	MS63	MS65
AH1400-1980	2,006,000	1.50	2.50	5.00	7.50	10.00

KM# 58 1/2 DINAR

9.68 g., Brass **Ruler:** Hussein **Obv:** Bust left **Rev:** Value in circle within artistic design **Edge:** Plain

Date	Mintage	VF20	XF40	MS60	MS63	MS65
AH1416-1996	—	1.50	2.50	3.50	5.00	7.50
AH1416-1996	—	PF60 7.00	PF63 8.50	PF65 10.00		

KM# 63 1/2 DINAR

Bi-Metallic Copper-Nickel center in Aluminum-Bronze ring **Ruler:** Hussein **Obv:** Bust left within circle **Rev:** Value in center of circled wreath **Edge:** Plain **Shape:** 7-sided

Date	Mintage	VF20	XF40	MS60	MS63	MS65
AH1417-1997	—	1.50	2.50	3.50	5.00	7.50

KM# 79 1/2 DINAR

9.67 g., Bi-Metallic Copper-Nickel center in Brass ring, 29 mm. **Ruler:** Abdullah II **Obv:** Bust right within circle **Rev:** Value in center of circled wreath **Edge:** Plain **Shape:** 7-sided

Date	Mintage	VF20	XF40	MS60	MS63	MS65
AH1421-2000	—	1.00	2.00	3.00	4.00	5.00

KM# 22 3/4 DINAR
30.00 g., 0.999 Silver 0.9636 oz. ASW, 45 mm. **Ruler:** Hussein **Obv:** Similar to 1/2 Dinar, KM#21 **Rev:** Shrine of the Nativity, Bethlehem **Edge:** Milled

Date	Mintage	VF20	XF40	MS60	MS63	MS65
AH1389//1969	5,800	PF60 70.00	PF63 80.00	PF65 95.00		

KM# 23 DINAR
40.00 g., 0.999 Silver 1.2847 oz. ASW, 55 mm. **Ruler:** Hussein **Obv:** Similar to 1/2 Dinar, KM#21 **Rev:** Temple Hill, Jerusalem **Edge:** Milled

Date	Mintage	VF20	XF40	MS60	MS63	MS65
AH1389//1969	6,800	PF60 95.00	PF63 120	PF65 135		

KM# 47 DINAR
14.00 g., Nickel-Bronze, 29 mm. **Ruler:** Hussein **Subject:** King Hussein's 50th Birthday **Obv:** Head right within beaded circle **Rev:** Crowned sun within 3/4 wreath flanked by dates **Edge:** Milled

Date	Mintage	VF20	XF40	MS60	MS63	MS65
AH1406-1985	—	—	—	5.00	7.00	12.00
AH1406-1985	5,000	PF60 15.00	PF63 20.00	PF65 25.00		

KM# 51.1 DINAR
15.00 g., 0.925 Silver 0.4461 oz. ASW, 30 mm. **Ruler:** Hussein **Subject:** 40th Year of Reign **Obv:** Uniformed bust facing **Rev:** Tughra **Edge:** Plain

Date	Mintage	VF20	XF40	MS60	MS63	MS65
AH1413-1992	4,900	PF60 30.00	PF63 35.00	PF65 45.00		

KM# 51.2 DINAR
15.00 g., 0.925 Silver 0.4461 oz. ASW, 30 mm. **Ruler:** Hussein **Subject:** King's 40th Anniversary of Reign **Obv:** Multicolor uniformed bust facing **Rev:** Tughra **Edge:** Plain

Date	Mintage	VF20	XF40	MS60	MS63	MS65
AH1413-1992	100	PF60 125	PF63 150	PF65 175		

KM# 52 DINAR
8.50 g., 0.917 Gold 0.2506 oz. AGW, 21 mm. **Ruler:** Hussein **Subject:** 40th Year of Reign **Obv:** Uniformed bust facing **Rev:** Tughra **Edge:** Milled

Date	Mintage	VF20	XF40	MS60	MS63	MS65
AH1413-1992	3,000	PF60 400	PF63 450	PF65 500		

KM# 62 DINAR
Brass **Ruler:** Hussein **Subject:** 50th Anniversary - F.A.O. **Obv:** Bust left **Rev:** F.A.O. logo within artistic design **Edge:** Plain **Shape:** 7-sided

Date	Mintage	VF20	XF40	MS60	MS63	MS65
AH1415-1995	—	5.00	7.00	9.00	10.00	12.00

KM# 59 DINAR
Brass **Ruler:** Hussein **Obv:** Bust left **Rev:** Value within center of artistic design **Edge:** Plain **Shape:** 7-sided

Date	Mintage	VF20	XF40	MS60	MS63	MS65
AH1416-1996	—	3.50	5.00	7.00	8.00	10.00
AH1416-1996	—	PF60 10.00	PF63 12.00	PF65 15.00		
AH1417-1997	—	3.50	5.00	7.00	8.00	10.00

KM# 68 DINAR
31.10 g., 0.999 Silver 0.999 oz. ASW, 40 mm. **Ruler:** Hussein **Subject:** 50 Years - Jordanian Independence **Obv:** Bust left **Rev:** Bust with headdress left with inscription at upper left **Edge:** Milled

Date	Mintage	VF20	XF40	MS60	MS63	MS65
ND-1996	Est. 2000	PF60 60.00	PF63 70.00	PF65 75.00		

KM# 64 DINAR
Brass **Ruler:** Hussein **Obv:** Bust left **Rev:** Value within ornamented circle **Edge:** Milled

Date	Mintage	VF20	XF40	MS60	MS63	MS65
AH1419-1998	—	2.00	3.00	5.50	6.50	8.00

KM# 65 DINAR
Brass **Ruler:** Hussein **Subject:** Human Rights **Obv:** Bust left **Rev:** Commemorative legend with value within ornamented circle **Edge:** Milled

Date	Mintage	VF20	XF40	MS60	MS63	MS65
AH1419-1998	—	3.50	5.00	7.00	8.00	10.00

KM# 24 2 DINARS
5.52 g., 0.900 Gold 0.1597 oz. AGW, 21 mm. **Ruler:** Hussein **Subject:** Forum in Jerash **Edge:** Milled

Date	Mintage	VF20	XF40	MS60	MS63	MS65
AH1389//1969	2,425	PF60 285	PF63 300	PF65 325		

KM# 31 2-1/2 DINARS
28.28 g., 0.925 Silver 0.841 oz. ASW, 38.61 mm. **Ruler:** Hussein **Subject:** Conservation **Obv:** Head right **Rev:** Rhim Gazelle **Edge:** Milled

Date	Mintage	VF20	XF40	MS60	MS63	MS65
AH1397-1977	6,265	—	—	27.00	30.00	35.00
AH1397-1977	5,011	PF60 32.00	PF63 37.00	PF65 40.00		

KM# 32 3 DINARS
35.00 g., 0.925 Silver 1.0409 oz. ASW, 42 mm. **Ruler:** Hussein **Subject:** Conservation **Obv:** Head right **Rev:** Palestine sunbird and flower **Edge:** Milled

Date	Mintage	VF20	XF40	MS60	MS63	MS65
AH1397-1977	6,263	—	—	35.00	37.00	40.00
AH1397-1977	4,897	PF60 38.00	PF63 42.00	PF65 45.00		

KM# 43 3 DINARS
23.33 g., 0.925 Silver 0.6938 oz. ASW, 38.61 mm. **Ruler:** Hussein **Subject:** International Year of the Child **Obv:** Bust left **Rev:** Palace of culture in Amman and two children within circle **Edge:** Milled

Date	Mintage	VF20	XF40	MS60	MS63	MS65
AH1401 (1981)	21,000	PF60 22.00	PF63 27.00	PF65 32.00		

KM# 25 5 DINARS
13.82 g., 0.900 Gold 0.3999 oz. AGW, 31 mm. **Ruler:** Hussein **Obv:** Bust left **Rev:** Treasury in Petra **Edge:** Milled

Date	Mintage	VF20	XF40	MS60	MS63	MS65
AH1389//1969	1,950	PF60 725	PF63 750	PF65 800		

KM# 57 5 DINARS
Copper-Nickel, 38.61 mm. **Ruler:** Hussein **Subject:** UN 50 Years **Obv:** Bust left **Rev:** Black iris **Edge:** Milled

Date	Mintage	VF20	XF40	MS60	MS63	MS65
ND(1995)	—	—	—	7.00	12.00	20.00

KM# 57a 5 DINARS
28.28 g., 0.925 Silver 0.841 oz. ASW, 38.61 mm. **Ruler:** Hussein **Subject:** UN 50 Years **Obv:** Bust left **Rev:** Black iris **Edge:** Milled

Date	Mintage	VF20	XF40	MS60	MS63	MS65
ND(1995)	100,000	PF60 32.00	PF63 37.00	PF65 45.00		

KM# 66 5 DINARS
28.28 g., 0.925 Silver 0.841 oz. ASW, 38.61 mm. **Ruler:** Hussein **Subject:** UNICEF: For the Children of the World **Obv:** Conjoined busts of King Hussein and Queen Noor right **Rev:** Boy, girl and UNICEF logo **Edge:** Milled

Date	Mintage	VF20	XF40	MS60	MS63	MS65
AH1419-1999	25,000	PF60 32.00	PF63 37.00	PF65 45.00		

KM# 71 5 DINARS
28.50 g., Brass, 40 mm. **Ruler:** Abdullah II **Subject:** Millennium and Baptism of Jesus **Obv:** Bust facing **Rev:** Baptism scene **Edge:** Milled

Date	Mintage	VF20	XF40	MS60	MS63	MS65
AH1420//2000 Prooflike	10,000	—	—	10.00	15.00	20.00

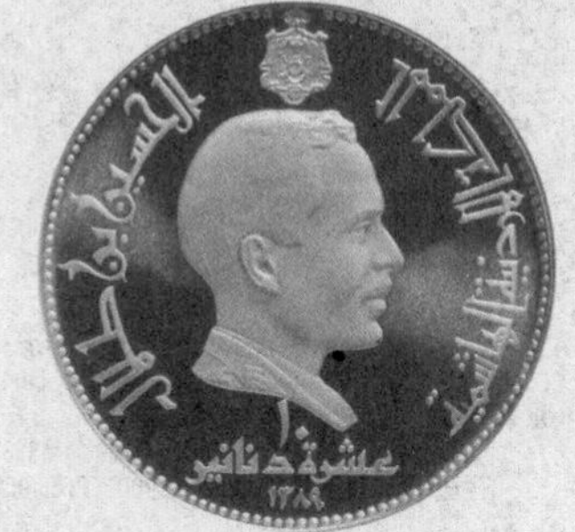

KM# 26 10 DINARS
27.64 g., 0.900 Gold 0.7998 oz. AGW, 40 mm. **Ruler:** Hussein **Subject:** Visit of Pope Paul VI **Obv:** Bust left **Rev:** Pope and church within circle above value

Date	Mintage	VF20	XF40	MS60	MS63	MS65
AH1389//1969	1,870	PF60 1,400	PF63 1,500	PF65 1,600		

KM# 44 10 DINARS
30.00 g., 0.925 Silver 0.8922 oz. ASW, 40 mm. **Ruler:** Hussein **Subject:** 15th century Hijrah calendar **Obv:** Bust 1/4 right **Rev:** Capitol building and sun within circle with sprig at left within larger circle **Edge:** Milled

Date	Mintage	VF20	XF40	MS60	MS63	MS65
AH1400-1980	17,000	PF60 35.00	PF63 40.00	PF65 50.00		

KM# 48 10 DINARS
15.20 g., 0.925 Silver 0.452 oz. ASW, 29 mm. **Ruler:** Hussein **Subject:** King's 50th Birthday **Obv:** Head right within beaded circle **Rev:** Crowned sun within 3/4 wreath above value **Edge:** Milled

Date	Mintage	VF20	XF40	MS60	MS63	MS65
AH1406-1985	—	PF60 25.00	PF63 30.00	PF65 40.00		

KM# 80 10 DINARS
31.10 g., 0.999 Silver 0.9989 oz. ASW, 40 mm. **Ruler:** Abdullah II **Subject:** Abdullah II's Accession to Throne **Obv:** Abdullah II **Rev:** Crowned and mantled arms **Edge:** Milled

Date	Mintage	VF20	XF40	MS60	MS63	MS65
AH1420-1999	2,000	PF60 40.00	PF63 45.00	PF65 50.00		

KM# 72 10 DINARS
31.00 g., 0.999 Silver 0.9957 oz. ASW, 40 mm. **Ruler:** Abdullah II **Subject:** Millennium and Baptism of Jesus **Obv:** Bust facing **Rev:** Baptism scene **Edge:** Milled **Note:** Issued in 1999.

Date	Mintage	VF20	XF40	MS60	MS63	MS65
AH1420 (2000)	5,000	—	—	35.00	40.00	50.00
Matte with Patina						
AH1420 (2000)	Inc. above	PF60 35.00	PF63 40.00	PF65 50.00		

KM# 27 25 DINARS
69.11 g., 0.900 Gold 1.9997 oz. AGW, 48 mm. **Ruler:** Hussein **Obv:** Head right with crowned mantled arms above **Rev:** Dome of the Rock, Jerusalem, above value **Edge:** Milled

Date	Mintage	VF20	XF40	MS60	MS63	MS65
AH1389//1969	1,000	PF60 3,500	PF63 3,650	PF65 3,750		

Note: Individually numbered

KM# 33 25 DINARS
15.00 g., 0.917 Gold 0.4422 oz. AGW, 29.01 mm. **Ruler:** Hussein **Subject:** 25th Anniversary of Reign **Obv:** Bust right **Rev:** Crowned mantled arms above dates **Edge:** Milled

Date	Mintage	VF20	XF40	MS60	MS63	MS65
AH1397-1977 FM	4,724	PF60 750	PF63 775	PF65 800		

KM# 45 40 DINARS
14.31 g., 0.917 Gold 0.4219 oz. AGW, 27 mm. **Ruler:** Hussein **Subject:** 15th century Hijrah calendar **Obv:** Bust facing 1/4 right **Rev:** Sun rays, cloud, domed building and box within flower design and circle **Edge:** Milled

Date	Mintage	VF20	XF40	MS60	MS63	MS65
AH1400-1980	9,500	PF60 650	PF63 700	PF65 750		

KM# 50 50 DINARS
15.98 g., 0.917 Gold 0.4711 oz. AGW, 28.40 mm. **Ruler:** Hussein **Subject:** Five-Year Plan **Obv:** Head right with crowned mantled arms above **Rev:** Fruit flanked by sprigs within circled gear with writing within chain wreath **Edge:** Milled

Date	Mintage	VF20	XF40	MS60	MS63	MS65
AH1396-1976	250	800	850	1,000	1,250	1,500
AH1396-1976	Inc. above	PF60 1,250	PF63 1,350	PF65 1,500		

KM# 34 50 DINARS
33.44 g., 0.900 Gold 0.9675 oz. AGW, 34 mm. **Ruler:** Hussein **Subject:** Conservation **Obv:** Head right **Rev:** Bird facing left **Edge:** Milled

Date	Mintage	VF20	XF40	MS60	MS63	MS65
AH1397-1977	829	—	—	1,700	1,750	1,850
AH1397-1977	287	PF60 1,750	PF63 1,900	PF65 2,000		

KM# 49 50 DINARS
17.00 g., 0.917 Gold 0.5012 oz. AGW, 29 mm. **Ruler:** Hussein **Subject:** King Hussein's 50th Birthday **Obv:** Head right within beaded circle **Rev:** Crown above rising sun within wreath **Edge:** Reeded

Date	Mintage	VF20	XF40	MS60	MS63	MS65
AH1406-1985	2,029	PF60 850	PF63 900	PF65 950		

KM# 69 50 DINARS
16.96 g., 0.9166 Gold 0.4998 oz. AGW, 30 mm. **Ruler:** Hussein **Subject:** 50 Years - Jordanian Independence **Obv:** Bust facing **Rev:** Portrait of King Abdullah

Date	Mintage	VF20	XF40	MS60	MS63	MS65
ND-1996	Est. 1000	PF60 850	PF63 900	PF65 950		

KM# 67 50 DINARS
6.22 g., 0.999 Gold 0.1998 oz. AGW, 22 mm. **Ruler:** Hussein **Subject:** UNICEF: For the Children of the World **Obv:** Hussein Ibn Talal and Noor Al-Hussein **Rev:** Boy, girl and UNICEF logo

Date	Mintage	VF20	XF40	MS60	MS63	MS65
AH1419-1999	10,000	PF60 375	PF63 400	PF65 425		

KM# 81 50 DINARS
16.96 g., 0.9166 Gold 0.4998 oz. AGW, 30 mm. **Ruler:** Abdullah II **Subject:** Abdullah II's Accession to the Throne **Obv:** Abdullah II **Rev:** Crowned and mantled arms **Edge:** Milled

Date	Mintage	VF20	XF40	MS60	MS63	MS65
AH1420-1999	1,750	PF60 825	PF63 875	PF65 900		

KM# 82 50 DINARS
16.96 g., 0.9166 Gold 0.4998 oz. AGW, 30 mm. **Ruler:** Abdullah II **Subject:** Millennium and Baptism of Jesus **Obv:** Abdullah II **Rev:** River baptism scene **Edge:** Milled

Date	Mintage	VF20	XF40	MS60	MS63	MS65
AH1420-2000	3,500	PF60 800	PF63 850	PF65 875		

KM# 46 60 DINARS
17.17 g., 0.917 Gold 0.5062 oz. AGW, 27 mm. **Ruler:** Hussein **Subject:** International Year of the Child **Obv:** Head right **Rev:** Palace of Culture in Amman and two children within circle **Edge:** Milled

Date	Mintage	VF20	XF40	MS60	MS63	MS65
AH1401-1981	20,000	PF60 650	PF63 725	PF65 800		

PATTERNS

Including off metal strikes

KM#	Date	Mintage	Identification	Mkt Val
Pn1	AH1387 (1968)	50	Fils. Gold. KM14.	400
Pn2	AH1387 (1968)	50	5 Fils. Gold. KM15.	850
Pn3	AH1387 (1968)	50	10 Fils. Gold. KM16.	1,400
Pn4	AH1387 (1968)	50	25 Fils. Gold. KM17.	675
Pn5	AH1387 (1968)	50	50 Fils. Gold. KM18.	1,000
Pn6	AH1387 (1968)	50	Dirham. Gold. KM19.	1,750
Pn7	AH1395 (1975)	170	Fils. Gold. As KM14.	350
Pn8	AH1395 (1975)	170	5 Fils. Gold. As KM15.	700
Pn9	AH1395 (1975)	170	10 Fils. Gold. As KM16.	1,100
Pn10	AH1395 (1975)	170	25 Fils. Gold. As KM17.	550
Pn11	AH1395 (1975)	170	50 Fils. Gold. As KM18.	850
Pn12	AH1395 (1975)	170	Dirham. Gold. As KM19.	1,400

Pn13	AH1395 (1975)	110	1/4 Dinar. Gold. As KM28.	2,000
PnA7	1976	—	50 Dinars. Bronze. KM#50.	1,500
PnA14	1980	—	10 Dinars. Copper Gilt. KM44.	—
Pn14	AH1412-1992	3	2-1/2 Piastres. Nickel Plated Steel. as KM-53, denomination not frosted.	—
Pn15	AH1412-1992	3	5 Piastres. Nickel Plated Steel. as KM-54, denomination not frosted.	—
Pn16	AH1412-1992	3	10 Piastres. Nickel Plated Steel. as KM-55, denomination not frosted.	—
Pn17	AH1415-1995(1996)	1	1/4 Dinar. Nickel-Brass. Similar to KM-61, never released in circulation with the "1995" date.	—
Pn18	AH1415-1995(1996)	1	1/2 Dinar. Brass. Similar to KM-58, never released in circulation with the "1995" date.	—
Pn19	AH1415-1995(1996)	3	Dinar. Brass. as KM-62, lighter metal.	—
Pn20	AH1417-1997	2	1/2 Dinar. Bi-Metallic. as KM-63, metal lighter in color.	—
Pn21	AH1418-1998	2	1/4 Dinar. (No Composition). Similar to KM#61 but with large center circle. Unadopted design.	—
Pn22	AH1420-2000	2	1/2 Dinar. Similar to KM79 but with AH date 1420. The issued coin was 2000//AH1421.	—

PIEDFORT

KM#	Date	Mintage	Identification	Mkt Val
P1	1981	Est. 2050	3 Dinars. Silver. KM43.	1,000
P2	1981	61	60 Dinars. Gold. KM46.	2,500
P3	1985	700	50 Dinars. Gold. KM49.	1,500
Note: Majority melted down; about 100 pcs. remain today				
P4	AH1413-1992	500	Dinar. 0.9167. Gold. Broad piefort of KM-52.	1,000
P5	ND-1996	400	50 Dinars. 0.9166. Gold. Milled. Similar to KM#69, with 40mm diameter.	1,500

MINT SETS

KM#	Date	Mintage	Identification	Issue Price	Mkt Val
MS1	1985 (8)	—	KM35-41, 47	10.75	35.00
MS2	1949-1964 (6)	—	KM5 (1949), 8 (1963), 9 (1962), 10-11 (1964), 12 (1962), mixed dates	—	35.00
MS3	1996 (8)	—	KM#53-56, 58-61	—	30.00
MS4	2000-2004 (5)	—	KM#73-74, 78.1, 79, 83, mixed dates	—	20.00

PROOF SETS

KM#	Date	Mintage	Identification	Issue Price	Mkt Val
PS1	1949 (6)	25	KM2-7	—	4,500
PS2	1965 (6)	10,000	KM8-13	14.40	40.00
PS3	1969 (7)	—	KM21-27	396	5,100
PS4	1969 (6)	—	KM21-26	—	2,225
PS5	1969 (4)	—	KM24-27	—	4,900
PS6	1969 (3)	5,800	KM21-23	36.00	250
PS6A	1974 (2)	100	KM#29-29a	—	2,200
PS7	1977 (3)	1,000	KM31, 32, 34	780	1,700
PS8	1977 (2)	9,000	KM31-32	60.00	75.00
PS9	1978 (7)	20,000	KM35-41	27.00	35.00
PS10	1980 (2)	—	KM44, 45	365	650
PS11	1985 (8)	5,000	KM35-41, 47	31.00	50.00
PS12	1996 (3)	50	KM#68, 69, P5	—	2,100
PS13	1996 (8)	—	KM#53-56, 58-61	30.00	55.00

SPECIMEN SETS (SS)

KM#	Date	Mintage	Identification	Issue Price	Mkt Val
SS1	1964 (6)	3,000	KM8-13	—	35.00
SS2	1965 (6)	5,000	KM8-13	—	35.00
SS3	1968 (6)	50	KM14-19	—	300
SS4	1968 (6)	50	KMPn1-6	—	6,100
SS5	1975 (7)	110	KMPn7-13	—	7,000

KATANGA

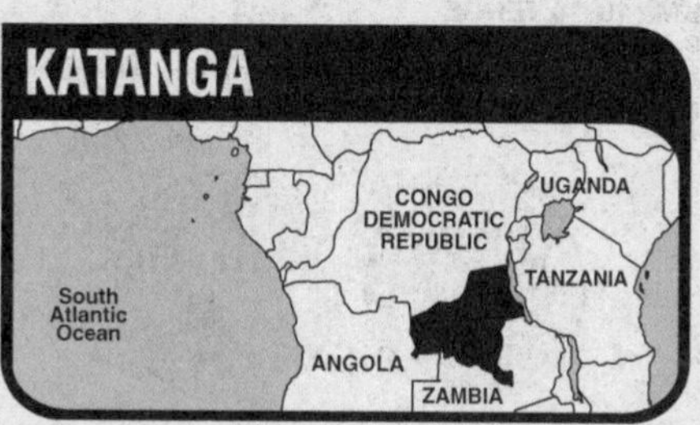

Katanga, the southern province of the former Belgian Congo, had an area of 191,873 sq. mi. (496,951 sq. km.) and was noted for its mineral wealth.

MONETARY SYSTEM

100 Centimes = 1 Franc

PROVINCE

DECIMAL COINAGE

KM# 1 FRANC

4.70 g., Bronze **Obv:** Bananas (musax paradisiaca-Musaceae) within circle **Rev:** Cross, value and date within circle

Date	Mintage	VF20	XF40	MS60	MS63	MS65
1961	—	1.25	2.00	4.00	6.00	9.00

KM# 2 5 FRANCS

6.54 g., Bronze, 26.3 mm. **Obv:** Bananas (musax paradisiaca-Musaceae) within circle **Rev:** Cross, value and date within circle

Date	Mintage	VF20	XF40	MS60	MS63	MS65
1961	—	2.25	3.50	5.00	7.00	10.00

KM# 2a 5 FRANCS

13.33 g., 0.900 Gold 0.3857 oz. AGW **Obv:** Bananas within circle **Rev:** Cross, value and date within circle

Date	Mintage	VF20	XF40	MS60	MS63	MS65
1961	20,000	—	—	525	575	675

KAZAKHSTAN

The Republic of Kazakhstan (formerly Kazakhstan S.S.R.) is bordered to the west by the Caspian Sea and Russia, to the north by Russia, in the east by the Peoples Republic of China and in the south by Uzbekistan and Kirghizia. It has an area of 1,049,155 sq. mi. (2,717,300 sq. km.) and a population of 16.7 million. Capital: Astana. Rich in mineral resources including coal, tungsten, copper, lead, zinc and manganese with huge oil and natural gas reserves. Agriculture is very important, (it previously represented 20 percent of the total arable acreage of the combined U.S.S.R.) Non-ferrous metallurgy, heavy engineering and chemical industries are leaders in its economy.

The Kazakh Autonomous Soviet Socialist Republic was proclaimed on Aug. 26, 1920 within the R.S.F.S.R. Russian and Ukrainian colonization continued while 2 purges in 1927 and 1935 quelled any Kazakh feelings of priority in the matters of their country. On Dec. 5, 1936 Kazakhstan qualified for full status as an S.S.R. and held its first congress in 1937. Independence was declared on Dec. 16, 1991 and Kazakhstan joined the C.I.S.

MONETARY SYSTEM

100 Tyin = 1 Tenge

REPUBLIC

DECIMAL COINAGE

KM# 1 2 TYIN

1.90 g., Yellow Brass, 17.2 mm. **Obv:** National emblem **Rev:** Star design divides date with value within

Date	Mintage	VF20	XF40	MS60	MS63	MS65
1993	—	—	—	0.25	0.45	0.75

KM# 1a 2 TYIN

2.20 g., Copper Clad Brass, 17.2 mm. **Obv:** National emblem **Rev:** Star design divides date with value within **Edge:** Plain

Date	Mintage	VF20	XF40	MS60	MS63	MS65
1993	—	—	—	0.25	0.45	0.75

KM# 2 5 TYIN

1.90 g., Yellow Brass, 17.2 mm. **Obv:** National emblem **Rev:** Star design divides date with value within

Date	Mintage	VF20	XF40	MS60	MS63	MS65
1993	—	—	—	0.30	0.60	1.00

KM# 2a 5 TYIN

2.24 g., Copper Clad Brass, 17.2 mm. **Obv:** National emblem **Rev:** Star design divides date with value within **Edge:** Plain

Date	Mintage	VF20	XF40	MS60	MS63	MS65
1993	—	—	—	0.30	0.60	1.00

KM# 3 10 TYIN

3.30 g., Yellow Brass, 19.95 mm. **Obv:** National emblem **Rev:** Star design divides date with value within **Edge:** Plain

Date	Mintage	VF20	XF40	MS60	MS63	MS65
1993	—	—	—	0.40	0.80	1.50

KM# 3a 10 TYIN

3.10 g., Copper Clad Brass, 19.6 mm. **Obv:** National emblem **Rev:** Star design divides date with value within

Date	Mintage	VF20	XF40	MS60	MS63	MS65
1993	—	—	—	0.40	0.80	1.50

KM# 4 20 TYIN

4.52 g., Brass Plated Zinc, 22 mm. **Obv:** National emblem **Rev:** Star design divides date with value within

Date	Mintage	VF20	XF40	MS60	MS63	MS65
1993	—	—	—	0.60	1.25	2.00

KM# 4a 20 TYIN

4.52 g., Copper Plated Zinc, 22 mm. **Obv:** National emblem **Rev:** Star design divides sate with value within

Date	Mintage	VF20	XF40	MS60	MS63	MS65
1993	—	—	—	0.60	1.25	2.00

KM# 5 50 TYIN

6.80 g., Brass Plated Zinc, 25.1 mm. **Obv:** National emblem **Rev:** Star design divides date with value within

Date	Mintage	VF20	XF40	MS60	MS63	MS65
1993	—	—	—	0.75	1.50	2.50

KM# 5a 50 TYIN

6.80 g., Copper Plated Zinc, 25.1 mm. **Obv:** National emblem **Rev:** Star design divides date with value within

Date	Mintage	VF20	XF40	MS60	MS63	MS65
1993	—	—	—	0.75	1.50	2.50

KM# 6 TENGE

Copper-Nickel, 17.3 mm. **Obv:** Mythical animal **Rev:** Star design with value and date within

Date	Mintage	VF20	XF40	MS60	MS63	MS65
1992	—	—	—	0.50	1.00	1.75
1993	—	—	—	0.25	0.50	0.85

KM# 23 TENGE

1.60 g., Nickel-Brass, 15 mm. **Obv:** National emblem **Rev:** Value flanked by designs **Edge:** Plain

Date	Mintage	VF20	XF40	MS60	MS63	MS65
1997	—	—	—	0.25	0.50	0.85
2000	—	—	—	0.25	0.50	0.85

KM# 8 3 TENGE

3.43 g., Copper-Nickel, 19.6 mm. **Obv:** Mythical animal within circle **Rev:** Star design with value and date within

Date	Mintage	VF20	XF40	MS60	MS63	MS65
1993	—	—	—	0.35	0.75	1.25

KM# 9 5 TENGE

Copper-Nickel **Obv:** Mythical animal within circle **Rev:** Star design with date and value within

Date	Mintage	VF20	XF40	MS60	MS63	MS65
1993	—	—	—	0.60	1.25	2.00

KM# 24 5 TENGE

2.20 g., Nickel-Brass, 17.3 mm. **Obv:** National emblem **Rev:** Value flanked by designs

Date	Mintage	VF20	XF40	MS60	MS63	MS65
1997	—	—	—	0.25	0.50	0.85
2000	—	—	—	0.25	0.50	0.85

KM# 10 10 TENGE

Copper-Nickel **Obv:** National emblem above value **Rev:** Stylized double headed eagle within circle above date

Date	Mintage	VF20	XF40	MS60	MS63	MS65
1993	—	—	—	1.00	2.00	3.50

KM# 25 10 TENGE

2.80 g., Nickel-Brass, 19.6 mm. **Obv:** National emblem **Rev:** Value above design

Date	Mintage	VF20	XF40	MS60	MS63	MS65
1997	—	—	—	0.35	0.75	1.25
2000	—	—	—	0.35	0.75	1.25

KM# 11 20 TENGE

Copper-Nickel **Obv:** National emblem above value **Rev:** Turbaned head 1/4 right within circle

Date	Mintage	VF20	XF40	MS60	MS63	MS65
1993	—	—	—	1.50	2.50	4.00

KM# 12 20 TENGE

Copper-Nickel **Subject:** 50th Anniversary - United Nations **Obv:** National emblem above value **Rev:** UN logo and anniversary dates within circle

Date	Mintage	VF20	XF40	MS60	MS63	MS65
1995	—	—	—	1.50	2.50	4.00

KM# 18 20 TENGE

Copper-Nickel **Subject:** 150th Anniversary - Jambyl **Obv:** National emblem above value **Rev:** Man with stringed instrument

Date	Mintage	VF20	XF40	MS60	MS63	MS65
1996	—	—	—	1.50	2.50	4.00

KM# 19 20 TENGE

Copper-Nickel **Subject:** 5th Anniversary - Independence **Obv:** National emblem above value **Rev:** Monument and buildings

Date	Mintage	VF20	XF40	MS60	MS63	MS65
1996	—	—	—	1.50	2.50	4.00

KM# 20 20 TENGE

Copper-Nickel **Subject:** Centennial - Birth of Muchtar Auezov **Obv:** National emblem above value **Rev:** Head facing divides dates

Date	Mintage	VF20	XF40	MS60	MS63	MS65
ND-1997	—	—	—	1.50	2.50	4.00

KM# 21 20 TENGE

Copper-Nickel **Subject:** Year of Peace and Harmony **Obv:** National emblem above value **Rev:** Stylized dove

Date	Mintage	VF20	XF40	MS60	MS63	MS65
1997	—	—	—	1.50	2.50	4.00

KM# 26 20 TENGE

2.90 g., Copper-Nickel-Zinc, 18.3 mm. **Obv:** National emblem **Rev:** Value above design **Edge:** Segmented reeding **Edge Lettering:** * СТО TENGE * Y 3 TENGE

Date	Mintage	VF20	XF40	MS60	MS63	MS65
1997	—	—	—	0.50	1.00	1.75
2000	—	—	—	0.50	1.00	1.75

KM# 22 20 TENGE

Copper-Nickel **Subject:** New Capital - Astana **Obv:** National emblem above value **Rev:** Flower-like design

Date	Mintage	VF20	XF40	MS60	MS63	MS65
1998	—	—	—	1.50	2.50	4.00

KM# 28 20 TENGE

Copper-Nickel **Subject:** 100th Birthday - K.I. Satbaev **Obv:** National emblem above value **Rev:** Head facing

Date	Mintage	VF20	XF40	MS60	MS63	MS65
1999	—	—	—	2.00	3.00	5.00

KM# 27 50 TENGE
4.70 g., Copper-Nickel-Zinc, 23 mm. **Obv:** National emblem **Rev:** Value above design

Date	Mintage	VF20	XF40	MS60	MS63	MS65
1997	—	—	—	1.00	2.00	3.50
2000	—	—	—	1.00	2.00	3.50

KM# 30 50 TENGE
Copper-Nickel **Subject:** Millennium **Obv:** National emblem above value **Rev:** Rising sun above three blocks

Date	Mintage	VF20	XF40	MS60	MS63	MS65
1999	—	—	—	1.50	2.50	4.00

KM# 31 50 TENGE
10.70 g., Copper-Nickel, 31 mm. **Subject:** Victorious conclusion of World War II **Obv:** National emblem above value **Rev:** Soldiers celebrating **Edge:** Reeded and plain sections

Date	Mintage	VF20	XF40	MS60	MS63	MS65
ND-2000	—	—	—	2.00	3.00	5.00

KM# 33 50 TENGE
11.50 g., Copper-Nickel **Obv:** National emblem above value **Rev:** Bust 1/4 left **Edge:** Reeded and plain sections

Date	Mintage	VF20	XF40	MS60	MS63	MS65
2000	—	—	—	2.00	3.00	5.00

KM# 48 50 TENGE
11.06 g., Copper-Nickel, 31 mm. **Subject:** 1500th Anniversary of Akhmet Yasaui Kesenesi Mosque **Obv:** National emblem above value **Rev:** Mosque **Edge:** Reeded and plain sections

Date	Mintage	VF20	XF40	MS60	MS63	MS65
2000	—	—	—	1.50	2.50	4.00

KM# 13 100 TENGE
24.00 g., 0.925 Silver 0.7137 oz. ASW, 37 mm. **Subject:** 150th Anniversary - Birth of Abaj Kunabaev **Obv:** Mother and child within circle **Rev:** Head left flanked by dates above small assorted figures **Edge:** Plain

Date	Mintage	VF20	XF40	MS60	MS63	MS65
1995	6,000	PF65 75.00	PF67 95.00			

KM# 14 100 TENGE
24.00 g., 0.925 Silver 0.7137 oz. ASW, 37 mm. **Subject:** 150th Anniversary - Birth of Abaj Kunabaev **Obv:** Bust left **Rev:** Falconer **Edge:** Plain

Date	Mintage	VF20	XF40	MS60	MS63	MS65
1995	6,000	PF65 75.00	PF67 95.00			

KM# 15 100 TENGE
24.00 g., 0.925 Silver 0.7137 oz. ASW, 37 mm. **Subject:** 150th Anniversary - Birth of Abaj Kunabaev **Obv:** Bust left **Rev:** Couple on swings **Edge:** Plain

Date	Mintage	VF20	XF40	MS60	MS63	MS65
1995	6,000	PF65 75.00	PF67 95.00			

KM# 16 100 TENGE
24.00 g., 0.925 Silver 0.7137 oz. ASW, 37 mm. **Subject:** 150th Anniversary - Birth of Abaj Kunabaev **Obv:** Bust left **Rev:** Town view **Edge:** Plain

Date	Mintage	VF20	XF40	MS60	MS63	MS65
1995	6,000	PF65 75.00	PF67 95.00			

KM# 17 100 TENGE
24.00 g., 0.925 Silver 0.7137 oz. ASW, 37 mm. **Subject:** 150th Anniversary - Birth of Abaj Kunabaev **Obv:** Bust left **Rev:** Elderly man **Edge:** Plain

Date	Mintage	VF20	XF40	MS60	MS63	MS65
1995	6,000	PF65 75.00	PF67 95.00			

KM# 32 100 TENGE
24.00 g., 0.925 Silver 0.7137 oz. ASW, 37 mm. **Subject:** Millennium **Obv:** National emblem within design **Rev:** Ancient and modern technologies **Edge:** Plain

Date	Mintage	XF40	MS60	MS63	MS65	MS66
1999	—	PF67 325	PF69 400			

KM# 34 100 TENGE
24.00 g., 0.925 Silver 0.7137 oz. ASW, 37 mm. **Subject:** Turkestan City, 1500th Anniversary **Obv:** Value **Rev:** Domed building **Edge:** Plain

Date	Mintage	XF40	MS60	MS63	MS65	MS66
2000	—	PF67 125	PF69 175			

KM# 35 500 TENGE
24.00 g., 0.925 Silver 0.7137 oz. ASW, 37 mm. **Subject:** Snow Leopard **Obv:** Value **Rev:** Prowling leopard **Edge:** Plain

Date	Mintage	XF40	MS60	MS63	MS65	MS66
2000	3,000	PF67 275	PF69 350			

KM# 36 500 TENGE
24.00 g., 0.925 Silver 0.7137 oz. ASW, 36.9 mm.

Date	Mintage	XF40	MS60	MS63	MS65	MS66
2000	3,000	PF67 250	PF69 300			

KM# 111 500 TENGE
7.77 g., 0.999 Gold 0.2496 oz. AGW, 21.9 mm. **Subject:** Turkistan City, 1500th Anniversary **Obv:** Value **Rev:** Building facade

Date	Mintage	XF40	MS60	MS63	MS65	MS66
2000	—	PF67 400	PF69 475			

KM# 29 1000 TENGE
3.12 g., 0.9999 Gold 0.1003 oz. AGW **Subject:** Silk Road **Obv:** Value in ornamental frame **Rev:** Caravan of camels around lined cross within circle

Date	Mintage	XF40	MS60	MS63	MS65	MS66
1995	—	—	—	180	200	250

KM# 45 2500 TENGE

7.78 g., 0.9999 Gold 0.2501 oz. AGW, 20 mm. **Subject:** The Silk Road **Obv:** Value in ornamental frame **Rev:** Caravan of camels around lined cross within circle **Edge:** Reeded

Date	Mintage	XF40	MS60	MS63	MS65	MS66
1995	—	—	—	—	425	500

KM# 46 5000 TENGE

15.55 g., 0.9999 Gold 0.4999 oz. AGW, 25 mm. **Subject:** The Silk Road **Obv:** Value in ornamental frame **Rev:** Caravan of camels around lined cross within circle **Edge:** Reeded

Date	Mintage	XF40	MS60	MS63	MS65	MS66
1995	—	—	—	—	800	850

KM# 47 10000 TENGE

31.10 g., 0.9999 Gold 0.9998 oz. AGW, 32 mm. **Subject:** The Silk Road **Obv:** Value in ornamental frame **Rev:** Caravan of camels around lined cross within circle **Edge:** Reeded

Date	Mintage	XF40	MS60	MS63	MS65	MS66
1995	—	—	—	—	1,500	1,650

PROBAS

KM#	Date	Mintage	Identification	Mkt Val
Pr1	1992	—	Tenge. Copper-Nickel. 17.3mm.	—
Pr2	1992	—	50 Tenge. Copper-Nickel.	—
Pr3	1992	—	50 Tenge. Copper.	—
Pr4	1992	—	50 Tenge. Brass.	—
Pr5	1992	—	50 Tenge. Aluminum.	—

KEELING COCOS

The Territory of Cocos (Keeling) Islands, an Australian territory, comprises a group of 27 coral islands located (see arrow on map of Australia) in the Indian Ocean 1,300 miles northwest of Australia. Only Direction and Home Islands are regularly inhabited. The group has an area of 5.4 sq. mi. and a population of about 569. Calcium, phosphate and coconut products are exported.

The islands were discovered by Capt. William Keeling of the British East India Co. in 1609. Alexander Hare, an English adventurer, established a settlement on one of the southern islands in 1823, but it lasted less than a year. A permanent settlement was established on Direction Island in 1827 by Hare and Capt. John Clunies Ross, a Scot, for the purpose of storing East Indian spices for reshipment to Europe during periods of shortage. When the experiment in spice futures did not develop satisfactorily, Hare left the islands (1829 or 1830), leaving Ross as sole owner. The coral group became a British protectorate in 1856; was attached to the colony of Ceylon in 1878; and was placed under the administration of the Straits Settlements in 1882. In 1903 the group was annexed to the Straits Settlements and incorporated into the colony of Singapore until November of 1955, when it was placed under the administration of Australia.

RULER
British

MONETARY SYSTEM
100 Cents = 1 Rupee

BRITISH TERRITORY

TOKEN COINAGE

Tn1-Tn7 were all issued with individual serial numbers. Examples which have had their ink retouched are worth approximately 50% less than listed values.

Plastic Ivory

KM# Tn1 5 CENTS

Date	Mintage	VG8	F12	VF20	XF40	MS60
1913	5,000	65.00	120	240	450	600

KM# Tn2 10 CENTS

Date	Mintage	VG8	F12	VF20	XF40	MS60
1913	5,000	50.00	90.00	180	375	525

KM# Tn3 25 CENTS

Date	Mintage	VG8	F12	VF20	XF40	MS60
1913	5,000	25.00	36.00	60.00	125	260

KM# Tn4 50 CENTS

Date	Mintage	VG8	F12	VF20	XF40	MS60
1913	2,000	80.00	150	325	675	800

KM# Tn5 RUPEE

Date	Mintage	VG8	F12	VF20	XF40	MS60
1913	2,000	30.00	48.00	90.00	175	280

KM# Tn6 2 RUPEES

Date	Mintage	VG8	F12	VF20	XF40	MS60
1913	1,000	40.00	60.00	110	195	325

KM# Tn7 5 RUPEES

Date	Mintage	VG8	F12	VF20	XF40	MS60
1913	1,000	40.00	60.00	120	230	350

TOKEN COINAGE

Modern Plastic

KM# Tn8 CENT

Note: Aqua plastic.

Date	Mintage	VF20	XF40	MS60	MS63	MS65
1968	—	—	—	—	—	150

KM# Tn9 5 CENTS

Note: Aqua plastic.

Date	Mintage	VF20	XF40	MS60	MS63	MS65
1968	—	—	—	—	—	150

KM# Tn10 10 CENTS

Note: Aqua plastic.

Date	Mintage	VF20	XF40	MS60	MS63	MS65
1968	—	—	—	—	—	160

KM# Tn11 25 CENTS

Note: Aqua plastic.

Date	Mintage	VF20	XF40	MS60	MS63	MS65
1968	—	—	—	—	—	180

KM# Tn12 50 CENTS

Note: Aqua plastic.

Date	Mintage	VF20	XF40	MS60	MS63	MS65
1968	—	—	—	—	—	200

KM# Tn13 RUPEE

Note: Red plastic.

Date	Mintage	VF20	XF40	MS60	MS63	MS65
1968	—	—	—	—	—	220

KM# Tn14 2 RUPEES

Note: Red plastic.

Date	Mintage	VF20	XF40	MS60	MS63	MS65
1968	—	—	—	—	—	240

KM# Tn15 5 RUPEES
Note: Red plastic.

Date	Mintage	VF20	XF40	MS60	MS63	MS65
1968	—	—	—	—	—	280

KM# Tn16 10 RUPEES
Note: Red plastic.

Date	Mintage	VF20	XF40	MS60	MS63	MS65
1968	—	—	—	—	—	320

KM# Tn17 25 RUPEES
Note: Red plastic.

Date	Mintage	VF20	XF40	MS60	MS63	MS65
1968	—	—	—	—	—	385

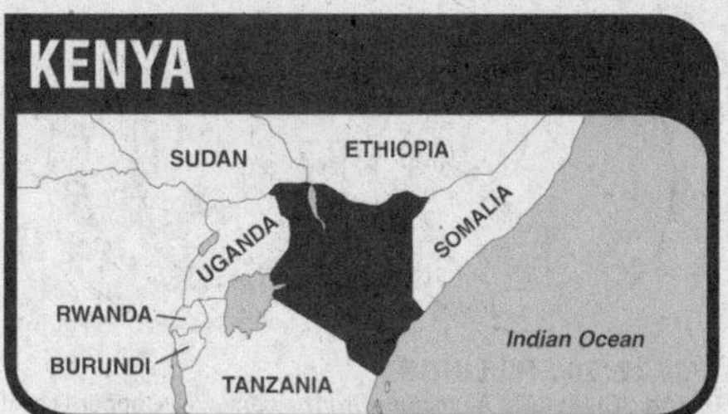

The Republic of Kenya, located on the east coast of Central Africa, has an area of 224,961 sq. mi. (582,650 sq. km.) and a population of 20.1 million. Capital: Nairobi. The predominantly agricultural country exports coffee, tea and petroleum products.

The Arabs came to the coast of Kenya in the 8th century and established posts to conduct an ivory and slave trade. The Portuguese followed in the 16th century. After a lengthy and bitter struggle with the sultans of Zanzibar who controlled much of the southeastern coast of Africa, the Portuguese were driven away (late 17th century) and for many years Kenya was simply a port of call on the route to India. German and British interests in the 19th century produced agreements defining their respective spheres of influence. The British sphere was administrated by the Imperial East Africa Co. until 1895, when the British government purchased the company's rights in the East Africa Protectorate which, in 1920, was designated as Kenya Colony and protectorate - the latter being a 10-mile-wide coastal strip together with Mombasa, Lamuand other small islands nominally retained by the Sultan of Zanzibar. Kenya achieved self-government in June of 1963 as a consequence of the 1952-60 Mau Mau terrorist campaign to secure land reforms and political rights for Africans. Independence was attained on Dec. 12, 1963. Kenya became a republic in 1964. It is a member of the Commonwealth of Nations. The president is Chief of State and Head of Government.

RULER
British, until 1964

MONETARY SYSTEM
100 Cents = 1 Shilling

REPUBLIC

STANDARD COINAGE

KM# 1 5 CENTS
Nickel-Brass, 25.5 mm. **Obv:** Arms with supporters above value **Rev:** Bust left

Date	Mintage	VF20	XF40	MS60	MS63	MS65
1966	28,000,000	0.25	0.50	0.65	1.00	2.00
1966	27	PF63 80.00				
1967	9,600,000	0.25	0.50	0.65	1.00	2.00
1968	12,000,000	0.25	0.50	0.65	1.00	2.00

KM# 10 5 CENTS
5.70 g., Nickel-Brass, 25.5 mm. **Obv:** Arms with supporters divide date above value **Rev:** Bust left

Date	Mintage	VF20	XF40	MS60	MS63	MS65
1969	800,000	0.50	1.00	1.25	2.25	4.00
1969	15	PF63 110				
1970	10,000,000	0.15	0.25	0.50	1.00	1.50
1971	29,680,000	0.15	0.25	0.50	1.00	1.50
1973	500	PF63 25.00				
1974	5,599,000	0.15	0.25	0.50	1.00	1.50
1975	28,000,000	0.15	0.25	0.50	1.00	1.50
1978	23,168,000	0.15	0.25	0.50	1.00	1.50

KM# 17 5 CENTS
5.60 g., Nickel-Brass, 25.5 mm. **Obv:** Arms with supporters divide date above value **Rev:** Bust right

Date	Mintage	VF20	XF40	MS60	MS63	MS65
1978	—	PF63 10.00				
1980	—	0.15	0.25	0.50	1.00	1.50
1981	—	PF63 20.00				
1984	—	0.15	0.25	0.50	1.00	1.50
1986	—	0.15	0.25	0.50	1.00	1.50
1987	—	0.15	0.25	0.50	1.00	1.50
1989	—	0.15	0.25	0.40	0.75	1.25
1990	—	0.15	0.25	0.40	0.75	1.25
1990	Est. 2	PF63 150	PF65 350			
1991	—	0.15	0.25	0.40	0.75	1.25

KM# 2 10 CENTS
9.00 g., Nickel-Brass, 30.8 mm. **Obv:** Arms with supporters divide date above value **Rev:** Bust left

Date	Mintage	VF20	XF40	MS60	MS63	MS65
1966	26,000,000	0.50	1.00	1.50	2.50	3.50
1966	27	PF63 80.00				
1967	7,300,000	0.50	1.00	1.50	2.50	3.50
1968	12,000,000	0.50	1.00	1.50	2.50	3.50

KM# 11 10 CENTS
9.00 g., Nickel-Brass, 30.8 mm. **Obv:** Arms with supporters divide date above value **Rev:** Bust left

Date	Mintage	VF20	XF40	MS60	MS63	MS65
1969	3,900,000	0.15	0.25	0.50	1.00	1.50
1969	15	PF63 110				
1970	7,200,000	0.15	0.25	0.50	1.00	1.50
1971	32,400,000	0.15	0.25	0.40	0.75	1.25
1973	3,000,000	0.15	0.25	0.50	1.00	1.50
1973	500	PF63 25.00				
1974	3,000,000	0.15	0.25	0.50	1.00	1.50
1975	3,000,000	0.15	0.25	0.50	1.00	1.50
1977	45,600,000	0.15	0.25	0.40	0.75	1.25
1978	22,600,000	0.15	0.25	0.40	0.75	1.25

KM# 18 10 CENTS
9.00 g., Nickel-Brass, 30.8 mm. **Obv:** Arms with supporters divide date above value **Rev:** Bust right

Date	Mintage	VF20	XF40	MS60	MS63	MS65
1978	—	PF63 15.00				
1980	—	0.15	0.25	0.75	1.50	2.50
1981	—	PF63 30.00				
1984	—	0.15	0.25	1.00	2.00	3.00
1986	—	0.15	0.25	1.00	2.00	3.00
1987	—	0.15	0.25	1.00	2.00	3.00
1989	—	0.15	0.25	0.75	1.50	2.50
1990	—	0.15	0.25	0.75	1.50	2.50
1990	Est. 2	PF63 150	PF65 350			
1991	—	0.15	0.25	0.65	1.25	2.00

KM# 18a 10 CENTS
9.30 g., Brass Plated Steel, 30.8 mm. **Obv:** Arms with supporters divide date above value **Rev:** Bust right

Date	Mintage	VF20	XF40	MS60	MS63	MS65
1994	—	0.20	0.30	0.50	1.00	1.50

KM# 31 10 CENTS
2.17 g., Brass Plated Steel **Obv:** Value above national arms **Rev:** Bust of President Daniel Toroitich Arap Moi right

Date	Mintage	VF20	XF40	MS60	MS63	MS65
1995	—	0.10	0.15	0.25	0.45	0.60

KM# 3 25 CENTS
Copper-Nickel, 18 mm. **Obv:** Arms with supporters divide date above value **Rev:** Bust left

Date	Mintage	VF20	XF40	MS60	MS63	MS65
1966	4,000,000	1.00	1.50	2.00	3.50	5.00
1966	—	PF63 100				
1967	4,000,000	1.00	1.50	2.00	3.50	5.00

KM# 12 25 CENTS
Copper-Nickel, 18 mm. **Obv:** Arms with supporters divide date above value **Rev:** Bust left

Date	Mintage	VF20	XF40	MS60	MS63	MS65
1969	200,000	1.00	2.50	5.00	10.00	15.00
1969	15	PF63 125				
1973	500	PF63 35.00				

KM# 4 50 CENTS

4.00 g., Copper-Nickel, 21 mm. **Obv:** Arms with supporters divide date above value **Rev:** Bust left **Edge:** Reeded

Date	Mintage	VF20	XF40	MS60	MS63	MS65
1966	4,000,000	0.40	1.00	2.50	4.50	6.00
1966	27	PF63 100				
1967	5,120,000	0.40	0.85	2.00	4.00	6.00
1968	6,000,000	0.40	0.85	1.75	3.50	5.00

KM# 13 50 CENTS

4.00 g., Copper-Nickel, 21 mm. **Obv:** Arms with supporters divide date above value **Rev:** Bust left **Edge:** Reeded

Date	Mintage	VF20	XF40	MS60	MS63	MS65
1969	400,000	0.75	1.00	1.50	3.00	5.00
1969	15	PF63 125				
1971	9,600,000	0.20	0.35	0.50	1.00	1.50
1973	3,360,000	0.35	0.75	1.00	1.75	2.50
1973	500	PF63 25.00				
1974	12,640,000	0.20	0.35	0.50	1.00	1.50
1975	8,000,000	0.20	0.35	0.50	1.00	1.50
1977	16,000,000	0.20	0.35	0.50	1.00	1.50
1978	20,480,000	0.20	0.35	0.50	1.00	1.50

KM# 19 50 CENTS

4.00 g., Copper-Nickel, 21 mm. **Obv:** National arms above value **Rev:** Bust of President Daniel Toroitich Arap Moi right **Edge:** Reeded

Date	Mintage	VF20	XF40	MS60	MS63	MS65
1978	—	PF63 20.00				
1980	—	0.15	0.25	0.40	0.75	1.00
1981	—	PF63 40.00				
1989	—	0.15	0.25	0.40	0.75	1.00

KM# 19a 50 CENTS

Nickel Plated Steel, 21 mm. **Obv:** National arms above value **Rev:** Bust of President Daniel Toroitich Arap Moi right

Date	Mintage	VF20	XF40	MS60	MS63	MS65
1994	—	0.20	0.30	0.50	1.00	1.50

KM# 28 50 CENTS

3.10 g., Brass Plated Steel, 17.9 mm. **Obv:** Value above national arms **Rev:** Bust of President Daniel Toroitich Arap Moi right

Date	Mintage	VF20	XF40	MS60	MS63	MS65
1995	—	0.10	0.15	0.25	0.50	1.00
1997	—	0.10	0.15	0.25	0.50	1.00

KM# 5 SHILLING

8.00 g., Copper-Nickel, 27.8 mm. **Obv:** Arms with supporters divide date above value **Rev:** Bust left **Edge:** Reeded

Date	Mintage	VF20	XF40	MS60	MS63	MS65
1966	20,000,000	0.50	1.00	2.00	3.00	5.00
1966	27	PF63 100				
1967	4,000,000	0.50	1.00	1.50	2.75	4.50
1968	8,000,000	0.40	0.80	1.25	2.25	4.00

KM# 14 SHILLING

8.00 g., Copper-Nickel, 27.8 mm. **Obv:** Arms with supporters divide date above value **Rev:** Bust left **Edge:** Reeded

Date	Mintage	VF20	XF40	MS60	MS63	MS65
1969	15	PF63 125				
1969	4,000,000	0.30	0.75	1.25	2.25	4.00
1971	24,000,000	0.30	0.65	1.00	2.00	3.50
1973	500	PF63 30.00				
1973	2,480,000	0.40	0.80	1.25	2.75	4.50
1974	13,520,000	0.30	0.65	1.00	2.00	3.50
1975	40,856,000	0.30	0.65	1.00	2.00	3.50
1978	20,000,000	0.30	0.65	1.00	2.00	3.50

KM# 20 SHILLING

8.00 g., Copper-Nickel, 27.8 mm. **Obv:** National arms above value **Rev:** Bust of President Daniel Toroitich Arap Moi 2right **Edge:** Reeded

Date	Mintage	VF20	XF40	MS60	MS63	MS65
1978	—	PF63 30.00				
1980	—	0.30	0.60	0.80	1.50	2.00
1981	—	PF63 60.00				
1989	—	0.30	0.60	0.80	1.50	2.00

KM# 20a SHILLING

8.00 g., Nickel Plated Steel, 27.8 mm. **Obv:** National arms above value **Rev:** Bust of President Daniel Toroitich Arap Moi right

Date	Mintage	VF20	XF40	MS60	MS63	MS65
1994	—	0.35	0.70	1.00	1.75	2.50

KM# 29 SHILLING

4.35 g., Brass Plated Steel, 22 mm. **Obv:** Value above national arms **Rev:** Bust of President Daniel Toroitich Arap Moi right **Edge:** Segmented reeding

Date	Mintage	VF20	XF40	MS60	MS63	MS65
1995	—	0.20	0.35	0.50	0.75	1.00
1997	—	0.20	0.35	0.50	0.75	1.00
1998	—	0.20	0.35	0.50	0.75	1.00

KM# 6 2 SHILLINGS

Copper-Nickel, 32.3 mm. **Obv:** Arms with supporters divide date above value **Rev:** Bust left **Note:** Similar to KM#2.

Date	Mintage	VF20	XF40	MS60	MS63	MS65
1966	3,000,000	2.00	3.00	5.00	7.00	12.00
1966	27	PF63 120				
1968	1,100,000	2.75	4.50	6.00	10.00	15.00

KM# 15 2 SHILLINGS

Copper-Nickel, 32.3 mm. **Obv:** Arms with supporters divide date above value **Rev:** Bust left **Note:** Similar to KM#11.

Date	Mintage	VF20	XF40	MS60	MS63	MS65
1969	100,000	4.00	8.00	10.00	12.50	17.50
1969	15	PF63 150				
1971	1,920,000	1.25	3.50	5.00	7.50	12.50
1973	500	PF63 35.00				

KM# 16 5 SHILLINGS

14.00 g., Brass, 33 mm. **Subject:** 10th Anniversary of Independence **Obv:** National arms **Rev:** Bust of President Mzee Jomo Kenyatta left **Shape:** 9-sided

Date	Mintage	VF20	XF40	MS60	MS63	MS65
1973	100,000	8.00	15.00	18.00	22.50	45.00
1973	1,500	PF63 50.00				

KM# 23 5 SHILLINGS

13.50 g., Copper-Nickel, 30 mm. **Obv:** National arms **Rev:** Bust of President Daniel Toroitich Arap Moi right **Edge:** Plain **Shape:** 7-sided

Date	Mintage	VF20	XF40	MS60	MS63	MS65
1985	—	0.60	1.00	1.50	3.00	5.00

KM# 23a 5 SHILLINGS

Nickel Plated Steel **Obv:** National arms **Rev:** Bust of President Daniel Toroitich Arap Moi right **Edge:** Plain **Shape:** 7-sided

Date	Mintage	VF20	XF40	MS60	MS63	MS65
1994	—	0.75	1.50	2.00	3.50	6.00

KM# 30 5 SHILLINGS

3.75 g., Bi-Metallic Aluminum-Bronze center in Copper-Nickel ring, 19.5 mm. **Obv:** Value above national arms **Rev:** Bust of President Daniel Toroitich Arap Moi right **Edge:** Reeded

Date	Mintage	VF20	XF40	MS60	MS63	MS65
1995	—	0.90	1.80	2.50	4.50	6.00
1997	—	0.90	1.80	2.50	4.50	6.00

KM# 27 10 SHILLINGS

5.00 g., Bi-Metallic Copper-Nickel center in Aluminum-Bronze ring, 23 mm. **Obv:** Value above national arms **Rev:** Bust of President Daniel Toroitich Arap Moi right **Edge:** Reeded

Date	Mintage	VF20	XF40	MS60	MS63	MS65
1994	—	1.00	2.00	3.00	5.00	7.00
1995	—	1.00	2.00	3.00	5.00	7.00
1997	—	1.00	2.00	3.00	5.00	7.00

REPUBLIC OF KENYA
20
TWENTY SHILLINGS 1998
PRESIDENT DANIEL TOROITICH ARAP MOI

KM# 32 20 SHILLINGS

9.00 g., Bi-Metallic Aluminum-Bronze center in Copper-Nickel ring, 26 mm. **Obv:** Value above national arms **Rev:** Bust of President Daniel Toroitich Arap Moi right **Edge:** Segmented reeding

Date	Mintage	VF20	XF40	MS60	MS63	MS65
1998	—	1.50	2.50	4.00	6.00	9.00

KM# 7 100 SHILLINGS

7.60 g., 0.917 Gold 0.2241 oz. AGW **Subject:** 75th Anniversary - Birth of President Jomo Kenyatta **Obv:** Fly whisk above value and date **Rev:** Bust left

Date	Mintage	VF20	XF40	MS60	MS63	MS65
1966	—	—	—	—	325	425
1966	7,500	PF63 350	PF65 450	PF67 550		

KM# 21 200 SHILLINGS
28.28 g., 0.925 Silver 0.841 oz. ASW, 38 mm. **Obv:** President Moi **Rev:** Arms with supporters above value

Date	Mintage	VF20	XF40	MS60	MS63	MS65
1978	9,500	**PF63** 125	**PF65** 175			
1981	—	**PF63** 250	**PF65** 350			

KM# 8 250 SHILLINGS
19.00 g., 0.917 Gold 0.5602 oz. AGW **Subject:** 75th Anniversary - Birth of President Jomo Kenyatta **Obv:** Rooster with axe above value and date **Rev:** Bust left

Date	Mintage	VF20	XF40	MS60	MS63	MS65
1966	—	—	—	—	825	950
1966	1,000	**PF63** 900	**PF65** 1,000	**PF67** 1,150		

KM# 9 500 SHILLINGS
38.00 g., 0.917 Gold 1.1203 oz. AGW **Subject:** 75th Anniversary - Birth of President Jomo Kenyatta **Obv:** Mountain above value and date **Rev:** Bust left

Date	Mintage	VF20	XF40	MS60	MS63	MS65
1966	—	—	—	—	1,600	1,850
1966	500	**PF63** 1,700	**PF65** 1,900	**PF67** 2,150		

KM# 42 500 SHILLINGS
28.28 g., 0.925 Silver 0.841 oz. ASW, 38 mm. **Subject:** Central Bank of Kenya, 20th Anniversary **Obv:** Bust right **Rev:** National arms

Date	Mintage	VF20	XF40	MS60	MS63	MS65
1986	—	**PF63** 200	**PF65** 275			

KM# 24 500 SHILLINGS
28.28 g., 0.925 Silver 0.841 oz. ASW **Subject:** 10th Anniversary of Moi as President **Obv:** Bust right **Rev:** Arms with supporters above value **Shape:** 10-sided

Date	Mintage	VF20	XF40	MS60	MS63	MS65
1978-1988	—	**PF63** 150	**PF65** 250			

KM# 25 500 SHILLINGS
28.33 g., 0.925 Silver 0.8425 oz. ASW **Subject:** 25th Anniversary of Independence **Obv:** Bust right **Rev:** Arms with supporters above value

Date	Mintage	VF20	XF40	MS60	MS63	MS65
1963-1988	—	**PF63** 100	**PF65** 150			

KM# 26 1000 SHILLINGS
28.28 g., 0.925 Silver 0.841 oz. ASW **Subject:** Silver Jubilee of Central Bank **Obv:** Bust right **Rev:** Arms with supporters above value

Date	Mintage	VF20	XF40	MS60	MS63	MS65
1991	—	**PF63** 125	**PF65** 200			

KM# 22 3000 SHILLING
40.00 g., 0.917 Gold 1.1793 oz. AGW **Obv:** President Moi **Rev:** Arms with supporters above value

Date	Mintage	VF20	XF40	MS60	MS63	MS65
ND (1979)	2,000	**PF63** 1,850	**PF65** 2,150			

MINT SETS

KM#	Date	Mintage	Identification	Issue Price	Mkt Val
MS1	1966 (3)	—	KM7-9	—	3,450

PROOF SETS

KM#	Date	Mintage	Identification	Issue Price	Mkt Val
PS1	1966 (6)	27	KM1-6	—	600
PS2	1966 (3)	500	KM7-9	152	3,700
PS3	1969 (6)	15	KM10-15	—	750
PS4	1973 (7)	500	KM10-16	—	225
PS5	1978 (5)	9,500	KM#17-21	—	275
PS6	1981 (5)	—	KM#17-21	—	500
PS7	1986 (2)	—	KM#42, two examples	—	750

KIAU CHAU

Kiau Chau (Kiao Chau, Kiaochow, Kiautscho, now Jiaozhou), a former German trading enclave, including the port of Tsingtao (Qingdao), was located on the Shantung (Shandong) Peninsula of eastern China. Following the murder of two missionaries in Shantung in 1897, Germany occupied Kiaochow Bay, and during subsequent negotiations with the Chinese government obtained a 99-year lease on 177 sq. mi. of land. The enclave was established as a free port in 1899, and a customs house set up to collect tariffs on goods moving to and from the Chinese interior. The Japanese took siege to the port on Aug. 27, 1914, as their first action in World War I to deprive German sea marauders of their east Asian supply and refitting base. Aided by the British forces, the siege ended Nov. 7. Japan retained possession until 1922, when it was restored to China by the Washington Conference on China and naval armaments. It fell again to Japan in 1938, but not before the Chinese had destroyed its manufacturing facilities. It is presently a part of the Peoples Republic of China. The major city is Tsingtao (Qingdao) and is noted for its beer.

RULERS
Wilhelm II, 1897-1914
Japan, 1914-1922, 1938-1945

MONETARY SYSTEM
100 Cents = 1 Dollar

GERMAN OCCUPATION

STANDARD COINAGE

KM# 1 5 CENTS
Copper-Nickel, 18.5 mm. **Ruler:** Wilhelm II **Obv:** German Imperial Eagle **Obv. Legend:** DEUTSCH.KIAUTSHAU GEBIET **Rev:** Inscription within beaded circle **Rev. Inscription:** Kuang-hsü Yüan-pao **Note:** Prev. Y#1.

Date	Mintage	VF20	XF40	MS60	MS63	MS65
1909	610,000	90.00	165	300	550	1,250
1909	—	**PF65** 3,750	**PF67** 5,000			

KM# 2 10 CENTS
Copper-Nickel, 21.5 mm. **Ruler:** Wilhelm II **Obv:** German Imperial Eagle **Obv. Legend:** DEUTSCH.KIAUTSHAU GEBIET **Rev:** Inscription within beaded circle **Rev. Inscription:** Kuang-hsü Yüan-pao **Note:** Prev. Y#2.

Date	Mintage	VF20	XF40	MS60	MS63	MS65
1909	670,000	60.00	145	275	525	1,350
1909	—	**PF65** 4,000	**PF67** 5,500			

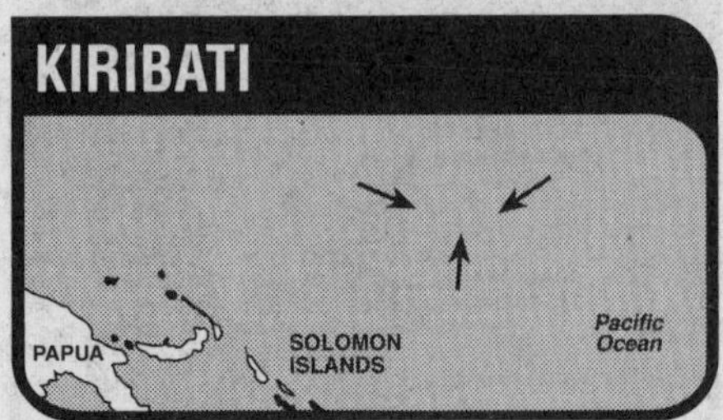

The Republic of Kiribati (formerly the Gilbert Islands), consists of 30 coral atolls and islands spread over more than one million sq. mi. (2,590,000 sq. km.) of the southwest Pacific Ocean, has an area of 332 sq. mi. (717 sq. km.) and a population of 64,200. Capital: Bairiki, on Tarawa. In addition to the Gilbert Islands proper, Kiribati includes Ocean Island, the Central and Southern Line Islands, and the Phoenix Islands, though possession of Canton and Enderbury of the Phoenix Islands is disputed with the United States. Most families engage in subsistence fishing. Copra and phosphates are exported, mostly to Australia and New Zealand.

The Gilbert Islands and the group formerly called the Ellice Islands (now Tuvalu) comprised a single British crown colony, the Gilbert and Ellice Islands.

Spanish mutineers first sighted the islands in 1537, succeeding visits were made by the English navigators John Byron (1764), James Cook (1777), and Thomas Gilbert and John Marshall (1788). An American, Edward Fanning, arrived in 1798. Britain declared a protectorate over the Gilbert and Ellice Islands, and in 1915 began the formation of a colony which was completed when the Phoenix Islands were added to the group in 1937. The Central and Southern Line Islands were administratively attached to the Gilbert and Ellice Islands colony in 1972, and remained attached to the Gilberts when Tuvalu was created in 1975. The colony became self-governing in 1971. Kiribati attained independence on July 12, 1979.

RULER
British, until 1979

MONETARY SYSTEM
100 Cents = 1 Dollar

REPUBLIC

DECIMAL COINAGE

KM# 1 CENT
2.60 g., Bronze, 17.5 mm. **Subject:** Christmas Island Frigate Bird **Obv:** National arms **Rev:** Frigate bird on branch

Date	Mintage	VF20	XF40	MS60	MS63	MS65
1979	90,000	—	0.15	0.25	0.50	1.00
1979	10,000	PF65 1.00				
1992	—	—	0.15	0.25	0.50	1.00

KM# 1a CENT
2.60 g., Bronze Plated Steel, 17.5 mm. **Obv:** National arms **Rev:** Frigate bird on branch

Date	Mintage	VF20	XF40	MS60	MS63	MS65
1992	—	—	—	0.25	0.50	1.00

KM# 2 2 CENTS
5.20 g., Bronze, 21.6 mm. **Obv:** National arms **Rev:** B'abal plant below value

Date	Mintage	VF20	XF40	MS60	MS63	MS65
1979	25,000	—	0.15	0.25	0.40	0.65
1979	10,000	PF65 1.25				
1992	—	—	0.15	0.25	0.40	0.65

KM# 3 5 CENTS
2.73 g., Copper-Nickel, 19.3 mm. **Obv:** National arms **Rev:** Stump-tailed Gecko below value **Edge:** Reeded

Date	Mintage	VF20	XF40	MS60	MS63	MS65
1979	20,000	0.15	0.30	0.75	1.50	2.50
1979	10,000	PF65 2.75				

KM# 3a 5 CENTS
Copper-Nickel Plated Steel, 19.3 mm. **Obv:** National arms **Rev:** Stump-tailed Gecko below value

Date	Mintage	VF20	XF40	MS60	MS63	MS65
1992	—	—	—	0.75	1.50	2.00

KM# 4 10 CENTS
5.70 g., Copper-Nickel, 23.6 mm. **Obv:** National arms **Rev:** Bread fruit above value

Date	Mintage	VF20	XF40	MS60	MS63	MS65
1979	20,000	0.15	0.25	0.65	1.25	1.50
1979	10,000	PF65 3.00				

KM# 5 20 CENTS
11.15 g., Copper-Nickel, 28.45 mm. **Obv:** National arms **Rev:** Dolphins above value

Date	Mintage	VF20	XF40	MS60	MS63	MS65
1979	20,000	0.60	1.50	2.50	3.50	5.00
1979	10,000	PF65 9.00				

KM# 6 50 CENTS
15.40 g., Copper-Nickel, 31.65 mm. **Obv:** National arms **Rev:** Panda nut above value

Date	Mintage	VF20	XF40	MS60	MS63	MS65
1979	20,000	0.50	1.00	2.00	3.00	4.50
1979	10,000	PF65 6.50				

KM# 7 DOLLAR
11.70 g., Copper-Nickel, 30 mm. **Obv:** National arms **Rev:** Outrigger sailboat above written value **Shape:** 12-sided

Date	Mintage	VF20	XF40	MS60	MS63	MS65
1979	20,000	0.85	1.25	2.50	4.00	5.00
1979	10,000	PF65 7.50				

KM# 46 DOLLAR
Copper-Nickel **Subject:** Queen Mother's 96th Birthday **Rev:** Windsor Castle

Date	Mintage	VF20	XF40	MS60	MS63	MS65
1996	—	PF65 12.00				

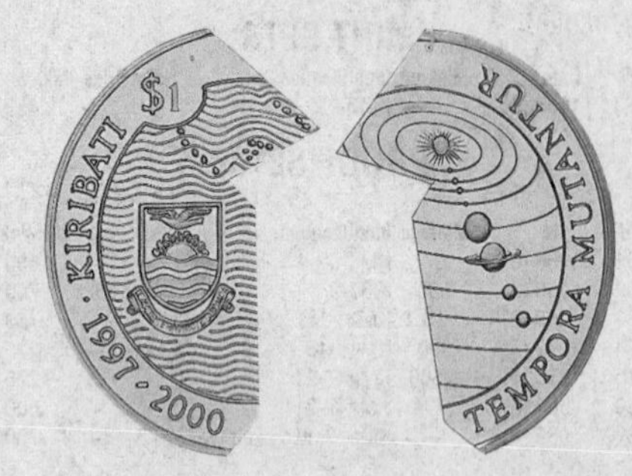

KM# 41 DOLLAR
12.40 g., Copper-Nickel, 25.8 x 38 mm. **Obv:** National arms **Rev:** Solar System **Edge:** Plain **Shape:** Irregular

Date	Mintage	VF20	XF40	MS60	MS63	MS65
ND (1997)	—	PF65 15.00				

KM# 14 2 DOLLARS
Nickel-Brass **Subject:** 10th Anniversary of Independence **Obv:** National arms above message within ribbon **Rev:** Meeting house with shell at lower left

Date	Mintage	VF20	XF40	MS60	MS63	MS65
1989	—	—	—	5.00	7.00	—

KM# 21 2 DOLLARS
10.00 g., 0.500 Silver 0.1608 oz. ASW **Subject:** Titanic sinking **Obv:** National arms

Date	Mintage	VF20	XF40	MS60	MS63	MS65
1998	—	PF63 12.00	PF65 15.00			

KM# 8 5 DOLLARS
28.16 g., 0.500 Silver 0.4527 oz. ASW **Subject:** Independence **Obv:** National arms **Rev:** Seated man with arms outstretched with written value below

Date	Mintage	VF20	XF40	MS60	MS63	MS65
1979	1,545	—	—	—	28.00	35.00

KM# 8a 5 DOLLARS
28.16 g., 0.925 Silver 0.8375 oz. ASW **Subject:** Independence **Obv:** National arms **Rev:** Seated man with arms outstretched above written value

Date	Mintage	VF20	XF40	MS60	MS63	MS65
1979	3,326	PF63 25.00	PF65 30.00			

KM# 10 5 DOLLARS
Copper-Nickel, 38.5 mm. **Subject:** 2nd Anniversary of Independence and Wedding of Prince Charles and Lady Diana **Obv:** National arms **Rev:** Wedding crown above value

Date	Mintage	VF20	XF40	MS60	MS63	MS65
1981	50,000	—	—	3.00	5.00	7.00

KM# 10a 5 DOLLARS
28.60 g., 0.925 Silver 0.8505 oz. ASW, 38.5 mm. **Subject:** 2nd Anniversary of Independence and Wedding of Prince Charles and Lady Diana **Obv:** National arms **Rev:** Wedding crown above value

Date	Mintage	VF20	XF40	MS60	MS63	MS65
1981	25,000	PF63 22.00	PF65 25.00			

KM# 12 5 DOLLARS
Copper-Nickel, 38.5 mm. **Subject:** Royal visit **Obv:** National arms **Rev:** Young bust right

Date	Mintage	VF20	XF40	MS60	MS63	MS65
1982	—	—	—	3.00	5.00	7.00

KM# 12a 5 DOLLARS
Silver, 38.5 mm. **Subject:** Royal visit **Obv:** National arms **Rev:** Young bust right

Date	Mintage	VF20	XF40	MS60	MS63	MS65
1982	—	PF63 25.00	PF65 30.00			

KM# 19 5 DOLLARS
31.47 g., 0.925 Silver 0.9359 oz. ASW **Obv:** National arms **Rev:** Standing figure and ship

Date	Mintage	VF20	XF40	MS60	MS63	MS65
1996	Est. 15000	PF65 30.00				

KM# 20 5 DOLLARS
31.47 g., 0.925 Silver 0.9359 oz. ASW **Subject:** OLYMPIC GAMES 2000 **Obv:** National arms **Obv. Legend:** KIRIBATI **Rev:** Two high divers

Date	Mintage	VF20	XF40	MS60	MS63	MS65
1996	40,000	PF63 25.00	PF65 30.00			

KM# 22 5 DOLLARS
15.55 g., 0.925 Silver 0.4625 oz. ASW **Subject:** Guerra & Paz **Obv:** National arms within wave-like designs **Rev:** Dove within wave-like designs **Shape:** Jagged half of coin **Note:** Half of two-part coin, combined with Samoa KM#115, issued in sets only. Value is determined by combining the two parts.

Date	Mintage	VF20	XF40	MS60	MS63	MS65
ND-1997	Est. 10000	PF65 25.00				

KM# 23 5 DOLLARS
15.55 g., 0.925 Silver 0.4625 oz. ASW **Subject:** Powerful empires **Obv:** National arms within wave-like designs **Rev:** Helmets and hats within wave-like designs **Shape:** Jagged half of coin **Note:** Half of two-part coin, combined with Western Samoa KM#116, issued in sets only. Value is determined by combining the two parts.

Date	Mintage	VF20	XF40	MS60	MS63	MS65
ND-1997	Est. 10000	PF65 25.00				

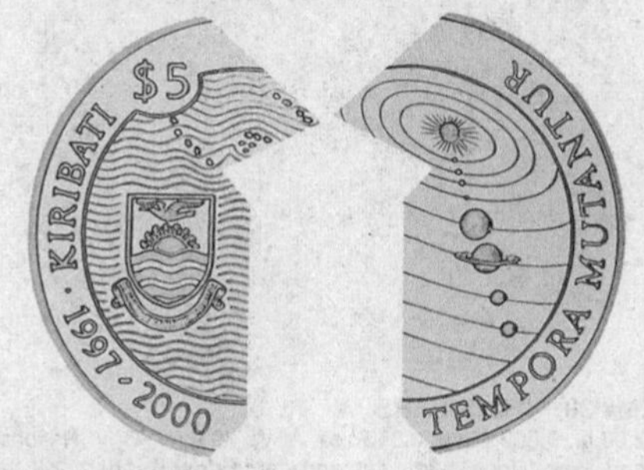

KM# 24 5 DOLLARS
15.55 g., 0.925 Silver 0.4625 oz. ASW **Subject:** Tempora Mutantur **Obv:** National arms within wave-like designs **Rev:** Solar system within wave-like designs **Shape:** Jagged half of coin **Note:** Half of two-part coin, combined with Samoa KM#117, issued in sets only. Value is determined by combining the two parts.

Date	Mintage	VF20	XF40	MS60	MS63	MS65
ND-1997	Est. 10000	PF65 25.00				

KM# 24a 5 DOLLARS
Copper-Nickel **Subject:** Tempora Mutantar **Obv:** National arms within wave-like designs **Rev:** Solar system within wave-like designs. **Shape:** Jagged half of coin **Note:** Half of two-part coin, combined with Samoa KM#117a. issued in pairs only. Value is determined by combining the two parts.

Date	Mintage	VF20	XF40	MS60	MS63	MS65
ND-1997	—	—	—	8.00	10.00	12.00

KM# 25 5 DOLLARS
15.55 g., 0.925 Silver 0.4625 oz. ASW **Subject:** People, monuments, column and compass within wave-like designs **Obv:** National arms within wave-like designs **Shape:** Jagged half of coin **Note:** Half of two-part coin, combined with Western Samoa KM#118, issued in sets only. Value is determined by combining the two parts.

Date	Mintage	VF20	XF40	MS60	MS63	MS65
ND-1997	Est. 10000	PF65 27.50				

KM# 31 5 DOLLARS
31.40 g., 0.925 Silver 0.9338 oz. ASW, 38.5 mm. **Subject:** British Queen Mother **Obv:** National arms **Rev:** Windsor Castle within beaded circle **Edge:** Reeded

Date	Mintage	VF20	XF40	MS60	MS63	MS65
1997	—	PF65 32.00				

KM# 30 5 DOLLARS
31.60 g., 0.925 Silver 0.9398 oz. ASW, 38.5 mm. **Subject:** Whaling Ship Potomac 1842 **Obv:** National arms **Rev:** Ship above sailors killing whale **Edge:** Reeded

Date	Mintage	VF20	XF40	MS60	MS63	MS65
1998	—	PF65 35.00				

KM# 42 5 DOLLARS
15.86 g., 0.925 Silver 0.4717 oz. ASW, 25.8 mm. **Obv:** National arms **Rev:** "POWERFUL EMPIRES" Charlemagne, Spanish ship, Soviet soldier with flag **Edge:** Plain **Shape:** Irregular

Date	Mintage	VF20	XF40	MS60	MS63	MS65
ND (1998)	—	PF65 25.00				

KM# 47 5 DOLLARS
16.00 g., 0.925 Silver 0.4758 oz. ASW **Subject:** Christian Millenium **Rev:** Times Change

Date	Mintage	VF20	XF40	MS60	MS63	MS65
1998	10,000	PF65 20.00				

KM# 48 5 DOLLARS
16.00 g., Silver **Subject:** Millennium - War and Peace

Date	Mintage	VF20	XF40	MS60	MS63	MS65
1998	10,000	PF65 20.00				

KM# 49 5 DOLLARS
16.00 g., Silver **Subject:** Millennium - people and monuments

Date	Mintage	VF20	XF40	MS60	MS63	MS65
1998	—	PF65 20.00				

KM# 50 5 DOLLARS
31.47 g., 0.925 Silver 0.9359 oz. ASW, 38 mm. **Subject:** Queen Mother's 98th Birthday, Prince Charles' 50th Birthday **Obv:** Shield **Rev:** Bust of Prince Charles right

Date	Mintage	VF20	XF40	MS60	MS63	MS65
1998	Est. 20000	PF65 32.00				

KM# 45 5 DOLLARS
31.38 g., 0.925 Silver 0.9332 oz. ASW, 38.6 mm. **Obv:** Shield **Rev:** Ship La Coquille **Edge:** Reeded

Date	Mintage	VF20	XF40	MS60	MS63	MS65
1999	—	PF65 30.00				

KM# 28 5 DOLLARS
31.30 g., 0.999 Silver 1.0053 oz. ASW, 38.6 mm. **Subject:** 10th Anniversary of Emperor Akihito's Reign **Obv:** National arms within circle **Rev:** Conjoined busts left **Edge:** Reeded

Date	Mintage	VF20	XF40	MS60	MS63	MS65
2000	2,000	PF63 80.00	PF65 120			

KM# 37 5 DOLLARS
24.20 g., Copper-Nickel, 39 mm. **Obv:** National arms **Rev:** "Harmony" earth, moon and sun **Edge:** Reeded

Date	Mintage	VF20	XF40	MS60	MS63	MS65
2000FM	—	PF63 7.00	PF65 9.00			

KM# 13 10 DOLLARS
28.28 g., 0.925 Silver 0.841 oz. ASW **Subject:** 5th Anniversary of Independence **Obv:** Value above national arms **Rev:** Geographical map

Date	Mintage	VF20	XF40	MS60	MS63	MS65
ND-1984	—	—	—	—	50.00	60.00
ND-1984	2,500	PF65 45.00				

KM# 13a 10 DOLLARS
47.52 g., 0.917 Gold 1.401 oz. AGW **Subject:** 5th Anniversary of Independence **Obv:** Value above national arms **Rev:** Geographical map

Date	Mintage	VF20	XF40	MS60	MS63	MS65
ND-1984	50	PF63 2,500	PF65 2,750			

KM# 27 10 DOLLARS
1.24 g., 0.999 Gold 0.040 oz. AGW **Subject:** Titanic **Obv:** National arms **Rev:** Sinking ships and lifeboats

Date	Mintage	VF20	XF40	MS60	MS63	MS65
1998	—	PF63 60.00	PF65 70.00			

KM# 43 10 DOLLARS
1.21 g., 0.999 Gold 0.0389 oz. AGW, 13.91 mm. **Obv:** National arms **Obv. Legend:** KIRIBATI **Rev:** Manger scene, birth of Jesus Christ in Bethlehem **Rev. Legend:** * CHRISTMAS ISLAND * KIRITIMATI * KIRIBATI **Edge:** Reeded

Date	Mintage	VF20	XF40	MS60	MS63	MS65
1998	—	PF63 55.00	PF65 65.00			

KM# 38 10 DOLLARS
22.00 g., 0.500 Silver 0.3537 oz. ASW, 39 mm. **Obv:** National arms **Rev:** "Hope" earth, sun and stars **Edge:** Reeded

Date	Mintage	VF20	XF40	MS60	MS63	MS65
2000FM	—	PF65 25.00				

KM# 44 10 DOLLARS
Gold, 13.90 mm. **Obv:** National arms **Obv. Legend:** KIRIBATI **Rev:** Shark-tooth sword across native cloak **Edge:** Reeded

Date	Mintage	VF20	XF40	MS60	MS63	MS65
2000	—	PF63 55.00	PF65 65.00			

KM# 17 20 DOLLARS
31.47 g., 0.925 Silver 0.9359 oz. ASW **Subject:** Barcelona Olympics - Sailing **Obv:** National arms above message within ribbon **Rev:** Radiant sun, sailboaters and seagull flying above

Date	Mintage	VF20	XF40	MS60	MS63	MS65
1992	40,000	PF65 25.00				

KM# 18 20 DOLLARS
31.47 g., 0.925 Silver 0.9359 oz. ASW **Subject:** Endangered Wildlife **Obv:** National arms above message within ribbon **Rev:** Frigate birds

Date	Mintage	VF20	XF40	MS60	MS63	MS65
1992	—	PF65 32.00				

KM# 15 20 DOLLARS
31.47 g., 0.925 Silver 0.9359 oz. ASW **Subject:** Soccer - World Cup '94 **Obv:** National arms **Rev:** Soccer players

Date	Mintage	VF20	XF40	MS60	MS63	MS65
1993	Est. 10000	PF65 28.00				

KM# 16 20 DOLLARS
31.47 g., 0.925 Silver 0.9359 oz. ASW **Subject:** First Space Walk **Obv:** National arms

Date	Mintage	VF20	XF40	MS60	MS63	MS65
1993	Est. 15000	PF65 22.00				

KM# 33 20 DOLLARS
3.11 g., 0.999 Gold 0.0999 oz. AGW, 18 mm. **Subject:** Christmas Island Holy Year 2000 **Obv:** National arms above name and date **Rev:** Angel in flight **Edge:** Reeded

Date	Mintage	VF20	XF40	MS60	MS63	MS65
1999	—	PF65 175				

KM# 39 20 DOLLARS
21.40 g., 0.925 Silver 0.6364 oz. ASW, 39 mm. **Obv:** National arms **Rev:** "Faith" hands below earth **Edge:** Reeded

Date	Mintage	VF20	XF40	MS60	MS63	MS65
2000FM	—	PF65 65.00				

KM# 26 50 DOLLARS
3.89 g., 0.999 Gold 0.1249 oz. AGW **Subject:** Tempora Mutantur **Obv:** National arms **Rev:** Solar system **Shape:** Jagged half of coin **Note:** Similar to KM#24. Half of two-part coin, combined with Western Samoa KM#119, issued in sets only. Value is determined by combining the two parts.

Date	Mintage	VF20	XF40	MS60	MS63	MS65
ND-1997	Est. 2500	PF65 175	PF67 225			

KM# 34 50 DOLLARS
7.78 g., 0.999 Gold 0.2498 oz. AGW, 22 mm. **Subject:** Christmas Island Holy Year 2000 **Obv:** National arms above name and date **Rev:** The three "Wise Men" on camels **Edge:** Reeded

Date	Mintage	VF20	XF40	MS60	MS63	MS65
1999	—	PF63 375	PF65 450	PF67 525		

KM# 51 50 DOLLARS
6.20 g., 0.999 Gold 0.1991 oz. AGW **Obv:** Shield **Rev:** Sun and planets

Date	Mintage	VF20	XF40	MS60	MS63	MS65
2000	—	PF63 300	PF65 400	PF67 475		

KM# 35 100 DOLLARS
15.55 g., 0.999 Gold 0.4994 oz. AGW, 30 mm. **Subject:** Christmas Island Holy Year 2000 **Obv:** National arms above name and date **Rev:** Mother and child **Edge:** Reeded

Date	Mintage	VF20	XF40	MS60	MS63	MS65
2000	—	PF65 800	PF67 850			

KM# 9 150 DOLLARS
15.98 g., 0.917 Gold 0.4711 oz. AGW **Subject:** Independence - Maneaba - a traditional meeting house **Obv:** National arms **Rev:** Maneaba - a traditional meeting house

Date	Mintage	XF40	MS60	MS63	MS65	MS66
1979	422	—	—	—	750	800
1979	386	PF65 825	PF67 875			

KM# 11 150 DOLLARS
15.98 g., 0.917 Gold 0.4711 oz. AGW **Subject:** 2nd Anniversary of Independence, and wedding of Prince Charles and Lady Diana **Obv:** National arms

Date	Mintage	XF40	MS60	MS63	MS65	MS66
1981	750	—	—	—	750	800
1981	1,500	PF65 825	PF67 875			

KM# 29 200 DOLLARS
31.30 g., 0.999 Gold 1.0053 oz. AGW, 35 mm. **Subject:** 10th Anniversary of Emperor Akihito's Reign **Obv:** National arms **Rev:** Conjoined busts left **Edge:** Reeded

Date	Mintage	VF20	XF40	MS60	MS63	MS65
2000	500	**PF65** 1,650	**PF67** 1,750			

KM# 32 200 DOLLARS
16.58 g., 0.999 Gold 0.5325 oz. AGW, 37.8x26.2 mm. **Subject:** People and Monuments **Obv:** National arms within wave-like designs **Rev:** Eiffel Tower **Edge:** Plain **Note:** Irregular shape

Date	Mintage	VF20	XF40	MS60	MS63	MS65
1999-2000	—	**PF67** 850				

KM# A35 200 DOLLARS
31.12 g., 0.999 Gold 0.9995 oz. AGW, 35 mm. **Subject:** Christmas Island Holy Year 2000 **Obv:** National arms above name and date **Rev:** Mother and child **Edge:** Reeded

Date	Mintage	VF20	XF40	MS60	MS63	MS65
2000	—	**PF65** 1,650	**PF67** 1,750			

KM# 36 500 DOLLARS
85.47 g., 0.999 Gold 2.7452 oz. AGW, 42.5 mm. **Obv:** National arms **Rev:** Doves, children, sword point and treaty **Edge:** Plain **Note:** Jagged coin half matching with Samoa KM-136

Date	Mintage	VF20	XF40	MS60	MS63	MS65
2000	99	**PF67** 4,500				

COMBINED PROOF SETS

KM#	Date	Mintage	Identification	Issue Price	Mkt Val
CPS1	1997 (4)	10,000	Kiribati KM#22-25, West Samoa KM#115-118	—	280

PROOF SETS

KM#	Date	Mintage	Identification	Issue Price	Mkt Val
PS1	1979 (7)	10,000	KM1-7	34.00	55.00
PS2	1981 (2)	—	KM10a, 11	—	935
PS3	1999 (3)	—	KM#33-35	—	1,650
PS4	2000 (3)	—	KM#37, 38, 39	—	150

KOREA

Korea, 'Land of the Morning Calm', occupies a mountainous peninsula in northeast Asia bounded by Manchuria, the Yellow Sea and the Sea of Japan.

According to legend, the first Korean dynasty, that of the House of Tangun, ruled from 2333 B.C. to 1122 B.C. It was followed by the dynasty of Kija, a Chinese scholar, which continued until 193 B.C. and brought a high civilization to Korea. The first recorded period in the history of Korea, the period of the Three Kingdoms, lasted from 57 B.C. to 935 A.D. and achieved the first political unification of the peninsula. The Kingdom of Koryo, from which Korea derived its name, was founded in 935 and continued until 1392, when the Yi Dynasty of King Yi superseded it. Sung Kye was to last until the Japanese annexation in 1910.

At the end of the 16th century Korea was invaded by Japan, a conflict lasting seven years. From 1627 until the late 19th century, Korea shared a friendly relationship with China, but was replaced by Japan as the predominant foreign influence at the end of the Sino-Japanese War (1894-95), only to find her position threatened by Russian influence from 1896 to 1904. The Russian threat was eliminated following the Russo-Japanese War (1904-05). In 1905 Japan established a direct protectorate over Korea. On Aug. 22,1910, the last Korean ruler signed the treaty that annexed Korea to Japan as a government generalcy in the Japanese Empire. Japanese suzerainty was maintained until the end of World War II.

From 1633 to 1891 the monetary system of Korea employed cast coins with a square center hole. Fifty-two agencies were authorized to procure these coins from a lesser number of coin foundries. They exist in thousands of varieties. Seed, or mother coins, were used to make the impressions in the molds in which the regular cash coins were cast. Czarist-Russian Korea experimented with Korean coins when Alexiev of Russia, Korea's Financial Advisor, founded the First Asian Branch of the Russo-Korean Bank on March 1, 1898, and authorized the issuing of a set of new Korean coins with a crowned Russian-style quasi-eagle. British-Japanese opposition and the Russo-Japanese War operated to end the Russian coinage experiment in 1904.

RULERS
Yi Hyong (Kojong), 1864-1897
as Emperor Kuang Mu, 1897-1907
Japanese Puppet
Yung Hi (Sunjong), 1907-1910

DATING

JAPANESE PROTECTORATE

MILLED COINAGE

Coinage Reform of 1902

KM# 1124 1/2 CHON
3.56 g., Bronze, 22 mm. **Ruler:** Kuang Mu **Obv:** Imperial eagle left within beaded circle **Rev:** Value within wreath below flower

Date	Mintage	VF20	XF40	MS60	MS63	MS65
10	24,000,000	15.00	50.00	150	250	450
10	—	**PF63** 3,000				

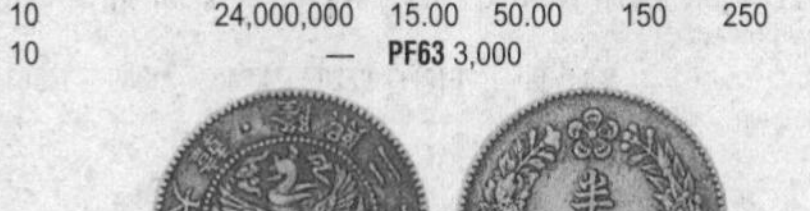

KM# 1136 1/2 CHON
2.10 g., Bronze, 19 mm. **Ruler:** Yung Hi (Sunjong) **Obv:** Imperial eagle facing left within beaded circle **Rev:** Value within wreath below flower

Date	Mintage	F12	VF20	XF40	MS60	MS63
1	Inc. above	175	350	750	1,850	—
Note: Mintage for year 1 is included in the mintage for Year 11 of KM#1124						
2	21,000,000	10.00	25.00	65.00	175	325
3	8,200,000	10.00	25.00	65.00	185	350
4	5,070,000	100	200	350	750	1,350

KM# 1145 1/2 CHON
2.10 g., Bronze **Ruler:** Kuang Mu

Date	Mintage	F12	VF20	XF40	MS60	MS63
11 Rare	—	—	—	—	—	—

KM# 1125 CHON
7.13 g., Bronze, 28 mm. **Ruler:** Kuang Mu **Obv:** Imperial eagle facing left within beaded circle **Rev:** Value within wreath below flower

Date	Mintage	VF20	XF40	MS60	MS63	MS65
9	11,800,000	25.00	50.00	100	200	1,000
10	Inc. above	20.00	50.00	100	200	1,000

KM# 1132 CHON
4.20 g., Bronze, 23.5 mm. **Ruler:** Kuang Mu **Obv:** Imperial eagle facing left within beaded circle **Rev:** Value within wreath below flower

Date	Mintage	F12	VF20	XF40	MS60	MS63
11	11,200,000	6.00	12.00	35.00	85.00	175

KM# 1137 CHON
4.20 g., Bronze, 24 mm. **Ruler:** Yung Hi (Sunjong) **Obv:** Imperial eagle facing left within beaded circle **Rev:** Value within wreath below flower

Date	Mintage	VF20	XF40	MS60	MS63	MS65
1	Inc. above	20.00	55.00	175	350	—
2	6,800,000	15.00	35.00	100	200	—
3	9,200,000	12.00	30.00	90.00	175	650
4	3,500,000	18.00	45.00	150	300	—

KM# 1126 5 CHON
4.50 g., Copper-Nickel, 21 mm. **Ruler:** Kuang Mu **Obv:** Imperial eagle facing left within beaded circle **Rev:** Value within wreath below flower

Date	Mintage	F12	VF20	XF40	MS60	MS63
9	20,000,000	6.00	15.00	35.00	60.00	120
9	—	**PF60** 1,500				
11	160,000,000	15.00	35.00	75.00	150	250

KM# 1138 5 CHON
4.50 g., Copper-Nickel, 21 mm. **Ruler:** Yung Hi (Sunjong)

Date	Mintage	F12	VF20	XF40	MS60	MS63
3	—	1,000	1,800	2,250	3,500	5,500

KM# 1127 10 CHON
2.70 g., 0.800 Silver 0.0694 oz. ASW, 18 mm. **Ruler:** Kuang Mu **Obv:** Dragon within beaded circle **Rev:** Value within wreath below flower **Note:** 1.5 millimeters thick

Date	Mintage	F12	VF20	XF40	MS60	MS63
10	2,000,000	24.00	45.00	80.00	150	250

KM# 1133 10 CHON
2.03 g., 0.800 Silver 0.0521 oz. ASW, 18 mm. **Ruler:** Kuang

Mu **Obv:** Dragon within beaded circle **Rev:** Value within wreath below flower **Note:** 1.0 millimeters thick

Date	Mintage	F12	VF20	XF40	MS60	MS63
11	2,400,000	28.00	50.00	90.00	175	300

KM# 1139 10 CHON
2.25 g., 0.800 Silver 0.0579 oz. ASW, 17 mm. **Ruler:** Yung Hi (Sunjong) **Obv:** Dragon within beaded circle **Rev:** Value within wreath below flower **Edge:** Reeded

Date	Mintage	F12	VF20	XF40	MS60	MS63
2	6,300,000	20.00	40.00	65.00	120	220
3 Rare	—	—	—	—	—	—
4	9,500,000	20.00	35.00	60.00	100	175

KM# 1128 20 CHON
5.39 g., 0.800 Silver 0.1386 oz. ASW, 22 mm. **Ruler:** Kuang Mu **Obv:** Dragon within beaded circle **Rev:** Value within wreath below flower

Date	Mintage	F12	VF20	XF40	MS60	MS63
9	1,000,000	45.00	85.00	145	220	375
9	—	PF63 2,250				
10	2,500,000	45.00	65.00	150	200	350
10	—	PF63 1,275				

KM# 1134 20 CHON
4.05 g., 0.800 Silver 0.1042 oz. ASW, 20 mm. **Ruler:** Kuang Mu **Obv:** Dragon within beaded circle **Rev:** Value within wreath below flower

Date	Mintage	F12	VF20	XF40	MS60	MS63
11	1,500,000	30.00	60.00	125	185	300

KM# 1140 20 CHON
4.05 g., 0.800 Silver 0.1042 oz. ASW, 20 mm. **Ruler:** Yung Hi (Sunjong) **Obv:** Dragon within beaded circle **Rev:** Value within wreath below flower

Date	Mintage	VF20	XF40	MS60	MS63	MS65
2	3,000,000	50.00	90.00	150	275	1,250
3	2,000,000	50.00	90.00	150	275	1,250
4	2,000,000	50.00	90.00	150	275	1,250

KM# 1129 1/2 WON
13.48 g., 0.800 Silver 0.3467 oz. ASW, 31 mm. **Ruler:** Kuang Mu **Obv:** Dragon within beaded circle **Rev:** Value within wreath below flower

Date	Mintage	VF20	XF40	MS60	MS63	MS65
9	600,000	150	250	350	750	3,000
9	—	PF63 1,850				
10	1,200,000	200	350	500	900	3,500

KM# 1135 1/2 WON
10.13 g., 0.800 Silver 0.2605 oz. ASW, 26.5 mm. **Ruler:** Kuang Mu **Obv:** Dragon within beaded circle **Rev:** Value within wreath below flower

Date	Mintage	F12	VF20	XF40	MS60	MS63
11	1,000,000	100	225	400	600	1,150

KM# 1141 1/2 WON
10.13 g., 0.800 Silver 0.2605 oz. ASW, 26 mm. **Ruler:** Yung Hi (Sunjong) **Obv:** Dragon within beaded circle **Rev:** Value within wreath below flower

Date	Mintage	F12	VF20	XF40	MS60	MS63
2	1,400,000	100	200	350	650	1,200

KM# 1142 5 WON
4.17 g., 0.900 Gold 0.1206 oz. AGW **Ruler:** Yung Hi (Sunjong) **Obv:** Dragon within beaded circle **Rev:** Value within wreath below flower

Date	Mintage	F12	VF20	XF40	MS60	MS63
2	10,000	14,000	30,000	45,000	65,000	95,000
Note: Heritage Piedmont sale 6-2000 Gem BU realized $86,250						
3 2 known	—	—	—	—	—	—

KM# 1130 10 WON
8.33 g., 0.900 Gold 0.2411 oz. AGW **Ruler:** Kuang Mu **Obv:** Dragon within beaded circle **Rev:** Value within wreath below flower

Date	Mintage	F12	VF20	XF40	MS60	MS63
10	5,012	—	12,500	17,500	35,000	65,000

KM# A1130 10 WON
8.33 g., 0.900 Gold 0.2411 oz. AGW **Ruler:** Yung Hi (Sunjong) **Obv:** Dragon within beaded circle **Rev:** Value within wreath below flower

Date	Mintage	F12	VF20	XF40	MS60	MS63
3 2 known	—	—	—	—	—	—

KM# 1131 20 WON
16.67 g., 0.900 Gold 0.4823 oz. AGW **Ruler:** Kuang Mu **Obv:** Dragon within beaded circle **Rev:** Value within wreath below flower

Date	Mintage	F12	VF20	XF40	MS60	MS63
10	2,506	—	—	45,000	70,000	115,000

KM# 1144 20 WON
16.67 g., 0.900 Gold 0.4823 oz. AGW **Ruler:** Yung Hi (Sunjong) **Obv:** Dragon within beaded circle **Rev:** Value within wreath

Date	Mintage	F12	VF20	XF40	MS60	MS63
2 Rare	—	—	—	—	—	—
3 2 known	—	—	—	—	—	—

Note: Reported mintages for Year 2 (1908) of 40,000 and Year 3 (1909) of 25,000 exist, but few are known today

KINGDOM

KM# 1116 5 FUN
17.20 g., Copper **Ruler:** Kuang Mu **Obv:** Encircled dragons within circle **Rev:** Value within wreath below flower

Date	Mintage	VF20	XF40	MS60	MS63	MS65
6	—	25.00	60.00	135	225	—

KM# 1117 1/4 YANG
Copper-Nickel **Ruler:** Kuang Mu **Obv:** Dragon within beaded circle **Rev:** Value within wreath below flower

Date	Mintage	F12	VF20	XF40	MS60	MS63
5	—	200	350	550	800	1,350

RUSSIAN DOMINATION

KM# 1121 CHON
6.80 g., Bronze **Ruler:** Kuang Mu **Obv:** Crowned imperial eagle within beaded circle **Rev:** Value within wreath below flower

Date	Mintage	VF20	XF40	MS60	MS63	MS65
6	3,001,000	8,500	15,500	27,500	85,000	165,000

KM# 1122 5 CHON
4.30 g., Copper-Nickel **Ruler:** Kuang Mu **Obv:** Crowned imperial eagle within beaded circle **Rev:** Value within wreath below flower

Date	Mintage	F12	VF20	XF40	MS60	MS63
6	2,800,000	3,500	7,000	14,000	25,000	—

KM# 1123 1/2 WON
13.50 g., 0.800 Silver 0.3472 oz. ASW **Ruler:** Kuang Mu **Obv:** Crowned imperial eagle within beaded circle **Rev:** Value within wreath below flower

Date	Mintage	F12	VF20	XF40	MS60	MS63
5	1,831,000	7,000	15,500	27,500	50,000	—

Note: Ponterio & Assoc. Witte Museum sale 8-89 choice BU realized $12,500; Heritage Piedmont sale 6-2000 choice BU realized $18,400

PATTERNS

Including off metal strikes

KM#	Date	Mintage	Identification	Mkt Val
Pn33	5 (1901)	—	5 Won. Copper.	—
Pn34	5 (1901)	—	10 Won. Copper.	—
Pn35	6 (1902)	—	20 Won. Copper.	100,000
Pn36	6 (1902)	—	20 Won. Copper.	—
Pn37	7 (1903)	—	5 Won. Copper.	—
Pn38	7 (1903)	—	5 Won. Copper.	—
Pn39	7 (1903)	—	10 Won. Copper.	90,000

The Democratic Peoples Republic of Korea, situated in northeastern Asia on the northern half of the Korean peninsula between the Peoples Republic of China and the Republic of Korea, has an area of 46,540 sq. mi. (120,540 sq. km.) and a population of 20 million. Capital: Pyongyang. The economy is based on heavy industry and agriculture. Metals, minerals and farm produce are exported.

Japan replaced China as the predominant foreign influence in Korea in 1895 and annexed the peninsular country in 1910. Defeat in World War II brought an end to Japanese rule. U.S. troops entered Korea from the south and Soviet forces entered from the north. The Cairo conference (1943) had established that Korea should be *free and independent*. The Potsdam conference (1945) set the 38th parallel as the line dividing the occupation forces of the United States and Russia. When Russia refused to permit a U.N. commission designated to supervise reunification elections to enter North Korea, an election was held in South Korea which established the Republic of Korea on Aug. 15,1948. North Korea held an unsupervised election on Aug. 25, 1948, and on Sept. 9, 1948, proclaimed the establishment of the Democratic Peoples Republic of Korea.

NOTE: For earlier coinage see Korea.

MONETARY SYSTEM
100 Chon = 1 Won

MINT:
Pyongyang

CIRCULATION RESTRICTIONS
W/o star: KM#1-4 - General circulation
1 star: KM#5-8 - Issued to visitors from Communist countries.
2 stars: KM#9-12 - Issued to visitors from hard currency countries.

PEOPLES REPUBLIC

DECIMAL COINAGE

KM# 1 CHON
0.64 g., Aluminum, 16 mm. **Obv:** National arms **Rev:** Value

Date	Mintage	VF20	XF40	MS60	MS63	MS65
1959	—	0.25	0.35	0.50	1.00	—
1970	—	0.35	0.50	0.75	1.50	—

KM# 5 CHON
0.62 g., Aluminum, 16 mm. **Obv:** National arms within circle **Rev:** Value flanked by stars

Date	Mintage	VF20	XF40	MS60	MS63	MS65
1959	—	—	0.50	0.75	1.00	—

KM# 9 CHON
Aluminum, 16 mm. **Obv:** National arms within circle **Rev:** Star to left of value

Date	Mintage	VF20	XF40	MS60	MS63	MS65
1959	—	—	0.50	0.75	1.00	—

KM# 2 5 CHON
0.81 g., Aluminum, 18 mm. **Obv:** National arms within circle **Rev:** Value

Date	Mintage	VF20	XF40	MS60	MS63	MS65
1959	—	0.75	1.00	1.25	2.00	—
1974	—	0.50	1.00	1.25	2.00	—

KM# 6 5 CHON
Aluminum, 18 mm. **Obv:** National arms within circle **Rev:** Value flanked by stars

Date	Mintage	VF20	XF40	MS60	MS63	MS65
1974	—	—	1.00	1.25	2.00	—

KM# 10 5 CHON
Aluminum, 18 mm. **Obv:** National arms within circle **Rev:** Star to left of value

Date	Mintage	VF20	XF40	MS60	MS63	MS65
1974	—	—	1.00	1.25	2.00	—

KM# 3 10 CHON
0.95 g., Aluminum, 20 mm. **Obv:** National arms within circle **Rev:** Value

Date	Mintage	VF20	XF40	MS60	MS63	MS65
1959	—	0.75	1.00	1.25	2.00	—

KM# 7 10 CHON
Aluminum, 20 mm. **Obv:** National arms within circle **Rev:** Value flanked by stars

Date	Mintage	VF20	XF40	MS60	MS63	MS65
1959	—	—	1.00	1.25	2.00	—

KM# 11 10 CHON
Aluminum, 20 mm. **Obv:** National arms within circle **Rev:** Star to left of value

Date	Mintage	VF20	XF40	MS60	MS63	MS65
1959	—	—	1.00	1.25	2.00	—

KM# 4 50 CHON
2.01 g., Aluminum, 25 mm. **Obv:** National arms within circle above value **Rev:** Leaping equestrian within radiant sun

Date	Mintage	VF20	XF40	MS60	MS63	MS65
1978	—	—	0.75	1.25	1.75	3.00

KM# 8 50 CHON
Aluminum, 25 mm. **Obv:** National arms within circle above value **Rev:** Leaping equestrian divides stars within radiant sun

Date	Mintage	VF20	XF40	MS60	MS63	MS65
1978	—	—	0.75	1.25	1.75	3.00

KM# 12 50 CHON
Aluminum, 25 mm. **Obv:** National arms within circle above value **Rev:** Star to left of leaping equestrian within radiant sun

Date	Mintage	VF20	XF40	MS60	MS63	MS65
1978	—	—	0.75	1.25	1.75	3.00

KM# 13 WON
Copper-Nickel **Obv:** National arms above date **Rev:** Kim Il Sung's birthplace among radiant sun

Date	Mintage	VF20	XF40	MS60	MS63	MS65
1987	—	—	—	—	2.50	4.00
1987	—	PF65 5.00				

KM# 14 WON
Copper-Nickel **Obv:** National arms above value divides date **Rev:** Kim Il Sung's Arch of Triumph within beaded circle

Date	Mintage	VF20	XF40	MS60	MS63	MS65
1987	—	—	—	—	2.50	4.00
1987	—	PF65 5.00				

KM# 15 WON
Copper-Nickel **Obv:** National arms above value **Rev:** Kim Il Sung's Tower of Juche within beaded circle

Date	Mintage	VF20	XF40	MS60	MS63	MS65
1987	—	—	—	—	2.50	4.00
1987	—	PF65 5.00				

KM# 18 WON
2.32 g., Aluminum, 27 mm. **Obv:** National arms above date **Rev:** Palace

Date	Mintage	VF20	XF40	MS60	MS63	MS65
1987	—	—	—	—	2.00	3.50

KM# 550 WON
31.11 g., 0.999 Silver 0.999 oz. ASW, 40 mm. **Obv:** National arms, name of the Central Bank flanked by 1 oz and .999 **Rev:** Panda in color

Date	Mintage	VF20	XF40	MS60	MS63	MS65
1995 Proof	—	—	—	—	—	—

KM# 534 WON
15.00 g., Brass, 34 mm. **Subject:** Nagano Olympics, 1998 **Obv:** National arms **Rev:** Two speed skaters

Date	Mintage	VF20	XF40	MS60	MS63	MS65
1998	—	PF65 12.50				

KM# 179 WON
6.70 g., Aluminum, 40 mm. **Subject:** Birds of Korea - Dryocopus Javensis **Obv:** National arms **Rev:** White-bellied woodpecker **Edge:** Plain

Date	Mintage	VF20	XF40	MS60	MS63	MS65
1999	—	PF65 16.00				

KM# 180 WON
6.70 g., Aluminum, 40 mm. **Subject:** Birds of Korea - Lyrurus Tetrix **Obv:** National arms **Rev:** Black grouse **Edge:** Plain

Date	Mintage	VF20	XF40	MS60	MS63	MS65
1999	—	PF65 16.00				

KM# 181 WON
6.70 g., Aluminum, 40 mm. **Subject:** Birds of Korea - Syrrhaptes Paradoxus **Obv:** National arms **Rev:** Pallas's sandgrouse at water's edge **Edge:** Plain

Date	Mintage	VF20	XF40	MS60	MS63	MS65
1999	—	PF65 16.00				

KM# 182 WON
6.70 g., Aluminum, 40 mm. **Subject:** Birds of Korea - Pitta Brachyura **Obv:** National arms **Rev:** Fairy pitta trilling on branch left **Edge:** Plain

Date	Mintage	VF20	XF40	MS60	MS63	MS65
1999	—	PF65 16.00				

KM# 613 WON
7.00 g., Aluminum, 40 mm. **Obv:** National arms **Rev:** Jeong Seongok, Marathon race champion

Date	Mintage	VF20	XF40	MS60	MS63	MS65
1999 Proof	—	—	—	—	—	—

KM# 614 WON
28.00 g., Brass, 40 mm. **Obv:** National arms **Rev:** Jeong Seongok, Marathon race champion

Date	Mintage	VF20	XF40	MS60	MS63	MS65
1999 Proof	—	—	—	—	—	—

KM# 126 WON
Copper-Nickel, 32 mm. **Obv:** National arms **Rev:** Hyonmu **Edge:** Reeded

Date	Mintage	VF20	XF40	MS60	MS63	MS65
2000	—	—	—	—	8.00	12.00

KM# 126a WON
3.94 g., Aluminum, 32 mm. **Obv:** National arms **Rev:** Hyonmu **Edge:** Plain

Date	Mintage	VF20	XF40	MS60	MS63	MS65
2000	—	PF65 16.00				

KM# 127 WON
Copper-Nickel, 35 mm. **Subject:** Blue Dragon **Obv:** National arms **Rev:** Dragon above mountains **Edge:** Reeded

Date	Mintage	VF20	XF40	MS60	MS63	MS65
2000	—	—	—	—	9.00	15.00

KM# 127a WON
5.20 g., Aluminum, 35 mm. **Obv:** National arms **Rev:** Blue Dragon **Edge:** Plain

Date	Mintage	VF20	XF40	MS60	MS63	MS65
2000	—	PF65 16.00				

KM# 128 WON
22.00 g., Copper-Nickel, 35 mm. **Subject:** Tiger **Obv:** Tiger in mountains **Rev:** Tiger head **Edge:** Plain

Date	Mintage	VF20	XF40	MS60	MS63	MS65
ND-1998 Proof	5,000	—	—	—	—	15.00

KM# 155 WON
16.20 g., Brass, 35 mm. **Subject:** Seafaring Ships **Obv:** National arms **Rev:** German school ship, Prinzess Eitel Friedrich with furled sails **Edge:** Plain

Date	Mintage	VF20	XF40	MS60	MS63	MS65
ND-2000	—	PF65 10.00				

KM# 155a WON
17.00 g., Copper-Nickel, 35 mm. **Subject:** School Ships **Obv:** National arms **Rev:** German school ship, Prinzess Eitel Friedrich with furled sails **Edge:** Plain

Date	Mintage	VF20	XF40	MS60	MS63	MS65
ND-2000	200	PF65 100				

KM# 156 WON
16.86 g., Copper-Nickel, 35 mm. **Subject:** Seafaring Ships **Obv:** National arms **Rev:** German school ship, Grossherzogin Elisabeth under full sail right **Edge:** Plain

Date	Mintage	VF20	XF40	MS60	MS63	MS65
ND-2000	—	PF65 10.00				

KM# 162 WON
6.70 g., Aluminum, 40 mm. **Subject:** 3,000 Years of Korean History **Obv:** National arms **Rev:** Radiant map and landmarks **Edge:** Plain

Date	Mintage	VF20	XF40	MS60	MS63	MS65
2000	—	PF65 9.00				

KM# 162a WON
26.75 g., Brass, 40.2 mm. **Subject:** 3,000 Years of Korean History **Obv:** National arms **Rev:** Radiant Korean map and landmarks **Edge:** Plain

Date	Mintage	VF20	XF40	MS60	MS63	MS65
2000	—	PF65 17.50				

KM# 198 WON
17.00 g., Copper-Nickel, 35 mm. **Subject:** School Ships **Obv:** National arms **Rev:** SS Grossherzog Friedrich August **Edge:** Plain

Date	Mintage	VF20	XF40	MS60	MS63	MS65
ND-2000	200	PF65 100				

KM# 263 WON
14.31 g., Brass, 34.2 mm. **Obv:** National arms **Rev:** Flying squirrel **Edge:** Segmented reeding

Date	Mintage	VF20	XF40	MS60	MS63	MS65
ND(2000)	—	PF65 25.00				

KM# 273 WON
28.20 g., Brass, 40.1 mm. **Obv:** National arms **Rev:** Kim Jong Il greeting diplomat, half length figures, Korean legend **Edge:** Plain

Date	Mintage	VF20	XF40	MS60	MS63	MS65
2000	—	PF65 22.00				

KM# 274 WON
28.20 g., Brass, 40.1 mm. **Obv:** National arms **Rev:** Kim Jong Il greeting diplomat, full length figures **Edge:** Plain

Date	Mintage	VF20	XF40	MS60	MS63	MS65
2000	—	PF65 22.00				

KM# 275 WON
28.20 g., Brass, 40.1 mm. **Obv:** National arms **Rev:** Kim Jong Il greeting diplomat, half length figures, Cyrillic legend **Edge:** Plain

Date	Mintage	VF20	XF40	MS60	MS63	MS65
2000	—	PF65 22.00				

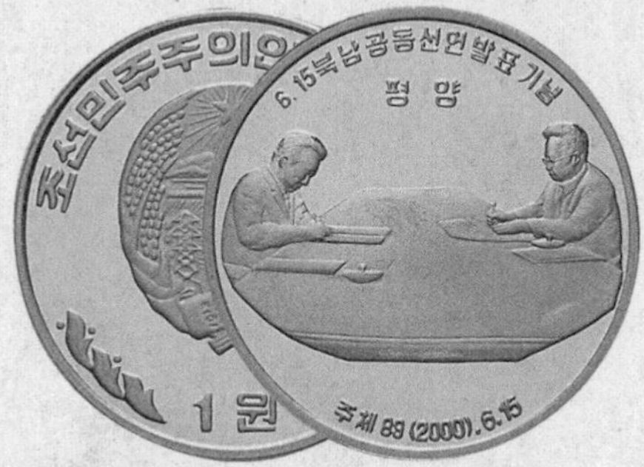

KM# 277 WON
28.20 g., Brass, 40.1 mm. **Obv:** National arms **Rev:** Treaty signing scene **Edge:** Plain

Date	Mintage	VF20	XF40	MS60	MS63	MS65
2000	—	PF65 22.00				

KM# 455 WON
Brass, 35 mm. **Subject:** Tall ships **Obv:** Arms **Rev:** Prinzess Eitel Friedrich

Date	Mintage	VF20	XF40	MS60	MS63	MS65
2000	—	PF65 8.00				

KM# 456 WON
Brass, 35 mm. **Subject:** Tall ships **Obv:** Arms **Rev:** Grosseherzogin Elizabeth

Date	Mintage	VF20	XF40	MS60	MS63	MS65
2000	—	PF65 8.00				

KM# 457 WON
Brass, 35 mm. **Subject:** Tall ships **Obv:** Arms **Rev:** Grossherzog Friedrich August

Date	Mintage	VF20	XF40	MS60	MS63	MS65
2000	—	PF65 8.00				

KM# 662 WON
7.00 g., Aluminum, 40 mm. **Obv:** National arms, Central Bank name **Rev:** Map of Korea in circle

Date	Mintage	VF20	XF40	MS60	MS63	MS65
2000	—	PF65 6.00				

KM# 680 WON
16.00 g., Brass, 35 mm. **Obv:** National arms, Country name **Rev:** Sail training ship Grand Duchess Elisabeth currently known as Duchess Anne

Date	Mintage	VF20	XF40	MS60	MS63	MS65
2000	—	PF65 7.00				

KM# 681 WON
16.00 g., Brass, 35 mm. **Obv:** National arms, Country name **Rev:** Sail training ship Princess Eitel Friedrich currently known as Dar Pomorza

Date	Mintage	VF20	XF40	MS60	MS63	MS65
2000	—	PF65 7.00				

KM# 682 WON
16.00 g., Brass, 35 mm. **Obv:** National arms, Country name **Rev:** Sail training vessel Grand Duke Friedrich August now called Statsraad Lehmkuhl

Date	Mintage	VF20	XF40	MS60	MS63	MS65
2000	—	PF65 7.00				

KM# 686 2 WON
7.00 g., 0.999 Silver 0.2248 oz. ASW, 30 mm. **Obv:** National arms, Central Bank name **Rev:** Two pandas in color

Date	Mintage	VF20	XF40	MS60	MS63	MS65
2000	—	PF65 30.00				

KM# 687 2 WON
7.00 g., Silver, 30 mm. **Obv:** National arms, Central Bank name **Rev:** Chillon castle, Montreux, Lake Leman

Date	Mintage	VF20	XF40	MS60	MS63	MS65
2000	—	PF65 35.00				

KM# 688 2 WON
7.00 g., 0.999 Silver 0.2248 oz. ASW, 30 mm. **Subject:** World Cup Soccer, 2006 **Obv:** National emblem, Central Bank name **Rev:** Brandenburg gate in Berlin

Date	Mintage	VF20	XF40	MS60	MS63	MS65
2000	—	PF65 25.00				

KM# 22 5 WON
Copper-Nickel **Obv:** Value divides date below national arms **Rev:** Kim Il Sung's Arch of Triumph

Date	Mintage	VF20	XF40	MS60	MS63	MS65
1987	—	—	—	—	7.00	8.00
1987	—	PF65 10.00				

KM# 23 5 WON
Copper-Nickel **Obv:** Radiant national arms above date and value **Rev:** Kim Il Sung's Tower of Juche

Date	Mintage	VF20	XF40	MS60	MS63	MS65
1987	—	—	—	—	7.00	8.00
1987	—	PF65 10.00				

KM# 25 5 WON
Copper-Nickel **Obv:** National arms above date and value **Rev:** Kim Il Sung's birthplace

Date	Mintage	VF20	XF40	MS60	MS63	MS65
1987	—	—	—	—	7.00	8.00
1987	—	PF65 10.00				

KM# 19 5 WON
Copper-Nickel **Subject:** World Festival of Youth and Students **Obv:** National arms with D.P.R. of Korea written below, value at lower left **Rev:** Flower-like design

Date	Mintage	VF20	XF40	MS60	MS63	MS65
1989	—	—	—	—	7.00	8.00
1989	—	PF65 10.00				

KM# 92 5 WON
12.00 g., 0.999 Silver 0.3854 oz. ASW **Subject:** 50th Anniversary of Liberation **Obv:** National arms above oat sprigs and date **Rev:** Teapot in bowl

Date	Mintage	VF20	XF40	MS60	MS63	MS65
1995	300	PF65 50.00				

KM# 129 5 WON
13.00 g., Copper-Nickel **Subject:** 10th Singapore International Coin Show **Obv:** National arms above sprigs and date **Rev:** Multicolor logo within globe **Edge:** Plain

Date	Mintage	VF20	XF40	MS60	MS63	MS65
1996	1,000	—	—	—	—	20.00

KM# 130 5 WON
27.00 g., 0.999 Silver 0.8672 oz. ASW, 35 mm. **Subject:** Kaesong - Sinuiju Railroad **Obv:** National arms **Rev:** Multicolor train **Edge:** Plain

Date	Mintage	VF20	XF40	MS60	MS63	MS65
1996	2,000	—	—	—	—	45.00

KM# 131 5 WON
27.00 g., 0.999 Silver 0.8672 oz. ASW, 35 mm. **Subject:** 1st Beijing International Coin Show **Obv:** National arms **Rev:** Multicolor panda holding logo **Edge:** Plain

Date	Mintage	VF20	XF40	MS60	MS63	MS65
1996	6,000	—	—	—	—	37.50

KM# 100 5 WON
26.94 g., 0.999 Silver 0.8653 oz. ASW **Subject:** Olympics **Obv:** National arms **Rev:** Two speed skaters

Date	Mintage	VF20	XF40	MS60	MS63	MS65
1997	—	PF65 32.00				

KM# 132 5 WON
27.00 g., 0.999 Silver 0.8672 oz. ASW, 35 mm. **Subject:** 11th Singapore International Coin Show **Obv:** National arms **Rev:** Multicolor panda holding logo **Edge:** Plain

Date	Mintage	VF20	XF40	MS60	MS63	MS65
1997	1,000	—	—	—	—	40.00

KM# 133 5 WON
27.00 g., 0.999 Silver 0.8672 oz. ASW, 35 mm. **Subject:** World Cup Soccer **Obv:** National arms **Rev:** Soccer players **Edge:** Plain

Date	Mintage	VF20	XF40	MS60	MS63	MS65
1997	3,000	—	—	—	—	32.50

KM# 161 5 WON
26.84 g., 0.999 Silver 0.8621 oz. ASW, 40 mm. **Subject:** Korean War **Obv:** National arms **Rev:** Multicolor flags and flowers in front of monument **Edge:** Reeded

Date	Mintage	VF20	XF40	MS60	MS63	MS65
1998	—	PF65 35.00				

KM# 454 5 WON
26.87 g., 0.999 Silver 0.863 oz. ASW, 40.08 mm. **Subject:** Korean Folk IV **Obv:** National arms **Rev:** Girl on swing **Edge:** Plain

Date	Mintage	VF20	XF40	MS60	MS63	MS65
JU87-1998	—	PF65 45.00				

KM# 544 5 WON
27.00 g., Silver, 40 mm. **Obv:** National arms, name of the Central Bank **Rev:** Soldiers attack bridge over the Yalu river at Dandong (1951)

Date	Mintage	VF20	XF40	MS60	MS63	MS65
1998	—	PF65 55.00				

KM# 592 5 WON
27.00 g., 0.999 Silver 0.8672 oz. ASW, 40 mm. **Obv:** National arms, Central Bank name **Rev:** Dragon rising **Edge:** Plain

Date	Mintage	VF20	XF40	MS60	MS63	MS65
1998 Proof	—	—	—	—	—	—

KM# 593 5 WON
27.00 g., 0.999 Silver 0.8672 oz. ASW, 40 mm. **Obv:** National arms, Central Bank name **Rev:** Two girls on seasaw **Edge:** Plain

Date	Mintage	VF20	XF40	MS60	MS63	MS65
1998 Proof	—	—	—	—	—	—

KM# 594 5 WON
27.00 g., 0.999 Silver 0.8672 oz. ASW, 40 mm. **Obv:** National arms, Central Bank name **Rev:** Korean struggle

Date	Mintage	VF20	XF40	MS60	MS63	MS65
1998 Proof	—	—	—	—	—	—

KM# 595 5 WON
27.00 g., 0.999 Silver 0.8672 oz. ASW, 40 mm. **Obv:** National arms, Central Bank name **Rev:** Children skipping **Edge:** Plain

Date	Mintage	VF20	XF40	MS60	MS63	MS65
1998 Proof	—	—	—	—	—	—

KM# 123 5 WON
20.00 g., 0.999 Silver 0.6424 oz. ASW, 34.3 mm. **Subject:** History of Seafaring **Obv:** National arms **Rev:** Sailing Junk **Edge:** Reeded and plain sections

Date	Mintage	VF20	XF40	MS60	MS63	MS65
1999	—	PF65 35.00				

KM# 424 5 WON
27.00 g., 0.999 Silver 0.8672 oz. ASW, 40 mm. **Obv:** National arms **Rev:** Rocket and satellite above Eastern Asia **Edge:** Plain

Date	Mintage	VF20	XF40	MS60	MS63	MS65
1999	—	PF65 40.00				

KM# 611 5 WON
20.00 g., 0.999 Silver 0.6424 oz. ASW, 34 mm. **Obv:** National arms, Central Bank name **Rev:** Chinese Junk at sail

Date	Mintage	VF20	XF40	MS60	MS63	MS65
1999	—	PF65 35.00				

KM# 172 5 WON
20.00 g., 0.999 Silver 0.6424 oz. ASW, 40 mm. **Subject:** Endangered Wildlife **Obv:** National arms **Rev:** Siberian flying squirrel **Edge:** Reeded and plain sections

Date	Mintage	VF20	XF40	MS60	MS63	MS65
2000	5,000	PF65 35.00				

KM# 173 5 WON
27.00 g., 0.999 Silver 0.8672 oz. ASW, 40 mm. **Subject:** King Tongmyong **Obv:** Mythical bird **Rev:** Crowned bust facing **Edge:** Reeded and plain sections

Date	Mintage	VF20	XF40	MS60	MS63	MS65
2000	3,000	PF65 35.00				

KM# 174 5 WON
27.00 g., 0.999 Silver 0.8672 oz. ASW, 40 mm. **Subject:** Olympics **Obv:** National arms **Rev:** Female archer drawing back her bow **Edge:** Plain

Date	Mintage	VF20	XF40	MS60	MS63	MS65
2000	3,000	PF65 35.00				

KM# 175 5 WON
27.00 g., 0.999 Silver 0.8672 oz. ASW, 40 mm. **Subject:** Olympics **Obv:** National arms **Rev:** Handball player **Edge:** Reeded and plain sections

Date	Mintage	VF20	XF40	MS60	MS63	MS65
2000	3,000	PF65 35.00				

KM# 176 5 WON
27.00 g., 0.999 Silver 0.8672 oz. ASW, 40 mm. **Subject:** Olympics **Obv:** National arms **Rev:** Two wrestlers **Edge:** Plain

Date	Mintage	VF20	XF40	MS60	MS63	MS65
2000	3,000	PF65 35.00				

KM# 177 5 WON
27.00 g., 0.999 Silver 0.8672 oz. ASW, 40 mm. **Subject:** Mt. Kumgang **Obv:** Mythical bird **Rev:** Buddha statue facing **Edge:** Reeded and plain sections

Date	Mintage	VF20	XF40	MS60	MS63	MS65
2000	3,000	PF65 37.00				

KM# 199 5 WON
15.00 g., 0.999 Silver 0.4818 oz. ASW, 35 mm. **Subject:** School Ships **Obv:** National arms **Rev:** SS Grossherzogin Elisabeth **Edge:** Plain

Date	Mintage	VF20	XF40	MS60	MS63	MS65
ND-2000	500	PF65 75.00	PF67 90.00			

KM# 200 5 WON
15.00 g., 0.999 Silver 0.4818 oz. ASW, 35 mm. **Subject:** School Ships **Obv:** National arms **Rev:** SS Prinzess Eitel Friedrich **Edge:** Plain

Date	Mintage	VF20	XF40	MS60	MS63	MS65
ND-2000	500	PF65 75.00	PF67 90.00			

KM# 201 5 WON
15.00 g., 0.999 Silver 0.4818 oz. ASW, 35 mm. **Subject:** School Ships **Obv:** National arms **Rev:** SS Grossherzog Friedrich August **Edge:** Plain

Date	Mintage	VF20	XF40	MS60	MS63	MS65
ND-2000	500	PF65 75.00	PF67 90.00			

KM# 213 5 WON
15.00 g., 0.999 Silver 0.4818 oz. ASW, 35 mm. **Subject:** First Nobel Prize Winners Series - Sully Prudhomme **Obv:** National arms **Rev:** Writer's portrait **Edge:** Plain

Date	Mintage	VF20	XF40	MS60	MS63	MS65
ND-2000	—	PF65 100				

KM# 214 5 WON
15.00 g., 0.999 Silver 0.4818 oz. ASW, 35 mm. **Subject:** First Nobel Prize Winners Series - Wilhelm C. Roentgen **Obv:** National arms **Rev:** Portrait and lab scene **Edge:** Plain

Date	Mintage	VF20	XF40	MS60	MS63	MS65
ND-2000	—	PF65 100				

KM# 215 5 WON
15.00 g., 0.999 Silver 0.4818 oz. ASW, 35 mm. **Subject:** First Nobel Prize Winners Series - Emil A. von Behring **Obv:** National arms **Rev:** Two man lab scene **Edge:** Plain

Date	Mintage	VF20	XF40	MS60	MS63	MS65
ND-2000	—	PF65 100				

KM# 216 5 WON
15.00 g., 0.999 Silver 0.4818 oz. ASW, 35 mm. **Subject:** First Nobel Prize Winners Series - Henri Dunant **Obv:** National arms **Rev:** Portrait and war wounded scene **Edge:** Plain

Date	Mintage	VF20	XF40	MS60	MS63	MS65
ND-2000	—	PF65 100				

KM# 217 5 WON
15.00 g., 0.999 Silver 0.4818 oz. ASW, 35 mm. **Subject:** First Nobel Prize Winners Series - Jacobus Van't Hoff **Obv:** National arms **Rev:** Two chemists in lab scene **Edge:** Plain

Date	Mintage	VF20	XF40	MS60	MS63	MS65
ND-2000	—	PF65 100				

KM# 218 5 WON
15.00 g., 0.999 Silver 0.4818 oz. ASW, 35 mm. **Subject:** First Nobel Prize Winners Series - Frederic Passy **Obv:** National arms **Rev:** Portrait and allegorical scene **Edge:** Plain

Date	Mintage	VF20	XF40	MS60	MS63	MS65
ND-2000	—	PF65 100				

KM# 268 5 WON
14.96 g., 0.999 Silver 0.4805 oz. ASW, 35 mm. **Obv:** National arms **Rev:** Mountbatten SR-N4 hovercraft **Edge:** Plain

Date	Mintage	VF20	XF40	MS60	MS63	MS65
2000	—	PF65 30.00				

KM# 283 5 WON
15.00 g., 0.999 Silver 0.4818 oz. ASW, 35 mm. **Subject:** Arirang **Obv:** National arms **Rev:** Flying female flute player **Edge:** Segmented reeding

Date	Mintage	VF20	XF40	MS60	MS63	MS65
ND	—	PF65 30.00				

KM# 284 5 WON
15.00 g., 0.999 Silver 0.4818 oz. ASW, 35 mm. **Subject:** Arirang **Obv:** National arms **Rev:** Dancers holding globe over arena **Edge:** Segmented reeding

Date	Mintage	VF20	XF40	MS60	MS63	MS65
ND	—	PF65 30.00				

KM# 285 5 WON
15.00 g., 0.999 Silver 0.4818 oz. ASW, 35 mm. **Subject:** Arirang **Obv:** National arms **Rev:** Uniformed heads right and outline of dove **Edge:** Segmented reeding

Date	Mintage	VF20	XF40	MS60	MS63	MS65
ND	—	PF65 30.00				

KM# 286 5 WON
15.00 g., 0.999 Silver 0.4818 oz. ASW, 35 mm. **Subject:** Arirang **Obv:** National arms **Rev:** Monument **Edge:** Segmented reeding

Date	Mintage	VF20	XF40	MS60	MS63	MS65
ND	—	PF65 30.00				

KM# 287 5 WON
15.00 g., 0.999 Silver 0.4818 oz. ASW, 35 mm. **Subject:** Arirang **Obv:** National arms **Rev:** Dancer in radiant sunlight **Edge:** Segmented reeding

Date	Mintage	VF20	XF40	MS60	MS63	MS65
ND	—	PF65 30.00				

KM# 288 5 WON
15.00 g., 0.999 Silver 0.4818 oz. ASW, 35 mm. **Subject:** Arirang **Obv:** National arms **Rev:** Folk dancers **Edge:** Segmented reeding

Date	Mintage	VF20	XF40	MS60	MS63	MS65
ND	—	PF65 30.00				

KM# 289 5 WON
15.00 g., 0.999 Silver 0.4818 oz. ASW, 35 mm. **Subject:** Arirang **Obv:** National arms **Rev:** Arena **Edge:** Segmented reeding

Date	Mintage	VF20	XF40	MS60	MS63	MS65
ND	—	PF65 30.00				

KM# 635 5 WON
15.00 g., Brass, 34 mm. **Obv:** National arms, Central Bank name **Rev:** Asiatic Volant

Date	Mintage	VF20	XF40	MS60	MS63	MS65
2000	—	PF65 7.50				

KM# 639 5 WON
20.00 g., 0.999 Silver 0.6424 oz. ASW, 34 mm. **Obv:** National arms, Central Bank name **Rev:** Two Korean tigers

Date	Mintage	VF20	XF40	MS60	MS63	MS65
2000	—	PF65 150				

KM# 65 10 WON
Copper-Nickel **Subject:** 80th Birthday - Kim Il Sung **Obv:** National arms **Rev:** Kim Il Sung birthplace

Date	Mintage	VF20	XF40	MS60	MS63	MS65
1992	—	—	—	—	7.50	9.00

KM# 66 10 WON
Copper-Nickel **Subject:** 50th Birthday - Kim Il Jong **Obv:** National arms **Rev:** Bust facing

Date	Mintage	VF20	XF40	MS60	MS63	MS65
1992	—	—	—	—	7.50	9.00

KM# 73 10 WON
Copper-Nickel **Subject:** 80th Birthday - Kim Il Sung **Obv:** National arms **Rev:** Bust facing

Date	Mintage	VF20	XF40	MS60	MS63	MS65
1992	—	—	—	—	7.50	9.00

KM# 87.1 10 WON
Copper-Nickel, 30 mm. **Subject:** International Sport and Culture Festival **Obv:** National arms **Rev:** Multicolor cartoon cat **Edge:** Plain

Date	Mintage	VF20	XF40	MS60	MS63	MS65
1995	—	—	—	—	15.00	17.50

KM# 87.2 10 WON
12.90 g., Copper-Nickel, 30 mm. **Subject:** International Sport and Culture Festival **Obv:** National arms **Rev:** Multicolor cartoon cat **Edge:** Plain

Date	Mintage	VF20	XF40	MS60	MS63	MS65
1995	—	—	—	—	10.00	14.00

KM# 93 10 WON
28.00 g., Silver **Subject:** 50th Anniversary of Liberation **Obv:** National arms above sprigs and date **Rev:** Taedong gatehouse

Date	Mintage	VF20	XF40	MS60	MS63	MS65
1995	300	PF65 65.00	PF67 75.00			

KM# 134.1 10 WON
12.90 g., Copper-Nickel, 30 mm. **Subject:** International Sport and Culture Festival **Obv:** National arms **Rev:** Festival logo **Edge:** Plain

Date	Mintage	VF20	XF40	MS60	MS63	MS65
1995	—	—	—	—	10.00	12.00

KM# 134.2 10 WON
12.90 g., Copper-Nickel, 30 mm. **Subject:** International Sport and Culture Festival **Obv:** National arms **Rev:** Festival logo with pink flame **Edge:** Plain

Date	Mintage	VF20	XF40	MS60	MS63	MS65
1995	—	—	—	—	10.00	12.00

KM# 230 10 WON
31.00 g., 0.999 Silver 0.9957 oz. ASW, 40.1 mm. **Subject:** Brontosaurus **Obv:** National arms **Rev:** Two dinosaurs above value **Edge:** Plain

Date	Mintage	VF20	XF40	MS60	MS63	MS65
1995	—	PF65 40.00				

KM# 269 10 WON
31.00 g., 0.999 Silver 0.9957 oz. ASW, 40 mm. **Obv:** National arms **Rev:** Olympic horse jumping **Edge:** Plain

Date	Mintage	VF20	XF40	MS60	MS63	MS65
1995	—	PF65 40.00				

KM# 270 10 WON
31.00 g., 0.999 Silver 0.9957 oz. ASW, 40 mm. **Obv:** National arms **Rev:** Olympic runners **Edge:** Plain

Date	Mintage	VF20	XF40	MS60	MS63	MS65
1995	—	PF65 40.00				

KM# 546 10 WON
12.90 g., Copper-Nickel, 30 mm. **Obv:** National arms, name of the Central Bank **Rev:** Tiger in color

Date	Mintage	VF20	XF40	MS60	MS63	MS65
1995	Est. 10000	—	—	—	7.50	9.00

KM# 547 10 WON
12.90 g., Copper-Nickel, 30 mm. **Obv:** National arms, name of the Central Bank **Rev:** Logo for International sportsfest 1995 in color

Date	Mintage	VF20	XF40	MS60	MS63	MS65
1995	—	—	—	—	7.50	9.00

KM# 105 10 WON
31.10 g., 0.999 Silver 0.999 oz. ASW **Subject:** Fauna of Asia - Ducks **Obv:** National arms **Rev:** Multicolored pair of falcated ducks

Date	Mintage	VF20	XF40	MS60	MS63	MS65
1996	—	PF65 45.00				

KM# 115 10 WON
30.96 g., 0.999 Silver 0.9944 oz. ASW **Subject:** Fauna of Asia **Obv:** National arms **Rev:** Multicolored parrot

Date	Mintage	VF20	XF40	MS60	MS63	MS65
1996	—	PF65 50.00				

KM# 135 10 WON
31.10 g., 0.999 Silver 0.999 oz. ASW, 40 mm. **Subject:** Korean Workers' Party **Obv:** National arms **Rev:** Flag and radiant setting sun **Edge:** Plain

Date	Mintage	VF20	XF40	MS60	MS63	MS65
1996	1,000	—	—	—	—	45.00

KM# 271 10 WON
31.00 g., 0.999 Silver 0.9957 oz. ASW, 40.2 mm. **Obv:** National arms **Rev:** Two green Olympic gymnasts **Edge:** Plain

Date	Mintage	VF20	XF40	MS60	MS63	MS65
1996	—	PF65 45.00				

KM# 515 10 WON
8.80 g., Aluminum, 40 mm. **Obv:** National arms **Rev:** Panda and tiger in color

Date	Mintage	VF20	XF40	MS60	MS63	MS65
1996	—	PF65 10.00				

KM# 98 10 WON
31.00 g., 0.999 Silver 0.9957 oz. ASW **Subject:** Return of Hong Kong to China **Obv:** National arms **Rev:** Temple of Heaven above Hong Kong city view

Date	Mintage	VF20	XF40	MS60	MS63	MS65
1997	—	PF65 65.00				

KM# 99 10 WON
31.00 g., 0.999 Silver 0.9957 oz. ASW **Subject:** Ginseng **Obv:** National arms **Rev:** Multicolored ginseng plant including root, leaves and berries

Date	Mintage	VF20	XF40	MS60	MS63	MS65
1997	—	PF65 45.00				

KM# 101 10 WON
30.88 g., 0.999 Silver 0.9918 oz. ASW **Subject:** Shanghai Coin Show **Obv:** National arms **Rev:** Two multicolored pandas eating bamboo

Date	Mintage	VF20	XF40	MS60	MS63	MS65
1997	20,000	PF65 45.00				

KM# 120 10 WON
30.96 g., 0.999 Silver 0.9944 oz. ASW, 38.6 mm. **Subject:** Korean War **Obv:** National arms **Rev:** Multicolored flags before monument **Edge:** Reeded and plain sections

Date	Mintage	VF20	XF40	MS60	MS63	MS65
1997	—	PF65 37.50				

KM# 121 10 WON
30.96 g., 0.999 Silver 0.9944 oz. ASW, 40.3 mm. **Subject:** Korean War **Obv:** National arms **Rev:** Soldier watching bridge bombardment **Edge:** Reeded and plain sections

Date	Mintage	VF20	XF40	MS60	MS63	MS65
1997	—	PF65 42.50				

KM# 124 10 WON
30.95 g., 0.999 Silver 0.9941 oz. ASW, 40.3 mm. **Subject:** World of Adventure **Obv:** National arms **Rev:** Multicolor sailing scene **Edge:** Segmented reeding

Date	Mintage	VF20	XF40	MS60	MS63	MS65
1997	—	PF65 55.00				

KM# 136 10 WON
31.10 g., 0.999 Silver 0.999 oz. ASW, 40 mm. **Subject:** Chou En Lai Centennial of Birth **Obv:** National arms above value and date **Rev:** Head facing above dates flanked by sprigs **Edge:** Plain

Date	Mintage	VF20	XF40	MS60	MS63	MS65
1997	8,000	—	—	—	—	50.00

KM# 137 10 WON
31.10 g., 0.999 Silver 0.999 oz. ASW, 40 mm. **Subject:** Chinese National Flower **Obv:** National arms **Rev:** Multicolor flower **Edge:** Plain

Date	Mintage	VF20	XF40	MS60	MS63	MS65
1997	5,000	—	—	—	—	55.00

KM# 138.1 10 WON
31.10 g., 0.999 Silver 0.999 oz. ASW, 40 mm. **Subject:** Giant Panda **Obv:** National arms **Rev:** Multicolor seated panda **Edge:** Plain **Note:** Previous KM#138.

Date	Mintage	VF20	XF40	MS60	MS63	MS65
1997	10,000	—	—	—	—	50.00

KM# 222 10 WON
30.80 g., 0.999 Silver 0.9893 oz. ASW, 40.2 mm. **Subject:** Fauna of Asia **Obv:** National arms **Rev:** Two multicolor water birds **Edge:** Reeded

Date	Mintage	VF20	XF40	MS60	MS63	MS65
1997	—	PF65 50.00				

KM# 349 10 WON
31.00 g., 0.999 Silver 0.9957 oz. ASW, 40.2 mm. **Obv:** National arms **Rev:** Multicolor parrot **Edge:** Plain

Date	Mintage	VF20	XF40	MS60	MS63	MS65
1997	—	PF65 40.00				

KM# 102 10 WON
30.88 g., 0.999 Silver 0.9918 oz. ASW **Subject:** Year of the Tiger **Obv:** Tiger on mountain ledge **Rev:** Tiger head

Date	Mintage	VF20	XF40	MS60	MS63	MS65
1998	—	PF65 45.00				

Note: Date in Chinese numeral characters

KM# 110 10 WON
30.88 g., 0.999 Silver 0.9918 oz. ASW, 40 mm. **Subject:** Korean Folk IV **Obv:** National arms **Rev:** Girl on swing **Edge:** Segmented reeding **Note:** Large date.

Date	Mintage	VF20	XF40	MS60	MS63	MS65
JU87-1998	—	PF65 45.00				

KM# 111.1 10 WON
30.88 g., 0.999 Silver 0.9918 oz. ASW, 40 mm. **Subject:** Korean Folk I **Obv:** National arms **Rev:** Two children flying a kite **Edge:** Segmented reeding **Note:** Large date.

Date	Mintage	VF20	XF40	MS60	MS63	MS65
JU87-1998	—	PF65 45.00				

KM# 111.2 10 WON
30.88 g., 0.999 Silver 0.9918 oz. ASW, 40 mm. **Subject:** Korean Folk I **Obv:** National arms **Rev:** Two children flying a kite **Edge:** Plain **Note:** Small date.

Date	Mintage	VF20	XF40	MS60	MS63	MS65
JU87-1998	—	PF65 60.00				

KM# 112.1 10 WON
30.88 g., 0.999 Silver 0.9918 oz. ASW, 40 mm. **Subject:** Korean Folk II **Obv:** National arms **Rev:** Two girls see-sawing **Edge:** Segmented reeding **Note:** Large date.

Date	Mintage	VF20	XF40	MS60	MS63	MS65
JU87-1998	—	PF65 45.00				

KM# 112.2 10 WON
30.88 g., 0.999 Silver 0.9918 oz. ASW, 40 mm. **Subject:** Korean Folk II **Obv:** National arms **Rev:** Two girls see-sawing **Edge:** Plain **Note:** Small date.

Date	Mintage	VF20	XF40	MS60	MS63	MS65
JU87-1998	—	PF65 60.00				

KM# 113.1 10 WON
30.88 g., 0.999 Silver 0.9918 oz. ASW, 40 mm. **Subject:** Korean Folk III **Obv:** National arms **Rev:** Wrestling **Edge:** Segmented reeding **Note:** Large date.

Date	Mintage	VF20	XF40	MS60	MS63	MS65
JU87-1998	—	PF65 45.00				

KM# 113.2 10 WON
30.88 g., 0.999 Silver 0.9918 oz. ASW, 40 mm. **Subject:** Korean Folk III **Obv:** National arms **Rev:** Wrestling **Edge:** Plain **Note:** Small date

Date	Mintage	VF20	XF40	MS60	MS63	MS65
JU87-1998	—	PF65 60.00				

KM# 114.1 10 WON
30.88 g., 0.999 Silver 0.9918 oz. ASW, 40 mm. **Subject:** Korean Folk V **Obv:** National arms **Rev:** Three girls jumping rope **Edge:** Segmented reeding **Note:** Large date.

Date	Mintage	VF20	XF40	MS60	MS63	MS65
JU87-1998	—	PF65 45.00				

KM# 114.2 10 WON
30.88 g., 0.999 Silver 0.9918 oz. ASW, 40 mm. **Subject:** Korean Folk V **Obv:** National arms **Rev:** Three girls jumping rope **Edge:** Plain **Note:** Small date

Date	Mintage	VF20	XF40	MS60	MS63	MS65
JU87-1998	—	PF65 60.00				

KM# 138.2 10 WON
31.10 g., 0.999 Silver 0.999 oz. ASW, 40 mm. **Subject:** Giant Panda **Obv:** National arms **Rev:** Multicolor seated Panda **Edge:** Plain

Date	Mintage	VF20	XF40	MS60	MS63	MS65
1998	—	PF65 50.00				

KM# 163 10 WON
31.00 g., 0.999 Silver 0.9957 oz. ASW, 40 mm. **Subject:** Intrepid Symbol: Tiger **Obv:** National arms **Rev:** Snarling tiger right **Edge:** Reeded and plain sections

Date	Mintage	VF20	XF40	MS60	MS63	MS65
1998	2,000	PF65 40.00				

KM# 164 10 WON
31.00 g., 0.999 Silver 0.9957 oz. ASW, 40 mm. **Subject:** 50th Anniversary - People's Republic **Obv:** National arms **Rev:** Flag, dates and value below mountains **Edge:** Reeded and plain sections

Date	Mintage	VF20	XF40	MS60	MS63	MS65
1998	1,000	PF65 42.50				

KM# 170 10 WON
31.00 g., 0.999 Silver 0.9957 oz. ASW, 40 mm. **Subject:** First North Korean Space Satellite **Obv:** National arms **Rev:** Rocket **Edge:** Reeded and plain sections

Date	Mintage	VF20	XF40	MS60	MS63	MS65
1998	—	PF65 37.50				
1999	—	PF65 37.50				

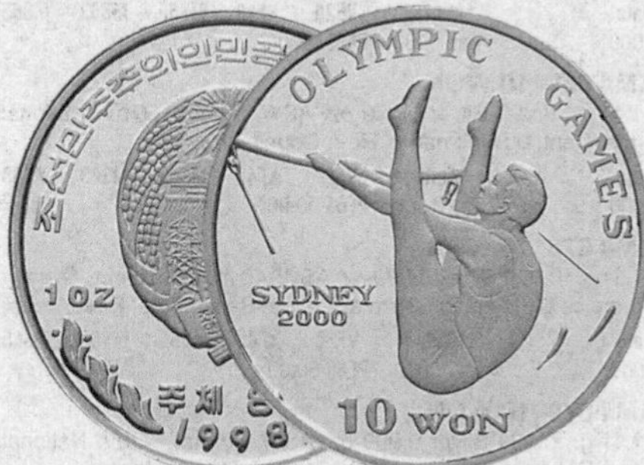

KM# 272 10 WON
31.00 g., 0.999 Silver 0.9957 oz. ASW, 40 mm. **Obv:** National arms **Rev:** Olympic gymnast on high bar **Edge:** Plain

Date	Mintage	VF20	XF40	MS60	MS63	MS65
1998	—	PF65 40.00				

KM# 103 10 WON
30.96 g., 0.999 Silver 0.9944 oz. ASW **Subject:** Year of the Rabbit **Obv:** National arms **Rev:** Multicolored rabbit with hearts with legend above

Date	Mintage	VF20	XF40	MS60	MS63	MS65
1999	—	PF65 42.50				

KM# 107 10 WON
30.96 g., 0.999 Silver 0.9944 oz. ASW **Subject:** Year of the Rabbit **Obv:** National arms **Rev:** Multicolored rabbits with hearts without legend above

Date	Mintage	VF20	XF40	MS60	MS63	MS65
1999	5,000	PF65 42.50				

KM# 108 10 WON
30.96 g., 0.999 Silver 0.9944 oz. ASW **Subject:** Blue dragon **Obv:** National arms **Rev:** Flying dragon above mountains

Date	Mintage	VF20	XF40	MS60	MS63	MS65
1999	—	PF65 45.00				

KM# 109.1 10 WON
30.96 g., 0.999 Silver 0.9944 oz. ASW **Subject:** Birds of Korea **Obv:** National arms **Rev:** White-bellied woodpecker on tree limb **Edge:** Segmented reeding **Note:** Prev. KM#109

Date	Mintage	VF20	XF40	MS60	MS63	MS65
1999	3,000	PF65 47.50				

KM# 109.2 10 WON
30.96 g., 0.999 Silver 0.9944 oz. ASW **Subject:** Birds of Korea **Obv:** National arms **Rev:** White-bellied woodpecker on tree limb **Edge:** Plain

Date	Mintage	VF20	XF40	MS60	MS63	MS65
1999	—	PF65 47.50				

KM# 166 10 WON
31.00 g., 0.999 Silver 0.9957 oz. ASW **Subject:** Birds of Korea **Obv:** National arms **Rev:** Fairy pitta on branch **Edge:** Reeded and plain sections

Date	Mintage	VF20	XF40	MS60	MS63	MS65
1999	2,000	PF65 45.00				

KM# 167 10 WON
31.00 g., 0.999 Silver 0.9957 oz. ASW, 40 mm. **Subject:** Olympic Games **Obv:** National arms **Rev:** Man jumping hurdles above kangaroo and value **Edge:** Reeded and plain sections

Date	Mintage	VF20	XF40	MS60	MS63	MS65
1999	3,000	PF65 40.00				

KM# 168 10 WON
31.00 g., 0.999 Silver 0.9957 oz. ASW, 40 mm. **Subject:** Olympic Games **Obv:** National arms **Rev:** Diver **Edge:** Reeded and plain sections

Date	Mintage	VF20	XF40	MS60	MS63	MS65
1999	3,000	PF65 40.00				

KM# 169 10 WON
31.00 g., 0.999 Silver 0.9957 oz. ASW, 40 mm. **Subject:** 7th World Track and Field Championships **Obv:** National arms **Rev:** Marathon winner Jong Song Ok **Edge:** Reeded and plain sections

Date	Mintage	VF20	XF40	MS60	MS63	MS65
1999	1,000	PF65 45.00				

KM# 171 10 WON
31.00 g., 0.999 Silver 0.9957 oz. ASW, 40 mm. **Subject:** Kim Il Sung and Zhou Enlai **Obv:** National arms **Rev:** Kim Il Sung and Zhou Enlai shaking hands **Edge:** Reeded and plain sections

Date	Mintage	VF20	XF40	MS60	MS63	MS65
1999	5,000	PF65 40.00				

KM# 223 10 WON
30.80 g., 0.999 Silver 0.9893 oz. ASW, 40.2 mm. **Subject:** Birds of Korea **Obv:** National arms **Rev:** Lyrurus Tetrix, bird on ground **Edge:** Reeded

Date	Mintage	VF20	XF40	MS60	MS63	MS65
1999	—	—	—	—	—	40.00

KM# 224 10 WON
30.80 g., 0.999 Silver 0.9893 oz. ASW, 40.2 mm. **Subject:** Birds of Korea **Obv:** National arms **Rev:** Syrrhaptes Paradoxus, bird on shore **Edge:** Reeded

Date	Mintage	VF20	XF40	MS60	MS63	MS65
1999	—	PF65 45.00				

KM# 125 10 WON
30.95 g., 0.999 Silver 0.9941 oz. ASW, 40.3 mm. **Subject:** One Korea: 3,000 Years of History **Obv:** National arms **Rev:** Radiant map and landmarks **Edge:** Segmented reeding

Date	Mintage	VF20	XF40	MS60	MS63	MS65
2000	—	PF65 45.00				

KM# 178 10 WON
31.00 g., 0.999 Silver 0.9957 oz. ASW, 40 mm. **Subject:** King Tangun **Obv:** National arms **Rev:** Bust facing **Edge:** Reeded and plain sections

Date	Mintage	VF20	XF40	MS60	MS63	MS65
2000	5,000	PF65 40.00				

KM# 228 10 WON
31.04 g., 0.999 Silver 0.997 oz. ASW, 40.3 mm. **Subject:** Hyonmu **Obv:** National arms and small legend **Rev:** Mythical creature **Edge:** Plain

Date	Mintage	VF20	XF40	MS60	MS63	MS65
2000	—	PF65 42.50				

KM# 229 10 WON
31.04 g., 0.999 Silver 0.997 oz. ASW, 40.3 mm. **Subject:** Hyonmu **Obv:** National arms with large legend **Rev:** Mythical creature **Edge:** Plain

Date	Mintage	VF20	XF40	MS60	MS63	MS65
2000	—	PF65 42.50				

KM# 276 10 WON
31.00 g., 0.999 Silver 0.9957 oz. ASW, 40.1 mm. **Obv:** National arms **Rev:** Kim greeting diplomat with Korean legend **Edge:** Plain **Note:** Similar to KM#273.

Date	Mintage	VF20	XF40	MS60	MS63	MS65
2000	—	PF65 42.50				

KM# 278 10 WON
31.00 g., 0.999 Silver 0.9957 oz. ASW, 40.1 mm. **Obv:** National arms **Rev:** Treaty signing scene **Edge:** Plain **Note:** Similar to KM#277.

Date	Mintage	VF20	XF40	MS60	MS63	MS65
2000	—	PF65 42.50				

KM# 279 10 WON
31.00 g., 0.999 Silver 0.9957 oz. ASW, 40.1 mm. **Obv:** National arms **Rev:** Kim Jong Il greeting diplomat, half length figures, Cyrillic legend **Edge:** Plain **Note:** Similar to KM#275.

Date	Mintage	VF20	XF40	MS60	MS63	MS65
2000	—	PF65 42.50				

KM# 280 10 WON
31.00 g., 0.999 Silver 0.9957 oz. ASW, 40.1 mm. **Obv:** National arms **Rev:** Kim greeting diplomat, full length view **Edge:** Plain

Date	Mintage	VF20	XF40	MS60	MS63	MS65
2000	—	PF65 42.50				

KM# 281 10 WON
31.00 g., 0.999 Silver 0.9957 oz. ASW, 40.1 mm. **Obv:** National arms **Rev:** Old couple embracing above dates and value **Edge:** Plain

Date	Mintage	VF20	XF40	MS60	MS63	MS65
2000	—	PF65 40.00				

KM# 282 10 WON
31.00 g., 0.999 Silver 0.9957 oz. ASW, 40.1 mm. **Obv:** National arms **Rev:** Two tigers **Edge:** Plain

Date	Mintage	VF20	XF40	MS60	MS63	MS65
2000	—	PF65 47.50				

KM# 348 10 WON
31.00 g., 0.999 Silver 0.9957 oz. ASW, 40.2 mm. **Obv:** National arms **Rev:** Olympic handball player **Edge:** Plain

Date	Mintage	VF20	XF40	MS60	MS63	MS65
2000	—	PF65 40.00				

KM# 350 10 WON
31.00 g., 0.999 Silver 0.9957 oz. ASW, 40.2 mm. **Obv:** National arms **Rev:** Radiant Korean map and landmarks **Edge:** Plain

Date	Mintage	VF20	XF40	MS60	MS63	MS65
2000	—	PF65 40.00				

KM# 658 10 WON
31.11 g., 0.999 Silver 0.999 oz. ASW, 40 mm. **Obv:** National arms, Central Bank name **Rev:** Two women standing nurturing young tree

Date	Mintage	VF20	XF40	MS60	MS63	MS65
2000	Est. 1000	PF65 60.00				

KM# 659 10 WON
31.11 g., 0.999 Silver 0.999 oz. ASW, 40 mm. **Obv:** National arms. Central Bank name **Rev:** Couple embrace

Date	Mintage	VF20	XF40	MS60	MS63	MS65
2000	Est. 1000	PF65 60.00				

KM# 678 10 WON
31.11 g., 0.999 Silver 0.999 oz. ASW, 40 mm. **Subject:** Sydney Olympics **Obv:** National arms, Central Bank name **Rev:** Archer

Date	Mintage	VF20	XF40	MS60	MS63	MS65
2000	Est. 3000	PF65 60.00				

KM# 679 10 WON
31.11 g., 0.999 Silver 0.999 oz. ASW, 40 mm. **Obv:** National arms, Central Bank name **Rev:** Korean Ribbon dancer

Date	Mintage	VF20	XF40	MS60	MS63	MS65
2000	Est. 3000	PF65 60.00				

KM# 689 10 WON
7.00 g., Aluminum, 40 mm. **Obv:** East gate of Pyeongyang **Rev:** Hyonmu

Date	Mintage	VF20	XF40	MS60	MS63	MS65
2000 Proof	—	—	—	—	—	—

KM# 20 20 WON
14.80 g., 0.999 Silver 0.4754 oz. ASW **Subject:** World Festival of Youth and Students **Obv:** National arms above D.P.R. of Korea, value, and date below **Rev:** Dove within circle of flower design

Date	Mintage	VF20	XF40	MS60	MS63	MS65
1989	—	PF65 28.00				

KM# 97.1 20 WON
31.10 g., 0.999 Silver 0.999 oz. ASW **Subject:** Kim Il Sung's death **Obv:** National arms above value **Rev:** Bust facing **Edge:** Plain **Note:** Prev. KM#97.

Date	Mintage	VF20	XF40	MS60	MS63	MS65
ND-1994	—	PF65 85.00				

KM# 97.2 20 WON
31.10 g., 0.999 Silver 0.999 oz. ASW **Subject:** Kim Il Sung's Death **Obv:** National arms **Rev:** Bust facing **Edge:** Reeded

Date	Mintage	VF20	XF40	MS60	MS63	MS65
ND-1994	—	PF65 50.00				

KM# 74 20 WON
Copper-Nickel **Subject:** 1998 World Cup Soccer **Obv:** National arms **Rev:** Soccer player in front of arch

Date	Mintage	VF20	XF40	MS60	MS63	MS65
1995	10,000	PF65 30.00				

KM# 94 20 WON
50.00 g., 0.999 Silver 1.6059 oz. ASW, 50 mm. **Subject:** 50th Anniversary of Liberation **Obv:** National arms **Rev:** Fairy of Mount Kumgang

Date	Mintage	VF20	XF40	MS60	MS63	MS65
1995	300	PF67 125				

Note: In proof sets only

KM# 139 20 WON
31.10 g., 0.999 Silver 0.999 oz. ASW, 40 mm. **Subject:** 50th Anniversary - Korean Workers' Party **Obv:** National arms **Rev:** Monument **Edge:** Plain

Date	Mintage	VF20	XF40	MS60	MS63	MS65
1995	—	—	—	—	—	45.00

KM# 140 20 WON
22.00 g., Copper-Nickel, 40 mm. **Subject:** 25th Basel International Coin Show **Obv:** National arms above phone fax and telex numbers **Rev:** Multicolor island and seascape **Edge:** Plain

Date	Mintage	VF20	XF40	MS60	MS63	MS65
1996	1,000	—	—	—	—	20.00

KM# 513 20 WON
22.00 g., Copper-Nickel, 40 mm. **Subject:** Singapore International Coin Show **Obv:** National arms **Rev:** Globe in color

Date	Mintage	VF20	XF40	MS60	MS63	MS65
1996	Est. 200	—	—	—	—	—

KM# 516 20 WON
31.11 g., 0.999 Silver 0.999 oz. ASW, 40 mm. **Obv:** National arms **Rev:** Star, wreath, torch, fields, power transmission tower and lines

Date	Mintage	VF20	XF40	MS60	MS63	MS65
1996	—	PF65 85.00				

KM# 683 20 WON
16.00 g., Brass, 35 mm. **Obv:** East gate of Pyeongyang **Rev:** Sail training ship Duchess Anne

Date	Mintage	VF20	XF40	MS60	MS63	MS65
2000	—	PF65 7.00				

KM# 684 20 WON
16.00 g., Brass, 35 mm. **Obv:** East gate of Pyeongyang **Rev:** Sail training vessel Dar Pomorza

Date	Mintage	VF20	XF40	MS60	MS63	MS65
2000	—	PF65 7.00				

KM# 685 20 WON
16.00 g., Brass, 35 mm. **Obv:** East gate of Pyeongyang **Rev:** Sail training vessel Statsraad Lehmkuhl

Date	Mintage	VF20	XF40	MS60	MS63	MS65
2000	—	PF65 7.00				

KM# 26 30 WON
17.02 g., 0.999 Silver 0.5467 oz. ASW **Subject:** Friendship Art Festival **Obv:** National arms **Rev:** Head 3/4 left with hand holding microphone

Date	Mintage	VF20	XF40	MS60	MS63	MS65
1989	—	PF65 40.00				

KM# 52 50 WON
17.02 g., 0.999 Silver 0.5467 oz. ASW **Subject:** 80th Birthday of Kim Il Sung **Obv:** National arms **Rev:** Kim Il Sung birthplace

Date	Mintage	VF20	XF40	MS60	MS63	MS65
1992	1,000	PF65 40.00				

KM# 54 50 WON
17.02 g., 0.999 Silver 0.5467 oz. ASW **Subject:** 80th Birthday of Kim Il Sung **Obv:** National arms **Rev:** Bust facing

Date	Mintage	VF20	XF40	MS60	MS63	MS65
1992	1,000	PF65 45.00				

KM# 56 50 WON
17.02 g., 0.999 Silver 0.5467 oz. ASW **Subject:** 50th Birthday of Kim Jong Il **Obv:** National arms **Rev:** Bust facing

Date	Mintage	VF20	XF40	MS60	MS63	MS65
1992	—	PF65 50.00				

KM# 88 50 WON
Copper-Nickel **Subject:** Sportsfest **Obv:** National arms **Rev:** Wrestlers

Date	Mintage	VF20	XF40	MS60	MS63	MS65
1995	—	—	—	—	22.50	25.00

KM# 141 50 WON
12.90 g., Copper-Nickel, 30 mm. **Subject:** International Friendship Exhibition **Obv:** National arms **Rev:** Building **Edge:** Plain

Date	Mintage	VF20	XF40	MS60	MS63	MS65
1995	—	—	—	—	10.00	12.00

KM# 142 50 WON
12.90 g., Copper-Nickel, 30 mm. **Subject:** May Day Stadium **Obv:** National arms **Rev:** Stadium **Edge:** Plain

Date	Mintage	VF20	XF40	MS60	MS63	MS65
1995	—	—	—	—	10.00	12.00

KM# 28 100 WON

3.13 g., 0.999 Gold 0.1005 oz. AGW **Subject:** 40th Anniversary of People's Republic **Obv:** National arms **Rev:** Leaping equestrian

Date	Mintage	VF20	XF40	MS60	MS63	MS65
1988	—	PF65 175	PF67 190			

KM# 70 100 WON

7.00 g., 0.999 Silver 0.2248 oz. ASW **Obv:** National arms **Rev:** Two multicolored Adelie penguins

Date	Mintage	VF20	XF40	MS60	MS63	MS65
1995	—	PF65 45.00				

KM# 71 100 WON

7.00 g., 0.999 Silver 0.2248 oz. ASW **Subject:** 1996 Olympics **Obv:** National arms **Rev:** Sprinter

Date	Mintage	VF20	XF40	MS60	MS63	MS65
1995	30,000	PF65 30.00				

KM# 72 100 WON

7.00 g., 0.999 Silver 0.2248 oz. ASW **Subject:** 1998 World Cup Soccer **Obv:** National arms **Rev:** Eiffel tower and soccer player

Date	Mintage	VF20	XF40	MS60	MS63	MS65
1995	30,000	PF65 30.00				

KM# 104 100 WON

7.00 g., 0.999 Silver 0.2248 oz. ASW **Subject:** Aix Galericulata **Obv:** National arms **Rev:** Multicolor pair of mandarin ducks

Date	Mintage	VF20	XF40	MS60	MS63	MS65
1995	Est. 30000	PF65 40.00				

KM# 122 100 WON

7.00 g., 0.999 Silver 0.2248 oz. ASW, 30 mm. **Subject:** Robinson Crusoe **Obv:** National arms **Rev:** Multicolor row boat scene **Edge:** Plain

Date	Mintage	VF20	XF40	MS60	MS63	MS65
1996	—	PF65 40.00				

KM# 422 100 WON

7.00 g., 0.999 Silver 0.2248 oz. ASW, 30 mm. **Subject:** Return of Hong Kong **Obv:** State emblem **Rev:** Houseboat **Edge:** Plain

Date	Mintage	VF20	XF40	MS60	MS63	MS65
1996	—	PF65 25.00				

KM# 517 100 WON

7.00 g., 0.999 Silver 0.2248 oz. ASW, 30 mm. **Obv:** National arms **Rev:** Koala in color

Date	Mintage	VF20	XF40	MS60	MS63	MS65
1996	Est. 10000	PF65 35.00				

KM# 518 100 WON

7.00 g., 0.999 Silver 0.2248 oz. ASW, 30 mm. **Obv:** National arms **Rev:** Two pandas in color

Date	Mintage	VF20	XF40	MS60	MS63	MS65
1996	Est. 10000	PF65 35.00				

KM# 519 100 WON

7.00 g., 0.999 Silver 0.2248 oz. ASW, 29 mm. **Obv:** National arms **Rev:** Robbin Hood in color

Date	Mintage	VF20	XF40	MS60	MS63	MS65
1996	—	PF65 35.00				

KM# 525 100 WON

7.00 g., 0.999 Silver 0.2248 oz. ASW, 30 mm. **Obv:** National arms **Rev:** Junk in Victoria Harbor and Hong Kong skyline in background

Date	Mintage	VF20	XF40	MS60	MS63	MS65
1996	Est. 10000	PF65 50.00				

KM# 529 100 WON

3.10 g., 0.999 Gold 0.0996 oz. AGW, 18 mm. **Obv:** National arms **Rev:** Houseboat before temple

Date	Mintage	VF20	XF40	MS60	MS63	MS65
1996	Est. 2500	PF67 275				

KM# 530 100 WON

3.10 g., 0.999 Gold 0.0996 oz. AGW, 18 mm. **Obv:** National arms **Rev:** Junk in Victoria Harbor with Hong Kong in background

Date	Mintage	VF20	XF40	MS60	MS63	MS65
1996	Est. 2500	PF67 275				

KM# 532 100 WON

3.10 g., 0.999 Gold 0.0996 oz. AGW, 18 mm. **Subject:** Kaesong - Sinuiju Railroad **Obv:** National arms **Rev:** Steam engine and mountains in color

Date	Mintage	VF20	XF40	MS60	MS63	MS65
1996	—	PF67 275				

KM# 449 100 WON

7.00 g., 0.999 Silver 0.2248 oz. ASW, 30.04 mm. **Obv:** National arms **Rev:** Olympic flame above kangeroo left on outlined map of Australia - multicolors **Rev. Legend:** XXVII JEUX OLYPIQUES SYDNEY 2000 **Edge:** Plain

Date	Mintage	VF20	XF40	MS60	MS63	MS65
1997	—	PF65 25.00	PF67 30.00			

KM# 450 100 WON

7.00 g., 0.999 Silver 0.2248 oz. ASW, 30.04 mm. **Obv:** National arms **Rev:** Olympic flame at center, kangeroo at left on large outlined map of Australia **Rev. Legend:** OLIMPIADA SYDNEY 2000 **Edge:** Plain

Date	Mintage	VF20	XF40	MS60	MS63	MS65
1997	—	PF65 25.00	PF67 30.00			

KM# 451 100 WON

7.00 g., 0.999 Silver 0.2248 oz. ASW, 30.04 mm. **Obv:** National arms **Rev:** Sydney Opera House at center right, bridge in background, multicolored **Rev. Legend:** OLYMPIC GAMES SYDNEY 2000 **Edge:** Plain

Date	Mintage	VF20	XF40	MS60	MS63	MS65
1997	—	PF65 25.00	PF67 30.00			

KM# 524 100 WON

7.00 g., 0.999 Silver 0.2248 oz. ASW, 30 mm. **Obv:** National arms **Rev:** Signing of the 1898 lease for Hong Kong

Date	Mintage	VF20	XF40	MS60	MS63	MS65
1997	Est. 10000	PF65 50.00				

KM# 528 100 WON

3.10 g., 0.999 Gold 0.0996 oz. AGW, 18 mm. **Obv:** National arms **Rev:** Signing of the 1898 lease for Hong Kong

Date	Mintage	VF20	XF40	MS60	MS63	MS65
1997	Est. 2500	PF67 275				

KM# 545 100 WON

7.00 g., 0.999 Silver 0.2248 oz. ASW, 30 mm. **Obv:** National arms, name of the Central Bank **Rev:** Two pandas in color

Date	Mintage	VF20	XF40	MS60	MS63	MS65
1997	Est. 10000	PF65 30.00				

KM# 596 100 WON

7.00 g., 0.999 Silver 0.2248 oz. ASW, 30 mm. **Obv:** National arms, Central Bank name **Rev:** Three pandas in color

Date	Mintage	VF20	XF40	MS60	MS63	MS65
1998	Est. 10000	PF65 30.00				

KM# 628 100 WON

7.00 g., 0.999 Silver 0.2248 oz. ASW, 30 mm. **Obv:** National arms, Central Bank name **Rev:** Polar bear and two cubs on ice flow in color

Date	Mintage	VF20	XF40	MS60	MS63	MS65
1999	Est. 10000	PF65 30.00				

KM# 629 100 WON

7.00 g., 0.999 Silver 0.2248 oz. ASW, 30 mm. **Obv:** National arms, Central Bank name **Rev:** Brown bear in color

Date	Mintage	VF20	XF40	MS60	MS63	MS65
1999	Est. 10000	PF65 35.00				

KM# 630 100 WON

7.00 g., 0.999 Silver 0.2248 oz. ASW, 30 mm. **Obv:** National arms, Central Bank name **Rev:** Black bear in color

Date	Mintage	VF20	XF40	MS60	MS63	MS65
1999	Est. 10000	PF65 35.00				

KM# 631 100 WON

7.00 g., 0.999 Silver 0.2248 oz. ASW, 30 mm. **Obv:** National arms, Central Bank name **Rev:** Panda on branch in color

Date	Mintage	VF20	XF40	MS60	MS63	MS65
1999	Est. 10000	PF65 30.00				

KM# 49 200 WON

14.97 g., 0.999 Silver 0.4808 oz. ASW **Subject:** Olympics **Obv:** Silver content statement divided by national arms **Rev:** Equestrian

Date	Mintage	VF20	XF40	MS60	MS63	MS65
1991	25,000	PF65 27.50				

KM# 50 200 WON
14.97 g., 0.999 Silver 0.4808 oz. ASW **Subject:** Olympics **Obv:** Silver content statement below national arms **Rev:** Equestrian

Date	Mintage	VF20	XF40	MS60	MS63	MS65
1991	Inc. above	PF65 25.00				

KM# 64 200 WON
15.00 g., 0.999 Silver 0.4818 oz. ASW **Subject:** Summer Olympic Games - Barcelona 1992 **Obv:** National arms **Rev:** Sprinter

Date	Mintage	VF20	XF40	MS60	MS63	MS65
1992	25,000	PF65 22.50				

KM# 95.1 200 WON
8.00 g., 0.999 Gold 0.2569 oz. AGW **Subject:** 50th Anniversary of Liberation **Obv:** National arms **Rev:** Turtle ship **Note:** Prev. KM#95.

Date	Mintage	VF20	XF40	MS60	MS63	MS65
1995	300	PF67 475				

KM# 95.2 200 WON
8.00 g., 0.999 Gold 0.2569 oz. AGW, 25 mm. **Subject:** 50th Anniversary of Liberation **Obv:** National arms with fineness closer to arms **Rev:** Turtle ship

Date	Mintage	VF20	XF40	MS60	MS63	MS65
1995	—	PF67 475				

KM# 29 250 WON
7.78 g., 0.999 Gold 0.2499 oz. AGW **Subject:** 40th Anniversary of People's Republic **Obv:** National arms **Rev:** Leaping equestrian

Date	Mintage	VF20	XF40	MS60	MS63	MS65
1988	—	PF67 450				

KM# 21 250 WON
7.77 g., 0.999 Gold 0.2496 oz. AGW **Subject:** World Festival of Youth and Students **Obv:** National arms above D.P.R. of Korea, value and date **Rev:** Flower design

Date	Mintage	VF20	XF40	MS60	MS63	MS65
1989	—	PF67 475				

KM# 423 250 WON
15.00 g., 0.999 Silver 0.4818 oz. ASW, 35.1 mm. **Subject:** Retrun of Hong Kong **Obv:** National arms **Rev:** Multicolor Junk and city view **Edge:** Plain

Date	Mintage	VF20	XF40	MS60	MS63	MS65
1996	—	PF65 35.00				

KM# 527 250 WON
15.00 g., 0.999 Silver 0.4818 oz. ASW, 35 mm. **Obv:** National arms **Rev:** Houseboat before temple, in color

Date	Mintage	VF20	XF40	MS60	MS63	MS65
1996	—	PF65 55.00				

KM# 533 250 WON
7.75 g., 0.999 Gold 0.2489 oz. AGW, 22 mm. **Subject:** Kaesong - Sinuiju Railroad **Obv:** National arms **Rev:** Steam locomotive and workers in valley in color

Date	Mintage	VF20	XF40	MS60	MS63	MS65
1996	Est. 1000	PF67 500				

KM# 526 250 WON
15.00 g., 0.999 Silver 0.4818 oz. ASW, 35 mm. **Obv:** National arms **Rev:** Signing of the 1898 lease for Hong Kong in color

Date	Mintage	VF20	XF40	MS60	MS63	MS65
1997	Est. 5000	PF65 55.00				

KM# 565 250 WON
15.00 g., 0.999 Silver 0.4818 oz. ASW, 35 mm. **Obv:** National arms, name of the Central Bank **Rev:** Kangaroo

Date	Mintage	VF20	XF40	MS60	MS63	MS65
1997	—	PF65 45.00				

KM# 566 250 WON
15.00 g., 0.999 Silver 0.4818 oz. ASW, 35 mm. **Obv:** National arms, name of the Central Bank **Rev:** Map of Australia

Date	Mintage	VF20	XF40	MS60	MS63	MS65
1997	—	PF65 45.00				

KM# 567 250 WON
15.00 g., 0.999 Silver 0.4818 oz. ASW, 35 mm. **Obv:** Naitonal arms, name of the Central Bank **Rev:** Sydney Opera house

Date	Mintage	VF20	XF40	MS60	MS63	MS65
1997	—	PF65 45.00				

KM# 116 250 WON
20.00 g., 0.999 Silver 0.6424 oz. ASW **Subject:** Millennium **Obv:** National arms above value **Rev:** Dragon **Shape:** Rectangular

Date	Mintage	VF20	XF40	MS60	MS63	MS65
1998//2000	—	PF65 45.00				

KM# 597 250 WON
15.00 g., 0.999 Silver 0.4818 oz. ASW, 35 mm. **Obv:** National arms **Rev:** Spring in color

Date	Mintage	VF20	XF40	MS60	MS63	MS65
1998	—	PF67 85.00				

KM# 598 250 WON
15.00 g., 0.999 Silver 0.4818 oz. ASW, 35 mm. **Obv:** National arms **Rev:** Summer in color

Date	Mintage	VF20	XF40	MS60	MS63	MS65
1998	—	PF67 85.00				

KM# 599 250 WON
15.00 g., 0.999 Silver 0.4818 oz. ASW, 35 mm. **Obv:** National arms **Rev:** Fall in color

Date	Mintage	VF20	XF40	MS60	MS63	MS65
1998	—	PF67 85.00				

KM# 600 250 WON
15.00 g., 0.999 Silver 0.4818 oz. ASW, 35 mm. **Obv:** National arms **Rev:** Winter in color

Date	Mintage	VF20	XF40	MS60	MS63	MS65
1998	—	PF67 85.00				

KM# 601 250 WON
15.50 g., 0.999 Silver 0.4978 oz. ASW **Obv:** National arms **Rev:** Greater pairis titmouse in color **Shape:** Rectangle

Date	Mintage	VF20	XF40	MS60	MS63	MS65
1998	—	PF67 110				

KM# 602 250 WON
15.50 g., 0.999 Silver 0.4978 oz. ASW **Obv:** National arms **Rev:** Black neck oriole in color **Shape:** Rectangle

Date	Mintage	VF20	XF40	MS60	MS63	MS65
1998	—	PF67 110				

KM# 603 250 WON
15.50 g., 0.999 Silver 0.4978 oz. ASW **Obv:** National arms **Rev:** Ruby-throated hummingbird in color **Shape:** Rectangle

Date	Mintage	VF20	XF40	MS60	MS63	MS65
1998	—	PF67 110				

KM# 604 250 WON
15.50 g., 0.999 Silver 0.4978 oz. ASW **Obv:** National arms **Rev:** Yellow helena in color **Shape:** Rectangle

Date	Mintage	VF20	XF40	MS60	MS63	MS65
1998	—	PF67 110				

KM# 605 250 WON
15.50 g., 0.999 Silver 0.4978 oz. ASW **Obv:** National arms **Rev:** Large aurorafalter in color **Shape:** Rectangle

Date	Mintage	VF20	XF40	MS60	MS63	MS65
1998	—	PF67 110				

KM# 606 250 WON
15.50 g., 0.999 Silver 0.4978 oz. ASW **Obv:** National arms **Rev:** Indian skipper butterfly in color **Shape:** Rectangle

Date	Mintage	VF20	XF40	MS60	MS63	MS65
1998	—	PF67 110				

KM# 607 250 WON
20.00 g., 0.999 Silver 0.6424 oz. ASW, 42x24 mm. **Obv:** National arms, Central Bank name **Rev:** Ship Hamburg **Shape:** Rectangle

Date	Mintage	VF20	XF40	MS60	MS63	MS65
1998	—	PF65 70.00				

KM# 225 250 WON
14.96 g., 0.999 Silver 0.4805 oz. ASW, 34.9 mm. **Subject:** Beethoven **Obv:** National arms **Rev:** Bust 3/4 left writing **Edge:** Plain

Date	Mintage	VF20	XF40	MS60	MS63	MS65
1999	—	PF65 35.00				

KM# 96 400 WON
16.00 g., Gold **Subject:** 50th Anniversary of Liberation **Obv:** National arms **Rev:** Lake on Mount Baektu

Date	Mintage	VF20	XF40	MS60	MS63	MS65
1995	100	PF67 875				

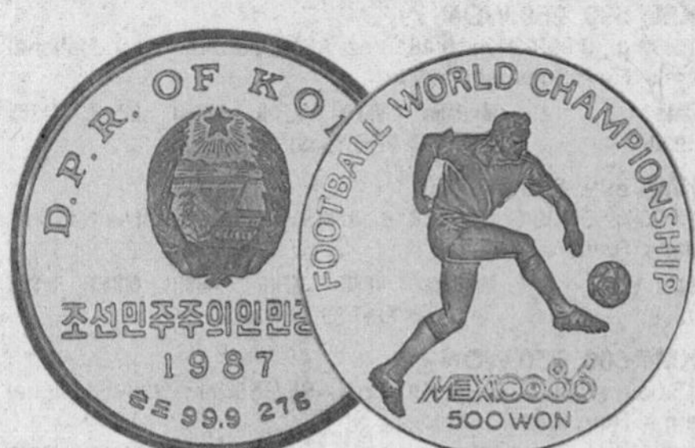

KM# 39 500 WON
27.00 g., 0.999 Silver 0.8672 oz. ASW **Subject:** World Championship Soccer - Mexico '96 **Obv:** National arms **Rev:** Soccer player

Date	Mintage	VF20	XF40	MS60	MS63	MS65
1987	—	PF65 37.50				

KM# 16 500 WON
27.00 g., 0.999 Silver 0.8672 oz. ASW **Series:** Winter Olympics **Subject:** Hockey **Obv:** National arms **Rev:** Hockey sticks and puck

Date	Mintage	VF20	XF40	MS60	MS63	MS65
1988	20,000	PF65 32.50				

KM# 17 500 WON
27.00 g., 0.999 Silver 0.8672 oz. ASW **Subject:** 30th Anniversary of Gorch Fock **Obv:** National arms **Rev:** Ship at sea **Edge:** Plain

Date	Mintage	VF20	XF40	MS60	MS63	MS65
1988	—	PF65 37.50				

KM# 24 500 WON
27.00 g., 0.999 Silver 0.8672 oz. ASW **Subject:** World Championship Soccer **Obv:** National arms above date and D.P.R. of Korea **Rev:** Soccer player

Date	Mintage	VF20	XF40	MS60	MS63	MS65
1988	—	PF65 30.00				

KM# 30 500 WON
15.57 g., 0.999 Gold 0.5001 oz. AGW **Subject:** 40th Anniversary of People's Republic **Obv:** National arms **Rev:** Leaping equestrian

Date	Mintage	VF20	XF40	MS60	MS63	MS65
1988	—	PF67 925				

KM# 36 500 WON
27.00 g., 0.999 Silver 0.8672 oz. ASW **Series:** F.A.O. **Subject:** Food for all **Obv:** National arms **Obv. Legend:** D.P.R. OF KOREA **Rev:** Farmer planting rice, FAO logo to right **Rev. Legend:** FOOD FOR ALL / 500 WON **Edge:** Plain

Date	Mintage	VF20	XF40	MS60	MS63	MS65
1988	Est. 2000	PF65 50.00				

KM# 27 500 WON
27.00 g., 0.999 Silver 0.8672 oz. ASW **Subject:** Amerigo Vespucci **Obv:** National arms **Rev:** Head left at right, map of 'Americas' at left

Date	Mintage	VF20	XF40	MS60	MS63	MS65
1989	—	PF65 42.50				

KM# 32 500 WON
31.82 g., 0.999 Silver 1.022 oz. ASW, 40 mm. **Obv:** National arms above date and sprigs **Rev:** Fairy of Mount Kumgang playing a flute **Edge:** Segmented reeding **Note:** Sectional reeding as follows - IIIIII II IIIIII II IIIIII.

Date	Mintage	VF20	XF40	MS60	MS63	MS65
1989	—	PF65 50.00				
Note: Number 1 in date without bottom serif						
1989	—	PF65 55.00				

KM# 32.1 500 WON
31.82 g., 0.999 Silver 1.022 oz. ASW, 40 mm. **Obv:** Number 1 in date without serifs **Rev:** Fairy of Mount Kumgang playing a flute **Edge:** Plain

Date	Mintage	VF20	XF40	MS60	MS63	MS65
1989	—	PF65 50.00				

KM# 33 500 WON
27.00 g., 0.999 Silver 0.8672 oz. ASW **Series:** Calgary Winter Olympics **Obv:** National arms **Rev:** Figure skater

Date	Mintage	VF20	XF40	MS60	MS63	MS65
1989	—	PF65 37.50				

KM# 34 500 WON
27.00 g., 0.999 Silver 0.8672 oz. ASW **Series:** Barcelona Summer Olympics **Obv:** National arms **Rev:** Discus thrower

Date	Mintage	VF20	XF40	MS60	MS63	MS65
1989	—	PF65 37.50				

KM# 37 500 WON
27.00 g., 0.999 Silver 0.8672 oz. ASW **Subject:** World Championship Soccer **Obv:** National arms **Rev:** Player kicking ball

Date	Mintage	VF20	XF40	MS60	MS63	MS65
1989	15,000	PF65 50.00				

KM# 38 500 WON
27.00 g., 0.999 Silver 0.8672 oz. ASW **Subject:** World Championship Soccer **Obv:** National arms **Rev:** Goalie

Date	Mintage	VF20	XF40	MS60	MS63	MS65
1989	—	PF65 30.00				

KM# 40 500 WON
31.82 g., 0.999 Silver 1.022 oz. ASW **Subject:** Olympic table tennis **Obv:** National arms **Rev:** Table tennis player

Date	Mintage	VF20	XF40	MS60	MS63	MS65
1990	15,000	PF65 38.00				

KM# 41 500 WON
31.82 g., 0.999 Silver 1.022 oz. ASW **Subject:** Endangered Wildlife **Obv:** National arms **Rev:** Red-crowned crane

Date	Mintage	VF20	XF40	MS60	MS63	MS65
1990	—	PF65 45.00				

KM# 44 500 WON
31.10 g., 0.999 Silver 0.9989 oz. ASW **Subject:** World Championship Table Tennis **Obv:** National arms **Rev:** Two male players on doubles team

Date	Mintage	VF20	XF40	MS60	MS63	MS65
1991	5,000	PF65 38.00				

KM# 45 500 WON
31.10 g., 0.999 Silver 0.9989 oz. ASW **Subject:** World Championship Table Tennis **Obv:** National arms **Rev:** Male player

Date	Mintage	VF20	XF40	MS60	MS63	MS65
1991	5,000	PF65 38.00				

KM# 46 500 WON
31.10 g., 0.999 Silver 0.9989 oz. ASW **Subject:** 41st World Table Tennis Championships **Obv:** National arms **Rev:** Table tennis player

Date	Mintage	VF20	XF40	MS60	MS63	MS65
1991	5,000	PF65 40.00				

KM# 47 500 WON
31.10 g., 0.999 Silver 0.9989 oz. ASW **Subject:** 41st World Table Tennis Championships **Obv:** National arms **Rev:** Three busts facing above trophy

Date	Mintage	VF20	XF40	MS60	MS63	MS65
1991	10,000	PF65 38.00				

KM# 48 500 WON
27.00 g., 0.999 Silver 0.8672 oz. ASW **Subject:** First Armoured Ship **Obv:** National arms **Rev:** First armoured ship above value

Date	Mintage	VF20	XF40	MS60	MS63	MS65
1991	Est. 10000	PF65 50.00				

KM# 63 500 WON
27.00 g., 0.999 Silver 0.8672 oz. ASW **Series:** Olympics **Obv:** National arms **Rev:** Women's volleyball

Date	Mintage	VF20	XF40	MS60	MS63	MS65
1991	15,000	PF65 37.50				

KM# 59 500 WON
27.00 g., 0.999 Silver 0.8672 oz. ASW **Subject:** Environmental Protection **Obv:** National arms **Rev:** Flowers

Date	Mintage	VF20	XF40	MS60	MS63	MS65
1992	1,000	PF65 55.00				

KM# 144 500 WON
27.00 g., 0.999 Silver 0.8672 oz. ASW, 35 mm. **Subject:** 1994 World Cup Soccer **Obv:** National arms **Rev:** Three soccer players **Edge:** Plain

Date	Mintage	VF20	XF40	MS60	MS63	MS65
1992	—	—	—	—	—	37.50

KM# 60 500 WON
27.00 g., 0.999 Silver 0.8672 oz. ASW **Series:** 1994 Olympics **Obv:** National arms **Rev:** Speed skating

Date	Mintage	VF20	XF40	MS60	MS63	MS65
1993	1,000	PF65 32.50				

KM# 61 500 WON
27.00 g., 0.999 Silver 0.8672 oz. ASW **Series:** 1994 Olympics **Obv:** National arms **Rev:** Two-man bobsled

Date	Mintage	VF20	XF40	MS60	MS63	MS65
1993	1,000	PF65 42.50				

KM# 62.1 500 WON
31.10 g., 0.999 Silver 0.999 oz. ASW, 40.3 mm. **Series:** Prehistoric Animals **Obv:** National arms **Rev:** Brontosaurus **Edge:** Reeded **Note:** Prev. KM#62.

Date	Mintage	VF20	XF40	MS60	MS63	MS65
1993	—	—	—	—	—	—
1993	—	PF65 42.50				

KM# 145 500 WON
31.10 g., 0.999 Silver 0.999 oz. ASW, 40 mm. **Subject:** 1994 World Cup Soccer **Obv:** National arms **Rev:** Two players and trophy cup **Edge:** Plain

Date	Mintage	VF20	XF40	MS60	MS63	MS65
1994	—	—	—	—	—	45.00

KM# 62.2 500 WON
31.10 g., 0.999 Silver 0.999 oz. ASW, 40.3 mm. **Series:** Prehistoric Animals **Obv:** National arms **Rev:** More vegetation by dinosaur's foot **Edge:** Reeded

Date	Mintage	VF20	XF40	MS60	MS63	MS65
1995	—	PF65 55.00				

KM# 67 500 WON
31.10 g., 0.999 Silver 0.999 oz. ASW **Series:** 1996 Atlanta Olympics **Obv:** National arms **Rev:** Relay racers

Date	Mintage	VF20	XF40	MS60	MS63	MS65
1995	—	PF65 42.50				

KM# 68 500 WON
31.10 g., 0.999 Silver 0.999 oz. ASW, 40 mm. **Series:** 1996 Atlanta Olympics **Obv:** National arms **Rev:** Equestrian **Edge:** Plain

Date	Mintage	VF20	XF40	MS60	MS63	MS65
1995	—	PF65 42.50				

KM# 69 500 WON
31.10 g., 0.999 Silver 0.999 oz. ASW **Subject:** Fauna of Asia **Obv:** National arms above date and sprigs **Rev:** Multicolor tiger

Date	Mintage	VF20	XF40	MS60	MS63	MS65
1995	20,000	PF65 45.00	PF67 50.00			

KM# 75 500 WON
31.10 g., 0.999 Silver 0.999 oz. ASW **Subject:** 1998 World Cup Soccer **Obv:** National arms **Rev:** Soccer player in front of arch

Date	Mintage	VF20	XF40	MS60	MS63	MS65
1995	10,000	PF65 45.00	PF67 50.00			

KM# 76 500 WON
31.10 g., 0.999 Silver 0.999 oz. ASW **Subject:** Fauna of Asia **Obv:** National arms **Rev:** Multicolor panda

Date	Mintage	VF20	XF40	MS60	MS63	MS65
1995	20,000	PF65 45.00	PF67 50.00			

KM# 77 500 WON
31.10 g., 0.999 Silver 0.999 oz. ASW **Subject:** Fauna of Asia **Obv:** National arms **Rev:** Multicolor parrot

Date	Mintage	VF20	XF40	MS60	MS63	MS65
1995	20,000	PF65 45.00	PF67 50.00			

KM# 78 500 WON
31.10 g., 0.999 Silver 0.999 oz. ASW **Subject:** Fauna of Asia **Obv:** National arms **Rev:** Multicolor eagle

Date	Mintage	VF20	XF40	MS60	MS63	MS65
1995	20,000	PF65 45.00	PF67 50.00			

KM# 79 500 WON
31.10 g., 0.999 Silver 0.999 oz. ASW **Subject:** Fauna of Asia **Obv:** National arms **Rev:** Multicolor Eurasian eagle owl

Date	Mintage	VF20	XF40	MS60	MS63	MS65
1995	20,000	PF65 50.00	PF67 55.00			

KM# 80 500 WON
31.10 g., 0.999 Silver 0.999 oz. ASW **Subject:** Fauna of Asia **Obv:** National arms **Rev:** Two multicolor falcated ducks **Note:** Enameled.

Date	Mintage	VF20	XF40	MS60	MS63	MS65
1995	20,000	PF65 45.00	PF67 50.00			

KM# 143 500 WON
31.10 g., 0.999 Silver 0.999 oz. ASW, 40 mm. **Subject:** International Sport and Culture Festival **Obv:** National arms **Rev:** Head facing **Edge:** Plain

Date	Mintage	VF20	XF40	MS60	MS63	MS65
1995	—	—	—	—	—	40.00

KM# 146 500 WON
17.00 g., 0.999 Silver 0.546 oz. ASW **Series:** F.A.O. **Subject:** F.A.O. 50 Years **Obv:** National arms **Rev:** F.A.O. logo above dates and value within chain-like sprigs **Edge:** Plain

Date	Mintage	VF20	XF40	MS60	MS63	MS65
1995	—	PF65 35.00				

KM# 510 500 WON
31.11 g., 0.999 Silver 0.999 oz. ASW, 40 mm. **Subject:** Atlanta Summer Olympics, 1996 **Obv:** National arms **Rev:** Torch relay in color

Date	Mintage	VF20	XF40	MS60	MS63	MS65
1995	Est. 20000	PF65 50.00	PF67 60.00			

KM# 89 500 WON
31.10 g., 0.999 Silver 0.999 oz. ASW multi-color **Series:** Olympics **Obv:** National arms **Rev:** Two eurythmic gymnasts

Date	Mintage	VF20	XF40	MS60	MS63	MS65
1996	1,000	—	—	—	—	65.00

KM# 90 500 WON
31.10 g., 0.999 Silver 0.999 oz. ASW **Series:** Olympics **Obv:** National arms **Rev:** Soccer

Date	Mintage	VF20	XF40	MS60	MS63	MS65
1996	30,000	—	—	—	—	45.00

KM# 91 500 WON
31.10 g., 0.999 Silver 0.999 oz. ASW **Subject:** Fauna of Asia **Obv:** National arms **Rev:** Multicolor holographic panda

Date	Mintage	VF20	XF40	MS60	MS63	MS65
1996	5,000	PF67 60.00				

KM# 106 500 WON
31.52 g., 0.999 Silver 1.0124 oz. ASW **Subject:** Fauna of Asia **Obv:** National arms **Rev:** Multicolor hologram of tiger

Date	Mintage	VF20	XF40	MS60	MS63	MS65
1996	—	PF67 60.00				

KM# 117 500 WON
31.10 g., 0.999 Silver 0.999 oz. ASW **Subject:** Fauna of Asia **Obv:** National arms **Rev:** Multicolor pearl gourami

Date	Mintage	VF20	XF40	MS60	MS63	MS65
1996	—	PF65 45.00	PF67 50.00			

KM# 118 500 WON
31.10 g., 0.999 Silver 0.999 oz. ASW **Subject:** Fauna of Asia **Obv:** National arms **Rev:** Multicolor clown loach

Date	Mintage	VF20	XF40	MS60	MS63	MS65
1996	—	PF65 45.00	PF67 50.00			

KM# 119 500 WON
31.10 g., 0.999 Silver 0.999 oz. ASW **Subject:** Fauna of Asia **Obv:** National arms **Rev:** Multicolor long-tailed angelfish

Date	Mintage	VF20	XF40	MS60	MS63	MS65
1996	—	PF65 45.00	PF67 50.00			

KM# 154 500 WON
27.00 g., 0.999 Silver 0.8672 oz. ASW, 35.2 mm. **Subject:** First Asian Gymnastic Championship **Obv:** National arms **Rev:** Multicolor panda holding logo **Edge:** Coarse and finely reeded sections

Date	Mintage	VF20	XF40	MS60	MS63	MS65
1996	—	PF67 60.00				

KM# 421 500 WON
31.10 g., 0.999 Silver 0.999 oz. ASW, 40 mm. **Obv:** National arms **Rev:** Multicolor lenticular hologram panda and tiger heads only one of which can be seen at a time **Edge:** Plain

Date	Mintage	VF20	XF40	MS60	MS63	MS65
1996	—	PF65 40.00	PF67 45.00			

KM# 511 500 WON
31.11 g., 0.999 Silver 0.999 oz. ASW, 40 mm. **Subject:** World Cup Soccer, 1998 **Obv:** National arms **Rev:** Player in front of the Eiffel Tower in color

Date	Mintage	VF20	XF40	MS60	MS63	MS65
1996	Est. 10000	PF65 45.00	PF67 50.00			

KM# 512 500 WON
31.11 g., 0.999 Silver 0.999 oz. ASW, 40 mm. **Obv:** National arms **Rev:** Sydney opera house in color

Date	Mintage	VF20	XF40	MS60	MS63	MS65
1996	Est. 20000	PF65 45.00	PF67 50.00			

KM# 520 500 WON
31.11 g., 0.999 Silver 0.999 oz. ASW, 40 mm. **Obv:** National arms **Rev:** Roald Amundsen and Robert Scott and South Pole in color

Date	Mintage	VF20	XF40	MS60	MS63	MS65
1996	Est. 10000	PF65 45.00	PF67 50.00			

KM# 521 500 WON
31.11 g., 0.999 Silver 0.999 oz. ASW, 40 mm. **Obv:** National arms **Rev:** Animal in color

Date	Mintage	VF20	XF40	MS60	MS63	MS65
1996	1,950	PF65 50.00	PF67 55.00			

KM# 522 500 WON
31.11 g., 0.999 Silver 0.999 oz. ASW, 40 mm. **Obv:** National arms **Rev:** Pennant fish in color

Date	Mintage	VF20	XF40	MS60	MS63	MS65
1996	1,950	PF65 50.00	PF67 55.00			

KM# 523 500 WON
31.11 g., 0.999 Silver 0.999 oz. ASW, 40 mm. **Obv:** National arms **Rev:** Pallets doctor fish in color

Date	Mintage	VF20	XF40	MS60	MS63	MS65
1996	1,950	PF65 50.00	PF67 55.00			

KM# 531 500 WON
27.00 g., 0.999 Silver 0.8672 oz. ASW, 35 mm. **Rev:** Panda mith written panel

Date	Mintage	VF20	XF40	MS60	MS63	MS65
1996	Est. 1000	PF65 55.00	PF67 60.00			

KM# 147 700 WON
31.10 g., 0.999 Gold 0.999 oz. AGW, 35 mm. **Subject:** Korean Workers' Party **Obv:** National arms **Rev:** Flag and radiant setting sun **Edge:** Plain

Date	Mintage	XF40	MS60	MS63	MS65	MS66
1996	100	—	—	—	1,850	1,900

KM# 165 700 WON
31.10 g., 0.999 Gold 0.9989 oz. AGW, 35 mm. **Subject:** 50th Anniversary of People's Republic **Obv:** National arms **Rev:** Flag **Edge:** Plain

Date	Mintage	VF20	XF40	MS60	MS63	MS65
1998	500	PF67 1,800				

KM# 571 700 WON
31.11 g., 0.999 Gold 0.999 oz. AGW **Obv:** Eastern gate in Pyeongyang **Rev:** Rocket and satellite

Date	Mintage	XF40	MS60	MS63	MS65	MS66
1998 Proof	—	—	—	—	1,950	2,000

KM# 615 700 WON
31.11 g., 0.999 Gold 0.999 oz. AGW **Obv:** National arms, Central Bank name **Rev:** Jeong Seongok, Marathon race champion **Shape:** 35

Date	Mintage	VF20	XF40	MS60	MS63	MS65
1999	Est. 500	PF67 1,800				

KM# 660 700 WON
31.11 g., 0.999 Gold 0.999 oz. AGW, 35 mm. **Obv:** National arms, Central Bank name **Rev:** Two females nurturing young tree

Date	Mintage	VF20	XF40	MS60	MS63	MS65
2000	Est. 500	PF67 1,800				

KM# 661 700 WON
31.11 g., 0.999 Gold 0.999 oz. AGW, 35 mm. **Obv:** National arms, Central Bank name **Rev:** Couple embrace

Date	Mintage	VF20	XF40	MS60	MS63	MS65
2000	—	PF67 1,800				

KM# 665 700 WON
31.11 g., 0.999 Gold 0.999 oz. AGW, 35 mm. **Obv:** National arms, Central Bank name **Rev:** Map of Korea in circle

Date	Mintage	VF20	XF40	MS60	MS63	MS65
2000	—	PF67 1,800				

KM# 669 700 WON
31.11 g., 0.999 Gold 0.999 oz. AGW, 40 mm. **Obv:** National arms, Central Bank name **Rev:** Couple embrace at reunion after 1945 division

Date	Mintage	VF20	XF40	MS60	MS63	MS65
2000	—	PF67 1,800				

KM# 673 700 WON
31.11 g., 0.999 Gold 0.999 oz. AGW, 40 mm. **Obv:** National arms, Central Bank name **Rev:** Kim Jeongil and Vladimir Putin

Date	Mintage	VF20	XF40	MS60	MS63	MS65
2000	Est. 300	PF67 1,800				

KM# 31 1000 WON
31.13 g., 0.999 Gold 0.9999 oz. AGW **Subject:** 40th Anniversary of People's Republic **Obv:** National arms **Rev:** Leaping equestrian

Date	Mintage	VF20	XF40	MS60	MS63	MS65
1988	—	PF67 1,800				

KM# 148 1000 WON

15.55 g., 0.999 Gold 0.4994 oz. AGW, 27 mm. **Subject:** Death of Kim Il Sung **Obv:** National arms **Rev:** Bust facing **Edge:** Plain

Date	Mintage	XF40	MS60	MS63	MS65	MS66
ND-1994	—	—	—	750	950	1,000

KM# 149 1000 WON

31.10 g., 0.999 Gold 0.999 oz. AGW, 35 mm. **Subject:** 50th Anniversary - Korean Workers' Party **Obv:** National arms **Rev:** Monument **Edge:** Plain

Date	Mintage	XF40	MS60	MS63	MS65	MS66
1995	—	—	—	1,650	1,750	1,850

KM# 58 1500 WON

8.00 g., 0.999 Gold 0.2569 oz. AGW **Series:** Olympics **Obv:** National arms **Rev:** Gymnast

Date	Mintage	VF20	XF40	MS60	MS63	MS65
1990	Est. 3000	PF65 425	PF67 475			

KM# 42 1500 WON

15.55 g., 0.999 Gold 0.4994 oz. AGW **Subject:** Inter-parliamentary Conference **Obv:** National arms **Rev:** Buildings

Date	Mintage	VF20	XF40	MS60	MS63	MS65
1991	1,000	PF67 900				

KM# 43 1500 WON

15.55 g., 0.999 Gold 0.4994 oz. AGW **Subject:** Inter-parliamentary Conference **Obv:** Wreath around original and date **Rev:** Buildings

Date	Mintage	VF20	XF40	MS60	MS63	MS65
1991	800	PF67 900				

KM# 51 1500 WON

8.00 g., 0.999 Gold 0.2569 oz. AGW, 25 mm. **Subject:** Soccer **Obv:** National arms **Rev:** Soccer player in mid-kick

Date	Mintage	VF20	XF40	MS60	MS63	MS65
1991	1,000	PF65 425	PF67 475			

KM# 498 1500 WON

8.00 g., 0.999 Gold 0.2569 oz. AGW, 22 mm. **Rev:** Soccer player bending back, kicking ball over head

Date	Mintage	VF20	XF40	MS60	MS63	MS65
1991	Est. 1000	PF65 475	PF67 500			

KM# 150 1500 WON

8.00 g., 0.999 Gold 0.2569 oz. AGW, 22 mm. **Series:** Olympics **Obv:** National arms **Rev:** Cyclists racing **Edge:** Plain

Date	Mintage	XF40	MS60	MS63	MS65	MS66
1993	—	—	—	—	425	475

KM# 500 1500 WON

8.00 g., 0.999 Gold 0.2569 oz. AGW, 25 mm. **Rev:** Two bicyclists

Date	Mintage	VF20	XF40	MS60	MS63	MS65
1993	Est. 500	PF67 1,100				

KM# 53 2000 WON

31.10 g., 0.999 Gold 0.9989 oz. AGW **Subject:** 80th Birthday of Kim Il Sung **Obv:** National arms **Rev:** Kim Il Sung birthplace

Date	Mintage	VF20	XF40	MS60	MS63	MS65
ND-1992	500	PF67 1,800				

KM# 55 2000 WON

31.10 g., 0.999 Gold 0.9989 oz. AGW **Subject:** 80th Birthday of Kim Il Sung **Obv:** National arms **Rev:** Bust facing

Date	Mintage	VF20	XF40	MS60	MS63	MS65
1992	500	PF67 1,800				

KM# 57 2000 WON

31.10 g., 0.999 Gold 0.9989 oz. AGW **Subject:** 50th Birthday of Kim Jong Il **Rev:** Bust facing

Date	Mintage	VF20	XF40	MS60	MS63	MS65
1992	500	PF67 1,800				

KM# 151 2000 WON

31.10 g., 0.999 Gold 0.999 oz. AGW, 40 mm. **Subject:** Death of Kim Il Sung **Obv:** National arms **Rev:** Bust facing **Edge:** Plain

Date	Mintage	XF40	MS60	MS63	MS65	MS66
ND-1994	—	—	—	1,650	1,750	1,850

KM# 992 2000 WON

31.11 g., 0.999 Gold 0.999 oz. AGW, 40 mm. **Obv:** Dokdo, rocky islands, Central Bank name **Rev:** Dome island

Date	Mintage	VF20	XF40	MS60	MS63	MS65
2000	—	PF67 1,900				

KM# 35 2500 WON

15.55 g., 0.999 Gold 0.4994 oz. AGW **Subject:** 30th Anniversary of Gorch Fock **Obv:** National arms **Rev:** Sailing ship

Date	Mintage	VF20	XF40	MS60	MS63	MS65
1988	Est. 500	PF65 800	PF67 925			

KM# 81 2500 WON

155.52 g., 0.999 Silver 4.995 oz. ASW, 65 mm. **Obv:** National arms **Rev:** Multicolor panda

Date	Mintage	VF20	XF40	MS60	MS63	MS65
1995	2,500	PF65 150	PF67 200			

KM# 82 2500 WON

155.52 g., 0.999 Silver 4.995 oz. ASW **Obv:** National arms **Rev:** Multicolor tiger

Date	Mintage	VF20	XF40	MS60	MS63	MS65
1995	2,500	PF65 150	PF67 200			

KM# 83 2500 WON

155.52 g., 0.999 Silver 4.995 oz. ASW **Obv:** National arms **Rev:** Multicolor parrot

Date	Mintage	VF20	XF40	MS60	MS63	MS65
1995	2,500	PF65 150	PF67 200			

KM# 84 2500 WON

155.52 g., 0.999 Silver 4.995 oz. ASW **Obv:** National arms **Rev:** Multicolor eagle

Date	Mintage	VF20	XF40	MS60	MS63	MS65
1995	2,500	PF65 150	PF67 200			

KM# 85 2500 WON

155.52 g., 0.999 Silver 4.995 oz. ASW **Obv:** National arms **Rev:** Multicolor eurasian eagle owl

Date	Mintage	VF20	XF40	MS60	MS63	MS65
1995	2,500	PF65 150	PF67 200			

KM# 86 2500 WON

155.52 g., 0.999 Silver 4.995 oz. ASW **Obv:** National arms **Rev:** Two multicolor falcated ducks

Date	Mintage	VF20	XF40	MS60	MS63	MS65
1995	2,500	PF65 150	PF67 200			

KM# 551 2500 WON

155.00 g., 0.999 Silver 4.9784 oz. ASW, 65 mm. **Obv:** National arms, name of the Central bank flanked by 5 oz and .999 **Rev:** Panda in color

Date	Mintage	VF20	XF40	MS60	MS63	MS65
1995	Est. 2500	PF65 150	PF67 200			

KM# 552 2500 WON

155.00 g., 0.999 Silver 4.9784 oz. ASW, 65 mm. **Obv:** National arms, name of the Central Bank **Rev:** Stone eagle in color

Date	Mintage	VF20	XF40	MS60	MS63	MS65
1995	—	PF65 175	PF67 225			

KM# 553 2500 WON

155.00 g., 0.999 Silver 4.9784 oz. ASW, 65 mm. **Obv:** National arms, name of the Central Bank **Rev:** Eagle owl in color

Date	Mintage	VF20	XF40	MS60	MS63	MS65
1995	—	PF65 175	PF67 225			

KM# 554 2500 WON

155.00 g., 0.999 Silver 4.9784 oz. ASW, 65 mm. **Obv:** National arms, name of the Central Bank **Rev:** Rainbow Lori in color

Date	Mintage	VF20	XF40	MS60	MS63	MS65
1995	—	PF65 175	PF67 225			

KM# 555 2500 WON

155.00 g., 0.999 Silver 4.9784 oz. ASW, 65 mm. **Obv:** National arms, name of the Central Bank **Rev:** Manderian duck in color

Date	Mintage	VF20	XF40	MS60	MS63	MS65
1995	—	PF65 175	PF67 225			

KM# 564 2500 WON

155.00 g., 0.999 Silver 4.9784 oz. ASW, 65 mm. **Obv:** National arms, name of Central Bank **Rev:** Tiger in color

Date	Mintage	VF20	XF40	MS60	MS63	MS65
1995	—	PF65 150	PF67 200			

PROOF SETS

KM#	Date	Mintage	Identification	Issue Price	Mkt Val
PS1	1995 (5)	300	KM92-96	—	1,600

KOREA-SOUTH

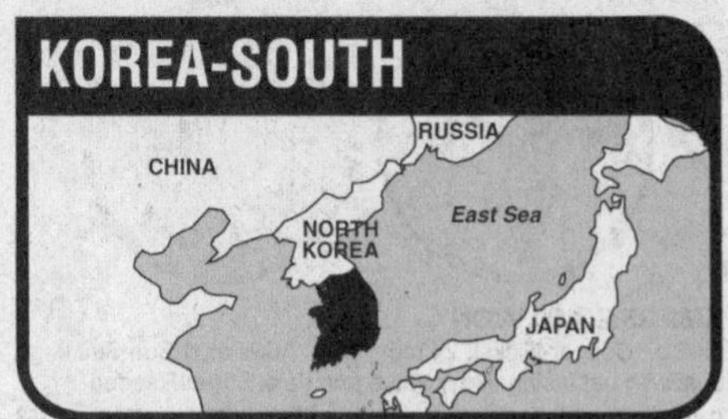

The Republic of Korea, situated in northeastern Asia on the southern half of the Korean peninsula between North Korea and the Korean Strait, has an area of 38,025 sq. mi. (98,480 sq. km.) and a population of 42.5 million. Capital: Seoul. The economy is based on agriculture and light and medium industry. Some of the world's largest oil tankers are built here. Automobiles, plywood, electronics, and textile products are exported.

Japan replaced China as the predominant foreign influence in Korea in 1895 and annexed the peninsular country in 1910. Defeat in World War II brought an end to Japanese rule. U.S. troops entered Korea from the south and Soviet forces entered from the north. The Cairo conference (1943) had established that Korea should be *free and independent*. The Potsdam conference (1945) set the 38th parallel as the line dividing the occupation forces of the United States and Russia. When Russia refused to permit a U.N. commission designated to supervise reunification elections to enter North Korea, an election was held in South Korea on May 10, 1948. By its determination, the Republic of Korea was inaugurated on Aug. 15,1948.

NOTE: For earlier coinage see Korea.

MONETARY SYSTEM

100 Chon = 1 Hwan

REPUBLIC

DECIMAL COINAGE

KM# 1 10 HWAN

2.46 g., Bronze, 19.1 mm. **Obv:** Value **Rev:** Rose of Sharon

Date	Mintage	F12	VF20	XF40	MS60	MS63
KE4292(1959)	100,000,000	2.00	5.00	20.00	50.00	90.00
Note: Issued 10-20-59						
KE4294(1961)	100,000,000	0.50	1.00	2.00	5.00	8.00

KM# 2 50 HWAN

3.69 g., Nickel-Brass, 22.86 mm. **Obv:** Value **Rev:** Iron-clad turtle boat

Date	Mintage	F12	VF20	XF40	MS60	MS63
KE4292(1959)	24,640,000	0.60	1.00	3.00	7.00	12.00
Note: Issued 10-20-59						
KE4294(1961)	20,000,000	0.60	1.00	3.00	5.00	10.00

KM# 3 100 HWAN

6.75 g., Copper-Nickel, 26 mm. **Obv:** Value flanked by phoenix **Rev:** Bust left **Edge:** Reeded

Date	Mintage	F12	VF20	XF40	MS60	MS63
KE4292(1959)	—	2.00	4.00	8.00	25.00	45.00

Note: Issued 10-30-59. Quantities of KM#1-3 dated 4292 in uncirculated condition were countermarked "SAMPLE" in Korean for distribution to government and banking agencies. See bank samples section at end of listing. KM#3 was withdrawn from circulation June 10, 1962, and melted; KM#1 and KM#2 continued to circulate as 1 Won and 5 Won coins for 13 years, respectively, until demonetized and withdrawn from circulation March 22, 1975.

REFORM COINAGE

10 Hwan = 1 Won

KM# 4 WON

1.70 g., Brass, 17.2 mm. **Obv:** Rose of Sharon **Rev:** Inscription, value and date

Date	Mintage	F12	VF20	XF40	MS60	MS63
1966	7,000,000	0.25	1.00	2.00	9.00	20.00
Note: Issued 8-16-66						
1967	48,500,000	0.10	0.50	1.00	2.00	5.00

KM# 4a WON

0.73 g., Aluminum, 17.2 mm. **Obv:** Rose of Sharon **Rev:** Inscription, value and date

Date	Mintage	F12	VF20	XF40	MS60	MS63
1968	66,500,000	—	0.25	1.00	2.00	3.50
Note: Issued 8-26-68						
1969	85,000,000	—	0.10	0.50	1.00	3.00
1970	45,000,000	—	0.10	0.50	1.00	3.00
1974	12,000,000	—	0.25	1.00	3.00	6.00
1975	10,000,000	—	0.10	0.75	1.50	4.00
1976	20,000,000	—	—	0.20	1.00	1.75
1977	30,000,000	—	—	0.20	1.00	1.75
1978	30,000,000	—	—	0.10	0.20	0.30
1979	30,000,000	—	—	0.10	0.20	0.30
1980	20,000,000	—	—	0.10	0.20	0.30
1981	20,000,000	—	—	0.10	0.20	0.30
1982	30,000,000	—	—	0.10	2.00	0.30
1982 Proof	2,000	—	—	—	—	—

KM# 31 WON

0.73 g., Aluminum, 17.2 mm. **Obv:** Rose of Sharon **Rev:** Value and date

Date	Mintage	F12	VF20	XF40	MS60	MS63
1983	40,000,000	—	—	—	0.15	0.25
Note: Issued 1-15-83						
1984	20,000,000	—	—	—	0.15	0.25
1985	10,000,000	—	—	—	0.15	0.25
1987	10,000,000	—	—	—	0.15	0.25
1988	6,500,000	—	—	—	0.15	0.25
1989	10,000,000	—	—	—	0.15	0.25
1990	6,000,000	—	—	—	0.15	0.25
1991	5,000,000	—	—	0.15	0.25	0.50
1995	15,000	—	—	—	0.15	0.25
1996	15,000	—	—	—	0.15	0.25
1997	15,000	—	—	—	0.15	0.25
1998	15,000	—	—	—	0.15	0.25
1999	15,000	—	—	—	0.15	0.25
2000	30,000	—	—	—	0.15	0.25

KM# 5 5 WON

2.95 g., Bronze, 20.4 mm. **Obv:** Iron-clad turtle boat **Rev:** Value, inscription and date

Date	Mintage	F12	VF20	XF40	MS60	MS63
1966	4,500,000	0.15	0.25	1.50	50.00	100
Note: Issued 8-16-66						
1967	18,000,000	0.15	0.25	1.00	60.00	120
1968	20,000,000	0.15	0.25	1.00	30.00	60.00
1969	25,000,000	—	0.10	0.25	10.00	20.00
1970	50,000,000	—	0.10	0.25	12.00	25.00

KM# 5a 5 WON

2.95 g., Brass, 20.4 mm. **Obv:** Iron-clad turtle boat **Rev:** Value, inscription and date

Date	Mintage	F12	VF20	XF40	MS60	MS63
1970	Inc. above	—	—	0.10	1.00	3.00
Note: Issued 7-16-70						
1971	64,038,000	—	—	—	0.25	0.20
1972	60,084,000	—	—	—	0.25	0.50
1977	1,000,000	—	—	0.10	0.65	0.50
1978	1,000,000	—	—	0.10	0.65	1.00
1979	1,000,000	—	—	0.10	0.65	1.00
1980	200,000	—	0.25	0.50	2.25	3.00
1981	200,000	—	0.25	0.50	1.50	2.00
1982 Proof	2,000	—	—	—	—	—
1982	200,000	—	0.25	0.50	1.50	2.00

KM# 32 5 WON

2.95 g., Brass, 20.4 mm. **Obv:** Iron-clad turtle boat **Rev:** Value and date **Edge:** Plain

Date	Mintage	F12	VF20	XF40	MS60	MS63
1983	6,000,000	—	—	0.10	0.20	0.30
Note: Issued 1-15-83						
1987	1,000,000	—	—	0.10	0.30	0.60
1988	500,000	—	—	0.50	1.00	2.00
1989	600,000	—	—	0.20	0.50	0.70
1990	600,000	—	—	0.20	0.50	0.70
1991	500,000	—	—	0.10	0.20	0.30
1995	15,000	—	—	0.10	0.20	0.30
1996	15,000	—	—	0.10	0.20	0.30
1997	15,000	—	—	0.10	0.20	0.30
1999	10,000	—	—	0.10	0.20	0.30
2000	30,000	—	—	0.10	0.20	0.30

KM# 6 10 WON

4.06 g., Bronze, 22.86 mm. **Obv:** Pagoda at Pul Guk Temple **Rev:** Value, inscription and date

Date	Mintage	F12	VF20	XF40	MS60	MS63
1966	10,600,000	0.15	0.25	1.50	75.00	175
Note: Issued 8-16-66						
1967	22,500,000	0.15	0.25	1.50	90.00	200
1968	35,000,000	0.15	0.25	1.50	35.00	75.00
1969	46,500,000	0.15	0.25	1.50	100	250
1970	157,000,000	0.15	0.25	1.50	150	350

KM# 6a 10 WON

4.06 g., Brass, 22.86 mm. **Obv:** Pagoda at Pul Guk Temple **Rev:** Value, inscription and date

Date	Mintage	F12	VF20	XF40	MS60	MS63
1970	Inc. above	—	0.35	1.25	40.00	120
Note: Issued 7-16-70						
1971	220,000,000	—	—	0.50	2.00	3.00
1972	270,000,000	—	—	0.50	2.00	3.00
1973	30,000,000	—	0.10	0.35	15.00	30.00
1974	15,000,000	—	0.10	1.00	7.00	15.00
1975	20,000,000	—	0.10	0.50	45.00	150
1977	1,000,000	—	0.10	0.35	3.50	8.00
1978	80,000,000	—	0.10	0.15	1.25	2.00
1979	200,000,000	—	—	0.10	0.55	1.00
1980	150,000,000	—	—	0.10	0.55	1.00
1981	100,000	—	0.25	0.75	4.00	10.00
1982 Proof	2,000	—	—	—	—	—
1982	20,000,000	—	—	0.10	0.60	1.10

KM# 33.1 10 WON

4.06 g., Brass, 22.86 mm. **Obv:** Pagoda at Pul Guk Temple **Rev:** Value below date

Date	Mintage	F12	VF20	XF40	MS60	MS63
1983	25,000,000	—	—	0.10	0.35	0.50
Note: Issued 1-15-83						
1985	35,000,000	—	—	0.10	0.35	0.50
1986	195,000,000	—	—	0.10	0.35	0.50
1987	155,000,000	—	—	0.10	0.35	0.50
1988	189,000,000	—	—	0.10	0.35	0.50
1989	310,000,000	—	—	0.10	0.35	0.50
1990	395,000,000	—	—	0.10	0.35	0.50
1991	300,000,000	—	—	0.10	0.35	0.50
1992	150,000,000	—	—	0.50	1.00	2.00
1993	110,000,000	—	—	0.75	1.50	3.00
1994	300,000,000	—	—	0.10	0.35	0.50
1995	380,000,000	—	—	0.10	0.35	0.50
1996	290,000,000	—	—	0.10	0.35	0.50
1997	177,000,000	—	—	0.10	0.35	0.50
1999	377,000,000	—	—	0.10	0.35	0.50
2000	335,000,000	—	—	0.10	0.35	0.50

KM# 33.2 10 WON
4.06 g., Brass **Obv:** Pagoda at Pul Guk Temple **Rev:** Thicker value below date

Date	Mintage	F12	VF20	XF40	MS60	MS63
1991	—	—	—	0.10	0.35	0.50
1997	—	—	—	0.10	0.35	0.50
1998	—	—	—	0.10	0.35	0.50
1999	—	—	—	0.10	0.35	0.50
2000	—	—	—	0.10	0.35	0.50

KM# 7 50 WON
2.80 g., 0.999 Silver 0.0899 oz. ASW, 16 mm. **Obv:** Arms within floral spray **Rev:** Half figure holding flag facing left

Date	Mintage	F12	VF20	XF40	MS60	MS63
KE4303-1970	4,350	PF65 50.00				
KE4304-1971 Rare	—	—	—	—	—	—

KM# 20 50 WON
4.16 g., Copper-Nickel-Zinc, 21.6 mm. **Series:** F.A.O. **Obv:** Text within sagging oat sprig **Rev:** Value below date **Edge:** Reeded

Date	Mintage	F12	VF20	XF40	MS60	MS63
1972	6,000,000	0.20	0.40	1.00	50.00	100
Note: Issued 12-1-72						
1973	40,000,000	—	0.15	0.25	20.00	50.00
1974	25,000,000	—	0.15	0.25	1.50	3.00
1977	1,000,000	—	0.15	0.25	5.00	10.00
1978	15,000,000	—	0.15	0.25	3.00	5.00
1979	20,000,000	—	0.10	0.20	3.00	5.00
1980	10,000,000	—	0.10	0.20	5.00	10.00
1981	25,000,000	—	0.10	0.20	2.00	3.00
1982	40,000,000	—	0.10	0.20	2.00	3.00
1982 Proof	2,000	—	—	—	—	—

KM# 34 50 WON
4.16 g., Copper-Nickel-Zinc, 21.6 mm. **Series:** F.A.O. **Obv:** Text below sagging oat sprig **Rev:** Value and date **Edge:** Reeded **Note:** Die varieties exist.

Date	Mintage	F12	VF20	XF40	MS60	MS63
1983	50,000,000	—	—	0.10	1.00	2.50
Note: Issued 1-15-83						
1984	40,000,000	—	—	0.10	1.00	2.50
1985	4,000,000	—	—	0.10	2.00	4.00
1987	32,000,000	—	—	0.10	1.00	2.50
1988	53,000,000	—	—	0.10	1.00	2.50
1989	70,000,000	—	—	0.10	1.00	2.50
1990	85,000,000	—	—	0.10	2.00	4.00
1991	80,000,000	—	—	0.10	1.00	3.00
1992	50,000,000	—	—	0.10	4.00	8.00
1993	5,000,000	—	—	0.10	25.00	45.00
1994	102,000,000	—	—	0.10	1.00	3.00
1995	98,000,000	—	—	0.10	1.00	3.00
1996	52,000,000	—	—	0.10	1.00	3.00
1997	129,000,000	—	—	0.10	1.00	3.00
1998	28,000,000	—	—	0.10	3.00	5.00
1999	15,000,000	—	—	0.10	1.00	3.00
2000	86,000,000	—	—	0.10	0.50	1.00

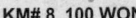

KM# 8 100 WON
5.60 g., 0.999 Silver 0.1799 oz. ASW, 21 mm. **Obv:** Arms within floral spray **Rev:** Standing figure and boat

Date	Mintage	F12	VF20	XF40	MS60	MS63
KE4303-1970	4,350	PF65 75.00				

KM# 9 100 WON
5.42 g., Copper-Nickel, 24 mm. **Obv:** Bust with hat facing **Rev:** Value and date within designed wreath **Edge:** Reeded

Date	Mintage	F12	VF20	XF40	MS60	MS63
1970	1,500,000	0.50	0.75	15.00	30.00	70.00
Note: Issued 11-30-70						
1971	13,000,000	0.15	0.25	20.00	35.00	75.00
1972	20,000,000	—	0.20	20.00	35.00	75.00
1973	80,000,000	—	0.15	3.00	5.00	9.00
1974	50,000,000	—	0.15	20.00	50.00	120
Note: Die varieties exist						
1975	75,000,000	—	0.15	6.00	10.00	20.00
Note: Die varieties exist						
1977	30,000,000	—	0.15	5.00	12.00	35.00
1978	50,000,000	—	0.15	2.00	4.00	6.00
1979	130,000,000	—	0.15	1.50	2.50	4.00
1980	60,000,000	—	0.15	3.00	5.00	10.00
1981	100,000	—	0.25	2.00	4.00	6.00
1982	70,000,000	—	0.15	1.00	2.00	3.50
1982 Proof	2,000	—	—	—	—	—

KM# 21 100 WON
12.00 g., Copper-Nickel, 30 mm. **Subject:** 30th Anniversary of Liberation **Obv:** Gate of Liberty **Rev:** Standing figures and value

Date	Mintage	F12	VF20	XF40	MS60	MS63
ND-1975	2,000	PF63 170				
ND-1975	4,998,000	0.30	0.50	0.75	1.25	2.50
Note: Issued 8-15-75						

KM# 24 100 WON
12.00 g., Copper-Nickel, 30 mm. **Subject:** 1st Anniversary of the 5th Republic **Obv:** Yin-yang symbol within rectangle above value flanked by flames **Rev:** Cluster of flowers

Date	Mintage	F12	VF20	XF40	MS60	MS63
1981	4,980,000	0.20	0.35	0.50	0.75	2.00
Note: Issued 8-81						
1981 Unfrosted, Proof	18,000	PF63 25.00				
1981	2,000	PF63 165				

KM# 35.1 100 WON
5.42 g., Copper-Nickel, 24 mm. **Obv:** Admiral Yi-Sun-Sin, small bust with hat facing **Rev:** Value and date **Edge:** Reeded

Date	Mintage	F12	VF20	XF40	MS60	MS63
1983	130,000,000	—	0.25	1.00	2.00	4.00
Note: Issued 1-15-83						

KM# 35.2 100 WON
5.42 g., Copper-Nickel, 24 mm. **Obv:** Admiral Yi-Sun-Sin, large bust with hat facing **Rev:** Value and date **Edge:** Reeded

Date	Mintage	F12	VF20	XF40	MS60	MS63
1984	40,000,000	—	0.25	1.00	2.00	4.00
Note: Issued 1-15-83						
1985	25,000,000	—	0.25	10.00	25.00	40.00
1986	131,000,000	—	0.25	2.00	3.00	5.00
1987	170,000,000	—	0.25	1.00	2.00	4.00
1988	298,000,000	—	0.25	1.00	2.00	4.00
1989	250,000,000	—	0.25	1.00	2.00	4.00
1990	185,000,000	—	0.25	1.00	2.00	4.00
1991	400,000,000	—	0.25	1.00	2.00	4.00
1992	425,000,000	—	0.25	3.00	4.00	6.00
1993	185,000,000	—	0.25	7.00	10.00	25.00
1994	401,000,000	—	0.25	1.00	2.00	4.00
1995	228,000,000	—	0.25	1.00	2.00	4.00
1996	447,000,000	—	0.25	0.50	1.50	3.00
1997	147,000,000	—	0.25	0.50	1.50	3.00
1998	5,000,000	—	—	5.00	10.00	30.00
1999	—	—	0.25	1.00	3.00	5.00
2000	—	—	0.25	0.50	1.00	3.00

KM# 10 200 WON
11.20 g., 0.999 Silver 0.3597 oz. ASW, 28 mm. **Obv:** Arms within floral spray **Rev:** Celadon vase

Date	Mintage	F12	VF20	XF40	MS60	MS63
KE4303-1970	4,200	PF65 100				

KM# 11 250 WON
14.00 g., 0.999 Silver 0.4497 oz. ASW, 30 mm. **Obv:** Arms above flower flanked by phoenix **Rev:** Bust facing

Date	Mintage	F12	VF20	XF40	MS60	MS63
KE4303-1970	4,100	PF65 125				

KM# 12 500 WON
28.00 g., 0.999 Silver 0.8993 oz. ASW, 40 mm. **Obv:** Arms within floral spray **Rev:** Half length female figure holding tea cup within circle

Date	Mintage	F12	VF20	XF40	MS60	MS63
KE4303-1970	4,700	PF65 125				

KM# 22 500 WON
17.00 g., Copper-Nickel, 32 mm. **Subject:** 42nd World Shooting Championships **Obv:** Symbol above value **Rev:** Marksman with text to right and below

Date	Mintage	F12	VF20	XF40	MS60	MS63
1978	980,000	0.35	0.50	1.00	2.00	3.00
1978 Unfrosted, proof	18,000	PF63 15.00	PF65 17.00			
1978	2,000	PF65 200				

KM# 27 500 WON
7.70 g., Copper-Nickel, 26.5 mm. **Obv:** Manchurian crane **Rev:** Value and date **Edge:** Reeded

Date	Mintage	F12	VF20	XF40	MS60	MS63
1982 Proof	2,000	—	—	—	—	—
1982	15,000,000	—	—	1.00	3.75	8.00
Note: Issued 6-12-82						
1983	64,000,000	—	—	1.00	2.50	5.00
1984	70,000,000	—	—	1.00	2.50	5.00
1987	1,000,000	—	—	2.00	5.00	12.00
1988	27,000,000	—	—	1.00	2.50	5.00
1989	25,000,000	—	—	1.00	2.50	5.00
1990	60,000,000	—	—	1.00	2.50	5.00
1991	90,000,000	—	—	1.00	2.50	5.00
1992	105,000,000	—	—	1.00	2.50	5.00
1993	32,000,000	—	—	1.00	2.50	5.00
1994	50,600,000	—	—	1.00	2.50	5.00
1995	87,000,000	—	—	1.00	2.50	5.00
1996	122,000,000	—	—	1.00	2.50	5.00
1997	62,000,000	—	—	1.00	2.50	5.00
1999	22,000,000	—	—	1.00	2.50	5.00
2000	128,000,000	—	—	1.00	2.50	5.00

KM# 13 1000 WON
56.00 g., 0.999 Silver 1.7986 oz. ASW, 55 mm. **Subject:** U.N. Forces in South Korea **Obv:** Arms within floral spray **Rev:** Korean and UN flags with four uniformed heads left within circle

Date	Mintage	F12	VF20	XF40	MS60	MS63
KE4303-1970	4,050	PF65 350				

KM# 14.1 1000 WON
3.87 g., 0.900 Gold 0.112 oz. AGW, 16 mm. **Obv:** Arms within floral spray **Rev:** Great South Gate in Seoul

Date	Mintage	F12	VF20	XF40	MS60	MS63
KE4303-1970	1,500	PF65 375				

KM# 14.2 1000 WON
3.87 g., 0.900 Gold 0.112 oz. AGW, 16 mm. **Obv:** Arms within floral spray **Rev:** Great South Gate in Seoul

Date	Mintage	F12	VF20	XF40	MS60	MS63
KE4303-1970 (a)	PF67 1250					

KM# 25 1000 WON
17.00 g., Nickel, 33 mm. **Subject:** 1st Anniversary of the 5th Republic **Obv:** Yin-yang symbol within rectangle above value flanked by flames **Rev:** Imaginary bird called Bong-hwang who represents a King

Date	Mintage	F12	VF20	XF40	MS60	MS63
1981	1,880,000	—	1.00	1.25	2.00	3.50
Note: Released in 8-81						
1981 Unfrosted, proof	18,000	PF63 15.00	PF65 17.00			
1981	2,000	PF65 250				

KM# 28 1000 WON
17.00 g., Copper-Nickel, 33 mm. **Series:** 1988 Olympics **Obv:** Dancers **Rev:** Flower design and value within sprigs

Date	Mintage	VF20	XF40	MS60	MS63	MS65
1982 Unfrosted, proof	10,000	PF63 12.00	PF65 15.00			
1982	1,980,000	—	—	1.50	3.00	—
1982	10,000	PF63 20.00	PF65 25.00			

KM# 36 1000 WON
17.00 g., Copper-Nickel, 33 mm. **Series:** 1988 Olympics **Obv:** Drummer within lined design **Rev:** Flower design and value within sprigs

Date	Mintage	VF20	XF40	MS60	MS63	MS65
1983	330,000	—	—	1.50	3.00	—
1983	101,000	PF63 15.00	PF65 20.00			
1983 Unfrosted, Proof	56,000	PF63 12.00	PF65 15.00			

KM# 39 1000 WON
17.00 g., Copper-Nickel, 33 mm. **Subject:** 200 Years of Catholic Church in Korea **Obv:** Cross above value **Rev:** Myung Dong Cathedral

Date	Mintage	VF20	XF40	MS60	MS63	MS65
1984	572,000	—	—	2.00	4.00	—

KM# 41 1000 WON
17.00 g., Copper-Nickel, 33 mm. **Subject:** 10th Asian Games **Obv:** Artistic design above flowers **Rev:** Lion dance

Date	Mintage	VF20	XF40	MS60	MS63	MS65
1986	930,000	—	—	1.50	3.00	—
1986	70,000	PF63 5.00	PF65 7.00			

KM# 46 1000 WON
12.00 g., Copper-Nickel, 30 mm. **Series:** 1988 Olympics **Obv:** Arms above floral spray **Rev:** Basketball players

Date	Mintage	VF20	XF40	MS60	MS63	MS65
1986	560,000	—	—	1.50	3.00	—
1986	140,000	PF63 7.00	PF65 10.00			

KM# 47 1000 WON
Copper-Nickel, 30 mm. **Series:** 1988 Olympics **Obv:** Arms above floral spray **Rev:** Tennis player

Date	Mintage	VF20	XF40	MS60	MS63	MS65
1987	560,000	—	—	1.50	3.00	—
1987	140,000	PF63 7.00	PF65 10.00			

KM# 48 1000 WON
12.00 g., Copper-Nickel, 30 mm. **Series:** 1988 Olympics **Obv:** Arms above floral spray **Rev:** Handball players

Date	Mintage	VF20	XF40	MS60	MS63	MS65
1987	560,000	—	—	1.50	3.00	—
1987	140,000	PF63 7.00	PF65 10.00			

KM# 49 1000 WON
Copper-Nickel, 30 mm. **Series:** 1988 Olympics **Obv:** Arms above floral spray **Rev:** Table tennis

Date	Mintage	VF20	XF40	MS60	MS63	MS65
1988	560,000	—	—	1.50	3.00	—
1988	140,000	PF63 7.00	PF65 10.00			

KM# 78 1000 WON
12.56 g., Copper-Nickel, 30 mm. **Subject:** Taejon International Exposition **Obv:** Circular symbols within circle **Rev:** Mascot of the Expo, Kumdori

Date	Mintage	VF20	XF40	MS60	MS63	MS65
1993	590,000	—	—	2.00	4.00	—

Note: Metal content is copper 94% and nickel 6% giving this coin a golden brass color

KM# 87 1000 WON
Copper-Nickel **Subject:** 50th Anniversary of U.N.

Date	Mintage	VF20	XF40	MS60	MS63	MS65
1995	1,000	—	—	—	10.00	—

KM# 50 2000 WON
17.00 g., Nickel, 33 mm. **Series:** 1988 Olympics **Obv:** Arms above floral spray **Rev:** Boxing

Date	Mintage	VF20	XF40	MS60	MS63	MS65
1986	560,000	—	—	3.00	5.00	—
1986	140,000	PF63 10.00	PF65 14.00			

KM# 51 2000 WON
17.00 g., Nickel, 33 mm. **Series:** 1988 Olympics **Obv:** Arms above floral spray **Rev:** Tae Kwon Do

Date	Mintage	VF20	XF40	MS60	MS63	MS65
1987	560,000	—	—	3.00	5.00	—
1987	140,000	PF63 8.00	PF65 12.00			

KM# 52 2000 WON
17.00 g., Nickel, 33 mm. **Series:** 1988 Olympics **Subject:** Wrestling **Obv:** Arms above floral spray **Rev:** Wrestlers

Date	Mintage	VF20	XF40	MS60	MS63	MS65
1987	560,000	—	—	3.00	5.00	—
1987	140,000	PF63 12.00	PF65 15.00			

KM# 53 2000 WON
17.00 g., Nickel, 33 mm. **Series:** 1988 Olympics **Subject:** Weight lifting **Obv:** Arms above floral spray **Rev:** Weight lifter

Date	Mintage	VF20	XF40	MS60	MS63	MS65
1988	560,000	—	—	3.00	5.00	—
1988	140,000	PF63 8.00	PF65 12.00			

KM# 88 2000 WON
10.70 g., Bi-Metallic Aluminum-Bronze center in Copper-Nickel ring, 28 mm. **Subject:** New Millennium **Obv:** Astronomical observation instrument **Rev:** Stylized design **Edge:** Reeded **Note:** Korea Minting and Security Printing Corp.

Date	Mintage	VF20	XF40	MS60	MS63	MS65
2000	—	—	—	5.00	7.00	—

KM# 15.1 2500 WON
9.68 g., 0.900 Gold 0.2801 oz. AGW, 26 mm. **Obv:** Arms within floral spray **Rev:** Crowned head and temple within circle

Date	Mintage	VF20	XF40	MS60	MS63	MS65
KE4303-1970	1,750	PF65 550	PF67 650			

KM# 15.2 2500 WON
9.68 g., 0.900 Gold 0.2801 oz. AGW **Obv:** Arms within floral spray **Rev:** Crowned head and temple within circle

Date	Mintage	VF20	XF40	MS60	MS63	MS65
KE4303-1970 (a)	100	PF67 1,500				

KM# 16.1 5000 WON
19.36 g., 0.900 Gold 0.5602 oz. AGW, 32 mm. **Obv:** Arms within floral spray **Rev:** Iron-clad turtle boats

Date	Mintage	VF20	XF40	MS60	MS63	MS65
KE4303-1970	670	PF67 1,850				

KM# 16.2 5000 WON
19.36 g., 0.900 Gold 0.5602 oz. AGW **Obv:** Arms within floral spray **Rev:** Iron-clad turtle boats

Date	Mintage	VF20	XF40	MS60	MS63	MS65
KE4303-1970 (a)	70	PF67 2,500				

KM# 23 5000 WON
23.00 g., 0.900 Silver 0.6655 oz. ASW, 35 mm. **Subject:** 42nd World Shooting Championships **Obv:** Artistic design above value **Rev:** Shilla hunter motif

Date	Mintage	VF20	XF40	MS60	MS63	MS65
1978	80,000	—	—	—	18.50	24.50
1978 Unfrosted, Proof	20,000	PF65 65.00	PF67 75.00			

KM# 54 5000 WON
16.81 g., 0.925 Silver 0.4999 oz. ASW, 32 mm. **Series:** 1988 Olympics **Obv:** Arms above floral spray **Rev:** Tiger mascot

Date	Mintage	VF20	XF40	MS60	MS63	MS65
1986	117,500	—	—	9.25	11.50	14.00
1986	227,500	PF65 12.50				

KM# 55 5000 WON
16.81 g., 0.925 Silver 0.4999 oz. ASW, 32 mm. **Series:** 1988 Olympics **Obv:** Arms above floral spray **Rev:** Tug of war

Date	Mintage	VF20	XF40	MS60	MS63	MS65
1986	117,500	—	—	9.25	11.50	14.00
1986	227,500	PF65 12.50				

KM# 60 5000 WON
16.81 g., 0.925 Silver 0.4999 oz. ASW, 32 mm. **Series:** 1988 Olympics **Obv:** Arms above floral spray **Rev:** Stadium

Date	Mintage	VF20	XF40	MS60	MS63	MS65
1987	117,500	—	—	9.25	11.50	14.00
1987	227,500	PF65 12.50				

KM# 61 5000 WON
16.81 g., 0.925 Silver 0.4999 oz. ASW, 32 mm. **Series:** 1988 Olympics **Obv:** Arms above floral spray **Rev:** Chegi - Kicking

Date	Mintage	VF20	XF40	MS60	MS63	MS65
1987	117,500	—	—	9.25	11.50	14.00
1987	227,500	PF65 12.50				

KM# 66 5000 WON
16.81 g., 0.925 Silver 0.4999 oz. ASW, 32 mm. **Series:** 1988 Olympics **Obv:** Arms above floral spray **Rev:** Tae Kwon Do

Date	Mintage	VF20	XF40	MS60	MS63	MS65
1987	117,500	—	—	9.25	11.50	14.00
1987	227,500	PF65 12.50				

KM# 67 5000 WON
16.81 g., 0.925 Silver 0.4999 oz. ASW, 32 mm. **Series:** 1988 Olympics **Obv:** Arms above floral spray **Rev:** Girls on swing

Date	Mintage	VF20	XF40	MS60	MS63	MS65
1987	117,500	—	—	9.25	11.50	14.00
1987	227,500	PF65 12.50				

KM# 70 5000 WON
16.81 g., 0.925 Silver 0.4999 oz. ASW, 32 mm. **Series:** 1988 Olympics **Obv:** Arms above floral spray **Rev:** Wrestling

Date	Mintage	VF20	XF40	MS60	MS63	MS65
1988	117,500	—	—	9.25	11.50	14.00
1988	227,500	PF65 12.50				

KM# 71 5000 WON
16.81 g., 0.925 Silver 0.4999 oz. ASW, 32 mm. **Series:** 1988 Olympics **Obv:** Arms above floral spray **Rev:** Boys spinning top

Date	Mintage	VF20	XF40	MS60	MS63	MS65
1988	117,500	—	—	9.25	11.50	14.00
1988	227,500	PF65 12.50				

KM# 79 5000 WON
16.81 g., 0.925 Silver 0.4999 oz. ASW, 32 mm. **Subject:** Taejon International Exposition **Obv:** Circular designs within dotted circle **Rev:** Seated figure spinning yarn

Date	Mintage	VF20	XF40	MS60	MS63	MS65
1993	120,000	—	—	9.25	11.50	14.00

KM# 80 5000 WON
16.81 g., 0.925 Silver 0.4999 oz. ASW, 32 mm. **Subject:** Taejon International Exposition **Obv:** Arms above floral spray **Rev:** Folk musicians

Date	Mintage	VF20	XF40	MS60	MS63	MS65
1993	120,000	—	—	9.25	11.50	14.00

KM# 85 5000 WON
16.00 g., 0.925 Silver 0.4758 oz. ASW, 32 mm. **Subject:** 50th Anniversary - Liberation from Japan **Obv:** Kim-Gu

Date	Mintage	VF20	XF40	MS60	MS63	MS65
1995	25,000	—	—	8.75	11.00	13.00

KM# 96 5000 WON
22.00 g., Bronze Enamel inlay, 38 mm. **Obv:** Head Office of the Bank of Korea old and new buildings **Rev:** 50th Anniversary of the Bank of Korea

Date	Mintage	VF20	XF40	MS60	MS63	MS65
2000	—	—	—	—	—	—

KM# 17.1 10000 WON
38.72 g., 0.900 Gold 1.1204 oz. AGW **Obv:** Arms above floral spray flanked by phoenix **Rev:** Bust facing

Date	Mintage	VF20	XF40	MS60	MS63	MS65
KE4303-1970	435	PF67 5,000				

KM# 17.2 10000 WON
38.72 g., 0.900 Gold 1.1204 oz. AGW **Obv:** Arms above floral spray flanked by phoenix **Rev:** Bust facing

Date	Mintage	VF20	XF40	MS60	MS63	MS65
KE4303-1970 (a)	55	PF67 6,000				

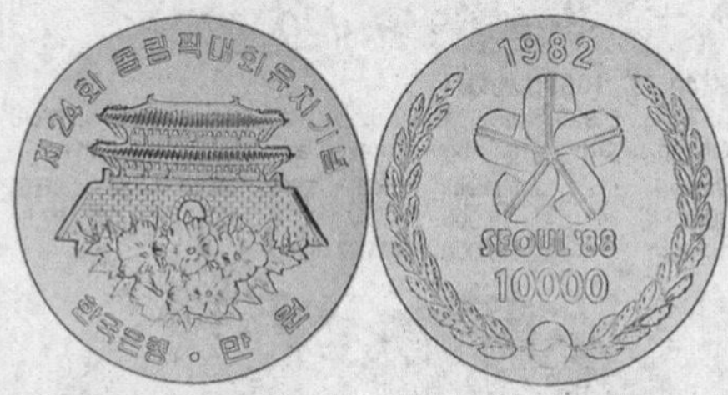

KM# 29 10000 WON
15.00 g., 0.900 Silver 0.434 oz. ASW, 30 mm. **Series:** 1988 Olympics **Obv:** Great South Gate, Seoul **Rev:** Stylized flower above value within wreath

Date	Mintage	VF20	XF40	MS60	MS63	MS65
1982	280,000	—	—	8.00	10.00	12.00
1982 Unfrosted, proof	10,000	PF65 17.00				
1982	10,000	PF65 22.00				

KM# 37 10000 WON
15.00 g., 0.900 Silver 0.434 oz. ASW, 30 mm. **Series:** 1988 Olympics **Obv:** Pavilion of Kyongbok Palace **Rev:** Stylized flower above value within wreath

Date	Mintage	VF20	XF40	MS60	MS63	MS65
1983	137,000	—	—	8.00	10.00	12.00
1983 Unfrosted, Proof	56,000	PF65 14.00				
1983	101,000	PF65 17.00				

KM# 40 10000 WON
22.30 g., 0.500 Silver 0.3585 oz. ASW, 36 mm. **Subject:** 200 Years of Catholic Church in Korea **Obv:** Cross within sectioned circle above value **Rev:** Standing haloed figures facing

Date	Mintage	VF20	XF40	MS60	MS63	MS65
1984	152,000	—	—	6.75	8.25	10.00

KM# 42 10000 WON
23.00 g., 0.900 Silver 0.6655 oz. ASW, 35 mm. **Subject:** 10th Asian Games **Obv:** Arms above floral spray **Rev:** Badminton

Date	Mintage	VF20	XF40	MS60	MS63	MS65
1986	130,000	—	—	12.50	15.50	18.50
1986	70,000	PF65 18.50				

KM# 43 10000 WON
23.00 g., 0.900 Silver 0.6655 oz. ASW, 35 mm. **Subject:** 10th Asian Games **Obv:** Arms above floral spray **Rev:** Soccer players

Date	Mintage	VF20	XF40	MS60	MS63	MS65
1986	130,000	—	—	12.50	15.50	18.50
1986	70,000	PF65 18.50				

KM# 56 10000 WON
33.62 g., 0.925 Silver 0.9998 oz. ASW, 40 mm. **Series:** 1988 Olympics **Obv:** Arms above floral spray **Rev:** Marathon runner

Date	Mintage	VF20	XF40	MS60	MS63	MS65
1986	117,500	—	—	18.50	23.00	27.50
1986	227,500	PF65 27.50				

KM# 57 10000 WON
33.62 g., 0.925 Silver 0.9998 oz. ASW, 40 mm. **Series:** 1988 Olympics **Subject:** Diving **Obv:** Arms above floral spray **Rev:** High diver

Date	Mintage	VF20	XF40	MS60	MS63	MS65
1987	117,500	—	—	18.50	23.00	27.50
1987	227,500	PF65 27.50				

KM# 62 10000 WON
33.62 g., 0.925 Silver 0.9998 oz. ASW, 40 mm. **Series:** 1988 Olympics **Subject:** Archery **Obv:** Arms above floral spray **Rev:** Archer

Date	Mintage	VF20	XF40	MS60	MS63	MS65
1987	117,500	—	—	18.50	23.00	27.50
1987	227,500	PF65 27.50				
1988	Inc. above	—	—	—	200	—
1988	Inc. above	PF65 50.00	PF67 60.00			

Note: 1988 is an error date

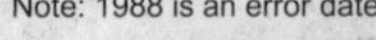

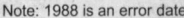

KM# 63 10000 WON
33.62 g., 0.925 Silver 0.9998 oz. ASW, 40 mm. **Series:** 1988 Olympics **Subject:** Volleyball **Obv:** Arms above floral spray **Rev:** Volleyball game

Date	Mintage	VF20	XF40	MS60	MS63	MS65
1987	117,500	—	—	18.50	23.00	27.50
1987	227,500	PF65 27.50				

KM# 74 10000 WON
33.62 g., 0.925 Silver 0.9998 oz. ASW, 40 mm. **Series:** 1988 Olympics **Subject:** Gymnastics **Obv:** Arms above floral spray **Rev:** Gymnast

Date	Mintage	VF20	XF40	MS60	MS63	MS65
1988	15,000	—	—	18.50	23.00	27.50
1988	110,000	PF65 27.50				

KM# 75 10000 WON
33.62 g., 0.925 Silver 0.9998 oz. ASW, 40 mm. **Series:** 1988 Olympics **Subject:** Equestrian events **Obv:** Arms above floral spray **Rev:** Equestrian jumping

Date	Mintage	VF20	XF40	MS60	MS63	MS65
1988	15,000	—	—	18.50	23.00	27.50
1988	110,000	PF65 27.50				

KM# 76 10000 WON
33.62 g., 0.925 Silver 0.9998 oz. ASW, 40 mm. **Series:** 1988 Olympics **Subject:** Cycling **Obv:** Arms above floral spray **Rev:** Cyclists

Date	Mintage	VF20	XF40	MS60	MS63	MS65
1988	15,000	—	—	18.50	23.00	27.50
1988	110,000	PF65 27.50				

KM# 77 10000 WON
33.62 g., 0.925 Silver 0.9998 oz. ASW, 40 mm. **Series:** 1988 Olympics **Obv:** Arms above floral spray **Rev:** Soccer players

Date	Mintage	VF20	XF40	MS60	MS63	MS65
1988	15,000	—	—	18.50	23.00	27.50
1988	110,000	PF65 27.50				

KM# 81 10000 WON
33.62 g., 0.925 Silver 0.9998 oz. ASW, 40 mm. **Subject:** Taejon International Exposition **Obv:** Stylized yin-yang within dotted circle **Rev:** Porcelain celadon

Date	Mintage	VF20	XF40	MS60	MS63	MS65
1993	100,000	—	—	20.50	25.00	30.50

KM# 86 10000 WON
23.00 g., 0.900 Silver 0.6655 oz. ASW, 35 mm. **Subject:** 50th Anniversary of Liberation from Japan **Obv:** Ahn Jong-Kun

Date	Mintage	VF20	XF40	MS60	MS63	MS65
1995	40,000	—	—	12.50	15.50	18.50

KM# 84 10000 WON
22.50 g., 0.925 Silver 0.6691 oz. ASW **Subject:** 50th Anniversary - Republic of Korea **Obv:** National yin-yang symbol within small circle above flowers **Rev:** Numeral 50 with doves on the 0 **Note:** With multicolor enamel and with gold-plated center insert.

Date	Mintage	VF20	XF40	MS60	MS63	MS65
ND-1998	100,000	—	—	12.50	15.50	18.50

KM# 18.1 20000 WON
77.40 g., 0.900 Gold 2.2396 oz. AGW, 55 mm. **Obv:** Arms within floral spray **Rev:** Gold crown - Silla Dynasty

Date	Mintage	VF20	XF40	MS60	MS63	MS65
KE4303-1970	382	PF67 8,750				

KM# 18.2 20000 WON
77.40 g., 0.900 Gold 2.2396 oz. AGW **Obv:** Arms within floral spray **Rev:** Gold Crown - Silla Dynasty

Date	Mintage	VF20	XF40	MS60	MS63	MS65
KE4303-1970 (a)	52	PF67 11,000				

KM# 26 20000 WON
22.53 g., 0.900 Silver 0.6519 oz. ASW, 35 mm. **Subject:** 1st Anniversary of the 5th Republic **Obv:** Arms above floral sprays **Rev:** Faint national yin-yang symbol above assorted uniformed busts left **Note:** Man, woman, laborer, soldier, student all symbolize the Korean will for unity.

Date	Mintage	VF20	XF40	MS60	MS63	MS65
1981	80,000	—	—	12.00	15.00	18.00
Note: Issued 8-81						
1981 Unfrosted, proof	18,000	PF65 18.00				
1981	2,000	PF65 125	PF67 150			

KM# 30 20000 WON
23.00 g., 0.900 Silver 0.6655 oz. ASW, 35 mm. **Series:** 1988 Olympics **Obv:** Stylized torch and flame within globe **Rev:** Stylized flower above value within wreath

Date	Mintage	VF20	XF40	MS60	MS63	MS65
1982	180,000	—	—	12.50	15.50	18.50
1982 Unfrosted, proof	10,000	PF65 23.50				
1982	10,000	PF65 26.50				

KM# 38 20000 WON

23.00 g., 0.900 Silver 0.6655 oz. ASW, 35 mm. **Series:** 1988 Olympics **Subject:** Wrestling **Obv:** Wrestlers **Rev:** Stylized flower above value within wreath

Date	Mintage	VF20	XF40	MS60	MS63	MS65
1983	123,000	—	—	12.50	15.50	18.50
1983 Unfrosted, proof	56,000	PF65 21.50				
1983	101,000	PF65 18.50				

KM# 44 20000 WON

28.00 g., 0.900 Silver 0.8102 oz. ASW, 38 mm. **Subject:** 10th Asian Games **Obv:** Artistic design above flowers **Rev:** Runner

Date	Mintage	VF20	XF40	MS60	MS63	MS65
1986	130,000	—	—	17.00	21.50	27.50
1986	70,000	PF65 24.50				

KM# 45 20000 WON

28.00 g., 0.900 Silver 0.8102 oz. ASW, 38 mm. **Subject:** 10th Asian Games **Obv:** Artistic design above flowers **Rev:** Pul Guk Temple - Kyong Ju City

Date	Mintage	VF20	XF40	MS60	MS63	MS65
1986	130,000	—	—	17.00	21.50	27.50
1986	70,000	PF65 24.50				

KM# 19.1 25000 WON

96.80 g., 0.900 Gold 2.801 oz. AGW, 60 mm. **Subject:** King Sejong The Great **Obv:** Arms within floral spray **Rev:** Seated figure facing reading from a book within circle **Note:** Illustration reduced.

Date	Mintage	VF20	XF40	MS60	MS63	MS65
KE4303-1970	325	PF67 14,000				

KM# 19.2 25000 WON

96.80 g., 0.900 Gold 2.801 oz. AGW, 60 mm. **Subject:** 10th Asian Games **Obv:** Arms within floral spray **Rev:** Seated figure facing reading from a book

Date	Mintage	VF20	XF40	MS60	MS63	MS65
KE4303-1970 (a)		PF67 17,500				

KM# 58 25000 WON

16.81 g., 0.925 Gold 0.4999 oz. AGW, 27 mm. **Series:** 1988 Olympics **Obv:** Arms above floral spray **Rev:** Folk dancing

Date	Mintage	XF40	MS60	MS63	MS65	MS66
1986	42,500	—	—	—	750	800
1986	117,500	PF65 750	PF67 825			

KM# 64 25000 WON

16.81 g., 0.925 Gold 0.4999 oz. AGW, 27 mm. **Series:** 1988 Olympics **Obv:** Arms above floral spray **Rev:** Fan dancing

Date	Mintage	XF40	MS60	MS63	MS65	MS66
1987	42,500	—	—	—	750	800
1987	117,500	PF65 750	PF67 825			

KM# 68 25000 WON

16.81 g., 0.925 Gold 0.4999 oz. AGW, 27 mm. **Series:** 1988 Olympics **Obv:** Arms above floral spray **Rev:** Kite flying

Date	Mintage	XF40	MS60	MS63	MS65	MS66
1987	47,500	—	—	—	750	800
1987	47,500	PF65 750	PF67 825			
1988	—	—	—	—	750	800
1988	—	PF65 750	PF67 825			

KM# 72 25000 WON

16.81 g., 0.925 Gold 0.4999 oz. AGW, 27 mm. **Series:** 1988 Olympics **Obv:** Arms above floral spray **Rev:** Korean Seesaw

Date	Mintage	XF40	MS60	MS63	MS65	MS66
1988	42,500	—	—	—	750	800
1988	117,500	PF65 750	PF67 825			

KM# 82 25000 WON

16.81 g., 0.925 Gold 0.4999 oz. AGW **Subject:** Taejon International Exposition **Obv:** Stylized yin-yang within multiple circles **Rev:** Celestial globe

Date	Mintage	XF40	MS60	MS63	MS65	MS66
1993	40,000	—	—	—	750	800

KM# 59 50000 WON

33.62 g., 0.925 Gold 0.9998 oz. AGW, 33 mm. **Series:** 1988 Olympics **Obv:** Arms above floral spray **Rev:** Turtle boat

Date	Mintage	XF40	MS60	MS63	MS65	MS66
1986	30,000	PF65 1,500	PF67 1,600			

KM# 65 50000 WON

33.62 g., 0.925 Gold 0.9998 oz. AGW, 33 mm. **Series:** 1988 Olympics **Obv:** Arms above floral spray **Rev:** Great South Gate

Date	Mintage	XF40	MS60	MS63	MS65	MS66
1987	30,000	PF65 1,500	PF67 1,600			

KM# 69 50000 WON

33.62 g., 0.925 Gold 0.9998 oz. AGW, 33 mm. **Series:** 1988 Olympics **Obv:** Arms above floral spray **Rev:** Stylized horse and rider

Date	Mintage	XF40	MS60	MS63	MS65	MS66
1987	30,000	PF65 1,500	PF67 1,600			

KM# 73 50000 WON

33.62 g., 0.925 Gold 0.9998 oz. AGW, 33 mm. **Series:** 1988 Olympics **Obv:** Arms above floral spray **Rev:** Pul Guk Temple

Date	Mintage	XF40	MS60	MS63	MS65	MS66
1988	30,000	PF65 1,500	PF67 1,600			

KM# 83 50000 WON

33.62 g., 0.925 Gold 0.9998 oz. AGW **Subject:** Taejon International Exposition **Obv:** Arms above floral spray **Rev:** Tower of Great Light

Date	Mintage	XF40	MS60	MS63	MS65	MS66
1993	10,000	—	—	—	1,600	1,700

BANK SAMPLES

Korean

KM#	Date	Mintage	Identification	Mkt Val
S1	KE4292 (1959)	—	10 Hwan. Bronze. KM1.	150
S2	KE4292 (1959)	—	50 Hwan. Nickel-Brass. KM2.	175
S3	KE4292 (1959)	—	100 Hwan. Copper-Nickel. KM3.	200
S4	1967	—	Won. Brass. KM4.	—
S5	1975	—	100 Won. Copper-Nickel. KM21.	—
S6	1978	—	500 Won. Copper-Nickel. KM22.	—
S7	1978	—	5000 Won. Silver. KM23.	—
S8	1984	—	20000 Won. Silver. KM26.	—
S9	1984	—	50000 Won. Silver. KM40.	—

MINT SETS

KM#	Date	Mintage	Identification	Issue Price	Mkt Val
MS1	Mixed dates (6)	75,000	KM6a(1980), 32, 34, 35.1 (1983), 27, 31 (1984) Issued as a presentation set for the World Bank Conference in Seoul, October 1985.	—	60.00
MS2	1983 (6)	—	KM27, 31-32, 33.1, 34, 35.1	—	60.00

MS3	1986 (5)	130,000	KM41-45	113	150
MSA4	1988 (8)	—	KM#46-53 Olympics	—	40.00
MS4	1991 (6)	—	KM27, 31-32, 33.1, 34, 35.2	—	14.00
MS5	1993 (6)	10,000	KM78-83	1,180	2,325
MS6	1993 (5)	30,000	KM78-82	443	825
MS7	1993 (4)	50,000	KM78-81	97.00	100

PROOF SETS

KM#	Date	Mintage	Identification	Issue Price	Mkt Val
PS1	1970 (12)	—	KM7-8, 10-13, 14.1-19.1	752	31,000
PS2	1970 (11)	—	KM7-8, 10-13, 14.2-18.2	—	22,500
PS3	1970 (6)	—	KM7-8, 10-13	53.50	850
PS4	1970 (6)	300	KM14.1-19.1	698	30,000
PS5	1970 (6)	25	KM14.2-19.2	—	38,500
PS6	1982 (6)	2,000	KM4a-6a, 9, 20, 27, (presentation set) Original, intact sets are worth substantially more than their individual components.	—	835
PS7	1986 (6)	350,000	KM#41, 50, 54-56, 58	275	875
PS8	1986 (5)	70,000	KM41-45	170	165
PSA9	1986 (6)	160,000	KM#46, 50, 54-56, 58	275	880
PS9	1986 (2)	—	KM46, 50	—	40.00

The State of Kuwait, a constitutional monarchy located on the Arabian Peninsula at the northwestern corner of the Persian Gulf, has an area of 6,880 sq. mi. (17,820 sq. km.) and a population of 1.7 million. Capital: Kuwait. Petroleum, the basis of the economy, provides 95 percent of the exports.

The modern history of Kuwait began with the founding of the city of Kuwait, 1740, by tribesmen who wandered northward from the region of the Qatar Peninsula of eastern Arabia. Fearing that the Turks would take over the sheikhdom, Sheikh Mubarak entered into an agreement with Great Britain, 1899, placing Kuwait under the protection of Britain and empowering Britain to conduct its foreign affairs. Britain terminated the protectorate on June 19, 1961, giving Kuwait its independence (by a simple exchange of notes) but agreeing to furnish military aid on request.

Kuwait was invaded and occupied by an army from neighboring Iraq Aug. 2, 1990. Soon thereafter Iraq declared that the country would become a province of Iraq. An international coalition of military forces primarily based in Saudi Arabia led by the United States under terms set by the United Nations, attacked Iraqi military installations to liberate Kuwait. This occurred Jan. 17, 1991. Kuwait City was liberated Feb. 27, and a cease-fire was declared Feb. 28. New paper currency was introduced March 24, 1991, to replace earlier notes.

TITLES

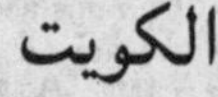

al-Kuwait

SOVEREIGN EMIRATE

MODERN COINAGE

KM# 2 FILS

2.00 g., Nickel-Brass, 17 mm. **Ruler:** Abdullah Ibn Salim **Obv:** Value within circle **Rev:** Ship with sails

Date	Mintage	VF20	XF40	MS60	MS63	MS65
AH1380-1961	60	**PF65** 30.00	**PF67** 45.00			
AH1380-1961	2,000,000	0.50	1.00	1.50	2.00	—

KM# 9 FILS

2.00 g., Nickel-Brass, 17 mm. **Ruler:** Jabir Ibn Ahmad **Obv:** Value within circle **Rev:** Ship with sails

Date	Mintage	VF20	XF40	MS60	MS63	MS65
AH1382-1962	60	**PF65** 30.00	**PF67** 45.00			
AH1382-1962	500,000	0.10	0.15	0.60	1.00	—
AH1384-1964	600,000	0.25	0.75	1.25	2.00	—
AH1385-1966	500,000	0.25	0.75	1.25	2.00	—
AH1386-1967	1,875,000	0.25	0.75	1.25	2.00	—
AH1389-1970	375,000	0.35	1.00	2.00	3.00	—
AH1391-1971	500,000	0.25	0.75	1.25	2.00	—
AH1390-1971	500,000	0.25	0.75	1.25	2.00	—
AH1392-1972	500,000	0.25	0.75	1.25	2.00	—
AH1393-1973	375,000	0.35	1.00	2.00	3.00	—
AH1395-1975	500,000	0.25	0.75	1.25	2.00	—
AH1396-1976	2,500,000	0.15	0.25	0.65	1.00	—
AH1397-1977	2,500,000	0.15	0.25	0.65	1.00	—
AH1399-1979	1,500,000	0.15	0.25	0.65	1.00	—
AH1400-1980	—	0.15	0.25	0.65	1.00	—
AH1403-1983	—	0.15	0.25	0.65	1.00	—
AH1407-1987	—	0.15	0.25	0.65	1.00	—
AH1408-1988	500,000	0.15	0.25	0.65	1.00	—

KM# 9a FILS

2.41 g., 0.925 Silver 0.0717 oz. ASW, 17 mm. **Ruler:** Jabir Ibn Ahmad **Obv:** Value within circle **Rev:** Ship with sails

Date	Mintage	VF20	XF40	MS60	MS63	MS65
AH1407-1987	—	**PF67** 95.00				

KM# 9b FILS

4.04 g., 0.917 Gold 0.1191 oz. AGW, 17 mm. **Ruler:** Jabir Ibn Ahmad **Obv:** Value within circle **Rev:** Ship with sails

Date	Mintage	XF40	MS60	MS63	MS65	MS66
AH1407-1987	—	**PF67** 280	**PF69** 360			

KM# 3 5 FILS

2.50 g., Nickel-Brass, 19.5 mm. **Ruler:** Abdullah Ibn Salim **Obv:** Value within circle **Rev:** Ship with sails

Date	Mintage	VF20	XF40	MS60	MS63	MS65
AH1380-1961	2,400,000	0.60	1.00	1.50	2.00	—
AH1380-1961	60	**PF65** 35.00	**PF67** 50.00			

KM# 10 5 FILS

2.50 g., Nickel-Brass, 19.5 mm. **Ruler:** Jabir Ibn Ahmad **Obv:** Value within circle **Rev:** Dhow, dates below

Date	Mintage	VF20	XF40	MS60	MS63	MS65
AH1382-1962	1,800,000	0.10	0.20	0.60	1.00	—
AH1382-1962	60	**PF65** 35.00	**PF67** 50.00			
AH1384-1964	600,000	0.30	0.75	1.50	3.00	—
AH1386-1967	1,600,000	0.20	0.35	0.75	1.50	—
AH1388-1968	800,000	0.30	0.75	1.25	2.25	—
AH1389-1969	—	0.30	0.75	1.25	2.25	—
AH1389-1970	600,000	0.30	0.75	1.25	2.25	—
AH1390-1971	600,000	0.30	0.75	1.25	2.25	—
AH1391-1971	600,000	0.30	0.75	1.25	2.25	—
AH1392-1972	800,000	0.25	0.65	1.25	1.75	—
AH1393-1973	800,000	0.25	0.65	1.25	1.75	—
AH1394-1974	1,200,000	0.10	0.20	0.60	1.00	—
AH1395-1975	5,020,000	0.10	0.20	0.60	1.00	—
AH1396-1976	180,000	0.35	1.00	2.00	3.00	—
AH1397-1977	4,000,000	0.10	0.20	0.50	0.70	—
AH1399-1979	6,700,000	0.10	0.20	0.50	0.70	—
AH1400-1980	—	0.10	0.20	0.50	0.70	—
AH1401-1981	7,000,000	0.10	0.20	0.50	0.70	—
AH1403-1983	—	0.10	0.20	0.50	0.70	—
AH1405-1985	—	0.10	0.20	0.50	0.70	—
AH1407-1987	—	0.10	0.20	0.50	0.70	—
AH1408-1988	3,000,000	0.10	0.20	0.50	0.70	—
AH1410-1990	—	0.10	0.20	0.50	0.70	—
AH1414-1993	—	0.10	0.20	0.50	0.70	—
AH1415-1994	—	0.10	0.20	0.50	0.70	—
Note: Varieties exist						
AH1415-1995	—	0.10	0.20	0.50	0.70	—
AH1417-1997	—	0.10	0.20	0.50	0.70	—

KM# 10a 5 FILS

3.01 g., 0.925 Silver 0.0895 oz. ASW, 19.5 mm. **Ruler:** Jabir Ibn Ahmad **Obv:** Value within circle **Rev:** Ship with sails

Date	Mintage	VF20	XF40	MS60	MS63	MS65
AH1407-1987	—	**PF67** 100				

KM# 10b 5 FILS

5.05 g., 0.917 Gold 0.1489 oz. AGW, 19.5 mm. **Ruler:** Jabir Ibn Ahmad **Obv:** Value within circle **Rev:** Ship with sails

Date	Mintage	XF40	MS60	MS63	MS65	MS66
AH1407-1987	—	**PF67** 280	**PF69** 360			

KM# 4 10 FILS

3.75 g., Nickel-Brass, 21 mm. **Ruler:** Abdullah Ibn Salim **Obv:** Value within circle **Rev:** Ship with sails

Date	Mintage	VF20	XF40	MS60	MS63	MS65
AH1380-1961	2,600,000	0.65	1.25	1.50	2.00	—
AH1380-1961	60	**PF65** 40.00	**PF67** 55.00			

KM# 11 10 FILS

3.75 g., Nickel-Brass, 21 mm. **Ruler:** Jabir Ibn Ahmad **Obv:** Value within circle **Rev:** Dhow, dates below

Date	Mintage	VF20	XF40	MS60	MS63	MS65
AH1382-1962	1,360,000	0.15	0.25	1.00	2.00	—
AH1382-1962	60	**PF65** 40.00	**PF67** 55.00			
AH1384-1964	800,000	0.35	0.85	1.50	2.50	—
AH1386-1967	1,360,000	0.30	0.75	1.50	2.50	—
AH1388-1968	672,000	0.35	0.85	1.50	2.50	—
AH1389-1969	480,000	0.50	1.00	1.75	2.75	—
AH1389-1970	640,000	0.35	0.85	1.50	2.50	—
AH1390-1971	480,000	0.50	1.00	1.75	2.75	—
AH1391-1971	800,000	0.35	0.85	1.50	2.50	—
AH1392-1972	1,120,000	0.15	0.40	1.00	2.00	—
AH1393-1973	1,440,000	0.15	0.40	1.00	2.00	—
AH1394-1974	1,280,000	0.15	0.40	1.00	2.00	—
AH1395-1975	5,280,000	0.15	0.25	0.75	1.25	—
AH1396-1976	2,400,000	0.15	0.25	0.75	1.25	—
AH1397-1977	—	0.15	0.25	0.75	1.25	—
AH1399-1979	6,160,000	0.15	0.25	0.75	1.25	—
AH1400-1980	—	0.15	0.25	0.75	1.25	—
AH1401-1981	8,320,000	0.15	0.25	0.75	1.25	—
AH1403-1983	—	0.15	0.25	0.75	1.25	—
AH1405-1985	—	0.15	0.25	0.75	1.25	—
AH1407-1987	—	0.15	0.25	0.75	1.25	—
AH1408-1988	5,000,000	0.15	0.25	0.75	1.25	—
AH1410-1990	—	0.15	0.25	0.75	1.25	—
Note: Varieties exist						
AH1415-1995	—	0.15	0.25	0.75	1.25	—
AH1417-1997	—	0.15	0.25	0.75	1.25	—
AH1418-1998	—	0.15	0.25	0.75	1.25	—

KM# 11a 10 FILS

4.35 g., 0.925 Silver 0.1294 oz. ASW, 21 mm. **Ruler:** Jabir Ibn Ahmad **Obv:** Value within circle **Rev:** Ship with sails

Date	Mintage	VF20	XF40	MS60	MS63	MS65
AH1407-1987	—	**PF67** 110				

KM# 11b 10 FILS

7.63 g., 0.917 Gold 0.2249 oz. AGW, 21 mm. **Ruler:** Jabir Ibn Ahmad **Obv:** Value within circle **Rev:** Ship with sails

Date	Mintage	XF40	MS60	MS63	MS65	MS66
AH1407-1987	—	**PF67** 400	**PF69** 480			

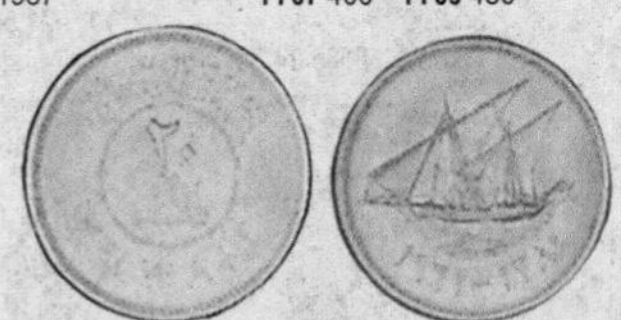

KM# 5 20 FILS

3.00 g., Copper-Nickel, 20 mm. **Ruler:** Abdullah Ibn Salim **Obv:** Value within circle **Rev:** Ship with sails **Edge:** Reeded

Date	Mintage	VF20	XF40	MS60	MS63	MS65
AH1380-1961	2,000,000	0.75	1.50	2.50	3.50	—
AH1380-1961	60	**PF65** 45.00	**PF67** 60.00			

KM# 12 20 FILS

3.00 g., Copper-Nickel, 20 mm. **Ruler:** Jabir Ibn Ahmad **Obv:** Value within circle **Rev:** Dhow, dates below **Edge:** Reeded **Note:** Varieties exist.

Date	Mintage	VF20	XF40	MS60	MS63	MS65
AH1382-1962	1,200,000	0.25	0.35	0.75	1.50	—
AH1382-1962	60	**PF65** 45.00	**PF67** 60.00			
AH1384-1964	480,000	0.50	1.00	2.00	3.00	—
AH1386-1967	1,280,000	0.35	0.85	1.25	2.00	—
AH1388-1968	672,000	0.35	0.85	1.50	2.50	—

Date	Mintage	VF20	XF40	MS60	MS63	MS65
AH1389-1969	800,000	0.35	0.85	1.50	2.50	—
AH1389-1970	480,000	0.50	1.00	2.00	3.00	—
AH1391-1971	960,000	0.35	0.85	1.25	2.00	—
AH1390-1971	480,000	0.50	1.00	2.00	3.00	—
AH1392-1972	1,440,000	0.20	0.45	1.00	2.00	—
AH1393-1973	1,280,000	0.20	0.45	1.00	2.00	—
AH1394-1974	1,600,000	0.20	0.45	0.85	1.75	—
AH1395-1975	2,400,000	0.20	0.30	0.75	1.50	—
AH1396-1976	3,200,000	0.20	0.30	0.75	1.50	—
AH1397-1977	3,400,000	0.20	0.30	0.75	1.50	—
AH1399-1979	5,520,000	0.20	0.30	0.75	1.50	—
AH1400-1980	—	0.20	0.30	0.65	1.25	—
AH1401-1981	8,960,000	0.20	0.30	0.65	1.25	—
AH1403-1983	—	0.20	0.30	0.65	1.25	—
AH1405-1985	—	0.20	0.30	0.65	1.25	—
AH1407-1987	—	0.20	0.30	0.65	1.25	—
AH1408-1988	5,000,000	0.20	0.30	0.65	1.25	—
AH1410-1990	—	0.20	0.30	0.65	1.25	—
AH1415-1995	—	0.20	0.30	0.65	1.25	—
AH1417-1997	—	0.20	0.45	1.00	2.00	—

KM# 12a 20 FILS

3.37 g., 0.925 Silver 0.1002 oz. ASW, 20 mm. **Ruler:** Jabir Ibn Ahmad **Obv:** Value within circle **Rev:** Dhow, dates below

Date	Mintage	VF20	XF40	MS60	MS63	MS65
AH1407-1987	—	PF67 115				

KM# 12b 20 FILS

5.67 g., 0.917 Gold 0.1672 oz. AGW, 20 mm. **Ruler:** Jabir Ibn Ahmad **Obv:** Value within circle **Rev:** Dhow, dates below

Date	Mintage	XF40	MS60	MS63	MS65	MS66
AH1407-1987	—	PF67 360	PF69 440			

KM# 6 50 FILS

4.50 g., Copper-Nickel, 23 mm. **Ruler:** Sabah Ibn Salim **Obv:** Value within circle **Rev:** Ship with sails **Edge:** Reeded

Date	Mintage	VF20	XF40	MS60	MS63	MS65
AH1380-1961	1,720,000	0.85	1.75	2.50	4.00	—
AH1380-1961	60	PF65 60.00	PF67 75.00			

KM# 13 50 FILS

4.50 g., Copper-Nickel, 23 mm. **Ruler:** Jabir Ibn Ahmad **Obv:** Value within circle **Rev:** Dhow, dates below **Edge:** Reeded

Date	Mintage	VF20	XF40	MS60	MS63	MS65
AH1382-1962	900,000	0.50	0.75	1.50	2.50	—
AH1382-1962	60	PF65 60.00	PF67 75.00			
AH1384-1964	300,000	0.75	1.50	2.50	4.00	—
AH1386-1966	800,000	0.40	0.85	2.00	3.50	—
AH1386-1967	—	0.50	0.75	1.50	2.50	—
AH1388-1968	200,000	1.00	2.00	4.00	6.00	—
AH1389-1969	500,000	0.50	1.00	2.00	3.00	—
AH1389-1970	—	1.00	2.00	4.00	6.00	—
AH1390-1970	300,000	1.00	2.00	4.00	6.00	—
AH1391-1971	500,000	0.50	1.00	2.00	3.00	—
AH1390-1971	—	0.75	1.50	2.50	4.00	—
AH1392-1972	900,000	0.50	0.85	1.25	2.50	—
AH1393-1973	800,000	0.50	0.85	1.25	2.50	—
AH1394-1974	1,000,000	0.35	0.50	1.00	2.00	—
AH1395-1975	1,950,000	0.35	0.50	1.00	2.00	—
AH1396-1976	2,250,000	0.25	0.35	1.00	2.00	—
AH1397-1977	6,000,000	0.25	0.35	0.75	1.50	—
AH1399-1979	6,050,000	0.25	0.35	0.75	1.50	—
AH1400-1980	—	0.25	0.35	0.75	1.50	—
AH1401-1981	3,000,000	0.25	0.35	0.75	1.50	—
AH1403-1983	—	0.25	0.35	0.75	1.50	—
AH1405-1985	—	0.25	0.35	0.75	1.50	—
AH1407-1987	2,000,000	0.25	0.35	0.75	1.50	—
AH1408-1988	3,000,000	0.25	0.35	0.75	1.50	—
AH1410-1990	—	0.25	0.35	0.75	1.50	—
AH1414-1993	—	0.25	0.35	0.75	1.50	—
AH1415-1995	—	0.20	0.35	0.75	1.50	—
AH1417-1997	—	0.25	0.35	0.75	1.50	—
AH1420-1999	—	0.25	0.35	0.75	1.50	—

KM# 13a 50 FILS

5.07 g., 0.925 Silver 0.1508 oz. ASW, 23 mm. **Ruler:** Jabir Ibn Ahmad **Obv:** Value within circle **Rev:** Ship with sails

Date	Mintage	VF20	XF40	MS60	MS63	MS65
AH1407-1987	—	PF67 120				

KM# 13b 50 FILS

8.52 g., 0.917 Gold 0.2512 oz. AGW, 23 mm. **Ruler:** Jabir Ibn Ahmad **Obv:** Value within circle **Rev:** Ship with sails

Date	Mintage	XF40	MS60	MS63	MS65	MS66
AH1407-1987	—	PF67 440	PF69 520			

KM# 7 100 FILS

6.50 g., Copper-Nickel, 26 mm. **Ruler:** Abdullah Ibn Salim **Obv:** Value within circle **Rev:** Ship with sails **Edge:** Reeded

Date	Mintage	VF20	XF40	MS60	MS63	MS65
AH1380-1961	1,260,000	1.00	2.00	5.00	—	—
AH1380-1961	60	PF65 90.00	PF67 110			

KM# 14 100 FILS

6.50 g., Copper-Nickel, 26 mm. **Ruler:** Jabir Ibn Ahmad **Obv:** Value within circle **Rev:** Dhow, dates below **Edge:** Reeded

Date	Mintage	VF20	XF40	MS60	MS63	MS65
AH1382-1962	640,000	0.50	0.65	3.50	—	—
AH1382-1962	60	PF65 90.00	PF67 110			
AH1384-1964	160,000	1.75	3.00	6.00	—	—
AH1386-1967	640,000	1.00	1.50	3.00	—	—
AH1388-1968	160,000	1.75	3.00	6.00	—	—
AH1389-1969	320,000	1.00	2.00	4.00	—	—
AH1391-1971	240,000	1.25	2.00	4.00	—	—
AH1392-1972	400,000	1.00	1.50	3.00	—	—
AH1393-1973	480,000	1.00	1.50	3.00	—	—
AH1394-1974	480,000	1.00	1.50	3.00	—	—
AH1395-1975	3,040,000	0.50	0.75	2.50	4.50	—
AH1396-1976	—	0.50	0.75	2.50	4.50	—
AH1397-1977	1,600,000	0.50	0.75	2.50	4.50	—
AH1399-1979	3,040,000	0.50	0.75	2.50	4.50	—
AH1400-1980	—	0.50	0.75	2.50	4.50	—
AH1401-1981	2,960,000	0.50	0.75	2.50	4.50	—
AH1403-1983	—	0.50	0.75	2.50	4.50	—
AH1405-1985	—	0.50	0.75	2.50	4.50	—
AH1407-1987	2,000,000	0.50	0.75	2.50	4.50	—
AH1408-1988	2,000,000	0.50	0.75	2.50	4.50	—
AH1410-1990	—	0.50	0.75	2.50	4.50	—
AH1415-1995	—	0.50	0.75	2.50	4.50	—
Note: Varieties exist						
AH1418-1998	—	0.50	0.75	2.50	4.50	—
AH1420-1999	—	0.50	0.75	1.75	3.00	—

KM# 14a 100 FILS

7.34 g., 0.925 Silver 0.2183 oz. ASW, 26 mm. **Ruler:** Jabir Ibn Ahmad **Obv:** Value within circle **Rev:** Ship with sails

Date	Mintage	VF20	XF40	MS60	MS63	MS65
AH1407-1987	—	PF67 125				

KM# 14b 100 FILS

12.33 g., 0.917 Gold 0.3635 oz. AGW, 26 mm. **Ruler:** Jabir Ibn Ahmad **Obv:** Value within circle **Rev:** Ship with sails

Date	Mintage	XF40	MS60	MS63	MS65	MS66
AH1407-1987	—	PF67 600	PF69 680			

KM# 15 2 DINARS

28.28 g., 0.500 Silver 0.4546 oz. ASW **Ruler:** Sabah Ibn Salim **Subject:** 15th Anniversary of Independence **Obv:** Conjoined busts with traditional gutra headdresses on facing 3/4 left **Rev:** Castle, tower and ships

Date	Mintage	VF20	XF40	MS60	MS63	MS65
ND-1976	70,000	—	—	28.00	38.00	45.00

KM# 15a 2 DINARS

28.28 g., 0.925 Silver 0.841 oz. ASW **Ruler:** Sabah Ibn Salim **Subject:** 15th Anniversary of Independence **Obv:** Castle, tower and ships **Rev:** Conjoined busts with traditional gutra headdresses on facing 3/4 left

Date	Mintage	VF20	XF40	MS60	MS63	MS65
ND-1976	53,000	PF65 60.00	PF67 70.00			

KM# 24 2 DINARS

28.28 g., 0.925 Silver 0.841 oz. ASW **Ruler:** Jabir Ibn Ahmad **Subject:** 50th Anniversary - United Nations **Obv:** Sailing ship within circle above dove with open wings within radiant circle **Rev:** United in peace written above designs, number 50, dates and emblem

Date	Mintage	VF20	XF40	MS60	MS63	MS65
ND-1995	Est. 110000	PF63 40.00	PF65 50.00			

KM# 8 5 DINARS

13.57 g., 0.917 Gold 0.4001 oz. AGW **Ruler:** Abdullah Ibn Salim **Obv:** Value in Arabic in center circle **Rev:** Dhow sailing left

Date	Mintage	VF20	XF40	MS60	MS63	MS65
AH1380-1961 Proof, Rare	Est. 1000	—	—	—	—	—

Note: Baldwin's Auction 101, 9-16, PF66 realized approximately $28,580

KM# 16 5 DINARS

28.28 g., 0.925 Silver 0.841 oz. ASW **Ruler:** Jabir Ibn Ahmad **Subject:** 15th Century of the Hijira **Obv:** Capital building within circle **Rev:** Courtyard within circle

Date	Mintage	VF20	XF40	MS60	MS63	MS65
AH1401-1981	10,000	PF65 65.00	PF67 75.00			

KM# 18 5 DINARS

28.28 g., 0.925 Silver 0.841 oz. ASW **Ruler:** Jabir Ibn Ahmad **Subject:** 20th Anniversary of Independence **Obv:** Building, crescent and captains wheel within circle **Rev:** Dates, building, towers and satellite dish within chained circle

Date	Mintage	VF20	XF40	MS60	MS63	MS65
ND-1981	10,000	PF65 65.00	PF67 75.00			

KM# 20 5 DINARS
33.63 g., 0.925 Silver 1.000 oz. ASW **Ruler:** Jabir Ibn Ahmad **Subject:** 25th Anniversary of Kuwait Currency **Obv:** Arabic value, buildings, port scene and refinery **Rev:** English legend, falcon, dhow, building and map on globe

Date	Mintage	VF20	XF40	MS60	MS63	MS65
ND (1986)	—	PF63 100	PF65 120	PF67 140		

KM# 21 50 DINARS
16.97 g., 0.917 Gold 0.5002 oz. AGW **Ruler:** Jabir Ibn Ahmad **Subject:** 25th Anniversary of Kuwait Independence **Obv:** Arabic legend, arched design, falcon, tent, dhow and pearl in a shell **Rev:** Radiant sun, mosque and assembly building with English and Arabic legend

Date	Mintage	VF20	XF40	MS60	MS63	MS65
AH1406-1986	—	PF63 950	PF65 1,000			

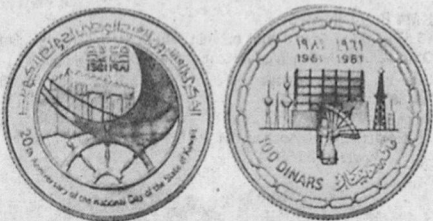

KM# 17 100 DINARS
15.98 g., 0.917 Gold 0.4711 oz. AGW **Ruler:** Jabir Ibn Ahmad **Subject:** 15th Century of the Hijira **Obv:** Building, crescent and captain's wheel within circle **Rev:** Dates, building, towers and satellite dish within chained circle

Date	Mintage	VF20	XF40	MS60	MS63	MS65
AH1401-1981	10,000	PF65 750	PF67 950			

KM# 19 100 DINARS
15.98 g., 0.917 Gold 0.4711 oz. AGW **Ruler:** Jabir Ibn Ahmad **Subject:** 20th Anniversary of Independence **Obv:** Capital building within circle **Rev:** Courtyard within circle

Date	Mintage	VF20	XF40	MS60	MS63	MS65
AH1401-1981	10,000	PF63 1,650	PF65 1,750			

MINT SETS

KM#	Date	Mintage	Identification	Issue Price	Mkt Val
MS1	1973 (6)	—	KM9-14	1.75	30.00

PROOF SETS

KM#	Date	Mintage	Identification	Issue Price	Mkt Val
PS1	1961 (6)	60	KM2-7	—	350
PS2	1962 (6)	60	KM9-14	—	350
PS3	1987 (6)	—	KM9a-14a	—	675
PS4	1987 (6)	—	KM9b-14b	—	2,850

KYRGYZSTAN

The Republic of Kyrgyzstan, (formerly Kirghiz S.S.R., a Union Republic of the U.S.S.R.), is an independent state since Aug. 31, 1991, a member of the United Nations and of the C.I.S. It was the last state of the Union Republics to declare its sovereignty. Capital: Bishkek (formerly Frunze).

Originally part of the autonomous Turkestan S.S.R. founded on May 1, 1918, the Kyrgyz ethnic area was established on October 14, 1924, as the Kara-Kirghiz Autonomous Region within the R.S.F.S.R. Then on May 25, 1925, the name Kara (black) was dropped. It became an A.S.S.R. on Feb. 1, 1926, and a Union Republic of the U.S.S.R. in 1936. On Dec. 12, 1990, the name was then changed to the Republic of Kyrgyzstan.

MONETARY SYSTEM
100 Tiyin = 1 Som

REPUBLIC

STANDARD COINAGE

KM# 1 10 SOM
28.28 g., 0.925 Silver 0.841 oz. ASW, 38.6 mm. **Subject:** Millennium of Manas **Obv:** Arms within circle above date flanked by sprigs **Rev:** Manas riding horse high above mountains

Date	Mintage	VF20	XF40	MS60	MS63	MS65
1995	5,000	PF63 75.00	PF65 85.00			

KM# 2 100 SOM
6.22 g., 0.999 Gold 0.1998 oz. AGW, 22 mm. **Subject:** Millennium of Manas **Obv:** Arms within circle above date flanked by sprigs **Rev:** Manas riding horse high above mountains

Date	Mintage	VF20	XF40	MS60	MS63	MS65
1995	1,000	PF63 325	PF65 375			

KM# 3 100 SOM
7.78 g., 0.916 Gold 0.2291 oz. AGW, 22 mm. **Subject:** OSH - 3000th Anniversary **Rev:** Davan Horses, Sulaiman mountain in background

Date	Mintage	VF20	XF40	MS60	MS63	MS65
2000	1,000	PF63 350	PF65 400			

LAO

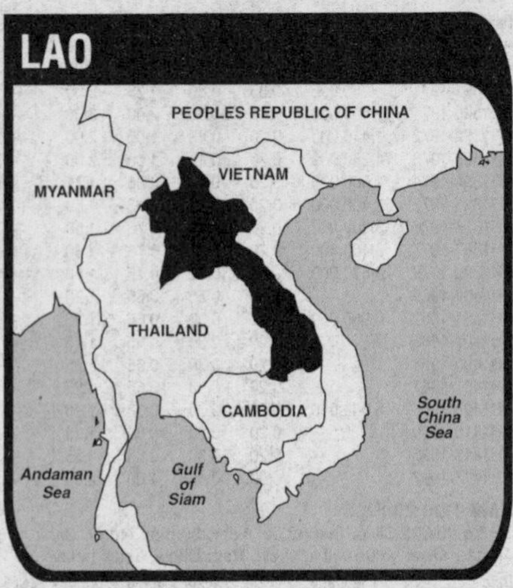

The Lao Peoples Democratic Republic, located on the Indo-Chinese Peninsula between the Socialist Republic of Vietnam and the Kingdom of Thailand, has an area of 91,428 sq. mi. (236,800 km.) and a population of 3.6 million. Capital: Vientiane. Agriculture employs 95 percent of the people. Tin, lumber and coffee are exported.

The first United Kingdom of Lan Xang (Million Elephants) was established in the mid-14th century by King Fa Ngum who ruled an area including present Laos, northeastern Thailand, and the southern part of China's Yunnan province from his capital at Luang Prabang. Thailand and Vietnam obtained control over much of the present Lao territory in the 18th century and remained dominant until France established a protectorate over the area in 1893 and incorporated it into the Union of Indo-China. The Independence of Laos was proclaimed in March of 1945, during the last days of the Japanese occupation of World War II. France reoccupied Laos in 1946, and established it as a constitutional monarchy within the French Union in 1949. In 1953 war erupted between the government and the Pathet Lao, a Communist movement supported by the Vietnamese Communist forces. Peace was declared in 1954 with Laos becoming fully independent in 1955 and the Pathet Lao being permitted to occupy two northern provinces. Civil war broke out again in 1960 with the United States supporting the government of the Kingdom of Laos and the North Vietnamese helping the Communist Pathet Lao, and continued, with intervals of truce and political compromise, until the formation of the Lao Peoples Democratic Republic on Dec. 2, 1975.

NOTE: For earlier coinage, see French Indo-China.

RULERS
Sisavang Vong, 1904-1959
Savang Vatthana, 1959-1975

MONETARY SYSTEM
100 Cents = 1 Piastre

Commencing 1955

100 Att = 1 Kip

MINT MARKS
(a) - Paris, privy marks only
Key - Havana
None - Berlin

NOTE: Private bullion issues previously listed here are now listed in *Unusual World Coins,* 5th Edition, Krause Publications, Inc., 2007.

KINGDOM

STANDARD COINAGE

KM# 4 10 CENTS
1.32 g., Aluminum, 23 mm. **Ruler:** Sisavang Vong **Obv:** Center hole in head right **Rev:** Center hole in flower design above date

Date	Mintage	VF20	XF40	MS60	MS63	MS65
1952 (a)	2,000,000	0.25	0.50	0.75	1.25	2.00

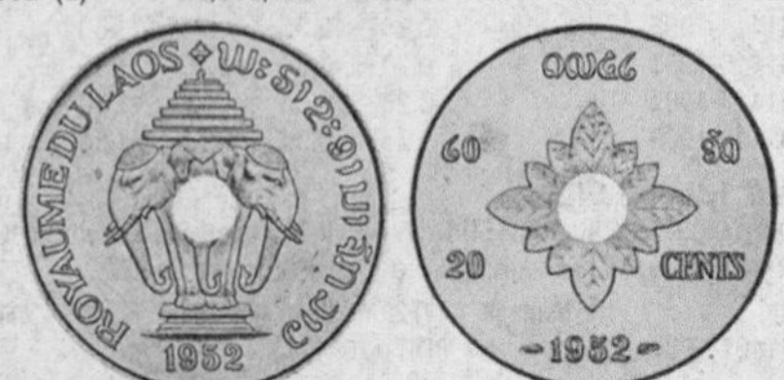

KM# 5 20 CENTS
2.23 g., Aluminum, 27 mm. **Ruler:** Sisavang Vong **Obv:** Center

hole within conjoined elephants above date **Rev:** Center hole within flower design above date

Date	Mintage	VF20	XF40	MS60	MS63	MS65
1952 (a)	3,000,000	0.35	0.60	1.00	1.50	2.50

KM# 6 50 CENTS
3.84 g., Aluminum, 31 mm. **Ruler:** Sisavang Vong **Obv:** Center hole within pedestal holding book divides radiant sun and date **Rev:** Center hole within flower design above date

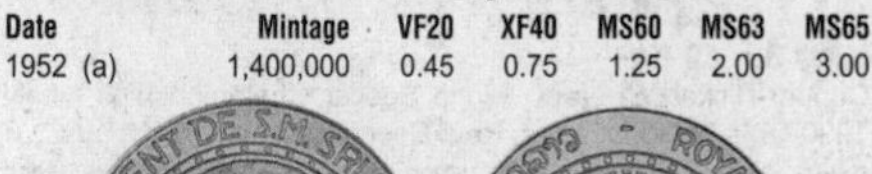

Date	Mintage	VF20	XF40	MS60	MS63	MS65
1952 (a)	1,400,000	0.45	0.75	1.25	2.00	3.00

KM# 7 1000 KIP
10.00 g., 0.925 Silver 0.2974 oz. ASW **Ruler:** Savang Vatthana **Subject:** King Savang Vatthana Coronation **Obv:** Head right within circle **Rev:** Radiant sun above statue dividing elephant heads with lamps flanking, all within circle

Date	Mintage	VF20	XF40	MS60	MS63	MS65
1971	—	—	—	25.00	28.00	32.00
1971	Est. 20000	PF65 40.00	PF67 45.00			

KM# 8 2500 KIP
20.00 g., 0.925 Silver 0.5948 oz. ASW **Ruler:** Savang Vatthana **Subject:** King Savang Vatthana Coronation **Obv:** Head right within circle **Rev:** Radiant sun above statue dividing elephant heads with lamps flanking, all within circle

Date	Mintage	VF20	XF40	MS60	MS63	MS65
1971	—	—	—	35.00	38.00	42.00
1971	Est. 20000	PF65 50.00	PF67 55.00			

KM# 9 4000 KIP
4.00 g., 0.900 Gold 0.1157 oz. AGW **Ruler:** Savang Vatthana **Subject:** King Savang Vatthana Coronation **Obv:** Head right within circle **Rev:** Radiant sun above statue dividing elephant heads with lamps flanking, all within circle

Date	Mintage	VF20	XF40	MS60	MS63	MS65
1971	10,000	PF65 185	PF67 225			

KM# 10 5000 KIP
40.00 g., 0.925 Silver 1.1896 oz. ASW **Ruler:** Savang Vatthana **Subject:** King Savang Vatthana Coronation **Obv:** Head right within circle **Rev:** Radiant sun above statue dividing elephant heads with lamps flanking, circle surrounds all

Date	Mintage	VF20	XF40	MS60	MS63	MS65
1971	—	—	—	100	110	120
1971	Est. 20000	PF65 120	PF67 135			

KM# 16.1 5000 KIP
11.70 g., 0.925 Silver 0.348 oz. ASW **Ruler:** Savang Vatthana **Subject:** Laotian maiden **Obv:** Head right above conjoined elephant heads flanked by lamps **Rev:** Head right above value **Note:** Hologram between denomination and "•" on reverse.

Date	Mintage	VF20	XF40	MS60	MS63	MS65
1975	400	—	—	—	130	140
1975	775	PF67 150				

KM# 16.2 5000 KIP
11.70 g., 0.925 Silver 0.348 oz. ASW **Ruler:** Savang Vatthana **Subject:** Laotian maiden **Obv:** Head right above conjoined elephant heads flanked by lamps **Rev:** Head right above value **Note:** .925 Counterstamp between "•" and "LAOS" on reverse.

Date	Mintage	VF20	XF40	MS60	MS63	MS65
ND-1975	—	—	—	90.00	100	110

KM# 17 5000 KIP
11.70 g., 0.925 Silver 0.348 oz. ASW **Ruler:** Savang Vatthana **Subject:** Wat Phra Kio Museum, Vientiane **Obv:** Head right above conjoined elephant heads flanked by lamps **Rev:** Museum

Date	Mintage	VF20	XF40	MS60	MS63	MS65
1975	400	—	—	—	125	130
1975	775	PF67 150				

KM# 11 8000 KIP
8.00 g., 0.900 Gold 0.2315 oz. AGW **Ruler:** Savang Vatthana **Subject:** King Savang Vatthana Coronation **Obv:** Head right within circle **Rev:** Radiant statue divides elephant heads with lamps flanking, all within circle

Date	Mintage	VF20	XF40	MS60	MS63	MS65
1971	10,000	PF65 400	PF67 450			

KM# 12 10000 KIP
80.00 g., 0.925 Silver 2.3792 oz. ASW **Ruler:** Savang Vatthana **Subject:** King Savang Vatthana Coronation **Obv:** Head right within circle **Rev:** Radiant sun above statue dividing elephant heads with lamps flanking, circle surrounds all

Date	Mintage	VF20	XF40	MS60	MS63	MS65
1971	—	—	—	150	165	180
1971	Est. 20000	PF65 245	PF67 275			

KM# 18 10000 KIP
23.50 g., 0.925 Silver 0.6989 oz. ASW **Ruler:** Savang Vatthana **Subject:** Wat Xieng - Thong Temple **Obv:** Head right above elephant statue and lamps **Rev:** Temple

Date	Mintage	VF20	XF40	MS60	MS63	MS65
1975	650	PF67 195				
1975	300	—	—	170	175	185

KM# 13 20000 KIP
20.00 g., 0.900 Gold 0.5787 oz. AGW **Ruler:** Savang Vatthana **Subject:** King Savang Vatthana Coronation **Obv:** Head right **Rev:** Elephant statue flanked by lamps

Date	Mintage	VF20	XF40	MS60	MS63	MS65
1971	Est. 10000	PF65 950	PF67 1,100			

KM# 14 40000 KIP
40.00 g., 0.900 Gold 1.1574 oz. AGW **Ruler:** Savang Vatthana **Subject:** King Savang Vatthana Coronation **Rev:** Elephant statue flanked by lamps

Date	Mintage	VF20	XF40	MS60	MS63	MS65
1971	Est. 10000	PF65 1,850	PF67 2,150			

KM# 19 50000 KIP
3.60 g., 0.900 Gold 0.1042 oz. AGW **Ruler:** Savang Vatthana **Obv:** Bust of King Savang Vatthana **Rev:** That Luang Temple

Date	Mintage	VF20	XF40	MS60	MS63	MS65
1975	100	—	—	—	275	285
1975	175	PF67 300				

KM# 20 50000 KIP
3.60 g., 0.900 Gold 0.1042 oz. AGW **Ruler:** Savang Vatthana **Obv:** Bust of King Savana Vatthana **Rev:** Bust of Laotion maiden 3/4 right

Date	Mintage	VF20	XF40	MS60	MS63	MS65
1975	100	—	—	—	275	285
1975	175	PF67 300				

KM# 15 80000 KIP
80.00 g., 0.900 Gold 2.3149 oz. AGW **Ruler:** Savang Vatthana **Subject:** King Savang Vatthana Coronation **Obv:** Similar to 20000 Kip, KM#13, head right

Date	Mintage	VF20	XF40	MS60	MS63	MS65
1971	—	PF65 3,700	PF67 4,200			

KM# 21 100000 KIP
7.32 g., 0.900 Gold 0.2118 oz. AGW **Ruler:** Savang Vatthana **Obv:** Bust of King Savang Vatthana **Rev:** Statue of Buddha

Date	Mintage	VF20	XF40	MS60	MS63	MS65
1975	100	—	—	—	450	475
1975	100	PF67 500				

PEOPLES DEMOCRATIC REPUBLIC

STANDARD COINAGE

KM# 22 10 ATT
1.20 g., Aluminum, 21 mm. **Obv:** National arms **Rev:** Half length figure facing holding wheat stalks divides sprigs with value above

Date	Mintage	VF20	XF40	MS60	MS63	MS65
1980	—	0.20	0.30	0.50	0.75	1.25

KM# 23 20 ATT
1.55 g., Aluminum, 23 mm. **Obv:** National arms **Rev:** Value flanked by designs above ox, man and plow

Date	Mintage	VF20	XF40	MS60	MS63	MS65
1980	—	0.20	0.30	0.50	0.75	1.25

KM# 24 50 ATT
2.50 g., Aluminum, 26 mm. **Obv:** National arms **Rev:** Value above fish and date flanked by palm trees

Date	Mintage	VF20	XF40	MS60	MS63	MS65
1980	—	0.25	0.35	0.65	1.00	1.50

KM# 37 KIP
Copper-Nickel **Subject:** 10th Anniversary of People's Democratic Republic **Obv:** National arms **Rev:** Value flanked by designs above date

Date	Mintage	VF20	XF40	MS60	MS63	MS65
1985	—	0.25	0.35	0.65	1.00	1.50

KM# 38 5 KIP
Copper-Nickel **Subject:** 10th Anniversary of People's Democratic Republic **Obv:** National arms **Rev:** Value flanked by designs above date

Date	Mintage	VF20	XF40	MS60	MS63	MS65
1985	—	0.25	0.35	0.75	1.25	2.00

KM# 39 10 KIP
Copper-Nickel **Subject:** 10th Anniversary of People's Democratic Republic **Obv:** National arms **Rev:** Value flanked by designs above date

Date	Mintage	VF20	XF40	MS60	MS63	MS65
1985	—	0.35	0.50	1.00	1.50	2.50

KM# 31 10 KIP
Copper-Nickel, 32.5 mm. **Obv:** National arms **Rev:** 5-masted clipper

Date	Mintage	VF20	XF40	MS60	MS63	MS65
1988	30,000	—	—	2.00	3.00	5.00

KM# 31a 10 KIP
Nickel Bonded Steel, 32.5 mm. **Obv:** National arms **Rev:** 5-masted clipper

Date	Mintage	VF20	XF40	MS60	MS63	MS65
1988	—	—	—	2.50	3.50	6.00

KM# 66 10 KIP
Copper **Obv:** National arms **Rev:** 5-masted clipper

Date	Mintage	VF20	XF40	MS60	MS63	MS65
1988	—	—	—	—	4.00	6.00
1988	100	PF65 75.00				

KM# 101 10 KIP
6.30 g., Copper-Nickel, 24.1 mm. **Rev:** Five-masted schooner

Date	Mintage	VF20	XF40	MS60	MS63	MS65
1988	—	—	—	—	5.00	7.00

KM# 30 10 KIP
Copper-Nickel **Subject:** World Soccer Championships - Italy 1990 **Obv:** National arms **Rev:** Soccer players

Date	Mintage	VF20	XF40	MS60	MS63	MS65
1989	2,000	—	—	3.00	6.00	9.00

KM# 46 10 KIP
Nickel Plated Steel **Series:** Olympics **Obv:** National arms **Rev:** Bicyclist

Date	Mintage	VF20	XF40	MS60	MS63	MS65
1991	5,000	—	—	—	10.00	12.50

KM# 51 10 KIP
Copper-Nickel **Series:** Endangered Wildlife **Obv:** National arms **Rev:** Tiger and cubs

Date	Mintage	VF20	XF40	MS60	MS63	MS65
1991	—	—	—	5.00	7.00	9.00

KM# 54 10 KIP
Copper **Series:** Endangered Wildlife **Obv:** National arms **Rev:** Tiger and cubs

Date	Mintage	VF20	XF40	MS60	MS63	MS65
1991	—	—	—	8.00	10.00	12.00

KM# 50 10 KIP
Copper-Nickel **Series:** Prehistoric Animals **Obv:** National arms **Rev:** Tyranosaurus Rex

Date	Mintage	VF20	XF40	MS60	MS63	MS65
1993	—	—	—	—	12.00	15.00

KM# 52 10 KIP
Copper-Nickel **Series:** Prehistoric Animals **Obv:** National arms **Rev:** Lufengosaurus

Date	Mintage	VF20	XF40	MS60	MS63	MS65
1994	—	—	—	—	12.00	15.00

KM# 61 10 KIP
Copper-Nickel, 38 mm. **Subject:** 1996 World Food Summit **Obv:** National arms **Rev:** Farmer plowing with water buffalo

Date	Mintage	VF20	XF40	MS60	MS63	MS65
1996	—	—	—	—	12.00	15.00

KM# 70 10 KIP
Copper-Nickel, 38 mm. **Series:** XXVII Olympiad **Subject:** Sydney 2000 **Obv:** National arms **Rev:** Sailboats, Neptune

Date	Mintage	VF20	XF40	MS60	MS63	MS65
1999	10,000	—	—	2.00	3.00	5.00

KM# 40 20 KIP
Copper-Nickel **Subject:** 10th Anniversary of People's Democratic Republic **Obv:** National arms within circle and wreath **Rev:** Value flanked by designs above date

Date	Mintage	VF20	XF40	MS60	MS63	MS65
1985	—	0.40	0.75	1.50	2.00	3.50

KM# 25 50 KIP
38.20 g., 0.900 Silver 1.1053 oz. ASW **Subject:** 10th Anniversary of People's Democratic Republic **Obv:** National arms **Rev:** Value flanked by designs below towered building

Date	Mintage	VF20	XF40	MS60	MS63	MS65
1985	2,000	PF63 45.00	PF65 60.00			

KM# 26 50 KIP
38.20 g., 0.900 Silver 1.1053 oz. ASW **Subject:** 10th Anniversary of People's Democratic Republic **Obv:** National arms **Rev:** Value flanked by designs below towered building

Date	Mintage	VF20	XF40	MS60	MS63	MS65
1985	2,000	PF63 45.00	PF65 60.00			

KM# 27 50 KIP
38.20 g., 0.900 Silver 1.1053 oz. ASW **Subject:** 10th Anniversary of People's Democratic Republic **Obv:** National arms **Rev:** Value flanked by designs below building

Date	Mintage	VF20	XF40	MS60	MS63	MS65
1985	2,000	PF63 45.00	PF65 60.00			

KM# 28 50 KIP
38.20 g., 0.900 Silver 1.1053 oz. ASW **Subject:** 10th Anniversary of People's Democratic Republic **Obv:** National arms **Rev:** Value flanked by designs below valley of jars

Date	Mintage	VF20	XF40	MS60	MS63	MS65
1985	2,000	PF63 45.00	PF65 60.00			

KM# 41 50 KIP
Copper-Nickel **Subject:** 10th Anniversary of People's Democratic Republic **Obv:** National arms within circle and wreath **Rev:** Value flanked by designs above date

Date	Mintage	VF20	XF40	MS60	MS63	MS65
1985	—	0.50	1.00	2.00	3.00	5.00

KM# 29 50 KIP
16.00 g., 0.999 Silver 0.5139 oz. ASW **Obv:** National arms **Rev:** 5-masted sailship "Prussia"

Date	Mintage	VF20	XF40	MS60	MS63	MS65
1988	2,000	PF63 25.00	PF65 30.00			

KM# 32 50 KIP
12.00 g., 0.999 Silver 0.3854 oz. ASW **Subject:** European Soccer Championship - Germany **Obv:** National arms **Rev:** Soccer players

Date	Mintage	VF20	XF40	MS60	MS63	MS65
1988	5,000	—	—	12.00	15.00	18.00

KM# 33 50 KIP
16.00 g., 0.999 Silver 0.5139 oz. ASW **Subject:** World Soccer Championship - Mexico 86 **Obv:** National arms **Rev:** Soccer players

Date	Mintage	VF20	XF40	MS60	MS63	MS65
ND-1988	5,000	PF63 22.00	PF65 27.00			

KM# 34 50 KIP

16.00 g., 0.999 Silver 0.5139 oz. ASW **Subject:** World Soccer Championship - Italy 1990 **Obv:** National arms **Rev:** Soccer players

Date	Mintage	VF20	XF40	MS60	MS63	MS65
1989	5,000	PF63 22.00	PF65 27.00			

KM# 35.1 50 KIP

16.00 g., 0.999 Silver 0.5139 oz. ASW **Series:** Winter Olympics **Subject:** Ice dancing **Obv:** National arms **Rev:** Ice dancers within design **Note:** Lightly frosted.

Date	Mintage	VF20	XF40	MS60	MS63	MS65
1989	—	PF63 22.00	PF65 28.00			

KM# 35.2 50 KIP

16.00 g., 0.999 Silver 0.5139 oz. ASW **Series:** Winter Olympics **Subject:** Ice dancing **Obv:** National arms **Rev:** Ice dancers within design **Note:** Extensive frosting.

Date	Mintage	VF20	XF40	MS60	MS63	MS65
1989	—	PF63 50.00	PF65 70.00			

KM# 36.1 50 KIP

16.00 g., 0.999 Silver 0.5139 oz. ASW **Series:** Summer Olympics **Subject:** Water polo **Obv:** National arms **Rev:** Water polo players within frosted water

Date	Mintage	VF20	XF40	MS60	MS63	MS65
1989	5,000	PF63 35.00	PF65 45.00			

KM# 36.2 50 KIP

16.00 g., 0.999 Silver 0.5139 oz. ASW **Series:** Summer Olympics **Subject:** Water polo **Obv:** National arms **Rev:** Water polo players within unfrosted water

Date	Mintage	VF20	XF40	MS60	MS63	MS65
1989	—	PF63 22.00	PF65 28.00			

KM# 44 50 KIP

12.00 g., 0.999 Silver 0.3854 oz. ASW **Subject:** World Cup Soccer **Obv:** National arms **Rev:** Soccer Ball

Date	Mintage	VF20	XF40	MS60	MS63	MS65
1991	—	—	—	12.00	15.00	18.00

KM# 45 50 KIP

20.00 g., 0.999 Silver 0.6424 oz. ASW **Subject:** Wildlife **Obv:** National arms **Rev:** Tiger and cubs

Date	Mintage	VF20	XF40	MS60	MS63	MS65
1991	100	—	—	—	125	175
1991	—	PF63 35.00	PF65 40.00			

KM# 47 50 KIP

20.00 g., 0.999 Silver 0.6424 oz. ASW **Subject:** Soccer **Obv:** National arms **Rev:** Goalie

Date	Mintage	VF20	XF40	MS60	MS63	MS65
1991	—	PF63 25.00	PF65 30.00			

KM# 48 50 KIP

20.00 g., 0.999 Silver 0.6424 oz. ASW **Subject:** Protection of Nature **Obv:** National arms **Rev:** Elephant

Date	Mintage	VF20	XF40	MS60	MS63	MS65
1993	—	PF63 35.00	PF65 40.00			

KM# 49 50 KIP

15.94 g., 0.999 Silver 0.512 oz. ASW **Series:** Prehistoric Animals **Obv:** National arms **Rev:** Sauroctonus

Date	Mintage	VF20	XF40	MS60	MS63	MS65
1993	—	PF63 32.00	PF65 38.00			

KM# 53 50 KIP

16.00 g., 0.999 Silver 0.5139 oz. ASW, 37.9 mm. **Subject:** Prehistoric Animals **Obv:** National arms **Rev:** Elasmosaurus fighting a Tylosaurus **Edge:** Plain

Date	Mintage	VF20	XF40	MS60	MS63	MS65
1994	—	PF63 40.00	PF65 45.00			

KM# 84 50 KIP

16.10 g., 0.999 Silver 0.5171 oz. ASW, 37.9 mm. **Obv:** National arms **Rev:** Megalosaurus

Date	Mintage	VF20	XF40	MS60	MS63	MS65
1994	—	PF65 37.00				

KM# 56 50 KIP

20.00 g., 0.999 Silver 0.6424 oz. ASW **Series:** Olympics **Obv:** National arms **Rev:** Javelin throwers

Date	Mintage	VF20	XF40	MS60	MS63	MS65
1995	Est. 15000	PF63 18.00	PF65 22.00			

KM# 57 50 KIP

20.00 g., 0.999 Silver 0.6424 oz. ASW **Subject:** World Cup Soccer **Obv:** National arms **Rev:** Player and cathedral

Date	Mintage	VF20	XF40	MS60	MS63	MS65
1996	100	—	—	—	75.00	95.00
1996	10,000	PF63 22.00	PF65 27.00			

KM# 58 50 KIP
20.00 g., 0.999 Silver 0.6424 oz. ASW **Subject:** World Cup Soccer **Obv:** National arms **Rev:** Stadium within map of France **Note:** Multicolor design.

Date	Mintage	VF20	XF40	MS60	MS63	MS65
1996	10,000	PF63 25.00	PF65 30.00			

KM# 62 50 KIP
20.00 g., 0.999 Silver 0.6424 oz. ASW **Series:** XXVII Olympiad **Obv:** National arms **Rev:** Archer - Diana, goddess of the hunt

Date	Mintage	VF20	XF40	MS60	MS63	MS65
1996	—	PF63 27.00	PF65 32.00			

KM# 63 50 KIP
20.00 g., 0.999 Silver 0.6424 oz. ASW **Series:** XXVII Olympiad **Obv:** National arms **Rev:** Multicolor torch and athletes **Note:** Multicolor design.

Date	Mintage	VF20	XF40	MS60	MS63	MS65
1996	—	PF63 27.00	PF65 32.00			

KM# 64 50 KIP
15.00 g., 0.999 Silver 0.4818 oz. ASW **Subject:** World of Adventure - Leif Ericson **Obv:** National arms **Rev:** Viking longship

Date	Mintage	VF20	XF40	MS60	MS63	MS65
1996	—	PF63 35.00	PF65 40.00			

KM# 79 50 KIP
15.00 g., 0.999 Silver 0.4818 oz. ASW, 35 mm. **Series:** World Cup Soccer **Obv:** National arms **Rev:** Soccer player with ball and map background **Edge:** Plain

Date	Mintage	VF20	XF40	MS60	MS63	MS65
1996	—	PF63 22.00	PF65 28.00			

KM# 97 50 KIP
Silver, 37 mm. **Subject:** World Food Summit - 1996 in Rome **Obv:** National arms **Rev:** Farmer plowing with ox **Edge:** Reeded

Date	Mintage	VF20	XF40	MS60	MS63	MS65
1996	—	—	—	25.00	30.00	35.00

KM# 82 50 KIP
15.00 g., 0.999 Silver 0.4818 oz. ASW partially gilt **Rev:** Buddah wheel and the teaching, gilt

Date	Mintage	VF20	XF40	MS60	MS63	MS65
1997	—	PF65 125	PF67 150			

KM# 42 100 KIP
3.15 g., 0.999 Gold 0.1012 oz. AGW **Obv:** National arms and legend above value **Rev:** 5-masted sailship "Prussia"

Date	Mintage	VF20	XF40	MS60	MS63	MS65
1988	500	—	—	—	170	220

KM# 43 100 KIP
3.15 g., 0.999 Gold 0.1012 oz. AGW **Subject:** 10th Anniversary of People's Democratic Republic **Obv:** National arms **Rev:** Radiant sun and temple

Date	Mintage	VF20	XF40	MS60	MS63	MS65
1990	—	—	—	—	175	225

KM# 69 500 KIP
20.00 g., 0.925 Silver 0.5948 oz. ASW **Subject:** Kouprey **Obv:** National arms **Rev:** Wild bull

Date	Mintage	VF20	XF40	MS60	MS63	MS65
1998	10,000	PF63 28.00	PF65 35.00			

KM# 111 500 KIP
20.00 g., 0.925 Silver 0.5948 oz. ASW, 34 mm. **Rev:** Lesser Panda on tree limb

Date	Mintage	VF20	XF40	MS60	MS63	MS65
2000	—	PF63 35.00	PF65 40.00			

KM# 156 1000 KIP
31.67 g., 0.999 Silver 1.0172 oz. ASW **Series:** Endangered Wildlife **Obv:** National arms **Rev:** Gibbon

Date	Mintage	VF20	XF40	MS60	MS63	MS65
1996	—	PF63 35.00	PF65 40.00			

KM# 67 1000 KIP
31.47 g., 0.925 Silver 0.9359 oz. ASW **Series:** Endangered Wildlife **Obv:** National arms **Rev:** Two long-horned saola

Date	Mintage	VF20	XF40	MS60	MS63	MS65
1997	15,000	PF65 35.00				

KM# 59 1200 KIP
Nickel Bonded Steel, 32 mm. **Subject:** Food for All, FAO 40th Anniversary **Obv:** National arms **Rev:** Three people harvesting rice below logo and dates

Date	Mintage	VF20	XF40	MS60	MS63	MS65
ND-1995	—	—	—	2.00	4.00	6.00

KM# 68 2000 KIP
1.24 g., 0.999 Gold 0.040 oz. AGW **Subject:** That Luang **Obv:** National arms **Rev:** Temple

Date	Mintage	VF20	XF40	MS60	MS63	MS65
1998	—	PF65 70.00	PF67 80.00			

KM# 109 2000 KIP
3.11 g., 0.585 Gold 0.0585 oz. AGW, 18.5 mm. **Subject:** Sydney Olympics, 2000 **Rev:** Archer

Date	Mintage	VF20	XF40	MS60	MS63	MS65
1998	Est. 3000	PF65 125	PF67 135			

KM# 112 2000 KIP
1.24 g., 0.999 Gold 0.0398 oz. AGW, 13.92 mm. **Subject:** Dynasty of a Million Elephants **Rev:** Elephants in mountain transport

Date	Mintage	VF20	XF40	MS60	MS63	MS65
2000	—	PF65 75.00	PF67 85.00			

KM# 72 3000 KIP

20.00 g., 0.925 Silver 0.5948 oz. ASW, 38.6 mm. **Subject:** Retrospection Rabbit **Obv:** National arms **Rev:** Multicolor rabbit looking back **Edge:** Reeded

Date	Mintage	VF20	XF40	MS60	MS63	MS65
1999	—	PF63 30.00	PF65 35.00			

KM# 73 3000 KIP

20.00 g., 0.925 Silver 0.5948 oz. ASW **Subject:** Anticipation Rabbit **Obv:** National arms **Rev:** Partially gold-plated rabbit with radiant sun background

Date	Mintage	VF20	XF40	MS60	MS63	MS65
1999	—	PF63 35.00	PF65 40.00			

KM# 91 3000 KIP

20.00 g., 0.925 Silver 0.5948 oz. ASW, 38.7 mm. **Subject:** Year of the Rabbit **Obv:** National arms **Rev:** Rabbit leaping to right over latent image date **Edge:** Reeded

Date	Mintage	VF20	XF40	MS60	MS63	MS65
1999	—	PF63 32.00	PF65 37.00			

KM# 60 5000 KIP

7.76 g., 0.5833 Gold 0.1455 oz. AGW **Series:** Olympics **Obv:** National arms **Rev:** Two boxers

Date	Mintage	VF20	XF40	MS60	MS63	MS65
1996	Est. 3000	—	—	—	250	300

KM# 80 5000 KIP

15.00 g., 0.999 Silver 0.4818 oz. ASW, 35 mm. **Series:** Olympics **Obv:** National arms **Rev:** Archer with statue in background **Edge:** Plain

Date	Mintage	VF20	XF40	MS60	MS63	MS65
1998	—	PF63 22.00	PF65 27.00			

KM# 81 5000 KIP

15.00 g., 0.999 Silver 0.4818 oz. ASW, 35 mm. **Obv:** National arms **Rev:** Multicolor torch and athletes **Edge:** Plain

Date	Mintage	VF20	XF40	MS60	MS63	MS65
1998	—	PF63 35.00	PF65 40.00			

KM# 108 5000 KIP

155.50 g., 0.999 Silver 4.9944 oz. ASW, 65 mm. **Rev:** That Luang temple in Vientiane

Date	Mintage	VF20	XF40	MS60	MS63	MS65
1998	Est. 1500	PF63 125	PF65 150			

KM# 71 5000 KIP

20.05 g., 0.999 Silver 0.644 oz. ASW **Series:** XXVII Olympiad **Subject:** Sydney 2000 **Obv:** National arms **Rev:** Sailboats, Neptune

Date	Mintage	VF20	XF40	MS60	MS63	MS65
1999	5,000	PF65 32.00				

KM# 92 5000 KIP

15.00 g., 0.999 Silver 0.4818 oz. ASW, 35.1 mm. **Obv:** National arms **Rev:** St. Thomas Aquinas **Edge:** Plain

Date	Mintage	VF20	XF40	MS60	MS63	MS65
1999	—	PF63 35.00	PF65 40.00			

KM# 74 5000 KIP

20.00 g., 0.925 Silver 0.5948 oz. ASW, 39 mm. **Subject:** Silver Dragon Fish **Obv:** National arms **Rev:** Fish **Edge:** Reeded

Date	Mintage	VF20	XF40	MS60	MS63	MS65
2000-2001	10,000	PF65 40.00				

Note: Latent image date

KM# 75 5000 KIP

20.00 g., 0.925 Silver 0.5948 oz. ASW, 39 mm. **Subject:** Red Dragon Fish **Obv:** National arms **Rev:** Red colored fish **Edge:** Reeded

Date	Mintage	VF20	XF40	MS60	MS63	MS65
2000-2001	10,000	PF65 40.00				

Note: Latent image date

KM# 76 5000 KIP

20.00 g., 0.925 Silver 0.5948 oz. ASW, 39 mm. **Subject:** Golden Dragon Fish **Obv:** National arms **Rev:** Jumping fish below gold cameo **Edge:** Reeded

Date	Mintage	VF20	XF40	MS60	MS63	MS65
2000-2001	Est. 4000	PF65 50.00				

Note: Latent image date

KM# 93 5000 KIP

15.14 g., 0.999 Silver 0.4863 oz. ASW, 35.1 mm. **Subject:** Third Millennium **Obv:** National arms **Rev:** World map with date 2000/1999 **Edge:** Plain

Date	Mintage	VF20	XF40	MS60	MS63	MS65
ND(2000)	—	PF63 35.00	PF65 40.00			

KM# 77 10000 KIP

1.24 g., 0.9999 Gold 0.040 oz. AGW, 14 mm. **Subject:** Golden Dragon Fish **Obv:** National arms **Rev:** Jumping fish **Edge:** Reeded **Note:** Date as a latent image.

Date	Mintage	VF20	XF40	MS60	MS63	MS65
2000-2001	—	—	—	—	75.00	85.00

KM# 110 20000 KIP

7.78 g., 0.999 Gold 0.2499 oz. AGW **Subject:** Year of the rabbit **Rev:** Rabbit

Date	Mintage	VF20	XF40	MS60	MS63	MS65
1999	—	PF65 425	PF67 475			

KM# 83 50000 KIP

7.78 g., 0.999 Gold 0.2497 oz. AGW, 32.2 mm. **Obv:** National arms **Rev:** Red Dragon Fish **Edge:** Reeded

Date	Mintage	VF20	XF40	MS60	MS63	MS65
2000-2001	3,000	PF65 400	PF67 450			

KM# 78 100000 KIP

15.55 g., 0.9999 Gold 0.500 oz. AGW, 27 mm. **Subject:** Golden Dragon Fish **Obv:** National arms **Rev:** Multicolored holographic jumping fish **Edge:** Reeded

Date	Mintage	VF20	XF40	MS60	MS63	MS65
2000-2001	3,000	PF65 800	PF67 875			

Note: Latent image date

ESSAIS

Standard metals unless otherwise noted

KM#	Date	Mintage	Identification	Mkt Val
E1	1952(a)	1,200	10 Cents.	50.00
E2	1952(a)	1,200	20 Cents.	55.00
E3	1952(a)	1,200	50 Cents.	60.00

PIEDFORT WITH ESSAI

Standard metals unless otherwise noted

KM#	Date	Mintage	Identification	Mkt Val
PE1	1952(a)	104	10 Cents.	225
PE2	1952(a)	104	20 Cents.	225
PE3	1952(a)	104	50 Cents.	250

PIEDFORT

KM#	Date	Mintage	Identification	Mkt Val
P1	1988	—	50 Kip. Silver.	85.00

MINT SETS

KM#	Date	Mintage	Identification	Issue Price	Mkt Val
MS1	1971 (4)	—	KM7, 8, 10, 12	—	350
MS2	1975 (6)	100	KM16-21	—	1,450
MS3	1975 (3)	300	KM16-18	—	450

PROOF SETS

KM#	Date	Mintage	Identification	Issue Price	Mkt Val
PS1	1971 (5)	Est. 10000	KM9, 11, 13-15	467	6,525
PS2	1971 (4)	Est. 20000	KM7, 8, 10, 12	163	475
PS3	1975 (6)	—	KM16-21	—	1,575
PS4	1975 (3)	650	KM16.1, 17, 18	—	475
PS5	1975 (3)	—	KM19-21	349	1,100
PS6	1985 (4)	2,000	KM25-28	—	240
PS7	2000-2001 (3)	3,500	KM#74-76	138	125
PS8	2000-2001 (4)	500	KM#74-77	213	200
PS9	2000-2001 (2)	800	KM#78, 83	—	1,100

LATVIA

The Republic of Latvia, the central Baltic state in east Europe, has an area of 24,749 sq. mi. (43,601 sq. km.) and a population of 2.6 million. Capital: Riga. Livestock raising and manufacturing are the chief industries. Butter, bacon, fertilizers and telephone equipment are exported.

The Latvians, of Aryan descent primarily from the German Order of Livonian Knights, were nomadic tribesmen who settled along the Baltic prior to the 13th century. Ideally situated as a trade route and lacking a central government, conquered in 1561 by Poland and Sweden. Following the third partition of Poland by Austria, Prussia and Russia in 1795, Latvia came under Russian domination and did not experience autonomy until the Russian Revolution of 1917 provided an opportunity for freedom. The Latvian Republic was established on Nov. 18, 1918. The republic was occupied by Soviet troops and annexed to the Soviet Union in 1940. Following the German occupation of 1941-44, it was retaken by Russia and reestablished as a member republic of the Soviet Union. Western countries, including the United States, did not recognize Latvia's incorporation into the Soviet Union.

The coinage issued during the early 20th Century Republic is now obsolete.

Latvia declared their independence from the U.S.S.R. on August 22, 1991.

MONETARY SYSTEM

100 Santimu = 1 Lats

FIRST REPUBLIC

1918-1939

STANDARD COINAGE

KM# 1 SANTIMS

1.65 g., Bronze, 17 mm. **Obv:** National arms above ribbon **Rev:** Value and date **Edge:** Plain **Note:** Struck at Huguenin Freres, Le Locle, Switzerland.

Date	Mintage	VF20	XF40	MS60	MS63	MS65
1922	5,000,000	5.00	7.00	12.00	16.00	—
1923	10	—	—	2,000	—	—
1924	4,990,000	5.00	7.00	12.00	16.00	—
1926	5,000,000	5.00	7.00	12.00	16.00	—
1928	5,000,000	5.00	7.00	12.00	16.00	—
Note: Mint name below ribbon						
1928	Inc. above	14.00	28.00	40.00	60.00	—
Note: Without mint name below ribbon						
1932	5,000,000	5.00	7.00	12.00	16.00	—
1932 Proof	—	—	—	—	—	—
1935	5,000,000	5.00	7.00	12.00	16.00	—

KM# 10 SANTIMS

1.80 g., Bronze, 17 mm. **Obv:** National arms above sprigs **Rev:** Value divides sprigs above date **Edge:** Plain

Date	Mintage	VF20	XF40	MS60	MS63	MS65
1937	2,700,000	5.00	8.00	14.00	20.00	—
1938	1,900,000	6.00	10.00	15.00	22.50	—
1939	3,400,000	—	5.00	7.00	9.00	12.00
Note: Most were never placed into circulation						

KM# 2 2 SANTIMI

2.00 g., Bronze, 19.5 mm. **Obv:** National arms above ribbon **Rev:** Value and date **Edge:** Plain

Date	Mintage	VF20	XF40	MS60	MS63	MS65
1922	10,000,000	5.00	10.00	15.00	25.00	—
Note: Mint name below ribbon						
1922	Inc. above	12.00	25.00	35.00	50.00	—
Note: Without mint name below ribbon						
1923	2	—	—	—	3,250	5,500
1926	5,000,000	5.00	9.00	15.00	20.00	—
1928	5,000,000	5.00	9.00	15.00	20.00	—
1932	5,000,000	5.00	9.00	15.00	20.00	—
1932 Proof	—	—	—	—	—	—

KM# 11.1 2 SANTIMI

2.00 g., Bronze, 19 mm. **Obv:** National arms above sprigs **Rev:** Value flanked by sprigs above date **Edge:** Plain

Date	Mintage	VF20	XF40	MS60	MS63	MS65
1937	45,000	35.00	50.00	70.00	100	—

KM# 11.2 2 SANTIMI

2.00 g., Bronze, 19.5 mm. **Obv:** National arms above sprigs **Rev:** Value flanked by sprigs above date **Edge:** Plain

Date	Mintage	VF20	XF40	MS60	MS63	MS65
1939	5,000,000	—	9.00	12.00	15.00	20.00
Note: Most were never placed in circulation						

KM# 3 5 SANTIMI

3.00 g., Bronze, 22 mm. **Obv:** National arms above ribbon **Rev:** Value and date

Date	Mintage	VF20	XF40	MS60	MS63	MS65
1922	15,000,000	4.00	7.00	12.00	16.00	—
Note: Mint name below ribbon						
1922	Inc. above	8.00	20.00	30.00	45.00	—
Note: Without name below ribbon						
1923	2	—	—	—	3,500	6,000

KM# 4 10 SANTIMU

3.00 g., Nickel, 19 mm. **Obv:** National arms above ribbon divides date **Rev:** Value above oat sprig **Edge:** Plain **Note:** Struck at Huguenin.

Date	Mintage	VF20	XF40	MS60	MS63	MS65
1922	15,000,000	4.00	7.00	12.00	17.00	—

KM# 5 20 SANTIMU

6.00 g., Nickel, 21 mm. **Obv:** National arms above ribbon divides date **Rev:** Value above oat sprig **Edge:** Plain **Note:** Struck at Huguenin.

Date	Mintage	VF20	XF40	MS60	MS63	MS65
1922	15,000,000	5.00	10.00	17.00	25.00	—

KM# 6 50 SANTIMU

6.50 g., Nickel, 25 mm. **Obv:** National arms above ribbon divides date **Rev:** Value to right of standing figure **Edge:** Plain **Note:** Struck at Huguenin.

Date	Mintage	VF20	XF40	MS60	MS63	MS65
1922	9,000,000	7.00	10.00	17.00	25.00	—

KM# 7 LATS

5.00 g., 0.835 Silver 0.1342 oz. ASW, 23 mm. **Obv:** Arms with supporters **Rev:** Value and date within wreath **Edge:** Milled

Date	Mintage	VF20	XF40	MS60	MS63	MS65
1923	—	—	—	—	900	1,100
1924	10,000,000	9.00	15.00	25.00	45.00	75.00

KM# 8 2 LATI

10.00 g., 0.835 Silver 0.2685 oz. ASW, 27 mm. **Obv:** Arms with supporters **Rev:** Value and date within wreath **Edge:** Milled

Date	Mintage	VF20	XF40	MS60	MS63	MS65
1925	6,386,000	7.00	12.00	20.00	35.00	60.00
1926	1,114,000	9.00	15.00	25.00	45.00	75.00

KM# 9 5 LATI

25.00 g., 0.835 Silver 0.6711 oz. ASW, 37 mm. **Obv:** Crowned head right **Rev:** Arms with supporters above value **Edge:** DIEVS *** SVETI *** LATVOJU ***

Date	Mintage	VF20	XF40	MS60	MS63	MS65
1929	1,000,000	25.00	35.00	55.00	75.00	95.00
1929 Proof	—	—	—	—	—	—
1931	2,000,000	25.00	35.00	50.00	65.00	85.00
1931 Proof	—	—	—	—	—	—
1932	600,000	30.00	45.00	60.00	85.00	110
1932	—	PF63 3,500				

MODERN REPUBLIC

1991-present

KM# 15 SANTIMS

1.60 g., Copper Clad Steel, 15.65 mm. **Obv:** National arms **Rev:** Value flanked by diamonds below lined arch **Edge:** Plain

Date	Mintage	VF20	XF40	MS60	MS63	MS65
1992	40,000,000	—	0.15	0.25	0.45	1.00
1997	40,000,000	—	0.10	0.20	0.30	1.00

KM# 21 2 SANTIMI

1.90 g., Copper Clad Steel, 17 mm. **Obv:** National arms **Rev:** Lined arch above value flanked by diamonds **Edge:** Plain

Date	Mintage	VF20	XF40	MS60	MS63	MS65
1992	35,000,000	0.10	0.25	0.50	0.75	1.25
2000	35,000,000	—	0.20	0.30	0.50	0.75

KM# 16 5 SANTIMI

2.50 g., Nickel-Brass, 18.5 mm. **Obv:** National arms **Obv. Legend:** LATVIJAS REPUBLIKA **Rev:** Lined arch above value flanked by diamonds **Edge:** Plain

Date	Mintage	VF20	XF40	MS60	MS63	MS65
1992	30,000,000	0.20	0.45	0.75	1.25	2.00

KM# 17 10 SANTIMU

3.25 g., Nickel-Brass, 19.9 mm. **Obv:** National arms **Rev:** Lined arch above value flanked by diamonds **Edge:** Plain

Date	Mintage	VF20	XF40	MS60	MS63	MS65
1992	30,000,000	0.25	0.50	1.00	1.50	2.50

KM# 22.1 20 SANTIMU

4.00 g., Nickel-Brass, 21.5 mm. **Obv:** National arms **Rev:** Lined arch above value flanked by diamonds **Edge:** Plain **Note:** 1.5mm thick.

Date	Mintage	VF20	XF40	MS60	MS63	MS65
1992	30,000,000	—	0.50	1.00	1.75	3.00

KM# 22.2 20 SANTIMU

4.00 g., Brass Plated Steel, 21.5 mm. **Note:** 1.65mm thick., Planchet for Geman 10 pfennig.

Date	Mintage	VF20	XF40	MS60	MS63	MS65
1992	—	—	100	500	—	—

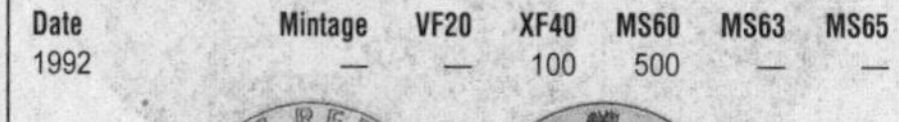

KM# 13 50 SANTIMU
3.50 g., Copper-Nickel, 18.8 mm. **Obv:** National arms **Rev:** Triple sprig above value **Edge:** Reeded

Date	Mintage	VF20	XF40	MS60	MS63	MS65
1992	15,000,000	—	1.00	1.50	3.50	5.00

KM# 12 LATS
4.80 g., Copper-Nickel, 21.75 mm. **Obv:** Arms with supporters **Rev:** Salmon above value **Edge Lettering:** LATVIJAS BANKA • LATVIJAS BANKA

Date	Mintage	VF20	XF40	MS60	MS63	MS65
1992	20,000,000	—	1.25	2.00	3.00	5.00

KM# 23 LATS
28.28 g., 0.925 Silver 0.841 oz. ASW **Series:** UN 50th Anniversary **Obv:** National arms **Rev:** Many people holding hands

Date	Mintage	VF20	XF40	MS60	MS63	MS65
1995	100,000	PF63 40.00	PF65 45.00			

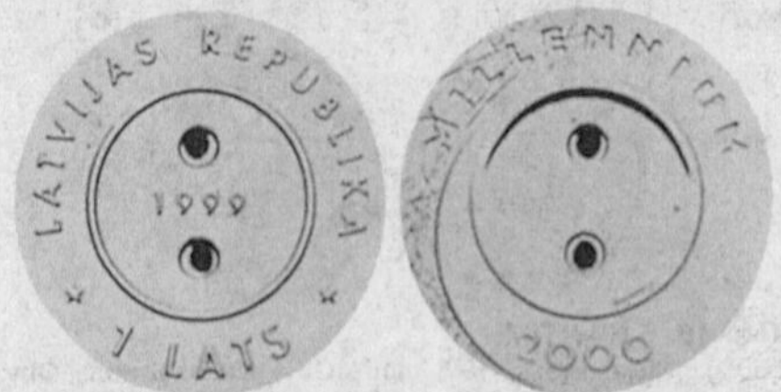

KM# 39 LATS
15.20 g., 0.925 Silver 0.452 oz. ASW **Subject:** Millennium **Obv:** Date divides holes within circle **Rev:** Vertical holes within circle, date on bottom **Note:** Button design.

Date	Mintage	VF20	XF40	MS60	MS63	MS65
1999-2000	—	PF63 50.00	PF65 55.00			

KM# 44 LATS
20.00 g., 0.925 Silver 0.5948 oz. ASW, 34 mm. **Series:** Olympics **Obv:** National arms **Rev:** Two cyclists **Edge:** Lettered

Date	Mintage	VF20	XF40	MS60	MS63	MS65
1999	—	PF63 30.00	PF65 35.00			

KM# 45 LATS
31.47 g., 0.925 Silver 0.9359 oz. ASW, 38.6 mm. **Subject:** European mink **Obv:** National arms **Rev:** Mink on rock **Edge:** Lettered

Date	Mintage	VF20	XF40	MS60	MS63	MS65
1999	—	PF63 40.00	PF65 45.00			

KM# 46 LATS
31.47 g., 0.925 Silver 0.9359 oz. ASW, 38.6 mm. **Subject:** Hanseatic City of Ventspils **Obv:** City arms above value **Rev:** Building and ship **Edge Lettering:** LATVIJAS REPUBLIKA LATVIJAS BANKA

Date	Mintage	VF20	XF40	MS60	MS63	MS65
2000	—	PF63 45.00	PF65 50.00			

KM# 47 LATS
31.47 g., 0.925 Silver 0.9359 oz. ASW, 38.6 mm. **Subject:** Earth - Roots **Obv:** Stylized "Roots" pattern **Rev:** Landscape and value **Edge:** Plain

Date	Mintage	VF20	XF40	MS60	MS63	MS65
2000	6,000	PF63 45.00	PF65 50.00			

KM# 48 LATS
31.47 g., 0.925 Silver 0.9359 oz. ASW, 38.6 mm. **Subject:** UNICEF **Obv:** National arms **Obv. Legend:** LATVIJAS REPUBLIXA above value **Rev:** Child art and logo **Edge Lettering:** "LATVIJAS BANKA" twice

Date	Mintage	VF20	XF40	MS60	MS63	MS65
2000	6,000	PF63 45.00	PF65 50.00			

KM# 14 2 LATI
6.00 g., Copper-Nickel, 24.35 mm. **Obv:** Arms with supporters **Rev:** Cow grazing above value **Edge Lettering:** LATVIJAS BANKA

Date	Mintage	VF20	XF40	MS60	MS63	MS65
1992	10,000,000	—	3.00	4.50	6.50	10.00

KM# 18 2 LATI
6.00 g., Copper-Nickel, 24.35 mm. **Subject:** 75th Anniversary - Declaration of Independence **Obv:** Arms with supporters **Rev:** Artistic lined art above value and dates **Edge Lettering:** LATVIJAS VALSTS 75 GADI

Date	Mintage	VF20	XF40	MS60	MS63	MS65
ND-1993	4,000,000	—	3.50	5.00	7.50	12.00
ND-1993	200,000	PF65 14.00				

KM# 38 2 LATI
9.50 g., Bi-Metallic Nickel-Brass center in Copper-Nickel ring, 26.3 mm. **Obv:** Arms with supporters within circle **Rev:** Cow above value within circle **Edge Lettering:** LATVIJAS BANKA

Date	Mintage	VF20	XF40	MS60	MS63	MS65
1999	5,000,000	—	3.00	4.50	7.50	12.00

KM# 19 10 LATU
25.18 g., 0.925 Silver 0.7487 oz. ASW, 36.07 mm. **Subject:** 75th Anniversary - Declaration of Independence **Obv:** Arms with supporters **Rev:** Artistic lines and design above value and dates

Date	Mintage	VF20	XF40	MS60	MS63	MS65
ND-1993	30,000	PF65 30.00				

KM# 24 10 LATU
31.47 g., 0.925 Silver 0.9359 oz. ASW **Series:** Olympics **Obv:** Arms with supporters **Rev:** Man paddling canoe

Date	Mintage	VF20	XF40	MS60	MS63	MS65
1994	30,000	PF65 45.00				

KM# 25 10 LATU
31.47 g., 0.925 Silver 0.9359 oz. ASW **Subject:** Julia Maria **Obv:** National arms **Rev:** 3-masted schooner

Date	Mintage	VF20	XF40	MS60	MS63	MS65
1995	20,000	PF65 45.00				

KM# 26 10 LATU
31.47 g., 0.925 Silver 0.9359 oz. ASW **Subject:** Riga 800 **Obv:** Standing figure in long robe with turban on head within warped circle **Rev:** First city seal within circle

Date	Mintage	VF20	XF40	MS60	MS63	MS65
1995 (1996)	Est. 8000	PF65 55.00				

KM# 27 10 LATU
31.47 g., 0.925 Silver 0.9359 oz. ASW **Subject:** 800th Anniversary - Riga **Obv:** Coat of arms from 1368 **Rev:** The Great Gould's coat of arms from 1354

Date	Mintage	VF20	XF40	MS60	MS63	MS65
1995 (1996)	—	PF65 45.00				

KM# 33 10 LATU
31.47 g., 0.925 Silver 0.9359 oz. ASW **Series:** Endangered Wildlife **Obv:** Arms with supporters **Rev:** Grieze bird **Edge:** Lettered **Edge Lettering:** LATVIJAS BANKA \ (2x)

Date	Mintage	VF20	XF40	MS60	MS63	MS65
1996	15,000	PF65 50.00				

KM# 34 10 LATU
31.47 g., 0.925 Silver 0.9359 oz. ASW **Subject:** Riga - XVI Century **Obv:** Old coin design above value **Rev:** Old city view

Date	Mintage	VF20	XF40	MS60	MS63	MS65
1996	—	PF65 50.00				

KM# 36 10 LATU
31.35 g., 0.999 Silver 1.0069 oz. ASW **Subject:** 800th Anniversary of Riga **Obv:** Old coin design with St. Christopher within warped circle **Rev:** Old coin design with city arms within partial circle **Edge:** Lettered **Edge Lettering:** LATVIJAS REPUBLIKA LATVIJAS BANKA

Date	Mintage	VF20	XF40	MS60	MS63	MS65
1996	—	PF65 50.00				

KM# 28 10 LATU
31.32 g., 0.925 Silver 0.9314 oz. ASW **Obv:** Arms with supporters **Rev:** 12th-century ship above its sunken remains **Edge:** Lettered **Edge Lettering:** LATIJAS BANKAS

Date	Mintage	VF20	XF40	MS60	MS63	MS65
1997	15,000	PF65 50.00				

KM# 35 10 LATU
31.47 g., 0.925 Silver 0.9359 oz. ASW **Subject:** Riga - XVII Century **Obv:** Old coin design of arms with supporters **Rev:** Aerial view of walled city

Date	Mintage	VF20	XF40	MS60	MS63	MS65
1997	—	PF65 50.00				

KM# 42 10 LATU
1.24 g., 0.999 Gold 0.040 oz. AGW, 13.92 mm. **Obv:** Arms with supporters **Rev:** Sailing ship "Julia Maria" **Edge:** Reeded

Date	Mintage	VF20	XF40	MS60	MS63	MS65
1997	—	PF65 60.00	PF67 70.00			

KM# 29 10 LATU
1.24 g., 0.9999 Gold 0.040 oz. AGW **Subject:** 800th Anniversary - Riga **Obv:** City arms on old coin design **Rev:** City arms and ship on old coin design

Date	Mintage	VF20	XF40	MS60	MS63	MS65
1998	—	PF65 60.00	PF67 70.00			

KM# 30 10 LATU
31.47 g., 0.925 Silver 0.9359 oz. ASW **Subject:** 800th Anniversary - Riga **Obv:** National song festival procession **Rev:** Crowned Riga city arms

Date	Mintage	VF20	XF40	MS60	MS63	MS65
1998	Est. 8000	PF65 50.00				

KM# 31 10 LATU
31.47 g., 0.925 Silver 0.9359 oz. ASW **Subject:** 800th Anniversary - Riga **Obv:** Liberty Monument **Rev:** City arms with supporters

Date	Mintage	VF20	XF40	MS60	MS63	MS65
1998	Est. 8000	PF65 50.00				

KM# 32 10 LATU
31.47 g., 0.925 Silver 0.9359 oz. ASW **Obv:** National arms **Rev:** 1925 Icebreaker "Krisjanis Valdemars"

Date	Mintage	VF20	XF40	MS60	MS63	MS65
1998	10,000	PF65 45.00				

KM# 43 10 LATU
3.11 g., 0.583 Gold 0.0583 oz. AGW, 18.5 mm. **Series:** Olympics **Obv:** Arms with supporters **Rev:** Javelin thrower **Edge:** Reeded

Date	Mintage	VF20	XF40	MS60	MS63	MS65
1999	—	PF67 100				

KM# 37 20 LATU
31.47 g., 0.925 Silver 0.9359 oz. ASW **Obv:** City arms **Rev:** Melngalvgu **Edge Lettering:** LATVIJAS REPUBLIKA LATVIJAS BANKA

Date	Mintage	VF20	XF40	MS60	MS63	MS65
1997	—	PF65 55.00				

KM# 41 20 LATU
7.78 g., 0.583 Gold 0.1458 oz. AGW, 25 mm. **Obv:** Arms with supporters **Rev:** Sailing ship "Gekronte Ehlendt" **Edge:** Reeded

Date	Mintage	VF20	XF40	MS60	MS63	MS65
1997	—	PF67 250				

KM# 20 100 LATU
13.34 g., 0.5833 Gold 0.2501 oz. AGW **Subject:** 75th Anniversary - Declaration of Independence **Obv:** National arms **Obv. Legend:** LATVIJAS - REPUBLIKA **Rev:** Artistic lined design above value and dates

Date	Mintage	VF20	XF40	MS60	MS63	MS65
ND-1993	5,000	PF67 450				

KM# 40 100 LATU
16.20 g., 0.999 Gold 0.5203 oz. AGW, 24 mm. **Subject:** Development **Obv:** Arms with supporters **Rev:** Partial circle within value **Edge:** Reeded and plain sections

Date	Mintage	VF20	XF40	MS60	MS63	MS65
1998	—	PF67 850				

PATTERNS

Including off metal strikes

KM#	Date	Mintage	Identification	Mkt Val
Pn1	1922	—	10 Santimu. Silver. KM4.	450
Pn2	1922	—	10 Santimu. Aluminum-Bronze. KM4.	500
Pn3	1924	—	2 Lati. Silver.	550
Pn4	1938	—	2 Santimi. Bronze. KM11.2.	850

MINT SETS

KM#	Date	Mintage	Identification	Issue Price	Mkt Val
MS1	1992 (8)	—	KM12-17, 21-22	—	50.00

PROOF SETS

KM#	Date	Mintage	Identification	Issue Price	Mkt Val
PS1	ND (1993) (3)	1,800	KM18-20	—	500

LEBANON

The Republic of Lebanon, situated on the eastern shore of the Mediterranean Sea between Syria and Israel, has an area of 4,015 sq. mi. (10,400 sq. km.) and a population of 3.5 million. Capital: Beirut. The economy is based on agriculture, trade and tourism. Fruit, other foodstuffs and textiles are exported.

Almost at the beginning of recorded history, Lebanon appeared as the well-wooded hinterland of the Phoenicians who exploited its famous forests of cedar. The mountains were a Christian refuge and a Crusader stronghold. Lebanon, the history of which is essentially the same as that of Syria, came under control of the Ottoman Turks early in the 16th century. Following the collapse of the Ottoman Empire after World War I, Lebanon, along with Syria, became a French mandate. The French drew a border around the predominantly Christian Lebanon *Sanjak* or administrative subdivision and on Sept. 1, 1920, proclaimed the area the State of Grand Lebanon (*Etat du Grand Liban*) a republic under French control. France announced the independence of Lebanon on Nov. 26, 1941, but the last British and French troops didn't leave until the end of August 1946.

TITLES

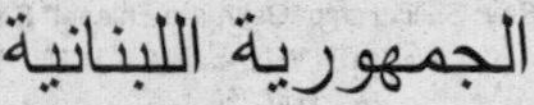

al-Jomhuriya(t) al-Lubnaniya(t)

MINT MARKS

(a) - Paris, privy marks only
(u) - Utrecht, privy marks only

MONETARY SYSTEM

100 Piastres = 1 Livre (Pound)

FRENCH PROTECTORATE

STANDARD COINAGE

KM# 9 1/2 PIASTRE
4.00 g., Copper-Nickel, 21 mm. **Obv:** Value within sprigs above date **Rev:** Value within roped wreath flanked by oat sprigs above date

Date	Mintage	F12	VF20	XF40	MS60	MS63
1934 (a)	200,000	8.00	20.00	50.00	100	200
1936 (a)	1,200,000	3.00	8.00	20.00	50.00	100

KM# 9a 1/2 PIASTRE
Zinc **Obv:** Value within sprigs above date **Rev:** Value within roped wreath flanked by oat sprigs above date

Date	Mintage	F12	VF20	XF40	MS60	MS63
1941 (a)	1,000,000	3.00	10.00	25.00	60.00	125

KM# 3 PIASTRE
5.00 g., Copper-Nickel, 24 mm. **Obv:** Hole in center of wreath **Rev:** Hole in center flanked by lion heads with value and date below

Date	Mintage	F12	VF20	XF40	MS60	MS63
1925 (a)	1,500,000	3.00	10.00	30.00	75.00	125
1931 (a)	300,000	6.00	20.00	50.00	125	225
1933 (a)	500,000	6.00	20.00	50.00	125	225
1936 (a)	2,200,000	3.00	10.00	25.00	60.00	100

KM# 3a PIASTRE
Zinc **Obv:** Hole in center of wreath **Rev:** Hole in center flanked by lion heads with value and date below

Date	Mintage	F12	VF20	XF40	MS60	MS63
1940 (a)	2,000,000	5.00	20.00	45.00	75.00	150

KM# 1 2 PIASTRES
2.00 g., Aluminum-Bronze **Obv:** Cedar tree within circle above date **Rev:** Value flanked by stars

Date	Mintage	F12	VF20	XF40	MS60	MS63
1924 (a)	1,800,000	3.00	8.00	30.00	90.00	225

KM# 4 2 PIASTRES
2.00 g., Aluminum-Bronze **Obv:** Cedar tree **Rev:** Ancient ship

Date	Mintage	F12	VF20	XF40	MS60	MS63
1925 (a)	1,000,000	12.00	25.00	60.00	125	275

KM# 10 2-1/2 PIASTRES
Aluminum-Bronze **Obv:** Hole in center of wreath **Rev:** Hole in center of flowered wreath

Date	Mintage	F12	VF20	XF40	MS60	MS63
1940 (a)	1,000,000	1.00	3.00	8.00	12.00	15.00

KM# 2 5 PIASTRES
Aluminum-Bronze **Obv:** Cedar tree within circle **Rev:** Value flanked by stars

Date	Mintage	F12	VF20	XF40	MS60	MS63
1924 (a)	1,000,000	3.00	8.00	30.00	90.00	225

KM# 5.1 5 PIASTRES
Aluminum-Bronze **Obv:** Cedar tree **Rev:** Ancient ship above value and dates

Date	Mintage	F12	VF20	XF40	MS60	MS63
1925 (a)	1,500,000	3.00	8.00	25.00	75.00	175

KM# 5.2 5 PIASTRES
4.10 g., Aluminum-Bronze **Obv:** Cedar tree **Rev:** Mint mark to the left and privy mark to the right of "5 Piastres"

Date	Mintage	F12	VF20	XF40	MS60	MS63
1925 (a)	Inc. above	3.00	8.00	25.00	75.00	175
1931 (a)	400,000	6.00	20.00	35.00	125	275
1933 (a)	500,000	6.00	20.00	35.00	125	275
1936 (a)	900,000	2.00	5.00	15.00	60.00	125
1940 (a)	1,000,000	2.00	3.00	12.00	50.00	90.00

KM# 6 10 PIASTRES
2.00 g., 0.680 Silver 0.0437 oz. ASW **Obv:** Cedar tree on rectangular box **Rev:** Crossed cornucopia above value

Date	Mintage	F12	VF20	XF40	MS60	MS63
1929	880,000	6.00	20.00	60.00	120	225

KM# 7 25 PIASTRES
5.00 g., 0.680 Silver 0.1093 oz. ASW **Obv:** Cedar tree on rectangular box **Rev:** Crossed cornucopia above value

Date	Mintage	F12	VF20	XF40	MS60	MS63
1929	600,000	10.00	25.00	75.00	150	275
1933 (a)	200,000	15.00	45.00	100	200	450
1936 (a)	400,000	12.00	35.00	90.00	175	350

KM# 8 50 PIASTRES
10.00 g., 0.680 Silver 0.2186 oz. ASW **Obv:** Cedar tree on rectangular box **Rev:** Crossed cornucopia with value above and below

Date	Mintage	F12	VF20	XF40	MS60	MS63
1929	500,000	20.00	50.00	125	275	500
1933 (a)	100,000	30.00	75.00	175	450	750
1936 (a)	100,000	25.00	60.00	150	375	650

WORLD WAR II COINAGE

KM# 11 1/2 PIASTRE
2.17 g., Brass **Obv:** Hole in center flanked by english value **Rev:** Hole in center flanked by value **Note:** Three varieties known. Usually crudely struck, off-center, etc. Perfectly struck, centered uncirculated specimens command a considerable premium. Finely struck coins appear with medal rotation while crude examples have coin rotation. Size of letters also vary.

Date	Mintage	F12	VF20	XF40	MS60	MS63
ND-1941	—	1.00	3.00	10.00	25.00	50.00

KM# 12 PIASTRE
Brass **Obv:** English value **Rev:** Value **Note:** Two varieties known. Usually crudely struck, off-center, etc. Perfectly struck, centered unc. specimens command a considerable premium.

Date	Mintage	F12	VF20	XF40	MS60	MS63
ND-1941	—	1.00	3.00	10.00	25.00	50.00

KM# 12a PIASTRE
Aluminum **Obv:** English value **Rev:** Value

Date	Mintage	F12	VF20	XF40	MS60	MS63
ND-1941	—	—	—	—	—	—

KM# 13 2-1/2 PIASTRES
Aluminum **Obv:** English value **Rev:** Value **Note:** Seven varieties known. Usually crudely struck, off-center, etc. Perfectly struck, centered unc. specimens command a considerable premium.

Date	Mintage	F12	VF20	XF40	MS60	MS63
ND-1941	—	1.00	3.00	8.00	25.00	50.00

KM# 13a 2-1/2 PIASTRES
Aluminum-Bronze **Obv:** English value **Rev:** Value

Date	Mintage	F12	VF20	XF40	MS60	MS63
ND-1941	—	—	—	—	—	—

KM# A14 5 PIASTRES
Aluminum **Obv:** English value **Rev:** Value **Note:** Did not enter circulation in significant numbers.

Date	Mintage	F12	VF20	XF40	MS60	MS63
ND-1941	—	—	—	2,000	3,000	—

REPUBLIC

STANDARD COINAGE

KM# 19 PIASTRE
2.04 g., Aluminum-Bronze, 17.5 mm. **Obv:** Wreath flanked by value above **Rev:** Wreath

Date	Mintage	VF20	XF40	MS60	MS63	MS65
1955 (a)	4,000,000	0.25	0.75	1.25	2.00	3.00

KM# 20 2-1/2 PIASTRES
2.70 g., Aluminum-Bronze, 20 mm. **Obv:** Hole in center of wreath flanked by value above **Rev:** Hole in center of wreath

Date	Mintage	VF20	XF40	MS60	MS63	MS65
1955 (a)	5,000,000	0.20	0.50	0.75	1.00	1.50

KM# 14 5 PIASTRES
Aluminum **Obv:** Cedar tree divides date **Rev:** Value below boat

Date	Mintage	VF20	XF40	MS60	MS63	MS65
1952 (a)	3,600,000	1.50	3.00	5.00	7.50	15.00

KM# 18 5 PIASTRES
Aluminum **Obv:** Cedar tree **Rev:** Wreath with value above and below

Date	Mintage	VF20	XF40	MS60	MS63	MS65
1954	4,440,000	0.50	1.00	2.50	5.00	8.00

KM# 21 5 PIASTRES
2.85 g., Aluminum-Bronze **Obv:** Cedar tree **Rev:** Lion head and value

Date	Mintage	VF20	XF40	MS60	MS63	MS65
1955 (a)	3,000,000	0.50	0.75	1.25	2.00	3.50
1961 (a)	—	0.40	0.60	1.00	1.50	3.00

KM# 25.1 5 PIASTRES
Nickel-Brass, 18 mm. **Obv:** Cedar tree above date **Rev:** Value within wreath

Date	Mintage	VF20	XF40	MS60	MS63	MS65
1968	2,000,000	0.10	0.15	0.50	1.00	1.50
1969	4,000,000	0.10	0.15	0.50	1.00	1.50
1970	—	0.10	0.15	0.50	1.00	1.50

KM# 25.2 5 PIASTRES
Nickel-Brass, 18 mm. **Obv:** Cedar tree above dates **Rev:** Value within wreath

Date	Mintage	VF20	XF40	MS60	MS63	MS65
1972 (a)	12,000,000	—	0.10	0.50	1.00	1.50
1975 (a)	—	—	0.10	0.50	1.00	1.50
1980	—	—	0.10	0.50	1.00	1.50

KM# 15 10 PIASTRES
1.27 g., Aluminum, 21.8 mm. **Obv:** Cedar tree above dates **Rev:** Lion head flanked by value

Date	Mintage	VF20	XF40	MS60	MS63	MS65
1952 (a)	3,600,000	1.50	3.00	7.00	20.00	30.00

KM# 22 10 PIASTRES
Aluminum-Bronze, 21.8 mm. **Obv:** Boat with sail above date **Rev:** Cedar tree above value

Date	Mintage	VF20	XF40	MS60	MS63	MS65
1955	2,175,000	1.00	3.00	5.00	12.50	18.50

KM# 23 10 PIASTRES
Aluminum-Bronze, 21.8 mm. **Obv:** Boat with sail above date with value at upper left **Rev:** Cedar tree above date

Date	Mintage	VF20	XF40	MS60	MS63	MS65
1955 (a)	6,000,000	0.35	0.50	1.00	2.00	4.00

KM# 24 10 PIASTRES
Copper-Nickel, 21.8 mm. **Obv:** Boat with sail above date with value at upper left **Rev:** Cedar tree above date

Date	Mintage	VF20	XF40	MS60	MS63	MS65
1961	7,000,000	0.15	0.35	1.00	1.50	3.00
1961 Proof	—	—	—	—	—	—

KM# 26 10 PIASTRES
Nickel-Brass, 21.8 mm. **Obv:** Cedar tree above dates **Rev:** Value within wreath

Date	Mintage	VF20	XF40	MS60	MS63	MS65
1968 (a)	2,000,000	0.15	0.25	1.00	1.50	2.50
1969 (a)	5,000,000	0.10	0.15	1.00	1.50	2.50
1970 (a)	8,000,000	0.10	0.15	1.00	1.50	2.50
1972 (a)	12,000,000	0.10	0.15	1.00	1.50	2.50
1975 (a)	—	0.10	0.15	1.00	1.50	2.50

KM# 16.1 25 PIASTRES
Aluminum-Bronze, 23.3 mm. **Obv:** Cedar tree **Rev:** Value within rectangular box divides wreath and dates

Date	Mintage	VF20	XF40	MS60	MS63	MS65
1952 (u)	7,200,000	0.35	0.50	1.00	2.00	3.50

KM# 16.2 25 PIASTRES
Aluminum-Bronze, 23.3 mm. **Obv:** Cedar tree **Rev:** Value within rectangular box divides wreath and dates **Note:** Different style of inscription and larger date.

Date	Mintage	VF20	XF40	MS60	MS63	MS65
1961 (u)	5,000,000	0.15	0.25	0.50	0.75	1.50

KM# 27.1 25 PIASTRES
4.00 g., Nickel-Brass, 23.3 mm. **Obv:** Cedar tree above dates **Rev:** Value within wreath **Edge:** Reeded

Date	Mintage	VF20	XF40	MS60	MS63	MS65
1968	1,500,000	0.15	0.25	1.00	1.50	3.00
1969	2,500,000	0.15	0.20	1.00	1.50	3.00
1970	—	0.15	0.20	1.00	1.50	3.00
1972	8,000,000	0.15	0.20	1.00	1.50	3.00
1975	—	0.15	0.20	1.00	1.50	3.00

KM# 27.2 25 PIASTRES
Nickel-Brass, 23.3 mm. **Obv:** Cedar tree above dates **Rev:** Value within wreath

Date	Mintage	VF20	XF40	MS60	MS63	MS65
1980	—	0.15	0.20	0.50	0.75	1.50

KM# 17 50 PIASTRES
4.90 g., 0.600 Silver 0.0945 oz. ASW, 24 mm. **Obv:** Cedar tree above dates **Rev:** Value within wreath

Date	Mintage	VF20	XF40	MS60	MS63	MS65
1952 (u)	7,200,000	1.70	5.00	8.00	12.00	15.00

KM# 28.1 50 PIASTRES
Nickel **Obv:** Cedar tree above dates **Rev:** Value within wreath

Date	Mintage	VF20	XF40	MS60	MS63	MS65
1968	2,000,000	0.40	0.60	1.25	1.75	3.50
1969	3,488,000	0.25	0.40	1.00	1.50	3.00
1970	2,000,000	0.25	0.40	1.00	1.50	3.00
1971	2,000,000	0.25	0.40	1.00	1.50	3.00
1975	—	0.25	0.40	1.00	1.50	3.00
1978	22,400,000	0.25	0.40	1.00	1.50	3.00

KM# 28.2 50 PIASTRES
Nickel **Obv:** Cedar tree above dates **Rev:** Value within wreath

Date	Mintage	VF20	XF40	MS60	MS63	MS65
1980	—	0.20	0.35	0.50	0.75	1.50

KM# 29 LIVRE
Nickel, 26 mm. **Series:** F.A.O. **Obv:** Cedar tree above dates **Rev:** Cluster of fruit above value

Date	Mintage	VF20	XF40	MS60	MS63	MS65
1968	300,000	0.35	0.75	1.50	3.00	5.00

KM# 30 LIVRE
7.20 g., Nickel, 27.3 mm. **Obv:** Cedar tree above dates **Rev:** Value within wreath **Note:** Varieties exist.

Date	Mintage	VF20	XF40	MS60	MS63	MS65
1975 (rm)	—	0.40	0.60	0.75	1.00	2.00
1975 (rm) Proof	—	—	—	—	—	—
1977 (rm)	8,000,000	0.40	0.60	0.75	1.00	2.00
1980 (rm)	12,000,000	0.40	0.60	0.75	1.00	2.00
1980 (a)	Inc. above	0.40	0.60	0.75	1.00	2.00
1981 (a)	—	0.40	0.60	0.75	1.00	2.00

KM# 32 LIVRE
Copper-Nickel **Series:** 1980 Winter Olympics **Subject:** Lake Placid

Date	Mintage	VF20	XF40	MS60	MS63	MS65
1980	40,000	PF60 5.00	PF63 8.00	PF65 15.00		

KM# 30a LIVRE
Nickel Clad Steel, 27.3 mm. **Obv:** Cedar tree above dates **Rev:** Value within wreath **Note:** Varieties exist.

Date	Mintage	VF20	XF40	MS60	MS63	MS65
1986	—	0.40	0.60	0.75	1.50	3.00

KM# 31 5 LIVRES
Nickel **Series:** F.A.O. **Obv:** Cedar tree above dates **Rev:** Cluster of fruit below radiant sun and value

Date	Mintage	VF20	XF40	MS60	MS63	MS65
1978	1,000,000	—	—	2.00	3.50	6.00

KM# 33 10 LIVRES
19.00 g., 0.500 Silver 0.3054 oz. ASW **Series:** 1980 Winter Olympics **Subject:** Lake Placid **Obv:** Olympic rings on top of design **Rev:** Stylized flame

Date	Mintage	VF20	XF40	MS60	MS63	MS65
1980	20,000	PF60 20.00	PF63 30.00	PF65 40.00		

KM# 35 10 LIVRES
Copper-Nickel **Series:** World Food Day **Obv:** Cedar tree above dates **Rev:** Man, oxen, radiant sun and value

Date	Mintage	VF20	XF40	MS60	MS63	MS65
1981	15,000	—	—	4.00	6.00	10.00

KM# 37 50 LIVRES
2.29 g., Stainless Steel, 18.35 mm. **Obv:** Arabic legend above large value on cedar tree within circle **Rev:** Large value "50" within circle **Rev. Legend:** BANQUE DU LIBAN **Edge:** Plain **Shape:** 8-sided

Date	Mintage	VF20	XF40	MS60	MS63	MS65
1996 (c)	—	—	0.50	0.70	1.20	1.80

KM# 38 100 LIVRES
4.00 g., Brass, 22.5 mm. **Obv:** Arabic legend above large value on cedar tree **Rev:** Stylized flag above large value "100" **Rev. Legend:** BANQUE DU LIBAN **Edge:** Plain

Date	Mintage	VF20	XF40	MS60	MS63	MS65
1995 (c)	—	—	0.65	0.85	1.50	2.00
1995 (c)	—	PF65 4.00				
1996 (c)	—	—	0.65	0.85	1.50	2.00
2000 (a)	—	—	0.65	0.85	1.50	2.00

KM# 36 250 LIVRES
5.00 g., Aluminum-Bronze, 23.5 mm. **Obv:** Arabic legend above large value on cedar tree **Rev:** Large 250 within eliptical border design **Edge:** Reeded

Date	Mintage	VF20	XF40	MS60	MS63	MS65
1995 (c)	—	—	0.75	0.95	1.85	2.50
1995 (c)	—	PF65 5.00				
1996 (c)	—	—	0.75	0.95	1.85	2.50
2000 (a)	—	—	0.75	0.95	1.85	2.50

KM# 34 400 LIVRES
8.00 g., 0.900 Gold 0.2315 oz. AGW **Series:** 1980 Winter Olympics **Subject:** Lake Placid **Obv:** Olympic rings on top of design **Rev:** Stylized flame

Date	Mintage	VF20	XF40	MS60	MS63	MS65
1980	1,000	PF65 900				

KM# 39 500 LIVRES
6.06 g., Nickel Plated Steel, 24.5 mm. **Obv:** Arabic legend above large value on cedar tree **Rev:** Large value "500", thick segmented circular border **Rev. Legend:** BANQUE DU LIBAN **Edge:** Plain

Date	Mintage	VF20	XF40	MS60	MS63	MS65
1995 (c)	—	—	0.90	1.50	2.25	3.00
1995 (c)	—	PF65 6.00				
1996 (c)	—	—	0.90	1.50	2.25	3.00
2000 (a)	—	—	0.90	1.50	2.25	3.00

ESSAIS

Standard metals unless otherwise noted

KM#	Date	Mintage	Identification	Mkt Val
E1	1924(a)	—	5 Piastres. Aluminum-Bronze. KM2.	400
E2	1925(a)	—	Piastre. Copper-Nickel. KM3.	300
E3	1925(a)	—	2 Piastres. Aluminum-Bronze. KM1.	500
E4	1925(a)	—	5 Piastres. Aluminum-Bronze. KM5.1.	400
E5	1929(a)	—	Piastre. Copper-Nickel. KM3.	400
E6	1929	—	10 Piastres. Silver. KM6.	750
E7	1929	—	25 Piastres. Silver. KM7.	850
E8	1929	—	50 Piastres. Silver. KM8.	1,000
E9	1934 A	—	1/2 Piastre. Copper-Nickel. Value within sprigs above date. Value within roped circle flanked by sprigs above date. KM9.	300
E10	1940(a)	—	2-1/2 Piastres. Aluminum-Bronze. KM10.	300
E11	1972	—	5 Piastres. Nickel-Brass. KM25.	50.00
E12	1972(a)	—	10 Piastres. Nickel-Brass. KM26.	50.00
E13	1980	—	25 Piastres. Nickel-Brass. KM27.	50.00
E14	1980	—	50 Piastres. Nickel. KM28.	50.00
E15	1980	—	Livre. Nickel. KM30.	50.00
E16	1981	—	10 Livres. Copper-Nickel. KM35.	75.00

PIEDFORT

KM#	Date	Mintage	Identification	Mkt Val
P1	1980	3,000	Livre. Copper-Nickel. KM32.	50.00
P2	1980	3,000	10 Livres. Silver. KM33.	125
P3	1980	750	400 Livres. Gold. KM34.	1,800

PROOF SETS

KM#	Date	Mintage	Identification	Issue Price	Mkt Val
PS1	1995 (3)	—	KM#36, 38, 39	—	15.00

LESOTHO

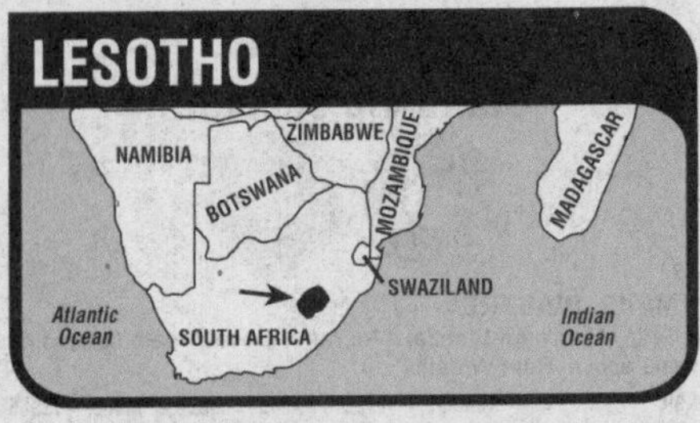

The Kingdom of Lesotho, a constitutional monarchy located within the east-central part of the Republic of South Africa, has an area of 11,720 sq. mi. (30,350 sq. km.) and a population of 1.5 million. Capital: Maseru. The economy is based on subsistence agriculture and livestock raising. Wool, mohair, and cattle are exported.

Lesotho (formerly Basutoland) was sparsely populated until the end of the 16th century. Between the 16th and 19th centuries an influx of refugees from tribal wars led to the development of a distinct Basotho group. During the reign of tribal chief Mashoeshoe I (1823-70), a series of wars with the Orange Free State resulted in the loss of large areas of territory to South Africa. Mashoeshoe appealed to the British for help, and Basutoland was constituted a native state under British protection. In 1871 it was annexed to Cape Colony, but was restored to direct control by the Crown in 1884. From 1884 to 1959 legislative and executive authority was vested in a British High Commissioner. The constitution of 1959 recognized the expressed wish of the people for independence, which was attained on Oct.4, 1966.

Lesotho is a member of the Commonwealth of Nations. The king is Head of State.

RULERS
Moshoeshoe II, 1966-1990
Letsie III, 1990-1995
Moshoeshoe II, 1995-

MONETARY SYSTEM
100 Licente/Lisente = 1 Maloti/Loti

KINGDOM

STANDARD COINAGE

100 Licente / Lisente = 1 Maloti / Loti

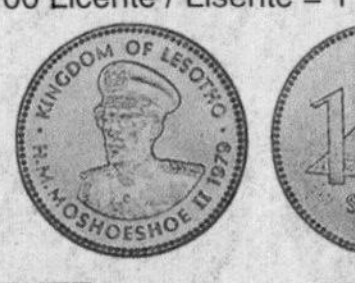

KM# 16 SENTE
1.50 g., Nickel-Brass, 16.5 mm. **Ruler:** Moshoeshoe II **Obv:** Uniformed bust 1/4 left **Rev:** Basotho hat and value

Date	Mintage	VF20	XF40	MS60	MS63	MS65
1979	4,500,000	—	0.15	0.40	0.60	1.25
1979	10,000	PF65 1.50				
1980	—	—	0.15	0.40	0.60	1.25
1980	10,000	PF65 1.50				
1981	2,500	PF65 1.50				
1983	—	—	0.15	0.40	0.60	1.25
1985	—	—	0.15	0.40	0.60	1.25
1989	—	—	0.15	0.40	0.60	1.25

KM# 54 SENTE
Brass, 16.5 mm. **Ruler:** Letsie III **Obv:** Arms with supporters **Rev:** Basotho hat and value

Date	Mintage	VF20	XF40	MS60	MS63	MS65
1992	—	—	0.15	0.75	1.00	2.00

KM# 54a SENTE
1.39 g., Brass Plated Steel, 16.5 mm. **Ruler:** Letsie III **Obv:** Arms with supporters **Rev:** Traditional house and value

Date	Mintage	VF20	XF40	MS60	MS63	MS65
1992	—	—	0.15	0.75	1.00	2.00

KM# 17 2 LISENTE
2.50 g., Nickel-Brass, 19.5 mm. **Ruler:** Moshoeshoe II **Obv:** Uniformed bust 1/4 left **Rev:** Steer and value

Date	Mintage	VF20	XF40	MS60	MS63	MS65
1979	3,000,000	—	0.20	0.50	0.75	1.50
1979	10,000	PF65 2.00				
1980	—	—	0.20	0.50	0.75	1.50
1980	10,000	PF65 2.00				
1981	2,500	PF65 2.00				
1985	—	—	0.20	0.50	0.75	1.50
1989	—	—	0.20	0.50	0.75	1.50

KM# 55 2 LISENTE
Brass, 19.5 mm. **Ruler:** Letsie III **Obv:** Arms with supporters **Rev:** Bull and value

Date	Mintage	VF20	XF40	MS60	MS63	MS65
1992	—	—	0.20	0.75	1.00	2.00

KM# 55a 2 LISENTE
2.25 g., Brass Plated Steel, 19.5 mm. **Ruler:** Letsie III **Obv:** Arms with supporters **Rev:** Bull and value **Edge:** Plain

Date	Mintage	VF20	XF40	MS60	MS63	MS65
1992	—	—	0.20	0.75	1.00	2.00

KM# 1 5 LICENTE (Lisente)
2.89 g., 0.900 Silver 0.0836 oz. ASW **Ruler:** Moshoeshoe II **Subject:** Independence attained **Obv:** Native bust right **Rev:** Arms with supporters above value flanked by stars

Date	Mintage	VF20	XF40	MS60	MS63	MS65
1966	5,000	PF63 17.00	PF65 20.00			

KM# 18 5 LICENTE (Lisente)
4.00 g., Nickel-Brass, 23.25 mm. **Ruler:** Moshoeshoe II **Obv:** Uniformed bust 1/4 left **Rev:** Single pine tree among hills, grass and value

Date	Mintage	VF20	XF40	MS60	MS63	MS65
1979	2,700,000	—	0.25	0.60	0.85	1.75
1979	10,000	PF65 2.00				
1980	—	—	0.25	0.60	0.85	1.75
1980	10,000	PF65 2.00				
1981	2,500	PF65 2.50				
1981	—	—	0.25	0.60	0.85	1.75
1989	—	—	0.25	0.60	0.85	1.75

KM# 56 5 LICENTE (Lisente)
Brass, 23.25 mm. **Ruler:** Letsie III **Obv:** Arms with supporters **Rev:** Single pine tree among grass, hills and value

Date	Mintage	VF20	XF40	MS60	MS63	MS65
1994	—	—	0.25	0.60	0.85	1.75

KM# 62 5 LICENTE (Lisente)
1.64 g., Brass Plated Steel, 15 mm. **Ruler:** Letsie III **Obv:** Arms with supporters **Rev:** Two pine trees among grass, hills and value

Date	Mintage	VF20	XF40	MS60	MS63	MS65
1998	—	—	0.25	0.60	0.85	1.75

KM# 2 10 LICENTE (Lisente)
5.68 g., 0.900 Silver 0.1644 oz. ASW **Ruler:** Moshoeshoe II **Subject:** Independence Attained **Obv:** Native bust right **Rev:** Arms with supporters above value flanked by stars

Date	Mintage	VF20	XF40	MS60	MS63	MS65
1966	5,000	PF63 20.00	PF65 25.00			

KM# 19 10 LICENTE (Lisente)
2.00 g., Copper-Nickel, 18.35 mm. **Ruler:** Moshoeshoe II **Obv:** Uniformed bust 1/4 left **Rev:** Angora goat

Date	Mintage	VF20	XF40	MS60	MS63	MS65
1979	2,000,000	0.15	0.30	1.00	1.50	3.00
1979	10,000	PF65 3.00				
1980	—	0.15	0.30	1.00	1.50	3.00
1980	10,000	PF65 3.00				
1981	2,500	PF65 3.00				
1983	—	0.15	0.30	1.00	1.50	3.00
1989	—	0.15	0.30	1.00	1.50	3.00

KM# 61 10 LICENTE (Lisente)
2.00 g., Copper-Nickel, 18.35 mm. **Ruler:** Letsie III **Obv:** Arms with supporters **Rev:** Angora goat

Date	Mintage	VF20	XF40	MS60	MS63	MS65
1992	—	—	—	1.00	1.50	3.00

KM# 63 10 LICENTE (Lisente)
1.96 g., Brass Plated Steel, 16 mm. **Ruler:** Moshoeshoe II **Obv:** Arms with supporters **Rev:** Angora goat

Date	Mintage	VF20	XF40	MS60	MS63	MS65
1998	—	—	—	1.00	1.50	3.00

KM# 3.1 20 LICENTE
11.28 g., 0.900 Silver 0.3264 oz. ASW **Ruler:** Moshoeshoe II **Subject:** Independence Attained **Obv:** Native bust right **Rev:** Small 900/1000 at right of date

Date	Mintage	VF20	XF40	MS60	MS63	MS65
1966	5,000	PF63 22.00	PF65 28.00			

KM# 3.2 20 LICENTE
11.28 g., 0.900 Silver 0.3264 oz. ASW **Ruler:** Moshoeshoe II **Subject:** Independence Attained **Obv:** Native bust right **Rev:** Large 900/1000 at right of date

Date	Mintage	VF20	XF40	MS60	MS63	MS65
1966	—	PF63 22.00	PF65 28.00			

KM# 64 20 LICENTE
2.67 g., Brass Plated Steel, 18 mm. **Ruler:** Moshoeshoe II **Obv:** Arms with supporters **Rev:** Flora

Date	Mintage	VF20	XF40	MS60	MS63	MS65
1998	—	—	—	0.75	1.00	2.00

KM# 20 25 LISENTE
3.50 g., Copper-Nickel, 21.7 mm. **Ruler:** Moshoeshoe II **Obv:** Uniformed bust 1/4 left **Rev:** Woman in native costume weaving baskets

Date	Mintage	VF20	XF40	MS60	MS63	MS65
1979	1,200,000	0.10	0.20	1.00	1.25	2.50
1979	10,000	PF65 2.75				
1980	—	0.10	0.20	1.00	1.25	2.50
1980	10,000	PF65 2.75				
1981	2,500	PF65 3.50				
1985	—	0.10	0.20	1.00	1.25	2.50
1989	—	0.10	0.20	1.00	1.25	2.50

KM# 4.1 50 LICENTE (Lisente)
28.10 g., 0.900 Silver 0.8131 oz. ASW, 35 mm. **Ruler:** Moshoeshoe II **Subject:** Independence Attained **Obv:** Native bust right **Rev:** 900/1000 to right of date

Date	Mintage	VF20	XF40	MS60	MS63	MS65
1966	17,500	—	—	—	18.00	22.00
1966	Inc. above	PF63 27.00	PF65 32.00			

KM# 4.2 50 LICENTE (Lisente)
28.10 g., 0.900 Silver 0.8131 oz. ASW, 35 mm. **Ruler:** Moshoeshoe II **Subject:** Independence Attained **Obv:** Native bust right **Rev:** Large 900/1000 to right of date

Date	Mintage	VF20	XF40	MS60	MS63	MS65
1966	—	—	—	—	18.00	22.00
1966	5,000	PF63 27.00	PF65 32.00			

KM# 4.3 50 LICENTE (Lisente)

28.10 g., 0.900 Silver 0.8131 oz. ASW **Ruler:** Moshoeshoe II **Subject:** Independence Attained **Obv:** Native bust right **Rev:** Mint mark and fineness below date

Date	Mintage	VF20	XF40	MS60	MS63	MS65
1966	—	—	—	—	18.00	22.00
1966	—	PF63 27.00	PF65 32.00			

KM# 21 50 LICENTE (Lisente)

5.50 g., Copper-Nickel, 25.5 mm. **Ruler:** Moshoeshoe II **Obv:** Uniformed bust 1/4 left **Rev:** Equestrian and value

Date	Mintage	VF20	XF40	MS60	MS63	MS65
1979	480,000	0.35	0.50	1.25	1.50	2.50
1979	10,000	PF65 3.00				
1980	—	0.35	0.50	1.25	1.50	2.50
1980	10,000	PF65 3.00				
1981	2,500	PF65 4.00				
1983	—	0.35	0.50	1.25	1.50	2.50
1989	—	0.35	0.50	1.25	1.50	2.50

KM# 65 50 LICENTE (Lisente)

3.40 g., Brass Plated Steel, 20 mm. **Ruler:** Moshoeshoe II

Date	Mintage	VF20	XF40	MS60	MS63	MS65
1998	—	—	—	1.00	1.25	2.50

KM# 5 LOTI

3.99 g., 0.917 Gold 0.1178 oz. AGW **Ruler:** Moshoeshoe II **Subject:** Independence Attained **Obv:** Native bust right **Rev:** Arms with supporters above value flanked by stars

Date	Mintage	VF20	XF40	MS60	MS63	MS65
1966	3,500	PF65 215				

KM# 8 LOTI

3.99 g., 0.917 Gold 0.1178 oz. AGW **Ruler:** Moshoeshoe II **Series:** F.A.O. **Obv:** Native bust right **Rev:** Equestrian

Date	Mintage	VF20	XF40	MS60	MS63	MS65
1969	3,000	PF65 185				

KM# 22 LOTI

11.30 g., Copper-Nickel, 28.5 mm. **Ruler:** Moshoeshoe II **Obv:** Uniformed bust 1/4 left **Rev:** Value at left of arms with supporters

Date	Mintage	VF20	XF40	MS60	MS63	MS65
1979	1,275,000	0.65	1.25	3.00	3.50	4.50
1979	10,000	PF65 5.00				
1980	—	0.75	1.50	4.00	4.50	5.00
1980	10,000	PF65 6.00				
1981	2,500	PF65 7.00				
1989	—	0.75	1.50	4.00	4.50	5.00

KM# 46 LOTI

11.31 g., 0.925 Silver 0.3364 oz. ASW **Ruler:** Moshoeshoe II **Subject:** Silver Jubilee of King Moshoeshoe II **Obv:** Uniformed bust 1/4 left **Rev:** Crown above arms with supporters flanked by dates

Date	Mintage	VF20	XF40	MS60	MS63	MS65
1985	2,500	PF63 22.00	PF65 25.00			

KM# 46a LOTI

18.98 g., 0.917 Gold 0.5596 oz. AGW **Ruler:** Moshoeshoe II **Subject:** Silver Jubilee of King Moshoeshoe II **Obv:** Uniformed bust 1/4 left **Rev:** Crown above arms with supporters flanked by dates

Date	Mintage	VF20	XF40	MS60	MS63	MS65
1985	500	PF63 850	PF65 950	PF67 1,000		

KM# 60 LOTI

Copper-Nickel **Ruler:** Letsie III **Series:** 50th Anniversary - UN

Date	Mintage	VF20	XF40	MS60	MS63	MS65
1995	—	—	—	7.00	8.00	10.00

KM# 66 LOTI

3.88 g., Nickel Plated Steel, 21 mm. **Ruler:** Letsie III **Obv:** Native seated right **Rev:** Value at left of arms with supporters

Date	Mintage	VF20	XF40	MS60	MS63	MS65
1998	—	—	—	1.50	2.00	3.00

KM# 6 2 MALOTI

7.99 g., 0.917 Gold 0.2355 oz. AGW **Ruler:** Moshoeshoe II **Obv:** Native bust right **Rev:** Arms with supporters above value flanked by stars

Date	Mintage	VF20	XF40	MS60	MS63	MS65
1966	—	PF65 475				

KM# 9 2 MALOTI

7.99 g., 0.917 Gold 0.2355 oz. AGW **Ruler:** Moshoeshoe II **Series:** F.A.O. **Obv:** Native bust right **Rev:** Figure on horseback left

Date	Mintage	VF20	XF40	MS60	MS63	MS65
1969	3,000	PF65 450				

KM# 58 2 MALOTI

4.49 g., Nickel Plated Steel, 22 mm. **Ruler:** Moshoeshoe II **Obv:** Arms with supporters **Rev:** Maize plants

Date	Mintage	VF20	XF40	MS60	MS63	MS65
1996	—	—	—	2.50	3.00	4.00
1998	—	—	—	2.00	2.50	3.50

KM# 7 4 MALOTI

15.98 g., 0.917 Gold 0.471 oz. AGW **Ruler:** Moshoeshoe II **Obv:** Native bust right **Rev:** Arms with supporters above value flanked by stars

Date	Mintage	VF20	XF40	MS60	MS63	MS65
1966	3,500	PF65 875				

KM# 10 4 MALOTI

15.98 g., 0.917 Gold 0.471 oz. AGW **Ruler:** Moshoeshoe II **Series:** F.A.O. **Obv:** Native bust right **Rev:** Figure on horseback left

Date	Mintage	VF20	XF40	MS60	MS63	MS65
1969	3,000	PF65 825				

KM# 67 5 MALOTI

5.46 g., Bi-Metallic Copper-Nickel center in Brass ring, 24 mm. **Ruler:** Moshoeshoe II **Subject:** 50th Anniversary of the United Nations **Obv:** National arms **Rev:** UN logo **Edge:** Reeded **Note:** 50th Anniversary of UN

Date	Mintage	VF20	XF40	MS60	MS63	MS65
1995	—	—	—	6.00	8.00	12.00

KM# 59 5 MALOTI

6.37 g., Nickel Plated Steel, 25 mm. **Ruler:** Moshoeshoe II **Obv:** Arms with supporters **Rev:** Wheat sprigs and value

Date	Mintage	VF20	XF40	MS60	MS63	MS65
1996	—	—	—	3.50	5.00	7.00
1998	—	—	—	2.50	4.00	6.00

KM# 11 10 MALOTI

39.94 g., 0.917 Gold 1.1775 oz. AGW **Ruler:** Moshoeshoe II **Series:** F.A.O. **Obv:** Arms with supporters **Rev:** Farmer leading two oxen

Date	Mintage	VF20	XF40	MS60	MS63	MS65
1969	3,000	PF65 2,250	PF67 2,500			

KM# 13 10 MALOTI
25.08 g., 0.925 Silver 0.7459 oz. ASW **Ruler:** Moshoeshoe II **Subject:** 10th Anniversary of Independence **Obv:** Uniformed bust 1/4 left divides dates **Rev:** Kneeling oriental woman with pottery within circle

Date	Mintage	VF20	XF40	MS60	MS63	MS65
1976	2,300	—	—	—	30.00	35.00
1976	2,100	PF63 37.00	PF65 45.00			

KM# 23 10 MALOTI
28.28 g., 0.925 Silver 0.841 oz. ASW **Ruler:** Moshoeshoe II **Subject:** Monument of King Moshoeshoe I **Obv:** Uniformed bust 1/4 left **Rev:** Native seated right

Date	Mintage	VF20	XF40	MS60	MS63	MS65
1979	10,000	—	—	—	17.00	22.00
1979	5,000	PF63 25.00	PF65 32.00			

KM# 23a 10 MALOTI
12.00 g., 0.500 Silver 0.1929 oz. ASW **Ruler:** Moshoeshoe II **Subject:** Monument of King Moshoeshoe I **Obv:** Uniformed bust 1/4 left **Rev:** Native seated right

Date	Mintage	VF20	XF40	MS60	MS63	MS65
1980	10,000	—	—	10.00	12.00	14.00
1980	5,000	PF65 15.00				

KM# 24 10 MALOTI
28.28 g., 0.925 Silver 0.841 oz. ASW **Ruler:** Moshoeshoe II **Series:** International Year of the Child **Obv:** Arms with supporters **Rev:** Busts of 3 children facing, logo below **Note:** Similar to 15 Maloti, KM#25.

Date	Mintage	VF20	XF40	MS60	MS63	MS65
1979 (1981)	—	—	—	16.00	20.00	25.00
1979 (1981)	37,000	PF63 25.00	PF65 30.00			

KM# 32 10 MALOTI
23.33 g., 0.925 Silver 0.6938 oz. ASW **Ruler:** Moshoeshoe II **Subject:** World Soccer Championship **Obv:** Arms with supporters **Rev:** Goalie in front of net

Date	Mintage	VF20	XF40	MS60	MS63	MS65
1982	3,582	PF63 27.00	PF65 35.00			

KM# 34 10 MALOTI
23.33 g., 0.925 Silver 0.6938 oz. ASW **Ruler:** Moshoeshoe II **Subject:** World Soccer Championship **Obv:** Arms with supporters **Rev:** Soccer players

Date	Mintage	VF20	XF40	MS60	MS63	MS65
1982	3,000	PF63 27.00	PF65 35.00			

KM# 40 10 MALOTI
31.10 g., 0.500 Silver 0.4999 oz. ASW **Ruler:** Moshoeshoe II **Subject:** George Washington **Obv:** Arms with supporters **Rev:** Bust left

Date	Mintage	VF20	XF40	MS60	MS63	MS65
1982	7,355	PF63 12.00	PF65 16.00			

KM# 41 10 MALOTI
31.10 g., 0.500 Silver 0.4999 oz. ASW **Ruler:** Moshoeshoe II **Subject:** George Washington **Obv:** Arms with supporters **Rev:** Washington on bended knee

Date	Mintage	VF20	XF40	MS60	MS63	MS65
1982	4,200	PF63 14.00	PF65 18.00			

KM# 42 10 MALOTI
31.10 g., 0.500 Silver 0.4999 oz. ASW **Ruler:** Moshoeshoe II **Subject:** George Washington **Obv:** Arms with supporters **Rev:** Washington crossing the Delaware

Date	Mintage	VF20	XF40	MS60	MS63	MS65
1982	Est. 15000	PF63 15.00	PF65 20.00			

KM# 52 10 MALOTI
28.28 g., Copper-Nickel, 38.61 mm. **Ruler:** Moshoeshoe II **Subject:** Los Angeles Olympics, 1984 **Rev:** Hurdlers

Date	Mintage	VF20	XF40	MS60	MS63	MS65
1984	—	PF65 2,800				

KM# 68 10 MALOTI
23.33 g., 0.925 Silver 0.6938 oz. ASW **Ruler:** Moshoeshoe II **Subject:** Los Angeles Olympics, 1984

Date	Mintage	VF20	XF40	MS60	MS63	MS65
1984 Proof	Est. 10000	—	—	—	—	—

KM# 49 10 MALOTI
23.33 g., 0.925 Silver 0.6938 oz. ASW **Ruler:** Moshoeshoe II **Subject:** Decade for Women **Obv:** Uniformed bust 1/4 left **Rev:** Half-figure of woman with basket on head left

Date	Mintage	VF20	XF40	MS60	MS63	MS65
1985	Est. 1000	PF63 45.00	PF65 60.00			

KM# 50 10 MALOTI
28.28 g., 0.925 Silver 0.841 oz. ASW **Ruler:** Moshoeshoe II **Subject:** Papal visit **Obv:** Arms with supporters **Rev:** Bust left

Date	Mintage	VF20	XF40	MS60	MS63	MS65
1988	Est. 15000	PF63 25.00	PF65 35.00			

KM# 71 10 MALOTI
28.28 g., 0.925 Silver 0.841 oz. ASW, 38.61 mm. **Ruler:** Letsie III **Obv:** National arms **Rev:** UN Seal

Date	Mintage	VF20	XF40	MS60	MS63	MS65
1995	—	—	—	—	—	65.00

KM# 25 15 MALOTI
33.40 g., 0.925 Silver 0.9933 oz. ASW **Ruler:** Moshoeshoe II **Series:** International Year of the Child **Obv:** Arms with supporters **Rev:** Busts of 3 children facing, logo below

Date	Mintage	VF20	XF40	MS60	MS63	MS65
1979	18,000	—	—	—	25.00	30.00
1979	7,500	PF63 30.00	PF65 35.00			

KM# 37 15 MALOTI
12.00 g., 0.500 Silver 0.1929 oz. ASW **Ruler:** Moshoeshoe II **Subject:** 15th Anniversary of Independence **Obv:** Uniformed bust 1/4 left **Rev:** Eagle with ribbon in talons

Date	Mintage	VF20	XF40	MS60	MS63	MS65
1981	2,500	PF65 40.00				

KM# 12 20 MALOTI
79.88 g., 0.917 Gold 2.3551 oz. AGW **Ruler:** Moshoeshoe II **Series:** F.A.O. **Obv:** Arms with supporters **Rev:** Grazing ewe and lamb

Date	Mintage	VF20	XF40	MS60	MS63	MS65
1969	3,000	PF65 3,750	PF67 4,000			

KM# 35 25 MALOTI
16.82 g., 0.925 Silver 0.5002 oz. ASW **Ruler:** Moshoeshoe II **Obv:** Arms with supporters **Rev:** Bust left

Date	Mintage	VF20	XF40	MS60	MS63	MS65
1981	5,000	PF65 32.00				

KM# 44 25 MALOTI
28.28 g., 0.925 Silver 0.841 oz. ASW **Ruler:** Moshoeshoe II **Series:** International Year of Disabled Persons **Obv:** Arms with supporters **Rev:** Inscription and disabled emblem divides map within circled grid

Date	Mintage	VF20	XF40	MS60	MS63	MS65
1983	—	—	—	—	37.00	42.00
1983	—	PF65 60.00				

KM# 53 25 MALOTI
28.28 g., 0.925 Silver 0.841 oz. ASW, 38.61 mm. **Ruler:** Moshoeshoe II **Subject:** Los Angles Olympics, 1984 **Rev:** Hurdlers

Date	Mintage	VF20	XF40	MS60	MS63	MS65
1984	—	PF65 3,250				

KM# 70 25 MALOTI
28.28 g., 0.925 Silver 0.841 oz. ASW, 38.61 mm. **Ruler:** Moshoeshoe II **Subject:** Los Angles Olympics **Rev:** Hurdler

Date	Mintage	VF20	XF40	MS60	MS63	MS65
1984	—	PF65 2,800				

KM# 30 30 MALOTI
0.925 Silver **Ruler:** Moshoeshoe II **Subject:** Wedding of Prince Charles and Lady Diana

Date	Mintage	VF20	XF40	MS60	MS63	MS65
1981	10,000	PF63 32.00	PF65 40.00			

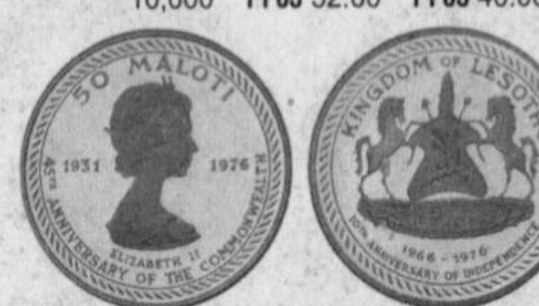

KM# 14 50 MALOTI
4.50 g., 0.900 Gold 0.1302 oz. AGW **Ruler:** Moshoeshoe II **Subject:** 10th Anniversary of Independence **Obv:** Arms with supporters within circle **Rev:** Young bust right divides dates

Date	Mintage	VF20	XF40	MS60	MS63	MS65
ND-1976	700	—	—	—	240	255
ND-1976	1,910	PF65 225				

KM# 27 50 MALOTI
33.62 g., 0.925 Silver 0.9998 oz. ASW **Ruler:** Moshoeshoe II **Subject:** 110th Anniversary - Death of King Moshoeshoe I **Obv:** Arms with supporters **Rev:** Hat within diamond at center, corn ear at left, alligator at right

Date	Mintage	VF20	XF40	MS60	MS63	MS65
1980	2,500	—	—	—	32.50	40.00
1980	1,400	PF63 65.00	PF65 75.00			

KM# 38 50 MALOTI
33.62 g., 0.925 Silver 0.9998 oz. ASW **Ruler:** Moshoeshoe II **Subject:** 15th Anniversary of Commonwealth Membership **Obv:** Arms with supporters **Rev:** Crowned bust right

Date	Mintage	VF20	XF40	MS60	MS63	MS65
1981	5,000	PF63 42.00	PF65 50.00			

KM# 15 100 MALOTI
9.00 g., 0.900 Gold 0.2604 oz. AGW **Ruler:** Moshoeshoe II **Subject:** 10th Anniversary of Independence **Obv:** Uniformed bust 1/4 left divides dates **Rev:** Equestrian and value within circle

Date	Mintage	VF20	XF40	MS60	MS63	MS65
ND-1976	450	—	—	—	475	500
ND-1976	1,410	PF65 465				

KM# 69 100 MALOTI
11.50 g., 0.916 Gold 0.3387 oz. AGW, 35 mm. **Ruler:** Moshoeshoe II **Subject:** Los Angles Olympics **Rev:** Female gymnastic floor exercises

Date	Mintage	VF20	XF40	MS60	MS63	MS65
1984	Est. 2	PF67 8,500				

KM# 45 200 MALOTI
15.98 g., 0.900 Gold 0.4624 oz. AGW **Ruler:** Moshoeshoe II **Series:** International Year of Disabled Persons **Obv:** Arms with supporters **Rev:** Disabled persons design within circle

Date	Mintage	XF40	MS60	MS63	MS65	MS66
1983	500	—	—	—	800	825
1983	500	PF67 850				

KM# 26 250 MALOTI
33.93 g., 0.917 Gold 1.0003 oz. AGW **Ruler:** Moshoeshoe II **Series:** International Year of the Child **Obv:** Native bust right **Rev:** Busts of 3 children facing with logo below

Date	Mintage	XF40	MS60	MS63	MS65	MS66
1979	2,500	—	—	—	1,650	1,700
1979	2,000	PF67 1,750				

KM# 28 250 MALOTI
31.10 g., 0.917 Gold 0.9169 oz. AGW **Ruler:** Moshoeshoe II **Subject:** 110th Anniversary - Death of King Moshoeshoe I **Obv:** Native bust right **Rev:** Hat within diamond at center, corn ear at left, alligator at right

Date	Mintage	XF40	MS60	MS63	MS65	MS66
1980	1,500	—	—	—	1,550	1,600
1980	3,000	PF67 1,650				

KM# 31 250 MALOTI
15.90 g., 0.917 Gold 0.4688 oz. AGW **Ruler:** Moshoeshoe II **Subject:** Wedding of Prince Charles and Lady Diana **Rev:** Conjoined busts left

Date	Mintage	XF40	MS60	MS63	MS65	MS66
1981	1,000	—	—	—	800	825
1981	1,500	PF67 850				

KM# 31a 250 MALOTI
15.75 g., 0.995 Platinum 0.5038 oz. APW **Ruler:** Moshoeshoe II **Subject:** Wedding of Prince Charles and Lady Diana **Obv:** Arms with supporters **Rev:** Conjoined busts left

Date	Mintage	XF40	MS60	MS63	MS65	MS66
1981	200	PF69 800				

KM# 36 250 MALOTI
16.96 g., 0.917 Gold 0.500 oz. AGW **Ruler:** Moshoeshoe II **Subject:** Duke of Edinburgh Youth Awards **Obv:** Arms with supporters **Rev:** Bust left

Date	Mintage	XF40	MS60	MS63	MS65	MS66
1981	1,500	PF67 850				

KM# 36a 250 MALOTI
15.75 g., 0.995 Platinum 0.5038 oz. APW **Ruler:** Moshoeshoe II **Subject:** Duke of Edinburgh Youth Awards **Obv:** Arms with supporters **Rev:** Bust left

Date	Mintage	XF40	MS60	MS63	MS65	MS66
1981	200	PF69 800				

KM# 33 250 MALOTI
7.13 g., 0.900 Gold 0.2063 oz. AGW **Ruler:** Moshoeshoe II **Subject:** Soccer Games **Obv:** Arms with supporters **Rev:** Goalie

Date	Mintage	XF40	MS60	MS63	MS65	MS66
1982	551	PF67 400	PF69 450			

KM# 51 250 MALOTI
15.98 g., 0.917 Gold 0.4711 oz. AGW **Ruler:** Moshoeshoe II **Subject:** Papal Visit **Obv:** Bust left **Rev:** Arms with supporters

Date	Mintage	XF40	MS60	MS63	MS65	MS66
1988	Est. 750	PF67 925				

KM# 72 250 MALOTI
15.98 g., 0.916 Gold 0.4706 oz. AGW, 28 mm. **Ruler:** Moshoeshoe II **Obv:** Bust 1/4 left **Rev:** National arms

Date	Mintage	XF40	MS60	MS63	MS65	MS66
1997	—	PF67 950				

KM# 29 500 MALOTI

33.93 g., 0.917 Gold 1.0003 oz. AGW **Ruler:** Moshoeshoe II **Subject:** 110th Anniversary - Death of King Moshoeshoe I **Obv:** Native bust right **Rev:** Hat within diamond at center, corn ear at left, alligator at right

Date	Mintage	XF40	MS60	MS63	MS65	MS66
1980	1,500	—	—	—	1,650	1,700
1980	3,000	PF65 1,750	PF67 1,800			

KM# 39 500 MALOTI

33.93 g., 0.917 Gold 1.0003 oz. AGW **Ruler:** Moshoeshoe II **Subject:** 15th Anniversary of Commonwealth Membership **Obv:** Arms with supporters **Rev:** Crowned bust right

Date	Mintage	XF40	MS60	MS63	MS65	MS66
1981	500	PF65 1,650	PF67 1,800			

KM# 39a 500 MALOTI

31.50 g., 0.995 Platinum 1.0077 oz. APW **Ruler:** Moshoeshoe II **Subject:** 15th Anniversary of Commonwealth Membership **Obv:** Arms with supporters **Rev:** Crowned bust right

Date	Mintage	XF40	MS60	MS63	MS65	MS66
1981	200	PF65 1,750	PF67 1,900			

KM# 57 500 MALOTI

33.93 g., 0.9166 Gold 0.9999 oz. AGW **Ruler:** Moshoeshoe II **Subject:** Royal Wedding of Prince Charles and Lady Diana **Obv:** Arms with supporters **Rev:** Conjoined busts left

Date	Mintage	XF40	MS60	MS63	MS65	MS66
ND-1981	—	PF65 1,600	PF67 1,750			

KM# 57a 500 MALOTI

33.48 g., 0.9995 Platinum 1.0759 oz. APW **Ruler:** Moshoeshoe II **Subject:** Royal Wedding **Obv:** Arms with supporters **Rev:** Conjoined bust left

Date	Mintage	XF40	MS60	MS63	MS65	MS66
ND-1981	—	PF65 1,900	PF67 2,000			

PATTERNS

Including off metal strikes

KM#	Date	Mintage	Identification	Mkt Val
Pn1	1966	2	5 Licente. 0.900. Silver.	—
Pn2	1966	2	10 Licente. 0.900. Silver.	—
Pn3	1966	2	20 Licente. 0.900. Silver.	—
Pn4	1966	2	50 Licente. 0.900. Silver.	—
Pn6	1966	7	2 Maloti. 0.916. Gold.	1,850
Pn7	1966	7	4 Maloti. 0.916. Gold.	2,150

KM#	Date	Mintage	Identification	Mkt Val
Pn8	1966	7	10 Maloti. 0.916. Gold. Head right. Arms with supporters above value and date.	2,650

KM#	Date	Mintage	Identification	Mkt Val
Pn9	1966	7	20 Maloti. 0.916. Gold.	3,350
Pn10.2a	1979	—	15 Maloti. 0.925. Silver.	—

KM#	Date	Mintage	Identification	Mkt Val
Pn10	1979	5	15 Maloti. Copper-Nickel. KM25. Medallic alignment.	125

KM#	Date	Mintage	Identification	Mkt Val
Pn11	1979	15	15 Maloti. Copper-Nickel. KM25. Coin alignment.	90.00

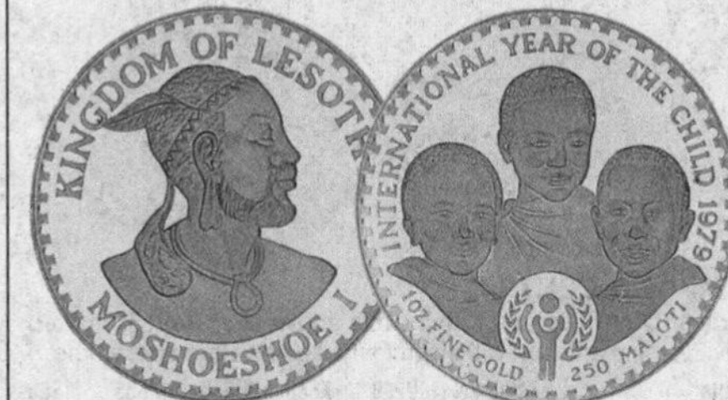

KM#	Date	Mintage	Identification	Mkt Val
Pn12	1979	15	250 Maloti. Brass. KM26.	85.00
Pn13	1979	5	250 Maloti. Copper-Nickel. KM26. Medallic alignment.	120
Pn14	1979	10	250 Maloti. Silver. KM26.	125

KM#	Date	Mintage	Identification	Mkt Val
Pn15	1980	10	50 Maloti. Copper-Nickel. KM27. Medallic alignment.	135
Pn16	1980	10	50 Maloti. Copper-Nickel. Coin alignment.	135

KM#	Date	Mintage	Identification	Mkt Val
Pn17	1980	10	250 Maloti. Brass. KM28. Coin alignment.	120
Pn18	1980	10	250 Maloti. Copper-Nickel. KM28. Medallic alignment.	110

KM#	Date	Mintage	Identification	Mkt Val
Pn19	1980	10	500 Maloti. Brass. KM29. Coin alignment.	120
Pn20	1980	10	500 Maloti. Copper-Nickel. KM29. Medallic alignment.	120

PIEDFORT

KM#	Date	Mintage	Identification	Mkt Val
P1	1979	50	10 Maloti. Silver. KM24.	375
P2	1981	—	250 Maloti. Gold. KM31.	950
P3	1983	—	25 Maloti. Silver. KM4.	125
P4	1983	100	200 Maloti. Gold. KM45.	1,000

MINT SETS

KM#	Date	Mintage	Identification	Issue Price	Mkt Val
MS1	1976 (3)	450	KM13-15	194	750
MS2	1989 (7)	—	KM16-22	—	11.50

PROOF SETS

KM#	Date	Mintage	Identification	Issue Price	Mkt Val
PS1	1966 (7)	1,500	KM1-7	301	1,625
PS2	1966 (4)	7	KMPn6-9	—	7,500
PS3	1966 (4)	2	KMPn1-4	—	—
PS4	1966 (4)	3,500	KM1, 2, 3.1, 4.1	28.00	65.00
PSA5	1966 (4)	—	KM1, 2, 3.2, 4.2	28.00	45.00
PS5	1966 (3)	2,000	KM5-7	301	1,550
PS6	1969 (5)	3,000	KM8-12	450	8,000
PS7	1976 (3)	1,410	KM13-15	285	750
PS8	1976 (2)	—	KM14, 15	270	700
PS9	1976 (2)	—	KM13, 14	—	280
PS10	1979 (7)	10,000	KM16-22	34.00	15.00
PS11	1980 (8)	10,000	KM16-22, 23a	51.00	30.00
PS12	1981 (8)	2,500	KM16-22, 37	55.00	45.00

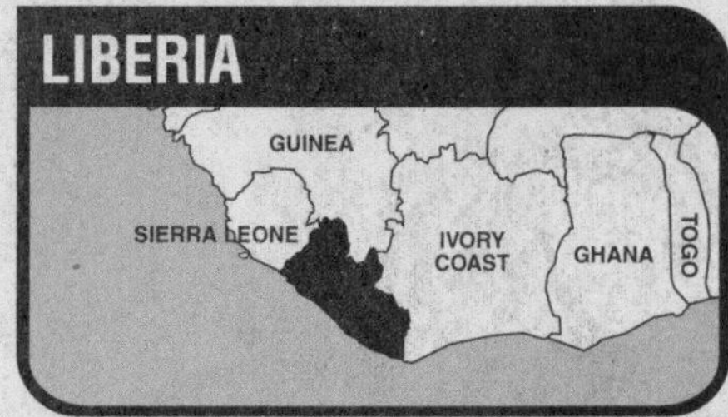

The Republic of Liberia, located on the southern side of the West African bulge between Sierra Leone and Ivory Coast, has an area of 38,250 sq. mi. (111,370 sq. km) and a population of 2.2 million. Capital: Monrovia. The major industries are agriculture, mining and lumbering. Iron ore, diamonds, rubber, coffee and coca are exported.

The Liberian coast was explored and charted by Portuguese navigator Pedro de Cintra in 1461. For the three centuries following Portuguese traders visited the area regularly to trade for gold, slaves and pepper. The modern country of Liberia, Africa's first republic, was settled in1822 by the American Colonization Society as a homeland for American freed slaves, with the U.S. government furnishing funds and assisting in negotiations for procurement of land from the native chiefs. The various settlements united in 1839 to form the Commonwealth of Liberia, and in 1847 established the country as a republic with a constitution modeled after that of the United States.

U.S. money was declared legal tender in Liberia in 1943, replacing British West African currency.

Most of the Liberian pattern series, particularly of the 1888-90 period, are acknowledged to have been "unofficial" privately sponsored issues, but many collectors of Liberian coins nonetheless, avidly collect them. The "K" number designations on these pieces refer to a listing of Liberian patterns compiled and published by Ernst Kraus.

MINT MARKS

B - Bern, Switzerland
H - Heaton, Birmingham
(l) – London
(d) – Denver, U.S.A.
(s) - San Francisco, U.S.
FM - Franklin Mint, U.S.A.*
PM - Pobjoy Mint

***NOTE:** From 1975-1985 the Franklin Mint produced coinage in up to 3 different qualities. Qualities of issue are designated in ( ) after each date and are defined as follows:

(M) MATTE - Normal circulation strike or a dull finish produced by sandblasting special uncirculated (polish finish) or proof quality dies.

(U) SPECIAL UNCIRCULATED - Polished or prooflike in appearance without any frosted features.

(P) PROOF - The highest quality obtainable having mirror-like fields and frosted features.

MONETARY SYSTEM

100 Cents = 1 Dollar

REPUBLIC

STANDARD COINAGE

100 Cents = 1 Dollar

KM# 10 1/2 CENT

2.42 g., Brass, 18 mm. **Obv:** Elephant striding left, star below **Rev:** Palm tree (Elaeis guineensis-Palmae) within circle flanked by stars

Date	Mintage	VF20	XF40	MS60	MS63	MS65
1937	1,000,000	0.25	0.40	1.25	2.50	5.00

KM# 10a 1/2 CENT

Copper-Nickel **Obv:** Elephant with star below **Rev:** Palm tree within circle flanked by stars

Date	Mintage	VF20	XF40	MS60	MS63	MS65
1941	250,000	0.35	0.55	1.50	2.50	5.00

KM# 5 CENT

Bronze **Obv:** Head laureate left above star **Obv. Legend:** REPUBLIC OF LIBERIA **Rev:** Palm tree divides ship and radiant sun within circle, 2 stars, date and value around border

Date	Mintage	F12	VF20	XF40	MS60	MS63
1906 H	180,000	4.50	10.00	25.00	50.00	75.00
1906 H	—	PF63 200	PF65 325			

KM# 11 CENT

5.19 g., Brass, 25.45 mm. **Obv:** Elephant within circle above star **Rev:** Palm tree within circle above date

Date	Mintage	VF20	XF40	MS60	MS63	MS65
1937	1,000,000	0.50	1.50	3.00	6.00	10.00

KM# 11a CENT

Copper-Nickel **Obv:** Elephant within circle above star **Rev:** Palm tree within circle above date

Date	Mintage	VF20	XF40	MS60	MS63	MS65
1941	250,000	7.00	12.00	25.00	45.00	—

KM# 13 CENT

2.60 g., Bronze, 18 mm. **Obv:** Elephant within circle above star **Rev:** Ship and bird to right of palm tree within 3/4 circle above date

Date	Mintage	VF20	XF40	MS60	MS63	MS65
1960	500,000	—	0.10	0.75	1.25	2.00
1961	7,000,000	—	0.10	0.75	1.25	2.00
1968 (l)	3,000,000	—	0.10	0.75	1.25	2.00
1968 (s)	14,000	PF65 1.25				
1969	5,056	PF65 1.25				
1970	3,464	PF65 1.25				
1971	3,032	PF65 1.25				
1972 (d)	10,000,000	—	0.10	0.75	1.25	2.00
1972 (s)	4,866	PF65 1.25				
1973	11,000	PF65 1.25				
1974	9,362	PF65 1.25				
1975	5,000,000	—	0.10	0.75	1.25	2.00
1975	4,056	PF65 1.25				
1976	2,131	PF65 1.25				
1977	2,500,000	—	0.10	0.75	1.25	2.00
1977	920	PF65 1.25				
1978 FM	7,311	PF65 1.25				
1983 FM	2,500,000	—	0.10	0.75	1.25	2.00
1984	2,500,000	—	0.10	0.75	1.25	2.00

KM# 13a CENT

Bronze **Obv:** Elephant left **Rev:** Palm tree, bird above ship at right **Edge Lettering:** O.A.U. July 1979

Date	Mintage	VF20	XF40	MS60	MS63	MS65
1979 FM	1,857	PF65 1.50				

KM# 6 2 CENTS

Bronze, 29 mm. **Obv:** Laureate head left above star **Obv. Legend:** REPUBLIC OF LIBERIA **Rev:** Palm tree divides ship and radiant sun within circle, 2 stars, date and value around border

Date	Mintage	F12	VF20	XF40	MS60	MS63
1906 H	108,000	5.00	12.00	40.00	60.00	85.00
1906 H	—	PF63 225	PF65 375			

KM# 12 2 CENTS

Brass **Obv:** Elephant within circle above star **Rev:** Palm tree divides ship and sun within circle flanked by stars above date

Date	Mintage	VF20	XF40	MS60	MS63	MS65
1937	1,000,000	0.35	1.00	3.00	6.00	10.00

KM# 12a 2 CENTS

Copper-Nickel **Obv:** Elephant within circle above star **Rev:** Palm tree divides sun and ship within circle flanked by stars above date

Date	Mintage	VF20	XF40	MS60	MS63	MS65
1941 (p)	810,000	0.25	0.50	2.50	5.00	8.00
1978 FM	7,311	PF65 2.00				

KM# 12b 2 CENTS

Copper-Nickel **Obv:** Elephant within circle above star **Rev:** Palm tree divides sun and ship within circle flanked by stars above date **Edge Lettering:** O.A.U. July 1979

Date	Mintage	VF20	XF40	MS60	MS63	MS65
1979 FM	1,857	PF65 4.00				

KM# 14 5 CENTS

4.10 g., Copper-Nickel, 20 mm. **Obv:** Elephant within circle above star **Rev:** Ship and bird to right of palm tree within 3/4 circle above date

Date	Mintage	VF20	XF40	MS60	MS63	MS65
1960	1,000,000	0.10	0.15	0.45	0.85	1.50
1961	3,200,000	0.10	0.15	0.45	0.85	1.50
1968	15,000	PF65 1.00				
1969	5,056	PF65 1.00				
1970	3,464	PF65 1.25				
1971	3,032	PF65 1.25				
1972 (d)	3,000,000	0.10	0.15	0.45	0.85	1.50
1972 (s)	4,866	PF65 1.00				
1973	11,000	PF65 1.00				
1974	9,362	PF65 1.00				
1975	3,000,000	0.10	0.15	0.45	0.85	1.50
1975	4,056	PF65 1.00				
1976	2,131	PF65 1.00				
1977	—	0.10	0.15	0.45	0.85	1.50
1977	920	PF65 1.00				
1978 FM	7,311	PF65 1.00				
1983 FM	1,000,000	0.10	0.15	0.45	0.85	1.50
1984	1,000,000	0.10	0.15	0.45	0.85	1.50

KM# 14a 5 CENTS

Copper-Nickel **Obv:** Elephant within circle above star **Rev:** Ship and bird to right of palm tree within 3/4 circle above date **Edge Lettering:** O.A.U. July 1979

Date	Mintage	VF20	XF40	MS60	MS63	MS65
1979 FM	1,857	PF65 2.00				

KM# 474 5 CENTS

2.25 g., Aluminum, 26.9 mm. **Obv:** National arms **Rev:** Dragon above value **Edge:** Plain

Date	Mintage	VF20	XF40	MS60	MS63	MS65
2000	—	—	—	1.00	1.25	1.75

KM# 7 10 CENTS

2.32 g., 0.925 Silver 0.069 oz. ASW **Obv:** Laureate head left above star **Obv. Legend:** REPUBLIC OF LIBERIA **Rev:** Value and date within wreath

Date	Mintage	F12	VF20	XF40	MS60	MS63
1906 H	35,000	6.00	25.00	50.00	125	175
1906 H	—	PF63 500	PF65 900			

KM# 15 10 CENTS

2.07 g., 0.900 Silver 0.0599 oz. ASW, 17 mm. **Obv:** Head with headdress left above star **Rev:** Value and date within wreath

Date	Mintage	VF20	XF40	MS60	MS63	MS65
1960	1,000,000	1.60	2.50	3.00	5.00	9.00
1961	1,200,000	1.60	2.50	3.00	5.00	9.00

KM# 15a.1 10 CENTS
2.10 g., Copper-Nickel **Obv:** Head with headdress left above star **Rev:** Value and date within wreath

Date	Mintage	VF20	XF40	MS60	MS63	MS65
1966	2,000,000	0.15	0.25	0.50	0.75	1.00

KM# 15a.2 10 CENTS
1.80 g., Copper-Nickel **Obv:** Head with headdress left above star **Rev:** Value and date within wreath

Date	Mintage	VF20	XF40	MS60	MS63	MS65
1968	14,000	PF65 1.25				
1969	5,056	PF65 1.25				
1970 (d)	2,500,000	0.15	0.25	0.50	0.75	1.00
1970 (s)	3,464	PF65 1.50				
1971	3,032	PF65 1.50				
1972	4,866	PF65 1.25				
1973	11,000	PF65 1.00				
1974	9,362	PF65 1.00				
1975	4,500	0.15	0.20	0.35	0.75	1.00
1975	4,056	PF65 1.00				
1976	2,131	PF65 1.00				
1977	—	0.15	0.25	0.75	1.25	1.50
1977	920	PF65 4.00				
1978 FM	7,311	PF65 1.00				
1983 FM	500,000	0.15	0.25	0.75	1.25	1.50
1984 FM	500,000	0.15	0.25	0.75	1.25	1.50
1987	10,000,000	0.15	0.25	0.75	1.25	1.50

KM# 15b 10 CENTS
1.80 g., Copper-Nickel **Obv:** Head with headdress left above star **Rev:** Value and date within wreath **Edge Lettering:** O.A.U. July 1979

Date	Mintage	VF20	XF40	MS60	MS63	MS65
1979 FM	1,857	PF65 2.00				

KM# 8 25 CENTS
5.80 g., 0.925 Silver 0.1725 oz. ASW **Obv:** Head laureate left above star **Obv. Legend:** REPUBLIC OF LIBERIA **Rev:** Value and date within wreath

Date	Mintage	F12	VF20	XF40	MS60	MS63
1906 H	34,000	12.00	35.00	75.00	150	250
1906 H	—	PF63 750	PF65 1,100			

KM# 16 25 CENTS
5.18 g., 0.900 Silver 0.1499 oz. ASW **Obv:** Head with headdress left above star **Rev:** Value and date within wreath

Date	Mintage	VF20	XF40	MS60	MS63	MS65
1960	900,000	—	3.25	5.00	7.50	10.00
1961	1,200,000	—	3.25	5.00	7.50	10.00

KM# 16a.1 25 CENTS
5.20 g., Copper-Nickel **Obv:** Head with headdress left above star **Rev:** Value and date within wreath

Date	Mintage	VF20	XF40	MS60	MS63	MS65
1966	800,000	0.25	0.65	1.00	1.25	2.00

KM# 16a.2 25 CENTS
4.80 g., Copper-Nickel, 23 mm. **Obv:** Head with headdress left above star **Rev:** Value and date within wreath **Note:** 1 and 1.15mm rim varieties exist.

Date	Mintage	VF20	XF40	MS60	MS63	MS65
1968 (d)	1,600,000	0.25	0.50	0.75	1.00	1.50
1968 (s)	14,000	PF65 1.50				
1969	5,056	PF65 1.50				
1970	3,464	PF65 1.75				
1971	3,032	PF65 1.75				
1972	4,866	PF65 1.50				
1973	2,000,000	0.25	0.50	0.75	1.00	1.50
1973	11,000	PF65 1.25				
1974	9,362	PF65 1.25				
1975	1,600,000	0.25	0.50	0.75	1.00	1.50
1975	4,056	PF65 1.25				

KM# 16a.3 25 CENTS
5.20 g., Copper-Nickel **Obv:** Head with headdress left above star **Rev:** Value and date within wreath **Rev. Legend:** Large letters, higher inscription **Note:** Struck in 1988.

Date	Mintage	VF20	XF40	MS60	MS63	MS65
1968 Restrike	2,400,000	0.25	0.50	0.75	1.00	1.50

KM# 30 25 CENTS
5.20 g., Copper-Nickel **Series:** F.A.O. **Obv:** Head 1/4 right flanked by stars **Rev:** Woman with basket of leaves on head divides date and value within circle

Date	Mintage	VF20	XF40	MS60	MS63	MS65
1976	800,000	0.25	0.75	1.25	1.75	3.00
1976	2,131	PF65 4.00				
1977	920	PF65 5.00				
1978 FM	7,311	PF65 2.50				

KM# 30a 25 CENTS
5.20 g., Copper-Nickel **Obv:** Head 1/4 right flanked by stars **Rev:** Woman with leaves in basket on head divides date and value within circle **Edge Lettering:** O.A.U. July 1979

Date	Mintage	VF20	XF40	MS60	MS63	MS65
1979 FM	1,857	PF65 3.50				

KM# 16b 25 CENTS
4.46 g., Nickel Clad Steel, 22.9 mm. **Obv:** Head with headdress left above star **Rev:** Value and date within wreath **Edge:** Reeded

Date	Mintage	VF20	XF40	MS60	MS63	MS65
2000	—	—	—	1.25	1.75	3.00

KM# 9 50 CENTS
11.60 g., 0.925 Silver 0.345 oz. ASW **Obv:** Laureate head left above star **Obv. Legend:** REPUBLIC OF LIBERIA **Rev:** Value and date within wreath

Date	Mintage	F12	VF20	XF40	MS60	MS63
1906 H	24,000	15.00	35.00	85.00	200	350
1906 H	—	PF63 1,250	PF65 2,000			

KM# 17 50 CENTS
10.37 g., 0.900 Silver 0.3001 oz. ASW **Obv:** Head with headdress left above star **Rev:** Value and date within wreath

Date	Mintage	VF20	XF40	MS60	MS63	MS65
1960	1,100,000	—	6.00	7.50	9.00	15.00
1961	800,000	—	6.00	7.50	9.00	15.00

KM# 17a.1 50 CENTS
10.40 g., Copper-Nickel **Obv:** Head with headdress left above star **Rev:** Value and date within wreath

Date	Mintage	VF20	XF40	MS60	MS63	MS65
1966	200,000	0.75	1.00	1.50	2.50	3.00

KM# 17a.2 50 CENTS
8.90 g., Copper-Nickel, 29 mm. **Obv:** Head with headdress left above star **Rev:** Value and date within wreath

Date	Mintage	VF20	XF40	MS60	MS63	MS65
1968 (l)	1,000,000	0.60	0.80	1.50	2.50	3.00
1968 (s)	14,000	PF65 1.50				
1969	5,056	PF65 1.50				
1970	3,464	PF65 2.50				
1971	3,032	PF65 2.50				
1972	4,866	PF65 1.50				
1973	1,000,000	0.60	0.75	1.25	2.00	2.50
1973	11,000	PF65 1.50				
1974	9,362	PF65 1.50				
1975	800,000	0.60	0.75	1.25	2.00	2.50
1975	4,056	PF65 1.50				

KM# 17b.2 50 CENTS
9.00 g., Nickel Clad Steel, 28 mm. **Obv:** Head with headdress left above star **Rev:** Value and date within wreath **Edge:** Reeded

Date	Mintage	VF20	XF40	MS60	MS63	MS65
2000	—	—	—	2.00	2.50	3.50

KM# 31 50 CENTS
8.90 g., Copper-Nickel **Obv:** Head 1/4 right flanked by stars **Rev:** National arms

Date	Mintage	VF20	XF40	MS60	MS63	MS65
1976	1,000,000	0.60	1.00	1.50	2.50	4.00
1976	2,131	PF65 5.50				
1977	920	PF65 6.50				
1978 FM	7,311	PF65 4.00				
1987	1,800,000	0.60	1.00	1.50	2.50	4.00

KM# 31a 50 CENTS
8.90 g., Copper-Nickel **Obv:** Head 1/4 right flanked by stars **Rev:** National arms **Edge Lettering:** O.A.U. July 1979

Date	Mintage	VF20	XF40	MS60	MS63	MS65
1979 FM	1,857	PF65 4.50				

KM# 18 DOLLAR
20.74 g., 0.900 Silver 0.6001 oz. ASW, 34 mm. **Obv:** Head with headdress left above star **Rev:** Value and date within wreath

Date	Mintage	VF20	XF40	MS60	MS63	MS65
1961	200,000	—	11.50	16.00	18.00	28.00
1962	1,000,000	—	11.50	14.00	16.00	25.00

KM# 18a.1 DOLLAR
20.70 g., Copper-Nickel, 34 mm. **Obv:** Head with headdress left above star **Rev:** Value and date within wreath

Date	Mintage	VF20	XF40	MS60	MS63	MS65
1966	1,000,000	1.00	1.50	2.00	2.50	3.50

KM# 18a.2 DOLLAR
18.00 g., Copper-Nickel, 34 mm. **Obv:** Head with headdress left above star **Rev:** Value and date within wreath

Date	Mintage	VF20	XF40	MS60	MS63	MS65
1968 (l)	1,000,000	1.00	1.50	2.00	2.50	3.50
1968 (s)	14,000	PF65 2.00				
1969	5,056	PF65 2.00				
1970 (d)	2,000,000	1.00	1.50	2.50	3.00	4.50
1970 (s)	3,464	PF65 6.00				
1971	3,032	PF65 4.50				
1972	4,866	PF65 4.50				
1973	11,000	PF65 3.00				
1974	9,362	PF65 3.00				
1975	400,000	1.25	1.75	2.50	3.00	4.50
1975	4,056	PF65 3.00				

KM# 32 DOLLAR
18.00 g., Copper-Nickel, 34 mm. **Obv:** Head 1/4 right flanked by stars **Rev:** Liberia, map and date within circle flanked by stars

Date	Mintage	VF20	XF40	MS60	MS63	MS65
1976	2,000,000	2.50	4.00	5.00	7.00	12.00
1976	2,131	PF65 12.00				
1977	920	PF65 13.50				
1978 FM	7,311	PF65 11.00				
1987	1,500,000	1.50	3.00	4.00	6.00	10.00

KM# 32a DOLLAR
18.00 g., Copper-Nickel, 34 mm. **Obv:** Head with headdress 1/4 right flanked by stars **Rev:** Liberia, map and date within circle flanked by stars **Edge Lettering:** O.A.U. July 1979

Date	Mintage	VF20	XF40	MS60	MS63	MS65
1979 FM	1,857	PF65 15.00				

KM# 98 DOLLAR
18.00 g., Copper-Nickel **Series:** Preserve Planet Earth **Obv:** National arms **Rev:** Protoceratops

Date	Mintage	VF20	XF40	MS60	MS63	MS65
1993	—	—	—	—	7.00	9.00

KM# 101 DOLLAR
18.00 g., Copper-Nickel **Subject:** Nolan Ryan **Obv:** National arms **Rev:** Nolan Ryan waving baseball cap **Note:** Similar to 10 Dollars, KM#102.

Date	Mintage	VF20	XF40	MS60	MS63	MS65
1993	—	—	—	—	4.00	6.00

KM# 109 DOLLAR
28.52 g., Copper-Nickel **Series:** Preserve Planet Earth **Obv:** National arms **Rev:** Corythosaurus

Date	Mintage	VF20	XF40	MS60	MS63	MS65
1993	—	—	—	—	7.00	9.00

KM# 112 DOLLAR
28.52 g., Copper-Nickel **Series:** Preserve Planet Earth **Obv:** National arms **Rev:** Atchaeopteryx **Note:** Incorrect spelling

Date	Mintage	VF20	XF40	MS60	MS63	MS65
1993	—	—	—	—	9.00	12.00

KM# 115 DOLLAR
28.52 g., Copper-Nickel **Series:** Preserve Planet Earth **Obv:** National arms **Rev:** Archaeopteryx **Note:** Correct spelling.

Date	Mintage	VF20	XF40	MS60	MS63	MS65
1994	—	—	—	—	12.00	12.00

KM# 118 DOLLAR
28.52 g., Copper-Nickel, 38.6 mm. **Series:** Preserve Planet Earth **Obv:** National arms **Rev:** Gorillas **Edge:** Reeded **Note:** Similar to 10 Dollars, KM#119.

Date	Mintage	VF20	XF40	MS60	MS63	MS65
1994	—	—	—	—	7.00	9.00

KM# 121 DOLLAR
28.52 g., Copper-Nickel **Series:** Preserve Planet Earth **Obv:** National arms **Rev:** Pygmy Hippopotami **Note:** Similar to 10 Dollars, KM#122.

Date	Mintage	VF20	XF40	MS60	MS63	MS65
1994	—	—	—	—	7.00	9.00

KM# 124 DOLLAR
28.52 g., Copper-Nickel **Series:** Preserve Planet Earth **Obv:** National arms **Rev:** Trionyx Turtle **Note:** Similar to 10 Dollars, KM#125.

Date	Mintage	VF20	XF40	MS60	MS63	MS65
1994	—	—	—	—	7.00	9.00

KM# 131 DOLLAR
28.52 g., Copper-Nickel **Subject:** Babe Ruth Sultan of Swat **Obv:** National arms **Rev:** Head 1/4 right divides date within circle

Date	Mintage	VF20	XF40	MS60	MS63	MS65
1994	—	—	—	—	4.00	6.00

KM# 131a DOLLAR
Copper-Nickel Gilt **Subject:** Babe Ruth Sultan of Swat **Obv:** National arms **Rev:** Head 1/4 right divides date within circle **Note:** Issued in a first day cover.

Date	Mintage	VF20	XF40	MS60	MS63	MS65
1994	—	—	—	—	—	20.00

KM# 139 DOLLAR
Copper-Nickel **Subject:** Damon Hill- Fomula One Race Car **Obv:** National arms **Rev:** Bust facing flanked by helmet and flag above car and value within sprigs

Date	Mintage	VF20	XF40	MS60	MS63	MS65
1994 Prooflike	—	—	—	—	3.00	5.00

KM# 248 DOLLAR
Copper-Nickel **Subject:** Hall of Fame - Roberto Clemente **Obv:** National arms **Rev:** Head facing

Date	Mintage	VF20	XF40	MS60	MS63	MS65
1994	—	—	—	—	4.00	6.00

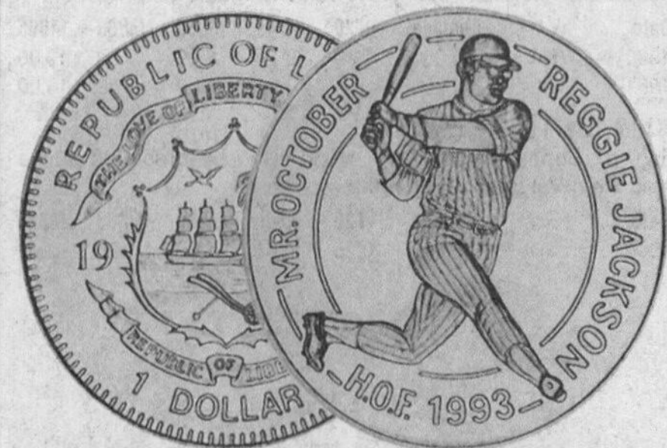

KM# 249 DOLLAR
Copper-Nickel **Subject:** Hall of Fame - Reggie Jackson **Obv:** National arms **Rev:** Baseball player divides circle above date

Date	Mintage	VF20	XF40	MS60	MS63	MS65
1994	—	—	—	—	4.00	6.00

KM# 411 DOLLAR

Copper-Nickel **Obv:** National arms **Rev:** Head left above small gazelle and value

Date	Mintage	VF20	XF40	MS60	MS63	MS65
1994	—	—	—	—	4.00	6.00

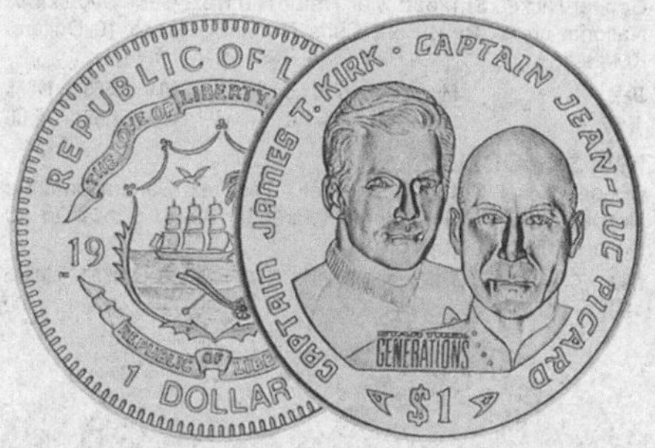

KM# 128 DOLLAR

Copper-Nickel **Subject:** Star Trek **Obv:** National arms **Rev:** Conjoined busts facing **Note:** Similar to 10 Dollars, KM#129.

Date	Mintage	VF20	XF40	MS60	MS63	MS65
1995	—	—	—	—	3.00	5.00

KM# 133 DOLLAR

Copper-Nickel **Series:** Preserve Planet Earth **Obv:** National arms **Rev:** Leopard

Date	Mintage	VF20	XF40	MS60	MS63	MS65
1995	—	—	—	—	7.00	9.00

KM# 136 DOLLAR

Copper-Nickel **Series:** Preserve Planet Earth **Obv:** National arms **Rev:** Storks

Date	Mintage	VF20	XF40	MS60	MS63	MS65
1995	—	—	—	—	4.00	6.00

KM# 140 DOLLAR

Copper-Nickel **Subject:** Sir Winston Churchill **Obv:** National arms **Rev:** Uniformed bust right with planes, army tanks and ship at right

Date	Mintage	VF20	XF40	MS60	MS63	MS65
1995	—	—	—	—	2.50	4.50

KM# 141 DOLLAR

Copper-Nickel **Subject:** President Franklin D. Roosevelt **Obv:** National arms **Rev:** President Roosevelt riding in jeep

Date	Mintage	VF20	XF40	MS60	MS63	MS65
1995	—	—	—	—	2.50	4.50

KM# 142 DOLLAR

Copper-Nickel **Subject:** General George Patton **Obv:** National arms **Rev:** General Patton in front of map

Date	Mintage	VF20	XF40	MS60	MS63	MS65
1995	—	—	—	—	2.50	4.50

KM# 143 DOLLAR

Copper-Nickel **Subject:** President Harry S. Truman **Obv:** National arms **Rev:** President Truman facing

Date	Mintage	VF20	XF40	MS60	MS63	MS65
1995	—	—	—	—	2.50	4.50

KM# 144 DOLLAR

Copper-Nickel **Subject:** President Charles de Gaulle **Obv:** National arms **Rev:** President on Champs Elysees

Date	Mintage	VF20	XF40	MS60	MS63	MS65
1995	—	—	—	—	2.50	4.50

KM# 158 DOLLAR

Copper-Nickel **Subject:** Dr. Sun Yat-sen **Obv:** National arms **Rev:** Uniformed bust facing

Date	Mintage	VF20	XF40	MS60	MS63	MS65
1995	—	—	—	—	3.00	5.00

KM# 161 DOLLAR

Copper-Nickel **Subject:** General Chiang Kai-shek **Obv:** National arms **Rev:** General Chiang kai-shek

Date	Mintage	VF20	XF40	MS60	MS63	MS65
1995	—	—	—	—	3.00	5.00

KM# 164 DOLLAR

Copper-Nickel **Subject:** Cairo Conference **Obv:** National arms **Rev:** Chiang kai-shek, Roosevelt and Churchill

Date	Mintage	VF20	XF40	MS60	MS63	MS65
1995	—	—	—	—	3.00	5.00

KM# 167 DOLLAR

Copper-Nickel **Subject:** 375th Anniversary - Pilgrim Fathers **Obv:** National arms **Rev:** The "Mayflower"

Date	Mintage	VF20	XF40	MS60	MS63	MS65
1995	—	—	—	—	2.50	4.50

KM# 168 DOLLAR

Copper-Nickel **Subject:** 375th Anniversary - Pilgrim Fathers **Obv:** National arms **Rev:** First Thanksgiving scene

Date	Mintage	VF20	XF40	MS60	MS63	MS65
1995	—	—	—	—	2.50	4.50

KM# 169 DOLLAR

Copper-Nickel **Subject:** 375th Anniversary - Pilgrim Fathers **Obv:** National arms **Rev:** Cape Cod and Pilgrims in skiff

Date	Mintage	VF20	XF40	MS60	MS63	MS65
1995	—	—	—	—	2.50	4.50

KM# 170 DOLLAR

Copper-Nickel **Subject:** 375th Anniversary - Pilgrim Fathers **Obv:** National arms **Rev:** Pilgrim landing party

Date	Mintage	VF20	XF40	MS60	MS63	MS65
1995	—	—	—	—	2.50	4.50

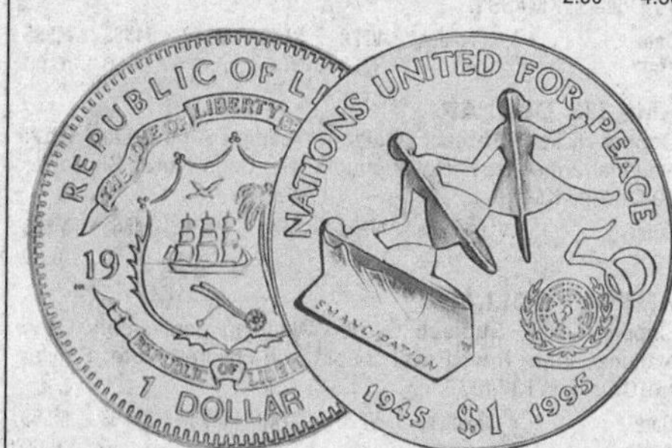

KM# 412 DOLLAR

Copper-Nickel **Subject:** Nations for Peace **Obv:** National arms **Rev:** Paper dolls, UN logo

Date	Mintage	VF20	XF40	MS60	MS63	MS65
1995	—	—	—	—	3.00	5.00

KM# 207 DOLLAR

Copper-Nickel **Subject:** Star Trek **Obv:** National arms **Rev:** Starships NCC-1701 and NCC-1701D **Note:** Similar to 10 Dollars, KM#208.

Date	Mintage	VF20	XF40	MS60	MS63	MS65
1996	—	—	—	—	3.00	5.00

KM# 210 DOLLAR

Copper-Nickel **Subject:** Star Trek **Obv:** National arms **Rev:** Conjoined busts facing **Note:** Similar to 10 Dollars, KM#211.

Date	Mintage	VF20	XF40	MS60	MS63	MS65
1996	—	—	—	—	3.00	5.00

KM# 213 DOLLAR

Copper-Nickel **Subject:** Star Trek **Obv:** National arms **Rev:** Conjoined busts facing **Note:** Similar to 10 Dollars, KM#214.

Date	Mintage	VF20	XF40	MS60	MS63	MS65
1996	—	—	—	—	3.00	5.00

KM# 216 DOLLAR

Copper-Nickel **Subject:** Star Trek **Obv:** National arms **Rev:** Spock and Uhura **Note:** Similar to 10 Dollars, KM#217.

Date	Mintage	VF20	XF40	MS60	MS63	MS65
1996	—	—	—	—	3.00	5.00

KM# 219 DOLLAR

Copper-Nickel **Subject:** Star Trek **Obv:** National arms **Rev:** Conjoined busts 1/4 left **Note:** Similar to 10 Dollars, KM#220.

Date	Mintage	VF20	XF40	MS60	MS63	MS65
1996	—	—	—	—	3.00	5.00

KM# 222 DOLLAR

Copper-Nickel **Series:** Preserve Planet Earth **Obv:** National arms **Rev:** Grey Parrot **Note:** Similar to 10 Dollars, KM#223.

Date	Mintage	VF20	XF40	MS60	MS63	MS65
1996	—	—	—	—	7.00	9.00

KM# 225 DOLLAR

Copper-Nickel **Series:** Preserve Planet Earth **Obv:** National arms **Rev:** Love Birds **Note:** Similar to 10 Dollars, KM#226.

Date	Mintage	VF20	XF40	MS60	MS63	MS65
1996	—	—	—	—	7.00	9.00

KM# 254 DOLLAR

Copper-Nickel **Subject:** Chairman Mao Zedong **Obv:** National arms **Rev:** Standing figure facing **Note:** Similar to 10 Dollars, KM#256. Issued in first day cover.

Date	Mintage	VF20	XF40	MS60	MS63	MS65
1996	20,000	—	—	—	3.00	5.00

KM# 260 DOLLAR

Copper-Nickel **Obv:** National arms **Rev:** Seated figures facing **Note:** Similar to 10 Dollars, KM#262. Issued in first day cover.

Date	Mintage	VF20	XF40	MS60	MS63	MS65
1996	20,000	—	—	—	3.00	5.00

KM# 263 DOLLAR

Copper-Nickel **Subject:** Pioneers of the West **Obv:** National arms **Rev:** Bust of Buffalo Bill facing at right of scene fighting indians **Note:** Similar to 10 Dollars, KM#264.

Date	Mintage	VF20	XF40	MS60	MS63	MS65
1996	—	—	—	—	3.00	5.00

KM# 266 DOLLAR

Copper-Nickel **Subject:** Pioneers of the West **Obv:** National arms **Rev:** Davy Crockett **Note:** Similar to 10 Dollars, KM#267.

Date	Mintage	VF20	XF40	MS60	MS63	MS65
1996	—	—	—	—	3.00	5.00

KM# 269 DOLLAR

Copper-Nickel **Subject:** Pioneers of the West **Obv:** National arms **Rev:** Jim Bowie in front of the Alamo **Note:** Similar to 10 Dollars, KM#270.

Date	Mintage	VF20	XF40	MS60	MS63	MS65
1996	—	—	—	—	3.00	5.00

KM# 272 DOLLAR

Copper-Nickel **Subject:** Pioneers of the West **Obv:** National arms **Rev:** Kit Carson **Note:** Similar to 10 Dollars, KM#273.

Date	Mintage	VF20	XF40	MS60	MS63	MS65
1996	—	—	—	—	3.00	5.00

KM# 275 DOLLAR
Copper-Nickel **Subject:** Pioneers of the West **Obv:** National arms **Rev:** Wild Bill Hickok **Note:** Similar to 10 Dollars, KM#276.

Date	Mintage	VF20	XF40	MS60	MS63	MS65
1996	—	—	—	—	3.00	5.00

KM# 278 DOLLAR
Copper-Nickel **Subject:** Pioneers of the West **Obv:** National arms **Rev:** Buffalo Bill **Note:** Similar to 10 Dollars, KM#279.

Date	Mintage	VF20	XF40	MS60	MS63	MS65
1996	—	—	—	—	3.00	5.00

KM# 560 DOLLAR
Silver **Obv:** National arms **Rev:** Multicolor fish

Date	Mintage	VF20	XF40	MS60	MS63	MS65
1996 B	—	PF65 25.00				

KM# 569 DOLLAR
24.61 g., Copper-Nickel, 38.6 mm. **Subject:** Marine Life Protection **Obv:** National arms **Rev:** Multicolor fish **Edge:** Reeded

Date	Mintage	VF20	XF40	MS60	MS63	MS65
1996	—	—	—	—	—	20.00

KM# 286 DOLLAR
Copper-Nickel **Subject:** WWII - Evacuation of Dunkirk **Obv:** National arms **Rev:** Star medal above dates to left of fighter planes and ships **Note:** Similar to 10 Dollars, KM#287.

Date	Mintage	VF20	XF40	MS60	MS63	MS65
1997	—	—	—	—	4.00	6.00

KM# 288 DOLLAR
Copper-Nickel **Subject:** WWII - Liberation of the Philippines **Obv:** National arms **Rev:** Medal to right of soldiers in water **Note:** Similar to 10 Dollars, KM#289.

Date	Mintage	VF20	XF40	MS60	MS63	MS65
1997	—	—	—	—	4.00	6.00

KM# 290 DOLLAR
Copper-Nickel **Subject:** WWII - Defense of Stalingrad **Obv:** National arms **Rev:** Soviet combat medal to left of war scene **Note:** Similar to 10 Dollars, KM#291.

Date	Mintage	VF20	XF40	MS60	MS63	MS65
1997	—	—	—	—	4.00	6.00

KM# 292 DOLLAR
Copper-Nickel **Subject:** WWII - Arnhem **Obv:** National arms **Rev:** Netherlands bronze lion cross to right of parachutists, bridge and soldier **Note:** Similar to 10 Dollars, KM#293.

Date	Mintage	VF20	XF40	MS60	MS63	MS65
1997	—	—	—	—	4.00	6.00

KM# 294 DOLLAR
Copper-Nickel **Subject:** WWII - Raid on the Dams **Obv:** National arms **Rev:** British distinguished flying medal **Note:** Similar to 10 Dollars, KM#295.

Date	Mintage	VF20	XF40	MS60	MS63	MS65
1997	—	—	—	—	4.00	6.00

KM# 296 DOLLAR
Copper-Nickel **Subject:** WWII - West African Campaign **Obv:** National arms **Rev:** WWII Victory medal **Note:** Similar to 10 Dollars, KM#297.

Date	Mintage	VF20	XF40	MS60	MS63	MS65
1997	—	—	—	—	4.00	6.00

KM# 298 DOLLAR
Copper-Nickel **Subject:** WWII - North African Campaign **Obv:** National arms **Rev:** British Africa star medal to right of tank in front of pyramid **Note:** Similar to 10 Dollars, KM#299.

Date	Mintage	VF20	XF40	MS60	MS63	MS65
1997	—	—	—	—	4.00	6.00

KM# 300 DOLLAR
Copper-Nickel **Subject:** WWII - The Dieppe Raid **Obv:** National arms **Rev:** British Victoria cross to right of plane over British tank **Note:** Similar to 10 Dollars, KM#301.

Date	Mintage	VF20	XF40	MS60	MS63	MS65
1997	—	—	—	—	4.00	6.00

KM# 302 DOLLAR
Copper-Nickel **Subject:** WWII - Iwo Jima **Obv:** National arms **Rev:** Purple Heart medal to upper left of damaged plane landing on a carrier **Note:** Similar to 10 Dollars, KM#303.

Date	Mintage	VF20	XF40	MS60	MS63	MS65
1997	—	—	—	—	4.00	6.00

KM# 304 DOLLAR
Copper-Nickel **Subject:** WWII - Battle of Britain **Obv:** National arms **Rev:** British distinguished flying cross to left of pilots running to board planes **Note:** Similar to 10 Dollars, KM#305.

Date	Mintage	VF20	XF40	MS60	MS63	MS65
1997	—	—	—	—	4.00	6.00

KM# 306 DOLLAR
Copper-Nickel **Subject:** WWII - Liberation of Paris **Obv:** National arms **Rev:** Croix de Guerre medal to right of soldiers in front of Arch de Triumph **Note:** Similar to 10 Dollars, KM#307.

Date	Mintage	VF20	XF40	MS60	MS63	MS65
1997	—	—	—	—	4.00	6.00

KM# 308 DOLLAR
Copper-Nickel **Subject:** WWII - Burma Campaign **Obv:** National arms **Rev:** British Burma star medal **Note:** Similar to 10 Dollars, KM#309.

Date	Mintage	VF20	XF40	MS60	MS63	MS65
1997	—	—	—	—	4.00	6.00

KM# 310 DOLLAR
Copper-Nickel **Subject:** Mahatma Gandhi **Obv:** National arms **Rev:** Seated figure facing left in front of Taj Mahal **Note:** Similar to 10 Dollars, KM#311.

Date	Mintage	VF20	XF40	MS60	MS63	MS65
1997	—	—	—	—	4.00	6.00

KM# 313 DOLLAR
Copper-Nickel **Subject:** Return of Hong Kong - Dragon **Obv:** National arms

Date	Mintage	VF20	XF40	MS60	MS63	MS65
1997	—	—	—	—	4.00	6.00

KM# 320 DOLLAR
Copper-Nickel **Subject:** Fiftieth Anniversary of the Kon-Tiki Expedition **Obv:** National arms **Rev:** Sailing ship within circle

Date	Mintage	VF20	XF40	MS60	MS63	MS65
1997	—	—	—	—	4.00	6.00

KM# 324 DOLLAR
Copper-Nickel **Subject:** Jurassic Park - Stegosaurus **Obv:** National arms **Rev:** Stegosaurus **Note:** Similar to 10 Dollars, KM#325.

Date	Mintage	VF20	XF40	MS60	MS63	MS65
1997	—	—	—	—	7.00	9.00

KM# 327 DOLLAR
Copper-Nickel **Subject:** Golden Wedding Anniversary **Obv:** National arms **Rev:** E & P initials above two shields **Note:** Similar to 10 Dollars, KM#328.

Date	Mintage	VF20	XF40	MS60	MS63	MS65
1997	—	—	—	—	4.50	6.00

KM# 330 DOLLAR
Copper-Nickel **Subject:** Golden Wedding Anniversary **Obv:** National arms **Rev:** Royal couple with horse **Note:** Similar to 10 Dollars, KM#331.

Date	Mintage	VF20	XF40	MS60	MS63	MS65
1997	—	—	—	—	4.50	6.00

KM# 333 DOLLAR
Copper-Nickel **Subject:** Golden Wedding Anniversary **Obv:** National arms **Rev:** Royal couple with dogs **Note:** Similar to 10 Dollars, KM#334.

Date	Mintage	VF20	XF40	MS60	MS63	MS65
1997	—	—	—	—	4.50	6.00

KM# 336 DOLLAR
Copper-Nickel **Subject:** Golden Wedding Anniversary **Obv:** National arms **Rev:** Royal couple with children **Note:** Similar to 10 Dollars, KM#337.

Date	Mintage	VF20	XF40	MS60	MS63	MS65
1997	—	—	—	—	4.50	6.00

KM# 344 DOLLAR
Copper-Nickel **Subject:** 150th Anniversary of Independence **Obv:** National arms **Rev:** The "Ashmon" **Note:** Similar to 10 Dollars, KM#345.

Date	Mintage	VF20	XF40	MS60	MS63	MS65
1997	—	—	—	—	5.50	7.00

KM# 368 DOLLAR
Copper-Nickel **Subject:** Star Trek - The Next Generation **Obv:** National arms **Rev:** Romulan Warbird **Note:** Similar to 10 Dollars, KM#369.

Date	Mintage	VF20	XF40	MS60	MS63	MS65
1997	—	—	—	—	4.50	6.00

KM# 371 DOLLAR
Copper-Nickel **Subject:** Star Trek - The Next Generation **Obv:** National arms **Rev:** Klingon Attack Cruiser **Note:** Similar to 10 Dollars, KM#372.

Date	Mintage	VF20	XF40	MS60	MS63	MS65
1997	—	—	—	—	4.50	6.00

KM# 374 DOLLAR
Copper-Nickel **Subject:** Star Trek - The Next Generation **Obv:** National arms **Rev:** U.S.S. Enterprise NCC-1701-D **Note:** Similar to 10 Dollars, KM#375.

Date	Mintage	VF20	XF40	MS60	MS63	MS65
1997	—	—	—	—	4.50	6.00

KM# 377 DOLLAR
Copper-Nickel **Subject:** Star Trek - The Next Generation **Obv:** National arms **Rev:** Klingon Bird of Prey **Note:** Similar to 10 Dollars, KM#378.

Date	Mintage	VF20	XF40	MS60	MS63	MS65
1997	—	—	—	—	4.50	6.00

KM# 380 DOLLAR
Copper-Nickel **Subject:** Star Trek - The Next Generation **Obv:** National arms **Rev:** Borg Cube **Note:** Similar to 10 Dollars, KM#381.

Date	Mintage	VF20	XF40	MS60	MS63	MS65
1997	—	—	—	—	4.50	6.00

KM# 383 DOLLAR
Copper-Nickel **Subject:** Star Trek - The Next Generation **Obv:** National arms **Rev:** Ferengi Marauder **Note:** Similar to 10 Dollars, KM#384.

Date	Mintage	VF20	XF40	MS60	MS63	MS65
1997	—	—	—	—	4.50	6.00

KM# 426 DOLLAR
13.94 g., Copper, 32 mm. **Subject:** AZA Species Survival Plan **Obv:** National arms **Rev:** Seated panda eating within circle **Edge:** Reeded

Date	Mintage	VF20	XF40	MS60	MS63	MS65
1997	—	—	—	—	4.00	6.00

KM# 570 DOLLAR
24.61 g., Copper-Nickel, 38.6 mm. **Subject:** Marine Life Protection **Obv:** National arms **Rev:** Multicolor fish **Edge:** Reeded

Date	Mintage	VF20	XF40	MS60	MS63	MS65
1997	—	—	—	—	—	20.00

KM# 386 DOLLAR
Copper-Nickel **Subject:** President Ronald Reagan **Obv:** National arms **Rev:** Lincoln Memorial below head right **Note:** Similar to 10 Dollars, KM#387.

Date	Mintage	VF20	XF40	MS60	MS63	MS65
1998	—	—	—	—	4.00	6.00

KM# 401 DOLLAR
Copper-Nickel **Subject:** Christopher Columbus **Obv:** National arms **Rev:** Bust 1/4 right above ship **Note:** Similar to 10 Dollars, KM#402.

Date	Mintage	VF20	XF40	MS60	MS63	MS65
1999	—	—	—	—	4.00	6.00

KM# 404 DOLLAR
Copper-Nickel **Subject:** Captain Cook **Obv:** National arms **Rev:** Portrait, ship and map **Note:** Similar to 10 Dollars, KM#405.

Date	Mintage	VF20	XF40	MS60	MS63	MS65
1999	—	—	—	—	4.00	6.00

KM# 407 DOLLAR
Copper-Nickel **Subject:** Return of Macao to China **Obv:** National arms **Rev:** Dragon and phoenix **Note:** Similar to 10 Dollars, KM#408.

Date	Mintage	VF20	XF40	MS60	MS63	MS65
1999	—	—	—	—	4.00	6.00

KM# 413 DOLLAR

Copper-Nickel **Subject:** The Wedding of Prince Edward **Obv:** National arms **Rev:** Couple in carriage **Note:** Similar to 10 Dollars, KM#413.

Date	Mintage	VF20	XF40	MS60	MS63	MS65
1999	—	—	—	—	4.00	6.00

KM# 571 DOLLAR

24.61 g., Copper-Nickel, 38.6 mm. **Subject:** Marine Life Protection **Obv:** National arms **Rev:** Multicolor fish **Edge:** Reeded

Date	Mintage	VF20	XF40	MS60	MS63	MS65
1999	—	—	—	—	—	20.00

KM# 442 DOLLAR

28.28 g., Copper-Nickel, 38.6 mm. **Subject:** Greenwich Meridian **Obv:** National arms **Rev:** World landmarks and fireworks **Edge:** Reeded

Date	Mintage	VF20	XF40	MS60	MS63	MS65
2000	—	—	—	—	7.00	9.00

KM# 612 DOLLAR

5.35 g., Copper-Nickel, 24.9 mm. **Subject:** Millennium - Year of the Dragon **Obv:** National arms within circle above date **Rev:** Chinese dragon within circle **Edge:** Reeded

Date	Mintage	VF20	XF40	MS60	MS63	MS65
2000	—	—	—	—	3.00	5.00

KM# 615 DOLLAR

5.35 g., Copper-Nickel, 24.9 mm. **Obv:** National arms within circle above date **Rev:** Dancing style dragon within circle **Edge:** Reeded

Date	Mintage	VF20	XF40	MS60	MS63	MS65
2000	—	—	—	—	3.00	5.00

KM# 635 DOLLAR

0.999 Silver, 21 mm. **Obv:** National arms **Rev:** American Quarter Horse

Date	Mintage	VF20	XF40	MS60	MS63	MS65
2000	—	PF65 27.00				

KM# 696 DOLLAR

31.10 g., 0.999 Silver 0.9989 oz. ASW, 39 mm. **Subject:** Millennium **Obv:** American style eagle **Rev:** Morgan dollar style Liberty head **Edge:** Reeded

Date	Mintage	VF20	XF40	MS60	MS63	MS65
2000	—	PF65 30.00				

KM# 47 2 DOLLARS

Copper-Nickel **Series:** F.A.O. **Subject:** World Fisheries Conference **Obv:** National arms **Rev:** Longneck croaker fish

Date	Mintage	VF20	XF40	MS60	MS63	MS65
1983	100,000	—	—	5.00	7.00	10.00

KM# 47a 2 DOLLARS

28.28 g., 0.925 Silver 0.841 oz. ASW **Subject:** World Fisheries Conference **Obv:** National arms **Rev:** Longneck croaker fish

Date	Mintage	VF20	XF40	MS60	MS63	MS65
1983	20,000	PF65 35.00				

KM# 47b 2 DOLLARS

47.54 g., Gold **Series:** F.A.O. **Subject:** World Fisheries Conference **Obv:** National arms **Rev:** Longneck croaker fish

Date	Mintage	VF20	XF40	MS60	MS63	MS65
1983	600	PF65 1,600				

KM# 24 2-1/2 DOLLARS

4.18 g., 0.900 Gold 0.1209 oz. AGW **Subject:** Inauguration of President Tolbert **Rev:** Capitol building

Date	Mintage	VF20	XF40	MS60	MS63	MS65
1972	—	PF65 215				

KM# 644 2-1/2 DOLLARS

11.80 g., Copper-Nickel, 29.5 mm. **Obv:** National arms divides date **Rev:** Olympic torch runner facing right **Edge:** Plain

Date	Mintage	VF20	XF40	MS60	MS63	MS65
1999	—	PF63 8.00	PF65 10.00			

KM# 62 5 DOLLARS

5.00 g., 0.900 Gold 0.1447 oz. AGW **Subject:** 25th Anniversary of Inter-Continental Hotels **Obv:** Value below hotel flanked by sprigs **Rev:** Letter I within football flanked by dates

Date	Mintage	VF20	XF40	MS60	MS63	MS65
ND-1971	—	PF65 250				

KM# 25 5 DOLLARS

8.36 g., 0.900 Gold 0.2419 oz. AGW **Subject:** Inauguration of President Tolbert **Rev:** Full masted ship at sea

Date	Mintage	VF20	XF40	MS60	MS63	MS65
1972	—	PF65 400				

KM# 29 5 DOLLARS

34.10 g., 0.900 Silver 0.9867 oz. ASW, 42 mm. **Obv:** National arms, value written on top, date on bottom **Rev:** Standing elephant looking 1/4 right above star

Date	Mintage	VF20	XF40	MS60	MS63	MS65
1973	500	—	—	—	37.00	—
1973	28,000	PF65 25.00				
1974	20,000	PF65 25.00				
1975	9,017	PF65 25.00				
1976	3,683	PF65 30.00				
1977	1,640	PF65 35.00				
1978 FM	7,311	PF65 25.00				

KM# 29a 5 DOLLARS

34.10 g., 0.900 Silver 0.9867 oz. ASW, 42 mm. **Obv:** National arms **Rev:** Standing elephant looking 1/4 right above star **Edge Lettering:** O.A.U. July 1979

Date	Mintage	VF20	XF40	MS60	MS63	MS65
1979	1,857	PF65 35.00				

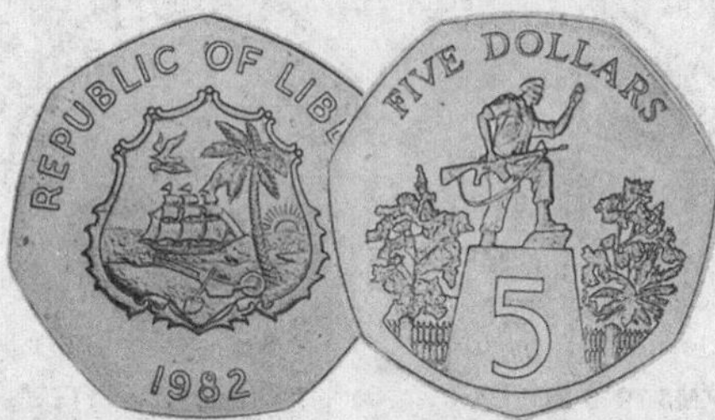

KM# 44 5 DOLLARS

Copper-Nickel **Subject:** Military Memorial **Obv:** National arms above date **Rev:** Memorial statue and value flanked by shrubs **Shape:** 7-sided

Date	Mintage	VF20	XF40	MS60	MS63	MS65
1982	4,000,000	—	—	2.00	4.00	6.00
1985	2,000,000	—	—	2.00	4.00	6.00

KM# 73 5 DOLLARS

15.55 g., 0.999 Silver 0.4994 oz. ASW **Subject:** Formula One - Gerhard Berger **Obv:** National arms divide date **Rev:** Head 1/4 right, racecar and flag

Date	Mintage	VF20	XF40	MS60	MS63	MS65
1992	—	PF65 14.50				

KM# 76 5 DOLLARS

15.55 g., 0.999 Silver 0.4994 oz. ASW **Subject:** Formula One - Nigel Mansell **Obv:** National arms **Rev:** Head right, racecar, date and flag above sprigs

Date	Mintage	VF20	XF40	MS60	MS63	MS65
1992	Est. 50000	PF65 14.50				

KM# 77 5 DOLLARS
15.55 g., 0.999 Silver 0.4994 oz. ASW **Subject:** Formula One - Aguri Suzuki **Obv:** National arms **Rev:** Racecar below bust at left **Note:** Similar to 10 Dollars, KM#84.

Date	Mintage	VF20	XF40	MS60	MS63	MS65
1992	Est. 50000	PF65 14.50				

KM# 78 5 DOLLARS
15.55 g., 0.999 Silver 0.4994 oz. ASW **Subject:** Formula One - Ayrton Senna **Obv:** National arms **Rev:** Bust 1/4 left above flag, racecar, dates and value

Date	Mintage	VF20	XF40	MS60	MS63	MS65
1992	Est. 50000	PF65 14.50				

KM# 79 5 DOLLARS
15.55 g., 0.999 Silver 0.4994 oz. ASW **Subject:** Formula One - Riccardo Patrese **Obv:** National arms **Rev:** Head 1/4 left to right of flag and racecar **Note:** Similar to 10 Dollars, KM#74.

Date	Mintage	VF20	XF40	MS60	MS63	MS65
1992	Est. 50000	PF65 14.50				

KM# 80 5 DOLLARS
15.55 g., 0.999 Silver 0.4994 oz. ASW **Subject:** Formula One - Michael Schumacher **Obv:** National arms **Rev:** Bust at right, car at left **Note:** Similar to 10 Dollars, KM#86.

Date	Mintage	VF20	XF40	MS60	MS63	MS65
1992	50,000	PF65 14.50				

KM# 81 5 DOLLARS
15.55 g., 0.999 Silver 0.4994 oz. ASW **Subject:** Formula One - Alain Prost **Obv:** National arms **Rev:** Head 3/4 left above flag, racecar, dates and value **Note:** Similar to 10 Dollars, KM#87.

Date	Mintage	VF20	XF40	MS60	MS63	MS65
1992	50,000	PF65 14.50				

KM# 82 5 DOLLARS
15.55 g., 0.999 Silver 0.4994 oz. ASW **Subject:** Formula One - Ukyo Katayama **Obv:** National arms **Rev:** Racecar below bust at left **Note:** Similar to 10 Dollars, KM#88.

Date	Mintage	VF20	XF40	MS60	MS63	MS65
1992	50,000	PF65 14.50				

KM# 67 5 DOLLARS
15.55 g., 0.999 Silver 0.4994 oz. ASW **Subject:** President Bill Clinton **Obv:** National arms **Rev:** Head right divides date and value above building **Note:** Similar to 10 Dollars, KM#68.

Date	Mintage	VF20	XF40	MS60	MS63	MS65
1993	50,000	PF65 18.50				

KM# 97 5 DOLLARS
15.55 g., 0.999 Silver 0.4994 oz. ASW **Subject:** Chancellor Willy Brandt **Obv:** National arms **Rev:** Horses pulling casket below head right dividing dates **Note:** Similar to 10 Dollars, KM#72.

Date	Mintage	VF20	XF40	MS60	MS63	MS65
1993	—	PF65 14.50				

KM# 103 5 DOLLARS
15.55 g., 0.999 Silver 0.4994 oz. ASW **Subject:** President John F. Kennedy **Obv:** National arms **Rev:** President Kennedy **Note:** Similar to 10 Dollars, KM#104.

Date	Mintage	VF20	XF40	MS60	MS63	MS65
1993	50,000	PF65 16.50				

KM# 179 5 DOLLARS
15.55 g., 0.999 Silver 0.4994 oz. ASW **Subject:** Formula One - Mika Hakkinen **Obv:** National arms **Rev:** Mike Hakkinen

Date	Mintage	VF20	XF40	MS60	MS63	MS65
1995	50,000	PF65 16.50				

KM# 182 5 DOLLARS
15.55 g., 0.999 Silver 0.4994 oz. ASW **Subject:** Formula One **Obv:** National arms **Rev:** Martin Brundle

Date	Mintage	VF20	XF40	MS60	MS63	MS65
1995	—	PF65 16.50				

KM# 185 5 DOLLARS
15.55 g., 0.999 Silver 0.4994 oz. ASW **Subject:** Formula One - Rubens Barrichello **Obv:** National arms **Rev:** Rubens Barrichello

Date	Mintage	VF20	XF40	MS60	MS63	MS65
1995	Est. 50000	PF65 16.50				

KM# 188 5 DOLLARS
15.55 g., 0.999 Silver 0.4994 oz. ASW **Subject:** Formula One - David Coulthard **Obv:** National arms **Rev:** David Coulthard

Date	Mintage	VF20	XF40	MS60	MS63	MS65
1995	Est. 50000	PF65 16.50				

KM# 191 5 DOLLARS
15.55 g., 0.999 Silver 0.4994 oz. ASW **Subject:** Formula One - Jean Alesi **Obv:** National arms **Rev:** Jean Alesi

Date	Mintage	VF20	XF40	MS60	MS63	MS65
1995	Est. 50000	PF65 16.50				

KM# 562 5 DOLLARS
15.50 g., 0.999 Silver 0.4978 oz. ASW **Obv:** National arms **Rev:** Benz Patent motor car

Date	Mintage	VF20	XF40	MS60	MS63	MS65
1995	—	PF65 20.50				

KM# 563 5 DOLLARS
15.50 g., 0.999 Silver 0.4978 oz. ASW, 32 mm. **Obv:** National arms **Rev:** Bughatti Royale

Date	Mintage	VF20	XF40	MS60	MS63	MS65
1995	—	—	—	—	—	20.50

KM# 195 5 DOLLARS
15.55 g., 0.999 Silver 0.4994 oz. ASW **Subject:** Formula One - Mark Blundell **Obv:** National arms **Rev:** Mark Brundell **Note:** Similar to 10 Dollars, KM#199.

Date	Mintage	VF20	XF40	MS60	MS63	MS65
1996	50,000	PF65 16.50				

KM# 196 5 DOLLARS
15.55 g., 0.999 Silver 0.4994 oz. ASW **Subject:** Formula One - Johnny Herbert **Obv:** National arms **Rev:** Johnny Herbert **Note:** Similar to 10 Dollars, KM#200.

Date	Mintage	VF20	XF40	MS60	MS63	MS65
1996	50,000	PF65 16.50				

KM# 197 5 DOLLARS
15.55 g., 0.999 Silver 0.4994 oz. ASW **Subject:** Formula One - Eddie Irvine **Obv:** National arms **Rev:** Eddie Irvine **Note:** Similar to 10 Dollars, KM#201.

Date	Mintage	VF20	XF40	MS60	MS63	MS65
1996	50,000	PF65 16.50				

KM# 198 5 DOLLARS
15.55 g., 0.999 Silver 0.4994 oz. ASW **Subject:** Formula One - Heinz Frentzen **Obv:** National arms **Rev:** Heinz Frentzen **Note:** Similar to 10 Dollars, KM#202.

Date	Mintage	VF20	XF40	MS60	MS63	MS65
1996	50,000	PF65 16.50				

KM# 228 5 DOLLARS
15.55 g., 0.999 Silver 0.4994 oz. ASW **Subject:** Formula One - Ayrton Senna **Obv:** National arms **Rev:** Ayrton Senna **Note:** Similar to 10 Dollars, KM#229.

Date	Mintage	VF20	XF40	MS60	MS63	MS65
1996	50,000	PF65 16.50				

KM# 255 5 DOLLARS
15.55 g., 0.999 Silver 0.4994 oz. ASW **Subject:** Chairman Mao Zedong **Obv:** National arms **Rev:** Standing figure facing above value **Note:** Similar to 10 Dollars, KM#256.

Date	Mintage	VF20	XF40	MS60	MS63	MS65
1996	20,000	PF65 16.50				
1996	20,000	PF65 16.50				

KM# 261 5 DOLLARS
15.55 g., 0.999 Silver 0.4994 oz. ASW **Subject:** Chairman Mao Zedong and President Nixon **Obv:** National arms **Rev:** Seated figures facing **Note:** Similar to 10 Dollars, KM#262.

Date	Mintage	VF20	XF40	MS60	MS63	MS65
1996	20,000	PF65 16.50				

KM# 351 5 DOLLARS
Copper-Nickel **Subject:** Chinese Astrology **Obv:** Seated Liberty **Rev:** Two rats and pumpkin

Date	Mintage	VF20	XF40	MS60	MS63	MS65
1997	Est. 4000	—	—	—	4.00	5.50

KM# 352 5 DOLLARS
Copper-Nickel **Subject:** Chinese Astrology **Obv:** Seated Liberty **Rev:** Ox

Date	Mintage	VF20	XF40	MS60	MS63	MS65
1997	Est. 4000	—	—	—	3.00	5.00

KM# 353 5 DOLLARS
Copper-Nickel **Subject:** Chinese Astrology **Obv:** Seated Liberty **Rev:** Tiger

Date	Mintage	VF20	XF40	MS60	MS63	MS65
1997	—	—	—	—	4.00	5.00

KM# 354 5 DOLLARS
Copper-Nickel **Subject:** Chinese Astrology **Obv:** Seated Liberty **Rev:** Rabbits

Date	Mintage	VF20	XF40	MS60	MS63	MS65
1997	Est. 4000	—	—	—	3.00	5.00

KM# 355 5 DOLLARS
Copper-Nickel **Subject:** Chinese Astrology **Obv:** Seated Liberty **Rev:** Dragon

Date	Mintage	VF20	XF40	MS60	MS63	MS65
1997	Est. 4000	—	—	—	4.00	5.50

KM# 356 5 DOLLARS
12.99 g., Copper-Nickel, 31.49 mm. **Subject:** Chinese Astrology **Obv:** Seated Liberty **Rev:** Snake **Edge:** Reeded

Date	Mintage	VF20	XF40	MS60	MS63	MS65
1997	—	—	—	—	3.00	4.00

KM# 357 5 DOLLARS
Copper-Nickel **Subject:** Chinese Astrology **Obv:** Seated Liberty **Rev:** Horse

Date	Mintage	VF20	XF40	MS60	MS63	MS65
1997	Est. 4000	—	—	—	4.00	5.00

KM# 358 5 DOLLARS
Copper-Nickel **Subject:** Chinese Astrology **Obv:** Seated Liberty **Rev:** Goat

Date	Mintage	VF20	XF40	MS60	MS63	MS65
1997	Est. 4000	—	—	—	3.00	4.00

KM# 359 5 DOLLARS
Copper-Nickel **Subject:** Chinese Astrology **Obv:** Seated Liberty **Rev:** Monkey

Date	Mintage	VF20	XF40	MS60	MS63	MS65
1997	—	—	—	—	3.00	4.00

KM# 360 5 DOLLARS
Copper-Nickel **Subject:** Chinese Astrology **Obv:** Seated Liberty **Rev:** Rooster

Date	Mintage	VF20	XF40	MS60	MS63	MS65
1997	—	—	—	—	3.00	5.00

KM# 361 5 DOLLARS
Copper-Nickel **Subject:** Chinese Astrology **Obv:** Seated Liberty **Rev:** Wrinkled seated dog

Date	Mintage	VF20	XF40	MS60	MS63	MS65
1997	Est. 4000	—	—	—	4.00	5.50

KM# 362 5 DOLLARS
Copper-Nickel **Subject:** Chinese Astrology **Obv:** Seated Liberty **Rev:** Pig

Date	Mintage	VF20	XF40	MS60	MS63	MS65
1997	—	—	—	—	3.00	5.00

KM# 441 5 DOLLARS
20.56 g., Copper-Nickel, 38.5 mm. **Obv:** National arms divide date **Rev:** Polar bear **Edge:** Reeded

Date	Mintage	VF20	XF40	MS60	MS63	MS65
1997	—	—	—	—	5.50	6.50

KM# 445 5 DOLLARS
25.10 g., Copper-Nickel, 38.5 mm. **Subject:** Princess Diana **Obv:** National arms divides date **Rev:** Crowned bust 3/4 left **Edge:** Reeded

Date	Mintage	VF20	XF40	MS60	MS63	MS65
1997	—	PF65 20.00				

KM# 446 5 DOLLARS
25.10 g., Copper-Nickel, 38.5 mm. **Subject:** Diana Series - Lady Spencer **Obv:** National arms **Rev:** Young girl's portrait **Edge:** Reeded

Date	Mintage	VF20	XF40	MS60	MS63	MS65
1997	—	—	—	—	8.00	10.00

KM# 447 5 DOLLARS
25.10 g., Copper-Nickel **Subject:** First TV Interview **Obv:** National arms **Rev:** Portrait of Diana with microphone

Date	Mintage	VF20	XF40	MS60	MS63	MS65
1997	—	—	—	—	8.00	10.00

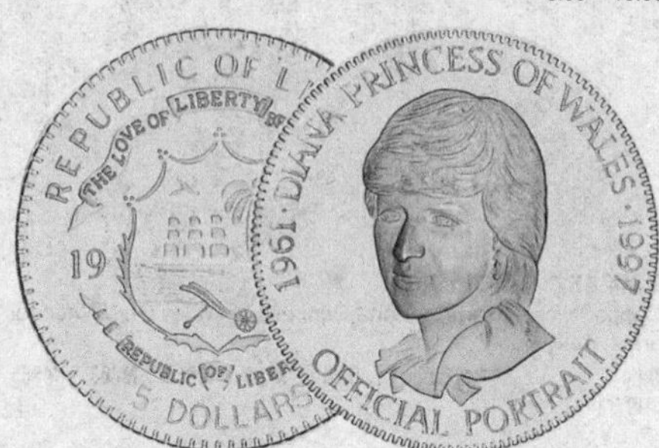

KM# 448 5 DOLLARS
Copper-Nickel **Subject:** Diana's Official Portrait **Obv:** National arms **Rev:** Portrait

Date	Mintage	VF20	XF40	MS60	MS63	MS65
1997	—	—	—	—	8.00	10.00

KM# 449 5 DOLLARS
Copper-Nickel **Subject:** Wedding Day **Obv:** National arms **Rev:** Diana in wedding dress

Date	Mintage	VF20	XF40	MS60	MS63	MS65
1997	—	—	—	—	8.00	10.00

KM# 450 5 DOLLARS

Copper-Nickel **Subject:** "People's Princess" - Diana **Obv:** National arms **Rev:** Formal portrait

Date	Mintage	VF20	XF40	MS60	MS63	MS65
1997	—	—	—	—	8.00	10.00

KM# 451 5 DOLLARS

Copper-Nickel **Subject:** England's Rose **Obv:** National arms **Rev:** Diana with bouquet of roses

Date	Mintage	VF20	XF40	MS60	MS63	MS65
1997	—	—	—	—	8.00	10.00

KM# A452 5 DOLLARS

Copper-Nickel **Subject:** Queen of Hearts **Obv:** National arms **Rev:** Diana wearing a choker

Date	Mintage	VF20	XF40	MS60	MS63	MS65
1997	—	—	—	—	10.00	12.00

KM# 452 5 DOLLARS

Copper-Nickel **Series:** Diana Princess of Wales **Obv:** National arms **Rev:** Head 3/4 left

Date	Mintage	VF20	XF40	MS60	MS63	MS65
1997	—	—	—	—	—	—

KM# 453 5 DOLLARS

Copper-Nickel **Subject:** Elegance **Obv:** National arms **Rev:** Diana wearing a high collar

Date	Mintage	VF20	XF40	MS60	MS63	MS65
1997	—	—	—	—	8.00	10.00

KM# 454 5 DOLLARS

Copper-Nickel **Subject:** Birth of William **Obv:** National arms **Rev:** Diana holding Prince William

Date	Mintage	VF20	XF40	MS60	MS63	MS65
1997	—	—	—	—	8.00	10.00

KM# 455 5 DOLLARS

Copper-Nickel **Subject:** William's Christening **Obv:** National arms **Rev:** Diana holding Prince William

Date	Mintage	VF20	XF40	MS60	MS63	MS65
1997	—	—	—	—	8.00	10.00

KM# 456 5 DOLLARS

Copper-Nickel **Subject:** Birth of Prince Harry **Obv:** National arms **Rev:** Diana holding Prince Harry

Date	Mintage	VF20	XF40	MS60	MS63	MS65
1997	—	—	—	—	8.00	10.00

KM# 457 5 DOLLARS

Copper-Nickel **Subject:** Loving Mother **Obv:** National arms **Rev:** Diana with Prince William and Prince Harry

Date	Mintage	VF20	XF40	MS60	MS63	MS65
1997	—	—	—	—	8.00	10.00

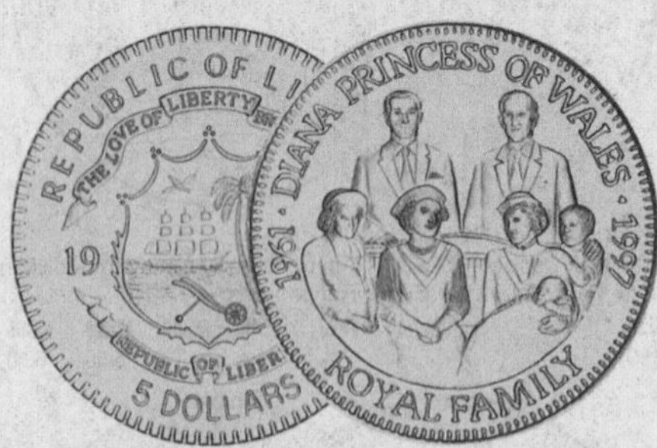

KM# 458 5 DOLLARS

Copper-Nickel **Subject:** Royal Family **Obv:** National arms **Rev:** Family portrait

Date	Mintage	VF20	XF40	MS60	MS63	MS65
1997	—	—	—	—	8.00	10.00

KM# 459 5 DOLLARS

Copper-Nickel **Subject:** Queen Elizabeth and Lady Diana **Obv:** National arms **Rev:** Conjoined crowned busts right

Date	Mintage	VF20	XF40	MS60	MS63	MS65
1997	—	—	—	—	8.00	10.00

KM# 460 5 DOLLARS

Copper-Nickel **Obv:** National arms **Rev:** Queen Mother and Diana

Date	Mintage	VF20	XF40	MS60	MS63	MS65
1997	—	—	—	—	8.00	10.00

KM# 461 5 DOLLARS

Copper-Nickel **Subject:** Visit to Wales **Obv:** National arms **Rev:** Charles and Diana

Date	Mintage	VF20	XF40	MS60	MS63	MS65
1997	—	—	—	—	8.00	10.00

KM# 462 5 DOLLARS

Copper-Nickel **Subject:** Australian Tour **Obv:** National arms **Rev:** Charles and Diana dancing

Date	Mintage	VF20	XF40	MS60	MS63	MS65
1997	—	—	—	—	8.00	10.00

KM# 463 5 DOLLARS

Copper-Nickel **Subject:** Tour of Japan **Obv:** National arms **Rev:** Half length figures looking right

Date	Mintage	VF20	XF40	MS60	MS63	MS65
1997	—	—	—	—	8.00	10.00

KM# 464 5 DOLLARS
Copper-Nickel, 38.5 mm. **Obv:** National arms **Rev:** Diana reading to child

Date	Mintage	VF20	XF40	MS60	MS63	MS65
1997	—	—	—	—	8.00	10.00

KM# 465 5 DOLLARS
Copper-Nickel **Subject:** Charity **Obv:** National arms **Rev:** Diana with poor child

Date	Mintage	VF20	XF40	MS60	MS63	MS65
1997	—	—	—	—	8.00	10.00

KM# 466 5 DOLLARS
Copper-Nickel **Obv:** National arms **Rev:** Diana with sick child

Date	Mintage	VF20	XF40	MS60	MS63	MS65
1997	—	—	—	—	8.00	10.00

KM# 467 5 DOLLARS
Copper-Nickel **Obv:** National arms **Rev:** Diana's casket on gun carriage

Date	Mintage	VF20	XF40	MS60	MS63	MS65
1997	—	—	—	—	8.00	10.00

KM# 496 5 DOLLARS
20.56 g., Copper-Nickel, 38.5 mm. **Obv:** National arms **Rev:** Giraffe **Edge:** Reeded

Date	Mintage	VF20	XF40	MS60	MS63	MS65
1997	—	—	—	—	3.00	5.00

KM# 566 5 DOLLARS
Copper-Nickel **Obv:** National arms **Rev:** Elephant

Date	Mintage	VF20	XF40	MS60	MS63	MS65
1997	—	—	—	—	2.50	4.00

KM# 578 5 DOLLARS
23.70 g., Copper-Nickel, 38.5 mm. **Subject:** Year of the Ox **Obv:** National arms **Rev:** Ox **Edge:** Reeded

Date	Mintage	VF20	XF40	MS60	MS63	MS65
1997	—	—	—	—	3.00	5.00

KM# 579 5 DOLLARS
21.30 g., Copper-Nickel, 38.4 mm. **Obv:** National arms **Rev:** Elephant **Edge:** Reeded

Date	Mintage	VF20	XF40	MS60	MS63	MS65
1997	—	—	—	—	4.00	5.50

KM# 580 5 DOLLARS
21.30 g., Copper-Nickel, 38.4 mm. **Obv:** National arms **Rev:** Lion **Edge:** Reeded

Date	Mintage	VF20	XF40	MS60	MS63	MS65
1997	—	—	—	—	4.00	5.50

KM# 581 5 DOLLARS
21.30 g., Copper-Nickel, 38.4 mm. **Obv:** National arms **Rev:** Rhinoceros **Edge:** Reeded

Date	Mintage	VF20	XF40	MS60	MS63	MS65
1997	—	—	—	—	4.00	5.50

KM# 582 5 DOLLARS
21.30 g., Copper-Nickel, 38.4 mm. **Obv:** National arms **Rev:** Zebra **Edge:** Reeded

Date	Mintage	VF20	XF40	MS60	MS63	MS65
1997	—	—	—	—	4.00	5.50

KM# 583 5 DOLLARS
21.30 g., Copper-Nickel, 38.4 mm. **Obv:** National arms **Rev:** Two kangaroos **Edge:** Reeded

Date	Mintage	VF20	XF40	MS60	MS63	MS65
1997	—	—	—	—	4.00	5.50

KM# 600 5 DOLLARS
21.30 g., Copper-Nickel, 38.5 mm. **Obv:** National arms **Rev:** Tiger at rest **Edge:** Reeded

Date	Mintage	VF20	XF40	MS60	MS63	MS65
1997	—	—	—	—	7.00	9.00

KM# 339 5 DOLLARS
Copper-Nickel **Subject:** Year of the Tiger **Obv:** National arms **Rev:** Tiger with three cubs

Date	Mintage	VF20	XF40	MS60	MS63	MS65
1998 (1997)	—	PF65 12.00				

KM# 363 5 DOLLARS
Copper-Nickel **Subject:** RMS Titanic **Obv:** National arms **Rev:** Cameo above sinking ship **Note:** Similar to 20 Dollars, KM#364.

Date	Mintage	VF20	XF40	MS60	MS63	MS65
1998	—	—	—	—	6.00	8.00

KM# 568 5 DOLLARS
14.63 g., Copper-Nickel, 33.1 mm. **Subject:** Battle of Gettysburg **Obv:** National arms **Rev:** Cannon and crossed flags divides busts facing **Edge:** Reeded **Note:** This also exists in an obverse denominated type for $2,000. Also see KM828.

Date	Mintage	VF20	XF40	MS60	MS63	MS65
1999 B	—	—	—	—	10.00	12.00
2000 B	—	—	—	—	10.00	12.00

KM# 572 5 DOLLARS
24.97 g., 0.925 Silver 0.7426 oz. ASW, 38.6 mm. **Subject:** Captain Cook **Obv:** National arms **Rev:** Seated Capt. Cook at right, his ship at left **Edge:** Reeded

Date	Mintage	VF20	XF40	MS60	MS63	MS65
1999	—	PF65 27.50				

KM# 593 5 DOLLARS
20.00 g., Copper-Nickel, 38 mm. **Subject:** John F. Kennedy Jr. **Obv:** National arms **Rev:** Two portraits, flag and the White House **Edge:** Reeded

Date	Mintage	VF20	XF40	MS60	MS63	MS65
1999	—	—	—	—	5.00	7.00

KM# 828 5 DOLLARS
14.68 g., Copper-Nickel, 33.1 mm. **Subject:** 1863 Gettysburg Battle **Obv:** National arms **Rev:** Crossed flags above cannon between busts of Generals George G. Meade and Robert E. lee **Edge:** Reeded

Date	Mintage	VF20	XF40	MS60	MS63	MS65
1999	—	—	—	—	3.00	5.00

KM# 427 5 DOLLARS
11.18 g., Copper-Nickel, 31.6 mm. **Series:** Millennium 2000 Zodiac **Obv:** National arms **Rev:** Snake **Edge:** Reeded

Date	Mintage	VF20	XF40	MS60	MS63	MS65
2000	—	—	—	—	2.00	4.00

KM# 428 5 DOLLARS
11.18 g., Copper-Nickel, 31.6 mm. **Series:** Millennium 2000 Zodiac **Obv:** National arms **Rev:** Two rats and pumpkin **Edge:** Reeded

Date	Mintage	VF20	XF40	MS60	MS63	MS65
2000	—	—	—	—	2.00	4.00

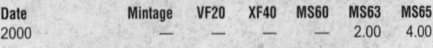

KM# 429 5 DOLLARS
11.18 g., Copper-Nickel, 31.6 mm. **Series:** Millennium 2000 Zodiac **Obv:** National arms **Rev:** Ox **Edge:** Reeded

Date	Mintage	VF20	XF40	MS60	MS63	MS65
2000	—	—	—	—	2.00	4.00

KM# 430 5 DOLLARS
11.18 g., Copper-Nickel, 31.6 mm. **Series:** Millennium 2000 Zodiac **Obv:** National arms **Rev:** Tiger **Edge:** Reeded

Date	Mintage	VF20	XF40	MS60	MS63	MS65
2000	—	—	—	—	2.00	4.00

KM# 431 5 DOLLARS
11.18 g., Copper-Nickel, 31.6 mm. **Series:** Millennium 2000 Zodiac **Obv:** National arms **Rev:** Horse **Edge:** Reeded

Date	Mintage	VF20	XF40	MS60	MS63	MS65
2000	—	—	—	—	2.00	4.00

KM# 432 5 DOLLARS
11.18 g., Copper-Nickel, 31.6 mm. **Series:** Millennium 2000 Zodiac **Obv:** National arms **Rev:** Goat **Edge:** Reeded

Date	Mintage	VF20	XF40	MS60	MS63	MS65
2000	—	—	—	—	2.00	4.00

KM# 433 5 DOLLARS
11.18 g., Copper-Nickel, 31.6 mm. **Series:** Millennium 2000 Zodiac **Obv:** National arms **Rev:** Monkey **Edge:** Reeded

Date	Mintage	VF20	XF40	MS60	MS63	MS65
2000	—	—	—	—	2.00	4.00

KM# 434 5 DOLLARS
11.18 g., Copper-Nickel, 31.6 mm. **Series:** Millennium 2000 Zodiac **Obv:** National arms **Rev:** Rooster **Edge:** Reeded

Date	Mintage	VF20	XF40	MS60	MS63	MS65
2000	—	—	—	—	2.00	4.00

KM# 435 5 DOLLARS
11.18 g., Copper-Nickel, 31.6 mm. **Series:** Millennium 2000 Zodiac **Obv:** National arms **Rev:** Dog **Edge:** Reeded

Date	Mintage	VF20	XF40	MS60	MS63	MS65
2000	—	—	—	—	2.00	4.00

KM# 436 5 DOLLARS
11.18 g., Copper-Nickel, 31.6 mm. **Series:** Millennium 2000 Zodiac **Obv:** National arms **Rev:** Pig **Edge:** Reeded

Date	Mintage	VF20	XF40	MS60	MS63	MS65
2000	—	—	—	—	2.00	4.00

KM# 437 5 DOLLARS
11.18 g., Copper-Nickel, 31.6 mm. **Series:** Millennium 2000 Zodiac **Obv:** National arms **Rev:** Rabbit **Edge:** Reeded

Date	Mintage	VF20	XF40	MS60	MS63	MS65
2000	—	—	—	—	2.00	4.00

KM# 438 5 DOLLARS
11.18 g., Copper-Nickel, 31.6 mm. **Series:** Millennium 2000 Zodiac **Obv:** National arms **Rev:** Dragon **Edge:** Reeded

Date	Mintage	VF20	XF40	MS60	MS63	MS65
2000	—	—	—	—	2.00	4.00

KM# 584 5 DOLLARS
8.54 g., 0.9999 Silver 0.2745 oz. ASW, 30.1 mm. **Subject:** Endangered Elephant **Obv:** National arms divide date **Rev:** Elephant and calf **Edge:** Reeded

Date	Mintage	VF20	XF40	MS60	MS63	MS65
2000	—	PF65 22.00				

KM# 589 5 DOLLARS
26.92 g., Copper-Nickel, 40.3 mm. **Subject:** First Man on Moon **Obv:** National arms **Rev:** Astronaut and American flag on moon **Edge:** Reeded

Date	Mintage	VF20	XF40	MS60	MS63	MS65
2000	—	—	—	—	8.00	10.00

KM# 651 5 DOLLARS

14.56 g., Copper-Nickel, 38 mm. **Obv:** National arms **Rev:** Japanese "Zero" flying over Pearl Harbor **Edge:** Reeded

Date	Mintage	VF20	XF40	MS60	MS63	MS65
2000	—	—	—	—	5.00	7.00

KM# 652 5 DOLLARS

27.33 g., Copper-Nickel, 40.2 mm. **Obv:** National arms **Rev:** Titanic sinking **Edge:** Reeded

Date	Mintage	VF20	XF40	MS60	MS63	MS65
2000	—	—	—	—	5.00	7.00

KM# 668 5 DOLLARS

26.15 g., 0.999 Silver Clad Copper-Nickel 0.8399 oz., 38.8 mm. **Subject:** Roy Rogers, King of the Cowboys **Obv:** National arms **Rev:** Roy Rogers wearing hat flanked by stars **Edge:** Plain

Date	Mintage	VF20	XF40	MS60	MS63	MS65
2000	—	PF65 30.00				

KM# 695 5 DOLLARS

27.25 g., Copper-Nickel, 40 mm. **Obv:** National arms **Rev:** The Mayflower ship **Edge:** Reeded

Date	Mintage	VF20	XF40	MS60	MS63	MS65
2000	—	PF65 10.00				

KM# 723 5 DOLLARS

12.00 g., Nickel-Silver, 31.5 mm. **Subject:** Year of the Dragon **Obv:** National arms **Obv. Legend:** MILLENNIUM **Rev:** Chinese Dragon, facing, type I **Edge:** Reeded

Date	Mintage	VF20	XF40	MS60	MS63	MS65
2000	—	—	—	—	3.00	5.00

KM# 735 5 DOLLARS

14.83 g., Copper-Nickel, 32.00 mm. **Subject:** XXVII Olympic Games - Sydney **Rev:** Javelin thrower **Edge:** Reeded

Date	Mintage	VF20	XF40	MS60	MS63	MS65
2000	20,000	—	—	—	7.00	9.00

KM# 778 5 DOLLARS

Nickel-Silver, 31.5 mm. **Subject:** Year of the Dragon **Obv:** National Arms **Obv. Legend:** MILLENNIUM **Rev:** Chinese Dragon, facing left, type II **Edge:** Reeded

Date	Mintage	VF20	XF40	MS60	MS63	MS65
2000	—	—	—	—	3.00	5.00

KM# 779 5 DOLLARS

Nickel-Silver, 31.5 mm. **Subject:** Year of the Dragon **Obv:** National Arms **Obv. Legend:** MILLENNIUM **Rev:** Chinese Dragon, facing right, type III **Edge:** Reeded

Date	Mintage	VF20	XF40	MS60	MS63	MS65
2000	—	—	—	—	3.00	5.00

KM# 805 5 DOLLARS

27.70 g., Copper-Nickel, 40.13 mm. **Series:** Wildlife of North America **Obv:** National arms **Rev:** Upper half of Bald Eagle - multicolor **Edge:** Reeded

Date	Mintage	VF20	XF40	MS60	MS63	MS65
2000	—	PF65 10.00				

KM# 836 5 DOLLARS

Copper-Nickel, 31.5 mm. **Obv:** U.S. Presidential Seal **Rev:** George Washington bust

Date	Mintage	VF20	XF40	MS60	MS63	MS65
2000	—	—	—	—	3.00	5.00

KM# 837 5 DOLLARS

Copper-Nickel, 31.5 mm. **Obv:** U.S. Presidential Seal **Rev:** George W. Bush bust

Date	Mintage	VF20	XF40	MS60	MS63	MS65
2000	—	—	—	—	3.00	5.00

KM# 840 5 DOLLARS

Copper-Nickel, 31.5 mm. **Obv:** U.S. Presidential Seal **Rev:** Thomas Jefferson bust

Date	Mintage	VF20	XF40	MS60	MS63	MS65
2000	—	—	—	—	3.00	5.00

KM# 912 5 DOLLARS

Copper-Nickel, 31.5 mm. **Obv:** U.S. Presidential Seal **Rev:** John Adams bust

Date	Mintage	VF20	XF40	MS60	MS63	MS65
2000	—	—	—	—	1.50	2.50

KM# 913 5 DOLLARS

Copper-Nickel, 31.5 mm. **Obv:** U.S. Presidential Seal **Rev:** Jame Madison bust

Date	Mintage	VF20	XF40	MS60	MS63	MS65
2000	—	—	—	—	1.50	2.50

KM# 914 5 DOLLARS

Copper-Nickel, 31.5 mm. **Obv:** U.S. Presidential Seal **Rev:** Jame Monroe bust

Date	Mintage	VF20	XF40	MS60	MS63	MS65
2000	—	—	—	—	1.50	2.50

KM# 915 5 DOLLARS

Copper-Nickel, 31.5 mm. **Obv:** U.S. Presidential Seal **Rev:** John Quincy Adams bust

Date	Mintage	VF20	XF40	MS60	MS63	MS65
2000	—	—	—	—	1.50	2.50

KM# 916 5 DOLLARS

Copper-Nickel, 31.5 mm. **Obv:** U.S. Presidential Seal **Rev:** Andrew Jackson bust

Date	Mintage	VF20	XF40	MS60	MS63	MS65
2000	—	—	—	—	1.50	2.50

KM# 917 5 DOLLARS

Copper-Nickel, 31.5 mm. **Obv:** U.S. Presidential Seal **Rev:** Martin van Buren bust

Date	Mintage	VF20	XF40	MS60	MS63	MS65
2000	—	—	—	—	1.50	2.50

KM# 918 5 DOLLARS

Copper-Nickel, 31.5 mm. **Obv:** U.S. Presidential Seal **Rev:** William Henry Harrison bust

Date	Mintage	VF20	XF40	MS60	MS63	MS65
2000	—	—	—	—	1.50	2.50

KM# 919 5 DOLLARS

Copper-Nickel, 31.5 mm. **Obv:** U.S. Presidential Seal **Rev:** John Tyler bust

Date	Mintage	VF20	XF40	MS60	MS63	MS65
2000	—	—	—	—	1.50	2.50

KM# 920 5 DOLLARS

Copper-Nickel, 31.5 mm. **Obv:** U.S. Presidential Seal **Rev:** James K. Polk bust

Date	Mintage	VF20	XF40	MS60	MS63	MS65
2000	—	—	—	—	1.50	2.50

KM# 921 5 DOLLARS

Copper-Nickel, 31.5 mm. **Obv:** U.S. Presidential Seal **Rev:** Zachary Taylor bust

Date	Mintage	VF20	XF40	MS60	MS63	MS65
2000	—	—	—	—	1.50	2.50

KM# 922 5 DOLLARS

Copper-Nickel, 31.5 mm. **Obv:** U.S. Presidential Seal **Rev:** Millard Fillmore bust

Date	Mintage	VF20	XF40	MS60	MS63	MS65
2000	—	—	—	—	1.50	2.50

KM# 923 5 DOLLARS

Copper-Nickel, 31.5 mm. **Obv:** U.S. Presidential Seal **Rev:** Franklin Pierce bust

Date	Mintage	VF20	XF40	MS60	MS63	MS65
2000	—	—	—	—	1.50	2.50

KM# 924 5 DOLLARS

Copper-Nickel, 31.5 mm. **Obv:** U.S. Presidential Seal **Rev:** James Buchanan bust

Date	Mintage	VF20	XF40	MS60	MS63	MS65
2000	—	—	—	—	1.50	2.50

KM# 925 5 DOLLARS

Copper-Nickel, 31.5 mm. **Obv:** U.S. Presidential Seal **Rev:** Abraham Lincoln bust

Date	Mintage	VF20	XF40	MS60	MS63	MS65
2000	—	—	—	—	1.50	2.50

KM# 926 5 DOLLARS

Copper-Nickel, 31.5 mm. **Obv:** U.S. Presidential Seal **Rev:** Andrew Johnson bust

Date	Mintage	VF20	XF40	MS60	MS63	MS65
2000	—	—	—	—	1.50	2.50

KM# 927 5 DOLLARS

Copper-Nickel, 31.5 mm. **Obv:** U.S. Presidential Seal **Rev:** Ulysses S. Grant bust

Date	Mintage	VF20	XF40	MS60	MS63	MS65
2000	—	—	—	—	1.50	2.50

KM# 928 5 DOLLARS

Copper-Nickel, 31.5 mm. **Obv:** U.S. Presidential Seal **Rev:** Rutherford B. Hayes bust

Date	Mintage	VF20	XF40	MS60	MS63	MS65
2000	—	—	—	—	1.50	2.50

KM# 929 5 DOLLARS

Copper-Nickel, 31.5 mm. **Obv:** U.S. Presidential Seal **Rev:** James A. Garfield bust

Date	Mintage	VF20	XF40	MS60	MS63	MS65
2000	—	—	—	—	1.50	2.50

KM# 930 5 DOLLARS

Copper-Nickel, 31.5 mm. **Obv:** U.S. Presidential Seal **Rev:** Chester Arthur bust

Date	Mintage	VF20	XF40	MS60	MS63	MS65
2000	—	—	—	—	1.50	2.50

KM# 931 5 DOLLARS
Copper-Nickel, 31.5 mm. **Obv:** U.S. Presidential Seal **Rev:** Grover Cleveland bust

Date	Mintage	VF20	XF40	MS60	MS63	MS65
2000	—	—	—	—	1.50	2.50

KM# 932 5 DOLLARS
Copper-Nickel, 31.5 mm. **Obv:** U.S. Presidential Seal **Rev:** Benjamin Harrison bust

Date	Mintage	VF20	XF40	MS60	MS63	MS65
2000	—	—	—	—	1.50	2.50

KM# 933 5 DOLLARS
Copper-Nickel, 31.5 mm. **Obv:** U.S. Presidential Seal **Rev:** William McKinley bust

Date	Mintage	VF20	XF40	MS60	MS63	MS65
2000	—	—	—	—	1.50	2.50

KM# 934 5 DOLLARS
Copper-Nickel, 31.5 mm. **Obv:** U.S. Presidential Seal **Rev:** Theodore Roosevelt bust

Date	Mintage	VF20	XF40	MS60	MS63	MS65
2000	—	—	—	—	1.50	2.50

KM# 935 5 DOLLARS
Copper-Nickel, 31.5 mm. **Obv:** U.S. Presidential Seal **Rev:** William Howard Taft bust

Date	Mintage	VF20	XF40	MS60	MS63	MS65
2000	—	—	—	—	1.50	2.50

KM# 936 5 DOLLARS
Copper-Nickel, 31.5 mm. **Obv:** U.S. Presidential Seal **Rev:** Woodrow Wilson bust

Date	Mintage	VF20	XF40	MS60	MS63	MS65
2000	—	—	—	—	1.50	2.50

KM# 937 5 DOLLARS
Copper-Nickel, 31.5 mm. **Obv:** U.S. Presidential Seal **Rev:** Warren G. Harding bust

Date	Mintage	VF20	XF40	MS60	MS63	MS65
2000	—	—	—	—	1.50	2.50

KM# 938 5 DOLLARS
Copper-Nickel, 31.5 mm. **Obv:** U.S. Presidential Seal **Rev:** Calvin Coolidge bust

Date	Mintage	VF20	XF40	MS60	MS63	MS65
2000	—	—	—	—	1.50	2.50

KM# 939 5 DOLLARS
Copper-Nickel, 31.5 mm. **Obv:** U.S. Presidential Seal **Rev:** Herbert Hoover bust

Date	Mintage	VF20	XF40	MS60	MS63	MS65
2000	—	—	—	—	1.50	2.50

KM# 940 5 DOLLARS
Copper-Nickel, 31.5 mm. **Obv:** U.S. Presidential Seal **Rev:** Franklin D. Roosevelt bust

Date	Mintage	VF20	XF40	MS60	MS63	MS65
2000	—	—	—	—	1.50	2.50

KM# 941 5 DOLLARS
Copper-Nickel, 31.5 mm. **Obv:** U.S. Presidential Seal **Rev:** Harry S Truman bust

Date	Mintage	VF20	XF40	MS60	MS63	MS65
2000	—	—	—	—	1.50	2.50

KM# 942 5 DOLLARS
Copper-Nickel, 31.5 mm. **Obv:** U.S. Presidential Seal **Rev:** Dwight D. Eisenhower bust

Date	Mintage	VF20	XF40	MS60	MS63	MS65
2000	—	—	—	—	1.50	2.50

KM# 943 5 DOLLARS
Copper-Nickel, 31.5 mm. **Obv:** U.S. Presidential Seal **Rev:** John F. Kennedy bust

Date	Mintage	VF20	XF40	MS60	MS63	MS65
2000	—	—	—	—	1.50	2.50

KM# 944 5 DOLLARS
Copper-Nickel, 31.5 mm. **Obv:** U.S. Presidential Seal **Rev:** Lyndon B. Johnson bust

Date	Mintage	VF20	XF40	MS60	MS63	MS65
2000	—	—	—	—	1.50	2.50

KM# 945 5 DOLLARS
Copper-Nickel, 31.5 mm. **Obv:** U.S. Presidential Seal **Rev:** Richard Nixon bust

Date	Mintage	VF20	XF40	MS60	MS63	MS65
2000	—	—	—	—	1.50	2.50

KM# 946 5 DOLLARS
Copper-Nickel, 31.5 mm. **Obv:** U.S. Presidential Seal **Rev:** Gerald R. Ford bust

Date	Mintage	VF20	XF40	MS60	MS63	MS65
2000	—	—	—	—	1.50	2.50

KM# 947 5 DOLLARS
Copper-Nickel, 31.5 mm. **Obv:** U.S. Presidential Seal **Rev:** Jimmy Carter bust

Date	Mintage	VF20	XF40	MS60	MS63	MS65
2000	—	—	—	—	1.50	2.50

KM# 948 5 DOLLARS
Copper-Nickel, 31.5 mm. **Obv:** U.S. Presidential Seal **Rev:** Ronald Regan bust

Date	Mintage	VF20	XF40	MS60	MS63	MS65
2000	—	—	—	—	1.50	2.50

KM# 949 5 DOLLARS
Copper-Nickel, 31.5 mm. **Obv:** U.S. Presidential Seal **Rev:** George W. Bush

Date	Mintage	VF20	XF40	MS60	MS63	MS65
2000	—	—	—	—	1.50	2.50

KM# 950 5 DOLLARS
Copper-Nickel, 31.5 mm. **Obv:** U.S. Presidential Seal **Rev:** Bill Clinton bust

Date	Mintage	VF20	XF40	MS60	MS63	MS65
2000	—	—	—	—	1.50	2.50

KM# 63 10 DOLLARS
11.72 g., 0.900 Gold 0.3391 oz. AGW **Subject:** 25th Anniversary of Inter-Continental Hotels **Obv:** Value below hotel building **Rev:** Letter I within football flanked by dates

Date	Mintage	VF20	XF40	MS60	MS63	MS65
1971	—	PF65 600				

KM# 26 10 DOLLARS
16.72 g., 0.900 Gold 0.4838 oz. AGW **Subject:** Inauguration of President Tolbert **Rev:** Head left

Date	Mintage	VF20	XF40	MS60	MS63	MS65
1972	—	PF65 850				

KM# 53 10 DOLLARS
23.33 g., 0.925 Silver 0.6938 oz. ASW **Subject:** Decade For Women **Obv:** National arms **Rev:** Coat of arms and value

Date	Mintage	VF20	XF40	MS60	MS63	MS65
1985	—	PF65 35.00				

KM# 54 10 DOLLARS
31.10 g., 0.999 Silver 0.9989 oz. ASW **Subject:** President John F. Kennedy **Obv:** National arms **Rev:** Head left

Date	Mintage	VF20	XF40	MS60	MS63	MS65
1988	25,000	PF65 27.50				

KM# 55 10 DOLLARS
31.10 g., 0.999 Silver 0.9989 oz. ASW **Subject:** President Samuel Kanyon Doe **Obv:** National arms **Rev:** President Samuel Kanyon Doe **Note:** Similar to 250 Dollars, KM#56.

Date	Mintage	VF20	XF40	MS60	MS63	MS65
1988	25,000	PF65 27.50				

KM# 57 10 DOLLARS
31.10 g., 0.999 Silver 0.9989 oz. ASW **Subject:** President George Bush **Obv:** National arms **Rev:** Head left **Note:** Similar to 250 Dollars, KM#58.

Date	Mintage	VF20	XF40	MS60	MS63	MS65
1989	25,000	PF65 27.50				

KM# 59 10 DOLLARS
31.10 g., 0.999 Silver 0.9989 oz. ASW **Subject:** Emperor Hirohito **Obv:** National arms **Rev:** Head facing divides dates **Note:** Similar to 250 Dollars, KM#60.

Date	Mintage	VF20	XF40	MS60	MS63	MS65
1989	25,000	PF65 25.00				

KM# 72 10 DOLLARS
31.10 g., 0.999 Silver 0.9989 oz. ASW **Subject:** Chancellor Willy Brandt - In Memorium **Obv:** National arms **Rev:** Head left, Chariot from Brandenburg Gate below

Date	Mintage	VF20	XF40	MS60	MS63	MS65
1992	—	PF65 27.50				

KM# 74 10 DOLLARS
31.10 g., 0.999 Silver 0.9989 oz. ASW **Subject:** Formula One **Obv:** National arms **Rev:** Ricardo Patrese

Date	Mintage	VF20	XF40	MS60	MS63	MS65
1992	25,000	PF65 32.50				

KM# 75 10 DOLLARS
31.10 g., 0.999 Silver 0.9989 oz. ASW **Subject:** Formula One **Obv:** National arms **Rev:** Nigel Mansell

Date	Mintage	VF20	XF40	MS60	MS63	MS65
1992	25,000	PF65 32.50				

KM# 83 10 DOLLARS
31.10 g., 0.999 Silver 0.9989 oz. ASW **Subject:** Formula One **Obv:** National arms **Rev:** Gerhard Berger

Date	Mintage	VF20	XF40	MS60	MS63	MS65
1992	25,000	PF65 32.50				

KM# 84 10 DOLLARS
31.10 g., 0.999 Silver 0.9989 oz. ASW **Subject:** Formula One **Obv:** National arms **Rev:** Aguri Suzuki

Date	Mintage	VF20	XF40	MS60	MS63	MS65
1992	25,000	PF65 32.50				

KM# 85 10 DOLLARS
31.10 g., 0.999 Silver 0.9989 oz. ASW **Subject:** Formula One **Obv:** National arms **Rev:** Ayrton Senna

Date	Mintage	VF20	XF40	MS60	MS63	MS65
1992	25,000	PF65 32.50				

KM# 86 10 DOLLARS
31.10 g., 0.999 Silver 0.9989 oz. ASW **Subject:** Formula One **Obv:** National arms **Rev:** Michael Schumacher

Date	Mintage	VF20	XF40	MS60	MS63	MS65
1992	25,000	PF65 32.50				

KM# 87 10 DOLLARS
31.10 g., 0.999 Silver 0.9989 oz. ASW **Subject:** Formula One **Obv:** National arms **Rev:** Alain Prost

Date	Mintage	VF20	XF40	MS60	MS63	MS65
1992	25,000	PF65 32.50				

KM# 88 10 DOLLARS
31.10 g., 0.999 Silver 0.9989 oz. ASW **Subject:** Formula One **Obv:** National arms **Rev:** Ukyo Katayama

Date	Mintage	VF20	XF40	MS60	MS63	MS65
1992	25,000	PF65 32.50				

KM# 68 10 DOLLARS
31.10 g., 0.999 Silver 0.9989 oz. ASW **Subject:** President Bill Clinton **Obv:** National arms **Rev:** Head right

Date	Mintage	VF20	XF40	MS60	MS63	MS65
1993	25,000	PF65 27.50				

KM# 99 10 DOLLARS
31.10 g., 0.999 Silver 0.9989 oz. ASW **Series:** Preserve Planet Earth **Obv:** National arms **Rev:** Protoceratops

Date	Mintage	VF20	XF40	MS60	MS63	MS65
1993	25,000	PF65 30.00				

KM# 102 10 DOLLARS
31.10 g., 0.999 Silver 0.9989 oz. ASW **Subject:** Baseball Hall of Fame **Obv:** National arms **Rev:** Nolan Ryan waving baseball cap

Date	Mintage	VF20	XF40	MS60	MS63	MS65
1993	—	PF65 27.50				

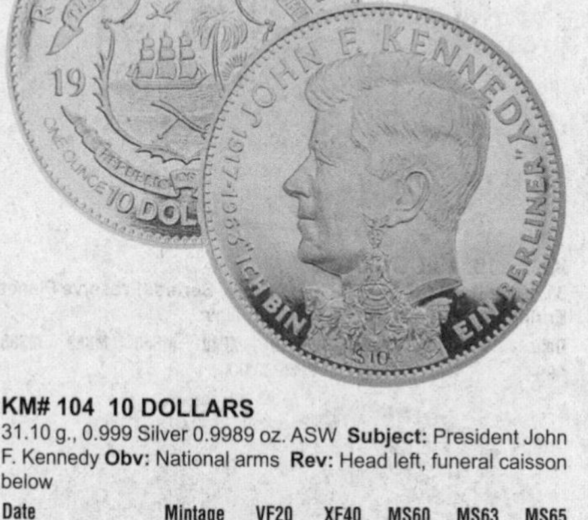

KM# 104 10 DOLLARS
31.10 g., 0.999 Silver 0.9989 oz. ASW **Subject:** President John F. Kennedy **Obv:** National arms **Rev:** Head left, funeral caisson below

Date	Mintage	VF20	XF40	MS60	MS63	MS65
1993	25,000	PF65 32.50				

KM# 110 10 DOLLARS
31.10 g., 0.999 Silver 0.9989 oz. ASW **Series:** Preserve Planet Earth **Obv:** National arms **Rev:** Corythosaurus

Date	Mintage	VF20	XF40	MS60	MS63	MS65
1993	25,000	PF65 27.50				

KM# 113 10 DOLLARS
31.10 g., 0.999 Silver 0.9989 oz. ASW **Series:** Preserve Planet Earth **Obv:** National arms **Rev:** Atchaeopteryx **Note:** Incorrect spelling.

Date	Mintage	VF20	XF40	MS60	MS63	MS65
1993	25,000	PF65 25.00				

KM# 116 10 DOLLARS
31.10 g., 0.999 Silver 0.9989 oz. ASW **Series:** Preserve Planet Earth **Obv:** National arms **Rev:** Archaeopteryx **Note:** Correct spelling.

Date	Mintage	VF20	XF40	MS60	MS63	MS65
1994	25,000	PF65 30.00				

KM# 119 10 DOLLARS
31.10 g., 0.999 Silver 0.9989 oz. ASW **Series:** Preserve Planet Earth **Obv:** National arms **Rev:** Gorillas

Date	Mintage	VF20	XF40	MS60	MS63	MS65
1994	25,000	PF65 30.00				

KM# 122 10 DOLLARS
31.10 g., 0.999 Silver 0.9989 oz. ASW **Series:** Preserve Planet Earth **Obv:** National arms **Rev:** Pygmy Hippopotami

Date	Mintage	VF20	XF40	MS60	MS63	MS65
1994	25,000	PF65 30.00				

KM# 125 10 DOLLARS
31.10 g., 0.999 Silver 0.9989 oz. ASW **Series:** Preserve Planet Earth **Obv:** National arms **Rev:** Nile Soft-shelled Turtle

Date	Mintage	VF20	XF40	MS60	MS63	MS65
1994	25,000	PF65 30.00				

KM# 127 10 DOLLARS
31.10 g., 0.999 Silver 0.9989 oz. ASW **Obv:** National arms **Rev:** Head left with small gazelle below

Date	Mintage	VF20	XF40	MS60	MS63	MS65
1994	25,000	PF65 27.50				

KM# 155 10 DOLLARS
31.10 g., 0.999 Silver 0.9989 oz. ASW **Obv:** National arms **Rev:** General Rommel, bust 1/4 left

Date	Mintage	VF20	XF40	MS60	MS63	MS65
1994	25,000	PF65 30.00				

KM# 156 10 DOLLARS
31.10 g., 0.999 Silver 0.9989 oz. ASW **Obv:** National arms **Rev:** Field Marshal Montgomery facing

Date	Mintage	VF20	XF40	MS60	MS63	MS65
1994	25,000	PF65 30.00				

KM# 157 10 DOLLARS
31.10 g., 0.999 Silver 0.9989 oz. ASW **Obv:** National arms **Rev:** General Dwight D. Eisenhower half left

Date	Mintage	VF20	XF40	MS60	MS63	MS65
1994	25,000	PF65 30.00				

KM# 281 10 DOLLARS
31.10 g., 0.999 Silver 0.9989 oz. ASW **Subject:** Baseball Hall of Fame, Reggie Jackson **Obv:** National arms **Rev:** Baseball player divides circle

Date	Mintage	VF20	XF40	MS60	MS63	MS65
1994	—	PF65 30.00				

KM# 282 10 DOLLARS
31.10 g., 0.999 Silver 0.9989 oz. ASW **Subject:** Baseball Hall of Fame **Obv:** National arms **Rev:** Roberto Clemente facing

Date	Mintage	VF20	XF40	MS60	MS63	MS65
1994	—	PF65 30.00				

KM# 347 10 DOLLARS
31.10 g., 0.999 Silver 0.9989 oz. ASW **Subject:** The History of the Motor Car **Obv:** National arms **Rev:** Mercedes-Benz C-Class car

Date	Mintage	VF20	XF40	MS60	MS63	MS65
1994	—	PF65 37.50				

KM# 561 10 DOLLARS
31.10 g., 0.999 Silver 0.999 oz. ASW **Obv:** National arms **Rev:** Mercedes Benz C-Class car

Date	Mintage	VF20	XF40	MS60	MS63	MS65
1994	Est. 25000	PF65 37.50				

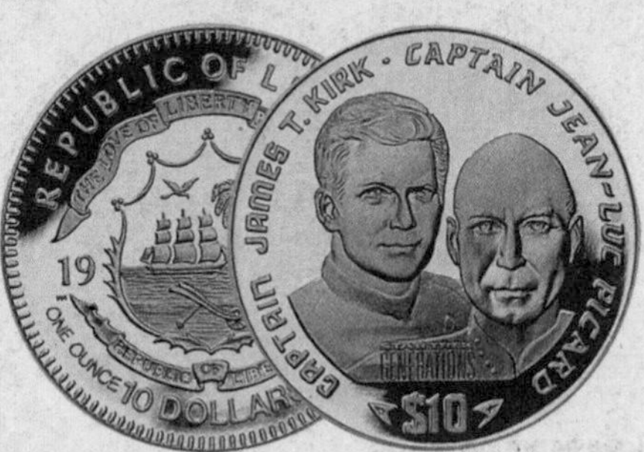

KM# 129 10 DOLLARS
31.10 g., 0.999 Silver 0.9989 oz. ASW **Subject:** Star Trek **Obv:** National arms **Rev:** Conjoined busts of Captain Kirk and Captian Picard

Date	Mintage	VF20	XF40	MS60	MS63	MS65
1995	—	PF65 37.50				

KM# 132 10 DOLLARS
31.10 g., 0.999 Silver 0.999 oz. ASW **Subject:** Centennial - Babe Ruth - Sultan of Swat **Obv:** National arms **Rev:** Head with cap 1/4 right divides dates within circle **Note:** Similar to 1 Dollar, KM#131.

Date	Mintage	VF20	XF40	MS60	MS63	MS65
1995	—	—	—	—	—	30.00

KM# 134 10 DOLLARS
31.10 g., 0.999 Silver 0.9989 oz. ASW **Series:** Preserve Planet Earth **Obv:** National arms **Rev:** Leopard

Date	Mintage	VF20	XF40	MS60	MS63	MS65
1995	25,000	PF65 30.00				

KM# 137 10 DOLLARS
31.10 g., 0.999 Silver 0.9989 oz. ASW **Series:** Preserve Planet Earth **Obv:** National arms **Rev:** Storks

Date	Mintage	VF20	XF40	MS60	MS63	MS65
1995	25,000	PF65 30.00				

KM# 145 10 DOLLARS
31.10 g., 0.999 Silver 0.9989 oz. ASW **Obv:** National arms **Rev:** Winston Churchill overlooking planes, tanks and ship

Date	Mintage	VF20	XF40	MS60	MS63	MS65
1995	25,000	PF65 30.00				

KM# 146 10 DOLLARS
31.10 g., 0.999 Silver 0.9989 oz. ASW **Obv:** National arms **Rev:** President Franklin D. Roosevelt riding in jeep

Date	Mintage	VF20	XF40	MS60	MS63	MS65
1995	25,000	PF65 30.00				

KM# 147 10 DOLLARS
31.10 g., 0.999 Silver 0.9989 oz. ASW **Obv:** National arms **Rev:** General George Patton in front of map

Date	Mintage	VF20	XF40	MS60	MS63	MS65
1995	25,000	PF65 30.00				

KM# 148 10 DOLLARS
31.10 g., 0.999 Silver 0.9989 oz. ASW **Obv:** National arms **Rev:** President Harry S. Truman facing

Date	Mintage	VF20	XF40	MS60	MS63	MS65
1995	25,000	PF65 30.00				

KM# 149 10 DOLLARS
31.10 g., 0.999 Silver 0.9989 oz. ASW **Obv:** National arms **Rev:** President Charles de Gaulle on Champs Elysees

Date	Mintage	VF20	XF40	MS60	MS63	MS65
1995	25,000	PF65 30.00				

KM# 159 10 DOLLARS
31.10 g., 0.999 Silver 0.9989 oz. ASW **Obv:** National arms **Rev:** Sun Yat Sen bust facing

Date	Mintage	VF20	XF40	MS60	MS63	MS65
1995	25,000	PF65 32.50				
1996	25,000	PF65 32.50				

KM# 162 10 DOLLARS
31.10 g., 0.999 Silver 0.9989 oz. ASW **Obv:** National arms **Rev:** General Chiang Kai-shek

Date	Mintage	VF20	XF40	MS60	MS63	MS65
1995	25,000	PF65 32.50				
1996	25,000	PF65 32.50				

KM# 165 10 DOLLARS
31.10 g., 0.999 Silver 0.9989 oz. ASW **Subject:** Cairo Conference **Obv:** National arms **Rev:** Chiang Kai-shek - Roosevelt - Churchill

Date	Mintage	VF20	XF40	MS60	MS63	MS65
1995	25,000	PF65 32.50				

KM# 171 10 DOLLARS
31.10 g., 0.999 Silver 0.9989 oz. ASW **Subject:** 375th Anniversary - Pilgrim Fathers **Obv:** National arms **Rev:** The "Mayflower"

Date	Mintage	VF20	XF40	MS60	MS63	MS65
1995	25,000	PF65 30.00				

KM# 172 10 DOLLARS
31.10 g., 0.999 Silver 0.9989 oz. ASW **Subject:** 375th Anniversary - Pilgrim Fathers **Obv:** National arms **Rev:** Pilgrims in skiff, Cape Cod map

Date	Mintage	VF20	XF40	MS60	MS63	MS65
1995	25,000	PF65 30.00				

KM# 173 10 DOLLARS
31.10 g., 0.999 Silver 0.9989 oz. ASW **Subject:** 375th Anniversary - Pilgrim Fathers **Obv:** National arms **Rev:** Pilgrim landing party

Date	Mintage	VF20	XF40	MS60	MS63	MS65
1995	25,000	PF65 30.00				

KM# 174 10 DOLLARS
31.10 g., 0.999 Silver 0.9989 oz. ASW **Subject:** 375th Anniversary - Pilgrim Fathers **Obv:** National arms **Rev:** First Thanksgiving scene

Date	Mintage	VF20	XF40	MS60	MS63	MS65
1995	25,000	PF65 30.00				

KM# 180 10 DOLLARS
31.10 g., 0.999 Silver 0.9989 oz. ASW **Subject:** Formula One **Obv:** National arms **Rev:** Mika Hakkinen

Date	Mintage	VF20	XF40	MS60	MS63	MS65
1995	25,000	PF65 32.50				

KM# 183 10 DOLLARS
31.10 g., 0.999 Silver 0.9989 oz. ASW **Subject:** Formula One **Obv:** National arms **Rev:** Martin Brundle

Date	Mintage	VF20	XF40	MS60	MS63	MS65
1995	25,000	PF65 32.50				

KM# 186 10 DOLLARS
31.10 g., 0.999 Silver 0.9989 oz. ASW **Subject:** Formula One **Obv:** National arms **Rev:** Rubens Barrichello

Date	Mintage	VF20	XF40	MS60	MS63	MS65
1995	25,000	PF65 32.50				

KM# 189 10 DOLLARS
31.10 g., 0.999 Silver 0.9989 oz. ASW **Subject:** Formula One **Obv:** National arms **Rev:** David Coulthard

Date	Mintage	VF20	XF40	MS60	MS63	MS65
1995	25,000	PF65 32.50				

KM# 192 10 DOLLARS
31.10 g., 0.999 Silver 0.9989 oz. ASW **Subject:** Formula One **Obv:** National arms **Rev:** Jean Alesi

Date	Mintage	VF20	XF40	MS60	MS63	MS65
1995	25,000	PF65 32.50				

KM# 194 10 DOLLARS
31.10 g., 0.999 Silver 0.9989 oz. ASW **Subject:** Nations United for Peace **Obv:** National arms divides date **Rev:** Logo, paper dolls

Date	Mintage	VF20	XF40	MS60	MS63	MS65
1995	25,000	PF65 27.50				

KM# 564 10 DOLLARS
31.10 g., 0.999 Silver 0.9989 oz. ASW, 38.6 mm. **Rev:** Bugatti Royale

Date	Mintage	VF20	XF40	MS60	MS63	MS65
1995	—	—	—	—	—	30.00

KM# 199 10 DOLLARS
31.10 g., 0.999 Silver 0.9989 oz. ASW **Subject:** Formula One **Obv:** National arms **Rev:** Mark Blundell

Date	Mintage	VF20	XF40	MS60	MS63	MS65
1996	25,000	PF65 32.50				

KM# 200 10 DOLLARS
31.10 g., 0.999 Silver 0.9989 oz. ASW **Subject:** Formula One **Obv:** National arms **Rev:** Johnny Herbert

Date	Mintage	VF20	XF40	MS60	MS63	MS65
1996	25,000	PF65 32.50				

KM# 201 10 DOLLARS
31.10 g., 0.999 Silver 0.9989 oz. ASW **Subject:** Formula One **Obv:** National arms **Rev:** Eddie Irvine

Date	Mintage	VF20	XF40	MS60	MS63	MS65
1996	25,000	PF65 32.50				

KM# 202 10 DOLLARS
31.10 g., 0.999 Silver 0.9989 oz. ASW **Subject:** Formula One **Obv:** National arms **Rev:** Heinz Frentzen

Date	Mintage	VF20	XF40	MS60	MS63	MS65
1996	25,000	PF65 32.50				

KM# 208 10 DOLLARS
31.10 g., 0.999 Silver 0.9989 oz. ASW **Subject:** Star Trek **Obv:** National arms **Rev:** Starships NCC-1701 and NCC-1701D

Date	Mintage	VF20	XF40	MS60	MS63	MS65
1996	25,000	PF65 37.50				

KM# 211 10 DOLLARS
31.10 g., 0.999 Silver 0.9989 oz. ASW **Subject:** Star Trek, Scott and McCoy **Obv:** National arms **Rev:** Conjoined busts facing

Date	Mintage	VF20	XF40	MS60	MS63	MS65
1996	25,000	PF65 37.50				

KM# 214 10 DOLLARS
31.10 g., 0.999 Silver 0.9989 oz. ASW **Subject:** Star Trek **Obv:** National arms **Rev:** LaForge and Data

Date	Mintage	VF20	XF40	MS60	MS63	MS65
1996	25,000	PF65 37.50				

KM# 217 10 DOLLARS
31.10 g., 0.999 Silver 0.9989 oz. ASW **Subject:** Star Trek **Obv:** National arms **Rev:** Spock and Uhura

Date	Mintage	VF20	XF40	MS60	MS63	MS65
1996	25,000	PF65 37.50				

KM# 220 10 DOLLARS
31.10 g., 0.999 Silver 0.9989 oz. ASW **Subject:** Star Trek **Obv:** National arms **Rev:** Worf and Dr. Crusher

Date	Mintage	VF20	XF40	MS60	MS63	MS65
1996	25,000	PF65 37.50				

KM# 223 10 DOLLARS
31.10 g., 0.999 Silver 0.9989 oz. ASW **Series:** Preserve Planet Earth **Obv:** National arms **Rev:** Grey Parrot

Date	Mintage	VF20	XF40	MS60	MS63	MS65
1996	25,000	PF65 30.00				

KM# 226 10 DOLLARS
31.10 g., 0.999 Silver 0.9989 oz. ASW **Series:** Preserve Planet Earth **Obv:** National arms **Rev:** Love Birds

Date	Mintage	VF20	XF40	MS60	MS63	MS65
1996	25,000	PF65 30.00				

KM# 229 10 DOLLARS
31.10 g., 0.999 Silver 0.9989 oz. ASW **Subject:** Formula One **Obv:** National arms **Rev:** Ayrton Senna

Date	Mintage	VF20	XF40	MS60	MS63	MS65
1996	25,000	PF65 32.50				

KM# 242 10 DOLLARS
31.10 g., 0.999 Silver 0.9989 oz. ASW **Subject:** President Chiang Ching-kuo **Obv:** National arms **Rev:** Bust 1/4 right

Date	Mintage	VF20	XF40	MS60	MS63	MS65
1996	25,000	PF65 32.50				

KM# 245 10 DOLLARS
31.10 g., 0.999 Silver 0.9989 oz. ASW **Obv:** National arms **Rev:** President Lee Ten-hui

Date	Mintage	VF20	XF40	MS60	MS63	MS65
1996	25,000	PF65 30.00				

KM# 256 10 DOLLARS
31.10 g., 0.999 Silver 0.9989 oz. ASW **Subject:** Chairman Mao Zedong **Obv:** National arms divides date **Rev:** Standing figure facing

Date	Mintage	VF20	XF40	MS60	MS63	MS65
1996	25,000	PF65 30.00				

KM# 257 10 DOLLARS
31.10 g., 0.999 Silver 0.9989 oz. ASW **Obv:** National arms **Rev:** Chairman Mao Zedong with gate of Heavenly Peace

Date	Mintage	VF20	XF40	MS60	MS63	MS65
1996	25,000	PF65 30.00				

KM# 258 10 DOLLARS
31.10 g., 0.999 Silver 0.9989 oz. ASW **Obv:** National arms **Rev:** Chairman Mao Zedong proclaiming People's Republic

Date	Mintage	VF20	XF40	MS60	MS63	MS65
1996	25,000	PF65 30.00				

KM# 262 10 DOLLARS
31.10 g., 0.999 Silver 0.9989 oz. ASW **Subject:** Chairman Mao Zedong and President Nixon **Obv:** National arms **Rev:** Seated figures facing

Date	Mintage	VF20	XF40	MS60	MS63	MS65
1996	25,000	PF65 30.00				

KM# 264 10 DOLLARS
31.10 g., 0.999 Silver 0.9989 oz. ASW **Series:** Pioneers of the West **Obv:** National arms **Rev:** Daniel Boone

Date	Mintage	VF20	XF40	MS60	MS63	MS65
1996	25,000	PF65 30.00				

KM# 267 10 DOLLARS
31.10 g., 0.999 Silver 0.9989 oz. ASW **Series:** Pioneers of the West **Obv:** National arms **Rev:** Davy Crockett

Date	Mintage	VF20	XF40	MS60	MS63	MS65
1996	25,000	PF65 30.00				

KM# 270 10 DOLLARS
31.10 g., 0.999 Silver 0.9989 oz. ASW **Series:** Pioneers of the West **Obv:** National arms **Rev:** Jim Bowie in front of the Alamo

Date	Mintage	VF20	XF40	MS60	MS63	MS65
1996	25,000	**PF65** 30.00				

KM# 273 10 DOLLARS
31.10 g., 0.999 Silver 0.9989 oz. ASW **Series:** Pioneers of the West **Obv:** National arms **Rev:** Kit Carson

Date	Mintage	VF20	XF40	MS60	MS63	MS65
1996	25,000	**PF65** 30.00				

KM# 276 10 DOLLARS
31.10 g., 0.999 Silver 0.9989 oz. ASW **Series:** Pioneers of the West **Obv:** National arms **Rev:** Wild Bill Hickok

Date	Mintage	VF20	XF40	MS60	MS63	MS65
1996	25,000	**PF65** 30.00				

KM# 279 10 DOLLARS
31.10 g., 0.999 Silver 0.9989 oz. ASW **Series:** Pioneers of the West **Obv:** National arms **Rev:** Buffalo Bill

Date	Mintage	VF20	XF40	MS60	MS63	MS65
1996	25,000	**PF65** 30.00				

KM# 284 10 DOLLARS
31.10 g., 0.999 Silver 0.9989 oz. ASW **Subject:** Return of Macao to China **Obv:** National arms **Rev:** City views, old and new

Date	Mintage	VF20	XF40	MS60	MS63	MS65
1996	Est. 6000	**PF65** 35.00				

KM# 285 10 DOLLARS
31.10 g., 0.999 Silver 0.9989 oz. ASW **Subject:** Return of Hong Kong to China **Obv:** National arms divide date above value **Rev:** City views, old and new **Shape:** Rectangular

Date	Mintage	VF20	XF40	MS60	MS63	MS65
1996	Est. 6000	**PF65** 32.50				

KM# 287 10 DOLLARS
31.10 g., 0.999 Silver 0.9989 oz. ASW **Series:** WWII **Subject:** Evacuation from Dunkirk **Obv:** National arms **Rev:** British 1939-45 Star Medal to left of fighter planes and ships

Date	Mintage	VF20	XF40	MS60	MS63	MS65
1997	25,000	**PF65** 27.50				

KM# 289 10 DOLLARS
31.10 g., 0.999 Silver 0.9989 oz. ASW **Series:** WWII **Subject:** Liberation of the Philippines **Obv:** National arms **Rev:** American Asian-Pacific campaign medal to right of soldiers in water

Date	Mintage	VF20	XF40	MS60	MS63	MS65
1997	25,000	**PF65** 27.50				

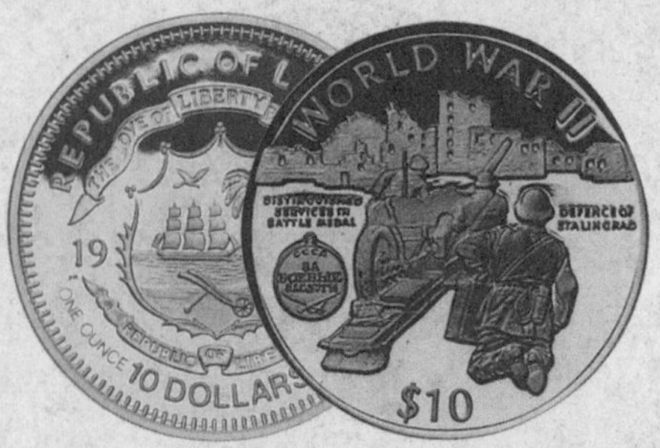

KM# 291 10 DOLLARS
31.10 g., 0.999 Silver 0.9989 oz. ASW **Series:** WWII **Subject:** Defense of Stalingrad **Obv:** National arms **Rev:** Soviet distinguished combat medal to left of war scene

Date	Mintage	VF20	XF40	MS60	MS63	MS65
1997	25,000	**PF65** 27.50				

KM# 293 10 DOLLARS
31.10 g., 0.999 Silver 0.9989 oz. ASW **Series:** WWII **Subject:** Arnhem **Obv:** National arms **Rev:** Netherlands bronze lion cross to right of parachutists, bridge and soldier

Date	Mintage	VF20	XF40	MS60	MS63	MS65
1997	25,000	**PF65** 27.50				

KM# 295 10 DOLLARS
31.10 g., 0.999 Silver 0.9989 oz. ASW **Series:** WWII **Subject:** Raid on the Dams **Obv:** National arms **Rev:** British distinguished flying medal

Date	Mintage	VF20	XF40	MS60	MS63	MS65
1997	25,000	**PF65** 27.50				

KM# 297 10 DOLLARS
31.10 g., 0.999 Silver 0.9989 oz. ASW **Series:** WWII **Subject:** West African Campaign **Obv:** National arms **Rev:** WWII Victory medal

Date	Mintage	VF20	XF40	MS60	MS63	MS65
1997	25,000	**PF65** 27.50				

KM# 299 10 DOLLARS
31.10 g., 0.999 Silver 0.9989 oz. ASW **Series:** WWII **Subject:** North African Campaign **Obv:** National arms **Rev:** British Africa star medal to right of tank in front of pyramid

Date	Mintage	VF20	XF40	MS60	MS63	MS65
1997	25,000	PF65 27.50				

KM# 301 10 DOLLARS
31.10 g., 0.999 Silver 0.9989 oz. ASW **Series:** WWII **Subject:** The Dieppe Raid **Obv:** National arms **Rev:** British Victoria cross to right of plane over half-track vehicle

Date	Mintage	VF20	XF40	MS60	MS63	MS65
1997	25,000	PF65 27.50				

KM# 303 10 DOLLARS
31.10 g., 0.999 Silver 0.9989 oz. ASW **Series:** WWII **Subject:** Iwo Jima **Obv:** National arms **Rev:** Purple Heart medal to upper left of damaged plane landing on a carrier

Date	Mintage	VF20	XF40	MS60	MS63	MS65
1997	25,000	PF65 27.50				

KM# 305 10 DOLLARS
31.10 g., 0.999 Silver 0.9989 oz. ASW **Series:** WWII **Subject:** Battle of Britain **Obv:** National arms **Rev:** British distinguished flying cross to left of pilots running to board planes

Date	Mintage	VF20	XF40	MS60	MS63	MS65
1997	25,000	PF65 27.50				

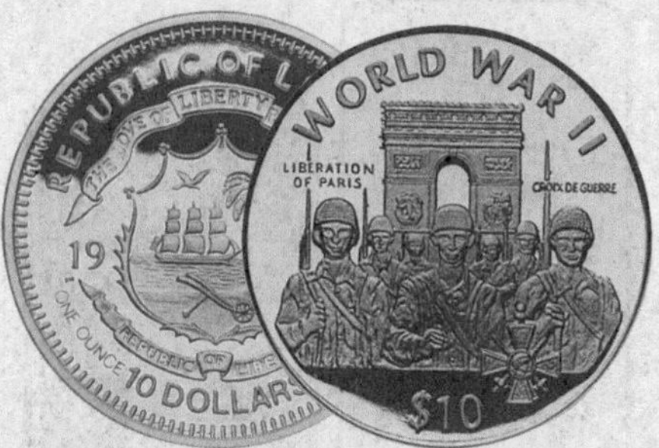

KM# 307 10 DOLLARS
31.10 g., 0.999 Silver 0.9989 oz. ASW **Series:** WWII **Subject:** Liberation of Paris **Obv:** National arms **Rev:** Croix de Guerre medal to right of soldiers in front of Arch de Triumph

Date	Mintage	VF20	XF40	MS60	MS63	MS65
1997	25,000	PF65 27.50				

KM# 309 10 DOLLARS
31.10 g., 0.999 Silver 0.9989 oz. ASW **Series:** WWII **Subject:** Burma Campaign **Obv:** National arms **Rev:** British Burma star medal

Date	Mintage	VF20	XF40	MS60	MS63	MS65
1997	25,000	PF65 27.50				

KM# 311 10 DOLLARS
31.10 g., 0.999 Silver 0.9989 oz. ASW **Subject:** Mahatma Gandhi **Obv:** National arms **Rev:** Seated figure facing left in front of Taj Mahal

Date	Mintage	VF20	XF40	MS60	MS63	MS65
1997	25,000	PF65 30.00				

KM# 314 10 DOLLARS
31.10 g., 0.999 Silver 0.9989 oz. ASW **Subject:** Return of Hong Kong **Obv:** National arms **Rev:** Dragon

Date	Mintage	VF20	XF40	MS60	MS63	MS65
1997	25,000	PF65 32.50				

KM# 321 10 DOLLARS
31.10 g., 0.999 Silver 0.9989 oz. ASW **Subject:** Fiftieth Anniversary of the Kon-Tiki Expedition **Obv:** National arms **Rev:** Mask within circle

Date	Mintage	VF20	XF40	MS60	MS63	MS65
1997	25,000	PF65 32.50				

KM# 325 10 DOLLARS
31.10 g., 0.999 Silver 0.9989 oz. ASW **Subject:** Jurassic Park **Obv:** National arms **Rev:** Stegosaurus

Date	Mintage	VF20	XF40	MS60	MS63	MS65
1997	10,000	PF65 30.00				

KM# 328 10 DOLLARS
31.10 g., 0.925 Gold Clad Silver 0.925 oz. **Subject:** Golden Wedding Anniversary **Obv:** National arms **Rev:** E & P initials above 2 shields

Date	Mintage	VF20	XF40	MS60	MS63	MS65
1997	10,000	PF65 37.50				

KM# 331 10 DOLLARS
31.10 g., 0.925 Gold Clad Silver 0.925 oz. **Subject:** Queen Elizabeth II and Prince Philip's Golden Wedding Anniversary **Obv:** National arms **Rev:** Royal couple with horse

Date	Mintage	VF20	XF40	MS60	MS63	MS65
1997	10,000	PF65 37.50				

KM# 334 10 DOLLARS
31.10 g., 0.925 Gold Clad Silver 0.925 oz. **Subject:** Queen Elizabeth II and Prince Philip's Golden Wedding Anniversary **Obv:** National arms **Rev:** Royal couple with dogs

Date	Mintage	VF20	XF40	MS60	MS63	MS65
1997	10,000	PF65 37.50				

KM# 337 10 DOLLARS
31.10 g., 0.925 Gold Clad Silver 0.925 oz. **Subject:** Queen Elizabeth II and Prince Philip's Golden Wedding Anniversary **Obv:** National arms **Rev:** Royal couple with children

Date	Mintage	VF20	XF40	MS60	MS63	MS65
1997	10,000	PF65 37.50				

KM# 345 10 DOLLARS
31.10 g., 0.999 Silver 0.999 oz. ASW **Subject:** 150th Anniversary - Independence of Liberia **Obv:** National arms **Rev:** Cameo to upper left of ship above small boat

Date	Mintage	VF20	XF40	MS60	MS63	MS65
1997	25,000	PF65 32.50				

KM# 346 10 DOLLARS
Copper-Nickel **Subject:** Famous Personalities of the World; Marilyn Monroe **Obv:** National arms with blank ribbons **Rev:** Head facing

Date	Mintage	VF20	XF40	MS60	MS63	MS65
ND-1997	—	PF65 15.00				

KM# 348 10 DOLLARS
31.10 g., 0.999 Silver 0.999 oz. ASW **Subject:** Return of Hong Kong to China **Obv:** National arms **Rev:** City view, old and new **Shape:** Rectangular

Date	Mintage	VF20	XF40	MS60	MS63	MS65
1997	Est. 8000	PF65 32.50				

KM# 349 10 DOLLARS
31.10 g., 0.999 Silver 0.999 oz. ASW **Subject:** Pending Return of Macao to China **Obv:** National arms **Rev:** City view within circle

Date	Mintage	VF20	XF40	MS60	MS63	MS65
1997	—	PF65 35.00				

KM# 350 10 DOLLARS
31.10 g., 0.999 Silver 0.999 oz. ASW **Subject:** Diana - The People's Princess **Obv:** National arms **Rev:** Princess Diana in minefield wearing protective gear

Date	Mintage	VF20	XF40	MS60	MS63	MS65
1997	—	PF65 32.50				

KM# 369 10 DOLLARS
31.10 g., 0.999 Silver 0.999 oz. ASW **Subject:** Star Trek - The Next Generation **Obv:** National arms **Rev:** Romulan Warbird

Date	Mintage	VF20	XF40	MS60	MS63	MS65
1997	25,000	PF65 32.50				

KM# 372 10 DOLLARS
31.10 g., 0.999 Silver 0.999 oz. ASW **Subject:** Star Trek - The Next Generation **Obv:** National arms. **Rev:** Klingon Attack Cruiser

Date	Mintage	VF20	XF40	MS60	MS63	MS65
1997	25,000	PF65 32.50				

KM# 375 10 DOLLARS
31.10 g., 0.999 Silver 0.999 oz. ASW **Subject:** Star Trek - The Next Generation **Obv:** National arms **Rev:** U.S.S. Enterprise NCC-1701-D

Date	Mintage	VF20	XF40	MS60	MS63	MS65
1997	25,000	PF65 32.50				

KM# 378 10 DOLLARS
31.10 g., 0.999 Silver 0.999 oz. ASW **Subject:** Star Trek - The Next Generation **Obv:** National arms **Rev:** Klingon Bird of Prey

Date	Mintage	VF20	XF40	MS60	MS63	MS65
1997	25,000	PF65 32.50				

KM# 381 10 DOLLARS
31.10 g., 0.999 Silver 0.999 oz. ASW **Subject:** Star Trek - The Next Generation **Obv:** National arms **Rev:** Borg Cube

Date	Mintage	VF20	XF40	MS60	MS63	MS65
1997	25,000	PF65 32.50				

KM# 384 10 DOLLARS
31.10 g., 0.999 Silver 0.999 oz. ASW **Subject:** Star Trek - The Next Generation **Obv:** National arms **Rev:** Ferengi Marauder

Date	Mintage	VF20	XF40	MS60	MS63	MS65
1997	25,000	PF65 32.50				

KM# 780 10 DOLLARS
31.98 g., 0.925 Silver 0.9511 oz. ASW, 38.75 mm. **Series:** World's Greatest Conquerors **Obv:** National arms **Rev:** Charles I **Edge:** Reeded

Date	Mintage	VF20	XF40	MS60	MS63	MS65
1997 FM	—	PF65 40.00				

KM# 781 10 DOLLARS
31.98 g., 0.925 Silver 0.9511 oz. ASW, 38.75 mm. **Series:** World's Greatest Conquerors **Obv:** National arms **Rev:** Genghis Khan **Edge:** Reeded

Date	Mintage	VF20	XF40	MS60	MS63	MS65
1997 FM	—	PF65 40.00				

KM# 782 10 DOLLARS
31.98 g., 0.925 Silver 0.9511 oz. ASW, 38.75 mm. **Series:** World's Greatest Conquerors **Obv:** National arms **Rev:** Tokugawa Ieyasu **Edge:** Reeded

Date	Mintage	VF20	XF40	MS60	MS63	MS65
1997 FM	—	PF65 40.00				

KM# 783 10 DOLLARS
31.98 g., 0.925 Silver 0.9511 oz. ASW, 38.75 mm. **Series:** World's Greatest Conquerors **Obv:** National arms **Rev:** Julius Caesar **Edge:** Reeded

Date	Mintage	VF20	XF40	MS60	MS63	MS65
1997 FM	—	PF65 40.00				

KM# 784 10 DOLLARS
31.98 g., 0.925 Silver 0.9511 oz. ASW, 38.75 mm. **Series:** World's Greatest Conquerors **Obv:** National arms **Rev:** Ramses II **Edge:** Reeded

Date	Mintage	VF20	XF40	MS60	MS63	MS65
1997 FM	—	PF65 40.00				

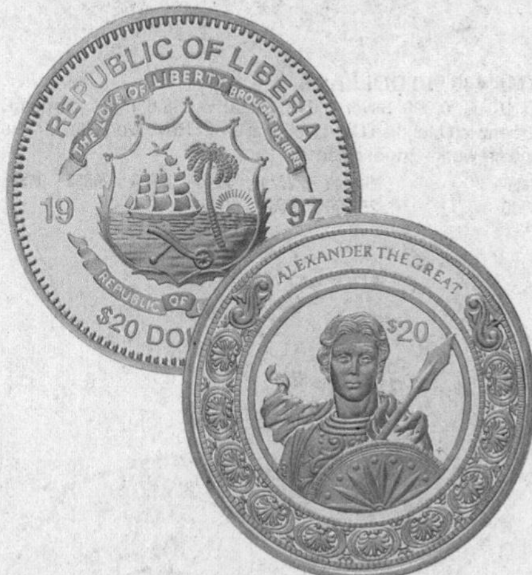

KM# 785 10 DOLLARS
31.98 g., 0.925 Silver 0.9511 oz. ASW, 38.75 mm. **Series:** World's Greatest Conquerors **Obv:** National arms **Rev:** 1/2 length figure of Alexander the Great standing facing holding spear and shield **Edge:** Reeded

Date	Mintage	VF20	XF40	MS60	MS63	MS65
1997 FM	—	PF65 40.00				

KM# 786 10 DOLLARS
31.98 g., 0.925 Silver 0.9511 oz. ASW, 38.75 mm. **Series:** World's Greatest Conquerors **Obv:** National arms **Rev:** Hannibal **Edge:** Reeded

Date	Mintage	VF20	XF40	MS60	MS63	MS65
1997 FM	—	PF65 40.00				

KM# 787 10 DOLLARS
31.98 g., 0.925 Silver 0.9511 oz. ASW, 38.75 mm. **Series:** World's Greatest Conquerors **Obv:** National arms **Rev:** 1/2 length figure of William the Conqueror standing facing holding sword **Edge:** Reeded

Date	Mintage	VF20	XF40	MS60	MS63	MS65
1997 FM	—	PF65 40.00				

KM# 788 10 DOLLARS
31.98 g., 0.925 Silver 0.9511 oz. ASW, 38.75 mm. **Series:** World's Greatest Conquerors **Obv:** National arms **Rev:** Constantine the Great seated facing 3/4 left **Edge:** Reeded

Date	Mintage	VF20	XF40	MS60	MS63	MS65
1997 FM	—	PF65 40.00				

KM# 789 10 DOLLARS
31.98 g., 0.925 Silver 0.9511 oz. ASW, 38.75 mm. **Series:** World's Greatest Conquerors **Obv:** National arms **Rev:** Kyros the Great **Edge:** Reeded

Date	Mintage	VF20	XF40	MS60	MS63	MS65
1997 FM	—	PF65 40.00				

KM# 790 10 DOLLARS
31.98 g., 0.925 Silver 0.9511 oz. ASW, 38.75 mm. **Series:** World's Greatest Conquerors **Obv:** National arms **Rev:** 1/2 length crowned armored bust of Attila the Hun facing 3/4 left **Edge:** Reeded

Date	Mintage	VF20	XF40	MS60	MS63	MS65
1997 FM	—	PF65 40.00				

KM# 791 10 DOLLARS
31.98 g., 0.925 Silver 0.9511 oz. ASW, 38.75 mm. **Series:** World's Greatest Conquerors **Obv:** National arms **Rev:** 1/2 length bust of Tamerlane the Great facing 3/4 right **Edge:** Reeded

Date	Mintage	VF20	XF40	MS60	MS63	MS65
1997 FM	—	PF65 40.00				

KM# 792 10 DOLLARS
31.98 g., 0.925 Silver 0.9511 oz. ASW, 38.75 mm. **Series:** World's Greatest Conquerors **Obv:** National arms **Rev:** Sultan Salah el-Din Yusuf bin-Ayyud **Edge:** Reeded

Date	Mintage	VF20	XF40	MS60	MS63	MS65
1997 FM	—	PF65 40.00				

KM# 793 10 DOLLARS
31.98 g., 0.925 Silver 0.9511 oz. ASW, 38.75 mm. **Series:** World's Greatest Conquerors **Obv:** National arms **Rev:** Edward the Black Prince horseback right **Edge:** Reeded

Date	Mintage	VF20	XF40	MS60	MS63	MS65
1997 FM	—	PF65 40.00				

KM# 794 10 DOLLARS
31.98 g., 0.925 Silver 0.9511 oz. ASW, 38.75 mm. **Series:** World's Greatest Conquerors **Obv:** National arms **Rev:** Henry V standing holding sword facing left, castle in background **Edge:** Reeded

Date	Mintage	VF20	XF40	MS60	MS63	MS65
1997 FM	—	PF65 40.00				

KM# 795 10 DOLLARS
31.98 g., 0.925 Silver 0.9511 oz. ASW, 38.75 mm. **Series:** World's Greatest Conquerors **Obv:** National arms **Rev:** Napoleon on rearing horse left **Edge:** Reeded

Date	Mintage	VF20	XF40	MS60	MS63	MS65
1997 FM	—	PF65 40.00				

KM# 796 10 DOLLARS
31.98 g., 0.925 Silver 0.9511 oz. ASW, 38.75 mm. **Series:** World's Greatest Conquerors **Obv:** National arms **Rev:** Duke of Marlborough **Edge:** Reeded

Date	Mintage	VF20	XF40	MS60	MS63	MS65
1997 FM	—	PF65 40.00				

KM# 387 10 DOLLARS
31.10 g., 0.999 Silver 0.999 oz. ASW **Subject:** President

Ronald Reagan **Obv:** National arms **Rev:** Lincoln Memorial below head right

Date	Mintage	VF20	XF40	MS60	MS63	MS65
1998	25,000	PF65 35.00				

KM# 402 10 DOLLARS
31.10 g., 0.999 Silver 0.999 oz. ASW **Subject:** Christopher Columbus **Obv:** National arms **Rev:** Bust 1/4 right above ship

Date	Mintage	VF20	XF40	MS60	MS63	MS65
1999	25,000	PF65 30.00				

KM# 405 10 DOLLARS
31.10 g., 0.999 Silver 0.999 oz. ASW **Subject:** Captain James Cook **Obv:** National arms **Rev:** Portrait, map and ship

Date	Mintage	VF20	XF40	MS60	MS63	MS65
1999	25,000	PF65 30.00				

KM# 408 10 DOLLARS
31.10 g., 0.999 Silver 0.999 oz. ASW **Subject:** Return of Macao to China **Obv:** National arms **Rev:** Dragon and phoenix

Date	Mintage	VF20	XF40	MS60	MS63	MS65
1999	25,000	PF65 30.00				

KM# 414 10 DOLLARS
31.10 g., 0.999 Silver 0.999 oz. ASW **Subject:** The Wedding of Prince Edward and Miss Sophie Rhys-Jones **Obv:** National arms **Rev:** Couple in carriage

Date	Mintage	VF20	XF40	MS60	MS63	MS65
1999	10,000	PF65 40.00				

KM# 424 10 DOLLARS
15.55 g., 0.999 Silver 0.4995 oz. ASW **Series:** Liberty **Subject:** John F. Kennedy and John Jr. **Obv:** National arms **Rev:** Conjoined heads left

Date	Mintage	VF20	XF40	MS60	MS63	MS65
1999	—	PF65 20.00				

KM# 468 10 DOLLARS
25.00 g., 0.925 Silver 0.7435 oz. ASW, 38.7 mm. **Obv:** National arms **Rev:** Sailing ship "Mayflower" **Edge:** Reeded

Date	Mintage	VF20	XF40	MS60	MS63	MS65
1999	—	PF65 32.00				

KM# 471 10 DOLLARS
30.75 g., 0.999 Silver 0.9876 oz. ASW, 37.9 mm. **Subject:** Transrapid-08 Hamburg-Berlin Monorail **Obv:** National arms **Rev:** Monorail train car **Edge:** Reeded

Date	Mintage	VF20	XF40	MS60	MS63	MS65
1999	—	PF65 38.00				

KM# 573 10 DOLLARS
25.10 g., 0.925 Silver 0.7465 oz. ASW, 38.6 mm. **Obv:** National arms **Rev:** Titanic steaming right **Edge:** Reeded

Date	Mintage	VF20	XF40	MS60	MS63	MS65
1999	—	PF65 32.00				

KM# 594 10 DOLLARS
31.00 g., 0.999 Silver 0.9957 oz. ASW, 40 mm. **Subject:** John F. Kennedy Jr. **Obv:** National arms **Rev:** Two portraits, flag and the White House **Edge:** Reeded

Date	Mintage	VF20	XF40	MS60	MS63	MS65
1999	—	PF65 37.00				

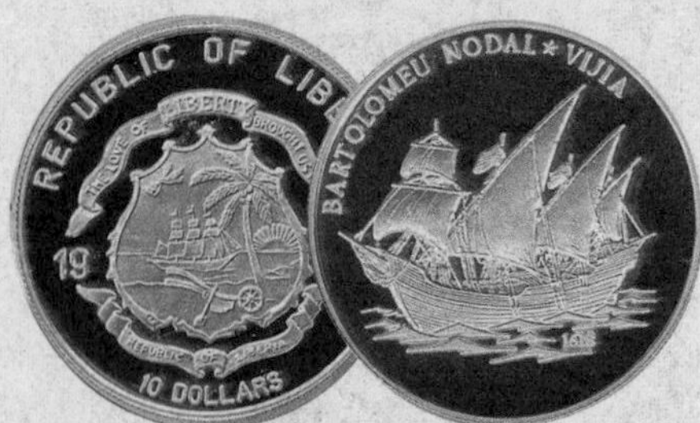

KM# 706 10 DOLLARS
20.10 g., 0.925 Silver 0.5978 oz. ASW, 34 mm. **Obv:** National arms **Rev:** Sail ship "Vijia" with captains name above **Edge:** Reeded

Date	Mintage	VF20	XF40	MS60	MS63	MS65
1999	—	PF65 25.00				

KM# 423 10 DOLLARS
31.10 g., 0.999 Silver 0.999 oz. ASW **Subject:** Millennium **Obv:** Liberty cap, crossed flags of USA and Liberia above national arms **Rev:** Morgan dollar Liberty head

Date	Mintage	VF20	XF40	MS60	MS63	MS65
2000	—	PF65 55.00				

KM# 443 10 DOLLARS
31.10 g., 0.999 Silver 0.999 oz. ASW, 38.6 mm. **Subject:** Greenwich Meridian **Obv:** National arms **Rev:** World landmarks and fireworks **Edge:** Reeded

Date	Mintage	VF20	XF40	MS60	MS63	MS65
2000	25,000	PF65 35.00				

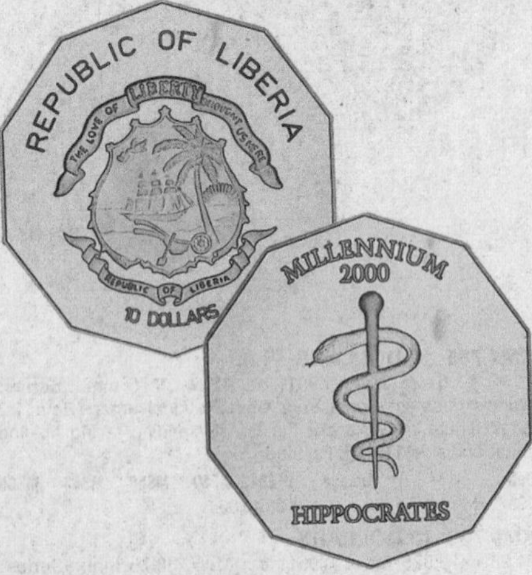

KM# 444 10 DOLLARS
25.00 g., 0.925 Silver 0.7435 oz. ASW, 36.8 mm. **Subject:** Millennium - Hippocrates **Obv:** National arms **Rev:** Caduceus **Edge:** Plain **Shape:** 10-sided

Date	Mintage	VF20	XF40	MS60	MS63	MS65
2000	10,000	PF65 32.00				

KM# 469 10 DOLLARS
20.50 g., 0.925 Silver 0.6097 oz. ASW, 38.6 mm. **Subject:** Millennium **Obv:** National arms **Rev:** Millennium Dome **Edge:** Reeded

Date	Mintage	VF20	XF40	MS60	MS63	MS65
2000	2,000	PF65 30.00				

KM# 470 10 DOLLARS
20.50 g., 0.925 Silver 0.6097 oz. ASW **Subject:** Mutiny on the Bounty **Obv:** National arms **Rev:** Mutineers setting ship's officers adrift

Date	Mintage	VF20	XF40	MS60	MS63	MS65
2000	2,000	PF65 30.00				

KM# 475 10 DOLLARS
8.45 g., 0.999 Silver 0.2714 oz. ASW, 30.1 mm. **Subject:** General Robert E. Lee **Obv:** National arms **Rev:** Equestrian left **Edge:** Reeded

Date	Mintage	VF20	XF40	MS60	MS63	MS65
2000	—	PF65 12.00				

KM# 476 10 DOLLARS
8.45 g., 0.999 Silver 0.2714 oz. ASW **Obv:** National arms **Rev:** Statue of Liberty

Date	Mintage	VF20	XF40	MS60	MS63	MS65
2000	—	PF65 12.00				

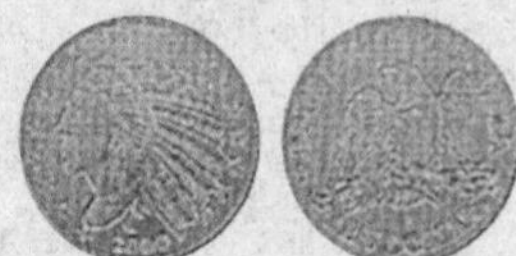

KM# 492 10 DOLLARS
3.39 g., 0.9167 Gold 0.100 oz. AGW, 16.5 mm. **Subject:** US Gold Indian Design Copy **Obv:** Incuse Indian design **Rev:** Incuse eagle design **Edge:** Reeded

Date	Mintage	VF20	XF40	MS60	MS63	MS65
2000	—	—	—	—	—	200

KM# 499 10 DOLLARS
20.15 g., 0.999 Silver 0.6472 oz. ASW, 34 mm. **Obv:** National arms **Rev:** Monkeys **Edge:** Reeded

Date	Mintage	VF20	XF40	MS60	MS63	MS65
2000	—	PF65 28.00				

KM# 500 10 DOLLARS
8.50 g., 0.999 Silver 0.273 oz. ASW, 30 mm. **Subject:** American History **Obv:** National arms **Rev:** Washington crossing the Delaware **Edge:** Reeded **Note:** The American Mint is not an actual mint.

Date	Mintage	VF20	XF40	MS60	MS63	MS65
2000	20,000	PF65 12.00				

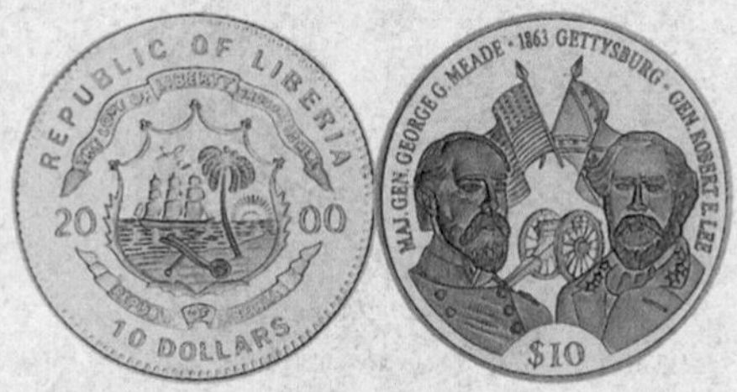

KM# 501 10 DOLLARS
8.55 g., 0.999 Silver 0.2746 oz. ASW, 30 mm. **Subject:** American History - Battle of Gettysburg **Obv:** National arms **Rev:** Flags and cannon divide uniformed busts **Edge:** Reeded **Note:** The American Mint is not an actual mint.

Date	Mintage	VF20	XF40	MS60	MS63	MS65
2000	20,000	PF65 12.00				

KM# 502 10 DOLLARS
8.55 g., 0.999 Silver 0.2746 oz. ASW, 30 mm. **Subject:** American History **Obv:** National arms **Rev:** B-17 Bomber in action **Edge:** Reeded **Note:** The American Mint is not an actual mint.

Date	Mintage	VF20	XF40	MS60	MS63	MS65
2000	20,000	PF65 12.00				

KM# 503 10 DOLLARS
8.55 g., 0.999 Silver 0.2746 oz. ASW, 30 mm. **Subject:** American History - First Man on the Moon **Obv:** National arms **Rev:** Astronaut on the moon with American flag **Edge:** Reeded **Note:** The American Mint is not an actual mint.

Date	Mintage	VF20	XF40	MS60	MS63	MS65
2000	20,000	PF65 12.00				

KM# 622 10 DOLLARS
21.00 g., Copper-Nickel, 37 mm. **Subject:** Millennium **Obv:** National arms **Rev:** Kneeling woman with hourglass **Edge:** Reeded

Date	Mintage	VF20	XF40	MS60	MS63	MS65
2000	—	—	—	—	3.00	5.00

KM# 645 10 DOLLARS
8.45 g., 0.999 Silver 0.2714 oz. ASW, 30 mm. **Obv:** National arms **Rev:** Boeing 707 **Edge:** Reeded

Date	Mintage	VF20	XF40	MS60	MS63	MS65
2000	—	PF65 12.00				

KM# 653 10 DOLLARS
14.60 g., Copper-Nickel, 33.1 mm. **Obv:** National arms **Rev:** Bust facing within U.S. flag **Edge:** Reeded

Date	Mintage	VF20	XF40	MS60	MS63	MS65
2000	—	—	—	—	3.00	5.00

KM# 698 10 DOLLARS
29.40 g., 0.999 Silver 0.9443 oz. ASW, 40 mm. **Obv:** National arms **Rev:** Multicolor cougar **Edge:** Reeded

Date	Mintage	VF20	XF40	MS60	MS63	MS65
2000	—	PF65 30.00				

KM# 699 10 DOLLARS
21.32 g., 0.999 Silver 0.6848 oz. ASW, 37.4 mm. **Obv:** National arms **Rev:** Three-dimensional multicolor timber wolf in winter **Edge:** Reeded

Date	Mintage	VF20	XF40	MS60	MS63	MS65
2000	—	—	—	—	—	25.00

KM# 700 10 DOLLARS
29.06 g., Copper-Nickel, 40 mm. **Obv:** National arms **Rev:** Multicolor timber wolf in summer **Edge:** Reeded

Date	Mintage	VF20	XF40	MS60	MS63	MS65
2000	—	PF65 12.00				

KM# 704 10 DOLLARS

Silver, 40 mm. **Subject:** Games of the XXVII Olympiad - Sydney 2000 **Obv:** National arms **Rev:** Map of Australia at upper left of man sailing **Edge:** Reeded

Date	Mintage	VF20	XF40	MS60	MS63	MS65
2000	—	PF65 35.00				

KM# 709 10 DOLLARS

0.50 g., 0.585 Gold 0.0094 oz. AGW, 11.1 mm. **Subject:** American Civil War **Obv:** National arms **Rev:** Battle of Gettysburg Generals Meade and Lee **Edge:** Reeded

Date	Mintage	VF20	XF40	MS60	MS63	MS65
2000	—	PF65 22.00				

KM# 821 10 DOLLARS

1.16 g., Gold, 13.89 mm. **Subject:** Liberian Art **Obv:** National arms **Rev:** Mask of the Dun **Edge:** Reeded

Date	Mintage	VF20	XF40	MS60	MS63	MS65
2000	—	PF65 65.00				

KM# 841 10 DOLLARS

20.00 g., Copper-Nickel **Subject:** First Man on the Moon

Date	Mintage	VF20	XF40	MS60	MS63	MS65
2000	—	—	—	—	3.00	5.00

KM# 842 10 DOLLARS

20.00 g., Copper-Nickel, 38 mm. **Rev:** Lucky symbols in color - Elephant with raised trunk, horseshoe, 7, 4-leaf clover.

Date	Mintage	VF20	XF40	MS60	MS63	MS65
2000	—	—	—	—	3.00	5.00

KM# 843 10 DOLLARS

0.73 g., 0.999 Gold 0.0234 oz. AGW, 11 mm. **Obv:** Arms **Rev:** John F. Kennedy head left

Date	Mintage	VF20	XF40	MS60	MS63	MS65
2000	20,000	PF63 50.00	PF65 55.00			

KM# 20 12 DOLLARS

6.00 g., 0.900 Gold 0.1736 oz. AGW **Subject:** 70th Birthday of President Tubman **Obv:** National arms **Rev:** Bust left

Date	Mintage	VF20	XF40	MS60	MS63	MS65
1965	400	PF65 375				

KM# 108 15 DOLLARS

1.00 g., 0.9999 Gold 0.0321 oz. AGW **Series:** Preserve Planet Earth **Obv:** National arms **Rev:** Compsognathus

Date	Mintage	VF20	XF40	MS60	MS63	MS65
1993	—	PF65 60.00				

KM# 19 20 DOLLARS

18.65 g., 0.900 Gold 0.5396 oz. AGW **Subject:** William Vacanarat Shadrach Tubman **Obv:** National arms **Rev:** Head 1/4 left above date flanked by stars

Date	Mintage	XF40	MS60	MS63	MS65	MS66
1964 B	10,000	—	—	—	750	850

KM# 19a 20 DOLLARS

18.38 g., 0.999 Gold 0.5903 oz. AGW **Obv:** National arms **Rev:** Head 1/4 left above date flanked by stars

Date	Mintage	VF20	XF40	MS60	MS63	MS65
1964 B L	100	PF65 1,100				

Note: Of the total issue, 10,200 were struck of .900 fine gold and bear the "B" mint mark of the Bern Mint below the date, while 100 were struck as proofs of .999 fine gold and are designated by the presence of a small "L" above the date

KM# 64 20 DOLLARS

15.81 g., 0.900 Gold 0.4575 oz. AGW **Subject:** 25th Anniversary of Inter-Continental Hotels **Obv:** Value below hotel building **Rev:** Letter I within football flanked by dates

Date	Mintage	VF20	XF40	MS60	MS63	MS65
1971	—	PF65 825				

KM# 27 20 DOLLARS

33.44 g., 0.900 Gold 0.9675 oz. AGW **Subject:** Inauguration of President Tolbert **Obv:** National arms **Rev:** Head left

Date	Mintage	VF20	XF40	MS60	MS63	MS65
1972	—	PF65 1,750				

KM# 45 20 DOLLARS

28.28 g., 0.925 Silver 0.841 oz. ASW **Subject:** Year of the Scout **Obv:** National arms **Rev:** Scouts at camp, three saluting, three seated

Date	Mintage	VF20	XF40	MS60	MS63	MS65
1983	10,000	—	—	—	22.00	28.00
1983	10,000	PF65 32.00				

KM# 48 20 DOLLARS

28.28 g., 0.925 Silver 0.841 oz. ASW **Series:** International Year of Disabled Persons **Obv:** National arms

Date	Mintage	VF20	XF40	MS60	MS63	MS65
1983	—	—	—	—	22.00	28.00
1983	—	PF65 32.00				

KM# 811 20 DOLLARS

1.24 g., Gold, 13.85 mm. **Subject:** In Memory of Willy Brant **Obv:** National arms **Rev:** Head of Brant right, statue at top of Brandenburg gate below **Edge:** Reeded

Date	Mintage	VF20	XF40	MS60	MS63	MS65
1992 PM	—	PF65 60.00				

KM# 812 20 DOLLARS

1.24 g., 0.9999 Gold 0.0399 oz. AGW, 13.91 mm. **Series:** Formula One **Obv:** National arms **Rev:** Head of Nigel Mansell right at left, race car at lower right **Edge:** Reeded

Date	Mintage	VF20	XF40	MS60	MS63	MS65
1992 PM	—	PF65 60.00				

KM# 813 20 DOLLARS

1.24 g., 0.9999 Gold 0.0399 oz. AGW, 13.91 mm. **Series:** Formula One **Obv:** National arms **Rev:** Head of Riccardo Patrese **Edge:** Reeded

Date	Mintage	VF20	XF40	MS60	MS63	MS65
1992 PM	—	PF65 60.00				

KM# 814 20 DOLLARS

1.24 g., 0.9999 Gold 0.0399 oz. AGW, 13.91 mm. **Series:** Formula One **Obv:** National arms **Rev:** Head of Gerhard Berger **Edge:** Reeded

Date	Mintage	VF20	XF40	MS60	MS63	MS65
1992 PM	—	PF65 60.00				

KM# 815 20 DOLLARS

1.24 g., 0.9999 Gold 0.0399 oz. AGW, 13.91 mm. **Series:** Formula One **Obv:** National arms **Rev:** Head of Ayrton Senna **Edge:** Reeded

Date	Mintage	VF20	XF40	MS60	MS63	MS65
1992 PM	—	PF65 60.00				

KM# 816 20 DOLLARS

1.24 g., 0.9999 Gold 0.0399 oz. AGW, 13.89 mm. **Series:** Formula One **Obv:** National arms **Rev:** Bust of Michael Schumacher 3/4 left at right, race car at lower left **Edge:** Reeded

Date	Mintage	VF20	XF40	MS60	MS63	MS65
1992 PM	—	PF65 60.00				

KM# 817 20 DOLLARS

1.24 g., 0.9999 Gold 0.0399 oz. AGW, 13.91 mm. **Series:** Formula One **Obv:** National arms **Rev:** Head of Alain Prost **Edge:** Reeded

Date	Mintage	VF20	XF40	MS60	MS63	MS65
1992 PM	—	PF65 60.00				

KM# 818 20 DOLLARS

1.24 g., 0.9999 Gold 0.0399 oz. AGW, 13.91 mm. **Series:** Formula One **Obv:** National arms **Rev:** Head of Aguri Suzuki **Edge:** Reeded

Date	Mintage	VF20	XF40	MS60	MS63	MS65
1992 PM	—	PF65 60.00				

KM# 819 20 DOLLARS

1.24 g., 0.9999 Gold 0.0399 oz. AGW, 13.91 mm. **Series:** Formula One **Obv:** National arms **Rev:** Head of Ukyo Katayami **Edge:** Reeded

Date	Mintage	VF20	XF40	MS60	MS63	MS65
1992 PM	—	PF65 60.00				

KM# 283 20 DOLLARS

1.27 g., 0.999 Gold 0.0408 oz. AGW **Subject:** Formula One **Obv:** National arms divide date **Rev:** Damon Hill

Date	Mintage	VF20	XF40	MS60	MS63	MS65
1994	25,000	PF65 60.00				

KM# 820 20 DOLLARS

1.24 g., 0.9999 Gold 0.0399 oz. AGW, 13.84 mm. **Subject:** In memory of John F. Kennedy's Visit to Berlin **Obv:** National arms **Rev:** Head of JFK left, statue at top of Brandenburg Gate below **Edge:** Reeded

Date	Mintage	VF20	XF40	MS60	MS63	MS65
1995 PM	—	PF65 60.00				

KM# 230 20 DOLLARS

1.27 g., 0.999 Gold 0.0408 oz. AGW **Subject:** Formula One **Obv:** National arms **Rev:** Ayrton Senna **Note:** Similar to 10 Dollars, KM#229.

Date	Mintage	VF20	XF40	MS60	MS63	MS65
1996	15,000	PF65 60.00				

KM# 250 20 DOLLARS

1.27 g., 0.999 Gold 0.0408 oz. AGW **Subject:** Dalai Lama **Obv:** National arms **Rev:** Bust with praying hands facing 1/4 left **Note:** Similar to 100 Dollars, KM#252.

Date	Mintage	VF20	XF40	MS60	MS63	MS65
1996	15,000	PF65 60.00				

KM# 315 20 DOLLARS

1.24 g., 0.999 Gold 0.0398 oz. AGW **Subject:** Return of Hong Kong to China **Obv:** National arms **Rev:** Dragon **Note:** Similar to 10 Dollars, KM#314.

Date	Mintage	VF20	XF40	MS60	MS63	MS65
1997	—	PF65 60.00				

KM# 340 20 DOLLARS
31.10 g., 0.999 Silver 0.999 oz. ASW **Subject:** Year of the Ox **Obv:** National arms **Rev:** Ox above value

Date	Mintage	VF20	XF40	MS60	MS63	MS65
1997	—	PF65 30.00				

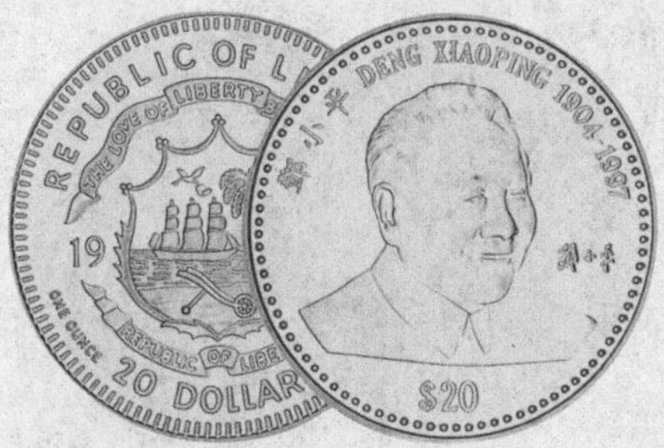

KM# 416 20 DOLLARS
31.35 g., 0.999 Silver 1.0069 oz. ASW **Subject:** Deng Xiaoping **Obv:** National arms **Rev:** Bust 1/4 right above value

Date	Mintage	VF20	XF40	MS60	MS63	MS65
1997	—	PF65 30.00				

KM# 417 20 DOLLARS
31.40 g., 0.999 Silver 1.0085 oz. ASW **Subject:** Princess Diana In Memoriam **Obv:** National arms **Rev:** Portrait and dates

Date	Mintage	VF20	XF40	MS60	MS63	MS65
1997	—	PF65 32.00				

KM# 498 20 DOLLARS
31.22 g., 0.999 Silver 1.0027 oz. ASW, 38.5 mm. **Subject:** Year of the Ox - Type II **Obv:** National arms **Rev:** Ox within inner circle with legend **Edge:** Reeded

Date	Mintage	VF20	XF40	MS60	MS63	MS65
1997	—	PF65 32.00				

KM# 515 20 DOLLARS
31.22 g., 0.999 Silver 1.0027 oz. ASW, 38.5 mm. **Subject:** Princess Diana **Obv:** National arms **Rev:** Diana as a young girl **Edge:** Reeded

Date	Mintage	VF20	XF40	MS60	MS63	MS65
1997	—	PF65 35.00				

KM# 518 20 DOLLARS
31.22 g., 0.999 Silver 1.0027 oz. ASW, 38.5 mm. **Subject:** Princess Diana **Obv:** National arms **Rev:** Diana in wedding dress **Edge:** Reeded

Date	Mintage	VF20	XF40	MS60	MS63	MS65
1997	—	PF65 35.00				

KM# 520 20 DOLLARS
31.22 g., 0.999 Silver 1.0027 oz. ASW, 38.5 mm. **Subject:** Princess Diana "England's Rose" **Obv:** National arms **Rev:** Diana with roses **Edge:** Reeded

Date	Mintage	VF20	XF40	MS60	MS63	MS65
1997	—	PF65 35.00				

KM# 523 20 DOLLARS
31.22 g., 0.999 Silver 1.0027 oz. ASW, 38.5 mm. **Subject:** Princess Diana **Obv:** National arms **Rev:** Diana with baby William **Edge:** Reeded

Date	Mintage	VF20	XF40	MS60	MS63	MS65
1997	—	PF65 35.00				

KM# 526 20 DOLLARS
31.22 g., 0.999 Silver 1.0027 oz. ASW, 38.5 mm. **Subject:** Princess Diana **Obv:** National arms **Rev:** Diana with two sons **Edge:** Reeded

Date	Mintage	VF20	XF40	MS60	MS63	MS65
1997	—	PF65 35.00				

KM# 527 20 DOLLARS
31.22 g., 0.999 Silver 1.0027 oz. ASW, 38.5 mm. **Subject:** Princess Diana **Obv:** National arms **Rev:** Royal family **Edge:** Reeded

Date	Mintage	VF20	XF40	MS60	MS63	MS65
1997	—	PF65 35.00				

KM# 528 20 DOLLARS
31.22 g., 0.999 Silver 1.0027 oz. ASW, 38.5 mm. **Subject:** Princess Diana **Obv:** National arms **Rev:** Queen Elizabeth II and Diana **Edge:** Reeded

Date	Mintage	VF20	XF40	MS60	MS63	MS65
1997	—	PF65 30.00				

KM# 533 20 DOLLARS
31.22 g., 0.999 Silver 1.0027 oz. ASW, 38.5 mm. **Subject:** Princess Diana **Obv:** National arms **Rev:** Diana teaching **Edge:** Reeded

Date	Mintage	VF20	XF40	MS60	MS63	MS65
1997	—	PF65 35.00				

KM# 535 20 DOLLARS
31.13 g., 0.999 Silver 0.9999 oz. ASW, 38.6 mm. **Subject:** Princess Diana - Compassion **Obv:** National arms **Rev:** Diana with sick child **Edge:** Reeded

Date	Mintage	VF20	XF40	MS60	MS63	MS65
1997	—	PF65 35.00				

KM# 592 20 DOLLARS
31.22 g., 0.999 Silver 1.0027 oz. ASW, 38.5 mm. **Subject:** Princess Diana **Obv:** National arms **Rev:** Mother Teresa and Diana **Edge:** Reeded

Date	Mintage	VF20	XF40	MS60	MS63	MS65
1997	—	PF65 35.00				

KM# 797 20 DOLLARS
31.98 g., 0.925 Silver 0.9511 oz. ASW, 38.75 mm. **Series:** World's Greatest Conquerors **Obv:** National arms **Rev:** Bust of Cortes facing 3/4 right **Edge:** Reeded

Date	Mintage	VF20	XF40	MS60	MS63	MS65
1997 FM	—	PF65 45.00				

KM# 798 20 DOLLARS
31.98 g., 0.925 Silver 0.9511 oz. ASW, 38.75 mm. **Series:** World's Greatest Conquerors **Obv:** National arms **Rev:** Pizarro in armor standing facing holding sword, sailing ship in background **Edge:** Reeded

Date	Mintage	VF20	XF40	MS60	MS63	MS65
1997 FM	—	PF65 45.00				

KM# 341 20 DOLLARS
31.10 g., 0.999 Silver 0.999 oz. ASW **Subject:** Year of the Tiger **Obv:** National arms **Rev:** Tiger in bamboo

Date	Mintage	VF20	XF40	MS60	MS63	MS65
1998 (1997)	—	PF65 35.00				

KM# 342 20 DOLLARS
24.94 g., Silver **Subject:** Year of the Tiger **Obv:** National arms **Rev:** Tiger lying in bamboo

Date	Mintage	VF20	XF40	MS60	MS63	MS65
1998 (1997)	—	PF65 35.00				

KM# 343 20 DOLLARS
24.94 g., Silver **Subject:** Year of the Tiger **Obv:** National arms **Rev:** Stalking tiger

Date	Mintage	VF20	XF40	MS60	MS63	MS65
1998 (1997)	—	PF65 35.00				

KM# 364 20 DOLLARS
31.10 g., 0.999 Silver 0.999 oz. ASW **Subject:** RMS Titanic **Obv:** National arms **Rev:** Cameo above sinking ship

Date	Mintage	VF20	XF40	MS60	MS63	MS65
1998	25,000	PF65 43.00				

KM# 585 20 DOLLARS
31.10 g., 0.999 Silver 0.999 oz. ASW, 38 mm. **Subject:** Year of the Tiger **Obv:** National arms **Rev:** Tiger above pineapple and flowers within beaded circle **Edge:** Reeded

Date	Mintage	VF20	XF40	MS60	MS63	MS65
1998	—	PF65 38.00				

KM# 586 20 DOLLARS
31.10 g., 0.999 Silver 0.999 oz. ASW, 38 mm. **Subject:** Year of the Tiger **Obv:** National arms **Rev:** Roaring tiger **Edge:** Reeded

Date	Mintage	VF20	XF40	MS60	MS63	MS65
1998	—	PF65 38.00				

KM# 587 20 DOLLARS
31.10 g., 0.999 Silver 0.999 oz. ASW, 38 mm. **Subject:** Year of the Tiger **Obv:** National arms **Rev:** Crouching tiger **Edge:** Reeded

Date	Mintage	VF20	XF40	MS60	MS63	MS65
1998	—	PF65 38.00				

KM# 389 20 DOLLARS
31.10 g., 0.999 Silver 0.999 oz. ASW **Subject:** Year of the Rabbit **Obv:** National arms **Rev:** Rabbit running left within dotted circle

Date	Mintage	VF20	XF40	MS60	MS63	MS65
1999	8,000	PF65 35.00				

KM# 390 20 DOLLARS
31.10 g., 0.999 Silver 0.999 oz. ASW **Subject:** Year of the Rabbit **Obv:** National arms **Rev:** Rabbit sitting

Date	Mintage	VF20	XF40	MS60	MS63	MS65
1999	8,000	PF65 35.00				

KM# 391 20 DOLLARS
31.10 g., 0.999 Silver 0.999 oz. ASW **Subject:** Year of the Rabbit **Obv:** National arms **Rev:** Rabbit running right

Date	Mintage	VF20	XF40	MS60	MS63	MS65
1999	8,000	PF65 35.00				

KM# 418 20 DOLLARS
1.24 g., 0.9999 Gold 0.040 oz. AGW **Subject:** Return of Macao to China **Obv:** National arms **Rev:** Dragon and phoenix **Note:** Similar to 10 Dollars, KM#408.

Date	Mintage	VF20	XF40	MS60	MS63	MS65
1999	25,000	PF65 42.00				

KM# 472 20 DOLLARS
20.17 g., 0.999 Silver 0.6478 oz. ASW, 40.3 mm. **Series:** American History **Obv:** National arms **Rev:** The Alamo and defenders **Edge:** Reeded

Date	Mintage	VF20	XF40	MS60	MS63	MS65
2000	—	PF65 25.00				

KM# 477 20 DOLLARS
20.04 g., 0.999 Silver 0.6437 oz. ASW, 40.3 mm. **Subject:** Admiral David G. Farragut **Obv:** National arms **Rev:** Uniformed bust 1/4 left within flag **Edge:** Reeded

Date	Mintage	VF20	XF40	MS60	MS63	MS65
2000	Est. 20000	PF65 25.00				

KM# 478 20 DOLLARS
20.04 g., 0.999 Silver 0.6437 oz. ASW **Subject:** Surrender of Appomattox **Obv:** National arms **Rev:** Surrender signing scene

Date	Mintage	VF20	XF40	MS60	MS63	MS65
2000	Est. 20000	PF65 25.00				

KM# 479 20 DOLLARS
20.04 g., 0.999 Silver 0.6437 oz. ASW, 39.95 mm. **Subject:** Abraham Lincoln **Obv:** National arms **Rev:** Bust 3/4 right **Edge:** Reeded

Date	Mintage	VF20	XF40	MS60	MS63	MS65
2000	20,000	PF65 22.50				

KM# 480 20 DOLLARS
20.04 g., 0.999 Silver 0.6437 oz. ASW **Subject:** Montgolfiere Balloon **Obv:** National arms **Rev:** First hot air balloon

Date	Mintage	VF20	XF40	MS60	MS63	MS65
2000	—	PF65 25.00				

KM# 481 20 DOLLARS
20.04 g., 0.999 Silver 0.6437 oz. ASW **Subject:** Concorde Supersonic Airliner **Obv:** National arms **Rev:** Plane in flight above runway

Date	Mintage	VF20	XF40	MS60	MS63	MS65
2000	Est. 20000	PF65 25.00				

KM# 482 20 DOLLARS
20.04 g., 0.999 Silver 0.6437 oz. ASW **Subject:** Apollo X **Obv:** National arms **Rev:** Rocket launch, space capsule, large X

Date	Mintage	VF20	XF40	MS60	MS63	MS65
2000	Est. 20000	PF65 25.00				

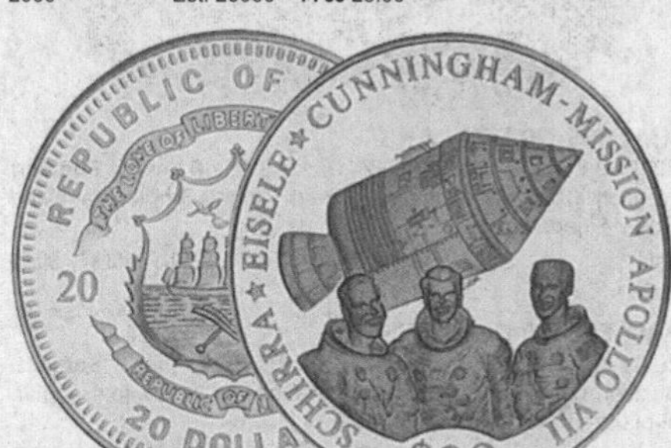

KM# 483 20 DOLLARS
20.04 g., 0.999 Silver 0.6437 oz. ASW **Subject:** Apollo VII **Obv:** National arms **Rev:** Space capsule above half-length busts of Schirra, Eisele, and Cunningham facing

Date	Mintage	VF20	XF40	MS60	MS63	MS65
2000	—	PF65 25.00				

KM# 484 20 DOLLARS
20.04 g., 0.999 Silver 0.6437 oz. ASW **Subject:** STS-1 **Obv:** National arms **Rev:** 3/4-length busts of Young and Crippen facing with shuttle model

Date	Mintage	VF20	XF40	MS60	MS63	MS65
2000	Est. 20000	PF65 25.00				

KM# 485 20 DOLLARS
20.04 g., 0.999 Silver 0.6437 oz. ASW **Subject:** Skylab I **Obv:** National arms **Rev:** Half-length busts of Conrad, Kerwin, and Weitz facing below Skylab

Date	Mintage	VF20	XF40	MS60	MS63	MS65
2000	Est. 20000	PF65 25.00				

KM# 486 20 DOLLARS
20.04 g., 0.999 Silver 0.6437 oz. ASW **Series:** Olympics **Obv:** National arms **Rev:** Hurdler

Date	Mintage	VF20	XF40	MS60	MS63	MS65
2000	Est. 20000	PF65 25.00				

KM# 487 20 DOLLARS
20.04 g., 0.999 Silver 0.6437 oz. ASW **Series:** Olympics **Obv:** National arms **Rev:** Equestrian

Date	Mintage	VF20	XF40	MS60	MS63	MS65
2000	Est. 20000	PF65 25.00				

KM# 488 20 DOLLARS
20.04 g., 0.999 Silver 0.6437 oz. ASW **Series:** Olympics **Obv:** National arms **Rev:** Two basketball players in front of flags

Date	Mintage	VF20	XF40	MS60	MS63	MS65
2000	Est. 20000	PF65 25.00				

KM# 489 20 DOLLARS
20.04 g., 0.999 Silver 0.6437 oz. ASW **Series:** Olympics **Obv:** National arms **Rev:** Three cyclists

Date	Mintage	VF20	XF40	MS60	MS63	MS65
2000	Est. 20000	PF65 25.00				

KM# 490 20 DOLLARS
20.04 g., 0.999 Silver 0.6437 oz. ASW **Series:** Olympics **Obv:** National arms **Rev:** Swimmer, cyclist, and speed walker

Date	Mintage	VF20	XF40	MS60	MS63	MS65
2000	Est. 20000	PF65 25.00				

KM# 504 20 DOLLARS
20.00 g., 0.999 Silver 0.6424 oz. ASW, 40.4 mm. **Subject:** American History **Obv:** National arms **Rev:** Treaty of Paris signing scene **Edge:** Reeded **Note:** The American Mint is not an actual mint.

Date	Mintage	VF20	XF40	MS60	MS63	MS65
2000	20,000	PF65 35.00				

KM# 505 20 DOLLARS
20.00 g., 0.999 Silver 0.6424 oz. ASW, 40.4 mm. **Subject:** American History - Civil War **Obv:** National arms **Rev:** Bombardment of Fort Sumter scene **Edge:** Reeded **Note:** The American Mint is not an actual mint.

Date	Mintage	VF20	XF40	MS60	MS63	MS65
2000	20,000	PF65 35.00				

KM# 506 20 DOLLARS
20.00 g., 0.999 Silver 0.6424 oz. ASW, 40.4 mm. **Subject:** American History **Obv:** National arms **Rev:** Bust facing **Edge:** Reeded **Note:** The American Mint is not an actual mint.

Date	Mintage	VF20	XF40	MS60	MS63	MS65
2000	20,000	PF65 32.00				

KM# 507 20 DOLLARS
20.00 g., 0.999 Silver 0.6424 oz. ASW, 40.4 mm. **Subject:** American History **Obv:** National arms **Rev:** Busts of astronauts Young and Crippen with Space Shuttle model **Edge:** Reeded **Note:** The American Mint is not an actual mint.

Date	Mintage	VF20	XF40	MS60	MS63	MS65
2000	20,000	PF65 35.00				

KM# 508 20 DOLLARS
31.10 g., 0.999 Silver 0.999 oz. ASW, 40.7 mm. **Subject:** Millennium **Obv:** Seated Liberty **Rev:** Y2K design **Edge:** Reeded **Note:** The American Mint is not an actual mint.

Date	Mintage	VF20	XF40	MS60	MS63	MS65
2000	2,000	—	—	—	—	37.00

KM# 509.1 20 DOLLARS
31.10 g., 0.999 Silver 0.999 oz. ASW, 39 mm. **Subject:** Millennium **Obv:** National arms **Rev:** Woman with hourglass and dove **Edge:** Reeded **Note:** The American Mint is not an actual mint.

Date	Mintage	VF20	XF40	MS60	MS63	MS65
2000	—	—	—	—	—	37.00

KM# 509.2 20 DOLLARS
31.10 g., 0.999 Silver 0.999 oz. ASW, 39 mm. **Subject:** Millennium **Obv:** National arms **Rev:** Multicolor woman with hourglass and dove **Edge:** Reeded **Note:** The American Mint is not an actual mint.

Date	Mintage	VF20	XF40	MS60	MS63	MS65
2000	—	—	—	—	—	40.00

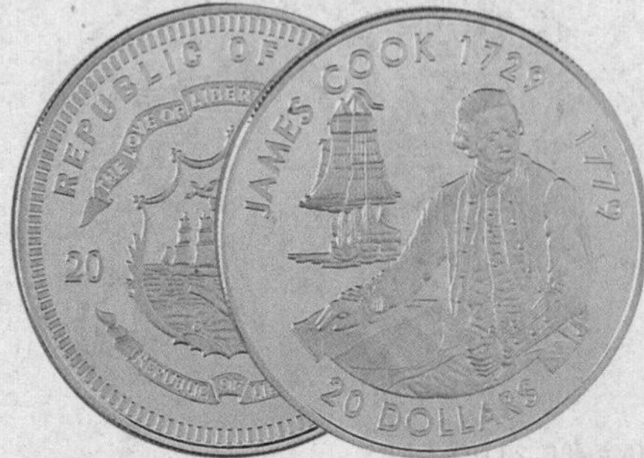

KM# 574 20 DOLLARS
20.00 g., 0.999 Silver 0.6424 oz. ASW, 40.1 mm. **Subject:** Captain Cook **Obv:** National arms **Rev:** Seated Capt. Cook at right, his ship at left **Edge:** Reeded

Date	Mintage	VF20	XF40	MS60	MS63	MS65
2000	—	PF65 25.00				

KM# 575 20 DOLLARS
31.00 g., 0.999 Silver 0.9957 oz. ASW, 38.7 mm. **Obv:** National arms **Rev:** Hippopotamus **Edge:** Reeded

Date	Mintage	VF20	XF40	MS60	MS63	MS65
2000	—	PF65 33.00				

KM# 576 20 DOLLARS
19.85 g., 0.999 Silver 0.6376 oz. ASW, 40.3 mm. **Subject:** Olympics **Obv:** National arms **Rev:** Volleyball player with city view behind **Edge:** Reeded

Date	Mintage	VF20	XF40	MS60	MS63	MS65
2000	—	PF65 27.00				

KM# 577 20 DOLLARS
19.85 g., 0.999 Silver 0.6376 oz. ASW, 40.3 mm. **Subject:** Olympics **Obv:** National arms **Rev:** High jumper and Australian map **Edge:** Reeded

Date	Mintage	VF20	XF40	MS60	MS63	MS65
2000	—	PF65 27.00				

KM# 590 20 DOLLARS
20.00 g., 0.999 Silver 0.6424 oz. ASW, 40 mm. **Obv:** National arms **Rev:** Titanic steaming right **Edge:** Reeded

Date	Mintage	VF20	XF40	MS60	MS63	MS65
2000	—	PF65 27.50				

KM# 591 20 DOLLARS
20.00 g., 0.999 Silver 0.6424 oz. ASW, 40 mm. **Subject:** Apollo XVIII and Soyuz XIX **Obv:** National arms **Rev:** Two space capsules about to link up **Edge:** Reeded

Date	Mintage	VF20	XF40	MS60	MS63	MS65
2000	—	PF65 27.50				

KM# 595 20 DOLLARS
20.00 g., 0.999 Silver 0.6424 oz. ASW, 40 mm. **Subject:** Aviation **Obv:** National arms **Rev:** Wright Brothers airplane **Edge:** Reeded

Date	Mintage	VF20	XF40	MS60	MS63	MS65
2000	20,000	PF65 27.50				

KM# 596 20 DOLLARS
20.00 g., 0.999 Silver 0.6424 oz. ASW, 40 mm. **Subject:** Aviation **Obv:** National arms **Rev:** Russian Witiaz four-engine bi-plane **Edge:** Reeded

Date	Mintage	VF20	XF40	MS60	MS63	MS65
2000	20,000	PF65 27.50				

KM# 597 20 DOLLARS
20.00 g., 0.999 Silver 0.6424 oz. ASW, 40 mm. **Subject:** Aviation **Obv:** National arms **Rev:** Curtiss R3C-2 floating bi-plane **Edge:** Reeded

Date	Mintage	VF20	XF40	MS60	MS63	MS65
2000	20,000	PF65 27.50				

KM# 598 20 DOLLARS
20.00 g., 0.999 Silver 0.6424 oz. ASW, 40 mm. **Subject:** Aviation **Obv:** National arms **Rev:** Grumman F3F bi-plane fighter **Edge:** Reeded

Date	Mintage	VF20	XF40	MS60	MS63	MS65
2000	20,000	PF65 35.00				

KM# 599 20 DOLLARS
20.00 g., 0.999 Silver 0.6424 oz. ASW, 40 mm. **Subject:** Aviation **Obv:** National arms **Rev:** Space Station **Edge:** Reeded

Date	Mintage	VF20	XF40	MS60	MS63	MS65
2000	20,000	PF65 27.50				

KM# 609 20 DOLLARS
19.90 g., 0.999 Silver 0.6392 oz. ASW, 40.2 mm. **Obv:** National arms **Rev:** United States Bill of Rights **Edge:** Reeded

Date	Mintage	VF20	XF40	MS60	MS63	MS65
2000	20,000	PF65 20.00				

KM# 610 20 DOLLARS
20.00 g., 0.999 Silver 0.6424 oz. ASW, 40.2 mm. **Obv:** National arms **Rev:** Louisiana Purchase map on flag behind portraits of Jefferson, Lewis and Clark **Edge:** Reeded

Date	Mintage	VF20	XF40	MS60	MS63	MS65
2000	—	PF65 20.00				

KM# 613 20 DOLLARS
31.10 g., 0.999 Silver 0.999 oz. ASW, 39 mm. **Subject:** "King of the Cowboys" Roy Rogers **Obv:** National arms **Obv. Legend:** ROY ROGERS, King of the Cowboys below **Rev:** Bust 1/4 left **Edge:** Reeded

Date	Mintage	VF20	XF40	MS60	MS63	MS65
2000	1,000	PF65 32.50				

KM# 614 20 DOLLARS
31.10 g., 0.999 Silver 0.999 oz. ASW, 39 mm. **Subject:** Roy Rogers **Obv:** National arms **Obv. Legend:** ROY ROGERS, Happy Trails to You! below **Rev:** Bust 1/4 left **Edge:** Reeded

Date	Mintage	VF20	XF40	MS60	MS63	MS65
2000	1,000	PF65 32.50				

KM# 636 20 DOLLARS
31.10 g., 0.999 Silver 0.9989 oz. ASW, 38.6 mm. **Obv:** National arms **Rev:** American Quarter Horse **Edge:** Reeded

Date	Mintage	VF20	XF40	MS60	MS63	MS65
2000	—	PF65 30.00				

KM# 637 20 DOLLARS
20.10 g., 0.999 Silver 0.6456 oz. ASW, 40.2 mm. **Obv:** National arms **Rev:** Berlin buildings **Edge:** Reeded

Date	Mintage	VF20	XF40	MS60	MS63	MS65
2000	—	PF65 27.50				

KM# 638 20 DOLLARS
20.10 g., 0.999 Silver 0.6456 oz. ASW, 40.2 mm. **Obv:** National arms **Rev:** Brussels landmarks **Edge:** Reeded

Date	Mintage	VF20	XF40	MS60	MS63	MS65
2000	—	PF65 27.50				

KM# 639 20 DOLLARS
20.10 g., 0.999 Silver 0.6456 oz. ASW, 20.1 mm. **Obv:** National arms **Rev:** London buildings **Edge:** Reeded

Date	Mintage	VF20	XF40	MS60	MS63	MS65
2000	—	PF65 27.50				

KM# 640 20 DOLLARS
20.10 g., 0.999 Silver 0.6456 oz. ASW, 40.2 mm. **Obv:** National arms **Rev:** Madrid buildings **Edge:** Reeded

Date	Mintage	VF20	XF40	MS60	MS63	MS65
2000	—	PF65 27.50				

KM# 641 20 DOLLARS
20.10 g., 0.999 Silver 0.6456 oz. ASW, 40.2 mm. **Obv:** National arms **Rev:** Rome buildings **Edge:** Reeded

Date	Mintage	VF20	XF40	MS60	MS63	MS65
2000	—	PF65 27.50				

KM# 642 20 DOLLARS
20.10 g., 0.999 Silver 0.6456 oz. ASW, 40.2 mm. **Obv:** National arms **Rev:** Stockholm buildings **Edge:** Reeded

Date	Mintage	VF20	XF40	MS60	MS63	MS65
2000	—	PF65 27.50				

KM# 646 20 DOLLARS
19.91 g., 0.999 Silver 0.6395 oz. ASW, 40 mm. **Obv:** National arms **Rev:** Sailing ship "Sovereign of the Seas" **Rev. Legend:** SOVEREIGN OF THE SEAS **Edge:** Reeded

Date	Mintage	VF20	XF40	MS60	MS63	MS65
2000	—	PF65 32.50				

KM# 647 20 DOLLARS
19.91 g., 0.999 Silver 0.6395 oz. ASW, 40 mm. **Obv:** National arms **Rev:** Sailing ship "Pamir" **Rev. Legend:** PAMIR **Edge:** Reeded

Date	Mintage	VF20	XF40	MS60	MS63	MS65
2000	—	PF65 32.50				

KM# 648 20 DOLLARS
19.91 g., 0.999 Silver 0.6395 oz. ASW, 40 mm. **Obv:** National arms **Rev:** HMS Victory, Nelson's flag ship **Edge:** Reeded

Date	Mintage	VF20	XF40	MS60	MS63	MS65
2000	—	PF65 32.50				

KM# 649 20 DOLLARS
19.91 g., 0.999 Silver 0.6395 oz. ASW, 40 mm. **Obv:** National arms **Rev:** LZ 127 Graf Zeppelin **Edge:** Reeded

Date	Mintage	VF20	XF40	MS60	MS63	MS65
2000	—	PF65 40.00				

KM# 655 20 DOLLARS
20.60 g., 0.999 Silver 0.6616 oz. ASW, 40.3 mm. **Obv:** National arms **Rev:** SS Europa **Edge:** Reeded

Date	Mintage	VF20	XF40	MS60	MS63	MS65
2000	—	PF65 22.50				

KM# 656 20 DOLLARS
20.60 g., 0.999 Silver 0.6616 oz. ASW, 40.3 mm. **Obv:** National arms **Rev:** "Royal William" ship **Edge:** Reeded

Date	Mintage	VF20	XF40	MS60	MS63	MS65
2000	—	PF65 22.50				

KM# 658 20 DOLLARS
20.60 g., 0.999 Silver 0.6616 oz. ASW, 40.3 mm. **Obv:** National arms **Rev:** The "Great Eastern" ship **Edge:** Reeded

Date	Mintage	VF20	XF40	MS60	MS63	MS65
2000	—	PF65 22.50				

KM# 660 20 DOLLARS
20.60 g., 0.999 Silver 0.6616 oz. ASW, 40.3 mm. **Obv:** National arms **Rev:** Signing of the Mayflower Compact **Edge:** Reeded

Date	Mintage	VF20	XF40	MS60	MS63	MS65
2000	—	PF65 22.50				

KM# 661 20 DOLLARS
20.60 g., 0.999 Silver 0.6616 oz. ASW, 40.3 mm. **Obv:** National arms **Rev:** R.M.S. Queen Mary **Edge:** Reeded

Date	Mintage	VF20	XF40	MS60	MS63	MS65
2000	—	PF65 24.00				

KM# 663 20 DOLLARS
20.22 g., 0.999 Silver 0.6494 oz. ASW, 40 mm. **Obv:** National arms **Rev:** Battle of the Monitor and the Virginia **Edge:** Reeded

Date	Mintage	VF20	XF40	MS60	MS63	MS65
2000	20,000	PF65 32.50				

KM# 697 20 DOLLARS
31.10 g., 0.999 Silver 0.999 oz. ASW, 39 mm. **Obv:** National arms **Rev:** Roy Rogers **Edge:** Reeded

Date	Mintage	VF20	XF40	MS60	MS63	MS65
2000	1,000	PF65 37.50				

KM# 707 20 DOLLARS
20.17 g., 0.999 Silver 0.6478 oz. ASW, 40.3 mm. **Obv:** National arms **Rev:** Boston Tea Party Scene **Edge:** Reeded

Date	Mintage	VF20	XF40	MS60	MS63	MS65
2000	—	PF65 27,50				

KM# 710 20 DOLLARS
20.00 g., 0.999 Silver 0.6424 oz. ASW, 40.3 mm. **Subject:** American History Series **Obv:** National arms **Rev:** Columbus going ashore **Edge:** Reeded

Date	Mintage	VF20	XF40	MS60	MS63	MS65
2000	20,000	PF65 22.50				

KM# 711 20 DOLLARS
20.00 g., 0.999 Silver 0.6424 oz. ASW, 40.3 mm. **Subject:** American History Series **Obv:** National arms **Rev:** Declaration of Independence signers with document in background **Edge:** Reeded

Date	Mintage	VF20	XF40	MS60	MS63	MS65
2000	20,000	PF65 22.50				

KM# 712 20 DOLLARS
20.00 g., 0.999 Silver 0.6424 oz. ASW, 40.3 mm. **Subject:** American History Series **Obv:** National arms **Rev:** Transcontinental Railroad Golden Spike ceremony scene **Edge:** Reeded

Date	Mintage	VF20	XF40	MS60	MS63	MS65
2000	20,000	PF65 22.50				

KM# 713 20 DOLLARS
20.00 g., 0.999 Silver 0.6424 oz. ASW, 40.3 mm. **Subject:** American History Series **Obv:** National arms **Rev:** Great Depression, Roosevelt visiting with people in a bread line **Edge:** Reeded

Date	Mintage	VF20	XF40	MS60	MS63	MS65
2000	20,000	PF65 22.50				

KM# 714 20 DOLLARS
20.00 g., 0.999 Silver 0.6424 oz. ASW, 40.3 mm. **Subject:** American History Series **Obv:** National arms **Rev:** Victory over Japan, surrender ceremony on the USS Missouri **Edge:** Reeded

Date	Mintage	VF20	XF40	MS60	MS63	MS65
2000	20,000	PF65 22.50				

KM# 728 20 DOLLARS
20.00 g., 0.999 Silver 0.6424 oz. ASW, 40 mm. **Rev:** Richard Nixon bust

Date	Mintage	VF20	XF40	MS60	MS63	MS65
2000	20,000	PF65 25.00				

KM# 729 20 DOLLARS
20.00 g., 0.999 Silver 0.6424 oz. ASW **Obv:** Shield **Rev:** George Washington bust

Date	Mintage	VF20	XF40	MS60	MS63	MS65
2000	20,000	PF65 22.50				

KM# 736 20 DOLLARS
Silver **Subject:** XXVII Olympic Games - Sydney **Rev:** Kayaker **Edge:** Reeded

Date	Mintage	VF20	XF40	MS60	MS63	MS65
2000	—	—	—	—	—	27.00

KM# 838 20 DOLLARS
31.11 g., 0.999 Silver 0.999 oz. ASW **Subject:** U.S. Civil War **Rev:** Battle of Shiloh, 1862

Date	Mintage	VF20	XF40	MS60	MS63	MS65
2000	—	PF65 27.00				

KM# 839 20 DOLLARS
31.11 g., 0.999 Silver 0.999 oz. ASW **Subject:** U.S. Civil War **Rev:** Crossed Confederate and U.S. Flags

Date	Mintage	VF20	XF40	MS60	MS63	MS65
2000	—	PF65 27.00				

KM# 870 20 DOLLARS
20.00 g., 0.999 Silver 0.6424 oz. ASW, 40 mm. **Rev:** John Adams bust

Date	Mintage	VF20	XF40	MS60	MS63	MS65
2000	20,000	PF65 22.50				

KM# 871 20 DOLLARS
20.00 g., 0.999 Silver 0.6424 oz. ASW, 40 mm. **Rev:** Thomas Jefferson bust

Date	Mintage	VF20	XF40	MS60	MS63	MS65
2000	20,000	PF65 22.50				

KM# 872 20 DOLLARS
20.00 g., 0.999 Silver 0.6424 oz. ASW, 40 mm. **Rev:** James Madison bust

Date	Mintage	VF20	XF40	MS60	MS63	MS65
2000	20,000	PF65 22.50				

KM# 873 20 DOLLARS
20.00 g., 0.999 Silver 0.6424 oz. ASW, 40 mm. **Rev:** James Monroe bust

Date	Mintage	VF20	XF40	MS60	MS63	MS65
2000	20,000	PF65 22.50				

KM# 874 20 DOLLARS
20.00 g., 0.999 Silver 0.6424 oz. ASW, 40 mm. **Rev:** John Quincey Adams bust

Date	Mintage	VF20	XF40	MS60	MS63	MS65
2000	20,000	PF65 22.50				

KM# 875 20 DOLLARS
20.00 g., 0.999 Silver 0.6424 oz. ASW, 40 mm. **Rev:** Andrew Jackson bust

Date	Mintage	VF20	XF40	MS60	MS63	MS65
2000	20,000	PF65 22.50				

KM# 876 20 DOLLARS
20.00 g., 0.999 Silver 0.6424 oz. ASW, 40 mm. **Rev:** Martin van Buren bust

Date	Mintage	VF20	XF40	MS60	MS63	MS65
2000	20,000	PF65 22.50				

KM# 877 20 DOLLARS
20.00 g., 0.999 Silver 0.6424 oz. ASW, 40 mm. **Rev:** William Henry Harrison bust

Date	Mintage	VF20	XF40	MS60	MS63	MS65
2000	20,000	PF65 22.50				

KM# 878 20 DOLLARS
20.00 g., 0.999 Silver 0.6424 oz. ASW, 40 mm. **Rev:** John Tyler bust

Date	Mintage	VF20	XF40	MS60	MS63	MS65
2000	20,000	PF65 22.50				

KM# 879 20 DOLLARS
20.00 g., 0.999 Silver 0.6424 oz. ASW, 40 mm. **Rev:** James K. Polk bust

Date	Mintage	VF20	XF40	MS60	MS63	MS65
2000	20,000	PF65 22.50				

KM# 880 20 DOLLARS
20.00 g., 0.999 Silver 0.6424 oz. ASW, 40 mm. **Rev:** Zachary Taylor bust

Date	Mintage	VF20	XF40	MS60	MS63	MS65
2000	20,000	PF65 22.50				

KM# 881 20 DOLLARS
20.00 g., 0.999 Silver 0.6424 oz. ASW, 40 mm. **Rev:** Millard Fillmore bust

Date	Mintage	VF20	XF40	MS60	MS63	MS65
2000	20,000	PF65 22.50				

KM# 882 20 DOLLARS
20.00 g., 0.999 Silver 0.6424 oz. ASW, 40 mm. **Rev:** Franklin Pierce bust

Date	Mintage	VF20	XF40	MS60	MS63	MS65
2000	20,000	PF65 22.50				

KM# 883 20 DOLLARS
20.00 g., 0.999 Silver 0.6424 oz. ASW, 40 mm. **Rev:** James Buchanan bust

Date	Mintage	VF20	XF40	MS60	MS63	MS65
2000	20,000	PF65 22.50				

KM# 884 20 DOLLARS
20.00 g., 0.999 Silver 0.6424 oz. ASW, 40 mm. **Rev:** Andrew Johnson bust

Date	Mintage	VF20	XF40	MS60	MS63	MS65
2000	20,000	PF65 22.50				

KM# 885 20 DOLLARS
20.00 g., 0.999 Silver 0.6424 oz. ASW, 40 mm. **Rev:** Ulysses S. Grant bust

Date	Mintage	VF20	XF40	MS60	MS63	MS65
2000	20,000	PF65 22.50				

KM# 886 20 DOLLARS
20.00 g., 0.999 Silver 0.6424 oz. ASW, 40 mm. **Rev:** Rutherford B. Hayes bust

Date	Mintage	VF20	XF40	MS60	MS63	MS65
2000	20,000	PF65 22.50				

KM# 887 20 DOLLARS
20.00 g., 0.999 Silver 0.6424 oz. ASW, 40 mm. **Rev:** James A. Garfield bust

Date	Mintage	VF20	XF40	MS60	MS63	MS65
2000	20,000	PF65 22.50				

KM# 888 20 DOLLARS
20.00 g., 0.999 Silver 0.6424 oz. ASW, 40 mm. **Rev:** Chester Arthur bust

Date	Mintage	VF20	XF40	MS60	MS63	MS65
2000	20,000	PF65 22.50				

KM# 889 20 DOLLARS
20.00 g., 0.999 Silver 0.6424 oz. ASW, 40 mm. **Rev:** Grover Cleveland bust

Date	Mintage	VF20	XF40	MS60	MS63	MS65
2000	20,000	PF65 22.50				

KM# 890 20 DOLLARS
20.00 g., 0.999 Silver 0.6424 oz. ASW, 40 mm. **Rev:** Benjamin Harrison bust

Date	Mintage	VF20	XF40	MS60	MS63	MS65
2000	20,000	PF65 22.50				

KM# 891 20 DOLLARS
20.00 g., 0.999 Silver 0.6424 oz. ASW, 40 mm. **Rev:** William McKinley bust

Date	Mintage	VF20	XF40	MS60	MS63	MS65
2000	20,000	PF65 22.50				

KM# 892 20 DOLLARS
20.00 g., 0.999 Silver 0.6424 oz. ASW, 40 mm. **Rev:** Theodore Roosevelt bust

Date	Mintage	VF20	XF40	MS60	MS63	MS65
2000	20,000	PF65 22.50				

KM# 893 20 DOLLARS
20.00 g., 0.999 Silver 0.6424 oz. ASW, 40 mm. **Rev:** William Howard Taft bust

Date	Mintage	VF20	XF40	MS60	MS63	MS65
2000	20,000	PF65 22.50				

KM# 894 20 DOLLARS
20.00 g., 0.999 Silver 0.6424 oz. ASW, 40 mm. **Rev:** Woodrow Wilson

Date	Mintage	VF20	XF40	MS60	MS63	MS65
2000	20,000	PF65 22.50				

KM# 895 20 DOLLARS
20.00 g., 0.999 Silver 0.6424 oz. ASW, 40 mm. **Rev:** Warren G. Harding bust

Date	Mintage	VF20	XF40	MS60	MS63	MS65
2000	20,000	PF65 22.50				

KM# 896 20 DOLLARS
20.00 g., 0.999 Silver 0.6424 oz. ASW, 40 mm. **Rev:** Calvin Coolidge bust

Date	Mintage	VF20	XF40	MS60	MS63	MS65
2000	20,000	PF65 22.50				

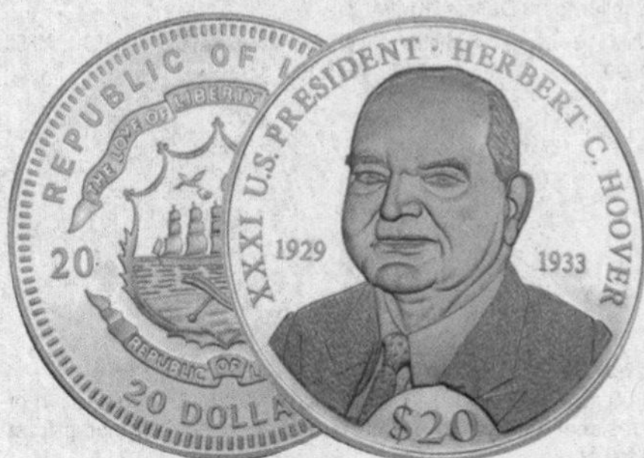

KM# 897 20 DOLLARS
20.00 g., 0.999 Silver 0.6424 oz. ASW, 40 mm. **Rev:** Herbert Hoover bust

Date	Mintage	VF20	XF40	MS60	MS63	MS65
2000	20,000	PF65 22.50				

KM# 898 20 DOLLARS
20.00 g., 0.999 Silver 0.6424 oz. ASW, 40 mm. **Rev:** Franklin D. Roosevelt bust

Date	Mintage	VF20	XF40	MS60	MS63	MS65
2000	20,000	PF65 22.50				

KM# 899 20 DOLLARS
20.00 g., 0.999 Silver 0.6424 oz. ASW, 40 mm. **Rev:** Dwight D. Eisenhower bust

Date	Mintage	VF20	XF40	MS60	MS63	MS65
2000	20,000	PF65 22.50				

KM# 900 20 DOLLARS
20.00 g., 0.999 Silver 0.6424 oz. ASW, 40 mm. **Rev:** John F. Kennedy bust

Date	Mintage	VF20	XF40	MS60	MS63	MS65
2000	20,000	PF65 22.50				

KM# 901 20 DOLLARS
20.00 g., 0.999 Silver 0.6424 oz. ASW, 40 mm. **Rev:** Lyndon B. Johnson bust

Date	Mintage	VF20	XF40	MS60	MS63	MS65
2000	20,000	PF65 22.50				

KM# 902 20 DOLLARS
20.00 g., 0.999 Silver 0.6424 oz. ASW, 40 mm. **Rev:** Gerald R. Ford bust

Date	Mintage	VF20	XF40	MS60	MS63	MS65
2000	20,000	PF65 22.50				

KM# 903 20 DOLLARS
20.00 g., 0.999 Silver 0.6424 oz. ASW, 40 mm. **Rev:** James E. Carter bust

Date	Mintage	VF20	XF40	MS60	MS63	MS65
2000	20,000	PF65 22.50				

KM# 904 20 DOLLARS
20.00 g., 0.999 Silver 0.6424 oz. ASW, 40 mm. **Rev:** Ronald Reagan bust

Date	Mintage	VF20	XF40	MS60	MS63	MS65
2000	20,000	PF65 22.50				

KM# 905 20 DOLLARS
20.00 g., 0.999 Silver 0.6424 oz. ASW, 40 mm. **Rev:** George H. W. Bush bust

Date	Mintage	VF20	XF40	MS60	MS63	MS65
2000	20,000	PF65 22.50				

KM# 906 20 DOLLARS
20.00 g., 0.999 Silver 0.6424 oz. ASW, 40 mm. **Rev:** Bill Clinton bust

Date	Mintage	VF20	XF40	MS60	MS63	MS65
2000	20,000	PF65 27.00				

KM# 907 20 DOLLARS
20.00 g., 0.999 Silver 0.6424 oz. ASW, 40 mm. **Subject:** Civil War - Flags of the C.S.A. **Rev:** Three flags

Date	Mintage	VF20	XF40	MS60	MS63	MS65
2000	20,000	PF65 22.50				

KM# 908 20 DOLLARS
20.00 g., 0.999 Silver 0.6424 oz. ASW, 40 mm. **Subject:** Civil War - Joseph E. Johnston **Rev:** Bust, flag in background

Date	Mintage	VF20	XF40	MS60	MS63	MS65
2000	20,000	PF65 22.50				

KM# 909 20 DOLLARS
20.00 g., 0.999 Silver 0.6424 oz. ASW, 40 mm. **Subject:** Civil War - Winfield S. Hancock **Rev:** Bust, flag in background

Date	Mintage	VF20	XF40	MS60	MS63	MS65
2000	20,000	PF65 22.50				

KM# 910 20 DOLLARS
20.00 g., 0.999 Silver 0.6424 oz. ASW, 40 mm. **Subject:** Civil War - George G. Meade **Rev:** Bust, flag in background

Date	Mintage	VF20	XF40	MS60	MS63	MS65
2000	20,000	PF65 22.50				

KM# 911 20 DOLLARS
20.00 g., 0.999 Silver 0.6424 oz. ASW, 40 mm. **Subject:** Civil War - Clarissa Barton **Rev:** Bust

Date	Mintage	VF20	XF40	MS60	MS63	MS65
2000	20,000	PF65 22.50				

KM# 1031 20 DOLLARS
20.11 g., 0.925 Silver 0.5981 oz. ASW, 40 mm. **Subject:** R.M.S. Mauretania

Date	Mintage	VF20	XF40	MS60	MS63	MS65
2000	—	PF65 27.00				

KM# 1032 20 DOLLARS
20.15 g., 0.925 Silver 0.5992 oz. ASW, 40 mm. **Subject:** R.M.S. Lucitania

Date	Mintage	VF20	XF40	MS60	MS63	MS65
2000	—	PF65 27.00				

KM# 21 25 DOLLARS
23.31 g., 0.900 Gold 0.6745 oz. AGW **Subject:** 70th Birthday of President Tubman **Obv:** Head 3/4 left above date flanked by stars **Rev:** Trees and sun above value flanked by stars

Date	Mintage	VF20	XF40	MS60	MS63	MS65
1965 B	3,000	—	—	—	1,000	1,100

KM# 21a 25 DOLLARS
23.31 g., 0.999 Gold 0.7487 oz. AGW **Obv:** Head 3/4 left above date flanked by stars **Rev:** Tree and sun above value flanked by stars

Date	Mintage	VF20	XF40	MS60	MS63	MS65
1965 B L	100	PF65 1,200				

KM# 23 25 DOLLARS
23.31 g., 0.900 Gold 0.6745 oz. AGW **Subject:** 75th Birthday of President Tubman **Obv:** Birthplace of President **Rev:** Head facing above dates

Date	Mintage	VF20	XF40	MS60	MS63	MS65
ND-1970 B	—	PF63 925	PF65 1,000			

KM# 28 25 DOLLARS
23.31 g., 0.900 Gold 0.6745 oz. AGW **Subject:** Sesquicentennial - Founding of Liberia **Obv:** Bust 1/4 left **Rev:** Man in canoe below tower and trees with value above

Date	Mintage	VF20	XF40	MS60	MS63	MS65
ND-1972 B	3,000	PF63 925	PF65 1,000			

KM# 323 25 DOLLARS
77.76 g., 0.999 Silver 2.4975 oz. ASW **Subject:** 25th Anniversary - Standard Catalog of World Coins **Obv:** National arms **Rev:** Children, globe and world coins

Date	Mintage	VF20	XF40	MS60	MS63	MS65
1997	2,500	PF65 90.00				

KM# 512 25 DOLLARS
0.73 g., 0.999 Gold 0.0234 oz. AGW, 11.1 mm. **Obv:** National arms **Rev:** Bust right **Rev. Legend:** NOFRETETE **Edge:** Reeded **Note:** The American Mint is not an actual mint.

Date	Mintage	VF20	XF40	MS60	MS63	MS65
2000	—	PF65 45.00				

KM# 623 25 DOLLARS
0.73 g., 0.999 Gold 0.0234 oz. AGW, 11.1 mm. **Obv:** National arms **Rev:** Martin Luther **Edge:** Reeded

Date	Mintage	VF20	XF40	MS60	MS63	MS65
2000	—	PF65 45.00				

KM# 624 25 DOLLARS
0.73 g., 0.999 Gold 0.0234 oz. AGW, 11.1 mm. **Obv:** National arms **Rev:** Queen Elizabeth II **Edge:** Reeded

Date	Mintage	VF20	XF40	MS60	MS63	MS65
2000	—	PF65 45.00				

KM# 625 25 DOLLARS
0.73 g., 0.999 Gold 0.0234 oz. AGW, 11.1 mm. **Obv:** National arms **Rev:** Mozart **Edge:** Reeded

Date	Mintage	VF20	XF40	MS60	MS63	MS65
2000	—	PF65 45.00				

KM# 626 25 DOLLARS
0.73 g., 0.999 Gold 0.0234 oz. AGW, 11.1 mm. **Obv:** National arms **Rev:** Christopher Columbus **Edge:** Reeded

Date	Mintage	VF20	XF40	MS60	MS63	MS65
2000	—	PF65 45.00				

KM# 627 25 DOLLARS
0.73 g., 0.999 Gold 0.0234 oz. AGW, 11.1 mm. **Obv:** National arms **Rev:** Tutankhamen **Edge:** Reeded

Date	Mintage	VF20	XF40	MS60	MS63	MS65
2000	—	PF65 45.00				

KM# 628 25 DOLLARS
0.73 g., 0.999 Gold 0.0234 oz. AGW, 11.1 mm. **Obv:** National arms **Rev:** Charlemagne **Edge:** Reeded

Date	Mintage	VF20	XF40	MS60	MS63	MS65
2000	—	PF65 45.00				

KM# 629 25 DOLLARS
0.73 g., 0.999 Gold 0.0234 oz. AGW, 11.1 mm. **Obv:** National arms **Rev:** Peter the Great **Edge:** Reeded

Date	Mintage	VF20	XF40	MS60	MS63	MS65
2000	—	PF65 45.00				

KM# 630 25 DOLLARS
0.73 g., 0.999 Gold 0.0234 oz. AGW, 11.1 mm. **Obv:** National arms **Rev:** Mikhail Gorbachev **Edge:** Reeded

Date	Mintage	VF20	XF40	MS60	MS63	MS65
2000	—	PF65 45.00				

KM# 631 25 DOLLARS
0.73 g., 0.999 Gold 0.0234 oz. AGW, 11.1 mm. **Obv:** National arms **Rev:** Julius Caesar **Edge:** Reeded

Date	Mintage	VF20	XF40	MS60	MS63	MS65
2000	—	PF65 45.00				

KM# 632 25 DOLLARS
0.73 g., 0.999 Gold 0.0234 oz. AGW, 11.1 mm. **Obv:** National arms **Rev:** George Washington **Edge:** Reeded

Date	Mintage	VF20	XF40	MS60	MS63	MS65
2000	—	PF65 45.00				

KM# 633 25 DOLLARS
0.73 g., 0.999 Gold 0.0234 oz. AGW, 11.1 mm. **Obv:** National arms **Rev:** Mahatma Gandhi **Edge:** Reeded

Date	Mintage	VF20	XF40	MS60	MS63	MS65
2000	—	PF65 45.00				

KM# 634 25 DOLLARS
0.73 g., 0.999 Gold 0.0234 oz. AGW, 11.1 mm. **Obv:** National arms **Rev:** Joan of Arc **Edge:** Reeded

Date	Mintage	VF20	XF40	MS60	MS63	MS65
2000	—	PF65 55.00				

KM# 22 30 DOLLARS
15.00 g., 0.900 Gold 0.434 oz. AGW **Subject:** 70th Birthday of President Tubman **Obv:** National arms **Rev:** Bust left

Date	Mintage	VF20	XF40	MS60	MS63	MS65
1965	400	PF65 700				

KM# 69 50 DOLLARS
155.52 g., 0.999 Silver 4.9949 oz. ASW **Subject:** President Bill Clinton **Obv:** National arms **Rev:** Head right divides date and value above building **Note:** Similar to 10 Dollars, KM#68.

Date	Mintage	VF20	XF40	MS60	MS63	MS65
1993	—	PF65 165				

KM# 231 50 DOLLARS
3.11 g., 0.999 Gold 0.0999 oz. AGW **Subject:** Formula One **Obv:** National arms **Rev:** Ayrton Senna **Note:** Similar to 10 Dollars, KM#229.

Date	Mintage	VF20	XF40	MS60	MS63	MS65
1996	10,000	PF65 175				

KM# 251 50 DOLLARS
3.11 g., 0.999 Gold 0.0999 oz. AGW **Subject:** Dalai Lama **Obv:** National arms **Rev:** Bust with praying hands 1/4 left **Note:** Similar to 100 Dollars, KM#252.

Date	Mintage	VF20	XF40	MS60	MS63	MS65
1996	10,000	PF65 175				

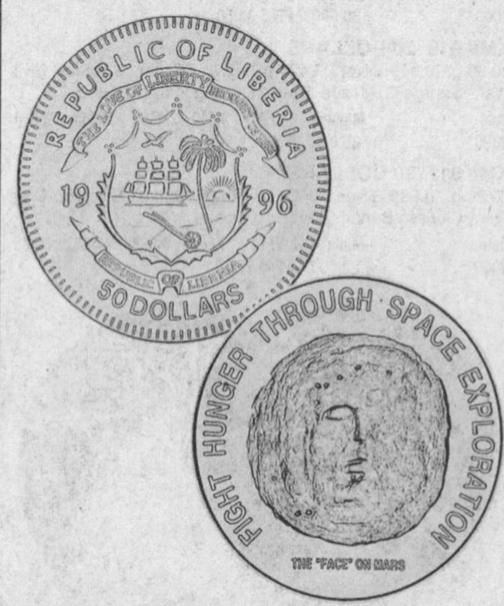

KM# 410.1 50 DOLLARS
Copper-Nickel **Obv:** National arms **Rev:** Face on Mars with rough texture

Date	Mintage	VF20	XF40	MS60	MS63	MS65
1996	—	—	—	—	3.00	5.00

KM# 410.2 50 DOLLARS
Copper-Nickel **Obv:** National arms **Rev:** Face on Mars with smooth texture

Date	Mintage	VF20	XF40	MS60	MS63	MS65
1996	—	—	—	—	3.00	5.00

KM# 316 50 DOLLARS
3.11 g., 0.999 Gold 0.0999 oz. AGW **Subject:** Return of Hong Kong to China **Obv:** National arms **Rev:** Dragon **Note:** Similar to 10 Dollars, KM#314.

Date	Mintage	VF20	XF40	MS60	MS63	MS65
1997	—	PF65 180				

KM# A366 50 DOLLARS
155.52 g., 0.999 Silver 4.9951 oz. ASW **Subject:** RMS Titanic **Obv:** National arms **Rev:** Cameo above sinking ship

Date	Mintage	VF20	XF40	MS60	MS63	MS65
1998	—	PF65 150				

KM# 366 50 DOLLARS
3.11 g., 0.999 Gold 0.0999 oz. AGW **Subject:** RMS Titanic **Obv:** National arms **Rev:** Ship sinking **Note:** Similar to 20 Dollars, KM#364.

Date	Mintage	VF20	XF40	MS60	MS63	MS65
1998	—	PF65 180				

KM# 419 50 DOLLARS
3.11 g., 0.999 Gold 0.0999 oz. AGW **Subject:** Return of Macao to China **Obv:** National arms **Rev:** Dragon and phoenix **Note:** Similar to 10 Dollars, KM#408.

Date	Mintage	VF20	XF40	MS60	MS63	MS65
1999	10,000	PF65 180				

KM# 33 100 DOLLARS
6.00 g., 0.900 Gold 0.1736 oz. AGW **Subject:** Inauguration of President Tolbert **Obv:** Bust facing **Rev:** Joined figures form a tower

Date	Mintage	VF20	XF40	MS60	MS63	MS65
1976	175	PF65 250	PF67 275			

KM# 36 100 DOLLARS
10.93 g., 0.900 Gold 0.3163 oz. AGW **Subject:** 130th Anniversary of the Republic **Obv:** Bust 3/4 left **Rev:** National arms

Date	Mintage	VF20	XF40	MS60	MS63	MS65
1977 FM (U)	787	—	—	—	525	550
1977 FM (P)	4,250	PF65 500				

KM# 37 100 DOLLARS
10.93 g., 0.900 Gold 0.3163 oz. AGW **Subject:** Organization of African Unity **Obv:** National arms above value flanked by stars **Rev:** Bust facing flanked by stars

Date	Mintage	VF20	XF40	MS60	MS63	MS65
1979 FM (P)	1,656	PF65 550				

KM# 38 100 DOLLARS
11.20 g., 0.900 Gold 0.3241 oz. AGW **Subject:** Organization of African Unity **Obv:** National arms **Rev:** Elephant

Date	Mintage	VF20	XF40	MS60	MS63	MS65
1979 FM (P)	—	PF65 450	PF67 475			

KM# 50 100 DOLLARS
10.93 g., 0.900 Gold 0.3163 oz. AGW **Subject:** 5th Anniversary of Government **Obv:** National arms **Rev:** Leopard

Date	Mintage	VF20	XF40	MS60	MS63	MS65
1985 FM (P)	409	PF65 600				

KM# 61 100 DOLLARS
7.13 g., 0.900 Gold 0.2063 oz. AGW **Series:** Decade For Women **Obv:** National arms **Rev:** Woman mashing grain

Date	Mintage	VF20	XF40	MS60	MS63	MS65
1985	318	PF65 375				

KM# 70 100 DOLLARS
311.03 g., 0.999 Silver 9.9898 oz. ASW **Subject:** President Bill Clinton **Obv:** National arms **Rev:** Head right flanked by value and date above building

Date	Mintage	VF20	XF40	MS60	MS63	MS65
1993	—	PF65 325				

KM# 100 100 DOLLARS
6.22 g., 0.999 Gold 0.1998 oz. AGW **Series:** Preserve Planet Earth **Obv:** National arms **Rev:** Protoceratops

Date	Mintage	VF20	XF40	MS60	MS63	MS65
1993	Est. 7500	PF65 325				

KM# 111 100 DOLLARS
6.22 g., 0.999 Gold 0.1998 oz. AGW **Series:** Preserve Planet Earth **Obv:** National arms **Rev:** Corythosaurus

Date	Mintage	VF20	XF40	MS60	MS63	MS65
1993	7,500	PF65 325				

KM# 114 100 DOLLARS
6.22 g., 0.999 Gold 0.1998 oz. AGW **Series:** Preserve Planet Earth **Obv:** National arms **Rev:** Atchaeopteryx **Note:** Incorrect spelling.

Date	Mintage	VF20	XF40	MS60	MS63	MS65
1993	Est. 7500	PF65 325				

KM# 117 100 DOLLARS
6.22 g., 0.999 Gold 0.1998 oz. AGW **Series:** Preserve Planet Earth **Obv:** National arms **Rev:** Archaeopteryx **Note:** Correct spelling.

Date	Mintage	VF20	XF40	MS60	MS63	MS65
1994	7,500	PF65 325				

KM# 120 100 DOLLARS
6.22 g., 0.999 Gold 0.1998 oz. AGW **Series:** Preserve Planet Earth **Obv:** National arms **Rev:** Gorillas **Note:** Similar to 10 Dollars, KM#120.

Date	Mintage	VF20	XF40	MS60	MS63	MS65
1994	Est. 7500	PF65 325				

KM# 123 100 DOLLARS
6.22 g., 0.999 Gold 0.1998 oz. AGW **Series:** Preserve Planet Earth **Obv:** National arms **Rev:** Pygmy Hippopotami **Note:** Similar to 10 Dollars, KM#122.

Date	Mintage	VF20	XF40	MS60	MS63	MS65
1994	Est. 7500	PF65 325				

KM# 126 100 DOLLARS
6.22 g., 0.999 Gold 0.1998 oz. AGW **Series:** Preserve Planet Earth **Obv:** National arms **Rev:** Trionyx Turtle **Note:** Similar to 10 Dollars, KM#125.

Date	Mintage	VF20	XF40	MS60	MS63	MS65
1994	Est. 7500	PF65 325				

KM# 130 100 DOLLARS
6.22 g., 0.999 Gold 0.1998 oz. AGW **Subject:** Star Trek **Obv:** National arms **Rev:** Captains Kirk and Picard **Note:** Similar to 10 Dollars, KM#129.

Date	Mintage	VF20	XF40	MS60	MS63	MS65
1995	—	PF65 325				

KM# 135 100 DOLLARS
6.22 g., 0.999 Gold 0.1998 oz. AGW **Series:** Preserve Planet Earth **Obv:** National arms **Rev:** Leopard

Date	Mintage	VF20	XF40	MS60	MS63	MS65
1995	Est. 7500	PF65 325				

KM# 138 100 DOLLARS
6.22 g., 0.999 Gold 0.1998 oz. AGW **Series:** Preserve Planet Earth **Obv:** National arms **Rev:** Storks

Date	Mintage	VF20	XF40	MS60	MS63	MS65
1995	Est. 7500	PF65 325				

KM# 150 100 DOLLARS
6.22 g., 0.999 Gold 0.1998 oz. AGW **Subject:** Sir Winston Churchill **Obv:** National arms **Rev:** Uniformed bust right, planes, army tanks and ship

Date	Mintage	VF20	XF40	MS60	MS63	MS65
1995	Est. 7500	PF65 325				

KM# 151 100 DOLLARS
6.22 g., 0.999 Gold 0.1998 oz. AGW **Subject:** President Franklin D. Roosevelt **Obv:** National arms **Rev:** President Roosevelt riding in jeep

Date	Mintage	VF20	XF40	MS60	MS63	MS65
1995	Est. 7500	PF65 325				

KM# 152 100 DOLLARS
6.22 g., 0.999 Gold 0.1998 oz. AGW **Subject:** General George Patton **Obv:** National arms **Rev:** General Patton in front of map

Date	Mintage	VF20	XF40	MS60	MS63	MS65
1995	Est. 7500	PF65 325				

KM# 153 100 DOLLARS
6.22 g., 0.999 Gold 0.1998 oz. AGW **Subject:** President Harry S. Truman **Obv:** National arms **Rev:** President Truman facing

Date	Mintage	VF20	XF40	MS60	MS63	MS65
1995	Est. 7500	PF65 325				

KM# 154 100 DOLLARS
6.22 g., 0.999 Gold 0.1998 oz. AGW **Subject:** President Charles de Gaulle **Obv:** National arms **Rev:** President de Gaulle on Champs Elysees

Date	Mintage	VF20	XF40	MS60	MS63	MS65
1995	Est. 7500	PF65 325				

KM# 160 100 DOLLARS
6.22 g., 0.999 Gold 0.1998 oz. AGW **Subject:** Dr. Sun Yat-Sen **Obv:** National arms **Rev:** Uniformed bust facing

Date	Mintage	VF20	XF40	MS60	MS63	MS65
1995	Est. 7500	PF65 325				

KM# 163 100 DOLLARS
6.22 g., 0.999 Gold 0.1998 oz. AGW **Subject:** General Chiang Kai-shek **Obv:** National arms **Rev:** General Chiang Kai-shek

Date	Mintage	VF20	XF40	MS60	MS63	MS65
1995	Est. 7500	PF65 325				

KM# 166 100 DOLLARS
6.22 g., 0.999 Gold 0.1998 oz. AGW **Subject:** Cairo Conference **Obv:** National arms **Rev:** Chiang Kai-shek, Roosevelt and Churchill

Date	Mintage	VF20	XF40	MS60	MS63	MS65
1995	Est. 7500	PF65 325				

KM# 175 100 DOLLARS
6.22 g., 0.999 Gold 0.1998 oz. AGW **Subject:** 375th Anniversary - Pilgrim Fathers **Obv:** National arms **Rev:** Mayflower

Date	Mintage	VF20	XF40	MS60	MS63	MS65
1995	7,500	PF65 325				

KM# 176 100 DOLLARS
6.22 g., 0.999 Gold 0.1998 oz. AGW **Subject:** 375th Anniversary - Pilgrim Fathers **Obv:** National arms **Rev:** Cape Cod and Pilgrims in skiff

Date	Mintage	VF20	XF40	MS60	MS63	MS65
1995	7,500	PF65 325				

KM# 177 100 DOLLARS
6.22 g., 0.999 Gold 0.1998 oz. AGW **Subject:** 375th Anniversary - Pilgrim Fathers **Obv:** National arms **Rev:** Pilgrim landing party

Date	Mintage	VF20	XF40	MS60	MS63	MS65
1995	7,500	PF65 325				

KM# 178 100 DOLLARS
6.22 g., 0.999 Gold 0.1998 oz. AGW **Subject:** 375th Anniversary - Pilgrim Fathers **Obv:** National arms **Rev:** First Thanksgiving scene

Date	Mintage	VF20	XF40	MS60	MS63	MS65
1995	7,500	PF65 325				

KM# 209 100 DOLLARS
6.22 g., 0.999 Gold 0.1998 oz. AGW **Subject:** Star Trek **Obv:** National arms **Rev:** Star ships NCC-1701 and NCC-1701D

Date	Mintage	VF20	XF40	MS60	MS63	MS65
1996	Est. 7500	PF65 325				

KM# 212 100 DOLLARS
6.22 g., 0.999 Gold 0.1998 oz. AGW **Subject:** Star Trek **Obv:** National arms **Rev:** Scott and McCoy

Date	Mintage	VF20	XF40	MS60	MS63	MS65
1996	7,500	PF65 325				

KM# 215 100 DOLLARS
6.22 g., 0.999 Gold 0.1998 oz. AGW **Subject:** Star Trek **Obv:** National arms **Rev:** LaForge and Data

Date	Mintage	VF20	XF40	MS60	MS63	MS65
1996	25,000	PF65 325				

KM# 218 100 DOLLARS
6.22 g., 0.999 Gold 0.1998 oz. AGW **Subject:** Star Trek **Obv:** National arms **Rev:** Spock and Uhura **Note:** Similar to 10 Dollars, KM#217.

Date	Mintage	VF20	XF40	MS60	MS63	MS65
1996	25,000	PF65 325				

KM# 221 100 DOLLARS
6.22 g., 0.999 Gold 0.1998 oz. AGW **Subject:** Star Trek **Obv:** National arms **Rev:** Worf and Dr. Crusher **Note:** Similar to 10 Dollars, KM#220.

Date	Mintage	VF20	XF40	MS60	MS63	MS65
1996	25,000	PF65 325				

KM# 224 100 DOLLARS
6.22 g., 0.999 Gold 0.1998 oz. AGW **Subject:** Preserve Planet Earth **Obv:** National arms **Rev:** Grey Parrot **Note:** Similar to 10 Dollars, KM#223.

Date	Mintage	VF20	XF40	MS60	MS63	MS65
1996	25,000	PF65 325				

KM# 227 100 DOLLARS
6.22 g., 0.999 Gold 0.1998 oz. AGW **Subject:** Preserve Planet Earth **Obv:** National arms **Rev:** Love Birds **Note:** Similar to 10 Dollars, KM#226.

Date	Mintage	VF20	XF40	MS60	MS63	MS65
1996	25,000	PF65 325				

KM# 232 100 DOLLARS
6.22 g., 0.999 Gold 0.1998 oz. AGW **Subject:** Formula One **Obv:** National arms **Rev:** Ayrton Senna **Note:** Similar to 10 Dollars, KM#229.

Date	Mintage	VF20	XF40	MS60	MS63	MS65
1996	20,000	PF65 325				

KM# 237 100 DOLLARS
6.22 g., 0.999 Gold 0.1998 oz. AGW **Subject:** Dr. Sun Yat-Sen

Date	Mintage	VF20	XF40	MS60	MS63	MS65
1996	Est. 7500	PF65 325				

KM# 240 100 DOLLARS
6.22 g., 0.999 Gold 0.1998 oz. AGW **Subject:** General Chiang Kai-shek **Obv:** National arms **Rev:** General Chiang kai-shek **Note:** Similar to 10 Dollars, KM#162.

Date	Mintage	VF20	XF40	MS60	MS63	MS65
1996	Est. 7500	PF65 325				

KM# 243 100 DOLLARS
6.22 g., 0.999 Gold 0.1998 oz. AGW **Subject:** President Chiang Ching-kuo **Obv:** National arms **Rev:** Bust facing **Note:** Similar to 10 Dollars, KM#242.

Date	Mintage	VF20	XF40	MS60	MS63	MS65
1996	—	PF65 325				

KM# 246 100 DOLLARS
6.22 g., 0.999 Gold 0.1998 oz. AGW **Subject:** President Lee Teng-hui **Obv:** National arms **Rev:** President Lee Ten-hui **Note:** Similar to 10 Dollars, KM#245.

Date	Mintage	VF20	XF40	MS60	MS63	MS65
1996	Est. 7500	PF65 325				

KM# 252 100 DOLLARS
6.22 g., 0.999 Gold 0.1998 oz. AGW **Subject:** Dalai Lama **Obv:** National arms **Rev:** Bust with praying hands facing 1/4 left

Date	Mintage	VF20	XF40	MS60	MS63	MS65
1996	Est. 7500	PF65 325				

KM# 253 100 DOLLARS
6.22 g., 0.999 Gold 0.1998 oz. AGW **Subject:** King Rama IX of Thailand **Obv:** National arms **Rev:** King seated on radiant throne

Date	Mintage	VF20	XF40	MS60	MS63	MS65
1996	Est. 7500	PF65 325				

KM# 259 100 DOLLARS
6.22 g., 0.999 Gold 0.1998 oz. AGW **Subject:** Mao Zedong Proclaiming People's Republic **Obv:** National arms **Rev:** Chairman Mao Zedong proclaiming People's Republic **Note:** Similar to 10 Dollars, KM#258.

Date	Mintage	VF20	XF40	MS60	MS63	MS65
1996	1,996	PF65 325				

KM# 312 100 DOLLARS
6.22 g., 0.999 Gold 0.1998 oz. AGW **Subject:** Mahatma Gandhi **Obv:** National arms **Rev:** Seated figure facing left in front of Taj Mahal **Note:** Similar to 10 Dollars, KM#311.

Date	Mintage	VF20	XF40	MS60	MS63	MS65
1997	Est. 5000	PF65 325				

KM# 317 100 DOLLARS
6.22 g., 0.999 Gold 0.1998 oz. AGW **Subject:** Return of Hong Kong to China **Obv:** National arms **Rev:** Dragon **Note:** Similar to 10 Dollars, KM#314.

Date	Mintage	VF20	XF40	MS60	MS63	MS65
1997	Est. 5000	PF65 325				

KM# 322 100 DOLLARS
6.22 g., 0.999 Gold 0.1998 oz. AGW **Subject:** Fiftieth Anniversary of the Kon-Tiki Expedition **Obv:** National arms **Rev:** Sailing ship within circle **Note:** Similar to 1 Dollar, KM#320.

Date	Mintage	VF20	XF40	MS60	MS63	MS65
1997	Est. 7500	PF65 325				

KM# 326 100 DOLLARS
6.22 g., 0.999 Gold 0.1998 oz. AGW **Subject:** Jurassic Park **Obv:** National arms **Rev:** Stegosaurus **Note:** Similar to 10 Dollars, KM#325.

Date	Mintage	VF20	XF40	MS60	MS63	MS65
1997	Est. 2500	PF65 325				

KM# 329 100 DOLLARS
6.22 g., 0.999 Gold 0.1998 oz. AGW **Subject:** Golden Wedding Anniversary **Obv:** National arms **Rev:** E & P initials above 2 shields **Note:** Similar to 10 Dollars, KM#328.

Date	Mintage	VF20	XF40	MS60	MS63	MS65
1997	Est. 3500	PF65 325				

KM# 332 100 DOLLARS
6.22 g., 0.999 Gold 0.1998 oz. AGW **Subject:** Golden Wedding Anniversary **Obv:** National arms **Rev:** Royal couple with horse **Note:** Similar to 10 Dollars, KM#331.

Date	Mintage	VF20	XF40	MS60	MS63	MS65
1997	Est. 3500	PF65 325				

KM# 335 100 DOLLARS
6.22 g., 0.999 Gold 0.1998 oz. AGW **Subject:** Golden Wedding Anniversary **Obv:** National arms **Rev:** Royal couple with dogs **Note:** Similar to 10 Dollars, KM#334.

Date	Mintage	VF20	XF40	MS60	MS63	MS65
1997	Est. 3500	PF65 325				

KM# 338 100 DOLLARS
6.22 g., 0.999 Gold 0.1998 oz. AGW **Subject:** Golden Wedding Anniversary **Obv:** National arms **Rev:** Royal couple with children **Note:** Similar to 10 Dollars, KM#337.

Date	Mintage	VF20	XF40	MS60	MS63	MS65
1997	Est. 3500	PF65 325				

KM# 370 100 DOLLARS
6.22 g., 0.999 Gold 0.1998 oz. AGW **Subject:** Star Trek - The Next Generation **Obv:** National arms **Rev:** Romulan Warbird **Note:** Similar to 10 Dollars, KM#369.

Date	Mintage	VF20	XF40	MS60	MS63	MS65
1997	Est. 7500	PF65 325				

KM# 373 100 DOLLARS
6.22 g., 0.999 Gold 0.1998 oz. AGW **Subject:** Star Trek - The Next Generation **Obv:** National arms **Rev:** Klingon Attack Cruiser **Note:** Similar to 10 Dollars, KM#372.

Date	Mintage	VF20	XF40	MS60	MS63	MS65
1997	Est. 7500	PF65 325				

KM# 376 100 DOLLARS
6.22 g., 0.999 Gold 0.1998 oz. AGW **Subject:** Star Trek - The Next Generation **Obv:** National arms **Rev:** U.S.S. Enterprise NCC-1701-D **Note:** Similar to 10 Dollars, KM#375.

Date	Mintage	VF20	XF40	MS60	MS63	MS65
1997	Est. 7500	PF65 325				

KM# 379 100 DOLLARS
6.22 g., 0.999 Gold 0.1998 oz. AGW **Subject:** Star Trek - The Next Generation **Obv:** National arms **Rev:** Klingon Bird of Prey **Note:** Similar to 10 Dollars, KM#378.

Date	Mintage	VF20	XF40	MS60	MS63	MS65
1997	Est. 7500	PF65 325				

KM# 382 100 DOLLARS
6.22 g., 0.999 Gold 0.1998 oz. AGW **Subject:** Star Trek - The Next Generation **Obv:** National arms **Rev:** Borg Cube **Note:** Similar to 10 Dollars, KM#381.

Date	Mintage	VF20	XF40	MS60	MS63	MS65
1997	—	PF65 325				

KM# 385 100 DOLLARS
6.22 g., 0.999 Gold 0.1998 oz. AGW **Subject:** Star Trek - The Next Generation **Obv:** National arms **Rev:** Ferengi Marauder **Note:** Similar to 10 Dollars, KM#384.

Date	Mintage	VF20	XF40	MS60	MS63	MS65
1997	—	PF65 325				

KM# 473 100 DOLLARS
6.22 g., 0.999 Gold 0.1998 oz. AGW **Subject:** Princess Diana in Memoriam **Obv:** National arms

Date	Mintage	VF20	XF40	MS60	MS63	MS65
1997	—	PF65 325				

KM# 365 100 DOLLARS
6.22 g., 0.999 Gold 0.1998 oz. AGW **Subject:** RMS Titanic **Obv:** National arms **Rev:** Ship sinking **Note:** Similar to 20 Dollars, KM#364.

Date	Mintage	VF20	XF40	MS60	MS63	MS65
1998	Est. 5000	PF65 325				

KM# 388 100 DOLLARS
6.22 g., 0.999 Gold 0.1998 oz. AGW **Subject:** President Ronald Reagan **Obv:** National arms **Rev:** Lincoln Memorial below head right **Note:** Similar to 10 Dollars, KM#387.

Date	Mintage	VF20	XF40	MS60	MS63	MS65
1998	Est. 7500	PF65 325				

KM# 392 100 DOLLARS
6.22 g., 0.999 Gold 0.1998 oz. AGW **Subject:** Year of the Rabbit **Obv:** National arms **Rev:** Rabbit running left **Note:** Similar to 20 Dollars, KM#389.

Date	Mintage	VF20	XF40	MS60	MS63	MS65
1999	5,000	PF65 325				

KM# 393 100 DOLLARS
6.22 g., 0.999 Gold 0.1998 oz. AGW **Subject:** Year of the Rabbit **Obv:** National arms **Rev:** Rabbit sitting **Note:** Similar to 20 Dollars, KM#390.

Date	Mintage	VF20	XF40	MS60	MS63	MS65
1999	5,000	PF65 325				

KM# 394 100 DOLLARS
6.22 g., 0.999 Gold 0.1998 oz. AGW **Subject:** Year of the Rabbit **Obv:** National arms **Rev:** Rabbit running right **Note:** Similar to 20 Dollars, KM#391.

Date	Mintage	VF20	XF40	MS60	MS63	MS65
1999	5,000	PF65 325				

KM# 403 100 DOLLARS
6.22 g., 0.999 Gold 0.1998 oz. AGW **Subject:** Christopher Columbus **Obv:** National arms **Rev:** Portrait, ship **Note:** Similar to 10 Dollars, KM#402.

Date	Mintage	VF20	XF40	MS60	MS63	MS65
1999	10,000	PF65 325				

KM# 406 100 DOLLARS
6.22 g., 0.999 Gold 0.1998 oz. AGW **Subject:** Captain James Cook **Obv:** National arms **Rev:** Portrait, ship, map **Note:** Similar to 10 Dollars, KM#405.

Date	Mintage	VF20	XF40	MS60	MS63	MS65
1999	10,000	PF65 325				

KM# 409 100 DOLLARS
6.22 g., 0.999 Gold 0.1998 oz. AGW **Subject:** Return of Macao to China **Obv:** National arms **Rev:** Dragon and phoenix **Note:** Similar to 10 Dollars, KM#408.

Date	Mintage	VF20	XF40	MS60	MS63	MS65
1999	10,000	PF65 325				

KM# 415 100 DOLLARS
6.22 g., 0.999 Gold 0.1998 oz. AGW **Subject:** The Wedding of Prince Edward and Miss Sophie Rhys-Jones **Obv:** National arms **Rev:** Couple in carriage **Note:** Similar to 10 Dollars, KM#414.

Date	Mintage	VF20	XF40	MS60	MS63	MS65
1999	Est. 5000	PF65 325				

KM# 106 150 DOLLARS
500.00 g., 0.999 Silver 16.0593 oz. ASW, 85 mm. **Subject:** Preserve Planet Earth **Obv:** National arms **Rev:** Two Brachiosauros **Note:** Illustration reduced.

Date	Mintage	VF20	XF40	MS60	MS63	MS65
1993	121	PF63 325	PF65 450			

KM# 34 200 DOLLARS
12.00 g., 0.900 Gold 0.3472 oz. AGW **Subject:** Inauguration of President Tolbert **Obv:** Bust facing flanked by stars **Rev:** Man holding horn within circle

Date	Mintage	VF20	XF40	MS60	MS63	MS65
1976	100	PF65 500	PF67 550			

KM# 46 200 DOLLARS
15.98 g., 0.917 Gold 0.4711 oz. AGW **Subject:** Year of the Scout **Obv:** National arms **Rev:** Saluting scout divides flags above dates

Date	Mintage	VF20	XF40	MS60	MS63	MS65
ND-1983	—	—	—	—	—	825
ND-1983	—	PF65 850				

KM# 49 200 DOLLARS
15.98 g., 0.900 Gold 0.4624 oz. AGW **Series:** International Year of Disabled Persons **Obv:** National arms **Rev:** Standing elderly figures above disability emblem

Date	Mintage	VF20	XF40	MS60	MS63	MS65
1983	500	—	—	—	—	800
1983	500	PF65 825				

KM# 395 200 DOLLARS
12.44 g., 0.9999 Gold 0.4001 oz. AGW **Subject:** Year of the Rabbit **Obv:** National arms **Rev:** Rabbit running left **Note:** Similar to 20 Dollars, KM#389.

Date	Mintage	VF20	XF40	MS60	MS63	MS65
1999	1,500	PF65 725				

KM# 396 200 DOLLARS
12.44 g., 0.9999 Gold 0.4001 oz. AGW **Subject:** Year of the Rabbit **Obv:** National arms **Rev:** Rabbit sitting **Note:** Similar to 20 Dollars, KM#390.

Date	Mintage	VF20	XF40	MS60	MS63	MS65
1999	1,500	PF65 725				

KM# 397 200 DOLLARS
12.44 g., 0.9999 Gold 0.4001 oz. AGW **Subject:** Year of the Rabbit **Obv:** National arms **Rev:** Rabbit running right **Note:** Similar to 20 Dollars, KM#391.

Date	Mintage	VF20	XF40	MS60	MS63	MS65
1999	1,500	PF65 725				

KM# 601 200 DOLLARS
500.00 g., 0.999 Silver 16.0593 oz. ASW, 89 mm. **Obv:** National arms **Rev:** Three facing elephants **Edge:** Reeded

Date	Mintage	VF20	XF40	MS60	MS63	MS65
2000	—	PF65 550				

KM# 52 250 DOLLARS
15.50 g., 0.999 Gold 0.4978 oz. AGW **Subject:** President John F. Kennedy **Obv:** National arms divides date **Rev:** Head left

Date	Mintage	VF20	XF40	MS60	MS63	MS65
1988	5,000	PF65 875				

KM# 56 250 DOLLARS
15.50 g., 0.999 Gold 0.4978 oz. AGW **Subject:** President Samuel Kanyon Doe **Obv:** National arms **Rev:** Head 3/4 facing

Date	Mintage	VF20	XF40	MS60	MS63	MS65
1988	Est. 5000	PF65 875				

KM# 58 250 DOLLARS
15.50 g., 0.999 Gold 0.4978 oz. AGW **Subject:** President George H. W. Bush **Obv:** National arms **Rev:** Head left

Date	Mintage	VF20	XF40	MS60	MS63	MS65
1989	600	PF65 900				

KM# 60 250 DOLLARS
15.50 g., 0.999 Gold 0.4978 oz. AGW **Subject:** Emperor Hirohito **Obv:** National arms **Rev:** Head facing divides dates

Date	Mintage	VF20	XF40	MS60	MS63	MS65
1989	600	PF65 925				

KM# 89 250 DOLLARS
15.50 g., 0.999 Gold 0.4978 oz. AGW **Subject:** Formula One **Obv:** National arms **Rev:** Nigel Mansell **Note:** Similar to 10 Dollars, KM#75.

Date	Mintage	VF20	XF40	MS60	MS63	MS65
1992	Est. 5000	PF65 800				

KM# 90 250 DOLLARS
15.50 g., 0.999 Gold 0.4978 oz. AGW **Subject:** Formula One **Obv:** National arms **Rev:** Gerhard Berger **Note:** Similar to 10 Dollars, KM#83.

Date	Mintage	VF20	XF40	MS60	MS63	MS65
1992	Est. 5000	PF65 800				

KM# 91 250 DOLLARS
15.50 g., 0.999 Gold 0.4978 oz. AGW **Subject:** Formula One **Obv:** National arms **Rev:** Aguri Suzuki **Note:** Similar to 10 Dollars, KM#84.

Date	Mintage	VF20	XF40	MS60	MS63	MS65
1992	Est. 5000	PF65 800				

KM# 92 250 DOLLARS
15.50 g., 0.999 Gold 0.4978 oz. AGW **Subject:** Formula One **Obv:** National arms **Rev:** Ayrton Senna **Note:** Similar to 10 Dollars, KM#85.

Date	Mintage	VF20	XF40	MS60	MS63	MS65
1992	—	PF65 800				

KM# 93 250 DOLLARS
15.50 g., 0.999 Gold 0.4978 oz. AGW **Subject:** Formula One **Obv:** National arms **Rev:** Ricardo Patrese **Note:** Similar to 10 Dollars, KM#74.

Date	Mintage	VF20	XF40	MS60	MS63	MS65
1992	Est. 5000	PF65 800				

KM# 94 250 DOLLARS
15.50 g., 0.999 Gold 0.4978 oz. AGW **Subject:** Formula One **Obv:** National arms **Rev:** Michael Schumacher **Note:** Similar to 10 Dollars, KM#86.

Date	Mintage	VF20	XF40	MS60	MS63	MS65
1992	—	PF65 800				

KM# 95 250 DOLLARS
15.50 g., 0.999 Gold 0.4978 oz. AGW **Subject:** Formula One **Obv:** National arms **Rev:** Alain Prost **Note:** Similar to 10 Dollars, KM#87.

Date	Mintage	VF20	XF40	MS60	MS63	MS65
1992	Est. 5000	PF65 800				

KM# 96 250 DOLLARS
15.50 g., 0.999 Gold 0.4978 oz. AGW **Subject:** Formula One **Obv:** National arms **Rev:** Ukyo Katayama **Note:** Similar to 10 Dollars, KM#88.

Date	Mintage	VF20	XF40	MS60	MS63	MS65
1992	Est. 5000	PF65 800				

KM# 71 250 DOLLARS
15.50 g., 0.999 Gold 0.4978 oz. AGW **Subject:** President Bill Clinton **Obv:** National arms **Rev:** Head right **Note:** Similar to 10 Dollars, KM#68.

Date	Mintage	VF20	XF40	MS60	MS63	MS65
1993	Est. 5000	PF65 800				

KM# 105 250 DOLLARS
15.50 g., 0.999 Gold 0.4978 oz. AGW **Subject:** President John F. Kennedy **Obv:** National arms **Rev:** Head left, funeral caisson below **Note:** Similar to 10 Dollars, KM#104.

Date	Mintage	VF20	XF40	MS60	MS63	MS65
1993	Est. 5000	PF65 800				

KM# 181 250 DOLLARS
15.50 g., 0.999 Gold 0.4978 oz. AGW **Subject:** Formula One **Obv:** National arms **Rev:** Mika Hakkinen

Date	Mintage	VF20	XF40	MS60	MS63	MS65
1995	Est. 5000	PF65 800				

KM# 184 250 DOLLARS
15.50 g., 0.999 Gold 0.4978 oz. AGW **Subject:** Formula One **Obv:** National arms **Rev:** Martin Brundle

Date	Mintage	VF20	XF40	MS60	MS63	MS65
1995	Est. 5000	PF65 800				

KM# 187 250 DOLLARS
15.50 g., 0.999 Gold 0.4978 oz. AGW **Subject:** Formula One **Obv:** National arms **Rev:** Rubens Barricchello

Date	Mintage	VF20	XF40	MS60	MS63	MS65
1995	Est. 5000	PF65 800				

KM# 190 250 DOLLARS
15.50 g., 0.999 Gold 0.4978 oz. AGW **Subject:** Formula One **Obv:** National arms **Rev:** David Coulthard

Date	Mintage	VF20	XF40	MS60	MS63	MS65
1995	Est. 5000	PF65 800				

KM# 193 250 DOLLARS
15.50 g., 0.999 Gold 0.4978 oz. AGW **Subject:** Formula One **Obv:** National arms **Rev:** Jean Alesi

Date	Mintage	VF20	XF40	MS60	MS63	MS65
1995	Est. 5000	PF65 800				

KM# 565 250 DOLLARS
15.50 g., 0.999 Gold 0.4978 oz. AGW, 33 mm. **Obv:** National arms **Rev:** Bugatti Royale

Date	Mintage	VF20	XF40	MS60	MS63	MS65
1995 B	—	—	—	—	—	900

KM# 203 250 DOLLARS
15.50 g., 0.999 Gold 0.4978 oz. AGW **Subject:** Formula One **Obv:** National arms **Rev:** Mark Blundell

Date	Mintage	VF20	XF40	MS60	MS63	MS65
1996	Est. 5000	PF65 800				

KM# 204 250 DOLLARS
15.50 g., 0.999 Gold 0.4978 oz. AGW **Subject:** Formula One **Obv:** National arms **Rev:** Johnny Herbert **Note:** Similar to 10 Dollars, KM#200.

Date	Mintage	VF20	XF40	MS60	MS63	MS65
1996	Est. 5000	PF65 800				

KM# 205 250 DOLLARS
15.50 g., 0.999 Gold 0.4978 oz. AGW **Subject:** Formula One **Obv:** National arms **Rev:** Eddie Irvine **Note:** Similar to 10 Dollars, KM#201.

Date	Mintage	VF20	XF40	MS60	MS63	MS65
1996	—	PF65 800				

KM# 206 250 DOLLARS
15.50 g., 0.999 Gold 0.4978 oz. AGW **Subject:** Formula One **Obv:** National arms **Rev:** Heinz Frentzen **Note:** Similar to 10 Dollars, KM#202.

Date	Mintage	VF20	XF40	MS60	MS63	MS65
1996	Est. 5000	PF65 800				

KM# 233 250 DOLLARS
15.50 g., 0.999 Gold 0.4978 oz. AGW **Subject:** Formula One **Obv:** National arms **Rev:** Ayrton Senna **Note:** Similar to 10 Dollars, KM#229.

Date	Mintage	VF20	XF40	MS60	MS63	MS65
1996	Est. 5000	PF65 800				

KM# 318 250 DOLLARS
15.50 g., 0.999 Gold 0.4978 oz. AGW **Subject:** Return of Hong Kong **Obv:** National arms **Rev:** Dragon **Note:** Similar to 10 Dollars, KM#314.

Date	Mintage	VF20	XF40	MS60	MS63	MS65
1997	—	PF65 800				

KM# 420 250 DOLLARS
15.50 g., 0.999 Gold 0.4978 oz. AGW **Subject:** Return of Macao to China **Obv:** National arms **Rev:** Dragon and phoenix **Note:** Similar to 10 Dollars, KM#408.

Date	Mintage	VF20	XF40	MS60	MS63	MS65
1999	—	PF65 800				

KM# 425 250 DOLLARS
15.50 g., 0.999 Gold 0.4978 oz. AGW **Subject:** Liberty **Obv:** National arms **Rev:** Conjoined heads left **Note:** Similar to 10 Dollars, KM#424.

Date	Mintage	VF20	XF40	MS60	MS63	MS65
1999	375	PF65 900				

KM# 439 250 DOLLARS
15.55 g., 0.9999 Gold 0.4999 oz. AGW, 27 mm. **Subject:** Taipai, Taiwan Rapid Transit System **Obv:** National arms above hole* and dragon **Rev:** Subway train, logo and tunnel hole* **Note:** Struck at Singapore Mint. *As first done on Albanian coins of 1988.

Date	Mintage	VF20	XF40	MS60	MS63	MS65
1999	2,000	PF65 875				

KM# 107 300 DOLLARS

1000.00 g., 0.999 Silver 32.1186 oz. ASW, 100 mm. **Series:** Preserve Planet Earth **Obv:** National arms **Rev:** Tyrannosaurus Rex attacking Triceratops **Note:** Illustration reduced.

Date	Mintage	VF20	XF40	MS60	MS63	MS65
1993	151	PF63 750	PF65 850			

KM# 367 300 DOLLARS

1000.00 g., 0.999 Silver 32.1186 oz. ASW **Subject:** RMS Titanic **Obv:** National arms **Rev:** Ship sinking **Note:** Similar to 20 Dollars, KM#364.

Date	Mintage	VF20	XF40	MS60	MS63	MS65
1998	Est. 500	PF65 1,000				

KM# 35 400 DOLLARS

24.00 g., 0.900 Gold 0.6945 oz. AGW **Subject:** Inauguration of President Tolbert **Obv:** Bust facing **Rev:** Liberia written within circle

Date	Mintage	VF20	XF40	MS60	MS63	MS65
1976	25	PF65 1,650				

KM# 234 500 DOLLARS

31.10 g., 0.999 Gold 0.999 oz. AGW **Subject:** Formula One **Obv:** National arms **Rev:** Ayrton Senna **Note:** Similar to 10 Dollars, KM#229.

Date	Mintage	VF20	XF40	MS60	MS63	MS65
1996	Est. 2500	PF65 1,750				

KM# 421 500 DOLLARS

31.10 g., 0.999 Gold 0.999 oz. AGW **Subject:** Return of Macao to China **Obv:** National arms **Rev:** Dragon and phoenix **Note:** Similar to 10 Dollars, KM#408.

Date	Mintage	VF20	XF40	MS60	MS63	MS65
1999	Est. 1000	PF65 1,800				

KM# 732 500 DOLLARS

373.24 g., 0.999 Bi-Metallic 11.9878 oz. Silver with .499 AGW Gold inlay center., 89.08 mm. **Subject:** JFK Memorial **Obv:** Arms with banners above and below **Obv. Legend:** REPUBLIC OF LIBERIA **Rev:** Conjoined heads of President John F. Kennedy and son John Jr. left **Rev. Legend:** Ask not what your country can do for you -. **Edge:** Reeded **Note:** Illustration reduced.

Date	Mintage	VF20	XF40	MS60	MS63	MS65
2000	300	PF65 1,250				

KM# 737 500 DOLLARS

0.585 Gold **Subject:** XXVII OLympic Games - Sydney **Rev:** Three sports figures **Edge:** Reeded

Date	Mintage	VF20	XF40	MS60	MS63	MS65
2000	2,000	—	—	—	—	—

KM# 235 2500 DOLLARS

155.52 g., 0.999 Gold 4.995 oz. AGW **Subject:** Formula One **Obv:** National arms **Rev:** Ayrton Senna **Note:** Similar to 10 Dollars, KM#229.

Date	Mintage	VF20	XF40	MS60	MS63	MS65
1996	Est. 250	PF65 8,000				

KM# 238 2500 DOLLARS

155.52 g., 0.999 Gold 4.995 oz. AGW **Subject:** Dr. Sun Yat-Sen

Date	Mintage	VF20	XF40	MS60	MS63	MS65
1996	Est. 250	PF65 8,000				

KM# 241 2500 DOLLARS

155.52 g., 0.999 Gold 4.995 oz. AGW **Subject:** General Chiang Kai-shek **Obv:** National arms **Rev:** General Chiang kai-shek **Note:** Similar to 10 Dollars, KM#162.

Date	Mintage	VF20	XF40	MS60	MS63	MS65
1996	Est. 250	PF65 8,000				

KM# 244 2500 DOLLARS

155.52 g., 0.999 Gold 4.995 oz. AGW **Subject:** President Chiang Ching-kuo **Obv:** National arms **Rev:** Bust facing **Note:** Similar to 10 Dollars, KM#242.

Date	Mintage	VF20	XF40	MS60	MS63	MS65
1996	Est. 250	PF65 8,000				

KM# 247 2500 DOLLARS

155.52 g., 0.999 Gold 4.995 oz. AGW **Subject:** President Lee Teng-hui **Obv:** National arms **Rev:** President Lee Teng-hui **Note:** Similar to 10 Dollars, KM#245.

Date	Mintage	VF20	XF40	MS60	MS63	MS65
1996	—	PF65 8,000				

KM# 319 2500 DOLLARS

155.52 g., 0.999 Gold 4.995 oz. AGW **Subject:** Return of Hong Kong **Obv:** National arms **Rev:** Dragon **Note:** Similar to 10 Dollars, KM#314.

Date	Mintage	VF20	XF40	MS60	MS63	MS65
1997	—	PF65 8,000				

KM# 588 2500 DOLLARS

155.52 g., 0.999 Gold 4.995 oz. AGW, 60 mm. **Subject:** Year of the Tiger **Obv:** National arms **Rev:** Tiger above pineapple and flowers within beaded circle **Edge:** Reeded **Note:** Illustration reduced.

Date	Mintage	VF20	XF40	MS60	MS63	MS65
1998	—	PF65 8,250				

KM# 398 2500 DOLLARS

155.52 g., 0.999 Gold 4.995 oz. AGW **Subject:** Year of the Rabbit **Obv:** National arms **Rev:** Rabbit running left **Note:** Similar to 20 Dollars, KM#389.

Date	Mintage	VF20	XF40	MS60	MS63	MS65
1999	88	PF65 8,250				

KM# 399 2500 DOLLARS

155.52 g., 0.999 Gold 4.995 oz. AGW **Subject:** Year of the Rabbit **Obv:** National arms **Rev:** Rabbit sitting **Note:** Similar to 20 Dollars, KM#390.

Date	Mintage	VF20	XF40	MS60	MS63	MS65
1999	88	PF65 8,250				

KM# 400 2500 DOLLARS

155.52 g., 0.999 Gold 4.995 oz. AGW **Subject:** Year of the Rabbit **Obv:** National arms **Rev:** Rabbit running right **Note:** Similar to 20 Dollars, KM#391.

Date	Mintage	VF20	XF40	MS60	MS63	MS65
1999	88	PF65 8,250				

KM# 422 2500 DOLLARS

155.52 g., 0.999 Gold 4.995 oz. AGW **Subject:** Return of Macau to China **Obv:** National arms **Rev:** Dragon and phoenix **Note:** Similar to 10 Dollars, KM#408.

Date	Mintage	VF20	XF40	MS60	MS63	MS65
1999	Est. 250	PF65 8,250				

KM# 440 2500 DOLLARS

155.52 g., 0.9999 Gold 4.9995 oz. AGW, 55 mm. **Subject:** Taipai, Taiwan Rapid Transit System **Obv:** National arms above dragon **Rev:** Dragon around subway train viewing sun with diamond inserts

Date	Mintage	VF20	XF40	MS60	MS63	MS65
ND-1999	50	PF65 8,500				

PATTERNS

Including off metal strikes

KM#	Date	Mintage	Identification	Mkt Val
Pn55	1976	—	100 Dollars. Bronze. KM#33.	185
Pn56	1976	—	200 Dollars. Bronze. KM#34.	215
Pn57	1976	—	400 Dollars. Bronze. KM#35.	245

PIEDFORT

KM#	Date	Mintage	Identification	Mkt Val
P1	1983	500	2 Dollars. Silver. KM#47a.	115
P2	1983	—	20 Dollars. Silver. KM#48.	150
P3	1983	100	200 Dollars. Gold. KM#49.	1,600

TRIAL STRIKES

KM#	Date	Mintage	Identification	Mkt Val
Ts8	2000	200	5 Dollars. 0.999. Silver. National arms in center of Millennium legend. Roy Rogers. Partially reeded and lettered. Roy Rogers, edge reads AG Trial Strike.	—

MINT SETS

KM#	Date	Mintage	Identification	Issue Price	Mkt Val
MS1	1997 (2)	4,000	KM#351, 352	50.00	60.00

PROOF SETS

KM#	Date	Mintage	Identification	Issue Price	Mkt Val
PS2	1906H (5)	—	KM#5-9	—	1,525
PS3	1968 (6)	14,396	KM#13, 14, 15a.2-18a.2	15.25	9.00
PS4	1969 (6)	5,056	KM#13, 14, 15a.2-18a.2	15.25	9.00
PS5	1970 (6)	3,464	KM#13, 14, 15a.2-18a.2	15.25	15.00
PS6	1971 (6)	3,032	KM#13, 14, 15a.2-18a.2	15.25	14.00
PS7	1972 (6)	4,866	KM#13, 14, 15a.2-18a.2	15.50	12.00
PS8	1972 (4)	—	KM#24-27	—	3,275
PS9	1973 (7)	10,542	KM#13, 14, 15a.2-18a.2, 29	27.00	45.00
PS10	1974 (7)	9,362	KM#13, 14, 15a.2-18a.2, 29	27.00	45.00
PS11	1975 (7)	4,056	KM#13, 14, 15a.2-18a.2, 29	31.50	42.50
PS12	1976 (7)	2,131	KM#13, 14, 15a.2, 29-32	45.00	65.00
PS13	1977 (7)	920	KM#13, 14, 15a.2, 29-32	45.00	75.00
PS14	1978 (8)	7,311	KM#12a, 13, 14, 15a.2, 29-32	47.00	60.00
PS16	1997 (3)	—	KM#417, 445, 473	—	440
PS17	1999 (2)	375	KM#424-425	345	980
PS18	2000 (2)	1,000	KM#613, 614	70.00	80.00

LIBYA

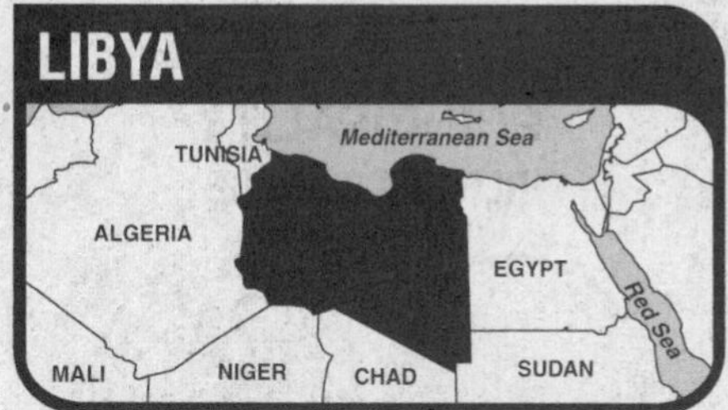

The Socialist People's Libyan Arab Jamahariya, located on the north-central coast of Africa between Tunisia and Egypt, has an area of 679,358 sq. mi. (1,759,540 sq. km.) and a population of 3.9 million. Capital: Tripoli. Crude oil, which accounts for 90 percent of the export earnings, is the mainstay of the economy.

Libya has been subjected to foreign rule throughout most of its history, various parts of it having been ruled by the Phoenicians, Carthaginians, Vandals, Byzantines, Greeks, Romans, Egyptians, and in the following centuries the Arabs' language, culture and religion were adopted by the indigenous population. Libya was conquered by the Ottoman Turks in 1553, and remained under Turkish domination, becoming a Turkish vilayet in 1835, until it was conquered by Italy and made into a colony in 1911. The name 'Libya', the ancient Greek name for North Africa exclusive of Egypt, was given to the colony by Italy in1934. Libya came under Allied administration after the fall of Tripoli on Jan. 23, 1943, divided into zones of British and French control. On Dec. 24, 1951, in accordance with a United Nations resolution, Libya proclaimed its independence as a constitutional monarchy, thereby becoming the first country to achieve independence through the United Nations. The monarchy was overthrown by a *coup d'etat* on Sept. 1, 1969, and Libya was established as a republic.

TITLES

المملكة الليبية

al-Mamlaka(t) al-Libiya(t)

الجمهورية الليبية

al-Jomhuriya(t) al-Arabiya(t) al-Libiya(t)

RULER

Idris I, 1951-1969

MONARCHY

STANDARD COINAGE

10 Milliemes = 1 Piastre; 100 Piastres = 1 Pound

KM# 1 MILLIEME

3.00 g., Bronze, 18 mm. **Ruler:** Idris I **Obv:** Bust right **Rev:** Crown divides wreath with value and date within **Note:** Date in Arabic.

Date	Mintage	F12	VF20	XF40	MS60	MS63
1952	7,750,000	—	0.15	0.25	0.75	1.50
1952	32	PF65 450				

KM# 6 MILLIEME

1.75 g., Nickel-Brass, 16.03 mm. **Ruler:** Idris I **Obv:** Crowned national arms above dates **Rev:** Value within wreath

Date	Mintage	F12	VF20	XF40	MS60	MS63
AH1385-1965	11,000,000	—	0.10	0.20	0.40	0.85

KM# 2 2 MILLIEMES

6.00 g., Bronze, 24 mm. **Ruler:** Idris I **Obv:** Bust right **Rev:** Crown divides wreath with value and date within **Note:** Date in Arabic.

Date	Mintage	F12	VF20	XF40	MS60	MS63
1952	6,650,000	—	0.15	0.35	1.00	2.00
1952	32	PF65 450				

KM# 3 5 MILLIEMES

10.00 g., Bronze **Ruler:** Idris I **Obv:** Bust right **Rev:** Crown divides wreath with value and date within **Note:** Date in Arabic.

Date	Mintage	F12	VF20	XF40	MS60	MS63
1952	7,680,000	—	0.25	0.50	1.50	3.00
1952	32	PF65 450				

KM# 7 5 MILLIEMES

Nickel-Brass **Ruler:** Idris I **Obv:** Crowned national arms above dates **Rev:** Value within 3/4 wreath

Date	Mintage	F12	VF20	XF40	MS60	MS63
AH1385-1965	8,500,000	—	0.15	0.25	0.50	1.00

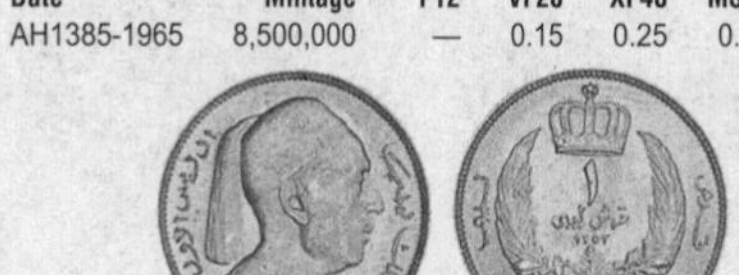

KM# 4 PIASTRE

3.75 g., Copper-Nickel **Ruler:** Idris I **Obv:** Bust right **Rev:** Crown divides wreath with value and date within **Edge:** Reeded **Note:** Date in Arabic.

Date	Mintage	F12	VF20	XF40	MS60	MS63
1952	10,200,000	—	0.35	0.60	1.25	2.50
1952	32	PF65 550				

KM# 5 2 PIASTRES

7.53 g., Copper-Nickel, 26 mm. **Ruler:** Idris I **Obv:** Bust right **Rev:** Crown divides wreath with value and dates within **Edge:** Reeded **Note:** Date in Arabic.

Date	Mintage	F12	VF20	XF40	MS60	MS63
1952	6,075,000	—	0.35	0.75	1.75	3.50
1952	32	PF65 600				

KM# 8 10 MILLIEMES

Copper-Nickel **Ruler:** Idris I **Obv:** Crowned national arms above dates **Rev:** Value within wreath

Date	Mintage	F12	VF20	XF40	MS60	MS63
AH1385-1965	17,000,000	—	0.15	0.25	0.50	1.00

KM# 9 20 MILLIEMES

Copper-Nickel **Ruler:** Idris I **Obv:** Crowned national arms above dates **Rev:** Value within wreath

Date	Mintage	F12	VF20	XF40	MS60	MS63
AH1385-1965	8,750,000	—	0.20	0.50	2.00	3.50

KM# 10 50 MILLIEMES

Copper-Nickel, 26 mm. **Ruler:** Idris I **Obv:** Crowned national arms above dates **Rev:** Value within wreath **Shape:** Scalloped

Date	Mintage	F12	VF20	XF40	MS60	MS63
AH1385-1965	8,000,000	—	0.35	0.75	3.00	5.00

KM# 11 100 MILLIEMES

Copper-Nickel **Ruler:** Idris I **Obv:** Crowned national arms above dates **Rev:** Value within wreath

Date	Mintage	F12	VF20	XF40	MS60	MS63
AH1385 (1965)	8,000,000	—	0.75	1.50	4.00	6.00

SOCIALIST PEOPLE'S REPUBLIC

STANDARD COINAGE

1000 Dirhams = 1 Dinar

KM# 12 DIRHAM

Brass Clad Steel, 15 mm. **Obv:** Eagle flanked by dates **Rev:** Value within wreath

Date	Mintage	F12	VF20	XF40	MS60	MS63
AH1395-1975	20,000,000	—	0.25	0.50	1.50	3.00

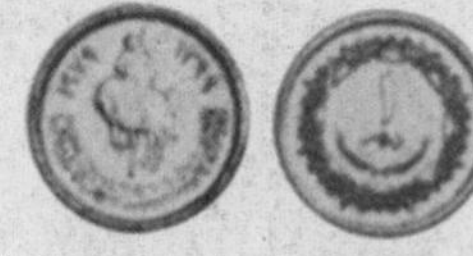

KM# 18 DIRHAM

Brass Clad Steel **Obv:** Armored equestrian **Rev:** Value within wreath

Date	Mintage	F12	VF20	XF40	MS60	MS63
AH1399-1979	1,000,000	—	0.50	1.00	3.00	5.00

KM# 13 5 DIRHAM

Brass Clad Steel **Obv:** Eagle flanked by dates **Rev:** Value above oat sprigs within wreath

Date	Mintage	F12	VF20	XF40	MS60	MS63
AH1395-1975	23,000,000	—	0.25	0.60	2.00	3.50

KM# 19 5 DIRHAM

Brass Clad Steel, 18 mm. **Obv:** Armored equestrian **Rev:** Value above oat sprigs within wreath

Date	Mintage	F12	VF20	XF40	MS60	MS63
AH1399-1979	2,000,000	—	0.75	2.00	4.00	6.00

KM# 14 10 DIRHAMS

Copper-Nickel Clad Steel **Obv:** Eagle flanked by dates **Rev:** Value above oat sprigs within wreath

Date	Mintage	F12	VF20	XF40	MS60	MS63
AH1395-1975	52,750,000	—	0.25	0.65	2.25	4.00

KM# 20 10 DIRHAMS

Copper-Nickel Clad Steel, 20 mm. **Obv:** Armored equestrian **Rev:** Value above oat sprigs within wreath

Date	Mintage	F12	VF20	XF40	MS60	MS63
AH1399-1979	4,000,000	—	1.00	2.00	4.00	6.00

KM# 15 20 DIRHAMS

5.66 g., Copper-Nickel Clad Steel, 24 mm. **Obv:** Eagle flanked by dates **Rev:** Value above oat sprigs within wreath

Date	Mintage	F12	VF20	XF40	MS60	MS63
AH1395-1975	25,500,000	—	0.50	1.75	3.00	5.00

KM# 21 20 DIRHAMS

Copper-Nickel Clad Steel **Obv:** Armored equestrian **Rev:** Value above oat sprigs within wreath

Date	Mintage	F12	VF20	XF40	MS60	MS63
AH1399-1979	6,000,000	—	1.00	2.00	4.00	6.00

KM# 16 50 DIRHAMS

6.25 g., Copper-Nickel, 25 mm. **Obv:** Eagle flanked by dates **Rev:** Value above oat sprigs within wreath

Date	Mintage	F12	VF20	XF40	MS60	MS63
AH1395-1975	25,640,000	—	1.00	2.50	6.00	8.00

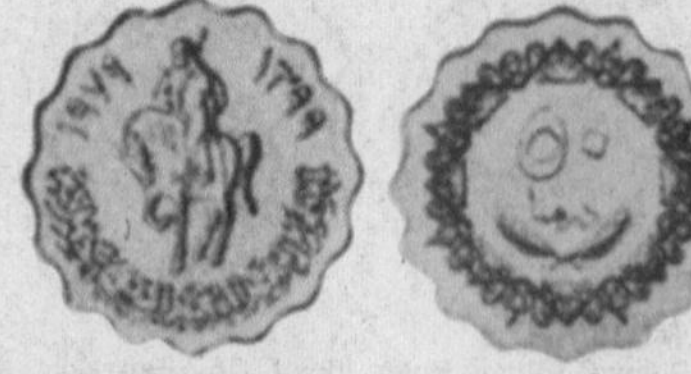

KM# 22 50 DIRHAMS

Copper-Nickel **Obv:** Armored equestrian **Rev:** Value above oat sprigs within wreath

Date	Mintage	F12	VF20	XF40	MS60	MS63
AH1399-1979	9,120,000	—	1.00	2.00	4.00	6.00

KM# 17 100 DIRHAMS

Copper-Nickel **Obv:** Eagle flanked by dates **Rev. Inscription:** Value above oat sprigs within wreath

Date	Mintage	F12	VF20	XF40	MS60	MS63
AH1395-1975	15,433,000	—	0.75	1.50	3.00	5.00

KM# 23 100 DIRHAMS

Copper-Nickel **Obv:** Armored equestrian **Rev:** Value above oat sprigs within wreath

Date	Mintage	F12	VF20	XF40	MS60	MS63
AH1399-1979	15,000,000	—	0.75	1.50	3.00	5.00

KM# 24 5 DINARS

28.28 g., 0.925 Silver 0.841 oz. ASW **Subject:** International Year of Disabled Persons **Obv:** Handicap symbol within center of helping hands **Rev:** Date and emblem within globe with legend above and below

Date	Mintage	VF20	XF40	MS60	MS63	MS65
1981	20,000	—	—	—	65.00	85.00
1981	21,000	PF63 75.00		PF65 95.00		

KM# 25 70 DINARS

15.98 g., 0.917 Gold 0.4711 oz. AGW **Subject:** International Year of Disabled Persons **Obv:** Handicap symbol within helping hands **Rev:** Date and emblem within globe with legend above and below

Date	Mintage	VF20	XF40	MS60	MS63	MS65
1981	4,000	—	—	—	1,500	1,700
1981	4,000	PF63 2,000		PF65 2,250		

PIEDFORT

KM#	Date	Mintage	Identification	Mkt Val
P1	1981	2,150	5 Dinars. Silver. KM24.	150
P2	1981	500	70 Dinars. Gold. KM25.	1,750

MINT SETS

KM#	Date	Mintage	Identification	Issue Price	Mkt Val
MS1	1975 (6)	—	KM12-17	—	23.00

PROOF SETS

KM#	Date	Mintage	Identification	Issue Price	Mkt Val
PS1	1952 (5)	32	KM1-5	—	510

LIECHTENSTEIN

The Principality of Liechtenstein, located in central Europe on the east bank of the Rhine between Austria and Switzerland, has an area of 62 sq. mi. (160 sq. km.) and a population of 27,200. Capital: Vaduz. The economy is based on agriculture and light manufacturing. Canned goods, textiles, ceramics and precision instruments are exported.

The lordships of Schellenburg and Vaduz were merged into the principality of Liechtenstein. It was a member of the Rhine Confederation from 1806 to 1815, and of the German Confederation from 1815 to 1866 when it became independent. Liechtenstein's long and close association with Austria was terminated by World War I. In 1921 it adopted the coinage of Switzerland, and two years later entered into a customs union with the Swiss, who also operated its postal and telegraph systems and represented it in international affairs. The tiny principality abolished its army in 1868 and has avoided involvement in all European wars since that time.

RULERS

Prince John II, 1858-1929
Prince Franz I, 1929-1938
Prince Franz Josef II, 1938-1990
Prince Hans Adam II, 1990-

MINT MARKS

A - Vienna
B - Bern
M - Munich (restrikes)

PRINCIPALITY

REFORM COINAGE

100 Heller = 1 Krone

Y# 2 KRONE

5.00 g., 0.835 Silver 0.1342 oz. ASW, 23 mm. **Ruler:** Prince John II **Obv:** Head left **Obv. Legend:** JOHANN II • FURST. **Rev:** Crowned shield within wreath divides value, date below

Date	Mintage	F12	VF20	XF40	MS60	MS63
1904	75,000	5.00	10.00	20.00	40.00	65.00
1910	50,000	5.00	10.00	20.00	40.00	65.00
1915	75,000	5.00	10.00	20.00	40.00	65.00

Y# 3 2 KRONEN

10.00 g., 0.835 Silver 0.2685 oz. ASW, 27 mm. **Ruler:** Prince John II **Obv:** Head left **Rev:** Crowned shield within wreath flanked by value and letters

Date	Mintage	F12	VF20	XF40	MS60	MS63
1912	50,000	12.00	20.00	35.00	65.00	85.00
1915	37,500	15.00	25.00	40.00	70.00	100

Y# 4 5 KRONEN
24.00 g., 0.900 Silver 0.6945 oz. ASW **Ruler:** Prince John II **Obv:** Head left **Obv. Legend:** JOHANN II. FURST. **Rev:** Crowned shield within wreath divides value above date

Date	Mintage	F12	VF20	XF40	MS60	MS63
1904	15,000	40.00	75.00	120	200	300
1910	10,000	50.00	90.00	160	245	350
1915	10,000	45.00	80.00	140	240	320

REFORM COINAGE

100 Rappen = 1 Frank

Y# 7 1/2 FRANK
2.50 g., 0.835 Silver 0.0671 oz. ASW, 18 mm. **Ruler:** Prince John II **Obv:** Head left **Rev:** Crowned shield within wreath flanked by value and letters **Note:** 15,745 were melted.

Date	Mintage	F12	VF20	XF40	MS60	MS63
1924	30,000	45.00	80.00	120	225	300

Y# 8 FRANK
5.00 g., 0.835 Silver 0.1342 oz. ASW, 23 mm. **Ruler:** Prince John II **Obv:** Head left **Rev:** Crowned shield within wreath flanked by value and letters **Note:** 45,355 were melted.

Date	Mintage	F12	VF20	XF40	MS60	MS63
1924	60,000	25.00	40.00	75.00	120	200

Y# 9 2 FRANKEN
10.00 g., 0.835 Silver 0.2685 oz. ASW, 27 mm. **Ruler:** Prince John II **Obv:** Head left **Rev:** Crowned shield within wreath flanked by value and letters **Note:** 41,707 were melted.

Date	Mintage	F12	VF20	XF40	MS60	MS63
1924	50,000	30.00	60.00	100	185	275

Y# 10 5 FRANKEN
25.00 g., 0.900 Silver 0.7234 oz. ASW **Ruler:** Prince John II **Obv:** Head left **Rev:** Crowned shield within wreath flanked by value and letters **Note:** 11,260 were melted.

Date	Mintage	F12	VF20	XF40	MS60	MS63
1924	15,000	120	225	375	700	1,000

Y# 11 10 FRANKEN
3.23 g., 0.900 Gold 0.0933 oz. AGW **Ruler:** Prince Franz I **Obv:** Bust right **Rev:** Crowned shield within wreath flanked by value and letters

Date	Mintage	VF20	XF40	MS60	MS63	MS65
1930	2,500	—	450	750	950	—

Y# 13 10 FRANKEN
3.23 g., 0.900 Gold 0.0933 oz. AGW **Ruler:** Prince Franz Josef II **Obv:** Head left **Rev:** Crowned shield within stars

Date	Mintage	VF20	XF40	MS60	MS63	MS65
1946 B	10,000	—	120	150	225	—

Y# 20 10 FRANKEN
30.00 g., 0.900 Silver 0.8681 oz. ASW **Ruler:** Prince Franz Josef II **Subject:** 50th Anniversary of Reign **Obv:** Head right **Rev:** Crowned shield

Date	Mintage	VF20	XF40	MS60	MS63	MS65
1988	35,000	PF65 27.00				

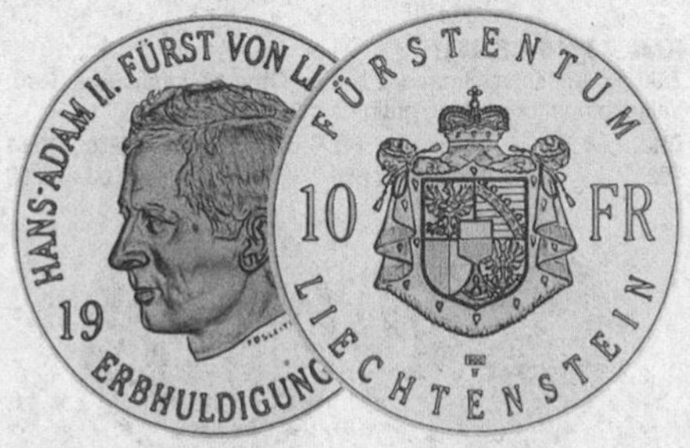

Y# 22 10 FRANKEN
30.00 g., 0.900 Silver 0.8681 oz. ASW **Ruler:** Prince Hans Adam II **Subject:** Succession of Hans Adam II **Obv:** Head left divides date **Rev:** Crowned mantled shield divides value and letters

Date	Mintage	VF20	XF40	MS60	MS63	MS65
1990	35,000	PF65 24.00				

Y# 12 20 FRANKEN
6.45 g., 0.900 Gold 0.1867 oz. AGW **Ruler:** Prince Franz I **Obv:** Bust right within circle **Rev:** Crowned shield within wreath divides value and letters

Date	Mintage	VF20	XF40	MS60	MS63	MS65
1930	2,500	—	600	1,000	1,250	—

Y# 14 20 FRANKEN
6.45 g., 0.900 Gold 0.1867 oz. AGW **Ruler:** Prince Franz Josef II **Obv:** Head left **Rev:** Crowned shield within stars

Date	Mintage	VF20	XF40	MS60	MS63	MS65
1946 B	10,000	—	—	237	285	380

Y# 15 25 FRANKEN
5.65 g., 0.900 Gold 0.1633 oz. AGW, 22 mm. **Ruler:** Prince Franz Josef II **Subject:** Franz Josef II and Princess Gina **Obv:** Conjoined busts left **Rev:** Crowned shield

Date	Mintage	VF20	XF40	MS60	MS63	MS65
1956	17,000	—	—	—	240	280

Y# 18 25 FRANKEN
5.65 g., 0.900 Gold 0.1633 oz. AGW **Ruler:** Prince Franz Josef II **Subject:** 100th Anniversary - National Bank **Obv:** Head right **Rev:** Crowned mantled shield

Date	Mintage	VF20	XF40	MS60	MS63	MS65
1961	20,000	—	—	—	230	260

Y# 16 50 FRANKEN
11.29 g., 0.900 Gold 0.3267 oz. AGW, 26 mm. **Ruler:** Prince Franz Josef II **Subject:** Franz Josef II and Princess Gina **Obv:** Conjoined busts left **Rev:** Crowned shield

Date	Mintage	VF20	XF40	MS60	MS63	MS65
1956	17,000	—	—	415	480	540

Y# 19 50 FRANKEN
11.29 g., 0.900 Gold 0.3267 oz. AGW **Ruler:** Prince Franz Josef II **Subject:** 100th Anniversary - National Bank **Obv:** Head right **Rev:** Crowned mantled shield

Date	Mintage	VF20	XF40	MS60	MS63	MS65
1961	20,000	—	—	415	460	500

Y# 21 50 FRANKEN
10.00 g., 0.900 Gold 0.2894 oz. AGW **Ruler:** Prince Franz Josef II **Subject:** 50th Anniversary of Reign **Obv:** Head right **Rev:** Crowned shield divides value and letters

Date	Mintage	VF20	XF40	MS60	MS63	MS65
1988	35,000	PF65 405				

Y# 23 50 FRANKEN
10.00 g., 0.900 Gold 0.2894 oz. AGW **Ruler:** Prince Hans Adam II **Subject:** Succession of Hans Adam II **Obv:** Head left divides date **Rev:** Crowned mantled shield divides value and letters

Date	Mintage	VF20	XF40	MS60	MS63	MS65
1990	25,000	PF65 405				

Y# 17 100 FRANKEN
32.26 g., 0.900 Gold 0.9334 oz. AGW, 36 mm. **Ruler:** Prince Franz Josef II **Subject:** Franz Josef II and Princess Gina **Obv:** Conjoined busts left **Rev:** Crowned shield

Date	Mintage	VF20	XF40	MS60	MS63	MS65
1952	4,000	—	—	1,850	2,750	3,500

MINT SETS

KM#	Date	Mintage	Identification	Issue Price	Mkt Val
MS1	1930 (2)	2,500	Y11-12	—	2,000
MS2	1946 (2)	10,000	Y13-14	—	600
MS3	1956 (2)	15,000	Y15-16	—	775
MS4	1961 (2)	20,000	Y18-19	—	675

PROOF SETS

KM#	Date	Mintage	Identification	Issue Price	Mkt Val
PS1	1988 (2)	35,000	Y20-21	—	470
PS2	1990 (2)	25,000	Y22-23	—	460

LITHUANIA

The Republic of Lithuania, southernmost of the Baltic states in east Europe, has an area of 25,174 sq. mi.(65,201 sq. km.) and a population of *3.6 million. Capital: Vilnius. The economy is based on livestock raising and manufacturing. Hogs, cattle, hides and electric motors are exported.

Lithuania emerged as a grand duchy in the 14th century. In the 15th century it was a major power of central Europe, stretching from the Baltic to the Black Sea. It was joined with Poland in 1569, but lost Smolensk, Chernihiv, and the right bank of the river Dnepr Ukraina in 1667, while the left bank remained under Polish – Lithuania rule until 1793. Following the third partition of Poland by Austria, Prussia and Russia, 1795, Lithuania came under Russian domination and did not regain its independence until shortly before the end of World War I when it declared itself a sovereign republic on Feb. 16, 1918. In fall of 1920, Poland captured Vilna (Vilnius). The republic was occupied by Soviet troops and annexed to the U.S.S.R. in 1940. Following the German occupation of 1941-44, it was retaken by Russia and reestablished as a member republic of the Soviet Union. Western countries, including the United States, did not recognize Lithuania's incorporation into the Soviet Union.

Lithuania declared its independence March 11, 1990 and it was recognized by the United States on Sept. 2, 1991, followed by the Soviet government in Moscow on Sept. 6. They were seated in the UN General Assembly on Sept. 17, 1991.

MINT MARKS

LMK – Vilna

REPUBLIC

1918-1940

STANDARD COINAGE

100 Centas = 1 Litas

KM# 71 CENTAS

1.60 g., Aluminum-Bronze, 16 mm. **Obv:** National arms **Rev:** Value within circle divides stem of flowers **Edge:** Plain

Date	Mintage	F12	VF20	XF40	MS60	MS63
1925	5,000,000	3.00	7.50	12.00	20.00	30.00

KM# 79 CENTAS

Bronze, 16.6 mm. **Obv:** National arms **Rev:** Large value with oat sprig at right **Edge:** Plain

Date	Mintage	F12	VF20	XF40	MS60	MS63
1936	9,995,000	3.00	7.50	12.00	20.00	30.00

KM# 80 2 CENTAI

2.30 g., Bronze, 18.5 mm. **Obv:** National arms **Rev:** Large value divides date within wreath **Edge:** Plain

Date	Mintage	F12	VF20	XF40	MS60	MS63
1936	4,951,000	3.00	7.50	12.00	25.00	40.00

KM# 72 5 CENTAI

Aluminum-Bronze, 19 mm. **Obv:** National arms **Rev:** Value within circle divides stem of flowers

Date	Mintage	F12	VF20	XF40	MS60	MS63
1925	12,000,000	3.00	7.50	12.00	20.00	30.00

KM# 81 5 CENTAI

2.50 g., Bronze, 20 mm. **Obv:** National arms **Rev:** Large value within wreath, date on top **Edge:** Plain

Date	Mintage	F12	VF20	XF40	MS60	MS63
1936	4,800,000	3.00	7.50	12.00	25.00	40.00

KM# 73 10 CENTŲ

3.00 g., Aluminum-Bronze, 21 mm. **Obv:** National arms **Rev:** Value to right of sagging grain ears **Edge:** Plain

Date	Mintage	F12	VF20	XF40	MS60	MS63
1925	12,000,000	1.50	3.00	7.50	20.00	30.00

KM# 74 20 CENTŲ

4.00 g., Aluminum-Bronze, 23 mm. **Obv:** National arms **Rev:** Value to right of sagging grain ears **Edge:** Plain

Date	Mintage	F12	VF20	XF40	MS60	MS63
1925	8,000,000	1.50	3.00	7.50	20.00	30.00

KM# 75 50 CENTŲ

5.00 g., Aluminum-Bronze, 25 mm. **Obv:** National arms **Rev:** Value to right of sagging grain ears **Edge:** Plain

Date	Mintage	F12	VF20	XF40	MS60	MS63
1925	5,000,000	3.00	5.00	10.00	20.00	35.00
1925	—	PF63 1,100				

KM# 76 LITAS

2.70 g., 0.500 Silver 0.0434 oz. ASW, 19 mm. **Obv:** National arms **Rev:** Value above oak leaves **Edge:** Milled **Note:** The knight riding a mare instead of stallion exist.

Date	Mintage	F12	VF20	XF40	MS60	MS63
1925	5,985,000	3.00	5.00	7.50	20.00	35.00
1925	—	PF63 1,100				

Note: Struck as proof record specimens by the Royal Mint, less than 12 were issued

KM# 77 2 LITŲ

5.40 g., 0.500 Silver 0.0868 oz. ASW, 22.9 mm. **Rev:** Denomination within wreath **Edge:** Milled

Date	Mintage	F12	VF20	XF40	MS60	MS63
1925	3,000,000	3.00	5.00	10.00	25.00	40.00
1925	—	PF63 1,100				

Note: Struck as proof record specimens by the Royal Mint, less than 12 were issued

KM# 78 5 LITAI

13.50 g., 0.500 Silver 0.217 oz. ASW, 29.5 mm. **Obv:** National arms **Rev:** Value within flowered flax wreath **Edge:** Milled

Date	Mintage	F12	VF20	XF40	MS60	MS63
1925	1,000,000	5.00	10.00	20.00	50.00	75.00
1925	—	PF63 1,100				

Note: Struck as proof record specimens by the Royal Mint, less than 12 were issued

KM# 82 5 LITAI

9.00 g., 0.750 Silver 0.217 oz. ASW, 27 mm. **Obv:** National arms **Rev:** Dr. Jonas Basanavicius left **Edge Lettering:** TAUTOS GEROVE TAVO GEROVE **Note:** Designer's initials below bust.

Date	Mintage	F12	VF20	XF40	MS60	MS63
1936	2,612,000	5.00	7.50	12.00	25.00	45.00

KM# 83 10 LITŲ

18.00 g., 0.750 Silver 0.434 oz. ASW, 32 mm. **Obv:** National arms **Rev:** Uytautas the Great, left **Edge Lettering:** VIENYBEJE TAUTOS JEGA **Note:** The knight riding a mare instead of stallion exist.

Date	Mintage	F12	VF20	XF40	MS60	MS63
1936	720,000	12.00	18.00	25.00	45.00	75.00

KM# 84 10 LITŲ

18.00 g., 0.750 Silver 0.434 oz. ASW, 32 mm. **Subject:** 20th Anniversary of Republic **Obv:** Columns of Gediminas above LIETUVA and dates 1918-1938 **Rev:** President Antanas Smetona left **Edge Lettering:** VIENYBEJE TAUTOS JEGA

Date	Mintage	F12	VF20	XF40	MS60	MS63
ND(1918-1938)	170,000	15.00	25.00	50.00	100	150

MODERN REPUBLIC

1991-present

REFORM COINAGE

100 Centas = 1 Litas

KM# 85 CENTAS

0.83 g., Aluminum, 18.75 mm. **Obv:** National arms **Rev:** Large value to right of design

Date	Mintage	VF20	XF40	MS60	MS63	MS65
1991	—	—	—	0.20	0.35	0.75

KM# 86 2 CENTAI

1.12 g., Aluminum, 21.75 mm. **Obv:** National arms **Rev:** Large value to right of design

Date	Mintage	VF20	XF40	MS60	MS63	MS65
1991	—	—	—	0.25	0.40	0.80

KM# 87 5 CENTAI

1.40 g., Aluminum, 24.4 mm. **Obv:** National arms **Rev:** Large value to right of artistic design on pole flanked by men blowing horns

Date	Mintage	VF20	XF40	MS60	MS63	MS65
1991	—	—	—	0.30	0.50	0.85

KM# 88 10 CENTŲ

1.40 g., Bronze, 16 mm. **Obv:** National arms **Rev:** Value **Note:** Varieties exist with thick or thin letters in the denomination name.

Date	Mintage	VF20	XF40	MS60	MS63	MS65
1991	—	—	—	1.00	1.25	2.00

KM# 106 10 CENTŲ

2.60 g., Nickel-Brass, 17 mm. **Obv:** National arms **Rev:** Value **Edge:** Reeded

Date	Mintage	VF20	XF40	MS60	MS63	MS65
1997	—	—	—	—	0.25	0.40
1998	—	—	—	—	0.25	0.40
1999	—	—	—	—	0.25	0.40
2000	—	—	—	—	0.25	0.40
2000 Prooflike	5,000	—	—	—	—	7.00

KM# 89 20 CENTŲ

2.10 g., Bronze, 17.5 mm. **Obv:** National arms **Rev:** Value

Date	Mintage	VF20	XF40	MS60	MS63	MS65
1991	—	—	—	1.00	1.25	2.00

KM# 107 20 CENTŲ

4.80 g., Nickel-Brass, 20.5 mm. **Obv:** National arms **Rev:** Value **Edge:** Reeded

Date	Mintage	VF20	XF40	MS60	MS63	MS65
1997	—	—	—	—	0.50	1.00
1998	—	—	—	—	0.50	1.00
1999	—	—	—	—	0.50	1.00
2000	—	—	—	—	0.50	1.00
2000	5,000	PF65 3.00				

KM# 90 50 CENTŲ

3.03 g., Bronze, 21 mm. **Obv:** National arms **Rev:** Value

Date	Mintage	VF20	XF40	MS60	MS63	MS65
1991	—	—	—	—	1.50	2.50

KM# 108 50 CENTŲ

6.00 g., Nickel-Brass, 23 mm. **Obv:** National arms **Rev:** Value within designed circle **Edge:** Reeded

Date	Mintage	VF20	XF40	MS60	MS63	MS65
1997	—	—	—	—	0.50	1.00
1998	—	—	—	—	0.50	1.00
1999	—	—	—	—	0.50	1.00
2000	—	—	—	—	0.50	1.00
2000	5,000	PF65 4.00				

KM# 91 LITAS

2.35 g., Copper-Nickel, 16.75 mm. **Obv:** National arms **Rev:** Value with lines above **Edge:** Reeded

Date	Mintage	VF20	XF40	MS60	MS63	MS65
1991	—	—	—	1.50	2.50	5.00

KM# 109 LITAS

6.25 g., Copper-Nickel, 22.3 mm. **Subject:** 75th Anniversary - Bank of Lithuania **Obv:** National arms above value **Rev:** Bust 1/4 right **Edge:** Segmented reeding

Date	Mintage	VF20	XF40	MS60	MS63	MS65
1997	200,000	—	—	3.00	5.00	10.00

KM# 109a LITAS

7.78 g., 0.999 Gold 0.2498 oz. AGW, 22.3 mm. **Subject:** 75th Anniversary - Bank of Lithuania **Obv:** National arms above value **Rev:** Bust 1/4 right

Date	Mintage	VF20	XF40	MS60	MS63	MS65
1997	1,500	PF65 725				

KM# 111 LITAS

6.25 g., Copper-Nickel, 22.3 mm. **Obv:** National arms **Rev:** Value within circle above lined designs **Edge:** Reeded

Date	Mintage	VF20	XF40	MS60	MS63	MS65
1998	—	—	—	—	0.75	1.50
1999	—	—	—	—	0.75	1.50
2000	—	—	—	—	0.75	1.50
2000	5,000	PF65 10.00				

KM# 117 LITAS

6.25 g., Copper-Nickel, 22.3 mm. **Subject:** The Baltic Highway **Obv:** National arms on shield within shaded circle divides date **Rev:** Six clasped hands within artistic design **Edge:** Segmented reeding

Date	Mintage	VF20	XF40	MS60	MS63	MS65
1999	1,000,000	—	—	1.00	1.50	2.50

KM# 92 2 LITAI

3.46 g., Copper-Nickel, 20.5 mm. **Obv:** National arms **Rev:** Value within design **Edge:** Reeded

Date	Mintage	VF20	XF40	MS60	MS63	MS65
1991	—	—	—	0.75	1.50	3.00

KM# 112 2 LITAI

7.50 g., Bi-Metallic Copper-Nickel center in Aluminum-Bronze ring, 25 mm. **Obv:** National arms within circle **Rev:** Value within circle **Edge:** Segmented reeding

Date	Mintage	VF20	XF40	MS60	MS63	MS65
1998	—	—	—	1.50	2.50	4.00
1999	—	—	—	1.50	2.50	4.00
2000	—	—	—	1.50	2.50	4.00
2000	5,000	PF65 8.00				

KM# 93 5 LITAI

4.36 g., Copper-Nickel, 23 mm. **Obv:** National arms **Rev:** Value within design **Edge:** Reeded

Date	Mintage	VF20	XF40	MS60	MS63	MS65
1991	—	—	—	2.00	4.00	7.00

KM# 113 5 LITAI

10.10 g., Bi-Metallic Aluminum-Bronze center in Copper-Nickel ring, 27.5 mm. **Obv:** National arms within circle **Rev:** Value within circle **Edge Lettering:** PENKI LITAI

Date	Mintage	VF20	XF40	MS60	MS63	MS65
1998	—	—	—	2.00	3.50	6.00
1999	—	—	—	2.00	3.50	6.00
2000	—	—	—	2.00	3.50	6.00
2000	5,000	PF65 15.00				

KM# 127 5 LITAI
28.28 g., 0.925 Silver 0.841 oz. ASW, 38.61 mm. **Series:** UNICEF **Subject:** For the Children of the World **Obv:** Hill of Gediminas Castle to right of national arms on shield above value and date **Rev:** Child with pinwheel **Edge Lettering:** LIETUVOS BANKAS

Date	Mintage	VF20	XF40	MS60	MS63	MS65
1998	—	PF65 300				

KM# 94 10 LITŲ
Copper-Nickel, 28.70 mm. **Subject:** 60th Anniversary - Darius and Girenas flight across the Atlantic **Obv:** National arms above value **Rev:** Conjoined pilot heads right **Edge Lettering:** SLOVE ATLANTO NUGALETOJAMS

Date	Mintage	VF20	XF40	MS60	MS63	MS65
ND-1993 LMK	4,500	—	—	—	50.00	80.00

KM# 95 10 LITŲ
Copper-Nickel, 28.70 mm. **Subject:** Papal visit **Rev:** Bust right **Edge Lettering:** TIKEJIMAS MEILE VILTIS

Date	Mintage	VF20	XF40	MS60	MS63	MS65
1993 LMK	5,000	—	—	—	40.00	70.00

KM# 96 10 LITŲ
Copper-Nickel, 28.70 mm. **Subject:** International Song Fest **Obv:** National arms and value **Rev:** Stringed instrument below design **Edge Lettering:** SKRISKIT SKAISCIOS DAINOS

Date	Mintage	VF20	XF40	MS60	MS63	MS65
1994 LMK	11,708	PF65 15.00				

KM# 97 10 LITŲ
Copper-Nickel, 28.70 mm. **Subject:** 5th World Sport Games **Obv:** National arms and value **Rev:** Runner with torch and design above divides globe **Edge Lettering:** LIETUVIAIS ESAME MES GIME

Date	Mintage	VF20	XF40	MS60	MS63	MS65
1995 LMK	10,000	PF65 30.00				

KM# 115 10 LITŲ
Copper-Nickel, 28.70 mm. **Obv:** Shielded arms divide date, value below **Rev:** Vilnus building tops as seen from ground level **Edge Lettering:** VILNIUS-LIETUVOS SOSTINE

Date	Mintage	VF20	XF40	MS60	MS63	MS65
1998	7,500	PF65 55.00				

KM# 116 10 LITŲ
Copper-Nickel, 28.70 mm. **Obv:** National arms above value **Rev:** Kaunas city arms on shield within buildings **Edge Lettering:** LAISVAS BUDAMAS, LAISVES NEISSIZADESI

Date	Mintage	VF20	XF40	MS60	MS63	MS65
1999	6,028	PF65 60.00				

KM# 120 10 LITŲ
1.24 g., 0.9999 Gold 0.040 oz. AGW, 28.70 mm. **Subject:** Lithuanian gold coinage **Obv:** National arms **Rev:** Medieval minter

Date	Mintage	VF20	XF40	MS60	MS63	MS65
1999	—	PF65 150				

KM# 98 50 LITŲ
23.30 g., 0.925 Silver 0.6929 oz. ASW, 34 mm. **Subject:** 5th Anniversary - Independence **Obv:** National arms flanked by ribbon with value below **Rev:** Oak tree stump with leafed branch flanked by dates above **Edge Lettering:** TEGUL MEILE LIETUVOS DEGA MUSU SIRDYSE

Date	Mintage	VF20	XF40	MS60	MS63	MS65
ND-1995 LMK	5,000	PF65 175				

KM# 99 50 LITŲ
23.30 g., 0.925 Silver 0.6929 oz. ASW, 34 mm. **Subject:** 120th Birth Anniversary Mikalojaus K. Ciurlionis **Obv:** National arms above date at right and an angel with big wings at left above value **Rev:** Head 3/4 right **Edge Lettering:** PASAULIS KAIP DIDELE SIMFONIJA

Date	Mintage	VF20	XF40	MS60	MS63	MS65
1995 LMK	6,514	PF65 125				

KM# 100 50 LITŲ
23.30 g., 0.925 Silver 0.6929 oz. ASW, 34 mm. **Subject:** 5th Anniversary - 13 January 1991 Assault **Obv:** National arms flanked by ribbon with value below **Rev:** Madonna holding man **Edge Lettering:** IR KRAUJU KRIKSTYTI TAMPA VEL GYUYBE

Date	Mintage	VF20	XF40	MS60	MS63	MS65
ND-1996	—	PF65 125				

KM# 101 50 LITŲ
23.30 g., 0.925 Silver 0.6929 oz. ASW, 34 mm. **Series:** Atlanta Olympics **Obv:** National arms flanked by sprigs **Rev:** Basketball players **Edge Lettering:** CITIUS. ALTIUS. FORTIUS.

Date	Mintage	VF20	XF40	MS60	MS63	MS65
1996 LMK	—	PF65 65.00				

KM# 102 50 LITŲ
23.30 g., 0.925 Silver 0.6929 oz. ASW, 34 mm. **Obv:** National arms at upper left within patterned circle, crown at lower right above lance **Rev:** Armored bust right **Edge Lettering:** IS PRAEITIES TAVO SUNUS TE STIPRYBE SEMIA

Date	Mintage	VF20	XF40	MS60	MS63	MS65
1996 LMK	—	PF65 95.00				

KM# 103 50 LITŲ
23.30 g., 0.925 Silver 0.6929 oz. ASW, 34 mm. **Obv:** National arms at upper left within patterned circle, crown at lower right above lance **Rev:** Armored bust 1/4 right **Edge Lettering:** IS PRAEITIES TAVO SUNUS TE STIPRYBE SEMIA

Date	Mintage	VF20	XF40	MS60	MS63	MS65
1996 LMK	—	PF65 95.00				

KM# 104 50 LITŲ
23.30 g., 0.925 Silver 0.6929 oz. ASW, 34 mm. **Subject:** 450th Anniversary - First Lithuanian Book **Obv:** National arms above date **Rev:** Page from book **Edge Lettering:** MARTYNAS MAZVYDAS IMKIT MANE IR SKAITYKIT

Date	Mintage	VF20	XF40	MS60	MS63	MS65
1997	—	PF65 125				

KM# 105 50 LITŲ
23.30 g., 0.925 Silver 0.6929 oz. ASW, 34 mm. **Subject:** 600th

Anniversary - Karaims and Tartars settlement in Lithuania **Obv:** National arms above value **Rev:** Standing figures facing with weapons **Edge Lettering:** LIETUVA TEVYNE MUSU

Date	Mintage	VF20	XF40	MS60	MS63	MS65
1997	—	PF65 250				

KM# 110 50 LITŲ

23.30 g., 0.925 Silver 0.6929 oz. ASW, 34 mm. **Obv:** National arms within patterned circle above date **Rev:** Armored bust facing holding scepter

Date	Mintage	VF20	XF40	MS60	MS63	MS65
1998	—	PF65 65.00				

KM# 114 50 LITŲ

23.30 g., 0.925 Silver 0.6929 oz. ASW, 34 mm. **Subject:** 200th Anniversary - Birth of Adomas Mickievicius **Obv:** Feather, denomination **Rev:** Laureated profile of Adomas Mickievicius, building

Date	Mintage	VF20	XF40	MS60	MS63	MS65
1998	—	PF65 145				

KM# 118 50 LITŲ

23.30 g., 0.925 Silver 0.6929 oz. ASW, 34 mm. **Subject:** Grand Duke Kestutis **Obv:** National arms within patterned circle **Rev:** Armored bust facing **Edge Lettering:** IS PRAEITIES TAVO SUNVS TE STIPRYBE SEMIA **Note:** Lithuanian Mint.

Date	Mintage	VF20	XF40	MS60	MS63	MS65
1999	—	PF65 250				

KM# 119 50 LITŲ

28.28 g., 0.925 Silver 0.841 oz. ASW, 38.6 mm. **Subject:** 100th Anniversary - Death of Vincas Kudirka **Obv:** National arms within stylized bell **Rev:** Head 1/4 left **Edge Lettering:** VARDAN TOS LIETUVOS VIENYBE TEZYDI **Note:** Lithuanian Mint.

Date	Mintage	VF20	XF40	MS60	MS63	MS65
1999	1,835	PF65 175				

KM# 123 50 LITŲ

28.28 g., 0.925 Silver 0.841 oz. ASW, 38.1 mm. **Subject:** 10th Anniversary - Baltic Way Highway **Obv:** National arms within circle divides date **Rev:** Three pairs of clasped hands **Edge Lettering:** VILNIUS RYGA TALINAS **Note:** Lithuanian Mint.

Date	Mintage	VF20	XF40	MS60	MS63	MS65
1999	—	PF65 200				

KM# 121 50 LITŲ

28.28 g., 0.925 Silver 0.841 oz. ASW, 38.61 mm. **Subject:** 350th Anniversary - The Great Art of Artillery Book **Obv:** National arms within frame **Rev:** Old rocket designs **Edge Lettering:** ARS MAGNA ARTILLERIAE * MDCL

Date	Mintage	VF20	XF40	MS60	MS63	MS65
2000	1,936	PF65 155				

KM# 122 50 LITŲ

28.28 g., 0.925 Silver 0.841 oz. ASW, 38.6 mm. **Subject:** 10th Anniversary of Independence **Obv:** National arms above value **Rev:** Radiant statue of independence **Edge Lettering:** LAISVE - AMZINOJI TAUTOS VERTYBE **Note:** Struck at Lietuvos Monetu Kalykla.

Date	Mintage	VF20	XF40	MS60	MS63	MS65
ND-2000	—	PF65 125				

KM# 124 50 LITŲ

28.28 g., 0.925 Silver 0.841 oz. ASW, 38.61 mm. **Series:** XXVII Summer Olympic Games **Obv:** National arms within lined diagonal design **Rev:** Man throwing discus, Olympic emblem and date **Edge Lettering:** NUGALI STIPRUS DVASIA IR KUNU

Date	Mintage	VF20	XF40	MS60	MS63	MS65
2000	—	PF65 35.00				

KM# 125 50 LITŲ

23.30 g., 0.925 Silver 0.6929 oz. ASW, 34 mm. **Subject:** Grand Duke Vytautas **Obv:** National arms on shield among other shields within patterned circle below design **Rev:** Crowned armored bust holding sword facing left **Edge Lettering:** IS PRAEITIES TAVO SUNUS TESTIPRYBE SEMIA

Date	Mintage	VF20	XF40	MS60	MS63	MS65
2000	2,500	PF65 250				

KM# 128 50 LITŲ

28.28 g., 0.925 Silver 0.841 oz. ASW, 38.61 mm. **Subject:** Millennium **Obv:** National arms within lined design with stars above value **Rev:** Radiant cross within arch **Edge Lettering:** SALVE NOVUM MILLENNIUM

Date	Mintage	VF20	XF40	MS60	MS63	MS65
2000	—	PF65 75.00				

KM# 126 100 LITŲ

7.78 g., 0.9999 Gold 0.2501 oz. AGW, 22.3 mm. **Subject:** Grand Duke Vytautas **Obv:** National arms above value **Rev:** Crowned armored bust right holding sword **Edge Lettering:** IS PRAEITIES TAVO SUNUS TE STIPRYBE SEMIA

Date	Mintage	VF20	XF40	MS60	MS63	MS65
2000	2,000	PF65 600				

PATTERNS

Including off metal strikes

KM#	Date	Mintage	Identification	Mkt Val
Pn3	1936	—	5 Litai. Silver. Plain. Coin struck.	2,000
Pn4	1936	—	5 Litai. Silver. Lettered. Coin struck.	2,000
Pn5	1936	—	5 Litai. Silver. Designer's name (J. ZIKARAS) below bust. Plain. KM82. Medal struck.	2,500
Pn6	1936	—	10 Litų. Silver. Plain. KM83.	3,500
Pn7	1938	—	2 Litai. Brass. Lettered.	2,800
Pn8	1938	—	2 Litai. Silver. Reeded.	3,000
Pn9	1938	—	2 Litai. Silver. Lettered.	3,000
Pn10	1938	—	2 Litai. Silver. Plain.	3,000
Pn11	1938	—	2 Litai. Silver. Plain.	3,000
Pn12	1938	—	2 Litai. Silver. Lettered.	3,000
Pn13	1938	—	10 Litų. Silver. Coin struck.	3,000
Pn14	1938	2	10 Litų. Gold. Lettered. Medal-struck presentation pieces.	—
Pn15	1994	234	50 Litų. Silver. Lettered.	5,000

TRIAL STRIKES

KM#	Date	Mintage	Identification	Mkt Val
TS1	1925	—	Centas. Aluminum-Bronze. Uniface. Obverse.	525
TS2	1925	—	Centas. Aluminum-Bronze. Uniface. Reverse.	525
TS3	1925	—	5 Centai. Aluminum-Bronze. Uniface. Obverse.	525
TS4	1925	—	5 Centai. Aluminum-Bronze. Uniface. Reverse.	525
TS5	1925	—	10 Centų. Aluminum-Bronze. Uniface. Obverse.	550
TS6	1925	—	10 Centų. Aluminum-Bronze. Uniface. Reverse.	550
TS7	1925	—	20 Centų. Aluminum-Bronze. Uniface. Obverse.	550
TS8	1925	—	20 Centų. Aluminum-Bronze. Uniface. Reverse.	550
TS9	1925	—	50 Centų. Aluminum-Bronze. Uniface. Obverse.	575
TS10	1925	—	50 Centų. Aluminum-Bronze. Uniface. Reverse.	575

MINT SETS

KM#	Date	Mintage	Identification	Issue Price	Mkt Val
MS1	1925 (5)	—	KM#71-75, 2 of each	—	3,800
MS2	1991 (9)	7,000	KM#85-93	7.50	30.00
MS3	2000 (6)	5,000	KM#106-108, 111-113	7.50	20.00

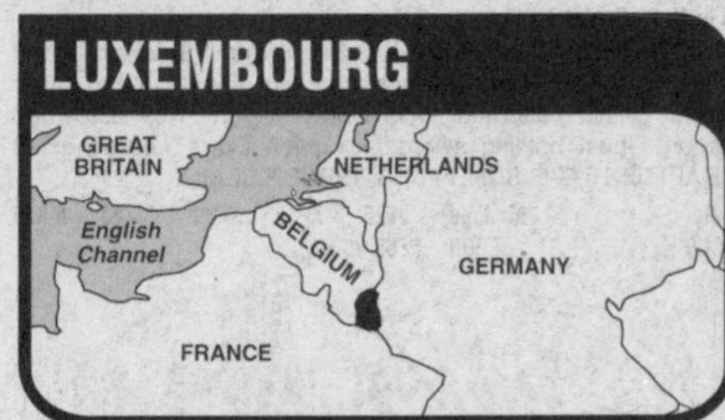

The Grand Duchy of Luxembourg is located in western Europe between Belgium, Germany and France, has an area of 1,103 sq. mi. (2,586 sq. km.) and a population of 377,100. Capital: Luxembourg. The economy is based on steel.

Founded about 963, Luxembourg was a prominent country of the Holy Roman Empire; one of its sovereigns became Holy Roman Emperor as Henry VII, 1308. After being made a duchy by Emperor Charles IV, 1354, Luxembourg passed under the domination of Burgundy, Spain, Austria and France, 1443-1815, regaining autonomy under the Treaty of Vienna, 1815, as a grand duchy in union with the Netherlands, though ostensibly a member of the German Confederation. When Belgium seceded from the Kingdom of the Netherlands, 1830, Luxembourg was forced to cede its greater western section to Belgium. The tiny duchy left the German Confederation in 1867 when the Treaty of London recognized it as an independent state and guaranteed its perpetual neutrality. Luxembourg was occupied by Germany and liberated by American troops in both World Wars.

RULERS

Adolphe, 1890-1905
William IV, 1905-1912
Marie Adelaide, 1912-1919
Charlotte, 1919-1964
Jean, 1964-2000
Henri, 2000-

MINT MARKS

A - Paris
(b) - Brussels, privy marks only
H – Gunzburg
(n) – lion - Namur
(u) - Utrecht, privy marks only

PRIVY MARKS

Angel's head, two headed eagle - Brussels
Sword, Caduceus - Utrecht (1846-74 although struck at Brussels until 1909)

NOTE: Beginning in 1994 the letters "qp" for quality proof appear on Proof coins.

GRAND DUCHY

STANDARD COINAGE RESUMED

100 Centimes = 1 Franc

KM# 21 2-1/2 CENTIMES

Bronze **Ruler:** William III **Obv:** Crowned ornate shield within rope wreath **Obv. Legend:** GRAND-DUCHE DE LUXEMBOURG **Rev:** Value and date within wreath

Date	Mintage	F12	VF20	XF40	MS60	MS63
1901 (u)	800,000	0.50	1.50	7.50	20.00	40.00
Note: BARTH on reverse						
1901 (u)	Inc. above	0.50	1.50	8.50	22.00	42.00
Note: BAPTH on reverse						
1908 (u)	400,000	0.50	1.50	9.50	25.00	45.00

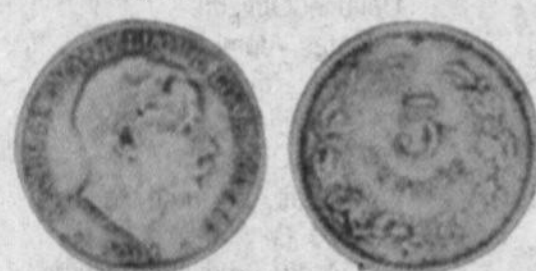

KM# 24 5 CENTIMES

1.95 g., Copper-Nickel, 17 mm. **Ruler:** Adolphe **Obv:** Head right **Rev:** Value within wreath

Date	Mintage	F12	VF20	XF40	MS60	MS63
1901	2,000,000	0.25	0.75	4.50	17.50	35.00

KM# 26 5 CENTIMES

Copper-Nickel **Ruler:** William IV **Obv:** Head right **Rev:** Value within wreath

Date	Mintage	F12	VF20	XF40	MS60	MS63
1908	1,500,000	0.35	1.00	6.50	20.00	40.00

KM# 27 5 CENTIMES

2.50 g., Zinc **Ruler:** Marie Adelaide **Obv:** Plain and beaded circle around hole in center with date below **Rev:** Value above hole in center with 1/2 wreath below

Date	Mintage	F12	VF20	XF40	MS60	MS63
1915	1,200,000	1.00	6.00	15.00	30.00	—

KM# 30 5 CENTIMES

Iron, 18 mm. **Ruler:** Charlotte **Obv:** National arms **Rev:** Value within wreath

Date	Mintage	F12	VF20	XF40	MS60	MS63
1918	1,200,000	1.00	4.00	8.00	30.00	—
1921	600,000	10.00	20.00	40.00	80.00	—
1922	400,000	15.00	30.00	80.00	120	—

KM# 33 5 CENTIMES

Copper-Nickel **Ruler:** Charlotte **Obv:** Crowned monogram **Rev:** Value within wreath

Date	Mintage	F12	VF20	XF40	MS60	MS63
1924	3,000,000	0.20	0.40	3.00	5.00	10.00

KM# 40 5 CENTIMES

2.50 g., Bronze **Ruler:** Charlotte **Obv:** Head left **Rev:** Value

Date	Mintage	F12	VF20	XF40	MS60	MS63
1930	5,000,000	0.10	0.25	2.00	4.00	7.50

KM# 25 10 CENTIMES

Copper-Nickel, 20 mm. **Ruler:** Adolphe **Obv:** Head right **Rev:** Value within wreath

Date	Mintage	F12	VF20	XF40	MS60	MS63
1901	4,000,000	0.25	0.75	6.00	14.00	30.00

KM# 28 10 CENTIMES

3.10 g., Zinc **Ruler:** Marie Adelaide **Obv:** Beaded circle around hole in center with date below **Rev:** Large value above hole in center with 1/2 wreath below

Date	Mintage	F12	VF20	XF40	MS60	MS63
1915	1,400,000	1.25	4.00	8.00	20.00	—

KM# 31 10 CENTIMES

Iron **Ruler:** Charlotte **Obv:** National arms **Rev:** Value within wreath

Date	Mintage	F12	VF20	XF40	MS60	MS63
1918	1,603,000	1.50	3.50	10.00	25.00	—
1921	626,000	2.00	10.00	20.00	40.00	—
1923	350,000	12.00	30.00	60.00	125	—

KM# 34 10 CENTIMES

Copper-Nickel **Ruler:** Charlotte **Obv:** Crowned monogram **Rev:** Value within wreath

Date	Mintage	F12	VF20	XF40	MS60	MS63
1924	3,500,000	0.25	0.50	2.00	5.00	8.00

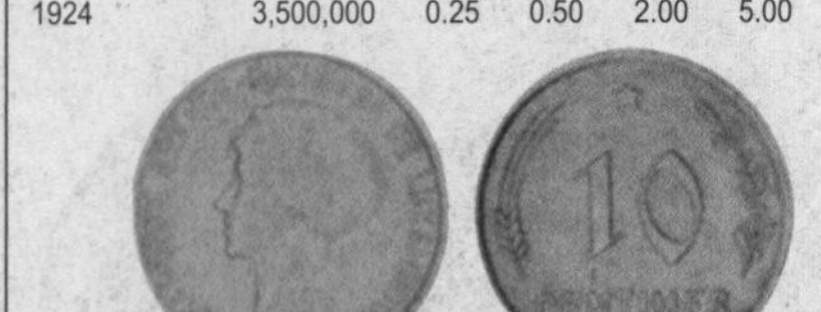

KM# 41 10 CENTIMES

4.00 g., Bronze, 22 mm. **Ruler:** Charlotte **Obv:** Head left **Rev:** Value flanked by sprigs with star above

Date	Mintage	F12	VF20	XF40	MS60	MS63
1930	5,000,000	0.10	0.25	2.00	5.00	9.00

KM# 29 25 CENTIMES

5.00 g., Zinc **Ruler:** Charlotte **Obv:** Beaded circle around hole in center with date below **Rev:** Large value above hole in center with wreath below

Date	Mintage	F12	VF20	XF40	MS60	MS63
1916	800,000	1.50	6.00	12.00	25.00	—
1920	—	200	400	600	1,000	—

KM# 32 25 CENTIMES

Iron **Ruler:** Charlotte **Obv:** National arms **Rev:** Value within wreath

Date	Mintage	F12	VF20	XF40	MS60	MS63
1919	804,000	2.75	6.50	12.50	35.00	—
1920	800,000	2.75	8.00	14.00	35.00	—
1922	600,000	2.75	8.50	16.00	40.00	—

KM# 37 25 CENTIMES

Copper-Nickel **Ruler:** Charlotte **Obv:** Crowned national arms flanked by stars **Rev:** Value and date to right of sprig

Date	Mintage	F12	VF20	XF40	MS60	MS63
1927	2,500,000	0.35	0.65	5.00	12.00	20.00

KM# 42 25 CENTIMES

Bronze **Ruler:** Charlotte **Obv:** Crowned national arms flanked by stars **Rev:** Value and date to right of sprig

Date	Mintage	F12	VF20	XF40	MS60	MS63
1930	1,000,000	0.35	1.00	8.00	15.00	25.00

KM# 42a.1 25 CENTIMES

Copper-Nickel, 25 mm. **Ruler:** Charlotte **Obv:** Crowned national arms flanked by stars **Rev:** Value and date to right of sprig **Note:** Coin alignment.

Date	Mintage	F12	VF20	XF40	MS60	MS63
1938	2,000,000	0.35	1.00	3.00	6.00	10.00

KM# 42a.2 25 CENTIMES

Copper-Nickel, 25 mm. **Ruler:** Charlotte **Obv:** Crowned national arms flanked by stars **Rev:** Value and date to right of sprig **Note:** Medal alignment.

Date	Mintage	F12	VF20	XF40	MS60	MS63
1938	Inc. above	50.00	75.00	100	200	—

KM# 45 25 CENTIMES

2.50 g., Bronze, 19 mm. **Ruler:** Charlotte **Obv:** Crowned national arms flanked by diamonds **Rev:** Value and date to right of sprig

Date	Mintage	VF20	XF40	MS60	MS63	MS65
1946	1,000,000	0.15	0.25	0.75	1.25	2.50
1947	1,000,000	0.15	0.25	0.75	1.25	2.50

KM# 45a.1 25 CENTIMES

0.76 g., Aluminum, 19 mm. **Ruler:** Jean **Obv:** Crowned national arms flanked by diamonds **Rev:** Value and date to right of sprig **Note:** Coin alignment.

Date	Mintage	VF20	XF40	MS60	MS63	MS65
1954	7,000,000	—	—	0.50	0.75	1.00
1957	3,020,000	—	—	0.50	0.75	1.00
1960	3,020,000	—	—	0.50	0.75	1.00
1963	4,000,000	—	—	0.50	0.75	1.00
1965	2,000,000	—	—	0.50	0.75	1.00
1967	3,000,000	—	—	0.50	0.75	1.00
1968	600,000	0.25	0.50	0.75	1.00	1.50
1970	4,000,000	—	—	0.50	0.75	1.00
1972	4,000,000	—	—	0.50	0.75	1.00

KM# 45a.2 25 CENTIMES

0.76 g., Aluminum, 19 mm. **Ruler:** Jean **Obv:** Crowned national arms flanked by diamonds **Rev:** Value and date to right of sprig **Note:** Medal alignment.

Date	Mintage	VF20	XF40	MS60	MS63	MS65
1954	Inc. above	20.00	30.00	40.00	—	—
1960	Inc. above	10.00	15.00	20.00	—	—
1963	Inc. above	10.00	15.00	20.00	—	—
1965	Inc. above	20.00	30.00	40.00	—	—
1967	Inc. above	20.00	30.00	40.00	—	—

KM# 45b 25 CENTIMES

2.96 g., 0.925 Silver 0.088 oz. ASW **Ruler:** Jean **Obv:** Crowned national arms flanked by diamonds **Rev:** Value and date to right of sprig

Date	Mintage	VF20	XF40	MS60	MS63	MS65
1980	3,000	PF65 15.00				

KM# 43 50 CENTIMES

Nickel **Ruler:** Charlotte **Obv:** Steelworker poking fire, date below **Rev:** Value divides wheat sprays

Date	Mintage	F12	VF20	XF40	MS60	MS63
1930	2,000,000	0.25	1.00	10.00	15.00	25.00

KM# 35 FRANC

5.10 g., Nickel, 23 mm. **Ruler:** Charlotte **Obv:** Crowned monogram **Rev:** Steelworker poking fire **Edge:** Reeded

Date	Mintage	F12	VF20	XF40	MS60	MS63
1924	1,000,000	0.25	1.50	10.00	15.00	25.00
1928	2,000,000	0.20	1.50	10.00	15.00	25.00
1935	1,000,000	0.25	2.00	14.00	20.00	30.00

KM# 44 FRANC

6.50 g., Copper-Nickel, 24 mm. **Ruler:** Charlotte **Obv:** Crowned monogram flanked by flower blossoms at top **Rev:** Woman figure divides date and value **Edge:** Reeded

Date	Mintage	F12	VF20	XF40	MS60	MS63
1939	5,000,000	0.25	0.75	1.50	3.00	7.50

KM# 46.1 FRANC

5.00 g., Copper-Nickel, 23 mm. **Ruler:** Charlotte **Obv:** Steelworker poking fire **Rev:** Crowned monogram divides value **Edge:** Reeded

Date	Mintage	F12	VF20	XF40	MS60	MS63
1946	4,000,000	0.15	0.35	0.50	1.50	3.00
1947	2,000,000	0.20	0.40	1.00	3.00	5.00

KM# 46.2 FRANC

4.00 g., Copper-Nickel, 21 mm. **Ruler:** Charlotte **Obv:** Steelworker poking fire **Rev:** Crowned monogram divides value **Edge:** Reeded

Date	Mintage	F12	VF20	XF40	MS60	MS63
1952	5,000,000	0.10	0.25	0.50	2.00	3.50
1953	2,000,000	0.10	0.25	0.50	1.50	3.00
1955	1,000,000	0.10	0.25	0.50	1.50	3.00
1957	2,000,000	—	0.10	0.25	1.00	2.50
1960	2,000,000	—	0.10	0.25	1.00	2.50
1962	2,000,000	—	0.10	0.25	1.00	2.50
1964	2,000,000	—	0.10	0.25	1.00	2.50

KM# 46.2a FRANC

4.45 g., 0.925 Silver 0.1323 oz. ASW, 21 mm. **Ruler:** Jean **Obv:** Steelworker poking fire **Rev:** Crowned monogram divides value

Date	Mintage	VF20	XF40	MS60	MS63	MS65
1980	—	PF65 22.00				

KM# 55 FRANC

4.00 g., Copper-Nickel, 21 mm. **Ruler:** Jean **Obv:** Head left **Rev:** Crown above value within wreath **Edge:** Reeded

Date	Mintage	VF20	XF40	MS60	MS63	MS65
1965	3,000,000	—	—	0.75	1.00	1.50
1966	1,000,000	—	—	0.75	1.00	1.50
1968	3,000,000	—	—	0.75	1.00	1.50
1970	3,000,000	—	—	0.75	1.00	1.50
1972	3,000,000	—	—	0.75	1.00	1.50
1973	3,000,000	—	—	0.75	1.00	1.50
1976	3,000,000	—	—	0.75	1.00	1.50
1977	1,000,000	—	—	0.75	1.00	1.50
1978	3,000,000	—	—	0.75	1.00	1.50
1979	2,000,000	—	—	0.75	1.00	1.50
1980	4,000,000	—	—	0.75	1.00	1.50
1981	5,000,000	—	—	0.75	1.00	1.50
1982	3,000,000	—	—	0.75	1.00	1.50
1983	3,000,000	—	—	0.75	1.00	1.50
1984	3,000,000	—	—	0.75	1.00	1.50

KM# 55a FRANC

4.47 g., 0.925 Silver 0.1329 oz. ASW, 21 mm. **Ruler:** Jean **Obv:** Head left **Rev:** Crown above value within wreath

Date	Mintage	VF20	XF40	MS60	MS63	MS65
1980	3,000	PF65 22.00				

KM# 59 FRANC

3.89 g., Copper-Nickel, 21 mm. **Ruler:** Jean **Obv:** Head left **Rev:** IML added

Date	Mintage	VF20	XF40	MS60	MS63	MS65
1986	3,000,000	—	—	0.75	1.00	1.50
1987	3,000,000	—	—	0.75	1.00	1.50

KM# 63 FRANC

2.75 g., Nickel Plated Steel, 18 mm. **Ruler:** Jean **Obv:** Head left **Rev:** Crown divides date above value

Date	Mintage	VF20	XF40	MS60	MS63	MS65
1988	10,000,000	—	—	0.75	1.00	1.50
1989	3,000,000	—	—	0.75	1.00	1.50
1990	25,010,000	—	—	0.75	1.00	1.50
1991	10,010,000	—	—	0.75	1.00	1.50
1992 Sets only	10,000	—	—	—	—	2.00
1993 Sets only	10,000	—	—	—	—	2.00
1994 Sets only	10,000	—	—	—	—	2.00
1995 Sets only	10,000	—	—	—	—	2.00

KM# 36 2 FRANCS

10.00 g., Nickel, 27 mm. **Ruler:** Charlotte **Obv:** Crowned monogram above sprig **Rev:** Steelworker poking fire **Edge:** Reeded

Date	Mintage	F12	VF20	XF40	MS60	MS63
1924	1,000,000	1.00	4.00	12.00	25.00	45.00

KM# 38 5 FRANCS

8.00 g., 0.625 Silver 0.1608 oz. ASW, 27.8 mm. **Ruler:** Charlotte **Rev:** Wing above national arms on shield divides value

Date	Mintage	F12	VF20	XF40	MS60	MS63
1929	2,000,000	3.00	6.00	12.00	20.00	30.00

KM# 50 5 FRANCS

7.00 g., Copper-Nickel **Ruler:** Charlotte **Obv:** Head left **Rev:** Value flanked by flowers below crown and ribbon **Edge:** Reeded

Date	Mintage	F12	VF20	XF40	MS60	MS63
1949	2,000,000	0.30	0.60	1.00	4.00	7.00

KM# 51 5 FRANCS

6.00 g., Copper-Nickel **Ruler:** Charlotte **Obv:** Head right **Rev:** Crowned arms divide value **Edge:** Reeded

Date	Mintage	VF20	XF40	MS60	MS63	MS65
1962	2,000,000	0.25	0.40	1.00	1.50	3.00

KM# 51a 5 FRANCS

6.74 g., 0.925 Silver 0.2004 oz. ASW **Ruler:** Jean **Obv:** Head right **Rev:** Crowned arms divide value

Date	Mintage	VF20	XF40	MS60	MS63	MS65
1980	3,000	PF63 22.50	PF65 27.50			

KM# 56 5 FRANCS

Copper-Nickel **Ruler:** Jean **Obv:** Head left **Rev:** Crown above value and date within sprigs

Date	Mintage	VF20	XF40	MS60	MS63	MS65
1971	1,000,000	—	—	1.00	2.00	3.50
1976	1,000,000	—	—	1.00	2.00	3.50
1979	1,000,000	—	—	1.00	2.00	3.50
1981	1,000,000	—	—	1.00	2.00	3.50

KM# 56a 5 FRANCS

6.78 g., 0.925 Silver 0.2016 oz. ASW **Ruler:** Jean **Obv:** Head left **Rev:** Crown above value and date within sprigs

Date	Mintage	VF20	XF40	MS60	MS63	MS65
1980	3,000	PF63 22.50	PF65 27.50			

KM# 60.1 5 FRANCS

5.50 g., Aluminum-Bronze, 24 mm. **Ruler:** Jean **Obv:** Head left **Rev:** Crown divides date above value within sprigs with IML added

Date	Mintage	VF20	XF40	MS60	MS63	MS65
1986	9,000,000	—	—	0.75	1.00	2.00

KM# 60.2 5 FRANCS

5.50 g., Aluminum-Bronze, 24 mm. **Ruler:** Jean **Obv:** Head left **Rev:** Larger crown divides date above value within sprigs

Date	Mintage	VF20	XF40	MS60	MS63	MS65
1986	Inc. above	—	—	2.00	4.00	8.50
1987	7,000,000	—	—	0.50	0.75	1.00
1988	2,000,000	—	—	0.75	1.00	1.50

KM# 65 5 FRANCS

5.50 g., Aluminum-Bronze, 24 mm. **Ruler:** Jean **Obv:** Head left **Rev:** Crown divides date above value

Date	Mintage	VF20	XF40	MS60	MS63	MS65
1989	2,000,000	—	—	0.75	1.00	1.50
1990	4,010,000	—	—	0.75	1.00	1.50
1991 Sets only	10,000	—	—	—	—	1.75
1992 Sets only	20,000	—	—	—	—	1.75
1993 Sets only	17,500	—	—	—	—	1.75
1994 Sets only	10,000	—	—	—	—	1.75
1995 Sets only	10,000	—	—	—	—	1.75

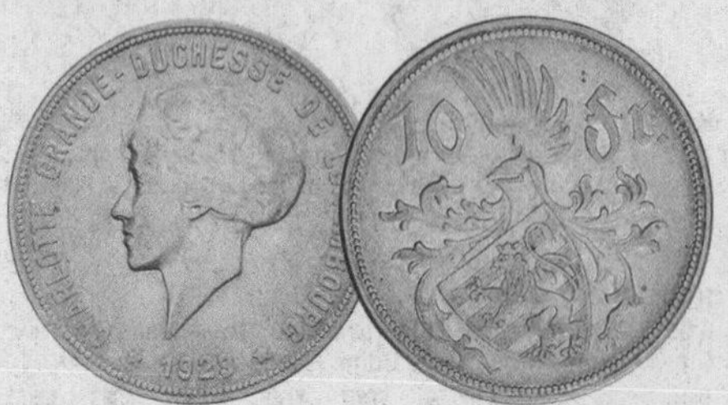

KM# 39 10 FRANCS

13.50 g., 0.750 Silver 0.3255 oz. ASW **Ruler:** Charlotte **Obv:** Head left **Rev:** Helmeted shield **Edge:** Reeded

Date	Mintage	F12	VF20	XF40	MS60	MS63
1929	1,000,000	6.00	12.50	20.00	35.00	60.00

KM# 57 10 FRANCS

8.00 g., Nickel, 27 mm. **Ruler:** Jean **Obv:** Head left **Rev:** Crown above value and date flanked by leaves

Date	Mintage	VF20	XF40	MS60	MS63	MS65
1971	3,000,000	—	—	1.00	1.50	3.00
1972	3,000,000	—	—	1.00	1.50	3.00
1974	3,000,000	—	—	1.00	1.50	3.00
1976	3,000,000	—	—	1.00	1.50	3.00
1977	1,000,000	—	—	1.00	1.50	3.00
1978	1,000,000	—	—	1.00	1.50	3.00
1979	1,000,000	—	—	1.00	1.50	3.00
1980	1,000,000	—	—	1.00	1.50	3.00

KM# 57a 10 FRANCS

8.79 g., 0.925 Silver 0.2614 oz. ASW **Ruler:** Jean **Obv:** Head left **Rev:** Crown above value and date flanked by leaves

Date	Mintage	VF20	XF40	MS60	MS63	MS65
1980	3,000	PF63 27.50	PF65 32.50			

KM# 47 20 FRANCS

8.50 g., 0.835 Silver 0.2282 oz. ASW, 27 mm. **Ruler:** Charlotte **Subject:** 600th Anniversary - John the Blind **Obv:** Head left flanked by shields **Rev:** Armored Knight on horse above dates

Date	Mintage	F12	VF20	XF40	MS60	MS63
ND-1946	100,000	4.25	8.50	12.50	22.00	25.00
ND-1946	100	PF63 200	PF65 220			

KM# 58 20 FRANCS

8.50 g., Aluminum-Bronze, 25.65 mm. **Ruler:** Jean **Obv:** Head left **Rev:** Crown above value flanked by sprigs **Edge:** Dashed

Date	Mintage	VF20	XF40	MS60	MS63	MS65
1980	3,000,000	—	—	1.50	2.00	3.50
1981	3,000,000	—	—	1.50	2.00	3.50
1982	3,000,000	—	—	1.50	2.00	3.50
1983	2,000,000	—	—	1.50	2.00	3.50

KM# 58a 20 FRANCS

10.21 g., 0.925 Silver 0.3036 oz. ASW, 25.5 mm. **Ruler:** Jean **Obv:** Head left **Rev:** Crown above value flanked by sprigs

Date	Mintage	VF20	XF40	MS60	MS63	MS65
1980	3,000	PF63 30.00	PF65 35.00			

KM# 64 20 FRANCS

6.22 g., 0.999 Gold 0.1998 oz. AGW **Ruler:** Jean **Subject:** 150th Anniversary of the Grand Duchy **Obv:** Head left **Rev:** Crowned national arms

Date	Mintage	VF20	XF40	MS60	MS63	MS65
ND-1989	50,000	PF63 280	PF65 305			

KM# 67 20 FRANCS

8.50 g., Aluminum-Bronze, 25.65 mm. **Ruler:** Jean **Obv:** Head left **Rev:** Crown divides date above value

Date	Mintage	VF20	XF40	MS60	MS63	MS65
1990	1,110,000	—	—	1.50	2.00	3.00
1991 Sets only	10,000	—	—	1.50	2.50	3.50
1992 Sets only	10,000	—	—	1.50	2.50	3.50
1993 Sets only	10,000	—	—	1.50	2.50	3.50
1994 Sets only	10,000	—	—	1.50	2.50	3.50
1995 Sets only	10,000	—	—	1.50	2.50	3.50

KM# 48 50 FRANCS

12.50 g., 0.835 Silver 0.3356 oz. ASW, 30 mm. **Ruler:** Charlotte **Subject:** 600th Anniversary - John the Blind

Date	Mintage	F12	VF20	XF40	MS60	MS63
ND-1946	100,000	—	12.50	15.00	25.00	35.00
ND-1946	100	PF63 225	PF65 245			

KM# 62 50 FRANCS

7.00 g., Nickel, 22.75 mm. **Ruler:** Jean **Obv:** Head left **Rev:** Crown divides date above value **Edge:** Reeded

Date	Mintage	VF20	XF40	MS60	MS63	MS65
1987	3,000,000	—	—	1.50	3.50	5.00
1988	1,000,000	—	—	1.50	3.50	5.00
1989	1,200,000	—	—	1.50	3.50	5.00

KM# 66 50 FRANCS

7.00 g., Nickel, 22.75 mm. **Ruler:** Jean **Obv:** Head left **Rev:** Small crown divides date above value **Edge:** Reeded **Note:** Similar to 5 Francs, KM#65.

Date	Mintage	VF20	XF40	MS60	MS63	MS65
1989	2,000,000	—	—	1.50	3.50	5.00
1990	2,010,000	—	—	1.50	3.50	5.00
1991 Sets only	10,000	—	—	—	—	6.00
1992 Sets only	10,000	—	—	—	—	6.00
1993 Sets only	10,000	—	—	—	—	6.00
1994 Sets only	10,000	—	—	—	—	6.00
1995 Sets only	10,000	—	—	—	—	6.00

KM# 49 100 FRANCS

25.00 g., 0.835 Silver 0.6711 oz. ASW, 37 mm. **Ruler:** Charlotte **Subject:** 600th Anniversary - John the Blind **Obv:** Head left flanked by crowned shields **Rev:** Armored Knight on horse above dates

Date	Mintage	F12	VF20	XF40	MS60	MS63
ND-1946	98,000	—	13.00	25.00	40.00	55.00
ND-1946	100	PF63 235	PF65 260			
ND-1946 Restrike	2,000	—	—	—	—	65.00

Note: Without designer's name

KM# 52 100 FRANCS
18.00 g., 0.835 Silver 0.4832 oz. ASW, 33.1 mm. **Ruler:** Charlotte **Obv:** Head right **Rev:** Crowned arms with supporters above value

Date	Mintage	VF20	XF40	MS60	MS63	MS65
1963	50,000	—	9.50	12.00	13.50	15.00

KM# 54 100 FRANCS
18.00 g., 0.835 Silver 0.4832 oz. ASW, 33.1 mm. **Ruler:** Charlotte **Rev:** Crowned mantled arms with supporters

Date	Mintage	VF20	XF40	MS60	MS63	MS65
1964	50,000	—	9.50	12.00	13.50	15.00

KM# 70 100 FRANCS
16.10 g., 0.925 Silver 0.4788 oz. ASW **Ruler:** Jean **Subject:** 50th Anniversary - United Nations **Obv:** Head left **Rev:** Emblem and numeral 50 to lower right of building, flags and gun

Date	Mintage	VF20	XF40	MS60	MS63	MS65
ND-1995 (qp)	110,000	PF63 30.00	PF65 35.00			

KM# 53.1 250 FRANCS
25.00 g., 0.835 Silver 0.6711 oz. ASW, 37 mm. **Ruler:** Charlotte **Subject:** Millennium of Luxembourg City **Obv:** Head right within circular inscriptions above dates **Rev:** City view above value

Date	Mintage	VF20	XF40	MS60	MS63	MS65
ND-1963	11,500	—	—	15.00	18.00	25.00

KM# 53.2 250 FRANCS
25.00 g., 0.835 Silver 0.6711 oz. ASW, 37 mm. **Ruler:** Charlotte **Subject:** Millennium of Luxembourg City **Obv:** Head right within circular inscriptions above dates **Rev:** City view above value **Note:** Darkly toned by the mint.

Date	Mintage	VF20	XF40	MS60	MS63	MS65
ND-1963	8,500	—	—	20.00	25.00	40.00

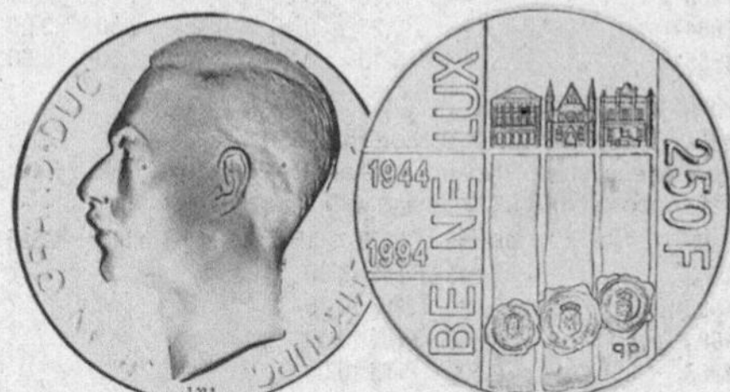

KM# 68 250 FRANCS
18.75 g., 0.925 Silver 0.5576 oz. ASW **Ruler:** Jean **Subject:** BE-NE-LUX Treaty **Obv:** Head left **Rev:** Houses above with flowers below dividing date and value

Date	Mintage	VF20	XF40	MS60	MS63	MS65
ND-1994 (qp)	30,000	PF63 22.50	PF65 27.50			

KM# 69 500 FRANCS
22.85 g., 0.925 Silver 0.6795 oz. ASW **Ruler:** Jean **Subject:** 50th Anniversary of Liberation **Obv:** Head left **Rev:** Flag design below with inscription above within circle

Date	Mintage	VF20	XF40	MS60	MS63	MS65
ND-1994	25,000	—	—	—	27.50	32.50
ND-1994 (qp)	25,000	PF63 35.00	PF65 45.00			

KM# 71 500 FRANCS
22.85 g., 0.925 Silver 0.6795 oz. ASW **Ruler:** Jean **Subject:** Luxembourg - European Cultural City **Obv:** Segmented head left **Rev:** Quartered cultural pictures

Date	Mintage	VF20	XF40	MS60	MS63	MS65
(19)95 (qp)	10,000	PF63 35.00	PF65 45.00			

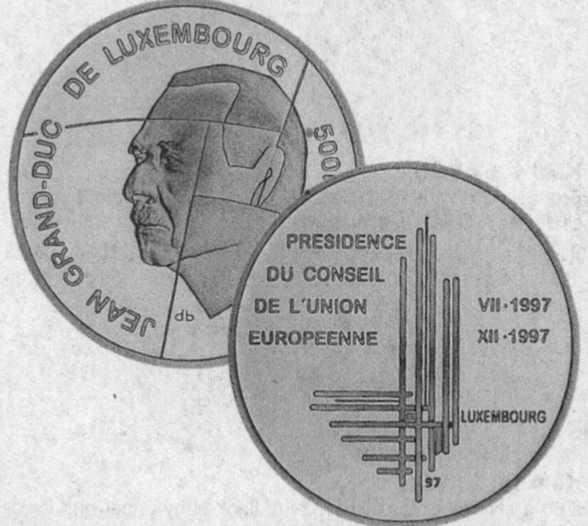

KM# 72 500 FRANCS
22.85 g., 0.925 Silver 0.6795 oz. ASW **Ruler:** Jean **Subject:** Presidency of the European Community **Obv:** Segmented portrait **Rev:** Symbolic design and dates

Date	Mintage	VF20	XF40	MS60	MS63	MS65
(19)97 (qp)	10,000	PF63 35.00	PF65 45.00			
(19)97 (qp)	10,000	PF63 30.00	PF65 40.00			

KM# 73 500 FRANCS
22.85 g., 0.925 Silver 0.6795 oz. ASW **Ruler:** Jean **Subject:** 1,300 years of Echternach **Obv:** Duke's segmented portrait **Rev:** City seal and anniversary dates

Date	Mintage	VF20	XF40	MS60	MS63	MS65
ND-1998 (qp)	10,000	PF63 30.00	PF65 40.00			

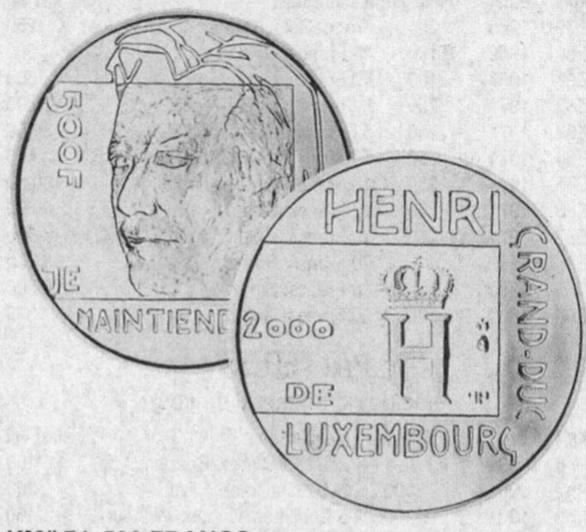

KM# 74 500 FRANCS
22.85 g., 0.925 Silver 0.6795 oz. ASW, 37 mm. **Ruler:** Jean **Subject:** Coronation of Henry III **Obv:** Head left **Rev:** Crowned "H"

Date	Mintage	VF20	XF40	MS60	MS63	MS65
2000 (qp)	10,000	PF63 35.00	PF65 45.00			

ESSAIS

KM#	Date	Mintage	Identification	Mkt Val
E22	1901	20	5 Centimes. Gold. Adolph.	1,250
E23	1901	—	10 Centimes. Gold. Adolph.	1,250
E24	1908	—	10 Centimes. Gold. Wilhelm.	1,250
E25	1914	100	50 Centimes. Copper.	75.00
E26	1914	Est. 3000	50 Centimes. Silver.	60.00
E27	1914	100	Franc. Copper. Bust left. Value and date within wreath.	75.00
E28	1914	Est. 3000	Franc. Silver.	60.00
E29	1914	100	2 Francs. Copper.	75.00
E30	1914	Est. 3000	2 Francs. Silver. Restruck after World War I.	60.00
E31	1927	—	25 Centimes. Gold.	—
E32	1929	50	5 Francs. Copper.	170
E33	1929	50	5 Francs. Bronze.	180
E34	1929	—	5 Francs. Gold.	2,500
E35	1929	50	10 Francs. Copper.	170
E36	1929	50	10 Francs. Bronze.	180
E37	1929	—	10 Francs. Silver.	1,250
E38	1929	—	10 Francs. Gold.	2,500
E39	1939	—	Franc. Gold.	1,850
E40	1945	100	25 Centimes. Copper. 25 at top.	40.00
E41	1945	100	25 Centimes. Copper. 25 at upper right.	40.00
E42	1946	100	25 Centimes. Copper.	30.00
E43	1946	500	25 Centimes. Copper.	30.00
E44	1946	500	25 Centimes. Silver.	40.00
E45	1946	500	Franc. Copper. Plain.	30.00
E46	1946	100	Franc. Copper. Milled.	35.00
E47	1946	500	Franc. Silver. Plain.	45.00
E48	1946	100	Franc. Silver. Milled.	55.00
E49	1946	100	Franc. Silver. Small letters.	55.00
E50	1946	100	20 Francs. Copper.	120
E51	1946	50	20 Francs. Silver.	220
E52	1946	25	20 Francs. Gold.	1,500
E53	1946	100	50 Francs. Copper.	145
E54	1946	50	50 Francs. Silver.	245
E55	1946	25	50 Francs. Gold.	2,500
E56	1946	100	100 Francs. Copper.	170
E57	1946	50	100 Francs. Silver. Head left. Crowned mantled arms with supporters divides date within circle.	345
E58	1946	25	100 Francs. Gold.	3,600
E59	1949	50	5 Francs. Copper.	65.00
E60	1949	50	5 Francs. Bronze-Aluminum.	65.00
E61	1962	75	5 Francs. Copper-Nickel.	45.00
E62	1962	50	5 Francs. Silver.	130
E63	1962	50	5 Francs. Gold.	1,250
E64	1963	250	20 Francs. Gold.	255
E65	1963	100	100 Francs. Bronze.	85.00
E66	1963	185	100 Francs. Silver.	75.00
E67	1963	50	100 Francs. Gold.	1,600
E68	ND-1963	—	250 Francs. Copper-Nickel.	65.00
E69	ND-1963	200	250 Francs. Bronze.	65.00
E70	ND-1963	200	250 Francs. Silver.	100
E71	ND-1963	200	250 Francs. Gold.	1,800
E72	1964	200	20 Francs. Gold.	255
E73	1964	200	100 Francs. Copper-Nickel. Head left.	35.00
E74	1964	200	100 Francs. Bronze.	35.00
E75	1964	200	100 Francs. Silver.	35.00
E76	1964	200	100 Francs. Gold.	1,000
E77	1965	200	Franc. Copper-Nickel.	30.00
E78	1965	200	Franc. Silver.	30.00

KM#	Date	Mintage	Identification	Mkt Val
E79	1965	200	Franc. Gold. KM55.	250
E80	1966	100	40 Francs. Gold.	500
E81	1967	100	40 Francs. Gold.	500
E82	1971	250	5 Francs. Copper-Nickel.	30.00
E83	1971	250	5 Francs. Silver.	30.00
E84	1971	250	5 Francs. Gold. KM56.	400
E85	1971	250	10 Francs. Copper-Nickel.	30.00
E86	1971	250	10 Francs. Silver.	30.00
E87	1971	250	10 Francs. Gold.	500
E88	1980	—	20 Francs. Bronze.	35.00
E89	1980	—	20 Francs. Silver.	60.00
E90	1980	500	20 Francs. Gold.	375

PATTERNS

Including off metal strikes

KM#	Date	Mintage	Identification	Mkt Val
Pn6	1901	—	2-1/2 Centimes. Copper.	160
Pn7	1901	100	2-1/2 Centimes. Silver.	200
Pn8	1901	100	5 Centimes. Copper. Without denomination.	160
Pn9	1901	100	5 Centimes. Copper-Nickel. Without denomination.	160
Pn10	1901	100	5 Centimes. Copper-Nickel. Without denomination.	—
Pn11	1901	50	5 Centimes. Silver. Without denomination.	185
Pn12	1901	20	5 Centimes. Gold. Without denomination.	1,520
Pn13	1901	100	10 Centimes. Copper. Without denomination.	125
Pn14	1901	100	10 Centimes. Copper-Nickel. Without denomination.	125
Pn15	1901	100	10 Centimes. Copper-Nickel. Plain. Large letters.	125
Pn16	1901	100	10 Centimes. Copper-Nickel. Milled. Large letters.	125
Pn17	1901	50	10 Centimes. Silver. Large letters.	185
Pn18	1901	20	10 Centimes. Gold. Without denomination.	1,520
Pn19	ND (1901)	50	Franc. Nickel. Head of William.	185
Pn20	1917	—	5 Centimes. Copper. Crossed L's.	185
Pn21	1917	—	10 Centimes. Copper.	185
Pn22	1923	100	Franc. Aluminum.	125
Pn23	1923	100	Franc. Bronze.	135
Pn24	1923	100	Franc. Nickel.	135
Pn25	1923	100	Franc. Silver.	170
Pn26	1923	100	2 Francs. Pewter.	160
Pn27	1923	100	2 Francs. Aluminum.	155
Pn28	1923	100	2 Francs. Bronze.	150
Pn29	1923	100	2 Francs. Nickel.	170
Pn30	1923	100	2 Francs. Silver.	185
Pn31	1924	—	Franc. Aluminum.	85.00
Pn32	1924	100	Franc. Copper.	145
Pn33	1924	100	Franc. Bronze.	145
Pn34	1924	100	Franc. Silver.	145
Pn35	1924	100	2 Francs. Copper.	135
Pn36	1924	100	2 Francs. Bronze.	145
Pn37	1930	—	5 Centimes. Copper. Crowned value.	125
Pn38	1930	—	5 Centimes. Copper.	110
Pn39	1930	—	10 Centimes. Copper.	160
Pn40	1930	—	50 Centimes. Copper-Nickel.	185
Pn41	1930	—	50 Centimes. Copper-Nickel.	195
Pn42	1939	50	Franc. Silver.	135
Pn43	1939	—	Franc. Gold.	750
Pn44	1942	—	5 Francs. Zinc.	135
Pn45	1942	—	5 Francs. Nickel.	135
Pn46	1947	100	2 Francs. Copper-Nickel.	115
Pn47	1947	100	5 Francs. Copper-Nickel.	125

PIEDFORT AND PIEDFORT WITH ESSAI

KM#	Date	Mintage	Identification	Mkt Val
PE4	1908	—	10 Centimes. Gold.	1,350
PE5	1927	100	25 Centimes. Bronze.	135
PE6	1938	100	25 Centimes. Copper-Nickel.	135

MINT SETS

KM#	Date	Mintage	Identification	Issue Price	Mkt Val
MS1	1990 (4)	10,000	KM63, 65-67	—	35.00
MS2	1991 (4)	10,000	KM63, 65-67	—	35.00
MS3	1992 (4)	10,000	KM63, 65-67	—	35.00
MS4	1993 (4)	10,000	KM63, 65-67	—	35.00
MS5	1994 (4)	10,000	KM63, 65-67	—	35.00
MS6	1995 (4)	10,000	KM63, 65-67 plus medal	—	65.00

PROOF SETS

KM#	Date	Mintage	Identification	Issue Price	Mkt Val
PS1	1980 (7)	3,000	KM#45b, 46, 3a, 51a, 55a-58a	—	175

MACAU

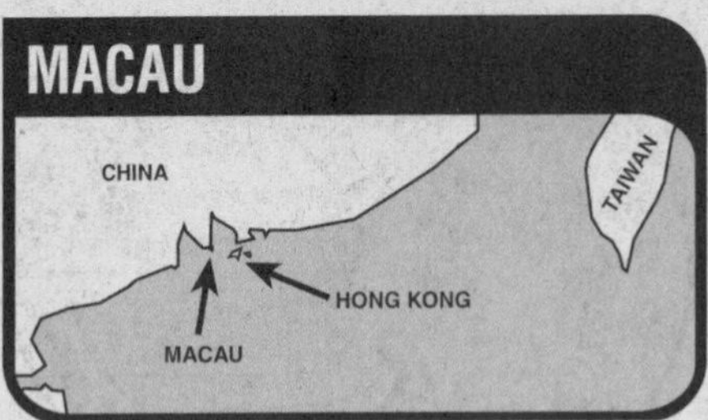

The Province of Macau, a Portuguese overseas province located in the South China Sea 40 miles southwest of Hong Kong, consists of the peninsula of Macau and the islands of Taipa and Coloane. It has an area of 6.2 sq. mi.(16 sq. km.) and a population of 500,000. Capital: Macau. Macau's economy is based on light industry, commerce, tourism, fishing, and gold trading - Macau is one of the entirely free markets for gold in the world. Cement, textiles, fireworks, vegetable oils, and metal products are exported.

Established by the Portuguese in 1557, Macau is the oldest European settlement in the Far East. The Chinese, while agreeing to Portuguese settlement, did not recognize Portuguese sovereign rights and the Portuguese remained largely under control of the Chinese until 1849, when the Portuguese abolished the Chinese customhouse and declared the independence of the port. The Manchu government formally recognized the Portuguese right to *perpetual occupation* of Macau in 1887.

In 1987, Portugal and China agreed that Macau would become a Chinese Territory in 1999. In December of 1999, Macau became a special administrative zone of China.

RULER

Portuguese 1887-1999

MINT MARKS

(p) - Pobjoy Mint
(s) - Singapore Mint

Pobjoy Mint

Singapore Mint

PORTUGUESE COLONY

STANDARD COINAGE

100 Avos = 1 Pataca

KM# 1 5 AVOS

Bronze **Obv:** Value flanked by upper and lower dots within circle **Rev:** Shield within crowned globe flanked by stars below

Date	Mintage	VF20	XF40	MS60	MS63	MS65
1952	500,000	3.50	15.00	30.00	50.00	70.00

KM# 1a 5 AVOS

2.60 g., Nickel-Brass **Obv:** Value flanked by upper and lower dots within circle **Rev:** Shield within crowned globe flanked by stars below

Date	Mintage	VF20	XF40	MS60	MS63	MS65
1967	5,000,000	0.50	1.00	3.00	6.00	10.00

KM# 2 10 AVOS

4.02 g., Bronze, 20.3 mm. **Obv:** Value flanked by upper and lower dots within circle **Rev:** Shield within crowned globe flanked by stars below

Date	Mintage	VF20	XF40	MS60	MS63	MS65
1952	12,500,000	0.30	0.80	1.50	3.50	8.00

KM# 2a 10 AVOS

4.50 g., Nickel-Brass, 22 mm. **Obv:** Value flanked by upper and lower dots within circle **Rev:** Shield within crowned globe flanked by stars below

Date	Mintage	VF20	XF40	MS60	MS63	MS65
1967	5,525,000	0.50	1.00	2.00	3.50	8.00
1968	6,975,000	0.25	1.00	2.00	3.50	8.00
1975	20,000,000	0.10	0.50	1.50	2.50	6.00
1976	Inc. above	0.10	0.50	1.50	2.50	6.00

KM# 20 10 AVOS

3.30 g., Brass, 19.1 mm. **Obv:** Portuguese shield flanked by stars below **Rev:** Value above building

Date	Mintage	VF20	XF40	MS60	MS63	MS65
1982	24,580,000	0.10	0.45	0.75	2.00	2.50
1983	—	0.10	0.25	0.50	1.50	2.00
1984	—	0.25	0.45	0.75	2.50	3.00
1985	—	0.10	0.25	0.50	1.50	2.00
1988	—	0.10	0.25	0.50	1.50	2.00

KM# 20a 10 AVOS

3.20 g., 0.925 Silver 0.0952 oz. ASW **Obv:** Portuguese shield flanked by stars below **Rev:** Value above building

Date	Mintage	VF20	XF40	MS60	MS63	MS65
1982	2,000	PF65 8.00				
1983	2,500	PF65 6.00				
1984	2,500	PF65 6.00				
1985	2,500	PF65 6.00				

KM# 20b 10 AVOS

4.00 g., 0.917 Gold 0.1179 oz. AGW **Obv:** Portuguese shield flanked by stars below (low star) **Rev:** Value above building

Date	Mintage	VF20	XF40	MS60	MS63	MS65
1982	150	PF65 225				

KM# 20c 10 AVOS

4.50 g., 0.950 Platinum 0.1374 oz. APW **Obv:** Portuguese shield flanked by stars below (low star) **Rev:** Value above building

Date	Mintage	VF20	XF40	MS60	MS63	MS65
1982	375	PF65 300				

KM# 21 20 AVOS

4.70 g., Brass, 21.1 mm. **Obv:** Portuguese shield flanked by stars below **Rev:** Value above block letter design within vertical rectangle

Date	Mintage	VF20	XF40	MS60	MS63	MS65
1982	9,960,000	0.10	0.25	0.50	1.50	2.00
1983	—	0.10	0.25	0.50	1.50	2.00
1984	—	0.25	0.45	0.75	2.50	3.00
1985	—	0.10	0.25	0.50	1.50	2.00

KM# 21a 20 AVOS

4.60 g., 0.925 Silver 0.1368 oz. ASW, 21.1 mm. **Obv:** Portuguese shield flanked by stars below above date **Rev:** Value above block letter design within vertical rectangle

Date	Mintage	VF20	XF40	MS60	MS63	MS65
1982	2,000	PF65 13.00				
1983	2,500	PF65 10.00				
1984	2,500	PF65 10.00				
1985	2,500	PF65 10.00				

KM# 21b 20 AVOS

5.50 g., 0.917 Gold 0.1622 oz. AGW, 21.1 mm. **Obv:** Portuguese shield flanked by stars, date below (low star) **Rev:** Value above block letter design within vertical rectangle

Date	Mintage	VF20	XF40	MS60	MS63	MS65
1982	150	PF65 350				

KM# 21c 20 AVOS

6.20 g., 0.950 Platinum 0.1894 oz. APW, 21.1 mm. **Obv:** Portuguese shield flanked by stars, date below (low star) **Rev:** Value above block letter design within vertical rectangle

Date	Mintage	VF20	XF40	MS60	MS63	MS65
1982	375	PF65 375				

KM# 71 20 AVOS

Brass, 20 mm. **Obv:** MACAU written over inner circle with date below **Rev:** Man standing above his crew on dragon boat flanked by mint marks with value above **Shape:** 12-sided

Date	Mintage	VF20	XF40	MS60	MS63	MS65
1993	—	—	—	0.35	1.00	1.75
1998	—	—	—	0.35	1.00	1.75

KM# 3 50 AVOS

Copper-Nickel, 20 mm. **Obv:** Portuguese shield within globe and cross **Rev:** Macau shield within crowned globe

Date	Mintage	VF20	XF40	MS60	MS63	MS65
1952	2,560,000	0.75	1.50	3.00	7.50	12.50

KM# 7 50 AVOS

5.80 g., Copper-Nickel, 23 mm. **Obv:** Portuguese shield within globe and cross **Rev:** Macau shield within crowned globe

Date	Mintage	VF20	XF40	MS60	MS63	MS65
1972	1,600,000	0.50	1.50	4.00	6.00	10.00
1973	4,840,000	0.50	1.00	3.00	5.00	9.00

KM# 9 50 AVOS

Copper-Nickel, 23 mm. **Obv:** Value and denomination flanked by upper and lower flower buds within circle **Rev:** Macau shield within crowned globe flanked by stars and mint marks

Date	Mintage	VF20	XF40	MS60	MS63	MS65
1978	3,000,000	0.50	0.75	1.50	3.00	5.00

KM# 22 50 AVOS

5.10 g., Brass, 23 mm. **Obv:** Portuguese shield flanked by stars below above date **Rev:** Value above fallen block letters within vertical rectangle

Date	Mintage	VF20	XF40	MS60	MS63	MS65
1982	16,952,000	—	0.50	1.00	1.50	3.00
1983	—	—	0.75	1.25	1.75	3.50
1984	—	—	0.75	1.25	1.75	3.50
1985	—	—	0.50	1.00	1.50	3.00

KM# 22a 50 AVOS

5.70 g., 0.925 Silver 0.1695 oz. ASW, 23 mm. **Obv:** Portuguese shield flanked by stars below above date **Rev:** Value above fallen block letters within vertical rectangle

Date	Mintage	VF20	XF40	MS60	MS63	MS65
1982	2,000	PF65 16.00				
1983	2,500	PF65 12.00				
1984	2,500	PF65 12.00				
1985	2,500	PF65 12.00				

KM# 22b 50 AVOS

7.40 g., 0.917 Gold 0.2182 oz. AGW, 23 mm. **Obv:** Portuguese shield flanked by stars, date below (low star) **Rev:** Value above fallen block letters within vertical rectangle

Date	Mintage	VF20	XF40	MS60	MS63	MS65
1982	150	PF65 450				

KM# 22c 50 AVOS

8.40 g., 0.950 Platinum 0.2566 oz. APW, 23 mm. **Obv:** Portuguese shield flanked by stars below above date (low star) **Rev:** Value above fallen block letters within vertical rectangle

Date	Mintage	VF20	XF40	MS60	MS63	MS65
1982	375	PF65 500				

KM# 4 PATACA

3.00 g., 0.720 Silver 0.0694 oz. ASW, 19 mm. **Obv:** Portuguese shield within globe and long cross **Rev:** Macau shield within crowned globe

Date	Mintage	VF20	XF40	MS60	MS63	MS65
1952	4,500,000	5.00	12.00	20.00	35.00	50.00

KM# 6 PATACA

10.60 g., Nickel, 28.5 mm. **Obv:** Portuguese shield within globe and long cross **Rev:** Macau shield within crowned globe **Edge:** Plain

Date	Mintage	VF20	XF40	MS60	MS63	MS65
1968	5,000,000	0.50	1.50	3.50	6.00	10.00
1975	6,000,000	0.50	1.50	3.50	6.00	10.00

KM# 6a PATACA

Copper-Nickel **Obv:** Portuguese shield within globe and long cross **Rev:** Macau shield within crowned globe

Date	Mintage	VF20	XF40	MS60	MS63	MS65
1980	—	—	1.50	3.00	6.00	10.00

KM# 23.1 PATACA

9.00 g., Copper-Nickel, 26 mm. **Obv:** Portuguese shield flanked by stars below above date (high stars) **Rev:** Artistic design flanked by upright fish **Edge:** Reeded

Date	Mintage	VF20	XF40	MS60	MS63	MS65
1982 (s)	6,427,000	—	1.00	2.00	3.50	5.00
1983 (s)	—	—	1.00	2.50	4.00	5.50
1984 (s)	—	—	1.50	3.00	4.50	6.00
1985 (s)	—	—	1.00	2.50	4.00	5.50

KM# 23.2 PATACA

9.00 g., Copper-Nickel, 26 mm. **Obv:** Portuguese shield flanked by stars below above date (low stars) **Rev:** Artistic design flanked by upright fish **Edge:** Reeded

Date	Mintage	VF20	XF40	MS60	MS63	MS65
1982 (p)	—	—	1.00	1.50	3.50	6.00
1983 (p)	—	1.00	1.50	2.50	4.50	7.00

KM# 23a.1 PATACA

9.00 g., 0.925 Silver 0.2677 oz. ASW, 26 mm. **Obv:** Portuguese shield flanked by stars below above date (high stars) **Rev:** Artistic design flanked by upright fish

Date	Mintage	VF20	XF40	MS60	MS63	MS65
1982 (s)	2,000	PF65 22.00				
1983 (s)	2,500	PF65 17.00				
1984 (s)	2,500	PF65 17.00				
1985 (s)	2,500	PF65 17.00				

KM# 23a.2 PATACA

5.70 g., 0.925 Silver 0.1695 oz. ASW, 26 mm. **Obv:** Portuguese shield flanked by stars below above date (low stars) **Rev:** Artistic design flanked by upright fish

Date	Mintage	VF20	XF40	MS60	MS63	MS65
1982	—	PF65 12.00				

KM# 23b.1 PATACA

11.60 g., 0.917 Gold 0.342 oz. AGW, 26 mm. **Obv:** Portuguese shield flanked by stars below above date (high stars) **Rev:** Artistic design flanked by upright fish

Date	Mintage	VF20	XF40	MS60	MS63	MS65
1982 (s)	150	PF65 750				

KM# 23c.1 PATACA

13.20 g., 0.950 Platinum 0.4032 oz. APW, 26 mm. **Obv:** Portuguese shield flanked by stars below above date (high stars) **Rev:** Artistic design flanked by upright fish

Date	Mintage	VF20	XF40	MS60	MS63	MS65
1982 (s)	375	PF65 720				

KM# 97 2 PATACAS

Nickel-Brass, 27.5 mm. **Obv:** MACAU written across center of globe above date **Rev:** Penha Church and Ama Temple **Edge:** Plain **Shape:** Octagonal

Date	Mintage	VF20	XF40	MS60	MS63	MS65
1998	—	—	—	1.00	2.00	3.50

KM# 5 5 PATACAS

15.00 g., 0.720 Silver 0.3472 oz. ASW **Obv:** Portuguese shield within globe and long cross **Rev:** Macau shield within crowned globe

Date	Mintage	VF20	XF40	MS60	MS63	MS65
1952	900,000	6.50	8.00	10.00	15.00	25.00

KM# 5a 5 PATACAS

10.00 g., 0.650 Silver 0.209 oz. ASW **Obv:** Portuguese shield within globe and long cross **Rev:** Macau shield within crowned globe

Date	Mintage	VF20	XF40	MS60	MS63	MS65
1971	500,000	3.75	5.25	12.00	17.00	27.00

KM# 24.1 5 PATACAS

10.70 g., Copper-Nickel, 29 mm. **Obv:** Portuguese shield flanked by stars below above date (high stars) **Rev:** Large stylized dragon above value

Date	Mintage	VF20	XF40	MS60	MS63	MS65
1982 (s)	1,102,000	—	—	1.00	3.00	5.00
1983 (s)	—	—	1.00	2.50	5.00	10.00
1984 (s)	—	1.00	2.00	5.00	15.00	25.00
1985 (s)	—	—	1.00	3.00	8.00	15.00
1988 (s)	—	—	1.00	2.00	5.00	7.50

KM# 24.2 5 PATACAS

10.70 g., Copper-Nickel, 29 mm. **Obv:** Portuguese shield flanked by stars below above date (low stars) **Rev:** Small stylized dragon above value

Date	Mintage	VF20	XF40	MS60	MS63	MS65
1982 (p)	—	—	—	1.00	3.00	5.00
1983 (p)	—	—	—	1.00	3.00	5.00

KM# 24a.1 5 PATACAS
10.70 g., 0.925 Silver 0.3182 oz. ASW, 29 mm. **Obv:** Portuguese shield flanked by stars below above date (high stars) **Rev:** Large stylized dragon above value

Date	Mintage	VF20	XF40	MS60	MS63	MS65
1982 (s)	2,000	PF65 47.00				
1983 (s)	2,500	PF65 35.00				
1984 (s)	2,500	PF65 35.00				
1985 (s)	2,500	PF65 35.00				

KM# 24a.2 5 PATACAS
10.70 g., 0.925 Silver 0.3182 oz. ASW, 29 mm. **Obv:** Portuguese shield flanked by stars below above date (low stars) **Rev:** Small stylized dragon above value

Date	Mintage	VF20	XF40	MS60	MS63	MS65
1982 (p)	—	PF65 18.00				

KM# 24b.1 5 PATACAS
16.30 g., 0.917 Gold 0.4806 oz. AGW, 29 mm. **Obv:** Portuguese shield flanked by stars below above date (high stars) **Rev:** Large stylized dragon above value

Date	Mintage	VF20	XF40	MS60	MS63	MS65
1982 (s)	150	PF65 1,200				

KM# 24c.1 5 PATACAS
18.40 g., 0.950 Platinum 0.562 oz. APW, 29 mm. **Obv:** Portuguese shield flanked by stars below above date (high stars) **Rev:** Large stylized dragon above value

Date	Mintage	VF20	XF40	MS60	MS63	MS65
1982 (s)	375	PF65 1,100				

KM# 83 10 PATACAS
Bi-Metallic Copper-Nickel center in Brass ring, 28 mm. **Obv:** MACAU written across center of globe within circle above date **Rev:** Church of St. Domingo within circle above value

Date	Mintage	VF20	XF40	MS60	MS63	MS65
1997	—	—	—	2.00	3.50	6.00

KM# 8 20 PATACAS
18.00 g., 0.650 Silver 0.3762 oz. ASW, 35 mm. **Obv:** Macau shield within globe **Rev:** Junk (ship) passing under Taipa bridge within circle

Date	Mintage	VF20	XF40	MS60	MS63	MS65
1974	1,000	—	10.00	20.00	30.00	45.00

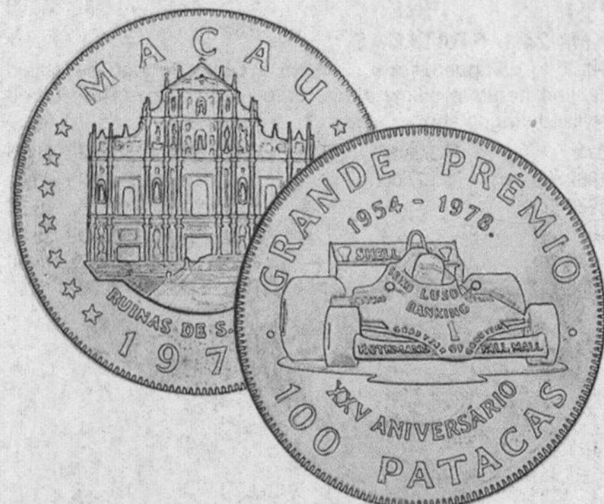

KM# 10 100 PATACAS
28.28 g., 0.925 Silver 0.841 oz. ASW **Subject:** 25th Anniversary of Grand Prix **Obv:** Church of St. Paul façade flanked by stars **Rev:** Race car with advertising logos

Date	Mintage	XF40	MS60	MS63	MS65	MS66
1978	610	PF65 235	PF67 475	PF69 800		

KM# 10a 100 PATACAS
Copper-Nickel **Subject:** 25th Anniversary of Grand Prix **Obv:** Church of St. Paul façade flanked by stars **Rev:** Race car with advertising logos

Date	Mintage	XF40	MS60	MS63	MS65	MS66
1978 Rare	—	—	—	—	2,250	—

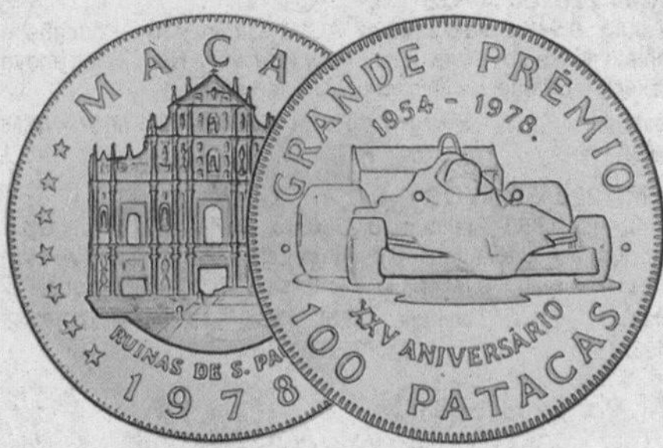

KM# 11 100 PATACAS
28.28 g., 0.925 Silver 0.841 oz. ASW **Obv:** Church of St. Paul façade flanked by stars **Rev:** Race car without advertising **Note:** Similar to KM#10, but reissued without advertising logos on the racecar.

Date	Mintage	VF20	XF40	MS60	MS63	MS65
1978	5,500	PF65 185	PF67 275			

KM# 14 100 PATACAS
28.28 g., 0.925 Silver 0.841 oz. ASW **Subject:** Year of the Goat **Obv:** Crowned arms with supporters **Rev:** Goat

Date	Mintage	VF20	XF40	MS60	MS63	MS65
1979 (s)	5,500	PF65 150	PF67 225			

KM# 16 100 PATACAS
28.28 g., 0.925 Silver 0.841 oz. ASW **Subject:** Year of the Monkey **Obv:** Crowned arms with supporters **Rev:** Monkey swinging on a rope

Date	Mintage	XF40	MS60	MS63	MS65	MS66
1980	1,000	—	—	—	200	—
1980	2,000	PF65 200	PF67 900	PF69 1,500		

KM# 18 100 PATACAS
28.28 g., 0.925 Silver 0.841 oz. ASW **Subject:** Year of the Rooster **Obv:** Crowned arms with supporters **Rev:** Rooster

Date	Mintage	VF20	XF40	MS60	MS63	MS65
1981 (p)	1,000	—	—	—	—	200
1981 (p)	1,000	PF65 225	PF67 345			

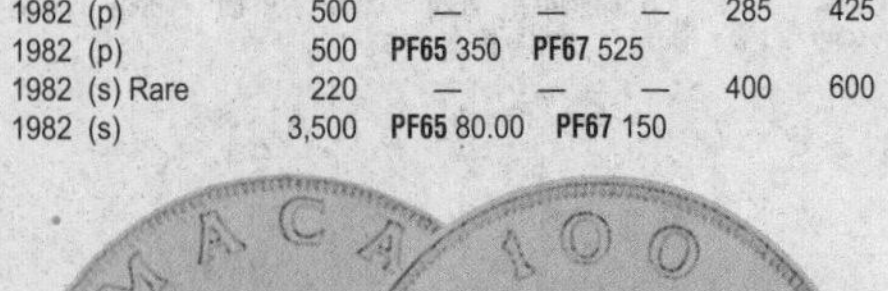

KM# 25 100 PATACAS
28.28 g., 0.925 Silver 0.841 oz. ASW **Subject:** Year of the Dog **Obv:** Crowned arms with supporters **Rev:** Dog

Date	Mintage	XF40	MS60	MS63	MS65	MS66
1982 (p)	500	—	—	—	285	425
1982 (p)	500	PF65 350	PF67 525			
1982 (s) Rare	220	—	—	—	400	600
1982 (s)	3,500	PF65 80.00	PF67 150			

KM# 27 100 PATACAS
28.28 g., 0.925 Silver 0.841 oz. ASW **Subject:** Year of the Pig **Obv:** Crowned arms with supporters **Rev:** Pig

Date	Mintage	XF40	MS60	MS63	MS65	MS66
1983 (s)	2,500	—	—	—	70.00	—
1983 (s)	2,500	PF65 90.00	PF67 200	PF69 500		

KM# 29 100 PATACAS
28.28 g., 0.925 Silver 0.841 oz. ASW **Subject:** Year of the Rat **Obv:** Crowned arms with supporters **Rev:** Rat

Date	Mintage	VF20	XF40	MS60	MS63	MS65
1984 (s)	2,000	—	—	—	—	120
1984 (s)	5,000	PF65 95.00	PF67 210			

KM# 31 100 PATACAS
28.28 g., 0.925 Silver 0.841 oz. ASW **Subject:** Year of the Ox **Obv:** Crowned arms with supporters **Rev:** Ox

Date	Mintage	VF20	XF40	MS60	MS63	MS65
1985 (s)	10,000	—	—	—	—	50.00
1985 (s)	5,000	PF65 75.00	PF67 135			

KM# 33 100 PATACAS
28.28 g., 0.925 Silver 0.841 oz. ASW **Subject:** Visit of Portugal's President Eanes **Obv:** Head left above date

Date	Mintage	VF20	XF40	MS60	MS63	MS65
1985 (s)	760	—	—	—	—	120
1985 (s)	2,000	PF65 80.00	PF67 150			

KM# 34 100 PATACAS
28.28 g., 0.925 Silver 0.841 oz. ASW **Subject:** Year of the Tiger **Obv:** Crowned arms with supporters **Rev:** Tiger

Date	Mintage	VF20	XF40	MS60	MS63	MS65
1986 (p)	760	—	—	—	—	120
1986 (p)	3,000	PF65 75.00	PF67 135			

KM# 36 100 PATACAS
28.28 g., 0.925 Silver 0.841 oz. ASW **Subject:** Year of the Rabbit **Obv:** Crowned arms with supporters **Rev:** Rabbit

Date	Mintage	VF20	XF40	MS60	MS63	MS65
1987 (p)	—	—	—	—	—	80.00
1987 (p)	5,000	PF65 65.00	PF67 115			

KM# 38 100 PATACAS
28.28 g., 0.925 Silver 0.841 oz. ASW **Subject:** Year of the Dragon **Obv:** Crowned arms with supporters **Rev:** Dragon **Note:** Similar to 1,000 Patacas, KM#39.

Date	Mintage	VF20	XF40	MS60	MS63	MS65
1988	—	—	—	—	—	125
1988	5,000	PF65 145	PF67 225			

KM# 40 100 PATACAS
28.28 g., 0.925 Silver 0.841 oz. ASW **Subject:** 35th Anniversary of Grand Prix **Obv:** Sailing ship within circle **Rev:** Race car and dates within circle

Date	Mintage	XF40	MS60	MS63	MS65	MS66
ND-1988	5,000	PF65 95.00	PF67 210			

KM# 40a 100 PATACAS
Platinum APW **Subject:** 35th Anniversary of Grand Prix **Obv:** Sailing ship within circle **Rev:** Race car within circle above dates

Date	Mintage	XF40	MS60	MS63	MS65	MS66
ND-1988	10	PF67 12,500				

KM# 40b 100 PATACAS
47.50 g., Gold **Subject:** 35th Anniversary of Grand Prix **Obv:** Sailing ship within circle **Rev:** Race car and dates within circle

Date	Mintage	XF40	MS60	MS63	MS65	MS66
ND-1988	10	PF67 14,500				

KM# 40c 100 PATACAS
Bronze **Subject:** 35th Anniversary of Grand Prix **Obv:** Sailing ship within circle **Rev:** Race car and dates within circle

Date	Mintage	XF40	MS60	MS63	MS65	MS66
ND-1988	10	PF67 4,000				

KM# 44 100 PATACAS
28.28 g., 0.925 Silver 0.841 oz. ASW **Subject:** Year of the Snake **Obv:** Crowned arms with supporters **Rev:** Coiled snake **Note:** Similar to 1,000 Patacas, KM#45.

Date	Mintage	VF20	XF40	MS60	MS63	MS65
1989 (s)	2,000	—	—	—	—	85.00
1989 (s)	3,000	PF65 95.00	PF67 210			

KM# 46 100 PATACAS
28.28 g., 0.925 Silver 0.841 oz. ASW **Subject:** Year of the Horse **Obv:** Crowned arms with supporters **Rev:** Horse

Date	Mintage	VF20	XF40	MS60	MS63	MS65
1990 (s)	1,000	—	—	—	—	125
1990 (s)	3,364	PF65 95.00	PF67 210			

KM# 48 100 PATACAS
28.28 g., 0.925 Silver 0.841 oz. ASW **Subject:** Year of the Goat **Obv:** Crowned arms with supporters **Rev:** Goat **Note:** Similar to KM#51.

Date	Mintage	VF20	XF40	MS60	MS63	MS65
1991 (s)	1,000	—	—	—	—	150
1991 (s)	Est. 4000	PF65 175	PF67 275			

KM# 52 100 PATACAS
28.28 g., 0.925 Silver 0.841 oz. ASW **Subject:** Year of the Monkey **Obv:** Crowned arms with supporters **Rev:** Monkey

Date	Mintage	VF20	XF40	MS60	MS63	MS65
1992 (s)	1,000	—	—	—	—	50.00
1992 (s)	Est. 4000	PF65 60.00	PF67 90.00			

KM# 58 100 PATACAS
28.28 g., 0.925 Silver 0.841 oz. ASW **Subject:** Year of the Rooster **Obv:** Church façade **Rev:** Rooster

Date	Mintage	VF20	XF40	MS60	MS63	MS65
1993	500	—	—	—	—	175
1993	Est. 4000	PF65 125	PF67 195			

KM# 62 100 PATACAS
28.28 g., 0.925 Silver 0.841 oz. ASW **Subject:** Macau Grand Prix **Obv:** Map above dates **Rev:** Checkered design divides race car and racing bike

Date	Mintage	VF20	XF40	MS60	MS63	MS65
ND-1993	5,000	PF65 60.00	PF67 90.00			

KM# 66 100 PATACAS
28.28 g., 0.925 Silver 0.841 oz. ASW **Subject:** Year of the Dog **Obv:** Church façade **Rev:** Dog

Date	Mintage	VF20	XF40	MS60	MS63	MS65
1994	1,000	—	—	—	—	60.00
1994	Est. 4000	PF65 90.00	PF67 135			

KM# 73 100 PATACAS
28.28 g., 0.925 Silver 0.841 oz. ASW **Subject:** Year of the Pig **Obv:** Church façade **Rev:** Pig

Date	Mintage	VF20	XF40	MS60	MS63	MS65
1995	1,000	—	—	—	—	70.00
1995	Est. 4000	PF65 90.00	PF67 135			

KM# 77 100 PATACAS
28.28 g., 0.925 Silver 0.841 oz. ASW **Subject:** Airport **Obv:** Value and date within circle **Rev:** Airport scene

Date	Mintage	VF20	XF40	MS60	MS63	MS65
1995	8,000	PF65 65.00	PF67 100			

KM# 79 100 PATACAS
28.28 g., 0.925 Silver 0.841 oz. ASW **Subject:** Year of the Rat **Obv:** Church façade **Rev:** Rat

Date	Mintage	VF20	XF40	MS60	MS63	MS65
1996	1,000	—	—	—	—	95.00
1996	Est. 4000	PF65 70.00	PF67 110			

KM# 84 100 PATACAS
28.28 g., 0.925 Silver 0.841 oz. ASW **Subject:** Year of the Ox **Obv:** Church façade **Rev:** Ox

Date	Mintage	VF20	XF40	MS60	MS63	MS65
1997	4,000	PF65 80.00	PF67 120			

KM# 88 100 PATACAS
28.28 g., 0.925 Silver 0.841 oz. ASW **Subject:** Year of the Tiger **Obv:** Church façade **Rev:** Tiger

Date	Mintage	VF20	XF40	MS60	MS63	MS65
1998	5,000	PF65 90.00	PF67 135			

KM# 106 100 PATACAS
28.40 g., 0.925 Silver 0.8446 oz. ASW, 38.4 mm. **Subject:** 19th East Asian Insurance Conference **Obv:** Church façade **Rev:** Two hands holding world within circle **Edge:** Reeded

Date	Mintage	VF20	XF40	MS60	MS63	MS65
1998	Est. 3000	PF65 85.00	PF67 125			

KM# 96 100 PATACAS
31.10 g., 0.925 Silver 0.925 oz. ASW **Subject:** Macau Returns to China **Obv:** Crowned arms with supporters **Rev:** Portuguese and Chinese ships below gold-plated cameo of the Gao Temple

Date	Mintage	VF20	XF40	MS60	MS63	MS65
1999	38,888	PF65 60.00	PF67 90.00			

KM# 98 100 PATACAS
28.28 g., 0.925 Silver 0.841 oz. ASW, 38.6 mm. **Subject:** Year of the Dragon **Obv:** Church façade **Rev:** Dragon **Edge:** Reeded

Date	Mintage	VF20	XF40	MS60	MS63	MS65
2000	1,000	—	—	—	—	95.00
2000	4,000	PF65 75.00	PF67 115			

KM# 49 250 PATACAS
3.99 g., 0.917 Gold 0.1176 oz. AGW **Subject:** Year of the Goat **Obv:** Crowned arms with supporters **Rev:** Goat **Note:** Similar to 1,000 Patacas, KM#51.

Date	Mintage	XF40	MS60	MS63	MS65	MS66
1991	Est. 2500	PF67 250	PF69 300			

KM# 53 250 PATACAS
3.99 g., 0.917 Gold 0.1176 oz. AGW **Subject:** Year of the Monkey **Obv:** Crowned arms with supporters **Rev:** Monkey **Note:** Similar to 1,000 Patacas, KM#51.

Date	Mintage	XF40	MS60	MS63	MS65	MS66
1992	—	PF67 250	PF69 300			

KM# 59 250 PATACAS
3.99 g., 0.917 Gold 0.1176 oz. AGW **Subject:** Year of the Rooster **Obv:** Crowned arms with supporters **Rev:** Rooster **Note:** Similar to 1,000 Patacas, KM#58.

Date	Mintage	XF40	MS60	MS63	MS65	MS66
1993	—	PF67 250	PF69 300			

KM# 67 250 PATACAS
3.99 g., 0.917 Gold 0.1176 oz. AGW **Subject:** Year of the Dog **Obv:** Church façade flanked by stars above date **Rev:** Dog **Note:** Similar to 1,000 Patacas, KM#69.

Date	Mintage	XF40	MS60	MS63	MS65	MS66
1994	Est. 2500	PF67 250	PF69 300			

KM# 74 250 PATACAS
3.99 g., 0.917 Gold 0.1176 oz. AGW **Subject:** Year of the Pig **Obv:** Church façade flanked by stars above date **Rev:** Pig

Date	Mintage	XF40	MS60	MS63	MS65	MS66
1995	—	PF67 275	PF69 325			

KM# 80 250 PATACAS
3.99 g., 0.917 Gold 0.1176 oz. AGW **Subject:** Year of the Rat **Obv:** Church façade flanked by stars above date **Rev:** Rat

Date	Mintage	XF40	MS60	MS63	MS65	MS66
1996	—	PF67 275	PF69 325			

KM# 85 250 PATACAS
3.99 g., 0.917 Gold 0.1176 oz. AGW **Subject:** Year of the Ox **Obv:** Church façade flanked by stars above date **Rev:** Ox **Note:** Similar to 100 Patacas, KM#84.

Date	Mintage	XF40	MS60	MS63	MS65	MS66
1997	Est. 2500	PF67 275	PF69 325			

KM# 89 250 PATACAS
3.99 g., 0.917 Gold 0.1176 oz. AGW **Subject:** Year of the Tiger **Obv:** Church façade flanked by stars above date **Rev:** Tiger **Note:** Similar to 100 Patacas, KM#88.

Date	Mintage	XF40	MS60	MS63	MS65	MS66
1998	Est. 2500	PF67 275	PF69 325			

KM# 93 250 PATACAS
3.99 g., 0.917 Gold 0.1176 oz. AGW **Subject:** Year of the Rabbit **Obv:** Church façade flanked by stars above value **Rev:** Rabbit

Date	Mintage	XF40	MS60	MS63	MS65	MS66
1999	Est. 2500	PF67 275	PF69 325			

KM# 99 250 PATACAS
3.99 g., 0.9167 Gold 0.1176 oz. AGW, 19.3 mm. **Subject:** Year of the Dragon **Obv:** Church façade flanked by stars above date **Rev:** Dragon **Edge:** Reeded

Date	Mintage	XF40	MS60	MS63	MS65	MS66
2000	2,500	PF67 350	PF69 425			

KM# 12 500 PATACAS
7.96 g., 0.917 Gold 0.2347 oz. AGW **Subject:** 25th Anniversary of Grand Prix **Obv:** Church façade flanked by stars above date **Rev:** Race car

Date	Mintage	XF40	MS60	MS63	MS65	MS66
1978	550	PF67 700	PF69 800			

KM# 13 500 PATACAS
7.96 g., 0.917 Gold 0.2347 oz. AGW **Obv:** Church façade flanked by stars above date **Rev:** Race car without advertising

Date	Mintage	XF40	MS60	MS63	MS65	MS66
1978	5,500	PF67 375	PF69 450			

KM# 15 500 PATACAS
7.96 g., 0.917 Gold 0.2347 oz. AGW **Subject:** Year of the Goat **Obv:** Crowned arms with supporters **Rev:** Goat

Date	Mintage	XF40	MS60	MS63	MS65	MS66
1979	5,500	PF67 375	PF69 450			

KM# 41 500 PATACAS
155.52 g., 0.999 Silver 4.9949 oz. ASW **Subject:** 35th Anniversary of Grand Prix **Obv:** Race car within circle **Rev:** Sailing ship within circle **Note:** Similar to KM#42.

Date	Mintage	XF40	MS60	MS63	MS65	MS66
1988	2,000	PF67 650	PF69 750			

KM# 42 500 PATACAS
7.99 g., 0.917 Gold 0.2355 oz. AGW **Subject:** 35th Anniversary of Grand Prix **Obv:** Sailing ship within circle **Rev:** Race car within circle

Date	Mintage	XF40	MS60	MS63	MS65	MS66
ND-1988	4,500	PF67 450	PF69 550			

KM# 50 500 PATACAS
7.99 g., 0.917 Gold 0.2355 oz. AGW **Subject:** Year of the Goat **Obv:** Crowned arms with supporters **Rev:** Goat **Note:** Similar to 1,000 Patacas, KM#51.

Date	Mintage	XF40	MS60	MS63	MS65	MS66
1991	Est. 2500	PF67 475	PF69 575			

KM# 54 500 PATACAS
7.99 g., 0.917 Gold 0.2356 oz. AGW **Subject:** Year of the Monkey **Obv:** Crowned arms with supporters **Rev:** Monkey **Note:** Similar to 1,000 Patacas, KM#51.

Date	Mintage	XF40	MS60	MS63	MS65	MS66
1992	Est. 2500	PF67 475	PF69 575			

KM# 60 500 PATACAS
7.99 g., 0.917 Gold 0.2356 oz. AGW **Subject:** Year of the Rooster **Obv:** Church façade flanked by stars above date **Rev:** Rooster **Note:** Similar to 100 Patacas, KM#58.

Date	Mintage	XF40	MS60	MS63	MS65	MS66
1993	Est. 2500	PF67 475	PF69 575			

KM# 63 500 PATACAS
155.60 g., 0.999 Silver 4.9976 oz. ASW **Subject:** Macau Grand Prix

Date	Mintage	XF40	MS60	MS63	MS65	MS66
1993	2,000	PF67 850	PF69 1,000			

KM# 64 500 PATACAS
7.99 g., 0.917 Gold 0.2356 oz. AGW **Subject:** Macau Grand Prix **Obv:** Map above dates **Rev:** Checkered design divides race car and racing bike

Date	Mintage	XF40	MS60	MS63	MS65	MS66
ND-1993	4,500	PF67 475	PF69 575			

KM# 68 500 PATACAS
7.99 g., 0.917 Gold 0.2356 oz. AGW **Subject:** Year of the Dog **Obv:** Church façade flanked by stars above date **Rev:** Dog **Note:** Similar to 1,000 Patacas, KM#69.

Date	Mintage	XF40	MS60	MS63	MS65	MS66
1994	Est. 2500	PF67 475	PF69 575			

KM# 75 500 PATACAS
7.99 g., 0.917 Gold 0.2356 oz. AGW **Subject:** Year of the Pig **Obv:** Church façade flanked by stars above date **Rev:** Pig

Date	Mintage	XF40	MS60	MS63	MS65	MS66
1995	Est. 2000	PF67 500	PF69 600			

KM# 81 500 PATACAS
7.99 g., 0.917 Gold 0.2356 oz. AGW **Subject:** Year of the Rat **Obv:** Church façade flanked by stars above date **Rev:** Rat

Date	Mintage	XF40	MS60	MS63	MS65	MS66
1996	—	PF67 500	PF69 600			

KM# 86 500 PATACAS
7.99 g., 0.917 Gold 0.2356 oz. AGW **Subject:** Year of the Ox **Obv:** Church façade flanked by stars above date **Rev:** Ox **Note:** Similar to 100 Patacas, KM#84.

Date	Mintage	XF40	MS60	MS63	MS65	MS66
1997	2,000	PF67 500	PF69 600			

KM# 90 500 PATACAS
7.99 g., 0.917 Gold 0.2356 oz. AGW **Subject:** Year of the Tiger **Obv:** Church façade flanked by stars above date **Rev:** Tiger **Note:** Similar to 100 Patacas, KM#88.

Date	Mintage	XF40	MS60	MS63	MS65	MS66
1998	2,500	PF67 550	PF69 650			

KM# 94 500 PATACAS
7.99 g., 0.917 Gold 0.2356 oz. AGW **Subject:** Year of the Rabbit **Obv:** Church façade flanked by stars above date **Rev:** Rabbit

Date	Mintage	XF40	MS60	MS63	MS65	MS66
1999	Est. 2500	PF67 550	PF69 650			

KM# 100 500 PATACAS
7.99 g., 0.9167 Gold 0.2355 oz. AGW, 22.05 mm. **Subject:** Year of the Dragon **Obv:** Church façade flanked by stars above date **Rev:** Dragon **Edge:** Reeded

Date	Mintage	XF40	MS60	MS63	MS65	MS66
2000	2,500	PF67 550	PF69 650			

KM# 17 1000 PATACAS
15.98 g., 0.917 Gold 0.471 oz. AGW **Subject:** Year of the Monkey **Obv:** Crowned arms with supporters **Rev:** Monkey

Date	Mintage	XF40	MS60	MS63	MS65	MS66
1980	5,500	PF67 1,150	PF69 1,250			

KM# 19 1000 PATACAS
15.98 g., 0.917 Gold 0.471 oz. AGW **Subject:** Year of the Rooster **Obv:** Crowned arms with supporters **Rev:** Rooster

Date	Mintage	XF40	MS60	MS63	MS65	MS66
1981	3,500	—	—	—	850	900
1981	Inc. above	PF67 900	PF69 1,000			

KM# 26 1000 PATACAS
15.98 g., 0.917 Gold 0.471 oz. AGW **Subject:** Year of the Dog **Obv:** Crowned arms with supporters **Rev:** Dog

Date	Mintage	XF40	MS60	MS63	MS65	MS66
1982	256	—	—	—	1,100	1,250
1982	255	PF67 1,350	PF69 1,500			

KM# 28 1000 PATACAS
15.98 g., 0.917 Gold 0.471 oz. AGW **Subject:** Year of the Pig **Obv:** Crowned arms with supporters **Rev:** Pig

Date	Mintage	XF40	MS60	MS63	MS65	MS66
1983	400	—	—	—	1,000	1,100
1983	500	PF67 1,150	PF69 1,250			

KM# 30 1000 PATACAS
15.98 g., 0.917 Gold 0.471 oz. AGW **Subject:** Year of the Rat **Obv:** Crowned arms with supporters **Rev:** Rat

Date	Mintage	XF40	MS60	MS63	MS65	MS66
1984	2,000	—	—	—	800	850
1984	3,000	PF67 850	PF69 950			

KM# 32 1000 PATACAS
15.98 g., 0.917 Gold 0.471 oz. AGW **Subject:** Year of the Ox **Obv:** Crowned arms with supporters **Rev:** Ox

Date	Mintage	XF40	MS60	MS63	MS65	MS66
1985	10,000	—	—	—	750	800
1985	5,000	PF67 800	PF69 900			

KM# 35 1000 PATACAS
15.98 g., 0.917 Gold 0.471 oz. AGW **Subject:** Year of the Tiger **Obv:** Crowned arms with supporters **Rev:** Tiger

Date	Mintage	XF40	MS60	MS63	MS65	MS66
1986 (p)	2,000	—	—	—	950	1,000
1986 (p)	3,000	PF67 1,000	PF69 1,100			

KM# 37 1000 PATACAS
15.98 g., 0.917 Gold 0.471 oz. AGW **Subject:** Year of the Rabbit **Obv:** Crowned arms with supporters **Rev:** Rabbit

Date	Mintage	XF40	MS60	MS63	MS65	MS66
1987 (p)	—	—	—	—	750	800
1987 (p)	5,000	PF67 800	PF69 900			

KM# 39 1000 PATACAS
15.98 g., 0.917 Gold 0.471 oz. AGW **Subject:** Year of the Dragon **Obv:** Crowned arms with supporters **Rev:** Dragon

Date	Mintage	XF40	MS60	MS63	MS65	MS66
1988	5,000	PF67 700	PF69 800			

KM# 45 1000 PATACAS
15.98 g., 0.917 Gold 0.471 oz. AGW **Subject:** Year of the Snake **Obv:** Crowned arms with supporters **Rev:** Snake

Date	Mintage	XF40	MS60	MS63	MS65	MS66
1989	2,000	—	—	—	800	850
1989	3,000	PF67 850	PF69 950			

KM# 47 1000 PATACAS
15.98 g., 0.917 Gold 0.471 oz. AGW **Subject:** Year of the Horse **Obv:** Crowned arms with supporters **Rev:** Horse

Date	Mintage	XF40	MS60	MS63	MS65	MS66
1990	2,000	—	—	—	750	800
1990	3,000	PF67 800	PF69 900			

KM# 51 1000 PATACAS
15.98 g., 0.917 Gold 0.471 oz. AGW **Obv:** Crowned arms with supporters **Rev:** Ram

Date	Mintage	XF40	MS60	MS63	MS65	MS66
1991	Est. 500	—	—	—	850	900
1991	—	PF67 900	PF69 1,000			

KM# 55 1000 PATACAS
15.98 g., 0.917 Gold 0.471 oz. AGW **Subject:** Year of the Monkey **Obv:** Crowned arms with supporters **Rev:** Monkey

Date	Mintage	XF40	MS60	MS63	MS65	MS66
1992	Est. 500	—	—	—	850	900
1992	Est. 4500	PF67 900	PF69 1,000			

KM# 61 1000 PATACAS
15.98 g., 0.917 Gold 0.471 oz. AGW **Subject:** Year of the Rooster **Obv:** Church façade flanked by stars above date **Rev:** Rooster

Date	Mintage	XF40	MS60	MS63	MS65	MS66
1993	Est. 500	—	—	—	850	900
1993	Est. 4500	PF67 900	PF69 1,000			

KM# 69 1000 PATACAS
15.98 g., 0.917 Gold 0.471 oz. AGW **Subject:** Year of the Dog

Obv: Church façade flanked by stars above date **Rev:** Dog

Date	Mintage	XF40	MS60	MS63	MS65	MS66
1994	Est. 500	—	—	—	850	900
1994	Est. 4500	PF67 900	PF69 1,000			

KM# 76 1000 PATACAS
15.98 g., 0.917 Gold 0.471 oz. AGW **Subject:** Year of the Pig **Obv:** Church façade flanked by stars above date **Rev:** Pig

Date	Mintage	XF40	MS60	MS63	MS65	MS66
1995	Est. 500	—	—	—	850	900
1995	Est. 4500	PF67 900	PF69 1,000			

KM# 78 1000 PATACAS
15.98 g., 0.917 Gold 0.471 oz. AGW **Subject:** Airport **Obv:** Stylized form **Rev:** City aerial view

Date	Mintage	XF40	MS60	MS63	MS65	MS66
1995	5,000	PF67 700	PF69 800			

KM# 82 1000 PATACAS
15.98 g., 0.917 Gold 0.471 oz. AGW **Subject:** Year of the Rat **Obv:** Church façade flanked by stars above date **Rev:** Rat

Date	Mintage	XF40	MS60	MS63	MS65	MS66
1996	—	PF67 1,200	PF69 1,350			

KM# 87 1000 PATACAS
15.98 g., 0.917 Gold 0.471 oz. AGW **Subject:** Year of the Ox **Obv:** Church façade flanked by stars above date **Rev:** Ox

Date	Mintage	XF40	MS60	MS63	MS65	MS66
1997	5,000	PF67 800	PF69 900			

KM# 91 1000 PATACAS
15.98 g., 0.917 Gold 0.471 oz. AGW **Subject:** Year of the Tiger **Obv:** Church façade flanked by stars above date **Rev:** Tiger

Date	Mintage	XF40	MS60	MS63	MS65	MS66
1998	5,000	PF67 800	PF69 900			

KM# 95 1000 PATACAS
15.98 g., 0.917 Gold 0.471 oz. AGW **Subject:** Year of the Rabbit **Obv:** Church façade flanked by stars above date **Rev:** Rabbit

Date	Mintage	XF40	MS60	MS63	MS65	MS66
1999	—	PF67 800	PF69 900			

KM# 101 1000 PATACAS
15.98 g., 0.9167 Gold 0.4709 oz. AGW, 28.4 mm. **Subject:** Year of the Dragon **Obv:** Church façade flanked by stars above date **Rev:** Dragon **Edge:** Reeded

Date	Mintage	XF40	MS60	MS63	MS65	MS66
2000	500	—	—	—	850	900
2000	4,000	PF67 900	PF69 1,000			

KM# 43 10000 PATACAS
155.52 g., 0.999 Gold 4.9949 oz. AGW, 69 mm. **Subject:** 35th Anniversary of Grand Prix **Obv:** Chinese junk within circle **Rev:** Race car above dates within circle **Note:** Similar to 500 Patacas, KM#42.

Date	Mintage	XF40	MS60	MS63	MS65	MS66
1988	500	PF67 6,700	PF69 7,300			

KM# 65 10000 PATACAS
155.52 g., 0.999 Gold 4.9949 oz. AGW **Subject:** Macau Grand Prix **Obv:** Map above dates **Rev:** Checkered design divides race car and racing bike **Note:** Similar to 500 Patacas, KM#64.

Date	Mintage	XF40	MS60	MS63	MS65	MS66
1993	500	PF67 6,700	PF69 7,300			

SPECIAL ADMINISTRATIVE REGION (S.A.R.)

KM# 70 10 AVOS
1.38 g., Brass, 17 mm. **Obv:** MACAU written at center with date below **Rev:** Crowned lion dance scene above value flanked by mint marks

Date	Mintage	VF20	XF40	MS60	MS63	MS65
1993	—	—	—	—	0.75	1.25
1998	—	—	—	—	0.75	1.25

KM# 111 10 AVOS
2.50 g., Brass, 17 mm. **Subject:** Macau's Return to China **Obv:** City arms **Rev:** Sun Yat Sen Memorial above clasped hands with building in background

Date	Mintage	VF20	XF40	MS60	MS63	MS65
1999	288,888	—	—	1.00	2.00	3.50

KM# 112 20 AVOS
3.26 g., Brass, 19.5 mm. **Subject:** Macau's Return to China **Obv:** City arms **Rev:** Monetary and Foreign Exchange Authority Building

Date	Mintage	VF20	XF40	MS60	MS63	MS65
1999	288,888	—	—	1.00	2.00	3.50

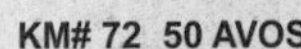

KM# 72 50 AVOS
4.59 g., Brass, 23 mm. **Obv:** MACAU written across center of globe with date below **Rev:** The dragon dance led by a man

Date	Mintage	VF20	XF40	MS60	MS63	MS65
1993	—	—	—	1.00	1.50	2.50

KM# 113 50 AVOS
4.54 g., Brass, 23 mm. **Subject:** Macau's Return to China **Obv:** City arms **Rev:** Jet above bridge and ship

Date	Mintage	VF20	XF40	MS60	MS63	MS65
1999	288,888	—	—	1.00	2.00	3.50

KM# 57 PATACA
9.18 g., Copper-Nickel, 25.98 mm. **Obv:** MACAU written across center of globe with date below **Rev:** Guia Fortress and Chapel of Our Lady of Guia **Edge:** Reeded

Date	Mintage	VF20	XF40	MS60	MS63	MS65
1992	—	—	0.50	1.00	1.50	2.50
1998	—	—	0.50	1.00	1.50	2.50

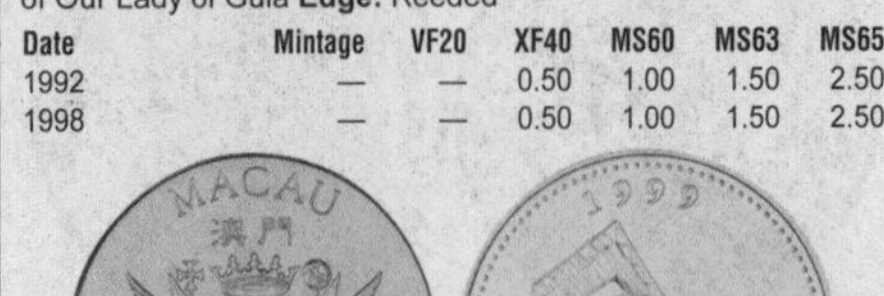

KM# 114 PATACA
6.05 g., Copper-Nickel, 25.9 mm. **Subject:** Macau's Return to China **Obv:** City arms **Rev:** Cultural and recreational center building

Date	Mintage	VF20	XF40	MS60	MS63	MS65
1999	288,888	—	—	3.00	5.00	10.00

KM# 115 2 PATACAS
5.58 g., Copper-Nickel, 25 mm. **Subject:** Macau's Return to China **Obv:** City arms **Rev:** Cathedral and race car

Date	Mintage	VF20	XF40	MS60	MS63	MS65
1999	288,888	—	—	3.00	5.00	10.00

KM# 56 5 PATACAS
10.10 g., Copper-Nickel **Obv:** MACAU written across center of globe with date below **Rev:** Chinese junk, ruins of St. Paul's Cathedral in background **Edge:** Plain **Shape:** 12-sided

Date	Mintage	VF20	XF40	MS60	MS63	MS65
1992	—	—	—	—	2.00	4.00

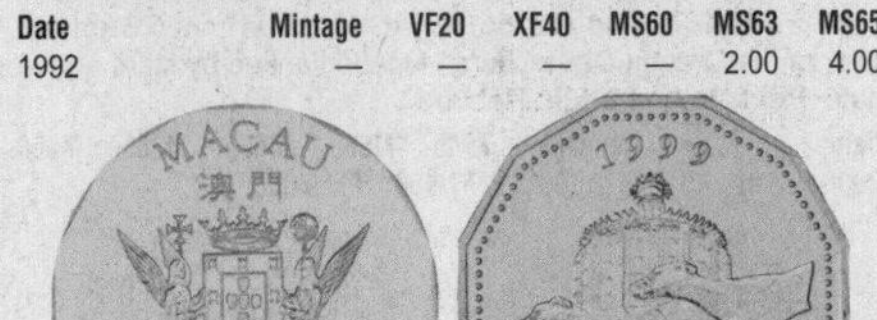

KM# 116 5 PATACAS
6.68 g., Copper-Nickel, 27 mm. **Subject:** Macau's Return to China **Obv:** City arms **Rev:** Racing dogs with Lisboa Hotel in background **Shape:** 12-sided

Date	Mintage	VF20	XF40	MS60	MS63	MS65
1999	288,888	—	—	4.00	6.00	12.00

KM# 117 10 PATACAS
7.20 g., Bi-Metallic Copper-Nickel center in Brass ring, 27.8 mm. **Subject:** Macau's Return to China **Obv:** City arms **Rev:** Government House Building **Edge:** Segmented reeding

Date	Mintage	VF20	XF40	MS60	MS63	MS65
1999	288,888	—	—	5.00	7.00	15.00

KM# 92 100 PATACAS
28.28 g., 0.925 Silver 0.841 oz. ASW, 38.5 mm. **Subject:** Year of the Rabbit **Obv:** Church façade **Rev:** Rabbit **Edge:** Reeded

Date	Mintage	VF20	XF40	MS60	MS63	MS65
1999	5,000	PF63 40.00	PF65 50.00			

KM# 127 1000 PATACAS
34.25 g., 0.9999 Gold 1.1012 oz. AGW **Subject:** Macau returns to China **Obv:** Harbor view including Luso International Bank, Bank of China, Lisboa Hotel, two flags below **Obv. Legend:** TERRITÓRIO DE MACAU **Rev:** Statue of Kun Iam at left of collage of historical sights, two flags below

Date	Mintage	VF20	XF40	MS60	MS63	MS65
1999	1,999	PF65 2,400				

PROVAS

Standard metals

KM#	Date	Mintage	Identification	Mkt Val
Pr1	1952	—	5 Avos.	55.00
Pr2	1952	—	10 Avos.	55.00
Pr3	1952	—	50 Avos.	65.00
Pr4	1952	—	Pataca.	70.00
Pr5	1952	—	5 Patacas.	80.00
Pr6	1967	—	5 Avos.	55.00
Pr7	1967	—	10 Avos.	55.00
Pr8	1968	—	10 Avos.	55.00
Pr9	1968	—	Pataca.	65.00
Pr10	1969	—	10 Avos.	35.00
Pr11	1971	—	5 Patacas.	65.00
Pr12	1972	—	50 Avos.	55.00
Pr13	1973	—	50 Avos.	55.00
Pr14	1974	—	20 Patacas.	85.00
Pr15	1975	—	Pataca.	65.00
Pr16	1988	1	10000 Patacas. 0.999. Silver. KM#43.	6,500

MINT SETS

KM#	Date	Mintage	Identification	Issue Price	Mkt Val
MS1	1999 (7)	288,888	KM#111-117	23.00	65.00

PROOF SETS

KM#	Date	Mintage	Identification	Issue Price	Mkt Val
PS1	1982 (5)	2,000	KM#20a-24a	—	120
PS1b	1982 (5)	150	KM#20b-24b	—	2,975
PS1c	1982 (5)	375	KM#20c-24c	—	3,000
PS2	1983 (5)	2,500	KM#20a-24a	55.00	85.00
PS3	1984 (5)	2,500	KM#20a-24a	55.00	85.00
PS4	1985 (5)	2,500	KM#20a-24a	55.00	85.00
PS5	1987 (2)	—	KM#36-37	—	1,025
PS6	1988 (2)	—	KM#38-39	—	1,025
PS7	1991 (3)	2,500	KM#49-51	775	1,725
PS8	1992 (3)	2,500	KM#53-55	825	1,725
PS9	1993 (3)	2,500	KM#59-61	830	1,725
PS10	1994 (3)	2,500	KM#67-69	825	1,725
PS11	1995 (3)	2,500	KM#74-76	825	1,775
PS12	1997 (3)	2,500	KM#85-87	849	1,725
PS13	1998 (3)	2,500	KM#89-91	855	1,775
PS14	1999 (3)	2,500	KM#93-95	850	1,775
PS15	2000 (3)	2,500	KM#99-101	849	1,900

The Republic of Macedonia is land-locked, and is bordered in the north by Yugoslavia, to the east by Bulgaria, in the south by Greece and to the west by Albania and has an area of 9,781 sq. mi. (25,713 sq. km.) and a population at the 1991 census was 2,038,847, of which the predominating ethnic groups were Macedonians. The capital is Skopje.

The Slavs settled in Macedonia since the 6th century, who had been Christianized by Byzantium, were conquered by the non-Slav Bulgars in the 7th century and in the 9th century formed a Macedo-Bulgarian empire, the western part of which survived until Byzantine conquest in 1014. In the 14th century, it fell to Serbia, and in1355 to the Ottomans. After the Balkan Wars of 1912-13 Turkey was ousted, and Serbia received the greater part of the territory, the balance going to Bulgaria and Greece. In 1918, Yugoslav Macedonia was incorporated into Serbia as "South Serbia", becoming a republic in the S.F.R. of Yugoslavia. Claims to the historical Macedonian territory have long been a source of contention between Bulgaria and Greece.

On Nov. 20, 1991, parliament promulgated a new constitution, and declared its independence on Nov.20, 1992, but failed to secure EC and US recognition owing to Greek objections to the use of the name *Macedonia*. On Dec. 11, 1992, the UN Security Council authorized the expedition of a small peacekeeping force to prevent hostilities spreading into Macedonia.

There is a 120-member single-chamber National Assembly.

REPUBLIC

STANDARD COINAGE

KM# 1 50 DENI

4.05 g., Brass, 21.5 mm. **Obv:** Black-headed gull flying offshore **Rev:** Radiant value

Date	Mintage	VF20	XF40	MS60	MS63	MS65
1993	11,051,000	0.10	0.30	0.50	0.75	1.50

KM# 2 DENAR

5.15 g., Brass, 23.7 mm. **Obv:** Macedonian sheepdog **Obv. Legend:** РЕПУБЛИКА МАКЕДОНИЈА **Rev:** Radiant value **Edge:** Plain

Date	Mintage	VF20	XF40	MS60	MS63	MS65
1993	21,040,000	0.20	0.35	0.75	1.50	3.00
1997	11,200,000	0.20	0.35	0.75	1.50	3.00

KM# 5 DENAR

5.15 g., Brass, 23.7 mm. **Series:** F.A.O. **Obv:** Pyrenean mountain dog **Rev:** Value below F.A.O logo

Date	Mintage	VF20	XF40	MS60	MS63	MS65
1995	2,314,000	—	—	1.00	2.00	3.50

KM# 5a DENAR

Copper-Nickel-Zinc, 23.7 mm. **Series:** F.A.O. **Obv:** Sheep dog **Rev:** F.A.O. logo above value

Date	Mintage	VF20	XF40	MS60	MS63	MS65
1995	1,001,000	—	—	1.00	2.00	3.50

KM# 8 DENAR

15.98 g., 0.9167 Gold 0.471 oz. AGW **Subject:** 5th Anniversary - UN Membership **Obv:** National emblem within circle **Rev:** White Storks within circle

Date	Mintage	XF40	MS60	MS63	MS65	MS66
ND-1996	1,100	PF67 775	PF69 850			

KM# 10 DENAR

8.00 g., 0.916 Gold 0.2356 oz. AGW, 23.3 mm. **Subject:** Macedonian Orthodox Church **Obv:** Half length figure of Saint facing **Rev:** Orthodox cathedral

Date	Mintage	VF20	XF40	MS60	MS63	MS65
1997	5,000	—	—	—	375	425

KM# 9 DENAR

5.10 g., Bronze, 23.8 mm. **Subject:** 2000 Years of Christianity **Obv:** Byzantine copper folis coin **Rev:** Ornamented cross **Edge:** Plain

Date	Mintage	VF20	XF40	MS60	MS63	MS65
2000	2,000	—	—	—	7.00	12.00

KM# 9a DENAR

7.00 g., 0.925 Silver 0.2082 oz. ASW, 23.8 mm. **Obv:** Byzantine copper folis coin **Rev:** Ornamented cross

Date	Mintage	VF20	XF40	MS60	MS63	MS65
2000	2,000	—	—	—	100	125

KM# 9b DENAR

8.00 g., 0.916 Gold 0.2356 oz. AGW, 23.8 mm. **Obv:** Byzantine copper folis coin **Rev:** Ornamented cross

Date	Mintage	VF20	XF40	MS60	MS63	MS65
2000	2,000	—	—	—	400	450

KM# 27 DENAR

5.10 g., Bronze, 23.8 mm. **Obv:** Byzantine copper folis coin design **Rev:** Radiant rising sun behind value **Edge:** Plain

Date	Mintage	VF20	XF40	MS60	MS63	MS65
2000	—	—	—	13.00	17.00	20.00

Note: Mule of KM-9 obverse and KM-2 reverse?

KM# 3 2 DENARI

5.15 g., Brass, 23.7 mm. **Obv:** Trout above water **Obv. Legend:** РЕПУБЛИКА МАКЕДОНИЈА **Rev:** Radiant value **Edge:** Plain

Date	Mintage	VF20	XF40	MS60	MS63	MS65
1993	8,998,000	—	0.50	0.75	1.50	3.00

KM# 6 2 DENARI

6.25 g., Brass, 25.5 mm. **Series:** F.A.O. **Obv:** Trout above water **Rev:** Value below F.A.O logo

Date	Mintage	VF20	XF40	MS60	MS63	MS65
1995	2,637,500	—	—	0.50	1.00	2.00

KM# 6a 2 DENARI

Copper-Nickel-Zinc, 25.5 mm. **Series:** F.A.O. **Obv:** Trout above water **Rev:** Value below F.A.O. logo

Date	Mintage	VF20	XF40	MS60	MS63	MS65
1995	1,000,000	—	—	0.75	1.50	3.00

KM# 12 2 DENARI

Silver, 23 mm. **Subject:** 50th Anniversary - Faculty of Economics **Obv:** Economics building **Rev:** Economics faculty logo

Date	Mintage	XF40	MS60	MS63	MS65	MS66
2000	—	PF65 125	PF67 150			

KM# 12a 2 DENARI
7.00 g., 0.916 Gold 0.2062 oz. AGW, 23 mm. **Subject:** 50th Anniversary - Faculty of Economics **Obv:** Economics building **Rev:** Economics faculty logo

Date	Mintage	XF40	MS60	MS63	MS65	MS66
2000	1,000	PF69 375				

KM# 4 5 DENARI
7.25 g., Brass, 27.5 mm. **Obv:** European lynx **Obv. Legend:** РЕПУБЛИКА МАКЕДОНИЈА **Rev:** Radiant value **Edge:** Plain

Date	Mintage	VF20	XF40	MS60	MS63	MS65
1993	12,330,000	0.35	0.50	0.85	1.75	3.50

KM# 7 5 DENARI
7.25 g., Brass, 27.5 mm. **Series:** F.A.O. **Obv:** European lynx **Rev:** Value below F.A.O logo

Date	Mintage	VF20	XF40	MS60	MS63	MS65
1995	3,123,000	—	—	0.65	1.25	2.50

KM# 7a 5 DENARI
Copper-Nickel-Zinc, 27.5 mm. **Series:** F.A.O. **Obv:** European lynx **Rev:** Value below F.A.O. logo

Date	Mintage	VF20	XF40	MS60	MS63	MS65
1995	1,000,000	—	—	0.85	1.75	3.50

KM# 20 5 DENARI
7.90 g., 0.916 Gold 0.2327 oz. AGW, 23.8 mm. **Subject:** 60th Anniversary - First session of Parliament **Obv:** Logo of Association of Refugees from Aegean part of Macedonia **Rev:** Refugee mother with three children

Date	Mintage	VF20	XF40	MS60	MS63	MS65
2000	1,500	—	—	—	400	450

KM# 11 10 DENARI
7.00 g., 0.916 Gold 0.2062 oz. AGW, 23 mm. **Subject:** Sts. Cyril and Methodus University **Obv:** Statue divides dates **Rev:** Macedonian Cyrillic alphabet

Date	Mintage	VF20	XF40	MS60	MS63	MS65
1999	2,000	—	—	—	350	400

MINT SETS

KM#	Date	Mintage	Identification	Issue Price	Mkt Val
MS1	1993 (4)	—	KM1-4	—	12.50
MS2	1995 (3)	—	KM5a-7a	—	13.50

MADAGASCAR

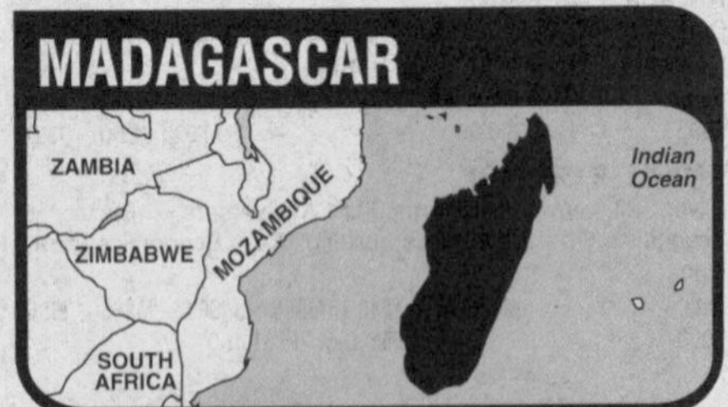

The Democratic Republic of Madagascar, an independent member of the French Community, located in the Indian Ocean 250 miles (402 km.) off the southeast coast of Africa, has an area of 226,656 sq. mi. (587,040 sq. km.) and a population of 10 million. Capital: Antananarivo. The economy is primarily agricultural; large bauxite deposits are being developed. Coffee, vanilla, graphite, and rice are exported.

Successive waves of immigrants from southeast Asia, Africa, Arabia and India populated Madagascar beginning about 2,000 years ago. Diago Diaz, a Portuguese navigator, sighted the island of Madagascar on Aug. 10, 1500, when his ship became separated from an India-bound fleet. Attempts at settlement by the British during the reign of Charles I and by the French during the 17th and 18th centuries were of no avail, and the island became a refuge and supply base for Indian Ocean pirates. Despite considerable influence on the island, the British accepted the imposition of a French protectorate in 1886 in return for French recognition of Britain's sphere of influence in Zanzibar. Madagascar was made a French colony in 1896 after absolute control had been established by military force. Britain occupied the island after the fall of France, 1942, to prevent its seizure by the Japanese, returning it to the Free French in 1943. On Oct. 14, 1958, following a decade of intermittent but bitter warfare, Madagascar, as the Malagasy Republic, became an autonomous state within the French Community. On June 27, 1960, it became a sovereign, independent nation, though remaining nominally within the French Community. The Malagasy Republic was renamed the Democratic Republic of Madagascar in 1975.

MONETARY SYSTEM
100 Centimes = 1 Franc

MINT MARKS
(a) - Paris, privy marks only
SA - Pretoria

FRENCH COLONY

TOKEN COINAGE

KM# Tn1 25 CENTIMES
Aluminum, 21 mm. **Issuer:** Societe des Mines d'Or de Andavakoera. **Obv:** Legend of issuer around value. **Rev:** Parakeet head left.

Date	Mintage	VG8	F12	VF20	XF40	MS60
ND-1920	—	10.00	20.00	50.00	150	340

KM# Tn2 50 CENTIMES
Aluminum, 28 mm. **Issuer:** Societe des Mines d'Or de Andavakoera **Note:** Similar to KM#Tn1.

Date	Mintage	VG8	F12	VF20	XF40	MS60
ND-1920	—	10.00	20.00	35.00	100	250

KM# Tn3 FRANC
Aluminum, 32 mm. **Issuer:** Societe des Mines d'Or de Andavakoera **Note:** Similar to KM#Tn1.

Date	Mintage	VG8	F12	VF20	XF40	MS60
ND-1920	—	9.00	18.00	35.00	100	210

STANDARD COINAGE

KM# 1 50 CENTIMES
Bronze **Obv:** Rooster **Rev:** Cross of Lorraine

Date	Mintage	VF20	XF40	MS60	MS63	MS65
1943 SA	2,000,000	2.50	10.00	25.00	65.00	125

KM# 2 FRANC
Bronze **Obv:** Rooster **Rev:** Cross of Lorraine

Date	Mintage	VF20	XF40	MS60	MS63	MS65
1943 SA	5,000,000	6.00	18.00	45.00	85.00	175

KM# 3 FRANC
1.30 g., Aluminum, 23 mm. **Obv:** Liberty bust left **Rev:** Conjoined ox heads flanked by sprigs, value within horns

Date	Mintage	VF20	XF40	MS60	MS63	MS65
1948 (a)	7,400,000	0.35	0.75	1.25	2.75	3.50
1958 (a)	2,600,000	0.35	0.75	1.25	2.75	3.50

KM# 4 2 FRANCS
Aluminum **Obv:** Liberty bust left **Rev:** Conjoined ox heads flanked by sprigs, value within horns

Date	Mintage	VF20	XF40	MS60	MS63	MS65
1948 (a)	10,000,000	0.45	0.85	1.25	2.50	3.50

KM# 5 5 FRANCS
Aluminum **Obv:** Liberty bust left **Rev:** Conjoined ox heads flanked by sprigs, value within horns

Date	Mintage	VF20	XF40	MS60	MS63	MS65
1953 (a)	30,012,000	0.55	1.00	1.75	3.00	5.00

KM# 6 10 FRANCS
Aluminum-Bronze, 20 mm. **Obv:** Liberty bust left **Rev:** Value within horns flanked by cluster of sprigs with shaded area above value

Date	Mintage	VF20	XF40	MS60	MS63	MS65
1953 (a)	25,000,000	0.65	1.25	2.00	3.50	6.00

KM# 7 20 FRANCS
4.00 g., Aluminum-Bronze **Obv:** Liberty bust left **Rev:** Value within horns flanked by cluster of sprigs with shaded area above value

Date	Mintage	VF20	XF40	MS60	MS63	MS65
1953 (a)	15,000,000	1.50	3.00	4.50	6.50	9.00

MALAGASY REPUBLIC

STANDARD COINAGE

1 Ariary = 100 Iraimbilanja

KM# 8 FRANC
2.40 g., Stainless Steel **Obv:** Poinsettia **Rev:** Value within horns of ox head above sprigs

Date	Mintage	VF20	XF40	MS60	MS63	MS65
1965 (a)	1,170,000	0.15	0.30	0.65	1.25	2.00

Date	Mintage	VF20	XF40	MS60	MS63	MS65
1966 (a)	—	0.15	0.30	0.65	1.25	2.00
1970 (a)	—	0.15	0.30	0.65	1.25	2.00
1974 (a)	1,250,000	0.15	0.30	0.65	1.25	2.00
1975 (a)	7,355,000	0.15	0.30	0.65	1.25	2.00
1976 (a)	—	0.15	0.30	0.65	1.25	2.00
1977 (a)	—	0.15	0.30	0.65	1.25	2.00
1979 (a)	—	0.15	0.30	0.65	1.25	2.00
1980 (a)	—	0.20	0.40	0.75	1.45	2.25
1981 (a)	—	0.20	0.40	0.75	1.45	2.25
1982 (a)	—	0.20	0.40	0.75	1.45	2.25
1983 (a)	—	0.20	0.40	0.75	1.45	2.25
1986 (a)	—	0.20	0.40	0.75	1.45	2.25
1987 (a)	—	0.20	0.40	0.75	1.45	2.25
1988 (a)	—	0.20	0.40	0.75	1.45	2.25
1989 (a)	—	0.20	0.40	0.75	1.45	2.25
1991 (a)	—	0.20	0.40	0.75	1.45	2.25
1993 (a)	—	0.20	0.40	0.75	1.45	2.25

KM# 9 2 FRANCS

3.40 g., Stainless Steel **Obv:** Poinsettia **Rev:** Value within horns of ox head above sprigs

Date	Mintage	VF20	XF40	MS60	MS63	MS65
1965 (a)	760,000	0.25	0.50	0.80	1.50	2.50
1970 (a)	—	0.25	0.45	0.65	1.25	2.00
1974 (a)	1,250,000	0.25	0.45	0.65	1.25	2.00
1975 (a)	8,250,000	0.25	0.45	0.65	1.25	2.00
1976 (a)	—	0.25	0.45	0.65	1.25	2.00
1977 (a)	—	0.25	0.45	0.65	1.25	2.00
1979 (a)	—	0.25	0.45	0.65	1.25	2.00
1980 (a)	—	0.25	0.45	0.65	1.25	2.00
1981 (a)	—	0.25	0.45	0.65	1.25	2.00
1982 (a)	—	0.25	0.45	0.65	1.25	2.00
1983 (a)	—	0.25	0.45	0.65	1.25	2.00
1984 (a)	—	0.25	0.45	0.65	1.25	2.00
1986 (a)	—	0.25	0.45	0.65	1.25	2.00
1987 (a)	—	0.25	0.45	0.65	1.25	2.00
1988 (a)	—	0.25	0.45	0.65	1.25	2.00
1989 (a)	—	0.25	0.45	0.65	1.25	2.00

KM# 10 5 FRANCS (Ariary)

5.00 g., Stainless Steel **Obv:** Poinsettia **Rev:** Value within horns of ox head above sprigs

Date	Mintage	VF20	XF40	MS60	MS63	MS65
1966 (a)	—	0.25	0.60	0.85	1.75	2.50
1967 (a)	—	0.25	0.60	0.85	1.75	2.50
1968 (a)	7,500,000	0.25	0.60	0.85	1.75	2.50
1970 (a)	—	0.25	0.60	0.85	1.75	2.50
1972 (a)	19,100,000	0.25	0.60	0.85	1.75	2.50
1976 (a)	—	0.25	0.60	0.85	1.75	2.50
1977 (a)	—	0.25	0.60	0.85	1.75	2.50
1979 (a)	—	0.25	0.60	0.85	1.75	2.50
1980 (a)	—	0.30	0.65	0.95	1.85	2.75
1981 (a)	—	0.30	0.65	0.95	1.85	2.75
1982 (a)	—	0.30	0.65	0.95	1.85	2.75
1983 (a)	—	0.30	0.65	0.95	1.85	2.75
1984 (a)	—	0.30	0.65	0.95	1.85	2.75
1986 (a)	—	0.30	0.65	0.95	1.85	2.75
1987 (a)	—	0.30	0.65	0.95	1.85	2.75
1988 (a)	—	0.30	0.65	0.95	1.85	2.75
1989 (a)	—	0.30	0.65	0.95	1.85	2.75

KM# 11 10 FRANCS (2 Ariary)

3.50 g., Aluminum-Bronze **Series:** F.A.O. **Obv:** Vanilla plant **Rev:** Value within horns of ox head flanked by sprigs and marks

Date	Mintage	VF20	XF40	MS60	MS63	MS65
1970 (a)	7,000,000	0.30	0.70	1.00	2.00	3.00
1971 (a)	10,000,000	0.30	0.70	1.00	2.00	3.00
1972 (a)	5,050,000	0.30	0.70	1.00	2.00	3.00
1973 (a)	3,000,000	0.30	0.70	1.00	2.00	3.00
1974 (a)	—	0.30	0.70	1.00	2.00	3.00
1975 (a)	—	0.30	0.70	1.00	2.00	3.00
1976 (a)	9,500,000	0.30	0.70	1.00	2.00	3.00
1977 (a)	—	0.30	0.70	1.00	2.00	3.00
1978 (a)	—	0.30	0.70	1.00	2.00	3.00
1979 (a)	—	0.30	0.70	1.00	2.00	3.00
1980 (a)	—	0.35	0.80	1.25	2.25	3.25
1981 (a)	—	0.35	0.80	1.25	2.25	3.25
1982 (a)	—	0.35	0.80	1.25	2.25	3.25
1983 (a)	—	0.35	0.80	1.25	2.25	3.25
1984 (a)	—	0.35	0.80	1.25	2.25	3.25
1986 (a)	—	0.35	0.80	1.25	2.25	3.25
1987 (a)	3,200,000	0.35	0.80	1.25	2.25	3.25
1988 (a)	—	0.35	0.80	1.25	2.25	3.25
1989 (a)	—	0.35	0.80	1.25	2.25	3.25

Note: Struck by Royal Canadian Mint.

KM# 11a 10 FRANCS (2 Ariary)

Copper Plated Steel **Series:** F.A.O. **Obv:** Vanilla plant **Rev:** Value within horns of ox head flanked by sprigs (without other marks)

Date	Mintage	VF20	XF40	MS60	MS63	MS65
1991	—	0.45	1.50	2.00	3.50	5.00

KM# 12 20 FRANCS (4 Ariary)

6.00 g., Aluminum-Bronze, 24.5 mm. **Series:** F.A.O. **Obv:** Cotton plant **Rev:** Value within horns of ox head above sprigs and marks

Date	Mintage	VF20	XF40	MS60	MS63	MS65
1970 (a)	4,000,000	0.35	0.75	1.50	2.50	3.50
1971 (a)	2,000,000	0.35	0.75	1.50	2.50	3.50
1972 (a)	2,000,000	0.40	0.80	1.75	2.75	3.75
1973 (a)	3,000,000	0.40	0.80	1.75	2.75	3.75
1974 (a)	—	0.40	0.80	1.75	2.75	3.75
1975 (a)	—	0.40	0.80	1.75	2.75	3.75
1976 (a)	2,700,000	0.40	0.80	1.75	2.75	3.75
1977 (a)	—	0.40	0.80	1.75	2.75	3.75
1978 (a)	—	0.40	0.80	1.75	2.75	3.75
1979 (a)	—	0.40	0.80	1.75	2.75	3.75
1980 (a)	—	0.45	0.85	1.85	3.00	4.00
1981 (a)	—	0.45	0.85	1.85	3.00	4.00
1982 (a)	—	0.45	0.85	1.85	3.00	4.00
1983 (a)	—	0.45	0.85	1.85	3.00	4.00
1984 (a)	—	0.45	0.85	1.85	3.00	4.00
1986 (a)	—	0.45	0.85	1.85	3.00	4.00
1987 (a)	5,200,000	0.45	0.85	1.85	3.00	4.00
1988 (a)	—	0.45	0.85	1.85	3.00	4.00
1989 (a)	—	0.45	0.85	1.85	3.00	4.00

Note: Struck by the Royal Canadian Mint

DEMOCRATIC REPUBLIC

KM# 17 5 ARIARY

4.50 g., Copper Plated Steel **Obv:** Star above value within 3/4 wreath **Rev:** Rice plant within circle **Rev. Legend:** Motto A

Date	Mintage	VF20	XF40	MS60	MS63	MS65
1992	—	—	0.50	1.00	3.00	5.00

KM# 13 10 ARIARY

Nickel **Series:** F.A.O. **Obv:** Star above value within 3/4 wreath **Rev:** Man cutting peat within circle **Rev. Legend:** Motto A

Date	Mintage	VF20	XF40	MS60	MS63	MS65
1978	8,001,000	—	1.00	2.00	4.00	7.00

KM# 13a 10 ARIARY

9.00 g., 0.925 Silver 0.2677 oz. ASW **Obv:** Star above value within 3/4 wreath **Rev:** Man cutting peat within circle **Rev. Legend:** Motto A

Date	Mintage	VF20	XF40	MS60	MS63	MS65
1978	—	PF63 12.00	PF65 15.00			

KM# 13b 10 ARIARY

Copper-Nickel **Obv:** Star above value within 3/4 wreath **Rev:** Man cutting peat within circle **Rev. Legend:** Motto A

Date	Mintage	VF20	XF40	MS60	MS63	MS65
1983	—	—	0.65	1.25	3.50	6.00

KM# 16 10 ARIARY

10.00 g., 0.917 Gold 0.2948 oz. AGW **Subject:** World Wildlife Fund **Obv:** Star above value within 3/4 wreath **Rev:** Ibis

Date	Mintage	VF20	XF40	MS60	MS63	MS65
1988	Est. 5000	PF65 525				

KM# 18 10 ARIARY

6.47 g., Stainless Steel, 23.5 mm. **Obv:** Star above value within 3/4 wreath **Rev:** Man cutting peat within circle **Rev. Legend:** Motto A **Shape:** 7-sided

Date	Mintage	VF20	XF40	MS60	MS63	MS65
1992	—	—	0.50	1.00	3.00	5.00

KM# 14 20 ARIARY

Nickel **Series:** F.A.O. **Obv:** Star above value within 3/4 wreath **Rev:** Farmer on tractor disking field **Rev. Legend:** Motto A

Date	Mintage	VF20	XF40	MS60	MS63	MS65
1978	8,001,000	—	1.50	3.00	5.00	8.00

KM# 14a 20 ARIARY

12.00 g., 0.925 Silver 0.3569 oz. ASW **Obv:** Star above value within 3/4 wreath **Rev:** Farmer on tractor disking field **Rev. Legend:** Motto A

Date	Mintage	VF20	XF40	MS60	MS63	MS65
1978	—	PF63 15.00	PF65 18.00			

KM# 14b 20 ARIARY

12.00 g., Copper-Nickel **Obv:** Star above value within 3/4 wreath **Rev:** Man on tractor disking field **Rev. Legend:** Motto A

Date	Mintage	VF20	XF40	MS60	MS63	MS65
1983	—	—	1.50	3.00	5.00	8.00

KM# 15 20 ARIARY

19.44 g., 0.925 Silver 0.5781 oz. ASW **Subject:** World Wildlife Fund **Obv:** Star above value within 3/4 wreath **Rev:** Lemur

Date	Mintage	VF20	XF40	MS60	MS63	MS65
1988	Est. 25000	PF63 20.00	PF65 25.00			

KM# 19 20 ARIARY
Stainless Steel **Obv:** Star above value within 3/4 wreath **Rev:** Farmer on tractor disking field **Rev. Legend:** Motto A

Date	Mintage	VF20	XF40	MS60	MS63	MS65
1992	—	—	0.50	1.00	3.00	5.00

KM# 26 20 ARIARY
19.44 g., 0.925 Silver 0.5781 oz. ASW **Series:** UNICEF **Obv:** Star above value within 3/4 wreath **Rev:** Child and ring-tailed lemur in tree

Date	Mintage	VF20	XF40	MS60	MS63	MS65
1996	—	PF63 30.00	PF65 35.00			

KM# 20 50 ARIARY
Stainless Steel **Obv:** Star above value within 3/4 wreath **Rev:** Avenue of Baobabs **Rev. Legend:** Motto A

Date	Mintage	VF20	XF40	MS60	MS63	MS65
1992	—	—	2.00	4.00	6.00	9.00

MADAGASIKARA REPUBLIC

STANDARD COINAGE

KM# 21 5 FRANCS (Ariary)
5.00 g., Stainless Steel, 22 mm. **Obv:** Poinsettia **Rev:** Value within horns of ox head flanked by sprigs

Date	Mintage	VF20	XF40	MS60	MS63	MS65
1996 (a)	—	—	—	0.50	1.00	1.50

KM# 22 10 FRANCS (2 Ariary)
Copper Plated Steel, 21 mm. **Obv:** Vanilla plant **Rev:** Value within horns of ox head flanked by sprigs

Date	Mintage	VF20	XF40	MS60	MS63	MS65
1996	—	—	—	0.50	1.00	1.50

KM# 23 5 ARIARY
4.70 g., Copper Plated Steel, 24 mm. **Obv:** Star above value within 3/4 wreath **Rev:** Rice plant within circle **Rev. Legend:** Motto B

Date	Mintage	VF20	XF40	MS60	MS63	MS65
1994	—	—	—	0.75	1.25	2.50
1996	—	—	—	0.75	1.25	2.50

KM# 27 10 ARIARY
Stainless Steel **Series:** F.A.O. **Obv:** Star above value within 3/4 wreath **Rev:** Man cutting peat **Rev. Legend:** Motto C **Edge:** Plain **Shape:** 7-sided

Date	Mintage	VF20	XF40	MS60	MS63	MS65
1999	—	—	—	1.00	2.00	3.50

KM# 24.1 20 ARIARY
Nickel Clad Steel, 28 mm. **Series:** F.A.O. **Obv:** Star above value within 3/4 wreath **Rev:** Farmer on tractor disking field **Rev. Legend:** Motto B

Date	Mintage	VF20	XF40	MS60	MS63	MS65
1994	—	—	—	1.00	2.00	3.50

KM# 24.2 20 ARIARY
9.15 g., Nickel Clad Steel, 28 mm. **Series:** F.A.O. **Obv:** Star above value within 3/4 wreath **Rev:** Man on tractor disking field **Rev. Legend:** Motto C

Date	Mintage	VF20	XF40	MS60	MS63	MS65
1999	—	—	—	1.00	2.00	3.50

KM# 25.1 50 ARIARY
Stainless Steel, 30.63 mm. **Obv:** Star above value within sprays **Rev:** Avenue of Baobabs **Rev. Inscription:** Motto B **Edge:** Plain **Shape:** 11-sided

Date	Mintage	VF20	XF40	MS60	MS63	MS65
1994	—	—	—	1.75	3.50	6.00
1996	—	—	—	1.75	3.50	6.00

ESSAIS

Standard metals unless otherwise noted

KM#	Date	Mintage	Identification	Mkt Val
E1	1948(a)	2,000	Franc. Copper-Nickel. KM3.	40.00
E2	1948	2,000	2 Francs. Copper-Nickel. KM4.	40.00
E3	1953(a)	1,200	5 Francs. Aluminum. KM5.	35.00
E4	1953(a)	1,200	10 Francs. Aluminum-Bronze. KM6.	35.00
E5	1953(a)	1,200	20 Francs. Aluminum-Bronze. KM7.	35.00
E6	1965(a)	—	Franc. Stainless Steel. KM8.	30.00
E7	1965(a)	—	2 Francs. Stainless Steel. KM9.	28.00
E8	1966(a)	—	5 Francs. Stainless Steel. KM10.	28.00
E9	1970(a)	—	10 Francs. Aluminum-Bronze. KM11.	28.00
E10	1970(a)	—	20 Francs. Aluminum-Bronze. KM12.	28.00

PIEDFORT WITH ESSAI

Double thickness; Standard metals unless otherwise noted

KM#	Date	Mintage	Identification	Mkt Val
PE1	1948(a)	104	Franc. Aluminum. KM3.	250
PE2	1948(a)	104	2 Francs. Aluminum. KM4.	250
PE3	1953(a)	104	5 Francs. Aluminum. KM5.	250
PE4	1953(a)	104	10 Francs. Aluminum-Bronze. KM6.	265
PE5	1953(a)	104	20 Francs. KM7.	265

FDC SETS

KM#	Date	Mintage	Identification	Issue Price	Mkt Val
SS1	1970 (5)	1,500	KM8-12	2.75	17.50

PROOF SETS

KM#	Date	Mintage	Identification	Issue Price	Mkt Val
PS1	1978 (2)	3,800	KM#13a, 14a	38.00	50.00

MADEIRA ISLANDS

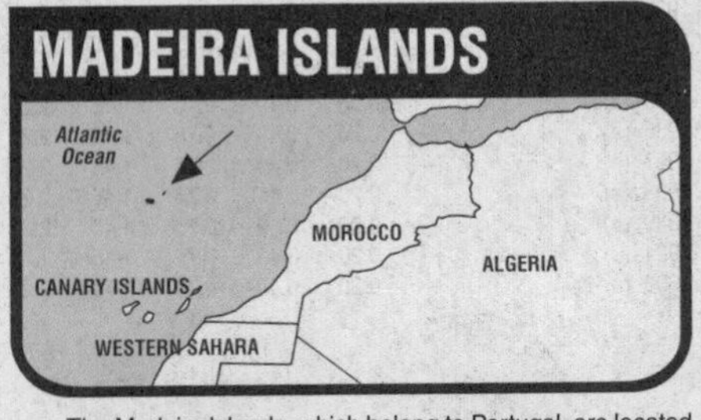

The Madeira Islands, which belong to Portugal, are located 360 miles (492 km.) off the northwest coast of Africa. They have an area of 307 sq. mi. (795 sq. km.). The group consists of two inhabited islands named Madeira and Porto Santo and two groups of uninhabited rocks named Desertas and Selvagens. Capital: Funchal. The two staple products are wine and sugar. Bananas and pineapples are also produced for export.

Although the evidence is insufficient, it is thought that the Phoenicians visited Madeira at an early period. It is also probable that the entire archipelago was explored by Genoese adventurers; an Italian map dated 1351 shows the Madeira Islands quite clearly. The Portuguese navigator Goncalvez Zarco first sighted Porto Santo in 1418, having been driven there by a storm while he was exploring the coast of West Africa. Madeira itself was discovered in 1420. The islands were uninhabited when visited by Zarco, but soon after 1418 Madeira was quickly colonized by Prince Henry the Navigator, aided by the knights of the Order of Christ. British troops occupied the islands in 1801, and again in 1807-14.

RULER
Portuguese

PORTUGUESE COLONY

MODERN COINAGE

KM# 4 25 ESCUDOS
11.00 g., Copper-Nickel, 28.5 mm. **Subject:** Autonomy of Madeira **Obv:** Shields above value **Rev:** Head facing

Date	Mintage	VF20	XF40	MS60	MS63	MS65
1981	750,000	—	—	3.00	5.00	8.00

KM# 4a 25 ESCUDOS
11.00 g., 0.925 Silver 0.3271 oz. ASW, 28.5 mm. **Subject:** Autonomy of Madeira **Obv:** Shields above value **Rev:** Head facing

Date	Mintage	VF20	XF40	MS60	MS63	MS65
1981	—	PF63 12.00	PF65 20.00			

KM# 5 100 ESCUDOS
Copper-Nickel, 33.8 mm. **Subject:** Autonomy of Madeira **Obv:** Shields above value **Rev:** Head facing

Date	Mintage	VF20	XF40	MS60	MS63	MS65
1981	250,000	—	—	5.00	7.50	10.00

KM# 5a 100 ESCUDOS
16.50 g., 0.925 Silver 0.4907 oz. ASW, 33.8 mm. **Subject:** Autonomy of Madeira **Obv:** Shields above value **Rev:** Head facing

Date	Mintage	VF20	XF40	MS60	MS63	MS65
1981	—	PF63 20.00	PF65 30.00			

PROVAS

KM#	Date	Mintage	Identification	Mkt Val
Pr1	1981	—	25 Escudos. Copper-Nickel. KM4.	45.00
Pr2	1981	—	100 Escudos. Copper-Nickel. KM5.	65.00

PROOF SETS

KM#	Date	Mintage	Identification	Issue Price	Mkt Val
PS1	1981 (2)	20,000	KM4a-5a	42.00	50.00

MALAWI

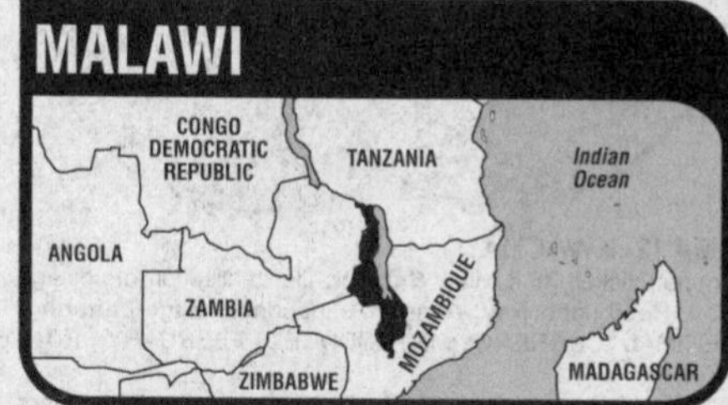

The Republic of Malawi (formerly Nyasaland), located in southeastern Africa to the west of Lake Malawi (Nyasa), has an area of 45,745 sq. mi. (118,480 sq. km.) and a population of 7 million. Capital: Lilongwe. The economy is predominantly agricultural. Tobacco, tea, peanuts and cotton are exported.

Although the Portuguese were the first Europeans to reach the Malawi area, the first meaningful contact was made by missionary-explorer Dr. David Livingstone. He arrived at Lake Malawi on Sept. 16, 1859, and remained to make extensive explorations in the 1860's. Subsequent clashes between settlements of Scottish missionaries and Arab slave traders, and the procurement of development rights by Cecil Rhodes, 1884, stimulated British interest and brought about the establishment of the Nyasaland protectorate in 1891. In 1953 Nyasaland reluctantly joined the Federation of Rhodesia and Nyasaland and, after prolonged protest, was granted self-government within the federation. Nyasaland became the independent nation of Malawi on July 6, 1964, and became a republic two years later. Malawi is a member of the Commonwealth of Nations. The president is the Chief of State and Head of Government.

NOTE: For earlier coinage see Rhodesia and Nyasaland.

MONETARY SYSTEM

12 Pence = 1 Shilling
2 Shillings = 1 Florin
5 Shillings = 1 Crown
20 Shillings = 1 Pound

REPUBLIC

STERLING COINAGE

KM# 6 PENNY
Bronze **Obv:** Malawi written above date and value **Rev:** Written and numeral value above designs

Date	Mintage	VF20	XF40	MS60	MS63	MS65
1967	6,000,000	0.65	1.25	2.50	5.00	10.00
1968	3,600,000	5.00	10.00	15.00	25.00	—

KM# 1 6 PENCE
2.79 g., Copper-Nickel-Zinc **Obv:** Head right **Rev:** Rooster

Date	Mintage	VF20	XF40	MS60	MS63	MS65
1964	14,800,000	0.50	0.75	1.25	2.50	4.00
1964	10,000	PF63 1.00	PF65 1.50			
1967	6,000,000	0.75	1.25	2.50	4.50	6.50

KM# 2 SHILLING
5.37 g., Copper-Nickel-Zinc, 23.5 mm. **Obv:** Head right **Rev:** Bundled corncobs

Date	Mintage	VF20	XF40	MS60	MS63	MS65
1964	11,900,000	0.50	0.75	1.25	2.50	3.50

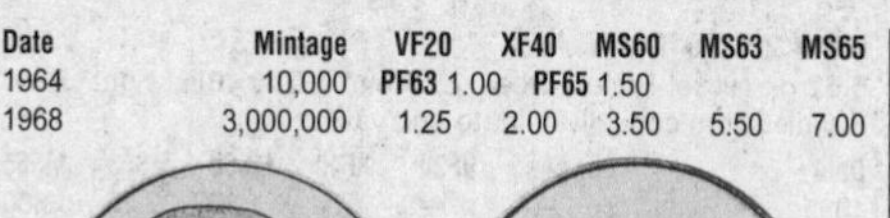

Date	Mintage	VF20	XF40	MS60	MS63	MS65
1964	10,000	PF63 1.00	PF65 1.50			
1968	3,000,000	1.25	2.00	3.50	5.50	7.00

KM# 3 FLORIN
11.31 g., Copper-Nickel-Zinc, 28 mm. **Obv:** Head right **Rev:** Elephants

Date	Mintage	VF20	XF40	MS60	MS63	MS65
1964	6,500,000	0.75	1.50	2.50	4.00	6.00
1964	10,000	PF63 2.50	PF65 4.50			

KM# 4 1/2 CROWN
Copper-Nickel-Zinc **Obv:** Head right **Rev:** Arms with supporters

Date	Mintage	VF20	XF40	MS60	MS63	MS65
1964	6,400,000	1.50	2.00	3.00	5.00	7.50
1964	10,000	PF63 2.50	PF65 4.50			

KM# 5 CROWN
Nickel-Brass **Subject:** Day of the Republic - July 6, 1966 **Obv:** Head right **Rev:** Arms with supporters

Date	Mintage	VF20	XF40	MS60	MS63	MS65
1966	20,000	PF63 4.50	PF65 7.50			

DECIMAL COINAGE

100 Tambala = 1 Kwacha

KM# 7.1 TAMBALA
1.76 g., Bronze, 17 mm. **Obv:** Head right **Rev:** Rooster

Date	Mintage	VF20	XF40	MS60	MS63	MS65
1971	15,000,000	0.20	0.40	0.60	0.75	1.50
1971	4,000	PF63 1.00	PF65 1.50			
1973	5,000,000	0.20	0.40	0.60	0.75	1.50
1974	12,500,000	0.20	0.40	0.60	0.75	1.50

KM# 7.2 TAMBALA
1.78 g., Bronze, 17 mm. **Obv:** Head right with accent mark above "W" in MALAWI **Rev:** Rooster

Date	Mintage	VF20	XF40	MS60	MS63	MS65
1975	10,000,000	0.20	0.40	0.60	0.75	1.50
1977	10,000,000	0.20	0.40	0.60	0.75	1.50
1979	15,000,000	0.20	0.40	0.60	0.75	1.50
1982	15,000,000	0.20	0.40	0.60	0.75	1.50

KM# 7.2a TAMBALA
1.80 g., Copper Plated Steel **Obv:** Head right **Rev:** Rooster divides value and date

Date	Mintage	VF20	XF40	MS60	MS63	MS65
1984	201,000	0.30	0.50	0.65	0.80	1.50
1985	10,000	PF63 2.00	PF65 3.00			
1987	—	0.30	0.50	0.65	0.80	1.50
1989	—	0.30	0.50	0.65	0.80	1.50
1991	—	0.30	0.50	0.65	0.80	1.50
1994	—	0.30	0.50	0.65	0.80	1.50

KM# 24 TAMBALA
1.80 g., Copper Plated Steel, 17.2 mm. **Obv:** Bust right **Rev:** Two Talapia fish

Date	Mintage	VF20	XF40	MS60	MS63	MS65
1995	—	—	—	0.50	1.00	1.50

KM# 33 TAMBALA
1.68 g., Bronze, 17.3 mm. **Obv:** Arms with supporters **Rev:** Two Talapia fish **Edge:** Plain

Date	Mintage	VF20	XF40	MS60	MS63	MS65
1995	—	—	—	0.50	1.00	1.50

KM# 8.1 2 TAMBALA
Bronze **Obv:** Head right **Rev:** Paradise whydah bird divides date and value

Date	Mintage	VF20	XF40	MS60	MS63	MS65
1971	10,000,000	0.40	0.75	1.00	1.50	2.00
1971	4,000	PF63 1.25	PF65 1.75			
1973	5,000,000	0.40	0.75	1.00	1.50	2.00
1974	5,000,000	0.40	0.75	1.00	1.50	2.00

KM# 8.2 2 TAMBALA
3.60 g., Bronze **Obv:** Head right with accent mark above "W" in MALAWI **Rev:** Paradise whydah bird divides date and value

Date	Mintage	VF20	XF40	MS60	MS63	MS65
1975	5,000,000	0.40	0.75	1.00	1.50	2.00
1977	5,000,000	0.40	0.75	1.00	1.50	2.00
1979	7,637,000	0.40	0.75	1.00	1.50	2.00
1982	15,000,000	0.40	0.75	1.00	1.50	2.00

KM# 8.2a 2 TAMBALA
3.46 g., Copper Plated Steel **Obv:** Head right **Rev:** Paradise whydah bird divides date and value

Date	Mintage	VF20	XF40	MS60	MS63	MS65
1984	150,000	0.50	0.85	1.25	2.00	3.00
1985	10,000	PF63 2.50	PF65 4.00			
1987	—	0.50	0.85	1.25	2.00	3.00
1989	—	0.50	0.85	1.25	2.00	3.00
1991	—	0.50	0.85	1.00	1.75	2.75
1994	—	0.50	0.85	1.00	1.75	2.75

KM# 25 2 TAMBALA
3.50 g., Copper Plated Steel, 20.3 mm. **Obv:** Bust right **Rev:** Paradise whydah bird divides date and value

Date	Mintage	VF20	XF40	MS60	MS63	MS65
1995	—	—	—	0.50	1.00	1.50

KM# 34 2 TAMBALA
3.50 g., Bronze, 20.3 mm. **Obv:** Arms with supporters **Rev:** Paradise whydah bird divides date and value **Edge:** Plain

Date	Mintage	VF20	XF40	MS60	MS63	MS65
1995	—	—	—	0.50	1.00	1.50

KM# 9.1 5 TAMBALA
2.86 g., Copper-Nickel **Obv:** Head right **Rev:** Purple heron and value

Date	Mintage	VF20	XF40	MS60	MS63	MS65
1971	7,000,000	0.45	0.85	1.00	1.75	2.00
1971	4,000	PF63 1.25	PF65 2.00			

KM# 9.2 5 TAMBALA

Copper-Nickel **Obv:** Head right with accent mark above "W" in MALAWI **Rev:** Purple heron and value

Date	Mintage	VF20	XF40	MS60	MS63	MS65
1985	10,000	PF63 3.00	PF65 5.00			

KM# 9.2a 5 TAMBALA

2.80 g., Nickel Clad Steel, 19.35 mm. **Obv:** Head right **Rev:** Purple heron and value

Date	Mintage	VF20	XF40	MS60	MS63	MS65
1989	—	0.50	0.85	1.25	2.00	3.00
1991	—	0.50	0.85	1.25	2.00	3.00
1994	—	0.50	0.85	1.25	2.00	3.00

KM# 26 5 TAMBALA

2.83 g., Nickel Plated Steel, 19.35 mm. **Obv:** Bust right **Rev:** Purple heron and value

Date	Mintage	VF20	XF40	MS60	MS63	MS65
1995	—	—	—	0.50	1.00	3.00

KM# 32.1 5 TAMBALA

Nickel Plated Steel, 19.35 mm. **Obv:** Arms with supporters **Rev:** Purple heron and value

Date	Mintage	VF20	XF40	MS60	MS63	MS65
1995	—	—	—	0.75	1.25	2.50

KM# 10.1 10 TAMBALA

Copper-Nickel, 23.6 mm. **Obv:** Head right **Rev:** Bundled corncob divides date and value

Date	Mintage	VF20	XF40	MS60	MS63	MS65
1971	4,000,000	0.50	1.00	1.25	2.25	3.00
1971	4,000	PF63 1.50	PF65 2.50			

KM# 10.2 10 TAMBALA

5.70 g., Copper-Nickel, 23.6 mm. **Obv:** Head right **Rev:** Bundled corncobs divide date and value

Date	Mintage	VF20	XF40	MS60	MS63	MS65
1985	10,000	PF63 4.00	PF65 6.00			
1989	—	0.80	1.50	2.00	2.75	3.50

KM# 10.2a 10 TAMBALA

5.60 g., Nickel Clad Steel, 23.6 mm. **Obv:** Head right **Rev:** Bundled cobs of corn divide value and date

Date	Mintage	VF20	XF40	MS60	MS63	MS65
1989	—	0.80	1.50	2.00	2.75	—

KM# 27 10 TAMBALA

5.62 g., Nickel Plated Steel, 23.6 mm. **Obv:** Bust right **Rev:** Bundled corn cobs divide date and value

Date	Mintage	VF20	XF40	MS60	MS63	MS65
1995	—	—	—	1.25	2.25	3.00

KM# 11.1 20 TAMBALA

10.97 g., Copper-Nickel, 26.5 mm. **Obv:** Head right **Rev:** Elephants

Date	Mintage	VF20	XF40	MS60	MS63	MS65
1971	3,000,000	0.80	1.50	2.00	3.00	5.00
1971	4,000	PF63 3.00	PF65 5.00			

KM# 11.2 20 TAMBALA

Copper-Nickel, 26.5 mm. **Obv:** Head right with accent mark above "W" in MALAWI **Rev:** Elephants

Date	Mintage	VF20	XF40	MS60	MS63	MS65
1985	10,000	PF63 5.00	PF65 7.00			

KM# 11.2a 20 TAMBALA

11.33 g., Nickel Clad Steel, 28.5 mm. **Obv:** Head right **Rev:** Elephants

Date	Mintage	VF20	XF40	MS60	MS63	MS65
1989	—	1.00	1.50	2.50	3.50	5.00
1994	—	1.00	1.50	2.50	3.50	5.00

KM# 29 20 TAMBALA

7.52 g., Nickel Clad Steel, 26.5 mm. **Obv:** Bust right **Rev:** Elephants

Date	Mintage	VF20	XF40	MS60	MS63	MS65
1996	—	—	—	2.50	4.00	6.00

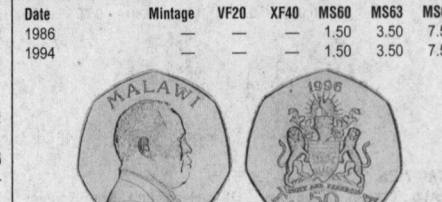

KM# 19 50 TAMBALA

11.35 g., Copper-Nickel-Zinc, 30 mm. **Obv:** Head right **Rev:** Arms with supporters **Note:** The 1989 date for this coin does not exist.

Date	Mintage	VF20	XF40	MS60	MS63	MS65
1986	—	—	—	1.50	3.50	7.50
1994	—	—	—	1.50	3.50	7.50

KM# 30 50 TAMBALA

4.40 g., Brass Plated Steel, 22 mm. **Obv:** Bust right **Rev:** Arms with supporters **Shape:** 7-sided

Date	Mintage	VF20	XF40	MS60	MS63	MS65
1996	—	—	—	2.00	3.50	5.00

KM# 12 KWACHA

Copper-Nickel, 38.8 mm. **Subject:** Decimalization of coinage **Obv:** Head right **Rev:** Arms with supporters **Edge Lettering:** DECIMAL CURRENCY INTRODUCED FEBRUARY 15TH, 1971

Date	Mintage	VF20	XF40	MS60	MS63	MS65
1971	20,000	—	1.50	3.00	5.00	9.00
1971	4,000	PF63 6.00	PF65 8.00			

KM# 20 KWACHA

9.40 g., Nickel-Brass, 26 mm. **Obv:** Head right **Rev:** Rooster

Date	Mintage	VF20	XF40	MS60	MS63	MS65
1992	—	1.00	1.50	3.00	5.00	7.50

KM# 28 KWACHA

9.00 g., Brass Plated Steel, 26 mm. **Obv:** Bust right **Rev:** Fish eagle

Date	Mintage	VF20	XF40	MS60	MS63	MS65
1996	—	—	1.00	1.50	3.00	5.00

KM# 15 5 KWACHA

28.28 g., 0.925 Silver 0.841 oz. ASW **Subject:** Conservation **Obv:** Head right **Rev:** Zebras running right

Date	Mintage	VF20	XF40	MS60	MS63	MS65
1978	4,048	—	—	—	25.00	28.00
1978	3,622	PF65 32.00				

KM# 23 5 KWACHA
Copper-Nickel **Subject:** United Nations 50th Anniversary **Obv:** Bust right **Rev:** Child reading and UN logo

Date	Mintage	VF20	XF40	MS60	MS63	MS65
ND-1995	—	—	—	—	7.00	9.00

KM# 23a 5 KWACHA
28.28 g., 0.925 Silver 0.841 oz. ASW **Subject:** United Nations 50th Anniversary **Obv:** Bust right **Rev:** Child reading and UN logo

Date	Mintage	VF20	XF40	MS60	MS63	MS65
ND-1995	—	PF65 30.00				

KM# 40 5 KWACHA
20.30 g., 0.925 Silver 0.6037 oz. ASW, 34 mm. **Obv:** Arms with supporters **Rev:** Elephant **Edge:** Reeded

Date	Mintage	VF20	XF40	MS60	MS63	MS65
1997	—	PF65 22.00				

KM# 41 5 KWACHA
28.50 g., 0.925 Silver 0.8476 oz. ASW, 38.5 mm. **Subject:** Queen's Golden Wedding Anniversary **Obv:** Arms with supporters **Rev:** Child giving flowers to Queen above gold plated arms with supporters **Edge:** Reeded

Date	Mintage	VF20	XF40	MS60	MS63	MS65
1997	—	PF65 35.00				

KM# 206 5 KWACHA
0.925 Silver, 34 mm. **Obv:** National arms **Rev:** Leopard reclining on branch

Date	Mintage	VF20	XF40	MS60	MS63	MS65
1997	—	PF63 30.00	PF65 35.00			

KM# 72 5 KWACHA
Gold **Subject:** Olympics **Rev:** Track and Field - Hurdler

Date	Mintage	VF20	XF40	MS60	MS63	MS65
1999	—	PF63 70.00	PF65 80.00			

KM# 114 5 KWACHA
1.24 g., 0.999 Gold 0.0398 oz. AGW, 13.92 mm. **Subject:** Sydney Olympics, 2000 **Rev:** Hurdler

Date	Mintage	VF20	XF40	MS60	MS63	MS65
1999	—	PF63 75.00	PF65 90.00			

KM# 116 5 KWACHA
1.24 g., 0.999 Gold 0.0398 oz. AGW, 13.92 mm. **Rev:** African Elephant

Date	Mintage	VF20	XF40	MS60	MS63	MS65
2000	Est. 25000	PF63 75.00	PF65 90.00			

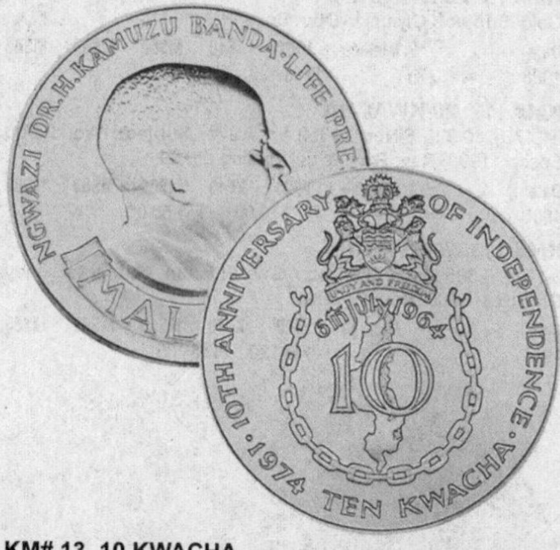

KM# 13 10 KWACHA
28.28 g., 0.925 Silver 0.841 oz. ASW, 39 mm. **Subject:** 10th Anniversary of Independence **Obv:** Head right **Rev:** Arms with supporters above value within chain links

Date	Mintage	VF20	XF40	MS60	MS63	MS65
1974	7,556	—	—	—	25.00	28.00
1974	4,937	PF63 30.00	PF65 35.00			

KM# 14 10 KWACHA
28.28 g., 0.925 Silver 0.841 oz. ASW **Subject:** 10th Anniversary of the Reserve Bank **Obv:** Head right **Rev:** Eagle with wings spread above lined design and value

Date	Mintage	VF20	XF40	MS60	MS63	MS65
ND-1975	6,870	—	—	—	25.00	28.00
ND-1975	Inc. above	PF63 30.00	PF65 35.00			

KM# 14a 10 KWACHA
0.900 Gold **Subject:** 10th Anniversary of the Reserve Bank **Obv:** Head right **Rev:** Eagle with wings spread above lined design and value

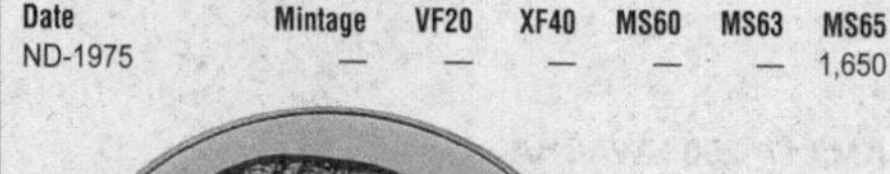

Date	Mintage	VF20	XF40	MS60	MS63	MS65
ND-1975	—	—	—	—	—	1,650

KM# 16 10 KWACHA
35.00 g., 0.925 Silver 1.0409 oz. ASW **Series:** Conservation **Obv:** Head right **Rev:** Sable antelope

Date	Mintage	VF20	XF40	MS60	MS63	MS65
1978	4,009	—	—	—	32.00	35.00
1978	3,416	PF63 35.00	PF65 40.00			

KM# 18 10 KWACHA
28.28 g., 0.925 Silver 0.841 oz. ASW **Subject:** 20th Anniversary - Reserve Bank **Obv:** Head right **Rev:** Eagle with wings spread above lined design and value

Date	Mintage	VF20	XF40	MS60	MS63	MS65
ND-1985	4,000	PF63 35.00	PF65 45.00			

KM# 18a 10 KWACHA
47.54 g., 0.917 Gold 1.4016 oz. AGW **Subject:** 20th Anniversary - Reserve Bank **Obv:** Head right **Rev:** Eagle with wings spread above lined design and value

Date	Mintage	VF20	XF40	MS60	MS63	MS65
ND-1985	50	PF63 2,250	PF65 2,500			

KM# 21 10 KWACHA
28.28 g., 0.925 Silver 0.841 oz. ASW **Series:** Save the Children **Subject:** Fishing **Obv:** Head right **Rev:** Children carrying fish, fishermen and sailboat in background

Date	Mintage	VF20	XF40	MS60	MS63	MS65
1992	20,000	PF63 30.00	PF65 35.00			

KM# 38 10 KWACHA
20.00 g., 0.925 Silver 0.5948 oz. ASW, 34 mm. **Subject:** Olympics **Obv:** Arms with supporters **Rev:** Two runners **Edge:** Reeded

Date	Mintage	VF20	XF40	MS60	MS63	MS65
1999	—	PF63 25.00	PF65 30.00			

KM# 22 20 KWACHA
10.00 g., 0.917 Gold 0.2948 oz. AGW **Series:** Save the Children **Subject:** Mother and children **Obv:** Head right **Rev:**

Mother and child facing left, buildings and athletic players in background

Date	Mintage	VF20	XF40	MS60	MS63	MS65
1992	—	PF63 500	PF65 525			

KM# 35 20 KWACHA
31.40 g., 0.925 Silver 0.9338 oz. ASW, 38.6 mm. **Series:** Endangered Wildlife **Subject:** The Romans **Obv:** Arms with supporters **Rev:** Female elephant with two calves in water **Edge:** Reeded

Date	Mintage	VF20	XF40	MS60	MS63	MS65
1996	—	PF63 45.00	PF65 50.00			

KM# 36 20 KWACHA
31.55 g., 0.925 Silver 0.9383 oz. ASW, 38.6 mm. **Subject:** Queen Mother **Obv:** Arms with supporters **Rev:** Queen Mother and two girl scouts within beaded circle **Edge:** Reeded

Date	Mintage	VF20	XF40	MS60	MS63	MS65
1997	—	PF63 35.00	PF65 40.00			

KM# 37 20 KWACHA
31.43 g., 0.925 Silver 0.9347 oz. ASW, 38.5 mm. **Subject:** British Queen Mother **Obv:** Arms with supporters **Rev:** Edward VIII making his abdication speech **Edge:** Reeded

Date	Mintage	VF20	XF40	MS60	MS63	MS65
1998	—	PF63 40.00	PF65 50.00			

KM# 73 20 KWACHA
Gold **Subject:** Olympics **Obv:** Boxer

Date	Mintage	VF20	XF40	MS60	MS63	MS65
1998	—	PF63 120	PF65 135			

KM# 112 20 KWACHA
31.47 g., 0.925 Silver 0.9359 oz. ASW **Subject:** World Cup Soccer, 1998 **Rev:** Players celebrating a goal

Date	Mintage	VF20	XF40	MS60	MS63	MS65
1998	—	PF63 50.00	PF65 55.00			

KM# 113 20 KWACHA
3.11 g., 0.585 Gold 0.0585 oz. AGW, 18.5 mm. **Subject:** Sidney Olympics, 2000 **Rev:** Boxers

Date	Mintage	VF20	XF40	MS60	MS63	MS65
1998	—	PF63 120	PF65 135			

KM# 31 20 KWACHA
31.53 g., 0.925 Silver 0.9377 oz. ASW **Subject:** Millennium **Obv:** Head right **Rev:** Year 2000 flanked by seated figures below trees all below ears of corn within vines **Shape:** Hexagon

Date	Mintage	VF20	XF40	MS60	MS63	MS65
1999	—	PF63 35.00	PF65 45.00			

KM# 115 20 KWACHA
31.47 g., 0.925 Silver 0.9359 oz. ASW, 38.61 mm. **Rev:** Relay race

Date	Mintage	VF20	XF40	MS60	MS63	MS65
1999	—	PF63 40.00	PF65 50.00			

KM# 17 250 KWACHA
33.44 g., 0.900 Gold 0.9675 oz. AGW **Series:** Conservation **Subject:** Nyala **Obv:** Head right **Rev:** Nyala (deer)

Date	Mintage	VF20	XF40	MS60	MS63	MS65
1978	566	—	—	—	1,700	1,850
1978	208	PF63 1,950	PF65 2,100			

PATTERNS

Including off metal strikes

KM#	Date	Mintage	Identification	Mkt Val
Pn1	1999	—	20 Kwacha. Silver Plated. National arms. Olympic relay runners. Reeded.	95.00

MINT SETS

KM#	Date	Mintage	Identification	Issue Price	Mkt Val
MS1	1971 (6)	10,000	KM7.1-11.1, 12	3.30	15.00
MS2	1978 (2)	—	KM15, 16	—	60.00

PROOF SETS

KM#	Date	Mintage	Identification	Issue Price	Mkt Val
PS1	1964 (4)	10,000	KM1-4	10.00	8.00
PS2	1971 (6)	4,000	KM7.1-11.1, 12	8.70	15.00
PS3	1978 (2)	—	KM15, 16	—	70.00
PS4	1985 (5)	10,000	KM7.2a-8.2a, 9.2-11.2	30.00	20.00

MALAY PENINSULA

KELANTAN

A state in northern Malaysia, colonized by the Javanese in 1300's. It was subject to Thailand from 1780 to 1909.

TITLES

كلنتن

Khalifa(t) Al-Mu'minin

MINT

خليفة المؤمنين

Kelantan

SULTAN
Muhammed IV, 1902-1919

SULTANATE

STANDARD COINAGE

KM# 12 PITIS
Tin, 24-29 mm. **Ruler:** Muhammed IV **Obv:** Arabic legend **Obv. Legend:** Belanjaan Negri Kelantan Adama Mulkahu **Rev:** Arabic legend **Rev. Legend:** Duriba Fi Dhul Hijja Sanat 1321

Date	Mintage	VG8	F12	VF20	XF40	MS60
AH1321	—	8.00	12.00	20.00	45.00	—

KM# 15 PITIS
Tin **Ruler:** Muhammed IV **Obv:** Arabic legend **Obv. Legend:** Belanjaan Kerajaan Kelan Tan **Rev:** Arabic legend **Rev. Legend:** Duriba Fi Dhul Hijja Sanat 1321

Date	Mintage	VG8	F12	VF20	XF40	MS60
AH1321	—	2.00	3.00	5.00	15.00	35.00

KM# 18 KEPING
Tin **Ruler:** Muhammed IV **Obv:** Arabic legend **Obv. Legend:** Negri Kelantan Satu Keping **Rev:** Uninscribed, but obverse legend shows through in negative form

Date	Mintage	VG8	F12	VF20	XF40	MS60
AH1323	—	15.00	25.00	40.00	75.00	—

KM# 20 10 KEPINGS
Tin **Ruler:** Muhammed IV **Obv:** Arabic legend **Obv. Legend:** Belanjaan Kerajaan Kelantin Sepuloh Keping **Rev:** Border of diamonds around Arabic legend **Rev. Legend:** Sunia Fi Dhul Hijja Sanat 1321

Date	Mintage	VG8	F12	VF20	XF40	MS60
AH1321	—	6.00	12.00	30.00	50.00	60.00

TRENGGANU

A state in eastern Malaysia on the shore of the south China Sea. Area of dispute between Malacca and Thailand with the latter emerging with possession. Trengganu became a British dependency in 1909.

TITLES

خليفة المؤمنين

Khalifa(t) al-Mu'minin

ترغكانو

Trengganu

SULTANS

Zainal Abidin III, 1881-1918

Muhammed, 1918-1920

Sulaiman, 1920-1942

SULTANATE

STANDARD COINAGE

KM# 17 1/4 CENT

Tin **Ruler:** Zainal Abidin III **Obv:** Legend within circle **Rev:** Value within circle **Note:** Similar to 1/2 Cent, KM#16.

Date	Mintage	F12	VF20	XF40	MS60	MS63
AH1325 Rare	—	—	—	—	—	—

KM# 16 1/2 CENT

Tin, 22 mm. **Ruler:** Zainal Abidin III **Obv:** Legend within circle **Rev:** Value within circle and wreath **Note:** Recast.

Date	Mintage	VG8	F12	VF20	XF40	MS60
AH1322	—	3.00	6.00	12.00	30.00	—

KM# 18 1/2 CENT

Tin, 22 mm. **Ruler:** Zainal Abidin III **Obv:** Legend within circle flanked by stars **Rev:** Value within circle and wreath **Note:** Recast. Originals are rare.

Date	Mintage	VG8	F12	VF20	XF40	MS60
AH1325	—	3.00	6.00	12.00	30.00	—

KM# 19 CENT

Tin, 29 mm. **Ruler:** Zainal Abidin III **Obv:** Legend within beaded circle flanked by stars **Rev:** Value within beaded circle and wreath

Date	Mintage	VG8	F12	VF20	XF40	MS60
AH1325	—	5.00	10.00	20.00	50.00	—

KM# 20 CENT

Tin, 29 mm. **Ruler:** Zainal Abidin III **Obv:** Legend within beaded circle flanked by stars **Rev:** Value flanked by stars within diamond shape within beaded circle and wreath **Note:** Although dated AH1325 (1907), this coin was actually struck in 1920 under Sultan Sulaiman. Authorized mintage was 1 million. Beware of thin lead counterfeits.

Date	Mintage	VG8	F12	VF20	XF40	MS60
AH1325	—	5.00	10.00	20.00	50.00	—

Malaya, a former member of the British Commonwealth located in the southern part of the Malay peninsula, consisted of 11 states: the un-federated Malay states of Johore, Kelantan, Kedah, Perlis and Trengganu; the federated Malay states of Negri-Sembilan, Pahang, Perakand Selangor; former members of the Straits Settlements Penang and Malacca. Malaya was occupied by the Japanese during the years 1942-1945. The only local opposition to the Japanese had come mainly from the Chinese Communists who then continued their guerilla operations after the war, finally being defeated in 1956. Malaya was granted full independence on Aug. 31, 1957, and became part of Malaysia in 1963.

RULER

British

MINT MARKS

I - Calcutta Mint (1941)

I - Bombay Mint (1945)

No Mint mark - Royal Mint

BRITISH COLONY

STANDARD COINAGE

100 Cents = 1 Dollar

KM# 1 1/2 CENT

2.91 g., Bronze **Obv:** Crowned head of King George VI left **Rev:** Value within beaded circle **Shape:** 4-sided **Note:** 18 mm x 18 mm.

Date	Mintage	VF20	XF40	MS60	MS63	MS65
1940	6,000,000	5.00	10.00	15.00	25.00	40.00
1940	—	PF63 600	PF65 1,000			

KM# 2 CENT

5.82 g., Bronze, 21 mm. **Obv:** Crowned head of King George VI left **Rev:** Value within beaded circle **Shape:** Square

Date	Mintage	VF20	XF40	MS60	MS63	MS65
1939	20,000,000	0.60	0.80	2.50	5.00	10.00
1939	—	PF63 600	PF65 1,000			
1940	23,600,000	0.60	0.80	2.50	5.00	10.00
1940	—	PF63 600	PF65 1,000			
1941 I	33,620,000	2.50	7.50	20.00	35.00	65.00

KM# 6 CENT

4.30 g., Bronze, 20 mm. **Obv:** Crowned head of King George VI left **Rev:** Value within beaded circle **Shape:** 4-sided **Note:** Reduced size.

Date	Mintage	VF20	XF40	MS60	MS63	MS65
1943	50,000,000	0.50	1.00	3.00	5.00	10.00
1943	—	PF63 500	PF65 900			
1945	40,033,000	0.50	1.00	3.00	5.00	10.00
1945	—	PF63 500	PF65 900			

KM# 3 5 CENTS

1.36 g., 0.750 Silver 0.0328 oz. ASW **Obv:** Crowned head of King George VI left **Rev:** Value within beaded circle

Date	Mintage	VF20	XF40	MS60	MS63	MS65
1939	2,000,000	1.50	3.00	5.00	15.00	22.00
1939	—	PF63 700	PF65 1,200			
1941	4,000,000	1.25	2.50	4.00	9.00	12.00
1941	—	PF63 700	PF65 1,200			
1941 I	Inc. above	1.25	2.50	4.00	9.00	12.00

KM# 3a 5 CENTS

1.36 g., 0.500 Silver 0.0219 oz. ASW **Obv:** Crowned head of King George VI left **Rev:** Value within beaded circle

Date	Mintage	VF20	XF40	MS60	MS63	MS65
1943	10,000,000	1.00	1.75	3.00	7.00	14.00
1943	—	PF63 700	PF65 1,200			
1945	8,800,000	1.00	1.75	3.00	7.00	14.00
1945 I	4,600,000	1.50	3.00	5.00	10.00	17.00

KM# 7 5 CENTS

1.41 g., Copper-Nickel, 16 mm. **Obv:** Crowned head of King George VI left **Rev:** Value within beaded circle **Edge:** Reeded

Date	Mintage	VF20	XF40	MS60	MS63	MS65
1948	30,000,000	0.25	2.00	3.00	5.00	10.00
1948	—	PF63 600	PF65 1,000			
1950	40,000,000	0.25	2.00	3.00	5.00	10.00

KM# 4 10 CENTS

2.71 g., 0.750 Silver 0.0653 oz. ASW, 18 mm. **Obv:** Crowned head of King George VI left **Rev:** Value within beaded circle

Date	Mintage	VF20	XF40	MS60	MS63	MS65
1939	10,000,000	2.25	3.00	4.00	8.00	12.00
1939	—	PF63 600	PF65 1,000			
1941	17,000,000	2.25	3.00	4.00	8.00	12.00
1941	—	PF63 600	PF65 1,000			
1941 I	—	—	4,000	5,000	—	—

KM# 4a 10 CENTS

2.71 g., 0.500 Silver 0.0436 oz. ASW **Obv:** Crowned head of King George VI left **Rev:** Value within beaded circle

Date	Mintage	VF20	XF40	MS60	MS63	MS65
1943	5,000,000	2.00	3.00	4.00	8.00	12.00
1943	—	PF63 600	PF65 1,000			
1945	3,152,000	3.00	5.00	10.00	25.00	45.00
1945 I	—	—	4,000	5,000	—	—

KM# 8 10 CENTS

2.83 g., Copper-Nickel, 19.5 mm. **Obv:** Crowned head of George VI left **Rev:** Value within beaded circle **Edge:** Reeded

Date	Mintage	VF20	XF40	MS60	MS63	MS65
1948	23,885,000	0.30	2.00	4.00	8.00	12.00
1948	—	PF63 600	PF65 1,000			
1949	26,115,000	0.50	3.00	6.00	12.00	25.00
1950	65,000,000	0.30	2.00	4.00	8.00	12.00
1950	—	PF63 600	PF65 1,000			

KM# 5 20 CENTS

5.43 g., 0.750 Silver 0.1309 oz. ASW **Obv:** Crowned head of King George VI left **Rev:** Value within beaded circle

Date	Mintage	VF20	XF40	MS60	MS63	MS65
1939	8,000,000	4.00	7.00	12.00	20.00	30.00
1939	—	PF63 600	PF65 1,000			

KM# 5a 20 CENTS
5.43 g., 0.500 Silver 0.0873 oz. ASW **Obv:** Crowned head of King George VI left **Rev:** Value within beaded circle

Date	Mintage	VF20	XF40	MS60	MS63	MS65
1943	5,000,000	3.00	5.00	8.00	15.00	22.00
1943	—	PF63 600	PF65 1,000			
1945	10,000,000	7.00	15.00	25.00	35.00	65.00
1945 I	—	—	4,000	5,000	—	—

KM# 9 20 CENTS
5.65 g., Copper-Nickel, 23.6 mm. **Obv:** Crowned head of King George VI left **Rev:** Value within beaded circle **Edge:** Reeded

Date	Mintage	VF20	XF40	MS60	MS63	MS65
1948	40,000,000	0.75	3.00	5.00	12.00	20.00
1948	—	PF63 600	PF65 1,000			
1950	20,000,000	0.75	3.00	5.00	12.00	20.00
1950	—	PF63 600	PF65 1,000			

MALAYA & BRITISH BORNEO

Malaya & British Borneo, a Currency Commission named the Board of Commissioners of Currency, Malaya and British Borneo, was initiated on Jan. 1, 1952, for the purpose of providing a common currency for use in Johore, Kelantan, Kedah, Perlis, Trengganu, Negri Sembilan, Pahang, Perak, Selangor, Penang, Malacca, Singapore, North Borneo, Sarawak and Brunei.

RULER
British

MINT MARKS
KN - King's Norton, Birmingham
H - Heaton, Birmingham
No Mint mark - Royal Mint

BRITISH COLONY

STANDARD COINAGE

100 Cents = 1 Dollar

KM# 5 CENT
4.27 g., Bronze **Obv:** Crowned bust of Queen Elizabeth II right **Rev:** Value within beaded circle **Shape:** 4-sided

Date	Mintage	VF20	XF40	MS60	MS63	MS65
1956	6,250,000	0.20	0.50	3.00	6.00	12.50
1956	—	PF63 1,200	PF65 2,500			
1957	12,500,000	0.20	0.50	3.00	6.00	12.50
1958	5,000,000	0.20	0.50	3.00	6.00	12.50
1958	—	PF63 1,000	PF65 2,000			
1961	10,000,000	0.20	0.50	3.00	6.00	12.50
1961	—	PF63 1,000	PF65 2,000			

KM# 6 CENT
1.96 g., Bronze, 18 mm. **Obv:** Value **Rev:** Crossed encased swords

Date	Mintage	VF20	XF40	MS60	MS63	MS65
1962	45,000,000	—	0.50	1.50	3.00	7.50
1962	Est. 25	PF63 2,500	PF65 3,000			

KM# 1 5 CENTS
1.41 g., Copper-Nickel, 16 mm. **Obv:** Crowned bust of Queen Elizabeth II right **Rev:** Value within beaded circle **Edge:** Reeded

Date	Mintage	VF20	XF40	MS60	MS63	MS65
1953	20,000,000	0.75	2.00	5.00	20.00	45.00
1953	—	PF63 1,000	PF65 2,000			
1957	10,000,000	0.75	2.00	5.00	20.00	45.00
1957 H	10,000,000	0.75	2.00	5.00	20.00	45.00
1957 H	—	PF63 950	PF65 1,850			
1957 KN	Inc. above	2.00	4.00	12.00	45.00	85.00
1958	10,000,000	1.00	2.00	5.00	20.00	45.00
1958	—	PF63 1,000	PF65 2,000			
1958 H	10,000,000	1.25	2.00	5.00	20.00	45.00
1961	90,000,000	0.60	1.50	4.00	18.00	35.00
1961	—	PF63 1,000	PF65 2,000			
1961 H	5,000,000	2.00	5.00	12.00	45.00	75.00
1961 KN	Inc. above	1.50	3.00	7.50	25.00	75.00

KM# 2 10 CENTS
2.83 g., Copper-Nickel, 19.5 mm. **Obv:** Crowned bust of Queen Elizabeth II right **Rev:** Value within beaded circle **Edge:** Reeded

Date	Mintage	VF20	XF40	MS60	MS63	MS65
1953	20,000,000	0.75	2.00	5.00	15.00	35.00
1953	—	PF63 1,200	PF65 2,500			
1956	10,000,000	0.75	2.00	5.00	15.00	35.00
1956	—	PF63 1,200	PF65 2,500			
1957 H	10,000,000	0.75	2.00	6.00	20.00	40.00
1957 H	—	PF63 1,000	PF65 2,000			
1957 KN	10,000,000	1.00	2.50	6.00	20.00	40.00
1958	10,000,000	1.00	2.50	6.00	20.00	40.00
1960	10,000,000	0.75	2.00	6.00	20.00	40.00
1960	—	PF63 1,000	PF65 2,000			
1961	60,784,000	0.40	0.60	4.00	12.00	25.00
1961	—	PF63 1,000	PF65 2,000			
1961 H	69,220,000	0.40	0.60	4.00	10.00	18.00
1961 KN	Inc. above	1.00	2.00	6.00	20.00	40.00

KM# 2a 10 CENTS
Silver, 19.5 mm. **Obv:** Crowned bust right **Rev:** Value within beaded circle **Note:** as KM#2

Date	Mintage	VF20	XF40	MS60	MS63	MS65
1953	—	PF65 5,000				

KM# 3 20 CENTS
5.65 g., Copper-Nickel, 23.51 mm. **Obv:** Crowned bust of Queen Elizabeth II right **Rev:** Value within beaded circle **Edge:** Reeded

Date	Mintage	VF20	XF40	MS60	MS63	MS65
1954	10,000,000	1.25	3.00	9.00	27.00	45.00
1954	—	PF63 1,200	PF65 2,500			
1956	5,000,000	1.00	3.00	10.00	32.00	60.00
1956	—	PF63 1,200	PF65 2,500			
1957 H	2,500,000	1.50	3.50	15.00	45.00	80.00
1957 H	—	PF63 1,000	PF65 2,000			
1957 KN	2,500,000	1.50	3.50	12.00	35.00	65.00
1961	32,000,000	0.75	4.00	6.00	15.00	30.00
1961	—	PF63 1,000	PF65 2,000			
1961 H	23,000,000	0.75	4.00	6.00	15.00	30.00

KM# 3a 20 CENTS
Silver **Obv:** Crowned bust right **Rev:** Value within beaded circle **Note:** as KM#3

Date	Mintage	VF20	XF40	MS60	MS63	MS65
1954	—	PF65 13,000				

KM# 4.1 50 CENTS
9.38 g., Copper-Nickel, 27 mm. **Obv:** Crowned bust of Queen Elizabeth II right **Rev:** Value within beaded circle **Edge:** Security

Date	Mintage	VF20	XF40	MS60	MS63	MS65
1954	8,000,000	2.50	5.00	12.00	35.00	125
1954	—	PF63 1,200	PF65 2,500			
1955 H	4,000,000	2.50	5.00	15.00	45.00	150
1956	3,440,000	2.50	5.00	15.00	45.00	150
1956	—	PF63 1,500	PF65 3,000			
1957 H	2,000,000	2.50	5.00	15.00	45.00	150
1957 H	—	PF63 1,200	PF65 2,500			
1957 KN	2,000,000	3.50	7.00	17.00	55.00	185
1958 H	4,000,000	2.50	5.00	15.00	45.00	150
1961	17,000,000	2.00	4.00	12.00	30.00	100
1961	—	PF63 1,300	PF65 2,700			
1961 H	4,000,000	2.50	5.00	12.00	30.00	125
1961 H	—	PF63 1,300	PF65 2,700			

KM# 4.2 50 CENTS
Copper-Nickel **Obv:** Crowned bust of Queen Elizabeth II right **Rev:** Value within beaded circle **Note:** Error, without security edge.

Date	Mintage	VF20	XF40	MS60	MS63	MS65
1954	Inc. above	300	550	1,100	—	—
1957 KN	Inc. above	300	550	1,100	—	—
1958 H	Inc. above	300	550	1,100	—	—
1961	Inc. above	300	550	1,100	—	—
1961 H	Inc. above	300	550	1,100	—	—

MALAYSIA

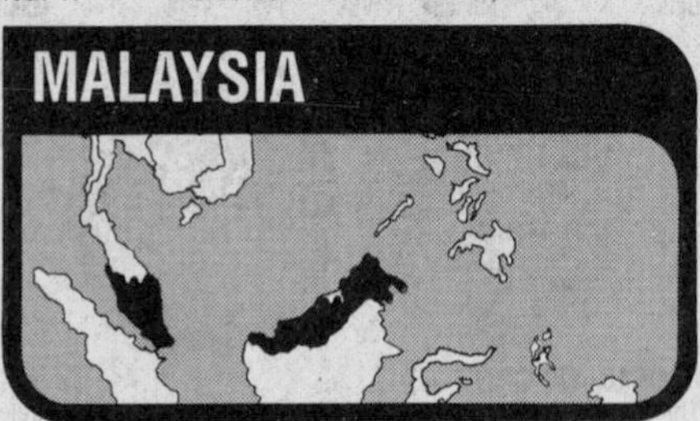

The independent limited constitutional monarchy of Malaysia, which occupies the southern part of the Malay Peninsula in Southeast Asia and the northern part of the island of Borneo, has an area of 127,316 sq. mi. (329,750 sq. km.) and a population of 15.4 million. Capital: Kuala Lumpur. The economy is based on agriculture, mining and forestry. Rubber, tin, timber and palm oil are exported.

Malaysia came into being on Sept. 16, 1963, as a federation of Malaya (Johore, Kelantan, Kedah, Perlis, Trengganu, Negri Sembilan, Pahang, Perak, Selangor, Penang, Malacca), Singapore, Sabah (British North Borneo) and Sarawak. Following two serious racial riots involving Malays and Chinese, Singapore withdrew from the federation on Aug. 9, 1965. Malaysia is a member of the Commonwealth of Nations.

MINT MARK
FM - Franklin Mint, U.S.A.

***NOTE:** From 1975-1985 the Franklin Mint produced coinage in up to 3 different qualities. Qualities of issue are designated in ( ) after each date and are defined as follows:

(M) MATTE - Normal circulation strike or a dull finish produced by sandblasting special uncirculated (polish finish) or proof quality dies.

(U) SPECIAL UNCIRCULATED - Polished or prooflike in appearance without any frosted features.

(P) PROOF - The highest quality obtainable having mirror-like fields and frosted features.

CONSTITUTIONAL MONARCHY

STANDARD COINAGE

100 Sen = 1 Ringgit (Dollar)

KM# 1 SEN
1.95 g., Bronze **Obv:** Value **Rev:** Parliament house **Note:** Varieties exist.

Date	Mintage	VF20	XF40	MS60	MS63	MS65
1967	45,000,000	—	0.50	1.00	3.00	5.00
1967	500	PF65 20.00				

Date	Mintage	VF20	XF40	MS60	MS63	MS65
1968	10,500,000	—	3.00	5.00	8.00	15.00
1970	2,535,000	—	7.00	12.00	16.00	20.00
1971	47,862,000	—	0.45	1.00	2.00	4.00
1973	21,400,000	—	0.25	0.75	1.50	3.00
1976	100	80.00	300	1,200	—	—
1980 FM (P)	5,000	**PF65** 3.00				
1981 FM (P)	6,628	**PF65** 3.00				

KM# 1a SEN

1.72 g., Copper Clad Steel, 17.69 mm. **Obv:** Value **Rev:** Parliament house

Date	Mintage	VF20	XF40	MS60	MS63	MS65
1973	Inc. above	—	0.65	1.50	3.00	5.00
1976	27,406,000	—	0.25	1.00	2.00	4.00
1977	21,751,000	—	0.25	0.75	1.50	3.00
1978	30,844,000	—	0.25	0.75	1.50	3.00
1979	15,714,000	—	0.25	0.75	1.50	3.00
1980	16,152,000	—	0.25	0.75	1.50	3.00
1981	24,633,000	—	0.25	0.75	1.50	3.00
1982	37,295,000	—	0.25	0.75	1.50	3.00
1983	19,333,000	—	0.25	0.75	1.25	2.00
1984	26,267,000	—	0.25	0.75	1.25	2.00
1985	52,402,000	—	0.25	0.75	1.25	2.00
1986	48,920,000	—	0.25	0.75	1.25	2.00
1987	35,284,000	—	0.25	0.50	1.00	1.50
1988	56,749,000	—	0.25	0.50	1.00	1.50

KM# 49 SEN

1.80 g., Bronze Clad Steel, 17.66 mm. **Obv:** Value divides date below flower blossom **Obv. Legend:** BANK NEGARA MALAYSIA **Rev:** Drum **Edge:** Plain

Date	Mintage	VF20	XF40	MS60	MS63	MS65
1989	28,429,000	—	—	0.25	0.35	0.50
1990	102,539,000	—	—	0.15	0.25	0.40
1991	100,314,734	—	—	0.15	0.25	0.40
1992	122,824,000	—	—	0.15	0.25	0.40
1993	153,805,875	—	—	0.15	0.25	0.40
1994	185,085,000	—	—	0.15	0.25	0.40
1995	208,611,295	—	—	0.15	0.25	0.40
1996	183,272,598	—	—	0.15	0.25	0.40
1997	172,215,681	—	—	0.15	0.25	0.40
1998	1,917,633,834	—	—	0.15	0.25	0.40
1999	265,502,565	—	—	0.15	0.25	0.40
2000	268,762,170	—	—	0.15	0.25	0.40

KM# 49a SEN

0.925 Silver **Obv:** Value divides date below flower blossom **Rev:** Drum

Date	Mintage	VF20	XF40	MS60	MS63	MS65
1992	—	**PF65** 20.00				

KM# 2 5 SEN

1.42 g., Copper-Nickel, 16.2 mm. **Obv:** Value **Rev:** Parliament house **Note:** Varieties exist.

Date	Mintage	VF20	XF40	MS60	MS63	MS65
1967	75,464,000	—	0.25	0.65	1.25	2.50
1967	500	**PF65** 25.00				
1968	74,536,000	—	0.25	0.65	1.25	2.50
1971	16,658,000	—	0.45	1.00	2.00	4.00
1973	102,942,000	—	0.25	0.65	1.25	2.50
1976	65,659,000	—	0.25	0.65	1.25	2.50
1977	10,609,000	—	0.30	0.85	1.75	3.50
1978	50,044,000	—	0.25	0.75	1.50	3.00
1979	38,824,000	—	0.25	0.75	1.50	3.00
1980	33,893,000	—	0.25	0.75	1.50	3.00
1980 FM (P)	6,628	**PF65** 5.00				
1981	51,490,000	—	0.25	0.65	1.25	2.50
1981 FM (P)	—	**PF65** 3.00				
1982	118,594,000	—	0.25	0.65	1.25	2.50
1985	15,553,000	—	0.25	0.65	1.25	2.50
1987	17,723,000	—	0.25	0.65	1.25	2.50
1988	26,788,000	—	0.25	0.65	1.25	2.50

KM# 50 5 SEN

1.40 g., Copper-Nickel, 16.25 mm. **Obv:** Value divides date below flower blossom **Obv. Legend:** BANK NEGARA MALAYSIA **Rev:** Top with string **Edge:** Reeded

Date	Mintage	VF20	XF40	MS60	MS63	MS65
1989	20,484,000	—	—	0.20	0.30	0.50
1990	58,909,000	—	—	0.20	0.30	0.50
1991	46,092,000	—	—	0.20	0.30	0.50
1992	67,844,000	—	—	0.20	0.30	0.50
1993	70,703,000	—	—	0.20	0.30	0.50
1994	83,026,000	—	—	0.20	0.30	0.50
1995	53,069,000	—	—	0.15	0.25	0.45
1996	51,812,529	—	—	0.15	0.25	0.45
1997	7,703,850	—	—	0.15	0.25	0.45
1998	1,293,910,233	—	—	0.15	0.25	0.45
1999	79,224,000	—	—	0.15	0.25	0.45
2000	61,198,528	—	—	0.15	0.25	0.45

KM# 50a 5 SEN

0.925 Silver, 16.3 mm. **Obv:** Value divides date below flower blossom **Rev:** Top with string

Date	Mintage	VF20	XF40	MS60	MS63	MS65
1992	—	**PF65** 10.00				

KM# 3 10 SEN

2.82 g., Copper-Nickel, 19.3 mm. **Obv:** Value **Rev:** Parliament house **Note:** Varieties exist.

Date	Mintage	VF20	XF40	MS60	MS63	MS65
1967	106,708,000	0.25	0.45	0.85	1.25	2.50
1967	500	**PF65** 45.00				
1968	128,292,000	0.25	0.45	0.85	1.25	2.50
1971	42,000	12.50	25.00	40.00	75.00	125
1973	214,832,000	0.10	0.30	0.50	1.00	2.00
1976	148,841,000	0.10	0.30	0.50	1.00	2.00
1977	52,720,000	0.10	0.30	0.65	1.25	2.50
1978	21,162,000	0.10	0.30	0.65	1.25	2.50
1979	50,633,000	0.10	0.25	0.65	1.25	2.50
1980	51,797,000	0.10	0.25	0.50	1.00	2.00
1980 FM (P)	6,628	**PF65** 6.00				
1981	236,639,000	0.10	0.25	0.50	1.00	2.00
1981 FM (P)	—	**PF65** 6.00				
1982	145,639,000	—	0.25	0.50	1.00	2.00
1983	30,832,000	—	0.25	0.50	1.00	2.00
1988	17,852,000	—	0.25	0.50	1.00	2.00

KM# 51 10 SEN

2.82 g., Copper-Nickel, 19.4 mm. **Obv:** Value divides date below flower blossom **Obv. Legend:** BANK NEGARA MALAYSIA **Rev:** Ceremonial table **Edge:** Reeded

Date	Mintage	VF20	XF40	MS60	MS63	MS65
1989	32,392,000	—	—	0.25	0.40	0.60
1990	132,982,000	—	—	0.25	0.40	0.60
1991	133,293,000	—	—	0.25	0.40	0.60
1992	89,919,000	—	—	0.25	0.40	0.60
1993	44,224,000	—	—	0.25	0.40	0.60
1994	7,122,000	—	—	0.30	0.50	0.70
1995	82,217,000	—	—	0.25	0.40	0.60
1996	77,347,125	—	—	0.25	0.40	0.60
1997	78,955,862	—	—	0.25	0.40	0.60
1998	1,966,056,746	—	—	0.25	0.40	0.60
1999	163,080,000	—	—	0.25	0.40	0.60
2000	162,940,000	—	—	0.25	0.40	0.60

KM# 51a 10 SEN

0.925 Silver, 19.3 mm. **Obv:** Value divides date below flower blossom **Rev:** Ceremonial table

Date	Mintage	VF20	XF40	MS60	MS63	MS65
1992	—	**PF65** 10.00				

KM# 4 20 SEN

Copper-Nickel, 23.4 mm. **Obv:** Value **Rev:** Parliament house **Note:** Varieties exist.

Date	Mintage	VF20	XF40	MS60	MS63	MS65
1967	49,560,000	0.25	0.75	1.50	3.00	5.00
1967	500	**PF65** 60.00				
1968	40,440,000	0.25	0.75	1.50	3.00	5.00
1969	15,000,000	0.25	1.00	2.50	5.00	10.00
1970	1,054,000	0.60	1.50	3.00	6.00	12.00
1971	9,958,000	0.25	0.50	1.50	3.00	5.00
1973	116,075,000	0.25	0.50	1.50	3.00	5.00
1976	47,396,000	0.25	0.50	1.50	3.00	5.00
1977	66,139,000	0.25	0.50	1.50	3.00	5.00
1978	6,847,000	0.25	0.50	1.50	3.00	5.00
1979	17,346,000	0.25	0.50	1.50	3.00	5.00
1980	32,837,000	0.15	0.30	1.50	3.00	5.00
1980 FM (P)	6,628	**PF65** 10.00				
1981	144,128,000	0.15	0.30	0.75	1.50	3.00
1981 FM (P)	—	**PF65** 5.00				
1982	97,905,000	—	0.25	0.75	1.50	3.00
1983	8,105,000	—	0.25	0.75	1.50	3.00
1987	26,225,000	—	0.25	0.75	1.50	3.00
1988	67,218,000	—	0.25	0.75	1.50	3.00

KM# 52 20 SEN

5.66 g., Copper-Nickel, 23.6 mm. **Obv:** Value divides date below flower blossom **Obv. Legend:** BANK NEGARA MALAYSIA **Rev:** Basket with food and utensils **Edge:** Reeded

Date	Mintage	VF20	XF40	MS60	MS63	MS65
1989	28,945,000	—	—	0.35	0.75	1.50
1990	56,249,000	—	—	0.35	0.75	1.50
1991	82,774,000	—	—	0.35	0.75	1.50
1992	48,975,000	—	—	0.35	0.75	1.50
1993	55,753,000	—	—	0.35	0.75	1.50
1994	2,680,000	—	—	0.65	1.25	2.50
1997	78,479,804	—	—	0.35	0.50	0.85
1998	1,161,791,361	—	—	0.35	0.50	0.85
2000	63,908,000	—	—	0.35	0.50	0.85

KM# 52a 20 SEN

0.925 Silver enameled, 23.5 mm. **Obv:** Value divides date below flower blossom **Rev:** Basket with food and utensils

Date	Mintage	VF20	XF40	MS60	MS63	MS65
1992	—	**PF65** 30.00				

KM# 5.1 50 SEN

Copper-Nickel, 27.8 mm. **Obv:** Value **Rev:** Parliament house

Date	Mintage	VF20	XF40	MS60	MS63	MS65
1967	15,000,000	—	0.50	1.00	3.00	5.00
1967	500	**PF65** 55.00				
1968	12,000,000	—	0.50	1.00	3.00	5.00
1969	2,000,000	5.00	10.00	15.00	30.00	50.00

KM# 5.2 50 SEN

Copper-Nickel, 27.8 mm. **Obv:** Value **Rev:** Parliament house **Note:** Error, no security edge.

Date	Mintage	VF20	XF40	MS60	MS63	MS65
1967	Inc. above	200	350	500	700	—
1968	Inc. above	200	350	500	700	—
1969	Inc. above	650	800	1,200	1,400	—

KM# 5.3 50 SEN

9.30 g., Copper-Nickel, 27.8 mm. **Obv:** Value **Rev:** Parliament house **Edge Lettering:** MALAYSIA BANK NEGARA (repeated)

Date	Mintage	VF20	XF40	MS60	MS63	MS65
1971	8,404,000	0.25	0.50	1.00	2.00	3.00
1973	50,135,000	0.25	0.50	1.00	2.00	3.00
1977	17,720,000	0.25	0.50	1.00	2.00	3.00
1978	11,033,000	0.25	0.50	1.00	2.00	3.00
1979	5,361,000	0.25	0.50	1.00	2.00	3.00
1980	15,911,000	0.25	0.50	1.00	2.00	3.00
1980 FM	6,628	**PF65** 4.50				
1981	22,969,000	0.25	0.50	1.00	2.00	3.00
1982	20,585,000	0.25	0.50	1.00	2.00	3.00
1983	11,560,000	0.25	0.50	1.00	2.00	3.00
1984	10,139,000	0.25	0.50	1.00	2.00	3.00
1985	7,115,000	0.25	0.50	1.00	2.00	3.00
1986	8,193,000	0.25	0.50	1.00	2.00	3.00
1987	7,696,000	0.25	0.50	1.00	2.00	3.00
1988	26,788,000	0.25	0.50	1.00	2.00	3.00

KM# 5.4 50 SEN

Copper-Nickel, 27.8 mm. **Obv:** Value **Rev:** Parliament house **Edge:** Plain

Date	Mintage	VF20	XF40	MS60	MS63	MS65
1981 FM (P)	—	**PF63** 15.00	**PF65** 20.00			

KM# 53 50 SEN

9.33 g., Copper-Nickel, 27.75 mm. **Obv:** Value divides date below flower blossom **Obv. Legend:** BANK NEGARA MALAYSIA **Rev:** Ceremonial kite **Edge Lettering:** BANK NEGARA MALAYSIA (twice)

Date	Mintage	VF20	XF40	MS60	MS63	MS65
1989	6,639,057	—	—	0.60	1.00	1.50
1990	26,276,464	—	—	0.60	1.00	1.50
1991	20,720,531	—	—	0.60	1.00	1.50
1992	15,134,992	—	—	0.60	1.00	1.50
1993	7,657,991	—	—	0.75	1.25	2.50
1994	6,565,914	—	—	0.75	1.25	2.50
1995	1,650,423	—	—	0.75	1.25	2.50
1996	7,475,790	—	—	0.75	1.25	2.50
1997	16,143,327	—	—	0.50	0.75	1.00
1998	401,622,135	—	—	0.50	0.75	1.00
1999	12,085,000	—	—	0.50	0.75	1.00
2000	48,206,000	—	—	0.50	0.75	1.00

KM# 53a 50 SEN

0.925 Silver, 28 mm. **Obv:** Value divides date below flower blossom **Rev:** Ceremonial kite

Date	Mintage	VF20	XF40	MS60	MS63	MS65
1992	—	PF65 30.00				

KM# 7 RINGGIT

Copper-Nickel, 33.5 mm. **Subject:** 10th Anniversary - Bank Negara **Obv:** Artistic value and dollar sign within 3/4 flower wreath **Rev:** Bust with headdress left

Date	Mintage	VF20	XF40	MS60	MS63	MS65
ND-1969	1,000,000	1.50	3.50	5.00	7.00	10.00

KM# 7a RINGGIT

19.92 g., 0.925 Silver 0.5924 oz. ASW, 33.5 mm. **Obv:** Artistic value and dollar sign within 3/4 flower wreath **Rev:** Bust with headdress left

Date	Mintage	VF20	XF40	MS60	MS63	MS65
ND-1969	1,000	PF63 350	PF65 500			

KM# 9.1 RINGGIT

16.90 g., Copper-Nickel, 33.4 mm. **Obv:** Artistic value and dollar sign above date **Rev:** Parliament house within cresent **Edge Lettering:** BANK NEGARA MALAYSIA

Date	Mintage	VF20	XF40	MS60	MS63	MS65
1971	2,378,995	0.50	1.00	2.00	3.00	6.00
1971	500	PF65 1,200				
1980	472,000	0.60	1.00	2.50	4.00	7.50
1980 FM (P)	6,628	PF65 8.00				
1981	765,000	0.60	1.00	2.50	4.00	7.50
1982	202,000	0.60	1.00	2.50	4.00	7.50
1984	355,000	0.60	1.00	2.50	4.00	7.50
1985	302,000	0.60	1.00	2.50	4.00	7.50
1986	253,000	0.60	1.00	2.50	4.00	7.50

KM# 9.2 RINGGIT

Copper-Nickel, 33.5 mm. **Obv:** Artistic value and dollar sign above value **Rev:** Parliament house within cresent **Edge:** Plain

Date	Mintage	VF20	XF40	MS60	MS63	MS65
1981 FM (P)	—	PF63 25.00	PF65 30.00			

KM# 12 RINGGIT

Copper-Nickel, 33.5 mm. **Subject:** Kuala Lumpur Anniversary **Obv:** Artistic value and dollar sign above date **Rev:** Artistic design **Edge Lettering:** MALAYSIA BANK NEGARA **Note:** Issued in 1973.

Date	Mintage	VF20	XF40	MS60	MS63	MS65
1972	500,000	—	—	2.50	3.50	5.00
1972	500	PF65 650				

KM# 13 RINGGIT

Copper-Nickel, 33.5 mm. **Subject:** 25th Anniversary - Employee Provident Fund **Obv:** Value **Rev:** Two upper circles among assorted heads

Date	Mintage	VF20	XF40	MS60	MS63	MS65
1976 FM (U)	500,000	—	—	1.25	2.00	3.00
1976 FM (P)	7,810	PF63 27.00	PF65 32.00			

KM# 16 RINGGIT

Copper-Nickel, 33 mm. **Subject:** 3rd Malaysian 5-Year Plan **Obv:** Arms with supporters **Rev:** Head with headdress facing within circle and block-like artistic design **Shape:** 14-sided

Date	Mintage	VF20	XF40	MS60	MS63	MS65
ND-1976	1,000,000	—	—	1.25	2.00	3.00
ND-1976 FM (P)	17,000	PF63 20.00	PF65 25.00			

KM# 22 RINGGIT

Copper-Nickel, 33.5 mm. **Subject:** 9th Southeast Asian Games **Obv:** Arms with supporters **Rev:** Kite flyer **Edge Lettering:** MALAYSIA BANK NEGARA

Date	Mintage	VF20	XF40	MS60	MS63	MS65
1977	1,000,000	—	—	1.75	2.50	3.50
1977 FM (P)	11,000	PF63 30.00	PF65 35.00			

KM# 25 RINGGIT

Copper-Nickel, 33.5 mm. **Subject:** 20th Anniversary of Independence **Obv:** Head facing **Rev:** Arms with supporters

Date	Mintage	VF20	XF40	MS60	MS63	MS65
ND-1977	500,000	—	—	2.00	3.00	4.50
ND-1977 FM (P)	3,100	PF63 45.00	PF65 55.00			

KM# 26 RINGGIT

Copper-Nickel, 33.5 mm. **Subject:** 100th Anniversary of Natural Rubber Production **Obv:** Value and dollar sign above dates **Rev:** Artistic design with a pair of hands **Edge Lettering:** MALAYSIA BANK NEGARA

Date	Mintage	VF20	XF40	MS60	MS63	MS65
ND-1977	500,000	—	—	1.25	2.00	3.00

KM# 27 RINGGIT

Copper-Nickel, 33.5 mm. **Subject:** 20th Anniversary of Bank Negara **Obv:** Value **Rev:** Building above dates

Date	Mintage	VF20	XF40	MS60	MS63	MS65
ND-1979	300,000	—	—	1.75	2.50	3.50

KM# 27a RINGGIT

17.00 g., 0.925 Silver 0.5056 oz. ASW, 33.5 mm. **Obv:** Value **Rev:** Building above dates

Date	Mintage	VF20	XF40	MS60	MS63	MS65
ND-1979	8,000	PF63 40.00	PF65 50.00			
ND-1979 FM (P)	6,628	PF63 25.00	PF65 35.00			

KM# 28 RINGGIT

Copper-Nickel, 33.5 mm. **Subject:** 15th Century of Hejira **Obv:** Value, date **Rev:** Design within spider web **Edge Lettering:** MALAYSIA BANK NEGARA

Date	Mintage	VF20	XF40	MS60	MS63	MS65
AH1401(1981)	500,000	—	—	1.00	1.50	2.50

KM# 29 RINGGIT

Copper-Nickel, 33.5 mm. **Subject:** 4th Malaysian Plan **Obv:** Arms with supporters **Rev:** Bust with headdress facing 1/4 right **Edge Lettering:** MALAYSIA BANK NEGARA **Note:** Tun Hussein Onn

Date	Mintage	VF20	XF40	MS60	MS63	MS65
ND-1981	1,000,000	—	—	1.25	2.00	3.00
ND-1981	10,000	PF63 15.00	PF65 20.00			

KM# 32 RINGGIT
Copper-Nickel, 33.5 mm. **Subject:** 25th Anniversary of Independence **Obv:** Star design and bust with headdress with left arm raised facing right **Rev:** Arms with supporters

Date	Mintage	VF20	XF40	MS60	MS63	MS65
ND-1982	1,500,000	—	—	1.25	2.00	3.00
ND-1982	15,000	PF63 12.00	PF65 18.00			

KM# 36 RINGGIT
Copper-Nickel **Subject:** 5th Malaysian 5-Year Plan **Obv:** Arms with supporters with value and dollar sign below **Rev:** Tractor tire, plants, scale and sun within circle

Date	Mintage	VF20	XF40	MS60	MS63	MS65
ND-1986	1,000,000	—	—	1.75	2.50	3.50
ND-1986	8,000	PF63 25.00	PF65 30.00			

KM# 39 RINGGIT
Copper-Nickel **Subject:** 35th Annual PATA Conference **Obv:** Value **Rev:** Standing turtle

Date	Mintage	VF20	XF40	MS60	MS63	MS65
ND-1986	500,000	—	—	2.50	4.00	5.00

KM# 39a RINGGIT
16.85 g., 0.500 Silver 0.2709 oz. ASW **Obv:** Value **Rev:** Standing turtle

Date	Mintage	VF20	XF40	MS60	MS63	MS65
ND-1986	11,000	PF63 12.00	PF65 16.00			

KM# 43 RINGGIT
Brass, 24 mm. **Subject:** 30th Anniversary of Independence **Obv:** Arms with supporters above value and dollar sign **Rev:** Numeral 30 divides dates below with flyin doves and sun above

Date	Mintage	VF20	XF40	MS60	MS63	MS65
ND-1987	20,000	PF63 15.00	PF65 20.00			
ND-1987	1,000,000	—	—	1.25	2.00	3.00

KM# 54 RINGGIT
9.40 g., Aluminum-Bronze, 24.8 mm. **Obv:** Value and dollar sign divide date with flower blossom above **Rev:** Native dagger and scabbard within designs **Edge:** Reeded **Note:** Varying degrees of filled die variations exist.

Date	Mintage	VF20	XF40	MS60	MS63	MS65
1989	20,410,000	—	—	0.50	1.00	2.00
1990	80,102,000	—	—	0.50	1.00	2.00
1991	169,001,000	—	—	0.35	0.75	1.50
1992	139,042,000	—	—	0.35	0.75	1.50
1993	178,894,000	—	—	0.35	0.75	1.50

KM# 54a RINGGIT
0.925 Silver, 24 mm. **Obv:** Value and dollar sign divide date below flower blossom **Rev:** Native dagger and scabbard within designs

Date	Mintage	VF20	XF40	MS60	MS63	MS65
1992	—	PF63 20.00	PF65 25.00			

KM# 64 RINGGIT
9.35 g., Aluminum-Bronze, 24.5 mm. **Obv:** Value divides date below flower blossom **Rev:** Native dagger and scabbard within designs

Date	Mintage	VF20	XF40	MS60	MS63	MS65
1993	Inc. above	—	—	0.50	1.00	2.00
1994	36,899,000	—	—	0.50	1.00	2.00
1995	132,173,000	—	—	0.50	1.00	2.00
1996	59,460,000	—	—	0.50	1.00	2.00

Note: Full mintage withdrawn

KM# 65 RINGGIT
8.15 g., Bi-Metallic Copper-Nickel center in Nickel-Brass ring, 26.5 mm. **Subject:** Thomas-Uber Cup **Obv:** City view within circle **Rev:** Two-handled cup on radiant background **Edge:** Reeded

Date	Mintage	VF20	XF40	MS60	MS63	MS65
2000	2,000,000	—	—	1.00	2.00	3.00

KM# 205 RINGGIT
8.15 g., Bi-Metallic Copper-Nickel center in Nickel-Brass ring, 26.5 mm. **Subject:** Pengisytiharan Bandaraya Shah Alam **Obv:** National Arms with supporters **Obv. Legend:** BANK NEGARA MALAYSIA **Rev:** City view **Rev. Legend:** SEMPENA PENGISYTIHARAN BANDARAYA SHAH ALAM 10 OKTOBER 2000

Date	Mintage	VF20	XF40	MS60	MS63	MS65
2000	10,000	PF63 8.00	PF65 12.00			

KM# 10 5 RINGGIT
Copper-Nickel, 38.1 mm. **Obv:** Prime Minister Abdul Rahman Putra al-Haj **Rev:** Government building in Kuala Lumpur

Date	Mintage	VF20	XF40	MS60	MS63	MS65
1971	2,000,000	—	—	2.00	3.50	5.00
1971	500	PF65 1,100				

KM# 40 5 RINGGIT
29.03 g., 0.500 Silver 0.4667 oz. ASW **Subject:** PATA Conference **Obv:** Value **Rev:** Standing turtle

Date	Mintage	VF20	XF40	MS60	MS63	MS65
ND-1986	11,000	PF63 50.00	PF65 70.00			

KM# 47 5 RINGGIT
Copper Plated Zinc **Subject:** 15th Southeast Asian Games **Obv:** Star design within small circle above value **Rev:** Soccer players below date and design

Date	Mintage	VF20	XF40	MS60	MS63	MS65
1989	500,000	—	—	1.00	2.00	3.00
1989	50,000	PF63 12.00	PF65 18.00			

KM# 55 5 RINGGIT
Copper Plated Zinc **Subject:** Commonwealth Heads of State Meeting **Obv:** Underlined Malaysia flanked by dots in center, arms with supporters above and value below **Rev:** City and towers with emblem at upper right

Date	Mintage	VF20	XF40	MS60	MS63	MS65
1989	150,000	—	—	1.50	3.00	5.00
1989	8,000	PF63 15.00	PF65 20.00			

KM# 59 5 RINGGIT
Copper Plated Zinc **Subject:** 100th Anniversary of Kuala Lumpur **Obv:** Artistic design within circle among horizontal lines with value below **Rev:** House and tower

Date	Mintage	VF20	XF40	MS60	MS63	MS65
ND-1990	100,000	—	—	1.25	2.50	4.00

KM# 61 5 RINGGIT
Brass **Series:** World Wildlife Fund **Obv:** Value and dollar sign flanked by flowers with WWF below design **Rev:** Stylized Milky stork above dates

Date	Mintage	VF20	XF40	MS60	MS63	MS65
ND-1992	—	—	—	1.50	2.25	3.50
ND-1992	3,000	PF63 8.00	PF65 12.00			

KM# 17 10 RINGGIT
10.82 g., 0.925 Silver 0.3218 oz. ASW **Subject:** 3rd Malaysian 5-Year Plan **Shape:** 14-sided

Date	Mintage	VF20	XF40	MS60	MS63	MS65
ND-1976 FM (U)	200,000	—	—	7.50	9.00	12.00
ND-1976 FM (P)	10,300	PF63 20.00	PF65 25.00			

KM# 44 10 RINGGIT
10.82 g., 0.500 Silver 0.1739 oz. ASW **Subject:** 30th Anniversary of Independence **Obv:** Dollar sign and value below arms with supporters **Rev:** Numeral 30 divides date below city view

Date	Mintage	VF20	XF40	MS60	MS63	MS65
ND-1987	50,000	—	—	5.00	7.50	10.00
ND-1987	10,000	PF63 20.00	PF65 25.00			

KM# 57 10 RINGGIT
13.60 g., 0.925 Silver 0.4045 oz. ASW **Subject:** Proclamation of Melaka as a Historical City **Obv:** Arms with supporters **Rev:** Oxen pulling covered cart

Date	Mintage	VF20	XF40	MS60	MS63	MS65
1989	20,000	PF63 20.00	PF65 25.00			

KM# 19 15 RINGGIT
28.28 g., 0.925 Silver 0.841 oz. ASW, 38.6 mm. **Series:** Conservation **Obv:** Arms with supporters **Rev:** Malaysian Gaur

Date	Mintage	VF20	XF40	MS60	MS63	MS65
1976	40,000	—	—	—	35.00	45.00
1976	8,113	PF65 100				

KM# 48 15 RINGGIT
16.73 g., 0.925 Silver 0.4975 oz. ASW **Subject:** 15th Southeast Asian Games **Obv:** Sun within small circle within horizontal lines above value within 3/4 circle **Rev:** Sport players below emblem and date

Date	Mintage	VF20	XF40	MS60	MS63	MS65
1989 Prooflike	50,000	—	—	—	20.00	25.00
1989	20,000	PF65 40.00				

KM# 68 15 RINGGIT
17.00 g., Copper-Nickel, 34 mm. **Subject:** First Malaysian Grand Prix **Obv:** Value **Rev:** Track route above island maps **Edge:** Reeded

Date	Mintage	VF20	XF40	MS60	MS63	MS65
1999	8,000	PF65 100				

KM# 30 20 RINGGIT
16.23 g., 0.500 Silver 0.2609 oz. ASW **Subject:** 4th Malaysian 5-Year Plan **Rev:** Tun Hussein Onn

Date	Mintage	VF20	XF40	MS60	MS63	MS65
ND-1981 FM (U)	100,000	—	—	—	18.00	22.00
ND-1981 FM (P)	5,000	PF65 45.00				

KM# 14 25 RINGGIT
35.00 g., 0.925 Silver 1.0409 oz. ASW, 42 mm. **Subject:** 25th Anniversary - Employee Provident Fund **Obv:** Value **Rev:** Two inner circles at top divide map of Malasia within globe

Date	Mintage	VF20	XF40	MS60	MS63	MS65
1976 FM (U)	100,000	—	—	—	20.00	25.00
1976 FM (P)	7,796	PF65 45.00				

KM# 20 25 RINGGIT
35.00 g., 0.925 Silver 1.0409 oz. ASW, 42 mm. **Series:** Conservation **Obv:** Arms with supporters **Rev:** Rhinoceros Hornbill flanked by sprigs

Date	Mintage	VF20	XF40	MS60	MS63	MS65
1976	40,000	—	—	—	35.00	45.00
1976	8,008	PF63 55.00	PF65 75.00			

KM# 23 25 RINGGIT
35.00 g., 0.925 Silver 1.0409 oz. ASW, 42 mm. **Subject:** 9th Southeast Asian Games **Obv:** Arms with supporters **Rev:** Olympic circles at upper right of mapped globe

Date	Mintage	VF20	XF40	MS60	MS63	MS65
1977 FM (U)	100,000	—	—	—	20.00	25.00
1977 FM (P)	5,877	PF63 40.00	PF65 60.00			

KM# 33 25 RINGGIT
35.00 g., 0.925 Silver 1.0409 oz. ASW, 42 mm. **Subject:** 25th Anniversary of Independence **Obv:** Star design and bust with headdress with arm holding dagger facing right **Rev:** Arms with supporters **Shape:** 14-sided

Date	Mintage	VF20	XF40	MS60	MS63	MS65
ND-1982	150,000	—	—	—	20.00	25.00
ND-1982	7,000	PF63 35.00	PF65 50.00			

KM# 35 25 RINGGIT
35.00 g., 0.500 Silver 0.5626 oz. ASW, 42 mm. **Subject:** 25th Anniversary of the National Bank **Obv:** Bust with headdress 1/4 left **Rev:** Animal figure within circle and sprigs with date and value below

Date	Mintage	VF20	XF40	MS60	MS63	MS65
ND-1984	98,000	—	—	—	22.50	27.50
ND-1984	10,000	PF63 35.00	PF65 50.00			

KM# 41 25 RINGGIT
23.33 g., 0.925 Silver 0.6938 oz. ASW **Subject:** Women's Decade **Obv:** Date to right of stylized design **Rev:** Animal figure within small circle at lower left within world globe

Date	Mintage	VF20	XF40	MS60	MS63	MS65
ND-1985	2,000	PF63 75.00	PF65 90.00			

KM# 37 25 RINGGIT
35.00 g., 0.500 Silver 0.5626 oz. ASW, 42 mm. **Subject:** 5th Malaysian 5-Year Plan **Obv:** Arms with supporters **Rev:** City scene from harbor

Date	Mintage	VF20	XF40	MS60	MS63	MS65
ND-1986	80,000	—	—	—	18.00	22.00
ND-1986	5,000	PF63 45.00	PF65 55.00			

KM# 56 25 RINGGIT
21.90 g., 0.925 Silver 0.6513 oz. ASW **Subject:** Commonwealth Heads of State Meeting **Obv:** Arms with supporters above lined Malaysia in center with value below **Rev:** Flag within 1/2 of world globe

Date	Mintage	VF20	XF40	MS60	MS63	MS65
1989	30,000	—	—	—	18.00	22.00
1989	8,000	PF63 35.00	PF65 45.00			

KM# 60 25 RINGGIT
21.90 g., 0.925 Silver 0.6513 oz. ASW **Subject:** 100th Anniversary of Kuala Lumpur **Obv:** Design within circle among horizontal lines with value below **Rev:** Castle and tower

Date	Mintage	VF20	XF40	MS60	MS63	MS65
ND-1990	25,000	—	—	—	18.00	22.00
ND-1990	25,000	PF63 35.00	PF65 45.00			

KM# 62 25 RINGGIT
21.77 g., 0.925 Silver 0.6474 oz. ASW **Series:** World Wildlife Fund **Subject:** 100th Anniversary of Kuala Lumpur **Obv:** Panda above value and dollar sign **Rev:** Stylized fish

Date	Mintage	VF20	XF40	MS60	MS63	MS65
ND-1992	—	PF63 35.00	PF65 45.00			

KM# 69 25 RINGGIT
21.77 g., 0.925 Silver 0.6474 oz. ASW, 36.25 mm. **Subject:** First Malaysian Grand Prix **Obv:** Value **Rev:** Trophy **Edge:** Reeded

Date	Mintage	VF20	XF40	MS60	MS63	MS65
1999	3,000	PF63 100	PF65 120			

KM# 46 30 RINGGIT
22.00 g., 0.925 Silver 0.6543 oz. ASW **Subject:** 30th Anniversary of the National Bank **Obv:** Value within circle **Rev:** City view with sun and crescent

Date	Mintage	VF20	XF40	MS60	MS63	MS65
1989	47,000	—	—	—	20.00	25.00
1989	10,000	PF63 40.00	PF65 50.00			

KM# 11 100 RINGGIT
18.66 g., 0.917 Gold 0.5501 oz. AGW **Subject:** Prime Minister Abdul Rahman Putra Al-haj **Obv:** Bust 3/4 facing **Rev:** Multi-storied building left of full sun

Date	Mintage	VF20	XF40	MS60	MS63	MS65
1971	100,000	—	—	—	1,100	1,200
1971	500	PF65 2,800				

KM# 18 200 RINGGIT
7.30 g., 0.900 Gold 0.2112 oz. AGW **Subject:** 3rd Malaysian 5-Year Plan **Shape:** 14-sided

Date	Mintage	VF20	XF40	MS60	MS63	MS65
1976 FM (U)	50,000	—	—	—	425	475
1976 FM (P)	—	PF65 650	PF67 750			

KM# 24 200 RINGGIT
7.22 g., 0.900 Gold 0.2089 oz. AGW **Subject:** 9th Southeast Asian Games **Obv:** Arms with supporters **Rev:** Man on horse right

Date	Mintage	VF20	XF40	MS60	MS63	MS65
1977 FM (U)	12,000	—	—	—	370	400
1977 FM (P)	—	PF65 650	PF67 750			

KM# 15 250 RINGGIT
10.11 g., 0.900 Gold 0.2925 oz. AGW **Subject:** 25th Anniversary - Employee Provident Fund **Obv:** Value **Rev:** Inscription within circle and design

Date	Mintage	VF20	XF40	MS60	MS63	MS65
1976 FM (U)	30,000	—	—	—	650	700
1976 FM (P)	7,706	PF65 850				

KM# 42 250 RINGGIT
8.10 g., 0.900 Gold 0.2344 oz. AGW **Series:** Womens' Decade **Obv:** Date below design **Rev:** World globe

Date	Mintage	VF20	XF40	MS60	MS63	MS65
1985	1,500	PF65 775				

KM# 45 250 RINGGIT
7.43 g., 0.900 Gold 0.215 oz. AGW **Subject:** 30th Anniversary of Independence **Obv:** Arms with supporters above value **Rev:** Numeral 30 divides dates below crossed encased swords, sun and building

Date	Mintage	VF20	XF40	MS60	MS63	MS65
1987	5,000	—	—	—	450	500
1987	1,000	PF65 650				

KM# 58 250 RINGGIT
7.13 g., 0.900 Gold 0.2063 oz. AGW **Subject:** 15th Southeast Asian Games **Obv:** Value below full sun on lined background **Rev:** Games logo and stylized swimmer

Date	Mintage	VF20	XF40	MS60	MS63	MS65
1989	2,500	PF65 550				

KM# 63 250 RINGGIT
8.60 g., 0.900 Gold 0.2488 oz. AGW **Series:** World Wildlife Fund **Obv:** Panda above World Wildlife Fund **Rev:** Clouded Leopard

Date	Mintage	VF20	XF40	MS60	MS63	MS65
1992	—	PF65 550				

KM# 21 500 RINGGIT
33.44 g., 0.900 Gold 0.9675 oz. AGW **Series:** Conservation **Obv:** Arms with supporters **Rev:** Malayan Tapir

Date	Mintage	VF20	XF40	MS60	MS63	MS65
1976	2,894	—	—	—	1,750	1,950
1976	508	PF63 4,250	PF65 5,250			

KM# 31 500 RINGGIT
10.26 g., 0.900 Gold 0.2969 oz. AGW **Subject:** 4th Malaysian 5-Year Plan **Obv:** Arms with supporters **Rev:** Bust 3/4 facing

Date	Mintage	VF20	XF40	MS60	MS63	MS65
ND-1981 FM (U)	20,000	—	—	—	650	700
ND-1981 FM (P)	1,000	PF65 800				

KM# 34 500 RINGGIT
10.26 g., 0.900 Gold 0.2969 oz. AGW **Subject:** 25th Anniversary of Independence **Obv:** Arms with supporters **Rev:** Bust upholding dagger facing right **Shape:** 14-sided **Note:** Similar to 1 Ringgit, KM#32.

Date	Mintage	VF20	XF40	MS60	MS63	MS65
1982	20,000	—	—	—	550	600
1982	1,000	PF65 750				

KM# 38 500 RINGGIT
10.26 g., 0.900 Gold 0.2969 oz. AGW **Subject:** 5th Malaysian 5-Year Plan **Obv:** Arms with supporters **Rev:** Sun, moon and gear-like designs within circle

Date	Mintage	VF20	XF40	MS60	MS63	MS65
ND-1986	10,000	—	—	—	550	600
ND-1986	1,000	PF65 750				

KM# 70 500 RINGGIT
25.00 g., 0.999 Gold 0.803 oz. AGW, 35.25 mm. **Subject:** Millennium **Obv:** Arms with supporters above value **Rev:** Flags within globe **Edge:** Reeded

Date	Mintage	VF20	XF40	MS60	MS63	MS65
1999	10,000	PF65 1,800				

BULLION COINAGE

KM# 121 50 RINGGIT
7.78 g., 0.9999 Gold 0.2499 oz. AGW **Obv:** Mouse deer running right **Obv. Legend:** BANK NEGARA MALAYSIA **Rev:** Flower

Date	Mintage	VF20	XF40	MS60	MS63	MS65
2000	—	—	—	—	—	415

KM# 122 100 RINGGIT
15.55 g., 0.9999 Gold 0.4999 oz. AGW **Obv:** Mousedeer running right **Obv. Legend:** BANK NEGARA MALAYSIA **Rev:** Flower

Date	Mintage	VF20	XF40	MS60	MS63	MS65
2000	—	—	—	—	—	760

KM# 123 200 RINGGIT
31.10 g., 0.9999 Gold 0.9999 oz. AGW **Obv:** Mousedeer running right **Obv. Legend:** BANK NEGARA MALAYSIA **Rev:** Flower

Date	Mintage	VF20	XF40	MS60	MS63	MS65
2000	—	—	—	—	—	1,400

PATTERNS

Including off metal strikes

KM#	Date	Mintage	Identification	Mkt Val
Pn1	SH2602(1942)	—	20 Cents. Aluminum. Cluster of leaves within beaded circle. Value above 1/2 flower wreath. Japanese occupation.	2,500
Pn2	SH2602(1942)	—	20 Cents. Aluminum. Japanese occupation.	2,500
Pn3	1966	Est. 6	Sen. Bronze. Cattle Egret.	—
Pn4	1966	—	Sen. Bronze. Single hibiscus flowers flank denomination. Parliament House.	—
Pn5	1966	—	5 Sen. Copper-Nickel. Malayan Tapir.	—
Pn6	1966	—	5 Sen. Copper-Nickel. Single hibiscus flowers flank denomination. Parliament House.	—
Pn7	1966	Est. 6	10 Sen. Copper-Nickel. Pangolin.	—
Pn8	1966	Est. 6	10 Sen. Copper-Nickel. Proboscis Monkey.	—
Pn9	1966	—	10 Sen. Copper-Nickel. Single hibiscus flowers flank denomination. Parliament House.	—
Pn10	1966	Est. 6	20 Sen. Copper-Nickel. Kijang with tall grass in background.	—
Pn11	1966	Est. 6	20 Sen. Copper-Nickel. Kijang with mountains in background.	—
Pn12	1966	Est. 6	20 Sen. Copper-Nickel. Kijang on mound.	—
Pn13	1966	—	20 Sen. Copper-Nickel. Single hibiscus flowers flank denomination. Parliament House.	—

MINT SETS

KM#	Date	Mintage	Identification	Issue Price	Mkt Val
MS1	1967 (5)	10,000	KM#1-5.1	—	70.00
MS2	1973 (5)	2,000	KM#1-4, 5.3	—	20.00
MS3	1980 (5)	2,000	KM#1a, 2-4, 5.3	—	20.00
MS4	1989 (6)	2,000	KM#49-54	—	15.00
MS5	1990 (6)	2,000	KM#49-54	—	15.00

PROOF SETS

KM#	Date	Mintage	Identification	Issue Price	Mkt Val
PS1	1967 (5)	500	KM#1-5.1	—	700
PS2	1976 (3)	508	KM#19-21	808	4,900
PS3	1976 (2)	7,500	KM#19-20	—	300
PS4	1976 (3)	2,641	KM#16-18	—	800
PS5	1976 (3)	1,000	KM#13-15	—	1,050
PS6	1977 (3)	975	KM#22-24	164	1,000
PS8	1981 (6)	—	KM#1-4, 5.4, 9.2 Minted and distributed by Franklin Mint.	—	75.00
PS9	1981 (3)	3,000	KM#29-31	—	950
PS10	1982 (3)	4,000	KM#32-34	—	900
PS11	1986 (3)	2,000	KM#36-38	—	925
PS12	1986 (2)	11,000	KM#39a, 40	—	100
PS13	1987 (3)	1,000	KM#43-45	—	800
PS14	1989 (3)	2,500	KM#47, 48, 58	—	700
PS15	1989 (2)	20,000	KM#47-48	—	450
PS16	1989 (2)	15,000	KM#55-56	—	60.00
PS17	1992 (6)	5,000	KM#49a-54a Minted by Bank of Negara Malaysia Mint Department and sold only to bank employees.	—	75.00
PS18	1992 (3)	3,000	KM#61-63	—	550

MALDIVE ISLANDS

The Republic of Maldives, an archipelago of 2,000 coral islets in the northern Indian Ocean 417 miles (671 km.) west of Ceylon, has an area of 116 sq. mi. (298 sq. km.)and a population of 189,000. Capital: Male. Fishing employs 95% of the male work force. Dried fish, copra and coir yarn are exported.

The Maldive Islands were visited by Arab traders and converted to Islam in 1153. After being harassed in the16th and 17th centuries by Mopla pirates of the Malabar coast and Portuguese raiders, the Maldivians voluntarily placed themselves under the suzerainty of Ceylon. In 1887 the islands became an internally self-governing British protectorate and a nominal dependency of Ceylon. Traditionally a sultanate, the Maldives became a republic in 1953 but restored the sultanate in 1954. The Sultanate of the Maldive Islands attained complete internal and external autonomy on July 26, 1965, and on Nov. 11, 1968, again became a republic. The Maldives is a member of the Commonwealth of Nations.

RULERS

Muhammad Imad al-Din V, AH1318-1322/1900-1904AD
Muhammad Shams al-Din III, AH1322-1353/1904-1935AD
Hasan Nur al-Din II, AH1353-1364/1935-1945AD
Abdul-Majid Didi, AH1364-1371/1945-1953AD
First Republic, AH1371-1372/1953-1954AD
Muhammad Farid Didi, AH1372-1388/1954-1968AD
Second Republic, AH1388 to date/1968AD to date*

MINT NAME

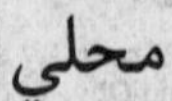

Mahle (Male)

MONETARY SYSTEM

100 Lari = 1 Rupee (Rufiyaa)

SULTANATE

Muhammad Imad al-Din V

AH 1318-22 / 1900-04 AD

STANDARD COINAGE

KM# 38 LARIN
Copper or Brass **Note:** Weight varies: 0.80-1.10 grams.

Date	Mintage	VF20	XF40	MS60	MS63	MS65
AH1318	—	1.50	2.00	4.00	—	—

Note: Die varieties exist

Date	Mintage	VF20	XF40	MS60	MS63	MS65
AH1319 (1901)	—	1.50	2.00	4.00	—	—

KM# 39 2 LARIAT
Copper-Brass, 13 mm. **Obv:** Legend **Rev:** Legend **Note:** 1.4-2.2 grams. Previously listed date AH1311 is merely poor die cutting of AH1319. Many die varieties exist.

Date	Mintage	VF20	XF40	MS60	MS63	MS65
AH1318	—	3.50	5.00	7.50	—	—
AH1319	—	3.50	5.00	7.50	—	—

KM# 40.1 4 LARIAT
Copper-Brass **Obv:** Legend **Rev:** Legend **Edge:** Plain or reeded **Note:** 2.5-4.5 grams. Many die varieties exist; size varies 17 - 18mm. Beware of coins which have been silver plated.

Date	Mintage	VF20	XF40	MS60	MS63	MS65
AH1320	—	2.50	4.50	8.00	—	—

KM# 40.2 4 LARIAT
Copper-Brass **Obv:** Legend **Rev:** Legend with Arabic "Sana(t)" below date **Note:** Silver strikes are most likely presentation pieces, but beware of silver plated pieces. Size varies 16.8-18mm.

Date	Mintage	VF20	XF40	MS60	MS63	MS65
AH1320	—	8.00	12.00	16.00	—	—

Muhammad Shams al-Din III

AH 1322-53 / 1904-35 AD

KM# 41 LARIN
0.90 g., Bronze, 13 mm. **Obv:** Legend **Rev:** Legend **Note:** Struck at Birmingham, England. Rare mint proof strikes in silver and gold exist.

Date	Mintage	VF20	XF40	MS60	MS63	MS65
AH1331	—	1.25	1.75	3.00	—	—

KM# 42 4 LARIAT
3.30 g., Bronze, 19 mm. **Obv:** Legend **Rev:** Legend **Note:** Struck at Birmingham, England. Rare mint proof strikes in silver and gold exist.

Date	Mintage	VF20	XF40	MS60	MS63	MS65
AH1331	—	1.50	2.75	6.00	—	—

2ND SULTANATE

Muhammad Farid Didi

AH 1372-88 / 1954-68 AD

KM# 43 LAARI
1.50 g., Bronze, 15 mm. **Obv:** National emblem divides dates above **Rev:** Value **Note:** Similar to Laari, KM#49.

Date	Mintage	VF20	XF40	MS60	MS63	MS65
AH1379-1960	300,000	0.25	0.50	1.00	1.50	3.00
AH1379-1960	1,270	PF65 3.00				

KM# 44 2 LAARI

3.15 g., Bronze, 18.2 mm. **Obv:** National emblem divides dates above **Rev:** Value **Shape:** 4-sided

Date	Mintage	VF20	XF40	MS60	MS63	MS65
AH1379-1960	600,000	0.35	0.65	1.00	1.50	3.00
AH1379-1960	1,270	PF65 3.50				

KM# 45 5 LAARI

2.60 g., Nickel-Brass, 20.4 mm. **Obv:** National emblem divides dates above **Rev:** Value **Shape:** Scalloped

Date	Mintage	VF20	XF40	MS60	MS63	MS65
AH1379-1960	300,000	0.40	0.75	1.25	1.75	3.50
AH1379-1960	1,270	PF65 4.00				

KM# 45a 5 LAARI

Bronze **Obv:** National emblem divides dates above **Rev:** Value

Date	Mintage	VF20	XF40	MS60	MS63	MS65
AH1379-1960	—	0.40	0.75	1.25	1.75	3.50

KM# 46 10 LAARI

5.20 g., Nickel-Brass, 23 mm. **Obv:** National emblem divides dates above **Rev:** Value **Shape:** Scalloped

Date	Mintage	VF20	XF40	MS60	MS63	MS65
AH1379-1960	600,000	0.75	1.00	1.50	2.00	4.00
AH1379-1960	1,270	PF65 5.00				

KM# 47.1 25 LAARI

4.10 g., Nickel-Brass, 20.4 mm. **Obv:** National emblem divides dates above **Rev:** Value **Edge:** Security

Date	Mintage	VF20	XF40	MS60	MS63	MS65
AH1379-1960	300,000	1.00	1.25	1.75	2.25	4.50
AH1379-1960	1,270	PF65 6.00				

KM# 47.2 25 LAARI

4.10 g., Nickel-Brass, 20.4 mm. **Obv:** National emblem divides dates above **Rev:** Value **Edge:** Reeded

Date	Mintage	VF20	XF40	MS60	MS63	MS65
AH1379-1960	—	2.50	3.00	3.50	5.00	7.00

KM# 48.1 50 LAARI

5.60 g., Nickel-Brass, 23.5 mm. **Obv:** National emblem divides dates above **Rev:** Value **Edge:** Security

Date	Mintage	VF20	XF40	MS60	MS63	MS65
AH1379-1960	300,000	1.75	2.25	2.50	3.50	5.00
AH1379-1960	1,270	PF65 8.00				

KM# 48.2 50 LAARI

Nickel-Brass, 23.5 mm. **Obv:** National emblem divides dates above **Rev:** Value **Edge:** Reeded

Date	Mintage	VF20	XF40	MS60	MS63	MS65
AH1379-1960	—	2.50	3.50	5.00	7.00	9.00

2ND REPUBLIC

STANDARD COINAGE

100 Laari = 1 Rufiyaa

KM# 49 LAARI

0.45 g., Aluminum, 15 mm. **Obv:** National emblem divides dates above **Rev:** Value **Edge:** Plain

Date	Mintage	VF20	XF40	MS60	MS63	MS65
AH1389-1970	500,000	0.10	0.20	0.30	0.40	0.50
AH1399-1979	—	0.10	0.20	0.30	0.40	0.50
AH1399-1979	100,000	PF65 1.25				

KM# 68 LAARI

0.46 g., Aluminum, 15 mm. **Obv:** Value **Rev:** Palm tree within circle **Edge:** Plain

Date	Mintage	VF20	XF40	MS60	MS63	MS65
AH1404-1984	—	—	0.10	0.15	0.25	0.35
AH1404-1984	2,500	PF65 2.50				

KM# 50 2 LAARI

Aluminum, 18.2 mm.

Date	Mintage	VF20	XF40	MS60	MS63	MS65
AH1389-1970	500,000	0.15	0.25	0.35	0.50	0.75
AH1389-1970 Proof	—	—	—	—	—	—
AH1399-1979	—	0.15	0.25	0.35	0.50	0.75
AH1399-1979	100,000	PF65 1.25				

KM# 45b 5 LAARI

Nickel-Brass, 20.4 mm. **Obv:** National emblem divides dates above **Shape:** Scalloped **Note:** Similar to 5 Laari, KM#45.

Date	Mintage	VF20	XF40	MS60	MS63	MS65
AH1389-1970	300,000	0.20	0.30	0.40	0.60	0.85
AH1389-1970	—	PF65 3.50				
AH1399-1979	—	—	0.10	0.20	0.30	0.50
AH1399-1979	—	PF65 2.50				

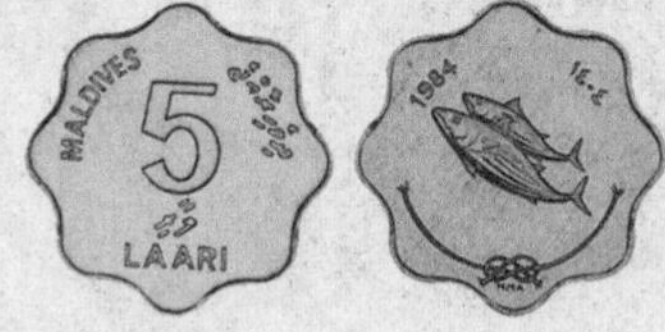

KM# 69 5 LAARI

1.00 g., Aluminum, 20.32 mm. **Obv:** Value **Rev:** Two Bonito fish swimming upward left **Shape:** Scalloped

Date	Mintage	VF20	XF40	MS60	MS63	MS65
AH1404-1984	—	—	0.10	0.25	0.35	1.00
AH1404-1984	2,500	PF65 3.00				
AH1411-1990	—	—	0.10	0.25	0.35	1.00

KM# 46a 10 LAARI

Aluminum, 23 mm. **Obv:** National emblem divides dates above **Shape:** Scalloped **Note:** Similar to 10 Laari, KM#46.

Date	Mintage	VF20	XF40	MS60	MS63	MS65
AH1399-1979	—	—	0.10	0.20	0.30	0.50
AH1399-1979	—	PF65 2.50				

KM# 70 10 LAARI

1.95 g., Aluminum, 23.11 mm. **Obv:** Value **Rev:** Maldivian sailing ship - Odi **Shape:** Scalloped

Date	Mintage	VF20	XF40	MS60	MS63	MS65
AH1404-1984	—	—	0.10	0.20	0.30	0.50
AH1404-1984	2,500	PF65 3.50				

KM# 47.3 25 LAARI

Nickel-Brass, 20.4 mm. **Obv:** National emblem divides dates above **Rev:** Palm tree **Note:** Similar to 25 Laari, KM#47.2.

Date	Mintage	VF20	XF40	MS60	MS63	MS65
AH1399-1979	—	—	0.10	0.20	0.30	0.50
AH1399-1979	100,000	PF65 3.50				

KM# 71 25 LAARI

4.15 g., Nickel-Brass, 20.2 mm. **Obv:** Value **Rev:** Mosque and minaret at Male **Edge:** Reeded

Date	Mintage	VF20	XF40	MS60	MS63	MS65
AH1404-1984	—	—	0.15	0.25	0.35	0.50
AH1404-1984	—	PF65 4.00				
AH1411-1990	—	—	0.15	0.25	0.35	0.50
AH1416-1996	—	—	0.15	0.25	0.35	0.50

KM# 48.3 50 LAARI

Nickel-Brass, 23.5 mm. **Obv:** National emblem divides dates above **Rev:** Palm tree **Note:** Similar to 50 Laari, KM#48.2.

Date	Mintage	VF20	XF40	MS60	MS63	MS65
AH1399-1979	—	0.10	0.20	0.30	0.40	0.60
AH1399-1979	100,000	PF65 6.50				

KM# 72 50 LAARI

5.66 g., Nickel-Brass, 23.6 mm. **Obv:** Value **Rev:** Loggerhead sea turtle **Edge:** Reeded

Date	Mintage	VF20	XF40	MS60	MS63	MS65
AH1404-1984	—	—	0.35	0.75	1.50	2.50
AH1404-1984	—	PF65 6.00				
AH1411-1990	—	—	0.35	0.75	1.50	2.50
AH1415-1995	—	—	0.35	0.75	1.50	2.50

KM# 73 RUFIYAA

Copper-Nickel Clad Steel, 25.9 mm. **Obv:** Value **Rev:** National emblem divides dates above

Date	Mintage	VF20	XF40	MS60	MS63	MS65
AH1402-1982	—	0.20	0.50	1.00	2.00	3.00

KM# 73a RUFIYAA

6.41 g., Copper-Nickel, 25.9 mm. **Obv:** Value **Rev:** National emblem divides dates above **Edge:** Reeded

Date	Mintage	VF20	XF40	MS60	MS63	MS65
AH1404-1984	—	0.20	0.50	1.00	2.00	3.00
AH1404-1984	—	PF65 9.00				
AH1411-1990	—	0.20	0.50	1.00	2.00	3.00
AH1416-1996	—	0.20	0.50	1.00	2.00	3.00

KM# 88 2 RUFIYAA

11.70 g., Nickel-Brass, 25.5 mm. **Obv:** Value **Rev:** Pacific triton sea shell **Edge:** Reeded and lettered **Edge Lettering:** REPUBLIC OF MALDIVES

Date	Mintage	VF20	XF40	MS60	MS63	MS65
AH1415-1995	—	—	2.25	3.50	5.50	7.50

KM# 55 5 RUFIYAA

Copper-Nickel **Series:** F.A.O. **Obv:** National emblem divides dates above **Rev:** Value below Bonito fish

Date	Mintage	VF20	XF40	MS60	MS63	MS65
AH1397-1977	15,000	—	3.50	4.50	6.50	10.00

KM# 57 5 RUFIYAA
Copper-Nickel, 36 mm. **Series:** F.A.O. **Obv:** National emblem divides dates above **Rev:** Spiny lobster divides circle

Date	Mintage	VF20	XF40	MS60	MS63	MS65
AH1398-1978	7,000	—	4.00	5.00	7.50	12.00

KM# 57a 5 RUFIYAA
19.15 g., 0.925 Silver 0.5695 oz. ASW **Series:** F.A.O. **Obv:** National emblem divides dates above **Rev:** Spiny lobster divides circle

Date	Mintage	VF20	XF40	MS60	MS63	MS65
AH1398-1978	1,887	PF63 35.00	PF65 45.00			

KM# 57b 5 RUFIYAA
18.95 g., 0.917 Gold 0.5587 oz. AGW **Series:** F.A.O. **Obv:** National emblem divides dates above **Rev:** Spiny lobster divides circle

Date	Mintage	VF20	XF40	MS60	MS63	MS65
AH1398-1978	200	PF63 850	PF65 950			

KM# 100 5 RUFIYAA
26.00 g., Copper-Nickel, 38.75 mm. **Subject:** International Year of the Reef **Obv:** National emblem divides dates above **Rev:** Multicolor fish scene **Edge:** Reeded

Date	Mintage	VF20	XF40	MS60	MS63	MS65
AH1419-1998	—	PF63 15.00	PF65 20.00			

KM# 59 10 RUFIYAA
Copper-Nickel **Series:** F.A.O. **Obv:** National emblem divides dates above **Rev:** Woman weaving

Date	Mintage	VF20	XF40	MS60	MS63	MS65
AH1399-1979	7,000	—	4.50	6.50	9.50	14.00

KM# 59a 10 RUFIYAA
25.00 g., 0.925 Silver 0.7435 oz. ASW **Series:** F.A.O. **Obv:** National emblem divides dates above **Rev:** Woman weaving

Date	Mintage	VF20	XF40	MS60	MS63	MS65
AH1399-1979	3,000	PF63 35.00	PF65 50.00			

KM# 62 10 RUFIYAA
Copper-Nickel **Series:** F.A.O. **Obv:** National emblem divides dates above **Rev:** Girl making embroidery

Date	Mintage	VF20	XF40	MS60	MS63	MS65
AH1400-1980	—	—	4.00	6.00	8.00	12.00

KM# 56 20 RUFIYAA
28.28 g., 0.500 Silver 0.4546 oz. ASW, 38.61 mm. **Series:** F.A.O. **Obv:** National emblem divides dates above **Rev:** Value flanked by fish

Date	Mintage	VF20	XF40	MS60	MS63	MS65
AH1397-1977	15,000	—	—	—	15.00	18.00

KM# 61 20 RUFIYAA
28.28 g., 0.925 Silver 0.841 oz. ASW, 38.61 mm. **Series:** International Year of the Child **Obv:** National emblem divides dates above **Rev:** Three children playing

Date	Mintage	VF20	XF40	MS60	MS63	MS65
AH1399-1979	12,000	PF63 25.00	PF65 30.00			

KM# 65 20 RUFIYAA
Copper-Nickel, 38.61 mm. **Subject:** World Fisheries Conference **Obv:** National emblem divides dates above **Rev:** Two tuna fish

Date	Mintage	VF20	XF40	MS60	MS63	MS65
AH1404-1984	100,000	—	—	12.00	15.00	22.00

KM# 65a 20 RUFIYAA
28.28 g., 0.925 Silver 0.841 oz. ASW, 38.61 mm. **Subject:** World Fisheries Conference **Obv:** National emblem divides dates above **Rev:** Two tuna fish

Date	Mintage	VF20	XF40	MS60	MS63	MS65
AH1404-1984	20,000	PF63 35.00	PF65 45.00			

KM# 74 20 RUFIYAA
19.44 g., 0.925 Silver 0.5781 oz. ASW **Series:** Decade for Women **Obv:** National emblem divides dates above **Rev:** Woman sewing lace on pillow

Date	Mintage	VF20	XF40	MS60	MS63	MS65
AH1405-1985	500	PF63 55.00	PF65 75.00			

KM# 97 20 RUFIYAA
31.22 g., 0.999 Silver 1.0027 oz. ASW, 30.3 mm. **Subject:** Millennium **Obv:** National emblem **Rev:** Multicolor design **Edge:** Reeded **Shape:** Square

Date	Mintage	VF20	XF40	MS60	MS63	MS65
AH1421-2000	—	PF63 45.00	PF65 55.00			

KM# 58 25 RUFIYAA
28.05 g., 0.500 Silver 0.4509 oz. ASW **Series:** F.A.O. **Obv:** National emblem divides dates above **Rev:** Sailing ship

Date	Mintage	VF20	XF40	MS60	MS63	MS65
AH1398-1978	7,140	—	—	—	20.00	25.00

KM# 58a 25 RUFIYAA
28.28 g., 0.925 Silver 0.841 oz. ASW **Series:** F.A.O. **Obv:** National emblem divides dates above **Rev:** Sailing ship

Date	Mintage	VF20	XF40	MS60	MS63	MS65
AH1398-1978	2,000	PF63 35.00	PF65 45.00			

KM# 58b 25 RUFIYAA
28.25 g., 0.917 Gold 0.8329 oz. AGW **Series:** F.A.O. **Obv:** National emblem divides dates above **Rev:** Sailing ship

Date	Mintage	VF20	XF40	MS60	MS63	MS65
AH1398-1978	200	PF63 1,350	PF65 1,550	PF67 1,700		

KM# 95 25 RUFIYAA
Copper-Nickel **Series:** 50th Anniversary - UN **Obv:** National emblem divides dates above **Rev:** UN building and logo

Date	Mintage	VF20	XF40	MS60	MS63	MS65
AH1416-1996	—	—	—	—	5.00	7.00

KM# 89 50 RUFIYAA
1.24 g., 0.9999 Gold 0.040 oz. AGW **Obv:** National emblem divides dates above **Rev:** Skylab space station

Date	Mintage	VF20	XF40	MS60	MS63	MS65
AH1415-1995	Est. 25000	—	—	—	65.00	75.00

KM# 90 50 RUFIYAA
10.00 g., 0.500 Silver 0.1608 oz. ASW **Series:** 1996 Olympics **Obv:** National emblem divides dates above **Rev:** Sailboat and map

Date	Mintage	VF20	XF40	MS60	MS63	MS65
AH1416-1996	Est. 10000	—	—	—	12.00	16.00

KM# 99 50 RUFIYAA
31.30 g., 0.925 Silver 0.9308 oz. ASW, 38.5 mm. **Subject:** Year of the Reef **Obv:** National emblem divides dates above **Rev:** Multicolor underwater scene **Edge:** Reeded

Date	Mintage	VF20	XF40	MS60	MS63	MS65
AH1419-1998	—	PF65 40.00				

KM# 60 100 RUFIYAA
28.28 g., 0.800 Silver 0.7274 oz. ASW **Series:** F.A.O. **Obv:** National emblem divides dates above **Rev:** Woman making mats

Date	Mintage	VF20	XF40	MS60	MS63	MS65
AH1399-1979	6,000	—	—	—	25.00	28.00

KM# 60a 100 RUFIYAA
28.28 g., 0.925 Silver 0.841 oz. ASW **Series:** F.A.O. **Obv:** National emblem divides dates above **Rev:** Woman making mats

Date	Mintage	VF20	XF40	MS60	MS63	MS65
AH1399-1979	8,000	PF65 35.00				

KM# 63 100 RUFIYAA
28.28 g., 0.800 Silver 0.7274 oz. ASW **Series:** F.A.O. **Obv:** National emblem divides dates above **Rev:** Crown of coconut and palm **Edge:** Reeded

Date	Mintage	VF20	XF40	MS60	MS63	MS65
AH1400-1980	6,501	—	—	—	30.00	35.00

KM# 63a 100 RUFIYAA
28.28 g., 0.925 Silver 0.841 oz. ASW **Series:** F.A.O. **Obv:** National emblem divides dates above **Rev:** Crown of coconut and palm

Date	Mintage	VF20	XF40	MS60	MS63	MS65
AH1400-1980	3,003	PF65 50.00				

KM# 64 100 RUFIYAA
28.28 g., 0.925 Silver 0.841 oz. ASW **Series:** World Food Day **Obv:** National emblem divides dates above **Rev:** Heads of 2 women working in a field

Date	Mintage	VF20	XF40	MS60	MS63	MS65
AH1401-1981	10,000	—	—	—	25.00	28.00
AH1401-1981	5,000	PF65 45.00				

KM# 66 100 RUFIYAA
28.28 g., 0.925 Silver 0.841 oz. ASW, 38.61 mm. **Series:** International Year of Disabled Persons **Obv:** National emblem divides dates above **Rev:** Stylized yin and yang symbol

Date	Mintage	VF20	XF40	MS60	MS63	MS65
AH1404-1984	—	—	—	—	22.00	25.00
AH1404-1984	—	PF65 42.00				

KM# 67 100 RUFIYAA
15.98 g., 0.917 Gold 0.4711 oz. AGW **Obv:** National emblem divides dates above **Rev:** Disabled figures within lower circle under 1/2 world globe

Date	Mintage	XF40	MS60	MS63	MS65	MS66
AH1404-1984	500	—	—	850	900	950
AH1404-1984	500	PF65 950	PF67 1,000			

KM# 75 100 RUFIYAA
15.98 g., 0.917 Gold 0.4711 oz. AGW **Subject:** Opening of Grand Mosque and Islamic Centre **Obv:** National emblem divides dates above

Date	Mintage	VF20	XF40	MS60	MS63	MS65
AH1405-1985	100	PF65 1,000	PF67 1,100			

KM# 78 100 RUFIYAA
28.28 g., 0.925 Silver 0.841 oz. ASW **Subject:** Opening of Grand Mosque and Islamic Centre **Obv:** National emblem divides dates above **Rev:** Building and tower

Date	Mintage	VF20	XF40	MS60	MS63	MS65
AH1405-1985	500	PF65 80.00	PF67 100			

KM# 76 100 RUFIYAA
28.28 g., 0.925 Silver 0.841 oz. ASW **Subject:** Commonwealth finance ministers meeting **Obv:** National emblem divides dates above **Rev:** Grand Mosque

Date	Mintage	VF20	XF40	MS60	MS63	MS65
ND(AH406)	300	PF65 100	PF67 120			

KM# 87 100 RUFIYAA
10.00 g., 0.500 Silver 0.1608 oz. ASW **Obv:** National emblem divides dates above **Rev:** Sailing ship "Cutty Sark"

Date	Mintage	VF20	XF40	MS60	MS63	MS65
AH1414-1993	Est. 25000	PF63 12.00	PF65 15.00			

KM# 98 100 RUFIYAA
20.00 g., 0.835 Silver 0.5369 oz. ASW, 34 mm. **Series:** Olympics **Obv:** National emblem divides dates above **Rev:** Swimmer within circle **Edge:** Reeded

Date	Mintage	VF20	XF40	MS60	MS63	MS65
AH1418-1998 Proof	30,000	—	—	—	27.00	30.00

KM# 102 100 RUFIYAA
Gold **Subject:** Millennium 2000

Date	Mintage	VF20	XF40	MS60	MS63	MS65
AH1421-2000	—	PF65 450	PF67 500			

KM# 80 250 RUFIYAA
31.47 g., 0.925 Silver 0.9359 oz. ASW **Series:** 1992 Olympics **Subject:** Swimming **Obv:** National emblem divides dates above **Rev:** Swimmer and diver

Date	Mintage	VF20	XF40	MS60	MS63	MS65
AH1410-1990	—	PF65 30.00				

KM# 81 250 RUFIYAA

31.47 g., 0.925 Silver 0.9359 oz. ASW, 38.61 mm. **Obv:** National emblem divides dates above **Rev:** Maldivian Schooner - Dhivehi-Odi

Date	Mintage	VF20	XF40	MS60	MS63	MS65
AH1410-1990	15,000	PF65 32.00				

KM# 82 250 RUFIYAA

31.47 g., 0.925 Silver 0.9359 oz. ASW, 38.61 mm. **Series:** World Football Championship **Obv:** National emblem divides dates above **Rev:** Soccer ball trailing an inscribed ribbon

Date	Mintage	VF20	XF40	MS60	MS63	MS65
AH1410-1990	—	PF65 35.00				

KM# 83 250 RUFIYAA

31.47 g., 0.925 Silver 0.9359 oz. ASW, 38.61 mm. **Subject:** World Cup '94 soccer **Obv:** National emblem divides dates above **Rev:** Two soccer players

Date	Mintage	VF20	XF40	MS60	MS63	MS65
AH1413-1993	25,000	PF65 35.00				

KM# 84 250 RUFIYAA

31.47 g., 0.925 Silver 0.9359 oz. ASW, 38.61 mm. **Obv:** National emblem divides dates above **Rev:** Skylab space station

Date	Mintage	VF20	XF40	MS60	MS63	MS65
AH1413-1993	1,440	PF65 45.00				

KM# 85 250 RUFIYAA

31.47 g., 0.925 Silver 0.9359 oz. ASW, 38.61 mm. **Series:** 1996 Olympics **Subject:** Sailing **Obv:** National emblem divides dates above **Rev:** Sailboat divides map

Date	Mintage	VF20	XF40	MS60	MS63	MS65
AH1414-1993	25,000	PF65 28.00				

KM# 86 250 RUFIYAA

31.47 g., 0.925 Silver 0.9359 oz. ASW, 38.61 mm. **Series:** Endangered Wildlife **Obv:** National emblem divides dates above **Rev:** Turtle

Date	Mintage	VF20	XF40	MS60	MS63	MS65
AH1414-1994	14,500	PF65 37.00				

KM# 96 250 RUFIYAA

31.24 g., 0.925 Silver 0.9291 oz. ASW, 38.61 mm. **Subject:** Ibn Battuta **Obv:** National emblem divides dates above **Rev:** Bust of Ibn Battuta, dhow and map

Date	Mintage	VF20	XF40	MS60	MS63	MS65
AH1416-1995	—	PF65 35.00				

KM# 101 250 RUFIYAA

28.50 g., 0.925 Silver 0.8476 oz. ASW, 38.6 mm. **Subject:** U N 50 Years **Obv:** National emblem divides dates above **Rev:** U N building and logo **Edge:** Reeded

Date	Mintage	VF20	XF40	MS60	MS63	MS65
AH1416-1996	—	PF65 75.00				

KM# 91 500 RUFIYAA

28.28 g., 0.925 Silver 0.841 oz. ASW, 38.61 mm. **Subject:** 25 Years of Independence

Date	Mintage	VF20	XF40	MS60	MS63	MS65
AH1410-1990	1,000	PF63 60.00	PF65 70.00			

KM# 92 500 RUFIYAA

28.28 g., 0.925 Silver 0.841 oz. ASW, 38.61 mm. **Subject:** 25 Years of Republic

Date	Mintage	VF20	XF40	MS60	MS63	MS65
AH1413-1993	500	PF63 65.00	PF65 75.00			

KM# 93 1000 RUFIYAA

15.98 g., 0.917 Gold 0.4711 oz. AGW, 28.4 mm. **Subject:** 25 Years of Independence

Date	Mintage	VF20	XF40	MS60	MS63	MS65
AH1410-1990	1,000	PF65 850	PF67 950			

KM# 94 1000 RUFIYAA

15.98 g., 0.917 Gold 0.4711 oz. AGW, 28.4 mm. **Subject:** 25 Years of Republic

Date	Mintage	VF20	XF40	MS60	MS63	MS65
AH1413-1993	500	PF65 1,000	PF67 1,100			

PIEDFORT

KM#	Date	Mintage	Identification	Mkt Val
P1	1979	100	20 Rufiyaa. Silver. National emblem - crescent moon, star and palm tree flanked by 2 flags. 3 children playing. KM61.	100
P2	1984	100	100 Rufiyaa. Silver. National emblem - crescent moon, star and palm tree flanked by 2 flags. Stylized Yin-Yang symbol. KM66.	120
P3	1984	100	100 Rufiyaa. Gold. National emblem - crescent moon, star and palm tree flanked by 2 flags. Disabled persons under an umbrella. KM67.	1,850

PATTERNS

Including off metal strikes

KM#	Date	Mintage	Identification	Mkt Val
Pn1	AH1319 (1901)	—	Larin. Silver. KM38.	—
Pn2	AH1319 (1901)	—	2 Lariat. Silver. KM39.	—
Pn3	AH1320 (1902)	—	4 Lariat. Silver. KM40.2.	—

MINT SETS

KM#	Date	Mintage	Identification	Issue Price	Mkt Val
MS1	1984 (6)	—	KM68-73	8.75	12.50

PROOF SETS

KM#	Date	Mintage	Identification	Issue Price	Mkt Val
PS1	1960 (6)	1,270	KM43-48	—	30.00
PS2	1979 (6)	—	KM45b, 46a, 47.3, 48.3, 49-50	30.00	18.00
PS3	1979 (2)	3,000	KM59a, 60a	—	70.00
PS4	1984 (6)	2,500	KM68-72, 73a	30.00	28.00

MALI

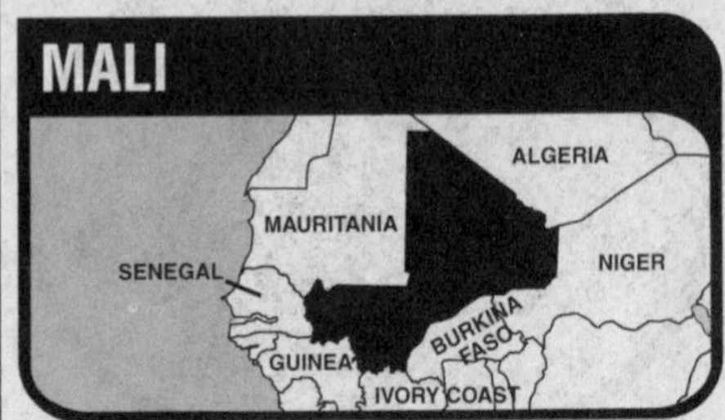

The Republic of Mali, a landlocked country in the interior of West Africa southwest of Algeria, has an area of 482,077 sq. mi. (1,240,000 sq. km.) and a population of 8.1 million. Capital: Bamako. Livestock, fish, cotton and peanuts are exported.

Malians are descendants of the ancient Malinke Kingdom of Mali that controlled the middle Niger from the 11th to the 17th centuries. The French penetrated the Sudan (now Mali) about 1880, and established their rule in 1898 after subduing fierce native resistance. In 1904 the area became the colony of Upper Senegal-Niger (changed to French Sudan in 1920), and became part of the French Union in 1946. In 1958 French Sudan became the Sudanese Republic with complete internal autonomy. Senegal joined with the Sudanese Republic in 1959 to form the Mali Federation which, in 1960, became a fully independent member of the French Community. Upon Senegal's subsequent withdrawal from the Federation, the Sudanese, on Sept. 22, 1960, proclaimed their nation the fully independent Republic of Mali and severed all ties with France.

MINT MARK

(a) - Paris, privy marks only

REPUBLIC

STANDARD COINAGE

KM# 2 5 FRANCS

1.00 g., Aluminum, 20 mm. **Obv:** Hippo facing **Rev:** Value above crossed leaves

Date	Mintage	VF20	XF40	MS60	MS63	MS65
1961	—	0.25	0.50	1.00	2.00	6.00

KM# 1 10 FRANCS
25.00 g., 0.900 Silver 0.7234 oz. ASW **Subject:** Independence **Obv:** Arms of Mali **Rev:** Bust facing

Date	Mintage	VF20	XF40	MS60	MS63	MS65
ND-1960	10,000	PF63 30.00	PF65 40.00			

KM# 3 10 FRANCS
1.55 g., Aluminum, 23.5 mm. **Obv:** Horse head left **Rev:** Value within leaf wreath

Date	Mintage	VF20	XF40	MS60	MS63	MS65
1961	—	1.00	1.50	3.00	5.00	7.00

KM# 5 10 FRANCS
3.20 g., 0.900 Gold 0.0926 oz. AGW **Subject:** President Modibo Keita **Obv:** Arms of Mali **Rev:** Bust facing **Note:** Similar to 25 Francs, KM#6.

Date	Mintage	VF20	XF40	MS60	MS63	MS65
1967	—	PF63 150	PF65 175			

KM# 11 10 FRANCS
1.55 g., Aluminum, 23.5 mm. **Obv:** Value flanked by triangles with date below **Rev:** Rice plants

Date	Mintage	VF20	XF40	MS60	MS63	MS65
1976 (a)	10,000,000	2.00	3.00	4.50	6.50	10.00

KM# 13 10 FRANCS
3.20 g., 0.900 Gold 0.0926 oz. AGW, 23.5 mm. **Subject:** Anniversary of Independence **Obv:** Designs within circle **Rev:** Bust with hat, facing **Note:** Similar to 50 Francs, KM#15.

Date	Mintage	VF20	XF40	MS60	MS63	MS65
ND (1976) Proof	—	—	—	—	—	—

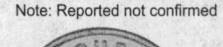

Note: Reported not confirmed

KM# 4 25 FRANCS
2.50 g., Aluminum, 27 mm. **Obv:** Lion's head facing **Rev:** Value within leaf wreath

Date	Mintage	VF20	XF40	MS60	MS63	MS65
1961	—	0.65	1.75	2.50	4.00	7.00

KM# 6 25 FRANCS
8.00 g., 0.900 Gold 0.2315 oz. AGW **Subject:** President Modibo Keita **Obv:** Arms of Mali **Rev:** Bust with hat, facing

Date	Mintage	VF20	XF40	MS60	MS63	MS65
1967	—	PF63 375	PF65 425			

KM# 12 25 FRANCS
2.50 g., Aluminum, 27 mm. **Obv:** Value flanked by triangles with date below **Rev:** Rice plants

Date	Mintage	VF20	XF40	MS60	MS63	MS65
1976 (a)	10,000,000	3.00	5.00	7.00	12.00	16.00

KM# 14 25 FRANCS
8.00 g., 0.900 Gold 0.2315 oz. AGW **Subject:** Anniversary of Independence **Obv:** Arms of Mali **Rev:** Bust with hat, facing

Date	Mintage	VF20	XF40	MS60	MS63	MS65
ND (1976)	—	PF63 400	PF65 450			

KM# 7 50 FRANCS
16.00 g., 0.900 Gold 0.463 oz. AGW **Subject:** President Modibo Keita **Obv:** Arms of Mali **Rev:** Bust with hat, facing

Date	Mintage	VF20	XF40	MS60	MS63	MS65
1967	—	PF63 750	PF65 800			

KM# 9 50 FRANCS
4.00 g., Nickel-Brass, 23.5 mm. **Series:** F.A.O. **Obv:** Value flanked by triangles with date below **Rev:** Millet plant

Date	Mintage	VF20	XF40	MS60	MS63	MS65
1975 (a)	10,000,000	0.50	1.00	2.00	3.00	4.50
1977 (a)	10,000,000	0.50	1.00	2.00	3.00	4.50

KM# 15 50 FRANCS
16.00 g., 0.900 Gold 0.463 oz. AGW **Subject:** Anniversary of Independence **Obv:** Arms of Mali **Rev:** Bust with hat, facing

Date	Mintage	VF20	XF40	MS60	MS63	MS65
ND (1977)	—	PF63 775	PF65 825			

KM# 8 100 FRANCS
32.00 g., 0.900 Gold 0.9259 oz. AGW **Subject:** President Modibo Keita **Obv:** Arms of Mali **Rev:** Bust with hat, facing

Date	Mintage	VF20	XF40	MS60	MS63	MS65
1967	—	PF63 1,350	PF65 1,450			

KM# 10 100 FRANCS
8.00 g., Nickel-Brass, 27.8 mm. **Series:** F.A.O. **Obv:** Value flanked by triangles with date below **Rev:** 3 Ears of corn

Date	Mintage	VF20	XF40	MS60	MS63	MS65
1975 (a)	23,000,000	1.00	2.00	2.75	4.50	6.50

KM# 16 100 FRANCS
32.00 g., 0.900 Gold 0.9259 oz. AGW **Subject:** Anniversary of Independence **Obv:** Arms of Mali **Rev:** Bust with hat, facing

Date	Mintage	VF20	XF40	MS60	MS63	MS65
ND (1975)	—	PF63 1,450	PF65 1,550			

ESSAIS

Standard metals unless otherwise noted

KM#	Date	Mintage	Identification	Mkt Val
E1	1975	—	50 Francs. Nickel-Brass. KM9.	70.00
E2	1975	—	100 Francs. Nickel-Brass. KM10.	65.00
E3	1976	—	10 Francs. Aluminum. KM11.	60.00
E4	1976	—	25 Francs. Aluminum. KM12.	60.00

PIEDFORT WITH ESSAI

Standard metals unless otherwise noted

KM#	Date	Mintage	Identification	Mkt Val
PE1	1960	10	10 Francs. Silver. KM1.	600

PROOF SETS

KM#	Date	Mintage	Identification	Issue Price	Mkt Val
PS1	1967 (4)	—	KM5-8	—	2,850

MALTA

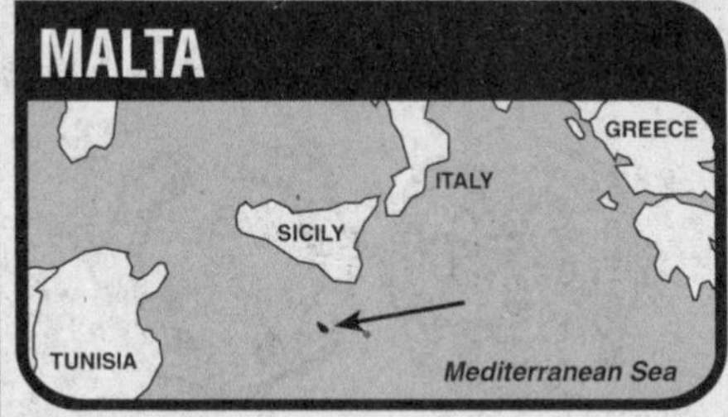

The Republic of Malta, an independent parliamentary democracy, is situated in the Mediterranean Sea between Sicily and North Africa. With the islands of Gozo and Comino, Malta has an area of 124 sq. mi. (320 sq. km.) and a population of 386,000. Capital: Valletta. Malta has no proven mineral resources, an agriculture insufficient to its needs, and a small, but expanding, manufacturing facility. Clothing, textile yarns and fabrics, and knitted wear are exported.

For more than 3,500 years Malta was ruled, in succession by Phoenicians, Carthaginians, Romans, Arabs, Normans, the Knights of Malta, France and Britain. Napoleon seized Malta by treachery in 1798. The French were ousted by a Maltese insurrection assisted by Britain, and in 1814 Malta, of its own free will, became a part of the British Empire. Malta obtained full independence in Sept., 1964; electing to remain within the Commonwealth with the British monarch as the nominal head of state.

Malta became a republic on Dec. 13, 1974, but remained a member of the Commonwealth of Nations. The president is Chief of State. The prime minister is the Head of Government.

RULER
British, until 1964

REPUBLIC

DECIMAL COINAGE

10 Mils = 1 Cent; 100 Cents = 1 Pound

KM# 5 2 MILS
0.95 g., Aluminum, 20.3 mm. **Obv:** Maltese cross **Rev:** Value within 3/4 wreath **Shape:** Scalloped

Date	Mintage	VF20	XF40	MS60	MS63	MS65
1972	30,000	—	1.00	2.00	3.00	3.50
1972	13,000	PF65 5.00				
1976 (M)	5,000	—	—	—	2.00	2.50
1976 (P)	26,000	PF65 5.00				
1977 (U)	5,252	—	—	—	1.00	1.50
1977 (P)	6,884	PF65 5.00				
1978 (U)	5,252	—	—	—	1.00	1.50
1978 (P)	3,244	PF65 5.00				

Date	Mintage	VF20	XF40	MS60	MS63	MS65
1979 (U)	537	—	—	—	3.00	4.00
1979 (P)	6,577	PF65 5.00				
1980 (U)	385	—	—	—	3.00	4.00
1980 (P)	3,451	PF65 5.00				
1981 (U)	444	—	—	—	3.00	4.00
1981 (P)	1,453	PF65 5.00				

KM# 54 2 MILS

0.95 g., Aluminum, 20.3 mm. **Subject:** 10th Anniversary of Decimalization **Obv:** Maltese cross **Rev:** Value within 3/4 wreath **Shape:** Scalloped

Date	Mintage	VF20	XF40	MS60	MS63	MS65
1982 (U)	850	—	—	—	—	15.00
1982 (P)	1,793	PF65 15.00				

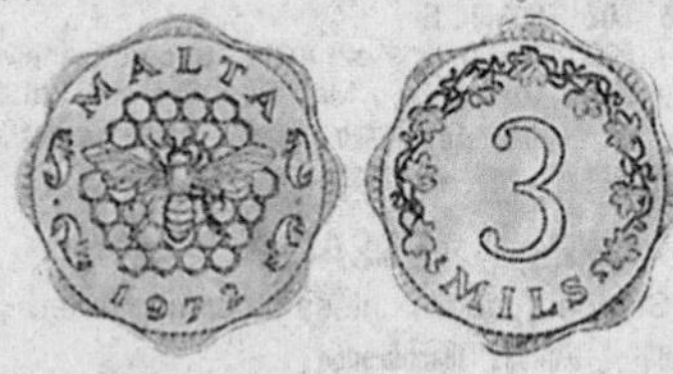

KM# 6 3 MILS

1.45 g., Aluminum, 23.25 mm. **Obv:** Bee and honeycomb **Rev:** Value within 3/4 wreath **Shape:** Scalloped

Date	Mintage	VF20	XF40	MS60	MS63	MS65
1972	—	—	1.00	2.00	3.00	4.00
1972	8,000	PF65 5.00				
1976 (M)	5,000	—	—	—	3.00	4.00
1976 (P)	26,000	PF65 5.00				
1977 (U)	5,252	—	—	—	3.00	4.00
1977 (P)	6,884	PF65 5.00				
1978 (U)	5,252	—	—	—	3.00	4.00
1978 (P)	3,244	PF65 5.00				
1979 (U)	537	—	—	—	5.00	6.00
1979 (P)	6,577	PF65 5.00				
1980 (U)	385	—	—	—	5.00	6.00
1980 (P)	3,451	PF65 5.00				
1981 (U)	449	—	—	—	5.00	6.00
1981 (P)	1,453	PF65 5.00				

KM# 55 3 MILS

1.45 g., Aluminum, 23.25 mm. **Subject:** 10th Anniversary of Decimalization **Obv:** Bee and honeycomb **Rev:** Value **Shape:** Scalloped

Date	Mintage	VF20	XF40	MS60	MS63	MS65
1982 (U)	850	—	—	—	4.00	5.00
1982 (P)	1,793	PF65 2.00				

KM# 7 5 MILS

2.10 g., Aluminum, 26 mm. **Obv:** Earthen lampstand **Rev:** Value within 3/4 wreath **Shape:** Scalloped

Date	Mintage	VF20	XF40	MS60	MS63	MS65
1972	4,320,000	—	1.00	2.00	3.00	3.50
1972	13,000	PF65 5.00				
1976 (M)	5,000	—	—	—	3.00	3.50
1976 (P)	26,000	PF65 5.00				
1977 (U)	5,252	—	—	—	3.00	3.50
1977 (P)	6,884	PF65 5.00				
1978 (U)	5,252	—	—	—	3.00	3.50
1978 (P)	3,244	PF65 5.00				
1979 (U)	537	—	—	—	7.00	8.00
1979 (P)	6,577	PF65 5.00				
1980 (U)	385	—	—	—	7.00	8.00
1980 (P)	3,451	PF65 5.00				
1981 (U)	449	—	—	—	7.00	8.00
1981 (P)	1,453	PF65 5.00				

KM# 56 5 MILS

2.10 g., Aluminum, 26 mm. **Subject:** 10th Anniversary of Decimalization **Obv:** Earthen lampstand **Rev:** Value **Shape:** Scalloped

Date	Mintage	VF20	XF40	MS60	MS63	MS65
1982 FM (U)	850	—	—	—	—	15.00
1982 FM (P)	1,793	PF65 15.00				

KM# 8 CENT

7.15 g., Bronze, 25.9 mm. **Obv:** The George Cross **Rev:** Value within 3/4 wreath

Date	Mintage	VF20	XF40	MS60	MS63	MS65
1972	5,650,000	—	0.25	0.50	1.00	1.50
1972	13,000	PF65 5.00				
1975	1,500,000	—	0.25	0.50	1.00	1.50
1976 (M)	5,000	—	—	—	5.00	5.50
1976 (P)	26,000	PF65 5.00				
1977	2,793,000	—	0.25	0.50	1.00	1.50
1977 (U)	5,252	—	—	—	4.50	5.50
1977 (P)	6,884	PF65 5.00				
1978 (U)	5,252	—	—	—	4.50	5.50
1978 (P)	3,244	PF65 5.00				
1979 (U)	537	—	—	—	9.00	10.00
1979 (P)	6,577	PF65 5.00				
1980 (U)	385	—	—	—	9.00	10.00
1980 (P)	3,451	PF65 5.00				
1981 (U)	449	—	—	—	9.00	10.00
1981 (P)	1,453	PF65 15.00				
1982	—	—	—	—	10.00	12.00

KM# 57 CENT

7.15 g., Bronze, 25.9 mm. **Subject:** 10th Anniversary of Decimalization **Obv:** The George cross **Rev:** Value

Date	Mintage	VF20	XF40	MS60	MS63	MS65
1982 FM (U)	850	—	—	—	—	15.00
1982 FM (P)	1,793	PF65 15.00				

KM# 9 2 CENTS

2.25 g., Copper-Nickel, 17.78 mm. **Subject:** Penthesilea, Queen of the Amazons **Obv:** Helmeted bust right **Rev:** Value within 3/4 wreath

Date	Mintage	VF20	XF40	MS60	MS63	MS65
1972	5,640,000	—	0.10	0.50	1.00	1.50
1972	13,000	PF65 5.00				
1976	1,000,000	—	1.50	2.00	2.50	3.00
1976 (M)	2,500	—	—	—	4.00	5.00
1976 (P)	—	PF65 5.00				
1977	6,105,000	—	1.50	2.00	2.50	3.00
1977 (U)	2,752	—	—	—	4.00	5.00
1977 (P)	—	PF65 5.00				
1978 (U)	2,752	—	—	—	4.00	5.00
1978 (P)	—	PF65 5.00				
1979 (U)	537	—	—	—	12.00	13.00
1979 (P)	—	PF65 5.00				
1980 (U)	385	—	—	—	12.00	13.00
1980 (P)	—	PF65 5.00				
1981 (U)	449	—	—	—	12.00	13.00
1981 (P)	1,453	PF65 5.00				
1982	—	—	0.10	0.15	0.30	0.50

KM# 58 2 CENTS

2.25 g., Copper-Nickel, 17.75 mm. **Subject:** 10th Anniversary of Decimalization **Obv:** Helmeted bust right **Rev:** Value **Edge:** Reeded

Date	Mintage	VF20	XF40	MS60	MS63	MS65
1982 (U)	850	—	—	—	—	12.00
1982 (P)	1,793	PF65 15.00				

KM# 10 5 CENTS

5.65 g., Copper-Nickel, 23.6 mm. **Obv:** Ritual altar in the Temple of Hagar Qim **Rev:** Value within 3/4 wreath

Date	Mintage	VF20	XF40	MS60	MS63	MS65
1972	4,180,000	—	3.00	4.00	5.00	5.50
1972	13,000	PF65 7.00				
1976	1,009,000	—	1.00	2.00	3.00	3.50
1976 (M)	2,500	—	—	—	5.00	5.50
1976 (P)	26,000	PF65 2.00				
1977	—	—	1.00	2.00	3.00	3.50
1977 (U)	2,752	—	—	—	4.50	5.50
1977 (P)	6,884	PF65 3.00				
1978 (U)	2,752	—	—	—	4.50	5.50
1978 (P)	3,244	PF65 3.00				
1979 (U)	537	—	—	—	15.00	17.00
1979 (P)	6,577	PF65 3.00				
1980 (U)	385	—	—	—	15.00	17.00
1980 (P)	3,451	PF65 3.00				
1981 (P)	1,453	PF65 3.00				
1981 (U)	449	—	—	—	15.00	17.00

KM# 59 5 CENTS

5.65 g., Copper-Nickel, 23.6 mm. **Subject:** 10th Anniversary of Decimalization **Obv:** Floral altar in the Temple of Hagar Qim **Rev:** Value

Date	Mintage	VF20	XF40	MS60	MS63	MS65
1982 (U)	850	—	—	—	—	15.00
1982 (P)	1,793	PF65 3.00				

KM# 11 10 CENTS

11.30 g., Copper-Nickel, 28.5 mm. **Obv:** Barge of the Grand Master **Rev:** Value within 3/4 wreath

Date	Mintage	VF20	XF40	MS60	MS63	MS65
1972	10,680,000	—	4.00	6.00	7.00	8.50
1972	13,000	PF65 2.25				
1976 (M)	1,000	—	—	—	7.00	8.50
1976 (P)	26,000	PF65 2.50				
1977 (U)	1,252	—	—	—	7.00	8.50
1977 (P)	6,884	PF65 3.50				
1978 (U)	1,252	—	—	—	7.00	8.50
1978 (P)	3,244	PF65 3.50				
1979 (U)	537	—	—	—	20.00	22.00
1979 (P)	6,577	PF65 3.50				
1980 (U)	385	—	—	—	20.00	22.00
1980 (P)	3,451	PF65 3.50				
1981 (U)	449	—	—	—	20.00	22.00
1981 (P)	1,453	PF65 3.50				

KM# 60 10 CENTS

11.30 g., Copper-Nickel, 28.5 mm. **Subject:** 10th Anniversary of Decimalization **Obv:** Barge of the grand master **Rev:** Value

Date	Mintage	VF20	XF40	MS60	MS63	MS65
1982 FM (U)	850	—	—	—	25.00	27.00
1982 FM (P)	1,793	PF65 30.00				

KM# 29 25 CENTS
10.55 g., Brass, 30 mm. **Subject:** 1st Anniversary - Republic of Malta **Obv:** Republic emblem within circle **Rev:** Value within 3/4 wreath **Shape:** 8-sided

Date	Mintage	VF20	XF40	MS60	MS63	MS65
1975	4,750,000	—	8.00	9.00	10.00	12.00
1975 Matte proof	—	PF63 200				

KM# 29a 25 CENTS
Bronze, 30 mm. **Obv:** Republic emblem within circle **Rev:** Value within 3/4 wreath

Date	Mintage	VF20	XF40	MS60	MS63	MS65
1975	6,000	PF65 25.00				

KM# 29b 25 CENTS
Copper-Nickel, 30 mm. **Obv:** Republic emblem within circle **Rev:** Value within 3/4 wreath

Date	Mintage	VF20	XF40	MS60	MS63	MS65
1976 FM (M)	300	—	—	—	40.00	45.00
1976 FM (P)	26,000	PF65 3.00				
1977 FM (U)	552	—	—	—	20.00	22.00
1977 FM (P)	6,884	PF65 4.50				
1978 FM (U)	552	—	—	—	20.00	22.00
1978 FM (P)	3,244	PF65 4.50				
1979 FM (U)	537	—	—	—	20.00	22.00
1979 FM (P)	6,577	PF65 4.50				
1980 FM (U)	385	—	—	—	20.00	22.00
1980 FM (P)	3,451	PF65 4.50				
1981 FM (U)	449	—	—	—	20.00	22.00
1981 FM (P)	1,453	PF65 4.50				

KM# 61 25 CENTS
Copper-Nickel, 30 mm. **Subject:** 10th Anniversary of Decimalization **Obv:** Republic emblem within circle **Rev:** Value **Shape:** Octagon

Date	Mintage	VF20	XF40	MS60	MS63	MS65
1982 FM (U)	850	—	—	—	35.00	37.00
1982 FM (P)	1,793	PF65 40.00				

KM# 12 50 CENTS
13.60 g., Copper-Nickel, 32.95 mm. **Obv:** Great Siege Monument **Rev:** Value within 3/4 wreath **Shape:** 10-sided

Date	Mintage	VF20	XF40	MS60	MS63	MS65
1972	5,500,000	—	9.00	12.00	15.00	16.00
1972	13,000	PF65 4.50				
1976 (M)	150	—	—	—	90.00	95.00
1976 (P)	26,000	PF65 5.00				
1977 (U)	402	—	—	—	25.00	27.00
1977 (P)	6,884	PF65 6.00				
1978 (U)	402	—	—	—	25.00	27.00
1978 (P)	3,244	PF65 6.00				
1979 (U)	537	—	—	—	25.00	27.00
1979 (P)	6,577	PF65 6.00				
1980 (U)	385	—	—	—	25.00	27.00
1980 (P)	3,451	PF65 6.00				
1981 (U)	449	—	—	—	25.00	27.00
1981 (P)	1,453	PF65 6.00				

KM# 62 50 CENTS
13.60 g., Copper-Nickel, 32.95 mm. **Subject:** 10th Anniversary of Decimalization **Obv:** Great Siege Monument **Rev:** Value **Shape:** 10-sided

Date	Mintage	VF20	XF40	MS60	MS63	MS65
1982 (U)	850	—	—	—	40.00	42.00
1982 (P)	1,793	PF65 40.00				

KM# 13 POUND
10.00 g., 0.987 Silver 0.3173 oz. ASW **Obv:** Crowned arms with supporters **Rev:** Bust left

Date	Mintage	VF20	XF40	MS60	MS63	MS65
1972	55,000	—	—	15.00	16.00	18.00

Note: Appears to be proof, but officially issued as "BU"

KM# 19 POUND
10.00 g., 0.987 Silver 0.3173 oz. ASW, 32 mm. **Obv:** Crowned arms with supporters **Rev:** Bust left **Edge:** Reeded

Date	Mintage	VF20	XF40	MS60	MS63	MS65
1973	30,000	—	—	15.00	16.00	18.00

KM# 45 POUND
5.66 g., 0.925 Silver 0.1683 oz. ASW **Obv:** Republic emblem within circle **Rev:** Dog

Date	Mintage	VF20	XF40	MS60	MS63	MS65
1977	66,000	—	—	30.00	35.00	45.00
1977	2,500	PF65 65.00				

KM# 51 POUND
5.66 g., 0.925 Silver 0.1683 oz. ASW **Subject:** Departure of foreign forces **Obv:** Republic emblem within circle **Rev:** Flames within helping hands divide date and value

Date	Mintage	VF20	XF40	MS60	MS63	MS65
1979 FM (U)	49,526	—	—	25.00	30.00	35.00
1979 FM (P)	7,871	PF65 45.00				

KM# 14 2 POUNDS
20.00 g., 0.987 Silver 0.6347 oz. ASW, 38 mm. **Obv:** Crowned arms with supporters **Rev:** Fort San Angelo

Date	Mintage	VF20	XF40	MS60	MS63	MS65
1972	53,000	—	—	30.00	35.00	40.00

Note: Appears to be proof, but officially issued as "BU"

KM# 20 2 POUNDS
20.00 g., 0.987 Silver 0.6347 oz. ASW, 38 mm. **Rev:** Tal-Imdina Gate

Date	Mintage	VF20	XF40	MS60	MS63	MS65
1973	30,000	—	—	35.00	40.00	45.00

KM# 24 2 POUNDS
10.00 g., 0.987 Silver 0.3173 oz. ASW **Obv:** Crowned arms with supporters **Rev:** Bust 1/4 left

Date	Mintage	VF20	XF40	MS60	MS63	MS65
1974	25,000	—	—	16.00	18.00	20.00
1974	—	PF65 25.00				

KM# 30 2 POUNDS
10.00 g., 0.987 Silver 0.3173 oz. ASW **Obv:** Crowned arms with supporters **Rev:** Bust left

Date	Mintage	VF20	XF40	MS60	MS63	MS65
1975	2,000	—	—	65.00	70.00	75.00

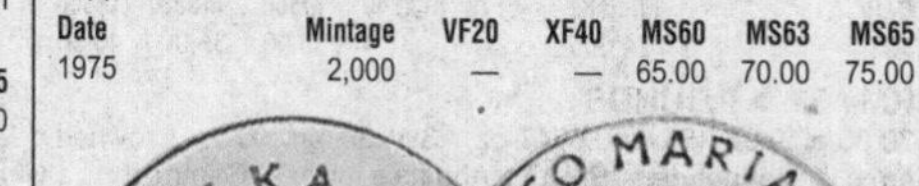

KM# 31 2 POUNDS
10.00 g., 0.987 Silver 0.3173 oz. ASW **Obv:** Republic emblem within circle **Rev:** Bust left

Date	Mintage	VF20	XF40	MS60	MS63	MS65
1975	18,000	—	—	16.00	18.00	20.00

KM# 40 2 POUNDS

10.00 g., 0.987 Silver 0.3173 oz. ASW **Obv:** Republic emblem within circle **Rev:** Bust 1/4 right

Date	Mintage	VF20	XF40	MS60	MS63	MS65
1976	11,000	—	—	20.00	23.00	25.00

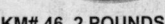

KM# 46 2 POUNDS

11.31 g., 0.925 Silver 0.3364 oz. ASW **Obv:** Republic emblem within circle **Rev:** Bust left

Date	Mintage	VF20	XF40	MS60	MS63	MS65
1977	15,000	—	—	—	35.00	40.00
1977	3,692	PF65 70.00				

KM# 52 2 POUNDS

11.31 g., 0.925 Silver 0.3364 oz. ASW **Series:** World Food Day **Obv:** Republic emblem within circle **Rev:** Men fishing in boat below small emblem

Date	Mintage	VF20	XF40	MS60	MS63	MS65
1981	1,500	—	—	—	22.00	25.00
1981	12,000	PF65 75.00				

KM# 25 4 POUNDS

20.00 g., 0.987 Silver 0.6347 oz. ASW, 38 mm. **Obv:** Crowned arms with supporters **Rev:** Cottonera Gate

Date	Mintage	VF20	XF40	MS60	MS63	MS65
1974	24,000	—	—	30.00	35.00	40.00

KM# 32 4 POUNDS

20.00 g., 0.987 Silver 0.6347 oz. ASW, 38 mm. **Obv:** Crowned arms with supporters **Rev:** St. Agatha's tower at Gammieh

Date	Mintage	VF20	XF40	MS60	MS63	MS65
1975	2,000	—	—	135	140	150

KM# 33 4 POUNDS

20.00 g., 0.987 Silver 0.6347 oz. ASW **Obv:** Republic emblem within circle **Rev:** St. Agatha's Tower at Gammieh

Date	Mintage	VF20	XF40	MS60	MS63	MS65
1975	18,000	—	—	30.00	35.00	40.00

KM# 41 4 POUNDS

20.00 g., 0.987 Silver 0.6347 oz. ASW **Obv:** Republic emblem **Rev:** Fort Manoel Gate

Date	Mintage	VF20	XF40	MS60	MS63	MS65
1976	10,000	—	—	35.00	40.00	45.00

KM# 15 5 POUNDS

3.00 g., 0.916 Gold 0.0884 oz. AGW **Obv:** Crowned arms with supporters **Rev:** Hand holding torch within map of Malta

Date	Mintage	VF20	XF40	MS60	MS63	MS65
1972	18,000	—	—	—	—	180

Note: Appears to be proof, but officially issued as "BU"

KM# 47 5 POUNDS

28.28 g., 0.925 Silver 0.841 oz. ASW **Obv:** Republic emblem **Rev:** Windmill divides date and value

Date	Mintage	VF20	XF40	MS60	MS63	MS65
1977	15,000	—	—	—	—	75.00
1977	3,938	PF65 150				

KM# 53 5 POUNDS

28.28 g., 0.925 Silver 0.841 oz. ASW **Subject:** International Youth Conference - UNICEF **Obv:** Republic emblem **Rev:** Kids playing game on numeral board flanked by UNICEF emblems

Date	Mintage	VF20	XF40	MS60	MS63	MS65
1981	11,000	PF65 120				

KM# 16 10 POUNDS

6.00 g., 0.917 Gold 0.1769 oz. AGW **Obv:** Crowned arms with supporters **Rev:** Kenur, a Maltese stone charcoal stove

Date	Mintage	VF20	XF40	MS60	MS63	MS65
1972	16,000	—	—	—	—	325

Note: Appears to be proof, but officially issued as "BU"

KM# 21 10 POUNDS

3.00 g., 0.917 Gold 0.0884 oz. AGW **Obv:** Crowned arms with supporters **Rev:** Watchtower

Date	Mintage	VF20	XF40	MS60	MS63	MS65
1973	9,078	—	—	—	—	175

KM# 26 10 POUNDS

3.00 g., 0.917 Gold 0.0884 oz. AGW **Obv:** Crowned arms with supporters **Rev:** Zerafa flower flanked by date and value

Date	Mintage	VF20	XF40	MS60	MS63	MS65
1974	9,124	—	—	—	—	175

KM# 34 10 POUNDS

3.00 g., 0.917 Gold 0.0884 oz. AGW **Obv:** Crowned arms with supporters **Rev:** Falcon

Date	Mintage	VF20	XF40	MS60	MS63	MS65
1975	2,000	—	—	—	—	175

KM# 35 10 POUNDS

3.00 g., 0.917 Gold 0.0884 oz. AGW **Obv:** Republic emblem within circle **Rev:** Maltese falcon

Date	Mintage	VF20	XF40	MS60	MS63	MS65
1975	6,448	—	—	—	—	175

KM# 42 10 POUNDS

3.00 g., 0.917 Gold 0.0884 oz. AGW **Obv:** Republic emblem within circle **Rev:** Swallowtail butterfly above value

Date	Mintage	VF20	XF40	MS60	MS63	MS65
1976	4,448	—	—	—	—	175

KM# 17 20 POUNDS

12.00 g., 0.917 Gold 0.3538 oz. AGW **Obv:** Crowned arms with supporters **Rev:** Merill bird

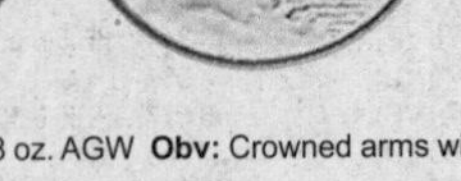

Date	Mintage	VF20	XF40	MS60	MS63	MS65
1972	16,000	—	—	—	—	700

Note: Appears to be proof, but officially issued as "BU"

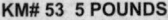

KM# 22 20 POUNDS
6.00 g., 0.917 Gold 0.1769 oz. AGW **Obv:** Crowned arms with supporters **Rev:** Dolphins Fountain at Floriana

Date	Mintage	VF20	XF40	MS60	MS63	MS65
1973	9,075	—	—	—	—	325

KM# 27 20 POUNDS
6.00 g., 0.917 Gold 0.1769 oz. AGW **Obv:** Crowned arms with supporters **Rev:** Gozo boat with lateen sails

Date	Mintage	VF20	XF40	MS60	MS63	MS65
1974	8,700	—	—	—	—	325

KM# 36 20 POUNDS
6.00 g., 0.917 Gold 0.1769 oz. AGW **Obv:** Crowned arms with supporters **Rev:** Freshwater crab

Date	Mintage	VF20	XF40	MS60	MS63	MS65
1975	2,000	—	—	—	—	350

KM# 37 20 POUNDS
6.00 g., 0.917 Gold 0.1769 oz. AGW **Obv:** Republic emblem within circle **Rev:** Fresh water crab

Date	Mintage	VF20	XF40	MS60	MS63	MS65
1975	5,698	—	—	—	—	335

KM# 43 20 POUNDS
6.00 g., 0.917 Gold 0.1769 oz. AGW **Obv:** Republic emblem within circle **Rev:** Storm petrel bird

Date	Mintage	VF20	XF40	MS60	MS63	MS65
1976	4,098	—	—	—	—	335

KM# 48 25 POUNDS
7.99 g., 0.917 Gold 0.2356 oz. AGW **Subject:** First Gozo coin **Obv:** Republic emblem within circle **Rev:** Figure holding lance facing right within circle

Date	Mintage	VF20	XF40	MS60	MS63	MS65
1977	4,000	—	—	—	—	550
1977	3,249	PF65 700				

KM# 18 50 POUNDS
30.00 g., 0.917 Gold 0.8845 oz. AGW **Obv:** Crowned arms with supporters **Rev:** Neptune divides date and value

Date	Mintage	VF20	XF40	MS60	MS63	MS65
1972	16,000	—	—	1,250	1,550	1,800

Note: Appears to be proof, but officially issued as "BU"

KM# 23 50 POUNDS
15.00 g., 0.917 Gold 0.4422 oz. AGW **Subject:** Auberge de Castille at Valletta **Obv:** Crowned arms with supporters **Rev:** Building with small flag on top above date and value

Date	Mintage	VF20	XF40	MS60	MS63	MS65
1973	9,075	—	—	—	—	800

KM# 28 50 POUNDS
15.00 g., 0.917 Gold 0.4422 oz. AGW **Subject:** First Maltese coin **Obv:** Crowned arms with supporters **Rev:** Design within wreath

Date	Mintage	VF20	XF40	MS60	MS63	MS65
1974	8,667	—	—	—	—	800

KM# 38 50 POUNDS
15.00 g., 0.917 Gold 0.4422 oz. AGW **Obv:** Crowned arms with supporters **Rev:** Ornamental stone balcony

Date	Mintage	VF20	XF40	MS60	MS63	MS65
1975	2,000	—	—	—	—	800

KM# 39 50 POUNDS
15.00 g., 0.917 Gold 0.4422 oz. AGW **Obv:** Republic emblem within circle **Rev:** Ornamental stone balcony

Date	Mintage	VF20	XF40	MS60	MS63	MS65
1975	5,500	—	—	—	—	800

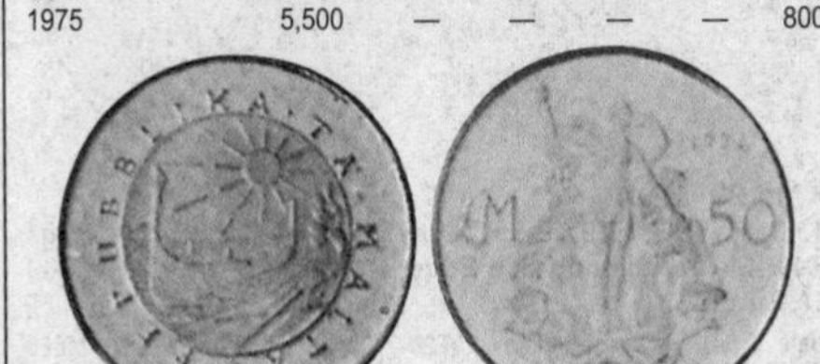

KM# 44 50 POUNDS
15.00 g., 0.917 Gold 0.4422 oz. AGW **Obv:** Republic emblem **Rev:** Ornamental door knocker

Date	Mintage	VF20	XF40	MS60	MS63	MS65
1976	3,748	—	—	—	—	800

KM# 49 50 POUNDS
15.98 g., 0.917 Gold 0.4711 oz. AGW **Subject:** Mnara **Obv:** Republic emblem within circle **Rev:** Mnara design flanked by value above date

Date	Mintage	VF20	XF40	MS60	MS63	MS65
1977	4,000	—	—	—	—	950
1977	846	PF65 1,250				

KM# 50 100 POUNDS
31.96 g., 0.917 Gold 0.9423 oz. AGW **Rev:** Father and two children sculpture above value

Date	Mintage	VF20	XF40	MS60	MS63	MS65
1977	4,000	—	—	—	—	1,850
1977	846	PF65 2,250				

REFORM COINAGE

1982 - Present;
10 Mils = 1 Cent; 100 Cents = 1 Lira

KM# 78 CENT
2.81 g., Nickel-Brass, 18.51 mm. **Obv:** Republic emblem within circle **Rev:** Common weasel (ballottra) below value **Edge:** Plain

Date	Mintage	VF20	XF40	MS60	MS63	MS65
1986	21,526,000	—	0.40	0.50	1.00	1.25
1986	10,000	PF65 5.00				

KM# 93 CENT
2.81 g., Nickel-Brass, 18.51 mm. **Obv:** Crowned shield within sprigs **Rev:** Common Weasel (ballottra) below value **Edge:** Plain

Date	Mintage	VF20	XF40	MS60	MS63	MS65
1991	—	—	0.40	0.50	1.00	1.25
1995	—	—	0.40	0.50	1.00	1.25
1998	—	—	0.40	0.50	1.00	1.25

KM# 79 2 CENTS
2.26 g., Copper-Nickel, 17.78 mm. **Obv:** Republic emblem within circle **Rev:** Zebbuga branch and value **Edge:** Reeded

Date	Mintage	VF20	XF40	MS60	MS63	MS65
1986	280,000	—	1.25	1.50	2.00	2.50
1986	10,000	PF65 6.00				

KM# 94 2 CENTS
2.26 g., Copper-Nickel, 17.78 mm. **Obv:** Crowned shield within sprigs **Rev:** Zebbuga branch and value **Edge:** Reeded

Date	Mintage	VF20	XF40	MS60	MS63	MS65
1991	—	—	0.75	1.00	1.25	1.50
1992	—	—	0.75	1.00	1.25	1.50
1993	—	—	0.75	1.00	1.25	1.50
1995	—	—	0.75	1.00	1.25	1.50
1998	—	—	0.75	1.00	1.25	1.50

KM# 77 5 CENTS

3.51 g., Copper-Nickel, 19.78 mm. **Obv:** Republic emblem within circle **Rev:** Freshwater crab (il-qobru) and value **Edge:** Reeded

Date	Mintage	VF20	XF40	MS60	MS63	MS65
1986	150,000	—	0.75	1.00	1.25	2.00
1986	10,000	PF65 7.00				

KM# 95 5 CENTS

3.51 g., Copper-Nickel, 19.78 mm. **Obv:** Crowned shield within sprigs **Rev:** Freshwater Crab (il-Qobru) and value **Edge:** Reeded

Date	Mintage	VF20	XF40	MS60	MS63	MS65
1991	—	—	0.75	1.00	1.25	2.00
1995	—	—	0.75	1.00	1.25	2.00
1998	—	—	0.75	1.00	1.25	2.00

KM# 76 10 CENTS

5.01 g., Copper-Nickel, 21.78 mm. **Obv:** Republic emblem within circle **Rev:** Lampuka and value **Edge:** Reeded

Date	Mintage	VF20	XF40	MS60	MS63	MS65
1986	4,188,000	—	1.25	1.50	2.00	2.50
1986	10,000	PF65 8.00				

KM# 96 10 CENTS

5.01 g., Copper-Nickel, 21.78 mm. **Obv:** Crowned shield within sprigs **Rev:** Lampuka and value **Edge:** Reeded

Date	Mintage	VF20	XF40	MS60	MS63	MS65
1991	—	—	1.25	1.50	2.00	2.50
1992	—	—	1.25	1.50	2.00	2.50
1995	—	—	1.25	1.50	2.00	2.50
1998	—	—	1.25	1.50	2.00	2.50

KM# 80 25 CENTS

6.19 g., Copper-Nickel, 24.95 mm. **Obv:** Republic embem within circle **Rev:** Ghirlanda flower and value

Date	Mintage	VF20	XF40	MS60	MS63	MS65
1986	3,090,000	—	5.00	8.00	10.00	12.00
1986	10,000	PF65 10.00				

KM# 97 25 CENTS

6.19 g., Copper-Nickel, 24.95 mm. **Obv:** Crowned shield within sprigs **Rev:** Ghirlanda flower and value

Date	Mintage	VF20	XF40	MS60	MS63	MS65
1991	—	—	2.25	2.50	3.00	3.50
1993	—	—	2.25	2.50	3.00	3.50
1995	—	—	2.25	2.50	3.00	3.50
1998	—	—	2.25	2.50	3.00	3.50

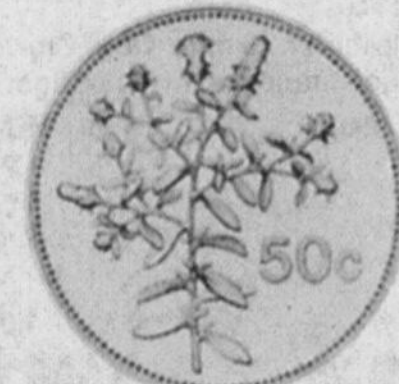

KM# 81 50 CENTS

8.00 g., Copper-Nickel, 27 mm. **Obv:** Republic emblem within circle **Rev:** Tulliera plant and value **Edge Lettering:** BANK CENTRALI TA' MALTA

Date	Mintage	VF20	XF40	MS60	MS63	MS65
1986	2,086,000	—	10.00	13.00	15.00	17.00
1986	10,000	PF65 15.00				

KM# 98 50 CENTS

8.00 g., Copper-Nickel, 27 mm. **Obv:** Crowned shield within sprigs **Rev:** Tulliera plant and value **Edge Lettering:** BANK CENTRALI TA' MALTA

Date	Mintage	VF20	XF40	MS60	MS63	MS65
1991	—	—	2.50	4.50	6.00	7.00
1992	—	—	2.50	4.50	6.00	7.00
1995	—	—	2.50	5.00	7.00	8.00
1998	—	—	2.50	5.00	7.00	8.00

KM# 63 LIRA

Copper-Nickel **Subject:** World Fisheries Conference **Rev:** Man in boat with fishing traps

Date	Mintage	VF20	XF40	MS60	MS63	MS65
ND-1984	120,000	—	—	—	20.00	22.00

KM# 82 LIRA

13.00 g., Nickel, 29.82 mm. **Obv:** Republic emblem within circle **Rev:** Merill bird and value **Edge Lettering:** BANK CENTRALI TA' MALTA

Date	Mintage	VF20	XF40	MS60	MS63	MS65
1986	2,272,000	—	—	14.00	16.00	18.00
1986	10,000	PF65 20.00				

KM# 99 LIRA

13.00 g., Nickel, 29.82 mm. **Obv:** Crowned shield within sprigs **Rev:** Merill bird and value **Edge Lettering:** BANK CENTRALI TA' MALTA

Date	Mintage	VF20	XF40	MS60	MS63	MS65
1991	—	—	—	4.00	6.00	9.00
1992	—	—	—	4.00	6.00	9.00
1994	—	—	—	4.00	6.00	9.00
1995	—	—	—	4.50	6.50	10.00
2000	—	—	—	4.50	6.50	10.00

KM# 88 2 LIRI

17.00 g., 0.925 Silver 0.5056 oz. ASW **Subject:** 25th Anniversary of Independence **Obv:** Crowned shield within sprigs **Rev:** Bust 1/4 right flanked by dates and value

Date	Mintage	VF20	XF40	MS60	MS63	MS65
1989	75,000	—	—	—	22.00	25.00
1989	7,500	PF65 65.00				

KM# 65 5 LIRI

28.28 g., 0.925 Silver 0.841 oz. ASW **Series:** International Year of Disabled Persons **Obv:** Republic emblem **Rev:** Disabled person design, date and value within

Date	Mintage	VF20	XF40	MS60	MS63	MS65
1983	—	—	—	—	40.00	65.00
1983	—	PF65 125				

KM# 64 5 LIRI

28.28 g., 0.925 Silver 0.841 oz. ASW **Subject:** World Fisheries Conference **Obv:** Republic emblem **Rev:** Man in boat with fishing traps

Date	Mintage	VF20	XF40	MS60	MS63	MS65
ND-1984	20,000	PF65 125				

KM# 67 5 LIRI

20.00 g., 0.925 Silver 0.5948 oz. ASW **Subject:** Maritime history "Strangier" (1813) **Obv:** Republic emblem within circle **Rev:** Saling ship among grid lines

Date	Mintage	VF20	XF40	MS60	MS63	MS65
1984 Prooflike	15,000	—	—	—	45.00	55.00

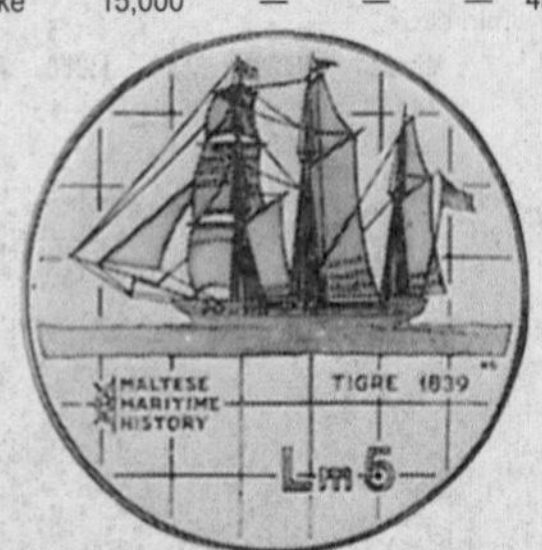

KM# 68 5 LIRI

20.00 g., 0.925 Silver 0.5948 oz. ASW, 34 mm. **Subject:** Maritime history **Obv:** Republic emblem **Rev:** "Tigre" (1839) **Edge:** Reeded

Date	Mintage	VF20	XF40	MS60	MS63	MS65
1984 Prooflike	15,000	—	—	—	45.00	55.00

KM# 69 5 LIRI

20.00 g., 0.925 Silver 0.5948 oz. ASW, 34 mm. **Subject:** Maritime history **Obv:** Republic emblem **Rev:** "Wignacourt" (1844) **Edge:** Reeded

Date	Mintage	VF20	XF40	MS60	MS63	MS65
1984 Prooflike	15,000	—	—	—	45.00	55.00

KM# 70 5 LIRI

20.00 g., 0.925 Silver 0.5948 oz. ASW, 34 mm. **Subject:** Maritime history **Obv:** Republic emblem **Rev:** "Providenza" (1848) **Edge:** Reeded

Date	Mintage	VF20	XF40	MS60	MS63	MS65
1984 Prooflike	15,000	—	—	—	45.00	55.00

KM# 71 5 LIRI

28.28 g., 0.925 Silver 0.841 oz. ASW **Series:** Decade for Women **Obv:** Republic emblem **Rev:** Woman weaving on board within circle

Date	Mintage	VF20	XF40	MS60	MS63	MS65
1984	17,000	PF65 75.00				

KM# 72 5 LIRI

20.00 g., 0.925 Silver 0.5948 oz. ASW **Subject:** Maritime history **Obv:** Republic emblem **Rev:** "Malta" (1862)

Date	Mintage	VF20	XF40	MS60	MS63	MS65
1985 Prooflike	15,000	—	—	—	45.00	55.00

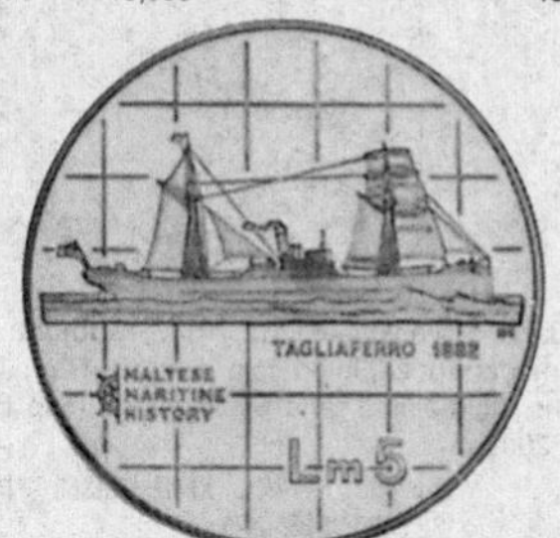

KM# 73 5 LIRI

20.00 g., 0.925 Silver 0.5948 oz. ASW **Subject:** Maritime history **Obv:** Republic emblem **Rev:** "Tagliaferro" (1882)

Date	Mintage	VF20	XF40	MS60	MS63	MS65
1985 Prooflike	15,000	—	—	—	45.00	55.00

KM# 74 5 LIRI

20.00 g., 0.925 Silver 0.5948 oz. ASW **Subject:** Maritime history **Obv:** Republic emblem **Rev:** "L'Isle Adam" (1883)

Date	Mintage	VF20	XF40	MS60	MS63	MS65
1985 Prooflike	15,000	—	—	—	45.00	55.00

KM# 75 5 LIRI

20.00 g., 0.925 Silver 0.5948 oz. ASW **Subject:** Maritime history **Obv:** Republic emblem **Rev:** "Maria Dacoutros" (1902)

Date	Mintage	VF20	XF40	MS60	MS63	MS65
1985 Prooflike	15,000	—	—	—	45.00	55.00

KM# 83 5 LIRI

20.00 g., 0.925 Silver 0.5948 oz. ASW **Subject:** Maritime history **Obv:** Republic emblem **Rev:** "Valetta City" (1917)

Date	Mintage	VF20	XF40	MS60	MS63	MS65
1986 Prooflike	15,000	—	—	—	45.00	55.00

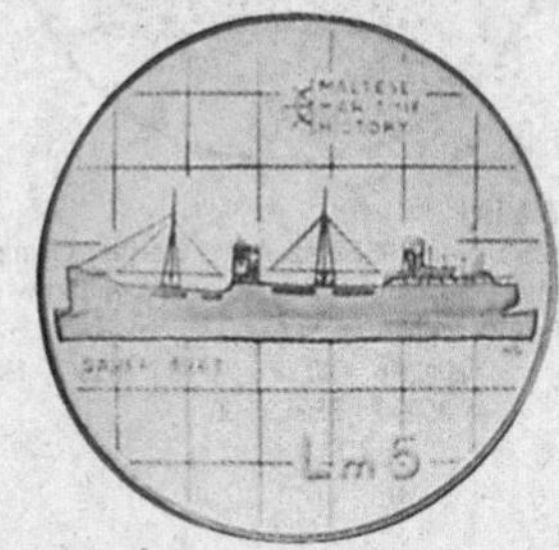

KM# 84 5 LIRI

20.00 g., 0.925 Silver 0.5948 oz. ASW **Subject:** Maritime history **Obv:** Republic emblem **Rev:** "Knight of Malta" (1929)

Date	Mintage	VF20	XF40	MS60	MS63	MS65
1986 Prooflike	15,000	—	—	—	45.00	55.00

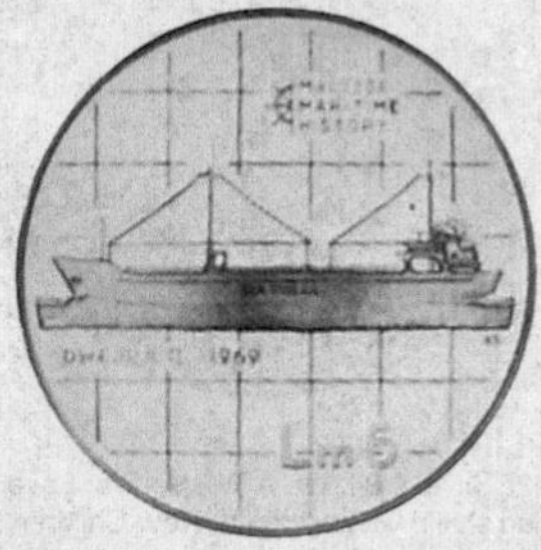

KM# 85 5 LIRI

20.00 g., 0.925 Silver 0.5948 oz. ASW **Subject:** Maritime history **Obv:** Republic emblem **Rev:** "Saver" (1943)

Date	Mintage	VF20	XF40	MS60	MS63	MS65
1986 Prooflike	15,000	—	—	—	45.00	55.00

KM# 86 5 LIRI

20.00 g., 0.925 Silver 0.5948 oz. ASW **Subject:** Maritime history **Obv:** Republic emblem **Rev:** "Dwejra II" (1969)

Date	Mintage	VF20	XF40	MS60	MS63	MS65
1986 Prooflike	15,000	—	—	—	45.00	55.00

KM# 87 5 LIRI

28.28 g., 0.925 Silver 0.841 oz. ASW **Subject:** 20th Anniversary - Central Bank of Malta **Obv:** Crowned arms with supporters **Rev:** Bank of Malta

Date	Mintage	VF20	XF40	MS60	MS63	MS65
1988	Est. 5000	—	—	—	—	60.00
1988	Est. 2000	PF65 110				

KM# 90 5 LIRI

28.60 g., 0.925 Silver 0.8505 oz. ASW **Subject:** Papal visit **Obv:** Crowned shield within sprigs **Rev:** Pope's hand with staff, city scene in background

Date	Mintage	VF20	XF40	MS60	MS63	MS65
1990	5,000	—	—	—	—	80.00
1990	4,000	PF65 150				

KM# 91 5 LIRI

28.28 g., 0.925 Silver 0.841 oz. ASW **Subject:** Entry of Malta to European Economic Community **Rev:** Two flags among the map of Malta

Date	Mintage	VF20	XF40	MS60	MS63	MS65
1990	—	—	—	—	—	50.00
1990	4,000	PF65 90.00				

KM# 92 5 LIRI
28.28 g., 0.925 Silver 0.841 oz. ASW **Series:** Save the Children **Obv:** Crowned shield within wreath **Rev:** Children playing

Date	Mintage	VF20	XF40	MS60	MS63	MS65
1991	20,000	PF65 90.00				

KM# 100 5 LIRI
28.28 g., 0.925 Silver 0.841 oz. ASW **Subject:** 50th Anniversary of George Cross Award **Obv:** Crowned shield within wreath **Rev:** George cross award

Date	Mintage	VF20	XF40	MS60	MS63	MS65
1992	—	—	—	—	—	70.00
1992	10,000	PF65 120				

KM# 102 5 LIRI
28.28 g., 0.925 Silver 0.841 oz. ASW **Subject:** 25th Anniversary of Central Bank **Obv:** Arms above Central Bank building **Rev:** Bust facing

Date	Mintage	VF20	XF40	MS60	MS63	MS65
ND (1993)	—	—	—	—	—	45.00
ND-1993	1,500	PF65 85.00				

KM# 106 5 LIRI
28.28 g., 0.925 Silver 0.841 oz. ASW **Subject:** 400th Anniversary - University of Malta **Obv:** University emblems above crowned shield within sprigs flanked by dates **Rev:** Conjoined armored busts left

Date	Mintage	VF20	XF40	MS60	MS63	MS65
ND-1993	Est. 1000	PF65 250				

KM# 107 5 LIRI
28.28 g., 0.925 Silver 0.841 oz. ASW **Subject:** World Cup Soccer **Obv:** Crowned shield within wreath **Rev:** Goalie catching ball

Date	Mintage	VF20	XF40	MS60	MS63	MS65
1993	Est. 20000	PF65 95.00				

KM# 108 5 LIRI
31.47 g., 0.925 Silver 0.9359 oz. ASW **Obv:** Crowned shield within wreath **Rev:** Sailing ship "Valletta" and fortress

Date	Mintage	VF20	XF40	MS60	MS63	MS65
1994	Est. 20000	PF65 125				

KM# 109 5 LIRI
28.28 g., 0.925 Silver 0.841 oz. ASW **Series:** 50th Anniversary - United Nations **Obv:** Crowned shield within wreath **Rev:** Small UN logo above two half figures shaking hands, all within circle

Date	Mintage	VF20	XF40	MS60	MS63	MS65
1995	125,000	PF65 95.00				

KM# 110 5 LIRI
31.47 g., 0.925 Silver 0.9359 oz. ASW **Series:** Olympic Games **Subject:** Water polo **Obv:** Crowned shield within wreath **Rev:** Men playing water volley ball

Date	Mintage	VF20	XF40	MS60	MS63	MS65
1996	Est. 35000	PF65 95.00				

KM# 115 5 LIRI
28.28 g., 0.925 Silver 0.841 oz. ASW, 38.6 mm. **Subject:** UNICEF **Obv:** Crowned shield within wreath **Rev:** Boy with dog and computer **Edge:** Reeded

Date	Mintage	VF20	XF40	MS60	MS63	MS65
1997	25,000	PF65 115				

KM# 111 5 LIRI
28.28 g., 0.925 Silver 0.841 oz. ASW **Obv:** Crowned shield within wreath **Rev:** Bank's pyramid fountain

Date	Mintage	VF20	XF40	MS60	MS63	MS65
1998	1,500	PF65 125				

KM# 112 5 LIRI
28.28 g., 0.925 Silver 0.841 oz. ASW **Subject:** 200th Anniversary - Anti-French Revolution **Obv:** National arms **Rev:** "Blockade" medal of 1798

Date	Mintage	VF20	XF40	MS60	MS63	MS65
1998	1,500	PF65 95.00				

KM# 113 5 LIRI
28.35 g., 0.925 Silver 0.8431 oz. ASW, 38.4 mm. **Subject:** Mattia Preti **Obv:** Crowned shield within wreath **Rev:** Portrait of Preti and John the Baptist **Edge:** Reeded

Date	Mintage	VF20	XF40	MS60	MS63	MS65
1999	5,000	PF65 125				

KM# 114 5 LIRI
15.00 g., 0.925 Silver 0.4461 oz. ASW **Subject:** Millennium **Obv:** Two modern gold-plated coin designs **Rev:** Two ancient coin designs, gold-plated, and Malta Island map **Edge:** Plain **Note:** 40 x 20mm.

Date	Mintage	VF20	XF40	MS60	MS63	MS65
2000	32,000	PF65 225				

KM# 101 25 LIRI
7.99 g., 0.917 Gold 0.2356 oz. AGW **Subject:** 50th Anniversary of George Cross Award **Obv:** Crowned shield within wreath **Rev:** George cross award

Date	Mintage	VF20	XF40	MS60	MS63	MS65
1992	Est. 500	PF65 700				

KM# 66 100 LIRI
15.98 g., 0.917 Gold 0.4711 oz. AGW **Series:** International Year of Disabled Persons **Obv:** Republic emblem within circle **Rev:** Puzzle head right with missing pieces on top

Date	Mintage	VF20	XF40	MS60	MS63	MS65
1983	700	—	—	—	—	850
1983	600	PF65 1,150				

KM# 89 100 LIRI
17.00 g., 0.917 Gold 0.5012 oz. AGW **Subject:** 25th Anniversary of Independence **Obv:** Crowned shield within sprigs **Rev:** Bust 1/4 right flanked by dates and value

Date	Mintage	VF20	XF40	MS60	MS63	MS65
1989	5,000	—	—	—	—	800
1989	2,500	PF65 950				

ECU / LIRA COINAGE

European Currency Unit

KM# 103 LIRA (2 Ecu)
Copper-Nickel **Subject:** Defense of Europe **Obv:** Crowned shield within sprigs **Rev:** Cluster of sailing ships within circle

Date	Mintage	VF20	XF40	MS60	MS63	MS65
1993	25,000	—	—	—	—	28.00

KM# 104 5 LIRI (10 Ecu)
25.00 g., 0.925 Silver 0.7435 oz. ASW **Subject:** Defense of Europe **Obv:** Crowned shield within wreath **Rev:** Ships at sea

Date	Mintage	VF20	XF40	MS60	MS63	MS65
1993	35,000	PF65 75.00				

KM# 105 25 LIRI (55 Ecu)
6.72 g., 0.900 Gold 0.1944 oz. AGW **Subject:** Defense of Europe

Date	Mintage	VF20	XF40	MS60	MS63	MS65
1993	2,500	PF65 450				

PIEDFORT

KM#	Date	Mintage	Identification	Mkt Val
P1	1981	177	5 Liri. 0.925. Silver. KM53.	525
P2	1983	700	5 Liri. 0.925. Silver. KM65.	425
P3	1983	—	100 Pounds. 0.917. Gold. KM66.	1,750
P4	1988	500	5 Liri. 0.925. Silver. KM87.	285

MINT SETS

KM#	Date	Mintage	Identification	Issue Price	Mkt Val
MS1	1972 (8)	8,000	KM5-12	—	35.00
MS2	1972 (4)	8,000	KM15-18	210	3,400
MS3	1972 (2)	—	KM13-14	8.50	45.00
MS4	1973 (3)	9,078	KM21-23	—	1,600
MS5	1973 (2)	—	KM19-20	—	55.00
MS6	1974 (3)	—	KM26-28	256	1,600
MS7	1974 (2)	—	KM24-25	19.60	55.00
MS8	1975 (5)	2,000	KM30, 32, 34, 36, 38	276	1,850
MS9	1975 (3)	—	KM34, 36, 38	256	1,600
MSA10	1975 (2)	—	KM31, 33	—	55.00
MS10	1975 (2)	2,000	KM30, 32	20.00	225
MS11	1975 (3)	—	KM35, 37, 39	—	1,600
MS12	1976 (3)	—	KM42-44	—	1,600
MS13	1976 (2)	—	KM40-41	—	75.00
MS14	1977 (9)	252	KM5-12, 29b	—	125
MS15	1977 (3)	4,000	KM48-50	610	4,350
MS16	1977 (3)	15,000	KM45-47	34.50	100
MS17	1978 (9)	252	KM5-12, 29b	—	125
MS18	1979 (9)	537	KM5-12, 29b	—	125
MS19	1980 (9)	385	KM5-12, 29b	11.00	125
MS20	1981 (9)	449	KM5-12, 29b	13.25	125
MS21	1982 (9)	850	KM54-62	13.25	175
MS22	1984 (4)	15,000	KM67-70	72.00	200
MS23	1985 (4)	15,000	KM72-75	72.00	200
MS24	1986 (4)	15,000	KM83-86	72.00	200
MS25	1995 (7)	—	KM#93-97, 99, 116	—	60.00

PROOF SETS

KM#	Date	Mintage	Identification	Issue Price	Mkt Val
PS1	1972 (8)	8,000	KM5-12; plastic case	—	55.00
PS2	1976 (9)	26,248	KM5-12, 29b	27.50	35.00
PS3	1977 (9)	6,884	KM5-12, 29b	31.50	55.00
PS4	1977 (3)	750	KM48-50	909	4,900
PS5	1977 (3)	2,500	KM45-47	72.00	225
PS6	1978 (9)	3,244	KM5-12, 29b	—	65.00
PS7	1979 (10)	6,577	KM5-12, 29b, 51	41.50	50.00
PS8	1980 (9)	3,451	KM5-12, 29b	30.00	65.00
PS9	1981 (9)	1,453	KM5-12, 29b	25.30	85.00
PS10	1982 (9)	1,793	KM54-62	32.00	150
PS11	1986 (7)	10,000	KM76-82	29.75	75.00

MARSHALL ISLANDS

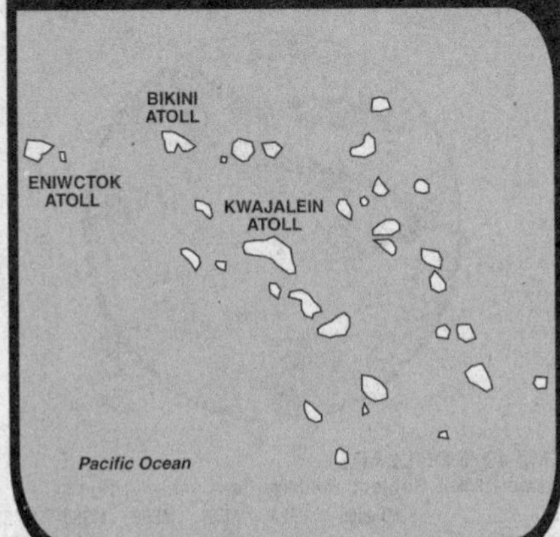

The Republic of the Marshall Islands, an archipelago which is one of the four island groups that make up what is commonly known as Micronesia, consists of 33 coral atolls comprised of over 1,150 islands or islets. It is located east of the Caroline Islands and west-northwest of the Gilbert Islands halfway between Hawaii and Australia. The Ratak chain to the east and the Ralik chain to the west comprise a total land area of 70 sq. mi. (181 sq. km.) with a population of 25,000 of which about 10 % includes Americans who work at the Kwajalein Missile Range. Majuro Atoll is the government and commercial center of the Republic.

Very little is known of the history of the islands before the 16th century. It is believed that many country's vessels visited the islands while searching for new trade routes to the East. In 1788, John Marshall, a British sea captain for whom the islands were named, explored them. The Islands have undergone successive domination by the Spanish, Germans, Japanese and Americans. It was the site of some of the fiercest fighting of the entire Pacific theater during World War II. At the conclusion of the war, the United States, under the direction of the United Nations administered the affairs of the Marshall Islands.

A constitutional government was formed on May 1,1979 with Amata Kabua being elected as the head of the government. On October 1, 1986, the United States notified the United Nations that the Marshall Islands were to be recognized as a separate nation.

The USA dollar is the current monetary system. Recently, the coinage has had limited redemption policies enforced.

MINT MARKS
M - Medallic Art Co.
R - Roger Williams Mint, Rhode Island
S - Sunshine Mining Co. Mint, Idaho

REPUBLIC

NON-CIRCULATING COLLECTOR COINAGE

The USA dollar is the current monetary system. Since May 1997, the coinage in the name of the Marshall Islands has had limited redemption policies enforced.

KM# 1 1/2 DOLLAR
15.55 g., 0.999 Silver 0.4995 oz. ASW **Rev:** Pandanus Fruit

Date	Mintage	VF20	XF40	MS60	MS63	MS65
1986	10,000	PF63 22.00	PF65 25.00	PF67 28.00		

KM# 2 DOLLAR
31.10 g., 0.999 Silver 0.999 oz. ASW **Obv:** Similar to 1/2 Dollar, KM#1 **Rev:** Triton Shell

Date	Mintage	VF20	XF40	MS60	MS63	MS65
1986	10,000	PF63 35.00	PF65 40.00	PF67 45.00		

KM# 293 DOLLAR
1.56 g., 0.999 Gold 0.050 oz. AGW **Obv:** Lion **Note:** Similar to 5 Dollars, KM#295.

Date	Mintage	VF20	XF40	MS60	MS63	MS65
1996	—	—	—	—	75.00	95.00

KM# 294 2-1/2 DOLLARS
3.11 g., 0.999 Gold 0.0999 oz. AGW **Obv:** Lion **Note:** Similar to 5 Dollars, KM#295.

Date	Mintage	VF20	XF40	MS60	MS63	MS65
1996	—	—	—	—	165	195

KM# 6 5 DOLLARS
Copper-Nickel **Subject:** U.S. Space Shuttle - Discovery

Date	Mintage	VF20	XF40	MS60	MS63	MS65
1988	756,000	—	—	—	2.50	4.00
1988 M	431,000	—	—	—	3.50	5.00

KM# 13 5 DOLLARS

Copper-Nickel **Subject:** 20th Anniversary - First Men on the Moon

Date	Mintage	VF20	XF40	MS60	MS63	MS65
1989	—	—	—	—	2.50	4.00

KM# 18 5 DOLLARS

Copper-Nickel **Subject:** To the Heroes of the Battle of Britain

Date	Mintage	VF20	XF40	MS60	MS63	MS65
1990 M	—	—	—	—	3.50	5.00

KM# 33 5 DOLLARS

Copper-Nickel **Subject:** German Unification

Date	Mintage	VF20	XF40	MS60	MS63	MS65
1990 M	—	—	—	—	3.50	5.00

KM# 38 5 DOLLARS

Copper-Nickel **Subject:** Dwight David Eisenhower **Obv:** Similar to KM#6 **Rev:** 1/2-length bust of Eisenhower saluting left

Date	Mintage	VF20	XF40	MS60	MS63	MS65
1990 M	—	—	—	—	3.50	5.00

KM# 35 5 DOLLARS

Copper-Nickel **Subject:** To the Heroes of Pearl Harbor

Date	Mintage	VF20	XF40	MS60	MS63	MS65
1991 M	—	—	—	—	4.00	6.00

KM# 37 5 DOLLARS

Copper-Nickel **Subject:** Space Shuttle Columbia

Date	Mintage	VF20	XF40	MS60	MS63	MS65
1991	—	—	—	—	3.50	5.00

KM# 40 5 DOLLARS

Copper-Nickel **Subject:** To the Heroes of Desert Storm

Date	Mintage	VF20	XF40	MS60	MS63	MS65
1991 R	—	—	—	—	4.00	6.00

KM# 49 5 DOLLARS

Copper-Nickel **Subject:** P-40 Warhawk of Flying Tigers

Date	Mintage	VF20	XF40	MS60	MS63	MS65
1991 M	—	—	—	—	3.50	5.00

KM# 81 5 DOLLARS

Copper-Nickel **Subject:** Reaching For New Horizons - Tipnol

Date	Mintage	VF20	XF40	MS60	MS63	MS65
1992 R	—	—	—	—	4.00	7.00

KM# 84 5 DOLLARS

Copper-Nickel **Subject:** To the Heroes of the First Air Raid on Tokyo - Doolittle **Rev:** Doolittle and the U.S.N. Hornet

Date	Mintage	VF20	XF40	MS60	MS63	MS65
1992 R	—	—	—	—	4.00	7.00

KM# 87 5 DOLLARS

Copper-Nickel **Subject:** To the Heroes of Corregidor

Date	Mintage	VF20	XF40	MS60	MS63	MS65
1992 R	—	—	—	—	5.00	7.00

KM# 90 5 DOLLARS

Copper-Nickel **Subject:** To the Heroes of Battle of Midway **Rev:** Carrier Akagi

Date	Mintage	VF20	XF40	MS60	MS63	MS65
1992 R	—	—	—	—	5.00	7.00

KM# 110 5 DOLLARS

Copper-Nickel **Subject:** Pacific Whales and Dolphins **Rev:** Humpback Whales

Date	Mintage	VF20	XF40	MS60	MS63	MS65
1993 R Prooflike	—	—	—	—	10.00	12.00

KM# 118 5 DOLLARS
Copper-Nickel **Subject:** To the Heroes of the North Atlantic **Rev:** Submarine

Date	Mintage	VF20	XF40	MS60	MS63	MS65
1993 R Prooflike	—	—	—	—	5.00	7.00

KM# 121 5 DOLLARS
Copper-Nickel **Subject:** To the Heroes of Guadalcanal **Rev:** Marine, battleship and airplanes

Date	Mintage	VF20	XF40	MS60	MS63	MS65
1993 R Prooflike	—	—	—	—	4.00	6.00

KM# 124 5 DOLLARS
Copper-Nickel **Rev:** Elvis Presley

Date	Mintage	VF20	XF40	MS60	MS63	MS65
1993 R Prooflike	—	—	—	—	4.00	6.00

KM# 126 5 DOLLARS
Copper-Nickel **Subject:** Pacific Whales and Dolphins **Rev:** Common Dolphin

Date	Mintage	VF20	XF40	MS60	MS63	MS65
1993 R Prooflike	—	—	—	—	10.00	12.00

KM# 144 5 DOLLARS
Copper-Nickel **Subject:** Christmas 1993

Date	Mintage	VF20	XF40	MS60	MS63	MS65
1993	—	—	—	—	4.00	6.00

KM# 148 5 DOLLARS
Copper-Nickel **Subject:** Flight at Kitty Hawk

Date	Mintage	VF20	XF40	MS60	MS63	MS65
1993	—	—	—	—	4.00	6.00

KM# 151 5 DOLLARS
Copper-Nickel **Subject:** First Men on the Moon

Date	Mintage	VF20	XF40	MS60	MS63	MS65
1994	—	—	—	—	4.00	6.00

KM# 179 5 DOLLARS
Copper-Nickel **Subject:** To the Heroes of D-Day - Normandy Invasion

Date	Mintage	VF20	XF40	MS60	MS63	MS65
1994	—	—	—	—	4.00	6.00

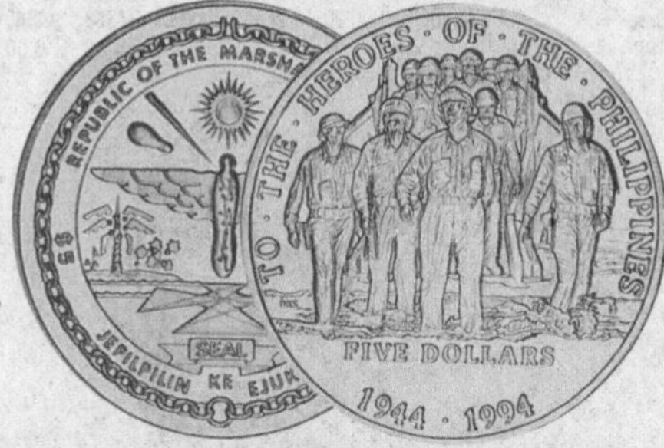

KM# 182 5 DOLLARS
Copper-Nickel **Subject:** To the Heroes of the Philippines **Rev:** MacArthur and staff

Date	Mintage	VF20	XF40	MS60	MS63	MS65
1994 R	—	—	—	—	4.00	6.00

KM# 187 5 DOLLARS
Copper-Nickel **Subject:** World Cup Soccer

Date	Mintage	VF20	XF40	MS60	MS63	MS65
1994	—	—	—	—	5.00	7.00

KM# 260 5 DOLLARS
Copper-Nickel **Subject:** Christmas - Cherub

Date	Mintage	VF20	XF40	MS60	MS63	MS65
1994	—	—	—	—	4.00	6.00

KM# 263 5 DOLLARS
Copper-Nickel **Subject:** To the Heroes of the Battle of The Bulge

Date	Mintage	VF20	XF40	MS60	MS63	MS65
1994 R	—	—	—	—	4.00	6.00

KM# 185 5 DOLLARS
Copper-Nickel **Rev:** F-100 Super Sabre

Date	Mintage	VF20	XF40	MS60	MS63	MS65
1995	—	—	—	—	4.00	6.00

KM# 186 5 DOLLARS
Copper-Nickel **Rev:** F-16 Fighting Falcon

Date	Mintage	VF20	XF40	MS60	MS63	MS65
1995	—	—	—	—	4.00	6.00

KM# 216 5 DOLLARS
Copper-Nickel **Subject:** Peace - Victory in Europe

Date	Mintage	VF20	XF40	MS60	MS63	MS65
1995 R	—	—	—	—	4.00	6.00

KM# 219 5 DOLLARS
Copper-Nickel **Subject:** To the Heroes of the Vietnam War

Date	Mintage	VF20	XF40	MS60	MS63	MS65
1995	—	—	—	—	4.00	6.00

KM# 222 5 DOLLARS
Copper-Nickel **Rev:** Elvis Presley

Date	Mintage	VF20	XF40	MS60	MS63	MS65
1995	—	—	—	—	4.00	6.00

KM# 225 5 DOLLARS
Copper-Nickel **Subject:** War in the Pacific **Note:** Similar to 10 Dollars, KM#226.

Date	Mintage	VF20	XF40	MS60	MS63	MS65
1995 R	—	—	—	—	4.00	6.00

KM# 253 5 DOLLARS
Copper-Nickel **Rev:** Head of Marilyn Monroe right, 1926-1962, actress

Date	Mintage	VF20	XF40	MS60	MS63	MS65
1995	—	—	—	—	5.00	7.00

KM# 257 5 DOLLARS
Copper-Nickel **Series:** 50th Anniversary United Nations **Subject:** Peace

Date	Mintage	VF20	XF40	MS60	MS63	MS65
1995	—	—	—	—	5.00	7.00

KM# 266 5 DOLLARS
Copper-Nickel **Subject:** Peace - VJ Day

Date	Mintage	VF20	XF40	MS60	MS63	MS65
1995	—	—	—	—	4.00	6.00

KM# 269 5 DOLLARS
Copper-Nickel **Rev:** Mirage 2000C Jet Fighter

Date	Mintage	VF20	XF40	MS60	MS63	MS65
1995	—	—	—	—	4.00	6.00

KM# 270 5 DOLLARS
Copper-Nickel **Rev:** Tornado F. MK 3 - Bomber

Date	Mintage	VF20	XF40	MS60	MS63	MS65
1995	—	—	—	—	4.00	6.00

KM# 271 5 DOLLARS
Copper-Nickel **Subject:** Christmas **Rev:** Cherub

Date	Mintage	VF20	XF40	MS60	MS63	MS65
1995	—	—	—	—	4.00	6.00

KM# 280 5 DOLLARS
Copper-Nickel **Subject:** Year of the Rat

Date	Mintage	VF20	XF40	MS60	MS63	MS65
1996	—	—	—	—	5.00	7.00

KM# 288 5 DOLLARS
Copper-Nickel **Rev:** Space Shuttle Columbia

Date	Mintage	VF20	XF40	MS60	MS63	MS65
1996	—	—	—	—	4.00	6.00

KM# 295 5 DOLLARS
7.78 g., 0.999 Gold 0.2498 oz. AGW **Obv:** State seal **Rev:** Lion

Date	Mintage	VF20	XF40	MS60	MS63	MS65
1996	—	—	—	—	—	420

KM# 297 5 DOLLARS
Copper-Nickel **Rev:** Tiger **Note:** Similar to 50 Dollars, KM#299.

Date	Mintage	VF20	XF40	MS60	MS63	MS65
1996	—	—	—	—	17.50	20.00

KM# 300 5 DOLLARS
Copper-Nickel **Rev:** Elvis Presley

Date	Mintage	VF20	XF40	MS60	MS63	MS65
1996	—	—	—	—	5.00	7.00

KM# 303 5 DOLLARS
Copper-Nickel **Rev:** James Dean

Date	Mintage	VF20	XF40	MS60	MS63	MS65
1996	—	—	—	—	5.00	7.00

KM# 308 5 DOLLARS
Copper-Nickel **Subject:** Classic Cars **Rev:** Ford Quadricycle
Note: Similar to 10 Dollars, KM#309.

Date	Mintage	VF20	XF40	MS60	MS63	MS65
1996	—	—	—	—	5.00	7.00

KM# 311 5 DOLLARS
Copper-Nickel **Subject:** Classic Cars **Rev:** Model A Ford

Date	Mintage	VF20	XF40	MS60	MS63	MS65
1996	—	—	—	—	5.00	7.00

KM# 314 5 DOLLARS
Copper-Nickel **Subject:** Classic Cars **Rev:** Model T Ford

Date	Mintage	VF20	XF40	MS60	MS63	MS65
1996	—	—	—	—	5.00	7.00

KM# 317 5 DOLLARS
Copper-Nickel **Subject:** Classic Cars **Rev:** 1955 Thunderbird

Date	Mintage	VF20	XF40	MS60	MS63	MS65
1996	—	—	—	—	5.00	7.00

KM# 320 5 DOLLARS
Copper-Nickel **Subject:** Classic Cars **Rev:** 1964 Mustang

Date	Mintage	VF20	XF40	MS60	MS63	MS65
1996	—	—	—	—	5.00	7.00

KM# 323 5 DOLLARS
Copper-Nickel **Subject:** Classic Cars **Rev:** Ford Taurus

Date	Mintage	VF20	XF40	MS60	MS63	MS65
1996	—	—	—	—	5.00	7.00

KM# 330 5 DOLLARS
Copper-Nickel **Subject:** Steam Locomotive **Rev:** Pennsylvania K4

Date	Mintage	VF20	XF40	MS60	MS63	MS65
1996	—	—	—	—	4.00	6.00

KM# 331 5 DOLLARS
Copper-Nickel **Subject:** Steam Locomotive **Rev:** Big Boy
Note: Similar to 50 Dollar, KM#292.

Date	Mintage	VF20	XF40	MS60	MS63	MS65
1996	—	—	—	—	4.00	6.00

KM# 344 5 DOLLARS
Copper-Nickel **Rev:** Lion

Date	Mintage	VF20	XF40	MS60	MS63	MS65
1996	—	—	—	—	10.00	12.00

KM# 345 5 DOLLARS
Copper-Nickel **Rev:** Cheetah

Date	Mintage	VF20	XF40	MS60	MS63	MS65
1996	—	—	—	—	10.00	12.00

KM# 346 5 DOLLARS
Copper-Nickel **Rev:** Jaguar

Date	Mintage	VF20	XF40	MS60	MS63	MS65
1996	—	—	—	—	10.00	12.00

KM# 353 5 DOLLARS
Copper-Nickel **Subject:** Christmas **Rev:** Two angels

Date	Mintage	VF20	XF40	MS60	MS63	MS65
1996	—	—	—	—	5.00	7.00

KM# 362 5 DOLLARS
Copper-Nickel **Subject:** Year of the Ox **Obv:** State seal **Rev:** Stylized Ox

Date	Mintage	VF20	XF40	MS60	MS63	MS65
1997	—	—	—	—	5.00	7.00

KM# 364 5 DOLLARS
Copper-Nickel **Rev:** Elvis Presley

Date	Mintage	VF20	XF40	MS60	MS63	MS65
1997	—	—	—	—	5.00	7.00

KM# 369 5 DOLLARS

Copper-Nickel **Subject:** The Last Supper **Obv:** State seal

Date	Mintage	VF20	XF40	MS60	MS63	MS65
1997	—	—	—	—	4.00	6.00

KM# 371 5 DOLLARS

Copper-Nickel **Subject:** To the Heroes of the Korean War **Obv:** State seal **Rev:** Soldier in poncho

Date	Mintage	VF20	XF40	MS60	MS63	MS65
1997	—	—	—	—	5.00	7.00

KM# 374 5 DOLLARS

Copper-Nickel **Obv:** State seal **Rev:** Gray wolf

Date	Mintage	VF20	XF40	MS60	MS63	MS65
1997	—	—	—	—	10.00	12.00

KM# 395 5 DOLLARS

Copper-Nickel **Obv:** State seal **Rev:** F-80 Shooting Star

Date	Mintage	VF20	XF40	MS60	MS63	MS65
1997	—	—	—	—	4.00	6.00

KM# 398 5 DOLLARS

Copper-Nickel **Subject:** History's Great Fighting Ships **Obv:** State seal **Rev:** USS Constitution

Date	Mintage	VF20	XF40	MS60	MS63	MS65
1997	—	—	—	—	5.00	7.00

KM# 403 5 DOLLARS

Copper-Nickel **Subject:** Christmas **Obv:** State seal **Rev:** Two cherubs

Date	Mintage	VF20	XF40	MS60	MS63	MS65
1997	—	—	—	—	4.00	6.00

KM# 407 5 DOLLARS

Copper-Nickel **Subject:** Sermon on the Mount **Obv:** State seal **Rev:** Jesus preaching

Date	Mintage	VF20	XF40	MS60	MS63	MS65
1997	—	—	—	—	4.00	6.00

KM# 413 5 DOLLARS

Copper-Nickel **Subject:** Year of the Tiger **Obv:** State seal **Rev:** Stylized tiger

Date	Mintage	VF20	XF40	MS60	MS63	MS65
1998	—	—	—	—	4.00	6.00

KM# 463 5 DOLLARS

Copper-Nickel **Subject:** History's Great Fighting Ships **Obv:** State seal **Rev:** USS Missouri

Date	Mintage	VF20	XF40	MS60	MS63	MS65
1998	—	—	—	—	4.00	6.00

KM# 464 5 DOLLARS

Copper-Nickel **Subject:** To the Heroes of the Berlin Airlift **Obv:** State seal **Rev:** C-54 landing

Date	Mintage	VF20	XF40	MS60	MS63	MS65
1998	—	—	—	—	4.00	6.00

KM# 466 5 DOLLARS

Copper-Nickel **Subject:** Classic Cars **Obv:** State seal **Rev:** 1912 Chevy Classic Six

Date	Mintage	VF20	XF40	MS60	MS63	MS65
1998	—	—	—	—	5.00	7.00

KM# 468 5 DOLLARS

Copper-Nickel **Subject:** Classic Cars **Obv:** State seal **Rev:** 1931 Chevy Roadster

Date	Mintage	VF20	XF40	MS60	MS63	MS65
1998	—	—	—	—	5.00	7.00

KM# 470 5 DOLLARS

Copper-Nickel **Subject:** Classic Cars **Obv:** State seal **Rev:** Cameo Carrier

Date	Mintage	VF20	XF40	MS60	MS63	MS65
1998	—	—	—	—	6.00	8.00

KM# 472 5 DOLLARS
Copper-Nickel **Subject:** Classic Cars **Obv:** State seal **Rev:** 1957 Chevy Bel Air

Date	Mintage	VF20	XF40	MS60	MS63	MS65
1998	—	—	—	—	6.00	8.00

KM# 474 5 DOLLARS
Copper-Nickel **Subject:** Classic Cars **Obv:** State seal **Rev:** 1957 Chevy Corvette

Date	Mintage	VF20	XF40	MS60	MS63	MS65
1998	—	—	—	—	7.00	9.00

KM# 476 5 DOLLARS
Copper-Nickel **Subject:** Classic Cars **Obv:** State seal **Rev:** 1967 Chevy Camaro

Date	Mintage	VF20	XF40	MS60	MS63	MS65
1998	—	—	—	—	6.00	8.00

KM# 478 5 DOLLARS
Copper-Nickel **Obv:** State seal **Rev:** Babe Ruth at bat

Date	Mintage	VF20	XF40	MS60	MS63	MS65
1998	—	—	—	—	5.00	7.00

KM# 481 5 DOLLARS
Copper-Nickel **Subject:** Christmas **Obv:** State seal **Rev:** Angel

Date	Mintage	VF20	XF40	MS60	MS63	MS65
1998	—	—	—	—	4.00	6.00

KM# 484 5 DOLLARS
Copper-Nickel, 39 mm. **Subject:** John Glenn returns to space **Rev:** Friendship 7 and Discovery blasting off **Edge:** Reeded

Date	Mintage	VF20	XF40	MS60	MS63	MS65
1998	—	—	—	—	4.00	6.00

KM# 486 5 DOLLARS
Copper-Nickel, 38.4 mm. **Subject:** USS United States **Obv:** National seal **Rev:** Sailing ship **Edge:** Reeded

Date	Mintage	VF20	XF40	MS60	MS63	MS65
1998	—	—	—	—	7.00	9.00

KM# 487 5 DOLLARS
Copper-Nickel, 38.4 mm. **Obv:** National seal **Rev:** USS Monitor and Merrimack battle scene **Edge:** Reeded

Date	Mintage	VF20	XF40	MS60	MS63	MS65
1998	—	—	—	—	10.00	11.00

KM# 488 5 DOLLARS
Copper-Nickel, 38.4 mm. **Subject:** USS Olympia **Obv:** National seal **Rev:** Battleship steaming left **Edge:** Reeded

Date	Mintage	VF20	XF40	MS60	MS63	MS65
1998	—	—	—	—	7.00	9.00

KM# 489 5 DOLLARS
Copper-Nickel, 38.4 mm. **Obv:** National seal **Rev:** USS Fanning and USS Nicholson **Edge:** Reeded

Date	Mintage	VF20	XF40	MS60	MS63	MS65
1998	—	—	—	—	7.00	9.00

KM# 490 5 DOLLARS
Copper-Nickel, 38.4 mm. **Obv:** National seal **Rev:** USS Enterprise **Edge:** Reeded

Date	Mintage	VF20	XF40	MS60	MS63	MS65
1998	—	—	—	—	7.00	9.00

KM# 491 5 DOLLARS
Copper-Nickel, 38.4 mm. **Obv:** National seal **Rev:** Battleship USS New Jersey **Edge:** Reeded

Date	Mintage	VF20	XF40	MS60	MS63	MS65
1998	—	—	—	—	7.00	9.00

KM# 492 5 DOLLARS
Copper-Nickel, 38.4 mm. **Obv:** National seal **Rev:** Heavy Cruiser USS Juneau **Edge:** Reeded

Date	Mintage	VF20	XF40	MS60	MS63	MS65
1998	—	—	—	—	7.00	9.00

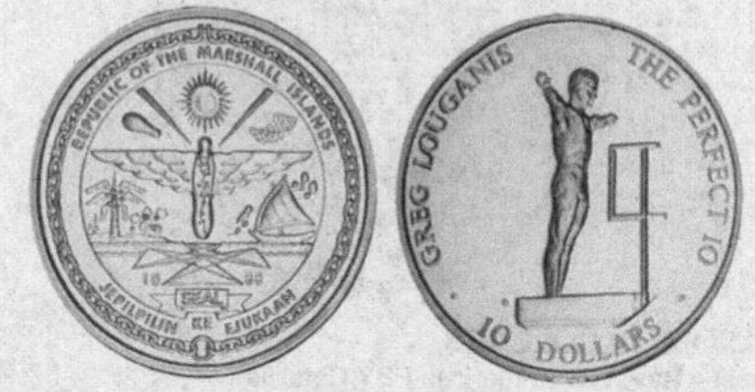

KM# 147 10 DOLLARS
11.00 g., 0.999 Silver 0.3533 oz. ASW **Rev:** Greg Louganis

Date	Mintage	VF20	XF40	MS60	MS63	MS65
1988	—	PF65 185	PF67 225			

KM# 41 10 DOLLARS
Brass **Subject:** To the Heroes of Desert Storm

Date	Mintage	VF20	XF40	MS60	MS63	MS65
1991 R	—	—	—	—	10.00	12.00

KM# 59 10 DOLLARS
Brass **Rev:** WWII American P-51 Mustang

Date	Mintage	VF20	XF40	MS60	MS63	MS65
1991 S Prooflike	Est. 50000	—	—	—	—	15.00

KM# 60 10 DOLLARS
Brass **Rev:** WWII American B-29 Superfortress

Date	Mintage	VF20	XF40	MS60	MS63	MS65
1991 S Prooflike	—	—	—	—	—	15.00

KM# 61 10 DOLLARS
Brass **Rev:** WWII American B-25 Mitchell

Date	Mintage	VF20	XF40	MS60	MS63	MS65
1991 S Prooflike	Est. 50000	—	—	—	—	15.00

KM# 62 10 DOLLARS
Brass **Rev:** WWII American PBY Catalina

Date	Mintage	VF20	XF40	MS60	MS63	MS65
1991 S Prooflike	Est. 50000	—	—	—	—	15.00

KM# 63 10 DOLLARS
Brass **Rev:** WWII German BF 109 Messerschmitt

Date	Mintage	VF20	XF40	MS60	MS63	MS65
1991 S Prooflike	Est. 50000	—	—	—	—	15.00

KM# 64 10 DOLLARS
Brass **Rev:** WWII British Spitfire

Date	Mintage	VF20	XF40	MS60	MS63	MS65
1991 S Prooflike	Est. 50000	—	—	—	—	15.00

KM# 65 10 DOLLARS
Brass **Rev:** WWII Japanaese A6M Reisen

Date	Mintage	VF20	XF40	MS60	MS63	MS65
1991 S Prooflike	Est. 50000	—	—	—	—	15.00

KM# 66 10 DOLLARS
Brass **Rev:** WWII American F6F Hellcat

Date	Mintage	VF20	XF40	MS60	MS63	MS65
1991 S Prooflike	Est. 50000	—	—	—	—	15.00

KM# 67 10 DOLLARS
Brass **Rev:** WWII Soviet Yak 9

Date	Mintage	VF20	XF40	MS60	MS63	MS65
1991 S Prooflike	—	—	—	—	—	15.00

KM# 68 10 DOLLARS
Brass **Rev:** WWII American B-17 Flying Fortress

Date	Mintage	VF20	XF40	MS60	MS63	MS65
1991 S Prooflike	Est. 50000	—	—	—	—	15.00

KM# 69 10 DOLLARS
Brass **Rev:** WWII British Hawker Hurricane

Date	Mintage	VF20	XF40	MS60	MS63	MS65
1991 S Prooflike	Est. 50000	—	—	—	—	15.00

KM# 70 10 DOLLARS
Brass **Rev:** WWII British Mosquito

Date	Mintage	VF20	XF40	MS60	MS63	MS65
1991 S Prooflike	Est. 50000	—	—	—	—	15.00

KM# 71 10 DOLLARS
Brass **Rev:** WWII British Lancaster

Date	Mintage	VF20	XF40	MS60	MS63	MS65
1991 S Prooflike	Est. 50000	—	—	—	—	15.00

KM# 73 10 DOLLARS
Brass **Subject:** To the Heroes of Pearl Harbor **Obv:** National seal

Date	Mintage	VF20	XF40	MS60	MS63	MS65
1991 Proofike	—	—	—	—	—	15.00

KM# 96 10 DOLLARS
Brass **Rev:** WWII American C-47 Skytrain

Date	Mintage	VF20	XF40	MS60	MS63	MS65
1991 S Prooflike	—	—	—	—	—	15.00

KM# 98 10 DOLLARS
Brass **Rev:** WWII American F4U Corsair

Date	Mintage	VF20	XF40	MS60	MS63	MS65
1991 S Prooflike	Est. 50000	—	—	—	—	15.00

KM# 101 10 DOLLARS
Brass **Rev:** WWII American P-38 Lightning

Date	Mintage	VF20	XF40	MS60	MS63	MS65
1991 Prooflike	Est. 50000	—	—	—	—	15.00

KM# 103 10 DOLLARS
Brass **Rev:** WWII Japanese G4M "Betty" Bomber

Date	Mintage	VF20	XF40	MS60	MS63	MS65
1991 S Prooflike	Est. 50000	—	—	—	—	15.00

KM# 107 10 DOLLARS
Brass **Rev:** WWII Japanese KI-61 Hien "Tony"

Date	Mintage	VF20	XF40	MS60	MS63	MS65
1991 S Prooflike	Est. 50000	—	—	—	—	15.00

KM# 109 10 DOLLARS
Brass **Rev:** WWII French D.520 Fighter

Date	Mintage	VF20	XF40	MS60	MS63	MS65
1991 S Prooflike	Est. 50000	—	—	—	—	15.00

KM# 125 10 DOLLARS
Brass **Rev:** WWII German FW 190 Fighters

Date	Mintage	VF20	XF40	MS60	MS63	MS65
1991 S Prooflike	Est. 50000	—	—	—	—	15.00

KM# 131 10 DOLLARS
Brass **Rev:** WWII American B-24 Liberator

Date	Mintage	VF20	XF40	MS60	MS63	MS65
1991 S Prooflike	Est. 50000	—	—	—	—	15.00

KM# 140 10 DOLLARS
Brass **Rev:** WWII Italian S.M. 79 Sparviero

Date	Mintage	VF20	XF40	MS60	MS63	MS65
1991 S Prooflike	Est. 50000	—	—	—	—	15.00

KM# 141 10 DOLLARS
Brass **Rev:** WWII German HE 111 Bombers

Date	Mintage	VF20	XF40	MS60	MS63	MS65
1991 S Prooflike	Est. 50000	—	—	—	—	15.00

KM# 142 10 DOLLARS
Brass **Rev:** WWII Soviet IL-2 Shturmovik ground attack

Date	Mintage	VF20	XF40	MS60	MS63	MS65
1991 S Prooflike	Est. 50000	—	—	—	—	15.00

KM# 82 10 DOLLARS
Brass **Subject:** Legends of Discovery **Rev:** Santa Maria

Date	Mintage	VF20	XF40	MS60	MS63	MS65
1992 R	—	—	—	—	—	15.00

KM# 85 10 DOLLARS
Brass **Subject:** First Air Raid on Tokyo **Rev:** Doolittle

Date	Mintage	VF20	XF40	MS60	MS63	MS65
1992 R	—	—	—	—	—	15.00

KM# 88 10 DOLLARS
Brass **Subject:** To the Heroes of Corregidor

Date	Mintage	VF20	XF40	MS60	MS63	MS65
1992 R	—	—	—	—	—	15.00

KM# 91 10 DOLLARS
Brass **Subject:** To the Heroes of Battle of Midway

Date	Mintage	VF20	XF40	MS60	MS63	MS65
1992 R	—	—	—	—	—	15.00

KM# 119 10 DOLLARS
Brass **Subject:** To the Heroes of the North Atlantic **Rev:** Submarine

Date	Mintage	VF20	XF40	MS60	MS63	MS65
1993 R Prooflike	—	—	—	—	—	17.00

KM# 122 10 DOLLARS
Brass **Subject:** To the Heroes of Guadalcanal **Rev:** Marine, battleship and airplanes

Date	Mintage	VF20	XF40	MS60	MS63	MS65
1993 R Prooflike	—	—	—	—	—	15.00

KM# 127 10 DOLLARS
Brass **Subject:** Pacific Whales and Dolphins **Rev:** Common Dolphin

Date	Mintage	VF20	XF40	MS60	MS63	MS65
1993 R Prooflike	—	—	—	—	—	17.00

KM# 129 10 DOLLARS
Brass **Rev:** Elvis Presley

Date	Mintage	VF20	XF40	MS60	MS63	MS65
1993 Prooflike	—	—	—	—	—	18.50

KM# 132 10 DOLLARS
Brass **Subject:** Pacific Whales and Dolphins **Rev:** Humpback Whales

Date	Mintage	VF20	XF40	MS60	MS63	MS65
1993	Est. 25000	—	—	—	—	17.00

KM# 133 10 DOLLARS
Brass **Subject:** Pacific Whales and Dolphins **Rev:** Risso's Dolphins

Date	Mintage	VF20	XF40	MS60	MS63	MS65
1993	—	—	—	—	—	17.00

KM# 134 10 DOLLARS
Brass **Subject:** Pacific Whales and Dolphins **Rev:** Beluga Whales

Date	Mintage	VF20	XF40	MS60	MS63	MS65
1993	Est. 25000	—	—	—	—	17.00

KM# 135 10 DOLLARS
Brass **Subject:** Pacific Whales and Dolphins **Rev:** Hector's Dolphins

Date	Mintage	VF20	XF40	MS60	MS63	MS65
1993	Est. 25000	—	—	—	—	17.00

KM# 136 10 DOLLARS
Brass **Subject:** Pacific Whales and Dolphins **Rev:** Blue Whale

Date	Mintage	VF20	XF40	MS60	MS63	MS65
1993	Est. 25000	—	—	—	—	17.00

KM# 137 10 DOLLARS
Brass **Subject:** Pacific Whales and Dolphins **Rev:** Bottlenose Dolphin

Date	Mintage	VF20	XF40	MS60	MS63	MS65
1993	Est. 25000	—	—	—	—	17.00

KM# 138 10 DOLLARS
Brass **Subject:** Pacific Whales and Dolphins **Rev:** Killer Whale

Date	Mintage	VF20	XF40	MS60	MS63	MS65
1993	Est. 25000	—	—	—	—	17.00

KM# 139 10 DOLLARS
Brass **Subject:** Pacific Whales and Dolphins **Rev:** Baiji Dolphins

Date	Mintage	VF20	XF40	MS60	MS63	MS65
1993	Est. 25000	—	—	—	—	15.00

KM# 145 10 DOLLARS
Brass **Subject:** Christmas 1993

Date	Mintage	VF20	XF40	MS60	MS63	MS65
1993	Est. 25000	—	—	—	—	15.00

KM# 149 10 DOLLARS
Brass **Subject:** Flight at Kitty Hawk

Date	Mintage	VF20	XF40	MS60	MS63	MS65
1993	—	—	—	—	—	15.00

KM# 408 10 DOLLARS
Brass **Subject:** Pacific Whales and Dolphins **Rev:** Indo-Pacific Humpbacked Dolphin

Date	Mintage	VF20	XF40	MS60	MS63	MS65
1993	Est. 25000	—	—	—	—	17.00

KM# 409 10 DOLLARS
Brass **Subject:** Pacific Whales and Dolphins **Obv:** State seal **Rev:** Long-Snouted Spinner Dolphin

Date	Mintage	VF20	XF40	MS60	MS63	MS65
1993	Est. 25000	—	—	—	—	17.00

KM# 410 10 DOLLARS
Brass **Subject:** Pacific Whales and Dolphins **Rev:** Two Sperm whales

Date	Mintage	VF20	XF40	MS60	MS63	MS65
1993	Est. 25000	—	—	—	—	17.00

KM# 411 10 DOLLARS
Brass **Subject:** Pacific Whales and Dolphins **Rev:** Minke Whale

Date	Mintage	VF20	XF40	MS60	MS63	MS65
1993	Est. 25000	—	—	—	—	17.00

KM# 152 10 DOLLARS
Brass **Subject:** First Men on the Moon

Date	Mintage	VF20	XF40	MS60	MS63	MS65
1994	—	—	—	—	—	17.00

KM# 155 10 DOLLARS
Brass **Subject:** Mythological Mother Earth

Date	Mintage	VF20	XF40	MS60	MS63	MS65
1994 R	—	—	—	—	—	17.00

KM# 156 10 DOLLARS
Brass **Rev:** The Sun

Date	Mintage	VF20	XF40	MS60	MS63	MS65
1994	—	—	—	—	—	16.50

KM# 157 10 DOLLARS
Brass **Rev:** The Moon

Date	Mintage	VF20	XF40	MS60	MS63	MS65
1994	—	—	—	—	—	16.00

KM# 158 10 DOLLARS
Brass **Rev:** Pluto

Date	Mintage	VF20	XF40	MS60	MS63	MS65
1994	—	—	—	—	—	16.00

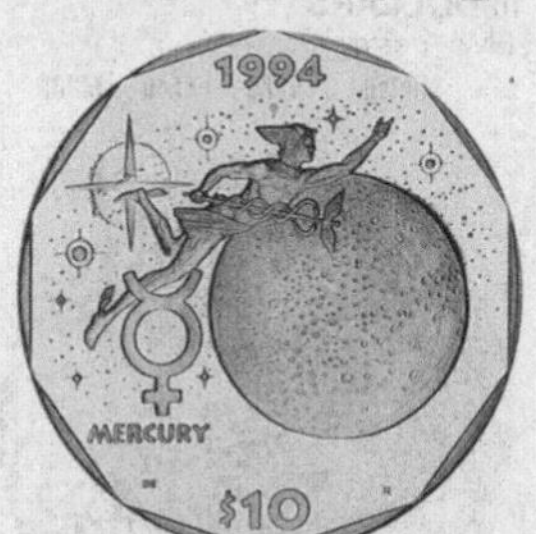

KM# 159 10 DOLLARS
Brass **Rev:** Mercury

Date	Mintage	VF20	XF40	MS60	MS63	MS65
1994	—	—	—	—	—	12.50

KM# 160 10 DOLLARS
Brass **Rev:** Venus

Date	Mintage	VF20	XF40	MS60	MS63	MS65
1994	—	—	—	—	—	17.50

KM# 161 10 DOLLARS
Brass **Rev:** Mars

Date	Mintage	VF20	XF40	MS60	MS63	MS65
1994	—	—	—	—	—	15.00

KM# 162 10 DOLLARS
Brass **Rev:** Saturn

Date	Mintage	VF20	XF40	MS60	MS63	MS65
1994	—	—	—	—	—	16.00

KM# 163 10 DOLLARS
Brass **Rev:** Jupiter

Date	Mintage	VF20	XF40	MS60	MS63	MS65
1994	—	—	—	—	—	16.50

KM# 164 10 DOLLARS
Brass **Rev:** Uranus

Date	Mintage	VF20	XF40	MS60	MS63	MS65
1994	—	—	—	—	—	12.50

KM# 165 10 DOLLARS
Brass **Rev:** Neptune

Date	Mintage	VF20	XF40	MS60	MS63	MS65
1994	—	—	—	—	—	16.50

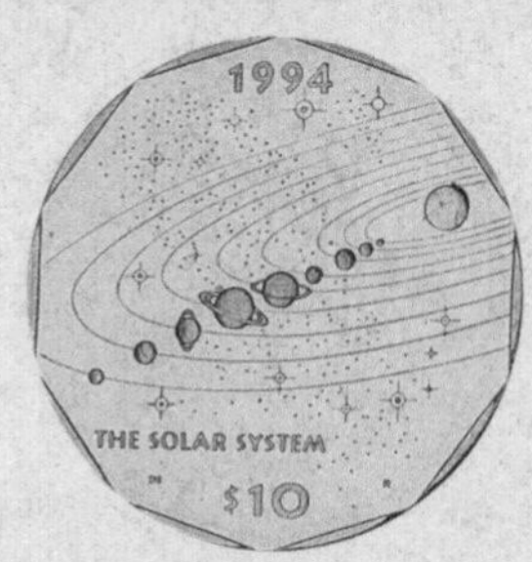

KM# 166 10 DOLLARS

Brass **Rev:** Solar System

Date	Mintage	VF20	XF40	MS60	MS63	MS65
1994	—	—	—	—	—	16.00

KM# 180 10 DOLLARS

Brass **Subject:** To the Heroes of D-Day - Normandy Invasion

Date	Mintage	VF20	XF40	MS60	MS63	MS65
1994 Prooflike	—	—	—	—	—	15.00

KM# 183 10 DOLLARS

Brass **Subject:** Heroes of the Philippines **Rev:** MacArthur and staff

Date	Mintage	VF20	XF40	MS60	MS63	MS65
1994 Prooflike	—	—	—	—	—	15.00

KM# 188 10 DOLLARS

Brass **Subject:** World Cup Soccer

Date	Mintage	VF20	XF40	MS60	MS63	MS65
1994	—	—	—	—	—	15.00

KM# 261 10 DOLLARS

Brass **Subject:** Christmas **Rev:** Cherub **Note:** Similar to 5 Dollars, KM#271.

Date	Mintage	VF20	XF40	MS60	MS63	MS65
1994	—	—	—	—	—	15.00

KM# 264 10 DOLLARS

Brass **Rev:** To the Heroes of the Battle of the Bulge

Date	Mintage	VF20	XF40	MS60	MS63	MS65
1994 Prooflike	—	—	—	—	—	15.00

KM# 217 10 DOLLARS

Brass **Subject:** Peace - Victory in Europe

Date	Mintage	VF20	XF40	MS60	MS63	MS65
1995 R	—	—	—	—	—	15.00

KM# 220 10 DOLLARS

Brass **Subject:** To the Heroes of Vietnam

Date	Mintage	VF20	XF40	MS60	MS63	MS65
1995 Prooflike	—	—	—	—	—	15.00

KM# 223 10 DOLLARS

Brass **Rev:** Elvis Presley

Date	Mintage	VF20	XF40	MS60	MS63	MS65
1995	—	—	—	—	—	15.00

KM# 226 10 DOLLARS

Brass **Subject:** To the Heroes of the War in the Pacific

Date	Mintage	VF20	XF40	MS60	MS63	MS65
1995 Prooflike	—	—	—	—	—	15.00

KM# 228 10 DOLLARS

Brass **Rev:** F-14 Tomcat

Date	Mintage	VF20	XF40	MS60	MS63	MS65
1995 R	Est. 25000	—	—	—	—	15.00

KM# 229 10 DOLLARS

Brass **Rev:** F-16 Fighting Falcon

Date	Mintage	VF20	XF40	MS60	MS63	MS65
1995 R	Est. 25000	—	—	—	—	15.00

KM# 230 10 DOLLARS

Brass **Rev:** Me 262A-1a Schwalbe

Date	Mintage	VF20	XF40	MS60	MS63	MS65
1995 R	—	—	—	—	—	15.00

KM# 231 10 DOLLARS

Brass **Rev:** F-104 Starfighter

Date	Mintage	VF20	XF40	MS60	MS63	MS65
1995 R	Est. 25000	—	—	—	—	15.00

KM# 232 10 DOLLARS

Brass **Rev:** Mirage 2000C

Date	Mintage	VF20	XF40	MS60	MS63	MS65
1995 R	—	—	—	—	—	15.00

KM# 233 10 DOLLARS

Brass **Rev:** F-4 Phantom II

Date	Mintage	VF20	XF40	MS60	MS63	MS65
1995 R	Est. 25000	—	—	—	—	15.00

KM# 234 10 DOLLARS
Brass **Rev:** Sea Harrier

Date	Mintage	VF20	XF40	MS60	MS63	MS65
1995 R	—	—	—	—	—	15.00

KM# 235 10 DOLLARS
Brass **Rev:** F-117 Nighthawk

Date	Mintage	VF20	XF40	MS60	MS63	MS65
1995 R	Est. 25000	—	—	—	—	15.00

KM# 236 10 DOLLARS
Brass **Rev:** F-100 Super Sabre

Date	Mintage	VF20	XF40	MS60	MS63	MS65
1995 R	—	—	—	—	—	15.00

KM# 237 10 DOLLARS
Brass **Rev:** F-86 Sabre

Date	Mintage	VF20	XF40	MS60	MS63	MS65
1995 R	Est. 25000	—	—	—	—	15.00

KM# 238 10 DOLLARS
Brass **Rev:** MIG-15

Date	Mintage	VF20	XF40	MS60	MS63	MS65
1995 R	Est. 25000	—	—	—	—	15.00

KM# 239 10 DOLLARS
Brass **Rev:** G91Y

Date	Mintage	VF20	XF40	MS60	MS63	MS65
1995 R	—	—	—	—	—	15.00

KM# 240 10 DOLLARS
Brass **Rev:** SAAB 35 Draken

Date	Mintage	VF20	XF40	MS60	MS63	MS65
1995 R	—	—	—	—	—	15.00

KM# 241 10 DOLLARS
Brass **Rev:** Meteor FMK8

Date	Mintage	VF20	XF40	MS60	MS63	MS65
1995 R	—	—	—	—	—	12.50

KM# 242 10 DOLLARS
Brass **Rev:** F-105 Thunderchief

Date	Mintage	VF20	XF40	MS60	MS63	MS65
1995 R	—	—	—	—	—	15.00

KM# 243 10 DOLLARS
Brass **Rev:** Tornado FMK3

Date	Mintage	VF20	XF40	MS60	MS63	MS65
1995 R	Est. 25000	—	—	—	—	15.00

KM# 254 10 DOLLARS
Brass **Rev:** Head of Marilyn Monroe right, 1926-1962, actress

Date	Mintage	VF20	XF40	MS60	MS63	MS65
1995	—	—	—	—	—	15.00

KM# 258 10 DOLLARS
Brass **Series:** 50th Anniversary United Nations **Subject:** Peace

Date	Mintage	VF20	XF40	MS60	MS63	MS65
1995	—	—	—	—	—	15.00

KM# 267 10 DOLLARS
Brass **Subject:** Peace - VJ Day

Date	Mintage	VF20	XF40	MS60	MS63	MS65
1995 R	—	—	—	—	—	15.00

KM# 272 10 DOLLARS
Brass **Subject:** Christmas **Rev:** Cherub

Date	Mintage	VF20	XF40	MS60	MS63	MS65
1995	—	—	—	—	—	16.50

KM# 282 10 DOLLARS
Brass **Subject:** Freedom / Liberty **Rev:** Torpedo Boat PT109

Date	Mintage	VF20	XF40	MS60	MS63	MS65
1995	—	—	—	—	—	15.00

KM# 283 10 DOLLARS
Brass **Subject:** Freedom / Liberty **Rev:** President John F. Kennedy takes oath of office

Date	Mintage	VF20	XF40	MS60	MS63	MS65
1995	—	—	—	—	—	15.00

KM# 284 10 DOLLARS
Brass **Subject:** Freedom / Liberty **Rev:** Peace Corps worker and native

Date	Mintage	VF20	XF40	MS60	MS63	MS65
1995	—	—	—	—	—	15.00

KM# 285 10 DOLLARS
Brass **Subject:** Freedom / Liberty **Rev:** Battleships under starry sky

Date	Mintage	VF20	XF40	MS60	MS63	MS65
1995	—	—	—	—	—	15.00

KM# 286 10 DOLLARS
Brass **Subject:** Freedom / Liberty **Rev:** President John F. Kennedy working at desk

Date	Mintage	VF20	XF40	MS60	MS63	MS65
1995	—	—	—	—	—	15.00

KM# 287 10 DOLLARS
Brass **Subject:** Freedom / Liberty **Rev:** President John F. Kennedy's Eternal Flame

Date	Mintage	VF20	XF40	MS60	MS63	MS65
1995	—	—	—	—	—	15.00

KM# 396 10 DOLLARS
Brass **Subject:** F-16 Fighting Falcon **Obv:** National seal **Rev:** Jet fighter

Date	Mintage	VF20	XF40	MS60	MS63	MS65
1995	Est. 25000	—	—	—	—	15.00

KM# 289 10 DOLLARS

Brass **Rev:** Space Shuttle Columbia

Date	Mintage	VF20	XF40	MS60	MS63	MS65
1996	—	—	—	—	—	15.00

KM# 298 10 DOLLARS

Brass **Rev:** Tiger **Note:** Similar to 50 Dollars, KM#299.

Date	Mintage	VF20	XF40	MS60	MS63	MS65
1996	—	—	—	—	—	16.00

KM# 301 10 DOLLARS

Brass **Rev:** Elvis Presley

Date	Mintage	VF20	XF40	MS60	MS63	MS65
1996	—	—	—	—	—	16.00

KM# 304 10 DOLLARS

Brass **Rev:** James Dean **Note:** Similar to 5 Dollars, KM#303.

Date	Mintage	VF20	XF40	MS60	MS63	MS65
1996	—	—	—	—	—	16.00

KM# 306 10 DOLLARS

Brass **Subject:** Steam Locomotive **Rev:** Pennsylvania K4

Date	Mintage	VF20	XF40	MS60	MS63	MS65
1996	Est. 250000	—	—	—	—	14.00

KM# 307 10 DOLLARS

Brass **Subject:** Steam Locomotive **Rev:** Big Boy

Date	Mintage	VF20	XF40	MS60	MS63	MS65
1996	Est. 25000	—	—	—	—	16.50

KM# 309 10 DOLLARS

Brass **Subject:** Classic Cars **Rev:** Ford Quadricycle

Date	Mintage	VF20	XF40	MS60	MS63	MS65
1996 Prooflike	—	—	—	—	—	15.00

KM# 312 10 DOLLARS

Brass **Subject:** Classic Cars **Rev:** Model A Ford

Date	Mintage	VF20	XF40	MS60	MS63	MS65
1996 Prooflike	—	—	—	—	—	15.00

KM# 315 10 DOLLARS

Brass **Subject:** Classic Cars **Rev:** Model T Ford **Note:** Similar to 5 Dollars, KM#314.

Date	Mintage	VF20	XF40	MS60	MS63	MS65
1996 Prooflike	—	—	—	—	—	15.00

KM# 318 10 DOLLARS

Brass **Subject:** Classic Cars **Rev:** 1955 Thunderbird **Note:** Similar to 5 Dollars, KM#317.

Date	Mintage	VF20	XF40	MS60	MS63	MS65
1996 Prooflike	—	—	—	—	—	16.00

KM# 321 10 DOLLARS

Brass **Subject:** Classic Cars **Rev:** 1964 Mustang

Date	Mintage	VF20	XF40	MS60	MS63	MS65
1996 Prooflike	—	—	—	—	—	15.00

KM# 324 10 DOLLARS

Brass **Subject:** Classic Cars **Rev:** Ford Taurus **Note:** Similar to 5 Dollars, KM#323.

Date	Mintage	VF20	XF40	MS60	MS63	MS65
1996 Prooflike	—	—	—	—	—	15.00

KM# 326 10 DOLLARS

Brass **Subject:** Steam Locomotive **Rev:** Mallard **Note:** Similar to 50 Dollars, KM#296.

Date	Mintage	VF20	XF40	MS60	MS63	MS65
1996	Est. 25000	—	—	—	—	16.50

KM# 336 10 DOLLARS

Brass **Rev:** Space Shuttle - Challenger

Date	Mintage	VF20	XF40	MS60	MS63	MS65
1996	—	—	—	—	—	15.00

KM# 337 10 DOLLARS

Brass **Rev:** Space Shuttle - Discovery

Date	Mintage	VF20	XF40	MS60	MS63	MS65
1996	—	—	—	—	—	15.00

KM# 338 10 DOLLARS

Brass **Rev:** Space Shuttle - Atlantis

Date	Mintage	VF20	XF40	MS60	MS63	MS65
1996	—	—	—	—	—	15.00

KM# 339 10 DOLLARS

Brass **Rev:** Space Shuttle - Endeavor

Date	Mintage	VF20	XF40	MS60	MS63	MS65
1996	—	—	—	—	—	12.50

KM# 347 10 DOLLARS

Brass **Rev:** Lion **Note:** Similar to 5 Dollars, KM#344.

Date	Mintage	VF20	XF40	MS60	MS63	MS65
1996	—	—	—	—	—	17.00

KM# 348 10 DOLLARS

Brass **Rev:** Cheetah **Note:** Similar to 5 Dollars, KM#345.

Date	Mintage	VF20	XF40	MS60	MS63	MS65
1996	—	—	—	—	—	17.00

KM# 349 10 DOLLARS

Brass **Rev:** Jaguar **Note:** Similar to 5 Dollars, KM#346.

Date	Mintage	VF20	XF40	MS60	MS63	MS65
1996	—	—	—	—	—	17.00

KM# 354 10 DOLLARS

Brass **Subject:** Christmas **Rev:** Two angels

Date	Mintage	VF20	XF40	MS60	MS63	MS65
1996	—	—	—	—	—	15.00

KM# 356 10 DOLLARS

Brass **Subject:** Steam Locomotive **Rev:** DB Class 01

Date	Mintage	VF20	XF40	MS60	MS63	MS65
1996	—	—	—	—	—	16.50

KM# 359 10 DOLLARS

Brass **Subject:** Steam Locomotive **Rev:** RENFE Class 242

Date	Mintage	VF20	XF40	MS60	MS63	MS65
1996	—	—	—	—	—	16.50

KM# 361 10 DOLLARS

Brass **Subject:** Steam Locomotive **Rev:** FS Group 691

Date	Mintage	VF20	XF40	MS60	MS63	MS65
1996	—	—	—	—	—	16.50

KM# 368 10 DOLLARS
Brass **Subject:** Steam Locomotive **Rev:** SNCF 232. U1

Date	Mintage	VF20	XF40	MS60	MS63	MS65
1996	Est. 25000	—	—	—	—	16.50

KM# 378 10 DOLLARS
Brass **Subject:** Steam Locomotive **Rev:** SAR 520 Class

Date	Mintage	VF20	XF40	MS60	MS63	MS65
1996	Est. 25000	—	—	—	—	16.50

KM# 379 10 DOLLARS
Brass **Subject:** Steam Locomotive **Rev:** Evening Star

Date	Mintage	VF20	XF40	MS60	MS63	MS65
1996	Est. 25000	—	—	—	—	16.50

KM# 393 10 DOLLARS
Brass **Subject:** Steam Locomotive **Rev:** QJ "Advance Forward"

Date	Mintage	VF20	XF40	MS60	MS63	MS65
1996	—	—	—	—	—	16.50

KM# 394 10 DOLLARS
Brass **Subject:** Steam Locomotive **Obv:** State seal **Rev:** Royal Hudson

Date	Mintage	VF20	XF40	MS60	MS63	MS65
1996	Est. 25000	—	—	—	—	16.50

KM# 402 10 DOLLARS
Brass **Subject:** Steam Locomotive **Obv:** State seal **Rev:** C62 "Swallow"

Date	Mintage	VF20	XF40	MS60	MS63	MS65
1996	Est. 25000	—	—	—	—	16.50

KM# 365 10 DOLLARS
Brass **Rev:** Elvis Presley **Note:** Similar to 5 Dollars, KM#364.

Date	Mintage	VF20	XF40	MS60	MS63	MS65
1997	—	—	—	—	—	15.00

KM# 372 10 DOLLARS
Brass **Subject:** To the Heroes of the Korean War **Note:** Similar to 5 Dollars, KM#371.

Date	Mintage	VF20	XF40	MS60	MS63	MS65
1997	Est. 25000	—	—	—	—	15.00

KM# 381 10 DOLLARS
Brass **Series:** Twelve Apostles **Obv:** State seal **Rev:** Andrew

Date	Mintage	VF20	XF40	MS60	MS63	MS65
1997	Est. 25000	—	—	—	—	15.00

KM# 382 10 DOLLARS
Brass **Series:** Twelve Apostles **Obv:** State seal **Rev:** Bartholomew

Date	Mintage	VF20	XF40	MS60	MS63	MS65
1997	Est. 25000	—	—	—	—	15.00

KM# 383 10 DOLLARS
Brass **Subject:** Twelve Apostles Series **Obv:** State seal **Rev:** James, Son of Zebedee

Date	Mintage	VF20	XF40	MS60	MS63	MS65
1997	—	—	—	—	—	15.00

KM# 384 10 DOLLARS
Brass **Subject:** Twelve Apostles Series **Obv:** State seal **Rev:** James, Son of Alphaeus

Date	Mintage	VF20	XF40	MS60	MS63	MS65
1997	Est. 25000	—	—	—	—	15.00

KM# 385 10 DOLLARS
Brass **Subject:** Twelve Apostles Series **Obv:** State seal **Rev:** John

Date	Mintage	VF20	XF40	MS60	MS63	MS65
1997	Est. 25000	—	—	—	—	15.00

KM# 386 10 DOLLARS
Brass **Subject:** Twelve Apostles Series **Obv:** State seal **Rev:** Paul

Date	Mintage	VF20	XF40	MS60	MS63	MS65
1997	—	—	—	—	—	15.00

KM# 387 10 DOLLARS
Brass **Subject:** Twelve Apostles Series **Obv:** State seal **Rev:** Matthew

Date	Mintage	VF20	XF40	MS60	MS63	MS65
1997	Est. 25000	—	—	—	—	12.00

KM# 388 10 DOLLARS
Brass **Subject:** Twelve Apostles Series **Obv:** State seal **Rev:** Peter

Date	Mintage	VF20	XF40	MS60	MS63	MS65
1997	Est. 25000	—	—	—	—	15.00

KM# 389 10 DOLLARS
Brass **Subject:** Twelve Apostles Series **Obv:** State seal **Rev:** Philip

Date	Mintage	VF20	XF40	MS60	MS63	MS65
1997	Est. 25000	—	—	—	—	15.00

KM# 390 10 DOLLARS
Brass **Subject:** Twelve Apostles Series **Obv:** State seal **Rev:** Simon

Date	Mintage	VF20	XF40	MS60	MS63	MS65
1997	Est. 25000	—	—	—	—	15.00

KM# 391 10 DOLLARS
Brass **Subject:** Twelve Apostles Series **Obv:** State seal **Rev:** Thaddaeus

Date	Mintage	VF20	XF40	MS60	MS63	MS65
1997	Est. 25000	—	—	—	—	15.00

KM# 392 10 DOLLARS
Brass **Subject:** Twelve Apostles Series **Obv:** State seal **Rev:** Thomas

Date	Mintage	VF20	XF40	MS60	MS63	MS65
1997	Est. 25000	—	—	—	—	15.00

KM# 400 10 DOLLARS
Brass **Obv:** State seal **Rev:** Deng Ziaoping

Date	Mintage	VF20	XF40	MS60	MS63	MS65
1997	—	—	—	—	—	15.00

KM# 404 10 DOLLARS
Brass **Subject:** Christmas **Obv:** State seal **Rev:** Two cherubs

Date	Mintage	VF20	XF40	MS60	MS63	MS65
1997	—	—	—	—	—	15.00

KM# 406 10 DOLLARS
Brass **Obv:** National seal **Rev:** Charging bull elephant

Date	Mintage	VF20	XF40	MS60	MS63	MS65
1997	—	—	—	—	—	16.00

KM# 415 10 DOLLARS
Brass **Subject:** History's Great Fighting Ships **Obv:** State seal **Rev:** Viking Longship

Date	Mintage	VF20	XF40	MS60	MS63	MS65
1998	Est. 25000	—	—	—	—	15.00

KM# 417 10 DOLLARS
Brass **Subject:** History's Great Fighting Ships **Obv:** State seal **Rev:** Greek Trireme

Date	Mintage	VF20	XF40	MS60	MS63	MS65
1998	Est. 25000	—	—	—	—	15.00

KM# 419 10 DOLLARS
Brass **Subject:** History's Great Fighting Ships **Obv:** State seal **Rev:** Roman Trireme

Date	Mintage	VF20	XF40	MS60	MS63	MS65
1998	Est. 25000	—	—	—	—	15.00

KM# 421 10 DOLLARS
Brass **Subject:** History's Great Fighting Ships **Obv:** State seal **Rev:** Chinese Ming Treasure Ship

Date	Mintage	VF20	XF40	MS60	MS63	MS65
1998	Est. 25000	—	—	—	—	15.00

KM# 423 10 DOLLARS
Brass **Subject:** History's Great Fighting Ships **Obv:** State seal **Rev:** Korean Turtle Ship

Date	Mintage	VF20	XF40	MS60	MS63	MS65
1998	Est. 25000	—	—	—	—	15.00

KM# 425 10 DOLLARS
Brass **Subject:** History's Great Fighting Ships **Obv:** State seal **Rev:** Fijan War Canoe

Date	Mintage	VF20	XF40	MS60	MS63	MS65
1998	Est. 25000	—	—	—	—	15.00

KM# 427 10 DOLLARS
Brass **Subject:** History's Great Fighting Ships **Obv:** State seal **Rev:** The Bismarck

Date	Mintage	VF20	XF40	MS60	MS63	MS65
1998	Est. 25000	—	—	—	—	15.00

KM# 429 10 DOLLARS
Brass **Subject:** History's Great Fighting Ships **Obv:** State seal **Rev:** The Graf Spee

Date	Mintage	VF20	XF40	MS60	MS63	MS65
1998	Est. 25000	—	—	—	—	15.00

KM# 431 10 DOLLARS
Brass **Subject:** History's Great Fighting Ships **Obv:** State seal **Rev:** The Yamato

Date	Mintage	VF20	XF40	MS60	MS63	MS65
1998	—	—	—	—	—	15.00

KM# 433 10 DOLLARS
Brass **Subject:** History's Great Fighting Ships **Obv:** State seal **Rev:** HMS Victory

Date	Mintage	VF20	XF40	MS60	MS63	MS65
1998	Est. 25000	—	—	—	—	15.00

KM# 435 10 DOLLARS
Brass **Subject:** History's Great Fighting Ships **Rev:** HMS Mary Rose

Date	Mintage	VF20	XF40	MS60	MS63	MS65
1998	Est. 25000	—	—	—	—	15.00

KM# 437 10 DOLLARS
Brass **Subject:** History's Great Fighting Ships **Rev:** HMS Dreadnought

Date	Mintage	VF20	XF40	MS60	MS63	MS65
1998	Est. 25000	—	—	—	—	15.00

KM# 439 10 DOLLARS
Brass **Subject:** History's Great Fighting Ships **Obv:** State Seal **Rev:** HMS Dorsetshire

Date	Mintage	VF20	XF40	MS60	MS63	MS65
1998	Est. 25000	—	—	—	—	15.00

KM# 441 10 DOLLARS
Brass **Subject:** History's Great Fighting Ships **Obv:** State Seal **Rev:** Nuestra Senora del Rosario

Date	Mintage	VF20	XF40	MS60	MS63	MS65
1998	Est. 25000	—	—	—	—	15.00

KM# 443 10 DOLLARS
Brass **Subject:** History's Great Fighting Ships **Obv:** State Seal **Rev:** Santisima Trinidad

Date	Mintage	VF20	XF40	MS60	MS63	MS65
1998	—	—	—	—	—	15.00

KM# 445 10 DOLLARS
Brass **Subject:** History's Great Fighting Ships **Obv:** State Seal **Rev:** USS Bonhomme Richard

Date	Mintage	VF20	XF40	MS60	MS63	MS65
1998	Est. 25000	—	—	—	—	15.00

KM# 447 10 DOLLARS
Brass **Subject:** History's Great Fighting Ships **Obv:** State Seal **Rev:** USS Constellation

Date	Mintage	VF20	XF40	MS60	MS63	MS65
1998	Est. 25000	—	—	—	—	15.00

KM# 449 10 DOLLARS
Brass **Subject:** History's Great Fighting Ships **Obv:** State Seal **Rev:** USS Hartford

Date	Mintage	VF20	XF40	MS60	MS63	MS65
1998	Est. 25000	—	—	—	—	15.00

KM# 451 10 DOLLARS
Brass **Subject:** History's Great Fighting Ships **Obv:** State Seal **Rev:** USS Hornet

Date	Mintage	VF20	XF40	MS60	MS63	MS65
1998	Est. 25000	—	—	—	—	15.00

KM# 453 10 DOLLARS
Brass **Subject:** History's Great Fighting Ships **Obv:** State Seal **Rev:** USS Missouri

Date	Mintage	VF20	XF40	MS60	MS63	MS65
1998	Est. 25000	—	—	—	—	15.00

KM# 455 10 DOLLARS
Brass **Subject:** History's Great Fighting Ships **Obv:** State Seal **Rev:** USS Tautog

Date	Mintage	VF20	XF40	MS60	MS63	MS65
1998	—	—	—	—	—	15.00

KM# 457 10 DOLLARS
Brass **Subject:** History's Great Fighting Ships **Obv:** State Seal. **Rev:** Brederode

Date	Mintage	VF20	XF40	MS60	MS63	MS65
1998	Est. 25000	—	—	—	—	15.00

KM# 459 10 DOLLARS
Brass **Subject:** History's Great Fighting Ships **Obv:** State Seal **Rev:** Ville de Paris

Date	Mintage	VF20	XF40	MS60	MS63	MS65
1998	Est. 25000	—	—	—	—	15.00

KM# 461 10 DOLLARS
Brass **Subject:** History's Great Fighting Ships **Obv:** State Seal **Rev:** Galera Veneziana

Date	Mintage	VF20	XF40	MS60	MS63	MS65
1998	Est. 25000	—	—	—	—	15.00

KM# 479 10 DOLLARS
Brass **Subject:** Babe Ruth at bat **Obv:** State Seal

Date	Mintage	VF20	XF40	MS60	MS63	MS65
1998	—	—	—	—	—	15.00

KM# 482 10 DOLLARS
Brass **Subject:** Christmas **Obv:** State Seal **Rev:** Angel

Date	Mintage	VF20	XF40	MS60	MS63	MS65
1998	—	—	—	—	—	12.00

KM# 3 20 DOLLARS
3.11 g., 0.999 Gold 0.0999 oz. AGW **Rev:** Sun

Date	Mintage	VF20	XF40	MS60	MS63	MS65
1986	Est. 5000	PF65 175	PF67 195			

KM# 153 20 DOLLARS
15.55 g., 0.999 Silver 0.4995 oz. ASW **Subject:** First Men on the Moon

Date	Mintage	VF20	XF40	MS60	MS63	MS65
1994	—	PF65 22.50				

KM# 189 20 DOLLARS
15.55 g., 0.999 Silver 0.4995 oz. ASW **Subject:** World Cup Soccer

Date	Mintage	VF20	XF40	MS60	MS63	MS65
1994	—	PF65 22.50				

KM# 255 20 DOLLARS
15.55 g., 0.999 Silver 0.4995 oz. ASW **Subject:** Head of Marilyn Monroe right, 1926-1962, actress

Date	Mintage	VF20	XF40	MS60	MS63	MS65
1995	—	PF65 25.00				

KM# 401 20 DOLLARS
10.37 g., 0.999 Silver 0.333 oz. ASW **Subject:** Deng Xiaoping **Obv:** State seal

Date	Mintage	VF20	XF40	MS60	MS63	MS65
1997	—	PF65 25.00				

KM# 20 25 DOLLARS
33.96 g., 0.925 Silver 1.010 oz. ASW **Subject:** Greg Louganis **Rev:** Back dive

Date	Mintage	VF20	XF40	MS60	MS63	MS65
1988	Est. 280000	—	—	90.00	100	120
1988	Est. 350000	PF63 130	PF65 150	PF67 170		

KM# 21 25 DOLLARS
33.96 g., 0.925 Silver 1.010 oz. ASW **Subject:** Greg Louganis **Rev:** Twister

Date	Mintage	VF20	XF40	MS60	MS63	MS65
1988	Est. 280000	—	—	90.00	100	120
1988	—	PF63 130	PF65 150	PF67 170		

KM# 22 25 DOLLARS
33.96 g., 0.925 Silver 1.010 oz. ASW **Subject:** Greg Louganis **Rev:** Jackknife

Date	Mintage	VF20	XF40	MS60	MS63	MS65
1988	Est. 280000	—	—	90.00	100	120
1988	Est. 350000	PF63 130	PF65 150	PF67 170		

KM# 4 50 DOLLARS
7.78 g., 0.999 Gold 0.2497 oz. AGW **Rev:** Coconut

Date	Mintage	VF20	XF40	MS60	MS63	MS65
1986	—	PF65 375	PF67 425			

KM# 7 50 DOLLARS
31.10 g., 0.999 Silver 0.9989 oz. ASW **Subject:** John Glenn in Space Orbit

Date	Mintage	VF20	XF40	MS60	MS63	MS65
1989	Est. 25000	PF65 32.50				
1989 S	Inc. above	PF65 30.00				

KM# 8 50 DOLLARS
31.10 g., 0.999 Silver 0.9989 oz. ASW **Subject:** Neil Armstrong on the Moon **Obv:** Similar to KM#12

Date	Mintage	VF20	XF40	MS60	MS63	MS65
1989	Est. 25000	PF65 32.50				
1989 S	Inc. above	PF65 30.00				

KM# 9 50 DOLLARS
31.10 g., 0.999 Silver 0.9989 oz. ASW **Subject:** American Space Station - Skylab **Obv:** Similar to KM#12

Date	Mintage	VF20	XF40	MS60	MS63	MS65
1989	Est. 25000	PF65 30.00				
1989 S	Inc. above	PF65 27.50				

KM# 10 50 DOLLARS

31.10 g., 0.999 Silver 0.9989 oz. ASW **Subject:** Apollo - Sojus Joint Mission

Date	Mintage	VF20	XF40	MS60	MS63	MS65
1989	Est. 25000	PF65 32.50				
1989 S	Inc. above	PF65 30.00				

KM# 11 50 DOLLARS

31.10 g., 0.999 Silver 0.9989 oz. ASW **Subject:** First Space Shuttle Flight

Date	Mintage	VF20	XF40	MS60	MS63	MS65
1989	Est. 25000	PF65 32.50				
1989 S	Inc. above	PF65 30.00				

KM# 12 50 DOLLARS

31.10 g., 0.999 Silver 0.9989 oz. ASW **Subject:** U.S. Space Shuttle - Discovery

Date	Mintage	VF20	XF40	MS60	MS63	MS65
1989	Est. 50000	PF65 27.50				
1989 S	Inc. above	PF65 30.00				

KM# 14 50 DOLLARS

31.10 g., 0.999 Silver 0.9989 oz. ASW **Subject:** 20th Anniversary - First Men on the Moon

Date	Mintage	VF20	XF40	MS60	MS63	MS65
1989	Est. 50000	PF65 27.50				
1989 S	Inc. above	PF65 30.00				

KM# 15 50 DOLLARS

31.10 g., 0.999 Silver 0.9989 oz. ASW **Subject:** First American Space Walk

Date	Mintage	VF20	XF40	MS60	MS63	MS65
1989	Est. 25000	PF65 32.50				
1989 S	Inc. above	PF65 30.00				

KM# 23 50 DOLLARS

31.10 g., 0.999 Silver 0.9989 oz. ASW **Subject:** First Docking In Space

Date	Mintage	VF20	XF40	MS60	MS63	MS65
1989	Est. 25000	PF65 32.50				
1989 S	Inc. above	PF65 30.00				

KM# 24 50 DOLLARS

31.10 g., 0.999 Silver 0.9989 oz. ASW **Subject:** First Man-made Satellite - 1957

Date	Mintage	VF20	XF40	MS60	MS63	MS65
1989	—	PF65 32.50				
1989 S	Inc. above	PF65 30.00				

KM# 25 50 DOLLARS

31.10 g., 0.999 Silver 0.9989 oz. ASW **Subject:** First Man In Space - 1961

Date	Mintage	VF20	XF40	MS60	MS63	MS65
1989	Est. 25000	PF65 32.50				
1989 S	Inc. above	PF65 30.00				

KM# 26 50 DOLLARS

31.10 g., 0.999 Silver 0.9989 oz. ASW **Subject:** First Woman In Space - 1963

Date	Mintage	VF20	XF40	MS60	MS63	MS65
1989	Est. 25000	PF65 32.50				
1989 S	Inc. above	PF65 30.00				

KM# 27 50 DOLLARS

31.10 g., 0.999 Silver 0.9989 oz. ASW **Subject:** First Rendezvous In Space - 1965

Date	Mintage	VF20	XF40	MS60	MS63	MS65
1989	Est. 25000	PF65 32.50				
1989 S	Inc. above	PF65 30.00				

KM# 28 50 DOLLARS

31.10 g., 0.999 Silver 0.9989 oz. ASW **Subject:** First Space Walk - 1965

Date	Mintage	VF20	XF40	MS60	MS63	MS65
1989	—	PF65 32.50				
1989 S	Inc. above	PF65 30.00				

KM# 29 50 DOLLARS

31.10 g., 0.999 Silver 0.9989 oz. ASW **Subject:** First Soft Landing on the Moon - 1966

Date	Mintage	VF20	XF40	MS60	MS63	MS65
1989	Est. 25000	PF65 32.50				
1989 S	Inc. above	PF65 30.00				

KM# 30 50 DOLLARS

31.10 g., 0.999 Silver 0.9989 oz. ASW **Subject:** First Probe of Venus - 1967

Date	Mintage	VF20	XF40	MS60	MS63	MS65
1989	Est. 25000	PF65 32.50				
1989 S	Inc. above	PF65 30.00				

KM# 31 50 DOLLARS
31.10 g., 0.999 Silver 0.9989 oz. ASW **Subject:** First Manned Orbit of the Moon - 1968

Date	Mintage	VF20	XF40	MS60	MS63	MS65
1989	Est. 25000	PF65 32.50				
1989 S	Inc. above	PF65 30.00				

KM# 32 50 DOLLARS
31.10 g., 0.999 Silver 0.9989 oz. ASW **Subject:** First Space Station Crew - 1971

Date	Mintage	VF20	XF40	MS60	MS63	MS65
1989	Est. 25000	PF65 32.50				
1989 S	Inc. above	PF65 30.00				

KM# 50 50 DOLLARS
31.10 g., 0.999 Silver 0.9989 oz. ASW **Subject:** First Manned Lunar Vehicle - 1971

Date	Mintage	VF20	XF40	MS60	MS63	MS65
1989	—	PF65 32.50				
1989 S	Inc. above	PF65 30.00				

KM# 51 50 DOLLARS
31.10 g., 0.999 Silver 0.9989 oz. ASW **Subject:** First American Satellite - 1958

Date	Mintage	VF20	XF40	MS60	MS63	MS65
1989 M	Est. 25000	PF65 32.50				
1989 S	Inc. above	PF65 30.00				

KM# 52 50 DOLLARS
31.10 g., 0.999 Silver 0.9989 oz. ASW **Subject:** First Liquid Fuel Rocket Launch - 1926

Date	Mintage	VF20	XF40	MS60	MS63	MS65
1989	Est. 25000	PF65 32.50				
1989 S	Inc. above	PF65 30.00				

KM# 53 50 DOLLARS
31.10 g., 0.999 Silver 0.9989 oz. ASW **Subject:** First Untethered Space Walk - 1984

Date	Mintage	VF20	XF40	MS60	MS63	MS65
1989	Est. 25000	PF65 32.50				
1989 S	Inc. above	PF65 30.00				

KM# 54 50 DOLLARS
31.10 g., 0.999 Silver 0.9989 oz. ASW **Subject:** First Landing on Mars - 1976

Date	Mintage	VF20	XF40	MS60	MS63	MS65
1989	—	PF65 32.50				
1989 S	Inc. above	PF65 30.00				

KM# 55 50 DOLLARS
31.10 g., 0.999 Silver 0.9989 oz. ASW **Subject:** First Flyby of Saturn - 1979

Date	Mintage	VF20	XF40	MS60	MS63	MS65
1989	Est. 25000	PF65 32.50				
1989 S	Inc. above	PF65 30.00				

KM# 56 50 DOLLARS
31.10 g., 0.999 Silver 0.9989 oz. ASW **Subject:** First Probe Beyond the Solar System - 1983

Date	Mintage	VF20	XF40	MS60	MS63	MS65
1989	Est. 25000	PF65 32.50				
1989 S	Inc. above	PF65 30.00				

KM# 57 50 DOLLARS
31.10 g., 0.999 Silver 0.9989 oz. ASW **Subject:** First Flyby of Jupiter - 1973

Date	Mintage	VF20	XF40	MS60	MS63	MS65
1989	Est. 25000	PF65 32.50				
1989 S	Inc. above	PF65 30.00				

KM# 19 50 DOLLARS
31.10 g., 0.999 Silver 0.9989 oz. ASW **Subject:** 50th Anniversary - Battle of Britain

Date	Mintage	VF20	XF40	MS60	MS63	MS65
1990 M	Est. 50000	PF65 35.00				

KM# 34 50 DOLLARS
31.10 g., 0.999 Silver 0.9989 oz. ASW **Subject:** German Unification

Date	Mintage	VF20	XF40	MS60	MS63	MS65
1990 M	—	PF65 45.00				

KM# 39 50 DOLLARS
31.10 g., 0.999 Silver 0.9989 oz. ASW **Subject:** Dwight David Eisenhower

Date	Mintage	VF20	XF40	MS60	MS63	MS65
1990 M	—	PF65 30.00				

KM# 36 50 DOLLARS
31.10 g., 0.999 Silver 0.9989 oz. ASW **Subject:** Pearl Harbor

Date	Mintage	VF20	XF40	MS60	MS63	MS65
1991 M	Est. 50000	PF65 32.50				

KM# 42 50 DOLLARS
31.10 g., 0.999 Silver 0.9989 oz. ASW **Subject:** To the Heroes of Desert Storm

Date	Mintage	VF20	XF40	MS60	MS63	MS65
1991 R	—	PF65 35.00				

KM# 43 50 DOLLARS
31.10 g., 0.999 Silver 0.9989 oz. ASW **Rev:** WWII American P-51 Mustang

Date	Mintage	VF20	XF40	MS60	MS63	MS65
1991	Est. 25000	PF65 35.00				

KM# 44 50 DOLLARS
31.10 g., 0.999 Silver 0.9989 oz. ASW **Rev:** WWII American B-29 Superfortress

Date	Mintage	VF20	XF40	MS60	MS63	MS65
1991 M	Est. 25000	PF65 37.50				

KM# 45 50 DOLLARS
31.10 g., 0.999 Silver 0.9989 oz. ASW **Rev:** WWII German BF-109 Messerschmitt

Date	Mintage	VF20	XF40	MS60	MS63	MS65
1991	—	PF65 35.00				

KM# 46 50 DOLLARS
31.10 g., 0.999 Silver 0.9989 oz. ASW **Rev:** WWII British Spitfire

Date	Mintage	VF20	XF40	MS60	MS63	MS65
1991 M	Est. 25000	PF65 35.00				

KM# 47 50 DOLLARS
31.10 g., 0.999 Silver 0.9989 oz. ASW **Rev:** WWII American PBY Catalina

Date	Mintage	VF20	XF40	MS60	MS63	MS65
1991 M	Est. 25000	PF65 37.50				

KM# 48 50 DOLLARS
31.10 g., 0.999 Silver 0.9989 oz. ASW **Rev:** WWII Japanese A6M Reisen

Date	Mintage	VF20	XF40	MS60	MS63	MS65
1991 M	—	PF65 27.50				

KM# 58 50 DOLLARS
31.10 g., 0.999 Silver 0.9989 oz. ASW **Rev:** WWII American P-40 Warhawk

Date	Mintage	VF20	XF40	MS60	MS63	MS65
1991 M	Est. 25000	PF65 35.00				

KM# 72 50 DOLLARS
31.10 g., 0.999 Silver 0.9989 oz. ASW **Rev:** Space Shuttle Columbia - 1981

Date	Mintage	VF20	XF40	MS60	MS63	MS65
1991	—	PF65 45.00				
Note: Smaller stars above moon						
1991 M	Est. 25000	PF65 45.00				

KM# 74 50 DOLLARS
31.10 g., 0.999 Silver 0.9989 oz. ASW **Rev:** WWII British Hurricane

Date	Mintage	VF20	XF40	MS60	MS63	MS65
1991 S	Est. 24000	PF65 35.00				

KM# 75 50 DOLLARS
31.10 g., 0.999 Silver 0.9989 oz. ASW **Rev:** WWII British Mosquito

Date	Mintage	VF20	XF40	MS60	MS63	MS65
1991 S	Est. 24000	**PF65** 35.00				

KM# 76 50 DOLLARS
31.10 g., 0.999 Silver 0.9989 oz. ASW **Rev:** WWII American B-24 Liberator

Date	Mintage	VF20	XF40	MS60	MS63	MS65
1991 S	Est. 25000	**PF65** 35.00				

KM# 77 50 DOLLARS
31.10 g., 0.999 Silver 0.9989 oz. ASW **Rev:** WWII American B-25 Mitchell

Date	Mintage	VF20	XF40	MS60	MS63	MS65
1991 S	Est. 25000	**PF65** 35.00				

KM# 78 50 DOLLARS
31.10 g., 0.999 Silver 0.9989 oz. ASW **Rev:** WWII American C-47 Skytrain

Date	Mintage	VF20	XF40	MS60	MS63	MS65
1991 S	—	**PF65** 35.00				

KM# 79 50 DOLLARS
31.10 g., 0.999 Silver 0.9989 oz. ASW **Rev:** WWII American B-17 Flying Fortress

Date	Mintage	VF20	XF40	MS60	MS63	MS65
1991 S	Est. 24000	**PF65** 37,50				

KM# 80 50 DOLLARS
31.10 g., 0.999 Silver 0.9989 oz. ASW **Rev:** WWII American F4U Corsair

Date	Mintage	VF20	XF40	MS60	MS63	MS65
1991 S	Est. 24000	**PF65** 35.00				

KM# 93 50 DOLLARS
31.10 g., 0.999 Silver 0.9989 oz. ASW **Rev:** WWII American P-38 Lightning

Date	Mintage	VF20	XF40	MS60	MS63	MS65
1991 S	—	**PF65** 35.00				

KM# 94 50 DOLLARS
31.10 g., 0.999 Silver 0.9989 oz. ASW **Rev:** WWII American F6F Hellcat

Date	Mintage	VF20	XF40	MS60	MS63	MS65
1991 S	Est. 24000	**PF65** 35.00				

KM# 95 50 DOLLARS
31.10 g., 0.999 Silver 0.9989 oz. ASW **Rev:** WWII Japanese G4M "Betty" Bomber

Date	Mintage	VF20	XF40	MS60	MS63	MS65
1991 S	Est. 25000	**PF65** 35.00				

KM# 97 50 DOLLARS
31.10 g., 0.999 Silver 0.9989 oz. ASW **Rev:** WWII Soviet Yak-9

Date	Mintage	VF20	XF40	MS60	MS63	MS65
1991 S	Est. 24000	**PF65** 35.00				

KM# 99 50 DOLLARS
31.10 g., 0.999 Silver 0.9989 oz. ASW **Rev:** WWII Japanese K1-61 Hien "Tony"

Date	Mintage	VF20	XF40	MS60	MS63	MS65
1991 S	—	**PF65** 35.00				

KM# 100 50 DOLLARS
31.10 g., 0.999 Silver 0.9989 oz. ASW **Rev:** WWII French D-520 Fighter

Date	Mintage	VF20	XF40	MS60	MS63	MS65
1991 S	Est. 25000	**PF65** 35.00				

KM# 102 50 DOLLARS
31.10 g., 0.999 Silver 0.9989 oz. ASW **Rev:** WWII German FW 190 Fighters

Date	Mintage	VF20	XF40	MS60	MS63	MS65
1991 S	Est. 24000	PF65 35.00				

KM# 104 50 DOLLARS
31.10 g., 0.999 Silver 0.9989 oz. ASW **Rev:** WWII British Lancaster

Date	Mintage	VF20	XF40	MS60	MS63	MS65
1991 S	Est. 25000	PF65 35.00				

KM# 105 50 DOLLARS
31.10 g., 0.999 Silver 0.9989 oz. ASW **Rev:** WWII Italian S.M. 79 Sparviero Bombers

Date	Mintage	VF20	XF40	MS60	MS63	MS65
1991 S	Est. 24000	PF65 37.50				

KM# 106 50 DOLLARS
31.10 g., 0.999 Silver 0.9989 oz. ASW **Rev:** WWII German HE 111 Bombers

Date	Mintage	VF20	XF40	MS60	MS63	MS65
1991 S	Est. 25000	PF65 35.00				

KM# 108 50 DOLLARS
31.10 g., 0.999 Silver 0.9989 oz. ASW **Rev:** WWII Soviet IL-2 Shturmovik

Date	Mintage	VF20	XF40	MS60	MS63	MS65
1991 S	Est. 24000	PF65 35.00				

KM# 83 50 DOLLARS
31.10 g., 0.999 Silver 0.9989 oz. ASW **Subject:** Reaching for the Stars **Rev:** Greek ship Argo

Date	Mintage	VF20	XF40	MS60	MS63	MS65
1992 R	—	—	—	—	—	32.50

KM# 86 50 DOLLARS
31.10 g., 0.999 Silver 0.9989 oz. ASW **Subject:** To the Heroes of the Raid on Tokyo - Doolittle

Date	Mintage	VF20	XF40	MS60	MS63	MS65
1992 R	—	—	—	—	—	42.50

KM# 89 50 DOLLARS
31.10 g., 0.999 Silver 0.9989 oz. ASW **Subject:** Heroes of Corregidor

Date	Mintage	VF20	XF40	MS60	MS63	MS65
1992 R	—	—	—	—	—	42.50

KM# 92 50 DOLLARS
31.10 g., 0.999 Silver 0.9989 oz. ASW **Subject:** To the Heroes of Battle of Midway

Date	Mintage	VF20	XF40	MS60	MS63	MS65
1992 R	—	—	—	—	—	37.50

KM# A69 50 DOLLARS
31.16 g., 0.999 Silver 1.0008 oz. ASW, 39 mm. **Obv:** State seal **Rev:** Long-Snouted Spinner Dolphins **Edge:** Reeded **Note:** Legal tender status questionable

Date	Mintage	VF20	XF40	MS60	MS63	MS65
1993 S	—	PF65 45.00				

KM# 111 50 DOLLARS
31.10 g., 0.999 Silver 0.9989 oz. ASW **Subject:** Pacific Whales and Dolphins **Rev:** Humpback Whale

Date	Mintage	VF20	XF40	MS60	MS63	MS65
1993 R	—	PF65 37.50				

KM# 112 50 DOLLARS
31.10 g., 0.999 Silver 0.9989 oz. ASW **Subject:** Pacific Whales and Dolphins **Rev:** Risso's Dolphins

Date	Mintage	VF20	XF40	MS60	MS63	MS65
1993 R	Est. 25000	PF65 37.50				

KM# 113 50 DOLLARS
31.10 g., 0.999 Silver 0.9989 oz. ASW **Subject:** Pacific Whales and Dolphins **Rev:** Beluga Whale

Date	Mintage	VF20	XF40	MS60	MS63	MS65
1993 R	—	PF65 35.00				

KM# 114 50 DOLLARS
31.10 g., 0.999 Silver 0.9989 oz. ASW **Subject:** Pacific Whales and Dolphins **Rev:** Hector's Dolphin

Date	Mintage	VF20	XF40	MS60	MS63	MS65
1993 R	Est. 25000	PF65 35.00				

KM# 115 50 DOLLARS
31.10 g., 0.999 Silver 0.9989 oz. ASW **Subject:** Pacific Whales and Dolphins **Rev:** Blue Whales

Date	Mintage	VF20	XF40	MS60	MS63	MS65
1993 R	Est. 25000	PF65 37.50				

KM# 116 50 DOLLARS
31.10 g., 0.999 Silver 0.9989 oz. ASW **Subject:** Pacific Whales and Dolphins **Rev:** Baiji Dolphins

Date	Mintage	VF20	XF40	MS60	MS63	MS65
1993 R	Est. 25000	PF65 37.50				

KM# 117 50 DOLLARS
31.10 g., 0.999 Silver 0.9989 oz. ASW **Subject:** Pacific Whales and Dolphins **Rev:** Killer Whales

Date	Mintage	VF20	XF40	MS60	MS63	MS65
1993 R	Est. 25000	PF65 37.50				

KM# 120 50 DOLLARS
31.10 g., 0.999 Silver 0.9989 oz. ASW **Subject:** To the Heroes of the North Atlantic **Rev:** Submarine

Date	Mintage	VF20	XF40	MS60	MS63	MS65
1993 R	—	PF65 45.00				

KM# 123 50 DOLLARS
31.10 g., 0.999 Silver 0.9989 oz. ASW **Subject:** To the Heroes of Guadalcanal **Rev:** Marine, battleship and airplanes

Date	Mintage	VF20	XF40	MS60	MS63	MS65
1993 R	—	PF65 45.00				

KM# 128 50 DOLLARS
31.10 g., 0.999 Silver 0.9989 oz. ASW **Subject:** Pacific Whales and Dolphins **Rev:** Common Dolphins

Date	Mintage	VF20	XF40	MS60	MS63	MS65
1993 R	—	PF65 37.50				

KM# 130 50 DOLLARS
31.10 g., 0.999 Silver 0.9989 oz. ASW **Rev:** Elvis Presley

Date	Mintage	VF20	XF40	MS60	MS63	MS65
1993 S	—	PF65 35.00				

KM# 146 50 DOLLARS
31.10 g., 0.999 Silver 0.9989 oz. ASW **Subject:** Christmas 1993

Date	Mintage	VF20	XF40	MS60	MS63	MS65
1993 R	—	PF65 32.50				

KM# 150 50 DOLLARS
31.10 g., 0.999 Silver 0.9989 oz. ASW **Subject:** Flight of the Kitty Hawk

Date	Mintage	VF20	XF40	MS60	MS63	MS65
1993	—	PF65 35.00				

KM# 493 50 DOLLARS
31.13 g., 0.999 Silver 0.9999 oz. ASW, 38.6 mm. **Subject:** Indo-Pacific Humpbacked Dolphin **Obv:** State seal **Rev:** Two dolphins and island **Edge:** Reeded **Note:** Legal tender status in question.

Date	Mintage	VF20	XF40	MS60	MS63	MS65
1993	25,000	PF65 45.00				

KM# 494 50 DOLLARS
31.13 g., 0.999 Silver 0.9999 oz. ASW, 38.6 mm. **Subject:** Minke Whale **Obv:** State seal **Rev:** Two Minke whales and ship with coastline in background **Edge:** Reeded **Note:** Legal tender status in question.

Date	Mintage	VF20	XF40	MS60	MS63	MS65
1993	25,000	PF65 45.00				

KM# 495 50 DOLLARS
31.16 g., 0.999 Silver 1.0008 oz. ASW, 39 mm. **Obv:** State seal **Rev:** Long-snouted Spinner Dolphins **Edge:** Reeded **Note:** Legal tender status questionable

Date	Mintage	VF20	XF40	MS60	MS63	MS65
1993 S	—	PF65 55.00				

KM# 154 50 DOLLARS
31.10 g., 0.999 Silver 0.9989 oz. ASW **Subject:** First Men on the Moon

Date	Mintage	VF20	XF40	MS60	MS63	MS65
1994	—	PF65 30.00				

KM# 167 50 DOLLARS
31.10 g., 0.999 Silver 0.9989 oz. ASW **Rev:** Mythological Mother Earth

Date	Mintage	VF20	XF40	MS60	MS63	MS65
1994	Est. 25000	PF65 32.50				

KM# 168 50 DOLLARS
31.10 g., 0.999 Silver 0.9989 oz. ASW **Rev:** Sun

Date	Mintage	VF20	XF40	MS60	MS63	MS65
1994	Est. 25000	PF65 32.50				

KM# 169 50 DOLLARS
31.10 g., 0.999 Silver 0.9989 oz. ASW **Rev:** Moon

Date	Mintage	VF20	XF40	MS60	MS63	MS65
1994	Est. 25000	PF65 32.50				

KM# 170 50 DOLLARS
31.10 g., 0.999 Silver 0.9989 oz. ASW **Rev:** Pluto

Date	Mintage	VF20	XF40	MS60	MS63	MS65
1994	Est. 25000	PF65 35.00				

KM# 171 50 DOLLARS
31.10 g., 0.999 Silver 0.9989 oz. ASW **Rev:** Mercury

Date	Mintage	VF20	XF40	MS60	MS63	MS65
1994	Est. 25000	PF65 32.50				

KM# 172 50 DOLLARS
31.10 g., 0.999 Silver 0.9989 oz. ASW **Rev:** Venus

Date	Mintage	VF20	XF40	MS60	MS63	MS65
1994	Est. 25000	PF65 37.50				

KM# 173 50 DOLLARS
31.10 g., 0.999 Silver 0.9989 oz. ASW **Rev:** Mars

Date	Mintage	VF20	XF40	MS60	MS63	MS65
1994	Est. 25000	PF65 32.50				

KM# 174 50 DOLLARS
31.10 g., 0.999 Silver 0.9989 oz. ASW **Rev:** Saturn

Date	Mintage	VF20	XF40	MS60	MS63	MS65
1994	—	PF65 32.50				

KM# 175 50 DOLLARS
31.10 g., 0.999 Silver 0.9989 oz. ASW **Rev:** Jupiter

Date	Mintage	VF20	XF40	MS60	MS63	MS65
1994	—	PF65 32.50				

KM# 176 50 DOLLARS
31.10 g., 0.999 Silver 0.9989 oz. ASW **Rev:** Uranus

Date	Mintage	VF20	XF40	MS60	MS63	MS65
1994	Est. 25000	PF65 32.50				

KM# 177 50 DOLLARS
31.10 g., 0.999 Silver 0.9989 oz. ASW **Rev:** Neptune

Date	Mintage	VF20	XF40	MS60	MS63	MS65
1994	Est. 25000	PF65 35.00				

KM# 178 50 DOLLARS
31.10 g., 0.999 Silver 0.9989 oz. ASW **Rev:** Solar System

Date	Mintage	VF20	XF40	MS60	MS63	MS65
1994	—	PF65 32.50				

KM# 181 50 DOLLARS
31.10 g., 0.999 Silver 0.9989 oz. ASW **Subject:** To the Heroes of D-Day - Normandy Invasion

Date	Mintage	VF20	XF40	MS60	MS63	MS65
1994	—	PF65 35.00				

KM# 184 50 DOLLARS
31.10 g., 0.999 Silver 0.9989 oz. ASW **Subject:** Heroes of the Philippines **Rev:** MacArthur and Staff

Date	Mintage	VF20	XF40	MS60	MS63	MS65
1994	—	PF65 42.50				

KM# 190 50 DOLLARS
31.10 g., 0.999 Silver 0.9989 oz. ASW **Subject:** World Cup Soccer

Date	Mintage	VF20	XF40	MS60	MS63	MS65
1994	—	PF65 37.50				

KM# 262 50 DOLLARS
31.10 g., 0.999 Silver 0.9989 oz. ASW **Subject:** Christmas **Rev:** Angel

Date	Mintage	VF20	XF40	MS60	MS63	MS65
1994	—	PF65 32.50				

KM# 265 50 DOLLARS
31.10 g., 0.999 Silver 0.9989 oz. ASW **Subject:** To the Heroes of Battle of the Bulge

Date	Mintage	VF20	XF40	MS60	MS63	MS65
1994	—	PF65 35.00				

KM# 191 50 DOLLARS
31.10 g., 0.999 Silver 0.9989 oz. ASW **Rev:** Jet Fighter - F-4 Phantom II

Date	Mintage	VF20	XF40	MS60	MS63	MS65
1995	25,000	PF65 37.50				

KM# 192 50 DOLLARS
31.10 g., 0.999 Silver 0.9989 oz. ASW **Rev:** Jet Fighter - F-100 Super Sabre

Date	Mintage	VF20	XF40	MS60	MS63	MS65
1995	25,000	PF65 35.00				

KM# 193 50 DOLLARS
31.10 g., 0.999 Silver 0.9989 oz. ASW **Rev:** Jet Fighter - Mirage 2000C

Date	Mintage	VF20	XF40	MS60	MS63	MS65
1995	25,000	PF65 35.00				

KM# 194 50 DOLLARS
31.10 g., 0.999 Silver 0.9989 oz. ASW **Rev:** Jet Fighter - F-14 Tomcat

Date	Mintage	VF20	XF40	MS60	MS63	MS65
1995	25,000	PF65 35.00				

KM# 195 50 DOLLARS

31.10 g., 0.999 Silver 0.9989 oz. ASW **Rev:** Jet Fighter - F-86 Sabre

Date	Mintage	VF20	XF40	MS60	MS63	MS65
1995	25,000	PF65 35.00				

KM# 196 50 DOLLARS

31.10 g., 0.999 Silver 0.9989 oz. ASW **Rev:** Jet Fighter - MIG 15

Date	Mintage	VF20	XF40	MS60	MS63	MS65
1995	25,000	PF65 35.00				

KM# 197 50 DOLLARS

31.10 g., 0.999 Silver 0.9989 oz. ASW **Rev:** Jet Fighter - G91R

Date	Mintage	VF20	XF40	MS60	MS63	MS65
1995	25,000	PF65 37.50				

KM# 198 50 DOLLARS

31.10 g., 0.999 Silver 0.9989 oz. ASW **Rev:** Jet Fighter - Saab J35 Draken

Date	Mintage	VF20	XF40	MS60	MS63	MS65
1995	25,000	PF65 35.00				

KM# 199 50 DOLLARS

31.10 g., 0.999 Silver 0.9989 oz. ASW **Rev:** Jet Fighter - Meteor F.MK8

Date	Mintage	VF20	XF40	MS60	MS63	MS65
1995	25,000	PF65 35.00				

KM# 200 50 DOLLARS

31.10 g., 0.999 Silver 0.9989 oz. ASW **Rev:** Jet Fighter - F-105 Thunderchief

Date	Mintage	VF20	XF40	MS60	MS63	MS65
1995	25,000	PF65 35.00				

KM# 201 50 DOLLARS

31.10 g., 0.999 Silver 0.9989 oz. ASW **Rev:** Jet Fighter - Tornado F.MK3

Date	Mintage	VF20	XF40	MS60	MS63	MS65
1995	25,000	PF65 35.00				

KM# 202 50 DOLLARS

31.10 g., 0.999 Silver 0.9989 oz. ASW **Rev:** Jet Fighter - F-16 Fighting Falcon

Date	Mintage	VF20	XF40	MS60	MS63	MS65
1995	25,000	PF65 35.00				

KM# 203 50 DOLLARS

31.10 g., 0.999 Silver 0.9989 oz. ASW **Rev:** Me 262A-la Schwable

Date	Mintage	VF20	XF40	MS60	MS63	MS65
1995	25,000	PF65 35.00				

KM# 204 50 DOLLARS

31.10 g., 0.999 Silver 0.9989 oz. ASW **Rev:** Sea Harrier FRS. MK 1

Date	Mintage	VF20	XF40	MS60	MS63	MS65
1995	25,000	PF65 35.00				

KM# 205 50 DOLLARS

31.10 g., 0.999 Silver 0.9989 oz. ASW **Rev:** F-117 Nighthawk

Date	Mintage	VF20	XF40	MS60	MS63	MS65
1995	25,000	PF65 37.50				

KM# 206 50 DOLLARS

31.10 g., 0.999 Silver 0.9989 oz. ASW **Rev:** MIG - 21MF

Date	Mintage	VF20	XF40	MS60	MS63	MS65
1995	25,000	PF65 37.50				

KM# 207 50 DOLLARS

31.10 g., 0.999 Silver 0.9989 oz. ASW **Rev:** F-104 Starfighter

Date	Mintage	VF20	XF40	MS60	MS63	MS65
1995	25,000	PF65 35.00				

KM# 208 50 DOLLARS

31.10 g., 0.999 Silver 0.9989 oz. ASW **Rev:** Sukhoi SU-27 UB

Date	Mintage	VF20	XF40	MS60	MS63	MS65
1995	25,000	PF65 37.50				

KM# 209 50 DOLLARS

31.10 g., 0.999 Silver 0.9989 oz. ASW **Rev:** F-80 Shooting Star

Date	Mintage	VF20	XF40	MS60	MS63	MS65
1995	25,000	PF65 35.00				

KM# 210 50 DOLLARS

31.10 g., 0.999 Silver 0.9989 oz. ASW **Rev:** Swedish Saab JA 37 Viggen

Date	Mintage	VF20	XF40	MS60	MS63	MS65
1995	25,000	PF65 35.00				

KM# 211 50 DOLLARS

31.10 g., 0.999 Silver 0.9989 oz. ASW **Rev:** F8U Crusader

Date	Mintage	VF20	XF40	MS60	MS63	MS65
1995	25,000	PF65 35.00				

KM# 212 50 DOLLARS

31.10 g., 0.999 Silver 0.9989 oz. ASW **Rev:** Fiat-G91Y Jet Fighter

Date	Mintage	VF20	XF40	MS60	MS63	MS65
1995	25,000	PF65 37.50				

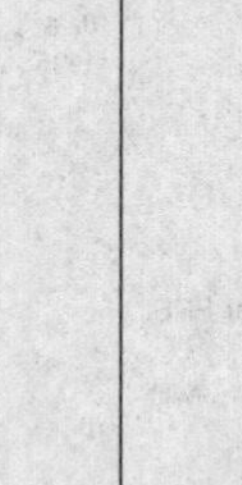

KM# 213 50 DOLLARS

31.10 g., 0.999 Silver 0.9989 oz. ASW **Rev:** Mirage FIC

Date	Mintage	VF20	XF40	MS60	MS63	MS65
1995	Est. 25000	PF65 35.00				

KM# 214 50 DOLLARS

31.10 g., 0.999 Silver 0.9989 oz. ASW **Rev:** F-15 Eagle

Date	Mintage	VF20	XF40	MS60	MS63	MS65
1995	Est. 25000	PF65 35.00				

KM# 215 50 DOLLARS

31.10 g., 0.999 Silver 0.9989 oz. ASW **Obv:** State seal **Rev:** F9F-2 Panther

Date	Mintage	VF20	XF40	MS60	MS63	MS65
1995	Est. 25000	PF65 35.00				

KM# 218 50 DOLLARS

31.10 g., 0.999 Silver 0.9989 oz. ASW **Subject:** Victory in Europe **Note:** Similar to 5 Dollars, KM#216.

Date	Mintage	VF20	XF40	MS60	MS63	MS65
1995	—	PF65 37.50				

KM# 221 50 DOLLARS

31.10 g., 0.999 Silver 0.9989 oz. ASW **Subject:** Vietnam Veterans **Note:** Similar to 5 Dollars, KM#219.

Date	Mintage	VF20	XF40	MS60	MS63	MS65
1995	—	PF65 27.50				

KM# 224 50 DOLLARS

31.10 g., 0.999 Silver 0.9989 oz. ASW **Rev:** Elvis Presley

Date	Mintage	VF20	XF40	MS60	MS63	MS65
1995	—	PF65 45.00				

KM# 227 50 DOLLARS

31.10 g., 0.999 Silver 0.9989 oz. ASW **Subject:** War in the Pacific **Note:** Similar to 10 Dollars, KM#226.

Date	Mintage	VF20	XF40	MS60	MS63	MS65
1995	—	PF65 35.00				

KM# 256 50 DOLLARS

31.10 g., 0.999 Silver 0.9989 oz. ASW **Rev:** Head of Marilyn Monroe right, 1926-1962, actress

Date	Mintage	VF20	XF40	MS60	MS63	MS65
1995	—	PF65 40.00				

KM# 259 50 DOLLARS

31.10 g., 0.999 Silver 0.9989 oz. ASW **Series:** 50th Anniversary United Nations **Subject:** Peace

Date	Mintage	VF20	XF40	MS60	MS63	MS65
1995	—	PF65 32.50				

KM# 268 50 DOLLARS

31.10 g., 0.999 Silver 0.9989 oz. ASW **Subject:** Peace - VJ Day

Date	Mintage	VF20	XF40	MS60	MS63	MS65
1995	—	PF65 40.00				

KM# 273 50 DOLLARS

31.10 g., 0.999 Silver 0.9989 oz. ASW **Subject:** Christmas **Rev:** Cherub

Date	Mintage	VF20	XF40	MS60	MS63	MS65
1995	—	PF65 37.50				

KM# 274 50 DOLLARS

31.10 g., 0.999 Silver 0.9989 oz. ASW **Subject:** Freedom / Liberty **Rev:** Torpedo Boat PT-109

Date	Mintage	VF20	XF40	MS60	MS63	MS65
1995	Est. 25000	PF65 45.00				

KM# 275 50 DOLLARS

31.10 g., 0.999 Silver 0.9989 oz. ASW **Subject:** Freedom / Liberty **Rev:** President John F. Kennedy takes oath of office

Date	Mintage	VF20	XF40	MS60	MS63	MS65
1995	Est. 25000	PF65 45.00				

KM# 276 50 DOLLARS

31.10 g., 0.999 Silver 0.9989 oz. ASW **Subject:** Freedom / Liberty **Rev:** Peace Corps worker and native

Date	Mintage	VF20	XF40	MS60	MS63	MS65
1995	Est. 25000	PF65 45.00				

KM# 277 50 DOLLARS
31.10 g., 0.999 Silver 0.9989 oz. ASW **Subject:** Freedom / LIberty **Rev:** Battleship and freighter

Date	Mintage	VF20	XF40	MS60	MS63	MS65
1995	Est. 25000	PF65 45.00				

KM# 278 50 DOLLARS
31.10 g., 0.999 Silver 0.9989 oz. ASW **Subject:** Freedom / Liberty **Rev:** President John F. Kennedy working at desk

Date	Mintage	VF20	XF40	MS60	MS63	MS65
1995	Est. 25000	PF65 45.00				

KM# 279 50 DOLLARS
31.10 g., 0.999 Silver 0.9989 oz. ASW **Subject:** Freedom / Liberty **Rev:** President John F. Kennedy's Eternal Flame

Date	Mintage	VF20	XF40	MS60	MS63	MS65
1995	Est. 25000	PF65 45.00				

KM# 367 50 DOLLARS
31.10 g., 0.999 Silver 0.9989 oz. ASW **Obv:** State seal **Rev:** F-102A Delta Dagger

Date	Mintage	VF20	XF40	MS60	MS63	MS65
1995	25,000	PF65 35.00				

KM# 397 50 DOLLARS
31.10 g., 0.999 Silver 0.9989 oz. ASW **Obv:** State seal **Rev:** B-52 Stratofortress

Date	Mintage	VF20	XF40	MS60	MS63	MS65
1995	25,000	PF65 35.00				

KM# 281 50 DOLLARS
31.10 g., 0.999 Silver 0.9989 oz. ASW **Subject:** Year of the Rat **Note:** Similar to 5 Dollars, KM#280.

Date	Mintage	VF20	XF40	MS60	MS63	MS65
1996	—	PF65 37.50				

KM# 290 50 DOLLARS
31.10 g., 0.999 Silver 0.9989 oz. ASW **Rev:** Space Shuttle Columbia

Date	Mintage	VF20	XF40	MS60	MS63	MS65
1996	—	PF65 42.50				

KM# 291 50 DOLLARS
31.18 g., 0.999 Silver 1.0015 oz. ASW, 38.68 mm. **Obv:** National arms **Rev:** "Pennsylvania K4" steam locomotive **Edge:** Reeded

Date	Mintage	VF20	XF40	MS60	MS63	MS65
1996	—	PF65 35.00				

KM# 292 50 DOLLARS
31.18 g., 0.999 Silver 1.0015 oz. ASW, 38.68 mm. **Obv:** National arms **Rev:** "Big Boy" steam locomotive **Edge:** Reeded

Date	Mintage	VF20	XF40	MS60	MS63	MS65
1996	—	PF65 35.00				

KM# 296 50 DOLLARS
31.18 g., 0.999 Silver 1.0015 oz. ASW, 38.68 mm. **Obv:** National arms **Rev:** "Mallard" steam locomotive **Edge:** Reeded

Date	Mintage	VF20	XF40	MS60	MS63	MS65
1996	—	PF65 35.00				

KM# 299 50 DOLLARS
31.10 g., 0.999 Silver 0.9989 oz. ASW **Rev:** Tiger

Date	Mintage	VF20	XF40	MS60	MS63	MS65
1996 In set only	—	—	—	—	—	40.00

KM# 302 50 DOLLARS
31.10 g., 0.999 Silver 0.9989 oz. ASW **Rev:** Elvis Presley

Date	Mintage	VF20	XF40	MS60	MS63	MS65
1996	—	PF65 40.00				

KM# 305 50 DOLLARS
31.10 g., 0.999 Silver 0.9989 oz. ASW **Rev:** James Dean **Note:** Similar to 5 Dollars, KM#303.

Date	Mintage	VF20	XF40	MS60	MS63	MS65
1996	—	PF65 40.00				

KM# 310 50 DOLLARS
31.10 g., 0.999 Silver 0.9989 oz. ASW **Subject:** Classic Cars **Rev:** Ford Quadricycle

Date	Mintage	VF20	XF40	MS60	MS63	MS65
1996	—	PF65 35.00				

KM# 313 50 DOLLARS
31.10 g., 0.999 Silver 0.9989 oz. ASW **Subject:** Classic Cars **Rev:** Model A Ford **Note:** Similar to 10 Dollars, KM#312.

Date	Mintage	VF20	XF40	MS60	MS63	MS65
1996	—	PF65 35.00				

KM# 316 50 DOLLARS
31.10 g., 0.999 Silver 0.9989 oz. ASW **Subject:** Classic Cars **Rev:** Model T Ford

Date	Mintage	VF20	XF40	MS60	MS63	MS65
1996	—	PF65 35.00				

KM# 319 50 DOLLARS
31.10 g., 0.999 Silver 0.9989 oz. ASW **Subject:** Classic Cars **Rev:** 1955 Thunderbird

Date	Mintage	VF20	XF40	MS60	MS63	MS65
1996	—	PF65 42.50				

KM# 322 50 DOLLARS
31.10 g., 0.999 Silver 0.9989 oz. ASW **Subject:** Classic Cars **Rev:** 1964 Mustang

Date	Mintage	VF20	XF40	MS60	MS63	MS65
1996	—	PF65 37.50				

KM# 325 50 DOLLARS
31.10 g., 0.999 Silver 0.9989 oz. ASW **Subject:** Classic Cars **Rev:** Ford Taurus

Date	Mintage	VF20	XF40	MS60	MS63	MS65
1996	—	PF65 32.50				

KM# 327 50 DOLLARS
31.18 g., 0.999 Silver 1.0015 oz. ASW, 38.68 mm. **Obv:** National arms **Rev:** "DB Class 01" steam locomotive **Edge:** Reeded

Date	Mintage	VF20	XF40	MS60	MS63	MS65
1996	Est. 25000	PF65 35.00				

KM# 328 50 DOLLARS
31.18 g., 0.999 Silver 1.0015 oz. ASW, 38.68 mm. **Obv:** National arms **Rev:** "RENFE Class 242" steam locomotive **Edge:** Reeded

Date	Mintage	VF20	XF40	MS60	MS63	MS65
1996	—	PF65 35.00				

KM# 329 50 DOLLARS
31.18 g., 0.999 Silver 1.0015 oz. ASW, 38.68 mm. **Obv:** National arms **Rev:** Steam locomotive "S Group 691" **Edge:** Reeded

Date	Mintage	VF20	XF40	MS60	MS63	MS65
1996	—	PF65 35.00				

KM# 340 50 DOLLARS
31.10 g., 0.999 Silver 0.9989 oz. ASW **Rev:** Space Shuttle Challenger **Note:** Similar to 10 Dollars, KM#336.

Date	Mintage	VF20	XF40	MS60	MS63	MS65
1996	—	PF65 42.50				

KM# 341 50 DOLLARS
31.10 g., 0.999 Silver 0.9989 oz. ASW **Rev:** Space Shuttle Discovery **Note:** Similar to 10 Dollars, KM#338.

Date	Mintage	VF20	XF40	MS60	MS63	MS65
1996	—	PF65 42.50				

KM# 342 50 DOLLARS
31.10 g., 0.999 Silver 0.9989 oz. ASW **Rev:** Space Shuttle Atlantis

Date	Mintage	VF20	XF40	MS60	MS63	MS65
1996	—	PF65 42.50				

KM# 343 50 DOLLARS
31.10 g., 0.999 Silver 0.9989 oz. ASW **Rev:** Space Shuttle Endeavor

Date	Mintage	VF20	XF40	MS60	MS63	MS65
1996	—	PF65 42.50				

KM# 350 50 DOLLARS
31.10 g., 0.999 Silver 0.9989 oz. ASW **Rev:** Lion **Note:** Similar to 5 Dollars, KM#344.

Date	Mintage	VF20	XF40	MS60	MS63	MS65
1996	—	PF65 40.00				

KM# 351 50 DOLLARS
31.10 g., 0.999 Silver 0.9989 oz. ASW **Rev:** Cheetah

Date	Mintage	VF20	XF40	MS60	MS63	MS65
1996	—	PF65 37.50				

KM# 352 50 DOLLARS
31.10 g., 0.999 Silver 0.9989 oz. ASW **Rev:** Jaguar **Note:** Similar to 5 Dollars, KM#346.

Date	Mintage	VF20	XF40	MS60	MS63	MS65
1996	—	PF65 30.00				

KM# 355 50 DOLLARS
31.10 g., 0.999 Silver 0.9989 oz. ASW **Subject:** Christmas **Rev:** Two angels

Date	Mintage	VF20	XF40	MS60	MS63	MS65
1996	—	PF65 35.00				

KM# 357 50 DOLLARS
31.10 g., 0.999 Silver 0.9989 oz. ASW **Subject:** Steam Locomotive **Rev:** SNCF 232.U1

Date	Mintage	VF20	XF40	MS60	MS63	MS65
1996	—	PF65 37.50				

KM# 358 50 DOLLARS
31.10 g., 0.999 Silver 0.9989 oz. ASW **Subject:** Steam Locomotive **Rev:** SAR 520 Class

Date	Mintage	VF20	XF40	MS60	MS63	MS65
1996	—	PF65 37.50				

KM# 360 50 DOLLARS
31.10 g., 0.999 Silver 0.9989 oz. ASW **Subject:** Steam Locomotive **Rev:** Evening Star

Date	Mintage	VF20	XF40	MS60	MS63	MS65
1996	—	PF65 37.50				

KM# 376 50 DOLLARS

31.10 g., 0.999 Silver 0.9989 oz. ASW **Subject:** Steam Locomotive **Rev:** C62 "Swallow"

Date	Mintage	VF20	XF40	MS60	MS63	MS65
1996	—	PF65 35.00				

KM# 377 50 DOLLARS

31.10 g., 0.999 Silver 0.9989 oz. ASW **Subject:** Steam Locomotive **Rev:** QJ "Advance Forward"

Date	Mintage	VF20	XF40	MS60	MS63	MS65
1996	—	PF65 35.00				

KM# 380 50 DOLLARS

31.10 g., 0.999 Silver 0.9989 oz. ASW **Subject:** Steam Locomotive **Rev:** Royal Hudson

Date	Mintage	VF20	XF40	MS60	MS63	MS65
1996	—	PF65 35.00				

KM# 363 50 DOLLARS

31.10 g., 0.999 Silver 0.9989 oz. ASW **Subject:** Year of the Ox **Obv:** State seal **Rev:** Stylized ox

Date	Mintage	VF20	XF40	MS60	MS63	MS65
1997	—	PF65 45.00				

KM# 366 50 DOLLARS

31.10 g., 0.999 Silver 0.9989 oz. ASW **Rev:** Elvis Presley **Note:** Similar to 5 Dollars, KM#362.

Date	Mintage	VF20	XF40	MS60	MS63	MS65
1997	—	PF65 45.00				

KM# 370 50 DOLLARS

31.10 g., 0.999 Silver 0.9989 oz. ASW **Subject:** The Last Supper **Note:** Similar to 5 Dollars, KM#369.

Date	Mintage	VF20	XF40	MS60	MS63	MS65
1997	—	PF65 40.00				

KM# 373 50 DOLLARS

31.10 g., 0.999 Silver 0.9989 oz. ASW **Subject:** To the Heroes of the Korean War **Note:** Similar to 5 Dollars, KM#371.

Date	Mintage	VF20	XF40	MS60	MS63	MS65
1997	—	PF65 32.50				

KM# 375 50 DOLLARS

31.10 g., 0.999 Silver 0.9989 oz. ASW **Rev:** Gray wolf

Date	Mintage	VF20	XF40	MS60	MS63	MS65
1997	—	PF65 45.00				

KM# 399 50 DOLLARS

31.10 g., 0.999 Silver 0.9989 oz. ASW **Subject:** History's Great Fighting Ships **Rev:** USS Constitution; ship, dates

Date	Mintage	VF20	XF40	MS60	MS63	MS65
1997	—	PF65 60.00				

KM# 405 50 DOLLARS

31.10 g., 0.999 Silver 0.9989 oz. ASW **Subject:** Christmas **Rev:** Two cherubs

Date	Mintage	VF20	XF40	MS60	MS63	MS65
1997	—	PF65 32.50				

KM# 414 50 DOLLARS

31.10 g., 0.999 Silver 0.9989 oz. ASW **Subject:** Year of the Tiger **Rev:** Stylized tiger

Date	Mintage	VF20	XF40	MS60	MS63	MS65
1998	—	PF65 40.00				

KM# 416 50 DOLLARS

31.10 g., 0.999 Silver 0.9989 oz. ASW **Subject:** History's Great Fighting Ships **Rev:** Viking Longship

Date	Mintage	VF20	XF40	MS60	MS63	MS65
1998 S	Est. 25000	PF65 60.00				

KM# 418 50 DOLLARS

31.10 g., 0.999 Silver 0.9989 oz. ASW **Subject:** History's Great Fighting Ships **Rev:** Greek Trireme

Date	Mintage	VF20	XF40	MS60	MS63	MS65
1998	Est. 25000	PF65 60.00				

KM# 420 50 DOLLARS

31.10 g., 0.999 Silver 0.9989 oz. ASW **Subject:** History's Great Fighting Ships **Rev:** Roman Trireme

Date	Mintage	VF20	XF40	MS60	MS63	MS65
1998	Est. 25000	PF65 60.00				

KM# 422 50 DOLLARS

31.10 g., 0.999 Silver 0.9989 oz. ASW **Subject:** History's Great Fighting Ships **Rev:** Chinese Ming Treasure Ship

Date	Mintage	VF20	XF40	MS60	MS63	MS65
1998	Est. 25000	PF65 60.00				

KM# 424 50 DOLLARS

31.10 g., 0.999 Silver 0.9989 oz. ASW **Subject:** History's Great Fighting Ships **Rev:** Korean Turtle Ship

Date	Mintage	VF20	XF40	MS60	MS63	MS65
1998	Est. 25000	PF65 40.00				

KM# 426 50 DOLLARS

31.10 g., 0.999 Silver 0.9989 oz. ASW **Subject:** History's Great Fighting Ships **Rev:** Fijan War Canoe

Date	Mintage	VF20	XF40	MS60	MS63	MS65
1998	Est. 25000	PF65 60.00				

KM# 428 50 DOLLARS

31.10 g., 0.999 Silver 0.9989 oz. ASW **Subject:** History's Great Fighting Ships **Rev:** The Bismarck

Date	Mintage	VF20	XF40	MS60	MS63	MS65
1998	Est. 25000	PF65 60.00				

KM# 430 50 DOLLARS

31.10 g., 0.999 Silver 0.9989 oz. ASW **Subject:** History's Great Fighting Ships **Rev:** The Graf Spee

Date	Mintage	VF20	XF40	MS60	MS63	MS65
1998	Est. 25000	PF65 60.00				

KM# 432 50 DOLLARS

31.10 g., 0.999 Silver 0.9989 oz. ASW **Subject:** History's Great Fighting Ships **Rev:** The Yamato

Date	Mintage	VF20	XF40	MS60	MS63	MS65
1998	Est. 25000	PF65 60.00				

KM# 434 50 DOLLARS

31.10 g., 0.999 Silver 0.9989 oz. ASW **Subject:** History's Great Fighting Ships **Rev:** HMS Victory

Date	Mintage	VF20	XF40	MS60	MS63	MS65
1998	—	PF65 60.00				

KM# 436 50 DOLLARS

31.10 g., 0.999 Silver 0.9989 oz. ASW **Subject:** History's Great Fighting Ships **Rev:** HMS Mary Rose

Date	Mintage	VF20	XF40	MS60	MS63	MS65
1998	Est. 25000	PF65 60.00				

KM# 438 50 DOLLARS

31.10 g., 0.999 Silver 0.9989 oz. ASW **Subject:** History's Great Fighting Ships **Rev:** HMS Dreadnought

Date	Mintage	VF20	XF40	MS60	MS63	MS65
1998	Est. 25000	PF65 60.00				

KM# 440 50 DOLLARS

31.10 g., 0.999 Silver 0.9989 oz. ASW **Subject:** History's Great Fighting Ships **Rev:** HMS Dorsetshire

Date	Mintage	VF20	XF40	MS60	MS63	MS65
1998	Est. 25000	PF65 60.00				

KM# 442 50 DOLLARS
31.10 g., 0.999 Silver 0.9989 oz. ASW **Subject:** History's Great Fighting Ships **Obv:** State seal **Rev:** Spanish Galleon Nuestra Senora del Rosario

Date	Mintage	VF20	XF40	MS60	MS63	MS65
1998	Est. 25000	PF65 60.00				

KM# 444 50 DOLLARS
31.10 g., 0.999 Silver 0.9989 oz. ASW **Subject:** History's Great Fighting Ships **Obv:** State seal **Rev:** Spanish Galleon Santisima Trinidad

Date	Mintage	VF20	XF40	MS60	MS63	MS65
1998	—	PF65 60.00				

KM# 446 50 DOLLARS
31.10 g., 0.999 Silver 0.9989 oz. ASW **Subject:** History's Great Fighting Ships **Obv:** State seal **Rev:** USS Bonhomme Richard

Date	Mintage	VF20	XF40	MS60	MS63	MS65
1998	Est. 25000	PF65 60.00				

KM# 448 50 DOLLARS
31.10 g., 0.999 Silver 0.9989 oz. ASW **Subject:** History's Great Fighting Ships **Obv:** State seal **Rev:** USS Constellation

Date	Mintage	VF20	XF40	MS60	MS63	MS65
1998	Est. 25000	PF65 60.00				

KM# 450 50 DOLLARS
31.10 g., 0.999 Silver 0.9989 oz. ASW **Subject:** History's Great Fighting Ships **Obv:** State seal **Rev:** USS Hartford

Date	Mintage	VF20	XF40	MS60	MS63	MS65
1998	Est. 25000	PF65 60.00				

KM# 452 50 DOLLARS
31.10 g., 0.999 Silver 0.9989 oz. ASW **Subject:** History's Great Fighting Ships **Obv:** State seal **Rev:** USS Hornet

Date	Mintage	VF20	XF40	MS60	MS63	MS65
1998	Est. 25000	PF65 60.00				

KM# 454 50 DOLLARS
31.10 g., 0.999 Silver 0.9989 oz. ASW **Subject:** History's Great Fighting Ships **Obv:** State seal **Rev:** USS Missouri

Date	Mintage	VF20	XF40	MS60	MS63	MS65
1998	Est. 25000	PF65 60.00				

KM# 456 50 DOLLARS
31.10 g., 0.999 Silver 0.9989 oz. ASW **Subject:** History's Great Fighting Ships **Obv:** State seal **Rev:** USS Tautog

Date	Mintage	VF20	XF40	MS60	MS63	MS65
1998	Est. 25000	PF65 60.00				

KM# 458 50 DOLLARS
31.10 g., 0.999 Silver 0.9989 oz. ASW **Subject:** History's Great Fighting Ships **Obv:** State seal **Rev:** Dutch Ship Brederode

Date	Mintage	VF20	XF40	MS60	MS63	MS65
1998	Est. 25000	PF65 60.00				

KM# 460 50 DOLLARS
31.10 g., 0.999 Silver 0.9989 oz. ASW **Subject:** History's Great Fighting Ships **Obv:** State seal **Rev:** French Ship Ville de Paris

Date	Mintage	VF20	XF40	MS60	MS63	MS65
1998	Est. 25000	PF65 60.00				

KM# 462 50 DOLLARS
31.10 g., 0.999 Silver 0.9989 oz. ASW **Subject:** History's Great Fighting Ships **Obv:** State seal **Rev:** Italian Ship Galera Veneziana

Date	Mintage	VF20	XF40	MS60	MS63	MS65
1998	Est. 25000	PF65 60.00				

KM# 465 50 DOLLARS
31.10 g., 0.999 Silver 0.9989 oz. ASW **Subject:** To the Heroes of the Berlin Airlift **Obv:** State seal **Rev:** C-54 Landing

Date	Mintage	VF20	XF40	MS60	MS63	MS65
1998	—	PF65 35.00				

KM# 467 50 DOLLARS
31.10 g., 0.999 Silver 0.9989 oz. ASW **Subject:** Classic Cars **Obv:** State seal **Rev:** 1912 Chevy Classic Six **Note:** Similar to 5 Dollars, KM#466.

Date	Mintage	VF20	XF40	MS60	MS63	MS65
1998	—	PF65 35.00				

KM# 469 50 DOLLARS
31.10 g., 0.999 Silver 0.9989 oz. ASW **Subject:** Classic Cars **Obv:** State seal **Rev:** 1931 Chevy Roadster **Note:** Similar to 5 Dollars, KM#468.

Date	Mintage	VF20	XF40	MS60	MS63	MS65
1998	—	PF65 40.00				

KM# 471 50 DOLLARS
31.10 g., 0.999 Silver 0.9989 oz. ASW **Subject:** Classic Cars **Obv:** State seal **Rev:** Cameo Carrier **Note:** Similar to 5 Dollars, KM#470.

Date	Mintage	VF20	XF40	MS60	MS63	MS65
1998	—	PF65 37.50				

KM# 473 50 DOLLARS
31.10 g., 0.999 Silver 0.9989 oz. ASW **Subject:** Classic Cars **Obv:** State seal **Rev:** 1957 Chevy Bel Air **Note:** Similar to 5 Dollars, KM#472.

Date	Mintage	VF20	XF40	MS60	MS63	MS65
1998	—	PF65 40.00				

KM# 475 50 DOLLARS
31.10 g., 0.999 Silver 0.9989 oz. ASW **Subject:** Classic Cars **Obv:** State seal **Rev:** 1957 Chevy Corvette **Note:** Similar to 5 Dollars, KM#474.

Date	Mintage	VF20	XF40	MS60	MS63	MS65
1998	—	PF65 40.00				

KM# 477 50 DOLLARS
31.10 g., 0.999 Silver 0.9989 oz. ASW **Subject:** Classic Cars **Obv:** State seal **Rev:** 1967 Chevy Camaro **Note:** Similar to 5 Dollars, KM#476.

Date	Mintage	VF20	XF40	MS60	MS63	MS65
1998	—	PF65 40.00				

KM# 480 50 DOLLARS
31.10 g., 0.999 Silver 0.9989 oz. ASW **Subject:** Babe Ruth at bat **Obv:** State seal

Date	Mintage	VF20	XF40	MS60	MS63	MS65
1998	—	PF65 35.00				

KM# 483 50 DOLLARS
31.10 g., 0.999 Silver 0.9989 oz. ASW **Subject:** Christmas **Obv:** State seal **Rev:** Angel

Date	Mintage	VF20	XF40	MS60	MS63	MS65
1998	—	PF65 35.00				

KM# 485 50 DOLLARS
31.10 g., 0.999 Silver 0.9989 oz. ASW **Rev:** Friendship 7 and Discovery blasting off **Edge:** Reeded

Date	Mintage	VF20	XF40	MS60	MS63	MS65
1998	—	PF65 45.00				

KM# 16 75 DOLLARS
155.67 g., 0.999 Silver 4.9999 oz. ASW, 65 mm. **Subject:** Greg Louganis - World's Greatest Diver **Note:** Illustration reduced. An actual mintage of 20 pieces has been reported for KM#16.

Date	Mintage	VF20	XF40	MS60	MS63	MS65
1988	Est. 175000	PF63 800	PF65 850	PF67 900		

KM# 17 100 DOLLARS
13.33 g., 0.583 Gold 0.2499 oz. AGW **Subject:** Greg Louganis - World's Greatest Diver **Obv:** State seal and legend **Rev:** Diver

Date	Mintage	VF20	XF40	MS60	MS63	MS65
1988	—	—	—	450	475	525
1988	Est. 350000	PF63 550	PF65 600	PF67 650		

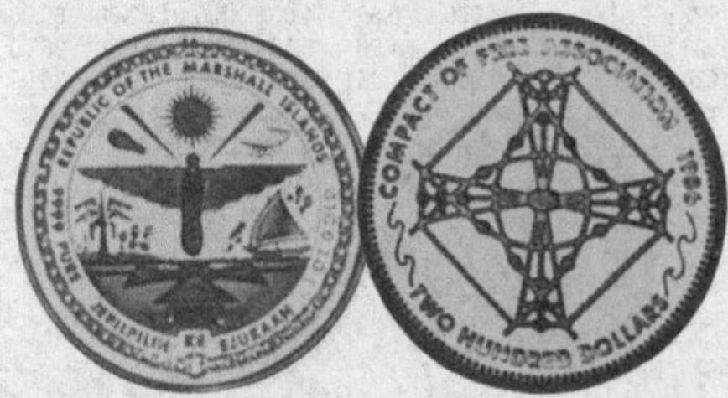

KM# 5 200 DOLLARS
31.10 g., 0.999 Gold 0.999 oz. AGW **Rev:** Stick chart

Date	Mintage	XF40	MS60	MS63	MS65	MS66
1986	Est. 5000	PF67 1,500	PF69 1,700			

MINT SETS

KM#	Date	Mintage	Identification	Issue Price	Mkt Val
MS1	1988 (3)	—	KM#20-22	—	275
MS2	1988 (4)	—	KM#17, 20-22	—	675
MS3	1992R (3)	—	KM#81-83	71.00	65.00
MS4	1992R (3)	—	KM#84-86	71.00	65.00
MS5	1992R (3)	—	KM#87-89	71.00	65.00
MS6	1992R (3)	—	KM#90-92	71.00	65.00
MS7	1992R (3)	—	KM#84, 87, 90	17.50	22.00
MS8	1992R (3)	—	KM#85, 88, 91	34.00	37.50
MS9	1992R (3)	—	KM#86, 89, 92	156	140
MS10	1995 (6)	—	KM#282-287	66.00	75.00
MS11	1998 (24)	25,000	KM#415, 417, 419, 421, 423, 425, 427, 429, 431, 433, 435, 437, 439, 441, 443, 445, 447, 449, 451, 453, 455, 457, 459, 461	288	290

PROOF SETS

KM#	Date	Mintage	Identification	Issue Price	Mkt Val
PS1	1986 (3)	5,000	KM#3-5	1,095	2,000
PS2	1986 (2)	10,000	KM#1-2	45.00	55.00
PS3	1988 (3)	—	KM#20-22	—	330
PS4	1988 (4)	—	KM#17, 20-22	—	775
PS5	1991 (3)	—	KM#40-42	71.00	75.00
PS6	1993 (3)	—	KM#124, 129-130	—	85.00
PS7	1994 (3)	—	KM#179-180 BU, 181	71.00	75.00
PS8	1994 (3)	—	KM#182 BU, 183 P/L, 184	71.00	75.00
PS9	1994 (3)	—	KM#260 BU, 261, 262	—	75.00
PS10	1994 (3)	—	KM#263 BU, 264, 265	—	75.00
PS11	1995 (6)	25,000	KM#274-279	—	345
PS12	1995 (3)	—	KM#216 BU, 217, 218	—	75.00
PS13	1995 (3)	—	KM#219 BU, 220, 221	—	75.00
PS14	1995 (3)	—	KM#222 BU, 223, 224	—	80.00
PS15	1995 (3)	—	KM#225 BU, 226, 227	—	75.00
PS16	1995 (3)	—	KM#253 BU, 254, 255	—	95.00
PS17	1995 (3)	—	KM#257 BU, 258, 259	—	75.00
PS18	1995 (3)	—	KM#266 BU, 267, 268	—	75.00
PS19	1996 (6)	—	KM#308, 311, 314, 317, 320, 323	33.00	47.50
PS20	1996 (6)	—	KM#309, 312, 315, 318, 321, 324	66.00	80.00
PS21	1996 (6)	—	KM#310, 313, 316, 319, 322, 325	306	250
PS22	1996 (3)	—	KM#288-290	71.00	75.00
PS23	1996 (3)	—	KM#297-299	71.00	78.00
PS24	1996 (3)	—	KM#300-302	71.00	78.00
PS25	1996 (3)	—	KM#303-305	71.00	75.00
PS26	1996 (3)	—	KM#308-310	71.00	75.00
PS27	1996 (3)	—	KM#311-313	71.00	75.00
PS28	1996 (3)	—	KM#314-316	71.00	75.00
PS29	1996 (3)	—	KM#317-319	71.00	75.00
PS30	1996 (3)	—	KM#320-322	71.00	75.00
PS31	1996 (4)	—	KM#322-325	71.00	100
PS32	1996 (3)	—	KM#353-355	71.00	75.00
PS33	1997 (2)	—	KM#362-363	61.00	67.50
PS34	1997 (3)	—	KM#364-366	71.00	80.00
PS35	1997 (2)	—	KM#369-370	61.00	62.50
PS36	1997 (3)	—	KM#371-373	71.00	75.00
PS37	1997 (2)	—	KM#374-375	61.00	70.00
PS38	1997 (2)	—	KM#398-399	61.00	62.50
PS40	1997 (3)	—	KM#403-405	71.00	75.00
PS41	1998 (24)	—	KM#416, 418, 420, 422, 424, 426, 428, 430, 432, 434, 436, 438, 440, 442, 444, 446, 448, 450, 452, 454, 456, 458, 460, 462	1,344	1,325
PS42	1998 (3)	—	KM#478-480	71.00	70.00
PS43	1998 (3)	—	KM#481-483	71.00	70.00

MARTINIQUE

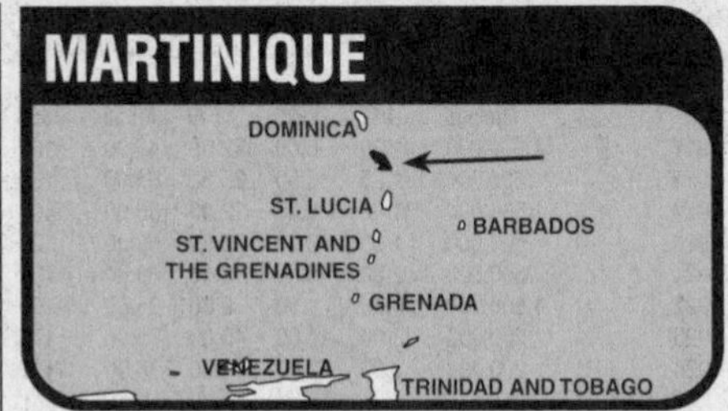

The French Overseas Department of Martinique, located in the Lesser Antilles of the West Indies between Dominica and Saint Lucia, has an area of 425 sq. mi.(1,100 sq. km.) and a population of 290,000. Capital: Fort-de-France. Agriculture and tourism are the major sources of income. Bananas, sugar, and rum are exported.

Christopher Columbus discovered Martinique, probably on June 15, 1502. France took possession on June 25, 1635, and has maintained possession since that time except for three short periods of British occupation during the Napoleonic Wars. A French department since 1946, Martinique voted a reaffirmation of that status in 1958, remaining within the new French Community. Martinique was the birthplace of Napoleon's Empress Josephine, and the site of the eruption of Mt. Pelee in 1902 that claimed 40,000 lives.

The official currency of Martinique is the French franc. The 1897-1922 coinage of the Colony of Martinique is now obsolete.

MONETARY SYSTEM
15 Sols = 1 Escalin
20 Sols = 1 Livre
66 Livres = 4 Escudos = 6400 Reis

FRENCH COLONY

DECIMAL COINAGE

KM# 40 50 CENTIMES
Copper-Nickel **Obv:** Bust left within circle with star above **Rev:** Value and date within wreath

Date	Mintage	F12	VF20	XF40	MS60	MS63
1922	500,000	55.00	85.00	175	250	650

KM# 41 FRANC
Copper-Nickel, 26 mm. **Obv:** Bust left of Josephine (Napoleon's first wife, who was born on Martinique) within circle with star above **Rev:** Value and date within wreath **Edge:** Plain

Date	Mintage	F12	VF20	XF40	MS60	MS63
1922	350,000	70.00	100	200	300	750

MAURITANIA

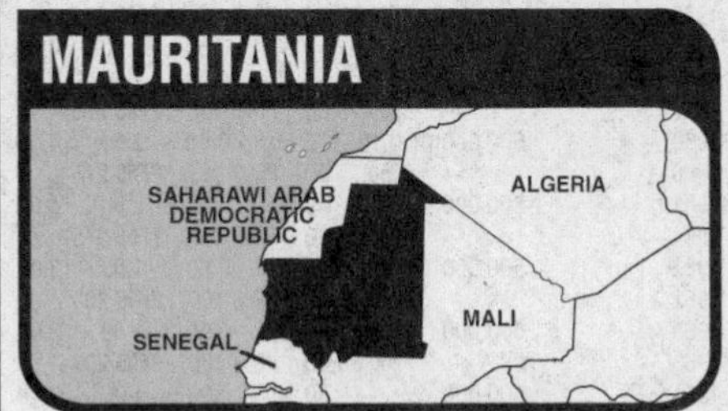

The Islamic Republic of Mauritania, located in northwest Africa bounded by Western Sahara, Mali, Algeria, Senegal and the Atlantic Ocean, has an area of 397,955 sq. mi.(1,030,700 sq. km.) and a population of 1.9 million. Capital: Nouakchott. The economy centers on herding, agriculture, fishing and mining. Iron ore, copper concentrates and fish products are exported.

The indigenous Negroid inhabitants were driven out of Mauritania by Berber invaders of the Islamic faith in the 11th century. The Berbers in turn were conquered by Arab invaders, the Beni Hassan, in the 16th century. Arab traders carried on a gainful trade in gum arabic, gold and slaves with Portuguese, Dutch, English and French traders until late in the 19th century when France took control of the area and made it a part of French West Africa, in 1920.Mauritania became a part of the French Union in 1946 and was made an autonomous republic within the new French Community in 1958, when the Islamic Republic of Mauritania was proclaimed. The republic became independent on November 28, 1960, and withdrew from the French Community in 1966.

On June 28, 1973, in a move designed to emphasize its non-alignment with France, Mauritania converted its currency from the old French-supported C.F.A. franc unit to a new unit called the Ouguiya.

MONETARY SYSTEM
5 Khoums = 1 Ouguiya

REPUBLIC

STANDARD COINAGE

KM# 1 1/5 OUGUIYA (Khoums)
Aluminum **Obv:** National emblem divides date above value **Obv. Legend:** BANQUE CENTRALE DE MAURITANIE **Rev:** Star and crescent divide sprigs within circle with legend around border

Date	Mintage	VF20	XF40	MS60	MS63	MS65
AH1393//1973	1,000,000	0.75	1.50	2.00	3.00	7.50

KM# 2 OUGUIYA
Aluminum-Bronze **Obv:** National emblem divides date above value **Obv. Legend:** BANQUE CENTRALE DE MAURITANIE **Rev:** Star and crescent divide sprigs below value within circle, legend around border

Date	Mintage	VF20	XF40	MS60	MS63	MS65
AH1393//1973	—	12.00	20.00	30.00	50.00	90.00

KM# 6 OUGUIYA
3.60 g., Aluminum-Bronze, 21 mm. **Obv:** National emblem divides date above value **Obv. Legend:** BANQUE CENTRALE DE MAURITANIE **Rev:** Star and crescent divide sprigs with legend below value, all within circle **Edge:** Reeded

Date	Mintage	VF20	XF40	MS60	MS63	MS65
AH1394//1974	—	5.00	7.00	10.00	15.00	25.00
AH1401//1981	—	2.50	3.50	5.00	7.00	10.00
AH1403//1983	—	1.50	2.50	3.50	6.50	10.00
AH1406//1986	—	1.50	2.00	2.50	5.00	9.00
AH1407//1987	—	1.00	1.50	2.00	4.00	7.50
AH1410//1990	—	1.00	1.50	2.00	4.00	7.50
AH1414//1993	—	1.00	1.50	2.00	4.00	7.50
AH1416//1995	—	1.00	1.50	2.00	4.00	7.50

KM# 3 5 OUGUIYA
5.88 g., Aluminum-Bronze, 25 mm. **Obv:** National emblem divides date above value **Obv. Legend:** BANQUE CENTRALE DE MAURITANIE **Rev:** Star and crescent divide sprigs below value within circle **Edge:** Plain

Date	Mintage	VF20	XF40	MS60	MS63	MS65
AH1393//1973	—	5.00	7.00	10.00	15.00	25.00
AH1394//1974	—	5.00	7.00	10.00	17.00	27.00
AH1401//1981	—	3.00	4.00	6.00	12.50	18.00
AH1404//1984	—	2.00	3.00	4.50	10.00	15.00
AH1407//1987	—	1.50	2.00	2.50	5.00	9.00
AH1410//1990	—	1.00	1.50	2.00	4.00	7.50
AH1414//1993	—	1.00	1.50	2.00	4.00	7.50
AH1416//1995	—	1.00	1.50	2.00	4.00	7.50
AH1418//1997	—	1.00	1.50	2.00	4.00	7.50
AH1420//1999	—	1.00	1.50	2.00	4.00	7.50

KM# 4 10 OUGUIYA
6.00 g., Copper-Nickel, 25 mm. **Obv:** National emblem divides date above value **Obv. Legend:** BANQUE CENTRALE DE MAURITANIE **Rev:** Crescent and star divide sprigs below value within circle **Edge:** Reeded

Date	Mintage	VF20	XF40	MS60	MS63	MS65
AH1393//1973	—	3.50	5.00	8.00	12.00	20.00

Date	Mintage	VF20	XF40	MS60	MS63	MS65
AH1394//1974	—	3.50	5.00	8.00	12.00	20.00
AH1401//1981	—	2.00	3.00	5.00	10.00	20.00
AH1403//1983	—	2.00	3.00	4.00	8.00	12.00
AH1407//1987	—	2.00	3.00	4.00	8.00	12.00
AH1410//1990	—	1.25	2.00	2.50	4.50	7.50
AH1411//1991	—	1.25	2.00	2.50	4.50	7.50
AH1414//1993	—	1.25	2.00	2.50	4.50	7.50
AH1416//1995	—	1.25	2.00	2.50	4.50	7.50
AH1418//1997	—	1.25	2.00	2.50	4.50	7.50
AH1420//1999	—	1.25	2.00	2.50	4.50	7.50

KM# 5 20 OUGUIYA

8.00 g., Copper-Nickel, 28 mm. **Obv:** National emblem divides date above value **Obv. Legend:** BANQUE CENTRALE DE MAURITANIE **Rev:** Star and crescent divide sprigs below value within circle **Edge:** Reeded

Date	Mintage	VF20	XF40	MS60	MS63	MS65
AH1393//1973	—	5.00	10.00	18.00	10.00	18.00
AH1394//1974	—	5.00	10.00	18.00	10.00	18.00
AH1403//1983	—	2.00	3.50	5.00	8.00	12.00
AH1407//1987	—	2.00	3.50	5.00	8.00	12.00
AH1410//1990	—	2.00	3.50	5.00	8.00	12.00
AH1414//1993	—	2.00	3.50	5.00	8.00	12.00
AH1416//1995	—	2.00	3.50	5.00	8.00	12.00
AH1418//1997	—	2.00	3.50	5.00	8.00	12.00
AH1420//1999	—	2.00	3.50	5.00	8.00	12.00

KM# 7 500 OUGUIYA

26.08 g., 0.920 Gold 0.7714 oz. AGW **Subject:** 15th Anniversary of Independence **Obv:** Star and crescent flanked by palm trees below dates **Rev:** Value in square flanked by a camel head and fish with design above

Date	Mintage	VF20	XF40	MS60	MS63	MS65
1975 (a)	1,800	—	—	—	2,600	2,800

MINT SETS

KM#	Date	Mintage	Identification	Issue Price	Mkt Val
MS1	1973 (5)	—	KM1-5, two each	20.00	275

MAURITIUS

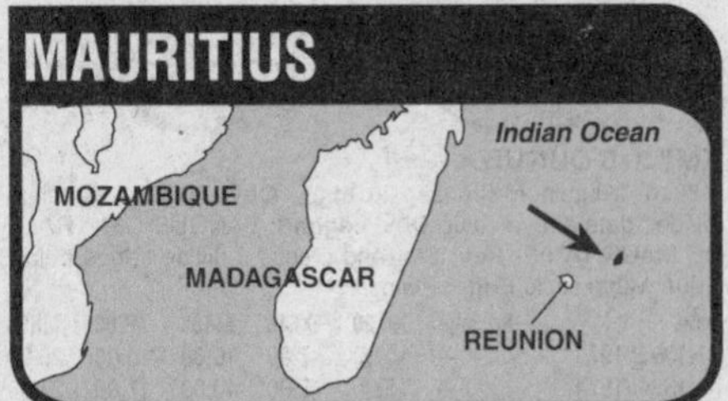

The Republic of Mauritius, is located in the Indian Ocean 500 miles (805 km.) east of Madagascar, has an area of 790 sq. mi. (1,860 sq. km.) and a population of 1 million. Capital: Port Louis. Sugar provides 90 percent of the export revenue.

Mauritius became independent on March 12, 1968. It is a member of the Commonwealth of Nations.

RULER

British, until 1968

MINT MARKS

H - Heaton, Birmingham
SA - Pretoria Mint

CROWN COLONY

STANDARD COINAGE

KM# 12 CENT

Bronze **Ruler:** George V **Obv:** Crowned bust left **Rev:** Value within beaded circle

Date	Mintage	F12	VF20	XF40	MS60	MS63
1911	1,000,000	1.00	6.00	22.00	40.00	100
1912	500,000	1.25	6.50	28.50	55.00	130
1917	500,000	1.00	6.00	22.00	35.00	75.00
1920	500,000	1.50	8.00	32.50	60.00	125
1921	500,000	2.00	8.00	32.50	60.00	120
1922	1,800,000	0.75	1.50	9.00	25.00	50.00
1923	200,000	3.00	17.00	45.00	75.00	175
1924	200,000	3.00	17.00	45.00	75.00	175

KM# 21 CENT

Bronze **Ruler:** George VI **Obv:** Crowned head left **Rev:** Value within beaded circle

Date	Mintage	F12	VF20	XF40	MS60	MS63
1943 SA	520,000	0.50	1.25	4.00	10.00	22.00
1944 SA	500,000	0.50	1.25	4.00	10.00	22.00
1945 SA	500,000	0.50	1.25	4.00	10.00	22.00
1946 SA	500,000	0.50	1.25	4.00	10.00	22.00
1947 SA	500,000	0.50	1.25	4.00	10.00	22.00

KM# 25 CENT

Bronze **Ruler:** George VI **Obv:** Crowned head left **Rev:** Value within beaded circle

Date	Mintage	F12	VF20	XF40	MS60	MS63
1949	500,000	0.75	1.25	2.50	7.50	15.00
1949	—	PF60 100		PF63 150	PF65 250	
1952	500,000	0.75	1.25	2.50	7.50	15.00
1952	—	PF60 150		PF63 250	PF65 400	

KM# 31 CENT

1.95 g., Bronze, 17.8 mm. **Ruler:** Elizabeth II **Obv:** Crowned head right **Rev:** Value within beaded circle

Date	Mintage	F12	VF20	XF40	MS60	MS63
1953	500,000	0.10	0.25	0.50	1.50	3.00
1953	—	PF60 75.00		PF63 150	PF65 275	
1955	501,000	0.10	0.25	0.50	2.50	4.00
1955	—	PF60 75.00		PF63 150	PF65 275	
1956	500,000	0.10	0.20	0.50	2.50	4.00
1956	—	PF60 75.00		PF63 150	PF65 275	
1957	501,000	0.10	0.20	0.50	2.50	4.00
1959	501,000	0.10	0.20	0.50	2.50	4.00
1959	—	PF60 75.00		PF63 150	PF65 275	
1960	500,000	0.10	0.20	0.50	2.50	4.00
1960	—	PF60 75.00		PF63 150	PF65 275	
1961	500,000	0.10	0.20	0.50	2.50	4.00
1961	—	PF60 75.00		PF63 150	PF65 275	
1962	500,000	0.10	0.20	0.50	1.50	3.00
1962	—	PF60 50.00		PF63 100	PF65 200	
1963	500,000	0.10	0.20	0.50	1.50	3.00
1963	—	PF60 50.00		PF63 100	PF65 200	
1964	1,500,000	—	0.10	0.20	1.00	3.00
1964	—	PF60 50.00		PF63 100	PF65 200	
1965	1,500,000	—	0.10	0.20	1.00	3.00
1969	500,000	—	0.10	0.20	1.00	3.00
1970	1,500,000	—	0.10	0.20	1.00	3.00
1971	1,000,000	—	0.10	0.20	1.00	3.00
1971	750	PF60 17.50		PF63 30.00	PF65 50.00	
1975	400,000	—	0.10	0.20	1.00	3.00
1978	—	—	0.10	0.20	1.00	3.00
1978	9,268	PF60 1.00		PF63 3.00	PF65 5.00	

KM# 13 2 CENTS

Bronze **Ruler:** George V **Obv:** Crowned bust left **Rev:** Value within beaded circle

Date	Mintage	F12	VF20	XF40	MS60	MS63
1911	500,000	2.00	12.00	25.00	40.00	85.00
1911	—	PF60 250		PF63 300	PF65 450	
1912	250,000	3.00	15.00	40.00	70.00	140
1917	250,000	1.25	14.50	22.00	50.00	80.00
1920	250,000	1.50	14.00	28.00	55.00	90.00
1921	250,000	1.50	10.00	28.00	55.00	90.00
1922	900,000	0.50	4.00	15.00	30.00	60.00
1923	400,000	1.25	5.50	28.50	55.00	95.00
1924	400,000	1.25	5.50	28.50	50.00	90.00

KM# 22 2 CENTS

3.85 g., Bronze **Ruler:** George VI **Obv:** Crowned head left **Rev:** Value within beaded circle

Date	Mintage	F12	VF20	XF40	MS60	MS63
1943 SA	290,000	0.75	2.00	4.00	10.00	22.00
1944 SA	500,000	0.75	2.00	4.00	10.00	22.00
1945 SA	250,000	0.75	2.00	4.00	10.00	22.00
1946 SA	400,000	0.75	2.00	4.00	10.00	22.00
1947 SA	250,000	0.75	2.00	4.00	10.00	22.00

KM# 26 2 CENTS

3.85 g., Bronze, 23.2 mm. **Ruler:** George VI **Obv:** Crowned head left **Rev:** Value within beaded circle

Date	Mintage	F12	VF20	XF40	MS60	MS63
1949	250,000	0.75	1.25	2.50	6.50	12.50
1949	—	PF60 175		PF63 225	PF65 350	
1952	250,000	0.75	1.25	2.50	6.50	12.50
1952	—	PF60 200		PF63 350	PF65 500	

KM# 32 2 CENTS

3.85 g., Bronze, 23.2 mm. **Ruler:** Elizabeth II **Obv:** Crowned head right **Rev:** Value within beaded circle

Date	Mintage	F12	VF20	XF40	MS60	MS63
1953	250,000	0.10	0.25	0.50	2.50	4.00
1953	—	PF60 100		PF63 200	PF65 375	
1954	—	PF60 300		PF63 600	PF65 800	
1955	501,000	0.10	0.25	0.50	2.50	4.00
1955	—	PF60 100		PF63 200	PF65 375	
1956	250,000	0.10	0.25	0.50	3.50	5.00
1956	—	PF60 100		PF63 200	PF65 375	
1957	501,000	0.10	0.25	0.50	3.50	5.00
1959	503,000	0.10	0.25	0.50	3.50	5.00
1959	—	PF60 100		PF63 200	PF65 375	
1960	250,000	0.10	0.25	0.50	3.50	5.00
1960	—	PF60 100		PF63 200	PF65 375	
1961	500,000	0.10	0.25	0.50	3.50	5.00
1961	—	PF60 100		PF63 200	PF65 375	
1962	500,000	0.10	0.25	0.50	1.50	3.00
1962	—	PF60 75.00		PF63 150	PF65 275	
1963	500,000	0.10	0.25	0.50	1.50	3.00
1963	—	PF60 75.00		PF63 150	PF65 275	
1964	1,000,000	—	0.10	0.25	1.00	3.00
1964	—	PF60 50.00		PF63 100	PF65 200	
1965	750,000	0.10	0.20	0.40	1.00	3.00
1966	500,000	0.10	0.20	0.40	1.00	3.00
1967	250,000	0.10	0.20	0.40	1.00	3.00
1969	500,000	0.10	0.20	0.40	1.00	3.00
1971	1,000,000	—	0.10	0.25	1.00	3.00
1971	750	PF60 17.50		PF63 30.00	PF65 50.00	
1975	5,200,000	—	0.10	0.25	1.00	3.00
1978	—	—	0.10	0.25	1.00	3.00
1978	9,268	PF60 1.50		PF63 3.00	PF65 5.00	

KM# 14 5 CENTS
9.70 g., Bronze, 28.4 mm. **Ruler:** George V **Obv:** Crowned bust left **Rev:** Value within beaded circle

Date	Mintage	F12	VF20	XF40	MS60	MS63
1917	600,000	2.00	24.50	57.50	80.00	165
1920	200,000	2.00	24.50	60.00	100	200
1921	100,000	3.00	26.50	65.00	120	250
1922	360,000	2.00	14.50	42.50	100	200
1923	400,000	3.00	16.50	45.00	120	250
1924	400,000	2.00	14.50	42.50	100	200

KM# 20 5 CENTS
9.70 g., Bronze, 28.4 mm. **Ruler:** George VI **Obv:** Crowned head left **Rev:** Value within beaded circle

Date	Mintage	F12	VF20	XF40	MS60	MS63
1942 SA	940,000	1.50	2.50	6.50	15.00	35.00
1944 SA	1,000,000	1.25	1.75	4.00	10.00	22.00
1945 SA	500,000	1.25	1.75	4.00	12.00	30.00

KM# 34 5 CENTS
9.70 g., Bronze, 28.4 mm. **Ruler:** Elizabeth II **Obv:** Crowned head right **Rev:** Value within beaded circle

Date	Mintage	F12	VF20	XF40	MS60	MS63
1956	201,000	0.25	0.50	0.75	5.00	7.50
1956	—	PF60 100	PF63 200	PF65 375		
1957	203,000	0.25	0.50	2.00	8.00	10.00
1957	—	PF60 100	PF63 200	PF65 375		
1959	801,000	0.25	0.50	1.00	4.00	7.50
1959	—	PF60 75.00	PF63 150	PF65 275		
1960	400,000	0.25	0.50	1.00	4.00	7.50
1960	—	PF60 75.00	PF63 150	PF65 275		
1963	200,000	0.25	0.50	1.00	2.50	5.00
1963	—	PF60 75.00	PF63 150	PF65 275		
1964	600,000	0.25	0.50	1.00	2.50	5.00
1964	—	PF60 75.00	PF63 150	PF65 275		
1965	200,000	0.25	0.50	0.75	2.50	5.00
1966	200,000	0.25	0.50	0.75	1.50	3.00
1967	200,000	0.25	0.50	0.75	1.50	3.00
1969	500,000	0.10	0.15	0.25	1.00	3.00
1970	800,000	0.10	0.15	0.25	1.00	3.00
1971	500,000	0.10	0.15	0.25	1.00	3.00
1971	750	PF60 17.50	PF63 30.00	PF65 50.00		
1975	3,700,000	0.10	0.15	0.25	1.00	3.00
1978	8,000,000	—	0.10	0.20	1.00	3.00
1978	9,268	PF60 2.00	PF63 4.00	PF65 7.00		

KM# 24 10 CENTS
5.15 g., Copper-Nickel, 23.5 mm. **Ruler:** George VI **Obv:** Crowned head left **Rev:** Value **Shape:** Scalloped

Date	Mintage	F12	VF20	XF40	MS60	MS63
1947	500,000	1.50	4.50	18.00	45.00	125
1947	—	PF60 200	PF63 400	PF65 750		

KM# 30 10 CENTS
5.15 g., Copper-Nickel, 23.5 mm. **Ruler:** George VI **Obv:** Crowned head left **Rev:** Value **Shape:** Scalloped

Date	Mintage	F12	VF20	XF40	MS60	MS63
1952	250,000	0.50	1.00	3.50	9.50	17.50
1952	—	PF60 150	PF63 300	PF65 550		

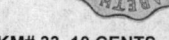

KM# 33 10 CENTS
5.15 g., Copper-Nickel, 23.5 mm. **Ruler:** Elizabeth II **Obv:** Crowned head right **Rev:** Value **Shape:** Scalloped

Date	Mintage	F12	VF20	XF40	MS60	MS63
1954	252,000	0.20	0.35	0.75	2.50	5.00
1954	—	PF60 150	PF63 300	PF65 550		
1957	250,000	0.20	0.35	0.75	2.50	5.00
1959	253,000	0.20	0.35	0.75	2.50	5.00
1959	—	PF60 175	PF63 350	PF65 650		
1960	50,000	0.20	0.35	0.75	2.00	5.00
1960	—	PF60 175	PF63 350	PF65 650		
1963	200,000	0.15	0.30	0.60	1.50	3.00
1963	—	PF60 175	PF63 350	PF65 650		
1964	200,000	0.15	0.30	0.60	1.00	3.00
1965	200,000	0.15	0.30	0.60	1.00	3.00
1966	200,000	0.10	0.25	0.50	1.00	3.00
1969	200,000	0.10	0.25	0.50	1.00	3.00
1970	500,000	0.10	0.25	0.50	1.00	3.00
1971	300,000	0.10	0.25	0.50	1.00	3.00
1971	750	PF60 17.50	PF63 30.00	PF65 50.00		
1975	6,675,000	0.10	0.25	0.50	1.00	3.00
1978	13,000,000	0.10	0.25	0.50	1.00	3.00
1978	9,268	PF60 2.50	PF63 5.00	PF65 9.00		

KM# 15 1/4 RUPEE
2.92 g., 0.916 Silver 0.086 oz. ASW, 19 mm. **Ruler:** George V **Obv:** Crowned bust left **Rev:** Crown above 3 emblems

Date	Mintage	F12	VF20	XF40	MS60	MS63
1934	400,000	3.00	12.00	32.50	70.00	165
1934	—	PF60 600	PF63 1,200			
1935	400,000	3.00	12.00	32.50	70.00	165
1935	—	PF60 750	PF63 1,500			
1936	400,000	3.00	12.00	32.50	70.00	165
1936	—	PF60 650	PF63 1,300			

KM# 18 1/4 RUPEE
2.92 g., 0.916 Silver 0.086 oz. ASW, 19 mm. **Ruler:** George VI **Obv:** Crowned bust left

Date	Mintage	F12	VF20	XF40	MS60	MS63
1938	2,000,000	5.00	17.00	46.00	100	185
1938	—	PF60 375	PF63 750			

KM# 18a 1/4 RUPEE
2.92 g., 0.500 Silver 0.0469 oz. ASW, 19 mm. **Ruler:** George VI **Obv:** Crowned bust left

Date	Mintage	F12	VF20	XF40	MS60	MS63
1946	2,000,000	10.00	35.00	75.00	125	225
1946	—	PF60 400	PF63 800			

KM# 27 1/4 RUPEE
2.95 g., Copper-Nickel, 19 mm. **Ruler:** George VI **Obv:** Crowned head left **Rev:** Crown above 3 emblems

Date	Mintage	F12	VF20	XF40	MS60	MS63
1950	2,000,000	0.50	1.00	2.00	9.50	18.00
1950	—	PF60 175	PF63 350	PF65 650		
1951	1,000,000	0.50	1.00	2.00	9.50	18.00
1951	—	PF60 175	PF63 350	PF65 650		

KM# 36 1/4 RUPEE
2.95 g., Copper-Nickel, 19 mm. **Ruler:** Elizabeth II **Obv:** Crowned head right **Rev:** Crown above 3 emblems

Date	Mintage	F12	VF20	XF40	MS60	MS63
1960	1,000,000	0.35	0.75	1.00	2.00	5.00
1960	—	PF60 100	PF63 200	PF65 350		
1964	400,000	0.25	0.50	0.75	1.50	3.00
1964	—	PF60 100	PF63 200	PF65 35.00		
1965	400,000	0.25	0.50	0.75	1.25	3.00
1970	400,000	0.20	0.35	0.65	1.25	3.00
1971	540,000	0.25	0.50	0.75	1.25	3.00
1971	750	PF60 17.50	PF63 30.00	PF65 50.00		

Date	Mintage	F12	VF20	XF40	MS60	MS63
1975	8,940,000	0.15	0.30	0.60	1.00	3.00
1978	8,800,000	0.15	0.30	0.60	1.00	3.00

Note: Variety exists with lower hole in 8 filled

Date	Mintage	F12	VF20	XF40	MS60	MS63
1978	9,268	PF60 3.50	PF63 7.50	PF65 15.00		

KM# 16 1/2 RUPEE
5.83 g., 0.916 Silver 0.1717 oz. ASW, 23.65 mm. **Ruler:** George V **Obv:** Crowned bust left **Rev:** Stag left **Edge:** Reeded with security

Date	Mintage	F12	VF20	XF40	MS60	MS63
1934	1,000,000	6.00	12.00	30.00	75.00	150
1934	—	PF60 450	PF63 850			

KM# 23 1/2 RUPEE
5.83 g., 0.500 Silver 0.0937 oz. ASW, 23.65 mm. **Ruler:** George VI **Obv:** Crowned head left **Rev:** Stag left

Date	Mintage	F12	VF20	XF40	MS60	MS63
1946	1,000,000	12.00	30.00	125	175	300
1946	—	PF60 700	PF63 1,200			

KM# 28 1/2 RUPEE
5.85 g., Copper-Nickel, 23.65 mm. **Ruler:** George VI **Obv:** Crowned head left **Rev:** Stag left

Date	Mintage	F12	VF20	XF40	MS60	MS63
1950	1,000,000	0.50	1.00	1.75	12.00	20.00
1950	—	PF60 175	PF63 350	PF65 650		
1951	570,000	0.75	1.25	2.00	14.00	25.00
1951	—	PF60 225	PF63 450	PF65 850		

KM# 37.1.1 1/2 RUPEE
5.85 g., Copper-Nickel, 23.65 mm. **Ruler:** Elizabeth II **Obv:** Crowned head right **Rev:** Stag left

Date	Mintage	F12	VF20	XF40	MS60	MS63
1965	200,000	0.50	1.00	2.00	9.00	16.00
1971	400,000	0.25	0.50	0.75	8.00	15.00
1971	750	PF60 22.50	PF63 45.00	PF65 75.00		
1975	4,160,000	0.25	0.50	0.75	8.00	15.00
1978	400,000	0.25	0.50	0.75	8.00	15.00
1978	9,268	PF60 6.00	PF63 10.00	PF65 20.00		

KM# 37.2.2 1/2 RUPEE
5.85 g., Copper-Nickel, 23.65 mm. **Ruler:** Elizabeth II **Obv:** Crowned head right **Rev:** Stag left **Edge:** Without security feature **Note:** Error.

Date	Mintage	F12	VF20	XF40	MS60	MS63
1971	Inc. above	—	—	—	—	—

KM# 17 RUPEE
11.66 g., 0.916 Silver 0.3434 oz. ASW **Ruler:** George V **Obv:** Crowned bust left **Rev:** National arms divide date above value **Edge:** Reeded with security

Date	Mintage	F12	VF20	XF40	MS60	MS63
1934	1,500,000	13.00	19.00	32.50	75.00	100
1934	—	PF60 600	PF63 900	PF65 1,500		

KM# 19 RUPEE

11.66 g., 0.916 Silver 0.3434 oz. ASW **Ruler:** George VI **Obv:** Crowned head left **Rev:** National arms divide date above value

Date	Mintage	F12	VF20	XF40	MS60	MS63
1938	200,000	15.00	22.00	60.00	125	225
1938	—	PF60 550	PF63 850	PF65 1,450		

KM# 29.1.1 RUPEE

11.70 g., Copper-Nickel, 29.6 mm. **Ruler:** George VI **Obv:** Crowned head left **Rev:** National arms divide date above value

Date	Mintage	F12	VF20	XF40	MS60	MS63
1950	1,500,000	0.75	1.50	3.00	16.00	30.00
1950	—	PF60 200	PF63 400	PF65 700		
1951	1,000,000	0.50	1.25	2.00	12.00	20.00
1951	—	PF60 300	PF63 600	PF65 1,000		

KM# 29.2.2 RUPEE

11.70 g., Copper-Nickel, 29.6 mm. **Ruler:** George VI **Obv:** Crowned head left **Rev:** National arms divide date above value **Edge:** Without security feature **Note:** Error.

Date	Mintage	F12	VF20	XF40	MS60	MS63
1951	Inc. above	—	—	—	—	—

KM# 35.1.1 RUPEE

11.70 g., Copper-Nickel, 29.6 mm. **Ruler:** Elizabeth II **Obv:** Crowned head right **Rev:** National arms divide date above value

Date	Mintage	F12	VF20	XF40	MS60	MS63
1956	1,000,000	0.25	0.75	1.50	7.50	12.00
1956	—	PF60 200	PF63 350	PF65 650		
1964	200,000	0.50	1.00	3.00	5.00	8.00
1971	600,000	0.25	0.60	1.00	2.00	5.00
1971	750	PF60 45.00	PF63 75.00	PF65 125		
1975	4,525,000	0.25	0.60	1.00	2.00	5.00
1978	2,000,000	0.25	0.60	1.00	2.00	5.00
1978	9,268	PF60 5.00	PF63 9.00	PF65 18.00		

KM# 35.2.2 RUPEE

11.70 g., Copper-Nickel, 29.6 mm. **Ruler:** Elizabeth II **Obv:** Crowned head right **Rev:** National arms divide date above value **Edge:** Without security feature **Note:** Error.

Date	Mintage	F12	VF20	XF40	MS60	MS63
1971	Inc. above	0.25	0.75	1.25	2.50	5.00

COMMONWEALTH

KM# 38 10 RUPEES

Copper-Nickel, 35 mm. **Ruler:** Elizabeth II **Subject:** Independence **Obv:** Crowned head right **Rev:** Dodo bird

Date	Mintage	VF20	XF40	MS60	MS63	MS65
1971	50,000	2.50	3.50	5.00	9.00	16.00

KM# 38a 10 RUPEES

20.00 g., 0.925 Silver 0.5948 oz. ASW, 35 mm. **Subject:** Independence **Obv:** Crowned head right **Rev:** Dodo bird

Date	Mintage	VF20	XF40	MS60	MS63	MS65
1971	750	PF63 70.00	PF65 85.00			

KM# 46 10 RUPEES

Copper-Nickel **Subject:** Wedding of Prince Charles and Lady Diana **Obv:** Young bust right **Rev:** Conjoined heads left

Date	Mintage	VF20	XF40	MS60	MS63	MS65
ND-1981	—	1.50	2.50	3.50	4.50	6.00

KM# 46a 10 RUPEES

28.28 g., 0.925 Silver 0.841 oz. ASW **Subject:** Wedding of Prince Charles and Lady Diana **Obv:** Young bust right **Rev:** Conjoined heads left

Date	Mintage	VF20	XF40	MS60	MS63	MS65
ND-1981	2,090	PF63 30.00	PF65 35.00			

KM# 48 10 RUPEES

28.28 g., 0.925 Silver 0.841 oz. ASW **Series:** World Food Day **Obv:** Young bust right **Rev:** Man harvesting sugar cane

Date	Mintage	VF20	XF40	MS60	MS63	MS65
1981	10,000	—	—	—	25.00	28.00
1981	5,000	PF63 27.00	PF65 30.00			

KM# 40 25 RUPEES

25.50 g., 0.500 Silver 0.4099 oz. ASW, 38.6 mm. **Series:** Conservation **Obv:** Young bust right **Rev:** Butterfly on flowers

Date	Mintage	VF20	XF40	MS60	MS63	MS65
1975	—	—	—	—	18.00	20.00

KM# 40a 25 RUPEES

28.28 g., 0.925 Silver 0.841 oz. ASW, 38 mm. **Series:** Conservation **Obv:** Young bust right **Rev:** Butterfly on flowers **Edge:** Reeded

Date	Mintage	VF20	XF40	MS60	MS63	MS65
1975	12	—	—	—	200	300
1975	9,869	PF63 25.00	PF65 30.00			

KM# 43 25 RUPEES

28.40 g., 0.500 Silver 0.4565 oz. ASW **Subject:** Queen's Silver Jubilee **Obv:** Young bust right **Rev:** Man harvesting sugar cane

Date	Mintage	VF20	XF40	MS60	MS63	MS65
ND-1977	—	—	—	—	14.00	16.00

KM# 43a 25 RUPEES

28.28 g., 0.925 Silver 0.841 oz. ASW **Subject:** Queen's Silver Jubilee **Obv:** Young bust right **Rev:** Man harvesting sugar cane

Date	Mintage	VF20	XF40	MS60	MS63	MS65
ND-1977	47,000	PF63 20.00	PF65 25.00			

KM# 44 25 RUPEES

28.28 g., 0.925 Silver 0.841 oz. ASW **Subject:** 10th Anniversary of Independence **Obv:** Similar to 1,000 Rupees, KM#45: bust right **Rev:** Building

Date	Mintage	VF20	XF40	MS60	MS63	MS65
1978	20,000	—	—	—	22.00	27.00
1978	5,100	PF63 30.00	PF65 40.00			

KM# 49 25 RUPEES

28.28 g., 0.925 Silver 0.841 oz. ASW **Series:** International Year of Disabled Persons **Obv:** Young bust right **Rev:** Disabled persons emblem to upper left of cluster of designs

Date	Mintage	VF20	XF40	MS60	MS63	MS65
1982	11,000	—	—	—	25.00	30.00
1982	10,000	PF63 30.00	PF65 35.00			

KM# 41 50 RUPEES

32.15 g., 0.500 Silver 0.5168 oz. ASW, 42 mm. **Series:** Conservation **Obv:** Young bust right **Rev:** Mauritius Kestrel

Date	Mintage	VF20	XF40	MS60	MS63	MS65
1975	—	—	—	—	20.00	22.00

KM# 41a 50 RUPEES

35.00 g., 0.925 Silver 1.0409 oz. ASW, 42 mm. **Series:** Conservation **Obv:** Young bust right **Rev:** Mauritius Kestrel **Edge:** Reeded

Date	Mintage	VF20	XF40	MS60	MS63	MS65
1975	12	PF65 350				
1975	9,513	PF63 28.00	PF65 32.00			

KM# 39 200 RUPEES

15.56 g., 0.917 Gold 0.4587 oz. AGW **Subject:** Independence **Obv:** Crowned head right **Rev:** Couple in the forest

Date	Mintage	VF20	XF40	MS60	MS63	MS65
1971	2,500	—	—	—	750	800
1971	750	PF65 900				

KM# 42 1000 RUPEES

33.44 g., 0.900 Gold 0.9675 oz. AGW **Series:** Conservation **Subject:** Mauritius flycatcher **Obv:** Young bust right **Rev:** Bird on nest in branch

Date	Mintage	VF20	XF40	MS60	MS63	MS65
1975	1,966	—	—	—	1,650	1,750
1975	716	PF65 1,750				

KM# 45 1000 RUPEES

15.98 g., 0.917 Gold 0.4711 oz. AGW **Subject:** 10th Anniversary of Independence **Obv:** Bust right **Rev:** Building

Date	Mintage	VF20	XF40	MS60	MS63	MS65
1978	1,000	—	—	—	775	825
1978	1,016	PF65 875				

KM# 47 1000 RUPEES

15.98 g., 0.917 Gold 0.4711 oz. AGW **Subject:** Wedding of Prince Charles and Lady Diana **Obv:** Young bust right **Rev:** Crowned monogram

Date	Mintage	VF20	XF40	MS60	MS63	MS65
ND-1981	28	—	—	—	900	950
ND-1981	22	PF65 1,000				

KM# 50 1000 RUPEES

15.98 g., 0.917 Gold 0.4711 oz. AGW **Series:** International Year of Disabled Persons **Obv:** Young bust right **Rev:** Disabled emblem within design

Date	Mintage	VF20	XF40	MS60	MS63	MS65
1982	45	—	—	—	825	875
1982	48	PF65 975				

GOLD BULLION COINAGE

KM# 57 100 RUPEES

3.41 g., 0.917 Gold 0.1006 oz. AGW **Obv:** Bust 1/4 left **Rev:** Dodo bird

Date	Mintage	VF20	XF40	MS60	MS63	MS65
1988	—	—	—	—	160	185

KM# 58 250 RUPEES

8.51 g., 0.917 Gold 0.251 oz. AGW **Obv:** Bust 1/4 left **Rev:** Dodo bird

Date	Mintage	VF20	XF40	MS60	MS63	MS65
1988	—	—	—	—	400	450

KM# 59 500 RUPEES

17.03 g., 0.917 Gold 0.5019 oz. AGW **Obv:** Bust 1/4 left **Rev:** Dodo bird

Date	Mintage	VF20	XF40	MS60	MS63	MS65
1988	—	—	—	—	825	875

KM# 60 1000 RUPEES

34.05 g., 0.917 Gold 1.0039 oz. AGW **Obv:** Bust 1/4 left **Rev:** Dodo bird

Date	Mintage	VF20	XF40	MS60	MS63	MS65
1988	—	—	—	—	1,650	1,750

REPUBLIC

STANDARD COINAGE

KM# 51 CENT

Copper Plated Steel **Obv:** Value within beaded circle **Rev:** Bust of Sir Seewoosagur Ramgoolam 3/4 right

Date	Mintage	VF20	XF40	MS60	MS63	MS65
1987	—	—	—	0.20	0.40	1.00
1987	Est. 2500	PF65 1.00				

KM# 52 5 CENTS

3.00 g., Copper Plated Steel **Obv:** Value within beaded circle **Rev:** Bust of Sir Seewoosagur Ramgoolam 3/4 right

Date	Mintage	VF20	XF40	MS60	MS63	MS65
1987	—	—	0.10	0.35	0.50	1.00
1987	Est. 2500	PF65 2.00				
1990	—	—	0.10	0.35	0.50	1.00
1991	—	—	0.10	0.35	0.50	1.00
1993	—	—	0.10	0.35	0.50	1.00
1994	—	—	0.10	0.35	0.50	1.00
1995	—	—	0.10	0.35	0.50	1.00
1996	—	—	0.10	0.35	0.50	1.00
1999	—	—	0.10	0.35	0.50	1.00

KM# 53 20 CENTS

3.00 g., Nickel Plated Steel, 19 mm. **Obv:** Value within beaded circle **Rev:** Bust of Sir Seewoosagur Ramgoolam 3/4 right

Date	Mintage	VF20	XF40	MS60	MS63	MS65
1987	—	—	0.20	0.50	0.75	1.25
1987	—	PF65 3.00				
1990	—	—	0.20	0.50	0.75	1.25
1991	—	—	0.20	0.50	0.75	1.25
1993	—	—	0.20	0.50	0.75	1.25
1994	—	—	0.20	0.50	0.75	1.25
1995	—	—	0.20	0.50	0.75	1.25
1996	—	—	0.20	0.50	0.75	1.25
1999	—	—	0.20	0.50	0.75	1.25

KM# 54 1/2 RUPEE

5.90 g., Nickel Plated Steel, 23.6 mm. **Obv:** Stag left **Rev:** Bust of Sir Seewoosagur Ramgoolam 3/4 right

Date	Mintage	VF20	XF40	MS60	MS63	MS65
1987	—	—	0.70	1.25	2.00	2.50
1987	Est. 2500	PF65 5.00				
1990	—	—	0.70	1.25	2.00	2.50
1991	—	—	0.70	1.25	2.00	2.50
1997	—	—	0.70	1.25	2.00	2.50
1999	—	—	0.70	1.25	2.00	2.50

KM# 55 RUPEE

7.50 g., Copper-Nickel, 26.6 mm. **Obv:** Shield divides date above value **Rev:** Bust of Sir Seewoosagur Ramgoolam 3/4 right **Edge:** Reeded

Date	Mintage	VF20	XF40	MS60	MS63	MS65
1987	—	—	0.65	1.25	2.25	2.75
1987	Est. 2500	PF65 10.00				
1990	—	—	0.65	1.25	2.25	2.75
1991	—	—	0.65	1.25	2.25	2.75
1993	—	—	0.65	1.25	2.25	2.75
1994	—	—	0.65	1.25	2.25	2.75
1996	—	—	0.65	1.25	2.25	2.75
1997	—	—	0.65	1.25	2.25	2.75
1999	—	—	0.65	1.25	2.25	2.75

KM# 56 5 RUPEES

12.40 g., Copper-Nickel, 31 mm. **Obv:** Value within palm trees **Rev:** Bust of Sir Seewoosagur Ramgoolam 3/4 right

Date	Mintage	VF20	XF40	MS60	MS63	MS65
1987	—	—	—	1.75	3.00	5.00
1987	Est. 2500	PF65 16.00				
1991	—	—	—	1.75	3.00	5.00
1992	—	—	—	1.75	3.00	5.00

KM# 61 10 RUPEES

10.10 g., Copper-Nickel, 28 mm. **Obv:** Sugar cane harvesting **Rev:** Bust of Sir Seewoosagur Ramgoolam 3/4 right **Shape:** 7-sided

Date	Mintage	VF20	XF40	MS60	MS63	MS65
1997	—	—	—	2.00	4.00	6.50
2000	—	—	—	2.00	4.00	6.50

KM# 62 10 RUPEES

28.28 g., 0.925 Silver 0.841 oz. ASW **Subject:** 150th Anniversary Chamber of Commerce and Industry **Obv:** National arms above Port Louis Harbor **Rev:** Chamber of Commerce and Industry seal

Date	Mintage	VF20	XF40	MS60	MS63	MS65
2000	1,000	PF63 65.00	PF65 75.00			

KM# 64 20 RUPEES

28.28 g., 0.925 Silver 0.841 oz. ASW, 38 mm. **Subject:** 50th Anniversary Birth of Prince Charles Philip **Obv:** Bust of Sir Seewoosagur Ramgoolam **Rev:** Elizabeth II seated holding Prince Charles Philip **Rev. Legend:** 1947 ELIZABETH AND PHILIP 1997

Date	Mintage	VF20	XF40	MS60	MS63	MS65
1997	30,000	PF63 45.00	PF65 55.00			

KM# 63 1000 RUPEES

17.00 g., 0.920 Gold 0.5028 oz. AGW **Subject:** 150th Anniversary Chamber of Commerce and Industry **Obv:** National arms above Port Louis Harbor **Rev:** Chamber of Commerce and Industry seal

Date	Mintage	VF20	XF40	MS60	MS63	MS65
2000	300	PF65 900				

PIEDFORT

KM#	Date	Mintage	Identification	Mkt Val
P2	1981	—	1000 Rupees. Gold. KM47.	1,250
P3	1982	1,100	25 Rupees. 0.925. Silver. KM49.	150
P4	1982	—	1000 Rupees. Gold. KM50.	2,100

MINT SETS

KM#	Date	Mintage	Identification	Issue Price	Mkt Val
MS1	1987 (6)	5,000	KM51-56	16.95	10.00
MS2	1988 (4)	—	KM57-60	1,250	3,200

PROOF SETS

KM#	Date	Mintage	Identification	Issue Price	Mkt Val
PS1	1934 (3)	20	KM15-17	—	1,650
PS2	1971 (9)	750	KM31-37, 38a, 39	200	1,175
PS3	1975 (2)	9,268	KM40a-41a	50.00	65.00
PS4	1978 (7)	30,000	KM31-37	22.00	15.00
PS5	1981 (2)	—	KM46a, 47	—	1,000
PS6	1987 (6)	2,500	KM51-56	36.95	27.00

MEXICO

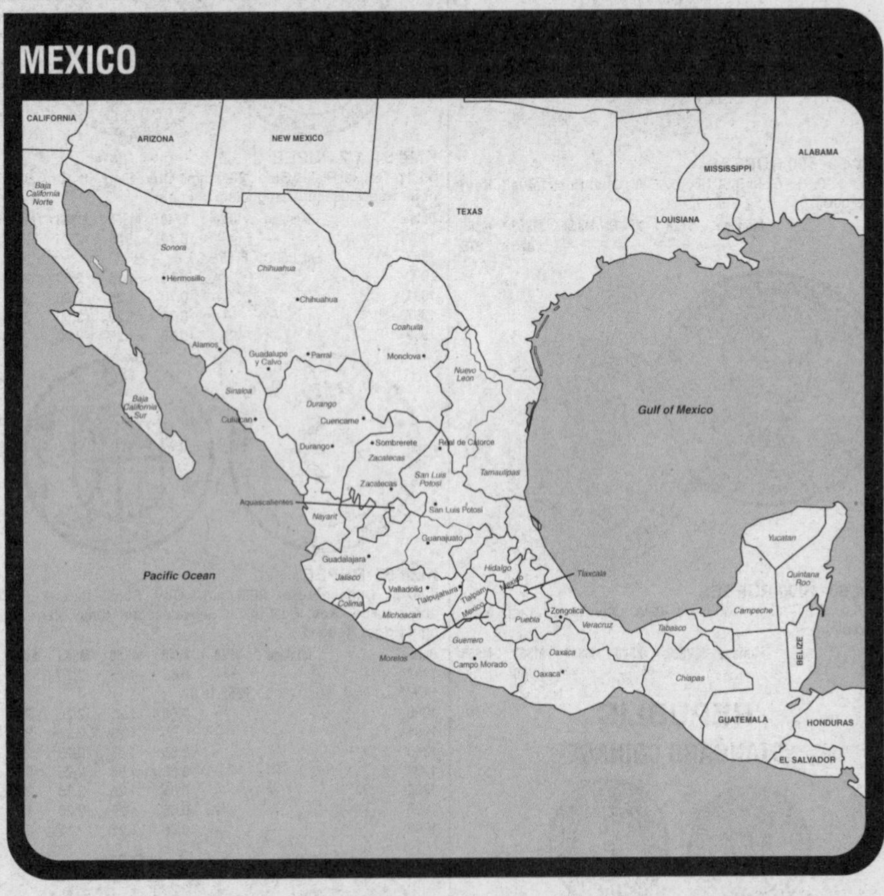

The United States of Mexico, located immediately south of the United States has an area of 759,529 sq. mi. (1,967,183 sq. km.) and an estimated population of 100 million. Capital: Mexico City. The economy is based on agriculture, manufacturing and mining. Oil, cotton, silver, coffee, and shrimp are exported.

Mexico was the site of highly advanced Indian civilizations 1,500 years before conquistador Hernando Cortes conquered the wealthy Aztec empire of Montezuma, 1519-21, and founded a Spanish colony, which lasted for nearly 300 years. During the Spanish period, Mexico, then called New Spain, stretched from Guatemala to the present states of Wyoming and California, its present northern boundary having been established by the secession of Texas during 1836 and the war of 1846-48 with the United States.

Independence from Spain was declared by Father Miguel Hidalgo on Sept. 16, 1810, (Mexican Independence Day) and was achieved by General Agustin de Iturbide in1821. Iturbide became emperor in 1822 but was deposed when a republic was established a year later. For more than fifty years following the birth of the republic, the political scene of Mexico was characterized by turmoil, which saw two emperors (including the unfortunate Maximilian), several dictators and an average of one new government every nine months passing swiftly from obscurity to oblivion. The land, social, economic and labor reforms promulgated by the Reform Constitution of Feb. 5, 1917 established the basis for sustained economic development and participative democracy that have made Mexico one of the most politically stable countries of modern Latin America.

Mintmarks: M (written as Mo in catalog) – Originally the mintmark of the Mexico City Mint. However, although mint headquarters are still in Mexico city, the mint itself was moved to San Luis Potosi in the early 1980s but the Mo mintmark was retained.

REPUBLIC

Second

DECIMAL COINAGE

100 Centavos = 1 Peso

KM# 394.1 CENTAVO

2.61 g., Copper **Obv:** Facing eagle, snake in beak **Obv. Legend:** REPUBLICA MEXICANA **Rev:** Value below date within wreath **Note:** Reduced size. Varieties exist.

Date	Mintage	F12	VF20	XF40	MS60	MS63
1901 M	1,494,000	3.00	8.00	25.00	100	—
1902/899 M	2,090,000	30.00	75.00	200	600	—
1902 M	Inc. above	2.25	4.00	10.00	40.00	—
1903 M	8,400,000	1.50	3.00	7.00	20.00	—
1904/3 M	10,250,000	1.50	10.00	20.00	55.00	—
1904 M	Inc. above	1.50	3.00	8.00	25.00	—
1905 M	3,643,000	2.25	4.00	10.00	40.00	—

KM# 394 CENTAVO

Copper **Obv:** National arms **Rev:** Value below date within wreath **Note:** Reduced size. Varieties exist.

Date	Mintage	F12	VF20	XF40	MS60	MS63
1901 C	220,000	15.00	22.50	60.00	150	—
1902 C	320,000	15.00	22.50	50.00	90.00	—
1903 C	536,000	7.50	12.50	20.00	50.00	—
1904/3 C	148,000	35.00	50.00	150	350	—
1905 C	110,000	100	150	300	600	—

KM# 400 5 CENTAVOS

1.35 g., 0.9027 Silver 0.0393 oz. ASW, 14 mm. **Obv:** Facing eagle, snake in beak **Obv. Legend:** REPUBLICA MEXICANA **Rev:** Value within 1/2 wreath **Note:** Varieties exist.

Date	Mintage	F12	VF20	XF40	MS60	MS63
1901 Cn Q	148,000	2.00	4.00	7.00	25.00	30.00
1902 Cn Q	262,000	2.00	4.00	7.00	20.00	25.00
Note: Narrow C, heavy serifs						
1902 Cn Q	Inc. above	2.00	4.00	7.00	20.00	25.00
Note: Wide C, light serifs						
1903/1 Cn Q	331,000	2.50	4.00	7.00	20.00	25.00
1903 Cn Q	Inc. above	2.00	3.00	5.00	18.00	23.00
1903 Cn V	Inc. above	2.00	3.00	5.00	18.00	23.00
1904 Cn H	352,000	2.00	2.75	6.00	20.00	25.00
1904 Cn H/C	—	2.00	3.00	6.00	20.00	25.00

KM# 400.2 5 CENTAVOS

1.35 g., 0.9027 Silver 0.0393 oz. ASW, 15 mm. **Obv:** Facing eagle, snake in beak **Rev:** Value within 1/2 wreath **Edge:** Reeded

Date	Mintage	F12	VF20	XF40	MS60	MS63
1901 Mo M	100,000	2.00	3.00	8.00	23.00	25.00
1902/1 Mo MoM	—	2.00	4.00	10.00	23.00	25.00
1902 Mo M	144,000	1.50	2.50	7.00	18.00	20.00
1903 Mo M	500,000	1.50	2.50	6.00	15.00	18.00
1904/804 Mo M	1,090,000	2.00	4.00	7.00	18.00	18.00
1904 Mo M	Inc. above	2.00	4.00	7.00	15.00	20.00
1905 Mo M	344,000	2.00	4.00	8.00	18.00	20.00

KM# 400.3 5 CENTAVOS

1.35 g., 0.9027 Silver 0.0393 oz. ASW **Obv:** Facing eagle, snake in beak **Rev:** Value within 1/2 wreath

Date	Mintage	F12	VF20	XF40	MS60	MS63
1901 Zs Z	40,000	2.50	5.00	11.00	30.00	35.00
1902/1 Zs Z	34,000	2.50	5.00	11.00	28.00	30.00
1902 Zs Z	Inc. above	2.00	5.00	11.00	35.00	40.00
1903 Zs Z	217,000	1.50	2.50	7.00	18.00	22.00
1904 Zs Z	191,000	2.00	3.00	7.00	18.00	22.00
1904 Zs M	Inc. above	4.00	10.00	18.00	60.00	75.00

Date	Mintage	F12	VF20	XF40	MS60	MS63
1905 Zs M	46,000	10.00	25.00	50.00	200	250
1905 Zs M Repullica; Rare	Inc. above	75.00	125	250	600	900

KM# 404 10 CENTAVOS

2.71 g., 0.903 Silver 0.0786 oz. ASW **Obv:** Facing eagle, snake in beak **Obv. Legend:** REPUBLICA MEXICANA **Rev:** Value within 1/2 wreath **Note:** Varieties exist.

Date	Mintage	F12	VF20	XF40	MS60	MS63
1901 Cn Q	235,000	2.75	3.25	7.00	25.00	28.00
1902 Cn Q	186,000	2.75	3.25	7.00	25.00	28.00
1903 Cn Q	256,000	2.75	3.25	7.00	25.00	28.00
1903 Cn V	Inc. above	2.75	3.25	7.00	25.00	28.00
1904 Cn H	307,000	2.75	3.25	7.00	25.00	28.00

KM# 404.2 10 CENTAVOS

2.71 g., 0.903 Silver 0.0786 oz. ASW **Obv:** Facing eagle, snake in beak **Obv. Legend:** REPUBLICA MEXICANA **Rev:** Value within 1/2 wreath

Date	Mintage	F12	VF20	XF40	MS60	MS63
1901 Mo M	80,000	2.75	3.50	8.00	27.00	30.00
1902 Mo M	181,000	2.75	3.50	8.00	25.00	28.00
1903 Mo M	581,000	2.75	3.50	8.00	22.00	25.00
1904 Mo MM (Error)	Inc. above	3.00	7.00	14.00	35.00	40.00
1904 Mo M	1,266,000	2.75	3.50	6.00	22.00	25.00
1905 Mo M	266,000	3.00	5.00	10.00	25.00	28.00

KM# 404.3 10 CENTAVOS

2.71 g., 0.902 Silver 0.0785 oz. ASW **Obv:** Facing eagle, snake in beak **Rev:** Value within 1/2 wreath

Date	Mintage	F12	VF20	XF40	MS60	MS63
1901 Zs Z	70,000	3.00	7.00	18.00	45.00	60.00
1902 Zs Z	120,000	3.00	7.00	14.00	30.00	35.00
1903 Zs Z	228,000	2.75	4.00	12.00	25.00	28.00
1904 Zs Z	368,000	2.75	4.00	12.00	25.00	28.00
1904 Zs M	Inc. above	2.75	4.00	15.00	60.00	85.00
1905 Zs M	66,000	10.00	27.50	70.00	200	275

KM# 405 20 CENTAVOS

5.42 g., 0.903 Silver 0.1572 oz. ASW **Obv:** Facing eagle, snake in beak **Rev:** Value within 1/2 wreath

Date	Mintage	F12	VF20	XF40	MS60	MS63
1901 Cn Q	185,000	6.00	12.00	25.00	130	150
1902/802 Cn Q	98,000	6.00	12.00	25.00	130	150
1902 Cn Q	Inc. above	6.00	12.00	25.00	130	150
1903 Cn Q	93,000	6.00	12.00	25.00	130	150
1904 Cn H	258,000	6.00	12.00	25.00	130	150

KM# 405.2 20 CENTAVOS

5.42 g., 0.903 Silver 0.1572 oz. ASW **Obv:** Facing eagle, snake in beak **Rev:** Value within 1/2 wreath **Note:** Varieties exist.

Date	Mintage	F12	VF20	XF40	MS60	MS63
1901 Mo M	110,000	6.00	12.00	25.00	110	125
1902 Mo M	120,000	6.00	12.00	25.00	110	125
1903 Mo M	213,000	6.00	12.00	25.00	110	125
1904 Mo M	276,000	6.00	12.00	25.00	110	125
1905 Mo M	117,000	6.00	20.00	45.00	160	190

KM# 405.3 20 CENTAVOS

5.42 g., 0.9027 Silver 0.1572 oz. ASW **Obv:** Facing eagle, snake in beak **Obv. Legend:** REPUBLICA MEXICANA **Rev:** Value within 1/2 wreath

Date	Mintage	F12	VF20	XF40	MS60	MS63
1901 Zs Z	Inc. above	6.00	12.00	25.00	130	150
1901/0 Zs Z	130,000	50.00	75.00	175	500	600
1902 Zs Z	105,000	6.00	12.00	50.00	400	550
1903 Zs Z	143,000	6.00	12.00	25.00	130	150
1904 Zs Z	246,000	6.00	12.00	25.00	130	150
1904 Zs M	Inc. above	6.00	15.00	40.00	300	350
1904/804 Zs	—	20.00	50.00	125	350	500
1905 Zs M	59,000	12.00	85.00	125	1,100	1,400

KM# 409 PESO

27.07 g., 0.903 Silver 0.786 oz. ASW, 39 mm. **Obv:** Facing eagle, snake in beak **Rev:** Radiant cap

Date	Mintage	F12	VF20	XF40	MS60	MS63
1901 Cn JQ	1,473,000	28.00	30.00	65.00	160	—
1902 Cn JQ	1,194,000	28.00	30.00	75.00	240	—
1903 Cn JQ	1,514,000	28.00	30.00	55.00	160	—
1903 Cn FV	Inc. above	40.00	80.00	175	425	—
1904 Cn MH	1,554,000	28.00	30.00	44.00	145	—
1904 Cn RP	Inc. above	80.00	160	265	650	—
1905 Cn RP	598,000	40.00	80.00	175	475	—

KM# 409.2 PESO

27.07 g., 0.9027 Silver 0.7857 oz. ASW, 39 mm. **Obv:** Facing eagle, snake in beak **Obv. Legend:** REPUBLICA MEXICANA **Rev:** Radiant cap **Note:** Varieties exist.

Date	Mintage	F12	VF20	XF40	MS60	MS63
1901 Mo AM	14,505,000	28.00	30.00	37.00	80.00	—
1902/1 Mo AM	16,224,000	240	475	875	1,800	—
1902 Mo AM	Inc. above	28.00	30.00	37.00	130	—
1903 Mo AM	22,396,000	28.00	30.00	37.00	130	—
1903 Mo MA (Error)	Inc. above	1,500	2,500	3,850	9,000	—
1904 Mo AM	14,935,000	28.00	30.00	37.00	130	—
1905 Mo AM	3,557,000	28.00	40.00	100	240	—
1908 Mo AM	7,575,000	28.00	30.00	37.00	115	—
1908 Mo GV	Inc. above	28.00	30.00	37.00	80.00	—
1909 Mo GV	2,924,000	28.00	30.00	37.00	80.00	—

KM# 409.3 PESO

27.07 g., 0.903 Silver 0.786 oz. ASW, 39 mm. **Obv:** Facing eagle, snake in beak **Rev:** Radiant cap **Note:** Mint mark Zs. Varieties exist.

Date	Mintage	F12	VF20	XF40	MS60	MS63
1901 Zs FZ	Inc. above	28.00	30.00	36.00	110	—
1901 Zs AZ	5,706,000	4,000	6,000	11,000	—	—
1902 Zs FZ	7,134,000	28.00	30.00	36.00	110	—
1903/2 Zs FZ	3,080,000	28.00	30.00	90.00	240	—
1903 Zs FZ	Inc. above	28.00	30.00	37.00	125	—
1904 Zs FZ	2,423,000	28.00	30.00	50.00	160	—
1904 Zs FM	Inc. above	28.00	30.00	45.00	145	—
1905 Zs FM	995,000	32.00	65.00	110	290	—

KM# 410.2 PESO

1.69 g., 0.875 Gold 0.0476 oz. AGW **Obv:** Facing eagle, snake in beak **Obv. Legend:** REPUBLICA MEXICANA **Rev:** Value within 1/2 wreath

Date	Mintage	F12	VF20	XF40	MS60	MS63
1901 Cn Q	Inc. above	90.00	110	150	225	325
1901/0 Cn Q	2,350	90.00	110	150	225	325
1902 Cn Q	2,480	90.00	110	150	225	325
1902 Cn/ MoQ/C	Inc. above	90.00	110	150	225	325
1904 Cn H	3,614	90.00	110	150	225	325
1904 Cn/ Mo/ H	Inc. above	90.00	110	150	250	350
1905 Cn P	1,000	—	—	—	—	—

Note: Requires Confirmation

KM# 410.5 PESO

1.69 g., 0.875 Gold 0.0476 oz. AGW **Obv:** Facing eagle, snake in beak **Obv. Legend:** REPUBLICA MEXICANA **Rev:** Value within 1/2 wreath

Date	Mintage	F12	VF20	XF40	MS60	MS63
1901 Mo M Small date	Inc. above	90.00	100	115	205	270
1901/801 Mo M Large date	8,293	90.00	100	115	205	270
1902 Mo M Large date	11,000	90.00	100	115	205	270
1902 Mo M Small date	Inc. above	90.00	100	115	205	270
1903 Mo M Large date	10,000	90.00	100	115	205	270
1903 Mo M Small date	Inc. above	90.00	100	145	220	325
1904 Mo M	9,845	90.00	100	115	205	270
1905 Mo M	3,429	90.00	100	115	205	270

KM# 412.2 5 PESOS

8.46 g., 0.875 Gold 0.238 oz. AGW **Obv:** Facing eagle, snake in beak **Obv. Legend:** REPUBLICA MEXICANA **Rev:** Radiant cap above scales

Date	Mintage	F12	VF20	XF40	MS60	MS63
1903 Cn Q	1,000	450	475	550	1,000	—

KM# 412.6 5 PESOS

8.46 g., 0.875 Gold 0.238 oz. AGW **Obv:** Facing eagle, snake in beak **Obv. Legend:** REPUBLICA MEXICANA **Rev:** Radiant cap above scales

Date	Mintage	F12	VF20	XF40	MS60	MS63
1901 Mo M	1,071	450	475	500	850	1,300
1902 Mo M	1,478	450	475	500	850	1,300
1903 Mo M	1,162	450	475	500	850	1,300
1904 Mo M	1,415	450	475	500	850	1,300
1905 Mo M	563	450	500	600	1,550	2,050

KM# 413.2 10 PESOS

16.92 g., 0.875 Gold 0.476 oz. AGW **Obv:** Facing eagle, snake in beak **Obv. Legend:** REPUBLICA MEXICANA **Rev:** Radiant cap above scales

Date	Mintage	F12	VF20	XF40	MS60	MS63
1903 Cn Q	774	875	950	1,100	2,100	—

KM# 413.7 10 PESOS
16.92 g., 0.875 Gold 0.476 oz. AGW **Obv:** Facing eagle, snake in beak **Obv. Legend:** REPUBLICA MEXICANA **Rev:** Radiant cap above scales

Date	Mintage	F12	VF20	XF40	MS60	MS63
1901 Mo M	562	875	900	950	1,600	—
1902 Mo M	719	875	900	950	1,600	2,800
1903 Mo M	713	875	900	950	1,600	2,800
1904 Mo M	694	875	900	950	1,600	—
1905 Mo M	401	875	900	1,100	1,800	—

KM# 414.2 20 PESOS
33.84 g., 0.875 Gold 0.952 oz. AGW **Obv:** Facing eagle, snake in beak **Obv. Legend:** REPUBLICA MEXICANA **Rev:** Radiant cap above scales

Date	Mintage	F12	VF20	XF40	MS60	MS63
1901 Cn Q	1,496	1,225	1,750	1,850	2,950	—
1901/0 Cn Q	Inc. above	—	—	—	—	—
1902 Cn Q	1,059	1,225	1,750	1,850	2,950	—
1903 Cn Q	1,121	1,225	1,750	1,850	2,950	—
1904 Cn H	4,646	1,225	1,750	1,700	2,950	—
1905 Cn P	1,738	1,225	1,750	1,850	3,150	—

KM# 414.6 20 PESOS
33.84 g., 0.875 Gold 0.952 oz. AGW **Obv:** Facing eagle, snake in beak **Obv. Legend:** REPUBLICA MEXICANA **Rev:** Radiant cap above scales

Date	Mintage	F12	VF20	XF40	MS60	MS63
1901 Mo M	29,000	1,225	1,750	1,850	2,450	—
1902 Mo M	38,000	1,225	1,750	1,850	2,450	—
1903/2 Mo M	31,000	1,225	1,750	1,850	2,450	—
1903 Mo M	Inc. above	1,225	1,750	1,850	2,450	—
1904 Mo M	52,000	1,225	1,750	1,850	2,450	—
1905 Mo M	9,757	1,225	1,750	1,850	2,450	—

ESTADOS UNIDOS MEXICANOS

DECIMAL COINAGE

100 Centavos = 1 Peso

KM# 415 CENTAVO
3.00 g., Bronze, 20 mm. **Obv:** National arms **Rev:** Value below date within wreath **Note:** Mint mark Mo.

Date	Mintage	F12	VF20	XF40	MS60	MS63
1905 Narrow date	6,040,000	4.00	6.50	14.00	75.00	—
1905 Wide date	—	4.00	6.50	14.00	75.00	—
1906 Narrow date	Est. 67505000	0.50	0.75	1.25	14.00	25.00

Note: 50,000,000 pcs. were struck at the Birmingham Mint

Date	Mintage	F12	VF20	XF40	MS60	MS63
1906 Wide date	Inc. above	0.75	1.50	2.50	22.00	—
1910 Narrow date	8,700,000	2.00	3.00	6.50	65.00	95.00
1910 Wide date	—	2.00	3.00	6.50	65.00	95.00
1911 Narrow date	16,450,000	0.60	1.00	2.75	22.50	—
1911 Wide date	Inc. above	0.75	1.00	4.00	35.00	—
1912	12,650,000	1.00	1.35	3.25	35.00	—
1913	12,850,000	0.75	1.25	3.00	35.00	—
1914 Narrow date	17,350,000	0.75	1.00	3.00	15.00	20.00
1914 Wide date	Inc. above	0.75	1.00	3.00	15.00	20.00
1915	2,277,000	11.00	25.00	65.00	250	—
1916	500,000	45.00	80.00	170	1,200	—
1920	1,433,000	22.00	50.00	115	400	—
1921	3,470,000	5.50	15.50	47.00	260	—
1922	1,880,000	9.00	17.00	50.00	240	—
1923	4,800,000	0.75	1.25	1.75	13.50	—
1924/3	2,000,000	65.00	170	275	525	—
1924	Inc. above	4.50	11.00	22.00	245	300
1925	1,550,000	4.50	10.00	25.00	215	—
1926	5,000,000	1.00	2.00	4.00	20.00	28.00
1927/6	6,000,000	25.00	40.00	65.00	175	—
1927	Inc. above	0.75	1.25	4.50	30.00	45.00
1928	5,000,000	0.75	1.00	3.25	16.50	28.00
1929	4,500,000	0.75	1.00	1.75	15.00	25.00
1930	7,000,000	0.75	1.00	2.50	20.00	—
1933	10,000,000	0.25	0.35	1.75	15.00	22.00
1934	7,500,000	0.25	0.95	3.25	40.00	—
1935	12,400,000	0.15	0.25	0.40	10.00	15.00
1936	20,100,000	0.15	0.20	0.30	9.00	—
1937	20,000,000	0.15	0.25	0.35	4.00	6.00
1938	10,000,000	0.10	0.15	0.30	2.00	3.00
1939	30,000,000	0.10	0.20	0.30	1.00	2.50
1940	10,000,000	0.20	0.30	0.60	4.50	8.50
1941	15,800,000	0.15	0.25	0.35	2.00	3.00
1942	30,400,000	0.15	0.20	0.30	1.25	2.00
1943	4,310,000	0.30	0.50	0.75	8.00	12.50
1944	5,645,000	0.15	0.25	0.50	5.50	8.50
1945	26,375,000	0.10	0.15	0.25	1.00	1.75
1946	42,135,000	—	0.15	0.20	0.60	1.50
1947	13,445,000	—	0.10	0.15	0.80	1.50
1948	20,040,000	0.10	0.15	0.30	1.10	2.25
1949	6,235,000	0.10	0.15	0.30	1.25	3.00

Note: Varieties exist

KM# 416 CENTAVO
1.50 g., Bronze, 16 mm. **Obv:** National arms **Rev:** Value below date within wreath **Note:** Zapata issue. Struck at Mexico City Mint, mint mark Mo. Reduced size. Weight varies 1.39-1.5g.

Date	Mintage	F12	VF20	XF40	MS60	MS63
1915	179,000	18.00	30.00	60.00	85.00	—

KM# 417 CENTAVO
2.00 g., Brass, 16 mm. **Obv:** National arms, eagle left **Rev:** Oat sprigs **Note:** Mint mark Mo.

Date	Mintage	F12	VF20	XF40	MS60	MS63
1950	12,815,000	—	0.15	0.35	1.65	2.25
1951	25,740,000	—	0.15	0.35	0.65	1.25
1952	24,610,000	—	0.10	0.25	0.40	0.85
1953	21,160,000	—	0.10	0.25	0.40	0.85
1954	25,675,000	—	0.10	0.15	0.85	1.50
1955	9,820,000	—	0.15	0.25	0.85	1.75
1956	11,285,000	—	0.15	0.25	0.80	1.75
1957	9,805,000	—	0.15	0.25	0.85	1.50
1958	12,155,000	—	0.10	0.25	0.45	0.75
1959	11,875,000	—	0.10	0.25	0.75	1.50
1960	10,360,000	—	0.10	0.15	0.40	0.65
1961	6,385,000	—	0.10	0.15	0.45	0.85
1962	4,850,000	—	0.10	0.15	0.55	0.90
1963	7,775,000	—	0.10	0.15	0.25	0.45
1964	4,280,000	—	0.10	0.15	0.20	0.30
1965	2,255,000	—	0.10	0.15	0.25	0.40
1966	1,760,000	—	0.10	0.25	0.60	1.00
1967	1,290,000	—	0.10	0.15	0.40	0.75
1968	1,000,000	—	0.10	0.20	0.85	1.45
1969	1,000,000	—	0.10	0.15	0.65	0.85

KM# 418 CENTAVO
1.50 g., Brass, 13 mm. **Obv:** National arms, eagle left **Rev:** Oat sprigs **Note:** Reduced size.

Date	Mintage	F12	VF20	XF40	MS60	MS63
1970 Mo	1,000,000	—	0.20	0.40	1.45	2.25
1972 Mo	1,000,000	—	0.20	0.45	2.50	4.00
1972/2 Mo	—	—	0.50	1.25	3.50	5.00
1973 Mo	1,000,000	—	1.65	2.75	8.50	17.50

KM# 419 2 CENTAVOS
6.00 g., Bronze, 25 mm. **Obv:** National arms **Rev:** Value below date within wreath **Note:** Mint mark Mo.

Date	Mintage	F12	VF20	XF40	MS60	MS63
1905	50,000	150	300	500	1,150	1,350
1906 Inverted 6	9,998,000	30.00	55.00	120	375	—
1906 Wide date	Inc. above	5.00	11.00	28.00	85.00	110
1906 Narrow date	Inc. above	6.50	14.00	30.00	95.00	—

Note: 5,000,000 pieces were struck at the Birmingham Mint

Date	Mintage	F12	VF20	XF40	MS60	MS63
1920	1,325,000	6.50	17.50	75.00	200	350
1921	4,275,000	2.50	4.75	15.00	100	—
1922	—	225	550	1,750	5,500	—
1924	750,000	8.50	27.50	75.00	450	—
1925	3,650,000	2.50	3.50	7.50	35.00	40.00
1926	4,750,000	1.00	2.25	5.50	40.00	—
1927	7,250,000	0.60	1.00	4.50	22.00	35.00
1928	3,250,000	0.75	1.50	4.75	25.00	38.00
1929	250,000	85.00	225	550	1,200	—
1935	1,250,000	4.25	9.25	65.00	195	275
1939	5,000,000	0.60	0.90	2.25	20.00	30.00
1941	3,550,000	0.45	0.60	1.25	18.00	28.00

KM# 420 2 CENTAVOS
3.00 g., Bronze, 20 mm. **Obv:** National arms **Rev:** Value below date within wreath **Note:** Zapata issue. Mint mark Mo. Reduced size. Weight varies 3-3.03g.

Date	Mintage	F12	VF20	XF40	MS60	MS63
1915	487,000	7.50	9.00	17.50	75.00	—

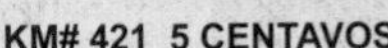

KM# 421 5 CENTAVOS
5.00 g., Nickel, 20 mm. **Obv:** National arms **Rev:** Value and date within beaded circle **Note:** Mint mark Mo. Varieties exist.

Date	Mintage	F12	VF20	XF40	MS60	MS63
1905	1,420,000	7.00	10.00	28.00	295	385
1906/5	10,615,000	13.00	30.00	70.00	375	—
1906	Inc. above	0.75	1.35	3.25	50.00	75.00
1907	4,000,000	1.25	4.00	35.00	350	450
1909	2,052,000	3.25	10.00	50.00	370	—
1910	6,181,000	1.30	3.50	9.00	75.00	125
1911 Narrow date	4,487,000	1.00	3.00	7.00	85.00	135
1911 Wide date	Inc. above	2.50	5.00	9.00	110	170
1912 Small mint mark	420,000	90.00	100	230	725	—
1912 Large mint mark	Inc. above	70.00	95.00	200	575	—
1913	2,035,000	1.75	4.25	30.00	200	300

Note: Wide and narrow dates exist for 1913

Date	Mintage	F12	VF20	XF40	MS60	MS63
1914	2,000,000	1.00	2.00	5.00	70.00	110

Note: 5,000,000 pieces appear to have been struck at the Birmingham Mint in 1914 and all of 1909-1911. The Mexican Mint report does not mention receiving the 1914 dated coins

KM# 422 5 CENTAVOS

9.00 g., Bronze, 28 mm. **Obv:** National arms **Rev:** Value below date within wreath

Date	Mintage	F12	VF20	XF40	MS60	MS63
1914 Mo	2,500,000	10.00	23.00	65.00	300	—
1915 Mo	11,424,000	3.00	5.00	35.00	165	265
1916 Mo	2,860,000	15.00	35.00	175	650	—
1917 Mo	800,000	75.00	225	400	900	—
1918 Mo	1,332,000	35.00	90.00	250	675	—
1919 Mo	400,000	115	225	360	950	—
1920 Mo	5,920,000	3.00	8.00	45.00	250	350
1921 Mo	2,080,000	10.00	24.00	75.00	275	—
1924 Mo	780,000	40.00	95.00	275	700	—
1925 Mo	4,040,000	5.50	11.00	45.00	225	—
1926 Mo	3,160,000	5.50	11.00	48.00	325	—
1927 Mo	3,600,000	4.00	7.00	35.00	230	350
1928 Mo Large date	1,740,000	11.00	18.00	65.00	250	375
1928 Mo Small date	Inc. above	30.00	45.00	100	385	—
1929 Mo	2,400,000	5.50	12.00	50.00	245	—
1930 Mo	2,600,000	5.00	8.00	28.00	225	—
Note: Large oval O in date						
1930 Mo	Inc. above	65.00	125	250	565	—
Note: Small square O in date						
1931 Mo	—	475	750	1,450	4,000	—
1933 Mo	8,000,000	1.50	2.25	3.50	27.50	45.00
1934 Mo	10,000,000	1.25	1.75	2.75	25.00	50.00
1935 Mo	21,980,000	0.75	1.20	2.50	22.50	40.00

KM# 423 5 CENTAVOS

4.00 g., Copper-Nickel, 20.5 mm. **Obv:** National arms, eagle left **Rev:** Value and date within circle

Date	Mintage	F12	VF20	XF40	MS60	MS63
1936 M	46,700,000	—	0.65	1.25	7.50	8.50
1937 M	49,060,000	—	0.50	1.00	7.00	8.00
1938 M	3,340,000	—	4.00	10.00	80.00	200
1940 M	22,800,000	—	0.75	1.25	8.00	10.00
1942 M	7,100,000	—	1.50	3.00	30.00	50.00

KM# 424 5 CENTAVOS

6.50 g., Bronze, 25.5 mm. **Obv:** National arms, eagle left **Rev:** Head left

Date	Mintage	F12	VF20	XF40	MS60	MS63
1942 Mo	900,000	—	25.00	75.00	375	550
1943 Mo	54,660,000	—	0.50	0.75	2.50	3.50
1944 Mo	53,463,000	—	0.25	0.35	0.75	1.00
1945 Mo	44,262,000	—	0.25	0.35	0.75	1.25
1946 Mo	49,054,000	—	0.50	1.00	2.00	3.00
1951 Mo	50,758,000	—	0.75	0.90	3.00	5.00
1952 Mo	17,674,000	—	1.50	2.50	9.50	11.50
1953 Mo	31,568,000	—	1.25	2.00	6.00	9.00
1954 Mo	58,680,000	—	0.40	1.00	2.75	4.00
1955 Mo	31,114,000	—	2.00	3.00	11.00	14.00

KM# 425 5 CENTAVOS

4.00 g., Copper-Nickel, 20.5 mm. **Obv:** National arms, eagle left **Rev:** Bust right flanked by date and value

Date	Mintage	F12	VF20	XF40	MS60	MS63
1950 Mo	5,700,000	—	0.75	1.50	6.00	7.00

Note: 5,600,000 pieces struck at Connecticut melted

KM# 426 5 CENTAVOS

4.00 g., Brass, 20.4 mm. **Obv:** National arms, eagle left **Rev:** Bust right

Date	Mintage	F12	VF20	XF40	MS60	MS63
1954 Mo Dot	—	—	10.00	50.00	290	375
1954 Mo Without dot	—	—	15.00	35.00	265	325
1955 Mo	12,136,000	—	0.75	1.50	7.50	12.50
1956 Mo	60,216,000	—	0.20	0.30	0.75	1.25
1957 Mo	55,288,000	—	0.15	0.20	0.90	1.50
1958 Mo	104,624,000	—	0.15	0.20	0.60	1.00
1959 Mo	106,000,000	—	0.15	0.25	0.75	1.25
1960 Mo	99,144,000	—	0.10	0.15	0.50	0.75
1961 Mo	61,136,000	—	0.10	0.15	0.50	0.75
1962 Mo	47,232,000	—	0.10	0.15	0.25	0.35
1963 Mo	156,680,000	—	—	0.15	0.25	0.40
1964 Mo	71,168,000	—	—	0.15	0.20	0.40
1965 Mo	155,720,000	—	—	0.15	0.25	0.35
1966 Mo	124,944,000	—	—	0.15	0.40	0.65
1967 Mo	118,816,000	—	—	0.15	0.25	0.40
1968 Mo	189,588,000	—	—	0.15	0.50	0.75
1969 Mo	210,492,000	—	—	0.15	0.55	0.80

KM# 426a 5 CENTAVOS

Copper-Nickel, 20.5 mm. **Obv:** National arms, eagle left **Rev:** Bust right

Date	Mintage	F12	VF20	XF40	MS60	MS63
1960 Mo	—	—	250	300	375	—
1962 Mo	19	—	250	300	375	—
1965 Mo	—	—	250	300	375	—

KM# 427 5 CENTAVOS

2.75 g., Brass, 18 mm. **Obv:** National arms, eagle left **Rev:** Bust right **Note:** Due to some minor alloy variations this type is often encountered with a bronze-color toning. Reduced size.

Date	Mintage	F12	VF20	XF40	MS60	MS63
1970 Mo	163,368,000	—	0.10	0.15	0.35	0.45
1971 Mo	198,844,000	—	0.10	0.15	0.25	0.30
1972 Mo	225,000,000	—	0.10	0.15	0.25	0.30
1973 Mo Flat top 3	595,070,000	—	0.10	0.15	0.25	0.40
1973 Mo Round top 3	Inc. above	—	0.10	0.15	0.20	0.30
1974 Mo	401,584,000	—	0.10	0.15	0.30	0.40
1975 Mo	342,308,000	—	0.10	0.15	0.25	0.35
1976 Mo	367,524,000	—	0.10	0.15	0.40	0.60

KM# 428 10 CENTAVOS

2.50 g., 0.800 Silver 0.0643 oz. ASW, 18 mm. **Obv:** National arms **Rev:** Value and date within 3/4 wreath with Liberty cap above **Note:** Mint mark Mo.

Date	Mintage	F12	VF20	XF40	MS60	MS63
1905	3,920,000	2.50	6.00	8.00	37.00	50.00
1906	8,410,000	2.50	5.50	7.50	27.00	40.00
1907/6	5,950,000	15.00	50.00	135	310	375
1907	Inc. above	2.50	5.50	6.25	35.00	50.00
1909	2,620,000	2.75	8.50	13.00	75.00	110
1910/00	3,450,000	3.00	10.00	25.00	60.00	85.00
1910	Inc. above	2.50	7.00	15.00	25.00	40.00
1911 Narrow date	2,550,000	3.00	11.00	17.00	80.00	125
1911 Wide date	Inc. above	2.50	7.50	10.00	45.00	65.00
1912	1,350,000	3.00	10.00	18.00	125	175
1912 Low 2	Inc. above	3.00	10.00	18.00	110	155
1913/2	1,990,000	3.00	10.00	25.00	40.00	70.00
1913	Inc. above	2.50	7.00	10.00	30.00	45.00
1914	3,110,000	2.50	5.50	7.00	15.00	25.00

Note: Wide and narrow dates exist for 1914

KM# 429 10 CENTAVOS

1.81 g., 0.800 Silver 0.0466 oz. ASW, 15 mm. **Obv:** National arms **Rev:** Value and date within 3/4 wreath with Liberty cap above **Note:** Mint mark Mo. Reduced size.

Date	Mintage	F12	VF20	XF40	MS60	MS63
1919	8,360,000	3.00	10.00	15.00	85.00	125

KM# 430 10 CENTAVOS

12.00 g., Bronze, 30.5 mm. **Obv:** National arms **Rev:** Value below date within wreath **Note:** Mint mark Mo.

Date	Mintage	F12	VF20	XF40	MS60	MS63
1919	1,232,000	7.00	25.00	85.00	455	550
1920	6,612,000	5.00	15.00	50.00	385	475
1921	2,255,000	10.00	35.00	95.00	650	800
1935	5,970,000	4.50	14.00	35.00	125	200

KM# 431 10 CENTAVOS

1.66 g., 0.720 Silver 0.0384 oz. ASW, 15 mm. **Obv:** National arms **Rev:** Value and date within wreath with Liberty cap above **Note:** Mint mark Mo.

Date	Mintage	F12	VF20	XF40	MS60	MS63
1925/15	5,350,000	10.00	30.00	75.00	115	175
1925/3	Inc. above	8.00	20.00	40.00	110	175
1925	Inc. above	0.70	2.00	5.00	40.00	50.00
1926/16	2,650,000	10.00	30.00	75.00	115	175
1926	Inc. above	1.80	3.50	7.50	60.00	95.00
1927	2,810,000	0.70	2.25	3.00	17.50	25.00
1928	5,270,000	0.70	2.00	2.75	13.50	20.00
1930	2,000,000	1.75	3.75	5.00	18.50	28.00
1933	5,000,000	0.70	1.50	3.00	10.00	17.00
1934	8,000,000	0.70	1.75	2.50	8.00	16.00
1935	3,500,000	1.50	2.75	5.00	11.00	18.00

KM# 432 10 CENTAVOS

5.50 g., Copper-Nickel, 23.5 mm. **Obv:** National arms, eagle left **Rev:** Value and date within circle **Note:** Mint mark Mo.

Date	Mintage	F12	VF20	XF40	MS60	MS63
1936	33,030,000	—	0.75	2.50	10.00	14.00
1937	3,000,000	2.00	10.00	50.00	200	250
1938	3,650,000	1.25	2.00	7.00	65.00	90.00
1939	6,920,000	—	1.00	3.50	27.50	35.00
1940	12,300,000	—	0.40	1.25	5.00	8.00
1942	14,380,000	—	0.60	1.50	7.00	12.00
1945	9,558,000	—	0.40	0.70	3.50	5.00
1946	46,230,000	—	0.40	0.60	2.50	4.00

KM# 433 10 CENTAVOS

5.50 g., Bronze, 23.5 mm. **Obv:** National arms, eagle left **Rev:** Bust left **Note:** Mint mark Mo.

Date	Mintage	F12	VF20	XF40	MS60	MS63
1955	1,818,000	—	0.75	3.25	22.00	35.00
1956	5,255,000	—	0.75	3.25	20.00	32.00
1957	11,925,000	—	0.20	0.40	5.00	9.00
1959	26,140,000	—	0.30	0.45	0.65	1.25
1966	5,873,000	—	0.15	0.25	1.00	1.75
1967	32,318,000	—	0.10	0.15	0.30	0.40

Sharp stem

KM# 434.1 10 CENTAVOS

1.50 g., Copper-Nickel **Obv:** National arms, eagle left **Rev:** Upright ear of corn **Edge:** Reeded **Note:** Variety I- Sharp stem and wide date

Date	Mintage	F12	VF20	XF40	MS60	MS63
1974 Mo	6,000,000	—	—	0.35	0.75	1.00
1975 Mo	5,550,000	—	0.10	0.35	0.75	1.00
1976 Mo	7,680,000	—	0.10	0.20	0.30	0.40
1977 Mo	144,650,000	—	1.25	2.25	3.50	5.50
1978 Mo	271,870,000	—	—	1.00	1.50	2.25
1979 Mo	375,660,000	—	—	0.50	1.00	1.75
1980/79 Mo	21,290,000	—	2.45	3.75	6.50	10.00
1980 Mo	Inc. above	—	1.50	2.00	4.50	7.00

Blunt stem

KM# 434.2 10 CENTAVOS

1.50 g., Copper-Nickel **Obv:** National arms, eagle left **Rev:** Upright ear of corn **Edge:** Reeded **Note:** Variety II- Blunt stem and narrow date

Date	Mintage	F12	VF20	XF40	MS60	MS63
1974 Mo	Inc. above	—	—	0.10	0.20	0.30
1977 Mo	Inc. above	—	0.15	0.50	1.25	2.25
1978 Mo	Inc. above	—	—	0.10	0.30	0.40
1979 Mo	Inc. above	—	0.15	0.35	0.85	1.50
1980 Mo	Inc. above	—	—	0.10	0.20	0.30

KM# 434.3 10 CENTAVOS

1.50 g., Copper-Nickel **Obv:** National arms, eagle left **Rev:** Upright ear of corn **Edge:** Reeded **Note:** Variety III- Blunt stem and wide date

Date	Mintage	F12	VF20	XF40	MS60	MS63
1980/79 Mo	—	—	—	2.50	7.00	9.00

KM# 434.4 10 CENTAVOS

1.50 g., Copper-Nickel **Obv:** National arms, eagle left **Rev:** Upright ear of corn **Edge:** Reeded **Note:** Variety IV- Sharp stem and narrow date

Date	Mintage	F12	VF20	XF40	MS60	MS63
1974 Mo	—	—	—	—	1.50	2.50
1979 Mo	—	—	—	—	1.50	2.50

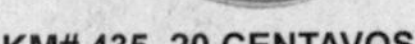

KM# 435 20 CENTAVOS

5.00 g., 0.800 Silver 0.1286 oz. ASW, 22 mm. **Obv:** National arms **Rev:** Value and date within wreath with Liberty cap above **Note:** Mint mark Mo.

Date	Mintage	F12	VF20	XF40	MS60	MS63
1905	2,565,000	5.00	12.00	25.00	145	195
1906	6,860,000	4.75	9.00	16.50	50.00	85.00
1907 Straight 7	4,000,000	5.00	11.50	22.00	65.00	125
1907 Curved 7	5,435,000	4.50	7.50	15.00	60.00	120
1908	350,000	50.00	95.00	250	1,800	—
1910	1,135,000	5.00	11.00	16.00	75.00	110
1911	1,150,000	12.00	15.00	40.00	125	175
1912	625,000	20.00	40.00	70.00	325	420
1913	1,000,000	5.00	14.50	30.00	85.00	125
1914	1,500,000	5.00	10.00	22.50	60.00	90.00

KM# 436 20 CENTAVOS

3.63 g., 0.800 Silver 0.0932 oz. ASW, 19 mm. **Obv:** National arms **Rev:** Value and date within wreath with Liberty cap above **Note:** Mint mark Mo. Reduced size.

Date	Mintage	F12	VF20	XF40	MS60	MS63
1919	4,155,000	10.00	30.00	65.00	185	275

KM# 437 20 CENTAVOS

15.00 g., Bronze, 32.5 mm. **Obv:** National arms **Rev:** Value below date within wreath **Note:** Mint mark Mo.

Date	Mintage	F12	VF20	XF40	MS60	MS63
1920	4,835,000	12.00	35.00	125	550	775
1935	20,000,000	2.00	6.00	10.00	75.00	145

KM# 438 20 CENTAVOS

3.33 g., 0.720 Silver 0.0772 oz. ASW, 19 mm. **Obv:** National arms **Rev:** Value and date within wreath with Liberty cap above **Note:** Mint mark Mo.

Date	Mintage	F12	VF20	XF40	MS60	MS63
1920	3,710,000	3.00	9.00	20.00	165	220
1921	6,160,000	3.00	7.00	14.00	90.00	150
1925	1,450,000	4.00	12.00	20.00	135	165
1926/5	1,465,000	7.00	20.00	70.00	335	375
1926	Inc. above	2.75	5.00	11.00	80.00	110
1927	1,405,000	2.75	5.00	12.00	85.00	115
1928	3,630,000	2.75	6.00	8.00	18.00	28.00
1930	1,000,000	2.75	8.00	12.00	28.00	42.00
1933	2,500,000	2.75	3.00	5.00	10.00	16.00
1934	2,500,000	2.75	3.00	6.00	12.00	20.00
1935	2,460,000	2.75	3.00	6.00	12.00	20.00
1937	10,000,000	1.50	2.75	3.00	6.00	9.00
1939	8,800,000	1.50	2.75	3.00	6.00	9.00
1940	3,000,000	1.50	2.75	3.00	5.00	9.00
1941	5,740,000	1.50	2.25	3.00	5.00	8.00
1942	12,460,000	1.50	2.25	3.00	5.00	8.00
1943	3,955,000	1.50	3.00	4.00	5.00	9.00

KM# 439 20 CENTAVOS

10.00 g., Bronze, 28.5 mm. **Obv:** National arms, eagle left **Rev:** Liberty cap divides value above Pyramid of the Sun at Teotihuacán, volcanos Ixtaccihuatl and Popocatepet in background **Edge:** Plain **Note:** Mint mark Mo.

Date	Mintage	F12	VF20	XF40	MS60	MS63
1943	46,350,000	—	1.25	3.00	18.00	28.00
1944	83,650,000	—	0.40	0.65	7.00	12.00
1945	26,801,000	—	1.25	3.50	8.50	15.00
1946	25,695,000	—	1.10	2.25	6.00	9.00
1951	11,385,000	0.50	3.00	8.75	85.00	120
1952	6,560,000	0.50	3.00	5.00	22.00	35.00
1953	26,948,000	—	0.35	0.80	7.00	15.00
1954	40,108,000	—	0.35	0.80	7.00	15.00
1955	16,950,000	0.50	2.75	7.00	55.00	75.00

KM# 440 20 CENTAVOS

10.00 g., Bronze, 28.5 mm. **Obv:** National arms, eagle left **Rev:** Liberty cap divides value above Pyramid of the Sun at Teotihuacán, volcanos Ixtaccihuatl and Popocatepet in background **Edge:** Plain **Note:** Mint mark Mo.

Date	Mintage	F12	VF20	XF40	MS60	MS63
1955 Inc.	Inc. above	—	0.75	1.75	16.00	22.00
KM#439						
1956	22,431,000	—	0.30	0.35	3.00	5.00
1957	13,455,000	—	0.45	1.25	7.00	13.00
1959	6,017,000	0.75	4.50	9.00	65.00	100
1960	39,756,000	—	0.15	0.25	0.75	1.00
1963	14,869,000	—	0.25	0.35	0.80	1.00
1964	28,654,000	—	0.25	0.40	0.90	1.25
1965	74,162,000	—	0.20	0.35	0.80	1.00
1966	43,745,000	—	0.15	0.25	0.75	1.00
1967	46,487,000	—	0.20	0.50	1.00	1.25
1968	15,477,000	—	0.30	0.55	1.35	1.65
1969	63,647,000	—	0.20	0.35	0.80	1.00
1970	76,287,000	—	0.15	0.20	0.90	1.30
1971	49,892,000	—	0.30	0.50	1.25	2.00

KM# 441 20 CENTAVOS

10.00 g., Bronze, 28.5 mm. **Obv:** National arms, eagle left **Rev:** Liberty cap divides value above Pyramid of the Sun at Teotihuacán, volcanos Ixtaccihuatl and Popocatepet in background **Edge:** Plain

Date	Mintage	F12	VF20	XF40	MS60	MS63
1971 Mo Inc.	Inc. above	—	0.20	0.35	1.85	2.50
KM#440						
1973 Mo	78,398,000	—	0.25	0.35	0.95	1.65
1974 Mo	34,200,000	—	0.20	0.35	1.25	2.00

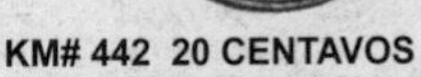

KM# 442 20 CENTAVOS

3.00 g., Copper-Nickel, 20 mm. **Obv:** National arms, eagle left **Rev:** Bust 3/4 facing flanked by value and date **Edge:** Reeded

Date	Mintage	F12	VF20	XF40	MS60	MS63
1974 Mo	112,000,000	—	0.10	0.15	0.25	0.30
1975 Mo	611,000,000	—	0.10	0.15	0.30	0.35
1976 Mo	394,000,000	—	0.10	0.15	0.35	0.45
1977 Mo	394,350,000	—	0.10	0.15	0.40	0.50
1978 Mo	527,950,000	—	0.10	0.15	0.25	0.30
1979 Mo	524,615,000	—	0.10	0.15	0.25	0.30
1979 Mo	—	—	1.25	2.00	4.00	8.00
Note: Doubled die obv. small letters						
1979 Mo	—	—	1.25	2.00	4.00	8.00
Note: Doubled die obv. large letters						
1980 Mo	326,500,000	—	0.15	0.20	0.30	0.40
1981 Mo Open 8	106,205,000	—	0.30	0.50	1.00	2.00
1981 Mo Closed 8, high date	248,500,000	—	0.30	0.50	1.00	2.00
1981 Mo Closed 8, low date	—	—	1.00	1.50	3.50	4.25
1981/1982 Mo	—	10.00	40.00	75.00	165	195
Note: The 1981/1982 overdate is often mistaken as 1982/1981						
1982 Mo	286,855,000	—	0.40	0.60	0.90	1.10
1983 Mo Round top 3	100,930,000	—	0.25	0.40	1.75	2.25
1983 Mo Flat top 3	Inc. above	—	0.25	0.50	1.25	1.75
1983 Mo	998	PF63 45.00				

KM# 491 20 CENTAVOS

3.00 g., Bronze, 20 mm. **Subject:** Olmec Culture **Obv:** National arms, eagle left **Rev:** Mask 3/4 right with value below

Date	Mintage	VF20	XF40	MS60	MS63	MS65
1983 Mo	260,000,000	0.20	0.25	1.25	1.75	—
1983 Mo	53	PF63 185				
1984 Mo	180,320,000	0.20	0.35	1.85	2.25	—

KM# 443 25 CENTAVOS

3.33 g., 0.300 Silver 0.0321 oz. ASW, 21.5 mm. **Obv:** National arms, eagle left **Rev:** Scale below Liberty cap **Edge:** Reeded **Note:** Mint mark Mo.

Date	Mintage	F12	VF20	XF40	MS60	MS63
1950	77,060,000	—	1.25	1.50	2.00	2.50
1951	41,172,000	—	1.25	1.50	2.00	2.50
1952	29,264,000	—	1.25	1.50	2.25	2.75
1953	38,144,000	—	1.25	1.25	2.00	2.50

KM# 444 25 CENTAVOS

5.50 g., Copper-Nickel, 23 mm. **Obv:** National arms, eagle left **Rev:** Bust 3/4 facing **Edge:** Reeded

Date	Mintage	F12	VF20	XF40	MS60	MS63
1964 Mo	20,686,000	—	—	0.15	0.20	0.30
1966 Mo Closed beak	180,000	—	0.75	1.25	3.00	4.50
1966 Mo Open beak	Inc. above	—	2.00	4.00	12.00	15.00

KM# 445 50 CENTAVOS

12.50 g., 0.800 Silver 0.3215 oz. ASW, 30 mm. **Obv:** National arms **Rev:** Value and date within 3/4 wreath with Liberty cap above **Note:** Mint mark Mo.

Date	Mintage	F12	VF20	XF40	MS60	MS63
1905	2,446,000	12.00	20.00	35.00	170	250
1906 Open 9	16,966,000	6.00	12.00	15.00	50.00	85.00
1906 Closed 9	Inc. above	6.00	9.50	14.00	48.00	70.00
1907 Straight 7	18,920,000	6.00	9.00	13.50	32.00	42.00
1907 Curved 7	14,841,000	6.00	9.50	14.00	35.00	45.00
1908	488,000	25.00	80.00	175	525	675
1912	3,736,000	12.00	22.50	20.00	50.00	85.00
1913/07	10,510,000	15.00	40.00	90.00	225	300
1913/2	Inc. above	11.00	20.00	27.50	70.00	100
1913	Inc. above	6.00	9.00	12.50	32.00	42.00
1914	7,710,000	6.00	12.50	20.00	42.00	65.00
1916 Narrow date	480,000	20.00	60.00	85.00	245	350
1916 Wide date	Inc. above	20.00	60.00	85.00	245	350
1917	37,112,000	6.00	9.50	14.00	27.00	33.00
1918	1,320,000	20.00	70.00	135	300	425

KM# 446 50 CENTAVOS

9.06 g., 0.800 Silver 0.2331 oz. ASW, 27 mm. **Obv:** National arms **Rev:** Value and date within 3/4 wreath with Liberty cap above **Note:** Mint mark Mo. Reduced size.

Date	Mintage	F12	VF20	XF40	MS60	MS63
1918/7	2,760,000	175	525	700	1,450	—
1918	Inc. above	9.00	20.00	70.00	325	450
1919	29,670,000	4.50	12.00	25.00	140	180

KM# 447 50 CENTAVOS

8.33 g., 0.720 Silver 0.1929 oz. ASW, 27 mm. **Obv:** National arms **Rev:** Value and date within 3/4 wreath with Liberty cap above **Edge Lettering:** INDEPENDENCIA Y LIBERTAD **Note:** Mint mark Mo.

Date	Mintage	F12	VF20	XF40	MS60	MS63
1919	10,200,000	3.75	12.00	22.00	95.00	130
1920	27,166,000	3.75	7.50	17.00	70.00	90.00
1921	21,864,000	3.75	7.50	17.00	90.00	120
1925	3,280,000	6.50	17.50	35.00	145	185
1937	20,000,000	3.75	6.00	9.00	13.00	18.00
1938	100,000	15.00	50.00	95.00	245	365
1939	10,440,000	3.75	6.00	9.00	16.00	25.00
1942	800,000	3.75	6.50	10.00	18.00	22.00
1943	41,512,000	3.75	6.00	9.00	12.00	15.00
1944	55,806,000	3.75	6.00	9.00	12.00	15.00
1945	56,766,000	3.75	6.00	9.00	12.00	15.00

KM# 448 50 CENTAVOS

7.97 g., 0.420 Silver 0.1077 oz. ASW, 27 mm. **Obv:** National arms **Rev:** Value and date within 3/4 wreath with Liberty cap above **Note:** Mint mark Mo.

Date	Mintage	F12	VF20	XF40	MS60	MS63
1935	70,800,000	2.75	4.00	5.00	9.00	12.00

KM# 449 50 CENTAVOS

6.66 g., 0.300 Silver 0.0642 oz. ASW, 26 mm. **Obv:** National arms, eagle left **Rev:** Head with head covering right **Note:** Mint mark Mo.

Date	Mintage	F12	VF20	XF40	MS60	MS63
1950	13,570,000	—	2.50	2.75	5.00	8.00
1951	3,650,000	—	3.00	4.00	6.00	9.00

KM# 450 50 CENTAVOS

14.00 g., Bronze, 33 mm. **Obv:** National arms, eagle left **Rev:** Head with headdress left **Edge:** Reeded **Note:** Mint mark Mo.

Date	Mintage	F12	VF20	XF40	MS60	MS63
1955	3,502,000	—	1.50	3.00	4.00	8.00
1956	34,643,000	—	0.75	1.50	7.00	9.00
1957	9,675,000	—	1.00	2.00	6.50	8.00
1959	4,540,000	—	0.50	0.75	2.00	3.50

KM# 451 50 CENTAVOS

6.50 g., Copper-Nickel, 25 mm. **Obv:** National arms, eagle left **Rev:** Head with headdress left **Edge:** Reeded

Date	Mintage	F12	VF20	XF40	MS60	MS63
1964 Mo	43,806,000	—	0.15	0.20	0.40	0.60
1965 Mo	14,326,000	—	0.20	0.25	0.45	0.65
1966 Mo	1,726,000	—	0.20	0.40	1.50	2.00
1967 Mo	55,144,000	—	0.20	0.30	0.75	1.25
1968 Mo	80,438,000	—	0.15	0.30	0.65	1.00
1969 Mo	87,640,000	—	0.20	0.35	0.80	1.25

KM# 452 50 CENTAVOS

6.50 g., Copper-Nickel, 25 mm. **Obv:** National arms, eagle left **Rev:** Head with headdress left **Edge:** Reeded **Note:** Coins dated 1975 and 1976 exist with and without dots in centers of three circles on plumage on reverse. Edge varieties exist.

Date	Mintage	F12	VF20	XF40	MS60	MS63
1970 Mo	76,236,000	—	0.15	0.20	0.80	1.35
1971 Mo	125,288,000	—	0.15	0.20	0.90	1.45
1972 Mo	16,000,000	—	1.25	2.00	3.50	5.50
1975 Mo Dots	177,958,000	—	0.65	1.75	3.50	6.00
1975 Mo No dots	Inc. above	—	0.15	0.20	0.75	1.25
1976 Mo Dots	37,480,000	—	0.75	1.50	5.00	7.00
1976 Mo No dots	Inc. above	—	0.15	0.20	0.50	0.90
1977 Mo	12,410,000	—	6.50	10.00	32.50	45.00
1978 Mo	85,400,000	—	0.15	0.25	0.50	1.20
1979 Mo Round 2nd 9 in date	229,000,000	—	0.15	0.25	0.50	1.00
1979 Mo Square 9's in date	Inc. above	—	0.20	0.40	1.60	2.25
1980 Mo Narrow date, square 9	89,978,000	—	0.45	0.75	1.75	2.50
1980 Mo Wide date, round 9	178,188,000	—	0.20	0.25	1.00	2.25
1981 Mo Rectangular 9, narrow date	142,212,000	—	0.50	0.75	1.75	2.50
1981 Mo Round 9, wide date	Inc. above	—	0.30	0.50	1.25	1.75
1982 Mo	45,474,000	—	0.20	0.40	1.95	1.75
1983 Mo	90,318,000	—	0.50	0.75	1.75	2.50
1983 Mo	998	PF63 45.00				

KM# 492 50 CENTAVOS

4.40 g., Stainless Steel, 22 mm. **Subject:** Palenque Culture **Obv:** National arms, eagle left **Rev:** Head with headdress 3/4 left

Date	Mintage	VF20	XF40	MS60	MS63	MS65
1983 Mo	99,540,000	—	0.30	1.50	2.50	—
1983 Mo	53	PF63 195				

KM# 453 PESO

27.07 g., 0.903 Silver 0.7859 oz. ASW, 39 mm. **Subject:** Caballito **Obv:** National arms **Rev:** Horse and rider facing left among sun rays **Note:** Mint mark Mo.

Date	Mintage	F12	VF20	XF40	MS60	MS63
1910	3,814,000	14.50	45.00	50.00	185	275
1911	1,227,000	14.50	45.00	75.00	200	300
Note: Long lower left ray on reverse						
1911	Inc. above	50.00	145	250	750	950
Note: Short lower left ray on reverse						
1912	322,000	35.00	100	210	365	500
1913/2	2,880,000	14.50	45.00	75.00	300	450
1913	Inc. above	14.50	45.00	70.00	195	300
Note: 1913 coins exist with even and unevenly spaced date						
1914	120,000	300	700	1,200	4,000	—

KM# 454 PESO

18.13 g., 0.800 Silver 0.4663 oz. ASW, 34 mm. **Obv:** National arms **Rev:** Value and date within 3/4 wreath with Liberty cap above **Note:** Mint mark Mo.

Date	Mintage	F12	VF20	XF40	MS60	MS63
1918/7	—	250	350	—	—	—
1918	3,050,000	20.00	45.00	150	1,350	2,500
1919	6,151,000	18.00	30.00	125	950	1,750

KM# 455 PESO

16.66 g., 0.720 Silver 0.3857 oz. ASW, 34 mm. **Obv:** National arms **Rev:** Value and date within 3/4 wreath with Liberty cap above **Edge Lettering:** INDEPENDENCIA Y LIBERTAD **Note:** Mint mark Mo.

Date	Mintage	F12	VF20	XF40	MS60	MS63
1920/10	8,830,000	18.00	50.00	90.00	325	—
1920	Inc. above	7.25	15.00	35.00	195	325
1921	5,480,000	7.25	15.00	35.00	195	275
1922	33,620,000	—	7.25	12.00	20.00	35.00
1923	35,280,000	—	7.25	12.00	20.00	35.00
1924	33,060,000	—	7.25	12.00	20.00	35.00
1925	9,160,000	—	7.25	12.00	60.00	85.00
1926	28,840,000	—	7.25	12.00	25.00	40.00
1927	5,060,000	7.25	12.00	16.00	70.00	90.00
1932 Open 9	50,770,000	—	—	7.25	12.00	16.00
1932 Closed 9	Inc. above	—	—	7.25	12.00	16.00
1933/2	43,920,000	14.00	20.00	35.00	100	—
1933	Inc. above	—	7.25	12.50	16.50	18.00
1934	22,070,000	—	—	7.25	15.00	22.00
1935	8,050,000	—	7.25	12.00	16.00	24.00
1938	30,000,000	—	—	7.25	12.00	16.50
1940	20,000,000	—	—	7.25	12.00	16.50
1943	47,662,000	—	—	7.25	12.00	16.50
1944	39,522,000	—	—	7.25	12.00	16.50
1945	37,300,000	—	—	7.25	12.00	16.50

KM# 456 PESO

14.00 g., 0.500 Silver 0.2251 oz. ASW, 32 mm. **Obv:** National arms, eagle left **Rev:** Head with headcovering right **Edge:** Reeded **Note:** Mint mark Mo.

Date	Mintage	F12	VF20	XF40	MS60	MS63
1947	61,460,000	—	—	4.25	7.00	10.00
1948	22,915,000	—	—	4.25	7.00	10.00
1949	—	PF63 4,500				
1949	4,000,000	350	650	1,300	1,700	2,700

Note: Not released for circulation

KM# 457 PESO

13.33 g., 0.300 Silver 0.1286 oz. ASW, 32 mm. **Obv:** National arms, eagle left **Rev:** Armored bust 3/4 left **Note:** Mint mark Mo.

Date	Mintage	F12	VF20	XF40	MS60	MS63
1950	3,287,000	—	5.00	6.00	10.00	15.00

KM# 458 PESO

16.00 g., 0.100 Silver 0.0514 oz. ASW, 34.5 mm. **Subject:** 100th Anniversary of Constitution **Obv:** National arms, eagle left within wreath **Rev:** Head left **Edge Lettering:** INDEPENDENCIA Y LIBERTAD **Note:** Mint mark Mo.

Date	Mintage	F12	VF20	XF40	MS60	MS63
1957	500,000	—	4.00	6.00	12.50	16.50

KM# 459 PESO

16.00 g., 0.100 Silver 0.0514 oz. ASW, 34.5 mm. **Obv:** National arms, eagle left within wreath **Rev:** Armored bust right within wreath **Edge Lettering:** INDEPENDENCIA Y LIBERTAD **Note:** Mint mark Mo.

Date	Mintage	F12	VF20	XF40	MS60	MS63
1957	28,273,000	—	1.00	2.00	3.00	10.00
1958	41,899,000	—	—	1.00	2.00	3.00
1959	27,369,000	—	1.00	2.00	5.50	8.00
1960	26,259,000	—	1.00	2.00	3.50	6.00
1961	52,601,000	—	—	1.00	2.50	5.00
1962	61,094,000	—	—	1.00	2.00	4.00
1963	26,394,000	—	—	1.00	2.00	2.50
1964	15,615,000	—	—	1.00	2.00	2.50
1965	5,004,000	—	—	1.00	2.00	2.50
1966	30,998,000	—	—	1.00	2.00	2.25
1967	9,308,000	—	—	1.00	2.75	4.50

Tall date

KM# 460 PESO

9.00 g., Copper-Nickel, 29 mm. **Obv:** National arms, eagle left **Rev:** Head left **Edge:** Reeded

Date	Mintage	F12	VF20	XF40	MS60	MS63
1970 Mo Narrow date	102,715,000	—	0.25	0.35	0.65	0.80
1970 Mo Wide date	Inc. above	—	1.25	2.50	7.50	10.00
1971 Mo	426,222,000	—	0.20	0.25	0.55	0.75
1972 Mo	120,000,000	—	0.20	0.25	0.40	0.65
1974 Mo	63,700,000	—	0.20	0.25	0.65	0.90
1975 Mo Tall narrow date	205,979,000	—	0.25	0.45	1.00	1.35
1975 Mo Short wide date	Inc. above	—	0.30	0.40	0.75	1.00
1976 Mo	94,489,000	—	0.15	0.20	0.50	0.75
1977 Mo Thick date close to rim	94,364,000	—	0.25	0.45	1.00	1.25
1977 Mo Thin date, space between sideburns and collar	Inc. above	—	1.00	2.50	8.50	16.50
1978 Mo Closed 8	208,300,000	—	0.20	0.30	1.00	1.50
1978 Mo Open 8	55,140,000	—	1.00	2.50	14.00	20.00
1979 Mo Thin date	117,884,000	—	0.20	0.30	1.15	1.50
1979 Mo Thick date	Inc. above	—	0.20	0.30	1.25	1.75
1980 Mo Closed 8	318,800,000	—	0.25	0.35	1.00	1.25
1980 Mo Open 8	23,865,000	—	0.75	1.50	8.00	15.00
1981 Mo Closed 8	413,349,000	—	0.20	0.30	0.75	0.90
1981 Mo Open 8	58,616,000	—	0.50	1.25	6.50	9.00
1982 Mo Closed 8	235,000,000	—	0.25	0.75	2.25	2.50
1982 Mo Open 8	—	—	0.75	1.50	8.00	15.00
1983 Mo Wide date	100,000,000	—	0.30	0.45	3.00	3.50
1983 Mo Narrow date	Inc. above	—	0.30	0.45	3.00	4.50
1983 Mo	1,051,000	PF63 38.00				

KM# 496 PESO

5.70 g., Stainless Steel, 24.5 mm. **Obv:** National arms, eagle left **Rev:** Armored bust right

Date	Mintage	VF20	XF40	MS60	MS63	MS65
1984 Mo	722,802,000	0.10	0.25	0.65	1.45	—
1985 Mo	985,000,000	0.10	0.25	0.50	1.25	—
1986 Mo	740,000,000	0.10	0.25	0.50	1.25	—
1987 Mo	250,000,000	0.10	0.25	0.50	1.25	—
1987 Mo Proof; 2 known	—	PF63 1,000				

KM# 461 2 PESOS

1.67 g., 0.900 Gold 0.0482 oz. AGW, 13 mm. **Obv:** National arms **Rev:** Date above value within wreath **Note:** Mint mark Mo.

Date	Mintage	F12	VF20	XF40	MS60	MS63
1919	1,670,000	—	65.00	90.00	110	—
1920/10	—	65.00	90.00	100	145	—
1920	4,282,000	—	65.00	90.00	110	—
1944	10,000	65.00	90.00	100	130	—
1945	Est. 140000	—	—	—	74.00	—
1946	168,000	65.00	90.00	110	165	—
1947	25,000	65.00	90.00	110	145	—
1948 No specimens known	45,000	—	—	—	—	—

Note: During 1951-1972 a total of 4,590,493 pieces were restruck, most likely dated 1945. In 1996 matte restrikes were produced. An additional 260,000 pieces dated 1945 were struck during 2000-2013

KM# 462 2 PESOS

26.67 g., 0.900 Silver 0.7716 oz. ASW, 39 mm. **Subject:** Centennial of Independence **Obv:** National arms, eagle left within wreath **Rev:** Winged Victory **Note:** Mint mark Mo.

Date	Mintage	F12	VF20	XF40	MS60	MS63
1921	1,278,000	25.00	40.00	75.00	400	675

KM# 463 2-1/2 PESOS

2.08 g., 0.900 Gold 0.0603 oz. AGW, 15.5 mm. **Obv:** National arms **Rev:** Miguel Hidalgo y Costilla **Note:** Mint mark Mo.

Date	Mintage	F12	VF20	XF40	MS60	MS63
1918	1,704,000	—	77.00	100	130	—
1919	984,000	—	77.00	100	130	—
1920/10	607,000	—	77.00	110	180	—
1920	Inc. above	—	77.00	100	125	—
1944	20,000	—	77.00	110	145	—
1945	Est. 180000	—	—	—	91.00	—
1946	163,000	—	77.00	110	145	—
1947	24,000	225	300	425	750	—
1948	63,000	—	77.00	110	145	—

Note: During 1951-1972 a total of 5,025,087 pieces were restruck, most likely dated 1945. In 1996 matte restrikes were produced. An additional 539,000 pieces dated 1945 were struck during 2000-2013

KM# 464 5 PESOS

4.17 g., 0.900 Gold 0.1206 oz. AGW, 19 mm. **Obv:** National arms **Rev:** Miguel Hidalgo y Costilla **Note:** Mint mark Mo.

Date	Mintage	F12	VF20	XF40	MS60	MS63
1905	18,000	200	230	325	700	—
1906	4,638,000	—	—	155	190	—
1907/6	—	—	—	—	—	—
1907	1,088,000	—	—	155	190	—
1910	100,000	—	—	155	210	—
1918/7	609,000	—	—	155	245	—
1918	Inc. above	—	—	155	210	—
1919	506,000	—	—	155	190	—
1920	2,385,000	—	—	155	190	—
1955	—	—	—	—	172	—

Note: During 1955-1972 a total of 1,767,645 pieces were restruck, most likely dated 1955. In 1996 matte restrikes were produced. An additional 96,300 pieces dated 1955 were struck during 2000-2013

KM# 465 5 PESOS

30.00 g., 0.900 Silver 0.8681 oz. ASW, 40 mm. **Obv:** National arms, eagle left **Rev:** Head with headdress left **Edge:** Reeded **Note:** Mint mark Mo.

Date	Mintage	F12	VF20	XF40	MS60	MS63
1947	5,110,000	—	—	16.00	28.00	32.00
1948	26,740,000	—	—	16.00	28.00	32.00

KM# 466 5 PESOS

27.78 g., 0.720 Silver 0.6431 oz. ASW, 40 mm. **Subject:** Opening of Southern Railroad **Obv:** National arms, eagle left **Rev:** Radiant sun flanked by palm trees above train **Edge Lettering:** COMERCIO - AGRICULTURA - INDUSTRIA **Note:** Mint mark Mo.

Date	Mintage	F12	VF20	XF40	MS60	MS63
1950	200,000	—	25.00	45.00	65.00	75.00

Note: It is recorded that 100,000 pieces were melted to be used for the 1968 Mexican Olympic 25 Pesos

KM# 467 5 PESOS

27.78 g., 0.720 Silver 0.6431 oz. ASW, 40 mm. **Obv:** National arms, eagle left **Rev:** Head left within wreath **Edge Lettering:** COMERCIO - AGRICULTURA - INDUSTRIA **Note:** Mint mark Mo.

Date	Mintage	F12	VF20	XF40	MS60	MS63
1951	4,958,000	—	—	12.00	20.00	23.00
1952	9,595,000	—	—	12.00	20.00	23.00
1953	20,376,000	—	—	12.00	20.00	23.00
1954	30,000	—	30.00	60.00	70.00	85.00

KM# 468 5 PESOS

27.78 g., 0.720 Silver 0.6431 oz. ASW, 40 mm. **Subject:** Bicentennial of Hidalgo's Birth **Obv:** National arms, eagle left **Rev:** Half-length figure facing to right of building and dates **Edge Lettering:** COMERCIO - AGRICULTURA - INDUSTRIA **Note:** Mint mark Mo.

Date	Mintage	F12	VF20	XF40	MS60	MS63
1953	1,000,000	—	—	12.00	22.00	25.00

KM# 469 5 PESOS

18.05 g., 0.720 Silver 0.4178 oz. ASW, 36 mm. **Obv:** National arms, eagle left **Rev:** Head left **Note:** Mint mark Mo.

Date	Mintage	F12	VF20	XF40	MS60	MS63
1955	4,271,000	—	—	7.75	13.50	17.00
1956	4,596,000	—	—	7.75	13.50	17.00
1957	3,464,000	—	—	7.75	13.50	17.00

KM# 470 5 PESOS

18.05 g., 0.720 Silver 0.4178 oz. ASW, 36 mm. **Subject:** 100th Anniversary of Constitution **Obv:** National arms, eagle left **Rev:** Head left **Edge Lettering:** INDEPENDENCIA Y LIBERTAD **Note:** Mint mark Mo.

Date	Mintage	F12	VF20	XF40	MS60	MS63
1957	200,000	—	7.75	13.00	16.00	18.00

KM# 471 5 PESOS

18.05 g., 0.720 Silver 0.4178 oz. ASW, 36 mm. **Subject:** Centennial of Carranza's Birth **Obv:** National arms, eagle left **Rev:** Head left **Edge:** Plain **Note:** Mint mark Mo.

Date	Mintage	F12	VF20	XF40	MS60	MS63
1959	1,000,000	—	—	7.75	13.50	17.00

Large date

KM# 472 5 PESOS

14.00 g., Copper-Nickel, 33 mm. **Obv:** National arms, eagle left **Rev:** Armored bust right **Edge Lettering:** INDEPENDENCIA Y LIBERTAD **Note:** Small date, large date varieties.

Date	Mintage	F12	VF20	XF40	MS60	MS63
1971 Mo	28,457,000	—	0.50	0.95	2.50	3.25
1972 Mo	75,000,000	—	0.60	1.25	2.00	2.50
1973 Mo	19,405,000	—	1.25	2.00	4.50	5.50
1974 Mo	34,500,000	—	0.50	0.80	1.75	2.25
1976 Mo Small date	26,121,000	—	0.75	1.45	3.25	4.00
1976 Mo Large date	121,550,000	—	0.35	0.50	1.50	1.75
1977 Mo	102,000,000	—	0.35	0.50	1.50	1.75
1978 Mo	25,700,000	—	1.00	1.50	4.50	6.25

KM# 485 5 PESOS

10.20 g., Copper-Nickel, 27 mm. **Subject:** Quetzalcoatl **Obv:** National arms, eagle left **Rev:** Native sculpture to lower right of value and dollar sign **Edge Lettering:** LIBERTAD Y INDEPENDENCIA **Note:** Inverted and normal edge legend varieties exist for the 1980 and 1981 dates.

Date	Mintage	VF20	XF40	MS60	MS63	MS65
1980 Mo	266,899,999	0.25	0.50	1.75	2.25	—
1981 Mo	30,500,000	0.45	0.65	2.75	3.25	—
1982 Mo	20,000,000	1.50	2.35	4.25	5.25	—
1982 Mo	1,051	PF63 50.00				
1983 Mo Proof; 7 known	—	PF63 1,200				
1984 Mo	16,300,000	1.25	2.00	4.75	6.00	—
1985 Mo	76,900,000	2.00	3.25	4.25	5.00	—

KM# 502 5 PESOS

3.10 g., Brass, 17 mm. **Obv:** National arms, eagle left **Rev:** Date and value **Edge:** Reeded

Date	Mintage	VF20	XF40	MS60	MS63	MS65
1985 Mo	30,000,000	—	0.15	0.35	0.50	—
1987 Mo	81,900,000	8.00	9.50	12.50	16.50	—
1988 Mo	76,600,000	—	0.10	0.25	0.35	—
1988 Mo Proof; 2 known	—	PF63 600				

KM# 473 10 PESOS

8.33 g., 0.900 Gold 0.2411 oz. AGW, 22.5 mm. **Obv:** National arms **Rev:** Miguel Hidalgo y Costilla **Note:** Mint mark Mo.

Date	Mintage	F12	VF20	XF40	MS60	MS63
1905	39,000	—	310	375	450	500
1906	2,949,000	—	310	375	450	500
1907	1,589,000	—	310	375	450	500
1908	890,000	—	310	375	450	500
1910	451,000	—	310	375	450	500
1916	26,000	—	310	420	475	525
1917	1,967,000	—	310	375	450	500
1919	266,000	—	310	375	450	500
1920	12,000	—	310	500	900	1,000
1959	Est. 50000	—	—	—	330	—

Note: *During 1961-1972 a total of 954,983 pieces were restruck, most likely dated 1959. In 1996 matte restrikes were produced. An additional 67,300 pieces dated 1959 were struck during 2000-2013

KM# 474 10 PESOS

28.89 g., 0.900 Silver 0.8359 oz. ASW, 40 mm. **Obv:** National arms **Rev:** Head left **Edge:** Reeded **Note:** Mint mark Mo.

Date	Mintage	F12	VF20	XF40	MS60	MS63
1955	585,000	—	—	15.50	30.00	35.00
1956	3,535,000	—	—	15.50	28.00	32.00

KM# 475 10 PESOS

28.88 g., 0.900 Silver 0.8357 oz. ASW, 40 mm. **Subject:** 100th Anniversary of Constitution **Obv:** National arms, eagle left **Rev:** Head left **Edge Lettering:** INDEPENDENCIA Y LIBERTAD **Note:** Mint mark Mo.

Date	Mintage	F12	VF20	XF40	MS60	MS63
1957	100,000	15.50	30.00	40.00	55.00	60.00

KM# 476 10 PESOS

28.89 g., 0.900 Silver 0.8359 oz. ASW, 40 mm. **Subject:** 150th Anniversary - War of Independence **Obv:** National arms, eagle left **Rev:** Conjoined busts facing flanked by dates **Edge:** Reeded **Note:** Mint mark Mo.

Date	Mintage	F12	VF20	XF40	MS60	MS63
1960	1,000,000	—	—	15.50	30.00	35.00

KM# 477.1 10 PESOS

10.00 g., Copper-Nickel, 30.5 mm. **Subject:** Miguel Hidalgo y Costilla **Obv:** National arms, eagle left **Rev:** Head left **Shape:** 7-sided **Note:** Thin flan - 1.6mm

Date	Mintage	F12	VF20	XF40	MS60	MS63
1974 Mo	3,900,000	—	0.50	1.00	3.00	4.50
1974 Mo	—	PF63 650				
1975 Mo	1,000,000	—	2.25	3.25	7.50	8.50
1976 Mo	74,500,000	—	0.25	0.75	1.75	2.75
1977 Mo	79,620,000	—	0.50	1.00	2.00	3.00

KM# 477.2 10 PESOS

11.50 g., Copper-Nickel, 30.5 mm. **Subject:** Miguel Hidalgo y Costilla **Obv:** National arms, eagle left **Rev:** Head left **Shape:** 7-sided **Note:** Thick flan - 2.3mm

Date	Mintage	F12	VF20	XF40	MS60	MS63
1978 Mo	124,850,000	—	0.50	0.75	2.50	2.75
1979 Mo	57,200,000	—	0.50	0.75	2.50	2.75
1980 Mo	55,200,000	—	0.50	0.75	2.50	3.75
1981 Mo	222,768,000	—	0.40	0.60	2.25	2.75
1982 Mo	151,770,000	—	0.50	0.80	2.50	3.50
1982 Mo	1,051	PF63 45.00				
1983 Mo Proof; 3 known	—	PF63 1,800				
1985 Mo	58,000,000	—	1.25	1.75	5.75	8.00

KM# 512 10 PESOS

3.84 g., Stainless Steel, 19 mm. **Obv:** National arms, eagle left **Rev:** Head facing with diagonal value at left **Note:** Date varieties exist.

Date	Mintage	VF20	XF40	MS60	MS63	MS65
1985 Mo	257,000,000	—	0.15	0.50	0.75	—
1986 Mo	392,000,000	—	0.15	0.50	1.50	—
1987 Mo	305,000,000	—	0.15	0.35	0.50	—
1988 Mo	500,300,000	—	0.15	0.25	0.35	—
1989 Mo	336,900,000	0.20	0.25	0.75	1.50	—
1990 Mo Proof; 2 known	—	PF63 550				
1990 Mo	101,000,000	—	0.25	0.75	1.25	—

KM# 478 20 PESOS

16.67 g., 0.900 Gold 0.4823 oz. AGW, 27.5 mm. **Obv:** National arms, eagle left **Rev:** Aztec Sunstone with denomination below **Edge:** Lettered **Edge Lettering:** INDEPEDENCIA Y LIBERTAD **Note:** Mint mark Mo.

Date	Mintage	VF20	XF40	MS60	MS63	MS65
1917	852,000	—	620	710	830	920
1918	2,831,000	—	620	710	830	920
1919	1,094,000	—	620	710	830	920
1920/10	462,000	—	620	710	830	920
1920	Inc. above	—	620	710	830	920
1921/11	922,000	—	620	710	830	920
1921/10	—	—	770	830	975	1,850
1921	Inc. above	—	620	710	830	920
1959	Est. 13000	—	—	640	—	—

Note: During 1960-1971 a total of 1,158,414 pieces were restruck, most likely dated 1959. In 1996 matte restrikes were produced. An additional 95,300 pieces dated 1959 were struck in 2000-2013

KM# 486 20 PESOS

15.20 g., Copper-Nickel, 32 mm. **Obv:** National arms, eagle left **Rev:** Figure with headdress facing left within circle **Edge Lettering:** INDEPENDENCIA Y LIBERTAD

Date	Mintage	VF20	XF40	MS60	MS63	MS65
1980 Mo	84,900,000	0.50	0.85	2.25	3.25	—
1981 Mo	250,573,000	0.60	0.80	2.25	3.25	—
1982 Mo	236,892,000	1.00	1.75	2.50	3.75	—
1982 Mo	1,051	PF63 50.00				
1983 Mo Proof; 3 known	—	PF63 575				
1984 Mo	55,000,000	1.00	1.50	2.50	4.75	—

KM# 508 20 PESOS

6.00 g., Brass, 21 mm. **Obv:** National arms, eagle left **Rev:** Bust facing with diagonal value at left **Edge:** Reeded

Date	Mintage	VF20	XF40	MS60	MS63	MS65
1985 Mo Wide date	25,000,000	0.10	0.20	1.00	1.50	—
1985 Mo Narrow date	Inc. above	0.10	0.25	1.50	2.25	—
1986 Mo	10,000,000	1.00	1.75	5.00	6.00	—
1988 Mo	355,200,000	0.10	0.20	0.45	0.75	—
1989 Mo	289,100,000	0.15	0.30	1.50	2.00	—
1990 Mo	126,550,000	0.15	0.30	1.50	2.50	—
1990 Mo Proof; 3 known	—	PF63 600				

Snake's tongue straight

KM# 479.1 25 PESOS

22.50 g., 0.720 Silver 0.5208 oz. ASW, 38 mm. **Obv:** National arms, eagle left **Rev:** Olympic rings below dancing native left, numeral design in background **Note:** Type I, Rings aligned.

Date	Mintage	F12	VF20	XF40	MS60	MS63
1968 Mo	27,182,000	—	—	9.75	16.00	20.00

KM# 479.2 25 PESOS

22.50 g., 0.720 Silver 0.5208 oz. ASW, 38 mm. **Subject:** Summer Olympics - Mexico City **Obv:** National arms, eagle left **Rev:** Olympic rings below dancing native left, numeral design in background **Note:** Type II, center ring low.

Date	Mintage	F12	VF20	XF40	MS60	MS63
1968 Mo	Inc. above	—	9.75	16.00	18.00	20.00

Snake's tongue curved

KM# 479.3 25 PESOS

22.50 g., 0.720 Silver 0.5208 oz. ASW, 38 mm. **Subject:** Summer Olympics - Mexico City **Obv:** National arms, eagle left **Rev:** Olympic rings below dancing native left, numeral design in background **Note:** Snake with long curved or normal tongue. Type III, center rings low.

Date	Mintage	F12	VF20	XF40	MS60	MS63
1968 Mo	Inc. above	—	9.75	16.00	20.00	22.50

KM# 480 25 PESOS

22.50 g., 0.720 Silver 0.5208 oz. ASW, 38 mm. **Obv:** National arms, eagle left **Rev:** Bust facing

Date	Mintage	F12	VF20	XF40	MS60	MS63
1972 Mo	2,000,000	—	9.75	16.00	18.00	20.00

KM# 497 25 PESOS

7.78 g., 0.720 Silver 0.180 oz. ASW **Subject:** 1986 World Cup Soccer Games **Obv:** National arms, eagle left **Rev:** Value above soccer ball with date below, with fineness

Date	Mintage	VF20	XF40	MS60	MS63	MS65
1985 Mo	473,605	—	—	—	10.00	—

KM# 503 25 PESOS

8.41 g., 0.925 Silver 0.250 oz. ASW **Subject:** 1986 World Cup Soccer Games **Obv:** National arms, eagle left **Rev:** Pre-Columbian hieroglyphs, ojo de buey, and soccer ball

Date	Mintage	VF20	XF40	MS60	MS63	MS65
1985 Mo	52,002	PF63 14.00				

KM# 514 25 PESOS

8.41 g., 0.925 Silver 0.250 oz. ASW **Subject:** 1986 World Cup Soccer Games **Obv:** National arms, eagle left **Rev:** Value above soccer ball

Date	Mintage	VF20	XF40	MS60	MS63	MS65
1985 Mo	21,260	PF63 14.00				

KM# 497a 25 PESOS

8.41 g., 0.925 Silver 0.250 oz. ASW **Subject:** 1986 World Cup Soccer Games **Obv:** National arms, eagle left **Rev:** Value above soccerball with date below **Note:** Without finess statement- reverse description

Date	Mintage	VF20	XF40	MS60	MS63	MS65
1986 Mo	22,552	PF63 14.00				

KM# 519 25 PESOS

8.41 g., 0.925 Silver 0.250 oz. ASW **Subject:** 1986 World Cup Soccer Games **Obv:** National arms, eagle left **Rev:** Soccer ball within net, date and value to left

Date	Mintage	VF20	XF40	MS60	MS63	MS65
1986 Mo	20,172	PF63 14.00				

KM# 481 50 PESOS

41.67 g., 0.900 Gold 1.2057 oz. AGW, 37 mm. **Subject:** Centennial of Independence **Obv:** National arms **Rev:** Winged Victory **Edge:** Reeded **Note:** During 1949-1972 a total of 3,975,654 pieces were restruck, most likely dated 1947 and an additional 388,800 pieces dated 1947 were struck during 2000-2013. In 1996 matte restrikes were produced. Mint mark Mo.

Date	Mintage	VF20	XF40	MS60	MS63	MS65
1921	180,000	—	1,545	1,700	2,000	2,650
1922	463,000	—	1,545	1,625	1,850	2,150
1923	432,000	—	1,545	1,625	1,850	2,150
1924	439,000	—	1,545	1,625	1,850	2,150
1925	716,000	—	1,545	1,625	1,850	2,150
1926	600,000	—	1,545	1,625	1,850	2,150
1927	606,000	—	1,545	1,625	1,850	2,150
1928	538,000	—	1,545	1,625	1,850	2,150
1929	458,000	—	1,545	1,625	1,850	2,150
1930	372,000	—	1,545	1,625	1,850	2,150
1931	137,000	—	1,545	1,625	1,900	2,250
1944	593,000	—	1,545	1,625	1,850	2,000
1945	1,012,000	—	1,545	1,625	1,850	2,000
1946	1,588,000	—	1,545	1,625	1,850	2,000
1947	309,000	—	—	—	1,625	—
1947 Specimen	—	—	—	—	—	—

Note: Value, $6,500

KM# 482 50 PESOS

41.67 g., 0.900 Gold 1.2057 oz. AGW, 37 mm. **Obv:** National arms **Rev:** Winged Victory

Date	Mintage	VF20	XF40	MS60	MS63	MS65
1943 Mo	89,000	—	—	1,625	1,850	2,000

KM# 481a 50 PESOS

Platinum APW **Subject:** Centennial of Independence **Obv:** National arms **Rev:** Winged Victory **Edge:** Reeded

Date	Mintage	VF20	XF40	MS60	MS63	MS65
1947 Mo	Est. 5	—	—	—	—	13,500

KM# 490 50 PESOS

19.84 g., Copper-Nickel, 39 mm. **Subject:** Coyolxauhqui **Obv:** National arms, eagle left **Rev:** Value to right of artistic designs **Edge:** Reeded **Note:** Doubled die examples of 1982 and 1983 dates exist.

Date	Mintage	VF20	XF40	MS60	MS63	MS65
1982 Mo	222,890,000	1.00	2.50	5.00	6.50	—
1983 Mo	45,000,000	1.50	3.00	6.00	7.00	—
1983 Mo	1,051	PF63 55.00				
1984 Mo	73,537,000	1.00	1.35	3.50	4.50	—
1984 Mo	—	PF63 750				

Proof; 4 known

KM# 495 50 PESOS

8.60 g., Copper-Nickel, 23.5 mm. **Subject:** Benito Juarez **Obv:** National arms, eagle left **Rev:** Bust 1/4 left with diagonal value at left **Edge:** Reeded

Date	Mintage	VF20	XF40	MS60	MS63	MS65
1984 Mo	94,216,000	0.65	1.25	2.70	3.25	—
1985 Mo	296,000,000	0.25	0.45	1.25	2.25	—
1986 Mo	50,000,000	6.00	10.00	12.00	14.00	—
1987 Mo	210,000,000	0.25	0.45	1.00	1.25	—
1988 Mo	80,200,000	6.25	9.00	13.50	16.00	—

KM# 495a 50 PESOS

7.10 g., Stainless Steel, 23.5 mm. **Subject:** Benito Juarez **Obv:** National arms, eagle left **Rev:** Bust 1/4 left with diagonal value at left **Edge:** Plain

Date	Mintage	VF20	XF40	MS60	MS63	MS65
1988 Mo	353,300,000	—	0.20	1.25	1.75	—
1989 Mo	20,000	—	—	—	—	—
Note: Reported not confirmed.						
1990 Mo	180,000,000	—	0.30	1.00	2.00	—
1992 Mo	84,520,000	—	0.25	1.00	2.75	—

KM# 498 50 PESOS
15.55 g., 0.720 Silver 0.360 oz. ASW **Subject:** 1986 World Cup Soccer Games **Obv:** National arms, eagle left **Rev:** Pair of feet and soccer ball, with fineness

Date	Mintage	VF20	XF40	MS60	MS63	MS65
1985 Mo	439,763	—	—	—	16.00	—

KM# 504 50 PESOS
16.83 g., 0.925 Silver 0.5005 oz. ASW **Subject:** 1986 World Cup Soccer Games **Obv:** National arms, eagle left **Rev:** Stylized athlete as soccer forerunner

Date	Mintage	VF20	XF40	MS60	MS63	MS65
1985 Mo	41,255	PF63 22.00				

KM# 515 50 PESOS
16.83 g., 0.925 Silver 0.5005 oz. ASW **Subject:** 1986 World Cup Soccer Games **Obv:** National arms, eagle left **Rev:** Value to right of soccer player

Date	Mintage	VF20	XF40	MS60	MS63	MS65
1985 Mo	24,907	PF63 22.00				

KM# 498a 50 PESOS
16.83 g., 0.925 Silver 0.5005 oz. ASW **Subject:** 1986 World Cup Soccer Games **Obv:** National arms, eagle left **Rev:** Without fineness statement

Date	Mintage	VF20	XF40	MS60	MS63	MS65
1986 Mo	19,564	PF63 22.00				

KM# 523 50 PESOS
16.83 g., 0.925 Silver 0.5005 oz. ASW **Subject:** 1986 World Cup Soccer Games **Obv:** National arms, eagle left **Rev:** Value to left of soccer balls

Date	Mintage	VF20	XF40	MS60	MS63	MS65
1986 Mo	18,653	PF63 22.00				

KM# 532 50 PESOS
15.55 g., 0.999 Silver 0.4994 oz. ASW **Subject:** 50th Anniversary - Nationalization of Oil Industry **Obv:** National arms, eagle left **Rev:** Monument

Date	Mintage	VF20	XF40	MS60	MS63	MS65
ND-1988 Mo	20,000	—	—	20.00	24.00	—

Low 7s

KM# 483.1 100 PESOS
27.77 g., 0.720 Silver 0.6428 oz. ASW, 39 mm. **Obv:** National arms, eagle left **Rev:** Bust facing, sloping right shoulder, round left shoulder with no clothing folds **Edge:** Reeded

Date	Mintage	F12	VF20	XF40	MS60	MS63
1977 Mo Low 7's	5,225,000	—	—	12.00	22.00	25.00
1977 Mo High 7's	Inc. above	—	—	12.00	22.00	25.00

High 7s

KM# 483.2 100 PESOS
27.77 g., 0.720 Silver 0.6428 oz. ASW, 39 mm. **Obv:** National arms, eagle left **Rev:** Bust facing, higher right shoulder, left shoulder with clothing folds. **Note:** Mintage inc. KM#483.1

Date	Mintage	F12	VF20	XF40	MS60	MS63
1977 Mo Date in line	—	—	—	12.00	22.00	25.00
1978 Mo	9,879,000	—	—	12.00	22.00	25.00
1979 Mo	784,000	—	—	12.00	22.00	25.00
1979 Mo	—	PF63 650				

KM# 493 100 PESOS
11.70 g., Aluminum-Bronze, 26.5 mm. **Obv:** National arms, eagle left **Rev:** Head 1/4 right with diagonal value at right **Edge:** Segmented reeding

Date	Mintage	VF20	XF40	MS60	MS63	MS65
1984 Mo	227,809,000	0.45	0.60	2.50	4.00	—
1985 Mo	377,423,000	0.30	0.50	2.00	3.00	—
1986 Mo	43,000,000	1.00	2.50	4.75	7.50	—
1987 Mo	165,000,000	0.60	1.25	2.25	3.00	—
1988 Mo	433,100,000	0.30	0.50	2.00	2.75	—
1989 Mo	135,630,000	0.35	0.65	2.00	2.75	—
1990 Mo	248,350,000	0.15	0.40	1.50	2.50	—
1990 Mo Proof; 1 known	—	PF63 650				
1991 Mo	189,900,000	0.15	0.25	1.00	2.50	—
1992 Mo	277,310,000	0.30	0.75	1.75	3.00	—

KM# 499 100 PESOS
31.10 g., 0.720 Silver 0.720 oz. ASW **Subject:** 1986 World Cup Soccer Games - Prehispanic **Obv:** National arms, eagle left **Rev:** Value above artistic designs and soccer ball

Date	Mintage	VF20	XF40	MS60	MS63	MS65
1985 Mo	449,247	—	—	—	27.00	—

KM# 499a 100 PESOS
32.63 g., 0.925 Silver 0.9702 oz. ASW **Subject:** 1986 World Cup Soccer Games - Prehispanic **Obv:** National arms, eagle left **Rev:** Without fineness statement

Date	Mintage	VF20	XF40	MS60	MS63	MS65
1985 Mo	26,964	PF63 47.00	PF65 52.00			

KM# 505 100 PESOS
32.63 g., 0.925 Silver 0.9702 oz. ASW, 38 mm. **Subject:** 1986 World Cup Soccer Games - Nat Player **Obv:** National arms, eagle left **Rev:** Without fineness statement

Date	Mintage	VF20	XF40	MS60	MS63	MS65
1985 Mo	71,718	PF63 42.00	PF65 47.00			

KM# 521 100 PESOS
32.63 g., 0.925 Silver 0.9702 oz. ASW **Subject:** 1986 World Cup Soccer Games - Goalkeeper **Obv:** National arms, eagle left **Rev:** Without fineness statement

Date	Mintage	VF20	XF40	MS60	MS63	MS65
1986 Mo	19,279	PF63 47.00	PF65 52.00			

KM# 524 100 PESOS
32.63 g., 0.925 Silver 0.9702 oz. ASW **Subject:** 1986 World Cup Soccer Games - Ball World **Obv:** National arms, eagle left **Rev:** Without fineness statement

Date	Mintage	VF20	XF40	MS60	MS63	MS65
1986 Mo	18,510	PF63 47.00	PF65 52.00			

KM# 537 100 PESOS
32.63 g., 0.720 Silver 0.7552 oz. ASW **Subject:** World Wildlife Fund **Obv:** National arms, eagle left **Rev:** Monarch butterflies

Date	Mintage	VF20	XF40	MS60	MS63	MS65
1987 Mo	28,500	PF63 57.00	PF65 62.00			

KM# 533 100 PESOS
31.10 g., 0.999 Silver 0.999 oz. ASW **Subject:** 50th Anniversary - Nationalization of Oil Industry **Obv:** National arms, eagle left **Rev:** Bust facing above sprigs and dates

Date	Mintage	VF20	XF40	MS60	MS63	MS65
1988 Mo	20,000	—	—	—	42.00	47.00

KM# 539 100 PESOS
33.63 g., 0.925 Silver 1.000 oz. ASW **Subject:** Save the Children **Obv:** National arms, eagle left **Rev:** Child flying kite, two others sitting and playing

Date	Mintage	VF20	XF40	MS60	MS63	MS65
1991 Mo	11,000	PF63 42.00	PF65 47.00			

KM# 540 100 PESOS
27.00 g., 0.925 Silver 0.803 oz. ASW, 40 mm. **Series:** Ibero - America **Obv:** National arms, eagle left within center of assorted arms **Rev:** Maps within circles flanked by pillars above sailboats

Date	Mintage	VF20	XF40	MS60	MS63	MS65
1991 Mo	30,000	PF63 77.00	PF65 82.00			
1992 Mo	20,000	PF63 32.00	PF65 37.00			

KM# 566 100 PESOS
31.10 g., 0.999 Silver 0.999 oz. ASW **Subject:** Save the Vaquita Porpoise **Obv:** National arms, eagle left **Rev:** Swimming vaquita porpoise

Date	Mintage	VF20	XF40	MS60	MS63	MS65
1992 Mo	28,007	PF63 52.00	PF65 57.00			

KM# 509 200 PESOS
Copper-Nickel, 29.5 mm. **Subject:** 175th Anniversary of Independence **Obv:** National arms, eagle left **Rev:** Conjoined busts left

Date	Mintage	VF20	XF40	MS60	MS63	MS65
1985 Mo	75,000,000	—	2.00	3.50	5.50	—

KM# 510 200 PESOS
Copper-Nickel, 29.5 mm. **Subject:** 75th Anniversary of 1910 Revolution **Obv:** National arms, eagle left **Rev:** Conjoined heads left below building

Date	Mintage	VF20	XF40	MS60	MS63	MS65
1985 Mo	98,590,000	—	2.00	4.00	6.00	—

KM# 525 200 PESOS
Copper-Nickel, 29.5 mm. **Subject:** 1986 World Cup Soccer Games **Obv:** National arms, eagle left **Rev:** Soccer players **Edge:** Reeded

Date	Mintage	VF20	XF40	MS60	MS63	MS65
1986 Mo	50,000,000	—	2.50	4.00	6.00	—

KM# 526 200 PESOS
62.21 g., 0.999 Silver 1.998 oz. ASW **Subject:** 1986 World Cup Soccer Games **Obv:** National arms, eagle left **Rev:** Value above 3 soccer balls

Date	Mintage	VF20	XF40	MS60	MS63	MS65
1986 Mo	23,489	—	—	—	75.00	85.00

KM# 500.1 250 PESOS
8.64 g., 0.900 Gold 0.250 oz. AGW **Subject:** 1986 World Cup Soccer Games **Obv:** National arms, eagle left **Rev:** Soccer ball within top 1/2 of design with value, date, and state below

Date	Mintage	VF20	XF40	MS60	MS63	MS65
1985 Mo	54,770	—	—	—	450	—
1986 Mo	Inc. above	—	—	—	450	—

KM# 500.2 250 PESOS
8.64 g., 0.900 Gold 0.250 oz. AGW **Subject:** 1986 World Cup Soccer Games **Obv:** National arms, eagle left **Rev:** Without fineness statement

Date	Mintage	VF20	XF40	MS60	MS63	MS65
1985 Mo	Incl. above	PF63 475				
1986 Mo	Inc. above	PF63 475				

KM# 506.1 250 PESOS
8.64 g., 0.900 Gold 0.250 oz. AGW **Subject:** 1986 World Cup Soccer Games **Obv:** National arms, eagle left **Rev:** Equestrian left within circle

Date	Mintage	VF20	XF40	MS60	MS63	MS65
1985 Mo	44,595	—	—	—	450	—

KM# 506.2 250 PESOS
8.64 g., 0.900 Gold 0.250 oz. AGW **Subject:** 1986 World Cup Soccer Games **Obv:** National arms, eagle left **Rev:** Without fineness statement

Date	Mintage	VF20	XF40	MS60	MS63	MS65
1985 Mo	Inc. above	PF63 450				

KM# 501.1 500 PESOS
17.28 g., 0.900 Gold 0.500 oz. AGW **Subject:** 1986 World Cup Soccer Games **Obv:** National arms, eagle left **Rev:** Soccer player to right within emblem

Date	Mintage	VF20	XF40	MS60	MS63	MS65
1985 Mo	51,776	—	—	—	900	—
1986 Mo	Inc. above	—	—	—	900	—

KM# 501.2 500 PESOS
17.28 g., 0.900 Gold 0.500 oz. AGW **Subject:** 1986 World Cup Soccer Games **Obv:** National arms, eagle left **Rev:** Without fineness statement

Date	Mintage	VF20	XF40	MS60	MS63	MS65
1985 Mo	Inc. above	PF63 900				
1986 Mo	Inc. above	PF63 900				

KM# 507.1 500 PESOS
17.28 g., 0.900 Gold 0.500 oz. AGW **Subject:** 1986 World Cup Soccer Games **Obv:** National arms, eagle left **Rev:** Soccer ball within emblem flanked by value and date

Date	Mintage	VF20	XF40	MS60	MS63	MS65
1985 Mo	6,267	—	—	—	900	—

KM# 507.2 500 PESOS
17.28 g., 0.900 Gold 0.500 oz. AGW **Subject:** 1986 World Cup Soccer Games **Obv:** National arms, eagle left **Rev:** Without fineness statement

Date	Mintage	VF20	XF40	MS60	MS63	MS65
1985 Mo	Inc. above	PF63 900				

KM# 511 500 PESOS
33.45 g., 0.925 Silver 0.9948 oz. ASW **Subject:** 75th Anniversary of 1910 Revolution **Obv:** National arms, eagle left **Rev:** Conjoined heads left below building

Date	Mintage	VF20	XF40	MS60	MS63	MS65
1985 Mo	40,002	PF65 60.00				

KM# 529 500 PESOS
12.60 g., Copper-Nickel, 28.5 mm. **Obv:** National arms, eagle left **Rev:** Head 1/4 right **Edge:** Reeded

Date	Mintage	VF20	XF40	MS60	MS63	MS65
1986 Mo	20,000,000	—	1.00	3.25	4.00	—
1987 Mo	180,000,000	—	0.75	2.25	3.00	—
1988 Mo	230,000,000	—	0.50	2.25	3.00	—
1988 Mo	—	PF63 650				
Proof; 2 known						
1989 Mo	40,000,000	—	0.75	2.25	3.50	—
1992 Mo	20,000,000	—	1.00	2.25	4.00	—

KM# 534 500 PESOS
17.28 g., 0.900 Gold 0.500 oz. AGW **Subject:** 50th Anniversary - Nationalization of Oil Industry **Obv:** National arms, eagle left **Rev:** Monument **Note:** Similar to 5000 Pesos, KM#531.

Date	Mintage	VF20	XF40	MS60	MS63	MS65
1988 Mo	611	—	—	—	925	—

KM# 513 1000 PESOS
17.28 g., 0.900 Gold 0.500 oz. AGW **Subject:** 175th Anniversary of Independence **Obv:** National arms, eagle left **Rev:** Conjoined heads left below value

Date	Mintage	VF20	XF40	MS60	MS63	MS65
1985 Mo	3,721	PF63 925				

KM# 527 1000 PESOS
31.11 g., 0.999 Gold 0.999 oz. AGW **Subject:** 1986 World Cup Soccer Games **Obv:** National arms, eagle left **Rev:** Value above soccer ball and two hemispheres

Date	Mintage	VF20	XF40	MS60	MS63	MS65
1986 Mo	1,279	—	—	—	1,800	1,950

KM# 535 1000 PESOS
34.56 g., 0.900 Gold 1.000 oz. AGW **Subject:** 50th Anniversary - Nationalization of Oil Industry **Obv:** National arms, eagle left **Rev:** Portrait of Cardenas **Note:** Similar to 5000 Pesos, KM#531.

Date	Mintage	VF20	XF40	MS60	MS63	MS65
1988 Mo	657	PF63 2,000				

KM# 536 1000 PESOS
15.00 g., Aluminum-Bronze, 30.5 mm. **Subject:** Juana de Asbaje **Obv:** National arms, eagle left **Rev:** Bust 1/4 left with diagonal value at left **Edge:** Reeded

Date	Mintage	VF20	XF40	MS60	MS63	MS65
1988 Mo	229,300,000	0.85	2.00	4.25	5.75	—
1989 Mo	215,716,000	0.85	2.00	4.25	5.75	—
1990 Mo	41,291,000	0.85	2.00	4.00	5.50	—
1990 Mo	—	PF63 550				
Proof; 2 known						
1991 Mo	42,468,000	1.00	2.00	3.00	7.00	—
1992 Mo	84,725,000	1.00	2.00	3.50	7.50	—

KM# 643 1000 PESOS
31.10 g., 0.999 Silver 0.999 oz. ASW **Rev:** Emiliano Zapata **Note:** Unissued type due to currency reform.

Date	Mintage	VF20	XF40	MS60	MS63	MS65
1990 Mo	—	PF63 1,500				

KM# 528 2000 PESOS
62.20 g., 0.999 Gold 1.9978 oz. AGW **Subject:** 1986 World Cup Soccer Games **Obv:** National arms, eagle left **Rev:** Value above soccer ball and two hemispheres

Date	Mintage	VF20	XF40	MS60	MS63	MS65
1986 Mo	964	—	—	—	3,750	4,000

KM# 531 5000 PESOS
Copper-Nickel, 33.5 mm. **Subject:** 50th Anniversary - Nationalization of Oil Industry **Obv:** National arms, eagle left **Rev:** Monument above dates with diagonal value at left

Date	Mintage	VF20	XF40	MS60	MS63	MS65
ND-1988 Mo	50,000,000	—	4.75	7.75	10.00	—

REFORM COINAGE

1 New Peso = 1000 Old Pesos; 100 centavos = 1 New Peso; 100 Centavos = 1 Peso

KM# 546 5 CENTAVOS
1.58 g., Stainless Steel, 15.5 mm. **Obv:** National arms **Rev:** Large value **Edge:** Plain

Date	Mintage	VF20	XF40	MS60	MS63	MS65
1992 Mo	136,800,000	—	0.15	0.20	0.50	—
1993 Mo	234,000,000	—	0.15	0.20	0.50	—
1994 Mo	125,000,000	—	0.15	0.20	0.50	—
1995 Mo	195,000,000	—	0.15	0.20	0.50	—
1995 Mo	6,981	PF63 2.00				
1996 Mo	104,831,000	—	0.15	0.20	0.50	—
1997 Mo	153,675,000	—	0.15	0.20	0.50	—
1998 Mo	64,417,000	—	0.15	0.20	0.50	—
1999 Mo	9,949,000	—	0.20	0.75	1.00	—
2000 Mo	10,871,000	—	0.20	0.75	1.00	—

KM# 547 10 CENTAVOS
2.08 g., Stainless Steel, 17 mm. **Obv:** National arms, eagle left **Rev:** Large value

Date	Mintage	VF20	XF40	MS60	MS63	MS65
1992 Mo	121,250,000	—	0.20	0.25	0.60	—
1993 Mo	755,000,000	—	0.20	0.25	0.60	—
1994 Mo	557,000,000	—	0.20	0.25	0.60	—
1995 Mo	560,000,000	—	0.20	0.25	0.60	—
1995 Mo	6,981	PF63 2.00				
1996 Mo	594,216,000	—	0.20	0.25	0.60	—
1997 Mo	581,622,000	—	0.20	0.25	0.60	—
1998 Mo	602,667,000	—	0.20	0.25	0.60	—
1999 Mo	488,346,000	—	0.20	0.25	0.60	—
2000 Mo	577,546,000	—	0.20	0.30	0.75	—

KM# 548 20 CENTAVOS
3.04 g., Aluminum-Bronze, 19.5 mm. **Obv:** National arms, eagle left **Rev:** Value and date within 3/4 wreath **Shape:** 12-sided

Date	Mintage	VF20	XF40	MS60	MS63	MS65
1992 Mo	95,000,000	—	0.25	0.35	1.00	—
1993 Mo	95,000,000	—	0.25	0.35	1.00	—
1994 Mo	105,000,000	—	0.25	0.35	11.00	—
1995 Mo	180,000,000	—	0.25	0.35	1.00	—
1995 Mo	6,981	PF63 3.00				
1996 Mo	54,896,000	—	0.25	0.35	1.00	—
1997 Mo	178,807,000	—	0.25	0.35	1.00	—
1998 Mo	223,847,000	—	0.25	0.35	1.00	—
1999 Mo	233,753,000	—	0.25	0.35	1.00	—
2000 Mo	223,973,000	—	0.25	0.35	1.00	—

KM# 549 50 CENTAVOS
4.39 g., Aluminum-Bronze, 22 mm. **Obv:** National arms, eagle left **Rev:** Value and date within 1/2 designed wreath **Shape:** 12-sided

Date	Mintage	VF20	XF40	MS60	MS63	MS65
1992 Mo	120,150,000	—	0.45	0.85	1.75	—
1993 Mo	330,000,000	—	0.45	0.75	1.50	—
1994 Mo	100,000,000	—	0.45	0.75	1.50	—
1995 Mo	60,000,000	—	0.45	0.75	1.50	—
1995 Mo	6,981	PF63 5.00				
1996 Mo	69,956,000	—	0.45	0.75	1.50	—
1997 Mo	129,029,000	—	0.45	0.75	1.50	—
1998 Mo	223,605,000	—	0.45	0.75	1.50	—
1999 Mo	89,516,000	—	0.45	0.75	1.50	—
2000 Mo	135,112,000	—	0.45	0.75	1.50	—

KM# 550 NUEVOS PESO
3.95 g., Bi-Metallic Aluminum-Bronze center in Stainless Steel ring, 21 mm. **Obv:** National arms, eagle left **Rev:** Value

Date	Mintage	VF20	XF40	MS60	MS63	MS65
1992 Mo	144,000,000	—	0.60	1.50	2.75	—
1993 Mo	329,860,000	—	0.60	1.50	2.75	—
1994 Mo	221,000,000	—	0.60	1.50	2.75	—
1995 Mo Small date	125,000,000	—	0.60	1.50	2.75	—
1995 Mo Large date	Inc. above	—	0.60	1.50	2.75	—
1995 Mo	6,981	PF63 6.00				

KM# 603 PESO
3.95 g., Bi-Metallic Aluminum-Bronze center in Stainless Steel ring, 21 mm. **Obv:** National arms, eagle left within circle **Rev:** Value and date within circle **Note:** Similar to KM#550 but without N.

Date	Mintage	VF20	XF40	MS60	MS63	MS65
1996 Mo	169,510,000	—	—	1.25	2.25	—
1997 Mo	222,870,000	—	—	1.25	2.25	—
1998 Mo	261,942,000	—	—	1.25	2.25	—
1999 Mo	99,168,000	—	—	1.25	2.25	—
2000 Mo	158,379,000	—	—	1.25	2.25	—

KM# 551 2 NUEVOS PESOS
5.19 g., Bi-Metallic Aluminum-Bronze center in Stainless Steel ring, 23 mm. **Obv:** National arms, eagle left within circle **Rev:** Value and date within circle with assorted emblems around border

Date	Mintage	VF20	XF40	MS60	MS63	MS65
1992 Mo	60,000,000	—	1.00	2.50	4.00	—
1993 Mo	77,000,000	—	1.00	2.50	4.00	—
1994 Mo	44,000,000	—	1.00	2.50	4.00	—
1995 Mo	20,000,000	—	1.00	2.50	4.00	—
1995 Mo	6,981	PF63 6.00				

KM# 604 2 PESOS
5.19 g., Bi-Metallic Aluminum-Bronze center in Stainless Steel ring, 23 mm. **Obv:** National arms, eagle left within circle **Rev:** Value and date within center circle of assorted emblems **Note:** Similar to KM#551, but denomination without N.

Date	Mintage	VF20	XF40	MS60	MS63	MS65
1996 Mo	24,902,000	—	—	2.50	4.00	—
1997 Mo	34,560,000	—	—	2.50	4.00	—
1998 Mo	104,138,000	—	—	2.50	4.00	—
1999 Mo	34,713,000	—	—	2.50	4.00	—
2000 Mo	69,322,000	—	—	2.50	4.00	—

KM# 552 5 NUEVOS PESOS
7.07 g., Bi-Metallic Aluminum-Bronze center in Stainless Steel ring, 25.5 mm. **Obv:** National arms, eagle left within circle **Rev:** Value and date within circle with bow below

Date	Mintage	VF20	XF40	MS60	MS63	MS65
1992 Mo	70,000,000	—	2.00	6.00	8.50	—
1993 Mo	168,240,000	—	2.00	6.00	8.50	—
1994 Mo	58,000,000	—	2.00	6.00	8.50	—
1995 Mo	6,981	PF63 25.00				

KM# 588 5 NUEVOS PESOS
27.00 g., 0.925 Silver 0.803 oz. ASW **Series:** Ibero-America **Subject:** Environmental Protection **Obv:** National arms, eagle left within center of past and present arms **Rev:** Pacific Ridley Sea Turtle

Date	Mintage	VF20	XF40	MS60	MS63	MS65
1994 Mo	11,005	PF65 47.00				

KM# 605 5 PESOS
7.07 g., Bi-Metallic Aluminum-Bronze center in Stainless Steel ring, 25.5 mm. **Obv:** National arms, eagle left within circle **Rev:** Value within circle **Note:** Similar to KM#552 but denomination without N.

Date	Mintage	VF20	XF40	MS60	MS63	MS65
1997 Mo	39,468,000	—	2.00	4.00	7.00	—
1998 Mo	103,729,000	—	2.00	4.00	7.00	—
1999 Mo	59,427,000	—	2.00	4.00	7.00	—
2000 Mo	20,869,000	—	2.00	4.50	7.00	—

KM# 627 5 PESOS
31.10 g., 0.999 Silver 0.999 oz. ASW **Subject:** World Wildlife Fund **Obv:** National arms, eagle left **Rev:** Wolf with pup

Date	Mintage	VF20	XF40	MS60	MS63	MS65
1997 Mo	—	—	—	—	—	—
1998 Mo	13,004	PF65 85.00				

KM# 629 5 PESOS
27.00 g., 0.925 Silver 0.803 oz. ASW, 40 mm. **Series:** Ibero-America **Subject:** Jarabe Tapatio **Obv:** National arms, eagle left within center of assorted arms **Rev:** Mexican dancers

Date	Mintage	VF20	XF40	MS60	MS63	MS65
1997 Mo	8,011	PF65 300				
1998 Mo	3,000	PF65 300				

KM# 630 5 PESOS
31.18 g., 0.999 Silver 1.0015 oz. ASW **Subject:** Millennium Series **Obv:** National arms, eagle left within center of past and present arms **Rev:** Butterfly flanked by sprigs above hands

Date	Mintage	VF20	XF40	MS60	MS63	MS65
1999-2000 Mo	47,435	PF65 55.00				

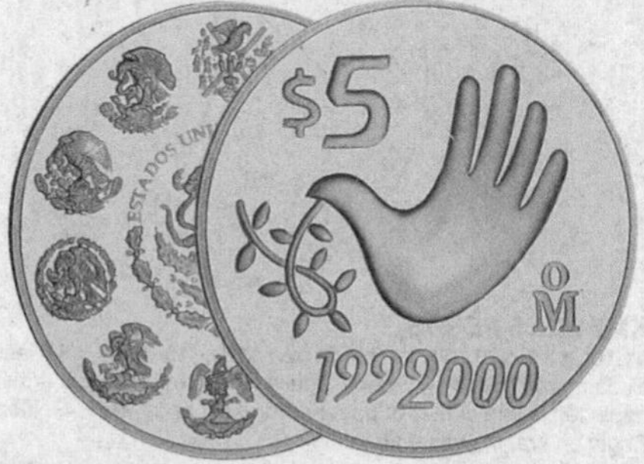

KM# 631 5 PESOS
31.18 g., 0.999 Silver 1.0015 oz. ASW **Subject:** Millennium Series **Obv:** National arms, eagle left within center of past and present arms **Rev:** Stylized dove as hand of peace

Date	Mintage	VF20	XF40	MS60	MS63	MS65
1999-2000 Mo	47,389	PF65 42.00				

KM# 632 5 PESOS
31.18 g., 0.999 Silver 1.0015 oz. ASW **Subject:** Millennium

Series **Obv:** National arms, eagle left within center of past and present arms **Rev:** Aztec bird design and value

Date	Mintage	VF20	XF40	MS60	MS63	MS65
1999-2000 Mo	48,080	PF65 42.00				

KM# 635 5 PESOS
19.60 g., 0.925 Silver 0.5829 oz. ASW **Subject:** Millennium Series **Obv:** National arms, eagle left **Rev:** Naval training ship Cuauhtemoc sailing into world globe

Date	Mintage	VF20	XF40	MS60	MS63	MS65
1999 Mo	15,504	PF65 35.00				

KM# 640 5 PESOS
31.10 g., 0.999 Silver 0.999 oz. ASW, 40 mm. **Subject:** UNICEF **Obv:** National arms, eagle left **Rev:** Two children flying kite **Edge:** Reeded

Date	Mintage	VF20	XF40	MS60	MS63	MS65
1999 Mo	4,010	PF65 60.00				

KM# 652 5 PESOS
31.10 g., 0.999 Silver 0.999 oz. ASW, 40 mm. **Series:** Endangered Wildlife **Subject:** Aguila Real **Obv:** National arms, eagle left within center of past and present arms **Rev:** Golden Eagle on branch, value and date

Date	Mintage	VF20	XF40	MS60	MS63	MS65
2000 Mo	30,000	—	—	—	40.00	45.00

KM# 655 5 PESOS
31.10 g., 0.999 Silver 0.999 oz. ASW, 40 mm. **Series:** Endangered Wildlife **Subject:** Cocodrilo de Rio **Obv:** National arms, eagle left within center of past and present arms **Rev:** American Crocodile, value and date

Date	Mintage	VF20	XF40	MS60	MS63	MS65
2000 Mo	30,000	—	—	—	40.00	45.00

KM# 656 5 PESOS
31.10 g., 0.999 Silver 0.999 oz. ASW, 40 mm. **Series:** Endangered Wildlife **Subject:** Nutria de Rio **Obv:** National arms, eagle left within center of past and present arms **Rev:** Neotropical River Otter, value and date

Date	Mintage	VF20	XF40	MS60	MS63	MS65
2000 Mo	30,000	—	—	—	40.00	45.00

KM# 657 5 PESOS
31.10 g., 0.999 Silver 0.999 oz. ASW, 40 mm. **Subject:** Endangered Wildlife - American Antelope **Obv:** National arms, eagle left within center of past and present arms **Rev:** Peninsular Pronghorn, giant cardon cactus in back, value and date

Date	Mintage	VF20	XF40	MS60	MS63	MS65
2000 Mo	30,000	—	—	—	40.00	45.00

KM# 670 5 PESOS
27.00 g., 0.925 Silver 0.803 oz. ASW, 40 mm. **Series:** Ibero-American **Obv:** National arms, eagle left within center of past and present arms **Rev:** Cowboy trick riding two horses **Edge:** Reeded

Date	Mintage	VF20	XF40	MS60	MS63	MS65
2000 Mo	9,000	PF65 95.00				

KM# 553 10 NUEVOS PESOS
11.18 g., Bi-Metallic 0.925 Silver center, .1667 oz. ASW within Aluminum-Bronze ring, 28 mm. **Obv:** National arms **Obv. Legend:** Estados Unidos Mexicanos **Rev:** Assorted shields within circle **Edge:** Reeded

Date	Mintage	VF20	XF40	MS60	MS63	MS65
1992 Mo	20,000,000	—	7.00	10.00	14.00	—
1993 Mo	47,981,000	—	7.00	10.00	14.00	—
1994 Mo	15,000,000	—	7.00	10.00	14.00	—
1995 Mo	15,000,000	—	7.00	10.00	14.00	—
1995 Mo	6,981	PF63 20.00				

KM# 616 10 PESOS
10.33 g., Bi-Metallic Copper-Nickel-Zinc center in Aluminum-Bronze ring, 28 mm. **Obv:** National arms **Obv. Legend:** ESTADOS UNIDOS MEXICANOS **Rev:** Aztec design of Tonatiuh with the Fire Mask

Date	Mintage	VF20	XF40	MS60	MS63	MS65
1997 Mo	44,837,000	—	2.50	4.00	8.00	—
1998 Mo	203,735,000	—	2.50	4.00	8.00	—
1999 Mo	29,842,000	—	2.50	4.00	8.00	—

KM# 633 10 PESOS
62.03 g., 0.999 Silver 1.9923 oz. ASW **Subject:** Millennium Series **Obv:** National arms, eagle left within center of past and present arms **Rev:** Ancient and modern buildings within circle

Date	Mintage	VF20	XF40	MS60	MS63	MS65
1999-2000 Mo	47,641	PF65 80.00				

KM# 636 10 PESOS
10.33 g., Bi-Metallic Copper-Nickel-Zinc center in Aluminum-Bronze ring, 28 mm. **Series:** Millennium **Obv:** National arms **Obv. Legend:** ESTADOS UNIDOS MEXICANOS **Rev:** Aztec carving **Edge Lettering:** ANO (year) repeated 3 times

Date	Mintage	VF20	XF40	MS60	MS63	MS65
2000 Mo	24,839,000	—	3.50	4.50	8.50	—

KM# 561 20 NUEVOS PESOS
16.92 g., Bi-Metallic 0.925 Silver (.250 oz. ASW) center within Aluminum-Bronze ring, 31.86 mm. **Obv:** National arms **Obv. Legend:** ESTADOS UNIDOS MEXICANOS **Rev:** Head of Hidalgo left within wreath **Edge:** Reeded

Date	Mintage	VF20	XF40	MS60	MS63	MS65
1993 Mo	25,000,000	—	10.00	12.00	15.00	—
1994 Mo	5,000,000	—	10.00	12.00	15.00	—
1995 Mo	5,000,000	—	10.00	12.00	15.00	—

KM# 641 20 PESOS
6.22 g., 0.999 Gold 0.1998 oz. AGW, 21.9 mm. **Subject:** UNICEF **Obv:** National arms, eagle left **Rev:** Child playing with lasso **Edge:** Reeded

Date	Mintage	VF20	XF40	MS60	MS63	MS65
1999 Mo	1,510	PF65 375				

KM# 637 20 PESOS
Bi-Metallic Copper-Nickel center within Brass ring, 32 mm. **Subject:** Xiuhtecuhtli **Obv:** National arms, eagle left within circle **Rev:** Aztec with torch within spiked circle

Date	Mintage	VF20	XF40	MS60	MS63	MS65
2000 Mo	14,850,000	2.50	3.50	15.00	18.50	—

KM# 638 20 PESOS
Bi-Metallic Copper-Nickel center within Brass ring, 32 mm. **Subject:** Octavio Paz **Obv:** National arms, eagle left within circle **Rev:** Head 1/4 right within circle

Date	Mintage	VF20	XF40	MS60	MS63	MS65
2000 Mo	14,943,000	2.50	3.50	15.00	18.50	—

KM# 571 50 NUEVOS PESOS
34.11 g., Bi-Metallic 0.925 Silver .500 ASW center within Brass ring, 38.87 mm. **Subject:** Nino Heroes **Obv:** National arms **Obv. Legend:** ESTADOS UNIDOS MEXICANOS **Rev:** Six heads facing with date at upper right, all within circle and 1/2 wreath **Edge:** Reeded

Date	Mintage	VF20	XF40	MS60	MS63	MS65
1993 Mo	2,000,000	—	18.00	25.00	32.50	—
1994 Mo	1,500,000	—	18.00	25.00	32.50	—
1995 Mo	1,500,000	—	18.00	25.00	32.50	—

SILVER BULLION COINAGE

Libertad Series

KM# 542 1/20 ONZA (1/20 Troy Ounce of Silver)
1.56 g., 0.999 Silver 0.0499 oz. ASW, 16 mm. **Obv:** National arms, eagle left **Rev:** Winged Victory

Date	Mintage	VF20	XF40	MS60	MS63	MS65
1991 Mo	50,017	—	—	—	—	5.50
1992 Mo	295,783	—	—	—	—	4.50
1992 Mo	5,000	PF65 10.00				
1993 Mo	100,000	—	—	—	—	4.50
1993 Mo	5,002	PF65 10.00				
1994 Mo	90,100	—	—	—	—	4.50
1994 Mo	5,002	PF65 10.00				
1995 Mo	50,000	—	—	—	—	5.50
1995 Mo	2,000	PF65 12.00				

KM# 609 1/20 ONZA (1/20 Troy Ounce of Silver)
1.56 g., 0.999 Silver 0.0499 oz. ASW, 16 mm. **Obv:** National arms, eagle left **Rev:** Winged Victory

Date	Mintage	VF20	XF40	MS60	MS63	MS65
1996 Mo	50,000	—	—	—	—	20.00
1996 Mo	1,000	PF65 30.00				
1997 Mo	20,000	—	—	—	—	20.00
1997 Mo	800	PF65 30.00				
1998 Mo	6,400	—	—	—	—	30.00
1998 Mo	300	PF65 37.00				
1999 Mo	8,001	—	—	—	—	25.00
1999 Mo	600	PF65 32.00				
2000 Mo	57,500	—	—	—	—	25.00
2000 Mo	900	PF65 32.00				

KM# 543 1/10 ONZA (1/10 Troy Ounce of Silver)
3.11 g., 0.999 Silver 0.0999 oz. ASW, 20 mm. **Obv:** National arms, eagle left **Rev:** Winged Victory

Date	Mintage	VF20	XF40	MS60	MS63	MS65
1991 Mo	50,017	—	—	—	—	7.50
1992 Mo	299,983	—	—	—	—	6.50
1992 Mo	5,000	PF65 12.00				
1993 Mo	100,000	—	—	—	—	6.50
1993 Mo	5,002	PF65 12.00				
1994 Mo	90,100	—	—	—	—	6.50
1994 Mo	5,002	PF65 12.00				
1995 Mo	50,000	—	—	—	—	7.50
1995 Mo	2,000	PF65 13.50				

KM# 610 1/10 ONZA (1/10 Troy Ounce of Silver)
3.11 g., 0.999 Silver 0.0999 oz. ASW, 20 mm. **Obv:** National arms, eagle left **Rev:** Winged Victory

Date	Mintage	VF20	XF40	MS60	MS63	MS65
1996 Mo	50,000	—	—	—	—	25.00
1996 Mo	1,000	PF65 35.00				
1997 Mo	20,000	—	—	—	—	25.00
1997 Mo	800	PF65 35.00				
1998 Mo	6,400	—	—	—	—	33.00
1998 Mo	300	PF65 45.00				
1999 Mo	8,000	—	—	—	—	27.50
1999 Mo	600	PF65 40.00				
2000 Mo	27,500	—	—	—	—	27.50
2000 Mo	1,000	PF65 40.00				

KM# 544 1/4 ONZA (1/4 Troy Ounce of Silver)
7.78 g., 0.999 Silver 0.2497 oz. ASW, 25 mm. **Obv:** National arms, eagle left **Rev:** Winged Victory

Date	Mintage	VF20	XF40	MS60	MS63	MS65
1991 Mo	50,017	—	—	—	—	11.50
1992 Mo	104,000	—	—	—	—	10.00
1992 Mo	5,000	PF65 16.50				
1993 Mo	90,500	—	—	—	—	10.00
1993 Mo	5,002	PF65 16.50				
1994 Mo	90,100	—	—	—	—	10.00
1994 Mo	5,002	PF65 16.50				
1995 Mo	50,000	—	—	—	—	11.50
1995 Mo	2,000	PF65 17.50				

KM# 611 1/4 ONZA (1/4 Troy Ounce of Silver)
7.78 g., 0.999 Silver 0.2497 oz. ASW, 27 mm. **Obv:** National arms, eagle left **Rev:** Winged Victory

Date	Mintage	VF20	XF40	MS60	MS63	MS65
1996 Mo	50,000	—	—	—	—	30.00
1996 Mo	1,000	PF65 40.00				
1997 Mo	20,000	—	—	—	—	32.00
1997 Mo	800	PF65 40.00				
1998 Mo	6,400	—	—	—	—	40.00
1998 Mo	300	PF65 65.00				
1999 Mo	7,000	—	—	—	—	35.00
1999 Mo	600	PF65 50.00				
2000 Mo	21,000	—	—	—	—	35.00
2000 Mo	700	PF65 50.00				

KM# 545 1/2 ONZA (1/2 Troy Ounce of Silver)
15.55 g., 0.999 Silver 0.4995 oz. ASW, 30 mm. **Obv:** National arms, eagle left **Rev:** Winged Victory

Date	Mintage	VF20	XF40	MS60	MS63	MS65
1991 Mo	50,618	—	—	—	—	24.00
1992 Mo	119,000	—	—	—	—	22.00
1992 Mo	5,000	PF65 27.00				
1993 Mo	90,500	—	—	—	—	22.00
1993 Mo	5,002	PF65 27.00				
1994 Mo	90,100	—	—	—	—	22.00
1994 Mo	5,002	PF65 27.00				
1995 Mo	50,000	—	—	—	—	22.00
1995 Mo	2,000	PF65 28.00				

KM# 612 1/2 ONZA (1/2 Troy Ounce of Silver)
15.55 g., 0.999 Silver 0.4995 oz. ASW, 33 mm. **Obv:** National arms, eagle left **Rev:** Winged Victory

Date	Mintage	VF20	XF40	MS60	MS63	MS65
1996 Mo	50,000	—	—	—	—	35.00
1996 Mo	1,000	PF65 60.00				
1997 Mo	20,000	—	—	—	—	40.00
1997 Mo	800	PF65 60.00				
1998 Mo	6,400	—	—	—	—	60.00
1998 Mo	2,500	PF65 90.00				
1999 Mo	2,000	—	—	—	—	45.00
1999 Mo	7,000	PF65 70.00				
2000 Mo	20,000	—	—	—	—	45.00
2000 Mo	700	PF65 70.00				

KM# 494.1 ONZA (Troy Ounce of Silver)
31.10 g., 0.999 Silver 0.9989 oz. ASW, 36 mm. **Subject:** Libertad **Obv:** National arms, eagle left **Rev:** Winged Victory **Edge:** Plain

Date	Mintage	VF20	XF40	MS60	MS63	MS65
1982 Mo	1,049,680	—	—	—	—	35.00
1983 Mo	1,001,768	—	—	—	—	35.00
1983 Mo	998	PF65 600				
1984 Mo	1,014,000	—	—	—	—	32.00
1985 Mo	2,017,000	—	—	—	—	32.00
1986 Mo	1,699,426	—	—	—	—	35.00
1986 Mo	30,006	PF65 45.00				
1987 Mo	500,000	—	—	—	—	70.00
1987 Mo Doubled die	Inc. above	—	—	—	—	70.00
1987 Mo	12,000	PF65 60.00				
1988 Mo	1,500,500	—	—	—	—	80.00
1989 Mo	1,396,500	—	—	—	—	45.00
1989 Mo	10,000	PF65 95.00				

KM# 494.2 ONZA (Troy Ounce of Silver)
31.10 g., 0.999 Silver 0.9989 oz. ASW, 36 mm. **Obv:** National arms, eagle left **Rev:** Winged Victory **Edge:** Reeded

Date	Mintage	VF20	XF40	MS60	MS63	MS65
1988 Mo	10,000	PF65 100				
1990 Mo	1,200,000	—	—	—	—	60.00
1990 Mo	10,000	PF65 90.00				
1991 Mo	1,650,518	—	—	—	—	52.00

KM# 494.5 ONZA (Troy Ounce of Silver)
31.10 g., 0.999 Silver 0.9989 oz. ASW **Subject:** Libertad **Obv:** National arms, eagle left, KM#494.3 **Rev:** Winged Victory, KM#494.2 **Edge:** Reeded **Note:** Mule

Date	Mintage	VF20	XF40	MS60	MS63	MS65
1991 Mo	10,000	PF65 85.00				

KM# 494.3 ONZA (Troy Ounce of Silver)
31.10 g., 0.999 Silver 0.9989 oz. ASW, 36 mm. **Subject:** Libertad **Obv:** National arms, eight dots below eagle's left talons **Rev:** Winged Victory with revised design and lettering **Edge:** Reeded

Date	Mintage	VF20	XF40	MS60	MS63	MS65
1991 Mo	Inc. above	—	—	—	—	50.00
1991 Mo	10,000	PF65 85.00				
1992 Mo	2,458,000	—	—	—	—	50.00
1992 Mo	10,000	PF65 85.00				

KM# 494.4 ONZA (Troy Ounce of Silver)
31.10 g., 0.999 Silver 0.9989 oz. ASW, 36 mm. **Subject:** Libertad **Obv:** National arms, Seven dots below eagle's left talon, dull claws on right talon, thick lettering **Rev:** Winged Victory with revised design and lettering **Edge:** Reeded

Date	Mintage	VF20	XF40	MS60	MS63	MS65
1993 Mo	1,000,000	—	—	—	—	45.00
1993 Mo	5,002	PF65 90.00				
1994 Mo	400,000	—	—	—	—	45.00
1994 Mo	5,002	PF65 85.00				
1995 Mo	500,000	—	—	—	—	45.00
1995 Mo	2,000	PF65 85.00				

KM# 613 ONZA (Troy Ounce of Silver)
31.11 g., 0.999 Silver 0.999 oz. ASW, 40 mm. **Obv:** National arms, eagle left **Rev:** Winged Victory

Date	Mintage	VF20	XF40	MS60	MS63	MS65
1996 Mo	300,000	—	—	—	—	48.00
1996 Mo	2,000	PF65 90.00				
1997 Mo	100,000	—	—	—	—	80.00
1997 Mo	1,500	PF65 70.00				
1998 Mo	67,000	—	—	—	—	135
1998 Mo	500	PF65 200				
1999 Mo	95,000	—	—	—	—	140
1999 Mo	600	PF65 95.00				

KM# 639 ONZA (Troy Ounce of Silver)
31.10 g., 0.999 Silver 0.9989 oz. ASW, 40 mm. **Subject:** Libertad **Obv:** National arms, eagle left within center of past and present arms **Rev:** Winged Victory **Edge:** Reeded

Date	Mintage	VF20	XF40	MS60	MS63	MS65
2000 Mo	340,000	—	—	—	—	55.00
2000 Mo	1,600	PF65 140				

KM# 614 2 ONZAS (2 Troy Ounces of Silver)
62.21 g., 0.999 Silver 1.998 oz. ASW, 48 mm. **Subject:** Libertad **Obv:** National arms, eagle left within center of past and present arms **Rev:** Winged Victory **Edge:** Reeded

Date	Mintage	VF20	XF40	MS60	MS63	MS65
1996 Mo	50,000	—	—	—	—	90.00
1996 Mo	1,200	PF65 275				
1997 Mo	15,000	—	—	—	—	100
1997 Mo	1,300	PF65 150				
1998 Mo	7,000	—	—	—	—	100
1998 Mo	400	PF65 450				
1999 Mo	5,000	—	—	—	—	110
1999 Mo	280	PF65 7,000				
2000 Mo	7,500	—	—	—	—	100
2000 Mo	500	PF65 300				

KM# 615 5 ONZAS (5 Troy Ounces of Silver)
155.52 g., 0.999 Silver 4.995 oz. ASW, 65 mm. **Subject:** Libertad **Obv:** National arms, eagle left within center of past and present arms **Rev:** Winged Victory **Edge:** Reeded **Note:** Illustration reduced.

Date	Mintage	VF20	XF40	MS60	MS63	MS65
1996 Mo	20,000	—	—	—	—	265
1996 Mo	1,200	PF65 295				
1997 Mo	10,000	—	—	—	—	265
1997 Mo	1,300	PF65 295				
1998 Mo	3,500	—	—	—	—	325
1998 Mo	400	PF65 1,000				
1999 Mo	2,800	—	—	—	—	255
1999 Mo	100	PF65 1,250				
2000 Mo	4,000	—	—	—	—	255
2000 Mo	500	PF65 375				

GOLD BULLION COINAGE

KM# 530 1/20 ONZA (1/20 Ounce of Pure Gold)
1.75 g., 0.900 Gold 0.0506 oz. AGW **Obv:** Winged Victory **Rev:** Calendar stone

Date	Mintage	VF20	XF40	MS60	MS63	MS65
1987 Mo	—	—	—	—	—	275
1988 Mo	—	—	—	—	—	—

KM# 589 1/20 ONZA (1/20 Ounce of Pure Gold)
1.56 g., 0.999 Gold 0.0499 oz. AGW, 13 mm. **Obv:** Winged Victory **Rev:** National arms, eagle left

Date	Mintage	VF20	XF40	MS60	MS63	MS65
1991 Mo	10,000	—	—	—	—	83.00
1992 Mo	65,225	—	—	—	—	83.00

Note: According to Mexican mint records combined mintages of 1991 and 1992 BU and proof coins are 73,858.

Date	Mintage	VF20	XF40	MS60	MS63	MS65
1993 Mo	10,000	—	—	—	—	83.00
1994 Mo	10,000	—	—	—	—	83.00

KM# 642 1/20 ONZA (1/20 Ounce of Pure Gold)
1.56 g., 0.999 Gold 0.0499 oz. AGW **Obv:** National arms, eagle left **Rev:** Native working

Date	Mintage	VF20	XF40	MS60	MS63	MS65
2000 Mo	—	PF65 100				

KM# 671 1/20 ONZA (1/20 Ounce of Pure Gold)
1.56 g., 0.999 Gold 0.0499 oz. AGW, 13 mm. **Obv:** National arms, eagle left **Rev:** Winged Victory **Edge:** Reeded **Note:** Design similar to KM#609. Value estimates do not include the high taxes and surcharges added to the issue prices by the Mexican Government.

Date	Mintage	VF20	XF40	MS60	MS63	MS65
2000 Mo	5,300	—	—	—	—	83.00

KM# 628 1/15 ONZA (1/15 Ounce of Pure Gold)
0.999 Gold **Obv:** Winged Victory above legend **Rev:** National arms, eagle left within circle

Date	Mintage	VF20	XF40	MS60	MS63	MS65
1987 Mo	—	—	—	—	—	250

KM# 541 1/10 ONZA (1/10 Ounce of Pure Gold)
3.11 g., 0.999 Gold 0.0999 oz. AGW, 16 mm. **Obv:** National arms, eagle left **Rev:** Winged Victory

Date	Mintage	VF20	XF40	MS60	MS63	MS65
1991 Mo	10,000	—	—	—	—	152
1992 Mo	50,777	—	—	—	—	152
1993 Mo	10,000	—	—	—	—	152
1994 Mo	10,000	—	—	—	—	152

Note: According to Mexican mint records combined mintages of 1991 and 1992 coins are 60,592.

KM# 672 1/10 ONZA (1/10 Ounce of Pure Gold)

3.11 g., 0.999 Gold 0.0999 oz. AGW, 16 mm. **Obv:** National arms, eagle left **Rev:** Winged Victory **Edge:** Reeded **Note:** Design similar to KM#610. Value estimates do not include the high taxes and surcharges added to the issue prices by the Mexican Government.

Date	Mintage	VF20	XF40	MS60	MS63	MS65
2000 Mo	3,500	—	—	—	—	152

KM# 487 1/4 ONZA (1/4 Ounce of Pure Gold)

8.64 g., 0.900 Gold 0.250 oz. AGW **Obv:** National arms, eagle left **Rev:** Winged Victory **Note:** Similar to KM#488.

Date	Mintage	VF20	XF40	MS60	MS63	MS65
1981 Mo	313,000	—	—	—	—	355
1982 Mo	—	—	—	—	—	355

KM# 590 1/4 ONZA (1/4 Ounce of Pure Gold)

7.78 g., 0.999 Gold 0.2497 oz. AGW, 23 mm. **Obv:** Winged Victory above legend **Rev:** National arms, eagle left

Date	Mintage	VF20	XF40	MS60	MS63	MS65
1991 Mo	10,000	—	—	—	—	355
1992 Mo	28,106	—	—	—	—	355
1993 Mo	2,500	—	—	—	—	355
1994 Mo	2,500	—	—	—	—	355

Note: According to Mexican mint records, combined mintages of 1991 and 1992 are 37,321.

KM# 673 1/4 ONZA (1/4 Ounce of Pure Gold)

7.78 g., 0.999 Gold 0.2497 oz. AGW, 23 mm. **Obv:** National arms, eagle left **Rev:** Winged Victory **Edge:** Reeded **Note:** Design similar to KM#611. Value estimates do not include the high taxes and surcharges added to the issue prices by the Mexican Government.

Date	Mintage	VF20	XF40	MS60	MS63	MS65
2000 Mo	2,500	—	—	—	—	355

KM# 488 1/2 ONZA (1/2 Ounce of Pure Gold)

17.28 g., 0.900 Gold 0.500 oz. AGW **Obv:** National arms, eagle left **Rev:** Winged Victory

Date	Mintage	VF20	XF40	MS60	MS63	MS65
1981 Mo	193,000	—	—	—	—	690
1982 Mo	—	—	—	—	—	690
1989 Mo	704	PF65 850				

KM# 591 1/2 ONZA (1/2 Ounce of Pure Gold)

15.55 g., 0.999 Gold 0.4995 oz. AGW, 29 mm. **Obv:** Winged Victory above legend **Rev:** National arms, eagle left

Date	Mintage	VF20	XF40	MS60	MS63	MS65
1991 Mo	10,000	—	—	—	—	690
1992 Mo	25,220	—	—	—	—	690
1993 Mo	2,500	—	—	—	—	690
1994 Mo	2,500	—	—	—	—	690

Note: According to Mexican mint records, combined mintages of 1981-1992 BU and proof coins are 35,047.

KM# 674 1/2 ONZA (1/2 Ounce of Pure Gold)

15.55 g., 0.999 Gold 0.4995 oz. AGW, 29 mm. **Obv:** National arms, eagle left **Rev:** Winged Victory **Edge:** Reeded **Note:** Design similar to KM#612. Value estimates do not include the high taxes and surcharges added to the issue prices by the Mexican Government.

Date	Mintage	VF20	XF40	MS60	MS63	MS65
2000 Mo	1,500	—	—	—	—	690

KM# 489 ONZA (Ounce of Pure Gold)

34.56 g., 0.900 Gold 1.000 oz. AGW **Obv:** National arms, eagle left **Rev:** Winged Victory **Note:** Similar to KM#488.

Date	Mintage	VF20	XF40	MS60	MS63	MS65
1981 Mo	596,000	—	—	—	—	1,325
1985 Mo	—	—	—	—	—	1,325
1988 Mo	—	—	—	—	—	1,325

KM# 592 ONZA (Ounce of Pure Gold)

31.10 g., 0.999 Gold 0.999 oz. AGW, 34.5 mm. **Obv:** Winged Victory above legend **Rev:** National arms, eagle left

Date	Mintage	VF20	XF40	MS60	MS63	MS65
1991 Mo	109,193	—	—	—	—	1,300
1992 Mo	46,281	—	—	—	—	1,300
1993 Mo	73,881	—	—	—	—	1,300
1994 Mo	1,000	—	—	—	—	1,325

Note: According to Mexican mint redords, combined mintages of 1981-1992 BU and proof coins are 90,384.

KM# 675 ONZA (Ounce of Pure Gold)

31.10 g., 0.999 Gold 0.999 oz. AGW, 34.5 mm. **Obv:** National arms, eagle left **Rev:** Winged Victory **Edge:** Reeded **Note:** Design similar to KM#639. Value estimates do not include the high taxes and surcharges added to the issue prices by the Mexican Government.

Date	Mintage	VF20	XF40	MS60	MS63	MS65
2000 Mo	2,370	—	—	—	—	1,300

PLATINUM BULLION COINAGE

KM# 538 1/4 ONZA (1/4 Ounce)

7.78 g., 0.999 Platinum 0.2498 oz. APW **Obv:** National arms, eagle left **Rev:** Winged Victory

Date	Mintage	VF20	XF40	MS60	MS63	MS65
1989 Mo	3,500	PF65 550				

BULLION COINAGE

These coins are still being minted. Mintage figures are through 2013.

Pre-Columbian • Aztec Series

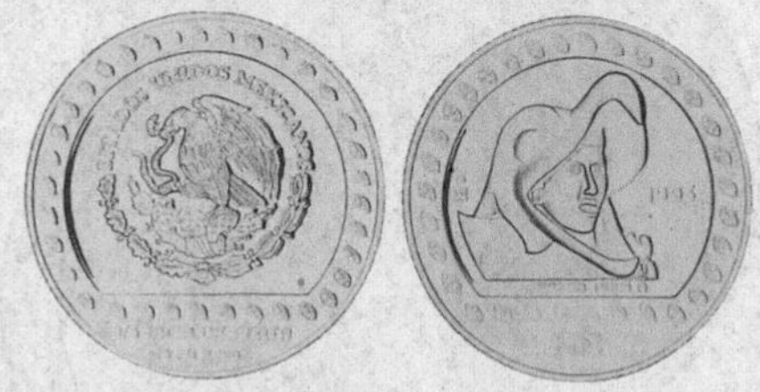

KM# 644 NUEVOS PESO

7.77 g., 0.999 Silver 0.2496 oz. ASW, 27 mm. **Subject:** Eagle Warrior **Obv:** National arms, eagle left within D-shaped circle and dotted border **Rev:** Eagle warrior within D-shaped circle and dotted border **Edge:** Reeded

Date	Mintage	VF20	XF40	MS60	MS63	MS65
1993 Mo	1,500	—	—	—	—	18.00
1993 Mo	900	PF65 30.00				

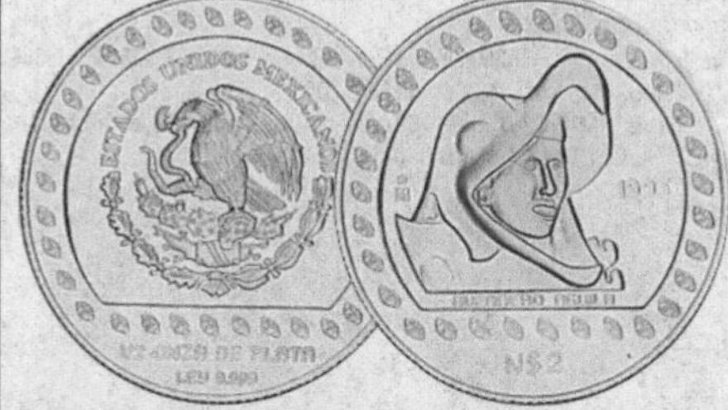

KM# 645 2 NUEVOS PESOS

15.42 g., 0.999 Silver 0.4953 oz. ASW, 33 mm. **Subject:** Eagle Warrior **Obv:** National arms, eagle left **Rev:** Eagle warrior **Edge:** Reeded

Date	Mintage	VF20	XF40	MS60	MS63	MS65
1993 Mo	1,500	—	—	—	—	20.00
1993 Mo	800	PF65 40.00				

KM# 646 5 NUEVOS PESOS

31.05 g., 0.999 Silver 0.9973 oz. ASW, 40 mm. **Subject:** Eagle Warrior **Obv:** National arms, eagle left **Rev:** Eagle warrior **Edge:** Reeded

Date	Mintage	VF20	XF40	MS60	MS63	MS65
1993 Mo	2,000	—	—	—	—	35.00
1993 Mo	1,000	PF65 70.00				

KM# 647 5 NUEVOS PESOS

31.00 g., 0.999 Silver 0.9957 oz. ASW, 40 mm. **Subject:** Xochipilli **Obv:** National arms, eagle left within D-shaped circle and flower blossom border **Rev:** Seated figure sculpture within D-shaped circle and flower blossom border **Edge:** Reeded

Date	Mintage	VF20	XF40	MS60	MS63	MS65
1993 Mo	2,000	—	—	—	—	35.00
1993 Mo	800	PF65 75.00				

KM# 648 5 NUEVOS PESOS

31.00 g., 0.999 Silver 0.9957 oz. ASW, 40 mm. **Subject:** Brasero Efigie **Obv:** National arms, eagle left within D-shaped circle and designed border **Rev:** Sculpture within D-shaped circle and designed border **Edge:** Reeded

Date	Mintage	VF20	XF40	MS60	MS63	MS65
1993 Mo	2,000	—	—	—	—	35.00
1993 Mo	500	PF65 75.00				

KM# 649 5 NUEVOS PESOS

31.00 g., 0.999 Silver 0.9957 oz. ASW, 40 mm. **Subject:** Huchucteotl **Obv:** National arms, eagle left within D-shaped circle and designed border **Rev:** Aztec sculpture within D-shaped circle and designed border **Edge:** Reeded

Date	Mintage	VF20	XF40	MS60	MS63	MS65
1993 Mo	5,000	—	—	—	—	25.00
1993 Mo	800	PF65 75.00				

KM# 650 10 NUEVOS PESOS

155.31 g., 0.999 Silver 4.9883 oz. ASW, 65 mm. **Subject:** Piedra de Tizoc **Obv:** National arms, eagle left **Rev:** Warrior capturing woman **Edge:** Reeded **Note:** Illustration reduced, similar to 100 Pesos, KM# 557

Date	Mintage	VF20	XF40	MS60	MS63	MS65
1992 Mo	—	PF65 300				
1993 Mo	1,000	—	—	—	—	175
1993 Mo	1,000	PF65 200				

KM# 554 25 PESOS

7.78 g., 0.999 Silver 0.2497 oz. ASW, 27 mm. **Obv:** National arms, eagle left within D-shaped circle and designed border **Rev:** Eagle warrior right within D-shaped circle and a designed border

Date	Mintage	VF20	XF40	MS60	MS63	MS65
1992 Mo	50,000	—	—	—	—	15.00
1992 Mo	3,000	PF65 30.00				

Note: Combined mintages of KM#554 and KM#644 through 2013 are 54,005 Unc. and 2,700 Proof.

KM# 555 50 PESOS

15.55 g., 0.999 Silver 0.4995 oz. ASW, 33 mm. **Obv:** National arms, eagle left within D-shaped circle designed border **Rev:** Eagle warrior right within D-shaped circle and designed border

Date	Mintage	VF20	XF40	MS60	MS63	MS65
1992 Mo	50,000	—	—	—	—	20.00
1992 Mo	3,000	PF65 40.00				

Note: Combined mintages for KM#555 and #645 through 2013 are 52,000 Unc. and 4,300 Proof.

KM# 556 100 PESOS

31.10 g., 0.999 Silver 0.999 oz. ASW, 40 mm. **Obv:** National arms, eagle left **Rev:** Eagle warrior

Date	Mintage	VF20	XF40	MS60	MS63	MS65
1992 Mo	205,000	—	—	—	—	35.00
1992	4,000	PF65 75.00				

Note: KM#556 and #646 have a combined mintage through 2013 of 208,400 Unc and 7,000 Proof.

KM# 562 100 PESOS

31.10 g., 0.999 Silver 0.999 oz. ASW, 40 mm. **Obv:** National arms, eagle left within D-shaped circle and designed border **Rev:** Seated figure sculpture within D-shaped circle and designed border

Date	Mintage	VF20	XF40	MS60	MS63	MS65
1992 Mo	4,000	PF65 90.00				

Note: KM#562 and #647 have a combined mintage through 2013 of 3,511 Unc and 6,200 Proof.

KM# 563 100 PESOS

31.10 g., 0.999 Silver 0.999 oz. ASW, 40 mm. **Obv:** National arms, eagle left within D-shaped circle and designed border **Rev:** Brasero Efigie - The God of Rain within D-shaped circle and designed border

Date	Mintage	VF20	XF40	MS60	MS63	MS65
1992 Mo	4,000	PF65 60.00				

Note: KM#563 and #648 have combined mintage through 2013 of 4,580 Unc. and 6,400 Proof.

KM# 564 100 PESOS

31.10 g., 0.999 Silver 0.999 oz. ASW, 40 mm. **Obv:** National arms, eagle left within D-shaped circle and designed border **Rev:** Huehueteotl - The God of Fire within D-shaped circle and designed border

Date	Mintage	VF20	XF40	MS60	MS63	MS65
1992 Mo	4,000	PF65 70.00				

Note: KM#564 and #649 have combined mintage through 2013 of 6,105 Unc. and 6,400 Proof.

KM# 558 250 PESOS

7.78 g., 0.999 Gold 0.2497 oz. AGW, 23 mm. **Subject:** Native Culture **Obv:** National arms, eagle left within D-shaped circle and designed border **Rev:** Sculpture of Jaguar head within D-shaped circle and designed border

Date	Mintage	VF20	XF40	MS60	MS63	MS65
1992 Mo	12,000	—	—	—	—	475
1992 Mo	2,000	PF65 450				

KM# 559 500 PESOS

15.55 g., 0.999 Gold 0.4995 oz. AGW, 29 mm. **Subject:** Native Culture **Obv:** National arms, eagle left within D-shaped circle and designed border **Rev:** Sculpture of Jaguar head within D-shaped circle and designed border

Date	Mintage	VF20	XF40	MS60	MS63	MS65
1992 Mo	12,000	—	—	—	—	900
1992 Mo	2,000	PF65 925				

KM# 560 1000 PESOS

31.10 g., 0.999 Gold 0.999 oz. AGW, 34.5 mm. **Subject:** Native Culture **Obv:** National arms, eagle left within D-shaped circle and designed border **Rev:** Sculpture of Jaguar head within D-shaped circle and designed border

Date	Mintage	VF20	XF40	MS60	MS63	MS65
1992 Mo	19,850	—	—	—	—	1,750
1992 Mo	2,000	PF65 1,800				

KM# 557 10000 PESOS

155.52 g., 0.999 Silver 4.995 oz. ASW, 64 mm. **Subject:** Pieora De Tizoc **Obv:** National arms, eagle left within D-shaped circle and designed border **Rev:** Native warriors within D-shaped circle and designed border **Note:** Similar to 10 Nuevo Pesos, KM#650

Date	Mintage	VF20	XF40	MS60	MS63	MS65
1992 Mo	51,900	—	—	—	—	175
1992 Mo	3,300	PF65 275				

Note: KM#557 and #650 have combined mintage through 2013 of 54,305 Unc. and 5,400 Proof.

Pre-Columbian • Central Veracruz Series

KM# 567 NUEVOS PESO

7.76 g., 0.999 Silver 0.2492 oz. ASW, 27 mm. **Subject:** Bajo relieve de el Tajin **Obv:** National arms, eagle left within D-shaped circle and designed border **Rev:** Design within D-shaped circle and designed border

Date	Mintage	VF20	XF40	MS60	MS63	MS65
1993 Mo	100,005	—	—	—	—	20.00
1993 Mo	4,305	PF65 35.00				

KM# 568 2 NUEVOS PESOS

15.55 g., 0.999 Silver 0.4995 oz. ASW, 33 mm. **Subject:** Bajo relieve de el Tajin **Obv:** National arms, eagle left within D-shaped circle and designed border **Rev:** Design within D-shaped circle and designed border

Date	Mintage	VF20	XF40	MS60	MS63	MS65
1993 Mo	100,005	—	—	—	—	25.00
1993 Mo	3,005	PF65 35.00				

KM# 569 5 NUEVOS PESOS

31.10 g., 0.999 Silver 0.999 oz. ASW, 40 mm. **Subject:** Bajo relieve de el Tajin **Obv:** National arms, eagle left within D-shaped circle and designed border **Rev:** Design within D-shaped circle and designed border

Date	Mintage	VF20	XF40	MS60	MS63	MS65
1993 Mo	101,005	—	—	—	—	37.50
1993 Mo	4,405	PF65 70.00				

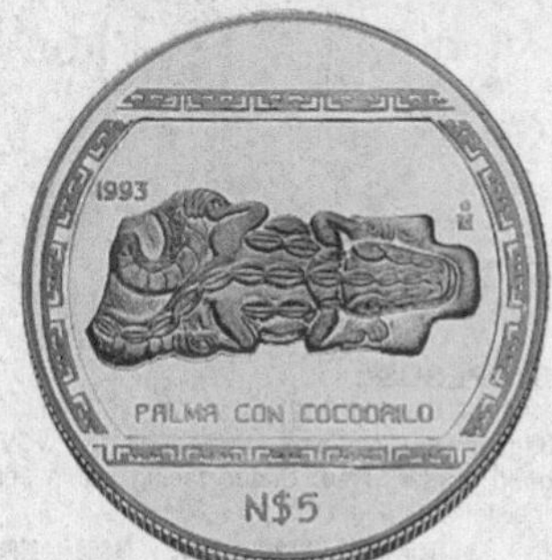

KM# 582 5 NUEVOS PESOS

31.10 g., 0.999 Silver 0.999 oz. ASW, 40 mm. **Subject:** Palma Con Cocodrilo **Obv:** National arms, eagle left within D-shaped circle and designed border **Rev:** Aerial view of crocodile within D-shaped circle and designed border

Date	Mintage	VF20	XF40	MS60	MS63	MS65
1993 Mo	5,105	—	—	—	—	37.50
1993 Mo	3,855	PF65 75.00				

KM# 583 5 NUEVOS PESOS

31.10 g., 0.999 Silver 0.999 oz. ASW, 40 mm. **Subject:** Anciano Con Brasero **Obv:** National arms, eagle left within D-shaped circle and designed border **Rev:** Kneeling figure sculpture within D-shaped circle and designed border

Date	Mintage	VF20	XF40	MS60	MS63	MS65
1993 Mo	3,800	—	—	—	—	37.50
1993 Mo	4,160	PF65 75.00				

KM# 584 5 NUEVOS PESOS

31.10 g., 0.999 Silver 0.999 oz. ASW, 40 mm. **Subject:** Carita Sonriente **Obv:** National arms, eagle left **Rev:** Sculptured head

Date	Mintage	VF20	XF40	MS60	MS63	MS65
1993 Mo	5,105	—	—	—	—	37.50
1993 Mo	4,705	PF65 75.00				

KM# 570 10 NUEVOS PESOS

155.52 g., 0.999 Silver 4.995 oz. ASW, 65 mm. **Subject:** Piramide Del El Tajin **Obv:** National arms, eagle left within flat shaped circle and designed border **Rev:** Pyramid within flat shaped circle and designed border **Note:** Illustration reduced.

Date	Mintage	VF20	XF40	MS60	MS63	MS65
1993 Mo	50,905	—	—	—	—	175
1993 Mo	4,148	PF65 190				

KM# 585 25 NUEVOS PESOS

7.78 g., 0.999 Gold 0.2497 oz. AGW, 23 mm. **Subject:** Hacha Ceremonial **Obv:** National arms, eagle left **Rev:** Mask left **Note:** Similar to 100 New Pesos, KM#587.

Date	Mintage	VF20	XF40	MS60	MS63	MS65
1993 Mo	15,508	—	—	—	—	475
1993 Mo	802	PF65 500				

KM# 586 50 NUEVOS PESOS

15.55 g., 0.999 Gold 0.4995 oz. AGW, 29 mm. **Subject:** Hacha Ceremonial **Obv:** National arms, eagle left **Rev:** Mask left **Note:** Similar to 100 New Pesos, KM#587.

Date	Mintage	VF20	XF40	MS60	MS63	MS65
1993 Mo	15,508	—	—	—	—	900
1993 Mo	802	PF65 925				

KM# 587 100 NUEVOS PESOS

31.10 g., 0.999 Gold 0.999 oz. AGW, 34.5 mm. **Subject:** Hacha Ceremonial **Obv:** National arms, eagle left **Rev:** Mask left

Date	Mintage	VF20	XF40	MS60	MS63	MS65
1993 Mo	7,160	—	—	—	—	1,800
1993 Mo	500	PF65 1,850				

Pre-Columbian • Mayan Series

KM# 572 NUEVOS PESO

7.76 g., 0.999 Silver 0.2492 oz. ASW, 27 mm. **Subject:** Chaac Mool **Obv:** National arms, eagle left within six sided shield and designed border **Rev:** Reclining figure within six sided shield and designed border

Date	Mintage	VF20	XF40	MS60	MS63	MS65
1994 Mo	53,505	—	—	—	—	20.00
1994 Mo	2,700	PF65 35.00				

KM# 573 2 NUEVOS PESOS

15.55 g., 0.999 Silver 0.4995 oz. ASW, 33 mm. **Subject:** Chaac Mool **Obv:** National arms, eagle left within six sided shield and designed border **Rev:** Reclining figure within six-sided shield and designed border

Date	Mintage	VF20	XF40	MS60	MS63	MS65
1994 Mo	51,500	—	—	—	—	25.00
1994 Mo	4,300	PF65 35.00				

KM# 574 5 NUEVOS PESOS

31.10 g., 0.999 Silver 0.999 oz. ASW, 40 mm. **Subject:** Chaac Mool **Obv:** National arms, eagle left within six-sided shield and designed border **Rev:** Reclining figure within six-sided shield and designed border

Date	Mintage	VF20	XF40	MS60	MS63	MS65
1994 Mo	208,300	—	—	—	—	37.00
1994 Mo	6,700	PF65 70.00				

KM# 575 5 NUEVOS PESOS
31.10 g., 0.999 Silver 0.999 oz. ASW, 40 mm. **Subject:** Chaac Mool **Obv:** National arms, eagle left within six-sided shield and designed border **Rev:** Tomb of Palenque Memorial Stone within six sided shield and designed border

Date	Mintage	VF20	XF40	MS60	MS63	MS65
1994 Mo	5,905	—	—	—	—	37.00
1994 Mo	6,300	PF65 70.00				

KM# 577 5 NUEVOS PESOS
31.10 g., 0.999 Silver 0.999 oz. ASW, 40 mm. **Subject:** Mascaron Del Dios Chaac **Rev:** Elaborately carved wall segment

Date	Mintage	VF20	XF40	MS60	MS63	MS65
1994 Mo	3,011	—	—	—	—	37.00
1994 Mo	6,300	PF65 70.00				

KM# 578 5 NUEVOS PESOS
31.10 g., 0.999 Silver 0.999 oz. ASW, 40 mm. **Subject:** Lintel 26 **Obv:** National arms, eagle left within six-sided shield and designed border **Rev:** Two seated figures wall carving within six sided shield and designed border

Date	Mintage	VF20	XF40	MS60	MS63	MS65
1994 Mo	4,080	—	—	—	—	45.00
1994 Mo	6,000	PF65 75.00				

KM# 676 10 NUEVOS PESOS
155.52 g., 0.999 Silver 4.995 oz. ASW, 65 mm. **Subject:** Piramide Del Castillo **Obv:** National arms, eagle left above metal content statement **Rev:** Pyramid above two-line inscription **Rev. Inscription:** PIRAMIDE DEL CASTILLO / CHICHEN-ITZA **Edge:** Reeded

Date	Mintage	VF20	XF40	MS60	MS63	MS65
1993 Mo	—	PF65 650				

KM# 576 10 NUEVOS PESOS
155.70 g., 0.999 Silver 5.0009 oz. ASW, 65 mm. **Subject:** Piramide del Castillo **Obv:** National arms, eagle left **Rev:** Pyramid **Note:** Illustration reduced.

Date	Mintage	VF20	XF40	MS60	MS63	MS65
1994 Mo	54,305	—	—	—	—	175
1994 Mo	5,500	PF65 225				

KM# 579 25 NUEVOS PESOS
7.78 g., 0.999 Gold 0.2497 oz. AGW, 23 mm. **Subject:** Personaje de Jaina **Rev:** Seated figure

Date	Mintage	VF20	XF40	MS60	MS63	MS65
1994 Mo	501	PF65 500				
1994 Mo	2,000	—	—	—	—	475

KM# 580 50 NUEVOS PESOS
15.55 g., 0.999 Gold 0.4995 oz. AGW, 29 mm. **Subject:** Personaje de Jaina **Rev:** Seated figure

Date	Mintage	VF20	XF40	MS60	MS63	MS65
1994 Mo	1,000	—	—	—	—	900
1994 Mo	501	PF65 925				

KM# 581 100 NUEVOS PESOS
31.10 g., 0.999 Gold 0.999 oz. AGW, 34.5 mm. **Subject:** Personaje de Jaina **Obv:** National arms, eagle left within six-sided shield and designed border **Rev:** Seated figure within six-sided shield and designed border

Date	Mintage	VF20	XF40	MS60	MS63	MS65
1994 Mo	1,000	—	—	—	—	1,800
1994 Mo	501	PF65 1,850				

Pre-Columbian • Olmec Series

KM# 593 PESO
7.78 g., 0.999 Silver 0.2497 oz. ASW, 27 mm. **Subject:** Senor De Las Limas **Obv:** National arms, eagle left within square and designed border **Rev:** Sitting figure facing within square and designed border **Note:** Similar to 5 Pesos, KM#595.

Date	Mintage	VF20	XF40	MS60	MS63	MS65
1996 Mo	6,400	—	—	—	—	20.00
1996 Mo	3,700	PF65 35.00				
1998 Mo Matte	2,400	—	—	—	—	22.00

KM# 594 2 PESOS
15.55 g., 0.999 Silver 0.4995 oz. ASW, 33 mm. **Subject:** Senor De Las Limas **Obv:** National arms, eagle left within square and designed border **Rev:** Sitting figure facing within square and designed border **Note:** Similar to 5 Pesos, KM#595.

Date	Mintage	VF20	XF40	MS60	MS63	MS65
1996 Mo	6,500	—	—	—	—	25.00
1996 Mo	2,200	PF65 35.00				
1998 Mo Matte	2,400	—	—	—	—	28.00

KM# 595 5 PESOS
31.10 g., 0.999 Silver 0.999 oz. ASW, 40 mm. **Subject:** Senor De Las Limas **Obv:** National arms, eagle left within square and designed border **Rev:** Seated figure facing within square and designed border

Date	Mintage	VF20	XF40	MS60	MS63	MS65
1996 Mo	9,200	—	—	—	—	37.50
1996 Mo	4,100	PF65 70.00				
1998 Matte	3,400	—	—	—	—	40.00

KM# 596 5 PESOS
31.10 g., 0.999 Silver 0.999 oz. ASW, 40 mm. **Subject:** Hombre Jaguar **Obv:** National arms, eagle left within square and designed border **Rev:** Statue facing within square and designed border

Date	Mintage	VF20	XF40	MS60	MS63	MS65
1996 Mo	6,000	—	—	—	—	90.00
1996 Mo	4,200	PF65 70.00				
1998 Mo Matte	6,000	—	—	—	—	37.50
1998 Mo	4,800	PF65 75.00				

KM# 597 5 PESOS

31.10 g., 0.999 Silver 0.999 oz. ASW, 40 mm. **Subject:** El Luchador **Obv:** National arms, eagle left **Rev:** El Luchador

Date	Mintage	VF20	XF40	MS60	MS63	MS65
1996 Mo	7,100	—	—	—	—	37.50
1996 Mo	3,800	PF65 70.00				
1998 Matte	2,000	—	—	—	—	40.00

KM# 598 5 PESOS

31.10 g., 0.999 Silver 0.999 oz. ASW, 40 mm. **Subject:** Hacha Ceremonial **Obv:** National arms, eagle left within square and designed border **Rev:** Statue within square and designed border

Date	Mintage	VF20	XF40	MS60	MS63	MS65
1996 Mo	7,500	—	—	—	—	37.50
1996 Mo	3,700	PF65 70.00				
1998 Mo Matte	2,000	—	—	—	—	40.00

KM# 599 10 PESOS

155.52 g., 0.999 Silver 4.995 oz. ASW, 65 mm. **Subject:** Cabeza Olmeca **Obv:** National arms, eagle left **Rev:** Native mask **Note:** Illustration reduced.

Date	Mintage	VF20	XF40	MS60	MS63	MS65
1996 Mo	5,560	—	—	—	—	180
1996 Mo	3,900	PF65 190				
1998 Matte	2,150	—	—	—	—	180

KM# 600 25 PESOS

7.78 g., 0.999 Gold 0.2497 oz. AGW, 23 mm. **Subject:** Sacerdote **Obv:** National arms, eagle left **Rev:** Sculpture **Note:** Similar to 100 Pesos, KM#602.

Date	Mintage	VF20	XF40	MS60	MS63	MS65
1996 Mo	500	—	—	—	—	475
1996 Mo	750	PF65 500				

KM# 601 50 PESOS

15.55 g., 0.999 Gold 0.4995 oz. AGW, 29 mm. **Subject:** Sacerdote **Obv:** National arms, eagle left **Rev:** Sculpture **Note:** Similar to 100 Pesos, KM#602.

Date	Mintage	VF20	XF40	MS60	MS63	MS65
1996 Mo	500	PF65 925				
1996 Mo	500	—	—	—	—	900

KM# 602 100 PESOS

31.10 g., 0.999 Gold 0.999 oz. AGW, 34.5 mm. **Subject:** Sacerdote **Obv:** National arms, eagle left within square and designed border **Rev:** Sculpture within square and designed border

Date	Mintage	VF20	XF40	MS60	MS63	MS65
1996 Mo	500	—	—	—	—	1,800
1996 Mo	500	PF65 1,850				

Pre-Columbian • Teotihuacan Series

KM# 617 PESO

7.78 g., 0.999 Silver 0.2498 oz. ASW, 27 mm. **Subject:** Disco De La Muerte **Obv:** National arms, eagle left within oblong circle and designed border **Rev:** Sculpture within oblong circle and designed border

Date	Mintage	VF20	XF40	MS60	MS63	MS65
1997 Mo	3,100	—	—	—	—	20.00
1997 Mo	1,906	PF65 35.00				
1998 Mo Matte	2,400	—	—	—	—	25.00
1998 Mo	500	PF65 45.00				

KM# 618 2 PESOS

15.55 g., 0.999 Silver 0.4995 oz. ASW, 33 mm. **Subject:** Disco De La Muerte **Obv:** National arms, eagle left within oblong circle and designed border **Rev:** Sculpture within oblong circle and designed border

Date	Mintage	VF20	XF40	MS60	MS63	MS65
1997 Mo	3,500	—	—	—	—	25.00
1997 Mo	1,606	PF65 35.00				
1998 Mo	2,400	—	—	—	—	30.00
1998 Mo	500	PF65 50.00				

KM# 619 5 PESOS

31.10 g., 0.999 Silver 0.999 oz. ASW, 40 mm. **Subject:** Teotihuacan - Disco de la Muerte **Obv:** National arms, eagle left within oblong circle and designed border **Rev:** Sculpture within oblong circle and designed border

Date	Mintage	VF20	XF40	MS60	MS63	MS65
1997 Mo	4,700	—	—	—	—	37.50
1997 Mo	3,206	PF65 75.00				
1998 Mo	3,400	—	—	—	—	40.00
1998 Mo	500	PF65 150				

KM# 620 5 PESOS

31.10 g., 0.999 Silver 0.999 oz. ASW, 40 mm. **Subject:** Teotihuacan - Mascara **Obv:** National arms, eagle left within oblong circle and designed border **Rev:** Face sculpture within oblong circle and designed border

Date	Mintage	VF20	XF40	MS60	MS63	MS65
1997 Mo	5,200	—	—	—	—	37.50
1997 Mo	2,906	PF65 75.00				
1998 Mo	2,000	—	—	—	—	40.00
1998 Mo	500	PF65 150				

KM# 621 5 PESOS

31.10 g., 0.999 Silver 0.999 oz. ASW, 40 mm. **Subject:** Teotihuacan - Vasija **Obv:** National arms, eagle left within oval and designed border **Rev:** Seated woman joined to pottery vase within oval and designed border

Date	Mintage	VF20	XF40	MS60	MS63	MS65
1997 Mo	3,006	PF65 75.00				
1997 Mo	5,300	—	—	—	—	42.00
1998 Mo Matte	2,000	—	—	—	—	42.00
1998 Mo	3,006	PF65 150				

KM# 622 5 PESOS

31.10 g., 0.999 Silver 0.999 oz. ASW, 40 mm. **Subject:** Teotihuacan - Jugador de Pelota **Obv:** National arms, eagle left

Date	Mintage	VF20	XF40	MS60	MS63	MS65
1997 Mo	5,400	—	—	—	—	37.50
1997 Mo	3,206	PF65 75.00				
1998 Mo Matte	2,000	—	—	—	—	40.00
1998 Mo	500	PF65 150				

KM# 623 10 PESOS
155.52 g., 0.999 Silver 4.995 oz. ASW, 65 mm. **Subject:** Piramide Del Sol **Obv:** National arms, eagle left within oblong circle and designed border **Rev:** Pyramid within oblong circle and designed border **Note:** Illustration reduced.

Date	Mintage	VF20	XF40	MS60	MS63	MS65
1997 Mo	3,136	—	—	—	—	200
1997 Mo	3,306	PF65 225				
1998 Mo Matte	2,150	—	—	—	—	200

KM# 624 25 PESOS
7.78 g., 0.999 Gold 0.2497 oz. AGW, 23 mm. **Subject:** Serpiente Emplumada **Obv:** National arms, eagle left **Note:** Similar to 100 Pesos, KM#626.

Date	Mintage	VF20	XF40	MS60	MS63	MS65
1997 Mo	500	—	—	—	—	475
1997 Mo	206	PF65 525				

KM# 625 50 PESOS
15.55 g., 0.999 Gold 0.4995 oz. AGW, 29 mm. **Subject:** Serpiente Emplumada **Obv:** National arms, eagle left **Note:** Similar to 100 Pesos, KM#626.

Date	Mintage	VF20	XF40	MS60	MS63	MS65
1997 Mo	500	—	—	—	—	925
1997 Mo	206	PF65 950				

KM# 626 100 PESOS
31.10 g., 0.999 Gold 0.999 oz. AGW, 24.5 mm. **Subject:** Teotihuacan - Serpiente Emplumada **Obv:** National arms, eagle left

Date	Mintage	VF20	XF40	MS60	MS63	MS65
1997 Mo	206	PF65 1,900				
1997 Mo	500	—	—	—	—	1,850

Pre-Columbian • Toltec Series

KM# 661 PESO
7.78 g., 0.999 Silver 0.2498 oz. ASW, 27 mm. **Subject:** Jaguar **Obv:** National arms, eagle left **Rev:** Jaguar carving **Edge:** Reeded

Date	Mintage	VF20	XF40	MS60	MS63	MS65
1998 Mo	6,400	—	—	—	—	20.00
1998 Mo	4,000	PF65 30.00				

KM# 662 2 PESOS
15.55 g., 0.999 Silver 0.4995 oz. ASW, 33 mm. **Subject:** Jaguar **Obv:** National arms, eagle left **Rev:** Jaguar carving **Edge:** Reeded

Date	Mintage	VF20	XF40	MS60	MS63	MS65
1998 Mo	6,600	—	—	—	—	25.00
1998 Mo	2,200	PF65 35.00				

KM# 663 5 PESOS
31.10 g., 0.999 Silver 0.999 oz. ASW, 40 mm. **Subject:** Jaguar **Obv:** National arms, eagle left within shield and designed border **Rev:** Jaguar carving within shield and designed border **Edge:** Reeded

Date	Mintage	VF20	XF40	MS60	MS63	MS65
1998 Mo	5,800	—	—	—	—	37.50
1998 Mo	4,300	PF65 75.00				

KM# 664 5 PESOS
31.10 g., 0.999 Silver 0.999 oz. ASW, 40 mm. **Obv:** National arms, eagle left **Rev:** Sacerdote sculpture **Edge:** Reeded

Date	Mintage	VF20	XF40	MS60	MS63	MS65
1998 Mo	7,800	—	—	—	—	35.00
1998 Mo	3,800	PF65 75.00				

KM# 665 5 PESOS
31.10 g., 0.999 Silver 0.999 oz. ASW, 40 mm. **Subject:** Quetzalcoatl **Obv:** National arms, eagle left **Rev:** Quetzalcoatl sculpture **Edge:** Reeded

Date	Mintage	VF20	XF40	MS60	MS63	MS65
1998 Mo	7,100	—	—	—	—	37.50
1998 Mo	3,900	PF65 75.00				

KM# 666 5 PESOS
31.10 g., 0.999 Silver 0.999 oz. ASW, 40 mm. **Subject:** Serpiente con Craneo **Obv:** National arms, eagle left **Rev:** Large sculpture **Edge:** Reeded

Date	Mintage	VF20	XF40	MS60	MS63	MS65
1998 Mo	8,700	—	—	—	—	37.50
1998 Mo	4,100	PF65 75.00				

KM# 634 10 PESOS
155.73 g., 0.999 Silver 5.0018 oz. ASW, 65 mm. **Subject:** Atlantes **Obv:** National arms, eagle left within shield and designed border **Rev:** Three carved statues within shield and designed border

Date	Mintage	VF20	XF40	MS60	MS63	MS65
1998 Mo	5,560	—	—	—	—	180
1998 Mo	3,650	PF65 200				

KM# 667 25 PESOS
7.78 g., 0.999 Gold 0.2498 oz. AGW, 23 mm. **Subject:** Aguila **Obv:** National arms, eagle left **Rev:** Eagle sculpture **Edge:** Reeded

Date	Mintage	VF20	XF40	MS60	MS63	MS65
1998 Mo	303	PF65 525				
1998 Mo	303	—	—	—	—	500

KM# 668 50 PESOS
15.55 g., 0.999 Gold 0.4995 oz. AGW, 29 mm. **Subject:** Aguila **Obv:** National arms, eagle left **Rev:** Eagle sculpture **Edge:** Reeded

Date	Mintage	VF20	XF40	MS60	MS63	MS65
1998 Mo	303	PF65 950				
1998 Mo	303	—	—	—	—	925

KM# 669 100 PESOS
31.10 g., 0.999 Gold 0.999 oz. AGW, 34.5 mm. **Subject:** Aguila **Obv:** National arms, eagle left within designed shield **Rev:** Eagle sculpture within designed shield **Edge:** Reeded

Date	Mintage	VF20	XF40	MS60	MS63	MS65
1998 Mo	303	PF65 1,900				
1998 Mo	303	—	—	—	—	1,850

MEDALLIC SILVER BULLION COINAGE

KM# M49a ONZA

33.63 g., 0.925 Silver 1.000 oz. ASW, 41 mm. **Obv:** Mint mark above coin press

Date	Mintage	VF20	XF40	MS60	MS63	MS65
1949	1,000,000	32.00	40.00	45.00	60.00	—

KM# M49b.1 ONZA

33.63 g., 0.925 Silver 1.000 oz. ASW, 41 mm. **Obv:** Wide spacing between DE MONEDA **Rev:** Mint mark below balance scale **Note:** Type I

Date	Mintage	VF20	XF40	MS60	MS63	MS65
1978 Mo	280,000	—	18.50	35.00	45.00	—

KM# M49b.2 ONZA

33.63 g., 0.925 Silver 1.000 oz. ASW, 41 mm. **Obv:** Close spacing between DE MONEDA **Rev:** Mint mark below balance scale **Note:** Type II

Date	Mintage	VF20	XF40	MS60	MS63	MS65
1978 Mo	Inc. above	—	18.50	36.00	48.00	—

KM# M49b.3 ONZA

33.63 g., 0.925 Silver 1.000 oz. ASW, 41 mm. **Obv:** Close spacing between DE MONEDA **Rev:** Left scale pan points to U in UNA **Note:** Type III

Date	Mintage	VF20	XF40	MS60	MS63	MS65
1979 Mo	4,508,000	—	18.50	35.00	42.00	—

KM# M49b.4 ONZA

33.63 g., 0.925 Silver 1.000 oz. ASW, 41 mm. **Obv:** Close spacing between DE MONEDA **Rev:** Left scale pan points between U and N of UNA **Note:** Type IV

Date	Mintage	VF20	XF40	MS60	MS63	MS65
1979 Mo	Inc. above	—	18.50	35.00	42.00	—

KM# M49b.5 ONZA

33.63 g., 0.925 Silver 1.000 oz. ASW, 41 mm. **Obv:** Close spacing between DE MONEDA **Rev:** Left scale pan points between U and N of UNA **Note:** Type V

Date	Mintage	VF20	XF40	MS60	MS63	MS65
1980/70 Mo	Inc. above	—	18.50	36.00	46.00	—
1980 Mo	6,104,000	—	18.50	35.00	42.00	—

MEDALLIC GOLD COINAGE

KM# M91a 10 PESOS

8.33 g., 0.900 Gold 0.2411 oz. AGW **Subject:** 200th Anniversary - Birth of Hidalgo

Date	Mintage	VF20	XF40	MS60	MS63	MS65
1953	—	—	—	315	425	

KM# M123a 10 PESOS

8.33 g., 0.900 Gold 0.2411 oz. AGW **Subject:** Centennial of Constitution

Date	Mintage	VF20	XF40	MS60	MS63	MS65
1957	—	—	—	315	425	

Note: Mintage includes #M122a

KM# M92a 20 PESOS

16.67 g., 0.900 Gold 0.4823 oz. AGW **Subject:** 200th Anniversary - Birth of Hidalgo

Date	Mintage	VF20	XF40	MS60	MS63	MS65
1953	—	—	—	620	800	

KM# M122a 50 PESOS

41.67 g., 0.900 Gold 1.2057 oz. AGW **Subject:** Centennial of Constitution

Date	Mintage	VF20	XF40	MS60	MS63	MS65
1957	—	—	—	1,550	2,000	

Note: Mintage included in total for KM#M123a

PATTERNS

Including off metal strikes

KM#	Date	Mintage	Identification	Mkt Val
Pn169	1901Cn Q	—	20 Centavos. Copper.	—

KM#	Date	Mintage	Identification	Mkt Val
Pn170	1901Cn Q	—	20 Centavos. Bronze.	425
Pn171	1904Zs FZ	—	Peso. Aluminum.	—
Pn172	1906Z	—	2 Centavos. Silver.	—

KM#	Date	Mintage	Identification	Mkt Val
Pn173	1907Mo	—	50 Centavos. Silver. Horse and rider facing left within sun rays. National arms. Plain.	8,500
Pn174	1907Mo	—	50 Centavos. Silver. Incuse lettered edge, matte Proof.	5,500
Pn175	1907	—	50 Centavos. Silver. Raised lettered edge, matte Proof.	3,750
Pn176	1908Mo	—	50 Centavos. Silver. Plain edge, Proof.	3,500
Pn177	1908Mo	—	Peso. Silver. Liberty on horseback, plain edge, Proof.	—

KM#	Date	Mintage	Identification	Mkt Val
Pn178	1909Mo	—	Peso. Silver. Plain edge, Proof.	8,500
Pn179	1909Mo	—	Peso. Silver. Incuse lettered edge, Proof.	12,500
Pn180	1909Mo	—	Peso. Brass. Incuse lettered edge, matte Proof.	3,700
Pn181	1909Mo	—	Peso. Brass. Raised lettered edge, matte Proof.	3,700
Pn182	1909Mo	—	Peso. Bronze Plated Lead. Raised lettered edge, matte Proof.	—
Pn183	1909Mo	—	Peso. Silver. Raised lettered edge, matte Proof.	—
Pn184	1910	—	2 Centavos. Bronze.	—
Pn185	1911Mo	—	Peso. Silver. Plain edge.	3,500
Pn186	1911Mo	—	Peso. Bronze. Plain edge.	3,000

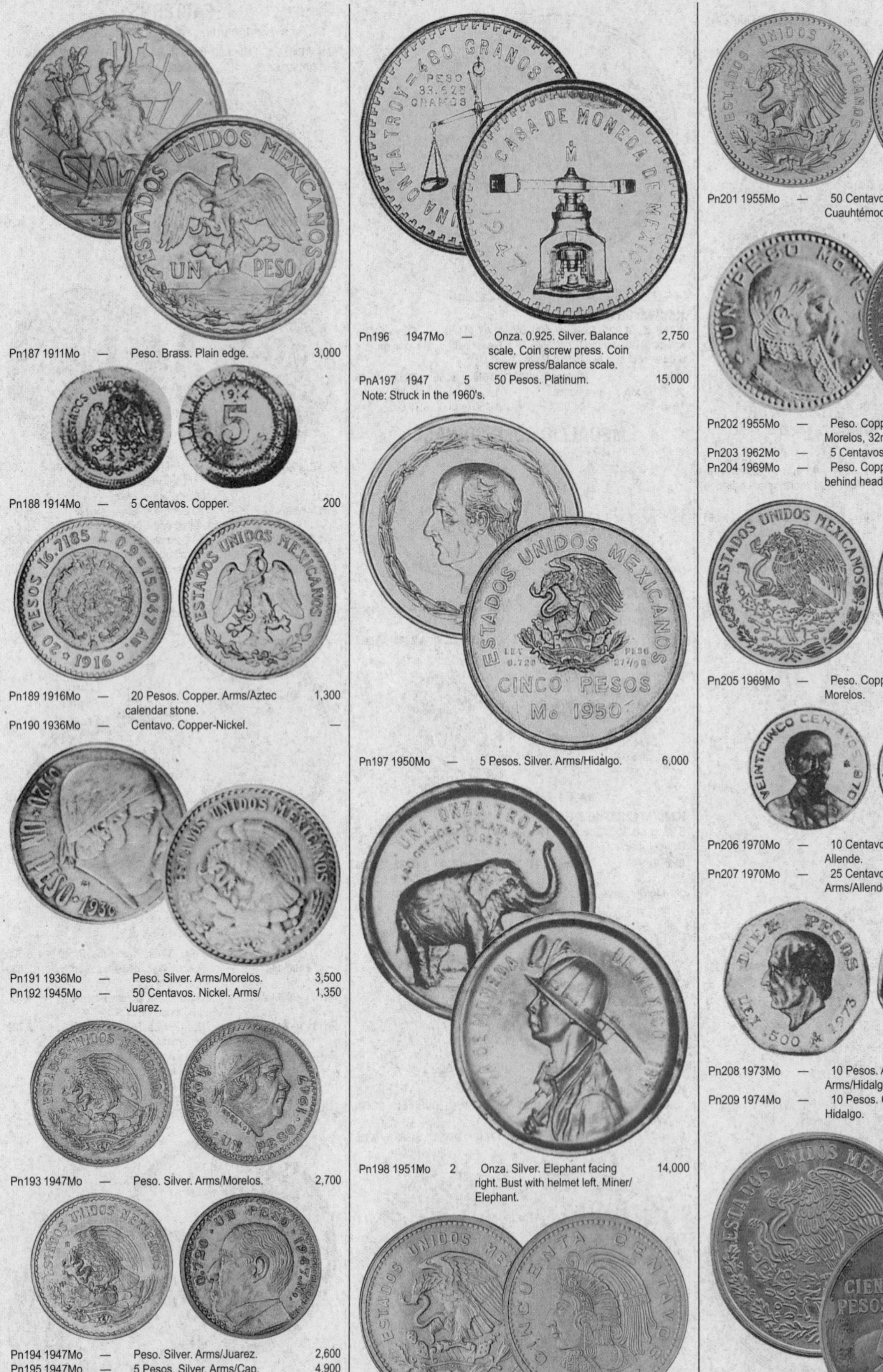

Pn187 1911Mo — Peso. Brass. Plain edge. 3,000

Pn188 1914Mo — 5 Centavos. Copper. 200

Pn189 1916Mo — 20 Pesos. Copper. Arms/Aztec calendar stone. 1,300

Pn190 1936Mo — Centavo. Copper-Nickel. —

Pn191 1936Mo — Peso. Silver. Arms/Morelos. 3,500

Pn192 1945Mo — 50 Centavos. Nickel. Arms/ Juarez. 1,350

Pn193 1947Mo — Peso. Silver. Arms/Morelos. 2,700

Pn194 1947Mo — Peso. Silver. Arms/Juarez. 2,600

Pn195 1947Mo — 5 Pesos. Silver. Arms/Cap, balance scale, scroll. 4,900

Pn196 1947Mo — Onza. 0.925. Silver. Balance scale. Coin screw press. Coin screw press/Balance scale. 2,750

PnA197 1947 5 50 Pesos. Platinum. 15,000

Note: Struck in the 1960's.

Pn197 1950Mo — 5 Pesos. Silver. Arms/Hidalgo. 6,000

Pn198 1951Mo 2 Onza. Silver. Elephant facing right. Bust with helmet left. Miner/ Elephant. 14,000

Pn199 1954Mo — 50 Centavos. Bronze. 33mm. Arms/Cuauhtémoc. —

Pn200 1954Mo — 50 Centavos. Copper-Nickel. Arms/Cuauhtémoc. —

Pn201 1955Mo — 50 Centavos. Bronze. Arms/ Cuauhtémoc. 625

Pn202 1955Mo — Peso. Copper-Nickel. Arms/ Morelos, 32mm. 1,800

Pn203 1962Mo — 5 Centavos. Copper-Nickel. 60.00

Pn204 1969Mo — Peso. Copper-Nickel. Value behind head. 2,000

Pn205 1969Mo — Peso. Copper-Nickel. Arms/ Morelos. 5,000

Pn206 1970Mo — 10 Centavos. Bronze. Arms/ Allende. 400

Pn207 1970Mo — 25 Centavos. Copper-Nickel. Arms/Allende. 750

Pn208 1973Mo — 10 Pesos. Aluminum-Bronze. Arms/Hidalgo. 800

Pn209 1974Mo — 10 Pesos. Copper-Nickel. Arms/ Hidalgo. 600

Pn210 1976Mo 16 100 Pesos. 0.720. Silver. Arms/ Morelos. 5,500

KM#	Date	Mintage	Identification	Mkt Val
Pn211	1978Mo	—	Onza. Silver. Coin screw press/ balance scale.	3,250

KM#	Date	Mintage	Identification	Mkt Val
Pn212	1978Mo	—	Onza. 0.925. Silver. Coin screw press / Coin belt powered press, Proof, PRUEBA.	2,750
Pn213	1978Mo	—	Onza. 0.925. Silver. Coin screw press / Coin belt powered press, Proof, PRUEBA.	—

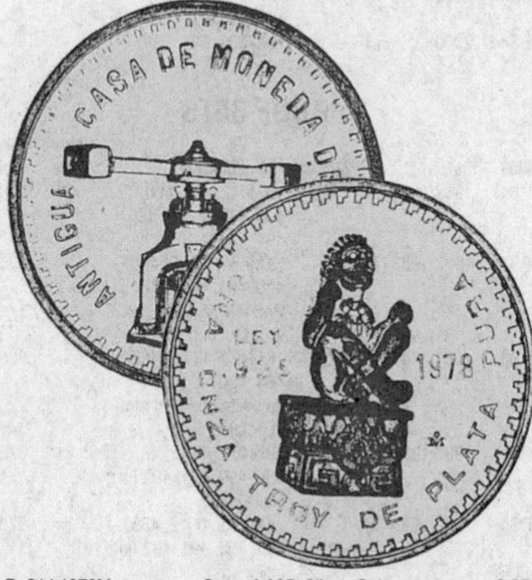

KM#	Date	Mintage	Identification	Mkt Val
Pn214	1978Mo	—	Onza. 0.925. Silver. Coin screw press / Native statue, Proof, PRUEBA.	2,250
Pn215	1978Mo	—	Onza. 0.925. Silver. Coin screw press / Native Statue, Proof, PRUEBA.	2,000
Pn216	1979Mo	—	Onza. 0.925. Silver.	2,250

KM#	Date	Mintage	Identification	Mkt Val
Pn217	1979Mo	—	20 Pesos. Bronze. Arms / Mayan art.	—
Pn218	1980Mo	8	20 Centavos. Copper-Nickel.	—

KM#	Date	Mintage	Identification	Mkt Val
Pn219	1980Mo	—	Peso. Brass. Arms / Mayan art.	350

KM#	Date	Mintage	Identification	Mkt Val
Pn220	1980Mo	—	10 Pesos. 0.500. Silver. Arms/ Mayan art.	—

KM#	Date	Mintage	Identification	Mkt Val
Pn221	1980Mo	—	10 Pesos. Bronze. Arms/ Mayan art.	750

KM#	Date	Mintage	Identification	Mkt Val
Pn222	1980Mo	—	20 Pesos. Copper-Nickel. Arms/ Mayan art. Large mint mark.	300

KM#	Date	Mintage	Identification	Mkt Val
Pn223	1980Mo	50	1/10 Onza. Silver. Arms/Radiant cap above mountain, Proof.	90.00

KM#	Date	Mintage	Identification	Mkt Val
Pn224	1981Mo	—	20 Centavos. Copper-Nickel. Small obverse design. Small arms design/Madero, Proof.	165
Pn225	1981Mo	—	20 Centavos. Copper-Nickel. Modified portrait. Small arms design/Modified portrait Madero, Proof.	135
Pn226	19xx (1981)	—	20 Centavos. Copper.	350

KM#	Date	Mintage	Identification	Mkt Val
PnA227	1982	—	50 Pesos.	—
Pn227	1983Mo	—	50 Centavos. Proof.	650
Pn228	1983Mo	12	Peso. Stainless Steel. Arms/ Morelos.	550

KM#	Date	Mintage	Identification	Mkt Val
Pn229	1983	—	5 Pesos. Bronze. Arms/Mayan art.	350

KM#	Date	Mintage	Identification	Mkt Val
Pn230	1983	—	Onza. Silver. Libertad.	1,400

KM#	Date	Mintage	Identification	Mkt Val
Pn231	1984Mo	—	50 Pesos. Copper-Nickel. Arms/ Juarez, Proof.	400

KM#	Date	Mintage	Identification	Mkt Val
Pn232	ND (1984)	—	50 Pesos. Gold. Arms/Juarez, w/o JUAREZ.	—
Pn233	1985Mo	—	Peso. Copper.	325
Pn234	1985Mo	10	Peso. Silver. SUD design divided from date and denomination.	—

KM#	Date	Mintage	Identification	Mkt Val
Pn235	1986Mo	33	Peso. Stainless Steel. SUD design w/date and denomination, no divider.	100

KM#	Date	Mintage	Identification	Mkt Val
Pn236	1986	—	500 Pesos. Stainless Steel. Proof.	500
Pn237	1987	3	100 Pesos. Copper. KM#537.	—
Pn238	1987	3	100 Pesos. Copper-Nickel. KM#537.	—

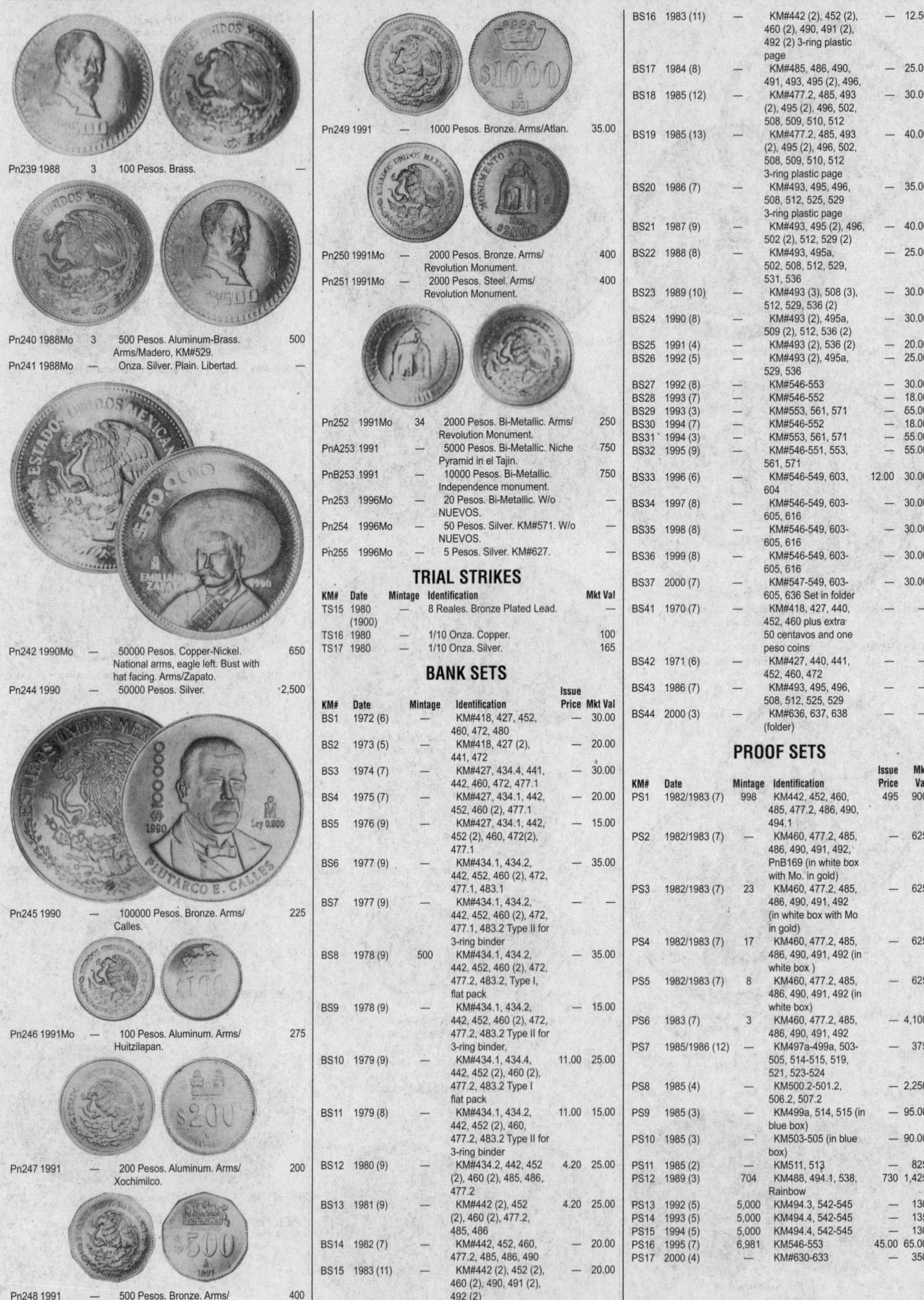

KM#	Date	Mintage	Identification	Mkt Val
Pn239	1988	3	100 Pesos. Brass.	—
Pn240	1988Mo	3	500 Pesos. Aluminum-Brass. Arms/Madero, KM#529.	500
Pn241	1988Mo	—	Onza. Silver. Plain. Libertad.	—
Pn242	1990Mo	—	50000 Pesos. Copper-Nickel. National arms, eagle left. Bust with hat facing. Arms/Zapato.	650
Pn244	1990	—	50000 Pesos. Silver.	2,500
Pn245	1990	—	100000 Pesos. Bronze. Arms/Calles.	225
Pn246	1991Mo	—	100 Pesos. Aluminum. Arms/Huitzilapan.	275
Pn247	1991	—	200 Pesos. Aluminum. Arms/Xochimilco.	200
Pn248	1991	—	500 Pesos. Bronze. Arms/Atenango.	400
Pn249	1991	—	1000 Pesos. Bronze. Arms/Atlan.	35.00
Pn250	1991Mo	—	2000 Pesos. Bronze. Arms/Revolution Monument.	400
Pn251	1991Mo	—	2000 Pesos. Steel. Arms/Revolution Monument.	400
Pn252	1991Mo	34	2000 Pesos. Bi-Metallic. Arms/Revolution Monument.	250
PnA253	1991	—	5000 Pesos. Bi-Metallic. Niche Pyramid in el Tajin.	750
PnB253	1991	—	10000 Pesos. Bi-Metallic. Independence monument.	750
Pn253	1996Mo	—	20 Pesos. Bi-Metallic. W/o NUEVOS.	—
Pn254	1996Mo	—	50 Pesos. Silver. KM#571. W/o NUEVOS.	—
Pn255	1996Mo	—	5 Pesos. Silver. KM#627.	—

TRIAL STRIKES

KM#	Date	Mintage	Identification	Mkt Val
TS15	1980 (1900)	—	8 Reales. Bronze Plated Lead.	—
TS16	1980	—	1/10 Onza. Copper.	100
TS17	1980	—	1/10 Onza. Silver.	165

BANK SETS

KM#	Date	Mintage	Identification	Issue Price	Mkt Val
BS1	1972 (6)	—	KM#418, 427, 452, 460, 472, 480	—	30.00
BS2	1973 (5)	—	KM#418, 427 (2), 441, 472	—	20.00
BS3	1974 (7)	—	KM#427, 434.4, 441, 442, 460, 472, 477.1	—	30.00
BS4	1975 (7)	—	KM#427, 434.1, 442, 452, 460 (2), 477.1	—	20.00
BS5	1976 (9)	—	KM#427, 434.1, 442, 452 (2), 460, 472(2), 477.1	—	15.00
BS6	1977 (9)	—	KM#434.1, 434.2, 442, 452, 460 (2), 472, 477.1, 483.1	—	35.00
BS7	1977 (9)	—	KM#434.1, 434.2, 442, 452, 460 (2), 472, 477.1, 483.2 Type II for 3-ring binder	—	—
BS8	1978 (9)	500	KM#434.1, 434.2, 442, 452, 460 (2), 472, 477.2, 483.2, Type I, flat pack	—	35.00
BS9	1978 (9)	—	KM#434.1, 434.2, 442, 452, 460 (2), 472, 477.2, 483.2 Type II for 3-ring binder,	—	15.00
BS10	1979 (9)	—	KM#434.1, 434.4, 442, 452 (2), 460 (2), 477.2, 483.2 Type I flat pack	11.00	25.00
BS11	1979 (8)	—	KM#434.1, 434.2, 442, 452 (2), 460, 477.2, 483.2 Type II for 3-ring binder	11.00	15.00
BS12	1980 (9)	—	KM#434.2, 442, 452 (2), 460 (2), 485, 486, 477.2	4.20	25.00
BS13	1981 (9)	—	KM#442 (2), 452 (2), 460 (2), 477.2, 485, 486	4.20	25.00
BS14	1982 (7)	—	KM#442, 452, 460, 477.2, 485, 486, 490	—	20.00
BS15	1983 (11)	—	KM#442 (2), 452 (2), 460 (2), 490, 491 (2), 492 (2)	—	20.00
BS16	1983 (11)	—	KM#442 (2), 452 (2), 460 (2), 490, 491 (2), 492 (2) 3-ring plastic page	—	12.50
BS17	1984 (8)	—	KM#485, 486, 490, 491, 493, 495 (2), 496,	—	25.00
BS18	1985 (12)	—	KM#477.2, 485, 493 (2), 495 (2), 496, 502, 508, 509, 510, 512	—	30.00
BS19	1985 (13)	—	KM#477.2, 485, 493 (2), 495 (2), 496, 502, 508, 509, 510, 512 3-ring plastic page	—	40.00
BS20	1986 (7)	—	KM#493, 495, 496, 508, 512, 525, 529 3-ring plastic page	—	35.00
BS21	1987 (9)	—	KM#493, 495 (2), 496, 502 (2), 512, 529 (2)	—	40.00
BS22	1988 (8)	—	KM#493, 495a, 502, 508, 512, 529, 531, 536	—	25.00
BS23	1989 (10)	—	KM#493 (3), 508 (3), 512, 529, 536 (2)	—	30.00
BS24	1990 (8)	—	KM#493 (2), 495a, 509 (2), 512, 536 (2)	—	30.00
BS25	1991 (4)	—	KM#493 (2), 536 (2)	—	20.00
BS26	1992 (5)	—	KM#493 (2), 495a, 529, 536	—	25.00
BS27	1992 (8)	—	KM#546-553	—	30.00
BS28	1993 (7)	—	KM#546-552	—	18.00
BS29	1993 (3)	—	KM#553, 561, 571	—	55.00
BS30	1994 (7)	—	KM#546-552	—	18.00
BS31	1994 (3)	—	KM#553, 561, 571	—	55.00
BS32	1995 (9)	—	KM#546-551, 553, 561, 571	—	55.00
BS33	1996 (6)	—	KM#546-549, 603, 604	12.00	30.00
BS34	1997 (8)	—	KM#546-549, 603-605, 616	—	30.00
BS35	1998 (8)	—	KM#546-549, 603-605, 616	—	30.00
BS36	1999 (8)	—	KM#546-549, 603-605, 616	—	30.00
BS37	2000 (7)	—	KM#547-549, 603-605, 636 Set in folder	—	30.00
BS41	1970 (7)	—	KM#418, 427, 440, 452, 460 plus extra 50 centavos and one peso coins	—	—
BS42	1971 (6)	—	KM#427, 440, 441, 452, 460, 472	—	—
BS43	1986 (7)	—	KM#493, 495, 496, 508, 512, 525, 529	—	—
BS44	2000 (3)	—	KM#636, 637, 638 (folder)	—	—

PROOF SETS

KM#	Date	Mintage	Identification	Issue Price	Mkt Val
PS1	1982/1983 (7)	998	KM442, 452, 460, 485, 477.2, 486, 490, 494.1	495	900
PS2	1982/1983 (7)	—	KM460, 477.2, 485, 486, 490, 491, 492, PnB169 (in white box with Mo. in gold)	—	625
PS3	1982/1983 (7)	23	KM460, 477.2, 485, 486, 490, 491, 492 (in white box with Mo in gold)	—	625
PS4	1982/1983 (7)	17	KM460, 477.2, 485, 486, 490, 491, 492 (in white box)	—	625
PS5	1982/1983 (7)	8	KM460, 477.2, 485, 486, 490, 491, 492 (in white box)	—	625
PS6	1983 (7)	3	KM460, 477.2, 485, 486, 490, 491, 492	—	4,100
PS7	1985/1986 (12)	—	KM497a-499a, 503-505, 514-515, 519, 521, 523-524	—	375
PS8	1985 (4)	—	KM500.2-501.2, 506.2, 507.2	—	2,250
PS9	1985 (3)	—	KM499a, 514, 515 (in blue box)	—	95.00
PS10	1985 (3)	—	KM503-505 (in blue box)	—	90.00
PS11	1985 (2)	—	KM511, 513	—	825
PS12	1989 (3)	704	KM488, 494.1, 538, Rainbow	730	1,425
PS13	1992 (5)	5,000	KM494.3, 542-545	—	130
PS14	1993 (5)	5,000	KM494.4, 542-545	—	135
PS15	1994 (5)	5,000	KM494.4, 542-545	—	130
PS16	1995 (7)	6,981	KM546-553	45.00	65.00
PS17	2000 (4)	—	KM#630-633	—	350

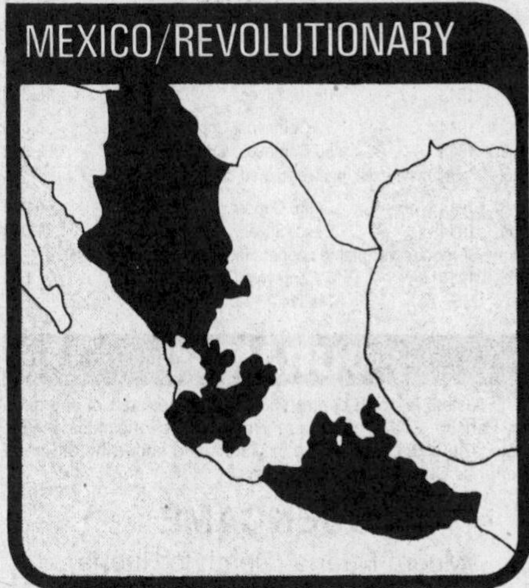

Revolution, 1910-1917

The Mexican independence movement, which is of interest and concern to collectors because of the warfare induced activity of local and state mints, began with the Sept. 16, 1810 march on the capital led by Father Miguel Hidalgo, a well-intentioned man of imagination and courage who proved to be an inept organizer and leader. Hidalgo was captured and executed within 10 months. His revolution, led by such as Morelos, Guerrero and Iturbide, continued and culminated in Mexican independence in 1821. Turbulent years followed. From 1821 to 1877 there were two emperors, several dictators and enough presidents to provide a change of government on the average of once every nine months. Porfirio Diaz, who had the longest tenure of any 19th century dictator in Latin American history, seized power in 1877 and did not relinquish it until 1911.

The final phase of Mexico's lengthy revolutionary period began in 1910 and lasted through the adoption of a liberal constitution and the election of a new congress in 1917. The 1910-1917 revolution was agrarian in character and intended to destroy the regime of Diaz and make Mexico economically and diplomatically independent. The republic experienced a state of upheaval that saw most of the leading figures of the revolution (Villa, Carranza, Obregon, Zapata, Calles) fighting each other at one time or another. Carranza eventually emerged as the most powerful figure of the early revolution. As *de-facto* president in 1916, he convened a constitutional convention, which produced a constitution in which the aims of the revolution were formulized. Obregon, perhaps the ablest general and wiliest politician of the lot, became Mexico's elected president in 1920, bringing the most disastrous but significant decade in Mexico's history to an end.

AGUASCALIENTES

Aguascalientes is a state in central Mexico. Its coin issues, struck by authority of Pancho Villa, represent his deepest penetration into the Mexican heartland. Lack of silver made it necessary to make all denominations in copper.

FRANCISCO PANCHO VILLA

REVOLUTIONARY COINAGE

KM# 601 CENTAVO

3.55 g., Copper, 17 mm. **Obv:** Liberty cap **Rev:** Value within 3/4 wreath below date **Note:** Large date weight 3.55g.

Date	Mintage	VG8	F12	VF20	XF40	MS60
1915	—	30.00	60.00	100	300	—
Note: Large date, reeded edge						
1915	—	30.00	60.00	100	300	—
Note: Small date, plain edge						
1915	—	250	350	450	—	—
Note: Large date, plain edge						
1915	—	30.00	60.00	80.00	250	—
Note: Small date, reeded edge						

KM# 602.1 2 CENTAVOS

4.28 g., Copper **Obv:** Liberty cap **Rev:** Value within 3/4 wreath below date

Date	Mintage	VG8	F12	VF20	XF40	MS60
1915	—	40.00	100	300	450	—
Note: Round front 2, plain edge						

KM# 602.2 2 CENTAVOS

3.35 g., Copper, 19 mm. **Obv:** Liberty cap **Rev:** Value within 1/2 wreath below date

Date	Mintage	VG8	F12	VF20	XF40	MS60
1915	—	35.00	60.00	85.00	300	—
Note: Square front 2, reeded edge						
1915 Plain edge	—	50.00	90.00	200	500	—
Note: Square front 2						

KM# 603 5 CENTAVOS

Copper, 25 mm. **Obv:** National arms **Rev:** Liberty cap and value above sprigs

Date	Mintage	VG8	F12	VF20	XF40	MS60
1915 Plain edge; Rare	—	—	—	—	—	—
1915 Reeded edge	—	10.00	20.00	30.00	75.00	—

KM# 604.1 5 CENTAVOS

7.13 g., Copper, 25 mm. **Obv:** National arms **Rev:** Vertically shaded 5 within sprigs

Date	Mintage	VG8	F12	VF20	XF40	MS60
1915	—	20.00	40.00	50.00	175	—
Note: Reeded edge						
1915	—	100	150	225	400	—
Note: Plain edge						

KM# 604.2 5 CENTAVOS

Copper, 25 mm. **Obv:** National arms **Rev:** Horizontally shaded 5 within sprigs

Date	Mintage	VG8	F12	VF20	XF40	MS60
1915	—	25.00	40.00	65.00	150	—
Note: Reeded edge						
1915	—	35.00	60.00	90.00	275	—
Note: Plain edge						

KM# 600 20 CENTAVOS

Copper **Obv:** National arms **Rev:** Value below Liberty cap within sprigs **Edge:** Reeded

Date	Mintage	VG8	F12	VF20	XF40	MS60
1915	—	15.00	20.00	50.00	100	—

Note: Varieties exist with both plain and milled edges and many variations in the shading of the numerals

KM# 605 20 CENTAVOS

Copper, 29 mm. **Obv:** National arms **Rev:** Value below Liberty cap within sprigs

Date	Mintage	VG8	F12	VF20	XF40	MS60
1915 Reeded edge	—	11.00	30.00	85.00	150	—

KM# 606 20 CENTAVOS

Copper, 29 mm. **Obv:** National arms **Rev:** Value below Liberty cap within sprigs

Date	Mintage	VG8	F12	VF20	XF40	MS60
1915 Reeded edge	—	10.00	20.00	60.00	100	—

PIEDFORT

KM#	Date	Mintage	Identification	Mkt Val
P1	1915	50	Centavo. Silver. Large date. Prev. KM#601a.	1,400
P2	1915	—	Centavo. Silver. Small date. Prev. KM#601a.	1,400
P3	1915	50	2 Centavos. Silver. Prev. KM#602a.	1,800
P4	1915	50	5 Centavos. Silver. Prev. KM#604a.	6,000
P5	1915	50	20 Centavos. Silver. Plain edge. Prev. KM#605a.	7,000
P6	1915	—	20 Centavos. Silver. Prev. KM#600a.	5,000

CHIHUAHUA

Chihuahua is a northern state of Mexico bordering the U.S. It was the arena that introduced Pancho Villa to the world. Villa, an outlaw, was given a title when asked by Madero to participate in maintaining order during Madero's presidency. After Madero's death in February 1913, Villa became a persuasive leader. Chihuahua was where he made his first coins - the Parral series. The *Army of the North* pesos also came from this state. This coin helped Villa recruit soldiers because of his ability to pay in silver while others were paying in worthless paper money.

ARMY OF THE NORTH

Ejercito Del Norte

REVOLUTIONARY COINAGE

KM# 619 PESO

29.27 g., Silver **Obv:** National arms **Rev:** Liberty cap

Date	Mintage	VG8	F12	VF20	XF40	MS60
1915	—	25.00	40.00	75.00	200	800

KM# 619a PESO

Copper **Obv:** National arms **Rev:** Liberty cap

Date	Mintage	VG8	F12	VF20	XF40	MS60
1915	—	500	1,000	1,500	3,500	—

KM# 619b PESO

Brass **Obv:** National arms **Rev:** Liberty cap **Note:** Uniface obverse

Date	Mintage	VG8	F12	VF20	XF40	MS60
1915 Rare	—	—	—	—	—	—

CONSTITUTIONALIST ARMY

Ejercito Constitucionalista

KM# 612 5 CENTAVOS

Copper **Obv:** Liberty cap **Rev:** Value above date

Date	Mintage	VG8	F12	VF20	XF40	MS60
1914	—	25.00	45.00	100	250	—

KM# 613 5 CENTAVOS

6.60 g., Copper, 25 mm. **Obv:** Liberty cap **Rev:** Value above date **Note:** Numerous varieties exist. Weight varies 6.3-6.93g.

Date	Mintage	VG8	F12	VF20	XF40	MS60
1914	—	1.00	2.50	4.00	10.00	—
1915	—	1.00	2.50	4.00	10.00	—

KM# 613a 5 CENTAVOS

Brass **Obv:** Liberty cap **Rev:** Value above date **Note:** Numerous varieties exist.

Date	Mintage	VG8	F12	VF20	XF40	MS60
1914	—	2.00	3.00	8.00	10.00	—
1915	—	2.00	3.00	8.00	10.00	—

KM# 613b 5 CENTAVOS

Cast Copper **Obv:** Liberty cap **Rev:** Value above date

Date	Mintage	VG8	F12	VF20	XF40	MS60
1914	—	75.00	200	300	450	—

KM# 614 5 CENTAVOS

Copper **Obv:** National arms **Rev:** Value below date within sprigs with double-lined V

Date	Mintage	VG8	F12	VF20	XF40	MS60
1915 SS Unique	—	—	—	—	—	—

KM# 614a 5 CENTAVOS

Copper **Obv:** National arms **Rev:** Value below date within sprigs with solid V

Date	Mintage	VG8	F12	VF20	XF40	MS60
1915 Rare	—	—	—	—	—	—

KM# 614b 5 CENTAVOS

Copper **Obv:** National arms **Rev:** Value above date **Note:** Mule.

Date	Mintage	VG8	F12	VF20	XF40	MS60
1915	—	—	500	—	—	—

KM# 614c 5 CENTAVOS

Copper **Obv:** National arms **Rev:** Liberty cap **Note:** Mule.

Date	Mintage	VG8	F12	VF20	XF40	MS60
1915 Rare	—	—	—	—	—	—

KM# 615 10 CENTAVOS

8.79 g., Copper, 27.5 mm. **Obv:** Liberty cap **Rev:** Value above date

Date	Mintage	VG8	F12	VF20	XF40	MS60
1915	—	1.25	2.50	3.50	8.00	20.00

KM# 615a 10 CENTAVOS

8.89 g., Brass, 27.5 mm. **Obv:** Liberty cap **Rev:** Value above date

Date	Mintage	VG8	F12	VF20	XF40	MS60
1915	—	5.00	10.00	30.00	50.00	—

Note: Many varieties exist

HIDALGO DEL PARRAL

Fuerzas Constitucionalistas

KM# 607 2 CENTAVOS

6.85 g., Copper, 25 mm. **Obv:** Liberty cap within circle flanked by sprigs **Rev:** Value flanked by sprigs within circle

Date	Mintage	VG8	F12	VF20	XF40	MS60
1913	—	5.00	10.00	25.00	50.00	—

KM# 607a 2 CENTAVOS

Brass **Obv:** Liberty cap within circle flanked by sprigs **Rev:** Value flanked by sprigs within circle

Date	Mintage	VG8	F12	VF20	XF40	MS60
1913	—	95.00	150	200	400	—

KM# 608 50 CENTAVOS

12.65 g., Silver **Obv:** Liberty cap **Rev:** Value flanked by sprigs below Liberty cap **Edge:** Reeded

Date	Mintage	VG8	F12	VF20	XF40	MS60
1913	—	18.00	40.00	80.00	150	—

KM# 609 50 CENTAVOS

12.17 g., Silver, 30 mm. **Edge:** Plain

Date	Mintage	VG8	F12	VF20	XF40	MS60
1913	—	50.00	70.00	125	250	—

KM# 609a 50 CENTAVOS

Copper **Edge:** Plain

Date	Mintage	VG8	F12	VF20	XF40	MS60
1913 rare	—	200	500	800	1,000	—

KM# 610 PESO

30.00 g., Silver **Obv:** Inscription **Rev:** 1 through PESO and small circle above sprigs **Note:** Weight varies 29.18-30.9g.

Date	Mintage	VG8	F12	VF20	XF40	MS60
1913	—	1,200	2,000	3,000	6,500	14,000

KM# 611 PESO

Silver, 38 mm. **Obv:** Inscription **Rev:** Value above sprigs **Note:** Well struck counterfeits of this coin exist with the dot at the end of the word Peso even with the bottom of the O. On legitimate pieces the dot is slightly higher. Weight varies 27.3-28.85g.

Date	Mintage	VG8	F12	VF20	XF40	MS60
1913	—	35.00	45.00	125	275	475

PATTERNS

Constitutionalist Army

KM#	Date	Mintage	Identification	Mkt Val
Pn1	1913	—	Peso. Silver.	15,000
Pn2.1	1914	—	50 Centavos. Copper. Reeded.	5,000
Pn2.2	1914	—	50 Centavos. Copper. Plain.	5,000
Note: Specimens exist in silver-plated copper				
Pn3	1914	—	Peso. Copper.	5,000
Pn4	1914	—	Peso. Silver.	31,000
Note: Silver or silver-plated copper pieces are modern fantasies				
Pn5	1915 MS	—	5 Centavos. Copper. Prev. KM#614.	600

DURANGO

A state in north central Mexico. Another area of operation for Pancho Villa. The *Muera Huerta* peso originates in this state. The coins were made in Cuencame under the orders of Generals Cemceros and Contreras.

CUENCAME

Muera Huerta (Death to Huerta)

REVOLUTIONARY COINAGE

KM# 620 PESO

Silver, 38 mm. **Obv:** National arms **Rev:** Liberty cap with written value flanked by stars

Date	Mintage	VG8	F12	VF20	XF40	MS60
1914	—	1,000	2,000	4,000	8,000	15,000

KM# 621 PESO

23.20 g., Silver, 39 mm. **Obv:** National arms with continuous border **Rev:** Liberty cap with continuous border

Date	Mintage	VG8	F12	VF20	XF40	MS60
1914	—	75.00	150	300	700	1,200

KM# 621a PESO

Copper **Obv:** National arms with continuous border **Rev:** Liberty cap with continuous border **Note:** Varieties exist.

Date	Mintage	VG8	F12	VF20	XF40	MS60
1914	—	400	600	2,000	3,000	—

KM# 621b PESO

Brass **Obv:** National arms **Rev:** Liberty cap

Date	Mintage	VG8	F12	VF20	XF40	MS60
1914	—	—	2,000	3,000	4,000	—

KM# 622 PESO
23.40 g., Silver, 38.5 mm. **Obv:** National arms with dot and dash border **Rev:** Liberty cap with continuous border **Note:** The so-called 20 Pesos gold Muera Huerta pieces are modern fantasies. Refer to Unusual World Coins, 4th edition, ©2005, KP Books, Inc.

Date	Mintage	VG8	F12	VF20	XF40	MS60
1914	—	65.00	120	300	600	1,100

ESTADO DE DURANGO

KM# 624 CENTAVO
Lead **Obv:** Date **Rev:** Value within wreath **Note:** Cast.

Date	Mintage	VG8	F12	VF20	XF40	MS60
1914	—	45.00	75.00	100	200	—

KM# 625 CENTAVO
3.29 g., Copper, 20 mm. **Obv:** Large date in center **Rev:** Value within wreath

Date	Mintage	VG8	F12	VF20	XF40	MS60
1914	—	2.00	4.00	10.00	20.00	—

KM# 625a CENTAVO
Brass **Obv:** Large date in center **Rev:** Value within wreath

Date	Mintage	VG8	F12	VF20	XF40	MS60
1914	—	75.00	200	400	500	—

KM# 625b CENTAVO
Lead **Obv:** Large date in center **Rev:** Value within wreath

Date	Mintage	VG8	F12	VF20	XF40	MS60
1914	—	20.00	40.00	65.00	90.00	—

KM# 625c CENTAVO
Copper **Obv:** Large date in center **Rev:** Value within wreath

Date	Mintage	VG8	F12	VF20	XF40	MS60
1914	—	25.00	50.00	80.00	125	—

KM# 626 CENTAVO
2.80 g., Copper, 20 mm. **Obv:** Date **Rev:** Value within wreath **Note:** Weight varies 2.46-2.78g.

Date	Mintage	VG8	F12	VF20	XF40	MS60
1914	—	15.00	20.00	40.00	50.00	—

KM# 626a CENTAVO
Brass **Obv:** Date **Rev:** Value within wreath

Date	Mintage	VG8	F12	VF20	XF40	MS60
1914	—	75.00	100	300	500	—

KM# 626b CENTAVO
Lead **Obv:** Date **Rev:** Value within wreath

Date	Mintage	VG8	F12	VF20	XF40	MS60
1914	—	20.00	40.00	70.00	125	—

Note: Varieties in size exist

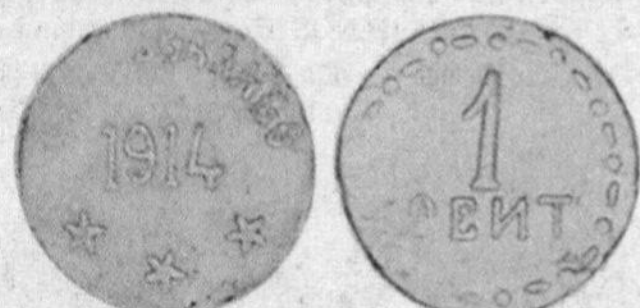

KM# 627 CENTAVO
Copper, 20 mm. **Obv:** Stars below date **Rev:** Value with retrograde N

Date	Mintage	VG8	F12	VF20	XF40	MS60
1914	—	6.00	12.00	30.00	45.00	—

KM# 627a CENTAVO
Lead, 20 mm. **Obv:** Stars below date **Rev:** Value with retrograde N

Date	Mintage	VG8	F12	VF20	XF40	MS60
1914	—	20.00	40.00	60.00	125	—

KM# 628 CENTAVO
Aluminum **Obv:** National arms within sprigs **Rev:** Value

Date	Mintage	VG8	F12	VF20	XF40	MS60
1914	—	0.65	1.00	2.00	4.00	12.00

KM# 629 5 CENTAVOS
6.20 g., Copper, 24 mm. **Obv:** Date above sprigs **Obv. Legend:** ESTADO DE DURANGO **Rev:** Value within designed wreath

Date	Mintage	VG8	F12	VF20	XF40	MS60
1914	—	2.00	3.00	8.00	15.00	—

KM# 630 5 CENTAVOS
Copper **Obv:** Date above sprigs **Obv. Legend:** E. DE DURANGO **Rev:** Value within designed wreath

Date	Mintage	VG8	F12	VF20	XF40	MS60
1914	—	125	275	450	700	—

KM# 631 5 CENTAVOS
5.05 g., Copper, 23.5 mm. **Obv:** Date above sprigs **Obv. Legend:** E. DE DURANGO **Rev:** Value within designed wreath

Date	Mintage	VG8	F12	VF20	XF40	MS60
1914	—	1.25	3.00	6.00	15.00	—

KM# 631a 5 CENTAVOS
Brass **Obv:** Date above sprigs **Obv. Legend:** E. DE DURANGO **Rev:** Value within designed wreath

Date	Mintage	VG8	F12	VF20	XF40	MS60
1914	—	30.00	40.00	70.00	100	—

KM# 631b 5 CENTAVOS
Lead **Obv:** Date above sprigs **Obv. Legend:** E. DE DURANGO **Rev:** Value within designed wreath

Date	Mintage	VG8	F12	VF20	XF40	MS60
1914	—	45.00	70.00	100	180	—

KM# 632 5 CENTAVOS
4.61 g., Copper, 23.5 mm. **Obv:** Date above sprigs **Obv. Legend:** E. DE DURANGO **Rev:** Roman numeral value

Date	Mintage	VG8	F12	VF20	XF40	MS60
1914	—	4.00	8.00	20.00	50.00	—

KM# 632a 5 CENTAVOS
Lead **Obv:** Date above sprigs **Obv. Legend:** E. DE DURANGO **Rev:** Roman numeral value

Date	Mintage	VG8	F12	VF20	XF40	MS60
1914	—	50.00	75.00	100	150	—

KM# 633 5 CENTAVOS
Lead **Obv:** Three stars below 1914 **Rev:** 5 CVS **Note:** Counterfeits are prevalent in the market

Date	Mintage	VG8	F12	VF20	XF40	MS60
1914	—	—	600	2,000	—	—

KM# 634 5 CENTAVOS
Brass **Obv:** National arms above sprigs **Obv. Legend:** REPUBLICA MEXICANA **Rev:** Value **Rev. Legend:** ESTADO DE DURANGO

Date	Mintage	VG8	F12	VF20	XF40	MS60
1914	—	0.50	1.00	2.50	6.00	12.00

KM# 634a 5 CENTAVOS
Copper **Obv:** National arms above sprigs **Obv. Legend:** REPUBLICA MEXICANA **Rev:** Value **Rev. Legend:** ESTADO DE DURANGO **Note:** There are numerous varieties of these general types of the Durango 1 and 5 Centavo pieces.

Date	Mintage	VG8	F12	VF20	XF40	MS60
1914	—	75.00	125	175	250	—

KM# 634b 5 CENTAVOS
6.89 g., Copper-Nickel, 25.53 mm. **Obv:** National arms above sprigs **Obv. Legend:** REPUBLICA MEXICANA **Rev:** Value **Rev. Legend:** ESTADO DE DURANGO **Edge:** Plain

Date	Mintage	F12	VF20	XF40	MS60	MS63
1914	—	25.00	50.00	85.00	135	200

GUERRERO

Guerrero is a state on the southwestern coast of Mexico. It was one of the areas of operation of Zapata and his forces in the south of Mexico. The Zapata forces operated seven different mints in this state. The date ranges were from 1914 to 1917 and denominations from 2 Centavos to 2 Pesos. Some were cast but most were struck and the rarest coin of the group is the Suriana 1915 2 Pesos.

EMILIANO ZAPATA

(General Salgado)

REVOLUTIONARY COINAGE

KM# 638 2 CENTAVOS
6.00 g., Copper, 22 mm. **Obv:** National arms **Obv. Legend:** REPUBLICA @XH@Z MEXICANA **Rev:** Value within wreath **Note:** Weight varies 5.4-6.03g.

Date	Mintage	VG8	F12	VF20	XF40	MS60
1915	—	75.00	125	175	250	—

KM# 635 3 CENTAVOS
Copper, 25 mm. **Obv:** National arms **Obv. Legend:** REPUBLICA MEXICANA **Rev:** Value within wreath **Note:** Weight varies 4.63-6.87g.

Date	Mintage	VG8	F12	VF20	XF40	MS60
1915	—	500	1,500	2,000	3,000	—

KM# 636 5 CENTAVOS
Copper, 26 mm. **Obv:** National arms **Rev:** Value within wreath

Date	Mintage	VG8	F12	VF20	XF40	MS60
1915 GRO	—	800	1,200	2,000	3,000	—

KM# 637.1 10 CENTAVOS
Copper, 27-28.5 mm. **Obv:** National arms, snake head ends at L in REPUBLICA **Obv. Legend:** REPUBLICA MEXICANA **Rev:** Date and value within wreath **Note:** Size varies.

Date	Mintage	VG8	F12	VF20	XF40	MS60
1915 GRO	—	600	1,000	1,500	2,000	—

KM# 637.2 10 CENTAVOS
Copper, 27-28.5 mm. **Obv:** National arms, snake head ends at C in REPUBLICA **Obv. Legend:** REPUBLICA MEXICANA **Rev:** Value within wreath **Note:** Size varies.

Date	Mintage	VG8	F12	VF20	XF40	MS60
1915 GRO	—	3.00	5.00	8.00	15.00	—

KM# 637.2a 10 CENTAVOS
8.23 g., Brass, 26 mm. **Obv:** National arms, snake head ends at C in REPUBLICA **Obv. Legend:** REPUBLICA MEXICANA **Rev:** Value within wreath

Date	Mintage	VG8	F12	VF20	XF40	MS60
1915 GRO	—	8.00	15.00	25.00	50.00	—

KM# 637.2b 10 CENTAVOS
Lead **Obv:** National arms, snake head ends at C in REPUBLICA **Obv. Legend:** REPUBLICA MEXICANA **Rev:** Value within wreath

Date	Mintage	VG8	F12	VF20	XF40	MS60
1915 GRO	—	50.00	75.00	175	275	—

KM# 637.3 10 CENTAVOS
Copper **Obv:** National arms, snake head ends before A in REPUBLICA **Obv. Legend:** REPUBLICA MEXICANA **Rev:** Date and value within wreath

Date	Mintage	VG8	F12	VF20	XF40	MS60
1915. GRO	—	3.00	5.00	8.00	15.00	—

KM# 637.3a 10 CENTAVOS
Brass **Obv:** National arms, snake head ends before A in REPUBLICA **Obv. Legend:** REPUBLICA MEXICANA **Rev:** Value and date within wreath

Date	Mintage	VG8	F12	VF20	XF40	MS60
1915. GRO	—	12.00	20.00	50.00	100	—

KM# 639 25 CENTAVOS
7.50 g., Silver, 25 mm. **Obv:** Liberty cap **Obv. Legend:** Mexicana REPUbLICA **Rev:** Value above date **Note:** Weight varies 7.41-7.5g.

Date	Mintage	VG8	F12	VF20	XF40	MS60
1915	—	125	300	800	1,200	—

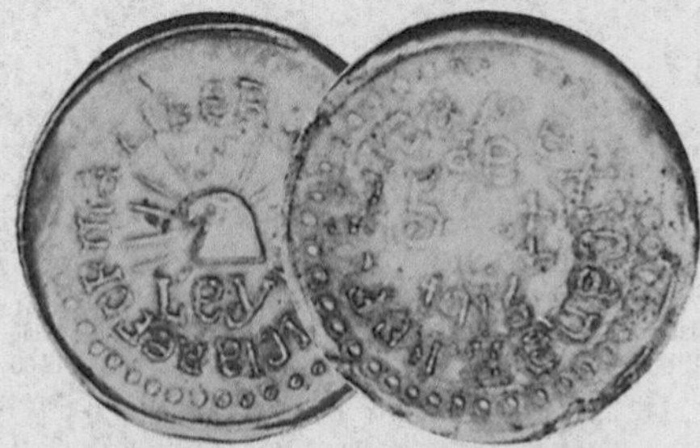

KM# 640 50 CENTAVOS
14.80 g., Silver, 34 mm. **Obv:** Liberty cap **Rev:** Date and value within beaded border **Note:** Weight varies 14.5-14.8g.

Date	Mintage	VG8	F12	VF20	XF40	MS60
1915	—	1,000	2,000	6,000	15,000	—

KM# 641 PESO (UN)
0.300 Gold with Silver, 29-31 mm. **Obv:** National arms **Obv. Legend:** REPUBLICA MEXICANA - ★ UN PESO **Rev:** Liberty cap and rays within sprigs **Rev. Legend:** REFORMA LIBERTAD JUSTICIA Y LEY **Rev. Inscription:** Oro: 0,300 **Note:** Many die varieties exist. Size varies. Weight varies 10.28-14.84g.

Date	Mintage	VG8	F12	VF20	XF40	MS60
1914 GRO	—	20.00	30.00	40.00	85.00	—

KM# 641a PESO (UN)
Copper **Obv:** National arms **Obv. Legend:** REPUBLICA MEXICANA - ★ UN PESO **Rev:** Liberty cap and rays within sprigs **Rev. Legend:** REFORMA LIBERTAD JUSTICIA Y LEY

Date	Mintage	G4	VG8	F12	VF20	XF40
1914 GRO	—	32.00	80.00	200	500	1,500

KM# 642 PESO (UN)
0.300 Gold with Silver, 30.5-31 mm. **Obv:** National arms **Obv. Legend:** REPUBLICA MEXICANA - ★ UN PESO (star) **Rev:** Liberty cap and rays within sprigs **Rev. Legend:** REFORMA. LIBERTAD.JUSTICIA Y LEY **Rev. Inscription:** Oro: 0,300 **Note:** Weight varies 12.93-14.66g.

Date	Mintage	VG8	F12	VF20	XF40	MS60
1914 GRO	—	50.00	75.00	100	180	—
1915 GRO	—	600	1,000	1,500	1,850	—

KM# 643 2 PESOS (Dos)
Gold with Silver, 38.25-39.6 mm. **Obv:** National arms **Obv. Legend:** REPUBLICA MEXICANA **Rev:** Radiant sun face above high mountain peaks **Rev. Legend:** "REFORMA LIBERTAD, JUSTICIA Y LEY", **Rev. Inscription:** Oro: 0,595 **Note:** Many varieties exist. Coin is 0.595g fine Gold.

Date	Mintage	VG8	F12	VF20	XF40	MS60
1914 GRO	—	25.00	45.00	125	200	600

KM# 643a 2 PESOS (Dos)
Copper, 38-38.5 mm. **Obv:** National arms **Obv. Legend:** REPUBLICA MEXICANA **Rev:** Radiant sun face above high mountain peaks **Rev. Legend:** REFORMA, LIBERTAD, JUSTICIA Y LEY **Note:** Size varies.

Date	Mintage	G4	VG8	F12	VF20	XF40
1914 GRO	—	—	—	1,400	1,800	4,000

KM# 644 2 PESOS (Dos)
Gold with Silver, 39-40 mm. **Obv:** National arms **Obv. Legend:** REPUBLICA MEXICANA **Rev:** Radiant sun face above high and low mountain peaks **Rev. Legend:** REFORMA, LIBERTAD, JUSTICIA Y LEY **Rev. Inscription:** Oro: 0,595 **Note:** Weight varies 21.71-26.54g. Coin is 0.595g fine Gold.

Date	Mintage	VG8	F12	VF20	XF40	MS60
1915 GRO	—	65.00	85.00	160	250	550

KM# 644a 2 PESOS (Dos)
Copper **Obv:** National arms **Obv. Legend:** REPUBLICA MEXICANA **Rev:** Radiant sun face above high and low mountain peaks **Rev. Legend:** REFORMA, LIBERTAD, JUSTICIA Y LEY

Date	Mintage	VG8	F12	VF20	XF40	MS60
1915 GRO	—	400	1,000	1,500	2,500	—

ATLIXTAC

KM# 645 10 CENTAVOS
Copper, 27.5-28 mm. **Obv:** National arms **Obv. Legend:** REPUBLICA MEXICANA **Rev:** Value within sprigs **Note:** Size varies. Weight varies 4.76-9.74g.

Date	Mintage	VG8	F12	VF20	XF40	MS60
1915	—	3.00	5.00	8.00	15.00	—

KM# 646 10 CENTAVOS
Copper, 27.55-28 mm. **Obv:** National arms **Obv. Legend:** REPUBLICA ★ Z MEXICANA **Rev:** Value within sprigs **Note:** Size varies. Weight varies 6.13-7.94g.

Date	Mintage	VG8	F12	VF20	XF40	MS60
1915	—	3.00	5.00	8.00	15.00	—

CACAHUATEPEC

KM# 648 5 CENTAVOS
12.19 g., Copper, 28 mm. **Obv:** National arms **Obv. Legend:** ESTADOS UNIDOS MEXICANOS **Rev:** Value within wreath

Date	Mintage	VG8	F12	VF20	XF40	MS60
1917	—	12.00	25.00	40.00	75.00	—

KM# 649 20 CENTAVOS
Silver, 21-23.8 mm. **Obv:** National arms **Obv. Legend:** ESTADOS UNIDOS MEXICANOS **Rev:** Value within sprigs below liberty cap and rays **Note:** Size varies. Weight varies 3.99-6.2g.

Date	Mintage	VG8	F12	VF20	XF40	MS60
1917	—	100	200	350	400	—

KM# 650 50 CENTAVOS

13.80 g., Silver, 30-30.3 mm. **Obv:** National arms **Obv. Legend:** ESTADOS UNIDOS MEXICANOS **Rev:** Value and date within sprigs below Liberty cap **Note:** Size varies. Weight varies 13.45-13.78g.

Date	Mintage	VG8	F12	VF20	XF40	MS60
1917	—	25.00	65.00	150	375	—

KM# 651 PESO (UN)

Silver, 38 mm. **Obv:** National arms **Rev:** Liberty cap **Note:** Weight varies 26.81-32.05g.

Date	Mintage	VG8	F12	VF20	XF40	MS60
1917 L.V. Go	—	2,000	4,000	10,000	12,000	—

CACALOTEPEC

KM# 652 20 CENTAVOS

Silver, 22.5 mm. **Obv:** National arms **Obv. Legend:** ESTADOS UNIDOS MEXICANOS **Rev:** Date and value within sprigs below Liberty cap and rays **Note:** Weight varies 3.89-5.73g.

Date	Mintage	VG8	F12	VF20	XF40	MS60
1917	—	1,000	1,800	4,000	8,000	—

CAMPO MORADO

KM# 653 5 CENTAVOS

4.37 g., Copper, 23.5-24 mm. **Obv:** National arms **Rev:** Value within wreath **Note:** Size varies.

Date	Mintage	VG8	F12	VF20	XF40	MS60
1915 C.M.	—	9.00	15.00	22.50	50.00	—

KM# 654 10 CENTAVOS

Copper, 25.25-26 mm. **Obv:** National arms **Rev:** Value and date within wreath **Note:** Size varies. Weight varies. 4.48-8.77g.

Date	Mintage	VG8	F12	VF20	XF40	MS60
1915 C.M. GRO	—	6.00	10.00	20.00	30.00	—

KM# 655 20 CENTAVOS

Copper, 28 mm. **Obv:** National arms **Rev:** Date above star and value within wreath **Note:** Weight varies 4.48-9g.

Date	Mintage	VG8	F12	VF20	XF40	MS60
1915 C.M..GRO	—	15.00	25.00	35.00	50.00	—

KM# 656 50 CENTAVOS

Copper, 29-31 mm. **Obv:** National arms **Rev:** Date and value within wreath **Note:** Size varies. Weight varies 9.81-16.77g.

Date	Mintage	VG8	F12	VF20	XF40	MS60
1915 C.M. GRO	—	12.00	20.00	30.00	60.00	—

KM# 657 50 CENTAVOS

Copper, 30-31 mm. **Obv:** National arms **Rev:** Date and value within wreath **Note:** Regular obverse. Size varies. Weight varies 6.49-13.19g.

Date	Mintage	VG8	F12	VF20	XF40	MS60
1915 C.M. GRO	—	6.00	10.00	15.00	50.00	—

KM# 657a 50 CENTAVOS

Billon **Obv:** National arms **Rev:** Date and value within wreath **Note:** Regular obverse.

Date	Mintage	VG8	F12	VF20	XF40	MS60
1915 C.M. GRO	—	200	300	500	1,000	—

KM# 658 PESO (UN)

Gold with Silver, 32-32.5 mm. **Obv:** National arms **Rev:** Liberty cap **Rev. Inscription:** Oro: 0,300 **Note:** Weight varies 12.42-16.5g. Coin is 0.300g fine Gold.

Date	Mintage	VG8	F12	VF20	XF40	MS60
1914 Co Mo Gro	—	500	600	1,000	1,200	—

KM# 658a PESO (UN)

Brass **Obv:** National arms **Rev:** Liberty cap

Date	Mintage	VG8	F12	VF20	XF40	MS60
1914 Co Mo Gro Unique	—	—	—	—	10,000	—

KM# 659 PESO (UN)

Gold with Silver, 30-31 mm. **Obv:** National arms **Rev:** Liberty cap within sprigs **Rev. Inscription:** Oro: 0,300 **Note:** Weight varies 12.26-15.81g. Coin is 0.300g fine Gold.

Date	Mintage	VG8	F12	VF20	XF40	MS60
1914 CAMPO Mo	—	20.00	35.00	50.00	85.00	—

KM# 660 2 PESOS (Dos)

Gold with Silver, 38.9-39 mm. **Obv:** National arms **Rev:** Sun over mountains **Rev. Inscription:** Oro: 0,595 **Note:** Weight varies 20.6-26.02g. Coin is 0.595g fine Gold.

Date	Mintage	VG8	F12	VF20	XF40	MS60
1915 Co. Mo.	—	18.00	22.00	40.00	85.00	425

KM# 660a 2 PESOS (Dos)

Copper **Obv:** National arms **Rev:** Sun over mountains

Date	Mintage	VG8	F12	VF20	XF40	MS60
1915 Co. Mo.	—	—	800	1,000	1,200	—

KM# 661 2 PESOS (Dos)

29.44 g., Gold with Silver, 39 mm. **Obv:** National arms **Rev:** Sun and mountains **Rev. Inscription:** Oro: 0,595 **Note:** Coin is 0.595g fine Gold.

Date	Mintage	VG8	F12	VF20	XF40	MS60
1915 Co. Mo.	—	2,500	5,000	9,000	15,000	—

KM# 662 2 PESOS (Dos)

0.60 g., 1.000 Gold with Silver 0.0191 oz., 34.5-35 mm. **Obv:** National arms **Rev:** Liberty cap **Note:** Size varies. Weight varies 18.27-20.08g.

Date	Mintage	VG8	F12	VF20	XF40	MS60
1915 C. M. GRO	—	25.00	35.00	65.00	125	—

KM# 662a.1 2 PESOS (Dos)

Copper **Obv:** National arms **Rev:** Liberty cap

Date	Mintage	VG8	F12	VF20	XF40	MS60
1915 C. M. GRO	—	—	—	—	1,200	—

KM# 662a.2 2 PESOS (Dos)

Copper **Obv:** National arms **Rev:** Liberty cap

Date	Mintage	VG8	F12	VF20	XF40	MS60
1915 C. M. GRO Unique	—	—	—	—	—	—

CHILPANCINGO

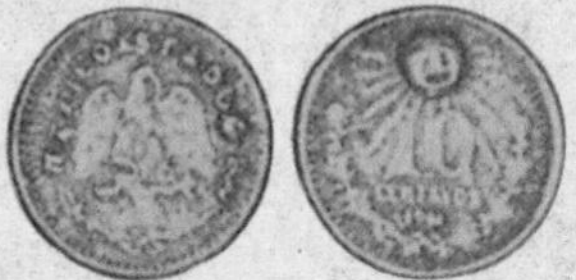

KM# 663 10 CENTAVOS

2.52 g., Cast Silver, 18 mm. **Obv:** National arms **Rev:** Sun above value and sprigs

Date	Mintage	VG8	F12	VF20	XF40	MS60
1914	—	700	1,000	1,200	1,500	—

Note: Many counterfeits exist

KM# 664 20 CENTAVOS
4.94 g., Cast Silver, 21.5 mm. **Obv:** National arms **Rev:** Sun above value and sprigs

Date	Mintage	VG8	F12	VF20	XF40	MS60
1914	—	700	1,000	1,200	1,500	—

Note: Many counterfeits exist

SURIANA

KM# 665 2 PESOS (Dos)
22.93 g., Gold with Silver, 39 mm. **Obv:** National arms **Rev:** Sun over mountains **Rev. Inscription:** Oro: 0,595 **Note:** Coin is 0.595g fine Gold.

Date	Mintage	VG8	F12	VF20	XF40	MS60
1915 Rare	—	—	—	20,000	35,000	—

Note: Ira & Larry Goldberg - Millenia sale, 5-08 AU-55 replica. Ponterio & Associates sale, 4-09 VF realized $17,000. Spink America Gerber sale part 2, 6-96 VF realized $16,500

TAXCO

KM# 667 2 CENTAVOS
Copper, 25.25-26 mm. **Obv:** National arms **Obv. Legend:** EDO.DE.GRO **Rev:** Value within sprigs **Note:** Size varies. Weight varies 6.81-8.55g.

Date	Mintage	VG8	F12	VF20	XF40	MS60
1915 O/T	—	25.00	40.00	60.00	90.00	—

KM# 668 5 CENTAVOS
Copper **Obv:** National arms **Obv. Legend:** REPUBLICA * MEXICANA **Rev:** Value within sprigs **Note:** Weight varies 7.13-7.39g.

Date	Mintage	VG8	F12	VF20	XF40	MS60
1915	—	10.00	20.00	40.00	80.00	—

KM# 669 10 CENTAVOS
Copper, 27-28 mm. **Obv:** National arms **Obv. Legend:** REPUBLICA * MEXICANA **Rev:** Date and value within sprigs **Note:** Size varies. Weight varies 7.51-8.67g.

Date	Mintage	VG8	F12	VF20	XF40	MS60
1915	—	9.00	20.00	35.00	50.00	—

KM# 670 50 CENTAVOS
5.45 g., Copper, 27-28 mm. **Obv:** National arms with legend in large letters **Rev:** Value within sprigs **Note:** Size varies.

Date	Mintage	VG8	F12	VF20	XF40	MS60
1915	—	15.00	25.00	50.00	65.00	—

KM# 671 50 CENTAVOS
Silver, 27.6-28 mm. **Obv:** National arms **Rev:** Sun above value and sprigs **Note:** Size varies. Weight varies 8.95-10.85g.

Date	Mintage	VG8	F12	VF20	XF40	MS60
1915	—	25.00	40.00	80.00	150	—

KM# 672 PESO (UN)
Gold with Silver, 30-31 mm. **Obv:** National arms **Rev:** Liberty cap within sprigs **Rev. Inscription:** Oro: 0,300 **Note:** Weight varies 30-31g. Coin is 0.300g fine Gold.

Date	Mintage	VG8	F12	VF20	XF40	MS60
1915	—	18.00	22.00	50.00	90.00	—

KM# 672a PESO (UN)
Brass **Obv:** National arms **Rev:** Liberty cap within sprigs

Date	Mintage	VG8	F12	VF20	XF40	MS60
1915	—	300	500	700	1,000	—

KM# 672b PESO (UN)
Lead **Obv:** National arms **Rev:** Liberty cap within sprigs

Date	Mintage	VG8	F12	VF20	XF40	MS60
1915	—	50.00	200	300	500	—

KM# 672c PESO (UN)
Copper **Obv:** National arms **Rev:** Liberty cap within sprigs

Date	Mintage	VG8	F12	VF20	XF40	MS60
1915	—	200	300	400	650	—

KM# 673 PESO (UN)
11.60 g., Gold with Silver, 30 mm. **Obv:** National arms **Rev:** Liberty cap within sprigs **Rev. Inscription:** Oro: 0,300 **Note:** Coin is 0.300g fine Gold.

Date	Mintage	VG8	F12	VF20	XF40	MS60
1915	—	250	500	800	1,000	—

KM# 674 PESO (UN)
Gold with Silver, 30 mm. **Obv:** National arms **Rev:** Liberty cap within sprigs **Rev. Inscription:** Oro: 0,300 **Note:** Weight varies 10.51-12.79g. Coin is 0.300g fine Gold.

Date	Mintage	VG8	F12	VF20	XF40	MS60
1915	—	100	200	300	550	—

PATTERNS

Including off metal strikes

KM#	Date	Mintage	Identification	Mkt Val
Pn647	1914	—	2 Pesos. Gold with Silver. Atlixtac.	—
Pn674	1914	—	2 Pesos. 1.000. Gold with Silver.	—

JALISCO

Jalisco is a state on the west coast of Mexico. The few coins made for this state show that the *Army of the North* did not restrict their operations to the northern border states. The coins were made in Guadalajara under the watchful eye of General Dieguez, commander of this segment of Villa's forces.

GUADALAJARA

REVOLUTIONARY COINAGE

KM# 675 CENTAVO
Copper **Obv:** Liberty cap **Rev:** Value

Date	Mintage	VG8	F12	VF20	XF40	MS60
1915	—	9.50	15.00	20.00	30.00	—

KM# 675a CENTAVO
Brass **Obv:** Liberty cap **Rev:** Value

Date	Mintage	VG8	F12	VF20	XF40	MS60
1915	—	—	—	400	550	—

KM# A676 CENTAVO
Copper **Obv:** Liberty cap **Rev:** Retrograde value **Note:** Varieties exist.

Date	Mintage	VG8	F12	VF20	XF40	MS60
1915	—	100	300	600	1,000	—

KM# 676.1 2 CENTAVOS
Copper, 20 mm. **Obv:** Liberty cap **Rev:** Value

Date	Mintage	VG8	F12	VF20	XF40	MS60
1915	—	10.00	18,00	20.00	35.00	—

Note: Varieties exist.

KM# 676.2 2 CENTAVOS
Copper **Obv:** Sm. Liberty cap **Rev:** Value

Date	Mintage	VG8	F12	VF20	XF40	MS60
1915	—	200	300	500	800	—

KM# 677 5 CENTAVOS
Copper, 24 mm. **Obv:** Liberty cap **Rev:** Value

Date	Mintage	VG8	F12	VF20	XF40	MS60
1915	—	6.50	20.00	40.00	60.00	—

KM# 677a 5 CENTAVOS
Brass **Obv:** Liberty cap **Rev:** Value

Date	Mintage	VG8	F12	VF20	XF40	MS60
1915 rare	—	—	—	—	—	—

KM# 678 10 CENTAVOS
Copper **Obv:** Liberty cap above value and date **Rev:** Crowned shield

Date	Mintage	VG8	F12	VF20	XF40	MS60
1915	—	—	—	5,000	12,000	—

KM# A678 PESO
Copper **Obv:** Liberty cap above value and date **Rev:** Crowned shield

Date	Mintage	VG8	F12	VF20	XF40	MS60
1915	—	—	—	—	20,000	—

MEXICO, ESTADO DE

Estado de Mexico is a state in central Mexico that surrounds the Federal District on three sides. The issues by the Zapata forces in this state have two distinctions – the Amecameca pieces are the crudest and the Toluca cardboard piece is the most unusual. General Tenorio authorized the crude incuse Amecameca pieces.

AMECAMECA

REVOLUTIONARY COINAGE

KM# 679 5 CENTAVOS
12.55 g., Brass, 24.5 mm. **Obv:** Legend **Obv. Legend:** EJERCITO CONVENCIONISTA **Rev:** Value above cent sign

Date	Mintage	VG8	F12	VF20	XF40	MS60
ND(1915) unique	—	—	—	—	—	—

KM# 680 5 CENTAVOS
12.77 g., Brass, 24.6 mm. **Obv:** National arms above RM **Rev:** Value above cent sign **Note:** Hand stamped.

Date	Mintage	VG8	F12	VF20	XF40	MS60
ND(1915)	—	300	500	800	1,000	—

KM# 681 10 CENTAVOS
15.00 g., Brass, 24.5-24.8 mm. **Obv:** National arms above RM **Rev:** Value above cent sign **Note:** Hand stamped. Varieties exist. Size varies.

Date	Mintage	VG8	F12	VF20	XF40	MS60
ND(1915)	—	60.00	90.00	150	200	—

KM# 681a 10 CENTAVOS
Copper **Obv:** National arms above RM **Rev:** Value above cent sign **Note:** Hand stamped.

Date	Mintage	VG8	F12	VF20	XF40	MS60
ND(1915)	—	75.00	125	225	350	—

KM# 682 20 CENTAVOS
Brass, 24-25 mm. **Obv:** National arms above RM **Rev:** Value above cent sign **Note:** Hand stamped. Varieties exist. Size varies. Weight varies 11.34-12.86g.

Date	Mintage	VG8	F12	VF20	XF40	MS60
ND(1915)	—	15.00	22.50	35.00	60.00	—

KM# 682a 20 CENTAVOS
Copper **Obv:** National arms above RM **Rev:** Value above cent sign **Note:** Hand stamped.

Date	Mintage	VG8	F12	VF20	XF40	MS60
ND(1915)	—	25.00	50.00	175	250	—

KM# 683 20 CENTAVOS
Copper, 19-20 mm. **Obv:** National arms above A. D. J. **Rev:** Value **Note:** Size varies. Weight varies 3.99-5.35g.

Date	Mintage	VG8	F12	VF20	XF40	MS60
ND(1915)	—	7.50	12.50	20.00	35.00	—

KM# 683a 20 CENTAVOS
Brass **Obv:** National arms above A. D. J. **Rev:** Value

Date	Mintage	VG8	F12	VF20	XF40	MS60
ND(1915)	—	—	—	300	500	—

KM# 684 25 CENTAVOS
Brass **Obv:** Legend **Obv. Legend:** EJERCITO CONVENCIONISTA **Rev:** Value above cent sign

Date	Mintage	VG8	F12	VF20	XF40	MS60
ND(1915) unique	—	—	—	—	—	—

KM# 685 25 CENTAVOS
Copper, 25 mm. **Obv:** National arms above sprigs **Rev:** Large numeral value **Note:** Hand stamped. Many modern counterfeits exist in all metals. Weight varies 6.32-6.99g.

Date	Mintage	VG8	F12	VF20	XF40	MS60
ND(1915)	—	15.00	20.00	30.00	40.00	—

KM# 685a 25 CENTAVOS
7.92 g., Brass, 25 mm. **Obv:** National arms above sprigs **Rev:** Large numeral value **Note:** Hand stamped.

Date	Mintage	VG8	F12	VF20	XF40	MS60
ND(1915)	—	—	—	100	300	—

KM# 685b 25 CENTAVOS
Silver **Obv:** National arms above sprigs **Rev:** Large numeral value **Note:** Hand stamped.

Date	Mintage	VG8	F12	VF20	XF40	MS60
ND(1915)	—	—	—	300	500	—

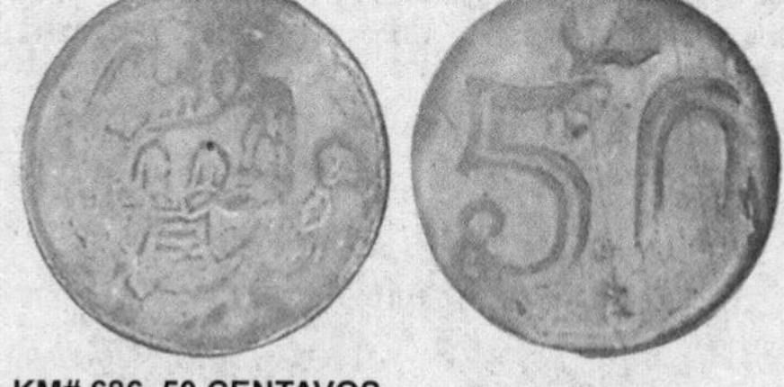

KM# 686 50 CENTAVOS
Copper, 28-28.5 mm. **Obv:** Eagle over sprays **Note:** Hand stamped. Size varies.

Date	Mintage	VG8	F12	VF20	XF40	MS60
ND(1915)	—	8.00	10.00	18.00	30.00	—

KM# 686a 50 CENTAVOS
16.04 g., Brass, 28.5 mm. **Obv:** National arms above sprigs **Rev:** Large numeral value **Note:** Hand stamped.

Date	Mintage	VG8	F12	VF20	XF40	MS60
ND(1915)	—	100	200	300	400	—

Note: Stem of "¢" above the 5

KM# 687 50 CENTAVOS
Copper, 23.5-29 mm. **Obv:** National arms above sprigs **Rev:** Large numeral value **Note:** Contemporary counterfeit, hand engraved. Size varies. Weight varies 8.8-10.8g.

Date	Mintage	VG8	F12	VF20	XF40	MS60
ND(1915)	—	12.00	30.00	50.00	80.00	—

Note: "¢" clears top of 5

TENANCINGO, TOWN

(Distrito Federal Mexico)

KM# 688.1 2 CENTAVOS
Copper **Obv:** National arms **Rev:** Value within wreath without TM below value

Date	Mintage	VG8	F12	VF20	XF40	MS60
1915	—	—	400	2,000	6,000	—

KM# 688.2 2 CENTAVOS
Copper **Obv:** National arms **Rev:** Value within wreath with TM below value

Date	Mintage	VG8	F12	VF20	XF40	MS60
1915	—	—	400	1,000	5,000	—

KM# 689.1 5 CENTAVOS
Copper, 19 mm. **Obv:** National arms **Rev:** Numeral value over lined C within wreath **Note:** Weight varies 2.83-2.84g.

Date	Mintage	VG8	F12	VF20	XF40	MS60
1915	—	10.00	20.00	40.00	60.00	—

KM# 689.2 5 CENTAVOS
Copper, 19 mm. **Obv:** National arms **Rev:** Numeral value over solid C within wreath **Note:** Weight varies 2.83-2.84g.

Date	Mintage	VG8	F12	VF20	XF40	MS60
1915	—	200	400	800	1,200	—

KM# 690.1 10 CENTAVOS
Copper, 25.25 mm. **Obv:** National arms **Rev:** Value over lined C within wreath below date **Note:** Weight varies 4.27-5.64g.

Date	Mintage	VG8	F12	VF20	XF40	MS60
1916	—	10.00	20.00	40.00	80.00	—

KM# 690.2 10 CENTAVOS
Copper, 25.25 mm. **Obv:** National arms **Rev:** Value over lined C within wreath **Note:** Weight varies 4.27-5.64g.

Date	Mintage	VG8	F12	VF20	XF40	MS60
1916	—	100	300	500	800	—

KM# 691 20 CENTAVOS
Copper, 27.5-28 mm. **Obv:** National arms **Rev:** Value and date above sprigs **Note:** Size varies. Weight varies 8.51-11.39g.

Date	Mintage	VG8	F12	VF20	XF40	MS60
1915	—	25.00	40.00	55.00	85.00	—

TOLUCA, CITY

(Distrito Federal Mexico)

KM# 692.1 5 CENTAVOS
Cardboard grey in color, 27-28 mm. **Obv:** Crowned shield within sprigs **Rev:** Banner across large numeral value **Note:** Size varies. Weight varies 1.04-1.16g.

Date	Mintage	VG8	F12	VF20	XF40	MS60
1915	—	15.00	30.00	50.00	100	—

KM# 692.2 5 CENTAVOS
Cardboard grey in color, 27-28 mm. **Obv:** Crowned shield within sprigs **Rev:** Banner accross large numeral value **Note:** Size varies. Weight varies 1.04-1.16g.

Date	Mintage	VG8	F12	VF20	XF40	MS60
1915	—	15.00	30.00	50.00	100	—

COUNTERMARKED COINAGE

KM# 693.1 20 CENTAVOS
Copper, 20 mm. **Obv:** National arms **Rev:** Numeral 20 within C and inner circle within sprigs **Countermark:** 20 within C **Note:** Countermark on 1 Centavo, KM#415. Varieties exist. Weight varies 2.65-2.95g.

CM Date	Host Date	VG8	F12	VF20	XF40	MS60
ND(1915)		20.00	40.00	55.00	95.00	—

KM# 693.2 20 CENTAVOS
Copper, 20 mm. **Obv:** National arms **Rev:** Numeral 20 within C and inner circle within 3/4 wreath **Countermark:** 20 within C **Note:** Countermark on 1 Centavo, KM#394.1. Weight varies 2.65-2.95g.

CM Date	Host Date	VG8	F12	VF20	XF40	MS60
ND(1915)	1904	30.00	50.00	90.00	165	—

KM# 694 40 CENTAVOS
5.86 g., Copper, 24.75-25 mm. **Obv:** National arms **Rev:** Numeral 40 within C and inner circle within wreath **Countermark:** 40 within C **Note:** Countermark on 2 Centavos, KM#419. Varieties exist. Size varies.

CM Date	Host Date	VG8	F12	VF20	XF40	MS60
ND(1915)		25.00	60.00	80.00	150	—

MORELOS

Morelos is a state in south central Mexico, adjoining the federal district on the south. It was the headquarters of Emiliano Zapata. His personal quarters were at Tlatizapan in Morelos. The Morelos coins from 2 Centavos to 1 Peso were all copper except one type of 1 Peso in silver. The two operating Zapatista mints in Morelos were Atlihuayan and Tlaltizapan.

EMILIANO ZAPATA

(Zapatista)

REVOLUTIONARY COINAGE

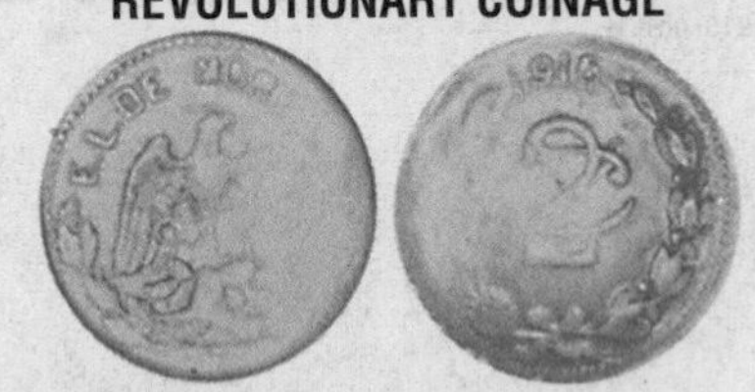

KM# 695 2 CENTAVOS
Copper, 23 mm. **Obv:** National arms **Obv. Legend:** E.L. DE MORELOS **Rev:** Value within wreath

Date	Mintage	VG8	F12	VF20	XF40	MS60
1915	—	1,000	1,400	1,800	2,750	—

KM# 696 5 CENTAVOS
9.00 g., Copper, 25.9 mm. **Obv:** National arms **Rev:** Value within 3/4 wreath **Rev. Legend:** E. DE MOR. 1915

Date	Mintage	VG8	F12	VF20	XF40	MS60
1915	—	300	800	2,000	5,000	—

KM# 697 10 CENTAVOS
8.69 g., Copper, 24 mm. **Obv:** National arms **Rev:** Value within lined C and wreath

Date	Mintage	VG8	F12	VF20	XF40	MS60
1915	—	12.00	20.00	30.00	40.00	—

KM# 698 10 CENTAVOS
Copper, 24-24.5 mm. **Obv:** National arms **Rev:** Value within lined C and wreath with date effaced from die **Note:** Size varies. Weight varies 4.83-6.8g.

Date	Mintage	VG8	F12	VF20	XF40	MS60
ND(1915)	—	12.00	20.00	35.00	55.00	—

KM# 699 10 CENTAVOS
Copper **Obv:** National arms **Rev:** Date and value within wreath **Rev. Legend:** E. DE MOR

Date	Mintage	VG8	F12	VF20	XF40	MS60
1915	—	1,000	2,000	3,000	8,000	—

KM# 700 10 CENTAVOS
Copper, 28 mm. **Obv:** National arms **Rev:** Date and value within wreath **Rev. Legend:** MOR **Note:** Weight varies 5.56-8.36g.

Date	Mintage	VG8	F12	VF20	XF40	MS60
1916	—	5.00	20.00	40.00	60.00	—

KM# 701 20 CENTAVOS
Copper, 23.75-24.75 mm. **Obv:** National arms **Rev:** Value within lined C and 3/4 wreath **Note:** Size varies. Weight varies 3.88-4.15g.

Date	Mintage	VG8	F12	VF20	XF40	MS60
1915	—	9.00	15.00	25.00	35.00	—

KM# 702 50 CENTAVOS
Copper, 28.8 mm. **Obv:** National arms with MOR beneath eagle **Rev:** 50C monogram

Date	Mintage	VG8	F12	VF20	XF40	MS60
1915	—	300	500	900	1,450	—

KM# 703 50 CENTAVOS
Copper, 28-29.5 mm. **Obv:** National arms **Rev:** Numeral value within lined C and 1/2 wreath **Note:** This coin exists with a silver and also a brass wash. Size varies. Weight varies 5.73-13.77g.

Date	Mintage	VG8	F12	VF20	XF40	MS60
1915	—	12.50	17.50	30.00	50.00	—

KM# 703a 50 CENTAVOS
Brass **Obv:** National arms above sprigs **Rev:** 50C monogram

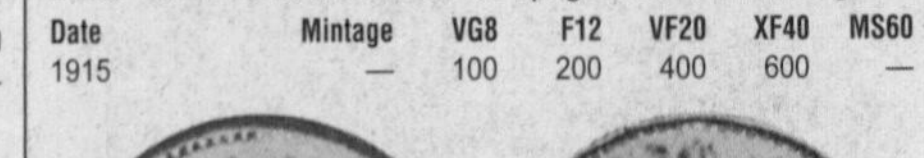

Date	Mintage	VG8	F12	VF20	XF40	MS60
1915	—	100	200	400	600	—

KM# 706 50 CENTAVOS
Copper, 28 mm. **Obv:** National arms **Rev:** Date above large numeral value **Rev. Legend:** REFORMA LIBERTAD JUSTICIA Y LEY

Date	Mintage	VG8	F12	VF20	XF40	MS60
1915	—	400	600	1,000	1,800	—

KM# 704 50 CENTAVOS
Copper, 29-30 mm. **Obv:** National arms with Morelos written below **Rev:** Value within wreath **Note:** Size varies. Weight varies 8.56-11.47g.

Date	Mintage	VG8	F12	VF20	XF40	MS60
1916	—	12.50	20.00	40.00	60.00	—

KM# 708 PESO (UN)
Silver **Obv:** National arms **Rev:** Liberty cap within wreath

Date	Mintage	VG8	F12	VF20	XF40	MS60
1916	—	450	750	1,150	1,850	—

KM# 708a PESO (UN)
10.00 g., Copper, 30 mm. **Obv:** National arms **Rev:** Liberty cap within wreath

Date	Mintage	VG8	F12	VF20	XF40	MS60
1916	—	500	1,000	1,200	2,300	—

PATTERNS

Including off metal strikes

KM#	Date	Mintage	Identification	Mkt Val
Pn1	1915	—	50 Centavos. Silver. KM#705.	2,000
Pn2	1915	—	50 Centavos. Copper. KM#705.	2,000
Pn3	191x (1915)	—	Peso. Silver. KM#707.	10,000
Pn4	191x (1915)	—	Peso. Copper. KM#707a.	10,000
Pn5	1916	—	Peso. Copper. KM#707b.	8,000

OAXACA

Oaxaca is one of the southern states in Mexico. The coins issued in this state represent the most prolific series of the Revolution. Most of the coins bear the portrait of Benito Juarez, have corded or plain edges and were issued by a provisional government in the state. The exceptions are the rectangular 1 and 3 Centavos pieces that begin the series.

PROVISIONAL GOVERNMENT

REVOLUTIONARY COINAGE

 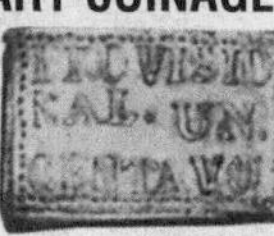

KM# 709 CENTAVO (UN)
Copper, 19 mm. **Obv:** Legend within beaded rectangle **Rev:** Legend within beaded rectangle **Note:** Rectangular flan.

Date	Mintage	VG8	F12	VF20	XF40	MS60
1915	—	90.00	125	400	650	—

KM# 710 CENTAVO (UN)
Copper, 18 mm. **Obv:** Bust left with date flanked by stars below **Rev:** Value within lined C and 1/2 wreath

Date	Mintage	VG8	F12	VF20	XF40	MS60
1915	—	12.00	17.50	25.00	40.00	—

KM# 710a CENTAVO (UN)
Brass **Obv:** Head left with date flanked by stars below **Rev:** Value within lined C and 1/2 wreath

Date	Mintage	VG8	F12	VF20	XF40	MS60
1915	—	50.00	100	200	350	—

KM# 711 3 CENTAVOS (Tres)
Copper, 24 mm. **Obv:** Legend within rectangle with date below, stars in corners **Rev:** Legend within rectangle with stars in corners **Rev. Legend:** PROVISIO... **Note:** Rectangular flan.

Date	Mintage	VG8	F12	VF20	XF40	MS60
1915	—	100	200	400	600	—

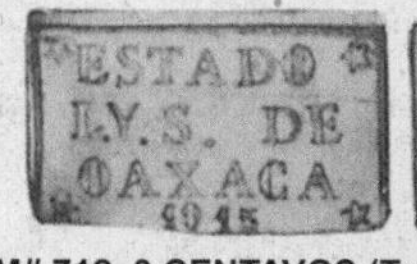 

KM# 712 3 CENTAVOS (Tres)
Copper **Obv:** Legend within rectangle with date below, stars in corners **Rev:** Legend within rectangle with stars in corners **Rev. Legend:** PROVISI... **Note:** Rectangular flan.

Date	Mintage	VG8	F12	VF20	XF40	MS60
1915	—	2,000	4,000	6,000	10,000	—

KM# 713.1 3 CENTAVOS (Tres)
2.25 g., Copper, 20 mm. **Obv:** Bust left flanked by stars below **Rev:** Value above sprigs **Note:** Without TM below value

Date	Mintage	VG8	F12	VF20	XF40	MS60
1915	—	3.00	5.00	12.00	50.00	—

KM# 713.2 3 CENTAVOS (Tres)
2.25 g., Copper, 20 mm. **Obv:** Bust left flanked by stars below **Rev:** Value above sprigs **Edge:** Plain **Note:** Without TM below value

Date	Mintage	VG8	F12	VF20	XF40	MS60
1915	—	—	—	70.00	100	—

KM# 713.3 3 CENTAVOS (Tres)
2.25 g., Copper, 20 mm. **Obv:** Bust left flanked by stars below **Rev:** Value above sprigs **Note:** With TM below value

Date	Mintage	VG8	F12	VF20	XF40	MS60
1915	—	100	200	500	600	—

KM# 714 3 CENTAVOS (Tres)
Copper, 20 mm. **Obv:** Bust left **Rev:** Value above sprigs **Note:** Small 3

Date	Mintage	VG8	F12	VF20	XF40	MS60
1915	—	6.00	10.00	15.00	30.00	—

KM# 715 5 CENTAVOS
Copper **Note:** JAN. 15 1915. incuse lettering

Date	Mintage	VG8	F12	VF20	XF40	MS60
1915 Rare	—	—	—	—	—	—

KM# 717 5 CENTAVOS
Copper, 22 mm. **Obv:** Low relief bust left with date flanked by stars below **Rev:** Value above sprigs **Note:** Low relief with long, pointed truncation

Date	Mintage	VG8	F12	VF20	XF40	MS60
1915	—	1.50	3.00	4.50	12.00	—

KM# 718 5 CENTAVOS
Copper, 22 mm. **Obv:** Raised bust left with date flanked by stars below **Rev:** Value above sprigs **Note:** Heavy with short unfinished lapels

Date	Mintage	VG8	F12	VF20	XF40	MS60
1915	—	1.50	2.50	4.00	12.00	—

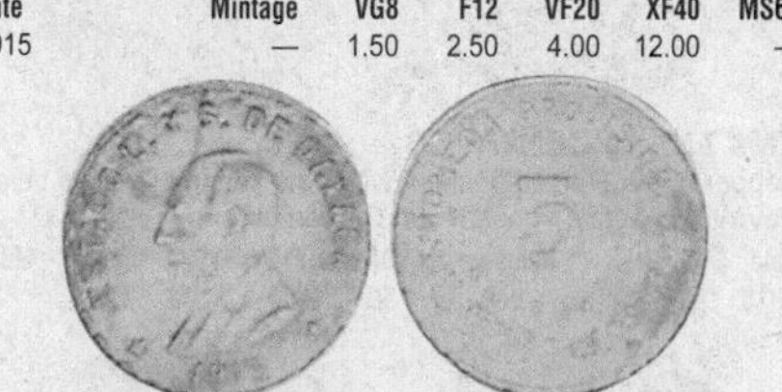

KM# 719 5 CENTAVOS
Copper, 22 mm. **Obv:** Raised bust left with date flanked by stars below **Rev:** Value above sprigs **Note:** Curved bottom

Date	Mintage	VG8	F12	VF20	XF40	MS60
1915	—	1.50	2.50	4.00	12.00	—

KM# 720 5 CENTAVOS
Copper, 22 mm. **Obv:** Bust left with date flanked by stars below **Rev:** Value above sprigs **Note:** Short truncation with closed lapels

Date	Mintage	VG8	F12	VF20	XF40	MS60
1915	—	1.50	3.00	4.50	12.00	—

KM# 721 5 CENTAVOS
Copper, 22 mm. **Obv:** Bust left with date flanked by stars below **Rev:** Value above sprigs **Note:** Short curved truncation

Date	Mintage	VG8	F12	VF20	XF40	MS60
1915	—	1.50	2.50	5.00	12.00	—

KM# 722 10 CENTAVOS
Copper **Obv:** Low relief bust left with date flanked by stars below **Rev:** Value above sprigs **Note:** Low relief with long pointed truncation

Date	Mintage	VG8	F12	VF20	XF40	MS60
1915	—	1.50	2.50	5.00	12.00	—

KM# 723 10 CENTAVOS
Copper **Obv:** Bust left with date flanked by stars below **Rev:** Value above sprigs **Note:** Obverse and reverse legend retrograde.

Date	Mintage	VG8	F12	VF20	XF40	MS60
1915 Rare	—	—	—	—	—	—

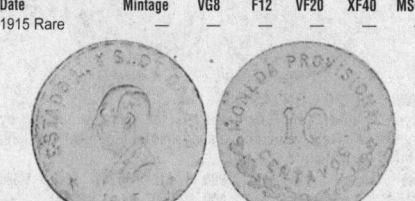

KM# 724 10 CENTAVOS
Copper, 26.5 mm. **Obv:** Raised bust left with date flanked by stars below **Rev:** Value above sprigs **Note:** Bold and unfinished truncation using 1 peso obverse die of KM#740

Date	Mintage	VG8	F12	VF20	XF40	MS60
1915	—	3.00	5.00	8.00	12.00	—

KM# 725 10 CENTAVOS

Copper, 26.5 mm. **Obv:** Bust left with date flanked by stars below **Rev:** Value above sprigs **Note:** Heavy with short unfinished lapels centered high

Date	Mintage	VG8	F12	VF20	XF40	MS60
1915	—	1.50	2.50	4.00	12.00	—

KM# 726 10 CENTAVOS

Copper **Obv:** Raised bust left with date flanked by stars below **Rev:** Value above sprigs **Note:** Curved bottom

Date	Mintage	VG8	F12	VF20	XF40	MS60
1915	—	1.50	2.50	4.00	12.00	—

KM# 727.1 10 CENTAVOS

Copper **Obv:** Raised bust left with date flanked by stars below **Rev:** Value above sprigs **Note:** Short truncation with closed lapels

Date	Mintage	VG8	F12	VF20	XF40	MS60
1915	—	1.50	2.50	4.00	12.00	—

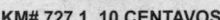

KM# 727.2 10 CENTAVOS

Copper **Obv:** Bust left with date flanked by stars below **Rev:** Value above sprigs **Note:** At present, only four pieces of this type are known. All are VF or better; T below bow with M below first leaf

Date	Mintage	VG8	F12	VF20	XF40	MS60
1915	—	—	—	500	700	—

KM# 727.3 10 CENTAVOS

Copper **Obv:** Raised bust left flanked by letters GV with date flanked by stars below **Rev:** Value above sprigs **Note:** This counterstamp appears on several different type host 10 cent coins.

Date	Mintage	VG8	F12	VF20	XF40	MS60
1915	—	100	200	400	500	—

Note: Letters GV correspond to General Garcia Vigil

KM# 728 20 CENTAVOS

Silver, 19 mm. **Obv:** Low relief bust left with date flanked by stars below **Rev:** Value above sprigs **Note:** Low relief with long pointed truncation

Date	Mintage	VG8	F12	VF20	XF40	MS60
1915	—	800	2,000	4,000	6,000	—

KM# 728a 20 CENTAVOS

Copper, 19 mm. **Obv:** Bust left with date flanked by stars below **Rev:** Value above sprigs **Note:** Low relief with long pointed truncation

Date	Mintage	VG8	F12	VF20	XF40	MS60
1915 Rare	—	—	—	—	—	—

KM# 729.1 20 CENTAVOS

Copper **Obv:** Raised bust left with date flanked by stars below **Rev:** Value above sprigs **Note:** Unfinished truncation using 1 peso obverse die

Date	Mintage	VG8	F12	VF20	XF40	MS60
1915	—	1.50	3.00	4.50	12.00	—

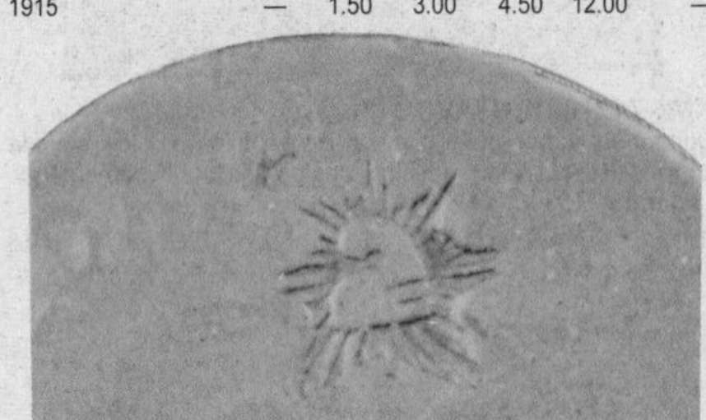

KM# 729.2 20 CENTAVOS

Copper **Obv:** Bust left with date flanked by stars below **Rev:** Value above sprigs **Note:** Counterstamp: Liberty cap and rays with bold unfinished truncation using 1 peso obverse die

Date	Mintage	VG8	F12	VF20	XF40	MS60
1915	—	100	150	300	375	—

KM# 730 20 CENTAVOS

Copper **Obv:** Bust left with date flanked by stars below **Rev:** Value above sprigs **Note:** 5th bust, heavy with short unfinished lapels using 20 Pesos obverse die

Date	Mintage	VG8	F12	VF20	XF40	MS60
1915	—	5.00	7.00	10.00	15.00	—

KM# 731.1 20 CENTAVOS

Copper, 31 mm. **Obv:** Raised bust left with date flanked by stars below **Rev:** Value above sprigs **Note:** Curved bottom

Date	Mintage	VG8	F12	VF20	XF40	MS60
1915	—	1.50	2.50	5.00	12.00	—

KM# 731.2 20 CENTAVOS

Copper **Obv:** Raised bust left with date flanked by stars below **Rev:** Value above sprigs **Note:** Similar to KM#731.1 but with fourth bust.

Date	Mintage	VG8	F12	VF20	XF40	MS60
1915 Unique	—	—	—	—	—	—

KM# 732 20 CENTAVOS

Copper **Obv:** Raised bust left with date flanked by stars below **Rev:** Value above sprigs

Date	Mintage	VG8	F12	VF20	XF40	MS60
1915	—	1.50	2.50	4.00	12.00	—

KM# 733 20 CENTAVOS

Copper **Obv:** Bust left with date flanked by stars below **Rev:** Value above sprigs **Note:** 7th bust, short truncation with closed lapels

Date	Mintage	VG8	F12	VF20	XF40	MS60
1915	—	1.50	3.00	4.50	12.00	—

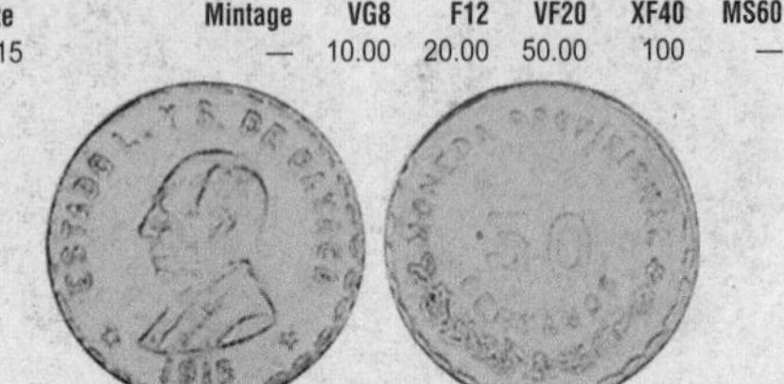

KM# 734 50 CENTAVOS

4.07 g., Silver, 22 mm. **Obv:** Raised bust left with date flanked by stars below **Rev:** Value above sprigs **Note:** Heavy with short unfinished lapels

Date	Mintage	VG8	F12	VF20	XF40	MS60
1915	—	10.00	20.00	50.00	100	—

KM# 735 50 CENTAVOS

Silver, 22 mm. **Obv:** Raised bust left with date flanked by stars below **Rev:** Value above sprigs **Note:** Curved bottom

Date	Mintage	VG8	F12	VF20	XF40	MS60
1915	—	8.00	15.00	30.00	75.00	—

KM# 736 50 CENTAVOS

Silver **Obv:** Bust left with date flanked by stars below **Rev:** Value above sprigs **Note:** Short truncation with closed lapels

Date	Mintage	VG8	F12	VF20	XF40	MS60
1915	—	8.00	15.00	30.00	75.00	—

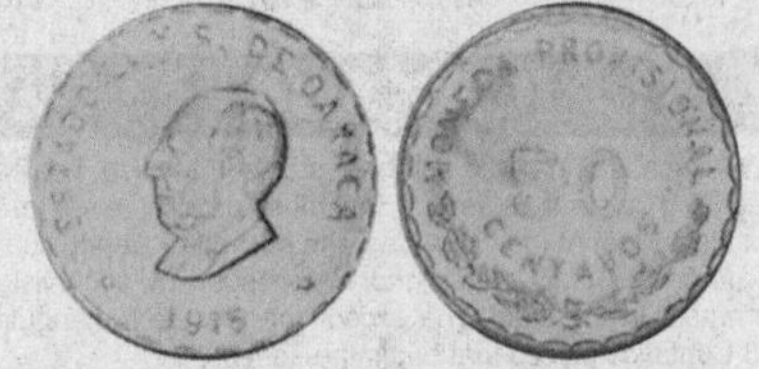

KM# 737 50 CENTAVOS

4.54 g., Silver, 22 mm. **Obv:** Bust left with date flanked by stars below **Rev:** Value above sprigs **Note:** Short truncation with pronounced curve

Date	Mintage	VG8	F12	VF20	XF40	MS60
1915	—	10.00	15.00	25.00	75.00	—

KM# 739 50 CENTAVOS

Billon, 28 mm. **Obv:** Raised bust left with date flanked by stars below **Rev:** Value above sprigs **Note:** Ninth bust, high nearly straight truncation

Date	Mintage	VG8	F12	VF20	XF40	MS60
1915	—	—	—	—	8,000	—

KM# 739a 50 CENTAVOS

Copper, 28 mm. **Obv:** Raised bust left with date flanked by stars below **Rev:** Value above sprigs **Note:** Ninth bust, high nearly straight truncation

Date	Mintage	VG8	F12	VF20	XF40	MS60
1915	—	—	—	—	8,000	—

KM# 740.1 PESO (UN)
Silver, 26 mm. **Obv:** Raised bust left with date flanked by stars below **Rev:** Written value above sprigs **Note:** Fourth bust with heavy unfinished truncation

Date	Mintage	VG8	F12	VF20	XF40	MS60
1915	—	7.00	12.00	30.00	50.00	—

KM# 740.2 PESO (UN)
Silver, 26 mm. **Obv:** Raised bust left with date flanked by stars below **Rev:** Written value above sprigs **Note:** Fourth bust with heavy unfinished truncation w/TM.

Date	Mintage	VG8	F12	VF20	XF40	MS60
1915	—	150	300	400	1,000	—

KM# 741 PESO (UN)
Silver **Obv:** Raised bust with date flanked by stars below **Rev:** Value above sprigs **Note:** Fifth bust, heavy with short unfinished lapels, centered high

Date	Mintage	VG8	F12	VF20	XF40	MS60
1915	—	8.00	10.00	35.00	45.00	—

KM# 742 PESO (UN)
Silver **Obv:** Low relief bust left with date flanked by stars below **Rev:** Value above sprigs **Note:** Sixth bust; curved bottom line

Date	Mintage	VG8	F12	VF20	XF40	MS60
1915	—	10.00	15.00	30.00	50.00	—

KM# 742a PESO (UN)
Copper **Obv:** Low relief bust left with date flanked by stars below **Rev:** Value above sprigs **Note:** Sixth bust; curved bottom line

Date	Mintage	VG8	F12	VF20	XF40	MS60
1915	—	—	—	—	600	—

KM# 743 PESO (UN)
Silver **Obv:** Low relief bust left with date flanked by stars below **Rev:** Value above sprigs **Note:** Seventh bust, short truncation with closed lapels

Date	Mintage	VG8	F12	VF20	XF40	MS60
1915	—	10.00	20.00	30.00	50.00	—

KM# 743a PESO (UN)
Silver **Obv:** Low relief bust left with date flanked by stars below **Rev:** Value above sprigs **Note:** Seventh bust, short truncation with closed lapels

Date	Mintage	VG8	F12	VF20	XF40	MS60
1915	—	35.00	75.00	150	200	—

KM# 744 2 PESOS (Dos)
Silver, 30 mm. **Obv:** Raised bust left with date flanked by stars below **Rev:** Value above sprigs **Note:** Fourth bust, using 1 peso obverse die

Date	Mintage	VG8	F12	VF20	XF40	MS60
1915	—	18.00	28.00	45.00	75.00	—

KM# 744a 2 PESOS (Dos)
Copper **Obv:** Raised bust left with date flanked by stars below **Rev:** Value above sprigs **Note:** Fourth bust, using 1 peso obverse die

Date	Mintage	VG8	F12	VF20	XF40	MS60
1915 Rare	—	—	—	—	—	—

KM# 745 2 PESOS (Dos)
Gold with Silver, 22 mm. **Obv:** Low relief bust left with date flanked by stars below **Rev:** Value above sprigs **Note:** 0.902 Silver, 0.010 Gold. Fifth bust, curved bottom 2 over pesos

Date	Mintage	VG8	F12	VF20	XF40	MS60
1915	—	15.00	25.00	50.00	110	—

KM# 745a 2 PESOS (Dos)
Copper **Obv:** Low relief bust left with date flanked by stars below **Rev:** Value above sprigs **Note:** Fifth bust, curved bottom 2 over pesos

Date	Mintage	VG8	F12	VF20	XF40	MS60
1915	—	75.00	100	200	400	—

KM# A746 2 PESOS (Dos)
Copper **Obv:** Raised bust left with date flanked by stars below **Rev:** Balance scale below liberty cap **Note:** Seventh bust, short truncation with closed lapels

Date	Mintage	VG8	F12	VF20	XF40	MS60
1915 Unique	—	—	—	—	—	—

KM# 746 2 PESOS (Dos)
Silver **Obv:** Raised bust left with date flanked by stars below **Rev:** Balance scale below liberty cap

Date	Mintage	VG8	F12	VF20	XF40	MS60
1915	—	22.00	28.00	50.00	75.00	—

KM# 746a 2 PESOS (Dos)
Copper **Obv:** Bust left with date flanked by stars below **Rev:** Balance scale below liberty cap

Date	Mintage	G4	VG8	F12	VF20	XF40
1915	—	—	150	200	600	1,000

KM# A747 2 PESOS (Dos)
Silver **Obv:** Bust left with date flanked by stars below **Rev:** Balance scale below liberty cap **Note:** Obverse die is free hand engraved.

Date	Mintage	VG8	F12	VF20	XF40	MS60
1915	—	—	—	185	275	—

KM# 747.1 2 PESOS (Dos)
13.44 g., Silver, 33 mm. **Obv:** Bust left with date flanked by stars below **Rev:** Balance scale below liberty cap

Date	Mintage	VG8	F12	VF20	XF40	MS60
1915	—	20.00	25.00	55.00	95.00	—

KM# 747.2 2 PESOS (Dos)
13.44 g., Silver, 33 mm. **Obv:** Bust left with date flanked by stars below **Rev:** Balance scale below liberty cap

Date	Mintage	VG8	F12	VF20	XF40	MS60
1915	—	22.00	28.00	60.00	100	—

KM# 747.3 2 PESOS (Dos)
13.44 g., Silver, 33 mm. **Obv:** Bust left with date flanked by stars below **Rev:** Balance scale below liberty cap

Date	Mintage	VG8	F12	VF20	XF40	MS60
1915	—	20.00	30.00	60.00	100	—

KM# 748 2 PESOS (Dos)
0.902 Silver, 22 mm. **Obv:** Bust left with date flanked by stars below **Rev:** Value above sprigs

Date	Mintage	VG8	F12	VF20	XF40	MS60
1915	—	20.00	30.00	60.00	100	—

KM# 749 2 PESOS (Dos)
Silver **Obv:** Head left with date flanked by stars below **Rev:** Value above sprigs

Date	Mintage	VG8	F12	VF20	XF40	MS60
1915 Unique	—	—	—	—	5,000	—

KM# 750 5 PESOS
0.175 Gold, 19 mm. **Obv:** Bust left **Rev:** Value above sprigs **Note:** Third bust, heavy, with short unfinished lapels

Date	Mintage	VG8	F12	VF20	XF40	MS60
1915	—	175	225	350	550	900

KM# 750a 5 PESOS
Copper **Obv:** Bust left **Rev:** Value above sprigs **Note:** Third bust, heavy, with short unfinished lapels

Date	Mintage	VG8	F12	VF20	XF40	MS60
1915 Unique	—	—	—	—	—	—

KM# 751 5 PESOS
16.77 g., Silver, 30 mm. **Obv:** Low relief bust left with date flanked by stars below **Rev:** Value above sprigs **Note:** Seventh bust, short truncation with closed lapels

Date	Mintage	VG8	F12	VF20	XF40	MS60
1915	—	50.00	80.00	175	275	—

KM# 751a 5 PESOS
Copper **Obv:** Low relief bust left with date flanked by stars below **Rev:** Value above sprigs **Note:** Seventh bust, short truncation with closed lapels

Date	Mintage	VG8	F12	VF20	XF40	MS60
1915	—	125	200	300	1,000	—

KM# A752 10 PESOS
0.150 Gold **Obv:** Bust left with date flanked by stars below **Rev:** Value above sprigs

Date	Mintage	VG8	F12	VF20	XF40	MS60
1915 Rare	—	—	—	—	—	—

KM# 752 10 PESOS
0.175 Gold, 23 mm. **Obv:** Bust left with date flanked by stars below **Rev:** Value above sprigs

Date	Mintage	VG8	F12	VF20	XF40	MS60
1915	—	225	350	450	650	1,000

KM# 752a 10 PESOS
Copper **Obv:** Bust left with date flanked by stars below **Rev:** Value above sprigs

Date	Mintage	VG8	F12	VF20	XF40	MS60
1915	—	800	1,500	2,000	4,000	—

KM# A753 20 PESOS
0.150 Gold **Obv:** Bust left with date flanked by stars below **Rev:** Value above sprigs **Note:** Fourth bust

Date	Mintage	VG8	F12	VF20	XF40	MS60
1915 Unique	—	—	—	—	—	—

KM# 753 20 PESOS
0.175 Gold **Obv:** Bust left with date flanked by stars below **Rev:** Value above sprigs

Date	Mintage	VG8	F12	VF20	XF40	MS60
1915	—	400	500	800	1,000	1,500

KM# 754 20 PESOS
0.175 Gold, 27 mm. **Obv:** Bust left with date flanked by stars below **Rev:** Value above sprigs

Date	Mintage	VG8	F12	VF20	XF40	MS60
1915	—	250	450	650	950	1,700

KM# 755 60 PESOS
50.00 g., 0.859 Gold 1.3809 oz. AGW **Obv:** Head left within 3/4 wreath **Rev:** Balance scale below liberty cap **Edge:** Reeded

Date	Mintage	F12	VF20	XF40	MS60	MS63
1916 Rare	—	—	10,000	20,000	35,000	—

KM# 755a 60 PESOS
Silver **Obv:** Head left within 3/4 wreath **Rev:** Balance scales below liberty cap **Edge:** Reeded

Date	Mintage	F12	VF20	XF40	MS60	MS63
1916	—	—	—	—	15,000	—

KM# 755b 60 PESOS
Copper **Obv:** Head left within 3/4 wreath **Rev:** Balance scales below liberty cap **Edge:** Plain

Date	Mintage	F12	VF20	XF40	MS60	MS63
1916	—	—	—	2,000	5,000	—

PUEBLA

A state of central Mexico. Puebla was a state that occasionally saw Zapata forces active within its boundaries. Also active, and an issuer of coins, was the Madero brigade who issued coins with their name two years after Madero's death. The state issue of 2, 5, 10 and 20 Centavos saw limited circulation and recent hoards have been found of some values.

CHICONCUAUTLA

Madero Brigade

REVOLUTIONARY COINAGE

KM# 756 10 CENTAVOS
6.73 g., Copper, 27 mm. **Obv:** Date below national arms **Rev:** Letters X and C entwined

Date	Mintage	VG8	F12	VF20	XF40	MS60
1915	—	7.50	12.50	17.50	25.00	—

KM# 757 20 CENTAVOS
Copper, 28 mm. **Obv:** Date below national arms **Rev:** Value **Note:** Varieties exist.

Date	Mintage	VG8	F12	VF20	XF40	MS60
1915	—	2.50	4.00	6.50	12.00	—

KM# 758 20 CENTAVOS
Copper, 28 mm. **Obv:** Date below national arms **Rev:** Value

Date	Mintage	VG8	F12	VF20	XF40	MS60
1915	—	2.50	4.00	6.50	12.00	—

TETELA DEL ORO Y OCAMPO

KM# 759 2 CENTAVOS
Copper, 16 mm. **Obv:** National arms above date **Rev:** Value

Date	Mintage	VG8	F12	VF20	XF40	MS60
1915	—	12.50	20.00	28.00	45.00	—
1915 Restrikes	—	—	1.00	1.50	2.00	—

KM# 760 2 CENTAVOS
Copper, 20 mm. **Obv:** National arms within beaded circle **Rev:** Value within beaded circle **Rev. Legend:** E. DE PU.

Date	Mintage	VG8	F12	VF20	XF40	MS60
1915	—	15.00	25.00	35.00	90.00	—

KM# 761 2 CENTAVOS
Copper, 20 mm. **Obv:** National arms within beaded circle **Rev:** Value within beaded circle **Rev. Legend:** E. DE PUE.

Date	Mintage	VG8	F12	VF20	XF40	MS60
1915	—	9.00	20.00	25.00	50.00	—

KM# 762 5 CENTAVOS
Copper, 21 mm. **Obv:** National arms within beaded circle **Rev:** Value within beaded circle

Date	Mintage	VG8	F12	VF20	XF40	MS60
1915	—	100	200	300	400	—

KM# 764 20 CENTAVOS
Copper, 24 mm. **Obv:** National arms **Rev:** Value above sprigs

Date	Mintage	VG8	F12	VF20	XF40	MS60
1915	—	50.00	100	150	225	—

TRIAL STRIKES

KM#	Date	Mintage	Identification	Mkt Val
TS1	1915	—	10 Centavos. Copper. Uniface, KM#763.	475
TS2	1915	—	10 Centavos. Brass. Uniface, KM#763.	750
TS3	1915	—	10 Centavos. Copper. KM#761. Eagle.	1,600

SINALOA

A state along the west coast of Mexico. The cast pieces of this state have been attributed to two people - Generals Rafael Buelna and Juan Carrasco. The cap and rays 8 Reales is usually attributed to General Buelna and the rest of the series to Carrasco. Because of their crude nature it is questionable whether separate series or mints can be determined.

BUELNA / CARRASCO

CAST COINAGE

Revolutionary

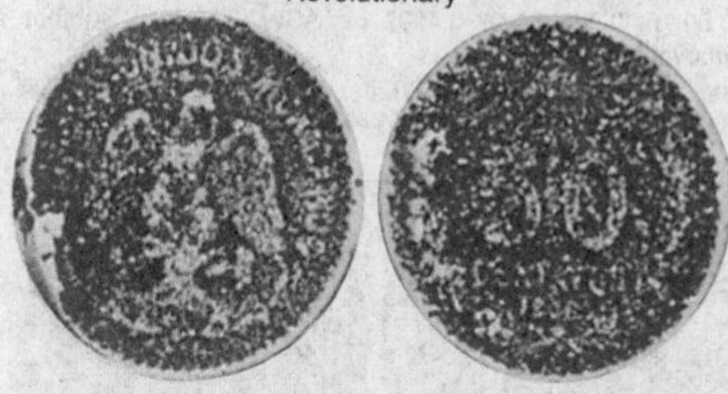

KM# 766 50 CENTAVOS
Cast Silver, 29-31 mm. **Obv:** National arms **Rev:** Numeral value within wreath **Note:** Sand molded using regular 50 Centavos, KM#445. Size varies. Weight varies 12.81-14.8g.

Date	Mintage	G4	VG8	F12	VF20	XF40
ND(1905-1918)	—	200	300	—	—	—

COUNTERMARKED COINAGE

These are all crude sand cast coins using regular coins to prepare the mold. Prices below give a range for how much of the original coin from which the mold was prepared is visible.

Revolutionary

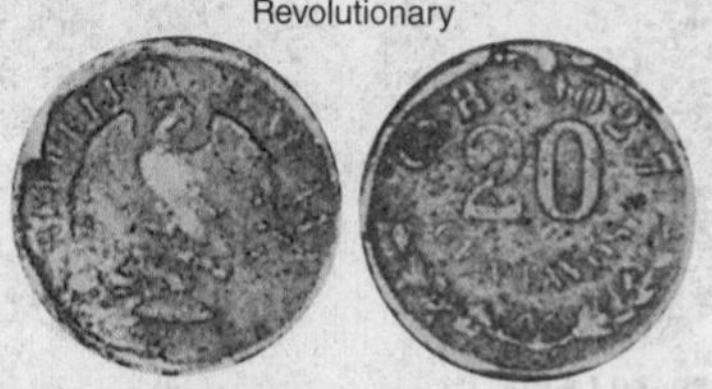

KM# 765 20 CENTAVOS
Cast Silver **Obv:** National arms within beaded circle **Rev:** Value within beaded circle **Note:** Sand molded using regular 20 Centavos.

Date	Mintage	G4	VG8	F12	VF20	XF40
ND(1898-1905)	—	200	300	—	—	—

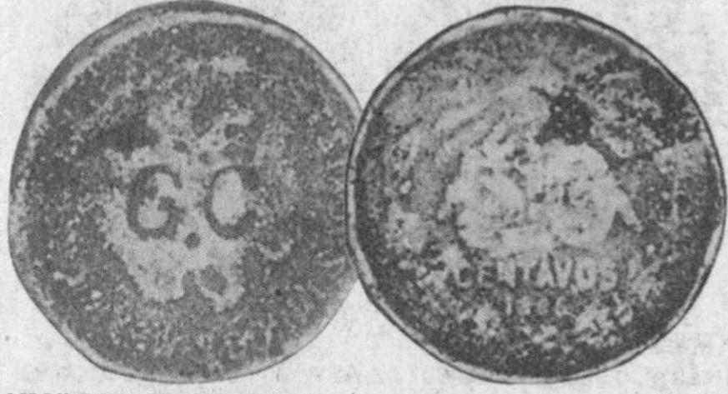

KM# 767 50 CENTAVOS
Cast Silver **Obv:** National arms with additional countermark **Rev:** Value and date within wreath with liberty cap above **Countermark:** G.C. **Note:** Sand molded using regular 50 Centavos, KM#445.

CM Date	Host Date	G4	VG8	F12	VF20	XF40
ND0	(1905-1918)	100	150	200	300	—

KM# 768.1 PESO
Cast Silver, 38.8-39 mm. **Note:** Sand molded using regular 8 Reales, KM#377. Size varies. Weight varies 26-33.67g.

Date	Mintage	G4	VG8	F12	VF20	XF40
ND(1824-97)	—	20.00	35.00	45.00	60.00	—

KM# 768.2 PESO
Cast Silver, 38.5-39 mm. **Obv:** With additional countermark **Countermark:** G.C. **Note:** Sand molded using regular 8 Reales, KM#377. Size varies. Weight varies 26-33.67g.

CM Date	Host Date	G4	VG8	F12	VF20	XF40
ND(ca.1915)	(1824-97)	25.00	45.00	100	150	—

KM# 769 PESO
Cast Silver **Note:** Sand molded using regular Peso, KM#409.

Date	Mintage	G4	VG8	F12	VF20	XF40
ND(1898-1909)	—	15.00	25.00	40.00	55.00	—

KM# 770 PESO
Cast Silver, 38.5 mm. **Obv:** National arms with additional countermark **Rev:** Liberty cap with additional countermark **Countermark:** G.C **Note:** Sand molded using regular Peso, KM#409.

CM Date	Host Date	G4	VG8	F12	VF20	XF40
ND(ca.1915)	(1898-1909)	35.00	65.00	150	185	—

Note: Many C/S counterfeits exist

MOLDOVA

The Republic of Moldova (formerly the Moldavian S.S.R.) is bordered in the north, east and south by the Ukraine and on the west by Romania. It has an area of 13,000 sq. mi. (33,700 sq. km.) and a population of 4.4 million. The capital is Chisinau. Agricultural products are mainly cereals, grapes, tobacco, sugar beets and fruits. Food processing, clothing, building materials and agricultural machinery manufacturing dominate the industry.

The historical Romanian principality of Moldova was established in the 14th century. It fell under Turkish suzerainty in the 16th century. From 1812 to 1918 Russians occupied the eastern portion of Moldova, which they named Bessarabia. In March 1918 the Bessarabian legislature voted in favor of reunification with Romania. At the Paris Peace Conference in 1920 United States, France, U.K., and Italy a.s.o officially recognized the union. The new Soviet government did not accept the union. In 1924, due to Soviet pressure against Romania a Moldavian Autonomous Soviet Socialist Republic (A.S.S.R.) was established within the USSR on the border strip that extends east of Nistru River (today it is Transdniestra or Transdniester).

Following the Molotov-Ribbentrop Pact (1939), the Soviet - German agreement, which divided Eastern Europe, the Soviet forces, reoccupied the region in June 1940 and the Moldavian S.S.R. was proclaimed. The Transdniestra region was transferred to the new republic, while Ukrainian S.S.R. obtained possession of southern part of Bessarabia. Romanian forces liberated the region in 1941. The Soviets reconquered the territory (in 1944).

A declaration of republican sovereignty was adopted in June 1990 and in Aug. 1991 the area was renamed Moldova, an independent republic. In Dec. 1991 Moldova became a member of the C.I.S. In 1992, as a result of Russian involvement, Transdniestra seceded from Moldova. In May 1992 fighting began between Moldavian separatists (Romanians) and rebels aided by contingents of Cossacks and the Russian14th Army. The Moldavian government made several futile requests for United Nations intervention. On July 3, 1992, Russian and Moldavian presidents agreed upon a neutral demarcation line with the withdrawal of Russian forces from Transdniestra. This status will remain until a more feasible constitution is proclaimed.

RULER
Romanian, until 1940

MONETARY SYSTEM
100 Bani = 1 Leu

REPUBLIC

DECIMAL COINAGE

KM# 1 BAN
0.67 g., Aluminum, 14.5 mm. **Obv:** National arms **Rev:** Value divides date above monogram **Edge:** Plain

Date	Mintage	VF20	XF40	MS60	MS63	MS65
1993	—	—	—	0.10	0.20	0.40
1995	—	—	—	0.10	0.20	0.40
1996	—	—	—	0.15	0.25	0.50
2000	—	—	—	0.15	0.25	0.50

KM# 2 5 BANI
0.75 g., Aluminum, 16 mm. **Obv:** National arms **Rev:** Monogram divides sprigs below value and date **Edge:** Plain

Date	Mintage	VF20	XF40	MS60	MS63	MS65
1993	—	—	0.15	0.25	0.35	0.50
1995	—	—	0.15	0.25	0.35	0.50
1996	—	—	0.15	0.25	0.35	0.50
1999	—	—	0.15	0.25	0.35	0.50
2000	—	—	0.15	0.25	0.35	0.50

KM# 7 10 BANI
0.85 g., Aluminum, 16.6 mm. **Obv:** National arms **Rev:** Value, date and monogram **Edge:** Plain

Date	Mintage	VF20	XF40	MS60	MS63	MS65
1995	—	—	—	0.25	0.40	0.60
1996	—	—	—	0.25	0.40	0.60
1997	—	—	—	0.25	0.40	0.60
1998	—	—	—	0.25	0.40	0.60
2000	—	—	—	0.25	0.40	0.60

KM# 3 25 BANI
0.95 g., Aluminum, 17.5 mm. **Obv:** National arms **Rev:** Monogram divides sprigs below value and date **Edge:** Plain

Date	Mintage	VF20	XF40	MS60	MS63	MS65
1993	—	—	0.20	0.30	0.50	0.75
1995	—	—	0.20	0.30	0.50	0.75
1999	—	—	0.20	0.30	0.50	0.75
2000	—	—	0.20	0.30	0.50	0.75

KM# 4 50 BANI
1.07 g., Aluminum, 19 mm. **Obv:** National arms **Rev:** Monogram divides sprigs below date and value

Date	Mintage	VF20	XF40	MS60	MS63	MS65
1993	—	—	—	0.35	0.75	1.00

KM# 10 50 BANI
3.10 g., Brass Clad Steel, 19 mm. **Obv:** National arms **Rev:** Value and date within grapevine **Edge:** Reeded

Date	Mintage	VF20	XF40	MS60	MS63	MS65
1997	—	—	—	0.75	1.50	2.00

KM# 5 LEU
Nickel Clad Steel **Obv:** National arms **Rev:** Value divides date with monogram above

Date	Mintage	VF20	XF40	MS60	MS63	MS65
1992	—	—	—	0.75	1.50	2.00

KM# 6 5 LEI
Nickel Clad Steel **Obv:** National arms **Rev:** Value flanked by monogram and date

Date	Mintage	VF20	XF40	MS60	MS63	MS65
1993	—	—	—	1.00	2.00	3.00

KM# 11 50 LEI
16.63 g., 0.985 Silver 0.5266 oz. ASW, 30 mm. **Subject:** Manastirea Rudi **Obv:** National arms **Rev:** Monastary building **Edge:** Plain

Date	Mintage	VF20	XF40	MS60	MS63	MS65
2000	1,000	PF65 50.00	PF67 65.00			

KM# 76 50 LEI
16.50 g., 0.925 Silver 0.4907 oz. ASW, 30 mm. **Subject:** Calarasauca Monastery

Date	Mintage	VF20	XF40	MS60	MS63	MS65
2000	Est. 1000	PF65 45.00	PF67 60.00			

KM# 77 50 LEI
16.50 g., 0.925 Silver 0.4907 oz. ASW, 30 mm. **Subject:** Capriana Monastery

Date	Mintage	VF20	XF40	MS60	MS63	MS65
2000	1,000	PF65 45.00	PF67 60.00			

KM# 78 50 LEI
16.50 g., 0.925 Silver 0.4907 oz. ASW, 30 mm. **Subject:** Condrita Monastery

Date	Mintage	VF20	XF40	MS60	MS63	MS65
2000	Est. 1000	PF65 45.00	PF67 60.00			

KM# 79 50 LEI
16.50 g., 0.925 Silver 0.4907 oz. ASW, 30 mm. **Subject:** Curchi Monastery

Date	Mintage	VF20	XF40	MS60	MS63	MS65
2000	Est. 1000	PF65 45.00	PF67 60.00			

KM# 80 50 LEI
16.50 g., 0.925 Silver 0.4907 oz. ASW, 30 mm. **Subject:** Cusilauca Monastery

Date	Mintage	VF20	XF40	MS60	MS63	MS65
2000	Est. 1000	PF65 45.00	PF67 60.00			

KM# 81 50 LEI
16.50 g., 0.925 Silver 0.4907 oz. ASW, 30 mm. **Subject:** Dobrusa Monastery

Date	Mintage	VF20	XF40	MS60	MS63	MS65
2000	Est. 1000	PF65 45.00	PF67 60.00			

KM# 82 50 LEI
16.50 g., 0.925 Silver 0.4907 oz. ASW, 30 mm. **Subject:** Frumoasa Monastery

Date	Mintage	VF20	XF40	MS60	MS63	MS65
2000	Est. 1000	PF65 45.00	PF67 60.00			

KM# 83 50 LEI
16.50 g., 0.925 Silver 0.4907 oz. ASW, 30 mm. **Subject:** Hincu Monastery

Date	Mintage	VF20	XF40	MS60	MS63	MS65
2000	Est. 1000	PF65 45.00	PF67 60.00			

KM# 84 50 LEI
16.50 g., 0.925 Silver 0.4907 oz. ASW, 30 mm. **Subject:** Hirbovat Monastery

Date	Mintage	VF20	XF40	MS60	MS63	MS65
2000	Est. 1000	PF65 45.00	PF67 60.00			

KM# 85 50 LEI
16.50 g., 0.925 Silver 0.4907 oz. ASW, 30 mm. **Subject:** Hirjauca Monastery

Date	Mintage	VF20	XF40	MS60	MS63	MS65
2000	Est. 1000	PF65 45.00	PF67 60.00			

KM# 86 50 LEI
16.50 g., 0.925 Silver 0.4907 oz. ASW, 30 mm. **Subject:** Hirova Monastery

Date	Mintage	VF20	XF40	MS60	MS63	MS65
2000	Est. 1000	PF65 45.00	PF67 60.00			

KM# 87 50 LEI
16.50 g., 0.925 Silver 0.4907 oz. ASW, 30 mm. **Subject:** Japca Monastery

Date	Mintage	VF20	XF40	MS60	MS63	MS65
2000	Est. 1000	PF65 45.00	PF67 60.00			

KM# 88 50 LEI
16.50 g., 0.925 Silver 0.4907 oz. ASW, 30 mm. **Subject:** Noul Neamt Monastery

Date	Mintage	VF20	XF40	MS60	MS63	MS65
2000	Est. 1000	PF65 45.00	PF67 60.00			

KM# 89 50 LEI
16.50 g., 0.925 Silver 0.4907 oz. ASW, 30 mm. **Subject:** Raciula Monastery

Date	Mintage	VF20	XF40	MS60	MS63	MS65
2000	Est. 1000	**PF65** 45.00	**PF67** 60.00			

KM# 90 50 LEI
16.50 g., 0.925 Silver 0.4907 oz. ASW, 30 mm. **Subject:** Rudi Monastery

Date	Mintage	VF20	XF40	MS60	MS63	MS65
2000	Est. 1000	**PF65** 45.00	**PF67** 60.00			

KM# 91 50 LEI
16.50 g., 0.925 Silver 0.4907 oz. ASW, 30 mm. **Subject:** Saharna Monastery

Date	Mintage	VF20	XF40	MS60	MS63	MS65
2000	Est. 1000	**PF65** 45.00	**PF67** 60.00			

KM# 92 50 LEI
16.50 g., 0.925 Silver 0.4907 oz. ASW, 30 mm. **Subject:** Suruceni Monastery

Date	Mintage	VF20	XF40	MS60	MS63	MS65
2000	Est. 1000	**PF65** 45.00	**PF67** 60.00			

KM# 93 50 LEI
16.50 g., 0.925 Silver 0.4907 oz. ASW, 30 mm. **Subject:** Tabara Monastery

Date	Mintage	VF20	XF40	MS60	MS63	MS65
2000	Est. 1000	**PF65** 45.00	**PF67** 60.00			

KM# 94 50 LEI
16.50 g., 0.925 Silver 0.4907 oz. ASW, 30 mm. **Subject:** Tiganesti Monastery

Date	Mintage	VF20	XF40	MS60	MS63	MS65
2000	Est. 1000	**PF65** 45.00	**PF67** 60.00			

KM# 95 50 LEI
16.50 g., 0.925 Silver 0.4907 oz. ASW, 30 mm. **Subject:** Varzaresti Monastery

Date	Mintage	VF20	XF40	MS60	MS63	MS65
2000	Est. 1000	**PF65** 45.00	**PF67** 60.00			

KM# 8 100 LEI
28.28 g., 0.925 Silver 0.841 oz. ASW, 38.61 mm. **Subject:** 5th Anniversary of Independence **Obv:** National arms **Rev:** Flying stork with grapes

Date	Mintage	VF20	XF40	MS60	MS63	MS65
1996	1,000	**PF65** 200	**PF67** 250			

KM# 9 100 LEI
28.28 g., 0.925 Silver 0.841 oz. ASW, 38.61 mm. **Subject:** First Olympic Games Participation **Obv:** National arms **Rev:** Two men in a canoe **Edge:** Reeded

Date	Mintage	VF20	XF40	MS60	MS63	MS65
1996	20,000	**PF65** 45.00	**PF67** 60.00			

KM# 15 100 LEI
31.10 g., 0.925 Silver 0.9249 oz. ASW, 37 mm. **Subject:** Effigy of King Alexandru the Good **Obv:** National arms **Rev:** Crowned bust facing flanked by dates and shield **Edge:** Plain

Date	Mintage	VF20	XF40	MS60	MS63	MS65
2000	1,000	**PF67** 80.00				

KM# 24 100 LEI
31.10 g., 0.925 Silver 0.9249 oz. ASW, 37 mm. **Subject:** Battle of Vaslui - 1475 **Obv:** National arms above value **Rev:** Battle scene, King on horse, soldiers at forefront, standard at top **Edge:** Plain

Date	Mintage	VF20	XF40	MS60	MS63	MS65
2000	1,000	**PF67** 80.00				

KM# 28 100 LEI
31.10 g., 0.925 Silver 0.9249 oz. ASW, 37 mm. **Subject:** 100th Anniversary - Birth of Stefan Neaga **Obv:** Arms, date divides legend above, value below **Obv. Legend:** REPUBLICA MOLDOVA **Rev:** Bust of Neaga facing, image of lyre at left, staff with musical notes at right **Rev. Legend:** STEFAN NEAGA **Edge:** Plain

Date	Mintage	VF20	XF40	MS60	MS63	MS65
2000	1,000	**PF67** 80.00				

KM# 75 100 LEI
31.10 g., 0.925 Silver 0.9249 oz. ASW, 37 mm. **Subject:** Mihai Eminescu, 150th Anniversary of Birth

Date	Mintage	VF20	XF40	MS60	MS63	MS65
2000	Est. 1000	**PF67** 80.00				

MONACO

The Principality of Monaco, located on the Mediterranean coast nine miles from Nice, has an area of 0.58 sq. mi. (1.9 sq. km.) and a population of 26,000. Capital: Monaco-Ville. The economy is based on tourism and the manufacture of cosmetics, gourmet foods and highly specialized electronics. Monaco also derives its revenue from a tobacco monopoly and the sale of postage stamps for philatelic purpose. Gambling in Monte Carlo accounts for only a small fraction of the country's revenue.

Monaco derives its name from Monoikos, the Greek surname for Hercules, the mythological strong man who, according to legend, formed the Monacan headland during one of his twelve labors. Monaco has been ruled by the Grimaldi dynasty since 1297 - Prince Albert II, the present and 32nd monarch of Monaco, is still of that line - except for a period during the French Revolution until Napoleon's downfall when the Principality was annexed to France. Since 1865, Monaco has maintained a customs union with France which guarantees its privileged position as long as the royal line remains intact. Under the new constitution proclaimed on December 17, 1962, the Prince shares his power with an 18-member unicameral National Council.

RULERS
Albert I, 1889-1922
Louis II, 1922-1949
Rainier III, 1949-2005

MINT MARKS
M - Monaco
A – Paris

MINT PRIVY MARKS
(a) - Paris (privy marks only)
(p) - Thunderbolt - Poissy

MONETARY SYSTEM
10 Centimes = 1 Decime
10 Decimes = 1 Franc

PRINCIPALITY

DECIMAL COINAGE

KM# 110 50 CENTIMES

Aluminum-Bronze **Ruler:** Louis II **Obv:** Hercules shooting bow to right **Rev:** Shield below value within circle

Date	Mintage	VF20	XF40	MS60	MS63	MS65
1924 (p)	150,000	8.00	18.00	50.00	100	200

KM# 113 50 CENTIMES

Aluminum-Bronze **Ruler:** Louis II **Obv:** Hercules shooting bow to right **Rev:** Shield below value within circle

Date	Mintage	VF20	XF40	MS60	MS63	MS65
1926 (p)	100,000	9.00	20.00	45.00	100	200

KM# 111 FRANC

Aluminum-Bronze **Ruler:** Louis II **Obv:** Hercules shooting bow to right **Rev:** Shield below value within circle

Date	Mintage	VF20	XF40	MS60	MS63	MS65
1924 (p)	150,000	7.00	14.00	45.00	90.00	180

KM# 114 FRANC

Aluminum-Bronze **Ruler:** Louis II **Obv:** Hercules shooting bow to right **Rev:** Shield below value within circle

Date	Mintage	VF20	XF40	MS60	MS63	MS65
1926 (p)	100,000	9.00	16.00	35.00	70.00	140

KM# 120 FRANC

1.25 g., Aluminum, 23 mm. **Ruler:** Louis II **Obv:** Head left **Rev:** Crowned mantled arms flanked by value below

Date	Mintage	VF20	XF40	MS60	MS63	MS65
ND-1943 (a)	2,500,000	12.00	15.00	20.00	30.00	60.00

KM# 120a FRANC

4.00 g., Aluminum-Bronze, 23 mm. **Ruler:** Louis II **Obv:** Head left **Rev:** Crowned mantled arms flanked by value below

Date	Mintage	VF20	XF40	MS60	MS63	MS65
ND-1945 (a)	1,509,000	1.00	2.00	5.00	10.00	25.00

KM# 112 2 FRANCS

Aluminum-Bronze, 27 mm. **Ruler:** Louis II **Obv:** Hercules shooting bow to right **Rev:** Shield below value within circle **Edge:** Reeded

Date	Mintage	VF20	XF40	MS60	MS63	MS65
1924 (p)	75,000	14.00	30.00	75.00	100	225

KM# 115 2 FRANCS

Aluminum-Bronze **Ruler:** Louis II **Obv:** Hercules shooting bow to right **Rev:** Shield below value within circle

Date	Mintage	VF20	XF40	MS60	MS63	MS65
1926 (p)	75,000	12.00	25.00	70.00	90.00	180

KM# 121 2 FRANCS

2.25 g., Aluminum, 27 mm. **Ruler:** Louis II **Obv:** Head left **Rev:** Crowned mantled arms flanked by value below

Date	Mintage	VF20	XF40	MS60	MS63	MS65
ND-1943 (a)	1,250,000	1.50	5.00	10.00	15.00	35.00

KM# 121a 2 FRANCS

8.00 g., Aluminum-Bronze, 27 mm. **Ruler:** Louis II **Obv:** Head left **Rev:** Crowned mantled arms flanked by value below

Date	Mintage	VF20	XF40	MS60	MS63	MS65
ND-1945 (a)	1,080,000	1.00	2.50	6.00	10.00	25.00

KM# 122 5 FRANCS

Aluminum **Ruler:** Louis II **Obv:** Head left **Rev:** Crowned mantled arms flanked by value below

Date	Mintage	VF20	XF40	MS60	MS63	MS65
1945 (a)	1,000,000	3.00	7.00	15.00	20.00	45.00

KM# 123 10 FRANCS

Copper-Nickel, 26 mm. **Ruler:** Louis II **Obv:** Bust left **Rev:** Crowned mantled arms above value flanked by sprigs

Date	Mintage	VF20	XF40	MS60	MS63	MS65
1946 (a)	1,000,000	3.00	6.00	12.50	20.00	45.00

KM# 130 10 FRANCS

Aluminum-Bronze **Ruler:** Rainier III **Obv:** Head left within circle **Rev:** Crowned shield flanked by value

Date	Mintage	VF20	XF40	MS60	MS63	MS65
1950 (a)	500,000	1.00	2.00	4.00	6.00	12.00
1951 (a)	500,000	1.00	2.00	4.00	6.00	12.00

KM# 124 20 FRANCS (Vingt)

Copper-Nickel **Ruler:** Louis II **Obv:** Bust left **Rev:** Crowned mantled arms above value flanked by sprigs

Date	Mintage	VF20	XF40	MS60	MS63	MS65
1947 (a)	1,000,000	4.00	8.00	20.00	30.00	50.00

KM# 131 20 FRANCS (Vingt)

Aluminum-Bronze **Ruler:** Rainier III **Obv:** Head left divides circle **Rev:** Crowned shield flanked by value

Date	Mintage	VF20	XF40	MS60	MS63	MS65
1950 (a)	500,000	1.25	2.50	5.00	7.00	15.00
1951 (a)	500,000	1.25	2.50	5.00	7.00	15.00

KM# 132 50 FRANCS (Cinquante)

Aluminum-Bronze **Ruler:** Rainier III **Obv:** Head left divides circle **Rev:** Armored equestrian divides circle above value

Date	Mintage	VF20	XF40	MS60	MS63	MS65
1950 (a)	500,000	3.00	5.00	12.00	15.00	30.00

KM# 105 100 FRANCS (Cent)

32.26 g., 0.900 Gold 0.9334 oz. AGW **Ruler:** Albert I **Obv:** Head left **Obv. Legend:** ALBERT I PRINCE. **Rev:** Crowned oval arms within wreath with ribbon above

Date	Mintage	VF20	XF40	MS60	MS63	MS65
1901 A	15,000	—	1,200	1,850	2,750	—
1904 A	10,000	—	1,200	1,850	2,750	—

KM# 133 100 FRANCS (Cent)

Copper-Nickel **Ruler:** Rainier III **Obv:** Head left divides circle **Rev:** Armored equestrian divides circle above value

Date	Mintage	VF20	XF40	MS60	MS63	MS65
1950 (a)	500,000	4.00	8.00	18.00	30.00	60.00

KM# 134 100 FRANCS (Cent)

Copper-Nickel **Ruler:** Rainier III **Obv:** Head left **Rev:** Value below crowned shield

Date	Mintage	VF20	XF40	MS60	MS63	MS65
1956 (a)	500,000	2.50	5.50	15.00	25.00	40.00

REFORM COINAGE

100 Old Francs = 1 New Franc

KM# 155 CENTIME

1.65 g., Stainless Steel, 15 mm. **Ruler:** Rainier III **Obv:** Crowned shield **Rev:** Sprig divides value and date **Edge:** Plain

Date	Mintage	VF20	XF40	MS60	MS63	MS65
1976 (a)	25,000	0.15	0.30	1.25	2.50	4.00
1977 (a)	25,000	0.15	0.30	1.25	2.50	4.00
1978 (a)	50,000	0.15	0.30	1.25	2.50	4.00
1979 (a)	50,000	0.15	0.30	1.25	2.50	4.00
1982 (a)	10,000	0.15	0.30	1.25	2.50	4.00
1995 (a)	—	0.15	0.30	1.25	2.50	4.00

KM# 156 5 CENTIMES

2.00 g., Aluminum-Bronze, 17 mm. **Ruler:** Rainier III **Obv:** Head right **Rev:** Figure with hand on shield divides crown and value **Edge:** Plain

Date	Mintage	VF20	XF40	MS60	MS63	MS65
1976 (a)	25,000	0.20	0.40	1.50	2.75	4.50
1977 (a)	25,000	0.20	0.40	1.50	2.75	4.50
1978 (a)	75,000	0.20	0.40	1.50	2.75	4.50
1979 (a)	75,000	0.20	0.40	1.50	2.75	4.50
1982 (a)	10,000	0.20	0.40	1.50	2.75	4.50
1995 (a)	—	0.20	0.40	1.50	2.75	4.50

KM# 142 10 CENTIMES

3.00 g., Aluminum-Bronze, 20 mm. **Ruler:** Rainier III **Obv:** Head right **Rev:** Figure with hand on shield divides crown and value **Edge:** Plain

Date	Mintage	VF20	XF40	MS60	MS63	MS65
1962 (a)	750,000	0.15	0.30	0.75	1.50	2.50
1974 (a)	172,000	0.15	0.30	0.75	1.50	2.50
1975 (a)	172,000	0.15	0.30	0.75	1.50	2.50
1976 (a)	172,000	0.15	0.30	0.75	1.50	2.50
1977 (a)	172,000	0.15	0.30	0.75	1.50	2.50
1978 (a)	300,000	0.15	0.30	0.75	1.50	2.50
1979 (a)	300,000	0.15	0.30	0.75	1.50	2.50
1982 (a)	100,000	0.15	0.30	0.75	1.50	2.50
1995 (a)	—	0.15	0.30	0.75	1.50	2.50

KM# 143 20 CENTIMES

4.00 g., Aluminum-Bronze, 23.5 mm. **Ruler:** Rainier III **Obv:** Head right **Rev:** Figure with hand on shield divides crown and value **Edge:** Plain

Date	Mintage	VF20	XF40	MS60	MS63	MS65
1962 (a)	750,000	0.25	0.50	1.00	1.75	3.00
1974 (a)	104,000	0.25	0.50	1.00	1.75	3.00
1975 (a)	97,000	0.25	0.50	1.00	1.75	3.00
1976 (a)	103,000	0.25	0.50	1.00	1.75	3.00
1977 (a)	97,000	0.25	0.50	1.00	1.75	3.00
1978 (a)	25,000	0.25	0.50	1.00	1.75	3.00
1979 (a)	25,000	0.25	0.50	1.00	1.75	3.00
1982 (a)	100,000	0.25	0.50	1.00	1.75	3.00
1995 (a)	30,000	0.25	0.50	1.00	1.75	3.00

KM# 144 50 CENTIMES

Aluminum-Bronze **Ruler:** Rainier III **Obv:** Head right **Rev:** Figure with hand on shield divides crown and value

Date	Mintage	VF20	XF40	MS60	MS63	MS65
1962 (a)	375,000	1.25	2.50	3.50	7.50	12.50

KM# 145 1/2 FRANC

4.50 g., Nickel, 19.5 mm. **Ruler:** Rainier III **Obv:** Head right **Rev:** Crown overlapping shield, value at lower left **Edge:** Reeded

Date	Mintage	VF20	XF40	MS60	MS63	MS65
1965 (a)	375,000	0.50	1.00	1.50	2.50	4.50
1968 (a)	125,000	0.50	1.00	1.50	2.50	4.50
1974 (a)	62,500	0.65	1.25	1.75	2.75	5.00
1975 (a)	62,500	0.65	1.25	1.75	2.75	5.00
1976 (a)	62,500	0.65	1.25	1.75	2.75	5.00
1977 (a)	62,500	0.65	1.25	1.75	2.75	5.00
1978 (a)	230,000	0.50	1.00	1.50	2.50	4.50
1979 (a)	230,000	0.50	1.00	1.50	2.50	4.50
1982 (a)	460,000	0.50	1.00	1.50	2.50	4.50
1989 (a)	10,000	0.50	1.00	1.50	2.50	4.60
1995 (a)	30,000	0.50	1.00	1.50	2.50	4.50

KM# 140 FRANC

6.00 g., Nickel, 24 mm. **Ruler:** Rainier III **Obv:** Head right **Rev:** Crown overlapping shield, value at lower left **Edge:** Reeded

Date	Mintage	VF20	XF40	MS60	MS63	MS65
1960 (a)	500,000	0.65	1.25	1.75	2.75	5.00
1966 (a)	175,000	0.75	1.50	2.00	3.00	5.50
1968 (a)	250,000	0.75	1.50	2.00	3.00	5.50
1974 (a)	194,000	0.75	1.50	2.00	3.00	5.50
1975 (a)	195,000	0.75	1.50	2.00	3.00	5.50
1976 (a)	193,000	0.75	1.50	2.00	3.00	5.50
1977 (a)	188,000	0.75	1.50	2.00	3.00	5.50
1978 (a)	280,000	0.75	1.50	2.00	3.00	5.50
1979 (a)	280,000	0.75	1.50	2.00	3.00	5.50
1982 (a)	525,000	0.75	1.50	2.00	3.00	5.50
1986 (a)	50,000	0.65	1.25	1.75	2.75	5.00
1989 (a)	50,000	0.65	1.25	1.75	2.75	5.00
1995 (a)	30,000	0.65	1.25	1.75	2.75	5.00

KM# 157 2 FRANCS

7.50 g., Nickel, 26.5 mm. **Ruler:** Rainier III **Obv:** Head right **Rev:** Monogram within crowned shield **Edge:** Reeded

Date	Mintage	VF20	XF40	MS60	MS63	MS65
1979 (a)	162,000	0.75	1.50	2.00	3.00	5.50
1981 (a)	275,000	0.75	1.50	2.00	3.00	5.50
1982 (a)	446,000	0.75	1.50	2.00	3.00	5.50

KM# 166 2 FRANCS

7.50 g., Nickel, 26.5 mm. **Ruler:** Rainier III **Obv:** Head left **Edge:** Reeded

Date	Mintage	VF20	XF40	MS60	MS63	MS65
1995 (a)	—	0.75	1.50	2.00	4.00	6.50

KM# 141 5 FRANCS

12.00 g., 0.835 Silver 0.3222 oz. ASW **Ruler:** Rainier III **Obv:** Head left **Rev:** Crowned arms with supporters flanked by value

Date	Mintage	VF20	XF40	MS60	MS63	MS65
1960 (a)	125,000	—	10.00	12.00	20.00	45.00
1966 (a)	125,000	—	10.00	12.00	20.00	45.00

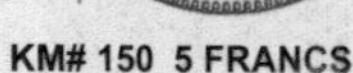

KM# 150 5 FRANCS

10.00 g., Copper-Nickel, 29 mm. **Ruler:** Rainier III **Obv:** Head right **Rev:** Value below monogram and crown, all flanked by lined designs **Edge:** Reeded

Date	Mintage	VF20	XF40	MS60	MS63	MS65
1971 (a)	250,000	1.50	2.50	4.50	6.50	12.00
1974 (a)	250,000	1.50	2.50	4.50	6.50	12.00
1975 (a)	14,000	2.50	6.00	12.50	16.00	20.00
1976 (a)	14,000	2.50	6.00	12.50	16.00	20.00
1977 (a)	14,500	2.00	4.00	8.00	12.00	16.00
1978 (a)	10,000	2.00	4.00	8.00	12.00	16.00
1979 (a)	10,000	2.00	4.00	8.00	12.00	16.00
1982 (a)	152,000	2.00	4.00	8.00	12.00	16.00
1989	35,000	2.00	4.00	8.00	12.00	16.00
1995 (a)	30,000	2.00	4.00	8.00	12.00	16.00

KM# 146 10 FRANCS

25.00 g., 0.900 Silver 0.7234 oz. ASW, 37 mm. **Ruler:** Rainier III **Subject:** 100th Anniversary - Accession of Charles III **Obv:** Head right **Rev:** Crowned shield

Date	Mintage	VF20	XF40	MS60	MS63	MS65
1966 (a)	62,500	—	—	25.00	40.00	70.00

KM# 151 10 FRANCS

10.20 g., Copper-Nickel-Aluminum **Ruler:** Rainier III **Subject:** 25th Anniversary of Reign **Obv:** Head left **Rev:** Monogram within crowned arms with supporters

Date	Mintage	VF20	XF40	MS60	MS63	MS65
ND-1974 (a)	25,000	—	2.50	4.00	8.00	16.00

KM# 154 10 FRANCS
Copper-Nickel-Aluminum **Ruler:** Rainier III **Obv:** Head left **Rev:** Monogram within crowned arms with supporters

Date	Mintage	VF20	XF40	MS60	MS63	MS65
1975 (a)	16,000	—	2.50	4.00	8.00	16.00
1976 (a)	16,000	—	2.75	4.50	9.00	18.00
1977 (a)	18,000	—	2.25	3.00	5.50	8.00
1978 (a)	190,000	—	2.25	3.00	5.50	8.00
1979 (a)	190,000	—	2.25	3.00	5.50	8.00
1981 (a)	230,000	—	2.25	3.00	5.50	8.00
1982 (a)	230,000	—	2.25	3.00	5.50	8.00

KM# 160 10 FRANCS
Copper-Nickel-Aluminum **Ruler:** Rainier III **Obv:** Head of Princess Grace left **Rev:** Single rose divides value

Date	Mintage	VF20	XF40	MS60	MS63	MS65
1982 (a)	30,000	—	—	7.50	12.50	25.00

KM# 162 10 FRANCS
10.00 g., Nickel-Aluminum-Bronze **Ruler:** Rainier III **Subject:** Prince Pierre Foundation **Obv:** Bust right and single sprig on paper to left of dates **Rev:** Small doubled wreath divides date on top of shield flanked by symbols

Date	Mintage	VF20	XF40	MS60	MS63	MS65
1989 (a)	100,000	—	—	4.00	7.00	12.00

KM# 163 10 FRANCS
6.50 g., Bi-Metallic Nickel center in Aluminum-Bronze ring, 23 mm. **Ruler:** Rainier III **Obv:** Value and monogram within circle **Rev:** Armored knight right within circle

Date	Mintage	VF20	XF40	MS60	MS63	MS65
1989 (a)	100,000	—	—	3.00	6.00	10.00
1991 (a)	250,000	—	—	7.00	12.00	15.00
1992 (a)	250,000	—	—	7.00	12.00	15.00
1993 (a)	250,000	—	—	7.00	12.00	15.00
1994 (a)	250,000	—	—	7.00	12.00	15.00
1995 (a)	250,000	—	—	3.00	6.00	10.00
1996 (a)	250,000	—	—	3.00	6.00	10.00
1997 (a)	250,000	—	—	3.00	6.00	10.00
1998 (a)	250,000	—	—	3.00	6.00	10.00
2000 (a)	240,000	—	—	3.00	6.00	10.00

KM# 165 20 FRANCS
9.00 g., Tri-Metallic Aluminum-Bronze center; Nickel ring; Aluminum-Bronze outer ring, 27 mm. **Ruler:** Rainier III **Obv:** Value and monogram within circle **Rev:** Prince's palace within circle with crown above

Date	Mintage	VF20	XF40	MS60	MS63	MS65
1992 (a)	100,000	—	—	7.50	13.00	17.00

Date	Mintage	VF20	XF40	MS60	MS63	MS65
1995 (a)	—	—	—	7.50	13.00	17.00
1997 (a)	120,000	—	—	7.50	13.00	17.00

KM# 152.1 50 FRANCS
30.00 g., 0.900 Silver 0.8681 oz. ASW, 41 mm. **Ruler:** Rainier III **Subject:** 25th Anniversary of Reign **Obv:** Bust right **Rev:** Crowned monograms divide diamonds **Edge:** Commemorative inscription

Date	Mintage	VF20	XF40	MS60	MS63	MS65
1974 (a)	25,000	—	—	35.00	75.00	165

KM# 152.2 50 FRANCS
30.00 g., 0.900 Silver 0.8681 oz. ASW, 41 mm. **Ruler:** Rainier III **Obv:** Bust right **Rev:** Crowned monograms divide diamonds **Edge:** Plain

Date	Mintage	VF20	XF40	MS60	MS63	MS65
1975 (a)	7,500	—	—	50.00	80.00	170
1976 (a)	6,000	—	—	55.00	85.00	175

KM# 161 100 FRANCS
15.00 g., 0.900 Silver 0.434 oz. ASW **Ruler:** Rainier III **Subject:** Heir Apparent Prince Albert **Obv:** Conjoined heads right **Rev:** Crowned arms with supporters

Date	Mintage	VF20	XF40	MS60	MS63	MS65
1982 (a)	30,000	—	—	35.00	65.00	150

KM# 164 100 FRANCS
15.00 g., 0.900 Silver 0.434 oz. ASW **Ruler:** Rainier III **Subject:** 40th Anniversary of Reign **Obv:** Head right **Rev:** Crowned monogram above value

Date	Mintage	VF20	XF40	MS60	MS63	MS65
1989 (a)	45,000	—	—	35.00	65.00	150

KM# 176 100 FRANCS
15.00 g., 0.950 Silver 0.4581 oz. ASW, 31 mm. **Ruler:** Rainier III **Subject:** 700th Anniversary - Grimaldi Dynasty **Obv:** Armored equestrian **Rev:** Robed figure drawing sword at castle drawbridge **Edge:** Plain

Date	Mintage	VF20	XF40	MS60	MS63	MS65
ND(1997)	30,000	—	—	35.00	65.00	150

KM# 175 100 FRANCS
15.00 g., 0.900 Silver 0.434 oz. ASW, 31 mm. **Ruler:** Rainier III **Subject:** 50th Anniversary of Reign - Prince Ranier III **Obv:** Head right **Rev:** Crowned monogram above value **Edge:** Plain

Date	Mintage	VF20	XF40	MS60	MS63	MS65
1999	20,000	—	—	35.00	65.00	150

PATTERNS

Including off metal strikes

KM#	Date	Mintage	Identification	Mkt Val
Pn15	1934A	15	500 Francs. 0.900. Gold.	6,500

ESSAIS

Standard metals unless otherwise noted

KM#	Date	Mintage	Identification	Mkt Val
E1	1924	—	50 Centimes. Gold. KM#110.	—
E2	1924	12	Franc. Aluminum-Bronze. KM111.	950
E3	1924	—	Franc. Gold. KM111.	1,200
E4	1924	12	2 Francs. Aluminum-Bronze. KM112.	1,000
E5	1924	—	2 Francs. Gold. Hercules shooting bow to right. Shield below value within circle. KM112.	—
E6	ND-1943 (1925) (a)	250	Franc. 0.900. Gold.	—
E7	ND-1943 (a)	1,100	Franc. Aluminum. KM120.	40.00
E8	ND-1943 (a)	—	Franc. Aluminum-Bronze. KM120.	50.00
E9	ND-1943 (a)	250	Franc. Silver. KM120.	150
E10	ND-1943 (a)	250	2 Francs. 0.900. Gold.	1,200
E11	ND-1943 (a)	1,100	2 Francs. Aluminum. KM121.	50.00
E13	ND-1943 (a)	250	2 Francs. Silver. KM121.	175
E12	ND-1945 (a)	1,100	2 Francs. Aluminum-Bronze. KM121.	50.00
E14	1945 (a)	250	5 Francs. 0.900. Gold.	1,300
E15	1945 (a)	1,100	5 Francs. Aluminum. KM122.	65.00
E16	1945 (a)	150	5 Francs. Aluminum-Bronze. KM122.	145
E17	1945 (a)	250	5 Francs. Silver. KM122.	225
E18	1945 (a)	1,100	10 Francs. Copper-Nickel. KM123.	45.00
E19	1945 (a)	250	10 Francs. Silver.	200
E20	1945 (a)	1,100	20 Francs. Copper-Nickel. KM124.	65.00
E21	1945 (a)	250	20 Francs. Silver.	200
E22	1946 (a)	250	10 Francs. 0.900. Gold.	1,400
E23	1947 (a)	250	20 Francs. 0.900. Gold.	1,400
E24	1950 (a)	1,100	10 Francs.	40.00
E25	1950 (a)	500	10 Francs. Silver.	60.00
E26	1950 (a)	500	10 Francs. 0.900. Gold.	800
E27	1950 (a)	1,700	20 Francs.	45.00
E28	1950 (a)	—	20 Francs. Silver.	75.00
E29	1950 (a)	500	20 Francs. 0.900. Gold.	725
E30	1950 (a)	1,700	50 Francs.	55.00
E31	1950 (a)	500	50 Francs. Silver.	100
E32	1950 (a)	500	50 Francs. 0.900. Gold.	925
E33	1950 (a)	1,700	100 Francs.	55.00
E34	1950 (a)	500	100 Francs. Silver.	125
E35	1950 (a)	500	100 Francs. 0.900. Gold. Head left divides circle. Armored knight on horse divides circle.	2,000
E36	1956 (a)	500	100 Francs. 0.900. Gold.	550
E37	1956 (a)	500	100 Francs. Silver. KM134.	170
E38	1960 (a)	—	Franc. Nickel. KM140.	75.00
E39	1960 (a)	500	Franc. Silver.	75.00
E40	1960 (a)	500	Franc. 0.920. Gold.	550
E41	1960 (a)	500	5 Francs. Silver.	120
E42	1960 (a)	500	5 Francs. 0.920. Gold.	725
E43	1962 (a)	1,200	10 Centimes.	25.00
E44	1962 (a)	502	10 Centimes. 0.950. Silver.	65.00
E45	1962 (a)	502	10 Centimes. 0.920. Gold. Head right. Figure with hand on shield divides crown and value.	300
E46	1962 (a)	1,200	20 Centimes.	45.00
E47	1962 (a)	502	20 Centimes. 0.950. Silver.	80.00
E48	1962 (a)	502	20 Centimes. 0.920. Gold.	350
E49	1962 (a)	1,200	50 Centimes.	65.00
E50	1962 (a)	502	50 Centimes. 0.950. Silver.	150
E51	1962 (a)	502	50 Centimes. 0.920. Gold.	500
E52	1965 (a)	2,000	1/2 Franc. Nickel.	45.00
E53	1965 (a)	1,000	1/2 Franc. Silver.	65.00

KM#	Date	Mintage	Identification	Mkt Val
E54	1965 (a)	1,000	1/2 Franc. 0.920. Gold.	325
E55	1966 (a)	500	5 Francs. 0.920. Gold.	650
E56	1966 (a)	100	10 Francs.	150
E57	1966 (a)	1,000	10 Francs. 0.920. Gold.	925
E58	1971 (a)	1,000	5 Francs.	50.00
E59	1971 (a)	1,000	5 Francs. Silver.	120
E60	1971 (a)	500	5 Francs. 0.920. Gold.	550
E61	1974 (a)	1,000	5 Francs. Silver.	75.00
E62	1974 (a)	1,000	5 Francs. Gold.	400
E63	1974 (a)	1,500	10 Francs.	50.00
E64	1974 (a)	1,000	10 Francs. Silver.	120
E65	1974 (a)	1,000	10 Francs. Gold.	425
E66	1974 (a)	1,000	50 Francs.	150
E67	1974 (a)	1,000	50 Francs. Gold.	1,400
E68	1976	1,600	Centime. Stainless Steel. KM155.	35.00
E69	1976	1,600	5 Centimes. Copper-Aluminum-Nickel. KM156.	40.00
E70	1976	1,600	10 Centimes. Aluminum-Bronze. KM142.	40.00
E71	1979	—	2 Francs. Nickel. KM157.	75.00
E72	1982 (a)	4,000	10 Francs. Nickel-Aluminum-Bronze.	50.00
E73	1982 (a)	30,000	10 Francs. Silver.	40.00
E74	1982 (a)	1,000	10 Francs. Gold.	475
E75	1982 (a)	1,000	100 Francs. 0.900. Silver. KM161.	65.00
E76	1982 (a)	1,000	100 Francs. Gold. Conjoined heads right. Crowned arms with supporters.	500

PIEDFORT

Double thickness; Standard metals unless otherwise stated

KM#	Date	Mintage	Identification	Mkt Val
P18a	1974 (a)	—	10 Francs. Gold. Without Essai.	850
P19a	1974 (a)	250	50 Francs. Gold. Without Essai.	2,500

PIEDFORT WITH ESSAI

Double thickness; Standard metals unless otherwise noted

KM#	Date	Mintage	Identification	Mkt Val
PE1	ND-1943 (a)	15	Franc. 0.900. Gold.	1,800
PE2	ND-1943 (a)	15	2 Francs. 0.900. Gold.	2,100
PE3	1945 (a)	15	5 Francs. 0.900. Gold.	2,250
PE4	1946 (a)	16	10 Francs. 0.900. Gold. Bust left. Crowned shield and value flanked by sprigs.	1,750
PE5	1947 (a)	16	20 Francs. 0.900. Gold.	2,200
PE6	1950 (a)	Est. 450	10 Francs. Silver.	85.00
PE6a	1950 (a)	325	10 Francs. 0.900. Gold.	500
PE7	1950 (a)	Est. 450	20 Francs. Silver.	90.00
PE7a	1950 (a)	325	20 Francs. 0.900. Gold.	475
PE8	1950 (a)	Est. 450	50 Francs. Silver.	170
PE8a	1950 (a)	325	50 Francs. 0.900. Gold.	2,000
PE9	1950 (a)	Est. 450	100 Francs. Silver.	170
PE9a	1950 (a)	325	100 Francs. 0.900. Gold.	750
PE10	1956 (a)	20	100 Francs. 0.900. Gold.	1,800
PE11	1960 (a)	25	Franc. 0.920. Gold.	975
PE12	1960 (a)	25	5 Francs. 0.920. Gold.	1,800
PE13	1962 (a)	100	10 Centimes. 0.950. Silver.	150
PE13a	1962 (a)	25	10 Centimes. 0.920. Gold.	1,100
PE14	1962 (a)	100	20 Centimes. 0.950. Silver.	150
PE14a	1962 (a)	25	20 Centimes. 0.920. Gold.	1,250
PE15	1962 (a)	100	50 Centimes. 0.950. Silver.	200
PE15a	1962 (a)	25	50 Centimes. 0.920. Gold.	1,350
PE16	1966 (a)	150	5 Francs. Nickel.	60.00
PE16a	1971 (a)	250	5 Francs. Silver.	160
PE16b	1971 (a)	250	5 Francs. 0.920. Gold.	950
PE17	1974 (a)	250	5 Francs. Silver.	160
PE17a	1974 (a)	250	5 Francs. Gold. Head right. Crowned monogram and value flanked by lined designs.	1,000
PE18	1974 (a)	250	10 Francs. Silver.	200
PE18a	1974 (a)	250	10 Francs. Gold.	950
PE19	1974 (a)	250	50 Francs. Without Essai.	170
PE19a	1974 (a)	250	50 Francs. Gold.	4,000
PE20	1982 (a)	250	10 Francs. Silver.	185
PE20a	1982 (a)	250	10 Francs. Gold.	600
PE21	1982 (a)	250	100 Francs. Silver.	275
PE21a	1982 (a)	250	100 Francs. Gold.	1,450

SPECIMEN SETS (SS)

KM#	Date	Mintage	Identification	Issue Price	Mkt Val
SS1	1974 (7)	7	KM140, 142, 143, 145, 150, 151, 152.1. 3,000 sets not released.	45.00	500
SS2	1975 (7)	8	KM140, 142, 143, 145, 150, 152.2, 154	—	200
SS3	1976 (9)	6,000	KM140, 142, 143, 145, 150, 152.2, 154-156	—	135
SS6	1982 (11)	10,000	KM140, 142, 143, 145, 150, 154-157, 160, 161	—	150
SS7	1995 (9)	—	KM140, 142, 143, 150, 155, 156, 163, 165, 166	—	120

MONGOLIA

The State of Mongolia, (formerly the Mongolian People's Republic) a landlocked country in central Asia between Russia and the People's Republic of China, has an area of 604,250 sq. mi. (1,565,000 sq. km.) and a population of 2.26 million. Capital: Ulaan Baator. Animal herds and flocks are the chief economic asset. Wool, cattle, butter, meat and hides are exported.

Mongolia (often referred to as Outer Mongolia), one of the world's oldest countries, attained its greatest power in the 13th century when Genghis Khan and his successors conquered all of China and extended their influence westward as far as Hungary and Poland. The empire dissolved in later centuries and in 1691 was brought under suzerainty of the Manchus, who had conquered China in 1644. Afterward the Chinese republican movement led by Sun Yat-sen overthrew the Manchus and set up the Chinese Republic in 1911. Mongolia, with the support of Russia, proclaimed their independence from China and, on March 13, 1921 a Provisional People's Government was established and later, on Nov. 26, 1924 the government proclaimed the Mongolian People's Republic.

Although nominally a dependency of China, Outer Mongolia voted at a plebiscite Oct. 20, 1945 to sever all ties with China and become an independent nation. Opposition to the communist party developed in late 1989 and after demonstrations and hunger strikes, the Politburo resigned on March 12, 1990 and the new State of Mongolia was organized.

On Feb. 12, 1992 it became the first to discard communism as the national political system by adopting a new constitution.

For earlier issues see Russia - Tannu Tuva.

MONETARY SYSTEM
100 Mongo = 1 Tugrik

PEOPLE'S REPUBLIC

DECIMAL COINAGE

KM# 1 MONGO

Copper, 21 mm. **Obv:** Soembo arms, text **Rev:** Value within 1/2 wreath

Date	Mintage	F12	VF20	XF40	MS60	MS63
AH15	—	5.00	8.00	15.00	55.00	125

KM# 9 MONGO

Aluminum-Bronze **Obv:** Soembo arms, text **Rev:** Value within 1/2 wreath

Date	Mintage	F12	VF20	XF40	MS60	MS63
AH27	—	2.50	3.50	7.50	18.50	25.00

KM# 15 MONGO

Aluminum-Bronze **Obv:** National arms within circle **Rev:** Value within 1/2 wreath

Date	Mintage	F12	VF20	XF40	MS60	MS63
AH35	—	2.00	3.00	5.50	14.00	20.00

KM# 21 MONGO

Aluminum **Obv:** Wreath around center hole with inscription around border **Rev:** Value above hole in center and 3/4 wreath

Date	Mintage	VF20	XF40	MS60	MS63	MS65
1959	9,000,000	0.60	1.00	1.50	2.50	3.50

KM# 27 MONGO

0.75 g., Aluminum, 17.5 mm. **Obv:** National arms **Rev:** Value above 1/2 wreath

Date	Mintage	VF20	XF40	MS60	MS63	MS65
1970	—	0.60	0.85	1.25	1.75	3.00
1977	—	0.60	0.85	1.25	1.75	3.00
1980	—	0.60	0.85	1.25	1.75	3.00
1981	—	0.60	0.85	1.25	1.75	3.00

KM# 2 2 MONGO

Copper, 24 mm. **Obv:** Soembo arms, text **Rev:** Value within 1/2 wreath

Date	Mintage	F12	VF20	XF40	MS60	MS63
AH15	—	3.50	6.50	12.00	55.00	150

KM# 10 2 MONGO

Aluminum-Bronze, 22 mm. **Obv:** Soembo, text **Rev:** Value within 1/2 wreath

Date	Mintage	F12	VF20	XF40	MS60	MS63
AH27	—	2.50	3.50	6.00	15.00	35.00

KM# 16 2 MONGO

Aluminum-Bronze **Obv:** National arms within circle **Rev:** Value within 1/2 wreath

Date	Mintage	F12	VF20	XF40	MS60	MS63
AH35	—	1.00	2.00	4.00	10.00	15.00

KM# 22 2 MONGO

Aluminum **Obv:** Wreath around center hole with inscription around border **Rev:** Value above center hole and 3/4 wreath

Date	Mintage	VF20	XF40	MS60	MS63	MS65
1959	4,000,000	0.65	1.50	2.50	3.50	5.00

KM# 28 2 MONGO

1.05 g., Aluminum, 20 mm. **Obv:** National arms above date **Rev:** Value within 1/2 wreath **Edge:** Plain

Date	Mintage	VF20	XF40	MS60	MS63	MS65
1970	—	0.65	1.00	1.50	2.50	3.50
1977	—	0.65	1.00	1.50	2.50	3.50
1980	—	0.65	1.00	1.50	2.50	3.50
1981	—	0.65	1.00	1.50	2.50	3.50

KM# 3.1 5 MONGO

Copper, 32 mm. **Obv:** Soembo arms, text **Rev:** Value within 1/2 wreath

Date	Mintage	F12	VF20	XF40	MS60	MS63
AH15	—	5.00	10.00	45.00	125	225

Note: Variety in obverse legend exists

KM# 3.2 5 MONGO

Copper, 32 mm. **Note:** Error: letter "m" looking like a horse's tail omitted in nayramdax (Vertically written word lower left of Soyombo)

Date	Mintage	F12	VF20	XF40	MS60	MS63
1925	—	—	—	—	100	—

KM# 11 5 MONGO

Aluminum-Bronze, 28 mm. **Obv:** Soembo arms, text **Rev:** Value within 1/2 wreath

Date	Mintage	F12	VF20	XF40	MS60	MS63
AH27	—	2.75	3.50	7.00	16.00	22.00

KM# 17 5 MONGO

Aluminum-Bronze **Obv:** National arms within circle **Rev:** Value within 1/2 wreath

Date	Mintage	F12	VF20	XF40	MS60	MS63
AH35	—	1.75	2.50	5.00	13.50	17.50

KM# 23 5 MONGO

0.87 g., Aluminum, 21 mm. **Obv:** Wreath around hole in center with inscription around border **Rev:** Value above hole in center and 1/2 wreath

Date	Mintage	VF20	XF40	MS60	MS63	MS65
1959	2,400,000	0.50	0.75	1.50	2.50	5.00

KM# 29 5 MONGO

1.70 g., Aluminum, 23 mm. **Obv:** Date below national arms **Rev:** Value within 1/2 wreath

Date	Mintage	VF20	XF40	MS60	MS63	MS65
1970	—	0.85	1.50	2.50	3.50	5.00
1977	—	0.85	1.50	2.50	3.50	5.00
1980	—	0.85	1.50	2.50	3.50	5.00
1981	—	0.85	1.50	2.50	3.50	5.00

KM# 4 10 MONGO

1.80 g., 0.500 Silver 0.0289 oz. ASW, 17 mm. **Obv:** Soembo arms, text **Rev:** Value within 1/2 wreath

Date	Mintage	F12	VF20	XF40	MS60	MS63
AH15	1,500,000	3.00	5.00	10.00	25.00	35.00

KM# 12 10 MONGO

Copper-Nickel **Obv:** Soembo arms, text **Rev:** Value within 1/2 wreath

Date	Mintage	F12	VF20	XF40	MS60	MS63
AH27	—	2.00	3.50	7.00	18.00	25.00

KM# 18 10 MONGO

Copper-Nickel **Obv:** National arms within circle **Rev:** Value within 1/2 wreath

Date	Mintage	F12	VF20	XF40	MS60	MS63
AH35	—	1.50	3.00	5.00	13.50	17.50

KM# 24 10 MONGO

Aluminum **Obv:** National arms within circle **Rev:** Value within 3/4 wreath

Date	Mintage	VF20	XF40	MS60	MS63	MS65
1959	3,000,000	1.25	2.00	3.50	6.50	9.00

KM# 30 10 MONGO

2.30 g., Copper-Nickel, 18.5 mm. **Obv:** Date below national arms **Rev:** Value within 1/2 wreath

Date	Mintage	VF20	XF40	MS60	MS63	MS65
1970	—	0.85	1.50	2.50	3.50	5.00
1977	—	0.85	1.50	2.50	3.50	5.00
1980	—	0.85	1.50	2.50	3.50	5.00
1981	—	0.85	1.50	2.50	3.50	5.00

KM# 5 15 MONGO

2.70 g., 0.500 Silver 0.0434 oz. ASW, 19 mm. **Obv:** Soembo arms, text **Rev:** Value within 1/2 wreath

Date	Mintage	F12	VF20	XF40	MS60	MS63
AH15	417,000	3.50	6.00	12.50	28.00	45.00

KM# 13 15 MONGO

Copper-Nickel **Obv:** Soembo arms, text **Rev:** Value within 1/2 wreath

Date	Mintage	F12	VF20	XF40	MS60	MS63
AH27	—	2.00	3.00	6.00	15.00	30.00

KM# 19 15 MONGO

Copper-Nickel **Obv:** National arms within circle **Rev:** Value within 3/4 wreath

Date	Mintage	F12	VF20	XF40	MS60	MS63
AH35	—	1.50	2.25	4.00	10.00	15.00

KM# 25 15 MONGO

Aluminum **Obv:** National arms within circle **Rev:** Value within 3/4 wreath

Date	Mintage	VF20	XF40	MS60	MS63	MS65
1959	4,600,000	0.85	1.50	2.50	3.50	5.00

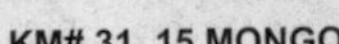

KM# 31 15 MONGO

4.05 g., Copper-Nickel, 22 mm. **Obv:** Date below national arms **Rev:** Value within 1/2 wreath

Date	Mintage	VF20	XF40	MS60	MS63	MS65
1970	—	0.65	1.00	1.25	1.75	3.00
1977	—	0.65	1.00	1.25	1.75	3.00
1980	—	0.65	1.00	1.25	1.75	3.00
1981	—	0.65	1.00	1.25	1.75	3.00

KM# 6 20 MONGO

3.60 g., 0.500 Silver 0.0579 oz. ASW, 22 mm. **Obv:** Soembo arms, text **Rev:** Value within 1/2 wreath

Date	Mintage	F12	VF20	XF40	MS60	MS63
AH15	1,625,000	4.00	7.50	16.00	35.00	55.00

KM# 14 20 MONGO

Copper-Nickel **Obv:** Soembo arms, text **Rev:** Value within 1/2 wreath

Date	Mintage	F12	VF20	XF40	MS60	MS63
AH27	—	2.50	4.50	10.00	22.00	35.00

KM# 20 20 MONGO

Copper-Nickel **Obv:** National arms within circle **Rev:** Value within 3/4 wreath

Date	Mintage	F12	VF20	XF40	MS60	MS63
AH35	—	1.50	2.50	5.00	13.50	20.00

KM# 26 20 MONGO

Aluminum **Obv:** National arms within circle **Rev:** Value within 3/4 wreath

Date	Mintage	VF20	XF40	MS60	MS63	MS65
1959	3,600,000	1.25	2.00	3.00	4.00	6.00

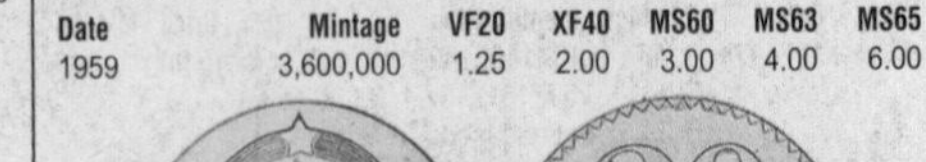

KM# 32 20 MONGO

5.90 g., Copper-Nickel, 25 mm. **Obv:** Date below national arms **Rev:** Value within 1/2 wreath

Date	Mintage	VF20	XF40	MS60	MS63	MS65
1970	—	0.80	1.50	2.50	3.50	5.00
1977	—	0.80	1.50	2.50	3.50	5.00
1980	—	0.80	1.50	2.50	3.50	5.00
1981	—	0.80	1.50	2.50	3.50	5.00

KM# 7 50 MONGO

10.00 g., 0.900 Silver 0.2893 oz. ASW, 27 mm. **Obv:** Soembo arms, text **Rev:** Value within 1/2 wreath

Date	Mintage	F12	VF20	XF40	MS60	MS63
AH15	920,000	11.00	16.00	25.00	40.00	60.00

KM# 33 50 MONGO

8.60 g., Copper-Nickel, 27.5 mm. **Obv:** Date below national arms **Rev:** Value within 1/2 wreath

Date	Mintage	VF20	XF40	MS60	MS63	MS65
1970	—	1.00	1.75	2.75	3.75	5.50
1977	—	1.00	1.75	2.75	3.75	5.50
1980	—	1.00	1.75	2.75	3.75	5.50
1981	—	1.00	1.75	2.75	3.75	5.50

KM# 8 TUGRIK

20.00 g., 0.900 Silver 0.5786 oz. ASW, 34 mm. **Obv:** Soembo arms, text **Rev:** Value within 1/2 wreath

Date	Mintage	F12	VF20	XF40	MS60	MS63
AH15	400,000	15.00	25.00	40.00	65.00	125

KM# 34 TUGRIK

14.90 g., Aluminum-Bronze, 32 mm. **Subject:** 50th Anniversary of the Revolution **Obv:** National arms **Rev:** Man on horse left within beaded circle **Edge Lettering:** ONE TUGRIK 1921 - 1971 **Note:** Date on edge.

Date	Mintage	VF20	XF40	MS60	MS63	MS65
ND-1971	—	—	—	4.00	6.00	10.00

KM# 34a TUGRIK

Copper-Nickel, 32 mm. **Obv:** National arms **Rev:** Man on horse left within beaded circle

Date	Mintage	VF20	XF40	MS60	MS63	MS65
ND-1971	—	—	—	7.00	12.00	18.00

KM# 34b TUGRIK

18.40 g., Silver, 32 mm. **Obv:** National arms **Rev:** Man on horse left within beaded circle

Date	Mintage	VF20	XF40	MS60	MS63	MS65
-1971	—	PF65 50.00				

KM# 34c TUGRIK

30.00 g., Gold, 32 mm. **Subject:** 50th Anniversary of the Revolution **Obv:** National arms **Rev:** Man on horse left within beaded circle **Note:** Mintage: 5-10 pieces.

Date	Mintage	VF20	XF40	MS60	MS63	MS65
-1971	—	PF65 4,000				

KM# 41 TUGRIK

14.90 g., Aluminum-Bronze, 32 mm. **Subject:** 60th Anniversary of the Revolution **Obv:** National arms **Rev:** Man on horse left within beaded circle **Edge:** Lettered

Date	Mintage	VF20	XF40	MS60	MS63	MS65
1981	—	—	—	4.00	7.50	9.00

KM# 42 TUGRIK

14.90 g., Aluminum-Bronze, 32 mm. **Subject:** Soviet - Mongolian Space Flight **Obv:** National arms **Rev:** Conjoined helmeted heads left with stars at upper left and date at lower right **Edge:** Smooth

Date	Mintage	VF20	XF40	MS60	MS63	MS65
1981	—	—	—	3.00	4.00	6.00

KM# 43 TUGRIK

14.90 g., Aluminum-Bronze, 32 mm. **Subject:** 60th Anniversary of the State Bank **Obv:** National arms **Rev:** Value within design with date within 1/2 wreath **Edge:** Lettered

Date	Mintage	VF20	XF40	MS60	MS63	MS65
1984	—	—	—	3.00	4.00	6.00

Note: Edge varieties exist

KM# 44 TUGRIK

14.90 g., Aluminum-Bronze, 32 mm. **Subject:** 60th Anniversary of the People's Republic **Obv:** National arms **Rev:** Soembo arms and value within 1/2 wreath **Edge:** Lettered

Date	Mintage	VF20	XF40	MS60	MS63	MS65
1984	—	—	—	3.00	5.50	7.50

KM# 48 TUGRIK

14.90 g., Aluminum-Bronze, 32 mm. **Subject:** Year of Peace **Obv:** National arms **Rev:** Dove above hands and 3/4 wreath **Edge:** Lettered

Date	Mintage	VF20	XF40	MS60	MS63	MS65
1986	—	—	—	3.50	5.00	7.50

KM# 49 TUGRIK

14.90 g., Aluminum-Bronze, 32 mm. **Subject:** 65th Anniversary of the Revolution **Obv:** National arms **Rev:** Bust left **Edge:** Lettered

Date	Mintage	VF20	XF40	MS60	MS63	MS65
1986	—	—	—	3.00	5.00	7.50

KM# 52 TUGRIK

14.90 g., Aluminum-Bronze, 32 mm. **Subject:** 170th Anniversary - Birth of Karl Marx **Obv:** National arms **Rev:** Head facing flanked by dates

Date	Mintage	VF20	XF40	MS60	MS63	MS65
ND-1988	—	—	—	4.00	6.50	12.50

KM# 35 10 TUGRIK

Copper-Nickel, 36.5 mm. **Subject:** 50th Anniversary of State Bank **Obv:** National arms **Rev:** State bank

Date	Mintage	VF20	XF40	MS60	MS63	MS65
ND-1974	—	—	—	3.50	6.00	9.00
ND-1974	—	—	—	3.50	6.00	9.00

KM# 36 25 TUGRIK

28.28 g., 0.925 Silver 0.841 oz. ASW **Subject:** Conservation **Obv:** National arms **Rev:** Arfali sheep

Date	Mintage	VF20	XF40	MS60	MS63	MS65
1976	5,348	—	—	—	30.00	32.00
1976	6,096	PF65 35.00				

KM# 39.1 25 TUGRIK
19.44 g., 0.925 Silver 0.5781 oz. ASW **Series:** International Year of the Child **Obv:** National arms **Rev:** Children riding camel

Date	Mintage	VF20	XF40	MS60	MS63	MS65
1980	14,000	PF65 25.00				

KM# 39.2 25 TUGRIK
19.26 g., 0.925 Silver 0.5728 oz. ASW, 36.1 mm. **Obv:** National arms **Rev:** Children riding camel, two countermarks at 5 o'clock **Edge:** Reeded

Date	Mintage	VF20	XF40	MS60	MS63	MS65
1980	—	PF63 35.00	PF65 50.00			

KM# 47 25 TUGRIK
19.44 g., 0.925 Silver 0.5781 oz. ASW **Series:** Decade for Women **Obv:** National arms **Rev:** Figure with hat holding child

Date	Mintage	VF20	XF40	MS60	MS63	MS65
1984	1,249	PF65 60.00	PF67 75.00			

KM# 50 25 TUGRIK
28.28 g., 0.925 Silver 0.841 oz. ASW **Series:** World Wildlife Fund **Obv:** National arms **Rev:** Snow leopard

Date	Mintage	XF40	MS60	MS63	MS65	MS66
1987 Matte	850	—	—	—	60.00	75.00
1987	25,000	PF65 30.00	PF67 35.00			

KM# 54 25 TUGRIK
28.28 g., 0.925 Silver 0.841 oz. ASW **Series:** Save the Children Fund **Obv:** National arms **Rev:** Child playing horse head fiddle

Date	Mintage	VF20	XF40	MS60	MS63	MS65
1989	20,000	PF65 30.00	PF67 35.00			

KM# 37 50 TUGRIK
35.00 g., 0.925 Silver 1.0409 oz. ASW **Subject:** Conservation **Obv:** National arms **Rev:** Camel running left above value flanked by bushes

Date	Mintage	VF20	XF40	MS60	MS63	MS65
1976	5,328	—	—	—	30.00	35.00
1976	5,900	PF65 40.00				

KM# 57 50 TUGRIK
31.10 g., 0.999 Silver 0.9989 oz. ASW **Subject:** Discovery of America **Obv:** National arms **Rev:** Portrait of Columbus and ship within circle and legend

Date	Mintage	VF20	XF40	MS60	MS63	MS65
1992	20,000	PF63 20.00	PF65 25.00			

KM# 170 50 TUGRIK
31.10 g., 0.999 Silver 0.9989 oz. ASW **Subject:** Year of the Monkey **Obv:** National arms **Rev:** Monkey

Date	Mintage	VF20	XF40	MS60	MS63	MS65
1992	Est. 20000	—	—	—	55.00	65.00

KM# 53 100 TUGRIK
28.00 g., 0.900 Silver 0.8102 oz. ASW **Subject:** Dinosaurs **Obv:** National arms **Rev:** Nemectosaurus

Date	Mintage	VF20	XF40	MS60	MS63	MS65
1989	1,000	—	—	—	80.00	100

KM# 55 100 TUGRIK
28.00 g., 0.900 Silver 0.8102 oz. ASW **Subject:** Secret history of the Mongols **Obv:** State emblem above denomination within English legend **Rev:** Portrait of Genghis Khan in light clothing

Date	Mintage	VF20	XF40	MS60	MS63	MS65
1990	4,000	—	—	—	50.00	60.00

KM# 58 100 TUGRIK
1.56 g., 0.999 Gold 0.0501 oz. AGW **Subject:** Discovery of America - Columbus **Obv:** National arms **Rev:** Portrait of Columbus and ship within circle and legend

Date	Mintage	VF20	XF40	MS60	MS63	MS65
1992	Est. 10000	PF65 95.00				

KM# 59 200 TUGRIK
3.11 g., 0.999 Gold 0.0999 oz. AGW **Subject:** Discovery of America - Columbus **Obv:** National arms **Rev:** Portrait of Columbus and ship within circle and legend

Date	Mintage	VF20	XF40	MS60	MS63	MS65
1992	Est. 10000	PF65 175				

KM# 45 250 TUGRIK
7.13 g., 0.900 Gold 0.2063 oz. AGW **Series:** Decade for Women **Obv:** National arms **Rev:** Figure on horseback left, value

Date	Mintage	VF20	XF40	MS60	MS63	MS65
1984	510	PF65 350				

KM# 72 300 TUGRIK
7.77 g., 0.999 Gold 0.2496 oz. AGW **Subject:** Japanese royal wedding **Obv:** National arms above value **Rev:** Royal couple facing each other

Date	Mintage	VF20	XF40	MS60	MS63	MS65
1993	Est. 500	PF65 425				

KM# 38 750 TUGRIK
33.44 g., 0.900 Gold 0.9675 oz. AGW **Subject:** Conservation **Rev:** Przewalski horses

Date	Mintage	VF20	XF40	MS60	MS63	MS65
1976	929	—	—	—	—	1,650
1976	374	PF65 1,750				

KM# 40 750 TUGRIK
18.79 g., 0.900 Gold 0.5437 oz. AGW **Series:** International Year of the Child **Obv:** National arms **Rev:** Children dancing

Date	Mintage	VF20	XF40	MS60	MS63	MS65
1980	32,000	PF65 950				

KM# 56 1000 TUGRIK
20.70 g., 0.900 Gold 0.599 oz. AGW **Subject:** Secret history of the Mongols **Obv:** State emblem above denomination within English legend **Rev:** Portrait of Genghis Khan in heavy clothing

Date	Mintage	VF20	XF40	MS60	MS63	MS65
1990	—	—	—	—	—	950

KM# 60 1000 TUGRIK
31.10 g., 0.999 Gold 0.9989 oz. AGW **Subject:** Discovery of America **Obv:** National arms divide date above value **Rev:** Portrait of Columbus and ship within circle and legend

Date	Mintage	VF20	XF40	MS60	MS63	MS65
1992	2,000	PF65 1,650				

KM# 171 1000 TUGRIK
31.10 g., 0.999 Gold 0.9989 oz. AGW **Subject:** Year of the Monkey **Obv:** National arms **Rev:** Monkey

Date	Mintage	VF20	XF40	MS60	MS63	MS65
1992	Est. 2000	—	—	—	—	1,600

STATE

KM# 122 20 TUGRIK
Aluminum **Obv:** Soembo arms, text **Rev:** Value

Date	Mintage	VF20	XF40	MS60	MS63	MS65
1994	—	—	—	1.00	1.50	1.75

KM# 84 50 TUGRIK
15.00 g., 0.999 Silver 0.4818 oz. ASW **Obv:** State emblem above value **Rev:** Bust with hat 1/4 left

Date	Mintage	VF20	XF40	MS60	MS63	MS65
1992	Est. 1000	PF65 35.00				

KM# 86 50 TUGRIK
31.10 g., 0.999 Silver 0.999 oz. ASW **Subject:** Year of the Monkey **Obv:** State emblem above value **Rev:** Sitting monkey

Date	Mintage	VF20	XF40	MS60	MS63	MS65
1992	20,000	PF65 42.00				

KM# 166 50 TUGRIK
31.10 g., 0.999 Silver 0.999 oz. ASW **Subject:** Discovery of America - Columbus **Obv:** State emblem above value **Rev:** Portrait of Columbus and ship within circle and legend

Date	Mintage	VF20	XF40	MS60	MS63	MS65
1992	—	PF65 40.00				

KM# 61 50 TUGRIK
31.10 g., 0.999 Silver 0.999 oz. ASW **Subject:** Year of the Rooster **Obv:** State emblem above value **Rev:** Rooster

Date	Mintage	VF20	XF40	MS60	MS63	MS65
1993	20,000	PF65 42.00				

KM# 69 50 TUGRIK
31.10 g., 0.999 Silver 0.999 oz. ASW **Subject:** Japanese Royal Wedding **Obv:** State emblem above value **Rev:** Busts facing each other

Date	Mintage	VF20	XF40	MS60	MS63	MS65
1993	1,962	PF65 75.00				

KM# 75 50 TUGRIK
31.10 g., 0.999 Silver 0.999 oz. ASW **Subject:** Year of the Dog **Obv:** State emblem above value **Rev:** Two dogs

Date	Mintage	VF20	XF40	MS60	MS63	MS65
1994	4,000	PF65 50.00				

KM# 123 50 TUGRIK
Aluminum **Obv:** Soembo arms, text **Rev:** Value within design

Date	Mintage	VF20	XF40	MS60	MS63	MS65
1994	—	—	—	1.25	1.75	2.00

KM# 94 50 TUGRIK
Copper-Nickel **Subject:** Year of the Pig **Obv:** State emblem above value **Rev:** Pig

Date	Mintage	VF20	XF40	MS60	MS63	MS65
1995	50,000	PF65 12.00				

KM# 104 50 TUGRIK
Copper-Nickel **Subject:** Year of the Rat **Obv:** Soembo arms within deigned circle **Rev:** Rat among flowers and plants

Date	Mintage	VF20	XF40	MS60	MS63	MS65
1996	50,000	PF65 18.00				

KM# 126 50 TUGRIK
Copper-Nickel **Subject:** Year of the Ox **Obv:** National emblem **Rev:** Ox

Date	Mintage	VF20	XF40	MS60	MS63	MS65
1997	25,000	PF65 15.00				

KM# 172 50 TUGRIK
Copper-Nickel **Subject:** Year of the Tiger **Obv:** National emblem **Rev:** Tiger

Date	Mintage	VF20	XF40	MS60	MS63	MS65
1998 Prooflike	25,000	—	—	—	10.00	12.00

KM# 159 50 TUGRIK
20.00 g., Copper-Nickel, 38 mm. **Subject:** Year of the Rabbit **Obv:** National emblem **Rev:** Rabbit **Edge:** Plain

Date	Mintage	VF20	XF40	MS60	MS63	MS65
1999 Prooflike	25,000	—	—	—	10.00	12.00

KM# 236 50 TUGRIK
Copper-Nickel **Obv:** Arms **Rev:** Dragon

Date	Mintage	VF20	XF40	MS60	MS63	MS65
2000	—	PF65 15.00				

KM# 87 100 TUGRIK
1.56 g., 0.999 Gold 0.0501 oz. AGW **Subject:** Year of the Monkey **Obv:** National emblem **Rev:** Monkey **Note:** Similar to 50 Tugrik, KM#86.

Date	Mintage	VF20	XF40	MS60	MS63	MS65
1992	10,000	PF65 85.00				

KM# 167 100 TUGRIK
1.56 g., 0.999 Gold 0.0501 oz. AGW **Subject:** Discovery of America - Columbus **Obv:** National emblem **Rev:** Portrait of Columbus and ship within circle and legend

Date	Mintage	VF20	XF40	MS60	MS63	MS65
1992	—	PF65 85.00				

KM# 62.1 100 TUGRIK
1.56 g., 0.999 Gold 0.0501 oz. AGW **Subject:** Year of the Rooster **Obv:** National emblem **Rev:** Rooster **Note:** Similar to 50 Tugrik, KM#61.

Date	Mintage	VF20	XF40	MS60	MS63	MS65
1993	30,000	PF65 85.00				

KM# 62.2 100 TUGRIK
1.56 g., 0.999 Gold 0.0501 oz. AGW **Obv:** National arms above value **Rev:** Rooster left **Note:** Handstruck.

Date	Mintage	VF20	XF40	MS60	MS63	MS65
1993	500	PF65 225				

Note: Strikes tend to be crude and do not have ".999" on them.

KM# 70 100 TUGRIK
1.56 g., 0.999 Gold 0.0501 oz. AGW **Subject:** Japanese Royal Wedding **Obv:** State emblem above value **Rev:** Busts facing each other **Note:** Similar to 50 Tugrik, KM#69.

Date	Mintage	VF20	XF40	MS60	MS63	MS65
1993	Est. 3000	PF65 85.00				

KM# 124 100 TUGRIK
Copper-Nickel **Obv:** Soembo arms, text **Rev:** Value below building

Date	Mintage	VF20	XF40	MS60	MS63	MS65
1994	—	—	—	1.50	2.00	3.00

KM# 88 200 TUGRIK
3.11 g., 0.999 Gold 0.0999 oz. AGW **Subject:** Year of the Monkey **Obv:** National emblem **Rev:** Seated monkey **Note:** Similar to 50 Tugrik, KM#86.

Date	Mintage	VF20	XF40	MS60	MS63	MS65
1992	—	PF65 185				

KM# 168 200 TUGRIK
3.11 g., 0.999 Gold 0.0999 oz. AGW **Subject:** Discovery of America - Columbus **Obv:** State emblem above value **Rev:** Portrait of Columbus and ship within circle and legend

Date	Mintage	VF20	XF40	MS60	MS63	MS65
1992	—	PF65 185				

KM# 63 200 TUGRIK
3.11 g., 0.999 Gold 0.0999 oz. AGW **Subject:** Year of the Rooster **Obv:** National emblem above value at left, country name at right **Rev:** Rooster **Note:** Similar to 50 Tugrik, KM#61.

Date	Mintage	VF20	XF40	MS60	MS63	MS65
1993	500	PF65 250				

KM# 71 200 TUGRIK
3.11 g., 0.999 Gold 0.0999 oz. AGW **Subject:** Japanese Royal Wedding **Obv:** National arms above value **Rev:** Busts facing each other **Note:** Similar to 50 Tugrik, KM#69.

Date	Mintage	VF20	XF40	MS60	MS63	MS65
1993	100	PF65 375				

KM# 76 200 TUGRIK
3.11 g., 0.999 Gold 0.0999 oz. AGW **Subject:** Year of the Dog. **Obv:** National emblem **Rev:** Dogs

Date	Mintage	VF20	XF40	MS60	MS63	MS65
1994	500	PF65 225				

KM# 125 200 TUGRIK
Copper-Nickel **Obv:** Soembo arms, text **Rev:** Value below building

Date	Mintage	VF20	XF40	MS60	MS63	MS65
1994	—	—	—	1.50	2.50	4.00

KM# 80 250 TUGRIK
31.47 g., 0.925 Silver 0.9359 oz. ASW **Subject:** Endangered Wildlife **Obv:** Soembo arms within 3/4 wreath **Rev:** Wolves

Date	Mintage	VF20	XF40	MS60	MS63	MS65
1993	Est. 15000	PF65 42.00	PF67 58.00			

Note: KM#89 previously listed here has been reported as never released.

Date	Mintage	VF20	XF40	MS60	MS63	MS65
1993	15,000	PF65 50.00	PF67 65.00			

Note: KM#89 previously listed here has been reported as never released

KM# 100 250 TUGRIK

31.47 g., 0.925 Silver 0.9359 oz. ASW **Subject:** Endangered Wildlife **Obv:** National emblem **Rev:** Przewalski's Horses

Date	Mintage	VF20	XF40	MS60	MS63	MS65
1992	20,000	PF65 40.00	PF67 55.00			

KM# 64 250 TUGRIK

155.50 g., 0.999 Silver 4.9944 oz. ASW **Subject:** Year of the Rooster **Obv:** National emblem **Rev:** Rooster **Note:** Similar to 50 Tugrik, KM#61.

Date	Mintage	VF20	XF40	MS60	MS63	MS65
1993	300	PF65 175	PF67 225			

KM# 110 250 TUGRIK

31.47 g., 0.925 Silver 0.9359 oz. ASW **Series:** Endangered Wildlife **Obv:** National emblem **Rev:** Saiga Antelope

Date	Mintage	VF20	XF40	MS60	MS63	MS65
1993	Est. 10000	PF65 40.00	PF67 55.00			

KM# 77 250 TUGRIK

155.50 g., 0.999 Silver 4.9944 oz. ASW, 65 mm. **Subject:** Year of the Dog **Obv:** National emblem **Rev:** Two Pekingese **Note:** Illustration reduced.

Date	Mintage	VF20	XF40	MS60	MS63	MS65
1994	200	PF65 275	PF67 325			

KM# 103 250 TUGRIK

31.47 g., 0.925 Silver 0.9359 oz. ASW **Subject:** World Cup soccer **Obv:** National arms **Rev:** Soccer players

Date	Mintage	VF20	XF40	MS60	MS63	MS65
1994	—	PF65 47.00	PF67 60.00			

KM# 111 250 TUGRIK

31.47 g., 0.925 Silver 0.9359 oz. ASW **Series:** Olympics **Subject:** Boxing **Obv:** National emblem

Date	Mintage	VF20	XF40	MS60	MS63	MS65
1994	Est. 5000	PF65 55.00	PF67 75.00			

KM# 112 250 TUGRIK

31.47 g., 0.925 Silver 0.9359 oz. ASW **Series:** Olympics **Subject:** Archery **Obv:** Soembo arms within wreath **Rev:** Archer

Date	Mintage	VF20	XF40	MS60	MS63	MS65
1994	—	PF65 42.00	PF67 58.00			
1995	Est. 40000	PF65 40.00	PF67 55.00			

KM# 186 250 TUGRIK

31.40 g., 0.925 Silver 0.9338 oz. ASW, 38.4 mm. **Subject:** Sojus 39 and Saljut 6 **Obv:** National arms **Rev:** 2 space capsules **Edge:** Reeded

Date	Mintage	VF20	XF40	MS60	MS63	MS65
1994	—	PF65 55.00	PF67 75.00			

KM# 73 500 TUGRIK

15.55 g., 0.999 Gold 0.4994 oz. AGW **Subject:** Japanese Royal Wedding **Obv:** State emblem above value **Rev:** Busts facing each other

Date	Mintage	VF20	XF40	MS60	MS63	MS65
1993	160	PF65 1,100	PF67 1,300			

KM# 95 500 TUGRIK

31.10 g., 0.999 Silver 0.999 oz. ASW **Subject:** Year of the Pig **Obv:** Soembo arms within circle **Rev:** Wild pig

Date	Mintage	VF20	XF40	MS60	MS63	MS65
1995	3,000	PF65 55.00	PF67 75.00			

KM# 101.1 500 TUGRIK

31.10 g., 0.999 Silver 0.999 oz. ASW, 40.1 mm. **Subject:** Moscow - Beijing Railroad **Obv:** National arms **Rev:** Map without trains

Date	Mintage	VF20	XF40	MS60	MS63	MS65
ND-1995	20,000	PF65 35.00	PF67 50.00			

KM# 101.2 500 TUGRIK

31.10 g., 0.999 Silver 0.999 oz. ASW, 40.1 mm. **Obv:** Soembo arms within circle **Rev:** Map with trains **Edge:** Plain

Date	Mintage	VF20	XF40	MS60	MS63	MS65
ND (1995)	—	PF65 45.00	PF67 60.00			

KM# 203 500 TUGRIK

31.15 g., 0.999 Silver 1.0005 oz. ASW, 38 mm. **Subject:** The Straits Times 150th Anniversary **Obv:** National emblem **Rev:** Rolled newspapers and logo **Edge:** Plain

Date	Mintage	XF40	MS60	MS63	MS65	MS66
ND(1995)	—	PF65 50.00	PF67 60.00			

KM# 105 500 TUGRIK

31.10 g., 0.999 Silver 0.999 oz. ASW **Subject:** Year of the Rat **Obv:** National emblem **Rev:** Rat **Note:** Similar to 50 Tugrik, KM#104, but with gold plated rat.

Date	Mintage	VF20	XF40	MS60	MS63	MS65
1996	500	PF65 80.00	PF67 95.00			

KM# 132 500 TUGRIK

25.00 g., 0.925 Silver 0.7435 oz. ASW **Subject:** Aquila Rapax **Obv:** Soembo arms above value **Rev:** Aquila rapax sitting among rocks

Date	Mintage	VF20	XF40	MS60	MS63	MS65
1996	3,500	PF65 35.00	PF67 45.00			

KM# 133 500 TUGRIK
25.00 g., 0.925 Silver 0.7435 oz. ASW **Subject:** Equus Ferus **Obv:** National emblem **Rev:** Horse running left

Date	Mintage	VF20	XF40	MS60	MS63	MS65
1996	3,500	PF65 35.00	PF67 45.00			

KM# 134 500 TUGRIK
25.00 g., 0.925 Silver 0.7435 oz. ASW **Subject:** Cameleus Ferus **Obv:** National emblem **Rev:** Camel right

Date	Mintage	VF20	XF40	MS60	MS63	MS65
1996	3,500	PF65 35.00	PF67 45.00			

KM# 135 500 TUGRIK
25.00 g., 0.925 Silver 0.7435 oz. ASW **Subject:** Panthera Tigris Altaica **Obv:** National emblem **Rev:** Three tigers

Date	Mintage	VF20	XF40	MS60	MS63	MS65
1996	3,500	PF65 35.00	PF67 45.00			

KM# 187 500 TUGRIK
31.60 g., 0.925 Silver 0.9398 oz. ASW **Series:** Endangered Wildlife **Obv:** National emblem **Rev:** Pelican

Date	Mintage	XF40	MS60	MS63	MS65	MS66
1996	—	PF65 35.00	PF67 45.00			

KM# 216 500 TUGRIK
1.18 g., 0.9999 Gold 0.0379 oz. AGW, 13.91 mm. **Subject:** 1996 Summer Olympics - Atlanta **Obv:** National emblem at left, value below **Rev:** Archer **Edge:** Reeded

Date	Mintage	XF40	MS60	MS63	MS65	MS66
1996	—	PF65 60.00	PF67 70.00			

KM# 127 500 TUGRIK
31.10 g., 0.999 Silver 0.999 oz. ASW with partial gold plating **Subject:** Year of the Ox **Obv:** National emblem **Rev:** Ox **Note:** Similar to 50 Tugrik, KM#126.

Date	Mintage	VF20	XF40	MS60	MS63	MS65
1997	3,000	PF65 40.00	PF67 50.00			

KM# 193 500 TUGRIK
19.44 g., 0.925 Silver 0.5781 oz. ASW, 36 mm. **Subject:** UNICEF **Obv:** National arms **Rev:** Three costumed children **Edge:** Reeded

Date	Mintage	XF40	MS60	MS63	MS65	MS66
1997	25,000	PF65 25.00	PF67 35.00			

KM# 155 500 TUGRIK
15.00 g., 0.925 Silver 0.4461 oz. ASW **Series:** 1988 Olympics **Obv:** Soembo arms **Rev:** Skier

Date	Mintage	VF20	XF40	MS60	MS63	MS65
1998	—	PF63 16.00	PF65 20.00			

KM# 156 500 TUGRIK
20.00 g., 0.500 Silver 0.3215 oz. ASW **Series:** 2000 Olympics **Obv:** National emblem **Rev:** 2 Wrestlers

Date	Mintage	VF20	XF40	MS60	MS63	MS65
1998	—	PF63 14.00	PF65 18.00			

KM# 157 500 TUGRIK
31.47 g., 0.999 Silver 1.0108 oz. ASW **Subject:** Endangered wildlife **Obv:** National emblem **Rev:** Tiger and cubs

Date	Mintage	XF40	MS60	MS63	MS65	MS66
1998	—	PF65 30.00	PF67 45.00			

KM# 158 500 TUGRIK
1.22 g., 0.999 Gold 0.0393 oz. AGW **Subject:** Buddhist Diety Maitreya **Obv:** National emblem **Rev:** Statue

Date	Mintage	XF40	MS60	MS63	MS65	MS66
1998	—	PF65 60.00	PF67 75.00			

KM# 173 500 TUGRIK
31.10 g., 0.999 Silver 0.999 oz. ASW **Subject:** Year of the Tiger **Obv:** National emblem **Rev:** Tiger

Date	Mintage	XF40	MS60	MS63	MS65	MS66
1998	25,000	—	—	25.00	35.00	—

KM# 173a 500 TUGRIK
31.10 g., 0.999 Silver 0.999 oz. ASW **Subject:** Year of the Tiger **Obv:** National emblem **Rev:** Tiger **Note:** Gold-plated tiger.

Date	Mintage	XF40	MS60	MS63	MS65	MS66
1998	3,000	—	—	50.00	60.00	—

KM# 174 500 TUGRIK
1.24 g., 0.999 Gold 0.040 oz. AGW **Subject:** Year of the Tiger **Obv:** National emblem **Rev:** Tiger

Date	Mintage	XF40	MS60	MS63	MS65	MS66
1998	—	PF65 70.00	PF67 80.00			

KM# 178 500 TUGRIK
31.61 g., 0.925 Silver 0.9401 oz. ASW **Subject:** Millennium 2000 **Obv:** National emblem **Rev:** Rider and multicolor speckled hologram

Date	Mintage	XF40	MS60	MS63	MS65	MS66
1998	Est. 10000	PF65 25.00	PF67 35.00			

KM# 197 500 TUGRIK
1.24 g., 0.999 Gold 0.0398 oz. AGW, 14 mm. **Subject:** 2000 Sydney Olympics **Obv:** National emblem **Rev:** Two Judo or Kickboxers

Date	Mintage	XF40	MS60	MS63	MS65	MS66
1998	—	PF65 60.00	PF67 70.00			

KM# 160 500 TUGRIK
31.10 g., 0.999 Silver 0.999 oz. ASW **Subject:** Year of the Rabbit **Obv:** Soembo arms within circle **Rev:** Rabbit running left

Date	Mintage	XF40	MS60	MS63	MS65	MS66
1999	3,000	—	—	40.00	50.00	—

KM# 160a 500 TUGRIK
31.10 g., 0.999 Silver 0.999 oz. ASW **Subject:** Year of the Rabbit **Obv:** Soembo arms within circle **Rev:** Rabbit running left **Note:** Gold plated rabbit.

Date	Mintage	XF40	MS60	MS63	MS65	MS66
1999	3,000	—	—	45.00	55.00	—

KM# 161 500 TUGRIK
1.24 g., 0.999 Gold 0.040 oz. AGW **Subject:** Year of the Rabbit **Obv:** Soembo arms within circle **Rev:** Rabbit running left

Date	Mintage	XF40	MS60	MS63	MS65	MS66
1999	5,000	—	—	75.00	80.00	—

KM# 179 500 TUGRIK
25.27 g., 0.925 Silver 0.7515 oz. ASW **Subject:** Sita Tara **Obv:** Soembo arms above value **Rev:** Seated figure facing

Date	Mintage	XF40	MS60	MS63	MS65	MS66
1999	2,500	PF65 35.00	PF67 45.00			

KM# 180 500 TUGRIK
25.00 g., 0.925 Bi-Metallic 0.7435 oz. Goldine center in Silver ring **Subject:** Genius of the Millennium - Gutenberg **Obv:** National emblem **Rev:** Open Bible, dates **Note:** Goldine center is square.

Date	Mintage	XF40	MS60	MS63	MS65	MS66
1999	2,500	PF65 35.00	PF67 45.00			

KM# 181 500 TUGRIK
25.00 g., 0.925 Bi-Metallic 0.7435 oz. Goldine center in Silver ring, 38.61 mm. **Subject:** Genius of the Millennium - Da Vinci **Obv:** National emblem **Obv. Legend:** MONGOLIA **Rev:** Male figure study **Rev. Legend:** LEONARDO DA VINCI **Edge:** Reeded **Note:** Goldine center is triangular.

Date	Mintage	XF40	MS60	MS63	MS65	MS66
1999	2,500	PF65 35.00	PF67 45.00			

KM# 181a 500 TUGRIK
25.00 g., 0.925 Bi-Metallic 0.7435 oz. Copper center in silver ring, 38.61 mm. **Subject:** Genius of the Millennium - Da Vinci **Obv:** National emblem **Obv. Legend:** MONGOLIA **Rev:** Male figure study **Rev. Legend:** LEONARDO DA VINCI **Edge:** Reeded **Note:** Copper center is triangular.

Date	Mintage	XF40	MS60	MS63	MS65	MS66
1999	—	PF65 40.00	PF67 50.00			

KM# 182 500 TUGRIK
25.00 g., 0.925 Bi-Metallic 0.7435 oz. Goldine center in Silver ring **Subject:** Genius of the Millennium - Newton **Obv:** National emblem **Rev:** Solar system diagram **Note:** Goldine center is round.

Date	Mintage	XF40	MS60	MS63	MS65	MS66
1999	2,500	PF65 35.00	PF67 45.00			

KM# 183 500 TUGRIK
25.00 g., 0.925 Bi-Metallic 0.7435 oz. Goldine center in Silver ring **Subject:** Genius of the Millennium - von Goethe **Obv:** National emblem **Rev:** Bust facing **Note:** Goldine center is round.

Date	Mintage	XF40	MS60	MS63	MS65	MS66
1999	2,500	PF65 35.00	PF67 45.00			

KM# 184 500 TUGRIK
25.00 g., 0.925 Bi-Metallic 0.7435 oz. Goldine center in Silver ring **Subject:** Genius of the Millennium - Edison **Obv:** National emblem **Rev:** Light bulb, telephone, record player **Note:** Goldine center is square.

Date	Mintage	XF40	MS60	MS63	MS65	MS66
1999	2,500	PF65 35.00	PF67 45.00			

Note: KM#90, previously listed here, has been reported as never released.

KM# 196 500 TUGRIK
19.82 g., 0.500 Silver 0.3186 oz. ASW, 34 mm. **Obv:** National emblem **Rev:** Two Bactrian camels **Edge:** Reeded

Date	Mintage	XF40	MS60	MS63	MS65	MS66
1999	—	PF65 35.00	PF67 45.00			

KM# 202 500 TUGRIK
31.44 g., 0.925 Silver 0.935 oz. ASW, 38.6 mm. **Subject:** Princess Diana **Obv:** National emblem **Rev:** Diana by minefield **Edge:** Plain

Date	Mintage	XF40	MS60	MS63	MS65	MS66
1999	—	PF65 45.00	PF67 55.00			

KM# 217 500 TUGRIK
1.21 g., Gold **Subject:** Troops of Chinggis Khan **Obv:** National emblem, value below **Rev:** Chinggis at right giving directions to charioteer at left

Date	Mintage	XF40	MS60	MS63	MS65	MS66
2000	—	PF65 60.00	PF67 70.00			

KM# 65 600 TUGRIK
373.20 g., 0.999 Silver 11.9867 oz. ASW **Subject:** Year of the Rooster **Obv:** National emblem **Rev:** Rooster **Note:** Similar to 50 Tugrik, KM#61

Date	Mintage	XF40	MS60	MS63	MS65	MS66
1993	200	PF65 750	PF67 850			

KM# 85 1000 TUGRIK
20.00 g., 0.900 Gold 0.5787 oz. AGW **Obv:** National arms above value **Rev:** Ugedei Khan, Son of Genghis

Date	Mintage	XF40	MS60	MS63	MS65	MS66
1992	500	PF65 1,150	PF67 1,350			

KM# 91 1000 TUGRIK
31.10 g., 0.999 Gold 0.9989 oz. AGW **Subject:** Year of the Monkey **Obv:** National emblem **Rev:** Monkey **Note:** Similar to 50 Tugrik, KM#86.

Date	Mintage	XF40	MS60	MS63	MS65	MS66
1992	2,000	PF65 1,650	PF67 1,850			

KM# 169 1000 TUGRIK
20.00 g., 0.900 Gold 0.5787 oz. AGW **Subject:** Discovery of America - Columbus **Obv:** State emblem above value **Rev:** Portrait of Columbus and ship within circle and legend

Date	Mintage	XF40	MS60	MS63	MS65	MS66
1992	Est. 2000	PF65 1,100	PF67 1,200			

KM# 66 1000 TUGRIK
31.10 g., 0.999 Gold 0.9989 oz. AGW **Subject:** Year of the Rooster **Obv:** National emblem above value at left, country name at right **Rev:** Rooster **Note:** Similar to 50 Tugrik, KM#61.

Date	Mintage	XF40	MS60	MS63	MS65	MS66
1993	1,000	PF65 1,700	PF67 1,900			

KM# 74 1000 TUGRIK
20.00 g., 0.900 Gold 0.5787 oz. AGW **Subject:** Japanese Royal Wedding **Obv:** State emblem above value **Rev:** Busts of couple facing each other

Date	Mintage	XF40	MS60	MS63	MS65	MS66
1993	145	PF65 1,250	PF67 1,500			

KM# 78 1000 TUGRIK
31.10 g., 0.999 Gold 0.999 oz. AGW **Subject:** Year of the Dog **Obv:** National emblem **Rev:** Pekingese

Date	Mintage	XF40	MS60	MS63	MS65	MS66
1994	500	PF65 1,750	PF67 1,950			

KM# 96 1000 TUGRIK
3.11 g., 0.999 Gold 0.0999 oz. AGW **Subject:** Year of the Pig **Obv:** National emblem **Rev:** Wild boar **Note:** Similar to 500 Tugrik, KM#95.

Date	Mintage	XF40	MS60	MS63	MS65	MS66
1995	500	PF65 250	PF67 300			

KM# 148 1000 TUGRIK
4.41 g., 0.900 Gold 0.1276 oz. AGW **Subject:** Moscow - Ulaan Blaatar - Bejing Railroad **Obv:** Soembo arms within circle **Rev:** Steam locomotive

Date	Mintage	XF40	MS60	MS63	MS65	MS66
1995	—	PF65 225	PF67 275			

KM# 106 1000 TUGRIK
3.11 g., 0.999 Gold 0.0999 oz. AGW **Subject:** Year of the Rat **Obv:** National emblem **Rev:** Rat **Note:** Similar to 50 Tugrik, KM#104.

Date	Mintage	XF40	MS60	MS63	MS65	MS66
1996	500	PF65 200	PF67 250			

KM# 115 1000 TUGRIK
156.61 g., 0.999 Silver 5.0301 oz. ASW, 65.5 mm. **Series:** Olympics **Obv:** Soembo arms **Rev:** Ancient runners within circle **Note:** With gold inlay. Illustration reduced.

Date	Mintage	XF40	MS60	MS63	MS65	MS66
1996 Matte	—	—	—	—	145	—

KM# 128 1000 TUGRIK
3.11 g., 0.999 Gold 0.0999 oz. AGW **Subject:** Year of the Ox **Obv:** National emblem **Rev:** Ox **Note:** Similar to 50 Tugrik, KM#126.

Date	Mintage	XF40	MS60	MS63	MS65	MS66
1997	500	PF65 175	PF67 225			

KM# 185 1000 TUGRIK
1.24 g., 0.9999 Gold 0.040 oz. AGW **Subject:** Genius of the Millennium - Da Vinci **Obv:** National arms **Rev:** Male figure study **Note:** Similar to 500 Tugrik, KM#181.

Date	Mintage	XF40	MS60	MS63	MS65	MS66
1999	25,000	PF65 75.00	PF67 80.00			

KM# 201 1000 TUGRIK
7.72 g., Gold, 24.8 mm. **Obv:** Soembo arms **Rev:** Tiger head with diamond inset eyes **Edge:** Reeded

Date	Mintage	XF40	MS60	MS63	MS65	MS66
1999	—	PF65 600	PF67 650			

KM# 234 1000 TUGRIK
7.77 g., 0.999 Gold 0.2496 oz. AGW **Obv:** Arms **Rev:** Cat head facing, diamond chip in eyes

Date	Mintage	XF40	MS60	MS63	MS65	MS66
1999	—	PF65 375	PF67 425			

KM# 235 1000 TUGRIK
7.77 g., 0.999 Gold 0.2496 oz. AGW **Obv:** Arms **Rev:** Tiger, diamond chip in eyes

Date	Mintage	XF40	MS60	MS63	MS65	MS66
1999	—	PF65 375	PF67 425			

KM# 237 1000 TUGRIK
7.77 g., 0.999 Gold 0.2496 oz. AGW **Rev:** Tiger, diamond chip in eyes

Date	Mintage	XF40	MS60	MS63	MS65	MS66
2000	—	PF65 375	PF67 425			

KM# 116 1200 TUGRIK
7.70 g., 0.999 Silver 0.2473 oz. ASW **Subject:** Chinggis Khan **Obv:** Soemba arms **Rev:** Bust 3/4 right, dates below **Note:** Similar to 5,000 Tugrik, KM#118.

Date	Mintage	XF40	MS60	MS63	MS65	MS66
1996	Est. 10000	—	—	12.00	15.00	—
1996	Est. 10000	PF65 17.00	PF67 20.00			

KM# 149 1200 TUGRIK
7.70 g., 0.999 Silver 0.2473 oz. ASW **Subject:** Ugedei Khan **Obv:** National emblem **Rev:** Head 3/4 facing, dates at right

Date	Mintage	XF40	MS60	MS63	MS65	MS66
1997	Est. 10000	PF65 17.00	PF67 20.00			

KM# 113 2000 TUGRIK
7.78 g., 0.583 Gold 0.1458 oz. AGW **Series:** Endangered Wildlife **Obv:** Soembo arms within wreath **Rev:** Snow leopard

Date	Mintage	XF40	MS60	MS63	MS65	MS66
1994	Est. 5000	PF65 275	PF67 325			

KM# 114 2000 TUGRIK
7.78 g., 0.583 Gold 0.1458 oz. AGW **Series:** Olympics **Obv:** Soembo arms within wreath **Rev:** Boxer

Date	Mintage	XF40	MS60	MS63	MS65	MS66
1994	Est. 5000	PF65 250	PF67 300			

KM# 175 2000 TUGRIK
7.78 g., 0.583 Gold 0.1458 oz. AGW **Subject:** Year of the Tiger **Obv:** National emblem **Rev:** Tiger

Date	Mintage	XF40	MS60	MS63	MS65	MS66
1998	—	PF67 350				

KM# 97 2500 TUGRIK
155.52 g., 0.999 Silver 4.9949 oz. ASW, 65 mm. **Subject:** Year of the Pig **Obv:** Soemba arms **Rev:** Wild pigs eating in the wild **Note:** Illustration reduced.

Date	Mintage	XF40	MS60	MS63	MS65	MS66
1995	300	PF65 250	PF67 300			

KM# 102 2500 TUGRIK
155.52 g., 0.999 Silver 4.9949 oz. ASW, 65.14 mm. **Subject:** Moscow - Ulaan Baatar - Beijing Railroad **Obv:** Soemba arms **Rev:** Passenger train crossing trestle left **Edge:** Plain **Note:** Illustration reduced.

Date	Mintage	XF40	MS60	MS63	MS65	MS66
1995	5,000	PF65 160	PF67 200			

KM# 107 2500 TUGRIK
155.52 g., 0.999 Silver 4.9949 oz. ASW, 65 mm. **Subject:** Year of the Rat **Obv:** Soemba arms **Rev:** Gold-plated rat

Date	Mintage	XF40	MS60	MS63	MS65	MS66
1996	300	PF65 225	PF67 275			

KM# 117 2500 TUGRIK
15.55 g., 0.999 Silver 0.4994 oz. ASW **Obv:** National emblem **Rev:** Chinggis Khan **Note:** Similar to 5000 Tugrik, KM#118

Date	Mintage	XF40	MS60	MS63	MS65	MS66
1996	Est. 10000	—	—	18.00	20.00	—
1996	Est. 10000	PF65 22.00	PF67 25.00			

KM# 129 2500 TUGRIK

155.52 g., 0.999 Silver 4.9949 oz. ASW with partial gold plating **Subject:** Year of the Ox **Obv:** National emblem **Rev:** Man riding ox, flowered spray around upper right

Date	Mintage	XF40	MS60	MS63	MS65	MS66
1997	300	PF65 250	PF67 300			

KM# 150 2500 TUGRIK

15.55 g., 0.999 Silver 0.4995 oz. ASW **Obv:** Soembo arms above value **Rev:** Bust with hat 1/4 left

Date	Mintage	XF40	MS60	MS63	MS65	MS66
1997	Est. 10000	PF65 18.00	PF67 22.00			

KM# 162 2500 TUGRIK

155.18 g., 0.999 Silver 4.984 oz. ASW, 65 mm. **Subject:** Year of the Rabbit **Obv:** National emblem **Rev:** Rabbit **Edge:** Plain **Note:** Struck at B.H. Mayer's.

Date	Mintage	XF40	MS60	MS63	MS65	MS66
1999	1,500	PF65 165	PF67 200			

KM# 163 2500 TUGRIK

7.78 g., 0.999 Gold 0.2498 oz. AGW, 22.5 mm. **Subject:** Year of the Rabbit **Obv:** National emblem **Rev:** Rabbit **Edge:** Plain **Note:** Struck at B.H. Mayer's.

Date	Mintage	XF40	MS60	MS63	MS65	MS66
1999	1,500	PF67 450				

KM# 81 4000 TUGRIK

15.59 g., 0.9999 Gold 0.5013 oz. AGW **Obv:** Soembo arms above value **Rev:** Horse and rider left

Date	Mintage	XF40	MS60	MS63	MS65	MS66
1992	Est. 9000	PF65 875	PF67 925			

KM# 67 5000 TUGRIK

155.50 g., 0.999 Gold 4.9944 oz. AGW **Subject:** Year of the Rooster **Obv:** National emblem above denomination at left, country name at right **Rev:** Rooster **Note:** Similar to 50 Tugrik, KM#51.

Date	Mintage	XF40	MS60	MS63	MS65	MS66
1993	50	PF67 9,000				

KM# 79 5000 TUGRIK

155.50 g., 0.999 Gold 4.9944 oz. AGW **Subject:** Year of the Dog **Obv:** National emblem **Rev:** Dog

Date	Mintage	XF40	MS60	MS63	MS65	MS66
1994	25	PF67 9,500				

KM# 118 5000 TUGRIK

31.00 g., 0.999 Silver 0.9957 oz. ASW **Obv:** Soembo arms above value **Rev:** Bust 3/4 facing, dates below

Date	Mintage	XF40	MS60	MS63	MS65	MS66
1996	Est. 10000	—	—	32.00	37.00	—
1996	Est. 10000	PF65 45.00	PF67 50.00			

KM# 136 5000 TUGRIK

155.52 g., 0.999 Silver 4.995 oz. ASW **Subject:** Aquila Rapax **Obv:** National emblem and value **Rev:** Bird standing on rock **Note:** Similar to 500 Tugrik, KM#132.

Date	Mintage	XF40	MS60	MS63	MS65	MS66
1997	750	PF65 145	PF67 185			

KM# 137 5000 TUGRIK

155.52 g., 0.999 Silver 4.995 oz. ASW **Subject:** Eguus Fergus **Obv:** National emblem and value **Rev:** Horse running left **Note:** Similar to 500 Tugrik, KM#133.

Date	Mintage	XF40	MS60	MS63	MS65	MS66
1997	750	PF65 145	PF67 185			

KM# 138 5000 TUGRIK

155.52 g., 0.999 Silver 4.995 oz. ASW **Subject:** Camelus Ferus **Obv:** National emblem and value **Rev:** Camel right **Note:** Similar to 500 Tugrik, KM#134.

Date	Mintage	XF40	MS60	MS63	MS65	MS66
1997	750	PF65 145	PF67 185			

KM# 139 5000 TUGRIK

155.52 g., 0.999 Silver 4.995 oz. ASW **Subject:** Panthera Tigris Altaica **Obv:** National emblem and value **Rev:** Tiger lying on rock **Note:** Similar to 500 Tugrik, KM#135.

Date	Mintage	XF40	MS60	MS63	MS65	MS66
1997	750	PF65 145	PF67 185			

KM# 151 5000 TUGRIK

31.10 g., 0.999 Silver 0.999 oz. ASW **Obv:** National emblem **Rev:** Ugedei Khan

Date	Mintage	XF40	MS60	MS63	MS65	MS66
1997	Est. 10000	PF65 32.00	PF67 45.00			

KM# 194 5000 TUGRIK

6.22 g., 0.999 Gold 0.1998 oz. AGW **Subject:** UNICEF **Obv:** National emblem and value **Rev:** Three costumed children **Edge:** Reeded

Date	Mintage	XF40	MS60	MS63	MS65	MS66
1997	10,000	PF65 325	PF67 375			

KM# 82 8000 TUGRIK

31.16 g., 0.9999 Gold 1.0018 oz. AGW **Obv:** Soembo arms above value **Rev:** Chinggis Khan standing

Date	Mintage	XF40	MS60	MS63	MS65	MS66
1992	Est. 3000	PF65 1,750	PF67 1,850			

KM# 98 10000 TUGRIK

31.10 g., 0.999 Gold 0.999 oz. AGW **Subject:** Year of the Pig **Obv:** National emblem **Rev:** Wild boar **Note:** Similar to 500 Tugrik, KM#95.

Date	Mintage	XF40	MS60	MS63	MS65	MS66
1995	300	PF65 1,900	PF67 2,000			

KM# 108 10000 TUGRIK

31.10 g., 0.999 Gold 0.999 oz. AGW **Subject:** Year of the Rat **Obv:** National emblem **Rev:** Rat **Note:** Similar to 50 Tugrik, KM#104.

Date	Mintage	XF40	MS60	MS63	MS65	MS66
1996	300	PF65 1,900	PF67 2,000			

KM# 140 10000 TUGRIK

1000.10 g., 0.999 Silver 32.1218 oz. ASW **Subject:** Aquila Rapax **Obv:** National emblem and value **Rev:** Bird standing on rock **Note:** Similar to 500 Tugrik, KM#132.

Date	Mintage	XF40	MS60	MS63	MS65	MS66
1996 Prooflike	450	—	—	—	—	750

KM# 141 10000 TUGRIK

1000.10 g., 0.999 Silver 32.1218 oz. ASW **Subject:** Equus Ferus **Obv:** National emblem and value **Rev:** Horse running left **Note:** Similar to 500 Tugrik, KM#133.

Date	Mintage	XF40	MS60	MS63	MS65	MS66
1996 Prooflike	450	—	—	—	—	750

KM# 142 10000 TUGRIK

1000.10 g., 0.999 Silver 32.1218 oz. ASW **Subject:** Camelus Ferus **Obv:** National emblem and value **Rev:** Camel right **Note:** Similar to 500 Tugrik, KM#134.

Date	Mintage	XF40	MS60	MS63	MS65	MS66
1996 Prooflike	450	—	—	—	—	750

KM# 143 10000 TUGRIK

1000.10 g., 0.999 Silver 32.1218 oz. ASW **Subject:** Panthera Tigris Alaica **Obv:** National emblem and value **Rev:** Tiger lying on rock **Note:** Similar to 500 Tugrik, KM#135.

Date	Mintage	XF40	MS60	MS63	MS65	MS66
1996 Prooflike	450	—	—	—	—	750

KM# 130 10000 TUGRIK

31.10 g., 0.999 Gold 0.999 oz. AGW **Subject:** Year of the Ox **Obv:** National emblem **Rev:** Ox **Note:** Similar to 2,500 Tugrik, KM#129.

Date	Mintage	XF40	MS60	MS63	MS65	MS66
1997	300	PF65 1,900	PF67 2,000			

KM# 176 10000 TUGRIK

31.10 g., 0.999 Gold 0.999 oz. AGW **Subject:** Year of the Tiger **Obv:** National emblem **Rev:** Tiger

Date	Mintage	XF40	MS60	MS63	MS65	MS66
1998	250	—	—	—	—	1,900

KM# 164 10000 TUGRIK

31.10 g., 0.999 Gold 0.999 oz. AGW **Subject:** Year of the Rabbit **Obv:** National emblem **Rev:** Rabbit

Date	Mintage	XF40	MS60	MS63	MS65	MS66
1999	250	—	—	—	—	1,800

KM# 68 12000 TUGRIK

373.20 g., 0.999 Gold 11.9867 oz. AGW **Subject:** Year of the Rooster **Obv:** National emblem above denomination at left, country name at right **Rev:** Rooster **Note:** Similar to 50 Tugrik, KM#61.

Date	Mintage	XF40	MS60	MS63	MS65	MS66
1993	25	PF67 22,000				

KM# 119 12000 TUGRIK

7.77 g., 0.9999 Gold 0.2498 oz. AGW **Subject:** Chinggis Khan **Obv:** National emblem and value **Rev:** Bust 3/4 facing **Note:** Similar to 50,000 Tugrik, KM#121.

Date	Mintage	XF40	MS60	MS63	MS65	MS66
1996 Rare	10	—	—	—	—	—
1996 Proof, rare	10	—	—	—	—	—

KM# 119a 12000 TUGRIK

7.77 g., 0.999 Gold 0.2496 oz. AGW **Subject:** Chinggis Khan **Obv:** National emblem and value **Rev:** Bust 3/4 facing

Date	Mintage	XF40	MS60	MS63	MS65	MS66
1996	Est. 10000	—	—	—	—	475
1996	Est. 10000	PF67 500				

KM# 152 12000 TUGRIK
7.78 g., 0.999 Gold 0.2497 oz. AGW **Obv:** Soembo arms above value **Rev:** Ugedei Khan with hat, facing

Date	Mintage	XF40	MS60	MS63	MS65	MS66
1997	Est. 10000	PF67 500				

KM# 120 25000 TUGRIK
15.55 g., 0.9999 Gold 0.4999 oz. AGW **Subject:** Chinggis Khan **Obv:** National emblem and value **Rev:** Bust 3/4 facing **Note:** Similar to 50,000 Tugrik, KM#121.

Date	Mintage	XF40	MS60	MS63	MS65	MS66
1996 Rare	10	—	—	—	—	—
1996 Proof, Rare	10	—	—	—	—	—

KM# 120a 25000 TUGRIK
15.55 g., 0.999 Gold 0.4994 oz. AGW **Subject:** Chinggis Khan **Obv:** National emblem and value **Rev:** Bust 3/4 facing

Date	Mintage	XF40	MS60	MS63	MS65	MS66
1996	Est. 10000	—	—	—	—	900
1996	Est. 10000	PF67 950				

KM# 144 25000 TUGRIK
15.59 g., 0.9999 Gold 0.5013 oz. AGW **Subject:** Aquila Rapaz **Obv:** National emblem and value **Rev:** Bird standing on rock **Note:** Similar to 500 Tugrik, KM#132.

Date	Mintage	XF40	MS60	MS63	MS65	MS66
1996	300	PF65 1,000	PF67 1,150			

KM# 145 25000 TUGRIK
15.59 g., 0.9999 Gold 0.5013 oz. AGW **Subject:** Equus Ferus **Obv:** National emblem and value **Rev:** Horse running left **Note:** Similar to 500 Tugrik, KM#133.

Date	Mintage	XF40	MS60	MS63	MS65	MS66
1996	300	PF65 1,000	PF67 1,150			

KM# 146 25000 TUGRIK
15.59 g., 0.9999 Gold 0.5013 oz. AGW **Subject:** Cameleus Ferus **Obv:** National emblem and value **Rev:** Camel right **Note:** Similar to 500 Tugrik, KM#134.

Date	Mintage	XF40	MS60	MS63	MS65	MS66
1996	300	PF65 1,000	PF67 1,150			

KM# 147 25000 TUGRIK
15.59 g., 0.9999 Gold 0.5013 oz. AGW **Subject:** Panthera Tigris Altaica **Obv:** National emblem and value **Rev:** Tiger lying on rock **Note:** Similar to 500 Tugrik, KM#135.

Date	Mintage	XF40	MS60	MS63	MS65	MS66
1996	300	PF65 1,000	PF67 1,150			

KM# 153 25000 TUGRIK
15.55 g., 0.999 Gold 0.4995 oz. AGW **Subject:** Ugedei Khan **Obv:** National arms **Rev:** Bust 1/4 left

Date	Mintage	XF40	MS60	MS63	MS65	MS66
1997	Est. 10000	PF65 950	PF67 1,000			

KM# 99 50000 TUGRIK
155.52 g., 0.999 Gold 4.9949 oz. AGW **Subject:** Year of the Pig **Obv:** National emblem **Rev:** Pigs in field **Note:** Similar to 2500 Tugrik, KM#97

Date	Mintage	XF40	MS60	MS63	MS65	MS66
1995	25	PF67 9,000				

KM# 109 50000 TUGRIK
155.52 g., 0.999 Gold 4.9949 oz. AGW **Subject:** Year of the Rat **Obv:** National emblem **Rev:** Rat **Note:** Similar to 50 Tugrik, KM#104.

Date	Mintage	XF40	MS60	MS63	MS65	MS66
1996	25	PF67 9,000				

KM# 121 50000 TUGRIK
31.10 g., 0.9999 Gold 0.9998 oz. AGW **Obv:** Soembo arms above value **Rev:** Chinggis Khan bust 3/4 facing

Date	Mintage	XF40	MS60	MS63	MS65	MS66
1996 Rare	10	—	—	—	—	—
1996 Proof, rare	10	—	—	—	—	—

KM# 121a 50000 TUGRIK
31.10 g., 0.999 Gold 0.9989 oz. AGW **Subject:** Chinggis Khan **Obv:** Soembo arms above value **Rev:** Bust 3/4 facing

Date	Mintage	XF40	MS60	MS63	MS65	MS66
1996	Est. 10000	—	—	—	—	1,850
1996	Est. 10000	PF67 1,900				

KM# 131 50000 TUGRIK
155.52 g., 0.9999 Gold 4.9994 oz. AGW **Subject:** Year of the Ox **Obv:** National emblem. **Rev:** Ox **Note:** Similar to 2,500 Tugrik, KM#129.

Date	Mintage	XF40	MS60	MS63	MS65	MS66
1997	25	PF67 9,000				

KM# 154 50000 TUGRIK
31.10 g., 0.999 Gold 0.999 oz. AGW **Obv:** Soembo arms above value **Rev:** Ugedei Khan bust 3/4 facing

Date	Mintage	XF40	MS60	MS63	MS65	MS66
1997	Est. 10000	PF67 1,850				

KM# 177 50000 TUGRIK
155.52 g., 0.9999 Gold 4.9994 oz. AGW **Subject:** Year of the Tiger **Obv:** National emblem **Rev:** Tiger

Date	Mintage	XF40	MS60	MS63	MS65	MS66
1998	99	—	—	—	—	8,250

KM# 165 50000 TUGRIK
155.52 g., 0.9999 Gold 4.9994 oz. AGW **Subject:** Year of the Rabbit **Obv:** National emblem **Rev:** Rabbit

Date	Mintage	XF40	MS60	MS63	MS65	MS66
1999	99	—	—	—	—	8,250

KM# 83 250000 TUGRIK
1000.10 g., 0.9999 Gold 32.1507 oz. AGW, 85 mm. **Subject:** Chinggis Khan **Obv:** Soemba arms **Rev:** Head facing

Date	Mintage	XF40	MS60	MS63	MS65	MS66
1992	Est. 300	PF67 55,000				

PIEDFORT

KM#	Date	Mintage	Identification	Mkt Val
P1	1980	92	25 Tugrik. Silver. KM39.	175
P2	1980	550	750 Tugrik. Gold. KM40.	1,900

MINT SETS

KM#	Date	Mintage	Identification	Issue Price	Mkt Val
MS1	1980 (8)	—	KM27-33, 41	—	25.00
MS2	1996 (3)	10,000	KM116-118	—	65.00
MS3	1996 (3)	10	KM119-121	—	—
MS4	1996 (3)	10,000	KM119a-121a	—	3,250

PROOF SETS

KM#	Date	Mintage	Identification	Issue Price	Mkt Val
PS1	1996 (3)	—	KM105, 106, 108	—	2,200
PS2	1996 (3)	10,000	KM116-118. The *10,000 mintage limit is per denomination including proof and BU single coins as well as coins included in sets.	—	95.00
PS3	1996 (3)	10	KM119-121	—	—
PS4	1996 (3)	10,000	KM119a-121a. The *10,000 mintage limit is per denomination including proof and BU single coins as well as coins included in sets.	—	3,350
PS5	1996 (4)	10	KM116-118, 121	—	—
PS6	1996 (4)	10,000	KM116-118, 121a. The *10,000 mintage limit is per denomination including proof and BU single coins as well as coins included in sets.	—	2,000
PS7	1996 (4)	10	KM118, 119-121	—	—
PS8	1996 (4)	10,000	KM118, 119a-121a. The *10,000 mintage limit is per denomination including proof and BU single coins as well as coins included in sets.	—	3,400
PS9	1997 (3)	10,000	KM149-151	—	90.00
PS10	1997 (3)	10,000	KM152-154	—	3,325

MONTENEGRO

The former independent kingdom of Montenegro, now one of the nominally autonomous federated units of Yugoslavia, was located in southeastern Europe north of Albania. As a kingdom, it had an area of 5,333 sq. mi. (13,812 sq. km.) and a population of about 250,000. Capital: Podgorica.

Montenegro became an independent state in 1355 following the break-up of the Serb empire. During the Turkish invasion of Albania and Herzegovina in the 15th century, the Montenegrins moved their capital to the remote mountain village of Cetinje where they maintained their independence through two centuries of intermittent attack, emerging as the only one of the Balkan states not subjugated by the Turks. When World War I began, Montenegro joined with Serbia and was subsequently invaded and occupied by the Austrians. Austria withdrew upon the defeat of the Central Powers, permitting the Serbians to move in and maintain the occupation. Montenegro then joined the kingdom of the Serbs, Croats and Slovenes, which later became Yugoslavia.

The coinage, issued under the autocratic rule of Prince Nicholas, is obsolete.

RULER
Nicholas I, as Prince, 1860-1910 as King, 1910-1918

MINT MARK
(a) - Paris, privy marks only

MONETARY SYSTEM
100 Para = 1 Perper

KINGDOM

STANDARD COINAGE

KM# 1 PARA
Bronze **Ruler:** Nicholas I **Obv:** Crowned arms **Rev:** Value

Date	Mintage	VF20	XF40	MS60	MS63	MS65
1906	200,000	8.00	15.00	25.00	45.00	75.00

KM# 16 PARA

Bronze **Ruler:** Nicholas I **Obv:** Crowned arms **Rev:** Value

Date	Mintage	F12	VF20	XF40	MS60	MS63
1913	100,000	12.00	20.00	50.00	90.00	125
1914	200,000	7.00	18.00	40.00	75.00	100
1914	—	PF63 675				

KM# 2 2 PARE

Bronze **Ruler:** Nicholas I **Obv:** Crowned arms **Rev:** Value

Date	Mintage	F12	VF20	XF40	MS60	MS63
1906	600,125	5.00	12.00	20.00	35.00	55.00
1908	250,000	7.00	15.00	30.00	45.00	75.00

KM# 17 2 PARE

Bronze **Ruler:** Nicholas I **Obv:** Crowned arms **Rev:** Value

Date	Mintage	F12	VF20	XF40	MS60	MS63
1913	500,000	5.00	8.00	16.00	25.00	45.00
1914	400,000	5.00	10.00	20.00	30.00	50.00
1914	—	PF63 1,000				

KM# 3 10 PARA

Nickel **Ruler:** Nicholas I **Obv:** Crowned arms **Rev:** Value

Date	Mintage	F12	VF20	XF40	MS60	MS63
1906	750,156	2.50	5.00	10.00	15.00	25.00
1906	—	PF63 850				
1908	250,000	3.00	5.50	12.00	18.00	30.00

KM# 18 10 PARA

Nickel **Ruler:** Nicholas I

Date	Mintage	F12	VF20	XF40	MS60	MS63
1913	200,000	3.50	7.00	15.00	30.00	40.00
1914	800,000	2.00	4.00	12.00	18.00	25.00

KM# 4 20 PARA

Nickel **Ruler:** Nicholas I **Obv:** Crowned arms **Rev:** Value

Date	Mintage	F12	VF20	XF40	MS60	MS63
1906	600,156	2.00	5.00	10.00	20.00	35.00
1908	400,000	3.00	7.00	14.00	25.00	40.00

KM# 19 20 PARA

Nickel **Ruler:** Nicholas I **Obv:** Crowned arms **Rev:** Value

Date	Mintage	F12	VF20	XF40	MS60	MS63
1913	200,000	4.00	7.00	15.00	30.00	45.00
1914	800,000	3.00	5.00	10.00	25.00	40.00

KM# 5 PERPER

5.00 g., 0.835 Silver 0.1342 oz. ASW **Ruler:** Nicholas I **Obv:** Head right **Rev:** Crowned mantled arms within sprigs above date and value **Note:** Approximately 30 percent melted.

Date	Mintage	F12	VF20	XF40	MS60	MS63
1909	500,018	10.00	15.00	30.00	75.00	125

KM# 14 PERPER

5.00 g., 0.835 Silver 0.1342 oz. ASW **Ruler:** Nicholas I **Obv:** Head right **Rev:** Crowned mantled arms within sprigs above value and date

Date	Mintage	F12	VF20	XF40	MS60	MS63
1912	520,008	9.00	16.00	30.00	60.00	90.00
1914	500,000	10.00	20.00	32.00	80.00	120

KM# 7 2 PERPERA

10.00 g., 0.835 Silver 0.2685 oz. ASW **Ruler:** Nicholas I **Obv:** Head right **Rev:** Crowned mantled arms within sprigs above date and value

Date	Mintage	F12	VF20	XF40	MS60	MS63
1910	300,006	12.00	32.00	70.00	125	185

KM# 20 2 PERPERA

10.00 g., 0.835 Silver 0.2685 oz. ASW **Ruler:** Nicholas I **Obv:** Head right **Rev:** Crowned mantled arms within sprigs above date and value

Date	Mintage	F12	VF20	XF40	MS60	MS63
1914	200,008	20.00	35.00	70.00	125	185

KM# 6 5 PERPERA

24.00 g., 0.900 Silver 0.6945 oz. ASW **Ruler:** Nicholas I **Obv:** Head right **Rev:** Crowned and mantled arms **Note:** Approximately 50 percent melted.

Date	Mintage	F12	VF20	XF40	MS60	MS63
1909	300,000	75.00	175	450	900	1,250

KM# 15 5 PERPERA

24.00 g., 0.900 Silver 0.6945 oz. ASW **Ruler:** Nicholas I **Obv:** Head right **Rev:** Crowned mantled arms within sprigs above date and value

Date	Mintage	F12	VF20	XF40	MS60	MS63
1912	40,002	75.00	150	300	575	900
1914	20,002	75.00	150	325	675	1,000

KM# 8 10 PERPERA

3.39 g., 0.900 Gold 0.098 oz. AGW **Ruler:** Nicholas I **Obv:** Head right **Rev:** Crowned mantled arms within sprigs above date and value

Date	Mintage	F12	VF20	XF40	MS60	MS63
1910	40,000	190	280	450	650	850

KM# 9 10 PERPERA

3.39 g., 0.900 Gold 0.098 oz. AGW **Ruler:** Nicholas I **Subject:** 50th Year of Reign **Obv:** Head laureate left **Rev:** Crowned mantled arms within sprigs above date and value

Date	Mintage	F12	VF20	XF40	MS60	MS63
1910	35,003	200	295	475	675	900

KM# 10 20 PERPERA

6.78 g., 0.900 Gold 0.196 oz. AGW **Ruler:** Nicholas I **Obv:** Head right **Rev:** Crowned mantled arms within sprigs above date and value

Date	Mintage	F12	VF20	XF40	MS60	MS63
1910	30,000	350	400	825	1,400	1,900

KM# 11 20 PERPERA

6.78 g., 0.900 Gold 0.196 oz. AGW **Ruler:** Nicholas I **Subject:** 50th Year of Reign **Obv:** Laureate head left **Rev:** Crowned mantled arms within sprigs above date and value

Date	Mintage	F12	VF20	XF40	MS60	MS63
1910	30,003	350	400	825	1,400	1,900

KM# 12 100 PERPERA

33.88 g., 0.900 Gold 0.9802 oz. AGW **Ruler:** Nicholas I **Obv:** Head right **Rev:** Crowned and mantled arms

Date	Mintage	F12	VF20	XF40	MS60	MS63
1910	301	—	5,000	8,000	15,000	20,000
1910	25	PF63 35,000				

KM# 13 100 PERPERA

33.88 g., 0.900 Gold 0.9802 oz. AGW **Ruler:** Nicholas I **Subject:** 50th Year of Reign **Obv:** Laureate head left **Rev:** Crowned mantled arms within sprigs above date and value

Date	Mintage	F12	VF20	XF40	MS60	MS63
1910	501	—	5,000	8,000	18,000	20,000
1910	Inc. above	PF63 20,000				

PATTERNS

KM#	Date	Mintage	Identification	Mkt Val
Pn1	1915	—	Para. With ESSAI. Struck at Paris.	1,500
Pn2	1915	—	2 Pare. With ESSAI. Struck at Paris.	1,500
Pn3	1915	—	10 Para. With ESSAI. Struck at Paris.	—
Pn4	1915	—	20 Para. With ESSAI. Struck at Paris.	—
Pn5	1915	—	Perper. With ESSAI. Struck at Paris.	1,800
Pn6	1915	—	2 Perpera. With ESSAI. Struck at Paris.	2,200
Pn7	1915	—	5 Perpera. With ESSAI. Struck at Paris. Bears the monogram EL for Edmond Lindauer, who copied the work of S. Schwarz of the Vienna Mint, where the regular issue coinage was struck.	8,500

TRIAL STRIKES

KM#	Date	Mintage	Identification	Mkt Val
TS1	ND-1910	—	100 Perpera. Hallmarked. Uniface.	6,500
TS2	ND-1910	—	100 Perpera. TITRE ZZK ESSAI.	5,500

MONTSERRAT

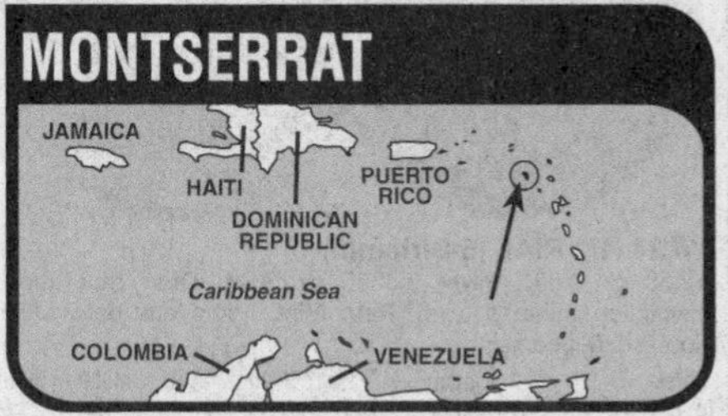

Montserrat, a British crown colony located in the Lesser Antilles of the West Indies 27 miles (43 km.) southwest of Antigua, has an area of 38 sq. mi. (100 sq. km.) and a population of 18,500. Capital: Plymouth. The island - actually a range of volcanic peaks rising from the Caribbean - exports cotton, limes and vegetables.

Columbus discovered Montserrat in 1493 and named it after Monserrado, a mountain in Spain. It was colonized by the English in 1632 and, except for brief periods of French occupancy in 1667 and 1782-83, has remained a British possession from that time. Currency of the British Caribbean Territories (Eastern Group) was used until later when the East Caribbean States coinage was introduced. Until becoming a separate colony in 1956, Montserrat was a presidency of the Leeward Islands.

The early 19th century countermarks of a crowned 3, 4, 7, 9 or 18 over M as documented by Major Pridmore have been more correctly listed under St. Bartholomew.

RULER
British

MONETARY SYSTEM
100 Cents = 1 Dollar

BRITISH COLONY

MODERN COINAGE

KM# 30 4 DOLLARS
28.30 g., Copper-Nickel, 38.5 mm. **Series:** F.A.O. **Obv:** National shield **Rev:** Value flanked by plants

Date	Mintage	VF20	XF40	MS60	MS63	MS65
1970	13,000	10.00	20.00	35.00	60.00	75.00
1970	2,000	PF63 65.00	PF65 85.00			

MOROCCO

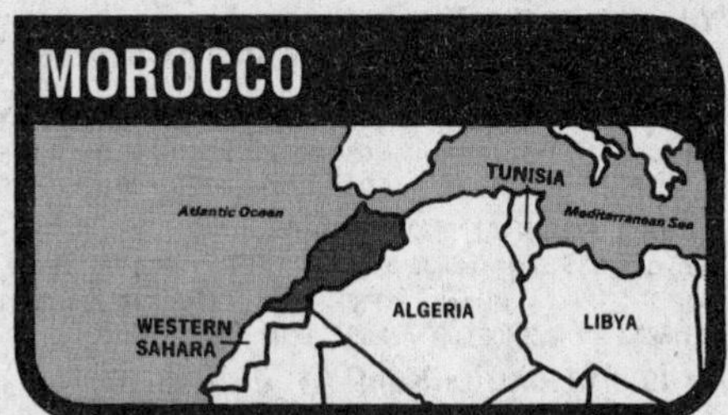

The Kingdom of Morocco, situated on the northwest corner of Africa, has an area of 432,620 sq. mi. (710,850 sq. km.) and a population of 36 million. Capital: Rabat. The economy is essentially agricultural. Phosphates, fresh and preserved vegetables, canned fish, and raw materials are exported.

Morocco's strategic position at the gateway to Western Europe has been the principal determinant of its violent, frequently unfortunate history. Time and again the fertile plain between the rugged Atlas Mountains and the sea has echoed the battle's trumpet as Phoenicians, Romans, Vandals, Visigoths, Byzantine Greeks and Islamic Arabs successively conquered and occupied the land. Modern Morocco is a remnant of an early empire formed by the Arabs at the close of the 7th century, which encompassed all of northwest Africa, and most of the Iberian Peninsula. During the 17th and 18th centuries, while under the control of native dynasties, it was the headquarters of the famous Sale pirates. Morocco's strategic position involved it in the competition of 19th century European powers for political influence in Africa, and resulted in the division of Morocco into French and Spanish spheres of interest, which were established as protectorates in 1912. Morocco became independent on March 2, 1956, after France agreed to end its protectorate. Spain signed similar agreements on April 7 of the same year.

TITLES

المغربية

Al-Maghribiya(t)

المملكة المغربية

Al-Mamlaka(t) al-Maghribiya(t)

المحمدية الشريفة

Al-Mohammediya(t) esh-Sherifiya(t)

RULERS

Filali (or 'Alawi) Sharifs
Abd al-Aziz, AH1311-1326/1894-1908AD
Abd al-Hafiz, AH1326-1330/1908-1912AD

French Protectorate, AH1330/1912AD
Yusuf, AH1330-1346/1912-1927AD
Mohammed V, AH1346-1375/1927-1955AD

Kingdom
Mohammed V, AH1376-1381/1956-1962AD
Al-Hasan II, AH1381-1420/1962-1999AD
Mohammed VI, AH1420- /1999- AD

MINTS
(a) - Paris privy marks only

Silver Coins　Bronze Coins

Bi - England (Birmingham)

بانكلند

Ln = bi-England (London)

باريز

Pa = bi-Bariz (Paris)

فاس

Fs = Fes (Fas, Fez)

Py - Poissy Inscribed "Paris" but with thunderbolt privy mark.

NOTE: Some of the above forms of the mintnames are shown as they appear on the coins, not in regular Arabic script.

NOTES

On the silver coins the denominations are written in words and each series has its own characteristic names:

Y#9-13 (1313-1319) Denomination in "Preferred" Dirhams.
Y#18-22 (1320-1323) Denomination in fractions of a Rial, but on the 3 larger sizes, the equivalent is given in "Urti parts", 1 Rial 20 = Urti parts.
Y#23-25 (1329) Denomination in Dirhams and in fraction of a Rial.
Y#30-33 (1331-1336) Denomination in Yusuti or "Treasury" Dirhams.

On most of the larger denominations, the denomination is given in the form of a rhymed couplet.

NOTE: Various copper and silver coins dated AH1297-1311 are believed to be patterns. Copper coins similar to Y#14-17, but without denomination on reverse, are patterns.

NOTE: 1, 2, 5 and 10 Mazunas of AH1320 Fes exist in medal alignment and coin alignment (rare). AH1321-1323 Fes strikes are medal alignment only.

KINGDOM

Filali Sharifs - Alawi Dynasty

'Abd al-Aziz

AH1311-1326/1894-1908AD

MILLED COINAGE

Y# 9.2 1/2 DIRHAM
1.46 g., 0.835 Silver 0.0391 oz. ASW, 14.5 mm. **Obv:** Seal of Solomon within inner circle flanked by arrow heads facing inwards **Rev:** Mint and Year. Seal of Solomon within inner circle flanked by arrow heads facing inwards

Date	Mintage	F12	VF20	XF40	MS60	MS63
AH1319	572,000	15.00	40.00	80.00	200	300

REFORM COINAGE

AH1320 / 1902AD

Y# 14.1 MUZUNA
1.00 g., Bronze **Obv:** Date within circle **Rev:** Value within circle

Date	Mintage	F12	VF20	XF40	MS60	MS63
AH1320 Bi	3,000,000	3.00	5.00	25.00	60.00	100
AH1321 Bi	900,000	5.00	10.00	40.00	75.00	175

Y# 14.2 MUZUNA
1.00 g., Bronze **Obv:** Date within circle **Rev:** Value within circle **Note:** Varieties exist.

Date	Mintage	F12	VF20	XF40	MS60	MS63
AH1320 Fs	—	50.00	150	300	500	—

Y# 15.1 2 MAZUNAS
2.00 g., Bronze, 21 mm. **Obv:** Date within circle **Rev:** Value within circle

Date	Mintage	F12	VF20	XF40	MS60	MS63
AH1320	1,500,000	3.00	5.00	20.00	60.00	90.00
AH1321	450,000	5.00	15.00	40.00	75.00	150

Y# 15.2 2 MAZUNAS
2.00 g., Bronze **Note:** Normal rim design; varieties exist.

Date	Mintage	F12	VF20	XF40	MS60	MS63
AH1320 Fs	—	20.00	75.00	175	300	—
AH1322 Fs	—	75.00	200	450	750	—
AH1323 Fs	—	25.00	150	350	650	—

Y# 15.3 2 MAZUNAS
2.00 g., Bronze, 21 mm. **Obv:** Date within circle **Rev:** Value within circle, rim design reversed

Date	Mintage	F12	VF20	XF40	MS60	MS63
AH1320 Fs Rare	—	—	—	—	—	—

Y# 15.4 2 MAZUNAS

2.00 g., Bronze, 20.1 mm. **Note:** Normal rim design.

Date	Mintage	F12	VF20	XF40	MS60	MS63
AH1321 Pa	6,500,000	2.00	5.00	15.00	45.00	75.00

Y# 16.1 5 MAZUNAS

5.00 g., Bronze **Obv:** Date within circle **Rev:** Value within circle

Date	Mintage	F12	VF20	XF40	MS60	MS63
AH1320 Bi	2,400,000	2.00	5.00	20.00	45.00	100
AH1321 Bi	720,000	4.00	10.00	30.00	75.00	175

Y# 16.2 5 MAZUNAS

5.00 g., Bronze **Obv:** Date within circle **Rev:** Value within circle **Note:** Varieties exist.

Date	Mintage	F12	VF20	XF40	MS60	MS63
AH1320 Fs	—	25.00	75.00	200	—	—
AH1322 Fs	—	40.00	125	350	—	—

Y# 16.3 5 MAZUNAS

5.00 g., Bronze **Obv:** Date within circle **Rev:** Value within circle

Date	Mintage	F12	VF20	XF40	MS60	MS63
AH1321 Pa	7,950,000	2.00	5.00	30.00	75.00	125

Y# 17.1 10 MAZUNAS

10.00 g., Bronze

Date	Mintage	F12	VF20	XF40	MS60	MS63
AH1320	2,400,000	2.00	5.00	25.00	75.00	125
AH1321	2,600,000	2.00	5.00	25.00	75.00	125

Y# 17.2 10 MAZUNAS

10.00 g., Bronze **Obv:** Date within circle **Rev:** Value within circle

Date	Mintage	F12	VF20	XF40	MS60	MS63
AH1320 Bi	1,200,000	3.00	6.00	25.00	90.00	150
AH1321 Bi	360,000	4.00	12.00	35.00	125	200

Y# 17.3 10 MAZUNAS

10.00 g., Bronze **Obv:** Date within circle **Rev:** Value within circle **Note:** Varieties exist.

Date	Mintage	F12	VF20	XF40	MS60	MS63
AH1320 Fs	—	75.00	125	—	—	—
Small letters						
AH1320 Fs	—	20.00	60.00	150	—	—
Large letters						
AH1321 Fs	—	18.00	50.00	150	—	—
AH1323 Fs	—	75.00	125	275	—	—
Large 10						
AH1323 Fs	—	85.00	145	325	—	—
Small 10						

Y# 18.1 1/20 RIAL (1/2 Dirham)

1.25 g., 0.835 Silver 0.0336 oz. ASW **Obv:** Inscription **Rev:** Value and date

Date	Mintage	F12	VF20	XF40	MS60	MS63
AH1320	3,920,000	4.00	12.00	40.00	90.00	175
AH1321	2,105,000	4.00	12.00	40.00	90.00	175

Y# 18.2 1/20 RIAL (1/2 Dirham)

1.25 g., 0.835 Silver 0.0336 oz. ASW

Date	Mintage	F12	VF20	XF40	MS60	MS63
AH1320 Pa	2,400,000	4.00	12.00	40.00	90.00	175

Y# 19 1/10 RIAL (Dirham)

2.50 g., 0.835 Silver 0.0671 oz. ASW, 16.5 mm.

Date	Mintage	F12	VF20	XF40	MS60	MS63
AH1320 Ln	2,940,000	4.00	12.00	60.00	90.00	200
AH1321 Ln	770,000	6.00	15.00	75.00	125	275

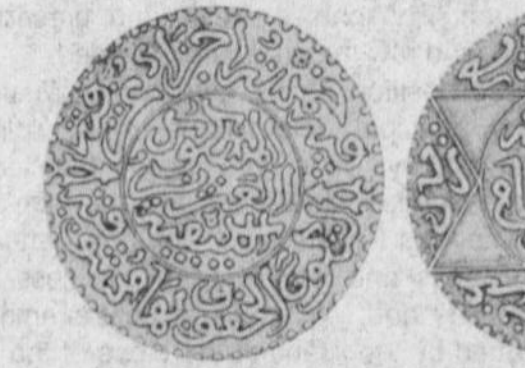

Y# 20.1 1/4 RIAL (2-1/2 Dirhams)

6.25 g., 0.835 Silver 0.1678 oz. ASW, 25 mm. **Obv:** Inscription within inner circle, legend around border **Rev:** Inscription and date within the Star of David, legend flanked by star points

Date	Mintage	F12	VF20	XF40	MS60	MS63
AH1320 Be	1,380,000	6.00	12.00	40.00	90.00	175
AH1320 Be	—	PF63 2,000				
AH1321 Be	4,450,000	6.00	12.00	40.00	90.00	175
AH1321 Be	5	—	—	—	—	—
Proof; Rare						

Y# 20.2 1/4 RIAL (2-1/2 Dirhams)

6.25 g., 0.835 Silver 0.1678 oz. ASW, 25 mm.

Date	Mintage	F12	VF20	XF40	MS60	MS63
AH1320 Ln	3,056,000	6.00	12.00	40.00	90.00	175
AH1321 Ln	1,889,000	6.00	12.00	40.00	90.00	175

Y# 20.3 1/4 RIAL (2-1/2 Dirhams)

6.25 g., 0.835 Silver 0.1678 oz. ASW, 25 mm.

Date	Mintage	F12	VF20	XF40	MS60	MS63
AH1320 Pa	480,000	12.00	20.00	90.00	200	400
AH1321 Pa	160,000	25.00	75.00	275	500	900

Y# 21.1 1/2 RIAL (5 Dirhams)

12.50 g., 0.835 Silver 0.3356 oz. ASW, 32 mm.

Date	Mintage	F12	VF20	XF40	MS60	MS63
AH1320 Be	2,510,000	12.00	25.00	60.00	125	225
AH1320 Be	—	PF63 2,000				

Y# 21.2 1/2 RIAL (5 Dirhams)

12.50 g., 0.835 Silver 0.3356 oz. ASW, 32 mm.

Date	Mintage	F12	VF20	XF40	MS60	MS63
AH1320 Ln	900,000	15.00	35.00	70.00	150	275
AH1321 Ln	1,041,000	12.00	25.00	60.00	125	225

Y# 21.3 1/2 RIAL (5 Dirhams)

12.50 g., 0.835 Silver 0.3356 oz. ASW, 32 mm.

Date	Mintage	F12	VF20	XF40	MS60	MS63
AH1321 Pa	1,800,000	12.00	25.00	60.00	125	225
AH1322 Pa	540,000	18.00	30.00	100	175	375
AH1323 Pa	1,090,000	10.00	15.00	75.00	150	275

Y# 22.1 RIAL (10 Dirhams)

25.00 g., 0.900 Silver 0.7234 oz. ASW, 37 mm.

Date	Mintage	F12	VF20	XF40	MS60	MS63
AH1320	330,000	30.00	50.00	125	200	425

Y# 22.2 RIAL (10 Dirhams)

25.00 g., 0.900 Silver 0.7234 oz. ASW, 37 mm. **Obv:** Inscription within circle, legend around border **Rev:** Inscription and date within the Star of David, legend flanked by star points

Date	Mintage	F12	VF20	XF40	MS60	MS63
AH1321 Pa	300,000	30.00	50.00	125	200	425

'Abd al-Hafiz
AH1326-1330/1908-1912AD

Y# 23 1/4 RIAL (2-1/2 Dirhams)

6.25 g., 0.835 Silver 0.1678 oz. ASW **Obv:** Inscription below star within sprays **Rev:** Mint, name and date within doubled tri-lobe star

Date	Mintage	F12	VF20	XF40	MS60	MS63
AH1329 Pa	3,900,000	10.00	15.00	45.00	90.00	200

Y# 24 1/2 RIAL (5 Dirhams)

12.50 g., 0.835 Silver 0.3356 oz. ASW **Obv:** Star above inscription within sprays **Rev:** Mint, name and date within doubled tri-lobe star

Date	Mintage	F12	VF20	XF40	MS60	MS63
AH1329 Pa	6,200,000	12.00	20.00	50.00	100	175

Y# 25 RIAL (10 Dirhams)

25.00 g., 0.900 Silver 0.7234 oz. ASW **Obv:** Star above inscription within sprays **Rev:** Mint, name and date within doubled tri-lobe star

Date	Mintage	F12	VF20	XF40	MS60	MS63
AH1329 Pa	10,100,000	20.00	25.00	50.00	125	350

PRIVATE TOKEN COINAGE

Enterprise Collet et Gouvernet

KM# Tn1 FRANC

Aluminum **Issuer:** Entreprise Collet et Gouvernet **Shape:** Hexagon

Date	Mintage	F12	VF20	XF40	MS60	MS63
ND (1912)	—	—	22.50	55.00	110	210

KM# Tn2 2 FRANCS

Aluminum **Shape:** Scalloped

Date	Mintage	F12	VF20	XF40	MS60	MS63
ND (1912)	—	—	27.50	60.00	130	270

KM# Tn3 5 FRANCS
Aluminum

Date	Mintage	F12	VF20	XF40	MS60	MS63
ND (1912)	—	—	42.00	70.00	175	325

KM# Tn4 5 FRANCS
Aluminum

Date	Mintage	F12	VF20	XF40	MS60	MS63
ND (1912)	—	—	42.00	70.00	175	325

Yusuf
AH1330-1346/1912-1927AD

REFORM COINAGE

AH1320 / 1902AD

Y# 26 MUZUNA
Bronze **Obv:** Value within star **Rev:** Mint name and date within doubled tri-lobe star

Date	Mintage	F12	VF20	XF40	MS60	MS63
AH1330 Pa	1,850,000	2.00	5.00	15.00	50.00	125

Y# 27 2 MAZUNAS
Bronze **Obv:** Value within star **Rev:** Mint name and date within doubled tri-lobe star

Date	Mintage	F12	VF20	XF40	MS60	MS63
AH1330 Pa	2,790,000	2.00	5.00	20.00	45.00	100

Note: Coins reportedly dated 1331Pa probably bore date AH1330

Y# 28.1 5 MAZUNAS
Bronze **Obv:** Value within star **Rev:** Mint name and date within doubled tri-lobe star

Date	Mintage	F12	VF20	XF40	MS60	MS63
AH1330 Pa	2,983,000	2.00	5.00	20.00	60.00	100
AH1340 Pa	2,000,000	2.00	5.00	15.00	45.00	75.00

Y# 28.2 5 MAZUNAS
Bronze **Obv:** Value within star **Rev:** Mint name and date within doubled tri-lobe star, with privy marks

Date	Mintage	F12	VF20	XF40	MS60	MS63
AH1340 Py	2,010,000	2.00	5.00	15.00	45.00	75.00

Y# 29.1 10 MAZUNAS
Bronze **Obv:** Value within star **Rev:** Mint name and date within doubled tri-lobe star

Date	Mintage	F12	VF20	XF40	MS60	MS63
AH1330 Pa	1,500,000	2.00	7.00	30.00	50.00	110
AH1340 Pa	1,000,000	2.00	7.00	20.00	45.00	90.00

Y# 29.2 10 MAZUNAS
Bronze **Obv:** Value within star **Rev:** Mint name and date within doubled tri-lobe star, privy marks

Date	Mintage	F12	VF20	XF40	MS60	MS63
AH1340 Py	1,000,000	2.00	7.00	20.00	45.00	90.00

Y# 30 1/10 RIAL (Dirham)
2.50 g., 0.835 Silver 0.0671 oz. ASW **Obv:** Inscription **Rev:** Mint name and date

Date	Mintage	F12	VF20	XF40	MS60	MS63
AH1331 Pa	500,000	20.00	35.00	60.00	150	250
AH1331 Pa	—	PF63 800				

Y# 31 1/4 RIAL (2-1/2 Dirhams)
6.25 g., 0.835 Silver 0.1678 oz. ASW **Obv:** Inscription and date within the Star of David, legend flanked by star points **Rev:** Mint name and date within circle

Date	Mintage	F12	VF20	XF40	MS60	MS63
AH1331 Pa	1,700,000	15.00	30.00	100	200	350

Y# 32 1/2 RIAL (5 Dirhams)
0.835 Silver **Obv:** Inscription and date within the Star of David, legend flanked by star points **Rev:** Mint name and date within circle

Date	Mintage	F12	VF20	XF40	MS60	MS63
AH1331 Pa	4,300,000	12.00	20.00	40.00	100	225
AH1336 Pa	7,200,000	12.00	20.00	35.00	75.00	175

Y# 33 RIAL (10 Dirhams)
25.00 g., 0.900 Silver 0.7234 oz. ASW **Obv:** Inscription and date within the Star of David, legend flanked by star points **Rev:** Mint name and date within circle

Date	Mintage	F12	VF20	XF40	MS60	MS63
AH1331 Pa	4,200,000	25.00	30.00	55.00	100	225
AH1336 Pa	2,500,000	27.00	32.00	75.00	125	250

FRENCH PROTECTORATE

STANDARD COINAGE

100 Centimes = 1 Franc

Y# 34.1 25 CENTIMES
Copper-Nickel, 24 mm. **Obv:** Hole in center of the star of David within circle, without privy marks **Rev:** Hole in center flanked by value within circle, without privy marks **Edge:** Plain

Date	Mintage	F12	VF20	XF40	MS60	MS63
ND (1921) Pa	8,000,000	1.00	2.00	15.00	35.00	100

Y# 34.2 25 CENTIMES
Copper-Nickel, 24 mm. **Obv:** Hole in center of the star of David within circle **Rev:** Hole in center flanked by value within circle **Edge:** Plain

Date	Mintage	F12	VF20	XF40	MS60	MS63
ND (1924) Py	2,037,000	2.00	4.00	15.00	35.00	100

Y# 34.3 25 CENTIMES
Copper-Nickel, 24 mm. **Rev:** Thunderbolt and torch at left and right of CENTIMES

Date	Mintage	F12	VF20	XF40	MS60	MS63
ND (1924) Py	Inc. above	2.00	4.00	15.00	35.00	100

Y# 35.1 50 CENTIMES
Nickel **Obv:** Star within circle ,without privy marks **Rev:** Value within artistic designed star, without privy marks

Date	Mintage	F12	VF20	XF40	MS60	MS63
ND (1921) Pa	7,976,000	0.50	1.00	15.00	35.00	100

Y# 35.2 50 CENTIMES
Nickel **Obv:** Star within circle **Rev:** Value within artistic designed star, thunderbolt at bottom

Date	Mintage	F12	VF20	XF40	MS60	MS63
ND (1924) Py	3,000,000	1.00	2.00	15.00	35.00	100

Y# 36.1 FRANC

7.84 g., Nickel, 27.2 mm. **Obv:** Star within circle, without privy marks **Rev:** Value within artistic designed star, without privy marks **Edge:** Reeded

Date	Mintage	VF20	XF40	MS60	MS63	MS65
ND (1921) Pa	8,325,000	3.00	20.00	45.00	125	—

Y# 36.2 FRANC

Nickel, 27 mm. **Obv:** Star within circle **Rev:** Value within artistic designed star, thunderbolt below 1 **Edge:** Reeded

Date	Mintage	VF20	XF40	MS60	MS63	MS65
ND (1924) Py	4,796,000	4.00	25.00	60.00	150	—

Mohammed V
AH1346-1381/1927-1962AD

Y# 40 50 CENTIMES

Aluminum-Bronze **Obv:** Star **Rev:** Value flanked by dates

Date	Mintage	VF20	XF40	MS60	MS63	MS65
AH1364-1945 (a)	24,000,000	0.50	1.00	3.00	8.00	15.00

Y# 41 FRANC

Aluminum-Bronze **Obv:** Legend around star **Rev:** Value flanked by dates

Date	Mintage	VF20	XF40	MS60	MS63	MS65
AH1364-1945 (a)	24,000,000	0.50	1.00	3.00	8.00	15.00

Y# 46 FRANC

Aluminum, 19.5 mm. **Obv:** Legend around star **Rev:** Value flanked by dates **Edge:** Plain

Date	Mintage	VF20	XF40	MS60	MS63	MS65
AH1370-1951 (a)	33,000,000	—	0.25	1.00	1.50	3.00

Note: Note: Y#46-51 were struck for more than 20 years without change of date, until a new currency was introduced in 1974

Y# 42 2 FRANCS

Aluminum-Bronze **Obv:** Legend around star **Rev:** Value flanked by dates

Date	Mintage	VF20	XF40	MS60	MS63	MS65
AH1364-1945 (a)	12,000,000	—	1.00	5.00	12.00	20.00

Y# 47 2 FRANCS

Aluminum, 22 mm. **Obv:** Legend around star **Rev:** Value flanked by dates **Edge:** Plain

Date	Mintage	VF20	XF40	MS60	MS63	MS65
AH1370-1951 (a)	20,000,000	—	0.25	1.00	1.50	3.00

Y# 37 5 FRANCS

5.00 g., 0.680 Silver 0.1093 oz. ASW **Obv:** Date within small circle of doubled tri-lobe star, all within circle **Rev:** Value within doubled square within circle

Date	Mintage	VF20	XF40	MS60	MS63	MS65
AH1347 (a)	4,000,000	5.00	12.00	35.00	50.00	—
AH1352 (a)	5,000,000	4.00	10.00	25.00	45.00	—

Y# 43 5 FRANCS

Aluminum-Bronze **Obv:** Date within small circle of doubled tri-lobe star, all within circle **Rev:** Value in doubled square within circle

Date	Mintage	VF20	XF40	MS60	MS63	MS65
AH1365 (a)	20,000,000	0.50	1.00	5.00	10.00	20.00

Y# 48 5 FRANCS

Aluminum, 25 mm. **Obv:** Date within small circle of doubled tri-lobe star, all within circle **Rev:** Value flanked by marks in doubled square within circle **Edge:** Plain

Date	Mintage	VF20	XF40	MS60	MS63	MS65
AH1370 (a)	23,000,000	0.50	1.00	3.00	5.00	7.50

Y# 38 10 FRANCS

10.00 g., 0.680 Silver 0.2186 oz. ASW, 27.7 mm. **Obv:** Date in small circle of doubled tri-lobe star, all within circle **Rev:** Date in doubled square within circle

Date	Mintage	VF20	XF40	MS60	MS63	MS65
AH1347 (a)	1,600,000	8.00	15.00	45.00	90.00	—
AH1352 (a)	2,900,000	8.00	15.00	30.00	75.00	—

Y# 44 10 FRANCS

Copper-Nickel **Obv:** Date in small circle of doubled tri-lobe star, all within circle **Rev:** Value in doubled square within circle

Date	Mintage	VF20	XF40	MS60	MS63	MS65
AH1366 (a)	20,000,000	0.50	1.00	3.00	7.50	15.00

Y# 49 10 FRANCS

3.00 g., Aluminum-Bronze, 20 mm. **Obv:** Star flanked by designs, date on bottom **Rev:** Value flanked by designs **Edge:** Plain

Date	Mintage	VF20	XF40	MS60	MS63	MS65
AH1371 (a)	40,000,000	0.50	1.00	3.00	5.00	7.50

Y# 39 20 FRANCS

20.00 g., 0.680 Silver 0.4372 oz. ASW, 35 mm. **Obv:** Date in inner circle of doubled tri-lobe star, all within circle **Rev:** Value in doubled square within circle

Date	Mintage	VF20	XF40	MS60	MS63	MS65
AH1347 (a)	177,000	20.00	45.00	175	350	—
AH1352 (a)	2,000,000	20.00	30.00	90.00	150	—

Y# 45 20 FRANCS

Copper-Nickel **Obv:** Date in inner circle of doubled tri-lobe star, all within circle **Rev:** Value in doubled square within circle

Date	Mintage	VF20	XF40	MS60	MS63	MS65
AH1366 (a)	6,000,000	0.50	1.00	3.00	7.50	12.00
AH1366 (a)	—	PF65 50.00				

Y# 50 20 FRANCS

4.00 g., Aluminum-Bronze, 23.8 mm. **Obv:** Star flanked by designs, date on bottom **Rev:** Value flanked by designs **Edge:** Plain

Date	Mintage	VF20	XF40	MS60	MS63	MS65
AH1371 (a)	20,000,000	0.50	1.00	3.00	7.50	12.00

Y# 51 50 FRANCS

Aluminum-Bronze, 27 mm. **Obv:** Date in inner circle of doubled tri-lobe star, all within circle **Rev:** Value in doubled square within circle **Edge:** Plain

Date	Mintage	VF20	XF40	MS60	MS63	MS65
AH1371 (a)	20,600,000	0.50	1.00	3.00	7.50	15.00

Y# 51a 50 FRANCS

Gold **Obv:** Date in inner circle of doubled tri-lobe star, all within circle **Rev:** Value within doubled square within circle

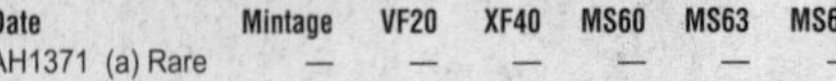

Date	Mintage	VF20	XF40	MS60	MS63	MS65
AH1371 (a) Rare	—	—	—	—	—	—

Y# A54 100 FRANCS
2.50 g., 0.720 Silver 0.0579 oz. ASW **Obv:** Star flanked by designs, date on bottom **Rev:** Value flanked by designs

Date	Mintage	VF20	XF40	MS60	MS63	MS65
AH1370 (a)	10,000,000	—	—	—	600	750

Note: Nearly all specimens were melted, only 100 known

Y# 52 100 FRANCS
4.00 g., 0.720 Silver 0.0926 oz. ASW **Obv:** Star within small circle in center of larger star with designs in points **Rev:** Value within beaded circle, legend around border

Date	Mintage	VF20	XF40	MS60	MS63	MS65
AH1372-1953 (a)	20,000,000	3.00	5.00	15.00	30.00	45.00

Y# 53 200 FRANCS
8.00 g., 0.720 Silver 0.1852 oz. ASW **Obv:** Star within small circle in center of larger star with designs in points **Rev:** Value and date within beaded circle

Date	Mintage	VF20	XF40	MS60	MS63	MS65
AH1372-1953 (a)	10,176,000	5.00	10.00	20.00	35.00	75.00

Y# 54 500 FRANCS
22.50 g., 0.900 Silver 0.6511 oz. ASW, 38 mm. **Obv:** Bust left within circle **Rev:** Crown in center of star flanked by dates and value

Date	Mintage	VF20	XF40	MS60	MS63	MS65
AH1376-1956 (a)	2,000,000	—	15.00	25.00	45.00	60.00

KINGDOM

1956-

REFORM COINAGE

100 Francs = 1 Dirham

Y# 55 DIRHAM
6.00 g., 0.600 Silver 0.1157 oz. ASW **Obv:** Head left **Rev:** Crowned arms with supporters flanked by dates above and value below

Date	Mintage	VF20	XF40	MS60	MS63	MS65
AH1380-1960 (a)	33,000,000	—	3.00	5.00	12.00	20.00

al-Hassan II

AH1381-1420/1962-1999AD

Y# 56 DIRHAM
6.00 g., Nickel, 24 mm. **Obv:** Head left **Rev:** Crowned arms with supporters **Edge:** Reeded

Date	Mintage	VF20	XF40	MS60	MS63	MS65
AH1384-1965 (a)	30,000,000	—	0.50	0.75	2.00	5.00
AH1388-1968 (a)	5,000,000	1.00	2.00	4.00	7.50	10.00
AH1389-1969 (a)	17,200,000	—	0.50	0.75	2.00	5.00

Y# 57 5 DIRHAMS
11.75 g., 0.720 Silver 0.272 oz. ASW **Obv:** Head left **Rev:** Crowned arms with supporters

Date	Mintage	VF20	XF40	MS60	MS63	MS65
AH1384-1965 (a)	200	PF65 120				
AH1384-1965 (a)	2,000,000	—	5.00	7.50	12.00	20.00

REFORM COINAGE

100 Santimat = 1 Dirham

Y# 58 SANTIM
0.70 g., Aluminum, 17 mm. **Obv:** Crowned arms with supporters **Rev:** Value flanked by designs

Date	Mintage	VF20	XF40	MS60	MS63	MS65
AH1394-1974	10,240,000	—	—	0.50	2.00	5.00

Y# 58a SANTIM
0.917 Gold, 17 mm. **Obv:** Crowned arms with supporters **Rev:** Value flanked by designs

Date	Mintage	VF20	XF40	MS60	MS63	MS65
AH1394-1974	30	PF65 450				

Y# 93 SANTIM
0.70 g., Aluminum, 17 mm. **Obv:** Crowned arms with supporters **Rev:** Fish above value

Date	Mintage	VF20	XF40	MS60	MS63	MS65
AH1407-1987	—	—	—	1.00	1.50	3.00

Y# 59 5 SANTIMAT
2.00 g., Aluminum-Bronze, 17.5 mm. **Series:** F.A.O. **Obv:** Crowned arms with supporters **Rev:** Value at lower right of captain's wheel **Edge:** Plain

Date	Mintage	VF20	XF40	MS60	MS63	MS65
AH1394-1974	54,820,000	—	—	0.15	1.00	2.00

Y# 59a 5 SANTIMAT
0.917 Gold, 17.5 mm. **Series:** F.A.O. **Obv:** Crowned arms with supporters **Rev:** Value at lower right of captain's wheel

Date	Mintage	VF20	XF40	MS60	MS63	MS65
AH1394-1974	30	PF65 500				

Y# 83 5 SANTIMAT
2.00 g., Aluminum-Bronze, 17.5 mm. **Series:** F.A.O. **Obv:** Crowned arms with supporters **Rev:** Value to upper left of center design **Edge:** Plain

Date	Mintage	VF20	XF40	MS60	MS63	MS65
AH1407-1987	—	—	—	0.50	1.00	2.00

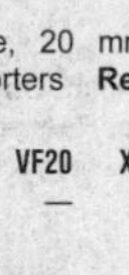

Y# 60 10 SANTIMAT
3.00 g., Aluminum-Bronze, 20 mm. **Series:** F.A.O. **Obv:** Crowned arms with supporters **Rev:** Value at lower left of designs **Edge:** Reeded

Date	Mintage	VF20	XF40	MS60	MS63	MS65
AH1394-1974	67,950,000	—	—	0.15	1.00	2.00

Y# 60a 10 SANTIMAT
0.917 Gold, 20 mm. **Series:** F.A.O. **Obv:** Crowned arms with supporters **Rev:** Value at lower left of designs

Date	Mintage	VF20	XF40	MS60	MS63	MS65
AH1394-1974	30	PF65 600				

Y# 84 10 SANTIMAT
3.00 g., Aluminum-Bronze, 20 mm. **Series:** F.A.O. **Obv:** Crowned arms with supporters **Rev:** Single ear of corn to left of value **Edge:** Reeded

Date	Mintage	VF20	XF40	MS60	MS63	MS65
AH1407-1987	—	—	—	0.50	1.00	2.00

Y# 61 20 SANTIMAT
4.00 g., Aluminum-Bronze, 23 mm. **Obv:** Head left **Rev:** Crowned arms with supporters, value below **Edge:** Reeded

Date	Mintage	VF20	XF40	MS60	MS63	MS65
AH1394-1974	59,840,000	—	0.30	0.40	1.00	2.00

Y# 61a 20 SANTIMAT
0.917 Gold, 23 mm. **Obv:** Head left **Rev:** Crowned arms with supporters

Date	Mintage	VF20	XF40	MS60	MS63	MS65
AH1394-1974	30	PF65 600				

Y# 85 20 SANTIMAT
4.00 g., Aluminum-Bronze, 23 mm. **Series:** F.A.O. **Obv:** Crowned arms with supporters **Rev:** Value to right of designs **Edge:** Reeded

Date	Mintage	VF20	XF40	MS60	MS63	MS65
AH1407-1987	—	—	—	0.50	1.00	2.00

Y# 62 50 SANTIMAT
4.00 g., Copper-Nickel, 21 mm. **Obv:** Head left **Rev:** Crowned arms with supporters, value below **Edge:** Reeded

Date	Mintage	VF20	XF40	MS60	MS63	MS65
AH1394-1974	40,380,000	—	0.20	0.40	1.00	2.00

Y# 62a 50 SANTIMAT
0.917 Gold, 21 mm. **Obv:** Head left **Rev:** Crowned arms with supporters

Date	Mintage	VF20	XF40	MS60	MS63	MS65
AH1394-1974	30	PF65 600				

Y# 87 1/2 DIRHAM
4.00 g., Copper-Nickel, 21 mm. **Obv:** Head left **Rev:** Crowned arms with supporters **Edge:** Reeded

Date	Mintage	VF20	XF40	MS60	MS63	MS65
AH1407-1987	—	—	—	0.50	1.00	1.50

Y# 63 DIRHAM
6.00 g., Copper-Nickel, 24 mm. **Obv:** Head left **Rev:** Crowned arms with supporters, value below **Edge:** Reeded

Date	Mintage	VF20	XF40	MS60	MS63	MS65
AH1394-1974	32,850,000	—	0.30	0.50	1.00	1.50

Y# 63a DIRHAM
0.917 Gold, 24 mm. **Obv:** Head left **Rev:** Crowned arms with supporters

Date	Mintage	VF20	XF40	MS60	MS63	MS65
AH1394-1974	30	PF65 725				

Y# 88 DIRHAM
6.00 g., Copper-Nickel, 24 mm. **Obv:** Head left **Rev:** Crowned arms with supporters, value below **Edge:** Reeded

Date	Mintage	VF20	XF40	MS60	MS63	MS65
AH1407-1987	—	—	—	1.00	1.50	2.50

Y# 64 5 DIRHAMS
Copper-Nickel **Series:** World Food Conference **Obv:** Head left **Rev:** Small value within center of designs

Date	Mintage	VF20	XF40	MS60	MS63	MS65
AH1395-1975	500,000	—	—	1.00	5.00	7.50
AH1395-1975	500	PF65 80.00				

Y# 64a 5 DIRHAMS
12.00 g., 0.925 Silver 0.3569 oz. ASW **Series:** World Food Conference **Obv:** Head left **Rev:** Small value within center of designs

Date	Mintage	VF20	XF40	MS60	MS63	MS65
AH1395-1975	200	PF65 150				

Y# 64b 5 DIRHAMS
23.65 g., 0.900 Gold 0.6843 oz. AGW **Series:** World Food Conference **Obv:** Head left **Rev:** Small value within center of designs

Date	Mintage	VF20	XF40	MS60	MS63	MS65
AH1395-1975	20	PF65 1,350				

Y# 72 5 DIRHAMS
12.00 g., Copper-Nickel, 29 mm. **Obv:** Head left **Rev:** Crowned arms with supporters **Edge:** Reeded

Date	Mintage	VF20	XF40	MS60	MS63	MS65
AH1400-1980	10,000,000	—	—	1.00	5.00	7.50

Y# 82 5 DIRHAMS
6.80 g., Bi-Metallic Aluminum-Bronze center in Stainless Steel ring, 26.2 mm. **Obv:** Head left within circle **Rev:** Crowned arms with supporters and value within circle **Edge:** Segmented reeding

Date	Mintage	VF20	XF40	MS60	MS63	MS65
AH1407-1987	—	—	1.00	1.50	3.00	5.00

Y# 92 10 DIRHAMS
12.00 g., Bi-Metallic Copper-Nickel center in Aluminum-Bronze ring, 28 mm. **Obv:** Hooded head left within circle with star below **Rev:** Crowned arms with supporters and value within circle with star above **Edge:** Reeded

Date	Mintage	VF20	XF40	MS60	MS63	MS65
AH1415-1995	—	—	—	3.00	5.00	7.50

Y# 65 50 DIRHAMS
35.00 g., 0.925 Silver 1.0409 oz. ASW, 42 mm. **Subject:** 20th Anniversary of Independence **Obv:** Head left **Rev:** Crowned arms with supporters **Edge:** Reeded

Date	Mintage	VF20	XF40	MS60	MS63	MS65
AH1395-1975	6,000	—	—	—	25.00	40.00
AH1395-1975	4,400	PF65 60.00				

Y# 65a 50 DIRHAMS
60.14 g., 0.900 Gold 1.7402 oz. AGW **Subject:** 20th Anniversary of Independence **Obv:** Head left **Rev:** Crowned arms with supporters

Date	Mintage	VF20	XF40	MS60	MS63	MS65
AH1395-1975	40	PF65 3,250				

Y# 67 50 DIRHAMS
35.00 g., 0.925 Silver 1.0409 oz. ASW **Series:** International Women's Year **Obv:** Head left **Rev:** Hand within circled design

Date	Mintage	VF20	XF40	MS60	MS63	MS65
AH1395-1975	6,000	—	—	—	25.00	40.00
AH1395-1975	4,400	PF65 60.00				

Y# 67a 50 DIRHAMS
60.14 g., 0.900 Gold 1.7402 oz. AGW **Series:** International Women's Year **Obv:** Head left **Rev:** Hand within circled design

Date	Mintage	VF20	XF40	MS60	MS63	MS65
AH1395-1975	20	PF65 3,500				

Y# 68 50 DIRHAMS
35.00 g., 0.925 Silver 1.0409 oz. ASW **Subject:** Green March in Spanish Sahara, 1st Anniversary **Obv:** Head left **Rev:** Stylized group of people marching forward

Date	Mintage	VF20	XF40	MS60	MS63	MS65
AH1396-1976	11,000	—	—	—	25.00	35.00
AH1396-1976	4,400	PF63 45.00	PF65 55.00			

Y# 68a 50 DIRHAMS
60.14 g., 0.900 Gold 1.7402 oz. AGW **Subject:** Green March in Spanish Sahara, 1st Anniversary **Obv:** Head left **Rev:** Stylized group of people marching forward

Date	Mintage	VF20	XF40	MS60	MS63	MS65
AH1396-1976	20	PF65 3,700				

Y# 143 50 DIRHAMS
35.00 g., 0.925 Silver 1.0409 oz. ASW, 42 mm. **Subject:** Green March in Spanish Sahara, 2nd Anniversary **Obv:** Head left **Rev:** Stylized group of people marching forward **Note:** Formerly listed as KM#68

Date	Mintage	VF20	XF40	MS60	MS63	MS65
1977	3,500	—	—	—	35.00	45.00
1977	200	PF65 250				

Y# 143a 50 DIRHAMS
60.14 g., 0.900 Gold 1.7402 oz. AGW **Subject:** Green March in Spanish Sahara, 2nd Anniversary **Obv:** Head left **Rev:** Stylized group of people marching forward **Note:** Formerly listed as KM#68a

Date	Mintage	VF20	XF40	MS60	MS63	MS65
AH1397-1977	20	PF65 3,700				

Y# 144 50 DIRHAMS
35.00 g., 0.925 Silver 1.0409 oz. ASW, 42 mm. **Subject:** Green March in the Spanish Sahara, 3rd Anniversary **Obv:** Head left **Rev:** Stylized group of people marching forward **Note:** Formerly listed as KM#68

Date	Mintage	VF20	XF40	MS60	MS63	MS65
AH1398-1978	5,000	—	—	—	30.00	40.00
1978	300	PF65 200				

Y# 144a 50 DIRHAMS
60.14 g., 0.900 Gold 1.7402 oz. AGW **Subject:** Green March in Spanish Sahara, 3rd Anniversary **Obv:** Head left **Rev:** Stylized group of people marching forward **Note:** Formerly listed as KM#68a

Date	Mintage	VF20	XF40	MS60	MS63	MS65
AH1398-1978	70	PF65 3,200				

Y# 70 50 DIRHAMS

35.00 g., 0.925 Silver 1.0409 oz. ASW **Series:** International Year of the Child **Obv:** Head left **Rev:** Design divides world globe flanked by dates

Date	Mintage	VF20	XF40	MS60	MS63	MS65
AH1399-1979	5,000	—	—	—	35.00	45.00
AH1399-1979	500	PF65 110				

Y# 70a 50 DIRHAMS

60.14 g., 0.900 Gold 1.7402 oz. AGW **Series:** International Year of the Child **Obv:** Head left **Rev:** Designs divide globe flanked by dates

Date	Mintage	VF20	XF40	MS60	MS63	MS65
AH1399-1979	70	PF65 3,200				

Y# 76 50 DIRHAMS

35.00 g., 0.925 Silver 1.0409 oz. ASW **Subject:** 50th Birthday - King Hassan **Obv:** Head left **Rev:** Crowned arms with supporters flanked by oat sprig, curvey line and dates with value below

Date	Mintage	VF20	XF40	MS60	MS63	MS65
AH1399-1979	5,000	—	—	—	35.00	45.00
AH1399-1979	500	PF65 110				

Y# 76a 50 DIRHAMS

60.14 g., 0.900 Gold 1.7402 oz. AGW **Subject:** 50th Birthday - King Hassan **Obv:** Head left **Rev:** Crowned arms with supporters flanked by oat sprig, curvy line and dates with value below

Date	Mintage	VF20	XF40	MS60	MS63	MS65
AH1399-1979	70	PF65 3,200				

Y# 145 50 DIRHAMS

35.00 g., 0.925 Silver 1.0409 oz. ASW, 42 mm. **Subject:** Green March in Spanish Sahara, 4th Anniversary **Obv:** Head left **Rev:** Stylized group of people marching forward **Note:** Formerly listed as KM#68

Date	Mintage	VF20	XF40	MS60	MS63	MS65
1979	3,000	—	—	—	40.00	50.00
1979	300	PF65 200				

Y# 145a 50 DIRHAMS

60.14 g., 0.900 Gold 1.7402 oz. AGW **Subject:** Green March in Spanish Sahara, 4th Anniversary **Obv:** Head left **Rev:** Stylized group of people marching forward **Note:** Formerly listed as KM#68a

Date	Mintage	VF20	XF40	MS60	MS63	MS65
AH1399-1979	70	PF65 3,200				

Y# 146 50 DIRHAMS

35.00 g., 0.925 Silver 1.0409 oz. ASW, 42 mm. **Subject:** Green March in Spanish Sahara, 5th Anniversary **Obv:** Head left **Rev:** Stylized group of people marching forward **Note:** Formerly listed as KM#68

Date	Mintage	VF20	XF40	MS60	MS63	MS65
1980	1,000	—	—	—	75.00	150
1980	200	PF65 300				

Y# 146a 50 DIRHAMS

60.14 g., 0.900 Gold 1.7402 oz. AGW **Subject:** Green March in Spanish Sahara, 5th Anniversary **Obv:** Head left **Rev:** Stylized group of people marching forward **Note:** Formerly listed as KM#68a

Date	Mintage	VF20	XF40	MS60	MS63	MS65
AH1400-1980	50	PF65 3,250				

Y# 75 100 DIRHAMS

25.00 g., 0.925 Silver 0.7435 oz. ASW **Subject:** 9th Mediterranean Games **Obv:** Head left **Rev:** Olympic circles flanked by dates

Date	Mintage	VF20	XF40	MS60	MS63	MS65
AH1403-1983	5,000	—	—	—	35.00	40.00
AH1403-1983	500	PF65 90.00				

Y# 77 100 DIRHAMS

15.00 g., 0.925 Silver 0.4461 oz. ASW **Series:** 6th Panarab Sports Games - Olympics **Obv:** Head left **Rev:** Olympic rings above map

Date	Mintage	VF20	XF40	MS60	MS63	MS65
AH1405-1985	2,300	—	—	—	40.00	50.00
AH1405-1985	300	PF65 150				

Y# 78 100 DIRHAMS

15.00 g., 0.925 Silver 0.4461 oz. ASW **Subject:** 10th Anniversary of Green March **Obv:** Seated figure right **Rev:** Crowned arms with supporters

Date	Mintage	VF20	XF40	MS60	MS63	MS65
AH1406-1985	1,200	—	—	—	50.00	80.00
AH1406-1985	200	PF65 220				

Y# 78a 100 DIRHAMS

21.50 g., 0.900 Gold 0.6221 oz. AGW **Subject:** 10th Anniversary of the Green March **Obv:** Seated figure right **Rev:** Crowned arms with supporters

Date	Mintage	VF20	XF40	MS60	MS63	MS65
AH1406-1985	30	PF65 1,250				

Y# 147 100 DIRHAMS

21.50 g., 0.900 Gold 0.6221 oz. AGW **Subject:** UN International Year of Youth **Rev:** Three youth

Date	Mintage	VF20	XF40	MS60	MS63	MS65
1985 Proof, rare	30	—	—	—	—	—

Y# 79 100 DIRHAMS

15.00 g., 0.925 Silver 0.4461 oz. ASW **Subject:** 25th Year - Reign of King Hassan **Obv:** Head left flanked by dates **Rev:** Cheering citizens

Date	Mintage	VF20	XF40	MS60	MS63	MS65
AH1406-1986	—	—	—	—	30.00	40.00
AH1406-1986	—	PF65 80.00				

Y# 80 100 DIRHAMS

15.00 g., 0.925 Silver 0.4461 oz. ASW **Subject:** Visit of Pope John Paul II **Obv:** Pope shaking hands local cleric **Rev:** Crowned arms with supporters

Date	Mintage	VF20	XF40	MS60	MS63	MS65
AH1406-1986	—	—	—	—	75.00	125
AH1406-1986	2,000	PF65 175				

Y# 86 100 DIRHAMS

15.00 g., 0.925 Silver 0.4461 oz. ASW **Subject:** Opening of the Rabat Mint **Obv:** Head left **Rev:** Cluster of square designs flanked by dates

Date	Mintage	VF20	XF40	MS60	MS63	MS65
AH1407-1987	—	—	—	—	30.00	40.00
AH1407-1987	—	PF65 80.00				

Y# 74 150 DIRHAMS

35.00 g., 0.925 Silver 1.0409 oz. ASW **Subject:** 15th Hejira Calendar Century **Obv:** Crowned arms with supporters flanked by dates **Rev:** Artistic design within circle flanked by dates

Date	Mintage	VF20	XF40	MS60	MS63	MS65
AH1401-1980	3,000	—	—	—	40.00	55.00
AH1401-1980	300	PF65 150				

Y# 74a 150 DIRHAMS

60.14 g., 0.900 Gold 1.7402 oz. AGW **Subject:** 15th Hejira Calendar Century **Obv:** Crowned arms with supporters flanked by dates **Rev:** Artistic design within circle flanked by dates

Date	Mintage	VF20	XF40	MS60	MS63	MS65
AH1401-1980	30	PF65 3,250				

Y# 73 150 DIRHAMS

35.00 g., 0.925 Silver 1.0409 oz. ASW **Subject:** 20th Anniversary - King Hassan's Coronation **Obv:** Crowned arms with supporters flanked by dates **Rev:** Crowned arms with supporters

Date	Mintage	VF20	XF40	MS60	MS63	MS65
AH1401-1981	3,000	—	—	—	40.00	55.00
AH1401-1981	300	PF65 150				

Y# 73a 150 DIRHAMS

60.14 g., 0.900 Gold 1.7402 oz. AGW **Subject:** 20th Anniversary - King Hassan's Coronation **Obv:** Head left **Rev:** Crowned arms with supporters flanked by dates

Date	Mintage	VF20	XF40	MS60	MS63	MS65
AH1401-1981	30	PF65 3,250				

Y# 81 200 DIRHAMS
15.00 g., 0.925 Silver 0.4461 oz. ASW **Subject:** Moroccan - American Friendship Treaty **Obv:** Head left **Rev:** Radiant sun behind crossed flags

Date	Mintage	VF20	XF40	MS60	MS63	MS65
AH1408-1987	Est. 5000	PF65 40.00				

Y# 81a 200 DIRHAMS
21.50 g., 0.900 Gold 0.6221 oz. AGW **Subject:** Moroccan - American Friendship Treaty **Obv:** Head left **Rev:** Radiant sun behind crossed flags

Date	Mintage	VF20	XF40	MS60	MS63	MS65
AH1408-1987	30	—	—	—	—	5,000

Y# 97 200 DIRHAMS
15.00 g., 0.925 Silver 0.4461 oz. ASW, 31.3 mm. **Subject:** African Cup Soccer Games **Obv:** Head left **Rev:** Games logo **Edge:** Reeded

Date	Mintage	VF20	XF40	MS60	MS63	MS65
AH1408-1988	—	—	—	—	45.00	60.00

Y# 91 200 DIRHAMS
15.00 g., 0.925 Silver 0.4461 oz. ASW **Subject:** First Francophone Games **Obv:** Head left **Rev:** Games emblem

Date	Mintage	VF20	XF40	MS60	MS63	MS65
AH1409-1989	5,000	—	—	—	25.00	35.00
AH1409-1989	500	PF65 95.00				

Y# 89 200 DIRHAMS
15.00 g., 0.925 Silver 0.4461 oz. ASW, 31.3 mm. **Subject:** 35th Anniversary of Independence **Obv:** Head left **Rev:** Crowned arms with supporters **Edge:** Reeded

Date	Mintage	VF20	XF40	MS60	MS63	MS65
AH1411-1990	—	—	—	—	50.00	60.00
AH1411-1990	—	PF65 90.00				

Y# 90 200 DIRHAMS
15.00 g., 0.925 Silver 0.4461 oz. ASW, 31.3 mm. **Subject:** King's Tunisian Visit **Obv:** Head left **Rev:** Inscription **Edge:** Reeded

Date	Mintage	VF20	XF40	MS60	MS63	MS65
AH1411-1990	—	PF65 85.00				
AH1411-1990	—	—	—	—	40.00	55.00

Y# 96 200 DIRHAMS
15.00 g., 0.925 Silver 0.4461 oz. ASW, 31.3 mm. **Subject:** 30th Anniversary of Reign **Obv:** Crowned arms with supporters **Rev:** King on horseback amidst crowd **Edge:** Reeded

Date	Mintage	VF20	XF40	MS60	MS63	MS65
AH1411-1991	—	PF65 85.00				
AH1411-1991	—	—	—	—	40.00	55.00

Y# 98 200 DIRHAMS
15.00 g., 0.925 Silver 0.4461 oz. ASW, 31.3 mm. **Subject:** Revolution, 40th Anniversary **Obv:** Head left **Rev:** Building within circle **Edge:** Reeded

Date	Mintage	VF20	XF40	MS60	MS63	MS65
AH1414-1993	2,000	—	—	—	40.00	55.00
AH1414-1993	300	PF65 100				

Y# 99 200 DIRHAMS
15.00 g., 0.925 Silver 0.4461 oz. ASW, 31.3 mm. **Subject:** 33rd Anniversary of Hassan's Inauguration **Obv:** Head left **Rev:** Mosque within circle **Edge:** Reeded

Date	Mintage	VF20	XF40	MS60	MS63	MS65
AH1414-1993	2,000	—	—	—	40.00	55.00
AH1414-1993	300	PF65 100				

Y# 100 200 DIRHAMS
15.00 g., 0.925 Silver 0.4461 oz. ASW, 31.3 mm. **Subject:** GATT Agreement **Obv:** Head left **Rev:** Tower within world globe **Edge:** Reeded

Date	Mintage	VF20	XF40	MS60	MS63	MS65
AH1414-1994	300	PF65 100				
AH1414-1994	2,000	—	—	—	40.00	55.00

Y# 100a 200 DIRHAMS
21.50 g., 0.900 Gold 0.6221 oz. AGW, 31.3 mm. **Subject:** GATT Agreement **Obv:** Head left **Rev:** Tower within world globe **Edge:** Reeded

Date	Mintage	VF20	XF40	MS60	MS63	MS65
AH1414-1994 Proof	—	—	—	—	—	—

Y# 101 200 DIRHAMS
15.00 g., 0.925 Silver 0.4461 oz. ASW, 31.3 mm. **Subject:** 40th Anniversary of Independence **Obv:** Head left **Rev:** Crowned arms with supporters **Edge:** Reeded

Date	Mintage	VF20	XF40	MS60	MS63	MS65
AH1416-1995	—	—	—	—	45.00	60.00
AH1416-1995	—	PF65 100				

Y# 102 200 DIRHAMS
15.00 g., 0.925 Silver 0.4461 oz. ASW, 31.3 mm. **Subject:** 50th Anniversary of United Nations **Obv:** Head left **Rev:** UN logo and value within circle **Edge:** Reeded

Date	Mintage	VF20	XF40	MS60	MS63	MS65
AH1416-1995	—	—	—	—	35.00	50.00
AH1416-1995	—	PF65 75.00				

Y# 103 200 DIRHAMS
15.00 g., 0.925 Silver 0.4461 oz. ASW, 31.3 mm. **Subject:** Rabat 800th Anniversary **Obv:** Head left **Rev:** City view within circle **Edge:** Reeded

Date	Mintage	VF20	XF40	MS60	MS63	MS65
AH1416-1995	—	—	—	—	45.00	60.00
AH1416-1995	—	PF65 100				

Y# 104 200 DIRHAMS
15.00 g., 0.925 Silver 0.4461 oz. ASW, 31.3 mm. **Subject:** 20th Anniversary of the Green March **Obv:** Head left **Rev:** Arabic inscription **Edge:** Reeded

Date	Mintage	VF20	XF40	MS60	MS63	MS65
AH1416-1995	—	—	—	—	45.00	60.00
AH1416-1995	—	PF65 100				

Y# 105 200 DIRHAMS
15.00 g., 0.925 Silver 0.4461 oz. ASW, 31.3 mm. **Subject:** 50th Anniversary Human Rights Declaration **Obv:** Head left **Rev:** Logo, legend and inscription **Edge:** Reeded

Date	Mintage	VF20	XF40	MS60	MS63	MS65
AH1419-1998	—	—	—	—	45.00	60.00

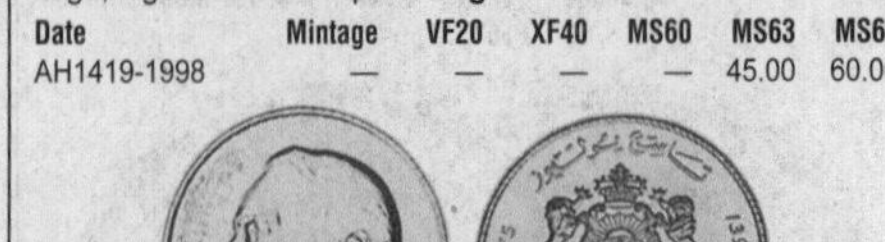

Y# 66 250 DIRHAMS
6.45 g., 0.900 Gold 0.1866 oz. AGW **Subject:** Birthday of King Hassan **Obv:** Head left **Rev:** Crowned arms with supporters flanked by dates

Date	Mintage	VF20	XF40	MS60	MS63	MS65
AH1395-1975	5,000	—	—	—	—	2,120
AH1395-1975	1,270	PF65 350				
AH1396-1976	3,200	—	—	—	—	360
AH1396-1976	450	PF65 345				
AH1397-1977	3,000	—	—	—	—	350
AH1397-1977	800	PF65 345				

Date	Mintage	VF20	XF40	MS60	MS63	MS65
AH1398-1978	2,000	—	—	—	—	375
AH1398-1978	150	PF65 360				

Y# 71 500 DIRHAMS

12.90 g., 0.900 Gold 0.3733 oz. AGW **Subject:** Birthday of King Hassan **Obv:** Head left **Rev:** Crowned arms with supporters flanked by oat sprig, curvy line and dates

Date	Mintage	VF20	XF40	MS60	MS63	MS65
AH1399-1979	3,000	—	—	—	—	625
AH1399-1979	300	PF65 645				
AH1400-1980	100	—	—	—	—	650
AH1400-1980	100	PF65 700				
AH1401-1981	100	—	—	—	—	650
AH1401-1981	100	PF65 700				
AH1402-1982	100	—	—	—	—	650
AH1402-1982	100	PF65 700				
AH1403-1983	2,500	—	—	—	—	625
AH1403-1983	Inc. above	PF65 650				
AH1404-1984	100	—	—	—	—	650
AH1404-1984	100	PF65 700				
AH1405-1985	275	—	—	—	—	635
AH1405-1985	125	PF65 675				
AH1406-1986	—	PF65 650				
AH1407-1987	—	PF65 650				
AH1408-1988	—	PF65 650				
AH1409-1989	—	PF65 650				
AH1410-1990	—	PF65 650				
AH1411-1991	—	PF65 650				
AH1412-1992	—	PF65 650				
AH1413-1993	—	PF65 650				

Y# 134 1000 DIRHAMS

21.50 g., 0.900 Gold 0.6221 oz. AGW, 31 mm. **Obv:** Head left

Date	Mintage	VF20	XF40	MS60	MS63	MS65
AH1415-1994	—	—	—	—	—	1,100
AH1415-1994	—	PF65 1,150				
AH1416-1995	—	—	—	—	—	1,100
AH1416-1995	—	PF65 1,150				
AH1417-1996	—	—	—	—	—	1,100
AH1417-1996	—	PF65 1,150				
AH1418-1997	—	—	—	—	—	1,100
AH1418-1997	—	PF65 1,150				
AH1419-1998	—	—	—	—	—	1,100
AH1419-1998	—	PF65 1,150				
AH1420-1999	—	—	—	—	—	1,100
AH1420-1999	—	PF65 1,150				

Mohammed VI
AH1420/1999AD

Y# 94 250 DIRHAMS

25.00 g., 0.925 Silver 0.7435 oz. ASW, 37 mm. **Subject:** First Anniversary of Mohammed VI's Enthronement **Obv:** Hooded bust left **Rev:** Crowned arms with supporters flanked by dates **Edge:** Reeded

Date	Mintage	VF20	XF40	MS60	MS63	MS65
AH1421-2000	—	—	—	—	45.00	60.00
AH1421-2000	—	PF65 100				

Y# 106 250 DIRHAMS

25.00 g., 0.925 Silver 0.7435 oz. ASW, 37 mm. **Subject:** Green March 25th Anniversary **Obv:** Head 3/4 left **Rev:** Map **Edge:** Reeded

Date	Mintage	VF20	XF40	MS60	MS63	MS65
AH1421-2000	—	—	—	—	45.00	60.00
AH1421-2000	—	PF65 100				

ESSAIS

KM#	Date	Mintage	Identification	Mkt Val
E1	AH1329 (1911) (a) (Pa)	—	5 Dirhams. Silver. Y24.	600
E2	AH1330 (1911) (a) (Pa)	—	Muzuna. Bronze. Y26.	300
E3	AH1330 (1911) (a) (Pa)	—	2 Mazunas. Bronze. Y27.	300
E4	AH1330 (1911) (a) (Pa)	—	5 Mazunas. Bronze. Value within star. Mint name and date within tri-lobe star. Y28.	350
E5	AH1330 (1911) (a) (Pa)	—	10 Mazunas. Bronze. Y29.	375
E6	AH1331 (1912) (a) (Pa)	—	5 Dirhams. Nickel.	750
E7	AH1331 (1912) (a) (Pa)	—	5 Dirhams. Aluminum-Bronze.	750
E8	AH1331 (1912) (a) (Pa)	—	5 Dirhams. Aluminum. Y32.	750
E10	ND (1921)(a) (Py)	—	50 Centimes. Star within circle. Value within artistic designed star.	175
E10a	ND (1921)Py	—	50 Centimes. Nickel. Y35.	—
E11	ND (1921)(a) (Py)	—	Franc. Nickel. Y36.	275
E12	AH1340 (1921) (a) (Py)	—	5 Mazunas. Bronze. Value within center of star. Mint name and date within doubled tri-lobe star. Y28.	450
E13	AH1340 (1921) (a) (a)	—	10 Mazunas. Bronze. Y29.	500
E9b	ND (1921)	—	25 Centimes. Hole in center flanked by value within circle. Incuse "Essai".	—
E9	ND (1924) (Py)	—	25 Centimes. Copper-Nickel. Without hole or ESSAI, Y34.	300
E9a	ND (1924)(a) (Py)	—	25 Centimes. Copper-Nickel. With hole, Y34.	300
E14	AH1346 (1927) (a) (Pa)	—	10 Francs. Nickel. Head laureate right. Value in doubled square within circle.	—
E15	AH1346 (1927) (a) (Pa)	—	10 Francs. Nickel. Without ESSAI.	—
E16	ND (1928)(a) (Pa)	—	5 Dirhams. Nickel. Head laureate right. Inscription within the star of David.	2,500
E17	ND (1928)(a) (Pa)	—	5 Dirhams. Nickel. Without ESSAI.	2,500
E18	ND (1928)(a) (Pa)	—	5 Dirhams. Aluminum-Bronze.	2,500
E19	ND (1928)(a) (Pa)	—	5 Dirhams. Aluminum-Bronze. Without ESSAI.	2,500
E20	AH1347 (1928) (a) (Pa)	—	5 Francs. Silver. Y37.	300
E21	AH1347 (1928) (a) (Pa)	—	10 Francs. Silver. Date in inner circle of doubled tri-lobe star, all within circle. Value in small circle among doubled square design, all within circle.	1,500
E22	AH1347 (1928) (a) (Pa)	—	10 Francs. Silver. Without ESSAI.	450
E23	AH1347 (1928) (a) (Pa)	—	10 Francs. Silver. Y38.	350
E24	AH1347 (1928) (a) (Pa)	—	20 Francs. Date in inner circle of doubled tri-lobe star, all within circle. Value in small circle of doubled square design, all within circle.	—
E25	AH1347 (1928) (a) (Pa)	—	20 Francs. Without ESSAI.	—
E26	AH1347 (1928) (a) (Pa)	—	20 Francs. Silver. Y39.	400
E28	AH1361 (1942) (a) (a)	—	50 Centimes. Aluminum-Bronze. Y40.	250
E29	AH1361 (1942) (a) (a)	—	Franc. Aluminum-Bronze. Y41.	250
E30	AH1361 (1942) (a) (a)	—	2 Francs. Aluminum-Bronze. Y42.	250
E31	AH1365 (1945) (a) (a)	—	50 Centimes. Aluminum-Bronze. Y40.	300
E32	AH1365 (1945) (a) (a)	—	Franc. Aluminum-Bronze. Y41.	200
E33	AH1365 (1945) (a) (a)	—	2 Francs. Aluminum-Bronze. Y42.	200
E34	AH1365 (1945) (a) (a)	—	5 Francs. Aluminum-Bronze. Y43.	80.00
E35	AH1366 (1946) (a) (a)	1,100	10 Francs. Copper-Nickel. Y44.	80.00
E36	AH1366 (1946) (a) (a)	1,100	20 Francs. Copper-Nickel. Y45.	80.00
E37	AH1370 (1950) (a) (a)	1,100	Franc. Aluminum. Y46.	50.00
E38	AH1370 (1950) (a) (a)	1,100	2 Francs. Aluminum. Y47.	50.00
E39	AH1370 (1950) (a) (a)	1,100	5 Francs. Aluminum. Y48.	60.00
E40	AH1370 (1950) (a) (a)	1,100	100 Francs. 0.720. Silver. Y-A54.	100

Note: KM#E37-E40 were issued in a set with Tunisia, KM#E28-E30.

KM#	Date	Mintage	Identification	Mkt Val
E41	AH1371 (1951) (a) (a)	1,100	10 Francs. Aluminum-Bronze. Y49.	60.00
E42	AH1371 (1951) (a) (a)	1,100	20 Francs. Aluminum-Bronze. Y50.	50.00
E43	AH1371 (1951) (a) (a)	1,100	50 Francs. Aluminum-Bronze. Value in doubled square design within circle. Date in small circle within doubled tri-lobe star, all within circle. Y51.	45.00

Note: KM#E41-43 also issued in 3-piece boxed sets.

KM#	Date	Mintage	Identification	Mkt Val
E44	AH1372 (1952) (a) (a)	1,100	100 Francs. Silver. Y52.	125
E45	AH1372 (1952) (a) (a)	1,100	200 Francs. Silver. Y53.	90.00
E46	AH1384 (1964)	—	5 Dirhams. Silver. Y#57.	—
E47	AH1384 (1964)	—	Dirham. Nickel. Y#56.	—

PATTERNS

Including off metal strikes

KM#	Date	Mintage	Identification	Mkt Val
Pn29	AH1319 (1901)Fs	—	1/4 Fals. Bronze. Machine struck.	—
Pn30	AH1319 (1901)Fs	—	1/2 Fals. Bronze.	—
Pn31	AH1319 (1901)Mr	—	1/2 Fals. Cast Bronze.	—
Pn32	AH1319 (1901)Fs	—	Fals. Bronze.	—
Pn33	AH1319 (1901)Mr	—	Fals. Cast Bronze.	—
Pn35	AH1319 (1901)Fs	—	4 Fulus. Bronze.	—
Pn36	AH1319 (1901)Mr	—	4 Fulus. Cast Bronze.	—
Pn34	AH1319 (1902)Mr	—	2 Fulus. Cast Bronze.	—
Pn37	AH1320 (1902)Fs	—	1/2 Fals. Bronze. Machine struck.	—
Pn38	AH1320 (1902)Fs	—	2 Fulus. Bronze. Machine struck.	—
Pn39	AH1320 (1902)Fs	—	4 Fulus. Bronze. Machine struck.	—
Pn40	AH1320 (1902)Be	—	Muzuna. Bronze.	4,500
Pn41	AH1320 (1902)Pa	—	Muzuna. Bronze.	—
Pn42	AH1320 (1902)Be	—	2 Mazunas. Bronze.	4,500
Pn43	AH1320 (1902)Fs	—	2 Mazunas. Bronze. Y#15.1 without "2".	—
Pn44	AH1320 (1902)Be	—	5 Mazunas. Bronze.	4,500
Pn45	AH1320 (1902)Fs	—	5 Mazunas. Bronze. Y#16.1 without "5".	—
Pn47	AH1320 (1902)Be	—	10 Mazunas. Bronze. Y#17.2.	4,500
Pn48	AH1320 (1902)Pa	—	10 Mazunas. Bronze.	—
Pn49	AH1320 (1902)Be	—	1/20 Rial. Silver.	6,000
Pn50	AH1320 (1902)Be	—	1/10 Rial. Silver.	6,000
Pn51	AH1320 (1902)Be	—	Rial. Silver.	25,000
Pn46	AH1320 (1903)Pa	—	5 Mazunas. Bronze.	—
Pn53	AH1321 (1903)Be	—	1/20 Rial. Silver.	—
Pn54	AH1321 (1903)Be	—	1/10 Rial. Silver.	—
Pn55	AH1321 (1903)Be	—	1/2 Rial. Silver.	—
Pn56	AH1321 (1903)Be	—	Rial. Silver.	—

PIEDFORT

Double thickness

KM#	Date	Mintage	Identification	Mkt Val
PA1	ND (1924)Py	—	Franc. Nickel. Y#36.2.	—
P1	AH1395 (1975)	10	5 Dirhams. Gold. Y64b.	1,200
P2	AH1395 (1975)	40	50 Dirhams. Silver. Y65.	400
P3	AH1395 (1975)	10	50 Dirhams. Gold. Y65a.	6,000
P4	AH1395 (1975)	10	50 Dirhams. Gold. Y67a.	6,000
P5	AH1395 (1975)	10	250 Dirhams. Gold. Y66.	400
P6	AH1395 (1976)	10	50 Dirhams. Gold. Y68a.	5,500
P7	AH1396 (1976)	10	250 Dirhams. Gold. Y66.	400
P8	AH1396 (1977)	10	50 Dirhams. Gold. Y143a.	5,500
P9	AH1397 (1977)	15	250 Dirhams. Gold. Y66.	375
P10	AH1397 (1978)	10	50 Dirhams. Gold. Y144a.	5,500
P11	AH1398 (1978)	20	250 Dirhams. Gold. Y66.	350
P12	AH1399 (1979)	20	50 Dirhams. Gold. Y145a.	5,250
P13	AH1399 (1979)	20	50 Dirhams. Silver. Y70.	500
P14	AH1399 (1979)	20	50 Dirhams. 0.925. Silver. Y76.	500
P15	AH1399 (1979)	20	50 Dirhams. Gold. Y76a.	5,000
P16	AH1399 (1979)	20	500 Dirhams. Gold. Y71.	800
P17	AH1400 (1980)	10	50 Dirhams. Gold. Y146a.	5,500
P18	AH1401 (1981)	10	150 Dirhams. 0.900. Gold. Y74a.	2,500
P19	AH1401 (1981)	10	150 Dirhams. 0.900. Gold. Y73a.	2,500

PIEDFORT WITH ESSAI

KM#	Date	Mintage	Identification	Mkt Val
PEC1	ND (1921)(a)	—	50 Centimes. Nickel. Y#35.1.	300
PED1	ND (1921)Pa	—	50 Centimes. Copper-Nickel. Star within circle. Value within artistic designed star. Small module with 12 sides.	1,500
PEE1	ND (1921)Pa	—	50 Centimes. Copper-Nickel. Star within circle. Value within artistic designed star. Large module with 12 sides.	1,500
PEF1	ND(AH1340) (1921)Py	—	5 Mazunas. Bronze. Y#28.2.	500
PEG1	ND(AH1340) (1921)Py	—	10 Mazunas. Bronze. Y#29.2.	600
PEB1	ND (1924)Py	—	25 Centimes. Copper-Nickel. Y#34.2; Without hole.	300
PEA1	AH1361 (1942)(a)	—	50 Centimes. Aluminum-Bronze. Y40.	175
PE1	AH1361 (1942) (a) (a)	—	Franc. Aluminum-Bronze. Y41.	300
PE2	AH1361 (1942) (a) (a)	—	2 Francs. Aluminum-Bronze. Y42.	350
PE3	AH1364 (1945) (a) (a)	104	50 Centimes. Aluminum-Bronze. Y40.	350
PE4	AH1364 (1945) (a)	104	Franc. Aluminum-Bronze. Y41.	300
PE5	AH1364 (1945) (a) (a)	104	2 Francs. Aluminum-Bronze. Y42.	375
PE6	AH1365 (1945) (a) (a)	104	5 Francs. Aluminum-Bronze. Y43.	350
PE7	AH1366 (1946) (a) (a)	104	10 Francs. Copper-Nickel. Y44.	350
PE8	AH1366 (1946) (a) (a)	104	20 Francs. Copper-Nickel. Y45.	350
PEB9	ND(AH1370) (1950)	—	Franc. Aluminum. Y#46.	175
PEB9	ND(AH1370) (1950)	—	2 Francs. Aluminum. Y#47.	200
PEC9	ND(AH1370) (1950)	—	5 Francs. Aluminum. Y#48.	200
PEG9	ND(AH1370) (1950)	—	100 Francs. Silver. Y#A54.	150
PED9	ND(AH1371) (1951)	—	10 Francs. Aluminum-Bronze. Y#49.	150
PEE9	ND(AH1371) (1951)	—	20 Francs. Aluminum-Bronze. Y#50.	150
PEF9	ND(AH1371) (1951)	—	50 Francs. Aluminum-Bronze. Y#51.	120
PE9	AH1372 (1953) (a) (a)	104	100 Francs. Copper-Nickel. Y52.	350
PE10	AH1372 (1953) (a) (a)	104	200 Francs. Silver. Y53.	400
PE11	AH1372 (1953) (a) (a)	—	200 Francs. Gold. Y53.	1,200

TRIAL STRIKES

Uniface

KM#	Date	Mintage	Identification	Mkt Val
TS1	AH1347 (1928)	—	10 Francs. Silver Plated Bronze.	800
TS2	AH1347 (1928)	—	10 Francs. Silver Plated Bronze. Value in doubled square design within circle. Uniface.	800
TS3	AH1347 (1928)	—	20 Francs. Silver Plated Bronze.	600
TS4	AH1347 (1928)	—	20 Francs. Silver Plated Bronze. Value in doubled square design within circle. Uniface.	600

MINT SETS

KM#	Date	Mintage	Identification	Issue Price	Mkt Val
MS1	AH1370-84 (8)	—	Y#46-48(AH1370), 49-51(AH1371), 56-57(AH1384)	—	175
MS2	1974-75 (7)	20,000	Y#58-63 (1974), Y#64 (1975)	20.00	25.00

PROOF SETS

KM#	Date	Mintage	Identification	Issue Price	Mkt Val
PS1	1974 (6)	30	Y#58a-63a	—	3,650

MOZAMBIQUE

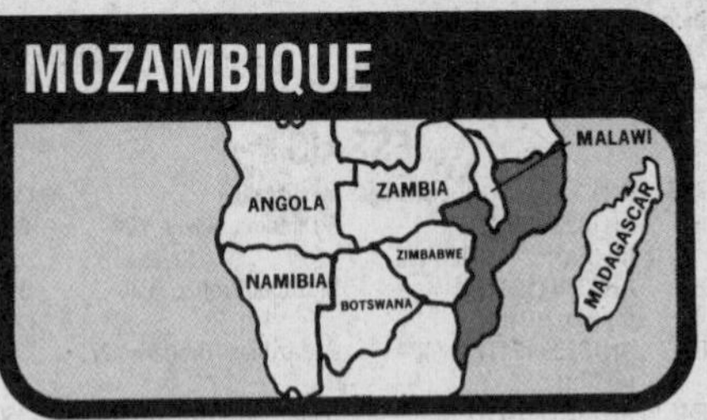

The Republic of Mozambique, a former overseas province of Portugal, stretches for 1,430 miles (2,301 km.) along the southeast coast of Africa, has an area of 302,330 sq. mi. (801,590 sq. km.) and a population of 14.1 million, 99 % of whom are native Africans of the Bantu tribes. Capital: Maputo. Agriculture is the chief industry. Cashew nuts, cotton, sugar, copra and tea are exported.

Vasco de Gama explored all the coast of Mozambique in 1498 and found Arab trading posts already established along the coast. Portuguese settlement dates from the establishment of the trading post of Mozambique in 1505. Within five years Portugal absorbed all the former Arab sultanates along the east African coast. The area was organized as a colony in 1907 and became an overseas province in 1952. In Sept. of 1974, after more than a decade of guerrilla warfare with the forces of the Mozambique Liberation Front, Portugal agreed to the independence of Mozambique, effective June 25, 1975. The Socialist party, led by President Joaquim Chissano was in power until the 2nd of November, 1990 when they became a republic.

Mozambique became a member of the Commonwealth of Nations in November 1995. The President is Head of State; the Prime Minister is Head of Government.

RULER

Portuguese, until 1975

MONETARY SYSTEM

100 Centavos = 1 Escudo

PORTUGUESE COLONY

DECIMAL COINAGE

100 Centavos = 1 Escudo

KM# 63 10 CENTAVOS

Bronze **Obv:** Value **Rev:** Arms

Date	Mintage	F12	VF20	XF40	MS60	MS63
1936	2,000,000	2.00	6.00	15.00	35.00	50.00

KM# 72 10 CENTAVOS

3.94 g., Bronze, 22.57 mm. **Obv:** Value **Rev:** Arms within crowned globe **Edge:** Plain

Date	Mintage	F12	VF20	XF40	MS60	MS63
1942	2,000,000	1.00	2.50	5.00	15.00	30.00

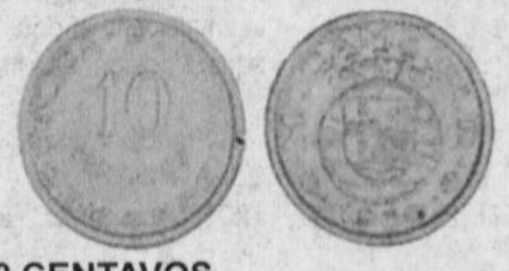

KM# 83 10 CENTAVOS

1.70 g., Bronze, 16 mm. **Obv:** Value **Rev:** Arms within crowned globe

Date	Mintage	F12	VF20	XF40	MS60	MS63
1960	3,750,000	—	0.25	1.00	2.50	5.00
1961	10,300,000	—	0.25	1.00	2.00	4.00

KM# 64 20 CENTAVOS

Bronze **Obv:** Value **Rev:** Arms

Date	Mintage	F12	VF20	XF40	MS60	MS63
1936	2,500,000	2.00	8.00	15.00	35.00	75.00

KM# 71 20 CENTAVOS

Bronze **Obv:** Value **Rev:** Arms within crowned globe

Date	Mintage	F12	VF20	XF40	MS60	MS63
1941	2,000,000	1.00	10.00	20.00	75.00	125

KM# 75 20 CENTAVOS

Bronze, 20.3 mm. **Obv:** Value **Rev:** Arms within crowned globe

Date	Mintage	F12	VF20	XF40	MS60	MS63
1949	8,000,000	—	1.00	3.00	7.00	15.00
1950	12,500,000	—	1.00	3.00	5.00	12.00

KM# 85 20 CENTAVOS

2.53 g., Bronze, 18 mm. **Obv:** Value **Rev:** Arms within crowned globe

Date	Mintage	F12	VF20	XF40	MS60	MS63
1961	12,500,000	—	—	0.50	1.00	3.00

KM# 88 20 CENTAVOS

1.80 g., Bronze, 16 mm. **Obv:** Value **Rev:** Arms within crowned globe **Edge:** Plain **Note:** Reduced size.

Date	Mintage	F12	VF20	XF40	MS60	MS63
1973	1,798,000	—	0.50	2.50	5.00	8.00
1974	13,044,000	—	0.50	2.50	5.00	8.00

KM# 65 50 CENTAVOS

Copper-Nickel **Obv:** Value **Rev:** Arms

Date	Mintage	F12	VF20	XF40	MS60	MS63
1936	2,500,000	5.00	15.00	50.00	125	225

KM# 73 50 CENTAVOS

4.00 g., Bronze **Obv:** Value **Rev:** Arms within crowned globe

Date	Mintage	F12	VF20	XF40	MS60	MS63
1945	2,500,000	0.25	2.50	12.00	32.00	75.00

KM# 76 50 CENTAVOS

Nickel-Bronze **Obv:** Value **Rev:** Arms within crowned globe

Date	Mintage	F12	VF20	XF40	MS60	MS63
1950	20,000,000	—	1.50	3.50	10.00	20.00
1951	16,000,000	—	1.50	3.50	10.00	20.00

KM# 81 50 CENTAVOS
Bronze **Obv:** Value **Rev:** Arms within crowned globe

Date	Mintage	F12	VF20	XF40	MS60	MS63
1953	5,010,000	—	1.00	3.00	6.00	12.00
1957	24,990,000	—	0.50	1.00	3.00	5.00

KM# 89 50 CENTAVOS
4.53 g., Bronze, 22.49 mm. **Obv:** Value **Rev:** Arms within crowned globe

Date	Mintage	F12	VF20	XF40	MS60	MS63
1973	6,841,000	—	0.50	1.00	3.00	4.50
1974	23,810,000	—	0.50	1.00	4.00	6.00

KM# 66 ESCUDO
8.00 g., Copper-Nickel **Obv:** Value **Rev:** Arms

Date	Mintage	F12	VF20	XF40	MS60	MS63
1936	2,000,000	4.00	10.00	50.00	125	250

KM# 74 ESCUDO
Bronze **Obv:** Value **Rev:** Arms within crowned globe

Date	Mintage	F12	VF20	XF40	MS60	MS63
1945	2,000,000	2.00	5.00	15.00	75.00	250

KM# 77 ESCUDO
Nickel-Bronze, 27 mm. **Obv:** Value **Rev:** Arms within crowned globe

Date	Mintage	VF20	XF40	MS60	MS63	MS65
1950	10,000,000	3.00	7.50	30.00	45.00	75.00
1951	10,000,000	3.00	7.00	12.00	25.00	45.00

KM# 82 ESCUDO
8.00 g., Bronze, 26 mm. **Obv:** Value **Rev:** Arms within crowned globe

Date	Mintage	VF20	XF40	MS60	MS63	MS65
1953	2,013,000	1.00	3.00	12.00	20.00	40.00
1957	2,987,000	1.00	3.00	12.00	20.00	35.00
1962	600,000	1.00	3.00	12.00	20.00	30.00
1963	3,258,000	0.25	1.00	5.00	7.50	15.00
1965	5,000,000	0.25	1.00	1.50	3.00	5.00
1968	4,500,000	0.25	1.00	1.50	3.00	5.00

Date	Mintage	VF20	XF40	MS60	MS63	MS65
1969	1,642,000	0.25	1.00	1.50	3.00	5.00
1973	501,000	0.25	1.25	2.00	3.50	6.00
1974	25,281,000	0.25	1.00	1.50	2.75	4.50

KM# 61 2-1/2 ESCUDOS
3.50 g., 0.650 Silver 0.0731 oz. ASW **Obv:** Shield within globe and maltese cross **Rev:** Arms

Date	Mintage	F12	VF20	XF40	MS60	MS63
1935	1,200,000	1.50	3.00	15.00	35.00	100

KM# 68 2-1/2 ESCUDOS
3.50 g., 0.650 Silver 0.0731 oz. ASW **Obv:** Shield within globe and maltese cross **Rev:** Arms within crowned globe

Date	Mintage	F12	VF20	XF40	MS60	MS63
1938	1,000,000	1.50	3.00	15.00	25.00	60.00
1942	1,200,000	1.50	3.00	15.00	25.00	60.00
1950	4,000,000	1.50	3.00	5.00	10.00	15.00
1951	4,000,000	1.50	3.00	7.50	15.00	30.00

KM# 78 2-1/2 ESCUDOS
3.50 g., Copper-Nickel **Obv:** Shield within globe and maltese cross **Rev:** Arms within crowned globe

Date	Mintage	VF20	XF40	MS60	MS63	MS65
1952	4,000,000	1.00	20.00	35.00	50.00	100
1953	4,000,000	1.00	10.00	20.00	35.00	75.00
1954	4,000,000	1.00	5.00	10.00	20.00	40.00
1955	4,000,000	1.00	5.00	20.00	35.00	75.00
1965	8,000,000	0.25	1.00	3.00	5.00	10.00
1973	1,767,000	0.25	1.00	3.00	5.00	12.00

KM# 62 5 ESCUDOS
7.00 g., 0.650 Silver 0.1463 oz. ASW, 26 mm. **Obv:** Shield within globe and maltese cross **Rev:** Arms **Edge:** Reeded

Date	Mintage	F12	VF20	XF40	MS60	MS63
1935	1,000,000	3.00	5.00	20.00	60.00	125

KM# 69 5 ESCUDOS
7.00 g., 0.650 Silver 0.1463 oz. ASW **Obv:** Shield within globe and maltese cross **Rev:** Arms within crowned globe

Date	Mintage	F12	VF20	XF40	MS60	MS63
1938	800,000	5.00	12.00	35.00	60.00	125
1949	8,000,000	3.00	.9.00	15.00	30.00	45.00

KM# 84 5 ESCUDOS
4.00 g., 0.650 Silver 0.0836 oz. ASW, 22 mm. **Obv:** Shield within globe and maltese cross **Rev:** Arms within crowned globe

Date	Mintage	F12	VF20	XF40	MS60	MS63
1960	8,000,000	1.00	2.00	3.00	5.00	7.50

KM# 86 5 ESCUDOS
Copper-Nickel **Obv:** Shield within globe and maltese cross **Rev:** Arms within crowned globe

Date	Mintage	VF20	XF40	MS60	MS63	MS65
1971	8,000,000	0.25	1.00	3.00	5.00	9.00
1973	3,352,000	0.25	1.00	3.00	5.00	9.00

KM# 67 10 ESCUDOS
12.50 g., 0.835 Silver 0.3356 oz. ASW **Obv:** Shield within globe and maltese cross **Rev:** Arms

Date	Mintage	F12	VF20	XF40	MS60	MS63
1936	497,000	8.00	12.00	35.00	75.00	150

KM# 70 10 ESCUDOS
12.50 g., 0.835 Silver 0.3356 oz. ASW **Obv:** Shield within globe and maltese cross **Rev:** Arms within crowned globe

Date	Mintage	F12	VF20	XF40	MS60	MS63
1938	530,000	8.00	12.00	35.00	85.00	175

KM# 79 10 ESCUDOS
5.00 g., 0.720 Silver 0.1157 oz. ASW, 24 mm. **Obv:** Shield within globe and maltese cross **Rev:** Arms within crowned globe

Date	Mintage	VF20	XF40	MS60	MS63	MS65
1952	1,503,000	2.00	4.00	9.00	15.00	30.00
1954	1,335,000	2.00	4.00	12.00	18.00	40.00
1955	1,162,000	2.00	4.00	9.00	15.00	30.00
1960	2,000,000	2.00	3.50	7.50	10.00	15.00

KM# 79a 10 ESCUDOS
5.00 g., 0.680 Silver 0.1093 oz. ASW **Obv:** Shield within globe and maltese cross **Rev:** Arms within crowned globe

Date	Mintage	VF20	XF40	MS60	MS63	MS65
1966	500,000	3.00	5.00	7.00	9.00	14.00

KM# 79b 10 ESCUDOS
9.01 g., Copper-Nickel, 28 mm. **Obv:** Shield within globe and maltese cross **Rev:** Arms within crowned globe

Date	Mintage	VF20	XF40	MS60	MS63	MS65
1968	5,000,000	0.50	1.50	3.00	5.00	9.00
1970	4,000,000	0.50	1.50	3.00	5.00	9.00
1974	3,366,000	0.50	1.50	3.00	5.00	9.00

KM# 80 20 ESCUDOS

10.00 g., 0.720 Silver 0.2315 oz. ASW **Obv:** Shield within globe and maltese cross **Rev:** Arms within crowned globe

Date	Mintage	VF20	XF40	MS60	MS63	MS65
1952	1,004,000	6.00	9.00	15.00	20.00	30.00
1955	996,000	6.00	9.00	15.00	20.00	30.00
1960	2,000,000	6.00	8.00	12.00	15.00	25.00

KM# 80a 20 ESCUDOS

10.00 g., 0.680 Silver 0.2186 oz. ASW **Obv:** Shield within globe and maltese cross **Rev:** Arms within crowned globe

Date	Mintage	VF20	XF40	MS60	MS63	MS65
1966	250,000	6.00	8.00	12.00	15.00	25.00

KM# 87 20 ESCUDOS

12.06 g., Nickel, 30 mm. **Obv:** Shield within globe **Rev:** Arms within circle

Date	Mintage	VF20	XF40	MS60	MS63	MS65
1971	2,000,000	0.50	1.50	3.00	5.00	9.00
1972	1,158,000	0.50	1.50	3.00	5.00	9.00

REPUBLIC

DECIMAL COINAGE

KM# 90 CENTIMO

Aluminum **Obv:** President Samora Machel head right **Rev:** Value and Angolan protea flower sprig

Date	Mintage	F12	VF20	XF40	MS60	MS63
1975	15,050,000	—	—	20.00	50.00	70.00

KM# 91 2 CENTIMOS

Brass **Obv:** President Samora Machel head right **Rev:** Value and Rain daisy flower sprig

Date	Mintage	F12	VF20	XF40	MS60	MS63
1975	8,242,000	—	—	20.00	50.00	70.00

KM# 92 5 CENTIMOS

Brass **Obv:** President Samora Machel head right **Rev:** Value and Purple dissotis flower sprig

Date	Mintage	F12	VF20	XF40	MS60	MS63
1975	14,898,000	—	—	20.00	50.00	70.00

KM# 93 10 CENTIMOS

Brass **Obv:** President Samora Machel head right **Rev:** Value and Sugar cane sprigs

Date	Mintage	F12	VF20	XF40	MS60	MS63
1975	18,000,000	—	—	15.00	35.00	55.00

KM# 94 20 CENTIMOS

Copper-Nickel **Obv:** President Samora Machel head right **Rev:** Value and Tea plant flower sprig

Date	Mintage	F12	VF20	XF40	MS60	MS63
1975	8,050,000	—	—	50.00	75.00	100

KM# 95 50 CENTIMOS

Copper-Nickel **Obv:** President Samora Machel head right **Rev:** Value and two and a half cashew nuts

Date	Mintage	F12	VF20	XF40	MS60	MS63
1975	3,050,000	—	—	65.00	100	125

KM# 96 METICA

Copper-Nickel **Obv:** President Samora Machel head right **Rev:** Sisal agave plant in vase

Date	Mintage	F12	VF20	XF40	MS60	MS63
1975	2,550,000	—	—	25.00	55.00	80.00

KM# 97 2-1/2 METICAIS

Copper-Nickel **Obv:** President Samora Machel head right **Rev:** Cotton plant **Shape:** 7-sided

Date	Mintage	F12	VF20	XF40	MS60	MS63
1975	1,500,000	—	—	75.00	125	175

REFORM COINAGE

100 Centavos = 1 Metical; 1980

KM# 98 50 CENTAVOS

1.40 g., Aluminum, 20 mm. **Obv:** Emblem **Rev:** Value above xylophone

Date	Mintage	VF20	XF40	MS60	MS63	MS65
1980	5,160,000	—	0.25	0.50	1.00	1.50
1981	—	—	—	—	—	—
1982	—	—	0.25	0.50	1.00	1.50

KM# 99 METICAL

8.00 g., Brass, 26 mm. **Obv:** Emblem **Rev:** Female student and value

Date	Mintage	VF20	XF40	MS60	MS63	MS65
1980	32,000	1.50	2.50	5.00	8.00	15.00
1981	—	—	—	—	—	—
1982	—	1.50	2.50	5.00	8.00	15.00

KM# 99a METICAL

Aluminum **Obv:** Emblem **Rev:** Female student and value

Date	Mintage	VF20	XF40	MS60	MS63	MS65
1986	—	—	0.35	0.75	1.00	1.50

KM# 100 2-1/2 METICAIS

Aluminum, 22.6 mm. **Obv:** Emblem **Rev:** Ship and crane in harbor **Note:** 1.80-2.00 grams.

Date	Mintage	VF20	XF40	MS60	MS63	MS65
1980	1,088,000	—	0.35	1.00	1.50	2.50
1981	—	—	—	—	—	—
1982	—	—	0.35	1.00	1.50	2.50
1986	—	—	0.35	1.00	1.50	2.50

Note: Edge varieties exist

KM# 101 5 METICAIS

2.60 g., Aluminum, 24.5 mm. **Obv:** Emblem **Rev:** Tractor and value

Date	Mintage	VF20	XF40	MS60	MS63	MS65
1980	7,736,000	—	0.35	1.00	1.50	2.50
1981	—	—	—	—	—	—
1982	—	—	0.35	1.00	1.50	2.50
1986	—	—	0.35	1.00	1.50	2.50

KM# 102 10 METICAIS

9.10 g., Copper-Nickel, 28 mm. **Obv:** Emblem **Rev:** Industrial skyline

Date	Mintage	VF20	XF40	MS60	MS63	MS65
1980	152,000	0.50	1.00	2.25	3.00	5.00
1981	—	0.50	1.00	2.25	3.00	5.00

KM# 102a 10 METICAIS

Aluminum, 28 mm. **Obv:** Emblem **Rev:** Industrial skyline

Date	Mintage	VF20	XF40	MS60	MS63	MS65
1986	—	0.25	0.35	1.00	1.50	2.50

KM# 103 20 METICAIS

12.00 g., Copper-Nickel, 30 mm. **Obv:** Emblem **Rev:** Armored personnel carrier

Date	Mintage	VF20	XF40	MS60	MS63	MS65
1980	78,000	1.00	2.00	4.00	5.00	7.50
1986	—	1.00	2.00	4.00	5.00	7.50

KM# 103a 20 METICAIS

Aluminum, 30 mm. **Obv:** Emblem **Rev:** Armored personnel carrier

Date	Mintage	VF20	XF40	MS60	MS63	MS65
1986	—	0.25	0.35	1.00	1.50	3.00

KM# 106 50 METICAIS

Copper-Nickel, 35 mm. **Subject:** World Fisheries Conference **Obv:** Emblem above value and date **Rev:** Traditional fishing raft

Date	Mintage	VF20	XF40	MS60	MS63	MS65
1983	130,000	—	1.50	3.00	6.00	10.00

KM# 106a 50 METICAIS

22.00 g., 0.925 Silver 0.6543 oz. ASW, 35 mm. **Subject:** World Fisheries Conference **Obv:** Emblem above value and date **Rev:** Traditional fishing raft

Date	Mintage	VF20	XF40	MS60	MS63	MS65
1983	21,000	PF63 25.00	PF65 35.00			

KM# 106b 50 METICAIS

22.00 g., 0.900 Gold 0.6366 oz. AGW **Subject:** World Fisheries Conference **Obv:** Emblem above value and date **Rev:** Traditional fishing raft

Date	Mintage	VF20	XF40	MS60	MS63	MS65
1983	135	PF63 1,100	PF65 1,200			

KM# 112 50 METICAIS

Aluminum **Obv:** Emblem **Rev:** Woman and soldier with provisions

Date	Mintage	VF20	XF40	MS60	MS63	MS65
1986	—	0.25	0.50	2.00	3.00	5.00

KM# 107 250 METICAIS

28.28 g., 0.925 Silver 0.841 oz. ASW **Subject:** 10th Anniversary of Independence **Obv:** Emblem **Rev:** Star and map divides circle, value within 1/2 circle

Date	Mintage	VF20	XF40	MS60	MS63	MS65
1985	2,000	PF63 40.00	PF65 45.00			

KM# 107a 250 METICAIS

28.28 g., Copper-Nickel, 38.61 mm. **Obv:** Emblem **Rev:** Star and map divides circle, value within 1/2 circle

Date	Mintage	VF20	XF40	MS60	MS63	MS65
1985	—	—	—	4.00	7.00	12.00

KM# 104 500 METICAIS

19.40 g., 0.800 Silver 0.499 oz. ASW **Subject:** 5th Anniversary of Independence **Obv:** Emblem above value **Rev:** 1/2 Figure, corn stalks and small building

Date	Mintage	VF20	XF40	MS60	MS63	MS65
1980	5,000	PF63 30.00	PF65 40.00			

KM# 110 500 METICAIS

16.00 g., 0.999 Silver 0.5139 oz. ASW **Subject:** Defense of Nature **Obv:** Emblem and value **Rev:** Lions

Date	Mintage	VF20	XF40	MS60	MS63	MS65
1989	2,500	PF63 20.00	PF65 25.00			

KM# 111 500 METICAIS

16.00 g., 0.999 Silver 0.5139 oz. ASW **Subject:** Defense of Nature **Obv:** Emblem and value **Rev:** Moorish Idol Fish

Date	Mintage	VF20	XF40	MS60	MS63	MS65
1989	2,000	PF63 20.00	PF65 25.00			

KM# 113 500 METICAIS

16.00 g., 0.999 Silver 0.5139 oz. ASW **Subject:** Defense of Nature **Obv:** Emblem and value **Rev:** Giraffes

Date	Mintage	VF20	XF40	MS60	MS63	MS65
1990	2,000	PF63 20.00	PF65 25.00			

KM# 109 1000 METICAIS

Copper-Nickel **Subject:** Visit of Pope John Paul II **Obv:** Emblem above value **Rev:** Bust right

Date	Mintage	VF20	XF40	MS60	MS63	MS65
1988	Est. 80000	—	—	2.00	4.00	7.00

KM# 109a 1000 METICAIS

28.28 g., 0.925 Silver 0.841 oz. ASW **Obv:** Emblem above value and date **Rev:** Bust right

Date	Mintage	VF20	XF40	MS60	MS63	MS65
1988	Est. 3500	PF63 30.00	PF65 35.00			

KM# 108 2000 METICAIS

17.50 g., 0.917 Gold 0.5159 oz. AGW **Subject:** 10th Anniversary of Independence **Obv:** Emblem above value **Rev:** Star and map divides circle, value at right

Date	Mintage	VF20	XF40	MS60	MS63	MS65
1985	100	PF63 850	PF65 950			

KM# 105 5000 METICAIS

17.28 g., 0.900 Gold 0.500 oz. AGW **Subject:** 5th Anniversary of Independence **Obv:** Emblem above value **Rev:** Figure at left, corn plants in background with tractor above

Date	Mintage	VF20	XF40	MS60	MS63	MS65
1980	2,000	PF63 800	PF65 900			

REFORM COINAGE

100 Centavos = 1 Metical; 1994

KM# 115 METICAL

Brass Clad Steel, 17 mm. **Obv:** Emblem **Rev:** Female student

Date	Mintage	VF20	XF40	MS60	MS63	MS65
1994	—	—	—	0.50	0.75	1.50

KM# 116 5 METICAIS

Brass Clad Steel **Obv:** Emblem **Rev:** Kingfisher

Date	Mintage	VF20	XF40	MS60	MS63	MS65
1994	—	—	—	1.00	1.25	2.00

KM# 117 10 METICAIS

Brass Clad Steel, 23 mm. **Obv:** Emblem **Rev:** Cotton plant

Date	Mintage	VF20	XF40	MS60	MS63	MS65
1994	—	—	—	0.50	0.75	1.50

KM# 118 20 METICAIS

Brass Clad Steel, 26 mm. **Obv:** Emblem **Rev:** Cashew tree branch and fruits

Date	Mintage	VF20	XF40	MS60	MS63	MS65
1994	—	—	—	0.50	0.75	1.50

KM# 119 50 METICAIS

5.06 g., Nickel Clad Steel, 24 mm. **Obv:** Emblem **Rev:** Leopard's head

Date	Mintage	VF20	XF40	MS60	MS63	MS65
1994	—	—	—	0.65	1.25	2.00

KM# 120 100 METICAIS

7.17 g., Nickel Clad Steel, 27 mm. **Obv:** Emblem **Rev:** Lobster

Date	Mintage	VF20	XF40	MS60	MS63	MS65
1994	—	—	—	0.75	1.50	3.00

KM# 121 500 METICAIS
12.05 g., Nickel Clad Steel, 32 mm. **Obv:** Emblem **Rev:** Building

Date	Mintage	VF20	XF40	MS60	MS63	MS65
1994	—	—	—	0.75	1.50	2.50

KM# 127 500 METICAIS
Nickel Clad Steel **Series:** 2000 Summer Olympics - Sydney

Date	Mintage	VF20	XF40	MS60	MS63	MS65
1998	10,000	PF63 5.00	PF65 7.50			

KM# 122 1000 METICAIS
11.60 g., Nickel Clad Steel, 32 mm. **Obv:** Emblem **Rev:** Building

Date	Mintage	VF20	XF40	MS60	MS63	MS65
1994	—	—	—	1.50	2.50	3.50

KM# 128 1000 METICAIS
24.62 g., 0.925 Silver 0.7322 oz. ASW **Series:** 2000 Summer Olympics - Sydney

Date	Mintage	VF20	XF40	MS60	MS63	MS65
1998	10,000	PF63 25.00	PF65 30.00			

KM# 125 5000 METICAIS
411.42 g., 0.999 Silver 13.2143 oz. ASW, 97 mm. **Obv:** National arms **Rev:** Rhinoceros right **Edge:** Reeded **Note:** Illustration reduced.

Date	Mintage	VF20	XF40	MS60	MS63	MS65
1997	2,000	PF65 275	PF67 325			

KM# 124 5000 METICAIS
14.00 g., Nickel Clad Steel, 28.5 mm. **Obv:** Emblem **Rev:** High power electric lines

Date	Mintage	VF20	XF40	MS60	MS63	MS65
1998	—	—	—	2.50	3.50	5.00

KM# 114.1 10000 METICAIS
20.00 g., 0.999 Silver 0.6424 oz. ASW **Subject:** World Cup Soccer **Obv:** Emblem **Rev:** Soccer player, 999 at right

Date	Mintage	VF20	XF40	MS60	MS63	MS65
1994	—	PF63 25.00	PF65 40.00			

KM# 114.2 10000 METICAIS
20.00 g., 0.999 Silver 0.6424 oz. ASW **Obv:** Emblem **Rev:** Soccer player without 999

Date	Mintage	VF20	XF40	MS60	MS63	MS65
1994	—	PF63 25.00	PF65 40.00			

KM# 123 10000 METICAIS
21.06 g., 0.999 Silver 0.6764 oz. ASW **Subject:** World Cup Soccer **Obv:** Emblem **Rev:** Soccer players and net, 999 at lower left

Date	Mintage	VF20	XF40	MS60	MS63	MS65
1994	—	PF63 25.00	PF65 40.00			

KM# 126 10000 METICAIS
822.84 g., 0.999 Silver 26.4286 oz. ASW, 100 mm. **Obv:** National arms **Rev:** Elephant charging **Edge:** Reeded **Note:** Illustration reduced.

Date	Mintage	VF20	XF40	MS60	MS63	MS65
1997	2,000	PF65 550	PF67 650			

KM# 129 10000 METICAIS
822.84 g., 0.999 Silver 26.4286 oz. ASW **Series:** 2000 Summer Olympics - Sydney

Date	Mintage	VF20	XF40	MS60	MS63	MS65
1998	2,000	PF65 625	PF67 725			

PATTERNS

Including off metal strikes

KM#	Date	Mintage	Identification	Mkt Val
Pn1	1994	—	10000 Meticais. Copper-Nickel. KM#114.1.	—
Pn2	1994	—	10000 Meticais. Copper-Nickel. KM#123.	—

PIEDFORT

KM#	Date	Mintage	Identification	Mkt Val
P1	1983	600	50 Meticais. 0.925. Silver.	90.00

PROVAS

Standard Metals

KM#	Date	Mintage	Identification	Mkt Val
Pr1	1935	—	2-1/2 Escudos. Silver. KM#61.	200
Pr2	1935	—	5 Escudos. Silver. KM62.	225
Pr3	1936	—	10 Centavos. Bronze. KM63.	100
Pr4	1936	—	20 Centavos. Bronze. KM64.	100
Pr5	1936	—	50 Centavos. Copper-Nickel. KM65.	100
Pr6	1936	—	Escudo. Copper-Nickel. KM66.	100
Pr7	1936	—	10 Escudos. Silver. KM67.	285
Pr8	1938	—	2-1/2 Escudos. Silver. KM61.	160
Pr9	1938	—	5 Escudos. Silver. KM69.	185
Pr10	1938	—	10 Escudos. Silver. KM70.	200
Pr11	1941	—	10 Centavos. Bronze. KM71.	100
Pr12	1942	—	10 Centavos. Bronze. KM72.	65.00
Pr13	1942	—	2-1/2 Escudos. Silver. KM68.	125
Pr14	1945	—	50 Centavos. Bronze. KM73.	65.00
Pr15	1945	—	Escudo. Bronze. KM74.	65.00
Pr16	1948	—	2-1/2 Escudos.	275
Pr17	1949	—	20 Centavos. Bronze. KM75.	65.00
Pr18	1949	—	5 Escudos. Silver. KM69.	125
PrA19	1950	—	20 Centavos. Bronze. KM75.	130
Pr19	1950	—	50 Centavos. Nickel-Bronze. KM76.	75.00
Pr20	1950	—	Escudo. Nickel-Bronze. KM77.	75.00
Pr21	1950	—	2-1/2 Escudos. Silver. KM68.	125
Pr22	1951	—	50 Centavos. Nickel-Bronze. KM76.	60.00
Pr23	1951	—	Escudo. Nickel-Bronze. KM77.	60.00
Pr24	1951	—	2-1/2 Escudos. Silver. KM68.	110
Pr25	1951	—	5 Escudos.	—
Pr26	1952	—	2-1/2 Escudos. Copper-Nickel. KM78.	100
Pr27	1952	—	5 Escudos.	—
Pr28	1952	—	10 Escudos. Silver. KM79.	110
Pr29	1952	—	20 Escudos. Silver. KM80.	125
Pr30	1953	—	50 Centavos. Bronze. KM81.	60.00
Pr31	1953	—	Escudo. Bronze. KM82.	60.00
Pr32	1953	—	2-1/2 Escudos. Copper-Nickel. KM78.	75.00
Pr34	1954	—	10 Escudos. Silver. KM79.	110
Pr35	1955	—	2-1/2 Escudos. Copper-Nickel. KM78.	75.00
Pr36	1955	—	10 Escudos. Silver. KM79.	110
Pr37	1955	—	20 Escudos. Silver. KM80.	110
Pr38	1957	—	50 Centavos. Bronze. KM81.	60.00
Pr39	1957	—	Escudo. Bronze. KM82.	60.00
Pr40	1960	—	10 Centavos. Bronze. KM83.	60.00
Pr41	1960	—	5 Escudos. Silver. KM84.	110
Pr42	1960	—	10 Escudos. Silver. KM79.	110
Pr43	1960	—	20 Escudos. Silver. KM80.	110
Pr44	1961	—	10 Centavos. Bronze. KM83.	60.00
Pr45	1961	—	20 Centavos. Bronze. KM85.	60.00
Pr46	1962	—	Escudo. Bronze. KM82.	60.00
Pr47	1963	—	Escudo. Bronze. KM82.	60.00

KM#	Date	Mintage	Identification	Mkt Val
Pr48	1965	—	Escudo. Bronze. KM82.	60.00
Pr49	1965	—	2-1/2 Escudos. Copper-Nickel. KM78.	75.00
Pr50	1966	—	10 Escudos. Silver. KM79a.	110
Pr51	1966	—	20 Escudos. Silver. KM80a.	125
Pr52	1968	—	Escudo. Bronze. KM82.	60.00
Pr53	1968	—	10 Escudos. Copper-Nickel. KM79b.	75.00
Pr54	1968	—	20 Escudos.	75.00
Pr55	1969	—	Escudo. Bronze. KM82.	60.00
Pr56	1969	—	20 Escudos.	75.00
Pr57	1970	—	10 Escudos. Copper-Nickel. KM79b.	75.00
Pr58	1970	—	20 Escudos.	75.00
Pr59	1971	—	5 Escudos. Copper-Nickel. KM86.	75.00
Pr60	1971	—	20 Escudos. Nickel. KM87.	75.00
Pr61	1972	—	20 Escudos. Nickel. KM87.	135
Pr62	1973	—	20 Centavos. Bronze. KM88.	100
Pr63	1973	—	50 Centavos. Bronze. KM89.	135
Pr64	1973	—	Escudo. Bronze. KM82.	100
Pr65	1973	—	2-1/2 Escudos. Copper-Nickel. KM78.	135
Pr66	1973	—	5 Escudos. Copper-Nickel. KM86.	135
Pr68	1974	—	20 Centavos. Bronze. KM88.	110
Pr69	1974	—	50 Centavos. Bronze. KM89.	135
Pr70	1974	—	Escudo. Bronze. KM82.	110

MINT SETS

KM#	Date	Mintage	Identification	Issue Price	Mkt Val
MS1	1980 (6)	—	KM#98-103	—	35.00

SPECIMEN SETS (SS)

KM#	Date	Mintage	Identification	Issue Price	Mkt Val
SS1	1975 (8)	—	KM#90-97	—	1,000

MUSCAT & OMAN

RULERS

al-Bu Sa'id Dynasty
Feisal ibn Turkee, AH1285-1332/1888-1913AD
Taimur ibn Faisal, AH1332-1351/1913-1932AD
Sa'id ibn Taimur, AH1351-1390/1932-1970AD

MONETARY SYSTEM

Until 1970

4 Baiza = 1 Anna
64 Baiza = 1 Rupee
200 Baiza = 1 Saidi (Dasin Dog)/Dhofari Rial
1970-1972
1000 (new) Baisa = 1 Saidi Rial

Commencing 1972

1000 Baisa = 1 Omani Rial
NOTE: For later coin issues, please refer to Oman.

SULTANATE

COUNTERMARKED COINAGE

1913 and 1932

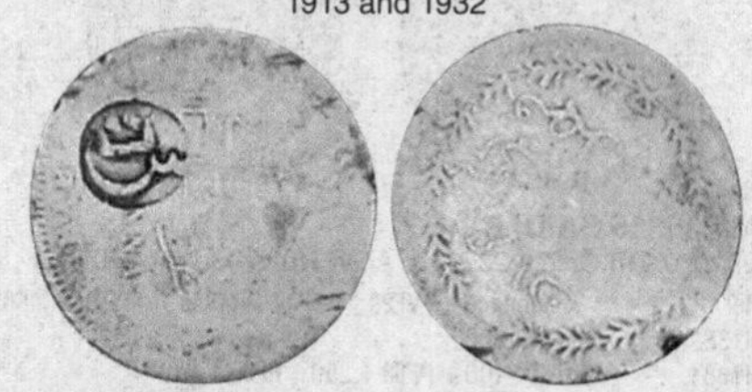

C# 19.1 1/4 ANNA

Copper **Ruler:** Faisal bin Turkee **Countermark:** ST **Note:** Countermark in Arabic on 1/4 Anna, KM#3.

CM Date	Host Date	G4	VG8	F12	VF20	XF40
1913	1315	15.00	30.00	60.00	150	600
1913	1315	15.00	30.00	60.00	150	600

C# 19.2 1/4 ANNA

Copper **Ruler:** Faisal bin Turkee **Countermark:** ST **Note:** Countermark in Arabic on 1/4 Anna, KM#8. Countermark for Sultan Taimur or Sayyid Taimur.

CM Date	Host Date	G4	VG8	F12	VF20	XF40
1913	1312	20.00	40.00	80.00	170	—

C# 20.1 1/4 ANNA

Copper **Ruler:** Faisal bin Turkee **Countermark:** SS **Note:** Large 10mm countermark in Arabic on 1/4 Anna, KM#3.

CM Date	Host Date	G4	VG8	F12	VF20	XF40
1932	1312	30.00	60.00	120	250	—
1932	1315	30.00	60.00	120	250	—

C# 20.2 1/4 ANNA

Copper **Ruler:** Faisal bin Turkee **Countermark:** SS **Note:** Large 10mm countermark in Arabic on 1/4 Anna, KM#8.

CM Date	Host Date	G4	VG8	F12	VF20	XF40
ND(1932)	1312	30.00	60.00	120	250	—

C# 21.1 1/4 ANNA

Copper **Ruler:** Faisal bin Turkee **Countermark:** SS **Note:** Small 8mm countermark in Arabic on 1/4 Anna, KM#3.

CM Date	Host Date	G4	VG8	F12	VF20	XF40
ND(1932)	1312	30.00	60.00	120	250	—

C# 21.2 1/4 ANNA

Copper **Ruler:** Faisal bin Turkee **Countermark:** SS **Note:** Small 8mm countermark in Arabic on 1/4 Anna, KM#8. Countermark for Sultan Sa'id or Sayyid Sa'id.

CM Date	Host Date	G4	VG8	F12	VF20	XF40
ND(1932)	1312	30.00	60.00	120	250	—

REFORM COINAGE

1000 (new) Baisa = 1 Saidi Rial

KM# 25 2 BAISA (Baiza)

Copper-Nickel **Ruler:** Sa'id bin Taimur **Obv:** Arms flanked by arabic "2" **Rev:** Arabic legend and inscription **Shape:** 4-sided

Date	Mintage	VF20	XF40	MS60	MS63	MS65
AH1365	1,500,000	5.00	12.00	17.00	35.00	60.00
AH1365 Restrike	—	PF65 35.00				

Note: Coins of AH1365 have the monetary unit spelled "Baiza", on all other coins it is spelled "Baisa". Most of the proof issues of the AH1359 and 1365 dated coins of Muscat and Oman now on the market are probably later restrikes produced by the Bombay Mint

KM# 36 2 BAISA (Baiza)

1.75 g., Bronze, 16 mm. **Ruler:** Sa'id bin Taimur **Obv:** Arms **Rev:** Value flanked by marks

Date	Mintage	VF20	XF40	MS60	MS63	MS65
AH1390	4,000,000	0.20	0.40	0.75	1.50	2.00
AH1390	—	PF65 2.50				

KM# 30 3 BAISA

Bronze, 20 mm. **Ruler:** Sa'id bin Taimur **Obv:** Arms **Rev:** Value flanked by marks

Date	Mintage	VF20	XF40	MS60	MS63	MS65
AH1378	8,000,000	0.75	1.25	2.00	3.50	5.00
AH1378 Proof	—	—	—	—	—	—

Note: Struck for use in Dhofar Province

KM# 32 3 BAISA

Bronze, 18 mm. **Ruler:** Sa'id bin Taimur **Obv:** Arms **Rev:** Value flanked by marks

Date	Mintage	VF20	XF40	MS60	MS63	MS65
AH1380	10,000,000	0.35	0.50	1.00	2.00	3.00
AH1380 Proof	Inc. above	—	—	—	—	—

Note: Struck for use in Muscat Province

KM# 26 5 BAISA (Baiza)

Copper-Nickel, 21 mm. **Ruler:** Sa'id bin Taimur **Obv:** Arms **Rev:** Arabic legend and inscription **Shape:** Scalloped

Date	Mintage	VF20	XF40	MS60	MS63	MS65
AH1365	3,849,000	8.00	15.00	25.00	50.00	75.00
AH1365 Restrike	—	PF65 40.00				

Note: Coins of AH1365 have the monetary unit spelled "Baiza", on all other coins it is spelled "Baisa"

KM# 33 5 BAISA (Baiza)

Copper-Nickel **Ruler:** Sa'id bin Taimur **Obv:** Arms **Rev:** Sailing ship within circle

Date	Mintage	VF20	XF40	MS60	MS63	MS65
AH1381	5,000,000	0.40	0.75	1.50	3.00	4.50
AH1381 Proof	Inc. above	—	—	—	—	—

Note: Struck for use in Muscat Province

KM# 37 5 BAISA (Baiza)

3.10 g., Bronze, 19 mm. **Ruler:** Sa'id bin Taimur **Obv:** Arms **Rev:** Value flanked by marks

Date	Mintage	VF20	XF40	MS60	MS63	MS65
AH1390	3,400,000	0.20	0.40	0.75	1.50	2.00
AH1390	—	PF65 2.50				

KM# 22 10 BAISA

Copper-Nickel **Ruler:** Sa'id bin Taimur **Obv:** Arms **Rev:** Inscription

Date	Mintage	VF20	XF40	MS60	MS63	MS65
AH1359	572,000	8.00	20.00	30.00	50.00	75.00
AH1359 Restrike	—	PF65 40.00				

Note: Struck for use in Dhofar Province

KM# 22a 10 BAISA

Gold **Ruler:** Sa'id bin Taimur **Obv:** Arms **Rev:** Inscription

Date	Mintage	VF20	XF40	MS60	MS63	MS65
AH1359	—	PF65 2,500				

KM# 38 10 BAISA

4.70 g., Bronze, 22.5 mm. **Ruler:** Sa'id bin Taimur **Obv:** Arms **Rev:** Value flanked by marks

Date	Mintage	VF20	XF40	MS60	MS63	MS65
AH1390	4,500,000	0.20	0.40	0.75	1.50	2.00
AH1390	—	PF65 2.75				

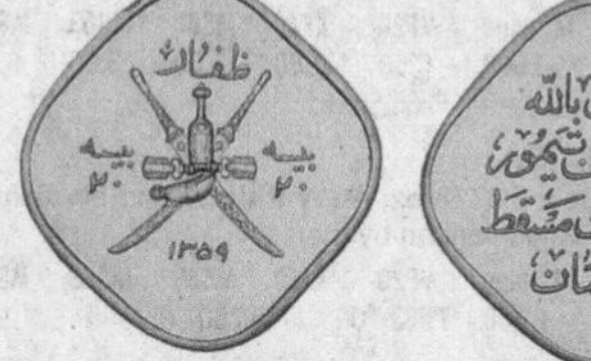

KM# 23 20 BAISA (Baiza)

Copper-Nickel **Ruler:** Sa'id bin Taimur **Obv:** Arms **Rev:** Inscription **Shape:** Square

Date	Mintage	VF20	XF40	MS60	MS63	MS65
AH1359	35,000	10.00	25.00	40.00	65.00	90.00
AH1359 Restrike	—	PF65 50.00				

Note: Struck for use in Dhofar Province

KM# 23a 20 BAISA (Baiza)
Gold **Ruler:** Sa'id bin Taimur **Obv:** Arms **Rev:** Inscription

Date	Mintage	VF20	XF40	MS60	MS63	MS65
AH1359	—	PF65 2,500				

KM# 27 20 BAISA (Baiza)
Copper-Nickel **Ruler:** Sa'id bin Taimur **Obv:** Arms **Rev:** Arabic legend and inscription **Shape:** Square

Date	Mintage	VF20	XF40	MS60	MS63	MS65
AH1365	1,135,000	12.00	25.00	40.00	65.00	90.00
AH1365 Restrike	—	PF65 60.00				

KM# 28 20 BAISA (Baiza)
Copper-Nickel **Ruler:** Sa'id bin Taimur **Obv:** Arms **Rev:** Inscription **Note:** Mule of obverse KM#23 and reverse KM#27

Date	Mintage	VF20	XF40	MS60	MS63	MS65
AH1359/1365 Restrike, Proof	—	—	—	—	—	—

KM# 39 25 BAISA
2.90 g., Copper-Nickel, 18 mm. **Ruler:** Sa'id bin Taimur **Obv:** Arms **Rev:** Value flanked by marks

Date	Mintage	VF20	XF40	MS60	MS63	MS65
AH1390	2,000,000	0.50	0.75	1.00	2.00	3.50
AH1390	—	PF65 3.50				

KM# 39a 25 BAISA
6.01 g., 0.916 Gold 0.177 oz. AGW **Ruler:** Sa'id bin Taimur **Obv:** Arms **Rev:** Value flanked by marks

Date	Mintage	VF20	XF40	MS60	MS63	MS65
AH1390	350	PF63 350	PF65 400			

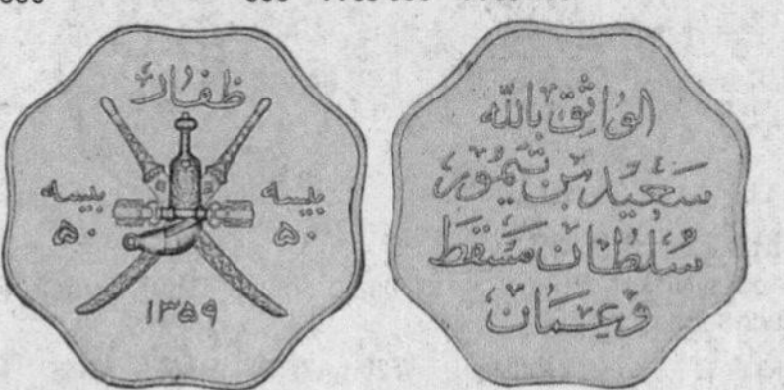

KM# 24 50 BAISA
Copper-Nickel **Ruler:** Sa'id bin Taimur **Obv:** Arms **Rev:** Inscription **Shape:** Scallop

Date	Mintage	VF20	XF40	MS60	MS63	MS65
AH1359	65,000	15.00	35.00	50.00	75.00	100
AH1359 Restrike	—	PF65 75.00				

Note: Struck for use in Dhofar Province

KM# 24a 50 BAISA
Gold **Ruler:** Sa'id bin Taimur **Obv:** Arms **Rev:** Inscription

Date	Mintage	VF20	XF40	MS60	MS63	MS65
AH1359	—	PF65 2,500				

KM# 40 50 BAISA
6.40 g., Copper-Nickel, 24 mm. **Ruler:** Sa'id bin Taimur **Obv:** Arms **Rev:** Value flanked by marks

Date	Mintage	VF20	XF40	MS60	MS63	MS65
AH1390	1,600,000	0.50	1.00	2.00	3.00	5.00
AH1390	—	PF65 5.00				

KM# 40a 50 BAISA
12.81 g., 0.916 Gold 0.3773 oz. AGW **Ruler:** Sa'id bin Taimur **Obv:** Arms **Rev:** Value flanked by marks

Date	Mintage	VF20	XF40	MS60	MS63	MS65
AH1390	350	PF63 700	PF65 750			

KM# 41 100 BAISA
Copper-Nickel **Ruler:** Sa'id bin Taimur **Obv:** Arms **Rev:** Value flanked by marks

Date	Mintage	VF20	XF40	MS60	MS63	MS65
AH1390	1,000,000	1.00	2.00	3.50	5.00	7.00
AH1390	—	PF65 9.00				

KM# 41a 100 BAISA
22.63 g., 0.916 Gold 0.6665 oz. AGW **Ruler:** Sa'id bin Taimur **Obv:** Arms **Rev:** Value flanked by marks

Date	Mintage	VF20	XF40	MS60	MS63	MS65
AH1390	350	PF63 1,250	PF65 1,300			

KM# 29 1/2 DHOFARI RIAL
14.03 g., 0.500 Silver 0.2255 oz. ASW **Ruler:** Sa'id bin Taimur **Obv:** Arms above sprig **Rev:** Inscription within circle and wreath

Date	Mintage	VF20	XF40	MS60	MS63	MS65
AH1367	200,000	12.00	25.00	45.00	75.00	125
AH1367 Restrike	—	PF63 200	PF65 250			

Note: Struck for use in Dhofar Province

KM# 29a 1/2 DHOFARI RIAL
24.03 g., 0.917 Gold 0.7085 oz. AGW **Ruler:** Sa'id bin Taimur **Obv:** Arms above sprig **Rev:** Inscription within circle and wreath

Date	Mintage	VF20	XF40	MS60	MS63	MS65
AH1367	2	PF65 26,000				

Note: Struck for presentation purposes

KM# 34 1/2 SAIDI RIAL
14.03 g., 0.500 Silver 0.2255 oz. ASW **Ruler:** Sa'id bin Taimur **Obv:** Arms **Rev:** Value

Date	Mintage	VF20	XF40	MS60	MS63	MS65
AH1380	300,000	8.00	15.00	25.00	65.00	100
AH1380	—	PF63 125	PF65 175			
AH1381	850,000	12.00	20.00	35.00	80.00	125

KM# 34a 1/2 SAIDI RIAL
25.60 g., 0.916 Gold 0.7539 oz. AGW **Ruler:** Sa'id bin Taimur **Obv:** Arms **Rev:** Value

Date	Mintage	VF20	XF40	MS60	MS63	MS65
AH1382	100	PF63 1,650	PF65 1,700			
AH1381	150	PF63 1,450	PF65 1,500			
AH1390	350	PF63 1,400	PF65 1,450			

Note: Struck for presentation purposes

KM# 31 SAIDI RIAL
28.07 g., 0.833 Silver 0.7518 oz. ASW, 38 mm. **Ruler:** Sa'id bin Taimur **Obv:** Arms within circle, designs around border **Rev:** Value and date

Date	Mintage	VF20	XF40	MS60	MS63	MS65
AH1378	1,000,000	20.00	30.00	40.00	75.00	95.00
AH1378	100	PF63 800	PF65 900			

KM# 31a SAIDI RIAL
28.07 g., 0.500 Silver 0.4512 oz. ASW, 38 mm. **Ruler:** Sa'id bin Taimur **Obv:** Arms within circle, designs around border **Rev:** Value and date

Date	Mintage	VF20	XF40	MS60	MS63	MS65
AH1378	400,000	9.00	15.00	20.00	35.00	50.00

KM# 31b SAIDI RIAL
46.65 g., 0.916 Gold 1.3738 oz. AGW, 33.7 mm. **Ruler:** Sa'id bin Taimur **Obv:** Arms within circle, designs around border **Rev:** Value and date

Date	Mintage	VF20	XF40	MS60	MS63	MS65
AH1378	100	PF63 2,800	PF65 3,000			
AH1390	350	PF63 2,600	PF65 2,800			

Note: Struck for presentation purposes

KM# 35 15 SAIDI RIALS
7.99 g., 0.916 Gold 0.2353 oz. AGW **Ruler:** Sa'id bin Taimur

Date	Mintage	VF20	XF40	MS60	MS63	MS65
AH1381	2,000	—	—	450	500	—
AH1381	100	PF63 1,250	PF65 1,400			

Note: Struck for presentation purposes

MINT SETS

KM#	Date	Mintage	Identification	Issue Price	Mkt Val
MS1	AH1390 (1970) (6)	5,500	KM#36-41	—	16.00

PROOF SETS

KM#	Date	Mintage	Identification	Issue Price	Mkt Val
PS1	AH1359, 65, 67 (1940, 45, 47) (6)		KM#22-26, 29, Restrikes	—	550
PS2	AH1359, 65, 67 (1940, 45, 47) (6)	—	KM#22, 24-27, 29, Restrikes	—	500
PS3	AH1390 (1970) (6)	2,102	KM#36-41	11.00	27.50
PS4	AH1390 (1970) (3)	350	KM#39a-41a	—	2,300

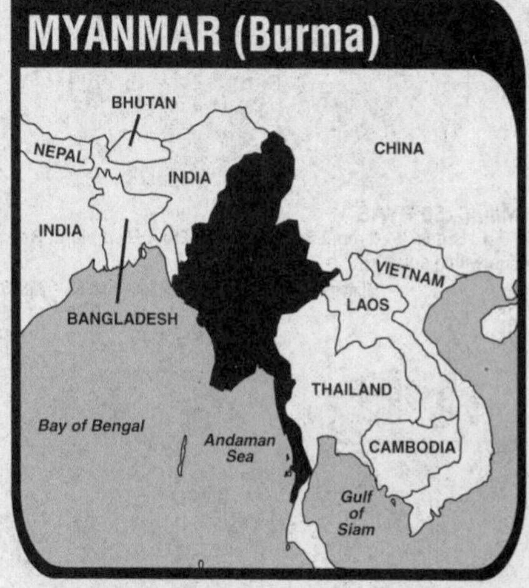

(BURMA)

The Republic of the Union of Myanmar, formerly Burma, a country of Southeast Asia fronting on the Bay of Bengal and the Andaman Sea, has an area of 261,218 sq. mi. (678,500 sq. km.) and a population of 38.8 million. Capital: Yangon (Rangoon) until 2005; followed thereafter by Naypyidaw. Myanmar is an agricultural country heavily dependent on its leading product (rice), which occupies two-thirds of the cultivated area and accounts for 40 % of the value of exports. Mineral resources are extensive, but production is low. Petroleum, lead, tin, silver, zinc, nickel cobalt, and precious stones are exported.

The British East India Company, while unsuccessful in its 1612 effort to establish posts along the Bay of Bengal, was enabled by the Anglo-Burmese Wars of 1824-86 to expand to the whole of Burma and to secure its annexation to British India. In 1937, Burma was separated from India, becoming a separate British colony with limited self-government. Burma became an independent nation outside the British Commonwealth on Jan. 4, 1948, the constitution of 1948 providing for a parliamentary democracy and the nationalization of certain industries. However, political and economic problems persisted, and on March 2, 1962, Gen. Ne Win took over the government, suspended the constitution, installed himself as chief of state, and pursued a socialistic program with nationalization of nearly all industry and trade. On Jan. 4, 1974, a new constitution adopted by referendum established Burma as a socialist republic under one-party rule. The country name was changed to Myanmar in 1989.

Burmese coins are frequently known by the equivalent Indian denominations, although their values are inscribed in Burmese units. Upper Burma was annexed in 1885 and the Burmese coinage remained in circulation until 1889, when Indian coins became current throughout Burma. Coins were again issued in the old Burmese denominations after independence in 1948, but decimal issues replaced these in 1952. The Chula-Sakarat (CS) dating is sometimes referred to as BE-Burmese Era and began in 638AD.

RULER

British, 1886-1948

MONETARY SYSTEM

(Until 1952)

4 Pyas = 1 Pe
2 Pe = 1 Mu
2 Mu = 1 Mat
5 Mat = 1 Kyat

NOTE: Originally 10 light Mu = 1 Kyat, eventually 8 heavy Mu = 1 Kyat.

Indian Equivalents

1 Silver Kyat = 1 Rupee = 16 Annas
1 Gold Kyat = 1 Mohur = 16 Rupees

UNION OF BURMA

STANDARD COINAGE

KM# 27 2 PYAS

Copper-Nickel **Obv:** Chinze **Rev:** Value and date flanked by sprays **Shape:** 4-sided

Date	Mintage	F12	VF20	XF40	MS60	MS63
1949	7,000,000	0.25	0.50	1.00	3.00	7.50
1949	100	PF65 100				

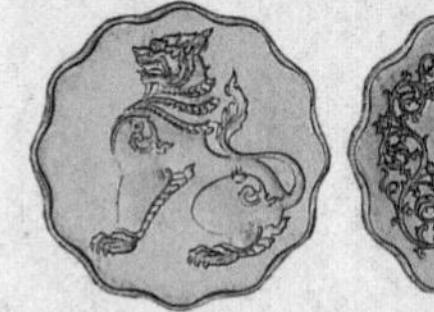

KM# 28 PE

Copper-Nickel **Obv:** Chinze **Rev:** Value and date flanked by sprays **Shape:** Scalloped

Date	Mintage	F12	VF20	XF40	MS60	MS63
1949	8,000,000	0.35	0.75	1.75	4.00	9.00
1949	100	PF65 100				
1950	9,500,000	0.35	0.75	1.75	4.00	9.00
1950 Proof	—	—	—	—	—	—
1951	6,500,000	0.50	1.00	2.00	5.00	10.00
1951 Proof	—	—	—	—	—	—

KM# 29 2 PE

Copper-Nickel **Obv:** Chinze **Rev:** Value and date flanked by sprays **Shape:** 4-sided

Date	Mintage	F12	VF20	XF40	MS60	MS63
1949	7,100,000	0.50	1.00	2.00	5.00	10.00
1949	100	PF65 100				
1950	8,500,000	0.50	1.00	2.00	5.00	10.00
1950 Proof	—	—	—	—	—	—
1951	7,480,000	0.50	1.00	2.00	5.00	10.00
1951 Proof	—	—	—	—	—	—

KM# 30 4 PE

Nickel **Obv:** Chinze **Rev:** Value and date flanked by sprays

Date	Mintage	F12	VF20	XF40	MS60	MS63
1949	6,500,000	1.25	2.50	5.00	10.00	15.00
1949	100	PF65 100				
1950	6,120,000	1.00	2.00	4.00	8.00	12.00

KM# 31 8 PE

Nickel Magnetic **Obv:** Chinze **Rev:** Value and date flanked by sprays

Date	Mintage	F12	VF20	XF40	MS60	MS63
1949	3,270,000	1.50	3.00	6.00	15.00	25.00
1949	100	PF65 100				
1950	3,900,000	1.25	2.50	5.00	12.00	20.00
1950 Proof	—	—	—	—	—	—

Note: 8 Pe 1950 (KM-31) coins made of copper nickel (non magnetic)have shown up in auctions. They were offered as new unlisted variety. These are counterfeit. The original coin is nickel and magnetic.

KM# 31a 8 PE

Copper-Nickel **Obv:** Chinze flanked by stars **Rev:** Value and date flanked by sprays

Date	Mintage	F12	VF20	XF40	MS60	MS63
CS1314-1952	1,642,000	50.00	100	150	200	300
CS1314-1952	—	PF65 400				

DECIMAL COINAGE

100 Pyas = 1 Kyat

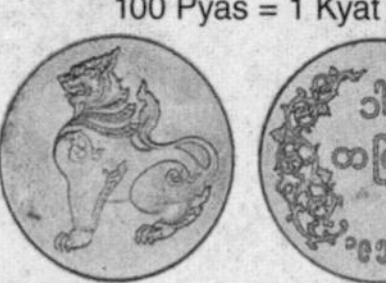

KM# 32 PYA

2.20 g., Bronze, 18 mm. **Obv:** Chinze **Rev:** Value and date flanked by sprays

Date	Mintage	F12	VF20	XF40	MS60	MS63
1952	500,000	0.10	0.15	0.20	0.25	0.35
1952	100	PF65 60.00				
1953	14,000,000	0.10	0.15	0.20	0.25	0.35
1953 Proof	—	—	—	—	—	—
1955	30,000,000	0.10	0.15	0.20	0.25	0.35
1955 Proof	—	—	—	—	—	—
1956	100	PF65 60.00				
1962	100	PF65 60.00				
1965	15,000,000	0.10	0.15	0.20	0.25	0.35
1965 Proof	—	—	—	—	—	—

KM# 38 PYA

0.60 g., Aluminum, 17 mm. **Subject:** Aung San **Obv:** Head 1/4 right flanked by stars below **Rev:** Value and date flanked by sprays

Date	Mintage	VF20	XF40	MS60	MS63	MS65
1966	8,000,000	0.10	0.15	0.25	0.35	0.65

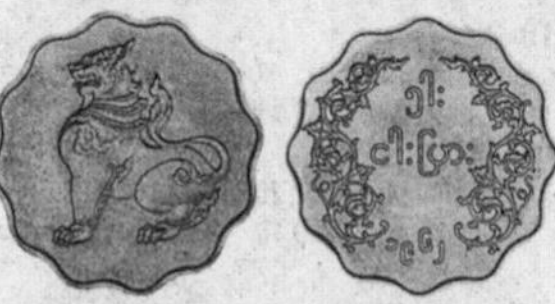

KM# 33 5 PYAS

3.17 g., Copper-Nickel **Obv:** Chinze **Rev:** Value and date flanked by sprays **Shape:** Scalloped

Date	Mintage	F12	VF20	XF40	MS60	MS63
1952	20,000,000	0.10	0.15	0.35	0.50	0.75
1952	100	PF65 65.00				
1953	59,700,000	0.10	0.15	0.35	0.50	0.75
1953 Proof	—	—	—	—	—	—
1955	40,272,000	0.10	0.15	0.35	0.50	0.75
1955 Proof	—	—	—	—	—	—
1956	20,000,000	0.10	0.15	0.35	0.50	0.75
1956	100	PF65 65.00				
1961	12,000,000	0.10	0.15	0.35	0.50	0.75
1961 Proof	—	—	—	—	—	—
1962	10,000,000	0.10	0.15	0.35	0.50	0.75
1962	100	PF65 65.00				
1963	40,400,000	0.10	0.15	0.25	0.35	0.60
1963 Proof	—	—	—	—	—	—
1965	43,600,000	0.10	0.15	0.20	0.30	0.40
1965 Proof	—	—	—	—	—	—
1966	20,000,000	0.10	0.15	0.20	0.30	0.40
1966 Proof	—	—	—	—	—	—

KM# 39 5 PYAS

0.90 g., Aluminum, 18.4 mm. **Subject:** Aung San **Obv:** Head 1/4 right flanked by stars below **Rev:** Value and date flanked by sprays **Shape:** Scalloped

Date	Mintage	VF20	XF40	MS60	MS63	MS65
1966	—	0.10	0.20	0.35	0.45	0.75

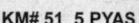

KM# 51 5 PYAS

Aluminum-Bronze **Series:** F.A.O. **Obv:** Rice plant **Rev:** Value and date within square

Date	Mintage	VF20	XF40	MS60	MS63	MS65
1987	—	0.20	0.40	0.60	1.00	—

KM# 34 10 PYAS

4.46 g., Copper-Nickel **Obv:** Chinze **Rev:** Value and date flanked by sprays **Shape:** 4-sided

Date	Mintage	F12	VF20	XF40	MS60	MS63
1952	20,000,000	0.10	0.20	0.40	0.60	1.00
1952	100	PF65 70.00				
1953	37,250,000	0.10	0.20	0.40	0.60	1.00
1953 Proof	—	—	—	—	—	—
1955	22,750,000	0.10	0.20	0.40	0.60	1.00
1955 Proof	—	—	—	—	—	—
1956	35,000,000	0.10	0.15	0.40	0.60	1.00
1956	100	PF65 70.00				
1962	6,000,000	0.10	0.20	0.40	0.60	1.00
1962	100	PF65 70.00				
1963	10,750,000	0.10	0.20	0.40	0.60	1.00
1963 Proof	10,750,000	—	—	—	—	—
1965	32,619,999	0.10	0.20	0.40	0.60	1.00
1965 Proof	—	—	—	—	—	—

KM# 40 10 PYAS

1.00 g., Aluminum **Subject:** Aung San **Obv:** Head 1/4 right flanked by stars below **Rev:** Value and date flanked by sprays **Shape:** Square

Date	Mintage	VF20	XF40	MS60	MS63	MS65
1966	—	0.15	0.25	0.45	0.65	1.25

KM# 49 10 PYAS

3.00 g., Brass, 20.45 mm. **Series:** F.A.O. **Obv:** Rice plant **Rev:** Value within square

Date	Mintage	VF20	XF40	MS60	MS63	MS65
1983	—	0.25	0.40	0.60	1.00	—

KM# 35 25 PYAS

Copper-Nickel **Obv:** Chinze flanked by stars **Rev:** Value and date flanked by sprays **Shape:** Scalloped

Date	Mintage	F12	VF20	XF40	MS60	MS63
1952	13,540,000	0.10	0.20	0.45	0.65	1.25
1952	100	PF65 75.00				
1954	18,000,000	0.10	0.20	0.45	0.65	1.25
1954 Proof	—	—	—	—	—	—
1955	—	PF65 75.00				
1956	14,000,000	0.10	0.20	0.45	0.65	1.25
1956	100	PF65 75.00				
1959	6,000,000	0.10	0.20	0.45	0.65	1.25
1959 Proof	—	—	—	—	—	—
1961	4,000,000	0.10	0.20	0.45	0.65	1.25
1961 Proof	—	—	—	—	—	—
1962	3,200,000	0.10	0.20	0.45	0.65	1.25
1962	100	PF65 75.00				
1963	16,000,000	0.10	0.15	0.25	0.45	0.75
1963 Proof	—	—	—	—	—	—
1965	26,000,000	0.10	0.15	0.25	0.45	0.75
1965 Proof	—	—	—	—	—	—

KM# 41 25 PYAS

1.80 g., Aluminum **Subject:** Aung San **Obv:** Head 1/4 right flanked by stars below **Rev:** Value and date flanked by sprays **Shape:** Scalloped

Date	Mintage	VF20	XF40	MS60	MS63	MS65
1966	—	0.15	0.25	0.45	0.65	1.25

KM# 48 25 PYAS

4.30 g., Bronze, 22.35 mm. **Series:** F.A.O. **Obv:** Rice plant **Rev:** Value and date within square

Date	Mintage	VF20	XF40	MS60	MS63	MS65
1980	—	0.15	0.25	0.40	0.60	1.00

KM# 50 25 PYAS

5.52 g., Bronze, 23.35 mm. **Series:** F.A.O. **Obv:** Rice plant **Rev:** Large value **Shape:** 6-sided

Date	Mintage	VF20	XF40	MS60	MS63	MS65
1986	—	—	0.15	0.25	0.35	0.60

KM# 36 50 PYAS

7.80 g., Copper-Nickel **Obv:** Chinze flanked by stars **Rev:** Value and date flanked by vine sprigs

Date	Mintage	F12	VF20	XF40	MS60	MS63
1952	2,500,000	0.20	0.50	0.75	1.25	1.75
1952	100	PF65 80.00				
1954	12,000,000	0.20	0.50	0.75	1.25	1.75
1954 Proof	—	—	—	—	—	—
1956	8,000,000	0.20	0.50	0.75	1.25	1.75
1956	100	PF65 80.00				
1961	2,000,000	0.15	0.40	0.75	1.25	1.75
1961 Proof	—	—	—	—	—	—
1962	600,000	0.25	0.75	1.25	1.75	2.25
1962	100	PF65 80.00				
1963	4,800,000	0.15	0.25	0.65	0.85	1.25
1963 Proof	—	—	—	—	—	—
1965	2,800,000	0.15	0.40	0.75	1.25	1.75
1965 Proof	—	—	—	—	—	—
1966	3,400,000	0.10	0.30	0.75	1.25	1.75
1966 Proof	—	—	—	—	—	—

KM# 42 50 PYAS

2.00 g., Aluminum **Subject:** Aung San **Obv:** Head 1/4 right flanked by stars below **Rev:** Value and date flanked by sprays

Date	Mintage	VF20	XF40	MS60	MS63	MS65
1966	—	0.40	0.60	0.75	1.25	2.25

KM# 46 50 PYAS

5.70 g., Brass, 24.6 mm. **Series:** F.A.O. **Obv:** Rice plant **Rev:** Value within square

Date	Mintage	VF20	XF40	MS60	MS63	MS65
1975	—	0.15	0.25	0.45	0.65	1.25
1976	—	0.15	0.25	0.45	0.65	1.25

KM# 37 KYAT

11.65 g., Copper-Nickel, 30.5 mm. **Obv:** Chinze flanked by stars **Rev:** Value and date flanked by sprays

Date	Mintage	F12	VF20	XF40	MS60	MS63
1952	2,500,000	0.35	0.75	1.25	2.00	3.00
1952	100	PF65 85.00				
1953	7,500,000	0.25	0.50	1.00	1.25	2.00
1953 Proof	—	—	—	—	—	—
1956	3,500,000	0.35	0.75	1.25	2.00	3.00
1956	100	PF65 85.00				
1962	100	PF65 85.00				
1965	1,000,000	0.35	0.75	1.25	2.00	3.00
1965 Proof	—	—	—	—	—	—

KM# 47 KYAT

7.20 g., Copper-Nickel, 26.45 mm. **Series:** F.A.O. **Obv:** Rice plant **Rev:** Value within square

Date	Mintage	VF20	XF40	MS60	MS63	MS65
1975	20,000,000	0.25	0.50	0.75	1.25	2.00

REVOLUTIONARY COINAGE

Patriotic Liberation Army

KM# 43 MU

2.00 g., 1.000 Gold 0.0643 oz. AGW **Obv:** Peacock **Rev:** Legend within star

Date	Mintage	VF20	XF40	MS60	MS63	MS65
1970-71	—	—	—	—	160	175

KM# 44 2 MU

4.00 g., 1.000 Gold 0.1286 oz. AGW **Obv:** Peacock **Rev:** Legend within star flanked by stars at points

Date	Mintage	VF20	XF40	MS60	MS63	MS65
1970-71	—	—	—	—	260	280

KM# 45 4 MU
8.00 g., 1.000 Gold 0.2572 oz. AGW **Obv:** Peacock **Rev:** Legend within star

Date	Mintage	VF20	XF40	MS60	MS63	MS65
1970-71	—	—	—	—	475	500

UNION OF MYANMAR

DECIMAL COINAGE

100 Pyas = 1 Kyat

KM# 57 10 PYAS
Brass **Obv:** Rice plant **Obv. Legend:** Myanmar Central Bank **Rev:** Value within square **Note:** Similar to KM#49.

Date	Mintage	VF20	XF40	MS60	MS63	MS65
1991	—	0.15	0.30	0.50	0.75	1.25

KM# 58 25 PYAS
5.00 g., Copper Plated Steel **Obv:** Rice plant **Obv. Legend:** Myanmar Central Bank **Rev:** Large value **Shape:** Hexagon

Date	Mintage	VF20	XF40	MS60	MS63	MS65
1991	—	0.15	0.30	0.50	0.75	1.25

KM# 59 50 PYAS
Brass, 24.6 mm. **Obv:** Rice plant **Obv. Legend:** Myanmar Central Bank **Rev:** Value within square **Edge:** Reeded

Date	Mintage	VF20	XF40	MS60	MS63	MS65
1991	—	0.25	0.50	0.75	1.00	1.50

KM# 60 KYAT
2.95 g., Bronze, 19.03 mm. **Obv:** Chinze flanked by stars **Rev:** Value **Edge:** Plain

Date	Mintage	VF20	XF40	MS60	MS63	MS65
1999	—	—	—	0.15	0.25	0.40

KM# 61 5 KYATS
2.73 g., Brass, 20 mm. **Obv:** Chinze flanked by stars **Rev:** Value **Edge:** Plain

Date	Mintage	VF20	XF40	MS60	MS63	MS65
1999	—	—	—	0.25	0.50	0.75

KM# 62 10 KYATS
4.45 g., Brass **Obv:** Chinze flanked by stars **Rev:** Value

Date	Mintage	VF20	XF40	MS60	MS63	MS65
1999	—	—	—	0.50	0.75	1.00

KM# 63 50 KYATS
5.06 g., Copper-Nickel, 23.85 mm. **Obv:** Chinze flanked by stars **Rev:** Value **Edge:** Reeded

Date	Mintage	VF20	XF40	MS60	MS63	MS65
1999	—	—	—	1.00	1.75	2.00

KM# 64 100 KYATS
7.52 g., Copper-Nickel, 26.8 mm. **Obv:** Chinze flanked by stars **Rev:** Value **Edge:** Reeded

Date	Mintage	VF20	XF40	MS60	MS63	MS65
1999	—	—	—	2.00	3.00	3.50

KM# A51 300 KYAT
1.24 g., 0.999 Gold 0.040 oz. AGW **Subject:** Year of the Tiger **Obv:** Lotus flower **Rev:** Tiger

Date	Mintage	VF20	XF40	MS60	MS63	MS65
1998	—	—	—	—	75.00	80.00

KM# 52 500 KYAT
20.00 g., 0.925 Silver 0.5948 oz. ASW **Subject:** Year of the Tiger **Obv:** Lotus flower **Rev:** Stalking tiger

Date	Mintage	VF20	XF40	MS60	MS63	MS65
1998	Est. 15000	PF63 35.00	PF65 45.00			

KM# 53 500 KYAT
20.00 g., 0.925 Silver 0.5948 oz. ASW **Subject:** Year of the Tiger **Obv:** Lotus flower **Rev:** Tiger drinking

Date	Mintage	VF20	XF40	MS60	MS63	MS65
1998	Est. 15000	PF63 35.00	PF65 45.00			

KM# 54 500 KYAT
20.00 g., 0.925 Silver 0.5948 oz. ASW **Subject:** Year of the Tiger **Obv:** Lotus flower **Rev:** Tiger

Date	Mintage	VF20	XF40	MS60	MS63	MS65
1998	Est. 15000	PF63 35.00	PF65 45.00			

KM# 55 2000 KYAT
7.78 g., 0.9999 Gold 0.250 oz. AGW **Subject:** Year of the Tiger **Obv:** Lotus flower **Rev:** Stalking tiger

Date	Mintage	VF20	XF40	MS60	MS63	MS65
1998	1,998	PF65 425				

KM# 56 5000 KYAT
15.55 g., 0.9999 Gold 0.500 oz. AGW **Subject:** Year of the Tiger **Obv:** Lotus flower **Rev:** Tiger

Date	Mintage	VF20	XF40	MS60	MS63	MS65
1998	5,798	PF65 850				

PATTERNS

Including off metal strikes

KM#	Date	Mintage	Identification	Mkt Val
Pn10	BE2602 (1949)	—	4 Annas. Aluminum.	—
Pn11	BE2602 (1949)	—	4 Annas. Aluminum.	—
Pn12	BE2602 (1949)	—	4 Annas. Aluminum.	—

PROOF SETS

KM#	Date	Mintage	Identification	Issue Price	Mkt Val
PS1	1949 (5)	100	KM#27-31	—	1,200
PS2	1952 (6)	100	KM#32-37	—	1,100
PS3	1956 (6)	100	KM#32-37	—	1,100
PS4	1962 (6)	100	KM#32-37	—	1,100
PS5	1998 (3)	3,998	KM#52-54	—	175
PS6	1998 (2)	1,998	KM#55-56	—	1,350

NAGORNO-KARABAKH

TURKEY
GEORGIA
RUSSIA
KAZAKHSTAN
ARMENIA
AZERBAIJAN
UZBEKISTAN
Caspian Sea
IRAN

Nagorno-Karabakh, an ethnically Armenian enclave inside Azerbaijan (pop., 1991 est.: 193,000), SW region. It occupies an area of 1,700 sq mi (4,400 square km) on the NE flank of the Karabakh Mountain Range, with the capital city of Stepanakert.

Russia annexed the area from Persia in 1813, and in 1923 it was established as an autonomous province of the Azerbaijan S.S.R. In 1988 the region's ethnic Armenian majority demonstrated against Azerbaijani rule, and in 1991, after the breakup of the U.S.S.R. brought independence to Armenia and Azerbaijan, war broke out between the two ethnic groups. On January 8, 1992 the leaders of Nagorno-Karabakh declared independence as the Republic of Mountainous Karabakh (RMK). Since 1994, following a cease-fire, ethnic Armenians have held Karabakh, though officially it remains part of Azerbaijan. Karabakh remains sovereign, but the political and military condition is volatile and tensions frequently flare into skirmishes.

Its marvelous nature and geographic situation, have all facilitated Karabakh to be a center of science, poetry and, especially, of the musical culture of Azerbaijan.

REPUBLIC

STANDARD COINAGE

KM# 1 25000 DRAMS

31.20 g., 0.999 Silver 1.0021 oz. ASW, 39 mm. **Obv:** National arms **Rev:** Head left above two fists **Edge:** Reeded **Note:** Struck at Lialoosin Inc., Los Angeles, CA.

Date	Mintage	VF20	XF40	MS60	MS63	MS65
1998	—	PF63 65.00	PF65 85.00			

KM# 1a 25000 DRAMS

Silver Gilt **Obv:** National arms **Rev:** Head left above two fists

Date	Mintage	VF20	XF40	MS60	MS63	MS65
1998	—	PF63 75.00	PF65 95.00			

KM# 5 25000 DRAMS

30.80 g., 0.999 Silver 0.9893 oz. ASW **Obv:** National arms **Rev:** Two stone faced monuments **Edge:** Plain **Note:** Struck at Lialoosin Inc., Los Angeles, CA.

Date	Mintage	VF20	XF40	MS60	MS63	MS65
1998(2000)	—	PF63 75.00	PF65 95.00			

KM# 5a 25000 DRAMS

Silver Gilt, 38.8 mm. **Obv:** National arms **Rev:** Two stone faced monuments

Date	Mintage	VF20	XF40	MS60	MS63	MS65
1998(2000)	—	PF63 85.00	PF65 100			

KM# 13 25000 DRAMS

31.22 g., 0.999 Silver 1.0027 oz. ASW, 38.9 mm. **Obv:** National arms **Rev:** Maps **Edge:** Plain

Date	Mintage	VF20	XF40	MS60	MS63	MS65
1998	—	PF63 75.00	PF65 95.00			

KM# 14 25000 DRAMS

31.22 g., 0.999 Silver 1.0027 oz. ASW, 38.9 mm. **Obv:** National arms **Rev:** "1700" in cross design with inscription 301AD **Edge:** Plain

Date	Mintage	VF20	XF40	MS60	MS63	MS65
1998	—	PF63 75.00	PF65 95.00			

KM# 15 25000 DRAMS

31.22 g., 0.999 Silver 1.0027 oz. ASW, 38.9 mm. **Subject:** 1700th Anniversary of Christianity in Armenia **Obv:** National arms **Rev:** Standing Saint and church **Edge:** Plain

Date	Mintage	VF20	XF40	MS60	MS63	MS65
1998	—	PF63 75.00	PF65 95.00			

KM# 16 25000 DRAMS

31.22 g., 0.999 Silver 1.0027 oz. ASW, 38.9 mm. **Obv:** National arms **Rev:** Head left **Edge:** Plain

Date	Mintage	VF20	XF40	MS60	MS63	MS65
1998	—	PF63 75.00	PF65 95.00			

KM# 16a 25000 DRAMS

31.22 g., 0.999 Silver Gilt 1.0027 oz., 38.9 mm. **Obv:** National arms **Rev:** Head left **Edge:** Plain

Date	Mintage	VF20	XF40	MS60	MS63	MS65
1998	—	PF63 85.00	PF65 100			

KM# 17 25000 DRAMS

31.22 g., 0.999 Silver 1.0027 oz. ASW, 38.9 mm. **Obv:** National arms **Rev:** Head right with laurels **Edge:** Plain

Date	Mintage	VF20	XF40	MS60	MS63	MS65
1998	—	PF63 75.00	PF65 95.00			

KM# 18 25000 DRAMS

31.22 g., 0.999 Silver 1.0027 oz. ASW, 38.9 mm. **Obv:** National arms **Rev:** Standing figure reading book right **Edge:** Plain

Date	Mintage	VF20	XF40	MS60	MS63	MS65
1998	—	PF63 75.00	PF65 95.00			

KM# 2 50000 DRAM

155.52 g., 0.999 Silver 4.995 oz. ASW, 63.8 mm. **Obv:** National arms **Rev:** Head left above two fists **Edge Lettering:** 5 T.O. .999 AG **Note:** Struck at Lialoosin Inc., Los Angeles, CA. Illustration reduced.

Date	Mintage	VF20	XF40	MS60	MS63	MS65
1998	—	PF65 400				

KM# 2a 50000 DRAM

Silver Gilt **Obv:** National arms **Rev:** Head left above two fists

Date	Mintage	VF20	XF40	MS60	MS63	MS65
1998	—	PF65 425				

KM# 3 50000 DRAM

7.80 g., 0.900 Gold 0.2257 oz. AGW, 22 mm. **Obv:** National arms **Rev:** Head left above two fists **Edge:** Plain **Note:** Struck at Lialoosin Inc., Los Angeles, CA.

Date	Mintage	VF20	XF40	MS60	MS63	MS65
1998	—	PF65 800				

KM# 4 50000 DRAM

155.52 g., 0.999 Silver 4.995 oz. ASW, 63.8 mm. **Obv:** National arms **Rev:** Two monumental portraits **Edge Lettering:** 5 T.O. .999 AG **Note:** Struck at Lialoosin Inc., Los Angeles, CA. Illustration reduced.

Date	Mintage	VF20	XF40	MS60	MS63	MS65
1998	—	PF65 400				

KM# 4a 50000 DRAM

Silver Gilt **Obv:** National arms **Rev:** Two monumental portraits

Date	Mintage	VF20	XF40	MS60	MS63	MS65
1998	—	PF65 425				

NAMIBIA

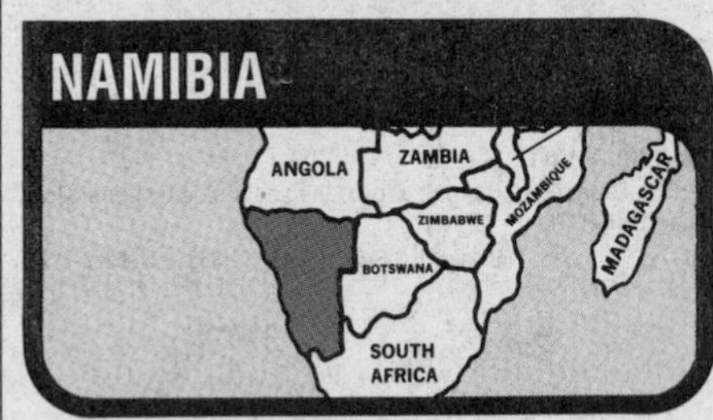

The Republic of Namibia, once the German colonial territory of German Southwest Africa, and later Southwest Africa, is situated on the Atlantic coast of southern Africa, bounded on the north by Angola, on the east by Botswana, and on the south by South Africa. It has an area of 318,261 sq. mi. (824,290 sq. km.) and a population of *1.4 million. Capital: Windhoek. Diamonds, copper, lead, zinc, and cattle are exported.

South Africa undertook the administration of Southwest Africa under the terms of a League of Nations mandate on Dec. 17, 1920. When the League of Nations was dissolved in 1946, its supervisory authority for Southwest Africa was inherited by the United Nations. In 1946 the UN denied South Africa's request to annex Southwest Africa. South Africa responded by refusing to place the territory under a UN trusteeship. In 1950 the International Court of Justice ruled that South Africa could not unilaterally modify the international status of Southwest Africa. A 1966 UN resolution declaring the mandate terminated was rejected by South Africa, and the status of the area remained in dispute. In June 1968 the UN General Assembly voted to rename the territory Namibia. In 1971 the International Court of Justice ruled that South Africa's presence in Namibia was illegal. In Dec. 1973 the UN appointed a UN Commissioner and a multi-racial Advisory Council was appointed. An interim government was formed in 1977 and independence was to be declared by Dec. 31, 1978. This resolution was rejected by major UN powers. In April 1978 South Africa accepted a plan for UN-supervised elections, which led to a political abstention by the

Southwest Africa People's Organization (SWAPO) party leading to dissolving of the Minister's Council and National Assembly in Jan. 1983. A Multi-Party Conference (MPC) was formed in May 1984, which held talks with SWAPO. The MPC petitioned South Africa for self-government and on June 17, 1985 the Transitional Government of National Unity was installed. Negotiations were held in 1988 between Angola, Cuba, and South Africa reaching a peaceful settlement on Aug. 5, 1988. By April 1989 Cuban troops were to withdraw from Angola and South African troops from Namibia. The Transitional Government resigned on Feb. 28, 1988 for the upcoming elections of the constituent assembly in Nov. 1989. Independence was finally achieved on March 12, 1990 within the Commonwealth of Nations. The President is the Head of State; the Prime Minister is Head of Government.

MONETARY SYSTEM
100 Cents = 1 Namibia Dollar
1 Namibia Dollar = 1 South African Rand

REPUBLIC

DECIMAL COINAGE

KM# 1 5 CENTS
2.20 g., Nickel Plated Steel, 17 mm. **Obv:** National arms **Rev:** Value left, aloe plant within 3/4 sun design

Date	Mintage	VF20	XF40	MS60	MS63	MS65
1993	—	—	—	0.20	0.50	0.75

KM# 16 5 CENTS
3.10 g., Stainless Steel, 20.03 mm. **Series:** F.A.O **Obv:** Arms with supporters **Rev:** Fish below value **Edge:** Plain

Date	Mintage	VF20	XF40	MS60	MS63	MS65
1999	—	—	—	0.50	1.00	1.50
2000	—	—	—	0.50	1.00	1.50

KM# 2 10 CENTS
3.40 g., Nickel Plated Steel, 21.5 mm. **Obv:** National arms **Rev:** Camelthorn tree right, partial sun design left, value below

Date	Mintage	VF20	XF40	MS60	MS63	MS65
1993	—	—	—	0.35	1.00	1.25
1996	—	—	—	0.35	1.00	1.25
1998	—	—	—	0.35	1.00	1.25

KM# 3 50 CENTS
4.43 g., Nickel Plated Steel, 24 mm. **Obv:** National arms **Rev:** Quiver tree right, partial sun design upper left, value below

Date	Mintage	VF20	XF40	MS60	MS63	MS65
1993	—	—	—	0.75	1.75	2.00
1996	—	—	—	0.75	1.75	2.00

KM# 4 DOLLAR
5.00 g., Brass, 22.4 mm. **Obv:** National arms **Rev:** Value divides Bateleur eagle at right, partial sun design at left

Date	Mintage	VF20	XF40	MS60	MS63	MS65
1993	—	—	—	1.25	3.50	6.00
1996	—	—	—	1.25	3.50	6.00
Note: Edge varieties exist for 1996						
1998	—	—	—	1.25	3.50	6.00

KM# 6 DOLLAR
Copper-Nickel **Subject:** 5th Year of Independence **Obv:** Arms with supporters within beaded border **Rev:** Hills within beaded border

Date	Mintage	VF20	XF40	MS60	MS63	MS65
1995	50,000	—	—	—	5.00	7.00

KM# 7 DOLLAR
Copper-Nickel, 37 mm. **Subject:** Miss Universe **Obv:** Arms with supporters within beaded border **Rev:** Multicolor gemsbok within beaded border **Edge:** Plain

Date	Mintage	VF20	XF40	MS60	MS63	MS65
1995	50,000	—	—	—	7.00	9.00

KM# 12 DOLLAR
Copper-Nickel **Subject:** Marine Life Protection **Obv:** Arms with supporters **Rev:** Multicolor whale and calf

Date	Mintage	VF20	XF40	MS60	MS63	MS65
1998	7,500	PF63 12.00	PF65 15.00			

KM# 5 5 DOLLARS
6.22 g., Brass, 24.9 mm. **Obv:** National arms **Rev:** Partial sun design at top, value at center, African fish eagle below

Date	Mintage	VF20	XF40	MS60	MS63	MS65
1993	—	—	—	1.50	2.50	5.00

KM# 18 5 DOLLARS
1.27 g., 0.9999 Gold 0.0408 oz. AGW, 13.9 mm. **Subject:** 10 Years of Independence **Obv:** Arms with supporters **Rev:** Two lions within circle **Edge:** Reeded

Date	Mintage	VF20	XF40	MS60	MS63	MS65
2000	8,000	PF63 65.00	PF65 70.00			

KM# 8 10 DOLLARS
25.00 g., 0.925 Silver 0.7435 oz. ASW, 37 mm. **Subject:** 5th Year of Independence **Obv:** Arms with supporters **Rev:** Multicolor desert view

Date	Mintage	VF20	XF40	MS60	MS63	MS65
1995	10,000	PF65 25.00				

KM# 9 10 DOLLARS
Copper-Nickel **Subject:** U.N. 50th Anniversary **Obv:** Arms with supporters **Rev:** Farm scene

Date	Mintage	VF20	XF40	MS60	MS63	MS65
1995	—	—	—	4.00	6.00	9.00

KM# 9a 10 DOLLARS
28.28 g., 0.925 Silver 0.841 oz. ASW **Subject:** U.N. 50th Anniversary **Obv:** Arms with supporters **Rev:** Farm scene

Date	Mintage	VF20	XF40	MS60	MS63	MS65
1995	—	PF63 25.00	PF65 30.00			

KM# 10 10 DOLLARS
25.00 g., 0.925 Silver 0.7435 oz. ASW **Subject:** Miss Universe **Obv:** Arms with supporters **Rev:** Multicolor leopard

Date	Mintage	VF20	XF40	MS60	MS63	MS65
1995	10,000	PF63 25.00	PF65 30.00			

KM# 11 10 DOLLARS
25.00 g., 0.925 Silver 0.7435 oz. ASW **Series:** Olympic Games 1996 **Obv:** Arms with supporters **Rev:** Runner and cheetah

Date	Mintage	VF20	XF40	MS60	MS63	MS65
1996	—	PF65 22.00				

KM# 13 10 DOLLARS
25.00 g., 0.925 Silver 0.7435 oz. ASW **Subject:** Marine Life Protection **Obv:** Arms with supporters **Rev:** Multicolor whale and calf **Note:** Similar to 1 Dollar, KM#12.

Date	Mintage	VF20	XF40	MS60	MS63	MS65
1998	—	PF65 50.00				

KM# 19 10 DOLLARS
25.00 g., 0.900 Silver 0.7234 oz. ASW, 37.3 mm. **Subject:** 10 Years of Independence **Obv:** Arms with supporters **Rev:** Two multicolor lions **Edge:** Reeded

Date	Mintage	VF20	XF40	MS60	MS63	MS65
2000	3,000	PF65 40.00				

KM# 20 10 DOLLARS
155.52 g., 0.999 Silver 4.9951 oz. ASW **Subject:** Independence, 10th Anniversary **Obv:** Arms **Rev:** Lion and lioness heads left, multicolor

Date	Mintage	VF20	XF40	MS60	MS63	MS65
2000	—	PF63 175	PF65 200			

KM# 14 20 DOLLARS
155.52 g., 0.999 Silver 4.995 oz. ASW **Obv:** Arms with supporters **Rev:** Multicolor whale and calf **Note:** Similar to 1 Dollar, KM#12.

Date	Mintage	VF20	XF40	MS60	MS63	MS65
1998	—	PF63 275	PF65 300			

KM# 17 100 DOLLARS

31.10 g., 0.9999 Gold 0.9999 oz. AGW **Series:** Olympic Games 1996 **Obv:** Arms with supporters **Rev:** Runner and cheetah **Note:** Similar to 10-Dollar, KM#11.

Date	Mintage	VF20	XF40	MS60	MS63	MS65
1996	400	PF63 1,650	PF65 1,750			

KM# 15 100 DOLLARS

31.10 g., 0.9999 Gold 0.9999 oz. AGW **Subject:** Marine Life Protection **Obv:** Arms with supporters **Rev:** Multicolor whale and calf **Note:** Similar to 1 Dollar, KM#12.

Date	Mintage	VF20	XF40	MS60	MS63	MS65
1998	125	PF63 1,750	PF65 1,850			

ESSAIS

KM#	Date	Mintage	Identification	Mkt Val
E1	1996	30	10 Dollars. Copper-Nickel. Multi-color, KM#11.	200
E2	1996	30	100 Dollars. Copper-Nickel. Multi-color, KM#17.	220

MINT SETS

KM#	Date	Mintage	Identification	Issue Price	Mkt Val
MS1	1993 (5)	—	KM#1-5	—	18.00

NAURU

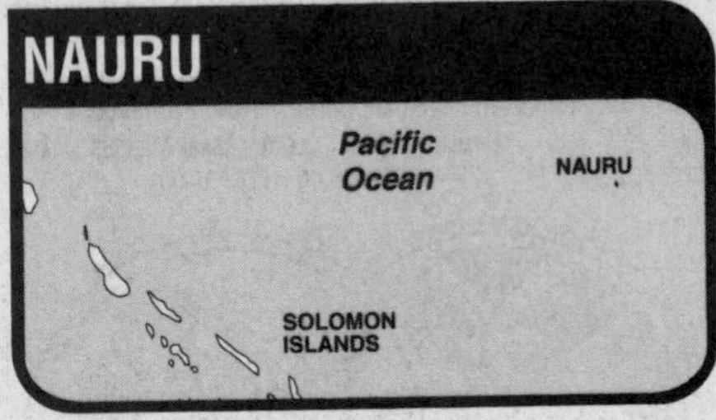

The Republic of Nauru, formerly Pleasant Island, is an island republic in the western Pacific Ocean west of the Gilbert Islands. It has an area of 8-1/2 sq. mi. and a population of 7,254. It is known for its phosphate deposits.

The island was discovered in 1798. It was annexed by Germany in 1888 and made a part of the Marshall Island protectorate. In 1914 the island was occupied by Australia and placed under mandate in 1919. During World War II it was seized by the Japanese in August, 1942. It became a joint Australian, British and New Zealand trust territory in 1947 and remained as such until it became an independent republic in 1968. Nauru has a unique relationship with the Commonwealth of Nations.

RULER

British, until 1968

MONETARY SYSTEM

100 Cents = 1 (Australian) Dollar

REPUBLIC

DECIMAL COINAGE

KM# 12 DOLLAR

Copper-Nickel, 38.6 mm. **Obv:** National arms **Obv. Legend:** BANK OF NAURU **Rev:** Queen Elizabeth and Winston Churchill standing facing while inspecting bomb damage to palace in 1940 **Rev. Legend:** QUEEN ELIZABETH THE QUEEN MOTHER **Edge:** Reeded

Date	Mintage	VF20	XF40	MS60	MS63	MS65
1996	—	PF63 6.00	PF65 9.00			

KM# 49 2 DOLLARS

15.98 g., 0.925 Silver 0.4752 oz. ASW, 28.4 mm. **Subject:** Queen Mother, 99th Birthday **Obv:** National arms **Rev:** Queen Mother and Churchill inspecting bombed Buckingham Palace during WWII

Date	Mintage	VF20	XF40	MS60	MS63	MS65
1999	50,000	PF65 40.00	PF67 45.00			

KM# 1 10 DOLLARS

38.70 g., 0.925 Silver 1.1509 oz. ASW **Subject:** Silver Jubilee of Independence **Obv:** National arms **Rev:** Island of Nauru value below

Date	Mintage	VF20	XF40	MS60	MS63	MS65
1993	1,000	PF65 350	PF67 375			

KM# 2 10 DOLLARS

31.47 g., 0.925 Silver 0.9359 oz. ASW **Subject:** Noah's Ark **Obv:** National arms **Rev:** Man, woman and animals in ark

Date	Mintage	VF20	XF40	MS60	MS63	MS65
1993	Est. 15000	PF65 40.00	PF67 45.00			

KM# 5 10 DOLLARS

31.47 g., 0.925 Silver 0.9359 oz. ASW **Series:** Endangered Wildlife **Obv:** National arms **Rev:** Songbirds

Date	Mintage	VF20	XF40	MS60	MS63	MS65
1993	Est. 10000	PF65 45.00	PF67 50.00			

KM# 3 10 DOLLARS

31.47 g., 0.925 Silver 0.9359 oz. ASW **Subject:** World Cup Soccer **Obv:** National arms **Rev:** Soccer player and soccer ball

Date	Mintage	VF20	XF40	MS60	MS63	MS65
1994	30,000	PF65 40.00	PF67 45.00			

KM# 6 10 DOLLARS

31.47 g., 0.925 Silver 0.9359 oz. ASW **Subject:** Queen Mother Visits Bombed Palace **Obv:** National arms **Rev:** Figures standing in front of bombed building

Date	Mintage	VF20	XF40	MS60	MS63	MS65
1994	Est. 30000	PF65 30.00	PF67 35.00			

KM# 7 10 DOLLARS

31.47 g., 0.925 Silver 0.9359 oz. ASW **Subject:** John Fearn **Obv:** National arms **Rev:** Ship

Date	Mintage	VF20	XF40	MS60	MS63	MS65
1994	Est. 15000	PF65 35.00	PF67 40.00			

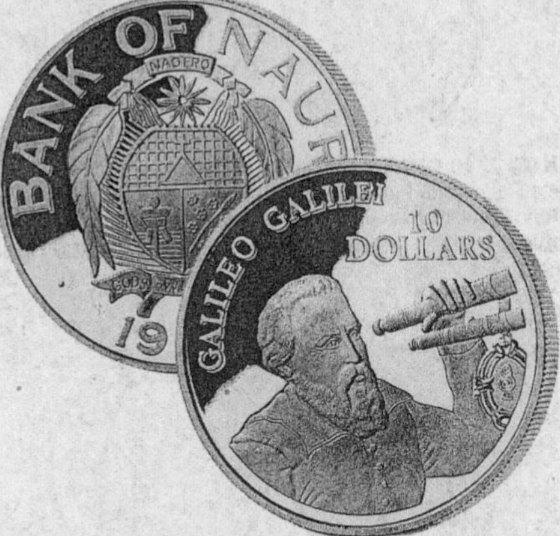

KM# 8 10 DOLLARS

31.47 g., 0.925 Silver 0.9359 oz. ASW **Obv:** National arms **Rev:** Bust with telescope facing right

Date	Mintage	VF20	XF40	MS60	MS63	MS65
1994	Est. 10000	PF65 45.00	PF67 50.00			

KM# 9 10 DOLLARS

31.47 g., 0.925 Silver 0.9359 oz. ASW, 38.61 mm. **Series:** Olympics **Obv:** National arms **Rev:** Weight lifter **Edge:** Reeded

Date	Mintage	VF20	XF40	MS60	MS63	MS65
1995	Est. 30000	PF65 30.00	PF67 35.00			

KM# 16 10 DOLLARS
Silver, 39 mm. **Obv:** National arms **Obv. Legend:** BANK OF NAURU **Rev:** Castle Mey in Scotland

Date	Mintage	VF20	XF40	MS60	MS63	MS65
1998	—	PF65 30.00	PF67 35.00			

KM# 48 10 DOLLARS
31.47 g., 0.925 Silver 0.9359 oz. ASW, 38.61 mm. **Subject:** Queen Mother, 98th Birthday

Date	Mintage	VF20	XF40	MS60	MS63	MS65
1998	—	PF65 40.00	PF67 45.00			

KM# 4 50 DOLLARS
8.05 g., 0.583 Gold 0.1509 oz. AGW **Series:** 1996 Olympics **Obv:** National arms **Rev:** Javelin throwing

Date	Mintage	VF20	XF40	MS60	MS63	MS65
1994	3,000	PF65 250	PF67 300			

KM# 10 50 DOLLARS
7.78 g., 0.5833 Gold 0.1458 oz. AGW **Obv:** National arms **Rev:** Crowned emblem above steamship

Date	Mintage	VF20	XF40	MS60	MS63	MS65
1994	—	PF65 225	PF67 275			

KM# 11 50 DOLLARS
7.78 g., 0.5833 Gold 0.1458 oz. AGW **Subject:** Endangered Wildlife **Obv:** National arms **Rev:** Sea otter

Date	Mintage	VF20	XF40	MS60	MS63	MS65
1995	Est. 2000	PF65 245	PF67 295			

KM# 17 50 DOLLARS
7.78 g., 0.583 Gold 0.1458 oz. AGW **Obv:** National arms **Obv. Legend:** BANK OF NAURU **Rev:** Queen Elizabeth and Winston Churchill standing facing while inspecting bomb damage to palace in 1940 **Rev. Legend:** QUEEN ELIZABETH THE QUEEN MOTHER

Date	Mintage	VF20	XF40	MS60	MS63	MS65
1998	—	PF65 225	PF67 275			

The Kingdom of Nepal, the world's only surviving Hindu kingdom, is a landlocked country occupying the southern slopes of the Himalayas. It has an area of 56,136 sq. mi. (140,800 sq. km.) and a population of 27 million. Capital: Kathmandu. Nepal has deposits of coal, copper, iron and cobalt, but they are largely unexploited. Agriculture is the principal economic activity. Rice, timber and jute are exported, with tourism being the other major foreign exchange earner.

Apart from a brief Muslim invasion in the 14th century, Nepal was able to avoid the mainstream of Northern Indian politics, due to its impregnable position in the mountains. It is therefore a unique survivor of the medieval Hindu and Buddhist culture of Northern India, which was largely destroyed by the successive waves of Muslim invasions.

Apart from agriculture, Nepal owed its prosperity to its position on one of the easiest trade routes between the great monasteries of central Tibet, and India. Nepal made full use of this, and a trading community was set up in Lhasa during the 16th century, and Nepalese coins became the accepted currency medium in Tibet.

A popular revolution in 1950 toppled the Rana family and reconstituted power in the throne. In 1959 King Mahendra declared Nepal a constitutional monarchy, and in 1962 a new constitution set up a system of *panchayat* (village council) democracy. In 1990, following political unrest, the king's powers were reduced. The country then adopted a system of parliamentary democracy.

On June 2, 2001 tragedy struck the royal family when Crown Prince Dipendra used an assault rifle to kill his father, mother and other members of the royal family as the result of a dispute over his current lady friend. He died 48 hours later, as King, from self inflicted gunshot wounds. Gyanendra began his second reign as King (his first was a short time as a toddler, 1950-51).

DATING

Saka Era (SE)

Up until 1888AD all coins of the Gorkha Dynasty were dated in the Saka era (SE). To convert from Saka to AD take Saka date and add 78 to arrive at the AD date. Coins dated with this era have SE before the date in the following listing.

Bikram Samvat Era (VS)

From 1888AD most copper coins were dated in the Bikram Samvat (VS) era. To convert take VS date - 57 =AD date. Coins with this era have VS before the year in the listing. With the exception of a few gold coins struck in 1890 & 1892, silver and gold coins only changed to the VS era in 1911AD, but now this era is used for all coins struck in Nepal.

RULERS

SHAH DYNASTY

पृथ्वी वीर विक्रम

Prithvi Bir Bikram
SE1803-1833/1881-1911AD, VS1938-1968/

लक्ष्मी दिव्येश्वरी

Queen of Prithvi Bir Bikram: Lakshmi Divyeswari

त्रिभुवनवीर विक्रम

Tribhuvana Bir Bikram
VS1968-2007, 2007-2011/1911-1950, 1951-1955AD (First reign)
VS2058-/2001-AD (Second reign)

ज्ञानेन्द्रवीर विक्रम

Gyanendra Bir Bikram
VS2007/1950-1951AD

महेन्द्रवीर विक्रम

Mahendra Bir Bikram
VS2012-2028/1955-1971AD

रत्न राज लक्ष्मी

Queen of Mahendra Bir Bikram: Ratna Rajya Lakshmi

वीरेन्द्र वीर विक्रम

Birendra Bir Bikram
VS2028-2058 /1971-2001AD

ऐश्वर्य राज्य लक्ष्मी देवी

Queen of Birendra Bir Bikram: Aishvarya Rajya Lakshmi
VS2028-2058 /1971-2001AD

MONETARY SYSTEM

Many of the mohars circulated in Tibet as well as in Nepal, and on a number of occasions coins were struck from bullion supplied by the Tibetan authorities. The smaller denominations never circulated in Tibet, but some of the mohars were cut for use as small change in Tibet.

In these listings only major changes in design have been noted. There are numerous minor varieties of ornamentation or spelling.

With a few exceptions, most all coins were struck at Kathmandu.

COPPER

Initially the copper paisa was not fixed in value relative to the silver coins, and generally fluctuated in value from1/32 mohar in 1865AD to around 1/50 mohar after 1880AD, and was fixed at that value in 1903AD.

4 Dam = 1 Paisa
2 Paisa = 1 Dyak, Adhani

COPPER and SILVER
Decimal Series

100 Paisa = 1 Rupee

Although the value of the copper paisa was fixed at 100 paisa to the rupee in 1903, it was not until 1932 that silver coins were struck in the decimal system.

GOLD COINAGE

Nepalese gold coinage, until recently, did not carry any denominations and was traded for silver, etc. at the local bullion exchange rate. The three basic weight standards used in the following listing are distinguished for convenience, although all were known as Asarphi (gold coin) locally as follows:

GOLD MOHAR
5.60 g multiples and fractions

TOLA
12.48 g multiples and fractions

GOLD RUPEE or ASHRPHI/ASARFI
11.66 g multiples and fractions
(Reduced to 10.00 g in 1966)

NOTE: In some instances the gold and silver issues were struck from the same dies.

NUMERALS

Nepal has used more variations of numerals on their coins than any other nation. The most common are illustrated in the numeral chart in the introduction. The chart below illustrates some variations encompassing the last four centuries.

1	2	3	4	5	6	7	8	9	0
१	२	३	४	५	६	७	८	९	०

NUMERICS

Half	आधा
One	एक
Two	दुइ
Four	चार
Five	पाच
Ten	दसा
Twenty	विसा

पचीसा
Twenty-five

पचासा
Fifty

सय
Hundred

DENOMINATIONS

पैसा
Paisa

दाम
Dam

मोरु
Mohar

रुपैयाँ
Rupee

असार्फी
Ashrapi

अश्रफी
Asarphi (Asarfi)

DIE VARIETIES

Although the same dies were usually used both for silver and gold minor denominations, the gold Mohar is easily recognized being less ornate. The following illustrations are of a silver Mohar, KM#602 and a gold Mohar KM#615 issued by Surendra Bikram Saha Deva in the period SE1769-1803/1847-1881AD. Note the similar reverse legend. The obverse usually will start with the character for the word Shri either in single or multiples, the latter as Shri Shri Shri or Shri 3.

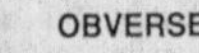

OBVERSE

SILVER SE1791 GOLD SE1793

LEGEND

श्री श्रीश्री सुरेन्द्र बिक्रम साहदेव

Shri Shri Shri Surendra Bikram Saha Deva (date).

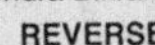

REVERSE

SILVER GOLD

LEGEND
(in center)

श्री ३ भवानी

Shri 3 Bhavani
(around outer circle)

श्री श्री श्री गोरषनाथ

Shri Shri Shri Gorakhanatha

SHAH DYNASTY

KINGDOM

Shah Dynasty

Prithvi Bir Bikram
VS1938-1968 / 1881-1911AD

COPPER COINAGE

With Arabic inscription. The Nepalese copper coins within the border of Nepal were struck in the Nepalese hills.

KM# 620.2 DAM
Copper **Rev. Inscription:** Sarkar

Date	Mintage	F12	VF20	XF40	MS60	MS63
VS(19)64	—	7.50	12.00	15.00	20.00	—

KM# 621 DAM
Copper

Date	Mintage	F12	VF20	XF40	MS60	MS63
VS(19)68	—	4.50	7.50	10.00	17.50	—
VS(19)68	—	PF60 55.00	PF63 60.00			

KM# 622 1/2 PAISA
Copper, 19 mm.

Date	Mintage	F12	VF20	XF40	MS60	MS63
VS(19)64	—	4.50	7.50	10.00	17.50	—
VS(19)68	—	4.50	7.50	10.00	17.50	—
VS(19)68	—	PF60 55.00	PF63 60.00			

KM# 628 PAISA
Copper **Obv:** Legend within sprays **Rev:** Legend within sprays **Note:** Varieties in sprays exist. Coin and medal alignment varieties exist. Also struck between VS1343-1357/1943-57AD.

Date	Mintage	G4	VG8	F12	VF20	XF40
VS1959	—	—	1.00	1.50	3.00	5.00
VS1960	—	—	1.00	1.50	3.00	5.00
VS1961	—	—	1.00	1.50	3.00	5.00
VS1962	—	—	1.00	1.50	3.00	5.00
VS(19)62	—	—	—	—	—	—
VS1963	—	—	1.00	1.50	3.00	5.00
VS1964	—	—	1.00	1.50	3.00	5.00
VS(19)64	—	—	—	—	—	—

KM# 629 PAISA
Copper **Obv:** Legend within squares **Rev:** Legend within squares

Date	Mintage	G4	VG8	F12	VF20	XF40
VS1959	—	—	1.00	1.50	2.50	4.00
VS1962	—	—	1.00	1.50	2.50	4.00
VS1963	—	—	1.00	1.50	2.50	4.00
VS1964	—	—	1.00	1.50	2.50	4.00
VS1965	—	—	1.00	1.50	2.50	4.00
VS1966	—	—	1.00	1.50	2.50	4.00
VS1967	—	—	1.00	1.50	2.50	4.00
VS1968	—	—	1.00	1.50	2.50	4.00

KM# 630 PAISA
Copper-Iron Alloy **Obv:** Legend within square **Rev:** Legend within circle **Note:** Magnetic and non-magnetic alloy.

Date	Mintage	G4	VG8	F12	VF20	XF40
VS1959	—	—	7.50	12.50	20.00	33.50

KM# 631 PAISA
Copper, 23 mm. **Note:** Also Tribhuvaua Bir Bikram struck a Paisa VS1968, see KM#685.1.

Date	Mintage	F12	VF20	XF40	MS60	MS63
VS1964	—	5.50	9.00	15.00	22.50	—
VS1968	—	8.50	13.50	20.00	30.00	—
VS1968	—	PF60 80.00	PF63 90.00			

KM# 633 2 PAISA (Dak)
Copper-Iron Alloy **Obv:** Legend within square **Rev:** Legend within circle **Note:** Magnetic and non-magnetic alloy. Similar to KM#630.

Date	Mintage	G4	VG8	F12	VF20	XF40
VS1959	—	—	12.50	17.50	25.00	50.00

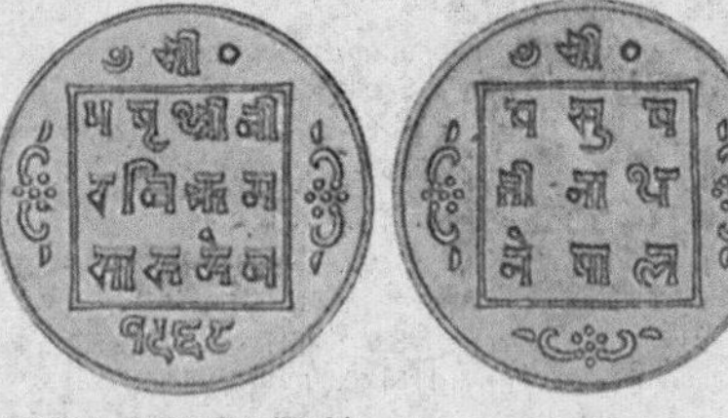

KM# 634 2 PAISA (Dak)
Copper, 26.5 mm.

Date	Mintage	F12	VF20	XF40	MS60	MS63
VS1964	—	8.50	13.50	20.00	30.00	—
VS1968	—	9.00	15.00	22.50	35.00	—
VS1968	—	PF60 100	PF63 115			

SILVER COINAGE

KM# 643 1/4 MOHAR
1.40 g., Silver **Rev:** Moon and dot for sun **Note:** Machine struck. Also struck between SE1804-1817.

Date	Mintage	F12	VF20	XF40	MS60	MS63
SE1827	—	2.25	5.00	7.00	9.00	15.00

KM# 644 1/4 MOHAR
1.40 g., Silver, 15.5 mm. **Note:** Machine struck.

Date	Mintage	F12	VF20	XF40	MS60	MS63
SE1833	—	2.25	5.00	7.00	9.00	15.00
SE1833	—	PF60 30.00	PF63 35.00			

KM# 647 1/2 MOHAR
2.77 g., Silver, 21 mm. **Edge:** Plain **Note:** Machine struck. Varieties exist. Also struck between SE1803-1817.

Date	Mintage	F12	VF20	XF40	MS60	MS63
SE1824	—	30.00	35.00	42.00	48.00	65.00

KM# 648 1/2 MOHAR
2.77 g., Silver, 21 mm. **Note:** Machine struck.

Date	Mintage	F12	VF20	XF40	MS60	MS63
SE1826	—	5.00	7.00	9.00	15.00	25.00
SE1827	—	5.00	7.00	9.00	15.00	25.00
SE1829	—	5.00	7.00	9.00	15.00	25.00

KM# 649 1/2 MOHAR

2.77 g., Silver, 19 mm. **Edge:** Milled **Note:** Machine struck.

Date	Mintage	F12	VF20	XF40	MS60	MS63
SE1832	—	30.00	35.00	42.00	48.00	65.00
SE1833	—	PF60 50.00	PF63 55.00			
SE1833	—	3.00	5.00	7.00	9.00	15.00

KM# 651.1 MOHAR

5.60 g., Silver, 26 mm. **Edge:** Plain **Note:** Machine struck. Also struck between SE1807-1822.

Date	Mintage	F12	VF20	XF40	MS60	MS63
SE1823	—	3.00	5.00	9.00	12.00	20.00
SE1824	—	3.00	5.00	9.00	12.00	20.00
SE1825	—	3.00	5.00	9.00	12.00	20.00
SE1826	—	3.00	5.00	9.00	12.00	20.00
SE1827	—	3.00	5.00	9.00	12.00	20.00

KM# 652 MOHAR

5.60 g., Silver, 26 mm. **Rev:** Gold die, in error

Date	Mintage	F12	VF20	XF40	MS60	MS63
SE1825	—	14.00	20.00	35.00	45.00	65.00

KM# 651.2 MOHAR

5.60 g., Silver, 26 mm. **Edge:** Milled **Note:** Machine struck.

Date	Mintage	F12	VF20	XF40	MS60	MS63
SE1826	—	3.00	5.00	9.00	12.00	20.00
SE1827	—	3.00	5.00	9.00	12.00	20.00
SE1828	—	3.00	5.00	9.00	12.00	20.00
SE1829	—	3.00	5.00	9.00	12.00	20.00
SE1830	—	3.00	5.00	9.00	12.00	20.00
SE1831	—	3.00	5.00	9.00	12.00	20.00
SE1832	—	3.00	5.00	9.00	12.00	20.00
SE1833	—	—	—	—	45.00	75.00

Note: The date SE1833 was only issued in presentation sets

KM# 655 2 MOHARS

11.20 g., Silver, 27 mm. **Edge:** Milled **Note:** Machine struck.

Date	Mintage	F12	VF20	XF40	MS60	MS63
SE1829	—	15.00	20.00	35.00	50.00	75.00
SE1831	—	9.00	13.00	17.00	30.00	45.00

KM# 656 2 MOHARS

Silver, 29 mm. **Note:** Machine struck.

Date	Mintage	F12	VF20	XF40	MS60	MS63
SE1832	—	5.00	10.00	15.00	20.00	35.00
SE1833	—	5.00	10.00	15.00	20.00	35.00
SE1833	—	PF60 100	PF63 115			

KM# 658 4 MOHARS

22.40 g., Silver, 29 mm. **Edge:** Milled

Date	Mintage	F12	VF20	XF40	MS60	MS63
SE1833	—	50.00	75.00	125	200	275
SE1833	—	PF63 625				

GOLD COINAGE

KM# 659 DAM

0.04 g., Gold **Obv:** Five characters around sword **Note:** Uniface.

Date	Mintage	F12	VF20	XF40	MS60	MS63
ND(1881-1911)	—	22.50	30.00	45.00	60.00	—

KM# 660 DAM

0.04 g., Gold **Obv:** Four characters around sword **Note:** Uniface.

Date	Mintage	F12	VF20	XF40	MS60	MS63
ND(1881-1911)	—	22.50	30.00	45.00	60.00	—

Actual Size 2 x Actual Size

KM# 661 DAM

0.04 g., Gold **Obv:** Circle around characters **Note:** Uniface.

Date	Mintage	F12	VF20	XF40	MS60	MS63
ND(1881-1911)	—	22.50	30.00	45.00	60.00	—

Actual Size 2 x Actual Size

KM# 662 DAM

0.04 g., Gold **Obv:** Two characters below sword **Note:** Uniface. Varieties exist.

Date	Mintage	F12	VF20	XF40	MS60	MS63
ND(1881-1911)	—	22.50	30.00	45.00	60.00	—

Actual Size 2 x Actual Size

KM# 663 1/64 MOHAR

0.09 g., Gold **Obv:** Four characters around sword **Note:** Uniface.

Date	Mintage	F12	VF20	XF40	MS60	MS63
ND(1881-1911)	—	27.50	37.50	50.00	65.00	—

Actual Size 2 x Actual Size

KM# 664 1/64 MOHAR

0.09 g., Gold **Obv:** Five characters around sword **Note:** Uniface.

Date	Mintage	F12	VF20	XF40	MS60	MS63
ND(1881-1911)	—	27.50	37.50	50.00	65.00	—

KM# 665 1/32 MOHAR

0.18 g., Gold **Obv:** Five characters around sword **Note:** Uniface.

Date	Mintage	F12	VF20	XF40	MS60	MS63
ND(1881-1911)	—	40.00	80.00	150	200	—

KM# 666 1/32 MOHAR

0.18 g., Gold **Obv:** Four characters around sword **Note:** Uniface.

Date	Mintage	F12	VF20	XF40	MS60	MS63
ND(1881-1911)	—	30.00	60.00	150	200	—

KM# 667 1/16 MOHAR

0.35 g., Gold

Date	Mintage	F12	VF20	XF40	MS60	MS63
ND(1881-1911)	—	30.00	80.00	150	200	—

KM# 668 1/16 MOHAR

0.35 g., Gold

Date	Mintage	F12	VF20	XF40	MS60	MS63
SE(18)33	—	—	38.00	75.00	190	255
SE(18)33 Proof	—	—	—	—	—	—

KM# 669.1 1/8 MOHAR

0.70 g., Gold **Obv:** Six characters

Date	Mintage	F12	VF20	XF40	MS60	MS63
ND (1881)	—	—	45.00	80.00	150	200

KM# 669.2 1/8 MOHAR

0.70 g., Gold **Obv:** Five characters **Note:** Varieties exist.

Date	Mintage	F12	VF20	XF40	MS60	MS63
ND (1881)	—	—	45.00	80.00	150	200

KM# 670 1/8 MOHAR

0.70 g., Gold

Date	Mintage	F12	VF20	XF40	MS60	MS63
SE(18)33	—	—	55.00	110	190	255

KM# 671.1 1/4 MOHAR

1.40 g., Gold

Date	Mintage	F12	VF20	XF40	MS60	MS63
SE1823	—	—	115	150	200	255
SE1829	—	—	110	125	150	200

KM# 671.2 1/4 MOHAR

1.40 g., Gold

Date	Mintage	F12	VF20	XF40	MS60	MS63
SE1833	—	—	110	125	150	200
SE1833 Proof	—	—	—	—	—	—

KM# 672.3 1/2 MOHAR
2.80 g., Gold

Date	Mintage	F12	VF20	XF40	MS60	MS63
SE1823	—	—	300	350	400	525

KM# 672.4 1/2 MOHAR
2.80 g., Gold

Date	Mintage	F12	VF20	XF40	MS60	MS63
SE1829	—	—	195	220	245	300

KM# 672.5 1/2 MOHAR
2.80 g., Gold

Date	Mintage	F12	VF20	XF40	MS60	MS63
SE1833	—	—	290	325	375	450
SE1833 Proof	—	—	—	—	—	—

KM# 673.1 MOHAR
5.60 g., Gold

Date	Mintage	F12	VF20	XF40	MS60	MS63
SE1823	—	300	350	450	550	725
SE1825	—	300	350	450	550	725
SE1826	—	300	350	450	550	725
SE1827	—	300	350	450	550	725

KM# 673.2 MOHAR
5.60 g., Gold **Edge:** Milled

Date	Mintage	F12	VF20	XF40	MS60	MS63
SE1828	—	300	350	450	550	725
SE1829	—	300	350	450	550	725
SE1831	—	300	350	450	550	725
SE1833	—	300	350	450	550	725
SE1833 Proof	—	—	—	—	—	—

KM# 674.3 TOLA
12.48 g., Gold **Edge:** Plain

Date	Mintage	F12	VF20	XF40	MS60	MS63
SE1823	—	—	625	650	700	750
SE1824	—	—	625	650	700	750
SE1825	—	—	625	650	700	750
SE1826	—	—	625	650	700	750

KM# 675.1 TOLA
12.48 g., Gold **Edge:** Vertical milling

Date	Mintage	F12	VF20	XF40	MS60	MS63
SE1828	—	—	625	650	700	750
SE1829	—	—	625	650	700	750
SE1831	—	—	625	650	700	750
SE1832	—	—	625	650	700	750
SE1833	—	—	625	650	700	750
SE1833 Proof	—	—	—	—	—	—

KM# 678 DUITOLA ASARPHI
23.32 g., Gold **Edge:** Plain

Date	Mintage	F12	VF20	XF40	MS60	MS63
SE1825	—	1,250	1,300	1,600	2,050	2,750

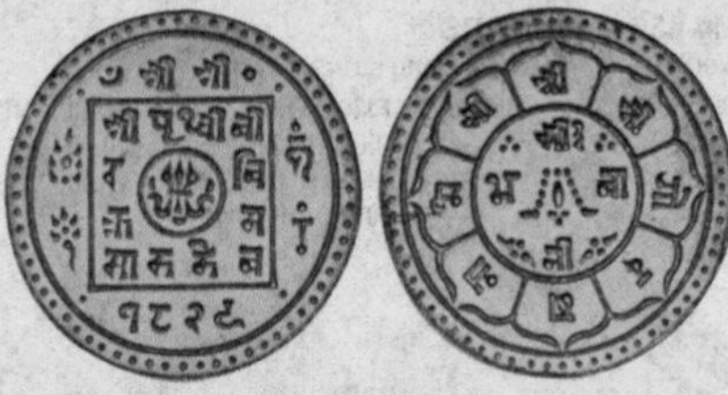

KM# 679 DUITOLA ASARPHI
23.32 g., Gold **Edge:** Milled

Date	Mintage	F12	VF20	XF40	MS60	MS63
SE1829	—	1,250	1,300	1,600	2,050	2,750

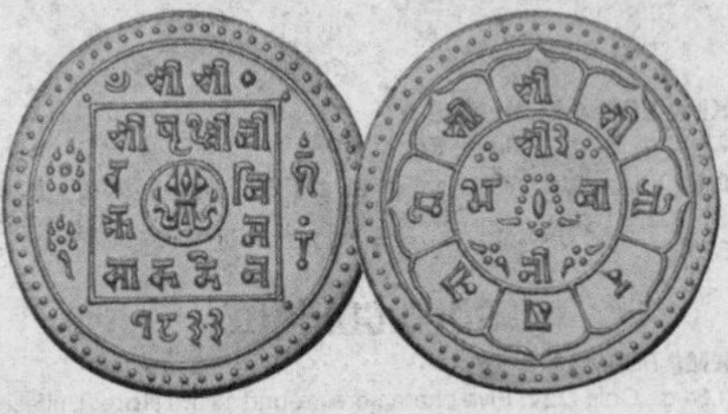

KM# 680 DUITOLA ASARPHI
23.32 g., Gold **Edge:** Milled

Date	Mintage	F12	VF20	XF40	MS60	MS63
SE1833	—	1,250	1,300	1,600	2,050	2,750
SE1833 Proof	—	—	—	—	—	—

Tribhuvana Bir Bikram
VS1968-2007 / 1911-1950AD

COPPER COINAGE

With Arabic inscription. The Nepalese copper coins within the border of Nepal were struck in the Nepalese hills.

KM# 684 1/2 PAISA
Copper **Note:** Struck only for presentation sets.

Date	Mintage	VF20	XF40	MS60	MS63	MS65
VS1978	—	—	—	—	50.00	75.00
VS1985	—	—	—	—	50.00	75.00

KM# 685.1 PAISA
Copper **Note:** Machine struck. Also Prithvi Bir Bikram struck a Paisa VS1968, see KM#631.

Date	Mintage	G4	VG8	F12	VF20	XF40
VS1968	—	—	—	—	10.00	20.00

KM# 685.2 PAISA
Copper **Note:** Hand struck. Many varieties exist.

Date	Mintage	G4	VG8	F12	VF20	XF40
VS1969	—	—	1.00	1.50	2.25	3.50
VS1970	—	—	1.00	1.50	2.25	3.50
VS1971	—	—	1.00	1.50	2.25	3.50
VS1972	—	—	1.00	1.50	2.25	3.50
VS1973	—	—	1.00	1.50	2.25	3.50
VS1974	—	—	1.00	1.50	2.25	3.50
VS1975	—	—	1.00	1.50	2.25	3.50
VS1976	—	—	1.00	1.50	2.25	3.50
VS1977	—	—	1.00	1.50	2.25	3.50

KM# 686.1 PAISA
5.20 g., Copper, 23.5 mm. **Rev:** Without "Nepal" below

Date	Mintage	F12	VF20	XF40	MS60	MS63
VS1975	—	—	—	37.50	50.00	75.00

KM# 686.2 PAISA
3.70 g., Copper, 21.5 mm. **Rev:** Without "Nepal" below

Date	Mintage	G4	VG8	F12	VF20	XF40
VS1975	—	—	—	—	—	—

Note: The above issues are believed to be patterns

KM# 687.1 PAISA
Copper, 21.5 mm. **Obv:** Outlined Khukris **Note:** Machine struck. Fine style. Weight varies: 3.50-3.80 g.

Date	Mintage	F12	VF20	XF40	MS60	MS63
VS1975 (1918)	—	—	6.00	8.00	12.00	25.00
VS1976 (1919)	—	—	6.00	8.00	12.00	25.00
VS1977 (1920)	—	—	3.00	5.00	8.00	15.00
Note: Inverted date						
VS1977 (1920)	—	—	3.00	5.00	8.00	15.00
VS1978 (1921)	—	—	3.00	5.00	8.00	15.00

KM# 687.4 PAISA
3.75 g., Brass **Obv:** Fine style crossed khukris

Date	Mintage	VG8	F12	VF20	XF40	MS60
VS1975	—	0.50	1.25	1.75	3.00	6.00
VS1976	—	0.50	1.25	1.75	3.00	6.00

KM# 687.2 PAISA
Copper, 22 mm. **Obv:** Outlined Khukris always right over left **Note:** Machine struck. Weight varies: 2.6-3.1 grams. Prev. KM#688.

Date	Mintage	F12	VF20	XF40	MS60	MS63
VS1978	—	1.25	1.75	3.00	6.00	—
VS1979	—	1.25	1.75	3.00	6.00	—
VS1980	—	1.50	3.00	5.00	10.00	—
VS1981	—	1.50	3.00	5.00	10.00	—
VS1982	—	1.25	1.75	3.00	6.00	—
VS1984	—	1.25	1.75	3.00	6.00	—
VS1985	—	1.25	1.75	3.00	6.00	—
VS1986	—	1.25	1.75	3.00	6.00	—
VS1987	—	1.25	1.75	3.00	6.00	—

KM# 687.3 PAISA
3.75 g., Copper, 21 mm. **Obv:** Outlined Khukris left over right and right over left **Note:** Crude, hand struck. Varieties of the Khukris exist

Date	Mintage	G4	VG8	F12	VF20	XF40
VS1978	—	2.00	3,00	4.50	7.50	—
VS1979	—	2.00	3.00	4.50	7.50	—
VS1980	—	4.00	5.00	7.50	12.50	—
VS1981	—	4.00	5.00	7.50	12.50	—
VS1982	—	4.00	5.00	7.50	12.50	—
VS1983	—	4.00	5.00	7.50	12.50	—

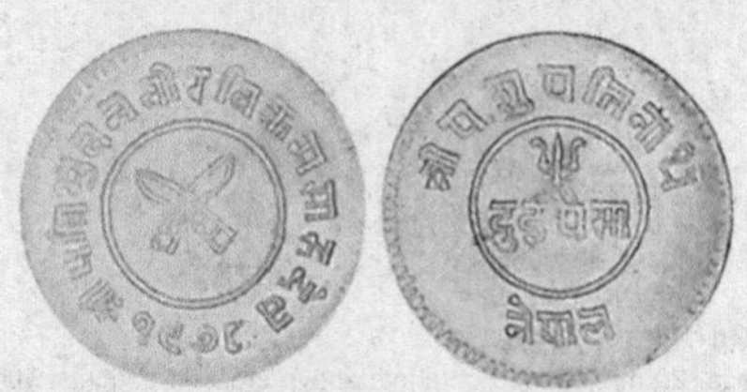

KM# 689.1 2 PAISA

Copper, 26 mm. **Obv:** Outlined Khukris **Note:** Machine struck. Varieties of the Khukris exist. Weight varies: 6.9-7.5 grams.

Date	Mintage	VG8	F12	VF20	XF40	MS60
VS1976	—	—	1.00	2.00	3.00	5.00
VS1977	—	—	1.00	2.00	3.00	5.00
VS1977	—	—	3.50	5.00	8.50	13.50
Inverted date						

KM# 689.4 2 PAISA

Brass **Obv:** Fine style crossed khukris

Date	Mintage	VG8	F12	VF20	XF40	MS60
VS1976	—	1.00	2.00	3.00	5.00	—

KM# 689.2 2 PAISA

Copper **Obv:** Outlined Khukris left over right and right over left **Note:** Crude struck. Varieties of the Khukris exist. Weight varies: 4.6-5.5 grams.

Date	Mintage	G4	VG8	F12	VF20	XF40
VS1978	—	—	1.00	2.00	3.50	6.50
VS1979	—	—	1.00	2.00	3.50	6.50
VS1980	—	—	1.00	2.00	3.50	6.50
VS1981	—	—	1.00	2.00	3.50	6.50
VS1982	—	—	1.00	2.00	3.50	6.50
VS1983	—	—	1.00	2.00	3.50	6.50
VS1984	—	—	1.00	2.00	3.50	6.50
VS1985	—	—	1.00	2.00	3.50	6.50
VS1986	—	—	1.50	2.50	4.00	7.50
VS1987	—	—	1.50	2.50	4.00	7.50
VS1988	—	—	2.00	3.00	5.00	9.00

KM# 689.3 2 PAISA

5.00 g., Copper **Obv:** Outlined Khukris always right over left **Note:** Machine struck. Weight varies: 5.00-5.700 grams.

Date	Mintage	VG8	F12	VF20	XF40	MS60
VS1978	—	1.00	2.00	3.00	4.50	—
VS1979	—	1.00	2.00	3.00	4.50	—
VS1980	—	1.00	2.00	3.00	4.50	—
VS1981	—	1.00	2.00	3.00	4.50	—
VS1982	—	1.00	2.00	3.00	4.50	—
VS1983	—	1.00	2.00	3.00	4.50	—
VS1984	—	1.00	2.00	3.00	4.50	—
VS1991	—	1.50	2.50	4.00	6.00	—

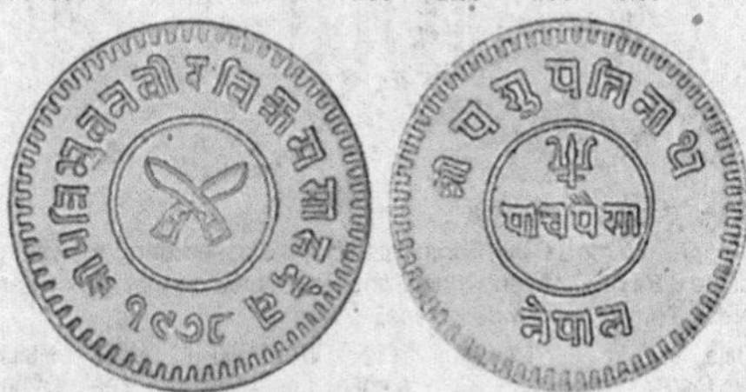

KM# 690.1 5 PAISA

Copper, 29.5 mm. **Obv:** Outlined Khukris **Note:** Weight varies: 18.1-18.8 g.

Date	Mintage	F12	VF20	XF40	MS60	MS63
VS1976	—	6.00	10.00	14.00	20.00	—
Note: Fine style						
VS1977	—	1.25	2.25	3.50	6.00	—
VS1977	—	3.00	5.00	8.50	12.50	—
Inverted date						

KM# 690.2 5 PAISA

Copper **Obv:** Outlined Khukris, left over right and right over left **Note:** Crude hand struck. Weight varies: 11.0-13.2 g. Size varies: 29.0-32.5mm.

Date	Mintage	F12	VF20	XF40	MS60	MS63
VS1978	—	1.75	3.00	5.00	8.00	—
VS1979	—	1.75	3.00	5.00	8.00	—
VS1980	—	1.75	3.00	5.00	8.00	—
VS1981	—	1.75	3.00	5.00	8.00	—
VS1982	—	1.75	3.00	5.00	8.00	—
VS1983	—	1.75	3.00	5.00	8.00	—
VS1984	—	1.75	3.00	5.00	8.00	—
VS1985	—	1.75	3.00	5.00	8.00	—
VS1986	—	1.75	3.00	5.00	8.00	—
VS1987	—	1.75	3.00	5.00	8.00	—
VS1988	—	6.00	10.00	14.00	20.00	—
VS1989	—	1.75	3.00	5.00	8.00	—

KM# 690.3 5 PAISA

14.00 g., Copper **Obv:** Outlined Khukris always right over left **Note:** Machine struck. Weight varies: 13.5-14.0 g. Varieties exist. Size varies: 29.0-30.0mm.

Date	Mintage	F12	VF20	XF40	MS60	MS63
VS1978	—	1.25	2.25	3.50	5.00	—
VS1979	—	1.25	2.25	3.50	5.00	—
VS1979	—	1.25	2.25	3.50	5.00	—
Backwards date						
VS1980	—	1.25	2.25	3.50	5.00	—
VS1981	—	1.25	2.25	3.50	5.00	—
VS1982	—	1.25	2.25	3.50	5.00	—
VS1983	—	1.25	2.25	3.50	5.00	—
VS1984	—	1.25	2.25	3.50	5.00	—
VS1991	—	15.00	20.00	25.00	30.00	—

SILVER COINAGE

KM# 691 DAM

0.04 g., Silver **Note:** Uniface.

Date	Mintage	F12	VF20	XF40	MS60	MS63
ND (1911)	—	20.00	32.00	40.00	65.00	—

KM# 692 1/4 MOHAR

1.40 g., Silver, 16 mm.

Date	Mintage	F12	VF20	XF40	MS60	MS63
VS1969	—	—	2.50	5.00	7.00	10.00
VS1970	—	—	2.50	5.00	7.00	10.00

KM# 693 1/2 MOHAR

2.80 g., Silver

Date	Mintage	F12	VF20	XF40	MS60	MS63
VS1968	—	—	3.00	5.00	7.00	10.00
VS1970	—	—	3.00	5.00	7.00	10.00
VS1971	—	—	3.00	5.00	7.00	10.00

KM# 681 1/2 MOHAR

2.77 g., Silver **Note:** In the name of "Queen Lakshmi Divyeswari" - Regent for Tribhuvana Bir Bikram.

Date	Mintage	F12	VF20	XF40	MS60	MS63
VS1971	—	—	6.00	9.00	13.00	16.00

KM# 694 MOHAR

5.60 g., Silver

Date	Mintage	F12	VF20	XF40	MS60	MS63
VS1968	—	—	7.00	9.00	12.00	15.00
VS1969	—	—	7.00	9.00	12.00	15.00
VS1971	—	—	7.00	9.00	12.00	15.00

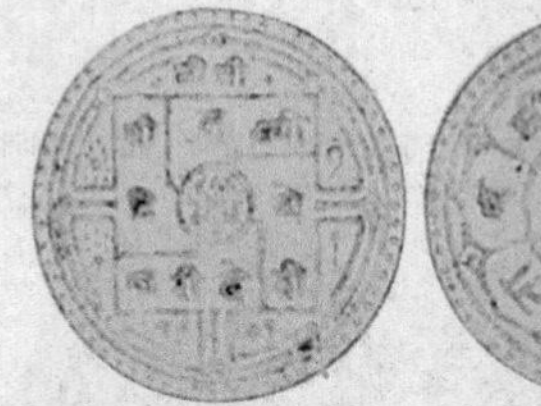

KM# 682 MOHAR

5.60 g., Silver **Note:** In the name of "Queen Lakshmi Divyeswari" - Regent for Tribhuvana Bir Bikram.

Date	Mintage	F12	VF20	XF40	MS60	MS63
VS1971	—	—	7.00	9.00	13.00	16.00

KM# 695 2 MOHARS

11.20 g., Silver, 29 mm. **Note:** Varieties exist for this type.

Date	Mintage	F12	VF20	XF40	MS60	MS63
VS1968	—	—	—	13.00	17.00	30.00
VS1969	—	—	—	13.00	17.00	30.00
VS1970	—	—	—	13.00	17.00	30.00
VS1971	—	—	—	13.00	17.00	30.00
VS1972	—	—	—	13.00	17.00	30.00
VS1973	—	—	—	13.00	17.00	30.00
VS1974	—	—	—	13.00	17.00	30.00
VS1975	—	—	—	13.00	17.00	30.00
VS1976	—	—	—	13.00	17.00	30.00
VS1977	—	—	—	13.00	17.00	30.00
VS1978	—	—	—	13.00	17.00	30.00
VS1979	—	—	—	13.00	17.00	30.00
VS1980	—	—	—	13.00	17.00	30.00
VS1982	—	—	—	13.00	17.00	30.00
VS1983	—	—	—	13.00	17.00	30.00
VS1984	—	—	—	13.00	17.00	30.00
VS1985	—	—	—	13.00	17.00	30.00
VS1986	—	—	—	13.00	17.00	30.00
VS1987	—	—	—	13.00	17.00	30.00
VS1988	—	—	—	13.00	17.00	30.00
VS1989	—	—	—	13.00	17.00	30.00

KM# 696 4 MOHARS

22.40 g., Silver

Date	Mintage	F12	VF20	XF40	MS60	MS63
VS1971	—	—	50.00	90.00	155	220

GOLD COINAGE

KM# 697 DAM

0.04 g., Gold **Note:** Uniface.

Date	Mintage	F12	VF20	XF40	MS60	MS63
ND (1911)	—	40.50	55.00	100	140	—

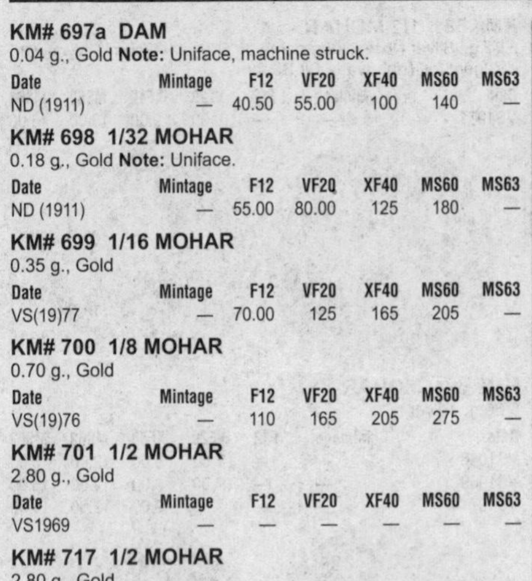

KM# 697a DAM
0.04 g., Gold **Note:** Uniface, machine struck.

Date	Mintage	F12	VF20	XF40	MS60	MS63
ND (1911)	—	40.50	55.00	100	140	—

KM# 698 1/32 MOHAR
0.18 g., Gold **Note:** Uniface.

Date	Mintage	F12	VF20	XF40	MS60	MS63
ND (1911)	—	55.00	80.00	125	180	—

KM# 699 1/16 MOHAR
0.35 g., Gold

Date	Mintage	F12	VF20	XF40	MS60	MS63
VS(19)77	—	70.00	125	165	205	—

KM# 700 1/8 MOHAR
0.70 g., Gold

Date	Mintage	F12	VF20	XF40	MS60	MS63
VS(19)76	—	110	165	205	275	—

KM# 701 1/2 MOHAR
2.80 g., Gold

Date	Mintage	F12	VF20	XF40	MS60	MS63
VS1969	—	—	—	—	—	—

KM# 717 1/2 MOHAR
2.80 g., Gold

Date	Mintage	F12	VF20	XF40	MS60	MS63
VS1995	—	—	—	—	—	—

KM# 702 MOHAR
5.60 g., Gold

Date	Mintage	F12	VF20	XF40	MS60	MS63
VS1969	—	295	325	325	350	500
VS1975	—	295	325	325	350	500
VS1978	—	295	325	325	350	500
VS1979	—	295	325	325	350	500
VS1981	—	295	325	325	350	500
VS1983	—	295	325	325	350	500
VS1985	—	295	325	325	350	500
VS1986	—	295	325	325	350	500
VS1987	—	295	325	325	350	500
VS1989	—	295	325	325	350	500
VS1990	—	295	325	325	350	500
VS1991	—	295	325	325	350	500
VS1998	—	295	325	325	350	500
VS1999	—	295	325	325	350	500
VS2000	—	295	325	325	350	500
VS2003	—	295	325	325	350	500
VS2005	—	295	325	325	350	500

KM# 683 MOHAR
5.60 g., Gold **Note:** In the name of "Queen Lakshmi Divyeswari" - Regent for Tribhuvana Bir Bikram.

Date	Mintage	F12	VF20	XF40	MS60	MS63
VS1971	—	—	300	325	350	375

KM# 722 MOHAR
5.60 g., Gold

Date	Mintage	F12	VF20	XF40	MS60	MS63
VS1993	376,000	—	—	—	—	—
VS1994	283,000	—	—	—	—	—

KM# 703.1 ASHRAPHI (Tola)
Gold **Rev:** Moon and sun in center **Rev. Legend:** SRI 3 BHAVANI

Date	Mintage	F12	VF20	XF40	MS60	MS63
VS1969	—	—	450	475	525	650
VS1974	—	—	450	475	525	650
VS1975	—	—	450	475	525	650
VS1976	—	—	450	475	525	650
VS1977	—	—	450	475	525	650
VS1978	—	—	450	475	525	650
VS1979	—	—	450	475	525	650
VS1980	—	—	450	475	525	650
VS1981	—	—	450	475	525	650
VS1982	—	—	450	475	525	650
VS1983	—	—	450	475	525	650
VS1984	—	—	450	475	525	650
VS1985	—	—	450	475	525	650
VS1986	—	—	450	475	525	650
VS1987	—	—	450	475	525	650
VS1988	—	—	450	475	525	650
VS1989	—	—	450	475	525	650
VS1990	—	—	450	475	525	650
VS1991	—	—	450	475	525	650
VS1998	—	—	450	475	525	650
VS1999	—	—	450	475	525	650
VS2000	—	—	450	475	525	650
VS2003	—	—	450	475	525	650

KM# 727 ASHRAPHI (Tola)
Gold **Obv:** Trident between moon and sun above crossed Khukris in center

Date	Mintage	F12	VF20	XF40	MS60	MS63
VS1992	—	475	475	550	700	800

KM# 703.2 ASHRAPHI (Tola)
Gold

Date	Mintage	F12	VF20	XF40	MS60	MS63
VS2005	—	—	450	475	525	650

KM# 703.3 ASHRAPHI (Tola)
Gold **Rev:** 3 dots each side in center **Rev. Legend:** SRI BHAVANI

Date	Mintage	F12	VF20	XF40	MS60	MS63
VS2033 (1976)	—	—	450	475	500	625

KM# 728 DUITOLA ASARPHI
Gold **Note:** Similar to 1 Tola, KM#703.

Date	Mintage	F12	VF20	XF40	MS60	MS63
VS2005	—	875	925	1,000	1,450	—

DECIMAL COINAGE

100 Paisa = 1 Rupee

KM# 704 1/4 PAISA
Copper, 14 mm. **Obv:** Footprints above crossed daggers within circle **Rev:** Crescent moon and star flank center dagger **Note:** Struck only for presentation sets.

Date	Mintage	F12	VF20	XF40	MS60	MS63
VS2000	—	—	—	—	35.00	40.00
VS2004	—	—	—	—	35.00	40.00

KM# 705 1/2 PAISA
Copper, 16 mm. **Obv:** Footprints above crossed daggers within circle **Rev:** Crescent moon and star flank dagger at center **Note:** Struck only for presentation sets.

Date	Mintage	F12	VF20	XF40	MS60	MS63
VS2004	—	—	—	—	35.00	40.00

KM# 706.1 PAISA
Copper, 23 mm. **Obv:** Footprints above crossed daggers within circle **Rev:** Right wreath with sharp end **Note:** Prev. KM#706.

Date	Mintage	F12	VF20	XF40	MS60	MS63
VS1990	—	0.75	1.50	3.00	5.00	7.00
VS1991	—	0.75	1.50	3.00	5.00	7.00
VS1992	—	0.75	1.50	3.00	5.00	7.00

KM# 706.2 PAISA
Copper, 23 mm. **Obv:** Footprints above crossed daggers within circle **Rev:** Right wreath with round end

Date	Mintage	F12	VF20	XF40	MS60	MS63
VS1993	—	0.75	1.50	3.00	5.00	7.00
VS1994	456,000	0.75	1.50	3.00	5.00	7.00
VS1995	—	0.75	1.50	3.00	5.00	7.00
VS1996	—	0.75	1.50	3.00	5.00	7.00

KM# 707a PAISA
Brass, 20 mm. **Obv:** Footprints above crossed daggers within circle **Rev:** Crescent moon and star flank dagger at center

Date	Mintage	F12	VF20	XF40	MS60	MS63
VS2001	—	0.30	0.50	0.75	1.00	1.50
VS2003	—	0.30	0.50	0.75	1.00	1.50
VS2004	—	3.00	5.00	7.00	10.00	15.00
VS2005	—	0.30	0.50	0.75	1.00	1.50
VS2006	—	0.60	1.00	1.25	1.75	3.00

KM# 707 PAISA
1.97 g., Brass, 20 mm.

Date	Mintage	F12	VF20	XF40	MS60	MS63
VS2005	—	0.75	1.25	1.75	2.50	4.00

KM# 708 2 PAISA
Copper, 27 mm. **Obv:** Footprints above crossed daggers within circle **Rev:** Crescent moon and star flank trident at center

Date	Mintage	VG8	F12	VF20	XF40	MS60
VS1992	—	3.00	5.00	8.50	13.50	—

KM# 709.1 2 PAISA
Copper, 27 mm. **Obv:** Footprints above crossed daggers within circle **Rev:** Crescent moon and star flank dagger at center **Note:** 2mm wide rim.

Date	Mintage	F12	VF20	XF40	MS60	MS63
VS1992	—	1.00	2.00	3.00	5.00	7.00
VS1993	473,000	1.00	2.00	3.00	5.00	7.00
VS1994	1,133,000	1.00	2.00	3.00	5.00	7.00
VS1995	—	1.00	2.00	3.00	5.00	7.00
VS1996	—	1.00	2.00	3.00	5.00	7.00
VS1997	—	1.00	2.00	3.00	5.00	7.00

KM# 709.2 2 PAISA
Copper, 25 mm. **Obv:** Footprints above crossed daggers within circle **Rev:** Crescent moon and star flank dagger at center **Note:** Rim is 1mm wide or less.

Date	Mintage	F12	VF20	XF40	MS60	MS63
VS1992	—	0.60	1.00	1.75	3.00	5.00
VS1993	—	0.60	1.00	1.75	3.00	5.00
VS1994	—	0.50	0.75	1.50	2.50	4.00
VS1995	—	2.00	3.50	5.00	7.50	10.00
VS1996	—	0.30	0.50	1.00	1.50	2.50
VS1997	—	0.50	0.75	1.50	2.50	4.00
VS1998	—	0.50	0.75	1.50	2.50	4.00
VS1999	—	0.50	0.75	1.50	2.50	4.00

KM# 710 2 PAISA

Copper, 23 mm. **Obv:** Footprints above crossed daggers within circle **Rev:** Crescent moon and star flank dagger at center

Date	Mintage	F12	VF20	XF40	MS60	MS63
VS1999	—	0.30	0.50	1.00	2.00	3.00
VS2000	—	0.30	0.50	1.00	2.00	3.00
VS2003	—	0.30	0.50	1.00	2.00	3.00
VS2005	—	3.00	5.00	7.00	10.00	12.00

KM# 710a 2 PAISA

Brass **Obv:** Footprints above crossed daggers within circle **Rev:** Crescent moon and star flank dagger at center

Date	Mintage	F12	VF20	XF40	MS60	MS63
VS1999	—	0.30	0.50	1.00	2.00	3.00
VS2000	—	0.30	0.50	1.00	2.00	3.00
VS2001	—	0.30	0.50	1.00	2.00	3.00
VS2005	—	1.75	3.00	5.00	7.50	10.00
VS2008	—	0.30	0.50	1.00	2.00	3.00
VS2009	—	0.30	0.50	1.00	2.00	3.00
VS2010	—	0.30	0.50	1.00	2.00	3.00

KM# 711 5 PAISA

Copper, 30 mm. **Obv:** Footprints above crossed daggers within circle **Rev:** Crescent moon and star flank trident at center

Date	Mintage	F12	VF20	XF40	MS60	MS63
VS1992	—	1.50	3.00	4.50	6.50	9.00
VS1993	878,000	1.50	3.00	4.50	6.50	9.00
VS1994	403,000	1.50	3.00	4.50	6.50	9.00
VS1995	—	1.00	2.00	3.00	5.00	7.00
VS1996	—	1.50	3.00	4.50	6.50	9.00
VS1997	—	1.50	3.00	4.50	6.50	9.00
VS1998	—	—	—	—	—	—

KM# 712 5 PAISA

Copper-Nickel-Zinc **Obv:** Lamp within center circle **Rev:** Crescent moon and star flank trident above inscription

Date	Mintage	F12	VF20	XF40	MS60	MS63
VS2000	—	0.65	1.00	1.50	2.50	4.00
VS2009	—	1.75	3.00	5.00	8.50	12.00
VS2010	—	1.25	2.00	3.00	5.00	7.00

KM# 712a 5 PAISA

Copper-Nickel **Obv:** Lamp within center circle **Rev. Inscription:** Crescent moon and star flank trident above inscription

Date	Mintage	F12	VF20	XF40	MS60	MS63
VS2010 Restrike	—	0.65	1.00	1.50	2.50	4.00

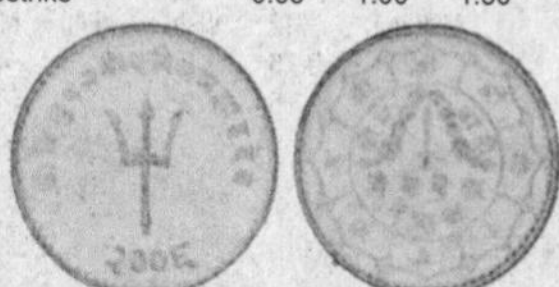

KM# 714 20 PAISA

2.22 g., 0.333 Silver 0.0237 oz. ASW **Obv:** Trident **Rev:** Dagger flanked by garlands from above

Date	Mintage	F12	VF20	XF40	MS60	MS63
VS1989	—	2.25	4.00	5.00	6.50	9.00
VS1991	—	1.75	3.50	4.50	6.00	8.50
VS1992	—	1.75	3.50	4.50	6.00	8.50
VS1993	—	1.75	3.50	4.50	6.00	8.50
VS1994	—	3.75	6.50	10.00	15.00	20.00
VS1995	—	1.75	3.50	4.50	6.00	8.50
VS1996	—	1.75	3.50	4.50	6.00	8.50
VS1997	—	1.75	3.50	4.50	6.00	8.50
VS1998	—	1.75	3.50	4.50	6.00	8.50
VS1999	—	1.75	3.50	4.50	6.00	8.50
VS2000	—	1.75	3.50	4.50	6.00	8.50
VS2001	—	1.75	3.50	4.50	6.00	8.50
VS2003	—	1.75	3.50	4.50	6.00	8.50
VS2004	—	1.75	3.50	4.50	6.00	8.50

KM# 715 20 PAISA

2.22 g., 0.333 Silver 0.0237 oz. ASW

Date	Mintage	F12	VF20	XF40	MS60	MS63
VS1989	—	2.25	4.00	6.00	8.50	12.50

Note: The date VS1989 is given in different style characters. Refer to 50 Paisa KM#719 and 1 Rupee, KM#724 for style

KM# 716 20 PAISA

2.22 g., 0.333 Silver 0.0237 oz. ASW

Date	Mintage	F12	VF20	XF40	MS60	MS63
VS2006	—	1.25	1.50	1.75	2.25	4.00
VS2007	—	—	—	—	—	—
VS2009	—	1.25	1.50	2.00	3.00	5.00
VS2010	—	1.25	1.50	2.00	3.00	5.00

KM# 718 50 PAISA

5.54 g., 0.800 Silver 0.1425 oz. ASW **Obv:** Trident within small center circle **Rev:** Dagger flanked by garlands from above

Date	Mintage	F12	VF20	XF40	MS60	MS63
VS1989	—	8.00	9.00	11.00	14.00	17.00
VS1991	—	5.00	7.00	10.00	12.00	15.00
VS1992	—	5.00	7.00	10.00	12.00	15.00
VS1993	—	5.00	7.00	10.00	12.00	15.00
VS1994	—	5.00	7.00	10.00	12.00	15.00
VS1995	—	5.00	7.00	10.00	12.00	15.00
VS1996	—	5.00	7.00	10.00	12.00	15.00
VS1997	—	5.00	7.00	10.00	12.00	15.00
VS1998	—	5.00	7.00	10.00	12.00	15.00
VS1999	—	5.00	7.00	10.00	12.00	15.00
VS2000	—	5.00	7.00	10.00	12.00	15.00
VS2001	—	5.00	7.00	10.00	12.00	15.00
VS2003	—	5.00	7.00	10.00	12.00	15.00
VS2004	—	5.00	7.00	10.00	12.00	15.00
VS2005	—	5.00	7.00	10.00	12.00	15.00

KM# 719 50 PAISA

5.54 g., 0.800 Silver 0.1425 oz. ASW **Obv:** Trident within small center circle **Rev:** Dagger flanked by garlands from above

Date	Mintage	F12	VF20	XF40	MS60	MS63
VS1989	—	4.50	6.50	9.50	11.50	15.00

Note: The date is given in different style characters

KM# 720 50 PAISA

5.54 g., 0.333 Silver 0.0593 oz. ASW **Obv:** Four dots around trident **Rev:** Dagger flanked by garlands from above

Date	Mintage	F12	VF20	XF40	MS60	MS63
VS2005	—	45.00	65.00	85.00	115	145

KM# 721 50 PAISA

5.54 g., 0.333 Silver 0.0593 oz. ASW **Obv:** Without dots around trident **Rev:** Dagger flanked by garlands from above

Date	Mintage	F12	VF20	XF40	MS60	MS63
VS2006	—	2.25	3.00	4.00	6.00	9.00
VS2007	—	2.25	3.00	4.00	6.00	9.00
VS2009/7	—	2.25	3.00	4.00	6.00	9.00
VS2009	—	2.25	3.00	4.00	6.00	9.00
VS2010	—	2.25	3.00	4.00	6.00	9.00

KM# 713 1/16 RUPEE

Silver **Obv:** Inscription **Rev:** Inscription

Date	Mintage	F12	VF20	XF40	MS60	MS63
VS(19)96	—	12.50	20.00	32.50	50.00	70.00

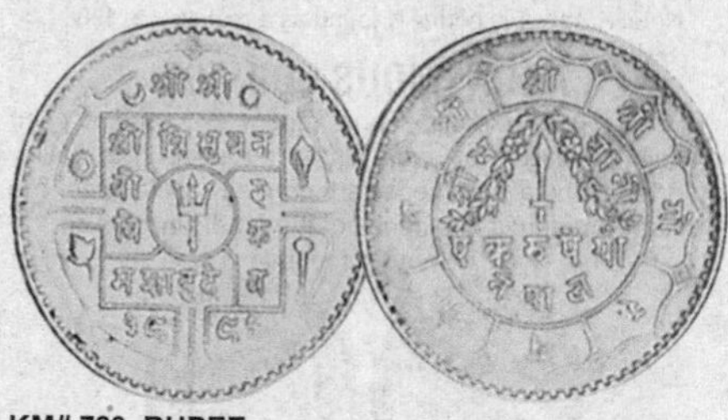

KM# 723 RUPEE

11.08 g., 0.800 Silver 0.285 oz. ASW **Obv:** Trident within small center circle **Rev:** Dagger flanked by garlands from above

Date	Mintage	F12	VF20	XF40	MS60	MS63
VS1989	—	10.00	12.00	15.00	20.00	28.00
VS1991	—	10.00	12.00	15.00	20.00	28.00
VS1992	—	10.00	12.00	15.00	20.00	28.00
VS1993	1,717,000	10.00	12.00	15.00	20.00	28.00
VS1994	2,097,000	10.00	12.00	15.00	20.00	28.00
VS1995	—	10.00	12.00	15.00	20.00	28.00
VS1996	—	10.00	12.00	15.00	20.00	28.00
VS1997	—	10.00	12.00	15.00	20.00	28.00
VS1998	—	10.00	12.00	15.00	20.00	28.00
VS1999	—	10.00	12.00	15.00	20.00	28.00
VS2000	—	10.00	12.00	15.00	20.00	28.00
VS2001	—	10.00	12.00	15.00	20.00	28.00
VS2003	—	10.00	12.00	15.00	20.00	28.00
VS2005	—	10.00	12.00	15.00	20.00	28.00

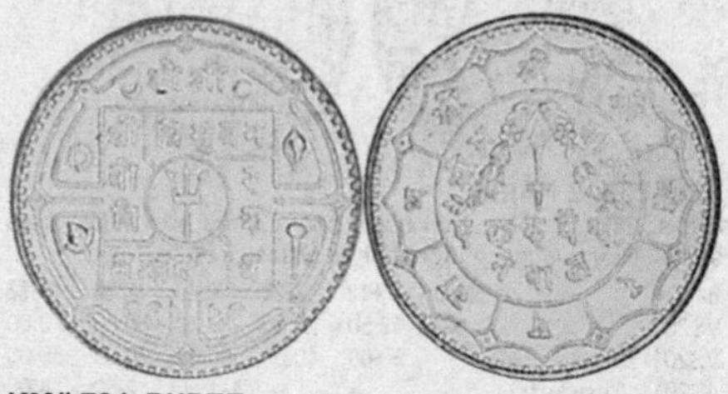

KM# 724 RUPEE

11.08 g., 0.800 Silver 0.285 oz. ASW **Obv:** Trident within small center circle **Rev:** Dagger flanked by garlands from above

Date	Mintage	F12	VF20	XF40	MS60	MS63
VS1989	—	13.00	15.00	18.00	22.00	30.00

Note: The date is given in different style characters

KM# 725 RUPEE

11.08 g., 0.333 Silver 0.1186 oz. ASW **Obv:** Four dots around trident **Rev:** Dagger flanked by garlands from above

Date	Mintage	F12	VF20	XF40	MS60	MS63
VS2005	—	7.00	9.00	14.00	18.00	22.00

KM# 726 RUPEE
11.08 g., 0.333 Silver 0.1186 oz. ASW **Obv:** Without dots around trident **Rev:** Dagger flanked by garlands from above

Date	Mintage	F12	VF20	XF40	MS60	MS63
VS2006	—	5.00	6.00	7.00	12.00	15.00
VS2007	—	5.00	6.00	7.00	12.00	15.00
VS2008	—	5.00	6.00	7.00	12.00	15.00
VS2009	—	5.00	6.00	7.00	12.00	15.00
VS2010	—	5.00	6.00	7.00	12.00	15.00

ASARFI GOLD COINAGE

Fractional designations are approximate for this series. Actual Gold Weight (AGW) is used to identify each type.

(Asarphi)

KM# 741 1/2 ASARPHI
5.80 g., Gold **Obv:** Head of Tribhuvan Bir Bikram right on 5-pointed star **Note:** Portrait type.

Date	Mintage	F12	VF20	XF40	MS60	MS63
VS2010	—	—	325	350	400	450

Note: KM#741 is normally found as a restrike ca. 1968

ANONYMOUS COINAGE

Fine copper pieces - non magnetic - and copper/iron alloy - magnetic - were produced in the hills. Mainly exported to India. The pieces are normally unstamped. The 4 Paisa sometimes has traces of the Arabic inscription.

Without inscription

KM# 733 PAISA
Brass, 18 mm. **Obv:** Sun rising above three hills within grain sprigs **Rev:** Dagger in front of hills within circle

Date	Mintage	F12	VF20	XF40	MS60	MS63
VS2010	—	8.00	15.00	20.00	25.00	32.00
VS2011	—	17.50	25.00	35.00	40.00	50.00
VS2012 Restrike	—	—	1.00	1.50	2.00	3.50

KM# 734 PAISA
Brass, 17.5 mm.

Date	Mintage	F12	VF20	XF40	MS60	MS63
VS2012	—	1.25	2.00	2.50	3.50	5.00

KM# 735 2 PAISA
Brass, 21 mm. **Obv:** Sun rising above three hills within grain sprigs **Rev:** Dagger in front of hills within circle

Date	Mintage	F12	VF20	XF40	MS60	MS63
VS2010	—	12.50	20.00	37.50	60.00	70.00
VS2011	—	30.00	40.00	50.00	70.00	80.00
VS2011 Restrike	—	—	—	1.50	2.50	4.00

KM# 749 2 PAISA
Brass, 19.5 mm. **Obv:** Sun rising above three hills within grain sprigs **Rev:** Dagger in front of hills within circle

Date	Mintage	F12	VF20	XF40	MS60	MS63
VS2012	—	0.30	0.50	0.75	1.50	2.50
VS2013	—	0.30	0.50	0.75	1.50	2.50
VS2014	—	0.30	0.50	0.75	1.50	2.50

KM# 754 4 PAISA
Brass **Obv:** Legend around center circle **Rev:** Date below center circle

Date	Mintage	F12	VF20	XF40	MS60	MS63
VS2012	—	1.00	1.75	3.00	5.00	7.00

KM# 736 5 PAISA
3.89 g., Bronze **Obv:** Sun rising above three hills within grain sprigs **Rev:** Hand divides date within decorative outline

Date	Mintage	F12	VF20	XF40	MS60	MS63
VS2010	—	2.75	4.50	7.00	10.00	12.00
VS2011	—	0.65	1.00	2.75	5.00	7.00
VS2012	—	0.30	0.50	0.75	1.25	2.00
VS2013	—	0.30	0.50	0.75	1.25	2.00
VS2014	—	0.30	0.50	0.75	1.25	2.00

KM# 736a 5 PAISA
4.04 g., Copper-Nickel **Obv:** Sun rising above three hills within grain sprigs **Rev:** Hand divides date within decorative outline

Date	Mintage	F12	VF20	XF40	MS60	MS63
VS2014	—	—	—	—	—	—

KM# 737 10 PAISA
Bronze **Obv:** Sun rising above three hills within grain sprigs **Rev:** Dagger in front of three hills within circle

Date	Mintage	F12	VF20	XF40	MS60	MS63
VS2010	—	2.75	4.50	7.00	10.00	12.00
VS2011	—	0.15	0.25	0.50	0.75	1.25
VS2011 Restrike	—	—	—	0.15	0.25	0.45
VS2012	—	0.15	0.25	0.50	0.75	1.25

KM# 738 20 PAISA
Copper-Nickel, 18 mm. **Obv:** Sun rising above three hills within grain sprigs **Rev:** Dagger in front of three hills within circle

Date	Mintage	F12	VF20	XF40	MS60	MS63
VS2010	—	12.50	20.00	30.00	40.00	50.00
VS2010 Restrike	—	—	—	2.50	3.00	5.00
VS2011	—	32.50	40.00	50.00	60.00	70.00

KM# 739 25 PAISA
Copper-Nickel, 19 mm. **Obv:** Sun rising above three hills within grain sprigs **Rev:** Dagger in front of three hills within circle

Date	Mintage	F12	VF20	XF40	MS60	MS63
VS2010	—	2.00	3.50	4.50	6.00	8.50
VS2011	—	2.00	3.50	4.50	6.00	8.50
VS2012	—	1.25	2.00	2.50	3.50	5.50
VS2014	—	1.25	2.00	2.50	3.50	5.50

KM# 768 1/5 ASARPHI
2.33 g., Gold

Date	Mintage	F12	VF20	XF40	MS60	MS63
VS2010	—	—	110	120	135	150

Note: Coins dated VS2010 are normally found as restrikes ca. 1968

Date	Mintage	F12	VF20	XF40	MS60	MS63
VS2012	—	—	—	—	—	—

KM# 774 1/4 ASARPHI
2.90 g., Gold

Date	Mintage	F12	VF20	XF40	MS60	MS63
VS2010	—	120	125	135	150	165

Note: Coins dated VS2010 are normally found as restrikes ca. 1968

Date	Mintage	F12	VF20	XF40	MS60	MS63
VS2012	—	—	—	—	—	—

Gyanendra Bir Bikram
VS2007 / 1950-51AD (first reign)

DECIMAL COINAGE

100 Paisa = 1 Rupee

KM# 729 50 PAISA
5.54 g., 0.333 Silver 0.0593 oz. ASW **Obv:** Trident within small center circle **Rev:** Dagger flanked by garlands from above

Date	Mintage	F12	VF20	XF40	MS60	MS63
VS2007	26	—	175	275	350	425

KM# 731 MOHAR
Gold

Date	Mintage	F12	VF20	XF40	MS60	MS63
VS2007 Rare	—	—	—	—	—	—

KM# 730 RUPEE
11.08 g., 0.333 Silver 0.1186 oz. ASW **Obv:** Trident within small center circle **Rev:** Dagger flanked by garlands from above

Date	Mintage	F12	VF20	XF40	MS60	MS63
VS2007	—	5.50	7.50	10.00	16.00	20.00

KM# 732 TOLA
Gold

Date	Mintage	F12	VF20	XF40	MS60	MS63
VS2007 Rare	—	—	—	—	—	—

Trivhuvan Bir Bikram
VS2007-2011 / 1951-1955AD (second reign)

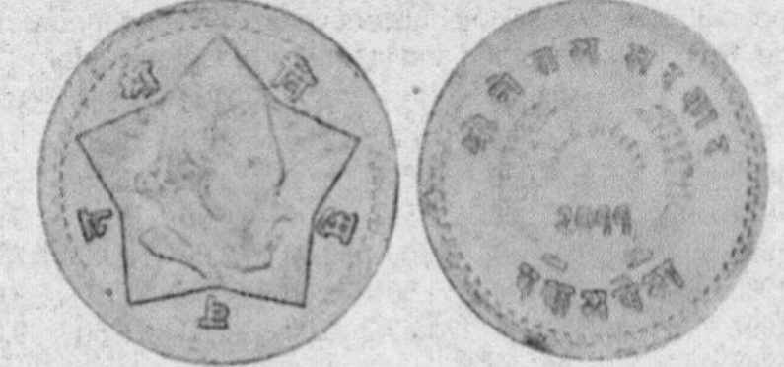

KM# 740 50 PAISA
Copper-Nickel, 25 mm. **Obv:** Head of Tribhuvan Bir Bikram right on 5-pointed star **Rev:** Sun rising back of hills, grain sprigs flank

Date	Mintage	F12	VF20	XF40	MS60	MS63
VS2010	—	0.50	1.00	2.00	4.00	7.00
VS2011	—	0.35	0.75	1.50	3.00	5.00

KM# 742 RUPEE
Copper-Nickel **Obv:** Head of Tribhuvan Bir Bikram right on 5-pointed star **Note:** Equal denticles at rim.

Date	Mintage	F12	VF20	XF40	MS60	MS63
VS2010	—	0.75	1.25	2.25	4.50	7.00
VS2011	—	0.75	1.25	2.25	4.50	7.00

KM# 743 RUPEE
Copper-Nickel **Obv:** Head of Tribhuvan Bir Bikram right on

5-pointed star **Rev:** Sun rising back of hills, grain sprigs flank **Note:** Unequal denticles at rim.

Date	Mintage	F12	VF20	XF40	MS60	MS63
VS2011	—	0.75	1.25	2.25	4.50	7.00

ASARFI GOLD COINAGE

Fractional designations are approximate for this series. Actual Gold Weight (AGW) is used to identify each type.

(Asarphi)

KM# 744 ASARPHI

11.66 g., Gold **Obv:** Head of Tribhuvan Bir Bikram right on 5-pointed star

Date	Mintage	F12	VF20	XF40	MS60	MS63
VS2010	—	—	600	625	650	700

Note: KM#744 normally found as a restrike ca. 1968

Mahendra Bir Bikram
VS2012-2028 / 1955-1971AD

DECIMAL COINAGE

100 Paisa = 1 Rupee

KM# 745.1 PAISA

Brass, 18 mm. **Subject:** Mahendra Coronation **Obv:** Crown **Rev:** Numeral at center, sprigs at sides **Note:** Prev. KM#745.

Date	Mintage	F12	VF20	XF40	MS60	MS63
VS2013	—	0.30	0.50	0.75	1.00	1.50

Narrow rim

KM# 746 PAISA

Brass, 16 mm. **Obv:** Crescent and star flank trident at center **Rev:** Numerals with shading

Date	Mintage	F12	VF20	XF40	MS60	MS63
VS2014	—	0.10	0.15	0.25	0.40	0.50
VS2015	—	0.10	0.15	0.25	0.40	0.50
VS2018	—	0.10	0.15	0.25	0.40	0.50
VS2019	—	0.10	0.15	0.25	0.40	0.50
VS2020	—	0.10	0.15	0.25	0.40	0.50

KM# 745.2 PAISA

Brass **Subject:** Mahendra coronation

Date	Mintage	F12	VF20	XF40	MS60	MS63
VS2013 Wide rim	—	0.30	0.50	0.75	1.00	1.50

KM# 747 PAISA

1.45 g., Brass, 16.5 mm. **Obv:** Crescent moon and star flank trident at center **Rev:** Numerals without shading

Date	Mintage	F12	VF20	XF40	MS60	MS63
VS2021	—	0.10	0.15	0.20	0.30	0.45
VS2022	—	0.10	0.15	0.25	0.40	0.50

KM# 748 PAISA

0.61 g., Aluminum, 16.6 mm. **Obv:** Trident with sun and moon flanking above hills **Rev:** National flower

Date	Mintage	F12	VF20	XF40	MS60	MS63
VS2023	—	—	0.10	0.15	0.25	0.35
VS2025	—	—	0.10	0.15	0.25	0.35
VS2026	—	—	0.10	0.15	0.25	0.35
VS2027	2,187	PF63 1.25				
VS2028	—	—	0.10	0.15	0.25	0.35
VS2028	2,380	PF63 1.25				

KM# 750.1 2 PAISA

Brass, 20.5 mm. **Subject:** Mahendra Coronation **Obv:** Crown **Rev:** Numeral at center **Note:** Narrow rim.

Date	Mintage	F12	VF20	XF40	MS60	MS63
VS2013	—	0.30	0.50	0.75	1.00	1.50

KM# 750.2 2 PAISA

Brass **Subject:** Mahendra coronation **Obv:** Crown **Rev:** Numeral at center **Note:** Wide rim.

Date	Mintage	F12	VF20	XF40	MS60	MS63
VS2013	—	0.30	0.50	0.75	1.00	1.50

KM# 751 2 PAISA

2.16 g., Brass, 19.1 mm. **Obv:** Crescent moon and sun flank trident **Rev:** Numerals with shading

Date	Mintage	F12	VF20	XF40	MS60	MS63
VS2014	—	0.10	0.15	0.25	0.40	0.50
VS2015	—	0.10	0.15	0.25	0.40	0.50
VS2016	—	0.10	0.15	0.25	0.40	0.50
VS2018	—	0.10	0.15	0.25	0.40	0.50
VS2019	—	0.10	0.15	0.25	0.40	0.50
VS2020	—	0.10	0.15	0.25	0.40	0.50

KM# 752 2 PAISA

Brass **Obv:** Crescent moon and sun flank trident at center **Rev:** Numerals wtihout shading

Date	Mintage	F12	VF20	XF40	MS60	MS63
VS2021	—	0.10	0.15	0.20	0.35	0.45
VS2022	—	0.10	0.15	0.25	0.50	0.75
VS2023	—	0.10	0.15	0.25	0.50	0.75

KM# 753 2 PAISA

0.91 g., Aluminum, 18.6 mm. **Obv:** Trident with sun and moon flanking above hills **Rev:** Himalayan Monal pheasant

Date	Mintage	F12	VF20	XF40	MS60	MS63
VS2023	—	—	0.10	0.15	0.75	1.25
VS2024	—	—	0.10	0.15	0.75	1.25
VS2025	—	—	0.10	0.15	0.75	1.25
VS2026	—	—	0.10	0.15	0.75	1.25
VS2027	—	—	0.10	0.15	0.75	1.25
VS2027	2,187	PF63 1.50				
VS2028	—	—	0.10	0.15	0.75	1.25
VS2028	2,380	PF63 1.50				

KM# 756.1 5 PAISA

Bronze, 22 mm. **Subject:** Mahendra Coronation **Obv:** Crown **Rev:** Numeral within floral outline **Note:** Wide rim with accent mark.

Date	Mintage	F12	VF20	XF40	MS60	MS63
VS2013	—	10.00	20.00	30.00	40.00	50.00

KM# 756.2 5 PAISA

Bronze, 22 mm. **Subject:** Mahendra coronation **Obv:** Crown **Rev:** Numeral within floral outline **Note:** Narrow rim.

Date	Mintage	F12	VF20	XF40	MS60	MS63
VS2013 Restrike	—	0.35	0.60	1.00	1.50	2.50

KM# 756.3 5 PAISA

Bronze, 22 mm. **Subject:** Mahendra coronation **Obv:** Crown **Rev:** Numeral within floral outline **Note:** Without accent mark.

Date	Mintage	F12	VF20	XF40	MS60	MS63
VS2013	—	1.00	2.00	3.00	5.00	7.00

KM# 757 5 PAISA

3.85 g., Bronze, 22.5 mm. **Obv:** Trident at center **Rev:** Numerals with shading

Date	Mintage	F12	VF20	XF40	MS60	MS63
VS2014	—	0.10	0.20	0.30	0.75	1.25
VS2015	—	0.10	0.20	0.30	0.75	1.25
VS2016	—	0.10	0.30	0.50	1.00	1.50
VS2017	—	0.10	0.20	0.30	0.75	1.25
VS2018	—	0.10	0.20	0.30	0.75	1.25
VS2019	—	0.10	0.20	0.30	0.75	1.25
VS2020	—	0.10	0.20	0.30	0.75	1.25

KM# 758 5 PAISA

Aluminum-Bronze, 22.5 mm. **Obv:** Crescent moon and sun flank trident at center **Rev:** Numerals without shading

Date	Mintage	F12	VF20	XF40	MS60	MS63
VS2021	—	0.50	1.00	1.50	2.50	4.00

KM# 758a 5 PAISA

3.08 g., Bronze, 21 mm. **Obv:** Crescent moon and sun flank trident at center **Rev:** Numeral within shaded floral outline

Date	Mintage	F12	VF20	XF40	MS60	MS63
VS2021	—	0.10	0.15	0.25	0.50	0.75
VS2022	—	0.10	0.15	0.30	0.60	0.85
VS2023	—	0.10	0.15	0.30	0.60	0.85

KM# 759 5 PAISA

Aluminum, 21 mm. **Obv:** Trident with sun and moon flanking above hills **Rev:** Ox left

Date	Mintage	F12	VF20	XF40	MS60	MS63
VS2023	—	—	0.15	0.25	1.00	1.50
VS2024	—	—	0.10	0.20	1.00	1.50
VS2025	—	—	0.10	0.20	1.00	1.50
VS2026	—	—	0.10	0.20	1.00	1.50
VS2027	—	—	0.10	0.20	1.00	1.50
VS2027	2,187	PF63 1.75				
VS2028	—	—	0.10	0.20	1.00	1.50
VS2028	2,038	PF63 1.75				

KM# 761 10 PAISA

Bronze, 24.5 mm. **Subject:** Mahendra Coronation **Obv:** Crown **Rev:** Shaded numeral

Date	Mintage	F12	VF20	XF40	MS60	MS63
VS2013	—	0.25	0.50	0.75	1.50	2.50

KM# 762 10 PAISA

6.30 g., Bronze, 25 mm. **Obv:** Crescent moon and sun flank trident **Rev:** Numerals with shading

Date	Mintage	F12	VF20	XF40	MS60	MS63
VS2014	—	2.75	4.50	7.00	10.00	15.00
VS2015	—	0.15	0.25	0.50	0.75	1.25
VS2016	—	3.00	5.00	7.00	10.00	15.00
VS2018	—	0.15	0.25	0.50	0.75	1.25
VS2019	—	0.15	0.25	0.50	0.75	1.25
VS2020	—	0.15	0.25	0.50	0.75	1.25

KM# 763 10 PAISA

Aluminum-Bronze **Obv:** Crescent moon and sun flank trident at center **Rev:** Numerals without shading

Date	Mintage	F12	VF20	XF40	MS60	MS63
VS2021	—	0.75	1.25	2.00	3.00	5.00

KM# 764 10 PAISA

4.93 g., Bronze, 25 mm. **Note:** Modified design.

Date	Mintage	F12	VF20	XF40	MS60	MS63
VS2021	—	0.10	0.15	0.25	0.50	0.75
VS2022	—	0.10	0.15	0.25	0.50	0.75
VS2023	—	0.10	0.15	0.25	0.50	0.75

KM# 765 10 PAISA

4.01 g., Brass, 21.2 mm. **Obv:** Trident with sun and moon flanking above hills **Rev:** Ox left

Date	Mintage	F12	VF20	XF40	MS60	MS63
VS2023	—	—	0.15	0.25	1.00	1.50
VS2024	—	—	0.15	0.25	1.00	1.50
VS2025	—	—	15.00	17.50	20.00	28.00
VS2026	—	—	0.10	0.20	1.00	1.50
VS2027	—	—	0.10	0.20	1.00	1.50
VS2027	2,187	**PF63** 2.00				
VS2028	—	—	0.10	0.20	1.00	1.50
VS2028	2,380	**PF63** 2.00				

Note: Birendra Bir Bikram also struck a 10 Paisa VS2028, see KM#806

KM# 766 10 PAISA

4.06 g., Brass, 21 mm. **Series:** F.A.O. **Obv:** Grain sprig at center **Rev:** Ox left

Date	Mintage	F12	VF20	XF40	MS60	MS63
VS2028	1,500,000	—	0.10	0.20	1.00	1.50

KM# 770 25 PAISA

Copper-Nickel **Subject:** Mahendra Coronation

Date	Mintage	F12	VF20	XF40	MS60	MS63
VS2013	—	0.30	0.50	0.70	1.00	1.50

KM# 771 25 PAISA

Copper-Nickel, 19 mm. **Obv:** Four characters in line above trident **Rev:** Small character at bottom (outer circle)

Date	Mintage	F12	VF20	XF40	MS60	MS63
VS2015	—	1.50	2.50	4.00	6.00	8.50
VS2018	—	0.25	0.40	0.60	0.80	1.35
VS2020	—	0.25	0.40	0.60	0.80	1.35
VS2021	—	0.30	0.50	0.75	1.00	1.50
VS2022	—	2.00	3.50	6.00	9.00	14.00

KM# 771a 25 PAISA

2.99 g., 0.084 Silver 0.0081 oz. ASW **Obv:** Trident within small center circle **Rev:** Dagger flanked by garlands from above

Date	Mintage	F12	VF20	XF40	MS60	MS63
VS6/5/2017	—	—	—	—	100	125

KM# 772 25 PAISA

3.05 g., Copper-Nickel, 19 mm. **Obv:** Trident within small center circle **Rev:** Large different character at bottom

Date	Mintage	F12	VF20	XF40	MS60	MS63
VS2021	—	0.30	0.50	0.70	1.00	1.50
VS2022	—	0.30	0.50	0.70	1.00	1.50
VS2023	—	0.30	0.50	0.70	1.00	1.50

KM# 773 25 PAISA

Copper-Nickel **Obv:** Five characters in line above trident **Rev:** Dagger flanked by garlands from above

Date	Mintage	F12	VF20	XF40	MS60	MS63
VS2024	—	—	0.35	0.50	0.75	1.25
VS2025	—	—	15.00	20.00	25.00	30.00
VS2026	—	—	0.35	0.50	0.75	1.25
VS2027	—	—	0.35	0.50	0.75	1.25
VS2027	2,187	**PF63** 2.50				
VS2028	—	—	0.35	0.50	0.75	1.25
VS2028	2,380	**PF63** 2.50				
VS2030	—	—	0.35	0.50	0.75	1.25

KM# 777 50 PAISA

Copper-Nickel, 25 mm. **Obv:** Trident within small center circle **Rev:** Small character at bottom

Date	Mintage	F12	VF20	XF40	MS60	MS63
VS2011	—	0.50	1.00	1.50	3.00	5.00
VS2012	—	0.25	0.50	0.75	1.00	1.50
VS2013	—	0.25	0.50	1.00	2.00	3.00
VS2014	—	0.25	0.50	1.00	2.00	3.00
VS2015	—	0.25	0.50	1.00	2.00	3.00
VS2016	—	0.25	0.50	1.00	2.00	3.00
VS2017	—	0.25	0.30	0.75	1.25	1.75
VS2018	—	0.25	0.50	1.00	2.00	3.00
VS2020	—	0.25	0.30	0.75	1.50	2.00

KM# 795 50 PAISA

Copper-Nickel **Obv:** Trident within small center circle **Rev:** Dagger flanked by garlands from above **Note:** In the name of "Queen Ratna Rajya Lakshmi".

Date	Mintage	F12	VF20	XF40	MS60	MS63
VS2012	—	—	100	125	150	200

KM# 776 50 PAISA

Copper-Nickel **Subject:** Mahendra Coronation **Obv:** Crown **Rev:** Dagger flanked by garlands from above

Date	Mintage	F12	VF20	XF40	MS60	MS63
VS2013	—	0.35	0.75	1.00	1.50	2.00

KM# 778 50 PAISA

Copper-Nickel, 25 mm. **Obv:** Trident within small center circle **Rev:** Large different character at bottom

Date	Mintage	F12	VF20	XF40	MS60	MS63
VS2021	—	0.25	0.35	0.50	0.75	1.25
VS2022	—	0.25	0.50	0.75	1.50	2.00
VS2023	—	0.25	0.50	0.75	1.00	1.50

KM# 779 50 PAISA

Copper-Nickel **Obv:** Four characters in line above trident **Rev:** Dagger flanked by garlands from above **Note:** Reduced size, 23.5mm.

Date	Mintage	F12	VF20	XF40	MS60	MS63
VS2023	—	0.25	0.50	0.75	1.50	2.00

KM# 780 50 PAISA

Copper-Nickel **Obv:** Five characters in line above trident **Rev:** Dagger flanked by garlands from above

Date	Mintage	F12	VF20	XF40	MS60	MS63
VS2025	—	—	0.30	0.50	1.00	—
VS2026	—	—	0.30	0.50	0.85	1.35
VS2027	2,187	**PF63** 3.00				
VS2028	2,380	**PF63** 3.00				
VS2030	—	—	0.30	0.50	0.85	1.35

KM# 784 RUPEE

Copper-Nickel, 30 mm.

Date	Mintage	F12	VF20	XF40	MS60	MS63
VS2011	—	1.25	2.25	3.50	5.50	8.50
VS2012	—	1.00	1.75	2.50	4.00	6.50

KM# 785 RUPEE

Copper-Nickel, 28.5 mm. **Obv:** Trident within center circle **Rev:** Small character at bottom **Note:** Reduced size.

Date	Mintage	F12	VF20	XF40	MS60	MS63
VS2012	—	0.50	0.85	1.25	1.75	2.50
VS2013	—	0.50	0.85	1.25	1.75	2.50
VS2014	—	0.50	0.85	1.25	1.75	2.50
VS2015	—	0.50	0.85	1.25	1.75	2.50
VS2016	—	0.50	0.85	1.25	1.75	2.50
VS2018	—	0.50	0.85	1.25	1.75	2.50
VS2020	—	0.50	0.85	1.25	1.75	2.50

KM# 797 RUPEE
Copper-Nickel **Obv:** Trident within center circle **Rev:** Dagger flanked by garlands from above **Note:** In the name of "Queen Ratna Rajya Lakshmi".

Date	Mintage	F12	VF20	XF40	MS60	MS63
VS2012	2,000	—	100	150	175	225

KM# 790 RUPEE
Copper-Nickel **Subject:** Mahendra Coronation **Obv:** Crown **Rev:** Dagger flanked by garlands from above

Date	Mintage	F12	VF20	XF40	MS60	MS63
VS2013	—	—	1.25	1.75	2.50	4.00

KM# 786 RUPEE
Copper-Nickel, 28.5 mm. **Obv:** Trident within center circle **Rev:** Large character at bottom

Date	Mintage	F12	VF20	XF40	MS60	MS63
VS2021	—	0.50	0.75	1.00	1.50	2.50
VS2022	—	0.50	1.00	1.50	2.50	4.00
VS2023	—	4.50	7.50	10.00	12.50	17.00

KM# 787 RUPEE
Copper-Nickel, 27 mm. **Obv:** Four characters in line above trident **Rev:** Dagger flanked by garlands from above **Note:** Reduced size.

Date	Mintage	F12	VF20	XF40	MS60	MS63
VS2023	—	0.75	1.00	1.35	2.00	3.50

KM# 788 RUPEE
Copper-Nickel **Obv:** Five characters in line above trident **Rev:** Dagger flanked by garlands from above

Date	Mintage	F12	VF20	XF40	MS60	MS63
VS2025	—	—	1.00	1.50	2.00	3.50
VS2026	—	—	1.00	1.40	2.00	3.50
VS2027	2,187	PF63 4.50				
VS2028	2,380	PF63 4.50				

KM# 794 10 RUPEE
15.60 g., 0.600 Silver 0.3009 oz. ASW **Series:** F.A.O. **Obv:** Bust of Mahendra Bir Bikram left **Rev:** Trident and 1/2 cogwheel above grain sprig

Date	Mintage	F12	VF20	XF40	MS60	MS63
VS2025	1,000,000	—	12.00	22.00	32.00	50.00

ASARFI GOLD COINAGE

Fractional designations are approximate for this series. Actual Gold Weight (AGW) is used to identify each type. (Asarphi)

KM# 767 1/6 ASARPHI
1.90 g., Gold **Subject:** Mahendra Coronation

Date	Mintage	F12	VF20	XF40	MS60	MS63
VS2013	—	—	105	115	150	170

KM# 775 1/4 ASARPHI
2.50 g., Gold **Obv:** Trident within small circle at center **Rev:** Dagger flanked by garlands from above **Note:** Reduced weight.

Date	Mintage	F12	VF20	XF40	MS60	MS63
VS2026	—	—	—	130	160	180

KM# 782 1/2 ASARPHI
5.80 g., Gold **Obv:** Trident within small circle at center **Rev:** Dagger flanked by garlands from above

Date	Mintage	F12	VF20	XF40	MS60	MS63
VS2012	—	—	290	300	350	400
VS2019	—	—	290	300	350	400

KM# 796 1/2 ASARPHI
Gold **Note:** In the name of "Queen Ratna Rajya Lakshmi".

Date	Mintage	F12	VF20	XF40	MS60	MS63
VS2012	—	—	—	—	—	—

KM# 781 1/2 ASARPHI
5.80 g., Gold **Subject:** Mahendra Coronation

Date	Mintage	F12	VF20	XF40	MS60	MS63
VS2013	—	—	290	300	350	400

KM# 783 1/2 ASARPHI
5.00 g., Gold **Subject:** Birendra Marriage

Date	Mintage	F12	VF20	XF40	MS60	MS63
VS2026	—	—	—	290	325	375

KM# 789 ASARPHI
Gold **Obv:** Trident within small center circle **Rev:** Dagger flanked by garlands from above

Date	Mintage	F12	VF20	XF40	MS60	MS63
VS2012	—	—	600	625	650	700
VS2019	—	—	600	625	650	700

KM# 798 ASARPHI
11.66 g., Gold **Note:** In the name of "Queen Ratna Rajya Lakshmi".

Date	Mintage	F12	VF20	XF40	MS60	MS63
VS2012	—	—	600	625	650	700
VS2018	—	—	600	625	650	700

KM# 791 ASARPHI
Gold **Subject:** Mahendra Coronation

Date	Mintage	F12	VF20	XF40	MS60	MS63
VS2013	—	—	600	625	650	700

KM# 792 ASARPHI
10.00 g., Gold **Obv:** Trident within small center circle **Rev:** Dagger flanked by garlands from above

Date	Mintage	F12	VF20	XF40	MS60	MS63
VS2026	—	—	600	625	650	700

KM# 793 2 ASARFI
Gold

Date	Mintage	F12	VF20	XF40	MS60	MS63
VS2012	—	—	1,150	1,250	1,350	1,500

Birendra Bir Bikram
VS2028-2058 / 1971-2001 AD

DECIMAL COINAGE

100 Paisa = 1 Rupee

KM# 799 PAISA
Aluminum **Obv:** Trident with sun and moon flanking above hills **Rev:** National flower

Date	Mintage	F12	VF20	XF40	MS60	MS63
VS2028	10,000	—	0.20	0.30	0.40	0.50
VS2029	3,036,000	—	0.10	0.15	0.25	0.35
VS2029	3,943	PF63 0.60				
VS2030	1,279,000	—	0.10	0.15	0.25	0.35
VS2030	8,891	PF63 0.50				
VS2031	430,000	—	0.10	0.15	0.25	0.35
VS2031	11,000	PF63 0.50				
VS2032	324,000	—	0.10	0.15	0.25	0.35
VS2033	217,000	—	—	0.10	0.25	0.35
VS2034	1,040,000	—	0.10	0.15	0.25	0.35
VS2035	394,000	—	0.10	0.15	0.25	0.35
VS2036	—	—	0.10	0.15	0.25	0.35

KM# 800 PAISA
Aluminum **Subject:** Birendra Coronation **Obv:** Crown

Date	Mintage	F12	VF20	XF40	MS60	MS63
VS2031	75,000	—	0.10	0.15	0.25	0.35

KM# 800a PAISA
Copper-Nickel **Subject:** Birendra Coronation **Obv:** Crown **Rev:** Dagger flanked by garlands from above

Date	Mintage	F12	VF20	XF40	MS60	MS63
VS2031	1,000	PF63 2.50				

KM# 1012 PAISA
Aluminum **Obv:** Crown **Rev:** Value

Date	Mintage	F12	VF20	XF40	MS60	MS63
VS2039	—	—	4.00	6.00	8.00	10.00
VS2040	42,000	—	—	—	—	—

KM# 801 2 PAISA
Aluminum, 20 mm. **Obv:** Flower above hills with sun and moon flanking **Rev:** Himalayan Monal pheasant

Date	Mintage	F12	VF20	XF40	MS60	MS63
VS2028	8,319	—	0.20	0.30	0.75	1.25
VS2029	5,206,000	—	0.10	0.15	0.75	1.25
VS2029	3,943	PF63 1.50				

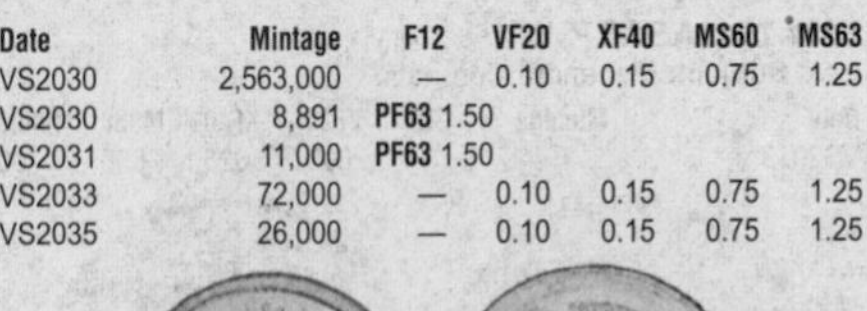

Date	Mintage	F12	VF20	XF40	MS60	MS63
VS2030	2,563,000	—	0.10	0.15	0.75	1.25
VS2030	8,891	PF63 1.50				
VS2031	11,000	PF63 1.50				
VS2033	72,000	—	0.10	0.15	0.75	1.25
VS2035	26,000	—	0.10	0.15	0.75	1.25

KM# 802 5 PAISA

1.14 g., Aluminum, 20.5 mm. **Obv:** Trident with sun and moon flanking above hills **Rev:** Ox left

Date	Mintage	F12	VF20	XF40	MS60	MS63
VS2028	3,700,000	—	0.10	0.20	0.75	1.25
VS2029	23,578,000	—	0.10	0.20	0.75	1.25
VS2029	3,943	PF63 1.50				
VS2030	12,320,000	—	0.10	0.20	0.75	1.25
VS2030	8,891	PF63 1.50				
VS2031	15,730,000	—	0.10	0.20	0.75	1.25
VS2031	11,000	PF63 1.50				
VS2032	19,747,000	—	0.10	0.20	0.75	1.25
VS2033	29,619,000	—	0.10	0.20	0.75	1.25
VS2034	27,222,000	—	0.10	0.20	0.75	1.25
VS2035	27,613,000	—	0.10	0.20	0.75	1.25
VS2036	—	—	0.10	0.20	0.75	1.25
VS2037	13,235,000	—	0.10	0.20	0.75	1.25
VS2038	15,137,000	—	0.10	0.20	0.75	1.25
VS2039	8,971,000	—	0.10	0.20	0.75	1.25

KM# 803 5 PAISA

1.23 g., Aluminum, 21 mm. **Series:** F.A.O. **Obv:** Value **Rev:** Irrigation dam

Date	Mintage	F12	VF20	XF40	MS60	MS63
VS2031	4,584,000	—	0.10	0.15	0.25	0.35

KM# 804 5 PAISA

Aluminum **Subject:** Birendra Coronation **Obv:** Crown **Rev:** Dagger flanked by garlands from above

Date	Mintage	F12	VF20	XF40	MS60	MS63
VS2031	2,869,000	—	0.10	0.25	0.50	0.75

KM# 804a 5 PAISA

Copper-Nickel **Subject:** Birendra Coronation **Obv:** Crown **Rev:** Dagger flanked by garlands from above

Date	Mintage	F12	VF20	XF40	MS60	MS63
VS2031	1,000	PF63 3.00				

KM# 1013 5 PAISA

0.85 g., Aluminum, 18 mm. **Obv:** Crown **Rev:** Value

Date	Mintage	F12	VF20	XF40	MS60	MS63
VS2039	8,971,000	—	7.00	10.00	15.00	20.00
VS2040	6,430,000	—	—	0.10	0.25	0.35
VS2041	9,634,000	—	—	0.10	0.25	0.35
VS2042	58,000	—	—	0.10	0.25	0.35
VS2043	2,937,000	—	—	0.10	0.25	0.35
VS2044	3,126,000	—	—	0.10	0.25	0.35
VS2045	1,030,000	—	—	0.10	0.25	0.35
VS2046	—	—	—	0.10	0.25	0.35
VS2047	—	—	—	0.10	0.25	0.35

KM# 806 10 PAISA

Brass **Obv:** Trident with sun and moon flanking above hills **Rev:** Ox left

Date	Mintage	F12	VF20	XF40	MS60	MS63
VS2028 Sets only	5,035	—	—	—	1.50	2.50

Note: Mahendra Bir Bikram also struck a 10 Paisa VS2028, see KM#765

KM# 807 10 PAISA

4.14 g., Brass, 21 mm. **Obv:** Trident with sun and moon flanking above hills **Rev:** Value with grain sprigs at sides of coin

Date	Mintage	F12	VF20	XF40	MS60	MS63
VS2029	3,297,000	—	0.15	0.25	0.40	0.50
VS2029	3,943	PF63 1.00				
VS2030	5,670,000	—	0.15	0.25	0.40	0.50
VS2030	8,891	PF63 0.70				
VS2031	11,000	PF63 0.70				

KM# 808 10 PAISA

Aluminum **Subject:** Birendra Coronation **Obv:** Crown **Rev:** Dagger flanked by garlands from above

Date	Mintage	F12	VF20	XF40	MS60	MS63
VS2031	192,000	—	0.10	0.20	0.35	0.45

KM# 808a 10 PAISA

Copper-Nickel **Subject:** Birendra Coronation **Obv:** Crown **Rev:** Dagger flanked by garlands from above

Date	Mintage	F12	VF20	XF40	MS60	MS63
VS2031	1,000	PF63 3.50				

KM# 809 10 PAISA

Brass **Series:** F.A.O. International Women's Year **Obv:** Busts left **Rev:** Value within grain sprigs

Date	Mintage	F12	VF20	XF40	MS60	MS63
VS2032	2,500,000	—	0.10	0.15	0.25	0.35

KM# 810 10 PAISA

Brass **Subject:** Agricultural Developement **Obv:** Sheep's head right **Rev:** Value

Date	Mintage	F12	VF20	XF40	MS60	MS63
VS2033	10,000,000	—	0.10	0.15	0.25	0.35

KM# 811 10 PAISA

Aluminum **Series:** International Year of the Child **Obv:** Trident within small circle at center **Rev:** Symbol at center, rising sun above

Date	Mintage	F12	VF20	XF40	MS60	MS63
VS2036	213,000	—	0.10	0.15	0.25	0.35

KM# 812 10 PAISA

Aluminum **Subject:** Education for Village Women **Obv:** Trident within small circle at center **Rev:** Open book

Date	Mintage	F12	VF20	XF40	MS60	MS63
VS2036	Inc. above	—	0.10	0.15	0.50	0.75

KM# 1014.1 10 PAISA

1.30 g., Aluminum, 21.5 mm. **Obv:** Crown **Rev:** Large ears of grain

Date	Mintage	F12	VF20	XF40	MS60	MS63
VS2039	796	—	7.00	10.00	15.00	20.00
VS2040	—	—	—	0.10	0.30	0.40
VS2041	7,834,000	—	—	0.10	0.30	0.40
VS2042	99,000	—	—	0.10	0.30	0.40

KM# 1014.2 10 PAISA

1.30 g., Aluminum, 21.5 mm. **Obv:** Crown **Rev:** Small ears of grain

Date	Mintage	F12	VF20	XF40	MS60	MS63
VS2041	—	—	—	0.10	0.30	0.40
VS2042	Inc. above	—	—	0.10	0.30	0.40
VS2043	10,000	—	—	0.10	0.30	0.40
VS2044	30,172,000	—	—	0.10	0.30	0.40
VS2045	4,140,000	—	—	0.10	0.30	0.40
VS2046	—	—	—	0.10	0.30	0.40
VS2047	—	—	—	0.10	0.30	0.40
VS2048	—	—	—	0.10	0.30	0.40
VS2049	—	—	—	0.10	0.30	0.40
VS2050	—	—	—	0.10	0.20	0.30

KM# 1014.3 10 PAISA

0.72 g., Aluminum, 17 mm. **Obv:** Crown **Rev:** Value, grain ears flank **Edge:** Plain **Note:** Reduced size.

Date	Mintage	F12	VF20	XF40	MS60	MS63
VS2051	—	—	—	0.10	0.30	0.40
VS2052	—	—	—	0.10	0.30	0.40
VS2053	—	—	—	0.10	0.30	0.40
VS2054	—	—	—	0.10	0.30	0.40
VS2055	—	—	—	0.10	0.30	0.40
VS2056	—	—	—	0.10	0.30	0.40
VS2057	—	—	—	0.10	0.30	0.40

KM# 813 20 PAISA

Brass **Series:** F.A.O. **Obv:** Trident within small circle at center

Date	Mintage	F12	VF20	XF40	MS60	MS63
VS2035	234,000	—	0.35	0.75	1.00	1.50

KM# 814 20 PAISA

Brass **Series:** International Year of the Child **Obv:** Trident within small center circle **Rev:** Emblem below rising sun

Date	Mintage	F12	VF20	XF40	MS60	MS63
VS2036	30,000	—	0.35	0.75	1.00	1.50

KM# 815 25 PAISA

3.00 g., Copper-Nickel **Obv:** Trident within small center circle **Rev:** Dagger flanked by garlands from above **Note:** Varieties exist.

Date	Mintage	F12	VF20	XF40	MS60	MS63
VS2028	5,691	—	0.40	0.60	0.80	1.35

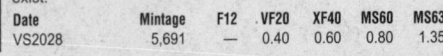

Date	Mintage	F12	VF20	XF40	MS60	MS63
VS2029	3,943	PF63 2.00				
VS2030	8,676,000	—	0.30	0.40	0.50	0.75
VS2030	8,891	PF63 1.25				
VS2031	1,172,000	—	0.35	0.50	0.75	1.25
VS2031	11,000	PF63 1.50				
VS2032	4,584,000	—	0.30	0.40	0.50	0.75
VS2033	1,837,000	—	0.30	0.40	0.50	0.75
VS2034	3,808,000	—	0.30	0.40	0.50	0.75
VS2035	5,964,000	—	0.30	0.40	0.50	0.75
VS2036	—	—	0.30	0.40	0.50	0.75
VS2037	2,047,000	—	0.30	0.40	0.50	0.75
VS2038	1,580,000	—	0.30	0.40	0.50	0.75
VS2039	7,185,000	—	0.30	0.40	0.50	0.75

KM# 815a 25 PAISA

Aluminum, 19 mm. **Obv:** Trident within small center circle **Rev:** Dagger flanked by garlands from above **Edge:** Reeded

Date	Mintage	F12	VF20	XF40	MS60	MS63
VS2030 (1973)	—	—	—	—	—	—

KM# 816.1.1 25 PAISA

2.93 g., Copper-Nickel, 18.8 mm. **Subject:** Birendra Coronation **Obv:** Crown **Rev:** Dagger flanked by garlands from above

Date	Mintage	F12	VF20	XF40	MS60	MS63
VS2031	431,000	—	0.35	0.50	0.75	1.25

KM# 816.2.2 25 PAISA

2.93 g., Copper-Nickel, 18.8 mm. **Subject:** Birendra Coronation **Obv:** Crown **Rev:** Dagger flanked by garlands from above **Edge:** Reeded

Date	Mintage	F12	VF20	XF40	MS60	MS63
VS2031	1,000	PF63 4.00				

KM# 817 25 PAISA

Brass **Series:** World Food Day **Obv:** Trident within small center circle **Rev:** Corn ear at left, logo at right

Date	Mintage	F12	VF20	XF40	MS60	MS63
VS2038	2,000,000	—	—	0.10	0.30	0.50

KM# 818 25 PAISA

Brass **Series:** International Year of Disabled Persons **Obv:** Trident within small center circle **Rev:** Emblem at center

Date	Mintage	F12	VF20	XF40	MS60	MS63
VS2038	Inc. above	—	0.10	0.25	0.50	0.75

KM# 1015.1 25 PAISA

1.80 g., Aluminum, 24.5 mm. **Obv:** Crown **Rev:** Value flanked by grain ears

Date	Mintage	F12	VF20	XF40	MS60	MS63
VS2039	—	—	4.00	6.00	8.00	12.00
VS2040	7,603,000	—	0.10	0.25	0.50	0.75
VS2041	15,534,000	—	0.10	0.25	0.50	0.75
VS2042	12,586,000	—	0.10	0.25	0.50	0.75
VS2043	54,000	—	0.10	0.25	0.50	0.75
VS2044	13,633,000	—	0.10	0.25	0.50	0.75
VS2045	13,046,000	—	0.10	0.25	0.50	0.75
VS2046	—	—	0.10	0.25	0.50	0.75

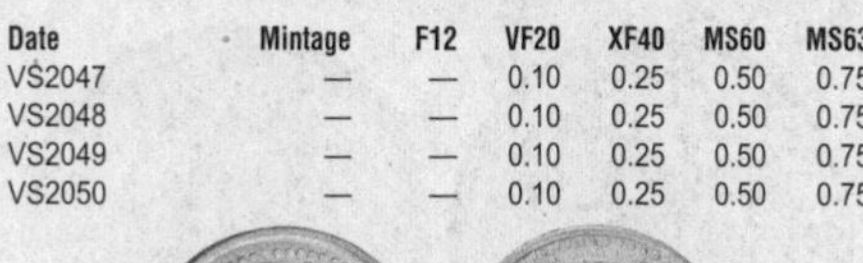

Date	Mintage	F12	VF20	XF40	MS60	MS63
VS2047	—	—	0.10	0.25	0.50	0.75
VS2048	—	—	0.10	0.25	0.50	0.75
VS2049	—	—	0.10	0.25	0.50	0.75
VS2050	—	—	0.10	0.25	0.50	0.75

KM# 1015.2 25 PAISA

1.50 g., Aluminum, 20 mm. **Obv:** Crown **Rev:** Value flanked by grain ears **Edge:** Plain **Note:** Reduced size.

Date	Mintage	F12	VF20	XF40	MS60	MS63
VS2051	—	—	0.10	0.25	0.50	0.75
VS2052	—	—	0.10	0.25	0.50	0.75
VS2053	—	—	0.10	0.25	0.50	0.75
VS2054	—	—	0.10	0.25	0.50	0.75
VS2055	—	—	0.10	0.25	0.50	0.75
VS2056	—	—	0.10	0.25	0.50	0.75
VS2057	—	—	0.10	0.25	0.50	0.75

KM# 821 50 PAISA

5.00 g., Copper-Nickel, 23.5 mm. **Obv:** Trident within small center circle **Rev:** Dagger flanked by garlands from above

Date	Mintage	F12	VF20	XF40	MS60	MS63
VS2028	5,343	—	0.35	0.50	1.00	—
VS2029	347,000	—	0.35	0.50	0.90	1.45
VS2029	3,943	PF63 2.00				
VS2030	998,000	—	0.35	0.50	0.90	1.45
VS2030	8,891	PF63 1.50				
VS2031	16,000	—	0.35	0.50	1.00	1.50
VS2031	11,000	PF63 1.50				
VS2032	227,000	—	0.35	0.50	0.90	1.45
Note: Dot in moon on reverse						
VS2033	3,446,000	—	0.35	0.50	0.75	1.25
VS2034	6,016,000	—	0.35	0.50	0.75	1.25
VS2035	2,355,000	—	0.35	0.50	0.75	1.25
VS2036	—	—	0.35	0.50	0.75	1.25
VS2037	4,861,000	—	0.35	0.50	0.75	1.25
VS2038	929,000	—	0.35	0.50	0.75	1.25
VS2039	2,954,000	—	0.35	0.50	0.75	1.25

KM# 821a 50 PAISA

5.09 g., Copper-Nickel, 20 mm. **Obv:** Trident within small center circle **Rev:** Dagger flanked by garlands from above

Date	Mintage	F12	VF20	XF40	MS60	MS63
VS2039	Inc. above	—	0.10	0.25	0.50	0.75
VS2040	72,000	—	0.10	0.25	0.50	0.75
VS2041	5,917,000	—	0.10	0.25	0.50	0.75

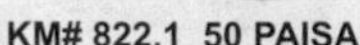

KM# 822.1 50 PAISA

Copper-Nickel **Subject:** Birendra Coronation **Obv:** Crown **Rev:** Dagger flanked by garlands from above **Note:** 1mm thick.

Date	Mintage	F12	VF20	XF40	MS60	MS63
VS2031	136,000	—	0.50	0.75	1.25	1.75

KM# 822.2 50 PAISA

Copper-Nickel **Subject:** Birendra Coronation **Edge:** Reeded **Note:** 1.5mm thick.

Date	Mintage	F12	VF20	XF40	MS60	MS63
VS2031	1,000	PF63 5.00				

KM# 846 50 PAISA

4.90 g., Copper-Nickel, 23.56 mm. **Obv:** Trident within small center circle **Rev:** Dagger flanked by garlands from above **Note:** In the name of Queen Aishvarya Rajya Lakshmi

Date	Mintage	F12	VF20	XF40	MS60	MS63
VS2031	—	—	—	—	1.00	1.50

KM# 823 50 PAISA

Copper-Nickel **Series:** World Food Day **Obv:** Trident within small center circle **Rev:** Corn ear at left, logo at right

Date	Mintage	F12	VF20	XF40	MS60	MS63
VS2038	2,000,000	—	0.10	0.30	0.60	0.90

KM# 824 50 PAISA

Copper-Nickel **Series:** International Year of Disabled Persons **Obv:** Trident within small center circle **Rev:** Emblem at center

Date	Mintage	F12	VF20	XF40	MS60	MS63
VS2038	Inc. above	—	0.50	0.75	1.25	1.75

KM# 1016 50 PAISA

3.00 g., Copper-Nickel, 20 mm. **Subject:** Family Planning **Obv:** Logo above inscription **Rev:** Value

Date	Mintage	F12	VF20	XF40	MS60	MS63
VS2041	—	—	0.10	0.25	0.50	0.75

KM# 1018 50 PAISA

Stainless Steel, 23.5 mm. **Obv:** Small trident in center **Rev:** Dagger flanked by garlands from above

Date	Mintage	F12	VF20	XF40	MS60	MS63
VS2044	6,341,000	—	0.10	0.25	0.50	0.75
VS2045	7,350,000	—	0.10	0.25	0.50	0.75
Note: Varieties with small and large Nepalese "5" exist						
VS2046	—	—	0.10	0.25	0.50	0.75
VS2049	—	—	0.10	0.25	0.50	0.75

KM# 1072 50 PAISA

1.41 g., Aluminum, 22.5 mm. **Obv:** Royal crown **Rev:** Crown **Edge:** Plain **Note:** Coins dated VS2051 exist in two minor varieties being struck at Kathmandu (round edge) and Singapore (sharp edge).

Date	Mintage	F12	VF20	XF40	MS60	MS63
VS2051	—	—	0.10	0.20	0.40	0.65
VS2052	—	—	0.10	0.20	0.40	0.65
VS2053	—	—	0.10	0.20	0.40	0.65
VS2054	—	—	0.10	0.20	0.40	0.65
VS2055	—	—	0.10	0.20	0.40	0.65
VS2056	—	—	0.10	0.20	0.40	0.65
VS2057	—	—	0.10	0.20	0.40	0.65

KM# 828.1 RUPEE

10.20 g., Copper-Nickel **Obv:** Trident within small center circle **Rev:** Dagger flanked by garlands from above

Date	Mintage	F12	VF20	XF40	MS60	MS63
VS2028	5,030	—	0.50	1.00	2.00	3.50
VS2029	22,000	—	0.50	1.00	1.50	2.50
VS2029	3,943	PF63 3.50				
VS2030	5,667	—	0.50	1.00	2.00	3.50
VS2030	8,891	PF63 2.50				
VS2031	11,000	PF63 2.00				

KM# 829.1 RUPEE

Copper-Nickel **Subject:** Birendra Coronation **Obv:** Crown at center of ornamental frame **Rev:** Dagger flanked by garlands from above **Note:** 2 millimeters thick.

Date	Mintage	F12	VF20	XF40	MS60	MS63
VS2031	—	—	0.75	1.25	1.75	2.75

KM# 829.2 RUPEE

Copper-Nickel **Subject:** Birendra Coronation **Obv:** Crown at center of ornamental frame **Rev:** Dagger flanked by garlands from above **Edge:** Reeded **Note:** 2.5 millimeters thick.

Date	Mintage	F12	VF20	XF40	MS60	MS63
VS2031	1,000	PF63 6.00				

KM# 848 RUPEE

Copper-Nickel **Obv:** Trident within small circle at center **Rev:** Dagger flanked by garlands from above **Note:** In the name of Queen Aishvarya Rajya Lakshmi.

Date	Mintage	F12	VF20	XF40	MS60	MS63
VS2031	—	—	—	—	150	180

KM# 831 RUPEE

Copper-Nickel **Series:** F.A.O. International Women's Year **Obv:** Busts left **Rev:** Value above logo, grain ears flank

Date	Mintage	F12	VF20	XF40	MS60	MS63
VS2032	1,500,000	—	0.25	0.50	1.25	2.00

KM# 828a RUPEE

7.50 g., Copper-Nickel, 27.5 mm. **Note:** Reduced weight. Coins dated VS2036 were struck at the Canberra Mint and have a very shiny surface. High quality examples of VS2034 were struck at Canberra Mint while dull surfaced examples were probably struck at Kathmandu Mint.

Date	Mintage	F12	VF20	XF40	MS60	MS63
VS2033	58,000	—	0.50	1.00	1.50	2.50
VS2034	30,000,000	—	0.25	0.50	1.00	1.50
VS2035	—	—	0.25	0.50	1.00	1.50
VS2036	30,000,000	—	0.25	0.50	1.00	1.50

KM# 828.2 RUPEE

Copper-Nickel **Note:** Reduced size: 23mm. Like 821a.

Date	Mintage	F12	VF20	XF40	MS60	MS63
VS2039 (1982)	—	—	0.25	0.50	1.00	1.50

KM# 1019 RUPEE

Copper-Nickel **Subject:** Family Planning **Obv:** Logo at center within design **Rev:** Value

Date	Mintage	F12	VF20	XF40	MS60	MS63
VS2041	21,000	—	—	—	0.75	1.25

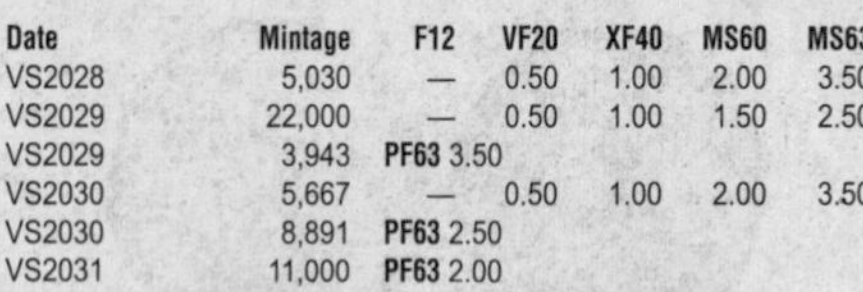

KM# 1061 RUPEE

6.75 g., Stainless Steel **Obv:** Small trident in center **Rev:** Dagger flanked by garlands from above

Date	Mintage	F12	VF20	XF40	MS60	MS63
VS2045 Prooflike	—	—	0.25	0.50	1.00	1.50
VS2048 Prooflike	—	—	0.25	0.50	1.00	1.50
Note: Varieties exist						
VS2049 Prooflike	—	—	0.25	0.50	1.25	2.00

KM# 1073 RUPEE

3.50 g., Brass Plated Steel, 22 mm. **Obv:** Small trident at center **Rev:** Large legends **Edge:** Plain **Note:** Sharp and round edge varieties.

Date	Mintage	F12	VF20	XF40	MS60	MS63
VS2051	—	—	0.25	0.50	1.00	1.50
VS2052	—	—	0.25	0.50	1.00	1.50

KM# 1073a RUPEE

4.08 g., Brass, 20 mm. **Obv:** Traditional design **Rev:** Small legends

Date	Mintage	F12	VF20	XF40	MS60	MS63
VS2052	—	—	—	—	1.00	1.50
VS2053	—	—	—	—	1.00	1.50
VS2054	—	—	—	—	1.00	1.50
VS2055	—	—	—	—	1.00	1.50
VS2056	—	—	—	—	1.00	1.50
VS2057	—	—	—	—	1.00	1.50

KM# 1092 RUPEE

Brass Plated Steel, 22 mm. **Series:** U.N. 50th Anniversary **Obv:** Traditional design **Rev:** UN logo and dates

Date	Mintage	F12	VF20	XF40	MS60	MS63
VS2052	—	—	—	—	1.75	2.75

KM# 1152 RUPEE

28.16 g., 0.999 Copper-Nickel 0.9045 oz., 38.5 mm. **Subject:** UN 50th Anniversary **Obv:** Traditional design **Rev:** UN 50 logo **Edge:** Reeded

Date	Mintage	F12	VF20	XF40	MS60	MS63
VS2052 (1995)	—	—	—	—	3.00	5.00

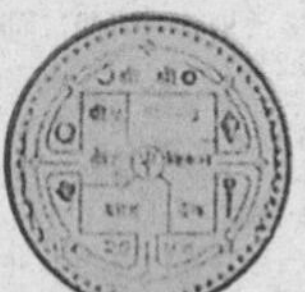

KM# 1115 RUPEE

Brass, 20 mm. **Subject:** Visit Nepal '98 **Obv:** Traditional design **Rev:** Moon and sun flanking mountaintop

Date	Mintage	F12	VF20	XF40	MS60	MS63
VS2054	—	—	—	—	1.00	1.50

KM# 1139 RUPEE

Brass, 20 mm. **Subject:** Gorkhapatra Centenary **Obv:** Traditional design **Rev:** Inscription within wreath of ten people reading newspapers **Rev. Inscription:** Gorkhapata 1958-VS2057

Date	Mintage	F12	VF20	XF40	MS60	MS63
VS2057	—	—	—	—	1.00	1.50

KM# 832 2 RUPEES

Copper-Nickel **Series:** World Food Day **Obv:** Trident within circle at center **Rev:** Corn ear at left, logo at right

Date	Mintage	F12	VF20	XF40	MS60	MS63
VS2038	1,000,000	—	0.50	0.75	1.50	2.50

KM# 1025 2 RUPEES

Copper-Nickel **Series:** F.A.O. **Obv:** Traditional design **Note:** Size of obverse square varies. With or without dot in reverse sun.

Date	Mintage	F12	VF20	XF40	MS60	MS63
VS2039	366,000	—	0.50	0.75	1.50	2.50

KM# 1020 2 RUPEES

Copper-Nickel **Subject:** Family Planning **Obv:** Emblem within decorative outlines **Rev:** Value

Date	Mintage	F12	VF20	XF40	MS60	MS63
VS2041	11,000	—	0.50	0.75	1.50	2.50

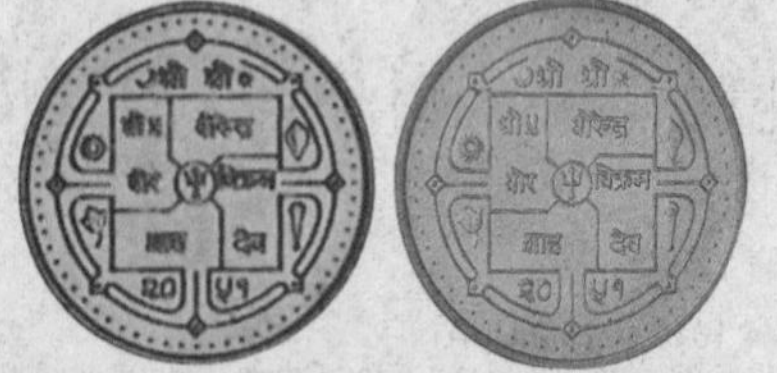

KM# 1074.1 2 RUPEES

4.96 g., Brass Plated Steel, 24.4 mm. **Obv:** Small trident at center **Rev:** Building above value **Edge:** Plain **Note:** Sharp and round edge varieties exist.

Date	Mintage	F12	VF20	XF40	MS60	MS63
VS2051	—	—	0.35	0.60	1.25	1.75
VS2052	—	—	0.35	0.60	1.25	1.75

KM# 1074.2 2 RUPEES

Brass, 25 mm.

Date	Mintage	F12	VF20	XF40	MS60	MS63
VS2053 (1996)	—	—	0.35	0.60	1.25	1.75
VS2055 (1998)	—	—	0.35	0.60	1.25	1.75
VS2056 (1999)	—	—	0.35	0.60	1.25	1.75
VS2057 (2000)	—	—	0.35	0.60	1.25	1.75

KM# 1116 2 RUPEES

Brass, 25 mm. **Subject:** Visit Nepal '98 **Obv:** Traditional design **Rev:** Moon and sun flanking mountaintop

Date	Mintage	F12	VF20	XF40	MS60	MS63
VS2053	—	—	—	—	1.25	1.75
VS2054	—	—	—	—	1.25	1.75

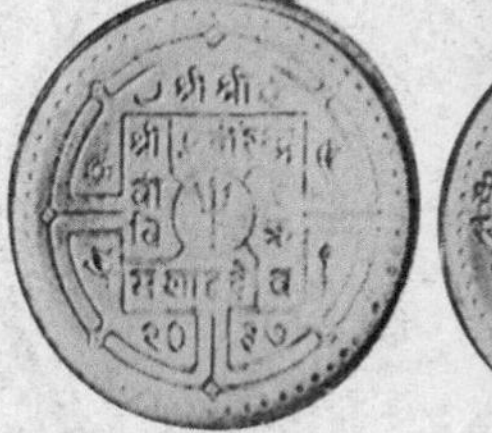

KM# 833 5 RUPEE

Copper-Nickel **Subject:** Rural Women's Advancement **Obv:** Trident within small circle at center

Date	Mintage	F12	VF20	XF40	MS60	MS63
VS2037	50,000	—	0.75	1.50	3.00	5.00

KM# 834 5 RUPEE

Copper-Nickel, 28.7-30.0 mm. **Subject:** National Bank Silver Jubilee **Obv:** Trident within small circle at center **Rev:** Small figurine of native god at center **Note:** Size varies.

Date	Mintage	F12	VF20	XF40	MS60	MS63
VS2038	64,000	—	0.75	1.50	3.00	5.00

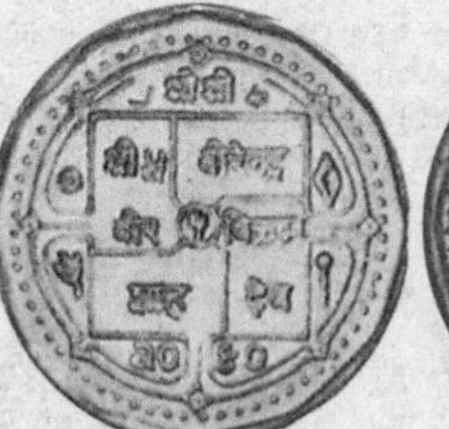

KM# 1009 5 RUPEE

Copper-Nickel **Obv:** Traditional design **Rev:** Dagger flanked by garlands from above **Note:** Circulation coinage

Date	Mintage	F12	VF20	XF40	MS60	MS63
VS2039	Inc. above	—	0.50	1.00	2.00	3.00
VS2040	478,000	—	0.30	0.50	1.00	1.50

KM# 1017 5 RUPEE

Copper-Nickel **Subject:** Family Planning **Obv:** Value **Rev:** Logo above inscription

Date	Mintage	F12	VF20	XF40	MS60	MS63
VS2041	458,000	—	0.50	1.00	2.00	3.00

KM# 1023 5 RUPEE

Copper-Nickel **Subject:** Year of Youth **Obv:** Value **Rev:** Emblem below hills

Date	Mintage	F12	VF20	XF40	MS60	MS63
VS2042	1,124,000	—	—	—	2.50	4.00

KM# 1047 5 RUPEE

Copper-Nickel **Subject:** Social Services **Obv:** Value **Rev:** Ox left within small center circle

Date	Mintage	F12	VF20	XF40	MS60	MS63
VS2042	Inc. above	—	—	—	3.50	6.00

KM# 1028 5 RUPEE

Copper-Nickel **Series:** World Food Day **Obv:** Traditional design **Rev:** Fish left below logo

Date	Mintage	F12	VF20	XF40	MS60	MS63
VS2043	99,000	—	—	—	3.50	6.00

KM# 1042 5 RUPEE

Copper-Nickel **Subject:** 15th World Buddhist Conference **Obv:** Value **Rev:** Figure at center of globe within ornamented circle **Note:** Two different obverse dies exist.

Date	Mintage	F12	VF20	XF40	MS60	MS63
VS2043//1986	135,000	—	—	—	3.50	6.00

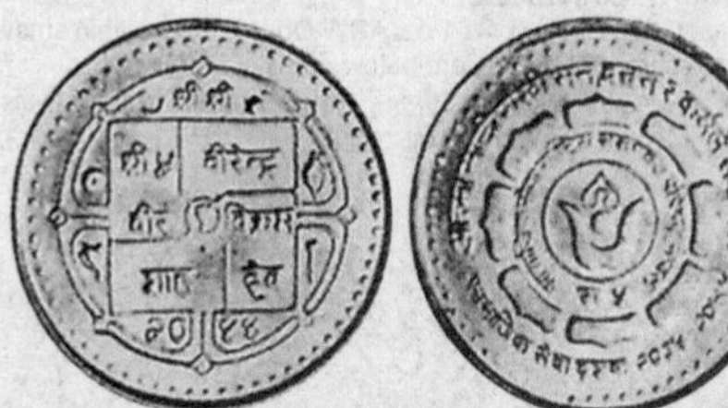

KM# 1030 5 RUPEE

Copper-Nickel **Subject:** 10th Year of National Social Security Administration **Obv:** Traditional design **Rev:** Emblem at center

Date	Mintage	F12	VF20	XF40	MS60	MS63
VS2044	104,000	—	—	—	3.50	6.00
VS2045	—	—	—	—	3.50	6.00

KM# 1043 5 RUPEE

Copper, 38.7 mm. **Subject:** 3rd SAARC Summit **Obv:** Traditional design **Rev:** Summit emblem

Date	Mintage	F12	VF20	XF40	MS60	MS63
VS2044	2,000	—	—	—	6.50	9.00

KM# 1053 5 RUPEE

Copper-Nickel **Series:** World Food Day **Obv:** Traditional design **Rev:** Emblem above symbols

Date	Mintage	F12	VF20	XF40	MS60	MS63
VS2047	—	—	—	—	4.00	7.00

KM# 1063 5 RUPEE

Copper-Nickel **Subject:** New Constitution **Obv:** Traditional design **Rev:** Flags above open book

Date	Mintage	F12	VF20	XF40	MS60	MS63
VS2047	—	—	—	—	3.25	6.00

KM# 1062 5 RUPEE

Copper-Nickel **Subject:** Parliament Session **Obv:** Traditional design **Rev:** Outlined drawings symbolizing figures of parliament

Date	Mintage	F12	VF20	XF40	MS60	MS63
VS2048	—	—	—	—	3.00	5.00

KM# 1075.1 5 RUPEE

6.52 g., Brass Plated Steel, 27 mm. **Obv:** Traditional design **Rev:** Temple **Edge:** Plain

Date	Mintage	F12	VF20	XF40	MS60	MS63
VS2051	—	—	—	—	1.50	2.00

KM# 1075.2 5 RUPEE

Brass, 25 mm. **Edge:** Reeded

Date	Mintage	F12	VF20	XF40	MS60	MS63
VS2053	—	—	—	—	1.50	2.00

KM# 1117 5 RUPEE
Copper, 25 mm. **Subject:** Visit Nepal '98 **Obv:** Traditional design **Rev:** Sun and moon flanking mountaintop **Edge:** Reeded

Date	Mintage	F12	VF20	XF40	MS60	MS63
VS2054	—	—	—	—	1.50	2.00

KM# 835 10 RUPEE
8.00 g., 0.250 Silver 0.0643 oz. ASW **Series:** F.A.O. **Obv:** Value and dates **Rev:** Family scene

Date	Mintage	F12	VF20	XF40	MS60	MS63
VS2031	39,000	—	—	5.00	7.00	9.00

KM# 1004 10 RUPEE
Copper-Nickel, 40 mm. **Subject:** 30th Anniversary - Ascent of Mt. Everest **Obv:** Traditional design **Rev:** Mount Everest

Date	Mintage	F12	VF20	XF40	MS60	MS63
VS2040	2,000	—	—	—	12.50	15.00

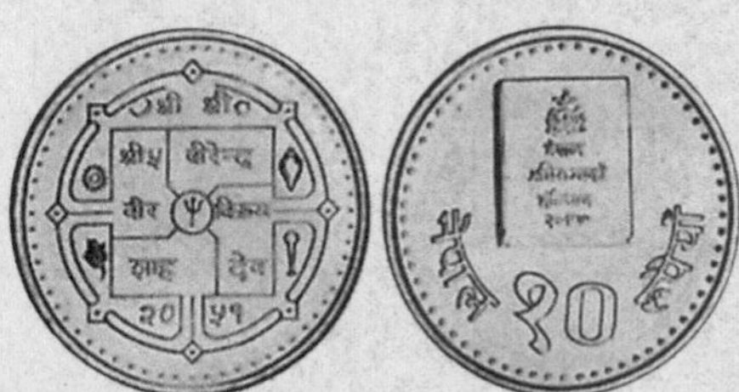

KM# 1076 10 RUPEE
8.00 g., Brass Plated Steel, 29 mm. **Obv:** Traditional design **Rev:** Closed book

Date	Mintage	F12	VF20	XF40	MS60	MS63
VS2051	—	—	—	—	2.50	4.00

KM# 1083 10 RUPEE
Copper-Nickel **Subject:** 75th Anniversary - International Labor Organization **Obv:** Traditional design **Rev:** Logo above legend

Date	Mintage	F12	VF20	XF40	MS60	MS63
VS2051	—	—	—	—	4.50	7.00

KM# 1089 10 RUPEE
Copper-Nickel, 29 mm. **Subject:** 50th Anniversary - F.A.O. Logo **Obv:** Traditional design **Rev:** Logo with grain ears flanking **Edge:** Plain

Date	Mintage	F12	VF20	XF40	MS60	MS63
VS2052	—	—	—	—	4.00	6.00

KM# 1118 10 RUPEE
Copper-Nickel, 25 mm. **Subject:** Visit Nepal '98 **Obv:** Traditional design **Rev:** Moon and sun flanking mountaintop **Edge:** Reeded

Date	Mintage	F12	VF20	XF40	MS60	MS63
VS2054	—	—	—	—	3.00	5.00

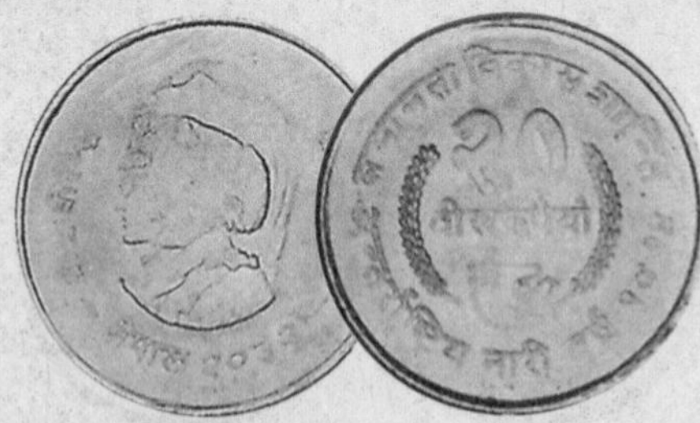

KM# 836 20 RUPEE
14.85 g., 0.500 Silver 0.2387 oz. ASW **Series:** F.A.O. International Women's Year **Obv:** Busts left **Rev:** Value within grain sprigs

Date	Mintage	VF20	XF40	MS60	MS63	MS65
VS2032	50,000	—	8.00	12.00	15.00	17.00

KM# 837 20 RUPEE
14.85 g., 0.250 Silver 0.1194 oz. ASW **Series:** International Year of the Child **Obv:** Trident within small circle at center **Rev:** Emblem below rising sun

Date	Mintage	VF20	XF40	MS60	MS63	MS65
VS2036	—	—	6.00	8.00	10.00	12.00

KM# 837a 20 RUPEE
15.00 g., 0.925 Silver 0.4461 oz. ASW **Obv:** Trident within small circle at center **Rev:** Emblem below rising sun

Date	Mintage	VF20	XF40	MS60	MS63	MS65
VS2036	1,000	PF65 35.00				

KM# 838 25 RUPEE
25.60 g., 0.500 Silver 0.4115 oz. ASW **Subject:** Birendra Coronation **Obv:** Crown **Rev:** Dagger flanked by garlands from above **Edge:** Reeded **Note:** 2mm thick.

Date	Mintage	VF20	XF40	MS60	MS63	MS65
VS2031	75,000	—	—	12.00	17.00	22.00

KM# 838a 25 RUPEE
28.28 g., 0.925 Silver 0.841 oz. ASW **Obv:** Crown **Rev:** Dagger flanked by garlands from above **Edge:** Reeded **Note:** 3mm thick.

Date	Mintage	VF20	XF40	MS60	MS63	MS65
VS2031	2,000	PF63 35.00	PF65 45.00			

KM# 839 25 RUPEE
25.60 g., 0.500 Silver 0.4115 oz. ASW **Series:** Conservation **Obv:** Bust of Birendra Bir Bikram right **Rev:** Himalayan Monal Pheasant

Date	Mintage	VF20	XF40	MS60	MS63	MS65
VS2031	11,000	—	—	13.00	18.00	27.00

KM# 839a 25 RUPEE
28.28 g., 0.925 Silver 0.841 oz. ASW **Obv:** Bust of Birendra Bir Bikram right **Rev:** Himalayan Monal Pheasant

Date	Mintage	VF20	XF40	MS60	MS63	MS65
VS2031	11,000	PF63 30.00	PF65 32.00			

KM# 1051 25 RUPEE
12.00 g., 0.250 Silver 0.0965 oz. ASW **Obv:** Crown **Rev:** Value

Date	Mintage	VF20	XF40	MS60	MS63	MS65
VS2041	—	—	—	—	12.00	15.00

KM# 1048.1 25 RUPEE
12.00 g., 0.250 Silver 0.0965 oz. ASW **Subject:** 25th Anniversary of Panchayat **Obv:** Thin 25 **Rev:** Small rosette

Note: Varieties exist with hollow or solid hand-like symbol below on obverse.

Date	Mintage	VF20	XF40	MS60	MS63	MS65
VS2042	9,962,000	—	—	—	8.00	10.00

KM# 1048.2 25 RUPEE

12.00 g., 0.250 Silver 0.0965 oz. ASW **Subject:** 25th Anniversary of Panchayat **Obv:** Thick 25 **Rev:** Large rosette **Note:** Varieties exist with hollow or solid hand-like symbol below on obverse.

Date	Mintage	VF20	XF40	MS60	MS63	MS65
VS2042 (1985)	Inc. above	—	—	—	8.00	10.00

KM# 1135 25 RUPEE

8.50 g., Copper-Nickel, 29 mm. **Subject:** Silver Jubilee of King's Accession **Obv:** Traditional design **Rev:** Crown on radiant emblem **Edge:** Plain

Date	Mintage	VF20	XF40	MS60	MS63	MS65
VS2053	—	—	—	—	3.50	5.00

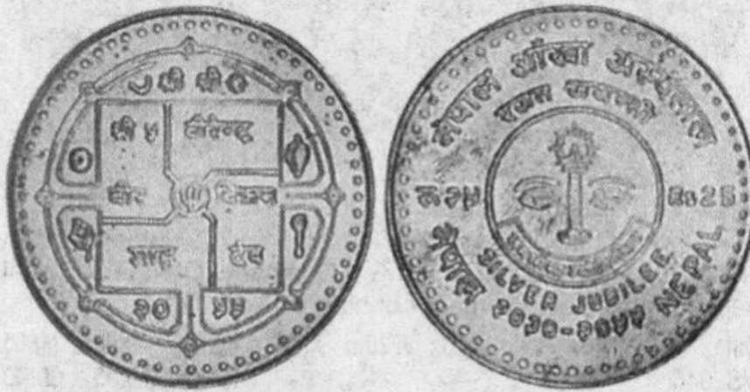

KM# 1126 25 RUPEE

Copper-Nickel **Subject:** Silver Jubilee **Obv:** Traditional design **Rev:** Stylized face design

Date	Mintage	VF20	XF40	MS60	MS63	MS65
VS2055	—	—	—	—	3.50	5.00

KM# 841 50 RUPEE

31.80 g., 0.500 Silver 0.5112 oz. ASW, 42 mm. **Series:** Conservation **Obv:** Bust right **Rev:** Red panda

Date	Mintage	VF20	XF40	MS60	MS63	MS65
VS2031	11,000	—	—	15.00	22.00	32.00

KM# 841a 50 RUPEE

35.00 g., 0.925 Silver 1.0409 oz. ASW, 42 mm. **Obv:** Bust right **Rev:** Red panda

Date	Mintage	VF20	XF40	MS60	MS63	MS65
VS2031	10,000	PF63 32.00	PF65 35.00			

KM# 842 50 RUPEE

25.00 g., 0.500 Silver 0.4019 oz. ASW **Subject:** Education for Village Women **Obv:** Traditional design **Rev:** Open book

Date	Mintage	VF20	XF40	MS60	MS63	MS65
VS2036	15,000	—	—	—	14.00	17.00

KM# 842a 50 RUPEE

25.00 g., 0.925 Silver 0.7435 oz. ASW **Obv:** Traditional design **Rev:** Open book

Date	Mintage	VF20	XF40	MS60	MS63	MS65
VS2036	1,000	PF63 45.00	PF65 55.00			

KM# A651 50 RUPEE

15.00 g., 0.400 Silver 0.1929 oz. ASW **Series:** International Year of the Child **Note:** Similar to 100 Rupee, KM#851.

Date	Mintage	VF20	XF40	MS60	MS63	MS65
VS2038	—	—	—	—	—	—

KM# 843 50 RUPEE

14.90 g., 0.500 Silver 0.2395 oz. ASW **Series:** International Year of Disabled Persons **Obv:** Traditional design **Rev:** Emblem within grain ears

Date	Mintage	VF20	XF40	MS60	MS63	MS65
VS2038	16,000	—	—	—	10.00	12.00

KM# 1046 50 RUPEE

15.00 g., 0.500 Silver 0.2411 oz. ASW **Subject:** 50th Anniversary of Kathmandu Mint **Obv:** Trident within small center circle **Rev:** Mint press

Date	Mintage	VF20	XF40	MS60	MS63	MS65
VS2039	8,765	—	—	12.00	14.00	18.00

KM# 1119 50 RUPEE

Bronze **Obv:** Traditional square in circle design **Rev:** Buddha's portrait and Ashoka pillar **Note:** Lord Buddha; Similar to 1500 Rupee, KM#1120.

Date	Mintage	VF20	XF40	MS60	MS63	MS65
VS2055	30,000	—	—	6.00	10.00	12.50

KM# 1136 50 RUPEE

Brass, 37.5 mm. **Subject:** 50th Anniversary - Radio Nepal **Obv:** Traditional design **Rev:** Stylized design **Edge:** Plain

Date	Mintage	VF20	XF40	MS60	MS63	MS65
VS2056	—	—	—	6.00	10.00	12.50

KM# 1127 50 RUPEE

Brass, 38.7 mm. **Subject:** Buddha **Obv:** Traditional square design **Rev:** Buddha and four figures **Edge:** Reeded

Date	Mintage	VF20	XF40	MS60	MS63	MS65
VS2057	30,000	—	—	6.00	10.00	12.50

KM# 1137 50 RUPEE

Brass, 37.5 mm. **Subject:** St. Xavier's Golden Jubilee **Obv:** Traditional design **Rev:** Coat of arms **Edge:** Plain

Date	Mintage	VF20	XF40	MS60	MS63	MS65
VS2057	—	—	—	6.00	10.00	12.50

KM# 1165 100 RUPEE

25.00 g., 0.500 Silver 0.4019 oz. ASW, 36 mm. **Obv:** Crown in square design **Rev:** Garland draped above sword **Edge:** Reeded

Date	Mintage	VF20	XF40	MS60	MS63	MS65
VS2031	1,000	PF63 45.00	PF65 50.00			

KM# 850.1 100 RUPEE

25.49 g., 0.500 Silver 0.4098 oz. ASW **Series:** World Food Day **Obv:** Traditional design **Rev:** Figure working in field

Date	Mintage	VF20	XF40	MS60	MS63	MS65
VS2038	18,000	—	—	15.00	18.00	22.00

KM# 850.2 100 RUPEE

25.49 g., 0.925 Silver 0.7581 oz. ASW **Series:** World Food Day **Obv:** Traditional design **Rev:** Figure working in field **Note:** Obverse and reverse are different.

Date	Mintage	VF20	XF40	MS60	MS63	MS65
VS2038	—	PF63 60.00	PF65 80.00			

KM# 851 100 RUPEE

19.44 g., 0.500 Silver 0.3125 oz. ASW **Series:** International

Year of the Child **Obv:** Crowned bust right **Rev:** Children filling water jug

Date	Mintage	VF20	XF40	MS60	MS63	MS65
VS2031(1974)	9,270	PF63 15.00	PF65 20.00			

Note: Struck in 1981

KM# 1005 100 RUPEE
31.10 g., 0.925 Silver 0.9249 oz. ASW, 38.6 mm. **Subject:** 30th Anniversary Ascent of Mt. Everest **Obv:** Trident within small circle at center **Rev:** Mount Everest

Date	Mintage	VF20	XF40	MS60	MS63	MS65
VS2040	1,500	PF63 65.00	PF65 75.00			

KM# 1024 100 RUPEE
15.00 g., 0.500 Silver 0.2411 oz. ASW **Subject:** Year of Youth **Obv:** Value **Rev:** Emblem below hills

Date	Mintage	VF20	XF40	MS60	MS63	MS65
VS2042	8,199	—	—	7.50	12.00	15.00

KM# 1114 100 RUPEE
12.04 g., 0.600 Silver 0.2323 oz. ASW **Series:** 50th Anniversary - F.A.O. **Obv:** Traditional design **Rev:** Logo at center, grain ears flank

Date	Mintage	VF20	XF40	MS60	MS63	MS65
VS2052	—	—	—	8.50	14.00	18.00

KM# 1102 100 RUPEE
Copper-Nickel **Series:** Nepal Wildlife **Rev:** Multicolor tiger

Date	Mintage	VF20	XF40	MS60	MS63	MS65
VS2054	25,000	—	—	—	16.00	22.00

KM# 1103 100 RUPEE
Copper-Nickel **Series:** Nepal Wildlife **Obv:** Traditional design **Rev:** Multicolor Great Indian rhino

Date	Mintage	VF20	XF40	MS60	MS63	MS65
VS2054-1998	25,000	—	—	—	16.00	22.00

KM# 1141 100 RUPEE
12.50 g., 0.500 Silver 0.2009 oz. ASW **Series:** International Year of Older Persons **Obv:** Traditional design **Rev:** Emblem and inscription

Date	Mintage	VF20	XF40	MS60	MS63	MS65
VS2056	—	—	—	6.00	10.00	12.00

KM# 1031 200 RUPEE
15.00 g., 0.600 Silver 0.2894 oz. ASW **Subject:** 10th Anniversary of National Social Security Administration **Obv:** Traditional design **Rev:** Emblem at center within small circle

Date	Mintage	VF20	XF40	MS60	MS63	MS65
VS2044	4,145	—	—	15.00	25.00	30.00

KM# 1007 250 RUPEE
28.28 g., 0.925 Silver 0.841 oz. ASW **Subject:** 10th Anniversary of Reign **Obv:** Conjoined busts left **Rev:** Value

Date	Mintage	VF20	XF40	MS60	MS63	MS65
VS2038	10,000	PF63 35.00	PF65 45.00			

KM# 1010 250 RUPEE
28.28 g., 0.925 Silver 0.841 oz. ASW **Subject:** Year of the Scout **Obv:** Traditional design **Rev:** Boy and girl scouts planting seedling

Date	Mintage	VF20	XF40	MS60	MS63	MS65
VS2039	10,000	—	—	—	35.00	40.00
VS2039	Inc. above	PF65 55.00				

KM# 1026 250 RUPEE
19.44 g., 0.925 Silver 0.5781 oz. ASW **Series:** Wildlife Preservation **Obv:** Traditional design **Rev:** Musk deer

Date	Mintage	VF20	XF40	MS60	MS63	MS65
VS2043	20,000	PF63 25.00	PF65 30.00			

KM# 1049 250 RUPEE
19.44 g., 0.925 Silver 0.5781 oz. ASW **Subject:** Silver Jubilee of Nepal Red Cross Society **Obv:** Traditional design **Rev:** Emblem at center

Date	Mintage	VF20	XF40	MS60	MS63	MS65
VS2045	6,360	—	—	15.00	25.00	30.00

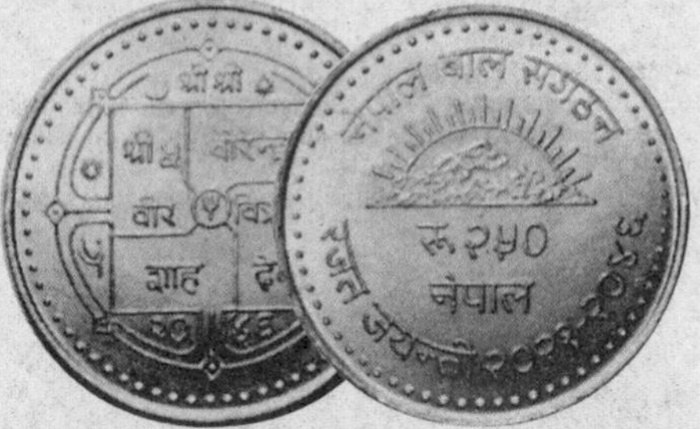

KM# 1052 250 RUPEE
19.44 g., 0.925 Silver 0.5781 oz. ASW **Subject:** 25th Anniversary of Nepalese Power Company **Obv:** Traditional design **Rev:** Rising sun back of hills

Date	Mintage	VF20	XF40	MS60	MS63	MS65
VS2046	—	—	—	15.00	25.00	30.00

KM# 1055 250 RUPEE
19.44 g., 0.925 Silver 0.5781 oz. ASW **Series:** Save the Children **Obv:** Traditional design **Rev:** Children dancing

Date	Mintage	VF20	XF40	MS60	MS63	MS65
VS2047	20,000	PF63 18.00	PF65 22.00			

KM# 1134.1 250 RUPEE
18.10 g., 0.925 Silver 0.5383 oz. ASW, 36 mm. **Subject:** Silver Jubilee - Nepal Disabled Association **Note:** Large figures, large inscriptions.

Date	Mintage	VF20	XF40	MS60	MS63	MS65
VS2052(1995)	—	PF63 20.00	PF65 25.00			

KM# 1134.2 250 RUPEE
17.70 g., 0.500 Silver 0.2845 oz. ASW, 36 mm. **Subject:** Nepal Disabled Association **Obv:** Traditional square design **Rev:** Human figures Logo and value **Edge:** Reeded **Note:** Small figures, small inscriptions

Date	Mintage	VF20	XF40	MS60	MS63	MS65
VS2052(1995)	—	—	—	12.00	22.00	30.00

KM# 1134.3 250 RUPEE
17.70 g., 0.500 Silver 0.2845 oz. ASW, 36 mm. **Subject:** Nepal Disabled Association **Obv:** Traditional square design with small inscriptions **Rev:** Human figures logo and value **Edge:** Reeded

Date	Mintage	VF20	XF40	MS60	MS63	MS65
VS2052(1995)	—	—	—	12.00	22.00	30.00

KM# 1029 300 RUPEE
25.29 g., 0.500 Silver 0.4065 oz. ASW **Subject:** First Scout

Jamboree in Nepal **Obv:** Traditional design **Rev:** Emblems within temple outline, hills in background

Date	Mintage	VF20	XF40	MS60	MS63	MS65
VS2043	6,967	—	—	—	25.00	32.00

KM# 1044 300 RUPEE
25.00 g., 0.925 Silver 0.7435 oz. ASW **Subject:** 3rd SAARC Summit **Obv:** Traditional design **Rev:** Summit emblem

Date	Mintage	VF20	XF40	MS60	MS63	MS65
VS2044	5,000	—	—	20.00	30.00	35.00

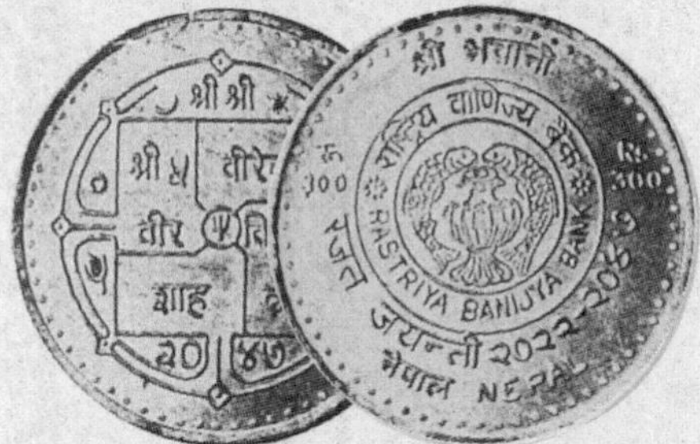

KM# 1057 300 RUPEE
18.05 g., 0.925 Silver 0.5368 oz. ASW **Obv:** Traditional design **Rev:** Rastriya Banijya Bank logo

Date	Mintage	VF20	XF40	MS60	MS63	MS65
VS2047	—	—	—	12.00	22.00	30.00

KM# 1064 300 RUPEE
18.32 g., 0.925 Silver 0.5447 oz. ASW **Subject:** New Constitution **Obv:** Traditional design **Rev:** Flags above open book

Date	Mintage	VF20	XF40	MS60	MS63	MS65
VS2047	—	—	—	12.00	22.00	30.00

KM# 1065 300 RUPEE
18.32 g., 0.925 Silver 0.5447 oz. ASW **Subject:** Parliament Session **Obv:** Traditional design **Rev:** Outlined figures symbolizing members of parliament

Date	Mintage	VF20	XF40	MS60	MS63	MS65
VS2048	—	—	—	12.00	22.00	30.00

KM# 1068 300 RUPEE
17.81 g., 0.925 Silver 0.5297 oz. ASW **Obv:** Traditional design **Rev:** Figure between hands holding grains, hills in background

Date	Mintage	VF20	XF40	MS60	MS63	MS65
VS2049	—	—	—	12.00	22.00	30.00

KM# 1094 300 RUPEE
18.13 g., 0.925 Silver 0.5392 oz. ASW **Subject:** Rastriya Beema Sansthan Silver Jubilee **Obv:** Traditional design **Rev:** Eyes below design

Date	Mintage	VF20	XF40	MS60	MS63	MS65
VS2049	—	—	—	12.00	22.00	30.00

KM# 1142 300 RUPEE
18.00 g., 0.925 Silver 0.5353 oz. ASW **Subject:** 75th Anniversary of I.L.O.

Date	Mintage	VF20	XF40	MS60	MS63	MS65
VS2051	—	—	—	12.00	22.00	30.00

KM# 1032 350 RUPEE
23.30 g., 0.500 Silver 0.3746 oz. ASW **Subject:** Crown Prince, Sacred Thread Ceremony **Obv:** Traditional design

Date	Mintage	VF20	XF40	MS60	MS63	MS65
VS2044	5,217	—	—	—	25.00	32.00

KM# 1035 500 RUPEE
35.00 g., 0.500 Silver 0.5626 oz. ASW **Subject:** 50th Anniversary of National Bank **Obv:** Traditional design **Rev:** Figure at center of designed globe

Date	Mintage	VF20	XF40	MS60	MS63	MS65
VS2044	19,000	—	—	—	35.00	40.00

KM# 1166 500 RUPEE
31.10 g., 0.999 Silver 0.9989 oz. ASW, 38.7 mm. **Obv:** Traditional design **Rev:** Ceremonial vase

Date	Mintage	VF20	XF40	MS60	MS63	MS65
VS2046(1989)	5,000	—	—	—	40.00	45.00

KM# 1058 500 RUPEE
31.47 g., 0.925 Silver 0.9359 oz. ASW **Subject:** 1992 Olympic games - Barcelona **Obv:** Traditional design **Rev:** Boxers

Date	Mintage	VF20	XF40	MS60	MS63	MS65
VS2049	Est. 40000	PF63 25.00	PF65 32.00			

KM# 1069 500 RUPEE
31.47 g., 0.925 Silver 0.9359 oz. ASW **Subject:** XV World Soccor Championship - USA **Rev:** Soccor goal being scored

Date	Mintage	VF20	XF40	MS60	MS63	MS65
VS2049	20,000	PF63 27.00	PF65 35.00			

KM# 1071 500 RUPEE
31.83 g., 0.925 Silver 0.9466 oz. ASW **Series:** 1992 Olympics - Ski Jumping **Obv:** Traditional design **Rev:** Ski jumper

Date	Mintage	VF20	XF40	MS60	MS63	MS65
VS2049	Est. 40000	PF63 25.00	PF65 32.00			

KM# 1090 500 RUPEE
31.47 g., 0.925 Silver 0.9359 oz. ASW **Series:** Endangered Wildlife **Obv:** Traditional design **Rev:** Red Panda

Date	Mintage	VF20	XF40	MS60	MS63	MS65
VS2049	Est. 15000	PF63 27.00	PF65 35.00			

KM# 1066 500 RUPEE
31.75 g., 0.925 Silver 0.9442 oz. ASW **Series:** 1994 Olympics **Obv:** Traditional design **Rev:** Cross-country skiing

Date	Mintage	VF20	XF40	MS60	MS63	MS65
VS2050	40,000	PF63 22.00	PF65 30.00			

KM# 1070 500 RUPEE
31.47 g., 0.925 Silver 0.9359 oz. ASW **Series:** Endangered Wildlife **Obv:** Traditional design **Rev:** Himalayan Black Bear

Date	Mintage	VF20	XF40	MS60	MS63	MS65
VS2050	10,000	PF63 27.00	PF65 35.00			

KM# 1084 500 RUPEE
28.28 g., 0.925 Silver 0.841 oz. ASW, 38.6 mm. **Subject:** 40th Anniversary - Conquest of Mt. Everest **Obv:** King's name above Nepelese calendar date surrounded by religious and cultural emblems **Rev:** Route taken by Sir Edmund Hillary and Sherpa Norgay Tensing's ascent in 1953 to the summit of the highest mountain in the world

Date	Mintage	VF20	XF40	MS60	MS63	MS65
VS2050	Est. 10000	PF63 25.00	PF65 32.00			

KM# 1091 500 RUPEE
31.47 g., 0.925 Silver 0.9359 oz. ASW **Series:** Endangered Wildlife **Rev:** Tiger

Date	Mintage	VF20	XF40	MS60	MS63	MS65
VS2050	Est. 15000	PF63 25.00	PF65 32.00			

KM# 1133 500 RUPEE
35.20 g., 0.900 Silver 1.0185 oz. ASW **Subject:** International Monetary Fund **Obv:** Traditional design **Rev:** Conjoined globes within rectangle above banner

Date	Mintage	VF20	XF40	MS60	MS63	MS65
VS2051	—	—	—	20.00	28.00	35.00

KM# 1192 500 RUPEE
35.00 g., 0.825 Silver 0.9284 oz. ASW **Subject:** 50th Anniversary World Bank **Obv:** Traditional design **Rev:** World Bank globe logo

Date	Mintage	VF20	XF40	MS60	MS63	MS65
VS2051(1994)	—	—	—	25.00	35.00	40.00

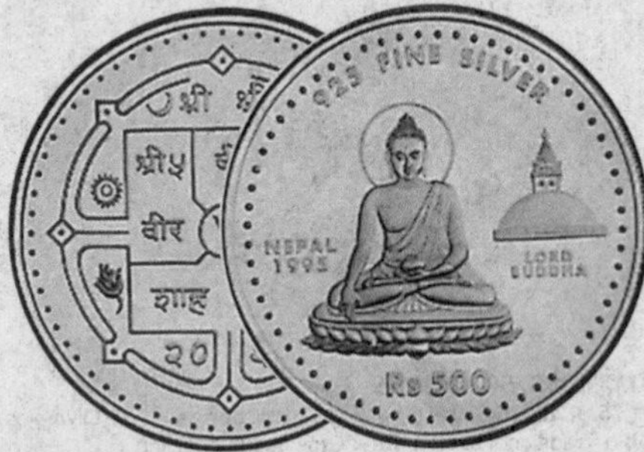

KM# 1077 500 RUPEE
31.10 g., 0.925 Silver 0.925 oz. ASW **Obv:** Traditional design **Rev:** Buddha

Date	Mintage	VF20	XF40	MS60	MS63	MS65
VS2052	15,000	PF63 25.00	PF65 30.00			

KM# 1125 500 RUPEE
31.35 g., 0.999 Silver 1.0069 oz. ASW **Obv:** Traditional design **Rev:** Gold-plated lotus flowers

Date	Mintage	VF20	XF40	MS60	MS63	MS65
VS2052	—	PF63 27.00	PF65 35.00			

KM# 1138 500 RUPEE
19.44 g., 0.925 Silver 0.5781 oz. ASW, 36 mm. **Series:** UNICEF **Obv:** Traditional design **Rev:** Standing girl serving seated boy **Edge:** Reeded

Date	Mintage	VF20	XF40	MS60	MS63	MS65
VS2054(1997)	25,000	PF63 22.00	PF65 28.00			

KM# 1143 500 RUPEE
25.20 g., 0.925 Silver 0.7494 oz. ASW **Subject:** 50th Anniversary of Universal Declaration of Human Rights **Obv:** Traditional design **Rev:** Logo above inscription

Date	Mintage	VF20	XF40	MS60	MS63	MS65
VS2055	—	—	—	—	22.00	28.00

KM# 1041 600 RUPEE
31.10 g., 0.999 Silver 0.999 oz. ASW **Subject:** 60th Birthday - Queen Mother **Obv:** Traditional design **Rev:** Bust left

Date	Mintage	VF20	XF40	MS60	MS63	MS65
VS2045	5,000	PF63 35.00	PF65 45.00			

KM# 844 1000 RUPEE
33.44 g., 0.900 Gold 0.9675 oz. AGW **Series:** Conservation **Obv:** Crowned bust right **Rev:** Great Indian Rhinoceros **Note:** Very small quantity restruck in 1979.

Date	Mintage	VF20	XF40	MS60	MS63	MS65
VS2031	2,176	—	—	—	—	1,700
VS2031	671	PF65 1,850				

KM# 1000 1000 RUPEE
33.44 g., 0.900 Gold 0.9675 oz. AGW **Subject:** Rural Women's Advancement

Date	Mintage	VF20	XF40	MS60	MS63	MS65
VS2038	500	PF65 1,900				

KM# 1036 1000 RUPEE
155.52 g., 0.999 Silver 4.9949 oz. ASW, 65 mm. **Obv:** Traditional design **Rev:** Snow Leopard **Note:** Illustration reduced.

Date	Mintage	VF20	XF40	MS60	MS63	MS65
VS2045	—	PF63 150	PF65 180			

KM# 1169 1000 RUPEE
40.00 g., 0.500 Silver 0.643 oz. ASW, 40 mm. **Obv:** Traditional square calendar with trident in circle at center **Rev:** Living Goddess Kumari **Edge:** Reeded

Date	Mintage	VF20	XF40	MS60	MS63	MS65
VS2057(2000)	—	—	—	—	35.00	45.00

KM# 1095 1500 RUPEE
31.10 g., 0.925 Silver 0.925 oz. ASW **Subject:** Buddha's Birth **Obv:** Traditional square in circle design **Rev:** Figure standing in center, cameo at right, small figure at left

Date	Mintage	VF20	XF40	MS60	MS63	MS65
VS2054	15,000	PF63 25.00	PF65 35.00			

KM# 1120 1500 RUPEE
20.00 g., 0.925 Silver 0.5948 oz. ASW **Subject:** Lord Buddha **Obv:** Traditional square in circle design **Rev:** Portrait of Buddha, Ashoka pillar, portrait halo glows under ultraviolet light

Date	Mintage	VF20	XF40	MS60	MS63	MS65
VS2055	15,000	PF63 25.00	PF65 35.00			

KM# 1168 1500 RUPEE
0.999 Silver, 38 mm. **Obv:** Traditional square design **Rev:** Tiger in tall grass **Edge:** Reeded

Date	Mintage	VF20	XF40	MS60	MS63	MS65
VS2054-1998	—	—	—	—	30.00	40.00

KM# 1128 1500 RUPEE
20.00 g., 0.925 Silver 0.5948 oz. ASW, 38.7 mm. **Subject:** Buddha **Obv:** Traditional square design **Rev:** Buddha with golden aura **Edge:** Reeded

Date	Mintage	VF20	XF40	MS60	MS63	MS65
2000	15,000	PF65 50.00				

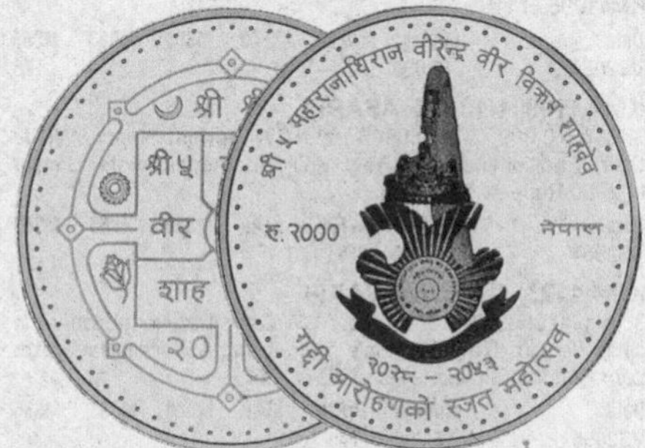

KM# 1100 2000 RUPEE
31.24 g., 0.999 Silver 1.0034 oz. ASW, 40 mm. **Subject:** Silver Jubilee of King's Accession **Obv:** Traditional design **Rev:** Multicolor crown

Date	Mintage	VF20	XF40	MS60	MS63	MS65
VS2053	Est. 5000	PF65 35.00				

KM# 1104 2000 RUPEE
31.17 g., 0.999 Silver 1.0011 oz. ASW **Series:** Nepal Wildlife **Obv:** Traditional design **Rev:** Multicolored leopard

Date	Mintage	VF20	XF40	MS60	MS63	MS65
VS2054-1998	8,000	PF65 40.00				

KM# 1105 2000 RUPEE
31.17 g., 0.999 Silver 1.0011 oz. ASW **Series:** Nepal Wildlife **Obv:** Traditional design **Rev:** Multicolor elephants

Date	Mintage	VF20	XF40	MS60	MS63	MS65
VS2054-1998	8,000	PF65 40.00				

KM# 1121 2000 RUPEE
20.00 g., 0.925 Silver 0.5948 oz. ASW with Gold inlay. **Obv:** Traditional square in circle design **Rev:** Buddha's portrait with gold insert halo, Ashoka pillar at right **Note:** Lord Buddha; Similar to 1500 Rupee, KM#1120.

Date	Mintage	VF20	XF40	MS60	MS63	MS65
VS2055	5,000	PF65 85.00				

KM# 1085 2500 RUPEE
155.51 g., 0.999 Silver 4.9948 oz. ASW **Subject:** Conquest of Mt. Everest **Obv:** Traditional design **Rev:** Busts facing in front of Mount Everest **Note:** Illustration reduced.

Date	Mintage	VF20	XF40	MS60	MS63	MS65
VS2050	Est. 3000	PF63 140	PF65 170			

KM# 1078 2500 RUPEE
155.51 g., 0.999 Silver 4.9948 oz. ASW **Obv:** Traditional design **Rev:** Buddha **Note:** Similar to 500 Rupee, KM#1077.

Date	Mintage	VF20	XF40	MS60	MS63	MS65
VS2052	3,000	PF63 150	PF65 180			

KM# 1101 5000 RUPEE
155.50 g., 0.999 Silver 4.9944 oz. ASW, 65 mm. **Subject:** Silver Jubilee of King's Accession **Obv:** Traditional design **Rev:** Multicolor crown

Date	Mintage	VF20	XF40	MS60	MS63	MS65
VS2053	—	PF65 200				

KM# 1106 5000 RUPEE
155.55 g., 0.999 Silver 4.9961 oz. ASW **Series:** Nepal Wildlife **Rev:** Multicolor elephants **Note:** Similar to 2000 Rupee, KM#1105.

Date	Mintage	VF20	XF40	MS60	MS63	MS65
VS2054	500	PF65 250				

ASARFI GOLD COINAGE

Fractional designations are approximate for this series. Actual Gold Weight (AGW) is used to identify each type.

(Asarphi)

KM# 1202 ASARPHI
1.24 g., 0.999 Gold 0.0398 oz. AGW, 13.92 mm. **Obv:** Arms **Rev:** Budda seated

Date	Mintage	VF20	XF40	MS60	MS63	MS65
1999	—	PF65 75.00				

KM# 1167 1/3 ASARFI
11.65 g., 0.900 Gold 0.3371 oz. AGW, 28.5 mm. **Obv:** Traditional design **Rev:** Ceremonial Vase **Note:** The Prince's Coming of Age

Date	Mintage	VF20	XF40	MS60	MS63	MS65
VS2046(1989)	1,000	—	—	—	550	600

KM# 1050a 0.3G ASARPHI
0.25 g., 0.999 Gold 0.008 oz. AGW

Date	Mintage	VF20	XF40	MS60	MS63	MS65
VS2051	—	—	—	—	—	40.00
VS2052	—	—	—	—	—	40.00
VS2053	—	—	—	—	—	35.00
VS2054	—	—	—	—	—	35.00
VS2055	—	—	—	—	—	35.00
VS2056	—	—	—	—	—	35.00
VS2057	—	—	—	—	—	35.00

KM# 1129 0.3G ASARPHI
0.30 g., 0.9999 Gold 0.0096 oz. AGW, 7 mm. **Subject:** Buddha **Obv:** Traditional square design **Rev:** Buddha with halo **Edge:** Reeded

Date	Mintage	VF20	XF40	MS60	MS63	MS65
VS2057	25,000	—	—	—	—	25.00

KM# 825 5.0G ASARPHI
5.00 g., 0.999 Gold 0.1606 oz. AGW

Date	Mintage	VF20	XF40	MS60	MS63	MS65
VS2028	4	—	—	—	—	—
VS2030	—	—	—	—	—	300
VS2031	—	—	—	—	—	300
VS2036	36	—	—	—	—	300
VS2037	45	—	—	—	—	300

Note: Reports indicate a mintage of 44 pieces struck in .960 gold in 1980

Date	Mintage	VF20	XF40	MS60	MS63	MS65
VS2038	—	—	—	—	—	300

KM# 822a 5.0G ASARPHI
5.00 g., 0.999 Gold 0.1606 oz. AGW **Subject:** Birendra Coronation **Obv:** Crown at center **Rev:** Dagger flanked by garlands from above

Date	Mintage	VF20	XF40	MS60	MS63	MS65
VS2031	500	—	—	—	—	300

KM# 1021 5.0G ASARPHI
5.00 g., 0.900 Gold 0.1447 oz. AGW **Obv:** Traditional design **Rev:** Dagger flanked by garlands from above

Date	Mintage	VF20	XF40	MS60	MS63	MS65
VS2039	23	—	—	—	—	275

KM# 1021a 5.0G ASARPHI
5.00 g., 0.999 Gold 0.1606 oz. AGW **Obv:** Traditiogal design **Rev:** Dagger flanked by garlands from above

Date	Mintage	VF20	XF40	MS60	MS63	MS65
VS2042	—	—	—	—	—	300
VS2043	—	—	—	—	—	300
VS2044	—	—	—	—	—	300
VS2045	—	—	—	—	—	375
VS2046	—	—	—	—	—	375
VS2048	—	—	—	—	—	285
VS2049	—	—	—	—	—	285
VS2050	—	—	—	—	—	375
VS2051	—	—	—	—	—	375
VS2052	—	—	—	—	—	375
VS2053	—	—	—	—	—	375
VS2054	—	—	—	—	—	375
VS2056	—	—	—	—	—	375

KM# 1060 5.0G ASARPHI
5.00 g., 0.999 Gold 0.1606 oz. AGW **Subject:** The New Constitution **Obv:** Traditional design **Rev:** Flags above open book **Note:** Similar to 10 Asarphi, KM#1054.

Date	Mintage	VF20	XF40	MS60	MS63	MS65
VS2047	—	—	—	—	—	300

KM# 1144 5.0G ASARPHI
5.00 g., 0.999 Gold 0.1606 oz. AGW **Subject:** New Parliament Session

Date	Mintage	VF20	XF40	MS60	MS63	MS65
VS2048	—	—	—	—	—	300

KM# 827 10.0G ASARPHI
10.00 g., 0.999 Gold 0.3212 oz. AGW **Obv:** Traditional design **Rev:** Dagger flanked by garlands from above

Date	Mintage	VF20	XF40	MS60	MS63	MS65
VS2028	Est. 4	—	—	—	—	—
VS2030	50	—	—	—	—	575
VS2031	—	—	—	—	—	575
VS2033	—	—	—	—	—	575
VS2035	—	—	—	—	—	575

Date	Mintage	VF20	XF40	MS60	MS63	MS65
VS2036	52	—	—	—	—	575
VS2037	30	—	—	—	—	575

Note: Reports indicate a mintage of 44 pieces struck in .960 gold in 1980

Date	Mintage	VF20	XF40	MS60	MS63	MS65
VS2038	—	—	—	—	—	575

KM# 829a 10.0G ASARPHI

10.00 g., 0.999 Gold 0.3212 oz. AGW **Subject:** Birendra Coronation **Obv:** Crown **Rev:** Dagger flanked by garlands from above

Date	Mintage	VF20	XF40	MS60	MS63	MS65
VS2031	Est. 500	PF65 550				

KM# 829b 10.0G ASARPHI

10.00 g., 0.500 White Gold 0.1608 oz.

Date	Mintage	VF20	XF40	MS60	MS63	MS65
VS2031	Est. 250	PF65 450				

Note: Sometimes referred to as 1000 Rupees

KM# 852 10.0G ASARPHI

11.66 g., 0.900 Gold 0.3374 oz. AGW **Series:** International Year of the Child **Obv:** Crowned bust right **Rev:** Child reading, emblems flank

Date	Mintage	VF20	XF40	MS60	MS63	MS65
VS2038	4,055	PF65 550				

Note: Struck in 1981

KM# 1022 10.0G ASARPHI

10.00 g., 0.900 Gold 0.2894 oz. AGW **Obv:** Traditional design **Rev:** Dagger flanked by garlands from above

Date	Mintage	VF20	XF40	MS60	MS63	MS65
VS2039	25	—	—	—	—	525

KM# 1006 10.0G ASARPHI

10.00 g., 0.500 Gold 0.1608 oz. AGW **Subject:** 30th Anniversary Ascent of Mt. Everest **Obv:** Trident within small circle at center **Rev:** Mount Everest

Date	Mintage	VF20	XF40	MS60	MS63	MS65
VS2040	350	PF65 325				

KM# 1022a 10.0G ASARPHI

10.00 g., 0.999 Gold 0.3212 oz. AGW

Date	Mintage	VF20	XF40	MS60	MS63	MS65
VS2042	—	—	—	—	—	575
VS2046	—	—	—	—	—	575
VS2048	—	—	—	—	—	575
VS2049	—	—	—	—	—	575
VS2050	—	—	—	—	—	575
VS2052	—	—	—	—	—	575
VS2054	—	—	—	—	—	575
VS2056	—	—	—	—	—	575

KM# 1034 10.0G ASARPHI

10.00 g., Gold **Subject:** Crown Prince, Sacred Thread Ceremony **Obv:** Traditional design

Date	Mintage	VF20	XF40	MS60	MS63	MS65
VS2044	1,962	—	—	—	—	575

KM# 1054 10.0G ASARPHI

10.00 g., 0.999 Gold 0.3212 oz. AGW **Subject:** The New Constitution **Obv:** Traditional design **Rev:** Flags above open book

Date	Mintage	VF20	XF40	MS60	MS63	MS65
VS2047	—	—	—	—	—	575

KM# 1145 10.0G ASARPHI

10.00 g., 0.999 Gold 0.3212 oz. AGW **Subject:** 50th Anniversary International Monetary Fund

Date	Mintage	VF20	XF40	MS60	MS63	MS65
VS2051	—	—	—	—	—	575

KM# 1146 10.0G ASARPHI

10.00 g., 0.999 Gold 0.3212 oz. AGW **Subject:** 50th Anniversary World Bank

Date	Mintage	VF20	XF40	MS60	MS63	MS65
VS2051	—	—	—	—	—	575

KM# 1147 10.0G ASARPHI

10.00 g., 0.999 Gold 0.3212 oz. AGW **Subject:** Queen Aishwariya Golden Anniversary

Date	Mintage	VF20	XF40	MS60	MS63	MS65
VS2056	—	—	—	—	—	575

KM# 1122 1/25-OZ. ASARFI

1.24 g., 0.9999 Gold 0.040 oz. AGW **Obv:** Traditional square in circle design **Rev:** Buddha's portrait and Ashoka pillar **Note:** Lord Buddha; Similar to Asarfi KM#1124.

Date	Mintage	VF20	XF40	MS60	MS63	MS65
VS2055	30,000	PF65 75.00				

KM# 1130 1/25-OZ. ASARFI

1.24 g., 0.9999 Gold 0.040 oz. AGW, 18 mm. **Subject:** Buddha **Obv:** Traditional square design **Rev:** Buddha with halo **Edge:** Reeded

Date	Mintage	VF20	XF40	MS60	MS63	MS65
VS2057	30,000	—	—	—	—	75.00

KM# 1033 1/20-OZ. ASARFI

5.83 g., 0.960 Gold 0.1799 oz. AGW **Subject:** Crown Prince, Sacred Thread Ceremony **Obv:** Traditional design

Date	Mintage	VF20	XF40	MS60	MS63	MS65
VS2044	2,774	—	—	—	—	325

KM# 1079 1/20-OZ. ASARFI

1.55 g., 0.999 Gold 0.0499 oz. AGW **Obv:** Traditional design **Rev:** Buddha **Note:** Similar to 1-oz. Asarfi, KM#1082.

Date	Mintage	VF20	XF40	MS60	MS63	MS65
VS2052	15,000	—	—	—	—	85.00

KM# 1096 1/20-OZ. ASARFI

1.55 g., 0.999 Gold 0.0499 oz. AGW **Subject:** Buddha's Birth **Obv:** Traditional design **Rev:** Standing figure at center, cameo at right, small figure at left **Note:** Similar to 1500 Rupee, KM#1095.

Date	Mintage	VF20	XF40	MS60	MS63	MS65
VS2054	15,000	—	—	—	—	85.00

KM# 1107 1/20-OZ. ASARFI

1.56 g., 0.999 Gold 0.050 oz. AGW **Series:** Nepal Wildlife **Obv:** Traditional design **Rev:** Multicolor leopard **Note:** Similar to 2000 Rupees, KM#1104.

Date	Mintage	VF20	XF40	MS60	MS63	MS65
VS2054	15,000	PF65 95.00				

KM# 1108 1/20-OZ. ASARFI

1.56 g., 0.999 Gold 0.050 oz. AGW **Series:** Nepal Wildlife **Obv:** Traditional design **Rev:** Multicolor tiger **Note:** Similar to 100 Rupees, KM#1102.

Date	Mintage	VF20	XF40	MS60	MS63	MS65
VS2054	15,000	PF65 95.00				

KM# 1050 1/10-OZ. ASARFI

2.50 g., 0.900 Gold 0.0723 oz. AGW

Date	Mintage	VF20	XF40	MS60	MS63	MS65
VS2039	11	—	—	—	—	200

KM# 1037 1/10-OZ. ASARFI

3.11 g., 0.999 Gold 0.0999 oz. AGW **Obv:** Traditional design **Rev:** Snow leopard **Note:** Similar to 1-oz. Asarphi, KM#1040.

Date	Mintage	VF20	XF40	MS60	MS63	MS65
VS2045	2,000	PF65 185				
VS2045	Est. 10000	—	—	—	—	175

KM# 1080 1/10-OZ. ASARFI

3.11 g., 0.999 Gold 0.0999 oz. AGW **Obv:** Traditional design **Rev:** Buddha **Note:** Similar to 1-oz. Asarphi, KM#1082.

Date	Mintage	VF20	XF40	MS60	MS63	MS65
VS2052	15,000	—	—	—	—	175

KM# 1097 1/10-OZ. ASARFI

3.11 g., 0.999 Gold 0.0999 oz. AGW **Subject:** Buddha's Birth **Obv:** Traditional design **Rev:** Standing figure at center, cameo at right, small figure at left **Note:** Similar to 1500 Rupee, KM#1095.

Date	Mintage	VF20	XF40	MS60	MS63	MS65
VS2054	15,000	—	—	—	—	175

KM# 1109 1/10-OZ. ASARFI

3.11 g., 0.999 Gold 0.0999 oz. AGW **Series:** Nepal Wildlife **Obv:** Traditional design **Rev:** Multicolor leopard **Note:** Similar to 2000 Rupees, KM#1104.

Date	Mintage	VF20	XF40	MS60	MS63	MS65
VS2054	10,000	PF65 175				

KM# 1123 1/10-OZ. ASARFI

3.11 g., 0.9999 Gold 0.100 oz. AGW **Obv:** Traditional square in circle design **Rev:** Buddha's portrait and Ashoka pillar **Note:** Lord Buddha; Similar to Asarfi KM#1124.

Date	Mintage	VF20	XF40	MS60	MS63	MS65
VS2055	15,000	PF65 175				

KM# 1131 1/10-OZ. ASARFI

3.11 g., 0.999 Gold 0.0999 oz. AGW, 18 mm. **Subject:** Buddha **Obv:** Traditional square design **Rev:** Buddha with halo **Edge:** Reeded

Date	Mintage	VF20	XF40	MS60	MS63	MS65
VS2057	30,000	—	—	—	—	180

KM# 819 1/4-OZ. ASARFI

2.50 g., 0.999 Gold 0.0803 oz. AGW **Obv:** Traditional design **Rev:** Dagger flanked by garlands from above

Date	Mintage	VF20	XF40	MS60	MS63	MS65
VS2028	4	—	—	—	—	—
VS2030	—	—	—	—	—	170
VS2031	—	—	—	—	—	170
VS2036	—	—	—	—	—	170
VS2037	48	—	—	—	—	170

KM# 816a 1/4-OZ. ASARFI

7.77 g., 0.999 Gold 0.2496 oz. AGW **Subject:** Birendra Coronation **Obv:** Crown **Rev:** Dagger flanked by garlands from above

Date	Mintage	VF20	XF40	MS60	MS63	MS65
VS2031	500	—	—	—	—	475

KM# 1038 1/4-OZ. ASARFI

7.77 g., 0.999 Gold 0.2496 oz. AGW **Obv:** Traditional design **Rev:** Snow leopard **Note:** Similar to 1-oz. Asarphi, KM#1040, Bullion Series.

Date	Mintage	VF20	XF40	MS60	MS63	MS65
VS2045	8,000	—	—	—	—	450
VS2045	—	PF65 475				

KM# 1056 1/4-OZ. ASARFI

11.66 g., 0.900 Gold 0.3374 oz. AGW **Series:** Save the Children **Obv:** Traditional design **Rev:** Older and younger children

Date	Mintage	VF20	XF40	MS60	MS63	MS65
VS2047	3,000	PF65 575				

KM# 1059 1/4-OZ. ASARFI

7.77 g., 0.999 Gold 0.2496 oz. AGW **Obv:** Traditional design **Rev:** Flags above open book **Note:** Similar to 1-oz. Asarphi, KM#1054.

Date	Mintage	VF20	XF40	MS60	MS63	MS65
VS2047	—	—	—	—	—	475

KM# 1081 1/4-OZ. ASARFI

7.78 g., 0.999 Gold 0.2498 oz. AGW **Obv:** Traditional design **Rev:** Buddha **Note:** Similar to 1-oz. Asarphi, KM#1082.

Date	Mintage	VF20	XF40	MS60	MS63	MS65
VS2052	15,000	—	—	—	—	450

KM# 1093 1/4-OZ. ASARFI

7.78 g., 0.999 Gold 0.2498 oz. AGW **Series:** Olympics **Obv:** Traditional design **Rev:** Runner and temple

Date	Mintage	VF20	XF40	MS60	MS63	MS65
VS2052	Est. 3000	—	—	—	—	475

KM# 1098 1/4-OZ. ASARFI

7.78 g., 0.999 Gold 0.2498 oz. AGW **Subject:** Buddha's Birth **Obv:** Traditional design **Rev:** Standing figure at center, cameo at right, small figure at left **Note:** Similar to 1500 Rupees, KM#1095.

Date	Mintage	VF20	XF40	MS60	MS63	MS65
VS2054	15,000	—	—	—	—	450

KM# 1110 1/4-OZ. ASARFI

7.78 g., 0.999 Gold 0.2498 oz. AGW **Series:** Nepal Wildlife **Obv:** Traditional design **Rev:** Multicolor elephants **Note:** Similar to 2000 Rupees, KM#1105.

Date	Mintage	VF20	XF40	MS60	MS63	MS65
VS2054	2,000	PF65 475				

KM# 1111 1/4-OZ. ASARFI

7.78 g., 0.999 Gold 0.2498 oz. AGW **Series:** Nepal Wildlife **Obv:** Traditional design **Rev:** Multicolor tiger **Note:** Similar to 100 Rupees, KM#1102.

Date	Mintage	VF20	XF40	MS60	MS63	MS65
VS2054	2,000	PF65 475				

KM# 1112 1/4-OZ. ASARFI

7.78 g., 0.999 Gold 0.2498 oz. AGW **Series:** Nepal Wildlife **Obv:** Traditional design **Rev:** Multicolor rhinoceros **Note:** Similar to 100 Rupees, KM#1103.

Date	Mintage	VF20	XF40	MS60	MS63	MS65
VS2054	2,000	PF65 475				

KM# 1113 1/4-OZ. ASARFI

7.78 g., 0.999 Gold 0.2498 oz. AGW **Series:** Nepal Wildlife **Obv:** Traditional design **Rev:** Multicolor leopard **Note:** Similar to 100 Rupees, KM#1104.

Date	Mintage	VF20	XF40	MS60	MS63	MS65
VS2054	2,000	PF65 475				

KM# 1008 1/2-OZ. ASARFI

15.98 g., 0.900 Gold 0.4624 oz. AGW **Subject:** 10th Anniversary of Reign **Rev:** Dagger flanked by garlands from above

Date	Mintage	VF20	XF40	MS60	MS63	MS65
VS2038	27	—	—	—	—	875
VS2038	5,092	PF65 825				

KM# 1011 1/2-OZ. ASARFI

15.98 g., 0.917 Gold 0.4711 oz. AGW **Series:** Year of the Scout **Obv:** Traditional design **Rev:** Girl scout filling water jug

Date	Mintage	VF20	XF40	MS60	MS63	MS65
VS2039	2,000	—	—	—	—	850

KM# 1045 1/2-OZ. ASARFI

15.00 g., 0.900 Gold 0.434 oz. AGW **Subject:** 3rd SAARC Summit **Obv:** Traditional design **Rev:** Summit emblem **Note:** Similar to 300 Rupees, KM#1044.

Date	Mintage	VF20	XF40	MS60	MS63	MS65
VS2044	1,000	—	—	—	—	775

KM# 1039 1/2-OZ. ASARFI

15.55 g., 0.999 Gold 0.4994 oz. AGW **Obv:** Traditional design **Rev:** Snow leopard **Note:** Similar to 1-oz. Asarphi, KM#1040.

Date	Mintage	VF20	XF40	MS60	MS63	MS65
VS2045	Est. 8000	—	—	—	—	875
VS2045	—	PF65 900				

KM# 1124 1/2-OZ. ASARFI

15.55 g., 0.9999 Gold 0.500 oz. AGW **Obv:** Traditional square in circle design **Rev:** Lord Buddha, Ashoka pillar

Date	Mintage	VF20	XF40	MS60	MS63	MS65
VS2055	2,500	PF65 900				

KM# 1132 1/2-OZ. ASARFI

15.55 g., 0.9999 Gold 0.500 oz. AGW, 27 mm. **Subject:** Buddha **Obv:** Traditional square design **Rev:** Buddha with halo **Edge:** Reeded

Date	Mintage	VF20	XF40	MS60	MS63	MS65
VS2057	—	PF65 900				

KM# 1027 1-OZ. ASARFI

31.10 g., 0.999 Gold 0.9989 oz. AGW **Series:** Wildlife Protection **Obv:** Traditional design **Rev:** Ganges River Dolphins

Date	Mintage	VF20	XF40	MS60	MS63	MS65
VS2043	5,000	PF65 1,750				

KM# 1040 1-OZ. ASARFI

31.10 g., 0.9999 Gold 0.9998 oz. AGW **Obv:** Traditional design **Rev:** Snow leopard

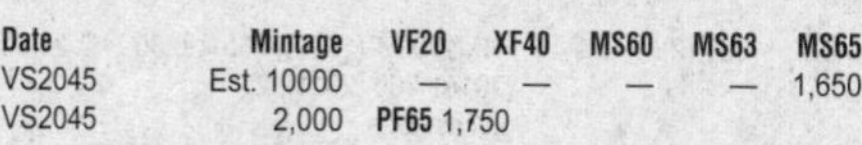

Date	Mintage	VF20	XF40	MS60	MS63	MS65
VS2045	Est. 10000	—	—	—	—	1,650
VS2045	2,000	PF65 1,750				

KM# 1082 1-OZ. ASARFI

31.10 g., 0.9999 Gold 0.9999 oz. AGW **Obv:** Traditional design **Rev:** Buddha

Date	Mintage	VF20	XF40	MS60	MS63	MS65
VS2052	2,500	PF65 1,800				

KM# 1099 1-OZ. ASARFI

31.10 g., 0.9999 Gold 0.9999 oz. AGW **Subject:** Buddha's Birth **Obv:** Traditional square in circle design **Rev:** Standing figure at center, cameo at right, small figure at left

Date	Mintage	VF20	XF40	MS60	MS63	MS65
VS2054	2,500	PF65 1,750				

KM# 1086 1-1/2 OZ. ASARFI

44.64 g., 0.9167 Gold 1.3157 oz. AGW **Subject:** Conquest of Mt. Everest **Obv:** Traditional design **Rev:** Mount Everest

Date	Mintage	VF20	XF40	MS60	MS63	MS65
VS2050	Est. 100	PF65 2,250				

PATTERNS

Including off metal strikes

KM#	Date	Mintage	Identification	Mkt Val
Pn3	VS1975 (1918)	—	5 Paisa. Copper. KM#690.1.	—

PIEDFORT

KM#	Date	Mintage	Identification	Mkt Val
P1	VS2038 (1981)	88	100 Rupee. Silver. KM#851.	150
P2	VS2039 (1982)	48	Asarphi.	1,650

MINT SETS

KM#	Date	Mintage	Identification	Issue Price	Mkt Val
MS1	1932 (0)	—	Set makeup requires confirmation	—	—
MS2	1949 (1)	—	KM#716, 718, 723 (restrikes)	—	8.00
MS3	1953 (8)	—	KM#733, 735-740, 742	—	160
MSA4	1953 (7)	—	KM#745.1, 750.1, 756.3, 761, 770, 776, 790 Coronation	—	14.00
MS4	1955 (3)	—	KM#712 (2000); 733; 749 (2012)	0.85	7.00
MS5	1956 (7)	—	KM#745.1, 750.1, 756.2, 761, 770, 776, 790	—	75.00
MS6	1956 (7)	—	KM#745.1, 750.1, 756.3, 761, 770, 776, 790 (restrikes)	—	15.00
MS7	1957 (4)	—	KM#740 (2011), 742, 738 (2010), 769 (2014)	2.00	95.00

KM#	Date	Mintage	Identification	Issue Price	Mkt Val
MS8	1957 (2)	—	KM#709.1 (1996), 755 (2014), 760 (2011); 2 pieces each	0.85	30.00
MS9	1964 (7)	—	KM#747, 752, 758, 763, 772, 778, 785	—	12.00
MS10	1964 (7)	—	KM#747, 752, 758a, 764, 772, 778, 785	—	50.00
MS11	1965 (7)	—	KM#747, 752 (2022), 758, 763, 772, 778, 786 (2021)	2.75	12.50
MS12	1966 (7)	—	KM#748, 753, 759, 765, 772, 779, 787	—	8.00
MS13	1967 (3)	—	KM#748, 753, 759, 765, 772, 779, 787	—	7.00
MS14	1971 (7)	—	KM#799, 801, 802, 806, 815, 821, 828.1	—	8.00
MS15	1974 (7)	—	KM#800, 804, 808, 816.1, 822.1, 829.1, 838	—	25.00
MS16	1974 (2)	—	KM#829.1, 841	32.50	40.00
MS17	1975 (5)	—	KM#808, 816.1, 822.1, 829.1, 838	—	25.00
MS18	1975 (3)	—	KM#809, 831, 836	—	12.50
MSA19	1996, 1995, 2011 (3)	—	KM#709.2 (1996); 711 (1995); 737 (2011)	—	8.00
MS19	1997 (3)	—	KM#1096-1098	—	600

PROOF SETS

KM#	Date	Mintage	Identification	Issue Price	Mkt Val
PS1	1911 (9)	—	KM621, 622, 631, 634, 644, 649, 651.2, 656, 658, Copper, Silver	—	1,150
PS2	1911 (6)	—	KM668, 671.2, 672.5, 673.2, 675.1, 680, Gold	—	—
PS3	1970 (7)	2,187	KM#748, 753, 759, 765, 773, 780, 788	10.00	25.00
PS4	1971 (7)	2,380	KM#748, 753, 759, 765, 773, 780, 788	10.00	25.00
PS5	1972 (7)	3,943	KM#799, 801, 802, 807, 815, 821, 828	10.00	9.00
PS6	1973 (7)	8,891	KM#799, 801, 802, 807, 815, 821, 828.1	10.00	7.50
PS7	1974 (7)	10,543	KM#799, 801, 802, 807, 815, 821, 828.1	10.00	7.00
PS8	1974 (2)	30,000	KM#839a, 841a	50.00	60.00
PS9	1981 (7)	1,000	KM#800a, 804a, 808a, 816.2, 822.2, 829.2, 838a Coins dated 2031 (1974) but this set was issued in 1981 to celebrate the 7th Anniversary of the Coronation.	62.00	62.50
PS10	1988 (4)	2,000	KM#1037-1040	—	2,800
PS11	1995-97 (2)	—	KM#1077, 1099	—	1,550

NETHERLANDS

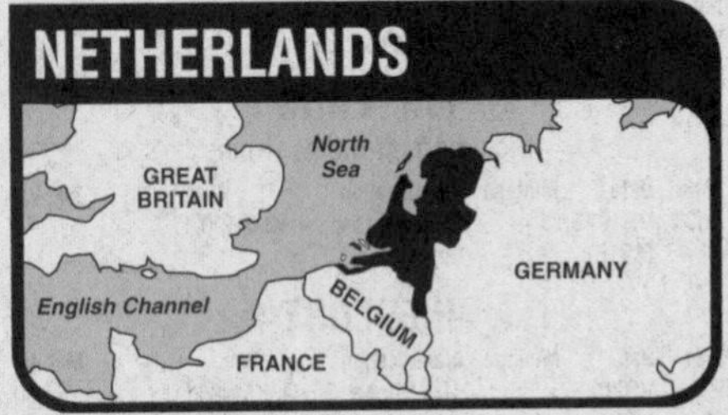

The Kingdom of the Netherlands, a country of western Europe fronting on the North Sea and bordered by Belgium and Germany, has an area of 15,770 sq. mi. (41,500 sq. km.) and a population of 16.4 million. Capital: Amsterdam, but the seat of government is at The Hague. The economy is based on dairy farming and a variety of industrial activities. Chemicals, yarns and fabrics, and meat products are exported.

After being a part of Charlemagne's empire in the 8th and 9th centuries, the Netherlands came under control of Burgundy and the Austrian Hapsburgs, and finally was subjected to Spanish dominion in the 16th century. Led by William of Orange, the Dutch revolted against Spain in 1568. The seven northern provinces formed the Union of Utrecht and declared their independence in 1581, becoming the Republic of the United Netherlands. In the following century, the *Golden Age* of Dutch history, the Netherlands became a great sea and colonial power, a patron of the arts and a refuge for the persecuted. The United Dutch Republic ended in 1795 when the French formed the Batavian Republic. Napoleon made his brother Louis, the King of Holland in 1806, however he abdicated in 1810 when Napoleon annexed Holland. The French were expelled in 1813, and all the provinces of Holland and Belgium were merged into the Kingdom of the United Netherlands under William I, in 1814. The Belgians withdrew in 1830 to form their own kingdom, the last substantial change in the configuration of European Netherlands. German forces invaded in 1940 as the royal family fled to England where a government-in-exile was formed.

WORLD WAR II COINAGE

U.S. mints in the name of the government in exile and its remaining Curacao and Suriname Colonies during the years 1941-45 minted coinage of the Netherlands Homeland Types -KM #152, 153, 163, 164, 161.1 and 161.2 -. The Curacao and Suriname strikes, distinguished by the presence of a palm tree in combination with a mint mark (P-Philadelphia; D-Denver; S-San Francisco) flanking the date, are incorporated under those titles in this volume. Pieces of this period struck in the name of the homeland bear an acorn and mint mark and are incorporated in the following tabulation.

NOTE: Excepting the World War II issues struck at U.S. mints, all of the modern coins were struck at the Utrecht Mint (or at the annex in the Birmingham Mint 1980-2000) and bear the caduceus mint mark of that facility. They also bear the mintmasters' marks.

RULERS

Wilhelmina I, 1890-1948
Juliana, 1948-1980
Beatrix, 1980-2013

MINT MARKS

D - Denver, 1943-1945
P - Philadelphia, 1941-1945
S - San Francisco, 1944-1945

MINT PRIVY MARKS

Utrecht

Date	Privy Mark
1806-present	Caduceus

MINTMASTERS' PRIVY MARKS

U. S. Mints

Date	Privy Mark
1941-45	Palm tree

Utrecht Mint

Date	Privy Mark
1888-1909	Halberd
1909	Halberd and star
1909-1933	Seahorse
1933-42	Grapes
1943-1945	No privy mark
1945-69	Fish
1969-79	Cock
1980	Cock and star (temporal)
1980-88	Anvil with hammer
1989-99	Bow and arrow
2000	Bow, arrow and star

NOTE: A star adjoining the privy mark indicates that the piece was struck at the beginning of the term of office of a successor. (The star was used only if the successor had not chosen his own mark yet.)

NOTE: Since October, 1999, the Dutch Mint has taken the title of Royal Dutch Mint.

MONETARY SYSTEM

Until January 29, 2002

100 Cents = 1 Gulden

KINGDOM

DECIMAL COINAGE

KM# 109.2 1/2 CENT

1.25 g., Bronze, 14 mm. **Ruler:** Wilhelmina I **Obv:** Crowned rampant lion left on field of 17 small shields all within beaded circle, date below **Obv. Legend:** KONINGRIJK DER NEDERLANDEN **Rev:** Crowned rampant lion left on field of 17 small shields all within beaded circle, date below **Edge:** Reeded **Note:** Privy mark: Halberd

Date	Mintage	F12	VF20	XF40	MS60	MS63
1901	6,000,000	4.00	7.00	12.00	30.00	45.00

KM# 133 1/2 CENT

1.25 g., Bronze, 14 mm. **Ruler:** Wilhelmina I **Obv:** Crowned arms with 15 small shields within beaded circle **Obv. Legend:** KONINGRIJK DER NEDERLANDEN **Rev:** Value within wreath **Edge:** Reeded

Date	Mintage	F12	VF20	XF40	MS60	MS63
1903	10,000,000	1.00	2.00	4.00	15.00	30.00
1906	10,000,000	1.00	2.00	4.00	15.00	30.00

KM# 138 1/2 CENT

1.25 g., Bronze, 14 mm. **Ruler:** Wilhelmina I **Obv:** Crowned arms with 15 large shields within beaded circle, date and legend **Rev:** Value within wreath **Edge:** Reeded

Date	Mintage	F12	VF20	XF40	MS60	MS63
1909	5,000,000	1.00	2.00	3.00	12.00	25.00
1911	5,000,000	1.00	2.00	3.00	12.00	25.00
1912	5,000,000	1.00	2.00	3.00	12.00	25.00
1914	5,000,000	1.00	2.00	3.00	12.00	25.00
1915	2,500,000	5.00	10.00	15.00	35.00	70.00
1916	4,000,000	2.00	4.00	7.00	15.00	30.00
1917	5,000,000	1.00	2.00	4.00	12.00	25.00
1921	1,500,000	5.00	10.00	15.00	30.00	60.00
1922/1	Inc. above	200	400	600	800	1,300
1922	2,500,000	5.00	10.00	15.00	25.00	45.00
1928	4,000,000	1.00	2.00	3.00	8.00	15.00
1930	6,000,000	1.00	1.50	2.50	6.00	10.00
1934	5,000,000	0.75	1.75	2.50	5.00	8.00
1936	5,000,000	0.75	1.75	2.50	5.00	8.00
1937	1,600,000	1.00	2.50	4.00	8.00	15.00
1938	8,400,000	0.75	1.50	2.00	3.00	5.00
1940	6,000,000	0.75	1.50	2.00	3.00	5.00

KM# 130 CENT

2.50 g., Bronze, 19 mm. **Ruler:** Wilhelmina I **Obv:** Crowned arms with 15 large shields within beaded circle **Obv. Legend:** KONINKRIJK DER NEDERLANDEN **Rev:** Value within wreath **Edge:** Reeded

Date	Mintage	F12	VF20	XF40	MS60	MS63
1901	10,000,000	1.00	2.50	5.00	20.00	50.00

KM# 131 CENT

2.50 g., Bronze, 19 mm. **Ruler:** Wilhelmina I **Obv:** Crowned arms with 10 large shields within beaded circle **Obv. Legend:** KONINGRIJK DER NEDERLANDEN **Rev:** Value within wreath **Edge:** Reeded

Date	Mintage	F12	VF20	XF40	MS60	MS63
1901	10,000,000	1.00	2.50	6.00	35.00	70.00

KM# 132.1 CENT

2.50 g., Bronze, 19 mm. **Ruler:** Wilhelmina I **Obv:** Crowned arms with 15 medium shields within beaded circle **Obv. Legend:** KONINGRIJK DER NEDERLANDEN **Rev:** Value within wreath **Edge:** Reeded

Date	Mintage	F12	VF20	XF40	MS60	MS63
1902	10,000,000	1.00	2.00	4.00	20.00	50.00
Note: Mint mark close to date						
1902	Inc. above	2.00	5.00	10.00	35.00	80.00
Note: Mint mark far from date						
1904	10,000,000	1.00	2.00	3.00	15.00	40.00
1905	10,000,000	1.00	2.00	3.00	15.00	40.00
1906	9,000,000	1.00	2.00	3.00	15.00	40.00
1907	6,000,000	6.00	12.00	30.00	60.00	150

KM# 132.2 CENT

2.50 g., Bronze, 19 mm. **Ruler:** Wilhelmina I **Obv:** 15 medium shields in field **Obv. Legend:** KONINGRIJK DER NEDERLANDEN **Rev:** Value within wreath **Edge:** Plain

Date	Mintage	F12	VF20	XF40	MS60	MS63
1906	—	PF63 875				

KM# 152 CENT

2.50 g., Bronze, 19 mm. **Ruler:** Wilhelmina I **Obv:** Crowned arms with 17 small shields within beaded circle **Rev:** Value within wreath **Edge:** Reeded

Date	Mintage	F12	VF20	XF40	MS60	MS63
1913	5,000,000	2.50	6.00	12.00	30.00	70.00
1914	9,000,000	1.00	2.00	3.00	15.00	40.00
1915	10,800,000	1.00	2.00	3.00	12.00	30.00
1916	21,700,000	0.75	1.00	2.00	10.00	30.00
1916	—	PF63 875				
1917	20,000,000	0.75	1.00	2.00	10.00	25.00
1918	10,000,000	1.00	2.00	4.00	12.00	30.00
1919	6,000,000	2.75	5.00	10.00	20.00	45.00
1920	11,400,000	0.75	1.50	2.00	10.00	25.00
1921	12,600,000	0.75	1.50	2.00	10.00	25.00

Date	Mintage	F12	VF20	XF40	MS60	MS63
1922	20,000,000	0.75	1.50	2.00	10.00	25.00
1924	1,400,000	12.00	25.00	55.00	110	230
1925	18,600,000	0.75	1.50	2.00	10.00	25.00
1926	10,000,000	1.00	3.00	6.00	15.00	40.00
1927	10,000,000	0.75	2.00	4.00	10.00	25.00
1928	10,000,000	0.75	1.00	2.00	10.00	25.00
1929	20,000,000	0.75	2.00	4.00	8.00	15.00
1930	10,000,000	0.75	1.50	2.00	8.00	15.00
1931	3,400,000	3.50	7.50	12.50	35.00	70.00
1937	10,000,000	0.50	1.00	1.50	5.00	8.00
1938	16,600,000	0.50	1.00	1.50	5.00	8.00
1939	22,000,000	0.50	1.00	1.50	5.00	7.00
1940	24,600,000	0.50	1.00	1.50	5.00	7.00
1941	66,600,000	0.25	0.60	1.00	2.50	4.00

Note: For similar coins dated 1942P see Curacao; 1943P, 1957-1960 see Suriname

KM# 170 CENT

2.00 g., Zinc, 17 mm. **Ruler:** Wilhelmina I **Obv:** Circled cross with banner below **Rev:** Value, waves, date and sprig **Edge:** Reeded

Date	Mintage	F12	VF20	XF40	MS60	MS63
1941	31,800,000	1.00	2.00	4.00	15.00	35.00
1942	241,200,000	0.25	0.50	1.00	3.00	8.00
1943	71,000,000	0.50	1.00	2.00	5.00	15.00
1943	—	PF63 1,250				
1944	29,600,000	1.00	2.00	4.00	15.00	35.00

KM# 175 CENT

2.00 g., Bronze, 14 mm. **Ruler:** Wilhelmina I **Obv:** Head left **Rev:** Value divides date **Edge:** Plain

Date	Mintage	F12	VF20	XF40	MS60	MS63
1948	175,000,000	0.05	0.10	0.50	3.50	15.00
1948 With PROEF in truncation	50	PF63 1,200				
1948	—	PF63 500				

KM# 180 CENT

2.00 g., Bronze, 14 mm. **Ruler:** Juliana **Obv:** Head right **Rev:** Value divides date

Date	Mintage	VF20	XF40	MS60	MS63	MS65
1950	46,400,000	0.20	2.00	5.00	9.00	15.00
1950	—	PF63 250				
1950 With PROEF in truncation	—	PF63 1,200				
1951	45,800,000	0.20	2.00	5.00	9.00	18.00
1951	—	PF63 200				
1952	—	PF63 200				
1952	68,000,000	0.20	2.00	5.00	9.00	15.00
1953	54,000,000	0.20	2.00	5.00	9.00	15.00
1953	—	PF63 200				
1954	—	PF63 200				
1954	54,000,000	0.20	2.00	5.00	9.00	15.00
1955	—	PF63 200				
1955	52,000,000	0.20	2.00	5.00	9.00	15.00
1956	34,800,000	0.20	2.00	5.00	9.00	18.00
1956	—	PF63 200				
1957	48,000,000	0.20	0.25	5.00	9.00	15.00
1957	—	PF63 200				
1958	34,000,000	0.20	0.25	5.00	9.00	15.00
1958	—	PF63 200				
1959	36,000,000	0.20	1.00	4.00	9.00	15.00
1959	—	PF63 200				
1960	40,000,000	0.20	1.00	4.00	6.00	10.00
1960	—	PF63 200				
1961	52,000,000	0.20	1.00	1.50	3.00	7.00
1961	—	PF63 200				
1962	—	PF63 200				
1962	57,000,000	0.20	1.00	1.50	3.00	7.00
1963	—	PF63 200				
1963	70,000,000	0.20	1.00	1.50	2.00	3.50
1964	73,000,000	0.20	1.00	1.50	2.00	3.50
1964	—	PF63 200				
1965	91,000,000	0.20	1.00	1.50	2.00	3.50
1965	—	PF63 200				
1966 large date	104,000,000	0.20	1.00	1.50	2.00	3.50
1966 Proof, large date	—	PF63 200				
1966 small date	Inc. above	0.20	1.00	1.50	2.00	3.50
1966 Proof, small date	—	PF63 200				
1967	140,000,000	0.20	1.00	1.50	2.00	3.50
1967	—	PF63 200				
1968	28,000,000	0.20	1.00	1.50	2.00	3.50
1968	—	PF63 200				
1969 fish privy mark	50,000,000	0.20	0.30	0.75	1.25	2.75
1969 Proof, fish privy mark	—	PF63 200				
1969 cock privy mark	50,000,000	0.20	0.30	0.75	1.25	2.75
1969 Proof, cock privy mark	—	PF63 200				
1970	100,000,000	0.20	0.30	0.75	1.25	2.75
1970	—	PF63 200				
1971	70,000,000	—	—	0.75	1.25	2.75
1971	—	PF63 350				
1972	40,000,000	—	—	0.75	1.25	2.75
1972	—	PF63 350				
1973	34,000,000	—	—	0.75	1.25	2.75
1973	—	PF63 350				
1974	46,000,000	—	—	0.75	1.25	2.75
1974	—	PF63 350				
1975	25,000,000	—	—	0.75	1.25	2.75
1975	—	PF63 350				
1976	15,000,000	—	—	0.75	1.25	2.75
1976	—	PF63 350				
1977	15,000,000	—	—	0.75	1.25	2.75
1977	—	PF63 350				
1978	15,000,000	—	—	0.75	1.25	2.75
1978	—	PF63 350				
1979	15,000,000	—	—	0.75	1.25	2.75
1979	—	PF63 350				
1980 cock and star privy mark	15,300,000	—	0.10	0.20	0.50	0.75
1980	—	PF63 350				

KM# 134 2-1/2 CENT

4.00 g., Bronze, 23.5 mm. **Ruler:** Wilhelmina I **Obv:** Crowned arms with 15 large shields within beaded circle **Obv. Legend:** KONINGRIJK DER NEDERLANDEN **Rev:** Value within wreath **Edge:** Reeded

Date	Mintage	F12	VF20	XF40	MS60	MS63
1903	4,000,000	2.00	3.50	7.50	30.00	70.00
1904	4,000,000	2.00	3.50	7.50	30.00	70.00
1905	4,000,000	2.00	3.50	7.50	30.00	70.00
1906	8,000,000	2.00	3.50	7.50	30.00	60.00

KM# 150 2-1/2 CENT

4.00 g., Bronze, 23.4 mm. **Ruler:** Wilhelmina I **Obv:** Crowned arms with 15 large shields within beaded circle **Obv. Legend:** KONINGRIJK. **Rev:** Value within wreath **Edge:** Reeded

Date	Mintage	F12	VF20	XF40	MS60	MS63
1912	2,000,000	4.00	8.00	25.00	75.00	180
1913	4,000,000	2.50	4.50	8.00	15.00	45.00
1914	2,000,000	4.00	8.00	25.00	75.00	180
1915	3,000,000	3.00	6.00	12.00	25.00	65.00
1916	8,000,000	2.00	3.50	6.00	15.00	40.00
1918	4,000,000	2.50	4.00	8.00	22.50	55.00
1919	2,000,000	3.00	6.00	12.00	25.00	60.00
1929	8,000,000	2.00	3.50	6.00	10.00	25.00
1941	19,800,000	1.25	2.00	3.00	6.00	9.00

KM# 171 2-1/2 CENT

2.80 g., Zinc, 20 mm. **Ruler:** Wilhelmina I **Obv:** Two swans on roof **Rev:** Value with four waves

Date	Mintage	F12	VF20	XF40	MS60	MS63
1941	27,600,000	1.00	3.00	6.00	25.00	60.00
1942	Est. 200000	2,000	5,000	10,000	17,500	25,000

Note: Almost entire issue melted, about 30 pieces known

KM# 137 5 CENTS

4.50 g., Copper-Nickel, 18 mm. **Ruler:** Wilhelmina I **Obv:** Crown flanked by sprigs **Rev:** Value within wreath

Date	Mintage	F12	VF20	XF40	MS60	MS63
1907	6,000,000	3.00	6.00	10.00	20.00	40.00
1908	5,430,000	4.00	8.00	12.50	22.50	45.00
1909	2,570,000	17.50	25.00	40.00	80.00	160

KM# 153 5 CENTS

4.50 g., Copper-Nickel, 21.3 mm. **Ruler:** Wilhelmina I **Obv:** Orange branch within circle **Rev:** Value within shells and beaded circle **Shape:** 4-sided

Date	Mintage	F12	VF20	XF40	MS60	MS63
1913	6,000,000	1.50	3.00	5.00	15.00	30.00
1913	—	PF63 1,250				
1914	7,400,000	1.50	3.00	5.00	15.00	30.00
1923	10,000,000	1.50	3.00	5.00	15.00	30.00
1929	8,000,000	1.50	3.00	5.00	15.00	30.00
1932	2,000,000	5.50	12.00	20.00	50.00	100
1933	1,400,000	17.50	25.00	50.00	80.00	160
1934	2,600,000	4.00	6.00	10.00	25.00	50.00
1936	2,600,000	4.00	6.00	10.00	25.00	50.00
1938	4,200,000	2.00	3.50	4.50	10.00	20.00
1939	4,600,000	2.00	3.50	4.50	10.00	20.00
1940	7,200,000	1.50	3.00	4.00	9.00	15.00

Note: For a similar coin dated 1943, see Curacao

KM# 172 5 CENTS

3.60 g., Zinc, 18 mm. **Ruler:** Wilhelmina I **Obv:** Two crossed horse heads and sun within square **Rev:** Value within circle flanked by nine waves and sprig **Shape:** 4-sided

Date	Mintage	F12	VF20	XF40	MS60	MS63
1941	32,200,000	1.00	2.50	6.00	20.00	50.00
1942	11,800,000	2.00	3.50	9.00	30.00	80.00
1943	7,000,000	5.00	8.00	20.00	50.00	140

KM# 176 5 CENTS

3.50 g., Bronze, 21 mm. **Ruler:** Wilhelmina I **Obv:** Head left **Rev:** Value divides date and orange branch

Date	Mintage	F12	VF20	XF40	MS60	MS63
1948	23,600,000	—	0.70	0.75	10.00	27.50
1948	—	PF63 800				
1948 With PROEF in truncation	50	PF63 1,800				

KM# 181 5 CENTS

3.50 g., Bronze, 21 mm. **Ruler:** Juliana **Obv:** Head right **Rev:** Value divides date and orange branch

Date	Mintage	VF20	XF40	MS60	MS63	MS65
1950	18,600,000	0.10	1.00	7.00	15.00	40.00
1950	—	PF63 250				
1950 With PROEF in truncation	—	PF63 1,800				
1951	16,200,000	0.10	1.00	10.00	20.00	100

Date	Mintage	VF20	XF40	MS60	MS63	MS65
1951	—	PF63 250				
1952	14,400,000	0.10	1.00	7.00	15.00	40.00
1952	—	PF63 250				
1953	12,000,000	0.10	1.00	7.00	15.00	40.00
1953	—	PF63 250				
1954	14,000,000	0.10	1.00	7.00	15.00	40.00
1954	—	PF63 250				
1955	11,400,000	0.10	1.00	7.00	15.00	100
1955	—	PF63 250				
1956	—	PF63 250				
1956	7,400,000	0.15	1.00	7.00	15.00	50.00
1957	—	PF63 250				
1957	16,000,000	0.10	1.00	7.00	15.00	85.00
1958	—	PF63 250				
1958	9,000,000	0.10	1.00	10.00	20.00	110
1960	—	PF63 250				
1960	11,000,000	0.10	1.00	5.00	10.00	30.00
1961	—	PF63 250				
1961	12,000,000	0.10	1.00	5.00	10.00	30.00
1962	15,000,000	0.10	0.25	2.00	4.00	15.00
1962	—	PF63 250				
1963	18,000,000	0.10	0.25	2.00	4.00	15.00
1963	—	PF63 250				
1964	21,000,000	0.10	0.25	2.00	4.00	15.00
1964	—	PF63 250				
1965	—	PF63 250				
1965	28,000,000	0.10	0.25	1.50	4.00	15.00
1966	—	PF63 250				
1966	22,000,000	0.10	0.25	2.00	4.00	15.00
1967 leaves far from rim	32,000,000	—	0.20	1.50	4.00	15.00
1967 Proof, leaves far from rim	—	PF63 250				
1967 leaves touching rim	Inc. above	0.15	0.50	1.50	4.00	15.00
1967 Proof, leaves touching rim	—	PF63 250				
1969 fish privy mark	5,000,000	0.15	1.00	5.00	10.00	30.00
1968	—	PF63 250				
1969 Proof, fish privy mark	—	PF63 250				
1969 cock privy mark	11,000,000	—	0.10	3.00	7.00	15.00
1969 Proof, cock privy mark	—	PF63 250				
1970	22,000,000	—	0.10	1.50	3.00	8.00
1970	—	PF63 250				
1970 date close to rim	Inc. above	—	0.10	1.50	3.00	8.00
1970 Proof, date close to rim	—	PF63 250				
1971	25,000,000	—	0.10	1.00	2.00	5.00
1971	—	PF63 450				
1972	25,000,000	—	0.10	1.00	2.00	5.00
1972	—	PF63 450				
1973	22,000,000	—	0.10	1.00	2.00	5.00
1973	—	PF63 450				
1974	20,000,000	—	—	0.75	2.00	5.00
1974	—	PF63 450				
1975	46,000,000	—	—	0.75	1.25	2.00
1975	—	PF63 450				
1976	50,000,000	—	—	0.75	1.25	2.00
1976	—	PF63 450				
1977	50,000,000	—	—	0.75	1.25	2.00
1977	—	PF63 450				
1978	60,000,000	—	—	0.75	1.25	2.00
1978	—	PF63 450				
1979	80,000,000	—	—	0.75	1.25	2.00
1979	—	PF63 450				
1980 cock and star privy mark	252,500,000	—	—	0.15	0.45	0.75
1980	—	PF63 450				

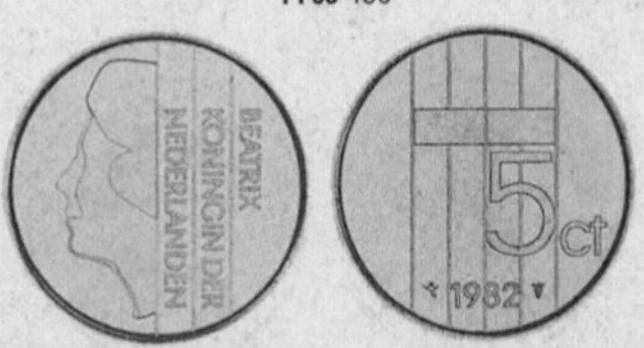

KM# 202 5 CENTS

3.50 g., Bronze, 21 mm. **Ruler:** Beatrix **Obv:** Head left with vertical inscription **Rev:** Value within vertical lines **Edge:** Plain

Date	Mintage	VF20	XF40	MS60	MS63	MS65
1982	47,100,000	—	—	0.20	0.50	1.00
1982	10,000	PF65 5.00				
1983	15,000	PF65 4.00				
1983	60,200,000	—	—	0.20	0.50	1.00
1984	20,000	PF65 3.00				
1984	70,700,000	—	—	0.20	0.50	1.00
1985	17,000	PF65 3.00				
1985	36,100,000	—	—	0.20	0.50	1.00
1986	19,700	PF65 3.00				
1986	7,700,000	—	—	0.50	1.00	3.00
1987	18,000	PF65 3.00				
1987	33,300,000	—	—	—	0.30	0.60
1988	22,600,000	—	—	—	0.30	0.60
1988	19,550	PF65 3.00				
1989	27,100,000	—	—	—	0.30	0.60
1989	15,300	PF65 4.00				
1990	39,200,000	—	—	—	0.30	0.60
1990	15,100	PF65 4.00				
1991	73,000,000	—	—	—	0.30	0.60
1991	14,000	PF65 4.00				
1992	52,600,000	—	—	—	0.30	0.60
1992	12,600	PF65 4.00				
1993	12,000	PF65 4.00				
1993	40,000,000	—	—	—	0.30	0.60
1994	12,500	PF65 4.00				
1994	13,900,000	—	—	—	0.75	1.50
1995	11,500	PF65 4.00				
1995	5,900,000	—	—	1.00	2.00	4.00
1996	13,500	PF65 4.00				
1996	39,900,000	—	—	—	0.35	0.70
1997	35,900,000	—	—	—	0.35	0.70
1997	12,000	PF65 4.00				
1998	65,000,000	—	—	—	0.35	0.70
1998	12,000	PF65 4.00				
1999	16,340,000	—	—	—	0.35	0.70
1999	15,000	PF65 4.00				
2000	15,000	PF65 4.00				
2000	29,900,000	—	—	—	0.35	0.70

KM# 119 10 CENTS

1.40 g., 0.640 Silver 0.0288 oz. ASW, 15 mm. **Ruler:** Wilhelmina I **Obv:** Small crowned head left divides legend **Obv. Legend:** WILHELMINA KONINGIN DER NEDERLANDEN **Rev:** Value and date within wreath **Edge:** Reeded **Note:** Privy mark: Halberd

Date	Mintage	F12	VF20	XF40	MS60	MS63
1901	2,000,000	25.00	60.00	120	250	350
1901	—	PF63 400				

KM# 135 10 CENTS

1.40 g., 0.640 Silver 0.0288 oz. ASW, 15 mm. **Ruler:** Wilhelmina I **Obv:** Head left **Rev:** Value in wreath

Date	Mintage	F12	VF20	XF40	MS60	MS63
1903	6,000,000	6.00	20.00	40.00	75.00	125

KM# 136 10 CENTS

1.40 g., 0.640 Silver 0.0288 oz. ASW, 15 mm. **Ruler:** Wilhelmina I **Obv:** Small head left with continous legend **Rev:** Value in wreath

Date	Mintage	F12	VF20	XF40	MS60	MS63
1904	3,000,000	6.00	20.00	40.00	80.00	150
1905	2,000,000	8.00	45.00	70.00	150	300
1906	4,000,000	4.00	17.50	30.00	60.00	125

KM# 145 10 CENTS

1.40 g., 0.640 Silver 0.0288 oz. ASW, 15 mm. **Ruler:** Wilhelmina I **Obv:** Small head left with continuous legend **Rev:** Value within wreath **Edge:** Reeded

Date	Mintage	F12	VF20	XF40	MS60	MS63
1910 High crown	2,250,000	10.00	30.00	60.00	120	250
1911	4,000,000	4.00	10.00	25.00	60.00	120
1912 Low crown	4,000,000	4.00	10.00	25.00	60.00	120
1912 High crown	Inc. above	40.00	100	250	500	1,000
1913	5,000,000	3.00	8.00	20.00	50.00	100
1914	9,000,000	1.50	4.00	15.00	30.00	60.00
1915	5,000,000	4.00	10.00	20.00	70.00	140
1916	5,000,000	4.00	10.00	20.00	70.00	140
1917	10,000,000	1.50	3.50	10.00	20.00	40.00
1918	20,000,000	1.25	2.50	6.00	15.00	35.00
1919	10,000,000	1.50	3.50	10.00	20.00	50.00
1921	5,000,000	2.00	6.00	15.00	35.00	80.00
1925	5,000,000	2.00	6.00	15.00	35.00	80.00

KM# 163 10 CENTS

1.40 g., 0.640 Silver 0.0288 oz. ASW, 15 mm. **Ruler:** Wilhelmina I **Obv:** Small head left with continuous legend **Rev:** Value within wreath **Edge:** Reeded

Date	Mintage	F12	VF20	XF40	MS60	MS63
1926	2,700,000	2.50	6.00	15.00	60.00	140
1927	2,300,000	2.50	6.00	15.00	65.00	150
1928	10,000,000	1.20	2.00	5.00	20.00	50.00
1930	5,000,000	1.50	3.50	10.00	30.00	60.00
1934	2,000,000	2.50	6.00	15.00	60.00	120
1935	8,000,000	1.00	1.50	3.50	10.00	25.00
1936	15,000,000	—	0.60	2.00	5.00	10.00
1937	18,600,000	—	0.60	2.00	3.50	5.00
1938	21,400,000	—	0.60	2.00	3.50	5.00
1939	20,000,000	—	0.60	2.00	3.50	5.00
1941	43,000,000	—	0.60	1.50	2.25	3.00
1943 P Acorn privy mark	—	—	0.60	6.50	15.00	40.00
1944 P Acorn privy mark	120,000,000	—	0.60	1.25	2.00	4.00
1944 D Acorn privy mark	25,400,000	—	—	7,500	15,000	25,000
Note: Almost entire issue melted						
1944 S Acorn privy mark	64,040,000	2.00	6.00	15.00	25.00	40.00
1944 S over P	2	—	600	1,000	2,000	3,000
1945 P Acorn privy mark	90,560,000	150	750	1,600	1,750	2,500

Note: For similar coins dated 1941P-1943P with palm tree privy mark, see Curacao and Suriname

KM# 173 10 CENTS

3.30 g., Zinc, 22 mm. **Ruler:** Wilhelmina I **Obv:** Three tulips flanked by dots within circle **Rev:** Value flanked by sprigs **Edge:** Reeded

Date	Mintage	F12	VF20	XF40	MS60	MS63
1941	29,800,000	0.75	1.50	3.50	15.00	35.00
1942	95,600,000	0.25	0.50	2.00	5.00	25.00
1943	29,000,000	0.75	1.50	3.50	15.00	35.00

KM# 177 10 CENTS

1.50 g., Nickel, 15 mm. **Ruler:** Wilhelmina I **Obv:** Head left **Rev:** Crowned value divides date **Edge:** Reeded

Date	Mintage	F12	VF20	XF40	MS60	MS63
1948	80,000,000	—	0.20	1.50	2.00	4.00
1948	—	PF63 500				
1948 With PROEF in truncation	50	PF63 1,200				

KM# 182 10 CENTS

1.50 g., Nickel, 15 mm. **Ruler:** Juliana **Obv:** Head right **Rev:** Crowned value divides date **Edge:** Reeded

Date	Mintage	VF20	XF40	MS60	MS63	MS65
1950	45,900,000	0.10	0.35	2.50	5.00	10.00
1950	—	PF63 250				
1950 With PROEF in truncation	—	PF63 1,200				
1951	—	PF63 200				
1951	54,200,000	0.10	0.35	2.50	5.00	10.00
1954	—	PF63 200				
1954	8,200,000	0.20	0.50	3.50	7.50	15.00
1955	—	PF63 200				
1955	18,200,000	0.10	0.35	2.50	5.00	10.00
1956	12,000,000	0.10	0.35	3.00	6.00	12.00
1956	—	PF63 200				
1957	—	PF63 200				

Date	Mintage	VF20	XF40	MS60	MS63	MS65
1957	18,600,000	0.10	0.35	2.00	4.00	8.00
1958	34,000,000	0.10	0.35	2.00	4.00	8.00
1958	—	PF63 200				
1959	44,000,000	0.10	0.35	2.00	4.00	8.00
1959	—	PF63 200				
1960	12,000,000	0.10	0.35	3.00	6.00	12.00
1960	—	PF63 200				
1961	25,000,000	—	0.15	1.00	2.00	8.00
1961	—	PF63 200				
1962	—	PF63 200				
1962	30,000,000	—	0.15	1.00	2.00	8.00
1963	—	PF63 200				
1963	35,000,000	—	0.15	1.00	2.00	8.00
1964	—	PF63 200				
1964	41,000,000	—	0.15	1.00	2.00	6.00
1965	59,000,000	—	0.15	1.00	2.00	6.00
1965	—	PF63 200				
1966	44,000,000	—	0.15	1.00	2.00	6.00
1966	—	PF63 200				
1967	39,000,000	—	0.10	0.50	1.00	3.00
1967	—	PF63 200				
1968	42,000,000	—	0.10	0.50	1.00	3.00
1968	—	PF63 200				
1969 fish privy mark	28,000,000	—	0.10	0.50	1.00	4.00
1969 Proof, fish privy mark	—	PF63 200				
1969 cock privy mark	24,000,000	—	0.10	0.50	1.00	4.00
1969 Proof, cock privy mark	—	PF63 200				
1970	—	PF63 200				
1970	50,000,000	—	—	0.20	0.50	1.50
1971	55,000,000	—	—	0.20	0.50	1.50
1971	—	PF63 350				
1972	60,000,000	—	—	0.20	0.50	1.50
1972	—	PF63 350				
1973	90,000,000	—	—	0.20	0.50	1.50
1973	—	PF63 350				
1974	75,000,000	—	—	0.20	0.50	1.50
1974	—	PF63 350				
1975	110,000,000	—	—	0.20	0.50	1.50
1975	—	PF63 350				
1976	85,000,000	—	—	0.10	0.20	1.00
1976	—	PF63 350				
1977	100,000,000	—	—	0.10	0.20	1.00
1977	—	PF63 350				
1978	110,000,000	—	—	0.10	0.20	1.00
1978	—	PF63 350				
1979	120,000,000	—	—	0.10	0.20	1.00
1979	—	PF63 350				
1980 cock and star privy mark	195,300,000	—	—	0.10	0.20	1.00
1980	—	PF63 350				

KM# 203 10 CENTS

1.50 g., Nickel, 15 mm. **Ruler:** Beatrix **Obv:** Head left with vertical inscription **Rev:** Value and vertical lines **Edge:** Reeded

Date	Mintage	VF20	XF40	MS60	MS63	MS65
1982	10,000	PF65 7.00				
1982	10,300,000	—	—	0.20	0.45	0.75
1983	38,200,000	—	—	—	—	0.75
1983	15,000	PF65 6.00				
1984	42,200,000	—	—	0.20	0.45	0.75
1984	20,000	PF65 3.00				
1985	17,000	PF65 3.00				
1985	29,100,000	—	—	0.20	0.45	0.75
1986	19,700	PF65 3.00				
1986	23,100,000	—	—	0.20	0.45	0.75
1987	21,700,000	—	—	0.20	0.45	0.75
1987	18,000	PF65 3.00				
1988	19,550	PF65 6.00				
1988	2,200,000	—	—	0.60	1.25	3.00
1989	5,300,000	—	—	0.35	0.75	1.50
1989	15,300	PF65 5.00				
1990	13,200,000	—	—	0.20	0.45	0.75
1990	15,100	PF65 4.00				
1991	41,000,000	—	—	0.20	0.45	0.75
1991	14,000	PF65 4.00				
1992	41,200,000	—	—	0.20	0.45	0.75
1992	12,600	PF65 4.00				
1993	12,000	PF65 4.00				
1993	30,100,000	—	—	0.20	0.45	0.75
1994	12,500	PF65 4.00				
1994	25,600,000	—	—	0.20	0.45	0.75
1995	11,500	PF65 4.00				
1995	31,000,000	—	—	0.20	0.45	0.75
1996	13,500	PF65 4.00				
1996	34,800,000	—	—	0.20	0.45	0.75
1997	20,000,000	—	—	0.20	0.45	0.75
1997	12,000	PF65 4.00				
1998	24,450,000	—	—	0.20	0.45	0.75
1998	12,000	PF65 4.00				
1999	49,900,000	—	—	0.20	0.45	0.75
1999	15,000	PF65 4.00				
2000	75,300,000	—	—	0.20	0.45	0.75
2000	15,000	PF65 4.00				

KM# 120.1 25 CENTS

3.58 g., 0.640 Silver 0.0736 oz. ASW, 19 mm. **Ruler:** Wilhelmina I **Obv:** Bust with wide truncation **Obv. Legend:** WILHELMINA KONINGIN DER NEDERLANDEN **Rev:** Value within wreath **Edge:** Reeded **Note:** Privy mark: Halberd

Date	Mintage	F12	VF20	XF40	MS60	MS63
1901 Wide neck	1,600,000	75.00	200	400	800	1,250

KM# 120.2 25 CENTS

3.58 g., 0.640 Silver 0.0736 oz. ASW, 19 mm. **Ruler:** Wilhelmina I **Obv:** Head left **Rev:** Value within wreath **Edge:** Reeded

Date	Mintage	F12	VF20	XF40	MS60	MS63
1901	3	PF63 1,500				
1901 Small neck	Inc. above	8.00	30.00	60.00	150	300

Note: Mintage included in KM#120.1

Date	Mintage	F12	VF20	XF40	MS60	MS63
1902	1,200,000	8.00	30.00	60.00	150	300
1903	1,200,000	8.00	30.00	60.00	150	300
1904	1,600,000	7.00	30.00	60.00	150	—
1905	1,200,000	8.00	40.00	80.00	160	300
1906	2,000,000	7.00	30.00	60.00	100	225

KM# 146 25 CENTS

3.58 g., 0.640 Silver 0.0736 oz. ASW, 19 mm. **Ruler:** Wilhelmina I **Obv:** Bust left, legend **Rev:** Value within wreath **Edge:** Reeded

Date	Mintage	F12	VF20	XF40	MS60	MS63
1910	—	PF63 800				
1910	880,000	18.00	60.00	120	200	450
1911	1,600,000	8.00	35.00	70.00	150	275
1912	1,600,000	8.00	35.00	70.00	150	300
1913	1,200,000	20.00	50.00	100	180	325
1914	5,600,000	3.50	15.00	35.00	75.00	125
1915	2,000,000	4.50	30.00	65.00	125	250
1916	2,000,000	4.50	30.00	65.00	125	250
1917	4,000,000	3.50	8.00	20.00	50.00	100
1918	6,000,000	2.50	6.00	15.00	35.00	75.00
1919	4,000,000	3.50	10.00	20.00	50.00	100
1925	2,000,000	4.50	20.00	40.00	100	175

KM# 164 25 CENTS

3.58 g., 0.640 Silver 0.0736 oz. ASW, 19 mm. **Ruler:** Wilhelmina I **Obv:** Small head left **Rev:** Value within wreath **Edge:** Reeded

Date	Mintage	F12	VF20	XF40	MS60	MS63
1926	2,000,000	6.00	20.00	60.00	120	240
1928	8,000,000	1.40	4.00	10.00	30.00	55.00
1939	4,000,000	1.40	2.50	3.00	7.00	15.00
1940	9,000,000	1.40	2.50	3.00	7.00	15.00
1941	40,000,000	—	1.40	2.50	5.00	7.00
1943 P acorn privy mark	—	1.40	2.50	3.50	15.00	30.00
1944 P acorn privy mark	40,000,000	—	1.40	2.50	5.00	10.00
1945 P acorn privy mark	92,000,000	50.00	150	300	350	500

Note: For similar coins dated 1941P and 1943P with palm tree privy mark, see Curacao

KM# 174 25 CENTS

5.00 g., Zinc, 26 mm. **Ruler:** Wilhelmina I **Obv:** Sailing boat **Rev:** Value flanked by sprigs

Date	Mintage	F12	VF20	XF40	MS60	MS63
1941	34,600,000	0.75	2.50	10.00	20.00	45.00
1942	27,800,000	0.75	2.50	10.00	20.00	45.00
1943	13,600,000	2.50	10.00	25.00	50.00	90.00

KM# 178 25 CENTS

3.00 g., Nickel, 19 mm. **Ruler:** Wilhelmina I **Obv:** Head left **Rev:** Crowned value divides date **Edge:** Reeded

Date	Mintage	F12	VF20	XF40	MS60	MS63
1948	32,000,000	—	0.50	2.50	15.00	25.00
1948	—	PF63 1,000				
1948 With PROEF in truncation	50	PF63 2,000				

KM# 183 25 CENTS

3.00 g., Nickel, 19 mm. **Ruler:** Juliana **Obv:** Head right **Rev:** Crowned value divides date **Edge:** Reeded

Date	Mintage	VF20	XF40	MS60	MS63	MS65
1950	38,400,000	0.20	0.50	2.50	5.00	20.00
1950	—	PF63 250				
1950 With PROEF in truncation	—	PF63 2,000				
1951	33,200,000	0.20	0.50	2.50	5.00	20.00
1951	—	PF63 250				
1954	6,400,000	0.50	2.50	5.00	10.00	40.00
1954	—	PF63 250				
1955	10,000,000	0.20	0.50	2.00	4.00	15.00
1955	—	PF63 250				
1956	8,000,000	0.20	0.50	2.00	4.00	15.00
1956	—	PF63 250				
1957	8,000,000	0.20	0.50	2.00	4.00	15.00
1957	—	PF63 250				
1958	15,000,000	0.20	0.50	2.00	4.00	12.00
1958	—	PF63 250				
1960	9,000,000	0.20	0.50	2.00	4.00	12.00
1960	—	PF63 250				
1961	6,000,000	0.40	1.25	2.50	5.00	20.00
1961	—	PF63 250				
1962	12,000,000	0.20	0.30	1.00	2.00	10.00
1962	—	PF63 250				
1963	18,000,000	0.20	0.30	1.00	2.00	10.00
1963	—	PF63 250				
1964	25,000,000	0.20	0.30	1.00	2.00	10.00
1964	—	PF63 250				
1965	18,000,000	0.20	0.30	1.00	2.00	10.00
1965	—	PF63 250				
1966	25,000,000	—	0.20	0.75	1.50	6.00
1966	—	PF63 250				
1967	18,000,000	—	0.20	0.75	1.50	6.00
1967	—	PF63 250				
1968	26,000,000	—	0.20	0.75	1.50	6.00
1968	—	PF63 250				
1969 fish privy mark	14,000,000	—	0.50	1.25	2.50	9.00
1969 Proof, fish privy mark	—	PF63 250				
1969 cock privy mark	21,000,000	—	0.50	1.00	2.00	6.00
1969 Proof, cock privy mark	—	PF63 250				
1970	39,000,000	—	0.20	0.30	1.00	2.00
1970	—	PF63 250				
1971	40,000,000	—	0.20	0.30	1.00	2.00
1971	—	PF63 450				
1972	50,000,000	—	0.20	0.30	0.50	1.00
1972	—	PF63 450				
1973	45,000,000	—	0.20	0.30	0.50	1.00
1973	—	PF63 450				
1974	10,000,000	—	0.20	0.60	1.25	2.50
1974	—	PF63 450				
1975	25,000,000	—	0.20	0.30	0.50	1.00
1975	—	PF63 450				
1976	64,000,000	—	0.20	0.30	0.50	1.00
1976	—	PF63 450				
1977	55,000,000	—	0.20	0.30	0.50	1.00
1977	—	PF63 450				
1978	35,000,000	—	0.20	0.30	0.50	1.00
1978	—	PF63 450				

Date	Mintage	VF20	XF40	MS60	MS63	MS65
1979	45,000,000	—	0.20	0.30	0.50	1.00
1979	—	PF63 450				
1980 cock and star privy mark	159,300,000	—	—	0.30	0.50	1.00
1980	—	PF63 450				

KM# 183a 25 CENTS

0.78 g., Aluminum **Ruler:** Juliana **Obv:** Head right **Rev:** Crowned value divides date **Note:** Thought by many sources to be a pattern.

Date	Mintage	VF20	XF40	MS60	MS63	MS65
1980	15	PF63 600				

KM# 204 25 CENTS

3.00 g., Nickel, 19 mm. **Ruler:** Beatrix **Obv:** Head left with vertical inscription **Obv. Inscription:** Beatrix/Konincin Der/ Nederlanden **Rev:** Value within vertical and horizontal lines **Edge:** Reeded

Date	Mintage	VF20	XF40	MS60	MS63	MS65
1982	18,300,000	—	—	0.30	0.50	1.00
1982	10,000	PF65 10.00				
1983	18,200,000	—	—	0.30	0.50	1.00
1983	15,000	PF65 8.00				
1984	19,200,000	—	—	0.30	0.50	1.00
1984	20,000	PF65 4.00				
1985	29,100,000	—	—	0.30	0.50	1.00
1985	17,000	PF65 4.00				
1986	20,300,000	—	—	0.30	0.50	1.00
1986	19,700	PF65 4.00				
1987	30,100,000	—	—	0.30	0.50	1.00
1987	18,000	PF65 4.00				
1988	17,400,000	—	—	0.30	0.50	1.00
1988	19,550	PF65 4.00				
1989	30,400,000	—	—	0.30	0.50	1.00
1989	15,300	PF65 5.00				
1990	23,000,000	—	—	0.30	0.50	1.00
1990	15,100	PF65 5.00				
1991	25,000,000	—	—	0.30	0.50	1.00
1991	14,000	PF65 5.00				
1992	41,500,000	—	—	0.30	0.50	1.00
1992	12,600	PF65 5.00				
1993	15,100,000	—	—	0.50	1.00	2.00
1993	12,000	PF65 5.00				
1994	1,560,000	—	—	1.25	2.50	5.00
1994	12,500	PF65 7.50				
1995	30,240,000	—	—	0.30	0.50	1.00
1995	11,500	PF65 5.00				
1996	24,840,000	—	—	0.30	0.50	1.00
1996	13,500	PF65 5.00				
1997	29,760,000	—	—	0.30	0.50	1.00
1997	12,000	PF65 5.00				
1998	69,560,000	—	—	0.30	0.50	1.00
1998	12,000	PF65 5.00				
1999	10,560,000	—	—	0.30	0.50	1.00
1999	15,000	PF65 5.00				
2000	31,000,000	—	—	0.30	0.50	1.00
2000	15,000	PF65 5.00				

KM# 121.2 1/2 GULDEN

5.00 g., 0.945 Silver 0.1519 oz. ASW, 22 mm. **Ruler:** Wilhelmina I **Obv:** Head left **Rev:** Crowned Arms without 50 C. below shield **Edge:** Reeded

Date	Mintage	F12	VF20	XF40	MS60	MS63
1904	1,000,000	30.00	90.00	200	300	500
1905	4,000,000	7.00	25.00	50.00	90.00	180
1906	1,000,000	30.00	90.00	200	300	500
1907	3,300,000	7.00	25.00	50.00	90.00	180
1907	—	PF63 2,500				
1908	4,000,000	7.00	25.00	50.00	90.00	180
1909	3,000,000	7.00	30.00	50.00	100	200

KM# 147 1/2 GULDEN

5.00 g., 0.945 Silver 0.1519 oz. ASW, 22 mm. **Ruler:** Wilhelmina I **Obv:** Head left **Rev:** Crowned Arms **Edge:** Reeded

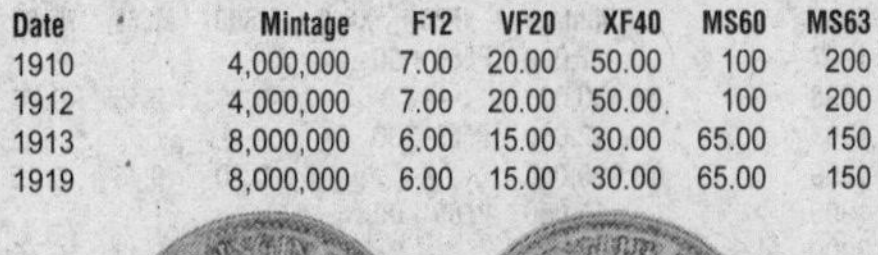

Date	Mintage	F12	VF20	XF40	MS60	MS63
1910	4,000,000	7.00	20.00	50.00	100	200
1912	4,000,000	7.00	20.00	50.00	100	200
1913	8,000,000	6.00	15.00	30.00	65.00	150
1919	8,000,000	6.00	15.00	30.00	65.00	150

KM# 160 1/2 GULDEN

5.00 g., 0.720 Silver 0.1157 oz. ASW, 22 mm. **Ruler:** Wilhelmina I **Obv:** Head left **Rev:** Crowned Arms **Edge:** Reeded

Date	Mintage	F12	VF20	XF40	MS60	MS63
1921	5,000,000	2.25	4.70	15.00	25.00	50.00
1921	—	PF63 250				
1922	11,240,000	2.25	4.50	12.50	20.00	40.00
1928	5,000,000	2.25	4.75	12.50	25.00	50.00
1929	9,500,000	—	2.25	5.00	12.00	18.00
Note: 3 pearls diadem under Gl						
1929	Inc. above	2.25	7.00	30.00	60.00	180
Note: 3 pearls under G						
1930	18,500,000	—	2.25	5.00	9.00	15.00

KM# 122.1 GULDEN

10.00 g., 0.945 Silver 0.3038 oz. ASW, 28 mm. **Ruler:** Wilhelmina I **Obv:** Crowned head left **Obv. Legend:** WILHELMINA KONINGIN DER NEDERLANDEN **Rev:** Crowned arms divide value **Rev. Legend:** (date) MUNT VAN HET KONINGRIJK DER NEDERLANDEN **Edge Lettering:** GOD*ZY* MET*ONS* **Note:** Privy mark: Halberd

Date	Mintage	F12	VF20	XF40	MS60	MS63
1901	—	PF63 1,000				
1901	2,000,000	25.00	100	200	400	550

KM# 122.2 GULDEN

10.00 g., 0.945 Silver 0.3038 oz. ASW **Ruler:** Wilhelmina I **Obv:** Head left **Rev:** Crowned arms without 100 C. below shield **Edge Lettering:** GOD * ZY * MET * ONS * **Shape:** 28

Date	Mintage	F12	VF20	XF40	MS60	MS63
1904	2,000,000	20.00	45.00	90.00	200	400
1904	—	PF63 2,500				
1905	1,000,000	25.00	85.00	150	300	650
1905	—	PF63 2,500				
1906	500,000	150	325	900	1,250	2,000
1906	—	PF63 4,000				
1907	5,100,000	12.00	25.00	45.00	100	150
1908	4,700,000	12.00	25.00	45.00	100	150
1908	—	PF63 3,000				
1909	2,000,000	20.00	60.00	150	250	500

KM# 148 GULDEN

10.00 g., 0.945 Silver 0.3038 oz. ASW, 28 mm. **Ruler:** Wilhelmina I **Obv:** Head left **Obv. Legend:** Crowned arms **Edge Lettering:** GOD * ZIJ * MET * ONS *

Date	Mintage	F12	VF20	XF40	MS60	MS63
1910	1,000,000	50.00	200	500	900	1,800
1910	—	PF63 2,200				
1911	2,000,000	40.00	160	250	400	600
1912	3,000,000	13.00	35.00	90.00	200	500
1913	8,000,000	12.00	25.00	60.00	100	175
1914	15,785,000	10.00	20.00	32.50	75.00	150
1915	14,215,000	10.00	20.00	35.00	75.00	150
1916	5,000,000	20.00	60.00	100	170	250
1917	2,300,000	20.00	70.00	110	200	300

KM# 161.1 GULDEN

10.00 g., 0.720 Silver 0.2315 oz. ASW, 28 mm. **Ruler:** Wilhelmina I **Obv:** Head left **Obv. Legend:** Ends below truncation **Rev:** Crowned arms **Edge Lettering:** GOD * ZIJ * MET * ONS *

Date	Mintage	F12	VF20	XF40	MS60	MS63
1922	9,550,000	4.25	7.75	15.00	40.00	75.00
1922	—	PF63 450				
1923	8,050,000	4.25	8.50	20.00	40.00	75.00
1924	8,000,000	4.25	10.00	25.00	40.00	75.00
1928	6,150,000	4.25	7.75	15.00	50.00	90.00
1929	32,350,000	—	4.25	8.00	10.00	18.00
1930	13,500,000	—	4.25	15.00	12.00	70.00
1931	38,100,000	—	4.25	8.00	10.00	15.00
1938	5,000,000	4.25	7.75	10.00	18.00	25.00
1939	14,200,000	—	4.25	8.00	10.00	15.00
1940	21,300,000	—	4.25	8.00	10.00	15.00
1940	—	PF63 200				
1944 P acorn privy mark	105,125,000	80.00	200	400	600	800
Note: EN under neck						

KM# 161.2 GULDEN

10.00 g., 0.720 Silver 0.2315 oz. ASW, 28 mm. **Ruler:** Wilhelmina I **Obv:** Head left **Obv. Legend:** Ends at right of truncation **Rev:** Crowned arms **Edge Lettering:** GOD * ZIJ * MET * ONS * **Note:** For similar coins dated 1943D with palm tree privy mark, see Netherlands East Indies

Date	Mintage	F12	VF20	XF40	MS60	MS63
1944 P acorn privy mark	Inc. above	10.00	20.00	35.00	60.00	125
Note: 'P' above 'EN'						
(1944) acorn privy mark	Inc. above	25.00	50.00	100	175	300
Note: 'P' above 'N'						
1945 P acorn privy mark	25,375,000	225	600	1,200	1,750	2,500
Note: Only a small number placed into circulation						

KM# 184 GULDEN

6.50 g., 0.720 Silver 0.1505 oz. ASW, 25 mm. **Ruler:** Juliana **Obv:** Head right **Rev:** Crowned arms divide date **Edge Lettering:** GOD * ZIJ * MET * ONS *

Date	Mintage	VF20	XF40	MS60	MS63	MS65
1954	6,600,000	—	2.75	6.00	10.00	15.00
1954	—	PF63 1,800				
1955	37,500,000	—	2.75	5.00	8.00	12.00
1955	—	PF63 350				
1956	38,900,000	—	2.75	5.00	8.00	12.00
1956	—	PF63 350				
1957	27,000,000	—	2.75	5.00	8.00	12.00
1957	—	PF63 350				
1958	30,000,000	—	2.75	7.00	12.00	20.00
1958	—	PF63 350				
1963	5,000,000	—	2.75	6.00	10.00	15.00
1963	—	PF63 350				
1964	9,000,000	—	2.75	5.00	8.00	12.00
1964	—	PF63 350				
1965	21,000,000	—	2.75	5.00	8.00	12.00
1965	—	PF63 350				
1966	5,000,000	—	2.75	5.00	8.00	12.00
1966	—	PF63 350				
1967	7,000,000	—	2.75	5.00	8.00	12.00
1967	—	PF63 350				

KM# 184a GULDEN
6.00 g., Nickel, 25 mm. **Ruler:** Juliana **Obv:** Head right **Rev:** Crowned arms divide date

Date	Mintage	VF20	XF40	MS60	MS63	MS65
1967	31,000,000	—	2.00	6.00	8.00	12.00
1967	—	PF63 350				
1968	61,000,000	—	2.00	5.00	7.50	12.00
1969 fish	27,500,000	—	2.50	6.00	9.00	15.00
1969 Proof, fish	—	PF63 350				
1969 cock	15,500,000	—	3.50	7.50	12.00	18.00
1969 Proof, cock	—	PF63 350				
1970	18,000,000	—	3.50	7.50	12.00	18.00
1970	—	PF63 350				
1971	50,000,000	—	—	2.75	6.00	10.00
1971	—	PF63 500				
1972	60,000,000	—	—	2.75	6.00	10.00
1972	—	PF63 500				
1973	27,000,000	—	—	2.75	6.00	10.00
1973	—	PF63 500				
1974	—	PF63 500				
1975	9,000,000	—	2.50	6.00	10.00	17.00
1975	—	PF63 500				
1976	32,000,000	—	—	1.00	2.00	4.00
1976	—	PF63 500				
1977	38,000,000	—	—	1.00	2.00	4.00
1977	—	PF63 500				
1978	30,000,000	—	—	0.75	1.50	3.00
1978	—	PF63 500				
1979	25,000,000	—	—	0.75	1.25	2.50
1979	—	PF63 500				
1980 cock and star privy mark	118,300,000	—	—	0.75	1.25	2.00
1980	—	PF63 500				

KM# 200 GULDEN
6.00 g., Nickel, 25 mm. **Ruler:** Beatrix **Subject:** Investiture of New Queen **Obv:** Conjoined heads left **Rev:** Crowned arms divide date **Edge Lettering:** GOD * ZIJ * MET * ONS *

Date	Mintage	VF20	XF40	MS60	MS63	MS65
1980	30,500,000	—	—	1.25	1.75	3.00

KM# 200a GULDEN
6.50 g., Silver, 25 mm. **Ruler:** Beatrix **Subject:** Investiture of New Queen **Obv:** Conjoined heads left **Rev:** Crowned arms divide date **Edge Lettering:** GOD * ZIJ * MET * ONS * **Note:** Z added (for silver).

Date	Mintage	VF20	XF40	MS60	MS63	MS65
1980	157	PF65 2,000				

KM# 200b GULDEN
Gold, 25 mm. **Ruler:** Beatrix **Subject:** Investiture of New Queen **Obv:** Conjoined heads left **Rev:** Crowned arms divide date **Note:** G added (for gold).

Date	Mintage	VF20	XF40	MS60	MS63	MS65
1980 Proof, Rare	7	PF65 25,000				

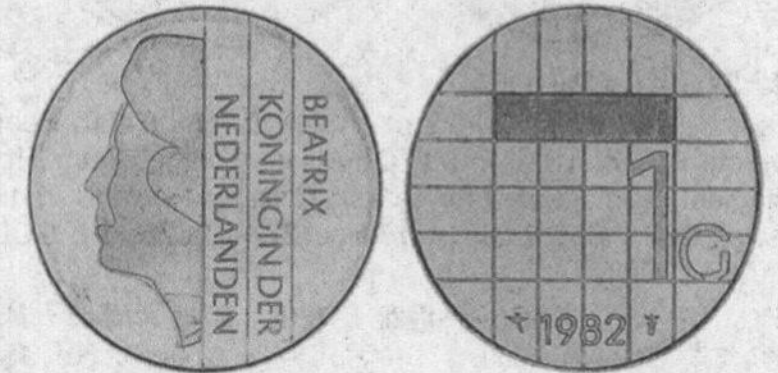

KM# 205 GULDEN
6.00 g., Nickel, 25 mm. **Ruler:** Beatrix **Obv:** Head left with vertical inscription **Rev:** Value within vertical and horizontal lines **Edge Lettering:** GOD * ZIJ * MET * ONS *

Date	Mintage	VF20	XF40	MS60	MS63	MS65
1982	31,300,000	—	—	0.60	1.25	2.50
1982	10,000	PF65 7.00				
1983	5,200,000	—	—	0.75	1.50	3.00
1983	15,000	PF65 5.00				
1984	4,200,000	—	—	0.75	1.50	3.00
1984	20,000	PF65 5.00				
1985	3,100,000	—	—	2.50	5.00	10.00
1985	17,000	PF65 5.00				
1986	12,100,000	—	—	0.75	1.50	3.00
1986	19,700	PF65 5.00				
1987	20,100,000	—	—	0.75	1.50	3.00
1987	18,000	PF65 5.00				
1988	13,600,000	—	—	0.75	1.50	3.00
1988	19,550	PF65 5.00				
1989	1,100,000	—	—	1.25	2.50	5.00
1989	15,300	PF65 5.00				
1990	1,000,000	—	—	1.25	2.50	5.00
1990	15,100	PF65 5.00				
1991	400,000	—	—	2.25	4.50	9.00
1991	14,000	PF65 5.00				
1992	10,000,000	—	—	0.50	1.00	1.50
1992	12,600	PF65 5.00				
1993	15,100,000	—	—	0.50	1.00	1.50
1993	12,000	PF65 5.00				
1994	16,600,000	—	—	0.50	1.00	1.50
1994	12,500	PF65 5.00				
1995	12,500,000	—	—	0.50	1.00	1.50
1995	11,500	PF65 5.00				
1996	6,500,000	—	—	0.50	1.00	1.50
1996	13,500	PF65 5.00				
1997	12,690,000	—	—	0.50	1.00	1.50
1997	12,000	PF65 5.00				
1998	15,000,000	—	—	0.50	1.00	1.75
1998	12,000	PF65 5.00				
1999	8,740,000	—	—	0.50	1.00	1.25
1999	15,000	PF65 5.00				
2000	37,500,000	—	—	0.50	1.00	1.25
2000	15,000	PF65 5.00				

KM# 230 GULDEN
11.00 g., 0.750 Gold 0.2652 oz. AGW, 25 mm. **Ruler:** Beatrix **Subject:** ERU, 175th Anniversary **Rev:** Small tulip, "750" added at lower right **Edge Lettering:** GOD ZIJ MET ONS **Note:** Similar to KM#205.

Date	Mintage	VF20	XF40	MS60	MS63	MS65
1999	1,000	PF65 1,500				

Note: Approximately 480 of the mintage were melted down

KM# 165 2-1/2 GULDEN
25.00 g., 0.720 Silver 0.5787 oz. ASW, 38 mm. **Ruler:** Wilhelmina I **Obv:** Head left **Rev:** Crowned arms divide value **Edge Lettering:** GOD * ZIJ * MET * ONS *

Date	Mintage	F12	VF20	XF40	MS60	MS63
1929	4,400,000	—	12.00	35.00	75.00	100
1930	11,600,000	—	12.00	30.00	30.00	50.00
1931	4,720,000	—	12.00	30.00	30.00	50.00
1932	6,000,000	—	12.00	30.00	30.00	50.00
1932 Deep hair lines	Inc. above	70.00	120	200	400	1,000
1933 Deep hair lines	3,560,000	—	12.00	30.00	30.00	60.00
1937	4,000,000	—	12.00	30.00	30.00	50.00
1938	2,000,000	12.00	25.00	35.00	35.00	60.00
1938 Deep hair lines	Inc. above	50.00	100	175	275	400
1939	3,760,000	—	12.00	30.00	30.00	40.00
1940	4,640,000	12.00	30.00	35.00	60.00	120

Note: For similar coins dated 1943D with palm tree privy mark, see Netherlands East Indies

KM# 185 2-1/2 GULDEN
15.00 g., 0.720 Silver 0.3472 oz. ASW, 33 mm. **Ruler:** Juliana **Obv:** Head right **Rev:** Crowned arms divide value **Edge Lettering:** GOD * ZIJ * MET * ONS *

Date	Mintage	VF20	XF40	MS60	MS63	MS65
1959	7,200,000	—	6.50	9.00	12.00	15.00
1959	—	PF63 450				
1960	12,800,000	—	6.50	9.00	12.00	15.00
1960	—	PF63 450				
1961	10,000,000	—	6.50	9.00	12.00	15.00
1961	—	PF63 450				
1962	5,000,000	—	6.50	9.00	12.00	15.00
1962	—	PF63 450				
1963	4,000,000	—	6.50	10.00	15.00	18.00
1963	—	PF63 450				
1964	2,800,000	—	6.50	10.00	17.00	30.00
1964	—	PF63 450				
1966	5,000,000	—	6.50	9.00	12.00	15.00
1966	—	PF63 450				

KM# 191 2-1/2 GULDEN
10.00 g., Nickel, 29 mm. **Ruler:** Juliana **Obv:** Head right **Rev:** Crowned arms divide value **Edge Lettering:** GOD * ZIJ * MET * ONS *

Date	Mintage	VF20	XF40	MS60	MS63	MS65
1969	1,200,000	—	1.50	3.00	7.00	15.00
Note: Fish privy mark						
1969	500	PF63 450				
Note: Fish privy mark with front hair lock						
1969 Proof, 2 known	—	PF63 3,500				
Note: Fish privy mark without front hair lock						
1969	15,600,000	—	1.00	3.00	7.50	16.00
Note: Cock privy mark						
1969	500	PF63 450				
Note: Cock privy mark						
1970	22,000,000	—	—	2.00	4.00	9.00
1970	500	PF63 450				
1971	8,000,000	—	—	1.50	3.00	6.00
1971	500	PF63 650				
1972	20,000,000	—	—	1.50	3.00	6.00
1972	500	PF63 650				
1973	500	PF63 650				
1974	500	PF63 650				
1975	500	PF63 650				
1976	500	PF63 650				
1977	500	PF63 650				
1978	5,000,000	—	—	1.50	3.00	6.00
1978	500	PF63 650				
1979	500	PF63 650				
1980	37,300,000	—	—	—	1.50	3.00
Note: Cock and star privy mark						
1980	500	PF63 650				

KM# 197 2-1/2 GULDEN
10.00 g., Nickel, 29 mm. **Ruler:** Juliana **Subject:** 400th Anniversary - The Union of Utrecht **Obv:** Head right **Rev:** Text, value and date **Edge Lettering:** GOD * ZIJ * MET * ONS *

Date	Mintage	VF20	XF40	MS60	MS63	MS65
1979	20,000,000	—	—	1.00	2.00	4.00

KM# 201 2-1/2 GULDEN
10.00 g., Nickel, 29 mm. **Ruler:** Beatrix **Subject:** Investiture of New Queen **Obv:** Conjoined heads left **Rev:** Crowned arms divide date **Edge Lettering:** GOD * ZIJ * MET * ONS *

Date	Mintage	VF20	XF40	MS60	MS63	MS65
1980	30,500,000	—	—	1.50	3.00	5.00

KM# 201a 2-1/2 GULDEN

Silver **Ruler:** Beatrix **Subject:** Investiture of New Queen **Obv:** Conjoined heads left **Rev:** Crowned arms divide date **Edge Lettering:** GOD * ZIJ * MET * ONS * **Note:** Z added (for silver).

Date	Mintage	VF20	XF40	MS60	MS63	MS65
1980	157	—	—	—	2,000	—

KM# 201b 2-1/2 GULDEN

Gold **Ruler:** Beatrix **Subject:** Investiture of New Queen **Obv:** Conjoined heads left **Rev:** Crowned arms divide date **Edge Lettering:** GOD * ZIJ * MET * ONS * **Note:** G added (for gold).

Date	Mintage	VF20	XF40	MS60	MS63	MS65
1980 Rare	7	—	—	—	25,000	—

KM# 206 2-1/2 GULDEN

10.00 g., Nickel, 29 mm. **Ruler:** Beatrix **Obv:** Head left with vertical inscription **Rev:** Value within horizontal, vertical and diagonal lines **Edge Lettering:** GOD * ZIJ * MET * ONS *

Date	Mintage	VF20	XF40	MS60	MS63	MS65
1982	14,300,000	—	—	1.00	2.00	2.50
1982	10,000	PF65 15.00				
1983	3,800,000	—	—	1.00	2.00	3.00
1983	15,000	PF65 12.50				
1984	5,200,000	—	—	1.00	2.00	3.00
1984	20,000	PF65 7.50				
1985	3,100,000	—	—	1.50	3.00	5.00
1985	17,000	PF65 7.50				
1986	5,800,000	—	—	1.50	2.50	4.50
1986	19,700	PF65 7.50				
1987	2,500,000	—	—	1.25	2.50	4.50
1987	18,000	PF65 7.50				
1988	6,200,000	—	—	1.25	2.50	4.50
1988	19,550	PF65 7.50				
1989	4,000,000	—	—	1.25	2.50	4.50
1989	15,300	PF65 7.50				
1990	1,000,000	—	—	1.25	2.50	4.50
1990	15,100	PF65 7.50				
1991	400,000	—	—	1.25	2.50	4.50
1991	14,000	PF65 7.50				
1992	400,000	—	—	1.50	3.00	5.00
1992	12,600	PF65 7.50				
1993	500,000	—	—	1.50	3.00	5.00
1993	12,000	PF65 7.50				
1994	420,000	—	—	1.50	3.00	5.00
1994	12,500	PF65 7.50				
1995	150,000	—	—	1.50	3.00	5.00
1995	11,500	PF65 7.50				
1996	150,000	—	—	1.50	3.00	5.00
1996	13,500	PF65 7.50				
1997	180,000	—	—	1.50	3.00	5.00
1997	12,000	PF65 7.50				
1998	200,000	—	—	1.50	3.00	5.00
1998	12,000	PF65 7.50				
1999	240,000	—	—	1.50	3.00	5.00
1999	15,000	PF65 7.50				
2000	300,000	—	—	1.50	3.00	5.00
2000	15,000	PF65 7.50				

KM# 151 5 GULDEN

3.36 g., 0.900 Gold 0.0972 oz. AGW, 18 mm. **Ruler:** Wilhelmina I **Obv:** Bust right **Rev:** Crowned arms divide value **Edge:** Reeded **Note:** Counterfeits are prevalent.

Date	Mintage	F12	VF20	XF40	MS60	MS63
1912	1,000,000	—	125	200	250	350
1912 Matte Proof	120	PF63 1,250				

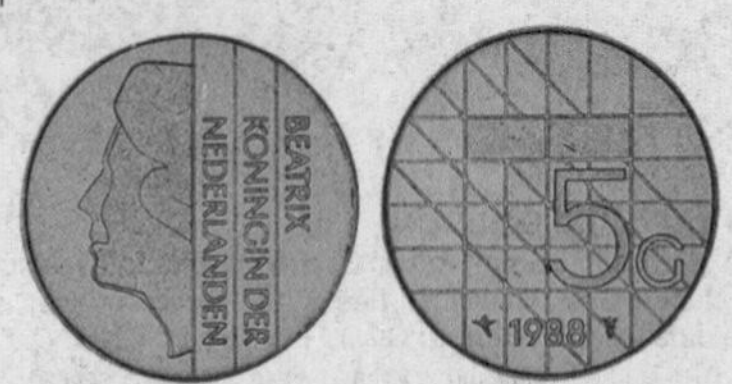

KM# 210 5 GULDEN

9.25 g., Bronze Clad Nickel, 23.5 mm. **Ruler:** Beatrix **Obv:** Head left with vertical inscription **Rev:** Value within horizontal, vertical and diagonal lines **Edge:** GOD * ZIJ * MET * ONS *

Date	Mintage	VF20	XF40	MS60	MS63	MS65
1987 Proof	2	—	—	—	—	—
1988	73,600,000	—	—	1.50	3.00	5.00
1988	19,550	PF65 7.00				
1989	69,000,000	—	—	1.50	3.00	5.00
1989	15,300	PF65 7.00				
1990	47,200,000	—	—	1.50	3.00	5.00
1990	15,100	PF65 7.00				
1991	17,000,000	—	—	1.50	3.00	5.00
1991	14,000	PF65 7.00				
1992	400,000	—	—	2.50	5.00	9.00
1992	12,600	PF65 7.00				
1993	5,400,000	—	—	1.50	3.00	5.00
1993	12,000	PF65 7.00				
1994	400,000	—	—	1.50	3.00	5.00
1994	12,500	PF65 7.00				
1995	400,000	—	—	1.50	3.00	5.00
1995	11,500	PF65 7.00				
1996	150,000	—	—	2.50	5.00	9.00
1996	13,500	PF65 7.00				
1997	170,000	—	—	2.50	5.00	9.00
1997	12,000	PF65 7.00				
1998	100,000	—	—	2.50	5.00	9.00
1998	12,000	PF65 7.00				
1999	120,000	—	—	2.50	5.00	9.00
1999	15,000	PF65 7.00				
2000	200,000	—	—	2.50	5.00	9.00
2000	15,000	PF65 7.00				

KM# 231 5 GULDEN

9.25 g., Brass Plated Nickel, 23.5 mm. **Ruler:** Beatrix **Subject:** Soccer **Obv:** Head left **Rev:** Value within soccerball **Edge:** Reeded **Edge Lettering:** GOD * ZIJ * MET * ONS * **Note:** A joint issue proof set exists containing the Netherlands KM#231, Belgium KM#213-214 plus a medal.

Date	Mintage	VF20	XF40	MS60	MS63	MS65
2000	Est. 1000	PF65 140				
Note: Small mintmark						
2000	2,500,000	—	—	1.50	3.00	5.00
2000	19,000	PF65 10.00				
Note: Large mintmark						

KM# 149 10 GULDEN

6.73 g., 0.900 Gold 0.1947 oz. AGW, 22.5 mm. **Ruler:** Wilhelmina I **Obv:** Head right **Rev:** Crowned arms divide value **Edge:** Reeded

Date	Mintage	F12	VF20	XF40	MS60	MS63
1911	774,544	—	—	—	250	400
1911	8	PF63 2,750				
1912	3,000,000	—	—	—	250	400
1912	20	PF63 2,500				
1913	1,133,476	—	—	—	250	400
1917	4,000,000	—	—	—	250	400
1917	—	PF63 3,500				

KM# 162 10 GULDEN

6.73 g., 0.900 Gold 0.1947 oz. AGW, 22.5 mm. **Ruler:** Wilhelmina I **Obv:** Head right **Rev:** Crowned arms divide value **Edge:** Reeded

Date	Mintage	F12	VF20	XF40	MS60	MS63
1925	2,000,000	—	—	—	250	400
1925	12	PF63 2,000				
1926	2,500,000	—	—	—	250	400
1926	—	PF63 1,300				
1927	1,000,000	—	—	—	250	400
1932	4,323,952	—	—	—	250	400
1933	2,462,101	—	—	—	250	400

KM# 195 10 GULDEN

25.00 g., 0.720 Silver 0.5787 oz. ASW, 38 mm. **Ruler:** Juliana **Subject:** 25th Anniversary of Liberation **Obv:** Head right within beaded border **Rev:** Head left within beaded border **Edge Lettering:** GOD * ZIJ * MET * ONS *

Date	Mintage	VF20	XF40	MS60	MS63	MS65
ND-1970	5,980,000	—	—	12.00	15.00	25.00
ND-1970 Prooflike	20,000	—	—	—	25.00	40.00
ND-1970	Est. 40	PF65 1,500				

KM# 196 10 GULDEN

25.00 g., 0.720 Silver 0.5787 oz. ASW, 38 mm. **Ruler:** Juliana **Subject:** 25th Anniversary of Reign **Obv:** Head right within beaded border **Rev:** Crowned arms divide date within beaded border **Edge Lettering:** GOD * ZIJ * MET * ONS *

Date	Mintage	VF20	XF40	MS60	MS63	MS65
1973	4,505,000	—	—	12.00	15.00	25.00
1973	105,570	PF65 28.00				

KM# 216 10 GULDEN

15.00 g., 0.720 Silver 0.3472 oz. ASW, 33 mm. **Ruler:** Beatrix **Subject:** BE-NE-LUX Treaty **Obv:** Head left. **Rev:** Three Parliament buildings on top, 3 designs in circles within vertical lines, all flanked by dates and value **Edge Lettering:** GOD * ZIJ * MET * ONS *

Date	Mintage	VF20	XF40	MS60	MS63	MS65
1994	2,000,000	—	—	6.50	12.00	15.00
Note: 100,000 pieces melted						
1994	66,500	PF65 20.00				
Note: 25,000 pieces issued in sets only						

KM# 220 10 GULDEN

15.00 g., 0.800 Silver 0.3858 oz. ASW, 33 mm. **Ruler:** Beatrix **Subject:** 300th Anniversary - Death of Hugo de Groot **Obv:** Head left **Rev:** Value and date above supine head facing upward **Edge Lettering:** GOD * ZIJ * MET * ONS *

Date	Mintage	VF20	XF40	MS60	MS63	MS65
1995	1,500,000	—	—	7.25	13.50	17.50
Note: 110,000 pieces melted						
1995	37,500	PF65 22.00				

KM# 223 10 GULDEN
15.00 g., 0.800 Silver 0.3858 oz. ASW, 33 mm. **Ruler:** Beatrix **Subject:** Artist Jan Steen - Lute Player **Obv:** Head left **Rev:** Jan Steen as lute player **Edge Lettering:** GOD * ZIJ * MET * ONS *

Date	Mintage	VF20	XF40	MS60	MS63	MS65
1996	1,526,000	—	—	7.25	13.50	17.50
Note: 395,000 pieces melted						
1996	25,000	PF65 22.00				

KM# 224 10 GULDEN
15.00 g., 0.800 Silver 0.3858 oz. ASW, 33 mm. **Ruler:** Beatrix **Subject:** Marshall Plan **Obv:** Head left **Rev:** Marshall head 3/4 left divides value **Edge Lettering:** GOD * ZIJ * MET * ONS *

Date	Mintage	VF20	XF40	MS60	MS63	MS65
1997	1,024,500	—	—	7.25	13.50	17.50
Note: 55,000 pieces melted						
1997	27,000	PF65 22.00				

KM# 228 10 GULDEN
15.00 g., 0.800 Silver 0.3858 oz. ASW, 33 mm. **Ruler:** Beatrix **Subject:** Millennium **Obv:** Head above 12 concentric rings within beaded border **Rev:** Head above 12 concentric rings within beaded border **Edge:** GOD ZIJ MET ONS

Date	Mintage	VF20	XF40	MS60	MS63	MS65
1999	1,250,000	—	—	7.25	13.50	17.50
1999	50,000	PF65 22.00				

KM# 207 50 GULDEN
25.00 g., 0.925 Silver 0.7435 oz. ASW, 38 mm. **Ruler:** Beatrix **Subject:** Dutch-American Friendship **Obv:** Head left **Rev:** Value within lion and eagle **Edge Lettering:** GOD * ZIJ * MET * ONS *

Date	Mintage	VF20	XF40	MS60	MS63	MS65
ND-1982	189,986	—	—	14.00	25.00	40.00
ND-1982 Prooflike	49,998	—	—	—	30.00	50.00

KM# 207a 50 GULDEN
Gold **Ruler:** Beatrix **Subject:** Dutch-American Friendship **Obv:** Head left **Rev:** Value within lion and eagle **Edge Lettering:** GOD ZIJ MET ONS

Date	Mintage	VF20	XF40	MS60	MS63	MS65
ND-1982 Rare	6	—	—	—	—	—

KM# 208 50 GULDEN
25.00 g., 0.925 Silver 0.7435 oz. ASW, 38 mm. **Ruler:** Beatrix **Subject:** 400th Anniversary - Death of William of Orange **Obv:** Head left **Rev:** Signature of William **Edge Lettering:** GOD * ZIJ * MET * ONS *

Date	Mintage	VF20	XF40	MS60	MS63	MS65
1984	1,000,000	—	—	14.00	20.00	35.00
Note: 145,000 pieces melted down						
1984 Prooflike	106,378	—	—	—	22.50	37.50
1984	56,200	PF65 40.00				

KM# 209 50 GULDEN
25.00 g., 0.925 Silver 0.7435 oz. ASW, 38 mm. **Ruler:** Beatrix **Subject:** Golden Wedding Anniversary - Queen Mother and Prince Bernhard **Obv:** Outlined profile left, triangular points at right **Rev:** Value within conjoined outlined heads right, 1/2 star border with letters within points **Edge Lettering:** GOD * ZIJ * MET * ONS *

Date	Mintage	VF20	XF40	MS60	MS63	MS65
1987	1,500,000	—	—	14.00	20.00	35.00
Note: 535,000 pieces melted down						
1987 Prooflike	80,400	—	—	—	22.50	37.50
1987	52,872	PF65 40.00				

KM# 212 50 GULDEN
25.00 g., 0.925 Silver 0.7435 oz. ASW, 38 mm. **Ruler:** Beatrix **Subject:** 300th Anniversary of William and Mary **Obv:** Patterned head left **Rev:** Conjoined heads right **Edge Lettering:** GOD * ZIJ * MET * ONS *

Date	Mintage	VF20	XF40	MS60	MS63	MS65
1988	900,000	—	—	14.00	20.00	35.00
Note: 235,000 pieces melted						
1988 Prooflike	52,500	—	—	—	25.00	40.00
1988	35,500	PF65 45.00				

KM# 212a 50 GULDEN
Gold **Ruler:** Beatrix **Subject:** 300th Anniversary of William and Mary **Obv:** Patterned head left **Rev:** Conjoined heads right **Edge Lettering:** GOD ZIJ MET ONS

Date	Mintage	VF20	XF40	MS60	MS63	MS65
1988 Rare	4	—	—	—	—	—

KM# 214 50 GULDEN
25.00 g., 0.925 Silver 0.7435 oz. ASW, 38 mm. **Ruler:** Beatrix **Subject:** 100 Years of Queens **Rev:** Heads of Queens Emma, Wilhelmina, Juliana, and Beatrix like rocks **Edge Lettering:** GOD * ZIJ * MET * ONS *

Date	Mintage	VF20	XF40	MS60	MS63	MS65
1990	800,000	—	—	14.00	20.00	35.00
Note: 210,000 pieces melted						
1990 Prooflike	50,400	—	—	—	25.00	40.00
1990	34,500	PF65 45.00				

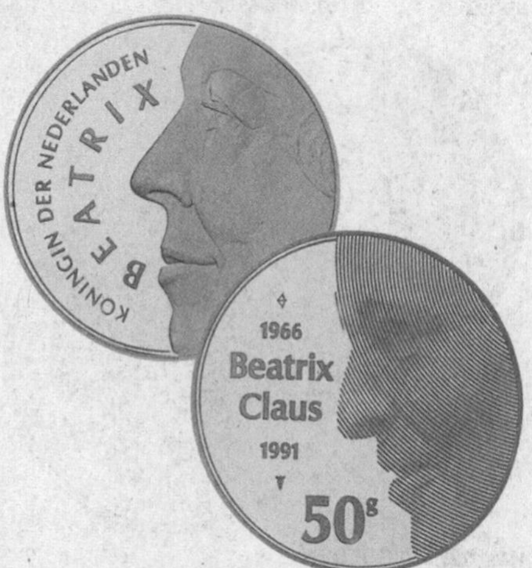

KM# 215 50 GULDEN
25.00 g., 0.925 Silver 0.7435 oz. ASW, 38 mm. **Ruler:** Beatrix **Subject:** Silver Wedding Anniversary **Obv:** Half face left **Rev:** Half face left **Edge Lettering:** GOD * ZIJ * MET * ONS *

Date	Mintage	VF20	XF40	MS60	MS63	MS65
1991	600,000	—	—	14.00	20.00	35.00
Note: 60,000 pieces melted						
1991 Prooflike	45,800	—	—	—	25.00	40.00
1991	34,700	PF65 45.00				

KM# 217 50 GULDEN
25.00 g., 0.925 Silver 0.7435 oz. ASW, 38 mm. **Ruler:** Beatrix **Subject:** Maastricht Treaty **Obv:** Head left with title within ribbon **Rev:** Value, date and name within rippled banner with stars **Edge Lettering:** GOD * ZIJ * MET * ONS *

Date	Mintage	VF20	XF40	MS60	MS63	MS65
1994	550,000	—	—	14.00	20.00	35.00
Note: 170,000 pieces melted						
1994 Prooflike	28,000	—	—	—	27.50	42.50
1994	24,500	PF65 55.00				

KM# 219 50 GULDEN
25.00 g., 0.925 Silver 0.7435 oz. ASW, 38 mm. **Ruler:** Beatrix **Subject:** 50th Anniversary of Liberation **Obv:** Head 1/4 left **Rev:** Large numeral value and legend **Edge Lettering:** GOD * ZIJ * MET * ONS *

Date	Mintage	VF20	XF40	MS60	MS63	MS65
ND-1995	650,000	—	—	14.00	20.00	35.00
Note: 220,000 pieces melted						
ND-1995 Prooflike	27,500	—	—	—	27.50	42.50
ND-1995	26,000	PF65 55.00				

KM# 227 50 GULDEN
25.00 g., 0.925 Silver 0.7435 oz. ASW, 38 mm. **Ruler:** Beatrix **Subject:** 350th Anniversary - Treaty of Munster **Obv:** Head 1/4 left within circle **Rev:** Head 1/4 right within circle **Edge Lettering:** GOD*ZIJ*MET*ONS*

Date	Mintage	VF20	XF40	MS60	MS63	MS65
1998	450,000	—	—	14.00	25.00	40.00
Note: 180,000 pieces melted						
1998 Prooflike	20,000	—	—	—	30.00	50.00
1998	20,000	PF65 65.00				

EURO COINAGE

European Union Issues

KM# 234 EURO CENT
2.30 g., Copper Plated Steel, 16.2 mm. **Ruler:** Beatrix **Obv:** Head left among stars **Rev:** Value and globe **Edge:** Plain

Date	Mintage	VF20	XF40	MS60	MS63	MS65
1999	47,800,000	—	—	0.50	0.75	1.00
1999 Proof	16,500	—	—	—	—	—
2000	276,800,000	—	—	0.35	0.50	0.75
2000 Proof	16,500	—	—	—	—	—

KM# 235 2 EURO CENT
3.06 g., Copper Plated Steel, 18.7 mm. **Ruler:** Beatrix **Obv:** Head left among stars **Rev:** Value and globe **Edge:** Grooved

Date	Mintage	VF20	XF40	MS60	MS63	MS65
1999	109,000,000	—	—	0.50	0.75	1.00
1999 Proof	16,500	—	—	—	—	—
2000	122,000,000	—	—	0.50	0.75	1.00
2000 Proof	16,500	—	—	—	—	—

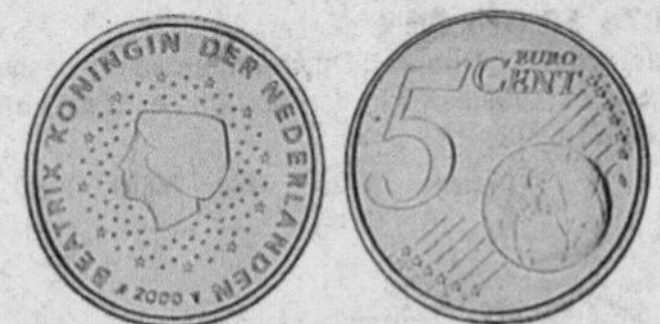

KM# 236 5 EURO CENT
3.92 g., Copper Plated Steel, 21.25 mm. **Ruler:** Beatrix **Obv:** Head left among stars **Rev:** Value and globe **Edge:** Plain

Date	Mintage	VF20	XF40	MS60	MS63	MS65
1999	213,000,000	—	—	0.50	0.75	1.00
1999 Proof	16,500	—	—	—	—	—
2000	184,200,000	—	—	0.50	0.75	1.00
2000 Proof	16,500	—	—	—	—	—

KM# 237 10 EURO CENT
4.10 g., Brass, 19.7 mm. **Ruler:** Beatrix **Obv:** Head left among stars **Rev:** Value and map

Date	Mintage	VF20	XF40	MS60	MS63	MS65
1999	149,700,000	—	—	0.75	1.00	1.50
1999 Proof	16,500	—	—	—	—	—
2000	156,700,000	—	—	0.75	1.00	1.50
2000 Proof	16,500	—	—	—	—	—

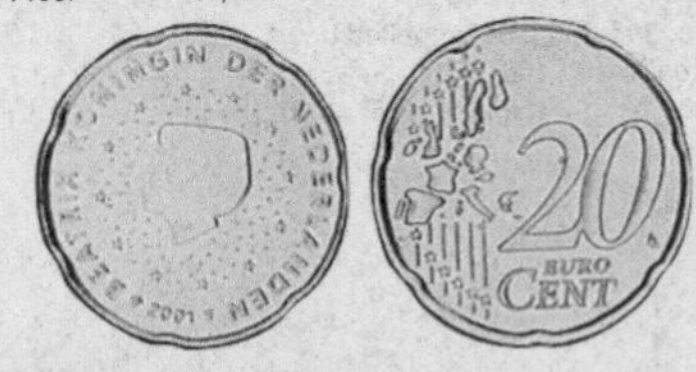

KM# 238 20 EURO CENT
5.74 g., Brass, 22.2 mm. **Ruler:** Beatrix **Obv:** Head left among stars **Rev:** Value and map **Edge:** Notched

Date	Mintage	VF20	XF40	MS60	MS63	MS65
1999	86,500,000	—	—	1.00	1.25	1.75
1999 Proof	16,500	—	—	—	—	—
2000	67,500,000	—	—	1.00	1.25	1.75
2000 Proof	16,500	—	—	—	—	—

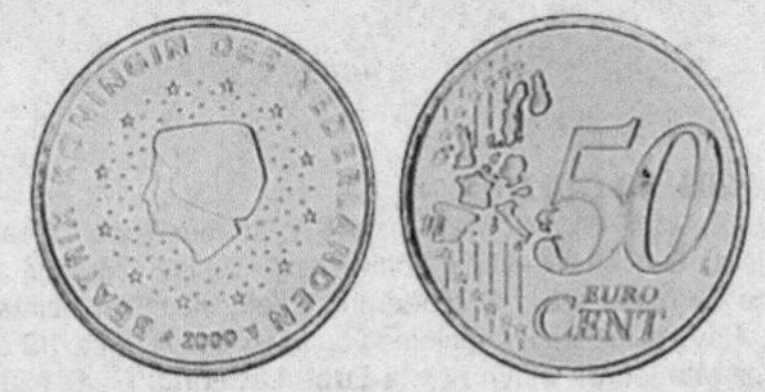

KM# 239 50 EURO CENT
7.80 g., Brass, 24.2 mm. **Ruler:** Beatrix **Obv:** Head left among stars **Rev:** Value and map **Edge:** Notched

Date	Mintage	VF20	XF40	MS60	MS63	MS65
1999	99,600,000	—	—	1.25	1.50	2.00
1999 Proof	16,500	—	—	—	—	—
2000	87,000,000	—	—	1.25	1.50	2.00
2000 Proof	16,500	—	—	—	—	—

KM# 240 EURO
7.50 g., Bi-Metallic Copper-Nickel center in Brass ring, 23.2 mm. **Ruler:** Beatrix **Obv:** Half head left within 1/2 circle and star border, name within vertical lines **Rev:** Value and map within circle **Edge:** Segmented reeding

Date	Mintage	VF20	XF40	MS60	MS63	MS65
1999	63,500,000	—	—	2.50	3.00	4.00
1999 Proof	16,500	—	—	—	—	—
2000	62,800,000	—	—	2.50	3.00	4.00
2000 Proof	16,500	—	—	—	—	—

KM# 241 2 EURO
8.50 g., Bi-Metallic Nickel-Brass center in Copper-Nickel ring, 25.75 mm. **Ruler:** Beatrix **Obv:** Profile left within 1/2 circle and star border, name within vertical lines **Rev:** Value and map within circle **Edge Lettering:** GOD * ZIJ * MET * ONS *

Date	Mintage	VF20	XF40	MS60	MS63	MS65
1999	9,900,000	—	—	—	6.00	10.00
1999 Proof	16,500	—	—	—	—	—
2000	24,400,000	—	—	—	5.00	6.00
2000 Proof	16,500	—	—	—	—	—

TRADE COINAGE

KM# 83.1a DUCAT
3.49 g., 0.983 Gold 0.1104 oz. AGW **Ruler:** Wilhelmina I **Obv:** Standing knight divides date **Obv. Legend:** CONCORDIA RES - PARVAE RESCUNT **Rev:** Inscription within ornamented square: MO.AUR./REG.BELGII/AD **Edge:** Slant-reeded **Shape:** 21 **Note:** Privy mark: Halberd

Date	Mintage	F12	VF20	XF40	MS60	MS63
1901	29,284	400	900	1,500	2,500	4,000
1903/1	90,824	450	1,400	2,000	3,200	6,000
1903	Inc. above	500	1,000	1,600	2,500	3,750
1905	87,995	140	600	850	1,200	2,200
1906	29,379	400	1,300	2,000	3,200	6,000
1908	91,006	140	650	900	1,200	2,000
1909	106,020	400	900	1,500	2,500	4,000
Note: Halberd with star privy mark						
1909	30,182	400	1,300	2,000	3,200	6,000
Note: Sea horse privy mark						
1910	421,447	140	500	800	1,000	1,700
1910 Proof	—	—	—	—	—	—
1912	147,860	140	400	550	1,000	1,700
1912 Proof	—	—	—	—	—	—
1913	205,464	140	400	550	1,000	1,700
1914	245,560	140	400	550	1,000	1,700
1916	116,997	140	400	550	1,000	1,700
1916 Proof	—	—	—	—	—	—
1917	216,892	—	—	—	140	225
1920	293,389	—	—	—	140	300
1920 Proof	—	—	—	—	—	—
1921	409,001	—	—	—	140	225
1922	49,837	200	350	500	900	1,600
1923	106,674	—	140	225	400	600
1924	84,206	—	140	225	400	600
1925	573,071	—	—	—	140	225
1925 Proof	Inc. above	—	—	—	—	—
1926	191,311	—	—	—	140	275
1927	654,424	—	—	—	140	225
1928	571,881	—	—	—	140	225
1932	88,268	350	750	1,500	2,600	4,200
1937	116,660	—	—	—	140	225

KM# 190.1 DUCAT
3.49 g., 0.983 Gold 0.1104 oz. AGW, 21 mm. **Ruler:** Beatrix **Obv:** Knight with right leg bent divides date **Rev:** Inscription within decorated square

Date	Mintage	VF20	XF40	MS60	MS63	MS65
1960	3,605	140	250	300	350	400
1972 Prooflike	29,205	—	—	—	140	225
1974 Prooflike	86,558	—	—	—	140	225
1974 Prooflike	Est. 2000	—	—	—	—	900
Note: Medal struck						
1975 Prooflike	204,788	—	—	—	140	225
1976 Prooflike	37,844	—	—	—	140	225
Note: Of 37,844 pieces struck, 32,000 were melted						
1978 Prooflike	29,305	—	—	—	140	225
1985	103,863	PF65 250				

KM# 190.2 DUCAT

3.49 g., 0.983 Gold 0.1104 oz. AGW **Ruler:** Beatrix **Obv:** Knight divides date with larger letters in legend **Rev:** Inscription within decorated square

Date	Mintage	VF20	XF40	MS60	MS63	MS65
1986	95,091	PF65 225				
1989	24,478	PF65 225				
1990	17,500	PF65 225				
1991	11,500	PF65 225				
1992	14,400	PF65 225				
1993	11,100	PF65 225				
1994	11,500	PF65 225				
1995	11,000	PF65 225				
1996	12,000	PF65 225				
1997	11,500	PF65 225				
1998	8,500	PF65 225				
1999	7,550	PF65 225				
2000	8,000	PF65 225				

KM# 211 2 DUCAT

6.99 g., 0.983 Gold 0.2208 oz. AGW, 26 mm. **Ruler:** Beatrix **Obv:** Knight divides date within beaded circle **Rev:** Inscription within decorated square

Date	Mintage	VF20	XF40	MS60	MS63	MS65
1988 B Proof	23,759	—	—	—	—	425
1989 B	17,862	PF65 425				
1991 B	10,000	PF65 425				
1992 B	11,800	PF65 425				
1996 B	10,500	PF65 425				
1999 B	6,250	PF65 425				
2000 B	7,000	PF65 425				

SILVER BULLION COINAGE

KM# 213 SILVER DUCAT

28.25 g., 0.873 Silver 0.7929 oz. ASW, 40 mm. **Ruler:** Beatrix **Obv:** Crowned arms divide date **Rev:** Knight standing with the arms of Utrecht

Date	Mintage	VF20	XF40	MS60	MS63	MS65
1989	35,797	PF65 22.00				
1992	17,200	PF65 25.00				
1993	12,500	PF65 30.00				

KM# 218 SILVER DUCAT

28.25 g., 0.873 Silver 0.7929 oz. ASW, 40 mm. **Ruler:** Beatrix **Subject:** Seven Provinces - Groningen **Obv:** Crowned arms divide date **Rev:** Knight standing with arms of Groningen

Date	Mintage	VF20	XF40	MS60	MS63	MS65
1994	11,000	PF65 40.00				

KM# 221 SILVER DUCAT

28.25 g., 0.873 Silver 0.7929 oz. ASW, 40 mm. **Ruler:** Beatrix **Subject:** Seven Provinces - Zeeland **Obv:** Crowned arms of the Netherlands **Rev:** Knight standing with arms of Zeeland

Date	Mintage	VF20	XF40	MS60	MS63	MS65
1995	11,000	PF65 30.00				

KM# 222 SILVER DUCAT

28.25 g., 0.873 Silver 0.7929 oz. ASW, 40 mm. **Ruler:** Beatrix **Subject:** Seven Provinces - Holland **Obv:** Crowned arms divide date **Rev:** Knight standing with arms of Holland

Date	Mintage	VF20	XF40	MS60	MS63	MS65
1996	12,500	PF65 30.00				

KM# 225 SILVER DUCAT

28.25 g., 0.873 Silver 0.7929 oz. ASW, 40 mm. **Ruler:** Beatrix **Subject:** Seven Provinces - Gelderland **Obv:** Crowned arms of the Netherlands **Rev:** Knight standing with arms of Gelderland

Date	Mintage	VF20	XF40	MS60	MS63	MS65
1997	11,500	PF65 30.00				

KM# 226 SILVER DUCAT

28.25 g., 0.873 Silver 0.7929 oz. ASW, 40 mm. **Ruler:** Beatrix **Subject:** Seven Provinces - Friesland **Obv:** Crowned arms of the Netherlands **Rev:** Knight standing with shield of Friesland

Date	Mintage	VF20	XF40	MS60	MS63	MS65
1998 B	11,100	PF65 30.00				

KM# 229 SILVER DUCAT

28.25 g., 0.873 Silver 0.7929 oz. ASW, 40 mm. **Ruler:** Beatrix **Subject:** Seven Provinces - Utrecht **Obv:** Crowned arms divide date **Rev:** Knight standing with arms of Utrecht

Date	Mintage	VF20	XF40	MS60	MS63	MS65
1999	9,500	PF65 30.00				

KM# 232 SILVER DUCAT

28.25 g., 0.873 Silver 0.7929 oz. ASW, 40 mm. **Ruler:** Beatrix **Subject:** Seven Provinces - Overijssel **Obv:** Crowned shield divides date **Rev:** Knight with crowned shield **Edge:** Reeded

Date	Mintage	VF20	XF40	MS60	MS63	MS65
2000 B	11,000	PF65 30.00				

PATTERNS

Including off metal strikes

KM#	Date	Mintage	Identification	Mkt Val
Pn95	190x (1901)	—	5 Cents. Nickel.	—
PnA101	190x (1901)	—	5 Cents. Small 5. Reverse small 5.	—
Pn101	190x (1901)	—	5 Cents. Bronze. Large 5. Reverse large 5.	—
Pn101a	190x (1901)	—	5 Cents. Silver.	—
PnA102	190x (1901)	—	5 Cents. Bronze.	—
Pn102	190x (1901)	—	5 Cents. Bronze.	—
Pn103	190x (1901)	—	10 Cents. Nickel.	—
Pn96	1902	—	Cent. Gold. KM132.	—
Pn97	1903	—	1/2 Cent. Gold. KM133.	—
Pn98	1903	—	2-1/2 Cent. Gold. KM134.	—
Pn99	1903	—	10 Cents. Gold. KM135.	—
Pn100	1903	—	25 Cents. Gold. KM120.2.	—
Pn104	1904	—	Cent. Bi-Metallic.	—
Pn105	1904	—	5 Cents. Bronze.	—
Pn106	1904	—	5 Cents. Bronze.	—
Pn107	1904	—	5 Cents. Bronze. Holed.	—
Pn108	1904	—	5 Cents. Nickel.	—
Pn109	1904	—	5 Cents. Nickel. Holed.	8,000
PnA110	1904	—	5 Cents.	—
Pn110	1905	—	1/2 Gulden. Gold. KM121.2.	—
PnA111	1906	—	5 Cents. Silver. Plain.	1,100
Pn111	1906	—	5 Cents. Bronze.	—
Pn112	1906	—	5 Cents. Nickel.	—
Pn113	1906	—	5 Cents. Nickel.	—
Pn114	1906	—	5 Cents. Nickel.	—
Pn115	1906	—	5 Cents. Silver.	—
Pn116	1906	—	10 Cents. Nickel.	—
PnA117	1906	—	10 Cents.	—
Pn117	1907	—	5 Cents. Bronze. Crown.	—
Pn118	1907	—	5 Cents. Nickel. Small crown.	—
PnA119	1907	—	5 Cents. Silver.	—
PnB119	1908	—	5 Cents. Silver.	—
PnC119	1908	—	5 Cents. Lead.	—
Pn119	1908	—	Gulden. Bronze. KM122.	—
PnD119	1909	—	5 Cents. Lead.	—
Pn120	1910	—	10 Cents. Gold. KM145.	—
PnA120	1911	—	1/2 Cent. Gold.	—
PnA121	1911	—	Gulden. Bronze.	1,100
PnB121	1911	2	Gulden. Gold.	—
PnC121	1912	—	5 Cents. Nickel. "Proof".	—
PnD121	1913	—	5 Cents. Gold.	—
PnE121	1913	—	5 Cents. Silver.	—
PnF121	1913	—	5 Cents. Bronze.	—
Pn121	1913	—	2-1/2 Gulden. Silver. KM148.	—
PnA122	1914	—	2 Cents.	—
Pn122	1928	—	Gulden. Silver.	350
PnA123	1928	—	Gulden. Gold.	700
Pn123	1928	—	Gulden. Silver.	250
PnA124	1928	—	Gulden. Gold.	550
Pn124	1929	—	Gulden. Silver.	—
PnA125	1929	—	Gulden. Nickel.	—
PnB125	1929	—	2-1/2 Gulden. Bronze.	1,250
Pn125	1929	—	2-1/2 Gulden. Silver.	550
PnA126	1929	—	2-1/2 Gulden. Gold.	1,300
Pn126	1934	—	10 Cents. Bronze. KM163.	—
PnA127	1935	—	5 Cents. Gold.	4,000
Pn127	1941	—	Cent. Zinc. KM170 with center hole.	550
Pn128	1941	—	2-1/2 Cent. Zinc. KM171 with center hole.	550
Pn129	1941	—	10 Cents. Zinc.	180
PnA130	1969	6	Cent. Nickel.	—
Pn130	1969	—	5 Cents. Nickel. Plain.	—
Pn131	1969	5	5 Cents. Nickel.	—
Pn132	1969	—	5 Cents. Aluminum.	—
Pn133	1969	4	5 Cents. Aluminum.	—
PnA134	1969	—	10 Cents. Nickel-Brass.	—
PnB134	1969	—	25 Cents. Brass.	—
PnC134	1970	—	Cent. Aluminum.	—
PnD134	1970	—	10 Gulden. Tin.	—
Pn134	1973	—	10 Gulden. Silver.	—
PnA135	1975	—	25 Cents. Aluminum. KM#183a.	—
PnB135	1977	—	25 Cents. Aluminum.	550
PnB135	1977	—	25 Cents. Aluminum.	550
Pn135	1979	—	10 Gulden. Nickel.	—
Pn136	1980	15	25 Cents. Aluminum. KM183a.	700
PnA138	1980	—	Gulden. Copper.	—
Pn138	1980	—	Gulden. Gold. KM200b.	—
Pn139	1980	—	Gulden. Silver. KM200a.	2,250
Pn140	1980	—	2-1/2 Gulden. Gold. KM201b.	—
Pn141	1980	—	2-1/2 Gulden. Silver. KM201a.	1,800
Pn142	1982	—	5 Cents. Bronze.	—
Pn143	1982	—	5 Cents. Tombac.	—
Pn144	1982	—	5 Cents. Brass.	—
Pn145	1982	—	5 Cents. Copper Clad Steel.	—
Pn146	1982	—	Gulden. Nickel.	—
Pn147	1982	—	50 Gulden. Gold. KM207.	—
Pn148	1984	—	5 Cents. Tombac.	200
Pn149	1984	—	10 Cents. Bronze.	200
Pn150	1985	—	5 Cents. Nickel. Plain.	200
PnA151	1985	—	25 Cents. Aluminum. KM204.	500
PnB151	1985	2	Gulden. Silver. KM#205.	—
Pn151	1986	—	25 Cents. Brass. KM204.	500
PnA152	1986	—	Gulden. Copper-Nickel. KM#206.	400
PnB152	1986	—	2-1/2 Gulden. Copper-Nickel. KM#206.	500
Pn152	1986	—	25 Cents. Aluminum. KM204.	500
Pn153	1986	—	Ducat. Tombac. KM190.2.	600
PnA154	1987	—	50 Gulden. Silver.	500
Pn154	1987	—	5 Cents. Nickel. KM202.	—
Pn155	1988	—	5 Cents. Nickel Clad Steel.	—
Pn156	1988	—	5 Cents. Copper Clad Steel.	—
Pn157	1988	—	5 Cents. Brass Clad Steel.	—
PnA158	1988	—	50 Gulden. Tombac.	750
PnB158	1988	—	50 Gulden. Silver.	1,000
Pn158	1988	—	50 Gulden. Gold. KM212.	—
Pn159	1990	—	5 Cents. Aluminum.	—
Pn160	1991	—	5 Cents. Nickel. KM202.	—

KM#	Date	Mintage	Identification	Mkt Val
Pn161	1991	—	50 Gulden. Silver. 1/4 Circle. Queen Beatrix and Prince Claus.	—
PnA162	1999	—	Euro Cent. Nickel.	100
PnB162	1999	—	50 Euro Cent. Bi-Metallic.	2,500
Pn162	1999	—	Euro. Brass.	250
Pn163	2000	110	2 Euro Cent. Copper-Nickel. KM#241.	450

PIEDFORT

KM#	Date	Mintage	Identification	Mkt Val
P19	1905	—	1/2 Gulden. Silver. KM121.2.	6,000
Note: Triple weight				
P20	1905	—	Gulden. Silver. KM122.2.	7,000
Note: Triple weight				
P21	1910	—	25 Cents. Bronze. KM146.	—
P22	1948	—	Cent. Silver. KM175.	—
P23	1948	—	5 Cents. Silver. KM176.	—
P24	1948	—	10 Cents. Silver. KM177.	—
P25	1948	—	25 Cents. Silver. KM178.	—
PA26	1956	—	Gulden. Silver. similar to KM#184.	—
P26	1958	—	Gulden. Silver. KM184.	—
P27	1995	—	10 Cents. Brass. KM203.	1,500
P28	1995	—	Gulden. Brass. KM205.	—

MINT SETS

KM#	Date	Mintage	Identification	Issue Price	Mkt Val
MS1	1999 (8)	65,000	KM#234-241 Charity set, Clinic Clowns	15.00	15.00
MS2	2000 (6)	50,000	KM#202-206, 210	12.00	25.00
MS3	2000 (8)	68,000	KM#234-241 Charity set, Nature Monuments	15.00	15.00
MS4	2000 (8)	13,850	KM#234-241 RABO Bank	—	40.00
MS107	2000 (6)	105,000	KM#202-206, 210 Introduction Euro-coins, no medal	15.00	30.00
MS108	2000 (8)	13,850	KM#234-241 RABO bank	—	30.00
MS109	2000 (8)	68,000	KM#234-241 Charity set, nature monuments	15.00	16.00

PROOF SETS

KM#	Date	Mintage	Identification	Issue Price	Mkt Val
PSA1	1928-29 (3)	—	PN122-123, 125	—	1,150
PSB1	1928-29 (3)	—	PnA123-A124, A126	—	2,600
PS1	1948 (4)	50	KM175-178 with PROEF	—	7,000
PS2	1948 (4)	50	KM175-178	—	3,000
PS3	1949 (3)	—	KM180-183, head left, rare.	—	—
PS4	1950 (4)	—	KM180-183 with PROEF	—	7,000
PS5	1950 (4)	—	KM180-183	—	1,000
PS6	1951 (4)	—	KM180-183	—	1,000
PS7	1952 (2)	—	KM180-181	—	700
PS8	1953 (2)	—	KM180-181	—	700
PS9	1954 (5)	—	KM180-184	—	3,000
PS10	1955 (5)	—	KM180-184	—	1,500
PS11	1956 (5)	—	KM180-184	—	1,500
PS12	1957 (5)	—	KM18-184	—	1,500
PS13	1958 (5)	—	KM180-184	—	1,500
PS14	1959 (3)	—	KM180, 182, 185	—	1,000
PS15	1960 (5)	—	KM180-183, 185	—	1,800
PS16	1961 (5)	—	KM180-183, 185	—	1,800
PS17	1962 (5)	40	KM180-183, 185	—	1,200
PS18	1963 (6)	40	KM180-185	—	2,400
PS19	1964 (6)	40	KM180-185	—	2,400
PS20	1965 (5)	—	KM180-184	—	2,000
PS21	1966 (6)	—	KM180-185	—	2,000
PS22	1967 (6)	—	KM180-184, 184a	—	1,800
PS23	1968 (5)	—	KM180-183, 184a	—	1,500
PS24	1969 (6)	—	KM180-183, 184a, 191. Cock.	—	2,000
PS25	1969 (6)	—	KM180-183, 184a, 191. Fish.	—	2,000
PSA26	1970 (1)	—	KM#195 10 Gulden 2x	—	3,000
PS26	1970 (6)	—	KM180-183, 184a, 191	—	2,000
PSA27	1971 (6)	500	KM180-183, 184a, 191	—	3,500
PSB27	1972 (6)	500	KM180-183, 184a, 191	—	3,500
PSC27	1973 (5)	500	KM180-183, 184a	—	2,500
PSD27	1974 (4)	500	KM180-183, 184a, 191	—	2,000
PSE27	1975 (5)	500	KM180-183, 184a, 191	—	2,500
PSF27	1976 (6)	500	KM180-183, 184a, 191	—	2,500
PSG27	1977 (5)	500	KM180-183, 184a	—	2,500
PSH27	1978 (6)	500	KM180-183, 184a, 191	—	3,500
PSI27	1979 (6)	500	KM180-183, 184a, 191	—	3,500
PSJ27	1980 (6)	500	KM180-183, 184a, 191	—	3,500
PSK27	1980 (2)	157	KM200-201	—	3,750
PS27	1982 (5)	10,000	KM202-206	35.00	35.00
PS28	1983 (5)	15,000	KM202-206	35.00	15.00
PS29	1984 (5)	20,000	KM202-206	35.00	15.00
PS30	1985 (5)	17,000	KM202-206	35.00	15.00
PS31	1986 (5)	19,700	KM202-206	35.00	15.00
PS32	1987 (5)	18,000	KM202-206, Utrecht medal	35.00	15.00
PS33	1988 (6)	19,550	KM202-206, 210, Groningen medal	38.00	20.00
PS34	1989 (6)	15,300	KM202-206,210, Flevoland medal	50.00	20.00
PS35	1989 (3)	6,400	KM190.2, 211, 213	260	575
PS36	1990 (6)	15,100	KM202-206, 210, N. Brabant medal. Set also includes 1974 25 Cents.	50.00	20.00
PS37	1991 (6)	14,000	KM202-206, 210, Drenthe medal	50.00	20.00
PS38	1992 (6)	12,600	KM202-206, 210, Zeeland medal	53.50	20.00
PS39	1992 (3)	6,300	KM190.2, 211, 213	270	575
PS40	1993 (6)	12,000	KM202-206, 210, Limburg medal	53.50	20.00
PS41	1994 (6)	12,500	KM202-206, 210, Friesland medal	59.50	20.00
PS42	1994 (3)	25,000	BE NE LUX, Belgium KM195, Netherlands KM216, Luxemburg KM68	65.00	45.00
PS43	1995 (6)	11,500	KM202-206, 210, Zuid-Holland medal	59.50	25.00
PS44	1996 (6)	13,500	KM202-206, 210 Booklet, 5 cents, Stuiver	60.00	30.00
PS45	1996 (2)	6,500	KM190.2, 211	247	550
PS46	1997 (6)	12,000	KM202-206, 210 Booklet, 10 Cents	60.00	30.00
PS47	1998 (7)	12,000	KM202-206, 210 Booklet, 25 Cents	60.00	40.00
PS48	1999 (6)	15,000	KM202-206, 210, Booklet, 1 Guilder	50.00	30.00
PS49	1999 (3)	2,500	KM190.2, 211, 229	—	575
PS50	1999 (2)	1,800	KM190.2, 211	—	550
PS51	2000 (6)	15,000	KM#202-206, 210 Booklet 2-1/2 Guilder	50.00	30.00
PS52	2000 (2)	500	KM#190.2, 211 Golden ducats	—	650
PS53	2000 (3)	1,000	KM#190.2, 211, 232 Golden Ducats and Silver Ducat	—	665
PS60	2000 (7)	15,000	KM#202-207, 210 Booklet 2 1/2 guilder	50.00	120
PS62	2000 (3)	1,000	KM#190.2, 211, 232 Golden ducats + silver ducat	—	665

PROOF-LIKE SETS (PL)

KM#	Date	Mintage	Identification	Issue Price	Mkt Val
PL1	1999 (8)	16,500	KM#234-241	50.00	25.00
PL2	2000 (8)	16,500	KM#234-241	50.00	25.00
PL10	1999 (8)	16,500	KM#234-241	50.00	25.00
PL11	2000 (8)	16,500	KM#234-241	50.00	25.00

SELECT SETS (FLEUR DE COIN)

KM#	Date	Mintage	Identification	Issue Price	Mkt Val
SS2	1971 (6)	1,000	KM180-183, 184a, 191	—	750
SS3	1972 (1)	2,000	KM191	—	25.00
SS4	1972 (5)	2,000	KM180-183, 184a	—	250
SS5	1973 (5)	10,000	KM180-183, 184a	—	50.00
SS6	1974 (3)	10,000	KM180-182	6.50	30.00
SS7	1975 (5)	12,000	KM180-183, 184a Set also includes 1974 25 cents.	6.50	50.00
SS8	1976 (5)	15,000	KM180-183, 184a	6.50	45.00
SS9	1977 (5)	17,000	KM180-183, 184a	6.50	35.00
SS10	1978 (6)	21,500	KM180-183, 184a, 191	6.50	20.00
SS11	1979 (6)	50,000	KM180-183, 184a, 197	6.50	10.00
SS12	1980 (6)	249,732	KM180-183, 184a, 191	6.50	7.50
SS13	1980 (2)	504,000	KM200-201	12.00	5.00
SS14	1980 (2)	157	KM200-201	—	3,000
SS15	1980 (2)	7	KM200b-201b. Gold.	—	60,000
SS16	1982 (5)	242,701	KM202-206	12.00	4.00
SS17	1983 (5)	156,165	KM202-206	12.00	6.00
SS18	1984 (5)	131,748	KM202-206	12.00	6.00
SS19	1985 (5)	113,079	KM202-206	12.00	10.00
SS20	1986 (5)	112,190	KM202-206	12.00	10.00
SS21	1987 (5)	120,850	KM202-206, Utrecht medal	15.00	8.00
SS22	1988 (6)	132,957	KM202-206, 210, Groningen medal	15.00	8.00
SS23	1988 (6)	5,000	KM202-206, 210, ERU medal	—	125
SS24	1989 (6)	103,607	KM202-206, 210, Flevoland medal	15.00	7.00
SS25	1990 (6)	102,750	KM202-206, 210, N-Brabant medal	15.00	7.00
SS26	1991 (6)	100,000	KM202-206, 210, Drenthe medal	15.00	8.00
SS27	1991 (6)	4,000	KM202-206, 210, RABO Bank medal	—	40.00
SS28	1992 (6)	94,000	KM202-206, 210, Zeeland medal	15.00	8.00
SS29	1992 (6)	3,000	KM202-206, 210, numismatic year medal	17.50	25.00
SS30	1993 (6)	87,000	KM202-206, 210, Limburg medal	15.00	10.00
SS31	1993 (6)	2,900	KM202-206, 210, V.O.C. medal	17.50	35.00
SS32	1994 (6)	85,000	KM202-206, 210, Friesland medal	15.00	8.00
SS33	1994 (6)	3,000	KM202-206, 210, millennium of mint	17.50	30.00
SS34	1995 (6)	81,000	KM202-206, 210, Zuid-Holland medal	15.00	8.00
SS35	1995 (6)	2,500	KM202-206, 210, Royal mint medal	17.50	30.00
SS36	1995 (6)	1,500	KM202-206, 210, Ehrbecker mint medal	—	30.00
SS37	1995 (6)	1,500	KM202-206, 210, Province of Utrecht medal	14.50	500
SS38	1995 (6)	800	KM202-206, 210, DeCampen medal, Lion Daalder from shipwreck	200	175
SS39	1996 (6)	1,500	KM202-206, 210, Utrecht: Town of the Mint medal	17.50	25.00
SS40	1996 (6)	80,000	KM202-206, 210, Overyssel medal	15.00	8.00
SS41	1996 (6)	3,000	KM202-206, 210, French Occupation (1795-1813) medal	17.50	20.00
SS42	1996 (6)	2,100	KM202-206, 210, Baby set	17.50	30.00
SS43	1996 (6)	350	KM202-206, 210, DeCampen medal, 1/2 Lion Daalder from shipwreck	240	300
SS44	1996 (6)	1,300	KM202-206, 210, Westpark I medal	—	25.00
SS45	1996 (6)	1,000	KM202-206, 210, Province of Utrecht II medal	—	750
SS46	1997 (6)	85,000	KM202-206, 210, Gelderland medal	15.00	8.00
SS47	1997 (6)	3,500	KM202-206, 210, King Willem I medal	17.50	30.00
SS48	1997 (6)	—	KM202-206, 210, Baby set	17.50	30.00
SS49	1997 (6)	1,430	KM202-206, 210, Ice skating/11 cities medal	45.00	30.00
SS50	1997 (6)	700	KM202-206, 210, Westpark II medal	—	40.00
SS51	1997 (6)	1,000	KM202-206, 210, Den Besterd I medal	—	30.00
SS52	1997 (6)	500	KM202-206, 210, Den Besterd II medal	—	75.00
SS53	1997 (6)	1,000	KM202-206, 210, Czar Peter medal	—	50.00
SS54	1997 (6)	500	KM202-206, 210, 't Vliegent heart medal, Ducaton from shipwreck	240	300
SS55	1997 (6)	1,150	KM202-206, 210, Royal Navy medal	—	175
SS56	1997 (6)	700	KM202-206, 210, BFBN medal	—	90.00
SS57	1997 (6)	1,500	KM202-206, 210, Maasdonk medal	50.00	20.00
SS58	1997 (6)	1,000	KM202-206, 210, BNN medal	75.00	60.00
SS59	1997 (6)	1,000	KM202-206, 210, Overyssel medal	—	750
SS60	1997 (6)	1,000	KM202-206, 210, Rembrandt medal	45.00	25.00
SS61	1997 (6)	1,000	KM202-206, 210, van Gogh I medal	45.00	25.00
SS62	1997 (6)	1,000	KM202-206, 210, Stuurman medal	75.00	50.00
SS63	1998 (7)	83,500	KM202-206, 210, N. Holland medal	15.00	10.00
SS64	1998 (6)	3,500	KM202-206, 210, King Willem II medal	17.50	30.00
SS65	1998 (6)	100	KM202-206, 210, 't Vliegent heart medal, Ducaton from shipwreck	1,000	1,000
SS66	1998 (6)	8,400	KM202-206, 210, Baby set	17.50	30.00
SS67	1998 (6)	1,000	KM202-206, 210, Rembrant II medal	40.00	35.00
SS68	1998 (6)	1,000	KM202-206, 210, van Gogh II medal	40.00	35.00

KM#	Date	Mintage	Identification	Issue Price	Mkt Val
SS69	1998 (6)	1,000	KM202-206, 210, Frans Hals medal	50.00	35.00
SS70	1998 (6)	1,000	KM202-206, 210, Statenjacht medal	—	25.00
SS71	1998 (6)	1,000	KM202-206, 210, Theo Peters medal	—	25.00
SS72	1998 (6)	1,000	KM202-206, 210, Vermeer medal	—	35.00
SS73	1998 (6)	1,000	KM202-206, 210, Knippenberg medal	—	35.00
SS74	1998 (6)	2,500	KM202-206, 210, Holland medal	40.00	20.00
SS75	1998 (6)	2,500	KM202-206, 210, Zeeland medal	40.00	20.00
SS76	1999 (6)	3,500	KM202-206, 210, King Willem III medal	17.50	35.00
SS77	1999 (6)	1,000	KM202-206, 210, Statenjacht medal	30.00	25.00
SS78	1999 (6)	1,000	KM202-206, 210, Friesland medal	40.00	20.00
SS79	1999 (6)	1,000	KM202-206, 210, West Friesland medal	40.00	20.00
SS80	1999 (6)	—	KM202-206, 210, Baby set	15.50	25.00
SS80A	1999 (6)	1,000	KM#202-206, 210 P.W.S.	75.00	70.00
SS81	1999 (6)	74	KM#202-206, 210, VOC ship "De Akerendam" with original golden ducat dated 1724 Utrecht (KM#7)	1,250	1,300
SS83	2000 (6)	3,500	KM202-206, 210, Queen Wilhelmina medal	17.50	25.00
SS84	2000 (6)	105,000	KM#202-206, 210 Introduction of Euro coins	15.00	12.00
SS85	2000 (6)	4,000	KM#202-206, 210 Netherland-Japan relations	17.50	20.00
SS86	2000 (6)	18,300	KM#202-206, 210 Baby set plus bear medal	15.50	25.00
SS87	2000 (6)	1,000	KM#202-206, 210 Gelderland medal	40.00	20.00
SS88	2000 (6)	1,000	KM#202-206, 210 Overijsel Medal	40.00	20.00
SS89	2000 (6)	1,000	KM#202-206, 210 Bouwers Met Visie	45.00	125

NETHERLANDS ANTILLES

Caribbean Sea
COLOMBIA
VENEZUELA

The Netherlands Antilles, comprises two groups of islands in the West Indies: Aruba (until 1986), Bonaire and Curacao and their dependencies near the Venezuelan coast and St. Eustatius, Saba, and the southern part of St. Martin (*St. Maarten*) southeast of Puerto Rico. The island group has an area of 371 sq. mi. (960 sq. km.) and a population of 225,000. Capital: Willemstad. Chief industries are the refining of crude oil and tourism. Petroleum products and phosphates are exported.

On Dec. 15, 1954, the Netherlands Antilles were given complete domestic autonomy and granted equality within the Kingdom with Surinam and the Netherlands. On Jan. l, 1986, Aruba achieved *status aparte* as the fourth part of the Dutch realm that was a step towards total independence.

The Netherlands Antilles was dissolved on Oct. 10, 2010, resulting in two new constituent countries, Curaçao and Sint Maarten, while the other islands (Bonaire, St. Eustatious and Saba) joining the Netherlands as "special municipalities". Since Jan. 1, 2011, the U.S. dollar has been the official currency on the "BES-islands", replacing the Netherlands Antillian guilder

RULERS

Juliana, 1948-1980
Beatrix, 1980-

MINT MARKS

Y – York Mint

Utrecht Mint (privy marks only)

Date	Privy Mark
1945-1969	Fish
1969	Fish with star
1970-1979	Cock
1980	Cock with star
1982-1988	Anvil with hammer
1988-1999	Bow and arrow
2000	Bow and arrow with star

FM - Franklin Mint, U.S.A.

NOTE: See Kingdom of the Netherlands for more details.

NOTE: From 1975-1985 the Franklin Mint produced coinage in up to 3 different qualities. Qualities of issue are designated in ( ) after each date and are defined as follows:

(M) MATTE - Normal circulation strike or a dull finish produced by sandblasting special uncirculated (polish finish) or proof quality dies.

(U) SPECIAL UNCIRCULATED - Polished or prooflike in appearance without any frosted features.

(P) PROOF - The highest quality obtainable having mirror-like fields and frosted features.

MONETARY SYSTEM

100 Cents = 1 Netherlands Antillian Gulden until 2013

DUTCH ADMINISTRATION

DECIMAL COINAGE

KM# 1 CENT

2.50 g., Bronze, 19 mm. **Ruler:** Juliana **Obv:** Rampant lion left **Rev:** Value within wreath **Edge:** Reeded

Date	Mintage	F12	VF20	XF40	MS60	MS63
1952	1,000,000	1.50	2.50	8.00	10.00	15.00
1952	100	**PF63** 150				
1954	1,000,000	1.50	2.50	5.00	7.00	12.50
1954	200	**PF63** 150				
1957	1,000,000	0.50	1.00	2.50	4.00	6.00
1957	250	**PF63** 150				
1959	1,000,000	0.50	1.00	2.50	3.50	5.00
1959	250	**PF63** 150				
1961	1,000,000	0.35	0.60	1.25	1.75	2.50
1961	—	**PF63** 100				
1963	1,000,000	0.35	0.60	1.25	1.75	2.50
1963	—	**PF63** 100				
1965	1,200,000	0.35	0.60	1.25	1.75	2.50
1965	—	**PF63** 100				
1967	850,000	0.35	0.60	1.25	1.75	2.50
1967	—	**PF63** 100				
1968 fish	900,000	1.50	2.50	5.00	9.00	15.00
1968 star and fish	700,000	1.50	2.50	5.00	9.00	15.00
Note: Struck in 1969						
1970	200,000	0.75	1.00	3.00	5.00	8.00
1970	—	**PF63** 40.00				

KM# 8 CENT

2.50 g., Bronze, 19 mm. **Ruler:** Juliana **Obv:** Crowned shield above date and ribbon **Rev:** Value flanked by stars **Edge:** Plain

Date	Mintage	VF20	XF40	MS60	MS63	MS65
1970	1,200,000	0.40	0.75	1.25	2.50	10.00
1970	—	**PF65** 25.00				
1971	3,000,000	0.40	0.75	1.00	1.50	3.00
1971	—	**PF65** 25.00				
1972	1,000,000	0.40	1.00	1.50	3.00	12.00
1973	3,000,000	0.20	0.40	0.60	0.80	2.00
1973	—	**PF65** 25.00				
1974	3,000,000	0.20	0.40	0.60	0.80	2.00
1974	—	**PF65** 25.00				
1975	2,000,000	0.20	0.40	0.60	0.80	2.00
1975	—	**PF65** 25.00				
1976	3,000,000	0.20	0.40	0.60	0.80	1.50
1977	4,000,000	0.20	0.40	0.60	0.80	1.50
1978	2,000,000	0.20	0.40	0.60	0.80	1.50

Note: 1969 date is now listed in the Patterns section

KM# 8a CENT

0.80 g., Aluminum, 18 mm. **Ruler:** Juliana **Obv:** Crowned shield above date and ribbon **Rev:** Value flanked by stars **Edge:** Plain

Date	Mintage	VF20	XF40	MS60	MS63	MS65
1979	7,512,000	0.10	0.25	0.35	0.50	1.00
1979	—	**PF65** 25.00				
1980	2,518,000	0.10	0.25	0.35	0.50	1.00
1981	2,423,000	0.10	0.25	0.35	0.50	1.00
1982	2,410,000	0.10	0.25	0.35	0.50	1.00
1983	2,925,000	0.10	0.25	0.35	0.50	1.00

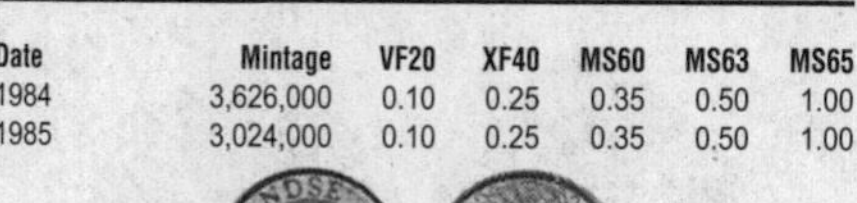

Date	Mintage	VF20	XF40	MS60	MS63	MS65
1984	3,626,000	0.10	0.25	0.35	0.50	1.00
1985	3,024,000	0.10	0.25	0.35	0.50	1.00

KM# 32 CENT

0.70 g., Aluminum, 14 mm. **Ruler:** Beatrix **Obv:** Orange blossom within circle **Rev:** Value within circle of geometric designed border **Edge:** Reeded

Date	Mintage	VF20	XF40	MS60	MS63	MS65
1989 (u)	1,365,000	—	0.10	0.15	0.25	0.50
1990 (u)	2,711,000	—	0.10	0.15	0.25	0.50
1991 (u)	4,016,000	—	0.10	0.15	0.25	0.50
1992 (u)	3,049,000	—	0.10	0.15	0.25	0.50
1993 (u)	3,997,000	—	0.10	0.15	0.25	0.50
1994 (u)	1,997,000	—	0.10	0.15	0.25	0.50
1995 (u)	997,000	—	0.10	0.15	0.25	1.00
1996 (u)	3,595,000	—	0.10	0.15	0.25	0.50
1997 (u)	4,107,000	—	0.10	0.15	0.25	0.50
1998 (u)	5,757,000	—	0.10	0.15	0.25	0.50
1999 (u)	15,876,000	—	0.10	0.15	0.25	0.50
2000 (u)	6,607,500	—	0.10	0.15	0.25	0.50

KM# 5 2-1/2 CENTS

4.00 g., Bronze, 23.5 mm. **Ruler:** Juliana **Obv:** Rampant lion left **Rev:** Value within orange wreath **Edge:** Reeded

Date	Mintage	F12	VF20	XF40	MS60	MS63
1956	400,000	0.50	1.25	2.50	4.00	10.00
1956	500	**PF63** 30.00				
1959	1,000,000	0.50	1.00	2.00	5.00	8.00
1959	250	**PF63** 40.00				
1965 fish	500,000	0.50	1.00	2.00	5.00	8.00
1965	—	**PF63** 40.00				
1965 fish and star	150,000	1.00	3.00	7.00	12.00	20.00

Note: Struck in 1969

KM# 9 2-1/2 CENTS

4.00 g., Bronze, 22 mm. **Ruler:** Juliana **Obv:** Crowned shield above date and ribbon **Rev:** Value flanked by stars **Edge:** Plain

Date	Mintage	VF20	XF40	MS60	MS63	MS65
1970	500,000	0.75	1.50	2.00	3.00	5.00
1970	—	**PF65** 30.00				
1971	3,000,000	0.25	0.50	1.00	2.00	4.00
1971	—	**PF65** 30.00				
1973	1,000,000	0.15	0.35	0.50	1.00	2.00
1973	—	**PF65** 30.00				
1974	1,000,000	0.15	0.35	0.50	1.00	2.00
1974	—	**PF65** 30.00				
1975	1,000,000	0.15	0.35	0.50	1.00	2.00
1976	1,000,000	0.15	0.35	0.50	1.00	2.00
1977	1,000,000	0.15	0.35	0.50	1.00	2.00
1978	1,500,000	0.15	0.35	0.50	1.00	2.00

Note: 1969 date is now found in the Patterns section

KM# 9a 2-1/2 CENTS

1.20 g., Aluminum, 23.5 mm. **Ruler:** Juliana **Obv:** Crowned shield above date and ribbon **Rev:** Value flanked by stars **Edge:** Plain

Date	Mintage	VF20	XF40	MS60	MS63	MS65
1979	2,012,000	0.10	0.25	0.35	0.50	1.50
1979	—	**PF65** 10.00				
1980	2,018,000	0.10	0.25	0.35	0.50	1.50
1981	1,023,000	0.10	0.25	0.35	0.50	1.00
1982	1,010,000	0.10	0.25	0.35	0.50	1.00
1983	1,025,000	0.10	0.25	0.35	0.50	1.00
1984	1,026,000	0.10	0.25	0.35	0.50	1.00
1985	1,024,000	0.10	0.25	0.35	0.50	1.00

KM# 6 5 CENTS

4.50 g., Copper-Nickel, 21.3 mm. **Ruler:** Juliana **Obv:** Orange blossom within circle **Rev:** Value within circle, pearls and shells around border **Edge:** Plain **Shape:** Square

Date	Mintage	F12	VF20	XF40	MS60	MS63
1957	500,000	0.50	1.25	2.50	3.50	5.00
1957	250	PF63 40.00				
1962	250,000	1.25	2.50	5.00	7.00	10.00
1962	200	PF63 30.00				
1963	400,000	0.35	0.75	1.50	2.00	3.00
1963	—	PF63 30.00				
1965	500,000	0.35	0.75	1.50	2.00	3.00
1965	—	PF63 30.00				
1967	600,000	0.35	0.75	1.50	2.00	3.00
1967	—	PF63 30.00				
1970	450,000	0.35	0.75	1.50	2.00	3.00
1970	—	PF63 30.00				

Note: KM#A13, previously listed here, is now under Patterns

KM# 13 5 CENTS

4.50 g., Copper-Nickel, 18.3 mm. **Ruler:** Juliana **Obv:** Crowned shield **Rev:** Value flanked by stars **Edge:** Plain **Shape:** 4-sided

Date	Mintage	VF20	XF40	MS60	MS63	MS65
1971	2,000,000	0.15	0.30	0.50	1.00	2.00
1971	—	PF65 22.50				
1974	500,000	0.60	1.25	2.50	5.00	10.00
1974	—	PF65 22.50				
1975	2,000,000	0.15	0.30	0.40	0.60	1.50
1975	—	PF65 22.50				
1976	1,500,000	0.15	0.30	0.40	0.60	1.50
1977	1,000,000	0.15	0.30	0.40	0.60	1.50
1978	1,500,000	0.15	0.30	0.40	0.60	1.50
1979	1,512,000	0.15	0.30	0.40	0.60	1.50
1980	1,518,000	0.15	0.30	0.40	0.60	1.50
1981	1,022,999	0.15	0.30	0.40	0.60	1.50
1982	1,010,000	0.15	0.30	0.40	0.60	1.50
1983	1,024,999	0.15	0.30	0.40	0.60	1.50
1984	1,526,000	0.15	0.30	0.40	0.60	1.50
1985	1,524,000	0.15	0.30	0.40	0.60	1.50

KM# 33 5 CENTS

1.16 g., Aluminum, 16 mm. **Ruler:** Beatrix **Obv:** Orange blossom within circle **Rev:** Value within circle, geometric designed border **Edge:** Reeded

Date	Mintage	VF20	XF40	MS60	MS63	MS65
1989	915,000	—	0.25	0.35	0.60	1.25
1990	1,811,000	—	0.25	0.35	0.60	1.25
1991	2,513,000	—	0.25	0.35	0.60	1.25
1992	1,599,000	—	0.25	0.35	0.60	1.25
1993	2,497,000	—	0.25	0.35	0.60	1.25
1994	1,497,000	—	0.25	0.35	0.60	1.25
1995	997,000	—	0.25	0.35	0.60	1.25
1996	796,000	—	0.25	0.35	0.60	1.25
1997	2,207,000	—	0.25	0.35	0.60	1.25
1998	2,507,000	—	0.25	0.35	0.60	1.25
1999	2,501,000	—	0.25	0.35	0.60	1.25
2000	1,007,500	—	0.25	0.35	0.60	1.25

KM# 3 1/10 GULDEN

1.40 g., 0.640 Silver 0.0288 oz. ASW, 15 mm. **Ruler:** Juliana **Obv:** Head right **Rev:** Value **Edge:** Reeded

Date	Mintage	F12	VF20	XF40	MS60	MS63
1954	200,000	1.75	3.00	8.00	16.00	35.00
1954	200	PF63 100				
1956	250,000	1.50	2.50	5.00	10.00	20.00
1956	500	PF63 80.00				
1957	250,000	1.50	2.50	4.00	6.00	10.00
1957	250	PF63 50.00				
1959	250,000	1.50	2.50	5.00	7.00	12.50
1959	250	PF63 60.00				
1960	400,000	1.00	1.25	2.50	3.50	5.00
1960	300	PF63 40.00				
1962	400,000	1.00	1.25	2.50	3.50	5.00
1962	200	PF63 35.00				
1963	900,000	1.00	1.25	2.50	3.50	5.00
1963	—	PF63 35.00				
1966 fish	1,000,000	1.00	1.25	2.00	3.00	4.00
1966 fish and star	200,000	1.50	2.00	3.75	5.00	7.50
Note: Struck in 1969						
1970	300,000	1.00	1.25	1.50	2.00	3.00
1970	—	PF63 35.00				

KM# 10 10 CENTS

2.00 g., Nickel, 15 mm. **Ruler:** Juliana **Obv:** Crowned shield above date and ribbon **Rev:** Value flanked by stars **Edge:** Reeded

Date	Mintage	VF20	XF40	MS60	MS63	MS65
1970	1,000,000	0.30	0.60	1.00	2.00	4.00
1970	—	PF65 25.00				
1971	3,000,000	0.10	0.25	0.50	1.00	2.00
1971	—	PF65 25.00				
1974	1,000,000	0.30	0.60	0.75	1.25	2.50
1974	—	PF65 25.00				
1975	1,500,000	0.10	0.25	0.50	1.00	2.00
1975	—	PF65 25.00				
1976	2,000,000	0.10	0.25	0.35	0.50	1.00
1977	1,000,000	0.10	0.25	0.35	0.50	1.00
1978	1,500,000	0.10	0.25	0.35	0.50	1.00
1979	1,512,000	0.10	0.25	0.35	0.50	1.00
1979	—	PF65 12.50				
1980	1,518,000	0.10	0.25	0.35	0.50	1.00
1981	1,022,999	0.10	0.25	0.35	0.50	1.00
1982	1,010,000	0.10	0.25	0.35	0.50	1.00
1983	1,024,999	0.10	0.25	0.35	0.50	1.00
1984	1,026,000	0.10	0.25	0.35	0.50	1.00
1985	1,024,000	0.10	0.25	0.35	0.50	1.00

Note: 1969 date of this variety is now in the Patterns section

KM# 34 10 CENTS

3.00 g., Nickel Bonded Steel, 18 mm. **Ruler:** Beatrix **Obv:** Orange blossom within circle **Rev:** Value within circle, geometric designed border **Edge:** Reeded

Date	Mintage	VF20	XF40	MS60	MS63	MS65
1989	915,000	—	0.20	0.30	0.50	1.00
1990	1,811,000	—	0.20	0.30	0.50	1.00
1991	2,513,000	—	0.20	0.30	0.50	1.00
1992	898,000	—	0.20	0.30	0.50	1.00
1993	1,996,000	—	0.20	0.30	0.50	1.00
1994	997,000	—	0.20	0.30	0.50	1.00
1995	97,000	—	0.50	0.75	1.25	2.00
1996	895,000	—	0.20	0.30	0.50	1.00
1997	1,607,000	—	0.20	0.30	0.50	1.00
1998	2,007,000	—	0.20	0.30	0.50	1.00
1999	1,501,000	—	0.20	0.30	0.50	1.00
2000	12,500	—	—	—	—	3.00

KM# 4 1/4 GULDEN

3.58 g., 0.640 Silver 0.0736 oz. ASW, 19 mm. **Ruler:** Juliana **Obv:** Head right **Rev:** Value **Edge:** Reeded

Date	Mintage	F12	VF20	XF40	MS60	MS63
1954	200,000	2.50	7.75	7.50	12.50	25.00
1954	200	PF63 80.00				
1956	200,000	2.50	3.00	5.00	8.00	15.00
1956	500	PF63 60.00				
1957	200,000	2.50	3.00	5.00	8.00	15.00
1957	250	PF63 60.00				
1960	240,000	1.40	2.50	3.00	5.00	7.00
1960	300	PF63 40.00				
1962	240,000	1.40	2.50	3.00	5.00	7.00
1962	200	PF63 45.00				
1963	300,000	1.40	2.50	3.00	5.00	7.00
1963	—	PF63 45.00				
1965	500,000	1.40	2.50	3.00	5.00	7.00
1965	—	PF63 45.00				
1967 fish	310,000	1.40	2.50	3.00	5.00	7.00
1967 Proof, fish	—	PF63 45.00				
1967 fish and star	200,000	1.40	2.50	3.50	6.00	8.00
1970	150,000	1.40	2.50	3.00	5.00	7.00
1970	—	PF63 35.00				

KM# 11 25 CENTS

3.50 g., Nickel, 19 mm. **Ruler:** Beatrix **Obv:** Crowned shield above date and value **Rev:** Value flanked by stars **Edge:** Reeded

Date	Mintage	F12	VF20	XF40	MS60	MS63	MS65
1970	750,000	0.50	1.00	2.50	4.00	8.00	
1970	—	PF65 30.00					
1971	3,000,000	0.15	0.30	0.40	0.60	2.00	
1971	—	PF65 30.00					
1975	—	PF65 30.00					
1975	1,000,000	0.15	0.30	0.40	0.60	2.00	
1976	1,000,000	0.15	0.30	0.40	0.60	1.00	
1977	1,000,000	0.15	0.30	0.40	0.60	1.00	
1978	1,000,000	0.15	0.30	0.40	0.60	1.00	
1979	1,012,000	0.15	0.30	0.40	0.60	1.00	
1979	—	PF65 17.50					
1980 cock and star	1,018,000	0.15	0.30	0.40	0.60	1.00	
1981	1,022,999	0.15	0.30	0.40	0.60	1.00	
1982	1,010,000	0.15	0.30	0.40	0.60	1.00	
1983	1,024,999	0.15	0.30	0.40	0.60	1.00	
1984	1,026,000	0.15	0.30	0.40	0.60	1.00	
1985	774,000	0.15	0.30	0.40	0.60	1.00	

KM# 35 25 CENTS

3.50 g., Nickel Bonded Steel, 20.2 mm. **Ruler:** Beatrix **Obv:** Orange blossom within circle **Rev:** Value within circle, geometric designed border **Edge:** Reeded

Date	Mintage	VF20	XF40	MS60	MS63	MS65
1989	915,000	—	0.30	0.40	0.60	1.00
1990	1,811,000	—	0.30	0.40	0.60	1.00
1991	2,013,000	—	0.30	0.40	0.60	1.00
1992	898,000	—	0.30	0.40	0.60	1.00
1993	997,000	—	0.30	0.40	0.60	1.00
1994	997,000	—	0.30	0.40	0.60	1.00
1995	297,000	—	0.30	0.40	0.60	1.00
1996	420,000	—	0.30	0.40	0.60	1.00
1997	1,297,000	—	0.30	0.40	0.60	1.00
1998	2,007,000	—	0.30	0.40	0.60	1.00
1999	1,501,000	—	0.30	0.40	0.60	1.00
2000	12,500	—	—	—	—	3.00

KM# 36 50 CENTS

5.00 g., Aureate Steel, 24 mm. **Ruler:** Beatrix **Obv:** Orange blossom within circle, designed border **Rev:** Value within circle of pearls and shell border **Edge:** Plain **Shape:** 4-sided

Date	Mintage	VF20	XF40	MS60	MS63	MS65
1989	315,000	—	0.50	0.65	1.00	3.00
1990	611,000	—	0.50	0.65	1.00	3.00
1991	513,000	—	0.50	0.65	1.00	3.00
1992	48,000	—	0.50	0.65	1.00	3.00
1993 In sets only	8,560	—	—	—	—	3.00
1994 In sets only	9,000	—	—	—	—	3.00
1995 In sets only	9,000	—	—	—	—	3.00
1996 In sets only	7,500	—	—	—	—	3.00
1997	9,500	—	—	—	—	3.00
1998	19,500	—	—	—	—	3.00
1999	11,000	—	—	—	—	3.00
2000	12,500	—	—	—	—	4.00

KM# 2 GULDEN
10.00 g., 0.720 Silver 0.2315 oz. ASW, 28 mm. **Ruler:** Juliana **Obv:** Head right **Rev:** Crowned arms **Edge Lettering:** GOD * ZIJ * MET * ONS *

Date	Mintage	VF20	XF40	MS60	MS63	MS65
1952	1,000,000	4.25	5.25	12.00	18.00	25.00
1952	100	PF63 300				
1963	100,000	5.25	12.00	14.00	22.00	30.00
1963	—	PF63 200				
1964 fish	300,000	4.25	5.25	9.00	12.00	20.00
1964	—	PF63 200				
1964 fish and star	200,000	5.25	12.00	18.00	25.00	40.00
Note: Struck in 1969						
1970	50,000	5.25	12.00	16.00	22.00	32.00
1970	—	PF63 200				

KM# 12 GULDEN
9.00 g., Nickel, 28 mm. **Ruler:** Juliana **Obv:** Head right **Rev:** Crowned shield above date and ribbon **Edge Lettering:** GOD * ZIJ * MET * ONS *

Date	Mintage	VF20	XF40	MS60	MS63	MS65
1970	500,000	0.60	1.25	2.50	4.00	8.00
1970	—	PF65 50.00				
1971	3,000,000	0.60	1.25	2.00	3.00	5.00
1971	—	PF65 50.00				
1978	500,000	0.50	0.75	1.25	2.00	4.00
1979	512,000	0.50	0.75	1.25	2.00	4.00
1979	—	PF65 25.00				
1980 cock and star	518,000	0.40	0.75	1.25	1.50	2.50

Note: 1969 date is now listed in the Patterns section

KM# 24 GULDEN
9.00 g., Nickel, 28 mm. **Ruler:** Beatrix **Obv:** Head left **Rev:** Crowned shield above date and ribbon **Edge Lettering:** GOD * ZIJ * MET * ONS *

Date	Mintage	VF20	XF40	MS60	MS63	MS65
1980 anvil	223,000	0.50	1.00	1.50	2.00	2.50
1981	223,000	0.50	1.00	1.50	2.00	2.50
1982	510,000	0.50	1.00	1.50	2.00	2.50
1983	525,000	0.50	1.00	1.50	2.00	2.50
1984	526,000	0.50	1.00	1.50	2.00	2.50
1985	424,000	0.50	1.00	1.50	2.00	2.50

KM# 37 GULDEN
6.00 g., Aureate Steel, 24 mm. **Ruler:** Beatrix **Obv:** Head left **Rev:** Crowned shield divides value above date and ribbon **Edge Lettering:** GOD * ZIJ * MET * ONS *

Date	Mintage	VF20	XF40	MS60	MS63	MS65
1989	715,000	—	1.00	1.50	2.00	4.00
1990	1,411,000	—	0.50	0.75	1.00	2.00
1991	2,013,000	—	0.50	0.75	1.00	2.00
1992	1,198,000	—	0.50	0.75	1.00	2.00
1993	1,986,000	—	0.50	0.75	1.00	2.00
1994	997,000	—	0.50	0.75	1.00	2.00
1995 In sets only	9,000	—	—	—	—	4.00
1996 In sets only	7,500	—	—	—	—	4.00
1997	9,500	—	—	—	—	4.00
1998	19,500	—	—	—	—	4.00
1999	11,000	—	—	—	—	4.00
2000	12,500	—	—	—	—	4.00

KM# 7 2-1/2 GULDEN
25.00 g., 0.720 Silver 0.5787 oz. ASW, 37 mm. **Ruler:** Juliana **Obv:** Head right **Rev:** Crowned arms **Edge Lettering:** GOD * ZIJ * MET * ONS *

Date	Mintage	VF20	XF40	MS60	MS63	MS65
1964	162,400	10.50	13.50	16.00	20.00	28.00
1964	—	PF63 250				

KM# 19 2-1/2 GULDEN
14.00 g., Nickel, 32 mm. **Ruler:** Juliana **Obv:** Head right **Rev:** Crowned shield above date and ribbon **Edge Lettering:** GOD * ZIJ * MET * ONS *

Date	Mintage	VF20	XF40	MS60	MS63	MS65
1978	100,000	—	2.50	3.50	5.00	7.00
1979	98,000	—	2.50	3.50	5.00	7.00
1979	—	PF65 35.00				
1980 cock and star	66,000	—	2.50	3.50	5.00	7.00

KM# 25 2-1/2 GULDEN
14.00 g., Nickel, 32 mm. **Ruler:** Beatrix **Obv:** Head left **Rev:** Crowned shield above date and ribbon **Edge Lettering:** GOD * ZIJ * MET * ONS *

Date	Mintage	VF20	XF40	MS60	MS63	MS65
1980 anvil & hammer	80,000	—	2.00	3.00	4.00	6.00
1981	30,000	—	2.00	3.00	4.00	6.00
1982	44,000	—	2.00	3.00	4.00	6.00
1984	12,500	—	3.00	4.00	6.00	7.00
1985	12,500	—	3.00	4.00	6.00	7.00

KM# 38 2-1/2 GULDEN
9.00 g., Aureate Steel, 28 mm. **Ruler:** Beatrix **Obv:** Head left **Rev:** Crowned shield divides value above date and ribbon **Edge Lettering:** GOD * ZIJ * MET * ONS *

Date	Mintage	VF20	XF40	MS60	MS63	MS65
1989	35,000	—	2.00	3.00	5.00	10.00
1990	60,000	—	2.00	3.00	5.00	9.00
1991	63,000	—	2.00	3.00	5.00	9.00
1992	23,000	—	2.00	3.00	5.00	9.00
1993 In sets only	8,560	—	—	—	—	9.00
1994 In sets only	9,000	—	—	—	—	9.00
1995 In sets only	9,000	—	—	—	—	9.00
1996 In sets only	7,500	—	—	—	—	9.00
1997	9,500	—	—	—	—	9.00
1998	19,500	—	1.00	2.00	4.00	9.00
1999	11,000	—	—	—	—	9.00
2000	12,500	—	—	—	—	6.00

KM# 26 5 GULDEN
3.36 g., 0.900 Gold 0.0972 oz. AGW, 18 mm. **Ruler:** Beatrix **Obv:** Head left **Rev:** Crown above joined arms of the Antilles and Netherlands **Edge:** Reeded

Date	Mintage	VF20	XF40	MS60	MS63	MS65
1980 Anvil & hammer	16,000	PF65 200				

KM# 43 5 GULDEN
14.00 g., Aureate Bonded Steel, 26 mm. **Ruler:** Beatrix **Obv:** Head left **Rev:** Crowned shield divides value above date and ribbon **Edge Lettering:** GOD * ZIJ * MET * ONS *

Date	Mintage	VF20	XF40	MS60	MS63	MS65
1998	607,000	—	2.00	3.00	4.50	5.00
1999	999,000	—	2.00	3.00	4.50	5.00
2000	10,500	—	—	—	—	10.00

KM# 20 10 GULDEN
25.00 g., 0.720 Silver 0.5787 oz. ASW, 38 mm. **Ruler:** Juliana **Subject:** 150th Anniversary of Bank **Obv:** Head right **Rev:** Crowned shield divides value **Edge Lettering:** * BANK VAN DE NEDERLANDSE ANTILLEN 1928-1978

Date	Mintage	VF20	XF40	MS60	MS63	MS65
1978	35,325	—	—	—	19.50	22.00
1978	14,675	PF65 25.00				

KM# 27 10 GULDEN
6.72 g., 0.900 Gold 0.1944 oz. AGW, 22.5 mm. **Ruler:** Beatrix **Obv:** Head left **Rev:** Crown above two shields dividing value **Edge:** Reeded

Date	Mintage	VF20	XF40	MS60	MS63	MS65
1980 Proof, anvil with hammer	6,000	PF65 400				

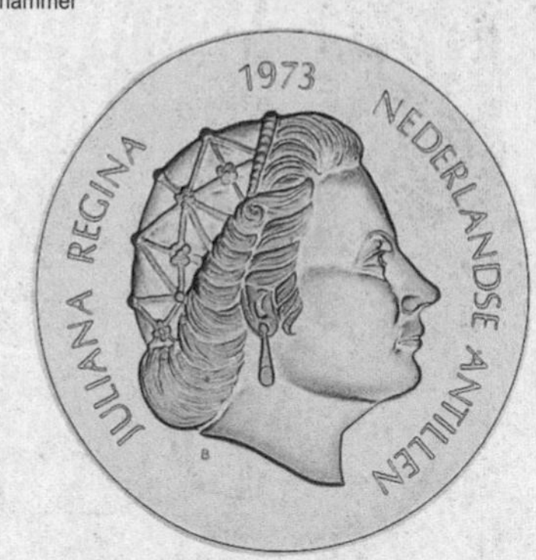

KM# 14 25 GULDEN
42.12 g., 0.925 Silver 1.2526 oz. ASW, 45 mm. **Ruler:** Juliana **Subject:** 25th Anniversary of Reign **Obv:** Head right **Rev:** Royal carriage on bridge **Edge:** DIOS KU NOS **Note:** Struck at the Ottawa Mint. Legend is in a creole version of Spanish, called Papiamento.

Date	Mintage	VF20	XF40	MS60	MS63	MS65
1973	40,188	—	—	—	35.00	40.00
1973	20,207	PF65 45.00				

KM# 15.1 25 GULDEN
42.12 g., 0.925 Silver 1.2526 oz. ASW, 45 mm. **Ruler:** Juliana **Subject:** U.S. Bicentennial **Obv:** Head right **Rev:** Saling ship Andrew Doria **Edge Lettering:** IN GOD WE TRUST ST. EUSTATIUS SALUTES FIRST AMERICAN FLAG

Date	Mintage	VF20	XF40	MS60	MS63	MS65
1976 FM(M)	200	—	—	—	220	200
1976 FM(U)	9,425	—	—	—	35.00	40.00
1976 FM(P)	12,788	PF65 55.00				

KM# 15.2 25 GULDEN
42.12 g., 0.925 Silver 1.2526 oz. ASW, 45 mm. **Ruler:** Juliana **Subject:** U.S. Bicentennial **Obv:** Head right **Rev:** Sailing ship Andrew Doria

Date	Mintage	VF20	XF40	MS60	MS63	MS65
1976 w/o edge lettering	—	—	—	—	—	550

KM# 17 25 GULDEN
42.12 g., 0.925 Silver 1.2526 oz. ASW, 45 mm. **Ruler:** Juliana **Subject:** Peter Stuyvesant **Obv:** Head right **Rev:** Standing statue left **Edge:** Plain

Date	Mintage	VF20	XF40	MS60	MS63	MS65
1977 FM	2,000	—	100	125	200	220

KM# 22 25 GULDEN
27.22 g., 0.925 Silver 0.8095 oz. ASW, 40 mm. **Ruler:** Juliana **Series:** International Year of the Child **Obv:** Head right **Rev:** Children dancing **Edge:** Plain

Date	Mintage	VF20	XF40	MS60	MS63	MS65
1979 (u)	1,000	—	—	—	100	—
1979 (u) Prooflike	4,000	—	—	—	—	45.00
1979 (u)	17,000	PF65 30.00				

KM# 39 25 GULDEN
25.00 g., 0.925 Silver 0.7435 oz. ASW, 39 mm. **Ruler:** Beatrix **Subject:** Visit of Pope John Paul II **Obv:** Head right **Rev:** Curacao map, Juliana bridge **Edge:** Plain

Date	Mintage	VF20	XF40	MS60	MS63	MS65
1990	10,000	—	—	—	30.00	35.00
1990	8,000	PF65 45.00				

KM# 40 25 GULDEN
25.00 g., 0.925 Silver 0.7435 oz. ASW **Ruler:** Beatrix **Subject:** First Amsterdam to Curacao Flight in 1934 **Obv:** Head left **Rev:** Folker FXVIII plane over route map **Edge:** Plain

Date	Mintage	VF20	XF40	MS60	MS63	MS65
1994	1,000	—	—	—	27.00	35.00
1994	5,300	PF65 40.00				

KM# 41 25 GULDEN
25.00 g., 0.925 Silver 0.7435 oz. ASW, 38 mm. **Ruler:** Beatrix **Series:** Olympics **Obv:** Crowned shield **Rev:** Weight lifter and dates **Edge:** Plain

Date	Mintage	VF20	XF40	MS60	MS63	MS65
1995	1,000	—	—	—	35.00	45.00
1995	2,500	PF65 50.00				

KM# 42 25 GULDEN
25.00 g., 0.925 Silver 0.7435 oz. ASW, 38 mm. **Ruler:** Juliana **Subject:** Fort Nassau 1797-1997 **Obv:** Head left **Rev:** Old steam sailship Curacao, dates **Edge:** Plain

Date	Mintage	VF20	XF40	MS60	MS63	MS65
ND-1997	1,000	—	—	—	35.00	40.00
ND-1997	15,000	PF65 42.00				

KM# 44 25 GULDEN
25.00 g., 0.925 Silver 0.7435 oz. ASW, 38 mm. **Ruler:** Juliana **Series:** World Wildlife Fund **Obv:** Crowned shield and value **Rev:** Whitetail buck and doe, WWF logo **Edge:** Plain

Date	Mintage	VF20	XF40	MS60	MS63	MS65
1998	500	—	—	—	37.50	45.00
1998	2,700	PF65 55.00				

KM# 45 25 GULDEN
25.00 g., 0.925 Silver 0.7435 oz. ASW, 38 mm. **Ruler:** Juliana **Subject:** 1499 Discovery of Curacao **Obv:** Crowned shield divides date within circle **Rev:** Sailing ship - Nina **Edge Lettering:** DIOS KU NOS **Note:** Edge inscription repeats three times.

Date	Mintage	VF20	XF40	MS60	MS63	MS65
1999	2,600	PF65 60.00				

KM# 48 25 GULDEN
25.00 g., 0.925 Silver 0.7435 oz. ASW, 38 mm. **Ruler:** Beatrix **Subject:** Olympics **Obv:** Crowned shield divides value **Rev:** Swimmer **Edge Lettering:** GOD*ZJ*MET*ONS

Date	Mintage	VF20	XF40	MS60	MS63	MS65
2000 (u)	3,500	PF65 50.00				

KM# 23 50 GULDEN
3.36 g., 0.900 Gold 0.0972 oz. AGW, 18 mm. **Ruler:** Juliana **Subject:** 75th Anniversary of the Royal Convenant **Obv:** Head right **Rev:** Crown above joined arms of the Antilles and Netherlands **Edge:** Reeded

Date	Mintage	VF20	XF40	MS60	MS63	MS65
1979	11,000	—	—	—	225	250
1979	64,000	PF65 250				

KM# 28 50 GULDEN
24.00 g., 0.500 Silver 0.3858 oz. ASW, 38 mm. **Ruler:** Beatrix **Obv:** Head left **Rev:** Crown above joined arms of the Antilles and Netherlands **Edge Lettering:** GOD * XIJ * MET * ONS *

Date	Mintage	VF20	XF40	MS60	MS63	MS65
1980 anvil and hammer	8,600	—	—	—	15.00	20.00
1980 Prooflike, anvil and hammer	16,400	—	—	—	—	20.00

KM# 30 50 GULDEN
25.00 g., 0.925 Silver 0.7435 oz. ASW, 38 mm. **Ruler:** Beatrix **Subject:** Dutch American Friendship **Obv:** Head left **Rev:** Bust facing above three flags as banners within circle **Edge Lettering:** DIOS KU NOS

Date	Mintage	VF20	XF40	MS60	MS63	MS65
1982 Y	40,000	PF65 30.00				

KM# 31 50 GULDEN
25.00 g., 0.925 Silver 0.7435 oz. ASW, 38 mm. **Ruler:** Beatrix **Obv:** Head left **Rev:** Mikve Israel Emanuel Synagogue

Date	Mintage	VF20	XF40	MS60	MS63	MS65
ND-1982 (u)	10,000	PF65 55.00				

KM# 47 75 GULDEN
19.40 g., Bi-Metallic Gold and Silver, 30 mm. **Ruler:** Beatrix **Subject:** Enkuentro Di Pueblonan **Obv:** Crowned shield divides date within circle **Rev:** World globe above five heads flanked by dates **Edge:** Plain

Date	Mintage	VF20	XF40	MS60	MS63	MS65
1999	750	PF65 600				

KM# 21 100 GULDEN
6.72 g., 0.900 Gold 0.1944 oz. AGW **Ruler:** Juliana **Subject:** 150th Anniversary of Bank **Obv:** Head right **Rev:** Head right **Edge:** Reeded

Date	Mintage	VF20	XF40	MS60	MS63	MS65
1978	26,500	—	—	—	—	375
1978	23,500	PF65 375				

KM# 46 100 GULDEN
7.77 g., 0.999 Gold 0.2496 oz. AGW, 22 mm. **Ruler:** Beatrix **Obv:** Crowned shield divides date within circle **Rev:** The Santa Maria **Rev. Legend:** YEGADA DI SPAÑÓNAN **Edge:** Plain

Date	Mintage	VF20	XF40	MS60	MS63	MS65
1999	850	PF65 475				

KM# 16 200 GULDEN
7.95 g., 0.900 Gold 0.230 oz. AGW **Ruler:** Juliana **Subject:** U.S. Bicentennial **Obv:** Head right **Rev:** The Andrew Doria **Edge:** IN GOD WE TRUST ST EUSTATIUS SALUTES FIRST AMERICAN FLAG **Shape:** Octagon

Date	Mintage	VF20	XF40	MS60	MS63	MS65
1976 FM(M)	100	—	—	—	—	600
1976 FM(U)	5,726	—	—	—	—	425
1976 FM(P)	15,442	PF65 425				

KM# 18 200 GULDEN
7.95 g., 0.900 Gold 0.230 oz. AGW **Ruler:** Juliana **Obv:** Head right **Rev:** Standing statue left **Edge:** Plain **Shape:** Octagon

Date	Mintage	VF20	XF40	MS60	MS63	MS65
1977 FM(M)	1,000	—	—	—	—	450
1977 FM(U)	654	—	—	—	—	475
1977 FM(P)	6,878	PF65 425				

KM# 29.1 300 GULDEN
5.04 g., 0.900 Gold 0.1458 oz. AGW **Ruler:** Juliana **Subject:** Abdication of Queen Juliana **Obv:** Head right **Rev:** Crown above joined arms of the Antilles and Netherlands **Edge:** Plain **Shape:** Square

Date	Mintage	VF20	XF40	MS60	MS63	MS65
1980 (u) cock and star	29,300	—	—	—	250	275
1980 (u) Proof, cock and star	12,000	PF65 275				

KM# 29.2 300 GULDEN
5.04 g., 0.900 Gold 0.1458 oz. AGW **Ruler:** Juliana **Subject:** Head right **Obv:** Queen Juliana **Rev:** Crown above joined arms of the Antilles and Netherlands **Edge:** Plain **Note:** Without mint mark or mintmaster's symbol

Date	Mintage	VF20	XF40	MS60	MS63	MS65
1980	Inc. above	PF65 475				

PATTERNS

Including off metal strikes

KM#	Date	Mintage	Identification	Mkt Val
Pn1	1969	210	Cent. Nickel. KM8.	400
Pn2	1969	210	2-1/2 Cents. Nickel. KM9.	400
Pn3	1969	210	5 Cents. Nickel. KMA13.	400
Pn4	1969	210	10 Cents. Nickel. KM10.	400
Pn5	1969	210	25 Cents. Nickel. KM11.	400
Pn6	1969	210	Gulden. Nickel. (KM12).	400
Pn7	1981 Y	—	125 Gulden. Bronze Gilt.	750
Pn8	1981 Y	—	125 Gulden. Gold.	3,500
Pn9	1981 Y	—	250 Gulden. Bronze Gilt.	850
Pn10	1981 Y	—	250 Gulden. Gold.	4,500
Pn11	1981 Y	—	500 Gulden. Bronze Gilt.	950
Pn12	1981 Y	—	500 Gulden. Gold.	5,500
Pn13	1983	18	50 Guilder. 0.925. Silver. Head of Beatrix left. Arms and banner above six islands of the Antilles, value 50G below. Struck at a private mint in Belgium.	—
PnA14	1983	20	50 Guilder. Brass. Head of Beatrix left. Arms and banner above six islands of the Antilles, value 50G below. Struck at a private mint in Belgium.	3,000
Pn14	1989	2	Cent. Lead. Value side, uniface.	—
Pn15	1989	2	5 Cents. Lead. Value side, uniface.	—
Pn16	1989	1	10 Cents. Lead. Value side, uniface.	—
Pn17	1989	2	50 Cents. Lead. Value side, uniface.	—
Pn18	1989	1	Gulden. Lead. Value side, uniface.	—
Pn19	1989	1	2-1/2 Gulden. Lead. Value side, uniface.	—

PIEDFORT

KM#	Date	Mintage	Identification	Mkt Val
P1	1998	200	5 Gulden. Brass Plated Steel. KM43.	800

MINT SETS

KM#	Date	Mintage	Identification	Issue Price	Mkt Val
MS1	1971 (7)	—	KM8-13 and Curacao KM46	—	22.00
MS2	1979 (7)	12,000	KM8a-9a, 10-13, 19	—	8.00
MS3	1980 (6)	18,000	KM8a-9a, 10-13, 19	—	5.00
MS4	1980 (2)	23,000	KM24-25	—	4.00
MS5	1981 (7)	23,000	KM8a-9a, 10-12, 24, 25	—	5.00
MS6	1982 (7)	10,000	KM8a-9a, 10-12, 24, 25	—	7.00

KM#	Date	Mintage	Identification	Issue Price	Mkt Val
MS7	1983 (6)	25,000	KM8a-9a, 10-12, 24 and medallion	14.00	5.00
MS8	1984 (7)	26,000	KM8a-9a, 10-12, 24, 25	14.50	7.00
MS9	1985 (7)	24,000	KM8a-9a, 10-12, 24, 25	—	7.00
MS10	1989 (7)	15,000	KM32-38	—	8.00
MS11	1990 (7)	10,000	KM32-38	13.00	8.00
MS12	1991 (7)	12,500	KM32-38	13.50	10.00
MS13	1992 (7)	10,500	MS32-38	—	10.00
MS14	1993 (7)	8,560	KM32-38	—	12.00
MS15	1994 (7)	9,000	KM32-38	17.00	12.00
MS16	1995 (7)	9,000	KM32-38	17.50	15.00
MS17	1996 (7)	7,500	KM32-38	18.50	15.00
MS18	1997 (7)	7,000	KM32-38	15.00	15.00
MS19	1998 (8)	7,000	KM32-38, 43	15.00	20.00
MS20	1999 (8)	6,000	KM32-38, 43	15.00	20.00
MS21	2000 (8)	7,500	KM32-38, 43	15.00	20.00

PROOF SETS

KM#	Date	Mintage	Identification	Issue Price	Mkt Val
PS1	1952 (2)	100	KM1-2	—	200
PS2	1954 (3)	200	KM1, 3-4	—	200
PS3	1956 (3)	500	KM3-5	—	150
PS4	1957 (4)	250	KM1, 3-4, 6	—	180
PS5	1959 (3)	250	KM1, 3, 5	—	130
PS6	1960 (3)	300	KM1, 3-4	—	125
PS7	1962 (3)	200	KM3-4, 6	—	125
PS8	1963 (5)	—	KM1-4, 6	—	250
PS9	1964 (3)	—	KM1-2, 7	—	350
PS10	1965 (4)	—	KM1, 4-6	—	140
PS11	1967 (3)	—	KM1, 4, 6	—	110
PS12	1969 (6)	200	KMPn1-Pn6, Pattern set	—	2,600
PS13	1970 (10)	—	KM1-4, 6, 8-12	—	400
PS14	1971 (6)	—	KM8-13	—	190
PS15	1973 (3)	—	KM8-9, 14	—	100
PS16	1974 (4)	—	KM8-10, 13	—	110
PS17	1975 (4)	—	KM8, 10-11, 13	—	125
PS18	1976 (2)	13,000	KM15-16	187	400
PS19	1979 (7)	—	KM8a-9a, 10-13, 19	—	120
PS20	1999 (3)	—	KM45-47, with Aruba KM18-19	—	900

Netherlands East Indies, (Kingdom of the Netherlands) is the world's largest archipelago extending for more than 3,000 mi. along the equator from the mainland of southeast Asia to Australia. At present time, since the late 1940's, it is known as Indonesia. The Dutch were in control until 1942 when the Japanese invaded. At the end of World War II, with Japanese encouragement, Indonesia declared its independence.

World War II Coinage

Netherlands and Netherlands East Indies coins of the 1941-45 period were struck at U.S. Mints (P - Philadelphia, D – Denver, S – San Francisco) and bear the mint mark and a palm tree (acorn on Homeland issues) flanking the date. The following issues, KM#330 and KM#331, are of the usual Netherlands type, being distinguished from similar 1944-45 issues produced in the name of the Homeland by the presence of the palm tree, but were produced for release in the colony. See other related issues under Curacao and Suriname.

RULER

Dutch, 1816-1942

MINT MARKS

Utrecht

Privy Marks
(a) – Halberd
(b) – Halberd and star
(c) – Sea horse
(d) - Grapes

KINGDOM OF NETHERLANDS

Dutch Administration 1817-1949

DECIMAL COINAGE

KM# 306 1/2 CENT

2.30 g., Copper, 17 mm. **Ruler:** William III **Obv:** Crowned arms divide date within circle **Obv. Legend:** NEDERLANDSCH INDIE **Rev:** Value and inscription within circle **Edge:** Plain

Date	Mintage	F12	VF20	XF40	MS60	MS63
1902 (u)	—	PF63 100				
1902 (u)	20,000,000	2.00	4.00	10.00	25.00	50.00
1908 (u)	—	PF63 200				
1908 (u)	10,600,000	3.00	6.25	17.50	40.00	100
1909 (u)	4,400,000	8.00	25.00	50.00	100	200

KM# 314.1 1/2 CENT

2.30 g., Bronze, 17 mm. **Ruler:** Wilhelmina I **Obv:** Crowned arms divide date within circle **Obv. Legend:** NEDERLANDSCH INDIE **Rev:** Value and inscription within circle **Edge:** Plain **Note:** Mintmaster's mark: Sea horse.

Date	Mintage	F12	VF20	XF40	MS60	MS63
1914 (u)	50,000,000	1.00	2.50	5.00	7.00	9.00
1916 (u)	10,000,000	1.50	3.00	6.00	12.00	15.00
1916 (u)	—	PF63 100				
1921 (u)	4,000,000	7.00	15.00	25.00	45.00	90.00
1932 (u)	10,000,000	1.50	3.00	6.00	12.00	15.00
1933 (u)	20,000,000	1.50	3.00	6.00	12.00	15.00

KM# 314.2 1/2 CENT

2.30 g., Bronze, 17 mm. **Ruler:** Wilhelmina I **Obv:** Crowned arms divide date within circle **Obv. Legend:** NEDERLANDSCH INDIE **Rev:** Inscription and value within circle **Edge:** Plain **Note:** Mintmaster's mark: Grapes.

Date	Mintage	F12	VF20	XF40	MS60	MS63
1933 (u)	Inc. above	25.00	50.00	100	200	300
1934 (u)	30,000,000	0.75	1.50	3.00	6.00	10.00
1935 (u)	14,000,000	1.50	2.50	5.00	10.00	12.00
1936 (u)	12,000,000	1.50	2.50	5.00	10.00	12.00
1936 (u)	—	PF63 50.00				
1937 (u)	8,400,000	1.50	2.50	5.00	10.00	30.00
1937 (u)	—	PF63 100				
1938 (u)	3,600,000	3.00	6.00	12.50	25.00	45.00
1939 (u)	2,000,000	6.00	12.50	25.00	45.00	80.00
1945 P High P	400,000,000	0.15	0.25	0.50	1.00	1.50
1945 P Low P	Inc. above	0.50	1.00	2.00	3.00	5.00

KM# 307.2 CENT

4.80 g., Copper, 23 mm. **Ruler:** Wilhelmina I **Obv:** Crowned Dutch arms in dotted circle, legend begins and ends beside date **Obv. Legend:** NEDERLANDSCH INDIE **Rev:** Value in Javanese and Malayan text **Edge:** Plain **Note:** Privy mark: halberd

Date	Mintage	F12	VF20	XF40	MS60	MS63
1901 (u)	15,000,000	5.00	15.00	30.00	55.00	110
1901 (u)	—	PF63 200				
1902 (u)	10,000,000	4.00	8.00	15.00	40.00	80.00
1907 (u)	7,500,000	5.00	10.00	20.00	50.00	100
1907 (u)	—	PF63 175				
1908 (u)	12,500,000	4.00	8.00	15.00	30.00	60.00
1908 (u)	—	PF63 165				
1909 (u)	7,500,000	7.00	20.00	40.00	80.00	120
1909 (u)	—	PF63 175				
1912 (u)	25,000,000	2.50	5.00	10.00	20.00	40.00

KM# 315 CENT

4.65 g., Bronze, 23 mm. **Ruler:** Wilhelmina I **Obv:** Crowned arms divide date within circle **Obv. Legend:** NEDERLANDSCH INDIE **Rev:** Inscription and value within circle

Date	Mintage	F12	VF20	XF40	MS60	MS63
1914 (u)	85,000,000	1.00	2.25	4.50	9.00	15.00
1914 (u)	—	PF63 55.00				
1916 (u)	16,440,000	2.00	4.00	8.00	16.00	25.00
1919 (u)	20,000,000	2.00	4.00	8.00	16.00	25.00
1919 (u)	—	PF63 100				
1920 (u)	120,000,000	1.00	2.25	4.50	9.00	12.00
1920 (u)	—	PF63 100				
1926 (u)	10,000,000	2.00	4.00	8.00	16.00	30.00
1929 (u)	50,000,000	1.00	2.50	5.00	10.00	15.00
1929 (u)	—	PF63 100				

KM# 317 CENT

4.80 g., Bronze, 23 mm. **Ruler:** Wilhelmina I **Obv:** 3/4 spray around hole in center with value below **Obv. Legend:** NEDERLANDSCH INDIE **Rev:** Inscription and flowers around hole in center **Edge:** Plain

Date	Mintage	F12	VF20	XF40	MS60	MS63
1936 (u)	52,000,000	0.50	1.00	1.75	3.50	12.00
1937 (u)	120,400,000	0.50	1.00	1.75	3.50	9.00
1937 (u)	—	PF63 75.00				
1938 (u)	150,000,000	0.50	1.00	1.75	3.50	7.50
1939 (u)	81,400,000	0.50	1.00	1.75	3.50	10.00
1942 P	100,000,000	0.10	0.25	0.50	1.25	2.00
1942 P Low P	Inc. above	0.50	0.75	1.50	2.50	4.50
1945 P High P	335,000,000	—	0.10	0.25	0.50	1.50
1945 P Low P	Inc. above	0.50	1.00	1.75	3.50	10.00
1945 D	133,800,000	0.10	0.25	0.50	1.25	2.00
1945 S	102,568,000	0.10	0.25	0.50	1.25	2.00

KM# 308.2 2-1/2 CENTS

12.50 g., Copper, 31 mm. **Ruler:** Wilhelmina I **Obv:** Crowned Dutch arms divide date **Obv. Legend:** NEDERLANDSCH INDIE **Rev:** Value in Javanese and Malayan text **Edge:** Plain

Date	Mintage	F12	VF20	XF40	MS60	MS63
1902	6,000,000	5.00	10.00	20.00	55.00	110
1907	3,000,000	6.50	20.00	40.00	80.00	160
1908	5,940,000	5.00	10.00	20.00	40.00	80.00
1908	—	PF63 200				
1909	3,060,000	15.00	30.00	60.00	90.00	170
1913	4,000,000	10.00	25.00	50.00	70.00	140
1913	—	PF63 160				

KM# 316 2-1/2 CENTS

12.00 g., Bronze, 31 mm. **Ruler:** Wilhelmina I **Obv:** Crowned Dutch arms divide date **Obv. Legend:** NEDERLANDSCH INDIE **Rev:** Inscription and value within beaded circle **Edge:** Plain

Date	Mintage	F12	VF20	XF40	MS60	MS63
1914 (u)	22,000,000	2.50	6.00	12.00	20.00	45.00
1914 (u)	—	PF63 165				
1915 (u)	6,000,000	5.00	10.00	20.00	45.00	100
1920 (u)	48,000,000	1.50	3.00	6.00	15.00	30.00
1920 (u)	—	PF63 165				
1945 P	200,000,000	0.25	0.50	1.00	2.00	4.00

KM# 313 5 CENTS

5.00 g., Copper-Nickel, 21 mm. **Ruler:** Wilhelmina I **Obv:** Crown above hole in center flanked by value and rice stalks **Obv. Legend:** NEDERLANDSCH INDIE **Rev:** Inscription around hole in center flanked by designs **Edge:** Plain

Date	Mintage	F12	VF20	XF40	MS60	MS63
1913 (u)	60,000,000	1.00	2.00	3.75	15.00	40.00
1913 (u)	—	PF63 500				
1921 (u)	40,000,000	1.50	3.00	6.00	20.00	50.00
1921 (u)	—	PF63 450				
1922 (u)	20,000,000	2.50	5.00	10.00	25.00	60.00
1922 (u)	—	PF63 400				

KM# 304.2 1/10 GULDEN

1.25 g., 0.720 Silver 0.0289 oz. ASW, 15 mm. **Ruler:** William III **Obv:** Crowned Dutch arms between value **Obv. Legend:** NEDERL INDIE **Rev:** Value in Javanese and Malayan text within circle **Note:** Privy mark: halberd

Date	Mintage	F12	VF20	XF40	MS60	MS63
1901 (u)	5,000,000	2.50	5.00	10.00	20.00	30.00
1901 (u)	—	PF63 100				

KM# 309 1/10 GULDEN

1.25 g., 0.720 Silver 0.0289 oz. ASW, 15 mm. **Ruler:** Wilhelmina I **Obv:** Crowned arms divide value **Obv. Legend:** NEDERL INDIE **Rev:** Inscription within circle **Edge:** Reeded

Date	Mintage	F12	VF20	XF40	MS60	MS63
1903 (u)	5,000,000	2.50	5.00	8.00	16.00	25.00
1903 (u)	—	PF63 110				
1904 (u)	5,000,000	2.50	5.00	8.00	16.00	25.00
1904 (u)	—	PF63 100				
1905 (u)	5,000,000	2.50	5.00	8.00	16.00	25.00
1906 (u)	7,500,000	1.00	2.50	5.00	10.00	20.00
1907 (u)	14,000,000	1.00	2.50	5.00	10.00	20.00
1907 (u)	—	PF63 80.00				
1908 (u)	3,000,000	2.50	5.00	10.00	20.00	40.00
1908 (u)	—	PF63 200				
1909 (u)	10,000,000	1.00	2.50	5.00	10.00	20.00
1909 (u)	—	PF63 110				

KM# 311 1/10 GULDEN

1.25 g., 0.720 Silver 0.0289 oz. ASW, 15 mm. **Ruler:** Wilhelmina I **Obv:** Crowned arms divide value **Obv. Legend:** NEDERL INDIE **Rev:** Inscription within circle **Edge:** Reeded **Note:** Wide rims.

Date	Mintage	F12	VF20	XF40	MS60	MS63
1910 (u)	15,000,000	1.50	3.50	8.00	15.00	30.00
1910 (u)	—	PF63 150				
1911 (u)	10,000,000	2.50	4.50	10.00	20.00	40.00
1912 (u)	25,000,000	1.00	2.00	3.50	7.00	12.50
1913 (u)	15,000,000	1.00	2.00	3.50	7.00	12.50
1914 (u)	25,000,000	1.00	2.00	3.50	7.00	12.50
1915 (u)	15,000,000	1.00	2.00	3.50	7.00	12.50
1918 (u)	30,000,000	1.00	2.00	3.50	7.00	12.50
1919 (u)	20,000,000	1.00	2.00	3.50	7.00	12.50
1920 (u)	8,500,000	1.00	2.50	4.50	8.00	15.00
1928 (u)	30,000,000	1.00	1.50	2.50	4.50	10.00
1930 (u)	15,000,000	1.00	1.50	2.50	4.50	10.00

KM# 318 1/10 GULDEN

1.25 g., 0.720 Silver 0.0289 oz. ASW, 15 mm. **Ruler:** Wilhelmina I **Obv:** Crowned arms divide value **Obv. Legend:** NEDERL INDIE **Rev:** Inscription within circle **Edge:** Reeded **Note:** Narrow rims.

Date	Mintage	F12	VF20	XF40	MS60	MS63
1937 (u)	20,000,000	1.00	1.25	2.00	3.00	4.50
1937 (u)	—	PF63 130				
1938 (u)	30,000,000	1.00	1.25	2.00	3.00	4.50
1939 (u)	5,500,000	1.00	1.50	3.00	10.00	20.00
1939 (u)	—	PF63 130				
1940 (u)	10,000,000	1.00	1.25	1.75	3.00	5.50
1941 P	41,850,000	0.50	1.00	1.50	2.50	3.50
1941 S	58,150,000	0.50	1.00	1.50	2.50	3.50
1942 S	75,000,000	0.50	1.00	1.50	2.50	3.50
1945 P	100,720,000	0.50	1.00	1.50	2.50	3.50
Note: Leg of mint mark P to the middle of 5 (normal)						
1945 P	Inc. above	3.00	10.00	15.00	25.00	35.00
Note: Mint mark slanted with three variations						
1945 P/P	Inc. above	5.00	15.00	20.00	30.00	50.00
1945 S	19,280,000	0.50	1.00	1.50	2.50	3.50

KM# 305.2 1/4 GULDEN

3.18 g., 0.720 Silver 0.0736 oz. ASW, 18.5 mm. **Ruler:** William III **Obv:** Crowned arms between value **Obv. Legend:** NEDERL INDIE **Rev:** Value in Javanese and Malayan text **Note:** Privy mark: halberd

Date	Mintage	F12	VF20	XF40	MS60	MS63
1901 (u)	2,000,000	10.00	20.00	35.00	75.00	100
1901 (u)	—	PF63 200				

KM# 310 1/4 GULDEN

3.18 g., 0.720 Silver 0.0736 oz. ASW, 15 mm. **Ruler:** Wilhelmina I **Obv:** Crowned arms divide value **Obv. Legend:** NEDERL INDIE **Rev:** Inscription within sun design flanked by small legends at points **Edge:** Reeded **Note:** Like KM#305 but with smaller privy mark and mint mark.

Date	Mintage	F12	VF20	XF40	MS60	MS63
1903 (u)	2,000,000	10.00	20.00	35.00	75.00	100
1903 (u)	—	PF63 200				
1904 (u)	2,000,000	3.00	8.00	15.00	30.00	60.00
1904 (u)	—	PF63 250				
1905 (u)	2,000,000	10.00	20.00	35.00	75.00	100
1905 (u)	—	PF63 200				
1906 (u)	4,000,000	10.00	20.00	35.00	75.00	100
1907 (u)	4,400,000	3.00	8.00	15.00	40.00	70.00
1907 (u)	—	PF63 130				
1908 (u)	2,000,000	4.00	10.00	20.00	50.00	90.00
1908 (u)	—	PF63 400				
1909 (u)	4,000,000	10.00	20.00	35.00	75.00	100
1909 (u)	—	PF63 110				

KM# 312 1/4 GULDEN

3.18 g., 0.720 Silver 0.0736 oz. ASW, 19 mm. **Ruler:** Wilhelmina I **Obv:** Crowned arms divide value **Obv. Legend:** NEDERL INDIE **Rev:** Inscription within sun design flanked by small legends at points **Edge:** Reeded

Date	Mintage	F12	VF20	XF40	MS60	MS63
1910 (u)	6,000,000	4.00	10.00	25.00	50.00	90.00
1910 (u)	—	PF63 150				
1911 (u)	4,000,000	4.00	15.00	30.00	60.00	100
1911 (u)	—	PF63 150				
1912 (u)	10,000,000	3.00	8.00	15.00	40.00	70.00
1912 (u)	—	PF63 400				
1913 (u)	6,000,000	4.00	10.00	25.00	50.00	90.00
1914 (u)	10,000,000	2.50	5.00	10.00	20.00	45.00
1915 (u)	6,000,000	2.50	5.00	10.00	20.00	45.00
1917 (u)	12,000,000	2.50	4.00	8.00	15.00	30.00
1919 (u)	6,000,000	3.00	8.00	15.00	40.00	70.00
1920 (u)	20,000,000	1.40	2.50	4.50	10.00	20.00
1920 (u)	—	PF63 300				
1921 (u)	24,000,000	1.40	2.50	4.50	10.00	20.00
1929 (u)	5,000,000	2.50	4.00	10.00	20.00	40.00
1930 (u)	7,000,000	2.50	4.00	8.00	15.00	30.00
1930 (u)	—	PF63 160				

KM# 319 1/4 GULDEN

3.18 g., 0.720 Silver 0.0736 oz. ASW, 18.9 mm. **Ruler:** Wilhelmina I **Obv:** Crowned arms divide value **Obv. Legend:** NEDERL INDIE **Rev:** Inscription within sun design flanked by small legends at points **Edge:** Reeded **Note:** Narrow rims.

Date	Mintage	F12	VF20	XF40	MS60	MS63
1937 (u)	8,000,000	1.40	2.50	3.00	7.00	15.00
1938 (u)	12,000,000	1.40	2.50	3.00	7.00	15.00
1939 (u)	10,400,000	1.40	2.50	3.00	7.00	15.00
1939 (u)	—	PF63 200				
1941 P	34,947,000	—	1.40	2.50	3.00	4.00
1941 S	5,053,000	1.40	2.50	3.50	8.00	20.00
1942 S	32,000,000	—	1.40	2.50	3.00	4.00
1945 S	56,000,000	—	1.40	2.50	3.00	4.00

KM# 330 GULDEN

10.00 g., 0.720 Silver 0.2315 oz. ASW, 28 mm. **Ruler:** Wilhelmina I **Obv:** Head left **Obv. Legend:** WILHELMINA KONINGIN DER NEDERLANDEN **Rev:** Crowned arms divide value **Rev. Legend:** MUNT VAN HET KONINGRIJK DER NEDERLANDEN **Edge Lettering:** GOD * ZIJ * MET * ONS *

Date	Mintage	F12	VF20	XF40	MS60	MS63
1943 D	20,000,000	4.50	8.00	12.00	20.00	30.00

KM# 331 2-1/2 GULDEN

25.00 g., 0.720 Silver 0.5787 oz. ASW, 38 mm. **Ruler:** Wilhelmina I **Obv:** Head left **Obv. Legend:** WILHELMINA KONINGIN DER NEDERLANDEN **Rev:** Crowned arms divide value **Rev. Legend:** MUNT VAN HET KONINGRIJK DER NEDERLANDEN **Edge Lettering:** GOD * ZIJ * MET * ONS *

Date	Mintage	F12	VF20	XF40	MS60	MS63
1943 D	2,000,000	—	19.00	25.00	50.00	70.00

TRADE COINAGE

These gold coins, intended primarily for circulation in the Netherlands East Indies, will be found listed as KM#83.1 in the Netherlands section.

KM# T1 DUCAT

3.49 g., 0.986 Gold 0.1108 oz. AGW, 21 mm. **Obv:** Standing knight with right leg bent **Rev:** Legend within square **Note:** See under the Netherlands KM#83.1

Date	Mintage	VG8	F12	VF20	XF40	MS60
ND(1901-37)	—	—	—	—	—	—

PATTERNS

Including off metal strikes

KM#	Date	Mintage	Identification	Mkt Val
Pn11	1902(u)	—	1/2 Cent. Silver. KM#306.	—
Pn12	1902(u)	—	1/2 Cent. Gold. KM#306.	—
Pn13	1902(u)	—	Cent. Silver. KM#307.	—
Pn14	1902(u)	—	Cent. Gold. KM#307.	—
Pn15	1902(u)	—	2-1/2 Cents. Silver. KM#308.	—
Pn16	1902(u)	—	2-1/2 Cents. Gold. KM#308.	—
Pn18	1903(u)	—	1/4 Gulden. Gold. KM#310.	—
Pn17	1908(u)	—	1/10 Gulden. Gold. KM#309.	—
Pn19	1908	—	1/2 Cent. Silver.	—
Pn20	1908	—	1/2 Cent. Gold.	—
Pn21	1908	—	Cent. Iron.	—
Pn22	1908	—	Cent. Silver.	—
Pn23	1908	—	Cent. Gold.	—
Pn24	1908	—	2-1/2 Cents. Silver. KM#308.	—
Pn25	1908	—	2-1/2 Cents. Gold. KM#308.	—
PnA27	1911	—	5 Cents. Copper-Nickel. with Proef under INDIE. similar to KM#313, with Proef under INDIE on obverse.	2,000
Pn27	1914	—	10 Sen. Tin.	—
Pn28	1914	—	5 Cents. Tin.	—
Pn29	1914	—	5 Cents. Gold.	—
Pn26	1934(u)	—	5 Cents. Copper-Nickel. KM#313.	—
PnA30	1934	—	1/4 Cent. Copper.	—
Pn30	1934	—	1/4 Cent. Copper. Holed.	—
Pn31	1934	—	1/2 Cent. Copper. KM#314.	—
Pn32	1934	—	1/4 Cent. Copper. KM#320.	—
Pn33	1945	—	1/4 Gulden. Gold. KM#319.	—

TRIAL STRIKES

KM#	Date	Mintage	Identification	Mkt Val
TS1	1941	1	1/10 Gulden. Silver. One side with value, Javanese and Malayan text. KM#318.	—
TS2	1941	—	1/4 Gulden. Silver. One side with value, KM#319.	—
TS3	1943	—	Gulden. Lead. One side with value, KM#330.	—
TS4	1943	—	2-1/2 Gulden. Lead. One side with value, KM#331.	—
TS5	1945	1	1/4 Cent. Lead. One side with value, KM#307.2.	—
TS6	1945	1	2-1/2 Cents. Lead. One side with value, KM#316.	—

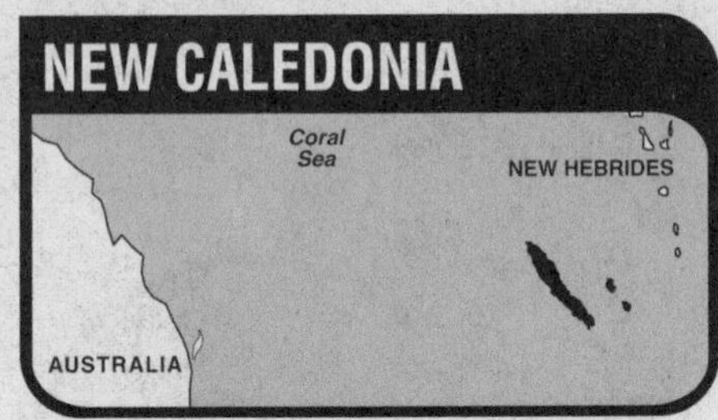

The French Overseas Territory of New Caledonia, is a group of about 25 islands in the South Pacific. They are situated about 750 miles (1,207 km.) east of Australia. The territory, which includes the dependencies of Isle des Pins, Loyalty Islands, Isle Huon, Isles Belep, Isles Chesterfield, Isle Walpole, Wallis and Futuna Islands and has a total land area of 7,358 sq. mi.(19,060 sq. km.) and a population of *156,000. Capital: Noumea. The islands are rich in minerals; New Caledonia has some of the world's largest known deposit of nickel. Nickel, nickel castings, coffee and copra are exported.

The first European to sight New Caledonia was the British navigator Capt. James Cook in 1774. The French took possession in 1853, and established a penal colony on the island in 1864. The European population of the colony remained disproportionately convict until 1897. New Caledonia became an overseas territory within the French Community in 1946, and in 1958 and 1972 chose to remain affiliated with France. Its status changed to that of a French Associated State after 1998.

MINT MARK
Paris, privy marks only

MONETARY SYSTEM
100 Centimes = 1 Franc

FRENCH OVERSEAS TERRITORY

1958-1998

DECIMAL COINAGE

KM# 1 50 CENTIMES

Aluminum, 18 mm. **Obv:** Seated figure holding torch **Rev:** Kagu bird within sprigs below value

Date	Mintage	F12	VF20	XF40	MS60	MS63
1949 (a)	1,000,000	—	0.50	1.00	3.50	7.50

KM# 2 FRANC

1.30 g., Aluminum, 23 mm. **Obv:** Seated figure holding torch **Rev:** Kagu bird within sprigs below value

Date	Mintage	F12	VF20	XF40	MS60	MS63
1949 (a)	4,000,000	—	0.25	0.75	2.00	5.00

KM# 8 FRANC

1.30 g., Aluminum, 23 mm. **Obv:** Seated figure holding torch **Rev:** Kagu bird within sprigs below value

Date	Mintage	VF20	XF40	MS60	MS63	MS65
1971 (a)	1,000,000	0.25	0.75	1.50	2.50	4.50

KM# 10 FRANC

1.30 g., Aluminum, 23 mm. **Obv:** Seated figure holding torch, legend added **Obv. Legend:** I. E. O. M. **Rev:** Kagu bird within sprigs below value

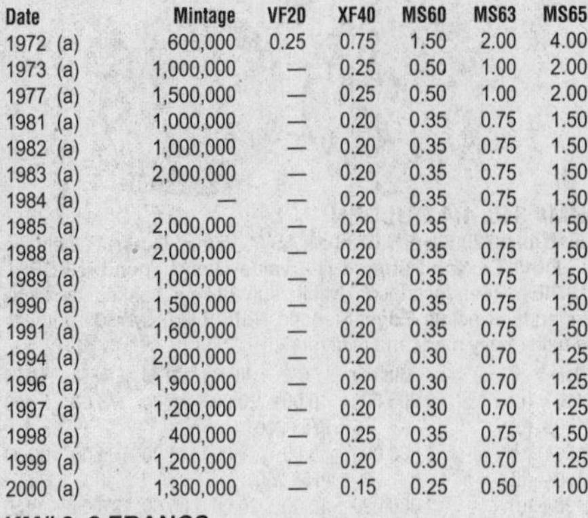

Date	Mintage	VF20	XF40	MS60	MS63	MS65
1972 (a)	600,000	0.25	0.75	1.50	2.00	4.00
1973 (a)	1,000,000	—	0.25	0.50	1.00	2.00
1977 (a)	1,500,000	—	0.25	0.50	1.00	2.00
1981 (a)	1,000,000	—	0.20	0.35	0.75	1.50
1982 (a)	1,000,000	—	0.20	0.35	0.75	1.50
1983 (a)	2,000,000	—	0.20	0.35	0.75	1.50
1984 (a)	—	—	0.20	0.35	0.75	1.50
1985 (a)	2,000,000	—	0.20	0.35	0.75	1.50
1988 (a)	2,000,000	—	0.20	0.35	0.75	1.50
1989 (a)	1,000,000	—	0.20	0.35	0.75	1.50
1990 (a)	1,500,000	—	0.20	0.35	0.75	1.50
1991 (a)	1,600,000	—	0.20	0.35	0.75	1.50
1994 (a)	2,000,000	—	0.20	0.30	0.70	1.25
1996 (a)	1,900,000	—	0.20	0.30	0.70	1.25
1997 (a)	1,200,000	—	0.20	0.30	0.70	1.25
1998 (a)	400,000	—	0.25	0.35	0.75	1.50
1999 (a)	1,200,000	—	0.20	0.30	0.70	1.25
2000 (a)	1,300,000	—	0.15	0.25	0.50	1.00

KM# 3 2 FRANCS

2.26 g., Aluminum, 27 mm. **Obv:** Seated figure holding torch **Rev:** Kagu bird within sprigs below value

Date	Mintage	F12	VF20	XF40	MS60	MS63
1949 (a)	3,000,000	—	0.35	1.00	2.50	5.50

KM# 9 2 FRANCS

2.20 g., Aluminum, 27 mm. **Obv:** Seated figure holding torch **Rev:** Kagu bird within sprigs below value

Date	Mintage	VF20	XF40	MS60	MS63	MS65
1971 (a)	1,000,000	0.35	0.75	1.25	2.25	3.50

KM# 14 2 FRANCS

2.20 g., Aluminum, 27 mm. **Obv:** Seated figure holding torch, legend added **Obv. Legend:** I. E. O. M. **Rev:** Kagu bird and value within sprigs

Date	Mintage	VF20	XF40	MS60	MS63	MS65
1973 (a)	400,000	0.20	0.65	1.00	2.00	3.00
1977 (a)	1,500,000	0.20	0.50	0.75	1.50	2.50
1982 (a)	1,000,000	0.20	0.35	0.50	1.00	2.25
1983 (a)	2,000,000	0.20	0.30	0.40	0.75	2.00
1987 (a)	2,000,000	0.20	0.30	0.40	0.75	2.00
1989 (a)	1,200,000	0.20	0.30	0.40	0.75	2.00
1990 (a)	1,500,000	0.20	0.30	0.40	0.75	2.00
1991 (a)	1,500,000	0.20	0.30	0.40	0.75	2.00
1995 (a)	400,000	0.20	0.30	0.40	0.75	2.00
1996 (a)	900,000	0.20	0.30	0.40	0.75	2.00
1997 (a)	400,000	0.20	0.30	0.40	0.75	2.00
1998 (a)	400,000	0.20	0.30	0.50	0.85	2.25
1999 (a)	800,000	0.20	0.30	0.50	0.85	2.25
2000 (a)	700,000	—	0.25	0.40	0.75	2.00

KM# 4 5 FRANCS

3.75 g., Aluminum, 31 mm. **Obv:** Seated figure holding torch **Rev:** Kagu bird and value within sprigs

Date	Mintage	F12	VF20	XF40	MS60	MS63
1952 (a)	4,000,000	—	0.50	1.50	3.50	8.00

KM# 16 5 FRANCS

3.75 g., Aluminum, 31 mm. **Obv:** Seated figure holding torch, legend added **Obv. Legend:** I. E. O. M. **Rev:** Kagu bird and value within sprigs

Date	Mintage	VF20	XF40	MS60	MS63	MS65
1983 (a)	500,000	0.45	0.75	1.25	2.50	4.50
1986 (a)	1,000,000	0.45	0.75	1.25	2.50	3.50
1989 (a)	500,000	0.45	0.75	1.25	2.50	3.50
1990 (a)	500,000	0.45	0.75	1.25	2.25	3.50
1991 (a)	480,000	0.45	0.75	1.25	2.25	3.50
1992 (a)	480,000	0.45	0.75	1.25	2.00	3.00
1994 (a)	1,200,000	0.45	0.75	1.25	2.00	3.00
1997 (a)	240,000	0.35	0.65	1.00	1.75	3.00
1998 (a)	120,000	0.35	0.65	1.00	1.75	3.00
1999 (a)	480,000	0.35	0.50	0.75	1.50	3.00
2000 (a)	400,000	0.35	0.50	0.75	1.50	3.00

KM# 5 10 FRANCS

6.00 g., Nickel, 24 mm. **Obv:** Liberty head left **Rev:** Sailboat above value

Date	Mintage	VF20	XF40	MS60	MS63	MS65
1967 (a)	400,000	1.00	1.50	2.00	4.00	7.00
1970 (a)	1,000,000	0.50	0.75	1.25	2.50	5.00

KM# 11 10 FRANCS

6.00 g., Nickel, 24 mm. **Obv:** Liberty head left **Obv. Legend:** I. E. O. M. **Rev:** Sailboat above value

Date	Mintage	VF20	XF40	MS60	MS63	MS65
1972 (a)	600,000	0.70	1.50	2.50	3.50	5.25
1973 (a)	400,000	0.70	1.00	1.75	2.50	4.25
1977 (a)	1,000,000	0.70	1.00	1.50	2.00	4.00
1983 (a)	800,000	0.60	0.85	1.50	2.00	4.00
1986 (a)	1,000,000	0.60	0.85	1.50	2.00	4.00
1989 (a)	500,000	0.60	0.85	1.50	2.00	4.00
1990 (a)	500,000	0.50	0.75	1.25	1.75	3.75
1991 (a)	500,000	0.50	0.75	1.25	1.75	3.75
1992 (a)	500,000	0.50	0.75	1.25	1.75	3.75
1995 (a)	200,000	0.50	0.75	1.25	2.00	3.50
1996 (a)	300,000	0.50	0.75	1.25	2.00	3.50
1997 (a)	300,000	0.50	0.75	1.25	2.00	3.50
1998 (a)	300,000	0.50	0.75	1.25	2.00	3.50
1999 (a)	500,000	0.50	0.75	1.25	2.00	3,50
2000 (a)	350,000	—	0.65	1.00	1.25	2.75

KM# 6 20 FRANCS

10.00 g., Nickel, 28.5 mm. **Rev:** Three zebu heads left

Date	Mintage	VF20	XF40	MS60	MS63	MS65
1967 (a)	300,000	1.25	2.50	3.50	5.00	8.50
1970 (a)	1,200,000	0.60	1.00	2.00	3.00	5.50

KM# 12 20 FRANCS

10.00 g., Nickel, 28.5 mm. **Obv:** Liberty head left **Obv. Legend:** I. O. E. M. **Rev:** Three ox heads above value

Date	Mintage	VF20	XF40	MS60	MS63	MS65
1972 (a)	700,000	0.85	1.50	2.00	3.00	5.00
1977 (a)	350,000	0.85	2.00	3.00	4.00	6.50
1983 (a)	600,000	0.75	1.50	2.00	3.00	5.00

Date	Mintage	VF20	XF40	MS60	MS63	MS65
1986 (a)	800,000	0.75	1.25	1.50	2.00	4.50
1990 (a)	500,000	0.75	1.25	1.50	2.00	4.50
1991 (a)	500,000	0.75	1.25	1.50	2.00	4.50
1992 (a)	500,000	0.75	1.25	1.50	2.00	4.50
1996 (a)	150,000	0.75	1.25	1.50	2.00	4.50
1997 (a)	—	0.75	1.25	1.50	1.75	3.25
1999 (a)	300,000	0.75	1.25	1.50	2.00	4.50
2000 (a)	250,000	0.75	1.25	1.50	2.00	4.50

KM# 7 50 FRANCS
15.00 g., Nickel, 33 mm. **Obv:** Liberty head left **Rev:** Small hut within pines and palm, value at bottom

Date	Mintage	VF20	XF40	MS60	MS63	MS65
1967 (a)	700,000	1.50	2.50	4.00	6.50	15.00

KM# 13 50 FRANCS
15.00 g., Nickel, 33 mm. **Obv:** Liberty head left **Obv. Legend:** I. E. O. M. **Rev:** Hut above value in center of palm and pine trees

Date	Mintage	VF20	XF40	MS60	MS63	MS65
1972 (a)	300,000	1.25	2.00	3.00	5.00	7.00
1983 (a)	300,000	1.25	2.00	2.75	4.50	6.50
1987 (a)	300,000	1.00	2.00	2.75	4.50	6.50
1991 (a)	450,000	1.00	1.85	2.25	3.00	4.25
1992 (a)	450,000	1.00	1.85	2.25	3.00	4.25
1996 (a)	—	1.00	1.75	2.25	3.00	4.25
1997 (a)	150,000	1.00	1.75	2.25	3.00	4.25
2000 (a)	1,000,000	1.00	1.75	2.25	3.00	4.25

KM# 15 100 FRANCS
10.00 g., Nickel-Bronze, 30 mm. **Obv:** Liberty head left **Rev:** Hut above value in center of palm and pine trees

Date	Mintage	VF20	XF40	MS60	MS63	MS65
1976 (a)	2,000,000	1.50	2.50	4.00	6.00	9.00
1984 (a)	600,000	1.50	2.50	4.00	6.00	8.50
1987 (a)	800,000	1.50	2.50	3.50	5.50	7.00
1988 (a)	—	1.50	2.50	3.50	5.50	7.00
1991 (a)	500,000	1.35	2.25	2.75	4.00	6.00
1992 (a)	500,000	1.35	2.25	2.75	4.00	6.00
1994 (a)	250,000	1.35	2.25	2.75	4.00	6.00
1995 (a)	—	1.35	2.00	2.50	3.50	5.50
1996 (a)	250,000	1.35	2.25	2.75	4.00	6.00
1997 (a)	190,000	1.35	2.00	2.50	3.50	5.50
1998 (a)	310,000	1.25	2.00	2.50	3.50	5.50
1999 (a)	400,000	1.25	2.00	2.50	3.50	5.50
2000 (a)	300,000	1.25	2.00	2.50	3.50	5.50

ESSAIS

KM#	Date	Mintage	Identification	Mkt Val
E1	1948(a)	1,100	50 Centimes. Nickel-Bronze. Sitting figure holding sprig. Bird with wings open. Incuse design, flat rim.	65.00
E1a	1948(a)	—	50 Centimes. Aluminum. Incuse design, flat rim.	75.00
E2	1948(a)	1,100	50 Centimes. Nickel-Bronze. Incuse design, raised rim.	55.00
E2a	1948(a)	—	50 Centimes. Aluminum. Incuse design, raised rim.	55.00
E3	1948(a)	1,100	Franc. Nickel-Bronze. Incuse design, flat rim.	40.00
E3a	1948(a)	—	Franc. Aluminum. Incuse design, flat rim.	65.00
E4	1948(a)	1,100	Franc. Nickel-Bronze. Incuse design, raised rim.	45.00
E4a	1948(a)	—	Franc. Aluminum. Incuse design, raised rim.	60.00
E5	1948(a)	1,100	2 Francs. Nickel-Bronze. Incuse design, flat rim.	45.00
E5a	1948(a)	—	2 Francs. Aluminum. Incuse design, flat rim.	70.00
E6	1948(a)	1,100	2 Francs. Nickel-Bronze. Incuse design, raised rim.	35.00
E6a	1948(a)	—	2 Francs. Aluminum. Incuse design, raised rim.	65.00
E7	1949(a)	2,000	50 Centimes. Copper-Nickel. KM1.	32.50
E8	1949(a)	2,000	Franc. Copper-Nickel. KM2.	35.00
E9	1949(a)	2,000	2 Francs. Copper-Nickel. KM3.	37.50
E10	1952(a)	1,200	5 Francs. Aluminum. KM4.	40.00
E11	1967(a)	1,700	10 Francs. Nickel. KM5.	30.00
E12	1967(a)	1,700	20 Francs. Nickel. KM6.	30.00
E13	1967(a)	1,700	50 Francs. Nickel. KM7.	30.00
E14	1976(a)	1,900	100 Francs. Nickel-Bronze. KM15.	45.00

PIEDFORT

KM#	Date	Mintage	Identification	Mkt Val
P1	1967(a)	500	10 Francs. Nickel. KM5.	125
P1a	1967(a)	50	10 Francs. 0.950. Silver. KM5.	425
P1b	1967(a)	20	10 Francs. 0.920. Gold. KM5.	2,000
P2	1967(a)	500	20 Francs. Nickel. KM6.	125
P2a	1967(a)	50	20 Francs. 0.950. Silver. KM6.	425
P2b	1967(a)	20	20 Francs. 0.920. Gold. KM6.	2,150
P3	1967(a)	500	50 Francs. Nickel. KM7.	275
P3a	1967(a)	50	50 Francs. 0.950. Silver. KM7.	550
P3b	1967(a)	20	50 Francs. 0.920. Gold. KM7.	3,850
P4	1979(a)	150	Franc. Aluminum. Similar to KM10.	200
P4a	1979(a)	250	Franc. 0.925. Silver. Similar to KM10.	275
P4b	1979(a)	200	Franc. 0.920. Gold. Similar to KM10.	1,400
P5	1979(a)	150	2 Francs. Aluminum. Similar to KM14.	275
P5a	1979(a)	250	2 Francs. 0.925. Silver. Similar to KM14.	350
P5b	1979(a)	200	2 Francs. 0.920. Gold. Similar to KM14.	1,850
P6	1979(a)	150	5 Francs. Aluminum. Similar to KM4.	275
P6a	1979(a)	250	5 Francs. 0.925. Silver. Similar to KM4.	300
P6b	1979(a)	200	5 Francs. 0.920. Gold. Similar to KM4.	2,750
P7	1979(a)	150	10 Francs. Nickel. Similar to KM11.	275
P7a	1979(a)	250	10 Francs. 0.925. Silver. Similar to KM11.	275
P7b	1979(a)	200	10 Francs. 0.920. Gold. Similar to KM11.	1,800
P8	1979(a)	150	20 Francs. Nickel. Similar to KM12.	275
P8a	1979(a)	250	20 Francs. 0.925. Silver. Similar to KM12.	300
P8b	1979(a)	200	20 Francs. 0.920. Gold. Liberty head left. Three ox heads, value at lower left. Similar to KM12.	2,400
P9	1979(a)	150	50 Francs. Nickel. Similar to KM13.	275
P9a	1979(a)	250	50 Francs. 0.925. Silver. Similar to KM13.	425
P9b	1979(a)	200	50 Francs. 0.920. Gold. Similar to KM13.	3,600
P10	1979(a)	150	100 Francs. Nickel-Bronze. Similar to KM15.	300
P10a	1979(a)	350	100 Francs. 0.925. Silver. Similar to KM15.	375
P10b	1979(a)	250	100 Francs. 0.920. Gold. Similar to KM15.	2,950

PIEDFORT WITH ESSAI

Double thickness

KM#	Date	Mintage	Identification	Mkt Val
PE1	1949(a)	104	50 Centimes. Aluminum. KM1.	195
PE2	1949(a)	104	Franc. Aluminum. KM2.	225
PE3	1949(a)	104	2 Francs. Aluminum. KM3.	255
PE4	1952(a)	104	5 Francs. Aluminum. KM4.	285

SPECIMEN SETS (SS)

KM#	Date	Mintage	Identification	Issue Price	Mkt Val
SS1	1967 (3)	2,200	KM5-7. This set issued with New Hebrides and French Polynesia 1967 set.	10.00	60.00

NEW GUINEA

Spanish navigator Jorge de Menezes, who landed on the northwest shore in 1527, discovered New Guinea, the world's largest island after Greenland. European interests, attracted by exaggerated estimates of the resources of the area, resulted in the island being claimed in part by Spain, the Netherlands, Great Britain and Germany.

RULER
German, 1884-1914
British, 1914-1952

MONETARY SYSTEM
12 Pence = 1 Shilling
20 Shillings = 1 Pound

AUSTRALIAN TERRITORY

STANDARD COINAGE

12 Pence = 1 Shilling; 20 Shillings = 1 Pound

KM# 1 1/2 PENNY
Copper-Nickel **Obv:** Hole in center flanked by scepters with crown above and value below **Rev:** Hole in center flanked by designs **Note:** Entire mintage returned to Melbourne Mint which later sold 400 pcs. in sets with KM#2. The balance of mintage was destroyed.

Date	Mintage	VF20	XF40	MS60	MS63	MS65
1929	25,000	—	275	495	650	—
1929	—	PF63 450	PF65 500	PF67 600		

KM# 1a 1/2 PENNY
Nickel **Obv:** Hole in center flanked by scepters with crown above and value below **Rev:** Hole in center flanked by designs

Date	Mintage	VF20	XF40	MS60	MS63	MS65
1929	—	PF65 800	PF67 900			

KM# 2 PENNY
Copper-Nickel **Obv:** Hole in center flanked by scepters with crown above and value below **Rev:** Hole in center flanked by designs **Note:** Entire mintage returned to Melbourne Mint which later sold 400 pcs. in sets with KM#1. The balance of mintage was destroyed.

Date	Mintage	VF20	XF40	MS60	MS63	MS65
1929	63,000	—	275	495	650	—
1929	—	PF63 550	PF65 600	PF67 700		

KM# 2a PENNY
Nickel **Obv:** Hole in center flanked by scepters with crown above and value below **Rev:** Hole in center flanked by designs

Date	Mintage	VF20	XF40	MS60	MS63	MS65
1929	—	PF65 800	PF67 900			

KM# 6 PENNY
Bronze **Obv:** Hole in center flanked by swimming birds with crown above and monogram below **Rev:** Artistic design around hole in center

Date	Mintage	VF20	XF40	MS60	MS63	MS65
1936	360,000	1.50	2.50	4.00	6.00	12.00
1936	—	PF63 300	PF65 350			

KM# 7 PENNY

Bronze **Obv:** Hole in center flanked by swimming birds with crown above and monogram below **Rev:** Artistic design around hole in center

Date	Mintage	VF20	XF40	MS60	MS63	MS65
1938	360,000	5.00	7.50	10.00	15.00	20.00
1944	240,000	3.00	5.00	7.00	10.00	15.00

KM# 3 3 PENCE

Copper-Nickel **Obv:** Hole in center divides date with crown above and monogram below **Rev:** Square-star design around hole in center

Date	Mintage	VF20	XF40	MS60	MS63	MS65
1935	1,200,000	5.00	10.00	20.00	30.00	45.00
1935	—	PF63 250	PF65 300			

KM# 10 3 PENCE

Copper-Nickel **Obv:** Hole in center divides date with crown above and monogram below **Rev:** Square-star design around hole in center

Date	Mintage	VF20	XF40	MS60	MS63	MS65
1944	500,000	4.00	8.00	20.00	30.00	45.00

KM# 4 6 PENCE

Copper-Nickel **Obv:** Hole in center divides date with crown above and monogram below **Rev:** Star design around hole in center

Date	Mintage	VF20	XF40	MS60	MS63	MS65
1935	2,000,000	4.00	8.00	22.50	32.50	47.50
1935	—	PF63 250	PF65 300			

KM# 9 6 PENCE

Copper-Nickel **Obv:** Hole in center divides date with crown above and monogram below **Rev:** Star design around hole in center

Date	Mintage	VF20	XF40	MS60	MS63	MS65
1943	130,000	6.00	15.00	40.00	55.00	90.00

KM# 5 SHILLING

5.38 g., 0.925 Silver 0.160 oz. ASW, 23.5 mm. **Obv:** Hole in center flanked by crossed scepters with crown above and star below **Rev:** Hole in center flanked by artistic designs

Date	Mintage	VF20	XF40	MS60	MS63	MS65
1935	2,100,000	3.00	4.50	6.50	9.00	12.00
1936	1,360,000	3.00	4.50	6.50	9.00	12.00

KM# 8 SHILLING

5.38 g., 0.925 Silver 0.160 oz. ASW, 23.5 mm. **Obv:** Hole in center flanked by crossed scepters with crown above and star below **Rev:** Hole in center flanked by artistic designs

Date	Mintage	VF20	XF40	MS60	MS63	MS65
1938	3,400,000	3.00	4.50	6.50	9.00	12.00
1945	2,000,000	3.00	4.50	6.50	9.00	12.00

PROOF SETS

KM#	Date	Mintage	Identification	Issue Price	Mkt Val
PS1	1929 (2)	—	KM#1, 2	—	1,400
PS2	1929 (2)	20	KM#1a, 2a	—	1,750

NEW HEBRIDES

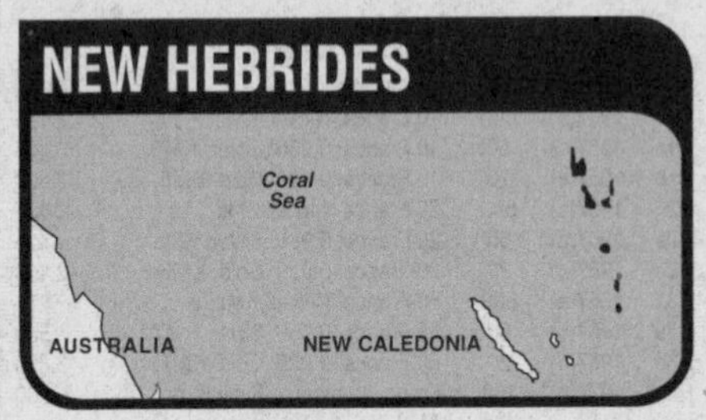

The New Hebrides were discovered by Portuguese navigator Pedro de Quiros in 1606, visited by French explorer Bougainville in 1768, and named by British navigator Capt. James Cook in 1774. Ships of all nations converged on the islands to trade for sandalwood, prompting France and Britain to relinquish their individual claims and declare the islands a neutral zone in 1878. The New Hebrides were placed under the control of a mixed Anglo-French commission of naval officers during the native uprisings of 1887, until achieving independence as Vanuatu, within the Commonwealth of nations on September 30, 1980.

MINT MARK

(a) - Paris, privy marks only

MONETARY SYSTEM

100 Centimes = 1 Franc

FRENCH/BRITISH CONDOMINIUM

(Jointly Governed Territory)

STANDARD COINAGE

KM# 4.1 FRANC

Nickel-Brass **Obv:** Liberty head left, date below **Obv. Legend:** REPVBLIQVE FRANCAISE **Rev:** Frigate bird above value

Date	Mintage	VF20	XF40	MS60	MS63	MS65
1970 (a)	435,000	0.25	0.50	0.85	1.75	2.50

KM# 4.2 FRANC

Nickel-Brass **Obv:** I.E.O.M. below head **Obv. Legend:** REPVBLIQVE FRANCAISE **Rev:** Frigate bird above value

Date	Mintage	VF20	XF40	MS60	MS63	MS65
1975 (a)	350,000	0.20	0.40	0.75	1.00	1.75
1978 (a)	200,000	0.20	0.40	0.75	1.00	1.75
1979 (a)	350,000	0.20	0.40	0.75	1.00	1.75
1982 (a)	—	—	—	50.00	75.00	125

Note: Issued briefly as an emergency coinage for Vanuatu. Most melted.

KM# 5.1 2 FRANCS

3.00 g., Nickel-Brass **Obv:** Liberty head left, date below **Obv. Legend:** REPVBLIQVE FRANCAISE **Rev:** Frigate bird above value

Date	Mintage	VF20	XF40	MS60	MS63	MS65
1970 (a)	264,000	0.50	0.75	1.50	2.50	5.00

KM# 5.2 2 FRANCS

Nickel-Brass **Obv:** Liberty head left, I.E.O.M. and date below head **Obv. Legend:** REPVBLIQVE FRANCAISE **Rev:** Frigate bird above value

Date	Mintage	VF20	XF40	MS60	MS63	MS65
1973 (a)	200,000	0.20	0.50	1.00	2.00	3.50
1975 (a)	300,000	0.20	0.50	1.00	2.00	3.50
1978 (a)	150,000	0.20	0.50	1.00	2.00	3.50
1979 (a)	250,000	0.20	0.50	1.00	2.00	3.50

KM# 6.1 5 FRANCS

Nickel-Brass **Obv:** Liberty head left, date below **Obv. Legend:** REPVBLIQVE FRANCAISE **Rev:** Frigate bird above value

Date	Mintage	VF20	XF40	MS60	MS63	MS65
1970 (a)	375,000	0.50	0.75	1.65	2.75	4.00

KM# 6.2 5 FRANCS

Nickel-Brass **Obv:** Liberty head left, I.E.O.M. and date below head **Obv. Legend:** REPVBLIQVE FRANCAISE **Rev:** Frigate bird above value

Date	Mintage	VF20	XF40	MS60	MS63	MS65
1975 (a)	350,000	0.30	0.75	1.25	2.00	3.50
1979 (a)	250,000	0.30	0.75	1.25	2.00	3.50
1982 (a)	—	—	—	50.00	75.00	125

Note: Issued briefly as an emergency coinage for Vanuatu. Most melted.

KM# 2.1 10 FRANCS

Nickel **Obv:** Liberty head left, date below **Obv. Legend:** REPVBLIQVE FRANCAISE **Rev:** Mask left flanked by designs with value below

Date	Mintage	VF20	XF40	MS60	MS63	MS65
1967 (a)	200,000	0.30	1.00	1.85	3.00	5.00
1970 (a)	400,000	0.30	1.00	1.85	3.00	5.00

KM# 2.2 10 FRANCS

6.00 g., Nickel **Obv:** Liberty head left, I.E.O.M. and date below head **Obv. Legend:** REPVBLIQVE FRANCAISE **Rev:** Mask left flanked by designs with value below

Date	Mintage	VF20	XF40	MS60	MS63	MS65
1973 (a)	200,000	0.30	1.15	1.85	2.75	4.50
1975 (a)	300,000	0.30	1.15	1.85	2.75	4.50
1977 (a)	200,000	0.30	1.15	1.85	2.75	4.50
1979 (a)	400,000	0.30	1.15	1.85	2.75	4.50

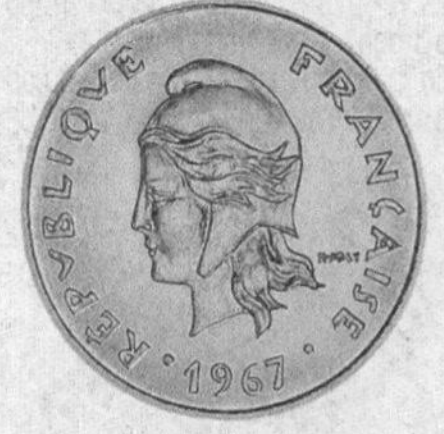

KM# 3.1 20 FRANCS

Nickel **Obv:** Liberty head left, date below **Obv. Legend:** REPVBLEQVE FRANCAISE **Rev:** Mask left flanked by designs with value below

Date	Mintage	VF20	XF40	MS60	MS63	MS65
1967 (a)	250,000	0.60	1.25	2.25	4.00	6.00
1970 (a)	300,000	0.60	1.25	2.25	4.00	6.00

KM# 3.2 20 FRANCS

Nickel **Obv:** Liberty head left, I.E.O.M. and date below head **Obv. Legend:** REPVBLIQVE FRANCAISE **Rev:** Mask left flanked by designs, value at bottom

Date	Mintage	VF20	XF40	MS60	MS63	MS65
1973 (a)	300,000	0.60	1.25	2.25	3.25	5.00
1975 (a)	150,000	0.60	1.25	2.25	3.25	5.00
1977 (a)	150,000	0.60	1.25	2.25	3.25	5.00
1979 (a)	300,000	0.60	1.25	2.25	3.25	5.00

KM# 7 50 FRANCS

Nickel **Obv:** Liberty head left, I.E.O.M. and date below head **Obv. Legend:** REPVBLIQVE FRANCAISE **Rev:** Scepter above value

Date	Mintage	VF20	XF40	MS60	MS63	MS65
1972 (a)	200,000	1.00	2.00	3.00	5.00	7.50

KM# 1 100 FRANCS

25.00 g., 0.835 Silver 0.6711 oz. ASW, 36 mm. **Obv:** Liberty head left, date below **Obv. Legend:** REPVBLIQVE FRANCAISE **Rev:** Scepter above value

Date	Mintage	VF20	XF40	MS60	MS63	MS65
1966 (a)	200,000	—	—	15.00	20.00	30.00

ESSAIS

KM#	Date	Mintage	Identification	Mkt Val
E1	1966(a)	3,000	100 Francs. Liberty head left, date below. Sword hilt above value.	150
E2	1967(a)	1,700	10 Francs.	35.00
E3	1967(a)	1,700	20 Francs.	35.00
E4	1970(a)	1,250	Franc.	35.00
E5	1970(a)	1,700	2 Francs.	35.00
E6	1970(a)	1,250	5 Francs.	35.00
E7	1972(a)	1,300	50 Francs.	37.00

PATTERNS

Including off metal strikes

KM#	Date	Mintage	Identification	Mkt Val
Pn1	1979	60	500 Francs. Copper-Nickel-Aluminum.	350
Pn2	1979	60	500 Francs. 0.999. Silver.	550
Pn3	1979	3	500 Francs. 0.999. Gold.	7,000
Pn4	1979	1	500 Francs. 0.999. Platinum.	10,000

PIEDFORT WITH ESSAI

Double thickness

KM#	Date	Mintage	Identification	Mkt Val
PE1	1966(a)	500	100 Francs.	200
PE2	1966(a)	50	100 Francs. 0.920. Gold.	8,000
PE3	1967(a)	500	10 Francs. Liberty head left, date below. Mask left, flanked by designs, value on bottom.	30.00
PE4	1967(a)	50	10 Francs. 0.950. Silver.	170
PE5	1967(a)	20	10 Francs. 0.920. Gold.	1,150
PE6	1967(a)	500	20 Francs.	30.00
PE7	1967(a)	50	20 Francs. 0.950. Silver.	270
PE8	1967(a)	20	20 Francs. 0.920. Gold.	1,500
PE10	1974(a)	500	100 Francs. 0.925. Silver.	150
PE11	1974(a)	119	100 Francs. 0.920. Gold.	6,500
PE12	1979(a)	150	Franc.	25.00
PE13	1979	250	Franc. 0.925. Silver.	50.00
PE14	1979(a)	123	Franc. 0.920. Gold.	600
PE15	1979(a)	150	2 Francs.	30.00
PE16	1979(a)	250	2 Francs. 0.925. Silver.	45.00
PE17	1979(a)	115	2 Francs. 0.920. Gold.	750
PE18	1979(a)	150	5 Francs.	30.00
PE19	1979(a)	250	5 Francs. 0.925. Silver.	45.00
PE20	1979(a)	116	5 Francs. 0.920. Gold.	1,350
PE21	1979(a)	150	10 Francs.	35.00
PE22	1979(a)	250	10 Francs. 0.925. Silver.	45.00
PE23	1979(a)	116	10 Francs. 0.920. Gold.	900
PE24	1979(a)	150	20 Francs.	35.00
PE25	1979(a)	250	20 Francs. 0.925. Silver.	55.00
PE26	1979(a)	115	20 Francs. 0.920. Gold.	1,500
PE27	1979(a)	150	50 Francs.	40.00
PE28	1979(a)	250	50 Francs. 0.925. Silver.	115
PE29	1979(a)	116	50 Francs. 0.920. Gold.	4,950

FDC SETS

KM#	Date	Mintage	Identification	Issue Price	Mkt Val
SS1	1966-67 (3)	2,200	KM#1, 2.1, 3.1	10.00	40.00

New Zealand, a parliamentary state located in the Southwest Pacific 1,250 miles (2,011 km.) east of Australia, has an area of 103,883 sq. mi. (268,680 sq. km.) and a population of *3.4 million. Capital: Wellington. Wool, meat, dairy products and some manufactured items are exported.

The first European to sight New Zealand was the Dutch navigator Abel Tasman in 1642. The islands were explored by British navigator Capt. James Cook who surveyed it in 1769 and annexed the land to Great Britain. The British government disavowed the annexation and for the next 70 years the only white settlers to arrive were adventurers attracted by the prospects of lumbering, sealing and whaling. Great Britain annexed the land in 1840 by treaty with the native chiefs and made it a dependency of New South Wales. The colony was granted self-government in1852, a ministerial form of government in 1856, and full dominion status on Sept. 26, 1907. Full internal and external autonomy, which New Zealand had in effect possessed for many years, was formally extended in 1947. New Zealand is a member of the Commonwealth of Nations. Elizabeth II is Head of State as Queen of New Zealand.

Prior to 1933 British coins were the official legal tender but Australian coins were accepted in small transactions. Currency fluctuations caused a distinctive New Zealand coinage to be introduced in 1933. The 1935 Waitangi crown and proof set were originally intended to mark the introduction but delays caused their date to be changed to 1935. The 1940 half crown marked the centennial of British rule, the 1949 and 1953 crowns commemorated Royal visits and the 1953 proof set marked the coronation of Queen Elizabeth.

Decimal Currency was introduced in 1967 with special sets commemorating the last issued of pound sterling (1965) and the first of the decimal issues. Since then dollars and set of coins have been issued nearly every year.

RULER

British

MINTS

(l) – British Royal Mint (Llantrisant)
(c) – Royal Australian Mint (Canberra)
(o) – Royal Canadian Mint, Ottawa or Winnepeg
(n) – Norwegian Mint
(m) – B.H. Meyer, Germany
(p) – South African Mint (Pretoria)
(v) – Valcambi SA, Switzerland
(w) – Perth Mint, Western Australia

MONETARY SYSTEM

4 Farthings = 1 Penny
12 Pence = 1 Shilling
20 Shillings = 1 Pound

STATE

1907 - present

POUND STERLING COINAGE

KM# 12 1/2 PENNY

5.60 g., Bronze, 25.4 mm. **Ruler:** George VI **Obv:** Head left **Rev:** Hei Tiki

Date	Mintage	VF20	XF40	MS60	MS63	MS65
1940	3,432,000	0.50	5.00	10.00	20.00	40.00
1940 Proof; 5 known	—	**PF63** 700	**PF65** 1,000			
1941	960,000	0.25	8.00	20.00	50.00	70.00
1941	—	**PF63** 195	**PF65** 275			
1942	1,920,000	2.50	20.00	50.00	100	230
1944	2,035,000	0.25	3.50	7.00	15.00	35.00
1945	1,516,000	0.25	3.50	7.00	15.00	35.00
1945	—	**PF63** 150	**PF65** 210			
1946	3,120,000	0.25	3.00	6.50	12.50	28.00
1946	—	**PF63** 150	**PF65** 210			
1947	2,726,400	0.25	3.00	6.50	12.50	22.00
1947	—	**PF63** 125	**PF65** 180			

KM# 20 1/2 PENNY

5.60 g., Bronze, 25.5 mm. **Ruler:** George VI **Obv:** Head left **Rev:** Hei Tiki

Date	Mintage	VF20	XF40	MS60	MS63	MS65
1949	1,766,400	0.25	3.00	6.50	12.50	22.00
1949	—	**PF63** 125	**PF65** 180			
1950	1,425,600	0.25	3.50	7.00	15.00	35.00
1950	—	**PF63** 150	**PF65** 210			
1951	2,342,400	0.25	2.00	4.00	8.00	12.00
1951	—	**PF63** 125	**PF65** 180			
1952	2,400,000	0.20	1.50	3.00	5.00	8.00
1952	—	**PF63** 125	**PF65** 180			

KM# 23.1 1/2 PENNY

5.60 g., Bronze, 25.4 mm. **Ruler:** Elizabeth II **Obv:** Laureate bust right without shoulder strap **Rev:** Hei Tiki

Date	Mintage	VF20	XF40	MS60	MS63	MS65
1953	720,000	0.50	3.00	6.50	12.50	20.00
1953	7,000	**PF63** 4.00	**PF65** 7.00			
1953 Matte proof	—	**PF63** 75.00	**PF65** 110			
1954	240,000	6.00	20.00	40.00	80.00	125
1954	—	**PF63** 120	**PF65** 170			
1955	240,000	6.00	20.00	40.00	80.00	125
1955	—	**PF63** 120	**PF65** 170			

KM# 23.2 1/2 PENNY

5.60 g., Bronze, 25.4 mm. **Ruler:** Elizabeth II **Obv:** Laureate bust right with shoulder strap **Rev:** Hei Tiki

Date	Mintage	VF20	XF40	MS60	MS63	MS65
1956	1,200,000	0.25	2.50	5.00	10.00	18.00
1956	—	**PF63** 100	**PF65** 150			
1957	1,440,000	0.25	2.50	5.00	10.00	18.00
1957	—	**PF63** 100	**PF65** 150			
1958	1,920,000	0.25	2.50	5.00	10.00	18.00
1958	—	**PF63** 100	**PF65** 150			
1959	1,920,000	0.20	2.00	4.00	8.00	17.00
1959	—	**PF63** 100	**PF65** 150			
1960	2,400,000	0.20	1.00	2.00	4.00	8.00
1960	—	**PF63** 100	**PF65** 150			
1961	2,880,000	0.15	1.50	3.50	7.00	10.00
1961	—	**PF63** 100	**PF65** 150			
1962	2,880,000	0.15	1.50	3.50	7.00	10.00
1962	—	**PF63** 100	**PF65** 150			
1963	1,680,000	0.15	0.30	0.50	1.00	2.00
1963	—	**PF63** 100	**PF65** 150			
1964	2,885,000	0.15	0.20	0.40	0.75	2.50
1964	—	**PF63** 70.00	**PF65** 100			
1965	5,200,000	0.15	0.20	0.30	0.50	2.50
1965 Prooflike	25,000	—	—	—	—	1.00
1965 Proof	10	—	—	—	—	—

KM# A23 1/2 PENNY

5.60 g., Bronze, 25.1 mm. **Ruler:** Elizabeth II **Obv:** Laureate bust right with shoulder strap, Latin legend. **Rev:** Hei Tiki **Note:** Mule. Obv. British Half Penny. Rev. New Zealand Half Penny

Date	Mintage	VF20	XF40	MS60	MS63	MS65
1965	—	—	—	—	7,250	—

KM# 13 PENNY

9.60 g., Bronze, 31 mm. **Ruler:** George VI **Obv:** Head left **Rev:** Tui bird sitting on branch

Date	Mintage	VF20	XF40	MS60	MS63	MS65
1940	5,424,000	0.50	6.00	12.50	25.00	45.00
1940	—	**PF63** 850	**PF65** 1,200			
Note: 5 known						
1941	1,200,000	0.50	25.00	50.00	100	175
1942	3,120,000	5.00	28.00	55.00	110	195
1942	—	**PF63** 250	**PF65** 400			
1943	8,400,000	0.40	5.00	12.00	25.00	45.00
1943	—	**PF63** 225	**PF65** 375			
1944	3,696,000	0.40	5.00	12.00	25.00	45.00
1944	—	**PF63** 225	**PF65** 375			
1945	4,764,000	0.40	5.00	12.00	25.00	45.00
1945	—	**PF63** 225	**PF65** 375			
1946	6,720,000	0.40	3.50	7.00	15.00	25.00
1946	—	**PF63** 225	**PF65** 375			
1947	5,880,000	0.40	3.00	6.00	12.50	22.00
1947	—	**PF63** 225	**PF65** 375			

KM# 13a PENNY

Bronze, 31 mm. **Ruler:** George VI **Obv:** Head left **Rev:** Tui bird sitting on branch **Note:** Burnished

Date	Mintage	VF20	XF40	MS60	MS63	MS65
1945	—	—	45.00	90.00	180	250

Note: Struck in error by the Royal Mint on Great Britain blanks

KM# 21 PENNY

9.60 g., Bronze, 31 mm. **Ruler:** George VI **Obv:** Head left **Rev:** Tui bird sitting on branch

Date	Mintage	VF20	XF40	MS60	MS63	MS65
1949	2,016,000	0.40	3.00	6.00	12.50	25.00
1949	—	**PF63** 250	**PF65** 425			
1950	5,784,000	0.40	3.00	6.00	12.50	20.00
1950	—	**PF63** 175	**PF65** 250			
1951	6,888,000	0.40	2.50	5.00	10.00	20.00
1951	—	**PF63** 175	**PF65** 250			
1952	10,800,000	0.40	2.50	5.00	10.00	20.00
1952	—	**PF63** 145	**PF65** 200			

KM# 24.1 PENNY

9.60 g., Bronze, 31 mm. **Ruler:** Elizabeth II **Obv:** Laureate bust right without shoulder strap **Rev:** Tui bird sitting on branch

Date	Mintage	VF20	XF40	MS60	MS63	MS65
1953	2,400,000	0.40	2.50	5.00	10.00	20.00
1953	7,000	**PF63** 7.00	**PF65** 10.00			
1953 Matte proof	—	**PF63** 75.00	**PF65** 110			
1954	1,080,000	3.00	12.50	25.00	50.00	120
1954	—	**PF63** 150	**PF65** 225			
1955	3,720,000	0.30	2.50	5.00	10.00	20.00
1955	—	**PF63** 250	**PF65** 425			
1956	Inc. below	45.00	175	350	700	1,100

KM# 24.2 PENNY

9.60 g., Bronze, 31 mm. **Ruler:** Elizabeth II **Obv:** Laureate bust right with shoulder strap **Rev:** Tui bird sitting on branch

Date	Mintage	VF20	XF40	MS60	MS63	MS65
1956	3,600,000	0.30	2.00	4.00	8.00	16.00
1956	—	**PF63** 175	**PF65** 300			
1957	2,400,000	0.30	2.00	4.00	8.00	16.00
1957	—	**PF63** 175	**PF65** 300			
1958	10,800,000	0.30	2.00	4.00	8.00	16.00
1958	—	**PF63** 175	**PF65** 300			
1959	8,400,000	0.30	2.00	4.00	8.00	16.00
1959	—	**PF63** 175	**PF65** 300			
1960	7,200,000	0.30	1.00	2.00	4.00	6.50
1960	—	**PF63** 200	**PF65** 350			
1961	7,200,000	0.30	0.50	1.00	2.00	4.00
1961	—	**PF63** 200	**PF65** 350			
1962	6,000,000	0.20	0.50	1.00	2.00	4.00
1962	—	**PF63** 200	**PF65** 350			
1963	2,400,000	0.20	0.30	0.50	1.00	2.50
1963	—	**PF63** 200	**PF65** 350			
1964	18,000,000	0.20	0.25	0.35	0.60	1.25
1964	—	**PF63** 200	**PF65** 350			
1965	200,000	—	1.25	2.50	5.00	6.00
1965 Prooflike	25,000	—	—	—	—	5.00
1965 Proof	10	—	—	—	—	—

KM# 1 3 PENCE

1.41 g., 0.500 Silver 0.0227 oz. ASW, 16.3 mm. **Ruler:** George V **Subject:** Crossed Patu **Obv:** Crowned bust left **Rev:** Crossed patu flanked by value and date

Date	Mintage	VF20	XF40	MS60	MS63	MS65
1933	6,000,000	3.00	5.00	10.00	20.00	40.00
1933	Est. 20	**PF63** 425	**PF65** 600			
1934	6,000,000	3.00	5.00	10.00	20.00	40.00
1934	Est. 20	**PF65** 1,750				
1935	40,000	175	225	450	900	1,250
1935	364	**PF63** 1,000	**PF65** 1,500			
1936	2,760,000	3.00	6.00	12.00	22.50	50.00
1936	—	**PF63** 425	**PF65** 600			

KM# 7 3 PENCE

1.41 g., 0.500 Silver 0.0227 oz. ASW, 16.3 mm. **Ruler:** George VI **Subject:** Crossed Patu **Obv:** Head left **Rev:** Crossed patu flanked by value and date

Date	Mintage	VF20	XF40	MS60	MS63	MS65
1937	2,880,000	3.00	5.00	10.00	20.00	45.00
1937	Est. 200	**PF63** 280	**PF65** 400			
1939	3,000,000	3.00	5.00	10.00	20.00	45.00
1939	—	**PF63** 385	**PF65** 550			
1940	2,000,000	3.00	6.00	12.50	25.00	50.00
1940	—	**PF63** 385	**PF65** 550			
1941	1,760,000	20.00	50.00	100	200	400
1941	—	**PF63** 350	**PF65** 500			
1942	3,120,000	3.00	5.00	10.00	20.00	40.00
1942 With 1 dot	—	40.00	90.00	200	400	600
1943	4,400,000	2.00	3.50	7.50	15.00	35.00
1944	2,840,000	2.00	3.50	7.50	15.00	35.00
1944	—	**PF63** 350	**PF65** 500			
1945	2,520,000	2.00	3.50	7.50	15.00	27.50
1945	—	**PF63** 350	**PF65** 500			
1946	6,080,000	2.00	3.50	7.50	15.00	25.00
1946	—	**PF63** 315	**PF65** 450			

KM# 7a 3 PENCE

1.41 g., Copper-Nickel, 16.3 mm. **Ruler:** George VI **Obv:** Head left **Rev:** Crossed patu flanked by value and date

Date	Mintage	VF20	XF40	MS60	MS63	MS65
1947	6,400,000	1.00	3.50	7.50	15.00	30.00
1947	Est. 20	**PF63** 280	**PF65** 400			

KM# 15 3 PENCE

1.41 g., Copper-Nickel, 16.3 mm. **Ruler:** George VI **Obv:** Head left **Rev:** Crossed patu flanked by value and date

Date	Mintage	VF20	XF40	MS60	MS63	MS65
1948	4,000,000	1.00	3.50	7.50	15.00	30.00
1948	—	**PF63** 175	**PF65** 250			
1950	800,000	7.50	20.00	50.00	100	200
1950	—	**PF63** 210	**PF65** 300			
1951	3,600,000	0.75	1.50	3.00	6.00	12.00
1951	—	**PF63** 160	**PF65** 225			
1952	8,000,000	0.75	1.50	3.00	6.00	10.00
1952	—	**PF63** 160	**PF65** 225			

KM# 25.1 3 PENCE

1.41 g., Copper-Nickel, 16.3 mm. **Ruler:** Elizabeth II **Obv:** Laureate bust right without shoulder strap **Rev:** Crossed patu flanked by value and date

Date	Mintage	VF20	XF40	MS60	MS63	MS65
1953	4,000,000	0.75	1.50	3.00	6.00	12.00
1953	7,000	**PF63** 5.00	**PF65** 7.00			
1953 Matte proof	—	**PF63** 90.00	**PF65** 130			
1954	4,000,000	0.75	1.50	3.00	6.00	10.00
1954	—	**PF63** 160	**PF65** 225			
1955	4,000,000	0.75	1.50	3.00	6.00	10.00
1955	—	**PF63** 160	**PF65** 225			
1956	—	**PF63** 210	**PF65** 300			
1956	Inc. below	6.00	50.00	110	220	400

KM# 25.2 3 PENCE
1.41 g., Copper-Nickel, 16.3 mm. **Ruler:** Elizabeth II **Obv:** Laureate bust right with shoulder strap **Rev:** Crossed patu flanked by value and date

Date	Mintage	VF20	XF40	MS60	MS63	MS65
1956	4,800,000	0.15	1.00	2.00	4.00	8.00
1956	—	PF63 160	PF65 225			
1957	8,000,000	0.15	0.50	1.00	2.00	4.00
1957	—	PF63 160	PF65 225			
1958	4,800,000	0.15	1.00	2.00	4.00	8.00
1958	—	PF63 160	PF65 225			
1959	4,000,000	0.15	1.00	2.00	4.00	8.00
1959	—	PF63 160	PF65 225			
1960	4,000,000	0.15	0.25	0.50	1.00	2.00
1960	—	PF63 160	PF65 225			
1961	4,800,000	0.15	0.50	1.00	2.00	4.00
1961	—	PF63 160	PF65 225			
1962	6,000,000	0.15	0.20	0.40	0.75	1.25
1962	—	PF63 160	PF65 225			
1963	4,000,000	0.15	0.20	0.40	0.75	1.25
1963	—	PF63 160	PF65 225			
1964	6,400,000	0.15	0.20	0.40	0.75	1.25
1964	—	PF63 125	PF65 175			
1965	4,200,000	0.10	0.15	0.25	0.50	1.00
1965 Prooflike	25,000	—	—	—	—	1.50
1965 Proof	10	—	—	—	—	—

KM# 2 6 PENCE
2.83 g., 0.500 Silver 0.0455 oz. ASW, 19.3 mm. **Ruler:** George V **Obv:** Crowned bust left **Rev:** Huia bird sitting on branch **Edge:** Reeded

Date	Mintage	VF20	XF40	MS60	MS63	MS65
1933	20	PF63 525	PF65 750			
1933	3,000,000	7.00	15.00	30.00	60.00	100
1934	3,600,000	7.00	15.00	30.00	60.00	100
1934	20	PF65 1,800				
1935	364	PF63 350	PF65 500			
1935	560,000	15.00	42.00	85.00	175	325
1936	1,480,000	9.00	17.50	35.00	70.00	125
1936 Proof	—	—	—	—	—	—

KM# 8 6 PENCE
2.83 g., 0.500 Silver 0.0455 oz. ASW, 19.3 mm. **Ruler:** George VI **Obv:** Head left **Rev:** Huia bird sitting on branch **Edge:** Reeded

Date	Mintage	VF20	XF40	MS60	MS63	MS65
1937	1,280,000	8.00	16.00	32.00	65.00	125
1937	—	PF63 245	PF65 350			
1939	700,000	9.00	17.50	35.00	70.00	150
1939	—	PF63 245	PF65 350			
1940	800,000	8.00	17.50	35.00	70.00	150
1940	—	PF63 245	PF65 350			
1941	440,000	25.00	50.00	90.00	200	425
1941	—	PF63 385	PF65 550			
1942	360,000	25.00	50.00	90.00	200	425
1943	1,800,000	6.00	12.00	22.50	45.00	75.00
1944	1,160,000	7.00	12.50	22.50	45.00	75.00
1944	—	PF63 210	PF65 300			
1945	940,000	7.00	12.50	22.50	45.00	75.00
1945	—	PF63 210	PF65 300			
1946	—	PF63 210	PF65 300			
1946	2,120,000	6.00	12.00	22.50	45.00	60.00

KM# 8a 6 PENCE
2.83 g., Copper-Nickel, 19.3 mm. **Ruler:** George VI **Obv:** Head left **Rev:** Huia bird sitting on branch **Edge:** Reeded

Date	Mintage	VF20	XF40	MS60	MS63	MS65
1947	3,200,000	5.00	10.00	20.00	40.00	80.00
1947	Est. 20	PF63 210	PF65 300			

KM# 16 6 PENCE
2.83 g., Copper-Nickel, 19.3 mm. **Ruler:** George VI **Obv:** Head left **Rev:** Huia bird sitting on branch **Edge:** Reeded

Date	Mintage	VF20	XF40	MS60	MS63	MS65
1948	2,000,000	5.00	10.00	22.50	45.00	85.00
1948	—	PF63 195	PF65 275			
1950	800,000	15.00	30.00	62.00	125	220
1950	—	PF63 195	PF65 275			
1951	1,800,000	0.50	1.00	2.00	4.00	6.00
1951	—	PF63 195	PF65 275			
1952	3,200,000	3.50	7.50	15.00	30.00	50.00
1952	—	PF63 160	PF65 225			

KM# 26.1 6 PENCE
2.83 g., Copper-Nickel, 19.3 mm. **Ruler:** Elizabeth II **Obv:** Laureate bust right without shoulder strap **Rev:** Huia bird sitting on branch **Edge:** Reeded

Date	Mintage	VF20	XF40	MS60	MS63	MS65
1953	1,200,000	2.00	3.75	7.50	15.00	22.50
1953	7,000	PF63 5.00	PF65 7.00			
1953 Matte proof	—	PF63 85.00	PF65 125			
1954	1,200,000	2.50	5.00	10.00	20.00	35.00
1954	—	PF63 125	PF65 175			
1955	1,600,000	2.50	5.00	10.00	20.00	35.00
1955	—	PF63 140	PF65 200			
1957	Inc. below	15.00	90.00	200	400	650
1957	—	PF63 420	PF65 600			

KM# 26.2 6 PENCE
2.83 g., Copper-Nickel, 19.3 mm. **Ruler:** Elizabeth II **Obv:** Laureate bust right with shoulder strap **Rev:** Huia bird sitting on branch **Edge:** Reeded

Date	Mintage	VF20	XF40	MS60	MS63	MS65
1956	2,000,000	1.25	2.50	5.00	10.00	22.50
1956	—	PF63 140	PF65 200			
1957	2,400,000	0.20	1.25	2.50	5.00	10.00
1957	—	PF63 140	PF65 200			
1958	3,000,000	0.20	1.25	2.50	5.00	10.00
1958	—	PF63 140	PF65 200			
1959	2,000,000	0.20	1.25	2.50	5.00	10.00
1959	—	PF63 140	PF65 200			
1960	1,600,000	0.15	0.50	1.00	2.00	4.00
1960	—	PF63 140	PF65 200			
1961	800,000	0.15	0.50	1.00	2.00	4.00
1961	—	PF63 140	PF65 200			
1962	1,200,000	0.15	0.60	1.25	2.50	6.00
1962	—	PF63 140	PF65 200			
1963	800,000	0.15	0.50	1.00	2.00	4.00
1963	—	PF63 140	PF65 200			
1964	3,800,000	0.10	0.15	0.25	0.50	6.00
1964	—	PF63 125	PF65 175			
1965	8,600,000	—	0.15	0.25	0.50	1.00
1965 Broken wing	Inc. above	3.50	7.50	15.00	30.00	40.00
1965 Prooflike	25,000	—	—	—	—	1.00
1965 Proof	10	—	—	—	—	—

KM# 3 SHILLING
5.65 g., 0.500 Silver 0.0908 oz. ASW, 23.62 mm. **Ruler:** George V **Obv:** Crowned bust left **Rev:** Crouched Maori warrior left **Edge:** Reeded

Date	Mintage	VF20	XF40	MS60	MS63	MS65
1933	2,000,000	10.00	25.00	55.00	110	225
1933	Est. 20	PF65 1,600				
1934	3,400,000	10.00	25.00	55.00	110	225
1934	Est. 20	PF65 2,500				
1935	1,680,000	20.00	50.00	100	200	400
1935	364	PF63 350	PF65 500			

KM# 9 SHILLING
5.65 g., 0.500 Silver 0.0908 oz. ASW, 23.62 mm. **Ruler:** George VI **Obv:** Head left **Rev:** Crouched Maori warrior left **Edge:** Reeded

Date	Mintage	VF20	XF40	MS60	MS63	MS65
1937	890,000	10.00	17.50	35.00	70.00	125
1937	Est. 200	PF63 385	PF65 550			
1940	500,000	12.00	22.50	45.00	90.00	200
1940	—	PF63 385	PF65 550			
1941	360,000	30.00	62.00	125	250	500
1941	—	PF63 385	PF65 550			
1942	240,000	30.00	62.00	125	250	500
1942 Broken back	Est. 80000	75.00	160	325	650	—
1943	900,000	6.50	12.50	25.00	50.00	100
1944	480,000	7.00	15.00	30.00	60.00	150
1944	—	PF63 385	PF65 550			
1945	1,030,000	5.00	10.00	20.00	40.00	75.00
1945	—	PF63 385	PF65 550			
1946	1,060,000	5.00	10.00	18.50	37.50	72.00
1946	—	PF63 385	PF65 550			

KM# 9a SHILLING
5.65 g., Copper-Nickel, 23.62 mm. **Ruler:** George VI **Obv:** Head left **Rev:** Crouched Maori warrior left **Edge:** Reeded

Date	Mintage	VF20	XF40	MS60	MS63	MS65
1947	2,800,000	7.00	20.00	40.00	80.00	230
1947	Est. 20	PF63 245	PF65 425			

KM# 17 SHILLING
5.65 g., Copper-Nickel, 23.62 mm. **Ruler:** George VI **Obv:** Head left **Rev:** Crouched Maori warrior left **Edge:** Reeded

Date	Mintage	VF20	XF40	MS60	MS63	MS65
1948	1,000,000	7.00	20.00	40.00	80.00	180
1948	—	PF63 245	PF65 425			
1950	600,000	7.00	20.00	40.00	80.00	200
1950	—	PF63 245	PF65 425			
1951	1,200,000	7.00	17.50	35.00	70.00	150
1951	—	PF63 245	PF65 425			
1952	600,000	10.00	20.00	40.00	80.00	160
1952	—	PF63 245	PF65 425			

KM# 27.1 SHILLING
5.65 g., Copper-Nickel, 23.62 mm. **Ruler:** Elizabeth II **Obv:** Laureate bust right without shoulder strap **Rev:** Crouched Maori warrior left **Edge:** Reeded

Date	Mintage	VF20	XF40	MS60	MS63	MS65
1953	200,000	3.50	6.50	12.50	25.00	45.00
1953	14,000	PF63 6.00	PF65 9.00			
1953 Matte proof	—	PF63 85.00	PF65 125			
1954 Proof	—	—	—	—	—	—
1955	200,000	15.00	30.00	60.00	120	220
1955	—	PF63 250	PF65 450	PF67 950		

KM# 27.2 SHILLING

5.65 g., Copper-Nickel, 23.62 mm. **Ruler:** Elizabeth II **Obv:** Laureate bust right with shoulder strap **Rev:** Crouched Maori warrior left **Edge:** Reeded

Date	Mintage	VF20	XF40	MS60	MS63	MS65
1956	800,000	1.00	3.50	7.50	15.00	27.50
1956	—	PF63 245	PF65 425			
1957	800,000	1.00	3.50	7.50	15.00	27.50
1957	—	PF63 245	PF65 425			
1958	1,000,000	1.00	3.50	7.50	15.00	25.00
1958	—	PF63 245	PF65 425			
1958 Broken back	—	15.00	30.00	60.00	120	220
1959	600,000	1.00	3.00	6.00	12.50	25.50
1959	—	PF63 245	PF65 425			
1960	600,000	1.00	3.00	6.00	12.50	22.50
1960	—	PF63 245	PF65 425			
1961	400,000	1.00	3.00	6.00	12.00	20.00
1961	—	PF63 245	PF65 425			
1962	1,000,000	0.30	0.50	1.25	2.50	5.00
1962	—	PF63 245	PF65 425			
1962 No Horizon	—	20.00	17.50	35.00	70.00	110
1963	600,000	0.25	0.60	1.25	2.50	7.50
1963	—	PF63 245	PF65 425			
1964	3,400,000	0.15	0.25	0.50	1.00	2.00
1964	—	PF63 245	PF65 425			
1965	3,500,000	0.15	0.25	0.50	1.00	2.00
1965 Prooflike	25,000	—	—	—	—	1.25
1965 Proof	10	—	—	—	—	—

KM# 4 FLORIN

11.31 g., 0.500 Silver 0.1818 oz. ASW, 28.58 mm. **Ruler:** George V **Obv:** Crowned bust left **Rev:** Kiwi bird

Date	Mintage	VF20	XF40	MS60	MS63	MS65
1933	2,100,000	12.50	27.50	55.00	110	250
1933	Est. 20	PF65 700				
1934	2,850,000	12.50	27.50	55.00	110	225
1934	Est. 20	PF65 2,200				
1935	755,000	22.00	45.00	95.00	190	500
1935	364	PF63 420	PF65 600			
1936	150,000	70.00	200	400	900	2,000
1936	—	PF63 850	PF65 1,250			

KM# 10.1 FLORIN

11.31 g., 0.500 Silver 0.1818 oz. ASW, 28.58 mm. **Ruler:** George VI **Obv:** Head left **Rev:** Kiwi bird with rounded back

Date	Mintage	VF20	XF40	MS60	MS63	MS65
1937	1,190,000	12.50	27.50	55.00	110	170
1937	Est. 200	PF63 420	PF65 600			
1940	500,000	30.00	60.00	125	250	650
1940	—	PF63 550	PF65 800			
1941	820,000	9.00	17.50	35.00	70.00	150
1941	—	PF63 420	PF65 600			
1942	150,000	12.00	25.00	50.00	100	190
1943	1,400,000	9.00	17.50	35.00	70.00	170
1944	140,000	27.00	55.00	110	220	500
1944	—	PF63 550	PF65 800			
1945	515,000	9.00	17.50	35.00	70.00	180
1945	—	PF63 450	PF65 650			
1946	1,200,000	8.00	15.00	30.00	60.00	125
1946	—	PF63 450	PF65 650			

KM# 10.2 FLORIN

11.31 g., 0.500 Silver 0.1818 oz. ASW, 28.58 mm. **Ruler:** George VI **Obv:** Head left **Rev:** Flat back on Kiwi

Date	Mintage	VF20	XF40	MS60	MS63	MS65
1946	Est. 300000	40.00	125	250	500	800

KM# 10.2a FLORIN

11.31 g., Copper-Nickel, 28.58 mm. **Ruler:** George VI **Obv:** Head left **Rev:** Kiwi bird **Edge:** Reeded

Date	Mintage	VF20	XF40	MS60	MS63	MS65
1947	2,500,000	7.00	15.00	35.00	70.00	175
1947	—	PF63 320	PF65 450			

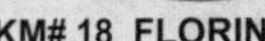

KM# 18 FLORIN

11.31 g., Copper-Nickel, 28.58 mm. **Ruler:** George VI **Obv:** Head left **Rev:** Kiwi bird

Date	Mintage	VF20	XF40	MS60	MS63	MS65
1948	1,750,000	7.00	15.00	35.00	70.00	175
1948	—	PF63 280	PF65 400			
1949	3,500,000	7.00	15.00	35.00	70.00	175
1949	—	PF63 280	PF65 400			
1950	3,500,000	2.50	5.00	10.00	20.00	35.00
1950	—	PF63 280	PF65 400			
1951	2,000,000	2.50	5.00	10.00	20.00	35.00
1951	—	PF63 280	PF65 400			

KM# 28.1 FLORIN

11.31 g., Copper-Nickel, 28.58 mm. **Ruler:** Elizabeth II **Obv:** Laureate bust right without shoulder strap **Rev:** Kiwi bird

Date	Mintage	VF20	XF40	MS60	MS63	MS65
1953	250,000	3.00	6.00	12.00	25.00	45.00
1953	7,000	PF63 9.00	PF65 13.00			
1953 Matte proof	—	PF63 125	PF65 180			
1954 Proof	—	—	—	—	—	—

KM# 28.2 FLORIN

11.31 g., Copper-Nickel, 28.58 mm. **Ruler:** Elizabeth II **Obv:** Laureate bust right with shoulder strap **Rev:** Kiwi bird

Date	Mintage	VF20	XF40	MS60	MS63	MS65
1961	1,500,000	1.50	2.50	5.00	10.00	20.00
1961	—	PF63 265	PF65 375			
1962	1,500,000	1.50	2.00	4.00	8.00	15.00
1962	—	PF63 265	PF65 375			
1963	100,000	1.50	2.50	5.00	10.00	20.00
1963	—	PF63 265	PF65 375			
1964	7,000,000	0.50	0.75	1.50	3.00	6.00
1964	—	PF63 265	PF65 375			
1965	9,450,000	0.25	0.35	0.50	1.00	1.50
1965 Prooflike	25,000	—	—	—	—	2.50
1965 Proof	10	—	—	—	—	—

KM# 5 1/2 CROWN

14.14 g., 0.500 Silver 0.2273 oz. ASW, 32 mm. **Ruler:** George V **Obv:** Crowned bust left **Rev:** Crowned shield within ornamental design

Date	Mintage	VF20	XF40	MS60	MS63	MS65
1933	2,000,000	20.00	45.00	100	200	325
1933	—	PF63 450	PF65 650			
1934	2,720,000	20.00	45.00	100	200	350
1934	Est. 20	PF65 2,350				
1935	612,000	40.00	80.00	175	350	650
1935	364	PF63 500	PF65 700			

KM# 11 1/2 CROWN

14.14 g., 0.500 Silver 0.2273 oz. ASW, 32 mm. **Ruler:** George VI **Obv:** Head left **Rev:** Crowned shield within ornamental design

Date	Mintage	VF20	XF40	MS60	MS63	MS65
1937	672,000	22.50	50.00	100	200	300
1937	200	PF63 500	PF65 700			
1941	776,000	12.50	25.00	50.00	100	200
1941	—	PF63 500	PF65 700			
1942	240,000	13.50	27.50	55.00	110	220
1943	1,120,000	9.00	17.50	37.50	75.00	150
1944	180,000	40.00	90.00	185	375	750
1944	—	PF63 500	PF65 700			
1945	420,000	15.00	30.00	60.00	120	240
1945	—	PF63 500	PF65 700			
1946	960,000	13.50	27.50	55.00	110	180
1946	—	PF63 500	PF65 700			

KM# 14 1/2 CROWN

14.14 g., 0.500 Silver 0.2273 oz. ASW, 32 mm. **Ruler:** George VI **Subject:** New Zealand Centennial **Obv:** Head left **Rev:** Radiant sun above city, standing figure in foreground

Date	Mintage	VF20	XF40	MS60	MS63	MS65
1940	100,800	7.00	12.00	20.00	35.00	60.00
1940	—	PF63 3,500	PF65 5,000			

KM# 11a 1/2 CROWN

Copper-Nickel, 32 mm. **Ruler:** George VI **Obv:** Head left **Rev:** Crowned shield within ornamental design

Date	Mintage	VF20	XF40	MS60	MS63	MS65
1947	1,600,000	5.00	30.00	60.00	120	200
1947	Est. 20	PF63 385	PF65 550			

KM# 19 1/2 CROWN
14.00 g., Copper-Nickel, 32 mm. **Ruler:** George VI **Obv:** Head left **Rev:** Crowned shield within ornamental design

Date	Mintage	VF20	XF40	MS60	MS63	MS65
1948	1,400,000	5.00	25.00	60.00	120	200
1948	—	**PF63** 350	**PF65** 500			
1949	2,800,000	5.00	25.00	60.00	120	200
1949	—	**PF63** 350	**PF65** 500			
1950	3,600,000	2.50	6.00	12.50	25.00	45.00
Note: K. G. close to dots						
1950	—	**PF63** 350	**PF65** 500			
1950	Inc. above	8.00	15.00	30.00	60.00	100
Note: K. G. close to rim						
1950	—	**PF63** 350	**PF65** 500			
1951	1,200,000	2.50	6.00	12.50	25.00	40.00
1951	—	**PF63** 350	**PF65** 500			

KM# 29.1 1/2 CROWN
Copper-Nickel, 32 mm. **Ruler:** Elizabeth II **Obv:** Laureate bust right without shoulder strap **Rev:** Crowned shield within ornamental design

Date	Mintage	VF20	XF40	MS60	MS63	MS65
1953	120,000	3.00	6.00	12.50	25.00	55.00
1953	7,000	**PF63** 15.00	**PF65** 20.00			
1953 Matte proof	—	**PF63** 175	**PF65** 245			

KM# 29.2 1/2 CROWN
Copper-Nickel, 32 mm. **Ruler:** Elizabeth II **Obv:** Laureate bust right with shoulder strap **Rev:** Crowned shield within ornamental design

Date	Mintage	VF20	XF40	MS60	MS63	MS65
1961	80,000	3.50	7.00	15.00	30.00	60.00
1961	—	**PF63** 315	**PF65** 450			
1962	600,000	1.00	1.25	2.50	4.50	8.00
1962	—	**PF63** 315	**PF65** 450			
1963	400,000	0.75	1.50	3.50	6.00	9.00
1963	—	**PF63** 315	**PF65** 450			
1965	200,000	1.00	1.25	2.50	4.00	6.00
1965 Prooflike	25,000	—	—	—	—	6.00
1965 Proof	10	—	—	—	—	—

KM# 6 CROWN
28.28 g., 0.500 Silver 0.4546 oz. ASW, 38.8 mm. **Ruler:** George V **Subject:** Treaty of Waitangi in 1840. **Obv:** Crowned bust left **Rev:** Crown above standing figures shaking hands **Note:** 364 Proofs issued in sets, 104 issued loose.

Date	Mintage	VF20	XF40	MS60	MS63	MS65
1935	660	2,000	3,000	3,500	4,000	5,500
1935	468	**PF63** 5,000	**PF65** 7,000	**PF67** 9,500		

KM# 22 CROWN
28.28 g., 0.500 Silver 0.4546 oz. ASW, 38.8 mm. **Ruler:** George VI **Subject:** Proposed Royal Visit **Obv:** Head left **Rev:** Silver fern leaf flanked by stars

Date	Mintage	VF20	XF40	MS60	MS63	MS65
1949	200,000	12.00	14.00	18.00	28.00	45.00
1949	Est. 3	**PF65** 12,500				

KM# 30 CROWN
Copper-Nickel, 38.8 mm. **Ruler:** Elizabeth II **Subject:** Queen Elizabeth II Coronation **Obv:** Laureate bust right **Rev:** Crowned monogram flanked by stars above design

Date	Mintage	VF20	XF40	MS60	MS63	MS65
1953	250,000	3.00	5.00	6.00	10.00	12.50
1953	7,000	**PF63** 60.00	**PF65** 90.00			
1953 Matte proof	—	**PF63** 450	**PF65** 650			
Note: Mintage: 4-10.						

DECIMAL COINAGE

100 Cents = 1 Dollar

KM# 31.1 CENT
2.07 g., Bronze, 17.53 mm. **Ruler:** Elizabeth II **Obv:** Young bust right **Rev:** Value within silver fern leaf **Note:** Rounded, high relief portrait.

Date	Mintage	VF20	XF40	MS60	MS63	MS65
1967 (l)	120,000,000	—	0.10	0.15	0.25	0.35
1967 (l) Prooflike	50,000	—	—	—	0.65	0.85
1967 Proof	10	—	—	—	—	—
1968	35,000	—	—	—	—	2.00
Note: Sets only.						
1968 Prooflike	40,000	—	—	—	—	2.50
1969	50,000	—	—	—	—	2.00
Note: Sets only						
1969 Prooflike	50,000	—	—	—	—	2.50
1970 (c)	10,060,000	—	0.10	0.25	0.50	1.00
1970 Prooflike	20,000	—	—	—	—	1.50
1970 Proof	10	—	—	—	—	—
1971 (c)	10,000,000	—	0.10	3.00	5.00	7.00
Note: Serifs on date numerals						
1971 (l) Sets only	15,000	—	—	—	—	5.00
Note: Without serifs						
1971 (l)	5,000	**PF65** 12.50				
1972 (c)	10,055,000	0.20	1.00	2.00	4.00	6.00
1972 (c)	8,045	**PF65** 5.00				
1973 (c)	15,055,000	—	0.10	2.00	4.00	6.00
1973 (c)	8,000	**PF65** 5.00				
1974 (c)	35,035,000	—	0.10	0.25	0.50	1.00
1974 (c)	8,000	**PF65** 4.00				
1975 (l)	60,015,000	—	0.10	0.25	0.50	1.00
1975 (l)	10,000	**PF65** 4.00				
1976 (l)	20,016,000	—	0.10	0.25	0.50	1.00
1976 (l)	11,000	**PF65** 4.00				
1977 Sets only	20,000	—	—	—	—	5.00
1977	12,000	**PF65** 6.00				
1978 (o)	15,023,000	—	0.10	0.25	0.50	1.00
1978 (o)	15,000	**PF65** 2.00				
1979 (o)	35,025,000	—	0.10	0.25	0.50	1.00
1979 (o)	16,000	**PF65** 2.00				
1980 (o)	40,000,000	—	0.10	0.25	0.50	1.00
Note: Oval 0 in date						
1980 (l)	27,000	—	—	0.25	0.50	1.00
Note: Round O in date. Sets only.						
1980 (l)	17,000	**PF65** 2.00				
Note: Round 0 in date.						
1981 (o)	10,000,000	—	0.10	0.25	0.50	1.00
Note: Oval hole in 8						
1981 (l)	25,000	—	—	0.25	0.50	1.00
Note: Round hole in 8. Sets only.						
1981 (l)	18,000	**PF65** 2.00				
Note: Round hole in 8						
1982 (o)	10,000,000	—	0.10	0.25	0.50	1.00
Note: Blunt-tipped 2						
1982 (l)	25,000	—	—	0.25	0.50	1.00
Note: Round-tipped 2. Sets only.						
1982 (l)	18,000	**PF65** 2.00				
Note: Round-tipped 2						
1983 (o)	40,000,000	—	0.10	0.25	0.50	1.00
Note: Round-top 3						
1983 (l)	25,000	—	0.10	0.25	0.50	1.00
Note: Flat-top 3. Sets only.						
1983 (l)	18,000	**PF65** 2.00				
Note: Flat-top 3						
1984 (l)	25,000	—	—	—	—	1.00
Note: Sets only.						
1984 (l)	15,000	**PF65** 2.00				
1985 (c)	20,000	—	—	—	—	1.00
Note: Sets only.						
1985 (c)	12,000	**PF65** 2.00				

KM# 31.2 CENT
2.07 g., Bronze, 17.53 mm. **Ruler:** Elizabeth II **Obv:** Crowned bust right **Rev:** Value within silver fern leaf **Note:** Die recut, low relief portrait.

Date	Mintage	VF20	XF40	MS60	MS63	MS65
1984 (o)	30,000,000	—	0.10	0.25	0.50	1.00
1985 (o)	40,000,000	—	0.10	0.25	0.50	1.00

KM# 58 CENT
2.07 g., Bronze, 17.53 mm. **Ruler:** Elizabeth II **Obv:** Crowned head right **Rev:** Value within silver fern leaf **Edge:** Plain

Date	Mintage	VF20	XF40	MS60	MS63	MS65
1986 (o)	25,000,000	—	0.10	0.25	0.50	1.00
1986 (l)	18,000	—	—	—	—	1.50
Note: Sets only.						
1986 (l)	10,000	**PF65** 1.00				
1987 (o)	27,500,000	—	0.10	0.25	0.50	1.00
1987 (l)	18,000	—	—	—	—	1.50
Note: Sets only.						
1987 (l)	10,000	**PF65** 1.00				
1988 (l)	15,000	—	—	—	—	6.50
Note: Sets only						
1988 (l)	9,000	**PF65** 2.00				

KM# 32.1 2 CENTS
4.14 g., Bronze, 21.08 mm. **Ruler:** Elizabeth II **Obv:** Young bust right **Rev:** Value within kowhai leaves **Note:** Rounded, high relief portrait.

Date	Mintage	VF20	XF40	MS60	MS63	MS65
1967 (l)	75,000,000	—	—	0.10	0.15	0.25
1967 (l) Prooflike	50,000	—	—	—	—	0.75
1967 (l) Proof	10	—	—	—	—	—
1968	35,000	—	—	—	—	3.00
Note: Sets only						
1968 Prooflike	40,000	—	—	—	—	1.25
1969 (c)	20,510,000	—	0.15	0.20	0.30	0.50
1969 Prooflike	50,000	—	—	—	—	1.25
1970 (c)	30,000	—	—	—	—	3.00
Note: Sets only						
1970 Prooflike	20,000	—	—	—	—	1.25
1970 Proof	10	—	—	—	—	—
1971 (c)	15,050,000	0.10	0.25	1.00	2.00	4.00
Note: Serifs on date numerals. Sets only.						
1971 (l)	15,000	—	—	2.00	3.00	5.00

Date	Mintage	VF20	XF40	MS60	MS63	MS65
Note: Without serifs						
1971 (l)	5,000	PF65 12.50				
1972 (c)	17,525,000	0.10	0.25	1.00	2.00	4.00
1972 (c)	8,045	PF65 5.00				
1973 (c)	38,565,000	0.10	0.25	1.00	2.00	4.00
1973 (c)	8,000	PF65 5.25				
1974 (c)	50,015,000	0.10	0.25	0.50	1.00	2.00
1974 (c)	8,000	PF65 3.00				
1975 (l)	20,015,000	—	0.10	0.25	1.00	1.50
1975 (l)	10,000	PF65 3.00				
1976 (l)	15,016,000	—	0.10	0.25	1.00	1.50
1976 (l)	11,000	PF65 3.00				
1977 (l)	20,000,000	—	0.10	0.25	1.00	1.50
1977 (l)	12,000	PF65 3.00				
1978 (o)	23,000	—	—	—	—	5.00
Note: Sets only						
1978 (o)	15,000	PF65 3.00				
1979 (o)	25,000	—	—	—	—	5.00
Note: Sets only						
1979 (o)	16,000	PF65 3.00				
1980 (o)	10,000,000	—	0.10	0.25	1.00	1.25
Note: Oval 0 in date						
1980 (l)	27,000	—	—	0.25	1.00	1.25
Note: Round O in date. Sets only.						
1980 (l)	17,000	PF65 3.00				
1981 (o)	25,000,000	—	0.10	0.25	1.00	1.25
Note: Oval hole in 8						
1981 (l)	25,000	—	—	0.25	1.00	1.25
Note: Round hole in 8. Sets only.						
1981 (l)	18,000	PF65 3.00				
1982 (o)	50,000,000	—	0.10	0.25	1.00	1.25
Note: Blunt open 2						
1982 (l)	25,000	—	—	0.25	1.00	1.25
Note: Pointed tight 2. Sets only.						
1982 (l)	18,000	PF65 3.00				
1983 (o)	15,000,000	—	0.10	0.25	1.00	1.25
Note: Round-topped 3						
1983 (l)	25,000	—	—	0.25	1.00	1.25
Note: Flat-topped 3. Sets only.						
1983 (l)	18,000	PF65 3.00				
1984 (l)	25,000	—	—	0.25	1.00	1.25
Note: Smooth shoulder folds. Sets only.						
1984 (l)	15,000	PF65 2.00				
1985 (c)	20,000	—	—	—	—	2.50
Note: Sets only.						
1985 (c)	12,000	PF65 2.00				

KM# 33 2 CENTS

4.14 g., Bronze, 21.08 mm. **Ruler:** Elizabeth II **Obv:** Young bust right **Rev:** Value within kowhai leaves **Note:** Mule with Bahamas KM#3.

Date	Mintage	VF20	XF40	MS60	MS63	MS65
ND-1967	Est. 50000	8.00	15.00	18.00	22.00	30.00

KM# 32.2 2 CENTS

4.14 g., Bronze, 21.08 mm. **Ruler:** Elizabeth II **Obv:** Crowned bust right **Rev:** Value within kowhai leaves **Note:** Die recut, low relief portrait.

Date	Mintage	VF20	XF40	MS60	MS63	MS65
1984 (o)	10,000,000	—	0.10	0.25	1.00	1.50
1985 (o)	22,500,000	—	0.10	0.25	1.00	1.50

KM# 59 2 CENTS

4.14 g., Bronze, 21.08 mm. **Ruler:** Elizabeth II **Obv:** Crowned head right **Rev:** Value within kowhai leaves

Date	Mintage	VF20	XF40	MS60	MS63	MS65
1986 (l)	18,000	—	—	—	—	6.50
Note: Sets only						
1986 (l)	10,000	PF65 7.50				
1987 (o)	36,250,000	—	0.10	0.25	1.00	1.25
1987 (l)	18,000	—	—	—	—	2.50
Note: Sets only.						
1987 (l)	10,000	PF65 2.00				
1988 (l)	15,000	—	—	—	—	6.50
Note: Sets only						
1988 (l)	9,000	PF65 1.25				

KM# 34.1 5 CENTS

2.83 g., Copper-Nickel, 19.43 mm. **Ruler:** Elizabeth II **Obv:** Young bust right **Rev:** Tuatara, value below **Edge:** Reeded **Note:** Rounded, high relief portrait. Many recalled and melted in 2006.

Date	Mintage	VF20	XF40	MS60	MS63	MS65
1967 (l)	26,000,000	—	0.10	0.15	0.20	0.50
1967 (l)	Inc. above	5.00	15.00	20.00	30.00	50.00
Note: Without sea line at right of Tuatara						
1967 (l)	Inc. above	5.00	15.00	20.00	30.00	50.00
Note: No tail triangle under chin						
1967 (l) Prooflike	50,000	—	—	—	—	1.00
1967 (l) Proof	10	—	—	—	—	—
1968	35,000	—	—	—	—	2.00
Note: Sets only						
1968 Prooflike	40,000	—	—	—	—	2.00
1969 (c)	10,260,000	—	0.10	0.20	0.50	1.00
1969 Prooflike	50,000	—	—	—	—	2.00
1970 (c)	11,202,000	—	0.10	0.20	0.50	1.00
1970 Prooflike	20,010	—	—	—	—	2.00
1970 Proof	10	—	—	—	—	—
1971 (c)	11,152,000	0.10	0.50	1.00	3.00	7.00
Note: Serifs on date numerals						
1971 (l)	15,000	—	0.50	1.00	3.00	6.00
Note: Without serifs						
1971 (l)	5,000	PF65 4.00				
1972 (c)	20,015,000	—	0.10	0.25	1.00	2.00
1972 (c)	8,000	PF65 4.00				
1973 (c)	4,038,999	—	0.10	0.25	1.00	2.00
Note: 2nd hardest date to find, after 2004						
1973 (c)	8,000	PF65 3.50				
1974 (c)	18,015,000	—	0.10	0.25	1.50	3.00
1974 (c)	8,000	PF65 3.50				
1975 (c)	32,015,000	—	0.10	0.20	0.50	1.00
1975 (c)	10,000	PF65 3.00				
1976 (l)	16,000	—	—	—	—	4.00
Note: Sets only						
1976 (l)	11,000	PF65 2.00				
1977 (l)	20,000	—	—	—	—	4.00
Note: Sets only						
1977 (l)	12,000	PF65 3.00				
1978 (o)	20,023,000	—	0.10	0.20	0.40	1.00
1978 (w)	15,000	PF65 3.00				
1979 (o)	25,000	—	—	—	—	4.00
Note: Sets only						
1979 (o)	16,000	PF65 3.00				
1980 (o)	12,000,000	—	0.10	0.20	0.50	1.00
Note: Oval 0 in date						
1980 (l)	27,000	—	—	0.20	0.50	1.00
Note: Round O in date. Sets only.						
1980 (l)	17,000	PF65 2.00				
1981 (o)	20,000,000	—	0.10	0.20	0.50	1.00
Note: Oval hole in 8						
1981 (l)	25,000	—	0.10	0.20	0.50	1.00
Note: Round hole in 8. Sets only.						
1981 (l)	18,000	PF65 2.00				
1982 (o)	50,000,000	—	0.10	0.20	0.50	1.00
Note: Blunt 2						
1982 (l)	25,000	—	0.25	0.50	1.00	2.00
Note: Pointed 2. Sets only.						
1982 (l)	18,000	PF65 2.00				
1983 (l)	25,000	—	—	—	—	3.00
Note: Sets only						
1983 (l)	18,000	PF65 3.00				
1984 (l)	25,000	—	—	—	—	3.00
Note: Sets only						
1984 (l)	15,000	PF65 3.00				
1985 (c)	20,000	—	—	—	—	2.00
Note: Sets only.						
1985 (c)	12,000	PF65 2.00				

KM# 64 5 CENTS

Copper-Nickel **Ruler:** Elizabeth II **Obv:** Young bust right **Rev:** Small ship **Note:** Mule with Canada KM#77.

Date	Mintage	VF20	XF40	MS60	MS63	MS65
1981 (o) Rare; Serif on 1	—	—	—	—	—	—

KM# 34.2 5 CENTS

2.83 g., Copper-Nickel, 19.43 mm. **Ruler:** Elizabeth II **Obv:** Crowned bust right **Rev:** Tuatara, value below **Edge:** Reeded **Note:** Die recut, low relief.

Date	Mintage	VF20	XF40	MS60	MS63	MS65
1985 (o)	14,000,000	—	0.10	0.25	0.50	1.00

KM# 60 5 CENTS

2.83 g., Copper-Nickel, 19.43 mm. **Ruler:** Elizabeth II **Obv:** Crowned head right **Rev:** Value below tuatara **Edge:** Reeded **Note:** Many recalled and melted in 2006.

Date	Mintage	VF20	XF40	MS60	MS63	MS65
1986 (o)	18,000,000	—	0.10	0.25	0.50	1.00
1986 (l)	18,000	—	—	—	—	2.00
Note: Sets only.						
1986 (l)	10,000	PF65 3.00				
1987 (o)	40,000,000	—	0.10	0.25	0.50	1.00
1987 (l)	18,000	—	—	—	—	2.50
Note: Sets only.						
1987 (l)	10,000	PF65 3.00				
1988 (c)	16,000,000	—	0.10	0.25	0.50	1.00
Note: Rounded relief						
1988 (l)	15,000	—	—	1.00	2.00	2.50
Note: Flat-topped relief. Sets only.						
1988 (l)	9,000	PF65 3.00				
1989 (o)	36,000,000	—	0.10	0.25	0.50	1.00
1989 (c)	15,000	—	—	—	—	1.50
Note: Sets only.						
1989 (c)	8,500	PF65 3.00				
1990 (c)	18,000	—	—	—	—	3.50
Note: Sets only						
1990 (c)	10,000	PF65 3.00				
1991 (c)	20,000	—	—	—	—	3.50
Note: Sets only						
1991 (c)	9,000	PF65 4.00				
1992 (l)	15,000	—	—	—	—	3.50
Note: Sets only						
1992 (l)	9,000	PF65 4.00				
1993 (l)	15,000	—	—	—	—	3.50
Note: Sets only						
1993 (l)	10,000	PF65 4.00				
1994 (l)	20,026,000	—	0.10	0.25	0.50	1.00
1994 (l)	10,000	PF65 3.00				
1995 (l)	40,010,000	—	0.10	0.25	0.50	1.00
1995 (l)	4,000	PF65 3.00				
1996 (n)	19,008,000	—	0.10	0.25	0.50	1.00
1996 (l)	4,000	PF65 3.00				
1997 (n)	14,000,000	—	0.10	0.25	0.50	1.00
1997 (l)	2,500	PF65 5.00				
1998 (p)	8,000,000	—	0.10	0.25	0.50	1.00
1998 (l)	2,000	PF65 3.00				

KM# 72 5 CENTS

2.83 g., Copper-Nickel, 19.43 mm. **Ruler:** Elizabeth II **Subject:** 1990 Anniversary Celebrations **Obv:** Crowned head right **Rev:** Stylized kotuku bird **Edge:** Reeded

Date	Mintage	VF20	XF40	MS60	MS63	MS65
1990	10,000	—	—	—	—	6.00
Note: Sets only.						

KM# 72a 5 CENTS

3.27 g., 0.925 Silver 0.0972 oz. ASW, 19.43 mm. **Ruler:** Elizabeth II **Obv:** Crowned head right **Rev:** Stylized kotuku bird

Date	Mintage	VF20	XF40	MS60	MS63	MS65
1990	7,000	PF65 12.00				

KM# 116 5 CENTS

2.83 g., Copper-Nickel, 19.43 mm. **Ruler:** Elizabeth II **Obv:** Head with tiara right **Rev:** Value below tuatara **Edge:** Reeded **Note:** Many recalled and melted in 2006.

Date	Mintage	VF20	XF40	MS60	MS63	MS65
1999 (p)	25,040,000	—	0.10	0.25	0.50	1.00
1999 (p) Wart on nose	—	—	—	1.50	3.50	6.50
Note: Die crack error						
1999 (l) Sets only	3,199	—	—	—	—	6.00
1999 (l)	1,800	PF65 3.00				
2000 (o)	26,000,000	—	0.10	0.25	0.50	1.00
2000 (c) Sets only	3,000	—	—	—	—	8.00
2000 (c)	1,500	PF65 14.00				

KM# 35 10 CENTS

5.66 g., Copper-Nickel, 23.62 mm. **Ruler:** Elizabeth II **Obv:** Young bust right **Rev:** Value above Maori mask, koruru **Edge:** Reeded **Note:** Many recalled and melted in 2006.

Date	Mintage	VF20	XF40	MS60	MS63	MS65
1967 (l)	17,000,000	—	0.10	0.15	0.25	0.50
1967 (l) Prooflike	50,000	—	—	—	—	1.00
1967 (l) Proof	10	—	—	—	—	—
1968	35,000	—	1.00	—	—	2.50
Note: Sets only						

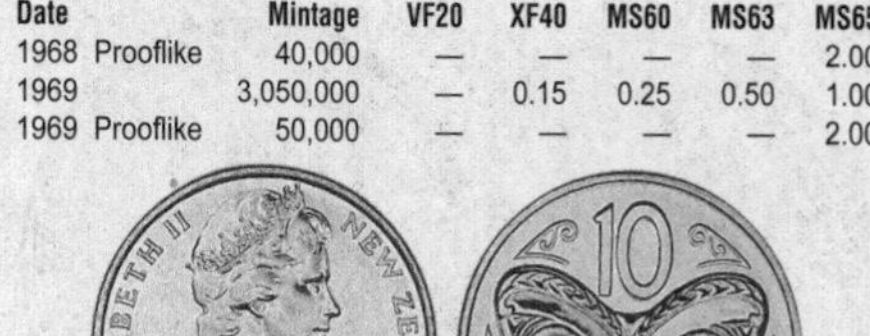

Date	Mintage	VF20	XF40	MS60	MS63	MS65
1968 Prooflike	40,000	—	—	—	—	2.00
1969	3,050,000	—	0.15	0.25	0.50	1.00
1969 Prooflike	50,000	—	—	—	—	2.00

KM# 41.1 10 CENTS

5.66 g., Copper-Nickel, 23.62 mm. **Ruler:** Elizabeth II **Obv:** Young bust right **Rev:** Value above Maori mask, koruru **Edge:** Reeded **Note:** Rounded, high relief portrait. Many recalled and melted in 2006.

Date	Mintage	VF20	XF40	MS60	MS63	MS65
1970	2,046,000	—	0.15	0.25	0.50	1.00
1970 Prooflike	20,000	—	—	—	—	1.50
1970 Proof	10	—	—	—	—	—
1971 (c)	2,800,000	0.10	5.00	10.00	20.00	35.00
Note: Serifs on date numerals						
1971 (l)	15,000	—	—	1.00	2.00	3.00
Note: Without serifs						
1971 (l)	5,000	PF65 5.00				
1972 (c)	2,039,000	—	0.15	0.25	1.00	2.00
1972 (c)	8,000	PF65 5.00				
1973 (c)	3,525,000	—	0.10	0.25	1.00	2.00
1973 (c)	8,000	PF65 3.00				
1974 (c)	4,619,000	—	0.10	0.25	1.00	2.00
1974 (c)	8,000	PF65 3.00				
1975 (l)	7,015,000	—	0.10	0.25	1.00	2.00
1975 (l)	10,000	PF65 3.00				
1976 (l)	5,016,000	—	0.10	0.25	1.00	2.00
1976 (l)	11,000	PF65 3.00				
1977 (l)	5,000,000	—	0.10	0.25	1.00	2.00
1977 (l)	12,000	PF65 3.00				
1978 (o)	16,023,000	—	0.10	0.25	1.00	2.00
1978 (o)	15,000	PF65 3.00				
1979 (o)	6,000,000	—	0.10	0.20	0.50	1.00
1979 (o)	16,000	PF65 3.00				
1980 (o)	28,000,000	—	0.10	0.20	0.50	1.00
Note: Oval 0 in date						
1980 (l)	27,000	—	—	0.20	0.50	1.00
Note: Round O in date. Sets only.						
1980 (l)	17,000	PF65 3.00				
1981 (o)	5,000,000	—	0.10	0.20	0.50	1.00
Note: Oval holes in 8						
1981 (l)	25,000	—	0.10	0.20	0.50	1.00
Note: Round holes in 8. Sets only.						
1981 (l)	18,000	PF65 3.00				
1982 (o)	18,000,000	—	0.10	0.20	0.50	1.00
Note: Blunt open 2						
1982 (l)	25,000	—	—	0.25	1.00	2.00
Note: Point-tipped 2. Sets only.						
1982 (l)	18,000	PF65 3.00				
1983 (l)	25,000	—	—	—	—	3.00
Note: Sets only						
1983 (l)	18,000	PF65 3.00				
1984 (l)	25,000	—	—	—	—	3.00
Note: Sets only						
1984 (l)	15,000	PF65 4.00				
1985 (c)	20,000	—	—	—	—	3.00
Note: Sets only.						
1985 (c)	12,000	PF65 4.00				

KM# 41.2 10 CENTS

5.66 g., Copper-Nickel, 23.62 mm. **Ruler:** Elizabeth II **Obv:** Crowned bust right **Rev:** Value above Maori mask, koruru **Edge:** Reeded **Note:** Recut due, low relief.

Date	Mintage	VF20	XF40	MS60	MS63	MS65
1985 (o)	8,000,000	—	—	0.50	1.00	2.00
Note: Wiry hair, bushy eyebrow						

KM# 61 10 CENTS

5.66 g., Copper-Nickel, 23.62 mm. **Ruler:** Elizabeth II **Obv:** Crowned head right **Rev:** Value above Maori mask, koruru **Edge:** Reeded **Note:** Many recalled and melted in 2006.

Date	Mintage	VF20	XF40	MS60	MS63	MS65
1986 (l)	18,000	—	—	—	—	2.50
Note: Sets only						
1986 (l)	10,000	PF65 4.00				
1987 (o)	21,000,000	—	0.10	0.20	0.50	1.00
1987 (l)	18,000	—	—	—	—	2.00
Note: Sets only.						
1987 (l)	10,000	PF65 3.00				
1988 (c)	26,702,000	—	0.10	0.20	0.50	1.00
Note: Rounded relief						
1988 (l)	15,000	—	—	0.25	1.00	2.00
Note: Flat relief. Sets only.						
1988 (l)	9,000	PF65 3.00				
1989 (o)	9,000,000	—	—	0.20	0.50	1.00
1989 (c)	14,600	—	—	—	—	2.50
Note: Sets only.						
1989 (c)	8,500	PF65 3.00				
1990 (c)	18,000	—	—	—	—	2.00
Note: Sets only						
1990 (c)	10,000	PF65 3.00				
1991 (c)	20,000	—	—	—	—	2.00
Note: Sets only						
1991 (c)	15,000	PF65 3.00				
1992 (l)	15,000	—	—	—	—	2.00
Note: Sets only						
1992 (l)	9,000	PF65 3.00				
1993 (l)	15,000	—	—	—	—	2.00
Note: Sets only						
1993 (l)	10,000	PF65 3.00				
1994 (l)	7,000	—	—	—	—	2.00
Note: Sets only						
1994 (l)	4,600	PF65 3.00				
1995 (l)	6,000	—	—	—	—	1.50
Note: Sets only						
1995 (l)	3,560	PF65 3.00				
1996	12,960,000	—	—	0.20	0.50	1.00
1996 (l)	2,569	PF65 3.00				
1997 (n)	8,000,000	—	—	0.20	0.50	1.00
1997 (l)	2,132	PF65 3.00				
1998	4,000	—	—	—	—	6.00
Note: Sets only						
1998 (l)	2,000	PF65 3.00				

KM# 73 10 CENTS

5.66 g., Copper-Nickel, 23.62 mm. **Ruler:** Elizabeth II **Subject:** 1990 Anniversary Celebrations **Obv:** Crowned head right **Rev:** Value above sailboats within rainbow design **Edge:** Reeded

Date	Mintage	VF20	XF40	MS60	MS63	MS65
1990 Sets only	10,000	—	—	—	—	5.00

KM# 73a 10 CENTS

6.53 g., 0.925 Silver 0.1942 oz. ASW, 23.62 mm. **Ruler:** Elizabeth II **Subject:** 1990 Anniversary Celebrations **Obv:** Crowned head right **Rev:** Value above sailboats within rainbow design

Date	Mintage	VF20	XF40	MS60	MS63	MS65
1990	7,000	PF65 10.00				

KM# 117 10 CENTS

5.66 g., Copper-Nickel, 23.62 mm. **Ruler:** Elizabeth II **Obv:** Head with tiara right **Rev:** Value above koruru **Edge:** Reeded **Note:** Many recalled and melted in 2006.

Date	Mintage	VF20	XF40	MS60	MS63	MS65
1999 (l) Sets only	3,199	—	—	—	—	6.00
1999 (l)	1,800	PF65 7.00				
2000 (o)	11,000,000	—	0.10	0.20	0.30	0.50
2000 (l) Sets only	4,500	—	—	—	—	7.00
2000 (l)	1,500	PF65 12.00				

KM# 36.1 20 CENTS

11.31 g., Copper-Nickel, 28.58 mm. **Ruler:** Elizabeth II **Obv:** Young bust right **Rev:** Value below Kiwi bird with sprigs above **Edge:** Reeded **Note:** Rounded, high relief portrait. Prev. KM#36. Many recalled and melted in 2006.

Date	Mintage	VF20	XF40	MS60	MS63	MS65
1967 (l)	13,000,000	—	0.20	0.30	0.50	1.00
1967 (l) Prooflike	50,000	—	—	—	—	1.00
1967 (l) Proof	10	—	—	—	—	—
1968	35,000	—	—	—	—	3.00
Note: Sets only						
1968 Prooflike	40,000	—	—	—	—	2.50
1969	2,500,000	—	0.20	0.50	1.00	1.50
1969 Prooflike	50,000	—	—	—	—	2.50
1970	30,000	—	—	—	—	3.00
Note: Sets only						
1970 Prooflike	20,000	—	—	—	—	3.00
1970 Proof	10	—	—	—	—	—
1971 (c)	1,600,000	1.00	5.00	—	20.00	30.00
Note: Serifs on date numerals						
1971 (l)	15,000	—	—	—	3.00	4.00
Note: Without serifs. Sets only.						
1971 (l)	5,000	PF65 10.00				
1972 (c)	1,531,000	—	0.20	0.50	1.00	2.00
1972 (c)	8,000	PF65 12.50				
1973 (c)	3,043,000	—	0.20	0.50	1.00	2.00
1973 (c)	8,000	PF65 7.00				
1974 (c)	4,527,000	—	0.20	1.00	2.00	5.00
1974 (c)	8,000	PF65 8.00				
1975 (l)	5,015,000	—	0.20	0.50	1.00	2.00
Note: About 15-20 examples are known struck on a Hong Kong $2 planchet						
1975 (l)	12,000	PF65 6.50				
1976 (l)	7,516,000	—	0.20	0.50	1.00	2.00
1976 (l)	11,000	PF65 6.00				
1977 (l)	7,500,000	—	0.20	0.50	1.00	2.00
1977 (l)	12,000	PF65 6.50				
1978 (o)	2,523,000	—	0.20	0.50	1.00	2.00
1978 (o)	15,000	PF65 5.00				
1979 (o)	8,025,000	—	0.20	0.50	1.00	2.00
1979 (o)	16,000	PF65 5.00				
1980 (o)	9,000,000	—	0.15	0.25	1.00	2.00
Note: Oval O in date						
1980 (l)	27,000	—	0.15	0.25	0.50	1.00
Note: Round O in date. Sets only.						
1980 (l)	17,000	PF65 5.00				
1981 (o)	7,500,000	—	0.15	0.25	0.50	1.00
Note: Oval holes in 8						
1981 (l)	25,000	—	—	0.50	1.00	2.00
Note: Round holes in 8. Sets only.						
1981 (l)	18,000	PF65 4.00				
1982 (o)	17,500,000	—	0.15	0.50	1.00	2.00
Note: Blunt 2						
1982 (l)	25,000	—	—	0.25	0.50	1.00
Note: Pointed 2. Sets only.						
1982 (l)	18,000	PF65 5.00				
1983 (o)	2,500,000	—	0.15	0.25	1.50	3.00
Note: Round topped 3						
1983 (l)	25,000	—	—	0.25	0.50	1.00
Note: Flat topped 3. Sets only.						
1983 (l)	18,000	PF65 4.00				
1984 (l)	25,000	—	—	—	—	1.00
Note: Sets only.						
1984 (l)	18,000	PF65 4.00				
1985 (c)	20,000	—	—	0.25	0.50	1.00
Note: Round tip 5. Sets only.						
1985 (c)	12,000	PF65 4.00				

KM# 36.2 20 CENTS

11.31 g., Copper-Nickel, 28.58 mm. **Ruler:** Elizabeth II **Obv:** Young bust right **Rev:** Value below Kiwi bird with sprigs above **Edge:** Reeded **Note:** Die recut, low relief. Many recalled and melted in 2006.

Date	Mintage	VF20	XF40	MS60	MS63	MS65
1984 (o)	1,500,000	—	0.15	0.25	1.00	2.00
1985 (o)	6,000,000	—	0.15	0.25	1.00	2.00

KM# 62 20 CENTS

11.31 g., Copper-Nickel, 28.58 mm. **Ruler:** Elizabeth II **Obv:** Crowned head right **Rev:** Value below Kiwi bird with sprigs above **Edge:** Reeded

Date	Mintage	VF20	XF40	MS60	MS63	MS65
1986 (o)	12,500,000	—	0.15	0.25	0.50	1.00
1986 (l)	18,000	—	—	—	—	2.00
Note: Sets only.						
1986 (l)	10,000	PF65 4.00				
1987 (o)	14,000,000	—	0.15	0.25	0.50	1.00
1987 (l)	18,000	—	—	—	—	2.00
Note: Sets only.						
1987 (l)	10,000	PF65 4.00				
1988 (c)	12,500,000	—	0.15	0.25	0.50	1.00
Note: Rounded relief.						
1988 (l)	15,000	—	—	0.25	1.00	2.00
Note: Flat releif. Sets only.						
1988 (l)	9,000	PF65 4.00				
1989 (o)	5,000,000	—	0.15	0.25	0.50	1.00
1989 (c)	8,500	PF65 4.00				
1989 (c)	15,000	—	—	—	—	2.00
Note: Sets only.						

KM# 74 20 CENTS

11.31 g., Copper-Nickel, 28.58 mm. **Ruler:** Elizabeth II **Subject:** 1990 Anniversary Celebrations **Obv:** Crowned head right **Rev:** Ship, H.M.S. Tory

Date	Mintage	VF20	XF40	MS60	MS63	MS65
1990 (c)	10,000	—	—	—	—	7.00
Note: Sets only.						

KM# 74a 20 CENTS

13.07 g., 0.925 Silver 0.3887 oz. ASW, 28.58 mm. **Ruler:** Elizabeth II **Subject:** 1990 Anniversary Celebrations **Obv:** Crowned head right **Rev:** Ship, H.M.S. Tory

Date	Mintage	VF20	XF40	MS60	MS63	MS65
1990 (c)	7,000	PF65 12.00				

KM# 81 20 CENTS

11.31 g., Copper-Nickel, 28.58 mm. **Ruler:** Elizabeth II **Obv:** Crowned head right **Rev:** Value below Pukaki **Edge:** Reeded **Note:** Many recalled and melted in 2006.

Date	Mintage	VF20	XF40	MS60	MS63	MS65
1990 (l)	5,000,000	—	0.20	0.30	0.50	1.00
1990 (c)	18,000	—	—	—	—	2.00
Note: Sets only.						
1990 (c)	10,000	PF65 4.00				
1991 (c)	20,000	—	—	—	—	3.00
Note: Sets only						
1991 (c)	15,000	PF65 4.00				
1992 (l)	15,000	—	—	—	—	3.50
Note: Sets only						
1992 (l)	9,000	PF65 4.00				
1993 (l)	15,000	—	—	—	—	3.50
Note: Sets only						
1993 (l)	10,000	PF65 4.00				
1994 (l)	7,000	—	—	—	—	3.50
Note: Sets only						
1994 (l)	4,600	PF65 5.00				
1995 (l)	6,000	—	—	—	—	3.50
Note: Sets only						
1995 (l)	3,560	PF65 7.00				
1996 (l)	5,150	—	—	—	—	4.00
Note: Sets only						
1996 (l)	2,569	PF65 5.00				
1997 (l)	4,150	—	—	—	—	4.00
Note: Sets only						
1997 (l)	2,132	PF65 8.00				
1998 (l)	4,000	—	—	—	—	4.00
Note: Sets only						
1998 (l)	2,000	PF65 7.00				

KM# 81a 20 CENTS

28.25 g., 0.925 Silver 0.8401 oz. ASW Piefort, 28.58 mm. **Ruler:** Elizabeth II **Subject:** Maori Language **Obv:** Crowned head right **Rev:** Value below Pukaki

Date	Mintage	VF20	XF40	MS60	MS63	MS65
1995 (l)	Est. 2500	PF65 45.00				

KM# 118 20 CENTS

11.31 g., Copper-Nickel, 28.58 mm. **Ruler:** Elizabeth II **Obv:** Head with tiara right **Rev:** Value below Pukaki **Edge:** Reeded **Note:** Many recalled and melted in 2006.

Date	Mintage	VF20	XF40	MS60	MS63	MS65
1999 (l) Sets only	3,199	—	—	—	—	7.00
1999 (l)	1,800	PF65 10.00				
2000 (l) Sets only	3,000	—	—	—	—	7.00
2000 (l)	1,500	PF65 10.00				

KM# 37.1 50 CENTS

13.61 g., Copper-Nickel, 31.75 mm. **Ruler:** Elizabeth II **Obv:** Young bust right **Rev:** H.M.S. Endeavour and value **Edge:** Segmented reeding **Note:** Rounded, high relief portrait. Many recalled and melted in 2006.

Date	Mintage	VF20	XF40	MS60	MS63	MS65
1967 (l)	10,000,000	—	0.30	0.50	1.00	1.50
1967 (l)	Est. 750000	4.00	7.00	12.00	25.00	75.00
Note: Dot above 1						
1967 (l) Prooflike	50,000	—	—	—	—	2.00
1967 (l) Proof	10	—	—	—	—	—
1968	35,000	—	—	—	—	2.00
Note: Sets only						
1968 Prooflike	40,000	—	—	—	—	3.00
1970	30,000	—	—	—	—	2.00
Note: Sets only						
1970 Prooflike	20,000	—	—	—	—	3.00
1970 Proof	10	—	—	—	—	—
1971 (c)	1,123,000	1.00	3.00	7.00	15.00	30.00
Note: Serifs on date numerals						
1971 (l)	15,000	—	0.50	1.00	2.00	4.00
Note: Without serifs. Sets only.						
1971 (l)	5,000	PF65 25.00				
1972 (c)	1,423,000	—	0.50	1.00	2.00	3.50
1972 (c)	8,045	PF65 10.00				
1973 (c)	2,523,000	—	0.50	1.00	2.00	3.50
1973 (c)	8,000	PF65 7.00				
1974 (c)	1,215,000	—	0.50	1.00	2.00	3.50
1974 (c)	8,000	PF65 7.00				
1975 (l)	3,815,000	—	0.50	0.75	1.50	3.00
1975 (l)	10,000	PF65 6.00				
1976 (l)	2,016,000	—	0.50	0.75	1.50	3.00
1976 (l)	11,000	PF65 6.00				
1977 (l)	2,000,000	—	0.50	0.75	1.50	3.00
1977 (l)	12,000	PF65 6.00				
1978 (o)	2,023,000	—	0.50	0.75	1.50	3.00
1978 (o)	15,000	PF65 5.00				
1979 (o)	2,425,000	—	0.50	0.75	1.50	3.00
1979 (o)	16,000	PF65 5.00				
1980 (o)	8,000,000	0.30	0.50	0.75	1.50	3.00
Note: Thin 8 in date						
1980 (l)	27,000	—	0.50	0.75	1.25	2.00
Note: Thick 8 in date. Sets only.						
1980 (l)	17,000	PF65 5.00				
1981 (o)	4,000,000	0.30	0.50	0.75	1.50	3.00
Note: Blunt end on 9, oval holes in 8						
1981 (l)	25,000	—	0.50	0.75	1.25	2.00
Note: Pointed end on 9, round holes in 8. Sets only.						
1981 (l)	18,000	PF65 5.00				
1982 (o)	6,000,000	—	0.50	0.75	1.50	3.00
Note: Blunt end on 2						
1982 (l)	25,000	—	0.50	0.75	1.50	3.00
Note: Pointed end on 2. Sets only.						
1982 (l)	18,000	PF65 5.00				
1983 (l)	25,000	—	—	0.75	1.50	3.00
Note: Sets only.						
1983 (l)	18,000	PF65 5.00				
1984 (l)	25,000	—	0.50	0.75	1.50	3.00
Note: Sets only.						
1984 (l)	15,000	PF65 5.00				
1985 (c)	20,000	—	0.50	0.75	1.50	3.00
Note: Sets only.						
1985 (c)	12,000	PF65 5.00				

KM# 39 50 CENTS

13.61 g., Copper-Nickel, 31.75 mm. **Ruler:** Elizabeth II **Subject:** 200th Anniversary - Captain Cook's Voyage **Obv:** Young bust right **Rev:** Ship, H.M.S. Endeavour **Edge Lettering:** Cook Bi-Centenary 1769-1969 **Note:** Similar to KM#37.

Date	Mintage	VF20	XF40	MS60	MS63	MS65
1969	50,000	—	—	1.00	1.50	3.00
1969 Prooflike	50,000	—	—	—	—	3.50

KM# 37.2 50 CENTS

13.61 g., Copper-Nickel, 31.75 mm. **Ruler:** Elizabeth II **Obv:** Crowned bust right **Rev:** H.M.S. Endeavour and value **Edge:** Segmented reeding **Note:** Recut die, low relief. Many recalled and melted in 2006.

Date	Mintage	VF20	XF40	MS60	MS63	MS65
1984 (o)	2,000,000	—	—	0.50	1.50	3.00
1985 (o)	2,000,000	—	—	0.50	1.50	3.00

KM# 95 50 CENTS

Nickel **Ruler:** Elizabeth II **Obv:** Young bust right **Rev:** Voyageur, date and value below **Note:** Mule with Canada Dollar, KM#120.

Date	Mintage	VF20	XF40	MS60	MS63	MS65
1985 6 known	—	1,200	1,900	—	—	—

KM# 63 50 CENTS

13.61 g., Copper-Nickel, 31.75 mm. **Ruler:** Elizabeth II **Obv:** Crowned head right **Rev:** H.M.S. Endeavour and value **Edge:** Segmented reeding **Note:** Many recalled and melted in 2006.

Date	Mintage	VF20	XF40	MS60	MS63	MS65
1986 (o)	5,200,000	—	0.50	0.65	1.20	2.00
1986 (l)	18,000	—	—	—	—	2.50
Note: Sets only.						
1986 (l)	10,000	PF65 5.00				
1987 (o)	3,600,000	—	0.50	0.65	1.20	2.00
1987 (l)	18,000	—	—	—	—	2.00
Note: Sets only.						
1987 (l)	10,000	PF65 5.00				
1988 (c)	8,800,000	—	0.50	0.65	1.20	2.00
Note: Rounded relief. Two die varieties known.						
1988 (l)	15,000	—	—	0.75	1.25	2.50
Note: Flat releif. Sets only.						
1988 (l)	9,000	PF65 5.00				
1989 (c)	15,000	—	—	—	—	2.50
Note: Sets only						
1989 (c)	8,500	PF65 5.00				
1990 (c)	18,000	—	—	—	—	3.50
Note: Sets only						
1990 (c)	10,000	PF65 5.00				
1991 (c)	20,000	—	—	—	—	2.50
Note: Sets only						
1991 (c)	15,000	PF65 5.00				
1992 (l)	15,000	—	—	—	—	3.50
Note: Sets only						
1992 (l)	9,000	PF65 5.00				
1993 (l)	15,000	—	—	—	—	3.50
Note: Sets only						
1993 (l)	10,000	PF65 5.00				
1995 (l)	10,000	—	—	—	—	3.50
Note: Sets only						
1995 (l)	4,000	PF65 5.00				
1996 (l)	5,150	—	—	—	—	3.50
Note: Sets only						
1996 (l)	2,569	PF65 5.00				
1997 (l)	4,150	—	—	—	—	3.50
Note: Sets only						
1997 (l)	2,132	PF65 5.00				
1998 (l)	4,000	—	—	—	—	3.50
Note: Sets only						
1998 (l)	2,000	PF65 5.00				

KM# 75 50 CENTS

13.61 g., Copper-Nickel, 31.75 mm. **Ruler:** Elizabeth II **Subject:** 1990 Anniversary Celebrations **Obv:** Crowned head right **Rev:** Child with shovel sitting beside tree, value slanted at right

Date	Mintage	VF20	XF40	MS60	MS63	MS65
1990 (c)	10,000	—	—	—	—	8.00
Note: Sets only.						

KM# 75a 50 CENTS
15.74 g., 0.925 Silver 0.4681 oz. ASW, 31.75 mm. **Ruler:** Elizabeth II **Subject:** 1990 Anniversary Celebrations **Obv:** Crowned head right **Rev:** Child with shovel sitting beside tree with slanted value at right

Date	Mintage	VF20	XF40	MS60	MS63	MS65
1990 (c)	7,000	PF65 20.00				

Note: Sets only.

KM# 90 50 CENTS
Bi-Metallic Aluminum-Bronze center in Copper-Nickel ring, 32 mm. **Ruler:** Elizabeth II **Subject:** H.M.S. Endeavour **Obv:** Crowned head right within circle **Rev:** Sailing ship within circle

Date	Mintage	VF20	XF40	MS60	MS63	MS65
1994	52,500	—	—	—	10.00	15.00

KM# 90a 50 CENTS
Bi-Metallic Aluminum-Bronze center in Silver ring., 32 mm. **Ruler:** Elizabeth II **Subject:** H.M.S. Endeavour **Obv:** Crowned head right within circle **Rev:** Sailing ship within circle

Date	Mintage	VF20	XF40	MS60	MS63	MS65
1994	10,000	PF65 25.00				

KM# 90b 50 CENTS
Bi-Metallic .916 Gold center in .375 Gold ring, 32 mm. **Ruler:** Elizabeth II **Subject:** H.M.S. Endeavour **Obv:** Crowned head right within circle **Rev:** Sailing ship within circle

Date	Mintage	VF20	XF40	MS60	MS63	MS65
1994	500	PF65 275				

KM# 119 50 CENTS
13.61 g., Copper-Nickel, 31.75 mm. **Ruler:** Elizabeth II **Obv:** Head with tiara right **Rev:** H.M.S. Endeavour and value **Edge:** Segmented reeding **Note:** Many recalled and melted in 2006.

Date	Mintage	VF20	XF40	MS60	MS63	MS65
1999 Sets only	3,199	—	—	—	—	6.00
1999	1,800	PF65 8.00				
2000 Sets only	3,000	—	—	—	—	6.00
2000	1,500	PF65 8.00				

KM# 38.1 DOLLAR
28.28 g., Copper-Nickel, 38.8 mm. **Ruler:** Elizabeth II **Subject:** Decimalization Commemorative **Obv:** Young bust right **Rev:** Crowned shield within silver fern leaves **Edge:** DECIMAL CURRENCY INTRODUCED JULY 10 1967

Date	Mintage	VF20	XF40	MS60	MS63	MS65
1967 (l)	250,000	—	—	0.75	1.00	2.00
1967 Prooflike	50,000	—	—	1.00	1.25	2.50
1967 Proof	10	—	—	—	—	—

KM# 38.2 DOLLAR
28.28 g., Copper-Nickel, 38.8 mm. **Ruler:** Elizabeth II **Obv:** Young bust right **Rev:** Crowned shield within silver fern leaves **Edge:** Reeded **Note:** Regular issue.

Date	Mintage	VF20	XF40	MS60	MS63	MS65
1971 (l)	45,000	—	—	1.00	1.25	2.50
1971	5,000	PF65 25.00				
1972 (c)	42,000	—	—	1.00	1.25	2.50
1972 (c)	8,045	PF65 10.00				
1972 (c) RAM case; Proof	3,000	PF65 30.00				
1973 (c)	37,000	—	—	1.00	1.50	3.00
1973	16,000	PF65 5.00				
1975 (l)	30,000	—	—	1.00	1.50	3.00
1975	20,000	PF65 5.00				
1976 (l)	36,000	—	—	1.00	1.50	3.00
1976	22,000	PF65 5.00				

KM# 40.1 DOLLAR
28.28 g., Copper-Nickel, 38.8 mm. **Ruler:** Elizabeth II **Subject:** 200th Anniversary - Captain Cook's Voyage **Obv:** Young bust right **Rev:** Map flanked by bust at left and ship at right **Edge:** COMMEMORATING COOK BI-CENTENARY 1769-1969

Date	Mintage	VF20	XF40	MS60	MS63	MS65
1969 (c)	450,000	—	—	1.00	1.25	2.50
1969 Prooflike	50,000	—	—	—	—	3.00

KM# 40.2 DOLLAR
28.28 g., Copper-Nickel, 38.8 mm. **Ruler:** Elizabeth II **Obv:** Young bust right **Rev:** Map flanked by bust at left and ship at right **Edge:** No hyphen in edge inscription

Date	Mintage	VF20	XF40	MS60	MS63	MS65
1969 (c)	Inc. above	—	—	—	—	4.00

KM# 40.3 DOLLAR
28.28 g., Copper-Nickel, 38.8 mm. **Ruler:** Elizabeth II **Obv:** Young bust right **Rev:** Map flanked by bust at left and ship at right **Edge Lettering:** No I in BI-CENTENARY

Date	Mintage	VF20	XF40	MS60	MS63	MS65
1969 (c)	Inc. above	—	—	—	—	—

KM# 42 DOLLAR
28.28 g., Copper-Nickel, 38.8 mm. **Ruler:** Elizabeth II **Subject:** Royal Visit **Obv:** Young bust right **Rev:** Mount Cook, known as Aorangi

Date	Mintage	VF20	XF40	MS60	MS63	MS65
1970 (c)	315,000	—	—	—	1.00	2.00
1970 Prooflike	20,000	—	—	—	—	2.50
1970 Proof	10	—	—	—	—	—

KM# 43 DOLLAR
28.28 g., Copper-Nickel, 38.8 mm. **Ruler:** Elizabeth II **Subject:** Cook Islands **Obv:** Young bust right **Rev:** Sailing ship to left of bust 1/4 left

Date	Mintage	VF20	XF40	MS60	MS63	MS65
1970	25,070	—	—	1.50	3.00	6.00
1970	5,030	PF65 25.00				

KM# 44 DOLLAR
28.28 g., Copper-Nickel, 38.8 mm. **Ruler:** Elizabeth II **Subject:** Commonwealth Games **Obv:** Young bust right **Rev:** Square emblem flanked by athletes

Date	Mintage	VF20	XF40	MS60	MS63	MS65
1974	515,000	—	—	1.00	1.50	2.50

KM# 44a DOLLAR
28.28 g., 0.925 Silver 0.841 oz. ASW, 38.8 mm. **Ruler:** Elizabeth II **Subject:** Commonwealth Games **Obv:** Young bust right **Rev:** Square emblem flanked by athletes

Date	Mintage	VF20	XF40	MS60	MS63	MS65
1974	18,000	PF65 25.00				

KM# 45 DOLLAR
28.28 g., Copper-Nickel, 38.8 mm. **Ruler:** Elizabeth II **Subject:** New Zealand Day **Obv:** Young bust right **Rev:** Great Egret

Date	Mintage	VF20	XF40	MS60	MS63	MS65
1974 (c)	50,000	—	—	2.00	4.00	6.00
1974	5,000	PF65 35.00				

KM# 46 DOLLAR
28.28 g., Copper-Nickel, 38.8 mm. **Ruler:** Elizabeth II **Subject:** Waitangi Day and Queen's Silver Jubilee **Obv:** Young bust right **Rev:** Treaty House **Edge:** Reeded

Date	Mintage	VF20	XF40	MS60	MS63	MS65
1977	90,000	—	—	1.00	2.00	3.00

KM# 46a DOLLAR

28.28 g., 0.925 Silver 0.841 oz. ASW, 38.8 mm. **Ruler:** Elizabeth II **Subject:** Waitangi Day and Queen's 25th Anniversary **Obv:** Young bust right **Rev:** Treaty House **Edge:** Reeded

Date	Mintage	VF20	XF40	MS60	MS63	MS65
1977	27,000	PF65 22.00				

KM# 47 DOLLAR

28.28 g., Copper-Nickel, 38.8 mm. **Ruler:** Elizabeth II **Subject:** 25th Anniversary of Coronation and Opening of Parliament Building **Obv:** Young bust right **Rev:** Parliament Building

Date	Mintage	VF20	XF40	MS60	MS63	MS65
1978 (l)	123,000	—	—	1.00	1.50	2.50

KM# 47a DOLLAR

27.22 g., 0.925 Silver 0.8094 oz. ASW, 38.8 mm. **Ruler:** Elizabeth II **Subject:** 25th Anniversary of Coronation and Opening of Parliament Building **Obv:** Young bust right **Rev:** Parliament Building

Date	Mintage	VF20	XF40	MS60	MS63	MS65
1978 (o)	33,000	PF65 22.00				

KM# 48 DOLLAR

28.28 g., Copper-Nickel, 38.8 mm. **Ruler:** Elizabeth II **Obv:** New head right **Rev:** Crowned shield within silver fern **Edge:** Reeded

Date	Mintage	VF20	XF40	MS60	MS63	MS65
1979 (o)	25,000	—	—	1.00	1.50	2.50
1979 (o)	85,000	PF65 3.00				

KM# 48a DOLLAR

27.22 g., 0.925 Silver 0.8094 oz. ASW, 38.8 mm. **Ruler:** Elizabeth II **Obv:** New head right **Rev:** Crowned shield within silver fern **Edge:** Reeded

Date	Mintage	VF20	XF40	MS60	MS63	MS65
1979 (o)	35,000	PF65 22.00				

KM# 49 DOLLAR

Copper-Nickel, 38.8 mm. **Ruler:** Elizabeth II **Obv:** New head right **Rev:** Fantail bird sitting on branch **Edge:** Reeded

Date	Mintage	VF20	XF40	MS60	MS63	MS65
1980 (l)	115,000	—	—	1.50	2.50	5.00

KM# 49a DOLLAR

27.22 g., 0.925 Silver 0.8094 oz. ASW, 38.8 mm. **Ruler:** Elizabeth II **Obv:** New head right **Rev:** Fantail bird sitting on branch **Edge:** Reeded

Date	Mintage	VF20	XF40	MS60	MS63	MS65
1980 (l)	44,000	PF65 25.00				

KM# 50 DOLLAR

Copper-Nickel, 38.8 mm. **Ruler:** Elizabeth II **Subject:** Royal Visit **Obv:** New head right **Rev:** English Oak **Edge:** Reeded

Date	Mintage	VF20	XF40	MS60	MS63	MS65
1981 (l)	100,000	—	—	1.00	1.50	2.50

KM# 50a DOLLAR

27.22 g., 0.925 Silver 0.8094 oz. ASW, 38.8 mm. **Ruler:** Elizabeth II **Subject:** Royal Visit **Obv:** New head right **Rev:** English Oak **Edge:** Reeded

Date	Mintage	VF20	XF40	MS60	MS63	MS65
1981 (l)	38,000	PF65 22.00				

KM# 51 DOLLAR

Copper-Nickel, 38.8 mm. **Ruler:** Elizabeth II **Obv:** New head right **Rev:** Takahe bird **Edge:** Reeded

Date	Mintage	VF20	XF40	MS60	MS63	MS65
1982 (l)	65,000	—	—	2.50	4.50	8.00

KM# 51a DOLLAR

27.22 g., 0.925 Silver 0.8094 oz. ASW, 38.8 mm. **Ruler:** Elizabeth II **Obv:** New head right **Rev:** Takahe bird **Edge:** Reeded

Date	Mintage	VF20	XF40	MS60	MS63	MS65
1982 (l)	35,000	PF65 25.00				

KM# 52 DOLLAR

Copper-Nickel, 38.8 mm. **Ruler:** Elizabeth II **Subject:** Royal Visit **Obv:** Young bust right **Rev:** Conjoined busts of Prince Charles and Lady Diana right **Edge:** Reeded

Date	Mintage	VF20	XF40	MS60	MS63	MS65
1983	40,000	—	—	1.00	1.50	2.50

KM# 52a DOLLAR

27.22 g., 0.925 Silver 0.8094 oz. ASW, 38.8 mm. **Ruler:** Elizabeth II **Subject:** Royal Visit **Obv:** Young bust right **Rev:** Conjoined busts of Prince Charles and Lady Diana right **Edge:** Reeded

Date	Mintage	VF20	XF40	MS60	MS63	MS65
1983	17,000	PF65 25.00				

KM# 53 DOLLAR

Copper-Nickel, 38.8 mm. **Ruler:** Elizabeth II **Subject:** 50 Years of New Zealand Coinage **Obv:** Young bust right **Rev:** Crowned arms with supporters above various coins **Edge:** Reeded

Date	Mintage	VF20	XF40	MS60	MS63	MS65
1983	65,000	—	—	1.25	2.50	4.50

KM# 53a DOLLAR

27.22 g., 0.925 Silver 0.8094 oz. ASW, 38.8 mm. **Ruler:** Elizabeth II **Subject:** 50 Years of New Zealand Coinage **Obv:** Young bust right **Rev:** Crowned arms with supporters above various coins **Edge:** Reeded

Date	Mintage	VF20	XF40	MS60	MS63	MS65
1983	35,000	PF65 22.00				

KM# 54 DOLLAR

Copper-Nickel, 38.8 mm. **Ruler:** Elizabeth II **Obv:** Young bust right **Rev:** Chatham Island Black Robin on branch **Edge:** Reeded

Date	Mintage	VF20	XF40	MS60	MS63	MS65
1984 (l)	65,000	—	—	2.50	4.50	8.00

KM# 54a DOLLAR

27.22 g., 0.925 Silver 0.8094 oz. ASW, 38.8 mm. **Ruler:** Elizabeth II **Subject:** Chatham Island **Obv:** Young bust right **Rev:** Black Robin on branch **Edge:** Reeded

Date	Mintage	VF20	XF40	MS60	MS63	MS65
1984 (l)	30,000	PF65 28.00				

KM# 55 DOLLAR

Copper-Nickel, 38.8 mm. **Ruler:** Elizabeth II **Subject:** Black Stilt **Obv:** Young bust right **Edge:** Reeded

Date	Mintage	VF20	XF40	MS60	MS63	MS65
1985 (c)	60,000	—	—	3.00	5.00	9.00

KM# 55a DOLLAR

27.22 g., 0.925 Silver 0.8094 oz. ASW, 38.8 mm. **Ruler:** Elizabeth II **Subject:** Black Stilt **Obv:** Young bust right **Rev:** Black stilt and chicks **Edge:** Reeded

Date	Mintage	VF20	XF40	MS60	MS63	MS65
1985 (c)	25,000	PF65 28.00				

KM# 56 DOLLAR
Copper-Nickel, 38.8 mm. **Ruler:** Elizabeth II **Subject:** Royal Visit **Obv:** Crowned head right **Rev:** Crowned E within wreath of houhere, clematis, Mt. Cook lilly, rata, pohutukawa, kowhai, kaka beak, manuka and fern fronds **Edge:** Reeded

Date	Mintage	VF20	XF40	MS60	MS63	MS65
1986 (l)	40,000	—	—	1.00	1.50	2.50

KM# 56a DOLLAR
27.22 g., 0.925 Silver 0.8094 oz. ASW, 38.8 mm. **Ruler:** Elizabeth II **Subject:** Royal Visit **Obv:** Crowned head right **Rev:** Crowned E within wreath of houhere, clematis, Mt. Cook lilly, rata, pohutukawa, kowhai, kaka beak, manuka and fern fronds **Edge:** Reeded

Date	Mintage	VF20	XF40	MS60	MS63	MS65
1986 (l)	12,500	PF65 25.00				

KM# 57 DOLLAR
Copper-Nickel, 38.8 mm. **Ruler:** Elizabeth II **Obv:** Crowned head right **Rev:** Kakapo bird **Edge:** Reeded

Date	Mintage	VF20	XF40	MS60	MS63	MS65
1986 (c)	53,000	—	—	3.00	5.00	9.00

KM# 57a DOLLAR
27.22 g., 0.925 Silver 0.8094 oz. ASW, 38.8 mm. **Ruler:** Elizabeth II **Obv:** Crowned head right **Rev:** Kakapo bird **Edge:** Reeded

Date	Mintage	VF20	XF40	MS60	MS63	MS65
1986 (l)	20,500	PF65 28.00				

KM# 65 DOLLAR
Copper-Nickel, 38.8 mm. **Ruler:** Elizabeth II **Subject:** National Parks Centennial **Obv:** Crowned head right **Rev:** Mountains within circular design **Edge:** Reeded

Date	Mintage	VF20	XF40	MS60	MS63	MS65
1987 (l)	53,000	—	—	1.50	2.50	4.50

KM# 65a DOLLAR
27.22 g., 0.925 Silver 0.8094 oz. ASW, 38.8 mm. **Ruler:** Elizabeth II **Subject:** National Parks Centennial **Obv:** Crowned head right **Rev:** Mountains within circular design **Edge:** Reeded

Date	Mintage	VF20	XF40	MS60	MS63	MS65
1987 (l)	20,500	PF65 25.00				

KM# 66 DOLLAR
Copper-Nickel, 38.8 mm. **Ruler:** Edward VIII **Obv:** Crowned head right **Rev:** Yellow-eyed Penguin

Date	Mintage	VF20	XF40	MS60	MS63	MS65
1988 (l)	45,000	—	—	4.00	7.00	12.00

KM# 66a DOLLAR
27.22 g., 0.925 Silver 0.8094 oz. ASW, 38.8 mm. **Ruler:** Elizabeth II **Obv:** Crowned head right **Rev:** Yellow-eyed Penguin

Date	Mintage	VF20	XF40	MS60	MS63	MS65
1988	18,500	PF65 30.00				

KM# 67 DOLLAR
28.28 g., Copper-Nickel, 38.8 mm. **Ruler:** Elizabeth II **Subject:** XIV Commonwealth Games **Obv:** Crowned head right **Rev:** Runner

Date	Mintage	VF20	XF40	MS60	MS63	MS65
1989 (c)	35,000	—	—	1.00	1.50	2.50

KM# 67a DOLLAR
27.22 g., 0.925 Silver 0.8094 oz. ASW, 38.8 mm. **Ruler:** Elizabeth II **Subject:** XIV Commonwealth Games **Obv:** Crowned head right **Rev:** Runner

Date	Mintage	VF20	XF40	MS60	MS63	MS65
1989	8,600	PF65 27.00				

KM# 68 DOLLAR
28.28 g., Copper-Nickel, 38.8 mm. **Ruler:** Elizabeth II **Subject:** XIV Commonwealth Games **Obv:** Crowned head right **Rev:** Gymnast

Date	Mintage	VF20	XF40	MS60	MS63	MS65
1989	35,000	—	—	1.00	1.50	2.50

KM# 68a DOLLAR
27.22 g., 0.925 Silver 0.8094 oz. ASW, 38.8 mm. **Ruler:** Elizabeth II **Subject:** XIV Commonwealth Games **Obv:** Crowned head right **Rev:** Gymnast

Date	Mintage	VF20	XF40	MS60	MS63	MS65
1989	8,600	PF65 27.00				

KM# 69 DOLLAR
28.28 g., Copper-Nickel, 38.8 mm. **Ruler:** Elizabeth II **Subject:** XIV Commonwealth Games **Obv:** Crowned head right **Rev:** Swimmer

Date	Mintage	VF20	XF40	MS60	MS63	MS65
1989	35,000	—	—	1.00	1.50	2.50

KM# 69a DOLLAR
27.22 g., 0.925 Silver 0.8094 oz. ASW, 38.8 mm. **Ruler:** Elizabeth II **Subject:** XIV Commonwealth Games **Obv:** Crowned head right **Rev:** Swimmer

Date	Mintage	VF20	XF40	MS60	MS63	MS65
1989	8,600	PF65 27.00				

KM# 70 DOLLAR
28.28 g., Copper-Nickel, 38.8 mm. **Ruler:** Elizabeth II **Subject:** XIV Commonwealth Games **Obv:** Crowned head right **Rev:** Weight lifter

Date	Mintage	VF20	XF40	MS60	MS63	MS65
1989	35,000	—	—	1.00	1.50	2.50

KM# 70a DOLLAR
27.22 g., 0.925 Silver 0.8094 oz. ASW, 38.8 mm. **Ruler:** Elizabeth II **Subject:** XIV Commonwealth Games **Obv:** Crowned head right **Rev:** Weight lifter

Date	Mintage	VF20	XF40	MS60	MS63	MS65
1989	8,600	PF65 27.00				

KM# 76 DOLLAR
Copper-Nickel, 38.8 mm. **Ruler:** Elizabeth II **Subject:** 1990 Anniversary Celebrations - Treaty of Waitangi **Obv:** Crowned head right **Rev:** Treaty signing scene

Date	Mintage	VF20	XF40	MS60	MS63	MS65
1990	40,000	—	—	1.50	2.50	4.00

KM# 76a DOLLAR
27.22 g., 0.925 Silver 0.8094 oz. ASW, 38.8 mm. **Ruler:** Elizabeth II **Subject:** 1990 Anniversary Celebrations - Treaty of Waitangi **Obv:** Crowned head right **Rev:** Treaty signing scene

Date	Mintage	VF20	XF40	MS60	MS63	MS65
1990	20,000	PF65 25.00				

KM# 78 DOLLAR

8.00 g., Aluminum-Bronze, 23 mm. **Ruler:** Elizabeth II **Obv:** Crowned head right **Rev:** Kiwi Bird with sprigs, value below **Edge:** Segmented reeding

Date	Mintage	VF20	XF40	MS60	MS63	MS65
1990 (c)	10,000	—	—	—	—	5.00
Note: Sets only.						
1990 (l)	40,000,000	—	—	1.00	2.00	3.50
1991 (l)	10,000,000	—	—	1.00	2.00	3.50
1991 (c)	20,000	—	—	—	—	5.00
Note: Sets only.						
1991 (c)	15,000	PF65 15.00				
1992 (l)	15,000	—	—	—	—	10.00
Note: Sets only						
1992 (l)	9,000	PF65 15.00				
1993 (l)	15,000	—	—	—	—	10.00
Note: Sets only						
1993 (l)	10,000	PF65 15.00				
1994 (l)	16,000	—	—	—	—	15.00
Note: Sets only						
1994 (l)	4,600	PF65 20.00				
1995 (l)	6,000	—	—	—	—	15.00
Note: Sets only						
1995 (l)	3,560	PF65 20.00				
1996 (l)	5,150	—	—	—	—	15.00
Note: Sets only						
1996 (l)	4,000	PF65 20.00				
1997 (l)	4,150	—	—	—	—	15.00
Note: Sets only						
1997 (l)	2,132	PF65 20.00				
1998 (l)	4,000	—	—	—	—	15.00
Note: Sets only						
1998 (l)	2,000	PF65 20.00				

KM# 78a DOLLAR

8.00 g., 0.925 Silver 0.2379 oz. ASW, 23 mm. **Ruler:** Elizabeth II **Obv:** Crowned head right **Rev:** Kiwi Bird

Date	Mintage	VF20	XF40	MS60	MS63	MS65
1990	10,000	PF65 25.00				

KM# 120 DOLLAR

8.00 g., Aluminum-Bronze, 23 mm. **Ruler:** Elizabeth II **Obv:** Head with tiara right **Rev:** Kiwi bird within sprigs, value below **Edge:** Segmented reeding

Date	Mintage	VF20	XF40	MS60	MS63	MS65
1999 Sets only	3,199	—	—	—	—	15.00
1999	1,800	PF65 15.00				
2000 (o)	5,000,000	—	—	1.00	1.50	3.00
2000	1,500	PF65 5.00				

KM# 79 2 DOLLARS

10.00 g., Aluminum-Bronze, 26.5 mm. **Ruler:** Elizabeth II **Obv:** Crowned head right **Rev:** Kotuku, white heron

Date	Mintage	VF20	XF40	MS60	MS63	MS65
1990 (l)	30,000,000	—	—	2.00	3.00	5.00
1990 (c)	18,000	—	—	—	—	5.50
Note: Sets only.						
1991 (l)	10,000,000	—	—	2.00	3.00	5.00
1991 (c)	20,000	—	—	—	—	5.50
Note: Sets only.						
1991 (c)	15,000	PF65 6.00				
1992 (l)	15,000	—	—	—	—	6.00
Note: Sets only						
1992 (l)	9,000	PF65 6,00				
1994 (l)	7,000	—	—	—	—	6.00
Note: Sets only						
1994 (l)	4,600	PF65 6.00				
1995 (l)	6,000	—	—	—	—	6.00
Note: Sets only						
1995 (l)	3,560	PF65 10.00				
1996 (l)	5,150	—	—	—	—	8.00
Note: Sets only						
1996 (l)	2,569	PF65 12.00				
1997 (l)	4,150	—	—	—	—	—
Note: Sets only.						
1997 (l)	2,132	PF65 12.00				
1997 (p)	1,000,000	—	—	2.00	3.00	5.00
Note: Entire mintage recalled, but many left in circulation						
1998 (p)	6,000,000	—	—	2.00	3.00	5.00
1998 (p)	2,000	PF65 6.00				

KM# 79a 2 DOLLARS

10.00 g., 0.925 Silver 0.2974 oz. ASW, 26.5 mm. **Ruler:** Elizabeth II **Obv:** Crowned head right **Rev:** Kotuku, white heron

Date	Mintage	VF20	XF40	MS60	MS63	MS65
1990	10,000	PF65 15.00				

KM# 87 2 DOLLARS

Aluminum-Bronze **Ruler:** Elizabeth II **Obv:** Crowned head right **Rev:** Sacred Kingfisher

Date	Mintage	VF20	XF40	MS60	MS63	MS65
1993	40,000	—	—	3.00	5.00	8.00

KM# 87a 2 DOLLARS

10.00 g., 0.925 Silver 0.2974 oz. ASW **Ruler:** Elizabeth II **Obv:** Crowned head right **Rev:** Sacred Kingfisher

Date	Mintage	VF20	XF40	MS60	MS63	MS65
1993	10,000	PF65 20.00				

KM# 121 2 DOLLARS

10.00 g., Aluminum-Bronze, 26.5 mm. **Ruler:** Elizabeth II **Obv:** Head with tiara right **Rev:** White heron (kotuku) above value **Edge:** Reeded with security groove

Date	Mintage	VF20	XF40	MS60	MS63	MS65
1999 (p)	5,050,000	—	—	2.00	3.00	5.00
1999 (l)	2,000	PF65 20.00				
2000 Sets only	3,000	—	—	—	—	5.00
2000 (l)	1,500	PF65 20.00				

KM# 71 5 DOLLARS

Aluminum-Bronze **Ruler:** Elizabeth II **Obv:** Crowned head right **Rev:** ANZAC Memorial

Date	Mintage	VF20	XF40	MS60	MS63	MS65
1990	60,000	PF65 17.50				
Note: Set only, issued with Australian 1990 $5 as pair						

KM# 80 5 DOLLARS

27.22 g., Copper-Nickel, 38.73 mm. **Ruler:** Elizabeth II **Subject:** Rugby World Cup **Obv:** Crowned head right **Rev:** Champion cup flanked by rugby players

Date	Mintage	VF20	XF40	MS60	MS63	MS65
1991 (c)	120,000	—	—	3.50	4.50	6.00

KM# 80a 5 DOLLARS

27.22 g., 0.925 Silver 0.8095 oz. ASW, 38.73 mm. **Ruler:** Elizabeth II **Subject:** Rugby World Cup **Obv:** Crowned head right **Rev:** Champion cup flanked by rugby players

Date	Mintage	VF20	XF40	MS60	MS63	MS65
1991 (c)	30,000	PF65 20.00				

KM# 82 5 DOLLARS

27.22 g., Copper-Nickel, 38.73 mm. **Ruler:** Elizabeth II **Subject:** 25th Anniversary of Decimal Currency **Obv:** Crowned head right **Rev:** Silver fern leaf above various coins

Date	Mintage	VF20	XF40	MS60	MS63	MS65
1992	34,000	—	—	3.50	4.50	6.00

KM# 82a 5 DOLLARS

27.22 g., 0.925 Silver 0.8095 oz. ASW **Ruler:** Elizabeth II **Subject:** 25th Anniversary of Decimal Currency **Obv:** Crowned head right **Rev:** Silver fern leaf above various coins

Date	Mintage	VF20	XF40	MS60	MS63	MS65
1992	17,000	PF65 20.00				

KM# 83 5 DOLLARS

27.22 g., Copper-Nickel, 38.73 mm. **Ruler:** Elizabeth II **Series:** The Discoverers **Subject:** Mythological Maori Hero - Kupe **Obv:** Crowned head right **Rev:** Bust right

Date	Mintage	VF20	XF40	MS60	MS63	MS65
1992	40,000	—	—	3.50	4.50	6.00

KM# 84 5 DOLLARS

27.22 g., Copper-Nickel, 38.73 mm. **Ruler:** Elizabeth II **Series:** The Discoverers **Subject:** Abel Tasman **Obv:** Crowned head right

Date	Mintage	VF20	XF40	MS60	MS63	MS65
1992	40,000	—	—	3.50	4.50	6.00

KM# 85 5 DOLLARS

27.22 g., Copper-Nickel, 38.73 mm. **Ruler:** Elizabeth II **Series:** The Discoverers **Subject:** Captain James Cook **Obv:** Crowned head right **Rev:** Bust 1/4 right

Date	Mintage	VF20	XF40	MS60	MS63	MS65
1992	40,000	—	—	3.50	4.50	6.00

KM# 86 5 DOLLARS
27.22 g., Copper-Nickel, 38.73 mm. **Ruler:** Elizabeth II **Series:** The Discoverers **Subject:** Christopher Columbus **Obv:** Crowned head right **Rev:** Bust 1/4 right

Date	Mintage	VF20	XF40	MS60	MS63	MS65
1992	40,000	—	—	3.50	4.50	6.00

KM# 88 5 DOLLARS
27.22 g., Copper-Nickel, 38.73 mm. **Ruler:** Elizabeth II **Subject:** 40th Anniversary of Coronation **Obv:** Crowned head right **Rev:** Coronation emblem within squares, all within artistic designed circle

Date	Mintage	VF20	XF40	MS60	MS63	MS65
1993	15,000	—	—	3.50	5.00	7.00

KM# 88a 5 DOLLARS
27.22 g., 0.925 Silver 0.8095 oz. ASW **Ruler:** Elizabeth II **Subject:** 40th Anniversary of Coronation **Obv:** Crowned head right **Rev:** Coronation emblem within squares, all within artistic designed circle

Date	Mintage	VF20	XF40	MS60	MS63	MS65
1993	15,000	PF65 30.00				

KM# 88b 5 DOLLARS
47.53 g., 0.917 Gold 1.4011 oz. AGW **Ruler:** Elizabeth II **Subject:** 40th Anniversary of Coronation **Obv:** Crowned head right **Rev:** Coronation emblem within squares, all within artistic designed circle

Date	Mintage	VF20	XF40	MS60	MS63	MS65
1993	210	PF65 2,500				

KM# 89 5 DOLLARS
31.47 g., 0.925 Silver 0.9359 oz. ASW **Ruler:** Elizabeth II **Subject:** Endangered Wildlife **Obv:** Crowned head right **Rev:** Hooker Sea Lions

Date	Mintage	VF20	XF40	MS60	MS63	MS65
1993	20,000	PF65 40.00				

KM# 91 5 DOLLARS
28.28 g., 0.925 Silver 0.841 oz. ASW **Ruler:** Elizabeth II **Obv:** Crowned head right **Rev:** Queen mother and infant Elizabeth within beaded circle

Date	Mintage	VF20	XF40	MS60	MS63	MS65
1994	34,600	PF65 28.00				

KM# 96 5 DOLLARS
31.47 g., 0.925 Silver 0.9359 oz. ASW **Ruler:** Elizabeth II **Series:** Winter Olympics - 1994 **Obv:** Crowned head right **Rev:** Downhill skier

Date	Mintage	VF20	XF40	MS60	MS63	MS65
1994	33,300	PF65 30.00				

KM# 92 5 DOLLARS
31.47 g., 0.925 Silver 0.9359 oz. ASW **Ruler:** Elizabeth II **Subject:** Antarctica **Obv:** Crowned head right **Rev:** James Clark Ross

Date	Mintage	VF20	XF40	MS60	MS63	MS65
1995	13,000	PF65 30.00				

KM# 93 5 DOLLARS
27.22 g., Copper-Nickel **Ruler:** Elizabeth II **Obv:** Crowned head right **Rev:** Tui bird sitting on branch

Date	Mintage	VF20	XF40	MS60	MS63	MS65
1995	11,000	—	—	—	7.00	12.00

KM# 93a 5 DOLLARS
28.28 g., 0.925 Silver 0.841 oz. ASW **Ruler:** Elizabeth II **Obv:** Crowned head right **Rev:** Tui bird sitting on branch

Date	Mintage	VF20	XF40	MS60	MS63	MS65
1995	7,000	PF65 28.00				

KM# 97 5 DOLLARS
27.22 g., Copper-Nickel, 38.61 mm. **Ruler:** Elizabeth II **Obv:** Crowned head right **Rev:** Kaka (Bush Parrot)

Date	Mintage	VF20	XF40	MS60	MS63	MS65
1996	11,000	—	—	—	10.00	15.00

KM# 97a 5 DOLLARS
28.28 g., 0.925 Silver 0.841 oz. ASW **Ruler:** Elizabeth II **Obv:** Crowned head right **Rev:** Kaka (Bush parrot)

Date	Mintage	VF20	XF40	MS60	MS63	MS65
1996	7,000	PF65 35.00				

KM# 99 5 DOLLARS
27.22 g., Copper-Nickel, 38.61 mm. **Ruler:** Elizabeth II **Subject:** Auckland City of Sails **Obv:** Crowned head right **Rev:** Bridge and boats

Date	Mintage	VF20	XF40	MS60	MS63	MS65
1996 (l)	6,000	—	—	—	5.00	9.00

KM# 99a 5 DOLLARS
28.28 g., 0.925 Silver 0.841 oz. ASW **Ruler:** Elizabeth II **Subject:** Auckland - City of Sails **Obv:** Crowned head right **Rev:** Bridge and boats

Date	Mintage	VF20	XF40	MS60	MS63	MS65
1996	3,000	PF65 40.00				

KM# 101 5 DOLLARS
28.28 g., 0.925 Silver 0.841 oz. ASW **Ruler:** Elizabeth II **Obv:** Crowned head right **Rev:** Crowned belt wreath flanked by flowers

Date	Mintage	VF20	XF40	MS60	MS63	MS65
1996 (l)	3,000	—	—	—	—	40.00

Note: Sets only with $20 commemorative banknote

KM# 102 5 DOLLARS
28.28 g., 0.925 Silver 0.841 oz. ASW **Ruler:** Elizabeth II **Subject:** De Heemskerck **Obv:** Crowned head right **Rev:** Sailship on globe with map

Date	Mintage	VF20	XF40	MS60	MS63	MS65
1996 (o)	18,000	PF65 42.00				

KM# 103 5 DOLLARS
27.22 g., Copper-Nickel, 38.61 mm. **Ruler:** Elizabeth II **Subject:** WWF Conserving Nature **Obv:** Crowned head right **Rev:** Saddleback bird

Date	Mintage	VF20	XF40	MS60	MS63	MS65
1997 (l)	8,000	—	—	—	5.00	9.00

KM# 103a 5 DOLLARS
28.28 g., 0.925 Silver 0.841 oz. ASW **Ruler:** Elizabeth II **Subject:** WWF Conserving Nature **Obv:** Crowned head right **Rev:** Saddleback bird

Date	Mintage	VF20	XF40	MS60	MS63	MS65
1997 (l)	19,000	PF65 30.00				

KM# 105 5 DOLLARS
27.22 g., Copper-Nickel **Ruler:** Elizabeth II **Subject:** Queen's Golden Wedding Anniversary **Obv:** Crowned head right **Rev:** Coronation scene

Date	Mintage	VF20	XF40	MS60	MS63	MS65
1997	9,000	—	—	—	10.00	15.00

KM# 105a 5 DOLLARS
28.28 g., 0.925 Silver 0.841 oz. ASW **Ruler:** Elizabeth II **Subject:** Queen's Golden Wedding Anniversary **Obv:** Crowned head right **Rev:** Coronation scene

Date	Mintage	VF20	XF40	MS60	MS63	MS65
1997	32,500	PF65 28.00				

KM# 106 5 DOLLARS
27.22 g., Copper-Nickel, 38.61 mm. **Ruler:** Elizabeth II **Subject:** City of Christchurch **Obv:** Crowned head right **Rev:** Value above church

Date	Mintage	VF20	XF40	MS60	MS63	MS65
1997	5,000	—	—	—	10.00	15.00

KM# 106a 5 DOLLARS
28.28 g., 0.925 Silver 0.841 oz. ASW **Ruler:** Elizabeth II **Subject:** City of Christchurch **Obv:** Crowned head right **Rev:** Value above church

Date	Mintage	VF20	XF40	MS60	MS63	MS65
1997	3,000	PF65 42.00				

KM# 107 5 DOLLARS
27.22 g., Copper-Nickel, 38.61 mm. **Ruler:** Elizabeth II **Obv:** Crowned head right **Rev:** Royal Albatross

Date	Mintage	VF20	XF40	MS60	MS63	MS65
1998	6,500	—	—	—	12.00	18.00

KM# 107a 5 DOLLARS
29.20 g., 0.925 Silver 0.8684 oz. ASW **Ruler:** Elizabeth II **Obv:** Crowned head right **Rev:** Royal Albatross

Date	Mintage	VF20	XF40	MS60	MS63	MS65
1998	2,500	PF65 65.00				

KM# 109 5 DOLLARS
27.22 g., Copper-Nickel, 38.61 mm. **Ruler:** Elizabeth II **Subject:** Pride in New Zealand **Obv:** Crowned head right **Rev:** Four stars

Date	Mintage	VF20	XF40	MS60	MS63	MS65
1998 (v) Sets only	2,000	—	—	—	—	9.00

KM# 109a 5 DOLLARS
6.00 g., 0.999 Silver 0.1927 oz. ASW **Ruler:** Elizabeth II **Subject:** Pride in New Zealand **Obv:** Crowned head right **Rev:** Four stars

Date	Mintage	VF20	XF40	MS60	MS63	MS65
1998 (v)	1,200	PF65 12.00				

KM# 110 5 DOLLARS
27.22 g., Copper-Nickel, 38.61 mm. **Ruler:** Elizabeth II **Subject:** Pride in New Zealand **Obv:** Crowned head right **Rev:** Fleece

Date	Mintage	VF20	XF40	MS60	MS63	MS65
1998 (v) Sets only	2,000	—	—	—	—	9.00

KM# 110a 5 DOLLARS
6.00 g., 0.999 Silver 0.1927 oz. ASW **Ruler:** Elizabeth II **Subject:** Pride in New Zealand **Obv:** Crowned head right **Rev:** Fleece

Date	Mintage	VF20	XF40	MS60	MS63	MS65
1998 (v)	1,200	PF65 12.00				

KM# 111 5 DOLLARS
27.22 g., Copper-Nickel, 38.61 mm. **Ruler:** Elizabeth II **Subject:** Pride in New Zealand **Obv:** Crowned head right **Rev:** Wheat sheaf

Date	Mintage	VF20	XF40	MS60	MS63	MS65
1998 (v) Sets only	2,000	—	—	—	—	9.00

KM# 111a 5 DOLLARS
6.00 g., 0.999 Silver 0.1927 oz. ASW **Ruler:** Elizabeth II **Subject:** Pride in New Zealand **Obv:** Crowned head right **Rev:** Wheat sheaf

Date	Mintage	VF20	XF40	MS60	MS63	MS65
1998 (v)	1,200	PF65 12.00				

KM# 112 5 DOLLARS
27.22 g., Copper-Nickel, 38.61 mm. **Ruler:** Elizabeth II **Subject:** Pride in New Zealand **Obv:** Crowned head right **Rev:** Crossed hammers

Date	Mintage	VF20	XF40	MS60	MS63	MS65
1998 (v) Sets only	2,000	—	—	—	—	9.00

KM# 112a 5 DOLLARS
6.00 g., 0.999 Silver 0.1927 oz. ASW **Ruler:** Elizabeth II **Subject:** Pride in New Zealand **Obv:** Crowned head right **Rev:** Crossed hammers

Date	Mintage	VF20	XF40	MS60	MS63	MS65
1998 (v)	1,200	PF65 12.00				

KM# 113 5 DOLLARS
27.22 g., Copper-Nickel, 38.61 mm. **Ruler:** Elizabeth II **Subject:** Dunedin **Obv:** Crowned head right **Rev:** Larnach Castle

Date	Mintage	VF20	XF40	MS60	MS63	MS65
1998 (v)	4,000	—	—	—	—	7.50

KM# 113a 5 DOLLARS
28.28 g., 0.925 Silver 0.841 oz. ASW **Ruler:** Elizabeth II **Subject:** Dunedin **Obv:** Crowned head right **Rev:** Larnach Castle

Date	Mintage	VF20	XF40	MS60	MS63	MS65
1998 (v)	2,500	PF65 30.00				

KM# 115 5 DOLLARS
27.22 g., Copper-Nickel, 38.61 mm. **Ruler:** Elizabeth II **Obv:** Head with tiara right **Rev:** Morepork on branch

Date	Mintage	VF20	XF40	MS60	MS63	MS65
1999	7,500	—	—	—	14.00	22.00

KM# 115a 5 DOLLARS
28.28 g., 0.999 Silver 0.9083 oz. ASW **Ruler:** Elizabeth II **Obv:** Head with tiara right **Rev:** Morepork

Date	Mintage	VF20	XF40	MS60	MS63	MS65
1999	7,000	PF65 45.00				

KM# 123 5 DOLLARS
27.22 g., Copper-Nickel, 38.61 mm. **Ruler:** Elizabeth II **Subject:** Wellington Harbour Capital **Obv:** Head with tiara right **Rev:** City view with ship

Date	Mintage	VF20	XF40	MS60	MS63	MS65
1999 (v)	—	—	—	—	12.00	20.00

KM# 123a 5 DOLLARS
31.05 g., 0.925 Silver 0.9234 oz. ASW, 38.7 mm. **Ruler:** Elizabeth II **Subject:** Wellington Harbour Capital **Obv:** Head with tiara right **Rev:** City view with ship **Edge:** Reeded

Date	Mintage	VF20	XF40	MS60	MS63	MS65
1999 (v)	2,500	PF65 32.00				

KM# 125 5 DOLLARS
32.20 g., Copper-Nickel, 38.6 mm. **Ruler:** Elizabeth II **Obv:** Head with tiara right **Rev:** Perching cormorant bird **Edge:** Reeded

Date	Mintage	VF20	XF40	MS60	MS63	MS65
2000 (v)	5,500	—	—	—	12.00	20.00
Frosted finish						

KM# 125a 5 DOLLARS
31.13 g., 0.999 Silver 0.9999 oz. ASW **Ruler:** Elizabeth II **Obv:** Head with tiara right **Rev:** Perching cormorant **Note:** Heavier than the official weight of 28.28 grams.

Date	Mintage	VF20	XF40	MS60	MS63	MS65
2000 (v)	5,000	PF65 35.00				

KM# 127 5 DOLLARS
32.20 g., Copper-Nickel, 38.6 mm. **Ruler:** Elizabeth II **Obv:** Queen's portrait from dies of Solomon Islands KM67-68 **Rev:** Pied Cormorant for dies of New Zealand KM125 **Edge:** Reeded **Note:** Mule.

Date	Mintage	VF20	XF40	MS60	MS63	MS65
2000 (v)	Est. 50	—	—	—	—	1,000

Note: This coin is included in a New Zealand mint set dated 2000

KM# 94 10 DOLLARS
Aluminum-Bronze **Ruler:** Elizabeth II **Obv:** Crowned head right **Rev:** Gold Prospector

Date	Mintage	VF20	XF40	MS60	MS63	MS65
1995 (l)	7,000	—	—	—	10.00	12.00

KM# 94a 10 DOLLARS
0.999 Gold **Ruler:** Elizabeth II **Obv:** Crowned head right **Rev:** Gold Prospector

Date	Mintage	VF20	XF40	MS60	MS63	MS65
1995 (l)	600	PF65 800				

KM# 98 10 DOLLARS
Aluminum-Bronze **Ruler:** Elizabeth II **Subject:** Sinking of General Grant **Obv:** Crowned head right **Rev:** Sinking ship above value

Date	Mintage	VF20	XF40	MS60	MS63	MS65
1996 (l) Prooflike	6,000	—	—	—	10.00	12.00

KM# 98a 10 DOLLARS
0.999 Gold **Ruler:** Elizabeth II **Subject:** Sinking of The General Grant **Obv:** Crowned head right **Rev:** Sinking ship above value

Date	Mintage	VF20	XF40	MS60	MS63	MS65
1996 (l)	650	PF65 800				

KM# 104 10 DOLLARS
Aluminum-Bronze **Ruler:** Elizabeth II **Subject:** Gabriel's Gully **Obv:** Crowned head right **Rev:** Prospector climbing hill with shovel in hand

Date	Mintage	VF20	XF40	MS60	MS63	MS65
1997 (l)	3,000	—	—	—	12.00	15.00

KM# 104a 10 DOLLARS
0.999 Gold **Ruler:** Elizabeth II **Subject:** Gabriel's Gully **Obv:** Crowned head right **Rev:** Prospector climbing hill with shovel in hand

Date	Mintage	VF20	XF40	MS60	MS63	MS65
1997 (l)	650	PF65 800				

KM# 114 10 DOLLARS
Brass **Ruler:** Elizabeth II **Subject:** Century of Motoring **Obv:** Crowned head right **Rev:** Karl Benz driving his automobile

Date	Mintage	VF20	XF40	MS60	MS63	MS65
1998 (v)	2,000	—	—	—	10.00	12.00

KM# 114a 10 DOLLARS
Copper-Nickel Gilt **Ruler:** Elizabeth II **Subject:** Century of Motoring **Obv:** Crowned head right **Rev:** Karl Benz driving his automobile

Date	Mintage	VF20	XF40	MS60	MS63	MS65
1998 (v)	1,500	PF65 40.00				

KM# 124 10 DOLLARS
15.45 g., 0.999 Silver 0.4962 oz. ASW, 29.9 mm. **Ruler:** Elizabeth II **Obv:** Crowned head right **Rev:** Kiwi bird below silver fern leaf **Edge:** Reeded

Date	Mintage	VF20	XF40	MS60	MS63	MS65
1998	1,500	—	—	—	75.00	90.00

KM# 122 10 DOLLARS
28.28 g., 0.925 Silver 0.841 oz. ASW, 38.8 mm. **Ruler:** Elizabeth II **Subject:** New Zealand - First to the Future **Obv:** Head with tiara right **Rev:** Gold-plated map of New Zealand, gold printed radiant sun **Edge:** Reeded

Date	Mintage	VF20	XF40	MS60	MS63	MS65
2000(1999)	33,000	PF65 65.00				

KM# 100 20 DOLLARS
31.10 g., 0.925 Silver 0.925 oz. ASW **Ruler:** Elizabeth II **Subject:** Salute to Bravery **Obv:** Crowned head right **Rev:** Cameo at left, Captain Charles Upham, Victoria Cross and Bar at right

Date	Mintage	VF20	XF40	MS60	MS63	MS65
1995	3,500	PF65 42.00				

KM# 108 20 DOLLARS
28.28 g., 0.925 Silver 0.841 oz. ASW **Ruler:** Elizabeth II **Subject:** Queen's Golden Wedding Anniversary **Obv:** Crowned head right **Rev:** Coronation scene **Note:** Similar to 5 Dollars, KM#105.

Date	Mintage	VF20	XF40	MS60	MS63	MS65
1997	32,500	PF65 38.00				

KM# 77 150 DOLLARS
16.95 g., 0.917 Gold 0.4997 oz. AGW **Ruler:** Elizabeth II **Obv:** Crowned head right **Rev:** Kiwi

Date	Mintage	VF20	XF40	MS60	MS63	MS65
1990	10,000	PF65 900				

KM# 126 150 DOLLARS
15.60 g., 0.995 Platinum 0.499 oz. APW, 30 mm. **Ruler:** Elizabeth II **Obv:** Crowned head right **Rev:** Two Kiwi and fern **Edge:** Reeded

Date	Mintage	VF20	XF40	MS60	MS63	MS65
1998	350	PF65 950				

PATTERNS

Including off metal strikes

KM#	Date	Mintage	Identification	Mkt Val
Pn2	1933	—	3 Pence. Silver.	20,000
Pn3	1933	—	Shilling. Silver.	50,000
Pn4	1935	—	Crown. Silver.	75,000

PIEDFORT

KM#	Date	Mintage	Identification	Mkt Val
P1	1992	5,000	Dollar. 0.925. Silver. KM78.	100

MINT SETS

KM#	Date	Mintage	Identification	Issue Price	Mkt Val
MSA1	1965 (7)	75,000	KM23.2-29.2, green label, flat pack	2.50	18.00
MS1	1965 (7)	100,000	KM23.2-29.2, pink label, flat pack	2.00	18.00
MS2	1967 (7)	250,000	KM31-32, 34-37, 38.1	4.50	9.00
MS4	1968 (6)	35,000	KM31-32, 34-37	2.15	14.00
MS5	1969 (7)	50,000	KM31-32, 34-36, 39-40.1	3.25	17.50
MS7	1970 (7)	30,000	KM31.1, 32.1, 34.1, 36.1, 37.1, 41.1, 42	3.50	17.50
MS10	1971 (6)	15,000	KM31.1, 32.1, 36.1, 37.1, 38.2, 41	3.50	22.00
MS12	1972 (7)	15,000	KM31.1, 32.1, 34.1, 36.1, 37.1, 38.2, 41.1	3.50	22.00
MS14	1973 (7)	15,000	KM31.1, 32.1, 34.1, 36.1, 37.1, 38.2, 41.1	3.50	22.00
MS17	1974 (7)	15,000	KM31.1, 32.1, 34.1, 36.1, 37.1, 41.1, 44	4.35	16.00
MS20	1975 (7)	15,000	KM31.1, 32.1, 34.1, 36.1, 37.1, 38.2, 41.1	4.50	12.00
MS22	1976 (7)	16,000	KM31.1, 32.1, 34.1, 36.1, 37.1, 38.2, 41	4.75	16.50
MS23	1977 (7)	20,000	KM31.1, 32.1, 34.1, 36.1, 37.1, 41.1, 46	4.75	20.00
MS24	1978 (7)	23,000	KM31.1, 32.1, 34.1, 36.1, 37.1, 41.1, 47	5.25	14.00
MS25	1979 (7)	25,000	KM31.1, 32.1, 34.1, 36.1, 37.1, 41.1, 48	5.50	17.00
MS26	1980 (7)	27,000	KM31.1, 32.1, 34.1, 36.1, 37.1, 41.1, 49	5.75	14.00
MS27	1981 (7)	25,000	KM31.1, 32.1, 34.1, 36.1, 37.1, 41.1, 50	5.75	14.00
MS28	1982 (7)	25,000	KM31.1, 32.1, 34.1, 36.1, 37.1, 41.1, 51	6.00	18.00
MS29	1983 (7)	25,000	KM31.1, 32.1, 34.1, 36.1, 37.1, 41.1, 53	6.25	17.00
MS30	1984 (7)	25,000	KM31.1, 32.1, 34.1, 36.1, 37.1, 41.1, 54	4.75	18.00
MS31	1985 (7)	20,000	KM31.1, 32.1, 34.1, 36.1, 37.1, 41.1, 55	4.00	16.00
MS32	1986 (7)	18,000	KM57-63	5.00	20.00
MS33	1987 (7)	18,000	KM58-63, 65	7.50	17.00
MS34	1988 (7)	15,000	KM58-63, 66	8.00	24.00
MS35	1989 (5)	14,600	KM60-63, 67	14.60	15.00
MS36	1990 (6)	18,000	KM60, 61, 63, 78, 79, 81	13.00	18.00
MS37	1990 (5)	10,000	KM72-76	11.00	36.00
MS38	1991 (7)	20,000	KM60, 61, 63, 78-81	16.00	22.00
MS39	1992 (7)	15,000	KM60, 61, 63, 78, 79, 81, 82	15.00	39.00
MS40	1992 (4)	40,000	KM83-86	—	25.00
MS41	1993 (6)	15,000	KM60, 61, 63, 78, 81, 87	—	30.00
MS42	1994 (6)	7,000	KM60, 61, 78, 79, 81, 90	20.00	47.50
MS43	1995 (7)	6,000	KM60, 61, 63, 78, 79, 81, 93	17.00	48.00
MS44	1996 (7)	5,150	KM60, 61, 63, 78, 79, 81, 97	17.00	62.00
MS45	1997 (7)	4,150	KM60, 61, 63, 78, 79, 81, 103	—	60.00
MS46	1998 (7)	4,000	KM60, 61, 63, 78, 79, 81, 107	15.00	105
MS47	1998 (4)	2,000	KM109-112	—	75.00
MS48	1999 (7)	3,199	KM115-121	20.00	150
MS49	2000 (7)	2,000	KM#KM116-121, 125.	18.00	210
MS49a	2000 (7)	50	KM116-121, 127mule	18.00	2,000

PROOF SETS

KM#	Date	Mintage	Identification	Issue Price	Mkt Val
PS1	1933 (5)	20	KM1-5	—	4,250
PS2	1934 (5)	20	KM1-5	—	10,250
PS3	1935 (6)	364	KM1-6	—	12,500
PS4	1937 (5)	200	KM7-9, 10.1, 11	—	2,700
PS5	1947 (5)	20	KM7a-9a, 10.2a, 11a	—	2,150
PSA6	1950 (7)	—	KM15-21	—	2,300
PS6	1953 (8)	7,000	KM23.1-29.1, 30	—	280
PS7	1953 (8)	—	KM23-30, Matte Proof	—	1,400
PS8	1954 (4)	—	KM23.1-26.1	—	800
PS9	1954 (6)	—	KM23.1-28.1	—	1,400
PS10	1965 (7)	10	KM23.2-29.2	—	—
PS11	1967 (7)	10	KM31-32,34-38, V.I.P. Set	—	—
PSA12	1970 (7)	10	KM#31.1-32.1, 34.1, 36.1-37.1, 41.1-42, official card, red plush case, V.I.P. set	—	—
PS12	1971 (7)	5,000	KM31.1, 32.1, 34.1, 36.1, 37.1, 38.2, 41.1	15.00	110
PS13	1972 (7)	8,000	KM31.1, 32.1, 34.1, 36.1, 37.1, 38.2, 41.1	16.00	57.50
PS14	1973 (7)	8,000	KM31.1, 32.1, 34.1, 36.1, 37.1, 38.2, 41.1	16.00	40.00
PS15	1974 (7)	8,000	KM31-32, 34, 36-37, 41, 44a	14.00	62.00
PS16	1975 (7)	10,000	KM31.1, 32.1, 34.1, 36.1, 37.1, 38.2, 41.1	18.50	35.00
PS17	1976 (7)	11,000	KM31.1, 32.1, 34.1, 36.1, 37.1, 38.2, 41.1	19.00	30.00
PS18	1977 (7)	12,000	KM31.1, 32.1, 34.1, 36.1, 37.1, 41.1, 46a	19.50	57.00
PS19	1977 (7)	10	KM31.1, 32.1, 34.1, 36.1, 37.1, 41.1, 46a, Official card, V.I.P set	—	85.00
PS20	1978 (7)	15,000	KM31.1, 32.1, 34.1, 36.1, 37.1, 41.1, 47a	23.50	50.00
PS21	1979 (7)	16,000	KM31.1, 32.1, 34.1, 36.1, 37.1, 41.1, 48a	25.50	50.00
PS22	1980 (7)	17,000	KM31.1, 32.1, 34.1, 36.1, 37.1, 41.1, 49a	42.00	50.00
PS23	1981 (7)	18,000	KM31.1, 32.1, 34.1, 36.1, 37.1, 41.1, 50a	37.00	48.00
PS24	1982 (7)	18,000	KM31.1, 32.1, 34.1 36.1, 37.1, 41.1, 51a	33.00	48.00
PS25	1983 (7)	18,000	KM31.1, 32.1, 34.1, 36.1, 37.1, 41.1, 53a	40.00	48.00
PS26	1984 (7)	15,000	KM31.1, 32.1, 34.1, 36.1, 37.1, 41.1, 54a	28.00	52.50
PS27	1985 (7)	11,500	KM31.1, 32.1, 34.1, 36.1, 37.1, 41.1, 55a	27.00	50.00
PS28	1986 (7)	10,000	KM57a, 58-63	30.00	57.50
PS29	1987 (7)	10,000	KM58-63, 65a	38.00	48.00
PS30	1988 (7)	9,000	KM58-63, 66a	43.00	50.00
PS31	1989 (5)	8,500	KM60-63, 67a	44.50	47.00
PS32	1989 (4)	8,600	KM67a-70a	132	128

KM#	Date	Mintage	Identification	Issue Price	Mkt Val
PS33	1990 (6)	10,000	KM60-61, 63, 78a-79a, 81	52.00	70.00
PS34	1990 (5)	7,000	KM72a-76a	110	95.00
PS35	1991 (7)	15,000	KM60-61, 63, 78-79, 80a, 81	61.00	72.00
PS36	1992 (7)	9,000	KM60-61, 63, 78-79, 81, 82a	58.00	72.00
PS37	1993 (6)	10,000	KM60-61, 63, 78, 81, 87a	75.00	58.00
PS38	1994 (6)	4,600	KM60-61, 78-79, 81, 90a	45.00	67.00
PS39	1995 (7)	3,560	KM60-61, 63, 78-79, 81, 93a	45.00	100
PS39A	1996 (7)	2,560	KM#60-61, 78-79, 81, 97a	—	100
PS40	1997 (7)	2,132	KM60, 61, 63, 78-79, 81, 103a	—	120
PS41	1998 (7)	2,000	KM60-61, 63, 78-79, 81, 107a	55.00	165
PS42	1998 (4)	1,200	KM109a-112a	—	120
PS43	1999 (7)	1,800	KM115a, 116-121	59.00	190
PS44	2000 (7)	1,500	KM116-121, 125a	40.00	450

PROOF-LIKE SETS (PL)

KM#	Date	Mintage	Identification	Issue Price	Mkt Val
PLS1	1965 (7)	25,000	KM23.2-29.2 flat pack, blue label	—	17.50
PLS2	1965 (7)	500	KM23.2-29.2 red plush case "Ballot sets"	—	300
PLS3	1967 (7)	49,500	KM31.1, 32.1, 34.1, 35, 36.1, 37.1, 38.1 flat pack, blue label	5.00	10.00
PLS4	1967 (6)	500	KM31.1-32.1, 34.1, 35, 36.1-38.1 blue plush case "Ballot sets"	—	220
PLS6	1968 (6)	40,000	KM31.1, 32.1, 34.1, 35, 36.1, 37.1 flat pack, blue label	5.00	12.50
PLS7	1968 (6)	Inc. above	KM31.1, 32.1, 34.1, 35, 36.1, 37.1 blue plush case	—	18.00
PLS8	1969 (7)	50,000	KM31.1, 32.1, 34.1, 35, 36.1, 39, 40.1 flat pack, blue label	5.00	15.50
PLS9	1969 (7)	Inc. above	KM31.1, 32.1, 34.1, 35, 36.1, 39, 40.1 blue plush case	—	18.00
PLS10	1970 (7)	20,000	KM31.1, 32.1, 34.1, 36.1, 37.1, 41.1, 42, flat pack, blue label	5.00	18.00
PLS11	1970 (7)	Inc. above	KM31.1, 32.1, 34.1, 36.1, 37.1, 41.1, 42, blue plush case	—	25.00

NICARAGUA

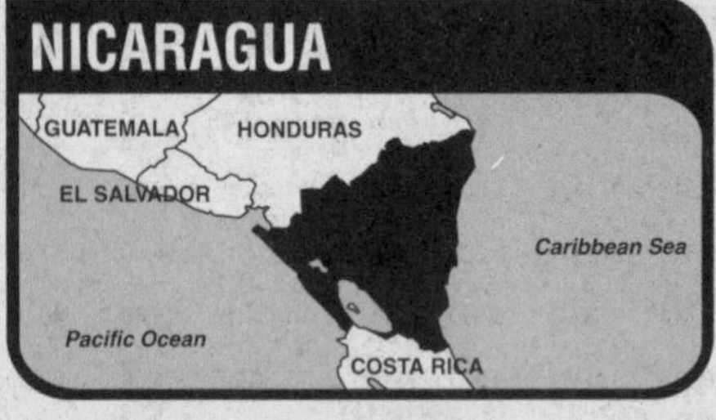

The Republic of Nicaragua, situated in Central America between Honduras and Costa Rica, has an area of 50,193 sq. mi. (129,494 sq. km.) and a population of *3.7 million. Capital: Managua. Agriculture, mining (gold and silver) and hardwood logging are the principal industries. Cotton, meat, coffee and sugar are exported.

Columbus sighted the coast of Nicaragua on Sept. 12,1502 during the course of his last voyage of discovery. It was first visited in 1522 by conquistadors from Panama, under the command of Gil Gonzalez. Francisco Hernandez de Cordoba established the first settlements in 1524 at Granada and Leon. Nicaragua was incorporated, for administrative purpose, in the Captaincy General of Guatemala, which included every Central American state but Panama. On September 15, 1821 the Captaincy General of Guatemala declared itself and all the Central American provinces independent of Spain. The next year Nicaragua united with the Mexican Empire of Augustin de Iturbide, only to join in 1823 the federation of the Central American Republic. Within Nicaragua rival cities or juntas such as Leon, Granada and El Viejo vied for power, wealth and influence, often attacking each other at will. To further prove their legitimacy as well as provide an acceptable circulating coinage in those turbulent times (1821-1825), provisional mints functioned intermittently at Granada, Leon and El Viejo. The early coinage reflected traditional but crude Spanish colonial cob-style designs. Nicaragua's first governor was Pedro Arias Davila, appointed on June 1, 1827. When the federation was dissolved, Nicaragua declared itself an independent republic on April 30, 1838.

Dissension between the Liberals and Conservatives of the contending cities kept Nicaragua in turmoil, which made it possible for William Walker to make himself President in 1855. The two major political parties finally united to drive him out and in 1857 he was expelled. A relative peace followed, but by 1912, Nicaragua had requested the U.S. Marines to restore order, which began a U.S. involvement that lasted until the Good Neighbor Policy was adopted in 1933. Anastasio Somoza Garcia assumed the Presidency in 1936. This family dynasty dominated Nicaragua until its overthrow in 1979. Formal elections in 1990 renewed a democratic government in power.

MINT MARKS

H - Heaton, Birmingham
HF - Huguenin Freres, Le Locle, Switzerland
Mo - Mexico City
-Philadelphia, Pa.
-Sherritt Mint, Canada
-Waterbury, Ct.

MONETARY SYSTEM

100 Centavos = 1 Peso

REPUBLIC

DECIMAL COINAGE

KM# 10 1/2 CENTAVO

Bronze, 17 mm. **Obv:** National emblem **Rev:** Value within sprigs **Note:** Minted at Heaton (1912-1916) and Philadelphia (1917-1937).

Date	Mintage	F12	VF20	XF40	MS60	MS63
1912	900,000	1.00	2.50	10.00	25.00	40.00
1912	—	PF63 275				
1915	320,000	1.50	4.00	15.00	60.00	90.00
1916	720,000	1.50	4.00	15.00	60.00	90.00
1917	720,000	1.50	4.00	10.00	50.00	75.00
1922	400,000	2.00	5.00	10.00	50.00	75.00
1924	400,000	1.00	3.00	7.00	50.00	75.00
1934	500,000	1.00	3.00	7.00	25.00	45.00
1936	600,000	0.50	0.75	5.00	20.00	35.00
1937	1,000,000	0.40	0.60	4.00	15.00	25.00

KM# 11 CENTAVO

4.00 g., Bronze, 20 mm. **Obv:** National emblem **Rev:** Value within sprigs

Date	Mintage	F12	VF20	XF40	MS60	MS63
1912 H	450,000	1.00	3.00	10.00	20.00	45.00
1912 H	—	PF63 275				
1914 H	300,000	1.00	5.00	15.00	50.00	85.00
1915 H	500,000	1.00	5.00	15.00	50.00	90.00
1916 H	450,000	1.00	5.00	15.00	50.00	90.00
1917	450,000	1.00	4.00	15.00	50.00	90.00
1919	750,000	1.00	3.00	12.00	30.00	50.00
1920	700,000	1.00	2.00	10.00	20.00	45.00
1922	500,000	1.00	2.00	10.00	20.00	45.00
1924	300,000	1.00	3.00	15.00	30.00	50.00
1927	250,000	1.00	3.00	15.00	35.00	60.00
1928	500,000	1.00	2.00	12.00	20.00	45.00
1929	500,000	1.00	2.00	10.00	20.00	45.00
1930	250,000	1.00	3.00	15.00	50.00	85.00
1934	500,000	1.00	2.00	8.00	20.00	45.00
1935	500,000	1.00	2.00	8.00	20.00	45.00
1936	500,000	1.00	2.00	5.00	20.00	45.00
1937	1,000,000	0.50	1.00	3.00	12.00	20.00
1938	2,000,000	0.50	1.00	3.00	10.00	20.00
1940	2,000,000	0.50	1.00	3.00	10.00	20.00

KM# 20 CENTAVO

Brass, 18 mm. **Obv:** National emblem **Rev:** Value within sprigs

Date	Mintage	F12	VF20	XF40	MS60	MS63
1943	1,000,000	0.50	1.00	3.00	10.00	25.00

KM# 12 5 CENTAVOS

5.00 g., Copper-Nickel, 21.2 mm. **Obv:** National emblem **Rev:** Value within sprigs

Date	Mintage	F12	VF20	XF40	MS60	MS63
1912 H	460,000	1.00	5.00	15.00	45.00	75.00
1912 H	—	PF63 300				
1914 H	300,000	1.00	5.00	15.00	45.00	75.00
1915 H	160,000	1.00	5.00	35.00	100	225
1919	100,000	1.00	5.00	20.00	60.00	100
1920	150,000	1.00	5.00	20.00	60.00	100
1927	100,000	1.00	5.00	20.00	60.00	100
1928	100,000	1.00	5.00	20.00	60.00	100
1929	100,000	1.00	5.00	25.00	65.00	120
1930	100,000	1.00	5.00	20.00	60.00	100
1934	200,000	1.00	5.00	15.00	60.00	100
1935	200,000	1.00	2.00	10.00	50.00	75.00
1936	300,000	0.50	1.00	10.00	50.00	75.00
1937	300,000	0.50	1.00	5.00	20.00	40.00
1938	800,000	0.50	1.00	5.00	15.00	25.00
1940	800,000	0.50	1.00	5.00	15.00	25.00

KM# 21 5 CENTAVOS

Brass, 21 mm. **Obv:** Bust facing within circle **Rev:** Radiant sun and hills within circle **Edge:** Plain

Date	Mintage	F12	VF20	XF40	MS60	MS63
1943	2,000,000	0.75	2.50	10.00	25.00	75.00

KM# 24.1 5 CENTAVOS

3.00 g., Copper-Nickel, 17 mm. **Obv:** Bust facing within circle **Rev:** Radiant sun and hills within circle **Edge Lettering:** B. N. N **Note:** Reduced size. Medal rotation.

Date	Mintage	F12	VF20	XF40	MS60	MS63
1946	4,000,000	0.10	0.25	1.00	10.00	20.00
1946	—	PF63 200				
1952	4,000,000	0.10	0.25	1.00	15.00	25.00
1952	—	PF63 250				
1954	4,000,000	0.10	0.15	0.25	2.00	5.00
1954	—	PF63 250				
1956	5,000,000	0.10	0.15	0.50	2.00	5.00
1956	—	PF63 250				

KM# 24.2 5 CENTAVOS

Copper-Nickel, 17 mm. **Obv:** Bust facing within circle **Rev:** Radiant sun and hills within circle **Edge Lettering:** B. C. N. **Note:** Medal rotation.

Date	Mintage	VF20	XF40	MS60	MS63	MS65
1962	3,000,000	0.10	0.15	0.75	1.25	2.00
1962	—	PF63 200				
1964	4,000,000	0.10	0.15	0.75	1.25	2.00
1965	10,000,000	0.10	0.15	0.75	1.25	2.00

KM# 24.2a 5 CENTAVOS

3.00 g., Nickel Clad Steel, 17 mm. **Obv:** Bust facing within circle **Rev:** Radiant sun and hills within circle **Note:** Medal rotation.

Date	Mintage	VF20	XF40	MS60	MS63	MS65
1972	10,020,000	—	0.10	0.25	0.50	0.75

KM# 24.3 5 CENTAVOS

3.00 g., Copper-Nickel **Obv:** Bust facing within circle **Rev:** Radiant sun and hills within circle **Edge:** Reeded **Note:** Coin rotation.

Date	Mintage	VF20	XF40	MS60	MS63	MS65
1972	20,000	PF65 2.50				

KM# 27 5 CENTAVOS

Aluminum, 21.5 mm. **Obv:** National emblem within circle **Rev:** Value within circle **Note:** Medal rotation.

Date	Mintage	VF20	XF40	MS60	MS63	MS65
1974	18,000,000	—	0.10	0.25	0.50	0.75

KM# 28 5 CENTAVOS

1.50 g., Aluminum, 21.5 mm. **Series:** F.A.O. **Obv:** National emblem within circle **Rev:** Value within circle **Edge:** Reeded **Note:** Medal rotation.

Date	Mintage	VF20	XF40	MS60	MS63	MS65
1974	2,000,000	—	0.40	0.50	0.75	1.00

KM# 49 5 CENTAVOS

1.04 g., Aluminum, 16.8 mm. **Obv:** Head with hat facing **Rev:** Value **Note:** Coin rotation.

Date	Mintage	VF20	XF40	MS60	MS63	MS65
1981	5,000,000	—	0.25	0.50	0.75	1.00

KM# 55 5 CENTAVOS

0.75 g., Aluminum, 15 mm. **Obv:** Hat above date and sprigs **Rev:** Value **Note:** Medal rotation.

Date	Mintage	VF20	XF40	MS60	MS63	MS65
1987	38,000,000	—	0.25	0.50	0.75	1.00

KM# 80 5 CENTAVOS

2.11 g., Chromium Plated Steel, 14.97 mm. **Obv:** National emblem **Rev:** Bird flying over map **Edge:** Plain **Note:** Coin rotation.

Date	Mintage	VF20	XF40	MS60	MS63	MS65
1994	20,000,000	—	—	0.50	0.75	1.00

KM# 13 10 CENTAVOS

2.50 g., 0.800 Silver 0.0643 oz. ASW, 18 mm. **Obv:** Bust facing within circle **Rev:** Radiant sun and hills within circle **Note:** All dates struck with medal rotation except 1935, which appears only in coin rotation.

Date	Mintage	F12	VF20	XF40	MS60	MS63
1912 H	230,000	2.00	3.00	25.00	75.00	120
1912 H	—	PF63 350				
1914 H	220,000	2.00	5.00	25.00	75.00	120
1914 H	—	PF63 450				
1927	500,000	2.00	3.00	15.00	60.00	100
1928	1,000,000	2.00	3.00	10.00	40.00	75.00
1930	150,000	2.00	3.00	20.00	75.00	125
1935	250,000	2.00	3.00	10.00	30.00	50.00
1936	250,000	2.00	3.00	10.00	20.00	35.00

KM# 17.1 10 CENTAVOS

4.00 g., Copper-Nickel, 20 mm. **Obv:** Bust facing within circle **Rev:** Radiant sun and hills within circle **Edge Lettering:** B.N.N **Note:** Medal rotation.

Date	Mintage	F12	VF20	XF40	MS60	MS63
1939	2,500,000	0.50	1.00	5.00	15.00	30.00
1939	—	PF63 250				
1946	2,000,000	0.50	1.00	5.00	15.00	30.00
1946	—	PF63 200				
1950	2,000,000	0.25	0.50	2.00	12.00	30.00
1950	—	PF63 200				
1952	1,500,000	0.25	0.50	2.00	15.00	30.00
1952	—	PF63 200				
1954	3,000,000	0.10	0.25	1.50	7.00	15.00
1954	—	PF63 200				
1956	5,000,000	0.10	0.20	1.00	3.00	5.00
1956	—	PF63 200				

KM# 17.2 10 CENTAVOS

3.91 g., Copper-Nickel, 20 mm. **Obv:** Bust facing within circle **Rev:** Radiant sun and hills within circle **Edge Lettering:** B.C.N **Note:** Medal rotation.

Date	Mintage	F12	VF20	XF40	MS60	MS63
1962	4,000,000	—	0.10	0.15	1.00	3.00
1962	—	PF63 225				
1964	4,000,000	—	0.10	0.15	1.00	3.00
1965	12,000,000	—	0.10	0.15	0.50	1.00

KM# 17.2a 10 CENTAVOS

Nickel Clad Steel, 20 mm. **Obv:** Bust facing within circle **Rev:** Radiant sun and hills within circle **Note:** Medal rotation. Previous KM#17.3a.

Date	Mintage	F12	VF20	XF40	MS60	MS63
1972	10,020,000	—	0.10	0.15	0.30	0.50

KM# 22 10 CENTAVOS

Brass, 20 mm. **Obv:** Bust facing within circle **Rev:** Radiant sun and hills within circle **Edge:** Reeded **Note:** Coin rotation.

Date	Mintage	F12	VF20	XF40	MS60	MS63
1943	2,000,000	0.50	1.00	5.00	20.00	50.00

KM# 17.3 10 CENTAVOS

Copper-Nickel, 17 mm. **Issuer:** Banco Central De Nicaragua **Obv:** Bust facing within circle - Francisco Hernandez de Cordoba **Obv. Legend:** Republica de Nicaragua **Rev:** Radiant sun and hills within circle, Seal of the Central America Federation **Rev. Legend:** In God We Trust (En Dios Confiamos) **Edge:** Reeded **Note:** Coin rotation.

Date	Mintage	VF20	XF40	MS60	MS63	MS65
1972	20,000	PF65 2.50				

Note: Sets only

KM# 29 10 CENTAVOS

Aluminum **Series:** F.A.O. **Obv:** Map within circle **Rev:** Value within circle **Note:** Medal rotation.

Date	Mintage	VF20	XF40	MS60	MS63	MS65
1974	2,000,000	—	0.10	0.50	0.75	1.00

KM# 30 10 CENTAVOS

Aluminum **Obv:** Map within circle **Rev:** Value within circle

Date	Mintage	VF20	XF40	MS60	MS63	MS65
1974	18,000,000	—	0.10	0.25	0.50	1.00

KM# 31 10 CENTAVOS

Copper-Nickel

Date	Mintage	VF20	XF40	MS60	MS63	MS65
1978	20,000,000	—	0.40	0.50	0.75	1.00

KM# 50 10 CENTAVOS

Aluminum **Obv:** Head with hat facing **Rev:** Value **Note:** Coin rotation.

Date	Mintage	VF20	XF40	MS60	MS63	MS65
1981	10,000,000	—	0.15	0.50	0.75	1.00

KM# 56 10 CENTAVOS

0.90 g., Aluminum, 17 mm. **Obv:** Hat above date and sprigs **Rev:** Value **Note:** Medal rotation.

Date	Mintage	VF20	XF40	MS60	MS63	MS65
1987	16,000,000	—	0.15	0.40	0.75	1.00

KM# 81 10 CENTAVOS

Chromium Plated Steel **Obv:** National emblem **Rev:** Bird flying above map **Note:** Coin rotation.

Date	Mintage	VF20	XF40	MS60	MS63	MS65
1994	6,439,000	—	—	0.25	0.65	1.00

KM# 14 25 CENTAVOS

6.25 g., 0.800 Silver 0.1608 oz. ASW, 24 mm. **Obv:** Bust facing within circle **Rev:** Radiant sun and hills within circle **Note:** Medal rotation.

Date	Mintage	F12	VF20	XF40	MS60	MS63
1912 H	320,000	5.50	8.00	25.00	50.00	125
1912 H	—	PF63 425				
1914 H	100,000	6.00	8.00	40.00	125	175
1928	200,000	5.50	8.00	25.00	60.00	100
1929	20,000	6.00	25.00	75.00	150	300
1930	20,000	6.00	25.00	75.00	150	300
1936	100,000	5.50	7.00	15.00	40.00	75.00

KM# 18.1 25 CENTAVOS

5.00 g., Copper-Nickel, 23 mm. **Obv:** Bust facing within circle **Rev:** Radiant sun and hills within circle **Edge Lettering:** B N N (repeated)

Date	Mintage	F12	VF20	XF40	MS60	MS63
1939	1,000,000	1.00	3.00	10.00	25.00	45.00
1939	—	PF63 300				
1946	1,000,000	1.00	3.00	8.00	20.00	40.00
1946	—	PF63 280				
1950	1,000,000	0.25	0.50	1.00	15.00	35.00
1950	—	PF63 300				
1952	1,000,000	0.25	0.50	1.00	15.00	35.00
1952	—	PF63 280				
1954	2,000,000	0.10	0.20	0.50	3.00	5.00
1954	—	PF63 280				
1956	3,000,000	0.10	0.20	0.50	3.00	5.00
1956	—	PF63 280				

KM# 23 25 CENTAVOS

Brass, 26.8 mm. **Obv:** Bust facing within circle **Rev:** Radiant sun and hills within circle **Edge:** Reeded **Note:** Coin rotation.

Date	Mintage	F12	VF20	XF40	MS60	MS63
1943 (no Mint Mark)	1,000,000	0.50	1.50	5.00	20.00	50.00

KM# 18.2 25 CENTAVOS

5.10 g., Copper-Nickel, 23 mm. **Obv:** Bust facing within circle **Rev:** Radiant sun and hills within circle **Edge Lettering:** B. C. N. **Note:** Medal rotation.

Date	Mintage	VF20	XF40	MS60	MS63	MS65
1964	3,000,000	0.20	0.40	1.50	2.00	3.00
1965	4,400,000	0.20	0.30	1.50	2.00	3.00

KM# 18.3 25 CENTAVOS
Copper-Nickel **Obv:** Bust facing within circle **Rev:** Radiant sun and hills within circle **Edge:** Reeded

Date	Mintage	VF20	XF40	MS60	MS63	MS65
1972	4,000,000	0.10	0.15	0.75	1.00	1.25
1972	20,000	PF65 2.50				
Note: Coin rotation						
1974	6,000,000	0.10	0.15	0.75	1.00	1.25
Note: Medal rotation						

KM# 51 25 CENTAVOS
3.40 g., Nickel Clad Steel **Obv:** Head with hat facing **Rev:** Value **Note:** Coin rotation

Date	Mintage	VF20	XF40	MS60	MS63	MS65
1981 (no Mint Mark)	10,000,000	—	0.25	0.75	1.00	1.25
1985 (no Mint Mark)	8,000,000	5.00	10.00	15.00	20.00	35.00

KM# 57 25 CENTAVOS
1.35 g., Aluminum, 19 mm. **Obv:** Hat above date and sprigs **Rev:** Value **Note:** Medal rotation.

Date	Mintage	VF20	XF40	MS60	MS63	MS65
1987	11,000,000	—	0.25	0.75	1.00	1.25

KM# 82 25 CENTAVOS
Chromium Plated Steel **Obv:** National emblem **Rev:** Bird flying above map **Note:** Coin rotation.

Date	Mintage	VF20	XF40	MS60	MS63	MS65
1994	2,500,000	—	—	0.50	0.75	1.00

KM# 15 50 CENTAVOS
12.50 g., 0.800 Silver 0.3215 oz. ASW, 30 mm. **Obv:** Bust facing within circle **Rev:** Radiant sun and hills within circle **Note:** Medal rotation.

Date	Mintage	F12	VF20	XF40	MS60	MS63
1912 H	260,000	8.00	12.00	50.00	125	250
1912 H	—	PF63 600				
1929	20,000	9.00	15.00	75.00	150	350

KM# 19.1 50 CENTAVOS
7.92 g., Copper-Nickel, 26 mm. **Obv:** Bust facing within circle **Rev:** Radiant sun and hills within circle **Edge Lettering:** B. N. N **Note:** Medal rotation.

Date	Mintage	F12	VF20	XF40	MS60	MS63
1939	1,000,000	1.00	3.00	10.00	35.00	60.00
1939	—	PF63 300				
1946	500,000	1.00	3.00	5.00	25.00	50.00
1946	—	PF63 300				
1950	500,000	1.00	2.00	5.00	25.00	50.00
1950	—	PF63 300				
1952	1,000,000	0.75	1.50	3.00	15.00	30.00
1952	—	PF63 300				
1954	2,000,000	0.50	1.00	4.00	8.00	15.00
1954	—	PF63 300				
1956	2,000,000	0.50	1.00	4.00	8.00	15.00
1956	—	PF63 300				

KM# 19.2 50 CENTAVOS
Copper-Nickel **Obv:** Bust facing within circle **Rev:** Radiant sun and hills within circle **Edge Lettering:** B. C. N

Date	Mintage	VF20	XF40	MS60	MS63	MS65
1965	600,000	0.75	1.50	3.50	7.00	15.00
1965	—	PF63 150				

KM# 19.3 50 CENTAVOS
Copper-Nickel **Obv:** Bust facing within circle **Rev:** Radiant sun and hills within circle **Edge:** Reeded

Date	Mintage	VF20	XF40	MS60	MS63	MS65
1972	—	—	—	—	—	—
1972	20,000	PF65 2.50				
Note: Coin rotation						
1974	2,000,000	0.25	0.50	1.25	2.00	3.00
Note: Medal rotation						

KM# 42 50 CENTAVOS
7.00 g., Copper-Nickel **Obv:** Head with hat facing **Rev:** Value **Note:** Coin rotation.

Date	Mintage	VF20	XF40	MS60	MS63	MS65
1980 Mo	15,000,000	0.25	0.50	1.00	1.25	1.50

KM# 42a 50 CENTAVOS
6.16 g., Nickel Clad Steel, 25.9 mm. **Obv:** Head with hat facing **Rev:** Value **Note:** Coin rotation.

Date	Mintage	VF20	XF40	MS60	MS63	MS65
1983	10,000,000	—	0.40	1.00	1.25	1.50
1985	10,000,000	3.00	7.00	10.00	12.00	20.00

KM# 58 50 CENTAVOS
4.85 g., Aluminum-Bronze, 22 mm. **Obv:** Hat above date and sprigs **Rev:** Value **Note:** Medal rotation.

Date	Mintage	VF20	XF40	MS60	MS63	MS65
1987	12,000,000	—	0.40	1.00	1.25	1.50

KM# 83 50 CENTAVOS
4.68 g., Chromium Plated Steel, 22 mm. **Obv:** National emblem **Rev:** Bird flying above map **Note:** Coin rotation.

Date	Mintage	VF20	XF40	MS60	MS63	MS65
1994	12,000,000	—	—	0.50	0.75	1.00

KM# 88 50 CENTAVOS
4.80 g., Nickel Clad Steel, 22 mm. **Obv:** National emblem **Rev:** Value above sprigs within circle, date flanked by stars

Date	Mintage	VF20	XF40	MS60	MS63	MS65
1997	24,000,000	—	—	0.50	0.75	1.00

KM# 16 CORDOBA
25.00 g., 0.900 Silver 0.7234 oz. ASW, 38 mm. **Obv:** Bust facing within circle **Rev:** Radiant sun and hills within circle **Note:** Medal rotation.

Date	Mintage	F12	VF20	XF40	MS60	MS63
1912 H	35,000	35.00	75.00	225	1,000	2,000
1912 H	—	PF63 2,850				

KM# 26 CORDOBA
9.45 g., Copper-Nickel, 28.9 mm. **Obv:** Bust facing within circle **Rev:** Radiant sun and hills within circle **Edge:** Reeded

Date	Mintage	VF20	XF40	MS60	MS63	MS65
1972	20,000,000	0.20	0.50	1.00	1.50	2.00
Note: Medal rotation						
1972	40,000	PF65 5.00				
Note: Coin rotation						

KM# 43 CORDOBA
8.84 g., Copper-Nickel **Obv:** Head with hat facing **Rev:** Value **Note:** Coin rotation.

Date	Mintage	VF20	XF40	MS60	MS63	MS65
1980 Mo	10,000,000	0.20	0.50	0.75	1.00	1.50
1983 Mo	10,000,000	0.20	0.50	0.75	1.00	1.50

KM# 43a CORDOBA
Nickel Clad Steel **Obv:** Head with hat facing **Rev:** Value **Note:** Coin rotation.

Date	Mintage	VF20	XF40	MS60	MS63	MS65
1984	10,000,000	0.10	0.50	0.75	1.00	1.50
1985	10,000,000	3.00	7.00	10.00	12.00	20.00

KM# 59 CORDOBA
6.15 g., Aluminum-Bronze, 24 mm. **Obv:** Hat above date and sprigs **Rev:** Value **Note:** Medal rotation.

Date	Mintage	VF20	XF40	MS60	MS63	MS65
1987	23,000,000	0.45	0.75	1.50	2.25	3.50

KM# 77 CORDOBA
27.00 g., 0.925 Silver 0.803 oz. ASW **Subject:** Ibero - American Series **Obv:** National emblem within assorted arms around border **Rev:** Map behind standing figures shaking hands within circle

Date	Mintage	VF20	XF40	MS60	MS63	MS65
1991	10,000	PF63 30.00	PF65 45.00			

KM# 84 CORDOBA
13.82 g., 0.925 Silver 0.411 oz. ASW **Subject:** National Ruben Dario Theater **Obv:** Dancing native and map **Rev:** Theatrical masks on theatre

Date	Mintage	VF20	XF40	MS60	MS63	MS65
1994	2,000	PF63 22.00	PF65 35.00			

KM# 85 CORDOBA
14.17 g., 0.925 Silver 0.4214 oz. ASW **Subject:** 100th Anniversary - City of Boaco **Obv:** National emblem **Rev:** Building

Date	Mintage	VF20	XF40	MS60	MS63	MS65
1995	1,000	PF63 35.00	PF65 45.00			

KM# 87 CORDOBA
13.96 g., 0.825 Silver 0.3703 oz. ASW **Subject:** 50th Anniversary - F.A.O **Obv:** National emblem **Rev:** F.A.O. logo within circle

Date	Mintage	VF20	XF40	MS60	MS63	MS65
1995	2,200	PF63 25.00	PF65 35.00			

KM# 89 CORDOBA
6.20 g., Nickel Clad Steel, 25 mm. **Obv:** National emblem **Rev:** Value above sprigs within circle **Edge:** Reeded

Date	Mintage	VF20	XF40	MS60	MS63	MS65
1997	39,000,000	—	—	1.00	1.50	2.00
2000	35,000,000	—	—	1.00	1.50	2.00

KM# 44 5 CORDOBAS
Copper-Nickel, 27 mm. **Obv:** Value **Rev:** Head with hat facing **Shape:** 7-sided **Note:** Medal rotation.

Date	Mintage	VF20	XF40	MS60	MS63	MS65
1980	10,000,000	0.25	0.50	1.00	1.50	2.00

KM# 44a 5 CORDOBAS
Nickel Clad Steel **Obv:** Value **Rev:** Head with hat facing **Shape:** 7-sided **Note:** Medal rotation.

Date	Mintage	VF20	XF40	MS60	MS63	MS65
1984	8,000,000	0.25	0.50	1.00	1.50	2.00

KM# 60 5 CORDOBAS
7.50 g., Aluminum-Bronze, 25.9 mm. **Obv:** Hat above date and sprigs **Rev:** Value

Date	Mintage	VF20	XF40	MS60	MS63	MS65
1987	23,000,000	0.50	1.00	2.00	3.00	5.00

KM# 86 5 CORDOBAS
27.00 g., 0.925 Silver 0.803 oz. ASW **Subject:** Wildlife Protection **Obv:** National emblem

Date	Mintage	VF20	XF40	MS60	MS63	MS65
1994	20,000	PF63 30.00	PF65 40.00			

KM# 90 5 CORDOBAS
7.80 g., Nickel Clad Steel, 27.8 mm. **Obv:** National emblem **Rev:** Value above sprigs within circle **Edge:** Reeded **Note:** Coin rotation.

Date	Mintage	VF20	XF40	MS60	MS63	MS65
1997	11,000,000	—	—	1.00	1.50	2.00
2000	25,000,000	—	—	1.00	1.50	2.00

KM# 96 5 CORDOBAS
27.00 g., 0.925 Silver 0.803 oz. ASW, 40 mm. **Subject:** Ibero-America **Obv:** National emblem within assorted arms border **Rev:** Two folk dancers **Edge:** Reeded

Date	Mintage	VF20	XF40	MS60	MS63	MS65
1997	1,000	PF63 35.00	PF65 45.00			

KM# 76 10 CORDOBAS
25.70 g., 0.999 Silver 0.8254 oz. ASW **Subject:** Soccer **Obv:** National emblem within circle **Rev:** Soccer champions with arms raised

Date	Mintage	VF20	XF40	MS60	MS63	MS65
1991	10,000	PF63 20.00	PF65 30.00			

KM# 78 10 CORDOBAS
19.95 g., 0.999 Silver 0.6408 oz. ASW **Subject:** Spanish Royal Visit **Obv:** National emblem within circle **Rev:** Heads 1/4 left on map

Date	Mintage	VF20	XF40	MS60	MS63	MS65
1991	5,000	PF63 30.00	PF65 42.00			

KM# 95 10 CORDOBAS
27.20 g., 0.925 Silver 0.8089 oz. ASW, 40 mm. **Subject:** Ibero-America Series **Obv:** National emblem within circle of assorted arms **Rev:** Man on horse with two milk cans **Edge:** Reeded

Date	Mintage	VF20	XF40	MS60	MS63	MS65
1999	—	PF63 40.00	PF65 55.00			

KM# 32 20 CORDOBAS
5.03 g., 0.925 Silver 0.1496 oz. ASW **Subject:** Earthquake Relief Issue **Obv:** National emblem **Rev:** Bird at center of cog wheel design, plant sprigs in sections

Date	Mintage	VF20	XF40	MS60	MS63	MS65
1975	1,750	PF63 18.00	PF65 22.00			
Note: Medal rotation						
1975	2,491	—	—	10.00	15.00	20.00

KM# 25 50 CORDOBAS
35.60 g., 0.900 Gold 1.0301 oz. AGW **Subject:** 100th Anniversary - Birth of Ruben Dario **Obv:** National emblem within circle **Rev:** Bust 3/4 facing within circle

Date	Mintage	VF20	XF40	MS60	MS63	MS65
1967 HF Prooflike	16,000	—	—	—	—	1,600

Note: 500 pieces were issued in blue boxes with certificates; Boxed examples command a premium

KM# 33 50 CORDOBAS
12.57 g., 0.925 Silver 0.3738 oz. ASW **Subject:** U.S. Bicentennial **Obv:** National emblem **Rev:** Liberty bell divides dates **Note:** Mintages are included with KM#34.

Date	Mintage	VF20	XF40	MS60	MS63	MS65
1975	—	—	—	12.00	17.00	20.00
1975	—	PF63 18.00	PF65 22.00			

Note: Medal rotation

KM# 34 50 CORDOBAS
12.57 g., 0.925 Silver 0.3738 oz. ASW **Subject:** Earthquake Relief Issue **Obv:** National emblem **Rev:** "The Bud" painting by Annigoni

Date	Mintage	VF20	XF40	MS60	MS63	MS65
1975	4,482	—	—	12.00	17.00	20.00
1975	3,500	PF63 18.00	PF65 22.00			

KM# 61 50 CORDOBAS
16.60 g., 0.825 Silver 0.4403 oz. ASW **Series:** Winter Olympics **Obv:** National emblem within circle **Rev:** Skier

Date	Mintage	VF20	XF40	MS60	MS63	MS65
1988	10,000	PF63 20.00	PF65 25.00			

KM# 62 50 CORDOBAS
16.60 g., 0.825 Silver 0.4403 oz. ASW **Series:** Olympics **Obv:** National emblem within circle **Rev:** Sailboat

Date	Mintage	VF20	XF40	MS60	MS63	MS65
1988	10,000	PF63 20.00	PF65 25.00			

KM# 91 50 CORDOBAS
27.00 g., 0.925 Silver 0.803 oz. ASW, 40 mm. **Subject:** Central Bank 40th Anniversary **Obv:** National emblem within circle and wreath **Rev:** Bust 1/4 left **Edge:** Reeded

Date	Mintage	VF20	XF40	MS60	MS63	MS65
2000	1,000	PF65 75.00				

KM# 35 100 CORDOBAS
25.14 g., 0.925 Silver 0.7476 oz. ASW **Subject:** U.S. Bicentennial **Obv:** National emblem **Rev:** Betsy Ross sewing flag on left, astronaut placing flag on moon on right **Note:** Mintages included with KM#36.

Date	Mintage	VF20	XF40	MS60	MS63	MS65
1975	—	—	—	25.00	35.00	45.00
1975	—	PF63 35.00	PF65 45.00			

Note: Medal rotation

KM# 36 100 CORDOBAS
25.14 g., 0.925 Silver 0.7476 oz. ASW **Subject:** Earthquake Relief Issue **Obv:** National emblem **Rev:** World globe in front of assorted flags

Date	Mintage	VF20	XF40	MS60	MS63	MS65
1975	4,682	—	—	22.00	32.00	42.00
1975	3,500	PF63 32.00	PF65 42.00			

Note: Medal rotation

KM# A91 100 CORDOBAS
27.00 g., 0.999 Gold 0.8672 oz. AGW **Subject:** Central Bank 40th Anniversary **Obv:** National emblem within circle and wreath **Rev:** Bust 1/4 left **Edge:** Reeded

Date	Mintage	VF20	XF40	MS60	MS63	MS65
2000	500	PF65 1,300				

KM# 37 200 CORDOBAS
2.10 g., 0.900 Gold 0.0608 oz. AGW **Subject:** Pieta by Michelangelo **Obv:** National emblem **Rev:** Sitting figure holding lying figure on lap within circle

Date	Mintage	VF20	XF40	MS60	MS63	MS65
1975	1,200	—	—	—	120	135
1975	1,650	PF65 140				

KM# 79 250 CORDOBAS
171.07 g., 0.999 Silver 5.4945 oz. ASW **Subject:** Spanish Royal Visit **Obv:** National emblem within circle **Rev:** Heads 1/4 left on map

Date	Mintage	VF20	XF40	MS60	MS63	MS65
1992	—	PF63 150	PF65 200			

KM# 38 500 CORDOBAS
5.40 g., 0.900 Gold 0.1563 oz. AGW **Subject:** Colonial Church, La Merced **Obv:** National emblem **Rev:** Colonial church within circle

Date	Mintage	VF20	XF40	MS60	MS63	MS65
1975	200	—	—	—	—	385
1975	100	PF65 650				

KM# 39 500 CORDOBAS
5.40 g., 0.900 Gold 0.1563 oz. AGW **Subject:** Earthquake Relief Issue **Obv:** National emblem **Rev:** "The Bud" by Annigoni

Date	Mintage	VF20	XF40	MS60	MS63	MS65
1975	1,750	—	—	—	—	385
1975	1,120	PF65 400				

KM# 45 500 CORDOBAS
14.00 g., 0.925 Silver 0.4164 oz. ASW **Obv:** Map **Rev:** Head with hat facing **Note:** Medal rotation.

Date	Mintage	VF20	XF40	MS60	MS63	MS65
1980 Mo	7,000	PF63 18.00	PF65 25.00			

KM# 46 500 CORDOBAS
14.00 g., 0.925 Silver 0.4164 oz. ASW **Obv:** Map **Rev:** Bust right **Note:** Medal rotation.

Date	Mintage	VF20	XF40	MS60	MS63	MS65
1980 Mo	7,000	PF63 18.00	PF65 25.00			

KM# 47 500 CORDOBAS
14.00 g., 0.925 Silver 0.4164 oz. ASW **Obv:** National emblem **Rev:** Bust of Rigoberto Lopez Perez 1/4 left **Note:** Medal rotation.

Date	Mintage	VF20	XF40	MS60	MS63	MS65
1980 Mo	7,000	PF63 18.00	PF65 25.00			

KM# 69 500 CORDOBAS
14.00 g., 0.999 Silver 0.4497 oz. ASW **Subject:** 50th Anniversary - A. C. Sandino **Obv:** National emblem **Rev:** Birthplace of Augusto Cesar Sandino

Date	Mintage	VF20	XF40	MS60	MS63	MS65
ND-1984	1,000	PF63 25.00	PF65 35.00			

KM# 70 500 CORDOBAS
14.00 g., 0.999 Silver 0.4497 oz. ASW **Subject:** 50th Anniversary - Sandono's Death **Obv:** National emblem **Rev:** Facing busts of Generals Sandino, Estrada and Umanzor

Date	Mintage	VF20	XF40	MS60	MS63	MS65
ND-1984	1,000	PF63 30.00	PF65 40.00			

KM# 73 500 CORDOBAS
14.00 g., 0.999 Silver 0.4497 oz. ASW **Subject:** 50th Anniversary - The Murder of General Augusto Cesar Sandino **Obv:** National emblem **Rev:** Bust with hat facing

Date	Mintage	VF20	XF40	MS60	MS63	MS65
ND-1984	1,000	PF63 30.00	PF65 40.00			

KM# 63 500 CORDOBAS
Aluminum **Obv:** Hat above date and sprigs **Rev:** Value

Date	Mintage	VF20	XF40	MS60	MS63	MS65
1987	—	—	—	2.50	3.50	6.00

KM# 40 1000 CORDOBAS
9.60 g., 0.900 Gold 0.2778 oz. AGW **Subject:** U.S. Bicentennial **Obv:** National emblem **Rev:** Liberty bell divides dates

Date	Mintage	VF20	XF40	MS60	MS63	MS65
1975	3,380	—	—	—	—	525
1975	2,270	PF65 550				

KM# 48 1000 CORDOBAS
20.00 g., 0.900 Gold 0.5787 oz. AGW **Subject:** 1st Anniversary of Revolution **Obv:** Three 1/2 figures with guns raised **Rev:** Busts of Sandino and Fonseca

Date	Mintage	VF20	XF40	MS60	MS63	MS65
1980 Mo	6,000	PF65 1,100				

KM# 52 1000 CORDOBAS
20.00 g., 0.917 Gold 0.5896 oz. AGW **Subject:** 50th Anniversary - The Murder of General Augusto Cesar Sandino **Obv:** National emblem **Rev:** Bust with hat facing

Date	Mintage	VF20	XF40	MS60	MS63	MS65
1984	1,000	PF65 1,200				

KM# 53 1000 CORDOBAS
20.00 g., 0.917 Gold 0.5896 oz. AGW **Obv:** National emblem **Rev:** Birthplace of Augusto Cesar Sandino

Date	Mintage	VF20	XF40	MS60	MS63	MS65
1984	1,000	PF65 1,200				

KM# 54 1000 CORDOBAS
20.00 g., 0.917 Gold 0.5896 oz. AGW **Obv:** National emblem **Rev:** Facing busts of Generals Sandino, Estrada and Umanzor

Date	Mintage	VF20	XF40	MS60	MS63	MS65
1984	1,000	PF65 1,200				

KM# 41 2000 CORDOBAS
19.20 g., 0.900 Gold 0.5556 oz. AGW **Subject:** U.S. Bicentennial **Obv:** National emblem **Rev:** Betsy Ross sewing flag on left, astronaut placing flag on moon on right

Date	Mintage	VF20	XF40	MS60	MS63	MS65
1975	320	—	—	—	—	1,100
1975	100	PF65 1,150				

KM# 65 2000 CORDOBAS
16.60 g., 0.825 Silver 0.4403 oz. ASW **Subject:** Soccer **Obv:** National emblem within circle **Rev:** Soccer player

Date	Mintage	VF20	XF40	MS60	MS63	MS65
1988	5,000	PF63 32.00	PF65 48.00			

KM# 64 10000 CORDOBAS
20.00 g., 0.999 Silver 0.6424 oz. ASW, 38 mm. **Subject:** Discovery of Nicaragua by Columbus **Obv:** National emblem **Rev:** Sailing ship and small boat **Edge:** Reeded

Date	Mintage	VF20	XF40	MS60	MS63	MS65
1989	Est. 10000	PF63 30.00	PF65 45.00			

KM# 66 10000 CORDOBAS
26.40 g., 0.999 Silver 0.8479 oz. ASW **Obv:** National emblem within circle **Rev:** Two soccer players

Date	Mintage	VF20	XF40	MS60	MS63	MS65
1990	5,000	PF63 35.00	PF65 50.00			

KM# 67 10000 CORDOBAS
26.00 g., 0.999 Silver 0.8351 oz. ASW **Subject:** Discovery of America **Obv:** National emblem within circle **Rev:** Sailing ship

Date	Mintage	VF20	XF40	MS60	MS63	MS65
1990	10,000	PF63 35.00	PF65 50.00			

KM# 68 10000 CORDOBAS
26.00 g., 0.999 Silver 0.8351 oz. ASW **Series:** 1992 Summer Olympics **Obv:** National emblem within circle **Rev:** Bicyclist

Date	Mintage	VF20	XF40	MS60	MS63	MS65
1990	10,000	PF63 30.00	PF65 45.00			

KM# 71 10000 CORDOBAS

26.00 g., 0.999 Silver 0.8351 oz. ASW **Subject:** Wildlife Protection **Obv:** National emblem within circle **Rev:** Ocelot

Date	Mintage	VF20	XF40	MS60	MS63	MS65
1990	5,000	PF63 40.00	PF65 55.00			

KM# 72.1 10000 CORDOBAS

20.40 g., 0.999 Silver 0.6552 oz. ASW **Series:** 1992 Summer Olympics **Obv:** National emblem within circle **Rev:** Horse jumping

Date	Mintage	VF20	XF40	MS60	MS63	MS65
1990	10,000	PF63 35.00	PF65 50.00			

KM# 72.2 10000 CORDOBAS

20.00 g., 0.999 Silver 0.6424 oz. ASW **Series:** 1992 Summer Olympics **Obv:** National emblem within circle **Rev:** Horse jumping, 999 added at 4 o'clock

Date	Mintage	VF20	XF40	MS60	MS63	MS65
1990	Inc. above	PF63 30.00	PF65 45.00			

KM# 74 10000 CORDOBAS

25.90 g., 0.999 Silver 0.8319 oz. ASW **Series:** 1992 Summer Olympics **Obv:** National emblem within circle **Rev:** Tennis player proclaiming victory

Date	Mintage	VF20	XF40	MS60	MS63	MS65
1990	10,000	PF63 35.00	PF65 50.00			

KM# 75 10000 CORDOBAS

20.00 g., 0.999 Silver 0.6424 oz. ASW **Series:** 1992 Winter Olympics **Obv:** National emblem within circle **Rev:** Figure skater

Date	Mintage	VF20	XF40	MS60	MS63	MS65
1990	10,000	PF63 30.00	PF65 45.00			

REVOLUTIONARY TOKEN COINAGE

KM# Tn1 10 PESOS

18.00 g., Lead **Issuer:** General Augusto Cesar Sandino

Date	Mintage	VG8	F12	VF20	XF40	MS60
ND-1927	—	500	750	1,250	2,700	—

PATTERNS

Including off metal strikes.

KM#	Date	Mintage	Identification	Mkt Val
Pn10	1912H	2	1/2 Centavo. Silver. KM10; 2 known.	—
Pn11	1912H	1	1/2 Centavo. Gold. KM10; unique.	—
Pn12	1912H	2	Centavo. Silver. KM11; 2 known.	4,000
Pn13	1912H	1	Centavo. Gold. KM#11.	—
Pn14	1912H	2	5 Centavos. Silver. KM12.	—
Pn15	1912H	1	5 Centavos. Gold. KM12.	—
Pn16	1912H	1	10 Centavos. Gold. KM13.	—
Pn17	1912H	1	25 Centavos. Gold. KM14.	—
Pn18	1912H	1	50 Centavos. Gold. KM#15.	—
Pn19	1912H	1	Cordoba. Gold. KM16.	—
Pn20	1975	—	20 Cordobas. Silver. KM32 with 4.65 gram Plata Fino, LEY 925 below date.	—
Pn21	1975	—	50 Cordobas. Silver. KM34 with 11.63 gram. Plata Fino, LEY 925 below date.	—
Pn22	1975	—	100 Cordobas. Silver. KM36 with 23.25 gram. Plata Fino, LEY 925 below date.	—

TRIAL STRIKES

KM#	Date	Mintage	Identification	Mkt Val
Ts1	ND-1912	—	10 Centavos. Aluminum. Obverse.	375
Ts2	ND-1912	—	10 Centavos. Aluminum. Bust facing within circle. Radiant sun and hills within circle. Reverse,.	375
Ts3	ND-1912	—	25 Centavos. Aluminum. Obverse.	385
Ts4	ND-1912	—	25 Centavos. Aluminum. Reverse.	385
Ts5	ND-1912	—	50 Centavos. Aluminum. Bust facing within circle. Radiant sun and hills within circle. Obverse.	400
Ts6	ND-1912	—	50 Centavos. Aluminum.	400
Ts7	ND-1912	—	Cordoba. 18.000. Aluminum. Obverse.	—
Ts8	ND-1912	—	Cordoba. 18.000. Aluminum. Reverse.	—
Ts9	1965	—	5 Centavos. Nickel. Raised "Trial" left of bust on obverse, above rays on reverse. KM24.2.	—
Ts10	1965	—	10 Centavos. Nickel. Raised "Trial" left of bust on obverse, above rays on reverse. KM17.2.	—

MINT SETS

KM#	Date	Mintage	Identification	Issue Price	Mkt Val
MS1	1975 (5)	—	KM37-41	—	2,900
MS2	1975 (5)	2,250	KM#32-36	—	150

PROOF SETS

KM#	Date	Mintage	Identification	Issue Price	Mkt Val
PS1	1912 (7)	10	KM10-16	—	5,100
PS2	1912 (3)	2	Pn10, Pn12, Pn14	—	—
PS3	1912 (7)	1	Pn11, Pn13, Pn15-19	—	—
PS4	1972 (5)	20,000	KM17.3-19.3, 24.3, 26	8.00	12.00
PS5	1975 (7)	—	KM32, 33, 35, 37, 38, 40, 41	—	2,650
PS6	1975 (5)	2,000	KM32-36	—	200
PS7	1975 (3)	—	KM32, 33, 35	115	130
PS8	1975 (3)	—	KM34, 36, 39	—	500
PS9	1975 (2)	—	KM37, 39	—	540

NIGER

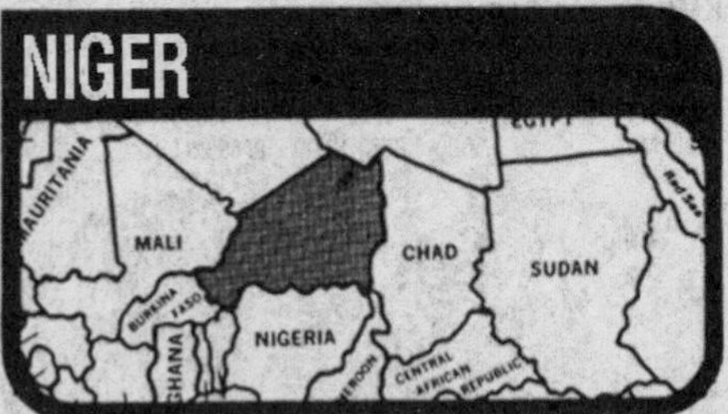

The Republic of Niger, located in West Africa's Sahara region 1,000 miles (1,609 km.) from the Mediterranean shore, has an area of 489,191 sq. mi. (1,267,000 sq. km.) and a population of *7.4 million. Capital: Niamey. The economy is based on subsistence agriculture and raising livestock. Peanuts, peanut oil, and livestock are exported.

Although four-fifths of Niger is arid desert, it was, some 6,000 years ago inhabited and an important economic crossroads. Its modern history began in the 19th century with the beginning of contacts with British and German explorers searching for the mouth of the Niger River. Niger was incorporated into French West Africa in 1896, but it was 1922 before all native resistance was quelled and Niger became a French colony. In 1958 the voters approved the new French Constitution and elected to become an autonomous republic within the French Community. On Aug. 3, 1960, Niger withdrew from the Community and proclaimed its independence.

REPUBLIC

DECIMAL COINAGE

KM# 1 10 FRANCS

4.20 g., 0.900 Gold 0.1215 oz. AGW **Subject:** Independence Commemorataive **Obv:** President Diori Hamani left **Rev:** Flagged arms

Date	Mintage	VF20	XF40	MS60	MS63	MS65
ND-1960	1,000	PF63 200	PF65 280			

KM# 7 10 FRANCS

3.20 g., 0.900 Gold 0.0926 oz. AGW **Obv:** Ostriches **Rev:** Flagged arms

Date	Mintage	VF20	XF40	MS60	MS63	MS65
1968	1,000	PF65 190				

KM# 8.1 10 FRANCS

20.00 g., 0.900 Silver 0.5787 oz. ASW, 36 mm. **Obv:** Lion **Rev:** Flagged arms **Note:** Sharp details, raised rim.

Date	Mintage	VF20	XF40	MS60	MS63	MS65
1968	1,000	PF63 75.00	PF65 120			

KM# 8.2 10 FRANCS

24.54 g., 0.900 Silver 0.7101 oz. ASW **Obv:** Exists with and without accent marks above first "E" in REPUBLIQUE **Rev:** Flagged arms **Note:** Dull details, machined-down rim

Date	Mintage	VF20	XF40	MS60	MS63	MS65
1968	—	PF63 30.00	PF65 45.00			

KM# 2 25 FRANCS

8.00 g., 0.900 Gold 0.2315 oz. AGW **Subject:** Independence Commemorative **Obv:** President Diori Hamani left **Rev:** Flagged arms

Date	Mintage	VF20	XF40	MS60	MS63	MS65
ND-1960	1,000	PF63 350	PF65 450			

KM# 9 25 FRANCS

8.00 g., 0.900 Gold 0.2315 oz. AGW **Obv:** Barbary sheep **Rev:** Flagged arms

Date	Mintage	VF20	XF40	MS60	MS63	MS65
1968	1,000	PF65 450				

KM# 3 50 FRANCS

16.00 g., 0.900 Gold 0.463 oz. AGW **Subject:** Independence Commemorative **Obv:** President Diori Hamani left **Rev:** Flagged arms

Date	Mintage	VF20	XF40	MS60	MS63	MS65
ND-1960	1,000	PF63 750	PF65 900			

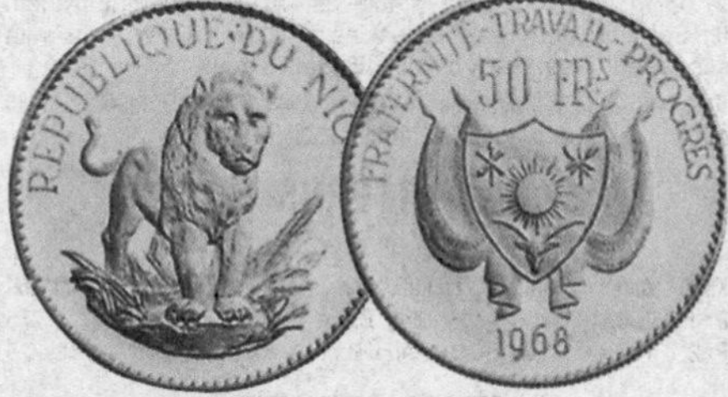

KM# 10 50 FRANCS

16.00 g., 0.900 Gold 0.463 oz. AGW **Subject:** Independence Commemorative **Obv:** Lion **Rev:** Flagged arms

Date	Mintage	VF20	XF40	MS60	MS63	MS65
1968	1,000	PF65 900				

KM# 4 100 FRANCS

32.00 g., 0.900 Gold 0.9259 oz. AGW **Subject:** Independence Commemorative **Obv:** President Diori Hamani left **Rev:** Flagged arms

Date	Mintage	VF20	XF40	MS60	MS63	MS65
ND-1960	1,000	PF63 1,350	PF65 1,750			

KM# 11 100 FRANCS

32.00 g., 0.900 Gold 0.9259 oz. AGW **Subject:** Independence Commemorative **Obv:** President Diori Hamani left **Rev:** Flagged arms

Date	Mintage	VF20	XF40	MS60	MS63	MS65
1968	1,000	PF65 1,750				

KM# 5 500 FRANCS

10.00 g., 0.900 Silver 0.2894 oz. ASW **Subject:** Independence Commemorative **Obv:** President Diori Hamani left **Rev:** Flagged arms

Date	Mintage	VF20	XF40	MS60	MS63	MS65
ND-1960	—	PF63 30.00	PF65 45.00			

KM# 6 1000 FRANCS

20.00 g., 0.900 Silver 0.5787 oz. ASW, 36 mm. **Subject:** Independence Commemorative **Obv:** President Diori Hamani left **Rev:** Flagged arms

Date	Mintage	VF20	XF40	MS60	MS63	MS65
ND-1960	—	PF63 50.00	PF65 65.00			

ESSAIS

KM#	Date	Mintage	Identification	Mkt Val
E1	1960	—	10 Francs. Silver. Lion facing. Arms. Thick planchet.	180
E2	1960	—	25 Francs.	200
E3	1960	—	50 Francs.	325
E4	1960	—	100 Francs.	500
E5	ND-1960	1,000	500 Francs. Silver. KM5.	50.00
E6	ND-1960	1,000	1000 Francs. Silver. KM6.	70.00
E7	1968	—	10 Francs. Gold. KM8.	2,400
E8	1968	—	10 Francs. Silver.	225
E9	1968	—	25 Francs. Silver.	55.00
E10	1968	—	50 Francs. Silver.	60.00
E11	1968	—	100 Francs. Silver.	160

PATTERNS

Including off metal strikes

KM#	Date	Mintage	Identification	Mkt Val
Pn1	1968	—	10 Francs. Copper. Reeded. KM8.1.	275

PROOF SETS

KM#	Date	Mintage	Identification	Issue Price	Mkt Val
PS1	1960 (4)	1,000	KM1-4	—	3,375
PS2	1968 (4)	—	KM7, 9-11	—	3,300

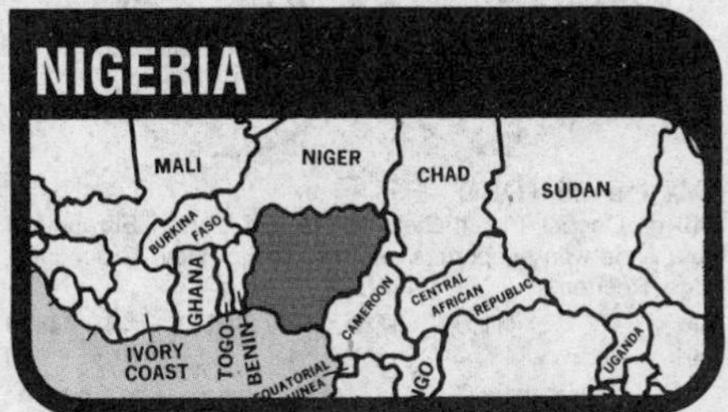

Nigeria, situated on the Atlantic coast of West Africa has an area of 356,669 sq. mi. (923,770 sq. km.).

Following the Napoleonic Wars, the British expanded their trade with the interior of Nigeria. The Berlin Conference of 1885 recognized British claims to a sphere of influence in that area, and in the following year the Royal Niger Company was chartered. Direct British control of the territory was initiated in 1900, and in 1914 the amalgamation of Northern and Southern Nigeria into the Colony and Protectorate of Nigeria was effected. In 1960, following a number of territorial and constitutional changes, Nigeria was granted independence within the British Commonwealth as a federation of the Northern, Western and Eastern regions. Nigeria altered its political relationship with Great Britain on Oct. 1, 1963, by proclaiming itself a republic. It did, however, elect to remain a member of the Commonwealth of Nations.

On May 30, 1967, the Eastern Region of the republic an area occupied principally by the proud and resourceful Ibo tribe – seceded from Nigeria and proclaimed itself the independent Republic of Biafra with Odumegwu Ojukwu as Chief of State. Civil war erupted and raged for 31 months. Casualties, including civilian, were about two million, the majority succumbing to malnutrition and disease. Biafra surrendered to the federal government on January 15, 1970.

For earlier coinage refer to British West Africa.

Arms Mottos

Short: Unity and faith

Long: Unity and Faith, Peace and Progress

BRITISH PROTECTORATE OF NIGERIA

POUND STERLING COINAGE

KM# 1 1/2 PENNY

Bronze, 21.6 mm. **Ruler:** Elizabeth II **Obv:** Crown above center hole flanked by curved sprig **Rev:** Star design around center hole

Date	Mintage	VF20	XF40	MS60	MS63	MS65
1959	52,800,000	0.25	0.45	0.75	1.50	5.00
1959	6,031	PF65 5.00				

KM# 2 PENNY

7.50 g., Bronze, 28 mm. **Ruler:** Elizabeth II **Obv:** Crown above center hole flanked by curved sprig **Rev:** Star design around center hole

Date	Mintage	VF20	XF40	MS60	MS63	MS65
1959	93,368,000	0.25	0.45	0.75	1.50	5.00
1959	6,031	PF65 5.00				

KM# 3 3 PENCE

3.25 g., Nickel-Brass, 19 mm. **Ruler:** Elizabeth II **Obv:** Crowned head right **Rev:** Cotton plant, date above, value below **Shape:** 12-sided

Date	Mintage	VF20	XF40	MS60	MS63	MS65
1959	52,000,000	0.50	1.00	1.50	3.00	5.00
1959	6,031	PF65 7.00				

KM# 4 6 PENCE

2.50 g., Copper-Nickel, 17.8 mm. **Ruler:** Elizabeth II **Obv:** Crowned head right **Rev:** Cocoa beans, date and value below

Date	Mintage	VF20	XF40	MS60	MS63	MS65
1959	35,000,000	0.50	1.00	1.50	3.00	5.00
1959	6,031	PF65 7.00				

KM# 5 SHILLING

5.00 g., Copper-Nickel, 23 mm. **Ruler:** Elizabeth II **Obv:** Crowned head right **Rev:** Palm divides date, value below

Date	Mintage	VF20	XF40	MS60	MS63	MS65
1959	18,000,000	0.65	1.45	2.25	3.50	6.00
1959	6,031	PF65 10.00				
1961	48,584,000	0.65	1.45	2.25	3.50	6.00
1962	39,416,000	0.65	1.45	2.25	3.50	6.00

KM# 6 2 SHILLING
10.00 g., Copper-Nickel, 27 mm. **Ruler:** Elizabeth II **Obv:** Crowned head right **Rev:** Peanut plant above value **Edge:** Security

Date	Mintage	VF20	XF40	MS60	MS63	MS65
1959	15,000,000	1.25	2.50	3.50	6.00	7.50
1959	6,031	PF65 15.00				

FEDERAL REPUBLIC

DECIMAL COINAGE

100 Kobo = 1 Naira

KM# 7 1/2 KOBO
3.53 g., Bronze **Ruler:** Elizabeth II **Obv:** Arms with supporters **Rev:** Value flanked by cotton plant

Date	Mintage	VF20	XF40	MS60	MS63	MS65
1973	166,618,000	0.45	1.00	1.50	2.00	3.50
1973	10,000	PF65 2.00				

KM# 8.1 KOBO
6.00 g., Bronze **Ruler:** Elizabeth II **Obv:** Arms with supporters and short motto **Rev:** Value flanked by oil derricks

Date	Mintage	VF20	XF40	MS60	MS63	MS65
1973	586,944,000	0.25	0.45	0.75	1.25	2.00
1973	10,000	PF65 2.00				
1974	14,500,000	0.25	0.45	1.00	1.50	3.00

KM# 8.2 KOBO
Bronze **Ruler:** Elizabeth II **Obv:** Arms with supporters and long motto **Rev:** Value flanked by oil derricks

Date	Mintage	VF20	XF40	MS60	MS63	MS65
1987	—	0.50	1.50	2.00	3.50	6.00
1988	—	0.50	1.50	2.00	3.50	6.00

KM# 8.2a KOBO
2.57 g., Copper Plated Steel, 17 mm. **Ruler:** Elizabeth II **Obv:** Arms with supporters and long motto **Rev:** Value flanked by oil derricks

Date	Mintage	VF20	XF40	MS60	MS63	MS65
1991	—	—	—	—	0.25	0.45

KM# 9.1 5 KOBO
Copper-Nickel **Ruler:** Elizabeth II **Obv:** Arms with supporters and short motto **Rev:** Cocoa beans

Date	Mintage	VF20	XF40	MS60	MS63	MS65
1973	10,000	PF65 3.00				
1973	96,920,000	0.35	0.75	1.25	1.75	2.75
1974	—	0.45	0.85	1.50	2.00	3.00
1976	9,800,000	0.45	0.85	1.50	2.00	3.00
1986	—	0.45	0.85	1.50	2.00	3.00

KM# 9.2 5 KOBO
Copper-Nickel **Ruler:** Elizabeth II **Obv:** Arms with supporters and long motto **Rev:** Cocoa beans

Date	Mintage	VF20	XF40	MS60	MS63	MS65
1987	—	0.65	1.25	2.00	3.00	5.00
1988	—	0.65	1.25	2.00	3.00	5.00
1989	—	0.65	1.25	2.00	3.00	5.00

KM# 10.1 10 KOBO
3.90 g., Copper-Nickel, 22.8 mm. **Ruler:** Elizabeth II **Obv:** Arms with supporters and short motto **Rev:** Value at left of oil palms

Date	Mintage	VF20	XF40	MS60	MS63	MS65
1973	10,000	PF65 3.00				
1973	340,870,000	0.50	1.00	1.50	2.25	3.50
1974	—	0.60	1.20	1.75	2.50	3.75
1976	7,000,000	0.60	1.20	1.75	2.50	3.75

KM# 10.2 10 KOBO
4.00 g., Copper-Nickel, 22.8 mm. **Ruler:** Elizabeth II **Obv:** Arms with supporters and long motto **Rev:** Value to left of oil palms

Date	Mintage	VF20	XF40	MS60	MS63	MS65
1987	—	0.50	1.00	1.50	2.00	3.00
1988	—	0.50	1.00	1.50	2.00	3.00
1989	—	0.50	1.00	1.50	2.00	3.00
1990	—	0.50	1.00	1.50	2.00	3.00

KM# 12 10 KOBO
3.48 g., Copper Plated Steel, 19.9 mm. **Ruler:** Elizabeth II **Obv:** Arms with supporters and long motto **Rev:** Value to left of oil palms **Shape:** 12-sided

Date	Mintage	VF20	XF40	MS60	MS63	MS65
1991	—	—	—	—	0.45	0.75

KM# 11 25 KOBO
Copper-Nickel **Ruler:** Elizabeth II **Obv:** Arms with supporters and short motto **Rev:** Groundnuts **Edge:** Security

Date	Mintage	VF20	XF40	MS60	MS63	MS65
1973	4,616,000	1.00	2.00	3.00	4.50	7.50
1973	10,000	PF65 5.00				
1975	—	1.00	2.00	3.00	4.50	7.50

KM# 11a 25 KOBO
4.49 g., Copper Plated Steel, 22.45 mm. **Ruler:** Elizabeth II **Obv:** Arms with supporters and long motto **Rev:** Groundnuts **Edge:** Reeded

Date	Mintage	VF20	XF40	MS60	MS63	MS65
1991	—	—	—	0.35	0.65	1.00

KM# 13.1 50 KOBO
5.50 g., Nickel Plated Steel, 24.72 mm. **Ruler:** Elizabeth II **Obv:** Arms with supporters with long motto **Rev:** Corn and value **Shape:** 12 rounded sides

Date	Mintage	VF20	XF40	MS60	MS63	MS65
1991	—	—	—	0.65	1.25	1.65

KM# 13.2 50 KOBO
5.53 g., Nickel Clad Steel, 24.72 mm. **Obv:** Arms with supporters with long motto **Rev:** Corn with value **Shape:** Round with a multi-sided inner rim

Date	Mintage	VF20	XF40	MS60	MS63	MS65
1993	—	—	—	0.75	1.35	1.75

KM# 14 NAIRA
12.15 g., Nickel Plated Steel, 27.5 mm. **Ruler:** Elizabeth II **Obv:** Arms with supporters and long motto **Rev:** Head 1/4 right

Date	Mintage	VF20	XF40	MS60	MS63	MS65
1991	—	—	—	1.00	1.75	2.25
1993	—	—	—	1.00	1.75	2.25

KM# 15 100 NAIRA
28.28 g., 0.925 Silver 0.841 oz. ASW **Ruler:** Elizabeth II **Subject:** 100 Years - Banking in Nigeria **Obv:** Arms with supporters **Rev:** Bank building **Edge:** Reeded

Date	Mintage	VF20	XF40	MS60	MS63	MS65
1994	5,000	PF65 650	PF67 750			

Note: Issue price at Bank in Lagos approximately $1,400

KM# 16 1000 NAIRA
47.54 g., 0.9166 Gold 1.401 oz. AGW **Ruler:** Elizabeth II **Subject:** 100 Years - Banking in Nigeria **Obv:** Arms with supporters **Rev:** Bank building **Edge:** Reeded

Date	Mintage	VF20	XF40	MS60	MS63	MS65
1994	100	PF65 2,250	PF67 2,550			

PATTERNS

Including off metal strikes

KM#	Date	Mintage	Identification	Mkt Val
Pn1	1962	—	Shilling. Bronze. KM5.	275
Pn2	1973	—	10 Kobo. Bronze. KM10.	225

TRIAL STRIKES

KM#	Date	Mintage	Identification	Mkt Val
TS1	1962	—	Shilling. Copper-Nickel. TRIAL" in field on obverse and reverse.	375

PROOF SETS

KM#	Date	Mintage	Identification	Issue Price	Mkt Val
PS1	1959 (6)	1,031	KM1-5, red case, originals	—	125
PS2	1959 (6)	5,000	KM1-5, blue case, restrikes	—	50.00
PS3	1973 (5)	102,000	KM7, 8.1-10.1,11	14.70	15.00

NIUE

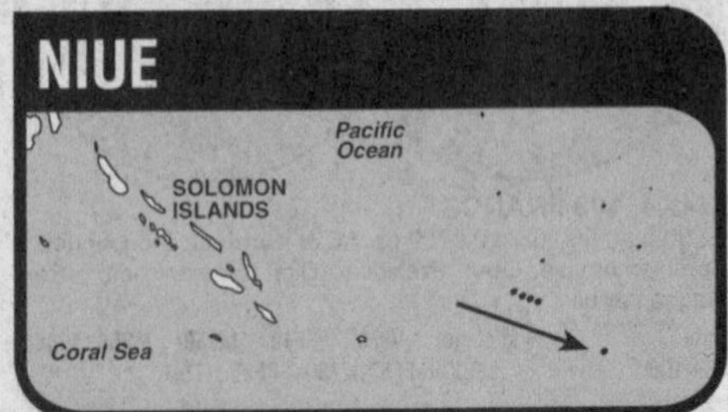

Niue, or Savage Island, a dependent state of New Zealand is located in the Pacific Ocean east of Tonga and southeast of Samoa. The size is 100 sq. mi. (260 sq. km.) with a population of *2,000. Chief village and port is Alofi. Bananas and copra are exported.

Discovered by Captain Cook in 1774, it was originally part of the Cook Islands administration but has been separate since 1922.a

MINT MARK
PM - Pobjoy Mint

NEW ZEALAND DEPENDENT STATE

DECIMAL COINAGE

KM# 85 DOLLAR

10.02 g., 0.500 Silver 0.1611 oz. ASW, 29 mm. **Ruler:** Elizabeth II **Obv:** Crowned arms within sprigs **Rev:** HMS Bounty, value and compass **Edge:** Reeded

Date	Mintage	VF20	XF40	MS60	MS63	MS65
1996	—	PF65 7.50				

KM# 113 DOLLAR

10.02 g., 0.500 Silver 0.1611 oz. ASW **Ruler:** Elizabeth II **Series:** Endangered Wildlife **Obv:** Crowned arms within sprigs **Rev:** Jaguar on tree limb

Date	Mintage	VF20	XF40	MS60	MS63	MS65
1996	—	PF65 12.00				

KM# 122 DOLLAR

10.00 g., 0.500 Silver 0.1608 oz. ASW, 30 mm. **Ruler:** Elizabeth II **Series:** Protect Our World **Obv:** Crowned arms within sprigs **Rev:** Oak tree **Edge:** Reeded

Date	Mintage	VF20	XF40	MS60	MS63	MS65
1996	—	PF65 7.00				

KM# 87 DOLLAR

Copper-Nickel **Ruler:** Elizabeth II **Obv:** Crowned arms within sprigs **Rev:** Bust facing **Rev. Legend:** . . . The People's Princess

Date	Mintage	VF20	XF40	MS60	MS63	MS65
1997	—	—	—	1.50	2.50	4.00

KM# 88 DOLLAR

Copper-Nickel **Ruler:** Elizabeth II **Obv:** Crowned arms within sprigs **Rev:** Bust facing **Rev. Legend:** . . . Princess of Wales **Note:** Similar to 10 Dollars, KM#91.

Date	Mintage	VF20	XF40	MS60	MS63	MS65
1997	—	—	—	1.50	2.50	4.00

KM# 89 DOLLAR

Copper-Nickel **Ruler:** Elizabeth II **Obv:** Crowned arms within sprigs **Rev:** Head left above sprigs **Rev. Legend:** . . . Princess of Wales **Note:** Similar to 10 Dollars, KM#92.

Date	Mintage	VF20	XF40	MS60	MS63	MS65
1997	—	—	—	1.50	2.50	4.00

KM# 102 DOLLAR

Copper-Nickel **Ruler:** Elizabeth II **Obv:** Crowned head right **Rev:** Bust facing **Rev. Legend:** . . . In Memoriam **Note:** Similar to 10 Dollars, KM#104.

Date	Mintage	VF20	XF40	MS60	MS63	MS65
1998	—	—	—	1.50	2.50	4.00

KM# 103 DOLLAR

Copper-Nickel **Ruler:** Elizabeth II **Obv:** Crowned head right **Rev:** Bust facing **Rev. Legend:** . . . Princess of Wales **Note:** Similar to 10 Dollars, KM#105.

Date	Mintage	VF20	XF40	MS60	MS63	MS65
1998	—	—	—	1.50	2.50	4.00

KM# 115 DOLLAR

Copper-Nickel **Ruler:** Elizabeth II **Subject:** 50th Anniversary of Peanuts **Obv:** Crowned head right **Rev:** Snoopy and Woodstock **Note:** Similar to 10 Dollars, KM#116.

Date	Mintage	VF20	XF40	MS60	MS63	MS65
2000	Est. 100000	—	—	5.00	7.00	10.00

KM# 174 DOLLAR

21.00 g., Copper-Nickel, 38.6 mm. **Ruler:** Elizabeth II **Subject:** Marine Life Protection **Obv:** Crowned head right **Rev:** Multicolor fish scene **Edge:** Reeded

Date	Mintage	VF20	XF40	MS60	MS63	MS65
2000	—	—	—	10.00	12.00	15.00

KM# 258 2 DOLLARS

31.47 g., 0.925 Silver 0.9359 oz. ASW **Ruler:** Elizabeth II **Rev:** Queen Mother and London bombings of 1940

Date	Mintage	VF20	XF40	MS60	MS63	MS65
1997	—	—	—	—	—	45.00

KM# 1 5 DOLLARS

Copper-Nickel **Ruler:** Elizabeth II **Series:** Olympics **Subject:** Tennis **Obv:** Crowned arms within sprigs **Rev:** Boris Becker

Date	Mintage	VF20	XF40	MS60	MS63	MS65
1987	80,000	—	—	3.00	5.00	7.00

KM# 5 5 DOLLARS

Copper-Nickel **Ruler:** Elizabeth II **Subject:** 24th Olympiad Tennis Games, Seoul 1988 **Obv:** Crowned arms within sprigs **Rev:** Steffi Graf

Date	Mintage	VF20	XF40	MS60	MS63	MS65
1987	50,000	—	—	3.00	5.00	7.00

KM# 11 5 DOLLARS

Copper-Nickel **Ruler:** Elizabeth II **Subject:** 24th Olympic Games, Seoul 1988 **Obv:** Crowned arms within sprigs **Rev:** 3/4 Tennis player with cup

Date	Mintage	VF20	XF40	MS60	MS63	MS65
1988	80,000	—	—	3.00	5.00	7.00

KM# 12 5 DOLLARS

Copper-Nickel **Ruler:** Elizabeth II **Series:** Olympics **Subject:** Soccer **Obv:** Crowned arms within sprigs **Rev:** Soccer player left of cameo

Date	Mintage	VF20	XF40	MS60	MS63	MS65
1988	50,000	—	—	3.00	5.00	7.00

KM# 15 5 DOLLARS

Copper-Nickel **Ruler:** Elizabeth II **Subject:** 24th Olympic Games, Seoul 1988 **Obv:** Crowned arms within sprigs **Rev:** Cameos of Navratilova, Graf and Evert, tennis champions

Date	Mintage	VF20	XF40	MS60	MS63	MS65
1988	80,000	—	—	3.00	5.00	7.00

KM# 17 5 DOLLARS

28.28 g., Copper-Nickel, 38.61 mm. **Ruler:** Elizabeth II **Subject:** John F. Kennedy, 25th Anniversary of Death **Obv:** Crowned arms within sprigs **Rev:** Head of John F. Kennedy left **Edge:** Reeded

Date	Mintage	VF20	XF40	MS60	MS63	MS65
1988	80,000	—	—	3.00	5.00	7.00

KM# 22 5 DOLLARS
Copper-Nickel **Ruler:** Elizabeth II **Obv:** Crowned arms within sprigs **Rev:** Head of General Douglas MacArthur 3/4 left **Edge:** Reeded

Date	Mintage	VF20	XF40	MS60	MS63	MS65
1989	—	—	—	2.00	4.00	6.00

KM# 24 5 DOLLARS
Copper-Nickel **Ruler:** Elizabeth II **Obv:** Crowned arms within sprigs **Rev:** Tennis player

Date	Mintage	VF20	XF40	MS60	MS63	MS65
1989	Est. 50000	—	—	2.00	4.00	6.00

KM# 67 5 DOLLARS
Copper-Nickel **Ruler:** Elizabeth II **Subject:** 24th Olympic Games, Seoul 1988 **Obv:** Crowned arms within sprigs. **Rev:** Steffi Graf

Date	Mintage	VF20	XF40	MS60	MS63	MS65
1989	—	—	—	2.00	4.00	6.00

KM# 29 5 DOLLARS
Copper-Nickel, 38.8 mm. **Ruler:** Elizabeth II **Obv:** Crowned arms within sprigs **Rev:** Bust of General Eisenhower facing within flags

Date	Mintage	VF20	XF40	MS60	MS63	MS65
1990	—	—	—	3.00	5.00	7.00

KM# 31 5 DOLLARS
Copper-Nickel, 38.8 mm. **Ruler:** Elizabeth II **Obv:** Crowned arms within sprigs **Rev:** General George S. Patton

Date	Mintage	VF20	XF40	MS60	MS63	MS65
1990	—	—	—	3.00	5.00	7.00

KM# 33 5 DOLLARS
Copper-Nickel, 38.8 mm. **Ruler:** Elizabeth II **Obv:** Crowned arms within sprigs **Rev:** Admiral William Halsey

Date	Mintage	VF20	XF40	MS60	MS63	MS65
1990	—	—	—	3.00	5.00	7.00

KM# 35 5 DOLLARS
Copper-Nickel, 38.8 mm. **Ruler:** Elizabeth II **Obv:** Crowned arms within sprigs **Rev:** Bust of Franklin D. Roosevelt facing above U.S.S. Arizona Memorial at Pearl Harbor **Edge:** Reeded

Date	Mintage	VF20	XF40	MS60	MS63	MS65
1990	—	—	—	3.00	5.00	7.00

KM# 37 5 DOLLARS
Copper-Nickel, 38.8 mm. **Ruler:** Elizabeth II **Obv:** Crowned arms within sprigs **Rev:** Sir Winston Churchill and Big Ben

Date	Mintage	VF20	XF40	MS60	MS63	MS65
1990	—	—	—	3.00	5.00	7.00

KM# 143 5 DOLLARS
28.34 g., Copper-Nickel, 38.6 mm. **Ruler:** Elizabeth II **Subject:** XIV Football World Championship Italy '90 **Obv:** Crowned arms within sprigs **Rev:** Head right at lower left of map and soccer player **Edge:** Reeded

Date	Mintage	VF20	XF40	MS60	MS63	MS65
1990	60,000	—	—	2.00	4.00	6.00

KM# 58 5 DOLLARS
9.93 g., 0.500 Silver 0.1596 oz. ASW **Ruler:** Elizabeth II **Series:** World Cup Soccer **Obv:** Crowned arms within sprigs **Rev:** Soccer player and Statue of Liberty

Date	Mintage	VF20	XF40	MS60	MS63	MS65
1991	150,000	PF65 10.00				

KM# 144 5 DOLLARS
28.15 g., Copper-Nickel, 38.5 mm. **Ruler:** Elizabeth II **Subject:** Basketball Centennial **Obv:** Crowned arms within sprigs **Rev:** Two female basketball players **Edge:** Reeded

Date	Mintage	VF20	XF40	MS60	MS63	MS65
1991	28,000	—	—	2.00	4.00	6.00

KM# 55 5 DOLLARS
10.00 g., 0.500 Silver 0.1608 oz. ASW **Ruler:** Elizabeth II **Obv:** Crowned arms within sprigs **Rev:** Ship, HMS Bounty

Date	Mintage	VF20	XF40	MS60	MS63	MS65
1992	Est. 150000	PF65 8.00				

KM# 60 5 DOLLARS
10.00 g., 0.500 Silver 0.1608 oz. ASW **Ruler:** Elizabeth II **Series:** Endangered Wildlife **Obv:** Crowned arms within sprigs **Rev:** Jaguar

Date	Mintage	VF20	XF40	MS60	MS63	MS65
1992	Est. 25000	PF65 15.00				

KM# 61 5 DOLLARS
10.00 g., 0.500 Silver 0.1608 oz. ASW **Ruler:** Elizabeth II **Series:** Olympics 1996 **Obv:** Crowned arms within sprigs **Rev:** Sprinter

Date	Mintage	VF20	XF40	MS60	MS63	MS65
1992	100,000	PF65 7.00				

KM# 68 5 DOLLARS
9.85 g., 0.500 Silver 0.1583 oz. ASW **Ruler:** Elizabeth II **Subject:** First Moon Landing **Obv:** Crowned arms within sprigs **Rev:** Man on moon

Date	Mintage	VF20	XF40	MS60	MS63	MS65
1992	—	PF65 7.00				

KM# 76 5 DOLLARS
10.00 g., 0.925 Silver 0.2974 oz. ASW **Ruler:** Elizabeth II **Obv:** Crowned arms within sprigs **Rev:** Kennedy, Brandenburg Gate

Date	Mintage	VF20	XF40	MS60	MS63	MS65
1992	Est. 50000	PF65 10.00				

KM# 80 5 DOLLARS
9.95 g., 0.500 Silver 0.1599 oz. ASW **Ruler:** Elizabeth II **Series:** Endangered Wildlife **Obv:** Crowned arms within sprigs **Rev:** Dolphins

Date	Mintage	VF20	XF40	MS60	MS63	MS65
1992	—	PF65 15.00				

KM# 62 5 DOLLARS
9.95 g., 0.500 Silver 0.1599 oz. ASW **Ruler:** Elizabeth II **Series:** Protect Our World **Obv:** Crowned arms within sprigs **Rev:** Oak tree

Date	Mintage	VF20	XF40	MS60	MS63	MS65
1993	—	PF65 12.00				

KM# 114 5 DOLLARS
31.32 g., 0.925 Silver 0.9314 oz. ASW, 38.51 mm. **Ruler:** Elizabeth II **Obv:** National arms **Rev:** Three-mast sailing ship H.M.S. Resolution facing right **Edge:** Reeded

Date	Mintage	VF20	XF40	MS60	MS63	MS65
1996	—	PF65 40.00				

KM# 175 5 DOLLARS
31.84 g., 0.925 Silver 0.9469 oz. ASW, 38.6 mm. **Ruler:** Elizabeth II **Subject:** Victorian Age **Obv:** Crowned head right **Rev:** Queen Victoria and Prince Albert wedding portrait **Edge:** Reeded

Date	Mintage	VF20	XF40	MS60	MS63	MS65
1996	—	PF65 37.00				

KM# 173 5 DOLLARS
31.22 g., 0.925 Silver 0.9285 oz. ASW, 38.6 mm. **Ruler:** Elizabeth II **Subject:** Queen Mother **Obv:** Crowned arms within sprigs **Rev:** Queen Mother viewing London bomb damage **Edge:** Reeded

Date	Mintage	VF20	XF40	MS60	MS63	MS65
1997	—	PF65 35.00				

KM# 145 5 DOLLARS
31.36 g., 0.925 Silver 0.9326 oz. ASW, 38.4 mm. **Ruler:** Elizabeth II **Subject:** Queen Mother **Obv:** Crowned head right **Rev:** Silver Wedding scene within circle **Edge:** Reeded

Date	Mintage	VF20	XF40	MS60	MS63	MS65
1998	—	PF65 35.00				

KM# 120 5 DOLLARS
31.42 g., 0.925 Silver 0.9344 oz. ASW **Ruler:** Elizabeth II **Subject:** Pterois Radiata **Obv:** Crowned head right **Rev:** Gold colored Clearfin lion fish **Edge:** Plain **Shape:** 7-sided

Date	Mintage	VF20	XF40	MS60	MS63	MS65
1999	—	PF63 60.00	PF65 70.00			

KM# 121 5 DOLLARS
31.42 g., 0.925 Silver 0.9344 oz. ASW **Ruler:** Elizabeth II **Subject:** Fourcipiger Longirostris **Obv:** Crowned head right **Rev:** Goldcolored big longnosed Butterfly fish **Edge:** Plain **Shape:** 7-sided

Date	Mintage	VF20	XF40	MS60	MS63	MS65
1999	—	PF63 60.00	PF65 70.00			

KM# 171 5 DOLLARS
31.25 g., 0.925 Silver 0.9294 oz. ASW, 35.5 mm. **Ruler:** Elizabeth II **Subject:** Pygoplites Diacantus **Obv:** Crowned head right **Rev:** Three gold-plated fish **Edge:** Plain **Shape:** 7-sided

Date	Mintage	VF20	XF40	MS60	MS63	MS65
1999	—	PF63 60.00	PF65 70.00			

KM# 172 5 DOLLARS
28.40 g., 0.925 Silver 0.8446 oz. ASW with gilt outer ring, 38.5 mm. **Ruler:** Elizabeth II **Subject:** Queen Mother **Obv:** Crowned head right **Rev:** Queen Mother's engagement portrait **Edge:** Reeded

Date	Mintage	VF20	XF40	MS60	MS63	MS65
2000	—	PF65 20.00				

KM# 260 5 DOLLARS
25.00 g., 0.999 Silver 0.803 oz. ASW, 38.6 mm. **Ruler:** Elizabeth II **Rev:** Kingfish

Date	Mintage	VF20	XF40	MS60	MS63	MS65
2000	—	PF63 55.00	PF65 60.00			

KM# 261 5 DOLLARS
31.47 g., 0.925 Silver 0.9359 oz. ASW **Ruler:** Elizabeth II **Subject:** John Williams, Messenger of Peace

Date	Mintage	VF20	XF40	MS60	MS63	MS65
2000	—	PF65 40.00				

KM# 46 10 DOLLARS

10.00 g., 0.925 Silver 0.2974 oz. ASW **Ruler:** Elizabeth II **Series:** Summer Olympics **Obv:** Crowned arms within sprigs **Rev:** Runners

Date	Mintage	VF20	XF40	MS60	MS63	MS65
1991	150,000	PF65 12.00				

KM# 56 10 DOLLARS

10.00 g., 0.925 Silver 0.2974 oz. ASW **Ruler:** Elizabeth II **Series:** Summer Olympics **Obv:** Crowned arms within sprigs **Rev:** Discus Thrower

Date	Mintage	VF20	XF40	MS60	MS63	MS65
1991	50,000	PF65 12.00				

KM# 59 10 DOLLARS

31.53 g., 0.9999 Silver 1.0136 oz. ASW **Ruler:** Elizabeth II **Series:** World Cup Soccer **Obv:** Crowned arms within sprigs **Rev:** Handshake above value with hands holding crowned arms below

Date	Mintage	VF20	XF40	MS60	MS63	MS65
1991	20,000	PF65 35.00				

KM# 257 10 DOLLARS

31.47 g., 0.925 Silver 0.9359 oz. ASW **Ruler:** Elizabeth II **Subject:** James Naismith, founder of Basketball

Date	Mintage	VF20	XF40	MS60	MS63	MS65
1991	—	—	—	—	—	35.00

KM# 69 10 DOLLARS

31.43 g., 0.9999 Silver 1.0104 oz. ASW **Ruler:** Elizabeth II **Subject:** Cook's Pacific Voyages **Obv:** Crowned arms within sprigs **Rev:** Cameo left of sailing ship

Date	Mintage	VF20	XF40	MS60	MS63	MS65
1992	—	PF65 32.00				

KM# 70 10 DOLLARS

31.43 g., 0.9999 Silver 1.0104 oz. ASW **Ruler:** Elizabeth II **Subject:** Moon Landing **Obv:** Crowned arms within sprigs **Rev:** Luna 9

Date	Mintage	VF20	XF40	MS60	MS63	MS65
1992	Est. 15000	PF65 32.00				

KM# 74 10 DOLLARS

31.47 g., 0.925 Silver 0.9359 oz. ASW **Ruler:** Elizabeth II **Series:** Endangered Wildlife **Obv:** Crowned arms within sprigs **Rev:** Whales

Date	Mintage	VF20	XF40	MS60	MS63	MS65
1992	25,000	PF65 38.00				

KM# 78 10 DOLLARS

31.47 g., 0.925 Silver 0.9359 oz. ASW **Ruler:** Elizabeth II **Subject:** The Resolution **Obv:** Crowned arms within sprigs **Rev:** Three-masted ship

Date	Mintage	VF20	XF40	MS60	MS63	MS65
1992	Est. 15000	PF65 35.00				

KM# 86 10 DOLLARS

31.04 g., 0.925 Silver 0.9231 oz. ASW **Ruler:** Elizabeth II **Obv:** Crowned arms within sprigs **Rev:** Head 1/4 left and rocket launch

Date	Mintage	VF20	XF40	MS60	MS63	MS65
1992	—	PF65 32.00				

KM# 81 10 DOLLARS

1.24 g., 0.999 Gold 0.040 oz. AGW, 13.9 mm. **Ruler:** Elizabeth II **Subject:** Liberty Gold Bullion **Obv:** Crowned head right **Rev:** Statue of Liberty

Date	Mintage	VF20	XF40	MS60	MS63	MS65
1997	—	PF63 70.00	PF65 75.00			

KM# 90 10 DOLLARS

28.28 g., 0.925 Silver 0.841 oz. ASW **Ruler:** Elizabeth II **Obv:** Crowned arms within sprigs **Rev:** Bust facing **Rev. Legend:** . . . The People's Princess

Date	Mintage	VF20	XF40	MS60	MS63	MS65
1997	Est. 10000	PF65 27.50				

KM# 91 10 DOLLARS

28.28 g., 0.925 Silver 0.841 oz. ASW **Ruler:** Elizabeth II **Obv:** Crowned arms within sprigs **Rev:** Bust facing **Rev. Legend:** . . . Princess of Wales

Date	Mintage	VF20	XF40	MS60	MS63	MS65
1997	Est. 10000	PF65 27.50				

KM# 92 10 DOLLARS

28.28 g., 0.925 Silver 0.841 oz. ASW **Ruler:** Elizabeth II **Obv:** Crowned arms within sprigs **Rev:** Head left above sprigs **Rev. Legend:** . . . Princess of Wales

Date	Mintage	VF20	XF40	MS60	MS63	MS65
1997	Est. 10000	PF65 27.50				

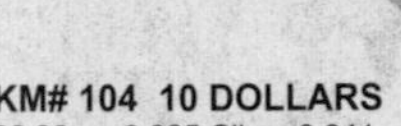

KM# 104 10 DOLLARS

28.28 g., 0.925 Silver 0.841 oz. ASW **Ruler:** Elizabeth II **Obv:** Crowned head right **Rev:** Bust facing **Rev. Legend:** . . . In Memoriam

Date	Mintage	VF20	XF40	MS60	MS63	MS65
1998	Est. 10000	PF65 27.50				

KM# 105 10 DOLLARS

28.28 g., 0.925 Silver 0.841 oz. ASW **Ruler:** Elizabeth II **Obv:** Crowned head right **Rev:** Bust facing **Rev. Legend:** . . . Princess of Wales

Date	Mintage	VF20	XF40	MS60	MS63	MS65
1998	Est. 10000	PF65 27.50				

KM# 116 10 DOLLARS
28.28 g., 0.925 Silver 0.841 oz. ASW **Ruler:** Elizabeth II **Subject:** 50th Anniversary of Peanuts **Obv:** Crowned head right **Rev:** Snoopy and Woodstock

Date	Mintage	VF20	XF40	MS60	MS63	MS65
2000	Est. 10000	PF65 30.00				

KM# 182 10 DOLLARS
1.24 g., Gold, 13.89 mm. **Ruler:** Elizabeth II **Obv:** National arms **Rev:** 2 Black and Gold Angelfish **Edge:** Reeded

Date	Mintage	VF20	XF40	MS60	MS63	MS65
2000	—	PF63 70.00	PF65 75.00			

KM# 57 20 DOLLARS
31.47 g., 0.925 Silver 0.9359 oz. ASW **Ruler:** Elizabeth II **Subject:** 40th Anniversary of Coronation **Obv:** Crowned head right **Rev:** Crowned monogram within 3/4 wreath with value and dates below

Date	Mintage	VF20	XF40	MS60	MS63	MS65
1993	Est. 10000	PF65 35.00				

KM# 63 20 DOLLARS
31.47 g., 0.925 Silver 0.9359 oz. ASW **Ruler:** Elizabeth II **Series:** Protect Our World **Obv:** Crowned arms within sprigs **Rev:** Hand holding seedling

Date	Mintage	VF20	XF40	MS60	MS63	MS65
1993	Est. 10000	PF65 35.00				

KM# 64 20 DOLLARS
31.47 g., 0.925 Silver 0.9359 oz. ASW **Ruler:** Elizabeth II **Obv:** Crowned arms within sprigs **Rev:** Bust right and Statue of Liberty

Date	Mintage	VF20	XF40	MS60	MS63	MS65
1993	—	PF65 37.00				

KM# 93 20 DOLLARS
1.24 g., 0.999 Gold 0.040 oz. AGW **Ruler:** Elizabeth II **Obv:** Crowned arms within sprigs **Rev:** Bust facing **Rev. Legend:** ...The People's Princess

Date	Mintage	VF20	XF40	MS60	MS63	MS65
1997	Est. 10000	PF65 60.00	PF67 70.00			

KM# 94 20 DOLLARS
1.24 g., 0.999 Gold 0.040 oz. AGW **Ruler:** Elizabeth II **Obv:** Crowned arms within sprigs **Rev:** Bust facing **Rev. Legend:** ...Princess of Wales

Date	Mintage	VF20	XF40	MS60	MS63	MS65
1997	Est. 10000	PF65 60.00	PF67 70.00			

KM# 95 20 DOLLARS
1.24 g., 0.999 Gold 0.040 oz. AGW **Ruler:** Elizabeth II **Obv:** Crowned arms within sprigs **Rev:** Head left above sprigs **Rev. Legend:** ...Princess of Wales

Date	Mintage	VF20	XF40	MS60	MS63	MS65
1997	Est. 10000	PF65 60.00	PF67 70.00			

KM# 106 20 DOLLARS
1.24 g., 0.999 Gold 0.040 oz. AGW **Ruler:** Elizabeth II **Obv:** Crowned head right **Rev:** Bust facing **Rev. Legend:** ...In Memoriam

Date	Mintage	VF20	XF40	MS60	MS63	MS65
1998	Est. 10000	PF65 60.00	PF67 70.00			

KM# 107 20 DOLLARS
1.24 g., 0.999 Gold 0.040 oz. AGW **Ruler:** Elizabeth II **Obv:** Crowned head right **Rev:** Bust facing **Rev. Legend:** ...Princess of Wales

Date	Mintage	VF20	XF40	MS60	MS63	MS65
1998	Est. 10000	PF65 60.00	PF67 70.00			

KM# 117 20 DOLLARS
1.24 g., 0.999 Gold 0.0398 oz. AGW **Ruler:** Elizabeth II **Subject:** 50th Anniversary of Peanuts **Obv:** Crowned head right **Rev:** Snoopy and Woodstock

Date	Mintage	VF20	XF40	MS60	MS63	MS65
2000	Est. 10000	PF65 60.00	PF67 70.00			

KM# 79 25 DOLLARS
1.24 g., 0.999 Gold 0.040 oz. AGW **Ruler:** Elizabeth II **Subject:** Death of John F. Kennedy **Obv:** National arms **Rev:** Half length figure of JFK left **Edge:** Reeded

Date	Mintage	VF20	XF40	MS60	MS63	MS65
1994	Est. 25000	PF65 60.00	PF67 70.00			

KM# 178 25 DOLLARS
1.23 g., 0.9999 Gold 0.0395 oz. AGW, 13.93 mm. **Ruler:** Elizabeth II **Obv:** National arms **Rev:** Sailing ship "H.M.S. Bounty" **Edge:** Reeded

Date	Mintage	VF20	XF40	MS60	MS63	MS65
1996	—	PF65 80.00	PF67 90.00			

KM# 179 25 DOLLARS
1.22 g., 0.9999 Gold 0.0392 oz. AGW, 13.86 mm. **Ruler:** Elizabeth II **Subject:** Protect our World **Obv:** National arms **Rev:** Tree **Edge:** Reeded

Date	Mintage	VF20	XF40	MS60	MS63	MS65
1996	—	PF65 75.00	PF67 85.00			

KM# 180 25 DOLLARS
1.24 g., Gold, 13.9 mm. **Ruler:** Elizabeth II **Subject:** Space rockets **Obv:** National arms **Rev:** Rocket and tower at left, head of Wernher von Braun 3/4 left at right **Edge:** Reeded

Date	Mintage	VF20	XF40	MS60	MS63	MS65
1996	—	PF65 75.00	PF67 85.00			

KM# 82 25 DOLLARS
3.10 g., 0.999 Gold 0.0996 oz. AGW **Ruler:** Elizabeth II **Series:** Liberty Gold Bullion **Obv:** Crowned head right **Rev:** Statue of Liberty

Date	Mintage	VF20	XF40	MS60	MS63	MS65
1997	—	—	—	—	—	200

KM# 96 25 DOLLARS
3.10 g., 0.999 Gold 0.0996 oz. AGW **Ruler:** Elizabeth II **Obv:** Crowned arms within sprigs **Rev:** Bust facing **Rev. Legend:** ...The People's Princess

Date	Mintage	VF20	XF40	MS60	MS63	MS65
1997	Est. 7500	PF63 140	PF65 155	PF67 175		

KM# 97 25 DOLLARS
3.10 g., 0.999 Gold 0.0996 oz. AGW **Ruler:** Elizabeth II **Obv:** Crowned arms within sprigs **Rev:** Bust facing **Rev. Legend:** ...Princess of Wales

Date	Mintage	VF20	XF40	MS60	MS63	MS65
1997	—	PF63 140	PF65 155	PF67 175		

KM# 98 25 DOLLARS
3.10 g., 0.999 Gold 0.0996 oz. AGW **Ruler:** Elizabeth II **Obv:** Crowned arms within sprigs **Rev:** Head left above sprigs **Rev. Legend:** . . . Princess of Wales

Date	Mintage	VF20	XF40	MS60	MS63	MS65
1997	Est. 7500	PF63 140	PF65 155	PF67 175		

KM# 259 25 DOLLARS
Gold **Ruler:** Elizabeth II **Subject:** 2000 Summer Olympics Sydney **Rev:** Kayaking

Date	Mintage	VF20	XF40	MS60	MS63	MS65
1998	—	PF67 450				

KM# 181 25 DOLLARS
1.24 g., Gold, 13.89 mm. **Ruler:** Elizabeth II **Subject:** Entering the New Century - For a Better World **Obv:** National arms **Rev:** 2 hands holding a plant **Edge:** Reeded

Date	Mintage	VF20	XF40	MS60	MS63	MS65
1999	—	PF65 75.00	PF67 85.00			

KM# 2 50 DOLLARS
27.10 g., 0.625 Silver 0.5446 oz. ASW **Ruler:** Elizabeth II **Series:** Olympics **Subject:** Tennis **Obv:** Crowned arms within sprigs **Rev:** Boris Becker

Date	Mintage	VF20	XF40	MS60	MS63	MS65
1987	20,000	PF65 35.00	PF67 48.00			

KM# 6 50 DOLLARS
27.10 g., 0.625 Silver 0.5446 oz. ASW **Ruler:** Elizabeth II **Subject:** 24th Olympiad Tennis Games, Seoul 1988 **Obv:** Crowned arms within sprigs **Rev:** Steffi Graf

Date	Mintage	VF20	XF40	MS60	MS63	MS65
1987	20,000	PF65 35.00	PF67 48.00			

KM# 13 50 DOLLARS
27.10 g., 0.625 Silver 0.5446 oz. ASW **Ruler:** Elizabeth II **Subject:** 24th Olympic Games, Seoul 1988 **Obv:** Crowned arms within sprigs **Rev:** Steffi Graf **Note:** Similar to 5 Dollars, KM#11.

Date	Mintage	VF20	XF40	MS60	MS63	MS65
1988	Est. 20000	PF65 37.00	PF67 50.00			

KM# 14 50 DOLLARS
27.10 g., 0.625 Silver 0.5446 oz. ASW **Ruler:** Elizabeth II **Series:** Olympics **Subject:** Soccer **Obv:** Crowned arms within sprigs **Rev:** Soccer player to left of cameo

Date	Mintage	VF20	XF40	MS60	MS63	MS65
1988	Est. 20000	PF65 25.00	PF67 30.00			

KM# 16 50 DOLLARS

27.10 g., 0.625 Silver 0.5446 oz. ASW **Ruler:** Elizabeth II **Subject:** 24th Olympic Games, Seoul 1988 **Obv:** Crowned arms within sprigs **Rev:** Cameos of Navratilova, Graf and Evert, tennis champions

Date	Mintage	VF20	XF40	MS60	MS63	MS65
1988	Est. 20000	PF65 27.00	PF67 32.00			

KM# 18 50 DOLLARS

28.28 g., 0.925 Silver 0.841 oz. ASW, 38.61 mm. **Ruler:** Elizabeth II **Subject:** John F. Kennedy, 25th Anniversary of Death **Obv:** Crowned arms within sprigs **Rev:** Kennedy head left

Date	Mintage	VF20	XF40	MS60	MS63	MS65
1988	20,000	PF65 27.50	PF67 32.50			

KM# 43 50 DOLLARS

28.28 g., 0.925 Silver 0.841 oz. ASW **Ruler:** Elizabeth II **Subject:** Soccer **Obv:** Crowned arms within sprigs **Rev:** Soccer players divide circle

Date	Mintage	VF20	XF40	MS60	MS63	MS65
1988	—	PF65 30.00	PF67 32.00			

KM# 23 50 DOLLARS

31.10 g., 0.999 Silver 0.999 oz. ASW **Ruler:** Elizabeth II **Obv:** Crowned arms within sprigs **Rev:** General Douglas MacArthur

Date	Mintage	VF20	XF40	MS60	MS63	MS65
1989	Est. 50000	PF65 32.00	PF67 37.00			

KM# 25 50 DOLLARS

28.28 g., 0.925 Silver 0.841 oz. ASW **Ruler:** Elizabeth II **Series:** Davis Cup Tennis **Obv:** Crowned arms within sprigs **Rev:** Conjoined busts of tennis players

Date	Mintage	VF20	XF40	MS60	MS63	MS65
1989	Est. 20000	PF65 37.50	PF67 42.50			

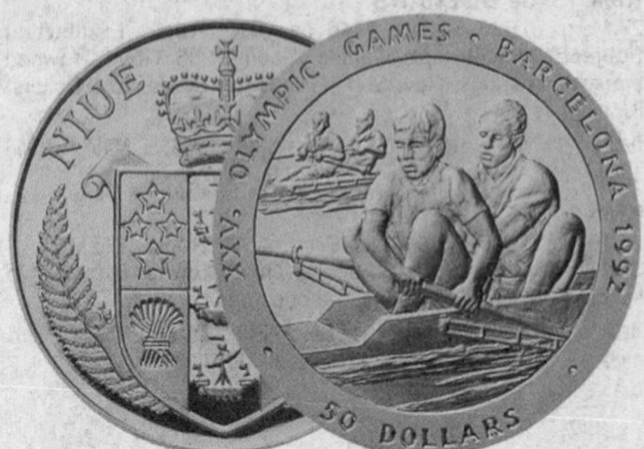

KM# 27 50 DOLLARS

28.28 g., 0.925 Silver 0.841 oz. ASW **Ruler:** Elizabeth II **Series:** 1992 Olympics **Subject:** Rowing **Obv:** Crowned arms within sprigs **Rev:** Men rowing boats within circle

Date	Mintage	VF20	XF40	MS60	MS63	MS65
1989	Est. 30000	PF65 27.50	PF67 32.50			

KM# 44 50 DOLLARS

28.28 g., 0.925 Silver 0.841 oz. ASW **Ruler:** Elizabeth II **Subject:** 24th Olympic Games, Seoul 1988 **Obv:** Crowned arms within sprigs **Rev:** Steffi Graf

Date	Mintage	VF20	XF40	MS60	MS63	MS65
1989	20,000	PF65 35.00	PF67 40.00			

KM# 30 50 DOLLARS

31.10 g., 0.999 Silver 0.999 oz. ASW **Ruler:** Elizabeth II **Obv:** Crowned arms within sprigs **Rev:** General Eisenhower within flags

Date	Mintage	VF20	XF40	MS60	MS63	MS65
1990	Est. 50000	PF65 30.00	PF67 32.00			

KM# 32 50 DOLLARS

31.10 g., 0.999 Silver 0.999 oz. ASW **Ruler:** Elizabeth II **Obv:** Crowned arms within sprigs **Rev:** General George S. Patton

Date	Mintage	VF20	XF40	MS60	MS63	MS65
1990	—	PF65 30.00	PF67 32.00			

KM# 34 50 DOLLARS

31.10 g., 0.999 Silver 0.999 oz. ASW **Ruler:** Elizabeth II **Obv:** Crowned arms within sprigs **Rev:** Admiral William Halsey

Date	Mintage	VF20	XF40	MS60	MS63	MS65
1990	—	PF65 30.00	PF67 32.00			

KM# 36 50 DOLLARS

31.10 g., 0.999 Silver 0.999 oz. ASW **Ruler:** Elizabeth II **Obv:** Crowned arms within sprigs **Rev:** President Franklin D. Roosevelt

Date	Mintage	VF20	XF40	MS60	MS63	MS65
1990	Est. 50000	PF65 30.00	PF67 32.00			

KM# 38 50 DOLLARS

31.10 g., 0.999 Silver 0.999 oz. ASW **Ruler:** Elizabeth II **Obv:** Crowned arms within sprigs **Rev:** Sir Winston Churchill

Date	Mintage	VF20	XF40	MS60	MS63	MS65
1990	Est. 50000	PF65 30.00	PF67 32.00			

KM# 47 50 DOLLARS

38.20 g., 0.925 Silver 1.136 oz. ASW **Ruler:** Elizabeth II **Subject:** Soccer **Obv:** Crowned arms within sprigs **Rev:** Player kicking soccer ball

Date	Mintage	VF20	XF40	MS60	MS63	MS65
1990	20,000	PF65 45.00	PF67 50.00			

KM# 75 50 DOLLARS

28.56 g., 0.925 Silver 0.8494 oz. ASW **Ruler:** Elizabeth II **Subject:** Soccer **Obv:** Crowned arms within sprigs **Rev:** Soccer players

Date	Mintage	VF20	XF40	MS60	MS63	MS65
1990	20,000	PF65 35.00	PF67 40.00			

KM# 71 50 DOLLARS
7.70 g., 0.583 Gold 0.1443 oz. AGW **Ruler:** Elizabeth II **Series:** Olympics **Obv:** Crowned arms within sprigs **Rev:** Discus thrower

Date	Mintage	VF20	XF40	MS60	MS63	MS65
1992	6,000	PF63 200	PF65 225	PF67 275		

KM# 65 50 DOLLARS
155.52 g., 0.999 Silver 4.995 oz. ASW **Ruler:** Elizabeth II **Obv:** Crowned arms within sprigs **Rev:** Head left with apollo rocket

Date	Mintage	VF20	XF40	MS60	MS63	MS65
1993	—	PF65 150	PF67 175			

KM# 66 50 DOLLARS
7.78 g., 0.583 Gold 0.1458 oz. AGW **Ruler:** Elizabeth II **Obv:** Crowned arms within sprigs **Rev:** Bust left and rocket launch

Date	Mintage	VF20	XF40	MS60	MS63	MS65
1993	—	PF63 200	PF65 225	PF67 275		

KM# 72 50 DOLLARS
156.17 g., 0.999 Silver 5.016 oz. ASW, 65 mm. **Ruler:** Elizabeth II **Series:** World Cup Soccer **Obv:** Crowned arms within sprigs **Rev:** Statue of Liberty, stars and various buildings within soccer ball design **Note:** Illustration reduced.

Date	Mintage	VF20	XF40	MS60	MS63	MS65
1994	Est. 3000	PF65 160	PF67 185			

KM# 83 50 DOLLARS
6.22 g., 0.999 Gold 0.1998 oz. AGW **Ruler:** Elizabeth II **Series:** Liberty Gold Bullion **Obv:** Crowned head right **Rev:** Statue of Liberty

Date	Mintage	VF20	XF40	MS60	MS63	MS65
1997	—	—	—	—	—	375

KM# 108 50 DOLLARS
3.11 g., 0.9999 Gold 0.100 oz. AGW **Ruler:** Elizabeth II **Obv:** Crowned head right **Rev:** Bust facing **Rev. Legend:** ...In Memoriam

Date	Mintage	VF20	XF40	MS60	MS63	MS65
1998	—	PF65 155	PF67 175			

KM# 109 50 DOLLARS
3.11 g., 0.9999 Gold 0.100 oz. AGW **Ruler:** Elizabeth II **Obv:** Crowned head right **Rev:** Bust facing **Rev. Legend:** ...Princess of Wales

Date	Mintage	VF20	XF40	MS60	MS63	MS65
1998	Est. 7500	PF65 155	PF67 175			

KM# 118 50 DOLLARS
3.11 g., 0.999 Gold 0.0999 oz. AGW **Ruler:** Elizabeth II **Subject:** 50th Anniversary of Peanuts **Obv:** Crowned head right **Rev:** Snoopy and Woodstock

Date	Mintage	VF20	XF40	MS60	MS63	MS65
2000	Est. 7500	PF65 155	PF67 175			

KM# 3 100 DOLLARS
155.52 g., 0.999 Silver 4.995 oz. ASW, 65 mm. **Ruler:** Elizabeth II **Series:** Olympics **Subject:** Tennis **Obv:** Crowned arms within sprigs **Rev:** Boris Becker **Note:** Illustration reduced.

Date	Mintage	VF20	XF40	MS60	MS63	MS65
1987	Est. 5000	PF65 150	PF67 175			

KM# 7 100 DOLLARS
155.52 g., 0.999 Silver 4.995 oz. ASW **Ruler:** Elizabeth II **Subject:** 24th Olympiad Tennis Games, Seoul 1988 **Obv:** Crowned arms within sprigs **Rev:** Steffi Graf

Date	Mintage	VF20	XF40	MS60	MS63	MS65
1987	—	PF65 150	PF67 175			

KM# 19 100 DOLLARS
173.00 g., 0.925 Silver 5.1449 oz. ASW **Ruler:** Elizabeth II **Obv:** Crowned arms within sprigs **Rev:** John Kennedy head left

Date	Mintage	VF20	XF40	MS60	MS63	MS65
1988	3,000	PF65 180	PF67 200			

KM# 21 100 DOLLARS
155.52 g., 0.999 Silver 4.995 oz. ASW **Ruler:** Elizabeth II **Subject:** Soccer **Obv:** Crowned arms within sprigs **Rev:** Soccer player

Date	Mintage	VF20	XF40	MS60	MS63	MS65
1988	3,000	PF65 160	PF67 175			

KM# 40 100 DOLLARS
155.52 g., 0.999 Silver 4.995 oz. ASW **Ruler:** Elizabeth II **Subject:** 24th Olympic Games, Seoul 1988 **Obv:** Crowned arms within sprigs **Rev:** Cameos of Navratilova, Graf and Evert, tennis champions

Date	Mintage	VF20	XF40	MS60	MS63	MS65
1988	—	PF65 170	PF67 185			

KM# 77 100 DOLLARS
Silver **Ruler:** Elizabeth II **Obv:** Crowned arms within sprigs **Rev:** Steffi Graf with cup **Note:** Similar to $5 KM#11.

Date	Mintage	VF20	XF40	MS60	MS63	MS65
1988	—	—	—	—	—	145

KM# 28 100 DOLLARS
155.52 g., 0.999 Silver 4.995 oz. ASW, 65 mm. **Ruler:** Elizabeth II **Subject:** 24th Olympic Games, Seoul 1988 **Obv:** Crowned arms within sprigs **Rev:** Steffi Graf **Note:** Illustration reduced.

Date	Mintage	VF20	XF40	MS60	MS63	MS65
1989	3,000	PF65 170	PF67 185			

KM# 73 100 DOLLARS
154.85 g., 0.999 Silver 4.9736 oz. ASW, 65 mm. **Ruler:** Elizabeth II **Subject:** Soccer **Obv:** Crowned arms within sprigs **Rev:** 1990 World Champion Italian soccer team **Note:** Illustration reduced.

Date	Mintage	VF20	XF40	MS60	MS63	MS65
1990	Est. 3000	PF65 170	PF67 185			

KM# 84 100 DOLLARS
15.55 g., 0.999 Gold 0.4995 oz. AGW **Ruler:** Elizabeth II **Series:** Liberty Gold Bullion **Obv:** Crowned head right **Rev:** Statue of Liberty

Date	Mintage	VF20	XF40	MS60	MS63	MS65
1997	—	PF65 765	PF67 800			

KM# 99 100 DOLLARS
6.22 g., 0.999 Gold 0.1998 oz. AGW **Ruler:** Elizabeth II **Obv:** Crowned arms within sprigs **Rev:** Bust facing **Rev. Legend:** ...The People's Princess

Date	Mintage	VF20	XF40	MS60	MS63	MS65
1997	Est. 5000	PF65 300	PF67 325			

KM# 100 100 DOLLARS
6.22 g., 0.999 Gold 0.1998 oz. AGW **Ruler:** Elizabeth II **Obv:** Crowned arms within sprigs **Rev:** Bust facing **Rev. Legend:** ...Princess of Wales

Date	Mintage	VF20	XF40	MS60	MS63	MS65
1997	Est. 5000	PF65 300	PF67 325			

KM# 101 100 DOLLARS
6.22 g., 0.999 Gold 0.1998 oz. AGW **Ruler:** Elizabeth II **Obv:** Crowned arms within sprigs **Rev:** Head left above sprigs **Rev. Legend:** ...Princess of Wales

Date	Mintage	VF20	XF40	MS60	MS63	MS65
1997	Est. 5000	PF65 300	PF67 325			

KM# 110 100 DOLLARS
6.22 g., 0.999 Gold 0.1998 oz. AGW **Ruler:** Elizabeth II **Obv:** Crowned head right **Rev:** Bust facing **Rev. Legend:** ...In Memoriam

Date	Mintage	VF20	XF40	MS60	MS63	MS65
1998	Est. 5000	PF65 300	PF67 325			

KM# 111 100 DOLLARS
6.22 g., 0.999 Gold 0.1998 oz. AGW **Ruler:** Elizabeth II **Obv:** Crowned head right **Rev:** Bust facing **Rev. Legend:** ...Princess of Wales

Date	Mintage	VF20	XF40	MS60	MS63	MS65
1998	—	PF65 300	PF67 325			

KM# 119 100 DOLLARS
6.22 g., 0.999 Gold 0.1998 oz. AGW **Ruler:** Elizabeth II **Subject:** 50th Anniversary of Peanuts **Obv:** Crowned head right **Rev:** Snoopy and Woodstock

Date	Mintage	VF20	XF40	MS60	MS63	MS65
2000	—	PF65 300	PF67 325			

KM# 4 200 DOLLARS
311.04 g., 0.999 Silver 9.990 oz. ASW **Ruler:** Elizabeth II **Series:** Olympics **Subject:** Tennis **Obv:** Crowned arms within sprigs **Rev:** Tennis player

Date	Mintage	VF20	XF40	MS60	MS63	MS65
1987	Est. 3000	PF65 300	PF67 325			

KM# 8 200 DOLLARS
311.04 g., 0.999 Silver 9.990 oz. ASW **Ruler:** Elizabeth II **Subject:** 24th Olympiad Tennis Games, Seoul 1988 **Obv:** Crowned arms within sprigs **Rev:** Tennis player

Date	Mintage	VF20	XF40	MS60	MS63	MS65
1987	Est. 3000	PF65 300	PF67 325			

KM# 42 200 DOLLARS
6.91 g., 0.900 Gold 0.200 oz. AGW **Ruler:** Elizabeth II **Obv:** Crowned arms within sprigs **Rev:** General Douglas MacArthur 1/4 left

Date	Mintage	VF20	XF40	MS60	MS63	MS65
1989	—	PF65 295	PF67 315			

KM# 50 200 DOLLARS
6.91 g., 0.900 Gold 0.200 oz. AGW **Ruler:** Elizabeth II **Obv:** Crowned arms within sprigs **Rev:** General George S. Patton

Date	Mintage	VF20	XF40	MS60	MS63	MS65
1989	—	PF65 295	PF67 315			

KM# 45 200 DOLLARS
6.91 g., 0.900 Gold 0.200 oz. AGW **Ruler:** Elizabeth II **Obv:** Crowned arms within sprigs **Rev:** General Dwight David Eisenhower in front of flags

Date	Mintage	VF20	XF40	MS60	MS63	MS65
1990	2,500	PF65 295	PF67 315			

KM# 51 200 DOLLARS
6.91 g., 0.900 Gold 0.200 oz. AGW **Ruler:** Elizabeth II **Obv:** Crowned arms within sprigs **Rev:** Admiral William Halsey

Date	Mintage	VF20	XF40	MS60	MS63	MS65
1990	—	PF65 295	PF67 315			

KM# 52 200 DOLLARS
6.91 g., 0.900 Gold 0.200 oz. AGW **Ruler:** Elizabeth II **Obv:** Crowned arms within sprigs **Rev:** President Franklin D. Roosevelt

Date	Mintage	VF20	XF40	MS60	MS63	MS65
1990	—	PF65 295	PF67 315			

KM# 53 200 DOLLARS
6.91 g., 0.900 Gold 0.200 oz. AGW **Ruler:** Elizabeth II **Obv:** Crowned arms within sprigs **Rev:** Sir.Winston Churchill

Date	Mintage	VF20	XF40	MS60	MS63	MS65
1990	—	PF65 295	PF67 315			

KM# 9 250 DOLLARS
8.48 g., 0.917 Gold 0.2501 oz. AGW **Ruler:** Elizabeth II **Series:** Olympics **Subject:** Tennis **Obv:** Crowned arms within sprigs **Rev:** Boris Becker

Date	Mintage	VF20	XF40	MS60	MS63	MS65
1987	1,000	PF65 375	PF67 400			

KM# 10 250 DOLLARS
8.48 g., 0.917 Gold 0.2501 oz. AGW **Ruler:** Elizabeth II **Subject:** 24th Olympiad Tennis Games, Seoul 1988 **Obv:** Crowned arms within sprigs **Rev:** Steffi Graf

Date	Mintage	VF20	XF40	MS60	MS63	MS65
1987	1,000	PF65 375	PF67 400			

KM# 20 250 DOLLARS
10.00 g., 0.917 Gold 0.2948 oz. AGW **Ruler:** Elizabeth II **Obv:** Crowned arms within sprigs **Rev:** John F. Kennedy left

Date	Mintage	VF20	XF40	MS60	MS63	MS65
1988	5,000	PF65 450	PF67 475			

KM# 39 250 DOLLARS
10.00 g., 0.917 Gold 0.2948 oz. AGW **Ruler:** Elizabeth II **Subject:** Soccer **Obv:** Crowned arms within sprigs **Rev:** Soccer player to left of cameo

Date	Mintage	VF20	XF40	MS60	MS63	MS65
1988	Est. 5000	PF65 450	PF67 475			

KM# 41 250 DOLLARS
10.00 g., 0.917 Gold 0.2948 oz. AGW **Ruler:** Elizabeth II **Subject:** 24th Olympic Games, Seoul 1988 **Obv:** Crowned arms within sprigs **Rev:** Cameos of Navratilova, Graf and Evert, tennis champions

Date	Mintage	VF20	XF40	MS60	MS63	MS65
1988	—	PF65 450	PF67 475			

KM# 48 250 DOLLARS
10.00 g., 0.917 Gold 0.2948 oz. AGW **Ruler:** Elizabeth II **Subject:** 24th Olympic Games, Seoul 1988 **Obv:** Crowned arms within sprigs **Rev:** Steffi Graf with cup

Date	Mintage	VF20	XF40	MS60	MS63	MS65
1988	5,000	PF65 450	PF67 475			

KM# 26 250 DOLLARS
10.00 g., 0.917 Gold 0.2948 oz. AGW **Ruler:** Elizabeth II **Series:** Davis Cup Tennis **Obv:** Crowned arms within sprigs **Rev:** Davis cup

Date	Mintage	VF20	XF40	MS60	MS63	MS65
1989	500	PF65 500	PF67 525			

KM# 49 250 DOLLARS
10.00 g., 0.917 Gold 0.2948 oz. AGW **Ruler:** Elizabeth II **Subject:** 24th Olympic Games, Seoul 1988 **Obv:** Crowned arms within sprigs **Rev:** Steffi Graf

Date	Mintage	VF20	XF40	MS60	MS63	MS65
1989	3,000	PF65 450	PF67 475			

KM# 54 250 DOLLARS
10.00 g., 0.917 Gold 0.2948 oz. AGW **Ruler:** Elizabeth II **Subject:** Soccer - Italian **Obv:** Crowned arms within sprigs

Date	Mintage	VF20	XF40	MS60	MS63	MS65
1990	Est. 2500	PF65 450	PF67 475			

KM# 112 250 DOLLARS
15.55 g., 0.9999 Gold 0.4999 oz. AGW **Ruler:** Elizabeth II **Obv:** Crowned head right **Rev:** Bust facing **Rev. Legend:** ...In Memoriam

Date	Mintage	VF20	XF40	MS60	MS63	MS65
1998	Est. 3000	PF65 765	PF67 800			

KM# A113 250 DOLLARS
15.55 g., 0.9999 Gold 0.4999 oz. AGW **Ruler:** Elizabeth II **Obv:** Crowned head right **Rev:** Bust facing **Rev. Legend:** . Princess of Wales

Date	Mintage	VF20	XF40	MS60	MS63	MS65
1998	—	PF65 765	PF67 800			

PATTERNS

Including off metal strikes

KM#	Date	Mintage	Identification	Mkt Val
Pn1	1990	2	5 Dollars. Silver. Silver Proof, KM33.	—
Pn2	1990	2	5 Dollars. Silver. Silver Proof, KM35.	—
Pn3	1990	2	5 Dollars. Silver. Silver Proof, KM37.	—

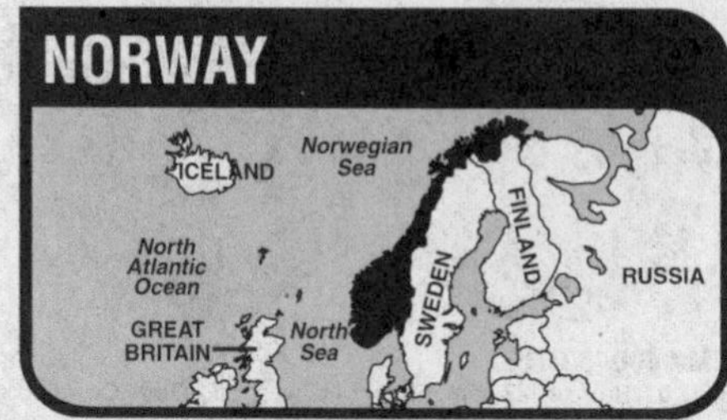

The Kingdom of Norway (*Norge, Noreg*), a constitutional monarchy located in northwestern Europe, has an area of 150,000sq. mi. (324,220 sq. km.), including the island territories of Spitzbergen (Svalbard) and Jan Mayen, and a population of *4.2 million. Capital: Oslo (Christiania). The diversified economic base of Norway includes shipping, fishing, forestry, agriculture, and manufacturing. Nonferrous metals, paper and paperboard, paper pulp, iron, steel and oil are exported.

A united Norwegian kingdom was established in the 9th century, the era of the indomitable Norse Vikings who ranged far and wide, visiting the coasts of northwestern Europe, the Mediterranean, Greenland and North America. In the 13th century the Norse kingdom was united briefly with Sweden, then passed through inheritance in 1380 to the rule of Denmark which was maintained until 1814. In 1814 Norway fell again under the rule of Sweden. The union lasted until 1905 when the Norwegian Parliament arranged a peaceful separation and invited a Danish prince (King Haakon VII) to ascend the throne of an independent Kingdom of Norway.

RULERS

Swedish, 1814-1905
Haakon VII, 1905-1957
Olav V, 1957-1991
Harald V, 1991-

MINT MARK

(h) - Crossed hammers – Kongsberg

MINT OFFICIALS' INITIALS

Letter	Date	Name
AB, B	1961-1980	Ame Jon Bakken
AB*	1980	Ole R. Kolberg
I, IT	1880-1918	Ivar Trondsen, engraver
IAR	*	Angrid Austlid Rise, engraver
K	1981	Ole R. Kolberg
OH	1959	Olvid Hansen, engraver

MONETARY SYSTEM

100 Ore = 1 Krone (30 Skilling)

KINGDOM

DECIMAL COINAGE

KM# 352 ØRE

2.00 g., Bronze **Obv:** Crowned arms divide monograms **Rev:** Value within wreath, crossed hammers divide date below **Note:** Varieties exist.

Date	Mintage	F12	VF20	XF40	MS60	MS63
1902	4,500,000	5.00	10.00	17.00	45.00	75.00

KM# 361 ØRE

2.00 g., Bronze **Ruler:** Haakon VII **Obv:** Crowned shield divides monogram **Rev:** Value within sprigs

Date	Mintage	F12	VF20	XF40	MS60	MS63
1906	3,000,000	2.00	3.00	12.00	17.00	27.50
1907	2,550,000	2.00	5.00	12.00	18.00	30.00

KM# 367 ØRE

2.00 g., Bronze, 16 mm. **Ruler:** Haakon VII **Obv:** Crowned monogram within circle **Rev:** Value **Edge:** Plain

Date	Mintage	F12	VF20	XF40	MS60	MS63
1908	1,450,000	11.00	22.50	45.00	100	165
1910	2,480,000	1.00	2.75	13.00	24.00	40.00
1911	3,270,000	1.50	2.75	17.00	45.00	75.00
1912	2,850,000	6.00	20.00	60.00	150	265
1913	2,840,000	1.00	2.75	12.00	35.00	60.00
1914	5,020,000	1.50	3.00	8.00	24.00	40.00
1915	1,540,000	20.00	35.00	60.00	200	350
1921	3,805,000	27.50	49.50	70.00	175	300
1922	Inc. above	1.00	5.00	10.00	30.00	55.00
1923	770,000	9.00	25.00	40.00	100	175
1925	3,000,000	0.60	1.75	12.00	35.00	60.00
1926	2,200,000	0.60	1.75	12.00	35.00	60.00
1927	800,000	8.00	11.00	33.00	100	165
1928	3,000,000	0.75	1.50	5.00	15.00	25.00
1929	4,990,000	0.30	0.80	4.00	12.00	20.00
1930 large date	2,009,999	0.60	1.00	5.00	16.00	27.50
1930 small date	Inc. above	0.60	1.00	5.00	16.00	27.50
1931	2,000,000	0.60	1.00	5.00	16.00	27.50
1932	2,500,000	0.60	1.00	5.00	15.00	25.00
1933	2,000,000	0.60	1.00	4.00	12.00	20.00
1934	2,000,000	0.60	1.00	5.00	15.00	25.00
1935	5,495,000	0.30	0.80	2.00	7.00	12.50
1936	6,855,000	0.30	0.80	2.00	7.00	12.50
1937	6,020,000	0.20	0.60	1.75	6.00	10.00
1938	4,920,000	0.20	0.60	1.75	6.00	10.00
1939	2,500,000	0.20	0.60	1.75	7.00	12.50
1940	5,010,000	0.20	0.60	1.00	6.00	10.00
1941	12,260,000	0.15	0.40	1.00	4.00	8.00
1946	2,200,000	0.25	0.75	2.00	7.00	12.00
1947	4,870,000	0.20	0.30	0.60	3.00	6.00
1948	9,405,000	0.20	0.30	0.60	3.00	5.00
1949	2,785,000	0.20	0.50	1.00	4.00	8.00
1950	5,730,000	0.20	0.30	0.60	3.00	5.00
1951	16,670,000	0.20	0.30	0.60	3.00	5.00
1952	Inc. above	0.20	0.50	0.90	2.00	4.00

KM# 367a ØRE

1.74 g., Iron, 15 mm. **Ruler:** Haakon VII **Obv:** Crowned monogram **Rev:** Value

Date	Mintage	F12	VF20	XF40	MS60	MS63
1918	6,000,000	5.00	8.00	14.00	40.00	70.00
1919	12,930,000	1.50	3.50	6.00	18.00	30.00
1920	4,445,000	6.00	12.50	35.00	100	175
1921	2,270,000	16.00	27.00	45.00	125	210

KM# 387 ØRE

1.74 g., Iron, 16 mm. **Ruler:** Haakon VII **Subject:** World War II German Occupation **Obv:** Shield **Rev:** Value **Edge:** Plain

Date	Mintage	F12	VF20	XF40	MS60	MS63
1941	13,410,000	0.15	0.50	1.75	7.00	12.50
1942	37,710,000	0.15	0.50	1.00	4.00	8.00
1943	33,030,000	0.15	0.35	0.60	3.00	6.00
1944	8,820,000	0.25	0.35	0.60	3.00	6.50
1945	1,740,000	3.00	5.00	9.00	21.00	35.00

KM# 398 ØRE

2.00 g., Bronze, 16 mm. **Ruler:** Haakon VII **Obv:** Crowned monogram divides date **Rev:** Value **Edge:** Plain

Date	Mintage	F12	VF20	XF40	MS60	MS63
1952	—	—	0.10	0.60	3.00	6.50
Note: Mintage included with KM#367						
1953	7,440,000	—	0.10	0.60	2.00	4.50
1954	7,650,000	—	0.10	0.75	4.00	8.00
1955	8,635,000	—	0.10	0.60	2.00	4.50
1956	11,705,000	—	0.10	0.60	2.00	4.50
1957	15,750,000	—	0.10	0.50	3.00	5.00

KM# 403 ØRE

2.00 g., Bronze, 16 mm. **Ruler:** Olav V **Obv:** Crowned monogram **Rev:** Squirrel and value **Edge:** Plain **Note:** Varieties exist.

Date	Mintage	F12	VF20	XF40	MS60	MS63
1958	2,820,000	0.25	0.50	1.00	4.00	8.00
1959	9,120,000	0.10	0.20	0.85	6.00	10.00
1960	7,890,000	—	0.10	0.30	1.00	3.00
1961	5,670,600	—	0.10	0.30	3.00	5.00
1962	12,180,000	—	0.10	0.25	1.00	3.00
1963	8,010,000	—	0.10	0.30	1.00	3.00
1964	11,020,000	—	—	0.10	0.45	0.75
1965	8,081,000	—	—	0.60	2.00	4.00
1966	12,431,000	—	—	0.15	0.75	1.25
1967	13,026,000	—	—	0.10	0.45	0.75
1968	125,500	0.50	1.00	2.00	5.00	9.00
1969	6,290,500	—	—	0.10	0.30	0.50
1970	6,607,500	—	—	0.10	0.30	0.50
1971	18,966,000	—	—	0.10	0.30	0.50
1972	21,102,984	—	—	0.10	0.30	0.50

KM# 353 2 ØRE

4.00 g., Bronze, 21 mm. **Obv:** Crowned arms divide monograms **Rev:** Value within wreath, crossed hammers divide date below

Date	Mintage	F12	VF20	XF40	MS60	MS63
1902	1,005,000	1.50	4.00	15.00	95.00	165

KM# 362 2 ØRE

4.00 g., Bronze, 21 mm. **Ruler:** Haakon VII **Obv:** Crowned shield **Rev:** Value within sprigs

Date	Mintage	F12	VF20	XF40	MS60	MS63
1906	500,000	5.00	15.00	50.00	175	325
1907	980,000	3.00	5.00	25.00	95.00	160

KM# 371 2 ØRE

4.00 g., Bronze, 21 mm. **Ruler:** Haakon VII **Obv:** Crowned monogram within circle **Rev:** Value **Edge:** Plain

Date	Mintage	F12	VF20	XF40	MS60	MS63
1909	520,000	7.00	22.50	50.00	150	250
1910	500,000	7.00	22.50	110	300	550
1911	195,000	7.00	19.00	85.00	225	400
1912	805,000	7.00	19.00	85.00	250	450
1913	2,010,000	0.80	2.25	13.00	80.00	135
1914	2,990,000	0.80	2.25	13.00	80.00	135
1915	Inc. above	6.00	22.50	105	300	550
1921	2,028,000	0.60	1.00	19.00	60.00	100
1922	2,288,000	0.60	1.00	16.00	45.00	80.00
1923	745,000	1.00	2.25	30.00	85.00	145
1928	2,250,000	0.60	1.00	14.00	45.00	75.00
1929	750,000	1.00	2.25	22.50	70.00	120
1931	1,570,000	0.60	1.00	17.00	45.00	75.00
1932	630,000	4.00	8.00	45.00	125	210
1933	750,000	0.60	1.75	11.00	45.00	75.00
1934	500,000	0.60	1.75	11.00	45.00	75.00
1935	2,223,000	0.30	1.00	8.00	27.00	45.00
1936	4,533,000	0.30	1.00	8.00	27.00	45.00
1937	3,790,000	0.20	0.60	3.00	12.00	20.00
1938	3,765,000	0.20	0.60	3.00	12.00	20.00
1939	4,420,000	0.20	0.60	3.00	12.00	20.00
1940	2,655,000	0.20	0.60	3.00	12.00	20.00
1946	1,575,000	0.20	0.60	4.00	12.00	20.00
1947	4,679,000	0.10	0.30	1.50	6.00	10.00
1948	1,002,999	1.00	2.00	3.00	7.00	12.50
1949	1,455,000	0.10	0.30	1.00	5.00	9.00
1950	5,790,000	0.10	0.30	1.00	3.00	6.00
1951	10,540,000	0.10	0.30	1.00	3.00	5.00
1952	Inc. above	0.10	0.30	1.00	3.00	5.00

KM# 371a 2 ØRE

3.48 g., Iron, 21 mm. **Ruler:** Haakon VII **Obv:** Crowned monogram **Rev:** Value

Date	Mintage	F12	VF20	XF40	MS60	MS63
1917	720,000	80.00	100	150	300	500
1918	1,280,000	35.00	50.00	75.00	150	250
1919	3,365,000	10.00	15.00	65.00	175	310
1920	2,635,000	10.00	15.00	65.00	175	300

KM# 394 2 ØRE
3.47 g., Iron, 21 mm. **Ruler:** Haakon VII **Obv:** Shield **Rev:** Value **Note:** World War II German occupation issue.

Date	Mintage	F12	VF20	XF40	MS60	MS63
1943	6,575,000	0.50	0.75	1.75	5.00	9.00
1944	9,805,000	0.50	0.75	1.75	5.00	9.00
1945	2,520,000	1.50	3.00	5.00	12.00	20.00

KM# 399 2 ØRE
4.00 g., Bronze, 21 mm. **Ruler:** Haakon VII **Obv:** Crowned monogram divides date **Rev:** Value **Edge:** Plain

Date	Mintage	F12	VF20	XF40	MS60	MS63
1952	Inc. above	—	0.10	0.85	6.00	10.00
1953	6,705,000	—	0.10	0.85	4.00	7.00
1954	2,805,000	—	0.10	0.85	6.00	10.00
1955	3,600,000	—	0.10	0.85	6.00	10.00
1956	6,780,000	—	0.10	0.85	4.00	7.00
1957	6,090,000	—	0.10	0.85	4.00	7.00

KM# 404 2 ØRE
4.00 g., Bronze, 21 mm. **Ruler:** Olav V **Obv:** Crowned monogram **Rev:** Moor hen and value, small lettering **Edge:** Plain

Date	Mintage	F12	VF20	XF40	MS60	MS63
1958	2,700,000	0.20	0.50	1.75	7.00	12.00

KM# 410 2 ØRE
4.00 g., Bronze, 21 mm. **Ruler:** Olav V **Obv:** Crowned monogram **Rev:** Moor hen and value, large lettering **Edge:** Plain

Date	Mintage	F12	VF20	XF40	MS60	MS63
1959	4,125,000	0.10	0.20	1.25	4.00	8.00
1960	3,735,000	—	0.10	0.85	12.00	20.00
1961	4,477,000	—	0.10	0.35	1.00	2.00
1962	6,205,000	—	0.10	0.35	1.00	2.00
1963	4,840,000	—	0.10	0.35	1.00	2.00
1964	7,250,000	—	0.10	0.20	0.90	1.50
1965	6,241,000	—	0.10	0.30	1.00	3.00
1966	10,485,000	—	—	0.15	1.00	2.50
1967	11,993,000	—	—	0.15	0.90	1.50
1968	3,467	—	—	—	600	1,000
Note: In mint sets only						
1969	315,600	0.50	0.75	1.25	3.00	6.00
1970	6,794,000	—	—	0.10	0.75	1.25
1971	15,462,000	—	—	0.10	0.60	1.00
1972	15,897,984	—	—	0.10	0.60	1.00

KM# 349 5 ØRE
8.00 g., Bronze, 27 mm. **Obv:** Crowned arms divide monograms **Rev:** Value within wreath, crossed hammers divide date below

Date	Mintage	F12	VF20	XF40	MS60	MS63
1902	705,000	2.50	6.00	55.00	225	400

KM# 364 5 ØRE
8.00 g., Bronze, 27 mm. **Ruler:** Haakon VII **Obv:** Crowned shield divides monogram **Rev:** Value within sprigs

Date	Mintage	F12	VF20	XF40	MS60	MS63
1907	200,000	3.50	12.50	60.00	175	300

KM# 368 5 ØRE
8.00 g., Bronze, 27 mm. **Ruler:** Haakon VII **Obv:** Crowned monogram within circle **Rev:** Numeral and written value **Edge:** Plain

Date	Mintage	F12	VF20	XF40	MS60	MS63
1908	600,000	27.50	49.50	100	350	600
1911	480,000	2.25	17.00	60.00	200	360
1912	520,000	7.00	27.50	150	450	825
1913	1,000,000	1.50	6.00	33.00	125	215
1914	1,000,000	1.50	6.00	33.00	125	215
1915	Inc. above	11.00	38.50	160	500	900
1916	300,000	7.00	17.00	65.00	250	450
1921	683,000	1.75	8.00	65.00	150	280
1922	2,296,000	1.50	6.00	33.00	95.00	165
1923	456,000	2.75	11.00	50.00	150	285
1928	848,000	0.70	3.00	24.00	65.00	110
1929	452,000	3.00	11.00	60.00	175	300
1930	1,292,000	0.70	2.75	30.00	90.00	150
1931	808,000	0.70	2.75	30.00	90.00	150
1932	500,000	3.00	17.00	45.00	125	225
1933	300,000	3.00	13.00	60.00	175	300
1935	496,000	1.75	6.00	27.50	100	180
1936	760,000	1.00	2.75	22.50	75.00	130
1937	1,552,000	0.60	1.75	13.00	35.00	60.00
1938	1,332,000	0.60	1.75	10.00	30.00	50.00
1939	1,370,000	0.60	1.75	10.00	30.00	50.00
1940	2,554,000	0.30	1.00	6.00	19.00	32.50
1941	3,576,000	0.30	1.00	6.00	19.00	32.50
1951	8,128,000	0.30	0.60	2.50	12.00	20.00
1952	Inc. above	1.75	4.00	10.00	30.00	50.00

KM# 368a 5 ØRE
6.69 g., Iron, 27 mm. **Ruler:** Haakon VII **Obv:** Crowned monogram within circle **Rev:** Numeral and written value

Date	Mintage	F12	VF20	XF40	MS60	MS63
1917	1,700,000	20.00	28.00	40.00	75.00	125
1918/7	432,000	125	175	250	500	850
1918	Inc. above	135	225	300	550	950
1919	3,464,000	12.00	30.00	70.00	150	250
1920	1,629,000	25.00	55.00	120	300	550

KM# 388 5 ØRE
6.94 g., Iron, 27 mm. **Ruler:** Haakon VII **Obv:** Shield **Rev:** Value **Edge:** Plain **Note:** World War II German occupation issue.

Date	Mintage	F12	VF20	XF40	MS60	MS63
1941	6,608,000	0.50	1.50	5.50	24.00	40.00
1942	10,312,000	0.50	1.50	5.00	12.00	20.00
1943	6,184,000	0.75	2.00	7.00	19.00	32.50
1944	4,256,000	1.25	3.00	7.00	19.00	32.50
1945	408,000	90.00	125	175	350	600

KM# 400 5 ØRE
8.00 g., Bronze, 27 mm. **Ruler:** Haakon VII **Obv:** Crowned monogram divides date **Rev:** Value **Edge:** Plain

Date	Mintage	F12	VF20	XF40	MS60	MS63
1952	—	0.10	0.50	2.50	21.00	35.00
Note: Mintage included with KM#368						
1953	6,216,000	0.10	0.35	2.25	12.00	20.00
1954	4,536,000	0.10	0.35	2.25	12.00	20.00
1955	6,570,000	0.10	0.35	2.25	12.00	20.00
1956	2,959,000	0.10	0.35	2.25	18.00	30.00
1957	5,624,000	0.10	0.35	2.25	7.00	12.50

KM# 405 5 ØRE
8.00 g., Bronze, 27 mm. **Ruler:** Olav V **Obv:** Head left **Rev:** Moose **Edge:** Plain

Date	Mintage	F12	VF20	XF40	MS60	MS63
1958	2,205,000	1.00	2.00	6.00	35.00	60.00
1959	3,208,000	0.10	0.50	2.25	15.00	25.00
1960	5,519,000	0.15	0.30	2.50	12.00	20.00
1961	4,554,000	0.15	0.30	2.50	15.00	25.00
1962	7,764,000	0.10	0.15	0.75	9.00	15.00
1963	3,204,000	0.15	0.25	1.00	12.00	20.00
1964	6,108,000	—	0.25	1.00	9.00	15.00
1965	6,841,000	—	0.10	0.50	7.00	12.00
1966	8,415,000	—	0.10	0.50	2.00	4.00
1967	9,071,000	—	0.10	0.45	2.00	4.00
1968	4,286,000	—	0.10	0.85	6.00	10.00
1969	4,328,000	—	0.10	0.35	1.00	2.00
1970	7,350,600	—	0.10	0.35	1.00	2.00
1971	13,450,100	—	0.10	0.35	1.00	2.00
1972	19,001,784	—	—	0.15	0.60	1.00
1973	9,584,175	—	—	0.15	0.60	1.00

KM# 415 5 ØRE
3.00 g., Bronze, 19 mm. **Ruler:** Olav V **Obv:** Arms **Rev:** Value **Edge:** Plain **Note:** Varieties exist.

Date	Mintage	VF20	XF40	MS60	MS63	MS65
1973	52,886,175	—	—	0.15	0.25	0.50
1974	37,150,223	—	—	0.15	0.25	0.50
1975	32,478,744	—	—	0.15	0.25	0.50
1976	24,232,824	—	—	0.15	0.25	0.50
1977	29,646,000	—	—	0.15	0.25	0.50
1978	13,838,000	—	—	0.15	0.25	0.50
1979	25,255,000	—	—	0.15	0.25	0.50
1980	12,315,000	—	—	0.15	0.25	0.50
1980 Without star	27,515,000	—	—	0.15	0.25	0.50
1981	24,529,000	—	—	0.15	0.25	0.50
1982	21,900,650	—	—	0.15	0.25	0.50

KM# 350 10 ØRE
1.50 g., 0.400 Silver 0.0193 oz. ASW, 15 mm. **Obv:** Crowned monogram **Obv. Legend:** BRODERFOLKENES VEL **Rev:** Crowned arms divide date

Date	Mintage	F12	VF20	XF40	MS60	MS63
1901	2,021,100	8.00	11.00	15.00	30.00	55.00
1903	1,500,700	10.00	18.00	25.00	45.00	60.00

KM# 372 10 ØRE

1.45 g., 0.400 Silver 0.0186 oz. ASW, 15 mm. **Ruler:** Haakon VII **Obv:** Crowned monogram **Rev:** Value

Date	Mintage	F12	VF20	XF40	MS60	MS63
1909	2,000,000	6.50	13.00	33.00	65.00	110
1911	1,650,000	9.00	22.00	65.00	125	220
1912	2,350,000	6.00	12.00	28.00	55.00	95.00
1913	2,000,000	6.00	11.00	25.00	45.00	75.00
1914	1,180,000	11.00	25.00	50.00	95.00	165
1915	2,820,000	3.00	5.00	14.00	65.00	110
1916	1,500,000	10.00	17.00	40.00	85.00	145
1917	5,950,000	1.50	3.00	6.00	13.00	22.50
1918/7	1,650,000	15.00	35.00	85.00	200	—
1918	Inc. above	3.00	5.00	14.00	35.00	65.00
1919	Inc. above	1.50	3.00	6.00	13.00	22.50
1919/7	7,800,000	15.00	35.00	85.00	200	—

KM# 378 10 ØRE

1.50 g., Copper-Nickel, 15 mm. **Ruler:** Haakon VII **Obv:** Crowned monogram **Rev:** Value flanked by designs

Date	Mintage	F12	VF20	XF40	MS60	MS63
1920	2,535,000	10.00	13.00	18.00	35.00	60.00
1921	6,465,000	7.00	11.00	15.00	30.00	55.00
1922	3,965,000	7.00	11.00	15.00	30.00	50.00
1923	7,135,000	8.00	11.00	15.00	30.00	55.00

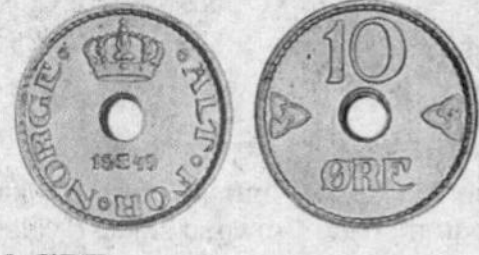

KM# 383 10 ØRE

1.50 g., Copper-Nickel, 15 mm. **Ruler:** Haakon VII **Obv:** Crown above center hole **Rev:** Value above center hole

Date	Mintage	F12	VF20	XF40	MS60	MS63
1924	12,079,100	0.30	0.75	10.00	24.00	40.00
1925	7,050,700	0.30	0.75	10.00	35.00	60.00
1926	11,764,200	0.30	0.75	10.00	24.00	40.00
1927	526,000	10.00	20.00	130	350	625
1937	5,000,000	0.30	0.75	6.00	24.00	40.00
1938	3,412,600	0.30	0.75	6.00	21.00	35.00
1939	1,538,400	1.00	2.50	10.00	40.00	70.00
1940	4,800,000	0.30	0.75	2.00	10.00	17.50
1941	10,150,000	0.30	0.75	2.00	6.00	10.00
1945	1,718,000	0.10	0.25	2.00	9.00	15.00
1946	3,723,200	0.10	0.25	2.00	5.00	9.00
1947	7,256,700	0.10	0.25	1.00	3.00	6.50
1948	3,104,500	0.10	0.25	2.25	4.00	7.00
1949	11,545,500	0.10	0.25	2.00	4.00	7.00
1951	5,150,000	0.10	0.25	2.00	4.00	7.00

KM# 389 10 ØRE

1.25 g., Zinc, 15 mm. **Ruler:** Haakon VII **Obv:** Shield flanked by designs **Rev:** Value flanked by designs **Edge:** Plain **Note:** World War II German occupation issue.

Date	Mintage	F12	VF20	XF40	MS60	MS63
1941	15,309,900	0.75	2.00	6.00	19.00	32.50
1942	50,387,600	0.35	1.00	3.50	7.00	12.50
1943	13,377,700	0.75	2.00	5.50	21.00	35.00
1944	3,549,400	7.50	12.50	30.00	80.00	135
1945	5,645,500	4.00	8.00	15.00	30.00	50.00

KM# 391 10 ØRE

1.15 g., Nickel-Brass, 15 mm. **Ruler:** Haakon VII **Obv:** Crown above center hole **Rev:** Value above center hole **Note:** World War II government in exile issue.

Date	Mintage	F12	VF20	XF40	MS60	MS63
1942	6,000,000	30.00	50.00	90.00	175	300

Note: All except 9,667 were melted

KM# 396 10 ØRE

1.50 g., Copper-Nickel, 15 mm. **Ruler:** Haakon VII **Obv:** Crowned monogram divides date **Rev:** Value flanked by designs **Edge:** Plain

Date	Mintage	F12	VF20	XF40	MS60	MS63
1951	17,400,000	0.10	0.30	2.50	40.00	70.00
1952	Inc. above	0.10	0.20	1.50	12.00	20.00
1953	7,700,000	0.10	0.20	1.50	12.00	20.00
1954	10,105,000	0.10	0.20	1.50	12.00	20.00
1955	9,829,500	0.10	0.20	1.50	30.00	50.00
1956	10,066,000	0.10	0.20	1.50	12.00	20.00
1957	22,900,000	0.10	0.20	1.50	7.00	12.00

KM# 406 10 ØRE

1.50 g., Copper-Nickel, 15 mm. **Ruler:** Olav V **Obv:** Crowned monogram **Rev:** Honey bee and value, small lettering **Edge:** Reeded

Date	Mintage	F12	VF20	XF40	MS60	MS63
1958	1,425,000	0.50	1.50	3.00	18.00	30.00

KM# 411 10 ØRE

1.50 g., Copper-Nickel, 15 mm. **Ruler:** Olav V **Obv:** Crowned monogram **Rev:** Honey bee and value, large lettering **Edge:** Reeded

Date	Mintage	F12	VF20	XF40	MS60	MS63
1959	2,500,000	—	0.75	3.00	12.00	20.00
1960	12,490,200	—	0.10	0.60	4.00	7.00
1961	10,385,000	—	0.10	0.60	12.00	20.00
1962	16,210,000	—	0.10	0.60	3.00	5.00
1963	17,560,000	—	0.10	0.60	3.00	5.00
1964	9,781,000	—	0.10	0.35	0.80	1.35
1965	10,561,000	—	0.10	0.60	9.00	15.00
1966	16,610,000	—	0.10	0.50	1.00	3.00
1967	18,243,000	—	0.10	0.35	3.00	5.00
1968	24,998,300	—	0.10	0.35	4.00	7.00
1969	27,157,200	—	0.10	0.25	1.00	2.25
1970	639,300	0.50	1.00	1.75	3.00	5.00
1971	8,903,800	—	0.10	0.25	0.80	1.35
1972	24,834,484	—	—	0.25	0.60	1.00
1973	22,300,925	—	—	0.25	0.60	1.00

KM# 416 10 ØRE

1.25 g., Copper-Nickel, 15 mm. **Ruler:** Olav V **Obv:** Crowned monogram divides date **Rev:** Value **Edge:** Plain **Note:** Varieties exist in monogram.

Date	Mintage	VF20	XF40	MS60	MS63	MS65
1974	30,995,223	—	—	0.15	0.30	0.60
1975	21,845,496	—	—	0.15	0.30	0.60
1976	42,403,074	—	—	0.15	0.25	0.40
1977	43,304,000	—	—	0.15	0.25	0.40
1978	37,395,000	—	—	0.15	0.25	0.40
1979	25,808,000	—	—	0.15	0.25	0.40
1980	28,620,000	—	—	0.15	0.25	0.40
1980 Without star	14,050,000	—	—	0.15	0.25	0.40
1981	43,083,400	—	—	0.15	0.25	0.40
1982	40,974,256	—	—	0.15	0.25	0.40
1983	45,637,300	—	—	0.15	0.25	0.40
1984	100,066,000	—	—	0.15	0.25	0.35
1985	103,108,000	—	—	0.15	0.25	0.35
1986	146,392,000	—	—	0.15	0.25	0.35
1987	166,040,000	—	—	0.15	0.25	0.35
1988	94,677,000	—	—	0.15	0.25	0.35
1989	97,273,500	—	—	0.15	0.25	0.35
1990	150,290,000	—	—	0.15	0.25	0.35
1991	79,597,000	—	—	0.10	0.25	0.35

KM# 360 25 ØRE

2.42 g., 0.600 Silver 0.0467 oz. ASW, 17 mm. **Obv:** Crowned arms within wreath **Obv. Legend:** BRODERFOLKENES VEL **Rev:** Value within wreath, crossed hammers divide date below

Date	Mintage	F12	VF20	XF40	MS60	MS63
1901	606,900	21.00	40.00	65.00	125	160
1902	611,700	21.00	40.00	65.00	125	160
1904	600,000	21.00	40.00	65.00	125	160

KM# 373 25 ØRE

2.42 g., 0.600 Silver 0.0467 oz. ASW **Ruler:** Haakon VII **Obv:** Arms flanked by designs **Rev:** Crowned cross with monogram

Date	Mintage	F12	VF20	XF40	MS60	MS63
1909	600,000	11.00	22.00	32.00	60.00	85.00
1911	400,000	22.00	32.00	65.00	125	155
1912	200,000	80.00	110	210	385	510
1913	400,000	14.00	25.00	49.00	100	125
1914	399,600	12.60	35.00	55.00	110	155
1915	1,032,300	7.50	12.00	35.00	70.00	100
1916	368,000	24.50	35.00	65.00	125	175
1917	400,000	22.00	32.00	50.00	110	155
1918/6	800,000	9.50	12.50	17.50	35.00	50.00
1918	Inc. above	9.00	16.00	35.00	70.00	100
1919	1,600,000	5.00	9.00	22.00	45.00	78.00

KM# 381 25 ØRE

4.40 g., Copper-Nickel, 17 mm. **Ruler:** Haakon VII **Obv:** Crowned monogram **Rev:** Arms flanked by designs

Date	Mintage	F12	VF20	XF40	MS60	MS63
1921	4,800,000	7.00	10.00	14.00	28.00	60.00
1922	14,200,000	7.00	10.00	14.00	28.00	60.00
1923	5,200,000	13.00	18.00	25.00	45.00	90.00

KM# 382 25 ØRE

2.40 g., Copper-Nickel, 17 mm. **Ruler:** Haakon VII **Obv:** Crowned monogram, hole in center **Rev:** Arms flanked by designs, hole in center

Date	Mintage	F12	VF20	XF40	MS60	MS63
1921	—	3.00	5.00	75.00	350	625
1922	—	3.00	4.00	45.00	225	375
1923	—	1.50	3.00	25.00	100	190

Note: Respective mintages included with KM#381

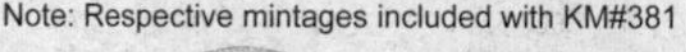

KM# 384 25 ØRE

2.40 g., Copper-Nickel, 17 mm. **Ruler:** Haakon VII **Obv:** Crowned cross with monogram, hole in center **Rev:** Center hole flanked by designs, crown above

Date	Mintage	F12	VF20	XF40	MS60	MS63
1924	4,000,000	0.50	2.00	7.00	35.00	65.00
1927	6,200,000	0.50	1.50	7.00	35.00	65.00
1929	800,000	1.50	6.00	42.00	150	275
1939	1,220,000	0.25	0.75	3.50	45.00	75.00
1940	1,160,000	0.25	0.75	3.50	30.00	55.00
1946	1,850,000	0.20	0.50	1.75	12.00	20.00
1947	2,592,000	0.20	0.50	1.75	9.00	15.00
1949	2,602,000	0.20	0.50	1.75	9.00	15.00
1950	2,800,000	0.20	0.50	1.75	9.00	15.00

KM# 392 25 ØRE

2.40 g., Nickel-Brass, 17 mm. **Ruler:** Haakon VII **Obv:** Crowned monograms form cross, hole at center **Rev:** Crown on top divides date, hole in center flanked by designs, value on bottom **Note:** World War II government in exile issue.

Date	Mintage	F12	VF20	XF40	MS60	MS63
1942	2,400,000	—	—	90.00	175	250

Note: All but 10,300 were melted

KM# 395 25 ØRE

2.00 g., Zinc, 17 mm. **Ruler:** Haakon VII **Obv:** Shield flanked by designs **Rev:** Value flanked by designs **Note:** World War II German occupation.

Date	Mintage	F12	VF20	XF40	MS60	MS63
1943	14,104,800	1.00	1.50	4.00	15.00	25.00
1944	3,030,500	4.00	7.50	18.00	35.00	50.00
1945	3,010,000	6.00	10.00	22.00	45.00	60.00

KM# 401 25 ØRE

2.40 g., Copper-Nickel, 17 mm. **Ruler:** Haakon VII **Obv:** Crowned monogram divides date **Rev:** Value flanked by designs **Edge:** Plain **Note:** Mint marks exist with mint mark on square or without square.

Date	Mintage	F12	VF20	XF40	MS60	MS63
1952	4,060,000	0.10	0.25	1.20	18.00	30.00
1953	3,320,000	0.10	0.25	1.20	24.00	40.00
1954	3,140,000	0.10	0.25	1.20	21.00	35.00
1955	2,000,000	0.10	0.25	1.20	45.00	75.00
1956	3,980,000	0.10	0.25	1.20	18.00	30.00
1957	7,660,000	0.10	0.25	1.20	12.00	20.00

KM# 407 25 ØRE

2.40 g., Copper-Nickel, 17 mm. **Ruler:** Olav V **Obv:** Head left **Rev:** Siberian tit above value **Edge:** Reeded

Date	Mintage	F12	VF20	XF40	MS60	MS63
1958	1,316,000	0.50	1.00	3.00	24.00	40.00
1959	1,184,000	0.50	1.00	3.00	21.00	35.00
1960	3,964,200	—	0.10	1.25	12.00	20.00
1961	4,656,000	—	0.10	1.00	4.00	7.50
1962	6,304,000	—	0.10	1.00	4.00	7.50
1963	3,640,000	—	0.10	1.00	4.00	7.50
1964	4,953,000	—	0.10	0.50	1.00	2.75
1965	2,798,000	—	0.10	0.65	18.00	30.00
1966	6,075,000	—	0.10	0.65	2.00	3.00
1967	6,641,000	—	0.10	0.65	2.00	3.00
1968	4,963,400	—	0.10	0.50	3.00	5.00
1969	12,426,500	—	0.10	0.15	1.00	2.00
1970	1,545,400	—	0.15	0.75	3.00	6.50
1971	5,247,200	—	—	0.10	0.75	1.25
1972	7,928,584	—	—	0.10	0.75	1.25
1973	8,516,175	—	—	0.10	0.75	1.25

KM# 417 25 ØRE

2.40 g., Copper-Nickel, 17 mm. **Ruler:** Olav V **Obv:** Crowned monograms in cross formation **Rev:** Value **Edge:** Reeded

Date	Mintage	VF20	XF40	MS60	MS63	MS65
1974	8,048,223	—	—	0.15	0.30	0.65
1975	15,594,696	—	—	0.15	0.30	0.65
1976	24,721,074	—	—	0.15	0.25	0.50
1977	20,150,000	—	—	0.15	0.25	0.50
1978	11,259,000	—	—	0.15	0.25	0.50
1979	16,666,000	—	—	0.15	0.25	0.50
1980	6,289,000	—	—	0.15	0.25	0.50
1980 Without star	8,176,000	—	—	0.15	0.25	0.50
1981	17,971,000	—	—	0.15	0.25	0.50
1982	16,862,650	—	—	0.15	0.25	0.50

KM# 356 50 ØRE

5.00 g., 0.600 Silver 0.0965 oz. ASW **Obv:** Head left **Obv. Legend:** OSCAR II NORGES. **Rev:** Crowned shield within wreath, crossed hammers divide date below

Date	Mintage	F12	VF20	XF40	MS60	MS63
1901	404,000	14.00	35.00	75.00	175	285
1902	301,200	14.00	35.00	75.00	175	285
1904	100,500	70.00	165	250	450	780

KM# 374 50 ØRE

5.00 g., 0.600 Silver 0.0965 oz. ASW **Ruler:** Haakon VII **Obv:** Head right **Rev:** Crowned shield flanked by designs

Date	Mintage	F12	VF20	XF40	MS60	MS63
1909	200,000	27.00	35.00	70.00	150	195
1911	200,000	40.00	60.00	100	200	275
1912	200,000	60.00	90.00	125	250	350
1913	200,000	40.00	60.00	100	200	275
1914	800,000	8.00	15.00	27.50	75.00	130
1915	300,000	23.00	40.00	65.00	125	165
1916	700,000	9.00	19.00	49.50	125	165
1918	3,090,000	5.00	8.00	13.00	65.00	110
1919	1,219,000	6.00	9.00	20.00	50.00	65.00

KM# 379 50 ØRE

4.80 g., Copper-Nickel, 22 mm. **Ruler:** Haakon VII **Obv:** Crowned monograms form cross **Rev:** Crowned shield flanked by designs

Date	Mintage	F12	VF20	XF40	MS60	MS63
1920	1,236,000	30.00	42.00	60.00	108	150
1921	7,345,000	10.00	21.50	30.00	55.00	75.00
1922	3,000,000	9.50	15.00	21.50	42.00	60.00
1923	4,540,000	60.00	80.00	110	180	225

KM# 380 50 ØRE

4.80 g., Copper-Nickel, 22 mm. **Ruler:** Haakon VII **Obv:** Crowned monograms form cross with hole in center **Rev:** Crowned shield flanked by designs, hole in center **Note:** Respective mintages are included with KM#379.

Date	Mintage	F12	VF20	XF40	MS60	MS63
1920	—	25.00	80.00	300	800	—
1921	—	4.75	12.00	110	360	600
1922	—	2.00	8.00	80.00	280	480
1923	—	2.50	4.75	55.00	160	280

KM# 386 50 ØRE

4.80 g., Copper-Nickel, 22 mm. **Ruler:** Haakon VII **Obv:** Crowned monograms form cross with hole in center **Rev:** Center hole flanked by designs, crown above, value below

Date	Mintage	F12	VF20	XF40	MS60	MS63
1926	2,000,000	0.25	1.00	12.50	38.00	67.50
1927	2,502,100	0.25	1.00	10.00	32.50	55.00
1928/7	1,458,200	0.50	2.50	14.00	45.00	80.00
1928	Inc. above	0.35	2.25	14.00	45.00	80.00
1929	600,000	2.25	5.50	50.00	245	420
1939	900,000	0.50	1.00	7.00	70.00	140
1940	2,193,000	0.20	0.50	2.50	22.00	35.00
1941	2,373,000	0.20	0.50	2.50	22.00	35.00
1945	1,354,000	0.20	0.50	1.75	13.50	22.50
1946	1,532,500	0.20	0.50	5.00	10.00	15.00
1947	2,465,300	0.20	0.50	4.50	8.40	11.50
1948	5,911,400	0.20	0.50	2.75	6.50	11.50
1949	1,029,600	0.35	0.75	3.50	10.00	17.50

KM# 390 50 ØRE

4.00 g., Zinc, 22 mm. **Ruler:** Haakon VII **Obv:** Shield flanked by designs **Rev:** Value flanked by designs **Edge:** Plain **Note:** World War II German occupation issue.

Date	Mintage	F12	VF20	XF40	MS60	MS63
1941	7,760,800	1.25	3.00	15.00	45.00	80.00
1942	7,605,550	1.00	2.50	7.00	30.00	50.00
1943	3,348,500	15.00	25.00	60.00	150	200
1944	1,542,400	10.00	15.00	25.00	50.00	65.00
1945	226,000	125	175	250	500	675

KM# 393 50 ØRE

4.80 g., Nickel-Brass, 22 mm. **Ruler:** Haakon VII **Obv:** Crowned monograms form cross with hole in center **Rev:** Center hole flanked by designs, crown above, value below **Note:** World War II government in exile issue.

Date	Mintage	F12	VF20	XF40	MS60	MS63
1942	1,600,000	—	—	125	250	350

Note: All but 9,238 were melted

KM# 402 50 ØRE

4.60 g., Copper-Nickel, 22 mm. **Ruler:** Haakon VII **Obv:** Crowned monogram **Rev:** Crowned shield divides date

Date	Mintage	F12	VF20	XF40	MS60	MS63
1953	2,370,000	0.20	0.45	1.25	14.50	24.50
1954	230,000	5.50	28.00	70.00	245	455
1955	1,930,000	0.20	0.35	5.50	31.50	52.50
1956	1,630,000	0.20	0.35	5.50	24.50	45.50
1957	1,800,000	0.20	0.35	5.50	14.50	24.50

KM# 408 50 ØRE

4.80 g., Copper-Nickel, 22 mm. **Ruler:** Olav V **Obv:** Head left **Rev:** Elkhound right divides date and value **Edge:** Reeded

Date	Mintage	F12	VF20	XF40	MS60	MS63
1958	1,560,000	1.00	1.50	8.00	50.00	90.00
1959	340,000	1.50	4.00	15.00	60.00	100
1960	1,584,200	—	0.10	1.75	12.00	20.00
1961	2,424,600	—	0.10	0.85	12.00	20.00
1962	3,064,000	—	0.10	0.85	7.00	12.50
1963	2,168,000	—	0.10	0.85	7.00	12.50
1964	2,692,000	—	0.10	0.60	4.00	8.00
1965	1,248,000	1.00	1.50	4.00	50.00	90.00
1966	4,262,000	—	0.10	0.50	4.00	8.00
1967	4,001,000	—	0.10	0.50	3.00	6.50
1968	5,430,800	—	0.10	0.50	7.00	12.50
1969	7,591,000	—	0.10	0.50	1.00	3.00
1970	481,000	1.00	1.50	5.00	9.00	16.00
1971	2,489,300	—	0.25	1.00	4.00	8.00
1972	4,452,784	—	0.10	0.50	1.00	3.00
1973	3,317,175	—	0.10	0.50	1.00	3.00

KM# 418 50 ØRE

4.80 g., Copper-Nickel, 22 mm. **Ruler:** Olav V **Obv:** Crowned shield divides date **Rev:** Value **Edge:** Reeded **Note:** Varieties in shield exist.

Date	Mintage	VF20	XF40	MS60	MS63	MS65
1974	8,494,223	—	—	0.15	0.25	1.00
1975	10,123,496	—	—	0.15	0.25	1.00
1976	15,177,324	—	—	0.15	0.25	1.00
1977	19,411,750	—	—	0.15	0.20	0.50
1978	15,305,000	—	—	0.15	0.20	0.50
1979	10,152,000	—	—	0.15	0.20	0.50
1980 Without star	7,066,000	—	—	0.15	0.20	0.50
1980	7,082,000	—	—	0.15	0.20	0.50
1981	3,402,000	—	—	0.15	0.20	0.50
1982	11,156,650	—	—	0.15	0.20	0.50

Date	Mintage	VF20	XF40	MS60	MS63	MS65
1983	15,762,300	—	—	0.15	0.20	0.50
1984	8,615,000	—	—	0.15	0.20	0.50
1985	4,444,000	—	—	0.15	0.20	0.50
1986	4,178,000	—	—	0.15	0.20	0.50
1987	5,167,000	—	—	0.15	0.20	0.50
1988	9,610,000	—	—	0.15	0.20	0.50
1989	5,785,000	—	—	0.15	0.20	0.50
1990	1,729,000	—	—	0.15	0.25	0.75
1991	2,924,008	—	—	0.15	0.20	0.50
1992	6,802,027	—	—	0.15	0.20	0.50
1992	20,000	PF65 10.00				
1993	8,056,000	—	—	0.15	0.15	0.50
1993 Proof	12,000	—	—	—	—	—
1994	7,173,000	—	—	0.15	0.15	0.50
1994	15,000	PF65 10.00				
1995	6,835,000	—	—	—	—	0.50
1995	15,000	PF65 10.00				
1996	4,500,000	—	—	—	—	1.00
1996	12,000	PF65 10.00				

KM# 460 50 ØRE

3.60 g., Bronze, 18.5 mm. **Ruler:** Harald V **Obv:** Crown **Rev:** Stylized animal and value **Edge:** Plain

Date	Mintage	VF20	XF40	MS60	MS63	MS65
1996	81,956,200	—	—	—	—	0.50
1997	24,089,873	—	—	—	—	0.50
1997	15,000	PF65 10.00				
1998	30,913,000	—	—	—	—	0.50
1998	14,097	PF65 10.00				
1999	25,314,273	—	—	—	—	0.50
1999	12,500	PF65 10.00				
2000	18,979,552	—	—	—	—	0.50
2000	13,500	PF65 10.00				

KM# 357 KRONE

7.50 g., 0.800 Silver 0.1929 oz. ASW **Obv:** Head left **Obv. Legend:** OSCAR II NORGES. **Rev:** Crowned arms within wreath, crossed hammers divide date below **Note:** Without 30 SK

Date	Mintage	F12	VF20	XF40	MS60	MS63
1901	151,800	45.00	70.00	200	400	540
1904	100,100	65.00	135	230	495	700

KM# 369 KRONE

7.50 g., 0.800 Silver 0.1929 oz. ASW **Ruler:** Haakon VII **Obv:** Head right **Rev:** Order of St. Olaf

Date	Mintage	F12	VF20	XF40	MS60	MS63
1908	180,000	50.00	80.00	125	250	325
Note: Crossed hammers on shield						
1908	170,000	40.00	60.00	100	200	260
Note: Crossed hammers without shield						
1910	100,000	150	200	350	600	800
1912	200,000	50.00	90.00	125	250	350
1913	230,000	65.00	90.00	125	250	350
1914	602,000	25.00	35.00	50.00	100	140
1915	498,000	25.00	45.00	65.00	125	150
1916	400,000	25.00	60.00	110	250	325
1917	600,000	25.00	35.00	45.00	80.00	110

KM# 385 KRONE

7.00 g., Copper-Nickel, 25 mm. **Ruler:** Haakon VII **Obv:** Crowned monograms form cross with hole in center **Rev:** Crowned order chain with hole in center

Date	Mintage	F12	VF20	XF40	MS60	MS63
1925	8,686,000	0.50	3.00	25.00	80.00	140
1926	1,984,000	0.75	4.00	35.00	125	240
1927	1,000,000	1.50	5.00	65.00	300	550
1936	700,000	2.00	6.00	65.00	300	500
1937	1,000,000	1.50	4.00	75.00	200	350
1938	926,000	1.50	4.50	20.00	90.00	150
1939	2,253,000	0.60	1.50	12.50	60.00	100
1940	3,890,000	0.50	1.50	12.00	45.00	75.00
1946	5,499,000	0.50	0.75	3.00	24.00	40.00
1947	802,000	2.00	3.00	20.00	40.00	70.00
1949	7,846,000	0.25	0.75	4.00	15.00	25.00
1950	9,942,000	0.25	0.75	4.00	15.00	25.00
1951	4,761,000	0.25	0.75	4.00	15.00	25.00

KM# 397.1 KRONE

7.00 g., Copper-Nickel, 25 mm. **Ruler:** Haakon VII **Obv:** Crowned monogram **Rev:** Crowned shield divides date **Note:** Thin border dentilations

Date	Mintage	F12	VF20	XF40	MS60	MS63
1951	3,819,000	0.25	0.75	3.50	35.00	45.00

KM# 397.2 KRONE

7.00 g., Copper-Nickel, 25 mm. **Ruler:** Haakon VII **Obv:** Crowned monogram **Rev:** Crowned shield divides date **Note:** Thick border dentilations.

Date	Mintage	F12	VF20	XF40	MS60	MS63
1953	1,465,000	0.25	1.00	5.00	40.00	70.00
1954	3,045,000	0.25	1.00	4.00	40.00	70.00
1955	1,970,000	0.25	1.00	5.00	60.00	100
1956	4,300,000	0.25	1.00	5.00	45.00	80.00
1957	7,630,000	0.25	1.00	4.00	35.00	65.00

KM# 409 KRONE

7.00 g., Copper-Nickel, 25 mm. **Ruler:** Olav V **Obv:** Head left **Rev:** Horse **Edge:** Reeded

Date	Mintage	F12	VF20	XF40	MS60	MS63
1958	540,000	3.00	10.00	50.00	200	325
1959	4,450,000	—	0.25	3.00	21.00	35.00
1960	1,790,200	—	2.50	5.00	21.00	35.00
1961	3,933,600	—	0.25	1.00	15.00	25.00
1962	6,015,000	—	0.25	1.00	9.00	15.00
1963	4,677,000	—	0.25	1.00	9.00	15.00
1964	3,469,000	—	0.25	1.00	4.00	7.50
1965	3,222,000	—	0.25	1.50	60.00	100
1966	3,084,000	—	0.25	1.25	24.00	40.00
1967	6,680,000	—	0.25	1.25	21.00	35.00
1968	6,149,200	—	0.25	1.50	40.00	70.00
1969	5,185,500	—	0.20	0.40	4.00	7.00
1970	8,637,900	—	0.20	0.50	18.00	30.00
1971	10,257,800	—	0.20	0.40	9.00	15.00
1972	13,179,394	—	0.20	0.40	2.00	4.75
1973	9,140,175	—	0.20	0.40	2.00	4.75

KM# 419 KRONE

7.00 g., Copper-Nickel, 25 mm. **Ruler:** Olav V **Obv:** Head left **Rev:** Value and date below crown **Edge:** Plain **Note:** Varieties with and without star mint mark exist.

Date	Mintage	VF20	XF40	MS60	MS63	MS65
1974	16,537,223	—	—	0.20	0.35	2.00
1975	26,043,966	—	—	0.20	0.35	2.00
1976	35,926,574	—	—	0.20	0.35	1.25
1977	26,263,500	—	—	0.20	0.35	1.00
1978	23,360,000	—	—	0.20	0.35	1.00
1979	15,896,500	—	—	0.20	0.35	1.00
1980	5,918,000	—	—	0.20	0.35	3.00
1981	16,308,150	—	—	0.20	0.35	0.75
1982	29,187,000	—	—	0.20	0.35	0.75
1983	24,293,300	—	—	0.20	0.35	0.75
1984	3,677,000	—	—	0.20	0.35	1.50
1985	10,985,000	—	—	0.20	0.35	0.75

Date	Mintage	VF20	XF40	MS60	MS63	MS65
1986	5,612,500	—	—	0.20	0.35	0.75
1987	11,015,500	—	—	0.20	0.35	0.75
1988	14,880,000	—	—	0.20	0.35	0.75
1989	5,605,000	—	—	0.20	0.35	0.65
1990	8,804,000	—	—	0.20	0.35	0.65
1990	15,110	PF65 85.00				
1991	21,064,500	—	—	0.20	0.35	0.65
1991	20,000	PF65 90.00				

KM# 436 KRONE

7.00 g., Copper-Nickel, 25 mm. **Ruler:** Harald V **Obv:** Head right **Rev:** Value and date below crown

Date	Mintage	VF20	XF40	MS60	MS63	MS65
1992	7,425,500	—	—	0.20	0.35	0.65
1992	20,000	PF65 10.00				
1993	12,295,000	—	—	0.20	0.35	0.65
1993 Proof	12,000	—	—	—	—	—
1994	25,951,000	—	—	0.20	0.35	0.65
1994	15,000	PF65 10.00				
1995	12,883,000	—	—	0.20	0.35	0.65
1995	14,459	PF65 10.00				
1996	20,844,000	—	—	0.20	0.35	0.65
1996	12,000	PF65 10.00				

KM# 462 KRONE

4.35 g., Copper-Nickel, 21 mm. **Ruler:** Harald V **Obv:** Crowned monograms form cross within circle with center hole **Rev:** Bird on vine above center hole date and value below

Date	Mintage	VF20	XF40	MS60	MS63	MS65
1997	141,099,873	—	—	—	—	0.65
1997	15,000	PF65 10.00				
1998	139,493,000	—	—	—	—	0.65
1998	14,097	PF65 10.00				
1999	74,454,273	—	—	—	—	0.65
1999	12,500	PF65 10.00				
2000	42,689,277	—	—	—	—	0.65
2000	13,500	PF65 10.00				

KM# 359 2 KRONER

15.00 g., 0.800 Silver 0.3858 oz. ASW, 31 mm. **Obv:** Head left **Obv. Legend:** OSCAR II NORGES. **Rev:** Crowned arms within wreath, crossed hammers divide date below **Note:** Restrikes are made by the Royal Mint, Norway, in gold, silver and bronze.

Date	Mintage	F12	VF20	XF40	MS60	MS63
1902	153,100	132	215	390	720	990
1904	75,600	155	260	420	720	990

KM# 363 2 KRONER

15.00 g., 0.800 Silver 0.3858 oz. ASW, 31 mm. **Ruler:** Haakon VII **Subject:** Norway Independence **Obv:** Crowned mantled shield **Rev:** Inscription and date within tree, wreath of grasped hands surround

Date	Mintage	F12	VF20	XF40	MS60	MS63
1906	100,000	50.00	90.00	125	250	350

KM# 365 2 KRONER

15.00 g., 0.800 Silver 0.3858 oz. ASW, 31 mm. **Ruler:** Haakon VII **Obv:** Crowned mantled shield **Rev:** Inscription and date within tree, wreath of grasped hands surround

Date	Mintage	F12	VF20	XF40	MS60	MS63
1907	54,600	58.00	80.00	115	200	270

KM# 366 2 KRONER

15.00 g., 0.800 Silver 0.3858 oz. ASW, 31 mm. **Ruler:** Haakon VII **Subject:** Border watch **Obv:** Crowned and mantled arms **Rev:** Inscription and date within tree, wreath of grasped hands surround

Date	Mintage	F12	VF20	XF40	MS60	MS63
1907	27,500	175	250	350	700	1,000

KM# 370 2 KRONER

15.00 g., 0.800 Silver 0.3858 oz. ASW, 31 mm. **Ruler:** Haakon VII **Obv:** Head right **Rev:** Crowned shield within designed circle, various emblems around border

Date	Mintage	F12	VF20	XF40	MS60	MS63
1908	200,000	52.00	72.00	100	200	280
1910	150,000	80.00	120	200	360	480
1912	150,000	72.00	100	160	360	480
1913	270,000	40.00	52.00	72.00	140	200
1914	255,000	48.00	72.00	100	160	225
1915	225,000	48.00	72.00	100	160	225
1916	250,000	65.00	95.00	120	240	320
1917	377,500	32.00	45.00	70.00	140	200

KM# 377 2 KRONER

15.00 g., 0.800 Silver 0.3858 oz. ASW, 31 mm. **Ruler:** Haakon VII **Subject:** Constitution centennial **Obv:** Crowned shield **Rev:** Standing figure facing right

Date	Mintage	F12	VF20	XF40	MS60	MS63
1914	225,600	50.00	65.00	90.00	175	250

KM# 412 5 KRONER

11.50 g., Copper-Nickel, 29.5 mm. **Ruler:** Olav V **Obv:** Head left **Rev:** Crowned shield divides value

Date	Mintage	F12	VF20	XF40	MS60	MS63
1963	7,074,000	—	1.00	3.50	30.00	50.00
1964	7,346,000	—	1.75	2.50	13.00	22.00
1965	2,233,000	—	1.50	5.00	60.00	100
1966	2,502,000	—	1.00	3.00	50.00	90.00
1967	583,000	1.50	2.00	7.00	45.00	80.00
1968	1,813,400	—	1.00	2.25	35.00	60.00
1969	2,403,700	—	1.00	2.50	15.00	25.00
1970	202,300	2.00	3.00	8.00	24.00	40.00
1971	177,900	3.00	8.00	15.00	30.00	50.00
1972	2,208,704	—	—	1.25	2.50	3.50
1973	2,778,055	—	—	2.00	6.00	10.00

KM# 420 5 KRONER

11.50 g., Copper-Nickel, 29.5 mm. **Ruler:** Olav V **Obv:** Head left **Rev:** Crowned shield divides date **Note:** Varieties exist with large and small shields.

Date	Mintage	VF20	XF40	MS60	MS63	MS65
1974	1,983,423	—	—	1.00	2.50	7.50
1975	2,946,442	—	—	1.00	2.50	6.00
1976	9,055,574	—	—	1.00	2.50	3.50
1977	4,629,600	—	—	1.00	2.50	3.50
1978	5,853,000	—	—	1.00	2.50	3.50
1979	6,818,000	—	—	1.00	2.50	3.50
1980	1,578,400	—	—	1.00	2.50	3.50
1981	1,104,800	—	—	1.00	2.50	3.50
1982	3,919,890	—	—	1.00	2.50	3.50
1983	2,932,260	—	—	1.00	2.50	3.50
1984	1,233,000	—	—	1.00	2.50	3.50
1985	1,399,600	—	—	1.00	2.50	3.50
1987	900,200	—	—	1.00	2.50	3.50
1988	865,200	—	—	1.00	2.50	3.50

KM# 421 5 KRONER

11.50 g., Copper-Nickel, 29.5 mm. **Ruler:** Olav V **Subject:** 100th Anniversary of Krone System **Obv:** Crowned shield divides value **Rev:** Balance scale and miner

Date	Mintage	VF20	XF40	MS60	MS63	MS65
ND-1975	1,191,813	—	—	0.90	1.50	5.00

KM# 422 5 KRONER

11.50 g., Copper-Nickel, 29.5 mm. **Ruler:** Olav V **Subject:** 150th Anniversary - Immigration to America **Obv:** Value below arms **Rev:** Sailing ship, The "Restaurasjonen"(Restoration)

Date	Mintage	VF20	XF40	MS60	MS63	MS65
ND-1975	1,222,827	—	—	1.00	2.00	8.00

KM# 423 5 KRONER

11.50 g., Copper-Nickel, 29.5 mm. **Ruler:** Olav V **Subject:** 350th Anniversary of Norwegian Army **Obv:** Value below arms **Rev:** Sword divides crowned monograms

Date	Mintage	VF20	XF40	MS60	MS63	MS65
ND-1978	2,989,768	—	—	0.90	1:50	4.00

KM# 428 5 KRONER

11.50 g., Copper-Nickel, 29.5 mm. **Ruler:** Olav V **Subject:** 300th Anniversary of the Mint **Obv:** Crossed mining tools below crown, circle surrounds **Rev:** Conjoined heads left and right within circle

Date	Mintage	VF20	XF40	MS60	MS63	MS65
1986	2,345,500	—	—	0.90	1.50	4.00
1986 Prooflike	5,000	—	—	—	—	35.00

KM# 430 5 KRONER

11.50 g., Copper-Nickel, 29.5 mm. **Ruler:** Olav V **Subject:** 175th Anniversary of the National Bank **Obv:** Arms **Rev:** Stein above date and inscription

Date	Mintage	VF20	XF40	MS60	MS63	MS65
1991	512,000	—	—	1.00	2.00	8.00
1991	20,000	PF65 70.00				

KM# 437 5 KRONER

11.50 g., Copper-Nickel, 29.5 mm. **Ruler:** Harald V **Obv:** Crowned shield divides date

Date	Mintage	VF20	XF40	MS60	MS63	MS65
1992	549,600	—	—	—	—	5.00
Note: 100,000 are in mint sets						
1992	20,000	PF65 10.00				
1993	509,600	—	—	—	—	3.50
1993	12,000	PF65 15.00				
1994	2,111,800	—	—	—	—	2.50
1994	15,000	PF65 12.00				

KM# 456 5 KRONER

11.50 g., Copper-Nickel, 29.5 mm. **Ruler:** Harald V **Obv:** Head right **Rev:** Old coin design divides value above legend and date **Note:** 1,000 years of Norwegian coinage

Date	Mintage	VF20	XF40	MS60	MS63	MS65
1995	500,000	—	—	1.00	2.00	8.00
1995	15,000	PF65 22.50				

KM# 458 5 KRONER

11.50 g., Copper-Nickel, 29.5 mm. **Ruler:** Harald V **Subject:** 50th Anniversary - United Nations **Obv:** Head right **Rev:** Standing figure with arms outstretched, children holding hands by tree

Date	Mintage	VF20	XF40	MS60	MS63	MS65
ND-1995	500,000	—	—	1.00	2.00	6.00

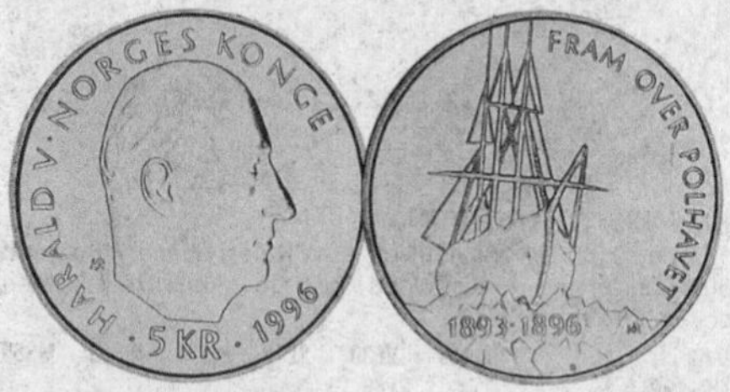

KM# 459 5 KRONER

11.50 g., Copper-Nickel, 29.5 mm. **Ruler:** Harald V **Subject:** Centennial - Nansen's Return From the Arctic **Obv:** Head right **Rev:** Sailing ship facing

Date	Mintage	VF20	XF40	MS60	MS63	MS65
1996	1,381,909	—	—	0.90	1.50	6.00
1996	12,000	PF65 22.50				

KM# 461 5 KRONER

11.50 g., Copper-Nickel, 29.5 mm. **Ruler:** Harald V **Subject:** 350th Anniversary - Norwegian Postal Service **Obv:** Arms **Rev:** Horse and rider left

Date	Mintage	VF20	XF40	MS60	MS63	MS65
ND-1997	1,742,073	—	—	0.60	1.00	4.00
ND-1997	15,000	PF65 12.00				

KM# 463 5 KRONER

7.85 g., Copper-Nickel, 26 mm. **Ruler:** Harald V **Subject:** Order of St. Olaf **Obv:** Hole at center of order chain **Rev:** Center hole divides sprigs, value above and date below **Edge:** Reeded

Date	Mintage	VF20	XF40	MS60	MS63	MS65
1998	47,701,000	—	—	—	—	1.50
1998	14,097	PF65 13.00				
1999	21,754,273	—	—	—	—	1.50
1999	12,500	PF65 13.00				
2000	9,691,387	—	—	—	—	1.50
2000	13,500	PF65 13.00				

KM# 358 10 KRONER

4.48 g., 0.900 Gold 0.1296 oz. AGW **Obv:** Head right **Obv. Legend:** OSCAR II NORGES. **Rev:** Crowned arms within wreath

Date	Mintage	F12	VF20	XF40	MS60	MS63
1902	24,100	280	560	1,450	4,000	—

KM# 375 10 KRONER

4.48 g., 0.900 Gold 0.1296 oz. AGW **Ruler:** Haakon VII **Obv:** Crowned head right **Rev:** King Olaf Haraldson, the Saint

Date	Mintage	F12	VF20	XF40	MS60	MS63
1910	52,600	240	320	640	1,200	1,600

KM# 413 10 KRONER

20.00 g., 0.900 Silver 0.5787 oz. ASW, 35 mm. **Ruler:** Haakon VII **Subject:** Constitution sesquicentennial **Obv:** Crowned shield **Rev:** Eidsval Mansion **Edge Lettering:** ENIGE OG TRO TIL DOVRE FALLER **Note:** Edge lettering varieties exist.

Date	Mintage	F12	VF20	XF40	MS60	MS63
ND-1964	1,408,000	—	—	11.50	14.00	20.00

KM# 427 10 KRONER

9.00 g., Nickel-Brass **Ruler:** Olav V **Obv:** Head left within circle **Rev:** Value within small circle at center of order chain

Date	Mintage	VF20	XF40	MS60	MS63	MS65
1983	20,193,060	—	—	1.50	2.75	6.00
1984	11,073,500	—	—	1.50	2.75	6.00
1985	22,457,550	—	—	1.50	2.50	5.00
1986	29,060,950	—	—	1.50	2.50	4.00
1987	8,809,750	—	—	1.50	2.25	3.25
1988	2,630,500	—	—	1.50	2.25	3.25
1989	3,259,000	—	—	1.50	2.25	3.25
1990	3,004,000	—	—	1.50	2.25	3.25
1991	20,287,150	—	—	1.50	2.00	2.75

KM# 457 10 KRONER

6.80 g., Nickel-Brass, 24 mm. **Ruler:** Harald V **Obv:** Head right **Rev:** Stylized church rooftop, value and date **Edge:** Segmented reeding

Date	Mintage	VF20	XF40	MS60	MS63	MS65
1995	60,740,000	—	—	—	1.25	2.50
1995	15,000	PF65 10.00				
1996	36,372,000	—	—	—	1.25	3.00
1996	12,000	PF65 10.00				
1997	1,229,873	—	—	1.25	2.00	3.50
1997	15,000	PF65 10.00				
1998	1,058,000	—	—	1.25	2.00	3.50
1998	14,097	PF65 10.00				
1999	1,059,273	—	—	1.25	2.00	3.50
1999	12,500	PF65 10.00				
2000	1,096,727	—	—	1.25	2.00	3.50
2000	13,500	PF65 10.00				

KM# 355 20 KRONER

8.96 g., 0.900 Gold 0.2593 oz. AGW **Obv:** Head right **Obv. Legend:** OSCAR II NORGES. **Rev:** Crowned arms within wreath

Date	Mintage	F12	VF20	XF40	MS60	MS63
1902	50,400	—	330	450	900	—

KM# 376 20 KRONER

8.96 g., 0.900 Gold 0.2593 oz. AGW **Ruler:** Haakon VII **Obv:** Crowned head right **Rev:** King Olaf II, the Saint

Date	Mintage	F12	VF20	XF40	MS60	MS63
1910	250,000	400	560	800	1,280	1,600

KM# 453 20 KRONER

9.90 g., Nickel-Brass, 27.5 mm. **Ruler:** Harald V **Obv:** Head right **Rev:** Value above 1/2 ancient boat

Date	Mintage	VF20	XF40	MS60	MS63	MS65
1994	18,598,000	—	—	2.50	3.00	6.50
1994	15,000	PF65 18.00				
1995	21,760,000	—	—	2.50	3.00	6.50
1995	15,000	PF65 18.00				
1996	1,519,500	—	—	2.50	3.00	6.50
1996	12,000	PF65 18.00				
1997	1,049,873	—	—	2.50	3.00	6.50
1997	15,000	PF65 18.00				
1998	5,007,000	—	—	2.50	3.00	6.50
1998	14,097	PF65 18.00				
1999	6,171,000	—	—	2.50	3.00	6.50
1999	12,500	PF65 18.00				
2000	11,113,370	—	—	2.50	3.00	6.50
2000	13,500	PF65 18.00				

KM# 464 20 KRONER

9.90 g., Nickel-Brass, 27.5 mm. **Ruler:** Harald V **Subject:** 700th Anniversary - Akershus Fortress **Obv:** Seal of King Hadon V **Rev:** Fortress

Date	Mintage	VF20	XF40	MS60	MS63	MS65
1999	5,121,986	—	—	2.50	4.00	8.00

KM# 465 20 KRONER

9.90 g., Nickel-Brass, 27.5 mm. **Ruler:** Harald V **Subject:** Vinland **Obv:** Head right **Rev:** Viking ship hull reflected

Date	Mintage	VF20	XF40	MS60	MS63	MS65
1999	1,048,700	—	—	3.00	5.00	12.00
1999	2,500	PF65 30.00				

KM# 468 20 KRONER

9.90 g., Nickel-Brass, 27.5 mm. **Ruler:** Harald V **Subject:** Millennium **Obv:** Head right **Rev:** Unknown road into the future

Date	Mintage	VF20	XF40	MS60	MS63	MS65
2000	1,032,307	—	—	3.00	5.00	14.00

KM# 414 25 KRONER
29.00 g., 0.875 Silver 0.8158 oz. ASW, 39 mm. **Ruler:** Olav V **Subject:** 25th Anniversary of Liberation **Obv:** Head right **Rev:** Crowned monogram **Edge:** Repeated pattern of circles and rectangles

Date	Mintage	F12	VF20	XF40	MS60	MS63
1970	1,203,700	—	—	—	18.00	28.00

KM# 424 50 KRONER
27.00 g., 0.925 Silver 0.803 oz. ASW **Ruler:** Olav V **Subject:** 75th Birthday of King Olav V **Obv:** Head left **Rev:** Single flowered stem divides signature and dates

Date	Mintage	F12	VF20	XF40	MS60	MS63
ND-1978	800,000	—	—	—	18.00	28.00

KM# 431 50 KRONER
16.81 g., 0.925 Silver 0.4999 oz. ASW **Ruler:** Olav V **Subject:** 1994 Olympics **Obv:** Head left **Rev:** Skiers within circle

Date	Mintage	VF20	XF40	MS60	MS63	MS65
1991	80,016	—	—	11.00	17.00	27.00

KM# 432 50 KRONER
16.81 g., 0.925 Silver 0.4999 oz. ASW **Ruler:** Olav V **Subject:** 1994 Olympics **Obv:** Head left **Rev:** Child skiing

Date	Mintage	VF20	XF40	MS60	MS63	MS65
1991	120,000	—	—	11.00	17.00	27.00

KM# 438 50 KRONER
16.81 g., 0.925 Silver 0.4999 oz. ASW **Ruler:** Harald V **Subject:** 1994 Olympics **Obv:** Head right **Rev:** Grandfather and child within circle

Date	Mintage	VF20	XF40	MS60	MS63	MS65
1992	74,000	—	—	11.00	17.00	27.00

KM# 439 50 KRONER
16.81 g., 0.925 Silver 0.4999 oz. ASW **Ruler:** Harald V **Subject:** 1994 Olympics **Obv:** Head right **Rev:** 2 children on sled

Date	Mintage	VF20	XF40	MS60	MS63	MS65
1992	88,000	—	—	11.00	17.00	27.00

KM# 447 50 KRONER
16.81 g., 0.925 Silver 0.4999 oz. ASW **Ruler:** Harald V **Subject:** 1994 Olympics **Obv:** Head right **Rev:** Cross-country skiers

Date	Mintage	VF20	XF40	MS60	MS63	MS65
1993	65,000	—	—	11.00	17.00	27.00

KM# 448 50 KRONER
16.81 g., 0.925 Silver 0.4999 oz. ASW **Ruler:** Harald V **Subject:** 1994 Olympics **Obv:** Head right **Rev:** Children ice skating within circle

Date	Mintage	VF20	XF40	MS60	MS63	MS65
1993	77,000	—	—	11.00	17.00	27.00

KM# 454 50 KRONER
16.81 g., 0.925 Silver 0.4999 oz. ASW **Ruler:** Harald V **Subject:** 50th Anniversary - United Nations **Obv:** Head right **Rev:** Standing figure facing, children holding hands under tree

Date	Mintage	VF20	XF40	MS60	MS63	MS65
ND-1995	200,000	PF65 32.50				

KM# 455 50 KRONER
16.81 g., 0.925 Silver 0.4999 oz. ASW **Ruler:** Harald V **Subject:** 50th Anniversary - End of World War II **Obv:** Arms **Rev:** Stylized dove above dates

Date	Mintage	VF20	XF40	MS60	MS63	MS65
ND-1995	50,000	PF65 35.00				

KM# 426 100 KRONER
24.73 g., 0.925 Silver 0.7355 oz. ASW **Ruler:** Olav V **Subject:** 25th Anniversary of King Olav's Reign **Obv:** Head left **Rev:** Tilted shield under artistic designed shield

Date	Mintage	VF20	XF40	MS60	MS63	MS65
1982	800,000	—	—	16.00	27.00	45.00

KM# 433 100 KRONER
33.62 g., 0.925 Silver 0.9998 oz. ASW **Ruler:** Olav V **Subject:** 1994 Olympics **Obv:** Head left **Rev:** Cross-country skier within circle

Date	Mintage	VF20	XF40	MS60	MS63	MS65
1991	88,000	—	—	19.00	32.00	55.00

KM# 434 100 KRONER
33.62 g., 0.925 Silver 0.9998 oz. ASW **Ruler:** Olav V **Subject:** 1994 Olympics **Obv:** Head left **Rev:** 2 speed skaters

Date	Mintage	VF20	XF40	MS60	MS63	MS65
1991	116,000	—	—	19.00	32.00	55.00

KM# 440 100 KRONER
33.62 g., 0.925 Silver 0.9998 oz. ASW **Ruler:** Harald V **Subject:** 1994 Olympics **Obv:** Head right **Rev:** Ski jumper within circle

Date	Mintage	VF20	XF40	MS60	MS63	MS65
1992	85,000	—	—	19.00	32.00	55.00

KM# 441 100 KRONER
33.62 g., 0.925 Silver 0.9998 oz. ASW **Ruler:** Harald V **Subject:** 1994 Olympics **Obv:** Head right **Rev:** Hockey players

Date	Mintage	VF20	XF40	MS60	MS63	MS65
1992	81,000	—	—	19.00	32.00	55.00

KM# 443 100 KRONER
33.62 g., 0.925 Silver 0.9998 oz. ASW **Ruler:** Harald V **Subject:** World Cycling Championships **Obv:** Arms **Rev:** Cyclist

Date	Mintage	VF20	XF40	MS60	MS63	MS65
1993	9,288	—	—	22.00	37.00	65.00

KM# 444 100 KRONER
33.62 g., 0.925 Silver 0.9998 oz. ASW **Ruler:** Harald V **Subject:** World Cycling Championships **Obv:** Arms **Rev:** 7 cyclists

Date	Mintage	VF20	XF40	MS60	MS63	MS65
1993	9,288	—	—	22.00	37.00	65.00

KM# 449 100 KRONER
33.62 g., 0.925 Silver 0.9998 oz. ASW **Ruler:** Harald V **Subject:** 1984 Olympics **Obv:** Head right **Rev:** Female figure skater within circle

Date	Mintage	VF20	XF40	MS60	MS63	MS65
1993	96,000	—	—	19.00	32.00	55.00

KM# 450 100 KRONER
33.62 g., 0.925 Silver 0.9998 oz. ASW **Ruler:** Harald V **Subject:** 1984 Olympics **Obv:** Head right **Rev:** Alpine skier

Date	Mintage	VF20	XF40	MS60	MS63	MS65
1993	85,000	—	—	19.00	32.00	55.00

KM# 466 100 KRONER
33.80 g., 0.925 Silver 1.0052 oz. ASW **Ruler:** Harald V **Subject:** Year 2000 **Obv:** National arms **Rev:** Cut tree trunk exposing rings

Date	Mintage	VF20	XF40	MS60	MS63	MS65
1999	—	PF65 65.00				

KM# 429 175 KRONER
26.50 g., 0.925 Silver 0.7881 oz. ASW **Ruler:** Olav V **Subject:** 175th Anniversary of Constitution **Obv:** Crowned arms within order chain **Rev:** Building

Date	Mintage	VF20	XF40	MS60	MS63	MS65
ND-1989	85,000	—	—	25.00	35.00	60.00
ND-1989	15,000	PF65 150				

KM# 425 200 KRONER
26.80 g., 0.625 Silver 0.5385 oz. ASW **Ruler:** Olav V **Subject:** 35th Anniversary of Liberation **Obv:** Arms **Rev:** Akershus Castle

Date	Mintage	VF20	XF40	MS60	MS63	MS65
1980	298,399	—	—	24.50	35.00	50.00

KM# 435 1500 KRONER
16.96 g., 0.917 Gold 0.500 oz. AGW, 27 mm. **Ruler:** Olav V **Subject:** 1994 Olympics **Obv:** Head left **Rev:** Ancient Norwegian skier

Date	Mintage	VF20	XF40	MS60	MS63	MS65
1991	20,960	PF65 900				

KM# 442 1500 KRONER
16.96 g., 0.917 Gold 0.500 oz. AGW, 27 mm. **Ruler:** Harald V **Subject:** 1994 Olympics **Obv:** Head right **Rev:** Birkebeiners

Date	Mintage	VF20	XF40	MS60	MS63	MS65
1992	18,267	PF65 900				

KM# 445 1500 KRONER
16.96 g., 0.917 Gold 0.500 oz. AGW, 27 mm. **Ruler:** Harald V **Subject:** World Cycling Championships **Obv:** Arms **Rev:** Two 19th century cyclists

Date	Mintage	VF20	XF40	MS60	MS63	MS65
1993	6,390	PF65 1,100				

KM# 446 1500 KRONER
16.96 g., 0.917 Gold 0.500 oz. AGW, 27 mm. **Ruler:** Harald V **Subject:** Edvard Grieg **Obv:** Crowned shield **Rev:** Figure playing piano

Date	Mintage	VF20	XF40	MS60	MS63	MS65
1993	5,139	PF65 2,400				

KM# 451 1500 KRONER
16.96 g., 0.917 Gold 0.500 oz. AGW, 27 mm. **Ruler:** Harald V **Subject:** 1994 Olympics **Obv:** Head right **Rev:** Telemark skier

Date	Mintage	VF20	XF40	MS60	MS63	MS65
1993	30,000	PF65 950				

KM# 452 1500 KRONER
16.96 g., 0.917 Gold 0.500 oz. AGW **Ruler:** Harald V **Subject:** Roald Amundsen **Obv:** Head right **Rev:** Bust left with skis on shoulder

Date	Mintage	VF20	XF40	MS60	MS63	MS65
1993	22,000	PF65 1,000				

KM# 467 1500 KRONER
16.96 g., 0.917 Gold 0.500 oz. AGW, 27 mm. **Ruler:** Harald V **Subject:** Year 2000 **Obv:** Head right **Rev:** Tree and roots

Date	Mintage	VF20	XF40	MS60	MS63	MS65
2000	7,500	PF65 1,400				

PATTERNS

Including off metal strikes

KM#	Date	Mintage	Identification	Mkt Val
Pn40	1958	6	Øre.	—

MINT SETS

KM#	Date	Mintage	Identification	Issue Price	Mkt Val
MS1	1960 (7)	200	KM#403, 405, 407-411	—	125
MS2	1961 (7)	475	KM#403, 405, 407-411	—	80.00
MS3	1962 (7)	570	KM#403, 405, 407-411	—	55.00
MS4	1963 (8)	430	KM#403, 405, 407-412	—	85.00
MS6	1964 (8)	1,200	KM#403, 405, 407-412	—	45.00
MS7	1965 (8)	1,800	KM#403, 405, 407-412. Plastic.	—	300
MS8	1966 (8)	1,400	KM#403, 405, 407-412. Plastic.	—	125
MS9	1967 (8)	2,400	KM#403, 405, 407-412. Soft plastic.	—	110
MS10	1967 (8)	—	KM403, 405, 407-412 Sandhill.	—	—
MS11	1968 (8)	1,167	KM#403, 405, 407-412. Soft plastic.	—	1,800
MS12	1968 (8)	2,300	KM#403, 405, 407-412. Sandhill.	—	1,800
MS13	1969 (8)	3,140	KM#403, 405, 407-412	—	40.00
MS14	1969 (8)	7,450	KM#403, 405, 407-412. Sandhill.	—	40.00
MS15	1970 (8)	2,005	KM#403, 405, 407-412. Soft plastic.	—	65.00
MS16	1970 (8)	7,311	KM#403, 405, 407-412. Sandhill.	—	150
MS17	1971 (8)	2,010	KM#403, 405, 407-412. Soft plastic.	—	50.00
MS18	1971 (8)	4,055	KM#403, 405, 407-412. Sandhill.	—	50.00
MS19	1972 (8)	6,549	KM#403, 405, 407-412. Soft plastic.	—	30.00
MS20	1972 (8)	6,435	KM#403, 405, 407-412. Sandhill.	—	20.00
MS21	1973 (7)	7,085	KM#405, 407-409, 411-412, 415. Soft plastic.	—	35.00
MS22	1973 (7)	13,090	KM#405, 407-409, 411-412, 415. Sandhill.	6.00	100
MS23	1974 (6)	10,275	KM#415-420. Soft plastic.	3.00	25.00
MS24	1974 (6)	29,695	KM#415-420. Sandhill.	—	75.00
MS25	1975 (8)	30,207	KM#415-422. Sandhill.	5.00	75.00
MS26	1975 (7)	5,287	KM#415-421. Soft plastic.	5.00	20.00
MS27	1976 (6)	5,000	KM#415-420. Soft plastic.	3.00	10.00
MS28	1976 (6)	25,000	KM#415-420. Sandhill.	3.00	100
MS29	1977 (6)	5,000	KM#415-420. Soft plastic.	3.40	25.00
MS30	1977 (6)	25,000	KM#415-420. Sandhill.	3.40	90.00
MS31	1978 (6)	5,000	KM#415-420. Soft plastic.	3.40	25.00
MS32	1978 (6)	30,000	KM#415-420. Sandhill.	3.40	85.00
MS33	1979 (6)	8,000	KM#415-420. Soft plastic.	3.40	25.00
MS34	1979 (6)	50,000	KM#415-420. Sandhill.	3.40	40.00
MS35	1980 (6)	10,000	KM#415-420. Soft plastic.	3.40	14.00
MS36	1980 (6)	70,000	KM#415-420. Sandhill.	3.40	30.00
MS37	1981 (6)	100,000	KM#415-420. Hard plastic.	4.25	24.00
MS38	1982 (6)	102,650	KM#415-420	4.50	33.00
MS39	1983 (4)	102,300	KM#416, 418-420	5.00	28.00
MS40	1984 (5)	101,000	KM#416, 418-420, 427	5.00	28.00
MS41	1985 (5)	110,000	KM#416, 418-420, 427	5.00	25.00
MS42	1986 (5)	100,000	KM#416, 418, 419, 427, 428	7.00	40.00
MS43	1987 (5)	85,000	KM#416, 418-420, 427	7.00	50.00
MS44	1988 (5)	102,000	KM#416, 418, 419, 420, 427	7.00	30.00
MS45	1989 (4)	101,000	KM#416, 418-419, 427	8.00	28.00
MS46	1990 (4)	103,000	KM#416, 418-419, 427, plus mint medal	8.00	28.00
MSA47	1991 (4)	100,000	KM#418, 419, 427, 430	—	32.00
MS47	1992 (5)	100,000	KM#416, 418, 427, 436, 437	—	30.00
MS48	1993 (5)	100,000	KM#416, 418, 427, 436, 437	—	28.00
MS49	1994 (4)	100,000	KM#418, 427, 436, 437, 453	—	28.00
MS50	1995 (5)	100,000	KM#418, 436, 453, 456, 457	—	22.50
MS51	1996 (5)	90,000	KM#418, 436, 453, 457, 459	—	32.00
MS52	1997 (5)	75,000	KM453, 457, 460, 461, 462	—	40.00
MS53	1998 (5)	58,000	KM453, 457, 460, 462, 463, Uncirculated set, classic version (hard plastic case)	—	40.00
MS54	1998 (5)	5,000	KM#453, 457, 460, 462, 463 (Uncirculated Set, Souvenir Version, Norwegian text)	—	35.00
MS55	1998 (5)	—	KM#453, 457, 460, 462, 463 (Uncirculated Set, Souvenir Version, English text). Mintage included with MS54.	—	35.00
MS56	1999 (5)	50,000	KM#453, 457, 460, 462, 463, Uncirculated set, classic version (hard plastic case)	—	75.00
MS57	1999 (5)	25,000	KM#453, 457, 460, 462, 463 (Uncirculated Set, Souvenir Version, English text)	—	30.00
MS58	1999 (5)	—	KM#457, 460 462-464. (Uncirculated set, souvenir version, Norwegian text). Mintage included with MS57.	13.00	20.00
MS59	1999 (5)	—	KM#457, 460, 462-464. Children's (baby) set.	14.30	20.00
MS60	1999 (5)	—	KM#457, 460, 462-464 plus medal.	26.00	20.00
MS61	2000 (5)	—	KM#453, 457, 460, 462, 463, Uncirculated set, classic version (hard plastic case)	—	65.00
MS62	2000 (5)	25,234	KM#453, 457, 460, 462, 463 (Uncirculated Set, Souvenir Version, Norwegian text)	—	30.00
MS63	2000 (5)	—	KM#453, 457, 460, 462, 463 (Uncirculated Set, Souvenir Version, English text). Mintage included with MS62.	—	30.00
MS64	2000 (5)	2,000	KM#453, 457, 460, 462, 463 plus Silver medal Children's (Baby) Set	—	70.00
MS65	2000 (5)	2,000	KM#453, 457, 460, 462, 463 plus Gold copy of 995 Olav Trygvason penning, the first Norwegian coin (Millennium Set)	—	750

PROOF SETS

KM#	Date	Mintage	Identification	Issue Price	Mkt Val
PS1	1991 (2)	20,000	KM#419, 430	—	110
PS2	1992 (3)	20,000	KM418, 436-437	—	90.00
PS3	1993 (3)	12,000	KM443-445	—	2,200
PS4	1993 (3)	12,000	KM#418, 436, 437	—	90.00
PS5	1994 (4)	15,000	KM418, 436, 437, 453	—	90.00
PS6	1995 (5)	14,459	KM418, 436, 453, 456, 457	—	80.00
PS7	1996 (5)	11,551	KM418, 436, 453, 457, 459	—	80.00
PS8	1997 (5)	15,000	KM453, 457, 460, 461, 462, (Norwegian Heritage Export/Proof Set).	—	65.00
PS9	1997 (5)	12,000	KM453, 457, 460, 461, 462, (Classic Proof Set)	—	90.00
PS10	1998 (5)	14,097	KM453, 457, 460, 462, 463, (Norwegian Heritage Export/Proof Set).	—	100
PS11	1998 (5)	12,000	KM#453, 457, 460, 462, 463 (Classic Proof Set)	—	90.00
PS12	1999 (5)	12,500	KM453, 457, 460, 462, 463 (Classic Proof Set)	60.00	80.00
PS13	1999 (5)	2,500	KM457, 460, 462-463, 465 (Norwegian Heritage Export/Proof Set).	—	225
PS14	2000 (5)	10,000	KM453, 457, 460, 462, 463 (Classic Proof Set)	—	100
PS15	2000 (5)	—	KM#453, 457, 460, 462, 463 (Norwegian Heritage (Export) Proof Set)	—	125

OMAN

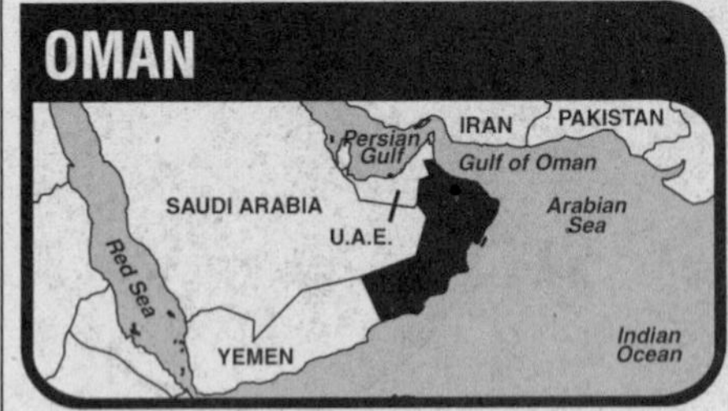

The Sultanate of Oman (formerly Muscat and Oman), an independent monarchy located in the southeastern part of the Arabian Peninsula, has an area of 82,030 sq. mi. (212,460 sq. km.) and a population of *1.3 million. Capital: Muscat. The economy is based on agriculture, herding and petroleum. Petroleum products, dates, fish and hides are exported.

The Portuguese who captured Muscat, the capital and chief port, in 1508, made the first European contact with Muscat and Oman. They occupied the city, utilizing it as a naval base and factory and holding it against land and sea attacks by Arabs and Persians until finally ejected by local Arabs in 1650. It was next occupied by the Persians who maintained control until 1741,when it was taken by Ahmed ibn Sa'id of the present ruling family. Muscat and Oman was the most powerful state in Arabia during the first half of the 19th century, until weakened by the persistent attack of interior nomadic tribes. British influence, initiated by the signing of a treaty of friendship with the Sultanate in 1798, remains a dominant fact of the civil and military phases of the government, although Britain recognizes the Sultanate as a sovereign state.

Sultan Sa'id bin Taimur was overthrown by his son, Qabus bin Sa'id, on July 23, 1970. The new sultan changed the nation's name to Sultanate of Oman.

TITLES

مسقط

Muscat

ملك نكر

Oman

SULTANATE

DECIMAL COINAGE

1000 Baisa = 1 Saidi Rial

KM# 42 1/2 SAIDI RIAL
25.60 g., 0.917 Gold 0.7547 oz. AGW **Ruler:** Qabus bin Sa'id **Obv:** National arms within circle **Rev:** Value and date

Date	Mintage	VF20	XF40	MS60	MS63	MS65
AH1391	100	PF65 1,700	PF67 2,200			

Note: Struck for presentation purposes

KM# 44 SAIDI RIAL
46.65 g., 0.917 Gold 1.3753 oz. AGW **Ruler:** Qabus bin Sa'id **Obv:** National arms within circle with star and moon border **Rev:** Value and date

Date	Mintage	VF20	XF40	MS60	MS63	MS65
AH1391	100	PF65 2,700	PF67 3,200			
AH1394	250	PF65 2,500	PF67 3,000			

Note: Struck for presentation purposes

KM# 43 15 SAIDI RIALS
5.81 g., 0.917 Gold 0.1713 oz. AGW **Ruler:** Qabus bin Sa'id **Obv:** National arms **Rev:** Value

Date	Mintage	VF20	XF40	MS60	MS63	MS65
AH1391	112	PF65 1,500	PF67 2,000			

Note: Struck for presentation purposes

KM# 53 15 SAIDI RIALS
7.98 g., 0.917 Gold 0.2353 oz. AGW **Ruler:** Qabus bin Sa'id **Obv:** National arms **Rev:** Value and date

Date	Mintage	VF20	XF40	MS60	MS63	MS65
AH1391	224	PF65 1,250	PF67 1,750			

Note: Struck for presentation purposes

REFORM COINAGE

1972; 1000 Baisa = 1 Omani Rial

KM# 50 5 BAISA
3.10 g., Bronze, 19 mm. **Ruler:** Qabus bin Sa'id **Obv:** National arms **Rev:** Value and date

Date	Mintage	VF20	XF40	MS60	MS63	MS65
AH1395 (1975)	6,000,000	0.10	0.30	0.75	1.00	1.50
AH1400 (1979)	3,000,000	0.10	0.30	0.75	1.00	1.50
AH1406 (1985)	2,000,000	0.10	0.30	0.75	1.00	1.50
AH1410 (1989)	5,000,000	0.10	0.30	0.75	1.00	1.50
AH1418 (1997)	—	0.10	0.30	0.75	1.00	1.50

KM# 76 5 BAISA
Bronze **Ruler:** Qabus bin Sa'id **Subject:** 20th National Day - Sultan Qaboos **Obv:** National emblem **Rev:** Sports Complex

Date	Mintage	VF20	XF40	MS60	MS63	MS65
AH1411	3,200	PF65 8.00				

KM# 150 5 BAISA
2.65 g., Bronze Clad Steel, 19 mm. **Ruler:** Qabus bin Sa'id **Obv:** National arms **Rev:** Value and dates

Date	Mintage	VF20	XF40	MS60	MS63	MS65
AH1418-1997	—	—	0.20	0.50	0.75	1.00
AH1420-1999	—	—	0.20	0.50	0.75	1.00

KM# 51 10 BAISA
4.70 g., Bronze, 22.5 mm. **Ruler:** Qabus bin Sa'id **Series:** F.A.O. **Obv:** Date palms **Rev:** Value and date

Date	Mintage	VF20	XF40	MS60	MS63	MS65
AH1395 (1975)	1,000,000	0.15	0.30	2.00	3.50	—

KM# 52 10 BAISA
4.70 g., Bronze, 22.5 mm. **Ruler:** Qabus bin Sa'id **Series:** F.A.O. **Obv:** National arms **Rev:** Value and date

Date	Mintage	VF20	XF40	MS60	MS63	MS65
AH1395 (1975)	6,000,000	0.15	0.40	1.00	1.35	1.65
AH1400 (1979)	5,250,000	0.15	0.40	1.00	1.35	1.65
AH1406 (1985)	3,000,000	0.15	0.40	1.00	1.35	1.65
AH1410 (1989)	6,000,000	0.15	0.40	1.00	1.35	1.65
AH1418 (1997)	—	0.15	0.40	1.00	1.35	1.65

KM# 77 10 BAISA
Bronze Clad Steel **Ruler:** Qabus bin Sa'id **Subject:** 20th National Day - Central Bank of Oman **Obv:** National emblem **Rev:** Central Bank building

Date	Mintage	VF20	XF40	MS60	MS63	MS65
AH1411	3,200	PF65 12.00				

KM# 94 10 BAISA
Bronze Clad Steel, 22.5 mm. **Ruler:** Qabus bin Sa'id **Series:** F.A.O. **Subject:** 50 Years **Obv:** National arms **Rev:** FAO symbol and dates

Date	Mintage	VF20	XF40	MS60	MS63	MS65
ND (1995)	—	—	—	6.00	8.00	—
ND-1995	224	—	—	6.00	8.00	—

KM# 151 10 BAISA
4.04 g., Bronze Clad Steel, 22.5 mm. **Ruler:** Qabus bin Sa'id **Obv:** National arms **Rev:** Value with both dates

Date	Mintage	VF20	XF40	MS60	MS63	MS65
AH1420-1999	—	—	0.30	0.75	1.00	1.50

KM# 75 15 BAISA
20.00 g., 0.925 Silver 0.5948 oz. ASW **Ruler:** Qabus bin Sa'id **Subject:** 15th Anniversary - Reign of Sultan **Obv:** Head 1/4 left within 3/4 wreath and circular design **Rev:** Crowned Arms over country map within circle

Date	Mintage	VF20	XF40	MS60	MS63	MS65
AH1406	2,000	PF65 200	PF67 275			

KM# 45 25 BAISA
5.96 g., 0.917 Gold 0.1757 oz. AGW, 18 mm. **Ruler:** Qabus bin Sa'id **Obv:** National arms **Rev:** Value and date

Date	Mintage	VF20	XF40	MS60	MS63	MS65
AH1392 (1972)	100	PF65 550	PF67 800			
AH1392 (1972)	50	PF65 600	PF67 850			
AH1394 (1974)	250	PF65 500	PF67 750			
AH1395 (1975)	250	PF65 500	PF67 750			

Note: Struck for presentation purposes

KM# 45a 25 BAISA
3.03 g., Copper-Nickel, 18 mm. **Ruler:** Qabus bin Sa'id **Obv:** National arms **Rev:** Value and date

Date	Mintage	VF20	XF40	MS60	MS63	MS65
AH1395 (1975)	4,500,000	0.20	0.50	1.20	1.60	2.00
AH1400 (1979)	5,250,000	0.20	0.50	1.20	1.60	2.00
AH1406 (1985)	4,000,000	0.20	0.50	1.20	1.60	2.00
AH1410 (1989)	7,000,000	0.20	0.50	1.20	1.60	2.00
AH1418 (1997)	—	0.20	0.50	1.20	1.60	2.00

KM# 78 25 BAISA
Copper-Nickel **Ruler:** Qabus bin Sa'id **Subject:** 20th National Day - Royal Hospital **Obv:** National emblem **Rev:** Royal Hospital building

Date	Mintage	VF20	XF40	MS60	MS63	MS65
AH1411	3,200	PF65 20.00				

KM# 152 25 BAISA
3.03 g., Copper-Nickel, 18 mm. **Ruler:** Qabus bin Sa'id **Obv:** National arms **Rev:** Value and both dates **Edge:** Reeded

Date	Mintage	VF20	XF40	MS60	MS63	MS65
AH1420-1999	—	0.15	0.35	0.90	1.35	2.25

KM# 46 50 BAISA
12.89 g., 0.917 Gold 0.380 oz. AGW **Ruler:** Qabus bin Sa'id **Obv:** National arms **Rev:** Value and date

Date	Mintage	VF20	XF40	MS60	MS63	MS65
AH1392 (1972)	200	PF65 900	PF67 1,150			
AH1392 (1972)	50	PF65 1,000	PF67 1,250			
AH1394 (1974)	250	PF65 850	PF67 1,100			
AH1395 (1975)	250	PF65 850	PF67 1,100			

Note: Struck for presentation purposes

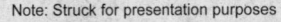

KM# 46a 50 BAISA
6.40 g., Copper-Nickel, 24 mm. **Ruler:** Qabus bin Sa'id **Obv:** National arms **Rev:** Value and date

Date	Mintage	VF20	XF40	MS60	MS63	MS65
AH1395 (1975)	2,500,000	0.30	0.70	1.80	2.40	3.50
AH1400 (1979)	2,750,000	0.30	0.70	1.80	2.40	3.50
AH1406 (1985)	4,000,000	0.30	0.70	1.80	2.40	3.50
AH1410 (1989)	4,000,000	0.30	0.70	1.80	2.40	3.50
AH1418 (1997)	—	0.30	0.70	1.80	2.40	3.50

KM# 79 50 BAISA
Copper-Nickel **Ruler:** Qabus bin Sa'id **Subject:** 20th National Day - Irrigation Canal **Obv:** National emblem **Rev:** Canal and palm trees

Date	Mintage	VF20	XF40	MS60	MS63	MS65
AH1411	3,200	PF65 25.00				

KM# 95 50 BAISA
6.40 g., Copper-Nickel, 24 mm. **Ruler:** Qabus bin Sa'id **Subject:** U.N. - 50 Years **Obv:** National arms **Rev:** UN symbol and anniversary dates

Date	Mintage	VF20	XF40	MS60	MS63	MS65
ND (1995)	—	—	—	2.00	4.00	7.00

KM# 153 50 BAISA
6.40 g., Copper-Nickel, 24 mm. **Ruler:** Qabus bin Sa'id **Obv:** National arms **Rev:** Value with both dates **Edge:** Reeded

Date	Mintage	VF20	XF40	MS60	MS63	MS65
AH1420-1999	—	0.25	0.60	1.50	2.00	3.00

KM# 47 100 BAISA
22.74 g., 0.917 Gold 0.6704 oz. AGW **Ruler:** Qabus bin Sa'id **Obv:** National arms **Rev:** Value and date

Date	Mintage	VF20	XF40	MS60	MS63	MS65
AH1392 (1972)	200	PF65 1,800	PF67 2,150			
AH1392 (1972)	50	PF65 1,900	PF67 2,250			
AH1394 (1974)	250	PF65 1,750	PF67 2,100			
AH1395 (1975)	250	PF65 1,750	PF67 2,100			

Note: Struck for presentation purposes

KM# 68 100 BAISA
4.20 g., Copper-Nickel, 21.5 mm. **Ruler:** Qabus bin Sa'id **Obv:** National arms **Rev:** Arms and date

Date	Mintage	VF20	XF40	MS60	MS63	MS65
AH1404-1983	4,000,000	—	0.40	1.50	2.50	4.00

KM# 80 100 BAISA
Copper-Nickel **Ruler:** Qabus bin Sa'id **Subject:** 20th National Day - Sultan Qaboos University **Obv:** National emblem **Rev:** University building

Date	Mintage	VF20	XF40	MS60	MS63	MS65
AH1411	3,200	PF65 30.00				

KM# 82 100 BAISA
Bi-Metallic Aluminumn-Bronze center in Copper-Nickel ring, 25 mm. **Ruler:** Qabus bin Sa'id **Subject:** 100 Years of Coinage **Obv:** Arms within circle **Rev:** Fortress within circle

Date	Mintage	VF20	XF40	MS60	MS63	MS65
AH1411-1991	—	1.00	1.50	3.50	6.50	12.50
AH1411-1991	1,000	PF65 40.00				

KM# 57 1/4 OMANI RIAL
12.89 g., 0.917 Gold 0.380 oz. AGW **Ruler:** Qabus bin Sa'id **Subject:** Fort al Hazam **Obv:** National arms **Rev:** Fort

Date	Mintage	VF20	XF40	MS60	MS63	MS65
AH1397	1,000	PF65 700	PF67 950			
AH1408	250	PF65 900	PF67 1,150			

KM# 66 1/4 OMANI RIAL
6.50 g., Aluminum-Bronze, 26 mm. **Ruler:** Qabus bin Sa'id **Obv:** National arms and dates **Rev:** Value

Date	Mintage	VF20	XF40	MS60	MS63	MS65
AH1400-1980	4,000,000	—	1.00	3.00	5.00	7.50

KM# 48 1/2 OMANI RIAL
25.60 g., 0.917 Gold 0.7547 oz. AGW **Ruler:** Qabus bin Sa'id **Obv:** National arms **Rev:** Value and date

Date	Mintage	VF20	XF40	MS60	MS63	MS65
AH1392 (1972)	124	PF65 2,400	PF67 2,850			
AH1394 (1974)	250	PF65 2,250	PF67 2,700			
AH1395 (1975)	250	PF65 2,250	PF67 2,700			

Note: Struck for presentation purposes

KM# 58 1/2 OMANI RIAL
19.67 g., 0.917 Gold 0.5799 oz. AGW **Ruler:** Qabus bin Sa'id **Subject:** Fort Mirbat **Obv:** National arms **Rev:** Fort

Date	Mintage	XF40	MS60	MS63	MS65	MS66
AH1397 (1976)	1,000	PF65 1,100	PF67 1,250	PF69 1,500		
AH1408 (1987)	250	PF65 1,200	PF67 1,500			

KM# 64 1/2 OMANI RIAL
Copper-Nickel **Ruler:** Qabus bin Sa'id **Series:** F.A.O. **Obv:** National arms flanked by dates **Rev:** Fruit above value **Shape:** 7-sided

Date	Mintage	VF20	XF40	MS60	MS63	MS65
AH1398-1978	15,000	—	3.00	5.00	7.50	13.50

KM# 69 1/2 OMANI RIAL
19.67 g., 0.917 Gold 0.5799 oz. AGW **Ruler:** Qabus bin Sa'id **Subject:** 10th National Day **Obv:** Crowned arms **Rev:** Value

Date	Mintage	VF20	XF40	MS60	MS63	MS65
AH1400-1979	600	PF65 950	PF67 1,150			

Note: Struck for presentation purposes

KM# 67 1/2 OMANI RIAL
10.00 g., Aluminum-Bronze, 30 mm. **Ruler:** Qabus bin Sa'id **Obv:** National arms and dates **Rev:** Value

Date	Mintage	VF20	XF40	MS60	MS63	MS65
AH1400-1980	2,000,000	6.00	1.50	4.00	6.50	10.00

KM# 87 1/2 OMANI RIAL
10.00 g., 0.917 Gold 0.2948 oz. AGW **Ruler:** Qabus bin Sa'id **Subject:** Youth Year **Obv:** National arms, date and value **Rev:** Youth with banner within sprigs

Date	Mintage	VF20	XF40	MS60	MS63	MS65
AH1403-1982	1,000	PF65 550	PF67 750			

KM# 85 1/2 OMANI RIAL
28.28 g., 0.925 Silver 0.841 oz. ASW **Ruler:** Qabus bin Sa'id

Subject: Year of Agriculture **Obv:** National arms within circle **Rev:** Dates within small circle, farm fields on top 1/2

Date	Mintage	VF20	XF40	MS60	MS63	MS65
AH1409-1988	300	PF63 225	PF65 300			

KM# 86 1/2 OMANI RIAL
28.28 g., 0.925 Silver 0.841 oz. ASW **Ruler:** Qabus bin Sa'id **Subject:** Year of Industry **Obv:** National arms **Rev:** Gears with map at center

Date	Mintage	VF20	XF40	MS60	MS63	MS65
AH1411	810	PF63 150	PF65 180			

KM# 91 1/2 OMANI RIAL
15.00 g., 0.925 Silver 0.4461 oz. ASW **Ruler:** Qabus bin Sa'id **Subject:** Youth Year **Obv:** National arms within circle flanked by stars **Rev:** Radiant design

Date	Mintage	VF20	XF40	MS60	MS63	MS65
AH1413	600	PF65 85.00				

KM# 134 1/2 OMANI RIAL
15.00 g., 0.925 Silver 0.4461 oz. ASW **Ruler:** Qabus bin Sa'id **Subject:** Youth Year **Obv:** Crowned arms **Rev:** Radiant design

Date	Mintage	VF20	XF40	MS60	MS63	MS65
AH1413 (1992) Proof; Rare	310	—	—	—	—	—

KM# 92 1/2 OMANI RIAL
28.28 g., 0.925 Silver 0.841 oz. ASW **Ruler:** Qabus bin Sa'id **Subject:** Heritage Year **Obv:** National arms within circle **Rev:** Radiant design

Date	Mintage	VF20	XF40	MS60	MS63	MS65
AH1414	840	PF63 150	PF65 180			

KM# 111 1/2 OMANI RIAL
28.28 g., 0.925 Silver 0.841 oz. ASW **Ruler:** Qabus bin Sa'id **Subject:** 250th Anniversary - Al Bu Sa'id Dynasty **Obv:** Bust facing flanked by dates **Rev:** National arms within artistic designed border

Date	Mintage	VF20	XF40	MS60	MS63	MS65
1994 (AH1414)	500	PF63 160	PF65 190			

KM# 54 OMANI RIAL
46.65 g., 0.917 Gold 1.3753 oz. AGW **Ruler:** Qabus bin Sa'id **Obv:** National arms **Rev:** Value and date **Note:** Similar to KM#44.

Date	Mintage	VF20	XF40	MS60	MS63	MS65
AH1392	124	PF67 3,750				
AH1394	250	PF67 3,450				
AH1395	250	PF67 3,450				

Note: Struck for presentation purposes

KM# 59 OMANI RIAL
25.60 g., 0.917 Gold 0.7547 oz. AGW **Ruler:** Qabus bin Sa'id **Subject:** Fort Buraimi **Obv:** National arms and value **Rev:** Fort

Date	Mintage	VF20	XF40	MS60	MS63	MS65
AH1397	1,000	PF65 1,350	PF67 1,500			
AH1408	250	PF65 1,600	PF67 1,850			

KM# 65 OMANI RIAL
15.00 g., 0.500 Silver 0.2411 oz. ASW **Ruler:** Qabus bin Sa'id **Series:** F.A.O. **Obv:** National arms flanked by dates **Rev:** Fish above value

Date	Mintage	VF20	XF40	MS60	MS63	MS65
AH1398-1978	15,000	—	12.00	16.00	20.00	—

KM# 70 OMANI RIAL
25.60 g., 0.917 Gold 0.7547 oz. AGW **Ruler:** Qabus bin Sa'id **Subject:** 10th National Day

Date	Mintage	VF20	XF40	MS60	MS63	MS65
AH1400	300	PF65 1,550	PF67 1,800			

Note: Struck for presentation purposes

KM# 84 OMANI RIAL
14.84 g., 0.925 Silver 0.4413 oz. ASW **Ruler:** Qabus bin Sa'id **Subject:** Youth Year **Obv:** National arms above value **Rev:** Youth with banner

Date	Mintage	VF20	XF40	MS60	MS63	MS65
AH1403-1982	1,200	PF65 120	PF67 150			

KM# 84a OMANI RIAL
20.00 g., 0.917 Gold 0.5896 oz. AGW, 30 mm. **Ruler:** Qabus bin Sa'id **Subject:** Youth Year **Obv:** National arms above value **Rev:** Youth with banner

Date	Mintage	VF20	XF40	MS60	MS63	MS65
AH1403	900	PF65 1,200	PF67 1,450			

KM# 112 OMANI RIAL
20.00 g., 0.917 Gold 0.5896 oz. AGW **Ruler:** Qabus bin Sa'id **Subject:** Youth Year **Obv:** National arms **Rev:** Radiant design **Note:** Similar to 1/2 Omani Rial, KM#91.

Date	Mintage	VF20	XF40	MS60	MS63	MS65
AH1413	900	PF65 1,150	PF67 1,450			

KM# 135 OMANI RIAL
20.00 g., 0.917 Gold 0.5896 oz. AGW **Ruler:** Qabus bin Sa'id **Subject:** Youth Year **Obv:** Crowned arms **Rev:** Radiant design **Note:** Similar to 1/2 Omani Rial, KM#91.

Date	Mintage	VF20	XF40	MS60	MS63	MS65
AH1413 (1992) Proof; Rare	110	—	—	—	—	—

KM# 93 OMANI RIAL
39.94 g., 0.9167 Gold 1.1771 oz. AGW **Ruler:** Qabus bin Sa'id **Subject:** Heritage Year **Obv:** National arms **Rev:** Radiant design **Note:** Similar to 1/2 Omani Rial, KM#92.

Date	Mintage	VF20	XF40	MS60	MS63	MS65
AH1414	1,000	PF65 2,250	PF67 2,500			

KM# 146 OMANI RIAL
39.94 g., 0.9167 Gold 1.1771 oz. AGW **Ruler:** Qabus bin Sa'id **Subject:** 250th Anniversary - Al Bu Sa'id Dynasty **Obv:** Portrait **Rev:** National arms and value **Note:** Similar to 1/2 Omani Rial, KM#111.

Date	Mintage	XF40	MS60	MS63	MS65	MS66
AH1414	500	PF67 2,250	PF69 2,500			

KM# 96 OMANI RIAL
10.00 g., 0.925 Silver 0.2974 oz. ASW, 30 mm. **Ruler:** Qabus bin Sa'id **Subject:** F.A.O. - 50 Years **Obv:** National arms within circle **Rev:** FAO symbol and anniversary dates

Date	Mintage	VF20	XF40	MS60	MS63	MS65
ND (1995)	—	PF65 25.00				

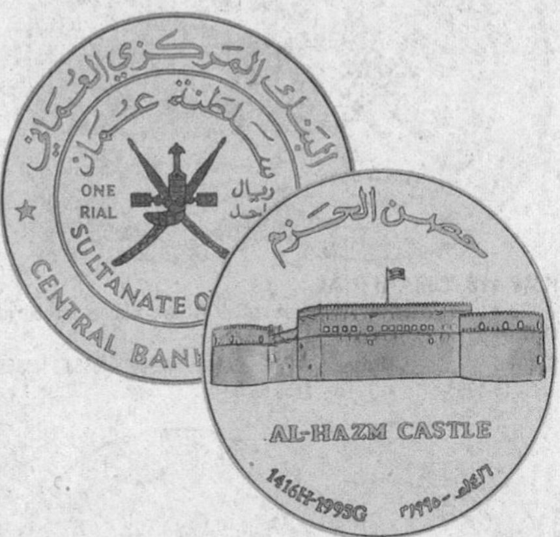

KM# 114 OMANI RIAL
28.28 g., 0.925 Silver 0.841 oz. ASW **Ruler:** Qabus bin Sa'id **Obv:** National arms within circle **Rev:** Al-Hazm castle

Date	Mintage	VF20	XF40	MS60	MS63	MS65
AH1416-1995	—	PF65 85.00				

KM# 115 OMANI RIAL
28.28 g., 0.925 Silver 0.841 oz. ASW **Ruler:** Qabus bin Sa'id **Obv:** National arms **Rev:** Al-Jalali fort

Date	Mintage	VF20	XF40	MS60	MS63	MS65
AH1416-1995	—	PF65 85.00				

KM# 116 OMANI RIAL
28.28 g., 0.925 Silver 0.841 oz. ASW **Ruler:** Qabus bin Sa'id
Obv: National arms **Rev:** Al-Mirani fort

Date	Mintage	VF20	XF40	MS60	MS63	MS65
AH1416-1995	—	PF65 85.00				

KM# 117 OMANI RIAL
28.28 g., 0.925 Silver 0.841 oz. ASW **Ruler:** Qabus bin Sa'id
Obv: National arms **Rev:** Al-Rustaq fort

Date	Mintage	VF20	XF40	MS60	MS63	MS65
AH1416-1995	—	PF65 85.00				

KM# 118 OMANI RIAL
28.28 g., 0.925 Silver 0.841 oz. ASW **Ruler:** Qabus bin Sa'id
Obv: National arms **Rev:** Al-Wafi castle

Date	Mintage	VF20	XF40	MS60	MS63	MS65
AH1416-1995	—	PF65 85.00				

KM# 119 OMANI RIAL
28.28 g., 0.925 Silver 0.841 oz. ASW **Ruler:** Qabus bin Sa'id
Obv: National arms **Rev:** Bait Al-Falaj fort

Date	Mintage	VF20	XF40	MS60	MS63	MS65
AH1416-1995	—	PF65 85.00				

KM# 120 OMANI RIAL
28.28 g., 0.925 Silver 0.841 oz. ASW **Ruler:** Qabus bin Sa'id
Obv: National arms **Rev:** Bait Al-Na'Aman castle

Date	Mintage	VF20	XF40	MS60	MS63	MS65
AH1416-1995	—	PF65 85.00				

KM# 121 OMANI RIAL
28.28 g., 0.925 Silver 0.841 oz. ASW **Ruler:** Qabus bin Sa'id
Obv: National arms **Rev:** Bahla fort

Date	Mintage	VF20	XF40	MS60	MS63	MS65
AH1416-1995	—	PF65 85.00				

KM# 122 OMANI RIAL
28.28 g., 0.925 Silver 0.841 oz. ASW **Ruler:** Qabus bin Sa'id
Obv: National arms **Rev:** Barka fort

Date	Mintage	VF20	XF40	MS60	MS63	MS65
AH1416-1995	—	PF65 85.00				

KM# 123 OMANI RIAL
28.28 g., 0.925 Silver 0.841 oz. ASW **Ruler:** Qabus bin Sa'id
Obv: National arms **Rev:** Barkat-Al-Mauz castle

Date	Mintage	VF20	XF40	MS60	MS63	MS65
AH1416-1995	—	PF65 85.00				

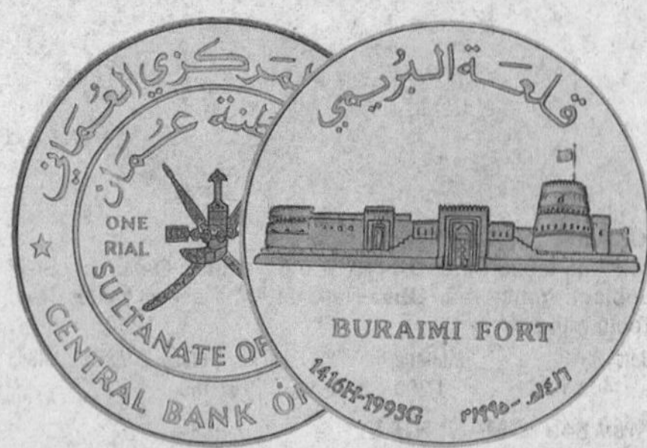

KM# 124 OMANI RIAL
28.28 g., 0.925 Silver 0.841 oz. ASW **Ruler:** Qabus bin Sa'id
Obv: National arms **Rev:** Buraimi fort

Date	Mintage	VF20	XF40	MS60	MS63	MS65
AH1416-1995	—	PF65 85.00				

KM# 125 OMANI RIAL
28.28 g., 0.925 Silver 0.841 oz. ASW **Ruler:** Qabus bin Sa'id
Obv: National arms **Rev:** Ja'Alan Bani Bu Hassan castle

Date	Mintage	VF20	XF40	MS60	MS63	MS65
AH1416-1995	—	PF65 85.00				

KM# 126 OMANI RIAL
28.28 g., 0.925 Silver 0.841 oz. ASW **Ruler:** Qabus bin Sa'id
Obv: National arms **Rev:** Jabrin castle

Date	Mintage	VF20	XF40	MS60	MS63	MS65
AH1416-1995	—	PF65 85.00				

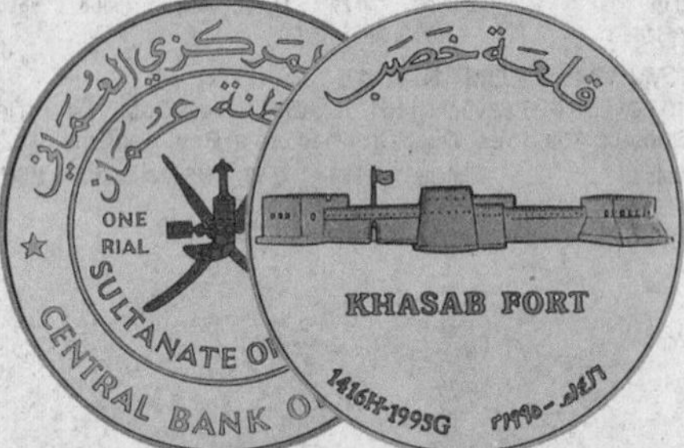

KM# 127 OMANI RIAL
28.28 g., 0.925 Silver 0.841 oz. ASW **Ruler:** Qabus bin Sa'id
Obv: National arms **Rev:** Khasab fort

Date	Mintage	VF20	XF40	MS60	MS63	MS65
AH1416-1995	—	PF65 85.00				

KM# 128 OMANI RIAL
28.28 g., 0.925 Silver 0.841 oz. ASW **Ruler:** Qabus bin Sa'id
Obv: National arms **Rev:** Matrah fort

Date	Mintage	VF20	XF40	MS60	MS63	MS65
AH1416-1995	—	PF65 85.00				

KM# 129 OMANI RIAL
28.28 g., 0.925 Silver 0.841 oz. ASW **Ruler:** Qabus bin Sa'id
Obv: National arms **Rev:** Mirbat castle

Date	Mintage	VF20	XF40	MS60	MS63	MS65
AH1416-1995	—	PF65 85.00				

KM# 130 OMANI RIAL
28.28 g., 0.925 Silver 0.841 oz. ASW **Ruler:** Qabus bin Sa'id
Obv: National arms **Rev:** Nakhl fort

Date	Mintage	VF20	XF40	MS60	MS63	MS65
AH1416-1995	—	PF65 85.00				

KM# 131 OMANI RIAL
28.28 g., 0.925 Silver 0.841 oz. ASW **Ruler:** Qabus bin Sa'id
Obv: National arms **Rev:** Nizwa fort

Date	Mintage	VF20	XF40	MS60	MS63	MS65
AH1416-1995	—	PF65 85.00				

KM# 132 OMANI RIAL
28.28 g., 0.925 Silver 0.841 oz. ASW **Ruler:** Qabus bin Sa'id
Obv: National arms **Rev:** Sohar fort

Date	Mintage	VF20	XF40	MS60	MS63	MS65
AH1416-1995	—	PF65 85.00				

KM# 133 OMANI RIAL
28.28 g., 0.925 Silver 0.841 oz. ASW **Ruler:** Qabus bin Sa'id
Obv: National arms **Rev:** Sur castle

Date	Mintage	VF20	XF40	MS60	MS63	MS65
AH1416-1995	—	PF65 85.00				

KM# 140 OMANI RIAL
13.90 g., 0.925 Silver 0.4134 oz. ASW **Ruler:** Qabus bin Sa'id
Subject: 25th National Day Anniversary - Burj Al Nahda **Obv:** National arms **Rev:** Burj Al Nahda

Date	Mintage	VF20	XF40	MS60	MS63	MS65
1995	—	PF65 90.00				

KM# 140a OMANI RIAL
22.80 g., 0.916 Gold 0.6715 oz. AGW **Ruler:** Qabus bin Sa'id
Subject: 25th National Day Anniversary - Burj Al Nahda **Obv:** National arms **Rev:** Burj Al Nahda

Date	Mintage	VF20	XF40	MS60	MS63	MS65
1995	—	PF65 1,250				

KM# 145 OMANI RIAL
28.28 g., 0.925 Silver 0.841 oz. ASW, 30 mm. **Ruler:** Qabus bin Sa'id **Subject:** U.N. - 50 Years **Obv:** National arms **Rev:** UN symbol and anniversary dates

Date	Mintage	VF20	XF40	MS60	MS63	MS65
ND-1995	25,000	PF63 55.00	PF65 60.00			

KM# 101 OMANI RIAL
31.47 g., 0.925 Silver 0.9359 oz. ASW **Ruler:** Qabus bin Sa'id
Subject: 26th National Day Anniversary - Sultanah **Obv:** National arms

Date	Mintage	VF20	XF40	MS60	MS63	MS65
1996	—	PF65 95.00				

KM# 102 OMANI RIAL
37.80 g., 0.916 Gold 1.1132 oz. AGW **Ruler:** Qabus bin Sa'id
Subject: 26th National Day Anniversary - Sultanah **Obv:** National arms **Rev:** Sailing ship - Sultanah within circle

Date	Mintage	VF20	XF40	MS60	MS63	MS65
1996	—	PF65 2,000	PF67 2,400			

KM# 103 OMANI RIAL
28.28 g., 0.925 Silver 0.841 oz. ASW **Ruler:** Qabus bin Sa'id
Subject: 26th National Day Anniversary - Al Battil **Obv:** National arms **Rev:** Sailing ship - Al Battil

Date	Mintage	VF20	XF40	MS60	MS63	MS65
1996	—	PF65 95.00				

KM# 104 OMANI RIAL
28.28 g., 0.925 Silver 0.841 oz. ASW **Ruler:** Qabus bin Sa'id
Subject: 26th National Day Anniversary - Al Badan **Obv:** National arms **Rev:** Sailing ship - Al Badan within circle

Date	Mintage	VF20	XF40	MS60	MS63	MS65
1996	—	PF65 95.00				

KM# 105 OMANI RIAL
28.28 g., 0.925 Silver 0.841 oz. ASW **Ruler:** Qabus bin Sa'id
Subject: 26th National Day Anniversary - Al Baghlah **Obv:** National arms **Rev:** Sailing ship - Al Baghlah

Date	Mintage	VF20	XF40	MS60	MS63	MS65
1996	—	PF65 95.00				

KM# 106 OMANI RIAL
28.28 g., 0.925 Silver 0.841 oz. ASW **Ruler:** Qabus bin Sa'id
Subject: 26th National Day Anniversary - Al Boum **Obv:** National arms **Rev:** Sailing ship - Al Boum within circle

Date	Mintage	VF20	XF40	MS60	MS63	MS65
1996	—	PF65 95.00				

KM# 107 OMANI RIAL
28.28 g., 0.925 Silver 0.841 oz. ASW **Ruler:** Qabus bin Sa'id
Subject: 26th National Day Anniversary - Al Jalbout **Obv:** National arms **Rev:** Sailing ship - Al Jalbout

Date	Mintage	VF20	XF40	MS60	MS63	MS65
1996	—	PF65 95.00				

KM# 108 OMANI RIAL
28.28 g., 0.925 Silver 0.841 oz. ASW **Ruler:** Qabus bin Sa'id
Subject: 26th National Day Anniversary - Al Sanbuq **Obv:** National arms **Rev:** Sailing ship - Al Sanbuq

Date	Mintage	VF20	XF40	MS60	MS63	MS65
1996	—	PF65 95.00				

KM# 109 OMANI RIAL

28.28 g., 0.925 Silver 0.841 oz. ASW **Ruler:** Qabus bin Sa'id **Subject:** 26th National Day Anniversary - Al Ghanjah **Obv:** National arms **Rev:** Sailing ship - Al Ghanjah within circle

Date	Mintage	VF20	XF40	MS60	MS63	MS65
1996	—	PF65 95.00				

KM# 110 OMANI RIAL

28.28 g., 0.925 Silver 0.841 oz. ASW **Ruler:** Qabus bin Sa'id **Subject:** 26th National Day Anniversary - Al Lateen **Obv:** National arms **Rev:** Sailing ship - Al Lateen

Date	Mintage	VF20	XF40	MS60	MS63	MS65
1996	—	PF65 95.00				

KM# 136 OMANI RIAL

28.28 g., 0.925 Silver 0.841 oz. ASW, 38.6 mm. **Ruler:** Qabus bin Sa'id **Subject:** 27th National Day Anniversary - Al Nahdha **Rev:** Al Nahdha Tower, coconut tree and Frankincense tree from the Dhofar Region

Date	Mintage	VF20	XF40	MS60	MS63	MS65
AH1418-1997	—	PF65 100				

KM# 136a OMANI RIAL

37.80 g., 0.9167 Gold 1.1141 oz. AGW, 38.6 mm. **Ruler:** Qabus bin Sa'id **Subject:** 27th National Day Anniversary - Al Nahdha **Rev:** Al Nahdha Tower, coconut tree and Frankincense tree from the Dhofar Region

Date	Mintage	VF20	XF40	MS60	MS63	MS65
AH1418-1997	—	PF65 2,200	PF67 2,500			

KM# 113 OMANI RIAL

28.28 g., 0.925 Silver 0.841 oz. ASW, 38.6 mm. **Ruler:** Qabus bin Sa'id **Series:** World Wildlife Fund **Obv:** National arms **Rev:** Mountain gazelle

Date	Mintage	VF20	XF40	MS60	MS63	MS65
1997	15,000	PF65 55.00				

KM# 138 OMANI RIAL

28.28 g., 0.925 Silver 0.841 oz. ASW **Ruler:** Qabus bin Sa'id **Series:** World Wildlife Fund **Obv:** National arms and value within circle **Rev:** Leopard

Date	Mintage	VF20	XF40	MS60	MS63	MS65
1997	15,000	PF65 60.00				

KM# 139 OMANI RIAL

28.28 g., 0.925 Silver 0.841 oz. ASW, 38.6 mm. **Ruler:** Qabus bin Sa'id **Subject:** 28th National Day Anniversary - Private Sector Year **Obv:** National arms within circle **Rev:** Radiant design

Date	Mintage	VF20	XF40	MS60	MS63	MS65
AH1418	—	PF65 110				

KM# 139a OMANI RIAL

37.80 g., 0.9167 Gold 1.1141 oz. AGW, 38.6 mm. **Ruler:** Qabus bin Sa'id **Subject:** 28th National Day Anniversary - Private Sector Year **Obv:** National arms **Rev:** Radiant design

Date	Mintage	VF20	XF40	MS60	MS63	MS65
AH1418	—	PF65 2,200	PF67 2,500			

KM# 149 OMANI RIAL

28.28 g., 0.925 Silver 0.841 oz. ASW, 38.61 mm. **Ruler:** Qabus bin Sa'id **Subject:** 29th National Day Anniversary - 1420/1999 **Obv:** National arms **Rev:** Palm tree (Khalas) and camels caravan

Date	Mintage	VF20	XF40	MS60	MS63	MS65
ND(1999)	—	PF63 120	PF65 135			

KM# 149a OMANI RIAL

37.80 g., 0.9167 Gold 1.1141 oz. AGW, 38.61 mm. **Ruler:** Qabus bin Sa'id **Subject:** 29th National Day Anniversary - 1420/1999 **Obv:** National arms **Rev:** Palm tree (Khalas) and camels caravan.

Date	Mintage	VF20	XF40	MS60	MS63	MS65
ND(1999)	—	PF65 2,200	PF67 2,500			

KM# 147 OMANI RIAL

27.87 g., 0.925 Silver 0.8288 oz. ASW, 38.61 mm. **Ruler:** Qabus bin Sa'id **Subject:** 30th National Day **Obv:** National arms **Rev:** Factory and symbols of commerce, value in center circle **Edge:** Reeded

Date	Mintage	VF20	XF40	MS60	MS63	MS65
2000	—	PF63 130	PF65 150			

KM# 147a OMANI RIAL

37.80 g., 0.916 Gold 1.1132 oz. AGW, 38.61 mm. **Ruler:** Qabus bin Sa'id **Subject:** 30th National Day **Obv:** National arms **Rev:** Factory and symbols of commerce, value in center circle **Edge:** Reeded

Date	Mintage	VF20	XF40	MS60	MS63	MS65
2000	—	PF65 2,200	PF67 2,500			

KM# 148 OMANI RIAL

27.87 g., 0.925 Silver 0.8288 oz. ASW, 38.6 mm. **Ruler:** Qabus bin Sa'id **Subject:** Central Bank's 25th Anniversary **Obv:** National arms **Rev:** Central Bank of Oman

Date	Mintage	VF20	XF40	MS60	MS63	MS65
ND(2000)	—	PF63 120	PF65 135			

KM# 81 2 OMANI RIALS

20.00 g., 0.925 Silver 0.5948 oz. ASW **Ruler:** Qabus bin Sa'id **Subject:** 20th National Day - Sultan Sa'id **Obv:** Crowned arms **Rev:** Head 1/4 left within circle

Date	Mintage	VF20	XF40	MS60	MS63	MS65
AH1411-1990	3,200	PF65 80.00	PF67 100			

KM# 60 2-1/2 OMANI RIALS

28.28 g., 0.925 Silver 0.841 oz. ASW **Ruler:** Qabus bin Sa'id **Subject:** Conservation **Obv:** National arms **Rev:** Caracal

Date	Mintage	XF40	MS60	MS63	MS65	MS66
AH1397 (1976)	4,539	—	—	40.00	50.00	60.00
AH1397 (1976)	4,407	PF65 55.00	PF67 65.00	PF69 75.00		

KM# 71 2-1/2 OMANI RIALS

28.28 g., 0.925 Silver 0.841 oz. ASW **Ruler:** Qabus bin Sa'id **Obv:** Crowned arms **Rev:** Verreaux's eagle in flight

Date	Mintage	VF20	XF40	MS60	MS63	MS65
AH1407-1986	—	—	—	—	—	—
Proof; Rare						

Note: Struck for presentation purposes

KM# 73 2-1/2 OMANI RIALS

28.28 g., 0.925 Silver 0.841 oz. ASW **Ruler:** Qabus bin Sa'id **Series:** World Wildlife Fund **Obv:** National arms **Rev:** Verreaux's eagle in flight

Date	Mintage	VF20	XF40	MS60	MS63	MS65
AH1407-1987	25,000	PF65 45.00	PF67 55.00			

KM# 83 2-1/2 OMANI RIALS
28.28 g., 0.925 Silver 0.841 oz. ASW **Ruler:** Qabus bin Sa'id **Series:** Save the Children **Obv:** Crowned arms **Rev:** Three children playing

Date	Mintage	VF20	XF40	MS60	MS63	MS65
AH1411-1991	Est. 20000	PF65 50.00	PF67 60.00			

KM# 97 2-1/2 OMANI RIALS
28.28 g., 0.925 Silver 0.841 oz. ASW **Ruler:** Qabus bin Sa'id **Obv:** Crowned arms **Rev:** Three children playing

Date	Mintage	VF20	XF40	MS60	MS63	MS65
AH1411-1991 Proof; Rare	—	—	—	—	—	—

Note: Struck for presentation purposes

KM# 61 5 OMANI RIALS
35.00 g., 0.925 Silver 1.0409 oz. ASW **Ruler:** Qabus bin Sa'id **Subject:** Conservation **Obv:** National arms **Rev:** Arabian White Oryx

Date	Mintage	XF40	MS60	MS63	MS65	MS66
AH1397	4,359	—	—	40.00	50.00	60.00
AH1397	4,401	PF65 55.00	PF67 65.00	PF69 75.00		

KM# 62 5 OMANI RIALS
45.65 g., 0.917 Gold 1.3459 oz. AGW **Ruler:** Qabus bin Sa'id **Subject:** 7th Anniversary - Reign of Sultan Qabus bin Sa'id **Obv:** National arms **Rev:** Bust 3/4 left

Date	Mintage	VF20	XF40	MS60	MS63	MS65
AH1397	1,000	PF65 2,500	PF67 3,000			
AH1408	250	PF65 3,000	PF67 3,500			

KM# 89 5 OMANI RIALS
20.00 g., 0.917 Gold 0.5896 oz. AGW **Ruler:** Qabus bin Sa'id **Subject:** Agricultural Year **Obv:** National arms **Rev:** Farm fields above dates within center circle **Note:** Similar to 1/2 Omani Rial, KM#85.

Date	Mintage	VF20	XF40	MS60	MS63	MS65
AH1409	200	PF65 1,350	PF67 165			

KM# 90 5 OMANI RIALS
20.00 g., 0.917 Gold 0.5896 oz. AGW **Ruler:** Qabus bin Sa'id **Subject:** Industry Year **Obv:** National arms **Rev:** Gears **Note:** Similar to 1/2 Omani Rial, KM#86.

Date	Mintage	VF20	XF40	MS60	MS63	MS65
AH1411-1991	410	PF65 1,250	PF67 1,550			

KM# 141 5 OMANI RIALS
18.80 g., 0.925 Silver 0.5591 oz. ASW **Ruler:** Qabus bin Sa'id **Subject:** 25th National Day Anniversary - Burj Al Sahwa **Obv:** National arms and value within circle **Rev:** Monument

Date	Mintage	VF20	XF40	MS60	MS63	MS65
1995	—	PF65 125	PF67 150			

KM# 141a 5 OMANI RIALS
31.00 g., 0.916 Gold 0.913 oz. AGW **Ruler:** Qabus bin Sa'id **Obv:** National arms and value within circle **Rev:** Monument

Date	Mintage	VF20	XF40	MS60	MS63	MS65
1995	—	PF65 1,650	PF67 1,850			

KM# 142 10 OMANI RIALS
23.20 g., 0.925 Silver 0.690 oz. ASW **Ruler:** Qabus bin Sa'id **Subject:** 25th National Day Anniversary - Central Bank **Obv:** National arms and value **Rev:** Central Bank of Oman

Date	Mintage	VF20	XF40	MS60	MS63	MS65
1995	—	PF65 125	PF67 150			

KM# 142a 10 OMANI RIALS
36.40 g., 0.916 Gold 1.072 oz. AGW **Ruler:** Qabus bin Sa'id **Subject:** 25th National Day Anniversary - Central Bank **Obv:** National arms and value **Rev:** Central Bank of Oman

Date	Mintage	VF20	XF40	MS60	MS63	MS65
1995	—	PF65 1,750	PF67 1,950			

KM# 49 15 OMANI RIALS
7.99 g., 0.917 Gold 0.2356 oz. AGW **Ruler:** Qabus bin Sa'id **Obv:** National arms **Rev:** Value

Date	Mintage	XF40	MS60	MS63	MS65	MS66
AH1392 (1972)	124	PF65 950	PF67 1,150			
AH1394 (1974)	300	—	—	—	650	750

Note: Struck for presentation purposes

KM# 55 15 OMANI RIALS
7.99 g., 0.917 Gold 0.2356 oz. AGW **Ruler:** Qabus bin Sa'id **Subject:** 10th National Day **Obv:** Crowned arms **Rev:** Value

Date	Mintage	VF20	XF40	MS60	MS63	MS65
AH1400	1,000	PF65 650	PF67 850			

Note: Struck for presentation purposes

KM# 56 15 OMANI RIALS
20.00 g., 0.917 Gold 0.5896 oz. AGW **Ruler:** Qabus bin Sa'id **Subject:** 15th Anniversary - Reign of Sultan **Obv:** Head 1/4 left within 3/4 wreath and designed border **Rev:** Crowned arms over country map within circle

Date	Mintage	VF20	XF40	MS60	MS63	MS65
AH1406	2,000	PF65 1,250	PF67 1,450			

KM# 56a 15 OMANI RIALS
31.01 g., 0.917 Gold 0.9142 oz. AGW **Ruler:** Qabus bin Sa'id **Subject:** 15th Anniversary - Reign of Sultan **Obv:** Head 1/4 left within 3/4 wreath and designed border **Rev:** Crowned arms over country map within circle

Date	Mintage	VF20	XF40	MS60	MS63	MS65
AH1406	200	PF65 1,750	PF67 1,950			

KM# 98 20 OMANI RIALS
20.00 g., 0.917 Gold 0.5896 oz. AGW **Ruler:** Qabus bin Sa'id **Subject:** 20th National Day - Sultan Sa'id **Obv:** National arms **Rev:** Bust 1/4 left within circle and designs around border **Note:** Similar to 2 Omani Rials, KM#81.

Date	Mintage	XF40	MS60	MS63	MS65	MS66
AH1411	1,200	PF67 1,250	PF69 1,450			

KM# 137.1 20 OMANI RIALS
48.65 g., 0.9167 Gold 1.4338 oz. AGW **Ruler:** Qabus bin Sa'id **Subject:** 2oth Anniversary of Sultan's Reign **Obv:** Crowned arms within designed circle, legend above and below **Rev:** Value within designed circle with dates below flanked by leaves

Date	Mintage	VF20	XF40	MS60	MS63	MS65
AH1411 (1990)	500	PF67 3,250				

KM# 137.2 20 OMANI RIALS
65.37 g., 0.917 Gold 1.9273 oz. AGW **Ruler:** Qabus bin Sa'id **Subject:** 20th Anniversary of Sultan's Reign **Obv:** Crowned arms within designed circle with legend above and below **Rev:** Value within designed circle above dates flanked by leaves **Note:** Prev. KM#137.

Date	Mintage	VF20	XF40	MS60	MS63	MS65
AH1411-1990	—	PF67 4,500				

KM# 143 20 OMANI RIALS
27.40 g., 0.925 Silver 0.8149 oz. ASW **Ruler:** Qabus bin Sa'id **Subject:** 25th National Day Anniversary **Obv:** National arms and value **Rev:** Radiant value within circle

Date	Mintage	VF20	XF40	MS60	MS63	MS65
1995	—	PF65 145	PF67 175			

KM# 143a 20 OMANI RIALS
41.20 g., 0.916 Gold 1.2133 oz. AGW **Ruler:** Qabus bin Sa'id **Subject:** 25th National Day Anniversary **Obv:** National arms and value **Rev:** Radiant value within circle

Date	Mintage	VF20	XF40	MS60	MS63	MS65
1995	—	PF65 2,250	PF67 2,750			

KM# 74 25 OMANI RIALS
10.00 g., 0.917 Gold 0.2948 oz. AGW **Ruler:** Qabus bin Sa'id **Series:** World Wildlife Fund **Obv:** National arms within circle **Rev:** Masked Booby

Date	Mintage	VF20	XF40	MS60	MS63	MS65
AH1407-1987	5,000	PF65 550	PF67 650			

KM# 99 25 OMANI RIALS
10.00 g., 0.917 Gold 0.2948 oz. AGW **Ruler:** Qabus bin Sa'id **Series:** World Wildlife Fund **Obv:** Crown above arms with legends above and below **Rev:** Masked booby

Date	Mintage	VF20	XF40	MS60	MS63	MS65
AH1407-1987 Proof; Rare	—	—	—	—	—	—

Note: Struck for presentation purposes

KM# 88 25 OMANI RIALS

10.00 g., 0.917 Gold 0.2948 oz. AGW **Ruler:** Qabus bin Sa'id **Series:** Save the Children **Obv:** National arms within circle **Rev:** School Master with pupils

Date	Mintage	VF20	XF40	MS60	MS63	MS65
AH1411-1991	Est. 3000	PF65 600	PF67 700			

KM# 100 25 OMANI RIALS

10.00 g., 0.917 Gold 0.2948 oz. AGW **Ruler:** Qabus bin Sa'id **Series:** Save the Children **Obv:** Crown above arms with legends above and below **Rev:** School Master with pupils

Date	Mintage	VF20	XF40	MS60	MS63	MS65
AH1411-1991 Proof; Rare	—	—	—	—	—	—

Note: Struck for presentation purposes

KM# 144 25 OMANI RIALS

31.70 g., 0.925 Silver 0.9427 oz. ASW **Ruler:** Qabus bin Sa'id **Subject:** 25th National Day Anniversary - Sultan Qaboos bin Said **Obv:** National arms and value **Rev:** Multicolor bust facing

Date	Mintage	XF40	MS60	MS63	MS65	MS66
1995	—	PF67 150	PF69 175			

KM# 144a 25 OMANI RIALS

50.20 g., 0.916 Gold 1.4784 oz. AGW **Ruler:** Qabus bin Sa'id **Subject:** 25th National Day Anniversary - Sultan Qaboos bin Said **Obv:** National arms and value **Rev:** Multicolor bust facing

Date	Mintage	XF40	MS60	MS63	MS65	MS66
1995	—	PF69 2,750				

KM# 63 75 OMANI RIALS

33.44 g., 0.900 Gold 0.9675 oz. AGW **Ruler:** Qabus bin Sa'id **Subject:** Conservation **Obv:** National arms above date **Rev:** Arabian Tahr

Date	Mintage	XF40	MS60	MS63	MS65	MS66
AH1397 (1976)	825	—	—	—	1,600	1,750
AH1397 (1976)	325	PF65 1,950	PF67 2,150	PF69 2,350		

PROOF SETS

KM#	Date	Mintage	Identification	Issue Price	Mkt Val
PS1	AH1394 (3)	250	KM#45-47	—	2,500
PS3	AH1397 (3)	—	KM#60, 61, 63	780	1,975
PS4	AH1397 (2)	—	KM#60, 61	60.00	75.00
PS5	AH1411 (6)	3,200	KM#76-81	84.50	160
PSA6	1996 (2)	—	KM#101-102	640	2,250
PS6	AH1416 (20)	—	KM#114-133	—	1,700
PS7	1996 (4)	—	KM#103-106	125	360
PS8	1996 (4)	—	KM#107-110	125	360
PS9	1996 (8)	—	KM#103-110	247	725

PAKISTAN

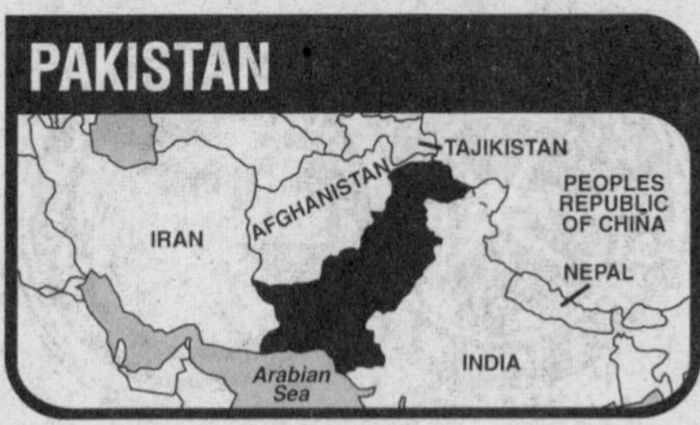

The Islamic Republic of Pakistan, located on the Indian sub-continent between India and Afghanistan, has an area of 310,404 sq. mi. (803,940 sq. km.) and a population of130 million. Capital: Islamabad. Pakistan is mainly an agricultural land although the industrial base is expanding rapidly. Yarn, textiles, cotton, rice, medical instruments, sports equipment and leather are exported.

Afghan and Turkish intrusions into northern India between the 11th and 18th centuries resulted in large numbers of Indians being converted to Islam. The idea of a separate Moslem state independent of Hindu India developed in the 1930's and was agreed to by Britain in 1946. The Islamic majority areas of India, consisting of the separate geographic entities known as East and West Pakistan, achieved self-government as Pakistan, with dominion status in the British Commonwealth, when the British withdrew from India on Aug. 14, 1947. Pakistan became a republic in 1956. When a basic constitutional crisis initiated by the election of Dec. 1, 1970 - the first direct general election in Pakistani history - could not be resolved by the leaders of East and West Pakistan, the East Pakistanis seceded from the Islamic Republic of Pakistan (March 26, 1971) and formed the independent People's Republic of Bangladesh. After many years of vacillation between civilian and military regimes, the people of Pakistan held a free national election in November, 1988 and installed the first of a series of democratic governments under a parliamentary system. Pakistan was a member of the Commonwealth of Nations, but was suspended from membership October 1999. In 2004, Pakistan was re-admitted.

TITLE

پاکستان

Pakistan

ISLAMIC REPUBLIC

STANDARD COINAGE

3 Pies = 1 Pice; 4 Pice = 1 Anna; 16 Annas = 1 Rupee

KM# 11 PIE

1.25 g., Bronze, 15.87 mm. **Obv:** Crescent and star above tughra **Rev:** Value and date flanked by stars within wreath **Edge:** Plain

Date	Mintage	VF20	XF40	MS60	MS63	MS65
1951	2,950,000	0.50	0.75	1.25	2.50	3.00
1951	—	PF63 4.00	PF65 6.00			
1953	110,000	3.00	5.00	7.00	9.00	12.00
1953	—	PF63 5.00	PF65 7.00			
1955	211,000	3.00	4.50	6.00	8.00	10.00
1955	—	PF63 13.00	PF65 15.00			
1956	3,390,000	0.50	1.00	1.25	2.50	3.00
1957	192,000	3.00	5.00	7.00	9.00	12.00

KM# 1 PICE

1.55 g., Bronze, 21.3 mm. **Obv:** Legend around center hole **Rev:** Crescent and star divides value around the top, center hole divides date **Note:** Varieties exist.

Date	Mintage	F12	VF20	XF40	MS60	MS63
1948	101,070,000	0.20	0.40	0.65	1.00	1.50
1948	—	PF63 2.00	PF65 3.00			
1949	25,740,000	0.20	0.40	0.65	1.00	1.50
1949	—	PF63 2.00	PF65 3.00			
1951	14,050,000	0.50	1.00	1.50	2.00	2.50
1952	41,680,000	0.20	0.40	0.65	1.00	1.50

KM# 12 PICE

2.30 g., Nickel-Brass, 20.59 mm. **Obv:** Crescent and star above tughra **Rev:** Value flanked by oat sprigs **Edge:** Plain

Date	Mintage	VF20	XF40	MS60	MS63	MS65
1953	47,540,000	0.30	0.50	0.75	1.00	1.25
1953	—	PF63 1.50	PF65 2.00			
1955	31,280,000	0.30	0.50	0.75	1.00	1.25
1956	9,710,000	0.70	1.00	1.25	1.75	2.50
1957	57,790,000	0.30	0.50	0.75	1.00	1.25
1958	52,470,000	0.30	0.50	0.75	1.00	1.25
1959	41,620,000	0.30	0.50	0.75	1.00	1.25

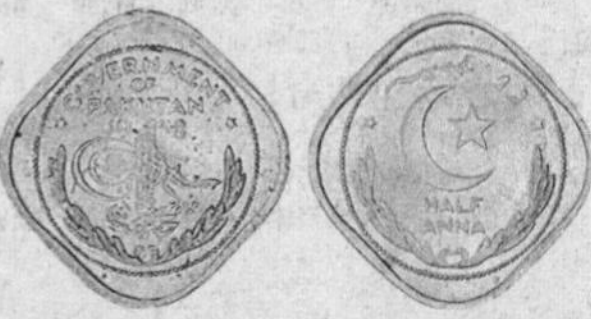

KM# 2 1/2 ANNA

2.90 g., Copper-Nickel, 19.8 mm. **Obv:** Tughra and date flanked by stars within sprigs, circle surrounds **Rev:** Crescent, stars and value above sprigs within circle **Shape:** 4-sided

Date	Mintage	F12	VF20	XF40	MS60	MS63
1948	73,920,000	0.50	0.75	1.00	1.50	1.75
1948	—	PF63 1.50	PF65 2.00			
1949 Dot after date	16,940,000	0.50	0.75	1.00	1.25	1.75
1951	75,360,000	0.50	0.75	1.00	1.50	1.75

KM# 13 1/2 ANNA

2.50 g., Nickel-Brass, 19.8 mm. **Obv:** Crescent and star above tughra **Rev:** Date divides wreath, value in center **Shape:** 4-sided

Date	Mintage	VF20	XF40	MS60	MS63	MS65
1953	8,350,000	0.35	0.60	0.80	1.15	1.50
1953	—	PF63 1.50	PF65 2.00			
1955	17,310,000	0.30	0.50	0.75	1.00	1.25
1958	38,250,000	0.30	0.50	0.75	1.00	1.25

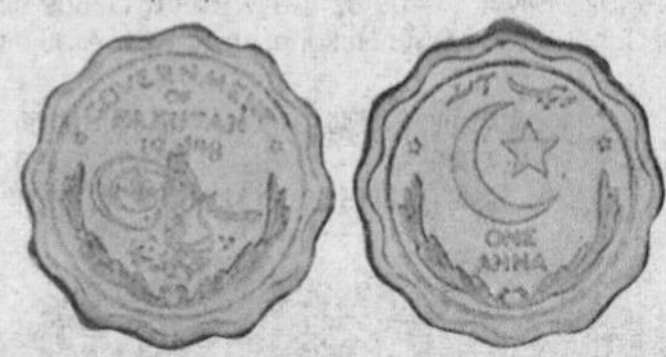

KM# 3 ANNA

3.75 g., Copper-Nickel, 21.0 mm. **Obv:** Tughra and date flanked by stars above sprigs within circle **Rev:** Crescent and star above sprigs within circle **Shape:** Scalloped

Date	Mintage	F12	VF20	XF40	MS60	MS63
1948	73,460,000	0.15	0.30	0.50	0.75	1.00
1948	—	PF63 1.50	PF65 2.00			
1949	11,140,000	0.20	0.35	0.60	0.80	1.15
1949 Dot after date	—	0.50	0.75	1.00	1.25	1.75

Note: Mintage included with KM#8.

Date	Mintage	F12	VF20	XF40	MS60	MS63
1951	40,800,000	0.15	0.30	0.50	0.75	1.00
1952	15,430,000	0.20	0.35	0.60	0.80	1.15

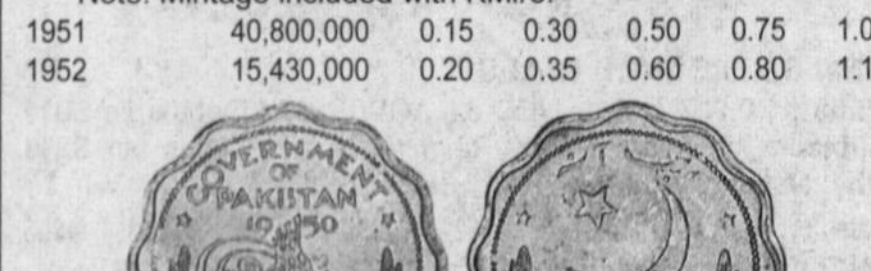

KM# 8 ANNA

3.75 g., Copper-Nickel, 21.0 mm. **Obv:** Tughra and date flanked by stars above sprigs within circle **Rev:** Crescent, stars and value above sprigs within circle **Shape:** Scalloped

Date	Mintage	F12	VF20	XF40	MS60	MS63
1950	94,830,000	3.00	4.00	5.00	7.00	9.00
1950	—	PF63 13.00	PF65 15.00			

KM# 14 ANNA

2.90 g., Copper-Nickel, 19.5 mm. **Obv:** Crescent and star above tughra **Rev:** Date divides wreath, value in center **Shape:** Scalloped

Date	Mintage	VF20	XF40	MS60	MS63	MS65
1953	9,350,000	0.30	0.50	0.75	1.00	1.25
1953	—	PF63 1.50	PF65 2.00			
1954	35,360,000	0.30	0.50	0.75	1.00	1.25
1955	6,230,000	0.35	0.60	0.80	1.15	1.50
1956	4,580,000	0.35	0.60	0.80	1.15	1.50
1957	12,500,000	0.30	0.50	0.75	1.00	1.25
1958	44,320,000	0.30	0.50	0.75	1.00	1.25

KM# 4 2 ANNAS

5.80 g., Copper-Nickel, 25.4 mm. **Obv:** Tughra and date flanked by stars above sprigs within circle **Rev:** Crescent, stars and value above sprigs within circle **Shape:** 4-sided

Date	Mintage	F12	VF20	XF40	MS60	MS63
1948	55,930,000	0.15	0.30	0.50	0.75	1.00
1948	—	PF63 1.50	PF65 2.00			
1949	19,720,000	0.20	0.35	0.60	0.80	1.15
1949 Dot after date	—	0.50	0.75	1.00	1.25	1.75

Note: Mintage included with KM#9.

Date	Mintage	F12	VF20	XF40	MS60	MS63
1951	33,130,000	0.15	0.30	0.50	0.75	1.00

KM# 9 2 ANNAS

5.80 g., Copper-Nickel, 25.4 mm. **Obv:** Tughra and date flanked by stars above sprigs within circle **Rev:** Crescent, stars and value above sprigs within circle **Shape:** 4-sided

Date	Mintage	F12	VF20	XF40	MS60	MS63
1950	21,190,000	3.50	4.50	6.00	8.00	10.00
1950	—	PF63 16.00	PF65 20.00			

KM# 15 2 ANNAS

5.80 g., Copper-Nickel, 25.4 mm. **Obv:** Crescent and star above tughra **Rev:** Date divides wreath, value in center **Shape:** 4-sided

Date	Mintage	VF20	XF40	MS60	MS63	MS65
1953	7,910,000	0.30	0.50	0.75	1.00	1.25
1953	—	PF63 1.50	PF65 2.00			
1954	5,740,000	0.30	0.50	0.75	1.00	1.25
1955	6,230,000	0.30	0.50	0.75	1.00	1.25
1956	1,370,000	0.35	0.60	0.80	1.15	1.50
1957	2,570,000	0.35	0.60	0.80	1.15	1.50
1958	6,200,000	0.30	0.50	0.75	1.00	1.25
1959	8,010,000	0.30	0.50	0.75	1.00	1.25

KM# 5 1/4 RUPEE

2.75 g., Nickel, 19 mm. **Obv:** Tughra and date flanked by stars above sprigs **Rev:** Crescent, stars and value above sprigs **Edge:** Reeded

Date	Mintage	F12	VF20	XF40	MS60	MS63
1948	52,680,000	0.20	0.30	0.50	0.75	1.00
1948	—	PF63 2.25	PF65 3.00			
1949	46,000,000	0.20	0.30	0.50	0.75	1.00
1951	19,120,000	0.20	0.35	0.60	0.80	1.15

KM# 10 1/4 RUPEE

2.75 g., Nickel, 19 mm. **Obv:** Tughra and date flanked by stars above sprigs **Rev:** Crescent, stars and value above sprigs **Edge:** Reeded

Date	Mintage	F12	VF20	XF40	MS60	MS63
1950	19,400,000	4.00	5.00	6.00	7.50	10.00
1950	—	PF63 25.00	PF65 27.00			

KM# 6 1/2 RUPEE

6.00 g., Nickel, 24 mm. **Obv:** Tughra and date flanked by stars above sprigs **Rev:** Crescent, stars and value above sprigs **Edge:** Reeded

Date	Mintage	F12	VF20	XF40	MS60	MS63
1948	33,260,000	0.40	0.60	0.75	1.25	1.75
1948	—	PF63 2.00	PF65 3.00			
1949	20,300,000	0.40	0.60	0.75	1.25	1.75
1951	11,430,000	0.40	0.65	0.90	1.35	1.85

KM# 7 RUPEE

11.50 g., Nickel, 28 mm. **Obv:** Tughra and date flanked by stars above sprigs **Rev:** Crescent, stars and value above sprigs **Edge:** Reeded **Note:** Varieties exist.

Date	Mintage	F12	VF20	XF40	MS60	MS63
1948	46,200,000	0.75	1.25	2.00	2.50	3.50
1948	—	PF63 5.00	PF65 6.00			
1949	37,100,000	0.75	1.25	2.00	2.50	3.50

DECIMAL COINAGE

100 Paisa = 1 Rupee

KM# 16 PICE

1.40 g., Bronze, 16 mm. **Obv:** Crescent and star above tughra **Rev:** Date and value flanked by oat sprigs

Date	Mintage	VF20	XF40	MS60	MS63	MS65
1961	74,910,000	0.30	0.50	0.75	1.00	1.25

KM# 17 PAISA

1.40 g., Bronze, 16 mm. **Obv:** Crescent and star above tughra **Rev:** Value and date flanked by oat sprigs

Date	Mintage	VF20	XF40	MS60	MS63	MS65
1961	134,650,000	0.25	0.40	0.60	0.85	1.00
1961	—	PF63 1.50	PF65 2.00			
1962	149,380,000	0.25	0.40	0.60	0.85	1.00
1963	127,810,000	0.25	0.40	0.60	0.85	1.00

KM# 24 PAISA

1.50 g., Bronze, 17 mm. **Obv:** Crescent and star above tughra **Rev:** Value flanked by oat sprigs

Date	Mintage	VF20	XF40	MS60	MS63	MS65
1964	39,890,000	0.35	0.50	0.75	1.00	1.25
1964	—	PF63 1.50	PF65 2.00			
1965	69,660,000	0.35	0.50	0.75	1.00	1.25

KM# 24a PAISA

1.50 g., Nickel-Brass, 17 mm. **Obv:** Crescent and star above tughra **Rev:** Value flanked by oat sprigs

Date	Mintage	VF20	XF40	MS60	MS63	MS65
1965	32,950,000	0.35	0.50	0.75	1.00	1.25
1966	179,370,000	0.25	0.40	0.60	0.85	1.00
1967	61,410,000	0.25	0.40	0.60	0.85	1.00

KM# 29 PAISA

0.60 g., Aluminum, 17 mm. **Obv:** Crescent and star above tughra **Rev:** Value flanked by oat sprigs

Date	Mintage	VF20	XF40	MS60	MS63	MS65
1967	170,070,000	0.20	0.40	0.50	0.75	1.00
1968	161,780,000	0.20	0.40	0.50	0.75	1.00
1969	160,230,000	0.20	0.40	0.50	0.75	1.00
1970	204,606,000	0.20	0.40	0.50	0.75	1.00
1971	191,880,000	0.20	0.40	0.50	0.75	1.00
1972	108,510,000	0.20	0.40	0.50	0.75	1.00
1973	9,370,000	0.20	0.40	0.50	0.75	1.00

KM# 33 PAISA

0.60 g., Aluminum, 17 mm. **Series:** F.A.O. **Obv:** Crescent within monument with star at upper left **Rev:** Value flanked by abstract cotton plant **Edge:** Plain

Date	Mintage	VF20	XF40	MS60	MS63	MS65
1974	14,230,000	0.20	0.40	0.50	0.75	1.00
1975	43,000,000	0.20	0.40	0.50	0.75	1.00
1976	49,180,000	0.20	0.40	0.50	0.75	1.00
1977	62,750,000	0.20	0.40	0.50	0.75	1.00
1978	20,380,000	0.20	0.40	0.50	0.75	1.00
1979	5,630,000	2.00	3.00	4.00	5.00	7.00

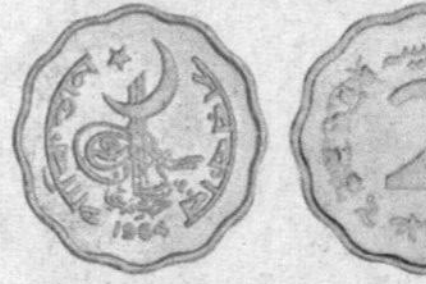

KM# 25 2 PAISA

2.25 g., Bronze, 18.0 mm. **Obv:** Crescent and star above tughra **Rev:** Value within sprigs **Shape:** Scalloped

Date	Mintage	VF20	XF40	MS60	MS63	MS65
1964	67,660,000	0.35	0.50	0.75	1.00	1.25
1964	—	PF63 1.50	PF65 2.00			
1965	27,880,000	0.35	0.50	0.75	1.00	1.25
1966	50,590,000	0.35	0.50	0.75	1.00	1.25

KM# 28 2 PAISA

0.75 g., Aluminum, 18 mm. **Obv:** Crescent and star above tughra **Rev:** Value within sprigs

Date	Mintage	VF20	XF40	MS60	MS63	MS65
1966	11,940,000	0.35	0.50	0.75	1.00	1.25
1967	73,970,000	0.35	0.50	0.75	1.00	1.25
1968	56,570,000	0.35	0.50	0.75	1.00	1.25

KM# 25a 2 PAISA

0.75 g., Aluminum, 18.0 mm. **Obv:** Crescent and star above tughra **Rev:** Value within sprigs **Shape:** Scalloped

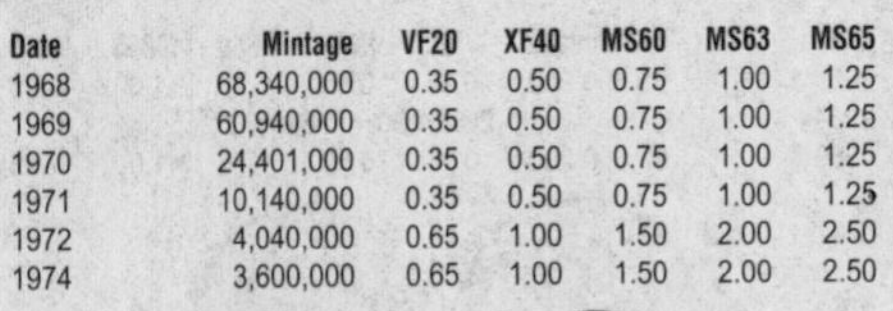

Date	Mintage	VF20	XF40	MS60	MS63	MS65
1968	68,340,000	0.35	0.50	0.75	1.00	1.25
1969	60,940,000	0.35	0.50	0.75	1.00	1.25
1970	24,401,000	0.35	0.50	0.75	1.00	1.25
1971	10,140,000	0.35	0.50	0.75	1.00	1.25
1972	4,040,000	0.65	1.00	1.50	2.00	2.50
1974	3,600,000	0.65	1.00	1.50	2.00	2.50

KM# 34 2 PAISA

1.00 g., Aluminum, 19.0 mm. **Series:** F.A.O. **Obv:** Crescent within monument with star at upper left **Rev:** Value flanked by rice plant **Shape:** Scalloped

Date	Mintage	VF20	XF40	MS60	MS63	MS65
1974	3,600,000	0.35	0.50	0.75	1.00	1.25
1975	4,020,000	0.35	0.50	0.75	1.00	1.25
1976	5,750,000	0.50	0.75	1.25	1.75	2.25

KM# 18 5 PICE

2.75 g., Nickel-Brass, 21 mm. **Obv:** Crescent and star above tughra **Rev:** Sailboat with value on sails **Shape:** 4-sided

Date	Mintage	VF20	XF40	MS60	MS63	MS65
1961	40,050,000	0.35	0.75	1.25	1.75	2.25

KM# 19 5 PAISA

2.75 g., Nickel-Brass, 21.0 mm. **Obv:** Crescent and star above tughra **Rev:** Sailboat with value on sails **Shape:** 4-sided

Date	Mintage	VF20	XF40	MS60	MS63	MS65
1961	40,790,000	0.35	0.75	1.25	1.75	2.25
1961	—	PF63 1.50	PF65 2.50			
1962	48,200,000	0.35	0.75	1.25	1.75	2.25
1963	45,020,000	0.35	0.75	1.25	1.75	2.25

KM# 26 5 PAISA

2.75 g., Nickel-Brass, 21.0 mm. **Obv:** Crescent and star above tughra **Rev:** Sailboat with value on the sails **Shape:** 4-sided

Date	Mintage	VF20	XF40	MS60	MS63	MS65
1964	82,730,000	0.35	0.50	0.75	1.00	1.25
1965	72,570,000	0.35	0.50	0.75	1.00	1.25
1966	32,900,000	0.35	0.50	0.75	1.00	1.25
1967	24,470,000	0.35	0.50	0.75	1.00	1.25
1968	34,650,000	0.35	0.50	0.75	1.00	1.25
1969	5,690,000	0.35	0.50	0.75	1.00	1.25
1970	24,655,000	0.35	0.50	0.75	1.00	1.25
1971	23,860,000	0.35	0.50	0.75	1.00	1.25
1972	40,345,000	0.35	0.50	0.75	1.00	1.25
1973	11,280,000	0.35	0.50	0.75	1.00	1.25
1974	7,695,000	1.00	2.00	3.00	4.00	5.00

KM# 35 5 PAISA

1.00 g., Aluminum, 21.0 mm. **Series:** F.A.O. **Obv:** Crescent within monument with star at upper left **Rev:** Value within sugar cane **Shape:** 4-sided

Date	Mintage	VF20	XF40	MS60	MS63	MS65
1974	23,395,000	0.35	0.50	0.75	1.00	1.25
1975	50,030,000	0.35	0.50	0.75	1.00	1.25
1976	58,255,000	0.35	0.50	0.75	1.00	1.25
1977	32,840,000	0.35	0.50	0.75	1.00	1.25
1978	61,940,000	0.35	0.50	0.75	1.00	1.25

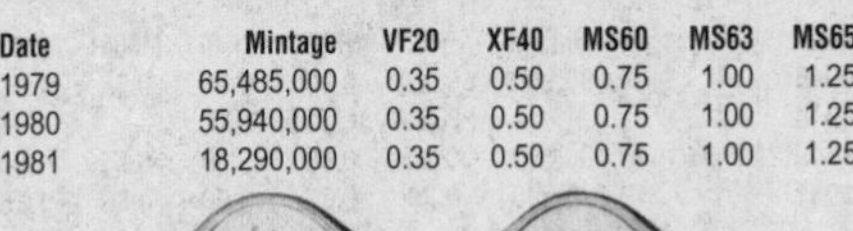

Date	Mintage	VF20	XF40	MS60	MS63	MS65
1979	65,485,000	0.35	0.50	0.75	1.00	1.25
1980	55,940,000	0.35	0.50	0.75	1.00	1.25
1981	18,290,000	0.35	0.50	0.75	1.00	1.25

KM# 52 5 PAISA

1.00 g., Aluminum, 19.12 mm. **Obv:** Crescent, star and date above sprigs **Rev:** Value within sugar cane flanked by stars **Edge:** Plain **Shape:** 4-sided

Date	Mintage	VF20	XF40	MS60	MS63	MS65
1981	16,730,000	0.35	0.50	0.75	1.00	1.25
1982	51,210,000	0.35	0.50	0.75	1.00	1.25
1983	42,915,000	0.35	0.50	0.75	1.00	1.25
1984	45,105,000	0.35	0.50	0.75	1.00	1.25
1985	46,555,000	0.35	0.50	0.75	1.00	1.25
1986	20,065,000	0.35	0.50	0.75	1.00	1.25
1987	37,710,000	0.35	0.50	0.75	1.00	1.25
1988	40,150,000	0.35	0.50	0.75	1.00	1.25
1989	50,460,000	0.35	0.50	0.75	1.00	1.25
1990	32,245,000	0.35	0.50	0.75	1.00	1.25
1991	22,780,000	0.35	0.50	0.75	1.00	1.25
1992	15,025,000	0.35	0.50	0.75	1.00	1.25

KM# 20 10 PICE

4.75 g., Copper-Nickel, 23.0 mm. **Obv:** Crescent and star above tughra **Rev:** Date divides wreath, value in center **Shape:** Scalloped

Date	Mintage	VF20	XF40	MS60	MS63	MS65
1961	22,230,000	0.35	0.50	0.75	1.00	1.25

KM# 21 10 PAISA

4.75 g., Copper-Nickel, 23.0 mm. **Obv:** Crescent and star above tughra **Rev:** Date divides wreath, value in center **Shape:** Scalloped

Date	Mintage	VF20	XF40	MS60	MS63	MS65
1961	31,090,000	0.35	0.50	0.75	1.00	1.25
1961	—	PF63 2.00	PF65 3.00			
1962	29,440,000	0.35	0.50	0.75	1.00	1.25
1963	19,760,000	0.35	0.50	0.75	1.00	1.25

KM# 27 10 PAISA

4.75 g., Copper-Nickel, 23.0 mm. **Obv:** Crescent and star above tughra **Rev:** Value within wreath **Shape:** Scalloped

Date	Mintage	VF20	XF40	MS60	MS63	MS65
1964	52,580,000	0.35	0.50	0.75	1.00	1.25
1965	41,450,000	0.35	0.50	0.75	1.00	1.25
1966	11,315,000	0.35	0.50	0.75	1.00	1.25
1967	16,430,000	0.35	0.50	0.75	1.00	1.25
1968	17,125,000	0.35	0.50	0.75	1.00	1.25

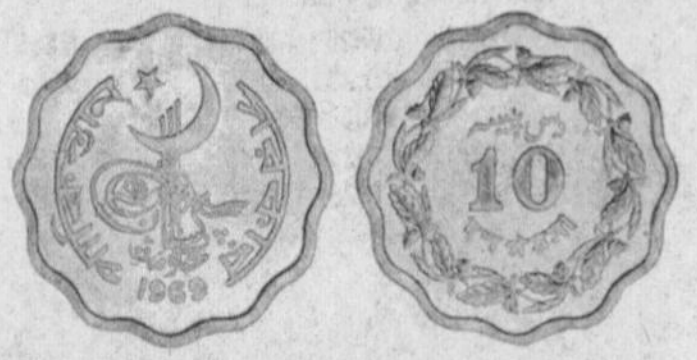

KM# 31 10 PAISA

4.00 g., Copper-Nickel, 22.0 mm. **Obv:** Crescent and star above tughra **Rev:** Value within wreath **Shape:** Scalloped **Note:** Reduced size.

Date	Mintage	VF20	XF40	MS60	MS63	MS65
1969	30,910,000	0.35	0.50	0.75	1.00	1.25

Date	Mintage	VF20	XF40	MS60	MS63	MS65
1970	30,250,000	0.35	0.50	0.75	1.00	1.25
1971	26,270,000	0.35	0.50	0.75	1.00	1.25
1972	24,845,000	0.35	0.50	0.75	1.00	1.25
1973	6,450,000	0.35	0.50	0.75	1.00	1.25
1974	4,780,000	0.35	0.50	0.75	1.00	1.25

KM# 36 10 PAISA

1.25 g., Aluminum, 22.0 mm. **Series:** F.A.O. **Obv:** Crescent within monument with star at upper left **Rev:** Value within wheat ears **Shape:** Scalloped

Date	Mintage	VF20	XF40	MS60	MS63	MS65
1974	18,640,000	0.35	0.50	0.75	1.00	1.25
1975	28,875,000	0.35	0.50	0.75	1.00	1.25
1976	43,755,000	0.35	0.50	0.75	1.00	1.25
1977	29,045,000	0.35	0.50	0.75	1.00	1.25
1978	55,185,000	0.35	0.50	0.75	1.00	1.25
1979	56,100,000	0.35	0.50	0.75	1.00	1.25
1980	40,985,000	0.35	0.50	0.75	1.00	1.25
1981	15,500,000	0.35	0.50	0.75	1.00	1.25

KM# 53 10 PAISA

1.25 g., Aluminum, 22 mm. **Obv:** Crescent, star and date above sprigs **Rev:** Value within square **Edge:** Plain **Shape:** Scalloped

Date	Mintage	VF20	XF40	MS60	MS63	MS65
1981	7,995,000	0.35	0.50	0.75	1.00	1.25
1982	39,770,000	0.35	0.50	0.75	1.00	1.25
1983	44,705,000	0.35	0.50	0.75	1.00	1.25
1984	35,255,000	0.35	0.50	0.75	1.00	1.25
1985	41,545,000	0.35	0.50	0.75	1.00	1.25
1986	43,280,000	0.35	0.50	0.75	1.00	1.25
1987	39,090,000	0.35	0.50	0.75	1.00	1.25
1988	42,510,000	0.35	0.50	0.75	1.00	1.25
1989	39,325,000	0.35	0.50	0.75	1.00	1.25
1990	37,750,000	0.35	0.50	0.75	1.00	1.25
1991	28,205,000	0.35	0.50	0.75	1.00	1.25
1992	11,600,000	0.35	0.50	0.75	1.00	1.25
1993	6,380,000	0.35	0.50	0.75	1.00	1.25

KM# 22 25 PAISA

2.90 g., Nickel, 19 mm. **Obv:** Crescent and star above tughra **Rev:** Value flanked by flower sprigs **Edge:** Reeded

Date	Mintage	VF20	XF40	MS60	MS63	MS65
1963	16,900,000	0.35	0.50	0.75	1.00	1.25
1964	7,990,000	0.35	0.50	0.75	1.00	1.25
1965	9,290,000	0.35	0.50	0.75	1.00	1.25
1966	6,650,000	0.35	0.50	0.75	1.00	1.25
1967	3,740,000	0.35	0.50	0.75	1.00	1.25

KM# 30 25 PAISA

4.00 g., Copper-Nickel, 20 mm. **Obv:** Crescent and star above tughra **Rev:** Value below flowers **Edge:** Reeded

Date	Mintage	VF20	XF40	MS60	MS63	MS65
1967	5,500,000	0.35	0.50	0.75	1.00	1.25
Note: Mintage unconfirmed						
1968	5,500,000	0.35	0.50	0.75	1.00	1.25
Note: Mintage unconfirmed						
1969	24,264,000	0.35	0.50	0.75	1.00	1.25
1970	30,392,000	0.35	0.50	0.75	1.00	1.25
1971	12,664,000	0.35	0.50	0.75	1.00	1.25
1972	10,824,000	0.35	0.50	0.75	1.00	1.25
1973	1,908,000	0.35	0.50	0.75	1.00	1.25
1974	9,756,000	0.35	0.50	0.75	1.00	1.25

KM# 37 25 PAISA

4.00 g., Copper-Nickel, 20 mm. **Obv:** Crescent within monument with star at upper left **Rev:** Value within flowers **Edge:** Reeded

Date	Mintage	VF20	XF40	MS60	MS63	MS65
1975	14,264,000	0.35	0.50	0.75	1.00	1.25
1976	20,440,000	0.35	0.50	0.75	1.00	1.25
1977	22,092,000	0.35	0.50	0.75	1.00	1.25
1978	33,544,000	0.35	0.50	0.75	1.00	1.25
1979	29,648,000	0.35	0.50	0.75	1.00	1.25
1980	49,556,000	0.35	0.50	0.75	1.00	1.25
1981	33,952,000	0.35	0.50	0.75	1.00	1.25

KM# 58 25 PAISA

2.50 g., Copper-Nickel, 18 mm. **Obv:** Crescent, star and date above sprigs **Rev:** Value within artistic designed wreath **Edge:** Reeded **Note:** Varieties in date and crescent size exist.

Date	Mintage	VF20	XF40	MS60	MS63	MS65
1981	5,648,000	0.35	0.50	0.75	1.00	1.25
1982	28,940,000	0.35	0.50	0.75	1.00	1.25
1983	40,844,000	0.35	0.50	0.75	1.00	1.25
1984	50,988,000	0.35	0.50	0.75	1.00	1.25
1985	53,748,000	0.35	0.50	0.75	1.00	1.25
1986	75,764,000	0.35	0.50	0.75	1.00	1.25
1987	53,560,000	0.35	0.50	0.75	1.00	1.25
1988	58,900,000	0.35	0.50	0.75	1.00	1.25
1989	60,272,000	0.35	0.50	0.75	1.00	1.25
1990	65,284,000	0.35	0.50	0.75	1.00	1.25
1991	56,264,000	0.35	0.50	0.75	1.00	1.25
1992	60,372,000	0.35	0.50	0.75	1.00	1.25
1993	57,344,000	0.35	0.50	0.75	1.00	1.25
1994	48,796,000	0.35	0.50	0.75	1.00	1.25
1995	38,964,000	0.35	0.50	0.75	1.00	1.25

KM# 23 50 PAISA

5.80 g., Nickel, 24 mm. **Obv:** Crescent and star above tughra **Rev:** Value flanked by flowers **Edge:** Reeded

Date	Mintage	VF20	XF40	MS60	MS63	MS65
1963	8,110,000	0.35	0.50	0.75	1.00	1.25
1964	4,580,000	0.35	0.50	0.75	1.00	1.25
1965	8,980,000	0.35	0.50	0.75	1.00	1.25
1966	2,860,000	0.35	0.50	0.75	1.00	1.25
1967	7,304,000	0.35	0.50	0.75	1.00	1.25
1968	2,252,000	0.35	0.50	0.75	1.00	1.25
1969	2,300,000	0.35	0.50	0.75	1.00	1.25

KM# 32 50 PAISA

5.00 g., Copper-Nickel, 22 mm. **Obv:** Crescent and star above tughra **Rev:** Value below flowers **Edge:** Reeded

Date	Mintage	VF20	XF40	MS60	MS63	MS65
1969	8,268,000	0.35	0.50	0.75	1.00	1.25
1970	9,160,000	0.35	0.50	0.75	1.00	1.25
1971	4,670,000	0.35	0.50	0.75	1.00	1.25
1972	4,900,000	0.35	0.50	0.75	1.00	1.25
1974	1,128,000	0.35	0.50	0.75	1.00	1.25

KM# 38 50 PAISA

5.00 g., Copper-Nickel, 23 mm. **Obv:** Crescent within monument with star at upper left **Rev:** Value within circle and designed wreath **Edge:** Reeded **Note:** Varieties in date size exist.

Date	Mintage	VF20	XF40	MS60	MS63	MS65
1975	9,180,000	0.35	0.50	0.75	1.00	1.25
1976	4,528,000	0.35	0.50	0.75	1.00	1.25
1977	5,548,000	0.35	0.50	0.75	1.00	1.25
1978	18,252,000	0.35	0.50	0.75	1.00	1.25
1979	14,596,000	0.35	0.50	0.75	1.00	1.25
1980	22,332,000	0.35	0.50	0.75	1.00	1.25
1981	13,552,000	0.35	0.50	0.75	1.00	1.25

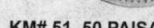

KM# 39 50 PAISA

5.83 g., Copper-Nickel, 24 mm. **Subject:** 100th Anniversary - Birth of Mohammad Ali Jinnah **Obv:** Value within circle and designed wreath **Rev:** Bust facing flanked by dates **Edge:** Reeded

Date	Mintage	VF20	XF40	MS60	MS63	MS65
1976	5,600,000	0.50	1.00	1.50	2.00	2.50

KM# 51 50 PAISA

5.00 g., Copper-Nickel, 23 mm. **Subject:** 1,400th Hejira Anniversary **Obv:** Crescent and star above design **Rev:** Value within wreath **Edge:** Reeded

Date	Mintage	VF20	XF40	MS60	MS63	MS65
AH1401	456,000	0.75	1.25	1.75	2.25	2.75

KM# 54 50 PAISA

4.00 g., Copper-Nickel, 21.1 mm. **Obv:** Crescent, star and date above sprigs **Rev:** Value within circle and leaf wreath **Edge:** Reeded

Date	Mintage	VF20	XF40	MS60	MS63	MS65
1981	4,612,000	0.35	0.50	0.75	1.00	1.25
1982	15,844,000	0.35	0.50	0.75	1.00	1.25
1983	9,608,000	0.35	0.50	0.75	1.00	1.25
1984	17,520,000	0.35	0.50	0.75	1.00	1.25
1985	20,144,000	0.35	0.50	0.75	1.00	1.25
1986	14,116,000	0.35	0.50	0.75	1.00	1.25
1987	23,044,000	0.35	0.50	0.75	1.00	1.25
1988	37,140,000	0.35	0.50	0.75	1.00	1.25
1989	33,956,000	0.35	0.50	0.75	1.00	1.25
1990	27,664,000	0.35	0.50	0.75	1.00	1.25
1991	30,376,000	0.35	0.50	0.75	1.00	1.25
1992	36,812,000	0.35	0.50	0.75	1.00	1.25
1993	37,079,000	0.35	0.50	0.75	1.00	1.25
1994	21,356,000	0.35	0.50	0.75	1.00	1.25
1995	35,968,000	0.35	0.50	0.75	1.00	1.25
1996	72,000	0.35	0.50	0.75	1.00	1.25

KM# 45 RUPEE

7.50 g., Copper-Nickel, 27.5 mm. **Subject:** Islamic Summit Conference **Obv:** Islamic summit minar flanked by designs **Rev:** Design within inner circle **Edge:** Reeded

Date	Mintage	VF20	XF40	MS60	MS63	MS65
1977	5,074,000	0.75	1.00	1.50	2.00	2.50

KM# 46 RUPEE

7.50 g., Copper-Nickel, 27.5 mm. **Subject:** 100th Anniversary - Birth of Allama Mohammad Iqbal **Obv:** Value and date above sprigs **Rev:** Head leaning on arm facing 1/4 left **Edge:** Reeded

Date	Mintage	VF20	XF40	MS60	MS63	MS65
1977	5,000,000	0.75	1.00	1.50	2.00	2.50

KM# 57.1 RUPEE

6.50 g., Copper-Nickel, 26.5 mm. **Obv:** Crescent, star and date above sprigs **Rev:** Value within sprigs **Edge:** Reeded

Date	Mintage	VF20	XF40	MS60	MS63	MS65
1979	—	0.40	0.55	0.80	1.15	1.50
1980	14,522,000	0.40	0.55	0.80	1.15	1.50
1981	12,038,000	0.40	0.55	0.80	1.15	1.50

KM# 55 RUPEE

6.50 g., Copper-Nickel, 26.5 mm. **Subject:** 1,400th Hejira Anniversary **Obv:** Crescent and star above design **Rev:** Value within wreath **Edge:** Reeded

Date	Mintage	VF20	XF40	MS60	MS63	MS65
AH1401	4,233,000	0.75	1.25	2.00	2.50	3.00

KM# 56 RUPEE

6.00 g., Copper-Nickel, 25 mm. **Series:** World Food Day **Obv:** Crescent, star and date above sprigs **Rev:** F.A.O. logo within circle **Edge:** Reeded

Date	Mintage	VF20	XF40	MS60	MS63	MS65
1981	1,267,000	0.75	1.50	2.25	3.00	3.50

KM# 57.2 RUPEE

6.00 g., Copper-Nickel, 25 mm. **Obv:** Crescent, star and date above sprigs **Rev:** Value within sprigs **Edge:** Reeded

Date	Mintage	VF20	XF40	MS60	MS63	MS65
1981	4,084,000	0.40	0.55	0.80	1.15	1.50
1982	27,878,000	0.35	0.50	0.75	1.00	1.25
1983	18,746,000	0.35	0.50	0.75	1.00	1.25
1984	14,562,000	0.35	0.50	0.75	1.00	1.25
1985	4,934,000	0.40	0.55	0.80	1.15	1.50
1986	11,840,000	0.35	0.50	0.75	1.00	1.25
1987	50,416,000	0.35	0.50	0.75	1.00	1.25
1988	10,644,000	0.35	0.50	0.75	1.00	1.25
1990	9,344,000	0.35	0.50	0.75	1.00	1.25
1991	1,394,000	0.35	0.50	0.75	1.00	1.25

KM# 62 RUPEE
4.00 g., Bronze, 20 mm. **Obv:** Head of Jinnah facing left **Rev:** Mosque above value **Edge:** Reeded

Date	Mintage	VF20	XF40	MS60	MS63	MS65
1998	42,292,000	0.25	0.35	0.50	0.65	0.75
1999	150,128,000	0.25	0.35	0.50	0.65	0.75
2000	72,600,000	0.25	0.35	0.50	0.65	0.75

KM# 63 2 RUPEES
4.00 g., Nickel-Brass, 22.5 mm. **Obv:** Crescent, star and date above sprigs **Rev:** Mosque **Edge:** Reeded

Date	Mintage	VF20	XF40	MS60	MS63	MS65
2014	—	0.25	0.35	0.50	0.65	0.75
2015	—	0.25	0.35	0.50	0.65	0.75

KM# 64 2 RUPEES
5.00 g., Nickel-Brass, 22.5 mm. **Obv:** Crescent, star and date above sprigs **Rev:** Value below mosque and clouds **Edge:** Reeded

Date	Mintage	VF20	XF40	MS60	MS63	MS65
1998	—	0.30	0.45	0.65	0.85	1.00
1999	—	—	—	1.00	1.50	2.50

KM# 59 5 RUPEES
20.00 g., Copper, 35 mm. **Subject:** United Nations 50th Year **Obv:** Crescent and star above grain sprigs **Rev:** 50, UN logo **Edge:** Reeded **Note:** Four die varieties are reported to exist.

Date	Mintage	VF20	XF40	MS60	MS63	MS65
2012	—	0.30	0.45	0.65	0.85	1.00

KM# 61 10 RUPEES
10.00 g., Copper-Nickel, 26 mm. **Subject:** 25th Anniversary - Pakistan's Senate **Obv:** Crescent, star and date above sprigs **Rev:** Shield within sprigs above banner and dates to left of numeral 25 **Edge:** Reeded

Date	Mintage	VF20	XF40	MS60	MS63	MS65
1998	100,000	—	—	3.00	4.50	6.50

KM# 60 50 RUPEES
20.00 g., Copper-Nickel, 35 mm. **Subject:** 50th Anniversary - National Independence **Obv:** Star and crescent **Rev:** Flag and dates **Edge:** Reeded

Date	Mintage	VF20	XF40	MS60	MS63	MS65
1997	500,000	—	—	3.50	5.00	7.50

KM# 40 100 RUPEES
28.28 g., 0.925 Silver 0.841 oz. ASW, 38.6 mm. **Series:** Conservation **Obv:** Crescent within monument with star at upper left **Rev:** Tropogan pheasant

Date	Mintage	VF20	XF40	MS60	MS63	MS65
1976	5,120	—	—	—	35.00	45.00
1976	5,837	PF63 40.00	PF65 50.00			

KM# 41 100 RUPEES
20.44 g., 0.925 Silver 0.6079 oz. ASW, 36 mm. **Subject:** 100th Anniversary - Birth of Mohammad Ali Jinnah **Obv:** Crescent and star **Rev:** Bust facing flanked by dates

Date	Mintage	VF20	XF40	MS60	MS63	MS65
ND-1976	1,300	—	—	—	45.00	50.00
ND-1976	2,800	PF63 60.00	PF65 75.00			

KM# 47 100 RUPEES
20.44 g., 0.925 Silver 0.6079 oz. ASW, 36 mm. **Subject:** Islamic Summit Conference **Obv:** Islamic building **Rev:** Islamic summit minar

Date	Mintage	VF20	XF40	MS60	MS63	MS65
1977	1,500	—	—	—	45.00	50.00
1977	2,500	PF63 55.00	PF65 65.00			

KM# 48 100 RUPEES
20.44 g., 0.925 Silver 0.6079 oz. ASW, 36 mm. **Subject:** 100th Anniversary - Birth of Allama Mohammad Iqbal **Obv:** Value and date above sprigs **Rev:** Head leaning on hand divides dates

Date	Mintage	VF20	XF40	MS60	MS63	MS65
1977	3,000	—	—	—	45.00	50.00
1977	300	PF65 225				

KM# 42 150 RUPEES
35.00 g., 0.925 Silver 1.0409 oz. ASW, 42 mm. **Series:** Conservation **Obv:** Crescent within monument with star at upper left **Rev:** Gavial crocodile and value

Date	Mintage	VF20	XF40	MS60	MS63	MS65
1976	5,119	—	—	—	55.00	70.00
1976	5,637	PF65 90.00				

KM# 43 500 RUPEES
4.50 g., 0.917 Gold 0.1327 oz. AGW, 19 mm. **Subject:** 100th Anniversary - Birth of Mohammad Ali Jinnah **Obv:** Crescent and star **Rev:** Bust facing flanked by dates

Date	Mintage	VF20	XF40	MS60	MS63	MS65
ND-1976	500	—	—	—	235	250
ND-1976	500	PF65 275				

KM# 49 500 RUPEES
3.64 g., 0.917 Gold 0.1073 oz. AGW, 19 mm. **Subject:** 100th Anniversary - Birth of Allama Mohammad Iqbal **Obv:** Value and date above sprigs **Rev:** Head leaning on hand flanked by dates

Date	Mintage	VF20	XF40	MS60	MS63	MS65
1977	500	—	—	—	195	225
1977	200	PF65 285				

KM# 50 1000 RUPEES
9.00 g., 0.917 Gold 0.2653 oz. AGW, 25 mm. **Subject:** Islamic Summit Conference **Obv:** Islamic summit minar **Rev:** Design within center circle

Date	Mintage	VF20	XF40	MS60	MS63	MS65
1977	400	—	—	—	485	600
1977	400	PF65 725				

KM# 44 3000 RUPEES
33.44 g., 0.900 Gold 0.9675 oz. AGW, 39 mm. **Obv:** Crescent within monument with star at upper left **Rev:** Astor Markhor and value

Date	Mintage	VF20	XF40	MS60	MS63	MS65
1976	902	—	—	—	—	1,650
1976	273	PF65 2,200				

PATTERNS

Including off-metal strikes

KM#	Date	Mintage	Identification	Mkt Val
Pn1	1947	—	Rupee. Nickel Alloy. Toughra within circle. Crescent and star, dates flanking.	—
Pn2	1947	—	Rupee. Nickel Alloy. Toughra within circle, dates below. Crescent with star.	—
Pn3	1947	—	Rupee. Nickel Alloy. Crescent and star, denomination and wreath below. Toughra, date at right, wreath below.	—
Pn4	ND-1995	—	Rupee. Copper Alloys. Crescent and star, wheat ears below. UN logo, large 50.	—

MINT SETS

KM#	Date	Mintage	Identification	Issue Price	Mkt Val
MS1	1948 (7)	—	KM1-7	—	12.50
MS2	1948, 1951, 1953 (8)	—	KM5-7 (1948), 11 (1951), 12-15 (1953). Restrikes have been issued.	4.00	13.50
MS3	1948, 1961 (6)	—	KM5-7 (1948), 17, 19, 21 (1961). Restrikes have been issued.	2.00	11.00
MS4	1948, 1964 (7)	—	KM7 (1948), 22-27 (1964). Restrikes have been issued.	2.00	10.00
MS5	1948, 1975 (7)	—	KM7 (1948), 33-38 (1975). Restrikes have been issued.	—	10.00
MS6	1951, 1953 (5)	—	KM11 (1951), 12-15 (1953). Restrikes have been issued.	—	8.00
MS7	1961 (3)	—	KM17, 19, 21	—	4.00
MS8	1976 (2)	—	KM41, 43	63.00	275
MS9	1976 (2)	—	KM40, 42	—	110
MS10	1977 (2)	—	KM47, 50	—	550

PROOF SETS

KM#	Date	Mintage	Identification	Issue Price	Mkt Val
PS1	1948 (7)	5,000	KM1-7	4.00	16.50
PS3	1950 (3)	—	KM8-10	—	60.00
PS4	1953 (5)	—	KM11-15	2.00	11.50
PS5	1961 (3)	—	KM17, 19, 21	1.00	5.00
PS6	1976 (2)	—	KM41, 43	90.50	320
PS7	1976 (2)	—	KM40, 42	—	125
PS8	1977 (2)	—	KM47, 50	—	775

PALAU

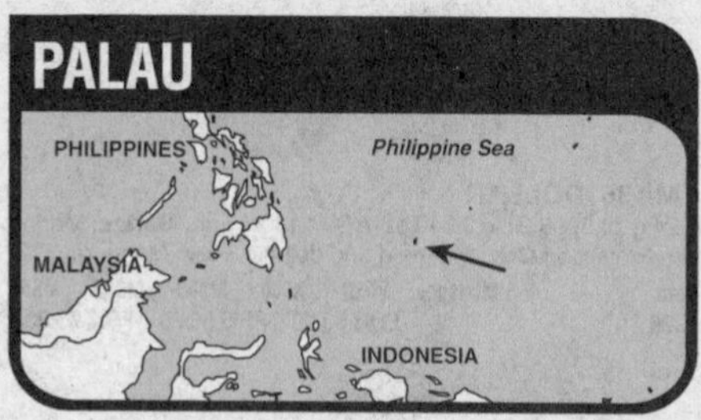

The Republic of Palau, a group of about 100 islands and islets, is generally considered a part of the Caroline Islands. It is located about 1,000 miles southeast of Manila and about the same distance southwest of Saipan and has an area of 179 sq. mi. and a population of 12,116. Capital: Koror.

The islands were administered as part of the Caroline Islands under the Spanish regime until they were sold to Germany in 1899. Seized by Japan in 1914, it was mandated to them in 1919 and Koror was made the administrative headquarters of all the Japanese mandated islands in 1921. During World War II the islands were taken by the Allies, in 1944, with the heaviest fighting taking place on Peleliu. They became part of the U.S. Trust Territory of the Pacific Islands in 1947. In 1980 they became internally self-governing and independent. Control over foreign policy, except defense, was approved in 1986. Palau became an independent nation in 1995.

REPUBLIC

MILLED COINAGE

KM# 1 DOLLAR
Copper-Nickel **Subject:** Year of Marine Life Protection **Obv:** Sailboat, mermaid and value within beaded circle **Rev:** Multicolor design within beaded circle

Date	Mintage	VF20	XF40	MS60	MS63	MS65
1992	Est. 50000	PF65 25.00				

KM# 3 DOLLAR
Copper-Nickel **Series:** Marine Life Protection **Obv:** Mermaid sitting upright **Rev:** Multicolor ocean scene

Date	Mintage	VF20	XF40	MS60	MS63	MS65
1993	50,000	PF65 27.00				

KM# 5 DOLLAR
Copper-Nickel **Series:** Marine Life Protection **Obv:** Ship, mermaid and value **Rev:** Multicolor ocean scene

Date	Mintage	VF20	XF40	MS60	MS63	MS65
1994	50,000	PF65 20.00				

KM# 8 DOLLAR
Copper-Nickel **Subject:** Independence **Obv:** Neptune and mermaid **Rev:** Multicolor ocean scene with a nautilus

Date	Mintage	VF20	XF40	MS60	MS63	MS65
1994	50,000	PF65 25.00				

KM# 11 DOLLAR
Copper-Nickel **Subject:** Marine Life Protection **Obv:** Mermaid with harp **Rev:** Multicolor seahorse and lion fish

Date	Mintage	VF20	XF40	MS60	MS63	MS65
1995	30,000	PF65 25.00				

KM# 14 DOLLAR
Copper-Nickel **Subject:** United Nations 50th Anniversary **Obv:** Mermaid above seahorses, value below **Rev:** Multicolor ocean scene with emblem on bottom

Date	Mintage	VF20	XF40	MS60	MS63	MS65
1995	30,000	PF65 25.00				

KM# 25 DOLLAR
Copper-Nickel **Series:** Marine Life Protection **Obv:** Two mermaids **Rev:** Multicolor high-relief dolphin

Date	Mintage	VF20	XF40	MS60	MS63	MS65
1998	13,000	PF65 25.00				

KM# 26 DOLLAR
1.24 g., 0.9999 Gold 0.040 oz. AGW, 13.94 mm. **Series:** Marine Life Protection **Obv:** Two mermaids **Rev:** Jumping dolphin

Date	Mintage	VF20	XF40	MS60	MS63	MS65
1998	10,000	PF63 60.00	PF65 65.00	PF67 75.00		

KM# 30 DOLLAR
Copper-Nickel **Series:** Marine Life Protection **Obv:** Mermaid with cockatoo **Rev:** Multicolor high-relief turtle

Date	Mintage	VF20	XF40	MS60	MS63	MS65
1998	—	PF65 35.00				

KM# 31 DOLLAR
1.24 g., 0.9999 Gold 0.040 oz. AGW, 13.94 mm. **Series:** Marine Life Protection **Obv:** Mermaid holding cockatoo **Rev:** Sea turtle

Date	Mintage	VF20	XF40	MS60	MS63	MS65
1998	—	PF63 60.00	PF65 65.00	PF67 75.00		

KM# 35 DOLLAR
Copper-Nickel **Series:** Marine Life Protection **Obv:** Mermaid and dolphin **Rev:** Multicolor high-relief manta ray

Date	Mintage	VF20	XF40	MS60	MS63	MS65
1999	—	PF65 32.00				

KM# 36 DOLLAR
1.24 g., 0.9999 Gold 0.040 oz. AGW, 13.94 mm. **Series:** Marine Life Protection **Obv:** Mermaid and dolphin **Rev:** Manta ray

Date	Mintage	VF20	XF40	MS60	MS63	MS65
1999	—	PF63 60.00	PF65 65.00	PF67 75.00		

KM# 40 DOLLAR
Copper-Nickel **Series:** Marine Life Protection **Obv:** Mermaid and sailboat **Rev:** Multicolor shark

Date	Mintage	VF20	XF40	MS60	MS63	MS65
1999	—	PF65 27.50				

KM# 82 DOLLAR
1.24 g., 0.9999 Gold 0.040 oz. AGW, 13.94 mm. **Obv:** Seated Mermaid and sailboat **Rev:** Shark **Edge:** Reeded

Date	Mintage	VF20	XF40	MS60	MS63	MS65
1999	—	PF63 60.00	PF65 65.00	PF67 75.00		

KM# 43 DOLLAR
26.65 g., Copper-Nickel **Series:** Marine Life Protection **Obv:** Mermaid and ship **Rev:** Multicolor fish and coral

Date	Mintage	VF20	XF40	MS60	MS63	MS65
2000	—	PF65 22.50				

KM# 58 DOLLAR
26.80 g., Copper-Nickel, 37.2 mm. **Obv:** Diving Mermaid **Rev:** Multicolor jumping swordfish **Edge:** Reeded

Date	Mintage	VF20	XF40	MS60	MS63	MS65
2000	—	PF65 27.50				

KM# 59 DOLLAR
26.80 g., Copper-Nickel, 37.2 mm. **Obv:** Seated Mermaid **Rev:** Multicolor fish and wreck **Edge:** Reeded

Date	Mintage	VF20	XF40	MS60	MS63	MS65
2000	—	PF65 22.50				

KM# 83 DOLLAR
1.24 g., 0.9999 Gold 0.040 oz. AGW, 13.94 mm. **Obv:** Diving Mermaid **Rev:** Jumping Swordfish **Edge:** Reeded

Date	Mintage	VF20	XF40	MS60	MS63	MS65
2000	—	PF63 60.00	PF65 65.00	PF67 75.00		

KM# 84 DOLLAR
1.24 g., 0.9999 Gold 0.040 oz. AGW, 13.94 mm. **Obv:** Seated Mermaid **Rev:** Multicolor fish and wreck **Edge:** Reeded

Date	Mintage	VF20	XF40	MS60	MS63	MS65
2000	—	PF63 60.00	PF65 65.00	PF67 75.00		

KM# 85 DOLLAR
1.24 g., 0.9999 Gold 0.040 oz. AGW, 13.94 mm. **Obv:** Seated Mermaid and ship **Rev:** Multicolor fish and coral **Edge:** Reeded

Date	Mintage	VF20	XF40	MS60	MS63	MS65
2000	—	PF63 60.00	PF65 65.00	PF67 75.00		

KM# 2 5 DOLLARS
25.00 g., 0.900 Silver 0.7234 oz. ASW **Series:** Marine Life Protection **Obv:** Neptune and spear **Rev:** Multicolor ocean scene

Date	Mintage	VF20	XF40	MS60	MS63	MS65
1992	Est. 6000	PF65 60.00	PF67 70.00			

KM# 4 5 DOLLARS
25.00 g., 0.900 Silver 0.7234 oz. ASW **Series:** Marine Life Protection **Obv:** Neptune in shell, horses, dolphin and value **Rev:** Multicolor ocean scene

Date	Mintage	VF20	XF40	MS60	MS63	MS65
1993	6,000	PF65 60.00	PF67 70.00			

KM# 6 5 DOLLARS
25.00 g., 0.900 Silver 0.7234 oz. ASW **Series:** Marine Life Protection **Obv:** Neptune and seascape **Rev:** Multicolor ocean scene

Date	Mintage	VF20	XF40	MS60	MS63	MS65
1994	10,000	PF65 55.00	PF67 65.00			

KM# 9 5 DOLLARS
25.00 g., 0.900 Silver 0.7234 oz. ASW **Series:** Independence **Obv:** Mermaid and Neptune **Rev:** Nautilus and seascape

Date	Mintage	VF20	XF40	MS60	MS63	MS65
1994	—	PF65 60.00	PF67 70.00			

KM# 12 5 DOLLARS
25.00 g., 0.900 Silver 0.7234 oz. ASW **Series:** Marine Life Protection **Rev:** Seahorse and lion fish

Date	Mintage	VF20	XF40	MS60	MS63	MS65
1995	7,500	PF65 60.00	PF67 70.00			

KM# 15 5 DOLLARS
25.00 g., 0.900 Silver 0.7234 oz. ASW **Subject:** United Nations 50th Anniversary **Obv:** Mermaid above seahorses **Rev:** Multicolor ocean scene

Date	Mintage	VF20	XF40	MS60	MS63	MS65
1995	5,500	PF65 55.00	PF67 65.00			

KM# 27 5 DOLLARS
24.64 g., 0.900 Silver 0.713 oz. ASW **Series:** Marine Life Protection **Obv:** Neptune and ship **Rev:** Multicolor dolphin jumping **Edge:** Reeded

Date	Mintage	VF20	XF40	MS60	MS63	MS65
1998	—	PF65 55.00	PF67 60.00			

KM# 32 5 DOLLARS
24.64 g., 0.900 Silver 0.713 oz. ASW **Series:** Marine Life Protection **Obv:** Neptune and two dolphins **Rev:** Multicolor sea turtle

Date	Mintage	VF20	XF40	MS60	MS63	MS65
1998	—	PF65 55.00	PF67 60.00			

KM# 46 5 DOLLARS
24.64 g., 0.900 Silver 0.713 oz. ASW **Series:** Marine Life Protection **Obv:** Mermaid and sailboat **Rev:** Multicolor shark

Date	Mintage	VF20	XF40	MS60	MS63	MS65
1998	—	PF65 50.00	PF67 55.00			
1999	—	PF65 50.00	PF67 55.00			

KM# 16 5 DOLLARS
25.00 g., 0.925 Silver 0.7435 oz. ASW **Series:** International Coins **Subject:** Spanish 5 Peseta - 1896-1899 **Obv:** Crowned Spanish arms **Rev:** Young head left

Date	Mintage	VF20	XF40	MS60	MS63	MS65
1999	—	PF63 27.00	PF65 30.00	PF67 35.00		

KM# 16a 5 DOLLARS
Gold **Series:** International Coins **Subject:** Spanish 5 Peseta - 1896-1899 **Obv:** Crowned Spanish arms **Rev:** Young head left

Date	Mintage	VF20	XF40	MS60	MS63	MS65
1999	5	PF67 2,250				

KM# 17 5 DOLLARS
25.00 g., 0.925 Silver 0.7435 oz. ASW **Series:** International Coins **Subject:** Prussian 5 Mark - 1891-1908 **Obv:** Crowned arms **Rev:** Head right

Date	Mintage	VF20	XF40	MS60	MS63	MS65
1999	—	PF63 25.00	PF65 30.00	PF67 35.00		

KM# 18 5 DOLLARS
25.00 g., 0.925 Silver 0.7435 oz. ASW **Series:** International Coins **Subject:** German East Africa **Obv:** Elephant above value **Rev:** Uniformed bust of Paul Emil von Lettow-Vorbeck facing, colonial arms at lower right

Date	Mintage	VF20	XF40	MS60	MS63	MS65
1999	—	PF63 30.00	PF65 35.00	PF67 40.00		

KM# 19 5 DOLLARS
25.00 g., 0.925 Silver 0.7435 oz. ASW **Series:** International Coins **Subject:** German Cameroon **Obv:** Kaiser Wilhelm I facing right **Rev:** Germania and colonial arms

Date	Mintage	VF20	XF40	MS60	MS63	MS65
1999	—	PF63 30.00	PF65 35.00	PF67 40.00		

KM# 20 5 DOLLARS
25.00 g., 0.925 Silver 0.7435 oz. ASW **Series:** International Coins **Subject:** Kiau Chau **Obv:** Ships in harbor **Rev:** Emblem based on 1909 coinage

Date	Mintage	VF20	XF40	MS60	MS63	MS65
1999	—	PF63 30.00	PF65 35.00	PF67 40.00		

KM# 21 5 DOLLARS
25.00 g., 0.925 Silver 0.7435 oz. ASW **Series:** International Coins **Subject:** German New Guinea **Obv:** Large ship **Rev:** Colonial arms

Date	Mintage	VF20	XF40	MS60	MS63	MS65
1999	—	PF63 30.00	PF65 35.00	PF67 40.00		

KM# 22 5 DOLLARS
25.00 g., 0.925 Silver 0.7435 oz. ASW **Series:** International Coins **Subject:** German Samoa **Obv:** Armored bust left of Kaiser Wilhelm II facing left **Rev:** Colonial arms

Date	Mintage	VF20	XF40	MS60	MS63	MS65
1999	—	PF63 30.00	PF65 35.00	PF67 40.00		

KM# 23 5 DOLLARS
25.00 g., 0.925 Silver 0.7435 oz. ASW **Series:** International Coins **Subject:** German South West Africa **Obv:** Whilhelm II portrait from Prussian 5 Mark coin of 1913-1914 **Rev:** Colonial arms and trooper on camel

Date	Mintage	VF20	XF40	MS60	MS63	MS65
1999	—	PF63 30.00	PF65 35.00	PF67 40.00		

KM# 24 5 DOLLARS
25.00 g., 0.925 Silver 0.7435 oz. ASW **Series:** International Coins **Subject:** German Togo **Obv:** Seated Germania **Rev:** Colonial arms

Date	Mintage	VF20	XF40	MS60	MS63	MS65
1999	—	PF63 25.00	PF65 30.00	PF67 35.00		

KM# 37 5 DOLLARS
24.64 g., 0.900 Silver 0.713 oz. ASW **Series:** Marine Life Protection **Obv:** Mermaid in profile, sailboat **Rev:** Multicolor manta ray

Date	Mintage	VF20	XF40	MS60	MS63	MS65
1999	—	PF65 55.00	PF67 60.00			

KM# 48 5 DOLLARS
24.64 g., 0.900 Silver 0.713 oz. ASW **Series:** Marine Life Protection **Obv:** Neptune seated **Rev:** Multicolor fish and coral

Date	Mintage	VF20	XF40	MS60	MS63	MS65
2000	—	PF65 50.00	PF67 55.00			

KM# 51 5 DOLLARS
24.94 g., 0.900 Silver 0.7217 oz. ASW, 38.6 mm. **Subject:** Our World - Our Future **Obv:** Half-length dancer with leis **Rev:** Multicolor world map **Edge:** Reeded

Date	Mintage	VF20	XF40	MS60	MS63	MS65
2000	—	PF65 35.00	PF67 40.00			

KM# 73 5 DOLLARS
25.00 g., 0.900 Silver 0.7234 oz. ASW, 37.2 mm. **Subject:** Marine Life Protection **Obv:** Neptune seated **Rev:** Multicolor jumping swordfish **Edge:** Reeded

Date	Mintage	VF20	XF40	MS60	MS63	MS65
2000	—	PF65 60.00	PF67 65.00			

KM# 74 5 DOLLARS
25.00 g., 0.900 Silver 0.7234 oz. ASW, 37.2 mm. **Subject:** Marine Life Protection **Obv:** Neptune behind ancient ship **Rev:** Multicolor fish and wreck **Edge:** Reeded

Date	Mintage	VF20	XF40	MS60	MS63	MS65
2000	—	PF65 60.00	PF67 65.00			

KM# 112 10 DOLLARS
1.49 g., 0.999 Gold 0.0479 oz. AGW, 11 x 19 mm. **Obv:** Value, date and inscription **Rev:** Mermaid **Edge:** Plain **Shape:** Rectangle

Date	Mintage	VF20	XF40	MS60	MS63	MS65
1995	—	PF63 80.00	PF65 90.00	PF67 100		

KM# 7 20 DOLLARS
155.52 g., 0.999 Silver 4.995 oz. ASW, 63.9 mm. **Subject:** Marine - Life Protection **Rev:** Multicolor ocean scene **Note:** Illustration reduced.

Date	Mintage	VF20	XF40	MS60	MS63	MS65
1994	3,000	PF65 145	PF67 165			

KM# 42 20 DOLLARS
155.52 g., 0.999 Silver 4.995 oz. ASW, 63.9 mm. **Subject:** Independence - October 1994 **Obv:** Mermaid and Neptune **Rev:** Multicolor seascape **Note:** Illustration reduced.

Date	Mintage	VF20	XF40	MS60	MS63	MS65
ND-1994	—	PF65 165	PF67 185			

KM# 13 20 DOLLARS
155.52 g., 0.999 Silver 4.995 oz. ASW **Series:** Marine Life Protection **Obv:** Seated mermaid with harp **Rev:** Seahorse and lion fish **Note:** Similar to Dollar, KM#11.

Date	Mintage	VF20	XF40	MS60	MS63	MS65
1995	3,000	PF65 145	PF67 165			

KM# 41 20 DOLLARS

155.52 g., 0.999 Silver 4.995 oz. ASW, 64.5 mm. **Series:** 50th Anniversary - United Nations Member **Obv:** Mermaid driving quadriga **Rev:** Multicolor seascape, globe of earth below **Note:** Illustration reduced.

Date	Mintage	VF20	XF40	MS60	MS63	MS65
1995	—	PF65 165	PF67 185			

KM# 28 20 DOLLARS

155.52 g., 0.999 Silver 4.995 oz. ASW **Series:** Marine Life Protection **Obv:** Two mermaids **Rev:** Multicolor high-relief dolphin **Note:** Similar to Dollar, KM#25.

Date	Mintage	VF20	XF40	MS60	MS63	MS65
1998	700	PF65 165	PF67 185			

KM# 33 20 DOLLARS

155.52 g., 0.999 Silver 4.995 oz. ASW **Series:** Marine Life Protection **Obv:** Mermaid with cockatoo **Rev:** Multicolor high-relief turtle **Note:** Similar to Dollar, KM#30.

Date	Mintage	VF20	XF40	MS60	MS63	MS65
1998	500	PF65 175	PF67 195			

KM# 38 20 DOLLARS

155.52 g., 0.999 Silver 4.995 oz. ASW **Series:** Marine Life Protection **Obv:** Mermaid with dolphin **Rev:** Multicolor high-relief manta ray **Note:** Similar to Dollar, KM#35.

Date	Mintage	VF20	XF40	MS60	MS63	MS65
1999	500	PF65 175	PF67 195			

KM# 49 20 DOLLARS

155.52 g., 0.999 Silver 4.995 oz. ASW **Series:** Marine Life Protection **Obv:** Seated mermaid and sailboat **Rev:** Multicolor shark **Edge:** Reeded

Date	Mintage	VF20	XF40	MS60	MS63	MS65
1999	500	PF65 175	PF67 195			

KM# 50 20 DOLLARS

155.52 g., 0.999 Silver 4.995 oz. ASW **Subject:** Marine - Life Protection **Obv:** Mermaid and ship **Rev:** Multicolor fish and coral **Note:** Illustration reduced.

Date	Mintage	VF20	XF40	MS60	MS63	MS65
2000	—	PF65 175	PF67 195			

KM# 54 20 DOLLARS

155.52 g., 0.999 Silver 4.995 oz. ASW, 64.5 mm. **Subject:** Marine Life Protection **Obv:** Seated mermaid **Rev:** Multicolor sunken ship and fish scene **Edge:** Reeded **Note:** Illustration reduced.

Date	Mintage	VF20	XF40	MS60	MS63	MS65
2000	500	PF65 175	PF67 195			

KM# 55 20 DOLLARS

155.52 g., 0.999 Silver 4.995 oz. ASW, 64.5 mm. **Subject:** Marine Life Protection **Obv:** Diving mermaid **Rev:** Multicolor jumping swordfish scene **Edge:** Reeded

Date	Mintage	VF20	XF40	MS60	MS63	MS65
2000	500	PF65 175	PF67 195			

KM# 10 200 DOLLARS

31.10 g., 0.999 Gold 0.999 oz. AGW **Subject:** Independence **Obv:** Mermaid and Neptune **Rev:** Nautilus and seascape

Date	Mintage	VF20	XF40	MS60	MS63	MS65
1994	—	PF65 1,650	PF67 1,750			

KM# 44 200 DOLLARS

31.11 g., 0.999 Gold 0.999 oz. AGW **Obv:** Neptune **Rev:** Palau seahorse

Date	Mintage	VF20	XF40	MS60	MS63	MS65
1995	Est. 500	PF65 1,700	PF67 1,800			

KM# 45 200 DOLLARS

31.11 g., 0.999 Gold 0.999 oz. AGW **Obv:** Neptune **Rev:** Dolphin and coral

Date	Mintage	VF20	XF40	MS60	MS63	MS65
1995	—	PF65 1,700	PF67 1,800			

KM# 29 200 DOLLARS

31.10 g., 0.999 Gold 0.999 oz. AGW **Subject:** Marine - Life Protection **Obv:** Two mermaids **Rev:** Multicolor high-relief dolphin **Note:** Similar to Dollar, KM#25.

Date	Mintage	VF20	XF40	MS60	MS63	MS65
1998	200	PF65 1,650	PF67 1,750			

KM# 34 200 DOLLARS

31.10 g., 0.999 Gold 0.999 oz. AGW **Subject:** Marine - Life Protection **Obv:** Mermaid with cockatoo **Rev:** Multicolor high-relief turtle **Note:** Similar to Dollar, KM#30.

Date	Mintage	VF20	XF40	MS60	MS63	MS65
1998	—	PF65 1,650	PF67 1,750			

KM# 39 200 DOLLARS

31.10 g., 0.999 Gold 0.999 oz. AGW **Subject:** Marine - Life Protection **Obv:** Mermaid with dolphin **Rev:** Multicolor high-relief manta ray **Note:** Similar to Dollar, KM#35.

Date	Mintage	VF20	XF40	MS60	MS63	MS65
1999	—	PF65 1,650	PF67 1,750			

KM# 47 200 DOLLARS

31.11 g., 0.999 Gold 0.999 oz. AGW **Rev:** Shark

Date	Mintage	VF20	XF40	MS60	MS63	MS65
1999	—	PF65 1,700	PF67 1,800			

KM# 328 200 DOLLARS

31.11 g., 0.999 Gold 0.999 oz. AGW **Rev:** Firefish

Date	Mintage	VF20	XF40	MS60	MS63	MS65
2000	Est. 200	PF65 1,700	PF67 1,800			

KM# 329 200 DOLLARS

31.11 g., 0.999 Gold 0.999 oz. AGW **Rev:** Blue marlin

Date	Mintage	VF20	XF40	MS60	MS63	MS65
2000	—	PF65 1,700	PF67 1,800			

KM# 330 200 DOLLARS

31.11 g., 0.999 Gold 0.999 oz. AGW **Rev:** Butterfly fish and shipwreck

Date	Mintage	VF20	XF40	MS60	MS63	MS65
2000	Est. 200	PF65 1,700	PF67 1,800			

ESSAIS

Standard metals unless otherwise noted

KM#	Date	Mintage	Identification	Mkt Val
E1	1992	—	Dollar. 0.999. Gold. Seated mermaid and sailboat. Multicolor sea life. KM1.	1,850
E2	1992	—	5 Dollars. 0.999. Gold. Seated Neptune and ship. Multicolor sea life. Reeded. KM2.	1,850
E3	1995	30	Dollar. Silver. KM41.	175
E4	1995	30	5 Dollars. Copper-Nickel. KM41.	125
E5	1995	30	200 Dollars. Copper-Nickel. KM41.	145
E6	1995	30	200 Dollars. Silver. KM41.	210
E7	1998	20	Dollar. Silver. KM25.	170
E8	1998	20	5 Dollars. Copper-Nickel. KM25.	170
E9	1998	20	200 Dollars. Silver. KM25.	170
E10	1999	—	200 Dollars. Copper-Nickel. Shark, m/c.	325
E11	2000	—	200 Dollars. Copper-Nickel. 3 fish, m/c.	325

PROOF SETS

KM#	Date	Mintage	Identification	Issue Price	Mkt Val
PS1	1992 (2)	—	KME1, E2	—	3,700
PS2	1995 (4)	20	KME3, E4, E5, E6	—	675
PS3	1998 (3)	20	KME7, E8, E9	—	525

PALESTINE

Palestine, which corresponds to Canaan of the Bible, was settled by the Philistines about the 12th century B.C. and shortly thereafter was settled by the Jews who established the kingdoms of Israel and Judah. Because of its position as part of the land bridge connecting Asia and Africa, Palestine was invaded and conquered by nearly all of the historic empires of ancient Europe and Asia. In the16th century it became a part of the Ottoman Empire. After falling to the British in World War I, it, together with Transjordan, was mandated to Great Britain by the League of Nations, 1922.

For more than half a century prior to the termination of the British mandate over Palestine, 1948, Zionist leaders had sought to create a Jewish homeland for Jews who were dispersed throughout the world. For almost as long, Jews fleeing persecution had immigrated to Palestine. The Nazi persecutions of the 1930s and 1940s increased the Jewish movement to Palestine and generated international support for the creation of a Jewish state, first promulgated by the Balfour Declaration of 1917, which asserted British support for the endeavor. The state of Israel was proclaimed as the Jewish state in the territory that was Palestine. The remainder of that territory was occupied by Jordanian and Egyptian armies. Israel demonetized the coins of Palestine on Sept. 15, 1948, the Jordan government declared Palestine currency no longer legal tender on June 30, 1951, and Egypt declared it no longer legal tender in Gaza on June 9, 1951.

TITLES

فاسطين

Filastin

פלשתינה (א"י).

Paleshtina (E.I.)

MONETARY SYSTEM

1000 Mils = 1 Pound

BRITISH ADMINISTRATION

MIL COINAGE

KM# 1 MIL

3.20 g., Bronze, 21 mm. **Obv:** Inscription PALESTINE, in English, Hebrew and Arabic **Rev:** Value, plant **Edge:** Plain

Date	Mintage	F12	VF20	XF40	MS60	MS63
1927	10,000,000	2.00	3.00	6.00	15.00	30.00
1927	68	PF63 1,000				
1935	704,000	3.00	5.00	10.00	35.00	65.00
1937	1,200,000	3.00	5.00	28.00	125	250
1939	3,700,000	2.00	4.00	8.00	40.00	65.00
1939 Proof; rare	—	—	—	—	—	—
1940	396,000	25.00	50.00	75.00	200	325
1941	1,920,000	2.00	3.00	10.00	35.00	50.00
1942	4,480,000	2.00	3.00	5.00	25.00	40.00
1943	2,800,000	2.00	3.00	5.00	30.00	45.00
1944	1,400,000	3.00	4.00	6.00	30.00	42.00
1946	1,632,000	5.00	8.00	12.00	45.00	75.00
1946 Proof; rare	—	—	—	—	—	—
1947	2,880,000	—	—	—	10,000	—

Note: Only 5 known; The entire issue was to be melted down

KM# 2 2 MILS

7.80 g., Bronze, 28 mm. **Obv:** Inscription PALESTINE, in English, Hebrew and Arabic **Rev:** Value, plant **Edge:** Plain

Date	Mintage	F12	VF20	XF40	MS60	MS63
1927	5,000,000	2.00	3.00	6.00	35.00	50.00
1927	68	PF63 1,000				
1941	1,600,000	2.00	3.00	6.00	50.00	100
1941 Proof; rare	—	—	—	—	—	—
1942	2,400,000	2.00	3.00	6.00	40.00	80.00
1945	960,000	6.00	10.00	25.00	150	225
1946	960,000	10.00	17.00	45.00	175	300
1947	480,000	—	—	—	—	—

Note: The entire issue was melted down, but at least one is reported to be in the British Museum's collection

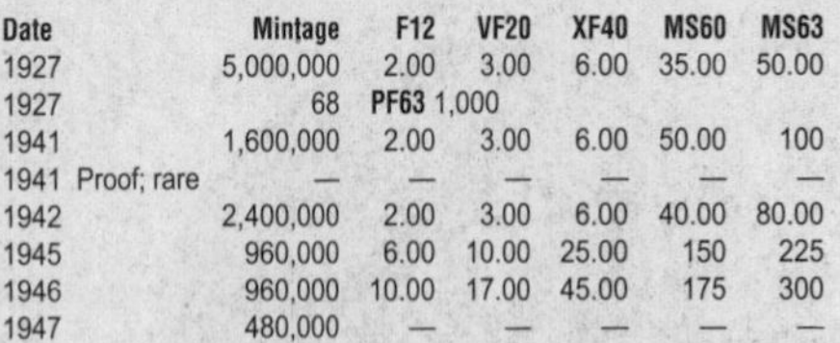

KM# 3 5 MILS

2.90 g., Copper-Nickel, 20 mm. **Obv:** Wreath around center hole, with enscription PALESTINE in English, Hebrew and Arabic **Rev:** Value above center hole **Edge:** Plain

Date	Mintage	F12	VF20	XF40	MS60	MS63
1927	10,000,000	3.00	5.00	8.00	40.00	65.00
1927	68	PF63 1,250				
1934	500,000	8.00	25.00	50.00	200	400
1935	2,700,000	3.00	5.00	10.00	75.00	150
1939	2,000,000	3.00	5.00	8.00	35.00	65.00
1939 Proof; rare	—	—	—	—	—	—
1941	400,000	12.00	40.00	70.00	250	500
1941 Proof; rare	—	—	—	—	—	—
1946	1,000,000	5.00	10.00	20.00	75.00	125
1946 Proof; rare	—	—	—	—	—	—
1947	1,000,000	—	—	—	—	25,000

Note: Almost the entire issue was melted down, with only 3 remaining pieces known to exist

KM# 3a 5 MILS

Bronze, 20 mm. **Obv:** Wreath around center hole, with inscription PALESTINE in English, Hebrew and Arabic **Rev:** Value above center hole **Edge:** Plain

Date	Mintage	F12	VF20	XF40	MS60	MS63
1942	2,700,000	4.00	7.00	12.00	75.00	150
1944	1,000,000	7.00	12.00	18.00	90.00	180

KM# 4 10 MILS

6.50 g., Copper-Nickel, 27 mm. **Obv:** Date above and below center hole, with inscription PALESTINE in English, Hebrew and Arabic **Rev:** Wreath around center hole with value above and below **Edge:** Plain

Date	Mintage	F12	VF20	XF40	MS60	MS63
1927	5,000,000	5.00	10.00	20.00	60.00	90.00
1927	68	PF63 1,250				
1933	500,000	12.00	30.00	75.00	400	600
1933 Proof; rare	—	—	—	—	—	—
1934	500,000	12.00	30.00	75.00	400	600
1934 Proof; rare	—	—	—	—	—	—
1935	1,150,000	5.00	15.00	50.00	300	500
1935 Proof; rare	—	—	—	—	—	—
1937	750,000	7.00	15.00	45.00	200	350
1937 Proof; rare	—	—	—	—	—	—
1939	1,000,000	4.00	7.00	15.00	100	175
1939 Proof; rare	—	—	—	—	—	—
1940	1,500,000	4.00	7.00	15.00	100	175
1940 Proof; rare	—	—	—	—	—	—
1941	400,000	15.00	30.00	60.00	250	400
1941 Proof; rare	—	—	—	—	—	—
1942	600,000	10.00	20.00	35.00	175	300
1946	1,000,000	10.00	20.00	30.00	125	200
1946 Proof; rare	—	—	—	—	—	—
1947	1,000,000	—	—	—	—	—

Note: The entire issue was melted down but at least one coin is reported to be in the British Museum's collection

KM# 4a 10 MILS

6.50 g., Bronze, 27 mm. **Obv:** Date above and below center hole, with inscription PALESTINE in English, Hebrew and Arabic **Rev:** Wreath around center hole with value above and below **Edge:** Plain

Date	Mintage	F12	VF20	XF40	MS60	MS63
1942	1,000,000	7.00	12.00	25.00	150	225
1943	1,000,000	7.00	18.00	40.00	225	325

KM# 5 20 MILS

11.30 g., Copper-Nickel, 30.5 mm. **Obv:** Wreath around center hole with dates below, with inscription PALESTINE in English, Hebrew and Arabic **Rev:** Value above and below center hole **Edge:** Plain

Date	Mintage	F12	VF20	XF40	MS60	MS63
1927	1,500,000	15.00	30.00	60.00	150	225
1927	68	PF63 1,500				
1933	250,000	35.00	55.00	120	400	750
1934	125,000	60.00	100	250	800	1,500
1934 Proof; rare	—	—	—	—	—	—
1935	575,000	20.00	40.00	75.00	350	750
1940	200,000	45.00	90.00	175	600	1,000
1940 Proof; rare	—	—	—	—	—	—
1941	100,000	75.00	125	250	1,250	2,500
1941 Proof; rare	—	—	—	—	—	—

KM# 5a 20 MILS

11.30 g., Bronze, 30.5 mm. **Obv:** Wreath around center hole with dates below, with inscription PALESTINE in English, Hebrew and Arabic **Rev:** Value above and below center hole **Edge:** Plain

Date	Mintage	F12	VF20	XF40	MS60	MS63
1942	1,100,000	20.00	40.00	80.00	275	450
1944	1,000,000	100	160	250	600	1,000

KM# 6 50 MILS

5.83 g., 0.720 Silver 0.135 oz. ASW, 23.5 mm. **Obv:** Plant flanked by dates within circle, with inscription PALESTINE in English, Hebrew and Arabic **Rev:** Written and numeric value **Edge:** Reeded

Date	Mintage	F12	VF20	XF40	MS60	MS63
1927	8,000,000	10.00	20.00	45.00	100	175
1927	68	PF63 1,500				
1931	500,000	75.00	150	250	1,250	2,500
1933	1,000,000	50.00	75.00	125	200	300
1934	398,861	70.00	90.00	150	225	350
1935	5,600,000	8.00	12.00	20.00	50.00	75.00
1939	3,000,000	10.00	15.00	22.00	50.00	75.00
1939 Proof; rare	—	—	—	—	—	—
1940	2,000,000	15.00	25.00	40.00	100	150
1940 Proof	—	—	—	—	—	—
1942	5,000,000	10.00	15.00	25.00	60.00	110

KM# 7 100 MILS

11.66 g., 0.720 Silver 0.270 oz. ASW, 29 mm. **Obv:** Plant flanked by dates, with inscription PALESTINE in English, Hebrew and Arabic **Rev:** Value within circle **Edge:** Reeded

Date	Mintage	F12	VF20	XF40	MS60	MS63
1927	2,000,000	25.00	50.00	75.00	125	175
1927	68	PF63 2,000				
1931	250,000	300	500	900	2,000	5,000
1931 Proof; rare	—	—	—	—	—	—
1933	500,000	100	135	250	600	1,250
1934	200,000	125	225	400	950	1,750
1935	2,850,000	22.00	35.00	50.00	100	175
1939	1,500,000	25.00	40.00	60.00	125	200
1939 Proof; rare	—	—	—	—	—	—
1940	1,000,000	25.00	40.00	70.00	150	225
1942	2,500,000	22.00	35.00	50.00	120	175

MINT SETS

KM#	Date	Mintage	Identification	Issue Price	Mkt Val
MS1	1927 (21)	—	KM1-7, two each	—	1,750

PROOF SETS

KM#	Date	Mintage	Identification	Issue Price	Mkt Val
PS1	1927 (14)	32	KM1-7, two each, original case. A 1928 British Royal Mint record indicates that 31 double proof sets (including one in a special case for King George V)	—	9,850
PS2	1927 (7)	4	KM1-7, original case	—	5,000

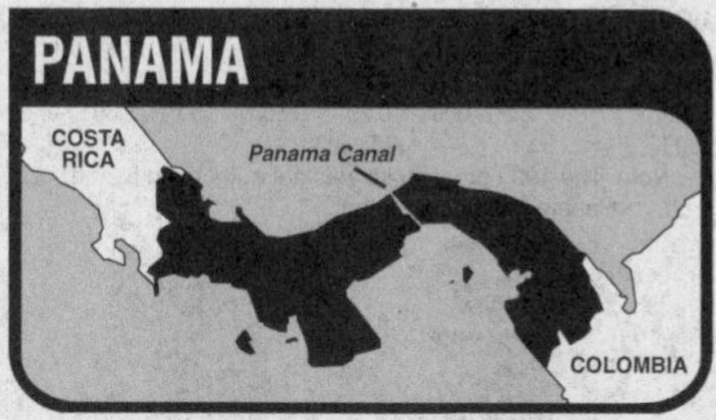

The Republic of Panama, a Central American Country situated between Costa Rica and Colombia, has an area of 29,762 sq. mi. (78,200 sq. km.) and a population of *2.4 million. Capital: Panama City. The Panama Canal is the country's biggest asset; servicing world related transit trade and international commerce. Bananas, refined petroleum, sugar and shrimp are exported.

Discovered in 1501 by the Spanish conquistador Rodrigo Galvan de Bastidas, the land of Panama was soon explored and after a few attempts at settlement was successfully colonized by the Spanish. It was in Panama in 1513 that Vasco Nunez de Balboa became the first European to see the Pacific Ocean. The first Pacific-coast settlement, founded in 1519 on the site of a village the natives called Panama, was named *Nuestra Senora de la Asuncion de Panama* (Our Lady of the Assumption of Panama). The settlement soon became a city and eventually, albeit briefly, an Audiencia (judicial tribunal).

In 1578 the city of Panama, being a primary transshipment center for treasure and supplies to and from Spain's South Pacific-coast colonies, was chosen for a new mint, and minting had begun there by 1580. By late 1582 or 1583 production was halted, possibly due to the fact that there were no nearby silver mines to sustain it. In it's brief operation, the Panama Mint must not have made many coins, as the corpus of surviving specimens known today from this colonial mint is less than 40.

The city of Panama, known today as the Old City of Panama, was sacked and burned in 1671 by the famous Henry Morgan in one of the greatest pirate victories against the Spanish Main.

Panama declared its independence in 1821 and joined the Confederation of Greater Colombia. In 1903, after Colombia rejected a treaty enabling the United States to build a canal across the Isthmus, Panama with the support of the United States proclaimed its independence from Colombia and became a sovereign republic.

The 1904 2-1/2 centesimos known as the 'Panama Pill' or 'Panama Pearl' is one of the world's smaller silver coins and a favorite with collectors.

MINT MARKS

FM - Franklin Mint, U.S.A.*
CHI in circle - Valcambi Mint, Balerna, Switzerland
RCM – Royal Canadian Mint

***NOTE:** From 1975-1985 the Franklin Mint produced coinage in up to 3 different qualities. Qualities of issue are designated in ( ) after each date and are defined as follows:

(M) MATTE - Normal circulation strike or a dull finish produced by sandblasting special uncirculated (polish finish) or proof quality dies.

(U) SPECIAL UNCIRCULATED - Polished or proof-like in appearance without any frosted features.

(P) PROOF - The highest quality obtainable having mirror-like fields and frosted features.

MONETARY SYSTEM

100 Centesimos = 1 Balboa

REPUBLIC

DECIMAL COINAGE

KM# 6 1/2 CENTESIMO

Copper-Nickel, 16 mm. **Obv:** Bust of Balboa left **Rev:** Written value **Note:** Previously listed re-engraved overdates were struck from very common doubled dies. The plain date in unc. is scarcer.

Date	Mintage	VF20	XF40	MS60	MS63	MS65
1907	1,000,000	3.00	5.00	10.00	15.00	20.00
1907	—	PF63 200				

KM# 14 CENTESIMO

Bronze, 19.05 mm. **Subject:** Uracca **Obv:** Written value above sprigs **Rev:** Bust with headcovering left

Date	Mintage	VF20	XF40	MS60	MS63	MS65
1935	200,000	7.00	18.00	25.00	45.00	90.00
1937	200,000	6.00	15.00	20.00	32.00	75.00

KM# 17 CENTESIMO

Bronze, 19.05 mm. **Subject:** 50th Anniversary of the Republic **Obv:** Written value above sprigs **Rev:** Bust of Uracca with headcovering left

Date	Mintage	VF20	XF40	MS60	MS63	MS65
1953	1,500,000	0.80	1.75	3.50	6.50	10.00

KM# 22 CENTESIMO

3.10 g., Bronze, 19.05 mm. **Obv:** Written value above sprigs with stars above **Obv. Legend:** Bust with headcovering left **Note:** Varieties exist.

Date	Mintage	VF20	XF40	MS60	MS63	MS65
1961	2,500,000	0.60	1.50	2.00	3.00	6.00
1962	2,000,000	0.60	1.00	2.00	3.00	6.00
1962	Est. 50	PF65 200				
1966	3,000,000	0.40	0.80	1.50	2.50	4.00
1966	13,000	PF65 2.00				
1967	7,600,000	0.40	0.80	1.50	2.50	5.00
1967	20,000	PF65 2.00				
1968	25,000,000	0.40	0.80	1.50	2.50	5.00
1968	23,000	PF65 6.00				
1969	14,000	PF65 6.00				
1970	9,528	PF65 6.00				
1971	11,000	PF65 6.00				
1972	13,000	PF65 6.00				
1973	17,000	PF65 6.00				
1974	Est. 10000000	0.20	0.80	1.50	3.00	5.00
Note: The 1974 circulation coins were stuck at West Point, NY.						
1974	Est. 18000	PF65 4.00				
Note: The 1974 proof coins were struck at San Francisco						
1975	10,000,000	0.40	0.80	1.50	3.00	6.00
1977	10,000,000	0.40	0.80	1.50	3.00	6.00
1978	10,000,000	0.40	0.80	1.50	3.00	6.00
1979	10,000,000	0.40	0.80	1.50	3.00	6.00
1980	20,500,000	0.40	0.80	1.25	2.50	4.00
1982	20,000,000	0.40	0.80	1.25	2.50	4.00
1983	5,000,000	0.40	0.80	1.50	3.00	6.00
1983	—	PF65 5.00				
1984	—	PF65 5.00				
1985	—	PF65 5.00				
Note: Unauthorized striking						
1986	20,000,000	0.25	0.80	1.25	2.00	4.00
1987	20,000,000	0.25	0.80	1.25	2.00	4.00

KM# 22a CENTESIMO

2.50 g., Copper Plated Zinc, 19.05 mm. **Obv:** Value above sprigs with stars above **Rev:** Covered head left

Date	Mintage	VF20	XF40	MS60	MS63	MS65
1983	45,000,000	0.50	1.00	1.50	3.00	5.00

KM# 33.1 CENTESIMO

2.50 g., Copper Plated Zinc, 19.05 mm. **Obv:** National coat of arms **Rev:** Covered head 1/4 left **Note:** Medal rotation.

Date	Mintage	VF20	XF40	MS60	MS63	MS65
1975 (c)	500,000	0.15	0.50	1.25	2.00	6.00
1975 (M)	125,000	0.25	0.75	1.50	3.00	7.00
1975 (U)	1,410	—	—	—	7.00	15.00
1975 FM (P)	41,000	PF65 5.00				
1976 (M)	63,000	0.15	0.50	2.00	4.00	8.00
1976 (P)	12,000	PF65 6.00				
1976 (c)	50,000	0.15	1.00	2.00	4.00	8.00
1977 (U)	63,000	0.25	1.00	2.00	4.00	8.00
1977 (P)	9,548	PF65 8.00				
1979 (U)	20,000	1.00	2.00	3.50	6.00	10.00
1979 (P)	5,949	PF65 10.00				
1980 (U)	40,000	0.25	0.50	1.75	3.50	7.50
1981 (P)	1,973	PF65 12.00				
1982 (U)	5,000	0.75	1.50	3.50	7.00	12.00
1982 FM (P)	1,480	PF65 15.00				

KM# 33.2 CENTESIMO

2.50 g., Copper Plated Zinc, 19.05 mm. **Obv:** National coat of arms **Rev:** Covered head of Urraca 1/4 left **Edge Lettering:** 1830 BOLIVAR 1980

Date	Mintage	VF20	XF40	MS60	MS63	MS65
1980 (P)	2,629	PF65 10.00				

KM# 45 CENTESIMO

2.50 g., Copper Plated Zinc, 19.05 mm. **Subject:** 75th Anniversary of Independence **Obv:** National coat of arms **Rev:** Covered head 1/4 left **Note:** Medal rotation.

Date	Mintage	VF20	XF40	MS60	MS63	MS65
1978 (U)	50,000	0.10	0.25	2.00	4.00	8.00
1978 (P)	11,000	PF65 10.00				

KM# 124 CENTESIMO

2.50 g., Copper Plated Zinc, 19.05 mm. **Obv:** Written value **Rev:** Covered head 1/4 left **Edge:** Plain

Date	Mintage	VF20	XF40	MS60	MS63	MS65
1991	—	—	—	0.50	1.00	2.00
1993	30,000,000	—	—	0.50	1.00	2.00

KM# 125 CENTESIMO

2.50 g., Copper Plated Zinc, 19.05 mm. **Obv:** Written value **Obv. Legend:** REPUBLICA DE PANAMA **Rev:** Native Urraca bust left **Edge:** Plain

Date	Mintage	VF20	XF40	MS60	MS63	MS65
1996 (c)	180,000,000	—	—	0.25	0.50	0.75

KM# 132 CENTESIMO

1.64 g., Aluminum, 22.8 mm. **Series:** F.A.O. **Subject:** XXI Century F.A.O. Food Security **Obv:** National coat of arms **Rev:** Ship in canal **Edge:** Plain **Note:** Medal rotation.

Date	Mintage	VF20	XF40	MS60	MS63	MS65
2000	1,000,000	—	—	3.00	6.00	9.00

KM# 15 1-1/4 CENTESIMOS

3.10 g., Bronze, 20 mm. **Obv:** Written value **Rev:** Uniformed bust left

Date	Mintage	VF20	XF40	MS60	MS63	MS65
1940	1,600,000	2.00	3.50	10.00	18.00	27.00

KM# 1 2-1/2 CENTESIMOS

1.25 g., 0.900 Silver 0.0362 oz. ASW, 10 mm. **Obv:** Uniformed bust left **Rev:** National coat of arms **Note:** This coin is popularly referred to as the "Panama Pill."

Date	Mintage	VF20	XF40	MS60	MS63	MS65
1904	400,000	20.00	25.00	35.00	45.00	55.00

KM# 7.1 2-1/2 CENTESIMOS

Copper-Nickel, 21 mm. **Obv:** National coat of arms **Rev:** Value above stars **Rev. Legend:** DOS Y MEDIOS

Date	Mintage	VF20	XF40	MS60	MS63	MS65
1907	800,000	7.00	22.00	45.00	75.00	100

KM# 7.2 2-1/2 CENTESIMOS

Copper-Nickel, 21 mm. **Obv:** National coat of arms **Rev:** Value above stars **Rev. Legend:** DOS Y MEDIO

Date	Mintage	VF20	XF40	MS60	MS63	MS65
1916	800,000	10.00	40.00	60.00	85.00	120
1918 7 Known	—	1,600	2,800	—	—	—

Note: Unauthorized issue, 1 million pieces were struck and nearly all were melted in June 1918.

KM# 8 2-1/2 CENTESIMOS

3.27 g., Copper-Nickel, 18 mm. **Obv:** Uniformed bust left **Rev:** Written value

Date	Mintage	VF20	XF40	MS60	MS63	MS65
1929	1,000,000	4.00	27.50	75.00	125	165
1929 Proof	—	—	—	—	—	—

KM# 16 2-1/2 CENTESIMOS

Copper-Nickel, 18 mm. **Obv:** Uniformed bust left **Rev:** Written value

Date	Mintage	VF20	XF40	MS60	MS63	MS65
1940	1,200,000	2.50	6.00	15.00	25.00	32.00

KM# 32 2-1/2 CENTESIMOS

1.65 g., Copper-Nickel Clad Copper, 15 mm. **Series:** F.A.O. **Obv:** National coat of arms **Rev:** Hand holding grain flanked by stars below

Date	Mintage	VF20	XF40	MS60	MS63	MS65
1973	2,000,000	0.25	0.50	0.75	1.00	1.50
1975	1,000,000	0.40	0.60	0.85	1.50	2.50

KM# 34.1 2-1/2 CENTESIMOS

1.25 g., Copper-Nickel Clad Copper, 10 mm. **Subject:** Victoriano Lorenzo **Obv:** National coat of arms, value below **Rev:** Head facing **Edge:** Plain **Note:** Medal rotation.

Date	Mintage	VF20	XF40	MS60	MS63	MS65
1975 (c)	40,000	1.50	2.50	4.00	6.00	9.00
1975 (M)	50,000	1.50	2.50	4.00	6.00	9.00
1975 (U)	1,410	2.50	3.50	5.00	7.00	12.00
1975 FM (P)	41,000	PF63 4.00	PF65 6.00			
1976 (c)	20,000	1.50	2.50	4.00	6.00	9.00
1976 (M)	25,000	1.50	2.50	4.00	6.00	9.00
1976 FM (P)	24,000	PF63 5.00	PF65 7.00			
1977 (U)	25,000	1.50	2.50	4.00	6.00	9.00
1977 FM (P)	9,548	PF63 6.00	PF65 8.00			
1979 (U)	12,000	2.50	4.00	6.00	8.00	12.00
1979 FM (P)	5,949	PF63 8.00	PF65 10.00			
1980 (U)	40,000	1.50	2.75	5.00	7.00	10.00
1981 FM (P)	1,973	PF63 10.00	PF65 12.00			
1982 FM (U)	2,000	2.50	4.00	6.00	8.00	12.00
1982 FM (P)	1,480	PF63 12.00	PF65 15.00			

KM# 34.2 2-1/2 CENTESIMOS

1.25 g., Copper-Nickel Clad Copper, 10 mm. **Subject:** Victoriano Lorenzo **Obv:** National coat of arms, value below **Rev:** Head facing **Edge Lettering:** 1830 BOLIVAR 1980

Date	Mintage	VF20	XF40	MS60	MS63	MS65
1980 (P)	2,629	PF65 8.00				

KM# 46 2-1/2 CENTESIMOS

1.25 g., Copper-Nickel Clad Copper, 10 mm. **Subject:** 75th Anniversary of Independence **Obv:** National coat of arms **Rev:** Head facing **Note:** Medal rotation.

Date	Mintage	VF20	XF40	MS60	MS63	MS65
1978 (U)	40,000	2.00	3.50	5.00	7.00	10.00
1978 (P)	11,000	PF65 8.00				

KM# 85 2-1/2 CENTESIMOS

1.25 g., Copper-Nickel Clad Copper, 10 mm. **Subject:** Victoriano Lorenzo **Obv:** National coat of arms **Rev:** Head facing

Date	Mintage	VF20	XF40	MS60	MS63	MS65
1983 FM	—	PF63 12.00	PF65 15.00			
1984 FM	—	PF63 20.00	PF65 25.00			
1985 FM	—	PF63 25.00	PF65 30.00			

Note: Unauthorized striking

KM# 2 5 CENTESIMOS

2.50 g., 0.900 Silver 0.0723 oz. ASW, 17.9 mm. **Obv:** Uniformed bust left **Rev:** National coat of arms **Edge:** Reeded

Date	Mintage	VF20	XF40	MS60	MS63	MS65
1904	1,500,000	7.00	15.00	25.00	45.00	60.00
1904	12	PF63 1,750				
1916	100,000	145	200	320	450	550

KM# 9 5 CENTESIMOS

5.00 g., Copper-Nickel, 21.2 mm. **Obv:** National coat of arms **Rev:** Numeric value

Date	Mintage	VF20	XF40	MS60	MS63	MS65
1929	500,000	7.00	25.00	45.00	75.00	100
1932	332,000	10.00	30.00	90.00	120	150

KM# 23.1 5 CENTESIMOS

5.00 g., Copper-Nickel, 21.2 mm. **Obv:** National coat of arms **Rev:** Numeric value

Date	Mintage	VF20	XF40	MS60	MS63	MS65
1961	1,000,000	1.00	3.00	6.00	12.00	20.00

KM# 23.2 5 CENTESIMOS

5.00 g., Copper-Nickel, 21.2 mm. **Obv:** National coat of arms **Rev:** Numeric value **Note:** The 1962 & 1966 Royal Mint strikes are normally sharper in detail. The stars on the reverse above the eagle are flat while previous dates are raised. Varieties exist.

Date	Mintage	VF20	XF40	MS60	MS63	MS65
1962	2,600,000	0.50	1.50	2.50	4.00	7.00
1962	Est. 25	PF63 350				
1966	4,900,000	0.15	1.00	2.00	3.00	7.00
1966	13,000	PF63 5.00	PF65 7.00			
1967	2,600,000	0.25	1.50	2.50	4.00	7.00
1967	20,000	PF63 5.00	PF65 7.00			
1968	6,000,000	0.10	1.00	2.00	3.00	6.00
1968	23,000	PF63 5.00	PF65 7.00			
1969	14,000	PF63 5.00	PF65 7.00			
1970	5,000,000	0.10	1.00	2.00	3.00	6.00
1970	9,528	PF63 5.00	PF65 7.00			
1971	11,000	PF63 5.00	PF65 7.00			
1972	13,000	PF63 5.00	PF65 7.00			
1973	5,000,000	0.10	1.00	2.00	3.00	6.00
1973	17,000	PF63 4.50	PF65 6.00			
1974	19,000	PF63 4.50	PF65 6.00			
1975	5,000,000	0.25	0.80	1.50	2.50	4.00
1982	8,000,000	0.25	0.80	1.50	2.50	4.00
1983	7,500,000	0.25	0.80	1.50	2.50	4.00
1993	6,000,000	0.25	0.80	1.50	2.50	4.00
1993	—	PF65 200				

Note: The 1993 proof strike was not authorized by the Panamanian government

KM# 35.1 5 CENTESIMOS

5.00 g., Copper-Nickel Clad Copper, 21.2 mm. **Subject:** Carlos J. Finlay **Obv:** National coat of arms **Rev:** Head 1/4 left **Note:** Medal rotation.

Date	Mintage	VF20	XF40	MS60	MS63	MS65
1975 (c)	80,000	0.15	0.30	1.25	2.50	6.00
1975 (M)	15,000	0.25	0.50	1.50	3.00	6.00
1975 (U)	1,410	—	—	7.00	12.00	15.00
1975 (P)	41,000	PF63 2.00	PF65 3.00			
1976 (c)	20,000	0.25	0.80	2.00	3.00	6.00
1976 (M)	13,000	0.25	0.80	2.00	3.00	6.00
1976 (P)	12,000	PF63 6.00	PF65 8.00			
1977 (U)	13,000	0.25	0.80	2.00	3.00	6.00
1977 (P)	9,548	PF63 7.00	PF65 9.00			
1979 (U)	12,000	0.25	0.80	2.00	3.00	6.00
1979 (P)	5,949	PF63 8.00	PF65 10.00			
1980 (U)	43,000	0.25	0.80	2.00	3.00	6.00
1981 (P)	1,973	PF63 10.00	PF65 12.00			
1982 (U)	3,000	10.00	20.00	25.00	30.00	35.00
1982 (P)	1,480	PF63 12.00	PF65 15.00			

KM# 35.2 5 CENTESIMOS

5.00 g., Copper-Nickel Clad Copper, 21.2 mm. **Obv:** National coat of arms **Rev:** Head 1/4 left **Edge Lettering:** 1830 BOLIVAR 1980 **Note:** Medal rotation.

Date	Mintage	VF20	XF40	MS60	MS63	MS65
1980 (P)	2,629	PF65 8.00				

KM# 47 5 CENTESIMOS

5.00 g., Copper-Nickel Clad Copper, 21.2 mm. **Subject:** 75th Anniversary of Independence **Obv:** National coat of arms **Rev:** Head 1/4 left **Note:** Medal rotation.

Date	Mintage	VF20	XF40	MS60	MS63	MS65
1978 (U)	30,000	0.40	0.60	1.25	2.00	5.00
1978 (P)	11,000	PF65 8.00				

KM# 86 5 CENTESIMOS

5.00 g., Copper-Nickel Clad Copper, 21.2 mm. **Obv:** National coat of arms **Rev:** Numeric value

Date	Mintage	VF20	XF40	MS60	MS63	MS65
1983 (P)	—	PF65 8.00				
1984 (P)	—	PF65 10.00				
1985 (P)	—	PF65 12.00				

Note: Unauthorized striking

KM# 126 5 CENTESIMOS

5.04 g., Copper-Nickel, 21.2 mm. **Obv:** National coat of arms **Rev. Legend:** Numeric value **Edge:** Plain

Date	Mintage	VF20	XF40	MS60	MS63	MS65
1996	4,000,000	—	—	0.60	1.25	2.00

KM# 3 10 CENTESIMOS

5.00 g., 0.900 Silver 0.1447 oz. ASW, 22 mm. **Obv:** Armored bust left **Rev:** National coat of arms

Date	Mintage	VF20	XF40	MS60	MS63	MS65
1904	1,100,000	16.00	35.00	75.00	125	165
1904	12	PF63 2,000				

KM# 36.1 10 CENTESIMOS

2.27 g., Copper-Nickel Clad Copper, 17.91 mm. **Subject:** Manuel E. Amador **Obv:** National coat of arms **Rev:** Head 1/4 right **Edge:** Reeded **Note:** Medal rotation.

Date	Mintage	VF20	XF40	MS60	MS63	MS65
1975 (c)	50,000	0.75	1.00	2.00	3.00	7.00
1975 FM (M)	13,000	1.00	2.50	3.50	5.00	9.00
1975 FM (U)	1,410	—	—	5.00	7.00	12.00
1975 FM (P)	41,000	PF63 3.00	PF65 4.00			
1976 (c)	20,000	0.75	1.25	2.50	4.00	8.00
1976 FM (M)	6,250	1.50	3.00	5.00	7.00	12.00
1976 FM (P)	12,000	PF63 4.00	PF65 6.00			
1977 FM (U)	6,250	1.25	2.50	4.00	6.00	10.00
1977 FM (P)	9,548	PF63 4.00	PF65 6.00			
1979 FM (U)	10,000	1.00	2.50	3.50	6.00	9.00
1979 FM (P)	5,949	PF63 4.00	PF65 6.00			
1980 FM (U)	40,000	0.75	1.00	2.50	5.00	7.00
1981 FM (P)	1,973	PF63 5.00	PF65 7.00			
1982 FM (U)	2,500	2.00	4.00	6.00	9.00	14.00
1982 FM (P)	1,480	PF63 6.00	PF65 8.00			

KM# 36.2 10 CENTESIMOS

2.27 g., Copper-Nickel Clad Copper, 17.91 mm. **Subject:** Manuel E. Amador **Obv:** National coat of arms **Rev:** Head 1/4 right **Edge Lettering:** 1830 BOLIVAR 1980 **Note:** Medal rotation.

Date	Mintage	VF20	XF40	MS60	MS63	MS65
1980 FM (P)	2,629	PF63 12.00	PF65 15.00			

KM# 48 10 CENTESIMOS

2.27 g., Copper-Nickel Clad Copper, 17.9 mm. **Subject:** 75th Anniversary of Independence **Obv:** National coat of arms **Rev:** Bust 1/4 right **Edge:** Reeded **Note:** Medal rotation.

Date	Mintage	VF20	XF40	MS60	MS63	MS65
1978 FM (U)	20,000	0.75	1.25	2.50	4.00	8.00
1978 FM (P)	11,000	PF65 8.00				

KM# 10.1 1/10 BALBOA

2.50 g., 0.900 Silver 0.0723 oz. ASW, 17.9 mm. **Obv:** National coat of arms **Rev:** Armored bust left **Edge:** Reeded **Note:** High relief.

Date	Mintage	VF20	XF40	MS60	MS63	MS65
1930	500,000	8.00	15.00	25.00	45.00	85.00
1930 Matte proof	20	PF63 1,000				
1931	200,000	20.00	35.00	65.00	120	160
1932	150,000	20.00	35.00	60.00	100	185
1933	100,000	37.00	85.00	165	210	485

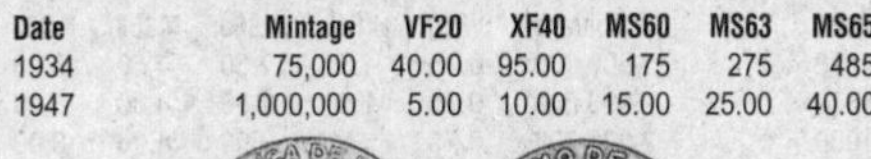

Date	Mintage	VF20	XF40	MS60	MS63	MS65
1934	75,000	40.00	95.00	175	275	485
1947	1,000,000	5.00	10.00	15.00	25.00	40.00

KM# 18 1/10 BALBOA

2.50 g., 0.900 Silver 0.0723 oz. ASW, 17.9 mm. **Subject:** 50th Anniversary of the Republic **Obv:** National coat of arms **Rev:** Armored bust left **Edge:** Reeded

Date	Mintage	VF20	XF40	MS60	MS63	MS65
1953	3,300,000	1.40	3.50	7.00	12.00	16.00

KM# 24 1/10 BALBOA

2.50 g., 0.900 Silver 0.0723 oz. ASW, 17.9 mm. **Obv:** National coat of arms **Rev:** Armored bust left **Edge:** Reeded

Date	Mintage	VF20	XF40	MS60	MS63	MS65
1961	2,500,000	1.40	3.00	6.00	9.00	12.00

KM# 10.2 1/10 BALBOA

2.50 g., 0.900 Silver 0.0723 oz. ASW, 17.9 mm. **Obv:** National coat of arms **Rev:** Armored bust left **Edge:** Reeded **Note:** Low relief.

Date	Mintage	VF20	XF40	MS60	MS63	MS65
1962	5,000,000	1.40	3.00	5.50	7.50	10.00
1962	Est. 25	PF65 500				

KM# 10 1/10 BALBOA

2.27 g., Copper-Nickel Clad Copper, 17.91 mm. **Obv:** National coat of arms **Rev:** Armored bust left **Edge:** Reeded

Date	Mintage	VF20	XF40	MS60	MS63	MS65
1966 Type 1	6,955,000	1.00	2.00	3.00	5.00	7.00

Note: The Type I is similar to the 1962 strike on a thick flan (London) with diamonds on both sides of DE

Date	Mintage	VF20	XF40	MS60	MS63	MS65
1966 Type 2	1,000,000	1.25	3.50	6.00	10.00	18.00

Note: The Type II strike similar to the 1947 strikes on a thin flan (U.S.) with elongated diamonds on both sides of DE

Date	Mintage	VF20	XF40	MS60	MS63	MS65
1966	13,000	PF65 10.00				

Note: Thick and thin planchets

Date	Mintage	VF20	XF40	MS60	MS63	MS65
1967	20,000	PF65 10.00				
1968	5,000,000	0.50	0.75	2.00	4.00	9.00
1968	23,000	PF65 10.00				
1969	14,000	PF65 10.00				
1970	7,500,000	0.25	0.50	1.50	4.00	9.00
1970	9,528	PF65 10.00				
1971	11,000	PF65 10.00				
1972	13,000	PF65 10.00				
1973	10,000,000	0.25	0.50	1.50	4.00	9.00
1973	17,000	PF65 10.00				
1974	18,000	PF65 10.00				
1975	500,000	0.50	1.00	2.00	4.00	12.00
1980	5,000,000	0.50	1.00	2.00	4.00	10.00
1982	7,740,000	0.50	1.00	2.00	4.00	8.00
1983 (c)	7,750,000	0.50	1.00	1.50	3.00	8.00
1986 (c)	1,000,000	0.50	1.00	1.50	3.00	8.00
1993	7,000,000	0.50	1.00	1.50	3.00	5.00
1993	—	PF65 300				

Note: Unauthorized striking

KM# 87 1/10 BALBOA

2.27 g., Copper-Nickel Clad Copper, 17.91 mm. **Obv:** National coat of arms **Rev:** Armored bust left **Edge:** Reeded **Note:** Medal rotation.

Date	Mintage	VF20	XF40	MS60	MS63	MS65
1983 FM (P)	—	PF65 12.00				
1984 FM (P)	—	PF65 12.00				
1985 FM (P)	—	PF65 15.00				

Note: Unauthorized striking

KM# 127 1/10 BALBOA

2.27 g., Copper-Nickel Clad Copper, 17.91 mm. **Obv:** National coat of arms **Obv. Legend:** REPUBLICA DE PANAMA **Rev:** Armored bust of Balboa left **Edge:** Reeded

Date	Mintage	VF20	XF40	MS60	MS63	MS65
1996 (c)	21,000,000	—	0.50	0.75	1.00	1.50

KM# 4 25 CENTESIMOS

12.50 g., 0.900 Silver 0.3617 oz. ASW, 30 mm. **Obv:** Armored bust left **Rev:** National coat of arms **Edge:** Reeded

Date	Mintage	VF20	XF40	MS60	MS63	MS65
1904	16,000,000	30.00	60.00	120	150	180
1904	12	PF63 3,000				

KM# 37.1 25 CENTESIMOS

5.67 g., Copper-Nickel Clad Copper, 24.26 mm. **Subject:** Justo Arosemena **Obv:** National coat of arms **Rev:** Head 1/4 left **Edge:** Reeded **Note:** Medal rotation.

Date	Mintage	VF20	XF40	MS60	MS63	MS65
1975 (c)	40,000	0.50	1.00	2.00	3.00	5.00
1975 FM (M)	5,000	2.50	3.50	5.00	7.00	12.00
1975 FM (U)	1,410	—	—	6.00	12.00	20.00
1975 FM (P)	41,000	PF65 3.00				
1976 (c)	12,000	1.50	2.50	3.50	6.00	10.00
1976 FM (M)	2,500	3.00	4.00	5.00	7.00	12.00
1976 FM (P)	12,000	PF65 8.00				
1977 FM (U)	2,500	3.00	4.00	5.00	7.00	12.00
1977 FM (P)	9,548	PF65 8.00				
1979 FM (U)	4,000	2.50	4.00	5.00	7.00	12.00
1979 FM (P)	5,949	PF65 8.00				
1980 FM (U)	4,000	2.50	4.00	5.00	7.00	12.00
1981 FM (P)	1,973	PF65 8.00				
1982 FM (U)	2,000	3.00	5.00	7.00	10.00	18.00
1982 FM (P)	1,480	PF65 8.00				

KM# 37.2 25 CENTESIMOS

5.67 g., Copper-Nickel Clad Copper, 24.26 mm. **Subject:** Justo Arosemena **Obv:** National coat of arms **Rev:** Head 1/4 left **Edge Lettering:** 1830 BOLIVAR 1980

Date	Mintage	VF20	XF40	MS60	MS63	MS65
1980 FM (P)	2,629	PF65 15.00				

KM# 49 25 CENTESIMOS

5.67 g., Copper-Nickel Clad Copper, 24.26 mm. **Subject:** 75th Anniversary of Independence **Obv:** National coat of arms **Rev:** Head 1/4 left **Edge:** Reeded **Note:** Medal rotation.

Date	Mintage	VF20	XF40	MS60	MS63	MS65
1978 FM (U)	8,000	2.00	4.00	5.00	7.00	12.00
1978 FM (P)	11,000	PF65 7.00				

KM# 11.1 1/4 BALBOA

6.25 g., 0.900 Silver 0.1808 oz. ASW, 24.3 mm. **Obv:** National coat of arms **Rev:** Armored bust left **Edge:** Reeded

Date	Mintage	VF20	XF40	MS60	MS63	MS65
1930	400,000	12.00	25.00	45.00	80.00	120
1930 Matte proof	20	**PF63** 2,000				
1931	48,000	100	300	600	1,100	2,000
1932	126,000	25.00	75.00	125	225	350
1933	120,000	20.00	50.00	200	300	480
1934	90,000	25.00	65.00	125	200	480
1947	700,000	12.00	15.00	25.00	40.00	80.00

KM# 19 1/4 BALBOA

6.25 g., 0.900 Silver 0.1808 oz. ASW, 24.3 mm. **Obv:** National coat of arms **Rev:** Armored bust left **Edge:** Reeded

Date	Mintage	VF20	XF40	MS60	MS63	MS65
1953	1,200,000	12.00	15.00	18.00	22.00	45.00
1953	Est. 5	**PF63** 1,350				

KM# 25 1/4 BALBOA

6.25 g., 0.900 Silver 0.1808 oz. ASW, 24.3 mm. **Obv:** National coat of arms **Rev:** Armored bust left **Edge:** Reeded

Date	Mintage	VF20	XF40	MS60	MS63	MS65
1961	2,000,000	7.00	10.00	12.00	20.00	30.00

KM# 11.2 1/4 BALBOA

6.25 g., 0.900 Silver 0.1808 oz. ASW, 24.3 mm. **Obv:** National coat of arms **Rev:** Armored bust left **Edge:** Reeded **Note:** Low relief.

Date	Mintage	VF20	XF40	MS60	MS63	MS65
1962	4,000,000	10.00	12.00	15.00	18.00	25.00
1962	25	**PF65** 500				

KM# 11.2a 1/4 BALBOA

5.67 g., Copper-Nickel Clad Copper, 24.3 mm. **Obv:** National coat of arms **Rev:** Armored bust left **Edge:** Reeded **Note:** Varieties exist.

Date	Mintage	VF20	XF40	MS60	MS63	MS65
1966	7,400,000	0.75	1.00	1.50	3.00	7.00
1966	13,000	**PF65** 10.00				
1967	20,000	**PF65** 10.00				
1968	23,000	**PF65** 10.00				
1968	1,200,000	1.00	2.00	3.00	6.00	10.00
1969	14,000	**PF65** 10.00				
1970	9,528	**PF65** 10.00				
1970	2,000,000	0.75	1.00	1.50	3.00	7.00
1971	11,000	**PF65** 10.00				
1972	13,000	**PF65** 10.00				
1973	17,000	**PF65** 10.00				
1973	800,000	0.75	1.00	1.50	3.00	7.00
1974	18,000	**PF65** 10.00				

Date	Mintage	VF20	XF40	MS60	MS63	MS65
1975	1,500,000	0.75	1.50	2.50	4.50	9.00
1979	2,000,000	0.75	1.50	2.00	4.00	8.00
1980	2,000,000	0.75	1.50	2.00	4.00	8.00
1982	3,000,000	0.75	1.50	2.00	4.00	8.00
1983 (c)	6,000,000	0.75	1.50	2.00	4.00	8.00
1986 (c)	3,000,000	0.75	1.50	2.00	4.00	8.00
1993	4,000,000	0.75	1.50	2.00	4.00	8.00
1993	—	**PF65** 350				

Note: The 1993 Proof strikes were not authorized by the Panamanian government

KM# 88 1/4 BALBOA

5.67 g., Copper-Nickel Clad Copper, 24.26 mm. **Obv:** National coat of arms **Rev:** Armored bust left **Edge:** Reeded **Note:** Medal rotation

Date	Mintage	VF20	XF40	MS60	MS63	MS65
1983 FM (P)	—	**PF65** 25.00				
1984 FM (P)	—	**PF65** 25.00				
1985 FM (P)	—	**PF65** 35.00				

Note: Unauthorized striking

KM# 128 1/4 BALBOA

5.67 g., Copper-Nickel Clad Copper, 24.26 mm. **Obv:** National coat of arms **Obv. Legend:** REPUBLICA DE PANAMA **Rev:** Armored bust of Balboa left **Edge:** Reeded

Date	Mintage	VF20	XF40	MS60	MS63	MS65
1996 (c)	7,200,000	—	—	0.50	1.00	2.00

KM# 5 50 CENTESIMOS

25.00 g., 0.900 Silver 0.7234 oz. ASW, 38.1 mm. **Obv:** Armored bust left **Rev:** National coat of arms **Edge:** Reeded

Date	Mintage	VF20	XF40	MS60	MS63	MS65
1904	12	**PF63** 6,000				
1904	1,800,000	75.00	125	175	275	450
1905	1,000,000	125	175	275	450	800

Note: 1,000,000 of both 1904 and 1905 dates were melted in 1931 for the metal to issue 1 Balboa coin at San Francisco Mint

KM# 38.1 50 CENTESIMOS

11.34 g., Copper-Nickel Clad Copper, 30.6 mm. **Subject:** Fernando de Lesseps **Obv:** National coat of arms **Rev:** Head 1/4 right **Edge:** Reeded **Note:** Medal rotation.

Date	Mintage	VF20	XF40	MS60	MS63	MS65
1975 (P)	41,000	**PF65** 10.00				
1975 (M)	2,000	1.50	2.50	4.00	6.00	15.00
1975 (U)	1,410	—	—	6.00	10.00	25.00

Date	Mintage	VF20	XF40	MS60	MS63	MS65
1975 (c)	20,000	1.50	2.00	3.00	5.00	10.00
1976 (P)	12,000	**PF65** 10.00				
1976 (M)	1,250	3.00	6.00	8.00	15.00	20.00
1976 (c)	12,000	2.00	3.00	5.00	8.00	15.00
1977 (U)	1,250	7.50	12.50	15.00	20.00	27.00
1977 (P)	9,548	**PF65** 11.00				
1979 (U)	2,000	6.00	8.00	12.00	15.00	22.00
1979 (P)	5,949	**PF65** 12.00				
1980 (U)	2,000	6.00	8.00	12.00	15.00	22.00
1980 (U) Error, without edge lettering	Inc. above	—	—	—	—	150
1981 (P)	1,973	**PF65** 18.00				
1982 (U)	1,000	7.00	12.00	15.00	20.00	32.00
1982 (P)	1,480	**PF65** 20.00				

KM# 38.2 50 CENTESIMOS

11.34 g., Copper-Nickel Clad Copper, 30.6 mm. **Subject:** Fernando de Lesseps **Obv:** National coat of arms **Rev:** Head 1/4 right **Edge Lettering:** 1830 BOLIVAR 1980 **Note:** Medal rotation.

Date	Mintage	VF20	XF40	MS60	MS63	MS65
1980 FM (P)	2,629	**PF65** 20.00				
1980	Inc. above	**PF65** 140				

Note: (error) without edge lettering

KM# 50 50 CENTESIMOS

11.34 g., Copper-Nickel Clad Copper, 30.6 mm. **Subject:** 75th Anniversary of Independence **Obv:** National coat of arms **Rev:** Bust 1/4 right **Edge:** Reeded **Note:** Medal rotation.

Date	Mintage	VF20	XF40	MS60	MS63	MS65
1978 (U)	8,000	5.00	7.00	9.00	12.00	20.00
1978 (P)	11,000	**PF65** 12.00				

KM# 12.1 1/2 BALBOA

12.50 g., 0.900 Silver 0.3617 oz. ASW, 30.6 mm. **Obv:** National coat of arms **Rev:** Armored bust left **Edge:** Reeded **Note:** High relief.

Date	Mintage	VF20	XF40	MS60	MS63	MS65
1930	300,000	20.00	40.00	70.00	120	150
1930 Matte proof	20	**PF63** 2,200				
1932	63,000	40.00	120	250	400	800
1933	120,000	30.00	60.00	175	300	500
1934	90,000	35.00	45.00	150	275	400
1947	450,000	22.00	30.00	40.00	60.00	100

KM# 20 1/2 BALBOA

12.50 g., 0.900 Silver 0.3617 oz. ASW, 30.6 mm. **Obv:** National coat of arms **Rev:** Armored bust left **Edge:** Reeded

Date	Mintage	VF20	XF40	MS60	MS63	MS65
1953	600,000	14.00	18.00	22.00	27.00	45.00
1953	Est. 5	**PF63** 1,850				

KM# 26 1/2 BALBOA

12.50 g., 0.900 Silver 0.3617 oz. ASW, 30.61 mm. **Obv:** National coat of arms **Rev:** Armored bust left **Edge:** Reeded

Date	Mintage	VF20	XF40	MS60	MS63	MS65
1961	350,000	14.00	17.00	20.00	25.00	35.00

KM# 12.2 1/2 BALBOA

12.50 g., 0.900 Silver 0.3617 oz. ASW, 30.6 mm. **Obv:** National coat of arms **Rev:** Armored bust left **Edge:** Reeded **Note:** Low relief.

Date	Mintage	VF20	XF40	MS60	MS63	MS65
1962	700,000	12.00	15.00	18.00	22.00	35.00
1962	25	PF65 750				

KM# 12a.1 1/2 BALBOA

11.50 g., 0.400 Silver 0.1479 oz. ASW Clad, 30.6 mm. **Obv:** National coat of arms **Rev:** Normal helmet **Edge:** Reeded **Note:** Varieties exist.

Date	Mintage	VF20	XF40	MS60	MS63	MS65
1966	1,000,000	2.75	8.00	10.00	12.00	15.00
1966	13,000	PF65 15.00				
1967	300,000	3.00	10.00	12.00	15.00	25.00
1967	20,000	PF65 12.00				
1968	1,000,000	2.75	8.00	10.00	12.00	15.00
1968	23,000	PF65 12.00				
1969	14,000	PF65 12.00				
1970	610,000	2.75	8.00	10.00	12.00	17.00
1970	9,528	PF65 15.00				
1971	11,000	PF65 15.00				
1972	13,000	PF65 15.00				
1993	—	PF65 300				

Note: The 1993 Proof strike was not authorized by the Panamanian government

KM# 12a.2 1/2 BALBOA

11.50 g., 0.400 Silver Clad 0.1479 oz., 30.6 mm. **Obv:** National coat of arms **Rev:** Error: Type II helmet rim incomplete. **Edge:** Reeded

Date	Mintage	VF20	XF40	MS60	MS63	MS65
1966	Inc. above	8.00	12.00	15.00	20.00	30.00

KM# 12b 1/2 BALBOA

11.34 g., Copper-Nickel Clad Copper, 30.6 mm. **Obv:** National coat of arms **Rev:** Armored bust left **Edge:** Reeded **Note:** Varieties exist.

Date	Mintage	VF20	XF40	MS60	MS63	MS65
1973	1,000,000	0.75	1.50	2.50	4.00	8.00
1973	17,000	PF65 5.00				
1974	18,000	PF65 5.00				
1975	1,200,000	0.75	1.50	2.50	4.00	8.00
1979	1,000,000	—	1.50	2.50	4.00	8.00
1980	400,000	—	1.50	2.00	3.50	10.00
1982	400,000	—	1.50	2.00	3.50	10.00
1983 (c)	1,850,000	—	1.50	2.00	3.00	10.00
1986 (c)	200,000	1.50	2.50	4.00	8.00	12.00
1993	600,000	0.75	1.50	2.50	4.00	7.00

KM# 89 1/2 BALBOA

11.34 g., Copper-Nickel Clad Copper, 30.6 mm. **Obv:** National coat of arms **Rev:** Armored bust left **Edge:** Reeded **Note:** Medal rotation.

Date	Mintage	VF20	XF40	MS60	MS63	MS65
1983 FM (P)	—	PF63 15.00	PF65 20.00			
1984 FM (P)	—	PF63 15.00	PF65 20.00			
1985 FM (P)	—	PF63 25.00	PF65 30.00			

Note: Unauthorized striking

KM# 129 1/2 BALBOA

11.34 g., Copper-Nickel Clad Copper, 30.61 mm. **Obv:** National coat of arms **Obv. Legend:** REPUBLICA DE PANAMA **Rev:** Armored bust of Balboa left **Edge:** Reeded

Date	Mintage	VF20	XF40	MS60	MS63	MS65
1996 (c)	200,000	1.50	3.50	5.00	8.00	10.00

KM# 13 BALBOA

26.73 g., 0.900 Silver 0.7734 oz. ASW, 38.1 mm. **Subject:** Vasco Nunez de Balboa **Obv:** Standing figure with arm on shield **Rev:** Armored bust left **Edge:** Reeded

Date	Mintage	VF20	XF40	MS60	MS63	MS65
1931	200,000	30.00	45.00	60.00	80.00	125
1931	20	PF63 3,000				
1934	225,000	30.00	45.00	60.00	80.00	125
1947	500,000	22.00	28.00	37.00	50.00	75.00

KM# 21 BALBOA

26.73 g., 0.900 Silver 0.7734 oz. ASW, 38.1 mm. **Subject:** 50th Anniversary of the Republic **Obv:** Standing figure with hand on shield **Rev:** Armored bust left **Edge:** Reeded

Date	Mintage	VF20	XF40	MS60	MS63	MS65
1953	50,000	35.00	45.00	65.00	90.00	135

KM# 27 BALBOA

26.73 g., 0.900 Silver 0.7734 oz. ASW, 38.1 mm. **Obv:** National coat of arms **Rev:** Armored bust left **Edge:** Reeded **Note:** More than 200,000 of 1966 dates were melted down in 1971 for silver for the 20 Balboas. Varieties exist.

Date	Mintage	VF20	XF40	MS60	MS63	MS65
1966	300,000	—	15.00	25.00	35.00	40.00
1966	13,000	PF63 35.00	PF65 40.00			
1967	20,000	PF63 30.00	PF65 35.00			
1968	23,000	PF63 30.00	PF65 35.00			
1969	14,000	PF63 30.00	PF65 35.00			
1970	13,000	PF63 35.00	PF65 40.00			
1971	18,000	PF63 35.00	PF65 40.00			
1972	10,081	PF63 40.00	PF65 45.00			
1973	30,000	PF63 30.00	PF65 35.00			
1974	30,000	PF63 30.00	PF65 35.00			

KM# 39.1 BALBOA

22.68 g., Copper-Nickel Clad Copper, 38.1 mm. **Obv:** National coat of arms **Rev:** Armored head 1/4 left **Edge:** Reeded

Date	Mintage	VF20	XF40	MS60	MS63	MS65
1975 FM (M)	4,035	—	—	—	25.00	35.00
1975 FM (U)	1,410	—	—	—	35.00	50.00
1976 FM (M)	625	—	—	—	125	150
1977 FM (U)	625	—	—	—	125	150
1979 FM (U)	1,000	—	—	—	90.00	120
1980 FM (U)	1,000	—	—	—	90.00	120
1982 FM (U)	500	—	—	—	150	175

KM# 39.1a BALBOA

26.73 g., 0.925 Silver 0.7949 oz. ASW, 38.1 mm. **Obv:** National coat of arms **Rev:** Armored head 1/4 left **Note:** Medal rotation.

Date	Mintage	VF20	XF40	MS60	MS63	MS65
1975 (P)	45,000	PF63 25.00	PF65 27.00			
1976 (P)	14,000	PF63 27.00	PF65 30.00			
1977 (P)	11,000	PF63 30.00	PF65 35.00			
1979 (P)	7,160	PF63 32.00	PF65 40.00			

KM# 39.2 BALBOA

22.68 g., Copper-Nickel Clad Copper, 38.1 mm. **Obv:** Erroneous silver content (LEY .925) below arms **Rev:** Armored head 1/4 left **Edge:** Reeded

Date	Mintage	VF20	XF40	MS60	MS63	MS65
1975 (c)	10,000	—	—	—	12.00	15.00
1976 (c)	12,000	—	—	—	12.00	15.00

KM# 51 BALBOA

Copper-Nickel Clad Copper, 38.1 mm. **Subject:** 75th Anniversary of Independence **Obv:** National coat of arms **Rev:** Armored head 1/4 left **Note:** Medal rotation.

Date	Mintage	VF20	XF40	MS60	MS63	MS65
1978 (U)	4,000	—	—	—	17.00	25.00

KM# 51a BALBOA

26.73 g., 0.925 Silver 0.7949 oz. ASW, 38.1 mm. **Obv:** National coat of arms **Rev:** Armored head 1/4 left **Edge:** Reeded

Date	Mintage	VF20	XF40	MS60	MS63	MS65
1978 (P)	13,000	PF63 30.00				

KM# 39.3 BALBOA

20.74 g., 0.500 Silver 0.3334 oz. ASW, 38.1 mm. **Obv:** National coat of arms **Rev:** Armored head 1/4 left **Edge Lettering:** 1830 BOLIVAR 1980

Date	Mintage	VF20	XF40	MS60	MS63	MS65
1980 (P)	2,629	PF63 27.00	PF65 35.00			

KM# 39.1b BALBOA

20.74 g., 0.500 Silver 0.3334 oz. ASW, 38.1 mm. **Obv:** National coat of arms **Rev:** Armored head 1/4 left

Date	Mintage	VF20	XF40	MS60	MS63	MS65
1981 (P)	2,633	PF63 35.00	PF65 40.00			
1982 (P)	1,837	PF63 35.00	PF65 40.00			

KM# 39.4 BALBOA

22.68 g., Copper-Nickel Clad Copper, 38.1 mm. **Obv:** Erroneous silver content (LEY .500) below arms **Rev:** Armored head 1/4 left **Edge:** Reeded

Date	Mintage	VF20	XF40	MS60	MS63	MS65
1982 FM (U)	11	—	—	—	1,250	1,500

KM# 76 BALBOA

22.68 g., Copper-Nickel Clad Copper, 38.1 mm. **Subject:** Death of General Omar Torrijos **Obv:** National coat of arms **Rev:** Uniformed bust right **Edge:** Reeded

Date	Mintage	VF20	XF40	MS60	MS63	MS65
1982	200	PF63 225	PF65 250			
Note: Frosted obverse and reverse						
1982	200,000	—	2.50	5.00	8.00	15.00
1982	50	PF63 325	PF65 350			
Note: Frosted obverse						
1983	200,000	—	2.50	5.00	8.00	15.00
1984	200,000	—	2.50	5.00	8.00	15.00

KM# 90 BALBOA

20.74 g., 0.500 Silver 0.3334 oz. ASW, 38.1 mm. **Obv:** National coat of arms **Rev:** Armored bust left

Date	Mintage	VF20	XF40	MS60	MS63	MS65
1983 FM (P)	1,602	PF63 40.00	PF65 45.00			
1984 FM (P)	1,044	PF63 50.00	PF65 60.00			
1985 FM (P)	954	PF63 70.00	PF65 80.00			

KM# 28 5 BALBOAS

35.70 g., 0.925 Silver 1.0617 oz. ASW, 39 mm. **Subject:** 11th Central American and Caribbean Games **Obv:** National coat of arms **Rev:** Discus thrower **Note:** Medal rotation.

Date	Mintage	VF20	XF40	MS60	MS63	MS65
1970	1,647,000	20.50	22.50	26.50	32.00	37.00
1970 (U)	603,000	20.50	22.50	26.50	32.00	37.00
1970 (P)	59,000	PF63 42.00	PF65 47.00			

KM# 30 5 BALBOAS

35.00 g., 0.900 Silver 1.0127 oz. ASW, 38.8 mm. **Subject:** F.A.O. **Obv:** National coat of arms **Rev:** Hand holding leafy plant

Date	Mintage	VF20	XF40	MS60	MS63	MS65
1972	70,000	19.50	21.50	25.50	32.00	37.00
1972	10,000	PF63 42.00	PF65 47.00			

KM# 40.1 5 BALBOAS

Copper-Nickel Clad Copper, 39 mm. **Subject:** Belisario Porras **Obv:** National coat of arms **Rev:** Head facing **Note:** Medal rotation.

Date	Mintage	VF20	XF40	MS60	MS63	MS65
1975 (M)	5,125	—	—	—	10.00	20.00
1975 (U)	1,410	—	—	—	20.00	35.00
1976 (M)	125	—	—	—	125	200
1977 (U)	125	—	—	—	125	200
1979 (U)	1,000	—	—	—	25.00	45.00
1980 (U)	1,000	—	—	—	25.00	45.00
1982 (U)	1,200	—	—	—	20.00	35.00

KM# 40.1a 5 BALBOAS

35.12 g., 0.925 Silver 1.0444 oz. ASW, 39 mm. **Obv:** National coat of arms **Rev:** Head facing

Date	Mintage	VF20	XF40	MS60	MS63	MS65
1975 (P)	41,000	PF63 32.00	PF65 42.00			
1976 (P)	12,000	PF63 50.00	PF65 60.00			
1977 (P)	9,548	PF63 60.00	PF65 80.00			
1979 (P)	5,949	PF63 80.00	PF65 100			

KM# 40.1b 5 BALBOAS

23.33 g., 0.500 Silver 0.375 oz. ASW, 39 mm. **Obv:** National coat of arms **Rev:** Head facing **Note:** Medal rotation.

Date	Mintage	VF20	XF40	MS60	MS63	MS65
1981 (P)	1,973	PF63 110	PF65 130			
1982 (P)	1,480	PF63 115	PF65 140			

KM# 40.2 5 BALBOAS

Copper-Nickel Clad Copper, 38.8 mm. **Obv:** Erroneous silver content (LEY .925) below arms **Rev:** Head facing

Date	Mintage	VF20	XF40	MS60	MS63	MS65
1975	4,000	—	—	—	17.00	25.00
1976	5,000	—	—	—	17.00	25.00

KM# 40.4 5 BALBOAS

23.33 g., 0.500 Silver 0.375 oz. ASW, 39 mm. **Obv:** Erroneous silver content (LEY .925) below arms **Rev:** Head facing

Date	Mintage	VF20	XF40	MS60	MS63	MS65
1982 (P)	—	PF63 110	PF65 130			

KM# 52 5 BALBOAS

Copper-Nickel Clad Copper **Subject:** 75th Anniversary of Independence **Obv:** National coat of arms **Rev:** Bust facing

Date	Mintage	VF20	XF40	MS60	MS63	MS65
1978 (U)	2,000	—	—	—	20.00	35.00

KM# 52a 5 BALBOAS

35.12 g., 0.925 Silver 1.0444 oz. ASW **Obv:** National coat of arms **Rev:** Bust facing

Date	Mintage	VF20	XF40	MS60	MS63	MS65
1978 (P)	11,000	PF63 40.00	PF65 45.00			

KM# 58 5 BALBOAS

35.12 g., 0.925 Silver 1.0444 oz. ASW **Subject:** Panama Canal Treaty Implementation **Obv:** National coat of arms **Rev:** Flag

Date	Mintage	VF20	XF40	MS60	MS63	MS65
1979 (P)	6,854	PF63 40.00	PF65 45.00			

KM# 40.3 5 BALBOAS

23.33 g., 0.500 Silver 0.375 oz. ASW, 39 mm. **Obv:** National coat of arms **Rev:** Head facing **Edge Lettering:** 1830 BOLIVAR 1980

Date	Mintage	VF20	XF40	MS60	MS63	MS65
1980 (P)	2,629	PF63 70.00	PF65 100			

KM# 63 5 BALBOAS

24.11 g., 0.500 Silver 0.3876 oz. ASW **Subject:** Champions of Boxing **Obv:** National coat of arms **Rev:** Boxer and flag

Date	Mintage	VF20	XF40	MS60	MS63	MS65
1980	1,261	PF63 57.00	PF65 65.00			

KM# 40.5 5 BALBOAS

Copper-Nickel Clad Copper, 39 mm. **Obv:** Erroneous silver content (LEY .500) below arms **Rev:** Head facing

Date	Mintage	VF20	XF40	MS60	MS63	MS65
1982 (U)	200	—	—	—	275	350

KM# 77 5 BALBOAS

24.16 g., 0.925 Silver 0.7185 oz. ASW **Subject:** Champions of Soccer **Obv:** National coat of arms **Rev:** Soccer ball and world globe

Date	Mintage	VF20	XF40	MS60	MS63	MS65
1982	9,446	PF63 35.00	PF65 50.00			

KM# 91 5 BALBOAS
23.33 g., 0.500 Silver 0.375 oz. ASW **Obv:** National coat of arms **Rev:** Armored bust left

Date	Mintage	VF20	XF40	MS60	MS63	MS65
1983 FM (P)	1,776	PF63 70.00	PF65 80.00			
1984 FM (P)	889	PF63 80.00	PF65 100			

KM# 104 5 BALBOAS
23.33 g., 0.500 Silver 0.375 oz. ASW **Subject:** Discovery of the Pacific Ocean **Obv:** National coat of arms **Rev:** Vasco Nunez de Balboa facing left

Date	Mintage	VF20	XF40	MS60	MS63	MS65
1985 (P)	765	PF63 175	PF65 225			

KM# 53 10 BALBOAS
42.48 g., 0.925 Silver 1.2633 oz. ASW, 45.6 mm. **Subject:** Panama Canal Treaty Ratification **Obv:** National coat of arms **Rev:** Map within circle

Date	Mintage	VF20	XF40	MS60	MS63	MS65
1978 (P)	12,000	PF63 45.00	PF65 50.00			
1978 (P) FDC	Inc. above	PF63 60.00	PF65 65.00			

KM# 53a 10 BALBOAS
42.38 g., Nickel, 45.6 mm. **Obv:** National coat of arms **Rev:** Map within circle

Date	Mintage	VF20	XF40	MS60	MS63	MS65
1978	300,000	—	7.00	12.00	18.00	25.00

KM# 59 10 BALBOAS
42.48 g., 0.925 Silver 1.2633 oz. ASW **Subject:** Panama Canal Treaty Implementation **Obv:** National coat of arms **Rev:** Ship and flag

Date	Mintage	VF20	XF40	MS60	MS63	MS65
1979 (P)	7,229	PF63 60.00	PF65 70.00	PF67 75.00		

KM# 64 10 BALBOAS
26.50 g., 0.500 Silver 0.426 oz. ASW **Subject:** Balseria Game **Obv:** National coat of arms **Rev:** Dancing figure

Date	Mintage	VF20	XF40	MS60	MS63	MS65
1980	1,267	PF65 75.00	PF67 85.00			

KM# 78 10 BALBOAS
26.50 g., 0.500 Silver 0.426 oz. ASW **Subject:** Champions of Soccer **Obv:** National coat of arms **Rev:** Soccer players

Date	Mintage	VF20	XF40	MS60	MS63	MS65
1982	9,076	PF63 45.00	PF65 50.00	PF67 55.00		

KM# 79 10 BALBOAS
26.50 g., 0.500 Silver 0.426 oz. ASW **Subject:** International Year of the Child **Obv:** National coat of arms **Rev:** Three dancing figures, 2 emblems on the bottom

Date	Mintage	VF20	XF40	MS60	MS63	MS65
1982	8,460	PF63 35.00	PF65 40.00	PF67 45.00		

KM# 130 10 BALBOAS
31.00 g., 0.925 Silver 0.9219 oz. ASW **Subject:** Panama Canal Transfer **Obv:** Bust left **Rev:** Ship in canal under Panamanian flag

Date	Mintage	VF20	XF40	MS60	MS63	MS65
1999	4,500	PF63 45.00	PF65 50.00	PF67 55.00		

KM# 29 20 BALBOAS
129.59 g., 0.925 Silver 3.8539 oz. ASW, 61 mm. **Subject:** 150th Anniversary of Central American Independence **Obv:** National coat of arms **Rev:** Head right **Note:** Illustration reduced.

Date	Mintage	VF20	XF40	MS60	MS63	MS65
1971 (U)	—	—	75.00	82.00	93.00	110
1971 (M)	69,000	—	75.00	82.00	93.00	110
1971 (P)	40,000	PF63 125	PF65 140	PF67 150		

KM# 31 20 BALBOAS

129.59 g., 0.925 Silver 3.8539 oz. ASW, 61 mm. **Subject:** Simon Bolivar 1783-1830 **Obv:** National coat of arms **Rev:** Head right, date below

Date	Mintage	VF20	XF40	MS60	MS63	MS65
1972 (M)	37,000	—	75.00	82.00	115	145
1972 (P)	48,000	PF63 110	PF65 125	PF67 140		
1973 (M)	94,000	—	75.00	82.00	100	117
1973 (P)	74,000	PF63 110	PF65 120	PF67 135		
1974 (M)	99,000	—	75.00	82.00	100	117
1974 (P)	161,000	PF63 110	PF65 120	PF67 130		
1975 (M)	2,500	86.00	115	140	170	220
1975 (U)	—	86.00	115	140	170	220
1975 (P)	62,000	PF63 120	PF65 130	PF67 145		
1976 (M)	2,500	86.00	115	140	170	220
Note: A substantial portion of the 1976 mintage was melted.						
1976 (P)	22,000	PF63 175	PF65 185	PF67 200		

KM# 44 20 BALBOAS

129.59 g., 0.925 Silver 3.8539 oz. ASW, 61 mm. **Subject:** Vasco Nunez de Balboa **Obv:** National coat of arms **Rev:** 3/4-length standing armored figure facing left, raised right arm holding sword, left arm a flag **Note:** Illustration reduced.

Date	Mintage	VF20	XF40	MS60	MS63	MS65
1977 (U)	2,879	82.00	110	135	170	220
1977 (P)	24,000	PF63 180	PF65 190	PF67 210		
1979 (U)	2,500	86.00	115	140	170	220
1979 (P)	13,000	PF63 215	PF65 235	PF67 250		

KM# 54 20 BALBOAS

129.59 g., 0.925 Silver 3.8539 oz. ASW, 61 mm. **Subject:** 75th Anniversary of Independence **Obv:** National coat of arms **Obv. Legend:** REPUBLICA DE PANAMA 75th ANIVERSARIO **Rev:** 3/4-length Balboa standing facing left, upraised right arm holding sword, left arm a flag **Note:** Illustration reduced.

Date	Mintage	VF20	XF40	MS60	MS63	MS65
1978 (U)	2,500	86.00	115	140	170	220
1978 (P)	23,000	PF63 165	PF65 175	PF67 195		

KM# 65 20 BALBOAS

119.88 g., 0.500 Silver 1.9271 oz. ASW, 61 mm. **Subject:** Sesquicentenarium - Death of Simon Bolivar **Obv:** National coat of arms **Rev:** Armored figure on horse **Note:** Illustration reduced.

Date	Mintage	VF20	XF40	MS60	MS63	MS65
1980 (U)	1,000	—	—	—	350	400
1980 (P)	3,714	PF63 135	PF65 145	PF67 165		

KM# 71 20 BALBOAS

118.57 g., 0.500 Silver 1.9061 oz. ASW, 61 mm. **Subject:** Simon Bolivar, El Libertador **Obv:** National coat of arms **Rev:** Armored figure on rearing horse in center of assorted flags **Note:** Illustration reduced.

Date	Mintage	VF20	XF40	MS60	MS63	MS65
1981 (U)	500	—	—	—	325	375
1981 (P)	3,528	PF63 215	PF65 235	PF67 250		

KM# 72 20 BALBOAS

2.14 g., 0.500 Gold 0.0344 oz. AGW **Obv:** National coat of arms **Rev:** Figure of Eight Butterfly

Date	Mintage	VF20	XF40	MS60	MS63	MS65
1981 (U)	205	—	—	—	—	450
1981 (P)	4,445	PF63 70.00	PF65 80.00	PF67 90.00		
1981 (P) FDC	Inc. above	PF63 80.00	PF65 90.00	PF67 100		

KM# 80 20 BALBOAS

119.88 g., 0.500 Silver 1.9271 oz. ASW, 61 mm. **Subject:** Balboa - Discoverer of the Pacific **Obv:** National coat of arms **Rev:** Standing armored figures **Note:** Illustration reduced.

Date	Mintage	VF20	XF40	MS60	MS63	MS65
1982 (P)	2,352	PF63 170	PF65 200	PF67 235		

KM# 81 20 BALBOAS

2.14 g., 0.500 Gold 0.0344 oz. AGW **Obv:** National coat of arms **Rev:** Hummingbird

Date	Mintage	XF40	MS60	MS63	MS65	MS66
1982 (U)	140	—	—	—	250	350
1982 (P)	3,445	PF65 140	PF67 165			
1982 (P) FDC	Inc. above	PF65 155	PF67 180			

KM# 92 20 BALBOAS

2.14 g., 0.500 0.0344 oz. **Obv:** National coat of arms **Rev:** Banded Butterfly fish

Date	Mintage	VF20	XF40	MS60	MS63	MS65
1983 (U)	—	—	—	—	—	225
1983 (P)	1,671	PF63 175	PF65 200	PF67 225		
1983 (P) FDC	Inc. above	PF63 195	PF65 225	PF67 250		

KM# 93 20 BALBOAS
118.57 g., 0.500 Silver 1.9061 oz. ASW, 61 mm. **Subject:** 200th Anniversary - Birth of Bolivar **Obv:** National coat of arms **Rev:** 1/2-Length bust left holding scroll **Note:** Illustration reduced.

Date	Mintage	VF20	XF40	MS60	MS63	MS65
1983 (U)	500	—	—	—	275	375
1983 (P)	3,186	PF63 220	PF65 240	PF67 260		

KM# 97 20 BALBOAS
2.14 g., 0.500 Gold 0.0344 oz. AGW **Obv:** National coat of arms **Rev:** Puma

Date	Mintage	XF40	MS60	MS63	MS65	MS66
1984 (U)	100	—	—	—	700	800
1984 (P)	357	PF65 375	PF67 425			
1984 (P) FDC	Inc. above	PF65 425	PF67 475			

KM# 98 20 BALBOAS
119.88 g., 0.500 Silver 1.9271 oz. ASW, 61 mm. **Obv:** National coat of arms **Rev:** Balboa and Indian guide **Note:** Illustration reduced.

Date	Mintage	VF20	XF40	MS60	MS63	MS65
1984 (P)	1,760	PF63 175	PF65 225	PF67 250		

KM# 102 20 BALBOAS
2.14 g., 0.500 Gold 0.0344 oz. AGW **Obv:** National coat of arms **Rev:** Harpy Eagle, flying to left

Date	Mintage	XF40	MS60	MS63	MS65	MS66
1985 (P)	817	PF65 275	PF67 300			
1985 (P) FDC	Inc. above	PF65 325	PF67 350			

KM# 105 20 BALBOAS
119.88 g., 0.500 Silver 1.9271 oz. ASW, 61 mm. **Subject:** Discovery of the Pacific Ocean **Obv:** National coat of arms **Rev:** Armored head and eagle facing left **Note:** Illustration reduced.

Date	Mintage	VF20	XF40	MS60	MS63	MS65
1985 (P)	1,402	PF63 240	PF65 260	PF67 300		

KM# 73 50 BALBOAS
5.37 g., 0.500 Gold 0.0863 oz. AGW **Subject:** Christmas 1981 **Obv:** National coat of arms **Rev:** Stylized dove flanked by flowers

Date	Mintage	XF40	MS60	MS63	MS65	MS66
1981 (U)	154	—	—	—	350	550
1981 (P)	1,940	PF65 200	PF67 225			
1981 (P) FDC	Inc. above	PF65 210	PF67 240			

KM# 82 50 BALBOAS
5.37 g., 0.500 Gold 0.0863 oz. AGW **Subject:** Christmas 1982 **Obv:** National coat of arms **Rev:** Star of Bethlehem flanked by flowers

Date	Mintage	XF40	MS60	MS63	MS65	MS66
1982 (U)	60	—	—	—	650	750
1982 (P)	1,361	PF65 210	PF67 240			
1982 (P) FDC	Inc. above	PF65 220	PF67 250			

KM# 94 50 BALBOAS
5.37 g., 0.500 Gold 0.0863 oz. AGW **Subject:** Christmas 1983 **Obv:** National coat of arms **Rev:** Poinsettia

Date	Mintage	XF40	MS60	MS63	MS65	MS66
1983 (U)	—	—	—	—	450	650
1983 (P)	1,283	PF65 230	PF67 280			
1983 (P) FDC	Inc. above	PF65 240	PF67 270			

KM# 99 50 BALBOAS
5.37 g., 0.500 Gold 0.0863 oz. AGW **Subject:** Peace at Christmas **Obv:** National coat of arms **Rev:** Lion and lamb

Date	Mintage	XF40	MS60	MS63	MS65	MS66
1984 (P)	—	PF67 800	PF69 900			
1984 (P) FDC	—	PF67 875	PF69 975			

KM# 55 75 BALBOAS
10.60 g., 0.500 Gold 0.1704 oz. AGW **Subject:** 75th Anniversary of Independence **Obv:** National coat of arms **Rev:** Flag flanked by dates, flowers and stars

Date	Mintage	VF20	XF40	MS60	MS63	MS65
ND1978 (U)	425	—	—	—	450	500
ND1978 (P)	9,161	PF63 225	PF65 285	PF67 325		
1978 (P) FDC	Inc. above	PF63 250	PF65 300	PF67 345		

KM# 41 100 BALBOAS
8.16 g., 0.900 Gold 0.2361 oz. AGW **Subject:** 500th Anniversary - Birth of Balboa **Obv:** National coat of arms **Rev:** Armored head 1/4 left

Date	Mintage	XF40	MS60	MS63	MS65	MS66
1975 (U)	44,000	—	—	—	360	405
1975 (P)	75,000	PF65 360	PF67 405			
1975 (P) FDC	Inc. above	PF65 375	PF67 420			
1976 (M)	50	—	—	—	1,000	1,250
1976 (U)	3,013	—	—	—	500	700
1976 (P)	11,000	PF65 405	PF67 450			
1976 (P) FDC	Inc. above	PF65 435	PF67 465			
1977 (M)	50	—	—	—	650	850
1977 (U)	324	—	—	—	550	750
1977 (P)	5,092	PF65 435	PF67 465			
1977 (P) FDC	Inc. above	PF65 450	PF67 480			

KM# 56 100 BALBOAS
8.16 g., 0.900 Gold 0.2361 oz. AGW **Subject:** Peace and Progress **Obv:** National coat of arms **Rev:** Dove orchid within circle

Date	Mintage	XF40	MS60	MS63	MS65	MS66
1978 (U)	300	—	—	—	450	650
1978 (M)	50	—	—	—	1,000	1,200
1978 (P)	6,086	PF65 450	PF67 475			
1978 (P) FDC	Inc. above	PF65 475	PF67 500			

KM# 60 100 BALBOAS
8.16 g., 0.900 Gold 0.2361 oz. AGW **Subject:** Pre-Columbian Art - Golden Turtle **Obv:** National coat of arms **Rev:** Stylized turtle

Date	Mintage	XF40	MS60	MS63	MS65	MS66
1979 (M)	50	—	—	—	1,000	1,200
1979 (U)	240	—	—	—	650	700
1979 (P)	4,829	PF65 475	PF67 500			
1979 (P) FDC	Inc. above	PF65 500	PF67 525			

KM# 66 100 BALBOAS
8.16 g., 0.900 Gold 0.2361 oz. AGW **Subject:** Pre-Columbian Art - Golden Condor **Obv:** National coat of arms **Rev:** Stylized condor within circle

Date	Mintage	XF40	MS60	MS63	MS65	MS66
1980 (U)	209	—	—	—	650	750
1980 (P)	2,411	PF65 525	PF67 550			
1980 (P) FDC	Inc. above	PF65 550	PF67 600			

KM# 67 100 BALBOAS
7.13 g., 0.500 Gold 0.1146 oz. AGW **Subject:** Panama Canal Centennial **Obv:** National coat of arms **Rev:** Bust 1/4 left

Date	Mintage	XF40	MS60	MS63	MS65	MS66
ND (1980) (U)	77	—	—	—	1,000	1,250
ND (1980) (P)	2,468	PF65 225	PF67 250			
ND (1980) (P) FDC	Inc. above	PF65 250	PF67 275			

KM# 74 100 BALBOAS

7.13 g., 0.500 Gold 0.1146 oz. AGW **Subject:** Pre-Columbian Art **Obv:** National coat of arms **Rev:** Cocie Peoples' Ceremonial Mask

Date	Mintage	XF40	MS60	MS63	MS65	MS66
1981 (U)	174	—	—	—	750	850
1981 (P)	1,841	PF65 250		PF67 275		
1981 (P) FDC	Inc. above	PF65 275		PF67 300		

KM# 83 100 BALBOAS

7.13 g., 0.500 Gold 0.1146 oz. AGW **Subject:** Pre-Columbian Art **Obv:** National coat of arms **Rev:** Native design within quartered circle

Date	Mintage	XF40	MS60	MS63	MS65	MS66
1982 (U)	26	—	—	—	3,750	4,250
1982 (P)	578	PF65 350		PF67 400		
1882 (P) FDC	Inc. above	PF65 360		PF67 420		

KM# 95 100 BALBOAS

7.13 g., 0.500 Gold 0.1146 oz. AGW **Subject:** Pre-Columbian Art **Obv:** National coat of arms **Rev:** Cocie style birds

Date	Mintage	XF40	MS60	MS63	MS65	MS66
1983 (U)	—	—	—	—	750	850
1983 (P)	1,308	PF65 300		PF67 350		
1983 (P) FDC	Inc. above	PF65 325		PF67 375		

KM# 100 100 BALBOAS

7.13 g., 0.500 Gold 0.1146 oz. AGW **Subject:** Pre-Columbian Art **Obv:** National coat of arms **Rev:** Native art

Date	Mintage	XF40	MS60	MS63	MS65	MS66
1984 (U)	—	—	—	—	450	500
1984 (P)	—	PF65 325		PF67 350		
1984 (P) FDC	—	PF65 350		PF67 375		

KM# 131 100 BALBOAS

8.30 g., 0.900 Gold 0.2402 oz. AGW **Subject:** Panama Canal Transfer **Obv:** Bust left **Rev:** Ship in canal under Panamanian flag

Date	Mintage	XF40	MS60	MS63	MS65	MS66
1999	1,000	PF65 425		PF67 450		

KM# 43 150 BALBOAS

9.30 g., 0.999 Platinum 0.2987 oz. APW **Subject:** 150th Anniversary - Pan Congress **Obv:** National coat of arms **Rev:** Bust left divides dates

Date	Mintage	XF40	MS60	MS63	MS65	MS66
ND (1976) (M)	30	—	—	—	2,200	2,700
ND (1976) (U)	510	—	—	—	750	900
ND (1976) (P)	13,000	PF65 450		PF67 500		
ND-1976 (P) FDC	Inc. above	PF65 475		PF67 525		

KM# 68 150 BALBOAS

7.67 g., 0.500 Gold 0.1233 oz. AGW **Subject:** Sesquicentenarium - Death of Simon Bolivar **Obv:** National coat of arms **Rev:** Armored bust 1/4 left

Date	Mintage	XF40	MS60	MS63	MS65	MS66
ND (1980) (U)	169	—	—	—	550	750
ND (1980) (P)	1,837	PF65 275		PF67 300		
ND-1980 (P) FDC	Inc. above	PF65 285		PF67 320		

KM# 61 200 BALBOAS

9.50 g., 0.980 Platinum 0.2993 oz. APW **Subject:** Panama Canal Treaty Implementation **Obv:** National coat of arms **Rev:** Flag above map

Date	Mintage	XF40	MS60	MS63	MS65	MS66
1979 (P)	2,178	PF65 550		PF67 600		
1979 (P) FDC	Inc. above	PF65 570		PF67 625		

KM# 69 200 BALBOAS

9.93 g., 0.980 Platinum 0.3129 oz. APW **Subject:** Champions of Boxing **Obv:** National coat of arms **Rev:** Boxer and flag

Date	Mintage	XF40	MS60	MS63	MS65	MS66
1980	219	PF67 1,100		PF69 1,250		

KM# 42 500 BALBOAS

41.70 g., 0.900 Gold 1.2066 oz. AGW **Subject:** 500th Anniversary - Birth of Balboa **Obv:** National coat of arms **Rev:** Kneeling armored figure, sword in right hand, flag in left hand

Date	Mintage	XF40	MS60	MS63	MS65	MS66
1975 (M)	10	—	—	—	—	9,000
1975 (U)	1,496	—	—	—	1,950	2,450
1975 (P)	9,824	PF65 1,850		PF67 1,950	PF69 2,150	
1975 (P) FDC	Inc. above	PF65 1,950		PF67 2,050	PF69 2,250	
1976 (M)	10	—	—	—	—	9,000
1976 (U)	160	—	—	—	2,150	2,650
1976 (P)	2,669	PF65 2,000		PF67 2,100	PF69 2,250	
1976 (P) FDC	Inc. above	PF65 2,050		PF67 2,150	PF69 2,300	
1977 (M)	10	—	—	—	—	8,000
1977 (U)	59	—	—	—	2,250	2,750
1977 (P)	1,980	PF65 2,150		PF67 2,250	PF69 2,400	
1977 (P) FDC	Inc. above	PF65 2,200		PF67 2,300	PF69 2,450	

KM# 57 500 BALBOAS

41.70 g., 0.900 Gold 1.2066 oz. AGW **Subject:** 30th Anniversary - Organization of American States **Obv:** Coat of arms and value **Rev:** Map of North America and South America in inner circle

Date	Mintage	XF40	MS60	MS63	MS65	MS66
ND-1978 (M)	10	—	—	—	—	5,500
ND-1978 (U)	106	—	—	—	2,000	2,500
ND-1978 (P)	2,009	PF65 2,150		PF67 2,250	PF69 2,400	
ND-1978 (P) FDC	Inc. above	PF65 2,250		PF67 2,350	PF69 2,500	

KM# 62 500 BALBOAS

41.70 g., 0.900 Gold 1.2066 oz. AGW **Obv:** National coat of arms **Rev:** Jaguar

Date	Mintage	XF40	MS60	MS63	MS65	MS66
1979 (U)	130	—	—	—	2,250	2,750
1979 (P)	1,657	PF65 2,450		PF67 2,550	PF69 2,700	
1979 (P) FDC	Inc. above	PF65 2,500		PF67 2,600	PF69 2,750	

KM# 70 500 BALBOAS

37.18 g., 0.500 Gold 0.5977 oz. AGW **Obv:** National coat of arms **Rev:** Great egrets

Date	Mintage	XF40	MS60	MS63	MS65	MS66
1980 (U)	54	—	—	—	2,150	2,650
1980 (P)	612	**PF65** 950	**PF67** 1,050	**PF69** 1,200		
1980 (P) FDC	Inc. above	**PF65** 1,000	**PF67** 1,100	**PF69** 1,250		

KM# 75 500 BALBOAS
37.18 g., 0.500 Gold 0.5977 oz. AGW **Obv:** National coat of arms **Rev:** Sailfish

Date	Mintage	XF40	MS60	MS63	MS65	MS66
1981 (U)	41	—	—	—	2,350	2,850
1981 (P)	487	**PF65** 1,050	**PF67** 1,150	**PF69** 1,300		
1981 (P) FDC	Inc. above	**PF65** 1,100	**PF67** 1,200	**PF69** 1,350		

KM# 84 500 BALBOAS
37.18 g., 0.500 Gold 0.5977 oz. AGW **Subject:** Death of General Omar Torrijos **Obv:** National coat of arms **Rev:** Uniformed bust right

Date	Mintage	XF40	MS60	MS63	MS65	MS66
1982 (U)	97	—	—	—	2,150	2,650
1982 (P)	398	**PF65** 1,150	**PF67** 1,250	**PF69** 1,300		
1982 (P) FDC	Inc. above	**PF65** 1,200	**PF67** 1,300	**PF69** 1,350		

KM# 96 500 BALBOAS
37.18 g., 0.500 Gold 0.5977 oz. AGW **Obv:** National coat of arms **Rev:** Owl Butterfly **Shape:** Scalloped

Date	Mintage	XF40	MS60	MS63	MS65	MS66
1983 (U)	73	—	—	—	2,000	2,250
1983 (P)	469	**PF65** 1,100	**PF67** 1,200	**PF69** 1,250		
1983 (P) FDC	Inc. above	**PF65** 1,150	**PF67** 1,250	**PF69** 1,300		

KM# 101 500 BALBOAS
37.12 g., 0.500 Gold 0.5967 oz. AGW **Subject:** Golden Eagle **Obv:** National coat of arms **Rev:** National eagle holding a ribbon, stars above

Date	Mintage	XF40	MS60	MS63	MS65	MS66
1984 (U)	10	—	—	—	—	9,500
1984 (P)	156	**PF67** 2,150	**PF69** 2,250			
1984 (P) FDC	Inc. above	**PF67** 2,200	**PF69** 2,300			

KM# 103 500 BALBOAS
37.18 g., 0.500 Gold 0.5977 oz. AGW **Subject:** National Eagle **Obv:** National coat of arms **Rev:** National eagle holding an ribbon, stars above **Shape:** Scalloped

Date	Mintage	XF40	MS60	MS63	MS65	MS66
1985 (P)	184	**PF67** 2,100	**PF69** 2,200			
1985 (P) FDC	Inc. above	**PF67** 2,150	**PF69** 2,250			

PATTERNS

Including off metal strikes.

KM#	Date	Mintage	Identification	Mkt Val
Pn1	1904	—	2-1/2 Centesimos. Silver.	1,500
Pn2	1907	—	Half Cent.	3,500
PnA3	1907	—	1/2 Centesimo. Bronze. KM6.	—
Pn3	1907	—	2-1/2 Centesimos. Silver.	—
PnB4	1953	—	Centesimo. Silver. 17a.	—
PnC4	1953	—	Centesimo. 0.900. Gold. 17b.	1,000
PnD4	1953	—	1/10 Balboa. Silver.	—
PnE4	1953	—	1/10 Balboa. 0.900. Gold. 18a.	—
PnF4	1953	—	1/4 Balboa. Silver.	—
PnG4	1953	—	1/4 Balboa. 0.900. Gold. 19a.	—
PnH4	1953	—	1/2 Balboa. Silver.	—
PnI4	1953	—	1/2 Balboa. 0.900. Gold. 20a.	—
PnA4	1953 (1986)	—	Centesimo. Copper. KM17.	—
Pn4	1986	10	Balboa. Copper-Nickel. No lines around the sun or near the moon. Small circles near the wheel of progress. No slanted lines in the upper circle of the helmet. Type I.	6,000
Pn5	1986	10	Balboa. Copper-Nickel. Lines around the sun, near the moon and in the right of the wheel of progress. 3 slanted lines in helmet in upper circle. Type II.	6,000
Pn6	1987	—	1/10 Balboa. Copper-Nickel Clad Copper. Similar to KM10.	1,000
Pn7	1987	—	1/4 Balboa. Copper-Nickel Clad Copper. Similar to KM11.	1,500
Pn8	1987	—	1/2 Balboa. Copper-Nickel Clad Copper. Similar to KM12.	2,000
Pn9	1988	—	1/10 Balboa. Copper-Nickel. KM24.	—
Pn10	1988	—	1/4 Balboa. Copper-Nickel. KM25.	1,500
Pn11	1988	—	1/2 Balboa. Copper-Nickel. KM26.	2,000

PIEDFORT

KM#	Date	Mintage	Identification	Mkt Val
P1	1982	Est. 15	Centesimo. 0.400. Gold. The 1982 series of 1-50 Centesimos were struck as pieforts in .400 Gold outside the normal minting facility without consent from the National Bank of Panama.	550
P2	1982	Est. 15	5 Centesimos. 0.400. Gold.	650
P3	1982	Est. 15	1/10 Balboa. 0.400. Gold.	750
P4	1982	20	1/4 Balboa. 0.400. Gold.	950
P5	1982	Est. 15	50 Centesimos. 0.400. Gold.	1,000

TRIAL STRIKES

KM#	Date	Mintage	Identification	Mkt Val
TS1	1982	Est. 15	Centesimo. 0.400. Gold. The 1982 series 1-50 Centesimos were struck as uniface trial strikes in .400 Gold outside the normal minting facility without consent from the National Bank or authorization from the Government of Panama. Reverse piefort.	450
TS2	1982	Est. 15	Centesimo. 0.400. Gold. Obverse piefort.	450
TS3	1982	Est. 15	5 Centesimos. 0.400. Gold. Reverse piefort.	500
TS4	1982	Est. 15	5 Centesimos. 0.400. Gold. Obverse piefort.	500
TS5	(1982)	—	1/10 Balboa. 0.400. Gold. Reverse piefort.	600
TS5	1982	Est. 15	1/10 Balboa. 0.400. Gold. Reverse piefort.	600
TS6	1982	Est. 15	1/10 Balboa. 0.400. Gold. Obverse piefort.	950
TS7	1982	Est. 15	1/4 Balboa. 0.400. Gold. Reverse piefort.	1,250
TS8	1982	Est. 15	1/4 Balboa. 0.400. Gold. Obverse piefort.	1,250
TS9	1982	Est. 15	50 Centesimos. 0.400. Gold. Reverse piefort.	1,350
TS10	1982	Est. 15	50 Centesimos. 0.400. Gold. Obverse piefort.	1,350
TS11	ND-1983 FM	—	1/4 Balboa. Copper-Nickel Clad Copper. Obverse, KM#88.	700
TS12	ND-1983 FM	—	1/2 Balboa. Copper-Nickel Clad Copper. Obverse, KM#89.	1,400

MINT SETS

KM#	Date	Mintage	Identification	Issue Price	Mkt Val
MS1	1975 (8)	1,410	KM33.1-40.1	25.00	150

PROOF SETS

KM#	Date	Mintage	Identification	Issue Price	Mkt Val
PS1	1904 (4)	12	KM2-5	—	13,000
PS2	1930 (3)	20	KM10.1-12.1	—	5,350
PS3	1962 (5)	25	KM10.2-12.2, 22, 23.2	—	2,500
PS4	1966 (6)	12,701	KM10-11, 12a.1, 22, 23.2, 27	15.25	85.00
PS5	1967 (6)	19,983	KM10-11, 12a.1, 22, 23.2, 27	15.25	75.00
PS6	1968 (6)	23,210	KM10-11, 12a.1, 22, 23.2, 27	15.25	80.00
PS7	1969 (6)	14,000	KM10-11, 12a.1, 22, 23.2, 27	15.25	80.00
PS8	1970 (6)	9,528	KM10-11, 12a.1, 22, 23.2, 27	15.25	90.00
PS9	1971 (6)	10,696	KM10-11, 12a.1, 22, 23.2, 27	15.25	90.00
PS10	1972 (6)	13,322	KM10-11, 12a.1, 22, 23.2, 27	15.25	95.00
PS11	1973 (6)	16,946	KM10-11, 12b, 22, 23.2, 27	17.50	75.00
PS12	1974 (6)	17,521	KM10-11, 12b, 22, 23.2, 27	17.50	75.00
PS13	1975 (9)	37,041	KM31, 33.1-38.1, 39.1a-40.1a	130	275
PS14	1975 (8)	4,057	KM33.1-38.1, 39.1a-40.1a	50.00	125
PS15	1976 (9)	10,610	KM31, 33.1-38.1, 39.1a-40.1a	102	355
PS16	1976 (8)	1,792	KM33.1-38.1, 39.1a-40.1a	50.00	165
PS17	1976 (2)	11,479	KM31, 34.1	51.00	200
PS18	1977 (9)	8,093	KM33.1-38.1, 39.1a-40.1a, 44	100	395
PS19	1977 (8)	1,455	KM33.1-38.1, 39.1a-40.1a	50.00	200

PS20	1978 (9)	9,667	KM45-50, 51a, 52a, 54	110	350
PS21	1978 (8)	1,122	KM45-50, 51a, 52a	—	165
PS22	1979 (9)	4,974	KM33.1-38.1, 39.1a-40.1a, 44	132	470
PS23	1979 (8)	975	KM33.1-38.1, 39.1a-40.1a	60.00	230
PS24	1979 (2)	1,775	KM58-59	125	135
PS25	1980 (9)	1,686	KM33.2-38.2, 39.3-40.3, 65	287	365
PS26	1980 (8)	943	KM33.2-38.2, 39.3-40.3	87.00	215
PS27	1981 (9)	1,279	KM33.1-38.1, 39.1b-40.1b, 71	212	515
PS28	1981 (8)	694	KM33.1-38.1, 39.1b-40.1b	87.00	265
PS29	1982 (9)	746	KM33.1-38.1, 39.1b-40.1b, 80	212	575
PS30	1982 (9)	—	Error set; KM33.1-38.1, 39.1b, 40.4, 80	212	600
PS31	1982 (8)	734	KM33.1-38.1, 39.1b, 40.1b	87.00	300
PS32	1982 (8)	—	Error set; KM33.1-38.1, 39.1b, 40.4	—	325
PS33	1983 (9)	—	KM22, 85-91, 93	87.00	535
PS34	1983 (8)	—	KM22, 85-91	—	260
PS35	1984 (9)	—	KM22, 85-91, 98	—	625
PS36	1984 (8)	—	KM22, 85-91	72.00	295
PS37	1985 (8)	765	KM22, 85-90, 104	72.00	520
PS39	1993 (4)	—	KM10-11, 12a.1, 23.2	—	1,250

PALO SECO

Palo Seco Leper Colony was established in Balboa, Canal Zone in 1907. It is known today as Palo Seco Hospital. The original issue of tokens totaled $1,800.00 of which $1,492.75 was destroyed on November 28, 1955. The issue was backed by United States Currency and was replaced by United States circulation coinage.

COLONY

LEPROSARIUM TOKEN COINAGE

KM# Tn1 CENT
Brass, 19 mm. **Obv:** Square center hole **Rev:** Square center hole divides values

Date	Mintage	VG8	F12	VF20	XF40	MS60
ND-1919	—	75.00	100	200	450	1,650

KM# Tn2 5 CENTS
Brass, 21 mm. **Obv:** Square center hole divides legend **Rev:** Square center hole divides values

Date	Mintage	VG8	F12	VF20	XF40	MS60
ND-1919	—	100	125	225	375	—

KM# Tn3 10 CENTS
Aluminum, 18 mm. **Obv:** Center hole divides legend **Rev:** Center hole divides values

Date	Mintage	VG8	F12	VF20	XF40	MS60
ND-1919	—	250	400	650	900	—

KM# Tn4 25 CENTS
Aluminum, 24 mm. **Obv:** Center hole divides legend **Rev:** Center hole divides values

Date	Mintage	VG8	F12	VF20	XF40	MS60
ND-1919	—	250	550	850	1,450	—

KM# Tn5 50 CENTS
Aluminum, 30.5 mm. **Obv:** Center hole divides legend **Rev:** Center hole divides values

Date	Mintage	VG8	F12	VF20	XF40	MS60
ND-1919	—	550	850	1,150	2,000	—

KM# Tn6 DOLLAR
Aluminum, 38 mm. **Obv:** Center hole divides legend **Rev:** Center hole divides values

Date	Mintage	VG8	F12	VF20	XF40	MS60
ND-1919	—	900	1,200	1,750	2,450	—

PAPUA NEW GUINEA

Papua New Guinea occupies the eastern half of the island of New Guinea. It lies north of Australia near the equator and borders on West Irian. The country, which includes nearby Bismark archipelago, Buka and Bougainville, has an area of 178,260 sq. mi. (461,690 sq. km.).and a population of 3.7 million that is divided into more than 1,000 separate tribes speaking more than 700 mutually unintelligible languages. Capital: Port Moresby. The economy is agricultural, and exports copra, rubber, cocoa, coffee, tea, gold and copper

In 1884 Germany annexed the area known as German New Guinea (also Neu Guinea or Kaiser Wilhelmsland) comprising the northern section of eastern New Guinea, and granted its administration and development to the Neu-Guinea Compagnie. Administration reverted to Germany in 1889 following the failure of the company to exercise adequate administration. While a German protectorate, German New Guinea had an area of 92,159 sq. mi. (238,692 sq. km.) and a population of about 250,000. Capital: Herbertshohe, 1 of 4 capitals of German New Guinea. The seat of government was transferred to Rabaul in 1910. Copra was the chief crop.

Australian troops occupied German New Guinea in Aug. 1914, shortly after Great Britain declared war on Germany. It was mandated to Australia by the League of Nations in 1920, known as the Territory of New Guinea. The territory was invaded and most of it was occupied by Japan in 1942. Following the Japanese surrender, it came under U.N. trusteeship, Dec. 13, 1946, with Australia as the administering power.

The Papua and New Guinea act, 1949, provided for the government of Papua and New Guinea as one administrative unit. On Dec. 1, 1973, Papua New Guinea became self-governing with Australia retaining responsibility for defense and foreign affairs. Full independence was achieved on Sept. 16, 1975. Papua New Guinea is a member of the Commonwealth of Nations. Elizabeth II is Head of State.

MINT MARK

FM - Franklin Mint, U.S.A.

NOTE: From 1975-1985 the Franklin Mint produced coinage in up to 3 different qualities. Qualities of issue are designated in ( ) after each date and are defined as follows:

(M) MATTE - Normal circulation strike or a dull finish produced by sandblasting special uncirculated (polish finish) or proof quality dies.

(U) SPECIAL UNCIRCULATED - Polished or prooflike in appearance without any frosted features.

(P) PROOF - The highest quality obtainable having mirror-like fields and frosted features.

MONETARY SYSTEM

100 Toea = 1 Kina

CONSTITUTIONAL MONARCHY

Commonwealth of Nations

STANDARD COINAGE

KM# 1 TOEA
2.00 g., Bronze, 17.65 mm. **Obv:** National emblem **Rev:** Butterfly and value **Edge:** Plain

Date	Mintage	VF20	XF40	MS60	MS63	MS65
1975	14,400,000	—	0.15	0.25	0.35	1.00
1975 FM (M)	83,000	—	—	0.30	0.45	1.00
1975 FM (U)	4,134	—	—	0.60	1.00	1.50
1975 FM (P)	67,000	PF65 1.00				
1976	25,175,000	—	—	0.20	0.35	1.00
1976 FM (M)	84,000	—	—	0.20	0.35	1.00
1976 FM (U)	976	—	—	0.60	1.00	1.50
1976 FM (P)	16,000	PF65 1.00				
1977 FM (M)	84,000	—	—	0.20	0.35	1.00
1977 FM (U)	603	—	—	0.80	1.50	2.50
1977 FM (P)	7,721	PF65 1.25				
1978	—	—	—	0.20	0.35	1.00
1978 FM (M)	83,000	—	—	0.20	0.35	1.00
1978 FM (U)	777	—	—	0.60	1.00	1.50
1978 FM (P)	5,540	PF65 1.50				
1979 FM (M)	84,000	—	—	0.20	0.35	1.00
1979 FM (U)	1,366	—	—	0.60	1.00	1.50
1979 FM (P)	2,728	PF65 1.50				
1980 FM (U)	1,160	—	—	0.60	1.00	1.50
1980 FM (P)	2,125	PF65 1.50				
1981	—	—	—	0.60	1.00	1.50
1981 FM (P)	10,000	PF65 1.25				
1981 FM (M)	—	—	—	0.20	0.35	1.00
1982 FM (M)	—	—	—	0.60	1.00	1.50
1982 FM (P)	—	PF65 2.25				
1983	—	—	—	0.30	0.45	1.25
1983 FM (U)	360	—	—	0.60	1.00	1.50
1983 FM (P)	—	PF65 2.25				
1984	—	—	—	0.30	0.45	1.25
1984 FM (P)	—	PF65 2.25				
1987	—	—	—	0.30	0.45	1.25
1990	—	—	—	0.30	0.45	1.25
1995	—	—	—	0.30	0.45	1.25
1996	—	—	—	0.30	0.45	1.25

KM# 2 2 TOEA
4.10 g., Bronze, 21.6 mm. **Obv:** National emblem **Rev:** Lion fish **Edge:** Plain

Date	Mintage	VF20	XF40	MS60	MS63	MS65
1975	11,400,000	—	0.10	0.40	0.60	1.00
1975 FM (M)	42,000	—	—	0.45	0.65	1.00
1975 FM (U)	4,134	—	—	0.60	1.00	1.50
1975 FM (P)	67,000	PF65 1.50				
1976	15,175,000	—	0.10	0.25	0.50	1.00
1976 FM (M)	42,000	—	—	0.25	0.50	1.00
1976 FM (U)	976	—	—	0.60	1.00	1.50
1976 FM (P)	16,000	PF65 1.50				
1977 FM (M)	42,000	—	—	0.25	0.50	1.00
1977 FM (U)	603	—	—	0.80	1.50	2.50
1977 FM (P)	7,721	PF65 1.75				
1978	—	—	—	0.25	0.50	1.00
1978 FM (M)	42,000	—	—	0.25	0.50	1.00
1978 FM (U)	777	—	—	0.60	1.00	1.50
1978 FM (P)	5,540	PF65 1.75				
1979 FM (M)	42,000	—	—	0.25	0.50	1.00
1979 FM (U)	1,366	—	—	0.60	1.00	1.50
1979 FM (P)	2,728	PF65 1.75				
1980 FM (U)	1,160	—	—	0.60	1.00	1.50
1980 FM (P)	2,125	PF65 1.75				
1981	—	—	—	0.25	0.50	1.25
1981 FM (P)	10,000	PF65 1.50				
1982 FM (M)	—	—	—	0.60	1.00	1.50
1982 FM (P)	—	PF65 2.50				
1983	—	—	—	0.25	0.50	1.25
1983 FM (U)	360	—	—	0.80	1.50	2.50
1983 FM (P)	—	PF65 2.50				
1984	—	—	—	0.25	0.50	1.25
1984	—	PF65 2.50				
1987	—	—	—	0.25	0.50	1.25
1990	—	—	—	0.25	0.50	1.25
1995	—	—	—	0.25	0.50	1.25
1996	—	—	—	0.25	0.50	1.25

KM# 3 5 TOEA
2.83 g., Copper-Nickel, 19.53 mm. **Obv:** National emblem **Rev:** Plateless turtle

Date	Mintage	VF20	XF40	MS60	MS63	MS65
1975	11,000,000	0.15	0.25	0.40	0.75	2.00
1975 FM (M)	17,000	—	—	0.40	0.75	2.00
1975 FM (U)	4,134	—	—	0.70	1.25	3.00
1975 FM (P)	67,000	PF65 2.00				
1976	24,000,000	0.15	0.25	0.40	0.75	2.00
1976 FM (M)	17,000	—	—	0.40	0.75	3.00
1976 FM (U)	976	—	—	0.70	1.25	3.00
1976 FM (P)	16,000	PF65 2.00				
1977 FM (M)	17,000	—	—	0.40	0.75	2.00
1977 FM (U)	603	—	—	1.00	1.75	3.00
1977 FM (P)	7,721	PF65 2.25				
1978	2,000	—	—	1.50	2.50	3.00
1978 FM (M)	17,000	—	—	0.40	0.75	2.00
1978 FM (U)	777	—	—	0.70	1.25	3.00
1978 FM (P)	5,540	PF65 2.25				
1979	—	—	—	0.40	0.75	2.00
1979 FM (M)	17,000	—	—	0.40	0.75	2.00
1979 FM (U)	1,366	—	—	0.70	1.25	2.00
1979 FM (P)	2,728	PF65 2.25				
1980 FM (U)	1,160	—	—	0.70	1.25	2.00
1980 FM (P)	2,125	PF65 2.25				
1981 FM (P)	10,000	PF65 2.00				
1982	—	—	—	0.40	0.75	2.00
1982 FM (M)	—	—	—	0.70	1.25	2.00
1982 FM (P)	—	PF65 3.00				
1983 FM (U)	360	—	—	1.25	2.25	5.00
1983 FM (P)	—	PF65 3.00				
1984	—	—	—	0.40	0.75	2.00
1984 FM (P)	—	PF65 3.00				
1987	—	—	—	0.40	0.75	2.00
1990	—	—	—	0.40	0.75	2.00
1995	—	—	—	0.40	0.75	2.00
1996	—	—	—	0.40	0.75	2.00
1998	—	—	—	0.40	0.75	2.00
1999	—	—	—	0.40	0.75	2.00

KM# 4 10 TOEA
5.65 g., Copper-Nickel, 23.72 mm. **Obv:** National emblem **Rev:** Cuscus and value **Edge:** Reeded

Date	Mintage	VF20	XF40	MS60	MS63	MS65
1975	8,600,000	0.20	0.35	0.45	0.65	1.50
1975 FM (M)	8,300	—	—	0.60	1.00	1.75
1975 FM (U)	4,134	—	—	0.80	1.50	2.00
1975 FM (P)	67,000	PF65 2.00				
1976	—	0.20	0.35	0.45	0.65	1.50
1976 FM (M)	8,300	—	—	0.60	1.00	1.75
1976 FM (U)	976	—	—	0.80	1.50	2.00
1976 FM (P)	16,000	PF65 2.00				
1977 FM (M)	8,300	—	—	0.60	1.00	1.75
1977 FM (U)	603	—	—	1.25	2.25	2.75
1977 FM (P)	7,721	PF65 2.50				
1978 FM (M)	8,300	—	—	0.60	1.00	1.75
1978 FM (U)	777	—	—	0.80	1.50	2.00
1978 FM (P)	5,540	PF65 2.75				
1979 FM (M)	8,300	—	—	0.60	1.00	1.75
1979 FM (U)	1,366	—	—	0.80	1.50	2.00
1979 FM (P)	2,728	PF65 2.75				
1980 FM (U)	1,160	—	—	0.80	1.50	2.00
1980 FM (P)	2,125	PF65 2.75				
1981 FM (P)	10,000	PF65 2.75				
1982 FM (M)	—	—	—	0.80	1.50	2.00
1982 FM (P)	—	PF65 3.50				
1983 FM (U)	360	—	—	1.50	2.50	3.00
1983 FM (P)	—	PF65 3.50				
1984 FM (P)	—	PF65 3.50				
1995	—	—	—	0.80	1.50	2.00
1996	—	—	—	0.80	1.50	2.00
1998	—	—	—	0.80	1.50	2.00
1999	—	—	—	0.80	1.50	2.00

KM# 5 20 TOEA
11.30 g., Copper-Nickel, 28.65 mm. **Obv:** National emblem **Rev:** Bennett's Cassowary and value

Date	Mintage	VF20	XF40	MS60	MS63	MS65
1975	15,500,000	—	—	0.70	1.25	1.75
1975 FM (M)	4,150	—	—	0.80	1.50	2.00
1975 FM (U)	4,134	—	—	0.80	1.50	2.00
1975 FM (P)	67,000	PF65 2.50				
1976 FM (M)	4,150	—	—	0.80	1.50	2.00
1976 FM (U)	976	—	—	1.00	1.75	2.25
1976 FM (P)	16,000	PF65 2.50				
1977 FM (M)	4,150	—	—	1.00	1.75	2.25
1977 FM (U)	603	—	—	1.25	2.25	2.75
1977 FM (P)	7,721	PF65 3.00				
1978	2,500,000	—	—	0.70	1.25	1.75
1978 FM (M)	4,150	—	—	0.80	1.50	2.00
1978 FM (U)	777	—	—	1.00	1.75	2.25
1978 FM (P)	5,540	PF65 3.00				
1979 FM (M)	4,150	—	—	0.80	1.50	2.00
1979 FM (U)	1,366	—	—	1.00	1.75	2.25
1979 FM (P)	2,728	PF65 3.00				
1980 FM (U)	1,160	—	—	1.00	1.75	2.25
1980 FM (P)	2,125	PF65 3.00				
1981	—	0.25	0.50	0.70	1.25	1.50
1981 FM (P)	10,000	PF65 2.50				
1982 FM (M)	—	—	—	1.00	2.00	2.25
1982 FM (P)	—	PF65 4.00				
1983 FM (U)	360	—	—	2.00	3.00	3.50
1983 FM (P)	—	PF65 4.00				
1984	—	0.25	0.50	0.70	1.25	1.50
1984 FM (P)	—	PF65 4.00				
1987	—	0.25	0.50	0.70	1.25	1.50
1990	—	0.25	0.50	0.70	1.25	1.50
1995	—	0.25	0.50	0.70	1.25	1.50
1998	—	0.25	0.50	0.70	1.25	1.50
1999	—	0.25	0.50	0.70	1.25	1.50

KM# 15 50 TOEA
13.50 g., Copper-Nickel, 30 mm. **Subject:** South Pacific Festival of Arts **Obv:** National emblem **Rev:** Design divides circles **Shape:** 7-sided

Date	Mintage	VF20	XF40	MS60	MS63	MS65
1980	—	1.25	1.50	2.00	3.00	5.00
1980 FM (U)	1,160	—	—	—	—	10.00
1980 FM (P)	2,125	PF65 6.50				

KM# 31 50 TOEA
13.50 g., Copper-Nickel, 30 mm. **Subject:** 9th South Pacific Games **Obv:** National emblem **Rev:** Games emblem **Shape:** 7-sided

Date	Mintage	VF20	XF40	MS60	MS63	MS65
1991	25,000	—	1.50	2.50	3.50	5.00

KM# 41 50 TOEA
13.50 g., Copper-Nickel, 30 mm. **Subject:** Silver Jubilee of Bank **Obv:** National emblem **Rev:** Symbolic design **Edge:** Reeded **Shape:** 7-sided

Date	Mintage	VF20	XF40	MS60	MS63	MS65
1998	—	—	2.00	3.00	4.00	6.00

KM# 49 50 TOEA
13.50 g., Copper-Nickel, 30 mm. **Subject:** 25th Anniversary of Statehood **Obv:** National Emblem **Rev:** Large 25 and bird in flight **Shape:** 7-sided

Date	Mintage	VF20	XF40	MS60	MS63	MS65
2000	—	—	2.00	3.00	4.00	6.00

KM# 50 50 TOEA
Copper-Nickel **Obv:** Bird of Paradise **Rev:** Tortoise and large 25 **Shape:** 7-sided

Date	Mintage	VF20	XF40	MS60	MS63	MS65
2000	—	—	1.50	2.50	3.50	5.00

KM# 6 KINA
14.52 g., Copper-Nickel, 23.72 mm. **Obv:** Symbolic design around center hole **Rev:** Crocodiles flank center hole

Date	Mintage	VF20	XF40	MS60	MS63	MS65
1975	2,000,000	1.35	2.00	2.50	3.50	7.50
1975 FM (M)	829	—	—	5.50	8.50	9.50
1975 FM (U)	4,134	—	—	2.50	3.50	7.50
1975 FM (P)	67,000	PF65 5.00				
1976 FM (M)	829	—	—	5.50	8.50	9.50
1976 FM (U)	976	—	—	2.50	3.50	7.50
1976 FM (P)	16,000	PF65 5.00				
1977 FM (M)	829	—	—	5.50	8.50	9.50
1977 FM (U)	603	—	—	—	12.50	13.50
1977 FM (P)	7,721	PF65 6.00				
1978 FM (M)	829	—	—	5.50	8.50	9.50
1978 FM (U)	777	—	—	2.50	3.50	6.00
1978 FM (P)	5,540	PF65 5.00				
1979 FM (M)	829	—	—	5.50	8.50	9.50
1979 FM (U)	1,366	—	—	2.50	3.50	6.50
1979 FM (P)	2,728	PF65 6.00				
1980 FM (U)	1,160	—	—	2.50	3.50	6.50
1980 FM (P)	2,125	PF65 5.00				
1981 FM (P)	10,000	PF65 5.00				
1982 FM (M)	—	—	—	2.50	3.50	6.50
1982 FM (P)	—	PF65 7.50				
1983 FM (U)	360	—	—	—	14.50	15.50
1983 FM (P)	—	PF65 7.00				
1984 FM (P)	—	PF65 7.00				
1995	—	—	—	2.50	3.50	6.00
1996	—	—	—	2.50	3.50	6.00
1998	—	—	—	2.50	3.50	6.00
1999	—	—	—	2.50	3.50	6.00

KM# 7 5 KINA
Copper-Nickel, 40 mm. **Obv:** National emblem **Rev:** New Guinea eagle

Date	Mintage	VF20	XF40	MS60	MS63	MS65
1975 FM (M)	166	—	—	—	32.00	35.00
1975 FM (U)	4,134	—	—	3.50	6.50	8.00
1976 FM (M)	166	—	—	—	32.00	35.00

Date	Mintage	VF20	XF40	MS60	MS63	MS65
1976 FM (U)	976	—	—	5.50	8.50	10.00
1977 FM (M)	166	—	—	—	32.00	35.00
1977 FM (U)	603	—	—	—	18.00	20.00
1978 FM (M)	166	—	—	—	32.00	35.00
1978 FM (U)	777	—	—	—	10.00	12.50
1979 FM (M)	166	—	—	—	32.00	35.00
1979 FM (U)	1,366	—	—	4.50	7.50	9.00
1980 FM (U)	1,160	—	—	4.50	7.50	9.00

KM# 7a 5 KINA
27.60 g., 0.500 Silver 0.4437 oz. ASW, 40 mm. **Obv:** National emblem **Rev:** New Guinea eagle

Date	Mintage	VF20	XF40	MS60	MS63	MS65
1975 FM (P)	67,000	PF63 15.00	PF65 17.00			
1976 FM (P)	16,000	PF63 15.00	PF65 17.00			
1977 FM (P)	7,721	PF63 16.00	PF65 20.00			
1978 FM (P)	5,540	PF63 16.00	PF65 20.00			
1979 FM (P)	2,728	PF63 18.00	PF65 20.00			
1980 FM (P)	2,125	PF63 18.00	PF65 20.00			

KM# 18 5 KINA
28.28 g., 0.500 Silver 0.4546 oz. ASW **Series:** International Year of the Child **Obv:** National emblem **Rev:** Kneeling figure holding fish

Date	Mintage	VF20	XF40	MS60	MS63	MS65
1981	8,775	PF63 16.00	PF65 20.00			

KM# 20 5 KINA
Copper-Nickel, 40 mm. **Subject:** Defense of the Kokoda Trail **Obv:** National emblem **Rev:** Standing figures

Date	Mintage	VF20	XF40	MS60	MS63	MS65
1982 FM (M)	—	—	—	2.50	3.50	5.00

KM# 20a 5 KINA
28.28 g., 0.925 Silver 0.841 oz. ASW, 40 mm. **Subject:** Defense of the Kokoda Trail **Obv:** National emblem **Rev:** Standing figures

Date	Mintage	VF20	XF40	MS60	MS63	MS65
1982 FM (P)	1,795	PF63 25.00	PF65 35.00			

KM# 23 5 KINA
Copper-Nickel, 40 mm. **Subject:** 10th Anniversary - Bank of Papua New Guinea **Obv:** National emblem **Rev:** Bank divides symbolic design above and value below

Date	Mintage	VF20	XF40	MS60	MS63	MS65
1983 FM (U)	360	—	—	4.50	7.50	9.00

KM# 23a 5 KINA
28.28 g., 0.925 Silver 0.841 oz. ASW, 40 mm. **Subject:** 10th Anniversary - Bank of Papua New Guinea **Obv:** National emblem **Rev:** Bank divides symbolic design above and value below

Date	Mintage	VF20	XF40	MS60	MS63	MS65
1983 FM (P)	673	PF63 42.00	PF65 45.00			

KM# 25 5 KINA
28.28 g., 0.925 Silver 0.841 oz. ASW, 40 mm. **Subject:** New Parliament Building **Obv:** National emblem **Rev:** Building **Note:** Prev. KM#25a.

Date	Mintage	VF20	XF40	MS60	MS63	MS65
1984 FM (P)	—	PF63 22.00	PF65 27.00			

KM# 28 5 KINA
28.28 g., 0.925 Silver 0.841 oz. ASW **Series:** Decade for Women **Obv:** National emblem **Rev:** Half-figure picking berries off branch

Date	Mintage	VF20	XF40	MS60	MS63	MS65
1984 FM	1,050	PF63 27.00	PF65 35.00			

KM# 34 5 KINA
23.33 g., 0.925 Silver 0.6938 oz. ASW **Obv:** National emblem **Rev:** Queen Alexandra butterfly (o. alexandrae)

Date	Mintage	VF20	XF40	MS60	MS63	MS65
1992 FM	500	—	—	—	50.00	60.00
1992 FM (P)	—	PF63 75.00	PF65 90.00			

KM# 37 5 KINA
27.78 g., 0.900 Silver 0.8038 oz. ASW **Subject:** Centennial of First Coinage **Obv:** National emblem within sprigs **Rev:** Raggiana Bird of Paradise

Date	Mintage	VF20	XF40	MS60	MS63	MS65
ND-1994	7,500	PF63 35.00	PF65 40.00			

KM# 39 5 KINA
31.47 g., 0.925 Silver 0.9359 oz. ASW **Series:** Endangered Wildlife **Obv:** National emblem **Rev:** Two Ribbon Sweetlips fish

Date	Mintage	VF20	XF40	MS60	MS63	MS65
1997	10,000	PF63 22.00	PF65 27.00			

KM# 40 5 KINA
20.00 g., 0.900 Silver 0.5787 oz. ASW **Series:** Olympic Games 2000 **Obv:** National emblem **Rev:** Sailboarder

Date	Mintage	VF20	XF40	MS60	MS63	MS65
1997	—	PF63 22.00	PF65 27.00			

KM# 43 5 KINA
31.50 g., 0.925 Silver 0.9368 oz. ASW, 38.6 mm. **Obv:** National emblem **Rev:** Sailing ship **Edge:** Reeded

Date	Mintage	VF20	XF40	MS60	MS63	MS65
1997	—	PF63 22.00	PF65 27.00			

KM# 44 5 KINA
31.43 g., 0.925 Silver 0.9347 oz. ASW, 38.6 mm. **Subject:** Green Tree Python **Obv:** National emblem **Rev:** Snake in tree **Edge:** Reeded

Date	Mintage	VF20	XF40	MS60	MS63	MS65
1997	—	—	—	—	—	—
1998	—	PF63 45.00	PF65 55.00			

KM# 47 5 KINA
31.35 g., 0.925 Silver 0.9323 oz. ASW, 38.6 mm. **Subject:** British Queen Mother **Obv:** National emblem **Rev:** Cameo above Sandringham Palace **Edge:** Reeded

Date	Mintage	VF20	XF40	MS60	MS63	MS65
1997	—	PF63 27.00	PF65 32.00			

KM# 45 5 KINA
31.85 g., 0.925 Silver 0.9472 oz. ASW, 38.6 mm. **Subject:** Queen Mother **Obv:** National emblem **Rev:** Investiture of Prince Charles **Edge:** Reeded

Date	Mintage	VF20	XF40	MS60	MS63	MS65
1998	—	PF63 27.00	PF65 32.00			

KM# 48 5 KINA
31.53 g., 0.925 Silver 0.9377 oz. ASW, 38.6 mm. **Subject:** Princess Diana **Obv:** National emblem **Rev:** Diana and Bishop Tutu **Edge:** Reeded

Date	Mintage	VF20	XF40	MS60	MS63	MS65
1998	—	PF63 27.00	PF65 32.00			

KM# 55 5 KINA
Silver, 39 mm. **Subject:** World Cup, 1998 **Obv:** National arms **Rev:** Soccer player

Date	Mintage	VF20	XF40	MS60	MS63	MS65
1998	—	PF63 32.00	PF65 42.00			

KM# 8 10 KINA
Copper-Nickel, 45 mm. **Obv:** National emblem **Rev:** Raggiana Bird of Paradise

Date	Mintage	VF20	XF40	MS60	MS63	MS65
1975 FM (M)	82	—	—	—	60.00	70.00
1975 FM (U)	4,134	—	—	—	10.00	12.50
1976 FM (M)	82	—	—	—	60.00	70.00
1976 FM (U)	976	—	—	—	14.00	18.00
1978 FM (M)	168	—	—	—	50.00	60.00
1978 FM (U)	777	—	—	—	15.00	20.00
1979 FM (M)	82	—	—	—	60.00	70.00
1979 FM (U)	1,366	—	—	—	12.00	16.00
1980 FM (U)	776	—	—	—	15.00	20.00
1983 FM (U)	360	—	—	—	18.00	25.00

KM# 8a 10 KINA
41.60 g., 0.925 Silver 1.2372 oz. ASW, 45 mm. **Obv:** National emblem **Rev:** Raggiana Bird of Paradise

Date	Mintage	VF20	XF40	MS60	MS63	MS65
1975 FM (P)	79,000	PF63 35.00	PF65 38.00			
1976 FM (P)	21,000	PF63 35.00	PF65 38.00			
1978 FM (P)	7,352	PF63 38.00	PF65 40.00			
1979 FM (P)	4,147	PF63 40.00	PF65 42.00			
1980 FM (P)	2,752	PF63 45.00	PF65 47.00			
1983 FM (P)	1,025	PF63 45.00	PF65 48.00			

KM# 8a.1 10 KINA
40.60 g., 0.925 Silver 1.2074 oz. ASW, 42 mm. **Subject:** Reduced size **Obv:** National emblem **Rev:** Raggiana Bird of Paradise **Edge:** Reeded

Date	Mintage	VF20	XF40	MS60	MS63	MS65
1983 FM	1,025	PF63 45.00	PF65 48.00			

KM# 11 10 KINA
Copper-Nickel, 45 mm. **Subject:** Silver Jubilee of Queen Elizabeth II **Obv:** National emblem **Rev:** Young bust right

Date	Mintage	VF20	XF40	MS60	MS63	MS65
1977 FM (M)	82	—	—	—	—	50.00
1977 FM (U)	603	—	—	—	—	25.00

KM# 11a 10 KINA
40.00 g., 0.925 Silver 1.1896 oz. ASW, 45 mm. **Subject:** Silver Jubilee of Queen Elizabeth II **Obv:** National emblem **Rev:** Young bust right

Date	Mintage	VF20	XF40	MS60	MS63	MS65
1977 FM (P)	14,000	PF63 40.00	PF65 42.00			

KM# 21 10 KINA
Copper-Nickel, 45 mm. **Subject:** Royal visit **Obv:** National emblem **Rev:** Conjoined heads right

Date	Mintage	VF20	XF40	MS60	MS63	MS65
1982 FM (M)	—	—	—	—	—	5.00

KM# 21a 10 KINA
40.50 g., 0.925 Silver 1.2044 oz. ASW, 45 mm. **Subject:** Royal visit **Obv:** National emblem **Rev:** Conjoined heads right

Date	Mintage	VF20	XF40	MS60	MS63	MS65
1982 FM (P)	1,185	PF63 52.00	PF65 55.00			

KM# 26 10 KINA
35.60 g., 0.925 Silver 1.0587 oz. ASW **Subject:** Papal visit **Obv:** National emblem **Rev:** Pope with arms outstretched with national arms above **Note:** Prev. KM#26a.

Date	Mintage	VF20	XF40	MS60	MS63	MS65
1984 FM (P)	597	PF63 70.00	PF65 75.00			

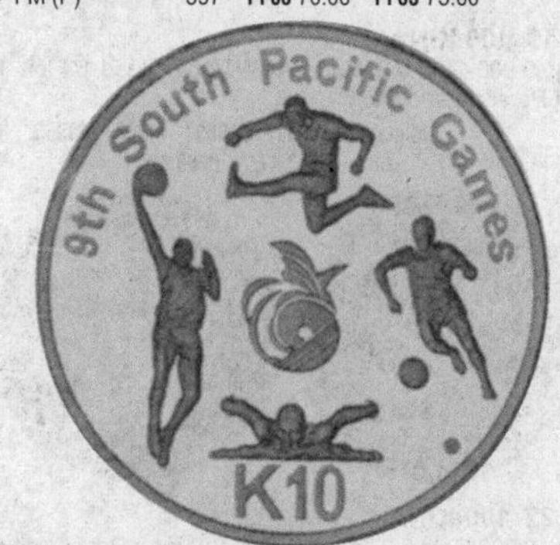

KM# 30 10 KINA
42.12 g., 0.925 Silver 1.2526 oz. ASW **Subject:** 9th South Pacific Games **Obv:** National emblem **Rev:** Assorted olympic athletes around emblem

Date	Mintage	VF20	XF40	MS60	MS63	MS65
1991	1,971	PF63 55.00	PF65 65.00			

KM# 33 10 KINA
1.57 g., 0.999 Gold 0.0505 oz. AGW **Obv:** National emblem **Rev:** Butterfly

Date	Mintage	XF40	MS60	MS63	MS65	MS66
1992	—	PF65 75.00	PF67 85.00	PF69 100		

KM# 33a 10 KINA
1.57 g., 0.995 Platinum 0.0503 oz. APW **Obv:** National emblem **Rev:** Butterfly

Date	Mintage	XF40	MS60	MS63	MS65	MS66
1992	—	PF65 80.00	PF67 90.00	PF69 110		

KM# 46 10 KINA
155.50 g., 0.999 Silver 4.9944 oz. ASW, 64.9 mm. **Subject:** Queen Mother **Obv:** National emblem **Rev:** Queen Mary with the Duchess of York **Edge:** Reeded **Note:** Illustration reduced.

Date	Mintage	VF20	XF40	MS60	MS63	MS65
1998	—	PF63 130	PF65 150			

KM# 52 20 KINA
1.24 g., 0.999 Gold 0.0398 oz. AGW, 13.92 mm. **Obv:** Bird of Paridise **Rev:** Queen Alexandria Wingbird butterfly

Date	Mintage	XF40	MS60	MS63	MS65	MS66
1998	—	PF65 60.00	PF67 75.00	PF69 90.00		

KM# 36 25 KINA
136.00 g., 0.925 Silver 4.0446 oz. ASW enameled, 63 mm. **Obv:** National emblem within wreath **Rev:** Raggiana Bird of Paradise **Note:** Illustration reduced.

Date	Mintage	VF20	XF40	MS60	MS63	MS65
ND-1994	1,000	PF63 165	PF65 180			

KM# 42 50 KINA
6.22 g., 0.900 Gold 0.180 oz. AGW, 21.9 mm. **Obv:** Crowned head right **Rev:** Golden butterfly and value **Edge:** Reeded

Date	Mintage	XF40	MS60	MS63	MS65	MS66
1993	—	PF67 275	PF69 375			

KM# 38 50 KINA
7.97 g., 0.900 Gold 0.2306 oz. AGW **Subject:** Centennial of First Coinage **Obv:** National emblem within wreath **Rev:** Bird of Paradise **Note:** Similar to 5 Kina, KM#37.

Date	Mintage	XF40	MS60	MS63	MS65	MS66
1994 Proof-like	100	—	—	—	450	550
1994	1,500	PF67 350	PF69 450			

KM# 9 100 KINA
9.57 g., 0.900 Gold 0.2769 oz. AGW **Subject:** Independence **Obv:** Head 3/4 left **Rev:** Bird of Paradise

Date	Mintage	XF40	MS60	MS63	MS65	MS66
1975 FM (M)	100	—	—	—	—	—
1975 FM (U)	8,081	—	—	—	375	475
1975 FM (P)	18,000	PF67 365	PF69 465			

KM# 10 100 KINA
9.57 g., 0.900 Gold 0.2769 oz. AGW **Subject:** 1st Anniversary of Independence **Obv:** Symbolic design around center hole **Rev:** National emblem above circular designs around center hole

Date	Mintage	XF40	MS60	MS63	MS65	MS66
1976 FM (M)	100	—	—	—	—	—
1976 FM (U)	250	—	—	—	550	650
1976 FM (P)	8,020	PF67 365	PF69 465			

KM# 12 100 KINA
9.57 g., 0.900 Gold 0.2769 oz. AGW **Obv:** National emblem **Rev:** Papuan hornbill

Date	Mintage	XF40	MS60	MS63	MS65	MS66
1977 FM (M)	100	—	—	—	—	—
1977 FM (U)	362	—	—	—	575	625
1977 FM (P)	3,460	PF67 425	PF69 475			

KM# 13 100 KINA
9.57 g., 0.900 Gold 0.2769 oz. AGW **Obv:** National emblem **Rev:** Bird-wing butterfly **Shape:** 7-sided

Date	Mintage	XF40	MS60	MS63	MS65	MS66
1978 FM (U)	400	—	—	—	525	600
1978 FM (P)	4,751	PF67 375	PF69 475			

KM# 14 100 KINA
9.57 g., 0.900 Gold 0.2769 oz. AGW **Obv:** National emblem **Rev:** Four Faces of the Nation

Date	Mintage	XF40	MS60	MS63	MS65	MS66
1979 FM (M)	102	—	—	—	—	—
1979 FM (U)	286	—	—	—	575	625
1979 FM (P)	3,492	PF67 375	PF69 475			

KM# 16 100 KINA
7.83 g., 0.500 Gold 0.1259 oz. AGW **Subject:** South Pacific Festival of Arts **Obv:** National emblem **Rev:** Design divides circle

Date	Mintage	XF40	MS60	MS63	MS65	MS66
1980	7,500	PF67 175	PF69 220			

KM# 17 100 KINA
9.57 g., 0.900 Gold 0.2769 oz. AGW **Subject:** 5th Anniversary of Independence **Obv:** National emblem **Rev:** Map and flag

Date	Mintage	XF40	MS60	MS63	MS65	MS66
1980 FM (M)	30	—	—	—	700	800
1980 FM (P)	1,118	PF67 450	PF69 500			

KM# 19 100 KINA
9.57 g., 0.900 Gold 0.2769 oz. AGW **Obv:** Head 1/4 left **Rev:** Bird of Paradise and stars

Date	Mintage	XF40	MS60	MS63	MS65	MS66
1981 FM (P)	685	PF67 475	PF69 525			

KM# 22 100 KINA
9.57 g., 0.900 Gold 0.2769 oz. AGW **Subject:** Royal Visit **Obv:** National emblem **Rev:** Conjoined heads right

Date	Mintage	XF40	MS60	MS63	MS65	MS66
1982 FM (P)	484	PF67 450	PF69 500			

KM# 24 100 KINA
9.57 g., 0.900 Gold 0.2769 oz. AGW **Subject:** 10th Anniversary - Bank of Papua New Guinea **Obv:** Symbol around center hole **Rev:** National emblem above center hole

Date	Mintage	XF40	MS60	MS63	MS65	MS66
1983 FM (P)	378	PF67 475	PF69 525			

KM# 27 100 KINA
9.57 g., 0.900 Gold 0.2769 oz. AGW **Subject:** 100th Anniversary - Founding of British and German Protectorates **Obv:** National emblem **Rev:** Value above flags

Date	Mintage	XF40	MS60	MS63	MS65	MS66
1984 FM (P)	274	PF67 485	PF69 535			

KM# 29 100 KINA
9.57 g., 0.900 Gold 0.2769 oz. AGW **Obv:** National emblem **Rev:** Queen Alexandra Butterfly **Shape:** 7-sided

Date	Mintage	XF40	MS60	MS63	MS65	MS66
1990	500	—	—	—	475	525
1990	Est. 5000	PF67 425	PF69 475			
1992	Est. 5000	PF67 425	PF69 475			

KM# 29a 100 KINA
9.57 g., 0.995 Platinum 0.3061 oz. APW **Obv:** National emblem **Rev:** Queen Alexandra butterfly

Date	Mintage	XF40	MS60	MS63	MS65	MS66
1992	500	—	—	—	700	800
1992	Est. 5000	PF67 575	PF69 625			

KM# 35 100 KINA
9.57 g., 0.900 Gold 0.2769 oz. AGW **Subject:** 9th South Pacific Games **Obv:** National emblem **Rev:** Artistic design **Shape:** 7-sided

Date	Mintage	XF40	MS60	MS63	MS65	MS66
1991	5,000	PF67 425	PF69 475			

KM# 32 100 KINA
9.57 g., 0.900 Gold 0.2769 oz. AGW **Subject:** 20th Anniversary of Independence **Obv:** National emblem **Rev:** Bird of Paradise with flag and flowers

Date	Mintage	XF40	MS60	MS63	MS65	MS66
1995 FM	—	PF67 500	PF69 550			

PIEDFORT

KM#	Date	Mintage	Identification	Mkt Val
P1	1982	39	5 Kina. Silver. KM18.	150

MINT SETS

KM#	Date	Mintage	Identification	Issue Price	Mkt Val
MS1	1975FM (8)	4,134	KM1-8	30.00	100
MS2	1976FM (8)	976	KM1-8	30.00	125
MS3	1977FM (8)	603	KM1-7, 11	30.00	110
MS4	1978FM (8)	777	KM#1-8	30.00	115
MS5	1979FM (8)	1,366	KM1-8	31.00	125
MS6	1980FM (9)	—	KM1-8, 15	35.00	55.00
MS7	1982FM (8)	—	KM1-6, 20, 21	36.00	30.00
MS8	1983FM (8)	360	KM1-6, 8, 23	36.00	50.00

PROOF SETS

KM#	Date	Mintage	Identification	Issue Price	Mkt Val
PS1	1975FM (8)	42,340	KM1-6, 7a, 8a	60.00	67.50
PS2	1976FM (8)	16,323	KM1-6, 7a, 8a	60.00	67.50
PS3	1977FM (8)	7,721	KM1-6, 7a, 11a	60.00	75.00
PS4	1978FM (8)	5,540	KM1-6, 7a, 8a	70.00	72.50
PS5	1979FM (8)	2,728	KM1-6, 7a, 8a	72.00	72.50
PS6	1980FM (9)	—	KM1-6, 7a, 8a, 15	130	80.00
PS7	1981FM (6)	10,000	KM1-6	29.00	15.00
PS8	1982FM (8)	—	KM1-6, 20a, 21a	92.00	95.00
PS9	1983FM (8)	—	KM1-6, 8a.1, 23a	132	95.00
PS10	1984FM (8)	—	KM1-6, 25, 26	133	97.50
PS11	1992 (4)	250	KM29a, 33, 33a, 34	—	925

PARAGUAY

The Republic of Paraguay, a landlocked country in the heart of South America surrounded by Argentina, Bolivia and Brazil, has an area of 157,048 sq. mi. (406,750 sq. km.) and a population of *4.5 million, 95 percent of whom are of mixed Spanish and Indian descent. Capital: Asuncion. The country is predominantly agrarian, with no important mineral deposits or oil reserves. Meat, timber, hides, oilseeds, tobacco and cotton account for 70 per-cent of Paraguay's export revenue.

Paraguay was first visited by a ship-wrecked Spaniard named Alejo Garcia, in 1524. The interior was explored by Sebastian Cabot in 1527 and 1528, when he sailed up the Parana and Paraguay rivers. Asuncion, which would become the center of a Spanish colonial province embracing much of southern South America, was established by the Spanish explorer Juan de Salazar on Aug. 15,1537. For 150 years the history of Paraguay was largely the history of the agricultural colonies established by the Jesuits in the south and east to Christianize the Indians. In 1811, following the outbreak of the South American wars of independence, Paraguayan patriots over-threw the local Spanish authorities and proclaimed their country's independence.

During the Triple Alliance War (1864-1870) in which Paraguay faced Argentina, Brazil and Uruguay, Asuncion's ladies gathered in an Assembly on Feb. 24, 1867 and decided to give up their jewelry in order to help the national defense. The President of the Republic, Francisco Solano Lopez accepted the offering and ordered one twentieth of it be used to mint the first Paraguayan gold coins according to the Decree of the 11th of Sept.,1867.

Two dies were made, one by Bouvet, and another by an American, Leonard Charles, while only the die made by Bouvet was eventually used.

MINT MARK

HF – LeLocle (Swiss)

REPUBLIC

DECIMAL COINAGE

KM# 6 5 CENTAVOS

Copper-Nickel, 17 mm. **Obv:** Seated lion with liberty cap on pole, date below **Obv. Legend:** REPUBLICA DEL PARAGUAY **Rev:** Value within wreath

Date	Mintage	F12	VF20	XF40	MS60	MS63
1900	600,000	2.00	9.00	30.00	100	150

KM# 9 5 CENTAVOS

Copper-Nickel, 17 mm. **Obv:** Radiant star within wreath **Rev:** Value within flower chain

Date	Mintage	F12	VF20	XF40	MS60	MS63
1908	400,000	2.50	8.00	15.00	35.00	75.00

KM# 7 10 CENTAVOS

Copper-Nickel, 19 mm. **Obv:** Seated lion with liberty cap on pole, date below **Obv. Legend:** REPUBLICA DEL PARAGUAY **Rev:** Value within wreath

Date	Mintage	F12	VF20	XF40	MS60	MS63
1900	1,200,000	2.00	7.00	20.00	80.00	150

KM# 10 10 CENTAVOS

Copper-Nickel, 19 mm. **Obv:** Radiant star within wreath **Rev:** Value within flower chain

Date	Mintage	F12	VF20	XF40	MS60	MS63
1908	800,000	2.50	6.50	15.00	35.00	75.00

KM# 8 20 CENTAVOS

Copper-Nickel, 21 mm. **Obv:** Seated lion with liberty cap on pole, date below **Obv. Legend:** REPUBLICA DEL PARAGUAY **Rev:** Value within wreath

Date	Mintage	F12	VF20	XF40	MS60	MS63
1900	750,000	2.00	5.00	25.00	100	150

KM# 11 20 CENTAVOS

Copper-Nickel, 21 mm. **Obv:** Radiant star within wreath **Rev:** Value

Date	Mintage	F12	VF20	XF40	MS60	MS63
1908	1,000,000	2.50	7.00	20.00	40.00	80.00

KM# 12 50 CENTAVOS

2.00 g., Copper-Nickel **Obv:** Radiant star within wreath **Rev:** Value

Date	Mintage	VF20	XF40	MS60	MS63	MS65
1925	4,000,000	1.00	2.00	5.00	10.00	15.00

KM# 15 50 CENTAVOS

0.90 g., Aluminum, 17.5 mm. **Obv:** Radiant star within wreath **Rev:** Value

Date	Mintage	VF20	XF40	MS60	MS63	MS65
1938	400,000	0.75	1.50	3.50	6.50	10.00

KM# 13 PESO

2.93 g., Copper-Nickel, 19 mm. **Obv:** Radiant star within wreath **Rev:** Value

Date	Mintage	VF20	XF40	MS60	MS63	MS65
1925	3,500,000	0.75	1.50	3.50	6.50	10.00

KM# 16 PESO

Aluminum **Obv:** Radiant star within wreath **Rev:** Value

Date	Mintage	VF20	XF40	MS60	MS63	MS65
1938	—	0.75	1.50	4.00	7.50	12.00

KM# 14 2 PESOS

4.00 g., Copper-Nickel, 22 mm. **Obv:** Radiant star within wreath **Rev:** Value

Date	Mintage	VF20	XF40	MS60	MS63	MS65
1925	2,500,000	0.75	1.50	3.50	6.50	10.00

KM# 17 2 PESOS

1.76 g., Aluminum, 22.5 mm. **Obv:** Radiant star within wreath **Rev:** Value

Date	Mintage	VF20	XF40	MS60	MS63	MS65
1938	—	0.75	1.50	3.50	6.50	10.00

KM# 18 5 PESOS

Copper-Nickel, 25.5 mm. **Obv:** Radiant star within wreath **Rev:** Value

Date	Mintage	VF20	XF40	MS60	MS63	MS65
1939	4,000,000	1.00	2.00	4.00	7.50	12.00

KM# 19 10 PESOS

Copper-Nickel, 28.5 mm. **Obv:** Radiant star within wreath **Rev:** Value

Date	Mintage	VF20	XF40	MS60	MS63	MS65
1939	4,000,000	1.00	2.00	5.00	10.00	15.00

REFORM COINAGE

100 Centimos = 1 Guarani

KM# 20 CENTIMO

2.00 g., Aluminum-Bronze, 17.5 mm. **Obv:** Flower within circle **Rev:** Value within wreath

Date	Mintage	VF20	XF40	MS60	MS63	MS65
1944	3,500,000	0.50	1.00	2.00	3.00	5.00
1948	2,000,000	0.50	1.00	2.00	3.00	5.00
1948 HF	—	0.50	1.00	2.00	3.00	5.00
1950	1,096,000	0.25	0.75	1.50	2.50	5.00
1950 HF	—	0.25	0.75	1.50	2.50	5.00

KM# 21 5 CENTIMOS

Aluminum-Bronze, 19 mm. **Obv:** Passion flower within circle **Rev:** Value within wreath

Date	Mintage	VF20	XF40	MS60	MS63	MS65
1944	2,195,000	0.50	1.00	2.00	4.00	7.50
1947 HF	13,111,000	0.20	0.50	1.00	2.00	5.00
1947	—	0.20	0.30	0.50	1.00	2.50

KM# 22 10 CENTIMOS

Aluminum-Bronze, 21 mm. **Obv:** Orchid within circle **Rev:** Value within wreath

Date	Mintage	VF20	XF40	MS60	MS63	MS65
1944	975,000	0.75	1.50	3.00	6.00	9.00
1947	6,656,000	0.25	0.50	1.00	3.00	7.50
1947 HF	—	0.50	1.00	2.00	5.00	8.00

KM# 25 10 CENTIMOS

Aluminum-Bronze, 19 mm. **Obv:** Seated lion with liberty cap on pole within circle **Rev:** Value within wreath **Shape:** Scalloped

Date	Mintage	VF20	XF40	MS60	MS63	MS65
1953	5,000,000	0.15	0.25	0.50	1.00	1.75
1953 Proof; 1 known	—	PF63 375				

Note: Medal die rotation

KM# 26 15 CENTIMOS

Aluminum-Bronze, 21 mm. **Obv:** Seated lion with liberty cap on pole within circle **Rev:** Value within wreath **Shape:** Scalloped

Date	Mintage	VF20	XF40	MS60	MS63	MS65
1953	5,000,000	0.15	0.25	0.50	1.00	1.75
1953 Proof; 1 known	—	PF63 375				

Note: Medal die rotation

KM# 23 25 CENTIMOS

Aluminum-Bronze, 23 mm. **Obv:** Orchid within circle **Rev:** Value within wreath

Date	Mintage	VF20	XF40	MS60	MS63	MS65
1944	700,000	0.75	1.50	3.00	6.00	12.00
1948 HF	600,000	0.60	1.25	2.50	5.00	8.00
1948	—	0.60	1.25	2.50	5.00	8.00
1951 HF	1,000,000	0.50	1.00	1.50	2.50	5.00
(1951)	—	0.60	1.25	2.50	5.00	8.00

KM# 27 25 CENTIMOS

Aluminum-Bronze, 23 mm. **Obv:** Seated lion with liberty cap on pole within circle **Rev:** Value within wreath **Shape:** Scalloped

Date	Mintage	VF20	XF40	MS60	MS63	MS65
1953	2,000,000	0.15	0.30	0.50	1.00	2.00
1953 Proof; 1 known	—	PF63 450				

Note: Medal die rotation

KM# 24 50 CENTIMOS

Aluminum-Bronze, 25 mm. **Obv:** Seated lion with liberty cap on pole within circle **Rev:** Value within wreath

Date	Mintage	VF20	XF40	MS60	MS63	MS65
1944	2,485,000	1.00	2.00	5.00	7.00	10.00
1951	2,893,000	0.50	1.25	2.00	3.00	5.00
(1951) HF	Inc. above	0.50	1.25	2.00	3.00	5.00

KM# 28 50 CENTIMOS

4.54 g., Aluminum-Bronze, 25 mm. **Obv:** Seated lion with liberty cap on pole within circle **Rev:** Value within wreath **Shape:** Scalloped

Date	Mintage	VF20	XF40	MS60	MS63	MS65
1953	2,000,000	0.15	0.30	0.50	1.00	2.50
1953 Proof; 1 known	—	PF63 450				

Note: Medal die rotation

KM# 151 GUARANI

2.90 g., Stainless Steel **Obv:** Soldier 3/4 facing **Rev:** Tobacco plant and value

Date	Mintage	VF20	XF40	MS60	MS63	MS65
1975	10,000,000	—	0.15	0.25	0.50	0.75
1975	1,000	PF65 6.00				
1976	12,000,000	—	0.10	0.20	0.40	0.65
1976	1,000	PF65 8.00				

KM# 151a GUARANI

6.99 g., Gold, 18 mm.

Date	Mintage	VF20	XF40	MS60	MS63	MS65
1976 Proof	10	—	—	—	—	2,000

KM# 165 GUARANI

2.60 g., Stainless Steel **Series:** F.A.O. **Obv:** Standing 3/4 figure facing **Rev:** Plant and value **Note:** Varieties exist.

Date	Mintage	VF20	XF40	MS60	MS63	MS65
1978	15,000,000	—	0.15	0.25	0.50	0.75
1978	—	PF65 6.00				
1980	13,000,000	—	0.15	0.25	0.50	0.75
1980	1,000	PF65 6.00				
1984	15,000,000	—	0.10	0.20	0.30	0.50
1986	15,000,000	—	0.10	0.20	0.30	0.50
1988	15,000,000	—	0.10	0.20	0.30	0.50

KM# 165a GUARANI

6.99 g., Gold, 18 mm.

Date	Mintage	VF20	XF40	MS60	MS63	MS65
1978 Proof	10	—	—	—	—	2,000
1980 Proof	10	—	—	—	—	2,000

KM# 192 GUARANI

1.50 g., Brass Plated Steel, 15.03 mm. **Series:** F.A.O. **Edge:** Reeded

Date	Mintage	VF20	XF40	MS60	MS63	MS65
1993	5,000,000	—	0.15	0.25	0.50	0.75

KM# 193 GUARANI

27.00 g., 0.925 Silver 0.803 oz. ASW **Subject:** Encuentro De Dos Mundos **Obv:** National arms within circle of assorted arms **Rev:** Dancer and artistic design within circle

Date	Mintage	VF20	XF40	MS60	MS63	MS65
1997	—	PF63 55.00	PF65 65.00			

KM# 196 GUARANI

27.10 g., 0.925 Silver 0.8059 oz. ASW, 40 mm. **Subject:** Ibero-America Series **Obv:** National arms within circle of assorted arms **Rev:** Cowboy on horse **Edge:** Reeded

Date	Mintage	VF20	XF40	MS60	MS63	MS65
2000	—	PF63 65.00	PF65 75.00			

KM# 152 5 GUARANIES

3.80 g., Stainless Steel, 20 mm. **Obv:** Half-length figure with jug looking right **Rev:** Cotton plant and value

Date	Mintage	VF20	XF40	MS60	MS63	MS65
1975	7,500,000	—	0.15	0.25	0.50	0.75
1975	1,000	PF65 6.00				

KM# 166 5 GUARANIES

3.80 g., Stainless Steel, 20 mm. **Series:** F.A.O. **Obv:** Half-length figure with jug looking right **Rev:** Cotton plant and value **Note:** Varieties exist.

Date	Mintage	VF20	XF40	MS60	MS63	MS65
1978	10,000,000	—	0.15	0.30	0.60	0.85
1978	—	PF65 6.00				
1980	12,000,000	—	0.15	0.30	0.60	0.85
1980	1,000	PF65 6.00				
1984	15,000,000	—	0.10	0.20	0.40	0.60
1986	15,000,000	—	0.10	0.20	0.40	0.60

KM# 166b 5 GUARANIES

Gold, 20 mm.

Date	Mintage	VF20	XF40	MS60	MS63	MS65
1978	10	PF65 2,200				
1980	10	PF65 2,200				

KM# 166a 5 GUARANIES

1.95 g., Nickel-Bronze, 16.97 mm. **Series:** F.A.O. **Obv:** Half-length figure with jug looking right **Rev:** Cotton plant and value **Edge:** Reeded

Date	Mintage	VF20	XF40	MS60	MS63	MS65
1992	15,000,000	—	0.10	0.15	0.30	0.50

KM# 153 10 GUARANIES

4.50 g., Stainless Steel, 22 mm. **Obv:** Bust 1/4 left **Rev:** Cow head left and value

Date	Mintage	VF20	XF40	MS60	MS63	MS65
1975	10,000,000	0.10	0.20	0.40	0.75	1.00
1975	1,000	PF65 8.00				
1976	10,000,000	0.10	0.20	0.40	0.75	1.00
1976	1,000	PF65 10.00				

KM# 153a 10 GUARANIES

Gold, 22 mm.

Date	Mintage	VF20	XF40	MS60	MS63	MS65
1976	10	PF65 2,200				

KM# 167 10 GUARANIES

4.50 g., Stainless Steel, 22 mm. **Series:** F.A.O. **Obv:** Bust 1/4 left **Rev:** Cow head left and value **Note:** Varieties exist.

Date	Mintage	VF20	XF40	MS60	MS63	MS65
1978	15,000,000	0.10	0.20	0.40	0.75	1.00
1978	—	PF65 8.00				
1980	15,000,000	0.10	0.20	0.40	0.75	1.00
1980	1,000	PF65 8.00				

Date	Mintage	VF20	XF40	MS60	MS63	MS65
1984	20,000,000	0.10	0.15	0.25	0.50	0.75
1986	35,000,000	0.10	0.15	0.25	0.50	0.75
1988	40,000,000	0.10	0.15	0.25	0.50	0.75

KM# 167a 10 GUARANIES
Gold, 22 mm.

Date	Mintage	VF20	XF40	MS60	MS63	MS65
1978	10	PF65 2,200				
1980	10	PF65 2,200				

KM# 178 10 GUARANIES
2.69 g., Nickel-Bronze, 19.34 mm. **Series:** F.A.O. **Obv:** Bust 1/4 left **Rev:** Cow head left and value **Edge:** Reeded

Date	Mintage	VF20	XF40	MS60	MS63	MS65
1990	40,000,000	—	0.10	0.20	0.40	0.60

KM# 178a 10 GUARANIES
Brass Plated Steel **Series:** F.A.O. **Obv:** Bust of Garay 1/4 left **Rev:** Cow's head left at left of value **Note:** Magnetic.

Date	Mintage	VF20	XF40	MS60	MS63	MS65
1996	20,000,000	—	0.10	0.20	0.40	0.60

KM# 154 50 GUARANIES
7.40 g., Stainless Steel, 26 mm. **Obv:** Uniformed bust facing **Rev:** Value above dam on the Acaray River

Date	Mintage	VF20	XF40	MS60	MS63	MS65
1975	9,500,000	0.40	0.60	0.75	1.25	1.50
1975	1,000	PF65 10.00				

KM# 169 50 GUARANIES
7.40 g., Stainless Steel, 26.1 mm. **Obv:** Bust of General Estigarribia facing **Obv. Legend:** REPUBLICA DEL PARAGUAY **Rev:** Acaray River Dam **Note:** Examples of each date differ slightly.

Date	Mintage	VF20	XF40	MS60	MS63	MS65
1980	10,700,000	0.40	0.60	0.75	1.25	1.50
1980	1,000	PF65 10.00				
1986	15,000,000	0.40	0.60	0.75	1.25	1.50
1988	25,000,000	0.30	0.45	0.65	1.00	1.25

KM# 169a 50 GUARANIES
Gold, 25 mm.

Date	Mintage	VF20	XF40	MS60	MS63	MS65
1980 Proof	10	—	—	—	—	—

KM# 191 50 GUARANIES
3.77 g., Copper-Nickel-Zinc, 21.69 mm. **Obv:** Bust of Major General J.F. Estigarribia facing **Obv. Legend:** REPUBLICA DEL PARAGUAY **Rev:** Acary River Dam **Rev. Legend:** REPRESA ACARAY **Edge:** Reeded

Date	Mintage	VF20	XF40	MS60	MS63	MS65
1992	35,000,000	—	—	0.50	0.75	1.00

KM# 191a 50 GUARANIES
Brass Plated Steel **Obv:** Uniformed bust facing **Rev:** Value above river dam **Note:** Magnetic

Date	Mintage	VF20	XF40	MS60	MS63	MS65
1995	25,000,000	—	—	0.50	0.75	1.00
1998	22,000,000	—	—	0.50	0.75	1.00

KM# 177 100 GUARANIES
10.45 g., Copper-Nickel-Zinc **Obv:** Bust of General Jose E. Dias facing **Obv. Legend:** REPUBLICA DEL PARAGUAY **Rev:** Ruins of Humaita **Rev. Inscription:** RUINAS DE HUMAITA 1865/70

Date	Mintage	VF20	XF40	MS60	MS63	MS65
1990	35,000,000	—	—	1.25	2.25	2.75

KM# 177a 100 GUARANIES
5.45 g., Brass Plated Steel **Obv:** Bust of General Jose E. Dias facing **Obv. Legend:** REPUBLICA DEL PARAGUAY **Rev:** Ruins of Humaita **Rev. Inscription:** RUINAS DE HUMAITA 1865/70 **Note:** Reduced weight and thickness.

Date	Mintage	VF20	XF40	MS60	MS63	MS65
1993	35,000,000	—	—	0.80	1.50	2.00
1995	10,000,000	—	—	0.80	1.50	2.00
1996	30,000,000	—	—	0.80	1.50	2.00

KM# 31 150 GUARANIES
25.00 g., 0.999 Silver 0.803 oz. ASW **Obv:** National arms **Rev:** Uniformed bust of General A. Stroessner facing

Date	Mintage	VF20	XF40	MS60	MS63	MS65
1972	Est. 10000	PF63 50.00	PF65 65.00			

KM# 32 150 GUARANIES
25.00 g., 0.999 Silver 0.803 oz. ASW **Subject:** Munich Olympics **Obv:** National arms **Rev:** Runner flanked by design and Olympic rings

Date	Mintage	VF20	XF40	MS60	MS63	MS65
1972	Est. 10000	PF63 60.00	PF65 75.00			

KM# 33 150 GUARANIES
25.00 g., 0.999 Silver 0.803 oz. ASW **Subject:** Munich Olympics **Obv:** National arms **Rev:** Broad jumper

Date	Mintage	VF20	XF40	MS60	MS63	MS65
1972	Est. 10000	PF63 60.00	PF65 75.00			

KM# 34 150 GUARANIES
25.00 g., 0.999 Silver 0.803 oz. ASW **Subject:** Munich Olympics **Obv:** National arms **Rev:** Soccer player

Date	Mintage	VF20	XF40	MS60	MS63	MS65
1972	Est. 10000	PF63 60.00	PF65 75.00			

KM# 35 150 GUARANIES
25.00 g., 0.999 Silver 0.803 oz. ASW **Subject:** Munich Olympics **Obv:** National arms **Rev:** Hurdler

Date	Mintage	VF20	XF40	MS60	MS63	MS65
1972	Est. 10000	PF63 60.00	PF65 75.00			

KM# 36 150 GUARANIES
25.00 g., 0.999 Silver 0.803 oz. ASW **Subject:** Munich Olympics **Obv:** National arms **Rev:** High jumper

Date	Mintage	VF20	XF40	MS60	MS63	MS65
1972	Est. 10000	PF63 60.00	PF65 75.00			

KM# 37 150 GUARANIES
25.00 g., 0.999 Silver 0.803 oz. ASW **Subject:** Munich Olympics **Obv:** National arms **Rev:** Boxer

Date	Mintage	VF20	XF40	MS60	MS63	MS65
1973	Est. 10000	PF63 60.00	PF65 75.00			

KM# 59 150 GUARANIES
25.00 g., 0.999 Silver 0.803 oz. ASW **Obv:** National arms **Rev:** Mariscal Jose F. Estigarribia

Date	Mintage	VF20	XF40	MS60	MS63	MS65
1973	Est. 10000	PF63 45.00	PF65 60.00			

KM# 60 150 GUARANIES
25.00 g., 0.999 Silver 0.803 oz. ASW **Obv:** National arms **Rev:** Mariscal Francisco Solano Lopez

Date	Mintage	VF20	XF40	MS60	MS63	MS65
1973	Est. 10000	PF63 45.00	PF65 60.00			

KM# 61 150 GUARANIES
25.00 g., 0.999 Silver 0.803 oz. ASW **Obv:** National arms **Rev:** General Jose E. Diaz

Date	Mintage	VF20	XF40	MS60	MS63	MS65
1973	Est. 10000	PF63 45.00	PF65 60.00			

KM# 62 150 GUARANIES
25.00 g., 0.999 Silver 0.803 oz. ASW **Obv:** National arms **Rev:** General Bernardino Cabaliero

Date	Mintage	VF20	XF40	MS60	MS63	MS65
1973	Est. 10000	PF63 45.00	PF65 60.00			

KM# 63 150 GUARANIES
25.00 g., 0.999 Silver 0.803 oz. ASW **Obv:** National arms **Rev:** Teotihucana Culture sculpture

Date	Mintage	VF20	XF40	MS60	MS63	MS65
1973	Est. 10000	PF63 40.00	PF65 55.00			

KM# 64 150 GUARANIES
25.00 g., 0.999 Silver 0.803 oz. ASW **Obv:** National arms **Rev:** Huasteca Culture sculpture

Date	Mintage	VF20	XF40	MS60	MS63	MS65
1973	Est. 10000	PF63 40.00	PF65 55.00			

KM# 65 150 GUARANIES
25.00 g., 0.999 Silver 0.803 oz. ASW **Obv:** National arms **Rev:** Mixteca Culture animal sculpture

Date	Mintage	VF20	XF40	MS60	MS63	MS65
1973	Est. 10000	PF63 45.00	PF65 60.00			

KM# 66 150 GUARANIES
25.00 g., 0.999 Silver 0.803 oz. ASW **Obv:** National arms **Rev:** Veracruz Ceramica Vase

Date	Mintage	VF20	XF40	MS60	MS63	MS65
1973	Est. 10000	PF63 45.00	PF65 60.00			

KM# 67 150 GUARANIES
25.00 g., 0.999 Silver 0.803 oz. ASW **Obv:** National arms **Rev:** Veracruz Culture sculpture facing

Date	Mintage	VF20	XF40	MS60	MS63	MS65
1973	Est. 10000	PF63 45.00	PF65 60.00			

KM# 68 150 GUARANIES
25.00 g., 0.999 Silver 0.803 oz. ASW **Obv:** National arms **Rev:** Albrecht Durer facing

Date	Mintage	VF20	XF40	MS60	MS63	MS65
1973	Est. 10000	PF63 50.00	PF65 65.00			

KM# 69 150 GUARANIES
25.00 g., 0.999 Silver 0.803 oz. ASW **Obv:** National arms **Rev:** Johann Wolfgang Goethe

Date	Mintage	VF20	XF40	MS60	MS63	MS65
1973	Est. 10000	PF63 50.00	PF65 65.00			

KM# 107 150 GUARANIES
25.00 g., 0.999 Silver 0.803 oz. ASW **Obv:** National arms **Rev:** Head of President Abraham Lincoln left

Date	Mintage	VF20	XF40	MS60	MS63	MS65
1974	Est. 10000	PF63 60.00	PF65 75.00			

KM# 108 150 GUARANIES
25.00 g., 0.999 Silver 0.803 oz. ASW **Obv:** National arms **Rev:** Ludwig van Beethoven

Date	Mintage	VF20	XF40	MS60	MS63	MS65
1974	Est. 10000	PF63 60.00	PF65 75.00			

KM# 109 150 GUARANIES
25.00 g., 0.999 Silver 0.803 oz. ASW **Obv:** National arms **Rev:** Head of Otto von Bismarck right

Date	Mintage	VF20	XF40	MS60	MS63	MS65
1974	Est. 10000	PF63 60.00	PF65 75.00			

KM# 110 150 GUARANIES
25.00 g., 0.999 Silver 0.803 oz. ASW **Obv:** National arms **Rev:** Head of Albert Einstein left

Date	Mintage	VF20	XF40	MS60	MS63	MS65
1974	Est. 10000	PF63 70.00	PF65 85.00			

KM# 111 150 GUARANIES
25.00 g., 0.999 Silver 0.803 oz. ASW **Obv:** National arms **Rev:** Head of Giuseppe Garibaldi facing

Date	Mintage	VF20	XF40	MS60	MS63	MS65
1974	Est. 10000	PF63 50.00	PF65 65.00			

KM# 112 150 GUARANIES
25.00 g., 0.999 Silver 0.803 oz. ASW **Obv:** National arms **Rev:** Head of Alessandro Manzoni facing

Date	Mintage	VF20	XF40	MS60	MS63	MS65
1974	Est. 10000	PF63 45.00	PF65 60.00			

KM# 113 150 GUARANIES
25.00 g., 0.999 Silver 0.803 oz. ASW **Obv:** National arms **Rev:** William Tell and son facing

Date	Mintage	VF20	XF40	MS60	MS63	MS65
1974	Est. 10000	PF63 45.00	PF65 60.00			

KM# 114 150 GUARANIES
25.00 g., 0.999 Silver 0.803 oz. ASW **Obv:** National arms **Rev:** Head of John F. Kennedy left

Date	Mintage	VF20	XF40	MS60	MS63	MS65
1974	Est. 10000	PF63 45.00	PF65 60.00			

KM# 115 150 GUARANIES
25.00 g., 0.999 Silver 0.803 oz. ASW **Obv:** National arms **Rev:** Head of Konrad Adenauer left

Date	Mintage	VF20	XF40	MS60	MS63	MS65
1974	Est. 10000	PF63 50.00	PF65 65.00			

KM# 116 150 GUARANIES
25.00 g., 0.999 Silver 0.803 oz. ASW **Obv:** National arms **Rev:** Head of Winston Churchill left

Date	Mintage	VF20	XF40	MS60	MS63	MS65
1974	Est. 10000	PF63 45.00	PF65 60.00			

KM# 117 150 GUARANIES
25.00 g., 0.999 Silver 0.803 oz. ASW **Obv:** National arms **Rev:** Head of Pope John XXIII left

Date	Mintage	VF20	XF40	MS60	MS63	MS65
1974	Est. 10000	PF63 50.00	PF65 65.00			

KM# 118 150 GUARANIES
25.00 g., 0.999 Silver 0.803 oz. ASW **Obv:** National arms **Rev:** Head of Pope Paul VI left

Date	Mintage	VF20	XF40	MS60	MS63	MS65
1974	Est. 10000	PF63 50.00	PF65 65.00			

KM# 155 150 GUARANIES
25.00 g., 0.999 Silver 0.803 oz. ASW **Obv:** National arms **Rev:** Parliament building

Date	Mintage	VF20	XF40	MS60	MS63	MS65
1975	Est. 10000	PF63 45.00	PF65 60.00			

KM# 156 150 GUARANIES
25.00 g., 0.999 Silver 0.803 oz. ASW **Subject:** Apollo 11 Mission **Obv:** National arms **Rev:** Eagle landing on moon with earth at left

Date	Mintage	VF20	XF40	MS60	MS63	MS65
1975	Est. 10000	PF63 50.00	PF65 65.00			

KM# 157 150 GUARANIES
25.00 g., 0.999 Silver 0.803 oz. ASW **Subject:** Apollo 15 Mission **Obv:** National arms **Rev:** Apollo mission design within circle

Date	Mintage	VF20	XF40	MS60	MS63	MS65
1975	Est. 10000	PF63 50.00	PF65 65.00			

KM# 158 150 GUARANIES
25.00 g., 0.999 Silver 0.803 oz. ASW **Obv:** National arms **Rev:** Friendship Bridge

Date	Mintage	VF20	XF40	MS60	MS63	MS65
1975	Est. 10000	PF63 45.00	PF65 60.00			

KM# 159 150 GUARANIES
25.00 g., 0.999 Silver 0.803 oz. ASW **Obv:** National arms **Rev:** Holy Trinity Church

Date	Mintage	VF20	XF40	MS60	MS63	MS65
1975	Est. 10000	PF63 45.00	PF65 60.00			

KM# 160 150 GUARANIES
25.00 g., 0.999 Silver 0.803 oz. ASW **Obv:** National arms **Rev:** Ruins of Humaita

Date	Mintage	VF20	XF40	MS60	MS63	MS65
1975	Est. 10000	PF63 45.00	PF65 60.00			

KM# 29 300 GUARANIES
26.60 g., 0.720 Silver 0.6158 oz. ASW, 38 mm. **Subject:** 4th Term of President Stroessner **Obv:** Seated lion with liberty cap on pole within circle **Rev:** Head left

Date	Mintage	VF20	XF40	MS60	MS63	MS65
1968	250,000	—	—	16.00	20.00	28.00

KM# 194 500 GUARANIES
Brass Plated Steel **Obv:** Head of General Bernardino Caballero facing **Rev:** Bank of Paraguay within circle

Date	Mintage	VF20	XF40	MS60	MS63	MS65
1997	20,000,000	—	—	1.50	2.25	3.00

KM# 195 500 GUARANIES
7.82 g., Brass Plated Steel **Obv:** Head of General Bernardino Caballero facing **Obv. Legend:** REPUBLICA DEL PARAGUAY **Rev:** Bank above value within circle **Rev. Legend:** BANCO CENTRAL DEL PARAGUAY

Date	Mintage	VF20	XF40	MS60	MS63	MS65
1997	—	—	—	20.00	35.00	50.00
1998	15,000,000	—	—	1.50	2.25	3.00

KM# 38 1500 GUARANIES
10.70 g., 0.900 Gold 0.3096 oz. AGW **Obv:** National arms **Rev:** Uniformed bust of General A. Stroessner facing

Date	Mintage	VF20	XF40	MS60	MS63	MS65
1972	Est. 1500	PF65 525				

KM# 39 1500 GUARANIES
10.70 g., 0.900 Gold 0.3096 oz. AGW **Subject:** Munich Olympics **Obv:** National arms **Rev:** Runner

Date	Mintage	VF20	XF40	MS60	MS63	MS65
1972	Est. 1500	PF65 700				

KM# 40 1500 GUARANIES
10.70 g., 0.900 Gold 0.3096 oz. AGW **Subject:** Munich Olympics **Obv:** National arms **Rev:** Broad jumper

Date	Mintage	VF20	XF40	MS60	MS63	MS65
1972	Est. 1500	PF65 700				

KM# 41 1500 GUARANIES
10.70 g., 0.900 Gold 0.3096 oz. AGW **Subject:** Munich Olympics **Obv:** National arms **Rev:** Soccer

Date	Mintage	VF20	XF40	MS60	MS63	MS65
1972	Est. 1500	PF65 700				

KM# 42 1500 GUARANIES
10.70 g., 0.900 Gold 0.3096 oz. AGW **Subject:** Munich Olympics **Obv:** National arms **Rev:** Hurdler

Date	Mintage	VF20	XF40	MS60	MS63	MS65
1972	Est. 1500	PF65 700				

KM# 43 1500 GUARANIES
10.70 g., 0.900 Gold 0.3096 oz. AGW **Subject:** Munich Olympics **Obv:** National arms **Rev:** High Jumper

Date	Mintage	VF20	XF40	MS60	MS63	MS65
1973	1,500	PF65 700				

KM# 44 1500 GUARANIES
10.70 g., 0.900 Gold 0.3096 oz. AGW **Subject:** Munich Olympics **Obv:** National arms **Rev:** Boxer

Date	Mintage	VF20	XF40	MS60	MS63	MS65
1973	Est. 1500	PF65 700				

KM# 70 1500 GUARANIES
10.70 g., 0.900 Gold 0.3096 oz. AGW **Obv:** National arms **Rev:** Mariscal Jose F. Estigarriba

Date	Mintage	VF20	XF40	MS60	MS63	MS65
1973	Est. 1500	PF65 550				

KM# 71 1500 GUARANIES
10.70 g., 0.900 Gold 0.3096 oz. AGW **Obv:** National arms **Rev:** Head of Mariscal Francisco Solano Lopez facing

Date	Mintage	VF20	XF40	MS60	MS63	MS65
1973	Est. 1500	PF65 550				

KM# 72 1500 GUARANIES
10.70 g., 0.900 Gold 0.3096 oz. AGW **Obv:** National arms **Rev:** Bust of General Jose E. Diaz facing

Date	Mintage	VF20	XF40	MS60	MS63	MS65
1973	Est. 1500	PF65 550				

KM# 73 1500 GUARANIES
10.70 g., 0.900 Gold 0.3096 oz. AGW **Obv:** National arms **Rev:** Head of General Bernardino Caballero facing

Date	Mintage	VF20	XF40	MS60	MS63	MS65
1973	Est. 1500	PF65 550				

KM# 74 1500 GUARANIES
10.70 g., 0.900 Gold 0.3096 oz. AGW **Obv:** National arms **Rev:** Teotihucana Culture sculpture facing

Date	Mintage	VF20	XF40	MS60	MS63	MS65
1973	Est. 1500	PF65 550				

KM# 75 1500 GUARANIES
10.70 g., 0.900 Gold 0.3096 oz. AGW **Obv:** National arms **Rev:** Huasteca Culture sculpture

Date	Mintage	VF20	XF40	MS60	MS63	MS65
1973	Est. 1500	PF65 550				

KM# 76 1500 GUARANIES
10.70 g., 0.900 Gold 0.3096 oz. AGW **Obv:** National arms **Rev:** Mixteca Culture sculpture

Date	Mintage	VF20	XF40	MS60	MS63	MS65
1973	Est. 1500	PF65 550				

KM# 77 1500 GUARANIES
10.70 g., 0.900 Gold 0.3096 oz. AGW **Obv:** National arms **Rev:** Veracruz Ceramica vase

Date	Mintage	VF20	XF40	MS60	MS63	MS65
1973	Est. 1500	PF65 550				

KM# 78 1500 GUARANIES
10.70 g., 0.900 Gold 0.3096 oz. AGW **Obv:** National arms **Rev:** Veracruz Culture sculpture

Date	Mintage	VF20	XF40	MS60	MS63	MS65
1973	Est. 1500	PF65 550				

KM# 79 1500 GUARANIES
10.70 g., 0.900 Gold 0.3096 oz. AGW **Obv:** National arms **Rev:** Bust of Albrecht Durer facing

Date	Mintage	VF20	XF40	MS60	MS63	MS65
1973	Est. 1500	PF65 550				

KM# 80 1500 GUARANIES
10.70 g., 0.900 Gold 0.3096 oz. AGW **Obv:** National arms **Rev:** Bust of Johann Wolfgang Goethe facing

Date	Mintage	VF20	XF40	MS60	MS63	MS65
1973	Est. 1500	PF65 550				

KM# 119 1500 GUARANIES
10.70 g., 0.900 Gold 0.3096 oz. AGW **Obv:** National arms **Rev:** Bust of President Abraham Lincoln left

Date	Mintage	VF20	XF40	MS60	MS63	MS65
1974	Est. 1500	PF65 550				

KM# 120 1500 GUARANIES
10.70 g., 0.900 Gold 0.3096 oz. AGW **Obv:** National arms **Rev:** Bust of Ludwig van Beethoven left

Date	Mintage	VF20	XF40	MS60	MS63	MS65
1974	Est. 1500	PF65 700				

KM# 121 1500 GUARANIES

10.70 g., 0.900 Gold 0.3096 oz. AGW **Obv:** National arms **Rev:** Head of Otto von Bismarck right

Date	Mintage	VF20	XF40	MS60	MS63	MS65
1974	Est. 1500	PF65 550				

KM# 122 1500 GUARANIES

10.70 g., 0.900 Gold 0.3096 oz. AGW **Obv:** National arms **Rev:** Head of Albert Einstein left

Date	Mintage	VF20	XF40	MS60	MS63	MS65
1974	Est. 1500	PF65 550				

KM# 123 1500 GUARANIES

10.70 g., 0.900 Gold 0.3096 oz. AGW **Obv:** National arms **Rev:** Giuseppe Garibaldi facing

Date	Mintage	VF20	XF40	MS60	MS63	MS65
1974	Est. 1500	PF65 550				

KM# 124 1500 GUARANIES

10.70 g., 0.900 Gold 0.3096 oz. AGW **Obv:** National arms **Rev:** Alessandro Manzoni facing

Date	Mintage	VF20	XF40	MS60	MS63	MS65
1974	Est. 1500	PF65 550				

KM# 125 1500 GUARANIES

10.70 g., 0.900 Gold 0.3096 oz. AGW **Obv:** National arms **Rev:** William Tell and son facing

Date	Mintage	VF20	XF40	MS60	MS63	MS65
1974	Est. 1500	PF65 550				

KM# 126 1500 GUARANIES

10.70 g., 0.900 Gold 0.3096 oz. AGW **Obv:** National arms **Rev:** Head of John F. Kennedy left

Date	Mintage	VF20	XF40	MS60	MS63	MS65
1974	Est. 1500	PF65 550				

KM# 127 1500 GUARANIES

10.70 g., 0.900 Gold 0.3096 oz. AGW **Obv:** National arms **Rev:** Head of Konrad Adenauer left

Date	Mintage	VF20	XF40	MS60	MS63	MS65
1974	Est. 1500	PF65 550				

KM# 128 1500 GUARANIES

10.70 g., 0.900 Gold 0.3096 oz. AGW **Obv:** National arms **Rev:** Head of Winston Churchill left

Date	Mintage	VF20	XF40	MS60	MS63	MS65
1974	Est. 1500	PF65 550				

KM# 129 1500 GUARANIES

10.70 g., 0.900 Gold 0.3096 oz. AGW **Obv:** National arms **Rev:** Head of Pope John XXIII left

Date	Mintage	VF20	XF40	MS60	MS63	MS65
1974	Est. 1500	PF65 550				

KM# 130 1500 GUARANIES

10.70 g., 0.900 Gold 0.3096 oz. AGW **Obv:** National arms **Rev:** Head of Pope Paul VI left

Date	Mintage	VF20	XF40	MS60	MS63	MS65
1974	Est. 1500	PF65 550				

KM# 179 1500 GUARANIES

10.70 g., 0.900 Gold 0.3096 oz. AGW **Obv:** National arms **Rev:** Parliament building

Date	Mintage	VF20	XF40	MS60	MS63	MS65
1975	1,500	PF65 550				

KM# 180 1500 GUARANIES

10.70 g., 0.900 Gold 0.3096 oz. AGW **Subject:** Apollo 11 Mission **Obv:** National arms **Rev:** Eagle landing on moon with earth at left

Date	Mintage	VF20	XF40	MS60	MS63	MS65
1975	1,500	PF65 600				

KM# 181 1500 GUARANIES

10.70 g., 0.900 Gold 0.3096 oz. AGW **Subject:** Apollo 15 Mission **Obv:** National arms **Rev:** Apollo mission design within circle

Date	Mintage	VF20	XF40	MS60	MS63	MS65
1975	1,500	PF65 600				

KM# 182 1500 GUARANIES

10.70 g., 0.900 Gold 0.3096 oz. AGW **Obv:** National arms **Rev:** Friendship Bridge

Date	Mintage	VF20	XF40	MS60	MS63	MS65
1975	1,500	PF65 550				

KM# 183 1500 GUARANIES

10.70 g., 0.900 Gold 0.3096 oz. AGW **Obv:** National arms **Rev:** Holy Trinity Chruch

Date	Mintage	VF20	XF40	MS60	MS63	MS65
1975	1,500	PF65 550				

KM# 184 1500 GUARANIES

10.70 g., 0.900 Gold 0.3096 oz. AGW **Obv:** National arms **Rev:** Ruins of Humaita

Date	Mintage	VF20	XF40	MS60	MS63	MS65
1975	Est. 1500	PF65 550				

KM# 45 3000 GUARANIES

21.30 g., 0.900 Gold 0.6163 oz. AGW **Obv:** National arms **Rev:** Uniformed bust of General A. Stroessner facing

Date	Mintage	VF20	XF40	MS60	MS63	MS65
1972	Est. 1500	PF65 950				

KM# 46 3000 GUARANIES

21.30 g., 0.900 Gold 0.6163 oz. AGW **Subject:** Munich Olympics **Obv:** National arms **Rev:** Runner

Date	Mintage	VF20	XF40	MS60	MS63	MS65
1972	Est. 1500	PF65 1,350				

KM# 47 3000 GUARANIES

21.30 g., 0.900 Gold 0.6163 oz. AGW **Subject:** Munich Olympics **Obv:** Radiant star within wreath **Rev:** Broad jumper

Date	Mintage	VF20	XF40	MS60	MS63	MS65
1972	Est. 1500	PF65 1,350				

KM# 48 3000 GUARANIES

21.30 g., 0.900 Gold 0.6163 oz. AGW **Subject:** Munich Olympics **Obv:** National arms **Rev:** Soccer

Date	Mintage	VF20	XF40	MS60	MS63	MS65
1972	Est. 1500	PF65 1,350				

KM# 49 3000 GUARANIES

21.30 g., 0.900 Gold 0.6163 oz. AGW **Subject:** Munich Olympics **Obv:** National arms **Rev:** Hurdler

Date	Mintage	VF20	XF40	MS60	MS63	MS65
1972	Est. 1500	PF65 1,350				

KM# 50 3000 GUARANIES

21.30 g., 0.900 Gold 0.6163 oz. AGW **Subject:** Munich Olympics **Obv:** National arms **Rev:** High jumper

Date	Mintage	VF20	XF40	MS60	MS63	MS65
1972	Est. 1500	PF65 1,350				

KM# 51 3000 GUARANIES
21.30 g., 0.900 Gold 0.6163 oz. AGW **Subject:** Munich Olympics **Obv:** National arms **Rev:** Boxer

Date	Mintage	VF20	XF40	MS60	MS63	MS65
1973	Est. 1500	PF65 1,350				

KM# 81 3000 GUARANIES
21.30 g., 0.900 Gold 0.6163 oz. AGW **Obv:** National arms **Rev:** Head of Mariscal Jose F. Estigarribia facing

Date	Mintage	VF20	XF40	MS60	MS63	MS65
1973	Est. 1500	PF65 1,000				

KM# 82 3000 GUARANIES
21.30 g., 0.900 Gold 0.6163 oz. AGW **Obv:** National arms **Rev:** Bust of Mariscal Francisco Solano Lopez facing

Date	Mintage	VF20	XF40	MS60	MS63	MS65
1973	Est. 1500	PF65 1,000				

KM# 83 3000 GUARANIES
21.30 g., 0.900 Gold 0.6163 oz. AGW **Obv:** National arms **Rev:** Bust of General Jose E. Diaz facing

Date	Mintage	VF20	XF40	MS60	MS63	MS65
1973	Est. 1500	PF65 1,000				

KM# 84 3000 GUARANIES
21.30 g., 0.900 Gold 0.6163 oz. AGW **Obv:** National arms **Rev:** Bust of General Bernardino Caballero facing

Date	Mintage	VF20	XF40	MS60	MS63	MS65
1973	Est. 1500	PF65 1,000				

KM# 85 3000 GUARANIES
21.30 g., 0.900 Gold 0.6163 oz. AGW **Obv:** National arms **Rev:** Teotihucana Culture sculpture facing

Date	Mintage	VF20	XF40	MS60	MS63	MS65
1973	Est. 1500	PF65 1,000				

KM# 86 3000 GUARANIES
21.30 g., 0.900 Gold 0.6163 oz. AGW **Obv:** National arms **Rev:** Huasteca Culture sculpture

Date	Mintage	VF20	XF40	MS60	MS63	MS65
1973	Est. 1500	PF65 1,000				

KM# 87 3000 GUARANIES
21.30 g., 0.900 Gold 0.6163 oz. AGW **Obv:** National arms **Rev:** Mixteca Culture sculpture

Date	Mintage	VF20	XF40	MS60	MS63	MS65
1973	Est. 1500	PF65 1,000				

KM# 88 3000 GUARANIES
21.30 g., 0.900 Gold 0.6163 oz. AGW **Obv:** National arms **Rev:** Veracruz Ceramica vase

Date	Mintage	VF20	XF40	MS60	MS63	MS65
1973	Est. 1500	PF65 1,000				

KM# 89 3000 GUARANIES
21.30 g., 0.900 Gold 0.6163 oz. AGW **Obv:** National arms **Rev:** Veracruz Culture sculpture facing

Date	Mintage	VF20	XF40	MS60	MS63	MS65
1973	Est. 1500	PF65 1,000				

KM# 90 3000 GUARANIES
21.30 g., 0.900 Gold 0.6163 oz. AGW **Obv:** National arms **Rev:** Bust of Albrecht Durer facing

Date	Mintage	VF20	XF40	MS60	MS63	MS65
1973	Est. 1500	PF65 950				

KM# 91 3000 GUARANIES
21.30 g., 0.900 Gold 0.6163 oz. AGW **Obv:** National arms **Rev:** Bust of Johann Wolfgang von Goethe facing

Date	Mintage	VF20	XF40	MS60	MS63	MS65
1973	Est. 1500	PF65 1,000				

KM# 131 3000 GUARANIES
21.30 g., 0.900 Gold 0.6163 oz. AGW **Obv:** National arms **Rev:** Bust of President Abraham Lincoln left

Date	Mintage	VF20	XF40	MS60	MS63	MS65
1974	Est. 1500	PF65 1,000				

KM# 132 3000 GUARANIES
21.30 g., 0.900 Gold 0.6163 oz. AGW **Obv:** National arms **Rev:** Bust of Ludwig van Beethoven left

Date	Mintage	VF20	XF40	MS60	MS63	MS65
1974	Est. 1500	PF65 1,200				

KM# 133 3000 GUARANIES
21.30 g., 0.900 Gold 0.6163 oz. AGW **Obv:** National arms **Rev:** Bust of Otto von Bismarck right

Date	Mintage	VF20	XF40	MS60	MS63	MS65
1974	Est. 1500	PF65 1,000				

KM# 134 3000 GUARANIES
21.30 g., 0.900 Gold 0.6163 oz. AGW **Obv:** National arms **Rev:** Head of Albert Einstein left

Date	Mintage	VF20	XF40	MS60	MS63	MS65
1974	Est. 1500	PF65 1,000				

KM# 135 3000 GUARANIES
21.30 g., 0.900 Gold 0.6163 oz. AGW **Obv:** National arms **Rev:** Head of Giuseppe Garibaldi facing

Date	Mintage	VF20	XF40	MS60	MS63	MS65
1974	Est. 1500	PF65 1,000				

KM# 136 3000 GUARANIES
21.30 g., 0.900 Gold 0.6163 oz. AGW **Obv:** National arms **Rev:** Bust of Alessandro Manzoni facing

Date	Mintage	VF20	XF40	MS60	MS63	MS65
1974	Est. 1500	PF65 1,000				

KM# 137 3000 GUARANIES
21.30 g., 0.900 Gold 0.6163 oz. AGW **Obv:** National arms **Rev:** William Tell and son facing

Date	Mintage	VF20	XF40	MS60	MS63	MS65
1974	Est. 1500	PF65 1,000				

KM# 138 3000 GUARANIES
21.30 g., 0.900 Gold 0.6163 oz. AGW **Obv:** National arms **Rev:** Head of President John F. Kennedy left

Date	Mintage	VF20	XF40	MS60	MS63	MS65
1974	Est. 1500	PF65 1,000				

KM# 139 3000 GUARANIES
21.30 g., 0.900 Gold 0.6163 oz. AGW **Obv:** National arms **Rev:** Head of Konrad Adenauer left

Date	Mintage	VF20	XF40	MS60	MS63	MS65
1974	Est. 1500	PF65 1,000				

KM# 140 3000 GUARANIES
21.30 g., 0.900 Gold 0.6163 oz. AGW **Obv:** National arms **Rev:** Head of Sir Winston Churchill left

Date	Mintage	VF20	XF40	MS60	MS63	MS65
1974	Est. 1500	PF65 1,000				

KM# 141 3000 GUARANIES
21.30 g., 0.900 Gold 0.6163 oz. AGW **Obv:** National arms **Rev:** Head of Pope John XXIII left

Date	Mintage	VF20	XF40	MS60	MS63	MS65
1974	Est. 1500	PF65 1,000				

KM# 142 3000 GUARANIES
21.30 g., 0.900 Gold 0.6163 oz. AGW **Obv:** National arms **Rev:** Head of Pope Paul VI left

Date	Mintage	VF20	XF40	MS60	MS63	MS65
1974	Est. 1500	PF65 1,000				

KM# 161 3000 GUARANIES
21.30 g., 0.900 Gold 0.6163 oz. AGW **Obv:** National arms **Rev:** Holy Trinity Chruch

Date	Mintage	VF20	XF40	MS60	MS63	MS65
1975	—	PF65 975				

KM# 162 3000 GUARANIES
21.30 g., 0.900 Gold 0.6163 oz. AGW **Obv:** National arms **Rev:** Parliament building

Date	Mintage	VF20	XF40	MS60	MS63	MS65
1975	—	PF65 975				

KM# 163 3000 GUARANIES
21.30 g., 0.900 Gold 0.6163 oz. AGW **Obv:** National arms **Rev:** Friendship bridge

Date	Mintage	VF20	XF40	MS60	MS63	MS65
1975	—	PF65 975				

KM# 164 3000 GUARANIES
21.30 g., 0.900 Gold 0.6163 oz. AGW **Obv:** National arms **Rev:** Humaita ruins

Date	Mintage	VF20	XF40	MS60	MS63	MS65
1975	—	PF65 975				

KM# 175 3000 GUARANIES
21.30 g., 0.900 Gold 0.6163 oz. AGW **Subject:** Apollo 11 Mission **Obv:** National arms **Rev:** Eagle landing on moon with earth at upper left

Date	Mintage	VF20	XF40	MS60	MS63	MS65
1975	—	PF65 1,000				

KM# 176 3000 GUARANIES
21.30 g., 0.900 Gold 0.6163 oz. AGW **Subject:** Apollo 15 Mission within circle **Obv:** National arms **Rev:** Apollo mission design within circle

Date	Mintage	VF20	XF40	MS60	MS63	MS65
1975	—	PF65 1,000				

KM# 52 4500 GUARANIES
31.90 g., 0.900 Gold 0.923 oz. AGW **Obv:** National arms **Rev:** General A. Stroessner

Date	Mintage	VF20	XF40	MS60	MS63	MS65
1972	Est. 1500	PF65 1,450				

KM# 53 4500 GUARANIES
31.90 g., 0.900 Gold 0.923 oz. AGW **Subject:** Munich Olympics **Obv:** National arms **Rev:** Runner

Date	Mintage	VF20	XF40	MS60	MS63	MS65
1972	Est. 1500	PF65 2,350				

KM# 54 4500 GUARANIES
31.90 g., 0.900 Gold 0.923 oz. AGW **Subject:** Munich Olympics **Obv:** National arms **Rev:** Broad jumper

Date	Mintage	VF20	XF40	MS60	MS63	MS65
1972	Est. 1500	PF65 2,350				

KM# 55 4500 GUARANIES
31.90 g., 0.900 Gold 0.923 oz. AGW **Subject:** Munich Olympics **Obv:** National arms **Rev:** Soccer

Date	Mintage	VF20	XF40	MS60	MS63	MS65
1972	Est. 1500	PF65 2,350				

KM# 56 4500 GUARANIES
31.90 g., 0.900 Gold 0.923 oz. AGW **Subject:** Munich Olympics **Obv:** National arms **Rev:** Hurdler

Date	Mintage	VF20	XF40	MS60	MS63	MS65
1972	Est. 1500	PF65 2,350				

KM# 57 4500 GUARANIES
31.90 g., 0.900 Gold 0.923 oz. AGW **Subject:** Munich Olympics **Obv:** National arms **Rev:** High jumper

Date	Mintage	VF20	XF40	MS60	MS63	MS65
1972	Est. 1500	PF65 2,350				

KM# 58 4500 GUARANIES
31.90 g., 0.900 Gold 0.923 oz. AGW **Subject:** Munich Olympics **Obv:** National arms **Rev:** Boxer

Date	Mintage	VF20	XF40	MS60	MS63	MS65
1973	Est. 1500	PF65 2,350				

KM# 92 4500 GUARANIES
31.90 g., 0.900 Gold 0.923 oz. AGW **Obv:** National arms **Rev:** Bust of Mariscal Jose F. Estigarribia facing

Date	Mintage	VF20	XF40	MS60	MS63	MS65
1973	Est. 1500	PF65 1,500				

KM# 93 4500 GUARANIES
31.90 g., 0.900 Gold 0.923 oz. AGW **Obv:** National arms **Rev:** Bust of Mariscal Francisco Solano Lopez facing

Date	Mintage	VF20	XF40	MS60	MS63	MS65
1973	Est. 1500	PF65 1,500				

KM# 94 4500 GUARANIES
31.90 g., 0.900 Gold 0.923 oz. AGW **Obv:** National arms **Rev:** Head of General Jose E. Diaz facing

Date	Mintage	VF20	XF40	MS60	MS63	MS65
1973	Est. 1500	PF65 1,500				

KM# 95 4500 GUARANIES
31.90 g., 0.900 Gold 0.923 oz. AGW **Obv:** National arms **Rev:** Head of General Bernardino Caballero facing

Date	Mintage	VF20	XF40	MS60	MS63	MS65
1973	Est. 1500	PF65 1,500				

KM# 96 4500 GUARANIES
31.90 g., 0.900 Gold 0.923 oz. AGW **Obv:** National arms **Rev:** Teotihucana Culture sculpture

Date	Mintage	VF20	XF40	MS60	MS63	MS65
1973	Est. 1500	PF65 1,500				

KM# 97 4500 GUARANIES
31.90 g., 0.900 Gold 0.923 oz. AGW **Obv:** National arms **Rev:** Huasteca Culture sculpture

Date	Mintage	VF20	XF40	MS60	MS63	MS65
1973	Est. 1500	PF65 1,500				

KM# 98 4500 GUARANIES
31.90 g., 0.900 Gold 0.923 oz. AGW **Obv:** National arms **Rev:** Mixteca Culture sculpture

Date	Mintage	VF20	XF40	MS60	MS63	MS65
1973	Est. 1500	PF65 1,500				

KM# 99 4500 GUARANIES
31.90 g., 0.900 Gold 0.923 oz. AGW **Obv:** National arms **Rev:** Veracruz Ceramica sculpture

Date	Mintage	VF20	XF40	MS60	MS63	MS65
1973	Est. 1500	PF65 1,500				

KM# 100 4500 GUARANIES
31.90 g., 0.900 Gold 0.923 oz. AGW **Obv:** National arms **Rev:** Veracruz Culture bust

Date	Mintage	VF20	XF40	MS60	MS63	MS65
1973	Est. 1500	PF65 1,500				

KM# 101 4500 GUARANIES
31.90 g., 0.900 Gold 0.923 oz. AGW **Obv:** National arms **Rev:** Bust of Albrecht Durer facing

Date	Mintage	VF20	XF40	MS60	MS63	MS65
1973	Est. 1500	PF65 1,500				

KM# 102 4500 GUARANIES
31.90 g., 0.900 Gold 0.923 oz. AGW **Obv:** National arms **Rev:** Johann Wolfgang Goethe facing

Date	Mintage	VF20	XF40	MS60	MS63	MS65
1973	Est. 1500	PF65 1,500				

KM# 103 4500 GUARANIES
31.90 g., 0.900 Gold 0.923 oz. AGW **Obv:** National arms **Rev:** Ludwig van Beethoven left

Date	Mintage	VF20	XF40	MS60	MS63	MS65
1974	Est. 1500	PF65 1,750				

KM# 104 4500 GUARANIES
31.90 g., 0.900 Gold 0.923 oz. AGW **Obv:** National arms **Rev:** Head of Otto von Biscarck right

Date	Mintage	VF20	XF40	MS60	MS63	MS65
1974	Est. 1500	PF65 1,500				

KM# 105 4500 GUARANIES
31.90 g., 0.900 Gold 0.923 oz. AGW **Obv:** National arms **Rev:** Giuseppe Garibaldi facing

Date	Mintage	VF20	XF40	MS60	MS63	MS65
1974	Est. 1500	PF65 1,500				

KM# 106 4500 GUARANIES
31.90 g., 0.900 Gold 0.923 oz. AGW **Obv:** National arms **Rev:** Alessandro Manzoni facing

Date	Mintage	VF20	XF40	MS60	MS63	MS65
1974	Est. 1500	PF65 1,500				

KM# 143 4500 GUARANIES
31.90 g., 0.900 Gold 0.923 oz. AGW **Obv:** National arms **Rev:** President Abraham Lincoln left

Date	Mintage	VF20	XF40	MS60	MS63	MS65
1974	Est. 1500	PF65 1,500				

KM# 144 4500 GUARANIES
31.90 g., 0.900 Gold 0.923 oz. AGW **Obv:** National arms **Rev:** Albert Einstein left

Date	Mintage	VF20	XF40	MS60	MS63	MS65
1974	Est. 1500	PF65 1,500				

KM# 145 4500 GUARANIES
31.90 g., 0.900 Gold 0.923 oz. AGW **Obv:** National arms **Rev:** William Tell and son facing

Date	Mintage	VF20	XF40	MS60	MS63	MS65
1974	Est. 1500	PF65 1,500				

KM# 146 4500 GUARANIES
31.90 g., 0.900 Gold 0.923 oz. AGW **Obv:** National arms **Rev:** President John F. Kennedy left

Date	Mintage	VF20	XF40	MS60	MS63	MS65
1974	Est. 1500	PF65 1,500				

KM# 147 4500 GUARANIES
31.90 g., 0.900 Gold 0.923 oz. AGW **Obv:** National arms **Rev:** Konrad Adenauer left

Date	Mintage	VF20	XF40	MS60	MS63	MS65
1974	Est. 1500	PF65 1,500				

KM# 148 4500 GUARANIES
31.90 g., 0.900 Gold 0.923 oz. AGW **Obv:** National arms **Rev:** Sir Winston Churchill left

Date	Mintage	VF20	XF40	MS60	MS63	MS65
1974	Est. 1500	PF65 1,500				

KM# 149 4500 GUARANIES
31.90 g., 0.900 Gold 0.923 oz. AGW **Obv:** National arms **Rev:** Pope JOhn XXIII left

Date	Mintage	VF20	XF40	MS60	MS63	MS65
1974	Est. 1500	PF65 1,500				

KM# 150 4500 GUARANIES
31.90 g., 0.900 Gold 0.923 oz. AGW **Obv:** National arms **Rev:** Pope Paul VI left

Date	Mintage	VF20	XF40	MS60	MS63	MS65
1974	Est. 1500	PF65 1,500				

KM# 185 4500 GUARANIES
31.90 g., 0.900 Gold 0.923 oz. AGW **Obv:** National arms **Rev:** Parliament building

Date	Mintage	VF20	XF40	MS60	MS63	MS65
1975	Est. 1500	PF65 1,500				

KM# 186 4500 GUARANIES
31.90 g., 0.900 Gold 0.923 oz. AGW **Subject:** Apollo 11 Mission **Obv:** National arms **Rev:** Eagle landing on moon with earth at upper left

Date	Mintage	VF20	XF40	MS60	MS63	MS65
1975	Est. 1500	PF65 1,500				

KM# 187 4500 GUARANIES
31.90 g., 0.900 Gold 0.923 oz. AGW, 19.5 mm. **Subject:** Apollo 15 Mission **Obv:** National arms **Rev:** Apollo mission designs within circle

Date	Mintage	VF20	XF40	MS60	MS63	MS65
1975	Est. 1500	PF65 1,500				

KM# 188 4500 GUARANIES
31.90 g., 0.900 Gold 0.923 oz. AGW **Obv:** National arms **Rev:** Friendship bridge

Date	Mintage	VF20	XF40	MS60	MS63	MS65
1975	Est. 1500	PF65 1,500				

KM# 189 4500 GUARANIES
31.90 g., 0.900 Gold 0.923 oz. AGW **Obv:** National arms **Rev:** Holy Trinity Church

Date	Mintage	VF20	XF40	MS60	MS63	MS65
1975	Est. 1500	PF65 1,500				

KM# 190 4500 GUARANIES
31.90 g., 0.900 Gold 0.923 oz. AGW **Obv:** National arms **Rev:** Ruins of Humaita

Date	Mintage	VF20	XF40	MS60	MS63	MS65
1975	Est. 1500	PF65 1,500				

KM# 30 10000 GUARANIES
46.01 g., 0.900 Gold 1.3313 oz. AGW **Subject:** 4th Term of President Stroessner **Obv:** Seated lion with liberty cap on pole within circle **Rev:** Head of President Stroessner left **Note:** Similar to 300 Guaranies KM#29. KM#30 struck for presentation.

Date	Mintage	VF20	XF40	MS60	MS63	MS65
ND-1968	Est. 50	PF63 6,000	PF65 6,500			

KM# 171 10000 GUARANIES
28.70 g., 0.999 Silver 0.9218 oz. ASW **Obv:** Bank building **Rev:** Conjoined busts of Caballero and Stroessner left

Date	Mintage	VF20	XF40	MS60	MS63	MS65
ND-1987	1,000	PF63 50.00	PF65 60.00			

KM# 173 10000 GUARANIES

28.70 g., 0.999 Silver 0.9218 oz. ASW **Subject:** 8th Term of President A. Stroessner **Obv:** Seated lion with Liberty cap on pole within circle **Rev:** Bust of President A. Stroessner left

Date	Mintage	VF20	XF40	MS60	MS63	MS65
ND-1988	1,000	PF63 50.00	PF65 60.00			

KM# 168 70000 GUARANIES

46.00 g., 0.900 Gold 1.331 oz. AGW **Subject:** 6th Term of President A. Stroessner **Obv:** Seated lion with Liberty cap on pole within circle **Rev:** Bust of President A. Stroessner left

Date	Mintage	VF20	XF40	MS60	MS63	MS65
ND-1978	300	PF63 2,600	PF65 2,800			

KM# 170 100000 GUARANIES

46.00 g., 0.900 Gold 1.331 oz. AGW **Subject:** 7th Term of President A. Stroessner **Obv:** Seated lion with Liberty cap on pole within circle **Rev:** Bust of President A. Stroessner left

Date	Mintage	VF20	XF40	MS60	MS63	MS65
ND-1983	300	PF63 2,600	PF65 2,800			

KM# 172 250000 GUARANIES

46.00 g., 0.917 Gold 1.3562 oz. AGW **Obv:** Bank building within circle **Rev:** Conjoined busts of Caballero and Stroessner left

Date	Mintage	VF20	XF40	MS60	MS63	MS65
ND-1987	—	PF63 2,450	PF65 2,650			

Note: 250 pieces remelted

KM# 174 300000 GUARANIES

46.00 g., 0.917 Gold 1.3562 oz. AGW. **Subject:** 8th Term of President A. Stroessner **Obv:** Seated lion with Liberty cap on pole within circle **Rev:** Bust of President A. Stroessner left

Date	Mintage	VF20	XF40	MS60	MS63	MS65
ND-1988	Est. 500	PF63 2,400	PF65 2,600			

Note: 250 pieces remelted

PATTERNS

Including off metal strikes

KM#	Date	Mintage	Identification	Mkt Val
Pn40	1925	—	2 Pesos. Aluminum. Narrow flan, KM14.	125
Pn41	1925	—	2 Pesos. Aluminum. Broad flan, KM14.	150
Pn42	1939	—	5 Pesos. Brass. KM#8.	200
Pn43	1939	—	5 Pesos. Copper. KM18.	200
Pn44	1976	10	Guarani. Gold.	500
Pn45	1976	10	10 Guaranies. Gold.	800
Pn46	1978	10	Guarani. Gold.	500
Pn47	1978	10	5 Guaranies. Gold.	600
Pn48	1978	10	10 Guaranies. Gold.	800
Pn49	1980	10	Guarani. Gold.	500
Pn50	1980	10	5 Guaranies. Gold.	600
Pn51	1980	10	10 Guaranies. Gold.	800
Pn52	1980	10	50 Guaranies. Gold.	1,150

PROOF SETS

KM#	Date	Mintage	Identification	Issue Price	Mkt Val
PS1	1953 (4)	1	KM25-28	—	1,650
PS2	1972 (24)	150	KM31-36, 38-43, 45-50, 52-57	—	27,750
PS3	1973 (48)	150	KM37, 44, 51, 58-102	—	38,000
PS4	1974 (48)	150	KM103-150	—	37,000
PS5	1975 (24)	150	KM155-164, 175-176, 179-190	—	17,900
PS6	1975 (4)	1,000	KM151-154	—	60.00
PS7	1976 (2)	1,000	KM151, 153	—	20.00
PS8	1976 (2)	—	KM#151a, 153a	—	—
PS9	1978 (3)	—	KM#165, 166, 167	—	20.00
PS10	1978 (3)	—	KM#165a, 166b, 167a	—	—
PS11	1980 (4)	1,000	KM165-167, 169	—	30.00
PS12	1980 (4)	—	KM#165a, 166b, 167a, 169a	—	—
PS13	1988 (3)	—	KM#165, 167, 169	—	20.00

PERU

The Republic of Peru, located on the Pacific coast of South America, has an area of 496,225 sq. mi. (1,285,220sq. km.) and a population of *21.4 million. Capital: Lima. The diversified economy includes mining, fishing and agriculture. Fishmeal, copper, sugar, zinc and iron ore are exported.

Once part of the great Inca Empire that reached from northern Ecuador to central Chile, the conquest of Peru by Francisco Pizarro began in 1531. Desirable as the richest of the Spanish viceroyalties, it was torn by warfare between avaricious Spaniards until the arrival in 1569 of Francisco de Toledo, who initiated 2-1/2 centuries of efficient colonial rule, which made Lima the most aristocratic colonial capital and the stronghold of Spain's American possessions. Jose de San Martin of Argentina proclaimed Peru's independence on July 28, 1821; Simon Bolivar of Venezuela secured it in December, 1824 when he defeated the last Spanish army in South America. After several futile attempts to re-establish its South American Empire, Spain recognized Peru's independence in 1879.

Andres de Santa Cruz, whose mother was a high-ranking Inca, was the best of Bolivia's early presidents, and temporarily united Peru and Bolivia 1836-39, thus realizing his dream of a Peruvian/Bolivian confederation. This prompted the separate coinages of North and South Peru. Peruvian resistance and Chilean intervention finally broke up the confederation, sending Santa Cruz into exile. A succession of military strongman presidents ruled Peru until Marshall Castilla revitalized Peruvian politics in the mid-19th century and repulsed Spain's attempt to reclaim its one-time colony. Subsequent loss of southern territory to Chile in the War of the Pacific, 1879-81, and gradually increasing rejection of foreign economic domination, combined with recent serious inflation, affected the country numismatically.

As a result of the discovery of silver at Potosi in 1545, a mint was eventually authorized in 1565 with the first coinage taking place in 1568. The mint had an uneven life span during the Spanish Colonial period from 1568-72. It was closed from 1573-76, reopened from 1577-88. It remained closed until 1659-1660 when an unauthorized coinage in both silver and gold were struck. After being closed in 1660, it remained closed until 1684 when it struck cob style coins until 1752.

MINT MARKS

AREQUIPA, AREQ = Arequipa
AYACUCHO = Ayacucho
(B) = Brussels
CUZCO (monogram), Cuzco, Co. Cuzco
L, LM, LIMAE (monogram), Lima
(monogram), LIMA = Lima
(L) = London
PASCO (monogram), Pasco, Paz, Po= Pasco
P, (P) = Philadelphia
S = San Francisco
(W) = Waterbury, CT, USA

MINT ASSAYERS' INITIALS

The letter(s) following the dates of Peruvian coins are the assayer's initials appearing on the coins. They generally appear at the 11 o'clock position on the Colonial coinage and at the 5 o'clock position along the rim on the obverse or reverse on the Republican coinage.

DATING

Peruvian 5, 10 and 20 centavos, issued from 1918-1944, bear the dates written in Spanish. The following table translates those written dates into numerals:

1918 - UN MIL NOVECIENTOS DIECIOCHO
1919 - UN MIL NOVECIENTOS DIECINUEVE
1920 - UN MIL NOVECIENTOS VEINTE
1921 - UN MIL NOVECIENTOS VEINTIUNO
1923 - UN MIL NOVECIENTOS VEINTITRES
1926 - UN MIL NOVECIENTOS VEINTISEIS
1934 - UN MIL NOVECIENTOS TREINTICUATRO
1935 - UN MIL NOVECIENTOS TREINTICINCO
1937 - UN MIL NOVECIENTOS TREINTISIETE
1939 - UN MIL NOVECIENTOS TREINTINUEVE
1940 - UN MIL NOVECIENTOS CUARENTA
1941 - UN MIL NOVECIENTOS CUARENTIUNO

U.S. Mints

1942 - MIL NOVECIENTOS CUARENTA Y DOS

Lima Mint

1942 - UN MIL NOVECIENTOS CUARENTIDOS

U.S. Mints

1943 - MIL NOVECIENTOS CUARENTA Y TRES
1944 - MIL NOVECIENTOS CUARENTA Y CUATRO

Lima Mint

1944 - MIL NOVECIENTOS CUARENTICUATRO

MONETARY SYSTEM

100 Centavos (10 Dineros) = 1 Sol
10 Soles = 1 Libra

REPUBLIC

DECIMAL COINAGE

KM# 208.1 CENTAVO

Bronze, 19.5 mm. **Obv:** Radiant star design around center circle with small date below and legend above **Rev:** Value within wreath, CENTAVO straight **Note:** Thick planchet.

Date	Mintage	VF20	XF40	MS60	MS63	MS65
1901	600,000	3.00	8.00	12.00	20.00	50.00
1904	1,000,000	15.00	25.00	35.00	60.00	75.00

KM# 208.2 CENTAVO

Bronze, 19.5 mm. **Obv:** Large date and legend **Rev:** CENTAVO straight **Note:** Thick planchet. Varieties exist.

Date	Mintage	VF20	XF40	MS60	MS63	MS65
1933	275,000	3.00	8.00	12.00	20.00	35.00
1934	1,185,000	2.00	5.00	8.00	15.00	25.00
1935	1,105,000	2.00	5.00	8.00	15.00	25.00
1936	565,000	3.00	8.00	12.00	20.00	35.00
1937/6	735,000	2.00	4.00	7.00	20.00	35.00
1937	Inc. above	1.50	2.50	5.00	15.00	25.00
1938	340,000	1.50	2.50	5.00	15.00	25.00
1939	1,225,000	3.00	5.50	10.00	20.00	35.00
1940	1,250,000	3.00	5.50	10.00	20.00	35.00
1941	2,593,000	0.75	1.50	4.00	10.00	15.00

KM# 208a CENTAVO

Bronze, 19.5 mm. **Obv:** Large date and legend **Rev:** Straight centavo **Note:** Thin planchet.

Date	Mintage	VF20	XF40	MS60	MS63	MS65
1941 Inc. KM#208.2	—	0.75	2.00	4.00	8.00	12.00
1942	2,865,000	1.00	2.50	5.00	10.00	15.00
1944	—	20.00	35.00	45.00	70.00	100

KM# 211 CENTAVO

Bronze, 19.5 mm. **Obv:** Radiant star design around center circle **Rev:** Value within wreath, CENTAVO curved **Note:** Thick planchet. Engravers initial R appears below ribbon on most or all new dies, but often became weak or filled. Most coins show at least a faint trace of an R. Date varieteis also exist.

Date	Mintage	VF20	XF40	MS60	MS63	MS65
1909/999 R	Inc. above	20.00	35.00	50.00	70.00	100
1909 R	Inc. above	20.00	35.00	50.00	70.00	100
1909	252,000	20.00	35.00	50.00	70.00	100
1915	250,000	6.00	10.00	20.00	30.00	50.00

Date	Mintage	VF20	XF40	MS60	MS63	MS65
1916	360,000	2.00	7.00	12.00	20.00	35.00
1916 R	Inc. above	2.00	6.00	9.00	15.00	30.00
1917	830,000	2.00	6.00	9.00	15.00	30.00
1917 R	Inc. above	2.00	6.00	9.00	15.00	30.00
1918	1,060,000	2.00	5.00	8.00	14.00	30.00
1918 R	Inc. above	2.00	5.00	8.00	14.00	30.00
1920	360,000	2.50	7.00	12.00	20.00	35.00
1920 R	Inc. above	2.50	7.00	12.00	20.00	35.00
1933 R Inc. KM208.2	—	2.50	7.00	12.00	20.00	35.00
1934 Inc. KM#208.2	—	8.00	16.00	25.00	40.00	75.00
1935 R Inc. KM#208.2	—	7.00	15.00	25.00	40.00	75.00
1936 R Inc. KM#208.2	—	3.50	7.00	12.00	20.00	35.00
1937	—	—	—	—	—	—
1937 R Inc. KM#208.2	—	3.50	7.00	12.00	20.00	35.00
1939 R Inc. KM#208.2	—	8.00	16.00	25.00	40.00	75.00

KM# 211a CENTAVO

Bronze, 19.5 mm. **Obv:** Radiant star design around center circle, large date and legend **Rev:** Value within wreath, CENTAVO curved **Note:** Thin planchet. Many varieties exist.

Date	Mintage	VF20	XF40	MS60	MS63	MS65
1941 Inc. KM#208.2	—	2.00	5.00	7.00	10.00	15.00
1942 Inc. KM#208a	—	1.00	3.00	5.00	7.50	12.00
1943	—	5.00	10.00	15.00	25.00	40.00
1944	2,490,000	0.40	1.00	2.00	4.00	7.50
1945	2,157,000	0.40	1.00	2.00	4.00	7.50
1946	3,198,000	0.40	1.00	2.00	4.00	7.50
1947	2,976,000	0.40	1.00	2.00	4.00	7.50
1948	3,195,000	0.40	1.00	2.00	4.00	7.50
1949	1,104,000	0.65	2.00	4.00	6.00	10.00

KM# 227 CENTAVO

1.02 g., Zinc, 14.98 mm. **Obv:** Radiant star design around center circle **Rev:** Value within wreath, curved centavo **Edge:** Plain **Note:** Varieties exist.

Date	Mintage	VF20	XF40	MS60	MS63	MS65
1950	3,196,000	0.25	1.25	2.00	3.00	—
1951	3,289,000	0.40	0.65	1.25	2.50	—
Note: Copper-plated examples of type dated 1951 are known						
1952	3,050,000	0.40	0.65	1.25	2.50	—
1953	3,260,000	0.60	1.00	2.00	3.00	—
1954	3,215,000	1.50	2.50	4.50	10.00	—
1955	3,400,000	0.40	0.65	1.50	3.00	—
1956 Pointed 6	2,500,000	0.40	0.65	1.50	3.00	—
1956 Knobbed 6	Inc. above	0.40	0.65	1.50	3.00	—
1957	4,400,000	0.85	2.00	4.00	7.00	—
1958/7	—	0.60	1.00	2.00	4.00	—
1958/8	3,200,000	1.00	2.00	4.00	7.00	—
1958	2,600,000	0.60	1.00	2.00	4.00	—
1959/8	Inc. above	0.75	1.50	3.00	5.00	—
1959	Inc. above	0.40	0.65	1.50	3.00	—
1960/50	3,060,000	0.60	1.00	2.00	4.00	—
1960	Inc. above	1.50	3.00	5.00	8.00	—
1961/51	2,600,000	0.40	1.00	2.00	3.00	—
1961	Inc. above	0.40	1.00	2.00	3.00	—
1962/52	2,600,000	0.40	1.00	2.00	3.00	—
1962	Inc. above	0.40	1.00	2.00	3.00	—
1963/53	2,400,000	0.40	1.00	2.00	3.00	—
1963	Inc. above	0.40	1.00	2.00	3.00	—
1965	360,000	1.50	3.00	6.00	10.00	—

KM# 187 CENTAVO

Bronze, 19.5 mm. **Obv:** Radiant star design around center circle **Rev:** Value within wreath **Note:** Earlier dates 1875-1878 are listed as KM#187.1a in our 19th Century book.

Date	Mintage	VF20	XF40	MS60	MS63	MS65
1919 (P)	4,000,000	1.00	2.50	3.50	5.00	12.00

KM# 212.1 2 CENTAVOS

Copper or Bronze, 24.5 mm. **Obv:** Date at bottom **Rev:** Curved "CENTAVOS" **Note:** Thick planchet. Engraver's initial C appeared below ribbon on most or all new dies, but often became weak or filled. Most coins show at least a faint trace of C. Other varieties also exist.

Date	Mintage	VF20	XF40	MS60	MS63	MS65
1917 C	73,000	6.50	15.00	25.00	40.00	100
1918/17	580,000	6.00	12.00	22.00	40.00	75.00
1918	Inc. above	6.00	15.00	25.00	40.00	75.00
1918/17 C	Inc. above	10.00	20.00	30.00	50.00	90.00
1918 C	Inc. above	6.00	15.00	25.00	40.00	75.00
1920/7 C	328,000	4.00	10.00	20.00	30.00	50.00
1920	Inc. above	2.00	5.00	9.00	15.00	25.00
1920 C	Inc. above	2.00	5.00	9.00	15.00	25.00
1933	285,000	2.00	5.00	9.00	15.00	25.00
1933 C	Inc. above	2.00	5.00	9.00	15.00	25.00
1934	973,000	1.50	4.00	8.00	15.00	25.00
1934 C	Inc. above	1.50	4.00	8.00	15.00	25.00
1935	950,000	1.50	4.00	8.00	15.00	25.00
1935 C	Inc. above	1.50	4.00	8.00	15.00	25.00
1936	763,000	1.50	4.00	8.00	15.00	25.00
1936/5 C	Inc. above	2.50	8.00	12.00	20.00	30.00
1936 C	Inc. above	1.25	3.00	6.00	12.00	25.00
1937	963,000	1.50	4.00	8.00	15.00	25.00
1937 C	Inc. above	1.50	4.00	8.00	15.00	25.00
1938 C	428,000	1.75	4.00	8.00	15.00	25.00
1939/8 C	—	—	—	—	—	—
Note: Requires Confirmation						
1939/8	—	2.50	8.00	12.00	20.00	30.00
1939 C Inverted A for V in CENTAVOS	783,000	1.50	4.00	8.00	15.00	25.00
1940	—	2.00	4.00	8.00	15.00	25.00
1940 C	565,000	1.75	4.00	8.00	15.00	25.00
1941/0	Inc. above	2.00	4.00	8.00	15.00	25.00
1941/0 C	Inc. above	2.00	4.00	8.00	15.00	25.00
1941/22	Inc. above	2.00	4.00	8.00	15.00	25.00
1941	Inc. above	2.00	4.00	8.00	15.00	25.00
1941 C	Inc. above	5.00	9.00	14.00	20.00	30.00

KM# A212 2 CENTAVOS

Copper or Bronze, 24.5 mm. **Obv:** Radiant star design around center circle **Rev:** Value within wreath **Note:** Sharper diework. Earlier date 1895 listed as KM#188.2 in 19th Century book.

Date	Mintage	VF20	XF40	MS60	MS63	MS65
1919 (P)	3,000,000	0.75	2.00	5.00	12.00	—

KM# 212.2 2 CENTAVOS

5.80 g., Copper or Bronze, 24.5 mm. **Obv:** Radiant star design around center circle **Rev:** Value within sprays **Edge:** Plain **Note:** Thin planchet. Varieties exist.

Date	Mintage	VF20	XF40	MS60	MS63	MS65
1941/33 C	Inc. above	2.00	3.50	5.00	7.00	10.00
1941/33	Inc. above	2.00	3.50	5.00	7.00	10.00
1941/38	Inc. above	2.00	3.50	5.00	7.00	10.00
1941/38 C	Inc. above	2.00	3.50	5.00	7.00	10.00
1941/39 C	Inc. above	2.00	3.50	5.00	7.00	10.00
1941/0	Inc. above	2.00	3.50	5.00	7.00	10.00
1941	Inc. above	1.00	2.00	4.00	10.00	15.00
1941/32	870,000	2.00	3.50	5.00	10.00	15.00
1942/22	4,418,000	0.50	1.00	2.00	3.00	5.00
1942/32	4,418,000	0.50	1.00	2.00	3.00	5.00
1942	Inc. above	0.50	1.00	2.00	3.00	5.00
1943/2	1,829,000	1.00	2.00	3.00	5.00	7.50
1943	Inc. above	1.00	2.00	3.00	5.00	7.50
1944	2,068,000	2.00	2.00	3.00	5.00	7.50
1945	2,288,000	2.00	2.00	3.00	5.00	7.50
1946	2,121,000	0.50	0.75	1.25	2.00	3.50
1947	1,280,000	0.50	0.75	1.25	2.00	3.50
1948	1,518,000	0.50	0.75	1.25	2.00	3.50
1949/8	938,000	0.60	1.00	3.00	5.00	7.50
1949	Inc. above	1.00	1.50	4.00	6.00	9.00

KM# 228 2 CENTAVOS

Zinc, 17 mm. **Obv:** Radiant star design around center circle **Rev:** Value within wreath

Date	Mintage	VF20	XF40	MS60	MS63	MS65
1950	1,702,000	0.50	0.75	1.25	3.00	—
1951	3,289,000	0.50	0.75	1.25	3.00	—
Note: Copper-plated examples of type dated 1951 exist						
1952	1,155,000	0.50	0.75	1.25	3.00	—
1953	1,150,000	0.60	0.85	1.50	4.00	—
1954	—	3.00	4.00	10.00	32.00	—
1955	1,185,000	0.50	0.75	1.25	3.00	—
1956	400,000	0.75	1.00	2.00	6.00	—
1957	520,000	2.00	3.00	6.00	27.50	—
1958	200,000	1.75	2.50	4.50	17.00	—

KM# 213.1 5 CENTAVOS

Copper-Nickel, 17 mm. **Obv:** Date: UN MIL NOVECIENTOS DIECIOCHO **Rev:** Value to right of sprig

Date	Mintage	VF20	XF40	MS60	MS63	MS65
1918	4,000,000	1.25	2.50	4.00	6.00	15.00
1919	10,000,000	0.75	1.25	2.00	3.50	12.00
1923	2,000,000	2.00	3.50	6.50	10.00	15.00
1926	4,000,000	3.00	6.00	10.00	15.00	25.00

KM# 213.2 5 CENTAVOS

3.00 g., Copper-Nickel, 17 mm. **Obv:** Head right **Rev:** Value to right of sprig

Date	Mintage	VF20	XF40	MS60	MS63	MS65
1934	—	PF63 200				
1934	4,000,000	2.00	3.00	5.00	9.00	15.00
1935	4,000,000	1.25	2.00	3.50	6.00	10.00
1935 Proof	—	—	—	—	—	—
1937	2,000,000	2.00	3.00	5.00	9.00	15.00
1937 Proof	—	—	—	—	—	—
1939	2,000,000	1.25	2.00	3.50	6.00	10.00
1939 Proof	—	—	—	—	—	—
1940	2,000,000	1.25	2.00	3.50	6.00	10.00
1940 Proof	—	—	—	—	—	—
1941	2,000,000	1.25	2.00	3.50	6.00	10.00
1941 Proof	—	—	—	—	—	—

KM# 213.2a1 5 CENTAVOS

Brass, 17 mm. **Obv:** Date: MIL NOVECIENTOS CUARENTA Y DOS **Rev:** Value to right of sprig

Date	Mintage	VF20	XF40	MS60	MS63	MS65
1942	4,000,000	3.00	5.00	8.00	15.00	35.00
1943	4,000,000	3.00	5.00	8.00	15.00	35.00
1944	4,000,000	2.75	4.50	7.50	15.00	35.00

KM# 213.2a2 5 CENTAVOS

Brass, 17 mm. **Obv:** Head right with date spelled out **Rev:** Value to right of sprig

Date	Mintage	VF20	XF40	MS60	MS63	MS65
1942 S	4,000,000	4.50	9.00	15.00	35.00	60.00
1943 S	4,000,000	4.50	7.50	12.00	25.00	50.00

KM# 213.2a3 5 CENTAVOS

Brass, 17 mm. **Obv:** Date: MIL NOVECIENTOS CUARENTICUATRO **Rev:** Value to right of sprig

Date	Mintage	VF20	XF40	MS60	MS63	MS65
1944	1,106,000	3.50	6.00	9.00	15.00	25.00

KM# 223.1 5 CENTAVOS

2.00 g., Brass, 17 mm. **Obv:** Head right with short legend **Rev:** Value to right of sprig **Note:** Thick planchet.

Date	Mintage	VF20	XF40	MS60	MS63	MS65
1945	2,768,000	0.75	1.50	2.50	4.00	10.00
1946/5	4,270,000	2.50	4.00	7.00	10.00	18.00
1946	Inc. above	0.50	1.00	2.00	4.00	7.50

KM# 223.3 5 CENTAVOS

Brass, 17 mm. **Obv:** Head right with long legend with 3mm gap above head **Rev:** Value to right of sprig **Note:** Thick planchet.

Date	Mintage	VF20	XF40	MS60	MS63	MS65
1947	7,683,000	0.50	1.00	2.00	3.00	5.00
1948	6,711,000	0.50	1.00	2.00	3.00	5.00
1949/8	5,550,000	2.00	3.00	5.00	9.00	15.00
1949	—	0.50	1.00	2.00	3.00	5.00

KM# 223.4 5 CENTAVOS

Brass, 17 mm. **Obv:** Head right **Rev:** Value to right of sprig **Note:** Thick planchet.

Date	Mintage	VF20	XF40	MS60	MS63	MS65
1949	Inc. above	2.00	3.00	5.00	10.00	15.00
1950	7,933,000	0.50	1.00	2.00	3.00	5.00
195.1	8,064,000	0.50	1.00	2.00	3.00	5.00
1951	Inc. above	2.00	4.00	6.00	15.00	25.00

KM# 223.2 5 CENTAVOS

1.85 g., Brass, 17 mm. **Obv:** Head right **Rev:** Value to right of sprig **Note:** Thin planchet. Varieties exist.

Date	Mintage	VF20	XF40	MS60	MS63	MS65
1951	Inc. above	0.25	0.50	2.00	6.00	10.00
1952	7,840,000	0.25	0.50	2.00	6.00	10.00
1953	6,976,000	0.25	0.50	2.00	6.00	10.00
1953 AFP	—	—	—	—	—	—
1954	6,244,000	0.20	0.40	0.60	1.00	3.00
1955	8,064,000	0.20	0.40	0.75	2.00	4.00
1956	16,200,000	0.10	0.35	0.75	1.50	3.50
1957 Small date	16,000,000	0.10	0.25	0.50	1.00	3.00
1957 Large date	Inc. above	0.10	0.25	0.50	1.00	3.00
1958	4,600,000	0.10	0.25	0.50	1.00	3.00
1959	8,300,000	0.10	0.25	0.50	1.00	3.00
1960/50	9,900,000	0.10	0.25	0.50	1.00	3.00
1960 Large date	Inc. above	0.10	0.25	0.50	1.00	3.00
1960 Small date	Inc. above	0.10	0.25	0.50	1.00	3.00
1961	10,200,000	0.10	0.20	0.50	1.00	3.00
1962 Curved 9	11,064,000	0.10	0.20	0.50	1.00	3.00
1962 Straight 9	Inc. above	0.10	0.20	0.50	1.00	3.00
1963	12,012,000	0.10	0.20	0.50	1.00	3.00
1964/3	12,304,000	0.10	0.35	0.75	1.50	3.50
1964	Inc. above	—	0.10	0.30	1.00	3.00
1965 Small date	12,500,000	—	0.10	0.30	1.00	3.00
1965 Large date	Inc. above	0.10	0.20	0.50	1.00	3.00
1965	—	PF65 20.00				

KM# 232 5 CENTAVOS

Brass, 17 mm. **Obv:** Head right **Rev:** Value to right of torch within chain circle

Date	Mintage	VF20	XF40	MS60	MS63	MS65
1954	2,080,000	2.00	3.00	5.00	8.00	10.00

KM# 290 5 CENTAVOS

1.44 g., Brass **Subject:** 400th Anniversary of Lima Mint **Obv:** National arms above value **Rev:** Pillars of Hercules within inner circle

Date	Mintage	VF20	XF40	MS60	MS63	MS65
1965	712,000	—	0.25	0.50	1.00	2.00
1965	—	PF65 100				

KM# 244.1 5 CENTAVOS

Brass **Obv:** National arms within circle above date **Rev:** Value to left of flower sprig

Date	Mintage	VF20	XF40	MS60	MS63	MS65
1966	14,620,000	—	0.10	0.20	0.35	0.50
Note: PAREJA in field at lower left of arms						
1966	1,000	PF65 15.00				
1967	14,088,000	—	0.10	0.20	0.35	0.50
1968	17,880,000	—	0.10	0.20	0.35	0.50

KM# 244.1a 5 CENTAVOS

Silver Plated Brass **Obv:** National arms within circle above date **Rev:** Value to left of flower sprig

Date	Mintage	VF20	XF40	MS60	MS63	MS65
1967	—	—	—	—	—	—

KM# 244.1b 5 CENTAVOS

Silver **Obv:** National arms within circle above date **Rev:** Value to left of flower sprig

Date	Mintage	VF20	XF40	MS60	MS63	MS65
1967	—	—	—	—	—	—

KM# 244.2 5 CENTAVOS

1.50 g., Brass **Obv:** National arms within circle **Rev:** Value to left of flower sprig **Edge:** Plain

Date	Mintage	VF20	XF40	MS60	MS63	MS65
1969	17,880,000	—	—	0.10	0.20	0.30
1970	—	—	—	0.10	0.20	0.30
1971	24,320,000	—	—	0.10	0.20	0.30
1972	24,342,000	—	—	0.10	0.20	0.30
1973	25,074,000	—	—	0.10	0.20	0.30

KM# 244.3 5 CENTAVOS

1.45 g., Brass, 14.8 mm. **Obv:** National arms within circle **Rev:** Value to left of flower sprig **Edge:** Plain

Date	Mintage	VF20	XF40	MS60	MS63	MS65
1973	Inc. above	—	—	0.10	0.20	0.30
1974	—	—	—	0.10	0.20	0.30
1975	—	—	—	0.10	0.20	0.30

KM# 206.2 1/2 DINERO

1.25 g., 0.900 Silver 0.0362 oz. ASW, 15.5 mm. **Obv:** National arms above date **Rev:** Seated Liberty flanked by shield and column **Note:** Most coins 1900-06 show faint to strong traces of 9/8 or 90/89 in date. Non-overdates without such traces are scarce. Most coins of 1907-17 have engraver's initial R at left of shield tip on reverse. Many other varieties exist.

Date	Mintage	VF20	XF40	MS60	MS63	MS65
1901/801 JF	500,000	2.00	3.00	6.00	9.00	15.00
1901/801/701 JF	Inc. above	2.00	3.00	6.00	9.00	15.00
1901/891/791	Inc. above	2.00	3.00	5.00	7.00	13.00
1901/891 JF	Inc. above	2.00	3.00	5.00	7.00	13.00
1901 JF	Inc. above	4.00	6.00	10.00	15.00	25.00
1902/802 JF	616,000	2.00	3.00	5.00	7.00	13.00
1902/892 JF	Inc. above	2.00	3.00	5.00	7.00	13.00
1902/92	Inc. above	2.00	3.00	5.00	7.00	13.00
1902 JF	Inc. above	4.00	6.00	10.00	15.00	25.00
1903/803 JF	1,798,000	2.50	5.00	8.00	12.00	22.50
1903/893 JF	Inc. above	2.50	5.00	8.00	12.00	22.50
1903/897 JF	Inc. above	2.50	4.00	6.00	10.00	18.00
1903 JF	Inc. above	3.00	5.00	8.00	12.00	25.00
1904/804 JF	723,000	2.00	3.00	5.00	7.00	13.00
1904/804 JF FFLIZ Error	Inc. above	12.00	16.00	30.00	45.00	60.00
1904/884 JF	Inc. above	2.00	3.00	5.00	7.00	14.00
1904/891 JF	Inc. above	2.00	3.00	5.00	7.00	14.00
1904/893 JF	Inc. above	2.00	3.00	5.00	7.00	13.00
1904/894 JF	Inc. above	2.00	3.00	5.00	7.00	13.00
1904/894 JF FFLIZ Error	Inc. above	7.00	12.00	18.00	22.00	27.50
1904 JF	Inc. above	4.00	6.00	10.00	15.00	25.00
1904 JF FFLIZ Error	Inc. above	7.00	12.00	18.00	22.00	27.50
1905/805 JF	1,400,000	4.00	6.00	10.00	15.00	20.00
1905/891 JF	Inc. above	4.50	7.00	12.00	18.00	27.50
1905/893 JF	Inc. above	4.50	7.00	12.00	18.00	27.50
1905/894	Inc. above	4.50	7.00	12.00	18.00	27.50
1905/895 JF	Inc. above	2.50	3.50	5.00	7.00	13.00
1905/3 JF	Inc. above	4.50	7.00	12.00	18.00	27.50
1905 JF	Inc. above	4.00	6.00	10.00	15.00	25.00
1906/806 JF	900,000	3.00	5.00	8.00	12.00	19.00
1906/886 JF	Inc. above	3.00	5.00	8.00	12.00	19.00
1906/895 JF	Inc. above	3.00	5.00	8.00	12.00	19.00
1906/896 JF	Inc. above	2.50	3.50	5.00	7.00	13.00
1906 JF	Inc. above	3.00	5.00	8.00	12.00	25.00
1907 FG	600,000	3.00	5.00	8.00	12.00	25.00
1908/7 FG	200,000	7.00	9.00	16.00	20.00	35.00
1908 FG	Inc. above	4.00	6.00	10.00	15.00	25.00
1909/7 FG	—	12.00	18.00	32.00	50.00	70.00
1909 FG	—	4.00	6.00	10.00	15.00	22.00
1910 FG	640,000	2.50	3.50	5.00	7.00	13.00
1911 FG	460,000	2.50	3.50	5.00	7.00	13.00
1912 FG	120,000	3.00	4.00	6.00	8.00	14.00
1913 FG	480,000	2.50	3.50	5.00	7.00	13.00
1914/3 FG	—	4.00	6.00	10.00	15.00	25.00
1914/03 FG	—	5.00	8.00	14.00	20.00	35.00
1914/04 FG	—	5.00	8.00	14.00	20.00	35.00
1914 FG	—	2.50	3.50	5.00	7.00	13.00
1916/3 FG	860,000	2.50	3.50	5.00	7.00	13.00
1916/3 FG FERUANA Error	—	4.00	7.00	11.00	18.00	27.50
1916 FG	Inc. above	2.00	3.00	4.00	6.00	12.00
1916/5 FG PERUANA Error	Inc. above	4.00	6.00	11.00	18.00	27.50
1916/5 FG FERUANA Error	Inc. above	4.00	6.00	11.00	18.00	27.50
1916/5 Without FERUANA	Inc. above	4.00	6.00	11.00	18.00	27.50
1916 FG FERUANA Error	Inc. above	4.00	6.00	12.00	20.00	35.00
1916 Matte	—	—	—	—	—	—
1917/87 FG	140,000	2.50	3.50	5.00	7.00	13.00
1917 FG	Inc. above	2.50	3.50	5.00	7.00	13.00

KM# 214.1 10 CENTAVOS

Copper-Nickel, 20 mm. **Obv:** Head right **Rev:** Value to right of sprig

Date	Mintage	VF20	XF40	MS60	MS63	MS65
1918	3,000,000	1.00	2.00	5.00	12.00	18.00
1919	2,500,000	1.00	2.00	5.00	12.00	18.00
1920	3,080,000	0.75	1.50	3.00	10.00	15.00
1921	6,920,000	0.75	1.50	3.00	10.00	15.00
1926	3,000,000	5.00	8.50	12.00	25.00	35.00

KM# 214.2 10 CENTAVOS

3.86 g., Copper-Nickel, 20 mm. **Obv:** Head right **Rev:** Value to right of sprig

Date	Mintage	VF20	XF40	MS60	MS63	MS65
1935	—	PF63 150				
1935	1,000,000	1.50	3.00	5.00	12.00	20.00
1937	1,000,000	1.00	2.00	4.00	10.00	15.00
1937 Proof	—	—	—	—	—	—
1939	2,000,000	0.75	1.25	3.00	7.50	12.00
1939 Proof	—	—	—	—	—	—
1940	2,000,000	0.75	1.25	3.00	7.50	12.00
1940	—	PF63 175				
1941	2,000,000	0.75	1.25	3.00	7.50	12.00
1941 Proof	—	—	—	—	—	—

KM# 214a.1 10 CENTAVOS

Brass, 20 mm. **Obv:** Head right, date begins MIL., spelled out w/a "Y" **Rev:** Value to right of sprig

Date	Mintage	VF20	XF40	MS60	MS63	MS65
1942	2,000,000	3.00	6.00	10.00	20.00	35.00
1943	2,000,000	3.00	6.00	10.00	20.00	35.00
1944	2,000,000	3.50	7.00	12.00	25.00	40.00

KM# 214a.2 10 CENTAVOS

Brass, 20 mm. **Obv:** Head right **Rev:** Value to right of sprig **Edge:** Plain

Date	Mintage	VF20	XF40	MS60	MS63	MS65
1942 S	2,000,000	12.00	15.00	25.00	50.00	75.00
1943 S	2,000,000	3.00	6.00	10.00	20.00	45.00

KM# 214a.3 10 CENTAVOS
Brass, 20 mm. **Obv:** Date behins MIL., spelled out with an "I" **Rev:** Value to right of sprig

Date	Mintage	VF20	XF40	MS60	MS63	MS65
1942	—	9.00	15.00	20.00	40.00	60.00

KM# 214a.4 10 CENTAVOS
Brass, 20 mm. **Obv:** Date behins MIL., spelled out with an "I" **Rev:** Value to right of sprig **Note:** Varieties exist.

Date	Mintage	VF20	XF40	MS60	MS63	MS65
1944	—	7.00	12.00	18.00	35.00	50.00

KM# 224.1 10 CENTAVOS
Brass, 20 mm. **Obv:** Head right with short legend **Rev:** Value to right of sprig **Note:** Thick planchet.

Date	Mintage	VF20	XF40	MS60	MS63	MS65
1945	2,810,000	0.50	1.50	2.50	4.00	7.50
1946/5	4,863,000	1.00	2.50	4.00	8.00	15.00
1946	Inc. above	0.75	2.00	3.50	7.00	12.00

KM# 226.1 10 CENTAVOS
3.89 g., Brass, 20 mm. **Obv:** Long legend with 3mm gap above head **Rev:** Value to right of sprig **Note:** Thick planchet.

Date	Mintage	VF20	XF40	MS60	MS63	MS65
1947	6,806,000	0.50	1.00	2.00	3.00	7.50
1948	5,771,000	0.50	1.25	2.50	4.00	7.50
1949/8	4,730,000	1.00	1.50	3.50	7.50	12.00

KM# 226.2 10 CENTAVOS
Brass, 20 mm. **Obv:** Head right **Rev:** Value to right of sprig

Date	Mintage	VF20	XF40	MS60	MS63	MS65
1949	Inc. above	0.50	1.00	3.00	5.00	7.50
1950 AFP	Inc. above	0.50	1.25	3.50	8.00	12.00
1950	5,298,000	0.40	0.80	2.00	4.00	7.50
1951	7,324,000	10.00	15.00	20.00	25.00	40.00
1951/0 AFP	—	0.50	1.00	2.00	4.00	4.50
1951 AFP	—	0.40	0.80	1.50	3.00	7.50

KM# 224.2 10 CENTAVOS
2.70 g., Brass, 20 mm. **Obv:** Head right **Rev:** Value to right of sprig **Note:** Thin planchet - 1.3mm. Date varieties exist.

Date	Mintage	VF20	XF40	MS60	MS63	MS65
1951	Inc. above	0.20	0.40	1.00	2.00	3.50
1951 AFP	—	0.20	0.40	1.00	2.00	3.50
1952	6,694,000	0.20	0.40	1.00	3.00	4.00
1952 AFP	—	0.20	0.40	1.00	3.00	4.00
1953	5,668,000	0.20	0.40	1.00	2.00	3.50
1953 AFP	—	0.20	0.40	1.00	2.00	3.50
1954	7,786,000	0.10	0.35	0.75	1.50	3.00
1954 AFP	—	0.10	0.35	0.75	1.50	3.00
1955	6,690,000	0.10	0.35	0.75	1.50	3.00
1955 AFP	—	0.10	0.35	0.75	1.50	3.00
1956/5	8,410,000	0.35	0.75	1.50	3.50	5.00
1956	Inc. above	0.10	0.25	0.50	1.00	3.00
1956 AFP	—	0.20	0.40	0.75	2.00	3.50
1957	8,420,000	0.10	0.25	0.50	1.00	3.00
1957 AFP	—	0.10	0.25	0.50	1.00	3.00
1958	10,380,000	0.10	0.25	0.50	1.00	3.00
1958 AFP	—	—	—	—	—	—
1959	8,300,000	0.10	0.25	0.50	1.00	3.00
1959 AFP	—	—	—	—	—	—
1960	12,600,000	0.10	0.25	0.50	1.00	3.00
1961	12,700,000	0.10	0.15	0.35	1.00	3.00
1962	14,598,000	0.10	0.15	0.35	1.00	3.00
1963	16,100,000	0.10	0.15	0.35	1.00	3.00
1964	16,504,000	0.10	0.15	0.35	1.00	3.00
1965	17,808,000	0.10	0.15	0.35	1.00	3.00
1965	—	PF65 25.00				

KM# 233 10 CENTAVOS
Brass, 20 mm. **Obv:** Head right **Rev:** Value to upper right of torch, all within chain circle

Date	Mintage	VF20	XF40	MS60	MS63	MS65
1954	1,818,000	0.75	1.50	3.00	6.00	12.00

KM# 237 10 CENTAVOS
2.10 g., Brass **Subject:** 400th Anniversary of Lima Mint **Obv:** National arms above value **Rev:** Pillars of Hercules within inner circle

Date	Mintage	VF20	XF40	MS60	MS63	MS65
1965	572,000	—	0.25	0.35	0.50	1.00
1965	—	PF65 150				

KM# 245.1 10 CENTAVOS
Brass **Obv:** National arms within circle **Rev:** Value to left of flower sprig **Edge:** Reeded **Note:** Date varieties exist.

Date	Mintage	VF20	XF40	MS60	MS63	MS65
1966	14,930,000	—	0.10	0.35	0.75	1.25
Note: PAREJA in field at lower left of arms						
1966	1,000	PF65 15.00				
1967	19,330,000	—	0.10	0.35	0.75	1.25
1968	24,390,000	—	0.10	0.35	0.75	1.25

KM# 245.1a 10 CENTAVOS
Silver Plated Brass **Obv:** National arms within circle **Rev:** Value to left of flower sprig

Date	Mintage	VF20	XF40	MS60	MS63	MS65
1967	—	—	—	—	—	—

KM# 245.2 10 CENTAVOS
2.17 g., Brass, 17.90 mm. **Obv:** National arms within circle **Rev:** Value to left of flower sprig **Edge:** Reeded **Note:** Date varieties exist.

Date	Mintage	VF20	XF40	MS60	MS63	MS65
1967	—	—	0.10	0.15	0.25	0.40
1968	—	—	—	0.10	0.20	0.35
1969	24,390,000	—	0.10	0.15	0.25	0.40
1970	29,110,000	—	—	0.10	0.20	0.35
1971	30,590,000	—	—	0.10	0.20	0.35
1972	34,442,000	—	—	0.10	0.20	0.35
1973	33,864,000	—	—	0.10	0.20	0.35

KM# 245.3 10 CENTAVOS
2.18 g., Brass **Obv:** National arms within circle **Rev:** Value to left of flower sprig **Edge:** Plain

Date	Mintage	VF20	XF40	MS60	MS63	MS65
1973	Inc. above	—	—	0.10	0.15	0.25
1974	—	—	—	0.10	0.15	0.25
1975	10,430,000	—	—	0.10	0.15	0.25

KM# 263 10 CENTAVOS
1.48 g., Brass, 14.8 mm. **Obv:** National arms within circle **Rev:** Value

Date	Mintage	VF20	XF40	MS60	MS63	MS65
1975	—	—	—	0.10	0.15	0.25

KM# 204.2 DINERO
2.50 g., 0.900 Silver 0.0723 oz. ASW, 18 mm. **Obv:** National arms above date **Rev:** Seated Liberty flanked by shield and column **Note:** Varieties exist.

Date	Mintage	VF20	XF40	MS60	MS63	MS65
1902/1 JF	375,000	7.00	9.00	12.00	22.00	37.00
1902/891 JF	Inc. above	7.00	9.00	12.00	22.00	37.00
1902/892 JF	Inc. above	7.00	9.00	12.00	22.00	37.00
1902/897 JF	Inc. above	7.00	9.00	12.00	22.00	37.00
1902 JF	Inc. above	8.00	10.00	13.00	25.00	45.00
1903/803 JF	887,000	7.00	9.00	12.00	22.00	37.00
1903/807 JF	Inc. above	7.00	9.00	12.00	22.00	37.00
1903/892 JF	Inc. above	6.00	8.00	10.00	18.00	30.00
1903/893 JF	Inc. above	6.00	8.00	10.00	18.00	30.00
1903/92 JF	Inc. above	6.00	8.00	10.00	18.00	30.00
1903 JF	Inc. above	7.00	9.00	12.00	22.00	37.00
1904 JF	380,000	7.00	9.00	12.00	23.00	38.00
1905/1 JF	700,000	7.00	9.00	12.00	23.00	38.00
1905/3 JF	Inc. above	7.00	9.00	12.00	23.00	38.00
1905 JF	Inc. above	7.00	9.00	12.00	22.00	37.00
1906 JF	826,000	7.00	9.00	12.00	22.00	37.00
1907 JF Rare	500,000	—	—	—	—	—
1907 FG/JF	Inc. above	8.00	10.00	14.00	25.00	40.00
1907 FG	Inc. above	5.00	7.00	10.00	20.00	30.00
1908/6 FG/JF	Inc. above	7.00	9.00	12.00	23.00	38.00
1908 FG/JF	200,000	7.00	9.00	12.00	23.00	38.00
1908 FG/GF	Inc. above	7.00	9.00	12.00	23.00	38.00
1908 FG	Inc. above	5.00	7.00	10.00	20.00	37.00
1909 FG	—	12.00	16.00	22.00	30.00	50.00
1909 FG/FO	—	12.00	16.00	22.00	30.00	50.00
1909 FG/FF	—	12.00	16.00	22.00	30.00	50.00
1910 FG	210,000	5.00	7.00	10.00	20.00	37.00
1910 FG/JF	Inc. above	7.00	9.00	12.00	25.00	45.00
1910 FG/JG	Inc. above	7.00	9.00	12.00	25.00	45.00
1911 FG	200,000	5.00	7.00	10.00	20.00	37.00
1911 FG/JF	Inc. above	7.00	9.00	12.00	25.00	45.00
1911 FG/JG	—	7.00	9.00	12.00	25.00	45.00
1912 FG	400,000	5.00	7.00	10.00	20.00	37.00
1912/02 FG/JF	Inc. above	7.00	9.00	12.00	25.00	45.00
1912 FG/JF	Inc. above	7.00	9.00	12.00	25.00	45.00
1912 FG/JG	Inc. above	7.00	9.00	12.00	25.00	45.00
1913/1 FG/JF	Inc. above	7.00	9.00	12.00	25.00	45.00
1913/2 FG	360,000	7.00	9.00	12.00	25.00	45.00
1913/7 FG/G	Inc. above	7.00	9.00	12.00	25.00	45.00
1913 FG	Inc. above	5.00	7.00	10.00	20.00	37.00
1913 FG/G	Inc. above	5.00	7.00	9.00	18.00	30.00
1913 FG/JB	Inc. above	9.00	12.00	18.00	30.00	50.00
1916 FG Large date	430,000	7.00	9.00	12.00	22.00	38.00
1916 FG Small date	Inc. above	4.50	5.00	7.00	10.00	15.00
1916 FG/JG	Inc. above	15.00	18.00	22.00	30.00	50.00
1916 FG/FF	Inc. above	15.00	18.00	22.00	30.00	50.00

KM# 215.1 20 CENTAVOS
7.00 g., Copper-Nickel, 24 mm. **Obv:** Date spelled: UN MIL NOVECIENTOS DIECIOCHO **Rev:** Value to right of sprig

Date	Mintage	VF20	XF40	MS60	MS63	MS65
1918	2,500,000	1.00	5.00	20.00	32.00	50.00
1919	1,250,000	2.50	5.00	20.00	32.00	50.00
1920	1,464,000	2.25	4.00	22.00	35.00	50.00
1921	8,536,000	3.00	6.00	22.00	35.00	50.00
1926	2,500,000	5.00	9.00	25.00	37.00	55.00

KM# 215.2 20 CENTAVOS
Copper-Nickel, 24 mm. **Obv:** Head right **Rev:** Value to right of sprig

Date	Mintage	VF20	XF40	MS60	MS63	MS65
1940	1,000,000	0.75	1.75	5.50	10.00	20.00
1940	—	PF63 175				
1941	1,000,000	1.00	2.50	7.50	12.00	22.00
1941	—	PF63 150				

KM# 215a.1 20 CENTAVOS
Brass, 24 mm. **Obv:** Date spelling: MIL NOVECIENTOS CUARENTA Y TRES **Rev:** Value to right of sprig

Date	Mintage	VF20	XF40	MS60	MS63	MS65
1942	500,000	6.00	13.50	30.00	60.00	90.00
1943	500,000	6.00	13.50	30.00	60.00	90.00
1944	500,000	7.50	16.50	32.00	65.00	95.00

KM# 215a.2 20 CENTAVOS
Brass, 24 mm. **Obv:** Head right **Rev:** Value to right of sprig

Date	Mintage	VF20	XF40	MS60	MS63	MS65
1942 S	500,000	12.00	35.00	75.00	150	200
1943 S	500,000	6.00	12.50	55.00	125	185

KM# 221.1 20 CENTAVOS
Brass, 24 mm. **Obv:** Head right, divided legend **Rev:** Value to right of sprig **Note:** Thick planchet.

Date	Mintage	VF20	XF40	MS60	MS63	MS65
1942	300,000	2.50	5.00	8.00	15.00	25.00
1943	1,900,000	1.50	2.50	5.50	9.00	18.00
1944	2,963,000	1.25	2.00	5.00	7.00	15.00

KM# 221.3 20 CENTAVOS
Brass **Obv:** Head right, continuous legend **Rev:** Value to right of sprig

Date	Mintage	VF20	XF40	MS60	MS63	MS65
1945	3,043,000	0.50	0.75	1.50	3.00	5.00
1946/5	Inc. above	0.65	1.00	2.00	3.50	6.00
1946	Inc. above	0.50	0.75	1.50	3.00	5.00

KM# 221.2 20 CENTAVOS
6.83 g., Brass, 24 mm. **Obv:** AFP on truncation, continuous legend **Rev:** Value to right of sprig

Date	Mintage	VF20	XF40	MS60	MS63	MS65
1946	3,410,000	0.50	0.85	1.50	3.50	7.50
1947	4,307,000	0.50	0.85	1.50	3.50	7.50
1948	3,578,000	0.50	0.85	1.50	3.50	7.50
1949/8	2,709,000	1.50	2.50	3.50	6.50	10.00

KM# 221.2a 20 CENTAVOS
Copper **Obv:** Head right **Rev:** Value to right of sprig

Date	Mintage	VF20	XF40	MS60	MS63	MS65
1947	300	—	—	100	150	250

KM# 221.4 20 CENTAVOS
Brass **Obv:** Different style legend **Rev:** Value to right of sprig

Date	Mintage	VF20	XF40	MS60	MS63	MS65
1949	Inc. above	1.00	1.50	2.50	4.00	8.50
1950	2,427,000	1.75	3.00	5.00	8.00	15.00
1951	2,941,000	7.00	12.00	18.00	25.00	50.00

KM# 221.2b 20 CENTAVOS
3.80 g., Brass, 23 mm. **Obv:** Head right **Rev:** Value to right of sprig **Note:** Thin planchet - 1.3mm. AFP. Date varieties exist.

Date	Mintage	VF20	XF40	MS60	MS63	MS65
1951	Inc. above	0.40	0.75	1.25	2.00	5.00
1951 Without AFP	—	—	—	—	—	—
1952	4,410,000	0.40	0.75	1.25	2.50	5.00
1952 Without AFP	Inc. above	—	—	—	—	—
1953	2,615,000	0.40	1.50	3.00	8.00	12.00
1954	1,816,000	2.50	4.00	6.00	12.00	18.00
1955 Large oval 9	4,050,000	0.15	0.30	0.75	1.50	3.00
1955 Small oval 9	Inc. above	0.40	1.50	3.00	8.00	15.00
1955 Round nine	Inc. above	—	—	—	—	—
1956	3,760,000	0.15	0.30	0.75	1.50	3.00
1957	3,680,000	0.15	0.30	0.50	1.00	3.00
1958	3,100,000	0.15	0.30	0.50	1.00	3.00
1959	5,450,000	0.10	0.20	0.40	1.00	3.00
1959 Without AFP	—	—	—	—	—	—
1960/90 Without AFP	—	—	—	—	—	—
1960/90 With AFP	—	—	—	—	—	—
1960	6,750,000	0.10	0.20	0.40	1.00	3.00
1960 Without AFP	—	0.75	1.50	2.50	4.00	7.50
1961	6,800,000	0.10	0.20	0.40	1.00	3.00
1961 Without AFP	—	—	—	—	—	—
1962	7,357,000	0.10	0.20	0.40	1.00	3.00
1963/2	8,843,000	0.25	0.50	1.00	2.00	5.00
1963	Inc. above	0.10	0.20	0.40	1.00	3.00
1964	9,550,000	0.10	0.20	0.40	1.00	3.00
1965 With inverted V for A in AFP	—	0.10	0.20	0.40	1.00	3.00
1965 Without AFP	—	0.15	0.30	0.50	1.00	3.00
1965	—	PF65 35.00				

KM# 234 20 CENTAVOS
Brass, 24 mm. **Subject:** President Castilla **Obv:** Head right **Rev:** Value to right of torch within chain circle **Edge:** Reeded **Note:** Thin planchet - 1.3mm. AFP.

Date	Mintage	VF20	XF40	MS60	MS63	MS65
1954	799,000	3.00	5.00	7.00	12.00	18.00

KM# 221.2c 20 CENTAVOS
Copper-Nickel **Obv:** Head right **Rev:** Value to right of sprig **Edge:** Reeded **Note:** Thin planchet - 1.3mm. AFP.

Date	Mintage	VF20	XF40	MS60	MS63	MS65
1958	—	—	—	—	150	—
1963	—	15.00	25.00	45.00	—	—
1965	—	PF65 30.00				

KM# 264 20 CENTAVOS
1.80 g., Brass, 16.2 mm. **Obv:** National arms within circle **Rev:** Value

Date	Mintage	VF20	XF40	MS60	MS63	MS65
1975	—	0.20	0.50	0.75	1.50	1.75

KM# 205.2 1/5 SOL
5.00 g., 0.900 Silver 0.1447 oz. ASW, 23.5 mm. **Obv:** National arms **Rev:** Libertad incuse **Edge:** Reeded **Note:** Die varieties exist. Some coins 1911-17 have engraver's initial R left of shield on reverse.

Date	Mintage	F12	VF20	XF40	MS60	MS63
1901 JF	638,000	4.00	7.00	11.00	23.00	36.00
1903/1 JF	702,000	9.00	12.00	14.00	25.00	55.00
1903/13 JF	Inc. above	5.00	8.00	13.00	23.00	45.00
1903 JF	Inc. above	5.00	8.00	13.00	23.00	36.00
1906 JF	660,000	5.00	8.00	13.00	23.00	36.00
1907 JF	1,370,000	4.00	7.00	11.00	14.00	30.00
1907 FG	Inc. above	5.00	8.00	13.00	23.00	36.00
1908/7 FG	560,000	5.00	8.00	13.00	23.00	45.00
1908 FG	Inc. above	5.00	8.00	13.00	23.00	45.00
1909 FG	42,000	9.00	12.00	14.00	35.00	85.00
1910/00 FG	165,000	10.00	15.00	25.00	55.00	115
1910 FG	Inc. above	10.00	15.00	25.00	42.00	80.00
1911 FG	250,000	5.00	8.00	13.00	23.00	30.00
1911 FG-R	Inc. above	5.00	8.00	13.00	23.00	30.00
1912 FG	300,000	4.00	7.00	11.00	14.00	25.00
1912 R	—	4.00	7.00	11.00	14.00	25.00
1912/1 FG-R	—	5.00	8.00	11.00	18.00	30.00
1912 FG-R	Inc. above	4.00	7.00	13.00	23.00	45.00
1913 FG	223,000	5.00	8.00	13.00	23.00	45.00
1913 FG-R	Inc. above	5.00	8.00	13.00	23.00	45.00
1914 FG	10,000	15.00	25.00	45.00	95.00	180
1915 FG	—	70.00	95.00	145	275	400
1916 FG	425,000	9.00	13.00	18.00	36.00	80.00
1916 FG-R	Inc. above	5.00	8.00	13.00	18.00	30.00
1917 FG-R	20,000	20.00	30.00	60.00	125	235

KM# 238 25 CENTAVOS
Brass, 25 mm. **Subject:** 400th Anniversary of Lima Mint **Obv:** National arms above value **Rev:** Pillars of Hercules within inner circle

Date	Mintage	VF20	XF40	MS60	MS63	MS65
ND (1965)	1,113,000	0.25	0.35	0.45	1.00	1.50
1965	—	PF65 200				

KM# 246.1 25 CENTAVOS
Brass **Obv:** PAREJA in field at lower left of arms **Rev:** Value to left of flower sprig **Edge:** Reeded

Date	Mintage	VF20	XF40	MS60	MS63	MS65
1966 PAREJA in field at lower left of arms	9,300,000	0.15	0.25	0.50	0.75	1.00
1966	1,000	PF65 15.00				
1967	8,150,000	0.15	0.25	0.50	0.75	1.00
1968	7,440,000	0.15	0.25	0.50	0.75	1.00

KM# 246.1a 25 CENTAVOS
Silver Plated Brass **Obv:** National arms within circle **Rev:** Value to left of flower sprig

Date	Mintage	VF20	XF40	MS60	MS63	MS65
1967	Inc. above	—	—	—	—	—

KM# 246.2 25 CENTAVOS
3.20 g., Brass, 21.03 mm. **Obv:** National arms within circle **Rev:** Value to left of flower sprig **Edge:** Reeded

Date	Mintage	VF20	XF40	MS60	MS63	MS65
1968 AP	Inc. above	0.15	0.25	0.50	0.75	1.00
1969 AP on reverse	7,440,000	0.20	0.40	1.00	1.50	2.00
1969 With inverted V for A in AP	Inc. above	0.20	0.40	1.00	1.50	2.00
1969 Without AP	Inc. above	0.15	0.25	0.50	0.75	1.00
1970	6,341,000	0.20	0.40	1.00	1.50	2.00
1971	3,196,000	0.20	0.40	1.00	1.50	2.00
1972	5,523,000	0.20	0.40	1.00	1.50	2.00
1973	7,492,000	0.15	0.25	0.50	0.75	1.00

KM# 259 25 CENTAVOS
3.10 g., Brass **Obv:** National arms within circle **Rev:** Value to left of flower sprig

Date	Mintage	VF20	XF40	MS60	MS63	MS65
1973	Inc. above	0.10	0.15	0.25	0.40	0.60
1974	—	0.10	0.15	0.25	0.40	0.60
1975	—	0.10	0.15	0.25	0.40	0.60

KM# 203 1/2 SOL

12.50 g., 0.900 Silver 0.3617 oz. ASW, 30 mm. **Obv:** National arms above date **Rev:** Seated Liberty flanked by shield and column **Note:** Mint mark: LIMA. Date varieties exist. Most coins have engraver's initials JR left of shield tip on reverse.

Date	Mintage	VF20	XF40	MS60	MS63	MS65
1907 LIMA FG-JR	1,000,000	13.00	15.00	20.00	35.00	—
1908/7 LIMA FG-JR	30,000	45.00	125	275	525	—
1908 LIMA FG-JR	Inc. above	43.25	115	175	300	—
1914 LIMA FG-JR	173,000	13.00	25.00	40.00	65.00	—
1915 LIMA FG-JR	570,000	13.00	15.00	20.00	30.00	—
1916 LIMA FG	384,000	13.00	15.00	20.00	30.00	—
1916 LIMA FG-JR	—	13.00	15.00	20.00	30.00	—
1917 LIMA FG-JR	178,000	13.00	17.00	22.00	35.00	—

KM# 216 1/2 SOL

12.50 g., 0.500 Silver 0.2009 oz. ASW, 30 mm. **Obv:** National arms above date **Rev:** Seated Liberty flanked by shield and column **Edge:** Reeded **Note:** Date varieties exist. Engraver's initials appear on stems of obverse wreath.

Date	Mintage	VF20	XF40	MS60	MS63	MS65
1922 LIMA LIBERTAD incuse, J.R. on reverse	465,000	14.00	45.00	90.00	150	—
1922 LIMA LIBERTAD in relief	Inc. above	14.00	45.00	90.00	150	—
1923 LIMA GM LIBER/TAD, round-top 3	2,520,000	8.00	18.00	35.00	55.00	—
1923/2 LIMA Flat-top 3	Inc. above	7.00	10.00	22.00	37.00	—
1923 LIMA Flat-top 3	Inc. above	7.00	13.00	27.00	45.00	—
1924 LIMA GM	238,000	13.00	35.00	55.00	90.00	—
1926 LIMA GM	694,000	7.00	13.00	27.00	45.00	—
1927 LIMA GM	2,640,000	7.00	10.00	20.00	30.00	—
1928/7 LIMA GM	3,028,000	—	—	—	—	—
1928 LIMA GM	Inc. above	7.00	10.00	20.00	30.00	—
1929 LIMA GM	3,068,000	7.00	10.00	20.00	30.00	—
1935 LIMA AP	2,653,000	7.00	9.00	18.00	27.00	—
1935 LIMA	—	—	—	—	—	—

KM# 220.1 1/2 SOL

Brass **Obv:** Five palm leaves point to llama on shield **Rev:** Value and legend

Date	Mintage	VF20	XF40	MS60	MS63	MS65
1935	10,000,000	1.25	2.25	4.50	7.00	12.00
1935	—	**PF63** 200				
1941	4,000,000	1.25	2.25	4.50	7.00	12.00

KM# 220.2 1/2 SOL

Brass **Obv:** Arms within wreath **Rev:** Value and legend

Date	Mintage	VF20	XF40	MS60	MS63	MS65
1942	4,000,000	3.00	5.00	10.00	20.00	35.00
1943 (P)	4,000,000	6.50	12.50	18.00	35.00	50.00
1944 (P)	Inc. above	3.00	5.00	10.00	20.00	35.00

KM# 220.4 1/2 SOL

7.32 g., Brass **Obv:** Three palm leaves point to llama on shield **Rev:** Value and legend **Note:** Dates 1941-44 have thick flat-top 4 without serifs. 1945 has narrow 4 like KM#220.5.

Date	Mintage	VF20	XF40	MS60	MS63	MS65
1941	2,000,000	6.00	12.00	18.00	35.00	50.00
1942	Inc. above	2.50	4.00	7.00	15.00	25.00
1942 AP	—	—	—	—	—	—
1943	2,000,000	1.00	2.00	6.00	12.00	20.00
1944	Inc. above	0.85	1.75	3.50	7.00	12.00
1944/2	4,000,000	—	—	—	—	—
1944 AP	Inc. above	—	—	—	—	—
1945	4,000,000	1.50	3.00	5.00	10.00	18.00

KM# 220.3 1/2 SOL

Brass **Obv:** National arms within wreath **Rev:** Value and legend **Note:** The coins struck in San Francisco have a serif on the "4" of the date; the Lima and London coins do not.

Date	Mintage	VF20	XF40	MS60	MS63	MS65
1942 S	1,668,000	2.50	4.00	7.00	15.00	25.00
1943 S	6,332,000	2.50	4.00	7.00	15.00	25.00

KM# 220.5 1/2 SOL

7.40 g., Brass, 27.1 mm. **Obv:** Three palm leaves point to llama on shield **Rev:** Value and legend **Note:** 1942, 1944 AP, and all 1945-49 have narrow 4 without serif on crossbar. 1944 without AP has flat-top 4 like KM#220.4. Engraver's initials AP appear on wreath stems of some 1944-45, all 1946 and some 1947 coins. Varieties exist, including narrow and wide dates for 1956 and 1961 issues.

Date	Mintage	VF20	XF40	MS60	MS63	MS65
1942 Long-top 2	Inc. above	2.50	4.00	7.00	15.00	25.00
1944	Inc. above	1.50	3.00	5.00	10.00	18.00
1944 AP	Inc. above	1.00	2.00	4.00	7.00	12.00
1945	Inc. above	1.50	3.00	5.00	10.00	15.00
1945 AP	Inc. above	1.50	3.00	5.00	10.00	15.00
1946/5 AP	3,744,000	3.50	6.50	9.00	17.50	28.00
1946 AP	Inc. above	0.75	1.25	3.50	7.00	12.00
1947 AP	6,066,000	0.75	1.25	3.50	7.00	12.00
1947	Inc. above	0.75	1.25	3.50	7.00	12.00
1948	3,324,000	0.75	1.25	3.50	7.00	12.00
1949/8	420,000	2.00	4.00	6.00	12.00	16.00
1949	Inc. above	3.00	6.00	9.00	18.00	28.00
1950	91,000	2.25	4.00	7.00	15.00	25.00
1951/8	930,000	1.00	2.00	4.00	7.00	10.00
1951	Inc. above	1.00	2.00	4.00	7.00	10.00
1952	935,000	1.50	3.00	5.00	10.00	15.00
1953	817,000	1.00	2.00	4.00	7.00	10.00
1954	637,000	1.50	3.00	5.00	10.00	15.00
1955	1,383,000	0.35	0.75	2.00	4.00	8.00
1956	2,309,000	0.25	0.40	0.75	1.50	3.00
1957	2,700,000	0.25	0.50	1.00	2.00	4.00
1958	2,691,000	0.25	0.40	0.75	1.50	3.00
1959	3,609,000	0.25	0.40	0.75	1.50	3.00
1960	5,600,000	0.20	0.35	0.50	0.75	1.50
1961 Narrow date	4,400,000	0.20	0.35	0.50	0.75	1.50
1961 Wide date	Inc. above	0.20	0.35	0.50	0.75	1.50
1962	3,540,000	0.20	0.35	0.65	1.00	2.00
1963	4,345,000	0.20	0.35	0.50	0.75	1.50
1964	5,315,000	0.20	0.35	0.50	0.75	1.50
1965	7,090,000	0.20	0.35	0.50	0.75	1.50
1965	—	**PF65** 75.00				

KM# 239 1/2 SOL

Brass **Subject:** 400th Anniversary of Lima Mint **Obv:** National arms above value **Rev:** Pillars of Hercules within inner circle

Date	Mintage	VF20	XF40	MS60	MS63	MS65
ND-1965	10,971,000	0.10	0.20	0.35	0.50	0.75
ND-1965	—	**PF65** 400				

KM# 247 1/2 SOL

Brass, 22.5 mm. **Obv:** National arms within circle **Rev:** Value to right of vicuña

Date	Mintage	VF20	XF40	MS60	MS63	MS65
1966	13,720,000	0.10	0.20	0.50	1.00	3.00
1966	1,000	**PF65** 20.00				
1967	15,500,000	0.10	0.20	0.50	1.00	3.00
1967 PAREJA on obverse and reverse	—	0.10	0.20	0.50	1.00	3.00
1968	13,890,000	7.00	12.00	18.00	32.00	—
1968 JAS	—	0.10	0.20	0.50	1.00	3.00
1969	13,890,000	0.10	0.20	0.50	1.00	3.00
1970	11,901,000	0.10	0.20	0.50	1.00	3.00
Note: Date varieties exist						
1971	7,524,000	0.15	0.20	0.50	1.00	3.00
1972	19,441,000	0.10	0.20	0.50	1.00	3.00
1973	14,951,000	0.10	0.20	0.50	1.00	3.00

KM# 247a 1/2 SOL

Silver Plated Brass **Obv:** National arms within circle **Rev:** Value to right of llama

Date	Mintage	VF20	XF40	MS60	MS63	MS65
1967	—	—	—	—	—	—

KM# 247b 1/2 SOL

Silver **Obv:** National arms within circle **Rev:** Value to right of llama

Date	Mintage	VF20	XF40	MS60	MS63	MS65
1967	—	—	—	—	—	—

KM# 260 1/2 SOL

4.16 g., Brass, 22.5 mm. **Obv:** National arms within circle **Rev:** Value to right of vicuña **Edge:** Reeded

Date	Mintage	VF20	XF40	MS60	MS63	MS65
1973	Inc. above	0.10	0.20	0.50	1.00	3.00
1974/1	Inc. below	0.10	0.20	0.50	1.00	3.00
1974	14,518,000	0.10	0.20	0.50	1.00	3.00
1975	14,039,000	0.10	0.20	0.50	1.00	3.00

KM# 265 1/2 SOL

2.10 g., Brass, 17.97 mm. **Obv:** National arms within circle **Rev:** Value **Edge:** Plain **Note:** Without mint mark.

Date	Mintage	VF20	XF40	MS60	MS63	MS65
1975	62,682,000	0.10	0.20	0.30	0.50	0.75
1976	168,414,000	0.10	0.20	0.30	0.50	0.75

KM# 268 1/2 SOL

9.35 g., 0.900 Gold 0.2705 oz. AGW **Subject:** 150th Anniversary - Battle of Ayacucho **Obv:** National arms **Rev:** Monument and value

Date	Mintage	VF20	XF40	MS60	MS63	MS65
1976	10,000	—	—	—	500	—

KM# 196.26 SOL

25.00 g., 0.900 Silver 0.7234 oz. ASW, 37 mm., **Obv:** National arms above date **Rev:** Libertad incuse **Note:** Type XII. Legends have smaller lettering. Varieties exist.

Date	Mintage	VF20	XF40	MS60	MS63	MS65
1914 FG	620,000	—	13.50	27.50	40.00	—
1915 FG	Inc. above	—	13.50	27.50	37.50	—

KM# 196.27 SOL

25.00 g., 0.900 Silver 0.7234 oz. ASW, 37 mm. **Obv:** National arms above date **Rev:** LIBERTAD incuse

Date	Mintage	VF20	XF40	MS60	MS63	MS65
1916 FG	1,927,000	—	13.50	27.50	37.50	—

KM# 196.28 SOL

25.00 g., 0.900 Silver 0.7234 oz. ASW, 37 mm. **Obv:** National arms above date **Rev:** LIBERTAD in relief **Note:** Type III.

Date	Mintage	VF20	XF40	MS60	MS63	MS65
1916 FG	Inc. above	—	13.50	27.50	37.50	—

KM# 217.1 SOL

25.00 g., 0.500 Silver 0.4019 oz. ASW, 37 mm. **Obv:** National arms, fineness omitted **Rev:** LEBERTAD in relief

Date	Mintage	VF20	XF40	MS60	MS63	MS65
1922 Rare	—	—	—	—	—	—
1923	3,600	30.00	70.00	180	275	—

KM# 217.2 SOL

25.00 g., 0.500 Silver 0.4019 oz. ASW, 37 mm. **Obv:** National arms above date **Rev:** LIBERTAD incuse

Date	Mintage	VF20	XF40	MS60	MS63	MS65
1923	1,400	75.00	165	300	475	—

KM# 218.1 SOL

25.00 g., 0.500 Silver 0.4019 oz. ASW, 37 mm. **Obv:** National arms **Rev:** Seated Liberty flanked by shield and column **Note:** Small letters. The Philadelphia and Lima strikings may be distinguished by the fact that the letters in the legends are smaller on those pieces produced at Philadelphia. All bear the name of the Lima Mint.

Date	Mintage	VF20	XF40	MS60	MS63	MS65
1923	Est. 2369000	14.00	20.00	25.00	30.00	—
1924/823	3,113,000	20.00	32.00	45.00	70.00	—
1924/824	Inc. above	20.00	32.00	45.00	70.00	—
1924	Inc. above	16.00	20.00	25.00	30.00	—
1925	1,291,000	16.00	22.50	28.00	38.00	—
1926	2,157,000	16.00	20.00	25.00	30.00	—

KM# 218.2 SOL

25.00 g., 0.500 Silver 0.4019 oz. ASW, 37 mm. **Obv:** National arms, engraver's initials GM on stems flanking date **Rev:** Seated Liberty flanked by shield and column **Edge:** Reeded **Note:** Large letters.

Date	Mintage	VF20	XF40	MS60	MS63	MS65
1924	96,000	14.00	25.00	50.00	75.00	—
1925	1,004,999	7.50	14.00	16.00	18.00	—
1930	76,000	9.50	15.00	18.00	25.00	—
1931	24,000	10.00	15.00	18.00	25.00	—
1933	5,000	14.00	22.50	30.00	45.00	—
1934/3	2,855,000	7.50	15.00	18.00	22.50	—
1934	Inc. above	7.50	14.00	16.00	18.00	—
1935	695,000	7.50	15.00	18.00	22.50	—

KM# 222 SOL

13.80 g., Brass, 33 mm. **Obv:** National arms **Rev:** Value within circle **Note:** Date varieties exist.

Date	Mintage	VF20	XF40	MS60	MS63	MS65
1943	10,000,000	1.25	3.00	5.00	8.00	16.00
1944	Inc. above	1.25	2.50	4.00	7.00	15.00
1945	—	1.50	3.50	6.00	9.00	17.00
1946	1,752,000	1.50	3.00	5.00	8.00	16.00
1947	3,302,000	1.00	2.00	3.50	6.00	10.00
1948	1,992,000	1.00	2.00	3.50	6.00	10.00
1949/8	751,000	4.00	7.00	12.00	20.00	35.00
1949	Inc. above	7.50	12.00	15.00	25.00	40.00
1950	1,249,000	10.00	15.00	18.00	25.00	40.00
1951/0	2,093,999	0.50	1.50	3.00	6.00	10.00
1951	Inc. above	0.50	1.50	3.00	6.00	10.00
1952	2,037,000	0.50	1.50	3.00	6.00	10.00
1953	1,243,000	6.00	10.00	15.00	25.00	40.00
1954	1,220,000	0.75	1.75	3.50	6.00	10.00
1955	1,323,000	0.75	1.75	3.50	6.00	10.00
1956	3,450,000	0.35	0.75	1.50	3.00	5.00
1957	3,086,000	0.35	1.00	2.00	5.00	8.00
1958 Wide date	3,390,000	0.35	0.75	1.50	3.00	5.00
1958 Narrow date	Inc. above	0.35	0.75	1.50	3.00	5.00
1959	4,975,000	0.35	1.00	2.00	5.00	8.00
1960	5,800,000	0.35	0.75	1.50	2.00	3.50
1961	5,200,000	0.35	0.75	1.50	2.50	4.00
1962	5,102,000	0.35	0.75	1.50	2.00	3.50
1963	5,499,000	0.35	0.75	1.50	2.50	4.00
1964 Wide date	5,888,000	0.35	0.75	1.50	2.50	4.00
1964 Narrow date	Inc. above	0.35	0.75	1.50	2.50	4.00
1965	5,504,000	0.35	0.75	1.50	2.50	4.00
1965	—	PF65 75.00				

KM# 240 SOL

Brass, 28 mm. **Subject:** 400th Anniversary of the Lima Mint **Obv:** National arms above value **Rev:** Pillars of Hercules within inner circle

Date	Mintage	VF20	XF40	MS60	MS63	MS65
ND-1965	3,103,000	0.35	0.75	1.25	1.75	3.00
ND-1965	—	PF65 500				

KM# 248 SOL

9.20 g., Brass, 28 mm. **Obv:** National arms **Rev:** Llama

Date	Mintage	VF20	XF40	MS60	MS63	MS65
1966	16,410,000	0.10	0.25	0.50	1.00	3.00
1966	1,000	PF65 25.00				
1967	13,920,000	0.10	0.25	0.50	1.00	3.00
1968	12,260,000	0.10	0.25	0.50	1.00	3.00
1969	12,260,000	0.10	0.25	0.50	1.00	3.00
1970	12,336,000	0.10	0.25	0.50	1.00	3.00
1971	11,927,000	0.10	0.25	0.50	1.00	3.00
1972	3,945,000	0.10	0.25	0.50	1.00	3.00
1973	12,856,000	0.10	0.25	0.50	1.00	3.00
1974	14,966,000	0.10	0.25	0.50	1.00	3.00
1975	—	0.10	0.25	0.50	1.00	3.00

KM# 248a SOL

Silver Plated Brass **Obv:** National arms **Rev:** Llama

Date	Mintage	VF20	XF40	MS60	MS63	MS65
1967	—	—	—	—	—	—

KM# 248b SOL

Silver **Obv:** National arms **Rev:** Llama

Date	Mintage	VF20	XF40	MS60	MS63	MS65
1967	—	—	—	—	—	—

KM# 266.1 SOL

3.24 g., Brass, 21 mm. **Obv:** National arms within circle **Rev:** Value **Edge:** Plain

Date	Mintage	VF20	XF40	MS60	MS63	MS65
1975	354,485,000	—	0.10	0.15	0.25	0.40
1976	114,660,000	—	0.10	0.15	0.25	0.40

KM# 269 SOL

23.40 g., 0.900 Gold 0.6771 oz. AGW **Subject:** 150th Anniversary - Battle of Ayacucho **Obv:** National arms within circle **Rev:** Monument divides value within circle **Note:** Mint mark in monogram.

Date	Mintage	VF20	XF40	MS60	MS63	MS65
1976 LIMA	10,000	—	—	—	1,000	1,250

KM# 266.2 SOL

2.00 g., Brass **Obv:** National arms within circle **Rev:** Value **Edge:** Plain **Note:** Mint mark in monogram.

Date	Mintage	VF20	XF40	MS60	MS63	MS65
1978 LIMA	9,000,000	—	0.15	0.25	0.35	0.50
1979 LIMA	4,842,000	—	0.15	0.25	0.35	0.50
1980 LIMA	28,830,000	—	0.15	0.25	0.35	0.50
1981 LIMA	55,786,000	—	0.15	0.25	0.35	0.50

KM# 235 5 SOLES

2.34 g., 0.900 Gold 0.0677 oz. AGW **Obv:** National arms above date **Rev:** Seated Liberty flanked by shield and column

Date	Mintage	VF20	XF40	MS60	MS63	MS65
1956	4,510	86.00	110	125	135	150
1957	2,146	86.00	115	130	140	160
1959	1,536	86.00	115	130	140	160
1960	8,133	86.00	110	125	135	150
1961	1,154	86.00	115	130	140	160
1962	1,550	86.00	115	130	140	160
1963	3,945	86.00	110	125	135	150
1964	2,063	86.00	115	130	140	160
1965	14,000	86.00	110	125	135	150
1966	4,738	86.00	110	125	135	150
1967	3,651	86.00	110	125	135	150
1969	127	86.00	250	400	550	650

KM# 252 5 SOLES

2.30 g., Copper-Nickel **Obv:** National arms within circle **Rev:** Value above designed Incan cup, written value around bottom half **Edge:** Reeded

Date	Mintage	VF20	XF40	MS60	MS63	MS65
1969	10,000,000	0.40	0.50	0.75	1.50	2.50

KM# 254 5 SOLES

Copper-Nickel **Subject:** 150th Anniversary of Independence **Obv:** National arms **Rev:** Bust of Tupac Amaru right **Note:** Mint mark in monogram.

Date	Mintage	VF20	XF40	MS60	MS63	MS65
1971 LIMA	3,480,000	0.40	0.50	0.75	1.50	2.50

KM# 257 5 SOLES

7.88 g., Copper-Nickel, 25.57 mm. **Obv:** National arms within circle **Rev:** Bust of Tupac Amaru **Edge:** Reeded **Note:** Mint mark in monogram.

Date	Mintage	VF20	XF40	MS60	MS63	MS65
1972	2,068,000	0.10	0.35	0.50	1.00	1.75
1973	475,000	0.10	0.35	0.50	1.00	2.00
1974	2,335,018	0.10	0.35	0.50	1.25	2.50
Note: Mintage is together with KM#258						
1975	4,650,605	0.10	0.35	0.50	1.25	2.50
Note: Mintage is together with KM#258 and 267						

KM# 267 5 SOLES

4.40 g., Copper-Nickel, 22 mm. **Obv:** National arms **Rev:** Bust of Tupac Amaru **Note:** Mint mark in monogram.

Date	Mintage	VF20	XF40	MS60	MS63	MS65
1975	—	0.10	0.35	0.50	0.75	1.25
Note: Mintage is included with KM#257						
1976	16,932,000	0.10	0.35	0.50	0.75	1.25
1977	94,272,000	0.10	0.35	0.50	0.75	1.25

KM# 271 5 SOLES

4.24 g., Brass, 22.49 mm. **Obv:** National arms within circle **Rev:** Value **Edge:** Plain **Note:** Mint mark in monogram.

Date	Mintage	VF20	XF40	MS60	MS63	MS65
1978	38,015,000	0.10	0.20	0.35	0.60	1.00
1979	64,524,000	0.10	0.20	0.35	0.60	1.00
1980	76,962,000	0.10	0.20	0.35	0.60	1.00
1981	31,632,000	0.10	0.20	0.35	0.60	1.00
1982	23,262,000	0.10	0.20	0.35	0.60	1.00
1983	650	30.00	40.00	60.00	—	—

Note: According to the 1983 Annual Report of the Central Reserve Bank of Peru, 12,720,000. 5 Soles coins were struck in 1983.

KM# 236 10 SOLES

4.69 g., 0.900 Gold 0.1356 oz. AGW **Obv:** National arms above date **Rev:** Seated Liberty flanked by shield and column

Date	Mintage	VF20	XF40	MS60	MS63	MS65
1956	5,410	172	180	225	250	280
1957	1,300	172	185	225	255	290
1959	1,103	172	185	225	255	290
1960	7,178	172	180	225	250	280
1961	1,634	172	185	225	255	290
1962	1,676	172	185	225	255	290
1963	3,372	172	180	225	250	280
1964	1,554	172	185	225	255	290
1965	14,000	172	175	225	250	280
1966	2,601	172	180	225	250	280
1967	3,002	172	180	225	250	280
1968	100	172	250	450	550	650
1969	100	172	250	450	550	650

KM# 253 10 SOLES

10.00 g., Copper-Nickel **Obv:** National arms within circle **Rev:** Stylized fish below value **Edge:** Reeded

Date	Mintage	VF20	XF40	MS60	MS63	MS65
1969	15,000,000	0.50	0.75	1.25	1.75	2.50

KM# 255 10 SOLES

Copper-Nickel **Subject:** 150th Anniversary of Independence **Obv:** National arms **Rev:** Bust of Tupac Amaru right **Note:** Mint mark in monogram.

Date	Mintage	VF20	XF40	MS60	MS63	MS65
1971 LIMA	2,460,000	0.50	1.00	1.50	2.50	3.50

KM# 258 10 SOLES

11.70 g., Copper-Nickel, 30.94 mm. **Obv:** National arms within circle **Rev:** Bust of Tupac Amaru right **Edge:** Reeded **Note:** Mint mark in monogram.

Date	Mintage	VF20	XF40	MS60	MS63	MS65
1972	2,235,000	0.10	0.40	0.65	1.25	2.00
1973	1,765,000	0.10	0.40	0.65	1.25	2.00
1974	—	0.10	0.40	0.65	1.25	2.00
Note: Mintage included with KM#257						
1975	—	0.10	0.40	0.65	1.25	2.00
Note: Mintage included with KM#257						

KM# 272.1 10 SOLES

Brass **Obv:** National arms, small letters: inner circle 18.1mm **Rev:** Head with hat 3/4 right **Edge:** Plain **Note:** Mint mark in monogram.

Date	Mintage	VF20	XF40	MS60	MS63	MS65
1978	46,970,000	0.10	0.35	0.50	0.85	1.50

KM# 272.2 10 SOLES

5.65 g., Brass, 24.48 mm. **Subject:** Tupac Amaru **Obv:** Small arms , large letters, inner circle 17.2mm **Rev:** Head with hat 3/4 right **Rev. Legend:** TUPAC AMARU, SOLES DE ORO **Edge:** Plain **Note:** Mint mark in monogram.

Date	Mintage	VF20	XF40	MS60	MS63	MS65
1978	Inc. above	0.10	0.35	0.50	0.85	1.50
1979	82,220,000	0.10	0.35	0.50	0.85	1.50
1980	99,595,000	0.10	0.35	0.50	0.85	1.50
1981	25,660,000	0.10	0.35	0.50	0.85	1.50
1982	61,035,000	0.10	0.35	0.50	0.85	1.50
1983	15,820,000	0.10	0.35	0.50	0.85	1.50

KM# 287 10 SOLES

Brass **Subject:** 150th Anniversary - Birth of Admiral Grau **Obv:** Value within circle **Rev:** Head 1/4 right **Note:** Mint mark in monogram.

Date	Mintage	VF20	XF40	MS60	MS63	MS65
1984	30,000,000	—	0.20	0.30	0.50	0.75

KM# 229 20 SOLES

9.36 g., 0.900 Gold 0.2709 oz. AGW, 22 mm. **Obv:** National arms **Rev:** Seated Liberty flanked by shield and column

Date	Mintage	VF20	XF40	MS60	MS63	MS65
1950	1,800	345	375	490	550	575
1951	9,264	345	360	475	525	550
1952	424	400	425	550	650	750
1953	1,435	345	375	490	550	575
1954	1,732	345	375	490	550	575
1955	1,971	345	375	490	550	575
1956	1,201	345	375	490	550	575
1957	11,000	345	360	475	550	575
1958	11,000	345	360	475	550	575
1959	12,000	345	360	475	550	575
1960	7,753	345	360	475	550	575
1961	1,825	345	375	490	550	575
1962	2,282	345	375	490	550	575
1963	3,892	345	375	490	550	575
1964	1,302	345	375	490	550	575
1965	12,000	345	360	475	550	575
1966	4,001	345	375	490	550	575
1967	5,003	345	375	490	550	575
1968	640	375	400	525	600	700
1969	640	375	400	525	600	700

KM# 241 20 SOLES

8.00 g., 0.900 Silver 0.2315 oz. ASW, 26 mm. **Subject:** 400th Anniversary of Lima Mint. **Obv:** National arms above value **Rev:** Pillars of Hercules within inner circle

Date	Mintage	VF20	XF40	MS60	MS63	MS65
ND-1965	150,000	—	4.50	6.00	8.00	10.00

KM# 249 20 SOLES

7.97 g., 0.900 Silver 0.2306 oz. ASW **Subject:** 100th Anniversary of Peru-Spain Naval Battle **Obv:** National arms above value **Rev:** Victory standing on globe flanked by dates

Date	Mintage	VF20	XF40	MS60	MS63	MS65
ND-1966	4,001	—	4.50	12.00	15.00	20.00

KM# 219 50 SOLES

33.44 g., 0.900 Gold 0.9675 oz. AGW **Obv:** Head with headdress left **Rev:** Sculpture

Date	Mintage	VF20	XF40	MS60	MS63	MS65
1930	5,584	1,235	1,750	2,500	2,800	3,250
1931	5,538	1,235	1,750	2,500	2,800	3,250
1967	10,000	1,235	1,500	1,900	2,350	2,700
1968	300	1,235	1,500	1,900	2,250	2,500
1969	403	1,235	1,500	1,900	2,150	2,400

KM# 230 50 SOLES

23.41 g., 0.900 Gold 0.6773 oz. AGW **Obv:** National arms **Rev:** Seated Liberty flanked by shield and column **Note:** Similar to KM#229.

Date	Mintage	VF20	XF40	MS60	MS63	MS65
1950	1,927	865	1,100	1,250	1,350	1,500
1951	5,292	865	1,100	1,250	1,350	1,500
1952	1,201	865	1,100	1,250	1,350	1,500
1953	1,464	865	1,100	1,250	1,350	1,500
1954	1,839	865	1,100	1,250	1,350	1,500
1955	1,898	865	1,100	1,250	1,350	1,500
1956	11,000	865	1,050	1,150	1,250	1,400
1957	11,000	865	1,050	1,150	1,250	1,400
1958	11,000	865	1,050	1,150	1,250	1,400
1959	5,734	865	1,100	1,250	1,350	1,500
1960	2,139	865	1,100	1,250	1,350	1,500
1961	1,110	865	1,100	1,250	1,350	1,500

Date	Mintage	VF20	XF40	MS60	MS63	MS65
1962	3,319	865	1,100	1,250	1,350	1,500
1963	3,089	865	1,100	1,250	1,350	1,500
1964/3	2,425	865	1,100	1,250	1,350	1,500
1964	Inc. above	865	1,100	1,250	1,350	1,500
1965	23,000	865	1,050	1,150	1,250	1,400
1966	3,409	865	1,100	1,250	1,350	1,500
1967	5,805	865	1,100	1,250	1,350	1,500
1968	443	975	1,100	1,300	1,400	1,600
1969	443	975	1,100	1,300	1,400	1,600
1970	553	975	1,100	1,300	1,400	1,600

KM# 242 50 SOLES

23.41 g., 0.900 Gold 0.6773 oz. AGW **Subject:** 400th Anniversary of Lima Mint **Obv:** National arms above value **Rev:** Pillars of Hercules within inner circle

Date	Mintage	VF20	XF40	MS60	MS63	MS65
ND-1965	17,000	865	1,100	1,250	1,350	1,500

KM# 250 50 SOLES

23.41 g., 0.900 Gold 0.6773 oz. AGW **Subject:** 100th Anniversary of Peru-Spain Naval Battle **Obv:** National arms above value **Rev:** Victory standing on globe divides dates

Date	Mintage	VF20	XF40	MS60	MS63	MS65
ND-1966	6,409	865	1,100	1,250	1,350	1,500

KM# 256 50 SOLES

21.45 g., 0.800 Silver 0.5517 oz. ASW, 37 mm. **Subject:** 150th Anniversary of Independence **Obv:** National arms within circle **Rev:** Bust of Tupac Amaru right **Note:** Mint mark in monogram.

Date	Mintage	VF20	XF40	MS60	MS63	MS65
1971 LIMA	100,000	—	10.00	12.00	15.00	18.00

KM# 273 50 SOLES

9.00 g., Aluminum-Bronze **Obv:** National arms **Rev:** Value within circle **Note:** Mint mark in monogram.

Date	Mintage	VF20	XF40	MS60	MS63	MS65
1979	1,323,000	0.15	0.30	0.50	1.00	1.50
1980	42,573,000	0.10	0.20	0.35	0.50	1.00
1981	19,923,000	0.10	0.20	0.35	0.50	1.00
1982 LIMA	18,471,000	0.10	0.20	0.35	0.50	1.00
1982 Without LIMA	Inc. above	0.15	0.30	0.50	1.00	1.50
1983	8,175,000	0.10	0.20	0.30	0.50	1.00

KM# 297 50 SOLES

Brass **Subject:** 150th Anniversary - Birth of Admiral Grau **Obv:** Value within circle **Rev:** Head 1/4 right **Note:** Mint mark in monogram.

Date	Mintage	VF20	XF40	MS60	MS63	MS65
1984	11,475,000	—	0.20	0.30	0.50	0.75

KM# 321 50 SOLES

1.70 g., Brass, 17 mm. **Subject:** Admiral Grau **Obv:** Value within circle **Rev:** Head 1/4 right **Edge:** Plain

Date	Mintage	VF20	XF40	MS60	MS63	MS65
1985 LIMAE	8,525,000	—	0.20	0.30	0.50	0.75

KM# 231 100 SOLES

46.81 g., 0.900 Gold 1.3544 oz. AGW **Obv:** National arms **Rev:** Seated Liberty flanked by shield and column

Date	Mintage	VF20	XF40	MS60	MS63	MS65
1950	1,176	—	1,725	2,200	2,450	2,600
1951	8,241	—	1,725	2,000	2,350	2,500
1952	126	1,725	2,200	2,500	3,000	3,600
1953	498	1,725	2,000	2,200	2,450	2,600
1954	1,808	—	1,725	2,200	2,450	2,600
1955	901	1,725	2,000	2,200	2,450	2,600
1956	1,159	—	1,725	2,200	2,450	2,600
1957	550	1,725	2,000	2,200	2,450	2,600
1958	101	1,725	2,500	3,000	4,000	4,600
1959	4,710	—	1,725	2,000	2,450	2,600
1960	2,207	—	1,725	2,200	2,450	2,600
1961	6,982	—	1,725	2,000	2,350	2,500
1962	9,678	—	1,725	2,000	2,350	2,500
1963	7,342	—	1,725	2,000	2,350	2,500
1964	11,000	—	1,725	2,000	2,350	2,500
1965	23,000	—	1,725	2,000	2,250	2,400
1966	3,409	—	1,725	2,200	2,450	2,600
1967	6,431	—	1,725	2,000	2,350	2,500
1968	540	1,725	2,000	2,200	2,450	2,600
1969	540	1,725	2,000	2,200	2,450	2,600
1970	425	1,725	2,000	2,200	2,450	2,600

KM# 243 100 SOLES

46.81 g., 0.900 Gold 1.3544 oz. AGW **Subject:** 400th Anniversary of Lima Mint **Obv:** National arms **Rev:** Pillars of Hercules within inner circle

Date	Mintage	VF20	XF40	MS60	MS63	MS65
ND-1965	27,000	—	1,725	2,200	2,450	2,600

KM# 251 100 SOLES

46.81 g., 0.900 Gold 1.3544 oz. AGW **Subject:** 100th Anniversary of Peru-Spain Naval Battle **Obv:** National arms **Rev:** Victory standing on globe divides dates

Date	Mintage	VF20	XF40	MS60	MS63	MS65
ND-1966	6,253	—	1,725	2,200	2,500	2,750

KM# 261 100 SOLES

22.45 g., 0.800 Silver 0.5774 oz. ASW, 37 mm. **Subject:** Centennial Peru-Japan Trade Relations **Obv:** National arms **Rev:** Value to left of flower sprig within circle **Edge:** Reeded **Note:** Mint mark in monogram.

Date	Mintage	VF20	XF40	MS60	MS63	MS65
1973 LIMA	375,000	—	10.50	14.00	18.00	22.00

KM# 283 100 SOLES

11.66 g., Copper-Nickel, 29.83 mm. **Obv:** National arms **Rev:** Value within circle **Edge:** Reeded **Note:** Without mint mark.

Date	Mintage	VF20	XF40	MS60	MS63	MS65
1980	100,000,000	—	0.20	0.40	1.50	2.00
1980	—	PF65 8.00				
1982	—	—	0.20	0.40	1.50	2.00

KM# 288 100 SOLES

3.00 g., Brass **Subject:** 150th Anniversary - Birth of Admiral Grau **Obv:** Value within circle **Rev:** Head 1/4 right **Note:** Mint mark in monogram.

Date	Mintage	VF20	XF40	MS60	MS63	MS65
1984 LIMA	20,000,000	—	0.15	0.35	1.00	1.50

KM# 262 200 SOLES

22.00 g., 0.800 Silver 0.5659 oz. ASW, 37 mm. **Subject:** Aviation Heroes - Chavez and Guinones **Obv:** National arms **Rev:** Conjoined heads left within circle **Edge:** Reeded **Note:** No mint mark.

Date	Mintage	VF20	XF40	MS60	MS63	MS65
1974	5,290	—	10.50	15.00	25.00	30.00
1975	109,710	—	10.50	13.00	16.00	20.00
1976	25,000	—	10.50	14.00	18.00	22.00
1977	3,000	—	10.50	16.50	27.00	32.00
1978	3,000	—	10.50	16.50	27.00	32.00

KM# 270 400 SOLES
28.10 g., 0.900 Silver 0.8131 oz. ASW, 37 mm. **Subject:** 150th Anniversary - Battle of Ayacucho **Obv:** National arms **Rev:** Monument divides value within circle **Edge:** Reeded **Note:** Mint mark in monogram.

Date	Mintage	VF20	XF40	MS60	MS63	MS65
1976 LIMA	350,000	—	15.00	18.00	30.00	35.00

KM# 289 500 SOLES
5.20 g., Brass **Subject:** 150th Anniversary - Birth of Admiral Grau **Obv:** Value within circle **Rev:** Head 1/4 right **Note:** Mint mark in monogram.

Date	Mintage	VF20	XF40	MS60	MS63	MS65
1984 LIMA	16,962,000	—	0.20	0.50	2.00	3.00

KM# 310 500 SOLES
5.12 g., Brass **Subject:** Admiral Grau **Obv:** National arms **Rev:** Head 1/4 right without date **Note:** Mint mark in monogram.

Date	Mintage	VF20	XF40	MS60	MS63	MS65
1985 LIMA	13,038,000	—	0.20	0.50	2.50	3.50

KM# 275 1000 SOLES
15.55 g., 0.500 Silver 0.250 oz. ASW, 30 mm. **Subject:** National Congress **Obv:** National arms within circle **Rev:** Building **Edge:** Smooth with incuse stars **Note:** Mint mark in monogram.

Date	Mintage	VF20	XF40	MS60	MS63	MS65
1979 LIMA	200,000	—	4.50	7.00	10.00	15.00

KM# 276 5000 SOLES
33.63 g., 0.925 Silver 1.0001 oz. ASW, 40 mm. **Subject:** 100th Anniversary - Battle of Iquique **Obv:** National arms **Rev:** Ship **Edge Lettering:** Reeded **Note:** Mint mark in monogram.

Date	Mintage	VF20	XF40	MS60	MS63	MS65
1979 LIMA	100,000	—	18.50	20.00	22.00	28.00

KM# 284 5000 SOLES
23.37 g., 0.925 Silver 0.695 oz. ASW **Subject:** Champions of Soccer **Obv:** National arms **Rev:** Soccer players **Note:** Mint mark in monogram.

Date	Mintage	VF20	XF40	MS60	MS63	MS65
1982 LIMA	—	PF63 17.00	PF65 25.00			

KM# 285 5000 SOLES
23.37 g., 0.925 Silver 0.695 oz. ASW **Subject:** Champions of Soccer **Obv:** National arms **Rev:** Soccer players in front of world globe **Note:** Mint mark in monogram.

Date	Mintage	VF20	XF40	MS60	MS63	MS65
1982 LIMA	—	PF63 17.00	PF65 25.00			

KM# 286 10000 SOLES
16.81 g., 0.925 Silver 0.4999 oz. ASW, 28 mm. **Subject:** Battle of La Brena and General Caceres **Obv:** National arms **Rev:** Head left **Edge:** Reeded **Note:** Mint mark in monogram.

Date	Mintage	VF20	XF40	MS60	MS63	MS65
1982 LIMA	100,000	—	9.25	13.00	17.00	22.00

KM# 277 50000 SOLES
16.86 g., 0.917 Gold 0.4971 oz. AGW **Subject:** Alfonso Urgarte **Obv:** National arms within circle **Rev:** Head left **Note:** Mint mark in monogram.

Date	Mintage	VF20	XF40	MS60	MS63	MS65
1979 LIMA	10,000	—	635	775	850	875

KM# 278 50000 SOLES
16.86 g., 0.917 Gold 0.4971 oz. AGW **Subject:** Elias Aguirre **Obv:** National arms within circle **Rev:** Head left **Note:** Mint mark in monogram.

Date	Mintage	VF20	XF40	MS60	MS63	MS65
1979 LIMA	10,000	—	635	775	850	875

KM# 279 50000 SOLES
16.86 g., 0.917 Gold 0.4971 oz. AGW **Subject:** F. Garcia Calderon **Obv:** National arms within circle **Rev:** Bust left **Note:** Mint mark in monogram.

Date	Mintage	VF20	XF40	MS60	MS63	MS65
1979 LIMA	10,000	—	635	775	850	875

KM# 280 100000 SOLES
33.90 g., 0.917 Gold 0.9994 oz. AGW **Subject:** Francisco Bolognese **Obv:** National arms within circle **Rev:** Bust left **Note:** Mint mark in monogram.

Date	Mintage	VF20	XF40	MS60	MS63	MS65
1979 LIMA	10,000	—	1,275	1,550	1,700	1,800

KM# 281 100000 SOLES
33.90 g., 0.917 Gold 0.9994 oz. AGW **Subject:** Andres A. Caceres **Obv:** National arms within circle **Rev:** Head left **Note:** Mint mark in monogram.

Date	Mintage	VF20	XF40	MS60	MS63	MS65
1979 LIMA	10,000	—	1,275	1,550	1,700	1,800

KM# 282 100000 SOLES
33.90 g., 0.917 Gold 0.9994 oz. AGW **Subject:** Miguel Grau **Obv:** National arms within circle **Rev:** Bust left **Note:** Mint mark in monogram.

Date	Mintage	VF20	XF40	MS60	MS63	MS65
1979 LIMA	10,000	—	1,275	1,550	1,700	1,800

REFORM COINAGE

1985; 1000 Soles de Oro = 1 Inti

KM# 291 CENTIMO
1.50 g., Brass, 15 mm. **Subject:** General Grau **Obv:** Value within circle **Rev:** Head 1/4 right **Note:** Mint mark: LIMA (monogram)

Date	Mintage	VF20	XF40	MS60	MS63	MS65
1985 LIMA	4,199,999	—	—	0.15	0.25	0.45

KM# 292 5 CENTIMOS
2.00 g., Brass, 17 mm. **Subject:** General Grau **Obv:** Value within circle **Rev:** Head 1/4 right **Note:** Mint mark: LIMA (monogram)

Date	Mintage	VF20	XF40	MS60	MS63	MS65
1985 LIMA	20,000,000	—	—	0.20	0.35	0.50

KM# 293 10 CENTIMOS
2.90 g., Brass, 19 mm. **Subject:** General Grau **Obv:** Value within circle **Rev:** Head 1/4 right **Rev. Legend:** GRAN ALMIRANTE MIGUEL GRAU **Edge:** Plain **Note:** Mint mark: LIMA (monogram)

Date	Mintage	VF20	XF40	MS60	MS63	MS65
1985 LIMA	143,900,000	—	—	0.25	0.50	0.85
1986 LIMA	48,730,000	—	—	0.30	0.65	1.00
1987 LIMA	42,370,000	—	—	0.30	0.65	1.00

KM# 294 20 CENTIMOS
4.06 g., Brass, 21 mm. **Subject:** General Grau **Obv:** Value within circle **Rev:** Head 1/4 right **Rev. Legend:** GRAN ALMIRANTE MIGUEL GRAU **Edge:** Plain **Note:** Mint mark: LIMA (monogram)

Date	Mintage	VF20	XF40	MS60	MS63	MS65
1985 LIMA	4,739,000	—	—	0.60	1.25	1.50
1986 LIMA	96,699,000	—	—	0.50	1.00	1.25
1987 LIMA	59,668,000	—	—	0.30	1.00	1.25

KM# 295 50 CENTIMOS
5.20 g., Brass, 23 mm. **Subject:** General Grau **Obv:** Value within circle **Rev:** Head 1/4 right **Note:** Mint mark: LIMA (monogram)

Date	Mintage	VF20	XF40	MS60	MS63	MS65
1985 LIMA	43,320,000	—	—	0.60	1.25	1.50
1986 LIMA	72,802,000	—	—	0.60	1.25	1.50
1987 LIMA	63,878,000	—	—	0.60	1.25	1.50
1988 LIMA	80,000,000	—	—	0.60	1.25	1.50

KM# 301 1/2 INTI
16.80 g., 0.925 Silver 0.4996 oz. ASW **Subject:** Pachacutec **Obv:** Map within design and stylized bow **Rev:** Native head left divides date **Note:** Mint mark: LIMA (monogram)

Date	Mintage	VF20	XF40	MS60	MS63	MS65
1989 LIMA	—	—	—	9.50	20.00	22.50

KM# 301a 1/2 INTI
Copper-Nickel **Subject:** Pachacutec **Obv:** Map within design and stylized bow **Rev:** Native head left divides date

Date	Mintage	VF20	XF40	MS60	MS63	MS65
1989	—	—	—	—	—	—

KM# 296 INTI
7.00 g., Copper-Nickel, 25 mm. **Subject:** Admiral Grau **Obv:** National arms **Rev:** Head 1/4 right **Rev. Legend:** GRAN ALMIRANTE MIGUEL GRAU, value **Edge:** Reeded **Note:** Mint mark: LIMA (monogram)

Date	Mintage	VF20	XF40	MS60	MS63	MS65
1985 LIMA	15,760,000	—	—	1.00	1.75	2.00
1986 LIMA	87,240,000	—	—	0.60	1.25	1.50
1987 LIMA	120,000,000	—	—	0.50	1.00	1.25
1988 LIMA	17,304,000	—	—	0.60	1.25	1.50

KM# 300 5 INTIS
8.20 g., Copper-Nickel, 27 mm. **Subject:** Admiral Grau **Obv:** National arms **Rev:** Head 1/4 right **Rev. Legend:** GRAN ALMIRANTE MIGUEL GRAU, value **Edge:** Reeded **Note:** Mint mark: LIMA (monogram)

Date	Mintage	VF20	XF40	MS60	MS63	MS65
1985 LIMA	3,972,000	—	—	—	—	—
1986 LIMA	28,028,000	—	—	0.75	1.50	3.00
1987 LIMA	20,106,000	—	—	0.60	1.25	2.50
1988 LIMA	34,084,000	—	—	0.60	1.25	2.50

KM# 298 100 INTIS
11.11 g., 0.925 Silver 0.3304 oz. ASW, 28 mm. **Subject:** 150th Anniversary - Birth of Marshal Caceres **Obv:** National arms above value **Rev:** Head right **Edge:** Reeded **Note:** Mint mark: LIMA (monogram)

Date	Mintage	VF20	XF40	MS60	MS63	MS65
ND-1986 LIMA	50,000	—	—	6.50	8.50	11.00

KM# 299 200 INTIS
22.04 g., 0.925 Silver 0.6555 oz. ASW, 33 mm. **Subject:** 150th Anniversary - Birth of Marshal Caceres **Obv:** National arms above value **Rev:** Head right **Edge:** Reeded **Note:** Mint mark: LIMA (monogram)

Date	Mintage	VF20	XF40	MS60	MS63	MS65
ND-1986 LIMA	25,000	—	—	12.50	17.50	22.50

REFORM COINAGE

1991; 1/M Intis = 1 Nuevo Sol;
100 (New) Centimos = 1 Nuevo Sol

KM# 303.1 CENTIMO
Brass, 16 mm. **Obv:** National arms **Rev:** Value flanked by designs **Note:** LIMA monogram is mint mark.

Date	Mintage	VF20	XF40	MS60	MS63	MS65
1991 LIMA CHAVEZ	6,000,000	—	—	0.15	0.35	0.50
1992 LIMA CHAVEZ	20,034,000	—	—	0.20	0.45	0.65
1993 LIMA CHAVEZ	3,859,000	—	—	0.15	0.35	0.50
1994 LIMA	765,000	—	—	1.00	2.50	3.00

KM# 303.2 CENTIMO
Brass **Obv:** National arms **Obv. Legend:** No accent in Peru **Rev:** Large braille, no accent mark above E in centimo, no Chavez **Note:** LIMA monogram is mint mark.

Date	Mintage	VF20	XF40	MS60	MS63	MS65
1997	100,000	—	1.00	2.00	4.00	5.00

KM# 303.3 CENTIMO
1.73 g., Brass, 15.94 mm. **Obv:** National arms **Obv. Legend:** Accent mark in Peru **Rev:** Large braille, accent mark in centimo, no Chavez **Edge:** Plain **Note:** LIMA monogram is mint mark.

Date	Mintage	VF20	XF40	MS60	MS63	MS65
1999 LIMA	1,362,000	—	—	0.50	1.00	2.00

KM# 304.1 5 CENTIMOS
2.26 g., Brass, 18 mm. **Obv:** National arms **Rev:** Value flanked by designs **Note:** LIMA monogram is mint mark.

Date	Mintage	VF20	XF40	MS60	MS63	MS65
1991 LIMA CHAVEZ	5,000,000	—	—	0.20	0.45	0.65
1992 LIMA CHAVEZ	42,200,000	—	—	0.20	0.50	0.75
1993 LIMA	40,000,000	—	—	0.20	0.45	0.65
1993 LIMA CHAVEZ	Inc. above	—	—	0.20	0.45	0.65
1994 LIMA	10,011,000	—	—	0.20	0.45	0.65
1995 LIMA	20,000,000	—	—	0.20	0.45	0.65
1996 LIMA	16,000,000	—	—	0.20	0.45	0.65

KM# 304.2 5 CENTIMOS
2.78 g., Brass, 18 mm. **Obv:** National arms **Rev:** Value flanked by designs. Small braille with no accent mark above E in centimos, no Chavez **Edge:** Plain **Note:** LIMA monogram is mint mark.

Date	Mintage	VF20	XF40	MS60	MS63	MS65
1997 LIMA	15,700,000	—	—	0.15	0.35	0.50
1998 LIMA	20,000,000	—	—	0.15	0.35	0.50

KM# 304.3 5 CENTIMOS
Brass, 18 mm. **Obv:** National arms **Rev:** Value flanked by designs. Small braille with accent mark above E in centimos **Note:** LIMA monogram is mint mark.

Date	Mintage	VF20	XF40	MS60	MS63	MS65
2000 LIMA	2,000,000	—	—	0.15	0.35	0.50

KM# 305.1 10 CENTIMOS
3.50 g., Brass, 20.5 mm. **Obv:** National arms within octagon **Rev:** Value flanked by designs within octagon **Edge:** Plain **Note:** LIMA monogram is mint mark.

Date	Mintage	VF20	XF40	MS60	MS63	MS65
1991 LIMA	12,400,000	—	—	0.30	0.65	0.85
1992 LIMA	45,100,000	—	—	0.35	0.75	1.00
1993 LIMA CHAVEZ	Inc. above	—	—	0.30	0.65	0.85
1993 LIMA	50,000,000	—	—	0.30	0.65	0.85
1994 LIMA	45,000,000	—	—	0.30	0.65	0.85
1995 LIMA	25,000,000	—	—	0.30	0.65	0.85
1996 LIMA	33,000,000	—	—	0.30	0.65	0.85

KM# 305.2 10 CENTIMOS

3.50 g., Brass, 20.5 mm. **Obv:** National arms within octagon **Rev:** Value flanked by designs within octagon **Note:** LIMA monogram mint mark.

Date	Mintage	VF20	XF40	MS60	MS63	MS65
1997 LIMA	13,000,000	—	—	0.30	0.65	0.85
1998 LIMA	33,000,000	—	—	0.30	0.65	0.85

KM# 305.3 10 CENTIMOS

3.50 g., Brass, 20.5 mm. **Obv:** National arms within octagon **Rev:** Value flanked by designs within octagon **Edge:** Plain **Note:** LIMA monogram is mint mark.

Date	Mintage	VF20	XF40	MS60	MS63	MS65
1999 LIMA	20,016,000	—	—	0.30	0.65	0.85
2000 LIMA	45,000,000	—	—	0.30	0.65	0.85

KM# 306.1 20 CENTIMOS

4.40 g., Brass, 23 mm. **Obv:** National arms **Rev:** Value **Edge:** Plain **Note:** LIMA monogram is mint mark. Varieties exist.

Date	Mintage	VF20	XF40	MS60	MS63	MS65
1991 LIMA CHAVEZ	35,000,000	—	—	0.35	0.85	1.20
1992 LIMA CHAVEZ	11,000,000	—	—	0.35	0.85	1.20
1993 LIMA CHAVEZ	30,000,000	—	—	0.35	0.85	1.20
1993 LIMA	Inc. above	—	—	0.35	0.85	1.20
1994 LIMA	20,000,000	—	—	0.35	0.85	1.20
1996 LIMA	10,000,000	—	—	0.35	0.85	1.20

KM# 306.2 20 CENTIMOS

4.40 g., Brass, 23 mm. **Obv:** National arms, accent above "u" **Rev:** Small braille dots, accent above "e" **Edge:** Plain **Note:** LIMA monogram is mint mark. Prev. KM#306.3.

Date	Mintage	VF20	XF40	MS60	MS63	MS65
2000 LIMA	7,000,000	—	—	0.35	0.85	1.20

KM# 307.1 50 CENTIMOS

5.45 g., Copper-Nickel-Zinc, 22 mm. **Obv:** National arms within octagon **Rev:** Value flanked by sprig and monogram within octagon **Edge:** Reeded **Note:** LIMA monogram is mint mark. Varieties exist.

Date	Mintage	VF20	XF40	MS60	MS63	MS65
1991 LIMA	42,265,000	—	—	0.75	1.25	1.75
1992 LIMA	8,400,000	—	—	1.00	1.50	2.00
1993 LIMA	8,660,000	—	—	0.75	1.25	1.75
1994 LIMA	45,000,000	—	—	0.75	1.25	1.75
1996 LIMA	5,000,000	—	—	0.75	1.25	1.75

KM# 307.2 50 CENTIMOS

5.45 g., Copper-Nickel-Zinc, 22 mm. **Obv:** National arms within octagon **Rev:** Value flanked by sprig and monogram within octagon **Edge:** Reeded **Note:** LIMA monogram is mint mark.

Date	Mintage	VF20	XF40	MS60	MS63	MS65
1997 LIMA	2,000,000	—	—	0.75	1.25	1.75
1998 LIMA	5,000,000	—	—	0.75	1.25	1.75

KM# 307.3 50 CENTIMOS

5.45 g., Copper-Nickel-Zinc, 22 mm. **Obv:** National arms within octagon **Rev:** Value flanked by sprig and monogram within octagon **Edge:** Reeded **Note:** LIMA monogram is mint mark.

Date	Mintage	VF20	XF40	MS60	MS63	MS65
2000 LIMA	8,000,000	—	—	0.75	1.25	1.75

KM# 302 NUEVO SOL

27.00 g., 0.925 Silver 0.803 oz. ASW, 40 mm. **Series:** Ibero - American **Subject:** Meeting of Two Worlds **Obv:** National arms within assorted emblems around border **Rev:** Supine conjoined heads with hands holding a cornstalk and cross **Edge:** Reeded

Date	Mintage	VF20	XF40	MS60	MS63	MS65
1991 (Mo)	Est. 5000	PF65 50.00				

KM# 308.1 NUEVO SOL

7.32 g., Copper-Nickel-Zinc, 25.5 mm. **Obv:** National arms within octagon **Rev:** Written value flanked by sprig and monogram within octagon **Edge:** Reeded **Note:** LIMA monogram is mint mark.

Date	Mintage	VF20	XF40	MS60	MS63	MS65
1991 LIMA	32,000,000	—	—	1.00	2.00	3.50
1992 LIMA	23,300,000	—	—	1.00	2.00	3.50
1993 LIMA	19,356,000	—	—	1.00	2.00	3.50
1994 LIMA	50,000,000	—	—	1.00	2.00	3.50
1995 LIMA	1,164,000	—	—	1.75	3.50	5.00
1996 LIMA	10,000,000	—	—	1.50	3.00	4.50

KM# 308.2 NUEVO SOL

7.32 g., Copper-Nickel-Zinc, 25.5 mm. **Obv:** National arms within octagon **Rev:** Written value flanked by sprig and monogram within octagon. F. Birz under sprig. **Edge:** Reeded **Note:** LIMA monogram is mint mark.

Date	Mintage	VF20	XF40	MS60	MS63	MS65
1991 LIMA	Inc. with KM#308.1	5.00	10.00	25.00	55.00	—

KM# 311 NUEVO SOL

33.63 g., 0.925 Silver 1.000 oz. ASW, 37 mm. **Subject:** Pre-Inca Moche Cultural Artifacts - Senor di Sipan **Obv:** National arms **Rev:** Cultural artifacts within designed circle **Edge:** Reeded **Note:** LIMA monogram is mint mark.

Date	Mintage	VF20	XF40	MS60	MS63	MS65
1994 LIMA	3,300	—	—	18.50	35.00	40.00
1994 LIMA	—	PF63 40.00	PF65 45.00			

KM# 312 NUEVO SOL

16.97 g., 0.916 Gold 0.4997 oz. AGW, 26 mm. **Obv:** National arms **Rev:** Cultural artifacts within circle **Edge:** Reeded **Note:** LIMA monogram is mint mark. Similar to KM#311.

Date	Mintage	VF20	XF40	MS60	MS63	MS65
1994 LIMA	899	—	640	750	850	1,000
1994 LIMA	100	PF65 2,000				

KM# 314 NUEVO SOL

20.00 g., 0.999 Silver 0.6424 oz. ASW, 36 mm. **Subject:** Environmental Protection **Obv:** National arms **Rev:** Two Young Vicunas **Edge:** Reeded

Date	Mintage	VF20	XF40	MS60	MS63	MS65
1994	Est. 10000	PF63 35.00	PF65 40.00			

KM# 317 NUEVO SOL

27.00 g., 0.925 Silver 0.803 oz. ASW, 40 mm. **Series:** Ibero-American **Subject:** Extinct Animals **Obv:** National arms **Rev:** Vicuña, monkey and crocodile **Edge:** Reeded

Date	Mintage	VF20	XF40	MS60	MS63	MS65
1994 (Mo)	Est. 5000	PF63 35.00	PF65 40.00			

KM# 325 NUEVO SOL

33.63 g., 0.925 Silver 1.000 oz. ASW, 37 mm. **Subject:** Centennial - Birth of Jose Carlos Mariategui **Obv:** National arms **Rev:** Bust half right **Edge:** Reeded **Note:** LIMA monogram is mint mark.

Date	Mintage	VF20	XF40	MS60	MS63	MS65
1994 LIMA	Est. 4000	—	—	—	35.00	40.00

KM# 318 NUEVO SOL

33.63 g., 0.925 Silver 1.000 oz. ASW, 37 mm. **Subject:** Centennial of Victor Raul Haya de la Torre **Obv:** National arms **Rev:** Head right **Note:** LIMA monogram is mint mark.

Date	Mintage	VF20	XF40	MS60	MS63	MS65
1995 LIMA	1,000	—	18.50	30.00	60.00	80.00

KM# 338 NUEVO SOL
33.63 g., 0.925 Silver 1.000 oz. ASW, 37 mm. **Obv:** National arms **Obv. Legend:** BANCO CENTRAL DE RESERVA DEL PERÚ **Rev:** Military bust of Grand Marshall Luis José de Orbegoso y Moncada 3/4 right **Rev. Legend:** PROCER de la INDEPENDENCIA y PRESIDENTE de la REPUBLICA **Edge:** Reeded

Date	Mintage	VF20	XF40	MS60	MS63	MS65
1995 LIMA	—	—	—	18.50	35.00	40.00

KM# 347 NUEVO SOL
16.97 g., 0.9167 Gold 0.5001 oz. AGW, 26 mm. **Subject:** Luis Hose de Orbegoso y Moncada, 150th Anniversary of Birth

Date	Mintage	VF20	XF40	MS60	MS63	MS65
1995 LIMA	Est. 1000	—	640	750	850	950

KM# 319 NUEVO SOL
33.63 g., 0.925 Silver 1.000 oz. ASW, 37 mm. **Subject:** National Mineral and Petroleum Society Centennial **Obv:** National arms **Rev:** Miner, oil derrick and cart **Edge:** Reeded **Note:** LIMA monogram is mint mark.

Date	Mintage	VF20	XF40	MS60	MS63	MS65
1996 LIMA	Est. 10000	—	—	18.50	30.00	50.00

KM# 328 NUEVO SOL
33.52 g., 0.925 Silver 0.9969 oz. ASW, 37 mm. **Subject:** Centennial - Birth of Raul Porras Barrenechea **Obv:** National arms **Rev:** Bust facing **Edge:** Reeded **Note:** LIMA monogram is mint mark.

Date	Mintage	VF20	XF40	MS60	MS63	MS65
1997 LIMA	Est. 1000	—	—	22.00	40.00	45.00

KM# 336 NUEVO SOL
33.63 g., 0.925 Silver 1.000 oz. ASW, 36.9 mm. **Subject:** Central Bank's 75th Anniversary **Obv:** National arms above date **Rev:** Radiant 75 design **Edge:** Reeded

Date	Mintage	VF20	XF40	MS60	MS63	MS65
1997 LIMA	Est. 5000	—	—	18.50	40.00	50.00

KM# 337 NUEVO SOL
33.63 g., 0.925 Silver 1.000 oz. ASW, 37 mm. **Obv:** National arms above date **Rev:** Grand Marshal Ramon Castilla **Edge:** Reeded

Date	Mintage	VF20	XF40	MS60	MS63	MS65
1997 LIMA	Est. 1000	—	—	22.00	55.00	60.00

KM# 348 NUEVO SOL
16.98 g., 0.916 Gold 0.500 oz. AGW, 26 mm. **Subject:** Central Bank, 75th anniversary **Edge:** Reeded

Date	Mintage	VF20	XF40	MS60	MS63	MS65
1997 LIMA	Est. 1000	—	640	750	850	1,000

KM# 349 NUEVO SOL
27.00 g., 0.925 Silver 0.803 oz. ASW, 40 mm. **Series:** Ibero-American **Obv:** National Arms **Rev:** Traditional dance **Rev. Legend:** DANZA DE LAS TIJERAS **Edge:** Reeded

Date	Mintage	VF20	XF40	MS60	MS63	MS65
1997 (Mo)	Est. 5000	**PF63** 40.00	**PF65** 45.00			

KM# 323 NUEVO SOL
33.63 g., 0.925 Silver 1.000 oz. ASW, 37 mm. **Subject:** Centennial of Chorrillos Military School **Obv:** National arms **Rev:** Monument and building divide dates **Edge:** Reeded **Note:** LIMA monogram is mint mark.

Date	Mintage	VF20	XF40	MS60	MS63	MS65
1998 LIMA	Est. 5000	—	—	22.00	45.00	50.00

KM# 350 NUEVO SOL
33.63 g., 0.925 Silver 1.000 oz. ASW, 37 mm. **Subject:** Juan Pablo Viscardo Guzmán, 250 Anniversary of Birth **Edge:** Reeded

Date	Mintage	VF20	XF40	MS60	MS63	MS65
1998 LIMA	Est. 1000	—	—	22.00	40.00	45.00

KM# 308.3 NUEVO SOL
7.32 g., Copper-Nickel-Zinc, 25.5 mm. **Obv:** National arms within octagon **Rev:** Value flanked by sprig and monogram within octagon **Edge:** Reeded **Note:** LIMA monogram is mint mark.

Date	Mintage	VF20	XF40	MS60	MS63	MS65
1999 LIMA	5,000,000	—	—	1.50	3.00	4.50
2000 LIMA	27,000,000	—	—	1.00	2.00	3.50

KM# 322 NUEVO SOL
33.63 g., 0.925 Silver 1.000 oz. ASW **Subject:** Centennial of Japanese Immigration **Obv:** National arms **Rev:** Radiant sun above maps **Edge:** Reeded **Note:** LIMA monogram is mint mark.

Date	Mintage	VF20	XF40	MS60	MS63	MS65
1999 LIMA	Est. 5000	—	—	22.00	40.00	45.00

KM# 351 NUEVO SOL
33.63 g., 0.925 Silver 1.000 oz. ASW, 37 mm. **Subject:** Ernest Malinowski, 100th Anniversary of Death **Rev:** Steam train on bridge in mountain pass **Edge:** Reeded

Date	Mintage	VF20	XF40	MS60	MS63	MS65
1999 LIMA	Est. 1000	—	—	22.00	50.00	55.00

KM# 352 NUEVO SOL
33.63 g., 0.925 Silver 1.000 oz. ASW, 37 mm. **Subject:** Peru Geological Society, 75th Anniversary **Edge:** Reeded

Date	Mintage	VF20	XF40	MS60	MS63	MS65
1999	Est. 1000	—	—	22.00	50.00	55.00

KM# 353 NUEVO SOL
33.63 g., 0.925 Silver 1.000 oz. ASW, 37 mm. **Subject:** 150th Anniversary Immigration of Chinese to Peru **Edge:** Reeded

Date	Mintage	VF20	XF40	MS60	MS63	MS65
1999 LIMA	Est. 5000	—	—	22.00	40.00	45.00

KM# 353a NUEVO SOL
57.39 g., 0.916 Gold 1.690 oz. AGW, 37 mm. **Subject:** Japanese Immigration to Peru, 100th Anniversary **Obv:** National arms **Rev:** Outline of Japan and Peru, radiant sun **Edge:** Reeded

Date	Mintage	VF20	XF40	MS60	MS63	MS65
1999	Est. 300	—	—	—	—	2,800

KM# 354 NUEVO SOL
33.63 g., 0.925 Silver 1.000 oz. ASW, 37 mm. **Subject:** Agreement between Ecuador and Peru by Brazil **Edge:** Reeded

Date	Mintage	VF20	XF40	MS60	MS63	MS65
1999 LIMA	Est. 5000	—	—	22.00	50.00	55.00

KM# 354a NUEVO SOL
57.39 g., 0.916 Gold 1.690 oz. AGW, 37 mm. **Subject:** Agreement between Peru and Ecuador by Brazil **Edge:** Reeded

Date	Mintage	VF20	XF40	MS60	MS63	MS65
1999 LIMA	Est. 300	—	2,150	2,500	2,800	3,000

KM# 326 NUEVO SOL
26.95 g., 0.925 Silver 0.8015 oz. ASW, 40 mm. **Series:** Ibero-American **Obv:** National arms within circle of assorted arms **Rev:** Horse and rider in courtyard **Edge:** Reeded

Date	Mintage	VF20	XF40	MS60	MS63	MS65
2000 (Mo)	Est. 5000	**PF63** 35.00	**PF65** 40.00			

KM# 355 NUEVO SOL
33.63 g., 0.925 Silver 1.000 oz. ASW, 37 mm. **Subject:** Naval Battle of Iquique, 120th Anniversary, Grand Admiral Miguel Grau **Edge:** Reeded

Date	Mintage	VF20	XF40	MS60	MS63	MS65
2000 LIMA	Est. 5000	—	—	22.00	50.00	55.00

KM# 313 2 NUEVOS SOLES

5.62 g., Bi-Metallic Nickel-Brass center in Stainless Steel ring, 22.2 mm. **Obv:** National arms within circle **Rev:** Stylized bird in flight to left of value within circle **Edge:** Plain **Note:** LIMA monogram is mint mark.

Date	Mintage	VF20	XF40	MS60	MS63	MS65
1994 LIMA	10,000,000	—	—	1.25	2.50	4.00
1995 LIMA	29,985,000	—	—	1.25	2.50	4.00

KM# 316 5 NUEVOS SOLES

6.67 g., Bi-Metallic Nickel-Brass center in Stainless Steel ring, 24.32 mm. **Obv:** National arms within circle **Rev:** Stylized bird in flight to left of value within circle **Edge:** Reeded **Note:** LIMA monogram is mint mark.

Date	Mintage	VF20	XF40	MS60	MS63	MS65
1994 LIMA	10,920,000	—	—	1.75	3.50	5.00
1995 LIMA	29,064,000	—	—	1.75	3.50	5.00
2000 LIMA	5,000,000	—	—	2.00	4.00	5.50

KM# 309 20 NUEVOS SOLES

33.63 g., 0.925 Silver 1.000 oz. ASW, 40 mm. **Subject:** Rio De Janeiro Protocal **Obv:** National arms **Rev:** Angel above map, dates at left **Edge:** Reeded **Note:** LIMA monogram is mint mark.

Date	Mintage	VF20	XF40	MS60	MS63	MS65
1992 LIMA	50,000	PF65 50.00				

KM# 315 20 NUEVOS SOLES

33.63 g., 0.925 Silver 1.000 oz. ASW **Obv:** National arms **Rev:** Head right **Edge:** Reeded **Note:** LIMA monogram is mint mark.

Date	Mintage	VF20	XF40	MS60	MS63	MS65
1992 LIMA	—	PF65 50.00				

KM# 320 50 NUEVOS SOLES

33.63 g., 0.925 Silver 1.000 oz. ASW **Subject:** Peru-Japan Commercial Exchange **Obv:** National arms **Rev:** Stylized bird design **Note:** LIMA monogram is mint mark.

Date	Mintage	VF20	XF40	MS60	MS63	MS65
1993 LIMA	Est. 4000	—	—	—	55.00	60.00

TRADE COINAGE

KM# 210 1/5 LIBRA (Pound)

1.60 g., 0.917 Gold 0.0471 oz. AGW **Obv:** Shield within sprigs with small radiant sun above **Rev:** Head with headband right **Note:** Struck at Lima.

Date	Mintage	VF20	XF40	MS60	MS63	MS65
1906 GOZF	106,000	60.00	80.00	110	120	140
1907 GOZF	31,000	60.00	80.00	115	125	145
1907 GOZG	—	60.00	80.00	110	120	140
1909 GOZG	—	60.00	80.00	110	120	140
1910 GOZG	—	60.00	80.00	110	120	140
1911 GOZG	—	60.00	80.00	110	120	140
1911 GOZF	62,000	60.00	80.00	110	120	140
1912 GOZG	—	60.00	80.00	110	120	140
1912 POZG	—	60.00	80.00	110	120	140
1913 POZG	60,000	60.00	80.00	110	120	140
1914 POZG	25,000	60.00	80.00	110	120	140
1914 PBLG	Inc. above	—	—	—	—	—
Note: Requires Confirmation						
1915	10,000	60.00	80.00	110	120	140
1916	13,000	60.00	—	—	—	—
Note: Requires Confirmation						
1917	3,896	60.00	85.00	120	130	150
1918	16,000	60.00	80.00	110	120	140
1919	10,000	60.00	80.00	110	120	140
1920	72,000	60.00	80.00	110	120	140
1922	8,110	60.00	80.00	110	120	140
1923	27,000	60.00	80.00	110	120	140
1924	—	60.00	80.00	110	120	140
1925	20,000	60.00	80.00	110	120	140
1926	11,000	60.00	80.00	110	120	140
1927	14,000	60.00	80.00	110	120	140
1928	9,322	60.00	80.00	110	120	140
1929	8,971	60.00	80.00	110	120	140
1930	9,991	60.00	80.00	110	120	140
1953 BBR	9,821	60.00	80.00	110	120	140
1955 ZBR	10,000	60.00	80.00	110	120	140
1958 ZBR	5,098	60.00	85.00	120	130	150
1959 ZBR	6,308	60.00	85.00	120	130	150
1960 ZBR	6,083	60.00	85.00	120	130	150
1961 ZBR	12,000	60.00	80.00	110	120	140
1962 ZBR	5,431	60.00	85.00	120	130	150
1963 ZBR	11,000	60.00	80.00	110	120	140
1964 ZBR	25,000	60.00	80.00	110	120	140
1965 ZBR	19,000	60.00	80.00	110	120	140
1966 ZBR	60,000	60.00	80.00	110	120	140
1967 BBR	9,914	60.00	80.00	110	120	140
1968 BBR	Inc. below	60.00	80.00	110	120	140
1968 BBB	4,781	60.00	80.00	110	120	140
1969 BBB	15,000	60.00	80.00	110	120	140

KM# 209 1/2 LIBRA (Pound)

3.99 g., 0.917 Gold 0.1178 oz. AGW **Obv:** Shield within sprigs with radiant sun above **Rev:** Head with headband right

Date	Mintage	VF20	XF40	MS60	MS63	MS65
1902 ROZF	7,800	150	220	250	275	300
1903 ROZF	7,245	150	220	250	275	300
1904 ROZF	8,360	150	220	250	275	300
1905 ROZF	8,010	150	220	250	275	300
1905 GOZF	Inc. above	150	220	250	275	300
1906 GOZF	9,176	150	220	250	275	300
1907 GOZG	—	150	220	250	275	300
1908 GOZG	8,180	150	220	250	275	300
1953 BBR	9,210	150	220	250	275	300
1955 ZBR	14,000	150	210	225	250	275
1961 ZBR	752	150	275	350	400	425
1962 ZBR	4,286	150	220	250	275	300
1963 ZBR	908	150	275	350	400	425
1964 ZBR	10,000	150	210	225	250	275
1965 ZBR	5,490	150	220	250	275	300
1966 ZBR	44,000	150	210	225	250	275
1967 BBR	Inc. above	150	210	225	250	275
1968 BBB	Inc. above	150	210	225	250	275
1968 BBR	Inc. above	150	210	225	250	275
1969 BBB	4,400	150	220	250	275	300

KM# 207 LIBRA (Pound)

7.99 g., 0.917 Gold 0.2355 oz. AGW **Obv:** Shield within sprigs with radiant sun above **Rev:** Head with headband right **Edge:** Reeded

Date	Mintage	VG8	F12	VF20	XF40	MS60
1901 ROZF	81,000	—	—	300	350	400
1902 ROZF	89,000	—	—	300	350	400
1903 ROZF	100,000	—	—	300	350	400
1904 ROZF	33,000	—	—	300	350	400
1905 ROZF	141,000	—	—	300	350	400
1905 GOZF	Inc. above	—	—	300	350	400
1906 GOZF	201,000	—	—	300	350	400
1907 GOZG	Inc. above	—	—	300	350	400
1908 GOZG	36,000	—	—	300	375	450
1909 GOZG	52,000	—	—	300	350	400
1910 GOZG	47,000	—	—	300	375	450
1911 GOZG	42,000	—	—	300	375	450
1912 GOZG	54,000	—	—	300	350	400
1912 POZG	Inc. above	—	—	300	350	400
1913 POZG	—	—	—	300	350	400
1914 PBLG	119,000	—	—	300	350	400
1914 POZG	Inc. above	—	—	300	350	400
1915 PVG	91,000	—	—	300	375	450
1915 PMGG	Inc. above	—	—	300	350	400
1915	Inc. above	—	—	300	350	400
1916	582,000	—	—	300	350	400
1917	1,928,000	—	—	300	350	400
1918	600,000	—	—	300	350	400
1919	Inc. above	—	—	300	350	400
1920	152,000	—	—	300	350	400
1921	Inc. above	—	—	300	350	400
1922	13,000	—	—	300	375	450
1923	15,000	—	—	300	375	450
1924	8,113	—	—	300	400	500
1925	9,068	—	—	300	375	450
1926	4,596	—	—	300	375	450
1927	8,360	—	—	300	375	450
1928	2,184	—	—	300	375	450
1929	3,119	—	—	300	375	450
1930	1,050	—	—	300	400	500
1959 ZBR	605	—	—	300	500	600
1961 ZBR	402	—	—	300	600	700
1962 ZBR	6,203	—	—	300	375	425
1963 ZBR	302	—	—	300	750	900
1964 ZBR	13,000	—	—	300	375	450
1965 ZBR	9,917	—	—	300	375	450
1966 ZBR	39,000	—	—	300	350	400
1967 BBR	2,002	—	—	300	375	450
1968 BBR	7,307	—	—	300	375	450
1968 BBB	Inc. above	—	—	300	375	450
1969 BBR	7,307	—	—	300	375	450

TOKEN COINAGE

KM# Tn3 50 CENTAVOS

Silver **Subject:** National Defense **Obv:** Inca warrior Cahuide attacking with war club

Date	Mintage	F12	VF20	XF40	MS60	MS63
1932	—	12.00	17.00	25.00	45.00	75.00

KM# Tn1 SOL

0.900 Silver **Note:** Medal rotation.

Date	Mintage	F12	VF20	XF40	MS60	MS63
1910	—	12.00	17.00	25.00	45.00	65.00

KM# Tn4 SOL

Silver **Subject:** National Defense **Obv:** Inca warrior Cahuide attacking with war club **Note:** Medal rotation.

Date	Mintage	F12	VF20	XF40	MS60	MS63
1932	—	9.00	16.00	22.50	45.00	75.00

KM# Tn2 5 SOLES

1.71 g., 0.900 Gold 0.0495 oz. AGW

Date	Mintage	F12	VF20	XF40	MS60	MS63
1910	—	120	130	150	190	220

KM# Tn5 5 SOLES

Silver **Subject:** National Defense **Obv:** Inca warrior Cahuide attacking with war club

Date	Mintage	F12	VF20	XF40	MS60	MS63
1932	—	20.00	30.00	42.50	70.00	120

KM# Tn6 10 SOLES

Silver Gilt **Subject:** National Defense **Obv:** Inca warrior Cahuide attacking with war club

Date	Mintage	F12	VF20	XF40	MS60	MS63
1932	—	22.50	32.50	55.00	75.00	125

PATTERNS

Including off metal strikes

KM#	Date	Mintage	Identification	Mkt Val
PnF26	1930	3	50 Soles. Native inscription.	—
PnG26	1932	—	50 Centavos.	—
Pn26	1932	—	Sol.	—
Pn27	1932	18,520,000	5 Soles.	—
PnA28	1932	—	10 Soles.	—
PnB28	1946	—	1/2 Sol. Copper-Nickel.	240
Pn28	1947	—	100 Soles. Bronze Gilt.	—
Pn29	1948	—	Sol. Aluminum.	—
PnA30	1949	—	Centavo. Zinc. KM#211.	150
PnB30	1949	—	2 Centavos. Zinc. KM#212.2.	120
Pn30	1952	—	1 Sol De Oro. Brass.	—
PnA31	1958	—	20 Centavos. Copper-Nickel.	120
Pn31	1958	—	50 Soles. Silver. With PRUEBA.	1,200
Pn32	1964	—	50 Soles. Silver. With PRUEBA.	1,200
PnA33	1965	—	5 Centavos. Copper-Nickel-Zinc. KM#290.	1,200
Pn33	1965	—	50 Soles. Silver. With PRUEBA.	1,200
Pn34	1966	200	Sol. Silver. With PAREJA.	—
Pn35	1967	—	1/2 Sol. With PAREJA.	—
Pn36	1967	7	50 Soles. Silver.	—
Pn37	1988	—	Inti. Brass. KM#296.	—
Pn38	198x (1988)	—	5 Intis. Copper-Nickel-Zinc. KM#300.	—
Pn39	1988	—	10 Intis. Brass.	—

TRIAL STRIKES

KM#	Date	Mintage	Identification	Mkt Val
TS4	1935	—	Sol. Silver. KM#218.1. Alloy percentage: N. 3/25, PLT/0, NKL 10 ZNC/55 CRE.	—
TS5	1935	—	Sol. Silver. KM#218.1. Alloy percentage: N. 4/20, PLT/15, NKL 10 ZNC/55 CRE.	—

PROOF SETS

KM#	Date	Mintage	Identification	Issue Price	Mkt Val
PS2	1965 (5)	10	KM#237-240, 290	—	1,350
PS3	1965 (5)	—	KM#220.5, 221.2b, 222, 223.2, 224.2	—	250
PS4	1966 (5)	1,000	KM244.1-246.1, 247-248	—	100

SPECIMEN SETS (SS)

KM#	Date	Mintage	Identification	Issue Price	Mkt Val
SS1	1964 (5)	—	KM220.5, 221.2b, 222, 223.2, 224.2	—	200
SS2	1965 (5)	—	KM220.5, 221.2b, 222, 223.2, 224.2	—	150
SS3	1965 (5)	—	KM220.5, 221.2b, 222, 223.2, 224.2	—	150
SS4	1966 (5)	—	KM244.1-246.1, 247-248	—	150

PHILIPPINES

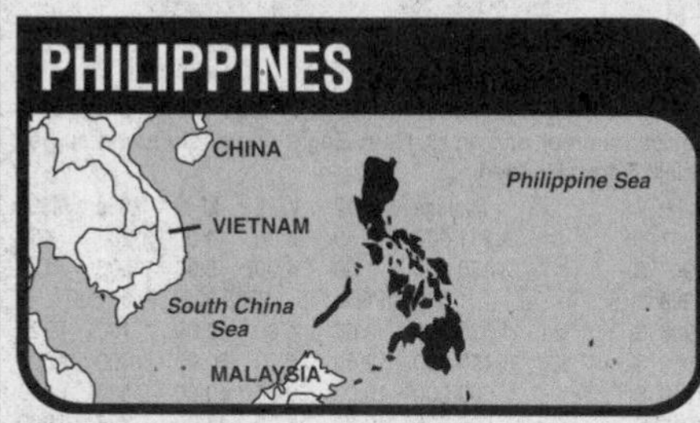

The Republic of the Philippines, an archipelago in the western Pacific 500 miles (805 km.) from the southeast coast of Asia, has an area of 115,830 sq. mi. (300,000 sq. km.) and a population of *64.9 million. Capital: Manila. The economy of the 7,000-island group is based on agriculture, forestry and fishing. Timber, coconut products, sugar and hemp are exported.

Migration to the Philippines began about 30,000 years ago when land bridges connected the islands with Borneo and Sumatra. Ferdinand Magellan claimed the islands for Spain in 1521. The first permanent settlement was established by Miguel de Legazpi at Cebu April 1565. Manila was established in 1572. A British expedition captured Manila and occupied the Spanish colony in October 1762, but returned it to Spain by the treaty of Paris, 1763. Spain held the Philippines despite growing Filipino nationalism until 1898 when they were ceded to the United States at the end of the Spanish-American War. The Philippines became a self-governing commonwealth under the United States in 1935, and attained independence as the Republic of the Philippines on July 4, 1946.

MINT MARKS

(b) Brussels, privy marks only
BSP - Bangko Sentral Pilipinas
D - Denver, 1944-1945
(Lt) - Llantrisant
M, MA - Manila
PM - Pobjoy Mint
S - San Francisco, 1903-1947
SGV - Madrid
(Sh) - Sherritt
(US) - United States
FM - Franklin Mint, U.S.A.*
(VDM) - Vereinigte Deutsche Metall
Werks; Altona, Germany
Star - Manila (Spanish) = Manila

***NOTE:** From 1975-1977 the Franklin Mint produced coinage in up to 3 different qualities. Beginning in 1978only (U) and (P) were struck. Qualities of issue are designated in ( ) after each date and are defined as follows:

(M) MATTE - Normal circulation strike or a dull finish produced by sandblasting special uncirculated (polish-finish) or proof quality dies.

(U) SPECIAL UNCIRCULATED - Polished or prooflike in appearance without any frosted features.

(P) PROOF - The highest quality obtainable having mirror-like fields and frosted features.

MONETARY SYSTEM
4 Quartos = 1 Real
8 Reales = 1 Peso

UNITED STATES ADMINISTRATION

1899-1946

DECIMAL COINAGE

KM# 162 1/2 CENTAVO

Bronze **Obv:** Man seated beside hammer and anvil **Rev:** Eagle above stars and striped shield

Date	Mintage	F12	VF20	XF40	MS60	MS63
1903	12,084,000	0.50	1.25	2.50	10.00	25.00
1903	2,558	PF60 50.00	PF63 110	PF65 150		
1904	5,654,000	1.00	1.75	3.50	20.00	50.00
1904	1,355	PF60 75.00	PF63 175	PF65 300		
1905	471	PF60 175	PF63 300	PF65 500		
1906	500	PF60 150	PF63 275	PF65 500		
1908	500	PF60 150	PF63 250	PF65 500		

KM# 163 CENTAVO

4.70 g., Bronze **Obv:** Man seated beside hammer and anvil **Rev:** Eagle above stars and striped shield

Date	Mintage	F12	VF20	XF40	MS60	MS63
1903	10,790,000	0.50	1.25	2.50	15.00	35.00
1903	2,558	PF60 70.00	PF63 100	PF65 190		
1904	17,040,000	0.50	1.25	2.75	20.00	45.00
1904	1,355	PF60 75.00	PF63 125	PF65 350		
1905	10,000,000	0.75	1.25	3.50	20.00	45.00
1905	471	PF60 175	PF63 300	PF65 750		
1906	500	PF60 150	PF63 275	PF65 700		
1908	500	PF60 150	PF63 275	PF65 700		
1908 S	2,187,000	2.50	4.00	8.00	40.00	100
1908 S/S	—	20.00	30.00	50.00	150	330
1909 S	1,738,000	7.00	10.00	20.00	100	225
1910 S	2,700,000	2.00	4.00	9.00	35.00	60.00
1911 S	4,803,000	1.00	2.50	5.00	30.00	60.00
1912 S	3,000,000	3.50	7.50	15.00	75.00	125
1913 S	5,000,000	2.00	4.00	7.00	25.00	75.00
1914 S	5,000,000	1.75	3.50	5.00	45.00	75.00
1915 S	2,500,000	30.00	40.00	90.00	550	1,250
1916 S	4,330,000	6.00	7.50	12.50	90.00	150
1917/6 S	7,070,000	40.00	55.00	160	500	750
1917 S	Inc. above	2.00	4.00	10.00	75.00	150
1918 S	11,660,000	2.00	5.00	12.50	100	200
1918 S Large S	Inc. above	125	150	250	1,000	1,900
1919 S	4,540,000	2.50	5.00	15.00	75.00	125
1920 S	2,500,000	4.50	3.50	20.00	50.00	175
1920	3,552,000	2.00	5.00	10.00	125	225
1921	7,283,000	1.00	2.50	5.00	35.00	85.00
1922	3,519,000	0.50	3.00	6.00	25.00	70.00
1925 M	9,332,000	0.50	2.50	7.50	35.00	85.00
1926 M	9,000,000	0.50	2.50	5.00	30.00	55.00
1927 M	9,270,000	0.50	2.50	5.00	25.00	45.00
1928 M	9,150,000	0.50	2.00	5.00	30.00	75.00
1929 M	5,657,000	1.00	3.00	6.00	40.00	85.00
1930 M	5,577,000	0.50	2.00	4.50	30.00	50.00
1931 M	5,659,000	0.50	2.25	5.00	35.00	60.00
1932 M	4,000,000	1.00	3.00	7.50	50.00	75.00
1933 M	8,393,000	0.25	2.00	3.00	20.00	50.00
1934 M	3,179,000	0.75	2.50	4.50	50.00	70.00
1936 M	17,455,000	0.50	2.50	4.00	35.00	65.00

KM# 164 5 CENTAVOS

5.25 g., Copper-Nickel, 21.3 mm. **Obv:** Man seated beside hammer and anvil **Rev:** Eagle above stars and striped shield

Date	Mintage	F12	VF20	XF40	MS60	MS63
1903	8,910,000	0.50	1.25	2.50	18.00	30.00
1903	2,558	PF60 75.00	PF63 135	PF65 250		
1904	1,075,000	0.75	2.50	5.00	20.00	45.00
1904	1,355	PF60 75.00	PF63 130	PF65 250		
1905	471	PF60 85.00	PF63 160	PF65 250		
1906	500	PF60 175	PF63 250	PF65 550		
1908	500	PF60 200	PF63 300	PF65 575		
1916 S	300,000	50.00	85.00	150	800	1,500
1917 S	2,300,000	2.25	5.00	12.50	130	300
1918 S/S	—	—	150	200	450	—
1918 S	2,780,000	3.00	8.00	15.00	140	300
1919 S	1,220,000	4.00	15.00	30.00	175	450
1920	1,421,000	3.00	8.50	30.00	175	375
1921	2,132,000	3.00	8.00	20.00	115	225
1925 M	1,000,000	8.00	20.00	30.00	175	300
1926 M	1,200,000	4.00	6.00	17.50	120	200
1927 M	1,000,000	2.50	5.00	10.00	70.00	110
1928 M	1,000,000	3.00	6.00	12.50	75.00	150

KM# 173 5 CENTAVOS

Copper-Nickel **Obv:** Man seated beside hammer and anvil **Rev:** Eagle above stars and striped shield **Note:** Mule.

Date	Mintage	F12	VF20	XF40	MS60	MS63
1918 S	—	175	475	1,200	4,500	9,500

KM# 175 5 CENTAVOS

4.75 g., Copper-Nickel, 19 mm. **Obv:** Man seated beside hammer and anvil **Rev:** Eagle above stars and striped shield

Date	Mintage	F12	VF20	XF40	MS60	MS63
1930 M	2,905,000	1.00	2.50	6.00	45.00	85.00
1931 M	3,477,000	1.00	2.50	7.50	70.00	150
1932 M	3,956,000	1.00	2.00	4.00	50.00	130
1934 M	2,154,000	1.00	3.50	9.00	75.00	200
1934 M recut 1	—	5.00	10.00	35.00	125	250
1935 M	2,754,000	1.00	2.50	8.00	85.00	220

KM# 165 10 CENTAVOS

2.69 g., 0.900 Silver 0.0779 oz. ASW **Obv:** Female standing beside hammer and anvil **Rev:** Eagle above stars and striped shield

Date	Mintage	F12	VF20	XF40	MS60	MS63
1903	5,103,000	2.50	4.00	5.00	35.00	75.00
1903	2,558	**PF60** 75.00		**PF63** 150	**PF65** 250	
1903 S	1,200,000	20.00	30.00	50.00	350	950
1904	11,000	20.00	30.00	55.00	90.00	150
1904	1,355	**PF60** 100		**PF63** 150	**PF65** 250	
1904 S	5,040,000	2.50	4.00	9.00	60.00	120
1905	471	**PF60** 150		**PF63** 325	**PF65** 650	
1906	500	**PF60** 135		**PF63** 225	**PF65** 625	

KM# 169 10 CENTAVOS

2.00 g., 0.750 Silver 0.0482 oz. ASW **Obv:** Female standing beside hammer and anvil **Rev:** Eagle above stars and striped shield **Edge:** Reeded

Date	Mintage	F12	VF20	XF40	MS60	MS63
1907	1,501,000	1.75	4.00	7.50	60.00	175
1907 S	4,930,000	1.75	2.00	5.00	40.00	90.00
1908	500	**PF60** 150		**PF63** 200	**PF65** 600	
1908 S	3,364,000	0.90	2.00	5.00	40.00	70.00
1909 S	312,000	25.00	30.00	65.00	450	1,200
1910 S	—	—	—	—	—	—
Note: Unknown in any collection. Counterfeits of the 1910S are commonly encountered						
1911 S	1,101,000	2.50	10.00	15.00	150	500
1912 S	1,010,000	2.50	6.00	12.00	125	275
1912 S S/S	—	—	50.00	75.00	200	500
1913 S	1,361,000	2.00	9.00	12.00	85.00	150
1914 S Short bar on "4"	1,180,000	2.00	6.00	15.00	175	350
1914 S Long bar on "4"	—	2.00	7.50	15.00	125	300
1915 S	450,000	12.50	25.00	45.00	250	750
1917 S	5,991,000	0.90	2.50	5.00	50.00	100
1918 S	8,420,000	—	2.00	3.00	20.00	50.00
1919 S	1,630,000	0.90	2.50	5.00	35.00	110
1920	520,000	3.00	6.00	15.00	100	200
1921	3,863,000	0.90	2.00	5.00	25.00	50.00
1929 M	1,000,000	0.90	2.00	5.00	25.00	45.00
1935 M	1,280,000	0.90	2.00	4.00	20.00	50.00

KM# 166 20 CENTAVOS

5.38 g., 0.900 Silver 0.1558 oz. ASW **Obv:** Female standing beside hammer and anvil **Rev:** Eagle above stars and striped shield **Edge:** Reeded

Date	Mintage	F12	VF20	XF40	MS60	MS63
1903	5,353,000	3.00	5.00	8.00	45.00	100
1903	2,558	**PF60** 100		**PF63** 150	**PF65** 250	
1903 S	150,000	15.00	25.00	50.00	600	1,900
1904	11,000	25.00	30.00	45.00	125	200
1904	1,355	**PF60** 110		**PF63** 175	**PF65** 275	
1904 S	2,060,000	5.00	7.00	11.00	100	200
1905	471	**PF60** 225		**PF63** 375	**PF65** 625	
1905 S	420,000	7.50	20.00	35.00	400	1,250
1906	500	**PF60** 175		**PF63** 325	**PF65** 600	

KM# 170 20 CENTAVOS

4.00 g., 0.750 Silver 0.0965 oz. ASW **Obv:** Female standing beside hammer and anvil **Rev:** Eagle above stars and striped shield **Edge:** Reeded

Date	Mintage	F12	VF20	XF40	MS60	MS63
1907	1,251,000	3.50	6.00	13.00	200	450
1907 S	3,165,000	1.80	4.00	5.00	75.00	175
1908	500	**PF60** 175		**PF63** 325	**PF65** 600	
1908 S	1,535,000	3.00	4.00	10.00	100	325
1909 S	450,000	12.50	25.00	50.00	400	1,500
1910 S	500,000	15.00	30.00	60.00	400	1,000
1911 S	505,000	10.00	25.00	45.00	325	900
1912 S	750,000	5.00	12.00	30.00	200	400
1913 S/S	949,000	7.50	12.50	35.00	200	350
1913 S	Inc. above	4.00	10.00	15.00	150	200
1914 S	795,000	4.50	10.00	30.00	150	450
1915 S	655,000	15.00	20.00	55.00	475	1,600
1916 S	1,435,000	6.00	10.00	25.00	150	500
1917 S	3,151,000	3.00	5.50	8.00	75.00	200
1918 S	5,560,000	3.00	4.50	6.00	50.00	125
1919 S	850,000	3.50	7.25	12.50	125	225
1920	1,046,000	4.00	8.00	20.00	125	225
1921	1,843,000	—	3.00	5.50	50.00	100
1929 M	1,970,000	—	3.00	5.00	40.00	100
1929 M 2/2/2002	—	—	—	100	250	400

KM# 174 20 CENTAVOS

4.00 g., 0.750 Silver 0.0965 oz. ASW **Obv:** Female standing beside hammer and anvil **Rev:** Eagle above stars and striped shield **Note:** Mule.

Date	Mintage	F12	VF20	XF40	MS60	MS63
1928 M	100,000	10.00	20.00	60.00	900	1,800

KM# 167 50 CENTAVOS

13.48 g., 0.900 Silver 0.390 oz. ASW **Obv:** Female standing beside hammer and anvil **Rev:** Eagle above stars and striped shield

Date	Mintage	F12	VF20	XF40	MS60	MS63
1903	3,102,000	—	10.00	15.00	70.00	125
1903	2,558	**PF60** 100		**PF63** 175	**PF65** 300	
1903 S 2 Known	—	—	—	22,000	—	—
1904	11,000	25.00	50.00	90.00	150	250
1904	1,355	**PF60** 150		**PF63** 400	**PF65** 550	
1904 S	2,160,000	—	12.00	25.00	125	225
1905	471	**PF60** 275		**PF63** 475	**PF65** 675	
1905 S	852,000	7.25	20.00	50.00	700	2,100
1906	500	**PF60** 225		**PF63** 425	**PF65** 575	

KM# 171 50 CENTAVOS

10.00 g., 0.750 Silver 0.2411 oz. ASW **Obv:** Female standing beside hammer and anvil **Rev:** Eagle above stars and striped shield **Edge:** Reeded

Date	Mintage	F12	VF20	XF40	MS60	MS63
1907	1,201,000	4.50	15.00	40.00	150	325
1907 S	2,112,000	4.50	11.00	30.00	150	325
1908	500	**PF60** 200		**PF63** 400	**PF65** 550	
1908 S	1,601,000	4.50	15.00	40.00	325	1,500
1909 S	528,000	10.00	20.00	60.00	350	850
1917 S	674,000	4.50	12.50	35.00	200	550
1918 S	2,202,000	4.50	7.50	15.00	125	190
1919 S	1,200,000	4.50	7.50	20.00	125	225
1920	420,000	4.50	7.50	11.00	70.00	100
1921	2,317,000	4.50	7.50	11.00	50.00	85.00

KM# 168 PESO

26.96 g., 0.900 Silver 0.780 oz. ASW **Obv:** Female standing beside hammer and anvil **Rev:** Eagle above stars and striped shield

Date	Mintage	F12	VF20	XF40	MS60	MS63
1903	2,791,000	25.00	35.00	45.00	190	550
1903	2,558	**PF60** 200		**PF63** 350	**PF65** 800	
1903 S	11,361,000	25.00	30.00	40.00	150	325
1904	11,000	65.00	80.00	115	300	625
1904	1,355	**PF60** 250		**PF63** 500	**PF65** 625	
1904 S	6,600,000	25.00	35.00	40.00	175	375
1905 S curved serif on 1	6,056,000	25.00	40.00	60.00	350	750
1905 S straight serif on 1	—	40.00	50.00	90.00	900	3,500
1905	471	**PF60** 700		**PF63** 1,500	**PF65** 2,000	
1906	500	**PF60** 700		**PF63** 1,200	**PF65** 1,500	
1906 S	201,000	1,000	1,500	3,000	17,500	32,500

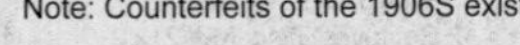
Note: Counterfeits of the 1906S exist

KM# 172 PESO

20.00 g., 0.800 Silver 0.5144 oz. ASW **Obv:** Female standing beside hammer and anvil **Rev:** Eagle above stars and striped shield **Edge:** Reeded

Date	Mintage	F12	VF20	XF40	MS60	MS63
1907 Proof, 2 known	—	**PF63** 165,000				
Note: Gem $165,000, 6/10/12 Pineda Sale.						
1907 S	10,276,000	14.00	17.50	22.00	90.00	250
1908	500	**PF60** 650		**PF63** 1,000	**PF65** 1,500	
1908 S	20,955,000	14.00	17.50	22.00	90.00	250
1909 S	7,578,000	18.00	24.00	30.00	115	300
1909 S S/S	—	—	—	100	225	450
1910 S	3,154,000	20.00	25.00	35.00	225	450
1911 S	463,000	30.00	40.00	75.00	750	4,250
1912 S	680,000	40.00	50.00	85.00	2,000	5,000

UNITED STATES ADMINISTRATION

Commonwealth

KM# 179 CENTAVO

5.30 g., Bronze, 25 mm. **Obv:** Male seated beside hammer and anvil **Rev:** Eagle above shield

Date	Mintage	VF20	XF40	MS60	MS63	MS65
1937 M	15,790,000	2.00	3.00	20.00	45.00	100
1938 M	10,000,000	1.50	2.50	15.00	35.00	65.00
1939 M	6,500,000	2.50	3.50	17.50	40.00	75.00
1940 M	4,000,000	1.25	3.00	15.00	25.00	75.00
1941 M	5,000,000	3.50	7.50	18.00	50.00	90.00
1944 S	58,000,000	0.25	0.50	2.00	4.00	35.00

KM# 180 5 CENTAVOS

4.80 g., Copper-Nickel **Obv:** Male seated beside hammer and anvil **Rev:** Eagle with wings open above shield

Date	Mintage	VF20	XF40	MS60	MS63	MS65
1937 M	2,494,000	5.00	7.50	50.00	75.00	125
1938 M	4,000,000	1.00	2.75	20.00	45.00	125
1941 M	2,750,000	4.00	8.00	70.00	150	375

KM# 180a 5 CENTAVOS

4.92 g., Copper-Nickel-Zinc, 19 mm. **Obv:** Male seated beside hammer and anvil **Rev:** Eagle with wings open above shield

Date	Mintage	VF20	XF40	MS60	MS63	MS65
1944	21,198,000	0.50	1.00	2.00	3.00	15.00
1944 S	14,040,000	0.25	0.50	1.00	2.00	12.00
1945 S	72,796,000	0.25	0.50	1.00	2.00	11.00

KM# 181 10 CENTAVOS

2.00 g., 0.750 Silver 0.0482 oz. ASW, 16.7 mm. **Obv:** Female standing beside hammer and anvil **Rev:** Eagle with wings open above shield **Edge:** Reeded

Date	Mintage	VF20	XF40	MS60	MS63	MS65
1937 M	3,500,000	2.25	3.50	15.00	30.00	90.00
1938 M	3,750,000	1.85	2.25	12.50	25.00	70.00
1941 M	2,500,000	1.85	2.25	7.50	15.00	50.00
1944 D	31,592,000	—	1.50	3.00	4.00	10.00
1945 D	137,208,000	—	1.50	3.00	4.00	10.00

Note: 1937, 1938, and 1941 dated strikes have inverted W's for M's

Date	Mintage	VF20	XF40	MS60	MS63	MS65
1945 D/D	—	8.50	15.00	30.00	50.00	100

KM# 182 20 CENTAVOS

4.00 g., 0.750 Silver 0.0965 oz. ASW, 21 mm. **Obv:** Female standing beside hammer and anvil **Rev:** Eagle with wings open above shield **Edge:** Reeded

Date	Mintage	VF20	XF40	MS60	MS63	MS65
1937 M	2,665,000	3.00	5.00	35.00	50.00	80.00
1938 M	3,000,000	3.00	3.75	15.00	30.00	50.00
1941 M	1,500,000	3.00	3.75	12.50	20.00	45.00
1944 D	28,596,000	—	2.00	3.00	5.00	7.00
1944 D/S	—	5.00	8.00	25.00	50.00	110
1945 D	82,804,000	—	2.00	3.00	5.00	7.00

KM# 176 50 CENTAVOS

10.00 g., 0.750 Silver 0.2411 oz. ASW, 27.5 mm. **Subject:** Establishment of the Commonwealth **Obv:** Murphy-Quezon busts facing each other **Rev:** Eagle above shield

Date	Mintage	VF20	XF40	MS60	MS63	MS65
1936	20,000	25.00	50.00	100	150	225

KM# 183 50 CENTAVOS

10.00 g., 0.750 Silver 0.2411 oz. ASW, 27.5 mm. **Obv:** Female standing beside hammer and anvil **Rev:** Eagle with wings open above shield **Edge:** Reeded

Date	Mintage	VF20	XF40	MS60	MS63	MS65
1944 S	19,187,000	5.00	6.00	8.50	12.50	50.00
1945 S	18,120,000	5.00	6.00	8.50	12.50	50.00
1945 S/S	—	12.00	30.00	80.00	180	240

KM# 177 PESO

20.00 g., 0.900 Silver 0.5787 oz. ASW, 35 mm. **Subject:** Establishment of the Commonwealth **Obv:** Roosevelt-Quezon conjoined busts left **Rev:** Eagle with wings open above shield

Date	Mintage	VF20	XF40	MS60	MS63	MS65
1936	10,000	70.00	85.00	200	300	450

KM# 178 PESO

20.00 g., 0.900 Silver 0.5787 oz. ASW, 35 mm. **Subject:** Establishment of the Commonwealth **Obv:** Murphy-Quezon conjoined busts left **Rev:** Eagle with wings open above shield

Date	Mintage	VF20	XF40	MS60	MS63	MS65
1936	10,000	70.00	85.00	200	300	450

REPUBLIC

KM# 186 CENTAVO

3.11 g., Bronze, 19 mm. **Obv:** Shield of arms **Rev:** Male seated beside hammer and anvil

Date	Mintage	VF20	XF40	MS60	MS63	MS65
1958	20,000,000	—	0.10	0.25	0.50	1.00
1960	40,000,000	—	0.10	0.15	0.35	1.00
1962	30,000,000	—	0.10	0.15	0.35	1.00
1963	130,000,000	—	0.10	0.15	0.25	1.00

KM# 187 5 CENTAVOS

4.80 g., Brass, 21 mm. **Obv:** Shield of arms **Rev:** Male seated beside hammer and anvil

Date	Mintage	VF20	XF40	MS60	MS63	MS65
1958	10,000,000	—	0.10	0.25	0.50	1.00
1959	10,000,000	—	0.10	0.20	0.50	1.00
1960	40,000,000	—	0.10	0.15	0.40	1.00
1962	40,000,000	—	0.10	0.15	0.40	1.00
1963	50,000,000	—	0.10	0.15	0.40	1.00
1964	100,000,000	—	—	0.10	0.40	1.00
1966	10,000,000	—	0.10	0.20	0.50	1.00

KM# 188 10 CENTAVOS

2.00 g., Copper-Nickel-Zinc, 18 mm. **Obv:** Shield of arms **Rev:** Female standing beside hammer and anvil **Edge:** Reeded

Date	Mintage	VF20	XF40	MS60	MS63	MS65
1958	10,000,000	—	0.15	0.25	0.50	1.00
1960	70,000,000	—	0.15	0.20	0.40	1.00
1962	50,000,000	—	0.15	0.20	0.40	1.00
1963	50,000,000	—	0.15	0.20	0.40	1.00
1964	100,000,000	—	0.10	0.20	0.40	1.00
1966	110,000,000	—	0.10	0.20	0.45	1.00

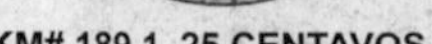

KM# 189.1 25 CENTAVOS

5.00 g., Copper-Nickel-Zinc, 23.5 mm. **Obv:** Shield of arms **Rev:** Female standing beside hammer and anvil, 8 smoke rings from volcano. **Edge:** Reeded

Date	Mintage	VF20	XF40	MS60	MS63	MS65
1958	10,000,000	—	0.25	0.50	0.75	1.25
1960	10,000,000	—	0.30	0.50	0.75	1.25
1962	40,000,000	—	0.25	0.50	0.75	1.25
1964	49,800,000	—	0.20	0.35	0.75	1.25
1966	50,000,000	0.25	0.50	1.00	1.25	1.50

KM# 189.2 25 CENTAVOS

5.00 g., Copper-Nickel-Zinc, 23.5 mm. **Obv:** Shield of arms **Rev:** Female standing beside hammer and anvil, 6 smoke rings **Edge:** Reeded

Date	Mintage	VF20	XF40	MS60	MS63	MS65
1966	40,000,000	—	0.25	0.50	1.25	1.50
1966 Matte finish	Inc. above	—	—	—	—	—

KM# 184 50 CENTAVOS

10.00 g., 0.750 Silver 0.2411 oz. ASW, 27.5 mm. **Obv:** Shield of arms above date and value **Rev:** Uniformed bust right

Date	Mintage	F12	VF20	XF40	MS60	MS63
1947 S	200,000	—	4.50	7.00	12.50	16.00

KM# 190 50 CENTAVOS
10.00 g., Copper-Nickel-Zinc, 30.3 mm. **Obv:** Shield of arms **Rev:** Female standing beside hammer and anvil **Edge:** Reeded

Date	Mintage	VF20	XF40	MS60	MS63	MS65
1958	5,000,000	0.25	0.45	0.75	1.00	1.25
1964	25,000,000	0.25	0.45	1.00	1.25	1.50

KM# 191 1/2 PESO
12.50 g., 0.900 Silver 0.3617 oz. ASW **Subject:** 100th Anniversary Birth of Dr. Jose Rizal **Obv:** Shield of arms **Rev:** Head left

Date	Mintage	VF20	XF40	MS60	MS63	MS65
ND-1961	100,000	—	7.00	8.00	9.00	12.50

KM# 185 PESO
20.00 g., 0.900 Silver 0.5787 oz. ASW, 35.5 mm. **Obv:** Shield of arms above date and value **Rev:** Uniformed bust right

Date	Mintage	F12	VF20	XF40	MS60	MS63
1947 S	100,000	—	11.00	12.50	20.00	25.00

KM# 192 PESO
26.00 g., 0.900 Silver 0.7523 oz. ASW **Subject:** 100th Anniversary Birth of Dr. Jose Rizal **Obv:** Shield of arms **Rev:** Bust 1/4 right divides dates

Date	Mintage	VF20	XF40	MS60	MS63	MS65
ND-1961	100,000	—	14.00	16.00	21.00	35.00

KM# 193 PESO
26.00 g., 0.900 Silver 0.7523 oz. ASW **Subject:** 100th Anniversary Birth of Andres Bonifacio **Obv:** Shield of arms **Rev:** Head 1/4 left divides dates **Edge:** Reeded

Date	Mintage	VF20	XF40	MS60	MS63	MS65
ND-1963	100,000	—	14.00	15.00	16.00	25.00

KM# 194 PESO
26.00 g., 0.900 Silver 0.7523 oz. ASW **Subject:** 100th Anniversary Birth of Apolinario Mabini **Obv:** Shield of arms **Rev:** Head 1/4 right divides dates

Date	Mintage	VF20	XF40	MS60	MS63	MS65
ND-1964	100,000	—	14.00	15.00	16.00	25.00

KM# 195 PESO
26.00 g., 0.900 Silver 0.7523 oz. ASW **Subject:** 25th Anniversary of Bataan Day **Obv:** Shield of arms **Rev:** Flaming broken sword flanked by sprigs, dates and stars **Edge:** Reeded

Date	Mintage	VF20	XF40	MS60	MS63	MS65
ND-1967	100,000	—	14.00	15.00	19.00	27.50

Note: KM#195 is a prooflike issue

REFORM COINAGE

100 Sentimos = 1 Piso

KM# 196 SENTIMO
Aluminum, 10 mm. **Obv:** Shield of arms **Rev:** Head left

Date	Mintage	VF20	XF40	MS60	MS63	MS65
1967	10,000,000	—	—	0.25	0.30	0.50
1968	27,940,000	—	—	0.10	0.20	0.30
1969/6	12,060,000	—	—	0.20	0.35	0.50
1970	130,000,000	—	—	0.10	0.15	0.25
1974	165,000,000	—	—	0.10	0.15	0.25
1974	10,000	PF65 3.50				

KM# 205 SENTIMO
1.22 g., Aluminum, 19 mm. **Obv:** Head 3/4 right **Rev:** Redesigned bank seal within circle **Edge:** Plain **Shape:** Square

Date	Mintage	VF20	XF40	MS60	MS63	MS65
1975 FM (M)	108,000	—	—	0.25	0.50	0.65
1975 FM (U)	5,875	—	—	1.00	2.00	3.00
1975 FM (P)	37,000	PF65 1.50				
1975 (Lt)	10,000,000	—	—	—	0.10	0.20
1975 (US)	60,190,000	—	—	—	0.10	0.20
1976 FM (M)	10,000	—	—	0.50	0.75	1.00
1976 FM (U)	1,826	—	1.00	1.25	2.50	3.50
1976 FM (P)	9,901	PF65 1.50				
1976 (US)	60,000,000	—	—	—	0.10	0.20
1977	4,808,000	—	—	0.15	0.25	0.35
1977 FM (M)	10,000	—	—	0.50	1.00	1.25
1977 FM (U)	354	—	—	3.00	4.00	5.00
1977 FM (P)	4,822	PF65 2.00				
1978	24,813,000	—	—	—	0.10	0.20
1978 FM (U)	10,000	—	—	0.75	1.00	1.50
1978 FM (P)	4,792	PF65 2.00				

KM# 224 SENTIMO
Aluminum **Obv:** Head 3/4 right **Rev:** Redesigned bank seal within circle **Shape:** Square **Note:** Varieties exist in date.

Date	Mintage	VF20	XF40	MS60	MS63	MS65
1979 BSP	—	—	—	0.15	0.25	0.35
1979 FM (U)	10,000	—	—	0.50	1.00	1.25
1979 FM (P)	—	PF65 2.00				
1980 BSP	12,601,000	—	—	0.15	0.25	0.35
1980 FM (U)	10,000	—	—	0.35	0.75	1.00
1980 FM (P)	—	PF65 2.00				
1981 BSP	33,391,000	—	—	0.10	0.20	0.35
1981 FM (U)	—	—	—	0.50	1.00	1.25
1981 FM (P)	—	PF65 2.00				
1982 BSP	51,730,000	—	—	—	0.10	0.20
1982 FM (P)	—	PF65 2.00				

KM# 238 SENTIMO
0.70 g., Aluminum, 15.5 mm. **Obv:** Lapu-Lapu head left **Rev:** Sea shell (Voluta imperalis) and value within circle

Date	Mintage	VF20	XF40	MS60	MS63	MS65
1983	62,090,000	—	—	0.25	0.50	0.65
1983	—	PF65 2.00				
1984	320,000	—	—	0.50	1.00	1.25
1985	16,000	—	—	1.50	3.00	3.50
1986	80,000	—	—	1.25	2.50	3.00
1987	13,570,000	—	—	0.35	0.75	1.00
1988	26,861,000	—	—	0.35	0.75	1.00
1989	—	—	—	0.35	0.75	1.00
1990	—	—	—	—	—	12.00
1991	—	—	—	—	—	20.00
1992	—	—	—	—	—	20.00
1993	—	2.00	4.00	7.00	10.00	16.50

KM# 273 SENTIMO
2.00 g., Copper Plated Steel, 15.5 mm. **Obv:** Value and date **Rev:** Central bank seal within circle and gear design, 1993 (date Central Bank was established) below **Rev. Legend:** BANGKO SENTRAL NG PILIPINAS - 1993

Date	Mintage	VF20	XF40	MS60	MS63	MS65
1995	—	—	—	0.25	0.35	0.75
1996	—	—	—	0.15	0.20	0.25
1997	—	—	—	0.15	0.20	0.25
1998	—	—	—	0.15	0.20	0.25
1999	—	—	—	0.15	0.20	0.25
2000	—	—	—	0.15	0.20	0.25

KM# 197 5 SENTIMOS
2.50 g., Brass, 18 mm. **Obv:** Shield above banner **Rev:** Head right

Date	Mintage	VF20	XF40	MS60	MS63	MS65
1967	40,000,000	—	—	0.15	0.30	0.50
1968	50,000,000	—	—	0.15	0.30	0.50
1970	5,000,000	—	—	1.00	2.00	3.00
1972	71,744,000	—	—	0.15	0.30	0.50
1974	90,025,000	—	—	0.15	0.30	0.50
1974	10,000	PF65 4.00				

KM# 206 5 SENTIMOS
2.40 g., Brass **Obv:** Head 3/4 left **Rev:** Redesigned bank seal within circle **Shape:** Scalloped

Date	Mintage	VF20	XF40	MS60	MS63	MS65
1975 FM (M)	104,000	—	—	0.25	0.50	0.75
1975 FM (U)	5,875	—	—	1.25	2.50	3.50
1975 FM (P)	37,000	PF65 2.00				
1975 (US)	98,928,000	—	—	—	0.10	0.20
1975 (Lt)	10,000,000	—	—	—	0.10	0.20
1976 FM (M)	10,000	—	—	0.75	1.50	2.00
1976 FM (U)	1,826	—	—	1.25	2.50	3.50
1976 FM (P)	9,901	PF65 1.50				
1976 (US)	98,000,000	—	—	—	0.20	0.30
1977	19,367,000	—	—	0.15	0.35	0.60
1977 FM (M)	10,000	—	—	0.65	1.25	2.00
1977 FM (U)	354	—	—	2.00	4.00	6.00
1977 FM (P)	4,822	PF65 2.50				
1978	61,838,000	—	—	0.10	0.20	0.30

Date	Mintage	VF20	XF40	MS60	MS63	MS65
1978 FM (U)	10,000	—	—	0.75	1.50	2.00
1978 FM (P)	4,792	**PF65** 2.50				

KM# 225 5 SENTIMOS

2.50 g., Brass **Obv:** Head 3/4 left **Rev:** Redesigned bank seal within circle **Shape:** Scalloped

Date	Mintage	VF20	XF40	MS60	MS63	MS65
1979 BSP	12,805,000	—	—	0.15	0.30	0.50
1979 FM (U)	10,000	—	—	0.65	1.25	2.00
1979 FM (P)	—	**PF65** 2.50				
1980 BSP	111,339,000	—	—	—	0.10	0.20
1980 FM (U)	—	—	—	0.75	1.50	2.00
1980 FM (P)	—	**PF65** 2.50				
1981 BSP	—	—	—	—	0.10	0.20
1981 FM (U)	—	—	—	0.65	1.25	2.00
1981 FM (P)	1,795	**PF65** 3.00				
1982 BSP	—	—	—	—	0.10	0.20
1982 FM (P)	—	**PF65** 3.00				

KM# 239 5 SENTIMOS

1.20 g., Aluminum, 17 mm. **Obv:** Melchora Aquino head right **Rev:** Waling-Waling orchid and value

Date	Mintage	VF20	XF40	MS60	MS63	MS65
1983	100,016,000	—	—	0.25	0.50	0.75
1983	—	**PF65** 2.00				
1984	141,744,000	—	—	0.20	0.40	0.60
1985	50,416,000	—	—	0.15	0.25	0.40
1986	11,664,000	—	—	0.20	0.35	0.50
1987	79,008,000	—	—	—	0.10	0.20
1988	90,487,000	—	—	—	0.10	0.20
1989	—	—	—	0.15	0.25	0.40
1990	—	—	—	0.15	0.25	0.40
1991	—	—	—	—	3.75	5.00
1992	—	—	—	0.15	0.25	0.40

KM# 268 5 SENTIMOS

1.90 g., Copper Plated Steel, 15.5 mm. **Obv:** Numeral value around center hole **Rev:** Hole in center with date, bank and name around border, 1993 (date Central Bank was established) below **Rev. Legend:** BANGKO CENTRAL NG PILIPINAS - 1993 **Edge:** Plain

Date	Mintage	VF20	XF40	MS60	MS63	MS65
1995	—	—	0.10	0.15	0.25	0.30
1996	—	—	0.10	0.15	0.25	0.30
1997	—	—	0.10	0.15	0.25	0.30
1998	—	—	0.10	0.15	0.25	0.30
1999	—	—	0.10	0.15	0.25	0.30
2000	—	—	0.10	0.15	0.25	0.30

KM# 198 10 SENTIMOS

2.00 g., Copper-Nickel, 17.5 mm. **Obv:** Shield of arms **Rev:** Bust left **Edge:** Reeded

Date	Mintage	VF20	XF40	MS60	MS63	MS65
1967	50,000,000	—	—	0.20	0.35	0.60
1968	60,000,000	—	—	0.20	0.35	0.60
1969	40,000,000	—	—	0.20	0.35	0.60
1970	50,000,000	—	—	0.20	0.35	0.60
1971	80,000,000	—	—	0.20	0.35	0.60
1972	121,390,000	—	—	0.20	0.35	0.60
1974	60,208,000	—	—	0.20	0.35	0.60
1974	10,000	**PF65** 2.00				

KM# 207 10 SENTIMOS

2.00 g., Copper-Nickel, 17.5 mm. **Obv:** Head 3/4 right **Rev:** Redesigned bank seal within circle **Edge:** Reeded

Date	Mintage	VF20	XF40	MS60	MS63	MS65
1975 FM (M)	104,000	—	—	0.25	0.50	0.75
1975 FM (U)	5,875	—	—	1.25	2.50	3.00
1975 FM (P)	37,000	**PF65** 2.50				
1975 (VDM)	10,000,000	—	—	0.15	0.25	0.35
1975 (US)	50,000,000	—	—	0.10	0.20	0.30
1976 FM (M)	10,000	—	—	0.25	0.50	0.75
1976 FM (U)	1,826	—	—	2.00	4.00	6.00
1976 FM (P)	9,901	**PF65** 2.00				
1976 (US)	50,000,000	—	—	0.10	0.20	0.30
1977	29,314,000	—	—	0.15	0.25	0.35
1977 FM (M)	10,000	—	—	0.75	1.50	2.50
1977 FM (U)	354	—	—	—	6.00	7.50
1977 FM (P)	4,822	**PF65** 3.00				
1978	60,042,000	—	—	—	0.10	0.20
1978 FM (U)	10,000	—	—	1.50	3.00	5.00
1978 FM (P)	4,792	**PF65** 3.00				

KM# 226 10 SENTIMOS

2.00 g., Copper-Nickel, 17.5 mm. **Obv:** Head 3/4 right **Rev:** Redesigned bank seal within circle **Edge:** Reeded **Note:** Varieties with thick and thin legends exist for coins with BSP mint mark.

Date	Mintage	VF20	XF40	MS60	MS63	MS65
1979 BSP	6,446,000	—	—	0.25	0.50	0.75
1979 FM (U)	10,000	—	—	1.25	2.75	4.00
1979 FM (P)	3,645	**PF65** 3.00				
1980 BSP	—	—	—	0.15	0.30	0.45
1980 FM (U)	10,000	—	—	0.75	1.50	2.50
1980 FM (P)	3,133	**PF65** 3.25				
1981 BSP	—	—	—	0.15	0.30	0.50
1981 FM (U)	—	—	—	0.50	1.00	1.50
1981 FM (P)	1,795	**PF65** 3.50				
1982 BSP	—	—	—	0.15	0.30	0.50
1982 FM (P)	—	**PF65** 3.50				
1982 FM (U)	—	**PF65** 23.00				

KM# 240.1 10 SENTIMOS

2.45 g., Aluminum, 18.95 mm. **Series:** F.A.O. **Subject:** World Conference on Fisheries **Obv:** Melchora Aquino head left **Rev:** Pygmy goby, world's smallest fish and value within circle **Edge:** Plain

Date	Mintage	VF20	XF40	MS60	MS63	MS65
1983	95,640,000	—	—	0.50	1.00	1.50
1983	—	**PF65** 10.00				
1986	—	—	—	0.50	1.00	1.50
1987	Inc. below	—	—	0.50	1.00	1.50

KM# 240.2 10 SENTIMOS

1.50 g., Aluminum, 19 mm. **Series:** F.A.O. **Subject:** World Conference on Fisheries **Obv:** Head left **Rev:** Pygmy goby, world's smallest fish and value within circle

Date	Mintage	VF20	XF40	MS60	MS63	MS65
1983	—	—	—	0.25	0.50	0.75
1984	235,900,000	—	—	0.20	0.35	1.00
1985	90,169,000	—	—	0.20	0.35	1.00
1986	4,270,000	—	—	0.25	0.50	0.75
1987	99,520,000	—	—	0.20	0.35	0.50
1988	117,166,000	—	—	0.20	0.35	0.50
1989	—	—	—	0.20	0.35	0.50
1990	—	—	—	0.20	0.35	0.50
1991	—	—	—	0.20	0.35	0.50
1992	—	—	—	0.20	0.35	0.50
1993	—	—	—	0.25	0.50	0.75
1994	—	—	—	0.25	0.50	0.75

KM# 270.1 10 SENTIMOS

2.50 g., Copper Plated Steel, 17 mm. **Obv:** Value and date **Rev:** Central Bank seal within circle and gear design, 1993 (date Central Bank was established) below **Rev. Legend:** BANGKO SENTRAL NG PILIPINAS - 1993 **Edge:** Reeded

Date	Mintage	VF20	XF40	MS60	MS63	MS65
1995	—	—	0.10	0.20	0.30	0.50
1996	—	—	0.40	0.60	1.00	1.50
1997	—	—	0.10	0.20	0.30	0.40
1998	—	—	0.10	0.20	0.30	0.40
1999	—	—	0.10	0.20	0.30	0.40

KM# 199 25 SENTIMOS

4.00 g., Copper-Nickel-Zinc, 21 mm. **Obv:** Shield of arms **Rev:** Head left **Edge:** Reeded

Date	Mintage	VF20	XF40	MS60	MS63	MS65
1967	40,000,000	—	0.10	0.25	0.50	0.75
1968	10,000,000	—	0.10	0.25	0.50	0.75
1969	10,000,000	—	0.10	0.25	0.50	0.75
1970	40,000,000	—	0.10	0.20	0.40	0.60
1971	60,000,000	—	0.10	0.20	0.40	0.60
1972	90,000,000	—	0.10	0.20	0.40	0.60
1974	10,000,000	—	0.10	0.25	0.50	0.75
1974	10,000	**PF65** 12.00				

KM# 208 25 SENTIMOS

4.00 g., Copper-Nickel, 21 mm. **Obv:** Head 3/4 left **Rev:** Redesigned bank seal within circle **Edge:** Reeded

Date	Mintage	VF20	XF40	MS60	MS63	MS65
1975 FM (M)	104,000	—	—	0.35	0.75	1.25
1975 FM (U)	5,875	—	—	2.00	4.00	6.00
1975 FM (P)	37,000	**PF65** 2.50				
1975 (US)	10,000,000	—	0.10	0.20	0.40	0.60
1975 (VDM)	10,000,000	—	0.15	0.25	0.50	0.75
1976 FM (M)	10,000	—	0.20	0.50	1.00	1.50
1976 FM (U)	1,826	—	—	3.00	5.00	7.00
1976 FM (P)	9,901	**PF65** 2.00				
1976 (US)	10,000,000	—	0.10	0.15	0.25	0.45
1977	24,654,000	—	0.10	0.15	0.25	0.45
1977 FM (M)	10,000	—	—	0.65	1.25	2.00
1977 FM (U)	354	—	—	3.00	5.00	7.00
1977 FM (P)	4,822	**PF65** 4.50				
1978	40,466,000	—	0.10	0.15	0.25	0.45
1978 FM (U)	10,000	—	—	2.00	3.50	5.00
1978 FM (P)	4,792	**PF65** 4.00				

KM# 227 25 SENTIMOS

4.00 g., Copper-Nickel, 21 mm. **Obv:** Head 3/4 left **Rev:** Redesigned bank seal within circle **Edge:** Reeded

Date	Mintage	VF20	XF40	MS60	MS63	MS65
1979 BSP	20,725,000	—	0.15	0.25	0.50	0.75
1979 FM (U)	10,000	—	—	1.00	2.00	4.00
1979 FM (P)	3,645	**PF65** 2.00				
1980 BSP	—	—	0.20	0.35	0.75	1.25
1980 FM (U)	10,000	—	—	0.65	1.25	2.00
1980 FM (P)	3,133	**PF65** 4.50				
1981 BSP	—	—	0.10	0.50	1.00	1.50
1981 FM (U)	—	—	—	1.50	3.00	5.00
1981 FM (P)	1,795	**PF65** 5.00				
1982 BSP	—	—	0.10	0.25	0.50	0.75
1982 FM (P)	—	**PF65** 5.00				
1982 FM (U)	—	**PF65** 34.00				

KM# 241.1 25 SENTIMOS

3.90 g., Brass, 21 mm. **Obv:** Juan Luna right **Rev:** Butterfly (Graphium idaeoides) **Edge:** Reeded

Date	Mintage	VF20	XF40	MS60	MS63	MS65
1983	92,944,000	—	0.15	0.50	1.00	2.00
1983	—	**PF65** 2.50				
1984	254,324,000	—	0.15	0.35	0.75	2.00
1985	84,922,000	—	0.15	0.35	0.75	1.25
1986	65,284,000	—	0.50	0.75	1.50	3.50

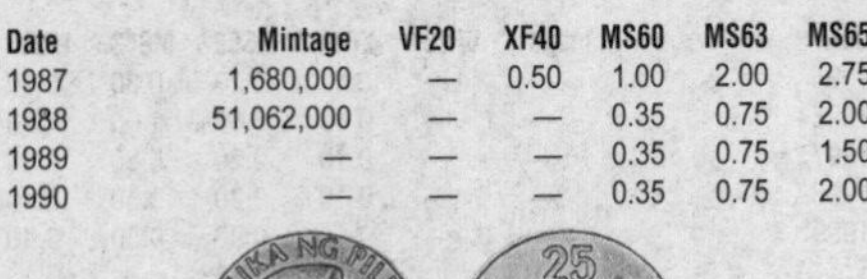

Date	Mintage	VF20	XF40	MS60	MS63	MS65
1987	1,680,000	—	0.50	1.00	2.00	2.75
1988	51,062,000	—	—	0.35	0.75	2.00
1989	—	—	—	0.35	0.75	1.50
1990	—	—	—	0.35	0.75	2.00

KM# 241.2 25 SENTIMOS

2.24 g., Brass, 16 mm. **Obv:** Juan Luna right **Rev:** Butterfly (Graphium idaeoides) **Edge:** Reeded **Note:** Reduced size.

Date	Mintage	VF20	XF40	MS60	MS63	MS65
1991	—	—	—	0.50	1.00	1.25
1992	—	—	—	0.50	1.00	1.25
1993	—	—	—	3.00	5.00	7.00
1994	—	—	—	1.25	2.50	3.00

KM# 271 25 SENTIMOS

3.80 g., Brass, 20 mm. **Obv:** Value and date **Rev:** Central Bank seal within circle and gear design, 1993 (date Central Bank was established) below **Rev. Legend:** BANGKO SENTRAL NG PILIPINAS - 1993 **Edge:** Plain

Date	Mintage	VF20	XF40	MS60	MS63	MS65
1995	—	0.15	0.30	0.50	0.75	1.00
1996	—	0.15	0.30	0.50	0.75	1.00
1997	—	0.15	0.30	0.50	0.75	1.00
1998	—	0.15	0.30	0.50	0.75	1.00
1999	—	0.15	0.30	0.50	0.75	1.00
2000	—	0.15	0.30	0.50	0.75	1.00

KM# 200 50 SENTIMOS

8.00 g., Copper-Nickel-Zinc, 27 mm. **Obv:** Shield of arms **Rev:** Marcelo H. del Pilar right **Edge:** Reeded

Date	Mintage	VF20	XF40	MS60	MS63	MS65
1967	20,000,000	0.10	0.25	0.50	0.75	1.25
1971	10,000,000	0.10	0.25	0.50	1.00	2.00
1972 Knob on 2	30,000,000	0.10	0.50	0.75	1.50	2.50
1972 Plain 2	20,517,000	0.10	0.45	0.65	1.25	2.00
1974	5,004,000	0.20	0.50	0.75	1.50	2.50
1974	10,000	PF65 20.00				
1975	5,714,000	0.10	0.20	0.50	1.00	2.00

KM# 242.1 50 SENTIMOS

6.00 g., Copper-Nickel, 25 mm. **Obv:** Head of Marcelo H. del Pilar left **Rev:** Pithecophaga (monkey eating eagle) attacking

Date	Mintage	VF20	XF40	MS60	MS63	MS65
1983	27,644,000	0.10	0.40	0.65	1.25	3.00
1983	—	PF65 4.25				
1984	121,408,000	0.10	0.20	0.50	1.00	2.00
1985	107,048,000	0.10	0.20	0.50	1.00	1.50
1986	120,000,000	0.10	0.20	0.35	0.75	0.75
1987	1,078,000	0.10	0.25	0.75	1.50	2.50
1988	24,008,000	0.10	0.20	0.50	1.00	1.50
1989	—	0.10	0.20	0.50	1.00	2.50
1990	—	0.10	0.20	0.50	1.00	1.50

KM# 242.2 50 SENTIMOS

6.00 g., Copper-Nickel, 25 mm. **Obv:** Head of Marcelo H. del Pilar left **Rev:** Pithecophaga (monkey eating eagle) attacking **Note:** Error eagle's name: PITHECOBHAGA

Date	Mintage	VF20	XF40	MS60	MS63	MS65
1983	Inc. above	2.00	2.50	5.00	7.50	10.00

KM# 242.3 50 SENTIMOS

3.00 g., Brass, 17.5 mm. **Obv:** Head of Marcelo H. Pilar left **Rev:** Pithecophaga (monkey eating eagle) attacking **Edge:** Reeded **Note:** Reduced size.

Date	Mintage	VF20	XF40	MS60	MS63	MS65
1991	—	—	0.25	0.75	1.50	2.00
1992	—	—	0.25	0.75	1.50	2.00
1993	—	—	—	2.75	3.00	6.00
1994	—	—	—	1.50	2.50	3.50

KM# 201 PISO

26.45 g., 0.900 Silver 0.7653 oz. ASW **Subject:** Centennial - Birth of Aguinaldo **Obv:** Shield of arms **Rev:** Bust facing divides dates

Date	Mintage	VF20	XF40	MS60	MS63	MS65
ND-1969 Prooflike	100,000	—	14.50	17.50	20.00	30.00

KM# 202 PISO

23.20 g., Nickel, 38.3 mm. **Subject:** Pope Paul VI Visit **Obv:** Bust of Ferdinand Marcos left **Rev:** Bust of Pope Paul VI right

Date	Mintage	VF20	XF40	MS60	MS63	MS65
1970	70,000	—	—	1.25	2.25	2.75
1970	—	PF65 15.00				

KM# 202a PISO

26.45 g., 0.900 Silver 0.7653 oz. ASW, 38.3 mm. **Subject:** Papal visit **Obv:** Bust of Ferdinand Marcos left **Rev:** Bust of Pope Paul VI right

Date	Mintage	VF20	XF40	MS60	MS63	MS65
1970	30,000	—	—	17.50	22.00	26.00

KM# 202b PISO

19.30 g., 0.917 Gold 0.569 oz. AGW, 38.3 mm. **Subject:** Papal visit **Obv:** Bust of Ferdinand Marcos left **Rev:** Bust of Pope Paul VI right

Date	Mintage	VF20	XF40	MS60	MS63	MS65
1970	1,000	—	—	—	—	1,100

KM# 203 PISO

15.00 g., Copper-Nickel-Zinc, 33 mm. **Obv:** Shield of arms **Rev:** Head of Jose Rizal left **Edge:** Reeded

Date	Mintage	VF20	XF40	MS60	MS63	MS65
1972	121,821,000	—	0.25	0.50	1.00	2.00
1974	45,631,000	—	0.25	0.50	1.00	2.00
1974	10,000	PF63 20.00	PF65 22.50			

KM# 209.1 PISO

9.50 g., Copper-Nickel, 29 mm. **Obv:** Head of Jose Rizal 1/4 right within octagon **Rev:** Shield of arms **Edge:** Reeded

Date	Mintage	VF20	XF40	MS60	MS63	MS65
1975 FM (M)	104,000	—	—	—	—	2.00
1975 FM (U)	5,877	—	—	—	—	5.50
1975 FM (P)	37,000	PF65 2.50				
1975 (VDM)	10,000,000	0.15	0.25	0.45	0.65	1.25
1975 (US)	30,000,000	0.15	0.25	0.35	0.50	0.75
1976 FM (M)	10,000	—	—	1.00	2.00	3.00
1976 FM (U)	1,826	—	—	3.50	4.50	8.00
1976 FM (P)	9,901	PF65 3.00				
1976 (US)	30,000,000	0.15	0.25	0.50	0.75	1.00
1977	14,771,000	0.15	0.25	0.50	0.75	1.00
1977 FM (M)	12,000	—	—	1.00	2.00	3.00
1977 FM (U)	354	—	—	3.00	5.00	10.00
1977 FM (P)	4,822	PF65 3.00				
1978	19,408,000	0.15	0.25	0.50	1.00	1.50
1978 FM (U)	10,000	—	—	2.00	3.00	5.00
1978 FM (P)	4,792	PF65 4.00				

KM# 209.2 PISO

9.50 g., Copper-Nickel, 29 mm. **Obv:** Head of Jose Rizal 1/4 right within octagon **Rev:** Shield of arms **Rev. Inscription:** ISANG BANSA ISANG DIWA

Date	Mintage	VF20	XF40	MS60	MS63	MS65
1979 BSP	321,000	0.15	0.35	0.75	1.50	2.00
1979 FM (U)	10,000	—	—	2.00	3.50	5.00
1979 FM (P)	3,645	PF65 3.00				
1980 BSP	19,693,000	0.15	0.25	0.50	0.75	1.00
1980 FM (U)	10,000	—	—	2.00	3.50	5.00
1980 FM (P)	3,133	PF65 8.50				
1981 BSP	7,944,000	0.15	0.25	0.50	1.00	1.50
1981 FM (U)	—	—	—	2.00	4.00	6.00
1981 FM (P)	1,795	PF65 6.00				
1982 FM (P)	—	PF65 7.00				
1982 BSP Large date	52,110,000	0.15	0.25	0.50	1.00	1.50
1982 BSP Small date	Inc. above	0.15	0.25	0.50	1.00	1.50

KM# 243.1 PISO

9.50 g., Copper-Nickel, 29 mm. **Obv:** Head of Jose Rizal right **Rev:** Tamaraw bull **Edge:** Reeded **Note:** Large legends and design elements.

Date	Mintage	VF20	XF40	MS60	MS63	MS65
1983	55,869,000	—	0.30	0.65	1.25	2.00
1983	—	PF65 6.50				
1984	4,997,000	—	0.50	1.50	3.00	3.50
1985	182,592,000	—	0.30	0.50	1.00	1.75
1986	19,072,000	—	0.30	0.65	1.25	2.25
1987	1,391,000	—	—	3.00	5.00	7.00
1988	54,636,000	—	0.30	0.50	1.00	1.50
1989	—	—	—	—	—	3.50

KM# 243.2 PISO

4.00 g., Stainless Steel, 21.6 mm. **Obv:** Head of Jose Rizal right **Rev:** Tamaraw bull **Edge:** Plain **Note:** Reduced size.

Date	Mintage	VF20	XF40	MS60	MS63	MS65
1991	—	—	0.50	0.65	1.25	2.25
1992	—	—	0.50	0.65	1.25	2.25
1993	—	—	0.30	0.50	1.00	2.00
1994	—	—	0.30	0.50	1.00	2.00

KM# 243.3 PISO

Copper-Nickel **Obv:** Head of Jose Rizal right **Rev:** Tamaraw bull **Note:** Smaller legends and design elements.

Date	Mintage	VF20	XF40	MS60	MS63	MS65
1989	—	—	0.30	0.50	1.00	1.50
1990 smaller legends	—					

KM# 251 PISO

Copper-Nickel, 28.5 mm. **Subject:** Philippine Cultures Decade **Obv:** Shield of arms divides date **Rev:** Three conjoined vertical busts right

Date	Mintage	VF20	XF40	MS60	MS63	MS65
1989	—	—	—	2.50	4.50	7.00
1989 Matte	—	—	—	—	7.00	9.00

KM# 257 PISO

Copper-Nickel **Obv:** Shield of arms **Rev:** Waterfall, ship, and flower within circle

Date	Mintage	VF20	XF40	MS60	MS63	MS65
ND-1991	—	—	—	0.65	1.25	2.00
ND-1991 Matte	1,000	—	—	—	6.00	8.00

Note: Special striking by CB

KM# 260 PISO

Nickel Clad Steel, 21.5 mm. **Subject:** 50th Anniversary - Battle of Kagitingan **Obv:** Shield of arms **Rev:** Military head left, cross, flag and dates

Date	Mintage	VF20	XF40	MS60	MS63	MS65
ND-1992	—	—	—	0.50	1.00	1.25

KM# 269 PISO

6.10 g., Copper-Nickel, 24 mm. **Obv:** Head of Jose Rizal right, value and date **Rev:** Bank seal within circle and gear design, 1993 (date Central Bank was established) below **Rev. Legend:** BANGKO SENTRAL NG PILIPINAS - 1993 **Edge:** Reeded

Date	Mintage	VF20	XF40	MS60	MS63	MS65
1995	—	0.20	0.35	0.50	0.75	1.00
1996	—	0.25	0.45	0.65	1.25	1.75
1997	—	0.25	0.45	0.65	1.25	1.75
1998	—	0.25	0.45	0.65	1.25	1.75
1999	—	0.25	0.45	0.65	1.25	1.75
2000	—	0.25	0.45	0.65	1.25	1.75

KM# 244 2 PISO

12.00 g., Copper-Nickel, 31 mm. **Obv:** Head of Andres Bonifacio left **Rev:** Coconut palm **Shape:** 10-sided

Date	Mintage	VF20	XF40	MS60	MS63	MS65
1983	15,640,000	—	0.35	1.25	2.50	3.50
1983	—	PF65 3.50				
1984	121,111,000	—	0.35	0.50	1.00	1.50
1985	115,211,000	—	0.35	0.65	1.25	1.50
1986	25,260,000	—	0.35	0.65	1.25	1.50
1987	2,196,000	—	—	5.00	8.00	10.00
1988	16,094,000	—	—	3.50	7.00	10.00
1989	—	—	—	0.65	1.25	1.50
1990	—	—	—	0.65	1.25	1.50

KM# 253 2 PISO

12.00 g., Copper-Nickel, 31 mm. **Obv:** Design within beaded circle **Rev:** Head of Elpidio Quirino right **Shape:** 10-sided

Date	Mintage	VF20	XF40	MS60	MS63	MS65
ND-1991	10,000,000	—	—	0.65	1.25	2.00
ND-1991 Matte	—	—	—	—	8.00	10.00

Note: Special striking by CB

KM# 258 2 PISO

5.00 g., Stainless Steel, 24 mm. **Obv:** Head of Andres Bonifacio left **Rev:** Coconut palm **Edge:** Reeded

Date	Mintage	VF20	XF40	MS60	MS63	MS65
1991	—	—	—	0.75	1.50	2.00
1992	—	—	—	0.75	1.50	2.00
1993	—	—	—	2.00	3.00	3.50
1994	—	—	—	1.50	2.50	3.00

KM# 256 2 PISO

Copper-Nickel **Obv:** Triangular design within circle **Rev:** Head of Jose Laurel right **Shape:** 10-sided

Date	Mintage	VF20	XF40	MS60	MS63	MS65
ND-1992	—	—	—	1.50	2.50	5.50
ND-1992 Matte	—	—	—	—	8.00	10.00

Note: Special striking by CB

KM# 261 2 PISO

Nickel Clad Steel, 23.5 mm. **Obv:** Design within beaded circle **Rev:** Head of Manuel A. Roxas right

Date	Mintage	VF20	XF40	MS60	MS63	MS65
ND-1992	—	—	—	1.25	2.00	2.50
ND-1992 Matte	—	—	—	—	—	10.00

Note: Special striking by CB

KM# 210.1 5 PISO

22.00 g., Nickel, 36.5 mm. **Obv:** Shield of arms above value **Rev:** Head of Ferdinand E. Marcos left

Date	Mintage	VF20	XF40	MS60	MS63	MS65
1975 FM (M)	3,850	—	—	—	—	14.00
1975 FM (U)	7,875	—	—	—	—	7.00
1975 FM (P)	39,000	PF65 4.00				
1975 (Sh)	20,000,000	0.40	0.60	0.80	1.25	1.75
1976 FM (M)	10,000	—	—	3.00	5.00	7.00
1976 FM (U)	1,826	—	—	—	—	17.00
1976 FM (P)	9,901	PF65 7.00				
1977 FM (M)	10,000	—	—	3.00	5.00	7.00
1977 FM (U)	354	—	—	—	—	12.00
1977 FM (P)	4,822	PF65 10.00				
1978 FM (U)	10,000	—	—	4.00	6.00	8.00
1978 FM (P)	4,792	PF65 14.00				
1982	—	0.60	0.90	1.25	1.75	3.00

KM# 210.2 5 PISO

22.00 g., Nickel, 36.5 mm. **Obv:** Shield of arms **Obv. Inscription:** ISANG BANSA ISANG DIWA below shield **Rev:** Head of Ferdinand E. Marcos left

Date	Mintage	VF20	XF40	MS60	MS63	MS65
1979 FM (U)	10,000	—	—	—	—	9.00
1979 FM (P)	3,645	PF65 9.00				
1980 FM (U)	10,000	—	—	—	—	8.50
1980 FM (P)	3,133	PF65 12.00				
1981 FM (U)	11,000	—	—	—	—	10.00
1981 FM (P)	1,795	PF65 12.00				
1982 FM (P)	—	PF65 12.00				
1982 FM (U); Prooflike	—	—	—	—	—	20.00

KM# 259 5 PISO

Nickel-Brass, 25.5 mm. **Obv:** Head of Emilio Aguinaldo right **Rev:** Pterocarpus Indicus Flower **Edge:** Reeded

Date	Mintage	VF20	XF40	MS60	MS63	MS65
1991	—	—	—	—	3.00	3.50
1992	—	—	—	—	3.50	4.50
1993	—	—	—	—	9.00	18.00
1994	—	—	—	—	10.00	15.00

KM# 262 5 PISO

Nickel-Brass, 25.5 mm. **Subject:** 30th Chess Olympiad **Obv:** Shield of arms **Rev:** Stylized horse head on chess board **Note:** Varieties exist.

Date	Mintage	VF20	XF40	MS60	MS63	MS65
1992	—	—	—	—	11.00	12.50

KM# 263 5 PISO

Nickel-Brass, 25.5 mm. **Subject:** Leyte Gulf Landings **Obv:** Shield of arms **Rev:** Standing figures

Date	Mintage	VF20	XF40	MS60	MS63	MS65
ND-1994	7,800	—	—	—	8.50	12.00

KM# 272 5 PISO

7.70 g., Nickel-Brass, 27 mm. **Obv:** Head of Emilio Aguinaldo right, value and date within scalloped border **Rev:** Central Bank seal within circle and gear design within scalloped border, 1993 (date Central Bank was established) below **Rev. Legend:** BANGKO SENTRAL NG PILIPINAS - 1993 **Edge:** Plain

Date	Mintage	VF20	XF40	MS60	MS63	MS65
1995	—	0.45	0.75	2.00	4.00	7.75
Note: Struck at Royal Canadian Mint, without designer initials						
1996	—	0.45	0.75	1.50	2.25	3.00
1997	—	0.35	0.70	1.00	1.75	2.50
Note: Struck at Royal Canadian Mint, without designer initials						
1997 BSP	—	0.35	0.70	1.00	1.75	2.50
Note: With designer initials below shoulder						
1998	—	—	—	1.25	2.00	3.00
Note: Struck at Royal Canadian Mint, without designer initials						
1998	—	0.35	0.70	1.00	1.75	2.50
Note: With designer initials below shoulder						
1999	—	0.35	0.70	1.00	1.75	2.50

KM# 278 10 PISO

8.70 g., Bi-Metallic Aluminum-Bronze center in Copper-Nickel ring, 26.5 mm. **Obv:** Conjoined heads right within circle **Rev:** Bank seal within circle and gear design, 1993 (date Central Bank was established) below **Rev. Legend:** BANGKO SENTRAL NG PILIPINAS - 1993 **Edge:** Segmented reeding

Date	Mintage	VF20	XF40	MS60	MS63	MS65
2000	—	0.75	1.50	2.25	3.75	5.00

KM# 204 25 PISO

26.40 g., 0.900 Silver 0.7639 oz. ASW **Subject:** 25th Anniversary of Bank **Obv:** Shield of arms **Rev:** Bank in front of clouds

Date	Mintage	VF20	XF40	MS60	MS63	MS65
ND-1974	90,000	—	—	—	20.00	25.00

KM# 204a 25 PISO

26.40 g., 0.900 Silver 0.7639 oz. ASW **Obv:** Shield of arms **Rev:** Bank in front of clouds

Date	Mintage	VF20	XF40	MS60	MS63	MS65
ND-1974	10,000	PF65 32.00				

KM# 211 25 PISO

25.00 g., 0.500 Silver 0.4019 oz. ASW **Obv:** Head of Emilio Aguinaldo 1/4 right **Rev:** Shield of arms

Date	Mintage	VF20	XF40	MS60	MS63	MS65
1975 FM (M)	10,000	—	—	—	14.00	17.00
1975 FM (U)	5,875	—	—	—	17.50	20.00
1975 FM (P)	37,000	PF65 17.00				

KM# 214 25 PISO

25.00 g., 0.500 Silver 0.4019 oz. ASW **Series:** F.A.O. **Obv:** Shield of arms **Rev:** Half figure with hat holding grain

Date	Mintage	VF20	XF40	MS60	MS63	MS65
1976 FM (M)	22,000	—	—	—	17.50	20.00
1976 FM (U)	1,826	—	—	—	20.00	22.50
1976 FM (P)	9,901	PF65 17.00				

KM# 250 10 PISO

22.00 g., Nickel, 36 mm. **Subject:** People Power Revolution **Obv:** Shield of arms divides date **Rev:** Group of people **Edge:** Reeded

Date	Mintage	VF20	XF40	MS60	MS63	MS65
1988	—	—	—	2.50	3.50	5.00

KM# 217 25 PISO

25.00 g., 0.500 Silver 0.4019 oz. ASW **Subject:** Banaue Rice Terraces **Obv:** Shield of arms **Rev:** Hilly designs within circle

Date	Mintage	VF20	XF40	MS60	MS63	MS65
1977 FM (M)	10,000	—	—	—	17.00	20.00
1977 FM (U)	354	—	—	—	35.00	40.00
1977 FM (P)	4,822	PF65 22.50				

KM# 221 25 PISO

25.00 g., 0.500 Silver 0.4019 oz. ASW **Subject:** 100th Anniversary - Birth of Quezon **Obv:** Shield of arms **Rev:** Monument divides dates within beaded circle

Date	Mintage	VF20	XF40	MS60	MS63	MS65
ND-1978 FM (U)	10,000	—	—	—	20.00	22.50
ND-1978 FM (P)	9,930	PF65 30.00				

KM# 228 25 PISO

25.00 g., 0.500 Silver 0.4019 oz. ASW **Subject:** UN Conference on Trade and Development **Obv:** Conference center buildings **Rev:** UN logo

Date	Mintage	VF20	XF40	MS60	MS63	MS65
1979 FM (U)	10,000	—	—	—	14.00	17.00
1979 FM (P)	7,093	PF65 22.50				

KM# 230 25 PISO

25.00 g., 0.500 Silver 0.4019 oz. ASW **Subject:** 100th Anniversary - Birth of Gen. Douglas MacArthur **Obv:** Uniformed figures **Rev:** Uniformed bust with pipe facing 1/4 left

Date	Mintage	VF20	XF40	MS60	MS63	MS65
ND-1980 FM (U)	9,800	—	—	22.50	30.00	40.00
ND-1980 FM (P)	6,318	PF65 55.00				

KM# 232 25 PISO
25.00 g., 0.500 Silver 0.4019 oz. ASW **Subject:** World Food Day **Obv:** Shield of arms **Rev:** Fish, corn, grain and fruit

Date	Mintage	VF20	XF40	MS60	MS63	MS65
1981 FM (U)	10,000	—	—	—	16.00	19.00
1981 FM (P)	3,033	PF65 31.75				

KM# 235 25 PISO
25.00 g., 0.500 Silver 0.4019 oz. ASW **Obv:** Shield of arms **Rev:** Conjoined heads of Marcos and Reagan right

Date	Mintage	VF20	XF40	MS60	MS63	MS65
1982	8,000	—	—	—	45.00	50.00
1982	250	PF65 450				

KM# 246 25 PISO
18.41 g., 0.925 Silver 0.5475 oz. ASW **Subject:** President Aquino's visit in Washington **Obv:** Head of President Aquino left **Rev:** Head of President Reagan right **Note:** Photo reduced.

Date	Mintage	VF20	XF40	MS60	MS63	MS65
1986	Est. 1000	PF63 225	PF65 250			

KM# 212 50 PISO
27.40 g., 0.925 Silver 0.8149 oz. ASW, 40 mm. **Subject:** 3rd Anniversary of the New Society **Obv:** Shield of arms **Rev:** Head of Marcos left

Date	Mintage	VF20	XF40	MS60	MS63	MS65
1975 FM (M)	10,000	—	—	—	27.00	32.00
1975 FM (U)	7,875	—	—	—	22.00	25.00
1975 FM (P)	54,000	PF65 25.00				

KM# 215 50 PISO
27.40 g., 0.925 Silver 0.8149 oz. ASW, 40 mm. **Subject:** I.M.F. Meeting **Obv:** Map **Rev:** Stylized star in center of world globe emblems

Date	Mintage	VF20	XF40	MS60	MS63	MS65
1976	5,477	PF65 37.00				
1976 FM (M)	10,000	—	—	—	20.00	25.00
1976 FM (U)	1,826	—	—	—	45.00	50.00
1976 FM (P)	15,000	PF65 32.00				

KM# 218 50 PISO
27.40 g., 0.925 Silver 0.8149 oz. ASW **Subject:** Inauguration of New Mint Facilities **Obv:** Shield of arms **Rev:** Two coins under star and building within circle

Date	Mintage	VF20	XF40	MS60	MS63	MS65
1977 FM (M)	10,000	—	—	25.00	32.00	35.00
1977 FM (U)	354	—	—	—	65.00	75.00
1977 FM (P)	6,704	PF65 32.50				

KM# 222 50 PISO
27.40 g., 0.925 Silver 0.8149 oz. ASW **Subject:** 100th Anniversary - Birth of Manuel L. Quezon **Obv:** Shield of arms **Rev:** Head right, dates and shield

Date	Mintage	VF20	XF40	MS60	MS63	MS65
ND-1978 FM (U)	10,000	—	—	—	32.50	35.00
ND-1978 FM (P)	9,969	PF65 37.00				

KM# 229 50 PISO
27.40 g., 0.925 Silver 0.8149 oz. ASW **Subject:** International Year of the Child **Obv:** Shield of arms **Rev:** Child's bust facing, logo at right

Date	Mintage	VF20	XF40	MS60	MS63	MS65
1979 FM (U)	10,000	—	—	—	30.00	32.50
1979 FM (P)	27,000	PF65 30.00				
1979 Piefort Proof	—	PF65 255				

KM# 233 50 PISO
27.40 g., 0.925 Silver 0.8149 oz. ASW **Subject:** Pope John Paul II Visit **Obv:** Standing figure praying **Rev:** Head 1/4 left

Date	Mintage	VF20	XF40	MS60	MS63	MS65
1981 FM (U)	10,000	—	—	—	60.00	75.00
1981 FM (P)	3,353	PF65 120				

KM# 236 50 PISO
27.40 g., 0.925 Silver 0.8149 oz. ASW **Subject:** 40th Anniversary of Bataan-Corregidor **Obv:** Shield of arms **Rev:** Conjoined military heads left

Date	Mintage	VF20	XF40	MS60	MS63	MS65
ND-1982 FM (U)	13,000	—	—	—	30.00	35.00
ND-1982 FM (P)	4,626	PF65 45.00				

KM# 245 100 PISO
25.00 g., 0.500 Silver 0.4019 oz. ASW **Subject:** 75th Anniversary - University of the Philippines **Obv:** Shield of arms **Rev:** Nude statue divides building above dates

Date	Mintage	VF20	XF40	MS60	MS63	MS65
ND-1983	15,000	—	—	—	32.00	35.00
ND-1983	2,000	PF65 46.00				

KM# 264 100 PISO
10.00 g., 0.925 Silver 0.2974 oz. ASW **Subject:** Papal Visit 1995-Pope John Paul II **Obv:** Shield of arms **Rev:** Head left

Date	Mintage	VF20	XF40	MS60	MS63	MS65
ND-1994	1,000	PF65 125				

KM# 279 100 PISO
16.73 g., 0.800 Silver 0.4303 oz. ASW **Subject:** Leyte Gulf Landing

Date	Mintage	VF20	XF40	MS60	MS63	MS65
ND(1994)	1,000	PF65 60.00				

KM# 254 150 PISO

16.82 g., 0.925 Silver 0.5002 oz. ASW **Subject:** Southeast Asian Games **Obv:** Shield of arms **Rev:** Official logo

Date	Mintage	VF20	XF40	MS60	MS63	MS65
1991 Prooflike	—	—	—	—	—	50.00
1991	5,000	PF65 45.00				

KM# 248 200 PISO

25.00 g., 0.925 Silver 0.7435 oz. ASW, 38 mm. **Subject:** World Wildlife Fund **Obv:** Shield of arms **Rev:** Mindoro Buffalo

Date	Mintage	VF20	XF40	MS60	MS63	MS65
1987	25,000	PF65 45.00				

KM# 252 200 PISO

25.00 g., 0.925 Silver 0.7435 oz. ASW **Subject:** Save the Children Fund **Obv:** Shield of arms **Rev:** Children playing

Date	Mintage	VF20	XF40	MS60	MS63	MS65
1990	Est. 20000	PF65 65.00				

KM# 265 200 PISO

15.56 g., 0.999 Silver 0.4998 oz. ASW **Subject:** Papal Visit 1995 **Obv:** Shield of arms **Rev:** Bust of John Paul II left **Note:** Similar to 100 Piso, KM#264.

Date	Mintage	VF20	XF40	MS60	MS63	MS65
ND-1994	1,000	PF65 150				

KM# 249 500 PISO

28.00 g., 0.925 Silver 0.8327 oz. ASW **Subject:** People Power Revolution **Obv:** Shield of arms divides date **Rev:** Group of people

Date	Mintage	VF20	XF40	MS60	MS63	MS65
1988	Est. 7500	PF65 70.00				

KM# 280 500 PISO

23.10 g., 0.925 Silver 0.687 oz. ASW **Subject:** Leyte Gulf Landing

Date	Mintage	VF20	XF40	MS60	MS63	MS65
ND(1994)	1,000	PF65 100				

KM# A276 500 PISO

28.28 g., 0.925 Silver 0.841 oz. ASW **Subject:** Centennial - Jose Rizal Martydom

Date	Mintage	VF20	XF40	MS60	MS63	MS65
ND1996	2,625	PF65 250				

KM# 276 500 PISO

28.28 g., 0.925 Silver 0.841 oz. ASW **Subject:** Centennial - Andres Bonifacio 1897-1997

Date	Mintage	VF20	XF40	MS60	MS63	MS65
ND-1997	2,625	PF65 125				
ND-1997 Prooflike	—	—	—	—	65.00	—

KM# 274 500 PISO

28.28 g., 0.925 Silver 0.841 oz. ASW **Subject:** Carlos P. Romulo Centennial **Obv:** Shield above value **Rev:** Bust left and dates

Date	Mintage	VF20	XF40	MS60	MS63	MS65
ND-1998	Est. 2100	PF65 80.00				

KM# 277 500 PISO

28.28 g., 0.925 Silver 0.841 oz. ASW **Subject:** Centennial - Emilio F. Aguinaldo 1898-1998

Date	Mintage	VF20	XF40	MS60	MS63	MS65
ND-1998	2,100	PF65 100				

KM# 275 500 PISO

28.28 g., 0.925 Silver 0.841 oz. ASW **Subject:** 50th Anniversary - Central Bank **Obv:** Old and new bank buildings **Rev:** Old and new bank seals

Date	Mintage	VF20	XF40	MS60	MS63	MS65
ND-1999	Est. 5000	PF65 50.00				

KM# 213 1000 PISO

9.95 g., 0.900 Gold 0.2879 oz. AGW **Subject:** 3rd Anniversary of the New Society **Obv:** Shield **Rev:** Head left

Date	Mintage	VF20	XF40	MS60	MS63	MS65
1975	23,000	—	—	—	400	475
1975	13,000	PF63 400	PF65 500			

KM# 281 1000 PISO

31.10 g., 0.999 Silver 0.9989 oz. ASW **Subject:** Leyte Gulf Landing

Date	Mintage	VF20	XF40	MS60	MS63	MS65
ND(1994)	1,000	PF65 125				

KM# 216 1500 PISO

20.55 g., 0.900 Gold 0.5946 oz. AGW **Subject:** I.M.F. Meeting **Obv:** Map **Rev:** Stylized star in center of world globe emblems

Date	Mintage	VF20	XF40	MS60	MS63	MS65
1976	5,500	—	—	—	—	1,150
1976	6,500	PF65 1,100				

KM# 219 1500 PISO

20.55 g., 0.900 Gold 0.5946 oz. AGW **Subject:** 5th Anniversary of the New Society **Obv:** Head facing **Rev:** Redesigned bank seal within circle

Date	Mintage	VF20	XF40	MS60	MS63	MS65
ND-1977	4,000	—	—	—	—	1,100
ND-1977	6,000	PF65 1,150				

KM# 223 1500 PISO

20.55 g., 0.900 Gold 0.5946 oz. AGW **Subject:** Inauguration of New Mint Facilities **Obv:** Flowers **Rev:** Bank, gold bars, paper money and coins

Date	Mintage	VF20	XF40	MS60	MS63	MS65
1978	3,000	—	—	—	—	1,100
1978	3,000	PF65 1,150				

KM# 234 1500 PISO

9.95 g., 0.900 Gold 0.2879 oz. AGW **Subject:** Pope John Paul II Visit **Obv:** Standing figure in prayer, crowd in background **Rev:** Bust 3/4 left

Date	Mintage	VF20	XF40	MS60	MS63	MS65
1980	—	PF65 1,825				
1981	1,000	PF65 1,100				
1982	—	PF65 1,200				

KM# 237 1500 PISO
9.78 g., 0.900 Gold 0.283 oz. AGW **Subject:** 40th Anniversary of Bataan-Corregidor **Obv:** Shield of arms **Rev:** Conjoined military heads left

Date	Mintage	VF20	XF40	MS60	MS63	MS65
ND-1982 FM (U)	1,000	—	—	—	—	525
ND-1982 FM (P)	445	PF65 575				

KM# 282 2000 PISO
10.00 g., 0.500 Gold 0.1608 oz. AGW, 27 mm. **Subject:** Asia Pacific Economic Cooperation **Obv:** Head of Fidel Ramos 3/4 right **Rev:** World globe logo and value **Edge:** Reeded

Date	Mintage	VF20	XF40	MS60	MS63	MS65
1996	3,000	PF65 300				

KM# 231 2500 PISO
14.57 g., 0.500 Gold 0.2342 oz. AGW **Subject:** 100th Anniversary - Birth of General Douglas MacArthur **Obv:** Military standing figures **Rev:** Uniformed bust with pipe facing 1/4 left

Date	Mintage	VF20	XF40	MS60	MS63	MS65
ND-1980 FM (P)	3,073	PF63 400	PF65 475			

KM# 247 2500 PISO
15.00 g., 0.500 Gold 0.2411 oz. AGW **Subject:** President Aquino's Visit in Washington **Obv:** Bust of President Aquino left **Rev:** Bust of President Reagan right

Date	Mintage	VF20	XF40	MS60	MS63	MS65
1986	Est. 250	PF63 725	PF65 800			

KM# 266 2500 PISO
7.98 g., 0.9167 Gold 0.2352 oz. AGW **Subject:** Papal Visit 1995 **Obv:** Shield of arms **Rev:** Pope John Paul II left **Note:** Similar to 100 Piso, KM#264.

Date	Mintage	VF20	XF40	MS60	MS63	MS65
ND-1994	—	PF65 600				

KM# 220 5000 PISO
68.74 g., 0.900 Gold 1.989 oz. AGW **Subject:** 5th Anniversary of the New Society **Obv:** Design within beaded circle **Rev:** Conjoined busts of Ferdindand and Imelda Marcos right

Date	Mintage	VF20	XF40	MS60	MS63	MS65
ND-1977 FM (U)	100	—	—	—	—	4,000
ND-1977 FM (P)	3,832	PF65 3,500				

KM# 267 5000 PISO
16.81 g., 0.925 Gold 0.4999 oz. AGW **Subject:** Papal Visit 1995 **Obv:** Shield of arms **Rev:** Bust of Pope John Paul II left **Note:** Similar to 100 Piso, KM#264.

Date	Mintage	VF20	XF40	MS60	MS63	MS65
ND-1994	—	PF65 925				

KM# 283 5000 PISO
Gold **Subject:** 50th Anniversary - Central Bank in the Philippines

Date	Mintage	VF20	XF40	MS60	MS63	MS65
1999	2,000	PF65 850				

KM# 255 10000 PESOS
33.55 g., 0.925 Gold 0.9978 oz. AGW **Subject:** People Power 1992 **Obv:** Bust of Aquino facing 3/4 right **Rev:** Map, scroll, dates and dove

Date	Mintage	VF20	XF40	MS60	MS63	MS65
ND-1992	1,600	PF65 1,850				

PATTERNS

Including off metal strikes

KM#	Date	Mintage	Identification	Mkt Val
Pn20	1922	—	Centavo. Silver. KM#163.	—
Pn21	ND(1965-66)	—	Peso. Silver. Marcos.	—
Pn22	1966	—	Centavo. Copper. Central Bank.	120
Pn23	1966	—	5 Centavos. Brass.	120
Pn24	1966	—	5 Centavos. Copper.	120
Pn25	1966	—	10 Centavos. Silver.	145
Pn26	1966	—	10 Centavos. Copper.	120
Pn27	1966	—	25 Centavos. Brass.	120
PnA28	1966	—	50 Centavos. Copper. Similar to Pn28. Conjoined busts of Ferdinand and Imelda Marcos.	110
PnB28	1966	—	50 Centavos. Copper. As Pn28.	110
Pn28	1966	—	50 Centavos. Silver.	220
Pn29	1966	—	Piso. Silver.	220
Pn30	1966	—	Peso. Silver. Ferd and Imelda Marcos.	—
PnA31	1966	—	Piso. Copper. Similar to Pn28. As Pn38.	170
PnB31	1966	—	Piso. Brass. Similar to Pn38 wtihout eagle and lion on arms.	170
Pn31	1967	—	Sentimo. Copper.	120
Pn32	1967	—	5 Sentimos.	145
Pn33	1967	—	5 Sentimos. Copper. Similar to Pn32. Similar to Pn27.	145
PnA34	1967	—	25 Centavos. Copper. Design similar to Pn28, legend as Pn34. Similar to Pn27.	120
PnB34	1967	—	10 Centavos. Bronze. Bust of Francisco Baltazar.	145
Pn34	1967	—	25 Sentimos. Silver.	145
PnA35	1967	—	50 Centavos. Copper. As Pn36. Small conjoined busts of Ferdinand and Imelda Marcos.	145
PnB35	1967	—	50 Sentimos. Bronze. Similar to Pn28. Bust of Juan Luna.	170
Pn35	1967	—	50 Sentimos. Copper. Large conjoined busts of Ferdinand and Imelda Marcos.	170
Pn36	1967	—	50 Sentimos. Silver. Del Pilar left. Del Pilar.	145
Pn37	1967	—	50 Sentimos. Copper. Del Pilar left. Del Pilar.	145
PnA38	1967	—	Peso. Copper. Similar to KM#195.	170
PnB38	1967	—	Peso. Brass. Similar to KM#195.	170
Pn38	1968	—	Peso. Silver. Sower walking left.	245
Pn39	1968	—	Piso. Silver. Sower walking right.	145
PnA40	1969	—	Peso. Copper. Similar to KM#195. As Pn40.	170
Pn40	1969	—	Piso. Silver. Dated 1966. Aquinaldo.	245
Pn41	ND-1970	—	Peso. Copper. Similar to KM#195. Conjoined busts of Marcos and Pope Paul VI left.	115
Pn42	1970	—	Peso. Copper. Similar to KM#195. Bust of Pope Paul VI 3/4 right.	115

PIEDFORT

All standard metals unless otherwise indicated

KM#	Date	Mintage	Identification	Mkt Val
P1	1979	—	50 Piso. Silver. KM#229.	225

TRIAL STRIKES

KM#	Date	Mintage	Identification	Mkt Val
TS8	1967	—	Peso. Brass. KM#195. Bataan Day.	120

MINT SETS

KM#	Date	Mintage	Identification	Issue Price	Mkt Val
MS1	1936 (3)	—	KM#176-178	—	700
MS2	1947 (2)	—	KM#184-185	—	40.00
MS3	1958 (4)	—	KM#186-190	—	3.50
MS4	1970 (2)	—	KM#202-202a	—	32.50
MS5	1975 (8)	5,877	KM#205-208, 209.1, 210.1, 211-212. Enclosed in Franklin Mint folder	33.50	55.00
MS6	1975 (8)	3,850	KM#205-208, 209.1, 210.1, 211-212, Specimen Set	—	70.00
MS7	1976 (8)	1,826	KM#205-208, 209.1, 210.1, 214-215. Enclosed in Franklin Mint folder	—	100
MS8	1976 (8)	10,000	KM#205-208, 209.1, 210.1, 214-215	—	55.00
MS9	1977 (8)	354	KM#205-208, 209.1, 210.1, 217-218; Enclosed in Franklin Mint folder.	—	100
MSA11	1977 (8)	10,000	KM#205-208, 209.1, 210.1, 217-218	—	55.00
MS11	1978 (2)	10,000	KM#205-210, 221-222	—	60.00
MS12	1979 (8)	10,000	KM#209.2-210.2, 224-229	—	62.50
MS13	1980 (7)	9,800	KM#209.2-210.2, 224-227, 230	—	50.00
MS14	1981 (8)	10,000	KM#209.2-210.2, 224-227, 232-233	—	100
MS15	1982 (5)	—	KM#209.2, 224-227	—	2.50
MS16	1983 (5)	—	KM#238-239, 240.2, 241, 242.1, 243-245BRM	—	35.00
MS17	1983 (5)	—	KM#238-239, 240.1, 241, 242.1, 243-244	—	15.00
MS18	1983 (7)	—	KM#238-239, 240.2, 241.1, 242.1, 243-244	—	10.00
MS19	1985 (6)	—	KM#238-239, 240.2, 241.1, 242.1, 243-244	—	10.00
MS20	1986 (7)	—	KM#238-239, 240.2, 241.1, 243-244	—	5.00
MS21	1987 (6)	—	KM#238-239, 240.2, 241.1, 242.1, 243-244	—	20.00
MS22	1988 (6)	—	KM#238-239, 240.2, 241.1, 242.1, 243-244	—	20.00
MS23	1989 (6)	—	KM#238-239, 240.2, 241.1, 242.1, 243-244	—	15.00
MS24	1989 (7)	—	KM#238-239, 240.2, 241, 242.1, 243-244	—	5.00
MS25	1990 (6)	—	KM#238-239, 240.2, 241.1, 242.1, 243-244	—	20.00
MS26	1990 (6)	—	KM#238-239, 240.2, 241.1, 242.1, 243-244	—	20.00
MS27	1991 (8)	—	KM#238-239, 240.2, 241.2, 242.3, 243.2, 258-259	—	35.00
MS28	1992 (8)	—	KM#238-239, 240.2, 241.2, 242.3, 243.2, 258-259	—	35.00

KM#	Date	Mintage	Identification	Issue Price	Mkt Val
MS29	1995 (6)	—	KM#268-273	—	12.00
MS30	1996 (6)	—	KM#268-273	—	12.00
MS31	1997 (6)	—	KM#268-273	—	20.00
MS32	1998 (5)	—	KM#268-269, 271-273	—	20.00
MS33	1999 (5)	—	KM#268-269, 271-273	—	20.00
MS34	2000 (5)	—	KM#268-269, 271, 273, 278	—	10.00

PROOF SETS

KM#	Date	Mintage	Identification	Issue Price	Mkt Val
PS1	1903 (7)	2,558	KM#162-168	—	1,900
PS1i	1903 (7)	Inc. above	KM#162-168 (impaired)	—	775
PS2	1904 (7)	1,355	KM#162-168	—	2,000
PS2i	1904 (7)	Inc. above	KM#162-168 (impaired)	—	950
PS3	1905 (7)	471	KM#162-168	—	4,250
PS3i	1905 (7)	Inc. above	KM#162-168 (impaired)	—	2,500
PS4	1906 (7)	500	KM#162-168	—	4,000
PS4i	1906 (7)	Inc. above	KM#162-168 (impaired)	—	2,080
PS5	1908 (7)	500	KM#162-164, 169-172	—	3,500
PS5i	1908 (7)	Inc. above	KM#162-164, 169-172 (impaired)	—	2,000
PS6	1958 (4)	—	KM#186-190, Not confirmed	—	5.00
PS7	1974 (6)	10,000	KM#196-200, 203; Not released to the general public	—	60.00
PS8	1975 (8)	36,516	KM#205-208, 209.1-210.1, 211-212	67.00	50.00
PS9	1975 (6)	—	KM#205-208, 209.1-210.1	—	16.00
PS10	1976 (8)	9,901	KM#205-208, 209.1-210.1, 214-215	67.00	60.00
PS11	1977 (8)	4,822	KM#205-208, 209.1-210.1, 217-218	70.00	70.00
PS12	1978 (8)	4,792	KM#205-208, 209.1-210.1, 220-221	70.00	2,950
PS13	1978 (2)	3,911	KM#221-222	46.00	60.00
PS14	1979 (8)	3,645	KM#209.2-210.2, 224-229	68.00	67.50
PS15	1979 (2)	2,448	KM#228-229	47.50	30.00
PS16	1980 (7)	3,133	KM#209.2-210.2, 224-227, 230	65.00	77.50
PS17	1981 (8)	1,795	KM#209.2-210.2, 224-227, 232-233	—	160
PS18	1981 (2)	—	KM#232, 233	—	130
PS19	1982 (7)	—	KM#209.2-210.2, 224-227, 236	52.00	82.00
PS20	1983 (6)	—	KM#238-239, 240.1, 241, 242.1, 243-245	50.00	65.00
PS21	1986 (2)	—	KM#246-247	—	950
PS22	ND(1994) (3)	—	KM264-265, 267 Papal Visit 1995	—	1,150
PS23	1994 (4)	—	KM#263, 279-281 50th Anniversary of Leyte Gulf Landings	—	300

CULION ISLAND

The Culion Leper Colony was established around 1903 on the island of Culion about 150 miles southeast of Manila by the Commission of Public Health. The first issue of coins valid only in the colony was produced by a private firm, Frank & Company. Later issues were struck at the Manila Mint.

MINT MARK

PM = Philippine Mint at Manila

MONETARY SYSTEM

100 Centavos = 1 Peso

CULION LEPER COLONY

Philippine Commission of Public Health

LEPROSARIUM COINAGE

KM# 1 1/2 CENTAVO

Aluminum, 19.5 mm. **Obv:** Value **Rev:** Caduceus

Date	Mintage	F12	VF20	XF40	MS60	MS63
1913	17,000	—	—	2.50	7.00	8.00

Note: Some authorities doubt that this coin circulated

KM# 2 CENTAVO

Aluminum, 22.8 mm.

Date	Mintage	G4	VG8	F12	VF20	XF40
1913	33,000	50.00	60.00	260	325	500

KM# 3 CENTAVO

Copper-Nickel, 21.2 mm. **Obv:** Bust 1/4 right **Rev:** Eagle above shield **Note:** Similar to KM#4 but first die, better strike.

Date	Mintage	G4	VG8	F12	VF20	XF40
1927 PM	30,000	10.00	15.00	30.00	60.00	130

Note: Type I - One-button coat, legible motto, "7" in date over "T" in Centavo, straight "S

KM# 4 CENTAVO

Copper-Nickel, 21.2 mm. **Obv:** Bust 1/4 right **Rev:** Eagle with wings open above shield **Note:** Second die, poor strike. This coin exists with thick and thin planchets. Telted "S" in shield.

Date	Mintage	G4	VG8	F12	VF20	XF40
1927 PM	Inc. above	12.00	15.00	30.00	75.00	125

Note: Type II - One-button coat, illegible motto, end of ribbon two widths from shield edge, "7" over "N"

KM# A5 CENTAVO

Copper-Nickel, 21.2 mm.

Date	Mintage	G4	VG8	F12	VF20	XF40
1927 PM	Inc. above	35.00	50.00	85.00	150	250

Note: Type III - Two-button coat, illegible motto, end of ribbon one width from shield edge, straight "S" in shield.

KM# 5 CENTAVO

Copper-Nickel **Obv:** Bust of Rizal in circle **Rev:** Legend **Rev. Legend:** PHILIPPINE HEALTH SERVICE/LEPER COIN ONE CENTAVO

Date	Mintage	G4	VG8	F12	VF20	XF40
1930 Unique	—	—	—	—	—	—

KM# 6 5 CENTAVOS

Aluminum, 26 mm. **Obv:** Value, legend **Rev:** Caduceus

Date	Mintage	G4	VG8	F12	VF20	XF40
1913	6,600	60.00	100	150	250	600

KM# 7 5 CENTAVOS

Copper-Nickel, 24.6 mm. **Obv:** Bust 1/4 right **Rev:** Eagle with wings open above shield

Date	Mintage	G4	VG8	F12	VF20	XF40
1927	16,000	3.00	5.00	10.00	25.00	40.00

KM# 8 10 CENTAVOS

Aluminum, 29 mm. **Obv:** Value **Rev:** Caduceus **Note:** Similar to 1/2 Centavo, KM#1.

Date	Mintage	G4	VG8	F12	VF20	XF40
1913	6,600	15.00	40.00	65.00	150	—

KM# 9 10 CENTAVOS

Aluminum, 29.8 mm. **Obv:** Value **Rev:** Caduceus **Note:** Similar to 1 Peso, KM#14.

Date	Mintage	G4	VG8	F12	VF20	XF40
1920	20,000	5.00	25.00	35.00	60.00	100

KM# 10 10 CENTAVOS

Copper-Nickel, 27 mm. **Obv:** Bust 1/4 left within circle **Rev:** Value within circle

Date	Mintage	VG8	F12	VF20	XF40	MS60
1930	17,000	—	5.00	15.00	22.00	100

Note: One pattern in copper, has been authenticated by ANACS

KM# 11 20 CENTAVOS

Aluminum, 32 mm. **Obv:** Value **Rev:** Caduceus **Note:** Similar to 1/2 Centavo, KM#1.

Date	Mintage	G4	VG8	F12	VF20	XF40
1913	10,000	35.00	80.00	100	150	1,000

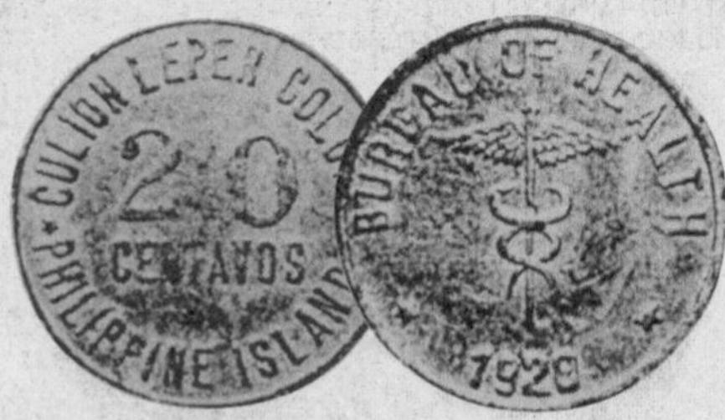

KM# 12 20 CENTAVOS

Aluminum, 32.3 mm. **Obv:** Value **Rev:** Caduceus

Date	Mintage	G4	VG8	F12	VF20	XF40
1920	10,000	8.00	25.00	35.00	70.00	175

KM# 13 20 CENTAVOS

Copper-Nickel, 31.8 mm. **Obv:** Value, legend **Rev:** Caduceus

Date	Mintage	VG8	F12	VF20	XF40	MS60
1922 PM	10,000	—	17.50	25.00	40.00	—

Note: This coin exists with thick and thin planchets, normal & recut dates.

KM# 14 PESO

Aluminum, 35.4 mm. **Obv:** Value **Rev:** Caduceus

Date	Mintage	VG8	F12	VF20	XF40	MS60
1913	8,600	10.00	17.50	35.00	45.00	—

Note: This coin exists with thick and thin planchets

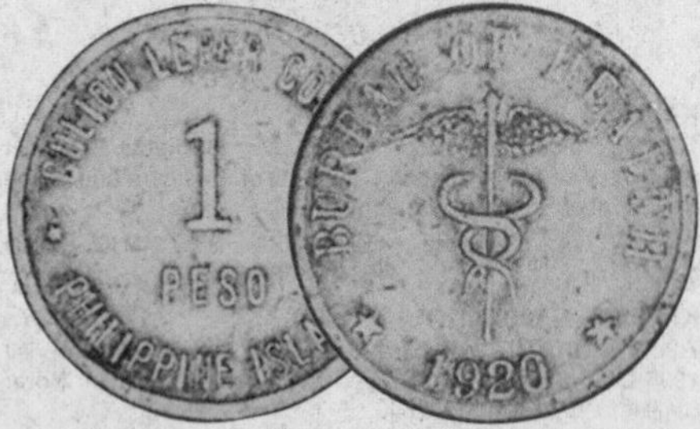

KM# 15 PESO

Aluminum, 35.4 mm. **Obv:** Value **Rev:** Caduceus

Date	Mintage	VG8	F12	VF20	XF40	MS60
1920	4,000	15.00	20.00	45.00	125	—

Note: Pointed serif on "1", (narrow numerals)

Date	Mintage	VG8	F12	VF20	XF40	MS60
1920	—	80.00	100	—	550	—

Note: Blunt serif on "1" (rounder numberals)

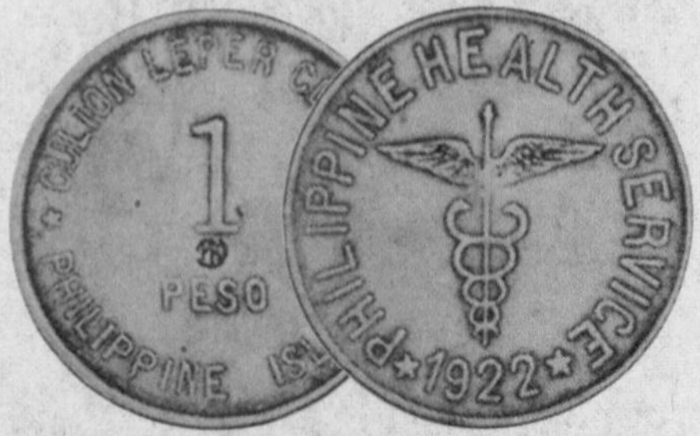

KM# 16 PESO
Copper-Nickel, 35.2 mm. **Obv:** Value **Rev:** Caduceus **Note:** Varieties exist.

Date	Mintage	VG8	F12	VF20	XF40	MS60
1922	8,280	—	10.00	30.00	60.00	—

KM# 17 PESO
Copper-Nickel, 35.2 mm. **Obv:** Value **Rev:** Caduceus with curved wings **Note:** Similar to KM#16, but caduceus has curved wings.

Date	Mintage	VG8	F12	VF20	XF40	MS60
1922 PM	Inc. above	—	—	300	375	—
Note: Curved Wing						

KM# 18 PESO
Copper-Nickel, 35.4 mm. **Obv:** Bust 3/4 right **Rev:** Eagle with wings open above shield

Date	Mintage	VG8	F12	VF20	XF40	MS60
1925	20,000	—	5.00	10.00	25.00	250

PITCAIRN ISLANDS

A small volcanic island, along with the uninhabited islands of Oeno, Henderson, and Ducie, constitute the British Colony of Pitcairn Islands. The main island has an area of about 2 sq. mi. (5 sq. km.) and a population of *68. It is located 1350 miles southeast of Tahiti. The islanders subsist on fishing, garden produce and crops. The sale of postage stamps and carved curios to passing ships brings cash income.

Discovered in 1767 by a British naval officer, Pitcairn was not occupied until 1790 when Fletcher Christian and nine mutineers from the British ship, *HMS Bounty*, along with some Tahitian men and women went ashore, and survived in obscurity until discovered by American whalers in 1808.

Adamstown is the chief settlement, located on the north coast, one of the few places that island-made longboats can land. The primary religion is Seventh-day Adventist and a public school provides basic education. In 1898 the settlement was placed under the jurisdiction of the Commissioner for the Western Pacific. Since 1970 this British settlement has been governed through a locally elected council under a governor.

New Zealand currency has been used since July 10, 1967.

BRITISH COLONY

REGULAR COINAGE

KM# 3 DOLLAR
Copper-Nickel, 38.5 mm. **Ruler:** Elizabeth II **Subject:** Drafting of Constitution, 1838-1988 **Obv:** Crowned bust right **Rev:** Sailing ship

Date	Mintage	VF20	XF40	MS60	MS63	MS65
ND-1988	—	—	—	2.00	4.00	6.00

KM# 3a DOLLAR
28.28 g., 0.925 Silver 0.841 oz. ASW, 38.5 mm. **Ruler:** Elizabeth II **Subject:** Drafting of constitution, 1838-1988 **Obv:** Crowned bust right **Rev:** Sailing ship

Date	Mintage	VF20	XF40	MS60	MS63	MS65
ND-1988	—	PF63 32.00	PF65 37.00	PF67 42.00		

KM# 4 DOLLAR
Copper-Nickel, 38.5 mm. **Ruler:** Elizabeth II **Subject:** HMAV Bounty, 1789-1989 **Obv:** Crowned bust right **Rev:** Sailing ship

Date	Mintage	VF20	XF40	MS60	MS63	MS65
ND-1989	50,000	—	—	2.00	4.00	6.00

KM# 4a DOLLAR
28.28 g., 0.925 Silver 0.841 oz. ASW, 38.5 mm. **Ruler:** Elizabeth II **Subject:** HMAV Bounty, 1789-1989 **Obv:** Crowned bust right **Rev:** Sailing ship

Date	Mintage	VF20	XF40	MS60	MS63	MS65
ND-1989	20,000	PF63 30.00	PF65 35.00	PF67 40.00		

KM# 7 DOLLAR
Copper-Nickel, 38.5 mm. **Ruler:** Elizabeth II **Subject:** Establishment of Settlement, 1790-1990 **Obv:** Crowned bust right **Rev:** Ship in flames

Date	Mintage	VF20	XF40	MS60	MS63	MS65
ND-1990	—	—	—	7.00	10.00	12.00

KM# 7a DOLLAR
28.28 g., 0.925 Silver 0.841 oz. ASW, 38.5 mm. **Ruler:** Elizabeth II **Subject:** Establishment of Settlement, 1790-1990 **Obv:** Crowned bust right **Rev:** Ship in flames

Date	Mintage	VF20	XF40	MS60	MS63	MS65
ND-1990	10,000	PF63 35.00	PF65 40.00	PF67 45.00		

KM# 10 DOLLAR
Copper-Nickel, 38.5 mm. **Ruler:** Elizabeth II **Subject:** British Queen Mother **Obv:** Crowned bust right **Rev:** Queen Mother at right, Order of the Garter at left within beaded circle **Note:** Struck at the British Royal Mint.

Date	Mintage	VF20	XF40	MS60	MS63	MS65
1997	—	—	—	3.00	5.00	7.00

KM# 11 5 DOLLARS
31.56 g., 0.925 Silver 0.9386 oz. ASW, 38.5 mm. **Ruler:** Elizabeth II **Subject:** Queen Mother **Obv:** Crowned bust right **Rev:** Queen Mother and the Order of the Garter at left within beaded circle **Edge:** Reeded

Date	Mintage	VF20	XF40	MS60	MS63	MS65
1997	—	PF63 30.00	PF65 35.00	PF67 40.00		

KM# 70 5 DOLLARS
Silver, 39 mm. **Ruler:** Elizabeth II **Subject:** Queen Mother **Obv:** Bust crowned right **Rev:** Earl of Strathmore's bust **Edge:** Reeded

Date	Mintage	VF20	XF40	MS60	MS63	MS65
1999	—	PF63 30.00	PF65 35.00	PF67 40.00		

KM# 13 10 DOLLARS
Silver **Ruler:** Elizabeth II **Subject:** 50th Wedding Anniversary of Queen Elizabeth II and Philip **Obv:** Bust right, legend above, date below, gold plate on shield **Rev:** Queen Elizabeth II and Philip with Prince Charles in baby buggy, legend above, value below

Date	Mintage	VF20	XF40	MS60	MS63	MS65
1997	—	PF63 45.00	PF65 50.00	PF67 60.00		

KM# 53 10 DOLLARS
28.28 g., 0.925 Silver 0.841 oz. ASW, 38.6 mm. **Ruler:** Elizabeth II **Subject:** 50th Wedding Anniversary **Rev:** Prince Edward in pram

Date	Mintage	VF20	XF40	MS60	MS63	MS65
1997	—	PF63 35.00	PF65 40.00	PF67 45.00		

KM# 1 50 DOLLARS
155.60 g., 0.999 Silver 4.9976 oz. ASW, 65 mm. **Ruler:** Elizabeth II **Subject:** Drafting of Constitution, 1838-1988 **Obv:** Crowned bust right **Rev:** Sailing ship **Note:** Illustration reduced.

Date	Mintage	VF20	XF40	MS60	MS63	MS65
ND-1988	10,000	PF63 120	PF65 140	PF67 170		

KM# 5 50 DOLLARS
155.60 g., 0.999 Silver 4.9976 oz. ASW, 65 mm. **Ruler:** Elizabeth II **Subject:** HMAV Bounty, 1789-1989 **Obv:** Crowned bust right **Rev:** Sailing ship **Note:** Similar to 250 Dollars, KM#6.

Date	Mintage	VF20	XF40	MS60	MS63	MS65
ND-1989	10,000	PF63 120	PF65 140	PF67 170		

KM# 8 50 DOLLARS

155.50 g., 0.999 Silver 4.9944 oz. ASW, 65 mm. **Ruler:** Elizabeth II **Subject:** Establishment of Settlement **Rev:** Burning of the Bounty **Note:** Illustration reduced

Date	Mintage	VF20	XF40	MS60	MS63	MS65
1990	2,500	PF63 150	PF65 170	PF67 200		

KM# 2 250 DOLLARS

15.98 g., 0.917 Gold 0.4711 oz. AGW **Ruler:** Elizabeth II **Subject:** Drafting of Constitution, 1838-1988 **Obv:** Crowned bust right **Rev:** Sailing ship

Date	Mintage	VF20	XF40	MS60	MS63	MS65
ND-1988	2,500	PF63 850	PF65 950	PF67 1,150		

KM# 6 250 DOLLARS

15.98 g., 0.917 Gold 0.4711 oz. AGW **Ruler:** Elizabeth II **Subject:** HMAV Bounty, 1789-1989 **Obv:** Crowned bust right **Rev:** Ship

Date	Mintage	VF20	XF40	MS60	MS63	MS65
ND-1989	2,500	PF63 800	PF65 900	PF67 1,100		

KM# 9 250 DOLLARS

15.98 g., 0.917 Gold 0.4711 oz. AGW **Ruler:** Elizabeth II **Subject:** Establishment of Settlement, 1790-1990 **Obv:** Crowned bust right **Rev:** Burning of the Bounty, ship in flames within circle

Date	Mintage	VF20	XF40	MS60	MS63	MS65
ND-1990	500	PF63 900	PF65 1,000	PF67 1,200		

POLAND

The Republic of Poland, located in central Europe, has an area of 120,725 sq. mi. (312,680 sq. km.) and a population of *38.2 million. Capital: Warszawa (Warsaw). The economy is essentially agricultural, but industrial activity provides the products for foreign trade. Machinery, coal, coke, iron, steel and transport equipment are exported.

Poland, which began as a Slavic duchy in the 10th century and reached its peak of power between the 14th and 16th centuries, has had a turbulent history of invasion, occupation or partition by Mongols, Turkey, Transylvania, Sweden, Austria, Prussia and Russia.

The first partition took place in 1772. Prussia took Polish Pomerania, Russia took part of the eastern provinces, and Austria occupied Galicia and its capital city Lwów. The second partition occurred in 1793 when Russia took another slice of the eastern provinces and Prussia took what remained of western Poland. The third partition, 1795, literally removed Poland from the map. Russia took what was left of the eastern provinces. Prussia seized most of central Poland, including Warsaw. Austria took what was left of the south. Napoleon restored to Poland much of the territory lost to Prussia and Austria, but after his defeat another partition returned the Duchy of Warsaw to Prussia, made Kraków into a tiny republic, and declared what remained to be the Kingdom of Poland under the czar and in permanent union with Russia.

Poland re-emerged as an independent state recognized by the Treaty of Versailles on June 28, 1919, and maintained its independence until 1939 when it was invaded by, and partitioned between, Germany and Russia. Poland's present boundaries were determined by the U.S.-British-Russian agreement of Aug. 16, 1945. The Government of National Unity was replaced when the Polish Communist-Socialist faction claimed victory at the polls in 1947 and established a Peoples Democratic Republic' of the Soviet type in 1952. On December 29, 1989 Poland was proclaimed as the Republic of Poland.

MINT MARKS

(b) - Basel
CHI - Valcambi, Switzerland
FF - Stuttgart Germany 1916-1917
(kr) - Kremnica
(lgd) - Leningrad
MV, MW, MW-monogram - Warsaw Mint, 1965-
(w) - Warsaw 1923-39 (opened officially in 1924)
arrow mintmark

Other letters appearing with date denote the Mintmaster at the time the coin was struck.

GERMAN OCCUPATION

REGENCY COINAGE

100 Fenigow = 1 Marka

Y# 4 FENIG

1.97 g., Iron, 15 mm. **Obv:** Value **Rev:** Crowned eagle with wings open

Date	Mintage	F12	VF20	XF40	MS60	MS63
1918 FF	51,484,000	0.50	1.00	3.00	10.00	35.00
1918 FF	—	PF63 200				

Y# 5 5 FENIGÓW

2.53 g., Iron, 18 mm. **Obv:** Value **Rev:** Crowned eagle with wings open

Date	Mintage	F12	VF20	XF40	MS60	MS63
1917 FF	18,700,000	0.25	0.75	1.50	5.00	10.00
1917 FF	—	PF63 100				
1918 FF	22,690,000	0.25	0.75	1.50	5.00	10.00
1918 FF	—	PF63 200				

Y# 6 10 FENIGÓW

3.56 g., Iron, 21 mm. **Obv:** Value **Rev:** Crowned eagle with wings open

Date	Mintage	F12	VF20	XF40	MS60	MS63
1917 FF	33,000,000	2.50	5.00	10.00	25.00	45.00
Note: Obverse legend touches edge						
1917 FF	—	PF63 100				
1917 FF	Inc. above	0.25	0.75	1.25	3.50	7.50
Note: Obverse legend away from edge						
1918 FF	14,990,000	0.50	1.00	2.00	5.00	10.00
Note: Obverse legend away from edge						
1918 FF	—	PF63 200				
Note: Obverse legend away from edge						

Y# 6a 10 FENIGÓW

3.56 g., Zinc, 21 mm. **Obv:** Value **Rev:** Crowned eagle with wings open **Note:** Error planchet.

Date	Mintage	F12	VF20	XF40	MS60	MS63
1917 FF	—	25.00	45.00	85.00	175	—

Y# 7 20 FENIGÓW

3.90 g., Iron, 23 mm. **Obv:** Value **Rev:** Crowned eagle with wings open

Date	Mintage	F12	VF20	XF40	MS60	MS63
1917 FF	1,900,000	2.00	4.00	6.00	9.00	20.00
1918 FF	19,260,000	0.75	1.25	2.50	6.50	12.00

Y# 7a 20 FENIGÓW

Zinc **Obv:** Value **Rev:** Crowned eagle with wings open **Note:** Error planchet.

Date	Mintage	F12	VF20	XF40	MS60	MS63
1917 FF	—	35.00	65.00	120	250	—

REPUBLIC

STANDARD COINAGE

100 Groszy = 1 Zloty

Y# 8 GROSZ

1.50 g., Brass, 14.7 mm. **Obv:** Crowned eagle with wings open **Rev:** Stylized value **Note:** Some authorities consider this strike a pattern.

Date	Mintage	F12	VF20	XF40	MS60	MS63
1923	—	—	—	—	150	275

Y# 8a GROSZ

1.50 g., Bronze, 14.7 mm. **Obv:** Crowned eagle with wings open **Rev:** Stylized value

Date	Mintage	F12	VF20	XF40	MS60	MS63
1923	30,000,000	0.50	1.00	4.00	16.00	28.00
1925 (w)	40,000,000	0.50	1.00	3.50	15.00	25.00
1927 (w)	17,000,000	0.50	1.00	4.00	16.00	28.00
1928 (w)	13,600,000	0.50	1.00	3.50	15.00	25.00
1930 (w)	22,500,000	3.00	9.00	25.00	45.00	150
1931 (w)	9,000,000	0.50	1.00	4.00	16.00	28.00
1932 (w)	12,000,000	0.50	1.00	4.00	16.00	28.00
1933 (w)	7,000,000	0.50	1.00	4.00	16.00	28.00
1934 (w)	5,900,000	0.50	1.00	4.50	17.00	30.00
1935 (w)	7,300,000	0.50	1.00	3.00	12.00	20.00
1936 (w)	12,600,000	0.50	1.00	2.50	5.00	7.50
1937 (w)	17,370,000	0.50	1.00	2.50	5.00	7.50
1938 (w)	20,530,000	0.50	1.00	2.50	5.00	7.50
1939 (w)	12,000,000	0.50	1.00	2.50	5.00	7.50

Y# 9 2 GROSZE

2.00 g., Brass, 17.6 mm. **Obv:** Crowned eagle with wings open **Rev:** Stylized value

Date	Mintage	F12	VF20	XF40	MS60	MS63
1923	20,500,000	2.50	5.00	15.00	35.00	75.00

Y# 9a 2 GROSZE

2.00 g., Bronze, 17.6 mm. **Obv:** Crowned eagle with wings open **Rev:** Stylized value

Date	Mintage	F12	VF20	XF40	MS60	MS63
1925 (w)	39,000,000	0.50	1.50	5.00	20.00	30.00
1927 (w)	15,300,000	0.50	1.50	5.00	20.00	30.00
1928 (w)	13,400,000	0.50	1.50	5.00	20.00	30.00
1930 (w)	20,000,000	0.50	1.50	5.00	20.00	30.00
1931 (w)	9,500,000	1.50	3.00	7.50	25.00	35.00
1932 (w)	6,500,000	2.00	4.00	9.00	35.00	50.00
1933 (w)	7,000,000	2.00	4.00	9.00	35.00	50.00
1934 (w)	9,350,000	2.00	4.00	9.00	35.00	50.00
1935 (w)	5,800,000	0.75	1.50	3.00	10.00	15.00
1936 (w)	5,800,000	0.75	1.50	3.00	10.00	15.00
1937 (w)	17,360,000	0.50	1.00	1.50	2.50	5.00
1938 (w)	20,530,000	0.50	1.00	1.50	2.50	5.00
1939 (w)	12,000,000	0.50	1.00	1.50	2.50	5.00

Y# 10 5 GROSZY

3.00 g., Brass, 20 mm. **Obv:** Crowned eagle with wings open **Rev:** Stylized value

Date	Mintage	F12	VF20	XF40	MS60	MS63
1923	32,000,000	3.00	5.00	15.00	35.00	75.00

Y# 10a 5 GROSZY

3.00 g., Bronze, 20 mm. **Obv:** Crowned eagle with wings open **Rev:** Stylized value

Date	Mintage	F12	VF20	XF40	MS60	MS63
1923	350	**PF63** 900				
1925 (w)	45,500,000	0.75	1.50	7.50	20.00	30.00
1928 (w)	8,900,000	0.75	1.50	8.00	22.00	40.00
1930 (w)	14,200,000	0.75	2.00	10.00	25.00	45.00
1931 (w)	1,500,000	1.00	3.00	12.00	35.00	50.00
1934 (w)	420,000	3.00	9.00	50.00	100	225
1935 (w)	4,660,000	0.50	1.50	2.50	12.00	15.00
1936 (w)	4,660,000	0.50	1.50	2.50	12.00	15.00
1937 (w)	9,050,000	0.50	1.50	2.50	3.50	5.00
1938 (w)	17,300,000	0.50	1.50	2.50	3.50	5.00
1939 (w)	10,000,000	0.50	1.50	2.50	3.50	5.00

Y# 11 10 GROSZY

2.00 g., Nickel, 17.7 mm. **Obv:** Crowned eagle with wings open **Rev:** Value within wreath

Date	Mintage	F12	VF20	XF40	MS60	MS63
1923	100,000,000	0.20	0.45	1.50	20.00	35.00

Y# 12 20 GROSZY

3.00 g., Nickel, 20 mm. **Obv:** Crowned eagle with wings open **Rev:** Value within wreath

Date	Mintage	F12	VF20	XF40	MS60	MS63
1923	150,000,000	0.35	0.75	1.25	7.50	12.00
1923	10	**PF63** 350				

Y# 13 50 GROSZY

5.00 g., Nickel, 23 mm. **Obv:** Crowned eagle with wings open **Rev:** Value within wreath

Date	Mintage	F12	VF20	XF40	MS60	MS63
1923	100,000,000	0.40	0.80	1.50	20.00	35.00
1923	10	**PF63** 400				

Y# 15 ZŁOTY

5.00 g., 0.750 Silver 0.1206 oz. ASW, 23 mm. **Obv:** Crowned eagle with wings open **Rev:** Bust left **Edge:** Reeded

Date	Mintage	F12	VF20	XF40	MS60	MS63
1924 (Paris)	16,000,000	5.00	12.00	35.00	75.00	125
Note: Torch and cornucopia flank date						
1924 (Birmingham); Proof	8	**PF63** 850				
1925 (London)	24,000,000	5.00	12.00	20.00	50.00	75.00
Note: Dot after date						
1925 (London); Proof	—	**PF63** 4,500				

Y# 14 ZŁOTY

7.00 g., Nickel, 25 mm. **Obv:** Crowned eagle with wings open **Rev:** Value within stylized design

Date	Mintage	F12	VF20	XF40	MS60	MS63
1929 (w)	32,000,000	0.75	1.50	15.00	35.00	50.00

Y# 16 2 ZŁOTE

10.00 g., 0.750 Silver 0.2411 oz. ASW, 27 mm. **Obv:** Crowned eagle with wings open **Rev:** Head left **Edge:** Reeded

Date	Mintage	F12	VF20	XF40	MS60	MS63
1924 (Paris)	8,200,000	10.00	15.00	25.00	75.00	125
Note: Torch and cornucopia flank date						
1924 H (Birmingham)	1,200,000	35.00	50.00	100	250	450
1924 (Birmingham); Proof	60	**PF63** 750				
1924 (Philadelphia)	800,000	15.00	25.00	40.00	100	175
Note: Without privy marks, coin alignment						
1925 (London)	11,000,000	10.00	15.00	25.00	75.00	125
Note: Dot after date						
1925 (Philadelphia)	5,200,000	10.00	15.00	25.00	75.00	125
Note: Without privy marks						

Y# 20 2 ZŁOTE

4.40 g., 0.750 Silver 0.1061 oz. ASW, 22 mm. **Obv:** National arms **Obv. Legend:** RRZECZPOSPOLITA POLSKA **Rev:** Radiant head of Queen Jadwiga left **Edge:** Milled

Date	Mintage	F12	VF20	XF40	MS60	MS63
1932 (w)	15,700,000	3.00	5.00	7.50	20.00	30.00
1933 (w)	9,250,000	3.00	5.00	7.50	20.00	30.00
1934 (w)	250,000	4.00	7.50	10.00	35.00	50.00

Y# 27 2 ZŁOTE

4.40 g., 0.750 Silver 0.1061 oz. ASW, 22 mm. **Obv:** Crowned eagle with wings open **Rev:** Head of Jozef Pilsudski left **Edge:** Reeded

Date	Mintage	F12	VF20	XF40	MS60	MS63
1934 (w)	10,425,000	3.00	5.00	10.00	45.00	75.00
1936 (w)	75,000	25.00	35.00	75.00	200	300

Y# 30 2 ZŁOTE

4.40 g., 0.750 Silver 0.1061 oz. ASW, 22 mm. **Subject:** 15th Anniversary of Gdynia Seaport **Obv:** Crowned eagle with wings open **Rev:** Sailing ship

Date	Mintage	F12	VF20	XF40	MS60	MS63
1936 (w)	3,918,000	2.00	5.00	9.00	20.00	30.00

Y# 17.1 5 ZŁOTYCH

25.00 g., 0.900 Silver 0.7234 oz. ASW, 37 mm. **Subject:** Adoption of the Constitution **Obv:** Crowned eagle with wings open **Rev:** 100 pearls in circle **Edge Lettering:** SALUS REIPUBLICAS SUPREMA LEX

Date	Mintage	F12	VF20	XF40	MS60	MS63
1925 (w)	100	550	1,250	3,200	6,750	10,000

Y# 17.1a 5 ZŁOTYCH

Gold **Obv:** Crowned eagle with wings open **Rev:** Adoption of the Constitution

Date	Mintage	F12	VF20	XF40	MS60	MS63
1925 (w)	2	—	—	—	100,000	—

Y# 17.2 5 ZŁOTYCH

25.00 g., 0.900 Silver 0.7234 oz. ASW, 37 mm. **Obv:** Without monogram by date **Rev:** Adoption of the Constitution

Date	Mintage	F12	VF20	XF40	MS60	MS63
1925 (w)	1,000	—	—	1,500	3,500	6,000

Y# 17.2a 5 ZŁOTYCH

Bronze, 37 mm. **Obv:** Crowned imperial eagle **Rev:** Adoption of the Constitution

Date	Mintage	F12	VF20	XF40	MS60	MS63
1925 (w)	100	—	—	800	1,750	3,000

Y# 17.2c 5 ZŁOTYCH

Gold, 37 mm. **Obv:** Without monogram by date **Rev:** Adoption of the Constitution

Date	Mintage	F12	VF20	XF40	MS60	MS63
1925 (w) Rare	1	—	—	—	—	—

Y# 17.3 5 ZŁOTYCH

25.00 g., 0.900 Silver 0.7234 oz. ASW, 37 mm. **Obv:** Monogram by date **Rev:** 81 pearls in circle

Date	Mintage	F12	VF20	XF40	MS60	MS63
1925 (w)	1,000	—	—	1,500	3,500	6,000

Y# 17.3a 5 ZŁOTYCH

43.33 g., 0.900 Gold 1.2538 oz. AGW, 37 mm. **Obv:** Crowned eagle with wings open, mint mark to right of date **Rev:** Adoption of the Constitution **Edge Lettering:** SALUS REIPUBLICAE SUPREMA LEX

Date	Mintage	F12	VF20	XF40	MS60	MS63
1925 (w) Rare	1	—	—	—	—	—

Y# 17.4 5 ZŁOTYCH

43.33 g., 0.900 Gold 1.2538 oz. AGW **Obv:** Without monogram by date, with mint mark **Rev:** Adoption of the Constitution

Date	Mintage	F12	VF20	XF40	MS60	MS63
1925 (w)	1	—	—	—	100,000	—

Y# 17.4a 5 ZŁOTYCH

Tombac **Obv:** Crowned imperial eagle **Rev:** Adoption of the Constitution

Date	Mintage	F12	VF20	XF40	MS60	MS63
1925 (w)	100	—	—	950	2,250	4,500

Y# 18 5 ZŁOTYCH

18.00 g., 0.750 Silver 0.434 oz. ASW, 33 mm. **Obv:** Crowned eagle with wings open **Rev:** Winged Victory right **Edge Lettering:** SALUS REIPUBLICAE SUPREMA LEX

Date	Mintage	F12	VF20	XF40	MS60	MS63
1928 (w)	7,500,000	25.00	50.00	100	600	1,200
Note: Conjoined arrow and K mint mark						
1928 Error	Inc. above	35.00	75.00	125	750	1,500
Note: "SUPRMA" edge inscription						
1928 Without mint mark	10,000,000	15.00	25.00	75.00	450	1,000
Note: 4,300,000 struck in London and 5,700,000 in Belgium						
1930 (w)	5,900,000	250	650	1,600	—	—
1931 (w)	2,200,000	350	800	1,750	—	—
1932 (w)	3,100,000	1,000	2,750	5,000	—	—

Y# 19.1 5 ZŁOTYCH

18.00 g., 0.750 Silver 0.434 oz. ASW, 33 mm. **Subject:** Centennial of 1830 Revolution **Obv:** Crowned eagle with wings open flanked by value **Rev:** Pole with flag and banner divides dates **Edge Lettering:** SALUS REIPUBLICAE SUPREMA LEX

Date	Mintage	F12	VF20	XF40	MS60	MS63
1930 (w)	1,000,000	20.00	35.00	75.00	150	250

Y# 19.2 5 ZŁOTYCH

18.00 g., 0.750 Silver 0.434 oz. ASW, 33 mm. **Obv:** Crowned imperial eagle **Rev:** Pole with flag and banner divides dates **Note:** High relief.

Date	Mintage	F12	VF20	XF40	MS60	MS63
1930 (w)	200	475	1,100	2,200	4,200	5,400

Y# 21 5 ZŁOTYCH

11.00 g., 0.750 Silver 0.2652 oz. ASW, 28 mm. **Obv:** National arms flanked by value **Obv. Legend:** RZECZPOSPOLITA POLSKA **Rev:** Radiant head of Queen Jadwiga left **Edge:** Reeded

Date	Mintage	F12	VF20	XF40	MS60	MS63
1932 (Warsaw : tiny arrow in space between talons of eagle's left claw)	1,000,000	37.50	95.00	400	1,050	1,250
1932 (London); without mint mark	3,000,000	5.00	6.00	10.00	75.00	125
1933 (w)	11,000,000	5.00	6.00	10.00	50.00	100
1933 (w) Proof	100	—	—	—	—	—
1934 (w)	250,000	5.00	6.00	10.00	50.00	100

Y# 25 5 ZŁOTYCH

11.00 g., 0.750 Silver 0.2652 oz. ASW, 28 mm. **Obv:** Rifle Corps symbol below eagle with wings open **Rev:** Head of Jozef Pilsudski left **Edge:** Reeded

Date	Mintage	F12	VF20	XF40	MS60	MS63
1934 (w)	300,000	7.50	10.00	20.00	75.00	150

Y# 28 5 ZŁOTYCH

11.00 g., 0.750 Silver 0.2652 oz. ASW, 28 mm. **Obv:** Radiant crowned eagle with wings open **Rev:** Head of Jozef Pilsudski left **Edge:** Reeded

Date	Mintage	F12	VF20	XF40	MS60	MS63
1934 (w)	6,510,000	5.00	6.00	10.00	50.00	75.00
1935 (w)	1,800,000	5.00	6.00	10.00	50.00	75.00
1936 (w)	1,800,000	5.00	6.00	10.00	50.00	75.00
1938 (w)	289,000	6.00	7.50	15.00	75.00	95.00

Y# 31 5 ZŁOTYCH

11.00 g., 0.750 Silver 0.2652 oz. ASW, 28 mm. **Subject:** 15th Anniversary of Gdynia Seaport **Obv:** Crowned eagle with wings open **Rev:** Sailing ship **Edge:** Reeded

Date	Mintage	F12	VF20	XF40	MS60	MS63
1936 (w)	1,000,000	10.00	18.00	35.00	100	225

Y# 32 10 ZŁOTYCH

3.23 g., 0.900 Gold 0.0933 oz. AGW, 19 mm. **Obv:** Crowned eagle with wings open **Rev:** Crowned head left **Note:** Never released into circulation; similar design to Y#33.

Date	Mintage	F12	VF20	XF40	MS60	MS63
ND (1925) (w)	50,350	—	120	125	200	325

Y# 22 10 ZŁOTYCH

22.00 g., 0.750 Silver 0.5305 oz. ASW, 34 mm. **Obv:** National arms **Obv. Legend:** RZECZPOSPOLITA POLSKA **Rev:** Radiant head of Queen Jadwiga left **Edge:** Reeded

Date	Mintage	F12	VF20	XF40	MS60	MS63
1932 (w)	3,100,000	9.75	12.00	18.00	100	175
Note: Warsaw Mint : tiny arrow in space between talons of eagle's left claw						
1932	6,000,000	9.75	12.00	18.00	100	175
Note: London Mint: without mint mark						
1932 (w) Proof	100	—	—	—	—	—
1933 (w)	2,800,000	9.75	12.00	20.00	125	200
1933 (w) Proof	100	—	—	—	—	—

Y# 23 10 ZŁOTYCH

22.00 g., 0.750 Silver 0.5305 oz. ASW, 34 mm. **Subject:** Jan III Sobieski's Victory Over the Turks **Obv:** Crowned eagle with wings open **Rev:** Uniformed bust right **Edge:** Reeded

Date	Mintage	F12	VF20	XF40	MS60	MS63
ND (1933) (w)	300,000	20.00	30.00	75.00	125	225
ND (1933) (w) Proof	100	—	—	—	—	—

Y# 24 10 ZŁOTYCH

22.00 g., 0.750 Silver 0.5305 oz. ASW, 34 mm. **Subject:** 70th Anniversary of 1863 Insurrection **Obv:** Crowned eagle with wings open **Rev:** Head of Romuald Traugutt 3/4 facing divides dates **Edge:** Reeded

Date	Mintage	F12	VF20	XF40	MS60	MS63
ND (1933) (w)	300,000	20.00	30.00	75.00	200	375
ND (1933) (w) Proof	100	—	—	—	—	—

Y# 26 10 ZŁOTYCH

22.00 g., 0.750 Silver 0.5305 oz. ASW, 34 mm. **Obv:** Rifle Corps symbol below eagle with wings open **Rev:** Head of Jozef Pilsudski left **Edge:** Reeded

Date	Mintage	F12	VF20	XF40	MS60	MS63
1934 (w)	300,000	15.00	25.00	75.00	225	450

Y# 29 10 ZŁOTYCH
22.00 g., 0.750 Silver 0.5305 oz. ASW, 34 mm. **Obv:** Eagle with wings open with no symbols below **Rev:** Head of Jozef Pilsudski left **Edge:** Reeded

Date	Mintage	F12	VF20	XF40	MS60	MS63
1934 (w)	200,000	15.00	25.00	45.00	175	350
1935 (w)	1,670,000	9.75	15.00	18.00	90.00	150
1936 (w)	2,130,000	9.75	15.00	18.00	90.00	150
1937 (w)	908,000	9.75	15.00	25.00	100	175
1938 (w)	234,000	12.00	20.00	35.00	125	225
1939 (w)	—	9.75	15.00	25.00	75.00	125

Y# 33 20 ZŁOTYCH
6.45 g., 0.900 Gold 0.1867 oz. AGW, 21 mm. **Obv:** Crowned eagle with wings open **Rev:** Crowned head of Boleslaw I left **Edge:** Reeded **Note:** Never released into circulation.

Date	Mintage	F12	VF20	XF40	MS60	MS63
ND (1925) (w)	27,240	—	237	250	300	400

WWII GERMAN OCCUPATION

OCCUPATION COINAGE

Y# 34 GROSZ
1.17 g., Zinc, 14.7 mm. **Obv:** Crowned eagle with wings open **Rev:** Stylized value

Date	Mintage	F12	VF20	XF40	MS60	MS63
1939 (w)	33,909,000	0.25	0.50	1.50	3.00	5.00

Y# 35 5 GROSZY
1.72 g., Zinc, 16 mm. **Obv:** Crowned eagle with wings open, hole in center **Rev:** Stylized value, hole in center

Date	Mintage	F12	VF20	XF40	MS60	MS63
1939 (w)	15,324,000	0.25	0.50	1.50	5.00	7.50

Y# 36 10 GROSZY
2.00 g., Zinc, 17.6 mm. **Obv:** Crowned imperial eagle **Rev:** Value

Date	Mintage	F12	VF20	XF40	MS60	MS63
1923 (w)	42,175,000	0.20	0.50	1.00	2.50	3.50

Note: Actually struck in 1941-44

Y# 37 20 GROSZY
2.97 g., Zinc, 20 mm. **Obv:** Crowned eagle with wings open **Rev:** Value within wreath

Date	Mintage	F12	VF20	XF40	MS60	MS63
1923 (w)	40,025,000	0.40	0.60	1.25	2.50	3.50

Note: Actually struck in 1941-44

Y# 38 50 GROSZY
5.00 g., Nickel Plated Iron, 23 mm. **Obv:** Crowned eagle with wings open **Rev:** Value within wreath

Date	Mintage	F12	VF20	XF40	MS60	MS63
1938 (w)	32,000,000	1.00	2.00	5.00	10.00	15.00

Y# 38a 50 GROSZY
Iron **Obv:** Crowned eagle with wings open **Rev:** Value within wreath

Date	Mintage	F12	VF20	XF40	MS60	MS63
1938 (w)	—	1.00	2.00	5.00	10.00	15.00

Note: Varieties exist

TOKEN COINAGE

A major industrial city in western Poland before World War II and site of the first wartime ghetto under German occupation (May 1940). It was also the last ghetto to close during the war (August 1944). Token coinage was struck in 1942 and 1943, in the name of the Jewish Elders of Litzmannstadt. This series has seen very little circulation, but is commonly found in conditions from slightly to badly corroded. The badly corroded specimens have the appearance of zinc.

Lodz Ghetto, 1942-1944

KM# Tn1 10 PFENNIG
Aluminum-Magnesium **Rev:** Value

Date	Mintage	VG8	F12	VF20	XF40	MS60
1942	Est. 100000	300	600	1,000	—	—

Note: Most were destroyed or remelted as the design was too similar to regular German coinage

KM# Tn5 10 PFENNIG
Aluminum-Magnesium **Obv:** Star in circle **Rev:** Value

Date	Mintage	VG8	F12	VF20	XF40	MS60
1942	100,000	35.00	75.00	150	300	—

Note: Off-metal strikes in silver and bronze are known

KM# Tn2 5 MARK
Aluminum **Obv:** Value **Rev:** Star at upper left, GETTO and date lower right

Date	Mintage	VG8	F12	VF20	XF40	MS60
1943	600,000	6.00	15.00	45.00	125	—

KM# Tn2a 5 MARK
Aluminum-Magnesium **Obv:** Value **Rev:** Star at upper left, GETTO and date lower right

Date	Mintage	VG8	F12	VF20	XF40	MS60
1943	Inc. above	20.00	45.00	115	225	—

KM# Tn3 10 MARK
Aluminum **Obv:** Value **Rev:** Star at upper left, GETTO and date lower right **Note:** Thick and thin planchets exist.

Date	Mintage	VG8	F12	VF20	XF40	MS60
1943	100,000	6.00	15.00	45.00	125	—

KM# Tn3a 10 MARK
Aluminum-Magnesium **Obv:** Value **Rev:** Star at upper left, GETTO and date lower right

Date	Mintage	VG8	F12	VF20	XF40	MS60
1943	Inc. above	25.00	55.00	130	240	—

KM# Tn4 20 MARK
Aluminum **Obv:** Value **Rev:** Star at upper left, GETTO and date lower right **Note:** Beware of numerous counterfeits.

Date	Mintage	VG8	F12	VF20	XF40	MS60
1943	600	175	350	650	1,250	—

REPUBLIC

Post War

STANDARD COINAGE

Y# 39 GROSZ
0.50 g., Aluminum, 14.7 mm. **Obv:** Eagle with wings open **Rev:** Value at upper right of sprig **Edge:** Reeded

Date	Mintage	VF20	XF40	MS60	MS63	MS65
1949	400,116,000	0.25	0.50	2.50	3.00	5.00

Note: 400000000 struck at Budapest Mint, 116,000 struck at Warsaw Mint at a later time

Y# 40 2 GROSZE
0.58 g., Aluminum, 16 mm. **Obv:** Eagle with wings open **Rev:** Value at upper right of sprig **Edge:** Reeded

Date	Mintage	VF20	XF40	MS60	MS63	MS65
1949	300,106,000	0.25	0.50	1.00	2.50	5.00

Note: 300000000 struck at Budapest Mint, 106,000 struck at Warsaw Mint

Y# 41 5 GROSZY
3.00 g., Bronze, 20 mm. **Obv:** Eagle with wings open **Rev:** Value at upper right of sprig

Date	Mintage	VF20	XF40	MS60	MS63	MS65
1949 (b)	300,000,000	0.25	0.50	2.50	5.00	7.50

Y# 41a 5 GROSZY
1.00 g., Aluminum, 20 mm. **Obv:** Eagle with wings open **Rev:** Value at upper right of sprig

Date	Mintage	VF20	XF40	MS60	MS63	MS65
1949 (kr)	200,000,000	0.25	0.50	1.50	3.00	5.00

Y# 42 10 GROSZY
2.00 g., Copper-Nickel, 17.6 mm. **Obv:** Eagle with wings open **Rev:** Value above sprig

Date	Mintage	VF20	XF40	MS60	MS63	MS65
1949 (kr)	200,000,000	0.40	1.00	3.00	9.00	15.00

Y# 42a 10 GROSZY
0.70 g., Aluminum, 17.6 mm. **Obv:** Eagle with wings open **Rev:** Value above sprig

Date	Mintage	VF20	XF40	MS60	MS63	MS65
1949 (w)	31,047,000	0.25	1.00	3.00	9.00	20.00

Y# 43 20 GROSZY
2.89 g., Copper-Nickel, 20 mm. **Obv:** Eagle with wings open **Rev:** Value above sprig

Date	Mintage	VF20	XF40	MS60	MS63	MS65
1949 (kr)	133,383,000	0.25	1.00	3.00	9.00	15.00

Y# 43a 20 GROSZY
1.00 g., Aluminum, 20 mm. **Obv:** Eagle with wings open **Rev:** Value above sprig

Date	Mintage	VF20	XF40	MS60	MS63	MS65
1949 (w)	197,472,000	0.25	1.00	3.00	12.00	25.00

Y# 44 50 GROSZY
5.00 g., Copper-Nickel, 23 mm. **Obv:** Eagle with wings open **Rev:** Value above sprig **Edge:** Reeded

Date	Mintage	VF20	XF40	MS60	MS63	MS65
1949 (kr)	109,000,000	0.25	1.00	3.00	12.00	25.00

Y# 44a 50 GROSZY
1.60 g., Aluminum, 23 mm. **Obv:** Eagle with wings open **Rev:** Value above sprig **Edge:** Reeded

Date	Mintage	VF20	XF40	MS60	MS63	MS65
1949 (w)	59,393,000	0.50	1.50	5.00	20.00	35.00

Y# 45 ZŁOTY
7.00 g., Copper-Nickel, 25 mm. **Obv:** Eagle with wings open **Rev:** Value within wreath **Edge:** Reeded

Date	Mintage	VF20	XF40	MS60	MS63	MS65
1949 (kr)	87,053,000	1.00	3.00	10.00	20.00	35.00

Y# 45a ZŁOTY
2.12 g., Aluminum, 25 mm. **Obv:** Eagle with wings open **Rev:** Value within wreath **Edge:** Reeded

Date	Mintage	VF20	XF40	MS60	MS63	MS65
1949 (w)	43,000,000	1.00	3.00	10.00	20.00	35.00

PEOPLES REPUBLIC

Y# A46 5 GROSZY
0.61 g., Aluminum, 16 mm. **Obv:** Eagle with wings open **Rev:** Value to upper right of sprig

Date	Mintage	VF20	XF40	MS60	MS63	MS65
1958	53,521,000	—	0.20	0.80	1.50	2.50
1959	28,564,000	—	0.20	0.60	1.25	1.85
1960	12,246,000	1.00	3.00	10.00	18.00	28.00
1961	29,502,000	—	0.20	0.80	1.50	2.50
1962	90,257,000	—	0.20	0.60	1.25	1.85
1963	20,878,000	—	0.20	0.60	1.25	1.85
1965 MW	5,050,000	1.50	4.00	12.00	20.00	35.00
1967 MW	10,056,000	1.50	4.00	12.00	20.00	35.00
1968 MW	10,196,000	1.50	4.00	12.00	20.00	35.00
1970 MW	20,095,000	—	0.20	0.30	0.50	1.00
1971 MW	20,000,000	—	0.20	0.30	0.50	1.00
1972 MW	10,000,000	—	0.20	0.30	0.50	1.00

Y# AA47 10 GROSZY
0.70 g., Aluminum, 17.6 mm. **Obv:** Eagle with wings open **Rev:** Value above sprig **Edge:** Plain **Note:** Varieties in date size exist.

Date	Mintage	VF20	XF40	MS60	MS63	MS65
1961 MW	73,400,000	1.50	5.00	14.00	22.00	38.00
1962 MW	25,362,000	4.00	10.00	32.00	50.00	90.00
1963 MW	40,434,000	—	1.00	4.00	7.00	12.00
1965 MW	50,521,000	0.50	2.00	5.00	9.00	16.00
1966 MW	70,749,000	—	1.00	4.00	7.00	12.00
1967 MW	62,059,000	—	1.00	4.00	7.00	12.00
1968 MW	62,204,000	—	1.00	4.00	7.00	12.00
1969 MW	71,566,000	—	1.00	3.00	6.00	10.00
1970 MW	38,844,000	—	0.20	0.70	1.50	2.50
1971 MW	50,000,000	—	0.20	0.70	1.50	2.50
1972 MW	60,000,000	—	0.20	0.70	1.50	2.50
1973 (kr) Rare	—	—	—	—	—	—
1973 MW	80,000,000	—	0.20	0.40	0.75	1.50
1974 (kr)	50,000,000	—	0.20	0.20	0.45	0.75
Note: Struck at Kremnica Mint						
1975 MW	50,000,000	—	0.20	0.20	0.45	0.75
1976 MW	100,000,000	—	—	0.20	0.45	0.75
1977 MW	100,000,000	—	—	0.20	0.45	0.75
1978 MW	71,204,000	—	—	0.20	0.45	0.75
1979 MW	73,191,000	—	—	0.20	0.45	0.75
1979 MW	5,000	PF65 1.00				
1980 MW	60,623,000	—	—	0.20	0.45	0.75
1980 MW	5,000	PF65 1.00				
1981 MW	70,000,000	—	—	0.20	0.45	0.75
1981 MW	5,000	PF65 1.00				
1983 MW	9,600,000	—	—	0.20	0.45	0.75
1985 MW	9,957,000	—	—	0.20	0.45	0.75

Y# A47 20 GROSZY
1.00 g., Aluminum, 20 mm. **Obv:** Eagle with wings open **Rev:** Value above sprig **Edge:** Plain **Note:** Date varieties exist.

Date	Mintage	VF20	XF40	MS60	MS63	MS65
1957	3,940,000	10.00	25.00	80.00	170	—
1961	53,108,000	4.00	8.00	18.00	28.00	45.00
1962	19,140,000	4.00	10.00	25.00	45.00	75.00
1963	41,217,000	—	1.00	3.00	7.00	16.00
1965 MW	32,022,000	—	1.00	3.00	7.00	16.00
1966 MW	23,860,000	—	1.00	3.00	7.00	16.00
1967 MW	29,099,000	—	2.00	12.00	22.00	40.00
1968 MW	29,191,000	—	2.00	12.00	22.00	40.00
1969 MW	40,227,000	—	1.00	4.00	7.00	12.00
1970 MW	20,028,000	—	0.20	2.00	5.00	9.00
1971 MW	20,000,000	—	0.20	2.00	5.00	9.00
1972 MW	60,000,000	—	0.20	2.00	5.00	9.00
1973 (kr)	50,000,000	—	0.20	0.70	1.50	2.50
1973 MW	65,000,000	—	0.20	0.70	1.50	2.50
1975 MW	50,000,000	—	0.20	0.70	1.50	2.50
1976 MW	100,000,000	—	0.20	0.70	1.50	2.50
Large date						
1976 MW	Inc. above	—	0.20	0.70	1.50	2.50
Small date						
1977 MW	80,730,000	—	0.20	0.30	0.50	1.00
1978 MW	50,730,000	—	0.20	0.30	0.50	1.00
1979 MW	45,252,000	—	0.20	0.30	0.50	1.00
1979 MW	5,000	PF65 1.00				
1980 MW	30,020,000	—	0.20	0.30	0.50	1.00
1980 MW	5,000	PF65 1.00				
1981 MW	60,082,000	—	0.20	0.30	0.50	1.00
1981 MW	5,000	PF65 1.00				
1983 MW	—	—	0.20	0.30	0.50	1.00
1985 MW	16,227,000	—	0.20	0.30	0.50	1.00

Y# 48.1 50 GROSZY
1.60 g., Aluminum, 23 mm. **Obv:** Eagle with wings open **Rev:** Value above sprig **Edge:** Reeded

Date	Mintage	VF20	XF40	MS60	MS63	MS65
1957	91,316,000	1.50	4.00	15.00	25.00	45.00
1965 MW	22,090,000	0.50	3.00	12.00	18.00	35.00
1967 MW	2,027,000	2.50	8.00	25.00	45.00	70.00
1968 MW	2,065,000	2.50	8.00	25.00	45.00	70.00
1970 MW	3,273,000	0.30	0.60	5.00	9.00	16.00
1971 MW	7,000,000	0.20	0.50	3.00	7.00	12.00
1972 MW	10,000,000	0.20	0.50	0.70	1.50	2.50
1973 MW	39,000	0.20	0.40	0.70	1.50	2.50
1974 MW	33,000,000	0.20	0.40	0.70	1.50	2.50
1975 (kr)	25,000,000	0.20	0.40	0.70	1.50	2.50
1976 (kr)	25,000,000	0.20	0.40	0.60	1.25	2.25
1977 MW	50,000,000	0.20	0.40	0.60	1.25	2.25
1978 (kr)	18,600,000	0.20	0.40	0.60	1.25	2.25
1978 MW	50,020,000	0.20	0.40	0.60	1.25	2.25
1982 MW	16,067,000	0.20	0.40	0.60	1.25	2.25
1982 MW	5,000	PF65 3.50				
1983 MW	39,667,000	0.20	0.40	0.60	1.25	2.25
1984 MW	44,217,000	0.20	0.40	0.60	1.25	2.25
1985 MW	49,052,000	0.20	0.40	0.60	1.25	2.25

Y# 48.2 50 GROSZY
1.60 g., Aluminum, 23 mm. **Obv:** Eagle with wings open **Rev:** Value above sprig **Edge:** Reeded

Date	Mintage	VF20	XF40	MS60	MS63	MS65
1986 MW	45,796,000	0.20	0.40	0.60	1.25	2.25
1986 MW	5,000	PF65 11.00				
1987 MW	21,257,000	0.20	0.40	0.60	1.25	2.25
1987 MW	5,000	PF65 11.00				

Y# 49.1 ZŁOTY
2.07 g., Aluminum, 25 mm. **Obv:** Eagle with wings open **Rev:** Value within wreath **Edge:** Reeded

Date	Mintage	VF20	XF40	MS60	MS63	MS65
1957 (w)	58,631,000	2.00	7.00	35.00	65.00	100
1965 MW	15,015,000	1.00	2.00	9.00	17.00	30.00
1966 MW	18,185,000	1.50	4.00	12.00	20.00	35.00
1967 MW	1,002,000	5.00	12.00	25.00	45.00	75.00
1968 MW	1,176,000	5.00	12.00	25.00	45.00	75.00
1969 MW	3,024,000	2.50	6.00	12.00	25.00	45.00
1970 MW	6,016,000	0.30	1.00	4.00	9.00	18.00
1971 MW	6,000,000	0.30	1.00	3.00	7.00	12.00
1972 MW	7,000,000	0.30	1.00	3.00	7.00	12.00
1973 MW	15,000,000	0.20	1.00	3.00	7.00	12.00
1974 MW	42,000,000	0.20	0.30	0.70	1.50	2.50
1975 (kr)	22,000,000	0.20	0.30	0.70	1.50	2.50
1975 MW	33,000,000	0.20	0.30	0.70	1.50	2.50
1976 (kr)	22,000,000	0.20	1.00	1.50	2.50	4.50
1977 MW	65,000,000	0.20	1.00	1.50	2.50	4.50
1978 (kr)	16,399,999	0.20	1.00	2.25	3.50	6.50
1978 MW	80,000,000	0.20	1.00	1.50	2.50	4.50
1980 MW	100,002,000	0.20	0.30	0.70	1.50	2.50
1980 MW	5,000	PF65 8.00				
1981 MW	4,082,000	0.20	0.30	1.50	2.50	4.50
1981 MW	5,000	PF65 8.00				
1982 MW	59,643,000	0.20	0.30	0.40	0.75	1.25
1982 MW	5,000	PF65 11.00				
1983 MW	49,636,000	0.20	0.30	0.40	0.75	1.25
1984 MW	61,036,000	0.20	0.30	0.40	0.75	1.25
1985 MW	167,939,000	0.20	0.30	0.40	0.75	1.25

Y# 49.2 ZŁOTY
2.20 g., Aluminum, 25 mm. **Obv:** Eagle with wings open **Rev:** Value within wreath **Edge:** Reeded

Date	Mintage	VF20	XF40	MS60	MS63	MS65
1986 MW	130,697,000	0.20	0.30	0.40	0.75	1.25
1986 MW	5,000	PF65 11.00				
1987 MW	100,081,000	0.20	0.30	0.40	0.75	1.25
1987 MW	5,000	PF65 11.00				
1988 MW	96,400,000	0.20	0.30	0.40	0.75	1.25
1988 MW	5,000	PF65 11.00				

Y# 49.3 ZŁOTY
0.57 g., Aluminum, 16 mm. **Obv:** Eagle with wings open **Rev:** Value within wreath **Edge:** Reeded

Date	Mintage	VF20	XF40	MS60	MS63	MS65
1989 MW	49,410,000	0.20	0.30	0.40	0.75	1.25
1989 MW	5,000	PF65 11.00				
1990 MW	30,667,000	0.20	0.30	0.40	0.75	1.25
1990 MW	5,000	PF65 11.00				

Y# 46 2 ZŁOTE
2.70 g., Aluminum, 27 mm. **Obv:** Eagle with wings open **Rev:** Value above design and fruit **Edge:** Reeded

Date	Mintage	VF20	XF40	MS60	MS63	MS65
1958 (w)	83,640,000	0.40	3.00	18.00	35.00	65.00
1959 (w)	7,170,000	1.00	8.00	35.00	65.00	100
1960 (w)	36,131,000	0.40	1.00	8.00	16.00	30.00
1970 MW	2,013,999	0.60	2.00	9.00	18.00	35.00

Date	Mintage	VF20	XF40	MS60	MS63	MS65
1971 MW	3,000,000	0.40	2.00	9.00	18.00	35.00
1972 MW	3,000,000	0.40	2.00	9.00	18.00	35.00
1973 MW	10,000,000	0.30	1.00	4.00	9.00	18.00
1974 MW	46,000,000	0.30	0.60	3.00	7.00	12.00

Y# 80.1 2 ZŁOTE

3.00 g., Brass, 21 mm. **Obv:** Eagle with wings open **Rev:** Value above design **Edge:** Reeded

Date	Mintage	VF20	XF40	MS60	MS63	MS65
1975	25,000,000	0.30	0.50	1.00	2.00	3.50
Note: Struck at Leningrad Mint						
1976	60,000,000	0.30	0.50	1.00	2.00	3.50
Note: Struck at Leningrad Mint						
1977	50,000,000	0.30	0.50	1.00	2.00	3.50
Note: Struck at Leningrad Mint						
1978	2,600,000	0.30	0.50	3.00	7.00	12.00
Note: Struck at Leningrad Mint						
1978 MW	2,382,000	0.30	0.50	3.00	7.00	12.00
1979 MW	85,752,000	0.30	0.50	1.00	2.00	3.50
1979 MW	5,000	PF65 8.00				
1980 MW	66,610,000	0.30	0.50	1.00	2.00	3.50
1980 MW	5,000	PF65 8.00				
1981 MW	40,306,000	0.30	0.50	1.00	2.00	3.50
1981 MW	5,000	PF65 8.00				
1982 MW	43,318,000	0.30	0.50	1.00	2.00	3.50
1982 MW	5,000	PF65 11.00				
1983 MW	35,244,000	0.30	0.50	1.00	2.00	3.50
1984 MW	59,999,000	0.30	0.50	1.00	2.00	3.50
1985 MW	100,300,000	0.30	0.50	1.00	2.00	3.50

Y# 80.2 2 ZŁOTE

3.00 g., Brass, 21 mm. **Obv:** Eagle with wings open **Rev:** Value above design **Edge:** Reeded

Date	Mintage	VF20	XF40	MS60	MS63	MS65
1986 MW	60,718,000	0.30	0.50	1.00	2.00	3.50
1986 MW	5,000	PF65 11.00				
1987 MW	44,673,000	0.30	0.50	1.00	2.00	3.50
1987 MW	5,000	PF65 11.00				
1988 MW	94,651,000	0.30	0.50	1.00	2.00	3.50
1988 MW	5,000	PF65 11.00				

Y# 80.3 2 ZŁOTE

0.71 g., Aluminum, 18 mm. **Obv:** Eagle with wings open **Rev:** Value above design **Edge:** Reeded

Date	Mintage	VF20	XF40	MS60	MS63	MS65
1989 MW	91,494,000	0.20	0.40	0.80	1.50	2.75
1989 MW	5,000	PF65 11.00				
1990 MW	40,723,000	0.20	0.40	0.80	1.50	2.75
1990 MW	5,000	PF65 11.00				

Y# 47 5 ZŁOTYCH

3.45 g., Aluminum, 29 mm. **Obv:** Eagle with wings open **Rev:** Fisherman with net **Edge:** Reeded

Date	Mintage	VF20	XF40	MS60	MS63	MS65
1958	1,328,000	15.00	25.00	65.00	125	200
Note: Two date varieties exist for strikes dated 1958						
1959	56,811,000	1.50	5.00	22.00	35.00	65.00
1960	16,300,999	0.50	3.00	12.00	25.00	50.00
1971 MW	1,000,000	15.00	25.00	65.00	125	200
1973 MW	5,000,000	0.40	2.00	12.00	25.00	45.00
1974 MW	46,000,000	0.40	1.00	7.00	18.00	30.00

Y# 81.1 5 ZŁOTYCH

5.00 g., Brass, 24 mm. **Obv:** Eagle with wings open **Rev:** Value **Edge:** Reeded **Note:** Varieties in the letter size exist.

Date	Mintage	VF20	XF40	MS60	MS63	MS65
1975 (lgd)	25,000,000	0.40	0.80	1.75	2.75	4.50
1976 (lgd)	60,000,000	0.40	0.80	1.75	2.75	4.50
1977 (lgd)	50,000,000	0.40	0.80	1.75	2.75	4.50
1978 Rare	—	—	—	—	—	—
1979 MW	5,098,000	0.40	0.80	2.00	5.00	9.00
1979 MW	5,000	PF65 11.00				
1980 MW	10,100,000	0.40	0.80	1.75	2.75	4.50
1980 MW	5,000	PF65 8.00				
1981 MW	4,008,000	0.40	0.80	3.00	7.00	12.00
1981 MW	5,000	PF65 8.00				
1982 MW	25,379,000	0.40	0.80	1.75	2.75	4.50
1982 MW	5,000	PF65 11.00				
1983 MW	30,531,000	0.40	0.80	1.75	2.75	4.50
1984 MW	85,598,000	0.40	0.80	1.75	2.75	4.50
1985 MW	20,501,000	0.40	0.80	1.75	2.75	4.50

Y# 81.2 5 ZŁOTYCH

5.00 g., Brass, 24 mm. **Obv:** Eagle with wings open **Rev:** Value **Edge:** Reeded

Date	Mintage	VF20	XF40	MS60	MS63	MS65
1986 MW	57,108,000	0.40	0.80	1.75	2.75	4.50
1986 MW	5,000	PF65 11.00				
1987 MW	58,843,000	0.40	0.80	1.75	2.75	4.50
1987 MW	5,000	PF65 11.00				
1988 MW	18,668,000	0.40	0.80	1.75	2.75	4.50
1988 MW	5,000	PF65 11.00				

Y# 81.3 5 ZŁOTYCH

0.88 g., Aluminum, 20 mm. **Obv:** Eagle with wings open **Rev:** Value **Edge:** Reeded

Date	Mintage	VF20	XF40	MS60	MS63	MS65
1989 MW	30,253,000	0.30	0.60	1.25	2.75	3.50
1989 MW	5,000	PF65 11.00				
1990 MW	38,248,000	0.30	0.60	1.25	2.75	3.50
1990 MW	5,000	PF65 11.00				

Y# 50 10 ZŁOTYCH

12.90 g., Copper-Nickel, 31 mm. **Obv:** Eagle with wings open **Rev:** Head of Tadeusz Kosciuszko left **Edge:** Reeded

Date	Mintage	VF20	XF40	MS60	MS63	MS65
1959	13,107,000	0.90	3.00	7.00	13.00	27.00
1960	27,551,000	0.90	3.00	7.00	13.00	27.00
1966 MW	4,157,000	1.50	12.00	20.00	35.00	60.00

Y# 50a 10 ZŁOTYCH

9.50 g., Copper-Nickel, 28 mm. **Obv:** Eagle with wings open **Rev:** Head of Tadeusz Kosciuszko left **Note:** Reduced size.

Date	Mintage	VF20	XF40	MS60	MS63	MS65
1969 MW	5,428,000	0.70	2.75	4.50	9.00	18.00
1970 MW	13,783,000	0.70	1.50	2.50	4.00	9.00
1971 MW	12,000,000	0.70	1.50	2.50	4.00	9.00
1972 MW	10,000,000	0.70	1.50	2.50	4.00	9.00
1973 MW	3,900,000	0.70	3.00	8.00	15.00	30.00

Y# 51 10 ZŁOTYCH

12.90 g., Copper-Nickel, 31 mm. **Obv:** Eagle with wings open **Rev:** Bust of Mikolaj Kopernik facing **Edge:** Reeded

Date	Mintage	VF20	XF40	MS60	MS63	MS65
1959	12,559,000	1.25	2.00	3.00	6.00	10.00
1965 MW	3,000,000	1.50	6.00	12.00	20.00	35.00

Y# 51a 10 ZŁOTYCH

9.50 g., Copper-Nickel, 28 mm. **Obv:** Eagle with wings open **Rev:** Bust of Mikolaj Kopernik facing **Note:** Reduced size.

Date	Mintage	VF20	XF40	MS60	MS63	MS65
1967 MW	2,128,000	1.25	3.00	7.00	12.00	25.00
1968 MW	9,389,000	1.25	2.00	3.00	5.00	10.00
1969 MW	8,612,000	1.25	2.00	3.50	6.00	12.00

Y# 52.1 10 ZŁOTYCH

12.90 g., Copper-Nickel, 31 mm. **Subject:** 600th Anniversary of Jagiello University **Obv:** Eagle with wings open **Rev:** Stylized crowned head left **Edge:** Reeded **Note:** Legends raised.

Date	Mintage	VF20	XF40	MS60	MS63	MS65
ND (1964)	2,610,000	0.50	1.50	2.50	5.00	10.00

Y# 52.2 10 ZŁOTYCH

12.90 g., Copper-Nickel, 31 mm. **Subject:** 600th Anniversary of Jagiello University **Obv:** Eagle with wings open **Rev:** Stylized crowned head left **Edge:** Reeded **Note:** Legends incuse.

Date	Mintage	VF20	XF40	MS60	MS63	MS65
ND (1964)	2,612,000	0.50	1.50	2.50	5.00	10.00

Y# 54 10 ZŁOTYCH

12.90 g., Copper-Nickel, 31 mm. **Subject:** 700th Anniversary of Warsaw **Obv:** Eagle with wings open **Rev:** Nike of Warsaw with sword **Edge:** Reeded

Date	Mintage	VF20	XF40	MS60	MS63	MS65
1965 MW	3,492,000	0.75	1.25	2.50	5.00	8.00

Y# 55 10 ZŁOTYCH

12.90 g., Copper-Nickel, 31 mm. **Subject:** 700th Anniversary of Warsaw **Obv:** Stylized eagle with wings open **Rev:** Sigismund Pillar **Edge:** Reeded

Date	Mintage	VF20	XF40	MS60	MS63	MS65
1965 MW	2,000,000	0.75	1.25	2.50	5.00	8.00

Y# 56 10 ZŁOTYCH

9.50 g., Copper-Nickel, 28 mm. **Subject:** 200th Anniversary of Warsaw Mint **Obv:** Stylized eagle with wings open **Rev:** Sigismund Pillar **Edge Lettering:** W DWUSETNA ROCZNICE MENNICY WARSZAWSKIEJ

Date	Mintage	VF20	XF40	MS60	MS63	MS65
1966 MW	102,000	2.50	6.50	17.00	32.00	60.00

Y# 58 10 ZŁOTYCH

9.50 g., Copper-Nickel, 28 mm. **Subject:** 20th Anniversary - Death of General Swierczewski **Obv:** Eagle with wings open **Rev:** Military head left **Edge:** Reeded

Date	Mintage	VF20	XF40	MS60	MS63	MS65
1967 MW	2,000,000	0.50	1.00	2.00	3.50	6.00

Y# 59 10 ZŁOTYCH

9.50 g., Copper-Nickel, 28 mm. **Subject:** Centennial - Birth of Marie Sklodowska Curie **Obv:** Eagle with wings open **Rev:** Head facing **Edge:** Reeded

Date	Mintage	VF20	XF40	MS60	MS63	MS65
1967 MW	2,000,000	0.50	1.00	2.00	3.50	6.00

Y# 60 10 ZŁOTYCH

9.50 g., Copper-Nickel, 28 mm. **Subject:** 25th Anniversary - Peoples Army **Obv:** Eagle with wings open standing on perch **Rev:** XXV and helmeted head right **Edge:** Reeded

Date	Mintage	VF20	XF40	MS60	MS63	MS65
1968 MW	2,000,000	0.50	1.00	2.00	3.50	6.00

Y# 61 10 ZŁOTYCH

9.50 g., Copper-Nickel, 28 mm. **Subject:** 25th Anniversary - Peoples Republic **Obv:** Eagle with wings open within circle **Rev:** Radiant design within circle **Edge:** Reeded

Date	Mintage	VF20	XF40	MS60	MS63	MS65
1969 MW	2,000,000	0.50	1.00	2.00	3.50	6.00

Y# 62 10 ZŁOTYCH

9.50 g., Copper-Nickel, 28 mm. **Subject:** 25th Anniversary - Provincial Annexations **Obv:** Eagle with wings open, shield divides value **Rev:** Assorted shields **Edge:** Reeded

Date	Mintage	VF20	XF40	MS60	MS63	MS65
1970 MW	2,000,000	0.50	1.00	2.00	3.50	6.00

Y# 63 10 ZŁOTYCH

9.50 g., Copper-Nickel, 28 mm. **Series:** F.A.O. **Obv:** Eagle with wings open on shield **Rev:** Atlantic turbot and ear of barley **Edge:** Reeded

Date	Mintage	VF20	XF40	MS60	MS63	MS65
1971 MW	2,000,000	0.75	1.50	2.50	5.00	8.00

Y# 64 10 ZŁOTYCH

9.50 g., Copper-Nickel, 28 mm. **Subject:** 50th Anniversary - Battle of Upper Silesia **Obv:** Eagle with wings open divides date **Rev:** Design and emblem **Edge:** Reeded

Date	Mintage	VF20	XF40	MS60	MS63	MS65
1971 MW	2,000,000	0.50	1.00	2.00	3.50	6.00

Y# 65 10 ZŁOTYCH

9.50 g., Copper-Nickel, 28 mm. **Subject:** 50th Anniversary - Gdynia Seaport **Obv:** Eagle with wings open **Rev:** Map and emblem **Edge:** Reeded

Date	Mintage	VF20	XF40	MS60	MS63	MS65
1972 MW	2,000,000	0.50	1.00	2.00	3.50	6.00

Y# 73 10 ZŁOTYCH

7.70 g., Copper-Nickel, 25 mm. **Obv:** Eagle with wings open divides date **Rev:** Head of Boleslaw Prus left **Edge:** Reeded

Date	Mintage	VF20	XF40	MS60	MS63	MS65
1975 MW	35,000,000	0.50	1.25	2.00	2.75	4.50
1976 MW	20,000,000	0.50	1.25	2.00	2.75	4.50
1977 MW	25,000,000	0.50	1.25	2.00	2.76	4.50
1978 MW	4,006,999	0.50	1.50	2.50	5.00	8.00
1981 MW	2,655,000	0.50	2.00	4.00	8.00	14.00
1981 MW	5,000	PF65 17.00				
1982 MW	16,341,000	0.50	1.25	2.00	2.75	4.50
1982 MW	5,000	PF65 20.00				
1983 MW	14,248,000	0.50	1.25	2.00	2.75	4.50
1984 MW	19,064,000	0.50	1.25	2.00	2.75	4.50

Y# 74 10 ZŁOTYCH

7.70 g., Copper-Nickel, 25 mm. **Obv:** Eagle with wings open **Rev:** Head of Adam Micklewicz left **Edge:** Reeded

Date	Mintage	VF20	XF40	MS60	MS63	MS65
1975 MW	35,000,000	0.25	0.65	1.25	2.50	4.50
1976 MW	20,000,000	0.25	0.65	1.25	2.50	4.50

Y# 152.1 10 ZŁOTYCH

7.70 g., Copper-Nickel, 25 mm. **Obv:** Eagle with wings open **Rev:** Value **Edge:** Reeded

Date	Mintage	VF20	XF40	MS60	MS63	MS65
1984 MW	15,756,000	0.40	0.75	1.50	2.25	4.00
1985 MW	5,282,000	0.40	0.75	1.50	2.25	4.00
1986 MW	31,043,000	0.40	0.75	1.50	2.25	4.00
1986 MW	5,000	PF65 12.00				
1987 MW	69,636,000	0.40	0.75	1.50	2.25	4.00
1987 MW	5,000	PF65 12.00				
1988 MW	102,493,000	0.40	0.75	1.50	2.25	4.00
1988 MW	5,000	PF65 12.00				

Y# 152.2 10 ZŁOTYCH

4.27 g., Brass, 22 mm. **Obv:** Imperial eagle **Rev:** Value **Edge:** Reeded

Date	Mintage	VF20	XF40	MS60	MS63	MS65
1989 MW	80,800,000	0.40	0.65	1.25	1.75	3.00
1989 MW	5,000	PF65 12.00				
1990 MW	106,892,000	0.40	0.65	1.25	1.75	3.00
1990 MW	5,000	PF65 12.00				

Y# 67 20 ZŁOTYCH

10.15 g., Copper-Nickel, 29 mm. **Obv:** Eagle with wings open within circle **Rev:** Value within designed waterfall **Edge:** Reeded

Date	Mintage	VF20	XF40	MS60	MS63	MS65
1973 (kr)	25,000,000	0.25	1.00	2.00	3.50	6.00
1974 (kr)	12,000,000	0.25	0.75	1.50	2.50	4.50
1976 (w)	20,000,000	0.25	0.75	1.50	2.50	4.50

Y# 69 20 ZŁOTYCH
10.15 g., Copper-Nickel, 29 mm. **Obv:** Eagle with wings open, value below **Rev:** Bust of Marceli Nowotko 1/4 left **Edge:** Reeded

Date	Mintage	VF20	XF40	MS60	MS63	MS65
1974 MW	10,000,000	0.25	1.00	2.00	4.00	7.00
1975 (kr)	10,000,000	0.25	0.75	1.50	3.00	5.00
1976 (kr)	20,000,000	0.25	0.75	1.25	2.25	4.00
1976 MW	30,000,000	0.25	0.75	1.25	2.25	4.00
1977 MW	16,000,000	0.25	0.75	1.50	3.00	5.00
1983 MW	152,000	0.25	2.50	6.00	12.50	22.00

Y# 70 20 ZŁOTYCH
10.15 g., Copper-Nickel, 29 mm. **Subject:** 25th Anniversary of the Comcon **Obv:** Imperial eagle above value **Rev:** Half sunflower, half cog wheel **Edge:** Reeded

Date	Mintage	VF20	XF40	MS60	MS63	MS65
1974 MW	2,000,000	0.75	1.25	2.00	4.00	6.00

Y# 75 20 ZŁOTYCH
10.15 g., Copper-Nickel, 29 mm. **Subject:** International Women's Year **Obv:** Polish eagle above value **Rev:** Stylized head left **Edge:** Reeded

Date	Mintage	VF20	XF40	MS60	MS63	MS65
1975 MW	2,000,000	0.75	1.25	2.00	4.00	6.00

Y# 95 20 ZŁOTYCH
10.15 g., Copper-Nickel, 29 mm. **Obv:** Imperial eagle above value **Rev:** Head of Maria Konopnicka facing **Edge:** Reeded

Date	Mintage	VF20	XF40	MS60	MS63	MS65
1978 MW	2,010,000	0.75	1.25	2.00	4.00	6.00

Y# 97 20 ZŁOTYCH
10.15 g., Copper-Nickel, 29 mm. **Subject:** First Polish Cosmonaut **Obv:** Imperial eagle above value **Rev:** Cosmonaut head 1/4 left **Edge:** Reeded

Date	Mintage	VF20	XF40	MS60	MS63	MS65
1978 MW	2,009,000	0.75	1.25	2.00	4.00	6.00

Y# 99 20 ZŁOTYCH
10.15 g., Copper-Nickel, 29 mm. **Series:** International Year of the Child **Obv:** Imperial eagle above value **Rev:** Children playing **Edge:** Reeded

Date	Mintage	VF20	XF40	MS60	MS63	MS65
1979 MW	2,007,000	1.00	1.50	3.00	5.00	7.00
1979 MW	5,000	**PF65** 12.00				

Y# 108 20 ZŁOTYCH
10.15 g., Copper-Nickel, 29 mm. **Series:** 1980 Olympics **Obv:** Imperial eagle above value **Rev:** Runner **Edge:** Reeded

Date	Mintage	VF20	XF40	MS60	MS63	MS65
1980 MW	2,012,000	1.00	1.50	3.00	5.00	7.00
1980 MW	5,000	**PF65** 12.00				

Y# 112 20 ZŁOTYCH
10.15 g., Copper-Nickel, 29 mm. **Subject:** 50th Anniversary - Training Ship Daru Pomorza **Obv:** Imperial eagle above value **Rev:** Sailing ship **Edge:** Reeded

Date	Mintage	VF20	XF40	MS60	MS63	MS65
1980 MW	2,069,200	1.00	1.50	2.50	3.50	5.00
1980 MW	5,000	**PF65** 10.00				

Y# 153.1 20 ZŁOTYCH
8.70 g., Copper-Nickel, 26.5 mm. **Obv:** Eagle with wings open **Rev:** Value **Edge:** Reeded **Note:** Circulation coinage.

Date	Mintage	VF20	XF40	MS60	MS63	MS65
1984 MW	12,703,000	0.50	0.75	1.25	2.50	3.00
1985 MW	15,514,000	0.50	0.75	1.25	2.50	3.00
1986 MW	37,959,000	0.50	0.75	1.25	2.50	3.00
1986 MW	5,000	**PF65** 12.00				
1987 MW	22,213,000	0.50	0.75	1.25	2.50	3.00
1987 MW	5,000	**PF65** 12.00				
1988 MW	14,994,000	0.50	0.75	1.25	2.50	3.00
1988 MW	5,000	**PF65** 12.00				

Y# 153.2 20 ZŁOTYCH
5.65 g., Copper-Nickel, 24 mm. **Obv:** Eagle with wings open **Rev:** Value **Edge:** Reeded **Note:** Reduced size.

Date	Mintage	VF20	XF40	MS60	MS63	MS65
1989 MW	95,974,000	0.50	0.70	1.00	1.50	2.00
1989 MW	5,000	**PF65** 12.00				
1990 MW	104,712,000	0.50	0.70	1.00	1.50	2.00
1990 MW	5,000	**PF65** 12.00				

Y# 66 50 ZŁOTYCH
12.75 g., 0.750 Silver 0.3074 oz. ASW, 30 mm. **Obv:** Eagle with wings open **Rev:** Head of Fryderyk Chopin left

Date	Mintage	VF20	XF40	MS60	MS63	MS65
1972	49,999	**PF63** 30.00	**PF65** 45.00			
1974	10,375	**PF63** 35.00	**PF65** 50.00			

Y# 100 50 ZŁOTYCH
11.70 g., Copper-Nickel, 30.5 mm. **Obv:** Imperial eagle above value **Rev:** Bust of Duke Mieszko I 3/4 left **Edge:** Reeded

Date	Mintage	VF20	XF40	MS60	MS63	MS65
1979 MW	2,640,000	1.00	2.00	3.00	5.00	7.00
1979 MW	5,000	**PF65** 15.00				

Y# 114 50 ZŁOTYCH
11.70 g., Copper-Nickel, 30.5 mm. **Obv:** Imperial eagle above value **Rev:** King Boleslaw I Chrobry **Edge:** Reeded

Date	Mintage	VF20	XF40	MS60	MS63	MS65
1980 MW	2,564,000	1.00	2.00	3.00	5.00	7.00
1980 MW	5,000	**PF65** 12.50				

Y# 117 50 ZŁOTYCH
11.70 g., Copper-Nickel, 30.5 mm. **Obv:** Imperial eagle above value **Rev:** Crowned bust of Duke Kazimierz I Odnowiciel facing **Edge:** Reeded

Date	Mintage	VF20	XF40	MS60	MS63	MS65
1980 MW	2,504,000	1.00	2.00	3.00	5.00	7.00
1980 MW	5,000	**PF65** 12.50				

Y# 122 50 ZŁOTYCH
11.70 g., Copper-Nickel, 30.5 mm. **Obv:** Imperial eagle above value **Rev:** General Broni Wladyslaw Sikorski left **Edge:** Reeded

Date	Mintage	VF20	XF40	MS60	MS63	MS65
1981 MW	2,505,000	1.00	2.00	4.00	6.00	8.00
1981 MW	5,000	**PF65** 12.50				

Y# 124 50 ZŁOTYCH

11.70 g., Copper-Nickel, 30.5 mm. **Obv:** Imperial eagle above value **Rev:** Crowned bust of King Boleslaw II Smialy 1/4 right **Edge:** Reeded

Date	Mintage	VF20	XF40	MS60	MS63	MS65
1981 MW	2,538,000	1.00	1.50	2.50	4.50	6.00
1981 MW	5,000	PF65 12.00				

Y# 127 50 ZŁOTYCH

11.70 g., Copper-Nickel, 30.5 mm. **Series:** F.A.O. - World Food Day **Obv:** Imperial eagle above value **Rev:** F.A.O. logo within circle **Edge:** Reeded

Date	Mintage	VF20	XF40	MS60	MS63	MS65
1981 MW	2,524,000	1.00	1.50	2.50	4.50	6.00
1981 MW	5,000	PF65 12.00				

Y# 128 50 ZŁOTYCH

11.70 g., Copper-Nickel, 30.5 mm. **Obv:** Imperial eagle above value **Rev:** Head of King Wladyslaw I Herman 3/4 left **Edge:** Reeded

Date	Mintage	VF20	XF40	MS60	MS63	MS65
1981 MW	2,500,000	1.00	1.50	2.50	4.50	6.00
1981 MW	5,000	PF65 12.00				

Y# 133 50 ZŁOTYCH

11.70 g., Copper-Nickel, 30.5 mm. **Obv:** Imperial eagle above value **Rev:** King Boleslaw III Krzywousty **Edge:** Reeded

Date	Mintage	VF20	XF40	MS60	MS63	MS65
1982 MW	2,616,000	1.00	1.50	2.50	4.50	6.00
1982 MW	5,000	PF65 12.50				

Y# 142 50 ZŁOTYCH

11.70 g., Copper-Nickel, 30.5 mm. **Subject:** 150th Anniversary of Great Theater **Obv:** Imperial eagle above value **Rev:** Theater building **Edge:** Reeded

Date	Mintage	VF20	XF40	MS60	MS63	MS65
1983 MW	615,000	1.00	3.00	5.00	8.00	10.00

Y# 145 50 ZŁOTYCH

11.70 g., Copper-Nickel, 30.5 mm. **Obv:** Imperial eagle above value **Rev:** King Jan III Sobieski facing **Edge:** Reeded

Date	Mintage	VF20	XF40	MS60	MS63	MS65
1983 MW	2,576,000	1.00	1.50	2.50	4.50	6.00

Y# 146 50 ZŁOTYCH

11.70 g., Copper-Nickel, 30.5 mm. **Obv:** Imperial eagle above value **Rev:** Bust of Ignacy Lukasiewicz right **Edge:** Reeded

Date	Mintage	VF20	XF40	MS60	MS63	MS65
1983 MW	612,000	1.00	3.00	5.00	8.00	10.00

Y# 57 100 ZŁOTYCH

20.00 g., 0.900 Silver 0.5787 oz. ASW, 35 mm. **Subject:** Polish Millennium **Obv:** Eagle with wings open within assorted shields around border **Rev:** Two figures standing behind shield within circle

Date	Mintage	VF20	XF40	MS60	MS63	MS65
1966 MW	196,859	—	20.00	30.00	45.00	75.00

Y# 68 100 ZŁOTYCH

16.50 g., 0.625 Silver 0.3316 oz. ASW, 32 mm. **Subject:** 500th Anniversary - Birth of Mikolaj Kopernik, scientist **Obv:** Eagle with wings open within circle **Rev:** Head of Mikolaj Kopernik 1/4 left

Date	Mintage	VF20	XF40	MS60	MS63	MS65
1973 MW	51,000	PF63 28.00	PF65 35.00			
1974 MW	50,000	PF63 28.00	PF65 35.00			

Y# 71 100 ZŁOTYCH

16.50 g., 0.625 Silver 0.3316 oz. ASW, 32 mm. **Subject:** 40th Anniversary - Death of Maria Sklodowska Curie **Obv:** Imperial eagle above value **Rev:** Profile of Curie left with radiation lines running from the symbol of the element at right

Date	Mintage	VF20	XF40	MS60	MS63	MS65
1974 MW	50,000	PF63 32.50	PF65 42.50			

Y# 76 100 ZŁOTYCH

16.50 g., 0.625 Silver 0.3316 oz. ASW, 32 mm. **Obv:** Imperial eagle above value **Rev:** Royal castle in Warsaw

Date	Mintage	VF20	XF40	MS60	MS63	MS65
1975 MW	50,177	PF63 30.00	PF65 40.00			

Y# 77 100 ZŁOTYCH

16.50 g., 0.625 Silver 0.3316 oz. ASW, 32 mm. **Obv:** Imperial eagle above value **Rev:** Ignacy Jan Paderewski, composer, left

Date	Mintage	VF20	XF40	MS60	MS63	MS65
1975 MW	60,184	PF63 22.50	PF65 32.50			

Y# 78 100 ZŁOTYCH

16.50 g., 0.625 Silver 0.3316 oz. ASW, 32 mm. **Obv:** Imperial eagle above value **Rev:** Bust of Helena Modrzejewska right

Date	Mintage	VF20	XF40	MS60	MS63	MS65
1975 MW	60,158	PF63 22.50	PF65 32.50			

Y# 82 100 ZŁOTYCH

16.50 g., 0.625 Silver 0.3316 oz. ASW, 32 mm. **Obv:** Imperial eagle above value **Rev:** Tadeusz Kosciuszko right

Date	Mintage	VF20	XF40	MS60	MS63	MS65
1976 MW	100,148	PF63 22.50	PF65 32.50			

Y# 84 100 ZŁOTYCH

16.50 g., 0.625 Silver 0.3316 oz. ASW, 32 mm. **Obv:** Imperial eagle above value **Rev:** Head of Kazimierz Pulaski left

Date	Mintage	VF20	XF40	MS60	MS63	MS65
1976 MW	100,334	PF63 22.50	PF65 32.50			

Y# 87 100 ZŁOTYCH
16.50 g., 0.625 Silver 0.3316 oz. ASW, 32 mm. **Series:** Environment Protection **Obv:** Imperial eagle above value **Rev:** Buffalo

Date	Mintage	VF20	XF40	MS60	MS63	MS65
1977 MW	30,050	**PF63** 60.00	**PF65** 75.00			

Y# 88 100 ZŁOTYCH
16.50 g., 0.625 Silver 0.3316 oz. ASW, 32 mm. **Obv:** Imperial eagle above value **Rev:** Henryk Sienkiewicz, Writer, left

Date	Mintage	VF20	XF40	MS60	MS63	MS65
1977 MW	20,000	**PF63** 40.00	**PF65** 55.00			

Y# 89 100 ZŁOTYCH
16.50 g., 0.625 Silver 0.3316 oz. ASW, 32 mm. **Obv:** Imperial eagle above value **Rev:** Head of Wladyslaw Reymont 1/4 right

Date	Mintage	VF20	XF40	MS60	MS63	MS65
1977 MW	20,150	**PF63** 30.00	**PF65** 40.00			

Y# 91 100 ZŁOTYCH
16.50 g., 0.625 Silver 0.3316 oz. ASW, 32 mm. **Obv:** Imperial eagle above value **Rev:** Castle

Date	Mintage	VF20	XF40	MS60	MS63	MS65
1977 MW	30,000	**PF63** 30.00	**PF65** 40.00			

Y# 92 100 ZŁOTYCH
16.50 g., 0.625 Silver 0.3316 oz. ASW, 32 mm. **Obv:** Imperial eagle above value **Rev:** Bust of Adam Mickiewicz facing

Date	Mintage	VF20	XF40	MS60	MS63	MS65
1978 MW	30,000	**PF63** 25.00	**PF65** 35.00			

Y# 93 100 ZŁOTYCH
16.50 g., 0.625 Silver 0.3316 oz. ASW, 32 mm. **Series:** Environment Protection **Obv:** Imperial eagle above value **Rev:** Moose heading left

Date	Mintage	VF20	XF40	MS60	MS63	MS65
1978 MW	30,000	**PF63** 50.00	**PF65** 65.00			

Y# 94 100 ZŁOTYCH
16.50 g., 0.625 Silver 0.3316 oz. ASW, 32 mm. **Subject:** 100th Anniversary - Birth of Janusz Korczak **Obv:** Imperial eagle above value **Rev:** Bust facing

Date	Mintage	VF20	XF40	MS60	MS63	MS65
1978 MW	30,000	**PF63** 25.00	**PF65** 35.00			

Y# 96 100 ZŁOTYCH
16.50 g., 0.625 Silver 0.3316 oz. ASW, 32 mm. **Series:** Environment Protection **Obv:** Imperial eagle above value **Rev:** Beaver

Date	Mintage	VF20	XF40	MS60	MS63	MS65
1978 MW	30,000	**PF63** 50.00	**PF65** 65.00			

Y# 98 100 ZŁOTYCH
16.50 g., 0.625 Silver 0.3316 oz. ASW, 32 mm. **Obv:** Imperial eagle above value **Rev:** Head of Henryk Wieniawski 3/4 left

Date	Mintage	VF20	XF40	MS60	MS63	MS65
1979 MW	30,000	**PF63** 25.00	**PF65** 35.00			

Y# 103 100 ZŁOTYCH
16.50 g., 0.625 Silver 0.3316 oz. ASW, 32 mm. **Obv:** Imperial eagle above value **Rev:** Ludwik Zamenhof left

Date	Mintage	VF20	XF40	MS60	MS63	MS65
1979 MW	30,000	**PF63** 25.00	**PF65** 35.00			

Y# 104 100 ZŁOTYCH
16.50 g., 0.625 Silver 0.3316 oz. ASW, 32 mm. **Series:** Environment Protection **Obv:** Imperial eagle above value **Rev:** Lynx

Date	Mintage	VF20	XF40	MS60	MS63	MS65
1979 MW	20,000	**PF63** 65.00	**PF65** 80.00			

Y# 105 100 ZŁOTYCH
16.50 g., 0.625 Silver 0.3316 oz. ASW, 32 mm. **Series:** Environment Protection **Obv:** Imperial eagle above value **Rev:** Chamois

Date	Mintage	VF20	XF40	MS60	MS63	MS65
1979 MW	20,000	**PF63** 65.00	**PF65** 80.00			

Y# 109 100 ZŁOTYCH
16.50 g., 0.625 Silver 0.3316 oz. ASW, 32 mm. **Series:** 1980 Olympics **Obv:** Imperial eagle above value **Rev:** Olympic rings and runner

Date	Mintage	VF20	XF40	MS60	MS63	MS65
1980 MW	10,000	**PF63** 75.00	**PF65** 90.00			

Y# 120 100 ZŁOTYCH
16.50 g., 0.625 Silver 0.3316 oz. ASW, 32 mm. **Subject:** 450th Anniversary - Birth of Jan Kochanowski, Poet **Obv:** Imperial eagle above value **Rev:** Bust of Jan Kochanowski 1/4 right

Date	Mintage	VF20	XF40	MS60	MS63	MS65
1980 MW	10,000	**PF63** 50.00	**PF65** 65.00			

Y# 121 100 ZŁOTYCH
16.50 g., 0.625 Silver 0.3316 oz. ASW, 32 mm. **Series:** Environment Protection **Obv:** Imperial eagle above value **Rev:** Cappercaillie

Date	Mintage	VF20	XF40	MS60	MS63	MS65
1980 MW	18,000	**PF63** 70.00	**PF65** 90.00			

Y# 123 100 ZŁOTYCH
16.50 g., 0.625 Silver 0.3316 oz. ASW, 32 mm. **Obv:** Imperial eagle above value **Rev:** General Broni Wladyslaw Sikorski left

Date	Mintage	VF20	XF40	MS60	MS63	MS65
1981 MW	12,000	**PF63** 45.00	**PF65** 60.00			

Y# 126 100 ZŁOTYCH
16.50 g., 0.625 Silver 0.3316 oz. ASW, 32 mm. **Series:** Environment Protection **Obv:** Imperial eagle above value **Rev:** Horse right

Date	Mintage	VF20	XF40	MS60	MS63	MS65
1981 MW	12,000	**PF63** 170	**PF65** 200			

Y# 136 100 ZŁOTYCH
14.15 g., 0.750 Silver 0.3412 oz. ASW, 30 mm. **Subject:** Visit of Pope John Paul II **Obv:** Imperial eagle above value **Rev:** Bust left

Date	Mintage	VF20	XF40	MS60	MS63	MS65
1982 CHI	8,700	—	—	—	225	—
1982 CHI	3,750	**PF65** 450				
1985 CHI Unique	—	—	—	—	—	—
1985 CHI Proof	5	—	—	—	—	—
1986 CHI	80	—	—	—	1,000	—
1986 CHI	128	**PF65** 1,150				

Y# 141 100 ZŁOTYCH
16.50 g., 0.625 Silver 0.3316 oz. ASW **Series:** Environment Protection **Obv:** Imperial eagle above value **Rev:** White Stork walking right

Date	Mintage	VF20	XF40	MS60	MS63	MS65
1982 MW	12,000	**PF63** 135	**PF65** 160			

Y# 147 100 ZŁOTYCH
16.50 g., 0.625 Silver 0.3316 oz. ASW, 32 mm. **Series:** Environment Protection **Obv:** Imperial eagle above value **Rev:** Bear walking right

Date	Mintage	VF20	XF40	MS60	MS63	MS65
1983 MW	8,000	**PF63** 245	**PF65** 280			

Y# 148 100 ZŁOTYCH
10.80 g., Copper-Nickel, 29.5 mm. **Obv:** Imperial eagle above value **Rev:** Wincenty Witos 3/4 facing **Edge:** Reeded

Date	Mintage	VF20	XF40	MS60	MS63	MS65
1984 MW	1,530,000	—	—	2.00	3.00	5.00

Y# 151 100 ZŁOTYCH
10.80 g., Copper-Nickel, 29.5 mm. **Subject:** 40th Anniversary of Peoples Republic **Obv:** Imperial eagle above value **Rev:** 40 PRL within design **Edge:** Reeded

Date	Mintage	VF20	XF40	MS60	MS63	MS65
1984 MW	2,595,000	—	—	2.00	3.00	5.00

Y# 155 100 ZŁOTYCH
10.80 g., Copper-Nickel, 29.5 mm. **Obv:** Imperial eagle above value **Rev:** King Przemyslaw II **Edge:** Reeded

Date	Mintage	VF20	XF40	MS60	MS63	MS65
1985 MW	2,924,000	—	—	2.00	3.00	5.00

Y# 157 100 ZŁOTYCH
9.60 g., Nickel Plated Steel, 29.5 mm. **Subject:** Polish Women's Memorial Hospital Center **Obv:** Imperial eagle above value **Rev:** Woman breastfeeding Child **Edge:** Reeded

Date	Mintage	VF20	XF40	MS60	MS63	MS65
1985 MW	1,927,000	—	—	2.00	3.00	5.00

Y# 160 100 ZŁOTYCH
10.80 g., Copper-Nickel, 29.5 mm. **Obv:** Imperial eagle above value **Rev:** Bust of King Wladyslaw I Lokietek 1/4 right **Edge:** Reeded

Date	Mintage	VF20	XF40	MS60	MS63	MS65
1986 MW	2,540,000	—	—	2.00	3.00	5.00
1986 MW	5,000	**PF65** 25.00				

Y# 167 100 ZŁOTYCH
10.80 g., Copper-Nickel, 29.5 mm. **Obv:** Imperial eagle above value **Rev:** King Kazimierz III half left **Edge:** Reeded

Date	Mintage	VF20	XF40	MS60	MS63	MS65
1987 MW	2,479,000	—	—	2.50	3.50	5.50
1987 MW	5,000	**PF65** 25.00				

Y# 182 100 ZŁOTYCH
10.80 g., Copper-Nickel, 29.5 mm. **Subject:** 70th Anniversary - Wielkopolskiego Insurrection **Obv:** Imperial eagle above value **Rev:** Uniformed conjoined busts left **Edge:** Reeded

Date	Mintage	VF20	XF40	MS60	MS63	MS65
1988 MW	2,513,000	—	—	2.00	3.00	5.00
1988 MW	5,000	**PF65** 25.00				

Y# 183 100 ZŁOTYCH
10.80 g., Copper-Nickel, 29.5 mm. **Obv:** Imperial eagle above value **Rev:** Queen Jadwiga 1384-1399 **Edge:** Reeded

Date	Mintage	VF20	XF40	MS60	MS63	MS65
1988 MW	2,469,000	—	—	2.00	3.00	5.00
1988 MW	5,000	**PF65** 25.00				

Y# 72 200 ZŁOTYCH
14.47 g., 0.625 Silver 0.2908 oz. ASW, 31 mm. **Subject:** 30th Anniversary - Polish Peoples Republic **Obv:** Eagle with wings open within square with value below **Rev:** XXX LAT PRL in square within shaded design **Edge:** Reeded

Date	Mintage	VF20	XF40	MS60	MS63	MS65
1974 MW	13,062,000	—	—	7.00	12.00	20.00
1974 MW	6,000	**PF63** 32.00	**PF65** 45.00			

Y# 79 200 ZŁOTYCH
14.47 g., 0.750 Silver 0.3489 oz. ASW, 31 mm. **Subject:** 30th Anniversary - Victory Over Fascism **Obv:** Eagle with wings open divides date **Rev:** Conjoined military heads left **Edge:** Reeded

Date	Mintage	VF20	XF40	MS60	MS63	MS65
1975 MW	1,826,000	—	—	10.00	15.00	20.00
1975 MW	2,600	**PF63** 35.00	**PF65** 48.00			

Y# 86 200 ZŁOTYCH
14.47 g., 0.625 Silver 0.2908 oz. ASW, 31 mm. **Series:** XXI Olympics **Obv:** Imperial eagle above value **Rev:** Rings and torch **Edge:** Reeded

Date	Mintage	VF20	XF40	MS60	MS63	MS65
1976 MW	2,072,000	—	—	8.00	13.00	20.00
1976 MW	11,000	**PF63** 35.00	**PF65** 40.00			

Y# 101 200 ZŁOTYCH
17.60 g., 0.750 Silver 0.4244 oz. ASW, 33 mm. **Obv:** Imperial eagle above value **Rev:** Uniformed bust of Duke Mieszko I 1/4 left

Date	Mintage	VF20	XF40	MS60	MS63	MS65
1979 MW	12,150	PF63 145	PF65 175			

Y# 110.1 200 ZŁOTYCH
17.60 g., 0.750 Silver 0.4244 oz. ASW, 33 mm. **Series:** Winter Olympics **Obv:** Imperial eagle above value **Rev:** Torch below ski jumper

Date	Mintage	VF20	XF40	MS60	MS63	MS65
1980 MW	32,040	PF63 50.00	PF65 60.00			

Y# 110.2 200 ZŁOTYCH
17.60 g., 0.750 Silver 0.4244 oz. ASW, 33 mm. **Series:** Winter Olympics **Obv:** Imperial eagle above value **Rev:** Ski jumper, no torch below

Date	Mintage	VF20	XF40	MS60	MS63	MS65
1980 MW	28,040	PF63 45.00	PF65 55.00			

Y# 115 200 ZŁOTYCH
17.60 g., 0.750 Silver 0.4244 oz. ASW, 33 mm. **Obv:** Imperial eagle above value **Rev:** King Boleslaw I Chrobry

Date	Mintage	VF20	XF40	MS60	MS63	MS65
1980 MW	12,000	PF63 145	PF65 165			

Y# 118 200 ZŁOTYCH
17.60 g., 0.750 Silver 0.4244 oz. ASW, 33 mm. **Obv:** Imperial eagle above value **Rev:** Bust of Duke Kazimierz I facing

Date	Mintage	VF20	XF40	MS60	MS63	MS65
1980 MW	12,000	PF63 80.00	PF65 100			

Y# 125 200 ZŁOTYCH
17.60 g., 0.750 Silver 0.4244 oz. ASW, 33 mm. **Obv:** Imperial eagle above value **Rev:** King Bolaslaw II Smialy 3/4 facing

Date	Mintage	VF20	XF40	MS60	MS63	MS65
1981 MW	12,000	PF63 80.00	PF65 100			

Y# 129 200 ZŁOTYCH
17.60 g., 0.750 Silver 0.4244 oz. ASW, 33 mm. **Obv:** Imperial eagle above value **Rev:** Bust of King Wladyslaw I Herman left within circle

Date	Mintage	VF20	XF40	MS60	MS63	MS65
1981 MW	12,000	PF63 80.00	PF65 100			

Y# 130 200 ZŁOTYCH
17.60 g., 0.750 Silver 0.4244 oz. ASW, 33 mm. **Subject:** World Soccer Championship Games in Spain **Obv:** Imperial eagle above value **Rev:** Stylized soccer player, date and names within grid-lined background

Date	Mintage	VF20	XF40	MS60	MS63	MS65
1982 MW	21,000	PF63 25.00	PF65 35.00			

Y# 132 200 ZŁOTYCH
17.60 g., 0.750 Silver 0.4244 oz. ASW, 33 mm. **Obv:** Imperial eagle above value **Rev:** King Boleslaw III Krzywousty

Date	Mintage	VF20	XF40	MS60	MS63	MS65
1982 MW	12,000	PF63 85.00	PF65 100			

Y# 137 200 ZŁOTYCH
28.30 g., 0.750 Silver 0.6824 oz. ASW, 40 mm. **Subject:** Visit of Pope John Paul II **Obv:** Imperial eagle above value **Rev:** Bust left

Date	Mintage	VF20	XF40	MS60	MS63	MS65
1982 CHI	3,000	—	—	—	475	575
1982 CHI	3,650	PF65 600				
1985 CHI Unique	—	—	—	—	—	—
1985 CHI Proof	5	—	—	—	—	—
1986 CHI	32	—	—	—	850	—
1986 CHI	75	PF65 900				

Y# 143 200 ZŁOTYCH
17.60 g., 0.750 Silver 0.4244 oz. ASW, 33 mm. **Obv:** Imperial eagle above value **Rev:** King Jan III Sobieski

Date	Mintage	VF20	XF40	MS60	MS63	MS65
1983 MW	11,000	PF63 80.00	PF65 95.00			

Y# 149 200 ZŁOTYCH
17.60 g., 0.750 Silver 0.4244 oz. ASW, 33 mm. **Series:** Winter Olympics **Obv:** Imperial eagle above value **Rev:** Ice skater

Date	Mintage	VF20	XF40	MS60	MS63	MS65
1984 MW	15,000	PF63 32.00	PF65 40.00			

Y# 150 200 ZŁOTYCH
17.60 g., 0.750 Silver 0.4244 oz. ASW, 33 mm. **Series:** Summer Olympics **Obv:** Imperial eagle above value **Rev:** Hurdler

Date	Mintage	VF20	XF40	MS60	MS63	MS65
1984 MW	16,000	PF63 32.00	PF65 37.00			

Y# 83 500 ZŁOTYCH
30.00 g., 0.900 Gold 0.8681 oz. AGW, 32 mm. **Obv:** Imperial eagle above value **Rev:** Head of Tadeusz Kosciuszko right

Date	Mintage	VF20	XF40	MS60	MS63	MS65
1976 MW	2,318	PF65 1,850				

Y# 85 500 ZŁOTYCH
30.00 g., 0.900 Gold 0.8681 oz. AGW, 32 mm. **Obv:** Imperial eagle above value **Rev:** Kazimierz Pulaski left

Date	Mintage	VF20	XF40	MS60	MS63	MS65
1976 MW	2,315	PF65 1,850				

Y# 154 500 ZŁOTYCH

16.50 g., 0.625 Silver 0.3316 oz. ASW, 32 mm. **Series:** Environment Protection **Obv:** Imperial eagle above value **Rev:** Swan and two chicks

Date	Mintage	VF20	XF40	MS60	MS63	MS65
1984 MW	10,000	PF63 170	PF65 200			

Y# 156 500 ZŁOTYCH

16.50 g., 0.750 Silver 0.3979 oz. ASW, 32 mm. **Obv:** Imperial eagle above value **Rev:** King Przemyslaw II

Date	Mintage	VF20	XF40	MS60	MS63	MS65
1985 MW	8,000	PF63 130	PF65 150			

Y# 158 500 ZŁOTYCH

16.50 g., 0.750 Silver 0.3979 oz. ASW, 32 mm. **Subject:** 40th Anniversary of United Nations **Obv:** Imperial eagle above value **Rev:** UN logo within sprigs

Date	Mintage	VF20	XF40	MS60	MS63	MS65
1985 MW	10,000	PF63 40.00	PF65 50.00			

Y# 159 500 ZŁOTYCH

16.50 g., 0.750 Silver 0.3979 oz. ASW, 32 mm. **Series:** Environmental Protection **Obv:** Imperial eagle above value **Rev:** Red squirrel

Date	Mintage	VF20	XF40	MS60	MS63	MS65
1985 MW	8,000	PF63 245	PF65 285			

Y# 161 500 ZŁOTYCH

16.50 g., 0.750 Silver 0.3979 oz. ASW, 32 mm. **Obv:** Imperial eagle above value **Rev:** King Wladyslaw I Lokietek half right

Date	Mintage	VF20	XF40	MS60	MS63	MS65
1986 MW	8,000	PF63 130	PF65 150			

Y# 162 500 ZŁOTYCH

16.50 g., 0.750 Silver 0.3979 oz. ASW, 32 mm. **Series:** Environment Protection **Obv:** Eagle with wings open divides date **Rev:** Owl with 2 chicks

Date	Mintage	VF20	XF40	MS60	MS63	MS65
1986 MW	12,000	PF63 115	PF65 140			

Y# 225 500 ZŁOTYCH

16.50 g., 0.750 Silver 0.3979 oz. ASW, 32 mm. **Obv:** Imperial eagle above value **Rev:** Soccer ball in net

Date	Mintage	VF20	XF40	MS60	MS63	MS65
1986 MW	16,000	PF63 40.00	PF65 50.00			

Y# 165 500 ZŁOTYCH

16.50 g., 0.750 Silver 0.3979 oz. ASW, 32 mm. **Series:** Olympics **Obv:** Imperial eagle above value **Rev:** Equestrian

Date	Mintage	VF20	XF40	MS60	MS63	MS65
1987 MW	15,000	PF63 40.00	PF65 50.00			

Y# 166 500 ZŁOTYCH

16.50 g., 0.750 Silver 0.3979 oz. ASW, 32 mm. **Subject:** European Championship Soccer Games **Obv:** Imperial eagle above value **Rev:** Soccer player

Date	Mintage	VF20	XF40	MS60	MS63	MS65
1987 MW	12,000	PF63 42.00	PF65 55.00			

Y# 172 500 ZŁOTYCH

16.50 g., 0.750 Silver 0.3979 oz. ASW, 32 mm. **Series:** Winter Olympics **Obv:** Imperial eagle above value **Rev:** Ice hockey goalie

Date	Mintage	VF20	XF40	MS60	MS63	MS65
1987 MW	15,000	PF63 30.00	PF65 40.00			

Y# 173 500 ZŁOTYCH

16.50 g., 0.750 Silver 0.3979 oz. ASW, 32 mm. **Obv:** Imperial eagle above value **Rev:** Bust of King Kazimierz III 3/4 facing

Date	Mintage	VF20	XF40	MS60	MS63	MS65
1987 MW	8,000	PF63 130	PF65 160			

Y# 181 500 ZŁOTYCH

16.50 g., 0.750 Silver 0.3979 oz. ASW, 32 mm. **Obv:** Imperial eagle above value **Rev:** Crowned bust of Queen Jadwiga facing

Date	Mintage	VF20	XF40	MS60	MS63	MS65
1988 MW	8,000	PF63 195	PF65 225			

Y# 184 500 ZŁOTYCH

16.50 g., 0.750 Silver 0.3979 oz. ASW, 32 mm. **Obv:** Imperial eagle above value **Rev:** Colosseum within split soccer ball

Date	Mintage	VF20	XF40	MS60	MS63	MS65
1988 MW	15,000	PF63 38.00	PF65 45.00			

Y# 185 500 ZŁOTYCH

10.80 g., Copper-Nickel, 29.5 mm. **Subject:** 50th Anniversary - Beginning of WWII **Obv:** Imperial eagle above value **Rev:** Infantry soldiers advancing **Edge:** Reeded

Date	Mintage	VF20	XF40	MS60	MS63	MS65
1989 MW	10,135,000	—	—	1.50	2.50	4.00
1989 MW	5,000	PF65 25.00				

Y# 194 500 ZŁOTYCH

10.80 g., Copper-Nickel, 29.5 mm. **Obv:** Imperial eagle above value **Rev:** Bust of King Wladyslaw II 1/4 left **Edge:** Reeded

Date	Mintage	VF20	XF40	MS60	MS63	MS65
1989 MW	2,544,000	—	—	2.00	3.00	5.00
1989 MW	5,000	PF65 25.00				

Y# 138 1000 ZŁOTYCH
3.40 g., 0.900 Gold 0.0984 oz. AGW, 18 mm. **Subject:** Visit of Pope John Paul II **Obv:** Eagle with wings open divides date **Rev:** 1/2 Figure of Pope 1/4 left

Date	Mintage	VF20	XF40	MS60	MS63	MS65
1982 CHI	900	—	—	—	—	1,250
1982 CHI	1,700	PF65 1,400				
1985 CHI Unique	—	—	—	—	—	—
1985 CHI Proof	2	—	—	—	—	—
1986 CHI	83	—	—	—	—	1,950
1986 CHI	53	PF65 2,400				

Y# 144 1000 ZŁOTYCH
14.50 g., 0.625 Silver 0.2914 oz. ASW, 31 mm. **Subject:** Visit of Pope John Paul II **Obv:** Imperial eagle above value **Rev:** Bust left

Date	Mintage	VF20	XF40	MS60	MS63	MS65
1982 MW	803,000	—	—	15.00	20.00	25.00
1983 MW	1,530,000	—	—	12.50	17.50	20.00
1983 MW	10,000	PF65 65.00				

Y# 168 1000 ZŁOTYCH
3.11 g., 0.999 Gold 0.0999 oz. AGW, 18 mm. **Subject:** Papal Visit in America **Obv:** Eagle above value **Rev:** Half figure of Pope 3/4 left **Note:** Similar to KM#163.

Date	Mintage	VF20	XF40	MS60	MS63	MS65
1987 MW	201	PF65 3,500				

Y# 174 1000 ZŁOTYCH
3.11 g., 0.999 Gold 0.0999 oz. AGW, 18 mm. **Subject:** 10th Anniversary of Pope John Paul II **Obv:** Imperial eagle above value **Rev:** Bust left **Note:** Similar to KM#177.

Date	Mintage	VF20	XF40	MS60	MS63	MS65
1988 MW	1,000	PF65 1,250				

Y# 186 1000 ZŁOTYCH
3.11 g., 0.999 Gold 0.0999 oz. AGW, 18 mm. **Subject:** Pope John Paul II **Obv:** Eagle above value **Rev:** Bust left on patterned background

Date	Mintage	VF20	XF40	MS60	MS63	MS65
1989 MW Sets only	Est. 1000	—	—	—	—	1,700

Y# 90 2000 ZŁOTYCH
8.00 g., 0.900 Gold 0 .2315 oz. AGW, 21 mm. **Obv:** Eagle with wings open divides date **Rev:** Head of Fryderyk Chopin left

Date	Mintage	VF20	XF40	MS60	MS63	MS65
1977 MW	4,000	PF65 650				

Y# 102 2000 ZŁOTYCH
8.00 g., 0.900 Gold 0.2315 oz. AGW, 21 mm. **Obv:** Eagle with wings open divides date **Rev:** Duke Mieszko I

Date	Mintage	VF20	XF40	MS60	MS63	MS65
1979 MW	3,000	PF65 800				

Y# 106 2000 ZŁOTYCH
8.00 g., 0.900 Gold 0.2315 oz. AGW, 21 mm. **Obv:** Eagle with wings open divides date **Rev:** Head of Mikolaj Kopernik 1/4 right

Date	Mintage	VF20	XF40	MS60	MS63	MS65
1979 MW	5,000	PF65 475				

Y# 107 2000 ZŁOTYCH
8.00 g., 0.900 Gold 0.2315 oz. AGW, 21 mm. **Obv:** Eagle with wings open divides date **Rev:** Profile of Maria Skiodowska Curie left, symbol at right

Date	Mintage	VF20	XF40	MS60	MS63	MS65
1979 MW	5,000	PF65 425				

Y# 111 2000 ZŁOTYCH
8.00 g., 0.900 Gold 0.2315 oz. AGW, 21 mm. **Series:** Winter Olympics **Obv:** Eagle above value **Rev:** Ski jumper

Date	Mintage	VF20	XF40	MS60	MS63	MS65
1980 MW	5,250	PF65 425				

Y# 116 2000 ZŁOTYCH
8.00 g., 0.900 Gold 0.2315 oz. AGW, 24 mm. **Obv:** Eagle above value **Rev:** King Boleslaw I Chrobry

Date	Mintage	VF20	XF40	MS60	MS63	MS65
1980 MW	2,500	PF65 1,200				

Y# 119 2000 ZŁOTYCH
8.00 g., 0.900 Gold 0.2315 oz. AGW, 21 mm. **Obv:** Eagle above value **Rev:** Kazimierz I

Date	Mintage	VF20	XF40	MS60	MS63	MS65
1980 MW	2,500	PF65 800				

Y# 131 2000 ZŁOTYCH
8.00 g., 0.900 Gold 0.2315 oz. AGW, 21 mm. **Obv:** Eagle above value **Rev:** Wladyslaw I Herman **Note:** Similar to 200 Zlotych, Y#129.

Date	Mintage	VF20	XF40	MS60	MS63	MS65
1981 MW	3,113	PF65 750				

Y# 135 2000 ZŁOTYCH
8.00 g., 0.900 Gold 0.2315 oz. AGW, 21 mm. **Obv:** Eagle above value **Rev:** Boleslaw II

Date	Mintage	VF20	XF40	MS60	MS63	MS65
1981 MW	—	PF65 750				

Y# 139 2000 ZŁOTYCH
6.80 g., 0.900 Gold 0.1968 oz. AGW, 23 mm. **Subject:** Visit of Pope John Paul II **Obv:** Eagle above value **Rev:** Half-figure of Pope 1/4 left

Date	Mintage	VF20	XF40	MS60	MS63	MS65
1982 CHI	500	—	—	—	—	2,500
1982 CHI	1,250	PF65 1,750				
1985 CHI Unique	—	—	—	—	—	—
1985 CHI Proof	Est. 2	—	—	—	—	—
1986 CHI	Est. 54	—	—	—	—	5,300
1986 CHI	Est. 79	PF65 4,900				

Y# 169 2000 ZŁOTYCH
7.77 g., 0.999 Gold 0.2496 oz. AGW, 22 mm. **Subject:** Papal Visit in America **Obv:** Eagle above value **Rev:** 1/2-figure of Pope with staff left **Note:** Similar to KM#163.

Date	Mintage	VF20	XF40	MS60	MS63	MS65
1987 MW	201	PF65 4,500				

Y# 175 2000 ZŁOTYCH
7.77 g., 0.999 Gold 0.2496 oz. AGW, 22 mm. **Subject:** 10th Anniversary of Pope John Paul II **Obv:** Eage above value **Rev:** Bust left **Note:** Similar to KM#177.

Date	Mintage	VF20	XF40	MS60	MS63	MS65
1988	1,000	PF65 2,000				

Y# 187 2000 ZŁOTYCH
7.77 g., 0.999 Gold 0.2496 oz. AGW, 22 mm. **Obv:** Eagle above value **Rev:** Bust left on patterned background **Note:** Pope John Paul II.

Date	Mintage	VF20	XF40	MS60	MS63	MS65
1989 MW	Est. 1000	—	—	—	—	1,950

Sets only

Y# 170 5000 ZŁOTYCH
15.55 g., 0.999 Gold 0.4994 oz. AGW, 27 mm. **Subject:** Papal Visit in America **Obv:** Eagle above value **Rev:** Half-figure of Pope with staff left **Note:** Similar to KM#163.

Date	Mintage	VF20	XF40	MS60	MS63	MS65
1987 MW	201	PF65 6,500				

Y# 176 5000 ZŁOTYCH
15.55 g., 0.999 Gold 0.4994 oz. AGW, 27 mm. **Subject:** 10th Anniversary of Pope John Paul II **Obv:** Eagle above value **Rev:** Bust left **Note:** Similar to KM#177.

Date	Mintage	VF20	XF40	MS60	MS63	MS65
1988 MW	1,000	PF65 3,000				

Y# 188 5000 ZŁOTYCH
15.55 g., 0.999 Gold 0.4994 oz. AGW, 27 mm. **Subject:** Pope John Paul II **Obv:** Eagle above value **Rev:** Bust left on patterned background

Date	Mintage	VF20	XF40	MS60	MS63	MS65
1989 MW	Est. 1000	—	—	—	—	3,000

Sets only

Y# 191 5000 ZŁOTYCH
16.50 g., 0.750 Silver 0.3979 oz. ASW, 32 mm. **Obv:** Eagle with wings open divides date **Rev:** Circular design in front of bust facing 1/4 left, building in background

Date	Mintage	VF20	XF40	MS60	MS63	MS65
1989 MW	20,000	PF63 40.00		PF65 50.00		

Y# 192 5000 ZŁOTYCH
16.50 g., 0.750 Silver 0.3979 oz. ASW, 32 mm. **Obv:** Imperial eagle above value **Rev:** Torunia Town Hall

Date	Mintage	VF20	XF40	MS60	MS63	MS65
1989 MW	20,000	PF63 40.00		PF65 50.00		

Y# 193 5000 ZŁOTYCH
16.50 g., 0.750 Silver 0.3979 oz. ASW, 32 mm. **Obv:** Imperial eagle above value **Rev:** Henryk Sucharski

Date	Mintage	VF20	XF40	MS60	MS63	MS65
1989 MW	25,000	PF63 35.00	PF65 45.00			

Y# 197 5000 ZŁOTYCH
16.50 g., 0.750 Silver 0.3979 oz. ASW, 32 mm. **Obv:** Imperial eagle above value **Rev:** Bust of King Wladyslaw II

Date	Mintage	VF20	XF40	MS60	MS63	MS65
1989 MW	8,000	PF63 130	PF65 155			

Y# 198 5000 ZŁOTYCH
16.50 g., 0.750 Silver 0.3979 oz. ASW, 32 mm. **Obv:** Imperial eagle above value **Rev:** Half-length portrait of King Wladyslaw II

Date	Mintage	VF20	XF40	MS60	MS63	MS65
1989 MW	2,500	PF63 600	PF65 650			

Y# 140 10000 ZŁOTYCH
34.50 g., 0.900 Gold 0.9983 oz. AGW, 40 mm. **Subject:** Visit of Pope John Paul II **Obv:** Eagle above value **Rev:** Half-figure of Pope 1/4 left

Date	Mintage	VF20	XF40	MS60	MS63	MS65
1982 CHI	200	—	—	—	—	7,000
1982 CHI	700	PF65 6,000				
1985 CHI Proof, unique	—	—	—	—	—	—
1986 CHI	Est. 6	—	—	—	—	—
1986 CHI Proof	Est. 13	—	—	—	—	—

Y# 399 10000 ZŁOTYCH
28.31 g., 0.900 Silver 0.8192 oz. ASW, 40.2 mm. **Subject:** Pope John Paul II **Obv:** Imperial eagle above value **Rev:** Bust of Pope left **Edge:** Plain

Date	Mintage	VF20	XF40	MS60	MS63	MS65
1986	—	PF65 3,250				

Y# 164 10000 ZŁOTYCH
19.30 g., 0.750 Silver 0.4654 oz. ASW, 35 mm. **Subject:** Papal Visit **Obv:** Imperial eagle above value **Rev:** 1/2 Figure of Pope 1/4 left

Date	Mintage	VF20	XF40	MS60	MS63	MS65
1987 MW	908,000	—	—	—	30.00	40.00
1987 MW	15,000	PF65 95.00				

Y# 171 10000 ZŁOTYCH
31.10 g., 0.999 Gold 0.999 oz. AGW, 32 mm. **Subject:** Papal Visit **Obv:** Eagle above value **Rev:** Half-figure of Pope left **Note:** Similar to KM#163.

Date	Mintage	VF20	XF40	MS60	MS63	MS65
1987 MW	201	PF65 8,500				

Y# 177 10000 ZŁOTYCH
31.10 g., 0.999 Gold 0.999 oz. AGW, 32 mm. **Subject:** 10th Anniversary of Pope John Paul II **Obv:** Eagle above value **Rev:** Bust left

Date	Mintage	VF20	XF40	MS60	MS63	MS65
1988 MW	1,000	—	—	—	—	5,000
1988 MW	1,000	PF65 5,500				

Y# 177a 10000 ZŁOTYCH
31.10 g., 0.999 Silver 0.999 oz. ASW, 32 mm. **Subject:** 10th Anniversary of Pope John Paul II **Obv:** Imperial eagle above value **Rev:** Bust left

Date	Mintage	VF20	XF40	MS60	MS63	MS65
1988 MW	5,000	—	—	—	—	—
1988 MW	—	PF63 700	PF65 800			

Y# 179 10000 ZŁOTYCH
31.10 g., 0.999 Silver 0.999 oz. ASW, 32 mm. **Subject:** Pope John Paul - Christmas **Obv:** Imperial eagle above value **Rev:** Bust of Pope left with right hand raised

Date	Mintage	VF20	XF40	MS60	MS63	MS65
1988 MW	5,000	PF63 400	PF65 450			

Y# 189 10000 ZŁOTYCH
31.10 g., 0.999 Gold 0.999 oz. AGW, 32 mm. **Subject:** Pope John Paul II **Obv:** Eagle above value **Rev:** Bust left on patterned background

Date	Mintage	VF20	XF40	MS60	MS63	MS65
1989 MW	Est. 2000	PF65 5,300				

Y# 189a 10000 ZŁOTYCH
31.10 g., 0.999 Silver 0.9989 oz. ASW, 32 mm. **Obv:** Imperial eagle above value **Rev:** Pope John Paul II

Date	Mintage	VF20	XF40	MS60	MS63	MS65
1989 MW	—	—	—	—	—	—
1989 MW	5,000	PF63 500	PF65 600			

Y# 237 10000 ZŁOTYCH
31.10 g., 0.999 Silver 0.9989 oz. ASW, 32 mm. **Obv:** Imperial eagle above value **Rev:** 3/4 Figure of Pope right

Date	Mintage	VF20	XF40	MS60	MS63	MS65
1989 MW	—	PF63 450	PF65 500			

Y# 223 20000 ZŁOTYCH
19.30 g., 0.750 Silver 0.4654 oz. ASW, 35 mm. **Obv:** Imperial eagle above value **Rev:** Soccer ball, map, and globe

Date	Mintage	VF20	XF40	MS60	MS63	MS65
1989 MW	25,000	PF63 35.00	PF65 45.00			

Y# 224 20000 ZŁOTYCH
19.30 g., 0.750 Silver 0.4654 oz. ASW, 35 mm. **Obv:** Eagle with wings open divides date **Rev:** Soccer player behind vertical lines, all within circle

Date	Mintage	VF20	XF40	MS60	MS63	MS65
1989 MW	25,000	PF63 35.00	PF65 45.00			

Y# 180 50000 ZŁOTYCH
19.30 g., 0.750 Silver 0.4654 oz. ASW, 35 mm. **Subject:** 70 Years of Polish Independence **Obv:** Imperial eagle above value **Rev:** Head of Pilsudski left **Edge:** Plain

Date	Mintage	VF20	XF40	MS60	MS63	MS65
1988 MW	1,000,000	—	—	—	25.00	30.00
1988 MW	20,000	PF63 80.00	PF65 95.00			

Y# 163 200000 ZŁOTYCH
373.24 g., 0.999 Gold 11.988 oz. AGW, 70 mm. **Subject:** Papal Visit **Obv:** Eagle above value **Rev:** Half-figure with staff left **Note:** Illustration reduced.

Date	Mintage	VF20	XF40	MS60	MS63	MS65
1987	101	PF65 25,000				

Y# 178 200000 ZŁOTYCH
373.24 g., 0.999 Gold 11.988 oz. AGW, 70 mm. **Subject:** 10th Anniversary of Pope John Paul II **Obv:** Eagle above value **Rev:** Bust with chin resting on thumbs left **Note:** Illustration reduced.

Date	Mintage	VF20	XF40	MS60	MS63	MS65
1988 MW	300	PF65 27,500				

Y# 190 200000 ZŁOTYCH
373.24 g., 0.999 Gold 11.988 oz. AGW, 70 mm. **Obv:** Eagle above value **Rev:** Pope John Paul II **Note:** Similar to KM#189.

Date	Mintage	VF20	XF40	MS60	MS63	MS65
1989 MW	Est. 200	PF65 30,000				

REPUBLIC

Democratic

Y# 216 50 ZŁOTYCH
6.80 g., Copper-Nickel, 26 mm. **Obv:** Crowned eagle with wings open, date below **Rev:** Value with sprig in 0

Date	Mintage	VF20	XF40	MS60	MS63	MS65
1990 MW	28,707,000	—	—	0.75	1.25	2.00
1990 MW	5,000	PF65 12.00				

Y# 214 100 ZŁOTYCH
7.68 g., Copper-Nickel, 28 mm. **Obv:** Crowned eagle with wings open **Rev:** Value with sprig in first 0

Date	Mintage	VF20	XF40	MS60	MS63	MS65
1990 MW	37,341,000	—	—	1.00	2.00	3.00
1990 MW	5,000	PF65 15.00				

Y# 195 10000 ZŁOTYCH
10.80 g., Copper-Nickel, 29.5 mm. **Subject:** 10th Anniversary of Solidarity **Obv:** Crowned eagle with wings open divides date **Rev:** Solidarity monument with city view background **Edge:** Reeded

Date	Mintage	VF20	XF40	MS60	MS63	MS65
1990 MW	15,164,000	—	—	2.50	4.50	6.00
1990 MW	5,000	PF65 16.50				

Y# 217 10000 ZŁOTYCH
9.47 g., Nickel Plated Steel, 29.5 mm. **Subject:** 200th Anniversary of Polish Constitution **Obv:** Crowned eagle with wings open divides date **Rev:** Crowned eagle above inscription, crowned monogram below **Edge:** Reeded

Date	Mintage	VF20	XF40	MS60	MS63	MS65
1991 MW	2,605,000	—	—	4.00	6.00	8.00

Y# 246 10000 ZŁOTYCH
10.80 g., Copper-Nickel, 29.5 mm. **Obv:** Crowned eagle with wings open divides date **Rev:** Wladyslaw III 3/4 left **Edge:** Reeded

Date	Mintage	VF20	XF40	MS60	MS63	MS65
1992 MW	2,500,000	—	—	2.50	3.50	5.00

Y# 219 20000 ZŁOTYCH
9.45 g., 0.999 Gold 0.3035 oz. AGW, 32.1 mm. **Subject:** 10th Anniversary of Solidarity **Obv:** Crowned eagle **Rev:** Solidarity monument with city view background **Edge:** alternating plain and reeded **Note:** SImilar to 10000 Zlotych, Y#195.

Date	Mintage	VF20	XF40	MS60	MS63	MS65
1990	1,004	PF65 2,250				

Y# 215 20000 ZŁOTYCH
9.45 g., Bi-Metallic Copper-Nickel center in Brass ring, 32 mm. **Subject:** 225th Anniversary of Warsaw Mint **Obv:** Crowned eagle with wings open divides date, all within circle **Rev:** Crowned monogram divides date, all within circle

Date	Mintage	VF20	XF40	MS60	MS63	MS65
1991 MW	100,000	PF65 22.00				

Y# 243 20000 ZŁOTYCH
10.80 g., Copper-Nickel, 29.5 mm. **Obv:** Imperial eagle above value **Rev:** Barn swallows **Edge:** Reeded

Date	Mintage	VF20	XF40	MS60	MS63	MS65
1993 MW	520,000	—	—	5.00	8.00	15.00

Y# 244 20000 ZŁOTYCH
10.80 g., Copper-Nickel, 29.5 mm. **Obv:** Crowned eagle with wings open divides date, all within circle **Rev:** Lancut Castle **Edge:** Reeded

Date	Mintage	VF20	XF40	MS60	MS63	MS65
1993 MW	500,000	—	—	2.50	4.50	6.00

Y# 256 20000 ZŁOTYCH
10.80 g., Copper-Nickel, 29.5 mm. **Obv:** Imperial eagle above value **Rev:** Kazimierz IV **Edge:** Reeded

Date	Mintage	VF20	XF40	MS60	MS63	MS65
1993 MW	1,500,000	—	—	2.50	4.50	6.00

Y# 261 20000 ZŁOTYCH
10.80 g., Copper-Nickel, 29.5 mm. **Series:** Olympics **Obv:** Crowned eagle with wings open divides date **Rev:** Slalom skier **Edge:** Reeded

Date	Mintage	VF20	XF40	MS60	MS63	MS65
1993 MW	988,000	—	—	3.50	7.50	10.00

Y# 265 20000 ZŁOTYCH
10.80 g., Copper-Nickel, 29.5 mm. **Subject:** 75th Anniversary - Disabled Association **Obv:** Crowned eagle with wings open divides date **Rev:** Shield and rose within designed circle **Edge:** Reeded

Date	Mintage	VF20	XF40	MS60	MS63	MS65
1994 MW	76,000	—	—	2.50	4.50	6.00

Y# 270 20000 ZŁOTYCH
10.80 g., Copper-Nickel, 29.5 mm. **Obv:** Crowned eagle with wings open divides date **Rev:** New mint building **Edge:** Reeded

Date	Mintage	VF20	XF40	MS60	MS63	MS65
1994	252,000	—	—	2.50	4.50	6.00

Y# 271 20000 ZŁOTYCH

10.80 g., Copper-Nickel, 29.5 mm. **Subject:** 200th Anniversary - Kosciuszko Insurrection **Obv:** Crowned eagle with wings open divides date **Rev:** Head left in circle within ship **Edge:** Milled

Date	Mintage	VF20	XF40	MS60	MS63	MS65
1994	100,000	—	—	3.00	5.00	7.00

Y# 272 20000 ZŁOTYCH

10.80 g., Copper-Nickel, 29.5 mm. **Obv:** Imperial eagle above value **Rev:** Zygmunt I, 1506-1548 **Edge:** Reeded

Date	Mintage	VF20	XF40	MS60	MS63	MS65
1994	1,500,000	—	—	2.50	4.50	6.00

Y# 220 50000 ZŁOTYCH

7.70 g., 0.999 Gold 0.2473 oz. AGW, 22 mm. **Subject:** 10th Anniversary of Solidarity **Obv:** Crowned eagle above value **Rev:** Solidarity monument with city view background **Note:** Similar to 10000 Zlotych, Y#195.

Date	Mintage	VF20	XF40	MS60	MS63	MS65
1990	1,001	PF63 3,000	PF65 3,500			

Y# 229 50000 ZŁOTYCH

11.30 g., Copper-Nickel, 32 mm. **Subject:** 200th Anniversary of Order Virtuti Militari **Obv:** Crowned eagle with wings open divides date, all within beaded circle **Rev:** Military medal and crowned monogram **Shape:** 8-sided

Date	Mintage	VF20	XF40	MS60	MS63	MS65
1992	125,000	PF65 12.50				

Y# 196.1 100000 ZŁOTYCH

31.10 g., 0.999 Silver 0.9989 oz. ASW, 32 mm. **Subject:** 10th Anniversary of Solidarity **Obv:** Imperial eagle above value **Rev:** Solidarity monument with city view background **Edge:** Plain

Date	Mintage	VF20	XF40	MS60	MS63	MS65
1990	520,000	—	—	—	37.00	42.00
1990	125,000	PF63 95.00	PF65 115			

Y# 196.2 100000 ZŁOTYCH

31.10 g., 0.999 Silver 0.9989 oz. ASW, 31.9 mm. **Subject:** 10th Anniversary of Solidarity **Obv:** Imperial eagle above value **Rev:** Solidarity monument with city view background **Note:** Reduced size.

Date	Mintage	VF20	XF40	MS60	MS63	MS65
1990	—	PF63 85.00	PF65 110			

Y# 199 100000 ZŁOTYCH

31.10 g., 0.999 Silver 0.9989 oz. ASW, 35 mm. **Obv:** Imperial eagle above value **Rev:** Fryderyk Chopin **Edge:** Reeded

Date	Mintage	VF20	XF40	MS60	MS63	MS65
1990	10,000	PF63 265	PF65 300			

Y# 200 100000 ZŁOTYCH

31.10 g., 0.999 Silver 0.9989 oz. ASW, 39 mm. **Obv:** Imperial eagle above value **Rev:** Uniformed figure on horse **Edge:** Milled

Date	Mintage	VF20	XF40	MS60	MS63	MS65
1990	10,000	PF63 265	PF65 300			

Y# 201 100000 ZŁOTYCH

31.10 g., 0.999 Silver 0.9989 oz. ASW, 39 mm. **Obv:** Imperial eagle above value **Rev:** Uniformed bust of Marszalek Pilsudski 1/4 left **Edge:** Reeded

Date	Mintage	VF20	XF40	MS60	MS63	MS65
1990	10,000	PF63 265	PF65 300			

Y# 221 100000 ZŁOTYCH

15.55 g., 0.999 Gold 0.4994 oz. AGW **Subject:** 10th Anniversary of Solidarity **Obv:** Crowned eagle above value **Rev:** Buildings, symbols **Note:** Similar to 10000 Zlotych, Y#195.

Date	Mintage	VF20	XF40	MS60	MS63	MS65
1990	Est. 1000	PF65 3,500				

Y# 235 100000 ZŁOTYCH

16.50 g., 0.750 Silver 0.3979 oz. ASW, 32 mm. **Series:** WWII **Obv:** Crowned eagle with wings open divides date **Rev:** Cavalry facing right, flanked by trees **Edge:** Reeded

Date	Mintage	VF20	XF40	MS60	MS63	MS65
1991	12,000	PF63 60.00	PF65 75.00			

Y# 236 100000 ZŁOTYCH

16.50 g., 0.750 Silver 0.3979 oz. ASW, 32 mm. **Series:** WWII **Subject:** Defense of Narvik **Obv:** Imperial eagle above value **Rev:** Polish troops **Edge:** Reeded

Date	Mintage	VF20	XF40	MS60	MS63	MS65
1991	12,000	PF63 60.00	PF65 75.00			

Y# 238 100000 ZŁOTYCH

16.50 g., 0.750 Silver 0.3979 oz. ASW, 32 mm. **Series:** WWII **Obv:** Imperial eagle above value **Rev:** Polish troops at Battle of Tobruk **Edge:** Reeded

Date	Mintage	VF20	XF40	MS60	MS63	MS65
1991	12,000	PF63 60.00	PF65 75.00			

Y# 239 100000 ZŁOTYCH

16.50 g., 0.750 Silver 0.3979 oz. ASW, 32 mm. **Series:** WWII **Obv:** Imperial eagle above value **Rev:** Polish pilots in Battle of Britain **Edge:** Reeded

Date	Mintage	VF20	XF40	MS60	MS63	MS65
1991	12,000	PF63 60.00	PF65 75.00			

Y# 227 100000 ZŁOTYCH

16.50 g., 0.750 Silver 0.3979 oz. ASW, 32 mm. **Subject:** Unification of Upper Silesia and Poland **Obv:** Imperial eagle above value **Rev:** Bust 3/4 left, inscription at left **Edge:** Reeded

Date	Mintage	VF20	XF40	MS60	MS63	MS65
1992	30,000	PF63 60.00	PF65 75.00			

Y# 268 100000 ZŁOTYCH

16.50 g., 0.900 Silver 0.4774 oz. ASW, 32 mm. **Subject:** Warsaw Uprising **Obv:** Imperial eagle above value **Rev:** Soldier with gun

Date	Mintage	VF20	XF40	MS60	MS63	MS65
1994	150,000	PF63 30.00	PF65 40.00			

Y# 202 200000 ZŁOTYCH
155.50 g., 0.999 Silver 4.9944 oz. ASW, 65 mm. **Obv:** Imperial eagle above value **Rev:** Fryderyk Chopin **Edge:** Reeded **Note:** Similar to 100,000 Zlotych, Y#199.

Date	Mintage	VF20	XF40	MS60	MS63	MS65
1990	10,000	PF63 2,000	PF65 2,250			

Y# 203 200000 ZŁOTYCH
155.50 g., 0.999 Silver 4.9944 oz. ASW, 65 mm. **Obv:** Imperial eagle above value **Rev:** Uniformed figure on horse **Edge:** Reeded **Note:** Similar to 100,000 Zlotych, Y#200.

Date	Mintage	VF20	XF40	MS60	MS63	MS65
1990	10,000	PF63 1,500	PF65 1,750			

Y# 204 200000 ZŁOTYCH
155.50 g., 0.999 Silver 4.9944 oz. ASW, 65 mm. **Obv:** Imperial eagle above value **Rev:** Bust of Marszalek Pilsudski 1/4 left **Note:** Similar to 100,000 Zlotych, Y#201.

Date	Mintage	VF20	XF40	MS60	MS63	MS65
1990	10,000	PF63 1,500	PF65 1,750			

Y# 205 200000 ZŁOTYCH
31.10 g., 0.999 Gold 0.9989 oz. AGW, 32 mm. **Obv:** Crowned eagle above value **Rev:** Fryderyk Chopin

Date	Mintage	VF20	XF40	MS60	MS63	MS65
1990	13,000	PF65 3,750				

Y# 206 200000 ZŁOTYCH
31.10 g., 0.999 Gold 0.9989 oz. AGW, 32 mm. **Obv:** Crowned eagle above value **Rev:** Tadeusz Kosciuszko

Date	Mintage	VF20	XF40	MS60	MS63	MS65
1990	13,000	PF65 3,750				

Y# 207 200000 ZŁOTYCH
31.10 g., 0.999 Gold 0.9989 oz. AGW, 32 mm. **Obv:** Crowned eagle above value **Rev:** Marszalek Pilsudski **Edge:** Reeded

Date	Mintage	VF20	XF40	MS60	MS63	MS65
1990	10,000	PF65 3,750				

Y# 222 200000 ZŁOTYCH
31.10 g., 0.999 Gold 0.9989 oz. AGW, 32 mm. **Subject:** Solidarity **Obv:** Crowned eagle **Rev:** Solidarity monument with city view background

Date	Mintage	VF20	XF40	MS60	MS63	MS65
1990	Est. 1000	PF65 6,000				

Y# 240 200000 ZŁOTYCH
19.36 g., 0.750 Silver 0.4668 oz. ASW, 35 mm. **Obv:** Imperial eagle above value **Rev:** Gen. Dyw. Stefan Rowecki "Grot" facing

Date	Mintage	VF20	XF40	MS60	MS63	MS65
1990 MW	25,000	PF63 60.00	PF65 70.00			
1991 MW	—	PF63 60.00	PF65 70.00			

Y# 250 200000 ZŁOTYCH
19.27 g., 0.999 Silver 0.6188 oz. ASW, 35 mm. **Obv:** Imperial eagle above value **Rev:** Bust of Gen. Komorowski facing

Date	Mintage	VF20	XF40	MS60	MS63	MS65
1990 MW	25,000	PF63 40.00	PF65 50.00			

Y# 218 200000 ZŁOTYCH
38.90 g., 0.999 Silver 1.2494 oz. ASW, 40 mm. **Subject:** 200th Anniversary of Polish Constitution **Obv:** Imperial eagle above value **Rev:** Crowned eagle perched on sprigs above engraved stone

Date	Mintage	VF20	XF40	MS60	MS63	MS65
1991	100,000	PF63 45.00	PF65 60.00			

Y# 226 200000 ZŁOTYCH
31.10 g., 0.925 Silver 0.9249 oz. ASW, 40 mm. **Series:** Albertville Olympics **Obv:** Imperial eagle above value **Rev:** Slalom skier

Date	Mintage	VF20	XF40	MS60	MS63	MS65
1991	20,000	PF63 45.00	PF65 60.00			

Y# 228 200000 ZŁOTYCH
31.10 g., 0.925 Silver 0.9249 oz. ASW, 40 mm. **Series:** Barcelona Olympics **Obv:** Imperial eagle above value **Rev:** Weight lifter

Date	Mintage	VF20	XF40	MS60	MS63	MS65
1991	20,000	PF63 70.00	PF65 85.00			

Y# 241 200000 ZŁOTYCH
31.16 g., 0.925 Silver 0.9267 oz. ASW, 40 mm. **Series:** Barcelona Olympics **Obv:** Imperial eagle above value **Rev:** Two sailboats

Date	Mintage	VF20	XF40	MS60	MS63	MS65
1991 MW	20,000	PF63 70.00	PF65 85.00			

Y# 242 200000 ZŁOTYCH
19.33 g., 0.750 Silver 0.4661 oz. ASW, 35 mm. **Subject:** 70th Anniversary of Poznan Fair **Obv:** Imperial eagle above value **Rev:** Monument and globe design, dates above and below

Date	Mintage	VF20	XF40	MS60	MS63	MS65
1991 MW	20,000	PF63 35.00	PF65 45.00			

Y# 251 200000 ZŁOTYCH
19.33 g., 0.750 Silver 0.4661 oz. ASW, 35 mm. **Obv:** Imperial eagle above value **Rev:** Bust of Gen. Okulicki 3/4 facing

Date	Mintage	VF20	XF40	MS60	MS63	MS65
1991 MW	25,000	PF63 45.00	PF65 55.00			

Y# 252 200000 ZŁOTYCH
19.33 g., 0.750 Silver 0.4661 oz. ASW, 35 mm. **Obv:** Imperial eagle above value **Rev:** Bust of Gen. Tokarzewski - Karaszewicz

Date	Mintage	VF20	XF40	MS60	MS63	MS65
1991 MW	25,000	PF63 45.00	PF65 55.00			

Y# 230 200000 ZŁOTYCH
31.10 g., 0.999 Silver 0.9989 oz. ASW, 40 mm. **Subject:** Discovery of America **Obv:** Imperial eagle above value **Rev:** Portrait and ship

Date	Mintage	VF20	XF40	MS60	MS63	MS65
1992	20,000	PF63 45.00	PF65 55.00			

Y# 231 200000 ZŁOTYCH
31.10 g., 0.999 Silver 0.9989 oz. ASW, 40 mm. **Subject:** Seville Expo '92 **Obv:** Imperial eagle above value **Rev:** Building facade and logo

Date	Mintage	VF20	XF40	MS60	MS63	MS65
1992	45,000	PF63 40.00	PF65 50.00			

Y# 232 200000 ZŁOTYCH

16.50 g., 0.750 Silver 0.3979 oz. ASW, 32 mm. **Series:** WWII **Obv:** Imperial eagle above value **Rev:** Polish protection of WWII sea convoys

Date	Mintage	VF20	XF40	MS60	MS63	MS65
1992	15,000	PF63 50.00	PF65 60.00			

Y# 233 200000 ZŁOTYCH

16.50 g., 0.750 Silver 0.3979 oz. ASW, 32 mm. **Obv:** Imperial eagle above value **Rev:** Bust of Stanislaw Staszic 3/4 left within sprigs

Date	Mintage	VF20	XF40	MS60	MS63	MS65
1992	20,000	PF63 25.00	PF65 35.00			

Y# 253 200000 ZŁOTYCH

16.50 g., 0.750 Silver 0.3979 oz. ASW, 32 mm. **Obv:** Imperial eagle above value **Rev:** Bust of Wladyslaw II 1/4 left

Date	Mintage	VF20	XF40	MS60	MS63	MS65
1992 MW	5,000	PF63 265	PF65 300			

Y# 254 200000 ZŁOTYCH

16.50 g., 0.750 Silver 0.3979 oz. ASW, 32 mm. **Obv:** Imperial eagle above value **Rev:** Bust of Wladyslaw III 1/4 left

Date	Mintage	VF20	XF40	MS60	MS63	MS65
1992 MW	20,000	PF63 70.00	PF65 95.00			

Y# 255 200000 ZŁOTYCH

16.50 g., 0.750 Silver 0.3979 oz. ASW, 32 mm. **Subject:** 750th Anniversary - City of Szczecin **Obv:** Imperial eagle above value **Rev:** Crowned griffin head within shield flanked by dates

Date	Mintage	VF20	XF40	MS60	MS63	MS65
1993 MW	20,000	PF63 40.00	PF65 50.00			

Y# 257 200000 ZŁOTYCH

16.50 g., 0.750 Silver 0.3979 oz. ASW, 32 mm. **Obv:** Imperial eagle above value **Rev:** Bust of Kazimierz IV 3/4 right

Date	Mintage	VF20	XF40	MS60	MS63	MS65
1993 MW	15,000	PF63 75.00	PF65 90.00			

Y# 258 200000 ZŁOTYCH

16.50 g., 0.750 Silver 0.3979 oz. ASW, 32 mm. **Obv:** Crowned eagle with wings open divides date **Rev:** Kazimierz IV enthroned

Date	Mintage	VF20	XF40	MS60	MS63	MS65
1993 MW	5,000	PF63 220	PF65 250			

Y# 259 200000 ZŁOTYCH

16.50 g., 0.750 Silver 0.3979 oz. ASW, 32 mm. **Series:** WWII **Obv:** Imperial eagle above value **Rev:** Polish partisans sabotaging railways

Date	Mintage	VF20	XF40	MS60	MS63	MS65
1993 MW	10,000	PF63 70.00	PF65 85.00			

Y# 262 200000 ZŁOTYCH

16.50 g., 0.750 Silver 0.3979 oz. ASW, 32 mm. **Series:** WWII **Obv:** Imperial eagle above value **Rev:** Battle of Monte Cassino

Date	Mintage	VF20	XF40	MS60	MS63	MS65
1994 MW	15,000	PF63 70.00	PF65 85.00			

Y# 266 200000 ZŁOTYCH

16.50 g., 0.750 Silver 0.3979 oz. ASW, 32 mm. **Subject:** 75th Anniversary - Disabled Association **Obv:** Imperial eagle above value **Rev:** Shield and rose within designed circle

Date	Mintage	VF20	XF40	MS60	MS63	MS65
1994 MW	15,000	PF63 50.00	PF65 65.00			

Y# 273 200000 ZŁOTYCH

16.50 g., 0.750 Silver 0.3979 oz. ASW, 32 mm. **Obv:** Imperial eagle above value **Rev:** Half-length figure of Zygmunt I 1/4 right

Date	Mintage	VF20	XF40	MS60	MS63	MS65
1994 MW	5,000	PF63 195	PF65 225			

Y# 274 200000 ZŁOTYCH

16.50 g., 0.750 Silver 0.3979 oz. ASW, 32 mm. **Obv:** Imperial eagle above value **Rev:** Bust of Zygmunt I facing

Date	Mintage	VF20	XF40	MS60	MS63	MS65
1994 MW	15,000	PF63 120	PF65 150			

Y# 275 200000 ZŁOTYCH

16.50 g., 0.750 Silver 0.3979 oz. ASW, 32 mm. **Subject:** 200th Anniversary - Kosciuszko Insurrection **Obv:** Imperial eagle above value **Rev:** Cameo bust left within ship

Date	Mintage	VF20	XF40	MS60	MS63	MS65
1994 MW	15,000	PF63 45.00	PF65 60.00			

Y# 245 300000 ZŁOTYCH

31.16 g., 0.925 Silver 0.9267 oz. ASW, 40 mm. **Subject:** 50th Anniversary of Warsaw Ghetto Uprising **Obv:** Imperial eagle above value **Rev:** Outreached arms above bricks

Date	Mintage	VF20	XF40	MS60	MS63	MS65
1993	30,000	PF63 50.00	PF65 65.00			

Y# 247 300000 ZŁOTYCH

31.16 g., 0.925 Silver 0.9267 oz. ASW, 40 mm. **Series:** 1994 Olympics **Obv:** Eagle with wings open divides date **Rev:** Lillehammer

Date	Mintage	VF20	XF40	MS60	MS63	MS65
1993	20,000	PF63 55.00	PF65 70.00			

Y# 248 300000 ZŁOTYCH

31.15 g., 0.999 Silver 1.0003 oz. ASW, 40 mm. **Obv:** Imperial eagle above value **Rev:** Barn swallow feeding young

Date	Mintage	VF20	XF40	MS60	MS63	MS65
1993	20,000	PF63 170	PF65 200			

Y# 249 300000 ZŁOTYCH

31.15 g., 0.999 Silver 1.0003 oz. ASW, 40 mm. **Obv:** Imperial eagle above value **Rev:** Lancut Castle

Date	Mintage	VF20	XF40	MS60	MS63	MS65
1993	20,000	PF63 90.00	PF65 110			

Y# 260 300000 ZŁOTYCH

31.10 g., 0.999 Silver 0.9989 oz. ASW, 40 mm. **Obv:** Imperial eagle above value **Rev:** Aerial view of Zamosc

Date	Mintage	VF20	XF40	MS60	MS63	MS65
1993	20,000	PF63 55.00	PF65 70.00			

Y# 263 300000 ZŁOTYCH

31.16 g., 0.925 Silver 0.9267 oz. ASW **Obv:** Imperial eagle above value **Rev:** St. Maksymilian Kolbe

Date	Mintage	VF20	XF40	MS60	MS63	MS65
1994	15,000	PF63 120	PF65 150			

Y# 264 300000 ZŁOTYCH

31.10 g., 0.925 Silver 0.9249 oz. ASW, 40 mm. **Subject:** 70th Anniversary - Polish National Bank **Obv:** Crowned eagle with wings open divides date **Rev:** Bust facing in front of buildings **Shape:** 7-sided

Date	Mintage	VF20	XF40	MS60	MS63	MS65
1994	20,880	PF63 65.00	PF65 85.00			

Y# 269 300000 ZŁOTYCH

31.10 g., 0.999 Silver 0.999 oz. ASW, 40 mm. **Subject:** Warsaw Uprising **Obv:** Imperial eagle above value **Rev:** Fighting soldiers, dates, designs and cross

Date	Mintage	VF20	XF40	MS60	MS63	MS65
1994	30,000	PF63 55.00	PF65 75.00			

Y# 208 500000 ZŁOTYCH

62.20 g., 0.999 Gold 1.9978 oz. AGW, 39 mm. **Obv:** Crowned eagle above value **Rev:** Fryderyk Chopin **Note:** Similar to 100,000 Zlotych, Y#199.

Date	Mintage	VF20	XF40	MS60	MS63	MS65
1990	16	PF65 5,000				

Y# 209 500000 ZŁOTYCH

62.20 g., 0.999 Gold 1.9978 oz. AGW, 39 mm. **Obv:** Crowned eagle above value **Rev:** Uniformed figure on horse **Note:** Similar to 100,000 Zlotych, Y#200.

Date	Mintage	VF20	XF40	MS60	MS63	MS65
1990	12	PF65 5,000				

Y# 210 500000 ZŁOTYCH

62.20 g., 0.999 Gold 1.9978 oz. AGW, 39 mm. **Obv:** Crowned eagle above value **Rev:** Bust of Marszalek Pilsudski 1/4 left **Note:** Similar to 100,000 Zlotych, Y#201.

Date	Mintage	VF20	XF40	MS60	MS63	MS65
1990	16	PF65 5,000				

Y# 211 1000000 ZŁOTYCH

373.20 g., 0.999 Gold 11.9867 oz. AGW, 65 mm. **Obv:** Crowned eagle above value **Rev:** Fryderyk Chopin **Note:** Similar to 100,000 Zlotych, Y#199.

Date	Mintage	VF20	XF40	MS60	MS63	MS65
1990	1	PF65 22,500				

Y# 212 1000000 ZŁOTYCH

373.20 g., 0.999 Gold 11.9867 oz. AGW, 65 mm. **Obv:** Crowned eagle above value **Rev:** Uniformed figure on horse **Note:** Similar to 100,000 Zlotych, Y#200.

Date	Mintage	VF20	XF40	MS60	MS63	MS65
1990	1	PF65 22,500				

Y# 213 1000000 ZŁOTYCH

373.20 g., 0.999 Gold 11.9867 oz. AGW, 65 mm. **Obv:** Imperial eagle above value **Rev:** Bust of Marszalek Pilsudski 1/4 left **Note:** Similar to 100,000 Zlotych, Y#201.

Date	Mintage	VF20	XF40	MS60	MS63	MS65
1990	1	PF65 22,500				

REFORM COINAGE

As far back as 1990, production was initiated for the new 1 Grosz - 1 Zlotych coins for a forthcoming monetary reform. It wasn't announced until the Act of July 7, 1994 and was enacted on January 1, 1995.

100 Old Zlotych = 1 Grosz; 10,000 Old Zlotych = 1 Zloty

Y# 276 GROSZ

1.64 g., Brass, 15.5 mm. **Obv:** National arms **Obv. Legend:** RZECZPOSPOLITA POLSKA **Rev:** Drooping oak leaf over value **Edge:** Reeded

Date	Mintage	VF20	XF40	MS60	MS63	MS65
1990 MW	29,140,000	—	—	0.25	0.50	0.75
1991 MW	79,000,000	—	—	0.15	0.30	0.50
1992 MW	362,000,000	—	—	0.10	0.20	0.40
1993 MW	80,780,000	—	—	0.15	0.30	0.50
1995 MW	102,280,109	—	—	0.10	0.20	0.40
1997 MW	103,080,002	—	—	0.10	0.20	0.40
1998 MW	257,640,003	—	—	0.10	0.20	0.40
1999 MW	203,970,000	—	—	0.10	0.20	0.40
2000 MW	210,100,000	—	—	0.10	0.20	0.40

Y# 277 2 GROSZE

2.13 g., Brass, 17.5 mm. **Obv:** National arms **Obv. Legend:** RZECZPOSPOLITA POLSKA **Rev:** Drooping oak leaves above value **Edge:** Plain

Date	Mintage	VF20	XF40	MS60	MS63	MS65
1990 MW	34,400,000	—	—	0.25	0.50	0.75
1991 MW	97,410,000	—	—	0.15	0.25	0.50
1992 MW	157,000,003	—	—	0.15	0.25	0.50
1997 MV	92,400,002	—	—	0.15	0.25	0.50
1998 MW	154,840,050	—	—	0.15	0.25	0.50
1999 MW	187,900,000	—	—	0.15	0.25	0.50
2000 MW	94,500,000	—	—	0.15	0.25	0.50

Y# 278 5 GROSZY

2.59 g., Brass, 19.5 mm. **Obv:** National arms **Obv. Legend:** RZECZPOSPOLITA POLSKA **Rev:** Value at upper left of oak leaves **Edge:** Segmented reeding

Date	Mintage	VF20	XF40	MS60	MS63	MS65
1990 MW	70,240,000	—	—	0.50	0.75	1.00
1991 MW	171,040,000	—	—	0.25	0.45	0.75
1992 MW	103,784,000	—	—	0.25	0.45	0.75
1993 MW	20,280,101	—	—	0.50	0.75	1.00
1998 MW	93,472,002	—	—	0.25	0.45	0.75
1999 MW	99,024,000	—	—	0.25	0.45	0.75
2000 MW	75,600,000	—	—	0.25	0.45	0.75

Y# 279 10 GROSZY

2.55 g., Copper-Nickel, 16.5 mm. **Obv:** National arms **Obv. Legend:** RZECZPOSPOLITA POLSKA **Rev:** Value within wreath

Date	Mintage	VF20	XF40	MS60	MS63	MS65
1990 MW	43,055,000	—	—	0.40	0.60	1.00
1991 MW	123,164,300	—	—	0.40	0.60	1.00
1992 MW	210,005,000	—	—	0.40	0.60	1.00
1993 MW	80,240,008	—	—	0.40	0.60	1.00
1998 MW	62,695,000	—	—	0.40	0.60	1.00
1999 MW	47,040,000	—	—	0.40	0.60	1.00
2000 MW	104,060,000	—	—	0.40	0.60	1.00

Y# 280 20 GROSZY

3.22 g., Copper-Nickel, 18.5 mm. **Obv:** National arms **Obv. Legend:** RZECZPOSPOLITA POLSKA **Rev:** Value within artistic design **Edge:** Reeded

Date	Mintage	VF20	XF40	MS60	MS63	MS65
1990 MW	25,100,000	—	—	1.00	1.50	2.00
1991 MW	75,400,000	—	—	0.65	0.85	1.25
1992 MW	106,100,001	—	—	0.65	0.85	1.25
1996 MW	29,745,000	—	—	0.65	0.85	1.25
1997 MW	59,755,000	—	—	0.65	0.85	1.25
1998 MW	52,500,000	—	—	0.65	0.85	1.25
1999 MW	25,985,000	—	—	0.65	0.85	1.25
2000 MW	52,135,000	—	—	0.65	0.85	1.25

Y# 281 50 GROSZY

3.94 g., Copper-Nickel, 20.5 mm. **Obv:** National arms **Obv. Legend:** RZECZPOSPOLITA POLSKA **Rev:** Value to right of sprig **Edge:** Reeded

Date	Mintage	VF20	XF40	MS60	MS63	MS65
1990 MW	29,152,000	—	—	1.25	1.50	2.00
1991 MW	99,120,000	—	—	1.00	1.25	1.75
1992 MW	116,000,000	—	—	1.00	1.25	1.75
1995 MW	101,600,113	—	—	1.00	1.25	1.75

Y# 282 ZŁOTY

5.03 g., Copper-Nickel, 23 mm. **Obv:** National arms **Obv. Legend:** RZECZPOSPOLITA POLSKA **Rev:** Value within wreath **Edge:** Segmented reeding

Date	Mintage	VF20	XF40	MS60	MS63	MS65
1990 MW	20,240,000	—	—	1.75	2.00	4.00
1991 MW	60,080,000	—	—	1.75	2.00	2.75
1992 MW	102,240,000	—	—	1.75	2.00	2.75
1993 MW	20,904,000	—	—	1.75	2.00	3.00
1994 MW	69,956,000	—	—	1.75	2.00	2.75
1995 MW	99,740,122	—	—	1.75	2.00	2.75

Y# 283 2 ZŁOTE

5.21 g., Bi-Metallic Copper-Nickel center in Aluminum-Bronze ring, 21.5 mm. **Obv:** National arms within circle **Obv. Legend:** RZECZPOSPOLITA POLSKA **Rev:** Value flanked by oak leaves **Edge:** Plain

Date	Mintage	VF20	XF40	MS60	MS63	MS65
1994 MW	79,644,000	—	—	4.00	4.50	5.50
1995 MW	122,880,020	—	—	4.00	4.50	5.50

Y# 285 2 ZŁOTE

10.80 g., Copper-Nickel, 29.5 mm. **Subject:** 55th Anniversary - Katyn Forest Massacre **Obv:** Crowned eagle with wings open divides date **Rev:** Burned forest

Date	Mintage	VF20	XF40	MS60	MS63	MS65
1995	300,000	—	—	3.50	5.50	7.50

Y# 289 2 ZŁOTE

10.80 g., Copper-Nickel, 29.5 mm. **Obv:** Crowned eagle with wings open **Rev:** Catfish

Date	Mintage	VF20	XF40	MS60	MS63	MS65
1995	300,000	—	—	15.00	25.00	30.00

Y# 297 2 ZŁOTE

10.80 g., Copper-Nickel, 26.8 mm. **Subject:** 75th Anniversary - Battle of Warsaw **Obv:** Crowned eagle with wings open divides date **Rev:** Armored figures behind figure with cross

Date	Mintage	VF20	XF40	MS60	MS63	MS65
1995	300,000	—	—	3.50	5.50	7.50

Y# 300 2 ZŁOTE

10.80 g., Copper-Nickel, 29.5 mm. **Series:** 1996 Olympic Games **Obv:** Crowned eagle with wings open divides date **Rev:** Centennial

Date	Mintage	VF20	XF40	MS60	MS63	MS65
1995	350,000	—	—	3.50	5.50	7.50

Y# 303 2 ZŁOTE

10.80 g., Copper-Nickel, 29.5 mm. **Series:** 1996 Olympics - Atlanta **Obv:** Crowned eagle with wings open divides date **Rev:** Wrestling

Date	Mintage	VF20	XF40	MS60	MS63	MS65
1995	300,000	—	—	3.50	5.50	7.50

Y# 310 2 ZŁOTE

10.80 g., Copper-Nickel, 29.5 mm. **Obv:** Crowned eagle with wings open divides date, all within circle **Rev:** Lazienki Royal Palace

Date	Mintage	VF20	XF40	MS60	MS63	MS65
1995	287,000	—	—	3.75	6.00	8.00

Y# 306 2 ZŁOTE

8.15 g., Brass, 27 mm. **Obv:** Imperial eagle above value **Rev:** Bust of Zygmunt II

Date	Mintage	VF20	XF40	MS60	MS63	MS65
1996	200,000	—	125	175	250	—

Y# 311 2 ZŁOTE

8.15 g., Brass, 27 mm. **Obv:** Crowned eagle with wings open **Rev:** Hedgehog with young

Date	Mintage	VF20	XF40	MS60	MS63	MS65
1996	300,000	—	16.00	28.00	45.00	—

Y# 313 2 ZŁOTE

8.15 g., Brass, 27 mm. **Obv:** Crowned eagle with wings open divides date, all within circle **Rev:** Castle and shield

Date	Mintage	VF20	XF40	MS60	MS63	MS65
1996	300,000	—	12.00	20.00	35.00	—

Y# 315 2 ZŁOTE

8.15 g., Brass, 27 mm. **Obv:** Crowned eagle with wings open divides date **Rev:** Heads opposite divide dates

Date	Mintage	VF20	XF40	MS60	MS63	MS65
1996	300,000	—	12.00	25.00	35.00	—

Y# 325 2 ZŁOTE

8.15 g., Brass, 27 mm. **Obv:** Crowned eagle with wings open divides date **Rev:** Head of Stefan Batory 1/4 right

Date	Mintage	VF20	XF40	MS60	MS63	MS65
1997	315,000	—	12.00	25.00	35.00	—

Y# 329 2 ZŁOTE

8.15 g., Brass, 27 mm. **Subject:** Jelonek Rogacz - Lucanus cervus. **Obv:** Crowned eagle with wings open **Rev:** Stag beetle

Date	Mintage	VF20	XF40	MS60	MS63	MS65
1997	315,000	—	14.00	28.00	40.00	—

Y# 331 2 ZŁOTE

8.15 g., Brass, 27 mm. **Obv:** Crowned eagle with wings open **Rev:** Zamek W Pieskowej Skale

Date	Mintage	VF20	XF40	MS60	MS63	MS65
1997	315,000	—	9.00	15.00	25.00	—

Y# 333 2 ZŁOTE
8.15 g., Brass, 27 mm. **Obv:** Crowned eagle with wings open divides date **Rev:** Head with headdress left, antelope and ostrich within globe design

Date	Mintage	VF20	XF40	MS60	MS63	MS65
1997	420,000	—	—	5.00	8.00	10.00

Y# 335 2 ZŁOTE
8.15 g., Brass, 26.8 mm. **Series:** Nagano Olympics **Obv:** Crowned eagle with wings open divides date **Rev:** Snow boarder

Date	Mintage	VF20	XF40	MS60	MS63	MS65
1998	400,000	—	6.00	12.00	20.00	25.00

Y# 336 2 ZŁOTE
8.15 g., Brass, 27 mm. **Obv:** Imperial eagle above value **Rev:** Sigismund III (1587-1632)

Date	Mintage	VF20	XF40	MS60	MS63	MS65
1998	400,000	—	6.00	12.00	20.00	25.00

Y# 340 2 ZŁOTE
8.15 g., Brass, 27 mm. **Obv:** Crowned eagle with wings open **Rev:** Toad right

Date	Mintage	VF20	XF40	MS60	MS63	MS65
1998	400,000	—	—	15.00	22.00	27.00

Y# 344 2 ZŁOTE
8.15 g., Brass, 27 mm. **Subject:** Discovery of Radium and Polomium **Obv:** Crowned eagle with wings open divides date **Rev:** Seated and standing figure among scientific figures of radium and polomium

Date	Mintage	VF20	XF40	MS60	MS63	MS65
1998	400,000	—	5.00	10.00	18.00	22.00

Y# 347 2 ZŁOTE
8.15 g., Brass, 26.8 mm. **Obv:** Imperial eagle above value **Rev:** Zamek W. Korniku - Palace

Date	Mintage	VF20	XF40	MS60	MS63	MS65
1998	400,000	—	5.00	10.00	18.00	22.00

Y# 349 2 ZŁOTE
8.15 g., Brass, 27 mm. **Subject:** 80th Anniversary - Polish Independence **Obv:** Crowned eagle with wings open divides date **Rev:** 1918 on flaming map

Date	Mintage	VF20	XF40	MS60	MS63	MS65
1998	400,000	—	5.00	10.00	18.00	22.00

Y# 352 2 ZŁOTE
8.15 g., Brass, 27 mm. **Subject:** 200th Birthday - Adam Mickiewicz **Obv:** Crowned eagle with wings open divides date **Rev:** Head of Adam Mickiewicz 3/4 facing **Note:** With and without dash between value and denomination.

Date	Mintage	VF20	XF40	MS60	MS63	MS65
1998	420,000	—	5.00	10.00	18.00	22.00

Y# 355 2 ZŁOTE
8.15 g., Brass, 27 mm. **Obv:** Crowned eagle with wings open **Rev:** Gray wolves and cubs **Edge Lettering:** POLSKI NARODOWY BANK

Date	Mintage	VF20	XF40	MS60	MS63	MS65
1999	420,000	—	—	15.00	25.00	30.00

Y# 356 2 ZŁOTE
8.15 g., Brass, 27 mm. **Obv:** Crowned eagle with wings open divides date **Rev:** Bust of Juliusz Slosacki 1/4 right

Date	Mintage	VF20	XF40	MS60	MS63	MS65
1999	420,000	—	4.00	8.00	16.00	20.00

Y# 357 2 ZŁOTE
8.15 g., Brass, 27 mm. **Subject:** Poland's Accession to NATO **Obv:** Crowned eagle with wings open divides date **Rev:** NATO globe, soldiers rappelling from helicopter **Edge Lettering:** NARODOWY BANK POLSKI

Date	Mintage	VF20	XF40	MS60	MS63	MS65
1999	400,000	—	4.00	8.00	16.00	20.00

Y# 358 2 ZŁOTE
8.15 g., Brass, 27 mm. **Obv:** Crowned eagle with wings open divides date **Rev:** Head of Ernest Malinowski facing above slanted text

Date	Mintage	VF20	XF40	MS60	MS63	MS65
1999	420,000	—	5.00	10.00	18.00	22.00

Y# 363 2 ZŁOTE
8.15 g., Brass, 27 mm. **Obv:** Crowned eagle with wings open divides date **Rev:** Laski and Erasmus **Edge Lettering:** NARODOWY BANK POLSKI

Date	Mintage	VF20	XF40	MS60	MS63	MS65
1999	420,000	—	4.00	8.00	16.00	20.00

Y# 365 2 ZŁOTE
8.15 g., Brass, 27 mm. **Obv:** Imperial eagle above value **Rev:** Fryderyk Chopin with stylized piano and music score **Edge Lettering:** NARODOWY BANK POLSKI

Date	Mintage	VF20	XF40	MS60	MS63	MS65
1999	420,000	—	6.00	12.00	20.00	25.00

Y# 368 2 ZŁOTE
8.15 g., Brass, 26.8 mm. **Obv:** Crowned eagle with wings open divides date **Rev:** Wladyslaw IV 1/4 right **Edge Lettering:** NARODOWY BANK POLSKI

Date	Mintage	VF20	XF40	MS60	MS63	MS65
1999	500,000	—	3.50	7.00	12.00	15.00

Y# 372 2 ZŁOTE
8.15 g., Brass, 26.8 mm. **Obv:** Crowned eagle with wings open divides date, all within circle **Rev:** Palace behind Potlocki family arms

Date	Mintage	VF20	XF40	MS60	MS63	MS65
1999	450,000	—	3.50	7.00	12.00	15.00

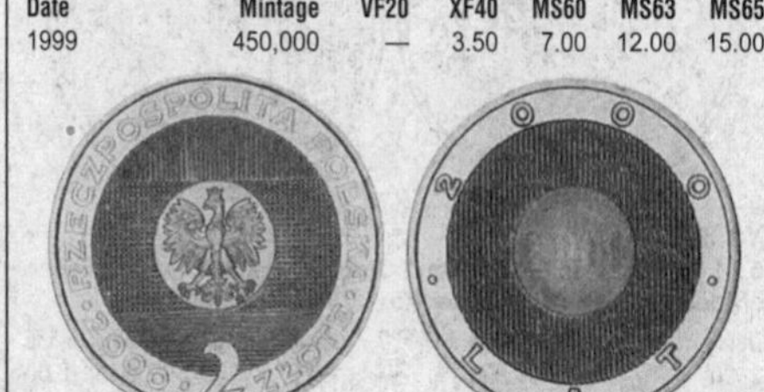

Y# 374 2 ZŁOTE
8.31 g., Bi-Metallic Copper-Nickel center in Brass ring, 26.8 mm. **Subject:** Millennium **Obv:** Crowned eagle in center **Rev:** Latent image dates in center **Edge Lettering:** NARODOWY BANK POLSKI

Date	Mintage	VF20	XF40	MS60	MS63	MS65
2000	2,000,000	—	—	3.00	5.00	7.00

Y# 376 2 ZŁOTE

8.15 g., Brass, 26.8 mm. **Subject:** Holy Year **Obv:** Crowned eagle with wings open divides date **Rev:** Cross with holy symbolic animals

Date	Mintage	VF20	XF40	MS60	MS63	MS65
2000	1,500,000	—	—	5.00	7.00	9.00

Y# 377 2 ZŁOTE

8.15 g., Brass, 26.8 mm. **Subject:** 1000th Anniversary - Gniezno Convention **Obv:** Crowned eagle with wings open divides date **Rev:** Denar coin design of Boleslaw Chrobry

Date	Mintage	VF20	XF40	MS60	MS63	MS65
2000	450,000	—	5.00	10.00	18.00	22.00

Y# 388 2 ZŁOTE

8.14 g., Brass, 26.8 mm. **Subject:** Dudek-Upupa epops **Obv:** Crowned eagle with wings open **Rev:** Long-billed Hoopoe **Edge Lettering:** NARODOWY BANK POLSKI

Date	Mintage	VF20	XF40	MS60	MS63	MS65
2000	500,000	—	5.00	10.00	18.00	22.00

Y# 389 2 ZŁOTE

8.14 g., Brass, 26.8 mm. **Subject:** 1000th Anniversary - Wroclaw (Breslau) **Obv:** Polish eagle **Rev:** St. John the Baptist standing with lamb, city view in background

Date	Mintage	VF20	XF40	MS60	MS63	MS65
2000	500,000	—	3.50	7.00	12.00	15.00

Y# 390 2 ZŁOTE

8.14 g., Brass, 26.8 mm. **Obv:** Crowned eagle with wings open divides date, all within circle **Rev:** Wilanowie Palace

Date	Mintage	VF20	XF40	MS60	MS63	MS65
2000	500,000	—	3.50	7.00	12.00	15.00

Y# 394 2 ZŁOTE

8.15 g., Brass, 26.8 mm. **Subject:** Solidarity **Obv:** Crowned eagle with wings open divides date **Rev:** Solidarity logo, map, children **Edge Lettering:** NARODOWY BANK POLSKI

Date	Mintage	VF20	XF40	MS60	MS63	MS65
2000	750,000	—	—	3.00	5.00	7.00

Y# 398 2 ZŁOTE

8.15 g., Brass, 26.8 mm. **Subject:** Jan II Kazimierz - 1648-68. **Obv:** Crowned eagle with wings open divides date **Rev:** Bust of Kazimierz facing 1/4 left **Edge Lettering:** POLSKA NARODOWY BANK

Date	Mintage	VF20	XF40	MS60	MS63	MS65
2000	450,000	—	5.00	10.00	18.00	22.00

Y# 404 2 ZŁOTE

8.15 g., Brass, 26.7 mm. **Subject:** Workers revolt in December 1970 **Obv:** Crowned eagle **Rev:** Fist **Edge:** "NBP" repeatedly

Date	Mintage	VF20	XF40	MS60	MS63	MS65
2000	750,000	—	—	3.00	5.00	7.00

Y# 284 5 ZŁOTYCH

6.54 g., Bi-Metallic Aluminum-Bronze center in Copper-Nickel ring, 24 mm. **Obv:** National arms within circle **Obv. Legend:** RZECZPOSPOLITA POLSKA **Rev:** Value within circle flanked by oak leaves

Date	Mintage	VF20	XF40	MS60	MS63	MS65
1994 MW	112,896,033	—	—	3.00	4.00	10.00
1996 MW	52,940,003	—	—	3.00	4.00	10.00

Y# 287 10 ZŁOTYCH

16.55 g., 0.750 Silver 0.3991 oz. ASW, 32 mm. **Obv:** Crowned eagle with wings open divides date **Rev:** Capture of Berlin

Date	Mintage	VF20	XF40	MS60	MS63	MS65
1995	12,000	PF65 265				

Y# 301 10 ZŁOTYCH

16.44 g., 0.925 Silver 0.4889 oz. ASW **Series:** 1996 Olympics **Obv:** Imperial eagle above value **Rev:** Centennial - Atlanta

Date	Mintage	VF20	XF40	MS60	MS63	MS65
1995	20,000	PF65 130				

Y# 305 10 ZŁOTYCH

16.50 g., 0.925 Silver 0.4907 oz. ASW **Subject:** Centennial of Organized Peasant Movement **Obv:** Imperial eagle above value **Rev:** Wincenty Witos

Date	Mintage	VF20	XF40	MS60	MS63	MS65
1995	20,000	PF65 85.00				

Y# 307 10 ZŁOTYCH

16.50 g., 0.925 Silver 0.4907 oz. ASW **Obv:** Imperial eagle above value **Rev:** Bust of Zygmunt II August left **Shape:** 32

Date	Mintage	VF20	XF40	MS60	MS63	MS65
1996	13,000	PF65 215				

Y# 308 10 ZŁOTYCH

16.50 g., 0.925 Silver 0.4907 oz. ASW **Obv:** Imperial eagle above value **Rev:** Half-length figure facing left

Date	Mintage	VF20	XF40	MS60	MS63	MS65
1996	5,000	PF65 840				

Y# 317 10 ZŁOTYCH

16.50 g., 0.925 Silver 0.4907 oz. ASW, 32 mm. **Obv:** Imperial eagle above value **Rev:** Stanislaw Mikolajczyk

Date	Mintage	VF20	XF40	MS60	MS63	MS65
1996	13,500	PF65 115				

Y# 318 10 ZŁOTYCH

16.50 g., 0.925 Silver 0.4907 oz. ASW, 32 mm. **Obv:** Imperial eagle above value **Rev:** Mazurka of Dabrowski

Date	Mintage	VF20	XF40	MS60	MS63	MS65
1996	14,000	PF65 190				

Y# 324 10 ZŁOTYCH

16.50 g., 0.925 Silver 0.4907 oz. ASW, 32 mm. **Subject:** 40th Anniversary - Poznan Workers Protest **Obv:** Crowned eagle with wings open **Rev:** Figures around inscription and date

Date	Mintage	VF20	XF40	MS60	MS63	MS65
1996	13,050	PF65 190				

Y# 321 10 ZŁOTYCH
16.50 g., 0.925 Silver 0.4907 oz. ASW **Subject:** St. Adalbert's Martyrdom **Obv:** Crowned eagle with wings open **Rev:** Baptism and funeral scenes **Edge Lettering:** 997-1997 (STAR) repeated 7 times

Date	Mintage	VF20	XF40	MS60	MS63	MS65
1997	25,000	PF65 115				

Y# 322 10 ZŁOTYCH
16.50 g., 0.925 Silver 0.4907 oz. ASW, 32 mm. **Subject:** 46th Eucharistic Congress **Obv:** Crowned eagle with wings open within design **Rev:** Pope left with arms raised **Edge Lettering:** MIEDZYNARODOWY KONGRES EUCHARYSTYCZNY - WROCLAW 1997

Date	Mintage	VF20	XF40	MS60	MS63	MS65
1997	—	PF65 80.00				

Y# 326 10 ZŁOTYCH
16.50 g., 0.925 Silver 0.4907 oz. ASW, 32 mm. **Obv:** Crowned eagle with wings open **Rev:** Stefan Batory 3/4 right

Date	Mintage	VF20	XF40	MS60	MS63	MS65
1997	5,250	PF65 740				

Y# 327 10 ZŁOTYCH
14.14 g., 0.925 Silver 0.4205 oz. ASW **Obv:** Crowned eagle with wings open **Rev:** Stefan Batory

Date	Mintage	VF20	XF40	MS60	MS63	MS65
1997	15,000	PF65 190				

Y# 334 10 ZŁOTYCH
14.14 g., 0.925 Silver 0.4205 oz. ASW **Obv:** Crowned eagle with wings open **Rev:** Pawel Edmund Strzelecki **Edge Lettering:** 200 LECIE URODZIN

Date	Mintage	VF20	XF40	MS60	MS63	MS65
1997	20,000	PF65 75.00				

Y# 337 10 ZŁOTYCH
14.14 g., 0.925 Silver 0.4205 oz. ASW, 32 mm. **Obv:** Crowned eagle with wings open **Rev:** Crowned bust of Zygmunt III 1/4 left

Date	Mintage	VF20	XF40	MS60	MS63	MS65
1998	22,000	PF65 110				

Y# 338 10 ZŁOTYCH
14.14 g., 0.925 Silver 0.4205 oz. ASW **Subject:** Sigismund III (1587-1632) **Obv:** Crowned eagle with wings open **Rev:** Seated King 1/4 left

Date	Mintage	VF20	XF40	MS60	MS63	MS65
1998	7,000	PF65 240				

Y# 341 10 ZŁOTYCH
14.14 g., 0.925 Silver 0.4205 oz. ASW, 32 mm. **Series:** 1998 Winter Olympics **Obv:** Crowned eagle with wings open **Rev:** Snowboarder

Date	Mintage	VF20	XF40	MS60	MS63	MS65
1998	30,000	PF65 65.00				

Y# 342 10 ZŁOTYCH
14.14 g., 0.925 Silver 0.4205 oz. ASW, 32 mm. **Obv:** Crowned eagle with wings open **Rev:** Brigadier General August Emil Fieldorf

Date	Mintage	VF20	XF40	MS60	MS63	MS65
1998	14,000	PF65 40.00				

Y# 345 10 ZŁOTYCH
14.14 g., 0.925 Silver 0.4205 oz. ASW, 32 mm. **Subject:** 20th Anniversary of Pontificate **Obv:** Value and eagles in cross design **Rev:** Pope John Paul II

Date	Mintage	VF20	XF40	MS60	MS63	MS65
1998	65,000	PF65 75.00				

Y# 350 10 ZŁOTYCH
14.14 g., 0.925 Silver 0.4205 oz. ASW, 32 mm. **Subject:** 80th Anniversary - Polish Independence **Obv:** Crowned eagle with wings open within stylized flames **Rev:** Anniversary dates

Date	Mintage	VF20	XF40	MS60	MS63	MS65
1998	16,000	PF65 85.00				

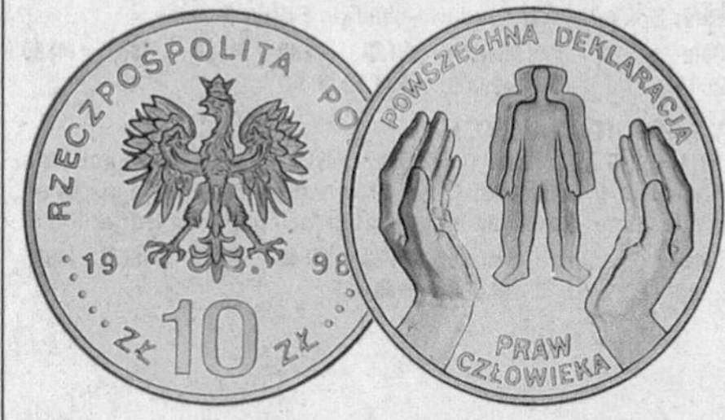

Y# 351 10 ZŁOTYCH
14.14 g., 0.925 Silver 0.4205 oz. ASW, 32 mm. **Subject:** Universal Declaration of Human Rights **Obv:** Crowned eagle with wings open divides date **Rev:** Human figure between two hands **Edge Lettering:** 50 ROCZNICA UCHWALENIA (three times)

Date	Mintage	VF20	XF40	MS60	MS63	MS65
1998	16,000	PF65 110				

Y# 359 10 ZŁOTYCH
14.14 g., 0.925 Silver 0.4205 oz. ASW, 32 mm. **Subject:** Poland's Accession to NATO **Obv:** Crowned eagle with wings open within quartered circle **Rev:** NATO globe, soldiers rapelling from helicopter

Date	Mintage	VF20	XF40	MS60	MS63	MS65
1999	16,000	PF65 50.00				

Y# 360 10 ZŁOTYCH
14.14 g., 0.925 Silver 0.4205 oz. ASW, 32 mm. **Obv:** Crucifix designs and crowned eagle **Rev:** Bust of Pope left and radiant dove

Date	Mintage	VF20	XF40	MS60	MS63	MS65
1999	70,000	PF65 75.00				

Y# 362 10 ZŁOTYCH
14.14 g., 0.925 Silver 0.4205 oz. ASW **Obv:** Crowned eagle with wings open **Rev:** Queen Jadwiga and coat of arms **Edge Lettering:** 1400-2000 (five times) **Shape:** 32 **Note:** Cracow University.

Date	Mintage	VF20	XF40	MS60	MS63	MS65
1999	22,000	PF65 85.00				

Y# 364 10 ZŁOTYCH
14.14 g., 0.925 Silver 0.4205 oz. ASW, 32 mm. **Obv:** Crowned eagle above windowed brick wall **Rev:** Laski with Erasmus in background **Edge Lettering:** 500 LECIE URODZIN (twice) **Note:** Jan Laski 1490-1560.

Date	Mintage	VF20	XF40	MS60	MS63	MS65
1999	15,000	PF65 85.00				

Y# 366 10 ZŁOTYCH
14.14 g., 0.925 Silver 0.4205 oz. ASW, 32 mm. **Obv:** Crowned eagle over twisted chords **Rev:** Head right with stylized design

Date	Mintage	VF20	XF40	MS60	MS63	MS65
1999	27,000	PF65 55.00				

Y# 369 10 ZŁOTYCH
14.14 g., 0.925 Silver 0.4205 oz. ASW **Obv:** Crowned eagle with wings open **Rev:** Portrait of Wladyslaw IV, dates

Date	Mintage	VF20	XF40	MS60	MS63	MS65
1999	20,000	PF65 110				

Y# 370 10 ZŁOTYCH
14.14 g., 0.925 Silver 0.4205 oz. ASW **Obv:** Crowned eagle with wings open **Rev:** Framed half-length portrait of Wladyslaw IV

Date	Mintage	VF20	XF40	MS60	MS63	MS65
1999	13,000	PF65 190				

Y# 378 10 ZŁOTYCH
14.14 g., 0.925 Silver 0.4205 oz. ASW, 32 mm. **Obv:** World globe and crowned eagle **Rev:** Bust of E. Malinowski facing, train in background **Edge Lettering:** 100-LECIE SMIERCI (twice)

Date	Mintage	VF20	XF40	MS60	MS63	MS65
1999	20,000	PF65 65.00				

Y# 379 10 ZŁOTYCH
14.14 g., 0.925 Silver 0.4205 oz. ASW, 32 mm. **Obv:** Inscription and crowned eagle **Rev:** Bust of Juliusz Slowacki 1/4 right **Edge:** Plain

Date	Mintage	VF20	XF40	MS60	MS63	MS65
1999	20,000	PF65 60.00				

Y# 380 10 ZŁOTYCH
14.14 g., 0.925 Silver 0.4205 oz. ASW **Subject:** Holy Year **Obv:** Crowned eagle in frame **Rev:** Cross with symbols of the evangelists **Edge Lettering:** WIELKI JUBILEUSZ ROKU 2000

Date	Mintage	VF20	XF40	MS60	MS63	MS65
2000	60,000	PF65 30.00				

Y# 381 10 ZŁOTYCH
14.14 g., 0.925 Silver 0.4205 oz. ASW **Subject:** 1000th Anniversary - Gniezno Convention **Obv:** Old coin designs in oxidized center, crowned eagle within circle **Rev:** Seated figures of Boleslaw Chrobry and Otto III in oxidized center **Edge:** Plain

Date	Mintage	VF20	XF40	MS60	MS63	MS65
2000	32,000	PF65 100				

Y# 392 10 ZŁOTYCH
14.20 g., 0.925 Silver 0.4223 oz. ASW **Subject:** 1000 Years Wroclaw (Breslau) **Obv:** Crowned eagle in front of city view **Rev:** City arms in arch **Edge:** Plain

Date	Mintage	VF20	XF40	MS60	MS63	MS65
2000	32,000	PF65 60.00				

Y# 395 10 ZŁOTYCH
14.22 g., 0.925 Silver 0.4229 oz. ASW, 32 mm. **Subject:** Solidarity **Obv:** Crowned eagle with wings open divides date **Rev:** Solidarity logo and two children **Edge:** Plain

Date	Mintage	VF20	XF40	MS60	MS63	MS65
2000	40,000	PF65 50.00				

Y# 400 10 ZŁOTYCH
14.14 g., 0.925 Silver 0.4205 oz. ASW, 32 mm. **Subject:** Jan Kazimierz II (1648-68) **Obv:** Crowned eagle with wings open divides date **Rev:** Half-length figure facing 1/4 left **Edge:** Plain

Date	Mintage	VF20	XF40	MS60	MS63	MS65
2000	14,000	PF65 165				

Y# 401 10 ZŁOTYCH
14.14 g., 0.925 Silver 0.4205 oz. ASW **Subject:** Jan Kazimierz II (1648-68) **Obv:** Crowned eagle **Rev:** Jan II Kazimierz 1/4 left

Date	Mintage	VF20	XF40	MS60	MS63	MS65
2000	20,000	PF65 110				

Y# 403 10 ZŁOTYCH
14.14 g., 0.925 Silver 0.4205 oz. ASW **Subject:** Rapperswil Polish Museum **Obv:** Crowned eagle and value between two buildings **Rev:** Eagle-topped column **Edge:** GDANSK GDYNIA SZCZECIN ELBLAG SLUPSK

Date	Mintage	VF20	XF40	MS60	MS63	MS65
2000	37,000	PF65 50.00				

Y# 405 10 ZŁOTYCH
14.14 g., 0.925 Silver 0.4205 oz. ASW **Subject:** Grudnia 1970 **Obv:** Two crowned eagles **Rev:** Shadow figures on pavement

Date	Mintage	VF20	XF40	MS60	MS63	MS65
2000	37,000	PF65 35.00				

Note: Antiqued finish

Y# 286 20 ZŁOTYCH
31.11 g., 0.925 Silver 0.9252 oz. ASW, 38.6 mm. **Subject:** Katyn Forest Massacre **Obv:** Crowned eagle with wings open divides date **Rev:** Burned forest

Date	Mintage	VF20	XF40	MS60	MS63	MS65
1995	30,000	PF65 110				

Y# 288 20 ZŁOTYCH
31.11 g., 0.999 Silver 0.9992 oz. ASW, 38.6 mm. **Subject:** 500th Anniversary - Plock Province **Obv:** Imperial eagle above value **Rev:** Eagle on shield divides dates, castle in background

Date	Mintage	VF20	XF40	MS60	MS63	MS65
1995	15,000	PF65 130				

Y# 290 20 ZŁOTYCH
31.11 g., 0.999 Silver 0.9992 oz. ASW **Obv:** Crowned eagle with wings open **Rev:** Catfish

Date	Mintage	VF20	XF40	MS60	MS63	MS65
1995	20,000	PF65 280				

Y# 291 20 ZŁOTYCH
31.11 g., 0.999 Silver 0.9992 oz. ASW **Subject:** 50th Anniversary - United Nations **Obv:** Imperial eagle above value **Rev:** ONZ in front of half globe with designs

Date	Mintage	VF20	XF40	MS60	MS63	MS65
1995	20,000	PF65 110				

Y# 296 20 ZŁOTYCH
31.17 g., 0.999 Silver 1.0011 oz. ASW **Obv:** Crowned eagle with wings open divides date, all within circle **Rev:** Royal Palace and swans

Date	Mintage	VF20	XF40	MS60	MS63	MS65
1995	20,000	PF65 110				

Y# 298 20 ZŁOTYCH
30.92 g., 0.925 Silver 0.9195 oz. ASW **Subject:** 75th Anniversary - Battle of Warsaw **Obv:** Imperial eagle above value **Rev:** Armored figures behind figure with cross

Date	Mintage	VF20	XF40	MS60	MS63	MS65
1995	20,000	PF65 100				

Y# 302 20 ZŁOTYCH
31.05 g., 0.925 Silver 0.9234 oz. ASW, 38.6 mm. **Obv:** Imperial eagle above value **Rev:** Copernicus and Ecu

Date	Mintage	VF20	XF40	MS60	MS63	MS65
1995	15,000	PF65 130				

Y# 304 20 ZŁOTYCH
31.10 g., 0.925 Silver 0.9249 oz. ASW, 38.6 mm. **Series:** 1996 Olympics - Atlanta **Obv:** Imperial eagle above value **Rev:** Wrestlers

Date	Mintage	VF20	XF40	MS60	MS63	MS65
1995	16,700	PF65 325				

Y# 309 20 ZŁOTYCH
31.10 g., 0.925 Silver 0.9249 oz. ASW, 38.6 mm. **Subject:** 400th Anniversary - Warsaw as Capital City **Obv:** Imperial eagle above value **Rev:** Buildings, statue and cross

Date	Mintage	VF20	XF40	MS60	MS63	MS65
1996	16,500	PF65 100				

Y# 312 20 ZŁOTYCH
31.10 g., 0.925 Silver 0.9249 oz. ASW, 38.6 mm. **Obv:** Crowned eagle with wings open **Rev:** Hedgehog with young

Date	Mintage	VF20	XF40	MS60	MS63	MS65
1996	18,000	PF65 450				

Y# 314 20 ZŁOTYCH
31.10 g., 0.925 Silver 0.9249 oz. ASW, 38.6 mm. **Obv:** Imperial eagle within circle outlined in crosses, value below **Rev:** Bishop's arms and Lidzibark Warminski castle

Date	Mintage	VF20	XF40	MS60	MS63	MS65
1996	15,000	PF65 130				

Y# 319 20 ZŁOTYCH
31.10 g., 0.925 Silver 0.9249 oz. ASW **Subject:** Millennium of Gdansk (Danzig) **Obv:** Imperial eagle above value **Rev:** Arms with supporters divide dates in front of city silhouette **Edge Lettering:** MONUMENTUM MILLENNII CIVITATIS GEDANENSIS

Date	Mintage	VF20	XF40	MS60	MS63	MS65
1996	20,000	PF65 100				

Y# 330 20 ZŁOTYCH
28.52 g., 0.925 Silver 0.8482 oz. ASW, 38.6 mm. **Obv:** Crowned eagle with wings open **Rev:** Stag beetle **Rev. Legend:** JELONEK ROGACZ - Lucanus cervus

Date	Mintage	VF20	XF40	MS60	MS63	MS65
1997	15,000	PF65 350				

Y# 332 20 ZŁOTYCH
28.28 g., 0.925 Silver 0.841 oz. ASW, 38.6 mm. **Obv:** Crowned eagle with wings open divides date, all within circle **Rev:** Zamek W Pieskowej Skale

Date	Mintage	VF20	XF40	MS60	MS63	MS65
1997	15,100	PF65 225				

Y# 343 20 ZŁOTYCH
28.28 g., 0.925 Silver 0.841 oz. ASW, 38.6 mm. **Obv:** Crowned eagle with wings open **Rev:** Ropucha Paskowka - Natterjack Toad

Date	Mintage	VF20	XF40	MS60	MS63	MS65
1998	20,000	PF65 250				

Y# 348 20 ZŁOTYCH

28.28 g., 0.925 Silver 0.841 oz. ASW, 38.6 mm. **Subject:** Zamek W. Koniku **Obv:** Crowned eagle with wings open **Rev:** Palace among diamond design

Date	Mintage	VF20	XF40	MS60	MS63	MS65
1998	20,000	PF65 100				

Y# 354 20 ZŁOTYCH

28.28 g., 0.925 Silver 0.841 oz. ASW, 38.6 mm. **Subject:** Discovery of Radium and Polonium **Obv:** Atom design **Rev:** Madame and Monsieur Curie and formulas

Date	Mintage	VF20	XF40	MS60	MS63	MS65
1998	20,000	PF65 85.00				

Y# 373 20 ZŁOTYCH

28.28 g., 0.925 Silver 0.841 oz. ASW **Subject:** Radzyn Podlaski Palace **Obv:** Crowned eagle within inner circle **Rev:** Palace behind sculptured arms

Date	Mintage	VF20	XF40	MS60	MS63	MS65
1999	15,000	PF65 160				

Y# 382 20 ZŁOTYCH

28.28 g., 0.925 Silver 0.841 oz. ASW, 38.6 mm. **Obv:** Imperial eagle above value **Rev:** Wolf family

Date	Mintage	VF20	XF40	MS60	MS63	MS65
1999	21,000	PF65 275				

Y# 387 20 ZŁOTYCH

28.37 g., 0.925 Silver 0.8437 oz. ASW **Obv:** Imperial eagle above value **Rev:** Dudek - Upupa epops - Eurasian Hoopoe

Date	Mintage	VF20	XF40	MS60	MS63	MS65
2000	24,000	PF65 250				

Y# 391 20 ZŁOTYCH

28.24 g., 0.925 Silver 0.8398 oz. ASW, 38.5 mm. **Obv:** Crowned eagle **Rev:** View of Palace through front gate **Edge:** Plain

Date	Mintage	VF20	XF40	MS60	MS63	MS65
2000	24,000	PF65 85.00				

Y# 328 100 ZŁOTYCH

8.00 g., 0.900 Gold 0.2315 oz. AGW, 24 mm. **Obv:** Crowned eagle with wings open divides date **Rev:** Bust of Stefan Batory 1/4 right

Date	Mintage	VF20	XF40	MS60	MS63	MS65
1997	2,000	PF65 1,350				

Y# 339 100 ZŁOTYCH

8.00 g., 0.900 Gold 0.2315 oz. AGW, 21 mm. **Obv:** Crowned eagle with wings open divides date **Rev:** Sigismund III 1/4 left

Date	Mintage	VF20	XF40	MS60	MS63	MS65
1998	2,000	PF65 1,000				

Y# 361 100 ZŁOTYCH

8.00 g., 0.900 Gold 0.2315 oz. AGW, 21 mm. **Obv:** Crowned eagle in inner circle **Rev:** Pope John Paul II left

Date	Mintage	VF20	XF40	MS60	MS63	MS65
1999	7,000	PF65 750				

Y# 371 100 ZŁOTYCH

8.00 g., 0.900 Gold 0.2315 oz. AGW, 21 mm. **Obv:** Crowned eagle with wings open divides date **Rev:** Wladyslaw IV in frame

Date	Mintage	VF20	XF40	MS60	MS63	MS65
1999	2,300	PF65 950				

Y# 383 100 ZŁOTYCH

8.00 g., 0.900 Gold 0.2315 oz. AGW **Obv:** Crowned eagle with wings open divides date **Rev:** Bust of Zygmunt II left

Date	Mintage	VF20	XF40	MS60	MS63	MS65
1999	2,000	PF65 1,200				

Y# 384 100 ZŁOTYCH

8.00 g., 0.900 Gold 0.2315 oz. AGW **Subject:** 100th Anniversary - Gniezno Convention **Obv:** Old coin designs **Rev:** Seated figures of Boleslaw Chrobry and Otto III

Date	Mintage	VF20	XF40	MS60	MS63	MS65
2000	2,200	PF65 825				

Y# 396 100 ZŁOTYCH

8.00 g., 0.900 Gold 0.2315 oz. AGW **Obv:** Crowned eagle with wings open divides date **Rev:** Queen Jadwiga facing **Edge:** Plain

Date	Mintage	VF20	XF40	MS60	MS63	MS65
2000	2,000	PF65 1,000				

Y# 402 100 ZŁOTYCH

8.00 g., 0.900 Gold 0.2315 oz. AGW, 21 mm. **Subject:** Jan Kazimierz II (1648-68) **Obv:** Crowned eagle with wings open **Rev:** Armored bust 1/4 left with names and dates on shoulder **Edge:** Plain

Date	Mintage	VF20	XF40	MS60	MS63	MS65
2000	—	PF65 950				

Y# 299 200 ZŁOTYCH

15.50 g., 0.900 Gold 0.4485 oz. AGW **Subject:** XII Chopin Piano Competition **Obv:** Crowned eagle with wings open divides date **Rev:** Bust of Chopin 1/4 right below tree **Edge:** Lettered

Date	Mintage	VF20	XF40	MS60	MS63	MS65
1995	500	PF65 11,500				

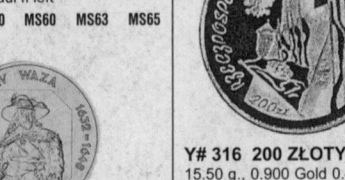

Y# 316 200 ZŁOTYCH

15.50 g., 0.900 Gold 0.4485 oz. AGW **Obv:** Stylized design to right of eagle **Rev:** Henryk Sienkiewicz

Date	Mintage	VF20	XF40	MS60	MS63	MS65
1996	Est. 1000	PF65 4,250				

Y# 320 200 ZŁOTYCH

15.50 g., 0.900 Gold 0.4485 oz. AGW **Subject:** Millennium of Gdansk (Danzig) **Obv:** Crowned eagle with wings open within shield **Rev:** City arms in old coin style

Date	Mintage	VF20	XF40	MS60	MS63	MS65
1996	2,000	PF65 2,250				

Y# 323 200 ZŁOTYCH

15.50 g., 0.900 Gold 0.4485 oz. AGW **Subject:** St. Adalbert's Martyrdom **Obv:** Crowned eagle with wings open within circle **Rev:** Figure standing within center design flanked by other figures

Date	Mintage	VF20	XF40	MS60	MS63	MS65
1997	2,000	PF65 2,250				

Y# 346 200 ZŁOTYCH

15.50 g., 0.900 Gold 0.4485 oz. AGW **Obv:** Imperial eagle above value **Rev:** Standing Pope with arms wide open

Date	Mintage	VF20	XF40	MS60	MS63	MS65
1998	5,000	PF65 1,500				

Y# 353 200 ZŁOTYCH

15.50 g., 0.900 Gold 0.4485 oz. AGW **Subject:** 200th Birthday - Adam Mickiewicz **Obv:** Small crowned eagle at lower right, quote written above **Rev:** Portrait with silhouette

Date	Mintage	VF20	XF40	MS60	MS63	MS65
1998	3,000	PF65 1,000				

Y# 367 200 ZŁOTYCH

15.50 g., 0.900 Gold 0.4485 oz. AGW **Obv:** Crowned eagle on sash, music design **Rev:** Head of Fryderyk Chopin 1/4 left with music background

Date	Mintage	VF20	XF40	MS60	MS63	MS65
1999	2,200	PF65 1,200				

Y# 385 200 ZŁOTYCH

15.50 g., 0.900 Gold 0.4485 oz. AGW **Obv:** Crowned eagle with wings open, feather at right **Rev:** Head of Juliusz Slowacki left

Date	Mintage	VF20	XF40	MS60	MS63	MS65
1999	1,900	PF65 1,500				

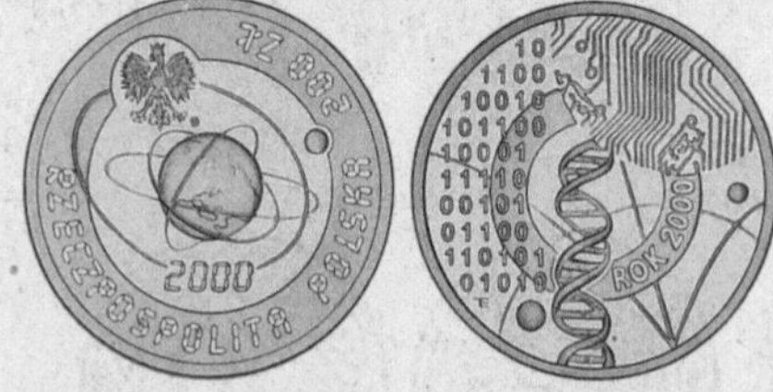

Y# 375 200 ZŁOTYCH

13.60 g., Gold and Silver **Subject:** Millennium **Obv:** Crowned eagle and world globe **Rev:** Various computer, DNA and atomic symbols **Note:** .900 Gold center in .925 Silver inner ring in a .900 Gold outer ring.

Date	Mintage	VF20	XF40	MS60	MS63	MS65
2000	6,000	PF65 550				

Y# 386 200 ZŁOTYCH

15.50 g., 0.900 Gold 0.4485 oz. AGW **Subject:** 1000th Anniversary - Gniezno Convention **Obv:** Old coin designs **Rev:** Seated figures of Boleslaw Chrobry and Otto III

Date	Mintage	VF20	XF40	MS60	MS63	MS65
2000	1,250	PF65 4,250				

Y# 393 200 ZŁOTYCH

15.50 g., 0.900 Gold 0.4485 oz. AGW, 27 mm. **Subject:** 1000 Years - Wroclzaw (Breslau) **Obv:** Crowned eagle with wings open within beaded circle **Rev:** Bust of Jesus facing, holding city arms **Edge:** Plain

Date	Mintage	VF20	XF40	MS60	MS63	MS65
2000	2,000	PF65 1,350				

Y# 397 200 ZŁOTYCH

23.32 g., 0.900 Gold 0.6748 oz. AGW, 32 mm. **Subject:** Solidarity **Obv:** Crowned eagle with wings open **Rev:** Multicolor Soldiarity logo, map and two children **Edge:** Plain

Date	Mintage	VF20	XF40	MS60	MS63	MS65
2000	2,500	PF65 2,250				

Y# 267 1000 ZŁOTYCH

27.95 g., 0.925 Silver 0.8312 oz. ASW **Subject:** World Cup Soccer **Rev:** Soccer stadium

Date	Mintage	VF20	XF40	MS60	MS63	MS65
1994 MW	10,000	PF65 175				

GOLD BULLION COINAGE

Y# 292 50 ZŁOTYCH

3.10 g., 0.9999 Gold 0.0997 oz. AGW, 18 mm. **Obv:** Crowned eagle with wings open, all within circle **Rev:** Golden eagle

Date	Mintage	VF20	XF40	MS60	MS63	MS65
1995	5,000	—	—	—	140	200
1996	2,500	—	—	—	140	200
1997	2,000	—	—	—	140	200
1998	1,500	—	—	—	140	200
1999	2,000	—	—	—	140	200
2000	2,000	—	—	—	140	200

Y# 293 100 ZŁOTYCH

7.78 g., 0.9999 Gold 0.2501 oz. AGW, 22 mm. **Obv:** Crowned eagle with wings open, all within circle **Rev:** Golden eagle

Date	Mintage	VF20	XF40	MS60	MS63	MS65
1995	3,000	—	—	—	350	475
1996	2,500	—	—	—	350	475
1997	2,000	—	—	—	350	475
1998	500	—	—	—	350	475
1999	1,000	—	—	—	350	475
2000	500	—	—	—	350	475

Y# 294 200 ZŁOTYCH

15.50 g., 0.900 Gold 0.4485 oz. AGW, 27 mm. **Obv:** Crowned eagle with wings open within beaded circle **Rev:** Golden eagle

Date	Mintage	VF20	XF40	MS60	MS63	MS65
1995	2,000	—	—	—	630	850
1996	2,500	—	—	—	630	850
1997	1,500	—	—	—	630	850
1998	500	—	—	—	630	850
1999	1,000	—	—	—	630	850
2000	500	—	—	—	630	850

Y# 295 500 ZŁOTYCH

31.10 g., 0.9999 Gold 0.9999 oz. AGW **Obv:** Crowned eagle with wings open within beaded circle **Rev:** Golden eagle

Date	Mintage	VF20	XF40	MS60	MS63	MS65
1995	2,500	—	—	—	1,400	1,850
1996	2,500	—	—	—	1,400	1,850
1997	3,500	—	—	—	1,400	1,850
1998	1,000	—	—	—	1,400	1,850
1999	1,500	—	—	—	1,400	1,850
2000	500	—	—	—	1,400	1,850

TRIAL STRIKES

KM#	Date	Mintage	Identification	Mkt Val
TS1	1923	—	Grosz. Copper. Uniface.	2,500
TS2	1923	—	Grosz. Copper. Uniface.	2,500

KM#	Date	Mintage	Identification	Mkt Val
TS3	1928	—	2 Złotych. Gold. Madonna. Uniface.	6,500

PATTERNS

Including off metal strikes

Pn232 1919 — 50 Groszy. Nickel. Small eagle. —

Pn233 1919 — 50 Groszy. Nickel. Large eagle. —

Pn234	1922	60	100 Marek. Copper.	4,500
Pn235	1922	100	100 Marek. Bronze.	3,900
Pn236	1922	10	100 Marek. Brass.	—
Pn237	1922	4	100 Marek. Tin.	—
Pn238	1922	50	100 Marek. Silver.	4,200
Pn239	1922	3	100 Marek. Gold.	—

Pn240	1923	120	50 Marek. Bronze.	2,700
Pn241	1923	12	50 Marek. Silver.	—
Pn242	1923	1	50 Marek. Gold.	—

Pn243 1923 30 Grosz. Bronze. —

Pn244	1923	125	2 Grosze. Bronze.	3,900
Pn245	1923	—	2 Grosze. Gold.	—

Pn246	1923	10	5 Groszy. Brass.	—
Pn247	1923	100	5 Groszy. Silver.	3,600

Pn248 1923 3 5 Groszy. Brass. —

Pn249 1923 30 20 Groszy. Brass. —

Pn250 1923 30 50 Groszy. Brass. —

Pn251	1923	—	50 Groszy. Nickel. HUGUENIN in 0 of 50.	—
Pn252	1924	10	20 Groszy. Nickel.	—

Pn253 1924 15 Złoty. Silver. ESSAI. —

Pn254	1924	40	Złoty. Silver. With torch.	4,500
Pn255	1924 H	8	Złoty. Silver.	—

Pn256	1924	40	2 Złote. Brass.	—
Pn257	1924	100	2 Złote. Brass. Rotated dies.	3,250

Pn258	1924	15	2 Złote. Silver. ESSAI. Paris Mint.	—
Pn259	1924 H	60	2 Złote. Silver.	4,500
Pn260	1924	10	2 Złote. Silver.	—

Pn261 1924 3 2 Złote. Silver. Larger eagle. —

Pn262	1924	120	20 Złotych. Bronze.	6,000
Pn263	1924	10	20 Złotych. Silver.	—
Pn264	1924	10	20 Złotych. Gold.	—

Pn265	1924	105	50 Złotych. Copper.	6,000
Pn266	1924	2	50 Złotych. Lead.	—
Pn267	1924	2	50 Złotych. Aluminum.	—
Pn268	1924	1	50 Złotych. Gold.	—
Pn269	1925	15	5 Groszy. Brass.	—

Pn272	1925	100	10 Złotych. Bronze.	4,750
Pn273	1925	50	10 Złotych. Silver.	6,000
Pn274	1925	1	10 Złotych. Gold.	—

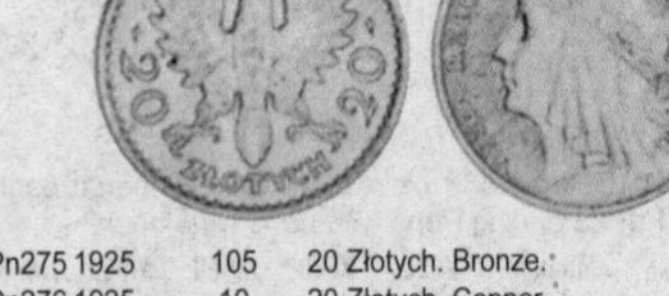

Pn275	1925	105	20 Złotych. Bronze.	4,250
Pn276	1925	10	20 Złotych. Copper.	—
Pn277	1925	12	20 Złotych. Silver.	—
Pn278	1925	5	20 Złotych. Gold.	—
Pn279	1925	35	20 Złotych. Brass. Boleslaus I, Y#33.	—
Pn280	1925	20	20 Złotych. Nickel. Boleslaus I, Y#33.	—

Pn281 1925 2 100 Złotych. Silver. Plain. —

Pn282 1925 100 100 Złotych. Silver. Edge lettering: SALUS REIPUBLICAE SUPREMA LEX. 6,500

Pn283 1925 100 100 Złotych. Bronze. Kopernik Commemorative. 5,400
Pn284 1925 50 100 Złotych. Silver. 4,200
Pn285 1925 1 100 Złotych. Gold. —

Pn286 1926 20 2 Grosze. Nickel. —
Pn287 1926 100 2 Grosze. Silver. 3,000
Pn288 1927 100 Grosz. Silver. 3,000
Pn289 1927 6 Grosz. Gold. —
Pn290 1927 100 2 Złote. 3,000

Pn291 1927 10 2 Złote. Bronze. With PROBA. —

Pn292 1927 100 2 Złote. Silver. Warsau Mint, with proba. 5,500

Pn293 1927 81 5 Złotych. Silver. With MM, PROBA. 6,000
Pn294 1927 20 5 Złotych. Silver. Without MM, without PROBA. —
Pn295 1927 100 5 Złotych. Silver. Without MM, with PROBA. 6,000

Pn296 1928 2 Złoty. Copper. —
Pn297 1928 2 Złoty. Tombac. —
Pn298 1928 25 Złoty. Nickel. —

Pn299 1928 110 Złoty. Nickel. 4,000
Pn300 1928 35 Złoty. Nickel. Mint mark. —
Pn301 1928 35 Złoty. Bronze. —

Pn302 1928 15 Złoty. Nickel. —
Pn303 1928 8 Złoty. Tombac. —
Pn304 1928 2 Złoty. Copper. —

Pn305 1928 125 Złoty. Bronze. 2,500
Pn306 1928 — Złoty. Nickel. Madonna. —
Pn307 1928 — 2 Złotych. Aluminum. Madonna. —
Pn308 1928 — 2 Złotych. Copper. Madonna. —
Pn309 1928 — 2 Złotych. Silver. Madonna. —

Pn310 1928 — 2 Złote. Gold. Madonna. 4,750
Pn311 1928 — 2 Złotych. Platinum. Madonna. 6,000

Pn312 1928 — 5 Złotych. Aluminum. Madonna. —
Pn313 1928 — 5 Złotych. Copper. Madonna. —
Pn314 1928 — 5 Złotych. Nickel. Madonna. —
Pn315 1928 — 5 Złotych. Silver. Madonna. —

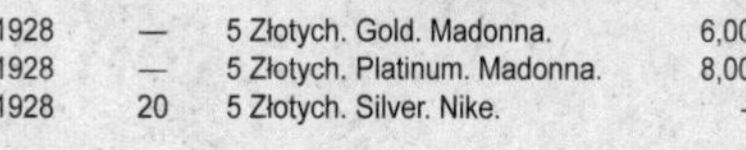

Pn316 1928 — 5 Złotych. Gold. Madonna. 6,000
Pn317 1928 — 5 Złotych. Platinum. Madonna. 8,000
Pn318 1928 20 5 Złotych. Silver. Nike. —

Pn319 1928 — 5 Złotych. Tombac. ESSAI/30. 3,000

Pn320 1928 20 5 Złotych. Tombac. Denticals instead of dots. 2,500

Pn321 1929 10 Złoty. Aluminum. —
Pn322 1929 12 Złoty. Bronze. —
Pn323 1929 115 Złoty. Nickel. Without PROBA. 1,800
Pn324 1930 20 5 Złotych. Bronze. PROBA. —
Pn325 1930 200 5 Złotych. Bronze. Without PROBA. 5,400
Pn326 1932 100 Złoty. Bronze. 3,900

Pn327 1932 120 Złoty. Silver. 3,950
Pn328 1932 100 2 Złote. Bronze. 3,250
Pn329 1932 110 2 Złote. Silver. 4,200

Pn330 1932 100 10 Złotych. Silver. 4,250
Pn331 1932 10 10 Złotych. Bronze. —
Pn332 1932 100 10 Złotych. Bronze. 3,500
PnA333 1933 — 2 Złote. Silver. PROBA. 3,750
Pn333 1933 100 5 Złotych. Bronze. 3,500
Pn334 1933 100 5 Złotych. Silver. 3,500
Pn335 1933 100 10 Złotych. Silver. 4,250

Pn336 1933 100 10 Złotych. Silver. PROBA, Y#23. 3,000

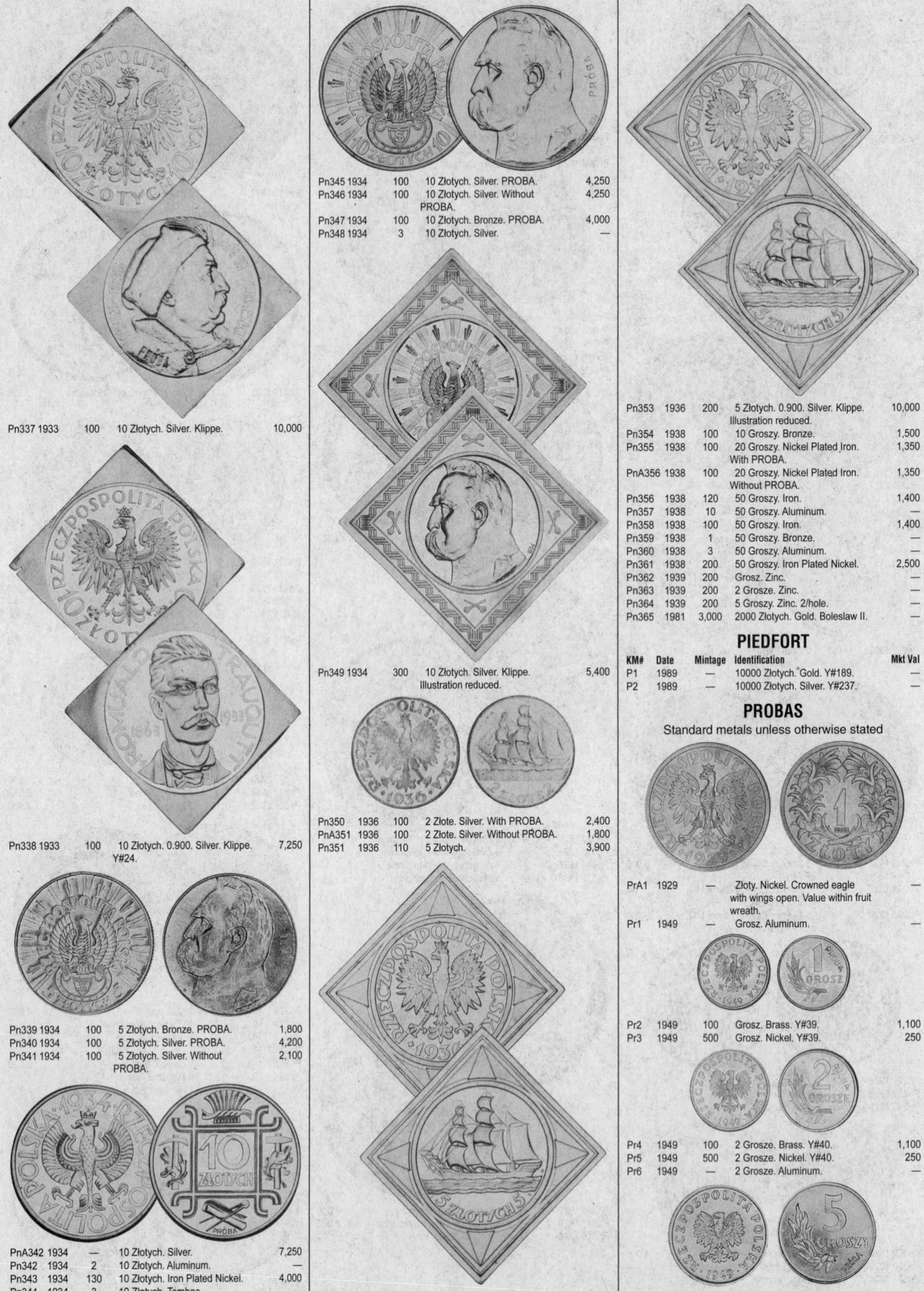

Pn337	1933	100	10 Złotych. Silver. Klippe.	10,000
Pn338	1933	100	10 Złotych. 0.900. Silver. Klippe. Y#24.	7,250
Pn339	1934	100	5 Złotych. Bronze. PROBA.	1,800
Pn340	1934	100	5 Złotych. Silver. PROBA.	4,200
Pn341	1934	100	5 Złotych. Silver. Without PROBA.	2,100
PnA342	1934	—	10 Złotych. Silver.	7,250
Pn342	1934	2	10 Złotych. Aluminum.	—
Pn343	1934	130	10 Złotych. Iron Plated Nickel.	4,000
Pn344	1934	3	10 Złotych. Tombac.	—
Pn345	1934	100	10 Złotych. Silver. PROBA.	4,250
Pn346	1934	100	10 Złotych. Silver. Without PROBA.	4,250
Pn347	1934	100	10 Złotych. Bronze. PROBA.	4,000
Pn348	1934	3	10 Złotych. Silver.	—
Pn349	1934	300	10 Złotych. Silver. Klippe. Illustration reduced.	5,400
Pn350	1936	100	2 Złote. Silver. With PROBA.	2,400
PnA351	1936	100	2 Złote. Silver. Without PROBA.	1,800
Pn351	1936	110	5 Złotych.	3,900
Pn352	1936	200	5 Złotych. Bronze. Klippe.	9,000
Pn353	1936	200	5 Złotych. 0.900. Silver. Klippe. Illustration reduced.	10,000
Pn354	1938	100	10 Groszy. Bronze.	1,500
Pn355	1938	100	20 Groszy. Nickel Plated Iron. With PROBA.	1,350
PnA356	1938	100	20 Groszy. Nickel Plated Iron. Without PROBA.	1,350
Pn356	1938	120	50 Groszy. Iron.	1,400
Pn357	1938	10	50 Groszy. Aluminum.	—
Pn358	1938	100	50 Groszy. Iron.	1,400
Pn359	1938	1	50 Groszy. Bronze.	—
Pn360	1938	3	50 Groszy. Aluminum.	—
Pn361	1938	200	50 Groszy. Iron Plated Nickel.	2,500
Pn362	1939	200	Grosz. Zinc.	—
Pn363	1939	200	2 Grosze. Zinc.	—
Pn364	1939	200	5 Groszy. Zinc. 2/hole.	—
Pn365	1981	3,000	2000 Złotych. Gold. Boleslaw II.	—

PIEDFORT

KM#	Date	Mintage	Identification	Mkt Val
P1	1989	—	10000 Złotych. Gold. Y#189.	—
P2	1989	—	10000 Złotych. Silver. Y#237.	—

PROBAS

Standard metals unless otherwise stated

PrA1	1929	—	Złoty. Nickel. Crowned eagle with wings open. Value within fruit wreath.	—
Pr1	1949	—	Grosz. Aluminum.	—
Pr2	1949	100	Grosz. Brass. Y#39.	1,100
Pr3	1949	500	Grosz. Nickel. Y#39.	250
Pr4	1949	100	2 Grosze. Brass. Y#40.	1,100
Pr5	1949	500	2 Grosze. Nickel. Y#40.	250
Pr6	1949	—	2 Grosze. Aluminum.	—
PrA7	1949	500	5 Groszy. Nickel. Y#41.	250

Pr7	1949	100	5 Groszy. Brass. Y#41.	1,150
Pr8	1949	100	5 Groszy. Brass.	—
Pr9	1949	—	5 Groszy. Aluminum. Eagle with wings open. Value at upper right of spray.	—
Pr10	1949	—	10 Groszy. Aluminum.	—
Pr11	1949	100	10 Groszy. Brass. Y#42.	1,100
Pr12	1949	500	10 Groszy. Nickel. Y#42.	250
Pr13	1949	100	20 Groszy. Brass. Y#43.	1,100
Pr14	1949	500	20 Groszy. Nickel. Y#43.	250
Pr15	1949	—	20 Groszy. Aluminum.	—
Pr16	1949	100	50 Groszy. Brass. Y#44.	1,100
Pr17	1949	20	50 Groszy. Tombac. Y#44.	—
Pr18	1949	500	50 Groszy. Nickel. Y#44.	250
Pr19	1949	—	50 Groszy. Aluminum.	—
Pr20	1949	100	Złoty. Brass. Y#45.	1,200
Pr21	1949	—	Złoty. Aluminum.	—
Pr22	1949	500	Złoty. Nickel. Y#45.	240
Pr23	1957	100	20 Groszy. Brass. Y#A47.	1,100

Pr24	1957	100	50 Groszy. Brass. Y#48.1.	1,200
Pr25	1957	500	50 Groszy. Nickel. Y#48.1.	240
Pr26	1957	100	Złoty. Brass. Y#49.1.	1,200
Pr27	1957	500	Złoty. Nickel. Y#49.1.	250
Pr28	1957	5	Złoty. Copper-Nickel-Zinc. Y#49.1 without PROBA.	—
Pr29	1958	100	5 Groszy. Brass. Y#A46.	—
Pr30	1958	245	50 Groszy. Aluminum. Eagle with wings open. Value above crossed hammers.	1,450
Pr31	1958	500	50 Groszy. Nickel. Crossed hammers.	550
Pr32	1958	198	50 Groszy. Aluminum. Eagle with wings open. Antenna below value.	1,500
Pr33	1958	500	50 Groszy. Nickel. Antenna below denomination.	550
Pr34	1958	212	50 Groszy. Aluminum. Eagle with wings open. Value above spears of grain.	1,400
Pr35	1958	500	50 Groszy. Nickel. 50 above spears of grain.	525
Pr36	1958	234	Złoty. Aluminum. Eagle with wings open. 1 Between spears of grain.	1,450
Pr37	1958	500	Złoty. Nickel. 1 between spears of grain.	550

Pr38	1958	235	Złoty. Aluminum. Eagle with wings open. Value in spears of grain within diamond shape design.	1,450
Pr39	1958	500	Złoty. Nickel. 1 within circle.	550
Pr40	1958	211	Złoty. Aluminum. Eagle with wings open. Value among acorns and oak leaves.	1,500
Pr41	1958	500	Złoty. Nickel. Acorns and oak leaves.	550
Pr42	1958	210	Złoty. Aluminum. Eagle with wings open. Value between doves, low relief.	1,450
Pr43	1958	53	Złoty. Aluminum. 1 between doves, high relief.	1,800
Pr44	1958	500	Złoty. Nickel. 1 between birds.	550
Pr45	1958	100	2 Złote. Brass. Y#46.	1,600
Pr46	1958	5	5 Złotych. Aluminum. Eagle with wings open. Hammer and shovel without PROBA.	—
Pr47	1958	5	5 Złotych. Brass. Eagle with wings open. Ship and value.	—
Pr48	1958	20	5 Złotych. Aluminum. Ship, without PROBA.	—

Pr49	1958	500	5 Złotych. Nickel. Ship.	725
Pr50	1958	10	5 Złotych. Aluminum. Without PROBA, reverse of Pr49.	—

Pr51	1958	5	10 Złotych. Aluminum. Eagle with wings open. Caliper and gear, without PROBA.	—

Pr52	1958	10	10 Złotych. Aluminum. Eagle with wings open. Kosciuszko with ornaments, without PROBA.	—
Pr53	1958	10	10 Złotych. Copper-Nickel. Eagle with wings open. Kosciuszko with ornaments, without PROBA.	—
Pr54	1958	5	10 Złotych. Aluminum. With ornaments and PROBA.	—
Pr55	1958	5	10 Złotych. Brass. Eagle with wings open. Kosciuszko with ornaments without PROBA.	—
Pr56	1958	5	10 Złotych. Copper-Nickel. Eagle with wings open. Kosciuszko with ornaments and PROBA.	—
Pr57	1958	10	10 Złotych. Aluminum.	—

Pr58	1958	5	10 Złotych. Copper-Nickel. Eagle with wings open. Without ornaments and PROBA, high relief.	—

Pr59	1959	500	2 Złote. Nickel. Y#46.	550

Pr60	1959	100	5 Złotych. Brass. Y#47.	1,100
Pr61	1959	500	5 Złotych. Nickel. Y#47.	550

Pr62	1959	500	5 Złotych. Nickel. Eagle with wings open. Value within industrial collage.	550

Pr63	1959	500	5 Złotych. Nickel. Eagle with wings open. Value to left of hammer and shovel.	550

Pr64	1959	10	10 Złotych. Aluminum. Y#51.	—
Pr65	1959	500	10 Złotych. Nickel. Y#51.	350
Pr66	1960	196	5 Złotych. Aluminum. Ship.	—

Pr67	1960	500	5 Złotych. Nickel. Eagle with wings open. Ship and value.	725

Pr68	1960	500	10 Złotych. Nickel. Eagle with wings open. Value above caliper and gear.	550

Pr69	1960	500	10 Złotych. Nickel. Eagle with wings open. Kosciuszko with ornaments and PROBA.	725

Pr70	1960	500	10 Złotych. Nickel. Eagle with wings open. Kosciuszko with PROBA in front of neck.	550

Pr71	1960	10	100 Złotych. Nickel. Y#57, with crosshatched field.	—
Pr72	1960	500	100 Złotych. Nickel. Y#57, with crosshatched field.	725
Pr73	1960	50	100 Złotych. 0.500. Silver. Without PROBA, Y#57 with crosshatched field.	—
Pr74	1960	20	100 Złotych. 0.750. Silver. Y#57, with crosshatched field.	—
Pr75	1960	500	100 Złotych. Nickel. Y#57.	725

Pr76	1960	12	100 Złotych. 0.750. Silver. Eagle with wings open flanked by shields. Conjoined heads right.	—
Pr77	1960	14	100 Złotych. 0.750. Silver.	—
Pr78	1960	4	100 Złotych. 0.700. Silver. High relief.	—
Pr79	1960	9	100 Złotych. 0.700. Silver. Flat relief.	—
Pr80	1960	20	100 Złotych. 0.500. Silver.	—

Pr81	1960	13	100 Złotych. 0.750. Silver. Eagle with wings open within circle, assorted shields around border. Conjoined heads right.	—

Pr82 1960 500 100 Złotych. Nickel. 725
Pr83 1960 5 100 Złotych. 0.750. Silver. —

Pr84 1960 500 100 Złotych. Nickel. 725
Pr85 1960 29 100 Złotych. 0.700. Silver. —

Pr86 1960 500 100 Złotych. Nickel. Eagle with wings open within circle. Conjoined heads left within circle. 725
Pr87 1960 12 100 Złotych. 0.750. Silver. —

Pr88 1960 500 100 Złotych. Nickel. Eagle with wings open. Conjoined heads right. 725
Pr89 1960 6 100 Złotych. 0.750. Silver. —

Pr90 1962 500 10 Groszy. Nickel. Y#AA47. 250

Pr91 1963 500 5 Groszy. Nickel. Y#A46. 250

Pr92 1963 500 20 Groszy. Nickel. Y#A47. 250

Pr93 1964 125 10 Złotych. Copper-Nickel. Raised legend, Y#52. 775

Pr94 1964 500 10 Złotych. Nickel. Y#52a. 350
Pr95 1964 125 10 Złotych. Copper-Nickel. Incuse legend, Y#52a. 775
Pr96 1964 5 10 Złotych. Tombac. Y#52a. —
Pr97 1964 500 10 Złotych. Nickel. Y#52a. 350

Pr98 1964 30 10 Złotych. Copper-Nickel-Zinc. Eagle with wings open. Seated King facing, PROBA raised. —
Pr99 1964 30,000 10 Złotych. Copper-Nickel. PROBA incuse. 36.00
Pr100 1964 Inc. above 10 Złotych. Copper-Nickel. Eagle with wings open. Without PROBA. 1,100
Pr101 1964 500 10 Złotych. Nickel. Eagle with wings open. PROBA raised. 425

Pr102 1964 500 10 Złotych. Nickel. Crowned eagle. Raised PROBA. 425
Pr103 1964 10 10 Złotych. Copper-Nickel. —

Pr104 1964 10 10 Złotych. Copper-Nickel. Shield on eagle with wings open. Standing figure holding spears of grain. —
Pr105 1964 500 10 Złotych. Nickel. 650

Pr106 1964 10 10 Złotych. Copper-Nickel. —

Pr107 1964 10 10 Złotych. Copper-Nickel. —

Pr108 1964 20 10 Złotych. Copper-Nickel. Eagle with wings open above inscription and date. Vertical inscription flanked by designs. —
Pr109 1964 500 10 Złotych. Nickel. 550

Pr110 1964 10 10 Złotych. Copper-Nickel. Eagle with wings open above inscription and date. Value below stylized tree. —

Pr111 1964 10 10 Złotych. Copper-Nickel. Eagle with wings open. Value below stylized tree. —
Pr112 1964 500 10 Złotych. Nickel. 650

Pr113 1964 10 10 Złotych. Copper-Nickel. Shield on eagle with wings open. Value below stylized tree. —

Pr114 1964 20 10 Złotych. Copper-Nickel. Eagle with wings open. Value below designs. —
Pr115 1964 500 10 Złotych. Nickel. 550

Pr116 1964 20 20 Złotych. Copper-Nickel. Shield on eagle with wings open. Standing figure holding spears of grain. —

Pr117 1964 500 20 Złotych. Nickel. 650

Pr118 1964 20 20 Złotych. Copper-Nickel. —

Pr119 1964 10 20 Złotych. Copper-Nickel. Eagle with wings open. Vertical inscription flanked by designs. —

Pr120 1964 20 20 Złotych. Copper-Nickel. Eagle with wings open above inscription and date. Vertical inscription flanked by designs. —

Pr121 1964 500 20 Złotych. Nickel. 550

Pr122 1964 20 20 Złotych. Copper-Nickel. Eagle with wings open. Value below tree. —

Pr123 1964 500 20 Złotych. Nickel. 650

Pr124 1964 20 20 Złotych. Copper-Nickel. Shield on eagle with wings open. Value below tree. —

Pr125 1964 20 20 Złotych. Copper-Nickel. Eagle with wings open. Value below designs. —

Pr126 1964 500 20 Złotych. Nickel. 550

Pr127 1965 20 10 Złotych. Copper-Nickel. —

Pr128 1965 500 10 Złotych. Nickel. —

Pr129 1965 20 10 Złotych. Copper-Nickel. Y#54. —

Pr130 1965 500 10 Złotych. Nickel. Y#54. 300

Pr131 1965 30,000 10 Złotych. Copper-Nickel. Eagle with wings open. Mermaid holding sword and shield. 20.00

Pr132 1965 500 10 Złotych. Nickel. 200

Pr133 1965 30,000 10 Złotych. Copper-Nickel. Eagle with wings open. Mermaid holding sword and shield flanked by ship and house, value at bottom. 20.00

Pr134 1965 500 10 Złotych. Nickel. 200

Pr135 1965 20 10 Złotych. Copper-Nickel. Eagle with wings open. Value, monument and flying birds. —

Pr136 1965 500 10 Złotych. Nickel. 300

Pr137 1965 5 10 Złotych. Aluminum. Kopernik. —

Pr138 1966 25 10 Złotych. Copper-Nickel. Eagle with wings open. Head left. —

Pr139 1966 500 10 Złotych. Nickel. 300

Pr140 1966 500 10 Złotych. Nickel. Eagle with wings open. Value, monument and flying birds. 425

Pr141 1966 10 10 Złotych. Copper-Nickel. —

Pr142 1966 10 100 Złotych. Copper-Nickel. —

Pr143 1966 10 100 Złotych. 0.750. Silver. —

Pr144 1966 500 100 Złotych. Nickel. Y#57. 725

Pr145 1966 500 100 Złotych. Nickel. 725

KM#	Date	Mintage	Identification	Mkt Val
Pr146	1966	31,000	100 Złotych. 0.900. Silver. Eagle with wings open within circle, assorted shields around border. Conjoined half figures facing right, flanked by value.	70.00

KM#	Date	Mintage	Identification	Mkt Val
Pr147	1966	500	100 Złotych. Nickel. Eagle with wings open. Conjoined heads right.	725
Pr148	1966	30,000	100 Złotych. 0.900. Silver. 2 heads.	70.00
Pr149	1967	10	10 Złotych. Copper-Nickel. Plain. Y#59.	—
Pr150	1967	16	10 Złotych. Copper-Nickel. Milled. Y#59.	—
Pr151	1967	500	10 Złotych. Nickel. Y#59.	250

KM#	Date	Mintage	Identification	Mkt Val
Pr152	1967	20	10 Złotych. Copper-Nickel. Eagle with wings open above inscription and value. Head facing 1/4 left.	—
Pr153	1967	500	10 Złotych. Nickel.	300

KM#	Date	Mintage	Identification	Mkt Val
Pr154	1967	16	10 Złotych. Copper-Nickel. Eagle with wings open. Head left.	—
Pr155	1967	10	10 Złotych. Plain.	—
Pr156	1967	500	10 Złotych. Nickel.	250

KM#	Date	Mintage	Identification	Mkt Val
Pr157	1967	25	10 Złotych. Copper-Nickel. Eagle with wings open. Head left.	—
Pr158	1967	500	10 Złotych. Nickel.	300
Pr159	1967	40	10 Złotych. Copper-Nickel.	—
Pr160	1967	500	10 Złotych. Nickel.	300

KM#	Date	Mintage	Identification	Mkt Val
Pr161	1967	17	10 Złotych. Aluminum. Kopernik.	—
Pr162	1967	1	10 Złotych. Copper-Nickel. Kopernik.	—
Pr163	1967	10	10 Złotych. Aluminum. Kopernik.	—

KM#	Date	Mintage	Identification	Mkt Val
Pr164	1968	20	10 Złotych. Copper-Nickel. Eagle with wings open perched on design. 1/4 helmeted head right, XXV to left.	—
Pr165	1968	500	10 Złotych. Nickel.	250

KM#	Date	Mintage	Identification	Mkt Val
Pr166	1969	20	10 Złotych. Copper-Nickel. Eagle with wings open within circle. Design divides date within radiant circle, PROBA at lower right.	—
Pr167	1969	500	10 Złotych. Nickel. PROBA at lower right.	250
Pr168	1969	5	10 Złotych. Gold. PROBA at lower right.	—

KM#	Date	Mintage	Identification	Mkt Val
Pr169	1969	20	10 Złotych. Copper-Nickel. Eagle with wings open within circle. PROBA at lower right.	—
Pr170	1969	500	10 Złotych. Nickel. PROBA at right.	—
Pr171	1969	500	10 Złotych. Nickel. Wthout PROBA.	250

KM#	Date	Mintage	Identification	Mkt Val
Pr172	1969	20	10 Złotych. Copper-Nickel. Eagle with wings open within circle, bold letters around border. 1/4 head right on mirror, bold letters around border.	—
Pr173	1969	500	10 Złotych. Nickel.	375

KM#	Date	Mintage	Identification	Mkt Val
Pr174	1969	20	10 Złotych. Copper-Nickel. Eagle with wings open within circle. Letters and numbers within blocks.	—
Pr175	1969	500	10 Złotych. Nickel.	375

KM#	Date	Mintage	Identification	Mkt Val
Pr176	1970	20	10 Złotych. Copper-Nickel. Eagle with wings open flanked by shields. Conjoined heads right. 25th Anniversary of Provincial Annexation.	—
Pr177	1970	500	10 Złotych. Nickel. 25th Anniversary of Provincial Annexation.	250
Pr178	1970	10	10 Złotych. Copper-Nickel. Without PROBA.	—

KM#	Date	Mintage	Identification	Mkt Val
Pr179	1970	20	10 Złotych. Copper-Nickel. Y#62.	—
Pr180	1970	500	10 Złotych. Nickel. Y#62.	250
Pr181	1970	300	10 Złotych. Silver. Y#62.	425
Pr182	1970	5	10 Złotych. Aluminum. Kopernik.	—
Pr183	1971	20	10 Złotych. Copper-Nickel. Y#63.	—
Pr184	1971	500	10 Złotych. Nickel. Y#63.	375

KM#	Date	Mintage	Identification	Mkt Val
Pr185	1971	51,000	10 Złotych. Copper-Nickel. Eagle with wings open. Baby nursing in front of world globe, FAO above.	15.00
Pr186	1971	500	10 Złotych. Nickel. FAO, baby nursing.	145

KM#	Date	Mintage	Identification	Mkt Val
Pr187	1971	52,000	10 Złotych. Copper-Nickel. Eagle with wings open. Spears of grain on top of globe, F.A.O. logo between spears.	15.00
Pr188	1971	500	10 Złotych. Nickel. FAO, wheat.	145

Pr189 1971 20 10 Złotych. Copper-Nickel. Y#64. —
Pr190 1971 500 10 Złotych. Nickel. Y#64. 200

Pr191 1971 20 10 Złotych. Copper-Nickel. Eagle with wings open within eagle with wings open, all within circle. Medal in front of inscription. —
Pr192 1971 500 10 Złotych. Nickel. Medal. 350

Pr193 1972 20 10 Złotych. Copper-Nickel. Y#65 but date inside legend. —
Pr194 1972 500 10 Złotych. Nickel. Y#65 but date inside legend. 200

Pr195 1972 20 10 Złotych. Copper-Nickel. Y#65. —
Pr196 1972 500 10 Złotych. Nickel. Y#65. 200
Pr197 1972 — 50 Złotych. Copper-Nickel. —
Pr198 1972 20 50 Złotych. 0.750. Silver. Y#66, Chopin. —
Pr199 1972 500 50 Złotych. Nickel. Y#66. 250
Pr200 1972 — 50 Złotych. Bronze. Chopin, without PROBA. —
Pr201 1972 20 50 Złotych. 0.750. Silver. Chopin, without PROBA. —

Pr202 1972 14,622 50 Złotych. 0.750, Silver. Stylized eagle with wings open within circle. Stylized head of Chopin 3/4 right. Chopin. 55.00
Pr203 1972 500 50 Złotych. Nickel. Chopin. 250

Pr204 1973 20 10 Złotych. Copper-Nickel. Eagle with wings open above inscription and date. Design above inscription and value. —
Pr205 1973 500 10 Złotych. Nickel. 350

Pr206 1973 20 10 Złotych. Copper-Nickel. Eagle with wings open. Design within dates. —
Pr207 1973 500 10 Złotych. Nickel. 350

Pr208 1973 10 10 Złotych. Copper-Nickel. Kopernik. —
Pr209 1973 500 10 Złotych. Nickel. Kopernik. 350
Pr210 1973 20 20 Złotych. Copper-Nickel. Plain. Without PROBA, Y#67. —

Pr211 1973 20 20 Złotych. Copper-Nickel. Eagle with wings open within circle. Value within designed waterfall. Ornamented. —

Pr212 1973 13,200 20 Złotych. Copper-Nickel. Milled. Y#67. 25.00
Pr213 1973 500 20 Złotych. Nickel. Y#67. 145

Pr214 1973 16,200 20 Złotych. Copper-Nickel. Tree. 35.00
Pr215 1973 500 20 Złotych. Nickel. Tree. 145
Pr216 1973 — 100 Złotych. Copper. Kopernik. —
Pr217 1973 20 100 Złotych. 0.625. Silver. Kopernik. —
Pr218 1973 500 100 Złotych. Nickel. Kopernik. 250

Pr219 1973 500 100 Złotych. Nickel. Y#68. 250
Pr220 1973 5,000 100 Złotych. 0.625. Silver. Y#68. 55.00

Pr221 1973 1,222 100 Złotych. 0.625. Silver. Eagle with wings open divides date. Head of Kopernik 1/4 right. 775
Pr222 1973 500 100 Złotych. Nickel. Kopernik. 550

Pr223 1974 40 10 Złotych. Copper-Nickel. Sienkiewicz. —
Pr224 1974 500 10 Złotych. Nickel. Sienkiewicz. 350

Pr225 1974 40 10 Złotych. Copper-Nickel. Y#74. —
Pr226 1974 500 10 Złotych. Nickel. Y#74. 240

Pr227 1974 10,000 20 Złotych. Copper-Nickel. Y#69. —
Pr228 1974 500 20 Złotych. Nickel. Y#69. 300

Pr229 1974 20 20 Złotych. Copper-Nickel. 4 laborers. —
Pr230 1974 500 20 Złotych. Nickel. 4 laborers. 350
Pr231 1974 20 20 Złotych. Copper-Nickel. —
Pr232 1974 500 20 Złotych. Nickel. 200

Pr233 1974 20 20 Złotych. Copper-Nickel. XXX LAT PRL. —
Pr234 1974 500 20 Złotych. Nickel. XXX LAT PRL. 210

Pr235	1974	20	20 Złotych. Copper-Nickel. Y#70.	—
Pr236	1974	500	20 Złotych. Nickel. Y#70.	250

Pr237	1974	20	20 Złotych. Copper-Nickel. Eagle with wings open above value. Letters within circle of 1/2 gear and 1/2 flower design.	—
Pr238	1974	500	20 Złotych. Nickel.	250

Pr239	1974	500	100 Złotych. Nickel. Eagle with wings open. Profile of Curie left, symbol at right.	250
Pr240	1974	10,041	100 Złotych. 0.625. Silver. Curie left.	40.00
Pr241	1974	500	100 Złotych. Nickel. Y#71.	250
Pr242	1974	10	100 Złotych. 0.625. Silver. Y#71.	—

Pr243	1974	500	100 Złotych. Nickel. Curie right.	250
Pr244	1974	10,131	100 Złotych. 0.625. Silver. Curie right.	40.00

Pr245	1974	500	100 Złotych. Nickel. Royal Castle in Warsaw.	250
Pr246	1974	20	100 Złotych. 0.625. Silver. Royal Castle in Warsaw.	—

Pr247	1974	500	200 Złotych. Nickel. Eagle with wings open within square. Triple x and letters within square.	250
Pr248	1974	20	200 Złotych. 0.625. Silver.	—
Pr249	1975	—	10 Złotych. Aluminum. Boleslaw Prus.	—
Pr250	1975	40	10 Złotych. Copper-Nickel. Boleslaw Prus.	—
Pr251	1975	500	10 Złotych. Nickel. Boleslaw Prus.	250

Pr252	1975	20	20 Złotych. Copper-Nickel. Year of the Woman.	—
Pr253	1975	500	20 Złotych. Nickel. Year of the Woman.	250

Pr254	1975	20	20 Złotych. Copper-Nickel. Eagle with wings open above value. Globe. Globe.	—
Pr255	1975	500	20 Złotych. Nickel. Globe.	550
Pr256	1975	5,000	100 Złotych. 0.625. Silver. Y#76.	30.00

Pr257	1975	500	100 Złotych. Nickel. Y#78.	—

Pr258	1975	20	100 Złotych. 0.625. Silver. Y#78.	—
Pr259	1975	500	100 Złotych. Nickel. Modrzeiewska.	300
Pr260	1975	20	100 Złotych. 0.625. Silver. Modrzeiewska.	—
Pr261	1975	500	100 Złotych. Nickel. Y#77.	250
Pr262	1975	20	100 Złotych. 0.625. Silver. Y#77.	—

Pr263	1975	500	100 Złotych. Nickel. Paderewski.	300
Pr264	1975	20	100 Złotych. 0.625. Silver. Paderewski.	—

Pr265	1975	500	200 Złotych. Nickel. Eagle with wings open above value. Name written in front of swords.	250
Pr266	1975	10,030	200 Złotych. 0.750. Silver.	55.00

Pr267	1975	500	200 Złotych. Nickel. Eagle with wings open. Hammer head flanked by dates with triple x on top.	250
Pr268	1975	10,054	200 Złotych. 0.750. Silver.	55.00
Pr269	1975	500	200 Złotych. Nickel. Y#79.	250
Pr270	1975	20	200 Złotych. 0.750. Silver. Y#79.	—
Pr271	1976	20	20 Złotych. Copper-Nickel. 30 Years of Budget Bill.	—
Pr272	1976	500	20 Złotych. Nickel. 30 Years of Budget Bill.	350
Pr273	1976	20	20 Złotych. Copper-Nickel. 30 Years of Budget Bill - PRL.	—
Pr274	1976	500	20 Złotych. Nickel. PRL.	350

Pr275	1976	500	100 Złotych. Nickel. Y#82.	250
Pr276	1976	20	100 Złotych. 0.625. Silver. Y#82.	—

Pr277 1976 3,000 100 Złotych. 0.625. Silver. Kosciuszko. 90.00
Pr278 1976 500 100 Złotych. Nickel. Kosciuszko. 250
Pr279 1976 20 100 Złotych. —

Pr280 1976 500 100 Złotych. Nickel. Pulaski. 250
Pr281 1976 3,000 100 Złotych. 0.625. Silver. Pulaski. 150

Pr282 1976 20 200 Złotych. 0.625. Silver. Olympics. —
Pr283 1976 500 200 Złotych. Nickel. Olympic rings and torch. 350

Pr284 1976 500 200 Złotych. Nickel. Y#86. 200
Pr285 1976 6,048 200 Złotych. 0.750. Silver. Y#86. 55.00

Pr286 1976 500 200 Złotych. Nickel. Eagle with wings open divides date. Stylized head with Olympic circles left. 200
Pr287 1976 6,060 200 Złotych. 0.625. Silver. 55.00
Pr288 1976 500 500 Złotych. Nickel. Y#83. 250
Pr289 1976 300 500 Złotych. 0.900. Gold. Y#83. 6,000
Pr290 1976 500 500 Złotych. Nickel. Kosciuszko. 250
Pr291 1976 500 500 Złotych. Nickel. Y#85. 250
Pr292 1976 300 500 Złotych. 0.900. Gold. Y#85. 6,000
Pr293 1976 500 500 Złotych. Nickel. Pulaski facing. 250
Pr294 1977 100 20 Złotych. Copper-Nickel. Y#96. 1,000
Pr295 1977 500 20 Złotych. Nickel. Y#96. 200

Pr296 1977 500 100 Złotych. Nickel. Y#88. 250

Pr297 1977 2,500 1000 Złotych. 0.625. Silver. Y#88. 150

Pr298 1977 500 100 Złotych. Nickel. Sienkiewicz facing. 250
Pr299 1977 3,000 100 Złotych. 0.625. Silver. Sienkiewicz facing. 95.00
Pr300 1977 500 100 Złotych. Nickel. Y#89. 250
Pr301 1977 3,100 100 Złotych. 0.625. Silver. Y#89. 75.00

Pr302 1977 500 100 Złotych. Nickel. Reymont profile left. 250
Pr303 1977 3,100 100 Złotych. 0.625. Silver. Reymont profile left. 75.00

Pr304 1977 500 100 Złotych. Nickel. Eagle with wings open divides date. Catfish. 425
Pr305 1977 5,100 100 Złotych. 0.625. Silver. Fish. 200

Pr306 1977 500 100 Złotych. Nickel. Y#91. 250
Pr307 1977 100 100 Złotych. 0.625. Silver. Y#91. —

Pr308 1977 500 100 Złotych. Nickel. Distant Krakow castle. 240
Pr309 1977 3,100 100 Złotych. 0.625. Silver. Distant Krakow castle. 210
Pr310 1977 500 100 Złotych. Nickel. Bison. 350
Pr311 1977 5,400 100 Złotych. 0.625. Silver. Bison. 145
Pr312 1977 6 2000 Złotych. Gold. Chopin. —
Pr313 1977 500 2000 Złotych. Nickel. Chopin. 350
Pr314 1978 100 20 Złotych. Copper-Nickel. Y#97. 1,200
Pr315 1978 500 20 Złotych. Nickel. Y#97. 175
Pr316 1978 100 20 Złotych. Copper-Nickel. Y#96. 1,200
Pr317 1978 500 20 Złotych. Nickel. Y#96. 175

Pr318 1978 100 100 Złotych. 0.625. Silver. Y#92. —
Pr319 1978 500 100 Złotych. Nickel. Y#92. 210
Pr320 1978 100 100 Złotych. 0.625. Silver. Similar to KM#PrM255 but with lock of hair at left of face. —
Pr321 1978 500 100 Złotych. Nickel. Similar to KM#PrK255, but with lock of hair at left of face. 240
Pr322 1978 500 100 Złotych. Nickel. Mickiewicz profile. 240

Pr323 1978 3,100 100 Złotych. 0.625. Silver. Eagle with wings open divides date. Head of Mickiewicz left. 100
Pr324 1978 100 100 Złotych. 0.625. Silver. Y#93. —
Pr325 1978 500 100 Złotych. Nickel. Y#93. 425
Pr326 1978 500 100 Złotych. Nickel. Elk head. 425

Pr327 1978 3,100 100 Złotych. 0.625. Silver. Eagle with wings open divides date. Moose head. 325
Pr328 1978 500 100 Złotych. Nickel. Beaver on wood. 425
Pr329 1978 100 100 Złotych. 0.625. Silver. Beaver on wood. —

Pr330	1978	500	100 Złotych. Nickel. Beaver on grass.	425
Pr331	1978	3,100	100 Złotych. 0.625. Silver. Beaver on grass.	350
Pr332	1978	100	100 Złotych. 0.625. Silver. Y#94.	—
Pr333	1978	500	100 Złotych. Nickel. Y#94.	240

Pr334	1978	500	100 Złotych. Nickel. Eagle with wings open divides date. Head of Korczak right.	240
Pr335	1978	3,100	100 Złotych. 0.625. Silver. Korczak.	95.00

Pr336	1978	500	100 Złotych. Nickel. Eagle with wings open divides date. Globe within legend.	240
Pr337	1978	3,100	100 Złotych. 0.625. Silver. Globe in legend.	80.00
Pr338	1979	500	2 Złotych. Nickel.	—
Pr339	1979	500	5 Złotych. Nickel.	—
Pr340	1979	500	20 Złotych. Nickel. I.Y.C., dancers.	210
Pr341	1979	4,200	20 Złotych. 0.625. Silver. I.Y.C.	85.00

Pr342	1979	500	20 Złotych. Nickel. I.Y.C. Health Center.	110
Pr343	1979	30,000	20 Złotych. Copper-Nickel. I.Y.C. Health Center.	17.50

Pr344	1979	100	50 Złotych. Copper-Nickel. Eagle with wings open divides date. Mieszko I.	1,200
Pr345	1979	500	50 Złotych. Nickel. Mieszko I.	425
Pr346	1979	100	100 Złotych. 0.625. Silver. Y#98.	—
Pr347	1979	500	100 Złotych. Nickel. Y#98.	200
Pr348	1979	500	100 Złotych. Nickel. Wieniawski profile.	240

Pr349	1979	3,100	100 Złotych. 0.625. Silver. Wieniawski profile.	80.00
Pr350	1979	100	100 Złotych. 0.625. Silver. Y#104.	—
Pr351	1979	500	100 Złotych. Nickel. Y#104.	200

Pr352	1979	500	100 Złotych. Nickel. Eagle with wings open divides date. Lynx.	425
Pr353	1979	4,100	100 Złotych. 0.625. Silver. Lynx.	325
Pr354	1979	100	100 Złotych. 0.625. Silver. Y#105.	—
Pr355	1979	500	100 Złotych. Nickel. Y#105.	—

Pr356	1979	500	100 Złotych. Nickel. Mountain goat on rock.	425
Pr357	1979	4,100	100 Złotych. 0.625. Silver. Mountain goat on rock.	240
Pr358	1979	100	100 Złotych. 0.625. Silver. Y#103.	—
Pr359	1979	500	100 Złotych. Nickel. Y#103.	425

Pr360	1979	500	100 Złotych. Nickel. Eagle with wings open divides date. Head of Zamenhof facing.	240
Pr361	1979	3,100	100 Złotych. 0.625. Silver. Zamenhof facing.	60.00
Pr362	1979	100	200 Złotych. 0.750. Silver. Y#101.	—
Pr363	1979	500	200 Złotych. Nickel. Y#101.	550
Pr364	1979	500	200 Złotych. Nickel. Mieszko.	450
Pr365	1979	4,100	200 Złotych. 0.750. Silver. Mieszko I.	325
Pr366	1979	5	2000 Złotych. 0.900. Gold. Y#106.	—
Pr367	1979	500	2000 Złotych. Nickel. Y#106.	350
Pr368	1979	6	2000 Złotych. 0.900. Gold. Y#107.	—
Pr369	1979	500	2000 Złotych. Nickel. Y#107.	300
Pr370	1979	4	2000 Złotych. 0.900. Gold. Y#102.	—
Pr371	1979	12	2000 Złotych. Bronze. Y#102.	—
Pr372	1979	500	2000 Złotych. Nickel. Y#102.	450
Pr373	1979	4	2000 Złotych. 0.900. Gold. Mieszko I, PrG266.	—
Pr374	1979	—	2000 Złotych. Bronze. PrG266.	—
Pr375	1979	500	2000 Złotych. Nickel. PrG266.	550
Pr376	1980	100	20 Złotych. 0.625. Silver. Y#108.	1,200
Pr377	1980	500	20 Złotych. Nickel. Y#108.	210

PrA378	1980	500	20 Złotych. Nickel. Eagle with wings open divides date. Stylized runner with torch, Olympic rings at right.	160
Pr378	1980	20	20 Złotych. Copper-Nickel. Y#112.	—
Pr379	1980	500	20 Złotych. Nickel. Y#112.	240
Pr380	1980	20	20 Złotych. Copper-Nickel. Date even with top sails of ship.	—
Pr381	1980	500	20 Złotych. Nickel. Date even with top sails of ship.	240

Pr382	1980	500	20 Złotych. Nickel. 1905-Lodz.	175
Pr383	1980	10,000	20 Złotych. Copper-Nickel. 1905-Lodz.	27.50
Pr384	1980	20	20 Złotych. Copper-Nickel. 75th Anniversary of Lodz riots.	—
Pr385	1980	500	20 Złotych. Nickel. 75th Anniversary of Lodz riots.	350
Pr386	1980	20	50 Złotych. Copper-Nickel. Y#114.	—
Pr387	1980	500	50 Złotych. Nickel. Reeded. Y#114.	350
Pr388	1980	20	50 Złotych. Copper-Nickel. Boleslaw I inscription below.	—
Pr389	1980	500	50 Złotych. Nickel. Boleslaw I, inscription below.	350
Pr390	1980	20	50 Złotych. Copper-Nickel. Y#117.	—

Pr391	1980	500	100 Złotych. Nickel. Eagle with wings open divides date. Ship.	250
Pr392	1980	4,000	100 Złotych. 0.625. Silver. Ship.	55.00
Pr393	1980	100	100 Złotych. Copper-Nickel. Olympic flame and rings.	—

Pr394	1980	500	100 Złotych. Nickel. Eagle with wings open divides date. Stylized runner holding torch, Olympic rings at right.	200
Pr395	1980	4,100	100 Złotych. 0.625. Silver. Olympic flame and rings.	80.00

PrA396 1980 500 100 Złotych. Nickel. Y#109. 200
Pr396 1980 20 100 Złotych. 0.625. Silver. Y#121. —
Pr397 1980 500 100 Złotych. Nickel. Y#121. 425

Pr398 1980 500 100 Złotych. Nickel. Eagle with wings open divides date. Birds. 425
Pr399 1980 4,018 100 Złotych. 0.625. Silver. Birds. 180
Pr400 1980 100 100 Złotych. 0.625. Silver. Y#120. —
Pr401 1980 500 100 Złotych. Nickel. 240

Pr402 1980 500 100 Złotych. Nickel. Larger head of Kochanowski. 240
Pr403 1980 4,100 100 Złotych. 0.625. Silver. Larger head of Kochanowski. 55.00
Pr404 1980 100 200 Złotych. 0.750. Silver. Y#110. —
Pr405 1980 500 200 Złotych. Nickel. Y#110. 210
Pr406 1980 100 200 Złotych. 0.750. Silver. Y#110a. —
Pr407 1980 500 200 Złotych. Nickel. Y#110a. 210

Pr408 1980 500 200 Złotych. Nickel. Eagle with wings open divides date. Olympic skier with torch mm. 210
Pr409 1980 3,620 200 Złotych. 0.750. Silver. Olympic skier with torch mm. 75.00
Pr410 1980 500 200 Złotych. Nickel. Olympic skier without mm. 250
Pr411 1980 3,620 200 Złotych. 0.750. Silver. Olympic skier without mm. 90.00
Pr412 1980 20 200 Złotych. 0.750. Silver. Y#115. —
Pr413 1980 500 200 Złotych. Nickel. Y#115. 550
Pr414 1980 500 200 Złotych. Nickel. Boleslaw I torso. 550
Pr415 1980 4,020 200 Złotych. 0.750. Silver. Boleslaw I torso. 325
Pr416 1980 20 200 Złotych. 0.750. Silver. Y#118. —
Pr417 1980 500 200 Złotych. Nickel. Y#118. 425
Pr418 1980 500 200 Złotych. Nickel. Kazimierz I torso. 425
Pr419 1980 4,020 200 Złotych. 0.750. Silver. Kazimierz I torso. 160
Pr420 1980 3 2000 Złotych. 0.900. Gold. Y#111. —
Pr421 1980 — 2000 Złotych. Bronze. Y#111. —

Pr422 1980 500 2000 Złotych. Nickel. Y#111. 350
Pr423 1980 6 2000 Złotych. 0.900. Gold. Y#116. —
Pr424 1980 500 2000 Złotych. Nickel. Y#116. 350
Pr425 1980 6 2000 Złotych. 0.900. Gold. Odnowiciel. —
Pr426 1980 500 2000 Złotych. Nickel. Odnowiciel. 550
Pr427 1980 500 2000 Złotych. Nickel. Olympic skier without torch mm. —

Pr428 1980 1,500 2000 Złotych. 0.900. Gold. Eagle with wings open divides date. Olympic skier without torch mm. 550
Pr429 1981 500 20 Złotych. Nickel. Restoration of Krakow. 175

Pr430 1981 30,040 20 Złotych. Copper-Nickel. Restoration of Krakow. 17.50
Pr431 1981 20 50 Złotych. Copper-Nickel. Y#122. —
Pr432 1981 500 50 Złotych. Nickel. Y#122. 250
Pr433 1981 20 50 Złotych. Copper-Nickel. Y#124. —
Pr434 1981 500 50 Złotych. Nickel. Y#124. 350
Pr435 1981 20 50 Złotych. Copper-Nickel. Y#128. —
Pr436 1981 500 50 Złotych. Nickel. Y#128. 350
Pr437 1981 20 50 Złotych. Copper-Nickel. Y#127. —
Pr438 1981 500 50 Złotych. Nickel. Y#127. 250
Pr439 1981 120 100 Złotych. 0.625. Silver. Y#123. —
Pr440 1981 500 100 Złotych. Nickel. Y#123. 250

Pr441 1981 500 100 Złotych. Nickel. Sikorski. 250
Pr442 1981 5,020 100 Złotych. 0.625. Silver. Sikorski. 50.00

Pr443 1981 500 100 Złotych. Nickel. St. Mary's Church. 250
Pr444 1981 4,020 100 Złotych. 0.625. Silver. St. Mary's Church. 55.00
Pr445 1981 20 100 Złotych. 0.625. Silver. Y#126. —
Pr446 1981 500 100 Złotych. Nickel. Y#126. 425

Pr447 1981 500 100 Złotych. Nickel. 425
Pr448 1981 4,020 100 Złotych. 0.625. Silver. Horses. 175
Pr449 1981 20 200 Złotych. 0.750. Silver. Y#125. —
Pr450 1981 500 200 Złotych. Nickel. Y#125. —
Pr451 1981 500 200 Złotych. Nickel. Boleslaw II. 425
Pr452 1981 4,020 200 Złotych. 0.750. Silver. Boleslaw II. 200
Pr453 1981 20 200 Złotych. 0.750. Silver. Y#129. —
Pr454 1981 500 200 Złotych. Nickel. Y#129. 425

Pr455 1981 500 200 Złotych. Nickel. Wladyslaw I Herman. 425
Pr456 1981 4,020 200 Złotych. 0.750. Silver. 210
Pr457 1981 — 200 Złotych. 0.750. Silver. Wladyslaw I. —
Pr458 1981 4 2000 Złotych. 0.900. Gold. Y#126. —
Pr459 1981 500 2000 Złotych. Nickel. Y#126. 550
Pr460 1981 4 2000 Złotych. 0.900. Gold. Y#131. —
Pr461 1981 500 2000 Złotych. 0.900. Gold. Y#131. 550
Pr462 1982 20 50 Złotych. Copper-Nickel. Y#133. —
Pr463 1982 500 50 Złotych. Nickel. Y#133. 350
Pr464 1982 500 100 Złotych. Nickel. Y#141. 425

Pr465 1982 500 100 Złotych. Nickel. Eagle with wings open divides date. Storks. 425
Pr466 1982 4,000 100 Złotych. 0.625. Silver. Storks. 240

Pr467 1982 20 200 Złotych. 0.750. Silver. Y#132. —
Pr468 1982 500 200 Złotych. Nickel. Y#132. 425
Pr469 1982 500 200 Złotych. Nickel. 425
Pr470 1982 3,000 200 Złotych. 0.750. Silver. 180
Pr471 1982 6,000 200 Złotych. 0.750. Silver. Soccer player leaning right. 55.00
Pr472 1982 6,002 200 Złotych. 0.750. Silver. Soccer player leaning left. 70.00

KM#	Date	Mintage	Identification	Mkt Val
Pr473	1982	500	200 Złotych. Nickel. Soccer player leaning right.	175
Pr474	1982	500	200 Złotych. Nickel. Without Espana 82, Y#130.	175

KM#	Date	Mintage	Identification	Mkt Val
Pr475	1982	500	200 Złotych. Nickel. Eagle with wings open divides date. Stylized soccer player leaning left.	200

KM#	Date	Mintage	Identification	Mkt Val
Pr476	1982	500	500 Złotych. Nickel. Eagle with wings open divides date. Ship.	240
Pr477	1982	25,000	500 Złotych. 0.625. Silver. Ship.	30.00

KM#	Date	Mintage	Identification	Mkt Val
Pr478	1982	10,000	1000 Złotych. 0.750. Silver. Pope John Paul II.	150
Pr479	1982	500	1000 Złotych. Nickel. Y#144.	725
Pr480	1982	500	1000 Złotych. Nickel.	725
Pr481	1983	20	50 Złotych. Copper-Nickel. Y#142.	—
Pr482	1983	500	50 Złotych. Nickel. Y#142.	240
Pr483	1983	20	50 Złotych. Copper-Nickel. Y#145.	—
Pr484	1983	500	50 Złotych. Nickel. Y#145.	350
Pr485	1983	20	50 Złotych. Copper-Nickel. Y#146.	—
Pr486	1983	500	50 Złotych. Nickel. Y#146.	240
Pr487	1983	500	100 Złotych. Nickel. Y#147.	425
Pr488	1983	500	100 Złotych. Nickel.	425

KM#	Date	Mintage	Identification	Mkt Val
Pr489	1983	3,000	100 Złotych. 0.625. Silver. Bears.	350
Pr490	1983	500	200 Złotych. Nickel. Y#143.	425

KM#	Date	Mintage	Identification	Mkt Val
Pr491	1983	500	200 Złotych. Nickel. Eagle with wings open divides date. Horse and rider rearing above fallen Indian.	400
Pr492	1983	4,000	200 Złotych. 0.750. Silver. Jan III Sobieski.	150

KM#	Date	Mintage	Identification	Mkt Val
Pr493	1983	500	500 Złotych. Nickel. Eagle with wings open divides date. Gymnast.	200
Pr494	1983	7,000	500 Złotych. 0.750. Silver. Gymnast.	55.00

KM#	Date	Mintage	Identification	Mkt Val
Pr495	1983	500	500 Złotych. Nickel. Eagle with wings open divides date. Speed skater within horizontal lines.	200
Pr496	1983	6,000	500 Złotych. 0.750. Silver. Speed skater.	55.00
Pr497	1984	500	10 Złotych. Nickel. Y#152.1.	130
Pr498	1984	500	20 Złotych. Nickel. Y#153.1.	145
Pr499	1984	500	100 Złotych. Nickel. Y#148.	200
Pr500	1984	500	100 Złotych. Nickel. Reeded. Y#151.	200
Pr501	1984	500	200 Złotych. Nickel. Y#149.	200
Pr502	1984	500	200 Złotych. Nickel. Y#150.	200
Pr503	1984	500	500 Złotych. Nickel. Y#154.	350

KM#	Date	Mintage	Identification	Mkt Val
Pr504	1984	500	1000 Złotych. Nickel. Wincenty Witos.	250
Pr505	1984	3,000	1000 Złotych. 0.625. Silver. Wincenty Witos.	100

KM#	Date	Mintage	Identification	Mkt Val
Pr506	1984	500	1000 Złotych. Nickel. PRL.	250
Pr507	1984	2,004	1000 Złotych. 0.625. Silver. 40th Anniversary of Peoples Republic.	90.00

KM#	Date	Mintage	Identification	Mkt Val
Pr508	1984	500	1000 Złotych. Nickel. Eagle with wings open divides date. Swan.	350
Pr509	1984	5,700	1000 Złotych. 0.625. Silver. Environment.	200
Pr510	1985	500	100 Złotych. Nickel. Y#155.	325
Pr511	1985	500	100 Złotych. Nickel. Y#157.	200

KM#	Date	Mintage	Identification	Mkt Val
Pr512	1985	500	200 Złotych. Nickel. Eagle with wings open divides date. Fallen soccer player within net design.	200
Pr513	1985	15,000	200 Złotych. Copper-Nickel.	20.00
Pr514	1985	500	200 Złotych. Nickel. Hospital Center.	175

KM#	Date	Mintage	Identification	Mkt Val
Pr515	1985	37,300	200 Złotych. Nickel Plated Iron. Hospital Center.	20.00
Pr516	1985	500	500 Złotych. Nickel. Y#156.	350
Pr517	1985	500	500 Złotych. Nickel. Y#158.	240
Pr518	1985	500	500 Złotych. Nickel. Y#159.	425

KM#	Date	Mintage	Identification	Mkt Val
Pr519	1985	500	1000 Złotych. Nickel. Przemyslaw II.	425
Pr520	1985	2,500	1000 Złotych. 0.750. Silver. Przemyslaw II.	240

KM#	Date	Mintage	Identification	Mkt Val
Pr521	1985	500	1000 Złotych. Nickel. Eagle with wings open divides date. Heart design. Hospital Center.	200
Pr522	1985	2,500	1000 Złotych. 0.750. Silver. Hospital Center.	90.00

Pr523	1985	500	1000 Złotych. Nickel. U.N.	240
Pr524	1985	2,500	1000 Złotych. 0.750. Silver. U.N.	145

Pr525	1985	500	1000 Złotych. Nickel. Eagle with wings open divides date. Squirrel.	425
Pr526	1985	2,500	1000 Złotych. 0.750. Silver. Squirrel.	240
Pr527	1986	500	50 Groszy. Nickel. Y#48.2.	145
Pr528	1986	500	Złoty. Nickel. Y#49.2.	150
Pr529	1986	500	2 Złote. Nickel. Y#80.2.	150
Pr530	1986	500	5 Złotych. Nickel. Y#81.2.	160
Pr531	1986	500	100 Złotych. Nickel. Y#160.	240

Pr532	1986	500	200 Złotych. Nickel. Y#162.	325
Pr533	1986	6,000	200 Złotych. Copper-Nickel. Y#162.	70.00

Pr534	1986	500	200 Złotych. Nickel. Wladyslaw.	210
Pr535	1986	10,000	200 Złotych. Copper-Nickel. Wladyslaw.	27.50
Pr536	1986	500	500 Złotych. Nickel. Y#161.	425
Pr537	1986	500	500 Złotych. Nickel. Y#162.	425
Pr538	1986	500	500 Złotych. Nickel. Y#166.	210

Pr539	1986	—	500 Złotych. Nickel. Y#225.	210
Pr540	1986	500	1000 Złotych. Nickel. Soccer.	210

Pr541	1986	9,000	1000 Złotych. 0.750. Silver. Eagle with wings open divides date. Soccer ball and globe.	55.00
Pr542	1986	500	1000 Złotych. Nickel. Education.	200
Pr543	1986	25,400	1000 Złotych. 0.625. Silver. Education.	27.50

Pr544	1986	22,000	1000 Złotych. 0.750. Silver. Hospital Center.	50.00

Pr545	1986	500	1000 Złotych. Nickel. Wladyslaw I.	—
Pr546	1986	2,500	1000 Złotych. 0.750. Silver. Wladyslaw I.	40.00

Pr547	1986	500	1000 Złotych. Nickel. Eagle with wings open divides date. Owl.	425
Pr548	1986	6,000	1000 Złotych. 0.750. Silver. Owl.	150

Pr549	1986	—	1000 Złotych. Nickel. Eagle with wings open divides date. School design.	200

Pr550	1986	—	1000 Złotych. 0.625. Silver. School aid.	200
Pr551	1987	500	100 Złotych. Nickel. Y#167.	425

Pr552	1987	500	200 Złotych. Nickel. Eagle with wings open divides date. Europe soccer.	200
Pr553	1987	15,000	200 Złotych. Copper-Nickel. Europe soccer.	39.00

Pr554	1987	500	200 Złotych. Nickel. Olympics - Tennis.	200
Pr555	1987	10,000	200 Złotych. Copper-Nickel. Olympics - Tennis.	55.00
Pr556	1987	500	500 Złotych. Nickel. Y#165.	200
Pr557	1987	500	500 Złotych. Nickel. Y#166.	200
Pr558	1987	500	500 Złotych. Nickel. Y#172.	200
Pr559	1987	500	500 Złotych. Nickel. Y#173.	425

Pr560	1987	500	1000 Złotych. Nickel. Wratislavia.	200
Pr561	1987	24,000	1000 Złotych. 0.750. Silver. Wratislavia.	27.50
Pr562	1987	500	1000 Złotych. Nickel. Slaskie Museum.	200
Pr563	1987	11,500	1000 Złotych. 0.750. Silver. Slaskie Museum.	30.00

Pr564	1987	500	1000 Złotych. Nickel. Olympic cross country skier.	210
Pr565	1987	10,000	1000 Złotych. 0.750. Silver. Olympic cross country skier.	45.00

Pr566	1987	500	1000 Złotych. Nickel. Eagle with wings open divides date. Olympic archery.	210
Pr567	1987	10,000	1000 Złotych. 0.750. Silver. Olympic archery.	80.00

Pr568	1987	500	1000 Złotych. Nickel. Eagle with wings open divides date. Kazimierz III.	425
Pr569	1987	2,500	1000 Złotych. 0.750. Silver. Kazimierz III.	250

Pr570	1987	9	1000 Złotych. Gold. Y#168.	450

Pr571	1987	9	2000 Złotych. Gold. Y#169; Similar design to Pr570.	—
Pr572	1987	9	5000 Złotych. Gold. Y#170; Similar design to Pr570.	—

Pr573	1987	9	10000 Złotych. Gold. Y#171; Similar design to Pr570.	—

Pr574	1987	5	200000 Złotych. Gold. Y#163; Similar design to Pr570. Photo reduced.	—

Pr575	1988	500	200 Złotych. Nickel. Eagle with wings open divides date. Soccer 1990.	175
Pr576	1988	10,000	200 Złotych. Copper-Nickel. Soccer 1990.	27.50
Pr577	1988	500	500 Złotych. Nickel. Soccer 1990, Y#184.	200

Pr578	1988	500	1000 Złotych. Nickel. Queen Jadwiga.	425
Pr579	1988	2,500	1000 Złotych. 0.750. Silver. Queen Jadwiga.	325

Pr580	1988	500	1000 Złotych. Nickel. Eagle with wings open divides date. Soccer 1990.	200
Pr581	1988	7,000	1000 Złotych. 0.750. Silver. Soccer 1990.	90.00

Pr582	1991	300	20000 Złotych. 0.999. Gold. Pope John Paul II right. Similar design to Pr583.	4,000
Pr583	1991	Est. 300	50000 Złotych. 0.999. Gold. Pope John Paul II right.	5,000

Pr584	1991	Est. 300	100000 Złotych. 0.999. Gold. Eagle with wings open divides date. Bust of Pope 1/4 right. Similar design to Pr583.	6,000
Pr585	1991	—	200000 Złotych. 0.999. Gold. Pope John Paul II right. Similar design to Pr583.	—

Pr586	1994	500	1000 Złotych. Copper-Nickel. Y#267.	300

BANK SETS

KM#	Date	Mintage	Identification	Issue Price	Mkt Val
BS1	1990-1994 (9)	—	Y#276-284 National Bank assembled mixed date set	—	20.00

MINT SETS

KM#	Date	Mintage	Identification	Issue Price	Mkt Val
MS1	1964 (2)	—	Y#52, 52a	—	15.00
MS2	1983 (11)	—	Y#AA47, A47, 48.1, 49.1, 69, 80.1, 81.1, 73, 142, 145, 146	—	40.00
MS3	1984 (9)	—	Y#48.1, 49.1, 80.1, 81.1, 73, 152.1, 153.1(Part 1), 148, 151 (Part 2)	—	18.50
MS4	1985 (10)	—	Y#AA47, A47, 48.1, 49.1, 73, 80.1, 81.1, 152.1, 153.1 (Part 1), 155, 157 (Part 2)	—	17.50

PROOF SETS

KM#	Date	Mintage	Identification	Issue Price	Mkt Val
PS1	1979 (6)	5,000	Y#AA47, A47, 80.1, 81.1, 99, 100	—	50.00
PS2	1980 (9)	5,000	Y#AA47, A47, 49.1, 80.1, 81.1, 108, 112, 114, 117	—	75.00
PS3	1981 (8)	5,000	Y#AA47, A47, 49.1, 80.1, 81.1, 73, 122, 124, 127, 128	—	72.50
PS4	1982 (6)	5,000	Y#48.1, 49.1, 80.1, 81.1, 73, 133	—	70.00
PS5	1986 (7)	5,000	Y#48.2, 49.2, 80.2, 81.2, 152.1, 153.1, 160	—	95.00
PS6	1987 (7)	5,000	Y#48.2, 49.2, 80.2, 81.2, 152.1, 153.1, 167	—	95.00
PS7	1988 (7)	5,000	Y#49.2, 80.2, 81.2, 152.1, 153.1, 182, 183 plus medal	—	110
PS8	1989 (7)	5,000	Y#49.3, 80.3, 81.3, 152.2, 153.2, 185, 194	—	110
PS9	1990 (8)	5,000	Y#49.3, 80.3, 81.3, 152.2, 153.2, 216, 214, 195	—	110

PORTUGAL

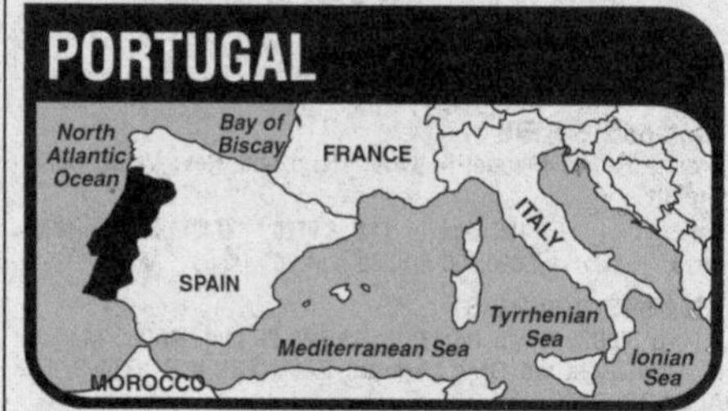

The Portuguese Republic, located in the western part of the Iberian Peninsula in southwestern Europe, has an area of 35,553 sq. mi. (92,080 sq. km.) and a population of *10.5 million. Capital: Lisbon. Portugal's economy is based on agriculture, tourism, minerals, fisheries and a rapidly expanding industrial sector. Textiles account for 33% of the exports and Portuguese wine is world famous. Portugal has become Europe's number one producer of copper and the world's largest producer of cork.

After centuries of domination by Romans, Visigoths and Moors, Portugal emerged in the 12th century as an independent kingdom financially and philosophically prepared for the great period of exploration that would soon follow. Attuned to the inspiration of Prince Henry the Navigator (1394-1460), Portugal's daring explorers of the15th and 16th centuries roamed the world's oceans from Brazil to Japan in an unprecedented burst of energy and endeavor that culminated in 1494 with Portugal laying claim to half the transoceanic world. Unfortunately for the fortunes of the tiny kingdom, the Portuguese population was too small to colonize this vast territory. Less than a century after Portugal laid claim to half the world, English, French and Dutch trading companies had seized the lion's share of the world's colonies and commerce, and Portugal's place as an imperial power was lost forever. The monarchy was overthrown in 1910 and a republic was established.

On April 25, 1974, the government of Portugal was seized by a military junta which reached agreements providing for independence for the Portuguese overseas provinces of Portuguese Guinea (*Guinea-Bissau*), Mozambique, Cape Verde Islands, Angola, and St. Thomas and Prince Islands (*Sao Tome and Principe*).

On January 1, 1986, Portugal became the eleventh member of the European Economic Community and in the first half of 1992 held its first EEC Presidency.

RULERS

Carlos I, 1889-1908
Manuel II, 1908-1910
Republic, 1910 to date

MONETARY SYSTEM

Beginning in 1836 all coins were expressed in terms of Reis and arranged in a decimal sequence (until 1910).

Commencing 1910
100 Centavos = 1 Escudo

KINGDOM

DECIMAL COINAGE

New denominations, all expressed in terms of Reis were introduced by Maria II in 1836, to bring Portugal's currency into decimal form. Some of the coins retained old names, as follows:

1000 Reis Silver - Coroa
100 Reis Silver - Tostao

The diameter of the new copper coins, first minted by Maria II in 1837, was smaller than the earlier coinage, but the weight was unaltered. However, in 1882, Luis I reduced the size and weight of the copper currency.

The Real and 2 Reis pieces dated 1853 were issued for circulation in Mozambique and will be found in those listings.

KM# 530 5 REIS

2.80 g., Bronze **Ruler:** Carlos I **Obv:** Head right **Obv. Legend:** CARLOS I REI. **Rev:** Value within wreath

Date	Mintage	F12	VF20	XF40	MS60	MS63
1901	1,070,000	2.50	12.50	45.00	100	—
1904	720,000	0.75	1.75	15.00	30.00	—
1905	1,340,000	0.75	1.50	5.00	15.00	—
1906/0	1,260	0.30	1.00	3.00	10.00	—
1906/9	Inc. above	0.25	0.75	2.50	8.00	—
1906	Inc. above	0.75	2.00	5.00	12.00	—

KM# 555 5 REIS

Bronze **Ruler:** Manuel II **Obv:** Head left **Rev:** Value within wreath

Date	Mintage	F12	VF20	XF40	MS60	MS63
1910	1,000,000	0.30	1.00	2.50	7.00	—

KM# 548 100 REIS

2.50 g., 0.835 Silver 0.0671 oz. ASW, 20 mm. **Ruler:** Manuel II **Obv:** Bust left **Obv. Legend:** EMANVEL II PORTVG: ET ALGARB: REX

Date	Mintage	F12	VF20	XF40	MS60	MS63
1909	6,363,000	3.50	9.50	15.50	55.00	—
1910	Inc. above	3.00	6.00	9.50	22.00	27.00

KM# 534 200 REIS

5.00 g., 0.917 Silver 0.1474 oz. ASW **Ruler:** Carlos I **Obv:** Head right **Obv. Legend:** CARLOS I. **Rev:** Value within wreath

Date	Mintage	VG8	F12	VF20	XF40	MS60
1901	205,000	40.00	125	250	550	—
1903	200,000	17.00	35.00	70.00	150	—

KM# 549 200 REIS

5.00 g., 0.835 Silver 0.1342 oz. ASW **Ruler:** Manuel II **Obv:** Head left **Obv. Legend:** EMANVEL II. **Rev:** Crown above value within wreath

Date	Mintage	VG8	F12	VF20	XF40	MS60
1909	7,656,000	6.00	9.00	12.00	20.00	40.00

KM# 535 500 REIS

12.50 g., 0.917 Silver 0.3685 oz. ASW, 30 mm. **Ruler:** Carlos I **Obv:** Head right **Obv. Legend:** CARLOS I. **Rev:** Crowned arms within wreath

Date	Mintage	VG8	F12	VF20	XF40	MS60
1901	1,050,000	22.00	54.00	96.00	180	360
1903	680,000	19.00	22.00	36.00	72.00	110
1906/3	240,000	36.00	84.00	168	138	600
1906	Inc. above	30.00	72.00	145	215	480
1907	384,000	17.00	19.00	30.00	45.00	85.00
1908	1,840,000	16.00	17.00	27.00	40.00	60.00

KM# 547 500 REIS

12.50 g., 0.917 Silver 0.3685 oz. ASW, 30 mm. **Ruler:** Manuel II **Obv:** Head left **Obv. Legend:** EMANVEL II. **Rev:** Crowned shield within sprigs

Date	Mintage	VG8	F12	VF20	XF40	MS60
1908	2,500,000	11.00	13.00	15.00	28.00	40.00
1909/8	1,513,000	15.00	30.00	55.00	100	200
1909	Inc. above	15.00	30.00	55.00	100	200

KM# 556 500 REIS

12.50 g., 0.917 Silver 0.3685 oz. ASW, 30 mm. **Ruler:** Manuel II **Subject:** Peninsular War Centennial **Obv:** Head left **Obv. Legend:** EMANVEL II. **Rev:** Crowned shield

Date	Mintage	VG8	F12	VF20	XF40	MS60
1910	200,000	15.00	30.00	45.00	75.00	150

KM# 557 500 REIS

12.50 g., 0.917 Silver 0.3685 oz. ASW, 30 mm. **Ruler:** Manuel II **Subject:** Marquis De Pombal **Obv:** Head left **Obv. Legend:** EMANVEL II. **Rev:** Seated Victory flanked by crowned shield and bust statue

Date	Mintage	VG8	F12	VF20	XF40	MS60
1910	400,000	13.00	18.00	25.00	40.00	80.00
1910	—	PF63 650				

KM# 558 1000 REIS

25.00 g., 0.917 Silver 0.7371 oz. ASW, 37 mm. **Ruler:** Manuel II **Subject:** Peninsular War Centennial **Obv:** Head left **Obv. Legend:** EMANVEL II. **Rev:** Crowned shield

Date	Mintage	VG8	F12	VF20	XF40	MS60
1910	200,000	28.00	55.00	90.00	150	250
1910	—	PF63 950				

REPUBLIC

KM# 565 CENTAVO

Bronze **Obv:** Value **Rev:** Shield within designed circle

Date	Mintage	F12	VF20	XF40	MS60	MS63
1917	2,250,000	0.50	1.00	2.00	4.00	6.00
1918	22,996,000	0.50	1.00	2.00	3.00	5.00
1920	12,535,000	0.50	1.00	2.50	5.00	7.00
1921	4,492,000	10.00	30.00	40.00	70.00	—
1922	Inc. above	—	—	150	350	—

KM# 567 2 CENTAVOS

Iron **Obv:** Value **Rev:** Shield within designed circle

Date	Mintage	F12	VF20	XF40	MS60	MS63
1918	170,000	125	225	400	900	—

Note: Most lower grades have oxidation and will sell for less

KM# 568 2 CENTAVOS

Bronze

Date	Mintage	F12	VF20	XF40	MS60	MS63
1918	4,295,000	0.50	0.75	2.00	4.00	6.00
1920	10,109,000	0.50	1.50	2.50	5.00	7.00
1921	679,000	25.00	50.00	100	150	—

KM# 566 4 CENTAVOS

Copper-Nickel **Obv:** Value **Rev:** Liberty head left

Date	Mintage	F12	VF20	XF40	MS60	MS63
1917	4,961,000	0.55	1.00	2.25	6.00	10.50
1919	10,067,000	0.55	1.00	2.70	6.75	12.00

KM# 569 5 CENTAVOS

Bronze **Obv:** Value **Rev:** Shield within designed circle

Date	Mintage	F12	VF20	XF40	MS60	MS63
1920	114,000	42.00	84.00	144	240	—
1921	5,916,000	0.75	2.00	4.00	7.00	9.00
1922	Inc. above	125	250	500	750	—

KM# 572 5 CENTAVOS
Bronze **Obv:** Value **Rev:** Liberty head left

Date	Mintage	F12	VF20	XF40	MS60	MS63
1924	6,480,000	0.50	1.50	4.50	10.00	—
1925	7,260,000	3.50	7.50	22.00	40.00	—
1927	26,320,000	0.25	0.75	1.50	5.00	10.00

KM# 563 10 CENTAVOS
2.50 g., 0.835 Silver 0.0671 oz. ASW **Obv:** Liberty head left **Rev:** Shield within designed circle within wreath

Date	Mintage	F12	VF20	XF40	MS60	MS63
1915	3,418,000	3.00	5.00	8.00	15.00	20.00

KM# 570 10 CENTAVOS
Copper-Nickel **Obv:** Value **Rev:** Liberty head left

Date	Mintage	F12	VF20	XF40	MS60	MS63
1920	1,120,000	3.50	7.00	13.00	22.00	—
1921	1,285,000	3.50	7.00	16.50	27.50	—

KM# 573 10 CENTAVOS
4.00 g., Bronze **Obv:** Value **Rev:** Liberty head left

Date	Mintage	F12	VF20	XF40	MS60	MS63
1924	1,210,000	4.00	16.00	56.00	125	—
1925	9,090,000	1.00	2.00	14.00	42.00	—
1926	26,250,000	1.00	3.50	19.00	50.00	—
1930	1,730,000	55.00	125	250	550	—
1938	2,000,000	6.00	25.00	50.00	125	—
1940	3,384,000	2.00	5.00	12.50	30.00	—

KM# 583 10 CENTAVOS
2.00 g., Bronze, 17 mm. **Obv:** Circles within cross **Rev:** Value above sprig

Date	Mintage	F12	VF20	XF40	MS60	MS63
1942	1,035,000	2.50	5.00	28.00	57.00	—
1943	18,765,000	2.50	6.25	12.50	50.00	—
1944	5,090,000	2.50	6.25	12.50	50.00	—
1945	6,090,000	2.50	6.00	12.50	42.00	—
1946	7,740,000	1.25	—	10.00	50.00	—
1947	9,283,000	1.25	2.50	6.50	25.00	40.00
1948	5,900,000	12.50	37.50	95.00	190	—
1949	15,240,000	0.50	1.25	6.00	18.00	25.00
1950	8,860,000	2.00	6.25	12.50	75.00	—
1951	5,040,000	2.00	6.25	19.00	95.00	—
1952	4,960,000	3.00	15.00	44.00	155	—
1953	7,548,000	2.00	3.75	6.00	12.50	20.00
1954	2,452,000	2.00	6.25	20.00	75.00	—
1955	10,000,000	0.15	0.50	3.00	7.50	12.00
1956	3,336,000	0.15	0.50	2.50	6.00	10.00
1957	6,654,000	0.15	0.50	2.50	6.00	9.00
1958	7,320,000	0.15	0.50	2.50	5.00	8.00
1959	7,140,000	0.15	0.50	2.50	5.00	8.00
1960	15,055,000	0.15	0.50	2.50	5.00	8.00
1961	5,020,000	—	0.15	2.00	5.00	8.00
1962	14,980,000	—	0.15	0.50	1.25	2.00
1963	5,393,000	—	0.15	2.00	3.00	5.00
1964	10,257,000	—	0.15	1.00	2.00	4.00
1965	15,550,000	—	0.15	1.00	2.00	4.00
1966	10,200,000	—	0.15	0.50	1.25	3.00
1967	18,592,000	—	0.15	0.50	1.25	2.00
1968	22,515,000	—	0.15	0.50	1.25	2.50
1969	3,871,000	0.15	0.50	1.50	3.00	5.00

KM# 594 10 CENTAVOS
0.50 g., Aluminum, 16 mm. **Obv:** Cross of five shields **Obv. Legend:** REPVBLICA PORTVGVESA **Rev:** Value above sprig **Edge:** Plain

Date	Mintage	F12	VF20	XF40	MS60	MS63
1969	—	700	1,250	1,950	3,500	—
1970 Rare	—	—	—	—	—	—
1971	25,673,000	—	—	0.50	1.00	1.50
1972	10,558,000	—	—	0.50	1.00	1.50
1973	3,149,000	—	—	1.25	3.50	6.00
1974	17,043,000	—	—	0.50	1.00	1.50
1975	22,410,000	—	—	0.50	1.00	1.50
1976	19,907,000	—	—	0.50	1.00	1.50
1977	8,431,000	—	—	0.50	1.00	1.50
1978	2,205,000	—	—	0.50	1.00	1.50
1979	9,083,000	—	—	1.00	2.50	4.00

KM# 562 20 CENTAVOS
5.00 g., 0.835 Silver 0.1342 oz. ASW **Obv:** Liberty head left **Rev:** Shield within designed circle and wreath

Date	Mintage	F12	VF20	XF40	MS60	MS63
1913	540,000	8.00	40.00	90.00	200	—
1916	706,000	6.00	35.00	50.00	125	—

KM# 571 20 CENTAVOS
Copper-Nickel **Obv:** Value and date within circle **Rev:** Liberty head left within circle

Date	Mintage	F12	VF20	XF40	MS60	MS63
1920	1,568,000	3.50	7.00	15.00	20.00	30.00
1921	3,030,000	4.00	8.00	14.00	22.50	35.00
1922	580,000	550	990	1,650	3,300	—

KM# 574 20 CENTAVOS
Bronze, 24 mm. **Obv:** Value **Rev:** Liberty head left

Date	Mintage	F12	VF20	XF40	MS60	MS63
1924	6,220,000	1.00	5.00	24.00	60.00	—
1925	10,580,000	1.00	5.00	24.00	60.00	—

KM# 584 20 CENTAVOS
3.20 g., Bronze, 21 mm. **Obv:** Circles within cross **Rev:** Value above sprig

Date	Mintage	F12	VF20	XF40	MS60	MS63
1942	10,170,000	2.00	4.00	28.00	65.00	—
1943	Inc. above	2.00	3.50	22.00	60.00	—
1944	7,290,000	2.00	3.50	22.00	60.00	—
1945	7,552,000	1.00	2.50	27.50	65.00	—
1948	2,750,000	3.00	13.00	39.00	150	—
1949	12,250,000	0.15	1.00	7.00	16.50	22.00
1951	3,185,000	0.50	2.50	22.00	165	—
1952	1,815,000	3.00	13.00	39.00	220	—
1953	9,426,000	—	1.00	4.00	9.00	13.00
1955	5,574,000	—	1.00	4.00	9.00	13.00
1956	6,450,000	—	1.00	3.00	7.00	8.00
1958	7,470,000	—	1.00	3.00	7.00	8.00
1959	4,780,000	—	1.00	3.00	7.00	8.00
1960	4,790,000	—	1.00	4.00	9.00	13.00
1961	5,180,000	—	1.00	4.00	9.00	13.00
1962	2,500,000	0.50	2.00	11.00	20.00	28.00
1963	7,990,000	—	0.50	2.00	4.00	6.00
1964	7,010,000	—	0.50	2.00	4.00	6.50
1965	7,365,000	—	0.50	1.00	3.00	5.00
1966	8,074,999	—	0.50	1.00	2.50	4.50
1967	9,220,000	—	0.50	1.00	2.50	4.50
1968	10,372,000	—	0.50	1.00	2.00	3.50
1969	8,657,000	—	0.50	1.00	3.50	6.00

KM# 595 20 CENTAVOS
1.80 g., Bronze, 16 mm. **Obv:** Circles within cross **Rev:** Value above sprig

Date	Mintage	F12	VF20	XF40	MS60	MS63
1969	10,891,000	—	0.25	0.75	2.50	4.50
1970	16,120,000	—	0.25	1.00	3.00	5.00
1971	1,933,000	—	1.00	2.50	5.50	9.00
1972	16,354,000	—	—	0.25	1.00	1.50
1973	4,900,000	—	—	0.25	1.00	1.50
1974	26,975,000	—	—	0.25	1.00	1.50

KM# 561 50 CENTAVOS
12.50 g., 0.835 Silver 0.3356 oz. ASW **Obv:** Liberty head left **Rev:** Shield within designed circle and wreath **Edge:** Reeded

Date	Mintage	F12	VF20	XF40	MS60	MS63
1912	1,695,000	11.00	18.00	30.00	65.00	—
1913	4,443,000	9.00	15.00	25.00	50.00	—
1914	4,992,000	11.00	18.00	30.00	65.00	—
1916	5,080,000	9.00	15.00	25.00	50.00	—

KM# 575 50 CENTAVOS
Aluminum-Bronze **Obv:** Seated figure **Rev:** Shield within designed circle and wreath

Date	Mintage	F12	VF20	XF40	MS60	MS63
1924	810,000	65.00	125	250	450	—
1925	—	1,000	1,500	3,500	7,000	12,000
1926	4,340,000	2.00	6.00	18.00	40.00	55.00

KM# 577 50 CENTAVOS
4.00 g., Copper-Nickel, 23 mm. **Obv:** Liberty head right **Rev:** Shield within designed circle and wreath above value **Edge:** Reeded

Date	Mintage	F12	VF20	XF40	MS60	MS63
1927	2,330,000	2.50	12.50	30.00	125	150
1928	6,823,000	2.50	12.50	30.00	175	200
1929	9,779,000	2.50	12.50	30.00	125	150
1930	1,116,000	3.00	25.00	250	400	—
1931	7,127,000	10.00	27.50	250	400	—
1935	902,000	31.00	69.00	375	600	—
Note: For exclusive use in Azores						
1938	923,000	31.00	69.00	375	1,000	—
1940	2,000,000	1.25	6.00	37.50	155	—
1944	2,974,000	0.50	1.25	9.00	25.00	37.50
1945	5,700,000	0.50	1.25	7.00	18.00	32.00
1946	4,334,000	—	2.50	12.50	42.00	57.00
1947	6,998,000	0.25	1.25	11.25	25.00	37.50
1951	4,610,000	—	0.50	4.00	12.50	20.00
1952	2,421,000	0.25	1.25	5.00	22.00	32.00
1953	2,369,000	0.25	1.25	16.00	63.00	95.00
1955	3,057,000	0.25	0.50	3.75	11.00	16.00
1956	3,003,000	—	0.50	4.00	8.00	10.00
1957	3,940,000	—	0.50	4.00	8.00	12.00
1958	2,687,000	—	0.50	5.00	11.00	16.00

Date	Mintage	F12	VF20	XF40	MS60	MS63
1959	4,027,000	—	0.50	2.50	8.00	10.00
1960	2,592,000	—	0.50	2.50	7.00	9.00
1961	3,324,000	—	0.50	2.50	5.00	8.00
1962	6,678,000	—	0.50	1.25	3.00	4.00
1963	2,346,000	—	0.50	4.00	11.00	16.00
1964	7,654,000	—	0.50	1.25	2.00	3.50
1965	3,366,000	—	0.50	1.25	3.00	4.50
1966	6,085,000	—	0.50	1.25	3.00	4.00
1967	19,391,000	—	0.50	1.00	2.50	3.50
1968	11,448,000	—	0.50	1.00	2.00	3.00

KM# 596 50 CENTAVOS

4.50 g., Bronze, 22.6 mm. **Obv:** Circles within cross **Obv. Legend:** REPVBLICA PORTVGVESA **Rev:** Value above spears of grain

Date	Mintage	F12	VF20	XF40	MS60	MS63
1969	3,481,000	—	—	1.00	3.50	5.00
1970	17,280,000	—	—	1.00	3.00	4.00
1971	9,139,000	—	—	1.00	3.00	4.00
1972	24,729,000	—	—	1.00	3.00	4.00
1973	35,588,000	—	—	0.75	2.50	3.50
1974	28,719,000	—	—	0.75	2.50	3.50
1975	17,793,000	—	—	0.75	2.50	3.50
1976	23,734,000	—	—	0.75	2.50	3.50
1977	16,340,000	—	—	0.75	2.50	3.50
1978	48,348,000	—	—	0.75	2.25	3.50
1979	61,652,000	—	—	0.75	2.00	3.00

KM# 560 ESCUDO

25.00 g., 0.835 Silver 0.6711 oz. ASW, 37 mm. **Subject:** October 5, 1910. Birth of the Republic **Obv:** Bust holding torch facing left **Obv. Legend:** REPUBLICA PORTUGUESA 5 de Outubro de 1910 **Rev:** Shield within designed circle and wreath

Date	Mintage	VF20	XF40	MS60	MS63	MS65
1910	1,000,000	195	295	455	—	—

Note: Struck in 1914

KM# 564 ESCUDO

25.00 g., 0.835 Silver 0.6711 oz. ASW, 37 mm. **Obv:** Liberty head left

Date	Mintage	VF20	XF40	MS60	MS63	MS65
1915	1,818,000	60.00	90.00	140	—	—
1916	1,405,000	75.00	100	155	—	—

KM# 576 ESCUDO

Aluminum-Bronze **Obv:** Sitting figure **Rev:** Shield within designed circle, value divides wreath

Date	Mintage	VF20	XF40	MS60	MS63	MS65
1924	2,709,000	27.00	50.00	100	—	—
1926	2,346,000	175	300	700	—	—

KM# 578 ESCUDO

7.50 g., Copper-Nickel, 26.7 mm. **Obv:** Liberty head right **Rev:** Shield within designed circle and wreath above value **Edge:** Reeded

Date	Mintage	VF20	XF40	MS60	MS63	MS65
1927	1,917,000	12.00	65.00	200	—	—
1928	7,462,000	5.00	35.00	225	—	—
1929	1,617,000	15.00	75.00	300	—	—
1930	1,911,000	25.00	250	650	950	—
1931	2,039,000	25.00	250	900	—	—
1935	—	300	1,000	5,000	7,000	—
Note: For exclusive use in Azores						
1939	304,000	85.00	300	550	700	—
1940	1,259,000	25.00	50.00	150	—	—
1944	993,000	100	250	350	500	—
1945	Inc. above	3.00	22.00	75.00	—	—
1946	2,507,000	3.00	12.50	75.00	—	—
1951	2,500,000	3.00	6.00	10.00	15.00	—
1952	2,500,000	4.00	45.00	125	—	—
1957	1,656,000	2.00	4.50	10.00	20.00	30.00
1958	1,447,000	2.00	4.50	12.00	22.00	32.00
1959	1,908,000	2.00	4.50	10.00	20.00	30.00
1961	2,505,000	2.00	3.00	5.00	7.00	9.00
1962	2,757,000	2.00	3.00	5.00	7.00	9.00
1964	1,611,000	2.00	3.00	5.00	7.00	9.00
1965	1,683,000	2.00	3.00	3.50	4.00	6.00
1966	2,607,000	2.00	3.00	4.00	4.00	6.00
1968	4,099,000	2.00	3.00	4.00	5.00	7.00

KM# 597 ESCUDO

8.00 g., Bronze, 26 mm. **Obv:** Circles within cross **Obv. Legend:** REPVBLICA PORTVGVESA **Rev:** Value above spears of grain **Edge:** Plain

Date	Mintage	VF20	XF40	MS60	MS63	MS65
1969	3,020,000	0.10	1.50	3.00	5.00	7.00
1970	6,009,000	0.10	1.50	2.00	4.00	6.00
1971	7,860,000	0.10	1.50	2.00	4.00	6.00
1972	3,815,000	0.10	1.50	2.50	4.50	7.00
1973	20,467,000	0.10	1.00	2.00	3.00	5.00
1974	11,444,000	0.10	1.00	2.00	3.00	5.00
1975	8,473,000	0.10	1.00	2.00	3.00	5.00
1976	7,353,000	0.10	0.50	1.00	2.00	4.00
1977	6,218,000	0.10	0.50	1.00	2.00	4.00
1978	7,061,000	0.10	0.50	1.00	2.00	4.00
1979	14,241,000	0.10	0.25	0.75	1.50	3.00

KM# 614 ESCUDO

3.00 g., Nickel-Brass, 18 mm. **Obv:** Shield **Rev:** Value **Note:** Prev. KM#611.

Date	Mintage	VF20	XF40	MS60	MS63	MS65
1981	30,165,000	—	0.10	0.50	1.00	2.00
1982	53,018,000	—	0.10	0.50	1.00	2.00
1983	53,165,000	—	0.10	0.25	0.50	1.00
1984	59,463,000	—	0.10	0.25	0.50	1.00
1985	46,832,000	—	0.10	0.25	0.50	1.00
1986	8,029,999	—	0.10	1.50	3.00	5.00
1987	21,922,000	—	0.10	0.20	0.35	0.50
1988	17,168,000	—	0.10	0.20	0.35	0.50
1989	17,194,000	—	0.10	0.20	0.35	0.50
1990	19,008,000	—	0.10	0.20	0.35	0.50
1991	21,500,000	—	0.10	0.20	0.35	0.50
1992	22,000,000	—	0.10	0.20	0.35	0.50
1993	10,505,000	—	0.10	0.20	0.35	0.50
1994	—	—	0.10	0.20	0.35	0.50
1994	—	PF65 0.50				
1995	—	—	—	—	—	0.50
Note: In Mint sets only						
1995	—	PF65 0.50				
1996	—	—	—	0.15	0.35	0.50
1996	7,000	PF65 0.50				
1997	—	—	—	0.15	0.35	0.50
1997	—	PF65 0.50				
1998	—	—	—	0.15	0.35	0.50
1998	—	PF65 2.00				
1999	—	—	—	0.15	0.35	0.50
2000	—	—	—	0.15	0.35	0.50

KM# 612 ESCUDO

Nickel-Brass, 18 mm. **Subject:** World Roller Hockey Championship Games **Obv:** Shield **Rev:** Hockey player

Date	Mintage	VF20	XF40	MS60	MS63	MS65
ND-1983	1,990,000	0.10	0.25	0.50	0.75	1.50

KM# 631 ESCUDO

1.69 g., Nickel-Brass, 16 mm. **Obv:** Design above shield **Rev:** Flower design above value **Edge:** Reeded

Date	Mintage	VF20	XF40	MS60	MS63	MS65
1986	14,882,000	—	0.10	0.20	0.35	0.50

KM# 580 2-1/2 ESCUDOS

3.50 g., 0.650 Silver 0.0731 oz. ASW, 20.41 mm. **Obv:** Early sailing ship **Rev:** Shield on globe **Edge:** Reeded

Date	Mintage	F12	VF20	XF40	MS60	MS63
1932	2,592,000	6.00	20.00	50.00	120	—
1933	2,457,000	15.00	40.00	100	200	—
1937	1,000,000	150	350	700	1,150	—
1940	2,763,000	7.00	15.00	25.00	70.00	—
1942	3,847,000	2.50	4.00	8.00	20.00	—
1943	8,302,000	2.00	2.75	4.00	10.00	15.00
1944	9,134,000	2.00	2.50	3.50	7.00	10.00
1945	6,316,000	2.50	5.00	11.00	20.00	30.00
1946	3,208,000	2.00	4.00	9.00	15.00	25.00
1947	2,610,000	2.00	4.00	9.00	15.00	25.00
1948	1,814,000	10.00	20.00	40.00	100	—
1951	4,000,000	2.25	2.50	3.00	6.00	8.00

KM# 590 2-1/2 ESCUDOS

3.50 g., Copper-Nickel, 20 mm. **Obv:** Ship **Rev:** Shield flanked by stars, value below **Edge:** Reeded

Date	Mintage	VF20	XF40	MS60	MS63	MS65
1963	12,711,000	0.50	20.00	32.00	45.00	—
1964	17,948,000	0.50	20.00	32.00	45.00	—
1965	19,512,000	0.25	5.00	11.00	15.00	—
1966	3,828,000	2.00	35.00	55.00	80.00	—
1967	5,545,000	0.25	7.00	18.00	—	—
1968	6,087,000	0.25	2.00	3.50	5.00	7.00
1969	9,969,000	0.25	1.75	3.00	4.00	6.00
1970	2,400,000	0.25	2.25	4.00	5.00	7.00
1971	6,791,000	0.25	1.50	3.00	4.00	6.00
1972	6,713,000	0.25	1.75	3.00	4.00	6.00
1973	9,104,000	0.25	1.00	2.00	3.00	5.00
1974	22,743,000	0.10	0.75	2.50	3.50	5.50
1975	16,623,999	0.10	0.50	1.50	2.00	3.50
1976	21,516,000	0.10	0.50	1.50	2.00	3.50
1977	45,726,000	0.10	0.50	1.50	2.00	3.50
1978	27,375,000	0.10	0.25	0.75	1.00	1.50
1979	44,804,000	0.10	0.25	0.75	1.00	1.50
1980	22,319,000	0.10	0.25	1.00	1.25	2.00
1981	25,420,000	0.10	0.20	1.00	1.25	2.00
1982	45,910,000	0.10	0.20	0.75	1.00	1.50
1983	62,946,000	0.10	0.20	0.75	1.00	1.50
1984	58,210,000	0.10	0.20	0.75	1.00	1.50
1985	60,142,000	0.10	0.20	0.75	1.00	1.50

KM# 605 2-1/2 ESCUDOS

3.50 g., Copper-Nickel, 20 mm. **Subject:** 100th Anniversary - Death of Alexandre Herculano, Poet **Obv:** Shield **Rev:** Bust facing flanked by dates

Date	Mintage	F12	VF20	XF40	MS60	MS63
ND-1977	10,000	PF65 3.50				
ND-1977	5,990,000	—	0.20	0.75	1.50	3.00

KM# 613 2-1/2 ESCUDOS

3.50 g., Copper-Nickel, 20 mm. **Subject:** World Roller Hockey Championship Games **Obv:** Shield **Rev:** Hockey player

Date	Mintage	F12	VF20	XF40	MS60	MS63
ND-1982	1,990,000	—	0.10	0.25	0.75	1.50

KM# 617 2-1/2 ESCUDOS

3.50 g., Copper-Nickel, 20 mm. **Series:** F.A.O. **Obv:** Shield **Rev:** Ear of corn, FAO and date

Date	Mintage	F12	VF20	XF40	MS60	MS63
1983	995,000	—	0.10	0.35	1.00	2.00

KM# 581 5 ESCUDOS

6.70 g., 0.650 Silver 0.140 oz. ASW, 28.4 mm. **Obv:** Ship **Rev:** Shield in front of circular design

Date	Mintage	F12	VF20	XF40	MS60	MS63
1932	800,000	15.00	35.00	200	780	—
1933	6,717,000	9.00	13.00	20.00	80.00	—
1934	1,012,000	10.00	20.00	50.00	155	—
1937	1,500,000	30.00	80.00	200	780	—
1940	1,500,000	10.00	20.00	50.00	156	—
1942	2,051,000	6.00	8.00	11.00	22.50	27.50
1943	1,354,000	8.00	22.50	60.00	125	—
1946	404,000	8.00	14.00	25.00	55.00	—
1947	2,420,000	6.00	8.00	10.00	14.00	—
1948	2,017,999	6.00	8.00	10.00	13.00	17.00
1951	966,000	6.00	8.00	10.00	13.00	17.00

KM# 587 5 ESCUDOS

7.00 g., 0.800 Silver 0.180 oz. ASW, 25 mm. **Subject:** 500th Anniversary - Death of Prince Henry the Navigator **Obv:** Shield **Rev:** Head with sombrero facing 1/4 left

Date	Mintage	F12	VF20	XF40	MS60	MS63
1960 INCM	800,000	—	7.00	8.00	12.00	16.00
1960 INCM Matte	—	—	—	—	75.00	—

Note: A small quantity of these coins were given a matte finish by the Lisbon Mint on private contract

KM# 591 5 ESCUDOS

7.00 g., Copper-Nickel, 24.5 mm. **Obv:** Ship **Obv. Legend:** REPUBLICA PORTUGUESA **Rev:** Shield flanked by stars, date below **Edge:** Reeded

Date	Mintage	VF20	XF40	MS60	MS63	MS65
1963	2,200,000	0.50	15.00	30.00	—	—
1964	4,268,000	0.50	12.50	25.00	35.00	—
1965	7,294,000	0.35	12.50	25.00	35.00	—
1966	8,119,999	0.35	10.00	25.00	35.00	—
1967	8,128,000	0.25	7.00	20.00	25.00	—
1968	5,023,000	0.25	3.00	5.00	10.00	15.00
1969	3,571,000	0.10	2.00	5.00	6.00	8.00
1970	1,200,000	0.10	2.50	5.50	7.00	9.00
1971	2,721,000	0.10	2.00	5.00	6.00	8.00
1972	1,880,000	0.10	2.00	6.00	8.00	12.00
1973	2,836,000	0.10	1.25	4.00	6.00	8.00
1974	3,984,000	0.10	1.00	3.50	5.00	7.00
1975	7,496,000	0.10	1.00	2.50	3.50	6.00
1976	11,379,000	0.10	1.00	2.50	3.50	6.00
1977	29,058,000	0.10	0.50	1.50	2.00	3.50
1978	672,000	2.00	5.00	10.00	—	—
1979	19,546,000	0.10	0.50	1.50	2.50	4.50
1980	46,244,000	0.10	0.50	1.50	2.00	3.50
1981	15,267,000	0.10	0.50	1.50	2.00	3.50
1982	31,318,000	0.10	0.50	1.50	2.00	3.50
1983	51,056,000	0.10	0.50	1.50	2.00	3.50
1984	46,794,000	0.10	0.50	1.50	2.00	3.50
1985	45,441,000	0.10	0.50	1.25	1.75	3.00
1986	18,753,000	0.10	0.50	1.50	2.50	4.50

KM# 606 5 ESCUDOS

7.00 g., Copper-Nickel, 24.5 mm. **Subject:** 100th Anniversary - Death of Alexandre Herculano, Poet **Obv:** Shield **Obv. Legend:** REPUBLICA PORTUGUESA **Rev:** Bust 1/4 right flanked by dates **Rev. Legend:** CENTENARIO DA MORTE DE ALEXANDRE HERCULANO 1877 1977

Date	Mintage	VF20	XF40	MS60	MS63	MS65
ND-1977 INCM	5,990,000	0.35	1.00	2.00	3.50	5.00
ND-1977 INCM	10,000	PF65 6.00				

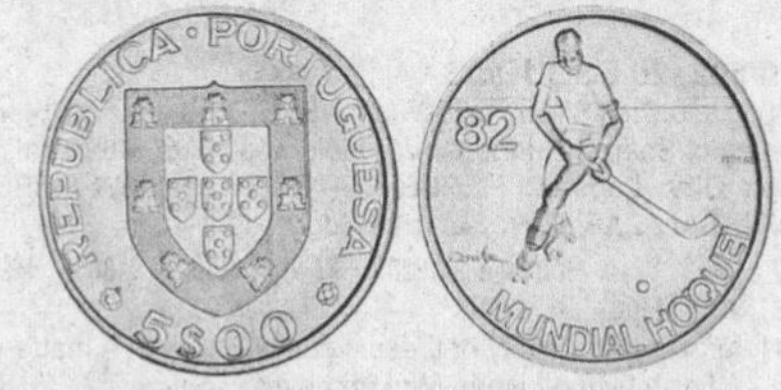

KM# 615 5 ESCUDOS

7.00 g., Copper-Nickel, 24.5 mm. **Subject:** World Roller Hockey Championship Games **Obv:** Shield **Rev:** Hockey player

Date	Mintage	VF20	XF40	MS60	MS63	MS65
ND-1983	1,990,000	0.25	0.50	1.00	1.50	2.50

KM# 618 5 ESCUDOS

7.00 g., Copper-Nickel, 24.5 mm. **Series:** F.A.O. **Obv:** Shield **Rev:** Bull

Date	Mintage	VF20	XF40	MS60	MS63	MS65
ND-1983	995,000	0.30	0.75	1.50	2.50	3.50

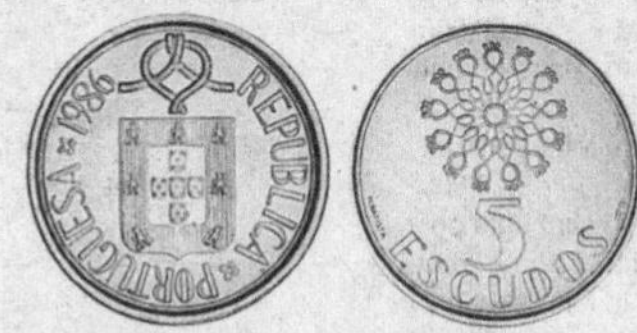

KM# 632 5 ESCUDOS

5.25 g., Nickel-Brass **Obv:** Design above shield **Rev:** Star design above value **Edge:** Reeded

Date	Mintage	VF20	XF40	MS60	MS63	MS65
1986	21,426,000	0.10	0.25	0.50	0.65	0.75
1987	40,548,000	0.10	0.25	0.50	0.65	0.75
1988	19,382,000	0.10	0.25	0.50	0.65	0.75
1989	27,641,000	0.10	0.25	0.50	0.65	0.75
1990	77,977,000	0.10	0.25	0.50	0.65	0.75
1991	32,000,000	—	—	0.50	0.65	0.75
1992	16,000,000	—	—	0.50	0.65	0.75
1993	8,300,000	—	—	0.50	0.65	0.75
1994	—	—	—	0.50	0.65	0.75
1994	—	PF65 0.75				
1995	—	—	—	0.50	0.65	0.75
1995	—	PF65 0.75				
1996	—	—	—	0.50	0.65	0.75
1996	7,000	PF65 0.75				
1997	—	—	—	0.50	0.65	0.75
1997	—	PF65 0.75				
1998	—	—	—	0.50	0.65	0.75
1998	—	PF65 0.75				
1999	—	—	—	0.50	0.65	0.75
2000	—	—	—	0.50	0.65	0.75

KM# 579 10 ESCUDOS

12.50 g., 0.835 Silver 0.3356 oz. ASW, 30 mm. **Subject:** Battle of Ourique **Obv:** Crowned shield flanked by value **Obv. Legend:** REPUBLICA PORTUGUESA **Rev:** Armored figure on horse holding sword **Rev. Legend:** Comemoração da Batalha de Ourique 1139

Date	Mintage	F12	VF20	XF40	MS60	MS63
1928	200,000	15.00	27.00	50.00	75.00	—

KM# 582 10 ESCUDOS

12.50 g., 0.835 Silver 0.3356 oz. ASW, 30 mm. **Obv:** Ship **Rev:** Shield in front of globe design

Date	Mintage	F12	VF20	XF40	MS60	MS63
1932	3,220,000	17.00	23.00	30.00	60.00	—
1933	1,780,000	30.00	70.00	175	450	—
1934	400,000	18.00	36.00	60.00	150	—
1937	500,000	60.00	150	350	500	—
1940	1,200,000	13.00	25.00	45.00	70.00	—
1942	186,000	200	400	600	750	1,000
1948	507,000	30.00	75.00	100	150	175

KM# 586 10 ESCUDOS

12.50 g., 0.835 Silver 0.3356 oz. ASW, 30 mm. **Obv:** Ship **Rev:** Shield above circular design flanked by value

Date	Mintage	F12	VF20	XF40	MS60	MS63
1954	5,764,000	—	6.50	9.00	15.00	20.00
1955	4,056,000	—	6.50	9.00	15.00	20.00

KM# 588 10 ESCUDOS

12.50 g., 0.800 Silver 0.3215 oz. ASW, 30 mm. **Subject:** 500th Anniversary - Death of Prince Henry the Navigator **Obv:** Shield flanked by designs **Rev:** Head with sombrero facing 1/4 left

Date	Mintage	F12	VF20	XF40	MS60	MS63
1960 INCM	200,000	—	7.50	20.00	35.00	50.00
1960 INCM Matte	—	—	—	—	75.00	—

Note: A small quantity of these coins were given a matte finish by the Lisbon Mint on private contract

KM# 600 10 ESCUDOS

10.00 g., Copper-Nickel Clad Nickel, 28 mm. **Obv:** Ship **Obv. Legend:** REPUBLICA PORTUGUESA **Rev:** Shield flanked by stars **Rev. Legend:** CONFIANCA ESPERANCA FRATERNIDADE **Note:** Edge lettering exists in both normal and upside down positions for all years.

Date	Mintage	VF20	XF40	MS60	MS63	MS65
1971	3,876,000	0.25	0.75	2.00	3.00	5.00
1972	2,694,000	0.25	1.00	2.50	3.50	6.00
1973	5,418,000	0.25	0.75	2.00	3.00	5.00
1974	4,043,000	0.25	0.75	2.00	3.00	5.00

KM# 633 10 ESCUDOS

7.50 g., Nickel-Brass **Obv:** Design above shield **Rev:** Artistic design above value **Edge:** Reeded

Date	Mintage	VF20	XF40	MS60	MS63	MS65
1986	12,818,000	0.20	0.40	1.00	1.50	2.00
1987	32,814,999	0.20	0.40	1.00	1.50	2.00
1988	32,579,000	0.20	0.40	1.00	1.50	2.00
1989	12,788,000	0.20	0.40	1.00	1.50	2.00
1990	26,500,000	0.20	0.40	1.00	1.50	2.00
1991	9,500,000	—	—	1.00	1.75	2.50
1992	5,600,000	—	—	1.00	1.75	2.50
1993	20,000	—	—	—	—	10.00
Note: In Mint sets only						
1994	20,000	—	—	—	—	10.00
Note: In Mint sets only						
1994	—	PF65 2.50				
1995	—	—	—	—	—	10.00
Note: In Mint sets only						
1995	—	PF65 2.50				
1996	—	—	—	—	1.00	1.50
1996	7,000	PF65 2.50				
1997	—	—	—	—	1.00	1.50
1997	—	PF65 2.50				
1998	—	—	—	—	1.00	1.50
1998	—	PF65 3.00				
1999	—	—	—	—	1.00	1.50
2000	—	—	—	—	1.00	1.50

KM# 638 10 ESCUDOS

7.40 g., Nickel-Brass **Subject:** Rural World **Obv:** Design above shield **Rev:** Hand holding sprig flanked by stars all around

Date	Mintage	VF20	XF40	MS60	MS63	MS65
1987	2,000,000	0.40	0.60	1.25	2.50	3.50

KM# 585 20 ESCUDOS

21.00 g., 0.800 Silver 0.5401 oz. ASW, 34 mm. **Subject:** 25th Anniversary of Financial Reform **Obv:** Shield above globe, value at left, all within circle **Rev:** Seated figure facing left reading a book

Date	Mintage	VF20	XF40	MS60	MS63	MS65
1953	1,000,000	10.50	16.50	18.50	22.00	27.00
1953 Matte	—	—	—	—	—	—

Note: A small quantity of these coins were given a matte finish by the Lisbon Mint on private contract

KM# 589 20 ESCUDOS

21.00 g., 0.800 Silver 0.5401 oz. ASW, 34 mm. **Subject:** 500th Anniversary - Death of Prince Henry the Navigator **Obv:** Shield flanked by designs **Rev:** Head with sombrero facing 1/4 left

Date	Mintage	VF20	XF40	MS60	MS63	MS65
1960	200,000	18.50	25.00	35.00	50.00	60.00
1960 Matte	—	—	—	75.00	—	—

Note: A small quantity of these coins were given a matte finish by the Lisbon Mint on private contract

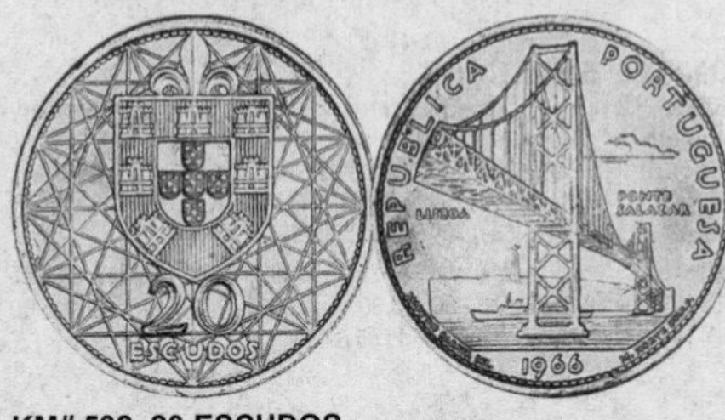

KM# 592 20 ESCUDOS

10.00 g., 0.650 Silver 0.209 oz. ASW, 30 mm. **Subject:** Opening of Salazar Bridge **Obv:** Shield and value within artistic design **Obv. Legend:** REPUBLICA PORTUGUESA LISBOA PONTE SALAZAR **Rev:** Salazar bridge

Date	Mintage	VF20	XF40	MS60	MS63	MS65
1966 INCM Matte	200	—	—	75.00	—	—
Note: A small quantity of these coins were given a matte finish by the Lisbon Mint on private contract						
1966 INCM	2,000,000	—	4.00	6.50	9.50	12.50

KM# 634.1 20 ESCUDOS

6.90 g., Copper-Nickel, 26.5 mm. **Obv:** Shield divides date with value below **Obv. Legend:** REPUBLICA PORTUGUESA **Rev:** Nautical windrose

Date	Mintage	VF20	XF40	MS60	MS63	MS65
1986 INCM	45,361,000	0.15	0.25	0.75	1.25	2.00
1987 INCM	68,216,000	0.15	0.25	0.75	1.25	2.00
1988 INCM	57,482,000	0.15	0.25	0.75	1.25	2.00
1989 INCM	25,060,000	0.15	0.25	0.75	1.25	2.00
1990 INCM	50,000	—	—	—	—	10.00
Note: In Mint sets only						
1991 INCM	50,000	—	—	—	—	10.00
Note: In Mint sets only						
1992 INCM	20,000	—	—	—	—	10.00
Note: In Mint sets only						
1993 INCM	20,000	—	—	—	—	10.00
Note: In Mint sets only						
1994 INCM	20,000	—	—	—	—	10.00
Note: In Mint sets only						
1994 INCM	—	PF65 2.50				
1995 INCM	—	—	—	—	—	10.00
Note: In Mint sets only						
1995 INCM	—	PF65 2.50				
1996 INCM	—	—	—	—	—	10.00
Note: In Mint sets only						
1996 INCM	7,000	PF65 2.50				
1997 INCM	—	—	—	—	—	10.00
Note: In Mint sets only						
1997 INCM	—	PF65 2.50				
1998 INCM	15,000,000	—	—	1.00	1.50	2.00
1999 INCM	20,000,000	—	—	1.00	1.50	2.00

KM# 634.2 20 ESCUDOS

Copper-Nickel **Obv:** Larger shield divides date with larger value below **Rev:** Nautical windrose

Date	Mintage	VF20	XF40	MS60	MS63	MS65
1998	—	PF65 4.00				
1998	—	—	—	1.00	2.00	—
1999	—	—	—	1.00	2.00	—
2000	—	—	—	1.00	2.00	—

KM# 607 25 ESCUDOS

Copper-Nickel **Obv:** Value to right of shield **Rev:** Head laureate left

Date	Mintage	VF20	XF40	MS60	MS63	MS65
1977	7,657,000	—	0.40	1.00	2.00	3.50
1978	12,277,000	—	0.40	1.50	3.00	6.00

KM# 608 25 ESCUDOS

9.50 g., Copper-Nickel, 26.5 mm. **Subject:** 100th Anniversary - Death of Alexandre Herculano, Poet **Obv:** Shield **Rev:** Bust flanked by dates facing 1/4 right

Date	Mintage	VF20	XF40	MS60	MS63	MS65
ND-1977	5,990,000	—	0.50	1.00	2.50	5.50
ND-1977	10,000	PF65 7.00				

KM# 609 25 ESCUDOS

Copper-Nickel **Subject:** International Year of the Child **Obv:** Shield **Rev:** Two faces, one facing left, the other 3/4 right

Date	Mintage	VF20	XF40	MS60	MS63	MS65
1979	990,000	—	0.50	1.00	2.50	5.50
1979 Prooflike	10,000	—	—	—	—	8.00

KM# 607a 25 ESCUDOS

10.80 g., Copper-Nickel, 28.5 mm. **Obv:** Value to right of shield **Rev:** Head laureate left **Note:** Increased size; prev. KM#610.

Date	Mintage	VF20	XF40	MS60	MS63	MS65
1980	750,000	—	0.40	0.80	1.50	5.00
1981	19,924,000	—	0.40	0.80	1.50	3.50
1982	12,158,000	—	0.40	0.80	1.50	3.50
1983	5,622,000	—	0.40	0.80	1.50	5.00
1984	3,453,000	—	0.40	1.00	3.00	6.00
1985	25,027,000	—	0.40	0.80	1.50	3.00
1986	—	—	0.50	1.00	4.00	7.00

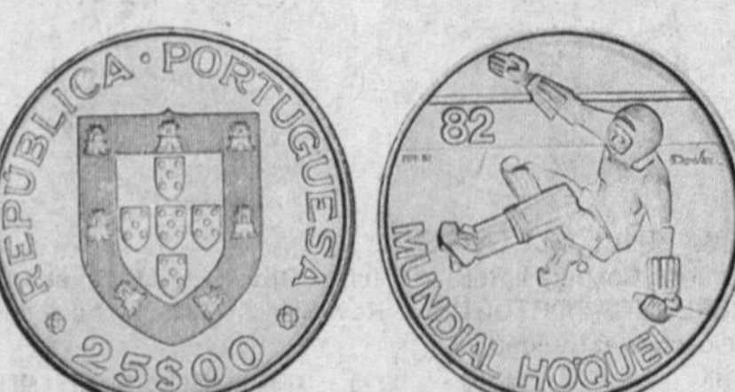

KM# 616 25 ESCUDOS

11.00 g., Copper-Nickel, 28.5 mm. **Subject:** World Roller Hockey Championship Games **Obv:** Shield **Rev:** Suited hockey player

Date	Mintage	VF20	XF40	MS60	MS63	MS65
ND-1982	1,990,000	—	0.50	1.00	2.00	2.50

KM# 619 25 ESCUDOS

Copper-Nickel, 28.5 mm. **Series:** F.A.O. **Obv:** Shield **Rev:** Fish, F.A.O. and date

Date	Mintage	VF20	XF40	MS60	MS63	MS65
1983	995,000	—	0.60	1.25	2.25	3.75

KM# 623 25 ESCUDOS

Copper-Nickel, 28.5 mm. **Subject:** 10th Anniversary of Revolution **Obv:** Waves breaking over shield **Rev:** Stylized 25

Date	Mintage	VF20	XF40	MS60	MS63	MS65
ND-1984	1,980,000	—	0.40	1.00	1.50	3.50

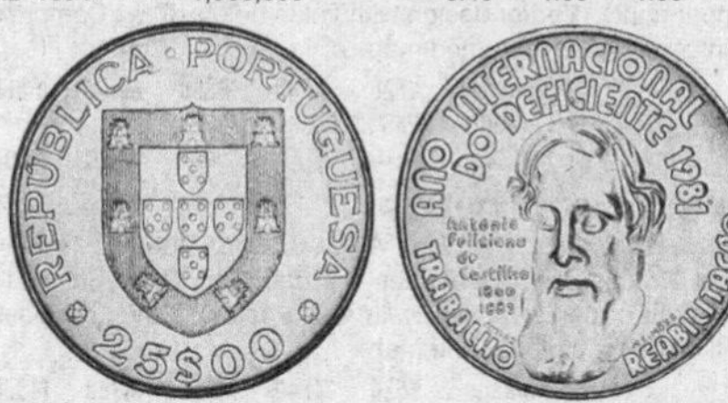

KM# 624 25 ESCUDOS

Copper-Nickel, 28.5 mm. **Subject:** International Year of Disabled Persons **Obv:** Shield **Rev:** Head 1/4 left with legend above

Date	Mintage	VF20	XF40	MS60	MS63	MS65
ND-1984	1,990,000	—	0.40	1.00	2.00	3.50

KM# 627 25 ESCUDOS

Copper-Nickel, 28.5 mm. **Subject:** 600th Anniversary - Battle of Aljubarrota **Obv:** Shield within circle **Rev:** Seated crowned figure flanked by shields

Date	Mintage	VF20	XF40	MS60	MS63	MS65
ND-1985	500,000	—	0.50	1.00	2.75	4.00

KM# 627a 25 ESCUDOS

10.83 g., 0.925 Silver 0.3221 oz. ASW, 28.5 mm. **Obv:** Shield within circle **Rev:** Seated crowned figure flanked by shields

Date	Mintage	VF20	XF40	MS60	MS63	MS65
ND-1985	5,000	PF65 40.00				
Note: In Proof sets only						
ND-1985	20,000	—	—	—	—	15.00
Note: In Mint sets only						

KM# 635 25 ESCUDOS

Copper-Nickel, 28.5 mm. **Subject:** Admission to European Common Market **Obv:** Shield **Rev:** Small square and lined design

Date	Mintage	VF20	XF40	MS60	MS63	MS65
1986	4,990,000	—	0.40	1.00	2.00	3.50

KM# 635a 25 ESCUDOS

11.00 g., 0.925 Silver 0.3271 oz. ASW, 28.5 mm. **Obv:** Shield **Rev:** Small square and lined design

Date	Mintage	VF20	XF40	MS60	MS63	MS65
1986	5,000	PF65 200				

KM# 593 50 ESCUDOS

18.00 g., 0.650 Silver 0.3762 oz. ASW **Subject:** 500th Anniversary - Birth of Pedro Alvares Cabral, Navigator, Discoverer of Brazil **Obv:** Crowned shield **Rev:** Bust with headdress right within circle

Date	Mintage	VF20	XF40	MS60	MS63	MS65
1968	1,000,000	—	—	—	14.00	16.00
1968 Matte	400	—	—	75.00	—	—

Note: A small quantity of these coins were given a matte finish by the Lisbon Mint on private contract

KM# 598 50 ESCUDOS

18.00 g., 0.650 Silver 0.3762 oz. ASW **Subject:** 500th Anniversary - Birth of Vasco daGama, Discoverer of the sea route to India **Obv:** Shield within maltese cross **Rev:** Head with headdress left

Date	Mintage	VF20	XF40	MS60	MS63	MS65
ND-1969	1,000,000	—	—	—	14.00	16.00
ND-1969 Matte	400	—	—	75.00	—	—

Note: A small quantity of these coins were given a matte finish by the Lisbon Mint on private contract

KM# 599 50 ESCUDOS

18.00 g., 0.650 Silver 0.3762 oz. ASW **Subject:** 100th Anniversary - Birth of Marechal Carmona, President **Obv:** Shield **Rev:** Uniformed bust 3/4 right

Date	Mintage	VF20	XF40	MS60	MS63	MS65
ND-1969 Matte	400	—	—	75.00	—	—
Note: A small quantity of these coins were given a matte finish by the Lisbon Mint on private contract						
ND-1969	500,000	—	—	—	14.00	16.00

KM# 601 50 ESCUDOS

18.00 g., 0.650 Silver 0.3762 oz. ASW **Subject:** 125th Anniversary - Bank of Portugal **Obv:** Circles within circled cross design **Rev:** Stylized tree

Date	Mintage	VF20	XF40	MS60	MS63	MS65
ND-1971	500,000	—	—	—	15.00	17.00
ND-1971 Matte	—	—	—	75.00	—	—

Note: A small quantity of these coins were given a matte finish by the Lisbon Mint on private contract

KM# 602 50 ESCUDOS

18.00 g., 0.650 Silver 0.3762 oz. ASW, 34.5 mm. **Subject:** 400th Anniversary of Heroic Epic 'Os Lusiadas' **Obv:** Book appears as part of Quinas Cross, all within circle **Rev:** Victory within design flanked by dates, all within circle

Date	Mintage	VF20	XF40	MS60	MS63	MS65
ND-1972	1,000,000	—	—	—	14.00	16.00
ND-1972 Matte	—	—	—	75.00	—	—

Note: A small quantity of these coins were given a matte finish by the Lisbon Mint on private contract

KM# 636 50 ESCUDOS

9.41 g., Copper-Nickel, 31 mm. **Obv:** Shield divides date with value below **Rev:** Sailboat, water and fish

Date	Mintage	VF20	XF40	MS60	MS63	MS65
1986	51,110,000	—	—	2.00	2.50	3.00
1987	28,248,000	—	—	2.00	2.50	3.00
1988	41,905,000	—	—	2.00	2.50	3.00
1989	18,327,000	—	—	2.00	2.50	3.00
1990 Sets only	50,000	—	—	—	—	15.00
1991	2,000,000	—	—	—	3.00	4.00
1992 Sets only	20,000	—	—	—	—	15.00
1993 Sets only	20,000	—	—	—	—	15.00
1994 Sets only	20,000	—	—	—	—	15.00
1994	—	PF65 5.00				
1995 Sets only	20,000	—	—	—	—	15.00
1996 Sets only	—	—	—	—	—	8.00
1996	7,000	PF65 5.00				
1997 Sets only	—	—	—	—	—	8.00
1997	—	PF65 5.00				
1998	6,000,000	—	—	—	3.00	4.00
1998	—	PF65 6.00				
1999	—	—	—	—	3.00	4.00
2000	—	—	—	—	3.00	4.00

KM# 603 100 ESCUDOS

18.00 g., 0.650 Silver 0.3762 oz. ASW, 32 mm. **Subject:** 1974 Revolution **Obv:** Small cross design within circle with numeral and written value above **Rev:** Inscription and date flanked by vertical block designs

Date	Mintage	VF20	XF40	MS60	MS63	MS65
ND-1976 INCM	1,000,000	—	—	7.25	15.00	17.00
ND-1976 INCM	—	PF65 20.00				

KM# 625 100 ESCUDOS

Copper-Nickel, 33.5 mm. **Subject:** International Year of Disabled Persons **Obv:** Shield **Rev:** Stylized head facing 1/4 right

Date	Mintage	VF20	XF40	MS60	MS63	MS65
ND-1984	990,000	—	0.75	1.50	2.50	3.50

KM# 628 100 ESCUDOS

Copper-Nickel, 33.5 mm. **Subject:** 50th Anniversary - Death of Fernando Pessoa - Poet **Obv:** Shield above value **Rev:** Four conjoined faces facing right and flying birds within circle

Date	Mintage	VF20	XF40	MS60	MS63	MS65
1985	480,000	—	0.75	2.00	3.50	4.50

KM# 628a 100 ESCUDOS

16.50 g., 0.925 Silver 0.4907 oz. ASW, 33.5 mm. **Obv:** Shield above value **Rev:** Four conjoined faces facing right and flying birds within circle

Date	Mintage	VF20	XF40	MS60	MS63	MS65
1985	5,000	PF65 250				

KM# 629 100 ESCUDOS

Copper-Nickel, 33.5 mm. **Subject:** 800th Anniversary - Death of King Alfonso Henriques **Obv:** Cross design within oblong circle flanked by designs, date and value **Rev:** Armored head left

Date	Mintage	VF20	XF40	MS60	MS63	MS65
1985	500,000	—	0.75	2.00	3.50	5.00

KM# 629a 100 ESCUDOS

16.50 g., 0.925 Silver 0.4907 oz. ASW, 33.5 mm. **Subject:** 800th Anniversary - Death of King Alfonso Henriques **Obv:** Cross design within oblong circle flanked by designs, date and value **Rev:** Armored head left

Date	Mintage	VF20	XF40	MS60	MS63	MS65
1985	20,000	—	—	—	—	30.00
1985	5,000	PF65 110				

KM# 630 100 ESCUDOS

Copper-Nickel, 33.5 mm. **Subject:** 600th Anniversary - Battle of Aljubarrota **Obv:** Shield within circle **Rev:** Standing figure facing within pillar arch **Edge:** Reeded

Date	Mintage	VF20	XF40	MS60	MS63	MS65
ND-1985	500,000	—	0.75	2.00	3.50	4.50

KM# 630a 100 ESCUDOS

16.50 g., 0.925 Silver 0.4907 oz. ASW, 33.5 mm. **Subject:** 600th Anniversary - Battle of Aljubarrota **Obv:** Shield within circle **Rev:** Standing figure facing within pillar arch

Date	Mintage	VF20	XF40	MS60	MS63	MS65
ND-1985	20,000	—	—	—	—	25.00
ND-1985	5,000	PF65 80.00				

KM# 637 100 ESCUDOS

15.00 g., Copper-Nickel, 33.5 mm. **Subject:** World Cup Soccer - Mexico 86 **Edge:** Reeded

Date	Mintage	VF20	XF40	MS60	MS63	MS65
1986 INCM	500,000	—	—	2.00	3.50	4.50

KM# 637a 100 ESCUDOS

16.50 g., 0.925 Silver 0.4907 oz. ASW, 33.5 mm. **Subject:** World Cup Soccer - Mexico 86 **Edge:** Reeded

Date	Mintage	VF20	XF40	MS60	MS63	MS65
1986	50,000	—	—	—	—	18.00
1986	20,000	PF65 30.00				

KM# 639 100 ESCUDOS

Copper-Nickel, 34 mm. **Subject:** Golden Age of Portuguese Discoveries - Gil Eanes **Obv:** Shield within circle **Rev:** Ship with flag on top of sails **Edge:** Reeded

Date	Mintage	VF20	XF40	MS60	MS63	MS65
1987	1,000,000	—	0.75	1.00	2.50	3.50

KM# 639a 100 ESCUDOS

16.50 g., 0.925 Silver 0.4907 oz. ASW, 34 mm. **Subject:** Golden Age of Portuguese Discoveries - Gil Eanes **Obv:** Shield within circle **Rev:** Ship with flag on top of sails

Date	Mintage	VF20	XF40	MS60	MS63	MS65
1987	22,000	PF65 25.00				
1987	50,000	—	—	—	16.50	18.50

KM# 639b 100 ESCUDOS

24.00 g., 0.917 Gold 0.7076 oz. AGW, 34 mm. **Subject:** Golden Age of Portuguese Discoveries - Gil Eanes **Obv:** Shield within circle **Rev:** Ship with flag on top of sails

Date	Mintage	VF20	XF40	MS60	MS63	MS65
1987	5,772	—	—	—	—	1,300

KM# 640 100 ESCUDOS

Copper-Nickel, 34 mm. **Subject:** Golden Age of Portuguese Discoveries - Nuno Tristao **Obv:** Shield flanked by crowns within circle **Rev:** Ship **Edge:** Reeded

Date	Mintage	VF20	XF40	MS60	MS63	MS65
1987	1,000,000	—	0.75	1.00	2.50	3.50

KM# 640a 100 ESCUDOS

16.50 g., 0.925 Silver 0.4907 oz. ASW, 34 mm. **Subject:** Golden Age of Portuguese Discoveries - Nuno Tristao **Obv:** Shield flanked by crowns within circle **Rev:** Ship

Date	Mintage	VF20	XF40	MS60	MS63	MS65
1987	50,000	—	—	—	18.00	20.00
1987	20,000	PF65 30.00				

KM# 640b 100 ESCUDOS

24.00 g., 0.917 Gold 0.7076 oz. AGW, 34 mm. **Subject:** Golden Age of Portuguese Discoveries - Nuno Tristao **Obv:** Shield flanked by crowns within circle **Rev:** Ship

Date	Mintage	VF20	XF40	MS60	MS63	MS65
1987	5,497	—	—	—	—	1,300

KM# 640c 100 ESCUDOS

31.12 g., 0.999 Palladium 0.9995 oz. APW **Subject:** Golden Age of Portuguese Discoveries - Nuno Tristao **Obv:** Shield flanked by crowns within circle **Rev:** Ship

Date	Mintage	VF20	XF40	MS60	MS63	MS65
1987	323	—	—	—	—	1,000
1987	2,000	PF65 850				

KM# 641 100 ESCUDOS

15.00 g., Copper-Nickel, 34 mm. **Series:** Portuguese Discoveries - Series I **Subject:** Golden Age of Portuguese Discoveries - Diogo Cao **Obv:** Shield to upper right of design with value below **Obv. Legend:** DIOGO CAO 1486 **Rev:** Compass within center of sailboat and map **Rev. Legend:** REPUBLICA PORTUGUESA **Edge:** Reeded

Date	Mintage	VF20	XF40	MS60	MS63	MS65
1987	1,000,000	—	1.50	3.00	6.00	7.50

KM# 641a 100 ESCUDOS

16.50 g., 0.925 Silver 0.4907 oz. ASW, 34 mm. **Subject:** Golden Age of Portuguese Discoveries - Diogo Cao **Obv:** Shield to upper right of center design with value below **Rev:** Compass within center of sailboat and map

Date	Mintage	VF20	XF40	MS60	MS63	MS65
1987	20,000	PF65 30.00				
1987	50,000	—	—	—	18.00	20.00

KM# 641b 100 ESCUDOS

24.00 g., 0.917 Gold 0.7076 oz. AGW, 34 mm. **Subject:** Golden Age of Portuguese Discoveries - Diogo Cao **Obv:** Shield to upper right of center design with value below **Rev:** Compass within center of sailboat and map

Date	Mintage	VF20	XF40	MS60	MS63	MS65
1987	5,387	PF65 1,300				
1987	5,256	—	—	—	—	1,300

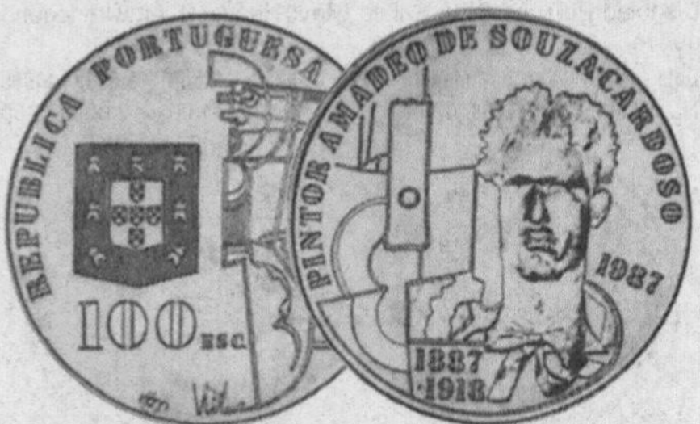

KM# 644 100 ESCUDOS

16.50 g., Copper-Nickel, 34 mm. **Subject:** Amadeo de Souza Cardoso **Obv:** Shield and value to left of design **Obv. Legend:** PINTOR AMADEO DE SOUZA CARDOSO1887-1918 1987 **Rev:** Head facing flanked by dates with design at left **Rev. Legend:** REPUBLICA PORTUGUESA **Edge:** Reeded

Date	Mintage	VF20	XF40	MS60	MS63	MS65
1987 INCM	800,000	—	1.50	3.50	5.50	8.00

KM# 644a 100 ESCUDOS

21.00 g., 0.925 Silver 0.6245 oz. ASW, 34 mm. **Subject:** Amadeo De Souza Cardoso **Obv:** Shield and value to left of design **Rev:** Head facing flanked by dates to right of design

Date	Mintage	VF20	XF40	MS60	MS63	MS65
1987	30,000	—	—	—	22.50	25.00
1987	15,000	PF65 32.50				

KM# 642 100 ESCUDOS

Copper-Nickel, 34 mm. **Subject:** Golden Age of Portuguese Discoveries - Bartolomeu Dias **Obv:** Shield within circle **Rev:** Stylized boat and map **Edge:** Reeded

Date	Mintage	VF20	XF40	MS60	MS63	MS65
ND-1988	1,000,000	—	0.75	1.00	2.50	3.50

KM# 642a 100 ESCUDOS
16.50 g., 0.925 Silver 0.4907 oz. ASW, 34 mm. **Subject:** Golden Age of Portuguese Discoveries - Bartolomeu Dias **Obv:** Shield within circle **Rev:** Stylized boat and map

Date	Mintage	VF20	XF40	MS60	MS63	MS65
ND-1988	20,000	PF65 25.00				
ND-1988	50,000	—	—	—	17.00	19.00

KM# 642b 100 ESCUDOS
24.00 g., 0.917 Gold 0.7076 oz. AGW, 34 mm. **Subject:** Golden Age of Portuguese Discoveries - Bartolomeu Dias **Obv:** Shield within circle **Rev:** Stylized boat and map

Date	Mintage	VF20	XF40	MS60	MS63	MS65
ND-1988	5,503	—	—	—	—	1,250

KM# 642c 100 ESCUDOS
31.12 g., 0.999 Platinum 0.9995 oz. APW **Subject:** Golden Age of Portuguese Discoveries - Bartolomeu Dias **Obv:** Shield within circle **Rev:** Stylized boat and map

Date	Mintage	VF20	XF40	MS60	MS63	MS65
ND-1988	2,000	PF65 1,900				
ND-1988	907	—	—	—	—	2,000

KM# 645.1 100 ESCUDOS
8.30 g., Bi-Metallic Aluminum-Bronze center in Copper-Nickel ring, 25.5 mm. **Obv:** Shield within globe above value within circle **Rev:** Armored 1/2 length figure holding globe facing left within circle **Edge:** Five reeded and five plain sections **Note:** Varieties exist with fine and bold letters.

Date	Mintage	VF20	XF40	MS60	MS63	MS65
1989	20,000,000	—	—	1.00	2.50	3.00
1990	52,000,000	—	—	1.00	2.50	3.00
1991	45,500,000	—	—	1.00	2.50	3.00
1992	14,500,000	—	—	1.00	2.50	3.00
1993	20,000	—	—	—	—	15.00
Note: In Mint sets only						
1994	20,000	—	—	—	—	15.00
Note: In Mint sets only						
1994	—	PF65 10.00				
1995	—	PF65 10.00				
1996	—	—	—	—	—	15.00
Note: In Mint sets only						
1996	7,000	PF65 10.00				
1997	—	—	—	—	2.50	3.50
1997	—	PF65 2.50				
1998	—	—	—	—	2.50	3.50
1998	—	PF65 10.00				
1999	—	—	—	—	2.50	3.50
2000	—	—	—	—	2.50	3.50

KM# 645.2 100 ESCUDOS
8.30 g., Bi-Metallic Aluminumn-Bronze center in Copper-Nickel ring, 25.1 mm. **Rev:** Pedro Nunes **Edge:** Six reeded and six plain sections

Date	Mintage	VF20	XF40	MS60	MS63	MS65
1989	Inc. above	—	1.00	1.50	3.00	5.00
1990	Inc. above	—	1.25	2.00	3.50	5.50
1991	Inc. above	—	1.00	1.50	3.00	5.00

KM# 646 100 ESCUDOS
Copper-Nickel, 34 mm. **Subject:** Discovery of the Canary Islands **Obv:** Shield with supporters above value **Rev:** Ship

Date	Mintage	VF20	XF40	MS60	MS63	MS65
1989	2,000,000	—	—	1.00	2.50	4.00

KM# 646a 100 ESCUDOS
21.00 g., 0.925 Silver 0.6245 oz. ASW, 34 mm. **Subject:** Discovery of the Canary Islands **Obv:** Shield with supporters above value **Rev:** Ship

Date	Mintage	VF20	XF40	MS60	MS63	MS65
1989	50,000	—	—	—	22.50	25.00
1989	23,000	PF65 32.50				

KM# 646b 100 ESCUDOS
24.00 g., 0.917 Gold 0.7076 oz. AGW **Subject:** Discovery of the Canary Islands **Obv:** Shield with supporters above value **Rev:** Ship

Date	Mintage	VF20	XF40	MS60	MS63	MS65
1989	2,981	PF65 1,300				

KM# 647 100 ESCUDOS
Copper-Nickel, 34 mm. **Subject:** Discovery of Madeira **Obv:** Cross and shield **Rev:** Ship **Edge:** Reeded

Date	Mintage	VF20	XF40	MS60	MS63	MS65
1989	2,000,000	—	—	1.00	2.50	4.00

KM# 647a 100 ESCUDOS
21.00 g., 0.925 Silver 0.6245 oz. ASW, 34 mm. **Subject:** Discovery of Madeira **Obv:** Cross and shield **Rev:** Ship

Date	Mintage	VF20	XF40	MS60	MS63	MS65
1989	50,000	—	—	—	22.50	25.00
1989	20,000	PF65 32.50				

KM# 647b 100 ESCUDOS
24.00 g., 0.917 Gold 0.7076 oz. AGW, 34 mm. **Subject:** Discovery of Madeira **Obv:** Cross and shield **Rev:** Ship

Date	Mintage	VF20	XF40	MS60	MS63	MS65
1989	2,996	PF65 1,300				

KM# 647c 100 ESCUDOS
31.12 g., 0.999 Palladium 0.9995 oz. APW **Subject:** Discovery of Madeira **Obv:** Cross and shield **Rev:** Ship

Date	Mintage	VF20	XF40	MS60	MS63	MS65
1989	2,500	PF65 850				

KM# 648 100 ESCUDOS
Copper-Nickel, 34 mm. **Subject:** Discovery of the Azores **Obv:** Shield at right within design **Rev:** Ship and stars within design

Date	Mintage	VF20	XF40	MS60	MS63	MS65
ND-1989	2,000,000	—	—	1.00	2.50	4.00

KM# 648a 100 ESCUDOS
21.00 g., 0.925 Silver 0.6245 oz. ASW, 34 mm. **Subject:** Discovery of the Azores **Obv:** Shield at right within design **Rev:** Ship and stars within design

Date	Mintage	VF20	XF40	MS60	MS63	MS65
ND-1989	20,000	PF65 32.50				
ND-1989	50,000	—	—	—	22.50	25.00

KM# 648b 100 ESCUDOS
24.00 g., 0.917 Gold 0.7076 oz. AGW **Subject:** Discovery of the Avores **Obv:** Shield to right within design **Rev:** Ship and stars within design

Date	Mintage	VF20	XF40	MS60	MS63	MS65
ND-1989	5,495	PF65 1,300				

KM# 649 100 ESCUDOS
Copper-Nickel, 34 mm. **Subject:** Celestial Navigation **Obv:** Value in center flanked by shield and circled star designs **Rev:** Artistic designs

Date	Mintage	VF20	XF40	MS60	MS63	MS65
1990	2,000,000	—	—	1.00	2.50	4.00

KM# 649a 100 ESCUDOS
21.00 g., 0.925 Silver 0.6245 oz. ASW, 34 mm. **Subject:** Celestial Navigation **Obv:** Value in center flanked by shield and circled star designs **Rev:** Artistic designs

Date	Mintage	VF20	XF40	MS60	MS63	MS65
1990	20,000	PF65 32.50				
1990	50,000	—	—	—	22.50	25.00

KM# 649b 100 ESCUDOS
24.00 g., 0.917 Gold 0.7076 oz. AGW, 34 mm. **Subject:** Celestial Navigation **Obv:** Value in center flanked by shield and circled star designs **Rev:** Artistic designs

Date	Mintage	VF20	XF40	MS60	MS63	MS65
1990	2,958	PF65 1,300				

KM# 649c 100 ESCUDOS
31.12 g., 0.999 Platinum 0.9995 oz. APW **Subject:** Celestial Navigation **Obv:** Value in center flanked by shield and circled star designs **Rev:** Artistic designs

Date	Mintage	VF20	XF40	MS60	MS63	MS65
1990	2,500	PF65 1,900				

KM# 651 100 ESCUDOS
Copper-Nickel, 33 mm. **Subject:** 350th Anniversary - Restoration of Portuguese Independence **Obv:** Shield within beaded circle **Rev:** Half length figure facing left holding sword under design **Edge:** Reeded

Date	Mintage	VF20	XF40	MS60	MS63	MS65
ND-1990	1,000,000	—	—	1.00	2.50	4.00

KM# 651a 100 ESCUDOS
18.50 g., 0.925 Silver 0.5502 oz. ASW, 33 mm. **Subject:** 350th Anniversary - Restoration of Portuguese **Obv:** Shield within beaded circle **Rev:** Half length figure facing left holding sword under design

Date	Mintage	VF20	XF40	MS60	MS63	MS65
ND-1990	10,000	PF65 40.00				
ND-1990	25,000	—	—	—	22.50	25.00

KM# 656 100 ESCUDOS
Copper-Nickel, 33 mm. **Rev:** Camilo Castelo Branco **Edge:** Reeded

Date	Mintage	VF20	XF40	MS60	MS63	MS65
1990	1,000,000	—	—	1.00	2.50	3.50

KM# 656a 100 ESCUDOS
18.50 g., 0.925 Silver 0.5502 oz. ASW, 33 mm. **Rev:** Camilo Castelo Branco

Date	Mintage	VF20	XF40	MS60	MS63	MS65
1990	10,000	PF65 42.00				
1990	25,000	—	—	—	22.50	25.00

KM# 664 100 ESCUDOS
Copper-Nickel, 33 mm. **Subject:** Centenary of the death of Antero de Quental **Obv:** Hand above national arms and value

Obv. Legend: REPUBLICA PORTUGUESA AÇORES **Rev:** Portrait, signature, life dates and name **Rev. Legend:** ANTERO DE QUENTAL 1842 1891 **Edge:** Reeded

Date	Mintage	VF20	XF40	MS60	MS63	MS65
1991 INCM	1,000,000	—	—	3.00	4.50	5.50

KM# 664a 100 ESCUDOS

26.50 g., 0.925 Silver 0.7881 oz. ASW, 36 mm. **Subject:** Antero DeQuental **Obv:** Hand above national arms and value **Rev:** Portrait, signature, name and life dates **Edge:** Reeded

Date	Mintage	VF20	XF40	MS60	MS63	MS65
1991 INCM	20,000	—	—	—	25.00	27.50
1991 INCM	—	PF65 45.00				

KM# 678 100 ESCUDOS

Bi-Metallic Aluminumn-Bronze center in Copper-Nickel ring, 25.5 mm. **Subject:** 50th Anniversary - F.A.O. **Obv:** Shield within globe above value within circle **Rev:** F.A.O. logo within oat wreath **Edge:** Segmented reeding

Date	Mintage	VF20	XF40	MS60	MS63	MS65
1995	500,000	—	—	2.00	5.00	7.00
1995	17,000	PF65 15.00				

KM# 680 100 ESCUDOS

Copper-Nickel, 33 mm. **Subject:** 400th Anniversary - Antonio Prior de Crato **Obv:** Bird, shield, cross and designs within circle **Rev:** Bust 1/4 right within circle

Date	Mintage	VF20	XF40	MS60	MS63	MS65
ND-1995	—	—	—	1.00	2.50	4.00

KM# 680a 100 ESCUDOS

18.50 g., 0.925 Silver 0.5502 oz. ASW, 33 mm. **Subject:** 400th Anniversary - Antonio Prior de Crato **Obv:** Bird, shield, cross and designs within circle **Rev:** Bust 1/4 right within circle

Date	Mintage	VF20	XF40	MS60	MS63	MS65
ND-1995	10,000	PF65 35.00				
ND-1995	5,000	—	—	—	—	32.00

KM# 693 100 ESCUDOS

Bi-Metallic Aluminumn-Bronze center in Copper-Nickel ring, 25.5 mm. **Subject:** Lisbon World Expo '98 **Obv:** Shield and flying bird above value **Rev:** Monk Seal

Date	Mintage	VF20	XF40	MS60	MS63	MS65
1997	—	—	—	2.00	5.00	9.00
1997	7,000	PF65 20.00				

KM# 722.1 100 ESCUDOS

Bi-Metallic Brass center in Copper-Nickel ring, 25 mm. **Obv:** National arms, value and country name **Obv. Legend:** REPUBLICA PORTUGUESA **Rev:** UNICEF logo **Edge:** Reeded and plain sections

Date	Mintage	VF20	XF40	MS60	MS63	MS65
1999 INCM	—	—	—	—	5.00	7.00

KM# 722.2 100 ESCUDOS

Bi-Metallic Brass center in Copper-Nickel ring, 25 mm. **Subject:** UNICEF **Obv:** Shield within globe in center circle, numeral and written value in outer circle **Obv. Legend:** REPUBLICA PORTUGUSA **Rev:** Silhouette heads of mother and baby and partial globe in center circle flanked by sprigs **Edge:** Reeded and plain sections **Note:** Legend Obverse with error. There is an "E" missing on the word PORTUGUESA.

Date	Mintage	VF20	XF40	MS60	MS63	MS65
1999 INCM	—	—	—	—	6.00	8.00

KM# 655 200 ESCUDOS

9.80 g., Bi-Metallic Copper-Nickel center in Aluminum-Bronze ring, 28 mm. **Obv:** Shield within globe above value **Obv. Legend:** REPUBLICA PORTUGUESA **Rev:** Armored 1/2 length bust right holding flower within circle **Rev. Legend:** GARCIA DE ORTA **Edge:** Segmented reeding

Date	Mintage	VF20	XF40	MS60	MS63	MS65
1991	33,000,000	—	—	1.50	2.50	4.00
1991	—	PF65 110				
1992	11,000,000	—	—	1.50	2.50	4.00
1993 Sets only	20,000	—	—	—	—	18.00
1996 Sets only	—	—	—	—	—	18.00
1996	7,000	PF65 20.00				
1997	5,000,000	—	—	1.50	3.00	5.00
1997	—	PF65 20.00				
1998	17,866,000	—	—	1.50	2.50	4.00
1998	—	PF65 20.00				
1999	5,998,000	—	—	1.50	2.50	4.00
2000	—	—	—	1.50	2.50	4.00

KM# 658 200 ESCUDOS

Copper-Nickel, 36 mm. **Subject:** Columbus and Portugal **Obv:** Shield and value to left of design **Rev:** Head left, map, cross, dates and 1/2 star design

Date	Mintage	VF20	XF40	MS60	MS63	MS65
1991	1,500,000	—	—	1.50	2.50	4.00

KM# 658a 200 ESCUDOS

26.50 g., 0.925 Silver 0.7881 oz. ASW, 36 mm. **Subject:** Columbus and Portugal **Obv:** Shield and value to left of design **Rev:** Head left, map, cross, dates and 1/2 star design

Date	Mintage	VF20	XF40	MS60	MS63	MS65
1991	10,000	—	—	—	27.00	30.00
1991	15,000	PF65 32.50				

KM# 658b 200 ESCUDOS

27.20 g., 0.917 Gold 0.8019 oz. AGW **Subject:** Columbus and Portugal **Obv:** Shield, value and date to left of design **Rev:** Head left, map, cross, dates and 1/2 star design

Date	Mintage	VF20	XF40	MS60	MS63	MS65
1991	3,500	PF65 1,450				

KM# 658c 200 ESCUDOS

31.12 g., 0.999 Platinum 0.9995 oz. APW **Subject:** Columbus and Portugal **Obv:** Shield, value and date to left of design **Rev:** Head left, map, cross, dates and 1/2 star design

Date	Mintage	VF20	XF40	MS60	MS63	MS65
1991	2,500	PF65 1,900				

KM# 658d 200 ESCUDOS

31.12 g., 0.999 Palladium 0.9995 oz. APW **Subject:** Columbus and Portugal **Obv:** Shield, value and date to left of design **Rev:** Head left, map, cross, dates and 1/2 star design

Date	Mintage	VF20	XF40	MS60	MS63	MS65
1991	2,500	PF65 875				

KM# 659 200 ESCUDOS

Copper-Nickel, 36 mm. **Subject:** Westward Navigation **Obv:** Shield and value within design **Rev:** Stylized ship

Date	Mintage	VF20	XF40	MS60	MS63	MS65
1991	1,500,000	—	—	2.00	4.00	6.00

KM# 659a 200 ESCUDOS

26.50 g., 0.925 Silver 0.7881 oz. ASW, 36 mm. **Subject:** Westward Navigation **Obv:** Shield and value within design **Rev:** Stylized ship

Date	Mintage	VF20	XF40	MS60	MS63	MS65
1991	10,000	—	—	—	27.00	30.00
1991	15,000	PF65 32.50				

KM# 659b 200 ESCUDOS

27.20 g., 0.917 Gold 0.8019 oz. AGW **Subject:** Westward Navigation **Obv:** Shield and value within design **Rev:** Stylized ship

Date	Mintage	VF20	XF40	MS60	MS63	MS65
1991	3,500	PF65 1,450				

KM# 659c 200 ESCUDOS

31.12 g., 0.999 Platinum 0.9995 oz. APW **Subject:** Westward Navigation **Obv:** Shield and value within design **Rev:** Stylized ship

Date	Mintage	VF20	XF40	MS60	MS63	MS65
1991	2,500	PF65 1,900				

KM# 659d 200 ESCUDOS

31.12 g., 0.999 Palladium 0.9995 oz. APW **Subject:** Westward Navigation **Obv:** Shield and value within design **Rev:** Stylized ship

Date	Mintage	VF20	XF40	MS60	MS63	MS65
1991	2,500	PF65 850				

KM# 660 200 ESCUDOS

Copper-Nickel, 36 mm. **Subject:** New World - America **Obv:** Shield within design **Rev:** Head 1/4 left and ships

Date	Mintage	VF20	XF40	MS60	MS63	MS65
ND-1992	1,300,000	—	—	1.50	3.50	5.00

KM# 660a 200 ESCUDOS

26.50 g., 0.925 Silver 0.7881 oz. ASW, 36 mm. **Subject:** New World - America **Obv:** Shield within design **Rev:** Head 1/4 left and ships

Date	Mintage	VF20	XF40	MS60	MS63	MS65
ND-1992	10,000	—	—	—	27.00	30.00
ND-1992	15,000	PF65 32.50				

KM# 660b 200 ESCUDOS

27.20 g., 0.917 Gold 0.8019 oz. AGW **Subject:** New World - America **Obv:** Shield within design **Rev:** Head 1/4 left and ships

Date	Mintage	VF20	XF40	MS60	MS63	MS65
ND-1992	6,000	PF65 1,450				

KM# 660c 200 ESCUDOS

31.12 g., 0.999 Platinum 0.9995 oz. APW **Subject:** New World - America **Obv:** Shield within design **Rev:** Head 1/4 left and ships

Date	Mintage	VF20	XF40	MS60	MS63	MS65
ND-1992	2,500	PF65 1,900				

KM# 660d 200 ESCUDOS

31.12 g., 0.999 Palladium 0.9995 oz. APW **Subject:** New World - America **Obv:** Shield within design **Rev:** Head 1/4 left and ships

Date	Mintage	VF20	XF40	MS60	MS63	MS65
ND-1992	2,500	PF65 850				

KM# 661 200 ESCUDOS

Copper-Nickel, 36 mm. **Obv:** Shield and value within thin-lined cross **Rev:** Standing figure and map

Date	Mintage	VF20	XF40	MS60	MS63	MS65
ND-1992	1,300,000	—	—	2.00	4.00	6.00

KM# 661a 200 ESCUDOS

26.50 g., 0.925 Silver 0.7881 oz. ASW, 36 mm. **Obv:** Shield and value within thin-lined cross **Rev:** Standing figure and map

Date	Mintage	VF20	XF40	MS60	MS63	MS65
ND-1992	10,000	—	—	—	27.00	30.00
ND-1992	15,000	PF65 32.50				

KM# 661b 200 ESCUDOS

27.20 g., 0.917 Gold 0.8019 oz. AGW **Obv:** Shield and value within thin-lined cross **Rev:** Standing figure and map

Date	Mintage	VF20	XF40	MS60	MS63	MS65
ND-1992	3,500	PF65 1,450				

KM# 661c 200 ESCUDOS

31.12 g., 0.999 Platinum 0.9995 oz. APW **Obv:** Shield and value within thin-lined cross **Rev:** Standing figure and map

Date	Mintage	VF20	XF40	MS60	MS63	MS65
ND-1992	2,500	PF65 1,900				

KM# 661d 200 ESCUDOS

31.12 g., 0.999 Palladium 0.9995 oz. APW **Obv:** Shield and value within thin-lined cross **Rev:** Standing figure and map

Date	Mintage	VF20	XF40	MS60	MS63	MS65
ND-1992	2,500	PF65 850				

KM# 662 200 ESCUDOS

Copper-Nickel, 36 mm. **Series:** Olympics **Rev:** Stylized runner

Date	Mintage	VF20	XF40	MS60	MS63	MS65
1992	1,000,000	—	—	2.00	4.00	6.00

KM# 662a 200 ESCUDOS

26.50 g., 0.925 Silver 0.7881 oz. ASW, 36 mm. **Series:** Olympics **Rev:** Stylized runner

Date	Mintage	VF20	XF40	MS60	MS63	MS65
1992	20,000	—	—	—	27.00	30.00
1992	30,000	PF65 32.50				

KM# 663 200 ESCUDOS

21.00 g., Copper-Nickel, 36 mm. **Subject:** Portugal's Presidency of the European Community **Obv:** Shield within wave-like design **Obv. Legend:** REPUBLICA PORTUGUESA **Rev:** Circle of stars within wave-like design **Rev. Legend:** PRESIDENCIA DA COMUNIDADE EUROPEIA - 1992 **Edge:** Reeded

Date	Mintage	VF20	XF40	MS60	MS63	MS65
1992 INCM	1,000,000	—	—	2.00	4.00	6.00

KM# 663a 200 ESCUDOS

26.50 g., 0.925 Silver 0.7881 oz. ASW, 36 mm. **Subject:** Portugal's Presidency of the European Community **Obv:** Shield within wave-like design **Rev:** Circle of stars within wave-like design

Date	Mintage	VF20	XF40	MS60	MS63	MS65
1992	20,000	—	—	—	27.00	30.00
1992	30,000	PF65 35.00				

KM# 665 200 ESCUDOS

Copper-Nickel, 36 mm. **Subject:** Tanegashima - Site 1st Portuguese Landing in Japan **Obv:** Shield **Rev:** Ship

Date	Mintage	VF20	XF40	MS60	MS63	MS65
ND-1993	1,000,000	—	—	2.00	4.00	6.00

KM# 665a 200 ESCUDOS

26.50 g., 0.925 Silver 0.7881 oz. ASW, 36 mm. **Subject:** Tanegashima - Site 1st Portuguese Landing in Japan **Obv:** Shield **Rev:** Ship

Date	Mintage	VF20	XF40	MS60	MS63	MS65
ND-1993	22,000	PF65 32.50				
ND-1993	30,000	—	—	—	27.00	30.00

KM# 665b 200 ESCUDOS

27.20 g., 0.917 Gold 0.8019 oz. AGW **Subject:** Tanegashima - 1st Portuguese Ship to Japan **Obv:** Shield **Rev:** Ship

Date	Mintage	VF20	XF40	MS60	MS63	MS65
ND-1993	7,000	PF65 1,450				

KM# 666 200 ESCUDOS

Copper-Nickel, 36 mm. **Subject:** Espingarda **Obv:** Inscription divides globe and shield **Rev:** Mounted cavalryman shooting rifle

Date	Mintage	VF20	XF40	MS60	MS63	MS65
1993	1,000,000	—	—	2.00	4.00	6.00

KM# 666a 200 ESCUDOS

26.50 g., 0.925 Silver 0.7881 oz. ASW, 36 mm. **Subject:** Espingarda **Obv:** Inscription divides globe and shield **Rev:** Mounted cavalryman shooting rifle

Date	Mintage	VF20	XF40	MS60	MS63	MS65
1993	20,000	PF65 35.00				
1993	30,000	—	—	—	27.00	30.00

KM# 666b 200 ESCUDOS

27.20 g., 0.917 Gold 0.8019 oz. AGW **Subject:** Espingarda **Obv:** Inscription divides globe and shield **Rev:** Mounted cavalryman shooting rifle

Date	Mintage	VF20	XF40	MS60	MS63	MS65
1993	7,000	PF65 1,450				

KM# 666c 200 ESCUDOS

31.12 g., 0.999 Palladium 0.9995 oz. APW **Subject:** Espingarda **Obv:** Inscription divides globe and shield **Rev:** Mounted cavalryman shooting rifle

Date	Mintage	VF20	XF40	MS60	MS63	MS65
1993	2,000	PF65 850				

KM# 667 200 ESCUDOS

Copper-Nickel, 36 mm. **Obv:** Ship at right of shield **Rev:** Armored busts and date to right of column

Date	Mintage	VF20	XF40	MS60	MS63	MS65
1993	1,000,000	—	—	2.00	4.00	6.00

KM# 667a 200 ESCUDOS

26.50 g., 0.925 Silver 0.7881 oz. ASW, 36 mm. **Obv:** Ship at right of shield **Rev:** Armored busts and date to right of column

Date	Mintage	VF20	XF40	MS60	MS63	MS65
1993	30,000	—	—	—	27.00	30.00
1993	20,000	PF65 35.00				

KM# 667b 200 ESCUDOS

27.20 g., 0.917 Gold 0.8019 oz. AGW **Obv:** Ship at right of shield **Rev:** Armored busts and date to right of column

Date	Mintage	VF20	XF40	MS60	MS63	MS65
1993	7,000	PF65 1,450				

KM# 668 200 ESCUDOS

Copper-Nickel, 36 mm. **Rev:** Arte Namban

Date	Mintage	VF20	XF40	MS60	MS63	MS65
1993	1,000,000	—	—	2.00	4.00	6.00

KM# 668a 200 ESCUDOS

26.50 g., 0.925 Silver 0.7881 oz. ASW, 36 mm. **Rev:** Arte Namban

Date	Mintage	VF20	XF40	MS60	MS63	MS65
1993	22,000	PF65 35.00				
1993	30,000	—	—	—	27.00	30.00

KM# 668b 200 ESCUDOS

27.20 g., 0.917 Gold 0.8019 oz. AGW **Rev:** Arte Namban

Date	Mintage	VF20	XF40	MS60	MS63	MS65
1993	7,000	PF65 1,450				

KM# 668c 200 ESCUDOS

31.12 g., 0.999 Platinum 0.9995 oz. APW **Rev:** Arte Namban

Date	Mintage	VF20	XF40	MS60	MS63	MS65
1993	2,000	PF65 1,900				

KM# 669 200 ESCUDOS

Bi-Metallic Copper-Nickel center in Aluminum-Bronze ring, 28 mm. **Subject:** Lisbon - European Cultural Capital **Obv:** Shield within globe above value within circle **Rev:** Cultural building within circle

Date	Mintage	VF20	XF40	MS60	MS63	MS65
1994	1,000,000	—	—	2.00	4.00	6.00
1994	7,000	PF65 20.00				

KM# 670 200 ESCUDOS

Copper-Nickel, 36 mm. **Obv:** Shield to left of ships **Rev:** Bust 1/4 right flanked by dates and symbol

Date	Mintage	VF20	XF40	MS60	MS63	MS65
ND-1994	750,000	—	—	—	4.00	6.00

KM# 670a 200 ESCUDOS

26.50 g., 0.925 Silver 0.7881 oz. ASW, 36 mm. **Obv:** Shield to upper left of ships **Rev:** Bust 1/4 right flanked by dates and symbol

Date	Mintage	VF20	XF40	MS60	MS63	MS65
ND-1994	20,000	—	—	—	27.00	30.00
ND-1994	13,000	PF65 32.50				

KM# 670b 200 ESCUDOS

27.20 g., 0.917 Gold 0.8019 oz. AGW **Obv:** Shield to upper left of ships **Rev:** Bust 1/4 right flanked by dates and symbol

Date	Mintage	VF20	XF40	MS60	MS63	MS65
ND-1994	2,000	PF65 1,450				

KM# 671 200 ESCUDOS

Copper-Nickel, 36 mm. **Subject:** Treaty of Tordesilhas **Obv:** Ship flanked by map, shield, designs and value **Rev:** Left 1/2 of coin is conjoined crowned heads right, arms above, right 1/2 of coin is crown head left, arms on bottom

Date	Mintage	VF20	XF40	MS60	MS63	MS65
ND-1994	750,000	—	—	—	5.00	7.00

KM# 671a 200 ESCUDOS

26.50 g., 0.925 Silver 0.7881 oz. ASW, 36 mm. **Subject:** Treaty of Tordesilhas **Obv:** Ship flanked by map, shield, designs and value **Rev:** Left 1/2 of coin is conjoined crowned heads right, arms above, right 1/2 of coin is crown head left, arms on bottom

Date	Mintage	VF20	XF40	MS60	MS63	MS65
ND-1994	20,000	—	—	—	27.00	30.00
ND-1994	13,000	PF65 32.50				

KM# 671b 200 ESCUDOS

27.20 g., 0.917 Gold 0.8019 oz. AGW **Subject:** Treaty of Tordesilhas **Obv:** Ship flanked by map, shield, designs and value **Rev:** Left 1/2 of coin is conjoined crowned heads right, arms above, right 1/2 of coin is crown head left, arms on bottom

Date	Mintage	VF20	XF40	MS60	MS63	MS65
ND-1994	2,000	PF65 1,450				

KM# 671c 200 ESCUDOS

31.12 g., 0.999 Palladium 0.9995 oz. APW **Subject:** Treaty of Tordesilhas **Obv:** Ship flanked by map, shield, designs and value **Rev:** Left 1/2 of coin is conjoined crowned heads right, arms above, right 1/2 of coin is crown head left, arms on bottom

Date	Mintage	VF20	XF40	MS60	MS63	MS65
ND-1994	1,000	PF65 850				

KM# 672 200 ESCUDOS

Copper-Nickel, 36 mm. **Subject:** Dividing Up The World **Obv:** Shield, map, value and date **Rev:** Ship, map and divided arms

Date	Mintage	VF20	XF40	MS60	MS63	MS65
1994	750,000	—	—	—	5.00	7.00

KM# 672a 200 ESCUDOS

26.50 g., 0.925 Silver 0.7881 oz. ASW, 36 mm. **Subject:** Dividing up the World **Obv:** Shield, value, date and map **Rev:** Ship, map and divided arms

Date	Mintage	VF20	XF40	MS60	MS63	MS65
1994	20,000	—	—	—	27.00	30.00
1994	12,000	PF65 32.50				

KM# 672b 200 ESCUDOS

27.20 g., 0.917 Gold 0.8019 oz. AGW **Subject:** Dividing Up The World **Obv:** Shield, map, value and date **Rev:** Ship, map and divided arms

Date	Mintage	VF20	XF40	MS60	MS63	MS65
1994	3,000	PF65 1,450				

KM# 673 200 ESCUDOS

Copper-Nickel, 36 mm. **Obv:** Water divides shield and design **Rev:** Crowned 1/2 length figure facing

Date	Mintage	VF20	XF40	MS60	MS63	MS65
ND-1994	750,000	—	—	—	5.00	7.00

KM# 673a 200 ESCUDOS

26.50 g., 0.925 Silver 0.7881 oz. ASW, 36 mm. **Obv:** Water divides shield and design **Rev:** Crowned 1/2 length figure facing

Date	Mintage	VF20	XF40	MS60	MS63	MS65
ND-1994	20,000	—	—	—	27.00	30.00
ND-1994	13,000	PF65 32.50				

KM# 673b 200 ESCUDOS

27.20 g., 0.917 Gold 0.8019 oz. AGW **Obv:** Water divides shield and design **Rev:** Crowned 1/2 length figure facing

Date	Mintage	VF20	XF40	MS60	MS63	MS65
ND-1994	2,000	PF65 1,450				

KM# 673c 200 ESCUDOS

31.12 g., 0.999 Platinum 0.9995 oz. APW **Obv:** Water divides shield and design **Rev:** Crowned 1/2 length figure facing

Date	Mintage	VF20	XF40	MS60	MS63	MS65
ND-1994	1,000	PF65 1,900				

KM# 679 200 ESCUDOS

Bi-Metallic Copper-Nickel center in Aluminum-Bronze ring, 28 mm. **Subject:** 50th Anniversary - United Nations **Obv:** Shield within globe above value **Rev:** Numeral 50 and emblem in center of puzzle pieces

Date	Mintage	VF20	XF40	MS60	MS63	MS65
1995	500,000	—	—	—	5.00	7.00
1995	17,000	PF65 20.00				

KM# 681 200 ESCUDOS

Copper-Nickel, 36 mm. **Obv:** Shield and globe above date and value **Rev:** Armored standing figure

Date	Mintage	VF20	XF40	MS60	MS63	MS65
1995	750,000	—	—	—	5.00	7.00

KM# 681a 200 ESCUDOS

26.50 g., 0.925 Silver 0.7881 oz. ASW, 36 mm. **Obv:** Shield and globe above date and value **Rev:** Armored standing figure

Date	Mintage	VF20	XF40	MS60	MS63	MS65
1995	20,000	—	—	—	27.00	30.00
1995	13,000	PF65 32.50				

KM# 681b 200 ESCUDOS

27.20 g., 0.917 Gold 0.8019 oz. AGW **Obv:** Shield and globe above date and value **Rev:** Armored standing figure

Date	Mintage	VF20	XF40	MS60	MS63	MS65
1995	4,000	PF65 1,450				

KM# 682 200 ESCUDOS

Copper-Nickel, 36 mm. **Obv:** Shield, value, fruit sprig and flower sprig **Rev:** Moluca Islands and ship

Date	Mintage	VF20	XF40	MS60	MS63	MS65
1995	750,000	—	—	—	5.00	7.00

KM# 682a 200 ESCUDOS

26.50 g., 0.925 Silver 0.7881 oz. ASW, 36 mm. **Obv:** Shield, value, fruit sprig and flower sprig **Rev:** Moluca Islands and ship

Date	Mintage	VF20	XF40	MS60	MS63	MS65
1995	20,000	—	—	—	27.00	30.00
1995	13,000	PF65 35.00				

KM# 682b 200 ESCUDOS

27.20 g., 0.917 Gold 0.8019 oz. AGW **Obv:** Shield, value, fruit sprig and flower sprig **Rev:** Moluca Islands and ship

Date	Mintage	VF20	XF40	MS60	MS63	MS65
1995	4,000	PF65 1,450				

KM# 682c 200 ESCUDOS

31.12 g., 0.9995 Palladium 1.000 oz. APW **Obv:** Shield, value, fruit sprig and flower sprig **Rev:** Moluca Islands and ship

Date	Mintage	VF20	XF40	MS60	MS63	MS65
1995	1,000	PF65 850				

KM# 683 200 ESCUDOS

Copper-Nickel, 36 mm. **Obv:** Tree, ship and shield **Rev:** Solor and Timor Islands

Date	Mintage	VF20	XF40	MS60	MS63	MS65
1995	750,000	—	—	—	5.00	7.00

KM# 683a 200 ESCUDOS

26.50 g., 0.925 Silver 0.7881 oz. ASW, 36 mm. **Obv:** Shield, tree and ship **Rev:** Solor and Timor Islands

Date	Mintage	VF20	XF40	MS60	MS63	MS65
1995	20,000	—	—	—	27.00	30.00
1995	13,000	PF65 35.00				

KM# 683b 200 ESCUDOS
27.20 g., 0.917 Gold 0.8019 oz. AGW **Obv:** Ship, tree and shield **Rev:** Solor and Timor Islands

Date	Mintage	VF20	XF40	MS60	MS63	MS65
1995	4,000	PF65 1,450				

KM# 684 200 ESCUDOS
Copper-Nickel, 36 mm. **Obv:** Shield, dates, globe and value **Rev:** Map and ships

Date	Mintage	VF20	XF40	MS60	MS63	MS65
1995	750,000	—	—	—	5.00	7.00

KM# 684a 200 ESCUDOS
26.50 g., 0.925 Silver 0.7881 oz. ASW, 36 mm. **Obv:** Shield, dates, globe and value **Rev:** Map and ships

Date	Mintage	VF20	XF40	MS60	MS63	MS65
1995	20,000	—	—	—	27.00	30.00
1995	13,000	PF65 35.00				

KM# 684b 200 ESCUDOS
27.20 g., 0.917 Gold 0.8019 oz. AGW **Obv:** Shield, dates, globe and value **Rev:** Map and ships

Date	Mintage	VF20	XF40	MS60	MS63	MS65
1995	4,000	PF65 1,450				

KM# 684c 200 ESCUDOS
31.12 g., 0.9995 Platinum 1.000 oz. APW **Obv:** Shield, dates, globe and value **Rev:** Map and ships

Date	Mintage	VF20	XF40	MS60	MS63	MS65
1995	1,000	PF65 1,900				

KM# 687 200 ESCUDOS
Bi-Metallic Copper-Nickel center in Brass ring, 28 mm. **Series:** Olympics **Subject:** XXVI Olympic Games Atlanta **Obv:** Shield, value and olympic circles **Obv. Legend:** REPUBLICA PORTUGUESA **Rev:** High jumper **Rev. Legend:** XXVI JOGOS OLIMPICOS 1896 Atlanta 1996 **Edge:** Segmented reeding

Date	Mintage	VF20	XF40	MS60	MS63	MS65
1996 INCM	1,000,000	—	—	3.00	5.00	7.00
1996 INCM	7,000	PF65 20.00				

KM# 687a 200 ESCUDOS
26.45 g., 0.925 Silver 0.7866 oz. ASW **Series:** Olympics **Obv:** Shield, value and olympic circles **Rev:** High jumper

Date	Mintage	VF20	XF40	MS60	MS63	MS65
1996	20,000	PF65 50.00				

KM# 689 200 ESCUDOS
Copper-Nickel, 36 mm. **Subject:** 1512 Portugal - Siam Alliance **Obv:** Ship, shield, dates and value **Rev:** Portuguese and Siamese arms

Date	Mintage	VF20	XF40	MS60	MS63	MS65
1996	—	—	—	—	5.00	7.00

KM# 689a 200 ESCUDOS
26.50 g., 0.925 Silver 0.7881 oz. ASW, 36 mm. **Subject:** 1512 Portugal - Siam Alliance **Obv:** Ship, shield, dates and value **Rev:** Portuguese and Siamese arms

Date	Mintage	VF20	XF40	MS60	MS63	MS65
1996	11,000	PF65 32.50				
1996	20,000	—	—	—	27.00	30.00

KM# 689b 200 ESCUDOS
27.20 g., 0.917 Gold 0.8019 oz. AGW **Subject:** 1512 Portugal - Siam Alliance **Obv:** Ship, shield, dates and value **Rev:** Portuguese and Siamese arms

Date	Mintage	VF20	XF40	MS60	MS63	MS65
1996	3,000	PF65 1,450				

KM# 690 200 ESCUDOS
Copper-Nickel, 36 mm. **Subject:** 1513 Portuguese Arrival in China **Obv:** Shield within globe flanked by leafy sprigs **Rev:** Ship, map and building

Date	Mintage	VF20	XF40	MS60	MS63	MS65
1996	—	—	—	—	5.00	7.00

KM# 690a 200 ESCUDOS
26.50 g., 0.925 Silver 0.7881 oz. ASW, 36 mm. **Subject:** 1513 Portuguese Arrival in China **Obv:** Shield within globe flanked by leafy sprigs **Rev:** Ship, map and building

Date	Mintage	VF20	XF40	MS60	MS63	MS65
1996	10,000	PF65 40.00				
1996	20,000	—	—	—	30.00	32.50

KM# 690b 200 ESCUDOS
27.20 g., 0.9166 Gold 0.8016 oz. AGW **Subject:** 1513 Portuguese Arrival in China **Obv:** Shield within globe flanked by leafy sprigs **Rev:** Ship, map and building

Date	Mintage	VF20	XF40	MS60	MS63	MS65
1996	3,000	PF65 1,450				

KM# 690c 200 ESCUDOS
31.12 g., 0.9995 Palladium 1.000 oz. APW **Subject:** 1513 Portuguese Arrival in China **Obv:** Shield within globe flanked by leafy sprigs **Rev:** Ship, map and building

Date	Mintage	VF20	XF40	MS60	MS63	MS65
1996	1,000	PF65 850				

KM# 691 200 ESCUDOS
Copper-Nickel, 36 mm. **Subject:** 1557 Portuguese Establishment in Macau **Obv:** Shield at upper left above building **Rev:** Building at upper left of ship

Date	Mintage	VF20	XF40	MS60	MS63	MS65
1996	—	—	—	—	5.00	7.00

KM# 691a 200 ESCUDOS
26.50 g., 0.925 Silver 0.7881 oz. ASW, 36 mm. **Subject:** 1557 Portuguese Establishment in Macau **Obv:** Shield at upper left above building **Rev:** Building at upper left of ship

Date	Mintage	VF20	XF40	MS60	MS63	MS65
1996	20,000	—	—	—	27.00	30.00
1996	10,000	PF65 32.50				

KM# 691b 200 ESCUDOS
27.20 g., 0.9166 Gold 0.8016 oz. AGW **Subject:** 1557 Portuguese establishment in Macau **Obv:** Shield at upper left above building **Rev:** Building at upper left of ship

Date	Mintage	VF20	XF40	MS60	MS63	MS65
1996	4,000	PF65 1,450				

KM# 692 200 ESCUDOS
Copper-Nickel, 36 mm. **Subject:** 1582 Portuguese Discovery of Taiwan **Obv:** Flower sprig to left of shield **Rev:** Ship

Date	Mintage	VF20	XF40	MS60	MS63	MS65
1996	—	—	—	—	5.00	7.00

KM# 692a 200 ESCUDOS
26.50 g., 0.925 Silver 0.7881 oz. ASW, 36 mm. **Subject:** 1582 Portuguese Discovery of Taiwan **Obv:** Flower sprig to left of shield **Rev:** Ship

Date	Mintage	VF20	XF40	MS60	MS63	MS65
1996	20,000	—	—	—	27.00	30.00
1996	10,000	PF65 32.50				

KM# 692b 200 ESCUDOS
27.20 g., 0.9166 Gold 0.8016 oz. AGW **Subject:** 1582 Portuguese Discovery of Taiwan **Obv:** Flower sprig to left of shield **Rev:** Ship

Date	Mintage	VF20	XF40	MS60	MS63	MS65
1996	3,000	PF65 1,450				

KM# 692c 200 ESCUDOS
31.12 g., 0.9995 Platinum 1.000 oz. APW **Subject:** 1582 Portuguese Discovery of Taiwan **Obv:** Flower sprig to left of shield **Rev:** Ship

Date	Mintage	VF20	XF40	MS60	MS63	MS65
1996	1,000	PF65 1,900				

KM# 694 200 ESCUDOS
9.73 g., Bi-Metallic Copper-Nickel center in Copper-Aluminum ring, 28 mm. **Subject:** Lisbon World Expo '98 **Obv:** Shield and value within circle **Obv. Legend:** REPUBLICA PORTUGUESA **Rev:** Dolphins **Rev. Legend:** EXPOSICÃO MUNDIAL DE LISBOA - EXPO'98 **Edge:** Segmented reeding

Date	Mintage	VF20	XF40	MS60	MS63	MS65
1997 INCM	—	—	—	—	5.00	7.00
1997 INCM	7,000	PF65 20.00				

KM# 697 200 ESCUDOS
Copper-Nickel, 36 mm. **Obv:** National arms **Rev:** S. Francisco Xavier

Date	Mintage	VF20	XF40	MS60	MS63	MS65
1997	—	—	—	—	5.00	7.00

KM# 697a 200 ESCUDOS
26.50 g., 0.925 Silver 0.7881 oz. ASW, 36 mm. **Obv:** National arms **Rev:** S. Francisco Xavier

Date	Mintage	VF20	XF40	MS60	MS63	MS65
1997	25,000	—	—	—	27.00	30.00
1997	25,000	PF65 32.50				

KM# 697b 200 ESCUDOS
27.20 g., 0.9167 Gold 0.8017 oz. AGW **Obv:** National arms **Rev:** St. Francis Xavier

Date	Mintage	VF20	XF40	MS60	MS63	MS65
1997	4,000	PF65 1,450				

KM# 698 200 ESCUDOS
Copper-Nickel, 36 mm. **Obv:** Shield to left of designs and value **Rev:** Two seated figures talking

Date	Mintage	VF20	XF40	MS60	MS63	MS65
1997	—	—	—	—	5.00	7.00

KM# 698a 200 ESCUDOS
26.50 g., 0.925 Silver 0.7881 oz. ASW, 36 mm. **Obv:** Shield to left of designs and value **Rev:** Two seated figures talking

Date	Mintage	VF20	XF40	MS60	MS63	MS65
1997	25,000	—	—	—	27.00	30.00
1997	24,000	PF65 32.50				

KM# 698b 200 ESCUDOS
27.20 g., 0.9167 Gold 0.8017 oz. AGW **Obv:** Shield to left of designs and value **Rev:** Two seated figures talking

Date	Mintage	VF20	XF40	MS60	MS63	MS65
1997	5,000	PF65 1,450				

KM# 699 200 ESCUDOS
Copper-Nickel, 36 mm. **Obv:** Shield and map of South America **Rev:** Bto. Jose de Anchieta

Date	Mintage	VF20	XF40	MS60	MS63	MS65
1997	650,000	—	—	—	5.00	7.00

KM# 699a 200 ESCUDOS
26.50 g., 0.925 Silver 0.7881 oz. ASW, 36 mm. **Obv:** Shield and map of South America **Rev:** Bto. Jose de Anchieta

Date	Mintage	VF20	XF40	MS60	MS63	MS65
1997	25,000	—	—	—	27.00	30.00
1997	24,000	PF65 32.50				

KM# 699b 200 ESCUDOS
27.20 g., 0.9167 Gold 0.8017 oz. AGW **Obv:** Shield and map of South America **Rev:** Bto. Jose de Anchieta

Date	Mintage	VF20	XF40	MS60	MS63	MS65
1997	4,000	PF65 1,450				

KM# 699c 200 ESCUDOS
31.12 g., 0.9995 Palladium 1.000 oz. APW **Obv:** Shield and map of South America **Rev:** Bto. Jose de Anchieta

Date	Mintage	VF20	XF40	MS60	MS63	MS65
1997	1,000	PF65 850				

KM# 700 200 ESCUDOS
Copper-Nickel, 36 mm. **Obv:** National cross and shield **Rev:** Irmao Bento de Gois, map of China's coast

Date	Mintage	VF20	XF40	MS60	MS63	MS65
1997	—	—	—	—	5.00	7.00

KM# 700a 200 ESCUDOS
26.50 g., 0.925 Silver 0.7881 oz. ASW, 36 mm. **Obv:** National cross and shield **Rev:** Irmao Bento de Gois, map of China's coast

Date	Mintage	VF20	XF40	MS60	MS63	MS65
1997	25,000	—	—	—	27.00	30.00
1997	24,000	PF65 32.50				

KM# 700b 200 ESCUDOS
27.20 g., 0.916 Gold 0.801 oz. AGW **Obv:** National cross and shield **Rev:** Irmao Bento de Gois, map of China's coast

Date	Mintage	VF20	XF40	MS60	MS63	MS65
1997	4,000	PF65 1,450				

KM# 700c 200 ESCUDOS
31.12 g., 0.9995 Platinum 1.000 oz. APW **Obv:** National cross and shield **Rev:** Irmao Bento de Gois, map of China's coast

Date	Mintage	VF20	XF40	MS60	MS63	MS65
1997	1,000	PF65 1,900				

KM# 706 200 ESCUDOS
Bi-Metallic Copper-Nickel center in Aluminum-Bronze ring, 28 mm. **Subject:** International Year of the Oceans Expo **Obv:** Small shield within sprigs above value **Rev:** Expo 98 and fish within sprigs

Date	Mintage	VF20	XF40	MS60	MS63	MS65
1998	Est. 50000	—	—	—	4.00	6.00
1998	Est. 20000	PF65 12.00				

KM# 709 200 ESCUDOS
Copper-Nickel, 36 mm. **Obv:** Three ships, shield, and value **Rev:** Portrait of Vasco Da Gama, dates

Date	Mintage	VF20	XF40	MS60	MS63	MS65
1998	—	—	—	—	5.00	7.00

KM# 709a 200 ESCUDOS
26.50 g., 0.925 Silver 0.7881 oz. ASW, 36 mm. **Obv:** Three ships, shield, and value **Rev:** Bust of Vasco da Gama left, dates

Date	Mintage	VF20	XF40	MS60	MS63	MS65
1998	—	—	—	—	27.00	30.00
1998	25,000	PF65 32.50				

KM# 709b 200 ESCUDOS
27.20 g., 0.9167 Gold 0.8017 oz. AGW **Obv:** Three ships, shield, and value **Rev:** Bust of Vasco da Gama left, dates

Date	Mintage	VF20	XF40	MS60	MS63	MS65
1998	5,000	PF65 1,450				

KM# 709c 200 ESCUDOS
31.12 g., 0.9995 Platinum 1.000 oz. APW **Obv:** Three ships, shield, and value **Rev:** Bust of Vasco da Gama, dates

Date	Mintage	VF20	XF40	MS60	MS63	MS65
1998	1,000	PF65 1,900				

KM# 710 200 ESCUDOS
Copper-Nickel, 36 mm. **Subject:** Discovery of Africa **Obv:** Shield, ship, and palm tree **Rev:** Ship, map, and hunter

Date	Mintage	VF20	XF40	MS60	MS63	MS65
1998	—	—	—	—	5.00	7.00

KM# 710a 200 ESCUDOS
26.50 g., 0.925 Silver 0.7881 oz. ASW, 36 mm. **Subject:** Discovery of Africa **Obv:** Shield, ship, and palm tree **Rev:** Ship, map, and hunter

Date	Mintage	VF20	XF40	MS60	MS63	MS65
1998	26,000	PF65 32.50				
1998	25,000	—	—	—	27.00	30.00

KM# 710b 200 ESCUDOS
27.20 g., 0.9167 Gold 0.8017 oz. AGW **Subject:** Discovery of Africa **Obv:** Shield, ship, and palm tree **Rev:** Ship, map, and hunter

Date	Mintage	VF20	XF40	MS60	MS63	MS65
1998	5,000	PF65 1,450				

KM# 711 200 ESCUDOS
Copper-Nickel, 36 mm. **Subject:** Mozambique **Obv:** Shield above mermaid **Rev:** Two ships and island map

Date	Mintage	VF20	XF40	MS60	MS63	MS65
1998	—	—	—	—	5.00	7.00

KM# 711a 200 ESCUDOS
26.50 g., 0.925 Silver 0.7881 oz. ASW, 36 mm. **Subject:** Mozambique **Obv:** Shield above mermaid **Rev:** Two ships and island map

Date	Mintage	VF20	XF40	MS60	MS63	MS65
1998	25,000	—	—	—	27.00	30.00
1998	25,000	PF65 32.50				

KM# 711b 200 ESCUDOS
27.20 g., 0.9167 Gold 0.8017 oz. AGW **Subject:** Mozambique **Obv:** Shield above mermaid **Rev:** Two ships and island map

Date	Mintage	VF20	XF40	MS60	MS63	MS65
1998	6,000	PF65 1,450				

KM# 712 200 ESCUDOS
Copper-Nickel, 36 mm. **Subject:** India 1498 **Obv:** Shield and sailing ship **Rev:** Ship and coastal map of India

Date	Mintage	VF20	XF40	MS60	MS63	MS65
1998	—	—	—	—	5.00	7.00

KM# 712a 200 ESCUDOS
26.50 g., 0.925 Silver 0.7881 oz. ASW, 36 mm. **Subject:** India 1498 **Obv:** Shield and sailing ship **Rev:** Ship and coastal map of India

Date	Mintage	VF20	XF40	MS60	MS63	MS65
1998	25,000	—	—	—	27.00	30.00
1998	25,000	PF65 32.50				

KM# 712b 200 ESCUDOS
27.20 g., 0.9167 Gold 0.8017 oz. AGW **Subject:** India 1498 **Obv:** Shield and sailing ship **Rev:** Ship and coastal map of India

Date	Mintage	VF20	XF40	MS60	MS63	MS65
1998	5,000	PF65 1,450				

KM# 712c 200 ESCUDOS
31.12 g., 0.9995 Palladium 1.000 oz. APW **Subject:** India 1498 **Obv:** Shield and sailing ship **Rev:** Ship and coastal map of India

Date	Mintage	VF20	XF40	MS60	MS63	MS65
1998	1,000	PF65 850				

KM# 716 200 ESCUDOS
Copper-Nickel, 36 mm. **Subject:** Death on the Sea **Obv:** Shield, globe and ropes **Rev:** Stylized sinking ship **Edge:** Reeded

Date	Mintage	VF20	XF40	MS60	MS63	MS65
1999 INCM	—	—	—	—	3.50	5.00

KM# 716a 200 ESCUDOS
26.50 g., 0.925 Silver 0.7881 oz. ASW, 36 mm. **Subject:** Death on the Sea **Obv:** Shield, globe and ropes **Rev:** Stylized sinking ship **Edge:** Reeded

Date	Mintage	VF20	XF40	MS60	MS63	MS65
1999 INCM	10,000	—	—	—	27.00	30.00
1999 INCM	10,000	PF65 35.00				

KM# 716b 200 ESCUDOS
27.20 g., 0.9167 Gold 0.8017 oz. AGW, 36 mm. **Subject:** Death on the Sea **Obv:** Shield, globe and ropes **Rev:** Stylized sinking ship **Edge:** Reeded

Date	Mintage	VF20	XF40	MS60	MS63	MS65
1999 INCM	1,000	PF65 1,450				

KM# 716c 200 ESCUDOS
31.12 g., 0.9995 Platinum 1.000 oz. APW, 36 mm. **Subject:** Portuguese Discoveries - Morte no Mar

Date	Mintage	VF20	XF40	MS60	MS63	MS65
1999	Est. 500	PF65 1,450				

KM# 717 200 ESCUDOS
Copper-Nickel, 36 mm. **Subject:** Pedro Alvares Cabral - Brasil 1500 **Obv:** Fleet of sailing ships **Rev:** Bust right superimposed on map of South American coastline, anchor marks spot of Porto Seguro **Edge:** Reeded

Date	Mintage	VF20	XF40	MS60	MS63	MS65
1999	—	—	—	—	3.50	5.00

KM# 717a 200 ESCUDOS
26.50 g., 0.925 Silver 0.7881 oz. ASW, 36 mm. **Subject:** Brasil 1500 **Obv:** Fleet of sailing ships **Rev:** Head right

Date	Mintage	VF20	XF40	MS60	MS63	MS65
1999	1,000	—	—	—	27.00	30.00
1999	1,000	PF65 35.00				

KM# 717b 200 ESCUDOS
27.20 g., 0.9167 Gold 0.8017 oz. AGW **Subject:** Brasil 1500 **Obv:** Fleet of sailing ships **Rev:** Head right

Date	Mintage	VF20	XF40	MS60	MS63	MS65
1999	1,000	PF65 1,450				

KM# 717c 200 ESCUDOS
31.12 g., 0.9995 Palladium 1.000 oz. APW, 36 mm. **Subject:** Portuguese discoveries - Brazil **Rev:** Pedro Alvares Cabral and outline map of Brazil

Date	Mintage	VF20	XF40	MS60	MS63	MS65
1999	Est. 500	PF65 1,450				

KM# 718 200 ESCUDOS
Copper-Nickel, 36 mm. **Subject:** Brasil **Obv:** Natives, palm trees, arms at right superimposed on coastline map of Brazil **Rev:** Ship, native, and map **Edge:** Reeded

Date	Mintage	VF20	XF40	MS60	MS63	MS65
1999	—	—	—	—	3.50	5.00

KM# 718a 200 ESCUDOS
26.50 g., 0.925 Silver 0.7881 oz. ASW, 36 mm. **Subject:** Brasil **Obv:** Natives, palm trees **Rev:** Ship, native, and map

Date	Mintage	VF20	XF40	MS60	MS63	MS65
1999	Est. 10000	—	—	—	27.00	30.00
1999	Est. 10000	PF65 35.00				

KM# 718b 200 ESCUDOS
27.20 g., 0.9167 Gold 0.8017 oz. AGW **Subject:** Brasil **Obv:** Natives and palm trees **Rev:** Ship, native, and map

Date	Mintage	VF20	XF40	MS60	MS63	MS65
1999	1,000	PF65 1,450				

KM# 719 200 ESCUDOS
Copper-Nickel, 36 mm. **Subject:** Duarte Pacheco Pereira **Obv:** Arms above sailing ships, value below **Rev:** Armored half-length bust facing **Edge:** Reeded

Date	Mintage	VF20	XF40	MS60	MS63	MS65
1999	—	—	—	—	3.50	5.00

KM# 719a 200 ESCUDOS
26.50 g., 0.925 Silver 0.7881 oz. ASW, 36 mm. **Subject:** Duarte Pacheco Pereira **Rev:** Armored half-length bust facing

Date	Mintage	VF20	XF40	MS60	MS63	MS65
1999	1,000	—	—	—	27.00	30.00
1999	1,000	PF65 35.00				

KM# 719b 200 ESCUDOS
27.20 g., 0.9167 Gold 0.8017 oz. AGW **Subject:** Duarte Pacheco Pereira **Rev:** Armored half-length bust facing

Date	Mintage	VF20	XF40	MS60	MS63	MS65
1999	1,000	PF65 1,450				

KM# 720 200 ESCUDOS
Bi-Metallic Copper-Nickel center in Brass ring, 28 mm. **Obv:** Shield within globe above value **Rev:** Stylized dove on wheels and logo **Edge:** Segmented reeding

Date	Mintage	VF20	XF40	MS60	MS63	MS65
1999 INCM	—	—	—	—	6.50	7.50

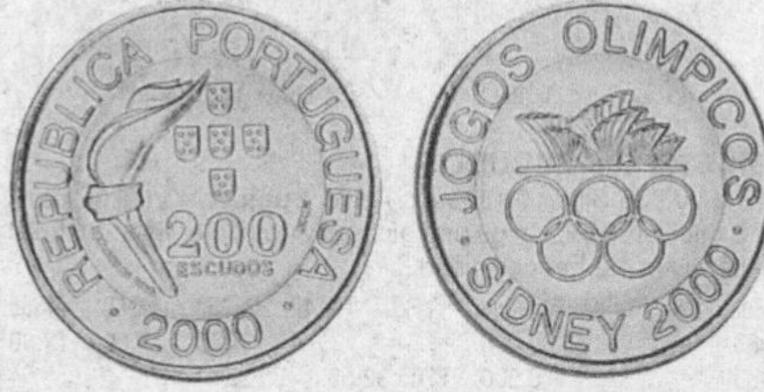

KM# 726 200 ESCUDOS
Bi-Metallic Copper-Nickel center in Nickel-Brass ring, 28 mm. **Obv:** Torch, cross design and value **Rev:** Olympic logo **Edge:** Reeded and plain sections

Date	Mintage	VF20	XF40	MS60	MS63	MS65
2000 INCM	10,000	—	—	—	3.50	5.00
2000 INCM	5,000	PF65 8.00				

KM# 728 200 ESCUDOS
21.10 g., Copper-Nickel, 36 mm. **Subject:** Terra Do Lavrado **Obv:** Compass and shield **Rev:** Labrador coast and ship **Edge:** Reeded

Date	Mintage	VF20	XF40	MS60	MS63	MS65
2000 INCM	—	—	—	—	3.50	5.00

KM# 728a 200 ESCUDOS
26.50 g., 0.925 Silver 0.7881 oz. ASW, 36 mm. **Subject:** Terra do Lavrado **Obv:** Shield and compass **Rev:** Labrador coast and ship **Edge:** Reeded

Date	Mintage	VF20	XF40	MS60	MS63	MS65
2000	Est. 10000	—	—	—	27.00	30.00
2000	Est. 10000	PF65 37.50				

KM# 728b 200 ESCUDOS
27.20 g., 0.9166 Gold 0.8016 oz. AGW, 36 mm. **Subject:** Terra do Lavrado **Obv:** Shield and compass **Rev:** Labrador coast and ship **Edge:** Reeded

Date	Mintage	VF20	XF40	MS60	MS63	MS65
2000	Est. 1375	PF65 1,450				

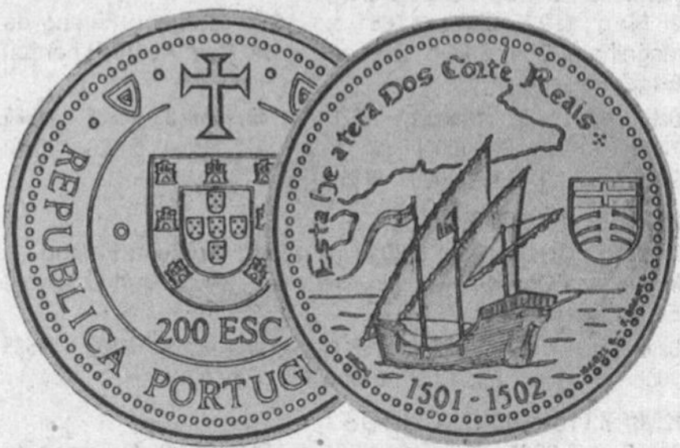

KM# 729 200 ESCUDOS
21.14 g., Copper-Nickel, 36 mm. **Subject:** Terra Dos Corte-Real **Obv:** Cross above shield **Rev:** Ship above 1501-1502 **Edge:** Reeded

Date	Mintage	VF20	XF40	MS60	MS63	MS65
2000 INCM	—	—	—	—	3.50	5.00

KM# 729a 200 ESCUDOS
26.50 g., 0.925 Silver 0.7881 oz. ASW, 36 mm. **Subject:** Terra Dos Corte-Real **Obv:** Cross above shield **Rev:** Ship above 1501-1502 **Edge:** Reeded

Date	Mintage	VF20	XF40	MS60	MS63	MS65
2000	Est. 10000	—	—	—	27.00	30.00
2000	Est. 10000	PF65 37.50				

KM# 729b 200 ESCUDOS
27.20 g., 0.9166 Gold 0.8016 oz. AGW **Subject:** Terra dos Corte-Real **Obv:** Cross above shield **Rev:** Ship above 1501-1502 **Edge:** Reeded

Date	Mintage	VF20	XF40	MS60	MS63	MS65
2000	Est. 1375	PF65 1,450				

KM# 729c 200 ESCUDOS
31.12 g., 0.9995 Palladium 1.000 oz. APW **Subject:** Terra Dos Corte-Real **Obv:** Cross above shield **Rev:** Ship above 1501-1502 **Edge:** Reeded

Date	Mintage	VF20	XF40	MS60	MS63	MS65
2000	Est. 250	PF65 900				

KM# 730 200 ESCUDOS

21.14 g., Copper-Nickel, 36 mm. **Subject:** Terra Florida **Obv:** Maltese crosses above compass **Rev:** Ship below maltese cross within map **Edge:** Reeded

Date	Mintage	VF20	XF40	MS60	MS63	MS65
2000 INCM	—	—	—	—	3.50	5.00

KM# 730a 200 ESCUDOS

26.50 g., 0.925 Silver 0.7881 oz. ASW **Subject:** Terra Florida **Obv:** Maltese crosses above compass **Rev:** Ship below maltese cross within map **Edge:** Reeded

Date	Mintage	VF20	XF40	MS60	MS63	MS65
2000	Est. 10000	—	—	—	27.00	30.00
2000	Est. 10000	PF65 37.50				

KM# 730b 200 ESCUDOS

27.20 g., 0.9166 Gold 0.8016 oz. AGW **Obv:** Maltese crosses above compass **Rev:** Ship below maltese cross within map **Edge:** Reeded **Edge Lettering:** Terra Florida

Date	Mintage	VF20	XF40	MS60	MS63	MS65
2000	Est. 1375	PF65 1,450				

KM# 731 200 ESCUDOS

21.14 g., Copper-Nickel, 36 mm. **Subject:** Fernao De Magalhaes **Obv:** Shield, ship, and value **Rev:** Bearded portrait **Edge:** Reeded

Date	Mintage	VF20	XF40	MS60	MS63	MS65
2000 INCM	—	—	—	—	3.50	5.00

KM# 731a 200 ESCUDOS

26.50 g., 0.925 Silver 0.7881 oz. ASW **Subject:** Fernao de Magalhaes **Obv:** Shield, ship, and value **Rev:** Bearded portrait **Edge:** Reeded

Date	Mintage	VF20	XF40	MS60	MS63	MS65
2000	Est. 10000	—	—	—	27.00	30.00
2000	Est. 10000	PF65 37.50				

KM# 731b 200 ESCUDOS

27.20 g., 0.9166 Gold 0.8016 oz. AGW **Subject:** Fernao de Magalhaes **Obv:** Shield, ship, and value **Rev:** Bearded portrait **Edge:** Reeded

Date	Mintage	VF20	XF40	MS60	MS63	MS65
2000	Est. 1375	PF65 1,450				

KM# 731c 200 ESCUDOS

31.12 g., 0.9995 Platinum 1.000 oz. APW **Subject:** Fernao de Magalhaes **Obv:** Shield, ship, and value **Rev:** Bearded portrait **Edge:** Reeded

Date	Mintage	VF20	XF40	MS60	MS63	MS65
2000	Est. 250	PF65 1,900				

KM# 604 250 ESCUDOS

25.00 g., 0.680 Silver 0.5466 oz. ASW, 37 mm. **Subject:** 1974 Revolution **Obv:** Value above cross design within circle **Rev:** Design flanked by dates with value above

Date	Mintage	VF20	XF40	MS60	MS63	MS65
ND-1976	1,000,000	—	—	12.00	20.00	22.00
ND-1976	—	PF65 30.00				

KM# 626 250 ESCUDOS

Copper-Nickel, 37 mm. **Subject:** World Fisheries Conference **Obv:** Shield within horizontal lines **Rev:** Cluster of fish within triangular design facing right **Rev. Legend:** FAO-CONFERENCIA MUNDIAL DE PESCAS 1983-84

Date	Mintage	VF20	XF40	MS60	MS63	MS65
ND-1984 INCM	200,000	—	—	—	22.00	28.00

KM# 626a 250 ESCUDOS

23.00 g., 0.925 Silver 0.684 oz. ASW, 37 mm. **Series:** World Fisheries Conference **Obv:** Shield within horizontal lines **Rev:** Cluster of fish within triangular design facing right **Edge:** Reeded

Date	Mintage	VF20	XF40	MS60	MS63	MS65
ND-1984	8,000	PF63 60.00	PF65 70.00			

KM# 643 250 ESCUDOS

Copper-Nickel, 37 mm. **Subject:** Seoul Olympics **Obv:** Shield in front of lined flower-like design **Rev:** Runners

Date	Mintage	VF20	XF40	MS60	MS63	MS65
1988	850,000	—	—	—	5.00	7.00

KM# 643a 250 ESCUDOS

28.00 g., 0.925 Silver 0.8327 oz. ASW, 37 mm. **Subject:** Seoul Olympics **Obv:** Shield in front of lined flower-like design **Rev:** Runners

Date	Mintage	VF20	XF40	MS60	MS63	MS65
1988	30,000	PF65 40.00				
1988	70,000	—	—	—	28.00	32.00

KM# 650 250 ESCUDOS

Copper-Nickel, 37 mm. **Subject:** 850th Anniversary - Founding of Portugal **Obv:** Small churches in cross formation at left of design **Rev:** Sword divides cresent flanked by dates below design within circle

Date	Mintage	VF20	XF40	MS60	MS63	MS65
1989	750,000	—	—	—	5.00	7.00

KM# 650a 250 ESCUDOS

28.00 g., 0.925 Silver 0.8327 oz. ASW, 37 mm. **Subject:** 850th Anniversary - Founding of Portugal **Obv:** Small churches in cross formation to left of design **Rev:** Sword divides cresent flanked by dates below design within circle

Date	Mintage	VF20	XF40	MS60	MS63	MS65
1989	15,000	—	—	—	28.00	32.00
1989	30,000	PF65 45.00				

KM# 620 500 ESCUDOS

7.00 g., 0.835 Silver 0.1879 oz. ASW **Subject:** XVII European Art Exhibition **Obv:** Cross and globe divides date **Rev:** Stylized castle within 1/2 beaded circle

Date	Mintage	VF20	XF40	MS60	MS63	MS65
1983	200,000	—	—	4.25	7.00	12.00
1983	8,500	PF65 32.50				

KM# 686 500 ESCUDOS

14.00 g., 0.500 Silver 0.2251 oz. ASW **Subject:** 800th Anniversary - Birth of Saint Anthony **Obv:** Castle to left of shield, date and value **Rev:** Seated figure holding cross and book within arch **Note:** Prev. KM686a

Date	Mintage	VF20	XF40	MS60	MS63	MS65
1995	—	—	—	5.00	8.50	10.00

KM# 686b 500 ESCUDOS

14.00 g., 0.925 Silver 0.4164 oz. ASW **Subject:** 800th Anniversary - Birth of Saint Anthony **Obv:** Church to left of shield, date and value **Rev:** Seated figure holding cross and book within arch

Date	Mintage	VF20	XF40	MS60	MS63	MS65
1995	10,000	PF65 45.00				

KM# 686c 500 ESCUDOS

17.50 g., 0.9177 Gold 0.5163 oz. AGW **Subject:** 800th Anniversary - Birth of Saint Anthony **Obv:** Church to left of shield, date and value **Rev:** Seated figure holding cross and book within arch

Date	Mintage	VF20	XF40	MS60	MS63	MS65
1995	5,000	PF65 900				

KM# 702 500 ESCUDOS

13.87 g., 0.500 Silver 0.223 oz. ASW **Obv:** Shield **Rev:** Bank seal - Banco de Portugal

Date	Mintage	VF20	XF40	MS60	MS63	MS65
ND-1996	—	—	—	5.00	8.50	10.00

KM# 701 500 ESCUDOS

14.00 g., 0.500 Silver 0.2251 oz. ASW **Obv:** Shield superimposed on radiant sun **Rev:** Head facing

Date	Mintage	VF20	XF40	MS60	MS63	MS65
ND-1997	—	—	—	5.00	8.50	10.00

KM# 701a 500 ESCUDOS

14.00 g., 0.925 Silver 0.4164 oz. ASW **Obv:** Shield superimposed on radiant sun **Rev:** Head facing

Date	Mintage	VF20	XF40	MS60	MS63	MS65
ND-1997	—	PF65 37.50				

KM# 701b 500 ESCUDOS

Silver and Gold **Obv:** Shield superimposed on radiant sun **Rev:** Head facing **Note:** 14.000 gram, .925 Silver, .4051 ounce with 3.100 gram .9167 gold, .0914 ounce lamination on reverse.

Date	Mintage	VF20	XF40	MS60	MS63	MS65
ND-1997	15,000	PF65 170				

KM# 705 500 ESCUDOS

14.00 g., 0.500 Silver 0.2251 oz. ASW **Obv:** Shield, design within circle and value **Rev:** Bridge

Date	Mintage	VF20	XF40	MS60	MS63	MS65
1998	—	—	—	5.00	8.50	10.00
1998	30,000	PF65 42.50				

KM# 705a 500 ESCUDOS

Bi-Metallic Gold center in Silver ring **Obv:** Shield, design within circle and value **Rev:** Bridge **Note:** 14.000 gram, .925 Silver, .4164 ounce with 3.100 gram .9167 gold, .0914 ounce lamination on reverse.

Date	Mintage	VF20	XF40	MS60	MS63	MS65
1998	15,000	PF65 165				

KM# 723 500 ESCUDOS

14.00 g., 0.500 Silver 0.2251 oz. ASW, 30 mm. **Subject:** Macao's Return to China **Obv:** Partial bridge above shield and value **Rev:** Bridge above monument **Edge:** Reeded

Date	Mintage	VF20	XF40	MS60	MS63	MS65
1999 INCM	—	—	—	5.00	8.50	10.00

KM# 725 500 ESCUDOS

14.00 g., 0.500 Silver 0.2251 oz. ASW **Subject:** Eca de Queiroz, death centennial **Obv:** Portuguese national shield in center flanked by laurel leaves **Obv. Legend:** REPUBLICA PORTUGUESA CENTENARIO DA MORTE DE EÇA DE QUEIROZ **Rev:** Portrait of Eça de Queiroz facing left **Rev. Legend:** EÇA DE QUEIROZ 1900 2000 **Edge:** Reeded

Date	Mintage	VF20	XF40	MS60	MS63	MS65
ND-2000 INCM	500,000	—	—	5.00	9.00	11.00
ND-2000 INCM	10,000	PF65 45.00				

KM# 725a 500 ESCUDOS

17.10 g., Bi-Metallic 14.000 gram, .925 Silver, .4164 ASW with 3.100 gram .9167 gold, .100 AGW lamination on reverse., 30 mm. **Subject:** Eca de Queiroz **Obv:** Shield flanked by sprigs above value **Rev:** Stylized portrait left **Edge:** Reeded

Date	Mintage	VF20	XF40	MS60	MS63	MS65
ND-2000	10,000	PF65 190				

KM# 621 750 ESCUDOS

12.50 g., 0.835 Silver 0.3356 oz. ASW **Subject:** XVII European Art Exhibition **Obv:** Cross and globe divides date **Rev:** Crowned shield within circle

Date	Mintage	VF20	XF40	MS60	MS63	MS65
1983	200,000	—	6.25	9.00	15.00	18.00
1983	8,500	PF65 40.00				

KM# 611 1000 ESCUDOS

17.00 g., 0.925 Silver 0.5056 oz. ASW, 34 mm. **Subject:** 400th Anniversary - Death of Louis de Camoes **Obv:** Shield within globe above sprig **Rev:** Armored bust 1/4 right flanked by dates **Rev. Legend:** IV CENTENARIO DA MORTE DE CAMOES

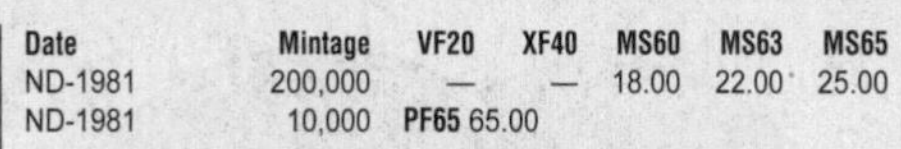

Date	Mintage	VF20	XF40	MS60	MS63	MS65
ND-1981	200,000	—	—	18.00	22.00	25.00
ND-1981	10,000	PF65 65.00				

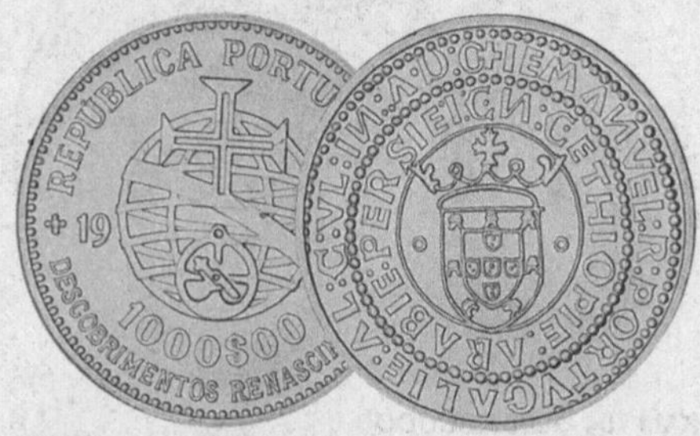

KM# 622 1000 ESCUDOS

21.00 g., 0.835 Silver 0.5638 oz. ASW **Subject:** XVII European Art Exhibition **Obv:** Cross and globe divides date **Rev:** Crowned shield within center circle

Date	Mintage	VF20	XF40	MS60	MS63	MS65
1983	200,000	—	—	18.00	22.00	25.00
1983	8,500	PF65 50.00				

KM# 657 1000 ESCUDOS

27.00 g., 0.500 Silver 0.434 oz. ASW **Series:** Ibero - American **Obv:** Shield within globe in center of assorted emblems around border **Rev:** Ship and assorted emblems within map and circle

Date	Mintage	VF20	XF40	MS60	MS63	MS65
ND-1992 INCM	326,000	—	—	18.00	22.00	25.00

KM# 657a 1000 ESCUDOS

27.00 g., 0.925 Silver 0.803 oz. ASW **Series:** Ibero - American **Obv:** Shield within globe in center of assorted emblems around border **Rev:** Ship and assorted emblems within circle

Date	Mintage	VF20	XF40	MS60	MS63	MS65
ND-1992	30,000	PF65 65.00				

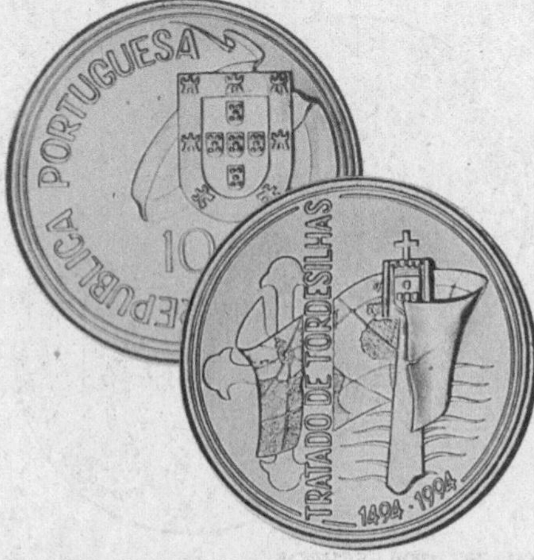

KM# 675 1000 ESCUDOS

28.00 g., 0.500 Silver 0.4501 oz. ASW, 40 mm. **Subject:** Treaty of Tordesilhas **Obv:** Upright design above value **Rev:** Cross on top of shield within mapped scroll

Date	Mintage	VF20	XF40	MS60	MS63	MS65
ND-1994 INCM	570,000	—	—	18.00	22.00	25.00

KM# 675a 1000 ESCUDOS

28.00 g., 0.925 Silver 0.8327 oz. ASW **Subject:** Treaty of Tordesilhas **Obv:** Upright design above value **Rev:** Cross on top of shield within mapped scroll

Date	Mintage	VF20	XF40	MS60	MS63	MS65
ND-1994	10,000	PF65 50.00				

KM# 676 1000 ESCUDOS

28.00 g., 0.500 Silver 0.4501 oz. ASW **Subject:** Endangered Wildlife **Obv:** Shield within globe in center of assorted emblems **Rev:** Gray wolves within circle

Date	Mintage	VF20	XF40	MS60	MS63	MS65
1994	70,000	—	—	—	125	145

KM# 676a 1000 ESCUDOS

28.00 g., 0.925 Silver 0.8327 oz. ASW **Subject:** Endangered Wildlife **Obv:** Shield within globe in center of assorted emblems **Rev:** Grey wolves within circle

Date	Mintage	VF20	XF40	MS60	MS63	MS65
1994	30,000	PF65 150				

KM# 685 1000 ESCUDOS

28.00 g., 0.500 Silver 0.4501 oz. ASW, 40 mm. **Subject:** 500th Anniversary - Death of John II **Obv:** Design within circle **Obv. Legend:** REPUBLICA PORTUGUESA **Rev:** Head right and 1/2 of ship **Rev. Legend:** D. JOÃO II : REI DE PORTUGAL : 1495-1995

Date	Mintage	VF20	XF40	MS60	MS63	MS65
ND-1995 INCM	600,000	—	—	18.00	22.00	25.00

KM# 685a 1000 ESCUDOS

28.00 g., 0.925 Silver 0.8327 oz. ASW **Subject:** 500th Anniversary - Death of John II **Obv:** Design within circle **Rev:** Head right and 1/2 of ship

Date	Mintage	VF20	XF40	MS60	MS63	MS65
ND-1995	15,000	PF65 45.00				

KM# 688 1000 ESCUDOS

28.00 g., 0.500 Silver 0.4501 oz. ASW **Subject:** Restoration of the Frigate Ferdinand II and Gloria **Obv:** Shield, figure head, ship's hull **Rev:** Ship below two facing busts

Date	Mintage	VF20	XF40	MS60	MS63	MS65
ND-1996	600,000	PF65 25.00				

KM# 688a 1000 ESCUDOS

28.00 g., 0.925 Silver 0.8327 oz. ASW **Subject:** Restoration of the Frigate Ferdinand II and Gloria **Obv:** Shield, figure head, ship's hull **Rev:** Two facing busts above ship

Date	Mintage	VF20	XF40	MS60	MS63	MS65
ND-1996	15,000	PF65 50.00				

KM# 696 1000 ESCUDOS
28.00 g., 0.500 Silver 0.4501 oz. ASW, 40 mm. **Subject:** N. S. Da Conceicao Padroeira de Portugal **Obv:** Shield **Obv. Legend:** REPUBLICA PORTUGUESA 1996 **Rev:** Madonna and child **Rev. Legend:** N.S.DA CONCEICAO PADROEIRA DE PORTUGAL

Date	Mintage	VF20	XF40	MS60	MS63	MS65
ND-1996 INCM	620,000	—	—	18.00	22.00	25.00

KM# 696a 1000 ESCUDOS
28.00 g., 0.925 Silver 0.8327 oz. ASW **Subject:** N. S. Da Conceicao Padroeira de Portugal **Obv:** Shield **Rev:** Madonna and child

Date	Mintage	VF20	XF40	MS60	MS63	MS65
ND(1996)	—	PF65 50.00				

KM# 695 1000 ESCUDOS
28.00 g., 0.500 Silver 0.4501 oz. ASW **Subject:** 100th Anniversary - Portuguese Oceanic Expedition **Obv:** Shield and fish **Rev:** Ship below two facing busts

Date	Mintage	VF20	XF40	MS60	MS63	MS65
1997	—	—	—	18.00	22.00	25.00

KM# 695a 1000 ESCUDOS
28.00 g., 0.925 Silver 0.8327 oz. ASW **Subject:** 100th Anniversary - Portuguese Oceanic Expedition **Obv:** Shield and fish **Rev:** Two busts above ship

Date	Mintage	VF20	XF40	MS60	MS63	MS65
1997	Est. 15000	PF65 55.00				

KM# 703 1000 ESCUDOS
28.00 g., 0.500 Silver 0.4501 oz. ASW, 40 mm. **Subject:** Credito Publico **Obv:** Shield within hexagonal design **Obv. Legend:** REPUBLICA PORTUGUESA **Rev:** Hexagonal design **Rev. Legend:** IGCP II CENTENÁRIO DO CRÉDITO PÚBLICO

Date	Mintage	VF20	XF40	MS60	MS63	MS65
1997 INCM	320,000	—	—	18.00	22.00	25.00

KM# 703a 1000 ESCUDOS
28.00 g., 0.925 Silver 0.8327 oz. ASW, 40 mm. **Subject:** Credito Publico **Obv:** Shield within hexagonal design **Obv. Legend:** REPUBLICA PORTUGUESA **Rev:** Hexagonal design **Rev. Legend:** IGCP II CENTENARIO DO CREDITO PUBLICO

Date	Mintage	VF20	XF40	MS60	MS63	MS65
1997 INCM	15,000	PF65 55.00				

KM# 704 1000 ESCUDOS
27.00 g., 0.500 Silver 0.434 oz. ASW **Obv:** Shield within circle of assorted shields **Rev:** Pauliteiros dancers

Date	Mintage	VF20	XF40	MS60	MS63	MS65
1997	—	—	—	18.00	22.00	25.00

KM# 704a 1000 ESCUDOS
27.00 g., 0.925 Silver 0.803 oz. ASW **Obv:** Shield within circle of assorted shields **Rev:** Pauliteiros dancers

Date	Mintage	VF20	XF40	MS60	MS63	MS65
1997	—	PF65 60.00				

KM# 707 1000 ESCUDOS
27.00 g., 0.500 Silver 0.434 oz. ASW, 40 mm. **Subject:** International Year of the Oceans Expo 98 **Obv:** Shield and logo **Rev:** Stylized expo designs

Date	Mintage	VF20	XF40	MS60	MS63	MS65
1998	1,000,000	—	—	18.00	22.00	25.00

KM# 707a 1000 ESCUDOS
27.00 g., 0.925 Silver 0.803 oz. ASW **Subject:** International Year of the Oceans Expo **Obv:** Shield and logo **Rev:** Stylized expo designs

Date	Mintage	VF20	XF40	MS60	MS63	MS65
1998	—	PF65 55.00				

KM# 708 1000 ESCUDOS
27.00 g., 0.500 Silver 0.434 oz. ASW **Subject:** 500th Anniversary - Misericordia Church **Obv:** Basket and rope design **Rev:** Crowned praying figure flanked by cherubs and other figures below

Date	Mintage	VF20	XF40	MS60	MS63	MS65
ND-1998	—	—	—	18.00	22.00	25.00

KM# 708a 1000 ESCUDOS
27.00 g., 0.925 Silver 0.803 oz. ASW **Subject:** 500th Anniversary - Misericordia Church **Obv:** Basket and rope design **Rev:** Crowned praying figure flanked by cherubs and other figures below

Date	Mintage	VF20	XF40	MS60	MS63	MS65
ND-1998	—	PF65 55.00				

KM# 713 1000 ESCUDOS
27.00 g., 0.500 Silver 0.434 oz. ASW **Obv:** Two ships, crowned shield, armillary sphere **Rev:** King Dom Manuel I seated on throne with sword

Date	Mintage	VF20	XF40	MS60	MS63	MS65
1998	—	—	—	18.00	22.00	25.00

KM# 713a 1000 ESCUDOS
27.00 g., 0.925 Silver 0.803 oz. ASW **Obv:** Two ships, crowned shield, armillary sphere **Rev:** King Dom Manuel I seated on throne with sword

Date	Mintage	VF20	XF40	MS60	MS63	MS65
1998	Est. 15000	PF65 55.00				

KM# 714 1000 ESCUDOS
27.00 g., 0.500 Silver 0.434 oz. ASW, 40 mm. **Subject:** 75th Anniversary - League of Combatants **Obv:** Stylized shield **Obv. Legend:** REPUBLICA PORTUGUESA **Rev:** Sword and laurel branch **Rev. Legend:** LIGA DOS COMBATENTES 1923 1998

Date	Mintage	VF20	XF40	MS60	MS63	MS65
1998 INCM	500,000	—	—	18.00	22.00	25.00

KM# 714a 1000 ESCUDOS
27.00 g., 0.925 Silver 0.803 oz. ASW **Subject:** 75th Anniversary - League of Combatants **Obv:** Stylized shield **Rev:** Sword and laurel branch

Date	Mintage	VF20	XF40	MS60	MS63	MS65
1998	—	PF65 55.00				

KM# 715 1000 ESCUDOS
27.00 g., 0.500 Silver 0.434 oz. ASW **Subject:** 25th Anniversary - Revolution of April 25 **Obv:** Circles within cross design above value and date **Rev:** Date and mirrored anniversary number

Date	Mintage	VF20	XF40	MS60	MS63	MS65
1999	—	—	—	18.00	22.00	25.00

KM# 715a 1000 ESCUDOS
27.00 g., 0.925 Silver 0.803 oz. ASW **Subject:** 25th Anniversary - Revolution of April 25 **Obv:** Circles within cross design above value and date **Rev:** Date and mirrored anniversary number

Date	Mintage	VF20	XF40	MS60	MS63	MS65
1999	Est. 15000	PF65 55.00				

KM# 721 1000 ESCUDOS
27.20 g., 0.500 Silver 0.4372 oz. ASW, 39 mm. **Subject:** Millennium of Atlantic Sailing **Obv:** Shield above logo **Rev:** Stylized face looking down on ship **Edge:** Reeded

Date	Mintage	VF20	XF40	MS60	MS63	MS65
1999 INCM	—	—	—	18.00	22.00	25.00

KM# 721a 1000 ESCUDOS
27.00 g., 0.925 Silver 0.803 oz. ASW **Subject:** Millennium of Atlantic Sailing **Obv:** Shield above logo **Rev:** Stylized face looking down on ship **Edge:** Reeded

Date	Mintage	VF20	XF40	MS60	MS63	MS65
1999 INCM	15,000	PF65 55.00				

KM# 724 1000 ESCUDOS
27.00 g., 0.500 Silver 0.434 oz. ASW, 40.2 mm. **Subject:** Presidency of the European Union **Obv:** Shield and cave drawings **Rev:** Stylized design **Edge:** Reeded

Date	Mintage	VF20	XF40	MS60	MS63	MS65
2000	450,000	—	—	18.00	22.00	25.00

KM# 724a 1000 ESCUDOS
27.05 g., 0.925 Silver 0.8045 oz. ASW **Obv:** Shield and cave drawings **Rev:** Stylized design

Date	Mintage	VF20	XF40	MS60	MS63	MS65
2000	10,000	PF65 75.00				

KM# 727 1000 ESCUDOS
27.00 g., 0.500 Silver 0.434 oz. ASW, 40 mm. **Series:** Ibero-America **Obv:** Shield within center of assorted shields **Rev:** Lusitano horses and rider **Edge:** Reeded

Date	Mintage	VF20	XF40	MS60	MS63	MS65
2000 INCM	—	—	—	22.50	25.00	28.00

KM# 727a 1000 ESCUDOS
27.00 g., 0.925 Silver 0.803 oz. ASW, 40 mm. **Series:** Ibero-America **Obv:** Shield within center of assorted shields **Rev:** Lusitano horses and rider **Edge:** Reeded

Date	Mintage	VF20	XF40	MS60	MS63	MS65
2000 Proof	Est. 20000	—	—	100	120	—

KM# 732 1000 ESCUDOS
27.00 g., 0.500 Silver 0.434 oz. ASW **Subject:** D. Joao De Castro **Obv:** Shield within globe above value **Rev:** Bearded styilized bust

Date	Mintage	VF20	XF40	MS60	MS63	MS65
2000	—	—	—	22.50	25.00	28.00

ESSAIS

KM#	Date	Mintage	Identification	Mkt Val
E1	1986	30	100 Escudos. Copper-Nickel. KM637.	—
E2	1998	—	100 Escudos. Silver. "ENSAIO" on obverse and reverse.	—
E3	1998	—	100 Escudos. Silver. "ENSAIO" on reverse only.	—

PATTERNS

Including off metal strikes

KM#	Date	Mintage	Identification	Mkt Val
Pn200	1903	—	2 Reis. Nickel. Plain royal arms.	—
Pn201	1903	—	20 Reis. Nickel. Royal arms with wreath.	800
Pn202	1903	—	20 Reis. Nickel. Plain. Without wreath.	800
Pn203	1903	—	20 Reis. Nickel. Reeded. Value on reeded edge.	650
Pn204	1903	—	20 Reis. Nickel. Plain. Value on plain edge.	650
Pn205	1903	—	100 Reis. Silver. Crowned value.	2,500
Pn206	1903	—	200 Reis. Silver. Crowned value.	3,500
Pn207	ND (1912)	—	20 Centavos. Silver. Two reverses.	1,000
Pn208	1912	—	50 Centavos. Copper. Plain. Type as adopted.	1,250
Pn209	1912	—	50 Centavos. Silver. Reeded. Type as adopted.	1,650
Pn210	1912	—	Escudo. Gold. 'October 5, 1910'.	—
Pn211	1912	—	Escudo. Gold. Obverse variety.	—
Pn212	1912	—	Escudo. Gold.	—
Pn213	1919	—	4 Centavos. Copper-Nickel. Plain. Wide border.	—
Pn214	1919	—	4 Centavos. Copper-Nickel. Reeded. Wide border.	—
Pn215	1919	—	4 Centavos. Copper-Nickel. Plain. Semi-wide border.	—
Pn216	1919	—	4 Centavos. Copper-Nickel. Alternate. Narrow border.	—
Pn217	1920	—	10 Centavos. Copper-Nickel. Plain. Larger type.	2,250
Pn218	1920	—	10 Centavos. Brass. Plain. Larger type.	—
Pn219	1920	—	5 Escudos. Copper. 'Abundance Through Labor'.	1,650
Pn220	1920	—	5 Escudos. Copper-Nickel. 'Abundance Through Labor'.	1,650
Pn221	1920	—	5 Escudos. Gold. 'Abundance Through Labor'.	—
Pn222	1921	—	10 Centavos. Bronze. Reeded. 19mm.	850
Pn223	1927	—	50 Centavos. Silver. Reeded. Large type.	850
Pn224	1927	—	50 Centavos. Silver. Obverse 1924 type.	850
Pn225	1927	—	Escudo. Silver. Reverse 1924 type.	—
Pn226	1928	—	Escudo. Brass.	1,100
Pn227	1928	—	10 Escudos. Copper. 'Battle of Orique'.	1,250
Pn228	1929	—	10 Escudos. Brass. 'Battle of Orique'.	—
Pn229	1932	—	5 Escudos. Copper-Nickel. Type adopted.	—
Pn230	1932	—	10 Escudos. Copper.	550
Pn231	1932	—	10 Escudos. Copper-Nickel. Type adopted.	550
Pn232	1940	—	10 Escudos. Copper-Nickel. Large type.	550
Pn233	1953	—	20 Escudos. Copper. 'National Revival'.	1,150
Pn234	1953	—	20 Escudos. Gold. 'National Revival'.	—
Pn235	1953	—	20 Escudos. Silver. Variety of type adopted.	1,650
Pn236	1961	—	2-1/2 Escudos. Nickel. Reeded.	—
Pn237	1961	—	2-1/2 Escudos. Nickel. Reeded.	—
Pn238	1961	—	2-1/2 Escudos. Copper-Nickel.	—
Pn239	1961	—	10 Escudos. Silver. Legend incuse.	950
Pn240	1961	—	10 Escudos. Copper-Nickel.	800
Pn241	1961	—	10 Escudos. Silver.	—
Pn242	1961	—	10 Escudos. Copper-Nickel. Legend in relief.	—
Pn243	ND (1961)	—	10 Centavos. Aluminum.	—
Pn244	ND (1961)	—	20 Centavos. Brass.	550
Pn245	ND (1961)	—	5 Escudos. Brass. Type adopted.	550
Pn246	ND (1961)	—	10 Escudos. Nickel. Reeded. Type adopted.	—
Pn247	ND (1961)	—	10 Escudos. Nickel. Plain. Type adopted.	—
Pn248	ND (1961)	—	10 Centavos. Bronze-Aluminum. Plain.	—
Pn249	1966	—	Escudo. Bronze-Aluminum.	500
Pn250	1966	—	Escudo. Bronze-Aluminum. Reeded.	500
Pn251	1966	—	20 Escudos. Nickel. Reeded.	800
Pn252	1968	—	10 Centavos. Aluminum. Similar to 1942 type.	550
Pn253	1969	—	10 Centavos. Aluminum. Large type as adopted.	—
Pn254	1970	—	Escudo. Nickel. Type adopted.	250
Pn255	1970	—	20 Escudos. Nickel. Reeded.	450
Pn256	1970	—	20 Escudos. Nickel. Plain.	450
Pn257	1970	—	20 Escudos. Nickel. Reeded.	450
Pn258	1970	—	20 Escudos. Nickel. Plain.	450
Pn259	1979	—	50 Centavos. Reeded.	300
Pn260	1979	—	Escudo. Reeded.	300
Pn261	1979	—	5 Escudos. Aluminum.	350
Pn262	ND (1985)	—	250 Escudos. Copper-Nickel. Decade of Women, United Nations.	—
Pn263	1989	—	100 Escudos.	2,000

PROVAS

Stamped

KM#	Date	Mintage	Identification	Mkt Val
PrA7	1942	—	10 Centavos. Bronze. KM583.	—
PrB7	1942	—	20 Centavos. Bronze. KM584.	475
Pr7	1943	—	5 Escudos. Silver. KM581.	300
Pr8	1943	—	10 Centavos. Bronze. KM583.	185
Pr9	1943	—	20 Centavos. Bronze. KM584.	185
Pr10	1960	—	5 Escudos. Silver. KM587.	150
Pr11	1960	—	10 Escudos. Silver. KM588.	185
PrA11	1960	—	5 Escudos. Silver. Matte, KM#587.	400
Pr12	1960	—	20 Escudos.	265
PrA13	1962	—	10 Centavos. Bronze. KM583.	—
PrB13	1962	—	20 Centavos. Bronze. KM584.	—
PrC13	1962	—	50 Centavos. Copper-Nickel. KM577.	—
PrD13	1962	—	Escudo. Copper-Nickel. KM578.	—
Pr13	1964	—	Escudo. Copper-Nickel. KM578.	—
PrE13	1964	—	5 Escudos. Copper-Nickel.	325
PrF13	1964	—	10 Centavos. Bronze. KM573.	450
PrG13	1964	—	50 Centavos. Copper-Nickel. KM577.	550
Pr14	1964	—	2-1/2 Escudos. Copper-Nickel. KM590.	—
PrA15	1965	—	50 Centavos. Copper-Nickel.	350
Pr15	1966	—	20 Centavos. Bronze. KM584.	—
PrB15	1966	—	10 Centavos. Bronze.	350
Pr16	1966	—	Escudo. Copper-Nickel. KM578.	—
Pr17	1966	—	2-1/2 Escudos. Copper-Nickel. KM590.	165
Pr18	1966	—	5 Escudos. Copper-Nickel. KM591.	145
Pr19	1966	—	20 Escudos. Silver. Salazar Bridge, KM592.	225
Pr20	1966	—	20 Escudos. Gold. Salazar Bridge, KM592.	3,500
Pr21	1968	—	50 Escudos. Silver. KM593.	265
PrA22	1968	—	Escudo. Copper-Nickel.	225
Pr22	1969	—	50 Escudos. Silver. KM598, 'Prova' incuse.	265
PrB22	1969	—	5 Escudos. Copper-Nickel.	325
PrC22	1969	—	20 Centavos. Bronze.	325
Pr23	1969	—	50 Escudos. Silver. KM598, 'Prova' in relief.	300
Pr24	1969	—	50 Escudos. Silver. KM599.	265
Pr25	1971	—	50 Escudos. Silver. KM601.	265
Pr26	1972	—	50 Escudos. Silver. KM602.	265
Pr27	ND-1984	100	25 Escudos. Copper-Nickel. Shield below wave-like design. Stylized value. KM623, Revolution.	145
Pr28	1985	5,000	100 Escudos. Copper-Nickel. KM629, Henrique.	—

TRIAL STRIKES

KM#	Date	Mintage	Identification	Mkt Val
TS19	1866	—	5000 Reis. Silver. Reverse, Charles Wiener.	200
TS33	1910	—	1000 Reis. Nickel Alloy. KM558; ALP.	650
TS34	1915	—	Escudo. Nickel Alloy. KM564; ALP.	650
TS35	1927	—	5 Centavos. Bronze. Reverse.	—
TS36	ND (1927)	—	20 Centavos. Brass. Reverse, Roman numeral.	—
TS36	ND-1963	—	20 Centavos. Brass. Reverse, Roman numeral.	—
TS37	ND-1927	—	50 Centavos. Brass. Reverse.	—
TS38	ND-1927	—	2 Escudos. Brass. Uniface, KM#591.	100

MINT SETS

KM#	Date	Mintage	Identification	Issue Price	Mkt Val
MS1	1960 (3)	—	KM587-589	—	125
MS2	1982 (4)	10,000	KM612-613, 615-616	3.00	7.50
MS3	1983 (3)	50,000	KM620-622	30.00	60.00
MS4	1983 (3)	5,000	KM617-619	4.00	7.50
MS5	1984 (2)	10,000	KM624-625	3.00	7.50

MSA6	1985 (2)	—	KM627, 630	—	7.50
MS6	1985 (2)	20,000	KM627a, 630a	20.00	45.00
MS7	1986 (5)	50,000	KM631-634, 636	6.00	10.00
MS10	1987 (6)	5,000	KM631-634, 636, 638	10.00	15.00
MS11	1988 (5)	30,000	KM631-634, 636	10.00	12.50
MS12	1989 (6)	50,000	KM631-634, 636, 645.1	12.00	15.00
MS13	1990 (6)	50,000	KM631-634, 636, 645.1	15.00	35.00
MS15	1991 (7)	—	KM631-634, 636, 645.1, 655	17.50	25.00
MS16	1992 (7)	—	KM631-634, 636, 645.1, 655	—	37.50
MS17	1993 (7)	—	KM631-634, 636, 645.1, 655	—	85.00
MS18	1993 (4)	30,000	KM665a-668a	79.50	110
MS19	1994 (7)	—	KM631-634, 636, 645.1, 669	—	65.00
MS20	1994 (4)	—	KM670a-673a	—	110
MS21	1995 (7)	—	KM631-634, 636, 678-679	—	55.00
MS22	1995 (4)	20,000	KM681a-684a	77.50	110
MS23	1995 (2)	5,000	KM678-679	—	20.00
MS24	1996 (8)	—	KM631-634, 636, 645.1, 655, 687	—	65.00
MS25	1996 (4)	10,000	KM689a, 690a, 691a, 692a	105	110
MS26	1997 (9)	20,000	KM631-634, 636, 645.1, 655, 693-694	32.50	45.00
MS27	1998 (8)	50,000	KM631-634, 636, 645.1, 655, 706	32.50	35.00
MS28	1998 (4)	25,000	KM709a-712a	95.00	110
MS29	1999 (9)	—	KM631-634, 636, 645.1, 655, 720, 722	—	35.00
MS30	1999 (4)	10,000	KM716a-719a	95.00	110
MS31	2000 (4)	10,000	KM#728a-731a	65.00	110

PROOF SETS

KM#	Date	Mintage	Identification	Issue Price	Mkt Val
PS1	1960 (3)	—	KM587-589; matte finish	—	150
PS2	1974 (2)	10,000	KM603-604	6.00	50.00
PS3	1977 (3)	10,000	KM605-606, 608	2.50	25.00
PS4	1983 (3)	8,500	KM620-622	60.00	125
PS5	1985 (2)	5,000	KM627a, 630a	40.00	125
PS6	1985 (2)	5,000	KM628, 628a	35.00	300
PS7	1987 (4)	20,000	KM639a-642a	128	110
PS15	1993 (7)	—	KM631-634, 636, 645.1, 655	—	80.00
PS16	1993 (4)	22,000	KM665a-668a	150	135
PS17	1993 (4)	5,000	KM665b-668b	1,980	3,900
PS18	1993 (4)	2,000	KM665a, 666c, 667b, 668c; Prestige	2,300	3,450
PS19	1994 (7)	—	KM631-633, 634.1, 636, 645.1, 669	—	70.00
PS20	1994 (4)	10,000	KM670a-673a	—	135
PS21	1994 (4)	—	KM670b-673b	—	4,800
PS22	1994 (4)	1,000	KM670a, 671c, 672b, 673c; Prestige	—	5,225
PS23	1995 (7)	7,000	KM631-633, 634.1, 636, 678, 679	47.50	60.00
PS24	1995 (4)	13,000	KM681a-684a	150	140
PS25	1995 (4)	2,000	KM681b-684b	1,980	4,800
PS26	1995 (4)	1,000	KM681a, 682c, 683b, 684c	1,800	4,100
PS27	1995 (2)	10,000	KM678, 679	—	35.00
PS28	1996 (8)	7,000	KM631-634, 636, 645.1, 655, 687	—	62.50
PS29	1996 (4)	10,000	KM689a, 690a, 691a, 692a	160	140
PS30	1996 (4)	2,000	KM689b, 690b, 691b, 692b	—	4,800
PS31	1996 (4)	1,000	KM689a, 690c, 691b, 692c	—	4,100
PS32	1997 (9)	7,000	KM631-634, 636, 645.1, 655, 693-694	55.00	75.00
PS33	1997 (4)	24,000	KM697a-700a	145	130
PS34	1997 (4)	4,000	KM697b-700b	1,980	4,500
PS35	1997 (4)	1,000	KM697a, 698b, 699c, 700c	2,000	4,000
PS36	1998 (8)	20,000	KM631-634, 636, 645.1, 655, 706	52.50	60.00
PS37	1998 (4)	25,000	KM709a-712a	150	125
PS38	1998 (4)	5,000	KM709b-712b	1,980	4,500
PS39	1998 (4)	1,000	KM709c, 710a, 711b, 712c	2,000	4,000
PS40	1999 (4)	10,000	KM716a-719a	145	150
PS41	1999 (4)	1,000	KM716b-719b	1,800	4,500
PS42	2000 (4)	10,000	KM#728a-731a	125	150
PS43	2000 (4)	1,000	KM#728b-731b	1,405	4,500
PS44	2000 (4)	250	KM#728a, 729c, 730b, 731c	2,988	4,000

QATAR

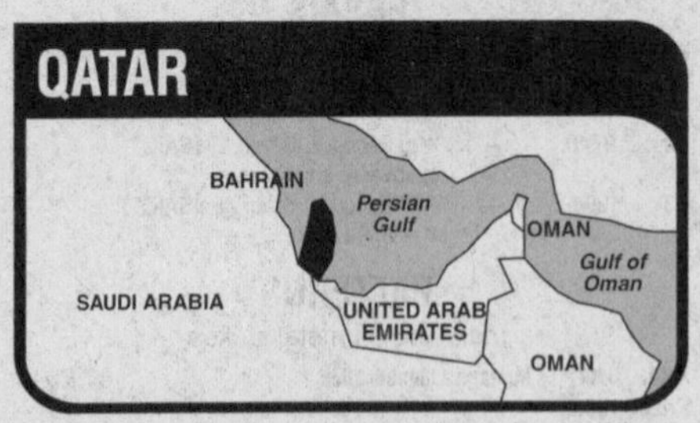

The State of Qatar, an emirate in the Persian Gulf between Bahrain and Trucial Oman, has an area of 4,247 sq. mi. (11,000 sq. km.) and a population of *469,000. Capital: Doha. Oil is the chief industry and export.

Qatar was under Turkish control from 1872 until the beginning of World War I when the Ottoman Turks evacuated the Qatar Peninsula. In 1916 Sheikh Abdullah placed Qatar under the protection of Great Britain and gave Britain responsibility for its defense and foreign relations. Qatar joined with Dubai in a Monetary Union and issued coins and paper money in 1966 and 1969. When Britain announced in 1968 that it would end treaty relationships with the Persian Gulf sheikhdoms in 1971, this union was dissolved; Qatar joined Bahrain and the seven trucial sheikhdoms (called the United Arab Emirates) in an effort to form a union of Arab Emirates. However the nine sheikhdoms were unable to agree on terms of union, and Qatar declared its independence as the State of Qatar on Sept. 3, 1971.

TITLES

دولة قطر

Daulat Qatar

RULERS

Al-Thani Dynasty

Qasim Bin Muhammad, 1876-1913
Abdullah Bin Qasim, 1913-1948
Ali Bin Abdullah, 1948-1960
Ahmad II, 1960-1972
Khalifah bin Hamad, 1972-1995
Hamad bin Khalifah, 1995-

MONETARY SYSTEM

100 Dirhem = 1 Riyal

STATE

STANDARD COINAGE

KM# 2 DIRHAM
1.50 g., Bronze, 15 mm. **Ruler:** Hamad bin Khalifa **Obv:** National arms **Rev:** Value

Date	Mintage	VF20	XF40	MS60	MS63	MS65
AH1393 - 1973	500,000	0.25	0.50	3.00	5.00	7.00

KM# 3 5 DIRHAMS
3.75 g., Bronze, 22 mm. **Ruler:** Hamad bin Khalifa **Obv:** National arms **Rev:** Value **Edge:** Plain

Date	Mintage	VF20	XF40	MS60	MS63	MS65
AH1393 - 1973	1,000,000	0.15	0.30	0.60	1.25	2.50
AH1398 - 1978	1,000,000	0.15	0.30	0.60	1.25	2.50

KM# 1 10 DIRHAMS
7.50 g., Bronze, 27 mm. **Ruler:** Hamad bin Khalifa **Obv:** National arms **Rev:** Value

Date	Mintage	VF20	XF40	MS60	MS63	MS65
AH1392 - 1972	1,500,000	0.50	1.00	2.00	3.50	5.00
AH1393 - 1973	1,500,000	0.25	0.50	1.50	3.00	4.50

KM# 4 25 DIRHAMS
3.50 g., Copper-Nickel, 20 mm. **Ruler:** Hamad bin Khalifa **Obv:** National arms **Rev:** Value **Edge:** Reeded

Date	Mintage	VF20	XF40	MS60	MS63	MS65
AH1393 - 1973	—	0.25	0.65	1.75	2.75	4.00
AH1396 - 1976	—	0.25	0.65	1.75	2.75	4.00
AH1401 - 1981	—	0.25	0.65	1.75	2.75	4.00
AH1407 - 1987	—	0.25	0.65	1.75	2.75	4.00
AH1410 - 1990	—	0.25	0.65	1.75	2.75	4.00
AH1414 - 1993	—	0.25	0.65	1.75	2.75	4.00
AH1419 - 1998	—	0.25	0.65	1.75	2.75	4.00

KM# 8 25 DIRHAMS
3.50 g., Copper-Nickel, 20 mm. **Ruler:** Hamad bin Khalifa **Obv:** National arms **Rev:** Value **Rev. Legend:** STATE OF QATAR **Edge:** Reeded

Date	Mintage	VF20	XF40	MS60	MS63	MS65
AH1421-2000	—	0.30	0.65	1.50	2.00	3.00

KM# 5 50 DIRHAMS
6.50 g., Copper-Nickel, 25 mm. **Ruler:** Hamad bin Khalifa **Obv:** National arms **Rev:** Value **Edge:** Reeded

Date	Mintage	VF20	XF40	MS60	MS63	MS65
AH1393 - 1973	1,500,000	0.40	0.85	2.00	3.00	5.00
AH1398 - 1978	2,000,000	0.40	0.85	2.00	3.00	5.00
AH1401 - 1981	—	0.40	0.85	2.00	3.00	5.00
AH1407 - 1987	—	0.40	0.85	2.00	3.00	5.00
AH1410 - 1990	—	0.40	0.85	2.00	3.00	5.00
AH1414 - 1993	—	0.40	0.85	2.00	3.00	5.00
AH1419 - 1998	—	0.40	0.85	2.00	3.00	5.00

KM# 9 50 DIRHAMS
6.50 g., Copper-Nickel, 25 mm. **Ruler:** Hamad bin Khalifa **Obv:** National arms **Rev:** Value **Edge:** Reeded

Date	Mintage	VF20	XF40	MS60	MS63	MS65
AH1421-2000	—	—	—	2.00	3.25	5.50

KM# 6 100 RIYALS
22.20 g., 0.925 Silver 0.6602 oz. ASW, 37 mm. **Ruler:** Hamad bin Khalifa **Subject:** Central Bank **Obv:** National arms **Rev:** Bank building **Edge:** Plain

Date	Mintage	VF20	XF40	MS60	MS63	MS65
ND-1998	—	PF65 400				

KM# 10 200 RIYALS
22.20 g., 0.925 Silver 0.6602 oz. ASW, 37 mm. **Ruler:** Hamad bin Khalifa **Subject:** Qatar University 25th Anniversary **Obv:** National arms **Rev:** University logo, value and dates **Edge:** Plain

Date	Mintage	VF20	XF40	MS60	MS63	MS65
ND(1998)	1,000	PF65 350				

KM# 7 500 RIYALS
17.00 g., 0.917 Gold 0.5012 oz. AGW, 31 mm. **Ruler:** Hamad bin Khalifa **Subject:** Central Bank **Obv:** National arms **Rev:** Bank building **Edge:** Plain

Date	Mintage	VF20	XF40	MS60	MS63	MS65
ND-1998	100	PF65 1,200				

PATTERNS

Including off metal strikes

KM#	Date	Mintage	Identification	Mkt Val
Pn1	AH1421-2000	—	Dirham. Bronze. National arms. Value on Central Bank building.	—
Pn2	AH1421 - 2000	—	5 Dirhams. Bronze. National arms. Value on Central Bank building.	—
Pn3	AH1421 - 2000	—	10 Dirhams. Bronze. National arms. Value on Central Bank building.	—
Pn4	AH1421 - 2000	—	25 Dirhams. Copper-Nickel. National arms. Value on Central Bank building.	—
Pn5	AH1421 - 2000	—	50 Dirhams. Copper-Nickel. National arms. Value on Central Bank building.	—
Pn6	AH1421 - 2000	—	Riyal. Bi-Metallic. National arms. Value on Central Bank building.	—

QATAR & DUBAI

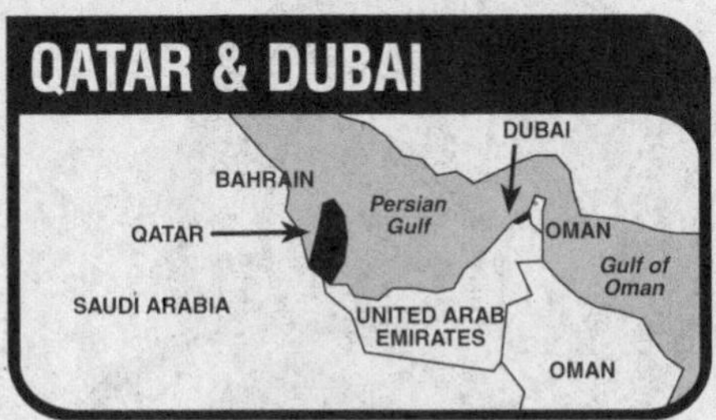

The State of Qatar, which occupies the Qatar Peninsula jutting into the Persian Gulf from eastern Saudi Arabia, has an area of 4,247 sq. mi. (11,000 sq. km.) and a population of *469,000. Capital: Doha. The traditional occupations of pearling, fishing, and herding have been replaced in economics by petroleum-related industries. Crude oil, petroleum products, and tomatoes are exported.

Dubai is one of the seven sheikhdoms comprising the United Arab Emirates (formerly Trucial States) located along the southern shore of the Persian Gulf. It has a population of about 60,000. Capital (of the United Arab Emirates): Abu Dhabi.

Qatar, which initiated protective treaty relations with Great Britain in 1916, achieved independence on Sept. 3, 1971, upon withdrawal of the British military presence from the Persian Gulf, and replaced its special treaty arrangement with Britain with a treaty of general friendship. Dubai attained independence on Dec. 1, 1971, upon termination of Britain's protective treaty with the crucial Sheikhdoms, and on Dec. 2, 1971, entered into the union of the United Arab Emirates.

Despite the fact that the Emirate of Qatar and the Sheikhdom of Dubai were merged under a monetary union, the two territories were governed independently from each other. Qatar now uses its own currency while Dubai uses the United Arab Emirates currency and coins.

TITLES

قطر و دبي

Qatar Wa Dubai

RULER
Ahmad II, 1960-1972

MONETARY SYSTEM
100 Dirhem = 1 Riyal

BRITISH PROTECTORATE

STANDARD COINAGE

KM# 1 DIRHEM
1.50 g., Bronze, 15 mm. **Ruler:** Ahmad II **Obv:** Value **Rev:** Goitered gazelle

Date	Mintage	VF20	XF40	MS60	MS63	MS65
AH1386 - 1966	1,000,000	2.00	4.00	8.00	16.00	30.00

KM# 2 5 DIRHEMS
3.75 g., Bronze, 22 mm. **Ruler:** Ahmad II **Obv:** Value **Rev:** Goitered gazelle

Date	Mintage	VF20	XF40	MS60	MS63	MS65
AH1386 - 1966	2,000,000	2.00	4.00	7.00	12.00	25.00
AH1389 - 1969	2,000,000	2.00	4.00	7.00	12.00	25.00

KM# 3 10 DIRHEMS
7.50 g., Bronze, 27 mm. **Ruler:** Ahmad II **Obv:** Value **Rev:** Goitered gazelle

Date	Mintage	VF20	XF40	MS60	MS63	MS65
AH1386 - 1966	2,000,000	3.00	5.00	9.00	15.00	28.00
AH1391 - 1971	1,500	—	—	—	550	750

Note: Official mintage figure reported for Qatar by British Royal Mint.

KM# 4 25 DIRHEMS
3.50 g., Copper-Nickel, 20 mm. **Ruler:** Ahmad II **Obv:** Value **Rev:** Goitered gazelle

Date	Mintage	VF20	XF40	MS60	MS63	MS65
AH1386 - 1966	2,000,000	4.00	7.00	12.00	20.00	35.00
AH1389 - 1969	2,000,000	4.00	7.00	12.00	20.00	35.00

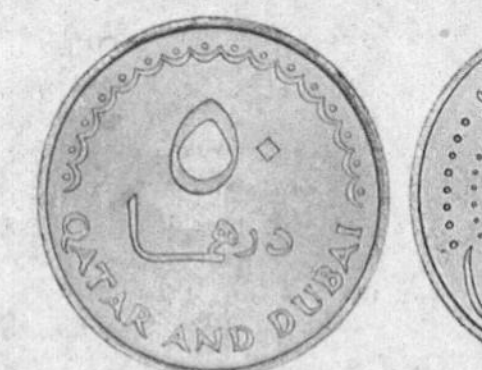

KM# 5 50 DIRHEMS
6.50 g., Copper-Nickel, 25 mm. **Ruler:** Ahmad II **Obv:** Value **Rev:** Goitered gazelle

Date	Mintage	VF20	XF40	MS60	MS63	MS65
AH1386 - 1966	2,000,000	5.00	9.00	15.00	25.00	40.00

RAS AL-KHAIMAH

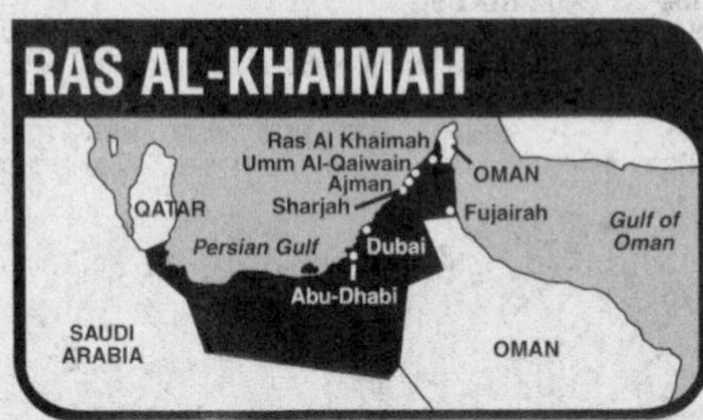

Ras al-Khaimah is only one of the coin issuing emirates that was not one of the original members of the United Arab Emirates. It was a part of Sharjah. It has an estimated area of 650 sq. mi. (1700 sq. km.) and a population of 30,000. Ras al Khaimah is the only member of the United Arab Emirates that has agriculture as its principal industry.

TITLES

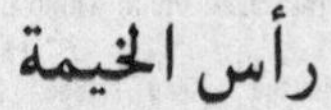

Ras al-Khaimah(t)

RULERS
Sultan bin Salim al-Qasimi,/1921-1948
Saqr Bin Muhammad al-Qasimi,/1948—

MONETARY SYSTEM
100 Dirhams = 1 Rial

UNITED ARAB EMIRATE

NON-CIRCULATING LEGAL TENDER COINAGE

KM# 28 50 DIRHAMS
Copper-Nickel **Ruler:** Saqr bin Muhammad al Qasimi **Obv:** Value within circle **Rev:** Falcon within circle flanked by stars

Date	Mintage	XF40	MS60	MS63	MS65	MS66
AH1390 - 1970	—	—	—	55.00	65.00	90.00

KM# 1 RIAL
3.95 g., 0.640 Silver 0.0813 oz. ASW **Ruler:** Saqr bin Muhammad al Qasimi **Obv:** Value within circle **Rev:** Crossed flags within wreath

Date	Mintage	XF40	MS60	MS63	MS65	MS66
AH1389 - 1969	—	—	—	15.00	25.00	55.00
AH1389 - 1969	1,500	PF65 50.00	PF67 70.00			

KM# 2 2 RIALS
6.45 g., 0.835 Silver 0.1732 oz. ASW **Ruler:** Saqr bin Muhammad al Qasimi **Obv:** Value within circle **Rev:** Crossed flags within wreath

Date	Mintage	XF40	MS60	MS63	MS65	MS66
AH1389 - 1969	—	—	—	20.00	30.00	65.00
AH1389 - 1969	1,500	PF65 60.00	PF67 80.00			

KM# 29 2-1/2 RIALS
7.50 g., 0.925 Silver 0.223 oz. ASW **Ruler:** Saqr bin Muhammad al Qasimi **Obv:** Head with headdress 1/4 right within circle flanked by stars **Rev:** Falcon within circle

Date	Mintage	XF40	MS60	MS63	MS65	MS66
AH1390 - 1970	—	—	—	75.00	90.00	120

KM# 3 5 RIALS
15.00 g., 0.835 Silver 0.4027 oz. ASW **Ruler:** Saqr bin Muhammad al Qasimi **Obv:** Value within circle **Rev:** Crossed flags within wreath

Date	Mintage	XF40	MS60	MS63	MS65	MS66
AH1389 - 1969	—	—	—	30.00	40.00	85.00
AH1389 - 1969	1,500	PF65 80.00	PF67 100			

KM# 5 7-1/2 RIYALS
22.50 g., 0.925 Silver 0.6691 oz. ASW **Ruler:** Saqr bin Muhammad al Qasimi **Obv:** Value within circle **Rev:** Head of Giacomo Agostini left

Date	Mintage	XF40	MS60	MS63	MS65	MS66
ND (1970)	—	PF65 200	PF67 350			

KM# 17 7-1/2 RIYALS
22.50 g., 0.925 Silver 0.6691 oz. ASW **Ruler:** Saqr bin Muhammad al Qasimi **Subject:** Centennial of Rome **Obv:** Value within circle **Rev:** Man plowing

Date	Mintage	XF40	MS60	MS63	MS65	MS66
1970	—	PF65 175	PF67 300			

KM# 30 7-1/2 RIYALS
22.50 g., 0.925 Silver 0.6691 oz. ASW, 39 mm. **Ruler:** Saqr bin Muhammad al Qasimi **Obv:** Head with headdress 1/4 right within circle flanked by stars **Rev:** Falcon within circle

Date	Mintage	XF40	MS60	MS63	MS65	MS66
AH1390	—	—	—	95.00	125	200

KM# 32 7-1/2 RIYALS
22.50 g., 0.925 Silver 0.6691 oz. ASW **Ruler:** Saqr bin Muhammad al Qasimi **Subject:** World Championship Football **Obv:** Value within circle **Rev:** Jules Rimet Cup flanked by shields

Date	Mintage	XF40	MS60	MS63	MS65	MS66
1970	Est. 2000	PF65 375	PF67 600			

KM# 6 10 RIYALS
30.00 g., 0.925 Silver 0.8922 oz. ASW **Ruler:** Saqr bin Muhammad al Qasimi **Subject:** World Championship Football **Obv:** Value within circle **Rev:** Jules Rimet Cup in front of soccer ball

Date	Mintage	XF40	MS60	MS63	MS65	MS66
1970	Est. 2000	PF65 300	PF67 500			

KM# 7 10 RIYALS
30.00 g., 0.925 Silver 0.8922 oz. ASW **Ruler:** Saqr bin Muhammad al Qasimi **Subject:** Felice Gimondi **Obv:** Value within circle **Rev:** Head left

Date	Mintage	XF40	MS60	MS63	MS65	MS66
ND (1970)	Est. 2000	PF65 350	PF67 550			

KM# 18 10 RIYALS
30.00 g., 0.925 Silver 0.8922 oz. ASW **Ruler:** Saqr bin Muhammad al Qasimi **Subject:** Centennial of Rome **Obv:** Value within circle **Rev:** Emperor standing with charging horses

Date	Mintage	XF40	MS60	MS63	MS65	MS66
1970	Est. 2000	PF65 185	PF67 300			

KM# 31 10 RIYALS
30.00 g., 0.925 Silver 0.8922 oz. ASW **Ruler:** Saqr bin Muhammad al Qasimi **Subject:** 1st Anniversary - Death of Dwight Eisenhower **Obv:** Value within circle **Rev:** Head left

Date	Mintage	XF40	MS60	MS63	MS65	MS66
1970	4,500	—	—	35.00	50.00	90.00
1970	1,400	PF65 100	PF67 150			

KM# 8 15 RIYALS
45.00 g., 0.925 Silver 1.3383 oz. ASW, 44 mm. **Ruler:** Saqr bin Muhammad al Qasimi **Subject:** Champions of Sport **Obv:** Value within circle **Rev:** Cluster of heads all facing left

Date	Mintage	XF40	MS60	MS63	MS65	MS66
ND-1970	Est. 2000	PF65 550	PF67 850			

KM# 19 15 RIYALS
45.00 g., 0.925 Silver 1.3383 oz. ASW, 44 mm. **Ruler:** Saqr bin Muhammad al Qasimi **Subject:** Centennial of Rome **Obv:** Value within circle **Rev:** Three heads facing right

Date	Mintage	XF40	MS60	MS63	MS65	MS66
1970	Est. 2000	PF65 245	PF67 400			

KM# 33 15 RIYALS
45.00 g., 0.925 Silver 1.3383 oz. ASW **Ruler:** Saqr bin Muhammad al Qasimi **Subject:** World Championship Football - Jules Rimet Cup **Obv:** Value within circle **Rev:** Jules Rimet Cup flanked by shields

Date	Mintage	XF40	MS60	MS63	MS65	MS66
1970	—	PF65 475	PF67 750			

KM# 10 50 RIYALS
10.35 g., 0.900 Gold 0.2995 oz. AGW **Ruler:** Saqr bin Muhammad al Qasimi **Subject:** Gigi Riva **Obv:** Value within circle **Rev:** Head left

Date	Mintage	XF40	MS60	MS63	MS65	MS66
ND (1970)	—	PF65 650	PF67 800			

KM# 21 50 RIYALS
10.35 g., 0.900 Gold 0.2995 oz. AGW **Ruler:** Saqr bin Muhammad al Qasimi **Subject:** Centennial of Italian Unification **Obv:** Value within circle **Rev:** Head left

Date	Mintage	XF40	MS60	MS63	MS65	MS66
1970	Est. 2000	PF65 625	PF67 750			

KM# 11 75 RIYALS
15.53 g., 0.900 Gold 0.4494 oz. AGW **Ruler:** Saqr bin Muhammad al Qasimi **Subject:** Gianni Rivera **Obv:** Value within circle **Rev:** Head left

Date	Mintage	XF40	MS60	MS63	MS65	MS66
ND (1970)	Est. 2000	PF65 900	PF67 1,100			

KM# 22 75 RIYALS
15.53 g., 0.900 Gold 0.4494 oz. AGW **Ruler:** Saqr bin Muhammad al Qasimi **Subject:** Centennial of Italian Unification, Rome as the Capital **Obv:** Value within circle **Rev:** Figure with gun walking left

Date	Mintage	XF40	MS60	MS63	MS65	MS66
1970	Est. 2000	PF65 875	PF67 1,050			

KM# 12 100 RIYALS
20.70 g., 0.900 Gold 0.599 oz. AGW **Ruler:** Saqr bin Muhammad al Qasimi **Subject:** World Chmapionship Football - Jules Rimet Cup **Obv:** Value within circle **Rev:** Jules Rimet Cup in front of soccer ball

Date	Mintage	XF40	MS60	MS63	MS65	MS66
1970	Est. 2000	PF65 1,400	PF67 1,700			

KM# 23 100 RIYALS
20.70 g., 0.900 Gold 0.599 oz. AGW **Ruler:** Saqr bin Muhammad al Qasimi **Subject:** Centennial of Italian Unification - WWI Victory

Date	Mintage	XF40	MS60	MS63	MS65	MS66
1970	Est. 2000	PF65 1,400	PF67 1,700			

KM# 13 150 RIYALS
31.05 g., 0.900 Gold 0.8985 oz. AGW **Ruler:** Saqr bin Muhammad al Qasimi **Series:** 1972 Munich Olympics **Obv:** Value within circle **Rev:** Figures within olympic circles and flaming torch

Date	Mintage	XF40	MS60	MS63	MS65	MS66
ND (1970)	3,060	PF65 2,250	PF67 2,500			

KM# 24 150 RIYALS
31.05 g., 0.900 Gold 0.8985 oz. AGW **Ruler:** Saqr bin Muhammad al Qasimi **Subject:** Centennial of Italian Unification **Rev:** Standing Italia

Date	Mintage	XF40	MS60	MS63	MS65	MS66
1970	Est. 2000	PF65 1,800	PF67 2,100			

KM# 14 200 RIYALS
41.40 g., 0.900 Gold 1.1979 oz. AGW **Ruler:** Saqr bin Muhammad al Qasimi **Subject:** Champions of Sport **Note:** Similar to KM#8.

Date	Mintage	XF40	MS60	MS63	MS65	MS66
ND (1970)	Est. 2000	PF65 2,400	PF67 2,700			

KM# 25 200 RIYALS
41.40 g., 0.900 Gold 1.1979 oz. AGW **Ruler:** Saqr bin Muhammad al Qasimi **Subject:** Centennial of Italian Unification - Romulus and Remus **Obv:** Value within circle **Rev:** Wolf within designed circle

Date	Mintage	XF40	MS60	MS63	MS65	MS66
1970	Est. 2000	PF65 2,250	PF67 2,500			

ESSAIS

KM#	Date	Mintage	Identification	Mkt Val
E1	1969	—	Riyal. Value within circle. Crossed flags within wreath. With ASSAY.	50.00
E2	1969	—	2 Riyals. Value within circle. Crossed flags within wreath. With ASSAY.	60.00
E3	1969	—	5 Riyals. Value within circle. Crossed flags within wreath. With ASSAY.	70.00
E4	1970	—	10 Riyals. With ASSAY.	90.00

MINT SETS

KM#	Date	Mintage	Identification	Issue Price	Mkt Val
MS1	1969 (3)	—	KM#1-3	—	100

PROOF SETS

KM#	Date	Mintage	Identification	Issue Price	Mkt Val
PS1	1969 (3)	1,500	KM#1-3	10.80	200
PS2	-1970 (9)	—	KM#5-8, 10-14	—	10,750
PS3	1970 (8)	—	KM#17-19, 21-25	—	9,000
PS4	-1970 (5)	—	KM#10-14	—	8,500
PS5	1970 (5)	—	KM#21-25	—	8,000
PS6	-1970 (4)	—	KM#5-8	41.50	2,250
PS7	1970 (3)	—	KM#17-19	—	1,000
PS8	1970 (4)	—	KM#6, 10-12	—	3,100

REUNION

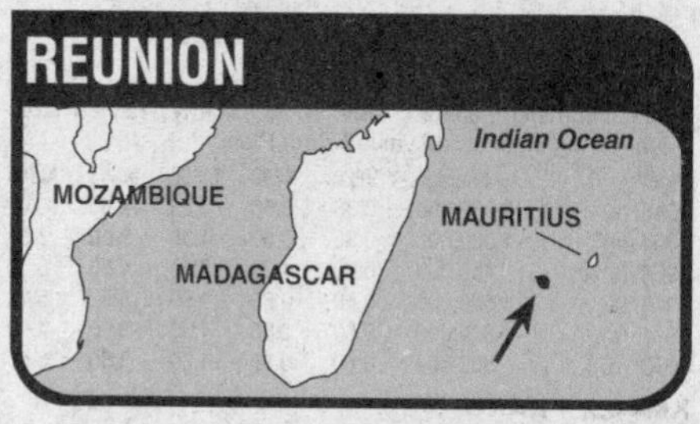

The Department of Reunion, an overseas department of France located in the Indian Ocean 400 miles (640 km.) east of Madagascar, has an area of 969 sq. mi. (2,510 sq. km.) and a population of *566,000. Capital: Saint-Denis. The island's volcanic soil is extremely fertile. Sugar, vanilla, coffee and rum are exported.

Although first visited by Portuguese navigators in the 16th century, Reunion was uninhabited when claimed for France by Capt. Goubert in 1638. The French first colonized the Isle de Bourbon in 1662 as a layover station for ships rounding the Cape of Good Hope to India. It was renamed Reunion in 1793. The island remained in French possession except for the period of 1810-15, when the British occupied it. Reunion became an overseas department of France in 1946, and in 1958 voted to continue that status within the new French Union.

During the first half of the 19th century, Reunion was officially known as Isle de Bonaparte (1801-14) and Isle de Bourbon (1814-48). Reunion coinage of those periods is so designated.

The world debut of the Euro was here on January 1, 2002.

MINT MARK
(a) – Paris, privy marks only

MONETARY SYSTEM
100 Centimes = 1 Franc

FRENCH OVERSEAS DEPARTMENT

TOKEN COINAGE

KM# Tn1 5 CENTIMES
Aluminum **Shape:** Hexagon **Note:** Bank token. Demonetized 1941.

Date	Mintage	F12	VF20	XF40	MS60	MS63
1920	500,000	50.00	125	290	670	950

KM# Tn2 10 CENTIMES
Aluminum **Shape:** Hexagon **Note:** Bank token. Demonetized 1941.

Date	Mintage	F12	VF20	XF40	MS60	MS63
1920	250,000	225	450	900	1,800	2,500

KM# Tn3 25 CENTIMES
Aluminum **Shape:** Hexagon **Note:** Bank token. Demonetized 1941.

Date	Mintage	F12	VF20	XF40	MS60	MS63
1920	120,000	200	400	800	1,500	2,000

STANDARD COINAGE

KM# 6.1 FRANC
0.90 g., Aluminum, 23 mm. **Obv:** Winged liberty head left **Rev:** Sugar cane plants divide value **Edge:** Plain

Date	Mintage	VF20	XF40	MS60	MS63	MS65
1948 (a)	3,000,000	0.35	0.60	1.25	2.50	10.00
1964 (a)	1,000,000	0.35	0.60	1.35	3.00	3.50
1968 (a)	450,000	0.60	1.25	2.50	4.50	6.00
1969 (a)	500,000	0.60	0.85	1.50	3.50	5.00
1971 (a)	800,000	0.60	0.85	1.50	3.00	4.50
1973 (a)	500,000	0.60	0.85	1.50	3.50	5.00

KM# 6.2 FRANC
Aluminum **Note:** Thinner planchet.

Date	Mintage	VF20	XF40	MS60	MS63	MS65
1969 (a)	Inc. above	0.75	1.50	3.00	5.00	7.00

KM# 7 FRANC
Aluminum **Obv:** Winged liberty head left **Rev:** Sugar cane plants divide value **Note:** Mule.

Date	Mintage	VF20	XF40	MS60	MS63	MS65
1948 (a)	Inc. above	—	—	1,250	1,800	2,700

KM# 8 2 FRANCS
Aluminum **Obv:** Winged liberty head left **Rev:** Sugar cane plants divide value

Date	Mintage	VF20	XF40	MS60	MS63	MS65
1948 (a)	2,000,000	0.35	0.85	1.75	3.50	10.00
1968 (a)	100,000	3.00	5.00	7.00	10.00	12.50
1969 (a)	150,000	1.75	3.50	4.50	6.50	9.00
1970 (a)	300,000	0.85	1.75	2.50	4.00	5.50
1971 (a)	300,000	0.85	1.75	2.50	4.00	5.50
1973 (a)	500,000	0.85	1.75	2.50	4.00	5.50

KM# 9 5 FRANCS
Aluminum, 31 mm. **Obv:** Winged liberty head left **Rev:** Sugar cane plants divides value

Date	Mintage	VF20	XF40	MS60	MS63	MS65
1955 (a)	3,000,000	0.60	1.00	1.50	3.00	4.00
1969 (a)	100,000	2.25	4.00	6.00	9.00	12.00
1970 (a)	200,000	1.75	3.50	5.00	6.50	9.00
1971 (a)	100,000	1.75	3.50	5.00	6.50	9.00
1972 (a)	300,000	0.85	1.75	2.25	3.50	5.00
1973 (a)	250,000	0.85	1.75	2.25	3.50	5.00

KM# 10 10 FRANCS
Aluminum-Bronze **Obv:** Winged liberty head left **Rev:** Crowned shield divides value

Date	Mintage	VF20	XF40	MS60	MS63	MS65
1955 (a)	1,500,000	0.45	0.75	1.50	3.00	3.50
1962 (a)	700,000	1.75	3.50	4.50	6.50	9.00
1964 (a)	1,000,000	0.45	0.75	1.50	3.00	3.50

KM# 10a 10 FRANCS
Aluminum-Nickel-Bronze **Obv:** Winged Liberty head left **Rev:** Crowned shield divides value

Date	Mintage	VF20	XF40	MS60	MS63	MS65
1964 (a)	Inc. above	0.45	0.75	1.50	3.00	3.50
1969 (a)	300,000	1.25	2.50	4.00	6.00	7.00
1970 (a)	300,000	1.25	2.50	3.50	5.00	6.00
1971 (a)	200,000	1.75	3.75	5.00	7.50	10.00
1972 (a)	400,000	1.25	2.50	4.00	6.00	7.00
1973 (a)	700,000	0.85	1.75	2.25	3.50	5.00

KM# 11 20 FRANCS
Aluminum-Bronze **Obv:** Winged liberty head left **Rev:** Crowned shield divides value

Date	Mintage	VF20	XF40	MS60	MS63	MS65
1955 (a)	1,250,000	0.75	1.50	2.50	4.00	5.50
1960 (a)	100,000	3.00	6.00	8.00	12.00	15.00
1961 (a)	300,000	2.50	4.50	6.00	8.00	10.00
1962 (a)	190,000	2.75	5.50	7.00	9.00	12.00
1964 (a)	750,000	0.75	1.50	2.50	3.50	5.00

KM# 11a 20 FRANCS
Aluminum-Nickel-Bronze **Obv:** Winged Liberty head left **Rev:** Crowned shield divides value

Date	Mintage	VF20	XF40	MS60	MS63	MS65
1969 (a)	200,000	2.75	5.50	7.00	9.00	12.00
1970 (a)	200,000	2.75	5.50	7.00	9.00	12.00
1971 (a)	200,000	2.75	5.50	7.00	9.00	12.00
1972 (a)	300,000	2.00	3.50	4.50	6.50	8.50
1973 (a)	550,000	0.75	1.50	2.50	3.50	5.00

KM# 12 50 FRANCS
Nickel **Obv:** Winged liberty head left **Rev:** Crowned shield divides value

Date	Mintage	VF20	XF40	MS60	MS63	MS65
1962 (a)	1,000,000	1.50	2.50	3.50	5.00	6.50
1964 (a)	500,000	2.00	3.00	4.00	6.00	7.50
1969 (a)	100,000	2.75	5.00	7.00	9.00	12.00
1970 (a)	100,000	2.75	5.00	7.00	9.00	12.00
1973 (a)	350,000	2.00	3.50	4.50	6.50	8.50

KM# 13 100 FRANCS
8.54 g., Nickel, 26.5 mm. **Obv:** Winged liberty head left **Rev:** Crowned shield divides value

Date	Mintage	VF20	XF40	MS60	MS63	MS65
1964 (a)	2,000,000	1.00	2.00	3.00	4.00	5.50
1969 (a)	200,000	2.25	4.50	5.50	7.50	10.00
1970 (a)	150,000	2.25	5.00	7.00	9.00	12.00
1971 (a)	200,000	2.75	6.00	8.00	12.00	15.00
1972 (a)	300,000	2.00	3.50	4.50	6.00	7.50
1973 (a)	550,000	2.25	4.50	5.50	7.50	10.00

ESSAIS

KM#	Date	Mintage	Identification	Mkt Val
E3	1948(a)	2,000	Franc. Copper-Nickel. KM6.1.	60.00
E4	1948(a)	2,000	2 Francs. Copper-Nickel. KM8.	60.00
E5	1955(a)	1,200	5 Francs. Aluminum. KM9.	45.00
E6	1955(a)	2,000	10 Francs. Aluminum-Bronze. KM10.	45.00
E7	1955(a)	1,200	20 Francs. Aluminum-Bronze. KM11.	50.00
E8	1962(a)	1,200	50 Francs. Nickel. KM12.	55.00
E9	1964(a)	2,000	50 Francs. Nickel. KM12.	55.00
E10	1964(a)	2,000	100 Francs. Nickel. KM13.	60.00

PIEDFORT WITH ESSAI

KM#	Date	Mintage	Identification	Mkt Val
PE3	1948(a)	104	Franc. Aluminum. KM6.1.	220
PE4	1948(a)	104	2 Francs. Aluminum. KM8.	240

FDC SETS

KM#	Date	Mintage	Identification	Issue Price	Mkt Val
SS1	1964 (5)	—	KM6.1, 10-13. Issued with Comoros set.	—	35.00

RHODESIA

The Republic of Rhodesia or Southern Rhodesia (now known as the Republic of Zimbabwe), located in the east-central part of southern Africa, has an area of 150,804 sq. mi. (390,580sq. km.) and a population of *10.1 million. Capital: Harare (formerly Salisbury). The economy is based on agriculture and mining. Tobacco, sugar, asbestos, copper, chrome, ore and coal are exported.

The Rhodesian area contains extensive evidence of the habitat of paleolithic man and earlier civilizations, notably the world-famous ruins of Zimbabwe, a gold-trading center that flourished about the 14th or 15th century A.D. The Portuguese of the 16th century were the first Europeans to attempt to develop south-central Africa, but it remained for Cecil Rhodes and the British South Africa Co. to open the hinterlands. Rhodes obtained a concession for mineral rights from local chiefs in 1888 and administered his African empire (named Southern Rhodesia in 1895) through the British South Africa Co. until 1923, when the British government annexed the area after the white settlers voted for existence as a separate entity, rather than for incorporation into the Union of South Africa. From Sept. of 1953 through 1963 Southern Rhodesia was joined with the British Protectorates of Northern Rhodesia and Nyasaland into a multiracial federation, known as the Federation of Rhodesia and Nyasaland. When the federation was dissolved at the end of 1963, Northern Rhodesia and Nyasaland became the independent states of Zambia and Malawi.

Britain was prepared to grant independence to Southern Rhodesia but declined to do so when the politically dominant white Rhodesians refused to give assurances of representative government. On Nov. 11, 1965, following two years of unsuccessful negotiation with the British government, Prime Minister Ian Smith issued an unilateral declaration of independence. Britain responded with economic sanctions supported by the United Nations. After further futile attempts to effect an accommodation, the Rhodesian Parliament severed all ties with Britain and on March 2, 1970, established the Republic of Rhodesia.

On March 3, 1978, Prime Minister Ian Smith and three moderate black nationalist leaders signed an agreement providing for black majority rule. The name of the country was changed to Zimbabwe Rhodesia. Following a conference in London in December 1979, the opposition government conceded and it was agreed that the British Government should resume control. A British Governor soon returned to Southern Rhodesia. One of his first acts was to affirm the nullification of the purported declaration of independence. On April 18, 1980 pursuant to an act of the British Parliament, the colony of Southern Rhodesia became independent as the Republic of Zimbabwe, which remains a member of the Commonwealth of Nations.

RULER

British, until 1966

MONETARY SYSTEM

12 Pence = 1 Shilling = 10 Cents
10 Shillings = 1 Dollar
20 Shillings = 1 Pound

BRITISH COLONY

Self-Governing

POUND COINAGE

KM# 8 3 PENCE = 2-1/2 CENTS

6.50 g., Copper-Nickel, 27 mm. **Ruler:** Elizabeth II **Obv:** Crowned bust right **Rev:** Three spear points divides date

Date	Mintage	VF20	XF40	MS60	MS63	MS65
1968	2,400,000	0.50	0.75	1.25	2.00	5.00
1968 Double shaft error	—	10.00	20.00	25.00	35.00	50.00
1968	10	PF65 1,200				

KM# 1 6 PENCE = 5 CENTS

Copper-Nickel, 19.5 mm. **Ruler:** Elizabeth II **Obv:** Crowned bust right **Rev:** Flame lily

Date	Mintage	VF20	XF40	MS60	MS63	MS65
1964	13,500,000	0.25	0.40	0.75	1.25	3.00
1964	2,060	PF65 15.00				

KM# 2 SHILLING = 10 CENTS

Copper-Nickel, 23.5 mm. **Ruler:** Elizabeth II **Obv:** Crowned bust right **Rev:** Shield

Date	Mintage	VF20	XF40	MS60	MS63	MS65
1964	15,500,000	0.25	0.65	1.00	1.50	3.50
1964	2,060	PF65 18.00				

KM# 3 2 SHILLINGS = 20 CENTS

Copper-Nickel **Ruler:** Elizabeth II **Obv:** Crowned bust right **Rev:** Native headdress

Date	Mintage	VF20	XF40	MS60	MS63	MS65
1964	10,500,000	0.50	1.25	2.00	3.00	5.00
1964	2,060	PF65 20.00				

KM# 4 2-1/2 SHILLINGS = 25 CENTS

14.00 g., Copper-Nickel, 32.5 mm. **Ruler:** Elizabeth II **Obv:** Crowned bust right **Rev:** Sable antelope

Date	Mintage	VF20	XF40	MS60	MS63	MS65
1964	11,500,000	1.00	2.00	3.00	4.50	6.00
1964	2,060	PF65 25.00				

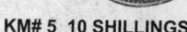

KM# 5 10 SHILLINGS

3.99 g., 0.916 Gold 0.1176 oz. AGW **Ruler:** Elizabeth II **Obv:** Crowned bust right **Rev:** Sable antelope

Date	Mintage	VF20	XF40	MS60	MS63	MS65
1966	6,000	PF65 200	PF67 250			

KM# 6 POUND

7.99 g., 0.916 Gold 0.2353 oz. AGW **Ruler:** Elizabeth II **Obv:** Crowned bust right **Rev:** Lion

Date	Mintage	VF20	XF40	MS60	MS63	MS65
1966	5,000	PF65 425	PF67 475			

KM# 7 5 POUNDS

39.94 g., 0.916 Gold 1.1762 oz. AGW **Ruler:** Elizabeth II **Obv:** Crowned bust right **Rev:** Arms with supporters divides date

Date	Mintage	VF20	XF40	MS60	MS63	MS65
1966	3,000	PF63 1,950	PF65 2,150	PF67 2,500		

REPUBLIC

DECIMAL COINAGE

KM# 9 1/2 CENT

Bronze, 20 mm. **Obv:** Value and date to upper left of sprig **Rev:** Arms with supporters

Date	Mintage	VF20	XF40	MS60	MS63	MS65
1970	10,000,000	0.10	0.25	0.50	1.00	3.00
1970	12	PF65 650				
1971	2,000,000	0.10	0.25	0.50	1.25	3.50
1972	2,000,000	0.10	0.25	0.50	1.25	3.50
1972	12	PF65 650				
1975	10,001,000	0.10	0.20	0.40	0.60	1.50
1975	10	PF65 650				
1977	—	—	350	500	800	1,500

Note: Circulation mintage melted, less than 10 surviving specimens known

Date	Mintage	VF20	XF40	MS60	MS63	MS65
1977 Proof	10	—	—	—	—	—

KM# 10 CENT

4.00 g., Bronze, 22.5 mm. **Obv:** Value and date to upper left of sprig **Rev:** Arms with supporters

Date	Mintage	VF20	XF40	MS60	MS63	MS65
1970	25,000,000	0.10	0.25	0.50	1.00	3.00
1970	12	PF65 750				
1971	15,000,000	0.10	0.25	0.50	1.00	3.00
1972	10,000,000	0.10	0.25	0.50	1.00	3.00
1972	12	PF65 750				
1973	5,000,000	0.10	0.25	0.50	1.50	3.50
1973	10	PF65 750				
1974	—	0.10	0.25	0.50	1.00	3.00
1975	10,000,000	0.10	0.25	0.50	1.00	3.00
1975	10	PF65 750				
1976	20,000,000	0.10	0.20	0.40	0.60	1.50
1976	10	PF65 750				
1977	10,000,000	0.10	0.20	0.40	0.60	1.50

KM# 11 2-1/2 CENTS

Copper-Nickel **Obv:** Three spear points divides date below value **Rev:** Arms with supporters

Date	Mintage	VF20	XF40	MS60	MS63	MS65
1970	4,000,000	0.25	0.45	0.75	1.50	3.50
1970	12	PF65 800				

KM# 12 5 CENTS

3.00 g., Copper-Nickel **Obv:** Flame lily divides date **Rev:** Arms with supporters

Date	Mintage	VF20	XF40	MS60	MS63	MS65
1973	—	0.45	0.75	1.50	3.00	5.00
1973	10	PF65 750				

KM# 13 5 CENTS

Copper-Nickel **Obv:** Flame lily **Rev:** Arms with supporters

Date	Mintage	VF20	XF40	MS60	MS63	MS65
1975	3,500,000	0.25	0.35	0.60	1.00	3.00
1975	10	PF65 800				
1976	8,038,000	0.25	0.35	0.60	1.00	3.00
1977	3,015,000	0.45	0.75	1.50	3.00	5.00

KM# 14 10 CENTS

Copper-Nickel **Obv:** Arms with supporters **Rev:** Shield, value and date

Date	Mintage	VF20	XF40	MS60	MS63	MS65
1975	2,003,000	0.25	0.35	0.75	1.50	3.50
1975	10	PF65 850				

KM# 15 20 CENTS
Copper-Nickel **Obv:** Arms with supporters **Rev:** Native headdress, value and date

Date	Mintage	VF20	XF40	MS60	MS63	MS65
1975	1,937,000	0.40	0.60	1.00	3.00	5.00
1975	10	PF65 900				
1977	—	0.45	0.75	1.50	3.50	6.00

KM# 16 25 CENTS
Copper-Nickel **Obv:** Arms with supporters **Rev:** Sable antelope, value and date

Date	Mintage	VF20	XF40	MS60	MS63	MS65
1975	1,011,000	1.00	2.00	3.00	5.00	7.50
1975	10	PF65 900				

PATTERNS

Including off metal strikes

KM#	Date	Mintage	Identification	Mkt Val
Pn1	1980	6	25 Cents. Copper-Nickel.	2,000

PROOF SETS

KM#	Date	Mintage	Identification	Issue Price	Mkt Val
PS1	1964 (8)	10	KM#1-4 Double set	—	250
PS2	1964 (4)	2,060	KM#1-4	—	80.00
PS3	1966 (3)	2,000	KM#5-7	280	2,875
PS4	1968 (1)	3	KM#8 Double set	—	2,400
PS5	1970 (3)	3	KM#9-11 Double set	—	5,700
PS6	1973 (1)	2	KM#12 Double set	—	1,900
PS7	1975 (4)	1	KM#13-16 Double set	—	7,500
PS8	1975 (6)	4	KM#9, 10, 13-16	—	5,650
PS9	1975 (4)	4	KM#13-16	—	3,750

RHODESIA & NYASALAND

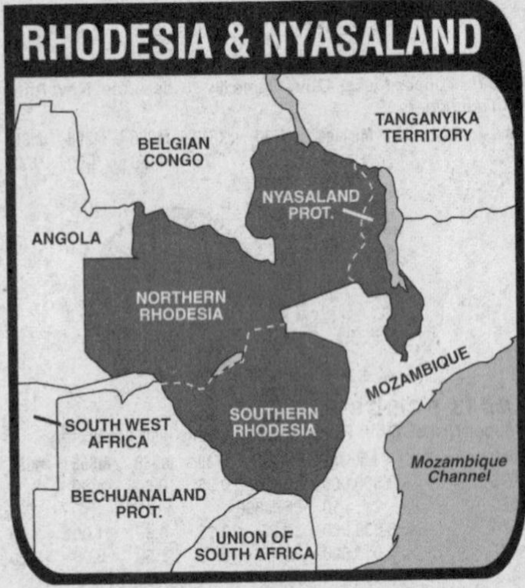

The Federation of Rhodesia and Nyasaland was located in the east-central part of southern Africa. The multiracial federation has an area of about 487,000 sq. mi. (1,261,330 sq. km.) and a population of 6.8 million. Capital: Salisbury, in Southern Rhodesia.

The geographical unity of the three British possessions suggested the desirability of political and economic union as early as 1924. Despite objections by the African constituency of Northern Rhodesia and Nyasaland, who feared that African self-determination would be retarded by the dominant influence of prosperous and self-governing Southern Rhodesia. The Central African Federation was established in Sept. of 1953. As feared by the European constituency, Southern Rhodesia despite the fact that the three component countries largely retained their pre-federation political structure effectively and profitably dominated the Federation. It was dissolved at the end of 1963, largely because of the effective opposition of the Nyasaland African Congress. Northern Rhodesia and Nyasaland became the independent states of Zambia and Malawi in 1964. Southern Rhodesia unilaterally declared its independence the following year, which was not recognized by the British Government.

For earlier coinage refer to Southern Rhodesia. For later coinage refer to Malawi, Zambia, Rhodesia and Zimbabwe.

RULER
Elizabeth II, 1952-1964

MONETARY SYSTEM
12 Pence = 1 Shilling
5 Shillings = 1 Crown
20 Shillings = 1 Pound

FEDERATION

STANDARD COINAGE

KM# 1 1/2 PENNY
Bronze, 21 mm. **Ruler:** Elizabeth II **Obv:** Hole in center flanked by giraffes with crown above **Rev:** Value around hole in center flanked by sprigs

Date	Mintage	VF20	XF40	MS60	MS63	MS65
1955	720,000	0.25	0.50	1.50	4.00	6.00
1955	2,010	PF65 20.00				
1956	480,000	0.50	1.00	2.00	4.00	6.00
1956	—	PF65 500				
1957	1,920,000	0.15	0.25	1.00	4.00	6.00
1957	—	PF65 450				
1958	2,400,000	0.15	0.25	1.00	4.00	6.00
1958	—	PF65 450				
1964	1,440,000	0.15	0.25	1.00	4.00	6.00

KM# 2 PENNY
6.30 g., Bronze **Ruler:** Elizabeth II **Obv:** Hole in center and crown flanked by elephants **Rev:** Value around hole in center flanked by sprigs

Date	Mintage	VF20	XF40	MS60	MS63	MS65
1955	2,040,000	0.25	0.75	1.50	4.50	7.50
1955	2,010	PF65 20.00				
1956	4,800,000	0.25	0.50	1.50	4.50	7.50
1956	—	PF65 500				
1957	7,200,000	0.15	0.25	1.50	4.50	7.50
1957 Proof	—	—	—	—	—	—
1958	2,880,000	0.15	0.25	1.50	4.50	7.50
1958	—	PF65 450				
1961	4,800,000	0.15	0.25	1.50	4.50	7.50
1961 Proof	—	—	—	—	—	—
1962	6,000,000	0.15	0.25	1.50	4.50	7.50
1963	6,000,000	0.15	0.25	1.50	4.50	7.50
1963	—	PF65 450				

KM# 3 3 PENCE
Copper-Nickel, 16.3 mm. **Ruler:** Elizabeth II **Obv:** Bust right **Rev:** Flame lily divides date

Date	Mintage	VF20	XF40	MS60	MS63	MS65
1955	1,200,000	0.50	0.75	1.50	4.50	7.50
1955	10	PF65 350				
1956	3,200,000	1.00	2.50	4.00	12.00	20.00
1956	—	PF65 600				
1957	6,000,000	0.50	0.75	1.50	3.00	5.00
1957	—	PF65 600				
1962	4,000,000	0.50	0.75	1.50	3.00	5.00
1962 Proof	—	—	—	—	—	—
1963	2,000,000	0.50	0.75	1.50	3.00	5.00
1963 Proof	—	—	—	—	—	—
1964	3,600,000	0.25	0.50	1.50	3.00	5.00

KM# 3a 3 PENCE
1.41 g., 0.500 Silver 0.0227 oz. ASW, 16.3 mm. **Ruler:** Elizabeth II **Obv:** Bust laureate right **Rev:** Flame lily divides date

Date	Mintage	VF20	XF40	MS60	MS63	MS65
1955	2,000	PF65 25.00				

KM# 4 6 PENCE
Copper-Nickel **Ruler:** Elizabeth II **Obv:** Bust right **Rev:** Lion standing on rock

Date	Mintage	VF20	XF40	MS60	MS63	MS65
1955	400,000	1.00	2.50	4.00	7.50	10.00
1955	10	PF65 400				
1956	800,000	2.00	7.00	12.00	25.00	40.00
1956	—	PF65 900				
1957	4,000,000	0.50	1.00	2.00	4.00	7.50
1957 Proof	—	—	—	—	—	—
1962	2,800,000	0.50	1.00	2.00	4.00	8.00
1962 Proof	—	—	—	—	—	—
1963	800,000	5.00	8.00	20.00	35.00	50.00
1963 Proof	—	—	—	—	—	—

KM# 4a 6 PENCE
2.83 g., 0.500 Silver 0.0455 oz. ASW **Ruler:** Elizabeth II **Obv:** Bust laureate right **Rev:** Lion standing on rock

Date	Mintage	VF20	XF40	MS60	MS63	MS65
1955	2,000	PF65 30.00				

KM# 5 SHILLING
Copper-Nickel **Ruler:** Elizabeth II **Obv:** Bust right **Rev:** Sable antelope

Date	Mintage	VF20	XF40	MS60	MS63	MS65
1955	200,000	2.50	4.50	7.00	10.00	18.00
1955	10	PF65 450				
1956	1,700,000	1.50	3.50	7.00	20.00	30.00
1956 Proof	—	—	—	—	—	—
1957	3,500,000	1.00	2.50	4.00	8.00	15.00
1957 Proof	—	—	—	—	—	—

KM# 5a SHILLING
5.66 g., 0.500 Silver 0.091 oz. ASW **Ruler:** Elizabeth II **Obv:** Bust laureate right **Rev:** Antelope

Date	Mintage	VF20	XF40	MS60	MS63	MS65
1955	2,000	PF65 40.00				

KM# 6 2 SHILLINGS
Copper-Nickel **Ruler:** Elizabeth II **Obv:** Bust right **Rev:** Eagle in flight left with fish in talons, flanked by ER

Date	Mintage	VF20	XF40	MS60	MS63	MS65
1955	1,750,000	2.50	5.00	7.50	12.50	20.00
1955	10	PF65 550				
1956	1,850,000	2.50	4.50	7.00	12.00	20.00
1956	—	PF65 1,000				
1957	1,500,000	2.50	4.50	7.00	12.00	20.00
1957 Proof	—	—	—	—	—	—

KM# 6a 2 SHILLINGS
11.31 g., 0.500 Silver 0.1818 oz. ASW **Ruler:** Elizabeth II **Obv:** Bust right **Rev:** Eagle with talons in fish

Date	Mintage	VF20	XF40	MS60	MS63	MS65
1955	2,000	PF65 50.00				

KM# 7 1/2 CROWN
Copper-Nickel **Ruler:** Elizabeth II **Obv:** Bust right **Rev:** Arms with supporters

Date	Mintage	VF20	XF40	MS60	MS63	MS65
1955	1,600,000	2.50	5.00	10.00	20.00	35.00
1955	10	PF65 600				
1956	160,000	15.00	35.00	75.00	165	250
1956 Proof	—	—	—	—	—	—
1957	2,400,000	7.50	12.00	20.00	35.00	100
1957	—	PF65 800				

KM# 7a 1/2 CROWN
14.14 g., 0.500 Silver 0.2273 oz. ASW **Ruler:** Elizabeth II **Obv:** Bust laureate right **Rev:** Arms with supporters

Date	Mintage	VF20	XF40	MS60	MS63	MS65
1955	2,000	PF65 60.00				

PROOF SETS

KM#	Date	Mintage	Identification	Issue Price	Mkt Val
PS1	1955 (7)	10	KM1-7, possibly in a blue case, confirmation required	—	2,500
PS2	1955 (7)	2,000	KM1-2, 3a-7a, in red case	—	250

ROMANIA

Romania (formerly the Socialist Republic of Romania), a country in southeast Europe, has an area of 91,699 sq. mi. (237,500 sq. km.) and a population of 23.2 million. Capital: Bucharest. Machinery, foodstuffs, raw minerals and petroleum products are exported. Heavy industry and oil have become increasingly important to the economy since 1959.

A new constitution was adopted in 1923. During this period in history, the Romanian government struggled with domestic problems, agrarian reform and economic reconstruction.

On August 23, 1944, King Mihai I proclaimed an armistice with the Allied Forces. The Romanian army drove out the Germans and Hungarians in northern Transylvania, but the country was subsequently occupied by the Soviet army. That monarchy was abolished on December 30, 1947, and Romania became a "People's Republic" based on the Soviet regime. The process of sovietization included Soviet regime. The anti-Communist combative resistance movement developed frequent purges of dissidents: mainly political but also clerical, cultural and peasants. Romanian elite disappeared into the concentration camps. The anti-Communist combative resistance movement developed in spite of the Soviet army presence until 1956. The partisans remained in the mountains until 1964. With the accession of N. Ceausescu to power, Romania began to exercise a considerable degree of independence, refusing to participate in the invasion of Czechoslovakia (August 1968). In 1965, it was proclaimed a "Socialist Republic". After 1977, an oppressed and impoverished domestic scene worsened.

On December 17, 1989, an anti-Communist revolt in Timisoara. On December 22, 1989 the Communist government was overthrown. Ceausescu and his wife were arrested and later executed. The new government established a republic, the constitutional name being Romania.

RULERS

Carol I (as Prince), 1866-81 (as King), 1881-1914
Ferdinand I, 1914-1927
Mihai I, 1927-1930
Carol II, 1930-1940
Mihai I, 1940-1947

MINT MARKS

(a) - Paris, privy marks only
(b) - Brussels, privy marks only
angel head (1872-1876),
no marks (1894-1924)
B - Bucharest (1870-1900)
B - Hamburg, Germany
C - Candescu, chief engineer of the Bucharest Mint (1870-)
FM - Franklin Mint, USA
H - Heaton, Birmingham, England
HF - Huguenin Freres & Co., Le Locle, Switzerland
J - Hamburg
KN - Kings Norton, Birmingham, England
(p) - Thunderbolt - Poissy, France
zig zag (1924)
V - Vienna, Austria
W - Watt (James Watt & Co.)
Huguenin - Le Locle, Switzerland
( ) - no marks, 1930 (10, 20 Lei), 1932 (100 Lei), Royal Mint – London

MINT OFFICIALS' INITIALS

Initials	Date	Name
Bassarab		Costache Bassarab
Ioana Bassarab	1941-45	Ioana Bassarab Starostescu
E.W. Becker	1939-40	E. W. Becker
(wing)		Lucien Bazor
P.M. Dammann	1922	P.M. Dammann
C.D.	1990	C. Dumitrescu
V.G.	1990	Vasile Gabor
H.I.; H. Ionescu	1939-52	Haralamb, Ionescu
I. Jalea	1935-41	Ion Jalea
Lavrillier	1930-32	A. Lavrillier
A.M.; A. Michaux	1906	Alfons Michaux
A. Murnu	1940	A. Murnu
(torch)		Henry Auguste Jules Patey
A. Romanescu	1946	A. Romanescu
A. Scharff	1894-1901	Anton Scharff
Tasset	1910-14	Ernst Paulini Tasset

MONETARY SYSTEM

100 Bani = 1 Leu

KINGDOM

STANDARD COINAGE

KM# 31 5 BANI

2.32 g., Copper-Nickel, 19 mm. **Ruler:** Carol I **Obv:** Crown above banner and hole in center **Rev:** Hole in center flanked by designs with value above and date below

Date	Mintage	F12	VF20	XF40	MS60	MS63
1905	2,000,000	1.00	2.50	4.50	12.00	25.00
1905	—	PF63 150				
1906	48,000,000	0.50	2.00	4.00	10.00	20.00
1906 J	24,000,000	0.50	1.50	3.00	6.00	20.00

KM# 32 10 BANI

4.00 g., Copper-Nickel, 22 mm. **Ruler:** Carol I **Obv:** Crown above banner and hole in center **Rev:** Hole in center flanked by designs with value above and date below

Date	Mintage	VF20	XF40	MS60	MS63	MS65
1905	10,820,000	4.00	9.00	18.00	50.00	75.00
1905	—	PF63 175				
1906	24,180,000	2.00	7.00	14.00	40.00	60.00
1906 J	17,000,000	1.50	6.00	12.00	35.00	50.00

KM# 33 20 BANI

5.90 g., Copper-Nickel, 25 mm. **Ruler:** Carol I **Obv:** Crown above banner and hole in center **Rev:** Hole in center flanked by designs with value above and date below

Date	Mintage	VF20	XF40	MS60	MS63	MS65
1905	2,500,000	7.00	15.00	32.00	75.00	125
1905	—	PF63 200				
1906	3,000,000	8.00	16.00	42.00	100	150
1906 J	2,500,000	7.00	12.00	32.00	75.00	125

KM# 44 25 BANI

0.90 g., Aluminum, 19 mm. **Ruler:** Ferdinand I **Obv:** Eagle above hole in center **Rev:** Hole in center of value with crown at right **Note:** Center hole sizes vary from 4 to 4.5mm.

Date	Mintage	VF20	XF40	MS60	MS63	MS65
1921	20,000,000	3.00	5.00	10.00	15.00	22.00

KM# 23 50 BANI

2.50 g., 0.835 Silver 0.0671 oz. ASW, 19 mm. **Ruler:** Carol I **Obv:** Head left **Rev:** Value, date within wreath **Edge:** Reeded

Date	Mintage	F12	VF20	XF40	MS60	MS63
1901	194,205	25.00	50.00	110	175	275

KM# 41 50 BANI

2.50 g., 0.835 Silver 0.0671 oz. ASW, 18 mm. **Ruler:** Carol I **Obv:** Head left **Rev:** Crown above design **Edge:** Reeded

Date	Mintage	VF20	XF40	MS60	MS63	MS65
1910	3,600,000	4.50	9.00	20.00	35.00	50.00
Note: Edge varieties (round or flat) exist						
1910	—	PF63 275				
1911	3,000,000	5.00	10.00	22.00	37.00	52.00
1912	1,800,000	6.00	12.00	25.00	40.00	55.00
1914	1,600,000	4.00	9.00	20.00	35.00	50.00
Note: Edge varieties (round or flat) exist						
1914	—	PF63 325				

KM# 45 50 BANI

1.20 g., Aluminum, 21 mm. **Ruler:** Ferdinand I **Obv:** Eagle above hole in center **Rev:** Hole in center of value with crown at right **Note:** Center hole size varies from 4 to 4.5mm.

Date	Mintage	VF20	XF40	MS60	MS63	MS65
1921	30,000,000	2.50	5.00	7.00	12.00	20.00

KM# 24 LEU

5.00 g., 0.835 Silver 0.1342 oz. ASW, 23 mm. **Ruler:** Carol I **Edge:** Reeded

Date	Mintage	F12	VF20	XF40	MS60	MS63
1901	369,614	15.00	60.00	175	400	650
1901	—	PF60 1,350	PF63 2,000			

KM# 34 LEU

5.00 g., 0.835 Silver 0.1342 oz. ASW, 23 mm. **Ruler:** Carol I **Subject:** 40th Anniversary - Reign of Carol I **Obv:** Bearded head left **Rev:** Head left **Edge:** Reeded **Note:** Designer's name below truncation on reverse.

Date	Mintage	VF20	XF40	MS60	MS63	MS65
ND-1906	2,500,000	12.00	18.00	35.00	75.00	125
ND-1906	—	PF63 320	PF65 500			

KM# 42 LEU

5.00 g., 0.835 Silver 0.1342 oz. ASW, 23 mm. **Ruler:** Carol I **Obv:** Bearded head left **Rev:** Standing figure walking right **Edge:** Reeded

Date	Mintage	VF20	XF40	MS60	MS63	MS65
1910	4,600,000	7.50	15.00	30.00	40.00	60.00
Note: Edge varieties (round or flat) exist						
1910	—	PF63 350	PF65 550			
1911	2,573,000	11.50	17.00	32.00	42.00	65.00
1912	3,540,000	11.50	17.00	32.00	42.00	65.00
1914	4,282,935	6.50	12.50	25.00	35.00	60.00
Note: Edge varieties (round or flat) exist						
1914	—	PF63 520				

KM# 46 LEU

3.50 g., Copper-Nickel, 21 mm. **Ruler:** Ferdinand I **Obv:** Crowned arms with supporters flanked by stars **Rev:** Value above sprig **Edge:** Reeded

Date	Mintage	VF20	XF40	MS60	MS63	MS65
1924 (b) Thin	100,000,000	1.75	3.50	10.00	15.00	25.00
1924 (p) Thick	100,006,000	1.75	3.50	10.00	15.00	25.00

KM# 56 LEU
2.75 g., Nickel-Brass, 18 mm. **Ruler:** Carol II **Obv:** Crown and date above sprig **Rev:** Ear of corn divides value **Edge:** Plain **Note:** Without mint mark.

Date	Mintage	VF20	XF40	MS60	MS63	MS65
1938	27,900,000	0.60	1.75	4.50	8.50	17.00
1939	21,000,000	0.50	1.50	3.50	7.50	15.00
1940	22,230,000	0.50	1.00	3.00	7.50	15.00
1941	20,250,000	0.50	1.50	3.50	7.50	15.00

KM# 25 2 LEI
10.00 g., 0.835 Silver 0.2685 oz. ASW, 27 mm. **Ruler:** Carol I **Obv:** Head left **Obv. Legend:** CAROL I. **Rev:** Crowned arms with supporters within crowned mantle, divided value **Edge:** Reeded

Date	Mintage	F12	VF20	XF40	MS60	MS63
1901	12,476	600	1,350	3,500	7,500	14,500

KM# 43 2 LEI
10.00 g., 0.835 Silver 0.2685 oz. ASW, 27 mm. **Ruler:** Carol I **Obv:** Bearded head left **Rev:** Standing figure walking right

Date	Mintage	VF20	XF40	MS60	MS63	MS65
1910	1,800,000	13.00	18.00	35.00	50.00	75.00
Note: Edge varieties (round and flat) exist						
1910	—	PF63 250	PF65 400			
1911	1,000,000	15.00	20.00	40.00	60.00	90.00
1912	1,500,000	16.00	22.00	45.00	65.00	100
1914	2,452,000	12.00	16.00	20.00	35.00	65.00
Note: Edge varieties (round and flat) exist						
1914	—	PF63 600				

KM# 47 2 LEI
7.00 g., Copper-Nickel, 25 mm. **Ruler:** Ferdinand I **Obv:** Crowned arms with supporters flanked by stars **Rev:** Value above sprig **Edge:** Reeded

Date	Mintage	VF20	XF40	MS60	MS63	MS65
1924 (b)	50,000,000	2.50	5.00	10.00	15.00	25.00
1924 (p)	50,008,000	2.50	5.00	10.00	15.00	25.00

KM# 58 2 LEI
3.20 g., Zinc, 20 mm. **Ruler:** Mihai I **Obv:** Crown above date **Rev:** Value within wreath

Date	Mintage	VF20	XF40	MS60	MS63	MS65
1941	101,778,000	3.00	7.00	20.00	40.00	—

KM# 17.2 5 LEI
25.00 g., 0.900 Silver 0.7234 oz. ASW, 38 mm. **Ruler:** Carol I **Obv:** Head left **Rev:** Crowned arms with supporters within crowned mantle, divided date **Edge:** Reeded

Date	Mintage	F12	VF20	XF40	MS60	MS63
1901 B	82,460	75.00	150	500	1,000	1,850
1901 B	—	PF63 5,500	PF65 9,500			

KM# 35 5 LEI
25.00 g., 0.900 Silver 0.7234 oz. ASW, 38 mm. **Ruler:** Carol I **Subject:** 40th Anniversary - Reign of Carol I **Obv:** Bearded head left **Rev:** Head left **Edge:** Reeded

Date	Mintage	VF20	XF40	MS60	MS63	MS65
ND-1906	200,000	140	450	800	1,500	—
ND-1906	—	PF63 1,800	PF65 3,000			

KM# 48 5 LEI
3.50 g., Nickel-Brass, 21 mm. **Ruler:** Mihai I **Obv:** Head left **Rev:** Crowned shield divides value flanked by stars **Edge:** Reeded

Date	Mintage	VF20	XF40	MS60	MS63	MS65
1930 H	15,000,000	4.50	12.50	25.00	45.00	75.00
1930 KN	15,000,000	6.00	18.00	35.00	75.00	125
1930 (a)	30,000,000	4.00	12.00	20.00	42.00	75.00

KM# 61 5 LEI
4.50 g., Zinc, 23 mm. **Ruler:** Mihai I **Obv:** Crown above date **Rev:** Oat sprigs to right of value

Date	Mintage	VF20	XF40	MS60	MS63	MS65
1942	140,000,000	2.50	6.00	18.00	35.00	—

KM# 49 10 LEI
5.00 g., Nickel-Brass, 23 mm. **Ruler:** Carol II **Obv:** Head left **Rev:** Crowned eagle with crowned shield on chest divides value **Edge:** Reeded

Date	Mintage	VF20	XF40	MS60	MS63	MS65
1930	15,000,000	10.00	20.00	35.00	75.00	150
1930	—	PF63 300				
1930 (a)	30,000,000	6.50	17.00	30.00	50.00	95.00
1930 H	7,500,000	7.00	18.00	30.00	50.00	95.00
1930 KN	7,500,000	15.00	25.00	45.00	85.00	160
1930 (a)	—	PF63 400				

KM# 36 12-1/2 LEI
4.03 g., 0.900 Gold 0.1167 oz. AGW, 19 mm. **Ruler:** Carol I **Subject:** 40th Anniversary - Reign of Carol I **Obv:** Bearded bust left **Rev:** Crowned eagle and banner

Date	Mintage	VF20	XF40	MS60	MS63	MS65
1906	32,000	177	350	550	900	—

KM# 37 20 LEI
6.45 g., 0.900 Gold 0.1867 oz. AGW, 20 mm. **Ruler:** Carol I **Subject:** 40th Anniversary - Reign of Carol I **Obv:** Bearded head left **Rev:** Head left **Edge:** Reeded

Date	Mintage	VF20	XF40	MS60	MS63	MS65
ND-1906 (b)	15,000	285	375	600	1,000	—

KM# 50 20 LEI
7.50 g., Nickel-Brass, 27 mm. **Ruler:** Mihai I **Obv:** Young head left **Rev:** Figures holding hands divides value **Edge:** Reeded

Date	Mintage	VF20	XF40	MS60	MS63	MS65
1930 London	40,000,000	7.00	15.00	30.00	50.00	95.00
1930	—	PF63 400				
1930 H	5,000,000	8.00	18.00	32.00	60.00	100
1930 KN	5,000,000	10.00	22.00	37.00	75.00	125

KM# 51 20 LEI
7.50 g., Nickel-Brass, 27 mm. **Ruler:** Carol II **Obv:** Head left **Rev:** Crowned eagle with crowned shield on chest divides value **Edge:** Reeded

Date	Mintage	VF20	XF40	MS60	MS63	MS65
1930	6,750,000	6.00	12.00	28.00	45.00	90.00
1930 Proof	—	—	—	—	—	—
1930 (a)	17,500,000	5.00	10.00	25.00	42.00	85.00
1930 (a)	—	PF63 1,000				
1930 KN	7,750,000	10.00	20.00	45.00	75.00	125
1930 KN	—	PF63 1,200				
1930 H	7,750,000	5.00	10.00	25.00	42.00	85.00
1930 H	—	PF63 1,000				

KM# 62 20 LEI
6.00 g., Zinc, 26.3 mm. **Ruler:** Mihai I **Obv:** Crown above date **Rev:** Value within wreath **Edge:** Reeded

Date	Mintage	VF20	XF40	MS60	MS63	MS65
1942	44,000,000	3.00	6.00	10.00	25.00	—
1943	25,783,000	3.00	7.00	12.00	27.00	—
1944	5,034,000	3.50	7.50	15.00	30.00	—

KM# 38 25 LEI
8.07 g., 0.900 Gold 0.2334 oz. AGW, 30 mm. **Ruler:** Carol I **Subject:** 40th Anniversary - Reign of Carol I **Obv:** Uniformed bust left **Rev:** Crowned eagle and banner

Date	Mintage	VF20	XF40	MS60	MS63	MS65
ND-1906 (b)	24,000	370	600	900	1,500	—

KM# 39 50 LEI
16.13 g., 0.900 Gold 0.4667 oz. AGW, 35 mm. **Ruler:** Carol I **Subject:** 40th Anniversary - Reign of Carol I **Obv:** Uniformed bust left **Rev:** Equestrian

Date	Mintage	VF20	XF40	MS60	MS63	MS65
ND-1906 (b)	28,000	740	1,450	2,850	4,500	—

KM# 55 50 LEI
5.83 g., Nickel, 24 mm. **Ruler:** Carol II **Obv:** Helmeted head left **Rev:** Crowned shield within sprigs divides value **Edge:** Reeded **Note:** 16,731 pieces melted.

Date	Mintage	VF20	XF40	MS60	MS63	MS65
1937	12,000,000	4.00	10.00	25.00	45.00	100
1938	8,000,000	7.00	15.00	45.00	85.00	125

KM# 40 100 LEI
32.26 g., 0.900 Gold 0.9335 oz. AGW, 36 mm. **Ruler:** Carol I **Subject:** 40th Anniversary - Reign of Carol I **Note:** Similar to KM#35.

Date	Mintage	VF20	XF40	MS60	MS63	MS65
ND-1906 (b)	3,000	1,750	3,250	6,500	12,000	—

KM# 52 100 LEI
14.00 g., 0.500 Silver 0.2251 oz. ASW, 31 mm. **Ruler:** Carol II **Obv:** Head right **Rev:** Crowned eagle divides wreath with value within **Edge:** Reeded

Date	Mintage	VF20	XF40	MS60	MS63	MS65
1932 (a)	2,000,000	20.00	40.00	100	225	600
1932	16,400,000	15.00	35.00	75.00	150	400
1932	—	PF63 1,400	PF65 2,700			

KM# 54 100 LEI
8.20 g., Nickel, 27 mm. **Ruler:** Carol II **Obv:** Head left **Rev:** Crowned shield within sprigs flanked by value **Edge:** Reeded **Note:** 17,030 pieces melted.

Date	Mintage	VF20	XF40	MS60	MS63	MS65
1936	20,230,000	8.00	18.00	65.00	100	—
1938	3,250,000	18.00	45.00	120	200	—

KM# 64 100 LEI
8.50 g., Nickel Clad Steel, 28 mm. **Ruler:** Mihai I **Obv:** Head right **Rev:** Crown divides wreath with date and value within **Edge:** Incuse lettering **Edge Lettering:** NIHIL SINE DEO

Date	Mintage	VF20	XF40	MS60	MS63	MS65
1943	40,590,000	1.00	3.00	8.00	15.00	30.00
Note: Portrait varieties exist						
1944	21,289,000	2.00	4.00	10.00	18.00	35.00

KM# 63 200 LEI
6.00 g., 0.835 Silver 0.1611 oz. ASW, 24 mm. **Ruler:** Mihai I **Obv:** Head right **Rev:** Crowned arms with supporters **Edge:** Incuse lettering **Edge Lettering:** NIHIL SINE DEO

Date	Mintage	VF20	XF40	MS60	MS63	MS65
1942	30,025,000	3.00	5.00	10.00	20.00	40.00

KM# 66 200 LEI
7.30 g., Brass, 27.2 mm. **Ruler:** Mihai I **Obv:** Head right **Rev:** Crown divides wreath with date and value within **Note:** Many were silver-plated privately.

Date	Mintage	VF20	XF40	MS60	MS63	MS65
1945	1,399,000	2.00	4.00	10.00	18.00	35.00

KM# 53 250 LEI
13.50 g., 0.750 Silver 0.3255 oz. ASW, 29 mm. **Ruler:** Carol II **Obv:** Head left **Rev:** Crowned eagle with shield on chest

Date	Mintage	VF20	XF40	MS60	MS63	MS65
1935	4,500,000	45.00	95.00	250	650	1,000

Note: Bank reports show that between 1937-39 4,490,670 pieces were withdrawn and remelted

KM# 57 250 LEI
12.00 g., 0.835 Silver 0.3222 oz. ASW, 30 mm. **Ruler:** Carol II **Obv:** Head right **Rev:** Crowned shield divides wreath with date and value within **Edge:** Incuse lettering, line interrupted by two rhombs **Edge Lettering:** MUNCA CREDINTA REGE NATIUNE

Date	Mintage	VF20	XF40	MS60	MS63	MS65
1939	10,000,000	6.00	15.00	35.00	75.00	150
1940	8,000,000	6.00	18.00	40.00	85.00	170

KM# 59.1 250 LEI
12.00 g., 0.835 Silver 0.3222 oz. ASW **Ruler:** Carol II **Obv:** Head left **Rev:** Date divided by portcullis **Edge:** Incuse lettering **Edge Lettering:** TOTUL PENTRU TARA **Note:** Mintage unissued and reportedly melted.

Date	Mintage	VF20	XF40	MS60	MS63	MS65
1940	—	—	—	—	6,000	9,500

Note: Deceptive fakes exist.

KM# 59.2 250 LEI
12.00 g., 0.835 Silver 0.3222 oz. ASW, 30 mm. **Ruler:** Mihai I **Obv:** Head left **Rev:** Crowned shield divides date with value and date within **Edge:** Incuse lettering **Edge Lettering:** TOTUL PENTRU TARA

Date	Mintage	VF20	XF40	MS60	MS63	MS65
1941	2,250,000	12.00	20.00	45.00	75.00	150

KM# 59.3 250 LEI
12.00 g., 0.835 Silver 0.3222 oz. ASW, 30 mm. **Ruler:** Mihai I **Obv:** Head left **Edge:** Lettered **Edge Lettering:** NIHIL SINE DEO

Date	Mintage	VF20	XF40	MS60	MS63	MS65
1941 B	13,750,000	6.00	10.00	18.00	25.00	45.00

KM# 60 500 LEI
25.00 g., 0.835 Silver 0.6711 oz. ASW, 37 mm. **Ruler:** Mihai I **Subject:** Basarabia Reunion **Obv:** Young head left **Rev:** Crowned kneeling figure presenting putna monastery to Lord **Edge:** Incuse lettering **Edge Lettering:** PRIN STATORNICIE LA IZBANADA +

Date	Mintage	VF20	XF40	MS60	MS63	MS65
1941	775,000	15.00	25.00	40.00	50.00	75.00

KM# 65 500 LEI
12.00 g., 0.700 Silver 0.2701 oz. ASW, 32 mm. **Ruler:** Mihai I **Obv:** Head left **Rev:** Crowned arms with supporters within crowned mantle divides date **Edge:** Incuse lettering **Edge Lettering:** NIHIL SINE DEO

Date	Mintage	VF20	XF40	MS60	MS63	MS65
1944	9,731,000	5.00	10.00	15.00	25.00	45.00

KM# 67 500 LEI
10.00 g., Brass, 30 mm. **Ruler:** Mihai I **Obv:** Head left **Rev:** Crowned arms with supporters within crowned mantle divides date **Edge:** Reeded **Note:** Many were silver-plated privately.

Date	Mintage	VF20	XF40	MS60	MS63	MS65
1945	3,422,000	3.50	7.00	12.00	20.00	37.00

KM# 68 500 LEI
1.50 g., Aluminum, 24 mm. **Ruler:** Mihai I **Obv:** Head right **Rev:** Value above sprig **Edge:** Reeded **Note:** Without designer's name, the result of a filled die.

Date	Mintage	VF20	XF40	MS60	MS63	MS65
1946	5,823,000	2.50	3.50	10.00	15.00	25.00

KM# 69 2000 LEI
5.10 g., Brass, 24 mm. **Ruler:** Mihai I **Obv:** Head right **Rev:** Crowned arms with supporters **Edge:** Incuse lettering **Edge Lettering:** NIHIL SINE DEO **Note:** Many were silver-plated privately.

Date	Mintage	VF20	XF40	MS60	MS63	MS65
1946	24,619,000	3.00	6.00	12.00	15.00	25.00

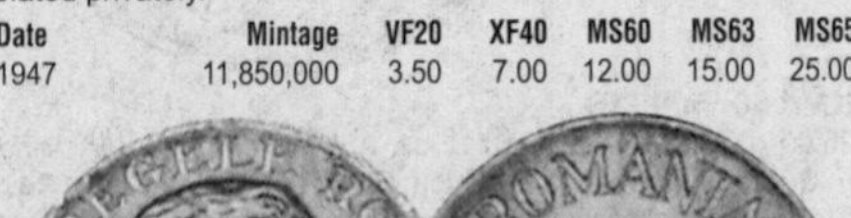

KM# 76 10000 LEI
10.00 g., Brass, 27 mm. **Ruler:** Mihai I **Obv:** Head right **Rev:** Crowned shield to left of value and sprigs **Edge:** Incuse lettering **Edge Lettering:** NIHIL SINE DEO **Note:** Many were silver-plated privately.

Date	Mintage	VF20	XF40	MS60	MS63	MS65
1947	11,850,000	3.50	7.00	12.00	15.00	25.00

KM# 70 25000 LEI
12.50 g., 0.700 Silver 0.2813 oz. ASW, 32 mm. **Ruler:** Mihai I **Obv:** Head right **Rev:** Crowned shield to left of value and sprigs **Edge:** Incuse lettering **Edge Lettering:** NIHIL SINE DEO

Date	Mintage	VF20	XF40	MS60	MS63	MS65
1946	2,372,000	5.25	8.00	12.50	20.00	30.00

KM# 71 100000 LEI
25.00 g., 0.700 Silver 0.5626 oz. ASW, 37 mm. **Ruler:** Mihai I **Obv:** Head right **Rev:** Standing figure releasing dove with crowned shield at lower right, value at lower left **Edge:** Incuse lettering **Edge Lettering:** NIHIL SINE DEO

Date	Mintage	VF20	XF40	MS60	MS63	MS65
1946	2,002,000	10.50	20.00	30.00	45.00	75.00

REFORM COINAGE

Aug. 15, 1947; 100 Bani = 1 Leu

KM# 72 50 BANI
1.70 g., Brass, 16.1 mm. **Ruler:** Mihai I **Obv:** Crown above date **Rev:** Value **Edge:** Plain

Date	Mintage	VF20	XF40	MS60	MS63	MS65
1947	13,266,000	3.00	3.00	10.00	25.00	—

KM# 73 LEU
2.50 g., Brass, 18 mm. **Ruler:** Mihai I **Obv:** Crowned shield **Rev:** Value within oat sprig **Edge:** Plain

Date	Mintage	VF20	XF40	MS60	MS63	MS65
1947	88,341,000	5.00	10.00	15.00	25.00	—

KM# 74 2 LEI
3.50 g., Bronze, 21 mm. **Ruler:** Mihai I **Obv:** Crowned shield and date **Rev:** Value within oat sprigs **Edge:** Plain

Date	Mintage	VF20	XF40	MS60	MS63	MS65
1947	40,000,000	5.00	10.00	15.00	25.00	—

KM# 75 5 LEI
1.50 g., Aluminum, 23 mm. **Ruler:** Mihai I **Obv:** Head right **Rev:** Value to left of oat sprig

Date	Mintage	VF20	XF40	MS60	MS63	MS65
1947	56,026,000	5.00	10.00	17.00	28.00	—

PEOPLE'S REPUBLIC

STANDARD COINAGE

KM# 78 LEU
1.83 g., Copper-Nickel-Zinc, 16 mm. **Obv:** Radiant sun and lighthouse **Rev:** Value and date **Edge:** Plain

Date	Mintage	VF20	XF40	MS60	MS63	MS65
1949	—	1.50	3.00	6.00	12.00	25.00
1950	—	1.50	4.00	8.00	14.00	35.00
1951	—	2.00	5.00	12.00	26.00	45.00

KM# 78a LEU
0.61 g., Aluminum, 16 mm. **Obv:** Radiant sun and lighthouse **Rev:** Value and date

Date	Mintage	VF20	XF40	MS60	MS63	MS65
1951	—	2.50	3.50	7.00	14.00	25.00
1952	—	7.00	15.00	30.00	75.00	150

KM# 79 2 LEI
2.44 g., Copper-Nickel-Zinc, 18 mm. **Obv:** Ear of corn flanked by oat and flower sprig **Rev:** Value and date **Edge:** Plain

Date	Mintage	VF20	XF40	MS60	MS63	MS65
1950	—	1.50	3.00	7.00	15.00	25.00
1951	—	2.00	4.00	8.00	16.00	27.00

KM# 79a 2 LEI
0.84 g., Aluminum, 18 mm. **Obv:** Ear of corn flanked by oat and flower sprig **Rev:** Value and date

Date	Mintage	VF20	XF40	MS60	MS63	MS65
1951	—	1.50	3.50	6.00	10.00	16.00
1952	—	15.00	25.00	50.00	100	225

KM# 77 5 LEI
1.50 g., Aluminum, 23 mm. **Obv:** National emblem **Rev:** Value within wreath **Edge:** Plain

Date	Mintage	VF20	XF40	MS60	MS63	MS65
1948	—	2.00	4.00	7.00	12.00	18.00
1949	—	1.50	3.00	6.00	12.00	17.00
1950	—	1.50	3.00	5.00	10.00	16.00
1951	—	1.50	3.00	6.00	12.00	20.00

KM# 80 20 LEI
2.12 g., Aluminum, 26 mm. **Obv:** National emblem **Rev:** Blacksmith at anvil, factory in background **Edge:** Plain

Date	Mintage	VF20	XF40	MS60	MS63	MS65
1951	—	6.00	12.00	20.00	35.00	65.00

REFORM COINAGE

Jan. 26, 1952; 20 "old" Lei + 1 "new" Lei; 100 Bani = 1 Leu

KM# 81.1 BAN
1.00 g., Copper-Nickel-Zinc, 16 mm. **Obv:** National emblem **Rev:** Value and date **Edge:** Reeded

Date	Mintage	VF20	XF40	MS60	MS63	MS65
1952	67,400,000	0.25	0.50	1.00	3.00	5.00

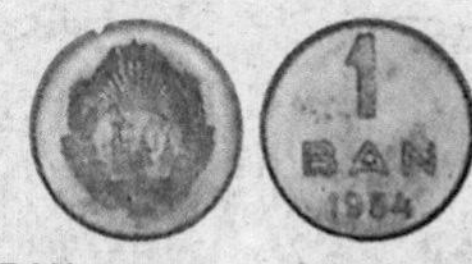

KM# 81.2 BAN
1.00 g., Copper-Nickel-Zinc, 15.2 mm. **Obv:** National emblem **Rev:** Value and date

Date	Mintage	VF20	XF40	MS60	MS63	MS65
1953	8,000,000	2.00	4.00	13.00	28.00	50.00
1954	15,300,000	2.00	3.50	12.00	25.00	45.00

KM# 82.1 3 BANI
2.00 g., Copper-Nickel-Zinc, 18 mm. **Obv:** National emblem **Rev:** Value and date **Edge:** Reeded

Date	Mintage	VF20	XF40	MS60	MS63	MS65
1952	26,100,000	1.00	2.00	7.00	15.00	25.00

KM# 82.2 3 BANI
2.00 g., Copper-Nickel-Zinc **Obv:** National emblem **Rev:** Value and date

Date	Mintage	VF20	XF40	MS60	MS63	MS65
1953	13,000,000	1.50	3.00	10.00	20.00	35.00
1954	33,400,000	10.00	20.00	35.00	75.00	150

KM# 83.1 5 BANI
2.40 g., Copper-Nickel-Zinc, 20 mm. **Obv:** National emblem **Rev:** Value and date **Edge:** Reeded

Date	Mintage	VF20	XF40	MS60	MS63	MS65
1952	78,400,000	0.50	1.00	3.00	9.00	18.00

KM# 83.2 5 BANI
2.40 g., Copper-Nickel-Zinc, 20 mm. **Obv:** National emblem **Rev:** Value and date

Date	Mintage	VF20	XF40	MS60	MS63	MS65
1953	54,600,000	2.00	3.50	7.00	12.00	25.00
1954	57,500,000	1.50	3.00	6.00	10.00	22.00
1955	38,100,000	1.50	3.00	6.00	10.00	22.00
1956	30,900,000	1.50	3.00	6.00	10.00	22.00
1957	—	1.50	3.00	6.00	10.00	20.00

KM# 89 5 BANI
1.70 g., Nickel Clad Steel, 16 mm. **Obv:** National emblem, RPR on ribbon **Rev:** Value and date **Edge:** Plain

Date	Mintage	VF20	XF40	MS60	MS63	MS65
1963	95,700,000	0.25	0.50	1.00	1.50	2.50

KM# 84.1 10 BANI
1.80 g., Copper-Nickel, 17 mm. **Obv:** National emblem **Rev:** Value and date within wreath **Edge:** Reeded

Date	Mintage	VF20	XF40	MS60	MS63	MS65
1952	37,900,000	2.00	4.00	8.00	17.00	35.00

KM# 84.2 10 BANI
1.80 g., Copper-Nickel, 17.5 mm. **Obv:** National emblem **Obv. Legend:** ROMANA **Rev:** Value and date within wreath

Date	Mintage	VF20	XF40	MS60	MS63	MS65
1954	1,600,000	6.00	12.00	25.00	35.00	75.00

KM# 84.3 10 BANI
1.80 g., Copper-Nickel, 17.5 mm. **Obv:** National emblem **Obv. Legend:** ROMINA **Rev:** Value and date within wreath

Date	Mintage	VF20	XF40	MS60	MS63	MS65
1955	4,100,000	6.00	12.00	25.00	35.00	75.00
1956	18,400,000	3.00	5.00	10.00	20.00	35.00

KM# 87 15 BANI
2.87 g., Nickel Clad Steel, 19.5 mm. **Obv:** National emblem **Rev:** Value within wreath **Edge:** Plain

Date	Mintage	VF20	XF40	MS60	MS63	MS65
1960	126,900,000	0.25	0.50	1.00	1.50	2.50

KM# 85.1 25 BANI
3.60 g., Copper-Nickel, 22 mm. **Obv:** National emblem **Rev:** Value and date within wreath **Edge:** Reeded

Date	Mintage	VF20	XF40	MS60	MS63	MS65
1952	43,600,000	3.00	5.00	10.00	20.00	35.00

KM# 85.2 25 BANI
3.60 g., Copper-Nickel, 22 mm. **Obv:** National emblem **Obv. Legend:** ROMANA **Rev:** Value and date within wreath

Date	Mintage	VF20	XF40	MS60	MS63	MS65
1953	1,100,000	6.00	12.00	25.00	45.00	75.00
1954	11,600,000	2.00	3.00	10.00	20.00	35.00

KM# 85.3 25 BANI
3.60 g., Copper-Nickel, 22 mm. **Obv:** National emblem **Obv. Legend:** ROMINA **Rev:** Value and date within wreath

Date	Mintage	VF20	XF40	MS60	MS63	MS65
1955	16,700,000	1.50	3.00	7.00	15.00	25.00

KM# 88 25 BANI
3.38 g., Nickel Clad Steel, 22 mm. **Obv:** National emblem **Rev:** Value above tractor **Edge:** Plain

Date	Mintage	VF20	XF40	MS60	MS63	MS65
1960	87,600,000	0.35	0.75	1.50	3.00	5.00

KM# 86 50 BANI
4.50 g., Copper-Nickel, 25.2 mm. **Obv:** National emblem **Rev:** Blacksmith at anvil, factory in background **Edge:** Reeded

Date	Mintage	VF20	XF40	MS60	MS63	MS65
1955	16,700,000	2.00	4.00	9.00	18.00	37.00
1956	16,700,000	2.00	4.00	10.00	20.00	40.00

KM# 90 LEU
5.06 g., Nickel Clad Steel, 24 mm. **Obv:** National emblem **Rev:** Tractor **Edge:** Plain

Date	Mintage	VF20	XF40	MS60	MS63	MS65
1963	71,910,000	0.35	0.75	1.50	3.00	5.00

KM# 91 3 LEI
5.86 g., Nickel Clad Steel, 27 mm. **Obv:** National emblem **Rev:** Oil refinery **Edge:** Plain

Date	Mintage	VF20	XF40	MS60	MS63	MS65
1963	18,436,000	0.50	1.00	2.00	4.00	6.00

SOCIALIST REPUBLIC

STANDARD COINAGE

KM# 92 5 BANI
1.70 g., Nickel Clad Steel, 16 mm. **Obv:** National emblem, ROMANIA on ribbon **Rev:** Value and date **Edge:** Plain

Date	Mintage	VF20	XF40	MS60	MS63	MS65
1966	106,881,000	0.25	0.50	1.00	1.50	2.50

KM# 92a 5 BANI
0.60 g., Aluminum, 16 mm. **Obv:** National emblem, ROMANIA on ribbon **Rev:** Value and date **Edge:** Plain

Date	Mintage	VF20	XF40	MS60	MS63	MS65
1975	—	0.25	0.50	1.00	1.50	2.50

KM# 93 15 BANI
2.88 g., Nickel Clad Steel, 19.5 mm. **Obv:** National emblem **Rev:** Value within wreath **Edge:** Plain

Date	Mintage	VF20	XF40	MS60	MS63	MS65
1966	41,165,000	0.25	0.50	1.00	1.50	2.50

KM# 93a 15 BANI
1.00 g., Aluminum, 19.5 mm. **Obv:** National emblem **Rev:** Value within wreath **Edge:** Plain

Date	Mintage	VF20	XF40	MS60	MS63	MS65
1975	—	0.25	0.50	1.00	1.50	2.50

KM# 94 25 BANI
3.38 g., Nickel Clad Steel, 22 mm. **Obv:** National emblem **Rev:** Value above tractor **Edge:** Plain

Date	Mintage	VF20	XF40	MS60	MS63	MS65
1966	18,955,000	0.25	0.50	1.00	1.50	2.50

KM# 94a 25 BANI
1.30 g., Aluminum, 22 mm. **Obv:** National emblem **Rev:** Value above tractor **Edge:** Plain

Date	Mintage	VF20	XF40	MS60	MS63	MS65
1982	—	0.25	0.50	1.00	1.50	2.50

KM# 95 LEU
5.06 g., Nickel Clad Steel, 24.6 mm. **Obv:** National emblem **Rev:** Tractor

Date	Mintage	VF20	XF40	MS60	MS63	MS65
1966	75,437,000	0.35	0.75	1.25	2.50	3.50

KM# 96 3 LEI
5.86 g., Nickel Clad Steel, 27 mm. **Obv:** National emblem **Rev:** Oil refinery **Edge:** Waves

Date	Mintage	VF20	XF40	MS60	MS63	MS65
1966	8,477,000	0.50	1.00	1.75	3.50	5.00

KM# 97 5 LEI
2.80 g., Aluminum, 29 mm. **Obv:** National emblem **Rev:** Value within design **Edge:** Security

Date	Mintage	VF20	XF40	MS60	MS63	MS65
1978	—	0.50	1.00	2.00	4.00	6.00

KM# 100 50 LEI
15.00 g., 0.925 Silver 0.4461 oz. ASW, 28 mm. **Subject:** 2,050th Anniversary of First Independent State **Obv:** National emblem **Rev:** Fighting figures within circle

Date	Mintage	VF20	XF40	MS60	MS63	MS65
1983 FM	7,000	—	—	—	—	650
1983 FM	1,000	PF65 1,350				

Note: Serially numbered on edges

KM# 98 100 LEI
30.00 g., 0.925 Silver 0.8922 oz. ASW, 37 mm. **Subject:** 2,050th Anniversary of First Independent State **Obv:** National emblem divides date **Rev:** Head with headdress left flanked by diamonds

Date	Mintage	VF20	XF40	MS60	MS63	MS65
1982 FM	7,500	—	—	—	—	650
1982 FM	—	PF65 900				
1983 FM	7,000	—	—	—	—	850
1983 FM	1,000	PF65 1,250				

Note: Serially numbered on edge

KM# 99 500 LEI
8.00 g., 0.900 Gold 0.2315 oz. AGW, 25 mm. **Subject:** 2,050th Anniversary of First Independent State **Obv:** National emblem divides date **Rev:** Fighting figures within circle

Date	Mintage	VF20	XF40	MS60	MS63	MS65
1982 FM	7,500	—	—	—	—	1,000
1982 FM	—	PF65 2,000				
1983 FM	7,000	—	—	—	—	3,000
1983 FM	1,000	PF65 6,000				

Note: Edge numbered

KM# 101 1000 LEI
16.00 g., 0.900 Gold 0.463 oz. AGW, 28 mm. **Subject:** 2,050th Anniversary of First Independent State **Obv:** National emblem divides date **Rev:** Head with headdress left flanked by diamonds

Date	Mintage	VF20	XF40	MS60	MS63	MS65
1983 FM	7,000	—	—	—	—	4,500
1983 FM	1,000	PF65 9,000				

Note: Edge numbered

REPUBLIC

KM# 113 LEU
2.50 g., Copper Clad Steel, 19 mm. **Subject:** National Bank of Romania **Obv:** Monogram above date and sprigs **Rev:** Value above oat sprigs **Edge:** Plain

Date	Mintage	VF20	XF40	MS60	MS63	MS65
1992	Est. 60000000	0.25	0.50	0.75	1.25	2.00

KM# 115 LEU
2.52 g., Copper Plated Steel, 19 mm. **Obv:** Value flanked by sprigs **Rev:** Shield divides date

Date	Mintage	VF20	XF40	MS60	MS63	MS65
1993	Est. 61000000	0.10	0.25	0.50	0.75	1.50
1994	Est. 10000000	0.10	0.25	0.50	0.75	1.50
1995	2,000,000	—	0.15	0.50	0.75	1.50
1996	272,000	0.50	1.00	2.00	3.00	5.00
2000	4,500	PF65 4.50				

KM# 112 5 LEI
3.35 g., Aluminum, 21 mm. **Subject:** Prince Mihai Viteazůl **Note:** Similar to 100 Lei, KM#111. Not released for circulation; majority were melted.

Date	Mintage	VF20	XF40	MS60	MS63	MS65
1991	—	—	—	—	75.00	150

KM# 114 5 LEI
3.30 g., Nickel Plated Steel, 21 mm. **Obv:** Value flanked by oak leaves **Rev:** Shield divides date **Edge:** Plain

Date	Mintage	VF20	XF40	MS60	MS63	MS65
1992 CD VG	Est. 30000000	0.25	0.50	0.75	1.50	3.00
1993 CD	Est. 70000000	—	0.30	0.50	1.00	2.00
1994	Est. 10000000	—	0.25	0.45	0.75	1.50
1995	25,000,000	—	0.20	0.30	0.50	1.00
1996	—	—	0.20	0.30	0.50	1.00
2000	4,500	PF65 4.50				

KM# 108 10 LEI
4.60 g., Nickel Clad Steel, 23.1 mm. **Subject:** Revolution Anniversary **Obv:** Flag and sprig **Rev:** Value within wreath **Edge:** Security scroll **Note:** Rotated die varieties exist.

Date	Mintage	VF20	XF40	MS60	MS63	MS65
1990	30,000,000	0.30	0.50	0.75	1.50	3.00
1991	31,303,000	0.25	0.40	0.60	1.00	2.00
1992	60,000,000	0.20	0.30	0.50	0.75	1.50

KM# 116 10 LEI
4.70 g., Nickel Clad Steel, 23 mm. **Obv:** Value within sprigs **Rev:** Shield divides date **Edge:** Plain

Date	Mintage	VF20	XF40	MS60	MS63	MS65
1993	Est. 6000000	0.30	0.50	0.75	1.50	3.00
1994	Est. 7000000	0.30	0.50	0.75	1.50	3.00
1995	30,000,000	—	0.30	0.50	0.75	1.50
1996	5,000	—	—	—	—	—
2000	4,500	PF65 5.50				

KM# 117.1 10 LEI
5.20 g., Nickel Plated Steel, 23.2 mm. **Series:** F.A.O. **Subject:** 50 Years - F.A.O. **Obv:** Shield flanked by sprigs and diamonds above value **Rev:** F.A.O logo and dates **Edge:** Plain

Date	Mintage	VF20	XF40	MS60	MS63	MS65
1995	200,000	—	1.00	2.00	3.00	5.00

KM# 117.2 10 LEI
Nickel Plated Steel, 23.3 mm. **Series:** F.A.O. **Subject:** 50 Years - F.A.O. **Obv:** Shield flanked by sprigs and diamonds **Rev:** F.A.O logo and dates **Note:** Obverse description: N in diamond at right for Numismatists

Date	Mintage	VF20	XF40	MS60	MS63	MS65
1995	30,000	—	1.25	2.50	4.00	7.00

KM# 120 10 LEI
Nickel Plated Steel **Series:** 1996 Olympic Games - U.S.A. **Obv:** Shield above sprigs flanked by value **Rev:** Swimmer

Date	Mintage	VF20	XF40	MS60	MS63	MS65
1996	10,000	—	—	2.50	4.00	6.50

KM# 121 10 LEI
Nickel Plated Steel **Series:** 1996 Olympic Games - U.S.A. **Obv:** Shield above sprig flanked by value **Rev:** Four Olympic scenes

Date	Mintage	VF20	XF40	MS60	MS63	MS65
1996	10,000	—	—	2.50	4.00	6.50

KM# 122 10 LEI
Nickel Plated Steel **Series:** 1996 Olympic Games - U.S.A. **Obv:** Shield above sprig flanked by value **Rev:** Windsurfer

Date	Mintage	VF20	XF40	MS60	MS63	MS65
1996	10,000	—	—	2.50	4.00	6.50

KM# 123 10 LEI
Nickel Plated Steel **Series:** 1996 Olympic Games - U.S.A. **Obv:** Shield above sprig flanked by value **Rev:** Sailboat with two racers

Date	Mintage	VF20	XF40	MS60	MS63	MS65
1996	10,000	—	—	2.50	4.00	6.50

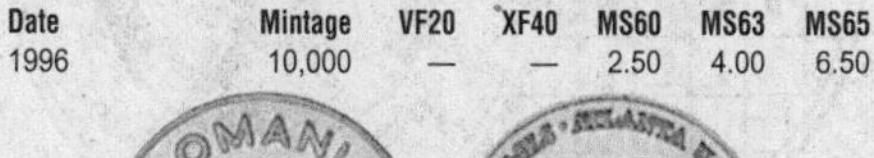

KM# 124 10 LEI
Nickel Plated Steel **Series:** 1996 Olympic Games - U.S.A. **Obv:** Shield above sprigs divide value **Rev:** Canoe with two racers

Date	Mintage	VF20	XF40	MS60	MS63	MS65
1996	10,000	—	—	2.50	4.00	6.50

KM# 125 10 LEI
Nickel Plated Steel **Series:** 1996 Olympic Games - U.S.A. **Obv:** Shield above sprigs divide value **Rev:** Scullcraft with racers

Date	Mintage	VF20	XF40	MS60	MS63	MS65
1996	10,000	—	—	2.50	4.00	6.50

KM# 126 10 LEI
Nickel Plated Steel **Subject:** World Food Summit - Rome **Obv:** Shield above value **Rev:** Logo above inscription

Date	Mintage	VF20	XF40	MS60	MS63	MS65
1996	50,000	—	—	1.00	2.00	4.00

KM# 134 10 LEI
Nickel Plated Steel **Subject:** Euro Soccer **Obv:** Shield divides value **Rev:** Stylized soccer players

Date	Mintage	VF20	XF40	MS60	MS63	MS65
1996	50,000	—	—	3.00	5.00	8.00

KM# 109 20 LEI
5.00 g., Brass Clad Steel, 24 mm. **Obv:** Crowned bust of Prince Stefan Cel Mare facing, flanked by dots **Rev:** Value and date within half sprigs and dots **Edge:** Plain **Note:** Date varieties exist.

Date	Mintage	VF20	XF40	MS60	MS63	MS65
1991	Est. 43200000	—	0.25	0.50	1.00	2.00
1992	Est. 48000000	—	0.25	0.50	1.00	2.00
1993	Est. 33800000	—	0.25	0.50	1.00	2.00
1994	5,000,000	—	0.35	0.75	1.50	3.00
1995	8,000,000	—	0.35	0.75	1.50	3.00
1996	500,000	0.50	1.00	2.00	3.00	7.00
2000	4,500	PF65 6.00				

KM# 110 50 LEI
5.90 g., Brass Clad Steel, 26 mm. **Obv:** Bust left flanked by dots **Rev:** Sprig divides date and value **Edge:** Plain

Date	Mintage	VF20	XF40	MS60	MS63	MS65
1991	Est. 29600000	—	0.35	0.75	1.50	3.00
1992	Est. 70800000	—	0.25	0.50	1.00	2.00
Note: 1992 date varieties exist						
1993	Est. 34600000	—	0.25	0.50	1.00	2.00
1994	Est. 30000000	—	0.25	0.50	1.00	2.00
1995	20,000,000	—	0.30	0.65	1.25	2.50
1996	4,900,000	—	0.50	1.00	2.00	4.00
2000	4,500	PF65 8.00				

KM# 111 100 LEI
8.75 g., Nickel Plated Steel, 29 mm. **Obv:** Bust with headdress 1/4 right **Rev:** Value within sprigs **Edge Lettering:** ROMANIA

Date	Mintage	VF20	XF40	MS60	MS63	MS65
1991	Est. 12600000	—	0.65	1.25	2.50	5.00
1992	Est. 70500000	—	0.50	0.75	1.50	3.00
Note: Reported edge varieties for 1992 with TOTUL PENTRU TARA; without ROMANIA are presumed essais						
1993	Est. 78000000	—	0.50	0.75	1.50	3.00
1994	Est. 125000000	—	0.45	0.65	1.25	2.50
1995	30,000,000	—	0.50	0.85	1.75	3.50
1996	11,000,000	—	0.75	1.50	3.00	6.00
2000	4,500	PF65 8.00				

KM# 118 100 LEI
27.50 g., 0.925 Silver 0.8178 oz. ASW, 37 mm. **Series:** F.A.O. **Subject:** 50 Years - F.A.O. **Obv:** Shield flanked by sprigs and diamonds above value **Rev:** F.A.O logo and dates **Edge:** Plain

Date	Mintage	VF20	XF40	MS60	MS63	MS65
1995	30,000	—	—	18.00	22.00	27.00

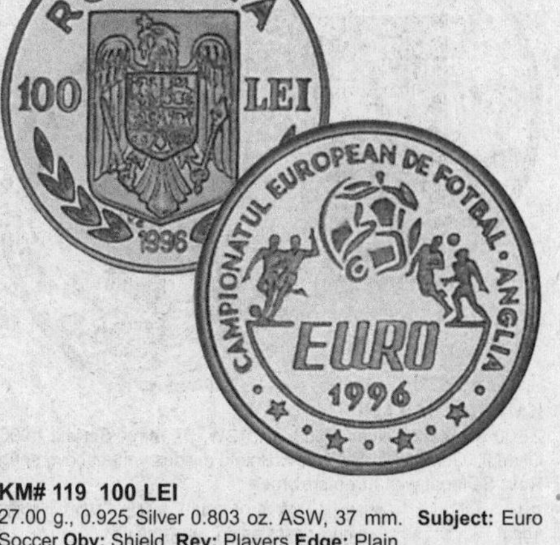

KM# 119 100 LEI
27.00 g., 0.925 Silver 0.803 oz. ASW, 37 mm. **Subject:** Euro Soccer **Obv:** Shield **Rev:** Players **Edge:** Plain

Date	Mintage	VF20	XF40	MS60	MS63	MS65
1996	12,000	PF63 25.00	PF65 30.00			

KM# 127 100 LEI
27.00 g., 0.925 Silver 0.803 oz. ASW, 37 mm. **Series:** 1996 Olympic Games - U.S.A. **Obv:** Shield divides value above sprig **Rev:** Swimmer **Edge:** Plain

Date	Mintage	VF20	XF40	MS60	MS63	MS65
1996	10,000	PF63 25.00	PF65 30.00			

KM# 128 100 LEI
27.00 g., 0.925 Silver 0.803 oz. ASW, 37 mm. **Series:** 1996 Olympic Games - U.S.A. **Obv:** Shield divides value above sprig **Rev:** Four olympic scenes **Edge:** Plain

Date	Mintage	VF20	XF40	MS60	MS63	MS65
1996	10,000	PF63 25.00	PF65 30.00			

KM# 129 100 LEI
27.00 g., 0.925 Silver 0.803 oz. ASW, 37 mm. **Series:** 1996 Olympic Games - U.S.A. **Obv:** Shield divides value above sprig **Rev:** Windsurfer

Date	Mintage	VF20	XF40	MS60	MS63	MS65
1996	10,000	PF63 25.00	PF65 30.00			

KM# 130 100 LEI

27.00 g., 0.925 Silver 0.803 oz. ASW, 37 mm. **Series:** 1996 Olympic Games - U.S.A. **Obv:** Shield divides value above sprig **Rev:** Sailboat with three crewmen

Date	Mintage	VF20	XF40	MS60	MS63	MS65
1996	10,000	PF63 25.00	PF65 30.00			

KM# 131 100 LEI

27.00 g., 0.925 Silver 0.803 oz. ASW, 37 mm. **Series:** 1996 Olympic Games - U.S.A. **Obv:** Shield divides value above sprig **Rev:** Canoe with two canoeists

Date	Mintage	VF20	XF40	MS60	MS63	MS65
1996	10,000	PF63 25.00	PF65 30.00			

KM# 132 100 LEI

27.00 g., 0.925 Silver 0.803 oz. ASW, 37 mm. **Series:** 1996 Olympic Games - U.S.A. **Obv:** Shield divides value above sprig **Rev:** Scullcraft with rowers

Date	Mintage	VF20	XF40	MS60	MS63	MS65
1996	10,000	PF63 27.00	PF65 32.00			

KM# 133 100 LEI

27.50 g., 0.925 Silver 0.8178 oz. ASW, 37 mm. **Subject:** World Food Summit - Rome **Edge:** Plain

Date	Mintage	VF20	XF40	MS60	MS63	MS65
1996	5,000	PF63 32.00	PF65 37.00			

KM# 135 100 LEI

27.00 g., 0.925 Silver 0.803 oz. ASW, 37 mm. **Subject:** 50th Anniversary - UNICEF **Obv:** Shield above value **Rev:** UNICEF logo on world globe **Edge:** Plain

Date	Mintage	VF20	XF40	MS60	MS63	MS65
1996	5,000	PF63 32.00	PF65 37.00			

KM# 138 100 LEI

27.00 g., 0.925 Silver 0.803 oz. ASW, 37 mm. **Subject:** 120th Anniversary of Independence **Obv:** Shield above value **Rev:** Three soldiers with flag behind cannon **Edge:** Plain

Date	Mintage	VF20	XF40	MS60	MS63	MS65
1998	Est. 5000	PF63 40.00	PF65 50.00			

KM# 139 100 LEI

27.00 g., 0.925 Silver 0.803 oz. ASW, 37 mm. **Subject:** Andrei Saguna **Obv:** Shield divides value **Rev:** Bust facing 1/4 right with dates and church towers **Edge:** Plain

Date	Mintage	VF20	XF40	MS60	MS63	MS65
1998	2,000	PF63 100	PF65 120			

KM# 140 100 LEI

27.00 g., 0.925 Silver 0.803 oz. ASW, 37 mm. **Series:** Olympic Games - Nagano 1998 **Obv:** Value above shield to right of stylized flame and snowflakes **Rev:** Bobsled **Edge:** Plain

Date	Mintage	VF20	XF40	MS60	MS63	MS65
1998	2,000	PF63 60.00	PF65 75.00			

KM# 141 100 LEI

27.00 g., 0.925 Silver 0.803 oz. ASW, 37 mm. **Series:** Olympic Games - Nagano 1998 **Rev:** Figure skaters

Date	Mintage	VF20	XF40	MS60	MS63	MS65
1998	2,000	PF63 60.00	PF65 75.00			

KM# 142 100 LEI

27.00 g., 0.925 Silver 0.803 oz. ASW, 37 mm. **Series:** Olympic Games - Nagano 1998 **Rev:** Slalom skier

Date	Mintage	VF20	XF40	MS60	MS63	MS65
1998	2,000	PF63 60.00	PF65 75.00			

KM# 143 100 LEI

27.00 g., 0.925 Silver 0.803 oz. ASW, 37 mm. **Subject:** World Cup Soccer - France 1998 **Obv:** Value within goal net with shield at right **Rev:** Eiffel Tower in front of soccer ball **Edge:** Plain

Date	Mintage	VF20	XF40	MS60	MS63	MS65
1998	5,000	PF63 25.00	PF65 35.00			

KM# 148 100 LEI

27.00 g., 0.925 Silver 0.803 oz. ASW, 37 mm. **Subject:** 100th Anniversary - Belgica Expedition **Obv:** Shield, birds and compas face **Rev:** The sailing ship Belgica and bust of scientist Emil Racoviţa **Edge:** Plain

Date	Mintage	VF20	XF40	MS60	MS63	MS65
1999	20,000	PF63 20.00	PF65 30.00			

KM# 149 100 LEI

27.00 g., 0.925 Silver 0.803 oz. ASW, 37 mm. **Subject:** Visit of Pope John Paul II - May 7-9, 1999 **Obv:** Shield on quatrefoil **Rev:** Portraits of Pope and Patriarch Theoctist **Edge:** Plain

Date	Mintage	VF20	XF40	MS60	MS63	MS65
1999	2,000	PF63 175	PF65 225			

KM# 152 100 LEI

1.22 g., 0.999 Gold 0.0393 oz. AGW, 13.92 mm. **Subject:** History of Gold **Obv:** Shield within ornamental circle above value **Rev:** Gold Dacian helmet found at Poiana Coţofeneşti

Date	Mintage	VF20	XF40	MS60	MS63	MS65
1999	25,000	PF65 100				

KM# 136 500 LEI
8.64 g., 0.900 Gold 0.250 oz. AGW, 24 mm. **Subject:** Revolution of 1848 **Obv:** Upper and lower shield divides value **Rev:** Half length figure with head facing right flanked by dates

Date	Mintage	VF20	XF40	MS60	MS63	MS65
1998	Est. 2000	PF65 1,000				

KM# 145 500 LEI
3.70 g., Aluminum, 25 mm. **Obv:** Shield within sprigs **Rev:** Value within 3/4 wreath **Edge:** Lettered **Edge Lettering:** ROMANIA (three times)

Date	Mintage	VF20	XF40	MS60	MS63	MS65
1998	—	—	0.50	0.75	1.25	2.00
1999	—	—	0.50	0.75	1.25	2.00
2000	—	—	0.50	0.75	1.25	2.00
2000	4,500	PF65 6.00				

KM# 146 500 LEI
3.60 g., Aluminum, 25 mm. **Obv:** Shield, value and date within design **Rev:** Solar eclipse **Edge:** Lettered **Edge Lettering:** ROMANIA (three times)

Date	Mintage	VF20	XF40	MS60	MS63	MS65
1999	4,000,000	—	0.75	1.25	2.50	4.00

KM# 147 500 LEI
3.70 g., Aluminum, 25 mm. **Obv:** Shield, eclipse and observatory **Rev:** Solar eclipse **Edge:** Lettered **Edge Lettering:** ROMANIA (three times)

Date	Mintage	VF20	XF40	MS60	MS63	MS65
1999	—	—	—	—	—	—

Note: This design never gained broad release and is considered to be a pattern by several authorities

KM# 154 500 LEI
27.00 g., 0.999 Silver 0.8672 oz. ASW, 37 mm. **Subject:** Alexander the Good of Moldavia **Obv:** Old seal design and value **Rev:** Crowned bust 1/4 left, church at left **Edge:** Plain

Date	Mintage	VF20	XF40	MS60	MS63	MS65
2000	Est. 1000	PF63 225	PF65 275			

KM# 137 1000 LEI
31.10 g., 0.999 Gold 0.999 oz. AGW, 35 mm. **Subject:** Revolution of 1848 **Obv:** Crossed flags and shield flanked by value **Rev:** Victory flanked by dates **Edge:** Plain

Date	Mintage	VF20	XF40	MS60	MS63	MS65
1998	Est. 1000	PF65 1,950				

KM# 144 1000 LEI
31.10 g., 0.999 Gold 0.999 oz. AGW, 35 mm. **Subject:** 80th Anniversary - Union of Transylvania **Obv:** Shield to right of value **Rev:** Large building and the arms of Wallachia, Moldova and Transylvania **Edge:** Plain

Date	Mintage	VF20	XF40	MS60	MS63	MS65
1998	2,000	PF65 1,850				

KM# 151 1000 LEI
31.10 g., 0.999 Gold 0.999 oz. AGW, 35 mm. **Subject:** Visit of Pope John Paul II - May 7-9, 1999 **Obv:** Shield **Rev:** Portraits of Pope and Patriarch Theoctist **Edge:** Plain

Date	Mintage	VF20	XF40	MS60	MS63	MS65
1999	1,000	PF65 2,350				

KM# 153 1000 LEI
2.00 g., Aluminum, 22 mm. **Subject:** Constantin Brancoveanu **Obv:** Value above shield within lined circle **Rev:** Bust with headdress facing **Edge:** Plain with serrated sections

Date	Mintage	VF20	XF40	MS60	MS63	MS65
2000	—	—	0.35	0.75	1.50	3.00
2000	—	PF65 10.00				

KM# 157 2000 LEI
31.10 g., 0.999 Gold 0.999 oz. AGW, 35 mm. **Subject:** 150th Anniversary - Birth of Mihai Eminesu, Poet **Obv:** Shield and quill within circle **Rev:** Bust 3/4 left **Edge:** Plain

Date	Mintage	VF20	XF40	MS60	MS63	MS65
2000	1,500	PF65 1,850				

KM# 155 5000 LEI
31.10 g., 0.999 Gold 0.999 oz. AGW, 35 mm. **Subject:** Michael the Brave's Unification of Romania in 1600 **Obv:** Shield and old seal within circle **Rev:** Bust with headdress and church **Edge:** Plain

Date	Mintage	VF20	XF40	MS60	MS63	MS65
2000	Est. 1500	PF65 1,850				

KM# 182 5000 LEI
31.10 g., 0.999 Gold 0.999 oz. AGW, 35 mm. **Subject:** 2000 Years of Christianity **Rev:** Jesus Christ

Date	Mintage	VF20	XF40	MS60	MS63	MS65
2000	Est. 1000	PF65 1,950				

ESSAIS

KM#	Date	Mintage	Identification	Mkt Val
E1	1905	—	10 Bani. Copper-Nickel. KM29. With center hole.	200

KM#	Date	Mintage	Identification	Mkt Val
E2	1910	—	50 Bani. Silver. Head left. Crown above sprigs.	350
E3	1910	—	Leu. Silver.	350
E4	1910	—	2 Lei. Silver.	350
E5	1914	—	50 Bani. Silver.	200
E6	1914	—	50 Bani. Silver. KM41.	150
E7	1914	—	Leu. Silver.	250
E8	1914	—	Leu. Silver. KM42.	—

KM#	Date	Mintage	Identification	Mkt Val
E9	1914	—	2 Lei. Silver. Head left. Crowned arms with supporters within crowned mantle flanked by value.	275
E10	1914	—	2 Lei. Silver. KM43.	—
E11	1924	—	2 Lei. Silver.	125

PATTERNS

Including off metal strikes

KM#	Date	Mintage	Identification	Mkt Val
Pn49	1905	—	5 Bani. White Metal. KM28.	100
Pn50	1905	—	5 Bani. Pewter. KM28.	—

KM#	Date	Mintage	Identification	Mkt Val
Pn51	1905	—	5 Bani. Aluminum. KM28.	—
Pn52	1905	—	5 Bani. Zinc. KM28.	—
Pn53	1905	—	5 Bani. Bronze. KM28.	—
Pn54	1905	—	5 Bani. Brass. KM28.	125
Pn55	1905	—	5 Bani. Copper. KM28. With center hole.	125
Pn56	1905	—	5 Bani. Copper. KM28.	500
Pn57	1905	—	5 Bani. Copper Gilt. KM28.	—
Pn58	1905	—	5 Bani. Silver. KM31. Without center hole.	1,500
Pn59	1905	—	5 Bani. Bronze. KM31. Without center hole.	—
Pn60	1905	—	5 Bani. Pewter. KM31. Without center hole.	100
Pn61	1905	—	5 Bani. Aluminum. KM31. Without center hole.	—
Pn62	1905	—	5 Bani. Zinc. KM31. Without center hole.	—
Pn63	1905	—	5 Bani. Copper-Nickel. KM31. Without center hole.	—
Pn64	1905	—	5 Bani. Gold. Without center hole.	2,000
Pn65	1905	—	5 Bani. Gold. Without center hole.	1,500
PnA66	1905	—	10 Bani. White Metal. With center hole.	—

KM#	Date	Mintage	Identification	Mkt Val
PnB66	1905	—	10 Bani. White Metal. Without center hole.	—
Pn66	1905	—	10 Bani. Pewter. KM29. With center hole.	125
Pn67	1905	—	10 Bani. Brass. KM29. With center hole.	125
Pn68	1905	—	10 Bani. Aluminum. KM29. With center hole.	75.00

PnA69 1905 — 10 Bani. Bronze. KM29. Red. With center hole. —

Pn69 1905 — 10 Bani. Bronze. KM29. Red. Without center hole. 100

Pn70 1905 — 10 Bani. Bronze. KM29. Green. Without center hole. 100

Pn71 1905 — 10 Bani. Zinc. KM29. 160

PnA72 1905 — 10 Bani. Bronze Gilt. KM29. With center hole. —

Pn72 1905 — 10 Bani. Bronze Gilt. KM29. Without center hole. 100

Pn73 1905 — 10 Bani. Copper-Nickel-Zinc. With center hole. 150

Pn74 1905 — 10 Bani. Nickel. KM29. With center hole. —

Pn75 1905 — 10 Bani. Silver. KM29. Without center hole. 400

Pn76 1905 — 10 Bani. Silver. KM29. With center hole. 400

PnA77 1905 — 10 Bani. Copper Gilt. With branches and small date. Without center hole. —

Pn77 1905 — 10 Bani. Copper. KM29. Without center hole. 100

Pn78 1905 — 10 Bani. Gold. Without branches. KM29. Without center hole. 1,800

Pn79 1905 — 10 Bani. Gold. KM29. With center hole. 1,500

Pn80 1905 — 10 Bani. Pewter. KM32. Without center hole. 150

Pn81 1905 — 10 Bani. Brass. KM32. Without center hole. 150

Pn82 1905 — 10 Bani. Aluminum. KM32. Without center hole. 100

Pn83 1905 — 10 Bani. Bronze. KM32. Without center hole. 125

Pn84 1905 — 10 Bani. Gold. KM32. Without center hole. 1,250

Pn85 1905 — 20 Bani. Lead. KM30. 100

Pn86 1905 — 20 Bani. Brass. KM30. 150

Pn87 1905 — 20 Bani. Copper. KM30. 125

Pn88 1905 — 20 Bani. Aluminum. KM30. 100

Pn89 1905 — 20 Bani. White Metal. KM30. 100

Pn90 1905 — 20 Bani. Zinc. KM30. —

Pn91 1905 — 20 Bani. Pewter. KM30. —

Pn92 1905 — 20 Bani. Bronze Gilt. KM30. 125

PnA93 1905 — 20 Bani. Bronze. KM30. —

Pn93 1905 — 20 Bani. Silver. KM30. 250

Pn94 1905 — 20 Bani. Gold. Without center hole. 1,750

Pn95 1905 — 20 Bani. Gold. With center hole. 1,500

Pn96 1905 — 20 Bani. Brass. KM33. Without center hole. —

Pn97 1905 — 20 Bani. Copper. KM33. Without center hole. 200

Pn98 1905 — 20 Bani. Aluminum. KM33. Without center hole. —

Pn99 1905 — 20 Bani. Pewter. KM33. Without center hole. 200

Pn100 1905 — 20 Bani. Silver. KM33. Without center hole. 400

Pn19 1906 — 12-1/2 Lei. Copper-Nickel. —

Pn101 1906 — Leu. White Metal. 125

Pn102 1906 — Leu. Brass. 150

Pn103 1906 — Leu. Aluminum. 100

Pn104 1906 — Leu. Copper. 125

Pn105 1906 — Leu. Bronze Gilt. 125

Pn106 1906 — Leu. Copper-Nickel. —

Pn107 1906 — Leu. Bronze Gilt. 125

Pn108 1906 — Leu. Silver. 250

Pn109 1906 — Leu. Gold. —

Pn110 1906 — 5 Lei. Silver. 4,500

Pn111 1906 — 12-1/2 Lei. Lead. 250

Pn112 1906 — 12-1/2 Lei. White Metal. 250

Pn113 1906 — 12-1/2 Lei. Brass. 250

Pn114 1906 — 12-1/2 Lei. Pewter. —

Pn115 1906 — 12-1/2 Lei. Bronze Gilt. 250

PnA116 1906 — 12-1/2 Lei. Bronze. Plain. 250

Pn116 1906 — 12-1/2 Lei. Aluminum. 250

Pn117 1906 — 12-1/2 Lei. Aluminum. Gilt. 250

Pn118 1906 — 12-1/2 Lei. Copper. 350

Pn120 1906 — 12-1/2 Lei. Silver. 550

Pn121 1906 — 12-1/2 Lei. Gold. 1,400

Pn122 1906 — 12-1/2 Lei. Gold. Pale. 2,500

Pn123 1906 — 20 Lei. Copper. 450

Pn124 1906 — 20 Lei. Bronze. 300

Pn125 1906 — 20 Lei. White Metal. —

Pn126 1906 — 20 Lei. White Metal. Gilt. —

Pn127 1906 — 20 Lei. Gold. 1,400

Pn128 1906 — 20 Lei. Gold. Pale. 2,500

Pn129 1906 — 25 Lei. Pewter. 250

Pn130 1906 — 25 Lei. Zinc. 400

Pn131 1906 — 25 Lei. Lead. 200

Pn132 1906 — 25 Lei. Copper. 175

Pn133 1906 — 25 Lei. Copper Gilt. —

Pn134 1906 — 25 Lei. Aluminum. 175

Pn135 1906 — 25 Lei. Brass. 175

Pn136 1906 — 25 Lei. Bronze. Antique. 175

Pn137 1906 — 25 Lei. Bronze Gilt. 175

Pn138 1906 — 25 Lei. Silver. 1,000

Pn139 1906 — 25 Lei. Gold. 2,650

Pn140 1906 — 25 Lei. Gold. Pale. 4,500

Pn141 1906 — 50 Lei. Aluminum. 350

Pn142 1906 — 50 Lei. Bronze. 400

Pn143 1906 — 50 Lei. White Metal. —

Pn144 1906 — 50 Lei. Pewter. 425

Pn145 1906 — 50 Lei. Brass. 400

Pn146 1906 — 50 Lei. Silver. 850

Pn148 1906 — 100 Lei. Copper. 650

Pn149 1906 — 100 Lei. Bronze. 650

Pn150 1906 — 100 Lei. Silver. —

Pn151 1906 — 100 Lei. Gold. 5,500

PnA152 1910 — 10 Bani. Zinc. —

Pn152 1910 — 10 Bani. Copper. —

Pn153 1910 — 50 Bani. Lead. —

Pn154 1910 — 50 Bani. Tin. —

PnA155 1910 — 50 Bani. Pewter. Plain. —

Pn155 1910 — 50 Bani. Pewter. Milled. 100

Pn156 1910 — 50 Bani. White Metal. 75.00

Pn157 1910 — 50 Bani. Aluminum. 60.00

Pn158 1910 — 50 Bani. Zinc. —

Pn159 1910 — 50 Bani. Copper. —

Pn160 1910 — 50 Bani. Copper-Nickel. —

Pn161 1910 — 50 Bani. Brass. 75.00

PnA162 1910 — 50 Bani. Bronze. Plain. Thin planchet. —

PnB162 1910 — 50 Bani. Bronze. Plain. Thick planchet. —

PnC162 1910 — 50 Bani. Bronze. Milled. Thin planchet. —

PnD162 1910 — 50 Bani. Bronze. Milled. Thick planchet. —

Pn162 1910 — 50 Bani. Nickel. 100

Pn163 1910 — Leu. Lead. 100

Pn164 1910 — Leu. Aluminum. 100

Pn165 1910 — Leu. Bronze. 100

Pn166 1910 — Leu. Bronze Gilt. 100

Pn167 1910 — Leu. Pewter. 125

Pn168 1910 — Leu. Zinc. —

PnA169 1910 — Leu. Copper Gilt. —

Pn169 1910 — Leu. Copper. —

Pn170 1910 — Leu. Copper-Nickel. —

Pn171 1910 — 2 Lei. Lead. 100

Pn172 1910 — 2 Lei. Tin. 150

Pn173 1910 — 2 Lei. Pewter. 150

Pn174 1910 — 2 Lei. Aluminum. 100

Pn175 1910 — 2 Lei. Brass. 100

PnA176 1910 — 2 Lei. Copper Gilt. —

Pn176 1910 — 2 Lei. Copper. —

Pn177 1910 — 2 Lei. Bronze Gilt. 100

PnA178 1910 — 2 Lei. Bronze. —

Pn178 1910 — 2 Lei. Nickel. —

PnA179 1910 — 2 Lei. Silver. —

PnB179 1914 — Leu. Silver. 350

PnC179 1914 — 2 Lei. Silver. 450

Pn179 1921 — 25 Bani. Aluminum. HF at left of date. 125

PnA180 1921 — 25 Bani. Bronze. HF at left of date. 200

PnB180 1921 — 25 Bani. Copper-Nickel. 185

PnC180 1921 — 25 Bani. Bronze. Without hole. 185

PnD180 1921 — 25 Bani. Nickel. 200

PnE180 1921 — 25 Bani. Copper. Without hole. 300

PnF180 1921 — 25 Bani. Bronze. With hole. 200

Pn180 1921 — 50 Bani. Nickel. With hole. 200

PnA181 1921 — 50 Bani. Bronze. Without hole. 300

PnB181 1921 — 50 Bani. Bronze. With hole. 200

PnC181 1921 — 50 Bani. Bronze. With hole. 200

PnD181 1921 — 1.25 Leu. Nickel. Without hole. 700

Pn181 1921 — 1.25 Leu. Nickel. With hole. 500

PnA182 1921 — 5 Lei. Billon. Arms, cornucopia. Hand numbered 1-15. Struck at Paris. —

Pn182 1921 — 5 Lei. Copper-Nickel. 450

Pn183 1921 — 5 Lei. Nickel. —

Pn184 1922 — 25 Bani. Aluminum. —

Pn185 1922 — 50 Bani. Aluminum. 175

Pn186 1922 — Leu. Bronze. 220

Pn187 1922 — Leu. Nickel. 250

Pn188 1922 — Leu. Copper-Nickel. 210

Pn189 1922 — 2 Lei. Bronze. 250

Pn190 1922 — 2 Lei. Nickel. 250

Pn191 1922 — 2 Lei. Brass. 150

Pn192 1922 — 5 Lei. Bronze. 300

Pn193 1922 — 5 Lei. Copper-Nickel. 300

Pn194	1922	—	5 Lei. Nickel.	300
PnA195	1922	—	5 Bani. Copper.	300
Pn195	1922	—	5 Lei. Brass.	300
Pn196	1922	—	5 Lei. Copper-Nickel.	300
Pn197	1922	—	20 Lei. Gold.	2,000
Pn198	1922	—	25 Lei. Gold.	2,750
Pn199	1922	—	50 Lei. Gold.	4,500

Pn200	1922	—	100 Lei. Gold.	6,000
PnC201	1922	—	100 Lei. Bronze.	—

PnA201	1923	—	Leu. Nickel.	275
PnB201	1923	—	2 Lei. Copper.	600
Pn201	1924	—	Leu. Nickel.	65.00
Pn202	1924	—	Leu. Aluminum.	45.00
Pn203	1924	—	Leu. Tin.	45.00
Pn204	1924	—	Leu. Zinc.	—
Pn205	1924	—	Leu. Copper.	—

Pn206	1924	—	Leu. Brass.	110
Pn207	1924	—	Leu. Bronze.	60.00
Pn208	1924	—	Leu. Bronze Gilt.	50.00
Pn209	1924	—	Leu. Silver. Plain.	125
Pn210	1924	—	Leu. Silver. Reeded.	125
Pn211	1924	—	2 Lei. Zinc.	75.00
Pn212	1924	—	2 Lei. Aluminum.	50.00
Pn213	1924	—	2 Lei. Tin.	—
Pn214	1924	—	2 Lei. Bronze.	240
Pn215	1924	—	2 Lei. Brass.	100

Pn216	1924	—	2 Lei. Copper.	65.00
PnA217	1924	—	2 Lei. Copper-Nickel.	—
Pn217	1924	—	2 Lei. Nickel.	75.00
Pn218	1924	—	2 Lei. Silver. Plain. Thick planchet.	200
PnA219	1930	—	10 Lei. Copper-Nickel. KM49.	100
Pn219	1930	—	20 Lei. Gold. Plain.	—
Pn220	1930	—	20 Lei. Gold. Ornamented.	—
Pn221	1930	—	100 Lei. Gold. Plain.	—
Pn222	1930	—	100 Lei. Gold. Ornamented.	—
Pn223	1931	—	20 Lei. Gold. Plain.	—
Pn224	1931	—	20 Lei. Gold. Ornamented.	—
Pn225	1931	—	100 Lei. Gold. Plain.	—
Pn226	1931	—	100 Lei. Gold. Ornamented.	—
Pn227	1932	—	20 Lei. Gold. Plain.	—
Pn228	1932	—	20 Lei. Gold. Ornamented.	—
Pn229	1932	—	100 Lei. Silver. Y62.	75.00
Pn230	1932	—	100 Lei. Gold. Plain.	—
Pn231	1932	—	100 Lei. Gold. Ornamented.	—
Pn232	1933	—	20 Lei. Gold. Plain.	—
Pn233	1933	—	20 Lei. Gold. Ornamented.	—
Pn234	1933	—	100 Lei. Gold. Plain.	—
Pn235	1933	—	100 Lei. Gold. Ornamented.	—
Pn236	1934	—	20 Lei. Gold. Plain.	—
Pn237	1934	—	20 Lei. Gold. Ornamented.	—
Pn238	1934	—	100 Lei. Gold. Plain.	—
Pn239	1934	—	100 Lei. Gold. Ornamented.	—
Pn240	1935	—	20 Lei. Gold. Plain.	—
Pn241	1935	—	20 Lei. Gold. Ornamented.	—
Pn242	1935	—	50 Lei. Silver.	—
Pn243	1935	—	100 Lei. Gold. Plain.	—
Pn244	1935	—	100 Lei. Gold. Ornamented.	—
PnA245	1935	—	250 Lei. Nickel.	—
PnB245	1935	—	250 Lei. Brass.	—

Pn245	1935	—	200 Lei. Silver.	450
Pn246	1936	—	20 Lei. Gold. Plain.	—
Pn247	1936	—	20 Lei. Gold. Ornamented.	—
Pn248	1936	—	50 Lei. Nickel.	—
Pn249	1936	—	100 Lei. Gold. Plain.	—
PnA250	1936	—	100 Lei. Copper.	500
Pn250	1936	—	100 Lei. Gold. Ornamented.	—
PnA251	1937	—	50 Lei. Nickel. KM55.	120
Pn251	1937	—	Leu. Copper-Nickel-Zinc.	250
Pn252	ND 1937	—	Leu. Copper-Nickel-Zinc.	—
Pn253	1937	—	2 Lei. Copper-Nickel-Zinc.	—
Pn254	1937	—	20 Lei. Gold. Plain.	—
Pn255	1937	—	20 Lei. Gold. Ornamented.	—
Pn256	1937	—	50 Lei. Copper-Nickel-Zinc.	240
Pn257	1937	—	100 Lei. Gold. Plain.	—
Pn258	1937	—	100 Lei. Gold. Ornamented.	—
Pn259	1938	—	Leu. Copper-Nickel-Zinc.	400
Pn260	1938	—	20 Lei. Gold. Plain.	—
Pn261	1938	—	20 Lei. Gold. Ornamented.	—
Pn262	1938	—	100 Lei. Gold. Plain.	—
Pn263	1938	—	100 Lei. Gold. Ornamented.	—
Pn264	1939	—	20 Lei. Gold. Plain.	—
Pn265	1939	—	20 Lei. Gold. Ornamented.	—
Pn266	1939	—	20 Lei. Gold. Arms.	—
Pn267	1939	—	20 Lei. Gold. Eagle.	—
Pn268	1939	—	100 Lei. Gold. Plain.	—
Pn269	1939	—	100 Lei. Gold. Ornamented.	—
Pn270	1939	—	100 Lei. Gold. Bust.	—
Pn271	1940	—	20 Lei. Gold. Plain.	3,300
Pn272	1940	—	20 Lei. Gold. Ornamented.	3,300
Pn273	1940	—	100 Lei. Gold. Plain.	—
Pn274	1940	—	100 Lei. Gold. Ornamented.	—
Pn275	1940	—	250 Lei. 0.750. Silver. Iron guard emblem.	9,000
Pn276	1941	—	Leu. Zinc.	—
Pn277	1941	—	Leu. Copper-Nickel-Zinc.	—
PnA278	1944	—	20 Lei. Copper Gilt.	200
Pn278	1944	—	20 Lei. Copper-Nickel-Zinc.	750
PnA279	1944	—	500 Lei. Silver. Plain.	180
Pn279	1944	—	500 Lei. Aluminum.	300
PnA280	1945	—	200 Lei. Aluminum.	—
Pn280	1945	—	100 Lei. Nickel Clad Steel.	125
Pn281	1945	—	500 Lei. Brass. Nickel plated.	125
Pn282	1945	—	2000 Lei. Brass. Nickel plated.	—

PnA283	1946	—	1000 Lei. Aluminum.	—
PnB283	1946	—	500 Lei. Aluminum.	—
PnC283	1946	—	25000 Lei. Silver. Without number.	5,000
Pn283	1946	—	25000 Lei. Silver. With number.	3,000
PnA284	1952	—	10 Bani. Copper-Nickel. With cogged wheel instead of wreath.	—
PnB284	1956	—	10 Bani. Aluminum.	100
PnC284	1956	—	50 Bani. Aluminum.	200
PnD284	ND 1958	—	5 Bani. Aluminum-Bronze.	—
Pn284	1958	—	5 Bani. Copper-Nickel-Zinc.	150
PnA285	1960	—	10 Bani. Nickel. 12 teeth to wheel.	400
Pn285	1960	—	10 Bani. Nickel. 20 teeth to wheel.	200
PnB285	1966	—	5 Bani. Aluminum.	—
PnC285	1966	—	15 Bani. Aluminum.	—
PnD285	1966	—	15 Bani. Brass.	—
PnE285	1966	—	15 Bani. Copper.	100
PnF285	1966	—	3 Lei. Silver.	7,500
PnG285	1966	—	5 Lei. Copper. Factory.	300
PnH285	1966	—	5 Lei. Copper.	300
PnI285	1966	—	5 Lei. Brass.	300
PnJ285	1984	—	100 Lei. Silver.	10,000

PnK285	ND (1984)	—	100 Lei. Silver.	10,000
PnL285	1987	—	2 Lei. Nickel Plated Steel.	250
Pn286	1987	—	10 Lei. Nickel. Steel plated.	75.00
Pn287	1987	—	10 Lei. Aluminum.	70.00

Pn288	1987	—	10 Lei. Aluminum.	70.00
Pn289	1987	—	10 Lei. Bronze.	80.00
PnA290	1987	—	10 Lei. Nickel Plated Steel.	—
PnB290	1987	—	10 Lei. Aluminum.	—
PnC290	1987	—	10 Lei. Brass.	—
Pn290	1987	—	10 Lei. Nickel. Steel plated.	75.00
Pn291	1988	—	10 Lei. Aluminum.	75.00

Pn292	1988	—	10 Lei. Aluminum.	75.00

PnA293	1990	—	10 Lei. Aluminum.	100
PnB293	1991	—	Leu. Copper-Nickel. 3 oak leaves.	60.00
Pn293	1991	—	5 Lei. Iron. Nickel clad. Similar to 100 Lei, KM#111.	70.00
Pn294	1991	—	5 Lei. Brass. Similar to 100 Lei, KM#111.	70.00
PnA296	1991	—	20 Lei. Aluminum.	70.00
PnB296	1991	—	20 Lei. Nickel Plated Steel. Similar to 100 Lei, KM#111.	95.00
PnC296	1991	—	50 Lei. Aluminum.	60.00
PnD296	1991	—	50 Lei. Copper-Nickel.	60.00
Pn296	1991	—	50 Lei. Silver. KM110.	250
PnA297	1991	—	100 Lei. Brass. King Stephen.	300
PnB297	1991	—	100 Lei. Brass. Prince M. Viteazul.	200
PnC297	1991	—	100 Lei. Aluminum. Prince M. Viteazul.	150
PnD297	1991	—	100 Lei. Nickel Plated Steel. Lettered.	180
PnE297	1991	—	100 Lei. Nickel Plated Steel. Sinus line.	90.00
PnF297	1991	—	100 Lei. Nickel Plated Steel. Lettered.	90.00
PnG297	1991	—	100 Lei. Nickel Plated Steel. Lettered.	90.00
PnH297	ND (1992)	—	Leu. Nickel.	80.00
Pn297	1992	—	Leu. Silver.	100
Pn298	ND (1992)	—	Leu. Nickel.	80.00
PnA299	1992	—	Leu. Silver.	100
PnB299	1992	—	5 Lei. Brass.	70.00
PnC299	1992	—	5 Lei. Copper-Nickel.	70.00
PnD299	1992	—	5 Lei. Nickel Plated Steel.	70.00
Pn299	1992	—	5 Lei. Aluminum.	50.00
PnA300	1993	—	Leu. Copper. Like KM#113.	80.00
PnB300	1995	—	100 Lei. Aluminum. KM#118.	40.00
Pn300	1996	—	10 Lei. Nickel Plated Steel. Similar to KM#117. KM#134.	35.00
Pn301	1996	—	100 Lei. Aluminum. KM#119.	45.00
Pn302	1996	—	100 Lei. Brass. KM#119.	50.00
Pn303	1996	—	100 Lei. Copper-Nickel. KM#127. Brass plated.	45.00
Pn304	1996	—	100 Lei. Aluminum. KM#127.	40.00
Pn305	1996	—	100 Lei. Copper-Nickel. KM#128. Brass plated.	45.00
Pn306	1996	—	100 Lei. Aluminum. KM#128.	40.00
Pn307	1996	—	100 Lei. Copper-Nickel. KM#129. Brass plated.	45.00
Pn308	1996	—	100 Lei. Aluminum. KM#129.	40.00
Pn309	1996	—	100 Lei. Copper-Nickel. KM#130. Brass plated.	45.00
Pn310	1996	—	100 Lei. Aluminum. KM#130.	40.00
Pn311	1996	—	100 Lei. Copper-Nickel. KM#131. Brass plated.	45.00
Pn312	1996	—	100 Lei. Aluminum. KM#131.	40.00
Pn313	1996	—	100 Lei. Copper-Nickel. KM#132. Brass plated.	45.00
Pn314	1996	—	100 Lei. Aluminum. KM#132.	40.00
PnA315c.1	1996	125	100 Lei. Bi-Metallic. Nationl arms. Gymnast on balance beam. Plain with denomination. Piefort version.	—
Pn316	1996	—	100 Lei. Aluminum. KM#133.	45.00
Pn317	1996	—	500 Lei. Brass. KM#135.	50.00
Pn318	1996	—	500 Lei. Brass. KM#147. Arms without outline.	90.00
Pn319	1996	—	500 Lei. Aluminum. KM#147. Arms without outline.	90.00
Pn320	1996	—	500 Lei. Nickel. KM#147. Arms without outline.	90.00
Pn321	1996	—	500 Lei. Aluminum. KM#147. Arms without outline. Bimetal.	100
Pn322	1996	—	3000 Lei. Copper. 1 ECU. Dracula.	100
Pn323	1996	—	3000 Lei. 1 ECU. Dracula. Golden brass.	100
Pn324	1996	—	3000 Lei. Silver. 1 ECU. Dracula.	150
Pn325	1996	—	3000 Lei. Aluminum. 1 ECU. Dracula.	120
PnB326	1996	125	100 Lei. Bronze.	30.00
PnA351	1996	—	100 Lei. Brass. National arms. Skier. Plain with denomination.	30.00
Pn326	1998	—	100 Lei. Silver. KM#119. Eiffel Tower. Golden brass.	60.00
Pn327	1998	—	100 Lei. Aluminum. KM#119. Eiffel Tower.	60.00
Pn328	1998	—	100 Lei. Brass. One player.	100
Pn329	1998	—	100 Lei. One player. Bimetal.	100
Pn330	1998	—	100 Lei. Brass. Two players.	60.00
Pn331	1998	—	100 Lei. Bi-Metallic. Two players.	100
Pn332	1998	—	100 Lei. Bi-Metallic. Gaelic cock.	100
Pn333	1998	—	500 Lei. Silver.	—
Pn334	1998	—	500 Lei. Golden brass.	—
Pn335	1998	—	500 Lei. Brass. KM#136.	25.00
Pn336	1998	—	1000 Lei. Silver. Arms at 6.	200
Pn337	1998	—	1000 Lei. Brass. Arms at 6.	80.00
Pn338	1998	—	1000 Lei. Arms at 9. Golden brass.	90.00
Pn339	1998	—	500 Lei. Brass. KM#147. Arms without outline.	90.00
Pn340	1998	—	500 Lei. Nickel. KM#147. Arms without outline.	40.00
Pn341	1998	—	500 Lei. Aluminum. KM#147. Arms without outline.	30.00
Pn342	1998	—	500 Lei. Aluminum. KM#147. Arms without outline. Bimetal.	45.00
Pn343	1998	—	100 Lei. Brass.	—
Pn344	1998	—	100 Lei. Bi-Metallic. KM#138.	—
Pn345	1998	—	100 Lei. Aluminum. KM#138.	—
Pn346	1998	—	100 Lei. Brass.	—
Pn347	1998	—	100 Lei. Silver.	—
Pn348	1998	—	100 Lei. Bi-Metallic.	—
Pn349	1998	—	100 Lei. Aluminum.	—
Pn350	1998	125	100 Lei. Aluminum. National arms. Two hockey players. Plain with denomination.	30.00
Pn350a	1998	—	100 Lei. Brass. Hockey.	35.00
Pn352	1998	—	100 Lei. Brass. Women single.	35.00
PnA353	1998	—	100 Lei. Brass. Ice dancing.	35.00
Pn353	1998	125	100 Lei. Aluminum. National arms. Two ice dancers. Plain with denomination.	30.00
Pn354	1998	—	100 Lei. Brass. Ice dancing, without inscription.	50.00
Pn355	1998	—	100 Lei. Brass. Bobsled, without inscription.	30.00
Pn356	1998	—	100 Lei. Brass. Slalom, without inscription.	50.00
Pn357	1998	—	1000 Lei. Brass. Large.	—
Pn358	1998	—	1000 Lei. Brass. Thin.	—
Pn359	1998	—	1000 Lei. Golden brass.	—
Pn360	1999	—	100 Lei. Brass. Young.	100
Pn361	1999	—	100 Lei. Brass. Old.	70.00
Pn362	1999	—	100 Lei. Brass.	—
Pn363	1999	—	100 Lei. Brass.	—
Pn364	1999	—	100 Lei. Aluminum. Plain. KM146.	100
Pn365	1999	—	100 Lei. Aluminum. Plain. KM147.	100
Pn366	1999	—	500 Lei. Aluminum. Solar Eclipse. Lettered edge. KM#147.	—

PIEDFORT

KM#	Date	Mintage	Identification	Mkt Val
P3	1905	—	20 Bani. Aluminum-Bronze.	250
P4	1905	—	20 Bani. Bronze.	250
P5	1906	—	12-1/2 Lei. Gold.	—
P6	1906	—	25 Lei. Gold.	—
P7	1906	—	50 Lei. Lead.	375
P8	1906	—	50 Lei. Copper.	375
P9	1906	—	50 Lei. Silver.	1,250
P10	1906	—	50 Lei. Gold.	—

TRIAL STRIKES

KM#	Date	Mintage	Identification	Mkt Val
TS1	1906	—	5 Lei. Silver.	5,000
TS2	1906	—	100 Lei. Silver.	400
TS3	1910	—	Leu. Pewter. Milled. Thin planchet.	—
TS4	1910	—	Leu. Pewter. Milled. Thick planchet.	—
TS5	1996	—	10 Lei. Nickel Plated Steel. KM#134.	100

MINT SETS

KM#	Date	Mintage	Identification	Issue Price	Mkt Val
MS1	1982FM (2)	—	KM#98-99	429	1,750
MS2	1983FM (4)	—	KM#98-101	850	9,500

PROOF SETS

KM#	Date	Mintage	Identification	Issue Price	Mkt Val
PS3	2000 (8)	—	KM109-111, 114-116, 145, 153 140th Anniversary Foundation Romanian Academy	—	50.00

Russia, formerly the central power of the Union of Soviet Socialist Republics and now of the Commonwealth of Independent States occupies the northern part of Asia and the eastern part of Europe, has an area of 17,075,400 sq. km. and a population of *146.2 million. Capital: Moscow. Exports include iron and steel, crude oil, timber, and nonferrous metals.

The first Russian dynasty was founded in Novgorod by the Viking Rurik in 862 A.D. under Yaroslav the Wise (1019-54). The subsequent Kievan state became one of the great commercial and cultural centers of Europe before falling to the Mongols of the Batu Khan, 13th century, who were suzerains of Russia until late in the 15th century when Ivan III threw off the Mongol yoke. The Russian Empire was enlarged, solidified and Westernized during the reigns of Ivan the Terrible, Peter the Great and Catherine the Great, and by 1881 extended to the Pacific and into Central Asia. Contemporary Russian history began in March of 1917 when Tsar Nicholas II abdicated under pressure and was replaced by a provisional government composed of both radical and conservative elements. This government rapidly lost ground to the Bolshevik wing of the Socialist Democratic Labor Party which attained power following the Bolshevik Revolution which began on Nov. 7, 1917. After the Russian Civil War, the regional governments, national states and armies became federal republics of the Russian Socialist Federal Soviet Republic. These autonomous republics united to form the Union of Soviet Socialist Republics that was established as a federation under the premiership of Lenin on Dec. 30, 1922.

In the fall of 1991, events moved swiftly in the Soviet Union. Estonia, Latvia and Lithuania won their independence and were recognized by Moscow, Sept. 6. The Commonwealth of Independent States was formed Dec. 8, 1991 in Mensk by Belarus, Russia and Ukraine. It was expanded at a summit Dec. 21, 1991 to include 11 of the 12 remaining republics (excluding Georgia) of the old U.S.S.R.

RULER

Nicholas II, 1894-1917

MINT MARKS

Л – Leningrad, 1991
М – Moscow, 1990
СП – St. Petersburg, 1999
СПБ – St. Petersburg, 1724-1914
СПМД – St. Petersburg, 1999

(sp) (l) – LMD (ЛМД) monogram in oval, (Leningrad), (St. Petersburg) 1977-1997

(m) – MMD (ММД) monogram in oval, Moscow, 1977-

MINT OFFICIALS' INITIALS

Leningrad Mint

Initials	Years	Mint Official
АГ	1921-22	A.F. Hartman
ПЛ	1922-27	P.V. Latishev

London Mint

Initials	Years	Mint Official
Т.Р.	1924	Thomas Ross
ФР	1924	Thomas Ross

St. Petersburg Mint

Initials	Years	Mint Official
ФЗ	1899-1901	Felix Zaleman
АР	1901-05	Alexander Redko
ЭБ	1906-13	Elikum Babayantz
ВС	1913-17	Victor Smirnov

NOTE: St. Petersburg Mint became Petrograd in 1914 and Leningrad in 1924. It was renamed St. Petersburg in 1991.

MONETARY SYSTEM

1/4 Kopek = Polushka ПОЛУШКА
1/2 Kopek = Denga, Denezhka ДЕНГА, ДЕНЕЖКА
Kopek = КОПЕЙКА
(2, 3 & 4) Kopeks КОПЕЙКИ
(5 and up) Kopeks КОПЕЕКЪ
(1924 – 5 and up) Kopeks КОПЕЕК
50 Kopeks = Poltina, Poltinnik ПОЛТИНА, ПОЛРУБЛЪ
100 Kopeks = Rouble, Ruble РУБЛЪ
10 Roubles = Imperial ИМПЕРIАЛЪ
10 Roubles = Chervonetz ЧЕРВОНЕЦ

NOTE: Mintage figures for years after 1885 are for fiscal years and may or may not reflect actual rarity, the commemorative and 1917 silver figures being exceptions.

EMPIRE

STANDARD COINAGE

Y# 47.2 POLUSHKA (1/4 Kopek)

0.80 g., Copper **Ruler:** Nicholas II **Obv:** Crowned monogram above sprays **Rev:** Value, date

Date	Mintage	F12	VF20	XF40	MS60	MS63
1915	500,000	200	300	500	1,000	—
1916	1,200,000	400	675	1,450	3,000	—

Y# 47.1 1/4 KOPEK

0.80 g., Copper **Ruler:** Nicholas II **Obv:** Crowned monogram above sprays **Rev:** Value, date **Edge:** Reeded

Date	Mintage	F12	VF20	XF40	MS60	MS63
1909 СПБ	2,000,000	25.00	40.00	50.00	70.00	—
1910 СПБ	8,000,000	40.00	60.00	90.00	250	—
1909-1910 Common date Proof	—	PF60 150				

Y# 48.1 1/2 KOPEK

1.60 g., Copper, 16 mm. **Ruler:** Nicholas II **Obv:** Crowned monogram above sprays **Rev:** Value and date **Edge:** Reeded

Date	Mintage	F12	VF20	XF40	MS60	MS63
1908 СПБ	8,000,000	15.00	20.00	30.00	40.00	—
1909 СПБ	49,500,000	7.00	15.00	20.00	40.00	—
1910 СПБ	24,000,000	15.00	20.00	30.00	40.00	50.00
1911 СПБ	35,800,000	15.00	20.00	30.00	40.00	50.00
1912 СПБ	28,000,000	15.00	20.00	30.00	40.00	50.00
1913 СПБ	50,000,000	8.00	10.00	15.00	20.00	30.00
1914 СПБ	14,000,000	15.00	20.00	30.00	40.00	50.00
1908-14 Common date Proof	—	PF60 200				

Y# 48.2 1/2 KOPEK

1.60 g., Copper **Ruler:** Nicholas II **Obv:** Crowned monogram above sprays **Rev:** Value and date **Note:** Struck at Petrograd without mint mark.

Date	Mintage	F12	VF20	XF40	MS60	MS63
1915	12,000,000	10.00	20.00	30.00	40.00	60.00
1916	9,400,000	10.00	20.00	30.00	40.00	60.00

Y# 9.2 KOPEK

3.30 g., Copper, 21.6 mm. **Ruler:** Nicholas II **Obv:** Crowned double-headed imperial eagle within circle **Rev:** Value flanked by stars within beaded circle **Edge:** Reeded

Date	Mintage	F12	VF20	XF40	MS60	MS63
1901 СПБ	30,000,000	3.00	4.00	6.00	15.00	—
1902 СПБ	20,000,000	200	400	700	1,000	—
1903 СПБ	74,400,000	4.00	6.00	8.00	15.00	—
1904 СПБ	30,600,000	4.00	6.00	8.00	15.00	—
1905 СПБ	23,000,000	6.00	8.00	15.00	35.00	—
1906 СПБ	20,000,000	10.00	20.00	30.00	45.00	—
1907 СПБ	20,000,000	10.00	20.00	30.00	45.00	—
1908 СПБ	40,000,000	3.00	4.00	6.00	15.00	—
1909 СПБ	27,500,000	3.00	4.00	6.00	15.00	—
1910 СПБ	36,500,000	3.00	4.00	6.00	15.00	—
1911 СПБ	38,150,000	3.00	4.00	6.00	15.00	—
1912 СПБ	31,850,000	3.00	4.00	6.00	15.00	—
1913 СПБ	61,500,000	3.00	4.00	6.00	15.00	—
1914 СПБ	32,500,000	3.00	4.00	6.00	15.00	—
1901-14 Common date Proof	—	PF60 600				

Y# 9.3 KOPEK

3.30 g., Copper **Ruler:** Nicholas II **Obv:** Crowned double-headed imperial eagle within circle **Rev:** Value flanked by stars within beaded circle **Note:** Struck at Petrograd without mint mark.

Date	Mintage	F12	VF20	XF40	MS60	MS63
1915	58,000,000	4.00	8.00	10.00	15.00	—
1916	46,500,000	5.00	8.00	10.00	16.00	—
1917 Unique	—	—	—	—	—	—

Y# 10.2 2 KOPEKS

6.60 g., Copper **Ruler:** Nicholas II **Obv:** Crowned double-headed imperial eagle within circle **Rev:** Value flanked by stars within circle **Edge:** Reeded

Date	Mintage	F12	VF20	XF40	MS60	MS63
1901 СПБ	20,000,000	4.00	6.00	20.00	40.00	—
1902 СПБ	10,000,000	50.00	150	225	340	—
1903 СПБ	29,200,000	4.00	6.00	13.00	100	—
1904 СПБ	13,300,000	4.00	6.00	25.00	55.00	—
1905 СПБ	15,000,000	4.00	6.00	13.00	25.00	—
1906 СПБ	6,250,000	4.00	6.00	30.00	65.00	—
1907 СПБ	7,500,000	4.00	6.00	30.00	300	—
1908 СПБ	19,000,000	4.00	6.00	13.00	25.00	—
1909 СПБ	16,250,000	5.00	10.00	25.00	50.00	—
1910 СПБ	12,000,000	5.00	10.00	25.00	50.00	—
1911 СПБ	17,200,000	4.00	6.00	13.00	100	—
1912 СПБ	17,050,000	4.00	6.00	13.00	25.00	—
1913 СПБ	26,000,000	4.00	6.00	13.00	25.00	—
1914 СПБ	20,000,000	4.00	6.00	13.00	30.00	—
1901-14 Common date proof	—	PF60 175				

Y# 10.3 2 KOPEKS

Copper **Ruler:** Nicholas II **Obv:** Crowned double-headed imperial eagle **Rev:** Value within circle **Note:** Struck at Petrograd without mint mark.

Date	Mintage	F12	VF20	XF40	MS60	MS63
1915	33,750,000	5.00	7.00	10.00	45.00	—
1916	31,500,000	7.00	8.00	12.00	55.00	—
1917 Rare	—	—	—	—	1,000	—

Y# 11.2 3 KOPEKS

8.00 g., Copper, 28 mm. **Ruler:** Nicholas II **Obv:** Crowned double imperial eagle within circle **Rev:** Value flanked by stars within beaded circle **Edge:** Reeded

Date	Mintage	F12	VF20	XF40	MS60	MS63
1901 СПБ	10,000,000	20.00	30.00	60.00	100	200
1902 СПБ	3,333,000	100	150	250	350	—
1903 СПБ	11,400,000	10.00	15.00	30.00	60.00	115
1904 СПБ	6,934,000	10.00	20.00	60.00	100	200
1905 СПБ	3,333,000	50.00	100	170	250	—
1906 СПБ	5,667,000	5.00	9.00	45.00	75.00	130
1907 СПБ	2,500,000	100	200	300	450	—
1908 СПБ	12,667,000	10.00	20.00	30.00	60.00	115
1909 СПБ	6,733,000	20.00	30.00	50.00	80.00	175
1910 СПБ	6,667,000	4.00	6.00	40.00	60.00	115
1911 СПБ	9,467,000	4.00	6.00	18.00	50.00	100
1912 СПБ	8,533,000	5.00	10.00	15.00	35.00	75.00
1913 СПБ	15,333,000	4.00	7.00	9.00	40.00	90.00
1914 СПБ	8,167,000	4.00	7.00	9.00	45.00	95.00
1901-14 СПБ Common date proof	—	PF60 1,000				

Y# 11.3 3 KOPEKS

Copper **Ruler:** Nicholas II **Obv:** Crowned double-headed imperial eagle **Rev:** Value flanked by stars within beaded circle **Note:** Struck at Petrograd without mint mark.

Date	Mintage	F12	VF20	XF40	MS60	MS63
1915	19,833,000	7.00	10.00	20.00	40.00	—
1916	25,667,000	7.00	10.00	20.00	60.00	—
1917 Rare	—	—	—	—	—	1,000

Y# 12.2 5 KOPEKS

16.40 g., Copper, 32.6 mm. **Ruler:** Nicholas II **Obv:** Crowned double-headed imperial eagle within circle **Rev:** Value flanked by stars within beaded circle **Edge:** Reeded

Date	Mintage	F12	VF20	XF40	MS60	MS63
1911 СПБ	3,800,000	50.00	100	300	475	—
1912 СПБ	2,700,000	100	200	450	600	—

Y# 19a.1 5 KOPEKS

0.90 g., 0.500 Silver 0.0145 oz. ASW **Ruler:** Nicholas II **Obv:** Crowned double-headed imperial eagle **Rev:** Crown above date and value within wreath **Edge:** Reeded

Date	Mintage	F12	VF20	XF40	MS60	MS63
1901 СПБ ФЗ	5,790,000	5.00	10.00	20.00	45.00	120
1901 СПБ АР	Inc. above	50.00	100	240	375	—
1902 СПБ АР	6,000,000	5.00	10.00	30.00	60.00	200
1903 СПБ АР	9,000,000	5.00	10.00	20.00	45.00	120
1904 СПБ АР Rare	9	—	9,000	37,500	—	—
1905 СПБ АР	10,000,000	8.00	12.00	30.00	60.00	200
1906 СПБ ЭБ	4,000,000	30.00	60.00	130	225	—
1908 СПБ ЭБ	400,000	8.00	12.00	55.00	85.00	225
1909 СПБ ЭБ	3,100,000	8.00	12.00	30.00	60.00	200
1910 СПБ ЭБ	2,500,000	8.00	12.00	30.00	60.00	200
1911 СПБ ЭБ	2,700,000	8.00	12.00	27.50	60.00	200
1912 СПБ ЭБ	3,000,000	8.00	15.00	30.00	60.00	200
1913 СПБ ЭБ Proof	Inc. below	—	400	1,300	—	—
1913 СПБ ВС	1,300,000	8.00	15.00	30.00	60.00	200
1914 СПБ ВС	4,200,000	8.00	15.00	30.00	60.00	200
1901-14 Common date proof	—	PF60 950				

Y# 19a.2 5 KOPEKS

0.90 g., 0.500 Silver 0.0145 oz. ASW **Ruler:** Nicholas II **Obv:** Crowned double-headed imperial eagle **Rev:** Crown above value and date within wreath **Note:** Struck at Petrograd without mint mark.

Date	Mintage	F12	VF20	XF40	MS60	MS63
1915 ВС	3,000,000	5.00	11.00	27.00	40.00	70.00

Y# 12.3 5 KOPEKS

Copper **Ruler:** Nicholas II **Obv:** Crowned double-headed imperial eagle **Rev:** Value flanked by stars within beaded circle **Note:** Struck at Petrograd without mint mark.

Date	Mintage	F12	VF20	XF40	MS60	MS63
1916	8,000,000	50.00	200	350	4,700	—
1917 Rare	—	—	—	—	—	1,000

Y# 20a.2 10 KOPEKS

1.80 g., 0.500 Silver 0.0289 oz. ASW **Ruler:** Nicholas II **Obv:** Crowned double-headed imperial eagle, ribbons on crown **Rev:** Crown above value and date within wreath **Edge:** Reeded

Date	Mintage	F12	VF20	XF40	MS60	MS63
1901 СПБ ФЗ	15,000,000	100	200	475	1,000	—
1901 СПБ АР	Inc. above	50.00	100	175	400	—
1902 СПБ АР	17,000,000	10.00	20.00	80.00	150	—
1903 СПБ АР	28,500,000	10.00	20.00	80.00	150	—
1904 СПБ АР	20,000,000	10.00	20.00	80.00	150	—
1905 СПБ АР	25,000,000	10.00	20.00	80.00	150	—
1906 СПБ ЭБ	17,500,000	10.00	20.00	80.00	150	—
1907 СПБ ЭБ	—	10.00	20.00	80.00	150	—
1908 СПБ ЭБ	8,210,000	20.00	40.00	110	200	—
1909 СПБ ЭБ	25,290,000	3.00	7.00	19.00	50.00	110
1910 СПБ ЭБ	20,000,000	3.00	7.00	19.00	50.00	110
1911 СПБ ЭБ	19,180,000	3.00	7.00	19.00	50.00	110
1912 СПБ ЭБ	20,000,000	3.00	7.00	19.00	50.00	110
1913 СПБ ЭБ	Inc. below	PF60 1,000				
1913 СПБ ВС	7,250,000	3.00	7.00	19.00	50.00	110
1914 СПБ ВС	51,250,000	3.00	7.00	19.00	50.00	110
1901-14 Common date proof	—	PF60 950				

Y# 20a.3 10 KOPEKS

1.80 g., 0.500 Silver 0.0289 oz. ASW **Ruler:** Nicholas II **Obv:** Crowned double-headed imperial eagle, ribbons on crown **Rev:** Crown above value and date within wreath **Edge:** Reeded **Note:** Struck at Petrograd without mintmaster initials.

Date	Mintage	F12	VF20	XF40	MS60	MS63
1915 ВС	82,500,000	4.00	5.00	7.00	80.00	—
1916 ВС	121,500,000	4.00	5.00	10.00	20.00	—
1917 ВС	17,600,000	30.00	60.00	110	160	—

Y# 20a.1 10 KOPEKS

1.80 g., 0.500 Silver 0.0289 oz. ASW **Ruler:** Nicholas II **Obv:** Crowned double-headed imperial eagle, ribbons on crown **Rev:** Crown above value and date within wreath **Note:** Struck at Osaka, Japan without mintmaster initials.

Date	Mintage	F12	VF20	XF40	MS60	MS63
1916	70,001,000	5.00	10.00	27.00	80.00	—

Y# 21a.2 15 KOPEKS

2.70 g., 0.500 Silver 0.0434 oz. ASW **Ruler:** Nicholas II **Obv:** Crowned double-headed imperial eagle, ribbons on crown **Rev:** Crown above date and value within wreath **Edge:** Reeded

Date	Mintage	F12	VF20	XF40	MS60	MS63
1901 СПБ ФЗ	6,670,000	20.00	50.00	100	200	—
1901 СПБ АР	Inc. above	50.00	100	150	300	—
1902 СПБ АР	28,667,000	20.00	50.00	100	200	—
1903 СПБ АР	16,667,000	30.00	60.00	130	250	—
1904 СПБ АР	15,600,000	30.00	60.00	130	250	—
1905 СПБ АР	24,000,000	30.00	60.00	130	250	—
1906 СПБ ЭБ	23,333,000	20.00	50.00	100	200	—
1907 СПБ ЭБ	30,000,000	10.00	30.00	70.00	150	—
1908 СПБ ЭБ	29,000,000	10.00	30.00	70.00	150	—
1909 СПБ ЭБ	21,667,000	4.00	8.00	19.00	50.00	—
1911 СПБ ЭБ	6,313,000	7.00	18.00	32.00	70.00	—
1912 СПБ ВС	Inc. above	—	2,300	5,000	—	—
1912 СПБ ЭБ	13,333,000	10.00	18.00	48.00	120	—
1913 СПБ ЭБ Proof	Inc. below	—	—	1,200	—	—
1913 СПБ ВС	5,300,000	7.00	14.00	30.00	70.00	—
1914 СПБ ВС	43,367,000	4.00	8.00	19.00	50.00	—
1901-14 Common date proof	—	PF60 1,000				

Y# 21a.3 15 KOPEKS

2.70 g., 0.500 Silver 0.0434 oz. ASW **Ruler:** Nicholas II **Obv:** Crowned double-headed imperial eagle, ribbons on crown **Rev:** Crown above value and date within wreath **Note:** Struck at Petrograd without mintmaster initials.

Date	Mintage	F12	VF20	XF40	MS60	MS63
1915 ВС	59,333,000	5.00	7.00	15.00	25.00	—
1916 ВС	96,773,000	3.00	5.00	10.00	20.00	—
1917 ВС	14,320,000	30.00	50.00	130	200	—

Y# 21a.1 15 KOPEKS

2.70 g., 0.500 Silver 0.0434 oz. ASW **Ruler:** Nicholas II **Obv:** Crowned double-headed imperial eagle, ribbons on crown **Rev:** Crown above value and date within wreath **Edge:** Reeded **Note:** Struck at Osaka, Japan without mintmaster initials.

Date	Mintage	F12	VF20	XF40	MS60	MS63
1916	96,666,000	3.00	8.00	18.00	100	130

Y# 22a.1 20 KOPEKS

3.60 g., 0.500 Silver 0.0579 oz. ASW, 22 mm. **Ruler:** Nicholas II **Obv:** Crowned double-headed imperial eagle, ribbons on crown **Rev:** Crown above value and date within wreath

Date	Mintage	F12	VF20	XF40	MS60	MS63
1901 СПБ ФЗ	7,750,000	10.00	22.00	150	240	—
1901 СПБ АР Proof	Inc. above	—	—	1,200	4,500	—
1902 СПБ АР	10,000,000	50.00	100	325	425	—
1903 СПБ АР	Inc. above	5.00	8.00	70.00	115	—
1904 СПБ АР	13,000,000	20.00	40.00	105	150	—
1905 СПБ АР	11,000,000	10.00	20.00	70.00	115	—
1906 СПБ ЭБ	15,000,000	10.00	20.00	70.00	115	—
1907 СПБ ЭБ	20,000,000	10.00	20.00	20.00	42.00	—
1908 СПБ ЭБ	5,000,000	5.00	10.00	25.00	42.00	—
1909 СПБ ЭБ	18,875,000	5.00	8.00	20.00	42.00	—
1910 СПБ ЭБ	11,000,000	5.00	8.00	20.00	42.00	—
1911 СПБ ЭБ	7,100,000	5.00	8.00	20.00	42.00	—
1912 СПБ ЭБ	15,000,000	5.00	8.00	20.00	42.00	—
1912 СПБ ВС Rare	Inc. above	—	800	3,300	—	—
1913 СПБ ЭБ Proof	Inc. below	—	500	2,200	—	—
1913 СПБ ВС	4,250,000	5.00	8.00	20.00	42.00	—
1914 СПБ ВС	52,750,000	4.00	8.00	15.00	30.00	50.00
1901-14 Common date proof	—	PF60 350				

Y# 22a.2 20 KOPEKS

3.60 g., 0.500 Silver 0.0579 oz. ASW **Ruler:** Nicholas II **Obv:** Crowned double-headed imperial eagle, ribbons on crown **Rev:** Crown above value and date within wreath **Note:** Struck at Petrograd without mint mark.

Date	Mintage	F12	VF20	XF40	MS60	MS63
1915 ВС	105,500,000	4.00	6.00	8.00	15.00	20.00
1916 ВС	131,670,000	8.00	10.00	15.00	30.00	40.00
1917 ВС	3,500,000	300	500	1,000	—	—
1915-17 Common date proof	—	PF60 400				

Y# 57 25 KOPEKS

5.00 g., 0.900 Silver 0.1446 oz. ASW **Ruler:** Nicholas II **Obv:** Head left **Rev:** Crowned double-headed imperial eagle, ribbons on crown **Note:** Struck at St. Petersburg without mint mark.

Date	Mintage	F12	VF20	XF40	MS60	MS63
1901	Est. 200	PF60 11,000				

Y# 58.2 50 KOPEKS

10.00 g., 0.900 Silver 0.2893 oz. ASW **Ruler:** Nicholas II **Obv:** Head left **Rev:** Crowned double-headed imperial eagle, ribbons on crown **Note:** Without mint mark, moneyer's initials on edge.

Date	Mintage	F12	VF20	XF40	MS60	MS63
1901 АР	412,000	130	600	1,900	3,000	—
1901 ФЗ	Inc. above	100	200	600	1,000	—

Date	Mintage	F12	VF20	XF40	MS60	MS63
1902 АР	36,000	300	460	700	2,000	—
1903 АР	—	PF60 1,900				
1904 АР	4,010,000	PF60 20,600				
1906 ЭБ	10,000	200	390	880	1,000	—
1907 ЭБ	200,000	50.00	130	600	950	—
1908 ЭБ	40,000	300	670	1,200	2,300	—
1909 ЭБ	50,000	350	600	900	1,500	—
1910 ЭБ	150,000	50.00	120	350	1,000	—
1911 ЭБ	800,000	100	65.00	245	850	—
1912 ЭБ	7,085,000	20.00	30.00	45.00	135	—
1913 ЭБ	6,420,000	100	200	300	430	—
1913 ВС	Inc. above	20.00	40.00	100	270	—
1914 ВС	1,200,000	50.00	150	400	500	—
1901-14 Common date proof	—	PF60 2,000				

Y# 59.3 ROUBLE

20.00 g., 0.900 Silver 0.5786 oz. ASW **Ruler:** Nicholas II **Obv:** Head left **Rev:** Crowned double-headed imperial eagle, ribbons on crown **Note:** Without mint mark, moneyer's initials on edge.

Date	Mintage	F12	VF20	XF40	MS60	MS63
1901 ФЗ	2,608,000	PF60 5,500				
1901 АР	Inc. above	120	650	700	1,250	4,000
1902 АР	140,000	PF60 11,000				
1903 АР	56,000	550	1,200	2,500	—	—
1904 АР	12,000	2,000	5,500	8,000	—	—
1905 АР	21,000	PF60 8,700				
1906 ЭБ	46,000	500	1,800	2,000	—	—
1907 ЭБ	400,000	200	500	1,300	2,950	4,500
1908 ЭБ	130,000	500	1,300	3,000	—	—
1909 ЭБ	51,000	150	640	1,500	—	—
1910 ЭБ	75,000	200	550	1,300	2,000	3,750
1911 ЭБ	129,000	PF60 4,100				
1912 ЭБ	2,111,000	100	280	430	750	1,250
1913 ЭБ	22,000	500	1,750	2,500	—	—
1913 ВС	Inc. above	500	2,000	3,300	—	—
1914 ВС	536,000	PF60 3,900				
1915 ВС	5,000	500	950	1,300	3,000	4,500

Note: Varieties exist with plain edge, these are mint errors and rare

Y# 68 ROUBLE

20.00 g., 0.900 Silver 0.5786 oz. ASW, 34 mm. **Ruler:** Nicholas II **Subject:** Centennial - Napolean's Defeat **Obv:** Crowned double-headed imperial eagle with various crowned shields **Rev:** Inscription and date within beaded circle

Date	Mintage	F12	VF20	XF40	MS60	MS63
1912 ЭБ	46,000	400	1,600	1,750	2,600	3,400
1912 ЭБ Proof	—	—	—	—	—	—

Y# 69 ROUBLE

20.00 g., 0.900 Silver 0.5786 oz. ASW, 34 mm. **Ruler:** Nicholas II **Subject:** Alexander III Memorial **Obv:** Head left **Rev:** Monument

Date	Mintage	F12	VF20	XF40	MS60	MS63
1912 ЭБ	2,100	800	8,500	10,300	13,200	15,300
1912 ЭБ Proof	—	—	—	—	—	—

Y# 70 ROUBLE

20.00 g., 0.900 Silver 0.5786 oz. ASW, 34 mm. **Ruler:** Nicholas II **Subject:** 300th Anniversary - Romanov Dynasty **Obv:** Conjoined heads facing 1/4 right **Rev:** Crowned double-headed imperial eagle **Note:** Struck at St. Petersburg without mint mark.

Date	Mintage	F12	VF20	XF40	MS60	MS63
1913 ВС	1,472,000	100	120	230	320	500

Y# 71 ROUBLE

20.00 g., 0.900 Silver 0.5786 oz. ASW, 34 mm. **Ruler:** Nicholas II **Subject:** 200th Anniversary - Battle of Gangut **Obv:** Armored bust right **Rev:** Crowned double-headed imperial eagle

Date	Mintage	F12	VF20	XF40	MS60	MS63
1914 ВС	Est. 30000	1,500	11,600	15,000	—	—

Note: Only 317 pieces were issued through 1917, but an unknown number of restrikes were made in the 1920's

Date	Mintage	F12	VF20	XF40	MS60	MS63
1914 ВС	—	PF60 23,800				

Y# 62 5 ROUBLES

4.30 g., 0.900 Gold 0.1245 oz. AGW, 18 mm. **Ruler:** Nicholas II **Obv:** Head left **Rev:** Crowned double-headed imperial eagle, ribbons on crown **Note:** Struck at St. Petersburg without mint mark.

Date	Mintage	F12	VF20	XF40	MS60	MS63
1901 ФЗ	7,500,000	190	300	400	520	600
1901 АР	Inc. above	190	300	400	520	600
1902 АР	6,240,000	190	300	400	520	600
1903 АР	5,148,000	190	300	400	520	600
1904 АР	2,016,000	190	300	400	520	600
1906 ЭБ	10	—	—	7,000	10,000	—
1907 ЭБ	109	—	—	4,000	7,500	—
1909 ЭБ	—	190	500	765	1,100	1,200
1910 ЭБ	200,000	190	800	1,450	2,700	3,200
1911 ЭБ	100,000	1,600	1,800	3,000	5,150	6,000
1901-11 Common date proof	—	PF60 4,000				

Y# 64 10 ROUBLES

8.60 g., 0.900 Gold 0.2489 oz. AGW **Ruler:** Nicholas II **Obv:** Head left **Rev:** Crowned double-headed imperial eagle, ribbons on crown **Note:** Without mint mark. Moneyer's initials on edge.

Date	Mintage	F12	VF20	XF40	MS60	MS63
1901 ФЗ	2,377,000	380	600	650	670	750
1901 АР	Inc. above	380	600	650	670	750
1902 АР	2,019,000	415	600	650	700	800
1903 АР	2,817,000	415	600	650	700	770
1904 АР Big head	1,025,000	415	600	650	750	800
1904 АР Small head	Inc. above	415	730	870	1,300	1,500
1906 ЭБ	10	PF60 35,000				
1909 ЭБ	50,000	445	650	700	800	900
1910 ЭБ	100,000	445	1,500	1,600	3,000	3,200
1911 ЭБ	50,000	445	1,200	1,400	1,680	2,000
1901-11 Common date proof	—	PF60 8,000				

Y# A65 25 ROUBLES

32.25 g., 0.900 Gold 0.9332 oz. AGW **Ruler:** Nicholas II **Obv:** Head left **Rev:** Crowned double imperial eagle, ribbons on crown, within circle flanked by rosettes **Rev. Legend:** 2-1/2 ИМПЕРІАЛЪА (IMPERIALS) **Note:** Struck at St. Petersburg without mint mark.

Date	Mintage	F12	VF20	XF40	MS60	MS63
1908	150	—	—	70,000	95,000	—
1908	—	PF60 100,000				

Y# B65 37 ROUBLES 50 KOPEKS

32.25 g., 0.900 Gold 0.9332 oz. AGW **Ruler:** Nicholas II **Obv:** Head left **Rev:** Crowned double-headed imperial eagle within beaded circle **Rev. Legend:** 100 ФРАНКОВЪ **Note:** Without mint mark.

Date	Mintage	F12	VF20	XF40	MS60	MS63
1902	225	—	—	100,000	150,000	—

Note: UBS sale #67 9-06, near Unc realized $68,750.

Date	Mintage	F12	VF20	XF40	MS60	MS63
1902	—	PF60 135,000				

Note: Impaired Proofs are valued at approximately $85,000.

Y# B65a 37 ROUBLES 50 KOPEKS

Copper-Nickel **Ruler:** Nicholas II **Obv:** Head left **Rev:** Crowned double headed imperial eagle within beaded circle **Rev. Inscription:** Letter "P" after "1902 G" **Edge:** Plain **Note:** Gold plated specimens were done outside the mint.

Date	Mintage	F12	VF20	XF40	MS60	MS63
1902 (1991) P Restrike	—	—	—	—	35.00	—

GOLD MINE INGOTS

During the late 19th and early 20th century, Russian law provided that gold mine owners who supplied gold to the mints should receive back whatever silver was recovered during refining of the gold. The silver was returned in the form of circular ingots of various weights which resembled coins. These pieces have often been erroneously described as Russian trade coins for use in Mongolia, China, and Turkestan.

Note: Both the Doyla and the Zolotnik are weights, not denominations.

KM# 1 24 DOLYA

1.07 g., 0.990 Silver 0.0339 oz. ASW **Ruler:** Nicholas II **Obv:** Crowned double-headed eagle within circle **Rev:** Value

Date	Mintage	F12	VF20	XF40	MS60	MS63
ND-1901	—	—	350	500	800	—

KM# 2 ZOLOTNIK

4.27 g., 0.990 Silver 0.1358 oz. ASW **Ruler:** Nicholas II **Obv:** Crowned double-headed eagle within small circle **Rev:** Value

Date	Mintage	F12	VF20	XF40	MS60	MS63
ND-1901	—	—	500	850	1,250	—

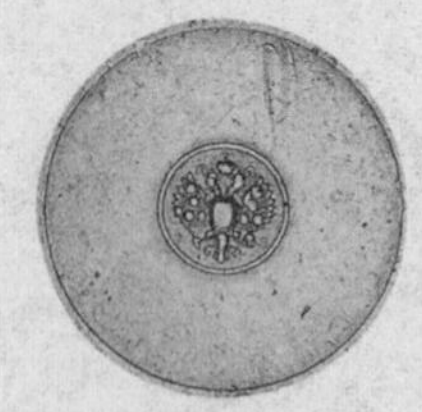

KM# 3 3 ZOLOTNIKS
12.80 g., 0.990 Silver 0.4073 oz. ASW **Ruler:** Nicholas II **Obv:** Crowned double-headed eagle within small circle **Rev:** Value

Date	Mintage	F12	VF20	XF40	MS60	MS63
ND-1901	—	—	1,150	1,950	2,750	—

KM# 4 10 ZOLOTNIKS
42.66 g., 0.990 Silver 1.3577 oz. ASW **Ruler:** Nicholas II **Obv:** Crowned double-headed eagle within small circle **Rev:** Value

Date	Mintage	F12	VF20	XF40	MS60	MS63
ND-1901	—	—	350	550	1,000	—

РСФСР (R.S.F.S.R.)

(Russian Soviet Federated Socialist Republic)

STANDARD COINAGE

Y# 80 10 KOPEKS
1.80 g., 0.500 Silver 0.0289 oz. ASW **Obv:** National arms **Rev:** Value and date within beaded circle, star on top divides wreath

Date	Mintage	F12	VF20	XF40	MS60	MS63
1921	950,000	20.00	50.00	80.00	120	300
1921	—	PF60 2,400				
1922	18,640,000	3.00	7.00	15.00	35.00	150
1922	—	PF60 550				
1923	33,424,000	3.00	5.00	7.00	25.00	125
1923	—	PF60 450				

Y# 81 15 KOPEKS
2.70 g., 0.500 Silver 0.0434 oz. ASW **Obv:** National arms within circle **Rev:** Value and date within beaded circle, star on top divides wreath

Date	Mintage	F12	VF20	XF40	MS60	MS63
1921	933,000	20.00	45.00	65.00	100	300
1921	—	PF60 2,400				
1922	13,633,000	5.00	10.00	15.00	45.00	200
1922	—	PF60 1,900				
1923	28,504,000	4.00	5.00	8.00	50.00	150
1923	—	PF60 400				

Y# 82 20 KOPEKS
3.60 g., 0.500 Silver 0.0579 oz. ASW **Obv:** National arms within circle **Rev:** Value and date within beaded circle, star on top divides wreath **Note:** Varieties exist.

Date	Mintage	F12	VF20	XF40	MS60	MS63
1921	825,000	20.00	45.00	60.00	110	300
1921	—	PF60 2,500				
1922	14,220,000	5.00	10.00	40.00	80.00	225
1922	—	PF60 550				
1923	27,580,000	10.00	20.00	30.00	50.00	175
1923	—	PF60 450				

Y# 83 50 KOPEKS
10.00 g., 0.900 Silver 0.2893 oz. ASW **Obv:** National arms within beaded circle **Rev:** Value in center of star within beaded circle **Edge Lettering:** Mintmaster's initials

Date	Mintage	F12	VF20	XF40	MS60	MS63
1921 АГ	1,400,000	30.00	40.00	50.00	100	300
1921 АГ	—	PF60 2,300				
1922 АГ	8,224,000	20.00	30.00	40.00	80.00	275
1922 АГ	—	PF60 1,750				
1922 ПЛ	Inc. above	20.00	30.00	40.00	60.00	250
1922 ПЛ	—	PF60 1,200				

Y# 84 ROUBLE
20.00 g., 0.900 Silver 0.5786 oz. ASW **Obv:** National arms within beaded circle **Rev:** Value in center of star within beaded circle **Edge Lettering:** Mintmaster's initials **Note:** Varieties exist.

Date	Mintage	F12	VF20	XF40	MS60	MS63
1921 АГ	1,000,000	100	150	200	300	500
1921 АГ	—	PF60 3,600				
1922 АГ	2,050,000	300	425	600	1,200	2,000
1922 АГ	—	PF60 3,000				
1922 ПЛ	Inc. above	200	300	400	650	900
1922 ПЛ	—	PF60 2,750				

TRADE COINAGE

Y# 85 CHERVONETZ (10 Roubles)
8.60 g., 0.900 Gold 0.2489 oz. AGW **Obv:** National arms, РСФСР below arms **Rev:** Standing figure with head right **Edge Lettering:** Mintmaster's initials

Date	Mintage	F12	VF20	XF40	MS60	MS63
1923 ПЛ	2,751,000	550	1,000	1,600	2,000	2,800
1923 ПЛ	—	PF60 44,000				
1975	250,000	—	—	—	350	—
1976 ЛМД	1,000,000	—	—	—	350	—
1976 Rare	—	—	—	—	—	1,000
1977 ММД	1,000,000	—	—	—	350	—
1977 ЛМД	1,000,000	—	—	—	350	—
1978 ММД	350,000	—	—	—	350	—
1979 ММД	1,000,000	—	—	—	350	—
1980 ЛМД	900,000	—	—	—	350	—
1980 ММД	—	—	—	—	—	—
1980 ММД	100,000	PF60 600				
1981 ММД	1,000,000	—	—	—	350	—
1981 ЛМД Rare	—	—	—	—	—	—
1982 ММД	65,000	—	—	—	350	—
1982 ЛМД Rare	—	—	—	—	—	10,000

Y# A86 CHERVONETZ (10 Roubles)
8.60 g., 0.900 Gold 0.2489 oz. AGW **Obv:** National arms with CCCP below **Rev:** Standing figure with head right

Date	Mintage	F12	VF20	XF40	MS60	MS63
1925 Unique	600,000	—	—	—	—	—

Note: Chervonetz were first struck in 1923 under the R.S.F.S.R. government; in 1925 the U.S.S.R. government attempted a new issue of these coins, of which only one remaining coin is known; from 1975 to 1982 the U.S.S.R. government continued striking the original type with new dates

CCCP (U.S.S.R.)

(Union of Soviet Socialist Republics)

STANDARD COINAGE

Y# 75 1/2 KOPEK
Copper **Obv:** CCCP within circle **Rev:** Value and date

Date	Mintage	F12	VF20	XF40	MS60	MS63
1925	45,380,000	20.00	30.00	40.00	70.00	—
1927	45,380,000	20.00	25.00	50.00	90.00	—
1927	—	PF60 350				
1928	—	50.00	70.00	130	200	—

Y# 76 KOPEK
3.20 g., Bronze **Obv:** National arms within circle **Rev:** Value and date within oat sprigs

Date	Mintage	F12	VF20	XF40	MS60	MS63
1924	34,705,000	10.00	20.00	30.00	60.00	—
Note: Reeded edge						
1924	—	PF60 400				
Note: Reeded edge						
1924	Inc. above	50.00	100	200	500	—
Note: Plain edge						
1925	141,806,000	PF60 17,400				

Y# 91 KOPEK
1.00 g., Aluminum-Bronze, 15.2 mm. **Obv:** National arms within circle **Rev:** Value and date within oat sprigs **Note:** Varieties exist.

Date	Mintage	F12	VF20	XF40	MS60	MS63
1926	87,915,000	4.00	10.00	15.00	25.00	—
1926	—	PF60 200				
1927	—	3.00	7.00	10.00	230	—
1928	—	2.00	5.00	9.00	18.00	—
1929	95,950,000	7.00	15.00	25.00	50.00	—
1930	85,351,000	10.00	20.00	35.00	230	—
1931	106,100,000	3.00	7.00	10.00	20.00	—
1932	56,900,000	6.00	12.00	15.00	35.00	—
1933	111,257,000	2.00	3.00	10.00	20.00	—
1934	100,245	3.00	7.00	10.00	20.00	—
1935	66,405,000	10.00	15.00	25.00	100	—

Y# 98 KOPEK
Aluminum-Bronze **Obv:** National arms **Rev:** Value and date within oat sprigs

Date	Mintage	F12	VF20	XF40	MS60	MS63
1935	—	17.00	35.00	50.00	120	—
Note: Mintage inc.Y91						
1936	132,204,000	2.00	4.00	7.00	12.00	—

Y# 105 KOPEK
1.00 g., Aluminum-Bronze, 15.2 mm. **Obv:** National arms **Rev:** Value and date within oat sprigs **Edge:** Reeded **Note:** Varieties exist.

Date	Mintage	F12	VF20	XF40	MS60	MS63
1937	—	2.00	4.00	6.00	10.00	—
1938	—	1.00	2.00	3.00	6.00	—
1939	—	2.00	3.00	5.00	9.00	—
1940	—	1.00	2.00	3.00	6.00	—
1941	—	5.00	10.00	17.00	24.00	—
1945	—	3.00	6.00	12.00	20.00	—
1946	—	0.50	1.00	4.00	9.00	—

Y# 112 KOPEK

1.00 g., Aluminum-Bronze **Obv:** National arms **Rev:** Value and date within oat sprigs **Edge:** Reeded **Note:** Varieties exist.

Date	Mintage	F12	VF20	XF40	MS60	MS63
1948	—	1.00	2.00	5.00	10.00	—
1949	—	0.50	1.00	4.00	9.00	—
1950	—	2.00	4.00	8.00	15.00	—
1951	—	3.00	5.00	9.00	18.00	—
1952	—	1.00	2.00	3.00	5.00	—
1953	—	1.00	2.00	3.00	5.00	—
1954	—	1.00	2.00	3.00	4.00	—
1955	—	1.00	2.00	3.00	4.00	—
1956	—	1.00	2.00	3.00	4.00	—
1957 Rare	—	**PF60** 1,000				

Y# 119 KOPEK

Aluminum-Bronze **Obv:** National arms **Rev:** Value and date within oat sprigs

Date	Mintage	F12	VF20	XF40	MS60	MS63
1957	—	2.00	4.00	8.00	16.00	—

Y# 126 KOPEK

Copper-Nickel **Obv:** National arms **Rev:** Value and date within oat sprigs

Date	Mintage	F12	VF20	XF40	MS60	MS63
1958	30,265,000	—	2,700	4,000	5,200	—

Note: Never officially released for circulation; majority of mintage remelted;Some pieces appeared in circulation in Ukraine

Y# 126a KOPEK

1.00 g., Brass, 15. mm. **Obv:** National arms **Rev:** Value and date above spray **Edge:** Reeded **Note:** Varieties exist.

Date	Mintage	VF20	XF40	MS60	MS63	MS65
1961	—	2.00	3.00	5.00	7.00	9.00
1962	—	2.00	3.00	5.00	7.00	9.00
1963	—	2.00	3.00	5.00	7.00	9.00
1964	—	5.00	10.00	15.00	22.00	30.00
1965	—	2.00	3.00	5.00	7.00	9.00
1966	—	3.00	5.00	7.00	9.00	12.00
1967	—	0.30	0.50	0.75	1.00	1.50
1968	—	0.30	0.50	0.75	1.00	1.50
1969	—	0.30	0.50	0.75	1.00	1.50
1970	—	0.30	0.50	0.75	1.00	1.50
1971	—	0.30	0.50	0.75	1.00	1.50
1972	—	0.30	0.50	0.75	1.00	1.50
1973	—	0.30	0.50	0.75	1.00	1.50
1974	—	0.30	0.50	0.75	1.00	1.50
1975	—	0.30	0.50	0.75	1.00	1.50
1976	—	0.30	0.50	0.75	1.00	1.50
1977	—	0.30	0.50	0.75	1.00	1.50
1978	—	0.30	0.50	0.75	1.00	1.50
1979	—	0.30	0.50	0.75	1.00	1.50
1980	—	0.30	0.50	0.75	1.00	1.50
1981	—	0.30	0.50	0.75	1.00	1.50
1982	—	0.30	0.50	0.75	1.00	1.50
1983	—	0.30	0.50	0.75	1.00	1.50
1984	—	0.30	0.50	0.75	1.00	1.50
1985	—	0.30	0.50	0.75	1.00	1.50
1986	—	0.30	0.50	0.75	1.00	1.50
1987	—	0.30	0.50	0.75	1.00	1.50
1988	—	0.30	0.50	0.75	1.00	1.50
1989	—	0.20	0.30	0.50	0.75	1.00
1990	—	0.20	0.30	0.50	0.75	1.00
1991 M	—	0.20	0.30	0.50	0.75	1.00
1991 Л	—	0.20	0.30	0.50	0.75	1.00

Y# 77 2 KOPEKS

Bronze **Obv:** National arms **Rev:** Value and date within oat sprigs **Note:** Varieties exist.

Date	Mintage	F12	VF20	XF40	MS60	MS63
1924	119,996,000	5.00	10.00	35.00	250	—
Note: Reeded edge						
1924	Inc. above	50.00	80.00	150	550	—
Note: Plain edge						
1925	Inc. above	1,700	3,200	4,000	4,700	—

Y# 92 2 KOPEKS

2.00 g., Aluminum-Bronze, 18.3 mm. **Obv:** National arms within circle **Rev:** Value and date within oat sprigs **Note:** Varieties exist.

Date	Mintage	F12	VF20	XF40	MS60	MS63
1926	105,053,000	3.00	4.00	7.00	14.00	—
1926	—	**PF60** 200				
1927	—	2,200	4,300	5,000	—	—
1928	—	2.00	3.00	5.00	10.00	—
1929	80,000,000	2.00	3.00	6.00	12.00	—
1930	134,186,000	1.00	2.00	5.00	8.00	—
1931	99,523,000	1.00	2.00	5.00	8.00	—
1932	39,573,000	2.00	4.00	7.00	15.00	—
1933	54,874,000	12.00	25.00	40.00	75.00	—
1934	61,574,000	2.00	3.00	4.00	8.00	—
1935	81,121,000	3.00	5.00	9.00	18.00	—

Y# 99 2 KOPEKS

Aluminum-Bronze **Obv:** National arms **Rev:** Value and date within oat sprigs **Note:** Varieties exist.

Date	Mintage	F12	VF20	XF40	MS60	MS63
1935	—	12.00	20.00	32.00	250	—
1936	94,354,000	1.00	2.00	5.00	10.00	—

Y# 106 2 KOPEKS

2.00 g., Aluminum-Bronze **Obv:** National arms **Rev:** Value and date within oat sprigs

Date	Mintage	F12	VF20	XF40	MS60	MS63
1937	—	1.00	2.00	4.00	7.00	—
1938	—	1.00	2.00	4.00	7.00	—
1939	—	2.00	4.00	8.00	16.00	—
1940	—	1.00	2.00	4.00	7.00	—
1941	—	2.50	5.00	10.00	20.00	—
1945	—	5.00	10.00	20.00	40.00	—
1946	—	2.00	3.00	4.00	7.00	—
1948	—	400	700	1,200	3,000	—

Note: Five ribbons on each wreath

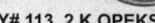

Y# 113 2 K OPEKS

1.80 g., Aluminum-Bronze **Obv:** National arms **Rev:** Value and date within oat sprigs **Edge:** Reeded **Note:** Varieties exist.

Date	Mintage	F12	VF20	XF40	MS60	MS63
1948	—	1.00	3.00	4.00	5.00	—
1949	—	1.00	3.00	4.00	5.00	—
1950	—	1.00	3.00	4.00	5.00	—
1951	—	5.00	11.00	16.00	30.00	—
1952	—	1.00	2.00	3.00	9.00	—
1953	—	1.00	2.00	3.00	9.00	—
1954	—	1.00	2.00	3.00	9.00	—
1955	—	1.00	2.00	3.00	9.00	—
1956	—	1.00	2.00	3.00	9.00	—

Y# 120 2 KOPEKS

Aluminum-Bronze **Obv:** National arms **Rev:** Value and date within oat sprigs

Date	Mintage	F12	VF20	XF40	MS60	MS63
1957	—	3.00	5.00	8.00	15.00	—

Y# 127 2 KOPEKS

Copper-Nickel **Obv:** National arms **Rev:** Value and date within sprays

Date	Mintage	F12	VF20	XF40	MS60	MS63
1958	39,591,000	—	3,000	4,000	6,000	—

Note: Never officially released for circulation; majority of mintage remelted; Some pieces appeared in circulation in Ukraine

Y# 127a 2 KOPEKS

2.00 g., Brass, 18 mm. **Obv:** National arms **Rev:** Value and date within sprays **Edge:** Reeded **Note:** Varieties exist.

Date	Mintage	VF20	XF40	MS60	MS63	MS65
1961	—	0.15	0.25	0.45	0.65	1.00
1962	—	0.15	0.25	0.45	0.65	1.00
1963	—	0.15	0.25	0.45	0.65	1.00
1964	—	10.00	15.00	20.00	25.00	45.00
1965	—	4.00	5.00	7.00	9.00	10.00
1966	—	4.00	5.00	9.00	12.00	18.00
1967	—	0.15	0.25	0.45	0.65	1.00
1968	—	0.15	0.25	0.45	0.65	1.00
1969	—	0.15	0.25	0.45	0.65	1.00
1970	—	0.15	0.25	0.45	0.65	1.00
1971	—	0.15	0.25	0.45	0.65	1.00
1972	—	0.15	0.25	0.45	0.65	1.00
1973	—	0.15	0.25	0.45	0.65	1.00
1974	—	0.15	0.25	0.45	0.65	1.00
1975	—	0.15	0.25	0.45	0.65	1.00
1976	—	0.15	0.25	0.45	0.65	1.00
1977	—	0.15	0.25	0.45	0.65	1.00
1978	—	0.15	0.25	0.45	0.65	1.00
1979	—	0.15	0.25	0.45	0.65	1.00
1980	—	0.15	0.25	0.45	0.65	1.00
1981	—	0.15	0.25	0.45	0.65	1.00
1982	—	0.15	0.25	0.45	0.65	1.00
1983	—	0.15	0.25	0.45	0.65	1.00
1984	—	0.15	0.25	0.45	0.65	1.00
1985	—	0.15	0.25	0.45	0.65	1.00
1986	—	0.15	0.25	0.45	0.65	1.00
1987	—	0.15	0.25	0.45	0.65	1.00
1988	—	0.15	0.25	0.45	0.65	1.00
1989	—	0.15	0.20	0.45	0.65	1.00
1990	—	0.15	0.20	0.45	0.65	1.00
1991 M	—	0.15	0.20	0.45	0.65	1.00
1991 Л	—	0.15	0.20	0.45	0.65	1.00

Y# 78 3 KOPEKS

Bronze **Obv:** National arms within circle **Rev:** Value and date within oat sprigs **Note:** Varieties exist.

Date	Mintage	F12	VF20	XF40	MS60	MS63
1924 Reeded edge	101,283,000	800	1,600	2,400	5,000	—
1924 Plain edge	Inc. above	10.00	20.00	40.00	200	—

Y# 93 3 KOPEKS

3.00 g., Aluminum-Bronze, 22.2 mm. **Obv:** National arms within circle **Rev:** Value and date within oat sprigs **Note:** Varieties exist.

Date	Mintage	F12	VF20	XF40	MS60	MS63
1926	19,940,000	4.00	8.00	10.00	15.00	—
1926	—	**PF60** 225				
1926 Rare	—	**PF60** 1,000				
Note: Obverse of Y#100						
1927	—	60.00	110	175	300	—

Date	Mintage	F12	VF20	XF40	MS60	MS63
1928	—	2.00	4.00	8.00	10.00	—
1929	50,150,000	2.00	4.00	7.00	14.00	—
1930	74,159,000	2.00	3.00	4.00	8.00	—
1931	121,168,000	2.00	3.00	4.00	8.00	—
1931 Rare	—	PF60 1,000				
Note: Without CCCP obverse						
1932	37,718,000	2.00	3.00	4.00	6.00	—
1933	44,764,000	3.00	7.00	10.00	20.00	—
1934	44,529,000	3.00	6.00	9.00	17.00	—
1935	58,303,000	3.00	5.00	8.00	15.00	—
1937 Rare	—	PF60 1,000				

Y# 100 3 KOPEKS

Aluminum-Bronze **Obv:** National arms **Rev:** Value and date within oat sprigs **Note:** Varieties exist.

Date	Mintage	F12	VF20	XF40	MS60	MS63
1935	—	4.00	9.00	17.00	30.00	—
1936	62,757,000	2.00	4.00	7.00	14.00	—

Y# 107 3 KOPEKS

3.00 g., Aluminum-Bronze **Obv:** National arms **Rev:** Value and date within oat sprigs **Note:** Varieties exist.

Date	Mintage	F12	VF20	XF40	MS60	MS63
1937	—	2.00	3.00	4.00	8.00	—
1938	—	2.00	3.00	4.00	8.00	—
1939	—	2.00	3.00	4.00	8.00	—
1940	—	2.00	3.00	4.00	12.00	—
1941	—	2.00	3.00	4.00	8.00	—
1943	—	2.00	3.00	4.00	8.00	—
1945	—	22.00	40.00	60.00	100	—
1946	—	2.00	3.00	4.00	8.00	—
1948	—	250	500	1,000	—	—
Note: Five ribbons on each wreath						

Y# 114 3 KOPEKS

Aluminum-Bronze **Obv:** National arms, 8 ribbons on the left and 7 on the right **Rev:** Value and date within oat sprigs **Edge:** Reeded **Note:** Varieties exist.

Date	Mintage	F12	VF20	XF40	MS60	MS63
1946 Rare	—	—	2,000	—	—	—
1948	—	2.00	3.00	4.00	8.00	—
1949	—	2.00	3.00	4.00	5.00	—
1950	—	2.00	3.00	4.00	5.00	—
1951	—	2.00	10.00	4.00	9.00	—
1952	—	2.00	3.00	4.00	5.00	—
1953	—	2.00	3.00	4.00	5.00	—
1954	—	2.00	3.00	4.00	5.00	—
1955	—	2.00	3.00	4.00	5.00	—
1956	—	2.00	3.00	4.00	5.00	—
1957	—	200	300	500	900	—

Y# 121 3 KOPEKS

Aluminum-Bronze **Obv:** National arms, 7 ribbons on each side **Rev:** Value and date within oat sprigs

Date	Mintage	F12	VF20	XF40	MS60	MS63
1957	—	2.00	3.00	6.00	12.00	—

Y# 128 3 KOPEKS

Brass **Obv:** National arms **Rev:** Value and date within sprigs

Date	Mintage	F12	VF20	XF40	MS60	MS63
1958	26,676,000	—	1,700	2,500	4,000	—

Note: Never officially released for circulation; majority of mintage remelted; Some pieces appeared in circulation in Ukraine

Y# 128a 3 KOPEKS

3.00 g., Aluminum-Bronze, 22 mm. **Obv:** National arms **Rev:** Value and date within sprigs **Edge:** Reeded **Note:** Varieties exist.

Date	Mintage	VF20	XF40	MS60	MS63	MS65
1961	—	0.15	0.25	0.50	0.75	1.25
1962	—	7.00	9.00	12.00	18.00	28.00
1965	—	11.00	14.00	16.00	22.00	35.00
1966	—	5.00	8.00	12.00	18.00	28.00
1967	—	0.15	0.25	0.50	0.75	1.25
1968	—	0.15	0.25	0.50	0.75	1.25
1969	—	0.15	0.25	0.50	0.75	1.25
1970	—	0.15	0.25	0.50	0.75	1.25
1971	—	0.15	0.25	0.50	0.75	1.25
1972	—	0.15	0.25	0.50	0.75	1.25
1973	—	0.15	0.25	0.50	0.75	1.25
1974	—	0.15	0.25	0.50	0.75	1.25
1975	—	1.50	2.00	3.00	3.50	4.00
1976	—	0.15	0.25	0.50	0.75	1.25
1977	—	1.00	1.50	2.00	2.50	3.00
1978	—	0.15	0.25	0.45	0.65	1.00
1979	—	0.15	0.25	0.45	0.65	1.00
1980	—	0.15	0.25	0.45	0.65	1.00
1981	—	0.15	0.25	0.45	0.65	1.00
1982	—	0.15	0.25	0.45	0.65	1.00
1983	—	0.15	0.25	0.45	0.65	1.00
1984	—	0.15	0.25	0.45	0.65	1.00
1985	—	0.15	0.25	0.45	0.65	1.00
1986	—	0.15	0.25	0.45	0.65	1.00
1987	—	0.15	0.25	0.45	0.65	1.00
1988	—	0.15	0.25	0.45	0.65	1.00
1989	—	0.15	0.20	0.35	0.50	0.75
1990	—	0.15	0.20	0.35	0.50	0.75
1991 M	—	0.15	0.20	0.35	0.50	0.75
1991 Л	—	0.15	0.20	0.35	0.50	0.75

Y# 79 5 KOPEKS

Bronze **Obv:** National arms within circle **Rev:** Value and date within oat sprigs **Note:** Varieties exist.

Date	Mintage	F12	VF20	XF40	MS60	MS63
1924 Reeded edge, Rare	88,510,000	—	—	—	—	—
1924 Plain edge	Inc. above	PF60 11,000				

Y# 94 5 KOPEKS

5.00 g., Aluminum-Bronze **Obv:** National arms **Rev:** Value and date **Note:** Varieties exist.

Date	Mintage	F12	VF20	XF40	MS60	MS63
1926	14,697,000	10.00	20.00	30.00	470	—
1926	—	PF60 1,150				

Date	Mintage	F12	VF20	XF40	MS60	MS63
1927	—	160	350	700	1,200	—
1928	—	3.00	7.00	15.00	25.00	—
1929	20,220,000	12.00	25.00	40.00	190	—
1930	44,490,000	3.00	4.00	7.00	10.00	—
1931	89,540,000	3.00	4.00	7.00	10.00	—
1932	65,100,000	5.00	10.00	15.00	25.00	—
1933	18,135,000	225	610	775	1,250	—
1934	5,354,000	150	300	450	900	—
1935	11,735,000	125	275	425	1,400	—

Y# 101 5 KOPEKS

Aluminum-Bronze **Obv:** National arms **Rev:** Value and date within oat sprigs **Note:** Varieties exist.

Date	Mintage	F12	VF20	XF40	MS60	MS63
1935	—	30.00	60.00	80.00	120	—
1936	5,242,000	20.00	45.00	60.00	950	—

Y# 108 5 KOPEKS

5.21 g., Aluminum-Bronze, 25.1 mm. **Obv:** National arms **Rev:** Value and date within oat sprigs **Note:** Varieties exist.

Date	Mintage	F12	VF20	XF40	MS60	MS63
1937	—	15.00	32.00	60.00	260	—
1938	—	11.00	30.00	35.00	60.00	—
1939	—	7.00	10.00	30.00	55.00	—
1940	—	2.00	5.00	9.00	18.00	—
1941	—	12.00	23.00	40.00	420	—
1943	—	3.00	5.00	10.00	20.00	—
1945	—	25.00	55.00	80.00	230	—
1946	—	2.00	3.00	5.00	10.00	—

Y# 115 5 KOPEKS

4.80 g., Aluminum-Bronze **Obv:** National arms **Rev:** Value and date withing oat sprigs **Note:** Varieties exist.

Date	Mintage	F12	VF20	XF40	MS60	MS63
1948	—	3.00	7.00	12.00	25.00	—
1949	—	1.00	2.00	4.00	8.00	—
1950	—	3.00	7.00	12.00	25.00	—
1951	—	12.00	25.00	45.00	200	—
1952	—	1.00	2.00	4.00	8.00	—
1953	—	1.00	2.00	4.00	8.00	—
1954	—	1.00	2.00	4.00	8.00	—
1955	—	1.00	2.00	4.00	8.00	—
1956	—	1.00	2.00	4.00	8.00	—

Y# 122 5 KOPEKS

4.90 g., Aluminum-Bronze **Obv:** National arms **Rev:** Value and date within oat sprigs **Note:** Varieties exist.

Date	Mintage	F12	VF20	XF40	MS60	MS63
1957	—	1.00	2.00	5.00	9.00	—

Y# 129 5 KOPEKS

Brass **Obv:** National arms **Rev:** Value and date within sprigs

Date	Mintage	F12	VF20	XF40	MS60	MS63
1958	61,119,000	—	4,750	6,000	8,000	—

Note: Never officially released for circulation; majority of mintage remelted; Some pieces appeared in circulation in Ukraine

Y# 129a 5 KOPEKS

5.00 g., Aluminum-Bronze, 25 mm. **Obv:** National arms **Rev:** Value and date within sprigs **Edge:** Reeded **Note:** Varieties exist.

Date	Mintage	VF20	XF40	MS60	MS63	MS65
1961	—	0.50	1.00	2.00	3.00	5.00
1962	—	0.50	1.00	2.00	3.00	5.00
1965	—	20.00	80.00	90.00	100	170
1966	—	20.00	80.00	90.00	100	170
1967	—	10.00	28.00	32.00	40.00	60.00
1968	—	10.00	30.00	45.00	150	200
1969	—	20.00	60.00	75.00	160	230
1970	—	60.00	140	250	450	850
1971	—	20.00	60.00	65.00	100	170
1972	—	20.00	60.00	65.00	170	290
1973	—	6.00	9.00	12.00	20.00	35.00
1974	—	0.20	0.50	0.75	1.00	1.50
1975	—	0.20	0.50	0.75	1.00	1.50
1976	—	0.20	0.30	0.50	0.75	1.00
1977	—	0.20	0.30	0.50	0.75	1.00
1978	—	0.20	0.30	0.50	0.75	1.00
1979	—	0.20	0.30	0.50	0.75	1.00
1980	—	0.20	0.30	0.50	0.75	1.00
1981	—	0.20	0.30	0.50	0.75	1.00
1982	—	0.20	0.30	0.50	0.75	1.00
1983	—	0.20	0.30	0.50	0.75	1.00
1984	—	0.20	0.30	0.50	0.75	1.00
1985	—	0.20	0.30	0.50	0.75	1.00
1986	—	0.20	0.30	0.50	0.75	1.00
1987	—	0.20	0.30	0.50	0.75	1.00
1988	—	0.20	0.30	0.50	0.75	1.00
1989	—	0.20	0.25	0.45	0.65	1.25
1990	—	0.25	0.45	0.65	1.00	1.50
1990 M	—	250	420	550	750	950
1991 M	—	0.15	0.25	0.45	0.65	1.25
1991	—	0.15	0.25	0.45	0.65	1.25

Y# 86 10 KOPEKS

1.80 g., 0.500 Silver 0.0289 oz. ASW **Obv:** National arms within circle **Rev:** Value and date within oat sprigs **Note:** Varieties exist.

Date	Mintage	F12	VF20	XF40	MS60	MS63
1924	67,351,000	5.00	8.00	12.00	18.00	—
1924	—	**PF60** 4,400				
1925	101,013,000	5.00	8.00	12.00	18.00	—
1925	—	**PF60** 225				
1927	—	3.00	5.00	10.00	15.00	—
1927	—	**PF60** 225				
1928	—	4.00	6.00	10.00	15.00	—
1929	64,900,000	4.00	6.00	10.00	15.00	—
1930	163,424,000	4.00	6.00	10.00	15.00	—
1931 Rare	8,791,000	**PF60** 1,000				

Y# 95 10 KOPEKS

1.82 g., Copper-Nickel, 17.4 mm. **Obv:** National arms within circle **Rev:** Value on shield held by figure at left looking right **Note:** Varieties exist.

Date	Mintage	F12	VF20	XF40	MS60	MS63
1931	122,511,000	4.00	8.00	10.00	20.00	—
1932	171,641,000	3.00	4.00	5.00	10.00	—
1933	163,125,000	3.00	4.00	5.00	10.00	—
1934	104,059,000	9.00	20.00	30.00	50.00	—

Y# 102 10 KOPEKS

1.80 g., Copper-Nickel **Obv:** National arms **Rev:** Value within octagon flanked by sprigs with date below

Date	Mintage	F12	VF20	XF40	MS60	MS63
1935	79,628,000	4.00	7.00	15.00	25.00	—
1936	122,260,000	2.00	3.00	4.00	8.00	—

Y# 109 10 KOPEKS

1.74 g., Copper-Nickel, 17.5 mm. **Obv:** National arms **Rev:** Value within octagon flanked by sprigs with date below **Edge:** Reeded **Note:** Varieties exist.

Date	Mintage	F12	VF20	XF40	MS60	MS63
1937	—	8.00	17.00	30.00	50.00	—
1938	—	3.00	7.00	12.00	20.00	—
1939	—	3.00	7.00	12.00	30.00	—
1940	—	3.00	7.00	12.00	20.00	—
1941	—	3.00	7.00	12.00	20.00	—
1942	—	150	335	400	600	—
1943	—	2.00	3.00	4.00	8.00	—
1944	—	60.00	120	200	350	—
1945	—	2.00	3.00	4.00	8.00	—
1946	—	2.00	3.00	4.00	8.00	—

Y# A110 10 KOPEKS

Copper-Nickel **Obv:** National arms **Rev:** Value within octagon flanked by sprigs **Note:** Mule.

Date	Mintage	F12	VF20	XF40	MS60	MS63
1946 Rare	—	**PF60** 1,000				

Y# 116 10 KOPEKS

1.80 g., Copper-Nickel **Obv:** National arms, 8 and 7 ribbons on wreath **Rev:** Value within octagon flanked by sprigs with date below **Note:** Varieties exist.

Date	Mintage	F12	VF20	XF40	MS60	MS63
1948	—	2.00	3.00	4.00	7.00	—
1949	—	2.00	3.00	4.00	7.00	—
1950	—	2.00	3.00	4.00	7.00	—
1951	—	3.00	4.00	6.00	8.00	—
1952	—	2.00	3.00	4.00	7.00	—
1953	—	1.00	2.00	3.00	4.00	—
1954	—	1.00	2.00	3.00	4.00	—
1955	—	1.00	2.00	3.00	4.00	—
1956	—	1.00	2.00	3.00	4.00	—
1956	—	400	800	1,000	2,000	—

Note: Reverse of Y#123

Y# 123 10 KOPEKS

1.80 g., Copper-Nickel **Obv:** National arms, 7 and 7 ribbons on wreath **Rev:** Value within octagon flanked by sprigs with date below

Date	Mintage	F12	VF20	XF40	MS60	MS63
1957	—	500	750	1,000	2,000	—
Note: Reverse of Y#116						
1957	—	3.00	4.00	5.00	10.00	—

Y# A130 10 KOPEKS

Copper-Nickel **Obv:** National arms **Rev:** Value and date within sprigs

Date	Mintage	F12	VF20	XF40	MS60	MS63
1958	108,023,000	—	1,000	1,500	2,500	—

Note: Never officially released for circulation; majority of mintage remelted; Some pieces appeared in circulation in Ukraine

Y# 130 10 KOPEKS

1.60 g., Copper-Nickel-Zinc, 17.35 mm. **Obv:** National arms **Rev:** Value and date flanked by sprigs **Edge:** Reeded

Date	Mintage	VF20	XF40	MS60	MS63	MS65
1961	—	0.30	0.50	0.75	1.00	1.50
1962	—	0.30	0.50	0.75	1.00	1.50
1965	—	50.00	80.00	100	110	175
1966	—	50.00	80.00	100	110	190
1967	—	4.00	25.00	32.00	40.00	60.00
1968	—	5.00	30.00	36.00	45.00	60.00
1969	—	1.00	2.00	3.00	5.00	7.00
1970	—	0.20	0.35	0.50	0.75	1.00
1971	—	0.20	0.35	0.50	0.75	1.00
1972	—	0.20	0.35	0.50	0.75	1.00
1973	—	0.20	0.35	0.50	0.75	1.00
1974	—	0.20	0.35	0.50	0.75	1.00
1975	—	0.20	0.35	0.50	0.75	1.00
1976	—	0.20	0.35	0.50	0.75	1.00
1977	—	0.20	0.35	0.50	0.75	1.00
1978	—	0.20	0.35	0.50	0.75	1.00
1979	—	0.20	0.35	0.50	0.75	1.00
1980	—	0.20	0.35	0.50	0.75	1.00
1981	—	0.20	0.35	0.50	0.75	1.00
1982	—	0.20	0.35	0.50	0.75	1.00
1983	—	0.20	0.35	0.50	0.75	1.00
1984	—	0.20	0.35	0.50	0.75	1.00
1985	—	0.20	0.35	0.50	0.75	1.00
1986	—	0.20	0.35	0.50	0.75	1.00
1987	—	0.20	0.35	0.50	0.75	1.00
1988	—	0.20	0.35	0.50	0.75	1.00
1989	—	0.20	0.30	0.50	0.75	1.00
1990	—	0.50	0.75	1.00	2.00	3.00
1990 M	—	250	420	500	600	650
1991	—	20.00	50.00	55.00	65.00	125
1991 Л	—	0.20	0.30	0.50	0.75	1.00
1991 M	—	0.20	0.30	0.50	0.75	1.00

Y# 136 10 KOPEKS

Copper-Nickel-Zinc, 17 mm. **Subject:** 50th Anniversary of Revolution **Obv:** National arms within radiant circle with dates at right **Rev:** Value above radiant sun and design

Date	Mintage	F12	VF20	XF40	MS60	MS63
1967	49,789,000	—	1.00	2.00	3.00	—
1967 Prooflike	211,000	—	—	—	—	5.00

Y# 87 15 KOPEKS

2.70 g., 0.500 Silver 0.0434 oz. ASW **Obv:** National arms within circle **Rev:** Value and date within oat sprigs **Note:** Varieties exist.

Date	Mintage	F12	VF20	XF40	MS60	MS63
1924	72,426,000	4.00	5.00	10.00	20.00	—
1924	—	**PF60** 1,900				
1925	112,709,000	3.00	4.00	7.00	14.00	—
1925	—	**PF60** 225				
1927	—	3.00	4.00	7.00	14.00	—
1927	—	**PF60** 225				
1928	—	3.00	4.00	7.00	14.00	—
1929	46,400,000	3.00	4.00	7.00	14.00	—
1930	79,868,000	3.00	4.00	7.00	14.00	—
1931 Rare	5,099,000	**PF60** 1,000				

Y# 96 15 KOPEKS

Copper-Nickel, 20 mm. **Obv:** National arms within circle **Rev:** Value on shield held by figure at left looking right **Note:** Varieties exist.

Date	Mintage	F12	VF20	XF40	MS60	MS63
1931	75,859,000	4.00	6.00	8.00	15.00	—
1932	136,046,000	3.00	4.00	5.00	9.00	—
1933	127,591,000	3.00	4.00	5.00	9.00	—
1934	58,367,000	10.00	21.00	25.00	220	—

Y# 103 15 KOPEKS

2.70 g., Copper-Nickel, 20 mm. **Obv:** National arms **Rev:** Value within octagon flanked by sprigs with date below

Date	Mintage	F12	VF20	XF40	MS60	MS63
1935	51,308,000	4.00	7.00	9.00	12.00	—
1936	52,183,000	4.00	5.00	7.00	10.00	—

Y# 110 15 KOPEKS

2.68 g., Copper-Nickel, 20 mm. **Obv:** National arms **Rev:** Value within octagon flanked by sprigs with date below **Edge:** Reeded **Note:** Varieties exist.

Date	Mintage	F12	VF20	XF40	MS60	MS63
1937	—	10.00	21.00	25.00	50.00	—
1938	—	3.00	5.00	7.00	15.00	—
1939	—	4.00	8.00	16.00	30.00	—
1940	—	3.00	5.00	7.00	15.00	—
1941	—	1.00	2.00	4.00	7.00	—
1942	—	150	300	400	700	—
1943	—	2.00	3.00	5.00	8.00	—
1944	—	7.00	15.00	20.00	65.00	—
1945	—	3.00	4.00	5.00	9.00	—
1946	—	3.00	4.00	5.00	9.00	—

Y# 117 15 KOPEKS

2.70 g., Copper-Nickel, 20 mm. **Obv:** National arms, 8 and 7 ribbons on wreath **Rev:** Value within octagon flanked by sprigs with date below **Note:** Varieties exist.

Date	Mintage	F12	VF20	XF40	MS60	MS63
1948	—	2.00	3.00	4.00	7.00	—
1949	—	7.00	15.00	25.00	50.00	—
1950	—	1.00	2.00	3.00	5.00	—
1951	—	2.00	5.00	7.00	10.00	—
1952	—	1.00	2.00	3.00	5.00	—
1953	—	1.00	2.00	3.00	5.00	—
1954	—	1.00	2.00	3.00	5.00	—
1955	—	1.00	2.00	3.00	5.00	—
1956	—	1.00	2.00	3.00	5.00	—

Y# 124 15 KOPEKS

2.70 g., Copper-Nickel, 20 mm. **Obv:** National arms **Rev:** Value within octagon flanked by sprigs with date below **Edge:** Reeded

Date	Mintage	F12	VF20	XF40	MS60	MS63
1957	—	2.00	3.00	6.00	10.00	—

Y# A131 15 KOPEKS

Copper-Nickel, 20 mm. **Obv:** National arms **Rev:** Value and date within sprigs

Date	Mintage	F12	VF20	XF40	MS60	MS63
1958	80,052,000	4,000	5,000	10,000	13,000	—

Note: Never officially released for circulation; majority of mintage remelted; Some pieces appeared in circulation in Ukraine

Y# 131 15 KOPEKS

2.50 g., Copper-Nickel-Zinc, 19.5 mm. **Obv:** National arms **Rev:** Value and date flanked by sprigs **Edge:** Reeded

Date	Mintage	VF20	XF40	MS60	MS63	MS65
1961	—	0.20	0.40	0.60	1.00	1.25
1962	—	0.20	0.40	0.60	1.00	1.25
1965	—	50.00	80.00	100	110	170
1966	—	50.00	80.00	100	120	220
1967	—	5.00	25.00	30.00	40.00	60.00
1968	—	10.00	30.00	40.00	50.00	170
1969	—	15.00	60.00	80.00	100	160
1970	—	100	280	400	575	950
1971	—	30.00	120	150	200	400
1972	—	30.00	120	150	200	400
1973	—	30.00	120	170	220	400
1974	—	10.00	35.00	55.00	70.00	140
1975	—	8.00	35.00	60.00	75.00	150
1976	—	1.00	2.00	3.00	4.00	6.00
1977	—	0.20	0.40	0.60	1.00	1.25
1978	—	0.20	0.40	0.60	1.00	1.25
1979	—	0.20	0.40	0.60	1.00	1.25
1980	—	0.20	0.40	0.60	1.00	1.25
1981	—	0.20	0.40	0.60	1.00	1.25
1982	—	0.20	0.40	0.60	1.00	1.25
1983	—	0.20	0.40	0.60	1.00	1.25
1984	—	0.20	0.40	0.60	1.00	1.25
1985	—	0.20	0.40	0.60	1.00	1.25
1986	—	0.20	0.40	0.60	1.00	1.25
1987	—	0.20	0.40	0.60	1.00	1.25
1988	—	0.20	0.40	0.60	1.00	1.25
1989	—	0.20	0.30	0.50	0.80	1.00
1990	—	0.20	0.30	0.50	0.80	1.00
1991 M	—	0.20	0.30	0.50	0.80	1.00
1991 Л	—	0.20	0.30	0.50	0.80	1.00

Y# 137 15 KOPEKS

Copper-Nickel-Zinc, 20 mm. **Subject:** 50th Anniversary of Revolution **Obv:** National arms above value **Rev:** Statue of Laborers and dates

Date	Mintage	F12	VF20	XF40	MS60	MS63
1967	49,789,000	1.00	1.50	2.00	6.00	—
1967 Prooflike	211,000	—	—	—	—	3.00

Y# 88 20 KOPEKS

3.60 g., 0.500 Silver 0.0579 oz. ASW, 22 mm. **Obv:** National arms within circle **Rev:** Value and date within oat sprigs

Date	Mintage	F12	VF20	XF40	MS60	MS63
1924	93,810,000	8.00	14.00	20.00	35.00	—
1924	—	**PF60** 4,400				
1925	135,188,000	4.00	7.00	15.00	30.00	—
1925	—	**PF60** 225				
1927	—	4.00	6.00	10.00	20.00	—
1928	—	4.00	6.00	10.00	20.00	—
1929	67,250,000	4.00	6.00	10.00	20.00	—
1930	125,658,000	4.00	5.00	7.00	12.00	—
1931	9,530,000	4,000	5,000	7,000	13,000	—

Y# 97 20 KOPEKS

3.48 g., Copper-Nickel, 22 mm. **Obv:** National arms within circle **Rev:** Value on shield held by figure at left looking right **Note:** Varieties exist.

Date	Mintage	F12	VF20	XF40	MS60	MS63
1931	82,200,000	3.00	4.00	6.00	12.00	—
1932	175,350,000	2.00	3.00	4.00	8.00	—
1933	143,927,000	2.00	3.00	4.00	8.00	—
1934 Rare	70,425,000	**PF60** 1,000				

Y# 104 20 KOPEKS

Copper-Nickel **Obv:** National arms **Rev:** Value within octagon flanked by sprigs with date below **Note:** Varieties exist.

Date	Mintage	F12	VF20	XF40	MS60	MS63
1935	125,165,000	2.00	3.00	4.00	7.00	—
1936	52,968,000	2.00	3.00	4.00	7.00	—
1941 Rare	—	**PF60** 1,000				

Y# 111 20 KOPEKS

3.61 g., Copper-Nickel, 22.5 mm. **Obv:** National arms **Rev:** Value within octagon flanked by sprigs with date below **Edge:** Reeded **Note:** Varieties exist.

Date	Mintage	F12	VF20	XF40	MS60	MS63
1937	—	4.00	7.00	15.00	30.00	—
1938	—	3.00	5.00	10.00	20.00	—
1939	—	6.00	12.00	25.00	50.00	—
1940	—	3.00	5.00	10.00	20.00	—
1941	—	2.00	3.00	4.00	7.00	—
1942	—	4.00	8.00	16.00	35.00	—
1943	—	2.00	3.00	4.00	7.00	—
1944	—	4.00	8.00	16.00	35.00	—
1945	—	2.00	3.00	4.00	7.00	—
1946	—	2.00	3.00	4.00	7.00	—

Y# 118 20 KOPEKS

3.60 g., Copper-Nickel **Obv:** National arms, 8 and 7 ribbons on wreath **Rev:** Value within octagon flanked by sprigs with date below **Note:** Varieties exist.

Date	Mintage	F12	VF20	XF40	MS60	MS63
1948	—	2.00	3.00	4.00	7.00	—
1949	—	2.00	3.00	4.00	7.00	—
1950	—	12.00	30.00	45.00	100	—
1951	—	2.00	3.00	4.00	10.00	—
1952	—	2.00	3.00	4.00	6.00	—
1953	—	2.00	3.00	4.00	6.00	—
1954	—	2.00	3.00	4.00	6.00	—
1955	—	2.00	3.00	4.00	6.00	—
1956	—	2.00	3.00	4.00	6.00	—

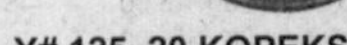

Y# 125 20 KOPEKS

Copper-Nickel **Obv:** National arms **Rev:** Value within octagon flanked by sprigs with date below

Date	Mintage	F12	VF20	XF40	MS60	MS63
1957	—	3.00	4.00	5.00	10.00	—

Y# A132 20 KOPEKS

Copper-Nickel **Obv:** National arms **Rev:** Value and date within sprigs

Date	Mintage	F12	VF20	XF40	MS60	MS63
1958	175,355,000	8,000	1,000	2,000	4,000	—

Note: Never officially released for circulation; majority of mintage remelted; Some pieces appeared in circulation in Ukraine

Y# 132 20 KOPEKS

3.30 g., Copper-Nickel-Zinc, 22 mm. **Obv:** National arms **Rev:** Value and date flanked by sprigs **Edge:** Reeded **Note:** Varieties exist.

Date	Mintage	VF20	XF40	MS60	MS63	MS65
1961	—	0.50	1.00	1.25	2.00	3.00
1962	—	0.50	1.00	1.25	2.00	3.00
1965	—	50.00	80.00	100	110	180
1966	—	50.00	80.00	100	120	190
1967	—	4.00	20.00	25.00	40.00	140
1968	—	4.00	30.00	35.00	45.00	150
1969	—	10.00	60.00	65.00	100	180
1970	—	40.00	95.00	220	300	650
1971	—	30.00	60.00	150	225	425
1972	—	30.00	70.00	165	260	500
1973	—	40.00	95.00	210	350	650
1974	—	15.00	25.00	60.00	80.00	150
1975	—	15.00	25.00	65.00	80.00	150
1976	—	30.00	65.00	140	250	475
1977	—	0.30	0.50	0.75	1.00	1.50
1978	—	0.30	0.50	0.75	1.00	1.50
1979	—	0.30	0.50	0.75	1.00	1.50
1980	—	0.30	0.50	0.75	1.00	1.50
1981	—	0.30	0.50	0.75	1.00	1.50
1982	—	0.30	0.50	0.75	1.00	1.50
1983	—	0.30	0.50	0.75	1.00	1.50
1984	—	0.30	0.50	0.75	1.00	1.50
1985	—	0.30	0.50	0.75	1.00	1.50
1986	—	0.30	0.50	0.75	1.00	1.50
1987	—	0.30	0.50	0.75	1.00	1.50
1988	—	0.30	0.50	0.75	1.00	1.50
1989	—	0.20	0.30	0.75	1.00	1.50
1990	—	0.20	0.30	0.75	1.00	1.50
1991	—	200	500	775	1,500	2,750
1991 M	—	0.20	0.30	0.75	1.00	1.50
1991 Л	—	0.20	0.30	0.75	1.00	1.50

Y# 138 20 KOPEKS

4.20 g., Copper-Nickel-Zinc **Subject:** 50th Anniversary of Revolution **Obv:** National arms flanked by dates with inscription below **Rev:** Navy Cruiser below value **Edge:** Reeded

Date	Mintage	F12	VF20	XF40	MS60	MS63
1967	49,789,000	2.00	3.00	4.00	6.00	—
1967 Prooflike	211,000	—	—	—	—	8.00

Y# 89.1 50 KOPEKS

10.00 g., 0.900 Silver 0.2893 oz. ASW **Obv:** National arms divide CCCP above inscription, circle surrounds all **Rev:** Blacksmith at anvil **Edge Lettering:** Weight shown in old Russian units

Date	Mintage	F12	VF20	XF40	MS60	MS63
1924 ПЛ	26,559,000	12.00	20.00	30.00	80.00	—
1924 ПЛ	—	PF60 850				
1924 TP	40,000,000	12.00	20.00	30.00	80.00	—

Y# 89.2 50 KOPEKS

10.00 g., 0.900 Silver 0.2893 oz. ASW **Obv:** National arms divide CCCP above inscription, circle surrounds all **Rev:** Blacksmith at anvil **Edge Lettering:** Weight shown in 18 ГРАММ (grams) only **Note:** Varieties exist.

Date	Mintage	F12	VF20	XF40	MS60	MS63
1925 ПЛ	43,558,000	18.00	30.00	60.00	80.00	120
1925 ПЛ	—	PF60 1,000				
1926 ПЛ	24,374,000	18.00	40.00	60.00	80.00	120
1926 ПЛ	—	PF60 400				
1927 ПЛ	—	20.00	35.00	60.00	90.00	160
1927 ПЛ	—	PF60 500				

Y# 133 50 KOPEKS

Copper-Nickel **Obv:** National arms **Rev:** Value and date within sprigs

Date	Mintage	F12	VF20	XF40	MS60	MS63
1958	40,600,000	8,000	8,300	14,000	20,000	—

Note: Never officially released for circulation; majority of mintage remelted; Some pieces appeared in circulation in Ukraine

Y# 133a.1 50 KOPEKS

4.60 g., Copper-Nickel-Zinc **Obv:** National arms **Rev:** Value and date within sprigs **Edge:** Plain **Note:** Varieties exist.

Date	Mintage	F12	VF20	XF40	MS60	MS63
1961	—	5.00	8.00	10.00	20.00	—

Y# 133a.2 50 KOPEKS

4.40 g., Copper-Nickel-Zinc, 24.05 mm. **Obv:** National arms **Rev:** Value and date within sprigs **Edge:** Lettered with date **Note:** Varieties exist for 1970, 1971, and 1975.

Date	Mintage	VF20	XF40	MS60	MS63	MS65
1964	—	0.25	0.50	0.75	1.00	2.00
1965	—	3.00	4.00	8.00	—	—
1966	—	0.25	0.50	0.75	1.00	2.00
1967	—	7.00	20.00	25.00	40.00	70.00
1968	—	0.25	0.35	0.50	0.75	1.50
1969	—	0.25	0.35	0.50	0.75	1.50
1970	—	50.00	100	125	225	425
1971	—	55.00	100	150	250	475
1972	—	3.00	5.00	7.00	12.00	22.00
1973	—	2.00	4.00	6.00	10.00	20.00
1974	—	0.50	1.00	2.00	3.50	6.50
1975	—	20.00	40.00	65.00	95.00	175
1976	—	7.00	15.00	22.00	32.00	65.00
1977	—	0.25	0.50	0.75	1.00	2.00
1978	—	0.50	1.00	2.00	3.00	5.00
1979	—	0.25	0.50	0.75	1.00	2.00
1980	—	0.25	0.50	0.75	1.00	2.00
1981	—	0.25	0.50	0.75	1.00	2.00
1982	—	0.25	0.50	0.75	1.00	2.00
1983	—	0.25	0.50	0.75	1.00	2.00
1984	—	0.25	0.50	0.75	1.00	2.00
1985	—	0.25	0.50	0.75	1.00	2.00
1986	—	60.00	120	200	350	600
Note: With 1985 on edge						
1986	—	—	0.25	0.45	0.75	1.50
1987	—	—	0.25	0.45	0.75	1.50
1988	—	20.00	30.00	60.00	100	200
Note: With 1987 on edge						
1988	—	—	0.25	0.45	0.75	1.50
1989	—	20.00	30.00	60.00	100	200
Note: With 1988 on edge						
1989	—	1.00	2.00	4.00	6.00	8.00
1990	—	1.00	2.00	4.00	6.00	8.00
1990 Rare	—	—	—	—	—	—
Note: With 1989 on edge						
1991 M	—	0.50	1.00	2.00	3.00	5.00
1991 Л	—	0.50	1.00	2.00	3.00	5.00

Y# 139 50 KOPEKS

Copper-Nickel-Zinc, 25 mm. **Subject:** 50th Anniversary of Revolution **Obv:** National arms **Rev:** Lenin with right arm raised facing left, star at upper left

Date	Mintage	F12	VF20	XF40	MS60	MS63
ND (1967)	49,789,000	—	3.00	4.00	8.00	—
ND (1967) Prooflike	—	—	—	—	5.00	—

Y# 90.1 ROUBLE

20.00 g., 0.900 Silver 0.5786 oz. ASW **Obv:** National arms divides circle with inscription within **Rev:** Two figures walking right, radiant sun rising at right **Edge Lettering:** 18 ГРАММ (grams) (43.21d) **Note:** Varieties exist.

Date	Mintage	F12	VF20	XF40	MS60	MS63
1924 ПЛ	12,998,000	40.00	60.00	80.00	170	275
1924 ПЛ	—	PF60 2,500				

Y# 90.2 ROUBLE

20.00 g., 0.900 Silver 0.5786 oz. ASW **Obv:** National arms divides circle holding inscription **Rev:** Two figures walking right, sun rising at right **Edge:** 4 Zolotniks 21 Dolyas

Date	Mintage	F12	VF20	XF40	MS60	MS63
1924 Rare	—	—	—	—	—	—

Y# 134 ROUBLE

Copper-Nickel **Obv:** National arms **Rev:** Value and date within sprigs

Date	Mintage	F12	VF20	XF40	MS60	MS63
1958	30,700,000	4,000	5,000	10,000	—	—

Note: Never officially released for circulation; majority of mintage remelted; Never appeared in circulation

Y# 134a.1 ROUBLE

Copper-Nickel-Zinc **Obv:** National arms within circle **Rev:** Value and date within sprigs **Edge:** Plain

Date	Mintage	F12	VF20	XF40	MS60	MS63
1961	—	4.00	8.00	16.00	30.00	—

Y# 134a.2 ROUBLE

7.40 g., Copper-Nickel-Zinc, 27 mm. **Obv:** National arms within circle **Rev:** Value and date within sprigs **Edge:** Lettered with date

Date	Mintage	VF20	XF40	MS60	MS63	MS65
1964	—	0.50	1.00	2.00	4.00	6.00
1965	—	5.00	7.00	12.00	20.00	30.00
1966	—	10.00	18.00	25.00	35.00	55.00
1967 Rare	—	—	—	—	—	—
Note: With 1966 on edge						
1967	—	12.00	20.00	30.00	45.00	65.00
1968	—	8.00	25.00	30.00	35.00	55.00
1969	—	8.00	30.00	32.00	35.00	55.00
1970	—	8.00	30.00	32.00	35.00	55.00
1971	—	8.00	30.00	32.00	35.00	55.00
1972	—	8.00	30.00	32.00	35.00	55.00
1973	—	8.00	30.00	32.00	35.00	55.00
1974	—	8.00	30.00	32.00	35.00	55.00
1975	—	8.00	30.00	32.00	35.00	55.00
1976	—	8.00	30.00	32.00	35.00	55.00
1976	—	75.00	150	250	400	600
Note: With 1975 on edge						
1977	—	8.00	30.00	32.00	35.00	55.00
1978	—	8.00	30.00	32.00	35.00	55.00
1979	—	12.00	30.00	32.00	45.00	65.00
1980	—	12.00	35.00	40.00	45.00	65.00
1981	—	12.00	30.00	32.00	45.00	65.00

Date	Mintage	VF20	XF40	MS60	MS63	MS65
1982	—	12.00	30.00	32.00	45.00	65.00
1983	—	12.00	30.00	32.00	45.00	65.00
1984	—	7.00	12.00	20.00	30.00	50.00
1985	—	7.00	12.00	20.00	30.00	50.00
1986	—	7.00	12.00	20.00	30.00	50.00
1987	—	7.00	12.00	20.00	30.00	50.00
1988	—	4.00	7.00	12.00	20.00	30.00
1988	—	75.00	150	250	400	600
Note: With 1989 on edge						
1989	—	4.00	7.00	12.00	20.00	30.00
1990	—	75.00	150	250	400	600
Note: With 1989 on edge						
1990	—	4.00	7.00	12.00	20.00	30.00
1991 M	—	3.50	6.00	12.00	20.00	30.00
1991 Л	—	3.00	5.00	10.00	15.00	25.00

Y# 135.1 ROUBLE

10.00 g., Copper-Nickel-Zinc, 31 mm. **Subject:** 20th Anniversary of World War II Victory **Obv:** National arms divide CCCP with inscription below **Rev:** Statue by Vouchetic

Date	Mintage	F12	VF20	XF40	MS60	MS63
1965	59,989,000	—	2.00	3.00	5.00	—
1965 Prooflike	—	—	—	—	15.00	—
1965	—	PF60 125				

Y# 135.2 ROUBLE

10.00 g., Copper-Nickel-Zinc, 31 mm. **Obv:** National arms divide CCCP with inscription below **Rev:** Victory monument **Edge Lettering:** 1988.N.

Date	Mintage	F12	VF20	XF40	MS60	MS63
1965 Proof, restrike	55,000	PF60 18.00				

Y# 140.1 ROUBLE

10.00 g., Copper-Nickel-Zinc, 31 mm. **Subject:** 50th Anniversary of Revolution **Obv:** National arms **Rev:** Lenin with right arm raised facing left, star at upper left **Edge:** Lettered, with date

Date	Mintage	F12	VF20	XF40	MS60	MS63
1967	52,289,000	—	3.00	4.00	8.00	—
1967 Prooflike	—	—	—	—	15.00	—
1967	—	PF60 125				

Y# 140.2 ROUBLE

10.00 g., Copper-Nickel-Zinc, 31 mm. **Obv:** National arms **Rev:** Lenin with right arm raised facing left, star at upper left **Edge Lettering:** 1988.N.

Date	Mintage	F12	VF20	XF40	MS60	MS63
1967 Proof, restrike	55,000	PF60 18.00				

Y# 141 ROUBLE

10.00 g., Copper-Nickel-Zinc, 31 mm. **Subject:** Centennial of Lenin's Birth **Obv:** National arms divide CCCP **Rev:** Head right

Date	Mintage	F12	VF20	XF40	MS60	MS63
ND (1970)	99,889,000	—	1.00	2.00	6.00	—
ND (1970) Prooflike	—	—	—	—	15.00	—
ND (1970)	—	PF60 805				

Y# 142.1 ROUBLE

10.00 g., Copper-Nickel-Zinc, 31 mm. **Subject:** 30th Anniversary of World War II Victory **Obv:** National arms divide CCCP **Rev:** Volgograd monument **Edge:** Date **Note:** Date appears on the edge in English and Russian as "9 March 1975". Varieties exist.

Date	Mintage	F12	VF20	XF40	MS60	MS63
1975	14,989,000	—	1.00	2.00	6.00	—
1975 Prooflike	—	—	—	—	15.00	—
1975	—	PF60 120				

Y# 142.2 ROUBLE

10.00 g., Copper-Nickel-Zinc, 31 mm. **Obv:** National arms divide CCCP, value below **Rev:** Volgograd monument **Edge Lettering:** 1988.N.

Date	Mintage	F12	VF20	XF40	MS60	MS63
ND (1975) Proof, restrike	55,000	PF60 18.00				

Y# 143.1 ROUBLE

10.00 g., Copper-Nickel-Zinc, 31 mm. **Subject:** 60th Anniversary of Bolshevik Revolution **Obv:** National arms divide CCCP **Rev:** Head left above ship, dates below

Date	Mintage	F12	VF20	XF40	MS60	MS63
ND (1977)	4,987,000	—	2.00	4.00	8.00	50.00
ND (1977) Prooflike	—	—	—	—	15.00	—
ND (1977)	—	PF60 120				

Y# 143.2 ROUBLE

10.00 g., Copper-Nickel-Zinc, 31 mm. **Obv:** National arms divide CCCP, value below **Rev:** Head left above ship, dates below **Edge Lettering:** 1988.N.

Date	Mintage	F12	VF20	XF40	MS60	MS63
ND (1977) Proof, restrike	55,000	PF60 18.00				

Y# A144 ROUBLE

10.00 g., Copper-Nickel-Zinc, 31 mm. **Obv:** National arms divide CCCP above value **Rev:** Design with star on top with Olympic rings below **Note:** Mule

Date	Mintage	F12	VF20	XF40	MS60	MS63
1977 Rare	Inc. below	—	—	—	—	—

Y# 144 ROUBLE

10.00 g., Copper-Nickel-Zinc, 31 mm. **Series:** 1980 Olympics **Obv:** National arms divide CCCP above value **Rev:** Design with star on top with Olympic rings below

Date	Mintage	F12	VF20	XF40	MS60	MS63
1977	8,665,000	—	1.00	2.00	3.00	—
1977 Prooflike	—	—	—	—	3.00	—
1977	—	PF60 49.00				

Y# 153.1 ROUBLE

10.00 g., Copper-Nickel-Zinc, 31 mm. **Series:** 1980 Olympics **Obv:** National arms divide CCCP with value below **Rev:** Moscow Kremlin with stars on top of steeples

Date	Mintage	F12	VF20	XF40	MS60	MS63
1978	6,490,000	—	1.00	2.00	3.00	—
1978 Prooflike	—	—	—	—	3.00	—
1978	—	PF60 390				

Y# 153.2 ROUBLE

10.00 g., Copper-Nickel-Zinc, 31 mm. **Obv:** National arms divide CCCP, value below **Rev:** Clock on tower shows Roman numeral 6 (VI) instead of 4 (IV)

Date	Mintage	F12	VF20	XF40	MS60	MS63
1978	Inc. above	—	8.00	16.00	25.00	—

Y# 164 ROUBLE

10.00 g., Copper-Nickel-Zinc, 31 mm. **Series:** 1980 Olympics **Obv:** National arms divide CCCP, value below **Rev:** Moscow University **Note:** Varieties in window arrangements exist.

Date	Mintage	F12	VF20	XF40	MS60	MS63
1979	4,665,000	—	1.00	2.00	3.00	—
1979 Prooflike	—	—	—	—	3.00	—
1979	—	PF60 38.00				

Y# 165 ROUBLE

10.00 g., Copper-Nickel-Zinc, 31 mm. **Series:** 1980 Olympics **Obv:** National arms divide CCCP, value below **Rev:** Monument, Sputnik and Sojuz

Date	Mintage	F12	VF20	XF40	MS60	MS63
1979	4,665,000	—	1.00	2.00	3.00	—
1979 Prooflike	—	—	—	—	3.00	—
1979	—	PF60 32.00				

Y# 177 ROUBLE

10.00 g., Copper-Nickel, 31 mm. **Series:** 1980 Olympics **Obv:** National arms divide CCCP with value below **Rev:** Dolgorukij Monument

Date	Mintage	F12	VF20	XF40	MS60	MS63
1980	4,490,000	—	1.00	2.00	3.00	—
1980 Prooflike	—	—	—	—	3.00	—
1980	—	PF60 40.00				

Y# 178 ROUBLE

10.00 g., Copper-Nickel, 31 mm. **Series:** 1980 Olympics **Obv:** National arms divide CCCP, value below **Rev:** Torch

Date	Mintage	F12	VF20	XF40	MS60	MS63
1980	4,490,000	—	1.00	2.00	3.00	—
1980 Prooflike	—	—	—	—	3.00	—
1980	—	PF60 40.00				

Y# 188.1 ROUBLE

10.00 g., Copper-Nickel, 31 mm. **Subject:** 20th Anniversary of Manned Space Flights **Obv:** National arms divide CCCP with value below **Rev:** Cosmonaut facing flanked by rockets, hammer and sickle above

Date	Mintage	F12	VF20	XF40	MS60	MS63
ND (1981)	3,962,000	—	1.00	2.00	3.00	—
ND (1981)	—	PF60 45.00				

Y# 188.2 ROUBLE

10.00 g., Copper-Nickel, 31 mm. **Subject:** 20th Anniversary of Manned Space Flights **Obv:** National arms divide CCCP, value below **Rev:** Cosmonaut facing flanked by rockets, hammer and sickle above **Edge Lettering:** 1988.N.

Date	Mintage	F12	VF20	XF40	MS60	MS63
ND (1981) Proof; restrike	55,000	PF60 20.00				

Y# 189.1 ROUBLE

Copper-Nickel, 31 mm. **Subject:** Russian-Bulgarian Friendship **Obv:** National arms divide CCCP with value below **Rev:** Grasped hands divide flags above and sprigs below within beaded circle **Edge Lettering:** Cyrillic lettering

Date	Mintage	F12	VF20	XF40	MS60	MS63
1981	1,984,000	—	1.00	5.00	6.00	—
1981	16,000	PF60 42.00				

Note: The same reverse die was used for both Russia 1 Rouble KM #189 and Bulgaria 1 Lev KM#119

Y# 189.2 ROUBLE

Copper-Nickel, 31 mm. **Subject:** Russian-Bulgarian Friendship **Obv:** National arms divide CCCP, value below **Rev:** Grasped hands divide flags above and sprigs below within beaded circle **Edge Lettering:** 1988.N.

Date	Mintage	F12	VF20	XF40	MS60	MS63
1981 Proof; restrike	55,000	PF60 13.00				

Note: The same reverse die was used for both Russia 1 Rouble KM#189 and Bulgaria 1 Lev KM#119

Y# 190.1 ROUBLE

Copper-Nickel, 31 mm. **Subject:** 60th Anniversary of the Soviet Union **Obv:** National arms divide CCCP with value below **Rev:** Radiant sun and standing statue facing left **Edge Lettering:** Cyrillic lettering

Date	Mintage	F12	VF20	XF40	MS60	MS63
ND (1982)	1,921,000	—	1.00	5.00	15.00	—
ND (1982)	—	PF60 13.00				

Y# 190.2 ROUBLE

Copper-Nickel, 31 mm. **Subject:** 60th Anniversary of the Soviet Union **Obv:** National arms divide CCCP, value below **Rev:** Radiant sun back of statue **Edge Lettering:** 1988.N.

Date	Mintage	F12	VF20	XF40	MS60	MS63
ND (1982) Proof; restrike	55,000	PF60 16.00				

Y# 191.1 ROUBLE

Copper-Nickel, 31 mm. **Subject:** Death of Karl Marx Centennial **Obv:** National arms divide CCCP with value below **Rev:** Bust 3/4 left and dates **Edge:** Cyrillic lettering

Date	Mintage	F12	VF20	XF40	MS60	MS63
1983	1,921,000	—	1.00	5.00	6.00	—
1983	—	PF60 13.50				

Y# 191.2 ROUBLE

Copper-Nickel, 31 mm. **Subject:** Death of Karl Marx Centennial **Obv:** National arms divide CCCP, value below **Rev:** Bust 3/4 left with dates **Edge Lettering:** 1988.N.

Date	Mintage	F12	VF20	XF40	MS60	MS63
1983 Proof; restrike	55,000	PF60 10.00				

Y# 192.1 ROUBLE

12.50 g., Copper-Nickel, 31 mm. **Subject:** 20th Anniversary of First Woman in Space **Obv:** National arms divide CCCP with value below **Rev:** Cosmonaut head facing flanked by stars

Date	Mintage	F12	VF20	XF40	MS60	MS63
1983	1,945,000	—	1.00	5.00	6.00	—
1983	—	PF60 32.00				

Y# 192.2 ROUBLE

Copper-Nickel, 31 mm. **Subject:** 20th Anniversary of First Woman in Space **Obv:** National arms divide CCCP, value below **Rev:** Cosmonaut head facing flanked by stars **Edge Lettering:** 1988.N.

Date	Mintage	F12	VF20	XF40	MS60	MS63
1983 Proof; restrike	55,000	PF60 14.00				

Y# 193.1 ROUBLE

Copper-Nickel, 31 mm. **Subject:** First Russian Printer **Obv:** National arms divide CCCP with value below **Rev:** Ivan Fedorov **Edge:** Cyrillic lettering

Date	Mintage	F12	VF20	XF40	MS60	MS63
1983	1,965,000	—	1.00	2.00	4.00	—
1983	—	PF60 48.00				

Y# 193.2 ROUBLE

Copper-Nickel, 31 mm. **Subject:** First Russian Printer **Obv:** National arms divide CCCP, value below **Rev:** Ivan Fedorov **Edge Lettering:** 1988.N.

Date	Mintage	F12	VF20	XF40	MS60	MS63
1983 Proof; restrike	55,000	PF60 14.00				

Y# 194.1 ROUBLE

Copper-Nickel, 31 mm. **Subject:** 150th Anniversary - Birth of Dmitri Ivanovich Mendeleyev **Obv:** National arms divide CCCP with value below **Rev:** Head facing and dates **Edge:** Cyrillic lettering

Date	Mintage	F12	VF20	XF40	MS60	MS63
1984	1,965,000	—	1.00	2.00	4.00	—
1984	—	PF60 42.00				

Y# 194.2 ROUBLE

Copper-Nickel, 31 mm. **Subject:** 150th Anniversary - birth of Dmitri Ivanovich Mendeleyev **Obv:** National arms divide CCCP, value below **Rev:** Head facing with dates at right **Edge Lettering:** 1988.N.

Date	Mintage	F12	VF20	XF40	MS60	MS63
1984 Proof; restrike	55,000	PF60 16.00				

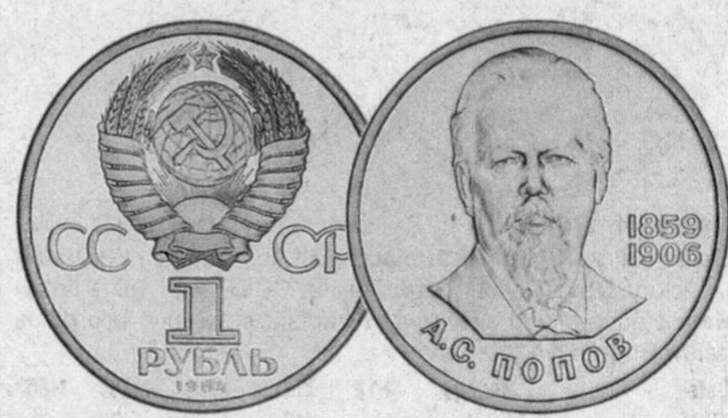

Y# 195.1 ROUBLE

Copper-Nickel, 31 mm. **Subject:** 125th Anniversary - Birth of Alexander Popov **Obv:** National arms divide CCCP with value below **Rev:** Head facing and dates **Edge:** Cyrillic lettering

Date	Mintage	F12	VF20	XF40	MS60	MS63
1984	1,965,000	—	1.00	2.00	4.00	—
1984	—	PF60 42.00				

Y# 195.2 ROUBLE

Copper-Nickel, 31 mm. **Subject:** 125th Anniversary - Birth of Alexander Popov **Obv:** National arms divide CCCP, value below **Rev:** Head facing with dates at right **Edge Lettering:** 1988.N.

Date	Mintage	F12	VF20	XF40	MS60	MS63
1984 Proof; restrike	55,000	PF60 16.00				

Y# 196.1 ROUBLE

Copper-Nickel, 31 mm. **Subject:** 185th Anniversary - Birth of Alexander Sergeyevich Pushkin **Obv:** National arms divide CCCP with value below **Edge:** Cyrillic lettering

Date	Mintage	F12	VF20	XF40	MS60	MS63
1984	1,965,000	—	1.00	2.00	5.00	—
1984	—	PF60 42.00				

Y# 196.2 ROUBLE

Copper-Nickel, 31 mm. **Subject:** 185th Anniversary - Birth of Alexander Sergeyevich Pushkin **Obv:** National arms divide CCCP, value below **Rev:** Head left with dates at right **Edge Lettering:** 1988.N.

Date	Mintage	F12	VF20	XF40	MS60	MS63
1984 Proof; restrike	55,000	PF60 16.00				
1985 Proof; Restrike/ Error	—	PF60 730				

Y# 197.1 ROUBLE

Copper-Nickel, 31 mm. **Subject:** 115th Anniversary - Birth of Vladimir Lenin **Obv:** National arms divide CCCP with value below **Rev:** Bust left with dates **Edge:** Cyrillic lettering

Date	Mintage	F12	VF20	XF40	MS60	MS63
1985	1,960,000	—	2.00	6.00	7.00	—
1985	—	PF60 49.00				

Y# 197.2 ROUBLE

Copper-Nickel, 31 mm. **Subject:** 115th Anniversary of Vladimir Lenin **Obv:** National arms divide CCCP, value below **Rev:** Bust left with dates **Edge Lettering:** 1988.N.

Date	Mintage	F12	VF20	XF40	MS60	MS63
1985 Proof; Restrike/Error	55,000	PF60 16.00				
1988 Error	—	PF60 9,700				

Y# 198.1 ROUBLE

Copper-Nickel, 31 mm. **Subject:** 40th Anniversary - World War II Victory **Obv:** National arms divide CCCP with value below **Rev:** Hammer and sickle within radiant star, sprig and dates below **Edge:** Cyrillic lettering

Date	Mintage	F12	VF20	XF40	MS60	MS63
1985	5,960,000	—	1.00	2.00	5.00	—
1985	—	PF60 39.00				

Y# 198.2 ROUBLE

Copper-Nickel, 33 mm. **Subject:** 40th Anniversary - World War II Victory **Obv:** National arms divide CCCP, value below **Rev:** Hammer and sickle within radiant star, sprig and dates below **Edge Lettering:** 1988.N.

Date	Mintage	F12	VF20	XF40	MS60	MS63
1985 Proof; restrike	55,000	PF60 16.00				

Y# 199.1 ROUBLE

Copper-Nickel, 31 mm. **Subject:** 12th World Youth Festival in Moscow **Obv:** National arms divide CCCP with value below **Rev:** Festival emblem **Edge:** Cyrillic lettering

Date	Mintage	F12	VF20	XF40	MS60	MS63
1985	5,960,000	—	2.00	3.00	5.00	—
1985	—	PF60 32.00				

Y# 199.2 ROUBLE

Copper-Nickel, 31 mm. **Subject:** 12th World Youth Festival in Moscow **Obv:** National arms divide CCCP, value below **Rev:** Festival emblem **Edge Lettering:** 1988.N.

Date	Mintage	F12	VF20	XF40	MS60	MS63
1985 Proof; restrike	55,000	PF60 10.00				

Y# 200.1 ROUBLE

Copper-Nickel, 31 mm. **Subject:** 165th Anniversary - Birth of Friedrich Engels **Obv:** National arms divide CCCP with value below **Rev:** Bust 3/4 left with dates

Date	Mintage	F12	VF20	XF40	MS60	MS63
1985	1,960,000	—	1.00	3.00	6.00	—
1985	—	PF60 26.00				

Y# 200.2 ROUBLE

Copper-Nickel, 31 mm. **Subject:** 165th Anniversary - Birth of Friedrich Engels **Obv:** National arms divide CCCP, value below **Rev:** Bust 3/4 left with dates **Edge Lettering:** 1988.N.

Date	Mintage	F12	VF20	XF40	MS60	MS63
1983 Proof; restrike	—	PF60 806				
Note: Error date						
1985 Proof; restrike	—	PF60 15.00				

Y# 201.1 ROUBLE

Copper-Nickel, 31 mm. **Subject:** International Year of Peace **Obv:** National arms divide CCCP with value below **Rev:** Hands within wreath releasing dove **Edge:** Cyrillic lettering **Note:** Rouble written with inverted "V" for ?.

Date	Mintage	F12	VF20	XF40	MS60	MS63
1986	—	—	—	—	15.00	—

Y# 201.2 ROUBLE

Copper-Nickel, 31 mm. **Subject:** International Year of Peace **Obv:** National arms divide CCCP with value below **Rev:** Hands within wreath releasing dove

Date	Mintage	F12	VF20	XF40	MS60	MS63
1986	3,955,000	—	2.00	3.00	6.00	—
1986	—	PF60 26.00				

Y# 201.4 ROUBLE

Copper-Nickel, 31 mm. **Subject:** International Year of Peace **Obv:** National arms divide CCCP, value below **Rev:** Hands within wreath releasing dove **Edge Lettering:** 1988.N.

Date	Mintage	F12	VF20	XF40	MS60	MS63
1986	—	—	2.00	3.00	7.00	—
1986 Proof, rare	—	—	—	—	—	—

Y# 202.1 ROUBLE

Copper-Nickel, 31 mm. **Subject:** 275th Anniversary - Birth of Mikhail Lomonosov **Obv:** National arms divide CCCP with value below **Rev:** Bust 1/4 left **Edge:** Cyrillic lettering

Date	Mintage	F12	VF20	XF40	MS60	MS63
1986	1,965,000	—	2.00	5.00	6.00	—
1986	—	PF60 26.00				

Y# 202.2 ROUBLE

Copper-Nickel, 31 mm. **Subject:** 275th Anniversary - Birth of Mikhail Lomonosov **Obv:** National arms divide CCCP, value below **Rev:** Bust looking left with dates at right **Edge Lettering:** 1988.N.

Date	Mintage	F12	VF20	XF40	MS60	MS63
1984 Error	—	—	4,900	—	—	—
1986 Proof; restrike	—	PF60 16.00				

Y# 203 ROUBLE

Copper-Nickel, 31 mm. **Subject:** 175th Anniversary - Battle of Borodino **Obv:** National arms with CCCP and value below **Rev:** Group of soldiers **Edge:** Cyrillic lettering **Note:** Varieties with wheat in coat of arms.

Date	Mintage	F12	VF20	XF40	MS60	MS63
1987	3,780,000	—	1.00	2.00	4.00	—
1987	—	PF60 6.00				

Y# 204 ROUBLE

Copper-Nickel, 31 mm. **Subject:** 175th Anniversary - Battle of Borodino **Obv:** National arms with CCCP and value below **Rev:** Kutuzov Monument **Edge:** Cyrillic lettering **Note:** Varieties with wheat in coat of arms.

Date	Mintage	F12	VF20	XF40	MS60	MS63
1987	3,780,000	—	1.00	2.00	4.00	—
1987	—	PF60 6.00				

Y# 205 ROUBLE

Copper-Nickel, 31 mm. **Subject:** 130th Anniversary - Birth of Constantin Tsiolkovsky **Obv:** National arms with CCCP and value below **Rev:** Seated figure facing left with stars and dates **Edge:** Cyrillic lettering

Date	Mintage	F12	VF20	XF40	MS60	MS63
1987	3,830,000	—	1.00	2.00	4.00	—
1987	170,000	PF60 6.00				

Y# 206 ROUBLE

Copper-Nickel, 31 mm. **Subject:** 70th Anniversary of Bolshevik Revolution **Obv:** National arms with CCCP and value below **Rev:** Hammer and sickle with ship on globe background at center of ribbon design, date and sprig below **Edge:** Cyrillic lettering **Note:** Varieties with wheat in coat of arms.

Date	Mintage	F12	VF20	XF40	MS60	MS63
1987	3,800,000	—	1.00	2.00	4.00	—
1987	—	PF60 7.00				

Y# 216 ROUBLE

Copper-Nickel, 31 mm. **Subject:** 160th Anniversary - Birth of Leo Tolstoi **Obv:** National arms with CCCP and value below **Rev:** Head facing **Edge:** Cyrillic lettering

Date	Mintage	F12	VF20	XF40	MS60	MS63
1987 Error	—	—	—	—	—	—
1988	3,775,000	—	1.00	2.00	5.00	—
1988	—	PF60 6.00				

Y# 209 ROUBLE

Copper-Nickel, 31 mm. **Subject:** 120th Anniversary - Birth of Maxin Gorky **Obv:** National arms with CCCP and value below **Rev:** Bust 1/4 right, designs and flying bird in background **Edge:** Cyrillic lettering

Date	Mintage	F12	VF20	XF40	MS60	MS63
1988	3,775,000	—	1.00	2.00	5.00	—
1988	—	PF60 6.00				

Y# 220 ROUBLE

Copper-Nickel, 31 mm. **Subject:** 150th Anniversary - Birth of Musorgsky **Obv:** National arms with CCCP and value below **Rev:** Head 3/4 left divides dates **Edge:** Cyrillic lettering

Date	Mintage	F12	VF20	XF40	MS60	MS63
1989	2,700,000	—	1.00	3.00	5.00	—
1989	—	PF60 5.50				

Y# 228 ROUBLE

Copper-Nickel, 31 mm. **Subject:** 175th Anniversary - Birth of M.Y. Lermontov **Obv:** National arms with CCCP and value below **Rev:** Head 1/4 left, quill below, dates at right **Edge:** Cyrillic lettering

Date	Mintage	F12	VF20	XF40	MS60	MS63
1989	2,700,000	—	1.00	3.00	5.00	—
1989	—	PF60 6.00				

Y# 232 ROUBLE

Copper-Nickel, 31 mm. **Subject:** 100th Anniversary - Birth of Hamza Hakim-zade Niyazi **Obv:** National arms with CCCP and value below **Rev:** Bust facing, dates at right **Edge:** Cyrillic lettering

Date	Mintage	F12	VF20	XF40	MS60	MS63
1989	1,800,000	—	2.00	4.00	7.00	—
1989	—	PF60 6.00				

Y# 233 ROUBLE

Copper-Nickel, 31 mm. **Subject:** 100th Anniversary - Death of Mihai Eminescu **Obv:** National arms with CCCP and value below **Rev:** Head 3/4 left flanked by dates **Edge:** Cyrillic lettering

Date	Mintage	F12	VF20	XF40	MS60	MS63
1989	1,800,000	—	2.00	4.00	7.00	—
1989	—	PF60 6.00				

Y# 235 ROUBLE

Copper-Nickel, 31 mm. **Subject:** 175th Anniversary - Birth of T.G. Shevchenko **Obv:** National arms with CCCP and value below **Rev:** Head looking down facing 3/4 left **Edge:** Cyrillic lettering

Date	Mintage	F12	VF20	XF40	MS60	MS63
1989	2,700,000	—	1.00	3.00	5.00	—
1989	—	PF60 5.50				

Y# 236 ROUBLE

Copper-Nickel, 31 mm. **Subject:** 100th Anniversary - Birth of Tschaikovsky - Composer **Obv:** National arms with CCCP and value below **Rev:** Seated figure left, musical notes in background **Edge:** Cyrillic lettering

Date	Mintage	F12	VF20	XF40	MS60	MS63
1990	2,600,000	—	—	—	5.00	—
1990	—	PF60 6.50				

Y# 237 ROUBLE

Copper-Nickel, 31 mm. **Subject:** Anniversary - Marshal Zhukov **Obv:** National arms with CCCP and value below **Rev:** Uniformed bust left **Edge:** Cyrillic lettering

Date	Mintage	F12	VF20	XF40	MS60	MS63
1990	1,600,000	—	—	6.00	16.00	—
1990	—	PF60 7.00				

Y# 240 ROUBLE

Copper-Nickel, 31 mm. **Subject:** 130th Anniversary - Birth of Anton Chekhov **Obv:** National arms with CCCP and value below **Rev:** Head 1/4 left divides design and dates **Edge:** Cyrillic lettering

Date	Mintage	F12	VF20	XF40	MS60	MS63
1990	2,600,000	—	—	—	5.00	—
1990	—	PF60 6.50				

Y# 257 ROUBLE

Copper-Nickel, 31 mm. **Subject:** 125th Anniversary - Birth of Janis Rainis **Obv:** National arms with CCCP and value below **Rev:** Head facing with dates at right **Edge:** Cyrillic lettering

Date	Mintage	F12	VF20	XF40	MS60	MS63
1990	2,600,000	—	—	—	5.00	—
1990	—	PF60 6.50				

Y# 258 ROUBLE

Copper-Nickel, 31 mm. **Subject:** 500th Anniversary - Birth of Francisk Scorina **Obv:** National arms with CCCP and value below **Rev:** Half figure facing **Edge:** Cyrillic lettering

Date	Mintage	F12	VF20	XF40	MS60	MS63
1990	2,600,000	—	—	—	5.00	—
1990	—	PF60 6.50				

Y# 260 ROUBLE

Copper-Nickel, 31 mm. **Subject:** 550th Anniversary - Birth of Alisher Navoi **Obv:** National arms with CCCP and value below **Rev:** Bust with hand on chin left **Edge:** Cyrillic lettering

Date	Mintage	F12	VF20	XF40	MS60	MS63
1990 Error	—	—	—	—	—	72.00
1991 Л	2,150,000	—	—	—	6.00	—
1991 Л	—	PF60 3.50				
1991 M	—	—	—	—	6.00	—
1991 M	—	PF60 3.50				

Y# 261 ROUBLE

Copper-Nickel, 31 mm. **Subject:** 125th Anniversary - Birth of P. N. Lebedev **Obv:** National arms with CCCP and value below **Rev:** Half figure right with hand on book, designs on bottom, dates and fomulas at right **Edge:** Cyrillic lettering

Date	Mintage	F12	VF20	XF40	MS60	MS63
1990 Error, rare	—	10,500	—	—	—	—
1991	2,150,000	—	—	—	5.00	—
1991	—	PF60 5.50				

Y# 263.1 ROUBLE

Copper-Nickel, 31 mm. **Subject:** 100th Birthday of Sergey Prokofiev **Obv:** National arms with CCCP and value below **Rev:** Head right **Edge:** Cyrillic lettering

Date	Mintage	F12	VF20	XF40	MS60	MS63
1991	2,150,000	—	—	—	3.00	—
1991	—	PF60 5.50				

Y# 263.2 ROUBLE

Copper-Nickel, 31 mm. **Subject:** 100th Birthday of Sergey Prokofiev **Obv:** National arms with CCCP and value below **Rev:** Head right, dates below **Note:** Error death date: 1952.

Date	Mintage	F12	VF20	XF40	MS60	MS63
1991 Rare	—	—	—	—	—	—

Y# 282 ROUBLE

Copper-Nickel, 31 mm. **Subject:** K.B. Ivanov **Obv:** National arms with CCCP and value below **Rev:** Head left **Edge:** Cyrillic lettering

Date	Mintage	F12	VF20	XF40	MS60	MS63
1991	3,150,000	—	—	—	5.00	—
1991	—	PF60 5.50				

Y# 283 ROUBLE
Copper-Nickel, 31 mm. **Subject:** Turkman Poet Makhtumkuli **Obv:** National arms with CCCP and value below **Rev:** Bust left **Edge:** Cyrillic lettering

Date	Mintage	F12	VF20	XF40	MS60	MS63
1991	2,150,000	—	—	—	6.00	—
1991	—	PF60 8.00				

Y# 284 ROUBLE
Copper-Nickel, 31 mm. **Subject:** 850th Anniversary - Birth of Nizami Gyanzhevi - Poet **Obv:** National arms with CCCP and value below **Rev:** Bust right writing with quill **Edge:** Cyrillic lettering

Date	Mintage	F12	VF20	XF40	MS60	MS63
1991	2,200,000	—	—	—	6.00	—
1991	—	PF60 5.50				

Y# 289 ROUBLE
Copper-Nickel, 31 mm. **Series:** 1992 Olympics **Obv:** National arms with CCCP and value below **Rev:** Wrestlers

Date	Mintage	F12	VF20	XF40	MS60	MS63
1991	250,000	PF60 7.50				

Y# 290 ROUBLE
Copper-Nickel, 31 mm. **Series:** 1992 Olympics **Obv:** National arms with CCCP and value below **Rev:** Javelin throwers

Date	Mintage	F12	VF20	XF40	MS60	MS63
1991	250,000	PF60 7.50				

Y# 291 ROUBLE
Copper-Nickel, 31 mm. **Series:** 1992 Olympics **Obv:** National arms with CCCP and value below **Rev:** Cyclist and charioteer

Date	Mintage	F12	VF20	XF40	MS60	MS63
1991	250,000	PF60 7.50				

Y# 299 ROUBLE
Copper-Nickel, 31 mm. **Series:** 1992 Olympics **Obv:** National arms with CCCP and value below **Rev:** Weight lifters

Date	Mintage	F12	VF20	XF40	MS60	MS63
1991	250,000	PF60 7.50				

Y# 300 ROUBLE
Copper-Nickel, 31 mm. **Series:** 1992 Olympics **Obv:** National arms with CCCP and value below **Rev:** Broad jumpers

Date	Mintage	F12	VF20	XF40	MS60	MS63
1991	250,000	PF60 7.50				

Y# 302 ROUBLE
Copper-Nickel, 31 mm. **Series:** 1992 Olympics **Obv:** National arms with CCCP and value below **Rev:** Runners

Date	Mintage	F12	VF20	XF40	MS60	MS63
1991	250,000	PF60 7.50				

Y# A134 2 ROUBLES
Copper-Nickel **Obv:** National arms **Rev:** Value above date within wreath

Date	Mintage	F12	VF20	XF40	MS60	MS63
1958	20,976,000	—	—	3,900	5,800	—

Note: Never officially released for circulation; majority of mintage remelted

Y# B134 3 ROUBLES
Copper-Nickel **Obv:** National arms **Rev:** Value above date within wreath

Date	Mintage	F12	VF20	XF40	MS60	MS63
1958	4,050,000	—	—	—	10,000	—

Note: Never officially released for circulation; majority of mintage remelted

Y# 207 3 ROUBLES
Copper-Nickel **Subject:** 70th Anniversary - Bolshevik Revolution **Obv:** National arms with CCCP and value below **Rev:** Date above three unifomed standing figures with weapons

Date	Mintage	F12	VF20	XF40	MS60	MS63
1987	2,300,000	—	—	—	8.00	9.00
1987	—	PF63 10.00				

Y# 210 3 ROUBLES
34.56 g., 0.900 Silver 1.000 oz. ASW **Subject:** 1000th Anniversary of Russian Architecture **Obv:** National arms with CCCP and value below **Rev:** Cathedral of St. Sophia in Kiev

Date	Mintage	F12	VF20	XF40	MS60	MS63
1988 (m)	Est. 35000	PF63 110				

Y# 211 3 ROUBLES
34.56 g., 0.900 Silver 1.000 oz. ASW **Subject:** 1000th Anniversary of Minting in Russian **Obv:** National arms with CCCP and value below **Rev:** Coin design of St. Vladimir, 977-1015

Date	Mintage	F12	VF20	XF40	MS60	MS63
1988 (l)	—	PF63 110				

Y# 222 3 ROUBLES
34.56 g., 0.900 Silver 1.000 oz. ASW **Subject:** 500th Anniversary United Russia **Obv:** National arms with CCCP and value below **Rev:** Kremlin

Date	Mintage	F12	VF20	XF40	MS60	MS63
1989 (l)	Est. 40000	PF63 70.00				

Y# 223 3 ROUBLES
34.56 g., 0.900 Silver 1.000 oz. ASW **Subject:** 500th Anniversary of the First All-Russian Coinage **Obv:** National arms with CCCP and value below **Rev:** Three ancient coins

Date	Mintage	F12	VF20	XF40	MS60	MS63
1989 (l)	Est. 40000	PF63 70.00				

Y# 234 3 ROUBLES

Copper-Nickel **Subject:** Armenian Earthquake Relief **Obv:** National arms with CCCP and value below **Rev:** Stylized hand with flame in palm, wings form mountains in background **Edge:** Cyrillic lettering

Date	Mintage	F12	VF20	XF40	MS60	MS63
1989	2,700,000	—	—	2.00	7.50	9.00
1989	—	PF63 11.50				

Y# 242 3 ROUBLES

34.56 g., 0.900 Silver 1.000 oz. ASW **Obv:** National arms with CCCP and value below **Rev:** Captain Cook on Unalaska Island

Date	Mintage	F12	VF20	XF40	MS60	MS63
1990 (l)	25,000	PF63 60.00				

Y# 247 3 ROUBLES

34.56 g., 0.900 Silver 1.000 oz. ASW **Subject:** World Summit for Children **Obv:** National arms with CCCP and value below **Rev:** Baby and flower within wreath above seated figures around v-shaped design

Date	Mintage	F12	VF20	XF40	MS60	MS63
1990 (l)	20,000	PF63 65.00				

Y# 248 3 ROUBLES

34.56 g., 0.900 Silver 1.000 oz. ASW **Obv:** National arms with CCCP and value below **Rev:** Peter the Great's Fleet

Date	Mintage	F12	VF20	XF40	MS60	MS63
1990 (m)	40,000	PF63 32.50				

Y# 249 3 ROUBLES

34.56 g., 0.900 Silver 1.000 oz. ASW **Obv:** National arms with CCCP and value below **Rev:** St. Peter and Paul Fortress in Leningrad

Date	Mintage	F12	VF20	XF40	MS60	MS63
1990 (l)	40,000	PF63 32.50				

Y# 262 3 ROUBLES

34.56 g., 0.900 Silver 1.000 oz. ASW **Obv:** National arms with CCCP and value below **Rev:** Yuri Gagarin Monument

Date	Mintage	F12	VF20	XF40	MS60	MS63
1991 (l)	35,000	PF63 40.00				

Y# 264 3 ROUBLES

34.56 g., 0.900 Silver 1.000 oz. ASW **Obv:** National arms with CCCP and value below **Rev:** Fort Ross in California

Date	Mintage	F12	VF20	XF40	MS60	MS63
1991 (l)	Est. 25000	PF63 45.00				

Y# 274 3 ROUBLES

34.56 g., 0.900 Silver 1.000 oz. ASW **Obv:** National arms with CCCP and value below **Rev:** Bolshoi Theater

Date	Mintage	F12	VF20	XF40	MS60	MS63
1991 (l)	40,000	PF63 35.00				

Y# 275 3 ROUBLES

34.56 g., 0.900 Silver 1.000 oz. ASW **Obv:** National arms with CCCP and value below **Rev:** Moscow's Arch of Triumph

Date	Mintage	F12	VF20	XF40	MS60	MS63
1991 (m)	40,000	PF63 35.00				

Y# 301 3 ROUBLES

Copper-Nickel **Subject:** 50th Anniversary - Defense of Moscow **Obv:** National arms with CCCP and value below **Rev:** Marching soldiers **Edge:** Cyrillic lettering

Date	Mintage	F12	VF20	XF40	MS60	MS63
1991	2,150,000	—	—	—	2.50	7.00
1991	—	PF60 4.00				

Y# C134 5 ROUBLES

Copper-Nickel, 33 mm. **Obv:** National arms **Rev:** Value and date within sprigs

Date	Mintage	F12	VF20	XF40	MS60	MS63
1958	5,150,000	—	—	2,650	5,800	—

Note: Never officially released for circulation; majority of mintage remelted

Y# 145 5 ROUBLES

16.67 g., 0.900 Silver 0.4824 oz. ASW **Series:** 1980 Olympics **Obv:** National arms flanked by CCCP with value below **Rev:** Scenes of Kiev

Date	Mintage	F12	VF20	XF40	MS60	MS63
1977 (l)	250,000	—	—	—	—	18.00
1977 (l) Frosted unc.	Inc. above	—	—	—	—	—
1977 (l)	121,000	PF63 18.00				
1977 (m)	—	PF63 18.00				

Y# 146 5 ROUBLES

16.67 g., 0.900 Silver 0.4824 oz. ASW **Series:** 1980 Olympics **Obv:** National arms divide CCCP with value below **Rev:** Scenes of Leningrad

Date	Mintage	F12	VF20	XF40	MS60	MS63
1977 (l)	250,000	—	—	—	—	22.00
1977 (l) Frosted unc.	Inc. above	—	—	—	—	—
1977 (l)	121,000	PF63 18.00				
1977 (m)	Inc. above	—	—	—	—	22.00
1977 (m)	—	PF63 18.00				

Y# 147 5 ROUBLES
16.67 g., 0.900 Silver 0.4824 oz. ASW **Series:** 1980 Olympics **Obv:** National arms divide CCCP with value below **Rev:** Scenes of Minsk

Date	Mintage	F12	VF20	XF40	MS60	MS63
1977 (l)	250,000	—	—	—	—	22.00
1977 (l)	121,000	**PF63** 16.50				
1977 (m)	—	**PF63** 16.50				

Y# 148 5 ROUBLES
16.67 g., 0.900 Silver 0.4824 oz. ASW **Series:** 1980 Olympics **Obv:** National arms divide CCCP with value below **Rev:** Scenes of Tallinn

Date	Mintage	F12	VF20	XF40	MS60	MS63
1977 (l)	252,000	—	—	—	—	22.00
1977 (l) Frosted	Inc. above	—	—	—	—	—
1977 (l)	—	**PF63** 18.00				
1977 (m)	Inc. above	—	—	—	—	22.00
1977 (m)	—	**PF63** 18.00				

Y# 154 5 ROUBLES
16.67 g., 0.900 Silver 0.4824 oz. ASW **Series:** 1980 Olympics **Obv:** National arms divide CCCP with value below **Rev:** Runner in front of stadium

Date	Mintage	F12	VF20	XF40	MS60	MS63
1978 (l)	227,000	—	—	—	—	22.00
1978 (m)	118,000	**PF63** 18.00				
1978 (l) Matte proof	—	**PF63** 30.00				

Y# 155 5 ROUBLES
16.67 g., 0.900 Silver 0.4824 oz. ASW **Series:** 1980 Olympics **Obv:** National arms divide CCCP with value below **Rev:** Swimming

Date	Mintage	F12	VF20	XF40	MS60	MS63
1978 (l)	227,000	—	—	—	—	22.00
1978 (l) Frosted	Inc. above	—	—	—	—	—
1978 (l)	118,000	**PF63** 18.00				
1978 (l) Matte proof	—	**PF63** 30.00				

Y# 156 5 ROUBLES
16.67 g., 0.900 Silver 0.4824 oz. ASW **Series:** 1980 Olympics **Obv:** National arms divide CCCP with value below **Rev:** High jumping

Date	Mintage	F12	VF20	XF40	MS60	MS63
1978 (l)	221,000	—	—	—	—	22.00
1978 (l)	119,000	**PF63** 18.00				
1978 (m)	Inc. above	—	—	—	—	22.00
1978 (m)	—	**PF63** 18.00				

Y# 157 5 ROUBLES
16.67 g., 0.900 Silver 0.4824 oz. ASW **Series:** 1980 Olympics **Obv:** National arms divide CCCP with value below **Rev:** Equestrian show jumping

Date	Mintage	F12	VF20	XF40	MS60	MS63
1978 (l)	221,000	—	—	—	—	22.00
1978 (l)	119,000	**PF63** 18.00				
1978 (m)	Inc. above	—	—	—	—	22.00
1978 (m)	—	**PF63** 18.00				

Y# 166 5 ROUBLES
16.67 g., 0.900 Silver 0.4824 oz. ASW **Series:** 1980 Olympics **Obv:** National arms divide CCCP with value below **Rev:** Weight lifting

Date	Mintage	F12	VF20	XF40	MS60	MS63
1979 (l)	207,000	—	—	—	—	22.00
1979 (l)	108,000	**PF63** 18.00				
1979 (m)	Inc. above	—	—	—	—	22.00
1979 (m)	—	**PF63** 18.00				

Y# 167 5 ROUBLES
16.67 g., 0.900 Silver 0.4824 oz. ASW **Series:** 1980 Olympics **Obv:** National arms divide CCCP with value below **Rev:** Hammer throw

Date	Mintage	F12	VF20	XF40	MS60	MS63
1979 (l)	207,000	—	—	—	—	22.00
1979 (l)	119,000	**PF63** 18.00				
1979 (m)	Inc. above	—	—	—	—	22.00
1979 (m)	—	**PF63** 18.00				

Y# 179 5 ROUBLES
16.67 g., 0.900 Silver 0.4824 oz. ASW **Series:** 1980 Olympics **Obv:** National arms divide CCCP with value below **Rev:** Archery

Date	Mintage	F12	VF20	XF40	MS60	MS63
1980 (l)	126,000	—	—	—	—	22.00
1980 (l)	—	**PF63** 18.00				
1980 (m)	Inc. above	—	—	—	—	22.00
1980 (m)	—	**PF63** 18.00				

Y# 180 5 ROUBLES
16.67 g., 0.900 Silver 0.4824 oz. ASW **Series:** 1980 Olympics **Obv:** National arms divide CCCP with value below **Rev:** Gymnastics

Date	Mintage	F12	VF20	XF40	MS60	MS63
1980 (l)	126,000	—	—	—	—	22.00
1980 (l)	—	**PF63** 18.00				
1980 (m)	Inc. above	—	—	—	—	22.00
1980 (m)	—	**PF63** 18.00				

Y# 181 5 ROUBLES
16.67 g., 0.900 Silver 0.4824 oz. ASW **Series:** 1980 Olympics **Subject:** Equestrian - Isindi **Obv:** National arms divide CCCP with value below **Rev:** Polo players

Date	Mintage	F12	VF20	XF40	MS60	MS63
1980 (l)	126,000	—	—	—	—	22.00
1980 (l)	—	**PF63** 18.00				

Y# 182 5 ROUBLES
16.67 g., 0.900 Silver 0.4824 oz. ASW **Series:** 1980 Olympics **Obv:** National arms divide CCCP with value below **Rev:** Gorodki - stick throwing

Date	Mintage	F12	VF20	XF40	MS60	MS63
1980 (l)	126,000	—	—	—	—	22.00
1980 (l)	—	**PF63** 18.00				

Y# 208 5 ROUBLES
Copper-Nickel **Subject:** 70th Anniversary - Bolshevik Revolution **Obv:** National arms with CCCP and value below **Rev:** Head left and date within banner

Date	Mintage	F12	VF20	XF40	MS60	MS63
1987	1,300,000	—	—	—	25.00	30.00
1987	—	PF63 28.00				

Y# 217 5 ROUBLES
Copper-Nickel, 35 mm. **Obv:** National arms with CCCP and value below **Rev:** Leningrad - Peter the Great

Date	Mintage	F12	VF20	XF40	MS60	MS63
1988	1,675,000	—	—	—	8.00	9.00
1988	—	PF63 8.00				

Y# 218 5 ROUBLES
Copper-Nickel, 35 mm. **Obv:** National arms with CCCP and value below **Rev:** Novgorood Monument to the Russian Millennium

Date	Mintage	F12	VF20	XF40	MS60	MS63
1988	1,675,000	—	—	—	8.00	9.00
1988	—	PF63 8.00				

Y# 219 5 ROUBLES
Copper-Nickel, 35 mm. **Obv:** National arms with CCCP and value below **Rev:** St. Sophia Cathedral in Kiev

Date	Mintage	F12	VF20	XF40	MS60	MS63
1988	1,675,000	—	—	—	8.00	9.00
1988	—	PF63 8.00				

Y# 221 5 ROUBLES
Copper-Nickel, 35 mm. **Obv:** National arms with CCCP and value below **Rev:** Pokrowsky Cathedral in Moscow

Date	Mintage	F12	VF20	XF40	MS60	MS63
1989	1,700,000	—	—	—	8.00	9.00
1989	—	PF63 12.00				

Y# 229 5 ROUBLES
Copper-Nickel, 35 mm. **Obv:** National arms with CCCP and value below **Rev:** Samarkand

Date	Mintage	F12	VF20	XF40	MS60	MS63
1989	1,700,000	—	—	—	6.00	7.00
1989	—	PF63 7.00				

Y# 230 5 ROUBLES
Copper-Nickel, 35 mm. **Obv:** National arms with CCCP and value below **Rev:** Cathedral of the Annunciation in Moscow

Date	Mintage	F12	VF20	XF40	MS60	MS63
1989	1,700,000	—	—	—	6.00	7.00
1989	—	PF63 8.00				

Y# 241 5 ROUBLES
Copper-Nickel, 35 mm. **Obv:** National arms with CCCP and value below **Rev:** St. Petersburg Palace

Date	Mintage	F12	VF20	XF40	MS60	MS63
1990	2,600,000	—	—	—	6.00	7.00
1990	—	PF63 10.00				

Y# 246 5 ROUBLES
Copper-Nickel, 35 mm. **Obv:** National arms with CCCP and value below **Rev:** Uspenski Cathedral **Edge:** Cyrillic lettering

Date	Mintage	F12	VF20	XF40	MS60	MS63
1990	2,600,000	—	—	—	6.00	7.00
1990	—	PF63 10.00				

Y# 259 5 ROUBLES
Copper-Nickel, 35 mm. **Obv:** National arms with CCCP and value below **Rev:** Matenadarin Depository of Ancient Armenian Manuscripts

Date	Mintage	F12	VF20	XF40	MS60	MS63
1990	2,600,000	—	—	—	6.00	7.00
1990	—	PF63 10.00				

Y# 268 5 ROUBLES
7.78 g., 0.999 Palladium 0.2497 oz. APW **Series:** Ballet **Obv:** National arms with CCCP and value below **Rev:** Ballerina

Date	Mintage	F12	VF20	XF40	MS60	MS63
1991 (l)	9,000	—	—	—	—	225

Y# 271 5 ROUBLES
Copper-Nickel, 35 mm. **Obv:** National arms with CCCP and value below **Rev:** Cathedral of the Archangel Michael in Moscow **Edge:** Cyrillic lettering

Date	Mintage	F12	VF20	XF40	MS60	MS63
1991	2,150,000	—	—	—	6.00	7.00
1991	—	PF63 10.00				

Y# 272 5 ROUBLES
Copper-Nickel, 35 mm. **Obv:** National arms with CCCP and value below **Rev:** State bank building in Moscow

Date	Mintage	F12	VF20	XF40	MS60	MS63
1991	2,600,000	—	—	—	6.00	7.00
1991	—	PF63 10.00				

Y# 273 5 ROUBLES
Copper-Nickel, 35 mm. **Obv:** National arms with CCCP and value below **Rev:** David of Sasun monument; Armenian epic hero **Edge:** Cyrillic lettering

Date	Mintage	F12	VF20	XF40	MS60	MS63
1991	2,150,000	—	—	—	6.00	7.00
1991	—	PF63 10.00				

Y# 149 10 ROUBLES
33.30 g., 0.900 Silver 0.9636 oz. ASW **Series:** 1980 Olympics **Obv:** National arms divide CCCP with value below **Rev:** Scenes of Moscow

Date	Mintage	F12	VF20	XF40	MS60	MS63
1977 (l)	250,000	—	—	—	40.00	45.00
1977 (l)	121,000	PF60 35.00		PF63 40.00		
1977 (m)	Inc. above	—	—	—	40.00	45.00
1977 (m)	—	PF60 35.00		PF63 40.00		

Y# 150 10 ROUBLES
33.30 g., 0.900 Silver 0.9636 oz. ASW **Series:** 1980 Olympics **Obv:** National arms divide CCCP with value below **Rev:** Map of USSR back of design above rings

Date	Mintage	F12	VF20	XF40	MS60	MS63
1977 (l)	250,000	—	—	—	40.00	45.00
1977 (l)	121,000	PF60 35.00		PF63 40.00		

Y# 158.1 10 ROUBLES
33.30 g., 0.900 Silver 0.9636 oz. ASW **Series:** 1980 Olympics **Obv:** National arms divide CCCP with value below **Rev:** Cycling

Date	Mintage	F12	VF20	XF40	MS60	MS63
1978 (l)	227,000	—	—	—	40.00	45.00
1978 (l)	118,000	PF60 35.00		PF63 40.00		

Y# 158.2 10 ROUBLES
33.30 g., 0.900 Silver 0.9636 oz. ASW **Series:** 1980 Olympics **Obv:** National arms divide CCCP with value below **Rev:** Without mint mark

Date	Mintage	F12	VF20	XF40	MS60	MS63
1978 Rare	—	—	—	—	—	—
1978 Proof, rare	100	—	—	—	—	—

Y# 159 10 ROUBLES
33.30 g., 0.900 Silver 0.9636 oz. ASW **Series:** 1980 Olympics **Obv:** National arms divide CCCP with value below **Rev:** Canoeing

Date	Mintage	F12	VF20	XF40	MS60	MS63
1978 (l) Rare	34,000	—	—	—	—	—
1978 (m)	192,000	—	—	—	40.00	45.00
1978 (m)	118,000	PF60 35.00		PF63 40.00		

Y# 160 10 ROUBLES
33.30 g., 0.900 Silver 0.9636 oz. ASW **Series:** 1980 Olympics **Obv:** National arms divide CCCP with value below **Rev:** Equestrian sports

Date	Mintage	F12	VF20	XF40	MS60	MS63
1978 (l) Rare	34,000	—	—	—	—	—
1978 (m)	192,000	—	—	—	40.00	45.00
1978 (m)	118,000	PF60 35.00		PF63 40.00		

Y# 161 10 ROUBLES
33.30 g., 0.900 Silver 0.9636 oz. ASW **Series:** 1980 Olympics **Obv:** National arms divide CCCP with value below **Rev:** Pole vaulting

Date	Mintage	F12	VF20	XF40	MS60	MS63
1978 (l)	221,000	—	—	—	40.00	45.00
1978 (l)	119,000	PF60 35.00		PF63 40.00		
1978 (m)	Inc. above	—	—	—	40.00	45.00
1978 (m)	—	PF60 35.00		PF63 40.00		

Y# 168 10 ROUBLES
33.30 g., 0.900 Silver 0.9636 oz. ASW **Series:** 1980 Olympics **Obv:** National arms divide CCCP with value below **Rev:** Basketball

Date	Mintage	F12	VF20	XF40	MS60	MS63
1979 (l)	221,000	—	—	—	40.00	45.00
1979 (l)	119,000	PF60 35.00		PF63 40.00		
1979 Rare	—	—	—	—	—	—

Y# 169 10 ROUBLES
33.30 g., 0.900 Silver 0.9636 oz. ASW **Series:** 1980 Olympics **Obv:** National arms divide CCCP with value below **Rev:** Volleyball

Date	Mintage	F12	VF20	XF40	MS60	MS63
1979 (l)	221,000	—	—	—	40.00	45.00
1979 (l)	119,000	PF60 35.00		PF63 40.00		

Y# 170 10 ROUBLES
33.30 g., 0.900 Silver 0.9636 oz. ASW **Series:** 1980 Olympics **Obv:** National arms divide CCCP with value below **Rev:** Boxing

Date	Mintage	F12	VF20	XF40	MS60	MS63
1979 (l)	207,000	—	—	—	40.00	45.00
1979 (l)	108,000	PF60 35.00		PF63 40.00		

Y# 171 10 ROUBLES
33.30 g., 0.900 Silver 0.9636 oz. ASW **Series:** 1980 Olympics **Obv:** National arms divide CCCP with value below **Rev:** Judo

Date	Mintage	F12	VF20	XF40	MS60	MS63
1979 (l)	207,000	—	—	—	40.00	45.00
1979 (l)	108,000	PF60 35.00		PF63 40.00		
1979 (m)	Inc. above	—	—	—	40.00	45.00
1979 (m)	—	PF60 35.00		PF63 40.00		

Y# 172 10 ROUBLES
33.30 g., 0.900 Silver 0.9636 oz. ASW **Series:** 1980 Olympics **Obv:** National arms divide CCCP with value below **Rev:** Weight lifting

Date	Mintage	F12	VF20	XF40	MS60	MS63
1979 (l)	207,000	—	—	—	40.00	45.00
1979 (l)	108,000	PF60 35.00		PF63 40.00		

Y# 183 10 ROUBLES
33.30 g., 0.900 Silver 0.9636 oz. ASW **Series:** 1980 Olympics **Obv:** National arms divide CCCP with value below **Rev:** Wrestlers

Date	Mintage	F12	VF20	XF40	MS60	MS63
1980 (l)	126,000	—	—	—	40.00	50.00
1980 (l)	—	PF60 35.00		PF63 40.00		
1980 (m)	Inc. above	—	—	—	40.00	45.00
1980 (m)	—	PF60 35.00		PF63 40.00		

Y# 184 10 ROUBLES
33.30 g., 0.900 Silver 0.9636 oz. ASW **Series:** 1980 Olympics **Obv:** National arms divide CCCP with value below **Rev:** Tug of war

Date	Mintage	F12	VF20	XF40	MS60	MS63
1980 (l)	126,000	—	—	—	40.00	45.00
1980 (l)	—	PF60 35.00		PF63 40.00		

Y# 185 10 ROUBLES
33.30 g., 0.900 Silver 0.9636 oz. ASW **Series:** 1980 Olympics **Obv:** National arms divide CCCP with value below **Rev:** Reindeer racing

Date	Mintage	F12	VF20	XF40	MS60	MS63
1980 (l)	126,000	—	—	—	40.00	45.00
1980 (l)	—	PF60 35.00	PF63 40.00			

Y# 238 10 ROUBLES
15.55 g., 0.999 Palladium 0.4994 oz. APW **Series:** Ballet **Obv:** National arms with CCCP and value below **Rev:** Ballerina

Date	Mintage	F12	VF20	XF40	MS60	MS63
1990 (l)	Est. 15000	—	—	—	—	400

Y# 269 10 ROUBLES
15.55 g., 0.999 Palladium 0.4994 oz. APW **Series:** Ballet **Obv:** National arms with CCCP and value below **Rev:** Ballerina

Date	Mintage	F12	VF20	XF40	MS60	MS63
1991 (l)	15,000	—	—	—	—	400

Y# 285 10 ROUBLES
2.66 g., 0.585 Gold 0.050 oz. AGW **Series:** Ballet **Obv:** National arms with CCCP and value below **Rev:** Ballerina

Date	Mintage	F12	VF20	XF40	MS60	MS63
1991 (l)	6,000	—	—	—	—	90.00

Y# 212 25 ROUBLES
31.10 g., 0.999 Palladium 0.9989 oz. APW **Subject:** Monument to Vladimir, Grand Duke of Kiev and Millennium of Christianity in Russia **Obv:** National arms with CCCP and value below **Rev:** Monument

Date	Mintage	F12	VF20	XF40	MS60	MS63
1988 (l)	7,000	—	—	—	—	775

Y# 224 25 ROUBLES
31.10 g., 0.999 Palladium 0.9989 oz. APW **Subject:** 500th Anniversary of Russian State **Obv:** National arms with CCCP and value below **Rev:** Ivan III on throne

Date	Mintage	F12	VF20	XF40	MS60	MS63
1989 (l)	Est. 12000	PF63 775				

Y# 231 25 ROUBLES
31.10 g., 0.999 Palladium 0.9989 oz. APW **Series:** Ballet **Obv:** National arms with CCCP and value below **Rev:** Ballerina

Date	Mintage	F12	VF20	XF40	MS60	MS63
1989 (l)	27,000	—	—	—	—	775
1989 (l)	—	PF63 825				
1989 (l) Matte proof	—	PF63 825				

Y# 239 25 ROUBLES
31.10 g., 0.999 Palladium 0.9989 oz. APW **Series:** Ballet **Obv:** National arms with CCCP and value below **Rev:** Ballerina

Date	Mintage	F12	VF20	XF40	MS60	MS63
1990 (l)	27,000	—	—	—	—	775
1990 (l)	—	PF63 825				

Y# 243 25 ROUBLES
31.10 g., 0.999 Palladium 0.9989 oz. APW **Subject:** 250th Anniversary - Discovery of Russian America **Obv:** National arms with CCCP and value below **Rev:** Ship, St. Peter

Date	Mintage	F12	VF20	XF40	MS60	MS63
1990 (l)	6,500	PF63 775				

Y# 244 25 ROUBLES
31.10 g., 0.999 Palladium 0.9989 oz. APW **Subject:** 250th Anniversary - Discovery of Russian America **Obv:** National arms with CCCP and value below **Rev:** Ship, St. Paul

Date	Mintage	F12	VF20	XF40	MS60	MS63
1990 (l)	6,500	PF63 775				

Y# 250 25 ROUBLES
31.10 g., 0.999 Palladium 0.9989 oz. APW **Subject:** 500th Anniversary of Russian State **Obv:** National arms with CCCP and value below **Rev:** Peter the Great

Date	Mintage	F12	VF20	XF40	MS60	MS63
1990 (l)	12,000	PF63 775				

Y# 265 25 ROUBLES
31.10 g., 0.999 Palladium 0.9989 oz. APW **Subject:** Three Saints Harbor - Russian settlement in America.

Date	Mintage	F12	VF20	XF40	MS60	MS63
1991 (l)	—	PF63 775				

Y# 266 25 ROUBLES
31.10 g., 0.999 Palladium 0.9989 oz. APW **Subject:** Novo Archangelsk 1799 - three-masted ship

Date	Mintage	F12	VF20	XF40	MS60	MS63
1991 (l)	Est. 6500	PF63 775				

Y# 270 25 ROUBLES
31.10 g., 0.999 Palladium 0.9989 oz. APW **Series:** Ballet **Obv:** National arms with CCCP and value below **Rev:** Ballerina

Date	Mintage	F12	VF20	XF40	MS60	MS63
1991 (l)	30,000	—	—	—	—	775
1991 (l)	—	PF63 775				

Y# 276 25 ROUBLES
31.10 g., 0.999 Palladium 0.9989 oz. APW **Subject:** 500th Anniversary of Russian State **Obv:** National arms with CCCP and value below **Rev:** Abolition of Serfdom in Russia

Date	Mintage	F12	VF20	XF40	MS60	MS63
1991 (l)	Est. 12000	PF63 775				

Y# 286 25 ROUBLES
5.32 g., 0.585 Gold 0.1001 oz. AGW **Series:** Ballet **Obv:** National arms with CCCP and value below **Rev:** Ballerina

Date	Mintage	F12	VF20	XF40	MS60	MS63
1991 (l)	5,000	—	—	—	—	175

Y# 286a 25 ROUBLES
3.11 g., 0.999 Gold 0.0999 oz. AGW **Series:** Ballet **Obv:** National arms with CCCP and value below **Rev:** Ballerina

Date	Mintage	F12	VF20	XF40	MS60	MS63
1991 (l)	1,500	PF63 225				

Y# 213 50 ROUBLES
8.64 g., 0.900 Gold 0.250 oz. AGW **Subject:** 1000th Anniversary of Russian Architecture **Obv:** National arms divide CCCP with value below **Rev:** Cathedral of St. Sophia in Novgorod

Date	Mintage	F12	VF20	XF40	MS60	MS63
1988 (m)	25,000	—	—	—	—	425

Y# 225 50 ROUBLES
8.64 g., 0.900 Gold 0.250 oz. AGW **Subject:** 500th Anniversary of Russian State **Obv:** National arms with CCCP and value below **Rev:** Cathedral of the Ascension

Date	Mintage	F12	VF20	XF40	MS60	MS63
1989 (m)	Est. 25000	PF63 425				

Y# 251 50 ROUBLES
8.64 g., 0.900 Gold 0.250 oz. AGW **Subject:** 500th Anniversary of Russian State **Obv:** National arms with CCCP and value below **Rev:** Moscow Church of the Archangel

Date	Mintage	F12	VF20	XF40	MS60	MS63
1990 (m)	25,000	PF63 425				

Y# 277 50 ROUBLES
8.64 g., 0.900 Gold 0.2501 oz. AGW **Subject:** 500th Anniversary of Russian State **Obv:** National arms with CCCP and value below **Rev:** St. Isaac Cathedral in St. Petersburg

Date	Mintage	F12	VF20	XF40	MS60	MS63
1991 (m)	25,000	PF63 425				

Y# 287 50 ROUBLES
13.30 g., 0.585 Gold 0.2501 oz. AGW **Subject:** Bolshoi Ballet **Obv:** National arms with CCCP and value below **Rev:** Ballerina

Date	Mintage	F12	VF20	XF40	MS60	MS63
1991 (l)	2,400	—	—	—	—	475

Y# 287a 50 ROUBLES
7.78 g., 0.999 Gold 0.2499 oz. AGW **Subject:** Bolshoi Ballet **Obv:** National arms with CCCP and value below **Rev:** Ballerina

Date	Mintage	F12	VF20	XF40	MS60	MS63
1991 (l)	1,500	PF63 500				

Y# A163 100 ROUBLES
17.28 g., 0.900 Gold 0.500 oz. AGW **Series:** 1980 Olympics **Obv:** National arms divide CCCP with value below **Rev:** Moscow Olympic's logo, sprig within world globe, olympic rings below

Date	Mintage	F12	VF20	XF40	MS60	MS63
1977 (l)	44,000	—	—	—	—	900
1977 (l)	—	PF63 875				
1977 (m)	Inc. above	—	—	—	—	900
1977 (m)	—	PF63 875				

Y# 151 100 ROUBLES
17.28 g., 0.900 Gold 0.500 oz. AGW **Series:** 1980 Olympics **Obv:** National arms divide CCCP with value below **Rev:** Lenin Stadium

Date	Mintage	F12	VF20	XF40	MS60	MS63
1978 (l)	62,000	—	—	—	—	900
1978 (l)	—	PF63 875				
1978 (m)	Inc. above	—	—	—	—	900
1978 (m)	—	PF63 875				

Y# 162 100 ROUBLES
17.28 g., 0.900 Gold 0.500 oz. AGW **Series:** 1980 Olympics **Obv:** National arms divide CCCP with value below **Rev:** Waterside Grandstand

Date	Mintage	F12	VF20	XF40	MS60	MS63
1978 Rare	—	—	—	—	—	—
1978 Proof, rare	—	—	—	—	—	—
1978 (l)	57,000	—	—	—	—	900
1978 (l)	—	PF63 875				
1978 (m) Rare	Inc. above	—	—	—	—	—
1978 (m) Proof, rare	—	—	—	—	—	—

Y# 173 100 ROUBLES
17.28 g., 0.900 Gold 0.500 oz. AGW **Series:** 1980 Olympics **Obv:** National arms divide CCCP with value below **Rev:** Velodrome Building

Date	Mintage	F12	VF20	XF40	MS60	MS63
1979 (l)	55,000	—	—	—	—	900
1979 (l)	—	PF63 875				
1979 (m) Rare	Inc. above	—	—	—	—	—
1979 (m)	—	PF63 875				

Y# 174 100 ROUBLES
17.28 g., 0.900 Gold 0.500 oz. AGW **Series:** 1980 Olympics **Obv:** National arms divide CCCP with value below **Rev:** Druzhba Sports Hall

Date	Mintage	F12	VF20	XF40	MS60	MS63
1979 (m)	54,000	—	—	—	—	900
1979 (l)	—	PF63 900				

Y# 186 100 ROUBLES
17.28 g., 0.900 Gold 0.500 oz. AGW **Series:** 1980 Olympics **Obv:** National arms divide CCCP with value below **Rev:** Torch

Date	Mintage	F12	VF20	XF40	MS60	MS63
1980 (m)	25,000	—	—	—	—	900
1980 (l)	—	PF63 900				

Y# 214 100 ROUBLES
17.28 g., 0.900 Gold 0.500 oz. AGW **Series:** 1980 Olympics **Subject:** 1000th Anniversary of Minting in Russia - Coin design of St. Vladimir (977-1015) **Obv:** National arms divide CCCP with value below **Rev:** Ancient coin design

Date	Mintage	F12	VF20	XF40	MS60	MS63
1988 (m)	14,000	—	—	—	—	900

Y# 226 100 ROUBLES
17.28 g., 0.900 Gold 0.500 oz. AGW **Series:** 1980 Olympics **Subject:** 500th Anniversary of Russian State **Obv:** National arms with CCCP and value below **Rev:** Seal of Ivan III

Date	Mintage	F12	VF20	XF40	MS60	MS63
1989 (m)	Est. 14000	PF63 900				

Y# 252 100 ROUBLES
17.28 g., 0.900 Gold 0.500 oz. AGW **Series:** 1980 Olympics **Subject:** 500th Anniversary of Russian State **Obv:** National arms divide CCCP with value below **Rev:** Peter the Great Monument

Date	Mintage	F12	VF20	XF40	MS60	MS63
1990 (m)	14,000	PF63 900				

Y# 278 100 ROUBLES
17.28 g., 0.900 Gold 0.500 oz. AGW **Series:** 1980 Olympics **Subject:** 500th Anniversary of Russian State **Obv:** National arms with CCCP and value below **Rev:** Tolstoi Monument

Date	Mintage	F12	VF20	XF40	MS60	MS63
1991 (m)	14,000	PF63 900				

Y# 288 100 ROUBLES
26.59 g., 0.585 Gold 0.5001 oz. AGW **Subject:** Bolshoi Ballet **Obv:** CCCP and value below building **Rev:** Ballerina

Date	Mintage	F12	VF20	XF40	MS60	MS63
1991 (l)	1,200	—	—	—	—	1,000

Y# 288a 100 ROUBLES
15.55 g., 0.999 Gold 0.4994 oz. AGW **Subject:** Bolshoi Ballet **Obv:** National arms with CCCP and value below **Rev:** Ballerina

Date	Mintage	F12	VF20	XF40	MS60	MS63
1991 (l)	1,500	PF63 950				

Y# 152 150 ROUBLES
15.54 g., 0.999 Platinum 0.4991 oz. APW **Series:** 1980 Olympics **Obv:** National arms divide CCCP with value below **Rev:** Moscow Olympic's logo within wreath, Olympic rings below

Date	Mintage	F12	VF20	XF40	MS60	MS63
1977 (l)	9,910	—	—	—	750	800
1977 (l)	—	PF63 800				

Y# 163 150 ROUBLES
15.54 g., 0.999 Platinum 0.4991 oz. APW **Series:** 1980 Olympics **Obv:** National arms divide CCCP with value below **Rev:** Throwing discus

Date	Mintage	F12	VF20	XF40	MS60	MS63
1978 (l)	13,000	—	—	—	750	800
1978 (l)	—	PF63 800				

Y# 175 150 ROUBLES
15.54 g., 0.999 Platinum 0.4991 oz. APW **Series:** 1980 Olympics **Obv:** National arms divide CCCP with value below **Rev:** Greek wrestlers

Date	Mintage	F12	VF20	XF40	MS60	MS63
1979 (l)	14,000	—	—	—	750	800
1979 (l)	19,000	PF63 800				

Y# 176 150 ROUBLES
15.54 g., 0.999 Platinum 0.4991 oz. APW **Series:** 1980 Olympics **Obv:** National arms divide CCCP with value below **Rev:** Roman chariot racers

Date	Mintage	F12	VF20	XF40	MS60	MS63
1979 (l)	9,728	—	—	—	750	800
1979 (l)	17,000	PF63 800				

Y# 187 150 ROUBLES
15.54 g., 0.999 Platinum 0.4991 oz. APW **Series:** 1980 Olympics **Obv:** National arms divide CCCP with value below **Rev:** Ancient Greek runners

Date	Mintage	F12	VF20	XF40	MS60	MS63
1980 (l)	7,820	—	—	—	750	800
1980 (l)	13,000	PF63 800				

Y# 215 150 ROUBLES
15.55 g., 0.999 Platinum 0.4994 oz. APW **Subject:** 1000th Anniversary of Russian Literature **Obv:** National arms with CCCP and value below **Rev:** Chronicler writing epic about Grand Duke Igor

Date	Mintage	F12	VF20	XF40	MS60	MS63
1988 (l)	16,000	PF63 750				

Y# 227 150 ROUBLES
15.55 g., 0.999 Platinum 0.4994 oz. APW **Subject:** 500th Anniversary of Russian State **Obv:** National arms with CCCP and value below **Rev:** Ugra River Encounter

Date	Mintage	F12	VF20	XF40	MS60	MS63
1989 (l)	Est. 16000	PF63 800				

Y# 245 150 ROUBLES
15.55 g., 0.999 Platinum 0.4994 oz. APW **Subject:** 250th Anniversary - Discovery of Russian America **Obv:** National arms with CCCP and value below **Rev:** Ship - St. Gavriil

Date	Mintage	F12	VF20	XF40	MS60	MS63
1990 (l)	6,500	PF63 900				

Y# 253 150 ROUBLES
15.55 g., 0.999 Platinum 0.4994 oz. APW **Subject:** 500th Anniversary of Russian State **Obv:** National arms with CCCP and value below **Rev:** Battle of Poltava River

Date	Mintage	F12	VF20	XF40	MS60	MS63
1990 (l)	16,000	PF63 800				

Y# 267 150 ROUBLES
15.55 g., 0.999 Platinum 0.4994 oz. APW **Subject:** 250th Anniversary - Discovery of Russian America **Obv:** National arms with CCCP and value below **Rev:** Bishop Veniaminov with ship in background

Date	Mintage	F12	VF20	XF40	MS60	MS63
1991 (l)	Est. 6500	PF63 900				

Y# 279 150 ROUBLES
17.50 g., 0.999 Platinum 0.5621 oz. APW **Subject:** 500th Anniversary of Russian State - War of Liberation Against Napoleon **Obv:** National arms with CCCP and value below **Rev:** Monument divides heads

Date	Mintage	F12	VF20	XF40	MS60	MS63
1991 (l)	16,000	PF63 950				

GOVERNMENT BANK ISSUES

Issued by Government Bank of the U.S.S.R but circulated only in Russian Federation

1991-1992

Y# 296 10 KOPEKS
2.00 g., Copper Clad Steel **Obv:** Kremlin Tower and Dome **Rev:** Value flanked by sprigs above date

Date	Mintage	F12	VF20	XF40	MS60	MS63
1991 M	—	0.30	0.50	1.00	2.00	—

Y# 292 50 KOPEKS
Copper-Nickel **Obv:** Kremlin Tower and Dome **Rev:** Value flanked by sprigs above date

Date	Mintage	F12	VF20	XF40	MS60	MS63
1991 Л	—	0.25	0.50	2.00	3.00	—

Y# 293 ROUBLE
Copper-Nickel **Obv:** Kremlin Tower and Dome **Rev:** Value flanked by sprigs above date

Date	Mintage	F12	VF20	XF40	MS60	MS63
1991 M	—	—	—	—	3.00	—

Y# 280 5 ROUBLES
Bi-Metallic Brass center in Copper-Nickel ring, 25 mm. **Series:** Wildlife **Obv:** Value flanked by sprigs within circle **Rev:** Owl flanked by grassy sprigs within circle **Edge:** Alternating reeded and smooth

Date	Mintage	F12	VF20	XF40	MS60	MS63
1991 Л	500,000	—	—	—	9.00	15.00

Y# 281 5 ROUBLES
Bi-Metallic Brass center in Copper-Nickel ring, 25 mm. **Series:** Wildlife **Obv:** Value flanked by sprigs within circle **Rev:** Mountain Goat within circle **Edge:** Alternating reeded and smooth

Date	Mintage	F12	VF20	XF40	MS60	MS63
1991 Л	500,000	—	—	—	9.00	15.00

Y# 294 5 ROUBLES
Copper-Nickel, 24 mm. **Obv:** Kremlin Tower and Dome **Rev:** Value flanked by sprigs above date **Edge:** Alternating reeded and smooth

Date	Mintage	F12	VF20	XF40	MS60	MS63
1991 Л	—	—	—	—	5.00	—
1991 M	—	—	—	—	7.00	—

Y# 295 10 ROUBLES
5.97 g., Bi-Metallic Aluminum-Bronze center in Copper-Nickel ring, 25 mm. **Obv:** Kremlin Tower and Dome **Rev:** Value flanked by sprigs above date **Edge:** Segmented reeding

Date	Mintage	F12	VF20	XF40	MS60	MS63
1991 LMD	—	0.50	2.00	3.00	5.00	—
1991 MMD	—	60.00	120	250	470	—
1992 Error	—	—	100	200	260	—

RUSSIAN FEDERATION

Issued by the Bank of Russia

STANDARD COINAGE

Y# 303 ROUBLE
Copper-Nickel, 31 mm. **Subject:** Rebirth of Russian Sovereignty and Democracy **Obv:** Tower and steeples, value below **Rev:** Winged Victory and small building with flag on top

Date	Mintage	VF20	XF40	MS60	MS63	MS65
1992 Л	700,000	—	—	—	2.50	—
1992 Л	—	PF63 5.00				

Y# 305 ROUBLE
Copper-Nickel, 31 mm. **Subject:** 110th Anniversary - Birth of Jacob Kolas **Obv:** Tower and steeples, value below **Rev:** Head 1/4 right **Edge:** Cyrillic lettering

Date	Mintage	VF20	XF40	MS60	MS63	MS65
1992 Л	700,000	—	—	—	3.00	—
1992 Л	300,000	PF63 5.00				

Y# 306 ROUBLE
Copper-Nickel, 31 mm. **Subject:** 190th Anniversary - Birth of Admiral Nakhimov **Obv:** Tower and steeples, value below **Rev:** Uniformed bust with back facing, ship at right **Edge:** Cyrillic lettering

Date	Mintage	VF20	XF40	MS60	MS63	MS65
1992 Л	700,000	—	—	—	3.00	—
1992 Л	—	PF63 5.00				

Y# 311 ROUBLE
3.30 g., Brass Clad Steel, 19.45 mm. **Obv:** Double headed eagle **Rev:** Value flanked by sprigs above date **Edge:** Plain

Date	Mintage	VF20	XF40	MS60	MS63	MS65
1992 ММД	—	—	0.50	1.00	2.00	—
1992 M	—	—	—	—	1.00	—
1992 Л	—	—	—	—	1.00	—

Y# 320 ROUBLE
Copper-Nickel, 31 mm. **Obv:** Tower and steeples, value below **Rev:** Head of Yanka Kupala left **Edge:** Cyrillic lettering

Date	Mintage	VF20	XF40	MS60	MS63	MS65
1992 Л	1,000,000	—	—	—	3.00	—
1992 Л Prooflike	200,000	—	—	—	—	3.50
1992 Л	—	PF65 5.00				

Y# 321 ROUBLE
Copper-Nickel, 31 mm. **Obv:** Double-headed eagle within beaded circle **Rev:** N.I. Lobachevsky 1/4 right

Date	Mintage	VF20	XF40	MS60	MS63	MS65
1992 M	1,000,000	—	—	—	3.00	—
1992 M Prooflike	500,000	—	—	—	—	3.50
1992 M	—	PF65 5.00				

Y# 319.1 ROUBLE
Copper-Nickel, 31 mm. **Subject:** Vladimir Ivanovich Vernadsky **Obv:** Double-headed eagle within beaded circle **Rev:** Head looking down with hand on head 1/4 right

Date	Mintage	VF20	XF40	MS60	MS63	MS65
1993 Л	450,000	—	—	—	3.00	—
1993	15,000	PF63 3.50				
1993 Л	—	PF63 5.50				

Y# 319.2 ROUBLE
Copper-Nickel, 31 mm. **Subject:** Vladimir Ivanovich Vernadsky **Obv:** Without mint mark below eagle's claw **Rev:** Head looking down with hand on head 1/4 right

Date	Mintage	VF20	XF40	MS60	MS63	MS65
1993	—	—	—	—	3.00	—
1993	—	PF63 15.00				

Y# 325 ROUBLE
Copper-Nickel, 31 mm. **Subject:** Gavrila Romanovich Derzhavin **Obv:** Double-headed eagle within beaded circle **Rev:** Bust 1/4 left above date and objects

Date	Mintage	VF20	XF40	MS60	MS63	MS65
1993 M	500,000	—	—	—	3.00	—
1993 M	—	PF65 5.00				

Y# 326 ROUBLE
Copper-Nickel, 31 mm. **Subject:** K.A. Timiryazev **Obv:** Double-headed eagle within beaded circle **Rev:** Bust facing, plant in vase at upper left

Date	Mintage	VF20	XF40	MS60	MS63	MS65
1993 M	500,000	—	—	—	3.00	—
1993 M	—	PF65 5.00				

Y# 327 ROUBLE
Copper-Nickel, 31 mm. **Subject:** V. Maikovski **Obv:** Kremlin Tower and Dome within beaded circle **Rev:** Head 1/4 left

Date	Mintage	VF20	XF40	MS60	MS63	MS65
1993 Л	500,000	—	—	—	3.00	—
1993 M	—	PF65 5.00				

Y# 335 ROUBLE
17.44 g., 0.900 Silver 0.5046 oz. ASW **Series:** Red Book Wildlife **Obv:** Double-headed eagle **Rev:** Tiger

Date	Mintage	VF20	XF40	MS60	MS63	MS65
1993	50,000	PF65 75.00				

Y# 336 ROUBLE

17.44 g., 0.900 Silver 0.5046 oz. ASW **Series:** Red Book Wildlife **Obv:** Double-headed eagle **Rev:** Owl flanked by grassy designs

Date	Mintage	VF20	XF40	MS60	MS63	MS65
1993	50,000	PF65 60.00				

Y# 337 ROUBLE

17.44 g., 0.900 Silver 0.5046 oz. ASW, 33 mm. **Series:** Red Book Wildlife **Obv:** Double-headed eagle **Rev:** Mountain goat

Date	Mintage	VF20	XF40	MS60	MS63	MS65
1993	50,000	PF65 60.00				

Y# 347 ROUBLE

Copper-Nickel, 31 mm. **Subject:** A.P. Borodin **Obv:** Double-headed eagle **Rev:** Bust facing 1/4 left, music notes and design in background

Date	Mintage	VF20	XF40	MS60	MS63	MS65
1993 M	500,000	—	—	—	3.00	—
1993 M	—	PF65 5.00				

Y# 348 ROUBLE

Copper-Nickel, 31 mm. **Subject:** I.S. Turgenev **Obv:** Double-headed eagle **Rev:** Head left

Date	Mintage	VF20	XF40	MS60	MS63	MS65
1993 Л	500,000	—	—	—	3.00	—
1993 Л	—	PF65 5.00				

Y# 372 ROUBLE

17.44 g., 0.900 Silver 0.5046 oz. ASW, 33 mm. **Series:** Wildlife **Obv:** Double-headed eagle **Rev:** Red-breasted Goose

Date	Mintage	VF20	XF40	MS60	MS63	MS65
1994	50,000	PF65 60.00				

Y# 373 ROUBLE

17.44 g., 0.900 Silver 0.5046 oz. ASW, 33 mm. **Series:** Wildlife **Obv:** Double-headed eagle **Rev:** Central Asia Cobra

Date	Mintage	VF20	XF40	MS60	MS63	MS65
1994	50,000	PF65 60.00				

Y# 374 ROUBLE

17.44 g., 0.900 Silver 0.5046 oz. ASW, 33 mm. **Series:** Wildlife **Obv:** Double-headed eagle **Rev:** Asiatic black bear

Date	Mintage	VF20	XF40	MS60	MS63	MS65
1994	50,000	PF65 50.00				

Y# 399 ROUBLE

Aluminum-Bronze, 19.5 mm. **Subject:** WWII Victory **Obv:** Double-headed eagle **Rev:** Mother Russia calling for volunteers

Date	Mintage	VF20	XF40	MS60	MS63	MS65
1995 (I) In sets only	200,000	—	—	—	2.00	—

Y# 446 ROUBLE

17.44 g., 0.900 Silver 0.5046 oz. ASW, 33 mm. **Series:** Wildlife **Obv:** Double-headed eagle **Rev:** Oriental Stork

Date	Mintage	VF20	XF40	MS60	MS63	MS65
1995	50,000	PF65 60.00				

Y# 447 ROUBLE

17.44 g., 0.900 Silver 0.5046 oz. ASW, 33 mm. **Series:** Wildlife **Obv:** Double-headed eagle **Rev:** Caucasian Black Grouse

Date	Mintage	VF20	XF40	MS60	MS63	MS65
1995	50,000	PF65 60.00				

Y# 448 ROUBLE

17.44 g., 0.900 Silver 0.5046 oz. ASW, 33 mm. **Series:** Wildlife **Obv:** Double-headed eagle **Rev:** Black Sea Dolphin

Date	Mintage	VF20	XF40	MS60	MS63	MS65
1995	50,000	PF65 60.00				

Y# 492 ROUBLE

17.44 g., 0.900 Silver 0.5046 oz. ASW, 33 mm. **Series:** Wildlife **Obv:** Double-headed eagle **Rev:** Peregrine Falcon

Date	Mintage	VF20	XF40	MS60	MS63	MS65
1996	50,000	PF65 60.00				

Y# 493 ROUBLE

17.44 g., 0.900 Silver 0.5046 oz. ASW, 33 mm. **Series:** Wildlife **Obv:** Double-headed eagle **Rev:** Turkmenistan Gecko

Date	Mintage	VF20	XF40	MS60	MS63	MS65
1996	50,000	PF65 60.00				

Y# 494 ROUBLE

17.44 g., 0.900 Silver 0.5046 oz. ASW, 33 mm. **Series:** Wildlife **Obv:** Double-headed eagle **Rev:** Blind Mole Rat

Date	Mintage	VF20	XF40	MS60	MS63	MS65
1996	50,000	PF65 60.00				

Y# 504 ROUBLE

Brass, 19.5 mm. **Subject:** 300th Anniversary - Russian Fleet **Obv:** Double-headed eagle **Rev:** Ship

Date	Mintage	VF20	XF40	MS60	MS63	MS65
1996 (I) In sets only	100,000	—	—	—	1.50	—

Y# 611 ROUBLE

17.44 g., 0.900 Silver 0.5046 oz. ASW, 33 mm. **Series:** Wildlife **Obv:** Double-headed eagle **Rev:** Two Lesser Flamingos

Date	Mintage	VF20	XF40	MS60	MS63	MS65
1996 (I) Proof	—	—	—	—	—	—
1997 (I)	15,000	PF65 60.00				

Y# 612 ROUBLE
17.44 g., 0.900 Silver 0.5046 oz. ASW, 33 mm. **Series:** Wildlife **Obv:** Double-headed eagle within beaded circle **Rev:** Mongolian Gazelle

Date	Mintage	VF20	XF40	MS60	MS63	MS65
1996 (l) Proof, rare	—	—	—	—	—	—
1997 (l)	15,000	PF65 60.00				

Y# 561 ROUBLE
8.53 g., 0.925 Silver 0.2537 oz. ASW, 25 mm. **Subject:** 850th Anniversary - Moscow **Obv:** Double-headed eagle within beaded circle **Rev:** Shield flanked by buildings

Date	Mintage	VF20	XF40	MS60	MS63	MS65
1997 (l)	20,000	—	—	—	—	12.00
1997 (m)	5,000	PF65 28.00				

Y# 562 ROUBLE
8.53 g., 0.925 Silver 0.2537 oz. ASW, 25 mm. **Subject:** 850th Anniversary - Moscow **Obv:** Double-headed eagle within beaded circle **Rev:** Cathedral of the Kazan Icon of the Holy Virgin

Date	Mintage	VF20	XF40	MS60	MS63	MS65
1997	20,000	—	—	—	—	12.00
1997 (m)	5,000	PF65 28.00				

Y# 563 ROUBLE
8.53 g., 0.925 Silver 0.2537 oz. ASW, 25 mm. **Subject:** 850th Anniversary - Moscow **Obv:** Double-headed eagle within beaded circle **Rev:** University and shield

Date	Mintage	VF20	XF40	MS60	MS63	MS65
1997 (l)	20,000	—	—	—	—	12.00
1997 (m)	5,000	PF65 28.00				

Y# 564 ROUBLE
8.53 g., 0.925 Silver 0.2537 oz. ASW, 25 mm. **Subject:** 850th Anniversary - Moscow **Obv:** Double-headed eagle within beaded circle **Rev:** Bolshoi Theatre and shield

Date	Mintage	VF20	XF40	MS60	MS63	MS65
1997	25,000	PF65 16.50				

Y# 565 ROUBLE
8.53 g., 0.925 Silver 0.2537 oz. ASW, 25 mm. **Subject:** 850th Anniversary - Moscow **Obv:** Double-headed eagle within beaded circle **Rev:** Resurrection Gate on Red Square

Date	Mintage	VF20	XF40	MS60	MS63	MS65
1997	25,000	PF65 16.50				

Y# 566 ROUBLE
8.53 g., 0.925 Silver 0.2537 oz. ASW, 25 mm. **Subject:** 850th Anniversary - Moscow **Obv:** Double-headed eagle within beaded circle **Rev:** Temple of Christ the Savior

Date	Mintage	VF20	XF40	MS60	MS63	MS65
1997	25,000	PF65 16.50				

Y# 576 ROUBLE
8.53 g., 0.925 Silver 0.2537 oz. ASW, 25 mm. **Subject:** World Soccer Championship - Paris 1998 **Obv:** Double-headed eagle **Rev:** Soccer players, Eiffel Tower and 1/2 globe

Date	Mintage	VF20	XF40	MS60	MS63	MS65
1997 (l)	20,000	PF65 16.50				

Y# 577 ROUBLE
8.53 g., 0.925 Silver 0.2537 oz. ASW, 25 mm. **Subject:** 1998 Winter Olympics **Obv:** Double-headed eagle within beaded circle **Rev:** Ice Hockey

Date	Mintage	VF20	XF40	MS60	MS63	MS65
1997 (m)	20,000	PF65 17.50				

Y# 578 ROUBLE
8.53 g., 0.925 Silver 0.2537 oz. ASW, 25 mm. **Subject:** 1998 Winter Olympics - Biathalon **Obv:** Double-headed eagle within beaded circle **Rev:** Skier within snow-flake design, marksman at left

Date	Mintage	VF20	XF40	MS60	MS63	MS65
1997 (m)	20,000	PF65 17.50				

Y# 579 ROUBLE
8.53 g., 0.925 Silver 0.2537 oz. ASW, 25 mm. **Subject:** 1897 Soccer **Obv:** Double-headed eagle within beaded circle **Rev:** Three soccer players

Date	Mintage	VF20	XF40	MS60	MS63	MS65
1997 (l)	25,000	PF65 17.50				

Y# 580 ROUBLE
8.53 g., 0.925 Silver 0.2537 oz. ASW, 25 mm. **Subject:** 1945 Soccer **Obv:** Double-headed eagle within beaded circle **Rev:** Goalie

Date	Mintage	VF20	XF40	MS60	MS63	MS65
1997 (l)	25,000	PF65 17.50				

Y# 581 ROUBLE
8.53 g., 0.925 Silver 0.2537 oz. ASW, 25 mm. **Subject:** 1956 Soccer **Obv:** Double-headed eagle within beaded circle **Rev:** Soccer players and kangaroo

Date	Mintage	VF20	XF40	MS60	MS63	MS65
1997 (l)	25,000	PF65 17.50				

Y# 582 ROUBLE
8.53 g., 0.925 Silver 0.2537 oz. ASW, 25 mm. **Subject:** 1960 Soccer **Obv:** Double-headed eagle within beaded circle **Rev:** Soccer players

Date	Mintage	VF20	XF40	MS60	MS63	MS65
1997 (l)	25,000	PF65 17.50				

Y# 583 ROUBLE
8.53 g., 0.925 Silver 0.2537 oz. ASW, 25 mm. **Subject:** 1988 Soccer **Obv:** Double-headed eagle **Rev:** Three players

Date	Mintage	VF20	XF40	MS60	MS63	MS65
1997 (l)	25,000	PF65 17.50				

Y# 613 ROUBLE
17.44 g., 0.900 Silver 0.5046 oz. ASW, 33 mm. **Series:** Wildlife **Obv:** Double-headed eagle **Rev:** European Bison

Date	Mintage	VF20	XF40	MS60	MS63	MS65
1997	15,000	PF63 60.00				

Y# 342 2 ROUBLES
15.87 g., 0.500 Silver 0.2551 oz. ASW **Subject:** Pavel Bazhov - Author of Ural Tales **Obv:** Double-headed eagle **Rev:** Head right

Date	Mintage	VF20	XF40	MS60	MS63	MS65
1994 (l)	250,000	PF63 12.50				

Y# 343 2 ROUBLES
15.87 g., 0.500 Silver 0.2551 oz. ASW **Subject:** Ivan Krylov - Author of Fables **Obv:** Double-headed eagle **Rev:** Head 1/4 left with assorted animals below

Date	Mintage	VF20	XF40	MS60	MS63	MS65
1994 (l)	250,000	PF63 12.50				

Y# 344 2 ROUBLES
15.87 g., 0.500 Silver 0.2551 oz. ASW **Subject:** Nikolai Gogol - Writer **Obv:** Double-headed eagle **Rev:** Head right

Date	Mintage	VF20	XF40	MS60	MS63	MS65
1994 (m)	250,000	PF63 12.50				

Y# 363 2 ROUBLES
15.87 g., 0.500 Silver 0.2551 oz. ASW **Obv:** Double-headed eagle within beaded circle **Rev:** Admiral Ushakov

Date	Mintage	VF20	XF40	MS60	MS63	MS65
1994 (m)	250,000	PF63 12.50				

Y# 364 2 ROUBLES
15.87 g., 0.500 Silver 0.2551 oz. ASW **Obv:** Double-headed eagle **Rev:** Ilya Repin, painter

Date	Mintage	VF20	XF40	MS60	MS63	MS65
1994 (m)	250,000	PF63 12.50				

Y# 377 2 ROUBLES
15.87 g., 0.500 Silver 0.2551 oz. ASW **Subject:** A.S. Griboyedov **Obv:** Double-headed eagle **Rev:** Bust 1/4 left divides dates

Date	Mintage	VF20	XF40	MS60	MS63	MS65
1995 (m)	200,000	PF63 14.50				

Y# A391 2 ROUBLES
15.87 g., 0.500 Silver 0.2551 oz. ASW **Obv:** Double-headed eagle **Rev:** Victory Parade **Note:** Mule of 1994 eagle obverse with Y#391 Victory Parade reverse.

Date	Mintage	VF20	XF40	MS60	MS63	MS65
1995	—	PF63 250				

Y# 391 2 ROUBLES
15.87 g., 0.500 Silver 0.2551 oz. ASW **Subject:** WWII Victory Parade **Obv:** Kremlin Tower and Dome within beaded circle **Rev:** Victory Parade

Date	Mintage	VF20	XF40	MS60	MS63	MS65
1995 (l)	200,000	PF63 30.00				

Y# 392 2 ROUBLES
15.87 g., 0.500 Silver 0.2551 oz. ASW **Series:** WWII **Obv:** Kremlin Tower and Dome within beaded circle **Rev:** Marshal Zhukov on horseback

Date	Mintage	VF20	XF40	MS60	MS63	MS65
1995 (m)	200,000	PF63 30.00				

Y# 393 2 ROUBLES
15.87 g., 0.500 Silver 0.2551 oz. ASW **Series:** WWII **Obv:** Kremlin Tower and Dome within beaded circle **Rev:** Nuremberg trial

Date	Mintage	VF20	XF40	MS60	MS63	MS65
1995 (l)	200,000	PF63 30.00				

Y# 414 2 ROUBLES
15.87 g., 0.500 Silver 0.2551 oz. ASW **Subject:** Sergei Esenin **Obv:** Double-headed eagle **Rev:** Head 1/4 right flanked by designs

Date	Mintage	VF20	XF40	MS60	MS63	MS65
1995 (l)	200,000	PF63 14.50				

Y# 415 2 ROUBLES
15.87 g., 0.500 Silver 0.2551 oz. ASW **Subject:** Field Marshal Kutuzov **Obv:** Double-headed eagle **Rev:** Bust 3/4 left

Date	Mintage	VF20	XF40	MS60	MS63	MS65
1995 (m)	200,000	PF63 13.50				

Y# 449 2 ROUBLES
15.87 g., 0.500 Silver 0.2551 oz. ASW **Subject:** Ivan Bunin **Obv:** Double-headed eagle **Rev:** Bust 1/4 right divides buildings and dates

Date	Mintage	VF20	XF40	MS60	MS63	MS65
1995 (m)	200,000	PF63 14.50				

Y# 514 2 ROUBLES
15.87 g., 0.500 Silver 0.2551 oz. ASW **Subject:** Nikolai Nekrasov **Obv:** Double-headed eagle **Rev:** Bust 1/4 right with building, horse in harness, book and quill

Date	Mintage	VF20	XF40	MS60	MS63	MS65
1996 (m)	50,000	PF63 25.00				

Y# 515 2 ROUBLES
15.87 g., 0.500 Silver 0.2551 oz. ASW **Subject:** Fyodor Dostoevsky **Obv:** Double-headed eagle **Rev:** Bust facing with standing figure holding child, building and dates

Date	Mintage	VF20	XF40	MS60	MS63	MS65
1996 (l)	50,000	PF63 25.00				

Y# 549 2 ROUBLES

15.87 g., 0.500 Silver 0.2551 oz. ASW **Subject:** N.E. Zhukovsky **Obv:** Double-headed eagle **Rev:** Head 1/4 left

Date	Mintage	VF20	XF40	MS60	MS63	MS65
1997 (l)	50,000	PF63 25.00				

Y# 550 2 ROUBLES

15.87 g., 0.500 Silver 0.2551 oz. ASW **Subject:** A.N. Skryabin - Musician **Obv:** Double-headed eagle **Rev:** Bust 3/4 right divides music notes and design

Date	Mintage	VF20	XF40	MS60	MS63	MS65
1997 (m)	50,000	PF63 25.00				

Y# 551 2 ROUBLES

15.87 g., 0.500 Silver 0.2551 oz. ASW **Subject:** A.L. Chizhevsky **Obv:** Double-headed eagle **Rev:** Bust with chin on hand 1/4 right, trees, sun and kneeling figure at right

Date	Mintage	VF20	XF40	MS60	MS63	MS65
1997 (m)	10,000	PF63 80.00				

Y# 558 2 ROUBLES

15.87 g., 0.500 Silver 0.2551 oz. ASW **Obv:** Double-headed eagle **Rev:** Sailing ship and Afanasi Nikitin

Date	Mintage	VF20	XF40	MS60	MS63	MS65
1997 (m)	7,500	PF63 150				

Y# 559 2 ROUBLES

15.87 g., 0.500 Silver 0.2551 oz. ASW **Subject:** Afanasi Nikitin - Indian Scene **Obv:** Double-headed eagle **Rev:** Head facing in center of assorted animal and ship designs

Date	Mintage	VF20	XF40	MS60	MS63	MS65
1997 (l)	7,500	PF63 155				

Y# 584 2 ROUBLES

15.87 g., 0.500 Silver 0.2551 oz. ASW **Subject:** A.K. Savrasov **Obv:** Double-headed eagle **Rev:** Head facing within square at upper left of church and trees

Date	Mintage	VF20	XF40	MS60	MS63	MS65
1997 (m)	15,000	PF63 40.00				

Y# 297 3 ROUBLES

Copper-Nickel, 33 mm. **Subject:** International Space Year **Obv:** Tower and steeples, value below **Rev:** Floating nude figure with planet at right **Edge:** Cyrillic lettering

Date	Mintage	VF20	XF40	MS60	MS63	MS65
1992 (m)	600,000	—	—	—	3.50	5.00
1992 (m)	—	PF63 6.50				

Y# 298 3 ROUBLES

Copper-Nickel, 33 mm. **Subject:** Battle of Chudskoye Lake **Obv:** Tower and steeples, value below **Rev:** Armored figures in battle **Edge:** Cyrillic lettering

Date	Mintage	VF20	XF40	MS60	MS63	MS65
1992 (l)	600,000	—	—	—	3.50	—
1992 (l)	—	PF63 5.50				

Y# 304 3 ROUBLES

Copper-Nickel, 33 mm. **Series:** WWII **Obv:** Tower and steeples, value below **Rev:** Allied supply convoys to Murmansk

Date	Mintage	VF20	XF40	MS60	MS63	MS65
1992 (l)	400,000	PF63 5.50				

Y# 317 3 ROUBLES

Copper-Nickel, 33 mm. **Subject:** 1st Anniversary - Defeat of Communist Attempted Coup **Obv:** Tower and steeples, value below **Rev:** Winged Victory holding harp-shaped shield above sprigs, building at right

Date	Mintage	VF20	XF40	MS60	MS63	MS65
1992 (m)	1,000,000	—	—	—	3.50	5.00
1992 (m) Prooflike	—	—	—	—	4.00	6.00
1992 (m)	—	PF63 6.50				

Y# 349 3 ROUBLES

34.56 g., 0.900 Silver 1.000 oz. ASW, 39 mm. **Obv:** Double-headed eagle **Rev:** St. Petersburg Trinity Cathedral

Date	Mintage	VF20	XF40	MS60	MS63	MS65
1992	40,000	PF63 42.50				

Y# 350 3 ROUBLES

34.56 g., 0.900 Silver 1.000 oz. ASW, 39 mm. **Obv:** Double-headed eagle **Rev:** St. Petersburg Academy of Science and ship

Date	Mintage	VF20	XF40	MS60	MS63	MS65
1992	40,000	PF63 42.50				

Y# 318 3 ROUBLES

Copper-Nickel, 33 mm. **Subject:** Battle of Stalingrad **Obv:** Kremlin Tower and Dome within beaded circle **Rev:** Half length figure looking right, monument at right

Date	Mintage	VF20	XF40	MS60	MS63	MS65
1993 (m)	150,000	—	—	—	3.50	—
1993 (m) Prooflike	—	—	—	—	4.00	—
1993 (m)	—	PF63 5.50				

Y# 323 3 ROUBLES

34.56 g., 0.900 Silver 1.000 oz. ASW, 39 mm. **Subject:** Bolshoi Ballet **Obv:** Double-headed eagle **Rev:** Ballet couple **Note:** Struck at Moscow without mint mark.

Date	Mintage	VF20	XF40	MS60	MS63	MS65
1993	125,000	—	—	—	35.00	—
1993	—	PF63 40.00				

Y# 328 3 ROUBLES
Copper-Nickel, 33 mm. **Subject:** 50th Anniversary - Battle of Kursk **Obv:** Kremlin Tower and Dome **Rev:** Armored tank and map **Edge:** Cyrillic lettering

Date	Mintage	VF20	XF40	MS60	MS63	MS65
1993 (l)	500,000	—	—	—	3.50	—
1993 (l)	—	PF63 5.50				

Y# 340 3 ROUBLES
Copper-Nickel, 33 mm. **Subject:** 50th Anniversary - Kiev's Liberation from German Fascists **Obv:** Kremlin Tower and Dome within beaded circle **Rev:** Variety of monuments

Date	Mintage	VF20	XF40	MS60	MS63	MS65
1993 (m)	500,000	—	—	—	3.50	—
1993 (m)	—	PF63 5.50				

Y# 351 3 ROUBLES
34.56 g., 0.900 Silver 1.000 oz. ASW, 39 mm. **Series:** Olympics **Obv:** Double-headed eagle **Rev:** Soccer

Date	Mintage	VF20	XF40	MS60	MS63	MS65
1993	40,000	PF63 42.50				

Y# 409 3 ROUBLES
34.56 g., 0.900 Silver 1.000 oz. ASW, 39 mm. **Series:** Wildlife **Obv:** Double-headed eagle **Rev:** Bear

Date	Mintage	VF20	XF40	MS60	MS63	MS65
1993	5,000	PF63 230				

Y# 450 3 ROUBLES
34.56 g., 0.900 Silver 1.000 oz. ASW, 39 mm. **Subject:** Ballet **Obv:** Double-headed eagle **Rev:** Ballerina and building

Date	Mintage	VF20	XF40	MS60	MS63	MS65
1993	45,000	PF63 50.00				

Y# 451 3 ROUBLES
34.56 g., 0.900 Silver 1.000 oz. ASW, 39 mm. **Subject:** Fedor Schalyapin **Obv:** Double-headed eagle **Rev:** Half-length bust left and building

Date	Mintage	VF20	XF40	MS60	MS63	MS65
1993	45,000	PF63 50.00				

Y# 456 3 ROUBLES
34.56 g., 0.900 Silver 1.000 oz. ASW, 39 mm. **Obv:** Double-headed eagle **Rev:** Vasilyblazheny Cathedral in Moscow

Date	Mintage	VF20	XF40	MS60	MS63	MS65
1993	30,000	PF63 35.00				

Y# 457 3 ROUBLES
34.56 g., 0.900 Silver 1.000 oz. ASW, 39 mm. **Obv:** Double-headed eagle **Rev:** Ivan the Great Cathedral, Moscow

Date	Mintage	VF20	XF40	MS60	MS63	MS65
1993	30,000	PF63 35.00				

Y# 464 3 ROUBLES
34.56 g., 0.900 Silver 1.000 oz. ASW, 39 mm. **Obv:** Double-headed eagle **Rev:** Ships Nadezhda and Neva on world voyage

Date	Mintage	VF20	XF40	MS60	MS63	MS65
1993	25,000	PF63 37.50				

Y# 465 3 ROUBLES
34.56 g., 0.900 Silver 1.000 oz. ASW, 39 mm. **Subject:** Russo-French Space Flight **Rev:** Cosmonauts holding flags above 1/4 globe

Date	Mintage	VF20	XF40	MS60	MS63	MS65
1993	40,000	PF63 37.50				

Y# 341 3 ROUBLES
Copper-Nickel, 33 mm. **Subject:** 50th Anniversary - Battle of Leningrad **Obv:** Kremlin Tower and Dome within beaded circle **Rev:** Soldiers, monument and tower

Date	Mintage	VF20	XF40	MS60	MS63	MS65
1994 (l)	500,000	PF63 5.50				

Y# 345 3 ROUBLES
34.56 g., 0.900 Silver 1.000 oz. ASW, 39 mm. **Obv:** Double-headed eagle **Rev:** Cathedral of the Nativity of the Mother of God

Date	Mintage	VF20	XF40	MS60	MS63	MS65
1994	30,000	PF63 35.00				

Y# 346 3 ROUBLES
Copper-Nickel **Subject:** 50th Anniversary - Liberation of Sevastopol from German Fascists **Obv:** Kremlin Tower and Dome within beaded circle **Rev:** Sevastopol scene, stylized soldier above

Date	Mintage	VF20	XF40	MS60	MS63	MS65
1994 (l)	250,000	PF63 5.50				

Y# 362 3 ROUBLES
Copper-Nickel, 33 mm. **Subject:** Normandy Invasion **Obv:** Kremlin Tower and Dome **Rev:** World globe with date in center divides designs

Date	Mintage	VF20	XF40	MS60	MS63	MS65
1994 (m)	250,000	PF63 5.50				

Y# 365 3 ROUBLES
Copper-Nickel, 33 mm. **Series:** WWII **Subject:** Partisans Activities **Obv:** Kremlin Tower and Dome within beaded circle **Rev:** Figures with weapons in bushes **Edge:** Cyrillic lettering

Date	Mintage	VF20	XF40	MS60	MS63	MS65
1994 (m)	250,000	PF63 5.50				

Y# 366 3 ROUBLES
Copper-Nickel, 33 mm. **Series:** WWII **Subject:** Liberation of Belgrade **Obv:** Kremlin Tower and Dome within beaded circle **Rev:** Armored figures marching, building in background

Date	Mintage	VF20	XF40	MS60	MS63	MS65
1994 (m)	250,000	PF63 5.50				

Y# 380 3 ROUBLES
Copper-Nickel, 33 mm. **Series:** WWII **Subject:** Capture of Konigsberg **Obv:** Kremlin Tower and Dome within beaded circle **Rev:** Crouched soldiers in front of building

Date	Mintage	VF20	XF40	MS60	MS63	MS65
1994 (m) Proof, error	—	PF63 50.00				
1995 (m)	200,000	PF63 6.50				

Y# 389 3 ROUBLES
34.56 g., 0.900 Silver 1.000 oz. ASW, 39 mm. **Subject:** Trans-Siberian railway **Obv:** Double-headed eagle **Rev:** Bridge, train and map

Date	Mintage	VF20	XF40	MS60	MS63	MS65
1994	25,000	PF63 40.00				

Y# 405 3 ROUBLES
34.56 g., 0.900 Silver 1.000 oz. ASW, 39 mm. **Subject:** Ballet **Obv:** Double-headed eagle **Rev:** Ballet couple

Date	Mintage	VF20	XF40	MS60	MS63	MS65
1994	40,000	PF63 40.00				

Y# 458 3 ROUBLES
34.56 g., 0.900 Silver 1.000 oz. ASW, 39 mm. **Obv:** Double-headed eagle **Rev:** Pocrov Church on the Neri

Date	Mintage	VF20	XF40	MS60	MS63	MS65
1994	30,000	PF63 40.00				

Y# 460 3 ROUBLES
34.56 g., 0.900 Silver 1.000 oz. ASW, 39 mm. **Series:** Wildlife **Obv:** Double-headed eagle **Rev:** Sable on tree limb

Date	Mintage	VF20	XF40	MS60	MS63	MS65
1994	10,000	PF63 65.00				

Y# 466 3 ROUBLES
34.56 g., 0.900 Silver 1.000 oz. ASW, 39 mm. **Subject:** Discovery of Antarctica **Rev:** Sailing ships Vostok and Mirny

Date	Mintage	VF20	XF40	MS60	MS63	MS65
1994	25,000	PF63 55.00				

Y# 513 3 ROUBLES
34.56 g., 0.900 Silver 1.000 oz. ASW, 39 mm. **Obv:** Double-headed eagle **Rev:** Smolny Institute & Monastery - St. Petersburg

Date	Mintage	VF20	XF40	MS60	MS63	MS65
1994	30,000	PF63 40.00				

Y# 520 3 ROUBLES
34.56 g., 0.900 Silver 1.000 oz. ASW, 39 mm. **Obv:** Double-headed eagle **Rev:** Ryazin Kremlin, city view

Date	Mintage	VF20	XF40	MS60	MS63	MS65
1994	30,000	PF63 40.00				

Y# 528 3 ROUBLES
34.56 g., 0.900 Silver 1.000 oz. ASW, 39 mm. **Subject:** Vassili Ivanovich Surikov **Obv:** Double-headed eagle **Rev:** Head facing above Siberian sled scene

Date	Mintage	VF20	XF40	MS60	MS63	MS65
1994	40,000	PF63 70.00				

Y# 529 3 ROUBLES
34.56 g., 0.900 Silver 1.000 oz. ASW, 39 mm. **Subject:** Alexander Andreyevich Ivannov **Obv:** Double-headed eagle **Rev:** Head facing 1/4 right above assorted figures

Date	Mintage	VF20	XF40	MS60	MS63	MS65
1994	40,000	PF63 70.00				

Y# 378 3 ROUBLES
Copper-Nickel, 33 mm. **Subject:** Liberation of Warsaw **Obv:** Kremlin Tower and Dome within beaded circle **Rev:** Standing figures holding flag

Date	Mintage	VF20	XF40	MS60	MS63	MS65
1995 (l)	200,000	PF63 6.00				

Y# 379 3 ROUBLES

Copper-Nickel, 33 mm. **Subject:** Liberation of Budapest **Obv:** Kremlin Tower and Dome within beaded circle **Rev:** Soldiers and building

Date	Mintage	VF20	XF40	MS60	MS63	MS65
1995 (m)	200,000	PF63 6.00				

Y# 381 3 ROUBLES

Copper-Nickel, 33 mm. **Series:** WWII **Subject:** Capture of Vienna **Obv:** Kremlin Tower and Dome within beaded circle **Rev:** Two uniformed figures with weapons, one holding flag, building in background

Date	Mintage	VF20	XF40	MS60	MS63	MS65
1995 (l)	200,000	PF63 6.50				

Y# 382 3 ROUBLES

Copper-Nickel, 33 mm. **Series:** WWII **Obv:** Kremlin Tower and Dome within beaded circle **Rev:** American and Russian soldiers **Note:** 50-star U.S.A. flag.

Date	Mintage	VF20	XF40	MS60	MS63	MS65
1995 (m)	200,000	PF63 6.00				

Y# 383 3 ROUBLES

Copper-Nickel, 33 mm. **Series:** WWII **Subject:** Capture of Berlin **Obv:** Kremlin Tower and Dome within beaded circle **Rev:** Soldiers in front of building

Date	Mintage	VF20	XF40	MS60	MS63	MS65
1995 (l)	200,000	PF63 6.50				

Y# 384 3 ROUBLES

Copper-Nickel, 33 mm. **Series:** WWII **Subject:** German Surrender **Obv:** Kremlin Tower and Dome within beaded circle **Rev:** Seated figures at table below flags

Date	Mintage	VF20	XF40	MS60	MS63	MS65
1995 (l)	200,000	PF63 6.50				

Y# 385 3 ROUBLES

Copper-Nickel, 33 mm. **Series:** WWII **Subject:** Liberation of Prague **Obv:** Kremlin Tower and Dome within beaded circle **Rev:** Armored tank divides building and standing figures

Date	Mintage	VF20	XF40	MS60	MS63	MS65
1995 (m)	200,000	PF63 6.50				

Y# 386 3 ROUBLES

Copper-Nickel, 33 mm. **Series:** WWII **Subject:** Surrender of Japanese Army in Kwantung **Obv:** Kremlin Tower and Dome within beaded circle **Rev:** Surrender scene

Date	Mintage	VF20	XF40	MS60	MS63	MS65
1995 (m)	200,000	PF63 6.50				

Y# 387 3 ROUBLES

Copper-Nickel, 33 mm. **Series:** WWII **Obv:** Kremlin Tower and Dome within beaded circle **Rev:** Japanese formal surrender on Battleship U.S.S. Missouri

Date	Mintage	VF20	XF40	MS60	MS63	MS65
1995 (l)	200,000	PF63 6.50				

Y# 388 3 ROUBLES

34.56 g., 0.900 Silver 1.000 oz. ASW, 39 mm. **Obv:** Double-headed eagle **Rev:** Vladimir's Golden Gate

Date	Mintage	VF20	XF40	MS60	MS63	MS65
1995	30,000	PF63 42.50				

Y# 394 3 ROUBLES

34.56 g., 0.900 Silver 1.000 oz. ASW, 39 mm. **Subject:** Ballet **Obv:** Double-headed eagle **Rev:** Scene from Sleeping Beauty

Date	Mintage	VF20	XF40	MS60	MS63	MS65
1995	40,000	PF63 45.00				

Y# 407 3 ROUBLES

34.56 g., 0.900 Silver 1.000 oz. ASW, 39 mm. **Subject:** 50th Anniversary - United Nations **Obv:** Double-headed eagle **Rev:** Blacksmith, UN logo at top, building at left

Date	Mintage	VF20	XF40	MS60	MS63	MS65
1995	20,000	PF63 47.50				

Y# 445 3 ROUBLES

34.56 g., 0.900 Silver 1.000 oz. ASW, 39 mm. **Obv:** Double-headed eagle **Rev:** Smolensk Kremlin

Date	Mintage	VF20	XF40	MS60	MS63	MS65
1995	30,000	PF63 40.00				

Y# 459 3 ROUBLES

34.56 g., 0.900 Silver 1.000 oz. ASW **Obv:** Double-headed eagle **Rev:** Kizhi Church on Onega Lake

Date	Mintage	VF20	XF40	MS60	MS63	MS65
1995	30,000	PF63 40.00				

Y# 461 3 ROUBLES
34.56 g., 0.900 Silver 1.000 oz. ASW **Subject:** Arctic Explorers 1733-43 **Obv:** Double-headed eagle **Rev:** Busts of arctic explorers, ship, map and sled dogs

Date	Mintage	VF20	XF40	MS60	MS63	MS65
1995	25,000	PF63 45.00				

Y# 462 3 ROUBLES
34.56 g., 0.900 Silver 1.000 oz. ASW **Subject:** Roald Amundsen - Arctic Explorer **Obv:** Double-headed eagle **Rev:** Head left, ship and designs

Date	Mintage	VF20	XF40	MS60	MS63	MS65
1995	25,000	PF63 45.00				

Y# 463 3 ROUBLES
34.56 g., 0.900 Silver 1.000 oz. ASW **Subject:** 200th Anniversary - Russian National Library **Obv:** Double-headed eagle **Rev:** Book, scroll and quill in front of building

Date	Mintage	VF20	XF40	MS60	MS63	MS65
1995	15,000	PF63 50.00				

Y# 467 3 ROUBLES
34.56 g., 0.900 Silver 1.000 oz. ASW **Subject:** Millennium of Belgorod **Obv:** Double-headed eagle **Rev:** Scroll and building below crowned shield

Date	Mintage	VF20	XF40	MS60	MS63	MS65
1995	30,000	PF63 37.50				

Y# 468 3 ROUBLES
34.56 g., 0.900 Silver 1.000 oz. ASW **Subject:** Russian Millennium **Obv:** Double-headed eagle within beaded circle **Rev:** Novgorod Kremlin

Date	Mintage	VF20	XF40	MS60	MS63	MS65
1995	40,000	PF63 37.50				

Y# 469 3 ROUBLES
34.56 g., 0.900 Silver 1.000 oz. ASW **Subject:** Russian Millennium **Obv:** Double-headed eagle **Rev:** Spaso-Preobrazhensky Cathedral

Date	Mintage	VF20	XF40	MS60	MS63	MS65
1995	40,000	PF63 35.00				

Y# 473 3 ROUBLES
34.56 g., 0.900 Silver 1.000 oz. ASW **Series:** Wildlife **Obv:** Double-headed eagle **Rev:** Sable on branch

Date	Mintage	VF20	XF40	MS60	MS63	MS65
1995 (l) Matte	500,000	—	—	60.00	—	—
1995 (m) Matte	500,000	—	—	60.00	—	—

Y# 474 3 ROUBLES
34.56 g., 0.900 Silver 1.000 oz. ASW **Series:** Wildlife **Obv:** Double-headed eagle **Rev:** Lynx

Date	Mintage	VF20	XF40	MS60	MS63	MS65
1995 (l)	25,000	PF63 75.00				

Y# 470 3 ROUBLES
34.56 g., 0.900 Silver 1.000 oz. ASW **Obv:** Double-headed eagle **Rev:** Ilya the Prophet's Church in Yaroslavl

Date	Mintage	VF20	XF40	MS60	MS63	MS65
1996	30,000	PF63 42.50				

Y# 477 3 ROUBLES
34.56 g., 0.900 Silver 1.000 oz. ASW **Subject:** Combat between Peresvet and Chelubey **Obv:** Double-headed eagle **Rev:** Two armored figures on rearing horses with swords

Date	Mintage	VF20	XF40	MS60	MS63	MS65
1996	40,000	PF63 35.00				

Y# 478 3 ROUBLES
34.56 g., 0.900 Silver 1.000 oz. ASW **Obv:** Double-headed eagle **Rev:** Old Testament Trinity icon

Date	Mintage	VF20	XF40	MS60	MS63	MS65
1996	40,000	PF63 35.00				

Y# 482 3 ROUBLES
34.56 g., 0.900 Silver 1.000 oz. ASW **Subject:** Ballet **Obv:** Double-headed eagle **Rev:** Nutcracker Ballet

Date	Mintage	VF20	XF40	MS60	MS63	MS65
1996	25,000	PF63 40.00				

Y# 483 3 ROUBLES
34.56 g., 0.900 Silver 1.000 oz. ASW **Subject:** Ballet - Nutcracker **Obv:** Double-headed eagle **Rev:** Duel with the Mouse King

Date	Mintage	VF20	XF40	MS60	MS63	MS65
1996	25,000	PF63 40.00				

Y# 490 3 ROUBLES
34.56 g., 0.900 Silver 1.000 oz. ASW **Obv:** Double-headed eagle **Rev:** Kremlin of Kazan

Date	Mintage	VF20	XF40	MS60	MS63	MS65
1996	25,000	PF63 45.00				

Y# 491 3 ROUBLES
34.56 g., 0.900 Silver 1.000 oz. ASW **Obv:** Double-headed eagle **Rev:** Kremlin of Tobolsk - city view

Date	Mintage	VF20	XF40	MS60	MS63	MS65
1996	25,000	PF63 42.50				

Y# 510 3 ROUBLES
34.56 g., 0.900 Silver 1.000 oz. ASW **Obv:** Double-headed eagle **Rev:** Alexander Column and Hermitage

Date	Mintage	VF20	XF40	MS60	MS63	MS65
1996	15,000	PF63 50.00				

Y# 511 3 ROUBLES
34.56 g., 0.900 Silver 1.000 oz. ASW **Subject:** 300th Anniversary - Russian Navy **Obv:** Double-headed eagle **Rev:** Icebreaker ship and bust left

Date	Mintage	VF20	XF40	MS60	MS63	MS65
1996	10,000	PF63 55.00				

Y# 512 3 ROUBLES
34.56 g., 0.900 Silver 1.000 oz. ASW **Subject:** 300th Anniversary - Russian Navy **Obv:** Double-headed eagle **Rev:** Carrier ship below bust facing

Date	Mintage	VF20	XF40	MS60	MS63	MS65
1996	10,000	PF63 55.00				

Y# 535 3 ROUBLES
34.56 g., 0.900 Silver 1.000 oz. ASW **Series:** Wildlife **Obv:** Double-headed eagle **Rev:** Tiger

Date	Mintage	VF20	XF40	MS60	MS63	MS65
1996	10,000	PF63 65.00				

Y# 552 3 ROUBLES
34.56 g., 0.900 Silver 1.000 oz. ASW **Subject:** 850th Anniversary - Moscow **Obv:** Double-headed eagle **Rev:** Workers building original Moscow, modern skyline behind

Date	Mintage	VF20	XF40	MS60	MS63	MS65
1997	40,000	PF63 37.50				

Y# 553 3 ROUBLES
34.56 g., 0.900 Silver 1.000 oz. ASW **Subject:** 850th Anniversary - Moscow **Obv:** Double-headed eagle **Rev:** Riverside city view

Date	Mintage	VF20	XF40	MS60	MS63	MS65
1997	40,000	PF63 37.50				

Y# 560 3 ROUBLES
34.56 g., 0.900 Silver 1.000 oz. ASW **Obv:** Double-headed eagle within beaded circle **Rev:** Monastery of the Saint Virgin in Yaroslavl

Date	Mintage	VF20	XF40	MS60	MS63	MS65
1997	15,000	PF63 45.00				

Y# 567 3 ROUBLES
34.56 g., 0.900 Silver 1.000 oz. ASW **Subject:** Ballet - Swan Lake **Obv:** Double-headed eagle **Rev:** Four ballerinas below crowned swan

Date	Mintage	VF20	XF40	MS60	MS63	MS65
1997	10,000	PF63 55.00				

Y# 568 3 ROUBLES
34.56 g., 0.900 Silver 1.000 oz. ASW **Subject:** Ballet - Swan Lake **Obv:** Double-headed eagle **Rev:** Rothbart and Prince Siegfried

Date	Mintage	VF20	XF40	MS60	MS63	MS65
1997	10,000	PF63 55.00				

Y# 575 3 ROUBLES

34.56 g., 0.900 Silver 1.000 oz. ASW **Subject:** First Anniversary - Russian-Belarus Treaty **Obv:** Double-headed eagle **Rev:** Two city views

Date	Mintage	VF20	XF40	MS60	MS63	MS65
1997	10,000	**PF63** 55.00				

Y# 585 3 ROUBLES

34.56 g., 0.900 Silver 1.000 oz. ASW **Subject:** Underroot Nativity of the Virgin Hermitage Monastery of Kursk **Obv:** Double-headed eagle **Rev:** Painting above monastery

Date	Mintage	VF20	XF40	MS60	MS63	MS65
1997	15,000	**PF63** 50.00				

Y# 586 3 ROUBLES

34.56 g., 0.900 Silver 1.000 oz. ASW **Subject:** Serge Julievich Witte **Obv:** Double-headed eagle **Rev:** Bust facing

Date	Mintage	VF20	XF40	MS60	MS63	MS65
1997	10,000	**PF63** 55.00				

Y# 587 3 ROUBLES

34.56 g., 0.900 Silver 1.000 oz. ASW **Subject:** Year of Reconciliation **Obv:** Double-headed eagle **Rev:** Standing figure facing holding quill and shield

Date	Mintage	VF20	XF40	MS60	MS63	MS65
1997	10,000	**PF63** 60.00				

Y# 591 3 ROUBLES

34.56 g., 0.900 Silver 1.000 oz. ASW **Obv:** Double-headed eagle **Rev:** Solovetski Monastery

Date	Mintage	VF20	XF40	MS60	MS63	MS65
1997	15,000	**PF63** 50.00				

Y# 593 3 ROUBLES

34.56 g., 0.900 Silver 1.000 oz. ASW **Series:** Wildlife **Obv:** Double-headed eagle **Rev:** Polar bear watching walrus

Date	Mintage	VF20	XF40	MS60	MS63	MS65
1997	10,000	**PF63** 100				

Y# 312 5 ROUBLES

4.10 g., Brass Clad Steel, 21.9 mm. **Obv:** Double-headed eagle **Rev:** Value flanked by sprigs above date

Date	Mintage	VF20	XF40	MS60	MS63	MS65
1992 ММД	—	—	—	3.00	—	—
1992 М	—	—	—	2.00	—	—
1992 Л	—	—	—	2.00	—	—

Y# 322 5 ROUBLES

Copper-Nickel, 35 mm. **Obv:** Value flanked by sprigs above date **Rev:** Kazakhstan

Date	Mintage	VF20	XF40	MS60	MS63	MS65
1992 (l)	300,000	—	—	4.00	5.00	—
1992 (l)	200,000	**PF63** 10.00				

Y# 324 5 ROUBLES

Copper-Nickel, 35 mm. **Subject:** Troitsk - Sergievsk Monastery **Obv:** Double-headed eagle **Rev:** Monastery

Date	Mintage	VF20	XF40	MS60	MS63	MS65
1993 (l)	500,000	—	—	6.00	7.00	—
1993 (l)	—	**PF63** 9.00				

Y# 339 5 ROUBLES

Copper-Nickel, 35 mm. **Subject:** 2500 Years of Merv Minaret, Turkmenistan **Obv:** Value flanked by sprigs above date **Rev:** Building

Date	Mintage	VF20	XF40	MS60	MS63	MS65
1993 (l)	500,000	—	—	4.00	5.00	—
1993 (l)	—	**PF63** 10.00				

Y# 420 5 ROUBLES

7.78 g., 0.999 Palladium 0.2497 oz. APW **Subject:** Ballet **Obv:** Double-headed eagle **Rev:** Ballerina

Date	Mintage	VF20	XF40	MS60	MS63	MS65
1993	6,000	—	—	—	275	375
1993	—	**PF63** 275	**PF65** 375			

Y# 431 5 ROUBLES

7.78 g., 0.999 Palladium 0.2497 oz. APW **Subject:** Ballet - Sleeping Beauty **Obv:** Double-headed eagle **Rev:** Ballerina

Date	Mintage	VF20	XF40	MS60	MS63	MS65
1994	4,000	—	—	—	275	375
1994	—	**PF63** 275	**PF65** 375			

Y# 400 5 ROUBLES

4.05 g., Aluminum-Bronze, 21.9 mm. **Series:** WWII **Obv:** Double-headed eagle **Rev:** Infantry officer leading attack

Date	Mintage	VF20	XF40	MS60	MS63	MS65
1995 (l) In sets only	200,000	—	—	—	2.00	—

Y# 435 5 ROUBLES

7.78 g., 0.999 Palladium 0.2497 oz. APW **Obv:** Double-headed eagle **Rev:** Ballerina

Date	Mintage	VF20	XF40	MS60	MS63	MS65
1995	4,000	**PF63** 250	**PF65** 350			

Y# 505 5 ROUBLES
4.05 g., Brass, 21.9 mm. **Subject:** 300th Anniversary - Russian Fleet **Obv:** Double-headed eagle **Rev:** Sailing ship

Date	Mintage	VF20	XF40	MS60	MS63	MS65
1996 (l) In sets only	100,000	—	—	—	3.00	—

Y# 307 10 ROUBLES
5.95 g., Bi-Metallic Aluminum-Bronze center in Copper-Nickel ring, 25 mm. **Series:** Wildlife **Obv:** Value **Rev:** Red-breasted Kazarka left **Edge:** Alternating reeded and smooth

Date	Mintage	VF20	XF40	MS60	MS63	MS65
1992 Л	300,000	—	—	9.00	15.00	—

Y# 308 10 ROUBLES
5.95 g., Bi-Metallic Aluminum-Bronze center in Copper-Nickel ring, 25 mm. **Series:** Wildlife **Obv:** Value **Rev:** Tiger **Edge:** Alternating reeded and smooth

Date	Mintage	VF20	XF40	MS60	MS63	MS65
1992 Л	300,000	—	—	9.00	15.00	—

Y# 309 10 ROUBLES
5.95 g., Bi-Metallic Aluminum-Bronze center in Copper-Nickel ring, 25 mm. **Series:** Wildlife **Obv:** Value **Rev:** Central Asia Cobra **Edge:** Alternating reeded and smooth

Date	Mintage	VF20	XF40	MS60	MS63	MS65
1992 Л	300,000	—	—	9.00	15.00	—

Y# 313 10 ROUBLES
3.65 g., Copper-Nickel, 21.1 mm. **Obv:** Double-headed eagle **Rev:** Value flanked by sprigs **Edge:** Reeded **Note:** St. Petersburg minted coins have a round-top 3 in date. Moscow minted coins have a flat-top 3 in date.

Date	Mintage	VF20	XF40	MS60	MS63	MS65
1992 Л	—	—	—	2.00	—	—
1992 M	—	—	—	2.00	—	—
1993 Л	—	—	—	670	—	—
1993 M	—	—	—	85.00	—	—

Y# 313a 10 ROUBLES
3.50 g., Copper-Nickel Clad Steel, 21.1 mm. **Obv:** Double-headed eagle **Rev:** Value flanked by sprigs **Edge:** Plain **Note:** St. Petersburg minted coins have a round-top 3 in date. Moscow minted coins have a flat-top 3 in date.

Date	Mintage	VF20	XF40	MS60	MS63	MS65
1992 ММД	—	—	—	700	—	—
1993 (sp)	—	—	—	2.00	3.00	—
1993 ММД	—	—	—	2.00	3.00	—

Y# 352 10 ROUBLES
15.67 g., 0.999 Palladium 0.5033 oz. APW **Series:** Olympics **Obv:** Double-headed eagle **Rev:** Cubertin and Butovsky and torch

Date	Mintage	VF20	XF40	MS60	MS63	MS65
1993	7,500	PF63 425	PF65 500			

Y# 416 10 ROUBLES
1.56 g., 0.999 Gold 0.050 oz. AGW **Subject:** Ballet **Obv:** Double-headed eagle **Rev:** Ballerina

Date	Mintage	VF20	XF40	MS60	MS63	MS65
1993	57,000	—	—	—	200	—
1993	11,500	PF63 85.00				

Y# 421 10 ROUBLES
15.55 g., 0.999 Palladium 0.4994 oz. APW **Subject:** Russian Ballet **Obv:** Double-headed eagle **Rev:** Ballerina

Date	Mintage	VF20	XF40	MS60	MS63	MS65
1993 (l)	4,000	—	—	—	425	500
1993 (l)	—	PF63 395	PF65 450			

Y# 424 10 ROUBLES
1.56 g., 0.999 Gold 0.050 oz. AGW **Subject:** Russian Ballet **Obv:** Double-headed eagle **Rev:** Ballerina

Date	Mintage	VF20	XF40	MS60	MS63	MS65
1994 (m)	7,000	PF63 90.00				

Y# 432 10 ROUBLES
15.55 g., 0.999 Palladium 0.4994 oz. APW **Subject:** Russian Ballet **Obv:** Double-headed eagle **Rev:** Ballerina

Date	Mintage	VF20	XF40	MS60	MS63	MS65
1994 (l)	3,000	—	—	—	500	600
1994 (l)	1,500	PF63 450	PF65 550			

Y# 401 10 ROUBLES
3.65 g., Copper-Nickel, 21.1 mm. **Series:** WWII **Obv:** Double-headed eagle **Rev:** Munitions workers

Date	Mintage	VF20	XF40	MS60	MS63	MS65
1995 (l) In sets only	200,000	—	—	—	3.00	—

Y# 436 10 ROUBLES
15.55 g., 0.999 Palladium 0.4994 oz. APW **Subject:** Ballet - Sleeping Beauty **Obv:** Double-headed eagle **Rev:** Ballerina

Date	Mintage	VF20	XF40	MS60	MS63	MS65
1995 (sp)	1,500	PF63 450	PF65 550			

Y# 438 10 ROUBLES
1.56 g., 0.999 Gold 0.050 oz. AGW **Subject:** Ballet - Sleeping Beauty **Obv:** Double-headed eagle **Rev:** Ballerina

Date	Mintage	VF20	XF40	MS60	MS63	MS65
1995 (m)	7,000	PF63 90.00				

Y# 484 10 ROUBLES
1.56 g., 0.999 Gold 0.050 oz. AGW **Subject:** Ballet - Nutcracker **Obv:** Double-headed eagle **Rev:** Nutcracker doll

Date	Mintage	VF20	XF40	MS60	MS63	MS65
1996 (m)	7,500	PF63 90.00				

Y# 506 10 ROUBLES
3.65 g., Copper-Nickel, 21.1 mm. **Subject:** 300th Anniversary - Russian Fleet **Obv:** Double-headed eagle **Rev:** Cargo ship

Date	Mintage	VF20	XF40	MS60	MS63	MS65
1996 (l) In sets only	100,000	—	—	—	3.00	—

Y# 569 10 ROUBLES
1.55 g., 0.999 Gold 0.0498 oz. AGW **Subject:** Ballet - Swan Lake **Obv:** Double-headed eagle **Rev:** Ballerina

Date	Mintage	VF20	XF40	MS60	MS63	MS65
1997 (sp)	2,500	PF63 90.00				

Y# 314 20 ROUBLES
5.25 g., Copper-Nickel, 24 mm. **Obv:** Double-headed eagle **Rev:** Value flanked by sprigs **Edge:** Alternating reeded and plain

Date	Mintage	VF20	XF40	MS60	MS63	MS65
1992 Л	—	—	—	3.00	4.00	—
1992 M	—	—	—	3.00	4.00	—
1993 Л	—	—	—	2,100	—	—
1993 M	—	—	—	230	—	—

Note: Plain edge

Y# 314a 20 ROUBLES
5.00 g., Copper-Nickel Clad Steel, 24.2 mm. **Obv:** Double-headed eagle **Rev:** Value flanked by sprigs **Edge:** Plain

Date	Mintage	VF20	XF40	MS60	MS63	MS65
1993 M	—	—	—	3.00	4.00	—

Y# 402 20 ROUBLES

5.60 g., Copper-Nickel, 24.1 mm. **Series:** WWII **Obv:** Double-headed eagle **Rev:** Soldiers and tanks

Date	Mintage	VF20	XF40	MS60	MS63	MS65
1995 (l) In sets only	200,000	—	—	—	3.00	—

Y# 507 20 ROUBLES

5.65 g., Copper-Nickel, 24.1 mm. **Subject:** 300th Anniversary - Russian Fleet **Obv:** Double-headed eagle **Rev:** Scientific research ship

Date	Mintage	VF20	XF40	MS60	MS63	MS65
1996 (l) In sets only	100,000	—	—	—	5.00	—

Y# 353 25 ROUBLES

31.10 g., 0.999 Palladium 0.999 oz. APW **Subject:** Age of enlightenment 17th century. **Obv:** Double-headed eagle **Rev:** Catherine the Great

Date	Mintage	VF20	XF40	MS60	MS63	MS65
1992 (l)	5,500	PF63 775	PF65 825			

Y# 395 25 ROUBLES

3.11 g., 0.999 Platinum 0.0999 oz. APW **Subject:** Russian Ballet **Obv:** Double-headed eagle **Rev:** Ballerina

Date	Mintage	VF20	XF40	MS60	MS63	MS65
1993 (l)	750	PF63 250	PF65 300			

Y# 406 25 ROUBLES

156.11 g., 0.999 Silver 5.014 oz. ASW, 60 mm. **Subject:** Russian Ballet **Obv:** Theatre within beaded circle **Rev:** Ballet couple

Date	Mintage	VF20	XF40	MS60	MS63	MS65
1993 (l)	—	PF63 150	PF65 175			
1993 (m)	10,000	PF63 150	PF65 175			

Y# 410 25 ROUBLES

3.11 g., 0.999 Gold 0.0999 oz. AGW **Series:** Wildlife **Obv:** Double-headed eagle **Rev:** Bear

Date	Mintage	VF20	XF40	MS60	MS63	MS65
1993 (m)	2,000	PF63 200				

Y# 417 25 ROUBLES

3.11 g., 0.999 Gold 0.0999 oz. AGW **Subject:** Russian Ballet **Obv:** Double-headed eagle **Rev:** Ballerina

Date	Mintage	VF20	XF40	MS60	MS63	MS65
1993 (m)	12,500	—	—	—	200	—
1993 (m)	—	PF63 185				

Y# 422 25 ROUBLES

31.10 g., 0.999 Palladium 0.999 oz. APW **Subject:** Russian Ballet **Obv:** Double-headed eagle **Rev:** Ballerina

Date	Mintage	VF20	XF40	MS60	MS63	MS65
1993 (l)	3,000	—	—	—	850	900
1993 (l)	—	PF63 800	PF65 850			

Y# 452 25 ROUBLES

31.10 g., 0.999 Palladium 0.999 oz. APW **Subject:** Russian and World Culture **Obv:** Double-headed eagle **Rev:** M.P. Musorgsky

Date	Mintage	VF20	XF40	MS60	MS63	MS65
1993 (m)	5,500	PF63 800	PF65 850			

Y# 517 25 ROUBLES

31.10 g., 0.999 Palladium 0.999 oz. APW, 37 mm. **Subject:** First Russian Global Circumnavigation **Obv:** Double-headed eagle **Rev:** Sloop Nadyezhda

Date	Mintage	VF20	XF40	MS60	MS63	MS65
1993 (l)	2,500	PF63 800	PF65 850			

Y# 518 25 ROUBLES

31.10 g., 0.999 Palladium 0.999 oz. APW, 37 mm. **Series:** First Russian Global Circumnavigation **Obv:** Double-headed eagle **Rev:** Sloop Neva

Date	Mintage	VF20	XF40	MS60	MS63	MS65
1993 (l)	25,000	PF63 800	PF65 850			

Y# 390 25 ROUBLES

173.29 g., 0.900 Silver 5.0143 oz. ASW, 60 mm. **Subject:** 100th Anniversary - Trans-Siberian Railroad **Rev:** Steam train, workers laying ties on track

Date	Mintage	VF20	XF40	MS60	MS63	MS65
1994 (l)	3,000	PF63 300	PF65 350			

Y# 423 25 ROUBLES

172.83 g., 0.900 Silver 5.0009 oz. ASW **Subject:** Russian Ballet

Date	Mintage	VF20	XF40	MS60	MS63	MS65
1994 (m)	7,500	PF63 225				

Y# 425 25 ROUBLES

3.11 g., 0.999 Gold 0.0999 oz. AGW **Subject:** Russian Ballet **Obv:** Double-headed eagle **Rev:** Ballerina

Date	Mintage	VF20	XF40	MS60	MS63	MS65
1994 (m)	5,000	PF63 200				

Y# 428 25 ROUBLES

3.11 g., 0.999 Platinum 0.0999 oz. APW **Subject:** Russian Ballet **Obv:** Double-headed eagle **Rev:** Ballerina

Date	Mintage	VF20	XF40	MS60	MS63	MS65
1994 (l)	900	PF63 225	PF65 275			

Y# 433 25 ROUBLES

31.10 g., 0.999 Palladium 0.999 oz. APW **Subject:** Russian Ballet **Obv:** Double-headed eagle **Rev:** Ballerina

Date	Mintage	VF20	XF40	MS60	MS63	MS65
1994 (l)	2,000	—	—	—	800	850
1994 (l)	1,500	PF63 850	PF65 900			

Y# 521 25 ROUBLES

31.10 g., 0.999 Palladium 0.999 oz. APW **Subject:** First Russian Antartic Expedition, 1819-21 **Obv:** Double-headed eagle **Rev:** Sloop Mirny

Date	Mintage	VF20	XF40	MS60	MS63	MS65
1994	4,000	PF63 800	PF65 850			

Y# 522 25 ROUBLES

31.10 g., 0.999 Palladium 0.999 oz. APW **Obv:** Double-headed eagle **Rev:** Sloop Vostok

Date	Mintage	VF20	XF40	MS60	MS63	MS65
1994	4,000	PF63 800	PF65 850			

Y# 524 25 ROUBLES

3.11 g., 0.999 Gold 0.0999 oz. AGW **Series:** Wildlife **Obv:** Double-headed eagle **Rev:** Sable's head

Date	Mintage	VF20	XF40	MS60	MS63	MS65
1994	4,000	PF63 200				

Y# 530 25 ROUBLES

31.10 g., 0.999 Palladium 0.999 oz. APW **Obv:** Double-headed eagle **Rev:** Andre Ruble

Date	Mintage	VF20	XF40	MS60	MS63	MS65
1994	6,000	PF63 800	PF65 850			

Y# 534 25 ROUBLES

4.32 g., 0.900 Gold 0.125 oz. AGW **Obv:** Double-headed eagle **Rev:** Baikal railroad tunnel

Date	Mintage	VF20	XF40	MS60	MS63	MS65
1994	3,000	PF63 250				

Y# 437 25 ROUBLES

31.10 g., 0.999 Palladium 0.999 oz. APW **Obv:** Double-headed eagle **Rev:** Ballerina

Date	Mintage	VF20	XF40	MS60	MS63	MS65
1995	1,500	PF63 800	PF65 850			

Y# 439 25 ROUBLES

3.11 g., 0.999 Gold 0.0999 oz. AGW **Obv:** Double-headed eagle **Rev:** Ballerina

Date	Mintage	VF20	XF40	MS60	MS63	MS65
1995	5,000	PF63 200				

Y# 442 25 ROUBLES

3.11 g., 0.999 Platinum 0.0999 oz. APW **Obv:** Double-headed eagle **Rev:** Ballerina

Date	Mintage	VF20	XF40	MS60	MS63	MS65
1995	900	PF63 225	PF65 276			

Y# 471 25 ROUBLES

173.29 g., 0.900 Silver 5.0143 oz. ASW, 60 mm. **Series:** Wildlife **Obv:** Double-headed eagle **Rev:** Lynx on log

Date	Mintage	VF20	XF40	MS60	MS63	MS65
1995	5,000	PF63 175	PF65 200			

Y# 472 25 ROUBLES

173.29 g., 0.900 Silver 5.0143 oz. ASW, 60 mm. **Subject:** First Station at North Pole **Obv:** Double-headed eagle **Rev:** Men, ship, and airplane

Date	Mintage	VF20	XF40	MS60	MS63	MS65
1995	5,000	PF63 185	PF65 220			

Y# 475 25 ROUBLES

31.10 g., 0.999 Palladium 0.999 oz. APW **Obv:** Double-headed eagle **Rev:** Alexander Nevski

Date	Mintage	VF20	XF40	MS60	MS63	MS65
1995	6,000	PF63 800	PF65 850			

Y# 479 25 ROUBLES

173.29 g., 0.900 Silver 5.0143 oz. ASW, 60 mm. **Obv:** Double-headed eagle **Rev:** Battle of Kulikova Plains

Date	Mintage	VF20	XF40	MS60	MS63	MS65
1996	5,000	PF63 225	PF65 275			

Y# 485 25 ROUBLES

173.29 g., 0.999 Silver 5.5658 oz. ASW, 60 mm. **Subject:** Ballet - Nutcracker **Obv:** Double-headed eagle **Rev:** Children dancing around tree

Date	Mintage	VF20	XF40	MS60	MS63	MS65
1996	5,000	PF63 225	PF65 275			

Y# 486 25 ROUBLES

3.11 g., 0.999 Gold 0.0999 oz. AGW **Subject:** Ballet - Nutcracker **Obv:** Double headed eagle **Rev:** Figure with nutcracker doll

Date	Mintage	VF20	XF40	MS60	MS63	MS65
1996	7,500	PF63 200				

Y# 536 25 ROUBLES

173.29 g., 0.900 Silver 5.0143 oz. ASW, 60 mm. **Series:** Wildlife **Obv:** Double-headed eagle **Rev:** Amur Tiger

Date	Mintage	VF20	XF40	MS60	MS63	MS65
1996	3,000	PF63 250	PF65 300			

Y# 542 25 ROUBLES

173.29 g., 0.900 Silver 5.0143 oz. ASW **Obv:** Double-headed eagle **Rev:** Battle of Gangut, 1714

Date	Mintage	VF20	XF40	MS60	MS63	MS65
1996	3,000	PF63 275	PF65 325			

Y# 543 25 ROUBLES

173.29 g., 0.900 Silver 5.0143 oz. ASW, 60 mm. **Subject:** Battle of Chesme, 1770 **Obv:** Double-headed eagle **Rev:** Battle of Chesme, 1770

Date	Mintage	VF20	XF40	MS60	MS63	MS65
1996	3,000	PF63 275	PF65 325			

Y# 544 25 ROUBLES

173.29 g., 0.900 Silver 5.0143 oz. ASW, 60 mm. **Obv:** Double-headed eagle **Rev:** Battle of Corfu, 1799

Date	Mintage	VF20	XF40	MS60	MS63	MS65
1996	3,000	PF63 275	PF65 325			

Y# 545 25 ROUBLES

173.29 g., 0.900 Silver 5.0143 oz. ASW, 60 mm. **Obv:** Double-headed eagle **Rev:** Battle of Sinop, 1853

Date	Mintage	VF20	XF40	MS60	MS63	MS65
1996	3,000	PF63 275	PF65 325			

Y# 554 25 ROUBLES

173.29 g., 0.900 Silver 5.0143 oz. ASW, 60 mm. **Subject:** 850th Anniversary - Moscow **Obv:** Double-headed eagle **Rev:** Monument flanked by trees

Date	Mintage	VF20	XF40	MS60	MS63	MS65
1997	5,000	PF63 200	PF65 250			

Y# 570 25 ROUBLES

173.29 g., 0.900 Silver 5.0143 oz. ASW, 60 mm. **Subject:** Ballet - Swan Lake **Obv:** Double-headed eagle **Rev:** Prince Siegfried dancing with Odile

Date	Mintage	VF20	XF40	MS60	MS63	MS65
1997	3,000	PF63 250	PF65 300			

Y# 571 25 ROUBLES

3.11 g., 0.999 Gold 0.0999 oz. AGW **Subject:** Ballet - Swan Lake **Obv:** Double-headed eagle **Rev:** Winged figure of Rothbart and Swan

Date	Mintage	VF20	XF40	MS60	MS63	MS65
1997	2,000	PF63 200				

Y# 592 25 ROUBLES

173.29 g., 0.900 Silver 5.0143 oz. ASW, 60 mm. **Series:** Wildlife **Obv:** Double-headed eagle **Rev:** Bear with cub

Date	Mintage	VF20	XF40	MS60	MS63	MS65
1997	1,000	PF63 350	PF65 400			

Y# 594 25 ROUBLES

173.29 g., 0.900 Silver 5.0143 oz. ASW, 60 mm. **Series:** Wildlife **Obv:** Double-headed eagle **Rev:** Polar bear, caribou, seal

Date	Mintage	VF20	XF40	MS60	MS63	MS65
1997	3,000	PF63 300	PF65 350			

Y# 622 25 ROUBLES

173.29 g., 0.900 Silver 5.0143 oz. ASW, 60 mm. **Series:** Wildlife **Obv:** Double-headed eagle **Rev:** Sable in tree

Date	Mintage	VF20	XF40	MS60	MS63	MS65
1997	1,000	PF63 350	PF65 400			

Y# 315 50 ROUBLES

5.95 g., Bi-Metallic Aluminum-Bronze center in Copper-Nickel ring, 25 mm. **Obv:** Double-headed eagle **Rev:** Value flanked by sprigs **Note:** Off-metal strikes exist from both mints. The strike is on the planchet reserved for Y#316, 100 Roubles.

Date	Mintage	VF20	XF40	MS60	MS63	MS65
1992 (sp)	—	1.00	2.00	4.00	—	—
1992 ММД	—	7.00	12.00	20.00	—	—
1993 (sp)	—	—	—	6,400	—	—

Y# 354 50 ROUBLES

8.64 g., 0.900 Gold 0.250 oz. AGW **Obv:** Double-headed eagle **Rev:** Moscow's Pashkov Palace

Date	Mintage	VF20	XF40	MS60	MS63	MS65
1992	7,500	PF63 475				

Y# 516 50 ROUBLES

8.64 g., 0.900 Gold 0.250 oz. AGW **Subject:** Yakutia. **Obv:** Double-headed eagle **Rev:** Chubuku (snow) ram on map

Date	Mintage	VF20	XF40	MS60	MS63	MS65
1992	25,000	PF63 425				

Y# 329.1 50 ROUBLES

6.50 g., Bronze, 25 mm. **Obv:** Double-headed eagle **Rev:** Value flanked by sprigs **Edge:** Segmented reeding

Date	Mintage	VF20	XF40	MS60	MS63	MS65
1993 ММД	—	—	—	3.00	—	—
1993 (SP)	—	—	—	3.00	—	—

Y# 329.2 50 ROUBLES

5.20 g., Brass Clad Steel, 25 mm. **Obv:** Double-headed eagle **Rev:** Value **Edge:** Plain **Note:** Released in 1996.

Date	Mintage	VF20	XF40	MS60	MS63	MS65
1993 ММД	—	—	—	3.00	—	—
1993 (sp)	—	—	—	4.00	—	—

Y# 330 50 ROUBLES

5.95 g., Bi-Metallic Aluminum-Bronze center in Copper-Nickel ring, 25 mm. **Series:** Wildlife **Obv:** Double-headed eagle **Rev:** Black bear **Edge:** Alternating reeded and smooth

Date	Mintage	VF20	XF40	MS60	MS63	MS65
1993 Л	300,000	—	—	12.00	20.00	—

Y# 331 50 ROUBLES

5.95 g., Bi-Metallic Aluminum-Bronze center in Copper-Nickel ring, 25 mm. **Series:** Wildlife **Obv:** Double-headed eagle **Rev:** Turkmenistan Gecko **Edge:** Alternating reeded and smooth

Date	Mintage	VF20	XF40	MS60	MS63	MS65
1993 Л	300,000	—	—	12.00	20.00	—

Y# 332 50 ROUBLES

5.95 g., Bi-Metallic Aluminum-Bronze center in Copper-Nickel ring, 25 mm. **Series:** Wildlife **Obv:** Double-headed eagle **Rev:** Grouse **Edge:** Alternating reeded and smooth

Date	Mintage	VF20	XF40	MS60	MS63	MS65
1993 Л	300,000	—	—	12.00	20.00	—

Y# 333 50 ROUBLES

5.95 g., Bi-Metallic Aluminum-Bronze center in Copper-Nickel ring, 25 mm. **Series:** Wildlife **Obv:** Double-headed eagle **Rev:** Oriental Stork **Edge:** Alternating reeded and smooth

Date	Mintage	VF20	XF40	MS60	MS63	MS65
1993 Л	300,000	—	—	20.00	30.00	—

Y# 334 50 ROUBLES

5.95 g., Bi-Metallic Aluminum-Bronze center in Copper-Nickel ring, 25 mm. **Series:** Wildlife **Obv:** Double-headed eagle **Rev:** Black Sea Porpoise **Edge:** Alternating reeded and smooth

Date	Mintage	VF20	XF40	MS60	MS63	MS65
1993 Л	300,000	—	—	20.00	30.00	—

Y# 355 50 ROUBLES

8.64 g., 0.900 Gold 0.250 oz. AGW **Series:** Olympics **Obv:** Double-headed eagle **Rev:** Figure skater

Date	Mintage	VF20	XF40	MS60	MS63	MS65
1993	7,500	PF63 475				

Y# 356 50 ROUBLES

7.78 g., 0.999 Platinum 0.2497 oz. APW **Series:** Olympics **Obv:** Double-headed eagle **Rev:** Formal riding

Date	Mintage	VF20	XF40	MS60	MS63	MS65
1993	7,500	PF63 450	PF65 500			

Y# 396 50 ROUBLES
7.78 g., 0.999 Platinum 0.2497 oz. APW **Subject:** Bolshoi Ballet **Obv:** Double-headed eagle **Rev:** Ballerina

Date	Mintage	VF20	XF40	MS60	MS63	MS65
1993	750	PF63 425	PF65 475			

Y# 411 50 ROUBLES
7.78 g., 0.999 Gold 0.2499 oz. AGW **Series:** Wildlife **Obv:** Double-headed eagle **Rev:** Bear between trees and sprigs

Date	Mintage	VF20	XF40	MS60	MS63	MS65
1993	1,480	PF63 550				

Y# 418 50 ROUBLES
7.78 g., 0.999 Gold 0.2499 oz. AGW **Subject:** Bolshoi Ballet **Obv:** Double-headed eagle **Rev:** Ballerina

Date	Mintage	VF20	XF40	MS60	MS63	MS65
1993	4,700	—	—	—	450	—
1993	1,500	PF63 450				

Y# 453 50 ROUBLES
7.78 g., 0.999 Gold 0.2499 oz. AGW **Subject:** Sergei Rachmaninov **Obv:** Double-headed eagle **Rev:** Head right

Date	Mintage	VF20	XF40	MS60	MS63	MS65
1993	7,500	PF63 450				

Y# 367 50 ROUBLES
5.95 g., Bi-Metallic Aluminum-Bronze center in Copper-Nickel ring, 25 mm. **Series:** Wildlife **Obv:** Double-headed eagle **Rev:** Blind mole rat **Edge:** Alternating reeded and smooth

Date	Mintage	VF20	XF40	MS60	MS63	MS65
1994 Л	300,000	—	—	30.00	50.00	—

Y# 368 50 ROUBLES
5.95 g., Bi-Metallic Aluminum-Bronze center in Copper-Nickel ring, 25 mm. **Series:** Wildlife **Obv:** Double-headed eagle **Rev:** Bison **Edge:** Alternating reeded and smooth

Date	Mintage	VF20	XF40	MS60	MS63	MS65
1994 Л	300,000	—	—	30.00	50.00	—

Y# 369 50 ROUBLES
5.95 g., Bi-Metallic Alunimum-Bronze center in Copper-Nickel ring, 25 mm. **Series:** Wildlife **Obv:** Double-headed eagle **Rev:** Mongolian Gazelle **Edge:** Alternating reeded and smooth

Date	Mintage	VF20	XF40	MS60	MS63	MS65
1994 Л	300,000	—	—	50.00	75.00	—

Y# 370 50 ROUBLES
5.95 g., Bi-Metallic Aluminum-Bronze center in Copper-Nickel ring, 25 mm. **Series:** Wildlife **Obv:** Double-headed eagle **Rev:** Peregrine Falcon **Edge:** Alternating reeded and smooth

Date	Mintage	VF20	XF40	MS60	MS63	MS65
1994 Л	300,000	—	—	30.00	50.00	—

Y# 371 50 ROUBLES
5.95 g., Bi-Metallic Aluminum-Bronze center in Copper-Nickel ring, 25 mm. **Series:** Wildlife **Obv:** Double-headed eagle **Rev:** Two flamingos **Edge:** Alternating reeded and smooth

Date	Mintage	VF20	XF40	MS60	MS63	MS65
1994 Л	300,000	—	—	30.00	50.00	—

Y# 426 50 ROUBLES
7.78 g., 0.999 Gold 0.2498 oz. AGW **Subject:** Bolshoi Ballet **Obv:** Double-headed eagle **Rev:** Ballerina

Date	Mintage	VF20	XF40	MS60	MS63	MS65
1994	2,500	PF63 450				

Y# 429 50 ROUBLES
7.78 g., 0.999 Platinum 0.2498 oz. APW **Subject:** Bolshoi Ballet **Obv:** Double-headed eagle **Rev:** Ballerina

Date	Mintage	VF20	XF40	MS60	MS63	MS65
1994	900	PF63 450	PF65 500			

Y# 525 50 ROUBLES
7.78 g., 0.999 Gold 0.2498 oz. AGW **Series:** Wildlife **Obv:** Double-headed eagle **Rev:** Sable in tree

Date	Mintage	VF20	XF40	MS60	MS63	MS65
1994	2,500	PF63 475				

Y# 531 50 ROUBLES
8.64 g., 0.900 Gold 0.250 oz. AGW, 22.6 mm. **Rev:** Dmitri Grigorievich Levitsky

Date	Mintage	VF20	XF40	MS60	MS63	MS65
1994	8,000	PF63 450				

Y# 403 50 ROUBLES
Aluminum-Bronze **Series:** WWII **Obv:** Double-headed eagle **Rev:** Two sailors, ship, and plane

Date	Mintage	VF20	XF40	MS60	MS63	MS65
1995 Л In sets only	200,000	—	—	5.00	—	—

Y# 408 50 ROUBLES
7.78 g., 0.999 Gold 0.2499 oz. AGW **Subject:** 50th Anniversary - United Nations **Obv:** Double-headed eagle **Rev:** Blacksmith with anvil at feet, UN logo at top, building at left **Note:** Similar to 3 Roubles, Y#407.

Date	Mintage	VF20	XF40	MS60	MS63	MS65
1995	5,000	PF63 450				

Y# 440 50 ROUBLES
7.78 g., 0.999 Gold 0.2499 oz. AGW **Subject:** Bolshoi Ballet - Sleeping Beauty **Obv:** Double-headed eagle **Rev:** Ballerina

Date	Mintage	VF20	XF40	MS60	MS63	MS65
1995	2,500	PF63 450				

Y# 443 50 ROUBLES
7.78 g., 0:999 Platinum 0.2498 oz. APW **Subject:** Bolshoi Ballet - Sleeping Beauty **Obv:** Double-headed eagle **Rev:** Male dancer

Date	Mintage	VF20	XF40	MS60	MS63	MS65
1995	900	PF63 450	PF65 500			

Y# A475 50 ROUBLES
7.78 g., 0.999 Gold 0.2499 oz. AGW **Series:** Wildlife **Obv:** Double-headed eagle **Rev:** Lynx

Date	Mintage	VF20	XF40	MS60	MS63	MS65
1995	10,000	PF63 425				

Y# 496 50 ROUBLES
8.64 g., 0.900 Gold 0.250 oz. AGW **Subject:** F. Nansen and the "Fram" **Obv:** Double-headed eagle **Rev:** F. Nansen and the "Fram"

Date	Mintage	VF20	XF40	MS60	MS63	MS65
1995	5,000	PF63 450				

Y# 480 50 ROUBLES
8.64 g., 0.900 Gold 0.250 oz. AGW, 22.6 mm. **Obv:** Double-headed eagle **Rev:** Dmitri Donskoy Monument

Date	Mintage	VF20	XF40	MS60	MS63	MS65
1996	10,000	PF63 425				

Y# 487 50 ROUBLES
7.78 g., 0.999 Gold 0.2499 oz. AGW **Subject:** Ballet - Nutcracker **Obv:** Double-headed eagle **Rev:** Marsha and Drosselmeyer with broken doll

Date	Mintage	VF20	XF40	MS60	MS63	MS65
1996	2,500	PF63 450				

Y# 501 50 ROUBLES
8.64 g., 0.900 Gold 0.250 oz. AGW **Obv:** Double-headed eagle **Rev:** Church of the Savior on the Nereditza River

Date	Mintage	VF20	XF40	MS60	MS63	MS65
1996	10,000	PF63 425				

Y# 508 50 ROUBLES
Aluminum-Bronze **Subject:** 300th Anniversary - Russian Fleet **Obv:** Double-headed eagle **Rev:** Submarine

Date	Mintage	VF20	XF40	MS60	MS63	MS65
1996 Л In sets only	100,000	—	—	10.00	—	—

Y# 537 50 ROUBLES
7.78 g., 0.999 Gold 0.2498 oz. AGW **Series:** Wildlife **Obv:** Double-headed eagle **Rev:** Tiger head

Date	Mintage	VF20	XF40	MS60	MS63	MS65
1996	1,500	PF63 550				

Y# 546 50 ROUBLES
8.64 g., 0.900 Gold 0.250 oz. AGW **Obv:** Double-headed eagle **Rev:** Cruiser Varyag 1904

Date	Mintage	VF20	XF40	MS60	MS63	MS65
1996	1,500	PF63 525				

Y# 555 50 ROUBLES
8.64 g., 0.900 Gold 0.250 oz. AGW **Subject:** 850th Anniversary - Moscow **Obv:** Double-headed eagle **Rev:** Shield flanked by designs

Date	Mintage	VF20	XF40	MS60	MS63	MS65
1997	10,000	PF63 425				

Y# 572 50 ROUBLES
7.78 g., 0.999 Gold 0.2498 oz. AGW **Subject:** Ballet - Swan Lake **Obv:** Double-headed eagle **Rev:** Prince Siegfried with crossbow and swan

Date	Mintage	VF20	XF40	MS60	MS63	MS65
1997	1,500	PF63 525				

Y# 595 50 ROUBLES
7.78 g., 0.999 Gold 0.2498 oz. AGW **Series:** Wildlife **Obv:** Double-headed eagle **Rev:** Polar bear

Date	Mintage	VF20	XF40	MS60	MS63	MS65
1997	1,500	PF63 525				

Y# 712 50 ROUBLES
8.64 g., 0.900 Gold 0.250 oz. AGW, 22.6 mm. **Series:** Three Millenniums **Subject:** Scientific and Technical Progress **Obv:** Double-headed eagle **Rev:** Icarus and space travel

Date	Mintage	VF20	XF40	MS60	MS63	MS65
2000 M	1,000	PF63 525				

Y# 316 100 ROUBLES
6.20 g., Bi-Metallic Copper-Nickel center in Aluminum-Bronze ring, 25 mm. **Obv:** Double-headed eagle **Rev:** Value flanked by sprigs **Edge:** Alternating reeded and plain **Note:** Off-metal strikes exist from the Moscow mint. The strike is on the planchet reserved for Y#315, 50 Roubles.

Date	Mintage	VF20	XF40	MS60	MS63	MS65
1992 (sp)	—	1.00	2.00	4.00	—	—
1992 ММД	—	6.00	11.00	20.00	—	—

Y# 357 100 ROUBLES
17.28 g., 0.900 Gold 0.500 oz. AGW, 30 mm. **Obv:** Double-headed eagle **Rev:** Michael Lomonossov

Date	Mintage	VF20	XF40	MS60	MS63	MS65
1992	5,700	PF63 900				

Y# 375 100 ROUBLES
17.28 g., 0.900 Gold 0.500 oz. AGW **Obv:** Double-headed eagle **Rev:** Wooly Mammoth within radiant map **Note:** Yakutia

Date	Mintage	VF20	XF40	MS60	MS63	MS65
1992	14,000	PF63 900				

Y# 338 100 ROUBLES
7.30 g., Copper-Nickel-Zinc, 27 mm. **Obv:** Double-headed eagle **Rev:** Value flanked by sprigs **Edge:** Alternating reeded and plain

Date	Mintage	VF20	XF40	MS60	MS63	MS65
1993 (sp)	—	0.75	1.75	3.00	—	—
1993 ММД	—	1.00	2.00	4.00	—	—

Y# 412 100 ROUBLES
15.55 g., 0.999 Gold 0.4994 oz. AGW **Series:** Wildlife **Obv:** Double-headed eagle **Rev:** Black bear

Date	Mintage	VF20	XF40	MS60	MS63	MS65
1993	1,400	PF63 925				

Y# 419 100 ROUBLES
15.55 g., 0.999 Gold 0.4994 oz. AGW **Subject:** Bolshoi Ballet **Obv:** Double-headed eagle **Rev:** Ballerina

Date	Mintage	VF20	XF40	MS60	MS63	MS65
1993	2,700	—	—	—	900	—
1993	1,500	PF63 825				

Y# 454 100 ROUBLES
17.28 g., 0.900 Gold 0.500 oz. AGW, 30 mm. **Obv:** Double-headed eagle **Rev:** Peter Tchaikovsky

Date	Mintage	VF20	XF40	MS60	MS63	MS65
1993	5,700	PF63 900				

Y# 427 100 ROUBLES
15.55 g., 0.999 Gold 0.4994 oz. AGW **Subject:** Bolshoi Ballet **Obv:** Double-headed eagle **Rev:** Ballerina

Date	Mintage	VF20	XF40	MS60	MS63	MS65
1994	2,500	PF63 900				

Y# 526 100 ROUBLES
15.55 g., 0.999 Gold 0.4994 oz. AGW **Series:** Wildlife **Obv:** Double-headed eagle **Rev:** Sable in tree

Date	Mintage	VF20	XF40	MS60	MS63	MS65
1994	2,500	PF63 925				

Y# 532 100 ROUBLES
17.45 g., 0.900 Gold 0.5049 oz. AGW, 30 mm. **Obv:** Double-headed eagle **Rev:** Vassili Vassilievich Kandinsky - The Blue Horse

Date	Mintage	VF20	XF40	MS60	MS63	MS65
1994	6,000	**PF63** 900				

Y# 376 100 ROUBLES
1111.12 g., 0.900 Silver 32.151 oz. ASW, 100 mm. **Series:** Wildlife **Obv:** Double-headed eagle **Rev:** Mother bear with cubs

Date	Mintage	VF20	XF40	MS60	MS63	MS65
1995	500	**PF63** 2,250	**PF65** 2,500			

Y# A387 100 ROUBLES
1111.12 g., 0.900 Silver 32.151 oz. ASW, 100 mm. **Subject:** WWII Victory **Rev:** Allied Commanders

Date	Mintage	VF20	XF40	MS60	MS63	MS65
1995	1,500	**PF63** 1,400	**PF65** 1,600			

Y# 404 100 ROUBLES
Copper-Nickel **Series:** WWII **Obv:** Double-headed eagle **Rev:** Berlin Soldier Monument

Date	Mintage	VF20	XF40	MS60	MS63	MS65
1995 Л In sets only	200,000	—	—	7.00	—	—

Y# 434 100 ROUBLES
1111.12 g., 0.900 Silver 32.151 oz. ASW, 100 mm. **Subject:** Ballet - Sleeping Beauty **Obv:** Building in back of double-headed eagle **Rev:** Theater above dancers

Date	Mintage	VF20	XF40	MS60	MS63	MS65
1995	1,000	**PF63** 1,400	**PF65** 1,600			

Y# 441 100 ROUBLES
15.55 g., 0.999 Gold 0.4994 oz. AGW **Subject:** Ballet - Sleeping Beauty **Obv:** Double-headed eagle **Rev:** Ballerina

Date	Mintage	VF20	XF40	MS60	MS63	MS65
1995	2,500	**PF63** 900				

Y# 497 100 ROUBLES
17.50 g., 0.900 Gold 0.5064 oz. AGW **Obv:** Double-headed eagle **Rev:** Icebreaker "Krassin"

Date	Mintage	VF20	XF40	MS60	MS63	MS65
1995	2,500	**PF63** 900				

Y# 498 100 ROUBLES
1111.12 g., 0.900 Silver 32.151 oz. ASW, 100 mm. **Series:** Wildlife **Obv:** Double-headed eagle **Rev:** Lynx with two kits

Date	Mintage	VF20	XF40	MS60	MS63	MS65
1995	500	**PF63** 1,150	**PF65** 1,350			

Y# 499 100 ROUBLES
17.50 g., 0.900 Gold 0.5064 oz. AGW **Series:** Wildlife **Obv:** Double-headed eagle **Rev:** Lynx

Date	Mintage	VF20	XF40	MS60	MS63	MS65
1995	3,500	**PF63** 900				

Y# 502 100 ROUBLES
17.50 g., 0.900 Gold 0.5064 oz. AGW **Obv:** Double-headed eagle **Rev:** Order of Alexander Nevsky

Date	Mintage	VF20	XF40	MS60	MS63	MS65
1995	5,000	**PF63** 900				

Y# 481 100 ROUBLES
17.50 g., 0.900 Gold 0.5064 oz. AGW **Obv:** Double-headed eagle **Rev:** All Saints Church in Kulishki

Date	Mintage	VF20	XF40	MS60	MS63	MS65
1996	5,000	**PF63** 900				

Y# 488 100 ROUBLES
1111.09 g., 0.900 Silver 32.150 oz. ASW, 100 mm. **Subject:** Ballet - Nutcracker **Obv:** Double-headed eagle **Rev:** Marsha cradling nutcracker doll

Date	Mintage	VF20	XF40	MS60	MS63	MS65
1996	1,000	**PF63** 1,300	**PF65** 1,500			

Y# 489 100 ROUBLES
15.55 g., 0.999 Gold 0.4995 oz. AGW **Subject:** Ballet - Nutcracker **Obv:** Double-headed eagle **Rev:** Dancing Prince

Date	Mintage	VF20	XF40	MS60	MS63	MS65
1996	2,500	**PF63** 900				

Y# 495 100 ROUBLES

1111.12 g., 0.900 Silver 32.151 oz. ASW, 100 mm. **Obv:** Double-headed eagle **Rev:** Sables around city

Date	Mintage	VF20	XF40	MS60	MS63	MS65
1996	500	PF63 1,400	PF65 1,600			

Y# 509 100 ROUBLES

Copper-Nickel **Subject:** 300th Anniversary - Russian Fleet **Obv:** Double-headed eagle **Rev:** Atlantic Icebreaker "Arctic"

Date	Mintage	VF20	XF40	MS60	MS63	MS65
1996 In sets only	100,000	—	—	9.00	—	—

Y# 538 100 ROUBLES

1111.09 g., 0.900 Silver 32.150 oz. ASW **Series:** Wildlife **Obv:** Double-headed eagle **Rev:** Tiger **Note:** Illustration reduced.

Date	Mintage	VF20	XF40	MS60	MS63	MS65
1996	1,000	PF63 1,300	PF65 1,500			

Y# 539 100 ROUBLES

15.55 g., 0.999 Gold 0.4995 oz. AGW **Series:** Wildlife **Obv:** Double-headed eagle **Rev:** Amur tiger

Date	Mintage	VF20	XF40	MS60	MS63	MS65
1996	1,000	PF63 925				

Y# 547 100 ROUBLES

1111.12 g., 0.900 Silver 32.151 oz. ASW, 100 mm. **Obv:** Double-headed eagle **Rev:** Warship Poltava, 1712

Date	Mintage	VF20	XF40	MS60	MS63	MS65
1996	3,000	PF63 1,200	PF65 1,400			

Y# 548 100 ROUBLES

17.50 g., 0.900 Gold 0.5064 oz. AGW **Subject:** Battleships of WWII **Obv:** Double-headed eagle **Rev:** Destroyers, "Gremysiy and Soobrazitelny"

Date	Mintage	VF20	XF40	MS60	MS63	MS65
1996	1,000	PF63 900				

Y# 556 100 ROUBLES

1111.09 g., 0.900 Silver 32.150 oz. ASW **Subject:** 850th Anniversary - Moscow **Obv:** Double-headed eagle **Rev:** Kuzma Minin and Dmitri Pozharsky Monument **Note:** Illustration reduced.

Date	Mintage	VF20	XF40	MS60	MS63	MS65
1997	1,000	PF63 1,400	PF65 1,600			

Y# 557 100 ROUBLES

17.29 g., 0.900 Gold 0.5003 oz. AGW **Subject:** 850th Anniversary - Moscow **Obv:** Double-headed eagle **Rev:** Yuri Dolgoruky Monument

Date	Mintage	VF20	XF40	MS60	MS63	MS65
1997	5,000	PF63 900				

Y# 573 100 ROUBLES

1111.09 g., 0.900 Silver 32.150 oz. ASW **Subject:** Ballet - Swan Lake **Obv:** Double-headed eagle **Rev:** Prince Siegfried dancing with Odette **Note:** Illustration reduced.

Date	Mintage	VF20	XF40	MS60	MS63	MS65
1997	1,000	PF63 1,400	PF65 1,600			

Y# 574 100 ROUBLES

15.55 g., 0.999 Gold 0.4995 oz. AGW **Subject:** Ballet - Swan Lake **Obv:** Double-headed eagle **Rev:** Prince Siegfried and Odette'd Duet

Date	Mintage	VF20	XF40	MS60	MS63	MS65
1997	1,500	PF63 900				

Y# 588 100 ROUBLES

1111.09 g., 0.900 Silver 32.150 oz. ASW **Obv:** Double-headed eagle **Rev:** 4-Masted Ship - "The Bark Krusenstern" **Note:** Illustration reduced.

Date	Mintage	VF20	XF40	MS60	MS63	MS65
1997	500	PF63 1,400	PF65 1,600			

Y# 596 100 ROUBLES

15.55 g., 0.999 Gold 0.4995 oz. AGW **Series:** Wildlife **Obv:** Double-headed eagle **Rev:** Polar bear on ice flow

Date	Mintage	VF20	XF40	MS60	MS63	MS65
1997	1,000	PF63 925				

Y# 597 100 ROUBLES

1111.09 g., 0.900 Silver 32.150 oz. ASW **Series:** Wildlife **Obv:** Double-headed eagle **Rev:** Two polar bears **Note:** Photo reduced.

Date	Mintage	VF20	XF40	MS60	MS63	MS65
1997	1,000	PF63 1,300	PF65 1,500			

Y# 623 100 ROUBLES

15.72 g., 0.999 Gold 0.5049 oz. AGW **Obv:** Double-headed eagle **Rev:** Serge Julievech Witte

Date	Mintage	VF20	XF40	MS60	MS63	MS65
1997	1,000	PF63 900				

Y# 699 100 ROUBLES

1111.12 g., 0.900 Silver 32.151 oz. ASW, 100 mm. **Subject:** Russian Ballet **Obv:** Double-headed eagle **Rev:** Raymonda wedding scene **Edge:** Reeded **Note:** Illustration reduced.

Date	Mintage	VF20	XF40	MS60	MS63	MS65
1999 (sp)	1,000	PF63 1,400	PF65 1,600			

Y# 358 150 ROUBLES

15.55 g., 0.999 Platinum 0.4995 oz. APW **Subject:** Naval Battle of Chesme **Obv:** Double-headed eagle **Rev:** Two battle ships

Date	Mintage	VF20	XF40	MS60	MS63	MS65
1992	3,000	PF63 950	PF65 1,150			

Y# 397 150 ROUBLES

15.55 g., 0.999 Platinum 0.4995 oz. APW **Subject:** Ballet **Obv:** Double-headed eagle **Rev:** Ballerina

Date	Mintage	VF20	XF40	MS60	MS63	MS65
1993	750	PF63 1,050	PF65 1,250			

Y# 455 150 ROUBLES

15.55 g., 0.999 Platinum 0.4995 oz. APW **Obv:** Double-headed eagle **Rev:** Igor Stravinsky

Date	Mintage	VF20	XF40	MS60	MS63	MS65
1993	3,000	PF63 950	PF65 1,150			

Y# 519 150 ROUBLES

15.55 g., 0.999 Platinum 0.4995 oz. APW **Subject:** First Global Circumnavigation **Obv:** Double-headed eagle **Rev:** Sloops - Nadyezdha and Neva

Date	Mintage	VF20	XF40	MS60	MS63	MS65
1993	2,500	PF63 950	PF65 1,150			

Y# 430 150 ROUBLES

15.55 g., 0.999 Platinum 0.4995 oz. APW **Subject:** Bolshoi Ballet **Obv:** Double-headed eagle **Rev:** Ballerina

Date	Mintage	VF20	XF40	MS60	MS63	MS65
1994	900	PF63 1,000	PF65 1,200			

Y# 523 150 ROUBLES

15.55 g., 0.999 Platinum 0.4995 oz. APW **Subject:** First Global Circumnavigation **Obv:** Double-headed eagle **Rev:** Sloops - "Mirny" and "Vostok"

Date	Mintage	VF20	XF40	MS60	MS63	MS65
1994	4,000	PF63 950	PF65 1,150			

Y# 533 150 ROUBLES

15.55 g., 0.999 Platinum 0.4995 oz. APW **Subject:** Michail Alexandrowich Vrubel - The Demon **Obv:** Double-headed eagle **Rev:** Michail Alexandrowich Vrubel - The Demon

Date	Mintage	VF20	XF40	MS60	MS63	MS65
1994	3,000	PF63 950	PF65 1,150			

Y# 444 150 ROUBLES

15.55 g., 0.999 Platinum 0.4995 oz. APW **Subject:** Ballet - Sleeping Beauty **Obv:** Double-headed eagle **Rev:** Male dancer

Date	Mintage	VF20	XF40	MS60	MS63	MS65
1995	900	PF63 1,000	PF65 1,200			

Y# 503 150 ROUBLES

15.55 g., 0.999 Platinum 0.4995 oz. APW **Subject:** Battle of the Neva River in 1240 **Obv:** Double-headed eagle **Rev:** Armored equestrians fighting

Date	Mintage	VF20	XF40	MS60	MS63	MS65
1995	3,000	PF63 950	PF65 1,150			

Y# 413 200 ROUBLES

31.10 g., 0.999 Gold 0.999 oz. AGW **Series:** Wildlife **Obv:** Double-headed eagle **Rev:** Bear with cub

Date	Mintage	VF20	XF40	MS60	MS63	MS65
1993	1,000	PF63 1,750				

Y# 527 200 ROUBLES

31.10 g., 0.999 Gold 0.999 oz. AGW **Series:** Wildlife **Obv:** Double-headed eagle **Rev:** Two sables

Date	Mintage	VF20	XF40	MS60	MS63	MS65
1994	2,000	PF63 1,750				

Y# 500 200 ROUBLES

31.10 g., 0.999 Gold 0.999 oz. AGW **Series:** Wildlife **Obv:** Double-headed eagle **Rev:** Seated lynx

Date	Mintage	VF20	XF40	MS60	MS63	MS65
1995	1,750	PF63 1,750				

Y# 540 200 ROUBLES
31.10 g., 0.999 Gold 0.999 oz. AGW **Series:** Wildlife **Obv:** Double-headed eagle **Rev:** Amur tiger

Date	Mintage	VF20	XF40	MS60	MS63	MS65
1996	1,000	PF63 1,750				

Y# 598 200 ROUBLES
31.10 g., 0.999 Gold 0.999 oz. AGW **Series:** Wildlife **Obv:** Double-headed eagle **Rev:** Seated polar bear

Date	Mintage	VF20	XF40	MS60	MS63	MS65
1997	1,000	PF63 1,750				

Y# 589 1000 ROUBLES
156.40 g., 0.999 Gold 5.0233 oz. AGW, 50 mm. **Obv:** Double-headed eagle **Rev:** The barque "Krusenstern" - 4-masted sailing ship

Date	Mintage	VF20	XF40	MS60	MS63	MS65
1997	250	PF65 9,000				

Y# 541 10000 ROUBLES
1111.09 g., 0.999 Gold 35.6865 oz. AGW, 100 mm. **Series:** Wildlife **Obv:** Double-headed eagle **Rev:** Amur tiger with two cubs **Note:** Illustration reduced.

Date	Mintage	VF20	XF40	MS60	MS63	MS65
1996	100	PF65 63,000				

Y# 599 10000 ROUBLES
1111.09 g., 0.999 Gold 35.6865 oz. AGW, 100 mm. **Series:** Wildlife **Obv:** Double-headed eagle **Rev:** Seated polar bear with two cubs **Note:** Illustration reduced.

Date	Mintage	VF20	XF40	MS60	MS63	MS65
1997	100	PF65 63,000				

REFORM COINAGE

1,000 Old Roubles = 1 New Rouble
January 1, 1998

Y# 600 KOPEK
1.50 g., Copper-Nickel Plated Steel, 15.5 mm. **Obv:** St. George **Obv. Legend:** БАНК РОССИИ **Rev:** Value above vine sprig **Edge:** Plain

Date	Mintage	VF20	XF40	MS60	MS63	MS65
1997 М	—	—	1.00	1.50	3.00	5.00
1997 СП	—	—	2.00	3.00	5.00	7.00
1998 М	—	—	—	0.30	0.40	0.60
1998 СП	—	—	1.00	1.50	3.00	5.00
1999 М	—	—	—	0.30	0.40	0.60
1999 СП	—	—	—	0.30	0.40	0.60
2000 М	—	—	—	0.30	0.40	0.60
2000 СП	—	—	—	0.30	0.40	0.60

Y# 601 5 KOPEKS
2.60 g., Copper-Nickel Clad Steel, 18.5 mm. **Obv:** St. George **Obv. Legend:** БАНК РОССИИ **Rev:** Value above vine sprig **Edge:** Plain

Date	Mintage	VF20	XF40	MS60	MS63	MS65
1997 М	—	—	—	0.35	0.50	0.75
1997 СП	—	—	—	0.35	0.50	0.75
1998 М	—	—	—	0.45	0.65	0.90
1998 СП	—	—	—	0.45	0.65	0.90
2000 М	—	—	—	0.35	0.50	0.75
2000 СП	—	—	—	0.35	0.50	0.75

Y# 602 10 KOPEKS
1.95 g., Brass, 17.5 mm. **Obv:** St. George horseback right slaying dragon **Rev:** Value above vine sprig **Edge:** Reeded

Date	Mintage	VF20	XF40	MS60	MS63	MS65
1997 М	—	—	—	0.50	0.75	1.00
1997 СП	—	—	—	0.50	0.75	1.00
1998 М	—	—	—	0.65	1.00	1.25
1998 СП	—	—	—	0.65	1.00	1.25
1999 М	—	—	—	0.50	0.75	1.00
1999 СП	—	—	—	0.50	0.75	1.00
2000 М	—	—	—	0.50	0.75	1.00
2000 СП	—	—	—	0.50	0.75	1.00

Y# 603 50 KOPEKS
2.90 g., Brass, 19.5 mm. **Obv:** St. George on horseback slaying dragon right **Rev:** Value above vine sprig **Edge:** Reeded

Date	Mintage	VF20	XF40	MS60	MS63	MS65
1997 М	—	—	—	0.75	1.00	1.25
1997 СП	—	—	—	0.75	1.00	1.25
1998 М	—	—	—	1.00	1.50	2.00
1998 СП	—	—	—	1.00	1.50	2.00
1999 М	—	—	—	3.00	5.00	7.00
1999 СП	—	—	—	3.00	5.00	7.00

Y# 604 ROUBLE
3.25 g., Copper-Nickel-Zinc, 20.5 mm. **Obv:** Double-headed eagle **Rev:** Value **Edge:** Reeded

Date	Mintage	VF20	XF40	MS60	MS63	MS65
1997 М	—	—	—	1.00	1.50	2.00
1997 СП	—	—	—	1.00	1.50	2.00
1998 М	—	—	—	1.00	1.50	2.00
1998 СМ	—	—	—	1.00	1.50	2.00
1999 М	—	—	—	1.50	3.00	5.00
1999 СМ	—	—	—	1.50	3.00	5.00

Y# 614 ROUBLE
8.53 g., 0.925 Silver 0.2537 oz. ASW **Series:** World Youth Games **Obv:** Double-headed eagle **Rev:** Female tennis player

Date	Mintage	VF20	XF40	MS60	MS63	MS65
1998	25,000	PF63 25.00				

Y# 615 ROUBLE
8.53 g., 0.925 Silver 0.2537 oz. ASW **Series:** World Youth Games **Obv:** Double-headed eagle **Rev:** Female-gymnast

Date	Mintage	VF20	XF40	MS60	MS63	MS65
1998	25,000	PF63 25.00				

Y# 616 ROUBLE
8.53 g., 0.925 Silver 0.2537 oz. ASW **Series:** World Youth Games **Obv:** Double-headed eagle **Rev:** Fencer

Date	Mintage	VF20	XF40	MS60	MS63	MS65
1998	25,000	PF63 25.00				

Y# 617 ROUBLE
8.53 g., 0.925 Silver 0.2537 oz. ASW **Series:** World Youth Games **Obv:** Double-headed eagle **Rev:** Hammer thrower

Date	Mintage	VF20	XF40	MS60	MS63	MS65
1998	25,000	PF63 25.00				

Y# 618 ROUBLE
8.53 g., 0.925 Silver 0.2537 oz. ASW **Series:** World Youth Games **Obv:** Double-headed eagle **Rev:** Female gymnast

Date	Mintage	VF20	XF40	MS60	MS63	MS65
1998	25,000	**PF63** 25.00				

Y# 619 ROUBLE
8.53 g., 0.925 Silver 0.2537 oz. ASW **Series:** World Youth Games **Obv:** Double-headed eagle **Rev:** Volleyball player

Date	Mintage	VF20	XF40	MS60	MS63	MS65
1998	25,000	**PF63** 25.00				

Y# 628 ROUBLE
17.44 g., 0.900 Silver 0.5046 oz. ASW, 33 mm. **Series:** Wildlife **Obv:** Double-headed eagle **Rev:** Far Eastern Skink

Date	Mintage	VF20	XF40	MS60	MS63	MS65
1998	15,000	**PF63** 70.00				

Y# 629 ROUBLE
17.44 g., 0.900 Silver 0.5046 oz. ASW, 33 mm. **Series:** Wildlife **Obv:** Double-headed eagle **Rev:** Lavtev Walrus

Date	Mintage	VF20	XF40	MS60	MS63	MS65
1998	15,000	**PF63** 70.00				

Y# 630 ROUBLE
17.44 g., 0.900 Silver 0.5046 oz. ASW, 33 mm. **Series:** Wildlife **Obv:** Double-headed eagle **Rev:** Emperor Goose

Date	Mintage	VF20	XF40	MS60	MS63	MS65
1998	15,000	**PF63** 70.00				

Y# 640 ROUBLE
Copper-Nickel-Zinc, 20.5 mm. **Obv:** Double-headed eagle **Rev:** Stylized head of Pushkin left **Edge:** Reeded

Date	Mintage	VF20	XF40	MS60	MS63	MS65
1999 M	5,000,000	—	—	5.00	8.00	10.00
1999 CM	5,000,000	—	—	5.00	8.00	10.00

Y# 641 ROUBLE
17.44 g., 0.900 Silver 0.5046 oz. ASW **Series:** Wildlife **Obv:** Double-headed eagle **Rev:** Daurian Hedgehog

Date	Mintage	VF20	XF40	MS60	MS63	MS65
1999	15,000	**PF63** 80.00				

Y# 642 ROUBLE
17.44 g., 0.900 Silver 0.5046 oz. ASW **Series:** Wildlife **Obv:** Double-headed eagle **Rev:** Caucasian viper

Date	Mintage	VF20	XF40	MS60	MS63	MS65
1999	15,000	**PF63** 80.00				

Y# 643 ROUBLE
17.44 g., 0.900 Silver 0.5046 oz. ASW **Series:** Wildlife **Obv:** Double-headed eagle **Rev:** Ross's Gull standing on shore

Date	Mintage	VF20	XF40	MS60	MS63	MS65
1999	15,000	**PF63** 80.00				

Y# 719 ROUBLE
17.44 g., 0.900 Silver 0.5046 oz. ASW, 33 mm. **Subject:** Wildlife **Obv:** Double-headed eagle **Rev:** Two Black-hooded cranes **Edge:** Reeded

Date	Mintage	VF20	XF40	MS60	MS63	MS65
2000 СП	3,000	**PF63** 400				

Y# 720 ROUBLE
17.44 g., 0.900 Silver 0.5046 oz. ASW **Obv:** Double-headed eagle **Rev:** Leopard Runner snake

Date	Mintage	VF20	XF40	MS60	MS63	MS65
2000 СП	3,000	**PF63** 500				

Y# 721 ROUBLE
17.44 g., 0.900 Silver 0.5046 oz. ASW **Obv:** Double-headed eagle **Rev:** Russian Desman

Date	Mintage	VF20	XF40	MS60	MS63	MS65
2000 СП	3,000	**PF63** 500				

Y# 605 2 ROUBLES
5.10 g., Copper-Nickel-Zinc, 23 mm. **Obv:** Double-headed eagle **Rev:** Value and vine sprig **Edge:** Segmented reeding

Date	Mintage	VF20	XF40	MS60	MS63	MS65
1997 M	—	—	—	2.00	3.00	5.00
1997 CM	—	—	—	2.00	3.00	5.00
1998 M	—	—	—	2.00	3.00	5.00
1998 CM	—	—	—	2.00	3.00	5.00
1999 M	—	—	—	3.00	6.00	9.00
1999 CM	—	—	—	3.00	6.00	9.00

Y# 607 2 ROUBLES
17.00 g., 0.925 Silver 0.5056 oz. ASW, 33 mm. **Subject:** 100th Anniversary - Sergei Eisenstein **Obv:** Double-headed eagle **Rev:** Head facing on movie screen with camera on stand at left

Date	Mintage	VF20	XF40	MS60	MS63	MS65
1998	15,000	—	—	25.00	27.50	32.50

Y# 608 2 ROUBLES
17.00 g., 0.925 Silver 0.5056 oz. ASW, 33 mm. **Subject:** 50th Anniversary - Sergei Eisenstein **Obv:** Double-headed eagle **Rev:** Figure looking at film strip, ship in background

Date	Mintage	VF20	XF40	MS60	MS63	MS65
1998	15,000	—	—	25.00	27.50	32.50

Y# 609 2 ROUBLES
17.00 g., 0.925 Silver 0.5056 oz. ASW, 33 mm. **Obv:** Double-headed eagle **Rev:** K.S. Stanslavski

Date	Mintage	VF20	XF40	MS60	MS63	MS65
1998	15,000	—	—	25.00	27.50	32.50

Y# 610 2 ROUBLES

17.00 g., 0.925 Silver 0.5056 oz. ASW, 33 mm. **Obv:** Double-headed eagle **Rev:** Maxim Gorky play - Stanislavsky method

Date	Mintage	VF20	XF40	MS60	MS63	MS65
1998	15,000	—	—	25.00	27.50	32.50

Y# 620 2 ROUBLES

17.00 g., 0.925 Silver 0.5056 oz. ASW **Obv:** Double-headed eagle **Rev:** Victor Mikhailovich Vasnetsov - 3 ancient warriors

Date	Mintage	VF20	XF40	MS60	MS63	MS65
1998	15,000	—	—	25.00	27.50	32.50

Y# 621 2 ROUBLES

17.00 g., 0.925 Silver 0.5056 oz. ASW **Obv:** Double-headed eagle **Rev:** Victor Mikhailovich Vasnetsov - 3 seated figures

Date	Mintage	VF20	XF40	MS60	MS63	MS65
1998	15,000	—	—	25.00	27.50	32.50

Y# 649 2 ROUBLES

17.00 g., 0.925 Silver 0.5056 oz. ASW **Subject:** K. L. Khetagurov 1859-1906 **Obv:** Double-headed eagle **Rev:** Portrait with mountain tops and buildings

Date	Mintage	VF20	XF40	MS60	MS63	MS65
1999	3,000	PF63 300				

Y# 650 2 ROUBLES

17.00 g., 0.925 Silver 0.5056 oz. ASW **Subject:** N. K. Rerikh 1874-1947 **Obv:** Double-headed eagle **Rev:** Painter with mountains in the background

Date	Mintage	VF20	XF40	MS60	MS63	MS65
1999	15,000	PF63 25.00	PF65 30.00			

Y# 651 2 ROUBLES

17.00 g., 0.925 Silver 0.5056 oz. ASW **Subject:** The Human Acts by Rerikh. **Obv:** Double-headed eagle **Rev:** Detail from painting, artist's portrait above

Date	Mintage	VF20	XF40	MS60	MS63	MS65
1999	15,000	PF63 25.00	PF65 30.00			

Y# 652 2 ROUBLES

17.00 g., 0.925 Silver 0.5056 oz. ASW **Subject:** K. P. Bryulov 1799-1852 **Obv:** Double-headed eagle **Rev:** Half length bust facing

Date	Mintage	VF20	XF40	MS60	MS63	MS65
1999	15,000	PF63 22.50	PF65 28.00			

Y# 653 2 ROUBLES

17.00 g., 0.925 Silver 0.5056 oz. ASW **Subject:** The Last Day of Pompei **Obv:** Double-headed eagle **Rev:** Detail from painting, portrait in exergue

Date	Mintage	VF20	XF40	MS60	MS63	MS65
1999	15,000	PF63 22.50	PF65 28.00			

Y# 654 2 ROUBLES

17.00 g., 0.925 Silver 0.5056 oz. ASW **Subject:** I.P. Pavlov **Obv:** Double-headed eagle **Rev:** Half bust 1/4 left, dog, books, cap, and gown

Date	Mintage	VF20	XF40	MS60	MS63	MS65
1999	15,000	PF63 20.00	PF65 25.00			

Y# 655 2 ROUBLES

17.00 g., 0.925 Silver 0.5056 oz. ASW **Subject:** I.P. Pavlov **Obv:** Double-headed eagle **Rev:** Seated figure left and silence tower

Date	Mintage	VF20	XF40	MS60	MS63	MS65
1999	15,000	PF63 20.00	PF65 25.00			

Y# 659 2 ROUBLES

17.00 g., 0.925 Silver 0.5056 oz. ASW **Subject:** Eugeny Abramovich Baratynsky **Obv:** Double-headed eagle **Rev:** Cameo to right of scenery **Edge:** Reeded

Date	Mintage	VF20	XF40	MS60	MS63	MS65
2000	—	PF63 75.00	PF65 85.00			

Y# 660 2 ROUBLES

17.00 g., 0.925 Silver 0.5056 oz. ASW **Subject:** F. A. Vassiliyev **Obv:** Double-headed eagle **Rev:** Cameo to right of scenery

Date	Mintage	VF20	XF40	MS60	MS63	MS65
2000	—	PF63 50.00	PF65 60.00			

Y# 662 2 ROUBLES

17.00 g., 0.925 Silver 0.5056 oz. ASW **Subject:** S. V. Kovaleuskaya **Obv:** Double-headed eagle **Rev:** Cameo to left of academic items

Date	Mintage	VF20	XF40	MS60	MS63	MS65
2000	—	PF63 45.00	PF65 55.00			

Y# 663 2 ROUBLES

5.10 g., Copper-Nickel-Zinc, 23 mm. **Series:** World War II **Obv:** Value **Rev:** Infantry assault at Stalingrad **Edge:** Segmented reeding

Date	Mintage	VF20	XF40	MS60	MS63	MS65
2000 СПМД	10,000,000	—	—	2.00	3.00	5.00

Y# 664 2 ROUBLES

5.10 g., Copper-Nickel-Zinc, 23 mm. **Obv:** Value at left of vine sprig **Rev:** Cannon manufacturing scene in Tula **Edge:** Segmented reeding

Date	Mintage	VF20	XF40	MS60	MS63	MS65
2000 ММД	10,000,000	—	—	2.00	3.00	5.00

Y# 665 2 ROUBLES

5.10 g., Copper-Nickel-Zinc, 23 mm. **Obv:** Value at left of vine sprig **Rev:** Truck-mounted rocket launchers in Smolensk **Edge:** Segmented reeding

Date	Mintage	VF20	XF40	MS60	MS63	MS65
2000 ММД	10,000,000	—	—	2.00	3.00	5.00

Y# 666 2 ROUBLES

5.10 g., Copper-Nickel-Zinc, 23 mm. **Obv:** Value at left of vine sprig **Rev:** Murmansk ship convoy **Edge:** Segmented reeding

Date	Mintage	VF20	XF40	MS60	MS63	MS65
2000 ММД	10,000,000	—	—	2.00	3.00	5.00

Y# 667 2 ROUBLES

5.10 g., Copper-Nickel-Zinc, 23 mm. **Obv:** Value at left of vine sprig **Rev:** Defense of Moscow scene **Edge:** Segmented reeding

Date	Mintage	VF20	XF40	MS60	MS63	MS65
2000 ММД	10,000,000	—	—	2.00	3.00	5.00

Y# 668 2 ROUBLES

5.10 g., Copper-Nickel-Zinc, 23 mm. **Obv:** Value at left of vine sprig **Rev:** Marine landing scene in Novorusiisk **Edge:** Segmented reeding

Date	Mintage	VF20	XF40	MS60	MS63	MS65
2000 СПМД	10,000,000	—	—	2.00	3.00	5.00

Y# 669 2 ROUBLES

5.10 g., Copper-Nickel-Zinc, 23 mm. **Obv:** Value at left of vine sprig **Rev:** Siege of Leningrad truck convoy scene **Edge:** Segmented reeding

Date	Mintage	VF20	XF40	MS60	MS63	MS65
2000 СПМД	10,000,000	—	—	2.00	3.00	5.00

Y# 704 2 ROUBLES

17.44 g., 0.925 Silver 0.5187 oz. ASW, 33 mm. **Subject:** M.I. Chigorin **Obv:** Double-headed eagle **Rev:** Cameo to left of chess pieces **Edge:** Reeded

Date	Mintage	VF20	XF40	MS60	MS63	MS65
2000 (sp)	5,000	PF63 45.00	PF65 55.00			

Y# 624 3 ROUBLES

34.88 g., 0.900 Silver 1.0093 oz. ASW, 39 mm. **Subject:** Russian Museum, 100th Anniversary **Obv:** Double-headed eagle **Rev:** Soldier Devydov

Date	Mintage	VF20	XF40	MS60	MS63	MS65
1998	15,000	PF63 50.00	PF65 60.00			

Y# 625 3 ROUBLES

34.88 g., 0.900 Silver 1.0093 oz. ASW, 39 mm. **Subject:** Russian Museum, 100th Anniversary **Obv:** Double-headed eagle **Rev:** "Russian Sosaveta" sculpture

Date	Mintage	VF20	XF40	MS60	MS63	MS65
1998	15,000	PF63 50.00	PF65 60.00			

Y# 626 3 ROUBLES

34.88 g., 0.900 Silver 1.0093 oz. ASW, 39 mm. **Subject:** Russian Museum, 100th Anniversary **Obv:** Double-headed eagle **Rev:** Archangel's head within square

Date	Mintage	VF20	XF40	MS60	MS63	MS65
1998	15,000	PF63 50.00	PF65 60.00			

Y# 627 3 ROUBLES

34.88 g., 0.900 Silver 1.0093 oz. ASW, 39 mm. **Subject:** Russian Museum, 100th Anniversary **Obv:** Double-headed eagle **Rev:** Merchant woman drinking tea within square

Date	Mintage	VF20	XF40	MS60	MS63	MS65
1998	15,000	PF63 50.00	PF65 60.00			

Y# 631 3 ROUBLES

34.56 g., 0.900 Silver 1.000 oz. ASW **Subject:** Nilo Stolobenskaya Hermitage **Obv:** Double-headed eagle **Rev:** Monastery, ships, boats and kneeling Saint at upper left

Date	Mintage	VF20	XF40	MS60	MS63	MS65
1998	15,000	PF63 70.00	PF65 80.00			

Y# 632 3 ROUBLES

34.56 g., 0.900 Silver 1.000 oz. ASW **Obv:** Double-headed eagle **Rev:** Church view from bell tower

Date	Mintage	VF20	XF40	MS60	MS63	MS65
1998	5,000	PF63 400				

Y# 633 3 ROUBLES

34.88 g., 0.900 Silver 1.0093 oz. ASW **Subject:** Russian Human Rights Year **Obv:** Double-headed eagle **Rev:** Document, people, and map **Edge:** Reeded

Date	Mintage	VF20	XF40	MS60	MS63	MS65
1998	15,000	PF63 45.00	PF65 55.00			

Y# 634 3 ROUBLES

34.77 g., 0.900 Silver 1.0061 oz. ASW **Subject:** 275th Anniversary - St. Petersburg University **Obv:** Double-headed eagle **Rev:** Four heads facing in front of building

Date	Mintage	VF20	XF40	MS60	MS63	MS65
1999	15,000	PF63 50.00	PF65 60.00			

Y# 635 3 ROUBLES

34.73 g., 0.900 Silver 1.0049 oz. ASW **Obv:** Double-headed eagle **Rev:** Mardjany Mosque in Kazan

Date	Mintage	VF20	XF40	MS60	MS63	MS65
1999	15,000	PF63 55.00	PF65 65.00			

Y# 636 3 ROUBLES

34.73 g., 0.900 Silver 1.0049 oz. ASW **Subject:** 200th Birthday - A. S. Pushkin **Obv:** Double-headed eagle **Rev:** Seated figure at desk facing 1/4 left

Date	Mintage	VF20	XF40	MS60	MS63	MS65
1999	15,000	PF63 50.00	PF65 60.00			

Y# 637 3 ROUBLES

34.73 g., 0.900 Silver 1.0049 oz. ASW **Subject:** 200th Birthday - A. S. Pushkin **Obv:** Double-headed eagle **Rev:** Standing 1/2 length figure right

Date	Mintage	VF20	XF40	MS60	MS63	MS65
1999	15,000	PF63 50.00	PF65 60.00			

Y# 638 3 ROUBLES

34.73 g., 0.900 Silver 1.0049 oz. ASW **Subject:** First Tibet Exhibition 1879-1880 **Obv:** Double-headed eagle **Rev:** Men on horseback, animals at corners

Date	Mintage	VF20	XF40	MS60	MS63	MS65
1999	15,000	PF63 40.00	PF65 50.00			

Y# 639 3 ROUBLES

34.73 g., 0.900 Silver 1.0049 oz. ASW **Subject:** Second Tibet Exhibition 1883-1885 **Obv:** Double-headed eagle **Rev:** Camp scene

Date	Mintage	VF20	XF40	MS60	MS63	MS65
1999	15,000	PF63 40.00	PF65 50.00			

Y# 644 3 ROUBLES

34.71 g., 0.900 Silver 1.0044 oz. ASW **Subject:** Science Academy. **Obv:** Double-headed eagle **Rev:** Allegorical figure, building, portraits, crowned double headed eagle

Date	Mintage	VF20	XF40	MS60	MS63	MS65
1999	5,000	PF63 275				

Y# 645 3 ROUBLES

34.71 g., 0.900 Silver 1.0044 oz. ASW **Subject:** Estada Kuskovo Palace **Obv:** Double-headed eagle **Rev:** Palace from three perspectives

Date	Mintage	VF20	XF40	MS60	MS63	MS65
1999	15,000	PF63 55.00	PF65 65.00			

Y# 646 3 ROUBLES

34.71 g., 0.900 Silver 1.0044 oz. ASW **Subject:** Juryev Monastery, Novgorod **Obv:** Double-headed eagle **Rev:** Building view and detail from interior

Date	Mintage	VF20	XF40	MS60	MS63	MS65
1999	15,000	PF63 70.00	PF65 80.00			

Y# 647 3 ROUBLES

34.88 g., 0.900 Silver 1.0093 oz. ASW **Subject:** 50th Anniversary - Diplomacy with China **Obv:** Double-headed eagle **Rev:** Moscow Kremlin and Tiananmen Gate

Date	Mintage	VF20	XF40	MS60	MS63	MS65
1999	3,000	PF63 400				

Y# 657 3 ROUBLES

34.73 g., 0.900 Silver 1.0049 oz. ASW **Subject:** Ballet **Obv:** Double-headed eagle **Rev:** Sword fight

Date	Mintage	VF20	XF40	MS60	MS63	MS65
1999	10,000	PF63 42.50	PF65 52.50			

Y# 658 3 ROUBLES

34.73 g., 0.900 Silver 1.0049 oz. ASW **Subject:** Ballet **Obv:** Double-headed eagle **Rev:** Couple dancing, Arabic soldiers in background

Date	Mintage	VF20	XF40	MS60	MS63	MS65
1999	10,000	PF63 42.50	PF65 52.50			

Y# 690 3 ROUBLES

34.73 g., 0.900 Silver 1.0049 oz. ASW, 38.8 mm. **Subject:** Ufa Friendship Monument **Obv:** Double-headed eagle **Rev:** Five figures and monument **Edge:** Reeded

Date	Mintage	VF20	XF40	MS60	MS63	MS65
1999	3,000	PF63 65.00	PF65 75.00			

Y# 661 3 ROUBLES
34.88 g., 0.900 Silver 1.0093 oz. ASW **Subject:** World Ice Hockey Championship **Obv:** Double-headed eagle **Rev:** Two hockey players **Edge:** Reeded

Date	Mintage	VF20	XF40	MS60	MS63	MS65
2000	—	PF63 500				

Y# 671 3 ROUBLES
34.76 g., 0.900 Silver 1.0058 oz. ASW **Series:** Olympics **Obv:** Double-headed eagle **Rev:** 2000 Olympic design in front of map **Edge:** Reeded

Date	Mintage	VF20	XF40	MS60	MS63	MS65
2000	5,000	PF63 150				

Y# 673 3 ROUBLES
34.67 g., 0.999 Silver 1.1136 oz. ASW **Subject:** Soccer **Obv:** Double-headed eagle **Rev:** Two soccer players, map, and net **Edge:** Reeded

Date	Mintage	VF20	XF40	MS60	MS63	MS65
2000	3,000	PF63 175				

Y# 674 3 ROUBLES
34.88 g., 0.900 Silver 1.0093 oz. ASW, 39 mm. **Subject:** 55th Anniversary - WWII **Obv:** Seated soldier **Rev:** Soviet Order of Glory **Edge Lettering:** BANK of RUSSIA THREE ROUBLES 2000

Date	Mintage	VF20	XF40	MS60	MS63	MS65
2000	5,000	PF63 75.00	PF65 85.00			

Y# 705 3 ROUBLES
34.88 g., 0.900 Silver 1.0093 oz. ASW, 39 mm. **Subject:** St. Nicholas Monastery **Obv:** Double-headed eagle **Rev:** Saint and buildings **Edge:** Reeded

Date	Mintage	VF20	XF40	MS60	MS63	MS65
2000 (m)	5,000	PF63 65.00	PF65 75.00			

Y# 706 3 ROUBLES
34.88 g., 0.900 Silver 1.0093 oz. ASW **Subject:** Novgorod Kremlin **Obv:** Double-headed eagle **Rev:** Buildings

Date	Mintage	VF20	XF40	MS60	MS63	MS65
2000 (m)	5,000	PF63 60.00	PF65 70.00			

Y# 707 3 ROUBLES
34.88 g., 0.900 Silver 1.0093 oz. ASW **Subject:** City of Pushkin **Obv:** Double-headed eagle **Rev:** Park and city view

Date	Mintage	VF20	XF40	MS60	MS63	MS65
2000 (m)	5,000	PF63 75.00	PF65 85.00			

Y# 708 3 ROUBLES
34.88 g., 0.900 Silver 1.0093 oz. ASW, 39 mm. **Series:** Third Millennium **Subject:** Science **Obv:** Double-headed eagle **Rev:** Astronaut, atomic elements chart, etc. **Edge:** Reeded

Date	Mintage	VF20	XF40	MS60	MS63	MS65
2000 (m)	5,000	PF63 50.00	PF65 60.00			

Y# 709 3 ROUBLES
34.88 g., 0.900 Silver 1.0093 oz. ASW **Series:** Third Millennium **Subject:** Human Role **Obv:** Double-headed eagle **Rev:** People between cog wheel and computer

Date	Mintage	VF20	XF40	MS60	MS63	MS65
2000 (m)	5,000	PF63 50.00	PF65 60.00			

Y# 714 3 ROUBLES
34.88 g., 0.900 Silver 1.0093 oz. ASW **Subject:** 140th Anniversary - State Bank of Russia **Obv:** Double-headed eagle **Rev:** Seated allegorical woman

Date	Mintage	VF20	XF40	MS60	MS63	MS65
2000 (m)	3,000	PF63 475				

Y# 716 3 ROUBLES
34.88 g., 1.0093 Silver 1.1318 oz. ASW **Subject:** Field Marshal Suvorov in Switzerland **Obv:** Double-headed eagle **Rev:** Battle scene

Date	Mintage	VF20	XF40	MS60	MS63	MS65
2000 (sp)	5,000	PF63 70.00	PF65 80.00			

Y# 722 3 ROUBLES
34.88 g., 0.900 Silver 1.0093 oz. ASW **Subject:** Snow Leopard **Obv:** Double-headed eagle **Rev:** Leopard on log

Date	Mintage	VF20	XF40	MS60	MS63	MS65
2000 (m)	5,000	PF63 75.00	PF65 85.00			

Y# 606 5 ROUBLES
6.45 g., Copper-Nickel Clad Copper, 25 mm. **Obv:** Double-headed eagle **Rev:** Value at left of vine sprig **Edge:** Segmented reeding

Date	Mintage	VF20	XF40	MS60	MS63	MS65
1997 ММД	—	—	—	3.00	4.00	—
1997 СПМД	—	—	—	3.00	4.00	—
1998 ММД	—	—	—	3.00	4.00	—
1998 СПМД	—	—	—	3.00	4.00	—
1999 СПМД	—	—	—	—	—	—

Unique

Y# 695 10 ROUBLES
1.55 g., 0.999 Gold 0.0498 oz. AGW, 12 mm. **Subject:** Russian Ballet **Obv:** Double-headed eagle **Rev:** Standing knight within flower wreath **Edge:** Reeded

Date	Mintage	VF20	XF40	MS60	MS63	MS65
1999 (m)	2,500	PF63 90.00				

Y# 670 10 ROUBLES
8.26 g., Bi-Metallic Copper-Nickel center in Brass ring, 27 mm. **Series:** WWII **Subject:** 55th Anniversary - Victorious Conclusion of WWII **Obv:** Value **Rev:** Infantry officer within star design **Edge:** Reeded and lettered

Date	Mintage	VF20	XF40	MS60	MS63	MS65
2000 (sp)	10,000,000	—	—	4.00	7.00	9.00
2000 (m)	10,000,000	—	—	4.00	7.00	9.00

Y# 691 25 ROUBLES
173.29 g., 0.900 Silver 5.0143 oz. ASW, 60 mm. **Subject:** Alexander Pushkin **Obv:** Double-headed eagle **Rev:** Walking figure with hat and cane **Edge:** Reeded

Date	Mintage	VF20	XF40	MS60	MS63	MS65
1999 (m)	3,000	PF63 225	PF65 275			

Y# 696 25 ROUBLES
173.29 g., 0.900 Silver 5.0143 oz. ASW, 60 mm. **Subject:** Russian Ballet **Obv:** Double-headed eagle **Rev:** Raymonda and the Knight dance scene **Edge:** Reeded

Date	Mintage	VF20	XF40	MS60	MS63	MS65
1999 (m)	3,000	PF63 225	PF65 275			

Y# 697 25 ROUBLES
3.20 g., 0.999 Gold 0.1028 oz. AGW, 16 mm. **Subject:** Russian Ballet **Obv:** Double-headed eagle **Rev:** Dancing Saracen. **Edge:** Reeded

Date	Mintage	VF20	XF40	MS60	MS63	MS65
1999 (sp)	2,000	PF63 200				

Y# 701 25 ROUBLES
173.29 g., 0.900 Silver 5.0143 oz. ASW, 60 mm. **Subject:** Russian Explorers: N.M. Przhevalsky **Obv:** Double-headed eagle **Rev:** Caravan in center of other designs **Edge:** Reeded

Date	Mintage	VF20	XF40	MS60	MS63	MS65
1999 (sp)	3,000	PF63 225	PF65 275			

Y# 710 25 ROUBLES
173.29 g., 0.900 Silver 5.0143 oz. ASW, 60 mm. **Series:** Third Millennium **Subject:** Education **Obv:** Double-headed eagle **Rev:** Ancient monk and modern student **Edge:** Reeded

Date	Mintage	VF20	XF40	MS60	MS63	MS65
2000 (m)	1,000	PF63 500	PF65 550			

Y# 715 25 ROUBLES
173.29 g., 0.900 Silver 5.0143 oz. ASW, 60 mm. **Subject:** State Bank of Russia, 140th Anniversary **Obv:** Double-headed eagle **Rev:** Document, portrait and building **Edge:** Reeded

Date	Mintage	VF20	XF40	MS60	MS63	MS65
2000 (m)	1,000	PF63 800	PF65 900			

Y# 717 25 ROUBLES
173.29 g., 0.900 Silver 5.0143 oz. ASW, 60 mm. **Obv:** Double-headed eagle **Rev:** Field Marshal Suvorov **Edge:** Reeded

Date	Mintage	VF20	XF40	MS60	MS63	MS65
2000 (m)	1,000	PF63 550	PF65 600			

Y# 723 25 ROUBLES
173.29 g., 0.900 Silver 5.0143 oz. ASW, 60 mm. **Obv:** Double-headed eagle **Rev:** Snow Leopard on branch **Edge:** Reeded

Date	Mintage	VF20	XF40	MS60	MS63	MS65
2000 (m)	1,000	PF63 450	PF65 500			

Y# 648 50 ROUBLES
8.75 g., 0.900 Gold 0.2532 oz. AGW **Subject:** 50th Anniversary - Diplomacy with China **Obv:** Double-headed eagle **Rev:** Moscow Kremlin and Tiananmen Gate

Date	Mintage	VF20	XF40	MS60	MS63	MS65
1999	1,000	PF63 475				

Y# 692 50 ROUBLES
8.75 g., 0.900 Gold 0.2532 oz. AGW, 22.6 mm. **Obv:** Double-headed eagle **Rev:** Alexander Pushkin **Edge:** Reeded

Date	Mintage	VF20	XF40	MS60	MS63	MS65
1999 (m)	1,500	PF63 450				

Y# 698 50 ROUBLES
8.75 g., 0.999 Gold 0.281 oz. AGW, 22.6 mm. **Subject:** Russian Ballet **Obv:** Double-headed eagle **Rev:** Dancing figures **Edge:** Reeded

Date	Mintage	VF20	XF40	MS60	MS63	MS65
1999 (m)	1,500	PF63 475				

Y# 702 50 ROUBLES
8.75 g., 0.900 Gold 0.2532 oz. AGW, 22.6 mm. **Subject:** Russian Explorer N.M. Przhevalsky **Obv:** Double-headed eagle **Rev:** Armored bust 1/4 right **Edge:** Reeded

Date	Mintage	VF20	XF40	MS60	MS63	MS65
1999 (sp)	1,500	PF63 450				

Y# 672 50 ROUBLES
8.71 g., 0.900 Gold 0.252 oz. AGW **Series:** Olympics **Obv:** Double-headed eagle **Rev:** Torch runner on map

Date	Mintage	VF20	XF40	MS60	MS63	MS65
2000	1,000	PF63 475				

Y# 718 50 ROUBLES
8.75 g., 0.900 Gold 0.2532 oz. AGW, 22.6 mm. **Subject:** Field Marshal Suvorov **Obv:** Double-headed eagle **Rev:** Cameo above cannons **Edge:** Reeded

Date	Mintage	VF20	XF40	MS60	MS63	MS65
2000 (sp)	500	PF63 475				

Y# 725 50 ROUBLES
7.89 g., 0.999 Gold 0.2534 oz. AGW, 22.6 mm. **Obv:** Double-headed eagle **Rev:** Snow leopard head **Edge:** Reeded

Date	Mintage	VF20	XF40	MS60	MS63	MS65
2000 (sp)	1,000	PF63 450				

Y# 693 100 ROUBLES
1111.12 g., 0.900 Silver 32.151 oz. ASW, 100 mm. **Subject:** Alexander Pushkin **Obv:** Double-headed eagle **Rev:** Statue, monuments and buildings **Edge:** Reeded

Date	Mintage	VF20	XF40	MS60	MS63	MS65
1999 (m)	1,000	PF63 1,000	PF65 1,100			

Y# 694 100 ROUBLES
17.45 g., 0.900 Gold 0.5049 oz. AGW, 30 mm. **Subject:** Alexander Pushkin **Obv:** Double-headed eagle **Rev:** Head 1/4 right, tree and scenes **Edge:** Reeded

Date	Mintage	VF20	XF40	MS60	MS63	MS65
1999	1,000	PF63 925				

Y# 700 100 ROUBLES
15.72 g., 0.999 Gold 0.5049 oz. AGW, 30 mm. **Subject:** Russian Ballet **Obv:** Double-headed eagle **Rev:** Ballerina **Edge:** Reeded

Date	Mintage	VF20	XF40	MS60	MS63	MS65
1999 (sp)	1,500	PF63 925				

Y# 703 100 ROUBLES
17.45 g., 0.900 Gold 0.5049 oz. AGW, 30 mm. **Subject:** Russian Explorer N.M. Przhevalsky **Obv:** Double-headed eagle **Rev:** Two men viewing lake **Edge:** Reeded

Date	Mintage	VF20	XF40	MS60	MS63	MS65
1999 (sp)	1,000	PF63 925				

Y# 711 100 ROUBLES
1111.12 g., 0.900 Silver 32.151 oz. ASW, 100 mm. **Subject:** Russian State **Obv:** Double-headed eagle **Rev:** Mother Russia, mythological bird and map **Edge:** Reeded

Date	Mintage	VF20	XF40	MS60	MS63	MS65
2000 (m)	500	PF63 1,350	PF65 1,450			

Y# 713 100 ROUBLES
17.45 g., 0.900 Gold 0.5049 oz. AGW, 30 mm. **Subject:** Department of Mining 300 Years **Obv:** Double-headed eagle **Rev:** Miner and equipment **Edge:** Reeded

Date	Mintage	VF20	XF40	MS60	MS63	MS65
2000 (m)	1,000	PF63 925				

Y# 724 100 ROUBLES
1111.12 g., 0.900 Silver 32.151 oz. ASW, 100 mm. **Obv:** Double-headed eagle **Rev:** Two snow leopards **Edge:** Reeded

Date	Mintage	VF20	XF40	MS60	MS63	MS65
2000 (sp)	500	PF63 1,250	PF65 1,350			

Y# 726 100 ROUBLES
15.72 g., 0.999 Gold 0.5049 oz. AGW, 30 mm. **Obv:** Double-headed eagle **Rev:** Snow leopard on branch **Edge:** Reeded

Date	Mintage	VF20	XF40	MS60	MS63	MS65
2000 (sp)	1,000	PF63 975				

Y# 729 100 ROUBLES

1111.12 g., 0.900 Silver 32.151 oz. ASW, 100 mm. **Subject:** WWII Victory 55th Anniversary **Obv:** Russian soldier writing on Reichstag building pillar **Rev:** Conference scene **Edge:** Reeded

Date	Mintage	VF20	XF40	MS60	MS63	MS65
2000 (sp)	500	PF63 1,350	PF65 1,450			

Y# 656 200 ROUBLES

3342.39 g., 0.900 Silver 96.7142 oz. ASW **Subject:** 275th Anniversary - St. Petersburg Mint **Obv:** Double-headed eagle **Rev:** Peter the Great, mint view, coin designs, and medal of the Imperial Order

Date	Mintage	VF20	XF40	MS60	MS63	MS65
1999	150	PF65 3,250				

Y# 727 200 ROUBLES

31.37 g., 0.999 Gold 1.0076 oz. AGW, 33 mm. **Obv:** Double-headed eagle **Rev:** Snow leopard on branch **Edge:** Reeded

Date	Mintage	VF20	XF40	MS60	MS63	MS65
2000 (sp)	500	PF63 1,875				

Y# 728 10000 ROUBLES

1001.10 g., 0.999 Gold 32.1539 oz. AGW, 100 mm. **Obv:** Double-headed eagle **Rev:** Snow leopard with two cubs **Edge:** Reeded

Date	Mintage	VF20	XF40	MS60	MS63	MS65
2000 (m)	100	PF63 48,000				

PATTERNS

Including off metal strikes

KM#	Date	Mintage	Identification	Mkt Val
Pn160	1911	—	5 Kopeks. Nickel.	16,500
Pn161	1911	—	10 Kopeks. Nickel.	15,000

KM#	Date	Mintage	Identification	Mkt Val
Pn162	1911	—	20 Kopeks. Nickel.	14,200
Pn163	1911	—	20 Kopeks. Nickel.	—
Pn164	1911	—	25 Kopeks. Nickel. Eagle, date below. 25 in circle.	—
Pn165	1916	—	Kopek. Copper. Dotted background in circle, date.	—
Pn166	1916	—	Kopek. Copper. Plain background.	—
Pn167	1916	—	Kopek. Copper. Value, date below.	—
Pn168	1916	—	2 Kopeks. Copper. Eagle in circle. 2 in circle, value, date below.	—
Pn169	1916	—	3 Kopeks. Copper. Eagle in circle. 3 in circle, value, date below.	—

KM#	Date	Mintage	Identification	Mkt Val
Pn170	1916	—	5 Kopeks. Copper.	—

KM#	Date	Mintage	Identification	Mkt Val
Pn171	1916	—	5 Roubles. Unknown Metal.	3,400

KM#	Date	Mintage	Identification	Mkt Val
Pn172	1917	—	3 Kopeks. Copper. Plain. 1/2mm larger than 1916.	3,500
Pn173	1922	—	20 Kopeks. Bronze. Y#82.	—
Pn174	1922	—	50 Kopeks. Silver. Plain. Y#89.	—
Pn175	1923	—	20 Kopeks. Bronze. Y#82.	475
Pn176	1923	—	20 Kopeks. Copper. Y#82.	475
Pn177	1924	—	Kopek. Copper-Aluminum. Y#76.	—
Pn178	1924	—	Kopek. Bronze. Y#76.	—
Pn179	1924	—	Kopek. Aluminum. Y#76.	—
Pn180	1924	—	Kopek. Copper-Nickel. Y#76.	—
Pn181	1924	—	Kopek. Brass. Y#76.	—

Note: Additional metals exist

KM#	Date	Mintage	Identification	Mkt Val
Pn182	1924	—	2 Kopeks. Copper-Aluminum. Y#77.	—
Pn183	1924	—	2 Kopeks. Bronze. Y#77.	—
Pn184	1924	—	2 Kopeks. Aluminum. Y#77.	—
Pn185	1924	—	2 Kopeks. Copper-Nickel. Y#77.	—
Pn186	1924	—	2 Kopeks. Brass. Y#77.	—

Note: Additional metals exist

KM#	Date	Mintage	Identification	Mkt Val
Pn187	1924	—	3 Kopeks. Copper-Aluminum. Y#78.	—
Pn188	1924	—	3 Kopeks. Bronze. Y#78.	—
Pn189	1924	—	3 Kopeks. Aluminum. Y#78.	—
Pn190	1924	—	3 Kopeks. Copper-Nickel. Y#78.	—
Pn191	1924	—	3 Kopeks. Brass. Y#78.	—

Note: Additional metals exist

KM#	Date	Mintage	Identification	Mkt Val
Pn192	1924	—	5 Kopeks. Unknown Metal.	—
Pn193	1924	—	5 Kopeks. Brass. Y#79.	—
Pn194	1924	—	5 Kopeks. Brass. Y#79.	—
Pn195	1924	—	5 Kopeks. Brass. Y#79.	—
Pn196	1924	—	10 Kopeks. Bronze. Y#86.	—
Pn197	1924	—	15 Kopeks. Bronze. Y#87.	—
Pn198	1924	—	15 Kopeks. Copper. Y#87.	—
Pn199	1924	—	20 Kopeks. Bronze. Y#88.	—
Pn200	1924	—	50 Kopeks. Bronze. Y#89.	—
Pn201	1924	—	50 Kopeks. Unknown Metal. Y#89.	—
Pn202	1924	—	50 Kopeks. Copper-Nickel. Plain. Y#89; London Mint.	1,250
Pn203	1924	—	50 Kopeks. Copper-Nickel. Plain. Y#89.	1,850
Pn204	1924	—	Rouble. Aluminum. Y#90.	—

Note: There are additional 1924 patterns but information is sketchy at present

KM#	Date	Mintage	Identification	Mkt Val
Pn205	1925	—	1/2 Kopek. Copper-Aluminum. Y#75.	—
Pn206	1925	—	1/2 Kopek. Aluminum. Y#75.	—
Pn207	1925	—	1/2 Kopek. Copper-Nickel. Y#75.	—
Pn208	1925	—	1/2 Kopek. Bronze. Y#75.	—
Pn209	1925	—	1/2 Kopek. Brass. Y#75.	—

Note: Additional metals exist

KM#	Date	Mintage	Identification	Mkt Val
Pn210	1925	—	10 Kopeks. Nickel. Y#86.	—
Pn211	1925	—	10 Kopeks. Aluminum-Bronze. Y#86.	—
Pn212	1925	—	15 Kopeks. Nickel. Y#87.	—
Pn213	1925	—	15 Kopeks. Copper. Y#87.	—
Pn214	1925	—	15 Kopeks. Aluminum-Bronze. Y#87.	—
Pn215	1925	—	20 Kopeks. Nickel. Y#88.	—
Pn216	1925	—	20 Kopeks. Copper. Y#88.	—
Pn217	1925	—	20 Kopeks. Aluminum-Bronze. Y#88.	—
Pn218	1925	—	50 Kopeks. Silver. Plain. Y#89.2.	—
Pn219	1925	—	50 Kopeks. Bronze. Y#89.2.	—
Pn220	1925	—	50 Kopeks. Lead. Y#89.2.	525
Pn221	1925	—	Chervonetz. Copper. Y#85.	—

KM#	Date	Mintage	Identification	Mkt Val
Pn222	1926	—	3 Kopeks. Aluminum.	—
Pn223	1926	—	3 Kopeks. Aluminum.	—
Pn224	1926	—	3 Kopeks. Unknown Metal. Y#100.	—

KM#	Date	Mintage	Identification	Mkt Val
Pn225	1929	—	10 Kopeks. Nickel.	—
Pn226	1929	—	15 Kopeks. Silver. 35% Silver; Y#87.	—

KM#	Date	Mintage	Identification	Mkt Val
Pn227	1929	—	50 Kopeks. Unknown Metal.	—
Pn228	1931	—	2 Kopeks. Copper. Y#92.	—
Pn229	1931	—	3 Kopeks. Copper. Y#93.	—
Pn230	1931	—	10 Kopeks. Unknown Metal. Y#93.	—
Pn231	1931	—	20 Kopeks. Bronze. Y#97.	—
Pn232	1932	—	3 Kopeks. Copper. KM#93.	—

Note: Additional metals exist

KM#	Date	Mintage	Identification	Mkt Val
Pn233	1932	—	15 Kopeks. Unknown Metal. Y#96.	—
Pn234	1933	—	10 Kopeks. Unknown Metal. Similar to Y#95.	—
Pn235	1934	—	2 Kopeks. Copper. Y#92.	—
Pn236	1934	—	3 Kopeks. Copper. Y#93.	—
Pn237	1936	—	20 Kopeks. Aluminum. Y#104.	—
Pn238	1937	—	20 Kopeks. Aluminum. Y#111.	—
Pn239	1938	—	5 Kopeks. Unknown Metal. Y#101.	—
Pn240	1938	—	15 Kopeks. Aluminum. Plain. Y#110.	—

Pn241 1941 — 3 Kopeks. Unknown Metal. Y#107. —

Pn242 1941 — 50 Kopeks. Unknown Metal. Similar to Y#109. —

Pn243 1943 — Rouble. Unknown Metal. Portrait Stalin. —

Pn244 1946 — 10 Kopeks. Unknown Metal. Y#102. —

Pn245 1946 — 20 Kopeks. Unknown Metal. Y#111. —

Pn246 1947 — Kopek. Aluminum-Bronze. Similar to Y#112; 16 bands on wreath. —

Pn247 1947 — 2 Kopeks. Aluminum-Bronze. Similar to Y#113; 16 bands on wreath. —

Pn248 1947 — 3 Kopeks. Unknown Metal. Similar to Y#114; 16 bands on wreath. —

Pn249 1947 — 5 Kopeks. Aluminum-Bronze. Similar to Y#115; 16 bands on wreath. —

Pn250 1947 — 10 Kopeks. Nickel. Similar to Y#116; 16 bands on wreath. —

Pn251 1947 — 15 Kopeks. Unknown Metal. Similar to Y#117; 16 bands on wreath. —

Pn252 1947 — 20 Kopeks. Nickel. Similar to Y#118; 16 bands on wreath. —

Pn253 1949 — Chervonetz. Copper. —

Pn254 1953 — Kopek. Copper-Nickel. With legend. Hammer and sickle, value above, date below. 850

Pn255 1953 — Kopek. Aluminum. —

Pn256 1953 — Kopek. Nickel. —

Note: Additional metals exist

Pn257 1953 — Kopek. Copper-Nickel. With legend. Hammer and sickle, value above, date below. —

Pn258 1953 — Kopek. Aluminum. —

Pn259 1953 — Kopek. Nickel. —

Note: Additional metals exist

Pn260 1953 — 2 Kopeks. Copper-Nickel. With legend. 850

Pn261 1953 — 2 Kopeks. Aluminum. —

Pn262 1953 — 2 Kopeks. Nickel. —

Note: Additional metals exist

Pn263 1953 — 2 Kopeks. Copper-Nickel. Without legend. 850

Pn264 1953 — 2 Kopeks. Aluminum. —

Pn265 1953 — 2 Kopeks. Nickel. —

Note: Additional metals exist

Pn266 1953 — 3 Kopeks. Copper-Nickel. With legend. 850

Pn267 1953 — 3 Kopeks. Aluminum. —

Pn268 1953 — 3 Kopeks. Nickel. —

Note: Additional metals exist

Pn269 1953 — 3 Kopeks. Copper-Nickel. Without legend. 850

Pn270 1953 — 3 Kopeks. Aluminum. —

Pn271 1953 — 3 Kopeks. Nickel. —

Note: Additional metals exist

Pn272 1953 — 5 Kopeks. Aluminum. With legend. —

Pn273 1953 — 5 Kopeks. Nickel. —

Note: Additional metals exist

Pn274 1953 — 5 Kopeks. Aluminum. Without legend. —

Pn275 1953 — 5 Kopeks. Nickel. —

Note: Additional metals exist

Pn276 1953 — 10 Kopeks. Aluminum. With legend. Value and date within wreath. —

Pn277 1953 — 10 Kopeks. Aluminum. Value, star above, date below. —

Pn278 1953 — 10 Kopeks. Aluminum. Value, date below. —

Pn279 1953 — 10 Kopeks. Aluminum. Value in wreath, star above date. —

Pn280 1953 — 10 Kopeks. Aluminum. Value in wreath, date incircle at bottom. —

Pn281 1953 — 10 Kopeks. Aluminum. Value in wreath in pellet border, date in circle at bottom. —

Pn282 1953 — 10 Kopeks. Aluminum. Oak leaves behind value. —

Pn283 1953 — 10 Kopeks. Aluminum. Without legend. Similar to KM#Pn276. —

Pn284 1953 — 10 Kopeks. Aluminum. Similar to KM#Pn277. —

Pn285 1953 — 10 Kopeks. Aluminum. Similar to KM#Pn278. —

Pn286 1953 — 10 Kopeks. Aluminum. Similar to KM#Pn279. —

Pn287 1953 — 10 Kopeks. Aluminum. Similar to KM#Pn280. —

Pn288 1953 — 10 Kopeks. Aluminum. Similar to KM#Pn281. —

Pn289 1953 — 10 Kopeks. Aluminum. Similar to KM#Pn282. —

Note: For Pn276-Pn289 at least four other base metal strikings exist of each

Pn290 1953 — 15 Kopeks. Aluminum. With legend. Value and date within wreath. —

Pn291 1953 — 15 Kopeks. Aluminum. Value, star above, date below. —

Pn292 1953 — 15 Kopeks. Aluminum. Value, date below. —

Pn293 1953 — 15 Kopeks. Aluminum. Value in wreath, star above date in circle at bottom. —

Pn294 1953 — 15 Kopeks. Aluminum. Value in wreath, date in circle at bottom. —

Pn295 1953 — 15 Kopeks. Aluminum. Value in wreath, pellet border, date in circle at bottom. —

Pn296 1953 — 15 Kopeks. Aluminum. Oak leaves behind value, date below. —

Pn297 1953 — 15 Kopeks. Aluminum. Legend. Similar to KM#Pn290. —

Pn298 1953 — 15 Kopeks. Aluminum. Similar to KM#Pn291. —

Pn299 1953 — 15 Kopeks. Aluminum. Similar to KM#Pn292. —

Pn300 1953 — 15 Kopeks. Aluminum. Similar to KM#Pn293. —

Pn301 1953 — 15 Kopeks. Aluminum. Similar to KM#Pn294. —

Pn302 1953 — 15 Kopeks. Aluminum. Similar to KM#Pn295. —

Pn303 1953 — 15 Kopeks. Aluminum. Similar to KM#Pn296. —

Note: Pn290-Pn303 exist in at least four other base metal strikings

Pn304 1953 — 20 Kopeks. Aluminum. With legend. Value and date within wreath. —

Pn305 1953 — 20 Kopeks. Aluminum. Value, star above, date below. —

Pn306 1953 — 20 Kopeks. Aluminum. Value, date below. —

Pn307 1953 — 20 Kopeks. Aluminum. Value in wreath, star above date in circle at bottom. —

Pn308 1953 — 20 Kopeks. Aluminum. Value in wreath, date in circle at bottom. —

Pn309 1953 — 20 Kopeks. Aluminum. Value in wreath, pellet border, date in circle at bottom. —

Pn310 1953 — 20 Kopeks. Aluminum. Oak leaves behind value, date below. —

Pn311 1953 — 20 Kopeks. Aluminum. Without legend. Similar to KM#Pn304. —

Pn312 1953 — 20 Kopeks. Aluminum. Similar to KM#Pn305. —

Pn313 1953 — 20 Kopeks. Aluminum. Similar to KM#Pn306. —

Pn314 1953 — 20 Kopeks. Aluminum. Similar to KM#Pn307. —

Pn315 1953 — 20 Kopeks. Aluminum. Similar to KM#Pn308. —

Pn316 1953 — 20 Kopeks. Aluminum. Similar to KM#Pn309. —

Pn317 1953 — 20 Kopeks. Aluminum. Similar to KM#Pn310. —

Note: Pn304-Pn317 exist in at least four additional metals

Pn318 1953 — 50 Kopeks. Bronze. —
Pn319 1953 — 50 Kopeks. Aluminum. —

Pn320 1953 — 50 Kopeks. Bronze. —
Pn321 1953 — 50 Kopeks. Aluminum. —

Pn322 1953 — 50 Kopeks. Bronze. —
Pn323 1953 — 50 Kopeks. Aluminum. —

Pn324 1953 — 50 Kopeks. Bronze. —
Pn325 1953 — 50 Kopeks. Aluminum. —

Note: Pn318-Pn325 exist in at least one other metal

Pn326 1955 — 25 Kopeks. Probably copper-nickel. —

Pn327 1956 — 10 Kopeks. Nickel. —
Pn328 1956 — 10 Kopeks. Brass. —
Pn329 1956 — 10 Kopeks. Copper. —
Pn330 1956 — 10 Kopeks. Aluminum. —

Pn331 1956 — 15 Kopeks. Nickel. —
Pn332 1956 — 15 Kopeks. Brass. —
Pn333 1956 — 15 Kopeks. Copper. —
Pn334 1956 — 15 Kopeks. Aluminum. —

Pn335 1956 — 20 Kopeks. Nickel. —
Pn336 1956 — 20 Kopeks. Brass. —
Pn337 1956 — 20 Kopeks. Copper. —
Pn338 1956 — 20 Kopeks. Aluminum. —

Pn339 1956 — 50 Kopeks. Nickel. —
Pn340 1956 — 50 Kopeks. Brass. —
Pn341 1956 — 50 Kopeks. Copper. —
Pn342 1956 — 50 Kopeks. Aluminum. —

Pn343 1956 — Rouble. Nickel. —
Pn344 1956 — Rouble. Brass. —
Pn345 1956 — Rouble. Copper. —
Pn346 1956 — Rouble. Aluminum. —

Pn347 1956 — 2 Roubles. Nickel. —
Pn348 1956 — 2 Roubles. Brass. —
Pn349 1956 — 2 Roubles. Copper. —
Pn350 1956 — 2 Roubles. Aluminum. —

Pn351 1956 — 3 Roubles. Nickel. —
Pn352 1956 — 3 Roubles. Brass. —
Pn353 1956 — 3 Roubles. Copper. —
Pn354 1956 — 3 Roubles. Aluminum. —

Pn355 1956 — 5 Roubles. Nickel. —
Pn356 1956 — 5 Roubles. Brass. —
Pn357 1956 — 5 Roubles. Copper. —

Pn358 1956 — 5 Roubles. Aluminum. —
Pn359 1957 — 10 Kopeks. Copper-Nickel. Y#123. —
Pn360 1957 — 10 Kopeks. Aluminum. Y#123. —
Pn361 1957 — 20 Kopeks. Copper-Nickel. Y#125. —

Pn362 1958 — Kopek. Aluminum. Y#126. —

Pn363 1958 — 2 Kopeks. Aluminum. Y#127. —

Pn364 1958 — 3 Kopeks. Aluminum. Y#128. —

Pn365 1958 — 5 Kopeks. Aluminum. Y#129. —

Pn366 1958 — 10 Kopeks. Aluminum. Y#A130. —

Pn367 1958 — 15 Kopeks. Aluminum. Y#A131. —

Pn368 1958 — 20 Kopeks. Aluminum. Y#A132. —

Pn369 1958 — 50 Kopeks. Aluminum. Y#133. —

Pn370 1958 — Rouble. Aluminum. Y#134. —

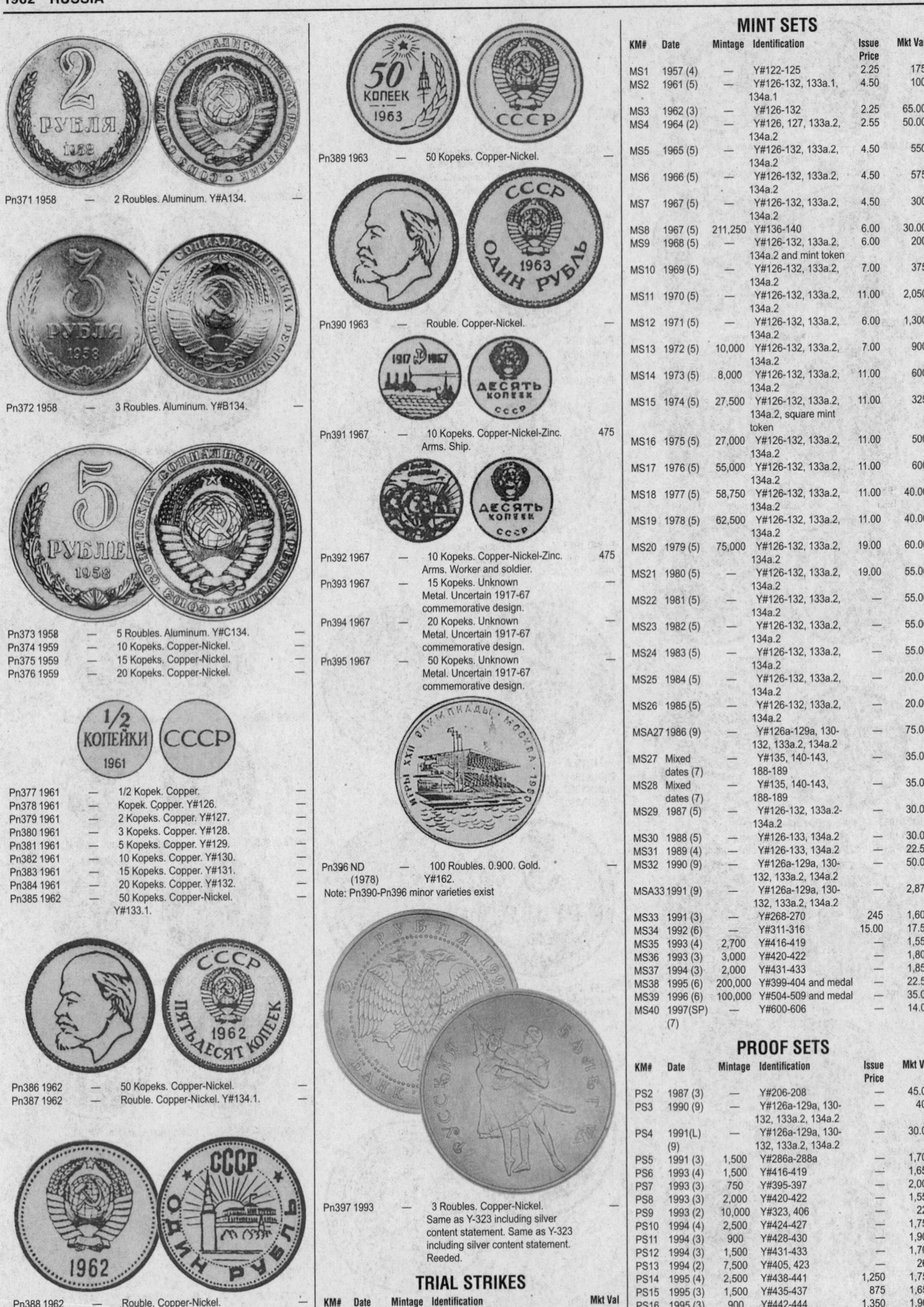

KM#	Date	Mintage	Identification	Mkt Val
Pn371	1958	—	2 Roubles. Aluminum. Y#A134.	—
Pn372	1958	—	3 Roubles. Aluminum. Y#B134.	—
Pn373	1958	—	5 Roubles. Aluminum. Y#C134.	—
Pn374	1959	—	10 Kopeks. Copper-Nickel.	—
Pn375	1959	—	15 Kopeks. Copper-Nickel.	—
Pn376	1959	—	20 Kopeks. Copper-Nickel.	—
Pn377	1961	—	1/2 Kopek. Copper.	—
Pn378	1961	—	Kopek. Copper. Y#126.	—
Pn379	1961	—	2 Kopeks. Copper. Y#127.	—
Pn380	1961	—	3 Kopeks. Copper. Y#128.	—
Pn381	1961	—	5 Kopeks. Copper. Y#129.	—
Pn382	1961	—	10 Kopeks. Copper. Y#130.	—
Pn383	1961	—	15 Kopeks. Copper. Y#131.	—
Pn384	1961	—	20 Kopeks. Copper. Y#132.	—
Pn385	1962	—	50 Kopeks. Copper-Nickel. Y#133.1.	—
Pn386	1962	—	50 Kopeks. Copper-Nickel.	—
Pn387	1962	—	Rouble. Copper-Nickel. Y#134.1.	—
Pn388	1962	—	Rouble. Copper-Nickel.	—
Pn389	1963	—	50 Kopeks. Copper-Nickel.	—
Pn390	1963	—	Rouble. Copper-Nickel.	—
Pn391	1967	—	10 Kopeks. Copper-Nickel-Zinc. Arms. Ship.	475
Pn392	1967	—	10 Kopeks. Copper-Nickel-Zinc. Arms. Worker and soldier.	475
Pn393	1967	—	15 Kopeks. Unknown Metal. Uncertain 1917-67 commemorative design.	—
Pn394	1967	—	20 Kopeks. Unknown Metal. Uncertain 1917-67 commemorative design.	—
Pn395	1967	—	50 Kopeks. Unknown Metal. Uncertain 1917-67 commemorative design.	—
Pn396	ND (1978)	—	100 Roubles. 0.900. Gold. Y#162.	—

Note: Pn390-Pn396 minor varieties exist

KM#	Date	Mintage	Identification	Mkt Val
Pn397	1993	—	3 Roubles. Copper-Nickel. Same as Y-323 including silver content statement. Same as Y-323 including silver content statement. Reeded.	—

TRIAL STRIKES

KM#	Date	Mintage	Identification	Mkt Val
TS1	1924	—	5 Kopeks. Copper. Y#79.	625
TS1	1924	—	5 Kopeks. Copper. Y#79.	625

MINT SETS

KM#	Date	Mintage	Identification	Issue Price	Mkt Val
MS1	1957 (4)	—	Y#122-125	2.25	175
MS2	1961 (5)	—	Y#126-132, 133a.1, 134a.1	4.50	100
MS3	1962 (3)	—	Y#126-132	2.25	65.00
MS4	1964 (2)	—	Y#126, 127, 133a.2, 134a.2	2.55	50.00
MS5	1965 (5)	—	Y#126-132, 133a.2, 134a.2	4.50	550
MS6	1966 (5)	—	Y#126-132, 133a.2, 134a.2	4.50	575
MS7	1967 (5)	—	Y#126-132, 133a.2, 134a.2	4.50	300
MS8	1967 (5)	211,250	Y#136-140	6.00	30.00
MS9	1968 (5)	—	Y#126-132, 133a.2, 134a.2 and mint token	6.00	200
MS10	1969 (5)	—	Y#126-132, 133a.2, 134a.2	7.00	375
MS11	1970 (5)	—	Y#126-132, 133a.2, 134a.2	11.00	2,050
MS12	1971 (5)	—	Y#126-132, 133a.2, 134a.2	6.00	1,300
MS13	1972 (5)	10,000	Y#126-132, 133a.2, 134a.2	7.00	900
MS14	1973 (5)	8,000	Y#126-132, 133a.2, 134a.2	11.00	600
MS15	1974 (5)	27,500	Y#126-132, 133a.2, 134a.2, square mint token	11.00	325
MS16	1975 (5)	27,000	Y#126-132, 133a.2, 134a.2	11.00	500
MS17	1976 (5)	55,000	Y#126-132, 133a.2, 134a.2	11.00	600
MS18	1977 (5)	58,750	Y#126-132, 133a.2, 134a.2	11.00	40.00
MS19	1978 (5)	62,500	Y#126-132, 133a.2, 134a.2	11.00	40.00
MS20	1979 (5)	75,000	Y#126-132, 133a.2, 134a.2	19.00	60.00
MS21	1980 (5)	—	Y#126-132, 133a.2, 134a.2	19.00	55.00
MS22	1981 (5)	—	Y#126-132, 133a.2, 134a.2	—	55.00
MS23	1982 (5)	—	Y#126-132, 133a.2, 134a.2	—	55.00
MS24	1983 (5)	—	Y#126-132, 133a.2, 134a.2	—	55.00
MS25	1984 (5)	—	Y#126-132, 133a.2, 134a.2	—	20.00
MS26	1985 (5)	—	Y#126-132, 133a.2, 134a.2	—	20.00
MSA27	1986 (9)	—	Y#126a-129a, 130-132, 133a.2, 134a.2	—	75.00
MS27	Mixed dates (7)	—	Y#135, 140-143, 188-189	—	35.00
MS28	Mixed dates (7)	—	Y#135, 140-143, 188-189	—	35.00
MS29	1987 (5)	—	Y#126-132, 133a.2-134a.2	—	30.00
MS30	1988 (5)	—	Y#126-133, 134a.2	—	30.00
MS31	1989 (4)	—	Y#126-133, 134a.2	—	22.50
MS32	1990 (9)	—	Y#126a-129a, 130-132, 133a.2, 134a.2	—	50.00
MSA33	1991 (9)	—	Y#126a-129a, 130-132, 133a.2, 134a.2	—	2,875
MS33	1991 (3)	—	Y#268-270	245	1,600
MS34	1992 (6)	—	Y#311-316	15.00	17.50
MS35	1993 (4)	2,700	Y#416-419	—	1,550
MS36	1993 (3)	3,000	Y#420-422	—	1,800
MS37	1994 (3)	2,000	Y#431-433	—	1,850
MS38	1995 (6)	200,000	Y#399-404 and medal	—	22.50
MS39	1996 (6)	100,000	Y#504-509 and medal	—	35.00
MS40	1997(SP) (7)	—	Y#600-606	—	14.00

PROOF SETS

KM#	Date	Mintage	Identification	Issue Price	Mkt Val
PS2	1987 (3)	—	Y#206-208	—	45.00
PS3	1990 (9)	—	Y#126a-129a, 130-132, 133a.2, 134a.2	—	400
PS4	1991(L) (9)	—	Y#126a-129a, 130-132, 133a.2, 134a.2	—	30.00
PS5	1991 (3)	1,500	Y#286a-288a	—	1,700
PS6	1993 (4)	1,500	Y#416-419	—	1,650
PS7	1993 (3)	750	Y#395-397	—	2,000
PS8	1993 (3)	2,000	Y#420-422	—	1,550
PS9	1993 (2)	10,000	Y#323, 406	—	220
PS10	1994 (4)	2,500	Y#424-427	—	1,750
PS11	1994 (3)	900	Y#428-430	—	1,900
PS12	1994 (3)	1,500	Y#431-433	—	1,700
PS13	1994 (2)	7,500	Y#405, 423	—	265
PS14	1995 (4)	2,500	Y#438-441	1,250	1,750
PS15	1995 (3)	1,500	Y#435-437	875	1,650
PS16	1995 (3)	900	Y#442-444	1,350	1,900

RUSSIAN CAUCASIA

Russian Caucasia, a natural area in Russia located between the Black and Caspian Seas, was a region of mystery and myth to the Ancient Greeks. It was there that Prometheus was bound for the eagle's torment and the Argonauts sought the Golden Fleece. For more than a thousand years Caucasia was the refuge for wave after wave of migrating peoples. Greeks, Romans, Persians, Turks, Huns, Mongols and finally the Russians invaded the treeless steppes and wooded highlands of this range-flanked granite bridge between Europe and Asia. Russian aggression, heroically resisted by the independent mountain races, began early in the 18th century and continued until the last opposition was stifled. The several states of Caucasia made a futile attempt to establish an independent federated republic during the Russian February Revolution of 1917, but were quickly re-conquered after the triumph of Bolshevism over the Kerensky administration.

The following area of Russian Caucasia was a coin-issuing entity of interest to numismatists.

ARMAVIR

Armavir is a city located in Krasnodar Territory, Southern Russia north of the Caucasus.

LOCAL CURRENCY UNDER THE WHITE RUSSIANS

CITY

KM# 1 ROUBLE
Copper **Obv:** Double-headed eagle with monogram below tail **Rev:** Value and date flanked by sprigs **Edge:** Reeded **Note:** Thin planchet.

Date	Mintage	VG8	F12	VF20	XF40	MS60
1918	—	150	200	350	600	—

KM# 2.1 3 ROUBLES
Copper, 28 mm. **Obv:** Double-headed eagle with monogram below tail **Rev:** Value and date flanked by sprigs **Edge:** Reeded **Note:** Varieties exist.

Date	Mintage	VG8	F12	VF20	XF40	MS60
1918	—	60.00	100	200	300	575

KM# 2.2 3 ROUBLES
Copper, 28 mm. **Obv:** Monogram below claw **Rev:** Value flanked by sprigs

Date	Mintage	VG8	F12	VF20	XF40	MS60
1918	—	75.00	110	200	350	—

KM# 3 5 ROUBLES
Copper, 31 mm. **Obv:** Double-headed eagle with monogram below tail **Rev:** Value and date flanked by sprigs

Date	Mintage	VG8	F12	VF20	XF40	MS60
1918	—	150	250	475	750	—

PATTERNS

Including off metal strikes

KM#	Date	Mintage	Identification	Mkt Val
Pn1	1918	—	Rouble. Copper. Reeded. Thin planchet. Y1.	—
Pn2	1918	—	Rouble. Copper. Plain. Thin planchet. Y1.	—
Pn3	1918	—	Rouble. Copper. Plain. Thick planchet. Y1.	—
Pn3a	1918	—	Rouble. Brass.	—
Pn4	1918	—	3 Roubles. Copper. Monogram under tail. Y2.1.	475
Pn5	1918	—	3 Roubles. Silver. Y2.1.	800
Pn6	1918	—	5 Roubles. Aluminum. Y3.	950

RWANDA

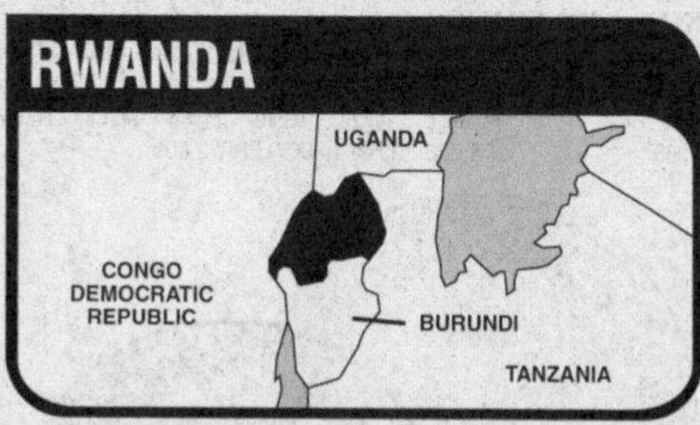

The Republic of Rwanda, located in central Africa between the Republic of the Congo and Tanzania, has an area of 10,169 sq. mi. (26,340 sq. km.) and a population of 7.3 million. Capital: Kigali. The economy is based on agriculture and mining. Coffee and tin are exported.

German Lieutenant Count von Goetzen was the first European to visit Rwanda, 1894. Four years later the court of the Mwami (the Tutsi king of Rwanda) willingly permitted the kingdom to become a protectorate of Germany. In 1916, during the African campaigns of World War I, Belgian troops from Congo occupied Rwanda. After the war it, together with Burundi, became a Belgian League of Nations mandate under the name of the Territory of Ruanda-Urundi. Following World War II, Ruanda-Urundi became a Belgian administered U.N. trust territory. The Tutsi monarchy was deposed by the U.N. supervised election of 1961, after which Belgium granted Rwanda internal autonomy. On July 1, 1962, the U.N. terminated the Belgian trusteeship and granted full independence to both Rwanda and Burundi.

For earlier coinage see Belgian Congo, and Rwanda and Burundi.

MINT MARKS
(a) - Paris, privy marks only
(b) - Brussels, privy marks only

MONETARY SYSTEM
100 Centimes = 1 Franc

REPUBLIC

STANDARD COINAGE

KM# 9 1/2 FRANC
0.70 g., Aluminum, 16.1 mm. **Obv:** Value divides design within circle **Rev:** Inscription within circle

Date	Mintage	VF20	XF40	MS60	MS63	MS65
1970	5,000,000	0.45	0.75	1.50	2.00	3.00

KM# 5 FRANC
3.00 g., Copper-Nickel, 21 mm. **Obv:** Head 1/4 right **Rev:** Value above flag-draped arms **Edge:** Plain

Date	Mintage	VF20	XF40	MS60	MS63	MS65
1964 (b)	3,000,000	5.00	10.00	20.00	30.00	50.00
1965 (b)	4,500,000	0.45	0.75	1.50	2.00	3.00

KM# 8 FRANC
1.09 g., Aluminum, 21.1 mm. **Obv:** Head right **Rev:** Value above flag-draped arms

Date	Mintage	VF20	XF40	MS60	MS63	MS65
1969	5,000,000	0.50	1.00	2.00	3.50	5.00

KM# 12 FRANC
1.02 g., Aluminum, 21.1 mm. **Obv:** Millet flower **Rev:** Value above flag-draped arms

Date	Mintage	VF20	XF40	MS60	MS63	MS65
1974	13,000,000	0.20	0.50	1.00	1.50	2.00
1977	15,000,000	0.15	0.25	0.75	1.25	1.75
1985	—	0.10	0.15	0.65	1.00	1.50

KM# 10 2 FRANCS
1.49 g., Aluminum, 23.5 mm. **Series:** F.A.O. **Obv:** Seated figure facing above monogramed banner **Rev:** Value above flag-draped arms **Shape:** Scalloped

Date	Mintage	VF20	XF40	MS60	MS63	MS65
1970	5,000,000	0.10	0.20	0.50	0.75	1.25

KM# 6 5 FRANCS
Bronze **Obv:** Gregoire Kayibanda head 3/4 right **Rev:** Value above flag-draped arms

Date	Mintage	VF20	XF40	MS60	MS63	MS65
1964 (b)	4,000,000	0.25	0.50	1.75	2.50	4.00
1965 (b)	3,000,000	5.00	10.00	18.00	28.00	45.00

KM# 13 5 FRANCS
5.00 g., Bronze, 26 mm. **Obv:** Coffee tree branch **Rev:** Value above flag-draped arms

Date	Mintage	VF20	XF40	MS60	MS63	MS65
1974	7,000,000	1.00	2.00	4.00	6.00	10.00
1977	7,002,000	1.00	2.00	3.00	5.00	8.00
1987	—	0.25	0.50	1.50	2.50	4.00

KM# 7 10 FRANCS
10.29 g., Copper-Nickel, 30.5 mm. **Obv:** Gregoire Kayibanda head 1/4 right **Rev:** Value above flag-draped arms

Date	Mintage	VF20	XF40	MS60	MS63	MS65
1964 (b)	6,000,000	1.00	2.00	4.00	7.00	9.00

KM# 1 10 FRANCS
3.00 g., 0.900 Gold 0.0868 oz. AGW **Obv:** Value above flag-draped arms **Rev:** Gregoire Kayibanda head 3/4 right

Date	Mintage	VF20	XF40	MS60	MS63	MS65
1965	10,000	—	—	—	175	200
1965	—	PF65 200	PF67 250			

KM# 14.1 10 FRANCS
10.50 g., Copper-Nickel, 30.1 mm. **Obv:** Coffee tree branch **Rev:** Value above flag-draped arms

Date	Mintage	VF20	XF40	MS60	MS63	MS65
1974	6,000,000	2.00	4.00	7.00	12.00	15.00

KM# 14.2 10 FRANCS
7.00 g., Copper-Nickel **Obv:** Coffee tree branch **Rev:** Value above flag-draped arms **Note:** Reduced size.

Date	Mintage	VF20	XF40	MS60	MS63	MS65
1985	—	0.45	0.75	1.50	2.50	3.00

KM# 15 20 FRANCS
7.95 g., Brass, 27 mm. **Obv:** Stalk of bananas and tree **Rev:** Value above flag-draped arms

Date	Mintage	VF20	XF40	MS60	MS63	MS65
1977 (a)	22,000,000	1.00	2.00	4.00	7.00	9.00

KM# 2 25 FRANCS
7.50 g., 0.900 Gold 0.217 oz. AGW **Obv:** Value above flag-draped arms **Rev:** Head 3/4 right **Note:** Similar to 10 Francs, KM#1.

Date	Mintage	VF20	XF40	MS60	MS63	MS65
1965	4,000	PF65 425	PF67 500			

KM# 3 50 FRANCS
15.00 g., 0.900 Gold 0.434 oz. AGW **Obv:** Value above flag-draped arms **Rev:** Head 3/4 right **Note:** Similar to 10 Francs, KM#1.

Date	Mintage	VF20	XF40	MS60	MS63	MS65
1965	3,000	PF65 850	PF67 975			

KM# 16 50 FRANCS
9.94 g., Brass, 28.88 mm. **Obv:** Leafy branch **Rev:** Value above flag-draped arms

Date	Mintage	VF20	XF40	MS60	MS63	MS65
1977 (a)	9,000,000	2.50	3.50	6.00	8.00	12.00

KM# 4 100 FRANCS
30.00 g., 0.900 Gold 0.8681 oz. AGW **Obv:** Value above flag-draped arms **Rev:** Gregoire Kayibanda head 3/4 right

Date	Mintage	VF20	XF40	MS60	MS63	MS65
1965	3,000	PF65 1,700	PF67 2,000			

KM# 18 100 FRANCS
31.23 g., 0.999 Silver 1.0031 oz. ASW **Subject:** Nelson Mandela **Obv:** Flag draped arms **Rev:** Head facing

Date	Mintage	VF20	XF40	MS60	MS63	MS65
1990	—	—	—	25.00	30.00	35.00
1990	Est. 50000	PF63 45.00	PF65 55.00			

KM# 21 100 FRANCS
31.10 g., 0.999 Silver 0.999 oz. ASW **Subject:** Environmental Protection **Obv:** Flag draped arms **Rev:** Gorilla

Date	Mintage	VF20	XF40	MS60	MS63	MS65
1993	Est. 20000	PF63 60.00	PF65 75.00			

KM# 11 200 FRANCS
18.00 g., 0.800 Silver 0.463 oz. ASW **Series:** F.A.O. **Subject:** 10th Anniversary of Independence **Obv:** Gregoire Kayibanda recieving the instruments of Independence **Rev:** Figure picking coffee beans, F.A.O logo within plants

Date	Mintage	VF20	XF40	MS60	MS63	MS65
1972	30,000	—	10.00	13.00	16.00	20.00

KM# 17 1000 FRANCS
28.47 g., 0.925 Silver 0.8467 oz. ASW, 38.47 mm. **Subject:** 25th Anniversary of National Bank **Obv:** Bust of President Juvénal Habyarimana facing **Rev:** National bank within circle **Edge:** Reeded

Date	Mintage	VF20	XF40	MS60	MS63	MS65
ND-1989	—	—	—	—	35.00	40.00

KM# 19 2000 FRANCS
7.80 g., 0.999 Gold 0.2505 oz. AGW **Subject:** Nelson Mandela **Obv:** Flag draped arms above value **Rev:** Head facing **Note:** Similar to 5,000 Francs, KM#20.

Date	Mintage	VF20	XF40	MS60	MS63	MS65
1990	Est. 50000	PF63 400	PF65 450	PF67 500		

KM# 20 5000 FRANCS
15.53 g., 0.999 Gold 0.4988 oz. AGW **Subject:** Nelson Mandela **Obv:** Value below flag-draped arms **Rev:** Head facing

Date	Mintage	VF20	XF40	MS60	MS63	MS65
1990	3,000	PF63 800	PF65 900	PF67 950		

ESSAIS

KM#	Date	Mintage	Identification	Mkt Val
E1	1964(b)	—	Franc. Aluminum.	50.00
E2	1964(b)	—	5 Francs. Bronze. Head 1/4 right. Value above flag-draped arms.	65.00
E3	1964(b)	—	10 Francs. Copper-Nickel.	80.00
E4	1977(a)	—	Franc. Aluminum.	35.00
E5	1977(a)	—	5 Francs. Bronze.	40.00
E6	1977(a)	—	20 Francs. Brass.	45.00
E7	1977(a)	—	50 Francs. Brass.	50.00

PROOF SETS

KM#	Date	Mintage	Identification	Issue Price	Mkt Val
PS1	1965(a) (4)	3,000	KM1-4	—	3,150

RWANDA-BURUNDI

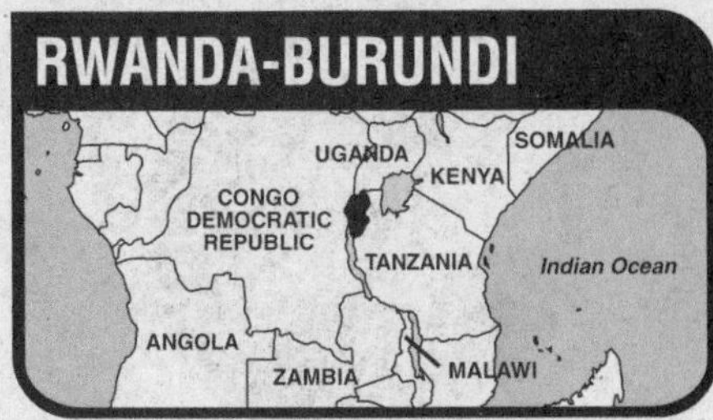

Rwanda-Burundi, a Belgian League of Nations mandate and United Nations trust territory comprising the provinces of Ruanda-Urundi of the former colony of German East Africa, was located in central Africa between the present Democratic Republic of the Congo, Uganda and mainland Tanzania. The mandate-trust territory had an area of 20,916 sq. mi. (54,272 sq. km.) and a population of 4.3 million.

For specific statistics and history of Ruanda and of Urundi see individual entries.

When Rwanda and Burundi were formed into a mandate for administration by Belgium, their names were combined as Ruanda-Urundi and they were organized as an integral part of the Belgian Congo. During the mandate-trust territory period, they utilized the coinage of the Belgian Congo, which from 1954 through 1960carried the appropriate dual identification. After the Belgian Congo acquired independence as the Democratic Republic of the Congo, the provinces of Ruanda and Urundi reverted to their former names of Rwanda and Burundi and utilized a common currency issued by a Central Bank (B.E.R.B.) established for that purpose until the time when, as independent republics, each issued its own national coinage.

For earlier coinage see Belgian Congo.

MONETARY SYSTEM
100 Centimes = 1 Franc

PROVINCES

STANDARD COINAGE

KM# 1 FRANC
Brass **Obv:** Value **Rev:** Lion (panthera leo-felidae)

Date	Mintage	VF20	XF40	MS60	MS63	MS65
1960	2,000,000	3.50	7.00	15.00	18.00	24.00
1961	16,000,000	0.50	1.00	2.00	3.50	7.00
1964	3,000,000	3.00	6.00	12.00	17.00	22.00

KM# 2 FRANC
Copper-Nickel **Obv:** Value **Rev:** Head left **Note:** Mule.

Date	Mintage	VF20	XF40	MS60	MS63	MS65
1961	50	—	—	650	950	1,250

ESSAIS

KM#	Date	Mintage	Identification	Mkt Val
E1	1960	—	Franc. Bronze. Crowned shield divides date. Palm tree divides value.	175
E2	1960	—	Franc. Brass. KM1.	70.00
E3	1960	—	Franc. Silver. KM1.	225

SAARLAND

The Saar, the 10th state of the German Federal Republic, is located in the coal-rich Saar basin on the Franco-German frontier, and has an area of 991 sq. mi. and a population of 1.2 million. Capital: Saarbrucken. It is an important center of mining and heavy industry.

From the late 14th century until the fall of Napoleon, the city of Saarbrucken was ruled by the counts of Nassau-Saarbrucken, but the surrounding territory was subject to the political and cultural domination of France. At the close of the Napoleonic era, the Saarland came under the control of Prussia. France was awarded the Saar coal mines following World War I, and the Saarland was made an autonomous territory of the League of Nations, its future political affiliation to be determined by referendum. The plebiscite, 1935, chose re-incorporation into Germany. France reoccupied the Saarland, 1945, establishing strong economic ties and assuming the obligation of defense and foreign affairs. After sustained agitation by West Germany, France agreed in 1955, to the return of the Saar to Germany by Jan. 1957.

MINT MARK
(a) - Paris - privy marks only

GERMAN REPUBLIC STATE

STANDARD COINAGE

KM# 1 10 FRANKEN
3.04 g., Aluminum-Bronze, 20 mm. **Obv:** Industrial scene, arms at center **Rev:** Value and date

Date	Mintage	VF20	XF40	MS60	MS63	MS65
1954 (a)	11,000,000	1.75	3.50	6.00	9.00	12.00

KM# 2 20 FRANKEN
4.00 g., Aluminum-Bronze, 23.5 mm. **Obv:** Industrial scene, arms at center **Rev:** Value and date **Edge:** Plain

Date	Mintage	VF20	XF40	MS60	MS63	MS65
1954 (a)	12,950,000	1.75	3.50	6.00	9.00	12.00

KM# 3 50 FRANKEN
8.00 g., Aluminum-Bronze **Obv:** Industrial scene, arms in center **Rev:** Value and date

Date	Mintage	VF20	XF40	MS60	MS63	MS65
1954 (a)	5,300,000	7.00	15.00	28.00	35.00	45.00

KM# 4 100 FRANKEN
6.04 g., Copper-Nickel, 24 mm. **Obv:** Arms within circular design **Rev:** Value and date

Date	Mintage	VF20	XF40	MS60	MS63	MS65
1955 (a)	11,000,000	4.00	7.00	15.00	22.00	32.00

ESSAIS

Standard metals unless otherwise noted

KM#	Date	Mintage	Identification	Mkt Val
E1	1954(a)	1,100	10 Franken. Aluminum-Bronze. KM1.	80.00
E2	1954(a)	Est. 50	10 Franken. Gold. KM1. Requires Confirmation.	—
E3	1954(a)	1,100	20 Franken. Aluminum-Bronze. KM2.	80.00
E4	1954(a)	50	20 Franken. Gold. KM2.	2,700
E5	1954(a)	1,100	50 Franken. Aluminum-Bronze. KM3.	80.00
E6	1954(a)	Est. 50	50 Franken. Gold. KM3. Requires Confirmation.	—
E7	1955(a)	50	100 Franken. Gold. Arms within circular design. Value. KM4.	3,200
E8	1955(a)	50	50 Franken. Gold.	2,500

SAHARAWI ARAB D.R.

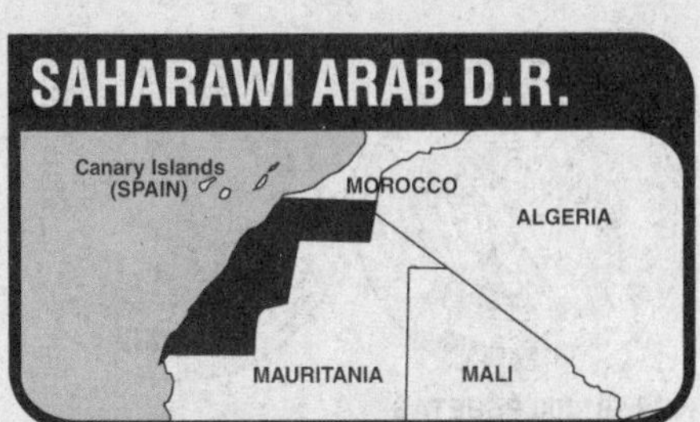

The Saharawi Arab Democratic Republic, located in northwest Africa has an area of 102,703 sq. mi. and a population (census taken 1974) of 76,425. Formerly known as Spanish Sahara, the area is bounded on the north by Morocco, on the east and southeast by Mauritania, on the northeast by Algeria, and on the west by the Atlantic Ocean. Capital: El Aaium. Agriculture, fishing and mining are the three main industries. Exports are barley, livestock and phosphates.

A Spanish trading post was established in 1476 but was abandoned in 1524. A Spanish protectorate for the region was proclaimed in 1884. The status of the Spanish Sahara changed from a colony to an overseas province in 1958. Spain relinquished its holdings in 1975. The SADR is a "government in exile" It currently controls about 20% of its claimed territory, the former Spanish colony of Western Sahara; Morocco controls and administers the majority of the territory as its Southern Provinces. SADR claims control over a zone largely bordering Mauritania, described as "the Free Zone," although characterized by Morocco as a buffer zone.

The official languages are Spanish and an Arab dialect: The Hassaniya.

DEMOCRATIC REPUBLIC

STANDARD COINAGE

KM# 14 PESETA
2.94 g., Copper-Nickel, 17.8 mm. **Obv:** National arms and value **Rev:** Arab and camel

Date	Mintage	VF20	XF40	MS60	MS63	MS65
1992	—	—	—	0.65	1.25	2.50

KM# 15 2 PESETAS
3.56 g., Copper-Nickel, 20 mm. **Obv:** National arms and value **Rev:** Arab and camel

Date	Mintage	VF20	XF40	MS60	MS63	MS65
1992	—	—	—	0.75	1.50	3.00

KM# 16 5 PESETAS
3.92 g., Copper-Nickel, 21.5 mm. **Obv:** National arms and value **Rev:** Arab and camel **Edge:** Plain

Date	Mintage	VF20	XF40	MS60	MS63	MS65
1992	—	—	—	1.00	2.00	4.00

KM# 1 50 PESETAS
Copper-Nickel **Obv:** National arms and value **Rev:** Arab and camel

Date	Mintage	VF20	XF40	MS60	MS63	MS65
1990	—	—	—	1.25	2.50	5.00

KM# 18 100 PESETAS

Copper-Nickel **Obv:** National arms and value **Rev:** Arab and sailing ship

Date	Mintage	VF20	XF40	MS60	MS63	MS65
1990	—	—	—	10.00	14.00	18.00

KM# 20 100 PESETAS

Copper, 38 mm. **Obv:** National arms and value **Rev:** Arab and camel

Date	Mintage	VF20	XF40	MS60	MS63	MS65
1990	—	—	—	13.00	18.00	23.00

KM# 25 100 PESETAS

Copper, 38 mm. **Obv:** National arms and value **Rev:** Arab and sailboat

Date	Mintage	VF20	XF40	MS60	MS63	MS65
1990	—	—	—	—	8.00	12.00
1990	—	PF65 55.00				

KM# 7 100 PESETAS

Nickel Plated Steel **Series:** Olympics **Obv:** National arms and value **Rev:** Equestrian event

Date	Mintage	VF20	XF40	MS60	MS63	MS65
1991	5,000	—	—	—	14.00	18.00

KM# 13 100 PESETAS

Copper-Nickel **Series:** Prehistoric Animals **Obv:** National arms and value **Rev:** Brontosaurus

Date	Mintage	VF20	XF40	MS60	MS63	MS65
1992	—	—	—	—	20.00	26.00

KM# 26 100 PESETAS

Nickel Plated Steel **Obv:** National arms and value **Rev:** Ship above Canary Islands map

Date	Mintage	VF20	XF40	MS60	MS63	MS65
1992	—	—	—	—	12.00	15.00

KM# 40 100 PESETAS

Copper **Subject:** Columbus' ship - Santa Maria **Obv:** National arms and value

Date	Mintage	VF20	XF40	MS60	MS63	MS65
1992	78	PF65 60.00				

KM# 19 100 PESETAS

Copper, 38 mm. **Series:** Prehistoric Animals **Obv:** National arms and value **Rev:** Tarbosaurus Bataar

Date	Mintage	VF20	XF40	MS60	MS63	MS65
1993	—	—	—	—	12.00	17.00

KM# 17 100 PESETAS

Nickel Clad Steel **Series:** Prehistoric Animals **Obv:** National arms and value **Rev:** Triceratops

Date	Mintage	VF20	XF40	MS60	MS63	MS65
1994	—	—	—	—	14.00	20.00

KM# 41 100 PESETAS

Nickel Clad Steel **Series:** Prehistoric Animals **Obv:** National arms and value **Rev:** Camarasaurus

Date	Mintage	VF20	XF40	MS60	MS63	MS65
1994	100	PF65 75.00				

KM# 23 100 PESETAS

Nickel Clad Steel **Obv:** National arms and value **Rev:** WWII British Spitfire MK II, enameled

Date	Mintage	VF20	XF40	MS60	MS63	MS65
1995	—	—	—	—	16.00	18.00

KM# 22 100 PESETAS

Copper, 38 mm. **Series:** Olympics **Obv:** National arms and value **Rev:** Wrestlers

Date	Mintage	VF20	XF40	MS60	MS63	MS65
1996	—	—	—	—	12.00	15.00

KM# 31 200 PESETAS

Copper **Subject:** 20th Anniversary - Proclamation of Republic **Obv:** National arms and value **Rev:** Armored standing figure facing

Date	Mintage	VF20	XF40	MS60	MS63	MS65
1996	—	PF65 55.00				

KM# 2 500 PESETAS

16.00 g., 0.999 Silver 0.5139 oz. ASW **Series:** Transportation **Obv:** National arms **Rev:** Arab walking camel

Date	Mintage	VF20	XF40	MS60	MS63	MS65
1990	—	—	—	—	22.00	32.00

KM# 3 500 PESETAS

16.00 g., 0.999 Silver 0.5139 oz. ASW **Obv:** National arms **Rev:** Arab and sailing ship

Date	Mintage	VF20	XF40	MS60	MS63	MS65
1990	—	—	—	—	37.00	47.00
1990	—	PF65 60.00				

KM# 42 500 PESETAS
Copper **Obv:** National arms **Rev:** Antique sailing ship

Date	Mintage	VF20	XF40	MS60	MS63	MS65
1990	13	PF65 1,450				

KM# 4 500 PESETAS
6.00 g., 0.999 Silver 0.1927 oz. ASW **Series:** 1992 Olympics **Obv:** National arms **Rev:** Tennis player, skier

Date	Mintage	VF20	XF40	MS60	MS63	MS65
1991	—	—	—	—	16.00	18.00

KM# 5 500 PESETAS
12.00 g., 0.999 Silver 0.3854 oz. ASW **Subject:** 1994 American States Games - Soccer **Obv:** National arms **Rev:** Player kicking ball

Date	Mintage	VF20	XF40	MS60	MS63	MS65
1991	—	—	—	—	33.00	38.00

KM# 8 500 PESETAS
15.84 g., 0.999 Silver 0.5088 oz. ASW **Subject:** Soccer **Obv:** National arms **Rev:** Ball divided by inscription

Date	Mintage	VF20	XF40	MS60	MS63	MS65
1991	15,000	—	—	—	28.00	33.00

KM# 9.1 500 PESETAS
20.00 g., 0.999 Silver 0.6424 oz. ASW **Subject:** Meeting of Two Worlds **Obv:** National arms **Rev:** Sailing ship above Canary Islands map **Note:** Thick letters.

Date	Mintage	VF20	XF40	MS60	MS63	MS65
1992	—	—	—	—	30.00	36.00
1992	—	PF65 50.00				

KM# 9.1a 500 PESETAS
Copper **Subject:** Meeting of Two Worlds **Obv:** National arms **Rev:** Sailing ship above Canary Islands map

Date	Mintage	VF20	XF40	MS60	MS63	MS65
1992	—	—	—	—	—	40.00
1992	—	PF65 1,250				

KM# 9.2 500 PESETAS
Copper **Subject:** Meeting of Two Worlds **Obv:** National arms **Rev:** Sailing ship above Canary Islands map **Note:** Thin letters.

Date	Mintage	VF20	XF40	MS60	MS63	MS65
1992	—	PF65 32.00				

KM# 11 500 PESETAS
Copper **Subject:** Defense of Nature **Obv:** National arms **Rev:** Elephant

Date	Mintage	VF20	XF40	MS60	MS63	MS65
1993	—	—	—	—	55.00	60.00

KM# 12 500 PESETAS
16.00 g., 0.999 Silver 0.5139 oz. ASW **Series:** Prehistoric Animals **Obv:** National arms **Rev:** Tarbosaurus Bataar

Date	Mintage	VF20	XF40	MS60	MS63	MS65
1993	—	PF65 40.00				

KM# 27 500 PESETAS
16.00 g., 0.999 Silver 0.5139 oz. ASW **Series:** Prehistoric Animals **Obv:** National arms **Rev:** Camarasaurus

Date	Mintage	VF20	XF40	MS60	MS63	MS65
1994	—	—	—	—	40.00	45.00

KM# 21 500 PESETAS
20.00 g., 0.999 Silver 0.6424 oz. ASW **Series:** 1996 Olympics **Obv:** National arms **Rev:** Wrestlers

Date	Mintage	VF20	XF40	MS60	MS63	MS65
1995	15,000	PF65 60.00				

KM# 24 500 PESETAS
20.00 g., 0.999 Silver 0.6424 oz. ASW **Obv:** National arms **Rev:** WWII British Spitfire MK II

Date	Mintage	VF20	XF40	MS60	MS63	MS65
1995	15,000	PF65 65.00				

KM# 28 500 PESETAS
16.00 g., 0.999 Silver 0.5139 oz. ASW **Series:** Prehistoric Animals **Obv:** National arms **Rev:** Plateosaurus

Date	Mintage	VF20	XF40	MS60	MS63	MS65
1995	—	PF65 90.00				

KM# 29 500 PESETAS
20.00 g., 0.999 Silver 0.6424 oz. ASW **Obv:** National arms **Rev:** Multicolor cheetah

Date	Mintage	VF20	XF40	MS60	MS63	MS65
1996	—	PF65 60.00				

KM# 32 500 PESETAS
20.00 g., 0.999 Silver 0.6424 oz. ASW **Subject:** XVI Copa Mundial - Francia 1998 - Soccer **Obv:** National arms **Rev:** Player kicking ball

Date	Mintage	VF20	XF40	MS60	MS63	MS65
1996	—	PF65 55.00				

KM# 33 500 PESETAS
20.00 g., 0.999 Silver 0.6424 oz. ASW **Subject:** XVI Copa Mundial - Francia 1998 - Soccer **Obv:** National arms **Rev:** Multicolor player kicking ball

Date	Mintage	VF20	XF40	MS60	MS63	MS65
1996	—	PF65 40.00				

KM# 30 500 PESETAS
16.00 g., 0.999 Silver 0.5139 oz. ASW **Series:** Sydney Olympics **Obv:** National arms **Rev:** Weight lifter

Date	Mintage	VF20	XF40	MS60	MS63	MS65
1997	—	PF65 50.00				

KM# 34 500 PESETAS
20.00 g., 0.999 Silver 0.6424 oz. ASW **Series:** XXVII Olympiada - Sydney 2000 **Obv:** National arms **Rev:** Multicolor kayaker

Date	Mintage	VF20	XF40	MS60	MS63	MS65
1997	—	PF65 55.00				

KM# 56 500 PESETAS
Silver, 29 mm. **Obv:** National arms **Rev:** Germany 20 mark coin, gilt, of Kaiser Wilhelm **Edge:** Plain

Date	Mintage	VF20	XF40	MS60	MS63	MS65
1997	—	PF63 45.00	PF65 55.00			

KM# 6 1000 PESETAS
3.10 g., 0.999 Gold 0.0996 oz. AGW **Series:** Transportation **Obv:** National arms **Rev:** Arab walking with camel **Note:** Similar to 500 Pesetas, KM#2.

Date	Mintage	VF20	XF40	MS60	MS63	MS65
1991	508	—	—	—	325	375

KM# 44 1000 PESETAS
30.50 g., 0.999 Silver 0.9796 oz. ASW **Subject:** Thor Heyerdahl **Obv:** National arms **Rev:** Multicolor reed boats **Edge:** Plain

Date	Mintage	VF20	XF40	MS60	MS63	MS65
1996	—	PF65 60.00				

KM# 45 1000 PESETAS
30.50 g., 0.999 Silver 0.9796 oz. ASW **Subject:** Horudsch Chaireddin **Obv:** National arms **Rev:** Multicolor pirates sailing vessels in background

Date	Mintage	VF20	XF40	MS60	MS63	MS65
1996	—	PF65 70.00				

KM# 37 1000 PESETAS
31.50 g., 0.999 Silver 1.0117 oz. ASW **Subject:** 15th Anniversary - Diplomacy between Venezuela and Arabic Sahara **Obv:** Pillar between national emblems **Rev:** Head facing and equestrian

Date	Mintage	XF40	MS60	MS63	MS65	MS66
1997	200	—	—	—	100	120
1997	800	PF65 85.00	PF67 100			

KM# 46 1000 PESETAS
14.94 g., 0.999 Silver 0.4799 oz. ASW, 35 mm. **Subject:** World Cup Soccer **Obv:** National arms **Rev:** Soccer ball and trophy **Edge:** Plain

Date	Mintage	VF20	XF40	MS60	MS63	MS65
1997	—	PF63 40.00	PF65 50.00			

KM# 47 1000 PESETAS
15.00 g., 0.999 Silver 0.4818 oz. ASW, 35 mm. **Obv:** National arms **Rev:** Multicolor Thompsons Gazelle **Edge:** Plain

Date	Mintage	VF20	XF40	MS60	MS63	MS65
1997	50	PF65 60.00				

KM# 53 1000 PESETAS
29.00 g., Copper-Nickel, 38.1 mm. **Obv:** National arms **Rev:** Multicolor Graf Ferdinand von Zeppelin and two Zeppelins in flight **Edge:** Reeded

Date	Mintage	VF20	XF40	MS60	MS63	MS65
ND (1997)	—	PF65 47.00				

KM# 57 1000 PESETAS
Silver, 35 mm. **Obv:** National arms **Rev:** Northern European sailing ship in color **Edge:** Plain

Date	Mintage	VF20	XF40	MS60	MS63	MS65
1997	—	PF65 60.00				

KM# 58 1000 PESETAS
Silver, 35 mm. **Obv:** National arms **Rev:** Early Russian sailing ship in color **Edge:** Plain

Date	Mintage	VF20	XF40	MS60	MS63	MS65
1997	—	PF65 60.00				

KM# 59 1000 PESETAS
Silver, 35 mm. **Obv:** National arms **Rev:** Ancient Egyptian sailing ship in color **Edge:** Plain

Date	Mintage	VF20	XF40	MS60	MS63	MS65
1997	—	PF65 60.00				

KM# 43 1000 PESETAS
Silver **Obv:** National emblem **Rev:** Viking ship

Date	Mintage	VF20	XF40	MS60	MS63	MS65
1998	100	PF65 100				

KM# 55 1000 PESETAS
15.48 g., 0.999 Silver 0.4972 oz. ASW, 35 mm. **Obv:** National arms **Rev:** Weight lifter **Edge:** Plain **Note:** Sydney Olympics

Date	Mintage	VF20	XF40	MS60	MS63	MS65
1998	—	PF65 55.00				

KM# 49 1000 PESETAS
15.00 g., 0.999 Silver 0.4818 oz. ASW, 35 mm. **Obv:** National arms **Rev:** Leonardo Da Vinci **Edge:** Plain

Date	Mintage	VF20	XF40	MS60	MS63	MS65
1999	—	PF65 22.50				

KM# 50 1000 PESETAS
15.00 g., 0.999 Silver 0.4818 oz. ASW, 35.1 mm. **Obv:** National arms **Rev:** Pedro Cabral, two sail ships and Brazilian map **Edge:** Plain

Date	Mintage	VF20	XF40	MS60	MS63	MS65
ND(2000)	—	PF65 22.50				

KM# 60 1000 PESETAS
Silver, 35 mm. **Subject:** Millennium **Obv:** National arms **Rev:** Spiral of years **Edge:** Plain

Date	Mintage	VF20	XF40	MS60	MS63	MS65
2000	—	PF63 45.00	PF65 50.00			

KM# 10 1000 PESETAS-10 ECU
31.00 g., 0.999 Silver 0.9957 oz. ASW **Subject:** European Community **Obv:** National arms **Rev:** Knight on horse and King

Date	Mintage	VF20	XF40	MS60	MS63	MS65
ND-1992	15,000	PF65 35.00				

KM# 35 5000 PESETAS
33.54 g., 0.920 Silver 0.9921 oz. ASW **Subject:** 20th Anniversary - Proclamation of Republic **Obv:** National arms **Rev:** Female guerilla with rifle

Date	Mintage	VF20	XF40	MS60	MS63	MS65
1996	—	PF65 125	PF67 150			

KM# 36 5000 PESETAS
33.54 g., 0.920 Silver 0.9921 oz. ASW **Subject:** 20th Anniversary - Proclamation of Republic **Obv:** National arms **Rev:** Land Rover with armed guerillas

Date	Mintage	VF20	XF40	MS60	MS63	MS65
1996	—	PF65 125	PF67 150			

KM# 38 40000 PESETAS
15.52 g., 0.900 Gold 0.4491 oz. AGW **Subject:** 20th Anniversary - Diplomacy between Venezuela and Saharawi Arab Democratic Republic **Obv:** Arms of Venezuela and Saharawi Arab Democratic Republic **Rev:** Bolivar and El Uali

Date	Mintage	XF40	MS60	MS63	MS65	MS66
1997	90	PF65 1,250	PF67 1,450	PF69 1,750		

KM# 38a 40000 PESETAS
15.50 g., 0.999 Gold 0.4978 oz. AGW **Subject:** 20th Anniversary - Diplomacy between Venezuela and Saharawi Arab Democratic Republic **Obv:** Arms of Venezuela and Saharawi Arab Democratic Republic **Rev:** Bolivar and El Uali

Date	Mintage	XF40	MS60	MS63	MS65	MS66
1997 Proof, Rare	10	—	—	—	—	—

ESSAIS

KM#	Date	Mintage	Identification	Mkt Val
E1	1997	8	1000 Pesetas. Copper. KM#37.	3,000

PATTERNS

KM#	Date	Mintage	Identification	Mkt Val
Pn2	1997	8	40000 Pesetas. Copper. KM#38.	3,000
Pn3	1997	8	40000 Pesetas. Silver. KM#38.	3,000

PIEDFORT

KM#	Date	Mintage	Identification	Mkt Val
P2	1997	8	40000 Pesetas. Gold. KM#38.	7,500
P3	1998	—	1000 Pesetas. 0.999. Silver. National arms. Viking ship. Plain.	—

SAINT HELENA

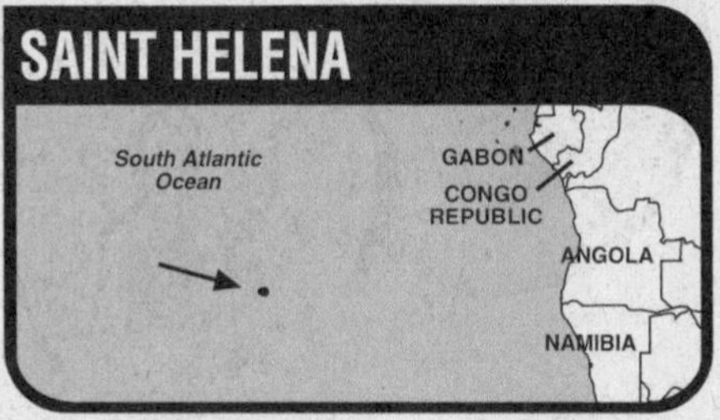

Saint Helena, a British colony located about 1,150 miles (1,850 km.) from the west coast of Africa, has an area of 47 sq. mi. (410 sq. km.) and a population of *7,000. Capital: Jamestown. Flax, lace, and rope are produced for export. Ascension and Tristan da Cunha are dependencies of Saint Helena.

The island was discovered and named by the Portuguese navigator Joao de Nova Castella in 1502. The Portuguese imported livestock, fruit trees, and vegetables but established no permanent settlement. The Dutch occupied the island temporarily, 1645-51. The original European settlement was founded by representatives of the British East India Company sent to annex the island after the departure of the Dutch. The Dutch returned and captured Saint Helena from the British on New Year's Day, 1673, but were in turn ejected by a British force under Sir Richard Munden. Thereafter Saint Helena was the undisputed possession of Great Britain. The island served as the place of exile for Napoleon, several Zulu chiefs, and an ex-sultan of Zanzibar.

RULER
British

MINT MARK
PM - Pobjoy Mint

MONETARY SYSTEM
12 Pence = 1 Shilling
100 Pence = 1 Pound

BRITISH COLONY

STANDARD COINAGE

KM# 5 25 PENCE (Crown)
27.90 g., Copper-Nickel, 38.6 mm. **Ruler:** Elizabeth II **Subject:** St. Helena Tercentenary **Obv:** Young bust right **Rev:** Sailing ship

Date	Mintage	XF40	MS60	MS63	MS65	MS66
ND-1973	100,000	—	—	1.50	2.50	—

KM# 5a 25 PENCE (Crown)
28.28 g., 0.925 Silver 0.841 oz. ASW, 38.5 mm. **Ruler:** Elizabeth II **Subject:** St. Helena Tercentenary **Obv:** Young bust right **Rev:** Sailing ship

Date	Mintage	XF40	MS60	MS63	MS65	MS66
ND-1973	10,000	PF65 30.00	PF67 35.00			

KM# 6 25 PENCE (Crown)
Copper-Nickel, 38.5 mm. **Ruler:** Elizabeth II **Subject:** Queen Elizabeth II Silver Jubilee **Obv:** Young bust right **Rev:** Aldabra giant tortoise

Date	Mintage	XF40	MS60	MS63	MS65	MS66
ND-1977	50,000	—	—	5.00	7.00	—

KM# 6a 25 PENCE (Crown)
28.28 g., 0.925 Silver 0.841 oz. ASW, 38.5 mm. **Ruler:** Elizabeth II **Subject:** Queen Elizabeth II Silver Jubilee **Obv:** Young bust right **Rev:** Aldabra giant tortoise

Date	Mintage	XF40	MS60	MS63	MS65	MS66
ND-1977	—	PF65 27.00	PF67 32.00			

KM# 7 25 PENCE (Crown)
Copper-Nickel, 38.5 mm. **Ruler:** Elizabeth II **Subject:** 25th Anniversary of Coronation **Obv:** Young bust right **Rev:** Crowned portrait with supporters

Date	Mintage	XF40	MS60	MS63	MS65	MS66
1978 PM	—	—	—	1.50	2.50	—

KM# 7a 25 PENCE (Crown)

28.28 g., 0.925 Silver 0.841 oz. ASW, 38.5 mm. **Ruler:** Elizabeth II **Subject:** 25th Anniversary of Coronation **Obv:** Young bust right **Rev:** Crowned portrait with supporters

Date	Mintage	XF40	MS60	MS63	MS65	MS66
1978 PM	70,000	—	—	20.00	25.00	—
1978 PM	—	PF65 30.00	PF67 35.00			

KM# 8 25 PENCE (Crown)

Copper-Nickel, 38.5 mm. **Ruler:** Elizabeth II **Subject:** Queen Mother's 80th Birthday **Obv:** Young bust right **Rev:** Cameo portrait above ship and hills

Date	Mintage	XF40	MS60	MS63	MS65	MS66
1980	100,000	—	—	1.50	2.50	—

KM# 8a 25 PENCE (Crown)

28.28 g., 0.925 Silver 0.841 oz. ASW, 38.5 mm. **Ruler:** Elizabeth II **Subject:** Queen Mother's 80th Birthday **Obv:** Young bust right **Rev:** Cameo portrait above hills

Date	Mintage	XF40	MS60	MS63	MS65	MS66
1980	—	PF65 30.00	PF67 35.00			

KM# 9 25 PENCE (Crown)

Copper-Nickel, 38.5 mm. **Ruler:** Elizabeth II **Subject:** Wedding of Prince Charles and Lady Diana **Obv:** Young bust right **Rev:** Nosegay separates facing heads of couple, ship above

Date	Mintage	XF40	MS60	MS63	MS65	MS66
ND-1981	50,000	—	—	1.50	2.50	—

KM# 9a 25 PENCE (Crown)

28.28 g., 0.925 Silver 0.841 oz. ASW, 38.5 mm. **Ruler:** Elizabeth II **Subject:** Wedding of Prince Charles and Lady Diana **Obv:** Young bust right **Rev:** Nosegay separates facing heads of couple, ship above

Date	Mintage	XF40	MS60	MS63	MS65	MS66
ND-1981	—	PF65 32.00	PF67 37.00			

KM# 10 25 PENCE (Crown)

28.28 g., 0.925 Silver 0.841 oz. ASW, 38.5 mm. **Ruler:** Elizabeth II **Series:** International Year of the Scout **Obv:** Young bust right **Rev:** Stylized value above dates

Date	Mintage	XF40	MS60	MS63	MS65	MS66
ND-1983	10,000	—	—	—	40.00	45.00
ND-1983	10,000	PF65 45.00	PF67 50.00			

KM# 12 50 PENCE

28.28 g., Copper-Nickel, 38.62 mm. **Ruler:** Elizabeth II **Subject:** 150th Anniversary - Saint Helena Colony **Obv:** Young bust right **Rev:** Half figure above crowned shield flanked by designs **Edge:** Reeded

Date	Mintage	XF40	MS60	MS63	MS65	MS66
ND-1984	10,000	—	—	2.50	3.50	—

KM# 12a 50 PENCE

28.28 g., 0.925 Silver 0.841 oz. ASW, 38.5 mm. **Ruler:** Elizabeth II **Subject:** 150th Anniversary - Saint Helena Colony **Obv:** Young bust right **Rev:** Half figure above crowned shield flanked by designs

Date	Mintage	XF40	MS60	MS63	MS65	MS66
ND-1984	—	PF65 42.00	PF67 47.00			

KM# 12b 50 PENCE

47.54 g., 0.917 Gold 1.4016 oz. AGW, 38.5 mm. **Ruler:** Elizabeth II **Subject:** 150th Anniversary - Saint Helena Colony **Obv:** Young bust right **Rev:** Half figure above crowned shield flanked by designs

Date	Mintage	XF40	MS60	MS63	MS65	MS66
ND-1984	150	PF65 2,200	PF67 2,400	PF69 2,800		

KM# 13 50 PENCE

Copper-Nickel, 38.5 mm. **Ruler:** Elizabeth II **Subject:** Royal Visit of Prince Andrew **Obv:** Young bust right **Rev:** Bust left

Date	Mintage	XF40	MS60	MS63	MS65	MS66
1984	125,000	—	—	1.50	2.50	—

KM# 13a 50 PENCE

28.28 g., 0.925 Silver 0.841 oz. ASW, 38.5 mm. **Ruler:** Elizabeth II **Subject:** Royal Visit of Prince Andrew **Obv:** Young bust right **Rev:** Bust left

Date	Mintage	XF40	MS60	MS63	MS65	MS66
1984	—	PF65 40.00	PF67 45.00			

KM# 14 50 PENCE

Copper-Nickel, 38.5 mm. **Ruler:** Elizabeth II **Subject:** Queen Mother **Obv:** Crowned bust right **Rev:** Queen Mother and equestrian within circle

Date	Mintage	XF40	MS60	MS63	MS65	MS66
1995	—	—	—	3.50	5.00	—

KM# 14a 50 PENCE

28.28 g., 0.925 Silver 0.841 oz. ASW, 38.5 mm. **Ruler:** Elizabeth II **Subject:** Queen Mother **Obv:** Crowned bust right **Rev:** Queen Mother and equestrian within circle

Date	Mintage	XF40	MS60	MS63	MS65	MS66
1995	10,000	PF65 42.00	PF67 47.00			

KM# 14b 50 PENCE

47.54 g., 0.916 Gold 1.4001 oz. AGW, 38.5 mm. **Ruler:** Elizabeth II **Subject:** Queen Mother **Obv:** Crowned bust right **Rev:** Queen Mother and equestrian within circle

Date	Mintage	XF40	MS60	MS63	MS65	MS66
1995	150	PF65 2,200	PF67 2,400	PF69 2,800		

KM# 15 50 PENCE

Copper-Nickel, 38.5 mm. **Ruler:** Elizabeth II **Subject:** Queen Elizabeth II's 70th Birthday **Obv:** Crowned bust right **Rev:** Mounted guardsman

Date	Mintage	XF40	MS60	MS63	MS65	MS66
1996	—	—	—	3.50	5.00	—

KM# 15a 50 PENCE

28.28 g., 0.925 Silver 0.841 oz. ASW, 38.5 mm. **Ruler:** Elizabeth II **Subject:** Queen Elizabeth II's 70th Birthday **Obv:** Crowned bust right **Rev:** Mounted guardsman

Date	Mintage	XF40	MS60	MS63	MS65	MS66
1996	—	PF65 45.00	PF67 50.00			

KM# 18 50 PENCE

Copper-Nickel, 38.5 mm. **Ruler:** Elizabeth II **Subject:** Elizabeth and Philip **Obv:** Crowned bust right **Rev:** Royal couple reviewing troops

Date	Mintage	XF40	MS60	MS63	MS65	MS66
ND-1997	—	—	—	3.50	5.00	—

KM# 16 50 PENCE

Copper-Nickel, 38.5 mm. **Ruler:** Elizabeth II **Series:** World Wildlife Fund **Subject:** Conserving Nature **Obv:** Crowned bust right **Rev:** Three blue whales

Date	Mintage	XF40	MS60	MS63	MS65	MS66
1998	—	—	—	7.00	12.00	14.00

KM# 16a 50 PENCE

28.28 g., 0.925 Silver 0.841 oz. ASW, 38.5 mm. **Ruler:** Elizabeth II **Series:** World Wildlife Fund **Subject:** Conserving Nature **Obv:** Crowned bust right **Rev:** Three Blue Whales

Date	Mintage	XF40	MS60	MS63	MS65	MS66
1998	—	PF65 50.00	PF67 55.00			

KM# 17 50 PENCE
Copper-Nickel, 38.5 mm. **Ruler:** Elizabeth II **Series:** World Wildlife Fund **Subject:** Conserving Nature **Obv:** Crowned bust right **Rev:** Rainpiper bird, shoreline, lily

Date	Mintage	XF40	MS60	MS63	MS65	MS66
1998	—	—	—	6.00	8.00	10.00

KM# 22 50 PENCE
28.28 g., Copper-Nickel, 38.6 mm. **Ruler:** Elizabeth II **Obv:** Crowned bust right **Rev:** Crowned bust of the Queen Mother right **Edge:** Reeded

Date	Mintage	XF40	MS60	MS63	MS65	MS66
ND(2000)	—	—	—	4.00	6.00	8.00

KM# 22a 50 PENCE
28.28 g., 0.925 Silver 0.841 oz. ASW, 38.6 mm. **Ruler:** Elizabeth II **Obv:** Crowned bust right **Rev:** Crowned bust of the Queen Mother right **Edge:** Reeded

Date	Mintage	XF40	MS60	MS63	MS65	MS66
ND(2000)	10,000	PF65 45.00	PF67 50.00			

KM# 22b 50 PENCE
47.54 g., 0.9166 Gold 1.401 oz. AGW, 38.6 mm. **Ruler:** Elizabeth II **Obv:** Crowned bust right **Rev:** Crowned bust of the Queen Mother right **Edge:** Reeded

Date	Mintage	XF40	MS60	MS63	MS65	MS66
ND(2000)	100	PF65 2,200	PF67 2,400	PF69 2,800		

KM# 21 POUND
4.20 g., Brass Plated Steel, 22 mm. **Ruler:** Elizabeth II **Obv:** Young bust right **Rev:** Coat of arms and value **Edge:** Reeded and plain sections

Date	Mintage	XF40	MS60	MS63	MS65	MS66
1980 PM	—	—	—	—	—	—

KM# 11 2 POUNDS
15.98 g., 0.917 Gold 0.4711 oz. AGW **Ruler:** Elizabeth II **Series:** International Year of the Scout **Obv:** Young bust right **Rev:** Scouts and tent

Date	Mintage	XF40	MS60	MS63	MS65	MS66
ND-1983	2,000	—	—	850	900	1,000
ND-1983	—	PF65 1,100	PF67 1,250			

PIEDFORT

KM#	Date	Mintage	Identification	Mkt Val
P1	1984	500	50 Pence. Silver. KM13a.	85.00
P2	1995	500	50 Pence. Silver. KM14a.	115

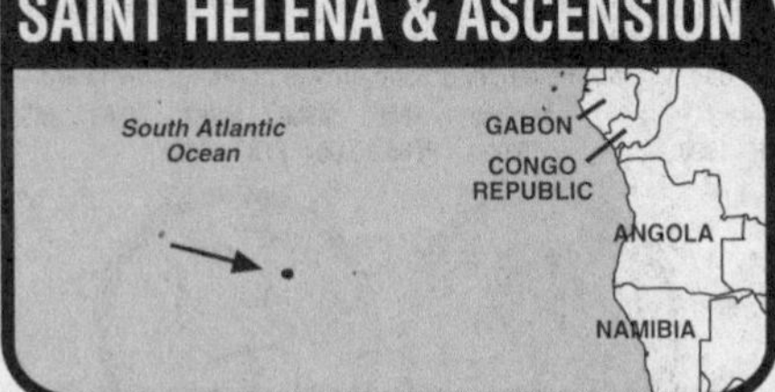

BRITISH OVERSEAS TERRITORY

STANDARD COINAGE

100 Pence = 1 Pound

KM# 1 PENNY
3.60 g., Bronze, 20.32 mm. **Ruler:** Elizabeth II **Obv:** Young bust right **Rev:** Tuna fish and value

Date	Mintage	VF20	XF40	MS60	MS63	MS65
1984	—	—	0.20	0.45	0.65	1.25
1984	10,000	PF65 1.50				

KM# 13 PENNY
3.60 g., Bronze, 20.32 mm. **Ruler:** Elizabeth II **Obv:** Crowned head right **Rev:** Tuna fish and value

Date	Mintage	VF20	XF40	MS60	MS63	MS65
1991	—	—	0.15	0.25	0.45	1.00

KM# 13a PENNY
3.50 g., Copper Plated Steel, 20.28 mm. **Ruler:** Elizabeth II **Obv:** Crowned head right **Rev:** Tuna above value **Edge:** Plain

Date	Mintage	VF20	XF40	MS60	MS63	MS65
1997	—	—	0.15	0.25	0.45	1.00

KM# 2 2 PENCE
7.10 g., Bronze, 25.9 mm. **Ruler:** Elizabeth II **Obv:** Young bust right **Rev:** Donkey with firewood

Date	Mintage	VF20	XF40	MS60	MS63	MS65
1984	—	—	0.25	0.45	0.65	1.25
1984	10,000	PF65 2.00				

KM# 12 2 PENCE
7.10 g., Bronze, 25.91 mm. **Ruler:** Elizabeth II **Obv:** Crowned head right **Rev:** Value below donkey

Date	Mintage	VF20	XF40	MS60	MS63	MS65
1991	—	—	0.20	0.40	0.70	1.50

KM# 12a 2 PENCE
Copper Plated Steel, 25.9 mm. **Ruler:** Elizabeth II **Obv:** Crowned head right **Rev:** Value below donkey

Date	Mintage	VF20	XF40	MS60	MS63	MS65
1998	—	—	0.20	0.40	0.60	1.25

KM# 3 5 PENCE
5.70 g., Copper-Nickel, 23.59 mm. **Ruler:** Elizabeth II **Obv:** Young bust right **Rev:** Rainpiper

Date	Mintage	VF20	XF40	MS60	MS63	MS65
1984	—	—	0.25	0.45	0.75	1.50
1984	—	PF65 2.00				

KM# 14 5 PENCE
Copper-Nickel, 18 mm. **Ruler:** Elizabeth II **Obv:** Crowned head right **Rev:** Value below rainpiper

Date	Mintage	VF20	XF40	MS60	MS63	MS65
1991	—	—	0.25	0.45	0.75	1.50

KM# 22 5 PENCE
3.25 g., Copper-Nickel, 18 mm. **Ruler:** Elizabeth II **Obv:** Crowned head right **Rev:** Giant tortoise

Date	Mintage	VF20	XF40	MS60	MS63	MS65
1998	—	—	1.00	1.50	2.50	5.00

KM# 4 10 PENCE
11.30 g., Copper-Nickel, 28.5 mm. **Ruler:** Elizabeth II **Obv:** Young bust right **Rev:** Value below arum lily

Date	Mintage	VF20	XF40	MS60	MS63	MS65
1984	—	—	0.50	0.75	1.25	2.00
1984	—	PF65 3.00				

KM# 15 10 PENCE
11.30 g., Copper-Nickel, 28.5 mm. **Ruler:** Elizabeth II **Obv:** Crowned head right

Date	Mintage	VF20	XF40	MS60	MS63	MS65
1991	—	—	0.30	0.50	1.00	1.50

KM# 23 10 PENCE
6.50 g., Copper-Nickel, 24.5 mm. **Ruler:** Elizabeth II **Obv:** Crowned head right **Rev:** Dolphins

Date	Mintage	VF20	XF40	MS60	MS63	MS65
1998	—	—	1.25	2.00	2.50	3.50

KM# 21 20 PENCE
5.00 g., Copper-Nickel, 21.4 mm. **Ruler:** Elizabeth II **Obv:** Crowned head right **Rev:** Ebony flower **Shape:** 7-sided

Date	Mintage	VF20	XF40	MS60	MS63	MS65
1998	—	—	0.65	1.25	1.50	2.50

KM# 5 50 PENCE
13.50 g., Copper-Nickel, 30 mm. **Ruler:** Elizabeth II **Obv:** Young bust right **Rev:** Green sea turtle **Shape:** 7-sided

Date	Mintage	VF20	XF40	MS60	MS63	MS65
1984	—	—	1.50	2.25	3.25	5.50
1984	—	PF65 7.50				

KM# 7 50 PENCE
Copper-Nickel, 38.5 mm. **Ruler:** Elizabeth II **Subject:** Wedding of Prince Andrew and Sarah Ferguson **Obv:** Crowned bust right **Rev:** Conjoined busts of couple right within circle

Date	Mintage	VF20	XF40	MS60	MS63	MS65
ND-1986	13,000	—	1.50	2.25	3.25	5.50

KM# 7a 50 PENCE
28.28 g., 0.925 Silver 0.841 oz. ASW, 38.5 mm. **Ruler:** Elizabeth II **Subject:** Wedding of Prince Andrew and Sarah Ferguson **Obv:** Crowned bust right **Rev:** Conjoined busts of couple right within circle

Date	Mintage	XF40	MS60	MS63	MS65	MS66
ND-1986	2,500	PF65 30.00	PF67 40.00			

KM# 7b 50 PENCE
47.54 g., 0.917 Gold 1.4016 oz. AGW, 38.5 mm. **Ruler:** Elizabeth II **Subject:** Wedding of Prince Andrew and Sarah Ferguson **Obv:** Crowned bust right **Rev:** Conjoined busts of couple right within circle

Date	Mintage	XF40	MS60	MS63	MS65	MS66
ND-1986	50	PF67 2,400	PF69 2,800			

KM# 8 50 PENCE
Copper-Nickel, 38.5 mm. **Ruler:** Elizabeth II **Subject:** 165th Anniversary of Napoleon's Death **Obv:** Crowned bust right **Rev:** Sailing ship and 1/2 figure facing right

Date	Mintage	VF20	XF40	MS60	MS63	MS65
1986	50,000	—	—	—	4.00	6.00

KM# 16 50 PENCE
13.50 g., Copper-Nickel, 30 mm. **Ruler:** Elizabeth II **Obv:** Crowned head right **Rev:** Green sea turtle **Shape:** 7-sided

Date	Mintage	VF20	XF40	MS60	MS63	MS65
1991	—	—	1.50	2.50	3.50	5.50

KM# 19 50 PENCE
Copper-Nickel, 38.5 mm. **Ruler:** Elizabeth II **Subject:** Normandy Invasion **Obv:** Crowned bust right **Rev:** Barbed wire above fence, artistic arrows pointing downward

Date	Mintage	VF20	XF40	MS60	MS63	MS65
ND-1994	—	—	—	—	5.00	7.00

KM# 19a 50 PENCE
28.28 g., 0.925 Silver 0.841 oz. ASW, 38.5 mm. **Ruler:** Elizabeth II **Subject:** Normandy Invasion **Obv:** Crowned bust right **Rev:** Barbed wire above fence, artistic arrows pointing downward

Date	Mintage	XF40	MS60	MS63	MS65	MS66
ND-1994	5,000	PF65 40.00	PF67 50.00			

KM# 6 POUND
9.50 g., Nickel-Brass, 22.5 mm. **Ruler:** Elizabeth II **Obv:** Young bust right **Rev:** Sooty terns (Wideawake birds)

Date	Mintage	VF20	XF40	MS60	MS63	MS65
1984	—	—	—	2.00	3.00	5.00
1984	—	PF65 8.00				

KM# 6a POUND
9.50 g., 0.925 Silver 0.2825 oz. ASW, 22.5 mm. **Ruler:** Elizabeth II **Obv:** Young bust right **Rev:** Sooty terns (Wideawake birds)

Date	Mintage	XF40	MS60	MS63	MS65	MS66
1984	10,000	PF65 20.00	PF67 25.00			

KM# 17 POUND
9.50 g., Nickel-Brass, 22.5 mm. **Ruler:** Elizabeth II **Obv:** Crowned head right **Rev:** Sooty terns (Wideawake birds)

Date	Mintage	VF20	XF40	MS60	MS63	MS65
1991	—	—	—	2.00	3.00	5.00

KM# 11 2 POUNDS
Copper-Nickel, 38.5 mm. **Ruler:** Elizabeth II **Subject:** Queen Mother **Obv:** Crowned bust right **Rev:** Crowned monogram flanked by flowers

Date	Mintage	VF20	XF40	MS60	MS63	MS65
ND-1990	—	—	—	—	8.00	10.00

KM# 18 2 POUNDS
28.28 g., 0.925 Silver 0.841 oz. ASW, 38.5 mm. **Ruler:** Elizabeth II **Subject:** 40th Anniversary - Coronation of Elizabeth II **Obv:** Crowned bust right **Rev:** Church figures

Date	Mintage	XF40	MS60	MS63	MS65	MS66
ND-1993	10,000	PF65 35.00	PF67 45.00			

KM# 24 5 POUNDS
28.28 g., 0.925 Silver 0.841 oz. ASW, 38.5 mm. **Ruler:** Elizabeth II **Subject:** Queen Mother **Obv:** Crowned bust right **Rev:** Queen Mother's monogram **Note:** Prev. KM#11a.

Date	Mintage	XF40	MS60	MS63	MS65	MS66
ND-1990	10,000	PF65 35.00	PF67 45.00			

KM# 9 25 POUNDS
155.00 g., 0.999 Silver 4.9784 oz. ASW, 65 mm. **Ruler:** Elizabeth II **Subject:** 165th Anniversary of Napoleon's Death **Obv:** Crowned bust right **Rev:** Sailing ship at right and 1/2 figure facing right **Note:** Illustration reduced.

Date	Mintage	XF40	MS60	MS63	MS65	MS66
1986	15,000	PF65 145	PF67 165			

KM# 20 25 POUNDS
155.52 g., 0.999 Silver 4.995 oz. ASW, 65 mm. **Ruler:** Elizabeth II **Subject:** 70th Birthday - Queen Elizabeth II **Obv:** Crowned bust right **Rev:** Mounted drummer and cameo head right **Note:** Illustration reduced.

Date	Mintage	XF40	MS60	MS63	MS65	MS66
1996	1,000	PF65 185	PF67 225			

KM# 10 50 POUNDS
32.26 g., 0.999 Platinum 1.0361 oz. APW **Ruler:** Elizabeth II **Subject:** 165th Anniversary of Napoleon's Death **Obv:** Crowned bust right **Rev:** Sailing ship at right and 1/2 figure at left looking right **Note:** Similar to KM#9.

Date	Mintage	XF40	MS60	MS63	MS65	MS66
1986	5,000	PF67 1,450	PF69 1,650			

PIEDFORT

KM#	Date	Mintage	Identification	Mkt Val
P1	1984	2,500	Pound. Silver. KM#6a.	50.00
P2	1986	250	50 Pence. Silver. KM#7a.	80.00
P3	1994	500	50 Pence. Copper-Nickel. KM#19.	60.00

MINT SETS

KM#	Date	Mintage	Identification	Issue Price	Mkt Val
MS1	1984 (6)	—	KM#1-6	—	20.00

PROOF SETS

KM#	Date	Mintage	Identification	Issue Price	Mkt Val
PS1	1984 (6)	—	KM#1-6	—	25.00

SAINT KITTS & NEVIS

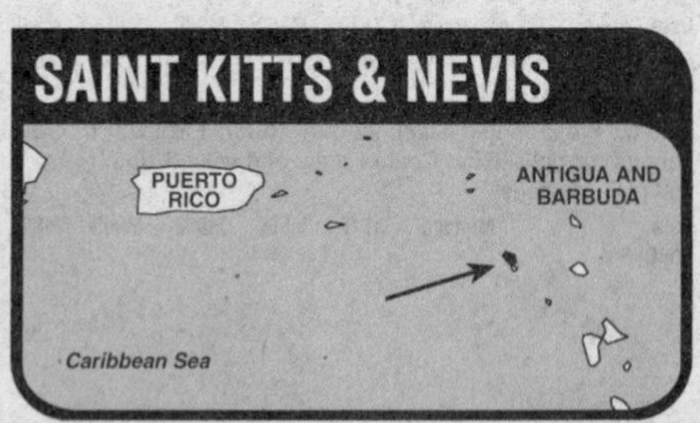

This independent state, located in the Leeward Islands of the West Indies, south of Puerto Rico, comprises the islands of St. Kitts, Nevis and Anguilla. The country has an area of 101 sq. mi. (261 sq. km.) and a population of 41,000. Capital: Basseterre, on St. Kitts (as it may be called in abbreviated form). The islands export sugar, cotton, lobsters, beverages and electrical equipment.

St. Kitts was discovered by Columbus in 1493 and was settled by Thomas Warner, an Englishman, in 1623. The Treaty of Utrecht, 1713, ceded the island to the British. France protested British occupancy, and on three occasions between 1616 and 1782 seized the island and held it for short periods. St. Kitts used the coins and currency of the British Caribbean Territories (Eastern Group).

In early 1967 the Colony was, together with the islands of Nevis and Anguilla, united politically as a self-governing British Associated State. However, in June 1967 Anguilla declared its independence, severing ties with Britain and established a so-called "Republic of Anguilla". Britain refused to accept this and established a Commissioner to govern Anguilla; this arrangement continues to the present time.

St. Kitts and Nevis became a member of the Commonwealth of Nations on Sept. 19, 1983. Queen Elizabeth II is Head of State.

From approximately 1750-1830, billon 2 sous of the French colony of Cayenne were countermarked SK' and used on St. Kitts. They were valued at 1-1/2 Pence Sterling. (St. Kitts and Nevis now use East Caribbean Currency.)

RULER
British

MONETARY SYSTEM
100 Cents = 1 East Caribbean Dollar

BRITISH ASSOCIATED STATE

STANDARD COINAGE

KM# 1 4 DOLLARS
Copper-Nickel, 38.5 mm. **Series:** F.A.O. **Obv:** Crowned arms with supporters **Rev:** Sugar cane and banana tree branch divided by value below

Date	Mintage	VF20	XF40	MS60	MS63	MS65
1970	13,000	6.00	10.00	22.00	35.00	50.00
1970	2,000	PF63 40.00	PF65 55.00	PF67 75.00		

KM# 3 10 DOLLARS
Copper-Nickel, 38.8 mm. **Subject:** Royal Visit **Obv:** Crowned bust right **Rev:** Crowned arms with supporters

Date	Mintage	VF20	XF40	MS60	MS63	MS65
1985	100,000	—	7.00	12.00	15.00	20.00

KM# 3a 10 DOLLARS
28.28 g., 0.925 Silver 0.841 oz. ASW, 38.8 mm. **Subject:** Royal Visit **Obv:** Crowned bust right **Rev:** Crowned arms with supporters

Date	Mintage	VF20	XF40	MS60	MS63	MS65
1985	5,000	PF63 35.00	PF65 40.00	PF67 45.00		

KM# 3b 10 DOLLARS
47.54 g., 0.917 Gold 1.4016 oz. AGW, 38.8 mm. **Subject:** Royal Visit **Obv:** Crowned bust right **Rev:** Crowned arms with supporters

Date	Mintage	VF20	XF40	MS60	MS63	MS65
1985	250	PF65 2,500	PF67 2,700			

KM# 4 20 DOLLARS
Copper-Nickel, 38.8 mm. **Subject:** 200th Anniversary - Battle of the Saints **Obv:** Crowned arms with supporters **Rev:** Dates above ship

Date	Mintage	VF20	XF40	MS60	MS63	MS65
ND-1982	—	—	—	20.00	30.00	45.00

KM# 4a 20 DOLLARS
28.28 g., 0.925 Silver 0.841 oz. ASW, 38.8 mm. **Subject:** 200th Anniversary - Battle of the Saints **Obv:** Crowned arms with supporters **Rev:** Dates above ship

Date	Mintage	VF20	XF40	MS60	MS63	MS65
ND-1982	2,500	PF63 45.00	PF65 50.00	PF67 60.00		

KM# 2 20 DOLLARS
28.28 g., Copper-Nickel, 38.61 mm. **Subject:** Attainment of Independence, September 19 **Obv:** Young bust right **Rev:** Ship, map and compass

Date	Mintage	VF20	XF40	MS60	MS63	MS65
1983	—	—	—	10.00	15.00	20.00

KM# 2a 20 DOLLARS
28.28 g., 0.925 Silver 0.841 oz. ASW **Subject:** Attainment of Independence, September 19 **Obv:** Young bust right **Rev:** Compass, ship and map

Date	Mintage	VF20	XF40	MS60	MS63	MS65
1983	5,000	PF63 40.00	PF65 45.00	PF67 50.00		

KM# 5 100 DOLLARS
7.99 g., 0.917 Gold 0.2356 oz. AGW **Subject:** 200th Anniversary - Siege of Brimstone Hill **Rev:** Brimstone Hill

Date	Mintage	XF40	MS60	MS63	MS65	MS66
ND-1982	250	—	—	1,350	1,650	2,000
ND-1982	15	PF67 2,350	PF69 2,500			

KM# 6 100 DOLLARS
129.59 g., 0.925 Silver 3.8539 oz. ASW, 63 mm. **Subject:** Tropical birds **Rev:** Green-throated Carib Hummingbird **Note:** Illustration reduced.

Date	Mintage	VF20	XF40	MS60	MS63	MS65
1988	Est. 10000	PF65 135	PF67 175			

SAINT LUCIA

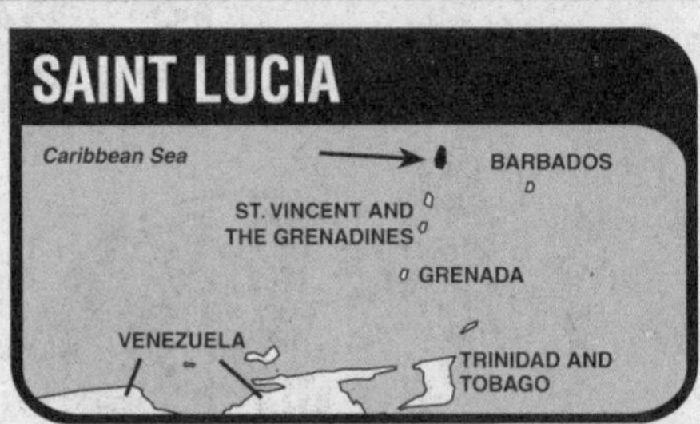

Saint Lucia, an independent island nation located in the Windward Islands of the West Indies between Saint Vincent and Martinique, has an area of 238 sq. mi. (620 sq. km.) and a population of *150,000. Capital: Castries. The economy is agricultural. Bananas, copra, cocoa, sugar and logwood are exported.

Columbus discovered Saint Lucia in 1502. The first attempts at settlement undertaken by the British in 1605 and 1638 were frustrated by sickness and the determined hostility of the fierce Carib inhabitants. The French settled it in 1650 and made a treaty with the natives. Until 1814, when the island became a definite British possession, it was the scene of a continuous conflict between the British and French, which saw the island change, hands on at least 14 occasions. In 1967, under the West Indies Act, Saint Lucia was established as a British associated state, self-governing in internal affairs. Complete independence was attained on February 22, 1979. Saint Lucia is a member of the Commonwealth of Nations. Elizabeth II is Head of State as Queen of Saint Lucia.

Prior to 1950, the island used sterling, which was superseded by the currency of the British Caribbean Territories (Eastern Group) and the East Caribbean State.

RULER
British

MONETARY SYSTEM
100 Cents = 1 Dollar

BRITISH ASSOCIATED STATE

MODERN COINAGE

KM# 11 4 DOLLARS
Copper-Nickel, 38.5 mm. **Series:** F.A.O. **Obv:** Crowned arms with supporters **Rev:** Sugar cane and banana tree branch divided by value below

Date	Mintage	VF20	XF40	MS60	MS63	MS65
1970	13,000	6.00	10.00	22.00	35.00	50.00
1970	2,000	PF63 40.00	PF65 55.00	PF67 75.00		

KM# 14 5 DOLLARS
Copper-Nickel **Subject:** Papal Visit - John Paul II **Obv:** Crowned arms with supporters **Obv. Legend:** • SAINT LUCIA • FIVE DOLLARS below **Rev:** Bust left **Rev. Legend:** • PAPAL VISIT JULY 1986 • JOHN PAUL II on shoulder

Date	Mintage	VF20	XF40	MS60	MS63	MS65
1986	—	—	—	10.00	15.00	25.00

KM# 14a 5 DOLLARS
28.28 g., 0.925 Silver 0.841 oz. ASW **Subject:** Papal Visit - John Paul II **Obv:** Crowned arms with supporters **Obv. Legend:** • SAINT LUCIA • FIVE DOLLARS below **Rev:** Bust left **Rev. Legend:** • PAPAL VISIT JULY 1986 • JOHN PAUL II on shoulder

Date	Mintage	VF20	XF40	MS60	MS63	MS65
1986	2,120	PF65 70.00	PF67 90.00			

KM# 12 10 DOLLARS
Copper-Nickel, 38.8 mm. **Subject:** 200th Anniversary - Battle of the Saints **Obv:** Crowned arms with supporters **Rev:** Dates above battleships

Date	Mintage	VF20	XF40	MS60	MS63	MS65
1982	—	—	—	15.00	25.00	45.00

KM# 12a 10 DOLLARS
28.28 g., 0.925 Silver 0.841 oz. ASW, 38.8 mm. **Subject:** 200th Anniversary - Battle of the Saints **Obv:** Crowned arms with supporters **Rev:** Dates above battleships

Date	Mintage	VF20	XF40	MS60	MS63	MS65
1982	2,500	PF65 60.00	PF67 70.00			

KM# 13 10 DOLLARS
Copper-Nickel, 38.8 mm. **Subject:** Royal Visit - Queen Elizabeth II **Obv:** Crowned bust right **Rev:** Crowned arms with supporters **Rev. Legend:** • ROYAL VISIT 1985 • TEN DOLLARS below

Date	Mintage	VF20	XF40	MS60	MS63	MS65
1985	100,000	—	—	5.00	9.00	12.00

KM# 13a 10 DOLLARS
28.28 g., 0.925 Silver 0.841 oz. ASW, 38.8 mm. **Subject:** Royal Visit - Queen Elizabeth II **Obv:** Crowned bust right **Rev:** Crowned arms with supporters **Rev. Legend:** • ROYAL VISIT 1985 • TEN DOLLARS below

Date	Mintage	VF20	XF40	MS60	MS63	MS65
1985	5,000	PF65 35.00	PF67 50.00			

KM# 13b 10 DOLLARS
47.54 g., 0.917 Gold 1.4016 oz. AGW, 38.8 mm. **Subject:** Royal Visit - Queen Elizabeth II **Obv:** Crowned bust right **Rev:** Crowned arms with supporters **Rev. Legend:** • ROYAL VISIT 1985 • TEN DOLLARS below

Date	Mintage	VF20	XF40	MS60	MS63	MS65
1985	250	PF65 2,400	PF67 2,700			

KM# 16 10 DOLLARS
28.28 g., 0.925 Silver 0.841 oz. ASW **Subject:** Commonwealth Finance Ministers' Meeting **Obv:** Monogram flanked by sprigs within circle **Rev:** Crowned arms with supporters above lake and mountains

Date	Mintage	VF20	XF40	MS60	MS63	MS65
1986	1,000	PF65 60.00	PF67 75.00			

KM# 17 100 DOLLARS
129.59 g., 0.925 Silver 3.8539 oz. ASW, 63 mm. **Subject:** Tropical Birds **Rev:** Two amazon parrots **Note:** Illustration reduced.

Date	Mintage	VF20	XF40	MS60	MS63	MS65
1988	Est. 10000	PF65 135	PF67 175			

KM# 15 500 DOLLARS
15.98 g., 0.917 Gold 0.4711 oz. AGW **Subject:** Papal Visit - John Paul II **Obv:** Crowned arms with supporters within circle **Rev:** Bust left **Rev. Legend:** • PAPAL VISIT JULY 1986 •

Date	Mintage	VF20	XF40	MS60	MS63	MS65
1986	100	PF65 1,300	PF67 1,500			

ST. PIERRE & MIQUELON

The Territorial Collectivity of Saint Pierre and Miquelon, a French overseas territory located 10 miles (16 km.) off the south coast of Newfoundland, has an area of 93 sq. mi. (242 sq. km.) and a population of *6,000. Capital: Saint Pierre. The economy of the barren archipelago is based on cod fishing and fur farming. Fish and fish products, and mink and silver fox pelts are exported.

The islands were occupied by the French in 1604, then were captured by the British in 1702 and held until 1763, at which time they were returned to the possession of France and employed as a fishing station. They passed between France and England on six more occasions between 1778 and 1814 when the Treaty of Paris awarded them permanently to France. The rugged, soil-poor granite islands, which will support only evergreen shrubs, are all that remain of France's extensive North American colonies. In 1958 Saint Pierre and Miquelon voted in favor of the new constitution of the Fifth Republic of France, thereby choosing to remain within the new French Community.

RULER
French

MINT MARK
(a) - Paris, privy marks only

MONETARY SYSTEM
100 Centimes = 1 Franc

FRENCH OVERSEAS DEPARTMENT

STANDARD COINAGE

KM# 1 FRANC
1.32 g., Aluminum, 22.56 mm. **Obv:** Winged Liberty head left **Rev:** Ship above value **Edge:** Plain

Date	Mintage	VF20	XF40	MS60	MS63	MS65
1948 (a)	600,000	1.00	2.00	5.00	10.00	20.00

KM# 2 2 FRANCS
2.14 g., Aluminum, 26.95 mm. **Obv:** Winged Liberty head left **Rev:** Ship above value **Edge:** Plain

Date	Mintage	VF20	XF40	MS60	MS63	MS65
1948 (a)	300,000	1.50	3.00	6.00	12.00	25.00

ESSAIS

Standard metals unless otherwise noted

KM#	Date	Mintage	Identification	Mkt Val
E1a	1948(a)	2,000	Franc. Copper-Nickel.	45.00
E2a	1948(a)	2,000	2 Francs. Copper-Nickel.	50.00

PIEDFORT WITH ESSAI

Double thickness, standard metals unless otherwise noted

KM#	Date	Mintage	Identification	Mkt Val
PE1	1948(a)	104	Franc.	250
PE2	1948(a)	104	2 Francs.	300

SAINT THOMAS & PRINCE

EQUATORIAL GUINEA
CAMEROON
CONGO REPUBLIC
GABON
South Atlantic Ocean

The Democratic Republic of St. Thomas & Prince (São Tomé e Príncipe) is located in the Gulf of Guinea 150 miles (241 km.) off the western coast of Africa. It has an area of 372 sq. mi. (960 sq. km.) and a population of *121,000. Capital: São Tomé. The economy of the islands is based on cocoa, copra and coffee.

Saint Thomas and Saint Prince were uninhabited when discovered by Portuguese navigators Joao de Santarem and Pedro de Escobar in 1470. After the failure of their initial settlement of 1485, the Portuguese successfully colonized St. Thomas with a colony of prisoners and exiled Jews in 1493. An initial prosperity based on the sugar trade gave way to a time of misfortune, 1567-1709, that saw the colony attacked and occupied or plundered by the French and Dutch, ravaged by the slave revolt of 1595; and finally rendered destitute by the transfer of the world sugar trade to Brazil. In the late 1800s, the colony turned from the production of sugar to cocoa, the basis of its present economy

The islands were designated a Portuguese overseas province in 1951. On April 25, 1974, the government of Portugal was seized by a military junta, which reached agreements providing for independence for the Portuguese overseas provinces of Portuguese Guinea (Guinea-Bissau), Mozambique, Cape Verde Islands, Angola, and Saint Thomas and Prince Islands. The Democratic Republic of São Tomé and Principe was declared on July 12, 1975.

RULERS
Portuguese, until 1975

MINT MARKS
R – Rio

MONETARY SYSTEM
100 Centavos = 1 Escudo

PORTUGUESE COLONY

REFORM COINAGE

100 Centavos = 1 Escudo

KM# 2 10 CENTAVOS
Nickel-Bronze **Obv:** Liberty head left **Rev:** Shield within globe above value

Date	Mintage	VF20	XF40	MS60	MS63	MS65
1929	500,000	3.00	10.00	25.00	35.00	50.00

KM# 15 10 CENTAVOS
Bronze **Obv:** Value **Rev:** Shield within crowned globe

Date	Mintage	VF20	XF40	MS60	MS63	MS65
1962	500,000	0.50	2.50	5.00	8.00	12.00

KM# 15a 10 CENTAVOS
Aluminum, 16 mm. **Obv:** Value **Rev:** Shield within crowned globe

Date	Mintage	F12	VF20	XF40	MS60	MS63
1971	1,000,000	—	0.25	1.00	2.00	3.00

KM# 3 20 CENTAVOS
Nickel-Bronze **Obv:** Liberty head left **Rev:** Shield within globe above value

Date	Mintage	VF20	XF40	MS60	MS63	MS65
1929	250,000	3.00	12.00	30.00	45.00	75.00

KM# 16.1 20 CENTAVOS
Bronze, 18 mm. **Obv:** Value **Rev:** Shield within crowned globe

Date	Mintage	VF20	XF40	MS60	MS63	MS65
1962	250,000	1.00	3.00	5.00	12.00	16.00

KM# 16.2 20 CENTAVOS
Bronze, 16 mm. **Obv:** Value **Rev:** Shield within crowned globe

Date	Mintage	VF20	XF40	MS60	MS63	MS65
1971	750,000	0.75	1.50	2.50	3.50	5.50

KM# 1 50 CENTAVOS
Nickel-Bronze **Obv:** Liberty head left **Rev:** Shield within globe above value

Date	Mintage	VF20	XF40	MS60	MS63	MS65
1928	—	50.00	250	450	750	—
1929	400,000	8.00	75.00	125	250	—

KM# 8 50 CENTAVOS
Nickel-Bronze **Obv:** Value **Rev:** Shield within crowned globe

Date	Mintage	VF20	XF40	MS60	MS63	MS65
1948	80,000	20.00	65.00	100	150	250

KM# 10 50 CENTAVOS
4.45 g., Copper-Nickel, 22.64 mm. **Obv:** Value **Rev:** Shield within crowned globe

Date	Mintage	VF20	XF40	MS60	MS63	MS65
1951	48,000	2.00	20.00	45.00	60.00	80.00

KM# 17.1 50 CENTAVOS
3.95 g., Bronze, 20 mm. **Obv:** Value **Rev:** Shield within crowned globe

Date	Mintage	F12	VF20	XF40	MS60	MS63
1962	480,000	—	0.25	1.00	2.50	3.50

KM# 17.2 50 CENTAVOS
Bronze, 22 mm. **Obv:** Value **Rev:** Shield within crowned globe

Date	Mintage	F12	VF20	XF40	MS60	MS63
1971	600,000	—	0.25	1.00	2.50	3.00

KM# 4 ESCUDO
Copper-Nickel **Obv:** Value **Rev:** Shield within crowned globe

Date	Mintage	VF20	XF40	MS60	MS63	MS65
1939	100,000	10.00	65.00	150	225	300

KM# 9 ESCUDO
Nickel-Bronze **Obv:** Value **Rev:** Shield within crowned globe

Date	Mintage	VF20	XF40	MS60	MS63	MS65
1948	60,000	20.00	75.00	150	225	325

KM# 11 ESCUDO
Copper-Nickel **Obv:** Value **Rev:** Shield within crowned globe

Date	Mintage	VF20	XF40	MS60	MS63	MS65
1951	18,000	8.00	45.00	100	150	200

KM# 18 ESCUDO
7.85 g., Bronze, 26 mm. **Obv:** Value **Rev:** Shield within crowned globe

Date	Mintage	F12	VF20	XF40	MS60	MS63
1962	160,000	—	1.00	8.00	15.00	20.00
1971	350,000	—	0.25	1.00	2.00	5.00

KM# 5 2-1/2 ESCUDOS
3.50 g., 0.650 Silver 0.0731 oz. ASW **Obv:** Shield within globe on cross **Rev:** Shield within crowned globe

Date	Mintage	VF20	XF40	MS60	MS63	MS65
1939	80,000	20.00	85.00	150	300	—
1948	120,000	20.00	65.00	125	250	—

KM# 12 2-1/2 ESCUDOS
3.50 g., 0.650 Silver 0.0731 oz. ASW **Obv:** Shield within globe on cross **Rev:** Shield within crowned globe

Date	Mintage	VF20	XF40	MS60	MS63	MS65
1951	64,000	5.00	20.00	45.00	75.00	100

KM# 19 2-1/2 ESCUDOS
Copper-Nickel **Obv:** Shield within globe on cross **Rev:** Shield within crowned globe

Date	Mintage	F12	VF20	XF40	MS60	MS63
1962	140,000	—	1.50	3.00	9.00	12.00
1971	250,000	—	1.00	2.50	5.00	8.00

KM# 6 5 ESCUDOS
7.00 g., 0.650 Silver 0.1463 oz. ASW **Obv:** Shield within globe on cross **Rev:** Shield within crowned globe

Date	Mintage	VF20	XF40	MS60	MS63	MS65
1939	60,000	20.00	45.00	125	225	325
1948	100,000	30.00	75.00	150	250	350

KM# 13 5 ESCUDOS
7.00 g., 0.650 Silver 0.1463 oz. ASW, 25 mm. **Obv:** Shield within globe on cross **Rev:** Shield within crowned globe

Date	Mintage	VF20	XF40	MS60	MS63	MS65
1951	72,000	5.00	15.00	30.00	45.00	65.00

KM# 20 5 ESCUDOS
4.00 g., 0.600 Silver 0.0772 oz. ASW, 22 mm. **Obv:** Shield within globe **Rev:** Shield within crowned globe

Date	Mintage	F12	VF20	XF40	MS60	MS63
1962	88,000	1.00	3.00	5.00	10.00	15.00

KM# 22 5 ESCUDOS
Copper-Nickel **Obv:** Shield within globe on cross **Rev:** Shield within crowned globe

Date	Mintage	F12	VF20	XF40	MS60	MS63
1971	100,000	—	1.00	3.00	5.00	8.00

KM# 7 10 ESCUDOS
12.50 g., 0.835 Silver 0.3356 oz. ASW **Obv:** Shield within globe on cross **Rev:** Shield within crowned globe

Date	Mintage	VF20	XF40	MS60	MS63	MS65
1939	40,000	25.00	60.00	125	200	275

KM# 14 10 ESCUDOS
12.50 g., 0.720 Silver 0.2894 oz. ASW **Obv:** Shield within globe on cross **Rev:** Shield within crowned globe

Date	Mintage	VF20	XF40	MS60	MS63	MS65
1951	40,000	7.00	12.00	16.00	20.00	30.00

KM# 23 10 ESCUDOS
Copper-Nickel **Obv:** Shield within globe on cross **Rev:** Shield within crowned globe

Date	Mintage	F12	VF20	XF40	MS60	MS63
1971	100,000	—	1.00	3.00	10.00	12.00

KM# 24 20 ESCUDOS
12.06 g., Nickel, 30 mm. **Obv:** Shield within globe **Rev:** Shield within circle

Date	Mintage	F12	VF20	XF40	MS60	MS63
1971	75,000	—	1.00	5.00	10.00	15.00

KM# 21 50 ESCUDOS
18.00 g., 0.650 Silver 0.3762 oz. ASW, 24 mm. **Subject:** 500th Anniversary of Discovery **Obv:** Cross within designed circle **Rev:** Double shields flanked by dates, star design at top

Date	Mintage	F12	VF20	XF40	MS60	MS63
1970	150,000	—	7.00	8.00	12.00	17.00
1970 Matte proof	Est. 200	PF60 100				

Note: Produced at the Lisbon Mint on private contract.

DEMOCRATIC REPUBLIC

STANDARD COINAGE

100 Centimos = 1 Dobra

KM# 25 50 CENTIMOS
Brass, 17 mm. **Series:** F.A.O. **Obv:** Arms with supporters **Rev:** Fish above value

Date	Mintage	F12	VF20	XF40	MS60	MS63
1977	2,000,000	—	0.10	0.20	0.75	1.00
1977	2,500	PF65 3.00				

KM# 26 DOBRA
Brass, 20 mm. **Series:** F.A.O. **Obv:** Arms with supporters **Rev:** Cocoa beans on stem and value

Date	Mintage	F12	VF20	XF40	MS60	MS63
1977	1,500,000	—	—	0.25	0.75	1.00
1977	2,500	PF65 3.00				

KM# 27 2 DOBRAS
Copper-Nickel, 18.5 mm. **Series:** F.A.O. **Obv:** Arms with supporters **Rev:** Goats

Date	Mintage	F12	VF20	XF40	MS60	MS63
1977	1,000,000	—	—	0.40	1.00	1.25
1977	2,500	PF65 3.50				

KM# 28 5 DOBRAS
Copper-Nickel, 24 mm. **Series:** F.A.O. **Obv:** Arms with supporters **Rev:** Corn and value

Date	Mintage	F12	VF20	XF40	MS60	MS63
1977	750,000	—	—	0.50	1.50	2.00
1977	2,500	PF65 5.00				

KM# 29 10 DOBRAS
6.40 g., Copper-Nickel, 26 mm. **Series:** F.A.O. **Obv:** Arms with supporters **Rev:** Eggs, turkey, chicken, rooster and duck

Date	Mintage	F12	VF20	XF40	MS60	MS63
1977	300,000	—	0.25	0.50	2.00	3.50
1977	2,500	PF65 7.00				

KM# 29a 10 DOBRAS
Copper-Nickel Clad Steel, 26 mm. **Series:** F.A.O. **Obv:** Arms with supporters **Rev:** Chickens with eggs in cartons

Date	Mintage	F12	VF20	XF40	MS60	MS63
1990	—	—	0.25	0.50	2.00	3.50

KM# 30 20 DOBRAS
7.90 g., Copper-Nickel Clad Steel, 29 mm. **Series:** F.A.O. **Obv:** Arms with supporters **Rev:** Logo and value to right of various plants and produce

Date	Mintage	F12	VF20	XF40	MS60	MS63
1977	500,000	—	0.25	1.00	3.00	5.00
1977	2,500	PF65 10.00				

KM# 52 50 DOBRAS
Copper-Nickel Clad Steel **Series:** F.A.O. **Obv:** Arms with supporters **Rev:** Value within octogon design with bird above and snake below

Date	Mintage	VF20	XF40	MS60	MS63	MS65
1990	—	—	—	2.00	3.00	5.00

KM# 41 100 DOBRAS
Copper-Nickel **Subject:** World Fisheries Conference **Obv:** Arms with supporters **Rev:** Figure standing in boat with fish net

Date	Mintage	VF20	XF40	MS60	MS63	MS65
ND-1984	1,000,000	—	—	4.00	6.00	9.00

KM# 41a 100 DOBRAS
28.28 g., 0.925 Silver 0.841 oz. ASW **Subject:** World Fisheries Conference **Obv:** Arms with supporters **Rev:** Figure standing in boat with fish net

Date	Mintage	F12	VF20	XF40	MS60	MS63
ND-1984	20,000	PF63 25.00	PF65 35.00			

KM# 41b 100 DOBRAS
47.54 g., 0.917 Gold 1.4016 oz. AGW **Subject:** World Fisheries Conference **Obv:** Arms with supporters **Rev:** Figure standing in boat with fish net

Date	Mintage	F12	VF20	XF40	MS60	MS63
ND-1984	100	PF63 2,500	PF65 2,700			

KM# 42 100 DOBRAS

Copper-Nickel **Subject:** 10th Anniversary of Independence **Obv:** Arms with supporters **Rev:** Value, stars and map

Date	Mintage	VF20	XF40	MS60	MS63	MS65
ND-1985	—	—	—	3.00	5.00	7.00

KM# 42a 100 DOBRAS

28.28 g., 0.925 Silver 0.841 oz. ASW **Subject:** 10th Anniversary of Independence **Obv:** Arms with supporters **Rev:** Value, stars and map

Date	Mintage	F12	VF20	XF40	MS60	MS63
ND-1985	1,000	PF63 35.00	PF65 45.00			

KM# 42b 100 DOBRAS

47.54 g., 0.917 Gold 1.4016 oz. AGW **Subject:** 10th Anniversary of Independence **Obv:** Arms with supporters **Rev:** Value, stars and map

Date	Mintage	F12	VF20	XF40	MS60	MS63
ND-1985	50	PF63 2,600	PF65 2,800			

KM# 87 100 DOBRAS

Chrome Clad Steel, 17.5 mm. **Obv:** Arms with supporters **Rev:** Value below bird

Date	Mintage	VF20	XF40	MS60	MS63	MS65
1997	—	—	—	0.75	1.25	1.75

KM# 31 250 DOBRAS

17.40 g., 0.925 Silver 0.5175 oz. ASW **Subject:** Independence **Obv:** Arms with supporters **Rev:** World population

Date	Mintage	XF40	MS60	MS63	MS65	MS66
1977	450	—	—	35.00	40.00	45.00
1977	750	PF65 35.00	PF67 40.00			

KM# 32 250 DOBRAS

17.40 g., 0.925 Silver 0.5175 oz. ASW **Subject:** Independence **Obv:** Arms with supporters **Rev:** World friendship

Date	Mintage	XF40	MS60	MS63	MS65	MS66
1977	450	—	—	35.00	40.00	45.00
1977	800	PF65 35.00	PF67 40.00			

KM# 33 250 DOBRAS

17.40 g., 0.925 Silver 0.5175 oz. ASW **Subject:** Independence **Obv:** Arms with supporters **Rev:** Folklore statue

Date	Mintage	XF40	MS60	MS63	MS65	MS66
1977	300	—	—	35.00	40.00	45.00
1977	600	PF65 35.00	PF67 40.00			

KM# 34 250 DOBRAS

17.40 g., 0.925 Silver 0.5175 oz. ASW **Subject:** Independence **Obv:** Arms with supporters **Rev:** World unity emblems

Date	Mintage	XF40	MS60	MS63	MS65	MS66
1977	400	—	—	35.00	40.00	45.00
1977	700	PF65 35.00	PF67 40.00			

KM# 35 250 DOBRAS

17.40 g., 0.925 Silver 0.5175 oz. ASW **Subject:** Independence **Obv:** Arms with supporters **Rev:** Mother and child

Date	Mintage	XF40	MS60	MS63	MS65	MS66
1977	350	—	—	35.00	40.00	45.00
1977	700	PF65 35.00	PF67 40.00			

KM# 88 250 DOBRAS

Chrome Clad Steel **Obv:** Arms with supporters **Rev:** Value above bird

Date	Mintage	VF20	XF40	MS60	MS63	MS65
1997	—	—	—	0.50	1.00	1.50

KM# 70 500 DOBRAS

Copper-Nickel **Obv:** Arms with supporters **Rev:** Elvis Presley

Date	Mintage	VF20	XF40	MS60	MS63	MS65
1993	—	—	—	—	5.00	7.00

KM# 89 500 DOBRAS

Chrome Clad Steel **Obv:** Arms with supporters **Rev:** Monkey in trees **Shape:** 7-sided

Date	Mintage	VF20	XF40	MS60	MS63	MS65
1997	—	—	—	0.65	1.25	2.50

KM# 126 500 DOBRAS

Copper-Nickel **Subject:** Princess Diana, death **Rev:** Diana and Dodi al Fayed

Date	Mintage	VF20	XF40	MS60	MS63	MS65
1997	—	—	—	—	—	20.00

KM# 44 1000 DOBRAS

23.33 g., 0.925 Silver 0.6938 oz. ASW **Subject:** Soccer **Obv:** Arms with supporters **Rev:** 2 players

Date	Mintage	VF20	XF40	MS60	MS63	MS65
1990	15,000	PF63 20.00	PF65 28.00			

KM# 45 1000 DOBRAS

23.33 g., 0.925 Silver 0.6938 oz. ASW **Subject:** Soccer **Obv:** Arms with supporters **Rev:** 2 players running

Date	Mintage	VF20	XF40	MS60	MS63	MS65
1990	15,000	PF63 20.00	PF65 28.00			

KM# 47 1000 DOBRAS

25.96 g., 0.999 Silver 0.8338 oz. ASW **Subject:** Soccer **Obv:** Arms with supporters **Rev:** Soccer player

Date	Mintage	VF20	XF40	MS60	MS63	MS65
1990	—	PF63 25.00	PF65 32.00			

KM# 48 1000 DOBRAS

25.96 g., 0.999 Silver 0.8338 oz. ASW **Subject:** Soccer **Obv:** Arms with supporters **Rev:** Soccer players

Date	Mintage	VF20	XF40	MS60	MS63	MS65
1990	—	PF63 25.00	PF65 32.00			

KM# 49 1000 DOBRAS

20.00 g., 0.999 Silver 0.6424 oz. ASW **Subject:** National independence **Obv:** Arms with supporters **Rev:** Cheering figures

Date	Mintage	VF20	XF40	MS60	MS63	MS65
1990	—	PF63 20.00	PF65 28.00			

KM# 50 1000 DOBRAS
20.00 g., 0.999 Silver 0.6424 oz. ASW **Subject:** Vasco de Gama **Obv:** Arms with supporters **Rev:** Cameo to right of ship

Date	Mintage	VF20	XF40	MS60	MS63	MS65
1990	—	PF63 18.00	PF65 22.00			

KM# 53 1000 DOBRAS
20.00 g., 0.999 Silver 0.6424 oz. ASW **Subject:** Olympics and Discovery of America **Obv:** Arms with supporters **Rev:** Seated figure, partial map and ship, book with Olympic circles on cover

Date	Mintage	VF20	XF40	MS60	MS63	MS65
1990	—	PF63 20.00	PF65 28.00			

KM# 73 1000 DOBRAS
23.74 g., 0.925 Silver 0.706 oz. ASW **Series:** 1992 Olympics **Obv:** Arms with supporters **Rev:** Date below flames and mountains

Date	Mintage	VF20	XF40	MS60	MS63	MS65
1990	10,000	PF63 17.00	PF65 22.00			

KM# 74 1000 DOBRAS
23.74 g., 0.925 Silver 0.706 oz. ASW **Series:** 1992 Olympics **Obv:** Arms with supporters **Rev:** Diver

Date	Mintage	VF20	XF40	MS60	MS63	MS65
1990	10,000	PF63 17.00	PF65 22.00			

KM# 115 1000 DOBRAS
12.00 g., Bronze, 30 mm. **Obv:** National arms **Rev:** William Tell monument in Altdorf

Date	Mintage	VF20	XF40	MS60	MS63	MS65
ND1990	5,050	—	—	—	—	25.00

KM# 116 1000 DOBRAS
31.11 g., 0.999 Silver 0.999 oz. ASW, 38.61 mm. **Obv:** National arms **Rev:** William Tell monument in Altdorf

Date	Mintage	VF20	XF40	MS60	MS63	MS65
1990	—	PF65 40.00				

KM# 54 1000 DOBRAS
Copper-Nickel **Series:** Atlanta Olympics **Obv:** Arms with supporters **Rev:** Wrestling

Date	Mintage	VF20	XF40	MS60	MS63	MS65
ND-1993	—	PF63 7.00	PF65 9.00			

KM# 55 1000 DOBRAS
Copper-Nickel **Series:** Atlanta Olympics **Obv:** Arms with supporters **Rev:** Soccer players

Date	Mintage	VF20	XF40	MS60	MS63	MS65
ND-1993	—	PF63 7.00	PF65 9.00			

KM# 56 1000 DOBRAS
Copper-Nickel **Series:** Atlanta Olympics **Obv:** Arms with supporters **Rev:** Boxer

Date	Mintage	VF20	XF40	MS60	MS63	MS65
ND-1993	—	PF63 7.00	PF65 9.00			

KM# 57 1000 DOBRAS
Copper-Nickel **Series:** Atlanta Olympics **Obv:** Arms with supporters **Rev:** Bicyclist

Date	Mintage	VF20	XF40	MS60	MS63	MS65
ND-1993	—	PF63 7.00	PF65 9.00			

KM# 58 1000 DOBRAS
Copper-Nickel **Series:** Atlanta Olympics **Obv:** Arms with supporters **Rev:** Karate competition

Date	Mintage	VF20	XF40	MS60	MS63	MS65
ND-1993	—	PF63 7.00	PF65 9.00			

KM# 59 1000 DOBRAS
Copper-Nickel **Series:** Atlanta Olympics **Obv:** Arms with supporters **Rev:** Runner

Date	Mintage	VF20	XF40	MS60	MS63	MS65
ND-1993	—	PF63 7.00	PF65 9.00			

KM# 60 1000 DOBRAS
Copper-Nickel **Series:** Atlanta Olympics **Obv:** Arms with supporters **Rev:** Field hockey players

Date	Mintage	VF20	XF40	MS60	MS63	MS65
ND-1993	—	PF63 7.00	PF65 9.00			

KM# 61 1000 DOBRAS
Copper-Nickel **Series:** Atlanta Olympics **Obv:** Arms with supporters **Rev:** Four track and field events

Date	Mintage	VF20	XF40	MS60	MS63	MS65
ND-1993	—	PF63 7.00	PF65 9.00			

KM# 62 1000 DOBRAS
Copper-Nickel **Series:** Atlanta Olympics **Obv:** Arms with supporters **Rev:** Surfer

Date	Mintage	VF20	XF40	MS60	MS63	MS65
ND-1993	—	PF63 7.00	PF65 9.00			

KM# 63 1000 DOBRAS
Copper-Nickel **Series:** Atlanta Olympics **Obv:** Arms with supporters **Rev:** Swimmers

Date	Mintage	VF20	XF40	MS60	MS63	MS65
ND-1993	—	PF63 7.00	PF65 9.00			

KM# 64 1000 DOBRAS
Copper-Nickel **Series:** Atlanta Olympics **Obv:** Arms with supporters **Rev:** Three gymnastic events

Date	Mintage	VF20	XF40	MS60	MS63	MS65
ND-1993	—	PF63 7.00	PF65 9.00			

KM# 65 1000 DOBRAS
Copper-Nickel **Series:** Atlanta Olympics **Obv:** Arms with supporters **Rev:** Tennis players

Date	Mintage	VF20	XF40	MS60	MS63	MS65
ND-1993	—	PF63 7.00	PF65 9.00			

KM# 71 1000 DOBRAS
25.00 g., 0.925 Silver 0.7435 oz. ASW **Obv:** Arms with supporters **Rev:** Elvis Presley

Date	Mintage	VF20	XF40	MS60	MS63	MS65
1993	—	PF65 20.00				

KM# 117 1000 DOBRAS
Brass, 38 mm. **Subject:** World Cup Soccer, 1994, USA

Date	Mintage	VF20	XF40	MS60	MS63	MS65
1993	2,100	PF65 25.00				

KM# 118.1 1000 DOBRAS
Copper-Nickel, 38 mm. **Subject:** World Cup Soccer 1994, USA **Obv:** National arms without border ornaments **Rev:** Far shot

Date	Mintage	VF20	XF40	MS60	MS63	MS65
1994	—	PF65 20.00				

KM# 118.1a 1000 DOBRAS
20.00 g., Silver, 38 mm. **Subject:** World Cup Soccer 1994, USA **Obv:** National arms with empty magazine belt and without border ornament **Rev:** Far shot

Date	Mintage	VF20	XF40	MS60	MS63	MS65
1994	—	PF65 25.00				

KM# 118.2 1000 DOBRAS
Copper-Nickel, 38 mm. **Subject:** World Cup Soccer 1994, USA **Obv:** National arms with border ornament **Rev:** Far shot

Date	Mintage	VF20	XF40	MS60	MS63	MS65
1994	—	PF65 30.00				

KM# 119 1000 DOBRAS
Copper-Nickel **Rev:** Steep pass **Note:** Edge marked EP.999, but coin is not plated silver

Date	Mintage	VF20	XF40	MS60	MS63	MS65
1994	—	PF65 10.00				

KM# 119a 1000 DOBRAS
20.00 g., 0.999 Silver 0.6424 oz. ASW **Rev:** Steep pass

Date	Mintage	VF20	XF40	MS60	MS63	MS65
1994	—	PF65 30.00				

KM# 76 1000 DOBRAS
25.00 g:, 0.925 Silver 0.7435 oz. ASW **Obv:** Arms with supporters **Rev:** Black Kite **Note:** Enamel.

Date	Mintage	VF20	XF40	MS60	MS63	MS65
1995	15,000	PF65 32.00				

KM# 77 1000 DOBRAS
25.00 g., 0.925 Silver 0.7435 oz. ASW **Obv:** Arms with supporters **Rev:** Porcelain rose **Note:** Enamel.

Date	Mintage	VF20	XF40	MS60	MS63	MS65
1995	15,000	PF65 32.00				

KM# 78 1000 DOBRAS
25.00 g., 0.925 Silver 0.7435 oz. ASW **Obv:** Arms with supporters **Rev:** Seahorse and crab **Note:** Enamel.

Date	Mintage	VF20	XF40	MS60	MS63	MS65
1995	15,000	PF65 35.00				

KM# 121 1000 DOBRAS
Copper-Nickel **Subject:** Summer Olympics, 1992, Barcelona

Date	Mintage	VF20	XF40	MS60	MS63	MS65
2013	—	PF65 35.00				

KM# 121a 1000 DOBRAS
20.00 g., 0.999 Silver 0.6424 oz. ASW **Subject:** Summer Olympics, 1992, Barcelona

Date	Mintage	VF20	XF40	MS60	MS63	MS65
1996	—	PF65 35.00				

KM# 85a 1000 DOBRAS
31.10 g., 0.999 Silver 0.999 oz. ASW **Subject:** Diana - Queen of the Hearts **Obv:** Arms with supporters **Rev:** Bust with hat left **Note:** Prev. KM#85.1.

Date	Mintage	VF20	XF40	MS60	MS63	MS65
1997	5,000	PF65 45.00				

KM# 90 1000 DOBRAS
6.30 g., Chrome Clad Steel **Obv:** Arms with supporters **Rev:** Flowers and value **Shape:** 7-sided

Date	Mintage	VF20	XF40	MS60	MS63	MS65
1997	—	—	—	1.50	2.00	3.00

KM# 102 1000 DOBRAS
1.25 g., 0.999 Gold 0.0401 oz. AGW **Subject:** Diana - Queen of the Hearts **Obv:** Arms with supporters **Rev:** Bust with hat left **Note:** Prev. KM#85.2.

Date	Mintage	VF20	XF40	MS60	MS63	MS65
1997	3,000	PF63 60.00	PF65 70.00			

KM# 79 1000 DOBRAS
31.10 g., 0.999 Silver 0.999 oz. ASW **Obv:** Arms with supporters **Rev:** Peacock hologram

Date	Mintage	VF20	XF40	MS60	MS63	MS65
1998(1997) Prooflike	10,000	—	—	—	—	45.00

KM# 80 1000 DOBRAS
31.10 g., 0.999 Silver 0.999 oz. ASW **Obv:** Arms with supporters **Rev:** Hummingbird hologram

Date	Mintage	VF20	XF40	MS60	MS63	MS65
1998(1997) Prooflike	10,000	—	—	—	—	45.00

KM# 81 1000 DOBRAS
31.10 g., 0.999 Silver 0.999 oz. ASW **Obv:** Arms with supporters **Rev:** Fish hologram

Date	Mintage	VF20	XF40	MS60	MS63	MS65
1998(1997) Prooflike	10,000	—	—	—	—	45.00

KM# 82 1000 DOBRAS
31.10 g., 0.999 Silver 0.999 oz. ASW **Obv:** Arms with supporters **Rev:** Butterfly hologram

Date	Mintage	VF20	XF40	MS60	MS63	MS65
1998(1997) Prooflike	10,000	—	—	—	—	45.00

KM# 92 1000 DOBRAS
Copper-Nickel **Subject:** Heidiland **Obv:** Arms with supporters **Rev:** Girl with goats

Date	Mintage	VF20	XF40	MS60	MS63	MS65
1998	15,000	—	—	3.50	5.00	7.00

KM# 93 1000 DOBRAS
25.00 g., 0.925 Silver 0.7435 oz. ASW **Subject:** Heidiland **Obv:** Arms with supporters **Rev:** Girl holding hat and flowers, bird, trees and mountains

Date	Mintage	VF20	XF40	MS60	MS63	MS65
1998	10,000	PF63 20.00	PF65 25.00			

KM# 94 1000 DOBRAS
25.14 g., 0.925 Silver 0.7476 oz. ASW **Subject:** World Cup Soccer - France 1998 **Obv:** Arms with supporters **Rev:** Soccer players and goalie net **Shape:** 10-sided

Date	Mintage	VF20	XF40	MS60	MS63	MS65
1998	10,000	PF63 30.00	PF65 35.00			

KM# 114 1000 DOBRAS
15.10 g., 0.999 Silver 0.485 oz. ASW, 30 mm. **Obv:** Arms with supporters **Rev:** Empress Elizabeth of Austria (1837-1898) **Edge:** Reeded

Date	Mintage	VF20	XF40	MS60	MS63	MS65
1998	—	PF63 17.00	PF65 22.00			

KM# 128 1000 DOBRAS
31.11 g., 0.999 Silver 0.999 oz. ASW, 38.61 mm. **Subject:** Year of the Tiger **Obv:** National arms **Rev:** Tiger advancing forward

Date	Mintage	VF20	XF40	MS60	MS63	MS65
1998	—	PF65 75.00				

KM# 129 1000 DOBRAS
31.11 g., 0.999 Silver 0.999 oz. ASW, 38.61 mm. **Subject:** Year of the Tiger **Obv:** National arms **Rev:** Two tigers

Date	Mintage	VF20	XF40	MS60	MS63	MS65
1998	—	PF65 70.00				

KM# 130 1000 DOBRAS
1.24 g., 0.999 Gold 0.0398 oz. AGW, 13.94 mm. **Rev:** Heidi in Alpine landscape in color

Date	Mintage	VF20	XF40	MS60	MS63	MS65
1998	—	PF65 75.00				

KM# 131 1000 DOBRAS
1.24 g., 0.999 Gold 0.0398 oz. AGW, 13.92 mm. **Rev:** Elizabeth of Hungary, 100th Anniversary of Death

Date	Mintage	VF20	XF40	MS60	MS63	MS65
1998	—	PF65 75.00				

KM# 132 1000 DOBRAS
31.11 g., 0.999 Silver 0.999 oz. ASW, 38.61 mm. **Subject:** Jubilee Year 2000 **Obv:** National arms within pentagon and oval star **Rev:** IHS within starburst

Date	Mintage	VF20	XF40	MS60	MS63	MS65
1998	Est. 7000	PF65 60.00				

KM# 99 1000 DOBRAS
36.55 g., 0.925 Silver 1.087 oz. ASW, 34.9 mm. **Subject:** Millennium **Obv:** Arms with supporters **Rev:** Perforated gold insert exposing digital clock **Edge:** Reeded **Note:** Gilt inset encased digital clock. 8.1mm thick.

Date	Mintage	VF20	XF40	MS60	MS63	MS65
1999	—	PF65 65.00				

KM# A120 2000 DOBRAS
8.00 g., 0.999 Gold 0.2569 oz. AGW, 28 mm. **Subject:** Year of the Rat - Happiness **Obv:** National arms **Rev:** Rat left

Date	Mintage	XF40	MS60	MS63	MS65	MS66
1996	—	PF67 500	PF69 600			

KM# B120 2000 DOBRAS
8.00 g., 0.999 Gold 0.2569 oz. AGW, 28 mm. **Subject:** Year of the Rat - Wealth **Obv:** National arms **Rev:** Rat

Date	Mintage	XF40	MS60	MS63	MS65	MS66
1996	—	PF67 500	PF69 600			

KM# 120 2000 DOBRAS
8.00 g., 0.999 Gold 0.2569 oz. AGW, 28 mm. **Subject:** Year of the Rat - Longevity **Obv:** National arms **Rev:** Rat facing

Date	Mintage	VF20	XF40	MS60	MS63	MS65
1996	—	PF67 500				

KM# 91 2000 DOBRAS
Chrome Clad Steel **Obv:** Arms with supporters **Rev:** Tropical food plants within circle **Shape:** 7-sided

Date	Mintage	VF20	XF40	MS60	MS63	MS65
1997	—	—	—	1.50	2.50	4.00

KM# A122 2000 DOBRAS
8.00 g., 0.999 Gold 0.2569 oz. AGW **Subject:** Year of the Ox - Happiness **Obv:** National arms **Rev:** Ox standing right, head turned left

Date	Mintage	XF40	MS60	MS63	MS65	MS66
1997	—	PF67 500	PF69 600			

KM# B122 2000 DOBRAS
8.00 g., 0.999 Gold 0.2569 oz. AGW **Subject:** Year of the Ox - Wealth **Obv:** National arms **Rev:** Ox

Date	Mintage	XF40	MS60	MS63	MS65	MS66
1997	—	PF67 500	PF69 600			

KM# 122 2000 DOBRAS
8.00 g., 0.999 Gold 0.2569 oz. AGW **Subject:** Year of the Ox - Wealth **Obv:** National arms **Rev:** Ox walking left, head facing

Date	Mintage	VF20	XF40	MS60	MS63	MS65
1997	—	PF67 500				

KM# 86 2000 DOBRAS
25.00 g., 0.925 Silver 0.7435 oz. ASW **Subject:** Third Christian millennium **Obv:** Arms with supporters **Rev:** Year 2000 CE calendar

Date	Mintage	VF20	XF40	MS60	MS63	MS65
1998	5,000	PF65 35.00				

KM# 86a 2000 DOBRAS
Copper-Nickel **Subject:** Third Christian millennium **Obv:** Arms with supporters **Rev:** Year 2000 CE calendar **Note:** Calendar detailing is acid etched, not struck.

Date	Mintage	VF20	XF40	MS60	MS63	MS65
1998 Prooflike	—	—	—	4.00	7.00	—

KM# 98 2000 DOBRAS
31.16 g., 0.999 Silver 1.0008 oz. ASW, 27.1x47.2 mm. **Subject:** Pseudo - Millennium **Obv:** Arms with supporters **Rev:** Multicolor world and year split **Edge:** Plain **Shape:** Rectangle

Date	Mintage	VF20	XF40	MS60	MS63	MS65
1998	—	PF65 35.00				

KM# 36 2500 DOBRAS
6.48 g., 0.900 Gold 0.1875 oz. AGW **Subject:** Independence **Obv:** Arms with supporters **Rev:** World friendship

Date	Mintage	XF40	MS60	MS63	MS65	MS66
1977	100	—	—	—	400	425
1977	170	PF67 375	PF69 400			

KM# 37 2500 DOBRAS
6.48 g., 0.900 Gold 0.1875 oz. AGW **Subject:** Independence - World Population **Obv:** Arms with supporters **Rev:** World population

Date	Mintage	XF40	MS60	MS63	MS65	MS66
1977	100	—	—	—	400	425

Date	Mintage	XF40	MS60	MS63	MS65	MS66
1977	170	PF67 375	PF69 400			

KM# 38 2500 DOBRAS
6.48 g., 0.900 Gold 0.1875 oz. AGW **Subject:** Independence **Obv:** Arms with supporters **Rev:** Folklore monument

Date	Mintage	XF40	MS60	MS63	MS65	MS66
1977	100	—	—	—	400	425
1977	170	PF67 375	PF69 400			

KM# 39 2500 DOBRAS
6.48 g., 0.900 Gold 0.1875 oz. AGW **Subject:** Independence **Obv:** Arms with supporters **Rev:** World unity

Date	Mintage	XF40	MS60	MS63	MS65	MS66
1977	100	—	—	—	400	425
1977	170	PF67 375	PF69 400			

KM# 40 2500 DOBRAS
6.48 g., 0.900 Gold 0.1875 oz. AGW **Subject:** Independence **Obv:** Arms with supporters **Rev:** Mother and child

Date	Mintage	XF40	MS60	MS63	MS65	MS66
1977	100	—	—	—	400	425
1977	170	PF67 375	PF69 400			

KM# C120 2500 DOBRAS
15.55 g., 0.999 Gold 0.4994 oz. AGW, 30 mm. **Subject:** Year of the Rat - Happiness **Obv:** National arms **Rev:** Rat left

Date	Mintage	XF40	MS60	MS63	MS65	MS66
1996	—	PF67 1,000	PF69 1,200			

KM# D120 2500 DOBRAS
15.55 g., 0.999 Gold 0.4994 oz. AGW, 30 mm. **Subject:** Year of the Rat - Wealth **Obv:** National arms **Rev:** Rat

Date	Mintage	XF40	MS60	MS63	MS65	MS66
1996	—	PF67 1,000	PF69 1,200			

KM# E120 2500 DOBRAS
15.55 g., 0.999 Gold 0.4994 oz. AGW, 30 mm. **Subject:** Year of the Rat - Longevity **Obv:** National arms **Rev:** Rat facing

Date	Mintage	XF40	MS60	MS63	MS65	MS66
1996	—	PF67 1,000	PF69 1,200			

KM# 123 2500 DOBRAS
15.55 g., 0.999 Gold 0.4994 oz. AGW, 30 mm. **Subject:** Year of the Ox - Happiness **Obv:** National arms **Rev:** Ox standing right, head turned left

Date	Mintage	VF20	XF40	MS60	MS63	MS65
1997	Est. 2000	PF67 1,000				

KM# A124 2500 DOBRAS
15.55 g., 0.999 Gold 0.4994 oz. AGW, 30 mm. **Subject:** Year of the Ox - Wealth **Obv:** National arms **Rev:** Ox

Date	Mintage	XF40	MS60	MS63	MS65	MS66
1997	—	PF67 1,000	PF69 1,200			

KM# 124 2500 DOBRAS
15.55 g., 0.999 Gold 0.4994 oz. AGW, 30 mm. **Subject:** Year of the Ox - Longevity **Obv:** National arms **Rev:** Ox standing left, head turned right

Date	Mintage	VF20	XF40	MS60	MS63	MS65
1997	—	PF67 1,000				

KM# 83 2500 DOBRAS
6.22 g., 0.9999 Gold 0.200 oz. AGW **Obv:** Arms with supporters **Rev:** Hummingbird hologram **Note:** Similar to 1,000 Dobras, KM#80.

Date	Mintage	VF20	XF40	MS60	MS63	MS65
1998(1997)	2,500	PF65 275	PF67 300			

KM# 84 2500 DOBRAS
6.22 g., 0.9999 Gold 0.200 oz. AGW **Obv:** Arms with supporters **Rev:** Butterfly hologram **Note:** Similar to 1,000 Dobras, KM#82.

Date	Mintage	VF20	XF40	MS60	MS63	MS65
1998(1997)	2,500	PF65 275	PF67 300			

KM# 133 2500 DOBRAS
3.11 g., 0.999 Gold 0.0999 oz. AGW, 17.95 mm. **Subject:** Jubilee Year 2000 **Obv:** National arms within pentagon and oval star **Rev:** IHS within starburst

Date	Mintage	VF20	XF40	MS60	MS63	MS65
1998	Est. 3000	PF65 180	PF67 200			

KM# 134 2500 DOBRAS
7.78 g., 0.999 Gold 0.2499 oz. AGW, 22 mm. **Subject:** Jubilee Year 2000 **Obv:** National arms within pentagon and oval star **Rev:** IHS within starburst

Date	Mintage	VF20	XF40	MS60	MS63	MS65
1998	Est. 1500	PF67 450				

KM# 46 3500 DOBRAS
136.08 g., 0.925 Silver 4.0469 oz. ASW, 63 mm. **Subject:** Wildlife Protection **Obv:** Arms with supporters **Rev:** Sea turtle **Note:** Illustration reduced.

Date	Mintage	VF20	XF40	MS60	MS63	MS65
1990	750	PF67 150				

KM# 135 5000 DOBRAS
15.55 g., 0.999 Gold 0.4994 oz. AGW, 30 mm. **Subject:** Jubilee Year 2000 **Obv:** National arms within pentagon and oval star **Rev:** IHS within starburst

Date	Mintage	VF20	XF40	MS60	MS63	MS65
1998	Est. 1000	PF67 950				

KM# 100 5000 DOBRAS
168.56 g., 0.999 5.4139 oz. **Subject:** Millennium **Obv:** Arms with supporters **Rev:** Perforated silver insert exposing digital clock **Edge:** Reeded **Note:** Silver shell with encased digital clock. 9mm thick.

Date	Mintage	VF20	XF40	MS60	MS63	MS65
1999	—	PF65 225				

KM# 51 10000 DOBRAS
7.78 g., 0.900 Gold 0.225 oz. AGW **Obv:** Arms with supporters **Rev:** Sea turtle

Date	Mintage	XF40	MS60	MS63	MS65	MS66
1992	500	PF67 475	PF69 550			

KM# 136 10000 DOBRAS
31.11 g., 0.999 Gold 0.999 oz. AGW, 38.61 mm. **Obv:** National arms within pentagon and oval star **Rev:** IHS within starburst

Date	Mintage	VF20	XF40	MS60	MS63	MS65
1998	Est. 1000	PF67 1,750				

KM# 72 25000 DOBRAS
15.55 g., 0.999 Gold 0.4994 oz. AGW **Obv:** Arms with supporters **Rev:** Elvis Presley

Date	Mintage	VF20	XF40	MS60	MS63	MS65
1993	—	PF65 950	PF67 1,000			

KM# A125 25000 DOBRAS
155.50 g., 0.999 Gold 4.9944 oz. AGW, 65 mm. **Subject:** Year of the Ox - Wealth **Obv:** National arms **Rev:** Ox

Date	Mintage	XF40	MS60	MS63	MS65	MS66
1997	—	PF67 8,500	PF69 9,000			

KM# B125 25000 DOBRAS
155.50 g., 0.999 Gold 4.9944 oz. AGW, 65 mm. **Subject:** Year of the Ox - Longevity **Obv:** National arms **Rev:** Ox standing left, head facing

Date	Mintage	XF40	MS60	MS63	MS65	MS66
1997	—	PF67 8,500	PF69 9,000			

KM# 125 25000 DOBRAS
155.50 g., 0.999 Gold 4.9944 oz. AGW, 65 mm. **Subject:** Year of the Ox - Happiness **Obv:** National arms **Rev:** Ox standing right, head turned left

Date	Mintage	VF20	XF40	MS60	MS63	MS65
1997	Est. 150	PF67 8,500				

DUAL DENOMINATED COINAGE

KM# 67 500 DOBRAS- 1 ECU
Copper-Nickel **Subject:** 15th Anniversary of Association With European Common Market **Obv:** Arms with supporters **Rev:** Circular star design above ships and city view

Date	Mintage	VF20	XF40	MS60	MS63	MS65
1993	20,000	—	—	—	10.00	12.00

KM# 68 2500 DOBRAS-5 ECU
25.00 g., 0.925 Silver 0.7435 oz. ASW **Subject:** 15th Anniversary of Association With European Common Market **Obv:** Arms with supporters **Rev:** Circular star design above ships and city view

Date	Mintage	VF20	XF40	MS60	MS63	MS65
1993	12,000	PF65 25.00				

KM# 69 25000 DOBRAS-50 ECU
6.72 g., 0.900 Gold 0.1944 oz. AGW **Subject:** 15th Anniversary of Association With European Common Market **Obv:** Arms with supporters **Rev:** Old harbor scene **Note:** Similar to 2500 Dobras, 5 Ecu, KM#68.

Date	Mintage	VF20	XF40	MS60	MS63	MS65
1993	1,000	PF67 350				

KM# 95 2000 DOBRAS-1 EURO
Copper-Nickel **Obv:** Arms with supporters **Rev:** Head left and multicolor Swiss flag in circle of stars, value at lower left

Date	Mintage	VF20	XF40	MS60	MS63	MS65
1997	5,000	PF63 12.50	PF65 15.00			

KM# 103 2000 DOBRAS-1 EURO
31.10 g., 0.925 Silver 0.9249 oz. ASW The Belgian one franc coin adds 2.74g for a total weight of 33.85g, 38.6 mm. **Subject:** Year of the Euro **Obv:** Arms with supporters **Rev:** Map with inset Belgian 1 franc coin **Edge:** Reeded

Date	Mintage	VF20	XF40	MS60	MS63	MS65
1999	—	PF63 35.00	PF65 40.00			

KM# 104 2000 DOBRAS-1 EURO
31.21 g., 0.925 Silver 0.9282 oz. ASW The Italian 50 lire adds 4.46g for a total weight of 35.67, 38.6 mm. **Subject:** Year of the Euro **Obv:** Arms with supporters **Rev:** Map with inset Italian 50 lire coin **Edge:** Reeded

Date	Mintage	VF20	XF40	MS60	MS63	MS65
1999	—	PF63 35.00	PF65 40.00			

KM# 105 2000 DOBRAS-1 EURO
30.95 g., 0.925 Silver 0.9204 oz. ASW The French 1/2 franc adds 4.5g for a total weight of 35.45g, 38.6 mm. **Subject:** Year of the Euro **Obv:** Arms with supporters **Rev:** Map with inset French 1/2 franc coin **Edge:** Reeded

Date	Mintage	VF20	XF40	MS60	MS63	MS65
1999	—	PF63 35.00	PF65 40.00			

KM# 106 2000 DOBRAS-1 EURO
31.10 g., 0.925 Silver 0.9249 oz. ASW, 38.5 mm. **Subject:** Year of the Euro **Obv:** Arms with supporters **Rev:** Austrian 50 groschen KM-2885 glued to map design **Edge:** Reeded **Note:** Total weight with Austrian coin 34.1g

Date	Mintage	VF20	XF40	MS60	MS63	MS65
1999	—	PF63 35.00	PF65 40.00			

KM# 107 2000 DOBRAS-1 EURO
31.10 g., 0.925 Silver 0.9249 oz. ASW, 38.5 mm. **Subject:** Year of the Euro **Obv:** Arms with supporters **Rev:** Finnland 10 penni KM-65 glued to map design **Edge:** Reeded **Note:** Total weight 32.84g with Finnish coin

Date	Mintage	VF20	XF40	MS60	MS63	MS65
1999	—	PF63 35.00	PF65 40.00			

KM# 108 2000 DOBRAS-1 EURO
31.10 g., 0.925 Silver 0.9249 oz. ASW, 38.5 mm. **Subject:** Year of the Euro **Obv:** Arms with supporters **Rev:** German 5 pfennig KM-107 glued to map design **Edge:** Reeded **Note:** Total weight 34.1g with German coin

Date	Mintage	VF20	XF40	MS60	MS63	MS65
1999	—	PF63 35.00	PF65 40.00			

KM# 109 2000 DOBRAS-1 EURO
31.10 g., 0.925 Silver 0.9249 oz. ASW, 38.5 mm. **Subject:** Year of the Euro **Obv:** Arms with supporters **Rev:** Irish 5 pence KM-28.1 glued to map design **Edge:** Reeded **Note:** Total weight 34.33g with Irish coin

Date	Mintage	VF20	XF40	MS60	MS63	MS65
1999	—	PF63 35.00	PF65 40.00			

KM# 110 2000 DOBRAS-1 EURO
31.10 g., 0.925 Silver 0.9249 oz. ASW, 38.5 mm. **Subject:** Year of the Euro **Obv:** Arms with supporters **Rev:** Luxembourg 25 centimes KM-45a.1 glued to map design **Edge:** Reeded **Note:** Total weight 31.83g with Luxembourg coin

Date	Mintage	VF20	XF40	MS60	MS63	MS65
1999	—	PF63 35.00	PF65 40.00			

KM# 111 2000 DOBRAS-1 EURO
31.10 g., 0.925 Silver 0.9249 oz. ASW, 38.5 mm. **Subject:** Year of the Euro **Obv:** Arms with supporters **Rev:** Netherlands 25 cents KM-183 glued to map design **Edge:** Reeded **Note:** Total weight 34.2g with Dutch coin

Date	Mintage	VF20	XF40	MS60	MS63	MS65
1999	—	PF63 35.00	PF65 40.00			

KM# 112 2000 DOBRAS-1 EURO
31.10 g., 0.925 Silver 0.9249 oz. ASW, 38.5 mm. **Subject:** Year of the Euro **Obv:** Arms with supporters **Rev:** Portuguese 1 escudo KM-631 glued to map design **Edge:** Reeded **Note:** Total weight 32.82g with Portuguese coin

Date	Mintage	VF20	XF40	MS60	MS63	MS65
1999	—	PF63 35.00	PF65 40.00			

KM# 113 2000 DOBRAS-1 EURO
31.10 g., 0.925 Silver 0.9249 oz. ASW, 38.5 mm. **Subject:** Year of the Euro **Obv:** Arms with supporters **Rev:** Spanish 5 pesetas KM-833 glued to map design **Edge:** Reeded **Note:** Total weight 34.14g with Spanish coin

Date	Mintage	VF20	XF40	MS60	MS63	MS65
1999	—	PF63 35.00	PF65 40.00			

KM# 96 10000 DOBRAS-5 EURO
25.00 g., 0.925 Silver 0.7435 oz. ASW **Obv:** Arms with supporters **Rev:** Head left and Swiss flag in star circle, date at lower left

Date	Mintage	VF20	XF40	MS60	MS63	MS65
1998	5,000	PF65 35.00				

KM# 127 10000 DOBRAS-5 EURO
6.72 g., 0.900 Gold 0.1944 oz. AGW **Obv:** National arms **Rev:** Vreneli before Swiss flag

Date	Mintage	VF20	XF40	MS60	MS63	MS65
Proof	Est. 300	PF67 425				

KM# 101 15000 DOBRAS-7.5 EURO
25.00 g., 0.925 Silver 0.7435 oz. ASW, 38.55 mm. **Subject:** Switzerland and the European **Obv:** Arms with supporters **Rev:** Helvetia viewing a Swiss flag within a circle of stars **Edge:** Reeded

Date	Mintage	VF20	XF40	MS60	MS63	MS65
1997	—	PF65 40.00				

PATTERNS

KM#	Date	Mintage	Identification	Mkt Val
Pn1	ND-1994	—	1000 Dobras. Copper-Nickel. 1 player.	85.00
Pn2	ND-1994	—	1000 Dobras. Copper-Nickel. With denticles.	85.00
Pn3	ND-1994	—	1000 Dobras. 0.999. Silver. With 999 CuNi in error.	100
Pn4	ND-1994	—	1000 Dobras. Copper-Nickel. 2 soccer players and E.P. 999.	90.00
Pn5	ND-1994	—	1000 Dobras. 0.999. Silver. E.P. 999.	100

PIEDFORT

KM#	Date	Mintage	Identification	Mkt Val
P1	1984	500	100 Dobras. Silver.	120

PROVAS

KM#	Date	Mintage	Identification	Mkt Val
Pr1	1928	—	50 Centavos. Nickel-Bronze. KM1.	250
Pr2	1929	—	10 Centavos. Nickel-Bronze. KM2.	65.00
Pr3	1929	—	20 Centavos. Nickel-Bronze. KM3.	65.00
Pr4	1929	—	50 Centavos. Nickel-Bronze. KM1.	160
Pr5	1939	—	Escudo. Silver. KM5.	275
Pr6	1939	—	2-1/2 Escudos. Silver. KM5.	215
Pr7	1939	—	5 Escudos. Silver. KM6.	225
Pr8	1939	—	10 Escudos. Silver. KM7.	300
Pr9	1948	—	50 Centavos. Nickel-Bronze. KM8.	135
Pr10	1948	—	Escudo. Nickel-Bronze. KM9.	135
Pr11	1948	—	2-1/2 Escudos. Silver. KM5.	165
Pr12	1948	—	5 Escudos. Silver. KM6.	175
Pr13	1951	—	50 Centavos. Copper-Nickel. KM10.	170
Pr14	1951	—	Escudo. Copper-Nickel. KM11.	250
Pr15	1951	—	2-1/2 Escudos. Silver. KM12.	100
Pr16	1951	—	5 Escudos. Silver. KM13.	135
Pr17	1951	—	10 Escudos. Silver. KM14.	265
Pr18	1962	—	10 Centavos. Bronze. KM15.	110
Pr19	1962	—	20 Centavos. Bronze. KM16.	120
Pr20	1962	—	50 Centavos. Bronze. KM17.	120
Pr21	1962	—	Escudo. Bronze. KM18.	130
Pr22	1962	—	2-1/2 Escudos. Copper-Nickel. KM19.	150
Pr23	1962	—	5 Escudos. Silver. KM20.	225
Pr24	1970	—	50 Escudos. Silver. KM21.	375
Pr25	1971	—	10 Centavos. Aluminum. KM15a.	100
Pr26	1971	—	20 Centavos. Bronze. KM16.2.	100
Pr27	1971	—	50 Centavos. Bronze. KM17.2.	100
Pr28	1971	—	Escudo. Bronze. KM18.	100
Pr29	1971	—	2-1/2 Escudos. Copper-Nickel. KM19.	115
Pr30	1971	—	5 Escudos. Copper-Nickel. KM22.	125
Pr31	1971	—	10 Escudos. Copper-Nickel. KM23.	145
Pr32	1971	—	20 Escudos. Nickel. KM24.	160

MINT SETS

KM#	Date	Mintage	Identification	Issue Price	Mkt Val
MS1	1977 (5)	—	KM31-35	71.00	225
MS2	1977 (5)	100	KM36-40	655	2,150

PROOF SETS

KM#	Date	Mintage	Identification	Issue Price	Mkt Val
PS1	1977 (5)	—	KM31-35	93.50	200
PS2	1977 (5)	170	KM36-40	805	2,000

SAINT VINCENT

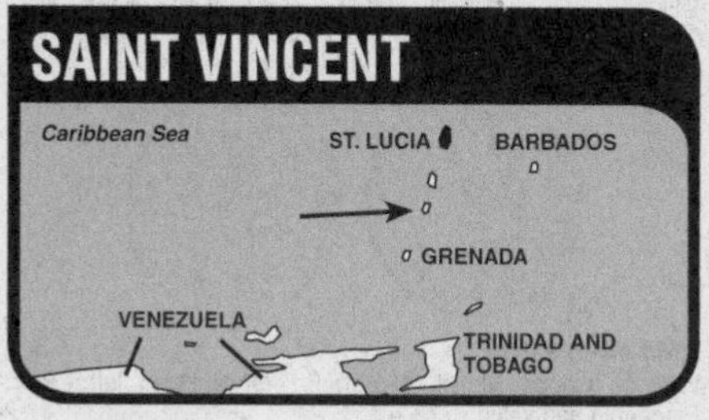

Saint Vincent and the Grenadines, consisting of the island of Saint Vincent and the northern Grenadines (a string of islets stretching southward from Saint Vincent), is located in the Windward Islands of the West Indies, West of Barbados and south of Saint Lucia. The tiny nation has an area of 150sq. mi. (340 sq. km.) and a population of *105,000.Capital: Kingstown. Arrowroot, cotton, sugar, molasses, rum and cocoa are exported. Tourism is a principal industry.

Saint Vincent was discovered by Columbus on Jan. 22,1498, but was left undisturbed for more than a century. The British began colonization early in the 18th century against bitter and prolonged Carib resistance. The island was taken by the French in 1779, but was restored to the British in 1783, at the end of the American Revolution. Saint Vincent and the northern Grenadines became a British associated state in Oct. 1969. Independence under the name of Saint Vincent and the Grenadines was attained at midnight of Oct. 26, 1979. The new nation chose to become a member of the Commonwealth of Nations with Elizabeth II as Head of State and Queen of Saint Vincent.

A local coinage was introduced in 1797, with the gold withdrawn in 1818 and the silver in 1823. This was replaced by sterling. From the mid-1950's, Saint Vincent used the currency of the British Caribbean Territories (Eastern Group), then that of the East Caribbean States.

RULER
British

MONETARY SYSTEM
Commencing 1979
100 Cents = 1 Dollar

BRITISH COLONY

MODERN COINAGE

KM# 13 4 DOLLARS
Copper-Nickel, 38.5 mm. **Series:** F.A.O. **Obv:** Flower above shield with banner and date below **Rev:** Value below divides sugar cane plant and banana tree branch

Date	Mintage	VF20	XF40	MS60	MS63	MS65
1970	13,000	6.00	10.00	22.00	35.00	55.00
1970	2,000	PF63 45.00	PF65 60.00	PF67 75.00		

KM# 14 10 DOLLARS
Copper-Nickel **Subject:** Royal Visit **Obv:** Crowned bust right **Rev:** Flower above shield within circle

Date	Mintage	VF20	XF40	MS60	MS63	MS65
1985	Est. 100000	—	—	25.00	45.00	75.00

KM# 14a 10 DOLLARS
28.28 g., 0.925 Silver 0.841 oz. ASW **Subject:** Royal Visit **Obv:** Crowned bust right **Rev:** Flower above shield within circle

Date	Mintage	VF20	XF40	MS60	MS63	MS65
1985	5,000	PF65 80.00	PF67 100			

KM# 14b 10 DOLLARS
47.54 g., 0.917 Gold 1.4016 oz. AGW **Subject:** Royal Visit **Obv:** Crowned bust right **Rev:** Flower above shield within circle

Date	Mintage	VF20	XF40	MS60	MS63	MS65
1985	250	PF65 2,400	PF67 2,700			

KM# 15 100 DOLLARS
129.59 g., 0.925 Silver 3.8539 oz. ASW, 63 mm. **Subject:** Tropical Birds - Pelican **Obv:** Coat of arms **Rev:** Pelican **Note:** Illustration reduced.

Date	Mintage	VF20	XF40	MS60	MS63	MS65
1988	Est. 10000	PF65 135	PF67 175			

SAMOA

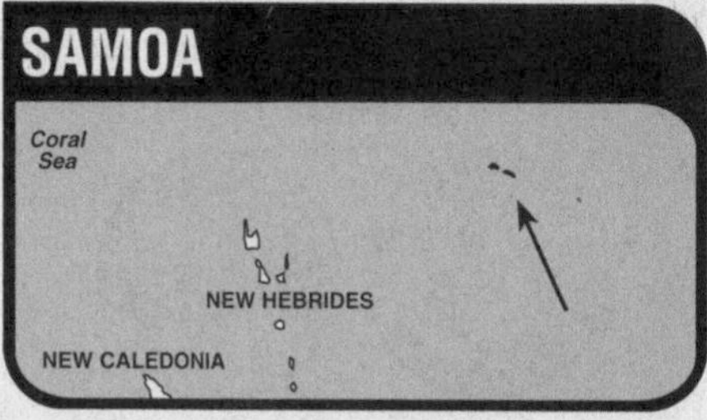

The Independent State of Samoa (formerly Western Samoa), located in the Pacific Ocean 1,600 miles (2,574 km.) northeast of New Zealand, has an area of 1,097 sq. mi. (2,860 sq. km.) and a population of *182,000. Capital: Apia. The economy is based on agriculture, fishing and tourism. Copra, cocoa and bananas are exported.

The first European to sight the Samoan group of islands was the Dutch navigator Jacob Roggeveen in 1722. Great Britain, the United States and Germany established consular representation at Apia in 1847, 1853 and 1861 respectively. The conflicting interests of the three powers produced the Berlin agreement of 1889, which declared Samoa neutral and had the effect of establishing a tripartite protectorate over the islands. A further agreement, 1899, recognized the rights of the United States in those islands east of 171 deg. west longitude (American Samoa) and of Germany in the other islands (Western Samoa).New Zealand occupied Western Samoa at the start of World War I and administered it as a League of Nations mandate and U. N. trusteeship until Jan. 1, 1962, when it became an independent state.

Samoa is a member of the Commonwealth of Nations. The Chief Executive is Chief of State. The prime minister is the Head of Government. The present Head of State, Malietoa Tanumafili II, holds his position for life. The Legislative Assembly will elect future Heads of State for 5-year terms.

Samoa, which had used New Zealand coinage, converted to a decimal coinage in 1967.

RULERS
British, until 1962
Malietoa Tanumafili II, 1962-

MONETARY SYSTEM
100 Sene = 1 Tala

CONSTITUTIONAL MONARCHY

Commonwealth of Nations

STANDARD COINAGE

KM# 1 SENE

1.75 g., Bronze, 17.5 mm. **Obv:** Head left **Rev:** Stars and value within wreath

Date	Mintage	VF20	XF40	MS60	MS63	MS65
1967	915,000	0.10	0.15	0.20	0.30	0.65
1967	15,000	PF65 0.50				

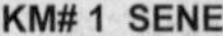

KM# 12 SENE

1.75 g., Bronze, 17.5 mm. **Obv:** Head left **Rev:** Coconut and value

Date	Mintage	VF20	XF40	MS60	MS63	MS65
1974	3,380,000	—	0.10	0.15	0.25	0.50
1987	—	—	0.10	0.15	0.25	0.50
1988	—	—	0.10	0.15	0.25	0.50
1993	—	—	0.10	0.15	0.25	0.50
1996	—	—	0.10	0.15	0.25	0.50

KM# 12a SENE

1.95 g., 0.925 Silver 0.058 oz. ASW, 17.5 mm. **Obv:** Head left **Rev:** Coconut and value

Date	Mintage	VF20	XF40	MS60	MS63	MS65
1974	5,578	PF65 3.00				

KM# 2 2 SENE

3.25 g., Bronze, 21.1 mm. **Obv:** Head left **Rev:** Stars and value within wreath

Date	Mintage	VF20	XF40	MS60	MS63	MS65
1967	465,000	0.10	0.20	0.30	0.40	0.85
1967	15,000	PF65 0.50				

KM# 13 2 SENE

3.25 g., Bronze, 21.1 mm. **Obv:** Head left **Rev:** Value below nut sprig

Date	Mintage	VF20	XF40	MS60	MS63	MS65
1974	1,640,000	0.10	0.15	0.20	0.30	0.65
1988	—	0.10	0.15	0.20	0.30	0.65
1996	—	0.10	0.15	0.20	0.30	0.65

KM# 13a 2 SENE

3.80 g., 0.925 Silver 0.113 oz. ASW, 21.1 mm. **Obv:** Head left **Rev:** Value below nut sprig

Date	Mintage	VF20	XF40	MS60	MS63	MS65
1974	5,578	PF65 5.00				

KM# 122 2 SENE

3.94 g., Bronze, 19.25 mm. **Series:** F.A.O. **Obv:** Head left **Rev:** Stars and value within wreath **Edge:** Plain

Date	Mintage	VF20	XF40	MS60	MS63	MS65
1999	—	—	—	0.25	0.35	0.75
2000	—	—	—	0.25	0.35	0.75

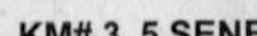

KM# 3 5 SENE

2.80 g., Copper-Nickel, 19.4 mm. **Obv:** Head left **Rev:** Value and stars

Date	Mintage	VF20	XF40	MS60	MS63	MS65
1967	495,000	0.15	0.25	0.35	0.50	0.75
1967	15,000	PF65 1.00				

KM# 14 5 SENE

2.80 g., Copper-Nickel, 19.4 mm. **Obv:** Head left **Rev:** Pineapple and value

Date	Mintage	VF20	XF40	MS60	MS63	MS65
1974	1,736,000	0.10	0.20	0.30	0.40	0.85
1987	—	0.10	0.20	0.30	0.40	0.85
1988	—	0.10	0.20	0.30	0.40	0.85
1993	—	0.10	0.20	0.30	0.40	0.85
1996	—	0.10	0.20	0.30	0.40	0.85
2000	—	0.10	0.20	0.30	0.40	0.85

KM# 14a 5 SENE

3.25 g., 0.925 Silver 0.0967 oz. ASW, 19.4 mm. **Obv:** Head left **Rev:** Pineapple and value

Date	Mintage	VF20	XF40	MS60	MS63	MS65
1974	5,578	PF65 4.50				

KM# 4 10 SENE

5.65 g., Copper-Nickel, 23.6 mm. **Obv:** Head left **Rev:** National arms

Date	Mintage	VF20	XF40	MS60	MS63	MS65
1967	400,000	0.20	0.35	0.45	0.70	1.50
1967	15,000	PF65 1.00				

KM# 15 10 SENE

5.65 g., Copper-Nickel, 23.6 mm. **Obv:** Head left **Rev:** Value to lower left of leafy plants

Date	Mintage	VF20	XF40	MS60	MS63	MS65
1974	1,580,000	0.15	0.30	0.40	0.60	1.25
1987	—	0.15	0.30	0.40	0.60	1.25
1988	—	0.15	0.30	0.40	0.60	1.25
1993	—	0.15	0.30	0.40	0.60	1.25
1996	—	0.15	0.30	0.40	0.60	1.25
2000	—	0.15	0.30	0.40	0.60	1.25

KM# 15a 10 SENE

6.37 g., 0.925 Silver 0.1894 oz. ASW, 23.6 mm. **Obv:** Head left **Rev:** Value to lower left of leafy plants

Date	Mintage	VF20	XF40	MS60	MS63	MS65
1974	5,578	PF65 8.00				

KM# 5 20 SENE

11.30 g., Copper-Nickel, 28.5 mm. **Obv:** Head left **Rev:** National arms

Date	Mintage	VF20	XF40	MS60	MS63	MS65
1967	400,000	0.25	0.35	0.65	1.25	2.50
1967	15,000	PF65 1.50				

KM# 16 20 SENE

11.30 g., Copper-Nickel, 28.5 mm. **Obv:** Head left **Rev:** Breadfruit and value

Date	Mintage	VF20	XF40	MS60	MS63	MS65
1974	1,380,000	0.20	0.30	0.40	0.80	1.60
1987	—	0.20	0.30	0.40	0.80	1.60
1988	—	0.20	0.30	0.40	0.80	1.60
1993	—	0.20	0.30	0.40	0.80	1.60
1996	—	0.20	0.30	0.40	0.80	1.60
2000	—	0.20	0.30	0.40	0.80	1.60

KM# 16a 20 SENE

12.70 g., 0.925 Silver 0.3777 oz. ASW, 28.5 mm. **Obv:** Head left **Rev:** Breadfruit and value

Date	Mintage	VF20	XF40	MS60	MS63	MS65
1974	5,578	PF65 15.00				

KM# 6 50 SENE

14.00 g., Copper-Nickel, 32.4 mm. **Obv:** Head left **Rev:** National arms

Date	Mintage	VF20	XF40	MS60	MS63	MS65
1967	80,000	0.50	0.75	1.25	2.00	3.50
1967	15,000	PF65 2.50				

KM# 17 50 SENE

14.00 g., Copper-Nickel, 32.4 mm. **Obv:** Head left **Rev:** Banana tree and value

Date	Mintage	VF20	XF40	MS60	MS63	MS65
1974	50,000	0.60	1.00	1.50	2.50	5.00
1988	—	0.60	1.00	1.50	2.50	5.00
1996	—	0.60	1.00	1.50	2.50	5.00
2000	—	0.60	1.00	1.50	2.50	5.00

KM# 17a 50 SENE

15.40 g., 0.925 Silver 0.458 oz. ASW, 32.4 mm. **Obv:** Head left **Rev:** Banana tree and value

Date	Mintage	VF20	XF40	MS60	MS63	MS65
1974	5,578	PF65 18.00				

KM# 80 50 SENE
14.00 g., Copper-Nickel, 32.4 mm. **Subject:** 25th Anniversary of Independence **Obv:** Head left **Rev:** National arms

Date	Mintage	VF20	XF40	MS60	MS63	MS65
1987	—	—	—	2.00	3.00	6.00

KM# 7 TALA
26.85 g., Copper-Nickel, 38.71 mm. **Obv:** Head of Malietoa Tanumafili II left **Rev:** National arms, value **Edge:** Lettered **Edge Lettering:** DECIMAL CURRENCY INTRODUCED 10 JULY 1967

Date	Mintage	VF20	XF40	MS60	MS63	MS65
1967	20,000	—	—	1.50	2.50	3.50
1967	15,000	PF65 5.00				

KM# 8 TALA
26.85 g., Copper-Nickel, 38.8 mm. **Subject:** 75th Anniversary - Death of Robert Louis Stevenson **Obv:** National arms **Rev:** Reclining figure holding pen and paper left

Date	Mintage	VF20	XF40	MS60	MS63	MS65
1969	25,000	—	—	1.50	2.50	3.50
1969	1,500	PF65 9.00				

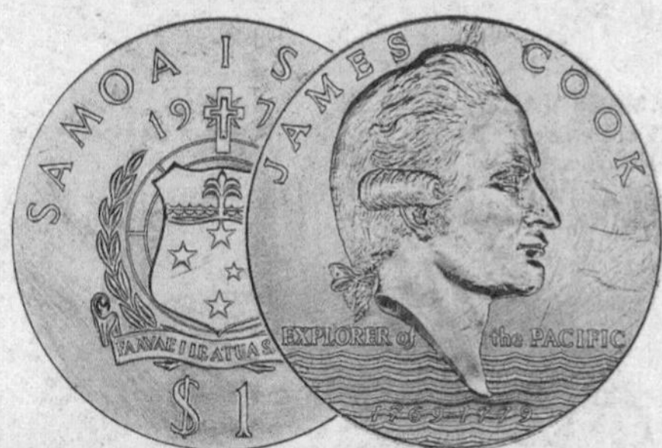

KM# 9 TALA
Copper-Nickel, 38.8 mm. **Subject:** 200th Anniversary - Capt. Cook voyages **Obv:** National arms **Rev:** Head right

Date	Mintage	VF20	XF40	MS60	MS63	MS65
1970	32,000	—	—	1.50	2.50	3.50
1970	3,000	PF65 7.50				

KM# 10 TALA
Copper-Nickel, 38.8 mm. **Subject:** Visit of Pope Paul VI **Obv:** National arms **Rev:** Bust right

Date	Mintage	VF20	XF40	MS60	MS63	MS65
1970	35,000	—	—	1.50	2.50	3.50
1970	3,000	PF65 8.00				

KM# 11 TALA
Copper-Nickel, 38.8 mm. **Subject:** Roggeveen's Pacific voyage **Obv:** National arms **Rev:** Sailing ship

Date	Mintage	VF20	XF40	MS60	MS63	MS65
1972	35,000	—	—	1.50	2.50	3.50
1972	3,000	PF65 9.50				

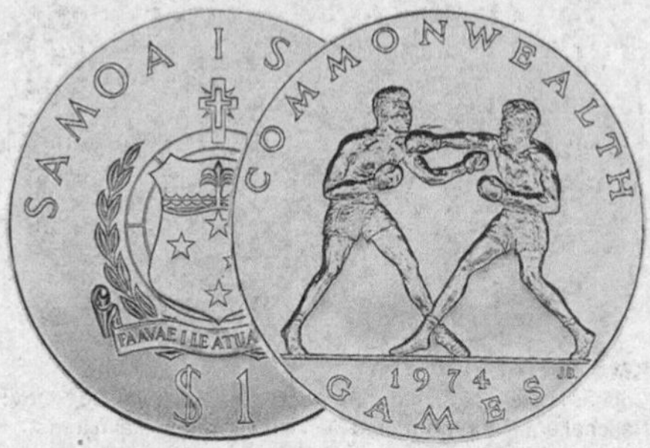

KM# 18 TALA
Copper-Nickel, 38.8 mm. **Subject:** 10th British Commonwealth Games **Obv:** National arms **Rev:** Boxing match

Date	Mintage	VF20	XF40	MS60	MS63	MS65
1974	40,000	—	—	1.50	2.50	3.50

KM# 18a TALA
27.70 g., 0.925 Silver 0.8238 oz. ASW, 38.8 mm. **Subject:** 10th British Commonwealth Games **Obv:** National arms **Rev:** Boxing match

Date	Mintage	VF20	XF40	MS60	MS63	MS65
1974	1,500	PF65 30.00				

KM# 19 TALA
Copper-Nickel, 38.8 mm. **Obv:** Head of Malietoa Tanumafili II left **Rev:** Coconut palm and value

Date	Mintage	VF20	XF40	MS60	MS63	MS65
1974	24,000	—	—	1.50	2.50	3.50

KM# 19a TALA
31.15 g., 0.925 Silver 0.9264 oz. ASW, 38.8 mm. **Obv:** Head of Malietoa Tanumafili II left **Rev:** Coconut palm and value

Date	Mintage	VF20	XF40	MS60	MS63	MS65
1974	11,000	PF65 25.00				

KM# 20 TALA
Copper-Nickel, 38.8 mm. **Subject:** U.S. Bicentennial **Obv:** Head of Malietoa Tanumafili II left **Rev:** Equestrian and USA map

Date	Mintage	VF20	XF40	MS60	MS63	MS65
ND-1976	40,000	—	—	1.50	2.50	3.50

KM# 20a TALA
30.40 g., 0.925 Silver 0.9041 oz. ASW, 38.8 mm. **Subject:** U.S. Bicentennial **Obv:** Head of Malietoa Tanumafili II left **Rev:** Equestrian and USA map

Date	Mintage	VF20	XF40	MS60	MS63	MS65
ND-1976	4,127	PF65 40.00				

KM# 22 TALA
Copper-Nickel, 38.8 mm. **Series:** Montreal Olympics **Obv:** National arms **Rev:** Weight lifter

Date	Mintage	VF20	XF40	MS60	MS63	MS65
1976	40,000	—	—	1.50	2.50	3.50

KM# 22a TALA
30.40 g., 0.925 Silver 0.9041 oz. ASW, 38.8 mm. **Series:** Montreal Olympics **Obv:** National arms **Rev:** Weight lifter

Date	Mintage	VF20	XF40	MS60	MS63	MS65
1976	6,000	PF65 32.00				

KM# 24 TALA
Copper-Nickel, 38.8 mm. **Subject:** Queen's Silver Jubilee **Obv:** National arms **Rev:** Cameo flanked by palm trees

Date	Mintage	VF20	XF40	MS60	MS63	MS65
1977	27,000	—	—	1.50	2.50	3.50

KM# 24a TALA
30.40 g., 0.925 Silver 0.9041 oz. ASW, 38.8 mm. **Subject:** Queen's Silver Jubilee **Obv:** National arms **Rev:** Cameo flanked by palm trees

Date	Mintage	VF20	XF40	MS60	MS63	MS65
1977	6,171	PF65 40.00				

KM# 26 TALA
Copper-Nickel, 38.8 mm. **Subject:** Lindbergh's New York to

Paris flight **Obv:** National arms **Rev:** Bust of Lindbergh at left, plane above, Eiffel tower at right, Statue of Liberty at left, ocean in background

Date	Mintage	VF20	XF40	MS60	MS63	MS65
1977	17,000	—	—	1.50	2.50	3.50

KM# 26a TALA

30.40 g., 0.925 Silver 0.9041 oz. ASW, 38.8 mm. **Subject:** Lindbergh's New York to Paris flight **Obv:** National arms **Rev:** Bust of Lindbergh at left, plane above, Eiffel tower at right, Statue of Liberty at left, ocean in background

Date	Mintage	VF20	XF40	MS60	MS63	MS65
1977	4,522	PF65 35.00				

KM# 28 TALA

Copper-Nickel, 38.8 mm. **Subject:** 50th Anniversary - First Transpacific Flight **Obv:** National arms **Rev:** Head left, map, plane and date

Date	Mintage	VF20	XF40	MS60	MS63	MS65
1978	20,000	—	—	1.50	2.50	3.50

KM# 28a TALA

30.40 g., 0.925 Silver 0.9041 oz. ASW, 38.8 mm. **Subject:** 50th Anniversary - First Transpacific Flight **Obv:** National arms **Rev:** Head left, map, plane and date

Date	Mintage	VF20	XF40	MS60	MS63	MS65
1978	5,000	PF65 35.00				

KM# 30 TALA

Copper-Nickel, 38.8 mm. **Subject:** XI Commonwealth Games **Obv:** National arms **Rev:** Runners

Date	Mintage	VF20	XF40	MS60	MS63	MS65
1978	7,710	—	—	1.50	2.50	3.50

KM# 30a TALA

30.40 g., 0.925 Silver 0.9041 oz. ASW, 38.8 mm. **Subject:** XI Commonwealth Games **Obv:** National arms **Rev:** Runners

Date	Mintage	VF20	XF40	MS60	MS63	MS65
1978	5,000	PF65 30.00				

KM# 32 TALA

Copper-Nickel, 38.8 mm. **Subject:** Bicentenary - Death of Capt. James Cook **Obv:** National arms **Rev:** Head right and sailing ship

Date	Mintage	VF20	XF40	MS60	MS63	MS65
1979	5,000	—	—	2.50	3.00	5.00

KM# 35 TALA

Copper-Nickel, 38.8 mm. **Series:** 1980 Olympics **Obv:** National arms **Rev:** Hurdles event

Date	Mintage	VF20	XF40	MS60	MS63	MS65
1980	5,000	—	—	2.50	3.00	5.00

KM# 38 TALA

Copper-Nickel, 38.8 mm. **Series:** F.A.O. **Obv:** National arms **Rev:** Coconut palm and value

Date	Mintage	VF20	XF40	MS60	MS63	MS65
1980	10,000	—	—	1.50	2.50	3.50

KM# 40 TALA

Copper-Nickel, 38.8 mm. **Subject:** Gov. Wilhelm Solf **Obv:** National arms **Rev:** Armored bust left flanked by palm trees

Date	Mintage	VF20	XF40	MS60	MS63	MS65
1980	5,000	—	—	2.00	3.00	5.00

KM# 43 TALA

Copper-Nickel, 38.8 mm. **Subject:** Wedding of Prince Charles and Lady Diana **Obv:** National arms **Rev:** Conjoined heads left

Date	Mintage	VF20	XF40	MS60	MS63	MS65
1981	12,000	—	—	1.50	2.75	4.00

KM# 47 TALA

Copper-Nickel, 38.8 mm. **Subject:** IYDP - President Franklin Roosevelt **Obv:** National arms **Rev:** Seated figure in wheelchair facing

Date	Mintage	VF20	XF40	MS60	MS63	MS65
1981	8,000	—	—	1.50	2.50	3.50

KM# 50 TALA

Copper-Nickel, 38.8 mm. **Subject:** Commonwealth Games **Obv:** National arms **Rev:** Javelin thrower

Date	Mintage	VF20	XF40	MS60	MS63	MS65
1982	6,000	—	—	1.50	2.50	3.50

KM# 53 TALA

Copper-Nickel, 38.8 mm. **Subject:** South Pacific Games **Obv:** National arms **Rev:** Runner

Date	Mintage	VF20	XF40	MS60	MS63	MS65
1983	8,000	—	—	1.50	2.50	3.50

KM# 57 TALA

9.50 g., Aluminum-Bronze, 30.6 mm. **Subject:** Circulation coinage **Obv:** Head left **Rev:** National arms **Shape:** 7-sided

Date	Mintage	VF20	XF40	MS60	MS63	MS65
1984	1,000,000	—	—	0.75	1.00	1.50

KM# 57a TALA

27.22 g., Copper-Nickel, 30 mm. **Obv:** Head left **Rev:** National arms **Edge:** Plain **Shape:** 7-sided

Date	Mintage	VF20	XF40	MS60	MS63	MS65
1984	5,000	—	—	2.00	3.50	5.00

KM# 58 TALA

Copper-Nickel, 38.8 mm. **Series:** Summer Olympics **Obv:** National arms **Rev:** Boxing match

Date	Mintage	VF20	XF40	MS60	MS63	MS65
1984	8,000	—	—	1.50	2.50	3.50

KM# 63 TALA
Copper-Nickel, 38.8 mm. **Subject:** Prince Andrew and Sarah Ferguson's Marriage **Obv:** National arms **Rev:** Conjoined busts

Date	Mintage	VF20	XF40	MS60	MS63	MS65
1986	10,000	—	—	1.50	2.50	3.50

KM# 74 TALA
Copper-Nickel, 38.8 mm. **Subject:** 25th Anniversary of World Wildlife Fund **Obv:** National arms **Rev:** Samoan Fantail bird

Date	Mintage	VF20	XF40	MS60	MS63	MS65
1986	—	—	—	3.50	5.00	7.00

KM# 88 TALA
Copper-Nickel, 38.8 mm. **Subject:** 40th Anniversary - Reign of Queen Elizabeth II **Obv:** National arms **Rev:** Cross in center circle, equestrians and chariot around border

Date	Mintage	VF20	XF40	MS60	MS63	MS65
ND-1992	—	—	—	1.50	2.50	3.50

KM# 111 TALA
Copper-Nickel, 38.8 mm. **Subject:** Queen Mother **Obv:** National arms **Rev:** Glamis Castle within beaded circle

Date	Mintage	VF20	XF40	MS60	MS63	MS65
1995	Est. 30000	—	—	1.50	2.50	3.50

KM# 112 TALA
10.00 g., 0.500 Silver 0.1608 oz. ASW **Series:** Olympics **Obv:** National arms **Rev:** Gymnast and pommel horse

Date	Mintage	VF20	XF40	MS60	MS63	MS65
1996	Est. 10000	—	—	5.00	7.50	10.00

KM# 175 TALA
Copper-Nickel, 39 mm. **Subject:** 1/2 of coin **Edge:** Plain

Date	Mintage	VF20	XF40	MS60	MS63	MS65
ND (1997)	—	—	—	—	7.00	10.00

KM# 176 2 TALA
Silver, 28 mm. **Subject:** Queen Mother **Obv:** National Arms **Rev:** Young Elizabeth on horseback **Edge:** Reeded

Date	Mintage	VF20	XF40	MS60	MS63	MS65
1997	—	PF65 30.00				

KM# 120 2 TALA
42.41 g., 0.925 Silver 1.2614 oz. ASW **Obv:** National arms **Rev:** Value and three scenes **Note:** Part of a tri-national, three-coin matching set with Cook Islands and Fiji.

Date	Mintage	VF20	XF40	MS60	MS63	MS65
1998	Est. 20000	PF65 45.00				

KM# 125 5 TALA
19.83 g., Copper-Nickel, 38.7 mm. **Subject:** Robert Louis Stevenson **Obv:** National arms **Rev:** Ship, portrait and pirate scene **Edge:** Reeded

Date	Mintage	VF20	XF40	MS60	MS63	MS65
ND(1994)	100,000	—	—	3.00	5.00	7.00

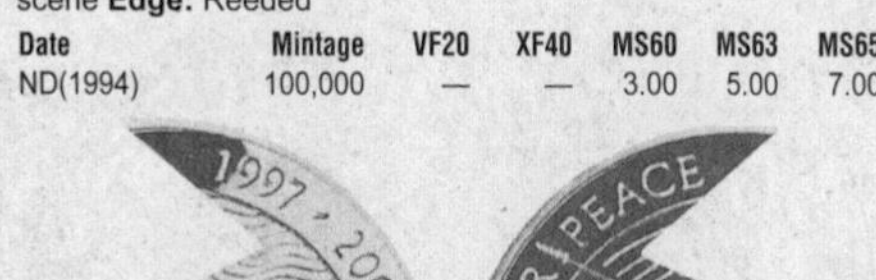

KM# 115 5 TALA
15.55 g., 0.925 Silver 0.4625 oz. ASW **Subject:** War and peace **Obv:** National arms **Rev:** Arrows and sword **Note:** 1/2 of 2-part coin, combined with Kiribati KM#22, issued in sets only. Value is determined by combining the 2 parts.

Date	Mintage	VF20	XF40	MS60	MS63	MS65
ND-1997	Est. 10000	PF65 27.00				

KM# 116 5 TALA
15.55 g., 0.925 Silver 0.4625 oz. ASW **Subject:** Epoch - making events **Obv:** National arms **Rev:** Helmet and crowns **Note:** 1/2 of 2-part coin, combined with Kiribati KM#23, issued in sets only. Value is determined by combining the 2 parts.

Date	Mintage	VF20	XF40	MS60	MS63	MS65
ND-1997	Est. 10000	PF65 27.00				

KM# 117 5 TALA
15.55 g., 0.925 Silver 0.4625 oz. ASW **Subject:** Tempora Mutantur **Obv:** National arms **Rev:** Man with torch **Note:** 1/2 of 2-part coin, combined with Kiribati KM#24, issued in sets only. Value is determined by combining the 2 parts.

Date	Mintage	VF20	XF40	MS60	MS63	MS65
ND-1997	Est. 10000	PF65 27.00				

KM# 117a 5 TALA
Copper-Nickel **Subject:** Tempora Mutantur **Obv:** National arms **Rev:** Man with torch **Note:** 1/2 of 2-part coin, combined with Kiribati KM#24a, issued in pairs only. Value is determined by combining the 2 parts.

Date	Mintage	VF20	XF40	MS60	MS63	MS65
ND-1997	—	—	—	—	10.00	12.50

KM# 118 5 TALA
15.55 g., 0.925 Silver 0.4625 oz. ASW **Subject:** People and buildings **Obv:** National arms **Rev:** Working hands **Note:** 1/2 of 2-part coin, combined with Kiribati KM#25, issued in sets only. Value is determined by combining the 2 parts.

Date	Mintage	VF20	XF40	MS60	MS63	MS65
ND-1997	Est. 10000	PF65 27.00				

KM# 138 5 TALA
14.80 g., 0.925 Silver 0.4401 oz. ASW, 24.5 mm. **Subject:** Epoch Making Events **Obv:** National arms **Rev:** Topless Marianne and Guru **Edge:** Pain **Shape:** Irregular

Date	Mintage	VF20	XF40	MS60	MS63	MS65
ND-1998	—	PF65 27.00				

KM# 33 10 TALA
31.33 g., 0.500 Silver 0.5036 oz. ASW **Subject:** Bicentenary - Death of Capt. James Cook **Obv:** National arms **Rev:** Head right and ship

Date	Mintage	VF20	XF40	MS60	MS63	MS65
1979	3,000	—	—	—	20.00	22.00

KM# 33a 10 TALA
31.47 g., 0.925 Silver 0.9359 oz. ASW **Subject:** Bicentenary - Death of Capt. James Cook **Obv:** National arms **Rev:** Head right and ship

Date	Mintage	VF20	XF40	MS60	MS63	MS65
1979	5,000	PF65 30.00				

KM# 36 10 TALA
31.33 g., 0.500 Silver 0.5036 oz. ASW **Series:** 1980 Olympics **Obv:** National arms **Rev:** Hurdles event

Date	Mintage	VF20	XF40	MS60	MS63	MS65
1980	3,000	—	—	—	20.00	22.00

KM# 36a 10 TALA
31.47 g., 0.925 Silver 0.9359 oz. ASW **Series:** 1980 Olympics **Obv:** National arms **Rev:** Hurdles event

Date	Mintage	VF20	XF40	MS60	MS63	MS65
1980	4,000	PF65 30.00				

KM# 39 10 TALA
31.33 g., 0.500 Silver 0.5036 oz. ASW, 38.8 mm. **Series:** F.A.O. **Obv:** National arms **Rev:** Palm tree with coconuts

Date	Mintage	VF20	XF40	MS60	MS63	MS65
1980	3,000	PF63 20.00	PF65 25.00			

KM# 41 10 TALA
31.33 g., 0.500 Silver 0.5036 oz. ASW **Subject:** Gov. Wilhelm Solf **Obv:** National arms **Rev:** Uniformed bust left flanked by palm trees

Date	Mintage	VF20	XF40	MS60	MS63	MS65
1980	3,000	—	—	—	20.00	22.00

KM# 41a 10 TALA
31.47 g., 0.925 Silver 0.9359 oz. ASW **Subject:** Gov. Wilhelm Solf **Obv:** National arms **Rev:** Uniformed bust left flanked by palm trees

Date	Mintage	VF20	XF40	MS60	MS63	MS65
1980	4,000	PF65 30.00				

KM# 44 10 TALA
31.47 g., 0.925 Silver 0.9359 oz. ASW **Subject:** Wedding of Prince Charles and Lady Diana **Obv:** National arms **Rev:** Conjoined busts left

Date	Mintage	VF20	XF40	MS60	MS63	MS65
1981	5,000	PF65 30.00				

KM# 48 10 TALA
31.47 g., 0.925 Silver 0.9359 oz. ASW **Subject:** IYDP - President Franklin Roosevelt **Obv:** National arms **Rev:** Seated figure in wheelchair facing

Date	Mintage	VF20	XF40	MS60	MS63	MS65
1981	5,000	PF65 30.00				

KM# 51 10 TALA
31.47 g., 0.925 Silver 0.9359 oz. ASW **Subject:** Commonwealth Games **Obv:** National arms **Rev:** Javelin thrower

Date	Mintage	VF20	XF40	MS60	MS63	MS65
1982	4,000	PF65 30.00				

KM# 54 10 TALA
31.47 g., 0.925 Silver 0.9359 oz. ASW **Subject:** South Pacific Games **Obv:** National arms **Rev:** Runner

Date	Mintage	VF20	XF40	MS60	MS63	MS65
1983	3,000	PF65 30.00				

KM# 59 10 TALA
31.47 g., 0.925 Silver 0.9359 oz. ASW **Series:** Summer Olympics **Obv:** National arms **Rev:** Boxing match

Date	Mintage	VF20	XF40	MS60	MS63	MS65
1984	3,000	PF65 30.00				

KM# 64 10 TALA
31.47 g., 0.925 Silver 0.9359 oz. ASW **Subject:** Prince Andrew and Sara Ferguson's Marriage **Obv:** National arms **Rev:** Conjoined busts left **Note:** Similar to Tala, KM#63.

Date	Mintage	VF20	XF40	MS60	MS63	MS65
1986	2,500	PF65 30.00				

KM# 72 10 TALA
31.47 g., 0.925 Silver 0.9359 oz. ASW **Subject:** 25th Anniversary of World Wildlife Fund **Obv:** National arms **Rev:** Samoan Fantail bird

Date	Mintage	VF20	XF40	MS60	MS63	MS65
1986	—	PF65 30.00				

KM# 66 10 TALA
31.10 g., 0.999 Silver 0.9989 oz. ASW **Subject:** America's Cup Race - 1987 Perth **Obv:** The Cup **Rev:** Sailing scene

Date	Mintage	VF20	XF40	MS60	MS63	MS65
1987	—	PF65 32.00				

KM# 70 10 TALA
31.10 g., 0.999 Silver 0.9989 oz. ASW **Series:** 1988 Olympics **Obv:** National arms **Rev:** Three torches and athletes

Date	Mintage	VF20	XF40	MS60	MS63	MS65
1988	20,000	—	—	—	20.00	22.00

KM# 75 10 TALA
31.10 g., 0.999 Silver 0.999 oz. ASW **Obv:** National arms **Rev:** Kon-Tiki raft and map

Date	Mintage	VF20	XF40	MS60	MS63	MS65
1988	Est. 16500	PF65 30.00				

KM# 79 10 TALA
31.47 g., 0.925 Silver 0.9359 oz. ASW, 38.7 mm. **Series:** Save the Children Fund **Obv:** National arms **Rev:** Two children flanked by palms leaves **Edge:** Reeded

Date	Mintage	VF20	XF40	MS60	MS63	MS65
1990	Est. 20000	PF65 27.00				

KM# 82 10 TALA
31.47 g., 0.925 Silver 0.9359 oz. ASW **Series:** Summer Olympics **Obv:** National arms **Rev:** Shot putter

Date	Mintage	VF20	XF40	MS60	MS63	MS65
1991	Est. 70000	PF65 25.00				

KM# 83 10 TALA
31.10 g., 0.925 Silver 0.925 oz. ASW **Subject:** RA expeditions **Obv:** National arms **Rev:** Map within circle to right of ship

Date	Mintage	VF20	XF40	MS60	MS63	MS65
1991	15,000	PF65 30.00				

KM# 85 10 TALA
31.47 g., 0.925 Silver 0.9359 oz. ASW **Series:** Olympics **Obv:** National arms **Rev:** Javelin thrower

Date	Mintage	VF20	XF40	MS60	MS63	MS65
1991	Est. 70000	PF65 27.00				

KM# 86 10 TALA
31.47 g., 0.925 Silver 0.9359 oz. ASW **Series:** Olympics **Obv:** National arms **Rev:** Hammer thrower

Date	Mintage	VF20	XF40	MS60	MS63	MS65
1992	Est. 70000	PF65 27.00				

KM# 89 10 TALA
31.86 g., 0.925 Silver 0.9475 oz. ASW **Subject:** World Cup Soccer **Obv:** National arms **Rev:** Arena behind player's legs kicking ball

Date	Mintage	VF20	XF40	MS60	MS63	MS65
1992	—	PF65 32.00				

KM# 93 10 TALA
31.47 g., 0.925 Silver 0.9359 oz. ASW **Subject:** Jakob Roggeveen **Obv:** National arms

Date	Mintage	VF20	XF40	MS60	MS63	MS65
1992	15,000	PF65 27.00				

KM# 98 10 TALA
31.35 g., 0.925 Silver 0.9323 oz. ASW **Series:** Endangered Wildlife **Obv:** National arms **Rev:** Pair of birds

Date	Mintage	VF20	XF40	MS60	MS63	MS65
1992	Est. 20000	PF65 35.00				

KM# 99 10 TALA
31.77 g., 0.925 Silver 0.9448 oz. ASW **Obv:** National arms **Rev:** Roggeveen's fleet

Date	Mintage	VF20	XF40	MS60	MS63	MS65
1992	Est. 15000	PF65 30.00				

KM# 109 10 TALA
31.47 g., 0.925 Silver 0.9359 oz. ASW **Subject:** 40th Anniversary - Reign of Queen Elizabeth II **Obv:** National arms **Rev:** Royal carriage and guard around Order of the Garter

Date	Mintage	VF20	XF40	MS60	MS63	MS65
1992	Est. 5000	PF65 32.00				

KM# 97 10 TALA
31.81 g., 0.925 Silver 0.946 oz. ASW **Series:** 1996 Olympics **Obv:** National arms **Rev:** Gymnast on pommel horse

Date	Mintage	VF20	XF40	MS60	MS63	MS65
1993	50,000	PF65 20.00				

KM# 91 10 TALA
31.81 g., 0.925 Silver 0.946 oz. ASW **Series:** Olympics **Obv:** National arms **Rev:** Diver

Date	Mintage	VF20	XF40	MS60	MS63	MS65
1994	Est. 50000	PF65 20.00				

KM# 94 10 TALA
31.10 g., 0.925 Silver 0.925 oz. ASW **Subject:** Tigris Expedition **Obv:** National arms **Rev:** Pyramid behind boat

Date	Mintage	VF20	XF40	MS60	MS63	MS65
1994	10,000	PF65 35.00				

KM# 95 10 TALA
31.10 g., 0.925 Silver 0.925 oz. ASW **Subject:** Tigris Expedition **Obv:** National arms **Rev:** Burning Tigris

Date	Mintage	VF20	XF40	MS60	MS63	MS65
1994	10,000	PF65 35.00				

KM# 100 10 TALA
31.77 g., 0.925 Silver 0.9448 oz. ASW **Obv:** National arms **Rev:** Two figures sighting land

Date	Mintage	VF20	XF40	MS60	MS63	MS65
1994	10,000	PF65 30.00				

KM# 101 10 TALA
31.23 g., 0.925 Silver 0.9288 oz. ASW **Series:** Endangered Wildlife **Obv:** National arms **Rev:** Flying bat

Date	Mintage	VF20	XF40	MS60	MS63	MS65
1994	Est. 20000	PF65 40.00				

KM# 102 10 TALA
31.47 g., 0.925 Silver 0.9359 oz. ASW **Subject:** Comte de la Perouse **Obv:** National arms **Rev:** World globe on stand flanked by figures, ship and date above

Date	Mintage	VF20	XF40	MS60	MS63	MS65
1994	—	PF65 30.00				

KM# 103 10 TALA
31.47 g., 0.925 Silver 0.9359 oz. ASW **Subject:** Protect Our World **Obv:** National arms **Rev:** Flowers

Date	Mintage	VF20	XF40	MS60	MS63	MS65
1994	Est. 10000	PF65 30.00				

KM# 104 10 TALA
31.47 g., 0.925 Silver 0.9359 oz. ASW **Subject:** Queen Mother **Obv:** National arms **Rev:** Glamis Castle within beaded circle

Date	Mintage	VF20	XF40	MS60	MS63	MS65
1994	Est. 30000	PF65 20.00				

KM# 121 10 TALA
31.23 g., 0.925 Silver 0.9288 oz. ASW, 38.6 mm. **Obv:** National arms **Rev:** Seated Robert Louis Stephenson **Edge:** Reeded

Date	Mintage	VF20	XF40	MS60	MS63	MS65
1994	10,000	PF65 40.00				

KM# 105 10 TALA
31.47 g., 0.925 Silver 0.9359 oz. ASW **Subject:** Edmond Halley **Obv:** National arms **Rev:** Bust 1/4 right

Date	Mintage	VF20	XF40	MS60	MS63	MS65
1995	10,000	PF65 30.00				

KM# 113 10 TALA
1.24 g., 0.9999 Gold 0.040 oz. AGW **Series:** Olympics **Obv:** National arms **Rev:** Discus thrower

Date	Mintage	VF20	XF40	MS60	MS63	MS65
1995	Est. 25000	—	—	—	—	71.00

KM# 124 10 TALA
31.62 g., 0.925 Silver 0.9404 oz. ASW, 38.5 mm. **Subject:** Queen Elizabeth - Queen Mother **Obv:** National arms **Rev:** Young Lady sitting on horse **Edge:** Reeded

Date	Mintage	VF20	XF40	MS60	MS63	MS65
1995	—	PF65 27.00				

KM# 144 10 TALA
1.26 g., 0.9999 Gold 0.0405 oz. AGW, 13.75 mm. **Obv:** National arms **Obv. Legend:** SAMOA - SISIFO **Rev:** Sailing ship "The Endeavour **Edge:** Reeded

Date	Mintage	VF20	XF40	MS60	MS63	MS65
1995	25,000	PF65 72.00				

KM# 114 10 TALA
31.70 g., 0.925 Silver 0.9427 oz. ASW **Subject:** Jakob le Maire **Obv:** National arms **Rev:** Sailing ship

Date	Mintage	VF20	XF40	MS60	MS63	MS65
1996	—	PF65 27.00				

KM# 127 10 TALA
31.80 g., 0.925 Silver 0.9457 oz. ASW, 38.6 mm. **Subject:** Victorian Age **Obv:** National arms **Rev:** Queen Victoria and family within circle **Edge:** Reeded

Date	Mintage	VF20	XF40	MS60	MS63	MS65
1996	—	PF65 27.00				

KM# 145 10 TALA
1:23 g., 0.9999 Gold 0.0395 oz. AGW, 13.91 mm. **Subject:** The Gold of Captain Flint - Treasue Island **Obv:** National arms **Obv. Legend:** SAMOA **Rev:** Treasure map **Edge:** Reeded

Date	Mintage	VF20	XF40	MS60	MS63	MS65
1997	25,000	PF65 71.00				

KM# 123 10 TALA
31.50 g., 0.925 Silver 0.9368 oz. ASW, 38.6 mm. **Subject:** Princess Diana **Obv:** National arms **Rev:** Diana holding child **Edge:** Reeded

Date	Mintage	VF20	XF40	MS60	MS63	MS65
1998	—	PF65 33.00				

KM# 128 10 TALA
31.80 g., 0.925 Silver 0.9457 oz. ASW, 38.6 mm. **Subject:** Queen Mother **Obv:** National arms **Rev:** Queen Mother presenting shamrocks to the Irish Guards **Edge:** Reeded

Date	Mintage	VF20	XF40	MS60	MS63	MS65
1998	—	PF65 27.00				

KM# 157 10 TALA
31.47 g., 0.925 Silver 0.9359 oz. ASW, 46 mm. **Obv:** National arms **Rev:** Soccer player and line drawing of rooster in background

Date	Mintage	VF20	XF40	MS60	MS63	MS65
1998	Est. 10000	PF65 45.00				

KM# 177 10 TALA
Silver, 28 mm. **Subject:** Queen Mother **Obv:** National arms **Rev:** Queen Mother receiving shamrocks form the Irish Guard **Edge:** Reeded

Date	Mintage	VF20	XF40	MS60	MS63	MS65
1998	—	PF65 35.00				

KM# 129 10 TALA
31.42 g., 0.925 Silver 0.9344 oz. ASW, 38.6 mm. **Subject:** Olympics **Obv:** National arms **Rev:** Two volleyball players **Edge:** Reeded

Date	Mintage	VF20	XF40	MS60	MS63	MS65
2000	—	PF65 40.00				

KM# 62 25 TALA
155.50 g., 0.999 Silver 4.9944 oz. ASW, 65 mm. **Subject:** Kon-Tiki **Obv:** National arms **Rev:** Sailing ship **Note:** Illustration reduced.

Date	Mintage	VF20	XF40	MS60	MS63	MS65
1986	—	PF65 125	PF67 175			

KM# 67 25 TALA
155.50 g., 0.999 Silver 4.9944 oz. ASW, 65 mm. **Subject:** America's Cup Race **Obv:** America's Cup trophy **Rev:** Sailing ship **Note:** Illustration reduced.

Date	Mintage	VF20	XF40	MS60	MS63	MS65
1987	—	PF65 125	PF67 175			

KM# 158 25 TALA
Silver **Obv:** National arms **Rev:** Soccer player and linear map of France in background

Date	Mintage	VF20	XF40	MS60	MS63	MS65
1998	Est. 5000	PF65 100	PF67 150			

KM# 76 50 TALA
31.10 g., 0.999 Palladium 0.999 oz. APW **Subject:** Kon-Tiki **Obv:** National arms **Rev:** Raft and bamboo poles

Date	Mintage	VF20	XF40	MS60	MS63	MS65
1988	—	PF65 775	PF67 825			

KM# 78 50 TALA
7.77 g., 0.999 Gold 0.2496 oz. AGW **Subject:** Trans-Antarctica Expedition **Obv:** Sled dogs and musher and single dog head facing left **Rev:** Six doves above snake on rock, value at upper left

Date	Mintage	VF20	XF40	MS60	MS63	MS65
1988	—	PF67 470				

KM# 90 50 TALA
7.78 g., 0.5833 Gold 0.1458 oz. AGW **Series:** 1996 Olympics **Obv:** National arms **Rev:** Discus thrower

Date	Mintage	VF20	XF40	MS60	MS63	MS65
1993	7,500	PF67 275				

KM# 92 50 TALA
7.78 g., 0.5833 Gold 0.1458 oz. AGW **Subject:** World Cup Soccer **Obv:** National arms **Rev:** Soccer players

Date	Mintage	VF20	XF40	MS60	MS63	MS65
1993	Est. 3000	PF67 275				

KM# 106 50 TALA
7.78 g., 0.5833 Gold 0.1458 oz. AGW **Obv:** National arms **Rev:** Portrait

Date	Mintage	VF20	XF40	MS60	MS63	MS65
1993	Est. 3000	PF67 275				

KM# 107 50 TALA
7.78 g., 0.5833 Gold 0.1458 oz. AGW **Subject:** The Endeavor **Obv:** National arms **Rev:** Sailing ship within radiant sun

Date	Mintage	VF20	XF40	MS60	MS63	MS65
1994	Est. 2500	PF67 275				

KM# 108 50 TALA
7.78 g., 0.5833 Gold 0.1458 oz. AGW **Series:** Endangered Wildlife **Obv:** National arms **Rev:** Dolphins

Date	Mintage	VF20	XF40	MS60	MS63	MS65
1995	Est. 2500	PF67 275				

KM# 119 50 TALA
3.89 g., 0.999 Gold 0.1249 oz. AGW **Subject:** Tempora Mutantur **Obv:** National arms **Rev:** Man with torch **Note:** 1/2 of 2-part coin, combined with Kiribati KM#26, issued in sets only; Value is determined by combining the 2 parts.

Date	Mintage	VF20	XF40	MS60	MS63	MS65
ND-1997	Est. 2500	PF67 250				

KM# 21 100 TALA
15.55 g., 0.917 Gold 0.4584 oz. AGW **Subject:** U.S. Bicentennial **Obv:** National arms **Rev:** Equestrian and USA map

Date	Mintage	VF20	XF40	MS60	MS63	MS65
1976	2,000	PF67 675				

KM# 23 100 TALA
15.55 g., 0.917 Gold 0.4584 oz. AGW **Series:** Montreal Olympics **Obv:** National arms **Rev:** Weight lifter

Date	Mintage	VF20	XF40	MS60	MS63	MS65
1976	2,500	PF67 675				

KM# 25 100 TALA
15.55 g., 0.917 Gold 0.4584 oz. AGW **Subject:** Queen's Silver Jubilee

Date	Mintage	VF20	XF40	MS60	MS63	MS65
1977	2,500	PF67 675				

KM# 27 100 TALA
15.55 g., 0.917 Gold 0.4584 oz. AGW **Subject:** Lindbergh's New York to Paris flight **Obv:** National arms **Rev:** Bust 1/4 right, plane, statue of Liberty, Eiffel tower and dates

Date	Mintage	VF20	XF40	MS60	MS63	MS65
1977	660	PF67 775				

KM# 29 100 TALA
15.55 g., 0.917 Gold 0.4584 oz. AGW **Subject:** 50th Anniversary - Transpacific Flight **Obv:** National arms **Rev:** Globe with plane flying across Pacific Ocean, portrait of Lindbergh facing left

Date	Mintage	VF20	XF40	MS60	MS63	MS65
1978	1,500	PF67 750				

KM# 31 100 TALA
15.55 g., 0.917 Gold 0.4584 oz. AGW **Subject:** XI Commonwealth Games **Obv:** National arms **Rev:** Runners

Date	Mintage	VF20	XF40	MS60	MS63	MS65
1978	1,000	PF67 775				

KM# 34 100 TALA
12.50 g., 0.917 Gold 0.3685 oz. AGW **Subject:** Bicentenary - death of Capt. James Cook **Obv:** National arms **Rev:** Portrait of Cook at left of sailing ship

Date	Mintage	VF20	XF40	MS60	MS63	MS65
1979	1,000	PF67 625				

KM# 37 100 TALA
7.50 g., 0.917 Gold 0.2211 oz. AGW **Series:** 1980 Moscow Olympics **Obv:** National arms **Rev:** Hurdles event, Moscow Olympic logo below

Date	Mintage	XF40	MS60	MS63	MS65	MS66
1980	250	—	—	—	—	450
1980	1,000	PF67 425				

KM# 42 100 TALA
7.50 g., 0.917 Gold 0.2211 oz. AGW **Subject:** Gov. Wilhelm Solf **Obv:** National arms **Rev:** Uniformed bust left flanked by huts and palm trees

Date	Mintage	XF40	MS60	MS63	MS65	MS66
1980	250	—	—	—	—	425
1980	1,000	PF67 450				

KM# 45 100 TALA
7.50 g., 0.917 Gold 0.2211 oz. AGW **Subject:** Wedding of Prince Charles and Lady Diana **Obv:** National arms **Rev:** Conjoined busts left

Date	Mintage	XF40	MS60	MS63	MS65	MS66
1981	250	—	—	—	—	450
1981	1,500	PF67 425				

KM# 49 100 TALA
7.50 g., 0.917 Gold 0.2211 oz. AGW **Subject:** IYDP - President Franklin Roosevelt **Obv:** National arms **Rev:** Seated figure in wheelchair facing

Date	Mintage	XF40	MS60	MS63	MS65	MS66
1981	250	—	—	—	—	450
1981	1,500	PF67 425				

KM# 52 100 TALA
7.50 g., 0.917 Gold 0.2211 oz. AGW **Subject:** Commonwealth Games **Obv:** National arms **Rev:** Javelin thrower

Date	Mintage	XF40	MS60	MS63	MS65	MS66
1982	250	—	—	—	—	450
1982	1,000	PF67 425				

KM# 55 100 TALA
7.50 g., 0.917 Gold 0.2211 oz. AGW **Subject:** South Pacific Games **Obv:** National arms **Rev:** Runner

Date	Mintage	XF40	MS60	MS63	MS65	MS66
1983	—	—	—	—	—	450
1983	1,000	PF67 425				

KM# 60 100 TALA
7.50 g., 0.917 Gold 0.2211 oz. AGW **Series:** Summer Olympics **Obv:** National arms **Rev:** Boxing match

Date	Mintage	XF40	MS60	MS63	MS65	MS66
1984	200	—	—	—	—	450
1984	500	PF67 450				

KM# 68 100 TALA
7.50 g., 0.900 Gold 0.217 oz. AGW **Subject:** America's Cup Race **Obv:** National arms **Rev:** Ship

Date	Mintage	VF20	XF40	MS60	MS63	MS65
1987	—	PF67 435				

KM# 77 100 TALA
7.50 g., 0.900 Gold 0.217 oz. AGW **Subject:** Kon-Tiki **Obv:** National arms **Rev:** Boat and inscription

Date	Mintage	VF20	XF40	MS60	MS63	MS65
1988	1,500	PF67 425				

KM# 81 100 TALA
7.50 g., 0.917 Gold 0.2211 oz. AGW **Series:** Save the Children **Obv:** National arms **Rev:** Children playing

Date	Mintage	VF20	XF40	MS60	MS63	MS65
1990	3,000	PF67 375				

KM# 84 100 TALA
7.50 g., 0.917 Gold 0.2211 oz. AGW **Subject:** RA expeditions **Obv:** National arms **Rev:** Ship (RA II)

Date	Mintage	VF20	XF40	MS60	MS63	MS65
1991	5,000	PF67 375				

KM# 87 100 TALA
7.50 g., 0.900 Gold 0.217 oz. AGW **Series:** Olympics **Obv:** National arms **Rev:** Torch runner

Date	Mintage	VF20	XF40	MS60	MS63	MS65
1991	—	PF67 425				

KM# 96 100 TALA
7.50 g., 0.917 Gold 0.2211 oz. AGW **Subject:** Tigris Expedition **Obv:** National arms **Rev:** Tigris sailing

Date	Mintage	VF20	XF40	MS60	MS63	MS65
1994	2,000	PF67 420				

KM# 126 100 TALA
7.50 g., 0.916 Gold 0.2209 oz. AGW, 28.5 mm. **Subject:** Robert Louis Stevenson **Obv:** National arms **Rev:** Ship and portrait **Edge:** Reeded

Date	Mintage	VF20	XF40	MS60	MS63	MS65
ND(1994)	—	PF67 425				

KM# 130 200 TALA
14.70 g., 0.999 Gold 0.4721 oz. AGW, 38.7x22.85 mm. **Subject:** People and Buildings **Obv:** National arms, value and dates **Rev:** Statue of Liberty **Edge:** Plain **Shape:** Coin halved, with jagged inside edge

Date	Mintage	VF20	XF40	MS60	MS63	MS65
1999-2000	—	PF67 825				

KM# 136 500 TALA
69.82 g., 0.999 Gold 2.2425 oz. AGW, 36.4 mm. **Obv:** National arms **Rev:** Dove and sword handle above two soldiers **Edge:** Plain **Note:** Jagged coin half matching with Kiribati KM#36

Date	Mintage	VF20	XF40	MS60	MS63	MS65
2000	99	PF67 3,500				

KM# 46 1000 TALA
33.95 g., 0.917 Gold 1.0009 oz. AGW **Subject:** Wedding of Prince Charles and Lady Diana **Obv:** National arms **Rev:** Conjoined busts left

Date	Mintage	VF20	XF40	MS60	MS63	MS65
1981	100	PF65 1,450	PF67 1,650			

KM# 56 1000 TALA
31.10 g., 0.917 Gold 0.9169 oz. AGW **Subject:** South Pacific Games **Obv:** National arms **Rev:** Runner

Date	Mintage	VF20	XF40	MS60	MS63	MS65
1983	100	PF65 1,350	PF67 1,500			

KM# 61 1000 TALA
31.10 g., 0.917 Gold 0.9169 oz. AGW **Series:** 1984 Olympics **Obv:** National arms **Rev:** Boxing match

Date	Mintage	VF20	XF40	MS60	MS63	MS65
1984	100	PF65 1,350				

KM# 65 1000 TALA
33.95 g., 0.917 Gold 1.0009 oz. AGW **Subject:** Prince Andrew and Sarah Fereguson's Marriage **Obv:** National arms **Rev:** Conjoined busts left

Date	Mintage	VF20	XF40	MS60	MS63	MS65
1986	50	PF65 1,600	PF67 1,800			

KM# 110 1000 TALA
33.95 g., 0.917 Gold 1.0009 oz. AGW **Subject:** 40th Anniversary - Reign of Queen Elizabeth II **Obv:** National arms **Rev:** Royal carriage and guard around Order of the Garter

Date	Mintage	VF20	XF40	MS60	MS63	MS65
1992	Est. 150	PF65 1,450	PF67 1,650			

PIEDFORT

KM#	Date	Mintage	Identification	Mkt Val
P1	1984	3,000	Tala. 0.925. Silver. KM57.	85.00
P2	1992	Est. 750	Tala. 0.925. Silver. KM109.	95.00

COMBINED PROOF SETS

KM#	Date	Mintage	Identification	Issue Price	Mkt Val
CPS1	1997 (4)	10,000	West Samoa KM#115-118, Kiribati KM#22-25	—	225

MINT SETS

KM#	Date	Mintage	Identification	Issue Price	Mkt Val
MS1	1967 (6)	—	KM1-6	—	5.00
MS2	1974 (7)	10,740	KM12-17, 19	5.30	7.50

PROOF SETS

KM#	Date	Mintage	Identification	Issue Price	Mkt Val
PS1	1967 (7)	15,000	KM1-7	10.00	12.00
PS2	1974 (7)	5,578	KM12a-17a, 19a	53.00	75.00
PS3	1988 (3)	—	KM75-77	—	1,450
PS4	1991 (2)	1,000	KM83-84	—	485
PS5	1994 (3)	500	KM94-96	—	525

SAN MARINO

The Republic of San Marino, the oldest and smallest republic in the world is located in north central Italy entirely surrounded by the Province of Emilia-Romagna. It has an area of 24 sq. mi. (60 sq. km.) and a population of *23,000. Capital: San Marino. The principal economic activities are farming, livestock raising, cheese making, tourism and light manufacturing. Building stone, lime, wheat, hides and baked goods are exported. The government derives most of its revenue from the sale of postage stamps for philatelic purposes.

According to tradition, San Marino was founded about 350AD by a Christian stonecutter as a refuge against religious persecution. While gradually acquiring the institutions of an independent state, it avoided the factional fights of the Middle Ages and, except for a brief period in fief to Cesare Borgia, retained its freedom despite attacks on its sovereignty by the Papacy, the Lords of Rimini, Napoleon and Mussolini. In 1862 San Marino established a customs union with, and put itself under the protection of, Italy. A Communist-Socialist coalition controlled the Government for 12 years after World War II. The Christian Democratic Party has been the core of government since 1957. In 1978 a Communist-Socialist coalition again came into power and remained in control until 1991.

San Marino has its own coinage, but Italian and Vatican City coins and currency are also in circulation.

MINT MARKS

M - Milan

R – Rome

MONETARY SYSTEM

100 Centesimi = 1 Lira

REPUBLIC

STANDARD COINAGE

KM# 12 5 CENTESIMI

3.20 g., Bronze, 19.5 mm. **Obv:** Crowned pointed arms within wreath **Rev:** Value and date

Date	Mintage	F12	VF20	XF40	MS60	MS63
1935 R	800,000	2.00	3.00	6.00	12.00	15.00
1936 R	400,000	2.00	3.00	6.00	12.00	15.00
1937 R	200,000	3.00	6.00	10.00	20.00	25.00
1938 R	200,000	3.00	6.00	10.00	20.00	25.00

KM# 13 10 CENTESIMI

5.30 g., Bronze, 22.5 mm. **Obv:** Crowned pointed arms within wreath **Rev:** Value and date

Date	Mintage	F12	VF20	XF40	MS60	MS63
1935 R	600,000	2.00	3.00	6.00	10.00	15.00
1936 R	300,000	2.00	3.00	6.00	10.00	15.00
1937 R	400,000	2.00	3.00	6.00	10.00	15.00
1938 R	400,000	2.00	3.00	6.00	10.00	15.00

KM# 4 LIRA

5.00 g., 0.835 Silver 0.1342 oz. ASW, 23 mm. **Obv:** Crowned arms within wreath **Obv. Legend:** RESPVBLICA S. MARINI **Rev:** Value, date within wreath

Date	Mintage	F12	VF20	XF40	MS60	MS63
1906 R	30,000	15.00	22.50	40.00	75.00	150

KM# 14 LIRA

Aluminum **Obv:** Bust of Saint 1/4 left **Rev:** Value above arms without shield

Date	Mintage	VF20	XF40	MS60	MS63	MS65
1972	291,000	—	—	0.10	0.20	0.30

KM# 22 LIRA

Aluminum **Obv:** Crowned shield **Rev:** Girl with national flag

Date	Mintage	VF20	XF40	MS60	MS63	MS65
1973	291,000	—	—	0.10	0.20	0.30

KM# 30 LIRA

Aluminum **Obv:** Ostrich feathers and towers within circle **Rev:** Ant

Date	Mintage	VF20	XF40	MS60	MS63	MS65
1974	276,000	—	—	0.25	1.25	2.50

KM# 40 LIRA

Aluminum **Obv:** Ostrich feathers and towers within circle **Rev:** Spiders in web

Date	Mintage	VF20	XF40	MS60	MS63	MS65
1975	291,000	—	—	0.25	1.25	2.50

KM# 51 LIRA

Aluminum **Obv:** Ostrich feathers and towers **Rev:** Crossed flags flanked by hands

Date	Mintage	VF20	XF40	MS60	MS63	MS65
1976	195,000	—	—	0.10	0.20	0.30

KM# 63 LIRA

0.65 g., Aluminum **Series:** F.A.O. **Obv:** Ostrich feathers and towers within circle **Rev:** Globe in center of star wreath

Date	Mintage	VF20	XF40	MS60	MS63	MS65
1977	1,180,000	—	—	0.10	0.20	0.30

KM# 76 LIRA

Aluminum **Obv:** Value below ostrich feathers and towers **Rev:** Sitting figure within spider web

Date	Mintage	VF20	XF40	MS60	MS63	MS65
1978	130,000	—	—	0.15	0.30	0.40

KM# 89 LIRA

Aluminum **Obv:** Crowned shield **Rev:** Sword handle divides value

Date	Mintage	VF20	XF40	MS60	MS63	MS65
1979	125,000	—	—	0.15	0.30	0.40

KM# 102 LIRA

Aluminum **Series:** 1980 Olympics **Obv:** Olympic circles and date to left of ostrich feathers and towers **Rev:** Ballerina

Date	Mintage	VF20	XF40	MS60	MS63	MS65
1980	125,000	—	—	0.15	0.30	0.40

KM# 116 LIRA

Aluminum **Obv:** Crowned shield **Rev:** Value within design

Date	Mintage	VF20	XF40	MS60	MS63	MS65
1981 R	100,000	—	—	0.15	0.30	0.40

KM# 131 LIRA

Aluminum **Subject:** Social conquest **Obv:** Crown above ostrich feathers and towers **Rev:** Back of standing figure divides date and value

Date	Mintage	VF20	XF40	MS60	MS63	MS65
1982 R	78,000	—	—	0.15	0.30	0.40

KM# 145 LIRA

Aluminum **Subject:** Nuclear war threat **Obv:** Crowned shield above sprig **Rev:** Beast of war

Date	Mintage	VF20	XF40	MS60	MS63	MS65
1983 R	72,000	—	—	0.20	0.40	0.50

KM# 159 LIRA

Aluminum **Obv:** Castle **Rev:** Bust facing flanked by value and caduceus

Date	Mintage	VF20	XF40	MS60	MS63	MS65
1984 R	65,000	—	—	0.20	0.40	0.50

KM# 173 LIRA
Aluminum **Subject:** War on drugs **Obv:** Shield **Rev:** Supine male 1/2 length figure below value and date

Date	Mintage	VF20	XF40	MS60	MS63	MS65
1985 R	60,000	—	—	0.10	0.25	0.35

KM# 187 LIRA
Aluminum **Subject:** Revolution of technology **Obv:** Crown above ostrich feathers and towers on rock **Rev:** Footprints on the moon

Date	Mintage	VF20	XF40	MS60	MS63	MS65
1986 R	50,000	—	—	0.10	0.25	0.35

KM# 201 LIRA
Aluminum **Subject:** 15th Anniversary - Resumption of Coinage **Obv:** Crowned pointed arms within sprigs **Rev:** Tree flanked by value

Date	Mintage	VF20	XF40	MS60	MS63	MS65
1987 R	83,000	—	—	0.10	0.25	0.35

KM# 218 LIRA
Aluminum **Subject:** Fortifications **Obv:** Crowned ornate arms on shield **Rev:** Corner Tower

Date	Mintage	VF20	XF40	MS60	MS63	MS65
1988 R	38,000	—	—	0.10	0.25	0.35

KM# 231 LIRA
Aluminum **Subject:** History **Obv:** Crowned shield **Rev:** Stone Age tool

Date	Mintage	VF20	XF40	MS60	MS63	MS65
1989 R	37,000	—	—	0.10	0.25	0.35

KM# 248 LIRA
Aluminum **Subject:** 1,600 Years of History **Obv:** Stylized towers **Rev:** Stylized Saint

Date	Mintage	VF20	XF40	MS60	MS63	MS65
1990 R	36,000	—	—	0.10	0.25	0.35

KM# 261 LIRA
Aluminum **Obv:** Date to upper left of ostrich feathers and towers **Rev:** Hands holding hammer and chisel below value

Date	Mintage	VF20	XF40	MS60	MS63	MS65
1991 R	—	—	—	0.10	0.25	0.35

KM# 278 LIRA
Aluminum **Subject:** Columbus **Obv:** Towers with feathers above within circle **Rev:** Potatoes and plant within design with value at left

Date	Mintage	VF20	XF40	MS60	MS63	MS65
ND-1992 R	—	—	—	0.10	0.25	0.35

KM# 293 LIRA
Aluminum **Obv:** Stylized ostrich feathers and towers **Rev:** Seedling divides date and value

Date	Mintage	VF20	XF40	MS60	MS63	MS65
1993 R	—	—	—	0.10	0.25	0.35

KM# 306 LIRA
Aluminum **Obv:** Bust facing with arms holding hammer and chisel, smoking towers at left **Rev:** Mother and child

Date	Mintage	VF20	XF40	MS60	MS63	MS65
1994 R	40,000	—	—	0.10	0.25	0.35

KM# 322 LIRA
Aluminum **Obv:** Banner around design **Rev:** Child on broken sword divides sprig and value

Date	Mintage	VF20	XF40	MS60	MS63	MS65
1995 R	—	—	—	0.10	0.25	0.35

KM# 349 LIRA
Aluminum **Subject:** Talete - Child of the Universe **Obv:** Bust facing with flame within hands **Rev:** Value and date at left of head facing

Date	Mintage	VF20	XF40	MS60	MS63	MS65
1996 R	32,000	—	—	0.10	0.25	0.35

KM# 359 LIRA
Aluminum **Subject:** The Arts - Prehistoric **Obv:** Bust facing with flame within hands **Rev:** Elk

Date	Mintage	VF20	XF40	MS60	MS63	MS65
1997 R	28,000	—	—	0.10	0.25	0.75

KM# 5 2 LIRE
10.00 g., 0.835 Silver 0.2685 oz. ASW, 27 mm. **Obv:** Crowned arms within wreath **Obv. Legend:** RESPVBLICA S. MARINI **Rev:** Value, date within wreath

Date	Mintage	F12	VF20	XF40	MS60	MS63
1906 R	15,000	25.00	35.00	50.00	100	175

KM# 15 2 LIRE
Aluminum, 18 mm. **Obv:** Value above stylized ostrich feathers and towers **Rev:** Bust of Saint 1/4 right

Date	Mintage	VF20	XF40	MS60	MS63	MS65
1972	291,000	—	—	0.10	0.30	0.40

KM# 23 2 LIRE
Aluminum, 18 mm. **Obv:** Crowned shield **Rev:** Pelican

Date	Mintage	VF20	XF40	MS60	MS63	MS65
1973	291,000	—	—	0.20	1.00	2.25

KM# 31 2 LIRE
Aluminum, 18 mm. **Obv:** Ostrich feathers and towers within circle **Rev:** Beetle

Date	Mintage	VF20	XF40	MS60	MS63	MS65
1974	276,000	—	—	0.25	1.25	2.50

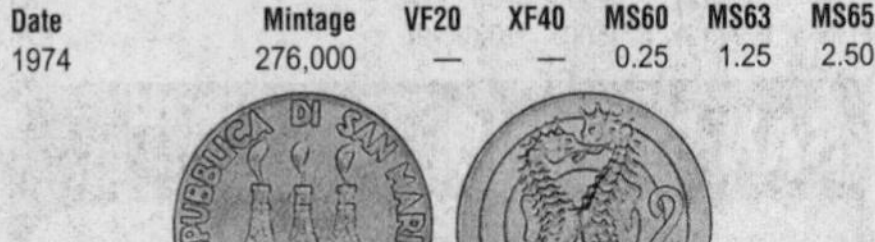

KM# 41 2 LIRE
Aluminum, 18 mm. **Obv:** Ostrich feathers and towers **Rev:** Seahorses

Date	Mintage	VF20	XF40	MS60	MS63	MS65
1975	291,000	—	—	0.25	1.25	2.25

KM# 52 2 LIRE
Aluminum, 18 mm. **Obv:** Ostrich feathers and towers **Rev:** Stylized sun, hills and sitting figure

Date	Mintage	VF20	XF40	MS60	MS63	MS65
1976	195,000	—	—	0.10	0.30	0.50

KM# 64 2 LIRE
Aluminum, 18 mm. **Obv:** Value and ostrich feathers and towers within circle **Rev:** Stars above wave-like designs within circle

Date	Mintage	VF20	XF40	MS60	MS63	MS65
1977	180,000	—	—	0.10	0.30	0.40

KM# 77 2 LIRE
Aluminum, 18 mm. **Obv:** Value below ostrich feathers and towers **Rev:** Standing figure working

Date	Mintage	VF20	XF40	MS60	MS63	MS65
1978	130,000	—	—	0.10	0.30	0.40

KM# 90 2 LIRE
Aluminum, 18 mm. **Obv:** Crowned shield **Rev:** Bugle with banner divides value

Date	Mintage	VF20	XF40	MS60	MS63	MS65
1979	125,000	—	—	0.10	0.30	0.40

KM# 103 2 LIRE

Aluminum, 18 mm. **Series:** 1980 Olympics **Obv:** Olympic rings and date to left of ostrich feathers and towers **Rev:** Soccer player

Date	Mintage	VF20	XF40	MS60	MS63	MS65
1980	125,000	—	—	0.25	0.45	0.75

KM# 117 2 LIRE

Aluminum, 18 mm. **Obv:** Crowned shield **Rev:** Small head and hand left, date and value at upper left

Date	Mintage	VF20	XF40	MS60	MS63	MS65
1981 R	100,000	—	—	0.10	0.30	0.40

KM# 132 2 LIRE

Aluminum, 18 mm. **Subject:** Social Conquests **Obv:** Crown above ostrich feathers and towers **Rev:** Value below stylized design

Date	Mintage	VF20	XF40	MS60	MS63	MS65
1982 R	78,000	—	—	0.10	0.30	0.40

KM# 146 2 LIRE

Aluminum, 18 mm. **Subject:** Nuclear war threat **Obv:** Crowned shield above sprig **Rev:** Two reaching arms

Date	Mintage	VF20	XF40	MS60	MS63	MS65
1983 R	72,000	—	—	0.20	0.40	0.50

KM# 160 2 LIRE

Aluminum, 18 mm. **Obv:** Castle **Rev:** Head facing

Date	Mintage	VF20	XF40	MS60	MS63	MS65
1984 R	65,000	—	—	0.20	0.40	0.50

KM# 174 2 LIRE

Aluminum, 18 mm. **Subject:** War on Drugs **Obv:** Shield **Rev:** Clenched fist

Date	Mintage	VF20	XF40	MS60	MS63	MS65
1985 R	60,000	—	—	0.10	0.25	0.35

KM# 188 2 LIRE

Aluminum, 18 mm. **Subject:** Revolution of Technology **Obv:** Crown above ostrich feathers and towers on rock **Rev:** Astronaut walking in space

Date	Mintage	VF20	XF40	MS60	MS63	MS65
1986 R	50,000	—	—	0.10	0.25	0.35

KM# 202 2 LIRE

Aluminum, 18 mm. **Subject:** 15th Anniversary - Resumption of Coinage **Obv:** Crowned pointed shield within sprigs **Rev:** Flower designs

Date	Mintage	VF20	XF40	MS60	MS63	MS65
1987 R	83,000	—	—	0.10	0.25	0.35

KM# 219 2 LIRE

Aluminum, 18 mm. **Subject:** Fortifications **Obv:** Crowned ornate arms on shield **Rev:** Fortified archway

Date	Mintage	VF20	XF40	MS60	MS63	MS65
1988 R	38,000	—	—	0.10	0.25	0.35

KM# 232 2 LIRE

Aluminum, 18 mm. **Subject:** History **Obv:** Crowned shield **Rev:** Value divides wheat stalk and olive branch

Date	Mintage	VF20	XF40	MS60	MS63	MS65
1989 R	37,000	—	—	0.10	0.25	0.35

KM# 249 2 LIRE

Aluminum, 18 mm. **Subject:** 1,600 Years of History **Obv:** Stylized towers **Rev:** Stylized figure with spear

Date	Mintage	VF20	XF40	MS60	MS63	MS65
1990 R	36,000	—	—	0.10	0.25	0.35

KM# 262 2 LIRE

Aluminum, 18 mm. **Obv:** Date to upper left of ostrich feathers and towers **Rev:** Hands with interlocked fingers below value

Date	Mintage	VF20	XF40	MS60	MS63	MS65
1991 R	—	—	—	0.10	0.25	0.35

KM# 279 2 LIRE

Aluminum, 18 mm. **Subject:** Columbus **Obv:** Towers with feathers above within circle **Rev:** Ear of corn to left of value within design

Date	Mintage	VF20	XF40	MS60	MS63	MS65
ND-1992 R	—	—	—	0.10	0.25	0.35

KM# 294 2 LIRE

Aluminum, 18 mm. **Obv:** Ostrich feathers and towers **Rev:** Rose

Date	Mintage	VF20	XF40	MS60	MS63	MS65
1993 R	—	—	—	0.10	0.25	0.35

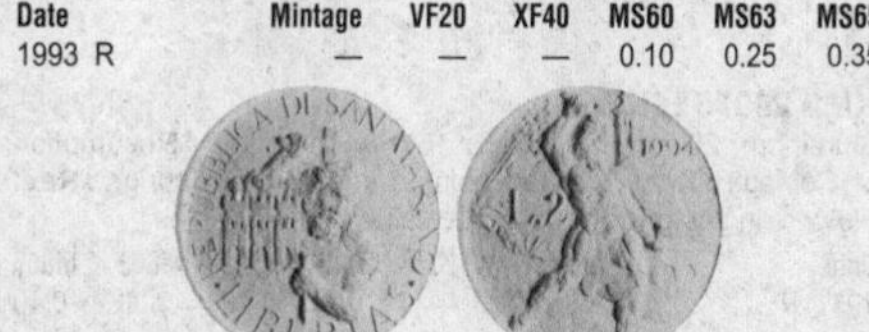

KM# 307 2 LIRE

Aluminum, 18 mm. **Obv:** Head with hands holding hammer and chisel, towers at left **Rev:** Standing stonecutter at work

Date	Mintage	VF20	XF40	MS60	MS63	MS65
1994 R	40,000	—	—	0.10	0.25	0.35

KM# 323 2 LIRE

Aluminum, 18 mm. **Obv:** Banner around bottom of design **Rev:** Child with toy castle

Date	Mintage	VF20	XF40	MS60	MS63	MS65
1995 R	—	—	—	0.10	0.25	0.35

KM# 350 2 LIRE

Aluminum, 18 mm. **Obv:** Bust facing with flame within hands **Rev:** Head of Socrates

Date	Mintage	VF20	XF40	MS60	MS63	MS65
1996 R	32,000	—	—	0.10	0.25	0.35

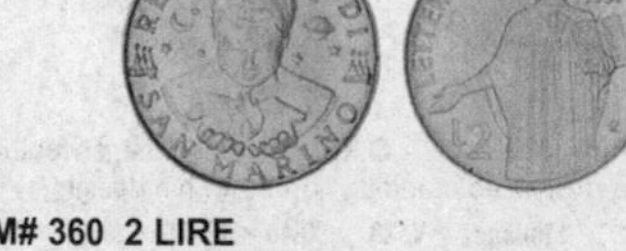

KM# 360 2 LIRE

Aluminum, 18 mm. **Subject:** The Arts - Literature **Obv:** Bust facing with flame within hands **Rev:** Dante holding Divine Comedy

Date	Mintage	VF20	XF40	MS60	MS63	MS65
1997 R	28,000	—	—	0.10	0.25	0.35

KM# 9 5 LIRE

5.00 g., 0.835 Silver 0.1342 oz. ASW, 23 mm. **Obv:** Bust left within beaded circle **Rev:** Plant divides value above plow

Date	Mintage	F12	VF20	XF40	MS60	MS63
1931 R	50,000	4.75	7.00	15.00	25.00	37.00
1932 R	50,000	4.75	7.00	15.00	25.00	37.00
1933 R	50,000	4.75	7.00	13.00	22.00	35.00
1935 R	200,000	4.50	6.50	12.00	15.00	20.00
1936 R	100,000	4.50	6.50	12.00	17.00	25.00
1937 R	100,000	4.50	6.50	12.00	17.00	25.00
1938 R	120,000	4.50	6.50	12.00	17.00	25.00

KM# 16 5 LIRE

Aluminum, 20 mm. **Obv:** Bust of Saint 1/4 left **Rev:** Value above stylized smoking towers

Date	Mintage	VF20	XF40	MS60	MS63	MS65
1972	291,000	—	—	0.10	0.35	0.45

KM# 24 5 LIRE

Aluminum, 20 mm. **Obv:** Crowned shield **Rev:** Five men rowing a boat, on a globe, under a starry sky

Date	Mintage	VF20	XF40	MS60	MS63	MS65
1973	291,000	—	—	0.10	0.35	0.45

KM# 32 5 LIRE

Aluminum, 20 mm. **Obv:** Ostrich feathers and towers within circle **Rev:** Porcupine

Date	Mintage	VF20	XF40	MS60	MS63	MS65
1974	276,000	—	—	0.25	1.25	2.50

KM# 42 5 LIRE
Aluminum, 20 mm. **Obv:** Ostrich feathers and towers **Rev:** Hedgehogs

Date	Mintage	VF20	XF40	MS60	MS63	MS65
1975	291,000	—	—	0.20	1.00	2.50

KM# 53 5 LIRE
Aluminum, 20 mm. **Series:** F.A.O. **Obv:** Stylized ostrich feathers and towers **Rev:** Stylized standing figures within design

Date	Mintage	VF20	XF40	MS60	MS63	MS65
1976	695,000	—	—	0.10	0.25	0.35

KM# 65 5 LIRE
Aluminum, 20 mm. **Obv:** Value below ostrich feathers and towers within circle **Rev:** Stars within circle

Date	Mintage	VF20	XF40	MS60	MS63	MS65
1977	180,000	—	—	0.10	0.35	0.45

KM# 78 5 LIRE
Aluminum, 20 mm. **Obv:** Value below ostrich feathers and towers **Rev:** Standing figure holding water hose

Date	Mintage	VF20	XF40	MS60	MS63	MS65
1978	130,000	—	—	0.10	0.35	0.45

KM# 91 5 LIRE
Aluminum, 20 mm. **Obv:** Crowned shield **Rev:** Crossbow divides value

Date	Mintage	VF20	XF40	MS60	MS63	MS65
1979	125,000	—	—	0.10	0.35	0.45

KM# 104 5 LIRE
Aluminum, 20 mm. **Series:** 1980 Olympics **Obv:** Olympic rings and date to left of ostrich feathers and towers **Rev:** Running figure right

Date	Mintage	VF20	XF40	MS60	MS63	MS65
1980	125,000	—	—	0.25	0.45	0.75

KM# 118 5 LIRE
Aluminum, 20 mm. **Obv:** Crowned shield **Rev:** Goat divides value and date

Date	Mintage	VF20	XF40	MS60	MS63	MS65
1981 R	100,000	—	—	0.25	0.75	2.50

KM# 133 5 LIRE
Aluminum, 20 mm. **Subject:** Social Conquests **Obv:** Crown above ostrich feathers and towers **Rev:** Stylized boats and plane

Date	Mintage	VF20	XF40	MS60	MS63	MS65
1982 R	78,000	—	—	0.10	0.30	0.40

KM# 147 5 LIRE
Aluminum, 20 mm. **Subject:** Nuclear War Threat **Obv:** Crown above shield and sprig **Rev:** Pair of reaching arms within barred window

Date	Mintage	VF20	XF40	MS60	MS63	MS65
1983 R	72,000	—	—	0.20	0.40	0.50

KM# 161 5 LIRE
Aluminum, 20 mm. **Obv:** Castle **Rev:** Bust of Galileo facing

Date	Mintage	VF20	XF40	MS60	MS63	MS65
1984 R	65,000	—	—	0.20	0.40	0.50

KM# 175 5 LIRE
Aluminum, 20 mm. **Subject:** War on Drugs **Obv:** Shield **Rev:** Face of addict

Date	Mintage	VF20	XF40	MS60	MS63	MS65
1985 R	60,000	—	—	0.10	0.30	0.40

KM# 189 5 LIRE
Aluminum, 20 mm. **Subject:** Revolution of Technology **Obv:** Crown above ostrich feathers and towers on rock **Rev:** Human figure operating larger robot

Date	Mintage	VF20	XF40	MS60	MS63	MS65
1986 R	50,000	—	—	0.10	0.30	0.40

KM# 203 5 LIRE
Aluminum, 20 mm. **Subject:** 15th Anniversary - Resumption of Coinage **Obv:** Crowned pointed shield within sprigs **Rev:** Flowers in designed vase divide value

Date	Mintage	VF20	XF40	MS60	MS63	MS65
1987 R	83,000	—	—	0.10	0.30	0.40

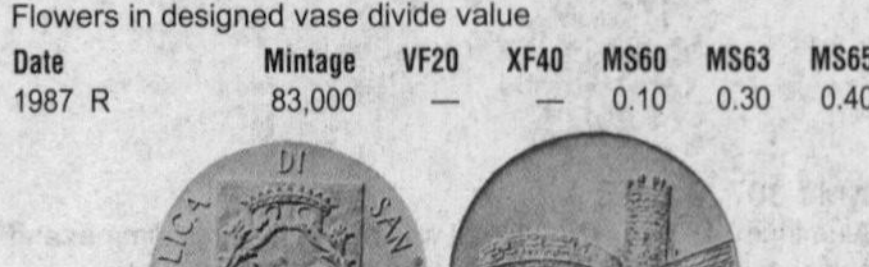

KM# 220 5 LIRE
Aluminum, 20 mm. **Subject:** Fortification **Obv:** Crowned ornate arms on shield **Rev:** Round corner tower

Date	Mintage	VF20	XF40	MS60	MS63	MS65
1988 R	38,000	—	—	0.10	0.30	0.40

KM# 233 5 LIRE
Aluminum, 20 mm. **Subject:** History **Obv:** Crowned shield **Rev:** Cluster of grapes divide value

Date	Mintage	VF20	XF40	MS60	MS63	MS65
1989 R	37,000	—	—	0.10	0.30	0.40

KM# 250 5 LIRE
Aluminum, 20 mm. **Subject:** 1,600 Years of History **Obv:** Stylized towers above design **Rev:** Two stylized facing figures

Date	Mintage	VF20	XF40	MS60	MS63	MS65
1990 R	36,000	—	—	0.10	0.30	0.40

KM# 263 5 LIRE
Aluminum, 20 mm. **Obv:** Date to upper left of ostrich feathers and towers **Rev:** Hand holding quill below value

Date	Mintage	VF20	XF40	MS60	MS63	MS65
1991 R	—	—	—	0.10	0.30	0.40

KM# 280 5 LIRE
Aluminum, 20 mm. **Subject:** Columbus **Obv:** Towers with feathers above within circle **Rev:** Cotton plants and value within design

Date	Mintage	VF20	XF40	MS60	MS63	MS65
ND-1992 R	—	—	—	0.10	0.30	0.40

KM# 295 5 LIRE
Aluminum, 20 mm. **Obv:** Ostrich feathers and towers **Rev:** Spade and hoe

Date	Mintage	VF20	XF40	MS60	MS63	MS65
1993 R	—	—	—	0.10	0.30	0.40

KM# 308 5 LIRE
Aluminum, 20 mm. **Obv:** Stone cutter holding hammer and chisel, towers at left **Rev:** Standing figures with tools

Date	Mintage	VF20	XF40	MS60	MS63	MS65
1994 R	40,000	—	—	0.10	0.30	0.40

KM# 324 5 LIRE
Aluminum, 20 mm. **Obv:** Banner wrapped around quills **Rev:** Child with 2 deer

Date	Mintage	VF20	XF40	MS60	MS63	MS65
1995 R	—	—	—	0.10	0.30	0.40

KM# 351 5 LIRE
Aluminum, 20 mm. **Obv:** Bust facing with flame within hands **Rev:** Plato

Date	Mintage	VF20	XF40	MS60	MS63	MS65
1996 R	32,000	—	—	0.10	0.30	0.40

KM# 361 5 LIRE
Aluminum, 20 mm. **Subject:** The Arts - Theater **Obv:** Bust facing with flame within hands **Rev:** Hamlet with skull

Date	Mintage	VF20	XF40	MS60	MS63	MS65
1997 R	28,000	—	—	0.10	0.30	0.40

KM# 7 10 LIRE
3.23 g., 0.900 Gold 0.0933 oz. AGW **Obv:** Stylized ostrich feathers and towers within circle **Rev:** Standing Saint facing divides value **Note:** 16,000 coins melted at the mint.

Date	Mintage	F12	VF20	XF40	MS60	MS63
1925 R	20,000	175	475	750	1,250	1,500

KM# 10 10 LIRE
10.00 g., 0.835 Silver 0.2685 oz. ASW, 27 mm. **Obv:** Nine sided shield divides value within circle, crown at top divides circle **Rev:** Facing figure holding crown divides date within circle

Date	Mintage	F12	VF20	XF40	MS60	MS63
1931 R	25,000	9.50	15.00	25.00	45.00	75.00
1932 R	25,000	9.50	15.00	25.00	45.00	75.00
1933 R	25,000	9.50	15.00	25.00	45.00	75.00
1935 R	30,000	8.50	12.50	22.00	40.00	65.00
1936 R	15,000	10.00	18.00	30.00	50.00	80.00
1937 R	20,000	8.50	12.50	22.00	40.00	65.00
1938 R	10,000	12.00	20.00	40.00	75.00	150

KM# 17 10 LIRE
1.60 g., Aluminum, 23.3 mm. **Obv:** Stylized ostrich feathers and towers **Rev:** Cow nursing calf

Date	Mintage	VF20	XF40	MS60	MS63	MS65
1972	291,000	—	0.10	0.20	0.50	2.50

KM# 25 10 LIRE
1.60 g., Aluminum, 23.3 mm. **Obv:** Crowned shield **Rev:** Hercules fighting the Hydra

Date	Mintage	VF20	XF40	MS60	MS63	MS65
1973	291,000	—	0.10	0.15	0.40	0.50

KM# 33 10 LIRE
1.60 g., Aluminum, 23.3 mm. **Series:** F.A.O. **Obv:** Ostrich feathers and towers within circle **Rev:** Bee

Date	Mintage	VF20	XF40	MS60	MS63	MS65
1974	1,276,000	—	—	0.15	0.45	1.50

KM# 43 10 LIRE
1.60 g., Aluminum, 23.3 mm. **Obv:** Ostrich feathers and towers **Rev:** Rats divide value

Date	Mintage	VF20	XF40	MS60	MS63	MS65
1975	291,000	—	0.10	0.25	1.00	2.50

KM# 54 10 LIRE
1.60 g., Aluminum, 23.3 mm. **Obv:** Stylized ostrich feathers and towers **Rev:** Fetus within circle, standing baby at left

Date	Mintage	VF20	XF40	MS60	MS63	MS65
1976	195,000	—	0.10	0.15	0.40	0.50

KM# 66 10 LIRE
1.60 g., Aluminum, 23.3 mm. **Obv:** Stylized ostrich feathers and towers within circle **Rev:** Foot above 1/2 designed star wreath

Date	Mintage	VF20	XF40	MS60	MS63	MS65
1977	180,000	—	0.10	0.15	0.40	0.50

KM# 79 10 LIRE
1.60 g., Aluminum, 23.3 mm. **Obv:** Value below ostrich feathers and towers **Rev:** Seated figure

Date	Mintage	VF20	XF40	MS60	MS63	MS65
1978	130,000	—	0.10	0.15	0.40	0.50

KM# 92 10 LIRE
1.60 g., Aluminum, 23.3 mm. **Obv:** Crowned shield **Rev:** Date flanked by two crowned shields on stands

Date	Mintage	VF20	XF40	MS60	MS63	MS65
1979	125,000	—	0.10	0.15	0.40	0.50

KM# 105 10 LIRE
1.60 g., Aluminum, 23.3 mm. **Series:** 1980 Olympics **Obv:** Olympic rings and date to left of ostrich feathers and towers **Rev:** Jumping equestrian

Date	Mintage	VF20	XF40	MS60	MS63	MS65
1980	125,000	0.25	0.50	0.80	1.50	—

KM# 119 10 LIRE
1.60 g., Aluminum, 23.3 mm. **Obv:** Crowned shield **Rev:** Value surrounded by nude figure

Date	Mintage	VF20	XF40	MS60	MS63	MS65
1981 R	100,000	—	0.10	0.20	0.50	0.60

KM# 134 10 LIRE
1.60 g., Aluminum, 23.3 mm. **Subject:** Social Conquests **Obv:** Crown above ostrich feathers and towers **Rev:** Stylized figures

Date	Mintage	VF20	XF40	MS60	MS63	MS65
1982 R	78,000	—	0.10	0.20	0.50	0.60

KM# 148 10 LIRE
1.60 g., Aluminum, 23.3 mm. **Subject:** Nuclear War Threat **Obv:** Crown above shield and sprig **Rev:** Vertical line within square divides reaching arms

Date	Mintage	VF20	XF40	MS60	MS63	MS65
1983 R	72,000	—	0.10	0.25	0.75	0.85

KM# 162 10 LIRE
1.60 g., Aluminum, 23.3 mm. **Subject:** Alessandro Volta **Obv:** Castle **Rev:** Bust 3/4 right

Date	Mintage	VF20	XF40	MS60	MS63	MS65
1984 R	65,000	—	0.10	0.25	0.75	0.85

KM# 176 10 LIRE
1.60 g., Aluminum, 23.3 mm. **Subject:** War on Drugs **Obv:** Shield **Rev:** Mother lecturing son

Date	Mintage	VF20	XF40	MS60	MS63	MS65
1985 R	60,000	—	—	0.10	0.35	0.45

KM# 190 10 LIRE
1.60 g., Aluminum, 23.3 mm. **Subject:** Revolution of Technology **Obv:** Crown above ostrich feathers and towers on rock **Rev:** Radio receiver

Date	Mintage	VF20	XF40	MS60	MS63	MS65
1986 R	50,000	—	—	0.10	0.35	0.45

KM# 204 10 LIRE
1.60 g., Aluminum, 23.3 mm. **Subject:** 15th Anniversary - Resumption of Coinage **Obv:** Crowned pointed shield within sprigs **Rev:** Tower divides value

Date	Mintage	VF20	XF40	MS60	MS63	MS65
1987 R	83,000	—	—	0.10	0.35	0.45

KM# 221 10 LIRE
1.60 g., Aluminum, 23.3 mm. **Subject:** Fortifications **Obv:** Crowned ornate arms on shield **Rev:** Sloping fortress wall

Date	Mintage	VF20	XF40	MS60	MS63	MS65
1988 R	38,000	—	—	0.10	0.35	0.45

KM# 234 10 LIRE
1.60 g., Aluminum, 23.3 mm. **Subject:** History **Obv:** Crowned shield **Rev:** Ancient pottery divides value

Date	Mintage	VF20	XF40	MS60	MS63	MS65
1989 R	37,000	—	—	0.10	0.35	0.45

KM# 251 10 LIRE
1.60 g., Aluminum, 23.3 mm. **Subject:** 1,600 Years of History **Obv:** Stylized towers above design **Rev:** Stylized soldier

Date	Mintage	VF20	XF40	MS60	MS63	MS65
1990 R	36,000	—	—	0.10	0.35	0.45

KM# 264 10 LIRE
1.60 g., Aluminum, 23.3 mm. **Obv:** Date at left of smoking towers **Rev:** Value above hand holding castle tower

Date	Mintage	VF20	XF40	MS60	MS63	MS65
1991 R	—	—	—	0.10	0.35	0.45

KM# 281 10 LIRE
1.60 g., Aluminum, 23.3 mm. **Subject:** Columbus **Obv:** Towers with feathers above within circle **Rev:** Dolphin, ship and value within globe design

Date	Mintage	VF20	XF40	MS60	MS63	MS65
ND-1992 R	—	—	—	0.20	0.75	2.00

KM# 296 10 LIRE
1.60 g., Aluminum, 23.3 mm. **Obv:** Ostrich feathers and towers **Rev:** Value above corinthian column

Date	Mintage	VF20	XF40	MS60	MS63	MS65
1993 R	—	—	—	0.10	0.35	0.45

KM# 309 10 LIRE
1.60 g., Aluminum, 23.3 mm. **Obv:** Stone cutter holding hammer and chisel, towers at left **Rev:** Marino and Leo working

Date	Mintage	VF20	XF40	MS60	MS63	MS65
1994 R	40,000	—	—	0.10	0.35	0.45

KM# 325 10 LIRE
1.60 g., Aluminum, 23.3 mm. **Obv:** Banner wrapped around bottom of design **Rev:** Child holding two urns within square

Date	Mintage	VF20	XF40	MS60	MS63	MS65
1995 R	—	—	—	0.10	0.35	0.45

KM# 352 10 LIRE
1.60 g., Aluminum, 23.3 mm. **Obv:** Bust facing with flame within hands **Rev:** Aristotle

Date	Mintage	VF20	XF40	MS60	MS63	MS65
1996 R	28,000	—	—	0.10	0.35	0.45

KM# 362 10 LIRE
1.60 g., Aluminum, 23.3 mm. **Subject:** The Arts - Architecture **Obv:** Bust facing with flame within hands **Rev:** Building on pillars

Date	Mintage	VF20	XF40	MS60	MS63	MS65
1997 R	28,000	—	—	0.10	0.35	0.45

KM# 378 10 LIRE
1.60 g., Aluminum, 23.3 mm. **Subject:** Mathematics **Rev:** Hand and geometric shape

Date	Mintage	VF20	XF40	MS60	MS63	MS65
1998 R	—	—	—	0.10	0.35	0.45

KM# 389 10 LIRE
1.60 g., Aluminum, 23.3 mm. **Subject:** Exploration **Obv:** Crowned shield **Rev:** Earth flat, as once envisioned

Date	Mintage	VF20	XF40	MS60	MS63	MS65
1999 R	—	—	—	0.10	0.35	0.45

KM# 399 10 LIRE
1.60 g., Aluminum, 23.3 mm. **Subject:** Love **Obv:** Bust facing with flame within hands **Rev:** Child within poinsettia and globe design **Edge:** Plain **Note:** Struck at Rome.

Date	Mintage	VF20	XF40	MS60	MS63	MS65
2000 R	—	—	—	0.10	0.35	0.45

KM# 8 20 LIRE
6.45 g., 0.900 Gold 0.1867 oz. AGW **Obv:** Smoking towers **Rev:** Standing Saint figure divides value **Note:** 7,334 coins were melted at the mint.

Date	Mintage	F12	VF20	XF40	MS60	MS63
1925 R	9,334	650	1,700	2,500	3,500	4,000

KM# 11 20 LIRE
15.00 g., 0.800 Silver 0.3858 oz. ASW **Obv:** Upright stylized ostrich feathers above value with crown above **Rev:** Half length figure holding smoking towers within circle

Date	Mintage	F12	VF20	XF40	MS60	MS63
1931 R	10,000	25.00	45.00	90.00	145	200
1932 R	10,000	35.00	60.00	110	185	240
1933 R	10,000	30.00	50.00	100	175	225
1935 R	10,000	30.00	50.00	100	175	225
1936 R	5,000	60.00	125	200	300	450

KM# 11a 20 LIRE
20.00 g., 0.800 Silver 0.5144 oz. ASW **Obv:** Stylized upright feathers above value with crown above **Rev:** Half length figure holding smoking towers within circle

Date	Mintage	F12	VF20	XF40	MS60	MS63
1935 R Rare	2	—	—	—	—	—
1937 R	5,100	100	120	200	450	800
1938 R	2,500	200	300	400	850	1,350

KM# 18 20 LIRE
3.60 g., Aluminum-Bronze, 21.25 mm. **Obv:** Stylized ostrich feathers and towers **Rev:** Standing figures

Date	Mintage	VF20	XF40	MS60	MS63	MS65
1972	291,000	—	0.10	0.25	0.60	0.70

KM# 26 20 LIRE
3.60 g., Aluminum-Bronze, 21.25 mm. **Obv:** Crowned shield **Rev:** Man rescuing old man and baby from fire

Date	Mintage	VF20	XF40	MS60	MS63	MS65
1973	291,000	—	0.10	0.25	0.60	0.70

KM# 34 20 LIRE
3.60 g., Aluminum-Bronze, 21.25 mm. **Obv:** Ostrich feathers and towers within circle **Rev:** Lobster

Date	Mintage	VF20	XF40	MS60	MS63	MS65
1974	276,000	—	0.10	0.30	1.50	2.50

KM# 44 20 LIRE
3.60 g., Aluminum-Bronze, 21.25 mm. **Series:** F.A.O. **Obv:** Ostrich feathers and towers **Rev:** Bird feeding its nestlings

Date	Mintage	VF20	XF40	MS60	MS63	MS65
1975	291,000	—	0.10	0.30	0.75	1.25

KM# 55 20 LIRE
3.60 g., Aluminum-Bronze, 21.25 mm. **Obv:** Stylized ostrich feathers and towers **Rev:** Design flanked by stylized hands

Date	Mintage	VF20	XF40	MS60	MS63	MS65
1976	195,000	—	0.10	0.25	0.60	0.70

KM# 67 20 LIRE
3.60 g., Aluminum-Bronze, 21.25 mm. **Obv:** Ostrich feathers and towers **Rev:** Circular pattern within stylized hand

Date	Mintage	VF20	XF40	MS60	MS63	MS65
1977	180,000	—	0.10	0.25	0.60	0.70

KM# 80 20 LIRE
3.60 g., Aluminum-Bronze, 21.25 mm. **Obv:** Value below ostrich feathers and towers **Rev:** Kneeling figure

Date	Mintage	VF20	XF40	MS60	MS63	MS65
1978	130,000	—	0.10	0.25	0.60	0.70

KM# 93 20 LIRE
3.60 g., Aluminum-Bronze, 21.25 mm. **Obv:** Crowned shield **Rev:** Crowned skeleton keys divide value

Date	Mintage	VF20	XF40	MS60	MS63	MS65
1979	125,000	—	0.10	0.30	0.60	0.70

KM# 106 20 LIRE
3.60 g., Aluminum-Bronze, 21.25 mm. **Series:** 1980 Olympics **Obv:** Olympic rings and date to left of ostrich feathers and towers **Rev:** Pole vaulter

Date	Mintage	VF20	XF40	MS60	MS63	MS65
1980	125,000	—	0.25	0.50	1.00	1.50

KM# 120 20 LIRE
3.60 g., Aluminum-Bronze, 21.25 mm. **Obv:** Crowned shield **Rev:** Value above bird

Date	Mintage	VF20	XF40	MS60	MS63	MS65
1981 R	100,000	—	0.10	0.30	0.75	2.00

KM# 135 20 LIRE
3.60 g., Aluminum-Bronze, 21.25 mm. **Subject:** Social conquests **Obv:** Crown above ostrich feathers and towers **Rev:** Standing figures within design

Date	Mintage	VF20	XF40	MS60	MS63	MS65
1982 R	78,000	—	0.10	0.25	0.60	0.75

KM# 149 20 LIRE
3.60 g., Aluminum-Bronze, 21.25 mm. **Subject:** Nuclear war threat **Obv:** Crown above shield and sprig **Rev:** Torch above man

Date	Mintage	VF20	XF40	MS60	MS63	MS65
1983 R	72,000	—	0.10	0.30	0.75	0.85

KM# 163 20 LIRE
3.60 g., Aluminum-Bronze, 21.25 mm. **Obv:** Castle **Rev:** Bust of Louis Pasteur facing

Date	Mintage	VF20	XF40	MS60	MS63	MS65
1984 R	65,000	—	0.10	0.30	0.75	0.85

KM# 177 20 LIRE
3.60 g., Aluminum-Bronze, 21.25 mm. **Subject:** War on drugs **Obv:** Shield **Rev:** Open hand flanked by value and date

Date	Mintage	VF20	XF40	MS60	MS63	MS65
1985 R	60,000	—	—	0.15	0.55	0.65

KM# 191 20 LIRE
3.60 g., Aluminum-Bronze, 21.25 mm. **Subject:** Revolution of technology **Obv:** Crown above ostrich feathers and towers on rock **Rev:** Stylized figure at lower right of computer flanked by value and date

Date	Mintage	VF20	XF40	MS60	MS63	MS65
1986 R	50,000	—	—	0.15	0.55	0.65

KM# 205 20 LIRE
3.60 g., Aluminum-Bronze, 21.25 mm. **Subject:** 15th Anniversary - Resumption of Coinage **Obv:** Crowned pointed arms within sprigs **Rev:** Volcanoes

Date	Mintage	VF20	XF40	MS60	MS63	MS65
1987 R	83,000	—	—	0.15	0.55	0.65

KM# 222 20 LIRE
3.60 g., Aluminum-Bronze, 21.25 mm. **Subject:** Fortifications **Obv:** Crowned ornate arms on shield **Rev:** Small fortified gate

Date	Mintage	VF20	XF40	MS60	MS63	MS65
1988 R	38,000	—	—	0.15	0.55	0.65

KM# 235 20 LIRE
3.60 g., Aluminum-Bronze, 21.25 mm. **Subject:** History **Obv:** Crowned shield **Rev:** Sword with value within flag

Date	Mintage	VF20	XF40	MS60	MS63	MS65
1989 R	37,000	—	—	0.15	0.55	0.65

KM# 252 20 LIRE
3.60 g., Aluminum-Bronze, 21.25 mm. **Subject:** 1,600 Years of History **Obv:** Stylized towers above design **Rev:** Stylized large figure straddling value

Date	Mintage	VF20	XF40	MS60	MS63	MS65
1990 R	96,000	—	—	0.15	0.55	0.65

KM# 265 20 LIRE
3.60 g., Aluminum-Bronze, 21.25 mm. **Obv:** Date at upper left of ostrich feathers and towers **Rev:** Value above gloved hand rejecting cardinal ring

Date	Mintage	VF20	XF40	MS60	MS63	MS65
1991 R	—	—	—	0.15	0.55	0.65

KM# 282 20 LIRE

3.60 g., Aluminum-Bronze, 21.25 mm. **Obv:** Towers with feathers above within circle **Rev:** Columbus landing on Hispaniola

Date	Mintage	VF20	XF40	MS60	MS63	MS65
1992 R	—	—	—	0.10	0.55	0.65

KM# 297 20 LIRE

3.60 g., Aluminum-Bronze, 21.25 mm. **Rev:** Scroll and arch **Edge:** Reeded

Date	Mintage	VF20	XF40	MS60	MS63	MS65
1993 R	—	—	—	0.10	0.55	0.65

KM# 310 20 LIRE

3.60 g., Aluminum-Bronze, 21.25 mm. **Obv:** Stone cutter **Rev:** Workers pulling stone

Date	Mintage	VF20	XF40	MS60	MS63	MS65
1994 R	40,000	—	—	0.10	0.55	0.65

KM# 326 20 LIRE

3.60 g., Aluminum-Bronze, 21.25 mm. **Obv:** Banner wrapped around quills **Rev:** Child straddling cornucopia

Date	Mintage	VF20	XF40	MS60	MS63	MS65
1995 R	—	—	—	0.10	0.55	0.65

KM# 353 20 LIRE

3.60 g., Aluminum-Bronze, 21.25 mm. **Obv:** Bust of Saint Thomas facing

Date	Mintage	VF20	XF40	MS60	MS63	MS65
1996 R	32,000	—	—	0.10	0.55	0.65

KM# 363 20 LIRE

3.60 g., Aluminum-Bronze, 21.25 mm. **Subject:** The Arts - Cinema **Obv:** Bust facing with flame within hands **Rev:** Film strips

Date	Mintage	VF20	XF40	MS60	MS63	MS65
1997 R	28,000	—	—	0.10	0.55	0.65

KM# 379 20 LIRE

3.60 g., Aluminum-Bronze, 21.25 mm. **Subject:** Communications **Rev:** Two profiles in silhouette left

Date	Mintage	VF20	XF40	MS60	MS63	MS65
1998 R	—	—	—	0.10	0.55	0.65

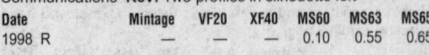

KM# 390 20 LIRE

3.60 g., Aluminum-Bronze, 21.25 mm. **Subject:** Exploration **Obv:** Crowned shield **Rev:** Earth as known today

Date	Mintage	VF20	XF40	MS60	MS63	MS65
1999 R	—	—	—	0.10	0.55	0.65

KM# 400 20 LIRE

3.60 g., Aluminum-Bronze, 21.22 mm. **Subject:** Solidarity **Obv:** Bust facing with flame within hands **Rev:** Two hands about to grasp, globe design in background **Edge:** Plain

Date	Mintage	VF20	XF40	MS60	MS63	MS65
2000 R	—	—	—	0.10	0.55	0.65

KM# 19 50 LIRE

6.20 g., Steel, 24.8 mm. **Obv:** Stylized ostrich feathers and towers **Rev:** Female kneeling before St. Marinus **Edge:** Reeded

Date	Mintage	VF20	XF40	MS60	MS63	MS65
1972	291,000	0.15	0.25	0.50	1.00	1.10

KM# 27 50 LIRE

6.20 g., Steel, 24.8 mm. **Obv:** Crowned shield **Rev:** Stylized standing figure with sword and scale **Note:** Depicts the balance of man, not as an individual but as a race

Date	Mintage	VF20	XF40	MS60	MS63	MS65
1973	291,000	0.15	0.25	0.50	1.00	1.10

KM# 35 50 LIRE

6.20 g., Steel, 24.8 mm. **Obv:** Ostrich feathers and towers within circle **Rev:** Stylized chicken

Date	Mintage	VF20	XF40	MS60	MS63	MS65
1974	276,000	0.15	0.25	0.60	1.25	2.50

KM# 45 50 LIRE

6.20 g., Steel, 24.8 mm. **Obv:** Ostrich feathers and towers **Rev:** Cluster of fish

Date	Mintage	VF20	XF40	MS60	MS63	MS65
1975	831,000	0.15	0.25	0.60	1.25	2.50

KM# 56 50 LIRE

6.20 g., Steel, 24.8 mm. **Obv:** Stylized ostrich feathers and towers **Rev:** Face forward within triangle flanked by pair of scales

Date	Mintage	VF20	XF40	MS60	MS63	MS65
1976	195,000	0.15	0.25	0.50	1.00	1.10

KM# 68 50 LIRE

6.20 g., Steel, 24.8 mm. **Obv:** Value below ostrich feathers and towers within circle **Rev:** Fingers in center of circle of stars

Date	Mintage	VF20	XF40	MS60	MS63	MS65
1977	180,000	0.15	0.25	0.50	1.00	1.10

KM# 81 50 LIRE

6.20 g., Steel, 24.8 mm. **Obv:** Value below ostrich feathers and towers **Rev:** Flowering plant below seated mother and child at desk

Date	Mintage	VF20	XF40	MS60	MS63	MS65
1978	130,000	0.15	0.25	0.50	1.00	1.10

KM# 94 50 LIRE

6.20 g., Steel, 24.8 mm. **Obv:** Crowned shield **Rev:** Liberty bell in front of building

Date	Mintage	VF20	XF40	MS60	MS63	MS65
1979	125,000	0.15	0.25	0.50	1.00	1.10

KM# 107 50 LIRE

6.20 g., Steel, 24.8 mm. **Series:** 1980 Olympics **Obv:** Olympic rings and date to upper left of ostrich feathers and towers **Rev:** Downhill skier

Date	Mintage	VF20	XF40	MS60	MS63	MS65
1980	125,000	0.15	0.25	0.50	1.00	1.25

KM# 121 50 LIRE

6.20 g., Steel, 24.8 mm. **Obv:** Crowned shield **Rev:** Value at left of dancing figure

Date	Mintage	VF20	XF40	MS60	MS63	MS65
1981 R	100,000	0.15	0.25	0.50	1.00	1.10

KM# 136 50 LIRE
6.20 g., Steel, 24.8 mm. **Subject:** Social conquests **Obv:** Crown above ostrich feathers and towers **Rev:** Standing figures within design

Date	Mintage	VF20	XF40	MS60	MS63	MS65
1982 R	78,000	0.15	0.25	0.50	1.00	1.25

KM# 150 50 LIRE
6.20 g., Steel, 24.8 mm. **Subject:** Nuclear war threat **Obv:** Crown above shield and sprig **Rev:** Beast of war above woman

Date	Mintage	VF20	XF40	MS60	MS63	MS65
1983 R	72,000	0.20	0.40	0.80	1.50	1.60

KM# 164 50 LIRE
6.20 g., Steel, 24.8 mm. **Obv:** Castle **Rev:** Pierre and Marie Curie

Date	Mintage	VF20	XF40	MS60	MS63	MS65
1984 R	65,000	0.20	0.40	0.80	1.50	1.60

KM# 178 50 LIRE
6.20 g., Steel, 24.8 mm. **Subject:** War on drugs **Obv:** Shield **Rev:** Stylized figures

Date	Mintage	VF20	XF40	MS60	MS63	MS65
1985 R	110,000	—	0.10	0.20	0.85	0.95

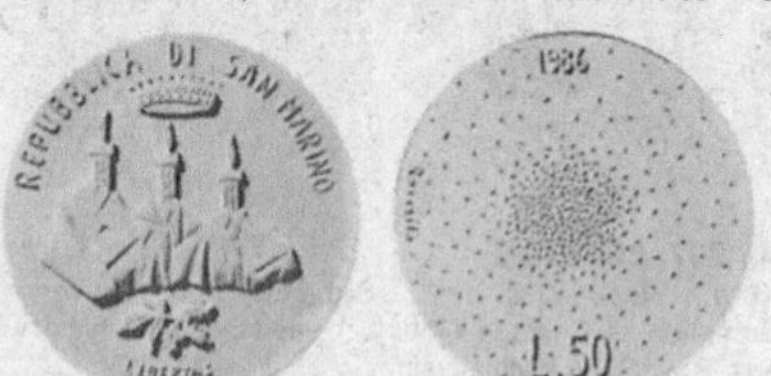

KM# 192 50 LIRE
6.20 g., Steel, 24.8 mm. **Subject:** Revolution of technology **Obv:** Crown above ostrich feathers and towers on rock **Rev:** Splitting the atom

Date	Mintage	VF20	XF40	MS60	MS63	MS65
1986 R	50,000	—	0.10	0.20	0.85	0.95

KM# 206 50 LIRE
6.20 g., Steel, 24.8 mm. **Subject:** 15th Anniversary - Resumption of Coinage **Obv:** Crowned pointed shield within sprigs **Rev:** Animal in front of rock with tower at top

Date	Mintage	VF20	XF40	MS60	MS63	MS65
1987 R	93,000	—	0.10	0.20	0.85	0.95

KM# 223 50 LIRE
6.20 g., Steel, 24.8 mm. **Subject:** Fortifications **Obv:** Crowned ornate arms on shield **Rev:** Ramp leading to gate house

Date	Mintage	VF20	XF40	MS60	MS63	MS65
1988 R	38,000	—	0.10	0.20	0.85	0.95

KM# 236 50 LIRE
6.20 g., Steel, 24.8 mm. **Subject:** History **Obv:** Crowned shield **Rev:** Crossbow divides value

Date	Mintage	VF20	XF40	MS60	MS63	MS65
1989 R	87,000	—	0.10	0.20	0.85	0.95

KM# 253 50 LIRE
Steel, 17 mm. **Subject:** 1,600 Years of History **Obv:** Stylized towers above design **Rev:** Stylized bird

Date	Mintage	VF20	XF40	MS60	MS63	MS65
1990 R	52,000	—	0.10	0.20	0.85	0.95

KM# 266 50 LIRE
Steel, 17 mm. **Obv:** Date at upper left of ostrich feathers and towers **Rev:** Value above hand holding cannon barrels and wheat stalks

Date	Mintage	VF20	XF40	MS60	MS63	MS65
1991 R	—	—	0.10	0.20	0.85	0.95

KM# 283 50 LIRE
Steel, 17 mm. **Subject:** Columbus **Obv:** Towers with feathers above within circle **Rev:** Flying seagulls within radiant sun flanked by dates

Date	Mintage	VF20	XF40	MS60	MS63	MS65
1992 R	—	—	0.10	0.20	0.85	1.25

KM# 298 50 LIRE
Steel, 17 mm. **Obv:** Stylized ostrich feathers within towers **Rev:** Wheat growing through barbed wire

Date	Mintage	VF20	XF40	MS60	MS63	MS65
1993 R	—	—	0.10	0.20	0.85	0.95

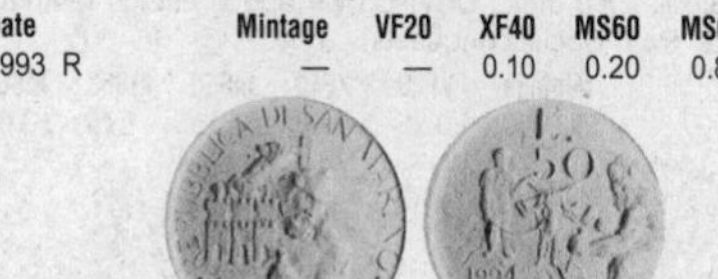

KM# 311 50 LIRE
Stainless Steel, 17 mm. **Obv:** Stonecutter holding hammer and chisel, ostrich feathers and towers at left **Rev:** Two stonecutters

Date	Mintage	VF20	XF40	MS60	MS63	MS65
1994 R	40,000	—	0.10	0.20	0.85	0.95

KM# 327 50 LIRE
Stainless Steel, 17 mm. **Obv:** Banner wrapped around bottom of design **Rev:** Child hugging bird

Date	Mintage	VF20	XF40	MS60	MS63	MS65
1995 R	—	—	0.10	0.20	0.85	0.95

KM# 354 50 LIRE
Stainless Steel, 17 mm. **Obv:** Bust facing with flame within hands **Rev:** Descartes

Date	Mintage	VF20	XF40	MS60	MS63	MS65
1996 R	32,000	—	0.10	0.20	0.85	0.95

KM# 364 50 LIRE
Stainless Steel, 19 mm. **Subject:** The Arts - Sculpture **Obv:** Bust facing with flame within hands **Rev:** Han Dynasty Horse statue

Date	Mintage	VF20	XF40	MS60	MS63	MS65
1997 R	28,000	—	0.15	0.25	1.00	2.00

KM# 380 50 LIRE
Copper-Nickel, 19 mm. **Subject:** Engineering **Rev:** Cogwheel mind

Date	Mintage	VF20	XF40	MS60	MS63	MS65
1998 R	—	—	0.10	0.20	0.85	0.95

KM# 391 50 LIRE
Copper-Nickel, 19 mm. **Subject:** Exploration **Obv:** Crowned shield **Rev:** Ship sail, sun and waves

Date	Mintage	VF20	XF40	MS60	MS63	MS65
1999 R	—	—	0.10	0.20	0.85	0.95

KM# 401 50 LIRE
4.50 g., Copper-Nickel, 19.2 mm. **Subject:** Equality **Obv:** Bust facing with flame within hands **Rev:** Five different plant leaves on 1 stem **Edge:** Plain **Note:** Struck at Rome.

Date	Mintage	VF20	XF40	MS60	MS63	MS65
2000 R	—	—	0.10	0.20	0.85	0.95

KM# 20 100 LIRE
8.00 g., Steel, 27.8 mm. **Obv:** Three ostrich feathers and towers **Rev:** St. Marinus in a small boat

Date	Mintage	VF20	XF40	MS60	MS63	MS65
1972	291,000	0.25	0.40	0.75	1.75	3.00

KM# 28 100 LIRE
8.00 g., Steel, 27.8 mm. **Obv:** Crowned shield **Rev:** Ulysses passing the pillars of Hercules

Date	Mintage	VF20	XF40	MS60	MS63	MS65
1973	291,000	0.25	0.40	0.75	1.75	3.00

KM# 36 100 LIRE
8.00 g., Steel, 27.8 mm. **Obv:** Ostrich feathers and towers within circle **Rev:** Goat

Date	Mintage	VF20	XF40	MS60	MS63	MS65
1974	276,000	0.25	0.40	0.75	1.75	3.00

KM# 46 100 LIRE
8.00 g., Steel, 27.8 mm. **Obv:** Ostrich feathers and towers **Rev:** Dog and cat lying together

Date	Mintage	VF20	XF40	MS60	MS63	MS65
1975	821,000	0.25	0.40	0.75	1.75	4.00

KM# 57 100 LIRE
8.00 g., Steel, 27.8 mm. **Obv:** Stylized ostrich feathers and towers **Rev:** Stylized seated figures within arch of building

Date	Mintage	VF20	XF40	MS60	MS63	MS65
1976	1,853,000	0.25	0.40	0.75	1.75	3.00

KM# 69 100 LIRE
8.00 g., Steel, 27.8 mm. **Obv:** Value below ostrich feathers and towers within circle **Rev:** Design within circular star wreath

Date	Mintage	VF20	XF40	MS60	MS63	MS65
1977	565,000	0.25	0.40	0.75	1.75	3.00

KM# 70 100 LIRE
8.00 g., Steel, 27.8 mm. **Obv:** Value below ostrich feathers and towers within circle **Rev:** Stylized fish

Date	Mintage	VF20	XF40	MS60	MS63	MS65
1977	565,000	0.25	0.40	0.75	1.75	3.00

KM# 82 100 LIRE
8.00 g., Steel, 27.8 mm. **Series:** F.A.O. **Obv:** Value below ostrich feathers and towers **Rev:** Standing figure using sickle

Date	Mintage	VF20	XF40	MS60	MS63	MS65
1978	875,000	0.25	0.40	0.75	1.75	3.00

KM# 95 100 LIRE
8.00 g., Steel, 27.8 mm. **Obv:** Crowned shield **Rev:** Spanish Conquistador helmet with assorted shields around border **Edge:** Reeded

Date	Mintage	VF20	XF40	MS60	MS63	MS65
1979	665,000	0.25	0.40	0.75	1.75	3.00

KM# 108 100 LIRE
8.00 g., Steel, 27.8 mm. **Series:** 1980 Olympics **Obv:** Olympic rings and date to upper left of ostrich feathers and towers **Rev:** Archery

Date	Mintage	VF20	XF40	MS60	MS63	MS65
1980	350,000	0.35	0.65	1.25	2.50	4.50

KM# 122 100 LIRE
8.00 g., Steel, 27.8 mm. **Obv:** Crowned shield **Rev:** Stylized draped figure to left of value

Date	Mintage	VF20	XF40	MS60	MS63	MS65
1981 R	512,000	0.25	0.40	0.75	1.75	3.00

KM# 137 100 LIRE
8.00 g., Steel, 27.8 mm. **Obv:** Crown above ostrich feathers and towers **Rev:** Social conquests

Date	Mintage	VF20	XF40	MS60	MS63	MS65
1982 R	178,000	0.25	0.40	0.75	1.75	3.00

KM# 151 100 LIRE
8.00 g., Steel, 27.8 mm. **Subject:** Nuclear War Threat **Obv:** Crown above shield and sprig **Rev:** Beast of war above man and woman

Date	Mintage	VF20	XF40	MS60	MS63	MS65
1983 R	172,000	0.25	0.40	0.75	1.75	3.00

KM# 165 100 LIRE
8.00 g., Steel, 27.8 mm. **Obv:** Castle **Rev:** Bust of Guglielmo Marconi left

Date	Mintage	VF20	XF40	MS60	MS63	MS65
1984 R	165,000	0.25	0.40	0.75	1.75	3.00

KM# 179 100 LIRE
8.00 g., Steel, 27.8 mm. **Subject:** War on Drugs **Obv:** Shield **Rev:** Three figures in discussion

Date	Mintage	VF20	XF40	MS60	MS63	MS65
1985 R	210,000	0.25	0.40	0.75	1.75	3.00

KM# 193 100 LIRE
8.00 g., Steel, 27.8 mm. **Subject:** Revolution of Technology **Obv:** Crown above ostrich feathers and towers on rock **Rev:** Satellite and receiving dishes divide date and value

Date	Mintage	VF20	XF40	MS60	MS63	MS65
1986 R	150,000	0.25	0.40	0.75	1.75	3.00

KM# 207 100 LIRE
8.00 g., Steel, 27.8 mm. **Subject:** 15th Anniversary - Resumption of Coinage **Obv:** Crowned pointed shield within sprigs **Rev:** Sprig divides value

Date	Mintage	VF20	XF40	MS60	MS63	MS65
1987 R	143,000	0.25	0.40	0.75	1.75	3.00

KM# 224 100 LIRE
8.00 g., Steel, 27.8 mm. **Subject:** Fortifications **Obv:** Crowned ornate arms on shield **Rev:** Gate tower

Date	Mintage	VF20	XF40	MS60	MS63	MS65
1988 R	38,000	0.25	0.40	0.75	1.75	3.00

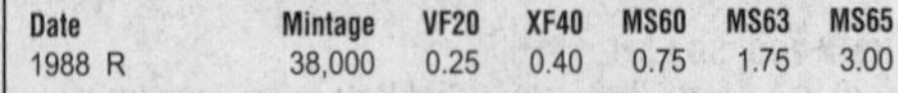

KM# 237 100 LIRE
8.00 g., Steel, 27.8 mm. **Subject:** History **Obv:** Crowned shield **Rev:** Teacher and student

Date	Mintage	VF20	XF40	MS60	MS63	MS65
1989 R	37,000	0.25	0.40	0.75	1.75	3.00

KM# 254 100 LIRE
Steel, 18 mm. **Subject:** 1,600 Years of History **Obv:** Towers above design **Rev:** Balance scales

Date	Mintage	VF20	XF40	MS60	MS63	MS65
1990 R	1,086,000	—	—	0.35	1.25	2.00

KM# 267 100 LIRE
Steel, 18 mm. **Obv:** Date at upper left of ostrich feathers and towers **Rev:** Value above clasped hands

Date	Mintage	VF20	XF40	MS60	MS63	MS65
1991 R	—	—	—	0.35	1.25	2.00

KM# 284 100 LIRE
Steel, 18 mm. **Subject:** Columbus **Obv:** Towers with feathers above within circle **Rev:** Value below three sailing ships

Date	Mintage	VF20	XF40	MS60	MS63	MS65
1992 R	—	—	—	0.35	1.25	2.00

KM# 299 100 LIRE
Copper-Nickel, 22 mm. **Obv:** Three towers above dentiled design **Rev:** Pan swallow above western Europe

Date	Mintage	VF20	XF40	MS60	MS63	MS65
1993 R	—	—	—	0.35	1.50	3.00

KM# 312 100 LIRE
Copper-Nickel, 22 mm. **Obv:** Stonecutter holding hammer and chisel, ostrich feathers and towers at left **Rev:** Two stonecutters

Date	Mintage	VF20	XF40	MS60	MS63	MS65
1994 R	40,000	—	—	0.35	1.25	2.00

KM# 328 100 LIRE
Copper-Nickel, 22 mm. **Obv:** Banner wrapped around quills **Rev:** Three children

Date	Mintage	VF20	XF40	MS60	MS63	MS65
1995 R	—	—	—	0.35	1.25	2.00

KM# 355 100 LIRE
Copper-Nickel, 22 mm. **Obv:** Bust facing with flame within hands **Rev:** Head of Rousseau 1/4 right

Date	Mintage	VF20	XF40	MS60	MS63	MS65
1996 R	32,000	—	—	0.35	1.25	2.00

KM# 365 100 LIRE
Copper-Nickel, 22 mm. **Subject:** The Arts - Dance **Obv:** Bust facing with flame within hands **Rev:** Ballet dancers

Date	Mintage	VF20	XF40	MS60	MS63	MS65
1997 R	28,000	—	—	0.35	1.25	2.00

KM# 381 100 LIRE
Copper-Nickel, 22 mm. **Subject:** Physics **Rev:** Human, crossbow

Date	Mintage	VF20	XF40	MS60	MS63	MS65
1998 R	—	—	—	0.35	1.25	2.00

KM# 392 100 LIRE
Copper-Nickel, 22 mm. **Subject:** Exploration **Obv:** Crowned shield **Rev:** Submarine below Arctic ice-cap

Date	Mintage	VF20	XF40	MS60	MS63	MS65
1999 R	—	—	—	0.35	1.25	2.00

KM# 402 100 LIRE
4.50 g., Copper-Nickel, 22 mm. **Subject:** Ecology **Obv:** Bust facing with flame within hands **Rev:** Outline of house in center of leaf design, globe design in background **Edge:** Reeded and plain sectioned

Date	Mintage	VF20	XF40	MS60	MS63	MS65
2000 R	—	—	—	0.35	1.25	2.00

KM# 83 200 LIRE
5.00 g., Aluminum-Bronze, 24 mm. **Obv:** Value below ostrich feathers and towers **Rev:** Seated figure weaving

Date	Mintage	VF20	XF40	MS60	MS63	MS65
1978	530,000	—	0.25	0.75	1.75	2.50

KM# 96 200 LIRE
5.00 g., Aluminum-Bronze, 24 mm. **Series:** F.A.O. **Obv:** Crowned shield **Rev:** Nude figure fighting lion flanked by value and date, F.A.O logo at upper right

Date	Mintage	VF20	XF40	MS60	MS63	MS65
1979	675,000	—	0.25	0.75	1.75	2.50

KM# 109 200 LIRE
5.00 g., Aluminum-Bronze, 24 mm. **Series:** 1980 Olympics **Obv:** Olympic rings and date to upper left of ostrich feathers and towers **Rev:** Wrestlers

Date	Mintage	VF20	XF40	MS60	MS63	MS65
1980	675,000	—	0.50	1.00	2.50	3.50

KM# 123 200 LIRE
5.00 g., Aluminum-Bronze, 24 mm. **Series:** F.A.O. **Obv:** Crowned shield **Rev:** Stylized animal divides date and value

Date	Mintage	VF20	XF40	MS60	MS63	MS65
1981 R	700,000	—	0.25	0.75	1.75	2.50

KM# 138 200 LIRE
5.00 g., Aluminum-Bronze, 24 mm. **Subject:** Social Conquests **Obv:** Crown above ostrich feathers and towers **Rev:** Stylized figure within design

Date	Mintage	VF20	XF40	MS60	MS63	MS65
1982 R	178,000	—	0.25	0.75	1.75	2.50

KM# 152 200 LIRE
5.00 g., Aluminum-Bronze, 24 mm. **Subject:** Nuclear War Threat **Obv:** Crown above shield and sprig **Rev:** Rider spearing victim

Date	Mintage	VF20	XF40	MS60	MS63	MS65
1983 R	172,000	—	0.25	0.75	1.75	2.50

KM# 166 200 LIRE
5.00 g., Aluminum-Bronze, 24 mm. **Obv:** Castle **Rev:** Bust of Enrico Fermi facing

Date	Mintage	VF20	XF40	MS60	MS63	MS65
1984 R	165,000	—	0.25	0.75	1.75	2.50

KM# 180 200 LIRE
5.00 g., Aluminum-Bronze, 24 mm. **Subject:** War on Drugs **Obv:** Shield **Rev:** Family group

Date	Mintage	VF20	XF40	MS60	MS63	MS65
1985 R	210,000	—	0.20	0.50	1.50	2.75

KM# 194 200 LIRE
5.00 g., Aluminum-Bronze, 24 mm. **Subject:** Revolution of Technology **Obv:** Crown above ostrich feathers and towers on rock **Rev:** Stylized hand holding microchip

Date	Mintage	VF20	XF40	MS60	MS63	MS65
1986 R	150,000	—	0.20	0.50	1.50	2.75

KM# 208 200 LIRE
5.00 g., Aluminum-Bronze, 24 mm. **Subject:** 15th Anniversary - Resumption of Coinage **Obv:** Crowned pointed shield within sprigs **Rev:** Building in front of smoking towers

Date	Mintage	VF20	XF40	MS60	MS63	MS65
1987 R	143,000	—	0.20	0.50	1.50	2.75

KM# 225 200 LIRE
5.00 g., Aluminum-Bronze, 24 mm. **Subject:** Fortifications **Obv:** Crowned ornate arms on shield **Rev:** Tower divides value **Edge:** Reeded

Date	Mintage	VF20	XF40	MS60	MS63	MS65
1988 R	38,000	—	0.20	0.50	1.50	2.75

KM# 238 200 LIRE
5.00 g., Aluminum-Bronze, 24 mm. **Subject:** History **Obv:** Crowned shield **Rev:** Stylized view of San Marino

Date	Mintage	VF20	XF40	MS60	MS63	MS65
1989 R	1,037,000	—	0.20	0.50	1.50	2.75

KM# 255 200 LIRE
5.00 g., Aluminum-Bronze, 24 mm. **Subject:** 1,600 Years of History **Obv:** Towers above design **Rev:** Stylized head left

Date	Mintage	VF20	XF40	MS60	MS63	MS65
1990 R	36,000	—	0.20	0.50	1.50	2.75

KM# 268 200 LIRE
5.00 g., Aluminum-Bronze, 24 mm. **Obv:** Date at upper left of ostrich feathers and towers **Rev:** Value above hand holding coin die

Date	Mintage	VF20	XF40	MS60	MS63	MS65
1991 R	—	—	0.20	0.50	1.50	2.75

KM# 285 200 LIRE
5.00 g., Aluminum-Bronze, 24 mm. **Obv:** Stylized feathers and towers within circle **Rev:** Columbus navigating by the stars

Date	Mintage	VF20	XF40	MS60	MS63	MS65
ND-1992 R	—	—	0.20	0.50	1.50	2.75

KM# 300 200 LIRE
5.00 g., Aluminum-Bronze, 24 mm. **Rev:** Door and arches

Date	Mintage	VF20	XF40	MS60	MS63	MS65
1993 R	—	—	0.20	0.50	1.50	2.75

KM# 313 200 LIRE
5.00 g., Aluminum-Bronze, 24 mm. **Obv:** Stonecutter holding hammer and chisel, ostrich feathers and towers at left **Rev:** Man and bear

Date	Mintage	VF20	XF40	MS60	MS63	MS65
1994 R	40,000	—	0.20	0.50	1.50	2.75

KM# 329 200 LIRE
5.00 g., Aluminum-Bronze, 24 mm. **Obv:** Banner wrapped around quills **Rev:** Two children playing

Date	Mintage	VF20	XF40	MS60	MS63	MS65
1995 R	—	—	0.20	0.50	1.50	2.75

KM# 356 200 LIRE
5.00 g., Aluminum-Bronze, 24 mm. **Subject:** Kant **Obv:** Bust facing with flame within hands **Rev:** Head of Kant right within square above value

Date	Mintage	VF20	XF40	MS60	MS63	MS65
1996 R	32,000	—	0.20	0.50	1.50	2.75

KM# 366 200 LIRE
5.00 g., Aluminum-Bronze, 24 mm. **Subject:** The Arts - Painting **Obv:** Bust facing with flame within hands **Rev:** Seated figure painting portrait of standing figure at left

Date	Mintage	VF20	XF40	MS60	MS63	MS65
1997 R	28,000	—	0.20	0.50	1.50	2.25

KM# 382 200 LIRE
5.00 g., Aluminum-Bronze, 24 mm. **Subject:** Zoology **Rev:** Stylized dolphins

Date	Mintage	VF20	XF40	MS60	MS63	MS65
1998 R	—	—	0.25	0.75	2.50	3.50

KM# 393 200 LIRE
5.00 g., Aluminum-Bronze, 24 mm. **Subject:** Exploration **Obv:** Crowned shield **Rev:** Stonehenge beneath the sun and stars

Date	Mintage	VF20	XF40	MS60	MS63	MS65
1999 R	—	—	0.20	0.50	1.50	2.25

KM# 403 200 LIRE
5.00 g., Aluminum-Bronze, 24 mm. **Subject:** Knowledge **Obv:** Bust facing with flame within hands **Rev:** Allegorical female head left within globe design **Edge:** Reeded **Note:** Struck at Rome.

Date	Mintage	VF20	XF40	MS60	MS63	MS65
2000 R	—	—	0.20	0.50	1.50	2.25

KM# 21 500 LIRE
11.00 g., 0.835 Silver 0.2953 oz. ASW, 29 mm. **Obv:** Three towers **Rev:** Mother lifting child in air **Note:** 22,374 coins melted at the mint.

Date	Mintage	VF20	XF40	MS60	MS63	MS65
1972	291,000	—	—	5.75	8.75	11.00

KM# 29 500 LIRE
11.00 g., 0.835 Silver 0.2953 oz. ASW, 29 mm. **Obv:** Crowned shield **Rev:** Child holding dove **Note:** 6,544 coins melted at the mint.

Date	Mintage	VF20	XF40	MS60	MS63	MS65
1973	291,000	—	—	5.75	8.75	11.00

KM# 37 500 LIRE
11.00 g., 0.835 Silver 0.2953 oz. ASW, 29 mm. **Obv:** Ostrich feathers and towers within circle **Rev:** Two stylized pigeons **Note:** 6,295 coins melted at the mint.

Date	Mintage	VF20	XF40	MS60	MS63	MS65
1974	276,000	—	—	5.75	8.75	11.00

KM# 47 500 LIRE
11.00 g., 0.835 Silver 0.2953 oz. ASW, 29 mm. **Obv:** Ostrich feathers and towers **Rev:** Seagulls flying over barbed wire **Note:** 119,743 coins melted at the mint.

Date	Mintage	VF20	XF40	MS60	MS63	MS65
1975	291,000	—	—	5.75	8.75	11.00

KM# 48 500 LIRE
11.00 g., 0.835 Silver 0.2953 oz. ASW, 29 mm. **Subject:** Numismatic Agency opening **Obv:** Value and date below ostrich feathers and towers **Rev:** Ancient stonecutter **Note:** 47,495 coins melted at the mint.

Date	Mintage	VF20	XF40	MS60	MS63	MS65
1975	200,000	—	—	5.75	8.75	11.00

KM# 58 500 LIRE
11.00 g., 0.835 Silver 0.2953 oz. ASW, 29 mm. **Obv:** Stylized ostrich feathers and towers **Rev:** Design **Note:** 40,509 coins melted at the mint.

Date	Mintage	VF20	XF40	MS60	MS63	MS65
1976	195,000	—	—	5.75	8.75	11.00

KM# 59 500 LIRE
11.00 g., 0.835 Silver 0.2953 oz. ASW, 29 mm. **Subject:** Social Security **Obv:** Stylized ostrich feathers and towers **Rev:** Standing figure holding blanket to cover man **Note:** 106,604 coins melted at the mint.

Date	Mintage	VF20	XF40	MS60	MS63	MS65
1976	195,000	—	—	5.75	8.75	11.00

KM# 71 500 LIRE
11.00 g., 0.835 Silver 0.2953 oz. ASW, 29 mm. **Obv:** Value below ostrich feathers and towers within circle **Rev:** Stylized upside-down bird among stars within circle **Note:** 45,483 coins melted at the mint.

Date	Mintage	VF20	XF40	MS60	MS63	MS65
1977	180,000	—	—	5.75	8.75	11.00

KM# 84 500 LIRE
11.00 g., 0.835 Silver 0.2953 oz. ASW, 29 mm. **Obv:** Value below ostrich feathers and towers **Rev:** Group of figures holding flags **Note:** 16,297 coins melted at the mint.

Date	Mintage	VF20	XF40	MS60	MS63	MS65
1978	130,000	—	—	5.75	8.75	11.00

KM# 97 500 LIRE
11.00 g., 0.835 Silver 0.2953 oz. ASW, 29 mm. **Obv:** Half length figure holding three towers with ostrich feathers **Rev:** Victory in a biga **Note:** 33,278 coins melted at the mint.

Date	Mintage	VF20	XF40	MS60	MS63	MS65
1979	125,000	—	—	5.75	8.75	11.00

KM# 110 500 LIRE
11.00 g., 0.835 Silver 0.2953 oz. ASW, 29 mm. **Series:** 1980 Olympics **Obv:** Olympic rings and date to upper left of ostrich feathers and towers **Rev:** Boxers **Note:** 47,724 coins melted at the mint.

Date	Mintage	VF20	XF40	MS60	MS63	MS65
1980	125,000	—	—	5.75	8.75	11.00

KM# 124 500 LIRE
11.00 g., 0.835 Silver 0.2953 oz. ASW, 29 mm. **Subject:** 2000th Anniversary - Virgil's Death **Obv:** Crowned shield within sprigs **Rev:** Seated figure playing flute under tree **Note:** 9,122 coins melted at the mint.

Date	Mintage	VF20	XF40	MS60	MS63	MS65
1981	75,000	—	—	5.75	8.75	11.00

KM# 125 500 LIRE
11.00 g., 0.835 Silver 0.2953 oz. ASW, 29 mm. **Subject:** 2,000th Anniversary - Virgil's Death **Obv:** Crowned shield within sprigs **Rev:** The seed sower **Note:** 9,122 coins melted at the mint.

Date	Mintage	VF20	XF40	MS60	MS63	MS65
1981	75,000	—	—	5.75	8.75	11.00

KM# 126 500 LIRE
11.00 g., 0.835 Silver 0.2953 oz. ASW, 29 mm. **Obv:** Crowned shield **Rev:** Value flanked by hands below head right **Note:** 21,124 coins melted at the mint.

Date	Mintage	VF20	XF40	MS60	MS63	MS65
1981 R	100,000	—	—	5.75	8.75	11.00

KM# 139 500 LIRE
11.00 g., 0.835 Silver 0.2953 oz. ASW, 29 mm. **Subject:** Centennial - Death of Garibaldi **Obv:** Crowned design above towers **Rev:** Head facing **Note:** 112 uncirculated and 369 proof coins melted at the mint.

Date	Mintage	VF20	XF40	MS60	MS63	MS65
ND-1982 R	48,000	—	—	5.75	8.75	11.00
ND-1982 R	13,000	PF65 20.00				

KM# 140 500 LIRE
6.80 g., Bi-Metallic Aluminum-Bronze center in Stainless Steel ring, 25.8 mm. **Subject:** Social Conquests **Obv:** Crown above ostrich feathers and towers within circle **Rev:** Stylized figures within circle **Edge:** Segmented reeding

Date	Mintage	VF20	XF40	MS60	MS63	MS65
1982 R	1,900,000	—	—	2.00	3.00	5.00

KM# 153 500 LIRE
6.80 g., Bi-Metallic Aluminum-Bronze center in Stainless Steel ring, 25.8 mm. **Subject:** Nuclear War Threat **Obv:** Crown above shield and sprig **Rev:** Three horses above two people **Edge:** Segmented reeding

Date	Mintage	VF20	XF40	MS60	MS63	MS65
1983 R	1,922,000	—	—	2.00	3.00	5.00

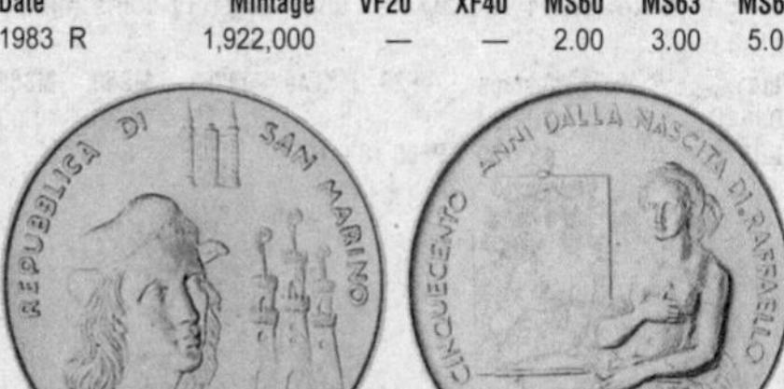

KM# 154 500 LIRE
11.00 g., 0.835 Silver 0.2953 oz. ASW, 29 mm. **Subject:** 500th Anniversary - Birth of Artist Raphael **Obv:** Head 3/4 right, ostrich feathers and towers at top and to right **Rev:** Seated figure looking at portrait **Note:** 80 uncirculated and 1,939 proof coins melted at the mint.

Date	Mintage	VF20	XF40	MS60	MS63	MS65
1983 R	42,000	—	—	5.75	8.75	11.00
1983 R	12,000	PF65 20.00				

KM# 167 500 LIRE
6.80 g., Bi-Metallic Aluminum-Bronze center in Stainless Steel ring, 25.8 mm. **Subject:** Albert Einstein, 105th Anniversary of Birth **Obv:** Castle within circle **Rev:** Bust facing within circle **Edge:** Segmented reeding

Date	Mintage	VF20	XF40	MS60	MS63	MS65
1984 R	2,633,000	—	—	2.00	3.00	5.00

KM# 168 500 LIRE
11.00 g., 0.835 Silver 0.2953 oz. ASW, 29 mm. **Series:** 1984 Summer Olympics **Obv:** Stylized ostrich feathers and towers **Rev:** Entwined vertical figures to left of Olympic rings, date and value **Note:** 2,920 uncirculated and 20 proof coins melted at the mint.

Date	Mintage	VF20	XF40	MS60	MS63	MS65
1984 R	52,000	—	—	5.75	8.75	11.00
1984 R	15,000	PF65 15.00				

KM# 181 500 LIRE
6.80 g., Bi-Metallic Aluminum-Bronze center in Stainless Steel ring, 25.8 mm. **Subject:** War on Drugs **Obv:** Stylized bending figure within circle **Rev:** Cured addict within circle **Edge:** Segmented reeding

Date	Mintage	VF20	XF40	MS60	MS63	MS65
1985 R	2,647,000	—	—	2.00	3.00	5.00

KM# 182 500 LIRE
11.00 g., 0.835 Silver 0.2953 oz. ASW, 29 mm. **Subject:** European Music Year, Bach Tercentenary **Rev:** Music seated at organ **Note:** 6,704 uncirculated and 122 proof coins melted at the mint.

Date	Mintage	VF20	XF40	MS60	MS63	MS65
1985 R	40,000	—	—	5.75	8.75	11.00
1985 R	12,000	PF65 18.00				

KM# 195 500 LIRE
6.80 g., Bi-Metallic Aluminum-Bronze center in Stainless Steel ring, 25.8 mm. **Subject:** Revolution of Technology **Obv:** Crown above ostrich feathers and towers on rock **Rev:** Human figure seated on console control panel

Date	Mintage	VF20	XF40	MS60	MS63	MS65
1986 R	3,111,000	—	—	2.00	3.00	5.00

KM# 196 500 LIRE
11.00 g., 0.835 Silver 0.2953 oz. ASW, 29 mm. **Subject:** Soccer **Obv:** Head left **Rev:** Field design **Note:** 5,212 uncirculated and 60 proof coins melted at the mint.

Date	Mintage	VF20	XF40	MS60	MS63	MS65
1986 R	45,000	—	—	5.75	8.75	11.00
1986 R	12,000	PF65 18.00				

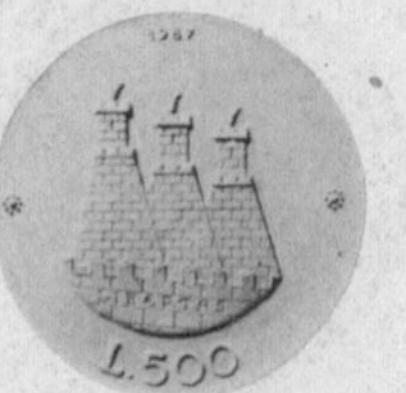

KM# 209 500 LIRE
6.80 g., Bi-Metallic Aluminum-Bronze center in Stainless Steel ring, 25.8 mm. **Subject:** 15th Anniversary - Resumption of Coinage **Obv:** Crowned pointed shield within sprigs **Rev:** Smoking towers

Date	Mintage	VF20	XF40	MS60	MS63	MS65
1987 R	3,063,000	—	—	2.00	3.00	5.00

KM# 213 500 LIRE
11.00 g., 0.835 Silver 0.2953 oz. ASW, 29 mm. **Subject:** Zagreb University Games **Rev:** Runner **Note:** 9,208 uncirculated and 1,206 proof coins melted at the mint.

Date	Mintage	VF20	XF40	MS60	MS63	MS65
1987 R	35,000	—	—	5.75	8.75	11.00
1987 R	10,000	PF65 18.00				

KM# 216 500 LIRE
11.00 g., 0.835 Silver 0.2953 oz. ASW, 29 mm. **Series:** Winter Olympics **Obv:** Stylized ostrich feathers and towers **Rev:** Downhill skier, oak leaf and Olympic rings **Note:** 146 uncirculated and 3 proof coins melted at the mint.

Date	Mintage	VF20	XF40	MS60	MS63	MS65
1988 R	32,000	—	—	5.75	8.75	11.00
1988 R	9,600	PF65 18.00				

KM# 226 500 LIRE
6.80 g., Bi-Metallic Aluminum-Bronze center in Stainless Steel ring, 25.8 mm. **Subject:** Fortifications **Obv:** Crowned ornate arms on shield **Rev:** Hilltop fortification

Date	Mintage	VF20	XF40	MS60	MS63	MS65
1988 R	3,526,000	—	—	2.00	3.00	5.00

KM# 239 500 LIRE
6.80 g., Bi-Metallic Aluminum-Bronze center in Stainless Steel ring, 25.8 mm. **Subject:** History **Obv:** Crowned shield **Rev:** Stone carver

Date	Mintage	VF20	XF40	MS60	MS63	MS65
1989 R	3,145,000	—	—	2.00	3.00	5.00

KM# 243 500 LIRE
11.00 g., 0.835 Silver 0.2953 oz. ASW, 29 mm. **Subject:** San Marino Grand Prix **Obv:** Stylized ostrich feathers and towers **Rev:** Vertical horse and rider above car **Note:** 5,180 coins melted at the mint.

Date	Mintage	VF20	XF40	MS60	MS63	MS65
1989 R	30,000	—	—	5.75	8.75	11.00
1989 R	8,000	PF65 22.00				

KM# 246 500 LIRE
11.00 g., 0.835 Silver 0.2953 oz. ASW, 29 mm. **Subject:** World Cup Soccer Championship Game **Obv:** Patterned design surrounds oval shield at center **Rev:** Cluster of stylized running figures

Date	Mintage	VF20	XF40	MS60	MS63	MS65
1990 R	40,000	—	—	5.75	8.75	11.00
1990 R	19,000	PF65 18.00				

KM# 256 500 LIRE
6.80 g., Bi-Metallic Aluminum-Bronze center in Stainless Steel ring, 25.8 mm. **Subject:** 1,600 Years of History **Obv:** Towers above design **Rev:** Birds and stamp

Date	Mintage	VF20	XF40	MS60	MS63	MS65
1990 R	—	—	—	2.00	3.00	5.00

KM# 269 500 LIRE
6.80 g., Bi-Metallic Aluminum-Bronze center in Stainless Steel ring, 25.8 mm. **Obv:** Date at left of ostrich featehrs towers within circle **Rev:** Value above hand holding flowers within circle

Date	Mintage	VF20	XF40	MS60	MS63	MS65
1991 R	3,580,563	—	—	2.00	3.00	5.00

KM# 271 500 LIRE

11.00 g., 0.835 Silver 0.2953 oz. ASW, 29 mm. **Series:** Barcelona Olympics **Obv:** Seated Saint facing with hammer in hand **Rev:** Priestess lighting fire with sunbeam

Date	Mintage	VF20	XF40	MS60	MS63	MS65
1991 R	Est. 60000	—	—	5.75	8.75	11.00
1991 R	Est. 8000	PF65 20.00				

KM# 276 500 LIRE

11.00 g., 0.835 Silver 0.2953 oz. ASW, 29 mm. **Series:** Olympics **Obv:** Three ostrich feathers and towers **Rev:** Chariot

Date	Mintage	VF20	XF40	MS60	MS63	MS65
1992 R	Est. 70000	—	—	5.75	8.75	11.00
1992 R	—	PF65 20.00				

KM# 286 500 LIRE

6.80 g., Bi-Metallic Aluminum-Bronze center in Stainless Steel ring, 25.8 mm. **Subject:** Columbus **Obv:** Ostrich feathers and towers within circle **Rev:** Winds blowing ship within circle **Edge:** Segmented reeding

Date	Mintage	VF20	XF40	MS60	MS63	MS65
1992 R	4,554,864	—	—	—	3.00	5.00

KM# 291 500 LIRE

11.00 g., 0.835 Silver 0.2953 oz. ASW, 29 mm. **Subject:** Wildlife protection **Obv:** Crowned pointed shield within sprigs **Rev:** Two European polecats

Date	Mintage	VF20	XF40	MS60	MS63	MS65
1993 R	Est. 35000	—	—	5.75	8.75	11.00
1993 R	—	PF65 22.00				

KM# 301 500 LIRE

6.80 g., Bi-Metallic Aluminum-Bronze center in Stainless Steel ring, 25.8 mm. **Obv:** Ostrich feathers and towers within circle **Rev:** Growth from a tree stump **Edge:** Segmented reeding

Date	Mintage	VF20	XF40	MS60	MS63	MS65
1993 R	4,200,000	—	—	—	3.00	5.00

KM# 314 500 LIRE

6.80 g., Bi-Metallic Aluminum-Bronze center in Stainless Steel ring, 25.8 mm. **Obv:** Stonecutter holding hammer and chisel, ostrich feathers and towers at left, all within circle **Rev:** St. Marino receiving Mount Titano within circle **Edge:** Segmented reeding

Date	Mintage	VF20	XF40	MS60	MS63	MS65
1994 R	40,000	—	—	—	3.00	5.00

KM# 317 500 LIRE

11.00 g., 0.835 Silver 0.2953 oz. ASW, 29 mm. **Subject:** World Cup Soccer **Obv:** Crowned pointed shield within sprigs **Rev:** Fallen soccer player

Date	Mintage	VF20	XF40	MS60	MS63	MS65
1994 R	—	PF65 16.00				

KM# 330 500 LIRE

6.80 g., Bi-Metallic Aluminum-Bronze center in Stainless Steel ring, 25.8 mm. **Series:** F.A.O. **Subject:** 50th Anniversary - F.A.O. **Obv:** Banner wrapped around bottom of design **Rev:** Kneeling figure under sprig **Edge:** Segmented reeding

Date	Mintage	VF20	XF40	MS60	MS63	MS65
1995 R	3,000,000	—	—	—	3.00	5.00

KM# 357 500 LIRE

6.80 g., Bi-Metallic Aluminum-Bronze center in Stainless Steel ring, 25.8 mm. **Obv:** Bust facing with flame within hands within circle **Rev:** Face within triangle and circle design **Edge:** Segmented reeding

Date	Mintage	VF20	XF40	MS60	MS63	MS65
1996 R	3,911,288	—	—	—	3.00	5.00

KM# 367 500 LIRE

6.80 g., Bi-Metallic Aluminum-Bronze center in Stainless Steel ring, 25.8 mm. **Subject:** The Arts - Music **Obv:** Bust facing with flame within hands within circle **Rev:** Woman playing pipes within circle **Edge:** Segmented reeding

Date	Mintage	VF20	XF40	MS60	MS63	MS65
1997 R	28,000	—	—	—	3.00	5.00

Note: In mint sets only

KM# 383 500 LIRE

6.80 g., Bi-Metallic Aluminum-Bronze center in Stainless Steel ring, 25.8 mm. **Subject:** Chemistry **Obv:** Bust facing with flame within hands within circle **Rev:** Laboratory

Date	Mintage	VF20	XF40	MS60	MS63	MS65
1998 R	1,300,000	—	—	—	3.00	5.00

KM# 394 500 LIRE

6.80 g., Bi-Metallic Aluminum-Bronze center in Stainless Steel ring, 25.86 mm. **Subject:** Exploration **Obv:** Bust facing with flame within hands within circle **Rev:** Moon's surface, radio waves and Saturn **Edge:** Segmented reeding

Date	Mintage	VF20	XF40	MS60	MS63	MS65
1999 R	2,000,000	—	—	—	3.00	5.00

KM# 404 500 LIRE

6.80 g., Bi-Metallic Aluminum-Bronze center in Stainless Steel ring, 25.8 mm. **Subject:** Work **Obv:** Bust facing with flames within hands within circle **Rev:** Spinning wheel design within circle **Edge:** Segmented reeding

Date	Mintage	VF20	XF40	MS60	MS63	MS65
2000 R	28,000	—	—	—	3.00	5.00

Note: In mint sets only

KM# 72 1000 LIRE

14.60 g., 0.835 Silver 0.3919 oz. ASW, 31.4 mm. **Subject:** 600th Anniversary - Birth of Brunelleschi- architect, author **Obv:** Standing figures on railed platform **Rev:** Head 3/4 left facing **Note:** 38,145 coins melted at the mint.

Date	Mintage	VF20	XF40	MS60	MS63	MS65
ND-1977	180,000	—	—	7.50	11.50	14.50

KM# 85 1000 LIRE

14.60 g., 0.835 Silver 0.3919 oz. ASW, 31.4 mm. **Subject:** 150th Anniversary - Birth of Tolstoy **Obv:** Ostrich feathers and towers **Rev:** Head left **Note:** 17,892 coins melted at the mint.

Date	Mintage	VF20	XF40	MS60	MS63	MS65
ND-1978	130,000	—	—	7.50	11.50	14.50

KM# 98 1000 LIRE

14.60 g., 0.835 Silver 0.3919 oz. ASW, 31.4 mm. **Subject:** European Unity **Obv:** Crown above stylized ostrich feathers and towers **Rev:** Seagulls above figure facing right **Note:** 14,945 coins melted at the mint.

Date	Mintage	VF20	XF40	MS60	MS63	MS65
1979	125,000	—	—	7.50	11.50	14.50

KM# 112 1000 LIRE

14.60 g., 0.835 Silver 0.3919 oz. ASW, 31.4 mm. **Subject:** 1,500th Anniversary - Birth of St. Benedict **Obv:** Ostrich feathers and towers **Rev:** Bust facing **Note:** 49,095 coins melted at the mint.

Date	Mintage	VF20	XF40	MS60	MS63	MS65
1980	125,000	—	—	7.50	11.50	14.50

KM# 127 1000 LIRE

14.60 g., 0.835 Silver 0.3919 oz. ASW, 31.4 mm. **Subject:** 200th Anniversary - Virgil's Death **Obv:** Crowned shield within sprigs **Rev:** Armored figure on horse **Note:** 9,122 coins melted at the mint.

Date	Mintage	VF20	XF40	MS60	MS63	MS65
1981	75,000	—	—	7.50	11.50	14.50

KM# 141 1000 LIRE

14.60 g., 0.835 Silver 0.3919 oz. ASW, 31.4 mm. **Subject:** Centennial - Garibaldi's Death **Obv:** Crowned design above towers **Rev:** Large head facing **Note:** 112 uncirculated and 369 proof coins melted at the mint.

Date	Mintage	VF20	XF40	MS60	MS63	MS65
ND-1982 R	48,000	—	—	7.50	11.50	14.50
ND-1982 R	13,000	PF65 25.00				

KM# 155 1000 LIRE

14.60 g., 0.835 Silver 0.3919 oz. ASW, 31.4 mm. **Subject:** 500th Anniversary - Birth of Artist Raphael **Obv:** Head 1/4 right, towers at top and right **Rev:** Standing figure facing divides date and value **Note:** 80 uncirculated and 1,939 proof coins melted at the mint.

Date	Mintage	VF20	XF40	MS60	MS63	MS65
1983 R	42,000	—	—	7.50	11.50	14.50
1983 R	12,000	PF65 25.00				

KM# 169 1000 LIRE

14.60 g., 0.835 Silver 0.3919 oz. ASW, 31.4 mm. **Series:** 1984 Summer Olympics **Obv:** Stylized ostrich feathers and towers **Rev:** Figures reaching wings of bird divide date and value with olympic rings below **Note:** 2,920 uncirculated and 20 proof coins melted at the mint.

Date	Mintage	VF20	XF40	MS60	MS63	MS65
1984 R	52,000	—	—	7.50	11.50	14.50
1984 R	15,000	PF65 22.50				

KM# 183 1000 LIRE

14.60 g., 0.835 Silver 0.3919 oz. ASW, 31.4 mm. **Subject:** European Music Year, Bach Tercentenary **Obv:** ostrich feathers and towers within crowned shield **Rev:** J.S. Bach **Note:** 6,704 uncirculated and 122 proof coins melted at the mint.

Date	Mintage	VF20	XF40	MS60	MS63	MS65
1985 R	40,000	—	—	7.50	11.50	14.50
1985 R	12,000	PF65 25.00				

KM# 197 1000 LIRE

14.60 g., 0.835 Silver 0.3919 oz. ASW, 31.4 mm. **Subject:** Soccer **Obv:** Head left **Rev:** Stylized flags **Note:** 5,212 uncirculated and 60 proof coins melted at the mint.

Date	Mintage	VF20	XF40	MS60	MS63	MS65
1986 R	45,000	—	—	7.50	11.50	14.50
1986 R	12,000	PF65 30.00				

KM# 210 1000 LIRE

14.60 g., 0.835 Silver 0.3919 oz. ASW, 31.4 mm. **Subject:** 15th Anniversary - Resumption of Coinage **Obv:** Crowned pointed shield within sprigs **Rev:** Standing Saint figure facing **Note:** 13 coins melted at the mint.

Date	Mintage	VF20	XF40	MS60	MS63	MS65
1987 R	43,000	—	—	7.50	11.50	14.50

KM# 214 1000 LIRE

14.60 g., 0.835 Silver 0.3919 oz. ASW, 31.4 mm. **Subject:** Zagreb University Games **Rev:** Pole vaulter **Note:** 9,207 uncirculated and 1,206 proof coins melted at the mint.

Date	Mintage	VF20	XF40	MS60	MS63	MS65
1987 R	35,000	—	—	7.50	11.50	14.50
1987 R	10,000	PF65 30.00				

KM# 217 1000 LIRE

14.60 g., 0.835 Silver 0.3919 oz. ASW, 31.4 mm. **Series:** Summer Olympics **Obv:** Stylized ostrich feathers and towers **Rev:** Diver **Note:** 146 uncirculated and 3 proof coins melted at the mint.

Date	Mintage	VF20	XF40	MS60	MS63	MS65
1988 R	32,000	—	—	7.50	11.50	14.50
1988 R	9,600	PF65 30.00				

KM# 227 1000 LIRE

14.60 g., 0.835 Silver 0.3919 oz. ASW, 31.4 mm. **Subject:** Fortifications **Obv:** Crowned ornate arms on shield **Rev:** Walls and towers

Date	Mintage	VF20	XF40	MS60	MS63	MS65
1988 R	38,000	—	—	7.50	11.50	14.50

KM# 240 1000 LIRE

14.60 g., 0.835 Silver 0.3919 oz. ASW, 31.4 mm. **Subject:** History **Obv:** Crowned shield **Rev:** Two men standing in boat

Date	Mintage	VF20	XF40	MS60	MS63	MS65
1989 R	32,000	—	—	7.50	11.50	14.50

KM# 244 1000 LIRE

14.60 g., 0.835 Silver 0.3919 oz. ASW, 31.4 mm. **Subject:** San Marino Grand Prix **Obv:** Stylized ostrich feathers and towers **Rev:** Date and value below race car **Note:** 5,180 coins melted at the mint.

Date	Mintage	VF20	XF40	MS60	MS63	MS65
1989 R	30,000	—	—	7.50	11.50	14.50
1989 R	8,000	PF65 35.00				

KM# 247 1000 LIRE
14.60 g., 0.835 Silver 0.3919 oz. ASW, 31.4 mm. **Subject:** World Cup Soccer Championship Games **Obv:** Patterned design surrounds oval shield at center **Rev:** Winged Victory divides value

Date	Mintage	VF20	XF40	MS60	MS63	MS65
1990 R	40,000	—	—	7.50	11.50	14.50
1990 R	19,000	PF65 30.00				

KM# 257 1000 LIRE
14.60 g., 0.835 Silver 0.3919 oz. ASW, 31.4 mm. **Subject:** 1,600 Years of History **Obv:** Towers above design **Rev:** Stylized hand and two figures

Date	Mintage	VF20	XF40	MS60	MS63	MS65
1990 R	36,000	—	—	7.50	11.50	14.50

KM# 270 1000 LIRE
14.60 g., 0.835 Silver 0.3919 oz. ASW, 31.4 mm. **Obv:** Date at upper left of ostrich featehrs and towers **Rev:** Large value above hand holding dove

Date	Mintage	VF20	XF40	MS60	MS63	MS65
1991 R	—	—	—	7.50	11.50	14.50

KM# 272 1000 LIRE
14.60 g., 0.835 Silver 0.3919 oz. ASW, 31.4 mm. **Series:** Barcelona Olympics **Rev:** Stylized runner and Olympic rings

Date	Mintage	VF20	XF40	MS60	MS63	MS65
1991 R	Est. 60000	—	—	7.50	11.50	14.50
1991 R	—	PF65 32.50				

KM# 277 1000 LIRE
14.60 g., 0.835 Silver 0.3919 oz. ASW, 31.4 mm. **Series:** Olympics **Obv:** Stylized ostrich feathers and towers **Rev:** Athletes

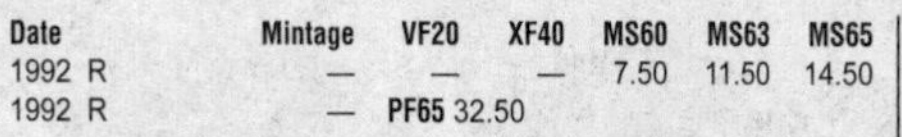

Date	Mintage	VF20	XF40	MS60	MS63	MS65
1992 R	—	—	—	7.50	11.50	14.50
1992 R	—	PF65 32.50				

KM# 287 1000 LIRE
14.60 g., 0.835 Silver 0.3919 oz. ASW, 31.4 mm. **Obv:** Ostrich feathers and towers within circle **Rev:** Columbus studying chart within circle

Date	Mintage	VF20	XF40	MS60	MS63	MS65
ND-1992 R	—	—	—	7.50	11.50	14.50

KM# 292 1000 LIRE
14.60 g., 0.835 Silver 0.3919 oz. ASW, 31.4 mm. **Series:** Wildlife Protection **Obv:** Crowned pointed shield within sprigs **Rev:** Falcon and Woodpecker

Date	Mintage	VF20	XF40	MS60	MS63	MS65
1993 R	—	—	—	7.50	11.50	14.50
1993 R	—	PF65 30.00				

KM# 302 1000 LIRE
14.60 g., 0.835 Silver 0.3919 oz. ASW, 31.4 mm. **Obv:** Ostrich feathers and towers **Rev:** Wing above globe

Date	Mintage	VF20	XF40	MS60	MS63	MS65
1993 R	—	—	—	7.50	11.50	14.50

KM# 315 1000 LIRE
14.60 g., 0.835 Silver 0.3919 oz. ASW, 31.4 mm. **Subject:** Founder Building First San Marino Church **Obv:** Stonecutter holding hammer and chisel, ostrich feathers and towers at left **Rev:** Seated stone cutter

Date	Mintage	VF20	XF40	MS60	MS63	MS65
1994 R	40,000	—	—	7.50	11.50	14.50

KM# 316 1000 LIRE
14.60 g., 0.835 Silver 0.3919 oz. ASW, 31.4 mm. **Series:** Olympics **Obv:** Crowned pointed shield within sprigs **Rev:** Ski jumper

Date	Mintage	VF20	XF40	MS60	MS63	MS65
1994 R	—	PF65 20.00				

KM# 318 1000 LIRE
14.60 g., 0.835 Silver 0.3919 oz. ASW, 31.4 mm. **Subject:** World Cup Soccer **Obv:** Crowned pointed shield within sprigs **Rev:** Soccer players

Date	Mintage	VF20	XF40	MS60	MS63	MS65
1994 R	—	PF65 27.50				

KM# 331 1000 LIRE
14.60 g., 0.835 Silver 0.3919 oz. ASW, 31.4 mm. **Obv:** Banner wrapped around quills **Rev:** Pyramid of children within value

Date	Mintage	VF20	XF40	MS60	MS63	MS65
1995 R	—	—	—	7.50	11.50	14.50

KM# 332 1000 LIRE
14.60 g., 0.835 Silver 0.3919 oz. ASW, 31.4 mm. **Series:** 1996 Olympics **Obv:** Crowned pointed shield within sprigs **Rev:** Pole vaulting and discus

Date	Mintage	VF20	XF40	MS60	MS63	MS65
1995 R	50,000	PF65 30.00				

KM# 358 1000 LIRE
14.60 g., 0.835 Silver 0.3919 oz. ASW, 31.4 mm. **Obv:** Bust facing with flame within hands **Rev:** Head of Popper facing

Date	Mintage	VF20	XF40	MS60	MS63	MS65
1996 R	32,000	—	—	7.50	11.50	14.50

KM# 368 1000 LIRE
8.82 g., Bi-Metallic Copper-Nickel center in Aluminum-Bronze ring, 27 mm. **Subject:** Millennium of building of the castle **Obv:** Heraldic lion within circle **Rev:** Statue, building and value within circle

Date	Mintage	VF20	XF40	MS60	MS63	MS65
1997 R	2,232,541	—	—	—	5.00	7.00

KM# 369 1000 LIRE
14.60 g., 0.835 Silver 0.3919 oz. ASW, 31.4 mm. **Subject:** The Arts - Interplanetary Communication **Obv:** Bust facing with flame within hands **Rev:** Nude couple from Pioneer 10 space probe plaque

Date	Mintage	VF20	XF40	MS60	MS63	MS65
1997 R	28,000	—	—	7.50	11.50	14.50

KM# 384 1000 LIRE
Bi-Metallic Copper-Nickel center in Aluminum-Bronze ring, 27 mm. **Subject:** Geology **Obv:** Child of the Universe **Rev:** Family standing on earth

Date	Mintage	VF20	XF40	MS60	MS63	MS65
1998 R	2,061,275	—	—	—	5.00	7.00

KM# 395 1000 LIRE
Bi-Metallic Copper-Nickel center in Aluminum-Bronze ring, 27 mm. **Subject:** Exploration **Obv:** Child of the Universe **Rev:** Radiant north star design

Date	Mintage	VF20	XF40	MS60	MS63	MS65
1999 R	1,836,495	—	—	—	5.00	7.00

KM# 405 1000 LIRE
Bi-Metallic Copper-Nickel center in Aluminum-Bronze ring, 27 mm. **Subject:** Liberty **Obv:** Child of the Universe **Rev:** Barn Swallow flying over world globe **Edge:** Reeded and plain sectioned **Note:** Struck at Rome.

Date	Mintage	VF20	XF40	MS60	MS63	MS65
2000 R	2,898,805	—	—	—	7.00	9.00

KM# 333 5000 LIRE
18.00 g., 0.835 Silver 0.4832 oz. ASW **Subject:** Sail Training Ship "Amerigo Vespucci" **Obv:** Crowned pointed shield within sprigs **Rev:** Sailing ship

Date	Mintage	VF20	XF40	MS60	MS63	MS65
1995 R	—	PF65 22.50				

KM# 340 5000 LIRE
18.00 g., 0.835 Silver 0.4832 oz. ASW **Series:** Wildlife Protection **Obv:** Crowned pointed shield within sprigs **Rev:** Falcons

Date	Mintage	VF20	XF40	MS60	MS63	MS65
1996	Est. 35000	PF65 35.00				

KM# 370 5000 LIRE
18.00 g., 0.835 Silver 0.4832 oz. ASW, 32 mm. **Obv:** Crowned pointed shield within sprigs **Rev:** Sailing ship and map of Africa **Rev. Legend:** VASCO DA GAMA 1497

Date	Mintage	VF20	XF40	MS60	MS63	MS65
1997 R	35,000	PF65 20.00				

KM# 385 5000 LIRE
18.00 g., 0.835 Silver 0.4832 oz. ASW **Subject:** Medicine **Obv:** Child of the Universe **Rev:** Emblem within circle of face outline left

Date	Mintage	VF20	XF40	MS60	MS63	MS65
1998 R	—	—	—	9.50	14.50	18.00

KM# 386 5000 LIRE
18.00 g., 0.835 Silver 0.4832 oz. ASW, 32 mm. **Subject:** Europe in the New Millennium **Obv:** Crowned pointed shield within sprigs **Rev:** Euro bridge with ivy, olive and oak trees **Edge:** Lettered **Edge Lettering:** RELINQUO VOS LIBEROS **Note:** Struck at Rome.

Date	Mintage	VF20	XF40	MS60	MS63	MS65
1998 R	—	PF65 22.50				

KM# 396 5000 LIRE
18.00 g., 0.835 Silver 0.4832 oz. ASW **Subject:** Exploration **Obv:** Crowned shield **Rev:** Solar system, European map and dish in human mind

Date	Mintage	VF20	XF40	MS60	MS63	MS65
1999 R	—	—	—	9.50	14.50	18.00

KM# 410 5000 LIRE
18.00 g., 0.835 Silver 0.4832 oz. ASW **Subject:** European Union **Obv:** Crowned pointed shield within sprigs **Rev:** Value above flags **Edge:** Lettered **Edge Lettering:** RELINQUO VOS LIBEROS

Date	Mintage	VF20	XF40	MS60	MS63	MS65
1999 R	—	PF65 30.00				

KM# 406 5000 LIRE
18.00 g., 0.835 Silver 0.4832 oz. ASW, 32 mm. **Subject:** Peace **Obv:** Child of the Universe **Rev:** Hawk and dove with same olive branch in their beaks **Edge:** Reeded and plain sectioned **Note:** Struck at Rome.

Date	Mintage	VF20	XF40	MS60	MS63	MS65
2000 R	—	—	—	9.50	14.50	18.00

KM# 421 5000 LIRE
18.00 g., 0.835 Silver 0.4832 oz. ASW **Subject:** First Holy Year Jubilee **Obv:** Crowned pointed shield within sprigs **Rev:** Pope Boniface VIII with two aides **Edge:** Lettered **Edge Lettering:** RELINQUO VOS LIBEROS

Date	Mintage	VF20	XF40	MS60	MS63	MS65
2000 R	—	PF65 22.50				

KM# 334 10000 LIRE
22.00 g., 0.835 Silver 0.5906 oz. ASW **Subject:** Amerigo Vespucci **Obv:** Crowned pointed shield within sprigs **Rev:** Cameo to upper left of ship

Date	Mintage	VF20	XF40	MS60	MS63	MS65
1995 R	Est. 35000	PF65 25.00				

KM# 341 10000 LIRE
22.00 g., 0.835 Silver 0.5906 oz. ASW **Series:** Wildlife Protection **Obv:** Crowned pointed shield within sprigs **Rev:** Wolves

Date	Mintage	VF20	XF40	MS60	MS63	MS65
1996	—	PF65 45.00				

KM# 342 10000 LIRE
22.00 g., 0.835 Silver 0.5906 oz. ASW **Subject:** Euro **Obv:** Crowned pointed shield within sprigs **Rev:** Parliament building and map

Date	Mintage	VF20	XF40	MS60	MS63	MS65
1996	—	PF65 30.00				

KM# 371 10000 LIRE
22.00 g., 0.835 Silver 0.5906 oz. ASW **Subject:** Giovanni Caboto 1497 **Obv:** Crowned pointed shield within sprigs **Rev:** Ship and Atlantic map

Date	Mintage	VF20	XF40	MS60	MS63	MS65
1997 R	35,000	PF65 28.00				

KM# 372 10000 LIRE
22.00 g., 0.835 Silver 0.5906 oz. ASW **Subject:** Euro - "Libertas" **Obv:** National arms above the 9 Casteli arms **Rev:** Head left within oval star design

Date	Mintage	VF20	XF40	MS60	MS63	MS65
1997 R	—	PF65 32.00				

KM# 376 10000 LIRE
22.00 g., 0.835 Silver 0.5906 oz. ASW **Subject:** Soccer World Championship **Obv:** Crowned pointed shield within sprigs **Rev:** Soccer players

Date	Mintage	VF20	XF40	MS60	MS63	MS65
1998 R	—	PF65 30.00				

KM# 377 10000 LIRE
22.00 g., 0.835 Silver 0.5906 oz. ASW, 34 mm. **Subject:** 50th Anniversary - Ferrari **Obv:** Crowned pointed shield within sprigs **Rev:** Race cars **Edge:** Reeded and plain sections

Date	Mintage	VF20	XF40	MS60	MS63	MS65
1998 R	—	PF65 27.50				

KM# 387 10000 LIRE
22.00 g., 0.835 Silver 0.5906 oz. ASW **Subject:** Europe in the New Millennium **Obv:** Crowned pointed shield within sprigs **Rev:** Child with flags

Date	Mintage	VF20	XF40	MS60	MS63	MS65
1998 R	—	PF65 28.50				

KM# 397 10000 LIRE
22.00 g., 0.835 Silver 0.5906 oz. ASW **Subject:** III Millennium **Obv:** Crowned pointed shield within sprigs **Rev:** Allegorical portrait of DNA unraveling from human mind

Date	Mintage	VF20	XF40	MS60	MS63	MS65
1999 R	Est. 25000	PF65 30.00				

KM# 398 10000 LIRE
22.00 g., 0.835 Silver 0.5906 oz. ASW **Series:** 2000 Olympics **Obv:** Crowned pointed shield within sprigs **Rev:** Prone shooter

Date	Mintage	VF20	XF40	MS60	MS63	MS65
1999 R	Est. 35000	PF65 27.50				

KM# 411 10000 LIRE
22.00 g., 0.835 Silver 0.5906 oz. ASW **Subject:** European Union **Obv:** Crowned pointed shield within sprigs **Rev:** Circle of paper dolls above value

Date	Mintage	VF20	XF40	MS60	MS63	MS65
1999 R	—	PF65 35.00				

KM# 419 10000 LIRE
22.00 g., 0.835 Silver 0.5906 oz. ASW, 34 mm. **Subject:** 17th Centennial of the Republic **Obv:** Crowned pointed shield within sprigs **Rev:** Bust of St. Marino facing

Date	Mintage	VF20	XF40	MS60	MS63	MS65
2000 R	18,000	PF65 25.00				

KM# 422 10000 LIRE
22.00 g., 0.835 Silver 0.5906 oz. ASW, 34 mm. **Subject:** Holy Year **Obv:** Crowned pointed shield within sprigs **Rev:** Pope kneeling before an open door **Edge:** Reeded and plain sections

Date	Mintage	VF20	XF40	MS60	MS63	MS65
2000 R	—	PF65 30.00				

KM# 423 10000 LIRE
22.00 g., 0.835 Silver 0.5906 oz. ASW, 34 mm. **Obv:** Crowned pointed shield within sprigs **Rev:** Michelangelo's Sacred Family Painting **Edge:** Reeded and plain sections

Date	Mintage	VF20	XF40	MS60	MS63	MS65
2000 R	—	PF65 30.00				

KM# 416 1/2 SCUDO
1.61 g., 0.900 Gold 0.0466 oz. AGW, 14 mm. **Subject:** Ilcenacolo **Obv:** Crowned pointed shield within sprigs **Rev:** Bearded bust facing **Edge:** Reeded **Note:** 1,915 coins melted at the mint.

Date	Mintage	VF20	XF40	MS60	MS63	MS65
1998	8,000	PF65 75.00				

KM# 413 1/2 SCUDO
1.61 g., 0.900 Gold 0.0466 oz. AGW **Subject:** Ritratto di Agnolo Doni **Obv:** Crowned pointed shield within sprigs **Rev:** Head 3/4 right

Date	Mintage	VF20	XF40	MS60	MS63	MS65
1999	—	PF65 75.00				

KM# 407 1/2 SCUDO
1.61 g., 0.900 Gold 0.0466 oz. AGW **Subject:** Ritratto di Giovane Donna **Obv:** Crowned pointed shield within sprigs **Rev:** Head left

Date	Mintage	VF20	XF40	MS60	MS63	MS65
2000	—	PF65 75.00				

KM# 38 SCUDO
3.00 g., 0.917 Gold 0.0884 oz. AGW **Obv:** Crowned pointed shield within sprigs **Rev:** Standing Saint facing **Note:** 2,491 coins melted at the mint.

Date	Mintage	VF20	XF40	MS60	MS63	MS65
1974	87,000	—	—	—	—	150

KM# 49 SCUDO

3.00 g., 0.917 Gold 0.0884 oz. AGW **Obv:** Crowned pointed shield within sprigs **Rev:** Value and date within wreath **Note:** 37,668 coins melted at the mint.

Date	Mintage	VF20	XF40	MS60	MS63	MS65
1975	90,000	—	—	—	—	150

KM# 60 SCUDO

3.00 g., 0.917 Gold 0.0884 oz. AGW **Obv:** Stylized ostrich feathers and towers **Rev:** Laureate head right **Note:** 30,026 coins melted at the mint.

Date	Mintage	VF20	XF40	MS60	MS63	MS65
1976	65,000	—	—	—	—	150

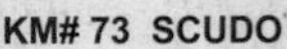

KM# 73 SCUDO

3.00 g., 0.917 Gold 0.0884 oz. AGW **Obv:** ostrich feathers and towers **Rev:** Democrazia **Note:** 1,839 coins melted at the mint.

Date	Mintage	VF20	XF40	MS60	MS63	MS65
1977	35,000	—	—	—	—	150

KM# 86 SCUDO

3.00 g., 0.917 Gold 0.0884 oz. AGW **Obv:** Ostrich feathers and towers **Rev:** Miss Liberta **Note:** 9,021 coins melted at the mint.

Date	Mintage	VF20	XF40	MS60	MS63	MS65
1978	38,000	—	—	—	—	150

KM# 99 SCUDO

3.00 g., 0.917 Gold 0.0884 oz. AGW **Obv:** Value within upright ostrich feathers **Rev:** Peace **Note:** 4,152 coins melted at the mint.

Date	Mintage	VF20	XF40	MS60	MS63	MS65
1979	38,000	—	—	—	—	150

KM# 113 SCUDO

3.00 g., 0.917 Gold 0.0884 oz. AGW **Rev:** Head on hands facing, dove at left **Note:** 10,309 coins melted at the mint.

Date	Mintage	VF20	XF40	MS60	MS63	MS65
1980 R	38,000	—	—	—	—	150

KM# 128 SCUDO

3.00 g., 0.917 Gold 0.0884 oz. AGW **Subject:** World Food Day **Obv:** Crowned pointed shield within sprigs above inscription **Rev:** Seated figure reading **Note:** 196 coins melted at the mint.

Date	Mintage	VF20	XF40	MS60	MS63	MS65
1981 R	31,000	—	—	—	—	150

KM# 142 SCUDO

3.00 g., 0.917 Gold 0.0884 oz. AGW **Obv:** Crowned shield **Rev:** Head left **Note:** 1,192 coins melted at the mint.

Date	Mintage	VF20	XF40	MS60	MS63	MS65
1982 R	17,000	—	—	—	—	150

KM# 156 SCUDO

2.00 g., 0.917 Gold 0.059 oz. AGW **Rev:** Perpetual Liberty **Note:** 917 coins melted at the mint.

Date	Mintage	VF20	XF40	MS60	MS63	MS65
1983 R	14,000	—	—	—	—	95.00

KM# 170 SCUDO

2.00 g., 0.917 Gold 0.059 oz. AGW **Subject:** Peace **Obv:** Crowned shield in front of city scene **Rev:** Half-figure holding laurel branch left **Note:** 979 coins melted at the mint.

Date	Mintage	VF20	XF40	MS60	MS63	MS65
1984 R	11,000	—	—	—	—	95.00

KM# 184 SCUDO

2.00 g., 0.917 Gold 0.059 oz. AGW **Subject:** International Year for Youth **Rev:** Head left **Note:** 1,162 coins melted at the mint.

Date	Mintage	VF20	XF40	MS60	MS63	MS65
1985 R	10,000	—	—	—	—	95.00

KM# 198 SCUDO

3.39 g., 0.917 Gold 0.100 oz. AGW **Subject:** Insects at Work **Rev:** Large ant **Note:** 1,308 coins melted at the mint.

Date	Mintage	VF20	XF40	MS60	MS63	MS65
1986 R	9,000	—	—	—	—	170

KM# 211 SCUDO

3.39 g., 0.917 Gold 0.100 oz. AGW **Subject:** European Year for Environment **Obv:** Robe-like design with seagull at right **Rev:** Nude children under sprig **Note:** 962 coins melted at the mint.

Date	Mintage	VF20	XF40	MS60	MS63	MS65
1987 R	8,000	—	—	—	—	170

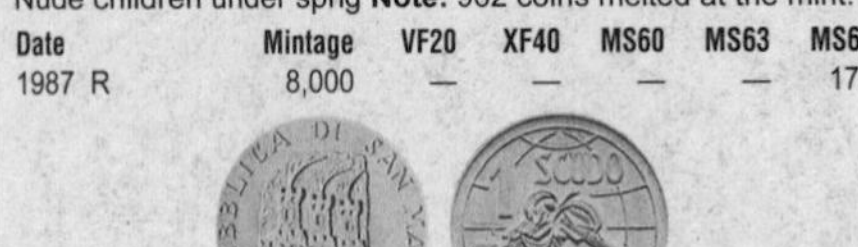

KM# 228 SCUDO

3.39 g., 0.917 Gold 0.100 oz. AGW **Subject:** Disarmament **Obv:** Stylized ostrich feathers and towers **Rev:** Design within globe **Note:** 873 coins melted at the mint.

Date	Mintage	VF20	XF40	MS60	MS63	MS65
1988 R	7,000	—	—	—	—	170

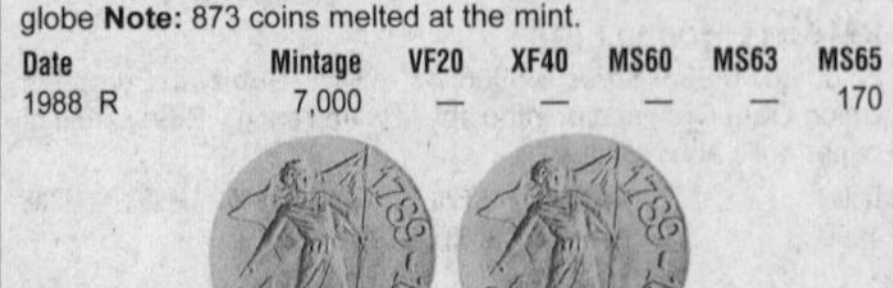

KM# 241 SCUDO

3.23 g., 0.900 Gold 0.0933 oz. AGW **Subject:** French Revolution **Rev:** Standing figure holding flag **Note:** 731 coins melted at the mint.

Date	Mintage	VF20	XF40	MS60	MS63	MS65
1989 R	7,500	—	—	—	—	160

KM# 258 SCUDO

3.23 g., 0.900 Gold 0.0933 oz. AGW **Subject:** San Marino's Presidency of the European Council **Obv:** Crowned pointed shield within sprigs **Rev:** Bust facing

Date	Mintage	VF20	XF40	MS60	MS63	MS65
1990 R	7,300	—	—	—	—	160

KM# 273 SCUDO

3.23 g., 0.900 Gold 0.0933 oz. AGW **Subject:** Peace **Obv:** Crowned pointed shield within sprigs **Rev:** Child fleeing

Date	Mintage	VF20	XF40	MS60	MS63	MS65
1991 R	Est. 7500	PF65 160				

KM# 288 SCUDO

3.23 g., 0.900 Gold 0.0933 oz. AGW **Subject:** San Marino's Entry Into the United Nations **Obv:** Crowned shield within sprigs **Rev:** UN logo

Date	Mintage	VF20	XF40	MS60	MS63	MS65
1992 R	8,500	PF65 160				

KM# 303 SCUDO

3.23 g., 0.900 Gold 0.0933 oz. AGW **Series:** International Monetary Fund **Rev:** Three standing figures within pointed oblong design **Note:** 455 coins melted at the mint.

Date	Mintage	VF20	XF40	MS60	MS63	MS65
1993 R	7,500	PF65 160				

KM# 319 SCUDO

3.23 g., 0.900 Gold 0.0933 oz. AGW **Series:** International Year of the Family **Obv:** Crowned shield within sprigs **Rev:** Couple facing each other **Note:** Sets only. 648 coins melted at the mint.

Date	Mintage	VF20	XF40	MS60	MS63	MS65
1994 R	7,500	PF65 160				

KM# 335 SCUDO

3.23 g., 0.900 Gold 0.0933 oz. AGW **Series:** 50th Anniversary - United Nations **Obv:** Crowned shield within sprigs **Rev:** Vertical dolphin and nude figure on triangle sides **Note:** Sets only. 494 coins melted at the mint.

Date	Mintage	VF20	XF40	MS60	MS63	MS65
1995 R	6,500	PF65 160				

KM# 338 SCUDO

3.23 g., 0.900 Gold 0.0933 oz. AGW **Series:** 1996 Olympics **Rev:** Boxers **Note:** 664 coins melted at the mint.

Date	Mintage	VF20	XF40	MS60	MS63	MS65
1996	7,000	PF65 160				

KM# 373 SCUDO

3.23 g., 0.900 Gold 0.0933 oz. AGW **Rev:** Michelangelo's

"Kneeling Angel **Note:** 412 coins melted at the mint.

Date	Mintage	VF20	XF40	MS60	MS63	MS65
1997	6,500	PF65 160				

KM# 417 SCUDO

3.23 g., 0.900 Gold 0.0933 oz. AGW, 15.9 mm. **Subject:** Canone Delle Proporzioni **Obv:** Crowned pointed shield within sprigs **Rev:** Anatomical drawing **Edge:** Reeded **Note:** 312 coins melted at the mint.

Date	Mintage	VF20	XF40	MS60	MS63	MS65
1998	6,000	PF65 160				

KM# 414 SCUDO

3.23 g., 0.900 Gold 0.0933 oz. AGW **Subject:** La Velata **Obv:** Crowned shield **Rev:** Head facing 1/4 left

Date	Mintage	VF20	XF40	MS60	MS63	MS65
1999	—	PF65 160				

KM# 408 SCUDO

3.23 g., 0.900 Gold 0.0933 oz. AGW **Obv:** Crowned shield **Rev:** La Primavera

Date	Mintage	VF20	XF40	MS60	MS63	MS65
2000	—	PF65 160				

KM# 39 2 SCUDI

6.00 g., 0.917 Gold 0.1769 oz. AGW **Obv:** Crowned pointed shield within wreath **Rev:** Standing figure facing **Note:** 1,637 coins melted at the mint.

Date	Mintage	VF20	XF40	MS60	MS63	MS65
1974	77,000	—	—	—	—	285

KM# 50 2 SCUDI

6.00 g., 0.917 Gold 0.1769 oz. AGW **Obv:** Crowned pointed shield within wreath **Rev:** Value and date within wreath **Note:** 3,373 coins melted at the mint.

Date	Mintage	VF20	XF40	MS60	MS63	MS65
1975	80,000	—	—	—	—	285

KM# 61 2 SCUDI

6.00 g., 0.917 Gold 0.1769 oz. AGW **Obv:** Stylized ostrich feathers and towers **Rev:** Head 3/4 right **Note:** 20,246 coins melted at the mint.

Date	Mintage	VF20	XF40	MS60	MS63	MS65
1976	55,000	—	—	—	—	285

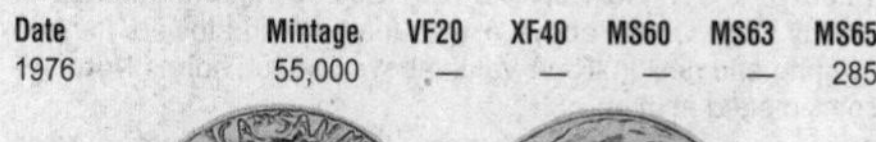

KM# 74 2 SCUDI

6.00 g., 0.917 Gold 0.1769 oz. AGW **Obv:** Date at right of ostrich feathers and towers **Rev:** Democrazia **Note:** 912 coins melted at the mint.

Date	Mintage	VF20	XF40	MS60	MS63	MS65
1977	34,000	—	—	—	—	285

KM# 87 2 SCUDI

6.00 g., 0.917 Gold 0.1769 oz. AGW **Obv:** Value at upper left of ostrich feathers and towers **Rev:** Libertas **Note:** 8,120 coins melted at the mint.

Date	Mintage	VF20	XF40	MS60	MS63	MS65
1978	37,000	—	—	—	—	285

KM# 100 2 SCUDI

6.00 g., 0.917 Gold 0.1769 oz. AGW **Subject:** Peace **Obv:** Three upright ostrich feathers **Rev:** Clasped hands **Note:** 3,238 coins melted at the mint.

Date	Mintage	VF20	XF40	MS60	MS63	MS65
1979	37,000	—	—	—	—	285

KM# 114 2 SCUDI

6.00 g., 0.917 Gold 0.1769 oz. AGW **Subject:** Justice **Obv:** Ostrich feathers and towers **Rev:** Mother holding 2 children **Note:** 9,340 coins melted at the mint.

Date	Mintage	VF20	XF40	MS60	MS63	MS65
1980 R	37,000	—	—	—	—	285

KM# 129 2 SCUDI

6.00 g., 0.917 Gold 0.1769 oz. AGW **Series:** World Food Day **Obv:** Crowned pointed arms within wreath above sprigs **Rev:** Seated nude figure with knees bent upright **Note:** 196 coins melted at the mint.

Date	Mintage	VF20	XF40	MS60	MS63	MS65
1981 R	30,000	—	—	—	—	285

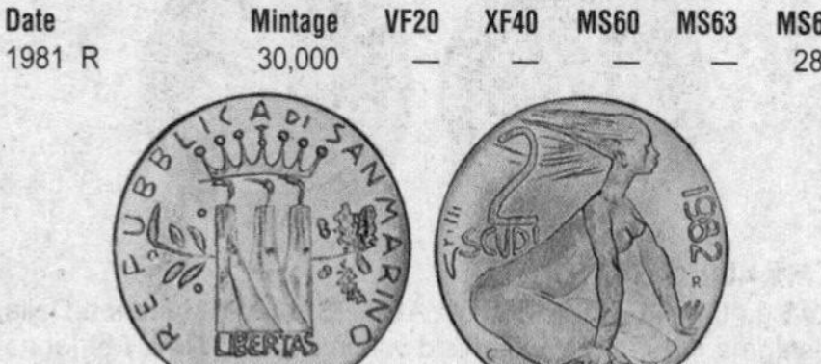

KM# 143 2 SCUDI

6.00 g., 0.917 Gold 0.1769 oz. AGW **Obv:** Crown above ostrich feathers and towers flanked by sprig and design **Rev:** Stylized seated nude right **Note:** 244 coins melted at the mint.

Date	Mintage	VF20	XF40	MS60	MS63	MS65
1982 R	16,000	—	—	—	—	285

KM# 157 2 SCUDI

4.00 g., 0.917 Gold 0.1179 oz. AGW **Subject:** Perpetual Liberty **Obv:** Inscription above crowned shield and sprig **Rev:** Smoking towers on top of head left **Note:** 17 coins melted at the mint.

Date	Mintage	VF20	XF40	MS60	MS63	MS65
1983 R	13,000	—	—	—	—	225

KM# 171 2 SCUDI

4.00 g., 0.917 Gold 0.1179 oz. AGW **Subject:** Liberty **Obv:** Crowned shield in front of city scene **Rev:** Standing figure with arms outstretched left **Note:** 12 coins melted at the mint.

Date	Mintage	VF20	XF40	MS60	MS63	MS65
1984 R	10,000	—	—	—	—	225

KM# 185 2 SCUDI

4.00 g., 0.917 Gold 0.1179 oz. AGW **Series:** International Year for Youth **Obv:** Crown above ostrich feathers and towers on rock flanked by sprigs **Rev:** Head right divides flower and date **Note:** 200 coins melted at the mint.

Date	Mintage	VF20	XF40	MS60	MS63	MS65
1985 R	9,000	—	—	—	—	225

KM# 199 2 SCUDI

6.78 g., 0.917 Gold 0.200 oz. AGW **Obv:** Crowned shield above view **Rev:** Spider within web divides 2S **Note:** 329 coins melted at the mint.

Date	Mintage	VF20	XF40	MS60	MS63	MS65
1986 R	8,000	—	—	—	—	335

KM# 212 2 SCUDI

6.78 g., 0.917 Gold 0.200 oz. AGW **Subject:** European Year for Envrionment **Rev:** Sprig divides dancing figures **Note:** 14 coins melted at the mint.

Date	Mintage	VF20	XF40	MS60	MS63	MS65
1987 R	7,000	—	—	—	—	335

KM# 229 2 SCUDI

6.78 g., 0.917 Gold 0.200 oz. AGW **Subject:** Disarmament **Rev:** Value above sprig within clasped hands, all within world globe design **Note:** 7 coins melted at the mint.

Date	Mintage	VF20	XF40	MS60	MS63	MS65
1988 R	6,000	—	—	—	—	335

KM# 242 2 SCUDI

6.45 g., 0.900 Gold 0.1867 oz. AGW **Subject:** French Revolution **Rev:** Dates above fortress

Date	Mintage	VF20	XF40	MS60	MS63	MS65
1989 R	6,500	—	—	—	—	320

KM# 259 2 SCUDI
6.45 g., 0.900 Gold 0.1867 oz. AGW **Subject:** San Marino's Presidency of the European Council **Obv:** Crowned shield within wreath **Rev:** World globe

Date	Mintage	VF20	XF40	MS60	MS63	MS65
1990 R	6,800	—	—	—	—	320

KM# 274 2 SCUDI
6.45 g., 0.900 Gold 0.1867 oz. AGW **Subject:** Peace **Obv:** Crowned shield within wreath **Rev:** New shoots growing from stump

Date	Mintage	VF20	XF40	MS60	MS63	MS65
1991 R	Est. 6500	PF65 320				

KM# 289 2 SCUDI
6.45 g., 0.900 Gold 0.1867 oz. AGW **Subject:** San Marino's Entry Into the United Nations **Obv:** Crowned shield within wreath **Rev:** UN logo above inscription

Date	Mintage	VF20	XF40	MS60	MS63	MS65
1992 R	7,500	PF65 320				

KM# 304 2 SCUDI
6.45 g., 0.900 Gold 0.1867 oz. AGW **Series:** International Monetary Fund **Obv:** Crowned shield within wreath **Rev:** Two stylized figures within globe design **Note:** 106 coins melted at the mint.

Date	Mintage	VF20	XF40	MS60	MS63	MS65
1993 R	6,500	PF65 320				

KM# 320 2 SCUDI
6.45 g., 0.900 Gold 0.1867 oz. AGW **Series:** International Year of the Family **Obv:** Crowned shield within wreath **Rev:** Family divides value **Note:** Sets only. 252 coins melted at the mint.

Date	Mintage	VF20	XF40	MS60	MS63	MS65
1994 R	6,500	PF65 320				

KM# 336 2 SCUDI
6.45 g., 0.900 Gold 0.1867 oz. AGW **Series:** 50th Anniversary - United Nations **Obv:** Crowned shield within wreath **Rev:** Seated figure with arms outstretched below value within triangular design **Note:** Sets only.

Date	Mintage	VF20	XF40	MS60	MS63	MS65
1995 R	Est. 7000	PF65 320				

KM# 339 2 SCUDI
6.45 g., 0.900 Gold 0.1867 oz. AGW **Series:** 1996 Olympics **Subject:** Track and Field **Obv:** Crowned shield within wreath **Rev:** Three athletes standing left **Note:** 1 coin melted at the mint.

Date	Mintage	VF20	XF40	MS60	MS63	MS65
1996	6,000	PF65 320				

KM# 374 2 SCUDI
6.45 g., 0.900 Gold 0.1867 oz. AGW **Rev:** Michelangelo's "David" **Note:** 124 coins melted at the mint.

Date	Mintage	VF20	XF40	MS60	MS63	MS65
1997	5,800	PF65 320				

KM# 418 2 SCUDI
6.45 g., 0.900 Gold 0.1867 oz. AGW, 21 mm. **Subject:** Vergine Delle Rocce **Obv:** Crowned shield within wreath **Rev:** Female Saint facing **Edge:** Reeded **Note:** 334 coins melted at the mint.

Date	Mintage	VF20	XF40	MS60	MS63	MS65
1998 R	5,500	PF65 320				

KM# 415 2 SCUDI
6.45 g., 0.900 Gold 0.1867 oz. AGW **Subject:** Sposalizio Della Vergine **Obv:** Crowned shield within wreath **Rev:** Three seated figures

Date	Mintage	VF20	XF40	MS60	MS63	MS65
1999	—	PF65 320				

KM# 409 2 SCUDI
6.45 g., 0.900 Gold 0.1867 oz. AGW **Subject:** Madonna Della Melagrna **Obv:** Crowned shield within wreath **Rev:** Madonna and child

Date	Mintage	VF20	XF40	MS60	MS63	MS65
2000	—	PF65 320				

KM# 62 5 SCUDI
15.00 g., 0.917 Gold 0.4422 oz. AGW **Obv:** Value below ostrich feathers and towers **Rev:** Head left **Note:** 25 coins melted at mint.

Date	Mintage	VF20	XF40	MS60	MS63	MS65
1976	8,000	—	—	—	—	700

KM# 75 5 SCUDI
15.00 g., 0.917 Gold 0.4422 oz. AGW **Subject:** Democrazia **Obv:** Value below ostrich feathers and towers **Rev:** Stylized head left **Note:** 29 coins melted at mint.

Date	Mintage	VF20	XF40	MS60	MS63	MS65
1977	16,000	—	—	—	—	700

KM# 101 5 SCUDI
15.00 g., 0.917 Gold 0.4422 oz. AGW **Subject:** Peace **Obv:** Value within upright ostrich feathers **Rev:** Stylized hands and arms **Note:** 161 coins melted at mint.

Date	Mintage	VF20	XF40	MS60	MS63	MS65
1979	24,000	—	—	—	—	700

KM# 115 5 SCUDI
15.00 g., 0.917 Gold 0.4422 oz. AGW **Subject:** Justice **Obv:** Ostrich feathers and towers **Rev:** Head at upper right of birds **Note:** 1,428 coins melted at mint.

Date	Mintage	VF20	XF40	MS60	MS63	MS65
1980 R	24,000	—	—	—	—	700

KM# 130 5 SCUDI
15.00 g., 0.917 Gold 0.4422 oz. AGW **Series:** World Food Day **Obv:** Crowned shield on sprigs above inscription **Rev:** Seated nude figure with knees bent upright **Note:** 33 coins melted at mint.

Date	Mintage	VF20	XF40	MS60	MS63	MS65
1981 R	24,000	—	—	—	—	700

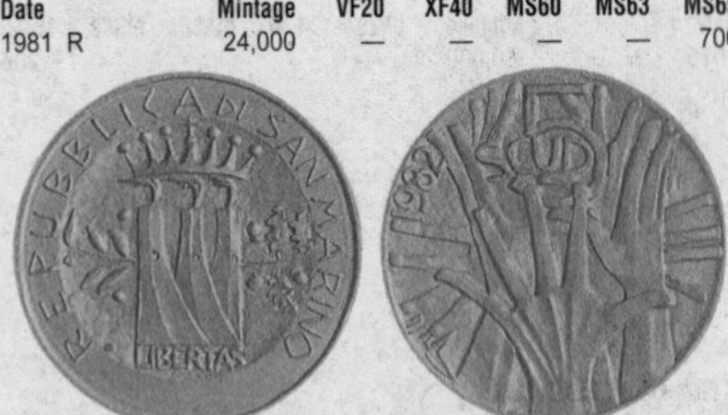

KM# 144 5 SCUDI
15.00 g., 0.917 Gold 0.4422 oz. AGW **Subject:** Defense of Liberty **Obv:** Crown above ostrich feathers and towers flanked by sprig and design **Rev:** Value above stylized hands **Note:** 19 coins melted at mint.

Date	Mintage	VF20	XF40	MS60	MS63	MS65
1982 R	15,000	—	—	—	—	700

KM# 158 5 SCUDI
10.00 g., 0.917 Gold 0.2948 oz. AGW **Subject:** Perpetual Liberty **Obv:** Inscription above crowned shield and sprig **Rev:** Standing figure and child walking right **Note:** 25 coins melted at mint.

Date	Mintage	VF20	XF40	MS60	MS63	MS65
1983 R	11,000	—	—	—	—	465

KM# 172 5 SCUDI
10.00 g., 0.917 Gold 0.2948 oz. AGW **Subject:** Justice **Obv:** Crowned shield in front of castle view **Rev:** Liberty walking on parapet of castle **Note:** 28 coins melted at mint.

Date	Mintage	VF20	XF40	MS60	MS63	MS65
1984 R	9,000	—	—	—	—	465

KM# 186 5 SCUDI
10.00 g., 0.917 Gold 0.2948 oz. AGW **Subject:** Libertas **Obv:** Crown above ostrich feathers and towers on rock flanked by sprigs **Rev:** Three nude dancing figures **Note:** 13 coins melted at mint.

Date	Mintage	VF20	XF40	MS60	MS63	MS65
1985 R	7,400	—	—	—	—	465

KM# 200 5 SCUDI
16.95 g., 0.917 Gold 0.4997 oz. AGW **Subject:** Work **Obv:** Crowned shield above view **Rev:** Bee within honey comb design divides value **Note:** 14 coins melted at mint.

Date	Mintage	VF20	XF40	MS60	MS63	MS65
1986 R	7,000	—	—	—	—	800

KM# 215 5 SCUDI
16.95 g., 0.917 Gold 0.4997 oz. AGW **Subject:** United Nations **Obv:** Crowned shield within wreath **Rev:** Value to left of building and tower **Note:** 49 coins melted at mint.

Date	Mintage	VF20	XF40	MS60	MS63	MS65
1987 R	6,000	—	—	—	—	800

KM# 230 5 SCUDI
16.95 g., 0.917 Gold 0.4997 oz. AGW **Subject:** Human Rights **Obv:** Crowned shield within wreath **Rev:** Stylized flame within wreath, value at upper left **Note:** 11 coins melted at mint.

Date	Mintage	VF20	XF40	MS60	MS63	MS65
1988 R	5,000	—	—	—	—	800

KM# 245 5 SCUDI
16.95 g., 0.917 Gold 0.4997 oz. AGW **Subject:** Entrance of San Marino in Common Market

Date	Mintage	VF20	XF40	MS60	MS63	MS65
1989 R	6,000	—	—	—	—	800

KM# 260 5 SCUDI
16.95 g., 0.917 Gold 0.4997 oz. AGW **Subject:** Founding of the Republic **Obv:** Doves in front of smoking towers **Rev:** Three kneeling figures to right of standing figure

Date	Mintage	VF20	XF40	MS60	MS63	MS65
1990 R	6,500	PF65 800				

KM# 275 5 SCUDI
16.95 g., 0.917 Gold 0.4997 oz. AGW **Subject:** Peace and Freedom **Obv:** Crowned shield within wreath **Rev:** Tree divides family

Date	Mintage	VF20	XF40	MS60	MS63	MS65
1991 R	7,000	PF65 800				

KM# 290 5 SCUDI
16.95 g., 0.917 Gold 0.4997 oz. AGW **Subject:** Customer Agreement with European Economic Community **Obv:** Crowned shield within wreath **Rev:** Value and oat sprig within center of circle of stars

Date	Mintage	VF20	XF40	MS60	MS63	MS65
1992 R	Est. 6500	PF65 800				

KM# 305 5 SCUDI
16.95 g., 0.917 Gold 0.4997 oz. AGW **Series:** International Monetary Fund **Obv:** Crowned shield within wreath **Rev:** Stylized figure holding scale above shield **Note:** 68 coins melted at the mint.

Date	Mintage	VF20	XF40	MS60	MS63	MS65
1993 R	5,500	PF65 800				

KM# 321 5 SCUDI
16.95 g., 0.917 Gold 0.4997 oz. AGW **Series:** International Year of the Family **Obv:** Crowned shield within wreath **Rev:** Family divides value **Note:** 207 coins melted at the mint.

Date	Mintage	VF20	XF40	MS60	MS63	MS65
1994 R	5,500	PF65 800				

KM# 337 5 SCUDI
16.95 g., 0.917 Gold 0.4997 oz. AGW **Series:** 50th Anniversary - United Nations **Obv:** Crowned shield within wreath **Rev:** Seated nude figure and squirrel flanked by dates above value **Note:** 65 coins melted at the mint.

Date	Mintage	VF20	XF40	MS60	MS63	MS65
1995 R	5,000	PF65 800				

KM# 343 5 SCUDI
16.95 g., 0.917 Gold 0.4997 oz. AGW **Obv:** Crowned shield within wreath **Rev:** The Pieta, Mary receives Jesus' body **Note:** 19 coins melted at the mint.

Date	Mintage	VF20	XF40	MS60	MS63	MS65
1996	5,840	PF65 800				

KM# 375 5 SCUDI
16.95 g., 0.917 Gold 0.4997 oz. AGW **Subject:** The Annunciation **Obv:** Crowned shield within wreath **Rev:** Angel **Note:** 469 coins melted at the mint.

Date	Mintage	VF20	XF40	MS60	MS63	MS65
1997	5,500	PF65 800				

KM# 412 5 SCUDI
16.96 g., 0.917 Gold 0.500 oz. AGW **Subject:** Madonna Della Seggiola **Obv:** Crowned shield within wreath **Rev:** Woman with 2 children **Note:** 1,151 coins melted at the mint.

Date	Mintage	VF20	XF40	MS60	MS63	MS65
1998 R	5,000	PF65 800				

KM# 388 5 SCUDI
16.96 g., 0.917 Gold 0.500 oz. AGW **Subject:** Birth of Venus **Obv:** Crowned shield within wreath **Rev:** Venus standing in shell

Date	Mintage	VF20	XF40	MS60	MS63	MS65
1999 R	—	PF65 800				

KM# 420 5 SCUDI
16.96 g., 0.917 Gold 0.500 oz. AGW **Subject:** Tiziano's painting "Rape of Europa" **Obv:** Crowned shield within wreath **Rev:** Europa on a bull's (Zeus) back

Date	Mintage	VF20	XF40	MS60	MS63	MS65
2000 R	4,486	PF65 800				

KM# 88 10 SCUDI
30.00 g., 0.917 Gold 0.8845 oz. AGW **Obv:** Ostrich feathers and towers within circle **Rev:** Head left **Note:** 54 coins melted at the mint.

Date	Mintage	VF20	XF40	MS60	MS63	MS65
1978	20,000	PF65 1,400				

PROVAS

KM#	Date	Mintage	Identification	Mkt Val
Pr1	1925R	75	20 Lire. Gold. KM8.	3,500
Pr2	1931R	—	5 Lire. Silver. KM9.	500
Pr3	1931R	—	10 Lire. Silver. KM10.	450
Pr4	1931R	—	20 Lire. Silver. KM11.	1,300

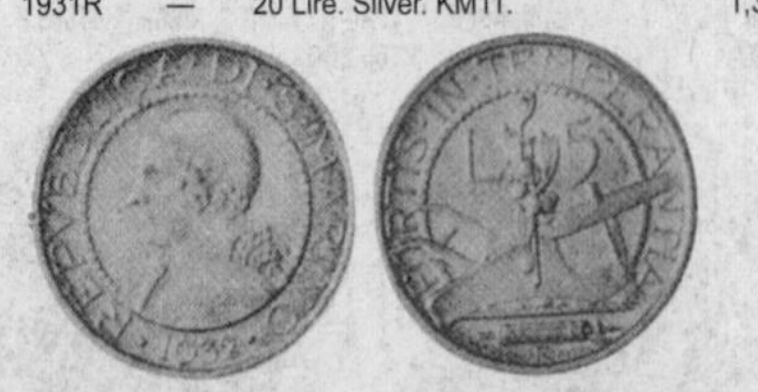

KM#	Date	Mintage	Identification	Mkt Val
Pr5	1932R	—	5 Lire. Silver. KM9.	1,750

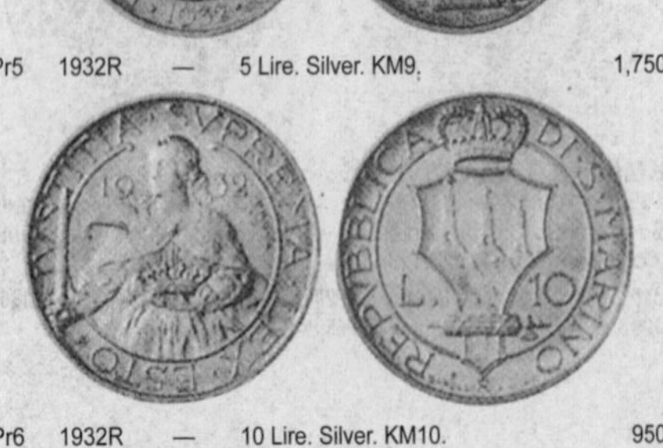

KM#	Date	Mintage	Identification	Mkt Val
Pr6	1932R	—	10 Lire. Silver. KM10.	950
Pr7	1933	—	5 Lire. Silver. KM9.	350

KM#	Date	Mintage	Identification	Mkt Val
Pr8	1933	—	10 Lire. Silver. KM10.	400
Pr9	1933	—	20 Lire. Silver. KM11.	550
Pr10	1935R	—	5 Lire. Silver. KM9.	650
Pr11	1935R	—	20 Lire. Silver. KM11.	1,150
PrA12	1936R	—	5 Lire. Silver. KM#9.	650

KM#	Date	Mintage	Identification	Mkt Val
Pr12	1937R	—	10 Lire. Silver. KM10.	850

KM#	Date	Mintage	Identification	Mkt Val
Pr13	1938R	—	10 Lire. 0.835. Silver. Crowned arms. Allegorical woman. Lettered.	950

MINT SETS

KM#	Date	Mintage	Identification	Issue Price	Mkt Val
MS1	1972 (8)	—	KM14-21	5.00	20.00
MS2	1973 (8)	—	KM22-29	6.00	20.00
MS3	1974 (8)	60,000	KM30-37	9.00	25.00
MS4	1974 (2)	60,000	KM38-39	—	380
MS5	1975 (7)	—	KM40-47	6.50	22.50
MS6	1975 (5)	—	KM40-44	—	8.00
MS7	1975 (2)	90,000	KM49-50	—	380
MS8	1976 (8)	—	KM51-58	6.00	20.00
MS9	1976 (2)	40,000	KM60-61	—	390
MS10	1977 (9)	—	KM63-71	—	20.00
MS11	1977 (2)	30,000	KM73-74	—	390
MS12	1978 (9)	—	KM76-84	—	20.00
MS13	1978 (2)	—	KM86-87	—	390
MS14	1979 (10)	—	KM89-98	—	40.00
MS15	1979 (2)	—	KM99-100	—	390
MS16	1980 (9)	—	KM102-110	—	25.00
MS17	1980 (2)	—	KM113-114	—	390
MS18	1981 (9)	—	KM116-123, 126	—	22.00
MS19	1981 (3)	—	KM124-125, 127	—	40.00
MS20	1981 (2)	—	KM128-129	—	410
MS21	1982 (9)	—	KM131-138, 140	6.00	20.00
MS22	1982 (2)	—	KM139, 141	—	25.00
MS23	1982 (2)	—	KM142-143	—	410
MS24	1983 (9)	—	KM145-153	5.50	20.00
MS25	1983 (2)	—	KM154-155	—	25.00
MS26	1983 (2)	—	KM156-157	—	265
MS27	1984 (9)	—	KM159-167	—	20.00
MS28	1984 (2)	—	KM168-169	—	22.00
MS29	1984 (2)	—	KM170-171	—	265
MS30	1985 (9)	—	KM173-181	—	20.00
MS31	1985 (2)	—	KM182-183	—	25.00
MS32	1985 (2)	—	KM184-185	—	270
MS33	1986 (9)	—	KM187-195	7.00	20.00
MS34	1986 (2)	—	KM196-197	—	25.00
MS35	1986 (2)	—	KM198-199	—	440
MS36	1987 (10)	43,000	KM201-210	—	30.00
MS37	1987 (2)	—	KM213-214	—	25.00
MS38	1987 (2)	—	KM211-212	—	440
MS39	1988 (10)	80,000	KM218-227	22.00	30.00
MS40	1988 (2)	—	KM216-217	—	25.00
MS41	1988 (2)	—	KM228-229	—	425
MS42	1989 (10)	32,000	KM231-240	—	30.00
MS43	1989 (2)	30,000	KM243-244	—	28.00
MS44	1989 (2)	6,500	KM241-242	—	425
MS45	1990 (10)	36,000	KM248-257	—	30.00
MS46	1990 (2)	40,000	KM246-247	—	28.00
MS47	1990 (2)	6,800	KM258-259	—	425
MS48	1991 (10)	36,000	KM261-270	—	30.00
MS49	1991 (2)	25,000	KM271-272	—	28.00
MS50	1992 (10)	45,000	KM278-287	—	32.00
MS51	1992 (2)	—	KM276-277	34.00	28.00
MS52	1993 (10)	—	KM293-302	18.00	30.00
MS53	1993 (2)	35,000	KM291-292	26.00	30.00
MS54	1994 (9)	40,000	KM307-315	18.00	30.00
MS55	1995 (10)	—	KM322-331	—	30.00
MS56	1996 (10)	32,000	KM349-358	18.00	30.00
MS57	1997 (9)	28,000	KM359-368	18.00	30.00
MS58	1998 (8)	—	KM378-385	18.00	38.00
MS59	1999 (7)	—	KM389-396	18.00	35.00
MS60	2000 (8)	28,000	KM399-406	18.00	38.00

PROOF SETS

KM#	Date	Mintage	Identification	Issue Price	Mkt Val
PS1	1989 (2)	8,000	KM243-244	55.00	50.00
PS2	1990 (2)	18,800	KM246-247	55.00	40.00
PS3	1991 (2)	8,000	KM271-272	55.00	45.00
PS4	1991 (2)	6,800	KM273-274	—	420
PS5	1993 (2)	—	KM303-304	158	215
PS6	1994 (2)	7,500	KM319-320	—	420
PS7	1995 (2)	—	KM333-334	31.00	35.00
PS8	1995 (2)	7,000	KM335-336	160	420
PS9	1996 (2)	—	KM340-341	35.00	110
PS10	1997 (2)	—	KM370-371	35.00	38.00
PSA11	1998 (2)	—	KM#386-387	—	—
PS11	1999 (2)	—	KM410-411	—	55.00
PS12	1999 (3)	8,000	KM413-415	178	500
PS13	2000 (3)	6,000	KM407-409	178	500

SARAWAK

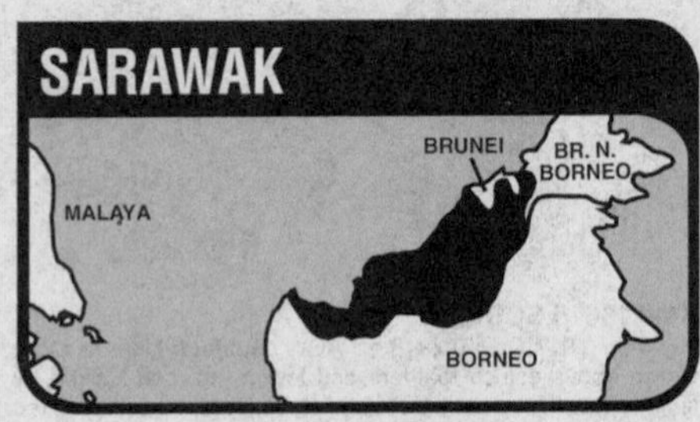

Sarawak is a former British protectorate located on the north-west coast of Borneo. The Japanese occupation during World War II so thoroughly devastated the economy that Rajah Sir Charles V. Brooke ceded it to Great Britain on July 1, 1946. In September, 1963 the colony joined the Federation of Malaysia. The capital is Kuching.

RULERS
Charles J. Brooke, Rajah, 1868-1917
Charles V. Brooke, Rajah, 1917-1946

BRITISH PROTECTORATE

STANDARD COINAGE

100 Cents = 1 Dollar

KM# 20 1/2 CENT
Bronze 0 **Ruler:** Charles V. Brooke **Obv:** Head right **Rev:** Value within wreath

Date	Mintage	VF20	XF40	MS60	MS63	MS65
1933 H	2,000,000	7.00	12.00	25.00	50.00	125
1933 H	—	PF63 800	PF65 1,600			

KM# 12 CENT
Copper-Nickel **Ruler:** Charles V. Brooke **Obv:** Head right **Rev:** Value within wreath

Date	Mintage	VF20	XF40	MS60	MS63	MS65
1920 H	5,000,000	10.00	20.00	35.00	75.00	150

KM# 18 CENT

Bronze **Ruler:** Charles V. Brooke **Obv:** Head right **Rev:** Value within wreath

Date	Mintage	VF20	XF40	MS60	MS63	MS65
1927 H	5,000,000	3.50	7.50	20.00	50.00	90.00
1929 H	2,000,000	3.50	7.50	20.00	50.00	90.00
1930 H	3,000,000	3.50	7.50	15.00	35.00	75.00
1937 H	3,000,000	3.50	7.50	15.00	30.00	65.00
1937 H	—	PF63 1,200	PF65 2,600			
1941 H	3,000,000	—	500	1,000	2,000	3,500

Note: Estimate 50 pieces exist

KM# 8 5 CENTS

1.35 g., 0.800 Silver 0.0347 oz. ASW **Ruler:** Charles J. Brooke **Obv:** Head left **Obv. Legend:** C. BROOKE RAJAH **Rev:** Value within roped wreath

Date	Mintage	VF20	XF40	MS60	MS63	MS65
1908 H	40,000	30.00	60.00	125	375	550
1908 H	—	PF63 1,000	PF65 2,000			
1911 H	40,000	30.00	60.00	125	375	550
1911 H	—	PF63 1,000	PF65 2,000			
1913 H	100,000	18.00	35.00	100	325	460
1913 H	—	PF63 1,000	PF65 2,000			
1915 H	100,000	18.00	35.00	100	325	460
1915 H	—	PF63 1,000	PF65 2,000			

KM# 13 5 CENTS

1.35 g., 0.400 Silver 0.0174 oz. ASW **Ruler:** Charles V. Brooke **Obv:** Head right **Rev:** Value within roped wreath

Date	Mintage	VF20	XF40	MS60	MS63	MS65
1920 H	100,000	65.00	125	275	475	—
1920 H	—	PF63 1,100	PF65 2,200			

KM# 14 5 CENTS

Copper-Nickel **Ruler:** Charles V. Brooke **Obv:** Head right **Rev:** Value within wreath

Date	Mintage	VF20	XF40	MS60	MS63	MS65
1920 H	400,000	4.00	8.00	15.00	30.00	65.00
1920 H	—	PF65 2,600				
1927 H	600,000	4.00	8.00	15.00	30.00	65.00
1927 H	—	PF63 650	PF65 950			

KM# 9 10 CENTS

2.71 g., 0.800 Silver 0.0697 oz. ASW **Ruler:** Charles J. Brooke **Obv:** Head left **Obv. Legend:** C. BROOKE RAJAH **Rev:** Value within roped wreath

Date	Mintage	F12	VF20	XF40	MS60	MS63
1906 H	50,000	20.00	40.00	100	165	350
1906 H	—	PF63 1,100	PF65 2,200			
1910 H	50,000	20.00	40.00	100	165	350
1910 H	—	PF63 1,100	PF65 2,200			
1911 H	100,000	12.00	25.00	75.00	145	325
1911 H	—	PF63 1,100	PF65 2,200			
1913 H	100,000	12.00	25.00	75.00	145	325
1913 H	—	PF63 1,100	PF65 2,200			
1915 H	100,000	25.00	55.00	125	250	575
1915 H	—	PF63 1,100	PF65 2,200			

KM# 15 10 CENTS

2.71 g., 0.400 Silver 0.0349 oz. ASW **Ruler:** Charles V. Brooke **Obv:** Head right **Rev:** Value within roped wreath

Date	Mintage	VF20	XF40	MS60	MS63	MS65
1920 H	150,000	45.00	75.00	150	275	550
1920 H	—	PF63 1,000	PF65 2,000			

KM# 16 10 CENTS

Copper-Nickel **Ruler:** Charles V. Brooke **Obv:** Head right **Rev:** Value within wreath

Date	Mintage	VF20	XF40	MS60	MS63	MS65
1920 H	800,000	4.00	8.00	17.00	45.00	100
1920 H	—	PF63 450	PF65 800			
1927 H	1,000,000	4.00	8.00	17.00	45.00	100
1927 H	—	PF63 450	PF65 800			
1934 H	2,000,000	3.00	7.00	15.00	40.00	90.00
1934 H	—	PF63 750	PF65 1,500			

KM# 10 20 CENTS

5.43 g., 0.800 Silver 0.1397 oz. ASW **Ruler:** Charles J. Brooke **Obv:** Head left **Obv. Legend:** C. BROOKE RAJAH **Rev:** Value within roped wreath

Date	Mintage	F12	VF20	XF40	MS60	MS63
1906 H	25,000	45.00	85.00	175	450	950
1906 H	—	PF63 1,500	PF65 4,000			
1910 H	25,000	45.00	85.00	175	450	950
1910 H	—	PF63 1,500	PF65 4,000			
1911 H	15,000	45.00	85.00	175	450	950
1913 H	25,000	45.00	85.00	175	450	950
1913 H	—	PF63 1,500	PF65 4,000			
1915 H	25,000	100	200	600	2,500	4,000
1915 H	—	PF63 6,000				

KM# 17 20 CENTS

5.43 g., 0.400 Silver 0.0698 oz. ASW **Ruler:** Charles V. Brooke **Obv:** Head right **Rev:** Value within roped wreath

Date	Mintage	F12	VF20	XF40	MS60	MS63
1920 H	25,000	50.00	100	250	750	1,950
1920 H	—	PF63 2,500				

KM# 17a 20 CENTS

5.08 g., 0.400 Silver 0.0653 oz. ASW **Ruler:** Charles V. Brooke **Obv:** Head right **Rev:** Value within roped wreath

Date	Mintage	F12	VF20	XF40	MS60	MS63
1927 H	250,000	20.00	40.00	80.00	200	325
1927 H	—	PF63 1,200				

KM# 11 50 CENTS

13.57 g., 0.800 Silver 0.349 oz. ASW **Ruler:** Charles V. Brooke **Obv:** Head left **Obv. Legend:** C. BROOKE RAJAH **Rev:** Value within roped wreath

Date	Mintage	F12	VF20	XF40	MS60	MS63
1906 H	10,000	200	350	550	2,000	4,500
1906 H	—	PF63 8,000	PF65 15,000			

KM# 19 50 CENTS

10.30 g., 0.500 Silver 0.1656 oz. ASW **Ruler:** Charles V. Brooke **Obv:** Head right **Rev:** Value within roped wreath

Date	Mintage	F12	VF20	XF40	MS60	MS63
1927 H	200,000	35.00	75.00	150	550	1,850
1927 H	—	PF63 4,500	PF65 8,500			

SAUDI ARABIA

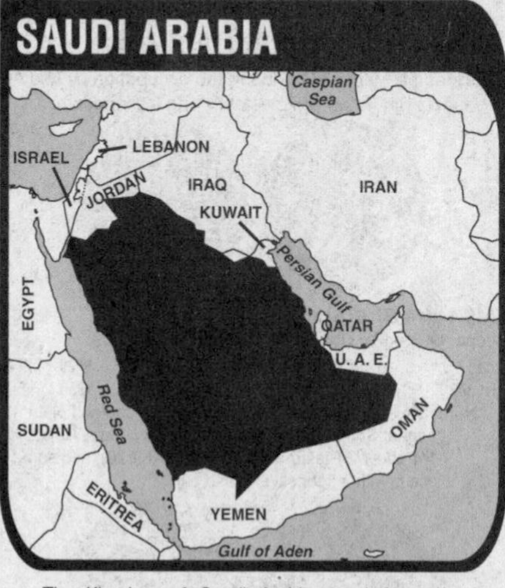

The Kingdom of Saudi Arabia, an independent and absolute hereditary monarchy comprising the former sultanate of Nejd, the old kingdom of Hejaz, Asir and Al Hasa, occupies four-fifths of the Arabian peninsula. The kingdom has an area of 830,000 sq. mi. (2,149,690 sq. km.) and a population of *16.1 million. Capital: Riyadh. The economy is based on oil, which provides 85 percent of Saudi Arabia's revenue.

Mohammed united the Arabs in the 7th century and his followers founded a great empire with its capital at Medina. The Turks established nominal rule over much of Arabia in the 16th and 17th centuries, and in the 18th century divided it into principalities.

The Kingdom of Saudi Arabia was created by King Abd Al-Aziz Bin Saud (1882-1953), a descendant of earlier Wahhabi rulers of the Arabian peninsula. In 1901 he seized Riyadh, capital of the Sultanate of Nejd, and in 1905 established himself as Sultan. In 1913 he captured the Turkish province of Al Hasa; took the Hejaz in 1925 and by 1926 most of Asir. In 1932 he combined Nejd and Hejaz into the single kingdom of Saudi Arabia. Asir was incorporated into the kingdom a year later.

TITLES

العربية السعودية

Al-Arabiya(t) as-Sa'udiya(t)

المملكة العربية السعودية

Al-Mamlaka(t) al-Arabiya(t) as-Sa'udiya(t)

RULERS

al Sa'ud Dynasty

Abd Al-Aziz Bin Sa'ud, (Ibn Sa'ud), AH1344-1373/1926-1953AD

Sa'ud bin Abd Al-Aziz, AH1373-1383/1953-1964AD

Faisal bin Abd Al-Aziz, AH1383-1395/1964-1975AD

Khalid bin Abd Al-Aziz, AH1395-1403/1975-1982AD

Fahad bin Abd Al-Aziz, AH1403-1426/1982-2005AD

Abdullah bin Abdul Aziz, AH1426-/2005AD

MONETARY SYSTEM

Until 1960

20-22 Ghirsh = 1 Riyal

40 Riyals = 1 Guinea

NOTE: Copper-nickel, reeded-edge coins dated AH1356 and silver coins dated AH1354 were struck at the U. S. Mint in Philadelphia between 1944-1949.

ROYAL TITLES

Appearing on coins

HEJAZ & NEJD

Mecca, the metropolis of Islam and the capital of Hejaz, is located inland from the Red Sea due east of the port of Jidda. A center of non-political commercial, cultural and religious activities, Mecca remained virtually independent until 1259. Two centuries of Egyptian rule were followed by four centuries of Turkish rule which lasted until the Arab revolts which extinguished pretensions to sovereignty over any part of the Arabian peninsula.

MINT NAME
Makkah, Mecca

RULERS
Sharifs of Mecca
Ghalib b. Ma'sud, AH1219-1229
Yahya b. Surer, AH1230-1240
Abdul Muttalib and Ibn Awn, AH1240-1248

KINGDOM AND SULTANATE

Abd Al-Aziz bin Sa'ud as King of Hejaz and Sultan of Nejd

TRANSITIONAL COINAGE

Struck at the Mecca Mint during the occupation by Abd Al-Aziz Bin Sa'ud while establishing his kingdom.

KM# 1 1/4 GHIRSH
Copper or Bronze **Obv:** Toughra **Rev:** Inscription

Date	Mintage	G4	VG8	F12	VF20	XF40
AH1343	—	—	75.00	125	250	500

Note: Several varieties exist, including reeded and plain edges; Some specimens struck over bronze Hejaz 1/4 and 1/2 Piastres (KM#23 and KM#26), and some occur with a light silver wash

KM# 2.1 1/2 GHIRSH
Copper or Bronze **Obv:** Toughra **Obv. Inscription:** Al-Faisal al Saud **Rev:** Inscription

Date	Mintage	G4	VG8	F12	VF20	XF40
AH1343	—	—	20.00	50.00	100	200

KM# 2.2 1/2 GHIRSH
Copper or Bronze **Obv:** Toughra **Obv. Inscription:** Al-Faisal **Rev:** Inscription

Date	Mintage	G4	VG8	F12	VF20	XF40
AH1343	—	—	150	300	750	1,500

KM# A3 1/2 GHIRSH
Bronze

Date	Mintage	F12	VF20	XF40	MS60	MS63
AH1344//2	—	30.00	60.00	125	—	—

REGULAR COINAGE

KM# 4 1/4 GHIRSH
Copper-Nickel **Obv:** Legend **Rev:** Value and date below legend

Date	Mintage	G4	VG8	F12	VF20	XF40
AH1344	—	—	4.00	8.00	12.00	40.00
AH1344	—	PF63 1,500				

KM# 5 1/2 GHIRSH
Copper-Nickel **Obv:** Legend **Rev:** Value and date below legend

Date	Mintage	G4	VG8	F12	VF20	XF40
AH1344	—	—	8.00	15.00	30.00	75.00
AH1344	—	PF63 1,500				

KM# 6 GHIRSH
Copper-Nickel, 26 mm. **Obv:** Legend **Rev:** Value and date below legend

Date	Mintage	G4	VG8	F12	VF20	XF40
AH1344	—	—	6.00	12.00	30.00	75.00
AH1344	—	PF63 1,500				

HEJAZ & NEJD SULTANATE

KINGDOM

REGULAR COINAGE

KM# 7 1/4 GHIRSH
Copper-Nickel **Obv:** Legend **Rev:** Value and date below legend

Date	Mintage	VG8	F12	VF20	XF40	MS60
AH1346	3,000,000	6.00	10.00	20.00	60.00	—
AH1346	—	PF63 1,500				

KM# 13 1/4 GHIRSH
Copper-Nickel **Obv:** Legend **Rev:** Value and date below legend

Date	Mintage	VG8	F12	VF20	XF40	MS60
AH1348	—	12.00	20.00	40.00	75.00	—
AH1348	—	PF63 1,750				

KM# 8 1/2 GHIRSH
Copper-Nickel

Date	Mintage	VG8	F12	VF20	XF40	MS60
AH1346	3,000,000	10.00	15.00	25.00	60.00	—
AH1346	—	PF63 1,500				

KM# 14 1/2 GHIRSH
Copper-Nickel **Obv:** Legend **Rev:** Value and date below legend

Date	Mintage	VG8	F12	VF20	XF40	MS60
AH1348	—	12.00	25.00	40.00	100	—
AH1348	—	PF63 1,750				

KM# 9 GHIRSH
Copper-Nickel **Obv:** Legend **Rev:** Value and date below legend

Date	Mintage	VG8	F12	VF20	XF40	MS60
AH1346	3,000,000	3.00	5.00	20.00	50.00	—
AH1346	—	PF63 1,500				

KM# 15 GHIRSH
Copper-Nickel **Obv:** Legend **Rev:** Value and date below inscription

Date	Mintage	VG8	F12	VF20	XF40	MS60
AH1348	—	12.00	20.00	30.00	75.00	—
AH1348	—	PF63 1,750				

KM# 10 1/4 RIYAL
6.05 g., 0.917 Silver 0.1784 oz. ASW, 24 mm. **Obv:** Inscription within beaded circle, legend above, crossed swords below within design flanked by palms trees **Rev:** Inscription within beaded circle, legend above, value below within design flanked by palm trees

Date	Mintage	VG8	F12	VF20	XF40	MS60
AH1346	400,000	40.00	80.00	225	400	—
AH1346	—	PF63 1,750				
AH1348	200,000	70.00	150	300	500	—
AH1348	—	PF63 2,500				

KM# 11 1/2 RIYAL
12.10 g., 0.917 Silver 0.3567 oz. ASW, 27 mm. **Obv:** Inscription within beaded circle, legend above, crossed swords below within design flanked by palm trees **Rev:** Inscription within beaded circle, legend above, value below within design flanked by palm trees and swords

Date	Mintage	F12	VF20	XF40	MS60
AH1346	200,000	100	225	350	750	—
AH1346	—	PF63 2,500				
AH1348	100,000	125	300	450	900	—
AH1348	—	PF63 3,500				

KM# 12 RIYAL
24.10 g., 0.917 Silver 0.7105 oz. ASW, 37 mm. **Obv:** Inscription within beaded circle, legend above, crossed swords below within design flanked by palm trees **Rev:** Inscription within beaded circle, legend above, value below within design flanked by palm trees

Date	Mintage	VG8	F12	VF20	XF40	MS60
AH1346	800,000	75.00	125	200	400	—

Date	Mintage	VG8	F12	VF20	XF40	MS60
AH1346	—	PF63 4,000				
AH1348	400,000	100	175	300	500	—
AH1348	—	PF63 5,000				

UNITED KINGDOMS

KINGDOM

STANDARD COINAGE

KM# 19.1 1/4 GHIRSH
Copper-Nickel **Obv:** Legend **Rev:** Value and date below legend **Edge:** Plain

Date	Mintage	VG8	F12	VF20	XF40	MS60
AH1356	1,000,000	2.00	5.00	10.00	35.00	—
AH1356	—	PF63 750				

KM# 19.2 1/4 GHIRSH
Copper-Nickel **Obv:** Legend **Rev:** Value and date below legend **Edge:** Reeded

Date	Mintage	VF20	XF40	MS60	MS63	MS65
AH1356	21,500,000	0.75	1.25	2.50	3.50	7.50

Note: Struck in 1947 (AH1366-67) at Philadelphia

KM# 20.1 1/2 GHIRSH
Copper-Nickel **Obv:** Legend **Rev:** Value and date below legend **Edge:** Plain

Date	Mintage	VG8	F12	VF20	XF40	MS60
AH1356	1,000,000	3.00	8.00	20.00	45.00	—
AH1356	—	PF63 750				

KM# 20.2 1/2 GHIRSH
Copper-Nickel **Obv:** Legend **Rev:** Value and date below legend **Edge:** Reeded

Date	Mintage	VF20	XF40	MS60	MS63	MS65
AH1356	10,850,000	1.00	2.00	3.00	4.50	10.00

Note: Struck in 1947 (AH1366-67) at Philadelphia

KM# 21.1 GHIRSH
Copper-Nickel **Obv:** Legend **Rev:** Value and date below legend **Edge:** Plain

Date	Mintage	VG8	F12	VF20	XF40	MS60
AH1356	4,000,000	3.00	8.00	15.00	40.00	—
AH1356	—	PF63 1,000				

KM# 21.2 GHIRSH
Copper-Nickel **Obv:** Legend **Rev:** Value and date below legend **Edge:** Reeded

Date	Mintage	VF20	XF40	MS60	MS63	MS65
AH1356	7,150,000	1.25	2.50	3.50	6.00	12.50

Note: Struck in 1947 (AH1366-67) at Philadelphia

KM# 40 GHIRSH
3.20 g., Copper-Nickel, 22 mm. **Obv:** Palm above crossed swords at center of legend **Rev:** Value and date below legend **Edge:** Reeded

Date	Mintage	VF20	XF40	MS60	MS63	MS65
AH1376	10,000,000	1.00	1.50	2.00	3.50	5.00
AH1378	50,000,000	1.00	1.50	2.00	3.00	3.75

KM# 41 2 GHIRSH
6.00 g., Copper-Nickel, 26.93 mm. **Obv:** Crossed swords below palm at center of legend **Rev:** Value and date below legend **Edge:** Reeded

Date	Mintage	VF20	XF40	MS60	MS63	MS65
AH1372	—	—	—	—	—	—
Note: Requires confirmation						
AH1376	50,000,000	1.50	2.25	3.00	—	—
AH1379	28,110,000	1.50	2.25	3.00	—	—

KM# 42 4 GHIRSH
12.00 g., Copper-Nickel, 30 mm. **Obv:** Crossed swords below palm at center of legend **Rev:** Value and date below legend **Edge:** Reeded

Date	Mintage	VF20	XF40	MS60	MS63	MS65
AH1376	49,100,000	0.50	1.00	1.75	3.75	6.00
AH1378	10,000,000	0.50	1.00	1.50	3.50	5.00

KM# 16 1/4 RIYAL
3.10 g., 0.917 Silver 0.0914 oz. ASW **Obv:** Inscription within beaded circle, legend above, crossed swords below within design flanked by palm trees **Rev:** Inscription within beaded circle, legend above, value below within design flanked by palm trees

Date	Mintage	VF20	XF40	MS60	MS63	MS65
AH1354	900,000	5.00	7.00	10.00	15.00	—
AH1354	—	PF63 1,500				

KM# 37 1/4 RIYAL
2.95 g., 0.917 Silver 0.087 oz. ASW **Obv:** Inscription within beaded circle, legend above, crossed swords below within design flanked by palm trees **Rev:** Inscription within beaded circle, legend above, value below within design flanked by palm trees

Date	Mintage	VF20	XF40	MS60	MS63	MS65
AH1374	4,000,000	3.50	5.00	9.00	12.00	—

KM# 17 1/2 RIYAL
5.85 g., 0.917 Silver 0.1725 oz. ASW **Obv:** Inscription within beaded circle, legend above, crossed swords below within design flanked by palm trees **Rev:** Inscription within beaded circle, legend above, value below within design flanked by palm trees

Date	Mintage	VF20	XF40	MS60	MS63	MS65
AH1354	950,000	6.50	12.00	25.00	35.00	—
AH1354	—	PF63 1,500				

KM# 38 1/2 RIYAL
5.95 g., 0.917 Silver 0.1754 oz. ASW **Obv:** Inscription within beaded circle, legend above, crossed swords below within design flanked by palm trees **Rev:** Inscription within beaded circle, legend above, value below within design flanked by palm trees

Date	Mintage	VF20	XF40	MS60	MS63	MS65
AH1374	2,000,000	6.50	10.00	18.00	25.00	—

KM# 18 RIYAL
11.60 g., 0.917 Silver 0.342 oz. ASW, 30.5 mm. **Obv:** Inscription within beaded circle, legend above, crossed swords below within design flanked by palm trees **Rev:** Inscription within beaded circle, legend above, value below within design flanked by palm trees **Edge:** Reeded

Date	Mintage	VF20	XF40	MS60	MS63	MS65
AH1354	60,000,000	13.00	15.50	20.00	28.00	—
AH1354	20,000,000	PF63 1,500				
AH1367	—	13.00	15.50	20.00	28.00	—
AH1370	—	13.00	16.00	22.50	30.00	—

KM# 39 RIYAL
11.60 g., 0.917 Silver 0.342 oz. ASW **Obv:** Inscription within beaded circle, legend above, crossed swords below within design flanked by palm trees **Rev:** Inscription within beaded circle, legend above, value below within design flanked by palm trees

Date	Mintage	VF20	XF40	MS60	MS63	MS65
AH1374	48,000,000	13.00	15.50	20.00	35.00	—

COUNTERMARKED COINAGE

The following pieces are countermarked examples of earlier types bearing the Arabic numerals 65. They were countermarked in a move to break money changers' monopoly on small coins in AH1365 (1946AD). These countermarks vary in size and are found with the Arabic numbers raised in a circle. Incuse countermarks are considered a recent fabrication.

70 = 65 Countermark

KM# 22 1/4 GHIRSH
Copper-Nickel **Countermark:** 65 **Note:** Countermark in Arabic numerals on 1/4 Ghirsh, KM#4.

CM Date	Host Date	G4	VG8	F12	VF20	XF40
AH1365	1344	6.00	12.00	30.00	65.00	—

KM# 23 1/4 GHIRSH
Copper-Nickel **Obv:** Countermark at center of legend **Rev:** Value and date below legend **Countermark:** 65 **Note:** Countermark in Arabic numerals on 1/4 Ghirsh, KM#7.

CM Date	Host Date	G4	VG8	F12	VF20	XF40
AH1365	1346	6.00	12.00	30.00	65.00	—

KM# 24 1/4 GHIRSH
Copper-Nickel **Countermark:** 65 **Note:** Countermark in Arabic numerals on 1/4 Ghirsh, KM#13.

CM Date	Host Date	G4	VG8	F12	VF20	XF40
AH1365	1348	20.00	30.00	50.00	100	—

KM# 25 1/4 GHIRSH

Copper-Nickel **Obv:** Countermark at center of legend **Rev:** Value and date below legend **Edge:** Plain **Countermark:** 65 **Note:** Countermark in Arabic numerals on 1/4 Ghirsh, KM#19.

CM Date	Host Date	G4	VG8	F12	VF20	XF40
AH1365	1356	2.50	5.00	15.00	30.00	—

KM# 26 1/2 GHIRSH

Copper-Nickel **Obv:** Countermark at center of legend **Rev:** Date below legend **Countermark:** 65 **Note:** Countermark in Arabic numerals on 1/2 Ghirsh, KM#5.

CM Date	Host Date	G4	VG8	F12	VF20	XF40
AH1365	1344	6.00	12.00	25.00	60.00	—

KM# 27 1/2 GHIRSH

Copper-Nickel **Obv:** Countermark at center of legend **Rev:** Date below legend **Countermark:** 65 **Note:** Countermark in Arabic numerals on 1/2 Ghirsh, KM#8.

CM Date	Host Date	G4	VG8	F12	VF20	XF40
AH1365	1346	6.00	12.00	25.00	60.00	—

KM# 28 1/2 GHIRSH

Copper-Nickel **Countermark:** 65 **Note:** Countermark in Arabic numerals on 1/2 Ghirsh, KM#14.

CM Date	Host Date	G4	VG8	F12	VF20	XF40
AH1365	1348	15.00	30.00	65.00	100	—

KM# 29 1/2 GHIRSH

Copper-Nickel **Obv:** Countermark at center of legend **Rev:** Date below legend **Edge:** Plain **Countermark:** 65 **Note:** Countermark in Arabic numerals on 1/2 Ghirsh, KM#20.1.

CM Date	Host Date	G4	VG8	F12	VF20	XF40
AH1365	1356	5.00	10.00	25.00	40.00	—

KM# 30 GHIRSH

Copper-Nickel **Obv:** Countermark at center of legend **Rev:** Value and date below legend **Countermark:** 65 **Note:** Countermark in Arabic numerals on 1 Ghirsh, KM#6.

CM Date	Host Date	G4	VG8	F12	VF20	XF40
AH1365	1344	6.00	12.00	35.00	65.00	—

KM# 31 GHIRSH

Copper-Nickel **Countermark:** 65 **Note:** Countermark in Arabic numerals on 1 Ghirsh, KM#9.

CM Date	Host Date	G4	VG8	F12	VF20	XF40
AH1365	1346	6.00	12.00	30.00	65.00	—

KM# 32 GHIRSH

Copper-Nickel, 25 mm. **Obv:** Countermark at center of legend **Rev:** Value and date below legend **Countermark:** 65 **Note:** Countermark in Arabic numerals on 1 Ghirsh, KM#15.

CM Date	Host Date	G4	VG8	F12	VF20	XF40
AH1365	1348	10.00	20.00	35.00	65.00	—

KM# 33 GHIRSH

Copper-Nickel **Edge:** Plain **Countermark:** 65 **Note:** Countermark in Arabic numerals on 1 Ghirsh, KM#21.

CM Date	Host Date	G4	VG8	F12	VF20	XF40
AH1365	1356	6.00	10.00	20.00	30.00	—

REFORM COINAGE

5 Halala = 1 Ghirsh; 100 Halala = 1 Riyal

KM# 44 HALALA

Bronze **Obv:** Crossed swords and palm tree at center, legend above and below **Rev:** Value and date below legend

Date	Mintage	VF20	XF40	MS60	MS63	MS65
AH1383	5,000,000	0.60	0.85	1.50	3.00	5.00

KM# 60 HALALA

Bronze **Obv:** Different legend **Rev:** Value and date below legend

Date	Mintage	VF20	XF40	MS60	MS63	MS65
AH1397	—	—	—	200	250	350

Note: Not released for circulation

KM# 45 5 HALALA (Ghirsh)

2.50 g., Copper-Nickel, 19.5 mm. **Obv:** Crossed swords and palm tree at center, legend above and below **Rev:** Legend above inscription in circle dividing value, date below **Edge:** Reeded

Date	Mintage	VF20	XF40	MS60	MS63	MS65
AH1392	130,000,000	0.50	1.50	2.00	2.50	3.00

KM# 53 5 HALALA (Ghirsh)

2.50 g., Copper-Nickel, 19.5 mm. **Obv:** Crossed swords and palm tree at center, legend above and below **Rev:** Legend above inscription in circle dividing value, date below **Edge:** Reeded

Date	Mintage	VF20	XF40	MS60	MS63	MS65
AH1397	20,000,000	0.50	1.00	1.50	2.25	3.00
AH1400	—	0.50	1.00	1.50	2.25	3.00

KM# 57 5 HALALA (Ghirsh)

2.50 g., Copper-Nickel, 19.5 mm. **Series:** F.A.O. **Obv:** Crossed swords and palm tree at center, legend above and below **Rev:** Legend above inscription in circle dividing value, date below **Edge:** Reeded

Date	Mintage	VF20	XF40	MS60	MS63	MS65
AH1398-1978	1,500,000	0.30	0.50	0.75	1.50	2.00

KM# 61 5 HALALA (Ghirsh)

2.50 g., Copper-Nickel, 19.5 mm. **Obv:** National emblem at center, legend above and below **Rev:** Legend above inscription in circle dividing value, date below **Edge:** Reeded

Date	Mintage	VF20	XF40	MS60	MS63	MS65
AH1408	80,000,000	0.15	0.30	0.45	0.75	1.50
AH1408	5,000	PF65 5.00				

KM# 46 10 HALALA (2 Ghirsh)

4.00 g., Copper-Nickel, 21 mm. **Obv:** Crossed swords and palm tree at center, legend above and below **Rev:** Legend above inscription in circle dividing value, date below **Edge:** Reeded

Date	Mintage	VF20	XF40	MS60	MS63	MS65
AH1392	55,000,000	1.00	1.50	2.00	2.50	3.00

KM# 54 10 HALALA (2 Ghirsh)

4.00 g., Copper-Nickel, 21 mm. **Obv:** Crossed swords and palm tree at center, legend above and below **Rev:** Legend above inscription in circle dividing value, date below **Edge:** Reeded

Date	Mintage	VF20	XF40	MS60	MS63	MS65
AH1397	50,000,000	1.25	1.75	2.00	3.00	4.00
AH1400	29,500,000	1.25	1.75	2.00	3.00	4.00

KM# 58 10 HALALA (2 Ghirsh)

4.00 g., Copper-Nickel, 21 mm. **Series:** F.A.O. **Obv:** Crossed swords and palm tree at center, legend above and below **Rev:** Legend above inscription in circle dividing value, date below **Edge:** Reeded

Date	Mintage	VF20	XF40	MS60	MS63	MS65
AH1398-1978	1,000,000	0.25	0.50	0.75	1.50	2.00

KM# 62 10 HALALA (2 Ghirsh)

4.00 g., Copper-Nickel, 21 mm. **Ruler:** Fahad Bin Abd Al-Aziz **Obv:** National emblem at center, legend above and below **Rev:** Legend above inscription in circle dividing value, date below **Edge:** Reeded

Date	Mintage	VF20	XF40	MS60	MS63	MS65
AH1408	100,000,000	0.50	0.75	1.25	1.75	2.50
AH1408	5,000	PF65 6.00				

KM# 47 25 HALALA (1/4 Riyal)

5.00 g., Copper-Nickel, 23 mm. **Obv:** Crossed swords and palm tree at center, legend above and below **Rev:** Legend above inscription in circle dividing value, date below **Edge:** Reeded **Note:** Error. Denomination in masculine gender.

Date	Mintage	VF20	XF40	MS60	MS63	MS65
AH1392	48,465,000	2.00	4.00	12.00	25.00	35.00

KM# 48 25 HALALA (1/4 Riyal)

5.00 g., Copper-Nickel, 23 mm. **Obv:** Crossed swords and palm tree at center, legend above and below **Rev:** Legend above inscription in circle dividing value, date below **Edge:** Reeded **Note:** Corrected denomination; feminine gender.

Date	Mintage	VF20	XF40	MS60	MS63	MS65
AH1392	48,465,000	0.50	1.50	2.50	3.50	5.00

KM# 49 25 HALALA (1/4 Riyal)
5.00 g., Copper-Nickel, 23 mm. **Series:** F.A.O. **Obv:** Crossed swords and palm tree at center, legend above and below **Rev:** Legend above inscription in circle dividing value, date below **Edge:** Reeded

Date	Mintage	VF20	XF40	MS60	MS63	MS65
AH1392-1973	200,000	0.20	0.50	1.50	2.50	3.50

KM# 55 25 HALALA (1/4 Riyal)
5.00 g., Copper-Nickel, 23 mm. **Obv:** Crossed swords and palm tree at center, legend above and below **Rev:** Legend above inscription in circle dividing value, date below **Edge:** Reeded

Date	Mintage	VF20	XF40	MS60	MS63	MS65
AH1397	20,000,000	0.50	1.00	2.00	3.00	4.50
AH1400	57,000,000	0.50	0.85	1.50	2.50	3.50

KM# 63 25 HALALA (1/4 Riyal)
5.00 g., Copper-Nickel, 23 mm. **Ruler:** Fahad Bin Abd Al-Aziz **Obv:** National emblem at center, legend above and below **Rev:** Legend above inscription in circle dividing value, date below **Edge:** Reeded

Date	Mintage	VF20	XF40	MS60	MS63	MS65
AH1408	100,000,000	0.50	1.00	1.50	—	—
AH1408	5,000	PF65 7.50				

KM# 50 50 HALALA (1/2 Riyal)
6.50 g., Copper-Nickel, 26 mm. **Series:** F.A.O. **Obv:** Crossed swords and palm tree at center, legend above and below **Rev:** Legend above inscription in circle dividing value, date below **Edge:** Reeded

Date	Mintage	VF20	XF40	MS60	MS63	MS65
AH1392	500,000	0.30	0.60	1.00	1.50	3.00

KM# 51 50 HALALA (1/2 Riyal)
6.50 g., Copper-Nickel, 26 mm. **Obv:** Crossed swords and palm tree at center, legend above and below **Rev:** Legend above inscription in circle dividing value, date below **Edge:** Reeded

Date	Mintage	VF20	XF40	MS60	MS63	MS65
AH1392	16,000,000	1.00	1.50	2.50	3.00	4.00

KM# 56 50 HALALA (1/2 Riyal)
6.50 g., Copper-Nickel, 26 mm. **Obv:** Crossed swords and palm tree at center, legend above and below **Rev:** Legend above inscription in circle dividing value, date below **Edge:** Reeded

Date	Mintage	VF20	XF40	MS60	MS63	MS65
AH1397	20,000,000	0.50	0.75	1.00	1.50	3.00
AH1400	21,600,000	0.35	0.65	1.25	1.75	3.50

KM# 64 50 HALALA (1/2 Riyal)
6.50 g., Copper-Nickel, 26 mm. **Ruler:** Fahad Bin Abd Al-Aziz **Obv:** National emblem at center, legend above and below **Rev:** Legend above inscription in circle dividing value, date below **Edge:** Reeded

Date	Mintage	VF20	XF40	MS60	MS63	MS65
AH1408	70,000,000	0.75	1.00	2.00	3.00	—
AH1408	5,000	PF65 15.00				

KM# 52 100 HALALA (1 Riyal)
9.30 g., Copper-Nickel, 30 mm. **Obv:** Crossed swords and palm tree at center, legend above and below **Rev:** Legend above inscription in circle dividing value, date below **Edge:** Reeded

Date	Mintage	VF20	XF40	MS60	MS63	MS65
AH1396	250,000	1.75	2.00	3.00	3.50	5.00
AH1400	30,000,000	0.65	1.25	1.75	2.75	4.00

KM# 59 100 HALALA (1 Riyal)
10.00 g., Copper-Nickel, 30 mm. **Series:** F.A.O. **Obv:** Crossed swords and palm tree at center flanked by dates, legend above and below **Rev:** Legend above inscription in circle dividing value, date below

Date	Mintage	VF20	XF40	MS60	MS63	MS65
AH1397 - 1977	—	—	20.00	25.00	30.00	35.00

Note: AH1397 date was struck as samples for the Saudi Arabia government by the British Royal Mint, but some escaped into circulation and hundreds are currently available in the numismatic market

Date	Mintage	VF20	XF40	MS60	MS63	MS65
AH1398 - 1978	10,000,000	0.75	1.50	2.00	3.00	5.00

KM# 65 100 HALALA (1 Riyal)
10.00 g., Copper-Nickel, 30 mm. **Obv:** National emblem at center, legend above and below **Rev:** Legend above inscription in circle dividing value, date below **Edge:** Reeded

Date	Mintage	VF20	XF40	MS60	MS63	MS65
AH1408	40,000,000	1.50	2.25	3.50	4.00	—
AH1408	5,000	PF65 22.00				
AH1414	—	1.50	2.25	3.50	4.00	—

KM# 66 100 HALALA (1 Riyal)
6.00 g., Bi-Metallic Brass center in Copper-Nickel ring, 23 mm. **Ruler:** Fahad Bin Abd Al-Aziz **Obv:** National emblem at center, legend above and below **Rev:** Inscription at center, value at left, legend above, date below **Edge:** Reeded

Date	Mintage	VF20	XF40	MS60	MS63	MS65
AH1419	—	1.75	3.00	4.50	6.00	—

KM# 67 100 HALALA (1 Riyal)
6.00 g., Bi-Metallic Brass center in Copper-Nickel ring, 23 mm. **Ruler:** Fahad Bin Abd Al-Aziz **Subject:** Centennial of Kingdom **Obv:** National emblem at center **Rev:** Inscription at center, legend above, value at left, date below **Edge:** Reeded

Date	Mintage	VF20	XF40	MS60	MS63	MS65
AH1419	—	2.50	3.50	5.00	7.00	—
AH1419	—	PF65 12.50				

TRADE COINAGE

KM# 36 GUINEA
7.99 g., 0.917 Gold 0.2355 oz. AGW **Obv:** Inscription within beaded circle, legend above, crossed swords below within design flanked by palm trees **Rev:** Inscription within beaded circle, legend above, value below within design flanked by palm trees

Date	Mintage	VF20	XF40	MS60	MS63	MS65
AH1370	2,000,000	—	300	400	425	450

KM# 43 GUINEA
7.99 g., 0.917 Gold 0.2355 oz. AGW

Date	Mintage	VF20	XF40	MS60	MS63	MS65
AH1377	1,579,000	—	300	400	425	600

BULLION COINAGE

Post WWII Issues

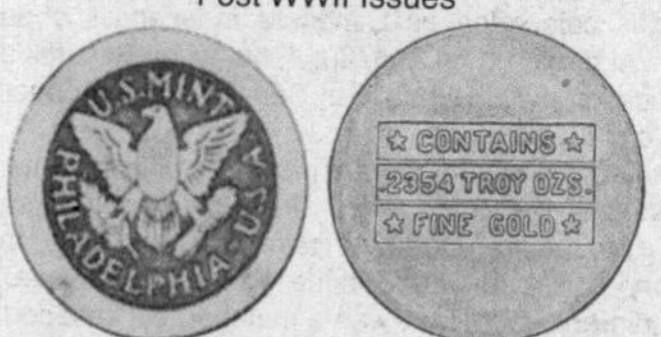

KM# 35 SOVEREIGN (Pound)
7.99 g., 0.917 Gold 0.2355 oz. AGW **Obv:** Eagle with wings open **Rev:** Three lined inscription within horizontal bars **Note:** KM#35 was struck at the Philadelphia Mint for a concession payment for oil to the Saudi Government. Most were melted into bullion.

Date	Mintage	VF20	XF40	MS60	MS63	MS65
ND-1947	123,000	750	1,250	1,450	1,750	2,750

KM# 34 4 POUNDS
31.95 g., 0.917 Gold 0.942 oz. AGW **Obv:** Eagle with wings open **Rev:** Three lined inscription within horizontal bars **Note:** KM#34 was struck at the Philadelphia Mint for a concession

payment for oil to the Saudi Government. Most were melted into bullion.

Date	Mintage	VF20	XF40	MS60	MS63	MS65
ND(1945-46)	91,000	1,750	1,850	2,000	2,250	3,000

PATTERNS

Including off metal strikes

KM#	Date	Mintage	Identification	Mkt Val
Pn4	AH1370 (1950)	—	Guinea. Aluminum. KM#36.	40,000
Pn5	AH1370 (1950)	—	Guinea. Bronze. KM#36, reeded edge, with Paris privy marks.	60,000
Pn6	AH1370 (1950)	—	Guinea. Gold. KM#36, reeded edge, with Paris privy marks, Rare.	—

Note: Different reverse legends. Baldwin's sale 4/12 realized approximately $193,800

KM#	Date	Mintage	Identification	Mkt Val
Pn1	AH1373 (1953)	—	1/4 Riyal. 0.917. Silver. As KM37.	—

Note: In the SAMA collection

KM#	Date	Mintage	Identification	Mkt Val
Pn2	AH1373 (1953)	—	1/2 Riyal. 0.917. Silver. As KM38.	—

Note: In the SAMA collection

KM#	Date	Mintage	Identification	Mkt Val
Pn3	AH1373 (1953)	—	Riyal. 0.917. Silver. As KM39.	—

Note: In the SAMA collection

MINT SETS

KM#	Date	Mintage	Identification	Issue Price	Mkt Val
MS1	AH1408(1988) (5)	—	KM#61-65	20.00	45.00

PROOF SETS

KM#	Date	Mintage	Identification	Issue Price	Mkt Val
PS1	AH1408(1988) (5)	5,000	KM#61-65	40.00	65.00

SENEGAL

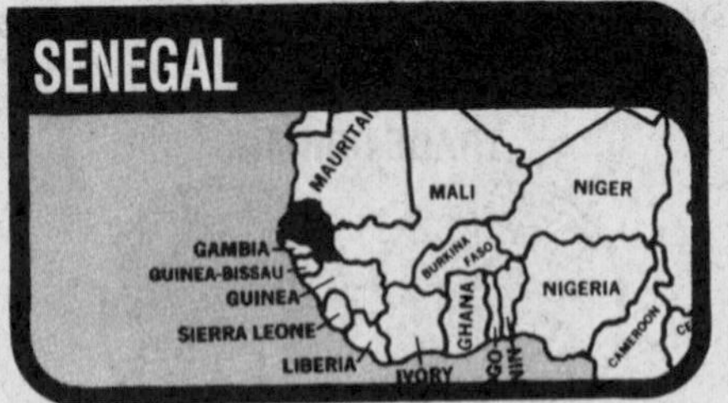

The Republic of Senegal, located on the bulge of West Africa between Mauritania and Guinea-Bissau, has an area of 75,750 sq. mi. (196,190 sq. km.) and a population of *7.5 million. Capital: Dakar. The economy is primarily agricultural. Peanuts and products, phosphates, and canned fish are exported.

An abundance of megalithic remains indicates that Senegal was inhabited in prehistoric times. The Portuguese had some trading stations on the banks of the Senegal River in the 15th century. French commercial establishments date from the 17th century. The French gradually acquired control over the interior regions, which were administered as a protectorate until 1920, and as a colony thereafter. After the 1958 French constitutional referendum, Senegal became a member of the French Community with virtual autonomy. In 1959 Senegal and the French Soudan merged to form the Mali Federation, which became fully independent on June 20, 1960. (April 4, the date the transfer of power agreement was signed with France, is celebrated as Senegal's independence day). The Federation broke up on Aug. 20, 1960, when Senegal seceded and proclaimed the Republic of Senegal. Soudan became the Republic of Mali a month later.

Senegal is a member of a monetary union of autonomous republics called the Monetary Union of West African States (*Union Monetaire Ouest-Africaine*). The other members are Ivory Coast, Benin, Burkina Faso (Upper Volta), Niger, Mauritania and Togo. Mali was a member, but seceded in1962. Some of the member countries have issued coinage in addition to the common currency issued by the Monetary Union of West African States.

REPUBLIC

TOKEN COINAGE

KM# Tn2 5 CENTIMES

Aluminum **Issuer:** Dakar

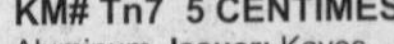

Date	Mintage	VG8	F12	VF20	XF40	MS60
1920	—	50.00	70.00	125	200	400

KM# Tn7 5 CENTIMES

Aluminum **Issuer:** Kayes

Date	Mintage	VG8	F12	VF20	XF40	MS60
1920	—	75.00	125	180	225	—

KM# Tn12 5 CENTIMES

Aluminum **Issuer:** Rufisque **Shape:** Octagon

Date	Mintage	VG8	F12	VF20	XF40	MS60
1920	—	50.00	70.00	125	200	400

KM# Tn3 10 CENTIMES

Aluminum **Issuer:** Dakar

Date	Mintage	VG8	F12	VF20	XF40	MS60
1920	—	40.00	60.00	90.00	150	—

KM# Tn4 10 CENTIMES

Brass **Issuer:** Dakar

Date	Mintage	VG8	F12	VF20	XF40	MS60
1920	—	50.00	70.00	100	150	250

KM# Tn8 10 CENTIMES

Aluminum **Issuer:** Kayes

Date	Mintage	VG8	F12	VF20	XF40	MS60
1920	—	100	150	200	300	550

KM# Tn13 10 CENTIMES

Aluminum **Issuer:** Rufisque

Date	Mintage	VG8	F12	VF20	XF40	MS60
1920	—	45.00	65.00	125	175	—

KM# Tn5 25 CENTIMES

Aluminum **Issuer:** Dakar

Date	Mintage	VG8	F12	VF20	XF40	MS60
1920	—	45.00	65.00	115	180	350

KM# Tn9 25 CENTIMES

Aluminum **Issuer:** Kayes

Date	Mintage	VG8	F12	VF20	XF40	MS60
1920	—	150	225	275	425	—

KM# Tn10 25 CENTIMES

Copper-Nickel **Issuer:** Kayes

Date	Mintage	VG8	F12	VF20	XF40	MS60
1920	—	150	200	300	400	—

KM# Tn14 25 CENTIMES

Aluminum **Issuer:** Rufisque

Date	Mintage	VG8	F12	VF20	XF40	MS60
1920	—	60.00	80.00	150	250	—

KM# Tn6 50 CENTIMES

Aluminum **Issuer:** Dakar **Shape:** Octagon

Date	Mintage	VG8	F12	VF20	XF40	MS60
1920	—	60.00	80.00	150	250	—

KM# Tn11 50 CENTIMES

Aluminum **Issuer:** Kayes

Date	Mintage	VG8	F12	VF20	XF40	MS60
1920	—	150	200	300	500	750

KM# Tn15 50 CENTIMES

Aluminum **Issuer:** Rufisque

Date	Mintage	VG8	F12	VF20	XF40	MS60
1920	—	60.00	80.00	150	250	—

KM# Tn16 50 CENTIMES

Brass **Issuer:** Rufisque

Date	Mintage	VG8	F12	VF20	XF40	MS60
1920	—	70.00	95.00	180	295	—

KM# Tn17 50 CENTIMES

Brass **Issuer:** Ziguinchor

Date	Mintage	VG8	F12	VF20	XF40	MS60
1921	—	70.00	95.00	180	285	550

KM# Tn18 FRANC

Brass **Issuer:** Ziguinchor

Date	Mintage	VG8	F12	VF20	XF40	MS60
1921	—	70.00	95.00	185	300	475

KM# Tn19 FRANC

Aluminum **Issuer:** Ziguinchor

Date	Mintage	VG8	F12	VF20	XF40	MS60
1921	—	40.00	80.00	175	350	500

STANDARD COINAGE

KM# 1 10 FRANCS

3.20 g., 0.900 Gold 0.0926 oz. AGW **Subject:** 8th Anniversary of Independence **Obv:** Star above shield within wreath **Rev:** Stars above value and date

Date	Mintage	VF20	XF40	MS60	MS63	MS65
1968	—	PF63 185	PF65 225			

KM# 2 25 FRANCS

8.00 g., 0.900 Gold 0.2315 oz. AGW **Subject:** 8th Anniversary of Independence **Obv:** Star above shield within wreath **Rev:** Stars above value and date

Date	Mintage	VF20	XF40	MS60	MS63	MS65
1968	—	PF63 400	PF65 450			

KM# 3 50 FRANCS

16.00 g., 0.900 Gold 0.463 oz. AGW **Subject:** 8th Anniversary of Independence **Obv:** Star above shield within wreath **Rev:** Stars above value and date

Date	Mintage	VF20	XF40	MS60	MS63	MS65
1968	—	PF63 775	PF65 850			

KM# 5 50 FRANCS

28.28 g., 0.925 Silver 0.841 oz. ASW **Subject:** 25th Anniversary of Eurafrique Program **Obv:** Sailboat at upper left of value and map **Rev:** Bust facing

Date	Mintage	VF20	XF40	MS60	MS63	MS65
1975	1,968	—	—	—	120	170
1975	18,032	PF63 75.00	PF65 95.00			

KM# 4 100 FRANCS
32.00 g., 0.900 Gold 0.9259 oz. AGW **Subject:** 8th Anniversary of Independence **Obv:** Star above shield within wreath **Rev:** Stars above value and date

Date	Mintage	VF20	XF40	MS60	MS63	MS65
1968	—	PF63 1,450	PF65 1,600			

KM# 6 150 FRANCS
79.97 g., 0.925 Silver 2.3783 oz. ASW, 48 mm. **Subject:** 25th Anniversary of Eurafrique Program **Obv:** Flying stork above value and map **Rev:** Bust facing

Date	Mintage	VF20	XF40	MS60	MS63	MS65
1975	1,075	—	—	—	140	190
1975	18,925	PF63 125	PF65 145			

KM# 7 250 FRANCS
3.98 g., 0.917 Gold 0.1173 oz. AGW **Subject:** 25th Anniversary of Eurafrique Program **Obv:** Star above shield within wreath **Rev:** Bust facing

Date	Mintage	VF20	XF40	MS60	MS63	MS65
1975	1,000	—	—	—	240	260
1975	1,250	PF63 240	PF65 260			

KM# 8 500 FRANCS
7.96 g., 0.917 Gold 0.2347 oz. AGW **Subject:** 25th Anniversary of Eurafrique Program **Obv:** Star above shield within wreath **Rev:** Bust facing

Date	Mintage	VF20	XF40	MS60	MS63	MS65
1975	500	—	—	—	425	475
1975	1,250	PF63 400	PF65 450			

KM# 9 1000 FRANCS
15.95 g., 0.916 Gold 0.4697 oz. AGW **Subject:** 25th Anniversary of Eurafrique Program **Obv:** Star above shield within wreath **Rev:** Bust facing

Date	Mintage	VF20	XF40	MS60	MS63	MS65
1975	217	—	—	—	950	1,000
1975	1,250	PF63 900	PF65 950			

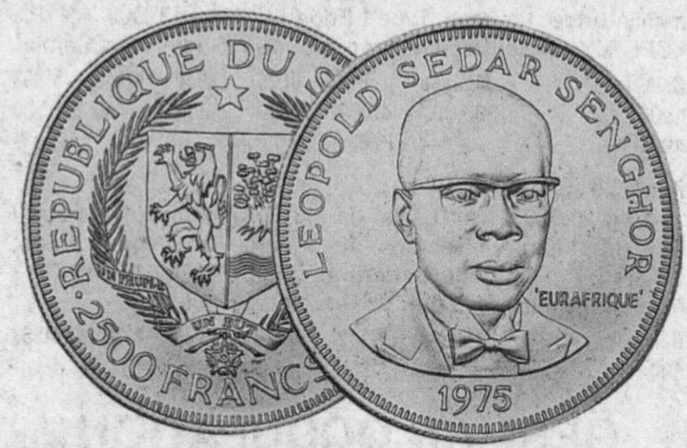

KM# 10 2500 FRANCS
39.93 g., 0.916 Gold 1.1759 oz. AGW **Subject:** 25th Anniversary of Eurafrique Program **Obv:** Star above shield within wreath **Rev:** Bust facing

Date	Mintage	VF20	XF40	MS60	MS63	MS65
1975	195	—	—	—	2,100	2,300
1975	1,250	PF63 1,950	PF65 2,150			

ESSAIS

Standard metals unless otherwise noted

KM#	Date	Mintage	Identification	Mkt Val
E1	1920	—	25 Centimes. Kayes. KM#Tn10.	275
E2	1921	—	50 Centimes. Brass. Zinguinchor. KMTn17.	325
E3	1921	—	Franc. Brass. Zinguinchor. KMTn18.	350

MINT SETS

KM#	Date	Mintage	Identification	Issue Price	Mkt Val
MS1	1975 (4)	195	KM#7-10	—	3,800

PROOF SETS

KM#	Date	Mintage	Identification	Issue Price	Mkt Val
PS1	1968 (4)	—	KM#1-4	—	3,275
PS2	1975 (2)	—	KM#5-6	—	240

Serbia, a former inland Balkan kingdom has an area of 34,116 sq. mi. (88,361 sq. km.). Capital: Belgrade.

Serbia emerged as a separate kingdom in the 12th century and attained its greatest expansion and political influence in the mid-14th century. After the Battle of Kosovo, 1389, Serbia became a vassal principality of Turkey and remained under Turkish suzerainty until it was re-established as an independent kingdom by the 1878 Treaty of Berlin. Following World War I, which had its immediate cause in the assassination of Austrian Archduke Francis Ferdinand by a Serbian nationalist, Serbia joined with the Croats and Slovenes to form the new Kingdom of the South Slavs with Peter I of Serbia as King. The name of the kingdom was later changed to Yugoslavia. Invaded by Germany during World War II, Serbia emerged as a constituent republic of the Socialist Federal Republic of Yugoslavia.

RULERS
Alexander I, 1889-1902
Peter I, 1903-1918

MINT MARKS
A - Paris
(a) - Paris, privy mark only
(g) - Gorham Mfg. Co., Providence, R.I.
H - Birmingham
V - Vienna
ÁÏ - (BP) Budapest

MONETARY SYSTEM
100 Para = 1 Dinara

DENOMINATIONS
ÏÀÐÀ = Para
ÏÀÐÅ = Pare
ÄÈÍÀÐ = Dinar
ÄÈÍÀÐÀ = Dinara

KINGDOM

STANDARD COINAGE

KM# 23 2 PARE
2.00 g., Bronze, 20 mm. **Ruler:** Peter I **Obv:** Crowned double-headed eagle **Rev:** Value **Note:** Medallic die alignment.

Date	Mintage	F12	VF20	XF40	MS60	MS63
1904	12,500,000	2.00	3.00	10.00	25.00	50.00

KM# 18 5 PARA
3.00 g., Copper-Nickel, 17 mm. **Ruler:** Milan I **Obv:** Crowned double-headed eagle **Rev:** Value **Note:** Medallic die alignment.

Date	Mintage	F12	VF20	XF40	MS60	MS63
1904	8,000,000	1.00	3.00	8.00	30.00	35.00
1904	Inc. above	PF63 300				
1912	10,500,032	1.00	3.00	6.00	12.00	20.00
1912	—	PF63 280				
1917 (g)	5,000,000	6.00	10.00	15.00	25.00	40.00

KM# 19 10 PARA
4.00 g., Copper-Nickel, 20 mm. **Ruler:** Milan I **Obv:** Crowned double-headed eagle **Rev:** Value **Note:** Medallic die alignment.

Date	Mintage	F12	VF20	XF40	MS60	MS63
1904	—	PF63 350				
1912	7,700,032	0.75	1.50	5.00	12.00	20.00
1912	—	PF63 160				
1917 (g)	5,000,000	20.00	30.00	40.00	80.00	120
1917 (g)	—	PF63 150				

KM# 20 20 PARA
5.60 g., Copper-Nickel, 22 mm. **Ruler:** Milan I **Obv:** Crowned double-headed eagle **Rev:** Value **Note:** Medallic die alignment.

Date	Mintage	F12	VF20	XF40	MS60	MS63
1904	—	PF63 400				
1912	5,650,035	1.00	2.00	5.00	12.00	20.00
1912	—	PF63 140				
1917 (g)	5,000,000	15.00	25.00	30.00	40.00	50.00

KM# 24.1 50 PARA
2.50 g., 0.835 Silver 0.0671 oz. ASW, 18 mm. **Ruler:** Peter I **Obv:** Head right with designer name **Rev:** Crown above value and date within wreath **Note:** Medallic die alignment.

Date	Mintage	F12	VF20	XF40	MS60	MS63
1904	1,400,031	2.00	3.00	10.00	20.00	35.00
1904	—	PF63 250				
1912	800,000	2.00	3.00	10.00	20.00	35.00
1915 (a)	12,137,928	2.00	3.00	5.00	12.00	15.00

KM# 24.2 50 PARA

2.50 g., 0.835 Silver 0.0671 oz. ASW, 18 mm. **Ruler:** Peter I **Obv:** Without designer's name **Rev:** Crown above value and date within wreath **Note:** Medallic die alignment

Date	Mintage	F12	VF20	XF40	MS60	MS63
1915	1,862,071	5.00	10.00	25.00	50.00	95.00

KM# 24.3 50 PARA

2.50 g., 0.835 Silver 0.0671 oz. ASW, 18 mm. **Ruler:** Peter I **Obv:** With designer's name **Rev:** Crown above value and date within wreath **Note:** Coin die alignment.

Date	Mintage	F12	VF20	XF40	MS60	MS63
1915 (a)	—	—	—	—	—	—

KM# 24.4 50 PARA

2.50 g., 0.835 Silver 0.0671 oz. ASW, 18 mm. **Ruler:** Peter I **Obv:** Without designer name **Rev:** Crown above value and date within wreath **Note:** Coin die alignment

Date	Mintage	F12	VF20	XF40	MS60	MS63
1915	—	—	—	—	—	—

KM# 24.5 50 PARA

2.50 g., 0.835 Silver 0.0671 oz. ASW, 18 mm. **Ruler:** Peter I **Obv:** With designer's signature **Rev:** Crown above value and date within wreath **Note:** Coin die alignment.

Date	Mintage	F12	VF20	XF40	MS60	MS63
1915 (a)	—	—	—	—	—	—

KM# 25.1 DINAR

5.00 g., 0.835 Silver 0.1342 oz. ASW, 22.5 mm. **Ruler:** Peter I **Obv:** Head right with designer's name below neck **Rev:** Crown above value and date within wreath **Note:** Medallic die alignment

Date	Mintage	F12	VF20	XF40	MS60	MS63
1904	2,000,086	5.00	9.00	20.00	50.00	75.00
1904	—	PF63 265				
1912	8,000,000	3.00	5.00	10.00	25.00	35.00
1915 (a)	10,688,711	3.00	5.00	8.00	15.00	25.00

KM# 25.2 DINAR

5.00 g., 0.835 Silver 0.1342 oz. ASW, 22.5 mm. **Ruler:** Peter I **Obv:** Without designer's name **Rev:** Crown above value and date within wreath **Note:** Medallic die alignment.

Date	Mintage	F12	VF20	XF40	MS60	MS63
1915	2,312,304	5.00	10.00	25.00	60.00	100

KM# 25.3 DINAR

5.00 g., 0.835 Silver 0.1342 oz. ASW, 23 mm. **Ruler:** Peter I **Obv:** With designer name **Rev:** Crown above value and date within wreath **Note:** Coin die alignment

Date	Mintage	F12	VF20	XF40	MS60	MS63
1915 (a)	—	—	—	—	—	—

KM# 25.4 DINAR

5.00 g., 0.835 Silver 0.1342 oz. ASW, 23 mm. **Ruler:** Peter I **Obv:** Without designer name **Rev:** Crown above value and date within wreath **Note:** Coin die alignment

Date	Mintage	F12	VF20	XF40	MS60	MS63
1915	—	—	—	—	—	—

KM# 26.1 2 DINARA

10.00 g., 0.835 Silver 0.2685 oz. ASW **Ruler:** Peter I **Obv:** Head right with designer's name below neck **Rev:** Crown above value and date within wreath **Note:** Medallic die alignment

Date	Mintage	F12	VF20	XF40	MS60	MS63
1904	1,150,044	7.00	10.00	20.00	50.00	95.00
1904	—	PF63 325				
1912	800,016	7.00	10.00	20.00	60.00	100
1915 (a)	4,174,142	7.00	10.00	15.00	30.00	45.00

KM# 26.2 2 DINARA

10.00 g., 0.835 Silver 0.2685 oz. ASW **Ruler:** Peter I **Obv:** Without designer's name **Rev:** Crown above value and date within wreath **Note:** Medallic die alignment.

Date	Mintage	F12	VF20	XF40	MS60	MS63
1915	825,858	10.00	20.00	45.00	125	200

KM# 26.3 2 DINARA

10.00 g., 0.835 Silver 0.2685 oz. ASW **Ruler:** Peter I **Obv:** With designer's name **Rev:** Crown above value and date within wreath **Note:** Coin die alignment.

Date	Mintage	VG8	F12	VF20	XF40	MS60
1915 (a)	Inc. above	—	9.00	15.00	22.00	48.00
1915 A	—	—	—	—	—	—

KM# 27 5 DINARA

25.00 g., 0.900 Silver 0.7234 oz. ASW, 37 mm. **Ruler:** Peter I **Subject:** 100th Anniversary - Karageorgevich Dynasty **Obv:** Conjoined heads right with designer name below neck **Rev:** Crowned double-headed eagle on shield within crowned mantle **Edge:** Lettered, Type I **Edge Lettering:** • БОГ • ЧУВА • СРБИЈУ • **Note:** Edge lettered in Cyrillic: God Protect Serbia

Date	Mintage	F12	VF20	XF40	MS60	MS63
1904	200,000	40.00	75.00	250	750	1,500
1904	—	PF63 2,200				

KM# 28 5 DINARA

25.00 g., 0.900 Silver 0.7234 oz. ASW, 37 mm. **Ruler:** Peter I **Subject:** 100th Anniversary - Karageorgevich Dynasty **Edge:** Lettered, Type II **Edge Lettering:** • БОГ • СРБИЈУ • ЧУВА • **Note:** Edge lettered in Cyrillic: God Serbia Protect

Date	Mintage	F12	VF20	XF40	MS60	MS63
1904	Inc. above	200	350	750	1,800	—

GERMAN OCCUPATION

World War II

OCCUPATION COINAGE

KM# 30 50 PARA

Zinc, 18 mm. **Obv:** Double-headed eagle **Rev:** Value and date within oat sprigs

Date	Mintage	F12	VF20	XF40	MS60	MS63
1942 БП (BP)	20,000,000	0.70	2.00	8.00	20.00	—

KM# 31 DINAR

Zinc, 20 mm. **Obv:** Double-headed eagle **Rev:** Value and date within oat sprigs

Date	Mintage	F12	VF20	XF40	MS60	MS63
1942 БП (BP)	50,000,000	0.70	2.00	8.00	20.00	—

KM# 32 2 DINARA

Zinc, 22 mm. **Obv:** Double-headed eagle **Rev:** Value and date within oat sprigs

Date	Mintage	F12	VF20	XF40	MS60	MS63
1942 БП (BP)	40,000,000	0.70	2.00	8.00	20.00	—

KM# 33 10 DINARA

Zinc, 26.5 mm. **Obv:** Double-headed eagle **Rev:** Value and date within oat sprigs

Date	Mintage	F12	VF20	XF40	MS60	MS63
1943 БП (BP)	50,000,000	1.00	2.50	9.00	22.00	—

PATTERNS

Including off metal strikes

KM#	Date	Mintage	Identification	Mkt Val
Pn14	1904	—	2 Dinara. Bronze.	1,600
Pn15	1904	4	5 Dinara. Gold.	—
Pn16	1917	—	5 Para. Gold.	—
Pn17	1917	—	10 Para. Gold.	—
Pn18	1917	—	20 Para. Gold.	—
Pn19	1917	—	20 Dinara. Gold.	—

SEYCHELLES

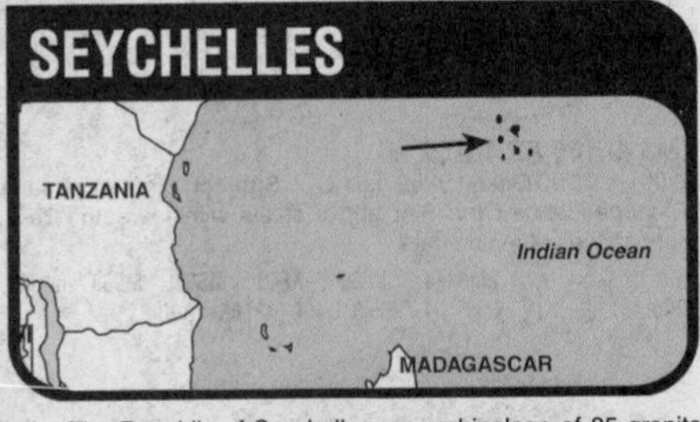

The Republic of Seychelles, an archipelago of 85 granite and coral islands situated in the Indian Ocean 600 miles (965 km.) northeast of Madagascar, has an area of 156 sq. mi. (455 sq. km.) and a population of *70,000. Among these islands are the Aldabra Islands, the Farquhar Group, and Ile Desroches, which the United Kingdom ceded to the Seychelles upon its independence. Capital: Victoria, on Mahe. The economy is based on fishing, a plantation system of agriculture, and tourism. Copra, cinnamon and vanilla are exported.

Although the Seychelles is marked on Portuguese charts of the early 16th century, the first recorded visit to the islands, by an English ship, occurred in 1609. The Seychelles were annexed to France by Captain Lazare Picault in 1743 and permanently settled in 1768, with the intention of establishing spice plantations to compete with the Dutch monopoly of the spice trade. British troops seized the islands in 1810, during the Napoleonic Wars; the Treaty of Paris, 1814, formally ceded them to Britain. The Seychelles was a dependency of Mauritius until Aug. 31, 1903, when they became a separate British Crown Colony. The colony was granted limited internal self-government in 1970, and attained independence on June 28, 1976, becoming Britain's last African possession to do so. Seychelles is a member of the Commonwealth of Nations. The president is the Head of State and of Government.

RULER

British, until 1976

MINT MARKS

(sa) - M in oval – South African Mint Co.
On coins dated 2000 and up in
Place of PM
PM - Pobjoy Mint
None - British Royal Mint

MONETARY SYSTEM

100 Cents = 1 Rupee

BRITISH CROWN COLONY

STANDARD COINAGE

KM# 5 CENT

Bronze **Obv:** Crowned head left **Rev:** Value within beaded circle

Date	Mintage	VF20	XF40	MS60	MS63	MS65
1948	300,000	0.25	0.50	1.00	1.75	5.00
1948	—	PF63 150	PF65 250	PF67 300		

KM# 14 CENT

Bronze **Obv:** Crowned head right **Rev:** Value within beaded circle

Date	Mintage	VF20	XF40	MS60	MS63	MS65
1959	30,000	0.75	1.50	2.00	3.00	5.00
1959 Proof	—	—	—	—	—	—
1961	30,000	0.50	1.00	1.50	2.25	5.00
1961 Proof	—	—	—	—	—	—
1963	40,000	0.50	0.75	1.00	1.50	5.00
1963 Proof	—	—	—	—	—	—
1965	20,000	0.75	1.00	1.50	3.00	5.00
1969	Est. 5000	5.00	7.00	15.00	30.00	60.00

Note: Latest reports indicate only 5,000 circulation strikes have been releasesd to date in addition to proof issues

Date	Mintage	VF20	XF40	MS60	MS63	MS65
1969	—	PF65 4.00				

KM# 17 CENT
0.70 g., Aluminum, 16 mm. **Series:** F.A.O. **Obv:** Young bust right **Rev:** Cow head **Edge:** Plain

Date	Mintage	VF20	XF40	MS60	MS63	MS65
1972	2,350,000	—	0.10	0.15	0.25	1.00

KM# 6 2 CENTS
6.44 g., Bronze, 23.1 mm. **Obv:** Crowned head left **Rev:** Value within beaded circle

Date	Mintage	VF20	XF40	MS60	MS63	MS65
1948	350,000	0.35	0.50	0.75	1.50	5.00
1948	—	PF63 225	PF65 375	PF67 425		

KM# 15 2 CENTS
Bronze, 23.1 mm. **Obv:** Crowned head right **Rev:** Value within beaded circle

Date	Mintage	VF20	XF40	MS60	MS63	MS65
1959	30,000	0.50	1.00	2.00	3.00	5.00
1959 Proof	—	—	—	—	—	—
1961	30,000	0.50	0.85	1.75	2.75	5.00
1961 Proof	—	—	—	—	—	—
1963	40,000	0.75	1.00	1.25	2.50	5.00
1963 Proof	—	—	—	—	—	—
1965	20,000	0.75	1.00	1.50	3.00	5.00
1968	20,000	0.75	1.00	1.50	3.00	5.00
1969	5,000	PF65 4.00				

KM# 7 5 CENTS
Bronze, 28.4 mm. **Obv:** Crowned head left **Rev:** Value within circle

Date	Mintage	VF20	XF40	MS60	MS63	MS65
1948	300,000	0.40	0.80	1.50	3.00	5.00
1948	—	PF63 350	PF65 500	PF67 550		

KM# 16 5 CENTS
Bronze, 28.4 mm. **Obv:** Crowned head right **Rev:** Value within beaded circle

Date	Mintage	VF20	XF40	MS60	MS63	MS65
1964	20,000	0.50	1.00	1.50	3.00	7.00
1964 Proof	—	—	—	—	—	—
1965	40,000	0.50	1.00	2.50	5.00	10.00
1967	20,000	0.50	1.00	1.50	3.00	5.00
1968	40,000	0.50	1.00	1.50	3.00	5.00
1969	100,000	0.50	1.00	1.50	3.00	5.00
1969	—	PF65 8.00				
1971	25,000	0.50	1.00	1.50	3.00	5.00

KM# 18 5 CENTS
0.77 g., Aluminum, 18.5 mm. **Series:** F.A.O. **Obv:** Young bust right **Rev:** Cabbage head **Shape:** Scalloped

Date	Mintage	VF20	XF40	MS60	MS63	MS65
1972	2,200,000	—	0.10	0.15	0.25	0.50
1975	1,200,000	—	0.10	0.15	0.25	0.50

KM# 1 10 CENTS
Copper-Nickel **Obv:** Crowned head left **Rev:** Value within sprig above date **Shape:** Scalloped

Date	Mintage	VF20	XF40	MS60	MS63	MS65
1939	36,000	10.00	15.00	22.00	45.00	100
1939	—	PF63 150				
1943	36,000	10.00	15.00	20.00	35.00	85.00
1944	36,000	10.00	15.00	20.00	35.00	85.00
1944	—	PF63 175				

KM# 8 10 CENTS
Copper-Nickel **Obv:** Crowned head left **Rev:** Value within sprig above date **Shape:** Scalloped

Date	Mintage	VF20	XF40	MS60	MS63	MS65
1951	36,000	3.00	10.00	15.00	20.00	50.00
1951	—	PF63 300	PF65 500			

KM# 10 10 CENTS
6.04 g., Nickel-Brass, 21.57 mm. **Obv:** Crowned head right **Rev:** Value within sprig above date **Shape:** 12-sided

Date	Mintage	VF20	XF40	MS60	MS63	MS65
1953	130,000	0.50	1.00	1.50	3.00	5.00
1953	—	PF65 100				
1965	40,000	0.50	1.00	2.50	5.00	10.00
1967	20,000	0.50	2.00	3.00	6.00	15.00
1968	50,000	0.25	1.00	2.00	4.00	8.00
1969	60,000	0.25	0.50	1.50	3.00	5.00
1969	—	PF65 2.00				
1970	75,000	0.15	0.25	0.50	1.00	2.00
1971	100,000	0.15	0.25	0.35	0.50	1.00
1972	120,000	0.15	0.25	0.35	0.50	1.00
1973	100,000	0.15	0.25	0.35	0.50	1.00
1974	100,000	0.15	0.25	0.35	0.50	1.00

KM# 2 25 CENTS
2.92 g., 0.500 Silver 0.0469 oz. ASW **Obv:** Crowned head left **Rev:** Value within sprig above date

Date	Mintage	VF20	XF40	MS60	MS63	MS65
1939	36,000	3.00	20.00	45.00	95.00	250
1939	—	PF63 200				
1943	36,000	3.00	20.00	45.00	95.00	250
1944	36,000	3.00	20.00	45.00	125	300
1944	—	PF63 225	PF65 350			

KM# 9 25 CENTS
Copper-Nickel **Obv:** Crowned head left **Rev:** Value within sprig above date

Date	Mintage	VF20	XF40	MS60	MS63	MS65
1951	36,000	1.00	5.00	10.00	20.00	50.00
1951	—	PF63 160				

KM# 11 25 CENTS
2.80 g., Copper-Nickel, 19 mm. **Obv:** Crowned head right **Rev:** Value within sprig above date

Date	Mintage	VF20	XF40	MS60	MS63	MS65
1954	124,000	0.50	0.75	1.50	3.00	5.00
1954	—	PF65 120				
1960	40,000	0.50	0.75	1.50	3.00	5.00
1960 Proof	—	—	—	—	—	—
1964	40,000	0.50	0.75	2.00	5.00	8.00
1965	40,000	0.50	0.75	2.00	5.00	8.00
1966	10,000	2.00	5.00	10.00	20.00	45.00
1967	20,000	1.50	3.00	6.00	10.00	30.00
1968	20,000	1.00	2.00	7.00	15.00	35.00
1969	100,000	0.25	0.75	1.00	1.50	2.00
1969	—	PF65 3.00				
1970	40,000	0.50	1.00	1.50	3.00	5.00
1972	120,000	0.25	0.75	1.00	1.50	2.00
1973	100,000	0.25	0.75	1.00	1.50	2.00
1974	100,000	0.25	0.75	1.00	1.50	2.00

KM# 3 1/2 RUPEE
5.83 g., 0.500 Silver 0.0937 oz. ASW **Obv:** Crowned head left **Rev:** Value within sprig above date

Date	Mintage	VF20	XF40	MS60	MS63	MS65
1939	36,000	10.00	20.00	40.00	70.00	150
1939	—	PF63 250				

KM# 12 1/2 RUPEE
Copper-Nickel **Obv:** Crowned head right **Rev:** Value within sprig above date

Date	Mintage	VF20	XF40	MS60	MS63	MS65
1954	72,000	0.25	1.00	1.50	3.00	5.00
1954	—	PF65 150				
1960	60,000	0.25	1.00	2.00	5.00	7.00
1960	—	PF65 150				
1966	15,000	3.00	5.00	10.00	20.00	45.00
1967	20,000	0.50	3.00	7.00	15.00	35.00
1968	20,000	0.50	3.00	10.00	20.00	45.00
1969	60,000	0.25	1.50	2.50	6.00	9.00
1969	—	PF65 3.00				
1970	50,000	0.25	0.50	1.50	3.00	5.00
1971	100,000	0.25	0.50	1.00	2.00	3.00
1972	120,000	0.25	0.50	0.75	1.00	1.50
1974	100,000	0.25	0.50	0.75	1.00	1.50

KM# 4 RUPEE
11.66 g., 0.500 Silver 0.1874 oz. ASW, 30 mm. **Obv:** Crowned head left **Rev:** Value within sprig above date **Edge:** Reeded

Date	Mintage	VF20	XF40	MS60	MS63	MS65
1939	90,000	15.00	75.00	100	125	225
1939	—	PF63 400				

KM# 13 RUPEE
11.64 g., Copper-Nickel, 30 mm. **Obv:** Crowned head right **Rev:** Value within sprig above date

Date	Mintage	VF20	XF40	MS60	MS63	MS65
1954	150,000	0.25	0.75	1.50	3.00	5.00
1954	—	PF65 200				
1960	60,000	0.25	0.75	1.50	3.00	5.00
1960 Proof	—	—	—	—	—	—
1966	45,000	0.25	0.75	1.50	3.00	5.00
1967	10,000	1.00	3.00	7.00	15.00	50.00
1968	40,000	0.50	1.50	5.00	10.00	35.00
1969	50,000	0.25	1.00	2.50	5.00	10.00
1969	—	PF65 12.50				
1970	50,000	0.25	1.00	1.50	3.00	10.00
1971	100,000	0.25	0.75	1.25	2.00	3.50
1972	120,000	0.25	0.75	1.00	1.50	2.00
1974	100,000	0.25	0.75	1.00	1.50	2.00

KM# 19 5 RUPEES
Copper-Nickel, 30 mm. **Obv:** Young bust right **Rev:** Palm tree, sailboats,giant tortoise and value **Edge:** Plain **Shape:** 7-sided

Date	Mintage	VF20	XF40	MS60	MS63	MS65
1972	220,000	0.25	1.00	2.00	3.00	9.00

KM# 19a 5 RUPEES
15.50 g., 0.925 Silver 0.461 oz. ASW, 30 mm. **Obv:** Young bust right **Rev:** Palm tree, boats and value **Shape:** 7-sided

Date	Mintage	VF20	XF40	MS60	MS63	MS65
1972	2,500	PF63 22.00	PF65 25.00			
1974	5,000	PF63 17.00	PF65 20.00			

KM# 20 10 RUPEES
Copper-Nickel, 38.5 mm. **Obv:** Young bust right **Rev:** Sea turtle and value

Date	Mintage	VF20	XF40	MS60	MS63	MS65
1974	—	1.50	2.50	4.00	6.00	9.00

KM# 20a 10 RUPEES
28.28 g., 0.925 Silver 0.841 oz. ASW **Obv:** Young bust right **Rev:** Green sea turtle

Date	Mintage	VF20	XF40	MS60	MS63	MS65
1974	25,000	PF63 20.00	PF65 25.00			

REPUBLIC

KM# 21 CENT
Aluminum, 16 mm. **Subject:** Declaration of Independence **Obv:** President James Mancham head right **Rev:** Boueteur fish and value

Date	Mintage	VF20	XF40	MS60	MS63	MS65
1976	109,000	0.10	0.20	0.35	0.75	1.00
1976	8,500	PF65 1.50				

KM# 30 CENT
0.70 g., Aluminum, 16 mm. **Obv:** Arms with supporters **Rev:** Boueteur fish and value

Date	Mintage	VF20	XF40	MS60	MS63	MS65
1977	—	—	0.15	0.35	0.75	1.00

KM# 46.1 CENT
Brass **Obv:** Arms with supporters **Rev:** Mud Crab and value

Date	Mintage	VF20	XF40	MS60	MS63	MS65
1982	500,000	—	0.15	0.25	0.50	1.50
1982	—	PF65 2.25				

KM# 46.2 CENT
1.43 g., Brass, 16.03 mm. **Obv:** Altered coat of arms **Rev:** Mud Crab **Edge:** Plain

Date	Mintage	VF20	XF40	MS60	MS63	MS65
1990	—	—	0.15	0.25	0.45	0.75
1992	—	—	0.15	0.25	0.45	0.75
1992	—	PF65 2.25				
1997	—	—	0.15	0.20	0.40	0.75

KM# 22 5 CENTS
Aluminum **Subject:** Declaration of Independence **Obv:** President James Mancham head right **Rev:** Bourgeois fish above value and sprigs **Shape:** Scalloped **Note:** Varieties exist.

Date	Mintage	VF20	XF40	MS60	MS63	MS65
1976	209,000	0.10	0.20	0.35	0.75	1.25
1976	8,500	PF65 1.50				

KM# 31 5 CENTS
Aluminum **Series:** F.A.O. **Obv:** Arms with supporters **Rev:** Bourgeois fish above value and sprigs **Shape:** Scalloped

Date	Mintage	VF20	XF40	MS60	MS63	MS65
1977	300,000	—	0.15	0.35	0.75	1.25

KM# 43 5 CENTS
1.95 g., Brass, 18 mm. **Series:** World Food Day **Obv:** Arms with supporters **Rev:** Value at lower left of tapioca plant

Date	Mintage	VF20	XF40	MS60	MS63	MS65
1981	720,000	—	0.15	0.25	0.45	1.00

KM# 47.1 5 CENTS
1.95 g., Brass, 18 mm. **Obv:** Arms with supporters **Rev:** Value at lower left of tapioca plant

Date	Mintage	VF20	XF40	MS60	MS63	MS65
1982	1,500,000	—	0.10	0.20	0.30	0.50
1982	Inc. above	PF65 2.50				

KM# 47.2 5 CENTS
2.00 g., Brass, 18 mm. **Obv:** Altered coat of arms **Rev:** Tapioca plant

Date	Mintage	VF20	XF40	MS60	MS63	MS65
1990	—	—	0.10	0.20	0.30	0.50
1992	—	—	0.10	0.20	0.30	0.50
1992	—	PF65 2.50				
1995	—	—	0.10	0.20	0.30	0.50
1997	—	—	0.10	0.20	0.30	0.50
1997	—	PF65 2.50				
2000 (sa)	—	—	0.10	0.20	0.30	0.50

KM# 23 10 CENTS
Nickel-Brass, 21 mm. **Subject:** Declaration of Independence **Obv:** Head right **Rev:** Sailfish and value **Edge:** Plain **Shape:** 12-sided

Date	Mintage	VF20	XF40	MS60	MS63	MS65
1976	209,000	0.20	0.50	0.75	1.50	2.50
1976	8,500	PF65 2.50				

KM# 32 10 CENTS
Nickel-Brass, 21 mm. **Series:** F.A.O. **Obv:** Arms with supporters **Rev:** Sailfish and value

Date	Mintage	VF20	XF40	MS60	MS63	MS65
1977	125,000	0.10	0.35	0.65	1.50	2.50

KM# 44 10 CENTS
3.25 g., Brass, 21 mm. **Series:** World Food Day **Obv:** Arms with supporters **Rev:** Yellowfin tuna and value

Date	Mintage	VF20	XF40	MS60	MS63	MS65
1981	145,000	0.10	0.25	0.50	1.00	1.50

KM# 48.1 10 CENTS
3.30 g., Brass, 21 mm. **Obv:** Arms with supporters **Rev:** Yellowfin tuna and value

Date	Mintage	VF20	XF40	MS60	MS63	MS65
1982	1,000,000	0.10	0.25	0.50	1.00	1.50
1982	Inc. above	PF65 2.75				

KM# 48.2 10 CENTS
3.34 g., Brass, 21 mm. **Obv:** Altered coat of arms **Rev:** Yellowfin tuna **Edge:** Plain

Date	Mintage	VF20	XF40	MS60	MS63	MS65
1990	—	0.10	0.25	0.50	1.00	1.50
1992	—	0.10	0.25	0.50	1.00	1.50
1992	—	PF65 2.75				
1994	—	0.10	0.25	0.50	1.00	1.50
1997	—	0.10	0.25	0.50	1.00	1.50
2000 (sa)	—	0.10	0.25	0.50	1.00	1.50

KM# 24 25 CENTS
2.90 g., Copper-Nickel, 19 mm. **Subject:** Declaration of Independence **Obv:** President James Mancham head right **Rev:** Black Parrot and value

Date	Mintage	VF20	XF40	MS60	MS63	MS65
1976	209,000	0.25	0.50	0.75	1.50	3.00
1976	8,500	PF65 3.50				

KM# 33 25 CENTS
2.90 g., Copper-Nickel, 19 mm. **Obv:** Arms with supporters **Rev:** Black Parrot and value

Date	Mintage	VF20	XF40	MS60	MS63	MS65
1977	—	0.25	0.50	0.75	1.50	3.00

KM# 49.1 25 CENTS
2.90 g., Copper-Nickel, 19 mm. **Obv:** Arms with supporters **Rev:** Black Parrot and value **Edge:** Reeded

Date	Mintage	VF20	XF40	MS60	MS63	MS65
1982	375,000	0.25	0.50	0.75	1.50	3.00
1982	Inc. above	PF65 4.00				

KM# 49.2 25 CENTS
2.90 g., Copper-Nickel, 19 mm. **Obv:** Arms with supporters **Rev:** Black Parrot and value

Date	Mintage	VF20	XF40	MS60	MS63	MS65
1989	1,500,000	0.25	0.50	0.75	1.50	4.00
1992 PM	—	0.25	0.50	0.75	1.50	4.00
1992 PM	—	PF65 5.00				

KM# 49a 25 CENTS
2.97 g., Nickel Clad Steel, 18.9 mm. **Obv:** National arms **Rev:** Black Parrot and value **Edge:** Plain

Date	Mintage	VF20	XF40	MS60	MS63	MS65
1993 PM	—	0.25	0.60	0.90	1.75	3.00
1997 PM	—	0.25	0.60	0.90	1.75	3.00

KM# 49b 25 CENTS
2.90 g., Stainless Steel, 19 mm. **Obv:** Arms with supporters **Rev:** Black Parrot and value

Date	Mintage	VF20	XF40	MS60	MS63	MS65
2000 (sa)	—	—	0.50	0.70	1.25	2.00

KM# 25 50 CENTS
5.80 g., Copper-Nickel, 23.6 mm. **Subject:** Declaration of Independence **Obv:** President James Mancham head right **Rev:** Vanilla orchid and value **Edge:** Reeded

Date	Mintage	VF20	XF40	MS60	MS63	MS65
1976	209,000	0.50	0.75	1.00	1.50	3.00
1976	8,500	PF65 5.00				

KM# 34 50 CENTS
5.80 g., Copper-Nickel, 23.6 mm. **Obv:** Arms with supporters **Rev:** Vanilla orchid and value

Date	Mintage	VF20	XF40	MS60	MS63	MS65
1977	—	0.20	0.45	0.65	1.00	1.50

KM# 26 RUPEE
11.65 g., Copper-Nickel, 30 mm. **Subject:** Declaration of Independence **Obv:** President James Mancham head right **Rev:** Triton Conch shell and value **Edge:** Reeded

Date	Mintage	VF20	XF40	MS60	MS63	MS65
1976	259,000	0.25	0.50	0.75	1.25	2.50
1976	8,500	PF65 3.50				

KM# 35 RUPEE
11.65 g., Copper-Nickel, 30 mm. **Obv:** Arms with supporters **Rev:** Triton Conch shell and value

Date	Mintage	VF20	XF40	MS60	MS63	MS65
1977	—	0.25	0.50	0.75	1.25	3.00

KM# 50.1 RUPEE
6.05 g., Copper-Nickel, 25.4 mm. **Obv:** Arms with supporters **Rev:** Triton Conch shell and value

Date	Mintage	VF20	XF40	MS60	MS63	MS65
1982	2,000,000	0.25	0.45	0.60	1.00	1.50
1982	Inc. above	PF65 5.00				
1983	—	0.25	0.45	0.60	1.00	1.50

KM# 50.2 RUPEE
6.18 g., Copper-Nickel, 25.46 mm. **Obv:** Altered coat of arms **Rev:** Triton Conch Shell **Edge:** Reeded

Date	Mintage	VF20	XF40	MS60	MS63	MS65
1992 PM	—	—	0.25	0.50	0.75	1.00
1992 PM	—	PF65 5.00				
1995 PM	—	—	0.25	0.50	0.75	1.00
1997 PM	—	—	0.25	0.50	0.75	1.00

KM# 85 RUPEE
Copper-Nickel **Series:** Queen Elizabeth The Queen Mother **Subject:** Wedding of Lady Elizabeth Bowes-Lyon: The Duke of York, 1923 **Obv:** Arms with supporters **Rev:** Royal couple facing on steps

Date	Mintage	VF20	XF40	MS60	MS63	MS65
1995	Est. 30000	—	—	2.00	4.00	6.00

KM# 27 5 RUPEES
13.50 g., Copper-Nickel, 30 mm. **Subject:** Declaration of Independence **Obv:** President James Mancham head right **Rev:** Palm tree and value **Shape:** 7-sided

Date	Mintage	VF20	XF40	MS60	MS63	MS65
1976	50,000	0.25	0.50	0.75	1.50	3.00
1976	—	PF65 375				

KM# 27a 5 RUPEES
15.50 g., 0.925 Silver 0.461 oz. ASW, 30 mm. **Subject:** Declaration of Independence **Obv:** President James Mancham head right **Rev:** Palm tree and value

Date	Mintage	VF20	XF40	MS60	MS63	MS65
1976	8,500	PF63 14.00	PF65 17.00			

KM# 36 5 RUPEES
13.50 g., Copper-Nickel, 30 mm. **Obv:** Arms with supporters **Rev:** Palm tree and value **Shape:** 7-sided

Date	Mintage	VF20	XF40	MS60	MS63	MS65
1977	—	0.25	0.50	0.75	1.50	3.00

KM# 51.1 5 RUPEES
8.90 g., Copper-Nickel, 28.9 mm. **Obv:** Arms with supporters **Rev:** Palm tree and value

Date	Mintage	VF20	XF40	MS60	MS63	MS65
1982	300,000	0.25	0.50	0.75	1.50	3.00
1982	Inc. above	PF65 5.00				

KM# 51.2 5 RUPEES
9.00 g., Copper-Nickel, 29 mm. **Obv:** Altered arms **Rev:** Fruit tree divides value **Edge:** Reeded

Date	Mintage	VF20	XF40	MS60	MS63	MS65
1992	—	—	0.50	0.75	1.00	1.50
1992	—	PF65 5.00				
1997	—	—	0.50	0.75	1.00	1.50
2000 (sa) Thicker lettering	—	—	0.50	0.75	1.00	1.50

KM# 89 5 RUPEES
Copper-Nickel **Series:** 50th Anniversary United Nations **Obv:** Arms with supporters **Rev:** Dove in flight over UN's logo, large 50 at right

Date	Mintage	VF20	XF40	MS60	MS63	MS65
ND-1995	—	—	—	2.00	4.00	6.00

KM# 109 5 RUPEES
Copper-Nickel **Subject:** Marriage of Prince Edward **Obv:** Arms with supporters **Rev:** Tied initials and birds **Note:** Similar to 25 Rupees, KM#110.

Date	Mintage	VF20	XF40	MS60	MS63	MS65
1999	—	—	—	2.00	4.00	6.00

KM# 112 5 RUPEES
Copper-Nickel **Subject:** Millennium **Obv:** Arms with supporters **Rev:** Latent image of 1999-2000 dates **Note:** Similar to 25 Rupees, KM#113.

Date	Mintage	VF20	XF40	MS60	MS63	MS65
2000 (sa) (sa)	—	—	—	2.00	4.00	6.00

KM# 114 5 RUPEES
Copper-Nickel **Subject:** British Queen Mother **Obv:** Arms with supporters **Rev:** Head with hat 1/4 right, dates at right **Edge:** Reeded

Date	Mintage	VF20	XF40	MS60	MS63	MS65
2000 (sa) (sa)	—	—	—	2.00	4.00	6.00

KM# 28 10 RUPEES
18.10 g., Copper-Nickel, 34.5 mm. **Subject:** Declaration of Independence **Obv:** President James Mancham head right **Rev:** Green sea turtle and value

Date	Mintage	VF20	XF40	MS60	MS63	MS65
1976	50,000	0.50	0.75	1.50	3.00	5.00

KM# 28a 10 RUPEES
28.28 g., 0.925 Silver 0.841 oz. ASW, 34.5 mm. **Subject:** Declaration of Independence **Obv:** President James Mancham head right **Rev:** Green sea turtle and value

Date	Mintage	VF20	XF40	MS60	MS63	MS65
1976	29,000	PF63 28.00	PF65 35.00			

KM# 37 10 RUPEES
18.10 g., Copper-Nickel, 34.5 mm. **Series:** F.A.O. **Obv:** Arms with supporters **Rev:** Green sea turtle and value

Date	Mintage	VF20	XF40	MS60	MS63	MS65
1977	—	—	—	2.00	4.00	7.00
1977	—	PF65 10.00				

KM# 64 10 RUPEES
10.00 g., 0.925 Silver 0.2974 oz. ASW **Series:** Endangered Wildlife **Obv:** Arms with supporters **Rev:** Magpie Robin **Note:** Similar to 25 Rupees, KM#65.

Date	Mintage	VF20	XF40	MS60	MS63	MS65
1993	Est. 20000	PF63 12.00	PF65 15.00			

KM# 87 10 RUPEES
10.00 g., 0.500 Silver 0.1608 oz. ASW **Subject:** 1996 Olympics **Obv:** Arms with supporters **Rev:** Cyclist

Date	Mintage	VF20	XF40	MS60	MS63	MS65
1996	Est. 10000	—	—	—	5.00	7.00

KM# 52 20 RUPEES
Copper-Nickel, 36 mm. **Subject:** 5th Anniversary of Central Bank **Obv:** Arms with supporters **Rev:** Turtle at center of symbols of commerce **Edge:** Reeded

Date	Mintage	VF20	XF40	MS60	MS63	MS65
1983	—	—	—	2.00	4.00	6.00

KM# 52a 20 RUPEES
19.44 g., 0.925 Silver 0.5781 oz. ASW **Subject:** 5th Anniversary of Central Bank **Obv:** Arms with supporters **Rev:** Turtle at center of symbols of commerce

Date	Mintage	VF20	XF40	MS60	MS63	MS65
1983	5,000	PF63 20.00	PF65 25.00			

KM# 52b 20 RUPEES
33.90 g., 0.917 Gold 0.9994 oz. AGW **Subject:** 5th Anniversary of Central Bank **Obv:** Arms with supporters **Rev:** Turtle at center of symbols of commerce

Date	Mintage	VF20	XF40	MS60	MS63	MS65
1983	50	PF63 1,750	PF65 1,850			

KM# 38 25 RUPEES
28.28 g., 0.500 Silver 0.4546 oz. ASW **Subject:** Queen's Silver Jubilee **Obv:** Head right **Rev:** Royal Orb at center of legends

Date	Mintage	VF20	XF40	MS60	MS63	MS65
ND-1977	17,000	—	—	10.00	12.00	15.00

KM# 38a 25 RUPEES
28.28 g., 0.925 Silver 0.841 oz. ASW **Subject:** Queen's Silver Jubilee **Obv:** Head right **Rev:** Royal Orb at center of legends

Date	Mintage	VF20	XF40	MS60	MS63	MS65
ND-1977	15,000	PF63 25.00	PF65 30.00			

KM# 53 25 RUPEES
Copper-Nickel **Series:** F.A.O. **Subject:** World Fisheries Conference **Obv:** Arms with supporters **Rev:** Fish trap

Date	Mintage	VF20	XF40	MS60	MS63	MS65
1983	100,000	—	—	2.00	3.50	5.50

KM# 53a 25 RUPEES
28.28 g., 0.925 Silver 0.841 oz. ASW **Series:** F.A.O. **Subject:** World Fisheries Conference **Obv:** Arms with supporters **Rev:** Fish trap

Date	Mintage	VF20	XF40	MS60	MS63	MS65
1983	20,000	PF63 25.00	PF65 30.00			

KM# 53b 25 RUPEES
47.54 g., 0.917 Gold 1.4016 oz. AGW **Series:** F.A.O. **Subject:** World Fisheries Conference **Obv:** Arms with supporters **Rev:** Fish trap

Date	Mintage	VF20	XF40	MS60	MS63	MS65
1983	100	PF65 2,400	PF67 2,700			

KM# 63 25 RUPEES
31.47 g., 0.925 Silver 0.9359 oz. ASW **Subject:** 40th Anniversary of Queen Elizabeth's Coronation **Obv:** Arms with supporters **Rev:** Royal carriage

Date	Mintage	VF20	XF40	MS60	MS63	MS65
1993	Est. 10000	PF63 27.00	PF65 32.00			

KM# 65 25 RUPEES
28.28 g., 0.925 Silver 0.841 oz. ASW **Series:** Endangered Wildlife **Obv:** Arms with supporters **Rev:** Magpie Robin

Date	Mintage	VF20	XF40	MS60	MS63	MS65
1993	Est. 20000	PF63 22.00	PF65 28.00			

KM# 67 25 RUPEES
31.46 g., 0.925 Silver 0.9356 oz. ASW **Subject:** World Cup Soccer **Obv:** Arms with supporters **Rev:** Goalie at net

Date	Mintage	VF20	XF40	MS60	MS63	MS65
1993	Est. 15000	PF63 27.00	PF65 32.00			

KM# 68 25 RUPEES

31.46 g., 0.925 Silver 0.9356 oz. ASW **Obv:** Arms with supporters **Rev:** Space shuttle

Date	Mintage	VF20	XF40	MS60	MS63	MS65
1993	Est. 10000	PF63 27.00	PF65 32.00			

KM# 69 25 RUPEES

31.46 g., 0.925 Silver 0.9356 oz. ASW **Subject:** First French Landing **Obv:** Arms with supporters **Rev:** Figure with flag in boat, ships in background

Date	Mintage	VF20	XF40	MS60	MS63	MS65
1993	Est. 10000	PF63 27.00	PF65 32.00			

KM# 70 25 RUPEES

31.46 g., 0.925 Silver 0.9356 oz. ASW **Series:** 1992 Olympics **Obv:** Arms with supporters **Rev:** Balance beam gymnasts

Date	Mintage	VF20	XF40	MS60	MS63	MS65
1993	Est. 40000	PF63 27.00	PF65 32.00			

KM# 71 25 RUPEES

31.46 g., 0.925 Silver 0.9356 oz. ASW **Series:** Protect Our World **Obv:** Arms with supporters **Rev:** Fish and coral

Date	Mintage	VF20	XF40	MS60	MS63	MS65
1993	Est. 10000	PF63 27.00	PF65 32.00			

KM# 72 25 RUPEES

19.44 g., 0.925 Silver 0.5781 oz. ASW **Subject:** 15th Anniversary - Central Bank **Obv:** Arms with supporters **Rev:** Turtle flanked by dates

Date	Mintage	VF20	XF40	MS60	MS63	MS65
1993	Est. 1000	PF63 45.00	PF65 55.00			

KM# 74 25 RUPEES

19.44 g., 0.925 Silver 0.5781 oz. ASW **Series:** Endangered Wildlife **Obv:** Arms with supporters **Rev:** Butterfly and value

Date	Mintage	VF20	XF40	MS60	MS63	MS65
1994 PM	20,000	PF63 20.00	PF65 26.00			

KM# 79 25 RUPEES

31.47 g., 0.925 Silver 0.9359 oz. ASW **Series:** Queen Elizabeth The Queen Mother **Subject:** Wedding of Lady Elizabeth Bowes-Lyon: The Duke of York, 1923 **Obv:** Arms with supporters **Rev:** Royal couple on steps

Date	Mintage	VF20	XF40	MS60	MS63	MS65
1994	50,000	PF63 27.00	PF65 32.00			

KM# 78 25 RUPEES

28.28 g., 0.925 Silver 0.841 oz. ASW **Series:** Endangered Wildlife **Obv:** Arms with supporters **Rev:** Kestrel

Date	Mintage	VF20	XF40	MS60	MS63	MS65
1995	Est. 20000	PF63 22.00	PF65 28.00			

KM# 80 25 RUPEES

28.28 g., 0.925 Silver 0.841 oz. ASW **Series:** Olympics **Obv:** Arms with supporters **Rev:** Figures sailing

Date	Mintage	VF20	XF40	MS60	MS63	MS65
1995	Est. 30000	PF63 22.00	PF65 28.00			

KM# 81 25 RUPEES

28.28 g., 0.925 Silver 0.841 oz. ASW **Subject:** Vasco da Gama **Obv:** Arms with supporters **Rev:** Horizontal line divides ship and palms from standing ship captain **Edge:** Reeding over lettering **Edge Lettering:** EXPLORERS OF THE WORLD

Date	Mintage	VF20	XF40	MS60	MS63	MS65
1995	Est. 10000	PF63 22.00	PF65 28.00			

KM# 97 25 RUPEES

31.47 g., 0.925 Silver 0.9359 oz. ASW **Series:** 1996 Olympic Games **Obv:** Arms with supporters **Rev:** Cyclist

Date	Mintage	VF20	XF40	MS60	MS63	MS65
1995	—	PF63 25.00	PF65 30.00			

KM# 108 25 RUPEES

28.28 g., 0.925 Silver 0.841 oz. ASW **Series:** 50th Anniversary U.N. **Obv:** Arms with supporters **Rev:** Flying bird above UN logo and numeral 50

Date	Mintage	VF20	XF40	MS60	MS63	MS65
1995	—	PF63 22.00	PF65 28.00			

KM# 83 25 RUPEES

28.28 g., 0.925 Silver 0.841 oz. ASW **Series:** Endangered Wildlife **Obv:** Arms with supporters **Rev:** Flycatcher bird feeding babies

Date	Mintage	VF20	XF40	MS60	MS63	MS65
1996	Est. 20000	PF63 27.00	PF65 32.00			

KM# 88 25 RUPEES
31.47 g., 0.925 Silver 0.9359 oz. ASW **Subject:** Foundation of the Commonwealth **Obv:** Arms with supporters **Rev:** Crown and assorted flags

Date	Mintage	VF20	XF40	MS60	MS63	MS65
1996	40,000	—	—	20.00	25.00	30.00

KM# 124 25 RUPEES
28.28 g., 0.925 Silver 0.841 oz. ASW, 39 mm. **Obv:** National arms **Rev:** Victoria Cross above advancing infantry **Edge:** Reeded

Date	Mintage	VF20	XF40	MS60	MS63	MS65
1996	—	PF63 32.00	PF65 42.00			

KM# 91 25 RUPEES
28.28 g., 0.925 Silver 0.841 oz. ASW **Subject:** Diana - The People's Princess **Obv:** Arms with supporters **Rev:** Head 1/4 right

Date	Mintage	VF20	XF40	MS60	MS63	MS65
1997	Est. 10000	PF63 25.00	PF65 30.00			

KM# 92 25 RUPEES
1.24 g., 0.999 Gold 0.0398 oz. AGW **Subject:** Diana - The People's Princess **Obv:** Arms with supporters **Rev:** Head 1/4 right **Note:** Similar to KM#91.

Date	Mintage	VF20	XF40	MS60	MS63	MS65
1997	Est. 10000	PF63 65.00	PF65 70.00			

KM# 95 25 RUPEES
28.28 g., 0.925 Silver 0.841 oz. ASW **Subject:** Diana - The People's Princess **Obv:** Arms with supporters **Rev:** Diana holding baby Prince William

Date	Mintage	VF20	XF40	MS60	MS63	MS65
1997	Est. 10000	PF63 25.00	PF65 30.00			

KM# 96 25 RUPEES
1.24 g., 0.999 Gold 0.0398 oz. AGW **Subject:** Diana - The People's Princess **Obv:** Arms with supporters **Rev:** Diana holding baby Prince William

Date	Mintage	VF20	XF40	MS60	MS63	MS65
1997	Est. 10000	PF63 65.00	PF65 70.00			

KM# 99 25 RUPEES
28.28 g., 0.925 Silver 0.841 oz. ASW **Subject:** Diana - The People's Princess **Obv:** Arms with supporters **Rev:** Bust left holding young cancer patient

Date	Mintage	VF20	XF40	MS60	MS63	MS65
1997	Est. 10000	PF63 25.00	PF65 30.00			

KM# 100 25 RUPEES
1.24 g., 0.999 Gold 0.0398 oz. AGW **Subject:** Diana - The People's Princess **Obv:** Arms with supporters **Rev:** Diana holding young cancer patient

Date	Mintage	VF20	XF40	MS60	MS63	MS65
1997	Est. 10000	PF63 80.00	PF65 85.00			

KM# 117 25 RUPEES
19.44 g., 0.925 Silver 0.5781 oz. ASW, 36 mm. **Subject:** UNICEF **Obv:** Arms with supporters **Rev:** Boy fishing **Edge:** Reeded

Date	Mintage	VF20	XF40	MS60	MS63	MS65
1997	25,000	PF63 16.00	PF65 20.00			

KM# 103 25 RUPEES
28.28 g., 0.925 Silver 0.841 oz. ASW **Subject:** Diana - The People's Princess **Obv:** Arms with supporters **Rev:** Diana in summer clothes

Date	Mintage	VF20	XF40	MS60	MS63	MS65
1998	Est. 10000	PF63 25.00	PF65 30.00			

KM# 104 25 RUPEES
1.24 g., 0.9999 Gold 0.040 oz. AGW **Subject:** Diana - The People's Princess **Obv:** Arms with supporters **Rev:** Diana in summer clothes

Date	Mintage	VF20	XF40	MS60	MS63	MS65
1998	Est. 10000	PF63 80.00	PF65 85.00			

KM# 110 25 RUPEES
28.28 g., 0.925 Silver 0.841 oz. ASW **Subject:** Marriage of Prince Edward and Miss Sophie Rhys-Jones **Obv:** Arms with supporters **Rev:** Tied vertical monograms flanked by doves

Date	Mintage	VF20	XF40	MS60	MS63	MS65
1999	Est. 10000	PF63 25.00	PF65 30.00			

KM# 113 25 RUPEES
1.24 g., 0.9999 Gold 0.040 oz. AGW, 13.9 mm. **Subject:** Millennium **Obv:** Arms with supporters **Rev:** Latent image of 1999-2000 dates

Date	Mintage	VF20	XF40	MS60	MS63	MS65
2000	Est. 10000	PF63 65.00	PF65 70.00			

KM# 115 25 RUPEES
1.24 g., 0.9999 Gold 0.040 oz. AGW, 13.9 mm. **Subject:** 100th Birthday - British Queen Mother **Obv:** Arms with supporters **Rev:** Head with hat 1/4 right **Edge:** Reeded

Date	Mintage	VF20	XF40	MS60	MS63	MS65
2000	Est. 10000	PF63 65.00	PF65 70.00			

KM# 39 50 RUPEES
28.28 g., 0.925 Silver 0.841 oz. ASW **Subject:** Conservation **Obv:** Arms with supporters **Rev:** Squirrel fish, coral and value

Date	Mintage	VF20	XF40	MS60	MS63	MS65
1978	4,453	—	—	22.00	25.00	30.00
1978	4,281	PF63 32.00	PF65 37.00			

KM# 42 50 RUPEES
19.44 g., 0.925 Silver 0.5781 oz. ASW **Series:** UNICEF and International Year of the Child **Obv:** Arms with supporters **Rev:** Figures below palm tree flanked by UNICEF logos

Date	Mintage	VF20	XF40	MS60	MS63	MS65
1980	10,000	PF63 17.00	PF65 20.00			

KM# 54 50 RUPEES
19.44 g., 0.925 Silver 0.5781 oz. ASW **Series:** Decade for Women **Obv:** Arms with supporters **Rev:** Map flanked by figures above value

Date	Mintage	VF20	XF40	MS60	MS63	MS65
1985	500	PF63 25.00	PF65 30.00			

KM# 75 50 RUPEES
1.24 g., 0.9999 Gold 0.040 oz. AGW **Series:** Endangered Wildlife **Obv:** Arms with supporters **Rev:** Milkweed Butterfly **Note:** Similar to 25 Rupees, KM#74.

Date	Mintage	VF20	XF40	MS60	MS63	MS65
1994 PM Prooflike	—	—	—	—	65.00	75.00

KM# 107 50 RUPEES
3.11 g., 0.5833 Gold 0.0583 oz. AGW **Series:** Olympics Games 2000 **Obv:** Arms with supporters **Rev:** Two divers

Date	Mintage	VF20	XF40	MS60	MS63	MS65
1997	5,000	PF63 110	PF65 120			

KM# 40 100 RUPEES
31.65 g., 0.925 Silver 0.9413 oz. ASW **Subject:** Conservation **Obv:** Arms with supporters **Rev:** White-tailed Tropic bird

Date	Mintage	VF20	XF40	MS60	MS63	MS65
1978	4,453	—	—	20.00	25.00	30.00
1978	4,075	PF63 30.00	PF65 35.00			

KM# 45 100 RUPEES
31.65 g., 0.925 Silver 0.9413 oz. ASW **Series:** World Food Day **Obv:** Arms with supporters **Rev:** Value and coconuts below seated figure flanked by palm trees

Date	Mintage	VF20	XF40	MS60	MS63	MS65
1981	6,000	—	—	20.00	25.00	30.00
1981	5,000	PF63 30.00	PF65 35.00			

KM# 45a 100 RUPEES
35.00 g., 0.500 Silver 0.5626 oz. ASW **Subject:** World Food Day **Obv:** Arms with supporters **Rev:** Value and coconuts below seated figure flanked by palm trees

Date	Mintage	VF20	XF40	MS60	MS63	MS65
1981	10,000	PF63 18.00	PF65 22.00			

KM# 55 100 RUPEES
19.44 g., 0.925 Silver 0.5781 oz. ASW **Subject:** 10th Anniversary of Independence **Obv:** Arms with supporters **Rev:** Design above shark tail design dividing dates

Date	Mintage	VF20	XF40	MS60	MS63	MS65
ND-1986	1,000	PF63 30.00	PF65 35.00			

KM# 57 100 RUPEES
19.44 g., 0.925 Silver 0.5781 oz. ASW **Subject:** 10th Anniversary of Liberation **Obv:** Arms with supporters **Rev:** Standing figure divides dates

Date	Mintage	VF20	XF40	MS60	MS63	MS65
ND-1987 PM	1,000	PF63 30.00	PF65 35.00			

KM# 59 100 RUPEES
19.40 g., 0.917 Silver 0.572 oz. ASW **Subject:** 10th Anniversary of Central Bank **Obv:** Arms with supporters **Rev:** Sea Turtle, dates below

Date	Mintage	VF20	XF40	MS60	MS63	MS65
ND-1988 PM	—	PF63 45.00	PF65 60.00			

KM# 60 100 RUPEES
1.70 g., 0.917 Gold 0.0501 oz. AGW **Subject:** 10th Anniversary of Central Bank **Obv:** Arms with supporters **Rev:** Sea turtle

Date	Mintage	VF20	XF40	MS60	MS63	MS65
ND-1988 PM	—	PF63 125	PF65 150			

KM# 76 100 RUPEES
3.11 g., 0.9999 Gold 0.100 oz. AGW **Series:** Endangered Wildlife **Obv:** Arms with supporters **Rev:** Milkweed Butterfly

Date	Mintage	VF20	XF40	MS60	MS63	MS65
1994 PM Prooflike	—	—	—	—	175	200

KM# 82 100 RUPEES
7.78 g., 0.583 Gold 0.1458 oz. AGW **Series:** Olympics **Obv:** Arms with supporters **Rev:** Sailboats

Date	Mintage	VF20	XF40	MS60	MS63	MS65
1995	Est. 3000	PF63 225	PF65 275			

KM# 86 100 RUPEES
7.78 g., 0.583 Gold 0.1458 oz. AGW **Subject:** British Queen Mother **Obv:** Arms with supporters **Rev:** Wedding portrait

Date	Mintage	VF20	XF40	MS60	MS63	MS65
1995	Est. 5000	PF63 225	PF65 275			

KM# 93 100 RUPEES
7.78 g., 0.583 Gold 0.1458 oz. AGW **Subject:** Diana - The People's Princess **Obv:** Arms with supporters **Rev:** Bust facing

Date	Mintage	VF20	XF40	MS60	MS63	MS65
1997	Est. 7500	PF63 225	PF65 275			

KM# A97 100 RUPEES
7.78 g., 0.583 Gold 0.1458 oz. AGW **Subject:** Diana - The People's Princess **Obv:** Arms with supporters **Rev:** Diana holding newborn Prince William

Date	Mintage	VF20	XF40	MS60	MS63	MS65
1997	—	PF63 225	PF65 275			

KM# 101 100 RUPEES
7.78 g., 0.583 Gold 0.1458 oz. AGW **Subject:** Diana - The People's Princess **Obv:** Arms with supporters **Rev:** Diana holding young cancer patient

Date	Mintage	VF20	XF40	MS60	MS63	MS65
1997	Est. 7500	PF63 225	PF65 275			

KM# 105 100 RUPEES
7.78 g., 0.583 Gold 0.1458 oz. AGW **Subject:** Diana - The People's Princess **Obv:** Arms with supporters **Rev:** Diana in summer clothes

Date	Mintage	VF20	XF40	MS60	MS63	MS65
1998	Est. 7500	PF63 225	PF65 275			

KM# 111 100 RUPEES
6.22 g., 0.9999 Gold 0.200 oz. AGW **Subject:** Marriage of Prince Edward **Obv:** Arms with supporters **Rev:** Tied monograms and birds

Date	Mintage	VF20	XF40	MS60	MS63	MS65
1999	Est. 2000	PF63 325	PF65 375			

KM# 116 100 RUPEES
6.22 g., 0.9999 Gold 0.200 oz. AGW, 22 mm. **Subject:** 100th Birthday Queen Mother **Obv:** Arms with supporters **Rev:** Queen Mother's portrait **Edge:** Reeded

Date	Mintage	VF20	XF40	MS60	MS63	MS65
2000	—	PF63 325	PF65 375			

KM# 66 250 RUPEES
6.22 g., 0.999 Gold 0.1998 oz. AGW **Series:** Endangered Wildlife **Obv:** Arms with supporters **Rev:** Magpie Robin

Date	Mintage	VF20	XF40	MS60	MS63	MS65
1993	—	PF63 325	PF65 375			

KM# 77 250 RUPEES
6.22 g., 0.999 Gold 0.1998 oz. AGW **Series:** Endangered Wildlife **Obv:** Arms with supporters **Rev:** Milkweed Butterfly

Date	Mintage	VF20	XF40	MS60	MS63	MS65
1993	—	PF63 325	PF65 375			
1994 PM	—	PF63 325	PF65 375			
1996 PM	5,000	PF63 325	PF65 375			

KM# 84 250 RUPEES
6.22 g., 0.999 Gold 0.1998 oz. AGW **Series:** Endangered Wildlife **Obv:** Arms with supporters **Rev:** Paradise Flycatcher Bird

Date	Mintage	VF20	XF40	MS60	MS63	MS65
1996	Est. 5000	PF63 325	PF65 375			

KM# 94 250 RUPEES
6.22 g., 0.999 Gold 0.1998 oz. AGW **Subject:** Diana - The People's Princess **Obv:** Arms with supporters **Rev:** Bust facing **Note:** Similar to 25 Rupees, KM#91.

Date	Mintage	VF20	XF40	MS60	MS63	MS65
1997	Est. 5000	PF63 325	PF65 375			

KM# 98 250 RUPEES
6.22 g., 0.999 Gold 0.1998 oz. AGW **Subject:** Diana - The People's Princess **Obv:** Arms with supporters **Rev:** Diana holding newborn Prince William

Date	Mintage	VF20	XF40	MS60	MS63	MS65
1997	—	PF63 325	PF65 375			

KM# 102 250 RUPEES
6.22 g., 0.999 Gold 0.1998 oz. AGW **Subject:** Diana - The People's Princess **Obv:** Arms with supporters **Rev:** Diana holding young cancer patient

Date	Mintage	VF20	XF40	MS60	MS63	MS65
1997	Est. 5000	PF63 325	PF65 375			

KM# 106 250 RUPEES
6.22 g., 0.999 Gold 0.1998 oz. AGW **Subject:** Diana - The People's Princess **Obv:** Arms with supporters **Rev:** Diana in summer dress

Date	Mintage	VF20	XF40	MS60	MS63	MS65
1998	Est. 5000	PF63 325	PF65 375			

KM# 62 500 RUPEES
7.13 g., 0.900 Gold 0.2063 oz. AGW **Series:** Decade for Women **Obv:** Arms with supporters **Rev:** Value below standing figures

Date	Mintage	VF20	XF40	MS60	MS63	MS65
1985	500	PF65 450	PF67 550			

KM# 29 1000 RUPEES
15.98 g., 0.917 Gold 0.4711 oz. AGW **Subject:** Declaration of Independence **Obv:** President Mancham **Rev:** Tortoise, date, value

Date	Mintage	XF40	MS60	MS63	MS65	MS66
1976	5,000	—	—	650	700	750
1976	1,000	PF65 800	PF67 850			

KM# 56 1000 RUPEES
15.98 g., 0.917 Gold 0.4711 oz. AGW **Subject:** 10th Anniversary of Independence **Obv:** Arms with supporters **Rev:** Design above shark tail design dividing dates

Date	Mintage	VF20	XF40	MS60	MS63	MS65
ND-1986	100	PF65 950	PF67 1,000			

KM# 58 1000 RUPEES
15.98 g., 0.917 Gold 0.4711 oz. AGW **Subject:** 10th Anniversary of Liberation **Obv:** Arms with supporters **Rev:** Standing figure divides dates

Date	Mintage	VF20	XF40	MS60	MS63	MS65
ND-1987 PM	100	PF65 950	PF67 1,000			

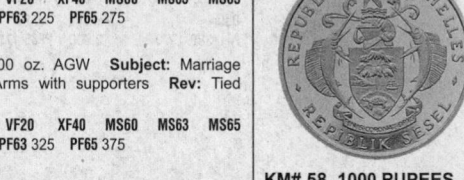

KM# 61 1000 RUPEES
15.94 g., 0.917 Gold 0.4699 oz. AGW **Subject:** 100th Anniversary of Central Bank **Obv:** Arms with supporters **Rev:** Sea turtle

Date	Mintage	VF20	XF40	MS60	MS63	MS65
ND-1988 PM	Est. 5000	PF63 850	PF65 900	PF67 950		

KM# 73 1000 RUPEES
15.98 g., 0.917 Gold 0.4711 oz. AGW **Subject:** Central Banking

Date	Mintage	VF20	XF40	MS60	MS63	MS65
1993	Est. 200	PF65 950	PF67 1,000			

KM# 41 1500 RUPEES
33.44 g., 0.900 Gold 0.9675 oz. AGW **Subject:** Conservation **Obv:** Arms with supporters **Rev:** Flycatcher birds

Date	Mintage	VF20	XF40	MS60	MS63	MS65
1978	683	—	—	—	1,850	2,000
1978	201	PF63 2,000	PF65 2,250			

PATTERNS

Including off metal strikes

KM#	Date	Mintage	Identification	Mkt Val
Pn1	1974	—	10 Rupees. Brass. KM#20.	—
Pn2	1974	—	10 Rupees. Bronze. KM#20.	—
Pn3	1974	—	10 Rupees. Copper-Nickel. KM#20.	—
Pn4	1974	—	10 Rupees. Silver. KM#20.	—
Pn5	1976	—	10 Cents. Silver. KM#23, thick planchet.	275
Pn6	1976	—	1000 Rupees. Bronze. KM#29.	—
Pn7	1985	—	500 Rupees. Copper. KM#62.	600

PIEDFORT

KM#	Date	Mintage	Identification	Mkt Val
P1	1980	78	50 Rupees. Silver. KM#42.	100
P2	1983	500	50 Rupees.	75.00
P3	1984	500	50 Rupees. 0.925. Silver.	75.00
P4	1984	100	50 Rupees. 0.900. Gold.	2,200

MINT SETS

KM#	Date	Mintage	Identification	Issue Price	Mkt Val
MS1	1972 (7)	—	KM#10-13, 17-19	—	20.00
MS2	1974 (5)	—	KM#10-13, 20	—	25.00
MS3	1976 (8)	—	KM#21-28	—	30.00
MS4	1977 (8)	—	KM#30-37	—	30.00
MS5	1982 (6)	—	KM#46.1-51.1	—	15.00
MS6	1992 (6)	—	KM#46.2, 47.2, 48.2, 49.2, 50.2, 51.2	12.00	12.00
MS7	Mixed dates (6)	—	KM#46.2 (1990), 47.2-51.2 (1997)	—	12.00

PROOF SETS

KM#	Date	Mintage	Identification	Issue Price	Mkt Val
PS1	1939 (4)	—	KM#1-4	—	1,000
PS2	1969 (7)	5,000	KM#10-16	8.40	20.00
PS3	1974 (2)	5,000	KM#19a, 20a	37.00	40.00
PS4	1976 (9)	1,000	KM#21-26 , 27a, 28a, 29	375	975
PS5	1976 (8)	7,500	KM#21-26, 27a, 28a	42.50	45.00
PS6	1982 (6)	5,000	KM#46.1-51.1	29.95	22.00
PS7	1992 (6)	—	KM#46.2-51.2	—	22.50

SHARJAH

Sharjah is the only one of the emirates that shares boundaries with all of the others plus Oman. It has an area of 1,000 sq. mi. (2,600 sq. km.) and a population of 40,000. Sharjah was an important pirate base in the 18th and early 19th centuries. Most of the treaties and diplomatic relations were with Great Britain.

TITLE
Ash-Sharqa(t)

RULERS
Saqr Bin Khalid al-Qasimi, 1883-1914
Khalid Bin Ahmad al-Qasimi, 1914-1924
Sultan Bin Saqr al-Qasimi, 1924-1951
Saqr Bin Sultan al-Qasimi, 1951-1965
Khalid Bin Muhammad al-Qasimi, 1965-1972 Sultan Bin Muhammad al-Qasimi,1972-

EMIRATE

NON-CIRCULATING LEGAL TENDER COINAGE

KM# 2 RIYAL
3.00 g., 1.000 Silver 0.0965 oz. ASW **Ruler:** Khalid bin Muhammad al-Qasimi **Subject:** Mona Lisa **Obv:** National arms **Rev:** Bust facing

Date	Mintage	VF20	XF40	MS60	MS63	MS65
AH1389-1970	3,850	PF65 85.00	PF67 110			

KM# 3 2 RIYALS
6.00 g., 1.000 Silver 0.1929 oz. ASW **Ruler:** Khalid bin Muhammad al-Qasimi **Subject:** Mexico World Soccer Cup **Obv:** National arms **Rev:** World soccer cup within globe design

Date	Mintage	VF20	XF40	MS60	MS63	MS65
AH1389-1970	4,500	PF65 135	PF67 175			

KM# 4 5 RIYALS
15.00 g., 1.000 Silver 0.4823 oz. ASW **Ruler:** Khalid bin Muhammad al-Qasimi **Subject:** Napoleon **Obv:** National arms **Rev:** Uniformed bust facing 1/4 left divides logo and dates

Date	Mintage	VF20	XF40	MS60	MS63	MS65
AH1389-1970	2,500	PF65 170	PF67 220			

KM# 5 10 RIYALS
30.00 g., 1.000 Silver 0.9645 oz. ASW, 44 mm. **Ruler:** Khalid bin Muhammad al-Qasimi **Subject:** Bolivar **Obv:** National arms **Rev:** Head right

Date	Mintage	VF20	XF40	MS60	MS63	MS65
AH1389-1970	3,200	PF65 200	PF67 250			

KM# 7 25 RIYALS
5.18 g., 0.900 Gold 0.1499 oz. AGW **Ruler:** Khalid bin Muhammad al-Qasimi **Subject:** Mona Lisa **Obv:** National arms **Rev:** Bust facing

Date	Mintage	VF20	XF40	MS60	MS63	MS65
AH1389-1970	6,775	PF65 350	PF67 500			

KM# 8 50 RIYALS
10.36 g., 0.900 Gold 0.2998 oz. AGW **Ruler:** Khalid bin Muhammad al-Qasimi **Subject:** Mexico World Soccer Cup **Obv:** National arms **Rev:** World soccer cup within globe design

Date	Mintage	VF20	XF40	MS60	MS63	MS65
AH1389-1970	1,815	PF65 475	PF67 675			

KM# 9 100 RIYALS
20.73 g., 0.900 Gold 0.5998 oz. AGW **Ruler:** Khalid bin Muhammad al-Qasimi **Subject:** Bicentennial - Napoleon **Obv:** National arms **Rev:** Uniformed bust facing 1/4 left divides logo and dates

Date	Mintage	VF20	XF40	MS60	MS63	MS65
AH1389-1970	—	PF65 1,350	PF67 1,550			

KM# 10 100 RIYALS
20.73 g., 0.900 Gold 0.5998 oz. AGW **Ruler:** Khalid bin Muhammad al-Qasimi **Subject:** Bolivar **Obv:** National arms **Rev:** Head right

Date	Mintage	VF20	XF40	MS60	MS63	MS65
AH1389-1970	—	PF65 1,450	PF67 1,750			

KM# 11 200 RIYALS
41.46 g., 0.900 Gold 1.1997 oz. AGW **Ruler:** Khalid bin Muhammad al-Qasimi **Subject:** Khalid III **Obv:** National arms **Rev:** Head facing

Date	Mintage	VF20	XF40	MS60	MS63	MS65
AH1389-1970	435	PF65 2,500	PF67 3,500			

PROOF SETS

KM#	Date	Mintage	Identification	Issue Price	Mkt Val
PS1	1970 (9)	—	KM#2-5, 7-11	—	6,225
PS2	1970 (5)	—	KM#7-11	—	6,850
PS3	1970 (4)	2,500	KM#2-5	25.30	585

SIERRA LEONE

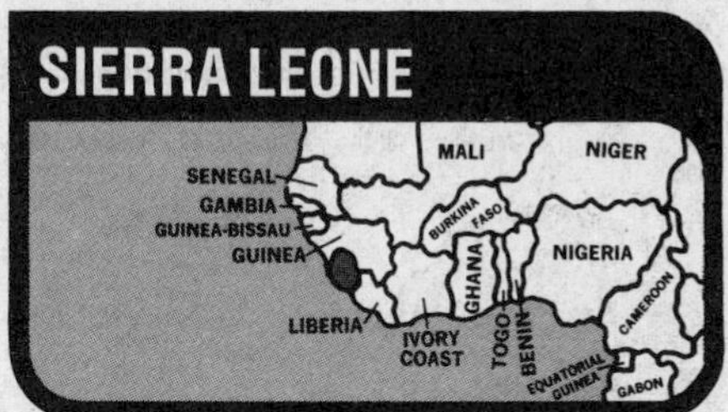

The Republic of Sierra Leone is located in western Africa between Guinea and Liberia, has an area of 27,699 sq. mi. (71,740 sq. km.) and a population of *4.1 million. Capital: Freetown. The economy is predominantly agricultural but mining contributes significantly to export revenues. Diamonds, iron ore, palm kernels, cocoa, and coffee are exported.

The coast of Sierra Leone was first visited by Portuguese and British slavers in the 15th and 16th centuries. The first settlement, at Freetown, 1787, was established as a refuge for freed slaves within the British Empire, runaway slaves from the United States and Negroes discharged from the British armed forces. The first settlers were virtually wiped out by tribal attacks and disease. The colony was re-established under the auspices of the Sierra Leone Company and transferred to the British Crown in 1807. The interior region was secured and established as a protectorate in 1896. Sierra Leone became independent on April 27, 1961, and adopted a republican constitution ten years later. It is a member of the Commonwealth of Nations. The president is Chief of State and Head of Government.

For similar coinage refer to British West Africa.

RULER
British, until 1961

MONETARY SYSTEM

Beginning 1964

100 Cents = 1 Leone

NOTE: Sierra Leone's official currency is the Leone. For previously listed Dollar Denominated Coinage, see the 5th Edition of Unusual World Coins.

REPUBLIC

STANDARD COINAGE

KM# 16 1/2 CENT
2.85 g., Bronze, 20.2 mm. **Obv:** Value divides fish **Rev:** Head of right Sir Milton Margai **Edge:** Plain

Date	Mintage	VF20	XF40	MS60	MS63	MS65
1964	600,000	—	0.15	0.25	0.45	0.75
1964	10,000	PF65 1.00				

KM# 16a 1/2 CENT
2.83 g., 0.925 Silver 0.0842 oz. ASW, 20.2 mm. **Obv:** Value divides fish **Rev:** Head of right Sir Milton Margai

Date	Mintage	VF20	XF40	MS60	MS63	MS65
1964	22	PF65 650				

KM# 31 1/2 CENT
2.85 g., Bronze, 20.2 mm. **Obv:** Value above arms **Rev:** Head of Dr. Siaka Stevens right

Date	Mintage	VF20	XF40	MS60	MS63	MS65
1980	—	0.15	0.30	0.45	0.75	1.25
1980	10,000	PF65 1.50				

KM# 17 CENT
5.70 g., Bronze, 25.45 mm. **Obv:** Value within palm sprigs **Rev:** Head of Sir Milton Margai right **Edge:** Plain

Date	Mintage	VF20	XF40	MS60	MS63	MS65
1964	35,000,000	—	0.15	0.25	0.45	0.75
1964	10,000	PF65 1.25				

KM# 17a CENT
5.67 g., 0.925 Silver 0.1686 oz. ASW, 25.45 mm. **Obv:** Value within palm sprigs **Rev:** Head of Sir Milton Margai right

Date	Mintage	VF20	XF40	MS60	MS63	MS65
1964	22	PF65 650				

KM# 32 CENT
5.70 g., Bronze, 25.45 mm. **Obv:** Value above arms **Rev:** Head of Sir Milton Margai right

Date	Mintage	VF20	XF40	MS60	MS63	MS65
1980	—	0.15	0.30	0.45	0.75	1.25
1980	10,000	PF65 1.50				

KM# 18 5 CENTS
2.50 g., Copper-Nickel, 17.8 mm. **Obv:** Tree divides date within circle **Rev:** Head of right Sir Milton Margai

Date	Mintage	VF20	XF40	MS60	MS63	MS65
1964	900,000	0.15	0.25	0.35	0.50	0.85
1964	10,000	PF65 1.50				

KM# 18a 5 CENTS
2.49 g., 0.925 Silver 0.0741 oz. ASW, 17.8 mm. **Obv:** Tree divides date within circle **Rev:** Head of right Sir Milton Margai

Date	Mintage	VF20	XF40	MS60	MS63	MS65
1964	22	PF65 650				

KM# 33 5 CENTS
2.50 g., Copper-Nickel, 17.7 mm. **Obv:** Value above arms **Rev:** Head of Dr. Siaka Stevens right

Date	Mintage	VF20	XF40	MS60	MS63	MS65
1980	—	0.15	0.30	0.45	0.75	1.50
1980	10,000	PF65 2.50				
1984	—	0.15	0.30	0.45	0.75	1.50

KM# 19 10 CENTS
4.90 g., Copper-Nickel, 22.9 mm. **Obv:** Value within cocoa bean wreath **Rev:** Head of right Sir Milton Margai

Date	Mintage	VF20	XF40	MS60	MS63	MS65
1964	24,000,000	0.25	0.40	0.60	0.80	1.75
1964	10,000	PF65 1.25				

KM# 19a 10 CENTS
4.92 g., 0.925 Silver 0.1463 oz. ASW, 22.9 mm. **Obv:** Value within cocoa bean wreath **Rev:** Head of right Sir Milton Margai

Date	Mintage	VF20	XF40	MS60	MS63	MS65
1964	22	PF65 650				

KM# 34 10 CENTS
4.90 g., Copper-Nickel, 22.9 mm. **Obv:** Value above arms **Rev:** Head of Dr. Siaka Stevens right

Date	Mintage	VF20	XF40	MS60	MS63	MS65
1978	200,000	0.25	0.50	0.75	1.00	1.85
1980	—	0.20	0.40	0.75	1.00	1.85
1980	10,000	PF65 2.50				
1984	—	0.20	0.40	0.75	1.00	1.85

KM# 20 20 CENTS
8.25 g., Copper-Nickel, 26.95 mm. **Obv:** Lion walking left **Rev:** Head of Sir Milton Margai right **Edge:** Reeded

Date	Mintage	VF20	XF40	MS60	MS63	MS65
1964	11,000,000	0.35	0.60	0.85	1.25	2.00
1964	10,000	PF65 2.50				

KM# 20a 20 CENTS
8.22 g., 0.925 Silver 0.2445 oz. ASW, 26.95 mm. **Obv:** Lion walking right **Rev:** Head of right Sir Milton Margai

Date	Mintage	VF20	XF40	MS60	MS63	MS65
1964	22	PF65 650				

KM# 30 20 CENTS
8.25 g., Copper-Nickel, 26.95 mm. **Obv:** Value above arms **Rev:** Head of Dr. Siaka Stevens right

Date	Mintage	VF20	XF40	MS60	MS63	MS65
1978	2,375,000	0.35	0.50	0.75	1.50	2.50
1980	—	0.35	0.50	0.65	1.25	1.75
1980	10,000	PF65 3.00				
1984	—	0.35	0.50	0.65	1.25	1.75

KM# 25 50 CENTS
11.60 g., Copper-Nickel, 30 mm. **Obv:** Value above arms **Rev:** Head of Dr. Siaka Stevens right

Date	Mintage	VF20	XF40	MS60	MS63	MS65
1972	1,000,000	0.75	1.25	1.75	3.00	4.50
1972	2,000	PF65 10.00				
1980	—	0.65	1.20	1.50	2.75	3.75
1980	10,000	PF65 5.00				
1984	—	0.65	1.20	1.50	2.75	3.75

KM# 21 LEONE
Copper-Nickel **Obv:** Value above arms **Rev:** Head of right Sir Milton Margai

Date	Mintage	VF20	XF40	MS60	MS63	MS65
1964	10,000	PF63 7.00	PF65 12.00			

KM# 21a LEONE
22.62 g., 0.925 Silver 0.6728 oz. ASW **Obv:** Value above arms **Rev:** Head of right Sir Milton Margai

Date	Mintage	VF20	XF40	MS60	MS63	MS65
1964	12	PF65 1,000				

KM# 21b LEONE
0.917 Gold **Obv:** Value above arms **Rev:** Head of right Sir Milton Margai

Date	Mintage	VF20	XF40	MS60	MS63	MS65
1964	10	PF65 2,750				

KM# 26 LEONE
Copper-Nickel, 38 mm. **Subject:** 10 Anniversary of Bank **Obv:** Lion right within circle **Rev:** Head of Dr. Siaka Stevens right

Date	Mintage	VF20	XF40	MS60	MS63	MS65
ND-1974	103,000	—	1.75	3.50	5.00	8.00

KM# 26a LEONE
28.28 g., 0.925 Silver 0.841 oz. ASW, 38 mm. **Obv:** Head of Dr. Siaka Stevens right **Rev:** Lion right within circle

Date	Mintage	VF20	XF40	MS60	MS63	MS65
ND-1974	22,000	PF63 30.00	PF65 35.00			

KM# 26b LEONE
Gold, 38 mm. **Subject:** 10 Anniversary of Bank **Obv:** Head of Dr. Siaka Stevens right **Rev:** Lion right within circle

Date	Mintage	VF20	XF40	MS60	MS63	MS65
ND(1974	100	—	—	1,750	1,800	1,850

KM# 36 LEONE
Copper-Nickel **Subject:** O.A.U. Summit Conference **Obv:** Map within circle **Rev:** Head of Dr. Siaka Stevens right

Date	Mintage	VF20	XF40	MS60	MS63	MS65
1980	75,000	—	1.75	2.75	5.00	9.00

KM# 36a LEONE
28.28 g., 0.925 Silver 0.841 oz. ASW **Obv:** Map within circle **Rev:** Head of Dr. Siaka Stevens right

Date	Mintage	VF20	XF40	MS60	MS63	MS65
1980	15,000	PF63 32.00	PF65 37.00			

KM# 40 LEONE
9.50 g., 0.925 Silver 0.2825 oz. ASW **Subject:** Freetown Bicentennial **Obv:** Numeral 200 within design **Rev:** Bust of Dr. Joseph Saidu Momoh left **Shape:** Octagon

Date	Mintage	VF20	XF40	MS60	MS63	MS65
1987	3,000	PF63 25.00	PF65 35.00			

KM# 40a LEONE
16.00 g., 0.917 Gold 0.4717 oz. AGW **Subject:** Freetown Bicentennial **Obv:** Numeral 200 within design **Rev:** Bust of Dr. Joseph Saidu Momoh left **Shape:** Octagon

Date	Mintage	VF20	XF40	MS60	MS63	MS65
1987	1,250	PF63 750	PF65 850			

KM# 43 LEONE
Nickel-Bronze **Obv:** Value above arms **Rev:** Bust of Dr. Joseph Saidu Momoh left **Shape:** Octagon

Date	Mintage	VF20	XF40	MS60	MS63	MS65
1987	—	—	0.50	0.75	1.50	2.50
1988	—	—	0.50	0.75	1.50	2.50

KM# 29 2 LEONES
Copper-Nickel, 30 mm. **Series:** F.A.O. **Subject:** Regional Conference for Africa **Obv:** Farmer tilling field **Rev:** Head of Dr. Siaka Stevens right **Edge:** Plain **Shape:** 7-sided

Date	Mintage	VF20	XF40	MS60	MS63	MS65
1976	20,000	—	1.25	2.00	3.50	6.00

KM# 38 10 LEONES
28.28 g., 0.925 Silver 0.841 oz. ASW **Series:** Year of the Scout **Obv:** Seated figure with hat within plants **Rev:** Head of Dr. Siaka Stevens right

Date	Mintage	VF20	XF40	MS60	MS63	MS65
ND-1983	10,000	—	—	—	22.00	28.00
ND-1983	10,000	PF63 30.00	PF65 35.00			

KM# 41 10 LEONES
28.28 g., 0.925 Silver 0.841 oz. ASW **Series:** World Wildlife Fund **Obv:** Pygmy Hippopotamus **Rev:** Bust of Dr. Joseph Saidu Momoh left

Date	Mintage	VF20	XF40	MS60	MS63	MS65
1987	25,000	PF63 25.00	PF65 30.00			

KM# 44 10 LEONES
2.50 g., Nickel Bonded Steel, 17.99 mm. **Obv:** Value divides fish **Rev:** Bust of Mammy Yoko facing within circle **Edge:** Plain

Date	Mintage	VF20	XF40	MS60	MS63	MS65
1996	—	—	—	0.50	0.75	1.00

KM# 45 50 LEONES
Nickel Bonded Steel **Obv:** Building above value **Rev:** Bust of Sir Henry Lightfoot facing **Shape:** Octagon

Date	Mintage	VF20	XF40	MS60	MS63	MS65
1996	—	—	—	0.75	1.25	1.50

KM# 39 100 LEONES
15.98 g., 0.917 Gold 0.4711 oz. AGW **Series:** Year of the Scout **Obv:** Lion within shield **Rev:** Head of Dr. Siaka Stevens right

Date	Mintage	VF20	XF40	MS60	MS63	MS65
ND-1983	2,000	—	—	—	800	850
ND-1983	2,000	PF63 825	PF65 875			

KM# 46 100 LEONES
Nickel Bonded Steel **Obv:** Cocoa pods and value within beaded circle **Rev:** Head of Naimbana facing within beaded circle

Date	Mintage	VF20	XF40	MS60	MS63	MS65
1996	—	—	—	1.25	1.75	2.00

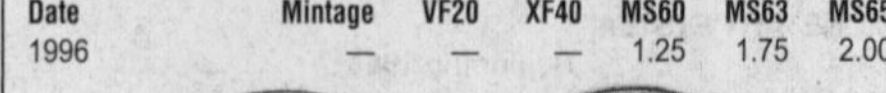

KM# 22 1/4 GOLDE
13.64 g., 0.900 Gold 0.3946 oz. AGW, 24 mm. **Subject:** 5th Anniversary of Independence **Obv:** Value within map **Rev:** Lion head facing

Date	Mintage	VF20	XF40	MS60	MS63	MS65
ND-1966	5,000	—	—	—	650	700

KM# 22a 1/4 GOLDE
15.00 g., 0.916 Gold 0.4418 oz. AGW **Subject:** 5th Anniversary of Independence **Obv:** Value within map **Rev:** Lion head facing

Date	Mintage	VF20	XF40	MS60	MS63	MS65
ND-1966	600	PF65 750	PF67 850			

KM# 22b 1/4 GOLDE
10.32 g., Palladium APW **Subject:** 5th Anniversary of Independence **Obv:** Value within map **Rev:** Lion head facing

Date	Mintage	VF20	XF40	MS60	MS63	MS65
ND-1966	100	PF65 400	PF67 450			

KM# 23 1/2 GOLDE
27.27 g., 0.900 Gold 0.7892 oz. AGW, 32 mm. **Subject:** 5th Anniversary of Independence **Obv:** Value within map **Rev:** Lion head facing

Date	Mintage	VF20	XF40	MS60	MS63	MS65
ND-1966	2,500	—	—	—	1,250	1,400

KM# 23a 1/2 GOLDE
30.00 g., 0.916 Gold 0.8835 oz. AGW **Subject:** 5th Anniversary of Independence **Obv:** Value within map **Rev:** Lion head facing

Date	Mintage	VF20	XF40	MS60	MS63	MS65
ND-1966	600	PF65 1,700	PF67 1,900			

KM# 23b 1/2 GOLDE
20.63 g., Palladium APW **Subject:** 5th Anniversary of Independence **Obv:** Value within map **Rev:** Lion head facing

Date	Mintage	VF20	XF40	MS60	MS63	MS65
ND-1966	100	PF65 850	PF67 1,000			

KM# 24 GOLDE
54.55 g., 0.900 Gold 1.5783 oz. AGW, 48 mm. **Subject:** 5th Anniversary of Independence **Obv:** Value within map **Rev:** Lion head facing

Date	Mintage	VF20	XF40	MS60	MS63	MS65
ND-1966	1,500	—	—	—	2,650	3,000

KM# 24a GOLDE
60.00 g., 0.916 Gold 1.767 oz. AGW **Subject:** 5th Anniversary of Independence **Obv:** Value within map **Rev:** Lion head facing

Date	Mintage	VF20	XF40	MS60	MS63	MS65
ND-1966	400	PF65 3,000	PF67 3,250			

KM# 24b GOLDE
41.26 g., Palladium APW **Subject:** 5th Anniversary of Independence **Obv:** Value within map **Rev:** Lion head facing

Date	Mintage	VF20	XF40	MS60	MS63	MS65
ND-1966	100	PF65 1,350	PF67 1,650			

KM# 24c GOLDE
41.26 g., Platinum APW **Subject:** 5th Anniversary of Independence **Obv:** Value within map **Rev:** Lion head facing

Date	Mintage	VF20	XF40	MS60	MS63	MS65
ND-1966	—	PF65 2,650	PF67 3,000			

KM# 37 5 GOLDE
15.98 g., 0.917 Gold 0.4711 oz. AGW **Subject:** O.A.U. Summit Conference **Obv:** Head of Dr. Siaka Stevens right **Rev:** Map within circle

Date	Mintage	VF20	XF40	MS60	MS63	MS65
1980	457	—	—	—	850	900
1980	325	PF63 875	PF65 950			

KM# 42 5 GOLDE
16.00 g., 0.917 Gold 0.4717 oz. AGW **Series:** World Wildlife Fund **Obv:** Bust of Dr. Joseph Saidu Momoh left **Rev:** Duiker Zebra

Date	Mintage	VF20	XF40	MS60	MS63	MS65
1987	—	PF65 800	PF67 875			

KM# 28 10 GOLDE
57.60 g., 0.916 Gold 1.6963 oz. AGW **Subject:** 70th Birthday - Dr. Siaka Stevens **Obv:** Lion facing right **Rev:** Head right

Date	Mintage	VF20	XF40	MS60	MS63	MS65
ND-1975	727	—	—	—	2,750	3,250
ND-1975	307	PF63 3,000	PF65 3,500			

DOLLAR DENOMINATED COINAGE

KM# 47 DOLLAR
Copper-Nickel **Obv:** Arms **Rev:** Crowned lion

Date	Mintage	VF20	XF40	MS60	MS63	MS65
1997	—	—	—	—	3.50	5.00

KM# 48 DOLLAR
Copper-Nickel **Obv:** Arms **Rev:** Unicorn

Date	Mintage	VF20	XF40	MS60	MS63	MS65
1997	—	—	—	—	3.50	5.00

KM# 53 DOLLAR
Copper-Nickel **Subject:** Golden Wedding Anniversary **Obv:** Arms **Rev:** E and P monogram

Date	Mintage	VF20	XF40	MS60	MS63	MS65
1997	—	—	—	—	6.00	8.00

KM# 56 DOLLAR
Copper-Nickel **Subject:** Golden Wedding Anniversary **Obv:** Arms **Rev:** Royal yacht

Date	Mintage	VF20	XF40	MS60	MS63	MS65
1997	—	—	—	—	3.00	4.50

KM# 59 DOLLAR
Copper-Nickel **Subject:** Golden Wedding Anniversary **Obv:** Arms **Rev:** Royal couple

Date	Mintage	VF20	XF40	MS60	MS63	MS65
1997	—	—	—	—	3.00	4.50

KM# 62 DOLLAR
Copper-Nickel **Subject:** Golden Wedding Anniversary **Obv:** Arms **Rev:** Fireworks above palace

Date	Mintage	VF20	XF40	MS60	MS63	MS65
1997	—	—	—	—	3.00	4.50

KM# 65 DOLLAR
Copper-Nickel **Subject:** Golden Wedding Anniversary **Obv:** Arms **Rev:** Queen with two children

Date	Mintage	VF20	XF40	MS60	MS63	MS65
1997	—	—	—	—	3.00	4.50

KM# 68 DOLLAR
Copper-Nickel **Subject:** Golden Wedding Anniversary **Obv:** Arms **Rev:** Royal couple with two children

Date	Mintage	VF20	XF40	MS60	MS63	MS65
1997	—	—	—	—	3.00	4.50

KM# 71 DOLLAR
Copper-Nickel **Subject:** Diana - The Peoples' Princess **Obv:** Arms **Rev:** Head 1/4 right

Date	Mintage	VF20	XF40	MS60	MS63	MS65
1997	—	—	—	—	4.00	5.00

KM# 77 DOLLAR
Copper-Nickel **Subject:** Diana - The Peoples' Princess **Obv:** Arms **Rev:** Diana with Mother Theresa

Date	Mintage	VF20	XF40	MS60	MS63	MS65
1997	—	—	—	—	5.00	6.00

KM# 83 DOLLAR
Copper-Nickel **Subject:** Diana - The Peoples' Princess **Obv:** Arms **Rev:** Diana and AIDS patient

Date	Mintage	VF20	XF40	MS60	MS63	MS65
1997	—	—	—	—	4.00	5.00

KM# 89 DOLLAR
Copper-Nickel **Subject:** Diana - The Peoples' Princess **Obv:** Arms **Rev:** Diana with sons William and Harry

Date	Mintage	VF20	XF40	MS60	MS63	MS65
1997	—	—	—	—	4.00	5.00

KM# 95 DOLLAR

Copper-Nickel **Subject:** Jurassic Park **Obv:** Arms **Rev:** Velociraptor

Date	Mintage	VF20	XF40	MS60	MS63	MS65
1997	—	—	—	—	6.00	9.00

KM# 103 DOLLAR

Copper-Nickel **Subject:** In Memoriam, Diana - The Peoples' Princess **Obv:** Arms **Rev:** Head 1/4 left

Date	Mintage	VF20	XF40	MS60	MS63	MS65
1998	—	—	—	—	4.00	5.00

KM# 109 DOLLAR

Copper-Nickel **Subject:** Dr. Livingston **Obv:** Arms **Rev:** Half length bust of David Livingstone at right above natives in longboat

Date	Mintage	VF20	XF40	MS60	MS63	MS65
1998	—	—	—	—	4.00	5.00

KM# 112 DOLLAR

Copper-Nickel **Subject:** Amerigo Vespucci **Obv:** Arms **Rev:** Ship and mountainous portrait

Date	Mintage	VF20	XF40	MS60	MS63	MS65
1999	—	—	—	—	4.00	5.00

KM# 115 DOLLAR

Copper-Nickel **Subject:** Charles Darwin **Obv:** Arms **Rev:** Ship at left, bust at right

Date	Mintage	VF20	XF40	MS60	MS63	MS65
1999	—	—	—	—	4.00	5.00

KM# 118 DOLLAR

Copper-Nickel **Subject:** China 2000 Series **Obv:** Arms **Rev:** Kneeling terracotta warrior

Date	Mintage	VF20	XF40	MS60	MS63	MS65
1999	—	—	—	—	4.50	6.00

KM# 121 DOLLAR

Copper-Nickel **Subject:** China 2000 Series - Ming Dynasty **Obv:** Arms **Rev:** Temple of Heaven

Date	Mintage	VF20	XF40	MS60	MS63	MS65
1999	—	—	—	—	4.50	6.00

KM# 124 DOLLAR

Copper-Nickel **Subject:** China 2000 Series **Obv:** Arms **Rev:** Portion of the Great Wall

Date	Mintage	VF20	XF40	MS60	MS63	MS65
1999	—	—	—	—	4.50	6.00

KM# 127 DOLLAR

Copper-Nickel **Subject:** China 2000 Series **Obv:** Arms **Rev:** Bronze chariot

Date	Mintage	VF20	XF40	MS60	MS63	MS65
1999	—	—	—	—	4.50	6.00

KM# 130 DOLLAR

Copper-Nickel **Subject:** China 2000 Series **Obv:** Arms **Rev:** First century armillary sphere

Date	Mintage	VF20	XF40	MS60	MS63	MS65
1999	—	—	—	—	4.50	6.00

KM# 133 DOLLAR

Copper-Nickel **Subject:** China 2000 Series **Obv:** Arms **Rev:** Tang Dynasty Royal Horse

Date	Mintage	VF20	XF40	MS60	MS63	MS65
1999	—	—	—	—	4.50	6.00

KM# 136 DOLLAR

Copper-Nickel **Subject:** Macau returns to China **Obv:** Arms **Rev:** Church, car, roulette wheel, and hands shaking

Date	Mintage	VF20	XF40	MS60	MS63	MS65
1999	—	—	—	—	5.00	7.00

KM# 139 DOLLAR

Copper-Nickel **Subject:** Prince Edward's Wedding **Obv:** Arms **Rev:** Symbolic wedding design

Date	Mintage	VF20	XF40	MS60	MS63	MS65
1999	—	—	—	—	4.50	6.00

KM# 142 DOLLAR

Copper-Nickel **Subject:** Year of the Dragon **Obv:** Arms **Rev:** Dragon

Date	Mintage	VF20	XF40	MS60	MS63	MS65
2000	—	—	—	—	6.50	9.00

KM# 150 DOLLAR

28.28 g., Copper-Nickel **Obv:** Arms **Rev:** Two Phoenix birds **Edge:** Reeded

Date	Mintage	VF20	XF40	MS60	MS63	MS65
2000	—	—	—	—	6.50	9.00

KM# 151 DOLLAR

Copper-Nickel **Obv:** Arms **Rev:** Chinese dragon

Date	Mintage	VF20	XF40	MS60	MS63	MS65
2000	—	—	—	—	6.50	9.00

KM# 152 DOLLAR

28.43 g., Copper-Nickel, 38.7 mm. **Obv:** Arms **Rev:** Chinese unicorn within circle **Edge:** Reeded

Date	Mintage	VF20	XF40	MS60	MS63	MS65
2000	—	—	—	—	6.00	8.00
1999	—	—	—	—	6.00	8.00

Note: Reported as an error date resulting from muled dies

KM# 174 DOLLAR

Copper-Nickel **Subject:** Buddha **Obv:** Arms **Rev:** Seated Buddha

Date	Mintage	VF20	XF40	MS60	MS63	MS65
2000	—	—	—	—	4.50	6.00

KM# 175 DOLLAR

Copper-Nickel **Obv:** Arms **Rev:** Goddess of Mercy

Date	Mintage	VF20	XF40	MS60	MS63	MS65
2000	—	—	—	—	4.50	6.00

KM# 176 DOLLAR

Copper-Nickel **Obv:** Arms **Rev:** Tzai-yen holding scroll

Date	Mintage	VF20	XF40	MS60	MS63	MS65
2000	—	—	—	—	6.00	8.00

KM# 98 5 DOLLARS

15.55 g., 0.999 Silver 0.4995 oz. ASW **Subject:** Shanghai Coin and Stamp Exposition **Obv:** Arms **Rev:** Standing crowned lion right

Date	Mintage	VF20	XF40	MS60	MS63	MS65
1997	Est. 10000	PF65 22.00				

KM# 99 5 DOLLARS

15.55 g., 0.999 Silver 0.4995 oz. ASW **Subject:** Shanghai Coin and Stamp Exposition **Obv:** Arms **Rev:** Standing unicorn left

Date	Mintage	VF20	XF40	MS60	MS63	MS65
1997	Est. 10000	PF65 18.00				

KM# 101 5 DOLLARS

15.55 g., 0.999 Silver 0.4995 oz. ASW **Subject:** Visit of President Clinton to China **Obv:** Arms **Rev:** Bust 1/4 right, tower at right

Date	Mintage	VF20	XF40	MS60	MS63	MS65
1998	Est. 10000	PF65 18.00				

KM# 102 5 DOLLARS

15.55 g., 0.999 Silver 0.4995 oz. ASW **Subject:** Visit of President Clinton to Beijing **Obv:** Arms **Rev:** Great Wall at left, bust 1/4 left

Date	Mintage	VF20	XF40	MS60	MS63	MS65
1998	Est. 10000	PF65 18.00				

KM# 49 10 DOLLARS

28.28 g., 0.925 Silver 0.841 oz. ASW **Obv:** Arms **Rev:** Standing crowned lion right

Date	Mintage	VF20	XF40	MS60	MS63	MS65
1997	Est. 10000	PF65 30.00				

KM# 50 10 DOLLARS

28.28 g., 0.925 Silver 0.841 oz. ASW **Obv:** Arms **Rev:** Standing unicorn left

Date	Mintage	VF20	XF40	MS60	MS63	MS65
1997	Est. 10000	PF65 30.00				

KM# 54 10 DOLLARS
28.28 g., 0.925 Silver 0.841 oz. ASW **Subject:** Golden Wedding Anniversary **Obv:** Arms **Rev:** E and P monogram within flower circle

Date	Mintage	VF20	XF40	MS60	MS63	MS65
1997	Est. 10000	**PF65** 32.00				

KM# 57 10 DOLLARS
28.28 g., 0.925 Silver 0.841 oz. ASW **Subject:** Golden Wedding Anniversary **Obv:** Arms **Rev:** Royal Yacht with cameo head facing at upper left

Date	Mintage	VF20	XF40	MS60	MS63	MS65
1997	Est. 10000	**PF65** 32.00				

KM# 60 10 DOLLARS
28.28 g., 0.925 Silver 0.841 oz. ASW **Subject:** Golden Wedding Anniversary **Obv:** Arms **Rev:** Royal couple

Date	Mintage	VF20	XF40	MS60	MS63	MS65
1997	Est. 10000	**PF65** 32.00				

KM# 63 10 DOLLARS
28.28 g., 0.925 Silver 0.841 oz. ASW **Subject:** Golden Wedding Anniversary **Obv:** Arms **Rev:** Fireworks above palace

Date	Mintage	VF20	XF40	MS60	MS63	MS65
1997	Est. 10000	**PF65** 32.00				

KM# 66 10 DOLLARS
28.28 g., 0.925 Silver 0.841 oz. ASW **Subject:** Golden Wedding Anniversary **Obv:** Arms **Rev:** Queen with two children

Date	Mintage	VF20	XF40	MS60	MS63	MS65
1997	Est. 10000	**PF65** 32.00				

KM# 69 10 DOLLARS
28.28 g., 0.925 Silver 0.841 oz. ASW **Subject:** Golden Wedding Anniversary **Obv:** Arms **Rev:** Royal couple with two children

Date	Mintage	VF20	XF40	MS60	MS63	MS65
1997	Est. 10000	**PF65** 32.00				

KM# 72 10 DOLLARS
28.28 g., 0.925 Silver 0.841 oz. ASW **Subject:** Diana - The Peoples' Princess **Obv:** Arms **Rev:** Head facing

Date	Mintage	VF20	XF40	MS60	MS63	MS65
1997	Est. 10000	**PF65** 24.00				

KM# 78 10 DOLLARS
28.28 g., 0.925 Silver 0.841 oz. ASW **Subject:** Diana - The Peoples' Princess **Obv:** Arms **Rev:** Diana with Mother Theresa

Date	Mintage	VF20	XF40	MS60	MS63	MS65
1997	Est. 10000	**PF65** 28.00				

KM# 84 10 DOLLARS
28.28 g., 0.925 Silver 0.841 oz. ASW **Subject:** Diana - The Peoples' Princess **Obv:** Arms **Rev:** Diana and AIDS patient

Date	Mintage	VF20	XF40	MS60	MS63	MS65
1997	Est. 10000	**PF65** 20.00				

KM# 90 10 DOLLARS
28.28 g., 0.925 Silver 0.841 oz. ASW **Subject:** Diana - The Peoples' Princess **Obv:** Arms **Rev:** Diana with sons William and Harry

Date	Mintage	VF20	XF40	MS60	MS63	MS65
1997	Est. 10000	**PF65** 22.00				

KM# 96 10 DOLLARS
28.28 g., 0.925 Silver 0.841 oz. ASW **Subject:** Jurassic Park **Obv:** Arms **Rev:** Velociraptor

Date	Mintage	VF20	XF40	MS60	MS63	MS65
1997	Est. 10000	**PF65** 30.00				

KM# 104 10 DOLLARS
28.28 g., 0.925 Silver 0.841 oz. ASW, 38.6 mm. **Subject:** In Memoriam, Diana - The Peoples' Princess **Obv:** Arms **Rev:** Head 1/4 left

Date	Mintage	VF20	XF40	MS60	MS63	MS65
1998	Est. 10000	**PF65** 24.00				

KM# A110 10 DOLLARS
28.28 g., 0.925 Silver 0.841 oz. ASW **Subject:** Dr. Livingstone **Obv:** Arms **Rev:** Standing figures rowing ancient boat, bust 1/4 left at upper right **Note:** Prev. KM#110.

Date	Mintage	VF20	XF40	MS60	MS63	MS65
1998	Est. 10000	PF65 34.00				

KM# 113 10 DOLLARS
28.28 g., 0.925 Silver 0.841 oz. ASW, 38.6 mm. **Subject:** Amerigo Vespucci **Obv:** Arms **Rev:** Ship and Vespucci portrait

Date	Mintage	VF20	XF40	MS60	MS63	MS65
1999	Est. 10000	PF65 34.00				

KM# 116 10 DOLLARS
28.28 g., 0.925 Silver 0.841 oz. ASW, 38.6 mm. **Subject:** Charles Darwin **Obv:** Arms **Rev:** Ship and bust facing at upper right

Date	Mintage	VF20	XF40	MS60	MS63	MS65
1999	Est. 10000	PF65 34.00				

KM# 119 10 DOLLARS
28.28 g., 0.925 Silver 0.841 oz. ASW, 38.6 mm. **Subject:** China 2000 Series **Obv:** Arms **Rev:** Kneeling Terracotta warrior

Date	Mintage	VF20	XF40	MS60	MS63	MS65
1999	Est. 10000	PF65 32.00				

KM# 122 10 DOLLARS
28.28 g., 0.925 Silver 0.841 oz. ASW, 38.6 mm. **Subject:** China 2000 Series - Ming Dynasty **Obv:** Arms **Rev:** Temple of Heaven

Date	Mintage	VF20	XF40	MS60	MS63	MS65
1999	Est. 10000	PF65 32.00				

KM# 125 10 DOLLARS
28.28 g., 0.925 Silver 0.841 oz. ASW, 38.6 mm. **Subject:** China 2000 Series **Obv:** Arms **Rev:** Portion of the Great Wall

Date	Mintage	VF20	XF40	MS60	MS63	MS65
1999	Est. 10000	PF65 32.00				

KM# 128 10 DOLLARS
28.28 g., 0.925 Silver 0.841 oz. ASW, 38.6 mm. **Subject:** China 2000 Series **Obv:** Arms **Rev:** Bronze chariot

Date	Mintage	VF20	XF40	MS60	MS63	MS65
1999	Est. 10000	PF65 32.00				

KM# 131 10 DOLLARS
28.28 g., 0.925 Silver 0.841 oz. ASW, 38.6 mm. **Subject:** China 2000 Series **Obv:** Arms **Rev:** First century armillary sphere

Date	Mintage	VF20	XF40	MS60	MS63	MS65
1999	Est. 10000	PF65 32.00				

KM# 134 10 DOLLARS
28.28 g., 0.925 Silver 0.841 oz. ASW, 38.6 mm. **Subject:** China 2000 Series **Obv:** Arms **Rev:** Tang Dynasty royal horse

Date	Mintage	VF20	XF40	MS60	MS63	MS65
1999	Est. 10000	PF65 32.00				

KM# 137 10 DOLLARS
28.28 g., 0.925 Silver 0.841 oz. ASW, 38.6 mm. **Subject:** Macau Return to China **Obv:** Arms **Rev:** Church, car, roulette wheel and clasped hands below

Date	Mintage	VF20	XF40	MS60	MS63	MS65
1999	Est. 10000	PF65 34.00				

KM# 140 10 DOLLARS
28.28 g., 0.925 Silver 0.841 oz. ASW, 38.6 mm. **Subject:** Prince Edward's Wedding **Obv:** Arms **Rev:** Symbolic wedding design

Date	Mintage	VF20	XF40	MS60	MS63	MS65
1999	Est. 10000	PF65 34.00				

KM# 143 10 DOLLARS
28.28 g., 0.925 Silver 0.841 oz. ASW, 38.6 mm. **Subject:** Year of the Dragon **Obv:** Arms **Rev:** Dragon

Date	Mintage	VF20	XF40	MS60	MS63	MS65
2000	—	PF65 30.00				

KM# 153 10 DOLLARS
28.28 g., 0.925 Silver 0.841 oz. ASW, 38.6 mm. **Obv:** Arms **Rev:** Two Phoenix birds

Date	Mintage	VF20	XF40	MS60	MS63	MS65
2000	Est. 10000	PF65 30.00				

KM# 154 10 DOLLARS

28.28 g., 0.925 Silver 0.841 oz. ASW, 38.6 mm. **Obv:** Arms **Rev:** Chinese dragon

Date	Mintage	VF20	XF40	MS60	MS63	MS65
2000	Est. 10000	PF65 30.00				

KM# 155 10 DOLLARS

28.28 g., 0.925 Silver 0.841 oz. ASW, 38.6 mm. **Obv:** Arms **Rev:** Chinese unicorn within circle

Date	Mintage	VF20	XF40	MS60	MS63	MS65
2000	Est. 10000	PF65 30.00				

KM# 177 10 DOLLARS

28.28 g., 0.925 Silver 0.841 oz. ASW, 38.6 mm. **Obv:** Arms **Rev:** Seated Buddha

Date	Mintage	VF20	XF40	MS60	MS63	MS65
2000	Est. 25000	PF65 32.00				

KM# 178 10 DOLLARS

28.28 g., 0.925 Silver 0.841 oz. ASW, 38.6 mm. **Obv:** Arms **Rev:** Goddess of Mercy

Date	Mintage	VF20	XF40	MS60	MS63	MS65
2000	Est. 25000	PF65 32.00				

KM# 179 10 DOLLARS

28.28 g., 0.925 Silver 0.841 oz. ASW, 38.6 mm. **Obv:** Arms **Rev:** Tzai-yen holding scroll

Date	Mintage	VF20	XF40	MS60	MS63	MS65
2000	Est. 25000	PF65 32.00				

KM# 73 20 DOLLARS

1.24 g., 0.999 Gold 0.040 oz. AGW, 13.9 mm. **Subject:** Diana - The Peoples' Princess **Obv:** Arms **Rev:** Head facing

Date	Mintage	VF20	XF40	MS60	MS63	MS65
1997	Est. 101000	PF65 65.00				

KM# 79 20 DOLLARS

1.24 g., 0.999 Gold 0.040 oz. AGW, 13.9 mm. **Subject:** Diana - The Peoples' Princess **Obv:** Arms **Rev:** Lady Diana and Mother Theresa

Date	Mintage	VF20	XF40	MS60	MS63	MS65
1997	Est. 101000	PF65 65.00				

KM# 85 20 DOLLARS

1.24 g., 0.999 Gold 0.040 oz. AGW, 13.9 mm. **Subject:** Diana - The Peoples' Princess **Obv:** Arms **Rev:** Lady Diana and AIDS patient

Date	Mintage	VF20	XF40	MS60	MS63	MS65
1997	Est. 101000	PF65 65.00				

KM# 91 20 DOLLARS

1.24 g., 0.999 Gold 0.040 oz. AGW, 13.9 mm. **Subject:** Diana - The Peoples' Princess **Obv:** Arms **Rev:** With sons William and Harry

Date	Mintage	VF20	XF40	MS60	MS63	MS65
1997	Est. 101000	PF65 65.00				

KM# 105 20 DOLLARS

1.24 g., 0.999 Gold 0.040 oz. AGW, 13.9 mm. **Subject:** In Memorium **Obv:** Arms **Rev:** Lady Diana

Date	Mintage	VF20	XF40	MS60	MS63	MS65
1998	Est. 10000	PF65 65.00				

KM# 144 20 DOLLARS

1.24 g., 0.999 Gold 0.040 oz. AGW, 13.9 mm. **Subject:** Year of the Dragon **Obv:** Arms **Rev:** Dragon

Date	Mintage	VF20	XF40	MS60	MS63	MS65
2000	Est. 15000	PF65 65.00				

KM# 180 20 DOLLARS

1.24 g., 0.999 Gold 0.0398 oz. AGW, 13.9 mm. **Subject:** Buddha **Obv:** Arms **Rev:** Seated Buddha **Edge:** Reeded **Note:** Struck at Pobjoy Mint.

Date	Mintage	VF20	XF40	MS60	MS63	MS65
2000	Est. 5000	PF65 75.00				

KM# 181 20 DOLLARS

1.24 g., 0.999 Gold 0.0398 oz. AGW, 13.9 mm. **Obv:** Arms **Rev:** Goddess of Mercy

Date	Mintage	VF20	XF40	MS60	MS63	MS65
2000	Est. 5000	PF65 75.00				

KM# 182 20 DOLLARS

1.24 g., 0.999 Gold 0.0398 oz. AGW, 13.9 mm. **Obv:** Arms **Rev:** Tzai-yen holding scroll

Date	Mintage	VF20	XF40	MS60	MS63	MS65
2000	Est. 5000	PF65 75.00				

KM# 74 50 DOLLARS

3.11 g., 0.999 Gold 0.0999 oz. AGW, 18 mm. **Subject:** Diana - The Peoples' Princess **Obv:** Arms **Rev:** Portrait of Lady Diana

Date	Mintage	VF20	XF40	MS60	MS63	MS65
1997	Est. 7500	PF65 175				

KM# 80 50 DOLLARS

3.11 g., 0.999 Gold 0.0999 oz. AGW, 18 mm. **Subject:** Diana - The Peoples' Princess **Obv:** Arms **Rev:** Lady Diana and Mother Theresa

Date	Mintage	VF20	XF40	MS60	MS63	MS65
1997	Est. 7500	PF65 175				

KM# 86 50 DOLLARS

3.11 g., 0.999 Gold 0.0999 oz. AGW, 18 mm. **Subject:** Diana - The Peoples' Princess **Obv:** Arms **Rev:** Lady Diana and AIDS patient

Date	Mintage	VF20	XF40	MS60	MS63	MS65
1997	Est. 7500	PF65 175				

KM# 92 50 DOLLARS

3.11 g., 0.999 Gold 0.0999 oz. AGW, 18 mm. **Subject:** Diana - The Peoples' Princess **Obv:** Arms **Rev:** With sons William and Harry

Date	Mintage	VF20	XF40	MS60	MS63	MS65
1997	Est. 7500	PF65 175				

KM# 106 50 DOLLARS

3.11 g., 0.999 Gold 0.0999 oz. AGW, 18 mm. **Subject:** Diana - The Peoples' Princess **Obv:** Arms **Rev:** Portrait of Lady Diana

Date	Mintage	VF20	XF40	MS60	MS63	MS65
1998	Est. 7500	PF65 175				

KM# 145 50 DOLLARS

3.11 g., 0.999 Gold 0.0999 oz. AGW, 18 mm. **Subject:** Year of the Dragon **Obv:** Arms **Rev:** Dragon

Date	Mintage	VF20	XF40	MS60	MS63	MS65
2000	Est. 20000	PF65 165				

KM# 183 50 DOLLARS

3.11 g., 0.999 Gold 0.0999 oz. AGW, 18 mm. **Obv:** Arms **Rev:** Seated Buddha **Edge:** Reeded

Date	Mintage	VF20	XF40	MS60	MS63	MS65
2000	—	PF65 175				

KM# 184 50 DOLLARS

3.11 g., 0.999 Gold 0.0999 oz. AGW, 18 mm. **Obv:** Arms **Rev:** Goddess of Mercy

Date	Mintage	VF20	XF40	MS60	MS63	MS65
2000	Est. 5000	PF65 180				

KM# 185 50 DOLLARS

3.11 g., 0.999 Gold 0.0999 oz. AGW, 18 mm. **Obv:** Arms **Rev:** Tzai-yen holding scroll

Date	Mintage	VF20	XF40	MS60	MS63	MS65
2000	Est. 5000	PF65 180				

KM# 51 100 DOLLARS

6.22 g., 0.9999 Gold 0.200 oz. AGW **Subject:** Shanghai Coin and Stamp Exposition **Obv:** Arms **Rev:** Crowned lion

Date	Mintage	VF20	XF40	MS60	MS63	MS65
1997	Est. 5000	PF65 375				

KM# 52 100 DOLLARS

6.22 g., 0.9999 Gold 0.200 oz. AGW **Subject:** Shanghai Coin and Stamp Exposition **Obv:** Arms **Rev:** Crowned lion

Date	Mintage	VF20	XF40	MS60	MS63	MS65
1997	—	PF65 375				

KM# 55 100 DOLLARS

6.22 g., 0.9999 Gold 0.200 oz. AGW **Subject:** Golden Wedding Anniversary **Obv:** Arms **Rev:** E and P monogram

Date	Mintage	VF20	XF40	MS60	MS63	MS65
1997	Est. 3500	PF65 425				

KM# 58 100 DOLLARS

6.22 g., 0.9999 Gold 0.200 oz. AGW **Subject:** Golden Wedding Anniversary **Obv:** Arms **Rev:** Yacht

Date	Mintage	VF20	XF40	MS60	MS63	MS65
1997	Est. 3500	PF65 425				

KM# 61 100 DOLLARS

6.22 g., 0.9999 Gold 0.200 oz. AGW **Subject:** Golden Wedding Anniversary **Obv:** Arms **Rev:** Royal couple

Date	Mintage	VF20	XF40	MS60	MS63	MS65
1997	Est. 10000	PF65 325				

KM# 64 100 DOLLARS

6.22 g., 0.9999 Gold 0.200 oz. AGW **Subject:** Golden Wedding Anniversary **Obv:** Arms **Rev:** Fireworks above palace

Date	Mintage	VF20	XF40	MS60	MS63	MS65
1997	Est. 3500	PF65 425				

KM# 67 100 DOLLARS

6.22 g., 0.9999 Gold 0.200 oz. AGW **Subject:** Golden Wedding Anniversary **Obv:** Arms **Rev:** Queen with two children

Date	Mintage	VF20	XF40	MS60	MS63	MS65
1997	Est. 3500	PF65 425				

KM# 70 100 DOLLARS

6.22 g., 0.9999 Gold 0.200 oz. AGW **Subject:** Golden Wedding Anniversary **Obv:** Arms **Rev:** Royal couple with two children

Date	Mintage	VF20	XF40	MS60	MS63	MS65
1997	Est. 3500	PF65 425				

KM# 75 100 DOLLARS

6.22 g., 0.9999 Gold 0.200 oz. AGW **Subject:** Diana - The Peoples' Princess **Obv:** Arms **Rev:** Portrait of Lady Diana

Date	Mintage	VF20	XF40	MS60	MS63	MS65
1997	Est. 5000	PF65 375				

KM# 81 100 DOLLARS

6.22 g., 0.9999 Gold 0.200 oz. AGW **Subject:** Diana - The Peoples' Princess **Obv:** Arms with supporters **Rev:** Diana with Mother Theresa

Date	Mintage	VF20	XF40	MS60	MS63	MS65
1997	Est. 5000	PF65 375				

KM# 87 100 DOLLARS

6.22 g., 0.9999 Gold 0.200 oz. AGW **Subject:** Diana - The Peoples' Princess **Obv:** Arms **Rev:** Lady Diana and AIDS patient

Date	Mintage	VF20	XF40	MS60	MS63	MS65
1997	Est. 5000	PF65 375				

KM# 93 100 DOLLARS

6.22 g., 0.9999 Gold 0.200 oz. AGW **Subject:** Diana - The Peoples' Princess **Obv:** Arms **Rev:** With sons William and Harry

Date	Mintage	VF20	XF40	MS60	MS63	MS65
1997	Est. 5000	PF65 375				

KM# 97 100 DOLLARS

6.22 g., 0.9999 Gold 0.200 oz. AGW **Subject:** Jurassic Park **Obv:** Arms **Rev:** Velociraptor

Date	Mintage	VF20	XF40	MS60	MS63	MS65
1997	Est. 5000	PF65 375				

KM# 100 100 DOLLARS
6.22 g., 0.9999 Gold 0.200 oz. AGW, 22 mm. **Subject:** Queen Victoria's Diamond Jubilee Centennial **Obv:** Arms **Rev:** Crowned bust with diamond necklace facing

Date	Mintage	VF20	XF40	MS60	MS63	MS65
1997	Est. 3500	PF65 425				

KM# 107 100 DOLLARS
6.22 g., 0.9999 Gold 0.200 oz. AGW, 22 mm. **Subject:** Diana - The People's Princess **Obv:** Arms **Rev:** Head half left

Date	Mintage	VF20	XF40	MS60	MS63	MS65
1998	—	PF65 375				

KM# 111 100 DOLLARS
6.22 g., 0.9999 Gold 0.200 oz. AGW, 22 mm. **Subject:** Dr. Livingstone **Obv:** Arms **Rev:** Dr. Livingstone above figures in boat

Date	Mintage	VF20	XF40	MS60	MS63	MS65
1998	—	PF65 375				

KM# 114 100 DOLLARS
6.22 g., 0.9999 Gold 0.200 oz. AGW, 22 mm. **Subject:** Amerigo Vespucci **Obv:** Arms **Rev:** Ship and mountainous portrait

Date	Mintage	VF20	XF40	MS60	MS63	MS65
1999	—	PF65 375				

KM# 117 100 DOLLARS
6.22 g., 0.9999 Gold 0.200 oz. AGW, 22 mm. **Subject:** Charles Darwin **Obv:** Arms **Rev:** Ship and portrait

Date	Mintage	VF20	XF40	MS60	MS63	MS65
1999	Est. 5000	PF65 375				

KM# 120 100 DOLLARS
6.22 g., 0.9999 Gold 0.200 oz. AGW, 22 mm. **Subject:** China 2000 Series **Obv:** Arms **Rev:** Kneeling terra cotta warrior

Date	Mintage	VF20	XF40	MS60	MS63	MS65
1999	—	PF65 375				

KM# 123 100 DOLLARS
6.22 g., 0.9999 Gold 0.200 oz. AGW, 22 mm. **Subject:** China 2000 Series - Ming Dynasty **Obv:** Arms **Rev:** Temple of Heaven

Date	Mintage	VF20	XF40	MS60	MS63	MS65
1999	Est. 5000	PF65 375				

KM# 126 100 DOLLARS
6.22 g., 0.9999 Gold 0.200 oz. AGW, 22 mm. **Subject:** China 2000 Series **Obv:** Arms **Rev:** Portion of the Great Wall

Date	Mintage	VF20	XF40	MS60	MS63	MS65
1999	Est. 5000	PF65 375				

KM# 129 100 DOLLARS
6.22 g., 0.9999 Gold 0.200 oz. AGW, 22 mm. **Series:** China 2000 **Obv:** Arms **Rev:** Bronze chariot

Date	Mintage	VF20	XF40	MS60	MS63	MS65
1999	—	PF65 375				

KM# 132 100 DOLLARS
6.22 g., 0.9999 Gold 0.200 oz. AGW, 22 mm. **Series:** China 2000 **Obv:** Arms **Rev:** First century armillary sphere

Date	Mintage	VF20	XF40	MS60	MS63	MS65
1999	Est. 5000	PF65 375				

KM# 135 100 DOLLARS
6.22 g., 0.9999 Gold 0.200 oz. AGW, 22 mm. **Series:** China 2000 **Obv:** Arms **Rev:** Tang Dynasty royal horse

Date	Mintage	VF20	XF40	MS60	MS63	MS65
1999	Est. 5000	PF65 375				

KM# 138 100 DOLLARS
6.22 g., 0.9999 Gold 0.200 oz. AGW, 22 mm. **Subject:** Macau Return to China **Obv:** Arms **Rev:** Church, car, roulette wheel, and hands shaking

Date	Mintage	VF20	XF40	MS60	MS63	MS65
1999	Est. 5000	PF65 375				

KM# 141 100 DOLLARS
6.22 g., 0.9999 Gold 0.200 oz. AGW, 22 mm. **Subject:** Prince Edward's Wedding **Obv:** Arms **Rev:** Symbolic wedding design

Date	Mintage	VF20	XF40	MS60	MS63	MS65
1999	Est. 5000	PF65 375				

KM# 146 100 DOLLARS
6.22 g., 0.9999 Gold 0.200 oz. AGW, 22 mm. **Subject:** Year of the Dragon **Obv:** Arms **Rev:** Dragon

Date	Mintage	VF20	XF40	MS60	MS63	MS65
2000	Est. 20000	PF65 325				

KM# 186 100 DOLLARS
6.22 g., 0.9999 Gold 0.200 oz. AGW, 22 mm. **Obv:** Arms **Rev:** Seated Buddha **Edge:** Reeded

Date	Mintage	VF20	XF40	MS60	MS63	MS65
2000	—	PF65 375				

KM# 187 100 DOLLARS
6.22 g., 0.9999 Gold 0.200 oz. AGW, 22 mm. **Obv:** Arms **Rev:** Goddess of Mercy

Date	Mintage	VF20	XF40	MS60	MS63	MS65
2000	Est. 5000	PF65 375				

KM# 188 100 DOLLARS
6.22 g., 0.9999 Gold 0.200 oz. AGW, 22 mm. **Obv:** Arms **Rev:** Tzai-yen holding scroll

Date	Mintage	VF20	XF40	MS60	MS63	MS65
2000	—	PF65 375				

KM# 76 250 DOLLARS
15.50 g., 0.999 Gold 0.4978 oz. AGW **Subject:** Diana - The Peoples' Princess **Obv:** Arms **Rev:** Portrait of Lady Diana

Date	Mintage	VF20	XF40	MS60	MS63	MS65
1997	—	PF65 800				

KM# 82 250 DOLLARS
15.50 g., 0.999 Gold 0.4978 oz. AGW **Subject:** Diana - The Peoples' Princess **Obv:** Arms **Rev:** Mother Theresa and Lady Diana

Date	Mintage	VF20	XF40	MS60	MS63	MS65
1997	Est. 3000	PF65 800				

KM# 88 250 DOLLARS
15.50 g., 0.999 Gold 0.4978 oz. AGW **Subject:** Diana - The Peoples' Princess **Obv:** Arms **Rev:** Lady Diana with AIDS patient

Date	Mintage	VF20	XF40	MS60	MS63	MS65
1997	—	PF65 800				

KM# 94 250 DOLLARS
15.50 g., 0.999 Gold 0.4978 oz. AGW **Subject:** Diana - The Peoples' Princess **Obv:** Arms **Rev:** Lady Diana with sons William and Harry

Date	Mintage	VF20	XF40	MS60	MS63	MS65
1997	Est. 3000	PF65 800				

KM# 240 250 DOLLARS
15.55 g., 0.9999 Gold 0.4999 oz. AGW, 29.9 mm. **Subject:** Centennial of Queen Victoria's Diamond Jubilee **Obv:** Arms **Rev:** Crowned bust with diamond necklace facing **Edge:** Reeded **Note:** The entire issue is reported to have been commissioned by and sold to a single purchaser.

Date	Mintage	VF20	XF40	MS60	MS63	MS65
1997	Est. 1000	PF65 850				

KM# 108 250 DOLLARS
15.50 g., 0.999 Gold 0.4978 oz. AGW **Subject:** Diana - The Peoples' Princess **Obv:** Arms **Rev:** Head half left

Date	Mintage	VF20	XF40	MS60	MS63	MS65
1998	Est. 3000	PF65 800				

KM# 147 250 DOLLARS
15.50 g., 0.999 Gold 0.4978 oz. AGW **Subject:** Year of the Dragon **Obv:** Arms **Rev:** Dragon

Date	Mintage	VF20	XF40	MS60	MS63	MS65
2000	Est. 5000	PF65 775				

KM# 189 250 DOLLARS
15.50 g., 0.999 Gold 0.4978 oz. AGW **Obv:** Arms **Rev:** Seated Buddha

Date	Mintage	VF20	XF40	MS60	MS63	MS65
2000	Est. 5000	PF65 775				

KM# 190 250 DOLLARS
15.55 g., 0.999 Gold 0.4994 oz. AGW **Obv:** Arms **Rev:** Goddess of Mercy

Date	Mintage	VF20	XF40	MS60	MS63	MS65
2000	Est. 5000	PF65 775				

KM# 191 250 DOLLARS
15.55 g., 0.999 Gold 0.4994 oz. AGW **Obv:** Arms **Rev:** Tzai-yen holding scroll

Date	Mintage	VF20	XF40	MS60	MS63	MS65
2000	—	PF65 800				

KM# 148 500 DOLLARS
31.10 g., 0.999 Gold 0.999 oz. AGW, 32.7 mm. **Subject:** Year of the Dragon **Obv:** Arms **Rev:** Dragon **Note:** Similar to 10 Dollars, KM#143.

Date	Mintage	VF20	XF40	MS60	MS63	MS65
2000	Est. 1000	PF65 1,750				

KM# 192 500 DOLLARS
31.10 g., 0.999 Gold 0.999 oz. AGW, 32.7 mm. **Obv:** Arms **Rev:** Seated Buddha **Edge:** Reeded

Date	Mintage	VF20	XF40	MS60	MS63	MS65
2000	Est. 5000	PF65 1,650				

KM# 193 500 DOLLARS
31.10 g., 0.999 Gold 0.999 oz. AGW, 32.7 mm. **Obv:** Arms **Rev:** Goddess of Mercy

Date	Mintage	VF20	XF40	MS60	MS63	MS65
2000	Est. 5000	PF65 1,650				

KM# 194 500 DOLLARS
31.10 g., 0.999 Gold 0.999 oz. AGW, 32.7 mm. **Obv:** Arms **Rev:** Tzai-yen holding scroll

Date	Mintage	VF20	XF40	MS60	MS63	MS65
2000	Est. 5000	PF65 1,650				

KM# 149 2500 DOLLARS
155.52 g., 0.999 Gold 4.995 oz. AGW, 50 mm. **Subject:** Year of the Dragon **Obv:** Arms **Rev:** Dragon

Date	Mintage	VF20	XF40	MS60	MS63	MS65
2000	250	PF65 8,500				

KM# 195 2500 DOLLARS
155.52 g., 0.999 Gold 4.995 oz. AGW, 50 mm. **Obv:** Arms **Rev:** Seated Buddha **Edge:** Reeded

Date	Mintage	VF20	XF40	MS60	MS63	MS65
2000	Est. 250	PF65 8,500				

KM# 196 2500 DOLLARS
155.52 g., 0.999 Gold 4.995 oz. AGW, 50 mm. **Obv:** Arms **Rev:** Goddess of Mercy

Date	Mintage	VF20	XF40	MS60	MS63	MS65
2000	Est. 250	PF65 8,500				

KM# 197 2500 DOLLARS
155.52 g., 0.999 Gold 4.995 oz. AGW, 50 mm. **Obv:** Arms **Rev:** Tzai-yen holding scroll

Date	Mintage	VF20	XF40	MS60	MS63	MS65
2000	—	PF65 8,500				

TRIAL STRIKES

KM#	Date	Mintage	Identification	Mkt Val
TS1	ND (1964)	—	5 Centesimos. Steel. Portrait of Milton Margai, Prime Minster. Uruguay 5 Centavos design with MBLAT top, HA in number 5. Reeded.	160
TS2	ND-1964	—	10 Cents. Brass. Head right. Value within wreath.	145
TS3	ND-1964	—	10 Cents. Aluminum. Reverse of KM#19. Uruguay 10 Centesimos.	145

MINT SETS

KM#	Date	Mintage	Identification	Issue Price	Mkt Val
MS1	1966 (3)	—	KM#22-24	—	3,200

PROOF SETS

KM#	Date	Mintage	Identification	Issue Price	Mkt Val
PS1	1964 (6)	10,000	KM#16-21	—	17.50
PS2	1964 (6)	12	KM#16a-20a, 21b	—	6,000
PS3	1964 (6)	10	KM#16a-21a	—	4,250
PS4	1966 (3)	400	KM#22a-24a	—	5,700
PS5	1972 (1)	1,000	KM25 (2 pieces with 50 cent bank note (0 serial#) in plush case	—	15.00
PS6	1980 (6)	10,000	KM25, 30-34	34.00	20.00

SINGAPORE

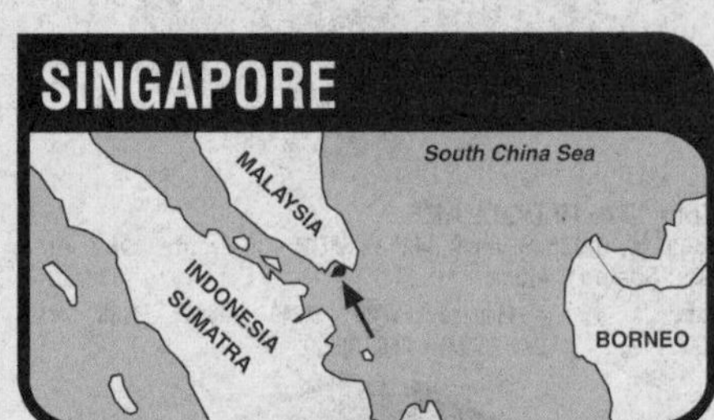

The Republic of Singapore, a member of the Commonwealth of Nations situated off the southern tip of the Malay peninsula, has an area of 224 sq. mi. (633 sq. km.) and a population of *2.7 million. Capital: Singapore. The economy is based on entrepôt trade, manufacturing and oil. Rubber, petroleum products, machinery and spices are exported.

Singapore's modern history - it was an important shipping center in the 14th century before the rise of Malacca and Penang - began in 1819 when Sir Thomas Stamford Raffles, an agent for the British East India Company, founded the town of Singapore. By 1825 its trade exceeded that of Malacca and Penang combined. The opening of the Suez Canal (1869) and the demand for rubber and tin created by the automobile and packaging industries combined to make Singapore one of the major ports of the world. In 1826 Singapore, Penang and Malacca were combined to form the Straits Settlements, which was made a Crown Colony in 1867. Singapore became a separate Crown Colony in 1946 when the Straits Settlements was dissolved. It joined in the formation of Malaysia in 1963, but broke away on Aug. 9, 1965, to become an independent republic. The President is Chief of State. The prime minister is Head of Government.

For earlier coinage see Straits Settlements, Malaya, Malaya and British Borneo.

MINT MARK

sm = *"sm"* - Singapore Mint monogram

MONETARY SYSTEM

100 Cents = 1 Dollar

REPUBLIC

STANDARD COINAGE

100 Cents = 1 Dollar

KM# 1 CENT

1.94 g., Bronze, 17.78 mm. **Obv:** Value **Rev:** Apartment building **Edge:** Plain

Date	Mintage	VF20	XF40	MS60	MS63	MS65
1967	7,508,000	—	0.30	0.60	1.00	2.00
1967	2,000	PF63 2.25	PF65 3.50			
1968	2,985,000	—	0.30	0.60	1.00	2.00
1968	5,000	PF63 2.00	PF65 3.00			
1969	7,234,000	—	1.20	2.00	3.00	5.00
1969	3,000	PF63 10.00	PF65 15.00			
1970	1,442,000	0.25	1.00	2.00	3.00	5.00
1971	9,731,000	—	0.25	0.60	1.00	2.00
1972	1,678,000	—	0.30	0.70	1.25	2.50
1972	749	PF63 20.00	PF65 25.00			
1973	6,392,000	—	0.20	0.30	0.50	1.00
1973	1,000	PF63 5.00	PF65 7.00			
1974	9,441,000	—	—	0.30	0.50	1.00
1974	1,500	PF63 4.00	PF65 6.00			
1975	24,256,000	—	—	0.30	0.50	1.00
1975	3,000	PF63 1.50	PF65 2.50			
1976	2,500,000	0.20	1.00	2.00	3.00	5.00
1976 sm	3,500	PF63 1.25	PF65 2.00			
1977 sm	3,500	PF63 1.25	PF65 2.00			
1978 sm	4,000	PF63 1.25	PF65 2.00			
1979 sm	3,500	PF63 1.25	PF65 2.00			
1980 sm	14,000	PF63 1.00	PF65 1.50			

KM# 1a CENT

1.74 g., Copper Clad Steel, 17.78 mm. **Obv:** Value **Rev:** Apartment building

Date	Mintage	VF20	XF40	MS60	MS63	MS65
1976	13,665,000	—	0.20	0.30	0.50	0.75
1977	13,980,000	—	0.20	0.30	0.50	0.75
1978	5,986,000	—	—	0.30	0.50	0.75
1979	12,051,000	—	—	0.25	0.45	0.65
1980	19,992,000	—	—	0.25	0.45	0.65
1981	38,194,000	—	—	0.25	0.45	0.65
1982	24,265,000	—	—	0.25	0.45	0.65
1983	2,354,000	—	—	0.25	0.45	0.65
1984	5,838,424	—	—	0.25	0.45	0.65
1985 Sets only	148,424	—	—	—	—	0.75

KM# 1b CENT

2.92 g., 0.925 Silver 0.0868 oz. ASW, 17.8 mm. **Obv:** Value **Rev:** Apartment building

Date	Mintage	VF20	XF40	MS60	MS63	MS65
1981 sm	30,000	PF65 2.50				
1982 sm	20,000	PF65 2.50				
1983 sm	15,000	PF65 2.50				
1984 sm	15,000	PF65 2.50				

KM# 49 CENT

1.53 g., Bronze, 15.9 mm. **Obv:** Arms with supporters **Rev:** Value divides national flower - Vanda Miss Joaquim **Edge:** Plain

Date	Mintage	VF20	XF40	MS60	MS63	MS65
1986	20,120,000	—	—	0.10	0.15	0.25
1987 Sets only	120,000	—	—	—	—	0.35
1988 Sets only	120,000	—	—	—	—	0.35
1989 Sets only	20,180,000	—	—	—	—	0.35
1990	10,100,000	—	—	0.10	0.15	0.25

KM# 49a CENT

1.81 g., 0.925 Silver 0.0538 oz. ASW, 15.9 mm. **Obv:** Arms with supporters **Rev:** Value divides national plant - Vanda Miss Joaquim

Date	Mintage	VF20	XF40	MS60	MS63	MS65
1985 sm	20,000	PF65 2.00				
1986 sm	15,000	PF65 2.00				
1987 sm	15,000	PF65 2.00				
1988	15,000	PF65 2.00				
1989	15,000	PF65 2.00				
1990	15,000	PF65 2.00				
1991	15,000	PF65 2.00				

KM# 49b CENT

1.24 g., Copper Plated Zinc, 15.9 mm. **Obv:** Arms with supporters **Rev:** Value divides plants

Date	Mintage	VF20	XF40	MS60	MS63	MS65
1991 Sets only	70,000	—	—	—	—	0.35

KM# 98 CENT

1.24 g., Copper Plated Zinc, 15.9 mm. **Obv:** National arms **Rev:** Value divides plants **Edge:** Plain **Note:** Similar to KM#49 but motto ribbon on arms curves down at center.

Date	Mintage	VF20	XF40	MS60	MS63	MS65
1992	20,055,000	—	—	0.10	0.15	0.25
1993	39,920,000	—	—	0.10	0.15	0.25
1994	130,910,200	—	—	0.10	0.15	0.25
1995	220,124,000	—	—	0.10	0.15	0.25
1996 Sets only	180,000	—	—	—	—	0.35
1997 Sets only	180,000	—	—	—	—	0.35
1998 Sets only	48,940,000	—	—	—	—	0.25
1999 Sets only	130,000	—	—	—	—	0.35
2000	50,150,000	—	—	0.10	0.15	0.25

KM# 98a CENT

1.81 g., 0.925 Silver 0.0538 oz. ASW, 15.9 mm. **Obv:** National arms **Rev:** Value divides plants

Date	Mintage	VF20	XF40	MS60	MS63	MS65
1992 sm	15,000	PF65 2.00				
1993 sm	15,000	PF65 2.00				
1994 sm	10,000	PF65 2.00				
1995 sm	10,000	PF65 2.00				
1996 sm	16,800	PF65 2.00				
1997 sm	18,000	PF65 2.00				
1998 sm	9,200	PF65 2.00				
1999 sm	9,200	PF65 2.00				
2000 sm	8,900	PF65 2.00				

KM# 2 5 CENTS

1.41 g., Copper-Nickel, 16.26 mm. **Obv:** Value and date **Rev:** Anhinga or Snake Bird **Edge:** Reeded

Date	Mintage	VF20	XF40	MS60	MS63	MS65
1967	28,008,000	—	0.20	0.35	0.65	1.25
1967	2,000	PF63 3.00	PF65 5.00			
1968	4,233,000	—	0.25	0.40	0.80	1.75
1968	5,000	PF63 3.00	PF65 5.00			
1969	14,792,000	—	0.10	0.35	0.65	1.25
1969	3,000	PF63 7.50	PF65 10.00			
1970	4,105,000	—	0.20	0.40	0.80	1.75
1971	13,202,000	—	0.10	0.35	0.65	1.00
1972	9,830,000	—	0.10	0.35	0.65	1.00
1972	749	PF63 25.00	PF65 30.00			
1973	2,995,000	0.50	1.50	2.25	—	—
1973	1,000	PF63 7.50	PF65 10.00			
1974	10,888,000	—	0.10	0.35	0.65	0.85
1974	1,500	PF63 6.50	PF65 9.00			
1975	1,759,000	—	0.40	1.00	1.25	1.50
1975	3,000	PF63 2.50	PF65 3.50			
1976	15,576,000	—	0.10	0.35	0.65	0.85
1976 sm	3,500	PF63 2.25	PF65 3.00			
1977	9,991,000	—	0.10	0.35	0.65	0.85
1977 sm	3,500	PF63 2.25	PF65 3.00			
1978	6,011,000	—	0.10	0.35	0.65	0.85
1978 sm	4,000	PF63 2.25	PF65 3.00			
1979	10,039,000	—	—	0.35	0.65	0.85
1979 sm	3,500	PF63 2.25	PF65 3.00			
1980	20,604,000	—	—	0.35	0.65	0.85
1980 sm	14,000	PF63 2.00	PF65 3.00			
1981	23,976,000	—	—	0.35	0.65	0.85
1982	24,573,000	—	—	0.35	0.65	0.85
1983	4,166,000	—	—	0.35	0.65	0.85
1984	19,040,000	—	—	0.35	0.65	0.85
1985 Sets only	148,424	—	—	—	—	1.00

KM# 8 5 CENTS

1.24 g., Aluminum, 21.23 mm. **Series:** F.A.O. **Obv:** Value and date **Rev:** Pomfret fish **Edge:** Reeded

Date	Mintage	VF20	XF40	MS60	MS63	MS65
1971	3,049,000	0.10	0.30	1.00	1.25	1.50

KM# 2a 5 CENTS

1.26 g., Copper-Nickel Clad Steel, 16.26 mm. **Obv:** Value **Rev:** Anhinga or Snake Bird **Edge:** Reeded

Date	Mintage	VF20	XF40	MS60	MS63	MS65
1980	12,001,000	—	—	0.35	0.50	0.65
1981	23,866,000	—	—	0.35	0.50	0.65
1982	24,413,000	—	—	0.35	0.50	0.65
1983	4,016,000	—	—	0.35	0.50	0.65
1984	—	—	—	0.35	0.50	0.65

KM# 2b 5 CENTS

1.57 g., 0.925 Silver 0.0467 oz. ASW, 16.26 mm. **Obv:** Value **Rev:** Anhinga or Snake Bird

Date	Mintage	VF20	XF40	MS60	MS63	MS65
1981 sm	30,000	PF65 2.00				
1982 sm	20,000	PF65 2.00				
1983 sm	15,000	PF65 2.00				
1984 sm	15,000	PF65 2.00				

KM# 50 5 CENTS

1.56 g., Aluminum-Bronze, 16.75 mm. **Obv:** Arms with supporters **Rev:** Fruit salad plant **Edge:** Reeded

Date	Mintage	VF20	XF40	MS60	MS63	MS65
1985	14,840,000	—	—	0.20	0.30	0.45
1986	15,600,000	—	—	0.20	0.30	0.45
1987	31,160,000	—	—	0.20	0.30	0.45
1988	45,300,000	—	—	0.20	0.30	0.45
1989	70,088,000	—	—	0.20	0.30	0.45
1990	26,152,000	—	—	0.20	0.30	0.45
1991 Sets only	70,000	—	—	—	—	0.50

KM# 50a 5 CENTS

2.00 g., 0.925 Silver 0.0595 oz. ASW, 16.75 mm. **Obv:** Arms with supporters **Rev:** Fruit salad plant

Date	Mintage	VF20	XF40	MS60	MS63	MS65
1985 sm	20,000	PF65 2.25				
1986 sm	15,000	PF65 2.25				
1987 sm	15,000	PF65 2.25				
1988	15,000	PF65 2.25				
1989	15,000	PF65 2.25				
1990	15,000	PF65 2.25				
1991	15,000	PF65 2.25				

KM# 99 5 CENTS

1.56 g., Aluminum-Bronze, 16.75 mm. **Obv:** National arms **Rev:** Fruit salad plant **Edge:** Reeded **Note:** Similar to KM#50 but motto ribbon on arms curves down at center.

Date	Mintage	VF20	XF40	MS60	MS63	MS65
1992 Sets only	55,000	—	—	—	—	0.50
1993	5,996,000	—	—	0.20	0.30	0.45
1994 Sets only	100,200	—	—	—	—	0.50
1995	90,124,000	—	—	0.20	0.30	0.45
1996 Sets only	180,000	—	—	—	—	0.50
1997	60,180,000	—	—	0.20	0.30	0.45
1998 Sets only	180,000	—	—	—	—	0.50
1999 Sets only	130,000	—	—	—	—	0.50
2000	30,150,000	—	—	0.20	0.30	0.45

KM# 99a 5 CENTS

2.00 g., 0.925 Silver 0.0595 oz. ASW, 16.75 mm. **Obv:** National arms **Rev:** Fruit salad plant

Date	Mintage	VF20	XF40	MS60	MS63	MS65
1992 sm	15,000	PF65 2.25				
1993 sm	15,000	PF65 2.25				
1994 sm	10,000	PF65 2.25				
1995 sm	10,000	PF65 2.25				
1996 sm	16,800	PF65 2.25				
1997 sm	18,000	PF65 2.25				
1998 sm	9,200	PF65 2.25				
1999 sm	9,200	PF65 2.25				
2000 sm	8,900	PF65 2.25				

KM# 3 10 CENTS

2.83 g., Copper-Nickel, 19.41 mm. **Obv:** Value and date **Rev:** Stylized Spotted Seahorse **Edge:** Reeded

Date	Mintage	VF20	XF40	MS60	MS63	MS65
1967	40,008,000	—	0.15	0.65	1.50	2.50
1967	2,000	PF63 5.00	PF65 7.00			
1968	36,277,000	—	0.20	0.65	1.50	2.50
1968	5,000	PF63 5.00	PF65 7.00			
1969	25,014,000	—	0.10	0.65	1.50	2.50
1969	3,000	PF63 10.00	PF65 12.00			
1970	21,344,000	—	0.20	0.65	1.50	2.00
1971	33,040,999	—	0.10	0.50	1.50	2.00
1972	2,688,000	0.20	0.75	1.50	2.00	3.00
1972	749	PF63 30.00	PF65 35.00			
1973	14,305,000	0.10	0.20	0.65	1.50	1.75
1973	1,000	PF63 5.00	PF65 7.00			
1974	13,470,000	0.10	0.20	0.65	1.50	1.75
1974	1,500	PF63 5.00	PF65 7.00			

Date	Mintage	VF20	XF40	MS60	MS63	MS65
1975	858,000	0.50	1.25	2.25	3.00	3.50
1975	3,000	PF63 4.00	PF65 6.00			
1976	29,753,000	—	0.15	0.35	1.50	1.75
1976 sm	3,500	PF63 3.50	PF65 5.00			
1977	11,816,000	—	0.10	0.35	1.50	1.75
1977 sm	3,500	PF63 3.50	PF65 5.00			
1978	5,991,000	—	0.10	0.35	1.50	1.75
1978 sm	4,000	PF63 3.50	PF65 5.00			
1979	12,066,000	—	0.10	0.35	1.50	1.75
1979 sm	3,500	PF63 3.50	PF65 5.00			
1980	40,369,000	—	0.10	0.35	1.50	1.75
1980 sm	14,000	PF63 3.00	PF65 5.00			
1981	58,710,000	—	0.10	0.35	1.50	1.75
1982	48,674,000	—	0.10	0.35	1.50	1.75
1983	10,565,000	—	0.10	0.35	1.50	1.75
1984	29,860,000	—	0.10	0.35	1.50	1.75
1985 Sets only	148,424	—	—	—	—	2.00

KM# 3a 10 CENTS

3.35 g., 0.925 Silver 0.0996 oz. ASW, 19.1 mm. **Obv:** Value and date **Rev:** Stylized Great Crowned Seahorse

Date	Mintage	VF20	XF40	MS60	MS63	MS65
1981 sm	30,000	PF65 3.50				
1982 sm	20,000	PF65 3.50				
1983 sm	15,000	PF65 3.50				
1984 sm	15,000	PF65 3.50				

KM# 51 10 CENTS

2.60 g., Copper-Nickel, 18.5 mm. **Obv:** Arms with supporters **Rev:** Star Jasmine plant above value **Edge:** Reeded

Date	Mintage	VF20	XF40	MS60	MS63	MS65
1985	45,040,000	—	—	0.20	0.30	0.45
1986	113,120,000	—	—	0.20	0.30	0.45
1987	90,120,000	—	—	0.20	0.30	0.45
1988	54,575,000	—	—	0.20	0.30	0.45
1989	134,290,000	—	—	0.20	0.30	0.45
1990	51,820,000	—	—	0.20	0.30	0.45
1991	159,840,000	—	—	0.20	0.30	0.45

KM# 51a 10 CENTS

2.93 g., 0.925 Silver 0.0871 oz. ASW, 18.5 mm. **Obv:** Arms with supporters **Rev:** Star Jasmine plant above value

Date	Mintage	VF20	XF40	MS60	MS63	MS65
1985 sm	20,000	PF65 3.25				
1986 sm	15,000	PF65 3.25				
1987 sm	15,000	PF65 3.25				
1988 sm	15,000	PF65 3.25				
1989 sm	15,000	PF65 3.25				
1990 sm	15,000	PF65 3.25				
1991 sm	15,000	PF65 3.25				

KM# 100 10 CENTS

2.60 g., Copper-Nickel, 18.5 mm. **Obv:** National arms **Rev:** Star Jasmine plant **Edge:** Reeded **Note:** Similar to KM#51 but motto ribbon on arms curves down at center.

Date	Mintage	VF20	XF40	MS60	MS63	MS65
1992 Sets only	55,000	—	—	—	—	0.50
1993	89,855,000	—	—	0.20	0.30	0.45
1994 Sets only	100,200	—	—	—	—	0.50
1995 Sets only	124,000	—	—	—	—	0.50
1996 Sets only	180,000	—	—	—	—	0.50
1997 Sets only	180,000	—	—	—	—	0.50
1998 Sets only	180,000	—	—	—	—	0.50
1999 Sets only	130,000	—	—	—	—	0.50
2000 Sets only	150,000	—	—	—	—	0.50

KM# 100a 10 CENTS

3.05 g., 0.925 Silver 0.0907 oz. ASW, 18.5 mm. **Obv:** National arms **Rev:** Star Jasmine plant **Edge:** Reeded

Date	Mintage	VF20	XF40	MS60	MS63	MS65
1992 sm	15,000	PF65 3.25				
1993 sm	15,000	PF65 3.25				
1994 sm	10,000	PF65 3.25				
1995 sm	10,000	PF65 3.25				
1996 sm	16,800	PF65 3.25				
1997 sm	18,000	PF65 3.25				
1998 sm	9,200	PF65 3.25				
1999 sm	9,200	PF65 3.25				
2000 sm	8,900	PF65 3.25				

KM# 4 20 CENTS

5.66 g., Copper-Nickel, 23.6 mm. **Obv:** Value and date **Rev:** Swordfish **Edge:** Reeded

Date	Mintage	VF20	XF40	MS60	MS63	MS65
1967	36,508,000	0.15	0.35	0.75	1.50	2.50
1967	2,000	PF63 7.00	PF65 9.00			
1968	10,950,000	0.15	0.35	0.75	1.50	2.50
1968	5,000	PF63 6.00	PF65 8.00			
1969	8,474,000	0.15	0.35	0.75	1.50	2.50
1969	3,000	PF63 30.00	PF65 35.00			
1970	3,290,000	0.15	0.30	0.80	1.50	2.00
1971	1,732,000	0.15	0.70	2.00	3.00	3.50
1972	9,120,000	0.15	0.30	0.80	1.50	1.75
1972	749	PF63 70.00	PF65 80.00			
1973	8,853,000	0.15	0.30	0.80	1.50	1.75
1973	1,000	PF63 17.50	PF65 20.00			
1974	4,587,000	0.15	0.30	0.75	1.50	1.75
1974	1,500	PF63 12.50	PF65 15.00			
1975	1,576,000	0.35	1.20	2.00	2.50	3.00
1975	3,000	PF63 6.50	PF65 9.00			
1976	19,795,000	0.20	0.50	0.85	1.50	1.75
1976 sm	3,500	PF63 6.00	PF65 8.00			
1977	7,114,000	0.15	0.50	0.85	1.50	1.75
1977 sm	3,500	PF63 6.00	PF65 8.00			
1978	4,505,000	0.15	0.50	0.85	1.50	1.75
1978 sm	4,000	PF63 6.00	PF65 8.00			
1979	14,930,000	0.15	0.50	0.85	1.50	1.75
1979 sm	3,500	PF63 6.00	PF65 8.00			
1980	27,973,000	—	0.25	0.60	1.50	1.75
1980 sm	14,000	PF63 5.00	PF65 7.00			
1981	47,107,000	—	0.25	0.60	1.50	1.75
1982	25,394,000	—	0.25	0.60	1.50	1.75
1983	6,574,000	—	0.25	0.60	1.50	1.75
1984	9,450,000	—	0.25	0.60	1.50	1.75
1985 Sets only	148,424	—	—	—	—	2.00

KM# 4a 20 CENTS

6.51 g., 0.925 Silver 0.1936 oz. ASW, 23.6 mm. **Obv:** Value and date **Rev:** Swordfish

Date	Mintage	VF20	XF40	MS60	MS63	MS65
1981 sm	30,000	PF65 6.50				
1982 sm	20,000	PF65 6.50				
1983 sm	15,000	PF65 6.50				
1984 sm	15,000	PF65 6.50				

KM# 52 20 CENTS

4.50 g., Copper-Nickel, 21.36 mm. **Obv:** Arms with supporters **Rev:** Powder-puff plant above value

Date	Mintage	VF20	XF40	MS60	MS63	MS65
1985	26,128,424	—	0.20	0.50	1.00	1.25
1986	47,680,000	—	0.20	0.50	1.00	1.25
1987	80,130,000	—	0.20	0.50	1.00	1.25
1988	35,903,000	—	0.20	0.50	1.00	1.25
1989	51,990,000	—	0.20	0.50	1.00	1.25
1990	59,058,000	—	0.20	0.50	1.00	1.25
1991	60,070,000	—	0.20	0.50	1.00	1.25

KM# 52a 20 CENTS

5.24 g., 0.925 Silver 0.1558 oz. ASW, 23.36 mm. **Obv:** Arms with supporters **Rev:** Powder puff plant above value

Date	Mintage	VF20	XF40	MS60	MS63	MS65
1985 sm	20,000	PF65 5.50				
1986 sm	15,000	PF65 5.50				
1987 sm	15,000	PF65 5.50				
1988 sm	15,000	PF65 5.50				
1989 sm	15,000	PF65 5.50				
1990 sm	15,000	PF65 5.50				
1991 sm	15,000	PF65 5.50				

KM# 101 20 CENTS

4.50 g., Copper-Nickel, 21.36 mm. **Obv:** National arms **Rev:** Powder-puff plant above value **Edge:** Reeded **Note:** Similar to KM#52 but motto ribbon on arms curves down at center.

Date	Mintage	VF20	XF40	MS60	MS63	MS65
1992 Sets only	55,000	—	—	—	—	1.50
1993	24,998,000	—	—	0.50	0.70	1.00
1994 Sets only	100,200	—	—	—	—	1.50
1995 Sets only	124,000	—	—	—	—	1.50
1996	45,180,000	—	—	0.50	0.70	1.00
1997	90,180,000	—	—	0.50	0.70	1.00
1998 Sets only	180,000	—	—	—	—	1.25
1999 Sets only	130,000	—	—	—	—	1.25
2000 Sets only	150,000	—	—	—	—	1.25

KM# 101a 20 CENTS

5.24 g., 0.925 Silver 0.1558 oz. ASW, 21.36 mm. **Obv:** National arms **Rev:** Powder puff plant above value **Edge:** Reeded

Date	Mintage	VF20	XF40	MS60	MS63	MS65
1992 sm	15,000	PF65 5.50				
1993 sm	15,000	PF65 5.50				
1994 sm	10,000	PF65 5.50				
1995 sm	10,000	PF65 5.50				
1996 sm	16,800	PF65 5.50				
1997 sm	18,000	PF65 5.50				
1998 sm	9,200	PF65 5.50				
1999 sm	9,200	PF65 5.50				
2000 sm	8,900	PF65 5.50				

KM# 5 50 CENTS

9.33 g., Copper-Nickel, 27.76 mm. **Obv:** Value and date **Rev:** Lion fish **Edge:** Reeded

Date	Mintage	VF20	XF40	MS60	MS63	MS65
1967	11,008,000	0.30	0.65	2.00	3.00	6.00
1967	2,000	PF63 6.00	PF65 8.00			
1968	3,205,000	0.30	0.80	2.00	3.00	6.00
1968	5,000	PF63 5.00	PF65 7.00			
1969	2,022,000	0.30	1.00	2.00	3.00	6.00
1969	3,000	PF63 15.00	PF65 20.00			
1970	3,142,000	0.30	0.65	2.00	3.00	5.00
1971	3,933,000	0.30	0.65	1.75	2.00	2.50
1972	5,440,000	0.30	0.65	1.65	1.85	2.25
1972	749	PF63 45.00	PF65 50.00			
1973	4,489,000	0.30	0.60	1.10	1.50	1.75
1973	1,000	PF63 15.00	PF65 20.00			
1974	11,570,000	—	0.60	1.10	1.50	1.75
1974	1,500	PF63 10.00	PF65 15.00			
1975	1,462,000	0.60	2.00	3.00	4.00	5.00
1975	3,000	PF63 6.00	PF65 8.00			
1976	5,763,000	0.30	0.65	1.20	1.75	2.00
1976 sm	3,500	PF63 5.00	PF65 7.00			
1977	6,993,000	—	0.65	1.20	1.75	2.00
1977 sm	3,500	PF63 5.00	PF65 7.00			
1978	3,989,000	—	0.65	1.20	1.75	2.00
1978 sm	4,000	PF63 5.00	PF65 7.00			
1979	8,526,000	—	0.65	1.20	1.75	2.00
1979 sm	3,500	PF63 5.00	PF65 7.00			
1980	14,787,000	—	0.65	1.20	1.75	2.00
1980 sm	14,000	PF63 5.00	PF65 7.00			
1981	29,652,000	—	0.60	1.10	1.75	2.00
1982	13,916,000	—	0.60	1.10	1.75	2.00
1983	4,632,000	—	0.85	1.50	1.85	2.25
1984	3,818,000	—	0.85	1.50	1.85	2.25
1985 Sets only	148,424	—	—	—	—	2.50

KM# 5a 50 CENTS

10.82 g., 0.925 Silver 0.3218 oz. ASW, 27.75 mm. **Obv:** Value and date **Rev:** Lion fish

Date	Mintage	VF20	XF40	MS60	MS63	MS65
1981 sm	30,000	PF65 11.00				
1982 sm	20,000	PF65 11.00				
1983 sm	15,000	PF65 11.00				
1984 sm	15,000	PF65 11.00				

KM# 53.1 50 CENTS

7.29 g., Copper-Nickel, 24.66 mm. **Obv:** Arms with supporters within designed circle **Rev:** Yellow Allamanda plant above value **Edge:** Reeded

Date	Mintage	VF20	XF40	MS60	MS63	MS65
1985	15,108,424	—	0.60	1.10	1.35	1.65
1986	15,142,000	—	0.60	1.10	1.35	1.65
1987	30,120,000	—	0.60	1.10	1.35	1.65
1988	25,120,000	—	0.60	1.10	1.35	1.65

KM# 53.1a 50 CENTS

8.56 g., 0.925 Silver 0.2546 oz. ASW, 24.66 mm. **Obv:** Arms with supporters within designed circle **Rev:** Yellow Allamanda plant above value

Date	Mintage	VF20	XF40	MS60	MS63	MS65
1985 sm	20,000	PF65 9.00				
1986 sm	15,000	PF65 9.00				
1987 sm	15,000	PF65 9.00				
1988 sm	15,000	PF65 9.00				

KM# 53.2 50 CENTS

7.29 g., Copper-Nickel, 24.66 mm. **Obv:** Arms with supporters **Rev:** Yellow Allamanda plant above value **Edge Lettering:** REPUBLIC OF SINGAPORE (lion's head)

Date	Mintage	VF20	XF40	MS60	MS63	MS65
1989	20,146,000	—	0.45	0.85	1.75	2.00
1990	19,840,000	—	0.45	0.75	1.50	1.75
1991	20,016,000	—	0.45	0.75	1.50	1.75

KM# 53.2a 50 CENTS

8.56 g., 0.925 Silver 0.2546 oz. ASW, 24.66 mm. **Obv:** Arms with supporters **Rev:** Yellow Allamanda plant above value

Date	Mintage	VF20	XF40	MS60	MS63	MS65
1989 sm	15,000	PF65 9.00				
1990 sm	15,000	PF65 9.00				
1991 sm	15,000	PF65 9.00				

KM# 102 50 CENTS

7.29 g., Copper-Nickel, 24.66 mm. **Obv:** National arms **Rev:** Yellow Allamanda plant above value **Edge Lettering:** REPUBLIC OF SINGAPORE (lion's head) **Note:** Similar to KM#53 but motto ribbon on arms curves down at center.

Date	Mintage	VF20	XF40	MS60	MS63	MS65
1992 Sets only	55,000	—	—	—	—	1.50
1993	4,878,000	—	—	0.75	1.00	1.25
1994 Sets only	100,200	—	—	—	—	1.50
1995	49,564,000	—	—	0.75	1.00	1.25
1996 Sets only	180,000	—	—	—	—	1.50
1997	30,180,000	—	—	0.75	1.00	1.25
1998 Sets only	180,000	—	—	—	—	1.50
1999 Sets only	130,000	—	—	—	—	1.50
2000 Sets only	150,000	—	—	—	—	1.50

KM# 102a 50 CENTS

8.56 g., 0.925 Silver 0.2546 oz. ASW, 24.66 mm. **Obv:** National arms **Rev:** Yellow Allamanda plant above value

Date	Mintage	VF20	XF40	MS60	MS63	MS65
1992 sm	15,000	PF65 9.00				
1993 sm	15,000	PF65 9.00				
1994 sm	10,000	PF65 9.00				
1995 sm	10,000	PF65 9.00				
1996 sm	16,800	PF65 9.00				
1997 sm	18,000	PF65 9.00				
1998 sm	9,200	PF65 9.00				
1999 sm	9,200	PF65 9.00				
2000 sm	8,900	PF65 9.00				

KM# 6 DOLLAR

16.85 g., Copper-Nickel, 33.32 mm. **Obv:** Value and date **Rev:** Statue of Singapore lion flanked by stalks of paddy **Edge:** Reeded

Date	Mintage	VF20	XF40	MS60	MS63	MS65
1967	3,008,000	1.00	1.50	2.50	4.00	6.00
1967	2,000	PF63 25.00	PF65 30.00			
1968	2,210,000	1.00	1.50	2.50	4.00	6.00
1968	5,000	PF63 10.00	PF65 12.00			
1969	1,885,000	1.00	1.75	3.00	4.50	7.00
1969	3,000	PF63 35.00	PF65 40.00			
1970	600,000	1.00	1.75	3.00	4.50	7.00
1971	900,000	1.00	1.75	3.00	4.50	7.00
1972	471,000	1.00	2.00	4.00	6.00	9.00
1972	749	PF63 75.00	PF65 85.00			
1973	356,000	1.00	2.00	3.50	5.00	8.00
1973	1,000	PF63 25.00	PF65 30.00			
1974	372,000	1.00	2.00	3.50	5.00	8.00
1974	1,500	PF63 25.00	PF65 30.00			
1975	460,000	1.00	2.00	3.50	5.00	8.00
1975	3,000	PF63 10.00	PF65 12.00			
1976	200,000	2.00	3.00	5.00	7.00	10.00
1976 sm	3,500	PF63 7.00	PF65 9.00			
1977	172,000	2.00	4.00	7.00	9.00	12.00
1977 sm	3,500	PF63 7.00	PF65 9.00			
1978	92,000	5.00	8.00	10.00	15.00	20.00
1978 sm	4,000	PF63 7.00	PF65 9.00			
1979	165,000	—	4.00	7.00	9.00	12.00
1979 sm	3,500	PF63 7.00	PF65 9.00			
1980	236,000	—	2.25	3.50	5.00	7.00
1980 sm	14,000	PF63 7.00	PF65 9.00			
1981	1,340,000	—	2.25	3.50	5.00	7.00
1982	1,240,000	—	2.25	3.50	5.00	7.00
1983	251,000	—	3.00	5.00	7.00	9.00
1984	330,000	—	3.00	4.50	6.00	8.00
1985 Sets only	148,424	—	—	—	—	10.00

KM# 6a DOLLAR

18.05 g., 0.925 Silver 0.5368 oz. ASW, 33.32 mm. **Obv:** Value and date **Rev:** Statue flanked by sprigs

Date	Mintage	VF20	XF40	MS60	MS63	MS65
1975	3,000	PF65 120				
1976 sm	10,000	PF65 55.00				
1977 sm	10,000	PF65 55.00				
1978 sm	10,000	PF65 75.00				
1979 sm	8,000	PF65 65.00				
1980 sm	15,000	PF65 55.00				
1981 sm	30,000	PF65 20.00				
1982 sm	20,000	PF65 22.00				
1983 sm	15,000	PF65 25.00				
1984 sm	15,000	PF65 25.00				

KM# 54 DOLLAR

10.03 g., Copper-Nickel, 26.5 mm. **Obv:** Arms with supporters **Rev:** Periwinkle flower

Date	Mintage	VF20	XF40	MS60	MS63	MS65
1985	—	—	—	1.75	2.50	3.50
1986 Sets only	120,000	—	—	—	—	4.00
1987 Sets only	120,000	—	—	—	—	4.00

KM# 54a DOLLAR

9.97 g., 0.925 Silver 0.2965 oz. ASW, 26.5 mm. **Obv:** Arms with supporters **Rev:** Periwinkle flower

Date	Mintage	VF20	XF40	MS60	MS63	MS65
1985 sm	20,000	PF65 10.00				
1986 sm	15,000	PF65 10.00				

KM# 54b DOLLAR

6.30 g., Aluminum-Bronze, 22.4 mm. **Obv:** Arms with supporters **Rev:** Periwinkle flower **Edge Lettering:** REPUBLIC OF SINGAPORE (lion's head)

Date	Mintage	VF20	XF40	MS60	MS63	MS65
1987	21,772,000	—	0.75	1.50	2.25	3.00
1988	59,452,000	—	0.75	1.50	2.25	3.00
1989	62,686,000	—	0.75	1.50	2.25	3.00
1990	37,708,000	—	0.75	1.50	2.25	3.00
1991 Sets only	70,000	—	—	—	—	3.50

KM# 54c DOLLAR

8.43 g., 0.925 Silver 0.2506 oz. ASW, 22.4 mm. **Obv:** Arms with supporters **Rev:** Periwinkle flower

Date	Mintage	VF20	XF40	MS60	MS63	MS65
1987 sm	15,000	PF65 9.00				
1988	15,000	PF65 9.00				
1989	15,000	PF65 9.00				
1990	15,000	PF65 9.00				
1991	15,000	PF65 9.00				

KM# 103 DOLLAR

6.30 g., Aluminum-Bronze, 22.4 mm. **Obv:** National arms **Rev:** Periwinkle flower **Edge:** Reeded **Note:** Similar to KM#54 but motto ribbon on arms curves down at center.

Date	Mintage	VF20	XF40	MS60	MS63	MS65
1992 Sets only	55,000	—	—	—	—	3.50
1993 Sets only	—	—	—	—	—	3.50
1994	5,108,200	—	—	1.50	2.25	3.00
1995	65,124,000	—	—	1.50	2.25	3.00
1996 Sets only	180,000	—	—	—	—	3.50
1997	130,036,000	—	—	1.50	2.25	3.00
1998	41,060,000	—	—	1.50	2.25	3.00
1999	38,460,000	—	—	1.50	2.25	3.00
2000	35,840,000	—	—	1.50	2.25	3.00

KM# 103a DOLLAR

8.05 g., 0.925 Silver 0.2394 oz. ASW, 22.4 mm. **Obv:** National arms **Rev:** Periwinkle flower

Date	Mintage	VF20	XF40	MS60	MS63	MS65
1992 sm	15,000	PF65 8.50				
1993 sm	15,000	PF65 8.50				
1994 sm	10,000	PF65 8.50				
1995 sm	10,000	PF65 8.50				
1996 sm	16,800	PF65 8.50				
1997 sm	18,000	PF65 8.50				
1998 sm	9,200	PF65 8.50				
1999 sm	9,200	PF65 8.50				
2000 sm	8,900	PF65 8.50				

KM# 29 2 DOLLARS

7.78 g., 0.999 Gold 0.2497 oz. AGW **Obv:** National arms **Rev:** Qilin

Date	Mintage	VF20	XF40	MS60	MS63	MS65
1983	20,000	—	—	—	—	355
1984	10,000	—	—	—	—	355

KM# 156 2 DOLLARS

20.00 g., 0.925 Silver 0.5948 oz. ASW **Series:** UNICEF **Obv:** Arms with supporters **Rev:** Children using computer below UNICEF logo within circle

Date	Mintage	VF20	XF40	MS60	MS63	MS65
1997	3,002	PF65 50.00				

KM# 10 5 DOLLARS

25.00 g., 0.500 Silver 0.4019 oz. ASW, 38 mm. **Subject:** 7th Southeast Asia Peninsular Games **Obv:** Arms with supporters **Rev:** Games logo above stadium

Date	Mintage	VF20	XF40	MS60	MS63	MS65
1973	250,000	—	—	—	20.00	30.00
1973	5,000	PF65 135				

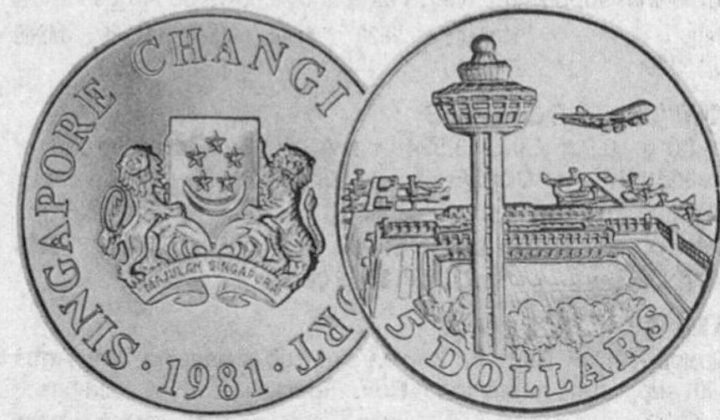

KM# 19 5 DOLLARS

Copper-Nickel, 33.5 mm. **Obv:** Arms with supporters **Rev:** Changi Airport **Edge:** Reeded

Date	Mintage	VF20	XF40	MS60	MS63	MS65
1981	220,000	—	—	4.00	8.00	—

KM# 19a 5 DOLLARS
18.05 g., 0.925 Silver 0.5368 oz. ASW, 33.5 mm. **Obv:** Arms with supporters **Rev:** Changi airport

Date	Mintage	VF20	XF40	MS60	MS63	MS65
1981 sm	20,000	PF65 45.00				

KM# 22 5 DOLLARS
Copper-Nickel, 33.5 mm. **Obv:** Arms with supporters **Rev:** Benjamin Shears Bridge

Date	Mintage	VF20	XF40	MS60	MS63	MS65
1982	260,000	—	—	5.00	10.00	—

KM# 22a 5 DOLLARS
18.05 g., 0.925 Silver 0.5368 oz. ASW, 33.5 mm. **Obv:** Arms with supporters **Rev:** Benjamin Shears Bridge

Date	Mintage	VF20	XF40	MS60	MS63	MS65
1982 sm	20,000	PF65 45.00				

KM# 25 5 DOLLARS
Copper-Nickel **Subject:** 12th SEA Games **Obv:** Arms with supporters **Rev:** Games logo above waves within circle, athletes around outer top half

Date	Mintage	VF20	XF40	MS60	MS63	MS65
1983	270,000	—	—	5.00	10.00	—

KM# 25a 5 DOLLARS
20.00 g., 0.925 Silver 0.5948 oz. ASW **Obv:** Arms with supporters **Rev:** Games logo above waves within circle, athletes around outer top half

Date	Mintage	VF20	XF40	MS60	MS63	MS65
1983 sm	20,000	PF65 35.00				

KM# 32 5 DOLLARS
Copper-Nickel **Subject:** 25 Years of Nation - Building **Obv:** Arms with supporters **Rev:** Value above flowered sprigs

Date	Mintage	VF20	XF40	MS60	MS63	MS65
ND-1984	270,000	—	—	5.00	10.00	—

KM# 32a 5 DOLLARS
20.00 g., 0.925 Silver 0.5948 oz. ASW **Subject:** 25 Years of Nation - Building **Obv:** Arms with supporters **Rev:** Value above flower sprigs

Date	Mintage	VF20	XF40	MS60	MS63	MS65
ND-1984 sm	20,000	PF65 55.00				

KM# 48 5 DOLLARS
Copper-Nickel **Subject:** 25 Years of Public Housing **Obv:** Arms with supporters and legend **Rev:** Figures in front of buildings

Date	Mintage	VF20	XF40	MS60	MS63	MS65
ND(1985)	117,000	—	—	5.00	10.00	—

KM# 48a 5 DOLLARS
20.00 g., 0.925 Silver 0.5948 oz. ASW **Obv:** Arms with supporters and legend **Rev:** Figures in front of buildings

Date	Mintage	VF20	XF40	MS60	MS63	MS65
ND(1985) sm	20,000	PF65 55.00				

KM# 68 5 DOLLARS
20.00 g., Copper-Nickel, 38.6 mm. **Subject:** 100th Anniversary of National Museum **Obv:** Arms with supporters **Rev:** Museum building

Date	Mintage	VF20	XF40	MS60	MS63	MS65
ND-1987	70,000	—	—	—	10.00	—

KM# 68a 5 DOLLARS
20.00 g., 0.925 Silver 0.5948 oz. ASW, 38.6 mm. **Subject:** 100th Anniversary of National Museum **Obv:** Arms with supporters **Rev:** Museum building

Date	Mintage	VF20	XF40	MS60	MS63	MS65
ND-1987 sm	25,000	PF65 45.00				

KM# 70 5 DOLLARS
Copper-Nickel **Subject:** 100th Anniversary of Singapore Fire Brigade **Obv:** Arms with supporters **Rev:** Pair of horses pulling wagon with equipment within circle

Date	Mintage	VF20	XF40	MS60	MS63	MS65
ND-1988	50,000	—	—	—	13.50	15.00

KM# 70a 5 DOLLARS
20.00 g., 0.925 Silver 0.5948 oz. ASW **Subject:** 100th Anniversary of Singapore Fire Brigade **Obv:** Arms with supporters **Rev:** Pair of horses pulling wagon with equipment within circle

Date	Mintage	VF20	XF40	MS60	MS63	MS65
ND-1988 sm	25,000	PF65 45.00				

KM# 74 5 DOLLARS
Copper-Nickel, 33.5 mm. **Subject:** Rapid Transit System **Obv:** Arms with supporters **Rev:** Train in city **Edge:** Reeded

Date	Mintage	VF20	XF40	MS60	MS63	MS65
1989	60,000	—	—	—	10.00	12.00

KM# 74a 5 DOLLARS
20.00 g., 0.925 Silver 0.5948 oz. ASW **Subject:** Rapid Transit System **Obv:** National arms **Rev:** Train in city

Date	Mintage	VF20	XF40	MS60	MS63	MS65
1989 sm	30,000	PF65 45.00				

KM# 77 5 DOLLARS
20.00 g., 0.925 Silver 0.5948 oz. ASW, 38.7 mm. **Series:** Save the Children Fund **Obv:** Arms with supporters **Rev:** Children, kayak, palm tree and value **Edge:** Reeded

Date	Mintage	VF20	XF40	MS60	MS63	MS65
1989 sm	20,000	PF65 42.50				

KM# 94 5 DOLLARS
Aluminum-Bronze **Subject:** 25th Anniversary of Independence **Obv:** Arms with supporters **Rev:** City view from water

Date	Mintage	VF20	XF40	MS60	MS63	MS65
1990	1,000,000	—	—	—	—	7.00

KM# 86 5 DOLLARS
Copper-Nickel **Subject:** Civil Defense **Obv:** Arms with supporters **Rev:** Working figures within circle

Date	Mintage	VF20	XF40	MS60	MS63	MS65
1991	55,000	—	—	—	—	9.00
1991	10,000	PF65 40.00				

KM# 86a 5 DOLLARS
20.00 g., 0.925 Silver 0.5948 oz. ASW **Subject:** Civil Defense **Obv:** Arms with supporters **Rev:** Working figures within circle

Date	Mintage	VF20	XF40	MS60	MS63	MS65
1991	20,000	PF65 40.00				

KM# 104.1 5 DOLLARS
6.70 g., Bi-Metallic Aluminum-Bronze center in Copper-Nickel ring, 23.3 mm. **Obv:** National arms **Rev:** Vanda Miss Joaquim flower and value within beaded circle **Shape:** Scalloped

Date	Mintage	VF20	XF40	MS60	MS63	MS65
1992 Mint sets only	55,000	—	—	—	—	10.00
1994 Mint sets only	100,200	—	—	—	—	10.00
1995 Mint sets only	124,000	—	—	—	—	10.00
1996 Mint sets only	180,000	—	—	—	—	10.00
1997 Mint sets only	180,000	—	—	—	—	10.00
1998 Mint sets only	180,000	—	—	—	—	10.00

KM# 104.1a 5 DOLLARS

8.25 g., 0.925 Silver 0.2454 oz. ASW, 23.3 mm. **Obv:** National arms **Rev:** Vanda Miss Joaquim flower and value within beaded circle

Date	Mintage	VF20	XF40	MS60	MS63	MS65
1992 sm	30,000	PF65 15.00				
1994 sm	10,000	PF65 15.00				
1995 sm	10,000	PF65 15.00				
1996 sm	16,800	PF65 15.00				
1997 sm	18,000	PF65 15.00				
1998 sm	9,200	PF65 15.00				

KM# 115 5 DOLLARS

Copper-Nickel **Subject:** XVII Sea Games **Obv:** Arms with supporters **Rev:** Martial arts

Date	Mintage	VF20	XF40	MS60	MS63	MS65
1993	23,000	—	—	—	—	9.00
1993	2,000	PF65 25.00				

KM# 115a 5 DOLLARS

20.00 g., 0.925 Silver 0.5948 oz. ASW **Subject:** XVII Sea Games **Obv:** Arms with supporters **Rev:** Martial arts

Date	Mintage	VF20	XF40	MS60	MS63	MS65
1993	10,000	PF65 52.50				

KM# 124 5 DOLLARS

Copper-Nickel **Subject:** Year of the Family **Obv:** Arms with supporters **Rev:** Stylized family and value

Date	Mintage	VF20	XF40	MS60	MS63	MS65
1994	20,000	—	—	—	12.00	14.00

KM# 124a 5 DOLLARS

20.00 g., 0.925 Silver 0.5948 oz. ASW **Subject:** Year of the Family **Obv:** Arms with supporters **Rev:** Stylized family and value

Date	Mintage	VF20	XF40	MS60	MS63	MS65
1994	40,000	PF65 52.50				

KM# 138 5 DOLLARS

Bi-Metallic Aluminum-Bronze center in Copper-Nickel ring **Series:** 50th Anniversary - United Nations **Obv:** Arms with supporters within beaded circle **Rev:** UN logo within artistic design **Shape:** Scalloped

Date	Mintage	VF20	XF40	MS60	MS63	MS65
1995	500,000	—	—	—	12.00	14.00

KM# 139 5 DOLLARS

20.00 g., 0.925 Silver 0.5948 oz. ASW **Series:** 50th Anniversary - United Nations **Obv:** Arms with supporters **Rev:** UN logo within artistic design

Date	Mintage	VF20	XF40	MS60	MS63	MS65
1995	9,000	PF65 45.00				

KM# 150 5 DOLLARS

20.00 g., Copper-Nickel, 38.7 mm. **Subject:** 30th Anniversary - Singapore's Independence **Obv:** Arms with supporters **Rev:** Globe on map

Date	Mintage	VF20	XF40	MS60	MS63	MS65
1995	20,000	—	—	—	12.00	15.00

KM# 150a 5 DOLLARS

20.00 g., 0.925 Silver 0.5948 oz. ASW **Subject:** 30th Anniversary - Singapore's Independence **Obv:** Arms with supporters **Rev:** Globe on map

Date	Mintage	VF20	XF40	MS60	MS63	MS65
1995 sm	8,000	PF65 50.00				

KM# 149 5 DOLLARS

Copper-Nickel **Subject:** World Trade Organization Conference **Obv:** Arms with supporters **Rev:** Value within stylized lion head

Date	Mintage	VF20	XF40	MS60	MS63	MS65
1996	23,800	—	—	—	8.00	—
1996 Proof	—	—	—	—	—	—

KM# 149a 5 DOLLARS

20.00 g., 0.925 Silver 0.5948 oz. ASW **Subject:** World Trade Organization Conference **Obv:** Arms with supporters with mintmark **Rev:** Value within stylized lion head

Date	Mintage	VF20	XF40	MS60	MS63	MS65
1996 sm	16,800	PF65 42.50				

KM# 151 5 DOLLARS

Copper-Nickel **Subject:** 50th Anniversary - Singapore Airlines **Obv:** Arms with supporters with no mint mark **Rev:** Plane in front of numeral 50

Date	Mintage	VF20	XF40	MS60	MS63	MS65
1997	24,688	—	—	—	17.00	—
1997 Proof	18,000	—	—	—	—	—

KM# 151a 5 DOLLARS

20.00 g., 0.925 Silver 0.5948 oz. ASW **Subject:** 50th Anniversary - Singapore Airlines **Obv:** Arms with supporters with mint mark **Rev:** Plane in front of numeral 50

Date	Mintage	VF20	XF40	MS60	MS63	MS65
1997 sm	18,000	PF65 50.00				

KM# 157 5 DOLLARS

7.78 g., 0.9999 Gold 0.250 oz. AGW, 22 mm. **Series:** UNICEF **Obv:** Arms with supporters **Rev:** Children using computer

Date	Mintage	VF20	XF40	MS60	MS63	MS65
1997 sm	10,000	PF65 425				

KM# 304 5 DOLLARS

7.77 g., 0.999 Gold 0.2496 oz. AGW, 22 mm. **Subject:** UNICEF **Obv:** Arms **Rev:** Children at computer

Date	Mintage	VF20	XF40	MS60	MS63	MS65
1997	551	PF65 450				

KM# 163 5 DOLLARS

20.00 g., Copper-Nickel, 38.7 mm. **Subject:** Charity Work in Singapore **Obv:** Arms with supporters **Rev:** Two hands holding heart-shaped fruit

Date	Mintage	VF20	XF40	MS60	MS63	MS65
1998	9,200	—	—	—	22.00	—

KM# 163a 5 DOLLARS

20.00 g., 0.925 Silver 0.5948 oz. ASW with .008 AGW Gold insert. **Subject:** Charity Work in Singapore **Obv:** Arms with supporters **Rev:** Two hands holding heart-shaped fruit

Date	Mintage	VF20	XF40	MS60	MS63	MS65
1998 sm	12,000	PF65 75.00				

KM# 104.2 5 DOLLARS

6.70 g., Bi-Metallic Aluminumn-Bronze center in Copper-Nickel ring, 23.3 mm. **Obv:** National arms, date and BCCS logo **Rev:** Canda Miss Joaquim flower above value **Edge:** Plain **Note:** Date in hologram

Date	Mintage	VF20	XF40	MS60	MS63	MS65
1999	430,000	—	—	—	—	12.00
2000 Sets only	150,000	—	—	—	—	12.00

KM# 104.2a 5 DOLLARS

8.25 g., 0.925 Silver 0.2454 oz. ASW, 23.3 mm. **Obv:** National arms, date and BCCS logo **Rev:** Vanda Miss Joaquim flower above value **Edge:** Plain

Date	Mintage	VF20	XF40	MS60	MS63	MS65
1999 sm	9,200	PF65 15.00				
2000 sm	8,900	PF65 15.00				

KM# 173 5 DOLLARS

20.00 g., Copper-Nickel, 38.7 mm. **Subject:** Parliament **Obv:** Arms with supporters **Rev:** Parliament building **Edge:** Reeded

Date	Mintage	VF20	XF40	MS60	MS63	MS65
1999	10,000	PF65 50.00				
1999	10,000	—	—	—	20.00	—

KM# 173a 5 DOLLARS

20.00 g., 0.925 Silver 0.5948 oz. ASW **Obv:** Arms with supporters **Rev:** Parliament building

Date	Mintage	VF20	XF40	MS60	MS63	MS65
1999 sm	10,000	PF65 45.00				

KM# 171 5 DOLLARS

Bi-Metallic Aluminum-Bronze center in Copper-Nickel ring **Obv:** Arms with supporters above latent date within beaded circle **Rev:** Millennium design **Edge:** Scalloped

Date	Mintage	VF20	XF40	MS60	MS63	MS65
2000	406,000	—	—	—	6.50	10.00

KM# 172 5 DOLLARS

31.10 g., 0.999 Gold 0.999 oz. AGW **Subject:** Millennium **Obv:** Arms with supporters above latent date within beaded circle **Rev:** Millennium design **Edge:** Scalloped

Date	Mintage	VF20	XF40	MS60	MS63	MS65
2000 sm	3,000	PF65 1,750				

KM# 9.1 10 DOLLARS
31.10 g., 0.900 Silver 0.8999 oz. ASW, 40 mm. **Obv:** Arms with supporters **Obv. Legend:** SINGAPORE inverted **Rev:** Hawk descending

Date	Mintage	VF20	XF40	MS60	MS63	MS65
1972	80,000	—	—	—	27.50	30.00
1972	3,000	PF65 115				

KM# 9.2 10 DOLLARS
31.10 g., 0.900 Silver 0.8999 oz. ASW, 40 mm. **Obv:** Arms with supporters **Rev:** Hawk descending

Date	Mintage	VF20	XF40	MS60	MS63	MS65
1973	80,000	—	—	—	27.50	30.00
1973	5,000	PF65 100				

KM# 9.2a 10 DOLLARS
31.10 g., 0.500 Silver 0.4999 oz. ASW, 40 mm. **Obv:** Arms with supporters **Rev:** Hawk descending

Date	Mintage	VF20	XF40	MS60	MS63	MS65
1974	100,000	—	—	—	17.50	20.00
1974	6,000	PF65 65.00				

KM# 11 10 DOLLARS
31.10 g., 0.500 Silver 0.4999 oz. ASW, 40 mm. **Subject:** 10th Anniversary of Independence **Obv:** Arms with supporters **Rev:** Value above ship

Date	Mintage	VF20	XF40	MS60	MS63	MS65
ND-1975	200,000	—	—	—	16.00	18.00
ND-1975	10,000	PF65 40.00				

KM# 15 10 DOLLARS
31.10 g., 0.500 Silver 0.4999 oz. ASW, 40 mm. **Subject:** 10th Anniversary of Independence **Obv:** Arms with supporters **Rev:** Ship in port

Date	Mintage	VF20	XF40	MS60	MS63	MS65
1976	150,000	—	—	—	16.00	18.00
1976 sm	10,000	PF65 40.00				
1977	150,000	—	—	—	16.00	18.00
1977 sm	10,000	PF65 40.00				

KM# 16 10 DOLLARS
31.10 g., 0.500 Silver 0.4999 oz. ASW **Subject:** ASEAN 10th Anniversary **Obv:** Arms with supporters **Rev:** Cluster of hands holding circled map

Date	Mintage	VF20	XF40	MS60	MS63	MS65
ND-1977	200,000	—	—	—	16.00	18.00
ND-1977 sm	10,000	PF65 60.00				

KM# 17.1 10 DOLLARS
31.10 g., 0.500 Silver 0.4999 oz. ASW, 40.7 mm. **Obv:** Arms with supporters **Rev:** Communications Satellites

Date	Mintage	VF20	XF40	MS60	MS63	MS65
1978	167,000	—	—	—	16.00	18.00
1978 sm	10,000	PF65 40.00				
1979	168,000	—	—	—	16.00	18.00
1979 sm	12,500	PF65 40.00				
1980	—	—	—	—	16.00	18.00

KM# 17.1a 10 DOLLARS
28.00 g., Nickel, 40.7 mm. **Obv:** Arms with supporters **Rev:** Communications Satellites

Date	Mintage	VF20	XF40	MS60	MS63	MS65
1980	120,000	—	—	—	13.50	16.50

KM# 17.2 10 DOLLARS
28.00 g., Nickel, 40.7 mm. **Obv:** Arms with supporters **Rev:** Communications Satellites **Note:** Different lettering style than 17.1a. Raised stars and moon in arms, frosted arms.

Date	Mintage	VF20	XF40	MS60	MS63	MS65
1980 sm	29,000	PF65 35.00				

KM# 20 10 DOLLARS
28.00 g., Nickel, 40.7 mm. **Subject:** Year of the Rooster **Obv:** Arms with supporters **Rev:** Rooster within circle, value below, various animals border

Date	Mintage	VF20	XF40	MS60	MS63	MS65
1981	180,000	—	—	—	45.00	55.00

KM# 20a 10 DOLLARS
31.10 g., 0.500 Silver 0.4999 oz. ASW **Obv:** Arms with supporters **Rev:** Rooster within circle, value below, various animals border

Date	Mintage	VF20	XF40	MS60	MS63	MS65
1981 sm	20,000	PF65 150				

KM# 23 10 DOLLARS
28.00 g., Nickel, 40.7 mm. **Subject:** Year of the Dog **Obv:** Arms with supporters **Rev:** Dog within circle, value below, various animals border

Date	Mintage	VF20	XF40	MS60	MS63	MS65
1982	210,000	—	—	—	25.00	40.00

KM# 23a 10 DOLLARS
31.10 g., 0.500 Silver 0.4999 oz. ASW **Obv:** Arms with supporters **Rev:** Dog within circle, value below, various animals border

Date	Mintage	VF20	XF40	MS60	MS63	MS65
1982 sm	20,000	PF65 110				

KM# 26 10 DOLLARS
28.00 g., Nickel, 40.7 mm. **Subject:** Year of the Pig **Obv:** Arms with supporters **Rev:** Pig within circle, value below, various animals border

Date	Mintage	VF20	XF40	MS60	MS63	MS65
1983	307,000	—	—	—	12.00	16.00

KM# 26a 10 DOLLARS
31.10 g., 0.500 Silver 0.4999 oz. ASW **Obv:** Arms with supporters **Rev:** Pig within circle, value below, various animals border

Date	Mintage	VF20	XF40	MS60	MS63	MS65
1983 sm	20,000	PF65 90.00				

KM# 33 10 DOLLARS
28.00 g., Nickel, 40.7 mm. **Subject:** Year of the Rat **Obv:** Arms with supporters **Rev:** Rat within circle, value below, various animals border

Date	Mintage	VF20	XF40	MS60	MS63	MS65
1984	300,000	—	—	—	12.00	16.00

KM# 33a 10 DOLLARS
31.10 g., 0.500 Silver 0.4999 oz. ASW **Obv:** Arms with supporters **Rev:** Rat within circle, value below, various animals border

Date	Mintage	VF20	XF40	MS60	MS63	MS65
1984 sm	20,000	PF65 70.00				

KM# 44 10 DOLLARS

28.00 g., Nickel, 40.7 mm. **Subject:** Year of the Ox **Obv:** Arms with supporters **Rev:** Ox within circle, value below, various animals border

Date	Mintage	VF20	XF40	MS60	MS63	MS65
1985	306,800	—	—	—	12.00	16.00

KM# 44a 10 DOLLARS

31.10 g., 0.500 Silver 0.4999 oz. ASW **Obv:** Arms with supporters **Rev:** Ox within circle, value below, various animals border

Date	Mintage	VF20	XF40	MS60	MS63	MS65
1985 sm	20,000	PF65 80.00				

KM# 59 10 DOLLARS

28.00 g., Nickel, 40.7 mm. **Subject:** Year of the Tiger **Obv:** Arms with supporters **Rev:** Tiger within circle, value below, various animals border

Date	Mintage	VF20	XF40	MS60	MS63	MS65
1986	300,000	—	—	—	12.00	16.00

KM# 59a 10 DOLLARS

31.10 g., 0.500 Silver 0.4999 oz. ASW **Obv:** Arms with supporters **Rev:** Tiger within circle, value below, various animals border

Date	Mintage	VF20	XF40	MS60	MS63	MS65
1986	20,000	PF65 70.00				

KM# 66 10 DOLLARS

28.00 g., Nickel, 40.7 mm. **Subject:** Year of the Rabbit **Obv:** Arms with supporters **Rev:** Rabbit within circle, value below, various animals border

Date	Mintage	VF20	XF40	MS60	MS63	MS65
1987	300,000	—	—	—	12.00	16.00

KM# 66a 10 DOLLARS

31.10 g., 0.500 Silver 0.4999 oz. ASW **Obv:** Arms with supporters **Rev:** Rabbit within circle, value below, various animals border

Date	Mintage	VF20	XF40	MS60	MS63	MS65
1987 sm	25,000	PF65 45.00				

KM# 67 10 DOLLARS

Copper-Nickel **Subject:** Association of Southeast Asian Nations **Obv:** Arms with supporters above 1967-1987 **Rev:** ASEAN logo within legend above value

Date	Mintage	VF20	XF40	MS60	MS63	MS65
ND(1987)	80,000	—	—	—	8.50	12.50

KM# 67a 10 DOLLARS

31.10 g., 0.500 Silver 0.500 oz. ASW **Subject:** Association of Southeast Asian Nations **Obv:** Arms with supporters above 1967-1987 **Rev:** ASEAN logo within legend above value

Date	Mintage	VF20	XF40	MS60	MS63	MS65
1987 sm	25,000	PF65 35.00				

KM# 69 10 DOLLARS

28.00 g., Nickel, 40.7 mm. **Subject:** Year of the Dragon **Obv:** Arms with supporters **Rev:** Dragon within circle, value below, various animals border

Date	Mintage	VF20	XF40	MS60	MS63	MS65
1988	300,000	—	—	—	15.00	20.00

KM# 69a 10 DOLLARS

31.10 g., 0.500 Silver 0.500 oz. ASW **Subject:** Year of the Dragon **Obv:** Arms with supporters **Rev:** Dragon within circle, value below, various animals border

Date	Mintage	VF20	XF40	MS60	MS63	MS65
1988	25,000	PF65 90.00				

KM# 71 10 DOLLARS

28.00 g., Nickel, 40.7 mm. **Subject:** Year of the Snake **Obv:** Arms with supporters **Rev:** Snake within circle, value below, various animals border

Date	Mintage	VF20	XF40	MS60	MS63	MS65
1989	250,000	—	—	—	12.00	16.00

KM# 71a 10 DOLLARS

31.10 g., 0.925 Silver 0.925 oz. ASW **Subject:** Year of the Snake **Obv:** Arms with supporters **Rev:** Snake within circle, value below, various animals border

Date	Mintage	VF20	XF40	MS60	MS63	MS65
1989	25,000	PF65 65.00				

KM# 75 10 DOLLARS

28.00 g., Nickel, 40.7 mm. **Subject:** Year of the Horse **Obv:** Arms with supporters **Rev:** Horse within circle with value and assorted animal border

Date	Mintage	VF20	XF40	MS60	MS63	MS65
1990	330,000	—	—	—	12.00	16.00

KM# 75a 10 DOLLARS

31.10 g., 0.925 Silver 0.925 oz. ASW **Subject:** Year of the Horse **Obv:** Arms with supporters **Rev:** Horse within circle, value below, various animals border

Date	Mintage	VF20	XF40	MS60	MS63	MS65
1990 sm	30,000	PF65 45.00				

KM# 95 10 DOLLARS

31.10 g., 0.925 Silver 0.925 oz. ASW **Subject:** 25th Anniversary of Independence **Obv:** Arms with supporters **Rev:** Stylized numeral 25 above city view and dates with value at right

Date	Mintage	VF20	XF40	MS60	MS63	MS65
1990 sm	50,000	PF65 60.00				

KM# 84 10 DOLLARS

28.00 g., Nickel, 40.7 mm. **Subject:** Year of the Goat **Obv:** Arms with supporters **Rev:** Goat within circle, value below, various animals border

Date	Mintage	VF20	XF40	MS60	MS63	MS65
1991	300,000	—	—	—	12.00	16.00

KM# 84a 10 DOLLARS

31.10 g., 0.925 Silver 0.925 oz. ASW **Subject:** Year of the Goat **Obv:** Arms with supporters **Rev:** Goat within circle, value below, various animals border

Date	Mintage	VF20	XF40	MS60	MS63	MS65
1991 sm	30,000	PF65 45.00				

KM# 92 10 DOLLARS

28.00 g., Nickel, 40.7 mm. **Subject:** Year of the Monkey **Obv:** Arms with supporters **Rev:** Monkey below value **Note:** Similar to 500 Dollars, KM#93.

Date	Mintage	VF20	XF40	MS60	MS63	MS65
1992	300,000	—	—	—	12.00	16.00

KM# 92a 10 DOLLARS

31.10 g., 0.925 Silver 0.925 oz. ASW **Obv:** Arms with supporters **Rev:** Monkey below value

Date	Mintage	VF20	XF40	MS60	MS63	MS65
1992	30,000	PF65 50.00				

KM# 105 10 DOLLARS

0.925 Silver **Subject:** 25th Anniversary - Board of Commissioners of Currency **Obv:** Arms with supporters **Rev:** Stylized dollar sign within circle **Note:** Piefort

Date	Mintage	VF20	XF40	MS60	MS63	MS65
1992	10,800	PF65 75.00				

KM# 113 10 DOLLARS
Copper-Nickel **Subject:** Year of the Rooster **Obv:** Arms with supporters **Rev:** Stylized rooster

Date	Mintage	VF20	XF40	MS60	MS63	MS65
1993 Prooflike	209,000	—	—	—	20.00	25.00

KM# 113a 10 DOLLARS
62.21 g., 0.999 Silver 1.998 oz. ASW **Subject:** Year of the Rooster **Obv:** Arms with supporters **Rev:** Stylized rooster **Note:** Piefort

Date	Mintage	VF20	XF40	MS60	MS63	MS65
1993	40,000	PF65 80.00				

KM# 122 10 DOLLARS
Copper-Nickel **Subject:** Year of the Dog **Obv:** Arms with supporters **Rev:** Stylized dog within designs

Date	Mintage	VF20	XF40	MS60	MS63	MS65
1994 Prooflike	215,000	—	—	—	20.00	25.00

KM# 122a 10 DOLLARS
62.21 g., 0.999 Silver 1.998 oz. ASW Piefort **Subject:** Year of the Dog **Obv:** Arms with supporters **Rev:** Stylized dog within designs

Date	Mintage	VF20	XF40	MS60	MS63	MS65
1994	35,000	PF65 80.00				

KM# 125 10 DOLLARS
Copper-Nickel **Subject:** Year of the Pig **Obv:** Arms with supporters **Rev:** Stylized pig

Date	Mintage	VF20	XF40	MS60	MS63	MS65
1995 Prooflike	210,000	—	—	—	17.50	22.50

KM# 125a 10 DOLLARS
62.21 g., 0.999 Silver 1.998 oz. ASW **Subject:** Year of the Pig **Obv:** Arms with supporters **Rev:** Stylized pig **Note:** Piefort

Date	Mintage	VF20	XF40	MS60	MS63	MS65
1995	35,000	PF65 85.00				

KM# 141 10 DOLLARS
Copper-Nickel **Subject:** Year of the Rat **Obv:** Arms with supporters **Rev:** Stylized rat within designs

Date	Mintage	VF20	XF40	MS60	MS63	MS65
1996 Prooflike	245,000	—	—	—	14.00	18.00

KM# 141a 10 DOLLARS
62.21 g., 0.999 Silver 1.998 oz. ASW **Subject:** Year of the Rat **Obv:** Arms with supporters **Rev:** Stylized rat within designs **Note:** Piefort

Date	Mintage	VF20	XF40	MS60	MS63	MS65
1996	35,000	PF65 85.00				

KM# 153 10 DOLLARS
Copper-Nickel **Subject:** Year of the Ox **Obv:** Arms with supporters **Rev:** Stylized ox within designs **Note:** Similar to KM#154.

Date	Mintage	VF20	XF40	MS60	MS63	MS65
1997 Prooflike	251,000	—	—	—	12.00	16.00

KM# 154 10 DOLLARS
62.21 g., 0.999 Silver 1.998 oz. ASW **Subject:** Year of the Ox **Obv:** Arms with supporters **Rev:** Stylized Ox within designs

Date	Mintage	VF20	XF40	MS60	MS63	MS65
1997	38,000	PF65 90.00				

KM# 164 10 DOLLARS
Copper-Nickel **Subject:** Year of the Tiger **Obv:** Arms with supporters **Rev:** Stylized tiger **Note:** Similar to KM#165.

Date	Mintage	VF20	XF40	MS60	MS63	MS65
1998 Prooflike	220,000	—	—	—	14.00	18.00

KM# 165 10 DOLLARS
62.21 g., 0.999 Silver 1.998 oz. ASW **Subject:** Year of the Tiger **Obv:** Arms with supporters **Rev:** Stylized tiger within designs

Date	Mintage	VF20	XF40	MS60	MS63	MS65
1998	38,000	PF65 75.00				

KM# 167 10 DOLLARS
28.00 g., Copper-Nickel **Subject:** Year of the Rabbit **Obv:** Arms with supporters **Rev:** Stylized rabbit within designs **Edge:** Reeded

Date	Mintage	VF20	XF40	MS60	MS63	MS65
1999	179,200	—	—	—	15.00	20.00

KM# 168 10 DOLLARS
62.21 g., 0.999 Silver 1.998 oz. ASW **Subject:** Year of the Rabbit **Obv:** Arms with supporters **Rev:** Rabbit **Note:** Piefort

Date	Mintage	VF20	XF40	MS60	MS63	MS65
1999	35,600	PF65 90.00				

KM# 174 10 DOLLARS
Copper-Nickel **Subject:** Year of the Dragon **Obv:** Arms with supporters **Rev:** Dragon **Edge:** Reeded

Date	Mintage	VF20	XF40	MS60	MS63	MS65
2000 Prooflike	210,000	—	—	—	12.00	16.00

KM# 175 10 DOLLARS
62.21 g., 0.999 Silver 1.998 oz. ASW, 40.7 mm. **Subject:** Year of the Dragon **Obv:** Arms with supporters **Rev:** Dragon **Edge:** Reeded **Note:** Piefort thickness.

Date	Mintage	VF20	XF40	MS60	MS63	MS65
2000	33,000	PF65 90.00				

KM# 18 50 DOLLARS
31.10 g., 0.500 Silver 0.4999 oz. ASW **Subject:** International Financial Center **Obv:** Arms with supporters **Rev:** Stylized letters and dollar sign

Date	Mintage	VF20	XF40	MS60	MS63	MS65
1980	25,000	—	—	—	45.00	50.00
1980 sm	15,000	PF63 75.00	PF65 85.00			
1981	50,000	—	—	—	45.00	50.00
1981 sm	20,000	PF63 75.00	PF65 85.00			

KM# 78 50 DOLLARS
10.00 g., 0.916 Gold 0.2945 oz. AGW **Series:** Save the Children Fund **Obv:** Arms with supporters **Rev:** Children, kayak, palm tree and value

Date	Mintage	VF20	XF40	MS60	MS63	MS65
1989	1,040	PF65 560				

KM# 140 50 DOLLARS
31.10 g., 0.9999 Gold 0.9999 oz. AGW **Series:** 50th Anniversary - United Nations **Obv:** Arms with supporters **Rev:** UN logo within design

Date	Mintage	VF20	XF40	MS60	MS63	MS65
1995	780	PF65 1,850				

KM# 152 50 DOLLARS
31.10 g., 0.9999 Gold 0.9999 oz. AGW **Subject:** 50th Anniversary - Singapore Airlines **Obv:** Arms with supporters **Rev:** Airplane in front of numeral 50

Date	Mintage	VF20	XF40	MS60	MS63	MS65
1997	2,188	PF65 1,850				

KM# 170 50 DOLLARS
31.10 g., 0.9999 Gold 0.9999 oz. AGW **Subject:** Parliament **Obv:** Arms with supporters **Rev:** Parliament buildings

Date	Mintage	VF20	XF40	MS60	MS63	MS65
1999	750	PF65 1,850				

KM# 12 100 DOLLARS
6.91 g., 0.900 Gold 0.200 oz. AGW **Subject:** 10th Anniversary of Independence **Obv:** Arms with supporters **Rev:** Building

Date	Mintage	VF20	XF40	MS60	MS63	MS65
1975	100,000	—	—	—	—	400
1975	3,000	PF65 450				

KM# 106 100 DOLLARS
31.10 g., 0.999 Gold 0.9989 oz. AGW **Subject:** 25th Anniversary - Board of Commissioners of Currency **Obv:** Arms with supporters **Rev:** Stylized dollar sign and value within circle

Date	Mintage	VF20	XF40	MS60	MS63	MS65
1992	759	PF65 1,850				

KM# 7 150 DOLLARS
24.88 g., 0.916 Gold 0.7328 oz. AGW **Subject:** 150th Anniversary - Founding of Singapore **Obv:** Arms with supporters **Rev:** Lighthouse and value

Date	Mintage	VF20	XF40	MS60	MS63	MS65
ND(1969)	198,000	—	—	—	—	1,350
ND(1969)	500	PF65 2,500				

KM# 107 200 DOLLARS
31.10 g., 0.999 Platinum 0.999 oz. APW **Subject:** 25th Anniversary - Board of Commissioners of Currency **Obv:** Arms with supporters **Rev:** Stylized dollar sign and value within circle **Note:** Similar to KM#106.

Date	Mintage	VF20	XF40	MS60	MS63	MS65
1992	300	PF65 1,950				

KM# 13 250 DOLLARS
17.28 g., 0.900 Gold 0.500 oz. AGW **Subject:** 10th Anniversary of Independence **Obv:** Arms with supporters **Rev:** Four grasped hands below value

Date	Mintage	VF20	XF40	MS60	MS63	MS65
ND(1975)	30,000	—	—	—	—	900
ND(1975)	2,000	PF65 925				

KM# 96 250 DOLLARS
31.10 g., 0.999 Gold 0.999 oz. AGW **Subject:** 25th Anniversary of Independence **Obv:** Arms with supporters **Rev:** Stylized numeral 25 above city view with value at lower right

Date	Mintage	VF20	XF40	MS60	MS63	MS65
1990	6,000	PF65 1,800				

KM# 114 250 DOLLARS
31.10 g., 0.999 Gold 0.999 oz. AGW **Subject:** Year of the Rooster **Obv:** Arms with supporters **Rev:** Stylized rooster

Date	Mintage	VF20	XF40	MS60	MS63	MS65
1993	8,900	PF65 1,400				

KM# 123 250 DOLLARS
31.10 g., 0.999 Gold 0.999 oz. AGW **Subject:** Year of the Dog **Obv:** Arms with supporters **Rev:** Stylized dog within designs

Date	Mintage	VF20	XF40	MS60	MS63	MS65
1994	7,250	PF65 1,400				

KM# 127 250 DOLLARS
31.10 g., 0.999 Gold 0.999 oz. AGW **Subject:** Year of the Pig **Obv:** Arms with supporters **Rev:** Stylized pig within design

Date	Mintage	VF20	XF40	MS60	MS63	MS65
1995	7,500	PF65 1,400				

KM# 143 250 DOLLARS
31.10 g., 0.999 Gold 0.999 oz. AGW **Subject:** Year of the Rat **Obv:** Arms with supporters **Rev:** Stylized rat within designs

Date	Mintage	VF20	XF40	MS60	MS63	MS65
1996	7,500	PF65 1,400				

KM# 155 250 DOLLARS
31.10 g., 0.999 Gold 0.999 oz. AGW **Subject:** Year of the Ox **Obv:** Arms with supporters **Rev:** Stylized ox within designs

Date	Mintage	VF20	XF40	MS60	MS63	MS65
1997	7,600	PF65 1,400				

KM# 166 250 DOLLARS
31.10 g., 0.999 Gold 0.999 oz. AGW **Subject:** Year of the Tiger **Obv:** Arms with supporters **Rev:** Stylized tiger

Date	Mintage	VF20	XF40	MS60	MS63	MS65
1998	6,800	PF65 1,400				

KM# 169 250 DOLLARS
31.10 g., 0.999 Gold 0.999 oz. AGW **Obv:** Arms with supporters **Rev:** Stylized rabbit within designs **Edge:** Reeded

Date	Mintage	VF20	XF40	MS60	MS63	MS65
1999	4,500	PF65 1,400				

KM# 176 250 DOLLARS
31.10 g., 0.999 Gold 0.999 oz. AGW, 32.12 mm. **Subject:** Year of the Dragon **Obv:** Arms with supporters **Rev:** Stylized dragon **Edge:** Reeded

Date	Mintage	VF20	XF40	MS60	MS63	MS65
2000	5,600	PF65 1,400				

KM# 14 500 DOLLARS

34.56 g., 0.900 Gold 1.000 oz. AGW **Subject:** 10th Anniversary of Independence **Obv:** Arms with supporters **Rev:** Lion head

Date	Mintage	VF20	XF40	MS60	MS63	MS65
ND-1975	30,000	—	—	—	1,400	1,475
ND-1975	2,000	PF65 2,250				

KM# 21 500 DOLLARS

16.97 g., 0.916 Gold 0.4996 oz. AGW **Subject:** Year of the Rooster **Obv:** Arms with supporters **Rev:** Rooster

Date	Mintage	VF20	XF40	MS60	MS63	MS65
1981 sm	12,000	PF63 900	PF65 1,000			

KM# 24 500 DOLLARS

16.97 g., 0.916 Gold 0.4996 oz. AGW **Subject:** Year of the Dog **Obv:** Arms with supporters **Rev:** Dog

Date	Mintage	VF20	XF40	MS60	MS63	MS65
1982 sm	5,500	PF63 900	PF65 1,000			

KM# 27 500 DOLLARS

16.97 g., 0.916 Gold 0.4996 oz. AGW **Subject:** Year of the Pig **Obv:** Arms with supporters **Rev:** Pig

Date	Mintage	VF20	XF40	MS60	MS63	MS65
1983 sm	5,000	PF63 950	PF65 1,100			

KM# 34 500 DOLLARS

16.97 g., 0.916 Gold 0.4996 oz. AGW **Subject:** Year of the Rat **Obv:** Arms with supporters **Rev:** Rat

Date	Mintage	VF20	XF40	MS60	MS63	MS65
1984 sm	4,000	PF63 950	PF65 1,100			

KM# 45 500 DOLLARS

16.97 g., 0.916 Gold 0.4996 oz. AGW **Subject:** Year of the Ox **Obv:** Arms with supporters **Rev:** Ox

Date	Mintage	VF20	XF40	MS60	MS63	MS65
1985 sm	4,000	PF63 900	PF65 950			

KM# 60 500 DOLLARS

16.97 g., 0.916 Gold 0.4996 oz. AGW **Subject:** Year of the Tiger **Obv:** Arms with supporters **Rev:** Tiger

Date	Mintage	VF20	XF40	MS60	MS63	MS65
1986 sm	3,000	PF63 1,350	PF65 1,500			

KM# 64 500 DOLLARS

16.97 g., 0.916 Gold 0.4996 oz. AGW **Subject:** Year of the Rabbit **Obv:** Arms with supporters **Rev:** Rabbit

Date	Mintage	VF20	XF40	MS60	MS63	MS65
1987 sm	2,400	PF63 2,350	PF65 2,650			

KM# 73 500 DOLLARS

16.97 g., 0.916 Gold 0.4996 oz. AGW **Subject:** Year of the Dragon **Obv:** Arms with supporters **Rev:** Dragon

Date	Mintage	VF20	XF40	MS60	MS63	MS65
1988 sm	4,000	PF63 1,200	PF65 1,350			

KM# 72 500 DOLLARS

16.97 g., 0.916 Gold 0.4996 oz. AGW **Subject:** Year of the Snake **Obv:** Arms with supporters **Rev:** Snake

Date	Mintage	VF20	XF40	MS60	MS63	MS65
1989 sm	2,500	PF63 1,850	PF65 2,000			

KM# 76 500 DOLLARS

16.97 g., 0.916 Gold 0.4996 oz. AGW **Subject:** Year of the Horse **Obv:** Arms with supporters **Rev:** Horse

Date	Mintage	VF20	XF40	MS60	MS63	MS65
1990 sm	5,000	PF63 900	PF65 1,000			

KM# 97 500 DOLLARS

31.10 g., 0.999 Platinum 0.999 oz. APW **Subject:** 25th Anniversary of Independence **Obv:** Arms with supporters **Rev:** Numeral 25 and value above city view

Date	Mintage	VF20	XF40	MS60	MS63	MS65
1990	2,000	PF63 1,900	PF65 2,000			

KM# 85 500 DOLLARS

16.97 g., 0.916 Gold 0.4996 oz. AGW **Subject:** Year of the Goat **Obv:** Arms with supporters **Rev:** Goat

Date	Mintage	VF20	XF40	MS60	MS63	MS65
1991 sm	5,000	PF63 850	PF65 950			

KM# 93 500 DOLLARS

16.97 g., 0.916 Gold 0.4996 oz. AGW **Subject:** Year of the Monkey **Obv:** Arms with supporters **Rev:** Monkey

Date	Mintage	VF20	XF40	MS60	MS63	MS65
1992 sm	5,000	PF63 850	PF65 950			

BULLION COINAGE

Lunar Year Issues

KM# 28 DOLLAR

3.11 g., 0.999 Gold 0.0999 oz. AGW **Obv:** National arms **Rev:** Carp and lotus flower

Date	Mintage	VF20	XF40	MS60	MS63	MS65
1983	20,000	—	—	—	147	160
1984	10,000	—	—	—	147	160

KM# 144 DOLLAR

1.56 g., 0.9999 Gold 0.050 oz. AGW, 13.92 mm. **Series:** Lunar **Subject:** Year of the Rat **Obv:** National arms **Rev:** Stylized lion's head right, rat privy mark at lower left

Date	Mintage	VF20	XF40	MS60	MS63	MS65
1996	1,920	—	—	—	80.00	92.00
1996	1,608	PF63 80.00	PF65 92.00			

KM# 158 DOLLAR

1.56 g., 0.9999 Gold 0.050 oz. AGW, 13.92 mm. **Series:** Lunar **Subject:** Year of the Ox **Obv:** National arms **Rev:** Stylized lion's head right, ox privy mark at lower left

Date	Mintage	VF20	XF40	MS60	MS63	MS65
1997	689	—	—	—	80.00	92.00
1997	864	PF63 80.00	PF65 92.00			

KM# 197 DOLLAR

1.56 g., 0.9999 Gold 0.050 oz. AGW, 13.92 mm. **Series:** Lunar **Subject:** Year of the Tiger **Obv:** National arms **Rev:** Stylized lion's head right, tiger privy mark at lower left

Date	Mintage	VF20	XF40	MS60	MS63	MS65
1998	450	—	—	—	80.00	92.00
1998	380	PF63 80.00	PF65 92.00			

KM# 202 DOLLAR

1.56 g., 0.9999 Gold 0.050 oz. AGW, 13.92 mm. **Series:** Lunar **Subject:** Year of the Rabbit **Obv:** National arms **Rev:** Stylized lion's head right, rabbit privy mark at lower left

Date	Mintage	VF20	XF40	MS60	MS63	MS65
1999	500	—	—	—	80.00	92.00
1999	700	PF63 80.00	PF65 92.00			

KM# 207 DOLLAR

1.56 g., 0.9999 Gold 0.050 oz. AGW, 13.92 mm. **Series:** Lunar **Subject:** Year of the Dragon **Obv:** National arms **Rev:** Stylized lion's head right, dragon privy mark at lower left

Date	Mintage	VF20	XF40	MS60	MS63	MS65
2000	225	—	—	—	80.00	92.00
2000	631	PF63 80.00	PF65 92.00			

KM# 30 5 DOLLARS
15.55 g., 0.999 Gold 0.4994 oz. AGW **Obv:** National arms **Rev:** Phoenix

Date	Mintage	VF20	XF40	MS60	MS63	MS65
1983	10,000	—	—	—	690	750
1984	10,000	—	—	—	690	750

KM# 79 5 DOLLARS
1.56 g., 0.9999 Gold 0.050 oz. AGW, 13.92 mm. **Obv:** National arms **Rev:** Stylized lion's head right

Date	Mintage	VF20	XF40	MS60	MS63	MS65
1990	8,000	—	—	—	76.00	89.00
1990	2,000	PF63 76.00	PF65 89.00			

KM# 87 5 DOLLARS
1.56 g., 0.9999 Gold 0.050 oz. AGW, 13.92 mm. **Series:** Lunar **Subject:** Year of the Goat **Obv:** National arms **Rev:** Stylized lion's head right, goat privy mark at lower left

Date	Mintage	VF20	XF40	MS60	MS63	MS65
1991	2,500	PF63 76.00	PF65 89.00			
1991	8,000	—	—	—	76.00	89.00

KM# 108 5 DOLLARS
1.56 g., 0.9999 Gold 0.050 oz. AGW, 13.92 mm. **Series:** Lunar **Subject:** Year of the Monkey **Obv:** National arms **Rev:** Stylized lion's head right, monkey privy mark at lower left

Date	Mintage	VF20	XF40	MS60	MS63	MS65
1992	4,298	—	—	—	76.00	89.00
1992	2,000	PF63 76.00	PF65 89.00			

KM# 117 5 DOLLARS
1.56 g., 0.9999 Gold 0.050 oz. AGW, 13.92 mm. **Series:** Lunar **Subject:** Year of the Rooster **Obv:** National arms **Rev:** Stylized lion's head right, rooster privy mark at lower left

Date	Mintage	VF20	XF40	MS60	MS63	MS65
1993	3,400	—	—	—	76.00	89.00
1993	1,500	PF63 76.00	PF65 89.00			

KM# 128 5 DOLLARS
1.56 g., 0.9999 Gold 0.050 oz. AGW, 13.92 mm. **Series:** Lunar **Subject:** Year of the Dog **Obv:** National arms **Rev:** Stylized lion's head right, dog privy mark at lower left

Date	Mintage	VF20	XF40	MS60	MS63	MS65
1994	1,900	—	—	—	76.00	89.00
1994	1,500	PF63 76.00	PF65 89.00			

KM# 133 5 DOLLARS
1.56 g., 0.9999 Gold 0.050 oz. AGW, 13.92 mm. **Series:** Lunar **Subject:** Year of the Boar **Obv:** National arms **Rev:** Stylized lion's head right, boar privy mark at lower left

Date	Mintage	VF20	XF40	MS60	MS63	MS65
1995	1,500	—	—	—	76.00	89.00
1995	1,500	PF63 76.00	PF65 89.00			

KM# 145 5 DOLLARS
3.11 g., 0.9999 Gold 0.100 oz. AGW, 17.95 mm. **Series:** Lunar **Subject:** Year of the Rat **Obv:** National arms **Rev:** Stylized lion's head right, rat privy mark at lower left

Date	Mintage	VF20	XF40	MS60	MS63	MS65
1996	1,597	—	—	—	152	177
1996	1,608	PF63 152	PF65 177			

KM# 159 5 DOLLARS
3.11 g., 0.9999 Gold 0.100 oz. AGW, 17.95 mm. **Series:** Lunar **Subject:** Year of the Ox **Obv:** National arms **Rev:** Stylized lion's head right, ox privy mark at lower left

Date	Mintage	VF20	XF40	MS60	MS63	MS65
1997	890	—	—	—	152	177
1997	864	PF63 152	PF65 177			

KM# 198 5 DOLLARS
3.11 g., 0.9999 Gold 0.100 oz. AGW, 17.95 mm. **Series:** Lunar **Subject:** Year of the Tiger **Obv:** National arms **Rev:** Stylized lion's head right, tiger privy mark at lower left

Date	Mintage	VF20	XF40	MS60	MS63	MS65
1998	600	—	—	—	152	177
1998	380	PF63 152	PF65 177			

KM# 203 5 DOLLARS
3.11 g., 0.9999 Gold 0.100 oz. AGW, 17.95 mm. **Series:** Lunar **Subject:** Year of the Rabbit **Obv:** National arms **Rev:** Stylized lion's head right, rabbit privy mark at lower left

Date	Mintage	VF20	XF40	MS60	MS63	MS65
1999	310	—	—	—	152	177
1999	700	PF63 152	PF65 177			

KM# 208 5 DOLLARS
3.11 g., 0.9999 Gold 0.100 oz. AGW, 17.95 mm. **Series:** Lunar **Subject:** Year of the Dragon **Obv:** National arms **Rev:** Stylized lion's head right, dragon privy mark at lower left

Date	Mintage	VF20	XF40	MS60	MS63	MS65
2000	270	—	—	—	160	177
2000	631	PF63 152	PF65 177			

KM# 31 10 DOLLARS
31.10 g., 0.999 Gold 0.9989 oz. AGW **Obv:** National arms **Rev:** Dragon

Date	Mintage	VF20	XF40	MS60	MS63	MS65
1983	10,000	—	—	—	1,400	1,525
1984	10,000	PF63 1,400	PF65 1,525			

KM# 80 10 DOLLARS
3.11 g., 0.9999 Gold 0.100 oz. AGW, 17.95 mm. **Obv:** National arms **Rev:** Stylized lion's head right

Date	Mintage	VF20	XF40	MS60	MS63	MS65
1990	5,000	—	—	—	147	160
1990	2,000	PF63 147	PF65 160			

KM# 88 10 DOLLARS
3.11 g., 0.9999 Gold 0.100 oz. AGW, 17.95 mm. **Series:** Lunar **Subject:** Year of the Goat **Obv:** National arms **Rev:** Stylized lion's head right, goat privy mark at lower left

Date	Mintage	VF20	XF40	MS60	MS63	MS65
1991	5,500	—	—	—	147	160
1991	2,500	PF63 147	PF65 160			

KM# 109 10 DOLLARS
3.11 g., 0.9999 Gold 0.100 oz. AGW, 17.95 mm. **Series:** Lunar **Subject:** Year of the Monkey **Obv:** National arms **Rev:** Stylized lion's head right, monkey privy mark at lower left

Date	Mintage	VF20	XF40	MS60	MS63	MS65
1992	3,284	—	—	—	147	160
1992	2,000	PF63 147	PF65 160			

KM# 118 10 DOLLARS
3.11 g., 0.9999 Gold 0.100 oz. AGW, 17.95 mm. **Series:** Lunar **Subject:** Year of the Rooster **Obv:** National arms **Rev:** Stylized lion's head right, rooster privy mark at lower left

Date	Mintage	VF20	XF40	MS60	MS63	MS65
1993	2,100	—	—	—	147	160
1993	1,500	PF63 147	PF65 160			

KM# 129 10 DOLLARS
3.11 g., 0.9999 Gold 0.100 oz. AGW, 17.95 mm. **Series:** Lunar **Subject:** Year of the Dog **Obv:** National arms **Rev:** Stylized lion's head right, dog privy mark at lower left

Date	Mintage	VF20	XF40	MS60	MS63	MS65
1994	1,900	—	—	—	147	160
1994	1,500	PF63 147	PF65 160			

KM# 134 10 DOLLARS
3.11 g., 0.9999 Gold 0.100 oz. AGW, 17.95 mm. **Series:** Lunar **Subject:** Year of the Boar **Obv:** National arms **Rev:** Stylized lion's head right, boar privy mark at lower left

Date	Mintage	VF20	XF40	MS60	MS63	MS65
1995	1,700	—	—	—	147	160
1995	1,500	PF63 152	PF65 165			

KM# 146 10 DOLLARS
7.78 g., 0.9999 Gold 0.250 oz. AGW, 21.96 mm. **Series:** Lunar **Subject:** Year of the Rat **Obv:** National arms **Rev:** Stylized lion's head right, rat privy mark at lower left **Note:** Year of the Rat privy mark.

Date	Mintage	VF20	XF40	MS60	MS63	MS65
1996	1,292	—	—	—	355	380
1996	1,608	PF63 365	PF65 400			

KM# 160 10 DOLLARS
7.78 g., 0.9999 Gold 0.250 oz. AGW, 21.96 mm. **Series:** Lunar **Subject:** Year of the ox **Obv:** National arms **Rev:** Stylized lion's head right, ox privy mark at lower left

Date	Mintage	VF20	XF40	MS60	MS63	MS65
1997	723	—	—	—	355	380
1997	864	PF63 365	PF65 400			

KM# 199 10 DOLLARS
7.78 g., 0.9999 Gold 0.250 oz. AGW, 21.96 mm. **Series:** Lunar **Subject:** Year of the Tiger **Obv:** National arms **Rev:** Stylized lion's head right, tiger privy mark at lower left

Date	Mintage	VF20	XF40	MS60	MS63	MS65
1998	450	—	—	—	365	400
1998	380	PF63 365	PF65 400			

KM# 204 10 DOLLARS
7.78 g., 0.9999 Gold 0.2499 oz. AGW, 21.96 mm. **Series:** Lunar **Subject:** Year of the Rabbit **Obv:** National arms **Rev:** Stylized lion's head right, rabbit privy mark at lower left

Date	Mintage	VF20	XF40	MS60	MS63	MS65
1999	360	—	—	—	365	400
1999	700	PF63 355	PF65 390			

KM# 209 10 DOLLARS
7.78 g., 0.9999 Gold 0.2499 oz. AGW, 21.96 mm. **Series:** Lunar **Subject:** Year of the Dragon **Obv:** National arms **Rev:** Stylized lion's head right, dragon privy mark at lower left

Date	Mintage	VF20	XF40	MS60	MS63	MS65
2000	215	—	—	—	365	400
2000	631	PF63 355	PF65 390			

KM# 147 20 DOLLARS
15.55 g., 0.9999 Gold 0.4999 oz. AGW, 27 mm. **Series:** Lunar **Subject:** Year of the Rat **Obv:** National arms **Rev:** Stylized lion's head right, rat privy mark at lower left

Date	Mintage	VF20	XF40	MS60	MS63	MS65
1996	996	—	—	—	710	760
1996	1,608	PF63 710	PF65 760			

KM# 161 20 DOLLARS
15.55 g., 0.9999 Gold 0.4999 oz. AGW, 27 mm. **Series:** Lunar **Subject:** Year of the Ox **Obv:** National arms **Rev:** Stylized lion's head right, ox privy mark at lower left

Date	Mintage	VF20	XF40	MS60	MS63	MS65
1997	589	—	—	—	710	760
1997	864	PF63 710	PF65 760			

KM# 200 20 DOLLARS
15.55 g., 0.9999 Gold 0.500 oz. AGW, 27 mm. **Series:** Lunar **Subject:** Year of the Tiger **Obv:** National arms **Rev:** Stylized lion's head right, tiger privy mark at lower left

Date	Mintage	VF20	XF40	MS60	MS63	MS65
1998	400	—	—	—	710	780
1998	380	PF63 710	PF65 780			

KM# 205 20 DOLLARS
15.55 g., 0.9999 Gold 0.500 oz. AGW, 27 mm. **Series:** Lunar **Subject:** Year of the Rabbit **Obv:** National arms **Rev:** Stylized lion's head right, rabbit privy mark at lower left

Date	Mintage	VF20	XF40	MS60	MS63	MS65
1999	210	—	—	—	730	800
1999	700	PF63 710	PF65 760			

KM# 210 20 DOLLARS
15.55 g., 0.9999 Gold 0.500 oz. AGW **Series:** Lunar **Subject:** Year of the Dragon **Obv:** National arms **Rev:** Stylized lion's head right, dragon privy mark at lower left

Date	Mintage	VF20	XF40	MS60	MS63	MS65
2000	200	—	—	—	730	800
2000	631	PF63 710	PF65 760			

KM# 81 25 DOLLARS
7.78 g., 0.9999 Gold 0.250 oz. AGW, 21.96 mm. **Obv:** National arms **Rev:** Stylized lion's head right

Date	Mintage	VF20	XF40	MS60	MS63	MS65
1990	Est. 5000	—	—	—	355	380
1990	Est. 2000	PF63 365	PF65 400			

KM# 89 25 DOLLARS
7.78 g., 0.9999 Gold 0.250 oz. AGW, 21.96 mm. **Series:** Lunar **Subject:** Year of the Goat **Obv:** National arms **Rev:** Stylized lion's head right, goat privy mark at lower left

Date	Mintage	VF20	XF40	MS60	MS63	MS65
1991	5,500	—	—	—	355	380
1991	2,500	PF63 365	PF65 400			

KM# 110 25 DOLLARS
7.78 g., 0.9999 Gold 0.250 oz. AGW, 21.96 mm. **Series:** Lunar **Subject:** Year of the Monkey **Obv:** National arms **Rev:** Stylized lion's head right, monkey privy mark at lower left

Date	Mintage	VF20	XF40	MS60	MS63	MS65
1992	4,000	—	—	—	355	380
1992	2,000	PF63 365	PF65 400			

KM# 119 25 DOLLARS
7.78 g., 0.9999 Gold 0.250 oz. AGW, 21.96 mm. **Series:** Lunar **Subject:** Year of the Rooster **Obv:** National arms **Rev:** Stylized lion's head right, rooster privy mark at lower left

Date	Mintage	VF20	XF40	MS60	MS63	MS65
1993	3,000	—	—	—	355	380
1993	Est. 1500	PF63 365	PF65 400			

KM# 130 25 DOLLARS
7.78 g., 0.9999 Gold 0.250 oz. AGW, 21.96 mm. **Series:** Lunar **Subject:** Year of the Dog **Obv:** National arms **Rev:** Stylized lion's head right, dog privy mark at lower left

Date	Mintage	VF20	XF40	MS60	MS63	MS65
1994	1,900	—	—	—	355	380
1994	1,500	PF63 365	PF65 400			

KM# 135 25 DOLLARS
7.78 g., 0.9999 Gold 0.250 oz. AGW, 21.96 mm. **Series:** Lunar **Subject:** Year of the Boar **Obv:** National arms **Rev:** Stylized lion's head right, boar privy mark at lower left

Date	Mintage	VF20	XF40	MS60	MS63	MS65
1995	1,700	—	—	—	355	380
1995	1,500	PF63 365	PF65 400			

KM# 82 50 DOLLARS
15.55 g., 0.9999 Gold 0.4999 oz. AGW, 27 mm. **Obv:** National arms **Rev:** Stylized lion's head right

Date	Mintage	VF20	XF40	MS60	MS63	MS65
1990	2,000	PF63 700	PF65 760			

KM# 90 50 DOLLARS
15.55 g., 0.9999 Gold 0.4999 oz. AGW, 27 mm. **Series:** Lunar **Subject:** Year of the Goat **Obv:** National arms **Rev:** Stylized lion's head right, goat privy mark at lower left

Date	Mintage	VF20	XF40	MS60	MS63	MS65
1991	5,500	—	—	—	700	760
1991	2,500	PF63 700	PF65 760			

KM# 111 50 DOLLARS
15.55 g., 0.9999 Gold 0.4999 oz. AGW, 27 mm. **Series:** Lunar **Subject:** Year of the Monkey **Obv:** National arms **Rev:** Stylized lion's head right, monkey privy mark at lower left

Date	Mintage	VF20	XF40	MS60	MS63	MS65
1992	3,204	—	—	—	700	760
1992	2,000	PF63 700	PF65 760			

KM# 120 50 DOLLARS
15.55 g., 0.9999 Gold 0.4999 oz. AGW, 27 mm. **Series:** Lunar **Subject:** Year of the Rooster **Obv:** National arms **Rev:** Stylized lion's head right, rooster privy mark at lower left

Date	Mintage	VF20	XF40	MS60	MS63	MS65
1993	2,600	—	—	—	700	760
1993	1,500	PF63 700	PF65 760			

KM# 131 50 DOLLARS
15.55 g., 0.9999 Gold 0.4999 oz. AGW, 27 mm. **Series:** Lunar **Subject:** Year of the Dog **Obv:** National arms **Rev:** Stylized lion's head right, dog privy mark at lower left

Date	Mintage	VF20	XF40	MS60	MS63	MS65
1994	1,400	—	—	—	700	760
1994	1,500	PF63 700	PF65 760			

KM# 136 50 DOLLARS
15.55 g., 0.9999 Gold 0.4999 oz. AGW, 27 mm. **Series:** Lunar **Subject:** Year of the Boar **Obv:** National arms **Rev:** Stylized lion's head right, boar privy mark at lower left

Date	Mintage	VF20	XF40	MS60	MS63	MS65
1995	1,500	—	—	—	700	760
1995	1,500	PF63 700	PF65 760			

KM# 148 50 DOLLARS
31.10 g., 0.9999 Gold 0.9999 oz. AGW, 32.12 mm. **Series:** Lunar **Subject:** Year of the Rat **Obv:** National arms **Rev:** Stylized lion's head right, rat privy mark at lower left

Date	Mintage	VF20	XF40	MS60	MS63	MS65
1996	1,013	—	—	—	1,375	1,425
1996	1,608	PF63 1,375	PF65 1,425			

KM# 162 50 DOLLARS
31.10 g., 0.9999 Gold 0.9999 oz. AGW, 32.12 mm. **Series:** Lunar **Subject:** Year of the Ox **Obv:** National arms **Rev:** Stylized lion's head right, ox privy mark at lower left

Date	Mintage	VF20	XF40	MS60	MS63	MS65
1997	624	—	—	—	1,375	1,425
1997	864	PF63 1,375	PF65 1,425			

KM# 201 50 DOLLARS
31.10 g., 0.9999 Gold 0.9999 oz. AGW, 32.12 mm. **Series:** Lunar **Subject:** Year of the Tiger **Obv:** National arms **Rev:** Stylized lion's head right, tiger privy mark at lower left

Date	Mintage	VF20	XF40	MS60	MS63	MS65
1998	700	—	—	—	1,375	1,425
1998	270	PF63 1,375	PF65 1,425			

KM# 206 50 DOLLARS
31.10 g., 0.9999 Gold 0.9999 oz. AGW, 32.12 mm. **Series:** Lunar **Subject:** Year of the Rabbit **Obv:** National arms **Rev:** Stylized lion's head right, rabbit privy mark at lower left

Date	Mintage	VF20	XF40	MS60	MS63	MS65
1999	310	—	—	—	1,375	1,425
1999	500	PF63 1,375	PF65 1,425			

KM# 211 50 DOLLARS
31.10 g., 0.9999 Gold 0.9999 oz. AGW, 32.12 mm. **Series:** Lunar **Subject:** Year of the Dragon **Obv:** National arms **Rev:** Stylized lion's head right, dragon privy mark at lower left

Date	Mintage	VF20	XF40	MS60	MS63	MS65
2000	200	—	—	—	1,375	1,425
2000	388	PF63 1,375	PF65 1,425			

KM# 83 100 DOLLARS
31.10 g., 0.9999 Gold 0.9998 oz. AGW, 32.12 mm. **Obv:** National arms **Rev:** Stylized lion's head right

Date	Mintage	VF20	XF40	MS60	MS63	MS65
1990	Est. 5000	—	—	—	1,350	1,400
1990	Est. 2000	PF63 1,350	PF65 1,400			

KM# 91 100 DOLLARS
31.10 g., 0.9999 Gold 0.9998 oz. AGW, 32.12 mm. **Series:** Lunar **Subject:** Year of the Goat **Obv:** National arms **Rev:** Stylized lion's head right, goat privy mark at lower left

Date	Mintage	VF20	XF40	MS60	MS63	MS65
1991	13,000	—	—	—	1,350	1,400
1991	2,500	PF63 1,350	PF65 1,400			

KM# 112 100 DOLLARS
31.10 g., 0.9999 Gold 0.9998 oz. AGW, 32.12 mm. **Series:** Lunar **Subject:** Year of the Monkey **Obv:** National arms **Rev:** Stylized lion's head right, monkey privy mark at lower left

Date	Mintage	VF20	XF40	MS60	MS63	MS65
1992	4,000	—	—	—	1,350	1,400
1992	2,000	PF63 1,350	PF65 1,400			

KM# 121 100 DOLLARS

31.10 g., 0.9999 Gold 0.9998 oz. AGW, 32.12 mm. **Series:** Lunar **Subject:** Year of the Rooster **Obv:** National arms **Rev:** Stylized lion's head right, rooster privy mark at lower left

Date	Mintage	VF20	XF40	MS60	MS63	MS65
1993	3,100	—	—	—	1,350	1,400
1993	Est. 1500	**PF63** 1,350	**PF65** 1,400			

KM# 132 100 DOLLARS

31.10 g., 0.9999 Gold 0.9998 oz. AGW, 32.12 mm. **Series:** Lunar **Subject:** Year of the Dog **Obv:** National arms **Rev:** Stylized lion's head right, dog privy mark at lower left

Date	Mintage	VF20	XF40	MS60	MS63	MS65
1994	1,600	—	—	—	1,350	1,400
1994	1,500	**PF63** 1,350	**PF65** 1,400			

KM# 137 100 DOLLARS

31.10 g., 0.9999 Gold 0.9998 oz. AGW, 32.12 mm. **Series:** Lunar **Subject:** Year of the Boar **Obv:** National arms **Rev:** Stylized lion's head right, boar privy mark at lower left

Date	Mintage	VF20	XF40	MS60	MS63	MS65
1995	1,600	—	—	—	1,350	1,400
1995	1,500	**PF63** 1,350	**PF65** 1,400			

MINT SETS

KM#	Date	Mintage	Identification	Issue Price	Mkt Val
MS1	1967 (6)	8,000	KM#1-6	1.50	35.00
MS2	1968 (6)	16,000	KM#1-6	1.50	30.00
MS3	1969 (6)	14,000	KM#1-6	1.50	35.00
MS4	1970 (6)	13,000	KM#1-6	1.50	70.00
MS5	1970 (6)	27,000	KM#1-6 Issued only in package of 3 sets plus KM#11, each set in plastic wallet for Expo'97 Osaka Japan	1.75	70.00
MS7	1972 (6)	13,000	KM#1-6	3.00	85.00
MS8	1973 (6)	15,000	KM#1-6	2.00	15.00
MS9	1974 (6)	20,000	KM#1-6	2.00	30.00
MS10	1975 (6)	30,000	KM#1-6	12.00	15.00
MS11	1975 (3)	30,000	KM#12-14	—	2,850
MS12	1976 (6)	35,000	KM#1-6	2.00	12.00
MS13	1977 (6)	40,000	KM#1a, 2-6	2.00	12.00
MS14	1978 (6)	55,000	KM#1a, 2-6	—	20.00
MS15	1979 (6)	65,000	KM#1a, 2-6	—	12.00
MS16	1980 (6)	70,000	kM#1a, 2-6	—	10.00
MS17	1981 (6)	110,000	KM#1a, 2-6	5.00	7.50
MS18	1982 (6)	160,000	KM#1a, 2-6	5.00	7.50
MS19	1983 (6)	40,000	KM#1a, 2-6 with Medallion, I.A.P.N.	—	9.00
MS20	1983 (6)	150,000	KM#1a, 2-6	5.00	9.00
MS21	1984 (6)	160,000	KM#1a, 2-6	3.75	9.00
MS22	1985 (6)	148,424	KM#1a, 2-6	—	20.00
MS23	1986 (6)	120,000	KM#49-52, 53.1, 54	—	12.00
MS24	1987 (6)	120,000	KM#49-52, 53.1, 54	—	12.00
MS25	1988 (6)	120,000	KM#49-52, 53.1, 54b	—	7.50
MS26	1989 (6)	100,000	KM#49-52, 53.2, 54b	—	7.50
MS27	1990 (6)	100,000	KM#49-52, 53.2, 54b	—	7.50
MS28	1990 (5)	5,000	KM#79-83	—	1,250
MS29	1991 (7)	70,000	KM#49b, 50-52, 53.2, 54b (1991), 94 (1990)	—	13.00
MS30	1992 (7)	55,000	KM#98-103, 104.1	—	12.00
MS32	1994 (7)	100,200	KM#98-103, 104.1	—	10.00
MS33	1995 (7)	124,000	KM#98-103, 104.1	—	10.00
MS34	1996 (7)	180,000	KM#98-103, 104.1	—	10.00
MS35	1997 (7)	180,000	KM#98-103, 104.1	—	10.00
MS36	1998 (7)	180,000	KM#98-103, 104.1	—	10.00
MS37	1999 (7)	130,000	KM#98-103, 104.2	—	12.00
MS38	2000 (7)	150,000	KM#98-103, 104.2	—	12.00

PROOF SETS

KM#	Date	Mintage	Identification	Issue Price	Mkt Val
PS1	1967 (6)	2,000	KM#1-6	25.00	75.00
PS2	1968 (6)	5,000	KM#1-6	25.00	55.00
PS3	1969 (6)	3,000	KM#1-6	25.00	180
PS4	1972 (6)	749	KM#1-6	25.00	325
PS5	1973 (6)	1,000	KM#1-6	32.00	100
PS6	1974 (6)	1,500	KM#1-6	34.00	85.00
PS7	1975 (6)	3,000	KM#1-6	35.00	40.00
PS8	1975 (3)	2,000	KM#12-14	—	3,500
PS9	1976 (6)	3,500	KM#1-6	37.00	40.00
PS10	1977 (6)	3,500	kM#1-6	—	40.00
PS11	1978 (6)	4,000	KM#1-6	—	40.00
PS12	1979 (7)	3,500	KM#1-6, 17.1	—	120
PS13	1980 (7)	14,000	KM#1-6, 17.2	64.00	50.00
PS14	1981 (6)	30,000	KM#1b-2b, 3a-6a, .925 Silver	82.00	60.00
PS15	1982 (6)	20,000	KM#1-5, 6a	52.00	35.00
PS16	1983 (6)	15,000	KM#1-5, 6a	52.00	30.00
PS17	1984 (6)	15,000	KM#1-5, 6a	52.00	30.00
PS18	1985 (6)	20,000	KM#49a-52a, 53.1a, 54a	40.00	30.00
PS19	1986 (6)	15,000	KM#49a-52a, 53.1a, 54a	—	28.00
PS20	1987 (6)	15,000	KM#49a-52a, 53.1a, 54c	42.00	28.00
PS21	1987 (5)	1,000	KM-MB28-MB32	1,400	1,650
PS22	1988 (6)	15,000	KM#49a-52a, 53.1a, 54c	—	20.00
PS23	1988 (5)	500	KM-MB41-45	—	1,650
PS24	1989 (6)	15,000	KM#49a-52a, 53.2a, 54c	—	30.00
PS25	1989 (5)	200	KM-MB51-55	—	1,975
PS26	1990 (6)	15,000	KM#49a-52a, 53.2a, 54c	—	35.00
PS27	1990 (5)	2,000	KM#79-83	—	850
PSA28	1990 (3)	1,000	KM#95-97	—	3,500
PS28	1991 (7)	15,000	KM#49a-52a, 53.2a, 54c, 86a	—	75.00
PS29	1991 (5)	2,500	KM#87-91	—	850
PS30	1991 (2)	5,000	KM#86, 86a	—	80.00
PS31	1992 (7)	15,000	KM#98a-103a, 104.1a	—	60.00
PS32	1992 (5)	2,000	KM#108-112 Ingot	—	850
PS33	1992 (3)	200	KM#105-107	—	3,900
PS34	1992 (6)	15,000	KM#98a-103a, 104.1a	—	60.00
PS35	1993 (5)	1,500	KM#117-121 Ingot	—	875
PS36	1993 (2)	2,000	KM#115, 115a	—	80.00
PS37	1994 (7)	10,000	KM#98a-103a, 104.1a	—	60.00
PS38	1994 (5)	1,500	KM#128-132 Ingot	—	875
PS39	1995 (7)	10,000	KM#98a-103a, 104.1a	—	55.00
PS41	1995 (5)	1,500	KM#133-137 Ingot	1,718	875
PS42	1995 (3)	2,689	KM#138-140	1,052	1,650
PS43	1996 (7)	16,800	KM#98a-103a, 104.1a	—	55.00
PS44	1996 (5)	2,688	KM#144-148 Ingot	—	900
PS45	1996 (2)	2,800	KM#149, 149a	66.00	50.00
PS46	1997 (7)	18,000	KM#98a-103a, 104.1a	90.00	120
PS47	1997 (2)	3,800	KM#151, 151a	—	55.00
PS48	1997 (3)	888	KM#151, 151a, 152 Ingot	—	1,650
PS49	1997 (5)	2,200	KM#158-162	—	—
PS50	1998 (3)	1,998	KM#164-166 Ingot	—	1,650
PS51	1998 (7)	9,200	KM#98a-103a, 104.1a	—	50.00
PS52	1998 (4)	1,000	KM#197-200	—	—
PS53	1998 (6)	500	KM#197-201 plus ingot	—	—
PS54	1999 (7)	9,200	KM#98a-103a, 104.2a	—	50.00
PS55	1999 (4)	1,000	KM#202-205	—	—
PS56	1999 (5)	500	KM#202-206 plus ingot	—	—
PS57	2000 (4)	—	KM#207-210	—	—
PS58	2000 (5)	—	KM#207-211	—	—
PS59	2000 (7)	8,900	KM#98a-103a, 104.2a	74.25	50.00
PS60	2000 (3)	2,000	KM#174-176, plus Ingot	—	1,775

SLOVAKIA

The Republic of Slovakia has an area of 18,923 sq. mi. (49,035 sq. km.) and a population of 4.9 million. Capital: Bratislava. Textiles, steel, and wood products are exported.

The Slovak lands were united with the Czechs and the Czechoslovak State came into existence on Oct. 28, 1918 upon the dissolution of Austro-Hungarian Empire at the close of World War I. In March 1939, the German-influenced Slovak government proclaimed Slovakia independent and Germany incorporated the Czech lands into the Third Reich as the "Protectorate of Bohemia and Moravia". A Czechoslovak government-in-exile was setup in London in July 1940. The Soviet and USA forces liberated the area by May, 1945. At the close of World War II, Communist influence increased steadily while pressure for liberalization culminated in the overthrow of the Stalinist leader Antonin Novotn'y and his associates in 1968. The Communist Party then introduced far reaching reforms which received warnings from Moscow, followed by occupation by Warsaw Pact forces resulting in stationing of Soviet forces. Mass civilian demonstrations for reform began in Nov.1989 and the Federal Assembly abolished the Communist Party's sole right to govern. New governments followed on Dec. 3 and Dec. 10 and the Czech and Slovak Federal Republic was formed. The Movement for Democratic Slovakia was apparent in the June 1992 elections with the Slovak National Council adopting a declaration of sovereignty. Later, a constitution for an independent Slovakia with the Federal Assembly voting for the dissolution of the Republic came into effect on Dec. 31, 1992, and two new republics came into being on Jan. 1, 1993.

MINT MARK

Kremnica Mint

REPUBLIC

1939-45

STANDARD COINAGE

100 Halierov = 1 Koruna Slovenska (Ks)

KM# 8 5 HALIEROV

0.94 g., Zinc, 14 mm. **Obv:** Double cross within shield **Rev:** Large value **Edge:** Plain

Date	Mintage	F12	VF20	XF40	MS60	MS63
1942	1,000,000	3.00	5.00	15.00	20.00	32.00

KM# 1 10 HALIEROV

1.66 g., Bronze, 16 mm. **Obv:** Double cross within shield above sprigs **Rev:** Castle and large value

Date	Mintage	F12	VF20	XF40	MS60	MS63
1939	15,000,000	1.50	2.00	3.00	5.00	9.00
1942	7,000,000	2.00	3.00	5.00	9.00	18.00

KM# 4 20 HALIEROV

2.50 g., Bronze, 18 mm. **Obv:** Double cross on shield within flower sprig **Rev:** Nitra Castle, large value **Edge:** Plain

Date	Mintage	F12	VF20	XF40	MS60	MS63
1940	10,972,000	1.25	2.00	3.00	5.00	8.00
1941	4,028,000	2.50	6.00	10.00	18.00	30.00
1942	6,474,000	10.00	15.00	25.00	35.00	65.00

KM# 4a 20 HALIEROV

0.65 g., Aluminum, 18 mm. **Obv:** Double cross on shield within flower sprigs **Rev:** Nitra castle and large value **Edge:** Plain **Note:** Varieties exist.

Date	Mintage	F12	VF20	XF40	MS60	MS63
1942	Inc. above	1.00	1.50	3.00	5.00	9.00
1943	15,000,000	1.00	1.50	3.00	5.00	9.00

KM# 5 50 HALIEROV

3.33 g., Copper-Nickel, 20 mm. **Obv:** Double cross on shield and date **Rev:** Value above plow **Edge:** Plain

Date	Mintage	F12	VF20	XF40	MS60	MS63
1940	Inc. above	25.00	35.00	50.00	70.00	120
1941	8,000,000	1.00	2.00	3.00	4.50	8.00

KM# 5a 50 HALIEROV

1.00 g., Aluminum, 20 mm. **Obv:** Double cross on shield and date **Rev:** Value above plow **Edge:** Milled

Date	Mintage	F12	VF20	XF40	MS60	MS63
1943	4,400,000	1.00	1.50	2.50	4.00	7.00
1944	2,621,000	5.00	10.00	15.00	20.00	32.00

KM# 6 KORUNA

5.00 g., Copper-Nickel, 22 mm. **Obv:** Double cross on shield within circle above date **Rev:** Value within oat sprigs and stalks **Edge:** Milled **Note:** Open and closed 4.

Date	Mintage	F12	VF20	XF40	MS60	MS63
1940	2,350,000	0.75	1.25	2.25	4.00	7.00
1941	11,650,000	0.50	1.00	2.00	3.00	5.00
1942	6,000,000	0.50	1.00	2.00	3.00	5.00
Note: Varieties exist of 1942, in the numeral 4						
1944	884,000	10.00	15.00	25.00	35.00	65.00
1945	3,321,000	0.75	1.25	2.25	4.00	7.00

KM# 2 5 KORUN

Nickel, 27 mm. **Obv:** Double cross on shield within wheat sprigs below value with date below **Rev:** Head left **Edge:** Milled **Note:** Pointed top or flat top to the letter A in NAROD.

Date	Mintage	F12	VF20	XF40	MS60	MS63
1939	5,101,000	1.50	2.00	3.50	7.00	12.00

Note: Approximately 2,000,000 pieces were melted down by the Czechoslovak National Bank in 1947

KM# 9.1 10 KORUN

7.00 g., 0.500 Silver 0.1125 oz. ASW, 29 mm. **Obv:** Double cross on shield within radiant circle **Rev:** Standing figures facing divide value **Edge:** Plain **Note:** Variety 1 - Cross atop church held by left figure.

Date	Mintage	F12	VF20	XF40	MS60	MS63
1944	1,381,000	5.00	6.00	8.00	12.00	18.00

KM# 9.2 10 KORUN

7.00 g., 0.500 Silver 0.1125 oz. ASW **Obv:** Double cross on shield within radiant circle **Rev:** Standing figure facing divides value **Note:** Variety 2 - Without cross atop church held by left figure.

Date	Mintage	F12	VF20	XF40	MS60	MS63
1944	Inc. above	5.00	7.00	10.00	15.00	20.00

KM# 3 20 KORUN

15.00 g., 0.500 Silver 0.2411 oz. ASW, 31 mm. **Obv:** Double cross on shield within wreath flanked by value **Rev:** Head right **Edge:** Milled

Date	Mintage	F12	VF20	XF40	MS60	MS63
1939	200,000	—	9.00	15.00	25.00	30.00

KM# 7.1 20 KORUN

15.00 g., 0.500 Silver 0.2411 oz. ASW, 31 mm. **Subject:** St. Kyrill and St. Methodius **Obv:** Double cross on shield within sprigs **Rev:** Standing figures flanked by value **Edge:** Milled

Date	Mintage	F12	VF20	XF40	MS60	MS63
1941	2,500,000	—	9.00	12.00	18.00	22.00

KM# 7.2 20 KORUN

15.00 g., 0.500 Silver 0.2411 oz. ASW, 31 mm. **Subject:** St. Kyrill and St. Methodius **Obv:** Double cross on shield within sprigs **Rev:** Variety 2 - Double bar cross

Date	Mintage	F12	VF20	XF40	MS60	MS63
1941	Inc. above	—	9.00	14.00	20.00	25.00

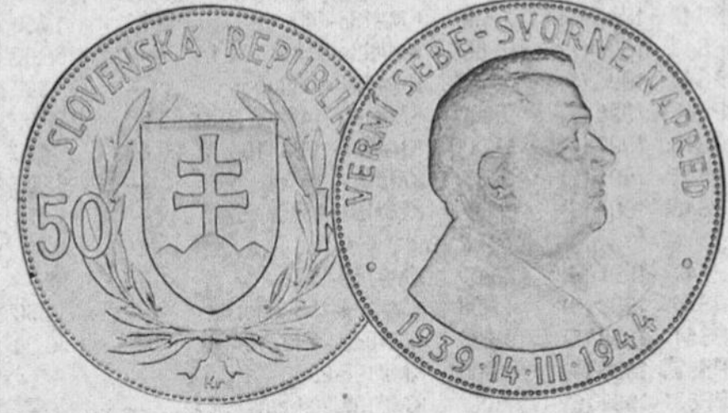

KM# 10 50 KORUN

16.50 g., 0.700 Silver 0.3713 oz. ASW, 34 mm. **Subject:** 5th Anniversary of Independence **Obv:** Double cross on shield within wreath flanked by value **Rev:** Head right **Edge:** Milled

Date	Mintage	F12	VF20	XF40	MS60	MS63
1944	2,000,000	—	12.00	15.00	22.50	30.00

REPUBLIC

STANDARD COINAGE

100 Halierov = 1 Slovak Koruna (Sk)

KM# 17 10 HALIEROV

0.72 g., Aluminum, 17 mm. **Obv:** Double cross on shield above inscription **Rev:** Church steeple **Edge:** Plain

Date	Mintage	VF20	XF40	MS60	MS63	MS65
1993	32,200,000	—	—	0.25	0.35	0.50
Note: Varieties of cross on state emblem						
1994	89,130,000	—	—	0.25	0.35	0.50
1995 Sets only	23,990,000	—	—	—	—	1.00
1996	31,540,000	—	—	0.25	0.35	0.50
1997	10,000,000	—	—	0.50	1.00	1.25
1998	30,260,000	—	—	0.25	0.35	0.50
1999	31,420,000	—	—	0.25	0.35	0.50
1999 Sets only	11,500	—	—	—	—	2.50
2000	30,600,000	—	—	0.25	0.35	0.50
2000	12,500	PF65 5.00				

KM# 18 20 HALIEROV

0.95 g., Aluminum, 19.5 mm. **Obv:** Double cross on shield above inscription **Rev:** Krivan Mountain and value **Edge:** Reeded

Date	Mintage	VF20	XF40	MS60	MS63	MS65
1993	37,410,000	—	—	0.35	0.45	0.60
1994	71,020,000	—	—	0.35	0.45	0.60
1995	32,390,000	—	—	0.35	0.45	0.60
1996	19,800,000	—	—	0.35	0.45	0.60
1997	10,000,000	—	—	0.35	0.45	0.60
1998	21,000,000	—	—	0.35	0.45	0.60
1999	15,710,000	—	—	0.35	0.45	0.60
1999 Sets only	11,500	—	—	—	—	2.50
2000	31,120,000	—	—	0.35	0.45	0.60
2000	12,500	PF65 5.00				

KM# 15 50 HALIEROV

1.20 g., Aluminum, 22 mm. **Obv:** Double cross on shield above inscription **Rev:** Watch tower and value **Edge:** Plain

Date	Mintage	VF20	XF40	MS60	MS63	MS65
1993	35,130,000	—	—	0.40	0.55	0.70
1994	19,020,000	—	—	0.45	0.60	0.75
1995 Sets only	12,000	—	—	—	—	1.50

KM# 35 50 HALIEROV

2.80 g., Copper Plated Steel, 18.75 mm. **Obv:** Double cross on shield above inscription **Rev:** Devin watch tower and value **Edge:** Segmented reeding

Date	Mintage	VF20	XF40	MS60	MS63	MS65
1996	39,640,000	—	—	0.40	0.55	0.70
1997 Sets only	11,500	—	—	—	—	1.50
1998	15,000,000	—	—	0.45	0.60	0.75
1999 Sets only	11,500	—	—	—	—	1.50
2000	20,212,000	—	—	0.45	0.60	0.75
2000	12,500	PF65 5.00				

KM# 12 KORUNA

3.85 g., Bronze Plated Steel, 21 mm. **Subject:** 15th Century of Madonna and Child **Obv:** Double cross on shield above inscription **Rev:** Madonna holding child and value **Edge:** Milled

Date	Mintage	VF20	XF40	MS60	MS63	MS65
1993	58,930,000	—	—	0.50	0.75	0.90
1994	44,320,000	—	—	0.50	0.75	0.90
1995	28,030,000	—	—	0.50	0.75	0.90
1996 Sets only	15,000	—	—	—	—	1.50
1997 Sets only	15,000	—	—	—	—	1.50
1998 Sets only	12,000	—	—	—	—	1.50
1999 Sets only	11,500	—	—	—	—	1.50
2000 Sets only	12,500	—	—	—	—	1.50
2000	900	PF65 10.00				

KM# 13 2 KORUNA

4.40 g., Nickel Plated Steel, 22.5 mm. **Obv:** Double cross on shield above inscription **Rev:** Venus statue and value

Date	Mintage	VF20	XF40	MS60	MS63	MS65
1993	36,810,000	—	—	0.60	0.85	1.00
Note: Varieties of artist's initials						
1994	24,720,000	—	—	0.60	0.85	1.00
1995	30,510,000	—	—	0.60	0.85	1.00

Date	Mintage	VF20	XF40	MS60	MS63	MS65
1996 Sets only	15,000	—	—	—	—	2.00
1997 Sets only	15,000	—	—	—	—	2.00
1998 Sets only	12,000	—	—	—	—	2.00
1999 Sets only	11,500	—	—	—	—	2.00
2000 Sets only	12,500	—	—	—	—	2.00
2000	900	PF65 10.00				

KM# 14 5 KORUNA

5.40 g., Nickel Plated Steel, 24.75 mm. **Obv:** Double cross on shield above inscription **Rev:** Celtic coin of BIATEC at upper left of value **Edge:** Milled

Date	Mintage	VF20	XF40	MS60	MS63	MS65
1993	36,200,000	—	—	0.75	1.25	1.50
Note: Varieties in artist's initials						
1994	26,140,000	—	—	0.75	1.25	1.50
1995	16,530,000	—	—	0.75	1.25	1.50
1996 Sets only	15,000	—	—	—	—	2.00
1997 Sets only	15,000	—	—	—	—	2.00
1998 Sets only	11,500	—	—	—	—	2.00
1999 Sets only	12,500	—	—	—	—	2.00
2000 Sets only	12,500	—	—	—	—	2.00
2000	900	PF65 20.00				

KM# 11 10 KORUNA

6.60 g., Aluminum-Bronze, 26.5 mm. **Obv:** Double cross on shield above inscription **Rev:** Bronze cross and value

Date	Mintage	VF20	XF40	MS60	MS63	MS65
1993	40,934,000	—	—	1.00	1.50	2.50
1994	14,360,000	—	—	1.00	1.50	2.50
1995	42,204,000	—	—	1.00	1.50	2.50
1996 Sets only	15,000	—	—	—	—	3.00
1997 Sets only	15,000	—	—	—	—	3.00
1998 Sets only	12,000	—	—	—	—	3.00
1999 Sets only	11,500	—	—	—	—	3.00
2000 Sets only	12,500	—	—	—	—	3.00
2000	900	PF65 35.00				

KM# 11a 10 KORUNA

8.50 g., 0.750 Silver 0.205 oz. ASW, 26.5 mm. **Obv:** Double cross on shield abov inscription **Rev:** Bronze cross and value

Date	Mintage	F12	VF20	XF40	MS60	MS63
1993	1,000	PF65 350				

Note: These coins are numbered and punched with an R

KM# 16 100 KORUN

13.00 g., 0.750 Silver 0.3135 oz. ASW, 29 mm. **Subject:** National Independence **Obv:** Double cross on shield above inscription and value **Rev:** Three doves below double cross within clouds **Edge:** Milled **Note:** 7,450 uncirculated pieces melted in 2002.

Date	Mintage	VF20	XF40	MS60	MS63	MS65
1993 MK	65,000	—	—	—	—	12.00
1993 MK	5,000	PF65 20.00				

KM# 19 200 KORUN

20.00 g., 0.750 Silver 0.4823 oz. ASW, 34 mm. **Subject:** 150th Anniversary of Slovak Language **Obv:** Double cross on shield above value **Rev:** Three heads facing above dates **Edge:** Plain with ornament **Note:** 6,182 uncirculated pieces melted.

Date	Mintage	VF20	XF40	MS60	MS63	MS65
1993 MK	35,000	—	—	—	—	25.00
1993 MK	2,000	PF65 32.50				

KM# 20 200 KORUN

20.00 g., 0.750 Silver 0.4823 oz. ASW, 34 mm. **Subject:** 200th Anniversary - Birth of Jan Kollar **Obv:** Double cross on shield above inscription, value at left **Rev:** Windswept head facing, name and dates at bottom **Edge Lettering:** SLAVME SLAVNE SLAVU SLAVOV SLAVNYCH **Note:** 10,065 uncirculated pieces melted in 2002.

Date	Mintage	VF20	XF40	MS60	MS63	MS65
1993 MK	35,000	—	—	—	—	25.00
1993 MK	2,000	PF65 37.50				

KM# 21 200 KORUN

20.00 g., 0.750 Silver 0.4823 oz. ASW, 34 mm. **Subject:** 100th Anniversary - Olympic Committee **Obv:** Olympic rings and double cross on shield within design, dates at upper left **Rev:** Value, hockey player and snow flake design below **Edge:** Snowflakes **Note:** 16,475 uncirculated pieces melted.

Date	Mintage	VF20	XF40	MS60	MS63	MS65
1994	45,000	—	—	—	—	25.00
1994	3,000	PF65 32.50				

KM# 22 200 KORUN

20.00 g., 0.750 Silver 0.4823 oz. ASW, 34 mm. **Subject:** 100th Anniversary - Birth of Poet and Painter Janko Alexy **Obv:** Small double cross on shield below value and head of young girl in winter **Rev:** Head 3/4 right **Edge:** Plain with ornament **Note:** 13,100 uncirculated pieces melted.

Date	Mintage	VF20	XF40	MS60	MS63	MS65
1994 MK	34,000	—	—	—	—	25.00
1994 MK	2,500	PF65 35.00				

KM# 23 200 KORUN

20.00 g., 0.750 Silver 0.4823 oz. ASW, 34 mm. **Subject:** 50th Anniversary - D-Day **Obv:** Double cross on shield within stylized leaves flanked by dates and value **Rev:** Crowned emblem within v-shaped design divides dates and symbol **Edge Lettering:** SLOVACI PROTI FASIZMU **Note:** 10,550 uncirculated pieces melted.

Date	Mintage	VF20	XF40	MS60	MS63	MS65
1994	35,000	—	—	—	—	25.00
1994	2,600	PF65 80.00				

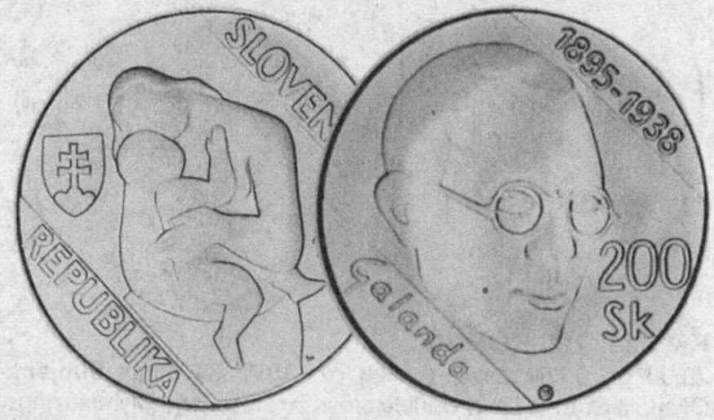

KM# 24 200 KORUN

20.00 g., 0.750 Silver 0.4823 oz. ASW, 34 mm. **Subject:** 200th Anniversary - Birth of Pavol Jozef Safarik **Obv:** Double cross on shield in center of inscription **Rev:** Head facing within inscription, value at bottom, dates diagonally at left **Edge Lettering:** ZAKLADATEL VEDECKEJ SLAVISTIKY **Note:** 8,700 uncirculated pieces melted in 2002.

Date	Mintage	VF20	XF40	MS60	MS63	MS65
1995 MK	23,500	—	—	—	—	28.00
1995 MK	1,500	PF65 45.00				

KM# 25 200 KORUN

20.00 g., 0.750 Silver 0.4823 oz. ASW, 34 mm. **Subject:** 100th Anniversary - Birth of Mikulas Galanda **Obv:** Double cross on shield to left of mother with child **Rev:** Head facing 3/4 right, dates diagonally at right, value at lower right **Edge Lettering:** MIKULAS GALANDA - MALIAR A GRAFIK **Note:** 10,700 uncirculated pieces melted.

Date	Mintage	VF20	XF40	MS60	MS63	MS65
1995	25,000	—	—	—	—	28.00
1995	1,500	PF65 45.00				

KM# 26 200 KORUN

20.00 g., 0.750 Silver 0.4823 oz. ASW, 34 mm. **Subject:** European Environmental Protection **Obv:** Double cross on shield above woodpecker feeding young **Rev:** Two storks and a flying swallow at right of flowers above value **Edge Lettering:** ENCY 1995 (3 fish) **Note:** 11,400 uncirculated pieces melted.

Date	Mintage	VF20	XF40	MS60	MS63	MS65
1995	28,000	—	—	—	—	28.00
1995	2,000	PF65 42.00				

KM# 27 200 KORUN

20.00 g., 0.750 Silver 0.4823 oz. ASW, 34 mm. **Subject:** Centennial of Bratislava Electric Tram **Obv:** Double cross on shield and date in center of inscription and value as a triangular design **Rev:** Two tram cars within triangular design **Edge Lettering:** HLAVNE NADRAZIE TEREZIANSKA STVRT **Note:** 9,300 uncirculated pieces melted.

Date	Mintage	VF20	XF40	MS60	MS63	MS65
1995	25,000	—	—	—	—	17.50
1995	1,600	PF65 140				

KM# 30 200 KORUN

20.00 g., 0.750 Silver 0.4823 oz. ASW, 34 mm. **Subject:** 200th Anniversary - Birth of Samuel Jurkovic **Obv:** Double cross on shield to left of design within lined square **Rev:** Half of head facing at left of lined square design **Edge Lettering:** V SLUZBACH NARODA **Note:** 11,100 uncirculated pieces melted.

Date	Mintage	VF20	XF40	MS60	MS63	MS65
1996 MK	26,000	—	—	—	—	17.50
1996 MK	1,600	PF65 50.00				

KM# 31 200 KORUN

20.00 g., 0.750 Silver 0.4823 oz. ASW, 34 mm. **Subject:** Olympic Games **Obv:** Double cross on shield and Olympic rings within square, date and inscription below **Rev:** Greek column within oval track, value below **Edge Lettering:** V DUCHU ODKAZU PIERRA DE COUBERTINA **Note:** 7,700 uncirculated pieces melted.

Date	Mintage	VF20	XF40	MS60	MS63	MS65
1996 MK	23,000	—	—	—	—	17.50
1996 MK	1,700	PF65 50.00				

KM# 32 200 KORUN

20.00 g., 0.750 Silver 0.4823 oz. ASW, 34 mm. **Subject:** 100th Anniversary - Birth of Jozef Ciger Hronsky **Obv:** Small double cross on shield within last O of value within square **Rev:** Half face with glasses and stylized sun within small squares flanked by dates and inscription **Edge Lettering:** NIET KRAJSICH SLOV AKO SKUTKY **Note:** 7,750 uncirculated pieces melted.

Date	Mintage	VF20	XF40	MS60	MS63	MS65
1996 MK	20,500	—	—	—	—	17.50
1996 MK	1,500	PF65 50.00				

KM# 33 200 KORUN

20.00 g., 0.750 Silver 0.4823 oz. ASW, 34 mm. **Subject:** Centennial - Mountain Railway to Strba Lake **Obv:** Double cross on shield above value, inscription and date **Rev:** Train and passenger car above dates and inscription **Edge Lettering:** VYSOKE TATRY VYSOKE TATRY **Note:** 6,050 uncirculated pieces melted.

Date	Mintage	VF20	XF40	MS60	MS63	MS65
1996	22,000	—	—	—	—	17.50
1996	1,600	PF65 225				

KM# 34 200 KORUN

20.00 g., 0.750 Silver 0.4823 oz. ASW, 34 mm. **Subject:** 200th Anniversary - Birth of Moric Benovsky **Obv:** Small double cross on shield at left of ship **Rev:** Bust facing **Edge Lettering:** IN ADVERSIS ET PROSPERIS **Note:** 5,050 uncirculated pieces melted in 2002.

Date	Mintage	VF20	XF40	MS60	MS63	MS65
1996	21,400	—	—	—	—	17.50
1996	2,000	PF65 40.00				

KM# 37 200 KORUN

20.00 g., 0.750 Silver 0.4823 oz. ASW, 34 mm. **Subject:** 150th Anniversary - Birth of Svetozar Hurban Vajansky 1847-1916 **Obv:** Double cross on shield **Rev:** Large head with beard and mustache **Edge Lettering:** POLITIK SPISOVATEL KRITIK NOVINAR **Note:** 4,600 uncirculated pieces melted.

Date	Mintage	VF20	XF40	MS60	MS63	MS65
1997	17,400	—	—	—	—	17.50
1997	1,800	PF65 40.00				

KM# 38 200 KORUN

20.00 g., 0.750 Silver 0.4823 oz. ASW, 34 mm. **Subject:** Banska Stiavnica - UNESCO **Obv:** Small double cross on shield at right of tower **Rev:** Baroque buildings **Edge Lettering:** PATRIMOINE MODIAL - WORLD HERITAGE **Note:** 1,900 Uncirculated pieces melted.

Date	Mintage	VF20	XF40	MS60	MS63	MS65
1997	16,500	—	—	—	—	17.50
1997	1,700	PF65 40.00				

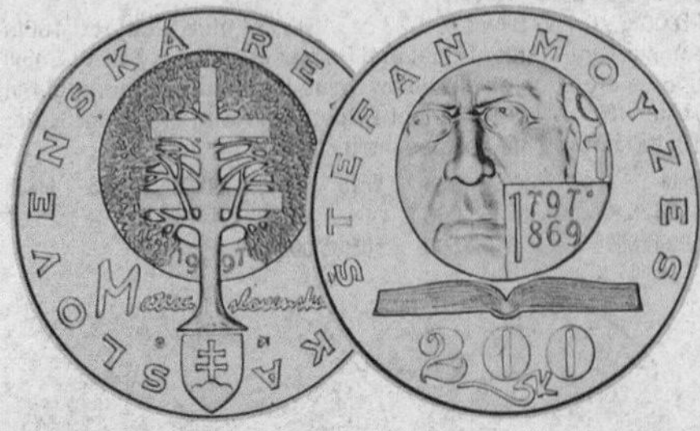

KM# 40 200 KORUN

20.00 g., 0.750 Silver 0.4823 oz. ASW, 34 mm. **Subject:** 200th Anniversary - Birth of Stefan Moyzes, 1797-1997 **Obv:** Stylized double cross in tree form with small double cross on shield below **Rev:** Head with glasses facing within circle above book and value **Edge Lettering:** PRVY PREDSEDA MATICE SLOVENSKEJ **Note:** 2,900 pieces melted.

Date	Mintage	VF20	XF40	MS60	MS63	MS65
1997	14,900	—	—	—	—	17.50
1997	1,500	PF65 100				

KM# 41 200 KORUN

20.00 g., 0.750 Silver 0.4823 oz. ASW, 34 mm. **Subject:** 50th Anniversary - Slovak National Gallery **Obv:** Crowned Madonna and child **Rev:** Daughters of King Lycomed **Edge Lettering:** GOTIKA A BAROK V ZBIERKACH SNG **Note:** 700 pieces melted.

Date	Mintage	VF20	XF40	MS60	MS63	MS65
1998	15,000	—	—	—	—	17.50
1998	1,600	PF65 50.00				

KM# 42 200 KORUN

20.00 g., 0.750 Silver 0.4823 oz. ASW, 34 mm. **Subject:** 150th Anniversary - 1st Railroad in Slovakia **Obv:** Small double cross on shield to right of train emerging from tunnel **Rev:** Bratislava Castle and locomotive **Edge Lettering:** 150 ROKOV ZELEZNIC NA SLOVENSKU **Note:** 200 pieces melted.

Date	Mintage	VF20	XF40	MS60	MS63	MS65
1998	14,000	—	—	—	—	17.50
1998	1,800	PF65 170				

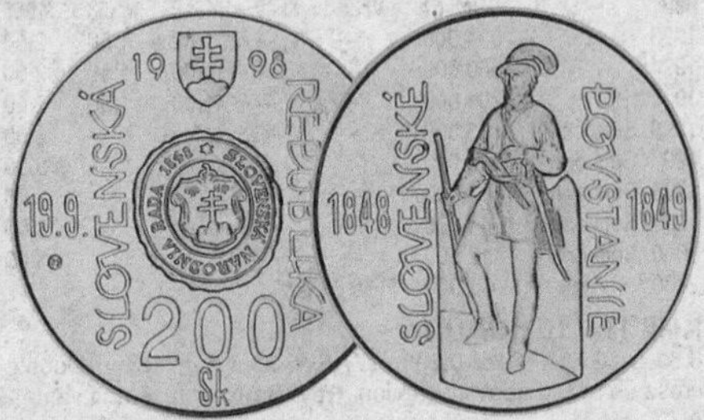

KM# 43 200 KORUN

20.00 g., 0.750 Silver 0.4823 oz. ASW **Subject:** 150th Anniversary - Slovak Revolt of 1848 **Obv:** Small double cross on shield divides date above emblem within circle flanked by vertical inscriptions **Rev:** Standing figure flanked by vertical inscriptions and dates **Edge Lettering:** ZA NARODNU SLOBODU **Note:** 1,900 pieces melted.

Date	Mintage	VF20	XF40	MS60	MS63	MS65
1998	13,400	—	—	—	—	17.50
1998	1,500	PF65 75.00				

KM# 44 200 KORUN

20.00 g., 0.750 Silver 0.4823 oz. ASW, 34 mm. **Subject:** UNESCO World Heritage site **Obv:** Cathedral towers **Rev:** Castle and gothic window arch **Edge Lettering:** PATRIMONIE MONDIAL WORLD HERITAGE **Note:** 700 pieces melted.

Date	Mintage	VF20	XF40	MS60	MS63	MS65
1998	13,500	—	—	—	—	17.50
1998	1,500	PF65 75.00				

KM# 45 200 KORUN
20.00 g., 0.750 Silver 0.4823 oz. ASW, 34 mm. **Subject:** Centennial - Birth of Jan Smrek **Obv:** Stylized seated female figure **Rev:** Half figure outline facing left **Edge Lettering:** BASNIK JAN SMREK 100 VYROCIE NARODENIA **Note:** 2,300 pieces melted.

Date	Mintage	VF20	XF40	MS60	MS63	MS65
1998	13,400	—	—	—	—	17.50
1998	1,500	**PF65** 50.00				

KM# 48 200 KORUN
20.00 g., 0.750 Silver 0.4823 oz. ASW, 34 mm. **Subject:** 150th Anniversary - Birth of Pavol Orszagh Hviezdoslav **Obv:** Portrait of face made with treetops **Rev:** Portrait of the artist **Edge Lettering:** HEROLD SVITAJUCICH CASOV **Note:** 800 pieces melted.

Date	Mintage	VF20	XF40	MS60	MS63	MS65
1999	12,700	—	—	—	—	17.50
1999	1,400	**PF65** 50.00				

KM# 49 200 KORUN
20.00 g., 0.750 Silver 0.4823 oz. ASW, 34 mm. **Subject:** 50th Anniversary - Slovac Philharmonic **Obv:** Pipe organ above double cross on shield flanked by value and date **Rev:** Reduta building bay window **Edge Lettering:** HUDBA-UNIVERZALNA REC LUDSTVA **Note:** 300 pieces melted.

Date	Mintage	VF20	XF40	MS60	MS63	MS65
1999 MK	12,700	—	—	—	—	17.50
1999 MK	1,400	**PF65** 50.00				

KM# 55 200 KORUN
20.00 g., 0.750 Silver 0.4823 oz. ASW, 33.9 mm. **Subject:** Juraj Fandly **Obv:** Radiant book above double cross on shield within design **Rev:** Half figure writing in book facing right **Edge Lettering:** NIE SILOU ANI MOCOU, ALE MOJIM DUCHOM **Note:** 700 pieces melted.

Date	Mintage	VF20	XF40	MS60	MS63	MS65
2000	10,600	—	—	—	—	20.00
2000	1,600	**PF65** 50.00				

KM# 28 500 KORUN
33.63 g., 0.925 Silver 1.0001 oz. ASW, 40 mm. **Subject:** Slovensky Raj National Park **Obv:** Double cross on shield, date, value and flowers **Rev:** Waterfall **Edge Lettering:** OCHRANA PRIRODY A. KRAJINY **Note:** 11,800 Uncirculated pieces melted in 2002.

Date	Mintage	VF20	XF40	MS60	MS63	MS65
1994	27,500	—	—	—	—	30.00
1994	2,400	**PF65** 60.00				

KM# 39 500 KORUN
33.63 g., 0.925 Silver 1.0001 oz. ASW, 40 mm. **Subject:** Pieninsky National Park **Obv:** Double cross on shield above butterfly within circle **Rev:** Park scene in circle within butterfly wings **Edge Lettering:** OCHRANA PRIRODY A KRAJINY **Note:** 2700 pieces uncirculated melted.

Date	Mintage	VF20	XF40	MS60	MS63	MS65
1997	14,500	—	—	—	—	65.00
1997	1,700	**PF65** 125				

KM# 47 500 KORUN
33.63 g., 0.925 Silver 1.0001 oz. ASW, 40 mm. **Subject:** Tatransky National Park **Obv:** Value, mountains, flowers and dates **Rev:** Chamois above flowers, date and double cross on shield **Edge Lettering:** OCHRANA PRIRODY A KRAJINY

Date	Mintage	VF20	XF40	MS60	MS63	MS65
1999	12,000	—	—	—	—	45.00
Note: 700 pieces uncirculated melted.						
1999	1,400	**PF65** 225				

KM# 50 500 KORUN
33.63 g., 0.925 Silver 1.0001 oz. ASW, 40 mm. **Subject:** 500th Anniversary - First Thalers of Kremnica **Obv:** Mining scene within beaded circle **Rev:** Old coin designs and city view within beaded circle **Edge Lettering:** GULDINER-PREDCHODCA TOLIARA

Date	Mintage	VF20	XF40	MS60	MS63	MS65
1999	12,000	—	—	—	—	45.00
1999	1,400	**PF65** 350				

KM# 53 500 KORUN
33.63 g., 0.925 Silver 1.0001 oz. ASW, 40 mm. **Subject:** 250th Anniversary - Death of Samuel Mikovini **Obv:** Armored bust right and cartographic instruments **Rev:** Allegorical scene and map **Edge Lettering:** KARTOGRAF - MATEMATIK - STAVITEL

Date	Mintage	VF20	XF40	MS60	MS63	MS65
2000	10,100	—	—	—	—	35.00
2000	1,500	**PF65** 120				

KM# 51 2000 KORUN
124.41 g., 0.999 Silver 3.996 oz. ASW, 65 mm. **Subject:** 2000 Bi-millennium **Obv:** Small double cross on shield, value and historical scenes **Rev:** Jesus within churches and value **Edge:** Plain **Shape:** Octagon

Date	Mintage	VF20	XF40	MS60	MS63	MS65
MM(2000)	3,000	**PF65** 600				

KM# 29 5000 KORUN
7.00 g., 0.900 Gold 0.2025 oz. AGW, 24 mm. **Subject:** 1100th Anniversary - Death of Moravian King Svatopluk **Obv:** Double cross on shield, value and date **Rev:** Head of Svatopluk and ruin of castle Devin **Edge:** Milled

Date	Mintage	VF20	XF40	MS60	MS63	MS65
1994	5,000	**PF65** 450				

KM# 36 5000 KORUN
9.50 g., 0.900 Gold 0.2749 oz. AGW, 26 mm. **Subject:** Banska Stiavnica Mines - UNESCO historic site **Obv:** Double cross on shield, value, date and upright design **Rev:** Steepled buildings **Edge:** Milled

Date	Mintage	VF20	XF40	MS60	MS63	MS65
1997	8,000	**PF65** 500				

KM# 46 5000 KORUN
9.50 g., 0.900 Gold 0.2749 oz. AGW, 26 mm. **Subject:** Spissky Castle - UNESCO historic site **Obv:** Double cross on shield and lion within design above date **Rev:** Scenic design and value **Edge:** Milled

Date	Mintage	VF20	XF40	MS60	MS63	MS65
1998	6,000	PF65 500				

KM# 54 5000 KORUN
9.50 g., 0.900 Gold 0.2749 oz. AGW, 26 mm. **Subject:** 500th Anniversary - Kremnica Mint **Obv:** Hungarian coin design **Rev:** Hungarian coin design **Edge:** Reeded

Date	Mintage	VF20	XF40	MS60	MS63	MS65
ND-1999	5,500	PF65 500				

KM# 52 10000 KORUN
19.00 g., 0.900 Gold 0.5498 oz. AGW, 34 mm. **Subject:** 2000 Bi-millennium **Obv:** Double cross on shield, value and historical scenes **Rev:** Jesus with churches **Edge:** Milled **Note:** Similar to 2000 Korun, KM#51.

Date	Mintage	VF20	XF40	MS60	MS63	MS65
MM(2000)	3,500	PF65 1,000				

ESSAIS

KM#	Date	Mintage	Identification	Mkt Val
E1	1939	—	20 Korun. 0.500. Silver. KM#7.	—
E2	1941	—	10 Korun. 0.500. Silver. KM#9.1.	—

MINT SETS

KM#	Date	Mintage	Identification	Issue Price	Mkt Val
MS1	1993 (7)	28,800	KM#11.1-15, 17-18, plus medal	—	10.00
MS2	1994 (7)	19,000	KM#11.1-15, 17-18, plus medal	—	10.00
MS3	1995 (7)	12,000	KM#11.1-15, 17-18, plus medal	—	10.00
MS4	1996 (7)	15,000	KM#11.1-14, 17-18, 35, plus medal	—	10.00
MS5	1997 (7)	15,000	KM#11.1-14, 17-18, 35, plus medal	—	12.50
MS6	1998 (7)	12,000	KM#11.1-14, 17-18, 35, plus medal	—	17.50
MS7	1999 (7)	11,500	KM#11.1-14, 17-18, 35, plus medal	—	12.00
MS8	2000 (7)	13,000	KM#11.1-14, 17-18, 35, plus medal	—	17.50

PROOF SETS

KM#	Date	Mintage	Identification	Issue Price	Mkt Val
PS1	2000 (7)	900	KM#11.1-14, 17-18, 35	—	125

SLOVENIA

The Republic of Slovenia is located northwest of Yugoslavia in the valleys of the Danube River. It has an area of 7,819 sq. mi. and a population of *1.9 million. Capital: Ljubljana. Agriculture is the main industry with large amounts of hops and fodder crops grown as well as many varieties of fruit trees. Sheep raising, timber production and the mining of mercury from one of the country's oldest mines are also very important to the economy.

Slovenia was important as a land route between Europe and the eastern Mediterranean region. The Roman Catholic Austro-Hungarian Empire gained control of the area during the 14th century and retained its dominance until World War I. The United Kingdom of the Serbs, Croats and Slovenes (Yugoslavia) was founded in 1918 and consisted of various groups of South Slavs.

In 1929, King Alexander declared his assumption of power temporarily, however he was assassinated in 1934. His son Peter's regent, Prince Paul tried to settle internal problems, however, the Slovenes denounced the agreement he made. He resigned in 1941 and Peter assumed the throne. Peter was forced to flee when Yugoslavia was occupied. Slovenia was divided between Germany and Italy. Even though Yugoslavia attempted to remain neutral, the Nazis occupied the country and were resisted by guerilla armies, most notably Marshal Josif Broz Tito.

Under Marshal Tito, the Constitution of 1946 established 6 constituent republics which made up Yugoslavia. Each republic was permitted Liberties under supervision of the Communist Party.

In Oct. 1989 the Slovene Assembly voted a constitutional amendment giving it the right to secede from Yugoslavia. A referendum on Dec. 23, 1990 resulted in a majority vote for independence, which was formally declared on Dec. 26.

On June 25 Slovenia declared independence, but agreed to suspend this for 3 months at peace talks sponsored by the EC. Federal troops moved into Slovenia on June 27 to secure Yugoslavia's external borders, but after some fighting withdrew by the end of July. The 3-month moratorium agreed at the EC having expired, Slovenia (and Croatia) declared their complete independence of the Yugoslav federation on Oct.8, 1991.

MINT MARKS
Based on last digit in date.
(K) - Kremnitz (Slovakia): open 4, upturned 5
(BP) - Budapest (Hungary): closed 4, downturned 5

MONETARY SYSTEM
100 Stotinov = 1 Tolar

REPUBLIC

STANDARD COINAGE

100 Stotinow = 1 Tolar

KM# 7 10 STOTINOV
0.55 g., Aluminum, 16 mm. **Obv:** Value within square **Rev:** Olm salamander **Edge:** Plain **Note:** Varieties exist.

Date	Mintage	VF20	XF40	MS60	MS63	MS65
1992	2,515,000	—	—	0.25	0.35	0.75
1992	1,000	PF65 5.00				
1993	2,515,000	—	—	0.25	0.35	0.75
1993	1,000	PF65 5.00				
1994 Sets only	1,000	—	—	—	—	3.00
1994	1,000	PF65 5.00				
1995 Sets only	1,000	—	—	—	—	3.00
1995	1,000	PF65 5.00				
1996 Sets only	1,000	—	—	—	—	3.00
1996	800	PF65 5.00				
1997 Sets only	1,000	—	—	—	—	3.00
1997	800	PF65 5.00				
1998 Sets only	1,000	—	—	—	—	3.00
1998	800	PF65 5.00				
1999 Sets only	1,000	—	—	—	—	3.00
1999	800	PF65 5.00				
2000 Sets only	1,000	—	—	—	—	3.00
2000	800	PF65 5.00				

KM# 8 20 STOTINOV
0.70 g., Aluminum, 18 mm. **Obv:** Value within square **Rev:** Barn owl and value **Edge:** Plain

Date	Mintage	VF20	XF40	MS60	MS63	MS65
1992	2,515,000	—	—	0.35	0.50	1.00
Note: Minor reverse varieties exist						
1992	1,000	PF65 6.00				
1993	2,515,000	—	—	0.35	0.50	1.00
Note: Minor reverse varieties exist						
1993	—	PF65 6.00				
1994 Sets only	1,000	—	—	—	—	4.00
1994	1,000	PF65 6.00				
1995 Sets only	1,000	—	—	—	—	4.00
1995	—	PF65 6.00				
1996 Sets only	1,000	—	—	—	—	4.00
1996	800	PF65 6.00				
1997 Sets only	1,000	—	—	—	—	4.00
1997	800	PF65 6.00				
1998 Sets only	1,000	—	—	—	—	4.00
1998	800	PF65 6.00				
1999 Sets only	1,000	—	—	—	—	4.00
1999	800	PF65 6.00				
2000 Sets only	1,000	—	—	—	—	4.00
2000	800	PF65 6.00				

KM# 3 50 STOTINOV
0.85 g., Aluminum, 20 mm. **Obv:** Value within square **Rev:** Bee and value **Edge:** Plain

Date	Mintage	VF20	XF40	MS60	MS63	MS65
1992	5,015,000	—	0.10	0.25	0.50	0.75
Note: Minor reverse varieties exist						
1992	1,000	PF65 7.50				
1993	18,315,000	—	0.10	0.25	0.50	0.75
1993	1,000	PF65 7.50				
1994 Sets only	1,000	—	—	—	—	6.00
1994	1,000	PF65 7.50				
1995	3,000,000	—	0.10	0.25	0.50	0.75
1995 Sets only	1,000	—	—	—	—	6.00
1995	1,000	PF65 7.50				
1996	3,000,000	—	0.10	0.25	0.50	0.75
1996	Est. 500	PF65 7.50				
1997 Sets only	1,000	—	—	—	—	6.00
1997	500	PF65 7.50				
1998 Sets only	1,000	—	—	—	—	6.00
1998	500	PF65 7.50				
1999 Sets only	1,000	—	—	—	—	6.00
1999	500	PF65 7.50				
2000 Sets only	1,000	—	—	—	—	6.00
2000	800	PF65 7.50				

KM# 4 TOLAR
4.50 g., Nickel-Brass, 22 mm. **Obv:** Value within circle **Rev:** Three brown trout **Rev. Legend:** SALMO TRUTTA FARIO **Edge:** Reeded **Note:** Date varieties exist: 1994 = closed or open "4"; 1995 = serif up and serif down in "5".

Date	Mintage	VF20	XF40	MS60	MS63	MS65
1992	10,015,000	—	0.20	0.45	0.85	1.50
1992	1,000	PF65 7.50				
1993	30,015,000	—	0.20	0.45	0.85	1.50
1993	1,000	PF65 7.50				
1994 (K)	10,000,000	—	—	0.50	0.75	1.50
Note: 4 open to the top						
1994 (K)	1,000	PF65 7.50				
Note: 4 open to right						
1994 (BP)	5,000,000	—	—	0.50	0.75	1.50
1995 (K)	10,000,000	—	—	0.50	0.75	1.50
1995 (K) Sets only	1,000	—	—	—	—	5.00
1995 (K)	1,000	PF65 7.50				
1995 (BP)	10,000,000	—	—	0.50	0.75	1.50
1996	Est. 21800000	—	—	0.50	0.75	1.50
1996	Est. 3000	PF65 7.50				
1997	8,000,000	—	—	0.50	0.75	1.50
1997	500	PF65 10.00				
1998	12,000,000	—	—	0.50	0.75	1.50
1998	500	PF65 10.00				
1999	8,000,000	—	—	0.50	0.75	1.50
1999	500	PF65 10.00				
2000	15,001,000	—	—	0.50	0.75	1.50
2000	800	PF65 7.50				

KM# 5 2 TOLARJA
5.40 g., Nickel-Brass, 24 mm. **Obv:** Value within circle **Rev:** Barn swallow in flight **Rev. Legend:** HIRUNDO RUSTICA **Edge:** Reeded **Note:** Date varieties exist: 1994 = closed or open "4"; 1995 = serif up and serif down in "5".

Date	Mintage	VF20	XF40	MS60	MS63	MS65
1992	5,015,000	—	0.25	0.45	0.85	1.75
1992	1,000	PF65 8.50				
1993	10,015,000	—	0.25	0.45	0.85	1.75
1993	1,000	PF65 8.50				
1994 (K)	10,000,000	—	—	0.45	0.75	1.75
Note: 4 open to the top						
1994 (K) Sets only	1,000	—	—	—	—	7.00
Note: 4 open to right						
1994 (K)	1,000	PF65 8.50				
Note: 4 open to right						
1994 (BP)	5,000,000	—	—	0.45	0.75	1.75
1995 (K) Sets only	1,000	—	—	—	—	7.00
1995 (K)	10,000,000	—	—	0.45	0.75	1.75
1995 (K)	1,000	PF65 8.50				
1995 (BP)	10,000,000	—	—	0.45	0.75	1.75
1996	Est. 16600000	—	—	0.45	0.75	1.75
1996	1,000	PF65 8.50				
1997	6,060,000	—	—	0.45	0.75	1.75
1997	500	PF65 12.00				
1998	5,000,000	—	—	0.45	0.75	1.75
1998	500	PF65 12.00				

Date	Mintage	VF20	XF40	MS60	MS63	MS65
1999	5,200,000	—	—	0.45	0.75	1.75
1999	500	PF65 12.00				
2000	15,001,000	—	—	0.45	0.75	1.75
2000	800	PF65 8.50				

KM# 6 5 TOLARJEV

6.44 g., Nickel-Brass, 26 mm. **Obv:** Value within circle **Rev:** Head and horns of ibex **Edge:** Reeded **Note:** Date varieties exist: 1994 = closed or open "4"; 1995 = serif up and serif down in "5".

Date	Mintage	VF20	XF40	MS60	MS63	MS65
1992	10,015,000	—	0.35	0.50	1.00	2.00
1992	1,000	PF65 10.00				
1993	1,000	PF65 10.00				
1993	10,015,000	—	0.35	0.50	1.00	2.00
1994 (K)	10,000,000	—	—	0.45	0.85	2.00
Note: 4 open to the top						
1994 (K)	1,000	—	—	—	—	8.00
Sets only						
Note: 4 open to right						
1994 (K)	1,000	PF65 10.00				
Note: 4 open to right						
1994 (BP)	5,000,000	—	—	0.45	0.85	2.00
1995 2 tip	—	—	—	0.45	0.85	2.00
1995	5,000,000	—	—	0.45	0.85	2.00
1995 (K)	1,000	PF65 10.00				
1996	6,000,000	—	—	0.45	0.85	2.00
1996	Est. 3000	PF65 10.00				
1997	8,000,000	—	—	0.45	0.85	2.00
1997	500	PF65 15.00				
1998	10,000,000	—	—	0.45	0.85	2.00
1998	500	PF65 15.00				
1999	6,403,000	—	—	0.45	0.85	2.00
1999	500	PF65 15.00				
2000	15,001,000	—	—	0.45	0.85	2.00
2000	800	PF65 10.00				

KM# 9 5 TOLARJEV

6.40 g., Nickel-Brass, 26 mm. **Subject:** 400th Anniversary - Battle of Sisek **Obv:** Value and date **Rev:** City view, arms, date, Andrej G. Turjaski **Edge:** Reeded

Date	Mintage	VF20	XF40	MS60	MS63	MS65
1993	100,000	—	—	1.25	1.65	2.25

KM# 12 5 TOLARJEV

6.40 g., Nickel-Brass, 26 mm. **Subject:** 300th Anniversary - Establishment of Operosorum Labacensium Academy **Obv:** Value and date **Rev:** Beehive and bees **Edge:** Reeded

Date	Mintage	VF20	XF40	MS60	MS63	MS65
1993	100,000	—	—	1.50	2.00	5.00

KM# 15 5 TOLARJEV

6.40 g., Nickel-Brass, 26 mm. **Subject:** 50th Anniversary - Slovenian Bank **Obv:** Value and date **Rev:** Linden leaf and seed pod **Edge:** Reeded

Date	Mintage	VF20	XF40	MS60	MS63	MS65
1994	100,000	—	—	1.25	1.65	2.25

KM# 16 5 TOLARJEV

6.40 g., Nickel-Brass, 26 mm. **Subject:** 1,000th Anniversary - Glagolitic Alphabet **Obv:** Value and date **Rev:** Feather **Edge:** Reeded

Date	Mintage	VF20	XF40	MS60	MS63	MS65
1994	200,000	—	—	1.25	1.65	2.25

KM# 21 5 TOLARJEV

6.40 g., Nickel-Brass, 26 mm. **Series:** F.A.O. **Subject:** 50th Anniversary - F.A.O. **Obv:** Value within circle **Rev:** Hands holding F.A.O. logo **Edge:** Reeded

Date	Mintage	VF20	XF40	MS60	MS63	MS65
ND-1995	500,000	—	—	1.25	1.65	2.25

KM# 22 5 TOLARJEV

6.40 g., Nickel-Brass, 26 mm. **Subject:** 50th Anniversary - Defeat of Fascism **Obv:** Value **Rev:** Vertical chain link design and dates **Edge:** Reeded

Date	Mintage	VF20	XF40	MS60	MS63	MS65
1995	200,000	—	—	1.25	1.65	2.25

KM# 26 5 TOLARJEV

6.40 g., Nickel-Brass, 26 mm. **Subject:** Aljazev Stolp **Obv:** Value within triangle design **Rev:** Head facing in front of mountains **Edge:** Reeded

Date	Mintage	VF20	XF40	MS60	MS63	MS65
1995	200,000	—	—	1.25	1.65	2.25

KM# 29 5 TOLARJEV

6.40 g., Nickel-Brass, 26 mm. **Subject:** 150th Anniversary - First Railway in Slovenia **Obv:** Date within design at upper right, value at far left **Rev:** Dates above train **Edge:** Reeded

Date	Mintage	VF20	XF40	MS60	MS63	MS65
1996	Est. 300000	—	—	1.25	1.65	2.25
1996	—	PF65 8.00				

KM# 32 5 TOLARJEV

6.40 g., Nickel-Brass, 26 mm. **Subject:** 5th Anniversary of Independence **Obv:** Value and date at left **Rev:** Pink Carnation and dates **Edge:** Reeded

Date	Mintage	VF20	XF40	MS60	MS63	MS65
1996	200,000	—	—	1.25	1.65	2.25
1996	—	PF65 8.00				

KM# 33 5 TOLARJEV

6.40 g., Nickel-Brass, 26 mm. **Series:** Olympics **Subject:** Olympics Centennial **Obv:** Value above olympic rings and flag **Rev:** Gymnast above dates **Edge:** Reeded

Date	Mintage	VF20	XF40	MS60	MS63	MS65
1996	200,000	—	—	1.25	1.65	2.25
1996	Est. 3000	PF65 8.00				

KM# 38 5 TOLARJEV

6.40 g., Nickel-Brass, 26 mm. **Subject:** Ziga Zois **Obv:** Value and date **Rev:** Name written within outline profile right, dates below **Edge:** Reeded

Date	Mintage	VF20	XF40	MS60	MS63	MS65
1997	200,000	—	—	1.25	1.65	2.25
1997 Proof	—	—	—	—	—	—

KM# 41 10 TOLARJEV

5.75 g., Copper-Nickel, 24 mm. **Obv:** Value within circle **Rev:** Stylized rearing horse **Rev. Legend:** EQUUS **Edge:** Reeded

Date	Mintage	VF20	XF40	MS60	MS63	MS65
2000	10,001,000	—	—	1.50	2.00	3.50
2000	800	PF65 12.00				

KM# 1 500 TOLARJEV

15.00 g., 0.925 Silver 0.4461 oz. ASW **Subject:** 1st Anniversary of Independence **Obv:** Value within circle at left, date at right **Rev:** Leaf, design and value **Note:** Eight minor obverse and reverse varieties exist.

Date	Mintage	VF20	XF40	MS60	MS63	MS65
1991	15,000	PF63 20.00	PF65 25.00			

KM# 10 500 TOLARJEV

15.00 g., 0.925 Silver 0.4461 oz. ASW, 32 mm. **Subject:** Battle of Sisek **Obv:** Value and date **Rev:** City view, arms and date

Date	Mintage	VF20	XF40	MS60	MS63	MS65
1993	5,000	PF63 25.00	PF65 28.00			

KM# 13 500 TOLARJEV
15.00 g., 0.925 Silver 0.4461 oz. ASW, 32 mm. **Subject:** 300th Anniversary - Establishment of Operasorum Labacensium Academy **Obv:** Value and date **Rev:** Dates above angel

Date	Mintage	VF20	XF40	MS60	MS63	MS65
1993	—	PF63 25.00	PF65 28.00			

KM# 17 500 TOLARJEV
15.00 g., 0.925 Silver 0.4461 oz. ASW, 32 mm. **Subject:** 50th Anniversary - Slovenian Bank **Obv:** Value **Rev:** Leaf and dates

Date	Mintage	VF20	XF40	MS60	MS63	MS65
1994	5,000	PF63 25.00	PF65 28.00			

KM# 19 500 TOLARJEV
15.00 g., 0.925 Silver 0.4461 oz. ASW, 32 mm. **Subject:** 1000th Anniversary - Bishop Abraham - Glagolistic Alphabet **Obv:** Value and date **Rev:** Feather and dates

Date	Mintage	VF20	XF40	MS60	MS63	MS65
1994	3,000	PF63 27.00	PF65 30.00			

KM# 23 500 TOLARJEV
15.00 g., 0.925 Silver 0.4461 oz. ASW, 32 mm. **Subject:** 50th Anniversary - Defeat of Fascism **Obv:** Stylized design **Rev:** Stylized design, dates and value

Date	Mintage	VF20	XF40	MS60	MS63	MS65
1995	3,000	PF63 27.00	PF65 30.00			

KM# 25 500 TOLARJEV
15.00 g., 0.925 Silver 0.4461 oz. ASW, 32 mm. **Series:** F.A.O. **Subject:** 50th Anniversary - F.A.O. **Obv:** Vertical value **Rev:** F.A.O. logo above weeds

Date	Mintage	VF20	XF40	MS60	MS63	MS65
1995	3,000	PF63 27.00	PF65 30.00			

KM# 27 500 TOLARJEV
15.00 g., 0.925 Silver 0.4461 oz. ASW, 32 mm. **Subject:** 100th Anniversary - Aljazev Stolp **Obv:** Value within triangle design below date **Rev:** Head facing in front of mountains

Date	Mintage	VF20	XF40	MS60	MS63	MS65
1995	3,000	PF63 27.00	PF65 30.00			

KM# 30 500 TOLARJEV
15.00 g., 0.925 Silver 0.4461 oz. ASW, 32 mm. **Subject:** 150th Anniversary - First Railway in Slovenia **Obv:** Large value **Rev:** Design within wheel designed circle

Date	Mintage	VF20	XF40	MS60	MS63	MS65
1996	4,000	PF63 27.00	PF65 30.00			

KM# 34 500 TOLARJEV
15.00 g., 0.925 Silver 0.4461 oz. ASW, 32 mm. **Subject:** 5th Anniversary of Independence **Obv:** Map of Slovenia divides date and value **Rev:** World globe and dates

Date	Mintage	VF20	XF40	MS60	MS63	MS65
1996	3,000	PF63 27.00	PF65 30.00			

KM# 36 500 TOLARJEV
15.00 g., 0.925 Silver 0.4461 oz. ASW, 32 mm. **Series:** Olympics **Obv:** Value above olympic rings and flag **Rev:** Gymnast and dates

Date	Mintage	VF20	XF40	MS60	MS63	MS65
1996	3,000	PF63 27.00	PF65 30.00			

KM# 39 500 TOLARJEV
15.00 g., 0.925 Silver 0.4461 oz. ASW, 32 mm. **Subject:** Zois Ziga

Date	Mintage	VF20	XF40	MS60	MS63	MS65
1997	3,000	PF63 27.00	PF65 30.00			

KM# 2.1 5000 TOLARJEV
7.00 g., 0.900 Gold 0.2025 oz. AGW **Subject:** 1st Anniversary of Independence **Obv:** Value within circle at left, date at right **Rev:** Bird's beak at center of spiral

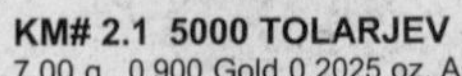

Date	Mintage	VF20	XF40	MS60	MS63	MS65
1991	2,000	PF63 325	PF65 375			

KM# 2.2 5000 TOLARJEV
7.00 g., 0.900 Gold 0.2025 oz. AGW **Obv:** Value within circle at left, date at right **Rev:** Bird's beak below center of spiral

Date	Mintage	VF20	XF40	MS60	MS63	MS65
1991	Inc. above	PF63 325	PF65 375			

KM# 11 5000 TOLARJEV
7.00 g., 0.900 Gold 0.2025 oz. AGW, 24 mm. **Subject:** Battle of Sisek **Obv:** Value below date **Rev:** City view, arms and date

Date	Mintage	VF20	XF40	MS60	MS63	MS65
1993	2,000	PF63 325	PF65 375			

KM# 14 5000 TOLARJEV
7.00 g., 0.900 Gold 0.2025 oz. AGW, 24 mm. **Subject:** 300th Anniversary - Establishment of Operosorum Labacensium Academy **Obv:** Value below date **Rev:** Beehive among bees

Date	Mintage	VF20	XF40	MS60	MS63	MS65
1993	—	PF63 325	PF65 375			

KM# 18 5000 TOLARJEV
7.00 g., 0.900 Gold 0.2025 oz. AGW, 24 mm. **Subject:** 50th Anniversary - Slovenian Bank **Obv:** Value and vertical date **Rev:** Leaf and dates

Date	Mintage	VF20	XF40	MS60	MS63	MS65
1994	2,000	PF63 325	PF65 375			

KM# 20 5000 TOLARJEV
7.00 g., 0.900 Gold 0.2025 oz. AGW **Subject:** 1000th Anniversary - Bishop Abraham - Glagolitic Alphabet **Obv:** Value **Rev:** Feather

Date	Mintage	VF20	XF40	MS60	MS63	MS65
1994	1,000	PF63 350	PF65 400			

KM# 24 5000 TOLARJEV
7.00 g., 0.900 Gold 0.2025 oz. AGW, 24 mm. **Subject:** 50th Anniversary - Defeat of Fascism **Obv:** Value **Rev:** Vertical chain link design and dates

Date	Mintage	VF20	XF40	MS60	MS63	MS65
1995	1,000	PF63 350	PF65 400			

KM# 28 5000 TOLARJEV
7.00 g., 0.900 Gold 0.2025 oz. AGW, 24 mm. **Subject:** Aljazev Stolp and Mountain Summit **Obv:** Value within triangle design **Rev:** Head facing in front of mountains

Date	Mintage	VF20	XF40	MS60	MS63	MS65
1995	1,000	PF63 350	PF65 400			

KM# 31 5000 TOLARJEV
7.00 g., 0.900 Gold 0.2025 oz. AGW, 24 mm. **Subject:** 100th Anniversary - First Railway in Slovenia **Obv:** Date within design at upper right, value at left **Rev:** Train below dates

Date	Mintage	VF20	XF40	MS60	MS63	MS65
1996	1,000	PF63 350	PF65 400			

KM# 35 5000 TOLARJEV
7.00 g., 0.900 Gold 0.2025 oz. AGW, 24 mm. **Subject:** 5th Anniversary of Independence **Obv:** Value above date **Rev:** Pink carnation above dates

Date	Mintage	VF20	XF40	MS60	MS63	MS65
1996	1,000	PF63 350	PF65 400			

KM# 37 5000 TOLARJEV
7.00 g., 0.900 Gold 0.2025 oz. AGW, 24 mm. **Series:** Olympics **Obv:** Value above olympic rings and flag **Rev:** Gymnast above dates

Date	Mintage	VF20	XF40	MS60	MS63	MS65
1996	1,000	PF63 350	PF65 400			

KM# 40 5000 TOLARJEV
7.00 g., 0.900 Gold 0.2025 oz. AGW, 24 mm. **Subject:** Zois Ziga

Date	Mintage	VF20	XF40	MS60	MS63	MS65
1997	1,000	PF63 350	PF65 400			

MINT SETS

KM#	Date	Mintage	Identification	Issue Price	Mkt Val
MS1	1992 (6)	—	KM#3-8	—	8.00
MS2	1992 (5)	15,000	KM#4-8	—	7.00
MS3	1993 (6)	—	KM#3-8	—	8.00
MS4	1993 (5)	15,000	KM#4-8	—	7.00
MS5	1994 (6)	1,000	KM#3-8	—	35.00
MS6	1995 (6)	1,000	KM#3-8	—	35.00
MS7	1996 (9)	300	KM#4-6, 29-30, 32-34, 36	—	100
MS9	2000 (7)	1,000	KM#3-8, 41	20.00	22.50

PROOF SETS

KM#	Date	Mintage	Identification	Issue Price	Mkt Val
PS1	1991 (2)	—	KM#1, 2.2	—	340
PS2	1992 (6)	1,000	KM#3-8	—	45.00
PS3	1992 (5)	1,000	KM#4-8	—	37.00
PS4	1993 (6)	1,000	KM#3-8	—	45.00
PS5	1993 (5)	1,000	KM#4-8	—	37.00
PS6	1994 (6)	1,000	KM#3-8	—	45.00
PS7	1995 (6)	1,000	KM#3-8	—	45.00
PS8	1996 (9)	3,000	KM#4-6, 29-30, 32-34, 36	—	140
PS9	1996 (28)	800	1996-99 KM#3-8, 1996 KM#29,32,33, 1997 KM#38	—	235
PS12	2000 (7)	800	KM#3-8, 41	—	57.50

SOLOMON ISLANDS

The Solomon Islands are made up of approximately 200 islands. They are located in the southwest Pacific east of Papua New Guinea, have an area of 10,983 sq. mi. (28,450 sq. km.) and a population of *552,000. Capital: Honiara. The most important islands of the Solomon chain are Guadalcanal (scene of some of the fiercest fighting of World War II), Malaitia, New Georgia, Florida, Vella Lavella, Choiseul, Rendova, San Cristobal, the Lord Howe group, the Santa Cruz islands, and the Duff group. Copra is the only important cash crop but it is hoped that timber will become an economic factor.

The Solomon Islands were discovered by Spanish navigator Alvaro de Mendana in 1567, and in 1569 he made an unsuccessful attempt to colonize them. European knowledge of the group would not be completed until the end of the 19th century. Germany declared a protectorate over the northern Solomon's in 1885. The British protectorate over the southern Solomons was established in 1893. In 1899 Germany transferred its claim to all Solomon Islands except Buka and Bougainville to Great Britain in exchange for recognition of German claims in Western Samoa. Australia occupied the two German islands in 1914, and administered them after 1920.

The Japanese invaded the Solomons during 1942-43, but were driven out by an American counteroffensive after a series of bloody clashes.

Following World War II, the islands returned to the status of a British protectorate. In 1976 the protectorate was abolished, and the Solomons became a self-governing dependency. Full independence was achieved on July 7,1978. Solomon Islands is a member of the Commonwealth of Nations. Queen Elizabeth II is Head of State, as Queen of the Solomon Islands.

RULER
British, until 1978
Queen Elizabeth II (see above)

MINT MARK
FM - Franklin Mint, U.S.A.*

NOTE: From 1977-1985 the Franklin Mint produced coinage in up to 3 different qualities. Qualities of issue are designated in ( ) after each date and are defined as follows:
(M) MATTE - Normal circulation strike or a dull finish produced by sandblasting special uncirculated (polish finish) or proof quality dies.
(U) SPECIAL UNCIRCULATED - Polished or proof-like in appearance without any frosted features.
(P) PROOF - The highest quality obtainable having mirror-like fields and frosted features.

MONETARY SYSTEM
100 Cents = 1 Dollar

COMMONWEALTH NATION

STANDARD COINAGE

KM# 1 CENT
2.60 g., Bronze, 17.53 mm. **Ruler:** Elizabeth II **Series:** F.A.O. **Obv:** Young bust right **Obv. Legend:** ELIZABETH II - SOLOMON ISLANDS **Rev:** Food bowl divides value **Edge:** Plain

Date	Mintage	VF20	XF40	MS60	MS63	MS65
1977	1,828,000	—	0.10	0.15	0.25	0.35
1977 FM (M)	6,000	—	—	0.50	0.60	0.75
1977 FM (U)	—	—	—	1.25	1.50	2.00
1977 FM (P)	14,000	PF65 1.00				
1978 FM (M)	6,000	—	—	0.50	0.60	0.75
1978 FM (U)	544	—	—	1.25	1.50	2.00
1978 FM (P)	5,122	PF65 1.00				
1979 FM (M)	6,000	—	—	0.50	0.60	0.75
1979 FM (U)	677	—	—	1.25	1.50	2.00
1979 FM (P)	2,845	PF65 1.50				
1980 FM (M)	6,000	—	—	0.50	0.60	0.75
1980 FM (U)	624	—	—	1.25	1.50	2.00
1980 FM (P)	1,031	PF65 1.50				
1981	—	—	—	0.50	0.60	0.75
1981 FM (M)	6,000	—	—	0.50	0.60	0.75
1981 FM (U)	212	—	—	2.00	2.50	3.00
1981 FM (P)	448	PF65 1.50				
1982 FM (U)	—	—	—	1.25	1.50	2.00
1982 FM (P)	—	PF65 1.50				
1983 FM (M)	—	—	—	0.50	0.60	0.75
1983 FM (U)	200	—	—	2.00	2.50	3.00
1983 FM (P)	—	PF65 1.50				

KM# 1a CENT
Bronze Plated Steel, 17.53 mm. **Series:** F.A.O. **Obv:** Young bust right **Rev:** Food bowl divides value **Edge:** Plain

Date	Mintage	VF20	XF40	MS60	MS63	MS65
1985	—	—	—	0.25	0.35	0.50

KM# 24 CENT
2.30 g., Bronze Plated Steel, 17.53 mm. **Ruler:** Elizabeth II **Obv:** Crowned head right **Obv. Legend:** ELIZABETH II - SOLOMON ISLANDS **Rev:** Food bowl divides value **Edge:** Plain

Date	Mintage	VF20	XF40	MS60	MS63	MS65
1987	—	—	—	0.35	0.50	0.75
1989	—	—	—	0.35	0.50	0.75
1996	—	—	—	0.35	0.50	0.75

KM# 2 2 CENTS
5.20 g., Bronze, 21.59 mm. **Subject:** Eagle Spirit of Malaita **Obv:** Young bust right **Rev:** Eagle spirit below value **Edge:** Plain

Date	Mintage	VF20	XF40	MS60	MS63	MS65
1977	2,400,000	—	0.10	0.25	0.50	0.50
1977 FM (M)	6,000	—	—	0.75	1.00	1.25
1977 FM (U)	—	—	—	1.50	2.00	2.50
1977 FM (P)	14,000	PF65 1.50				
1978 FM (M)	6,000	—	—	0.75	1.00	1.25
1978 FM (U)	544	—	—	1.50	2.00	2.50
1978 FM (P)	—	PF65 1.50				
1979 FM (M)	6,000	—	—	0.75	1.00	1.25
1979 FM (U)	677	—	—	1.50	2.00	2.50
1979 FM (P)	—	PF65 1.75				
1980 FM (M)	6,000	—	—	0.75	1.00	1.25
1980 FM (U)	624	—	—	1.50	2.00	2.50
1980 FM (P)	1,031	PF65 2.00				
1981 FM (M)	6,000	—	—	0.75	1.00	1.25
1981 FM (U)	212	—	—	1.50	2.00	2.50
1981 FM (P)	448	PF65 2.00				
1982 FM (U)	—	—	—	1.50	2.00	2.50
1982 FM (P)	—	PF65 2.00				
1983 FM (M)	—	—	—	0.75	1.00	1.25
1983 FM (U)	200	—	—	1.50	2.00	2.50
1983 FM (P)	—	PF65 2.00				

KM# 2a 2 CENTS
Bronze Plated Steel, 21.6 mm. **Ruler:** Elizabeth II **Subject:** Eagle Spirit of Malaita **Obv:** Crowned young bust right **Obv. Legend:** ELIZABETH II - SOLOMON ISLANDS **Rev:** Eagle spirit below value **Edge:** Plain

Date	Mintage	VF20	XF40	MS60	MS63	MS65
1985	—	0.75	1.50	2.50	3.00	4.00

KM# 25 2 CENTS
Bronze Plated Steel, 21.6 mm. **Ruler:** Elizabeth II **Obv:** Crowned head right **Obv. Legend:** ELIZABETH II - SOLOMON ISLANDS **Rev:** Eagle spirit below value **Edge:** Plain

Date	Mintage	VF20	XF40	MS60	MS63	MS65
1987	—	—	—	0.35	0.50	0.75
1989	—	—	—	0.35	0.50	0.75
1996	—	—	—	0.35	0.50	0.75

KM# 3 5 CENTS
2.80 g., Copper-Nickel, 19.4 mm. **Subject:** Santa Ysabel **Obv:** Young bust right **Rev:** Native mask and value **Edge:** Reeded

Date	Mintage	VF20	XF40	MS60	MS63	MS65
1977	1,200,000	—	0.15	0.35	0.50	0.75
1977 FM (U)	—	—	—	1.50	2.00	2.50
1977 FM (M)	6,000	—	—	1.00	1.25	1.50
1977 FM (P)	14,000	PF65 1.75				
1978 FM (M)	6,000	—	—	1.00	1.25	1.50
1978 FM (U)	544	—	—	1.50	2.00	2.50
1978 FM (P)	5,122	PF65 2.00				

Date	Mintage	VF20	XF40	MS60	MS63	MS65
1979 FM (M)	6,000	—	—	1.00	1.25	1.50
1979 FM (U)	677	—	—	1.50	2.00	2.50
1979 FM (P)	2,845	PF65 2.25				
1980	—	—	—	—	—	—
1980 FM (M)	6,000	—	—	1.00	1.25	1.50
1980 FM (U)	624	—	—	1.50	2.00	2.50
1980 FM (P)	1,031	PF65 2.50				
1981	—	—	—	—	—	—
1981 FM (M)	6,000	—	—	1.00	1.25	1.50
1981 FM (U)	212	—	—	1.50	2.00	2.50
1981 FM (P)	448	PF65 2.50				
1982 FM (U)	—	—	—	1.50	2.00	2.50
1982 FM (P)	—	PF65 2.50				
1983 FM (M)	—	—	—	1.00	1.25	1.50
1983 FM (U)	200	—	—	2.00	2.50	3.50
1983 FM (P)	—	PF65 2.50				
1985	—	—	—	0.30	0.40	0.50

KM# 26 5 CENTS

2.80 g., Copper-Nickel, 19.4 mm. **Ruler:** Elizabeth II **Obv:** Crowned head right **Obv. Legend:** ELIZABETH II - SOLOMON ISLANDS **Rev:** Native mask and value **Edge:** Reeded

Date	Mintage	VF20	XF40	MS60	MS63	MS65
1987	—	—	—	0.50	0.75	1.00
1988	—	—	—	0.50	0.75	1.00
1989	—	—	—	0.50	0.75	1.00

KM# 26a 5 CENTS

Nickel Plated Steel, 18.4 mm. **Ruler:** Elizabeth II **Obv:** Crowned bust right **Obv. Legend:** ELIZABETH II - SOLOMON ISLANDS **Rev:** Value at left, native mask at center right

Date	Mintage	VF20	XF40	MS60	MS63	MS65
1993	—	—	—	0.50	0.75	1.00
1996	—	—	—	0.50	0.75	1.00

KM# 4 10 CENTS

5.65 g., Copper-Nickel, 23.6 mm. **Subject:** Ngorieru **Obv:** Young bust right **Rev:** Sea spirit divides value **Edge:** Reeded

Date	Mintage	VF20	XF40	MS60	MS63	MS65
1977	3,600,000	—	0.20	0.50	0.60	0.75
1977 FM (M)	6,000	—	—	1.25	1.50	2.00
1977 FM (U)	—	—	—	2.50	3.00	4.00
1977 FM (P)	14,000	PF65 2.50				
1978 FM (M)	6,000	—	—	1.25	1.50	2.00
1978 FM (U)	544	—	—	2.50	3.00	4.00
1978 FM (P)	5,122	PF65 2.75				
1979 FM (M)	6,000	—	—	1.25	1.50	2.00
1979 FM (U)	677	—	—	2.50	3.00	4.00
1979 FM (P)	2,845	PF65 3.50				
1980 FM (M)	6,000	—	—	1.25	1.50	2.00
1980 FM (U)	624	—	—	2.50	3.00	4.00
1980 FM (P)	1,031	PF65 4.00				
1981 FM (M)	6,000	—	—	1.25	1.50	2.00
1981 FM (U)	212	—	—	2.50	3.00	4.00
1981 FM (P)	448	PF65 4.00				
1982 FM (U)	—	—	—	2.50	3.00	4.00
1982 FM (P)	—	PF65 4.00				
1983 FM (M)	—	—	—	1.25	1.50	2.00
1983 FM (U)	200	—	—	3.50	4.00	5.00
1983 FM (P)	—	PF65 4.00				

KM# 27 10 CENTS

5.65 g., Copper-Nickel, 23.6 mm. **Ruler:** Elizabeth II **Subject:** Ngorieru **Obv:** Crowned head right **Rev:** Sea spirit divides value **Edge:** Reeded

Date	Mintage	VF20	XF40	MS60	MS63	MS65
1988	—	—	—	0.65	0.80	1.00

KM# 27a 10 CENTS

Nickel Plated Steel, 23.6 mm. **Ruler:** Elizabeth II **Subject:** Ngorieru **Obv:** Crowned head right **Obv. Legend:** ELIZABETH II - SOLOMON ISLANDS **Rev:** Sea spirit divides value **Edge:** Reeded

Date	Mintage	VF20	XF40	MS60	MS63	MS65
1990	—	—	—	0.65	0.80	1.00
1993	—	—	—	0.65	0.80	1.00
1996	—	—	—	0.65	0.80	1.00
2000	—	—	—	0.65	0.80	1.00

KM# 5 20 CENTS

11.25 g., Copper-Nickel, 28.5 mm. **Obv:** Young bust right **Rev:** Malaita pendant design within circle, denomination appears twice in legend **Edge:** Reeded

Date	Mintage	VF20	XF40	MS60	MS63	MS65
1977	3,000,000	0.15	0.35	0.80	1.00	1.25
1977 FM (M)	5,000	—	—	2.50	3.00	3.50
1977 FM (P)	14,000	PF65 3.50				
1978	293,000	0.25	0.50	1.00	1.25	1.75
1978 FM (M)	5,000	—	—	2.50	3.00	3.50
1978 FM (U)	544	—	—	3.50	4.50	5.50
1978 FM (P)	5,122	PF65 3.75				
1979 FM (M)	5,000	—	—	2.50	3.00	3.50
1979 FM (U)	677	—	—	3.50	4.00	5.00
1979 FM (P)	2,845	PF65 3.75				
1980 FM (M)	5,000	—	—	2.50	3.00	3.50
1980 FM (U)	624	—	—	3.50	4.00	5.00
1980 FM (P)	1,031	PF65 3.75				
1981 FM (M)	5,000	—	—	2.50	3.00	3.50
1981 FM (U)	212	—	—	4.00	5.00	6.00
1981 FM (P)	448	PF65 4.00				
1982 FM (U)	—	—	—	4.00	5.00	6.00
1982 FM (P)	—	PF65 4.00				
1983 FM (M)	—	—	—	2.50	3.00	3.50
1983 FM (U)	200	—	—	5.00	6.00	7.00
1983 FM (P)	—	PF65 4.00				

KM# 28 20 CENTS

11.25 g., Nickel Plated Steel, 28.5 mm. **Ruler:** Elizabeth II **Obv:** Crowned head right **Obv. Legend:** ELIZABETH II - SOLOMON ISLANDS **Rev:** Malaita pendant design within circle, denomination appears twice in legend **Edge:** Reeded

Date	Mintage	VF20	XF40	MS60	MS63	MS65
1987	—	—	—	0.85	1.00	1.25
1989	—	—	—	0.85	1.00	1.25
1993	—	—	—	0.85	1.00	1.25
1996	—	—	—	0.85	1.00	1.25
1997	—	—	—	0.85	1.00	1.25
2000	—	—	—	0.85	1.00	1.25

KM# 82 20 CENTS

10.18 g., Nickel Alloy, 28.5 mm. **Ruler:** Elizabeth II **Subject:** FAO **Obv:** Head right **Rev:** Female with basket on head, FAO logo above **Edge:** Reeded

Date	Mintage	VF20	XF40	MS60	MS63	MS65
1995	20,000	—	—	20.00	22.00	25.00

KM# 23 50 CENTS

Copper-Nickel, 29.5 mm. **Subject:** 10th Anniversary of Independence **Obv:** Crowned head right **Rev:** Arms with supporters **Edge:** Plain **Shape:** 12-sided

Date	Mintage	VF20	XF40	MS60	MS63	MS65
1988	—	—	—	2.00	2.50	3.00

KM# 29 50 CENTS

10.00 g., Copper-Nickel, 29.5 mm. **Ruler:** Elizabeth II **Obv:** Crowned head right **Obv. Legend:** ELIZABETH II - SOLOMON ISLANDS **Rev:** Arms with supporters **Edge:** Plain **Shape:** 12-sided **Note:** Circulation type.

Date	Mintage	VF20	XF40	MS60	MS63	MS65
1990	—	—	—	2.00	2.50	3.00
1995	—	—	—	2.00	2.50	3.00
1996	—	—	—	2.00	2.50	3.00
1997	—	—	—	2.00	2.50	3.00

KM# 6 DOLLAR

13.40 g., Copper-Nickel, 30 mm. **Subject:** Nusu-Nusu head **Obv:** Young bust right **Rev:** Sea spirit statue divides value **Edge:** Plain **Shape:** 7-sided

Date	Mintage	VF20	XF40	MS60	MS63	MS65
1977	1,500,000	—	1.00	2.00	2.50	3.00
1977 FM (M)	3,000	—	—	3.00	4.00	5.00
1977 FM (P)	14,000	PF65 4.50				
1978 FM (M)	3,000	—	—	3.00	4.00	5.00
1978 FM (U)	544	—	—	—	5.00	7.00
1978 FM (P)	5,122	PF65 4.50				
1979 FM (M)	3,000	—	—	3.00	4.00	5.00
1979 FM (U)	677	—	—	—	5.00	7.00
1979 FM (P)	2,845	PF65 5.00				
1980 FM (M)	3,000	—	—	3.00	4.00	5.00
1980 FM (U)	624	—	—	—	5.00	7.00
1980 FM (P)	1,031	PF65 5.50				
1981 FM (M)	3,000	—	—	3.00	4.00	5.00
1981 FM (U)	212	—	—	—	8.00	10.00
1981 FM (P)	448	PF65 6.00				
1982 FM (U)	—	—	—	—	5.00	7.00
1982 FM (P)	—	PF65 6.00				
1983 FM (M)	—	—	—	—	5.00	7.00
1983 FM (U)	200	—	—	—	8.00	10.00
1983 FM (P)	—	PF65 5.50				

KM# 19 DOLLAR

Copper-Nickel **Series:** 1984 Olympics **Obv:** Young bust right **Rev:** Runners above torch and value

Date	Mintage	VF20	XF40	MS60	MS63	MS65
1984	5,000	—	—	3.50	4.00	6.00

KM# 30 DOLLAR
Copper-Nickel **Subject:** 50th Anniversary of Pearl Harbor **Obv:** Crowned head right **Rev:** Pearl Harbor war scene within circle

Date	Mintage	VF20	XF40	MS60	MS63	MS65
1991	—	—	—	2.00	3.00	5.00

KM# 30a DOLLAR
28.28 g., 0.925 Silver 0.841 oz. ASW **Subject:** 50th Anniversary of Pearl Harbor **Obv:** Crowned head right **Rev:** Pearl Harbor war scene

Date	Mintage	VF20	XF40	MS60	MS63	MS65
1991	Est. 25000	PF63 22.00	PF65 27.00			

KM# 35 DOLLAR
Copper-Nickel **Subject:** 50th Anniversary - Battle of the Coral Sea **Obv:** Crowned head right **Rev:** Planes bombing ship within circle

Date	Mintage	VF20	XF40	MS60	MS63	MS65
1992	—	—	—	2.00	3.00	5.00

KM# 35a DOLLAR
28.28 g., 0.925 Silver 0.841 oz. ASW **Subject:** 50th Anniversary - Battle of the Coral Sea **Obv:** Crowned head right **Rev:** War planes bombing ships within circle

Date	Mintage	VF20	XF40	MS60	MS63	MS65
1992	Est. 25000	PF63 22.00	PF65 27.00			

KM# 41 DOLLAR
Copper-Nickel **Subject:** 50th Anniversary - Battle of Guadalcanal **Obv:** Crowned head right **Rev:** Uniformed soldiers within circle

Date	Mintage	VF20	XF40	MS60	MS63	MS65
1992	—	—	—	2.00	3.00	5.00

KM# 41a DOLLAR
28.28 g., 0.925 Silver 0.841 oz. ASW **Subject:** 50th Anniversary - Battle of Guadalcanal **Obv:** Crowned head right **Rev;** Uniformed soldiers within circle

Date	Mintage	VF20	XF40	MS60	MS63	MS65
1992	Est. 25000	PF63 22.00	PF65 27.00			

KM# 77 DOLLAR
28.30 g., Copper-Nickel, 38.6 mm. **Subject:** Queen Mother **Obv:** Crowned head right **Rev:** Queen Mother's Coronation within beaded circle **Edge:** Reeded

Date	Mintage	VF20	XF40	MS60	MS63	MS65
1995	30,000	—	—	2.00	3.00	5.00

KM# 89 DOLLAR
28.28 g., 0.925 Silver 0.841 oz. ASW, 38.7 mm. **Ruler:** Elizabeth II **Series:** FAO - FOOD FOR ALL **Obv:** Bust right **Rev:** 2 palm trees on island divide value, FAO symbol above, inscription below **Edge:** Reeded

Date	Mintage	VF20	XF40	MS60	MS63	MS65
1995	2,200	—	50.00	60.00	70.00	85.00

KM# 72 DOLLAR
13.45 g., Copper-Nickel, 30 mm. **Ruler:** Elizabeth II **Obv:** Crowned head right **Obv. Legend:** ELIZABETH II - SOLOMON ISLANDS **Rev:** Sea spirit statue divides value **Edge:** Plain **Shape:** 7-sided

Date	Mintage	VF20	XF40	MS60	MS63	MS65
1996	—	—	—	1.50	2.00	3.00
1997	—	—	—	1.50	2.00	3.00

KM# 64 DOLLAR
Copper-Nickel **Subject:** World Wildlife Fund - Conserving Nature **Obv:** Crowned head right **Rev:** Eagle descending on fish

Date	Mintage	VF20	XF40	MS60	MS63	MS65
1998	—	—	—	3.00	5.00	7.00

KM# 64a DOLLAR
28.28 g., 0.925 Silver 0.841 oz. ASW **Subject:** World Wildlife Fund - Conserving Nature **Obv:** Crowned head right **Rev:** Eagle descending on fish

Date	Mintage	VF20	XF40	MS60	MS63	MS65
1998	—	PF63 25.00	PF65 30.00			

KM# 65 DOLLAR
32.55 g., Copper-Nickel, 38.62 mm. **Ruler:** Elizabeth II **Series:** Olympics 2000 **Obv:** Head with tiara right **Rev:** Multicolor koala swimming below torch within map **Edge:** Reeded

Date	Mintage	VF20	XF40	MS60	MS63	MS65
2000	—	PF63 6.00	PF65 8.50			

KM# 66 DOLLAR
32.55 g., Copper-Nickel, 38.62 mm. **Ruler:** Elizabeth II **Series:** Olympics 2000 **Obv:** Head with tiara right **Rev:** Multicolor kangaroo sail boarding **Edge:** Reeded

Date	Mintage	VF20	XF40	MS60	MS63	MS65
2000	—	PF63 6.00	PF65 8.50			

KM# 7 5 DOLLARS
28.28 g., 0.925 Silver 0.841 oz. ASW, 40 mm. **Obv:** Young bust right **Rev:** Fossilized clam shell on top of circle **Edge:** Reeded

Date	Mintage	VF20	XF40	MS60	MS63	MS65
1977 FM (U)	200	—	—	—	50.00	—
1977 FM (P)	15,000	PF65 25.00				
1978 FM (P)	5,148	PF65 28.00				
1979 FM (P)	2,845	PF65 35.00				
1980 FM (P)	1,031	PF65 37.50				
1981 FM (P)	448	PF65 45.00				
1983 FM (P)	339	PF65 45.00				

KM# 7a 5 DOLLARS
Copper-Nickel, 40 mm. **Obv:** Young bust right **Rev:** Fossilized clam shell on top of circle **Edge:** Reeded

Date	Mintage	VF20	XF40	MS60	MS63	MS65
1978 FM (M)	200	—	—	—	—	25.00
1978 FM (U)	544	—	—	—	—	15.00
1979 FM (M)	200	—	—	—	—	25.00
1979 FM (U)	677	—	—	—	—	14.00
1980 FM (M)	200	—	—	—	—	25.00
1980 FM (U)	624	—	—	—	—	14.00
1981 FM (M)	200	—	—	—	—	25.00
1981 FM (U)	212	—	—	—	—	25.00
1983 FM (U)	202	—	—	—	—	25.00

KM# 8 5 DOLLARS
28.28 g., 0.925 Silver 0.841 oz. ASW **Subject:** Coronation Jubilee **Obv:** Young bust right **Rev:** Crown flanked by supporters

Date	Mintage	VF20	XF40	MS60	MS63	MS65
1978	8,886	PF63 30.00	PF65 35.00			

KM# 13 5 DOLLARS
Copper-Nickel, 40 mm. **Ruler:** Elizabeth II **Subject:** Battle of Guadalcanal **Obv:** Young bust right **Rev:** Uniformed soldiers

Date	Mintage	VF20	XF40	MS60	MS63	MS65
1982 FM (U)	—	—	—	—	5.00	7.00

KM# 13a 5 DOLLARS
28.28 g., 0.925 Silver 0.841 oz. ASW, 40 mm. **Ruler:** Elizabeth II **Subject:** Battle of Guadalcanal **Obv:** Young bust right **Rev:** Uniformed soldiers

Date	Mintage	VF20	XF40	MS60	MS63	MS65
1982 FM (P)	1,368	PF63 50.00	PF65 65.00			

KM# 15 5 DOLLARS
28.28 g., 0.500 Silver 0.4546 oz. ASW, 38.61 mm. **Subject:** 30th Anniversary of Coronation **Obv:** Young bust right **Rev:** Crossed scepters divides dates, crown and cross on globe design **Edge:** Reeded

Date	Mintage	VF20	XF40	MS60	MS63	MS65
1983 FM (P)	2,944	PF63 22.00	PF65 28.00			

KM# 16 5 DOLLARS
28.28 g., 0.925 Silver 0.841 oz. ASW **Series:** International Year of the Child **Obv:** Young bust right **Rev:** Figures rowing boat divides emblems

Date	Mintage	VF20	XF40	MS60	MS63	MS65
1983	5,775	PF63 28.00	PF65 32.00			

KM# 22 5 DOLLARS
28.28 g., 0.925 Silver 0.841 oz. ASW **Series:** Decade for Women **Obv:** Crowned head right **Rev:** Teacher and student reading within circle

Date	Mintage	VF20	XF40	MS60	MS63	MS65
1985	1,050	PF63 50.00	PF65 65.00			

KM# 63 5 DOLLARS
10.00 g., 0.500 Silver 0.1608 oz. ASW **Subject:** Alvaro Mendana de Neyra **Obv:** Crowned head right **Rev:** Bust with hat facing, palm tree and ancient boat at left

Date	Mintage	VF20	XF40	MS60	MS63	MS65
1994	Est. 20000	PF63 7.00	PF65 10.00			

KM# 54 5 DOLLARS
Copper-Nickel **Subject:** MacArthur Accepting Japanese Surrender **Obv:** Crowned head right **Rev:** Uniformed bust left at far right

Date	Mintage	VF20	XF40	MS60	MS63	MS65
1995	—	—	—	3.00	5.00	7.00

KM# 54a 5 DOLLARS
28.28 g., 0.925 Silver 0.841 oz. ASW **Subject:** MacArthur Accepting Japanese Surrender **Obv:** Crowned head right **Rev:** Uniformed bust left at far right **Note:** Similar to 50 Dollars, KM#57.

Date	Mintage	VF20	XF40	MS60	MS63	MS65
1995	Est. 10000	PF63 30.00	PF65 35.00			

KM# 78 5 DOLLARS
28.20 g., 0.925 Silver 0.8387 oz. ASW, 38.6 mm. **Subject:** Queen's 70th Birthday **Obv:** Crowned bust right **Rev:** Royal yacht **Edge:** Reeded

Date	Mintage	VF20	XF40	MS60	MS63	MS65
1996	—	PF63 30.00	PF65 35.00			

KM# 80 5 DOLLARS
9.94 g., 0.525 Silver 0.1678 oz. ASW, 29.9 mm. **Obv:** Crowned head right **Rev:** Queen and Diana at the races **Edge:** Reeded

Date	Mintage	VF20	XF40	MS60	MS63	MS65
1998	—	PF63 9.00	PF65 13.00			

KM# 69 5 DOLLARS
20.10 g., 0.800 Silver 0.517 oz. ASW, 33.9 mm. **Subject:** Ship of Death **Obv:** Crowned head right **Rev:** Sailing ship **Edge:** Reeded

Date	Mintage	VF20	XF40	MS60	MS63	MS65
1999	Est. 20000	PF63 16.00	PF65 20.00			

KM# 67 5 DOLLARS
24.91 g., 0.925 Silver 0.7408 oz. ASW, 38.7 mm. **Series:** Olympics 2000 **Obv:** Head with tiara right **Rev:** Stylized multicolor koala tennis player below torch within map **Edge:** Reeded **Note:** Legend in block letters.

Date	Mintage	VF20	XF40	MS60	MS63	MS65
2000	15,000	PF63 27.00	PF65 32.00			

KM# 68 5 DOLLARS
24.91 g., 0.925 Silver 0.7408 oz. ASW **Series:** Olympics 2000 **Obv:** Crowned head right **Rev:** Stylized multicolored kangaroo bicyclist below torch within map

Date	Mintage	VF20	XF40	MS60	MS63	MS65
2000	15,000	PF63 27.00	PF65 32.00			

KM# 70 5 DOLLARS
32.20 g., Copper-Nickel, 38.6 mm. **Obv:** Head with tiara right **Obv. Inscription:** Portrait from dies of Solomon Islands KM# 67-68 **Rev:** Pied Cormorant **Rev. Inscription:** From dies from New Zealand KM#125 **Edge:** Reeded **Note:** Mule.

Date	Mintage	VF20	XF40	MS60	MS63	MS65
2000	—	PF65 1,300	PF67 1,600			

Note: This coin is included in a New Zealand Proof set dated 2000

KM# 10 10 DOLLARS
Copper-Nickel, 45 mm. **Obv:** Young bust right **Rev:** Flying frigate bird above value **Edge:** Reeded

Date	Mintage	VF20	XF40	MS60	MS63	MS65
1979 FM (M)	100	—	—	—	—	35.00
1979 FM (U)	777	—	—	—	—	16.00
1980 FM (M)	100	—	—	—	—	35.00
1980 FM (U)	624	—	—	—	—	16.00
1981 FM (M)	100	—	—	—	—	35.00
1981 FM (U)	212	—	—	—	—	18.50
1982 FM (U)	—	—	—	—	—	16.00

KM# 10a 10 DOLLARS
42.27 g., 0.925 Silver 1.2571 oz. ASW, 45 mm. **Obv:** Young bust right **Rev:** Frigate bird above value **Edge:** Reeded

Date	Mintage	VF20	XF40	MS60	MS63	MS65
1979 FM (P)	4,670	PF65 35.00				
1980 FM (P)	1,569	PF65 45.00				
1981 FM (P)	593	PF65 50.00				
1982 FM (P)	579	PF65 50.00				

KM# 17 10 DOLLARS
Copper-Nickel, 45 mm. **Subject:** 5th Anniversary of Independence **Obv:** Young bust right **Rev:** Arms with supporters in front of flag

Date	Mintage	VF20	XF40	MS60	MS63	MS65
1983 FM (U)	202	—	—	—	—	17.50

KM# 17a 10 DOLLARS
40.50 g., 0.925 Silver 1.2044 oz. ASW, 45 mm. **Subject:** 5th Anniversary of Independence **Obv:** Young bust right **Rev:** Arms with supporters in front of flag

Date	Mintage	VF20	XF40	MS60	MS63	MS65
1983 FM (P)	425	PF63 45.00	PF65 50.00	PF67 65.00		

KM# 20 10 DOLLARS
33.44 g., 0.925 Silver 0.9945 oz. ASW **Series:** 1984 Olympics **Obv:** Young bust right **Rev:** Runners above torch and value

Date	Mintage	VF20	XF40	MS60	MS63	MS65
1984	2,500	PF63 28.00	PF65 35.00	PF67 50.00		

KM# 31 10 DOLLARS
3.13 g., 0.999 Gold 0.1005 oz. AGW, 16.5 mm. **Subject:** 50th Anniversary of Pearl Harbor **Obv:** Crowned head right **Rev:** Map of Pearl Harbor

Date	Mintage	XF40	MS60	MS63	MS65	MS66
1991	Est. 500	PF67 170	PF69 200			

KM# 47 10 DOLLARS
31.80 g., 0.925 Silver 0.9457 oz. ASW **Subject:** Alvaro de Neyra **Obv:** Crowned head right **Rev:** Half figure with hat facing

Date	Mintage	VF20	XF40	MS60	MS63	MS65
1991	—	PF63 22.00	PF65 25.00	PF67 38.00		

KM# 48 10 DOLLARS
31.42 g., 0.925 Silver 0.9344 oz. ASW **Series:** 1992 Olympics **Obv:** Crowned head right **Rev:** Runner

Date	Mintage	VF20	XF40	MS60	MS63	MS65
1991	Est. 40000	PF63 22.00	PF65 25.00	PF67 38.00		

KM# 36 10 DOLLARS
3.13 g., 0.999 Gold 0.1005 oz. AGW, 16.5 mm. **Subject:** 50th Anniversary - Battle of the Coral Sea **Rev:** Planes dropping bombs within circle

Date	Mintage	XF40	MS60	MS63	MS65	MS66
1992	500	PF67 170	PF69 200			

KM# 40 10 DOLLARS
31.47 g., 0.925 Silver 0.9359 oz. ASW **Subject:** First Lunar Vehicle **Obv:** Crowned head right **Rev:** First lunar vehicle with astronaut

Date	Mintage	VF20	XF40	MS60	MS63	MS65
1992	Est. 10000	PF63 22.00	PF65 32.00	PF67 45.00		

KM# 42 10 DOLLARS
3.13 g., 0.999 Gold 0.1005 oz. AGW, 16.5 mm. **Subject:** 50th Anniversary - Battle of Guadalcanal **Rev:** Battle scene within circle

Date	Mintage	XF40	MS60	MS63	MS65	MS66
1992	500	PF67 170	PF69 200			

KM# 46 10 DOLLARS
31.47 g., 0.925 Silver 0.9359 oz. ASW **Subject:** 40th Anniversary - Queen Elizabeth's Coronation **Obv:** Crowned head right **Rev:** Crowned figure on throne facing

Date	Mintage	VF20	XF40	MS60	MS63	MS65
1992	Est. 50000	PF63 22.00	PF65 32.00	PF67 45.00		

KM# 50 10 DOLLARS
31.47 g., 0.925 Silver 0.9359 oz. ASW **Series:** 1992 Olympics **Obv:** Crowned head right **Rev:** Boxer

Date	Mintage	VF20	XF40	MS60	MS63	MS65
1992	40,000	PF63 22.00	PF65 25.00	PF67 38.00		

KM# 51 10 DOLLARS
31.47 g., 0.925 Silver 0.9359 oz. ASW **Series:** Endangered Wildlife **Obv:** Crowned head right **Rev:** Saltwater crocodile

Date	Mintage	VF20	XF40	MS60	MS63	MS65
1992	Est. 10000	PF63 25.00	PF65 28.00	PF67 35.00		

KM# 49 10 DOLLARS
28.28 g., 0.925 Silver 0.841 oz. ASW **Subject:** 100 Years as British Protectorate **Obv:** Crowned head right **Rev:** Cameo to upper left of ship

Date	Mintage	VF20	XF40	MS60	MS63	MS65
1993	5,000	PF63 35.00	PF65 38.00	PF67 50.00		

KM# 59 10 DOLLARS
31.47 g., 0.925 Silver 0.9359 oz. ASW **Subject:** Protect Our World **Obv:** Crowned head right **Rev:** Orchid and butterfly

Date	Mintage	VF20	XF40	MS60	MS63	MS65
1993	Est. 10000	PF63 25.00	PF65 30.00	PF67 42.00		

KM# 52 10 DOLLARS
28.28 g., 0.925 Silver 0.841 oz. ASW **Subject:** Sailing ship "Swallow" **Obv:** Crowned head right **Rev:** Ship divides cameos

Date	Mintage	VF20	XF40	MS60	MS63	MS65
1994	Est. 15000	PF63 20.00	PF65 22.00	PF67 30.00		

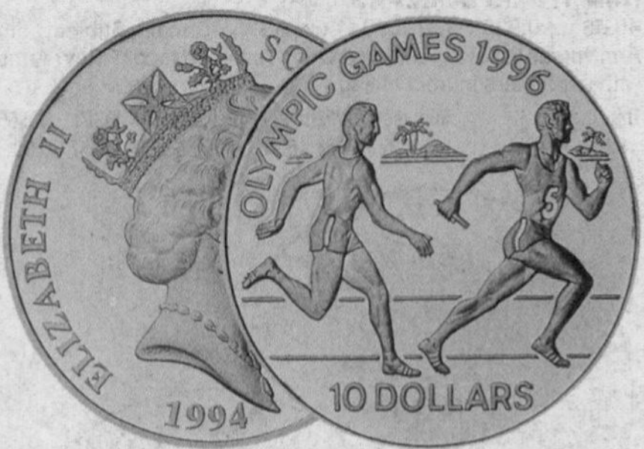

KM# 53 10 DOLLARS
28.28 g., 0.925 Silver 0.841 oz. ASW **Series:** 1996 Olympics **Obv:** Crowned head right **Rev:** Relay runners

Date	Mintage	VF20	XF40	MS60	MS63	MS65
1994	Est. 30000	PF63 20.00	PF65 22.00	PF67 30.00		

KM# 111 10 DOLLARS
31.47 g., 0.925 Silver 0.9359 oz. ASW, 38.61 mm. **Ruler:** Elizabeth II **Subject:** Elizabeth the Queen Mother, 94th Birthday

Date	Mintage	VF20	XF40	MS60	MS63	MS65
1994	20,000	PF63 35.00	PF65 40.00	PF67 55.00		

KM# 55 10 DOLLARS
3.13 g., 0.999 Gold 0.1005 oz. AGW, 16.5 mm. **Rev:** Marine and armored tank within circle

Date	Mintage	XF40	MS60	MS63	MS65	MS66
1995	Est. 500	PF67 170	PF69 200			

KM# 71 10 DOLLARS
31.44 g., 0.925 Silver 0.935 oz. ASW, 38.5 mm. **Subject:** Queen Mother **Obv:** Crowned head right **Rev:** Coronation scene within beaded circle **Edge:** Reeded

Date	Mintage	VF20	XF40	MS60	MS63	MS65
1995	—	PF63 25.00	PF65 30.00	PF67 42.00		

KM# 128 10 DOLLARS
28.28 g., 0.925 Copper-Nickel 0.841 oz., 38.61 mm. **Ruler:** Elizabeth II **Subject:** Elizabeth and Philip, 50th Wedding Anniversary

Date	Mintage	VF20	XF40	MS60	MS63	MS65
1997	—	—	—	—	5.00	7.00

KM# 128a 10 DOLLARS
28.28 g., 0.925 Silver 0.841 oz. ASW partially gilt, 38.61 mm. **Ruler:** Elizabeth II **Subject:** Elizabeth and Philip, 50th Wedding Anniversary

Date	Mintage	VF20	XF40	MS60	MS63	MS65
1997	—	PF63 35.00	PF65 40.00	PF67 55.00		

KM# 79 10 DOLLARS
31.60 g., 0.925 Silver 0.9398 oz. ASW, 38.6 mm. **Obv:** Crowned head right **Rev:** Queen Elizabeth and Diana at the races **Edge:** Reeded

Date	Mintage	VF20	XF40	MS60	MS63	MS65
1998	—	PF63 25.00	PF65 30.00	PF67 42.00		

KM# 73 10 DOLLARS
28.28 g., 0.925 Silver 0.841 oz. ASW with gilt outer ring, 38.61 mm. **Subject:** Queen Mother **Obv:** Crowned head right within beaded circle **Rev:** Inspecting the bombing of Buckingham Palace **Edge:** Reeded

Date	Mintage	VF20	XF40	MS60	MS63	MS65
2000	—	PF63 45.00	PF65 50.00	PF67 65.00		

KM# 74 10 DOLLARS
31.55 g., 0.925 Silver 0.9383 oz. ASW, 38.7 mm. **Obv:** Crowned head right **Rev:** Missionary ship **Edge:** Reeded

Date	Mintage	VF20	XF40	MS60	MS63	MS65
2000	—	PF63 25.00	PF65 30.00	PF67 42.00		

KM# 88 10 DOLLARS
1.20 g., 0.999 Gold 0.0385 oz. AGW, 13.91 mm. **Ruler:** Elizabeth II **Obv:** Crowned head right **Rev:** Statue of Nguzunguzu **Edge:** Reeded

Date	Mintage	XF40	MS60	MS63	MS65	MS66
2000	—	PF67 70.00	PF69 80.00			

KM# 32 25 DOLLARS
7.81 g., 0.999 Gold 0.2508 oz. AGW, 22 mm. **Subject:** 50th Anniversary - Pearl Harbor **Obv:** Crowned head right **Rev:** Pearl Harbor battle scene within circle

Date	Mintage	XF40	MS60	MS63	MS65	MS66
1991	Est. 3000	PF67 400	PF69 450			

KM# 37 25 DOLLARS
7.81 g., 0.999 Gold 0.2508 oz. AGW, 22 mm. **Subject:** 50th Anniversary - Battle of the Coral Sea **Rev:** Pearl Harbor battle scene within circle

Date	Mintage	XF40	MS60	MS63	MS65	MS66
1992	—	PF67 400	PF69 450			

KM# 43 25 DOLLARS
7.81 g., 0.999 Gold 0.2508 oz. AGW, 22 mm. **Subject:** 50th Anniversary - Battle of Guadalcanal **Rev:** Uniformed soldiers and armored tank in woods within circle

Date	Mintage	XF40	MS60	MS63	MS65	MS66
1992	—	PF67 400	PF69 450			

KM# 56 25 DOLLARS
7.81 g., 0.999 Gold 0.2508 oz. AGW, 22 mm. **Subject:** 50th Anniversary - Iwo Jima Flag Raising **Rev:** Uniformed soldiers raising flag within circle

Date	Mintage	XF40	MS60	MS63	MS65	MS66
1995	—	PF67 400	PF69 450			

KM# 81 25 DOLLARS
500.00 g., 0.999 Silver 16.0593 oz. ASW, 89 mm. **Subject:** Discovery of the Solomon Islands by Kermadec **Obv:** Crowned head right **Rev:** Sailing ship **Edge:** Reeded

Date	Mintage	XF40	MS60	MS63	MS65	MS66
2000	—	PF67 350	PF69 400			

KM# 33 50 DOLLARS
15.60 g., 0.999 Gold 0.501 oz. AGW, 27 mm. **Subject:** 50th Anniversary - Pearl Harbor **Obv:** Crowned head right **Rev:** Pearl Harbor battle scene within circle

Date	Mintage	XF40	MS60	MS63	MS65	MS66
1991	Est. 500	PF67 775	PF69 850			

KM# 38 50 DOLLARS
15.60 g., 0.999 Gold 0.501 oz. AGW, 27 mm. **Subject:** 50th Anniversary - Battle of the Coral Sea **Rev:** Planes bombing ship within circle

Date	Mintage	XF40	MS60	MS63	MS65	MS66
1992	—	PF67 775	PF69 850			

KM# 44 50 DOLLARS
15.60 g., 0.999 Gold 0.501 oz. AGW, 27 mm. **Subject:** 50th Anniversary - Battle of Guadalcanal **Rev:** Uniformed soldiers within circle

Date	Mintage	XF40	MS60	MS63	MS65	MS66
1992	Est. 500	PF67 775	PF69 850			

KM# 60 50 DOLLARS
7.76 g., 0.583 Gold 0.1455 oz. AGW **Series:** Endangered Wildlife **Obv:** Crowned head right **Rev:** Descending eagle

Date	Mintage	XF40	MS60	MS63	MS65	MS66
1993	—	PF67 245	PF69 275			

KM# 61 50 DOLLARS
155.52 g., 0.999 Silver 4.995 oz. ASW, 65 mm. **Subject:** Johannes Kepler **Obv:** Crowned bust right **Rev:** Bust 1/4 right **Note:** Illustration reduced.

Date	Mintage	XF40	MS60	MS63	MS65	MS66
1994	Est. 2000	PF67 120	PF69 140			

KM# 57 50 DOLLARS
15.61 g., 0.999 Gold 0.5014 oz. AGW, 27 mm. **Rev:** MacArthur accepting Japanese surrender

Date	Mintage	XF40	MS60	MS63	MS65	MS66
1995	500	PF67 775	PF69 850			

KM# 62 50 DOLLARS
31.47 g., 0.925 Silver 0.9359 oz. ASW **Rev:** MacArthur accepting Japanese surrender **Note:** Similar to 5 Dollars, KM#54.

Date	Mintage	VF20	XF40	MS60	MS63	MS65
1995	—	PF63 30.00	PF65 35.00	PF67 50.00		

KM# 112 50 DOLLARS
7.78 g., 0.583 Gold 0.1458 oz. AGW, 25 mm. **Ruler:** Elizabeth II **Subject:** Elizabeth, Queen Mother, 96th Birthday

Date	Mintage	XF40	MS60	MS63	MS65	MS66
1996	5,000	PF67 250	PF69 275			

KM# 129 50 DOLLARS
10.50 g., 0.999 Gold 0.3372 oz. AGW, 25 mm. **Ruler:** Elizabeth II **Subject:** Marathon **Rev:** Design in color **Note:** Legend in block letters.

Date	Mintage	XF40	MS60	MS63	MS65	MS66
2000	2,500	PF67 550	PF69 600			

KM# 9 100 DOLLARS
9.37 g., 0.900 Gold 0.2711 oz. AGW **Subject:** Attainment of Sovereignty **Obv:** Young bust right **Rev:** Arms with supporters

Date	Mintage	XF40	MS60	MS63	MS65	MS66
1978 FM (M)	50	—	—	—	525	600
1978 FM (U)	213	—	—	—	500	550
1978 FM (P)	3,159	PF67 450	PF69 500			

KM# 11 100 DOLLARS
7.64 g., 0.500 Gold 0.1228 oz. AGW **Ruler:** Elizabeth II **Subject:** Native Art **Obv:** Young bust right **Rev:** Artistic design in center of designed circles

Date	Mintage	XF40	MS60	MS63	MS65	MS66
1980 FM (U)	50	—	—	—	285	325
1980 FM (P)	7,500	PF67 220	PF69 245			

KM# 12 100 DOLLARS
7.64 g., 0.500 Gold 0.1228 oz. AGW **Ruler:** Elizabeth II **Obv:** Young bust right **Rev:** Shark

Date	Mintage	XF40	MS60	MS63	MS65	MS66
1981	675	PF67 225	PF69 250			

KM# 14 100 DOLLARS
9.37 g., 0.900 Gold 0.2711 oz. AGW **Ruler:** Elizabeth II **Subject:** Battle of Guadalcanal **Obv:** Young bust right **Rev:** Uniformed soldiers

Date	Mintage	XF40	MS60	MS63	MS65	MS66
1982 FM (P)	311	PF67 475	PF69 525			

KM# 18 100 DOLLARS

9.37 g., 0.900 Gold 0.2711 oz. AGW **Subject:** 5th Anniversary of Independence **Obv:** Young bust right within circle, radiant border **Rev:** Arms with supporters in front of flag within circle, radiant border **Shape:** Pentagon

Date	Mintage	XF40	MS60	MS63	MS65	MS66
1983 FM (P)	268	PF67 450	PF69 500			

KM# 21 100 DOLLARS

7.50 g., 0.917 Gold 0.2211 oz. AGW **Series:** 1984 Olympics **Rev:** Weightlifter

Date	Mintage	XF40	MS60	MS63	MS65	MS66
1984	500	PF67 350	PF69 425			

KM# 34 100 DOLLARS

31.21 g., 0.999 Gold 1.0024 oz. AGW, 32.7 mm. **Subject:** 50th Anniversary of Pearl Harbor **Obv:** Crowned head right **Rev:** Pearl Harbor battle scene within circle

Date	Mintage	XF40	MS60	MS63	MS65	MS66
1991	Est. 500	PF67 1,450	PF69 1,550			

KM# 39 100 DOLLARS

31.21 g., 0.999 Gold 1.0024 oz. AGW, 32.7 mm. **Subject:** 50th Anniversary - Battle of Coral Sea **Rev:** Soldiers in lifeboats, burning building and boat, all within circle

Date	Mintage	XF40	MS60	MS63	MS65	MS66
1992	Est. 500	PF67 1,450	PF69 1,550			

KM# 45 100 DOLLARS

31.21 g., 0.999 Gold 1.0024 oz. AGW, 32.69 mm. **Subject:** 50th Anniversary - Battle of Guadalcanal **Rev:** Planes bombing ship within circle

Date	Mintage	XF40	MS60	MS63	MS65	MS66
1992	Est. 500	PF67 1,450	PF69 1,550			

KM# 58 100 DOLLARS

31.21 g., 0.999 Gold 1.0024 oz. AGW, 32.69 mm. **Rev:** B-25 bomber and mushroom cloud within circle

Date	Mintage	XF40	MS60	MS63	MS65	MS66
1995	Est. 500	PF67 1,450	PF69 1,550			

PIEDFORT

KM#	Date	Mintage	Identification	Mkt Val
P1	1983	62	5 Dollars. Silver. KM16.	140

PATTERNS

Including off metal strikes

KM#	Date	Mintage	Identification	Mkt Val
Pn1	2000	1	Dollar. Copper-Nickel. Head with tiara right with italic legends. Cartoon kangaroo on sailboard. Reeded.	—
Pn2	2000	30	Dollar. Copper-Nickel. Head with tiara right italic legends. Cartoon kangaroo on sailboard. Reeded.	—
Pn3	2000	—	Dollar. Copper-Nickel. Head with tiara right with italic legend. Multicolor cartoon kangaroo on sailboard. Reeded.	—
Note: Mintage included in Pn2				
Pn4	2000	30	Dollar. Copper-Nickel. Head with tiara right with italic legends. Cartoon koala swimming. Reeded.	—
Pn5	2000	—	Dollar. Copper-Nickel. Head with tiara right. Multicolor cartoon koala swimming. Reeded.	—
Note: mintage included with Pn4				
Pn6	2000	1	5 Dollars. Copper-Nickel. Head with tiara right with italic legends. Cartoon koala playing tennis. Reeded.	—
Pn7	2000	30	5 Dollars. 0.925. Silver. Head with tiara right. Cartoon koala playing tennis. Reeded.	—
Pn8	2000	—	5 Dollars. 0.925. Silver. Head with tiara right with italic legends. Multicolor cartoon koala playing tennis. Reeded.	—
Note: mintage included with Pn7				
Pn9	2000	30	5 Dollars. 0.925. Silver. Head with tiara right with italic legends. Cartoon kangaroo on bicycle. Reeded.	—
Pn10	2000	—	5 Dollars. 0.925. Silver. Head with tiara right with italic legends. Multicolor cartoon kangaroo on bicycle. Reeded.	—
Note: mintage included with Pn9				
Pn11	2000	30	50 Dollars. 0.5833. Gold. Head with tiara right with italic legends. Multicolor cartoon emu running. Reeded.	—

MINT SETS

KM#	Date	Mintage	Identification	Issue Price	Mkt Val
MS1	1978 (7)	544	KM#1-6, 7a	22.00	35.00
MS2	1979 (8)	677	KM#1-6, 7a, 10	31.00	55.00
MS3	1980 (8)	624	KM#1-6, 7a, 10	35.00	55.00
MS4	1981 (8)	212	KM#1-6, 7a, 10	36.00	75.00
MS5	1982 (8)	—	KM#1-6, 10, 13	36.00	55.00
MS6	1983 (8)	192	KM#1-6, 7a, 17	36.00	75.00

PROOF SETS

KM#	Date	Mintage	Identification	Issue Price	Mkt Val
PS1	1977 (7)	72,748	KM#1-7	40.00	40.00
PSA2	1977 (6)	—	KM#1-6	—	16.50
PS2	1978 (7)	5,122	KM#1-7	45.00	50.00
PS3	1979 (8)	2,845	KM#1-7, 10a	77.00	85.00
PS4	1980 (8)	1,031	KM#1-7, 10a	135	90.00
PS5	1981 (8)	448	KM#1-7, 10a	137	100
PS6	1982 (8)	—	KM#1-6, 10a, 13a	87.00	100
PS7	1983 (8)	334	KM#1-7, 17a	137	115
PS8	1991 (4)	500	KM#31-34	1,650	3,000
PS9	1991 (2)	—	KM#30a, 32	—	540
PS10	1992 (4)	500	KM#36-39	1,595	3,000
PS11	1992 (4)	500	KM#42-45	1,595	3,000
PS12	1995 (4)	500	KM#55-58	1,595	3,000

SOMALIA

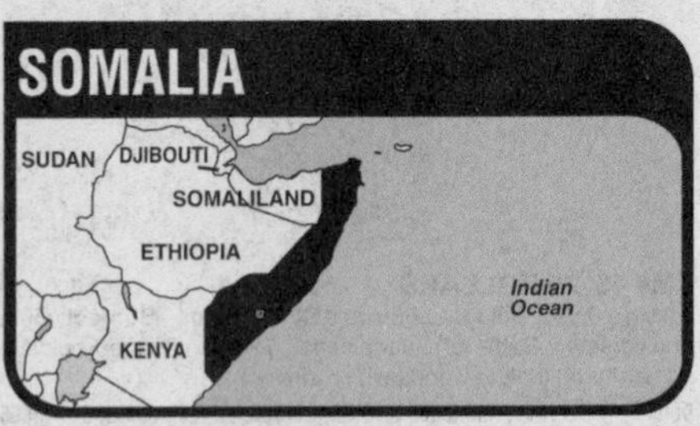

The Somali Democratic Republic, comprised of the former Italian Somaliland, is located on the coast of the eastern projection of the African continent commonly referred to as the "Horn". It has an area of 178,201 sq. mi. (461,657 sq. km.) and a population of *8.2 million. Capital: Mogadishu. The economy is pastoral and agricultural. Livestock, bananas and hides are exported.

The area of the British Somaliland Protectorate was known to the Egyptians at least 1,500 years B.C., and was occupied by the Arabs and Portuguese before British sea captains obtained trading and anchorage rights in 1827. The land of sandy clay and sporadic rainfall acquired a strategic importance with the opening of the Suez Canal in1869. After negotiating treaties with the tribes, Britain declared the area a protectorate in 1888. Italy acquired Italian Somaliland in 1895 by purchase from the Sultan of Zanzibar. Britain occupied Italian Somaliland in 1941 and administered it until April 1, 1950, when it was returned to Italy as a U.N. trusteeship. The British Somaliland protectorate became independent on June 26, 1960. Five days later it joined with Italian Somaliland to form the Somali Republic. The country was under a revolutionary military regime installed Oct. 21, 1969. After eleven years of civil war rebel forces fought their way into the capital. A.M. Muhammad became president in Aug. 1991,but inter-factional fighting continued. A UN-sponsored truce was signed in March 1992 and a peace plan and pact was signed Jan. 15, 1993.

The Northern Somali National Movement (SNM) declared a secession of the northwestern Somaliland Republic on May 17, 1991, which is not recognized by the Somali Democratic Republic.

TITLE

Al-Jumhuriya(t)as - Somaliya(t)

RULERS

Italian, until 1941
British, until 1950

MINT MARKS

Az - Arezzo (Italy)
R – Rome

U. N. TRUSTEESHIP UNDER ITALY

STANDARD COINAGE

KM# 1 CENTESIMO

3.00 g., Copper, 21 mm. **Obv:** African elephant **Rev:** Value within circle with star flanked by crescents above **Edge:** Plain

Date	Mintage	VF20	XF40	MS60	MS63	MS65
AH1369-1950	4,000,000	0.50	1.00	3.00	5.00	7.50

KM# 2 5 CENTESIMI

Copper, 25 mm. **Obv:** African elephant **Rev:** Value within circle with star flanked by crescents above

Date	Mintage	VF20	XF40	MS60	MS63	MS65
AH1369-1950	6,800,000	0.50	1.50	4.00	7.00	9.00

KM# 3 10 CENTESIMI
Copper, 30 mm. **Rev:** Value within circle with star flanked by crescents above **Edge:** African elephant

Date	Mintage	VF20	XF40	MS60	MS63	MS65
AH1369-1950	7,400,000	1.00	3.00	5.00	9.00	12.00

KM# 4 50 CENTESIMI
3.80 g., 0.250 Silver 0.0305 oz. ASW, 22 mm. **Obv:** Star flanked by crescents above lion **Rev:** Value within beaded circle

Date	Mintage	VF20	XF40	MS60	MS63	MS65
AH1369-1950	1,800,000	1.50	3.50	6.00	10.00	15.00

KM# 5 SOMALO
7.60 g., 0.250 Silver 0.0611 oz. ASW **Obv:** Star flanked by crescents above lion **Rev:** Value within beaded circle

Date	Mintage	VF20	XF40	MS60	MS63	MS65
AH1369-1950	11,480,000	2.50	4.50	7.50	15.00	25.00

SOMALI REPUBLIC

KM# 6 5 CENTESIMI
2.50 g., Brass **Obv:** Crowned arms with supporters **Rev:** Value and star within circle

Date	Mintage	VF20	XF40	MS60	MS63	MS65
1967	10,000,000	—	0.20	0.30	0.60	1.00

KM# 7 10 CENTESIMI
Brass **Obv:** Crowned arms with supporters **Rev:** Value and star within circle

Date	Mintage	VF20	XF40	MS60	MS63	MS65
1967	15,000,000	0.15	0.25	0.45	0.70	1.25

KM# 8 50 CENTESIMI
Copper-Nickel **Obv:** Crowned arms with supporters **Rev:** Value and star within beaded circle

Date	Mintage	VF20	XF40	MS60	MS63	MS65
1967	5,100,000	0.50	1.00	1.50	2.00	3.50

KM# 9 SCELLINO / SHILLING
7.63 g., Copper-Nickel, 26.7 mm. **Obv:** Arms with supporters **Rev:** Value within beaded circle

Date	Mintage	VF20	XF40	MS60	MS63	MS65
1967	8,150,000	0.75	1.50	3.00	5.00	7.00

KM# 10 20 SHILLINGS / SCELLINI
2.80 g., 0.900 Gold 0.081 oz. AGW **Subject:** 5th Anniversary of Independence **Obv:** Bust facing **Rev:** Crowned arms with supporters

Date	Mintage	VF20	XF40	MS60	MS63	MS65
1965 Az	6,325	PF65 125	PF67 135			
1966 Az	—	PF65 125	PF67 135			

KM# 11 50 SHILLINGS
7.00 g., 0.900 Gold 0.2025 oz. AGW **Subject:** 5th Anniversary of Independence **Obv:** Bust facing **Rev:** Crowned arms with supporters

Date	Mintage	VF20	XF40	MS60	MS63	MS65
1965 Az	6,325	PF65 305	PF67 325			
1966 Az	—	PF65 305	PF67 325			

KM# 12 100 SHILLINGS
14.00 g., 0.900 Gold 0.4051 oz. AGW **Subject:** 5th Anniversary of Independence **Obv:** Bust facing **Rev:** Crowned arms with supporters

Date	Mintage	VF20	XF40	MS60	MS63	MS65
1965 Az	6,325	PF65 590	PF67 630			
1966 Az	—	PF65 590	PF67 630			

KM# 13 200 SHILLINGS
28.00 g., 0.900 Gold 0.8102 oz. AGW **Subject:** 5th Anniversary of Independence **Obv:** Bust facing **Rev:** Arms with supporters **Note:** Similar to 100 Shillings, KM#12.

Date	Mintage	VF20	XF40	MS60	MS63	MS65
1965 Az	6,325	PF65 1,150	PF67 1,225			
1966 Az	—	PF65 1,150	PF67 1,225			

KM# 14 500 SHILLINGS
70.00 g., 0.900 Gold 2.0255 oz. AGW **Subject:** 5th Anniversary of Independence **Obv:** Bust facing **Rev:** Arms with supporters **Note:** Similar to 100 Shillings, KM#12.

Date	Mintage	VF20	XF40	MS60	MS63	MS65
1965 Az	6,325	PF65 2,850	PF67 2,950			
1966 Az	—	PF65 2,850	PF67 2,950			

DEMOCRATIC REPUBLIC

KM# 15 5 SHILLINGS
Copper-Nickel, 38 mm. **Subject:** 2nd F.A.O. Conference **Obv:** Crowned arms with supporters **Rev:** Cow, goat, sheep and fruit **Edge:** Reeded

Date	Mintage	VF20	XF40	MS60	MS63	MS65
1970	100,000	—	1.00	2.00	3.00	5.00
1970	1,000	PF63 20.00	PF65 25.00	PF67 30.00		

KM# 16 20 SHILLINGS
2.80 g., 0.900 Gold 0.081 oz. AGW **Subject:** 10th Anniversary of Independence **Obv:** Crowned arms with supporters **Rev:** Star-like design within circle

Date	Mintage	VF20	XF40	MS60	MS63	MS65
ND-1970	8,000	PF65 125	PF67 135			

KM# 17 50 SHILLINGS
7.00 g., 0.900 Gold 0.2025 oz. AGW **Subject:** 10th Anniversary of Independence **Obv:** Crowned arms with supporters **Rev:** Half-figure with bowl right

Date	Mintage	VF20	XF40	MS60	MS63	MS65
ND-1970	8,000	PF65 305	PF67 325			

KM# 18 50 SHILLINGS
7.00 g., 0.900 Gold 0.2025 oz. AGW **Subject:** 1st Anniversary of 1969 Revolution **Obv:** Crowned arms with supporters **Rev:** Wheat sprig

Date	Mintage	VF20	XF40	MS60	MS63	MS65
ND-1970	—	PF65 305	PF67 325			

KM# 19 100 SHILLINGS
14.00 g., 0.900 Gold 0.4051 oz. AGW **Subject:** 10th Anniversary of Independence **Obv:** Crowned arms with supporters flanked by dates **Rev:** Bust with headscarf and fruit basket on back left

Date	Mintage	VF20	XF40	MS60	MS63	MS65
ND-1970	8,000	PF65 590	PF67 630			

KM# 20 100 SHILLINGS
14.00 g., 0.900 Gold 0.4051 oz. AGW **Subject:** 1st Anniversary of the 1969 Revolution **Obv:** Crowned arms with supporters **Rev:** Hand, helmet and gun in front of design

Date	Mintage	VF20	XF40	MS60	MS63	MS65
ND-1970	—	PF65 590	PF67 630			

KM# 21 200 SHILLINGS
28.00 g., 0.900 Gold 0.8102 oz. AGW **Subject:** 10th Anniversary of Independence **Obv:** Crowned arms with supporters **Rev:** Supplies on camel

Date	Mintage	VF20	XF40	MS60	MS63	MS65
ND-1970	8,000	PF65 1,150	PF67 1,225			

KM# 22 200 SHILLINGS
28.00 g., 0.900 Gold 0.8102 oz. AGW **Subject:** 1st Anniversary of 1969 Revolution **Obv:** Crowned arms with supporters **Rev:** Monument

Date	Mintage	VF20	XF40	MS60	MS63	MS65
ND-1970	—	PF65 1,150	PF67 1,225			

KM# 23 500 SHILLINGS
70.00 g., 0.900 Gold 2.0255 oz. AGW **Subject:** 10th Anniversary of Independence **Obv:** Crowned arms with supporters **Rev:** Building within map

Date	Mintage	VF20	XF40	MS60	MS63	MS65
ND-1970	8,000	PF65 2,850	PF67 2,950			

REFORM COINAGE

KM# A24 5 SENTI
Aluminum **Series:** F.A.O. **Obv:** Value within circle **Rev:** Corn ears and flower flanked by dates **Shape:** Round

Date	Mintage	VF20	XF40	MS60	MS63	MS65
1976	—	—	—	—	—	1,500

KM# 24 5 SENTI
0.87 g., Aluminum, 20 mm. **Series:** F.A.O. **Obv:** Crowned arms with supporters **Rev:** Value above fruit, grains and bread **Shape:** 12-sided

Date	Mintage	VF20	XF40	MS60	MS63	MS65
1976	18,500,000	0.10	0.15	0.25	0.35	0.50

KM# 25 10 SENTI
1.39 g., Aluminum, 23.5 mm. **Series:** F.A.O. **Obv:** Crowned arms with supporters **Rev:** Lamb flanked by dates below value **Edge:** Plain **Shape:** 12-sided

Date	Mintage	VF20	XF40	MS60	MS63	MS65
1976	40,500,000	0.10	0.15	0.25	0.50	1.00

KM# 26 50 SENTI
3.80 g., Copper-Nickel, 21.1 mm. **Series:** F.A.O. **Obv:** Crowned arms with supporters **Rev:** Value above grains and dates

Date	Mintage	VF20	XF40	MS60	MS63	MS65
1976	10,080,000	0.15	0.25	0.35	0.75	1.00

KM# 26a 50 SENTI
3.81 g., Nickel Plated Steel, 21 mm. **Series:** F.A.O. **Obv:** Crowned arms with supporters **Rev:** Value above grains and dates

Date	Mintage	VF20	XF40	MS60	MS63	MS65
1984	—	0.35	0.75	1.50	2.50	4.00

KM# 27 SHILLING
6.22 g., Copper-Nickel, 25.5 mm. **Series:** F.A.O. **Obv:** Crowned arms with supporters **Rev:** Lamb flanked by dates below value

Date	Mintage	VF20	XF40	MS60	MS63	MS65
1976	20,040,000	0.25	0.65	1.00	1.50	2.00

KM# 27a SHILLING
6.19 g., Nickel Plated Steel, 25.42 mm. **Series:** F.A.O. **Obv:** Crowned arms with supporters **Rev:** Lamb flanked by dates below value

Date	Mintage	VF20	XF40	MS60	MS63	MS65
1984	—	0.75	1.50	2.50	4.50	7.00

KM# 28 10 SHILLINGS
Copper-Nickel, 39 mm. **Subject:** 10th Anniversary of Republic **Obv:** Crowned arms with supporters **Rev:** Workers

Date	Mintage	VF20	XF40	MS60	MS63	MS65
ND-1979	—	—	—	5.00	9.00	12.00

KM# 28a 10 SHILLINGS
28.28 g., 0.925 Silver 0.841 oz. ASW **Subject:** 10th Anniversary of Republic **Obv:** Crowned arms with supporters **Rev:** Workers

Date	Mintage	VF20	XF40	MS60	MS63	MS65
ND-1979	Est. 5000	PF63 35.00	PF65 45.00			

KM# 29 10 SHILLINGS
Copper-Nickel **Subject:** 10th Anniversary of Republic **Obv:** Crowned arms with supporters **Rev:** Seated figures in front of tents

Date	Mintage	VF20	XF40	MS60	MS63	MS65
ND-1979	—	—	—	5.00	9.00	12.00

KM# 29a 10 SHILLINGS
28.28 g., 0.925 Silver 0.841 oz. ASW **Subject:** 10th Anniversary of Republic **Obv:** Crowned arms with supporters **Rev:** Seated figures in front of tents

Date	Mintage	VF20	XF40	MS60	MS63	MS65
ND-1979	Est. 5000	PF63 35.00	PF65 45.00			

KM# 30 10 SHILLINGS
Copper-Nickel **Subject:** 10th Anniversary of Republic **Obv:** Crowned arms with supporters **Rev:** Lab workers

Date	Mintage	VF20	XF40	MS60	MS63	MS65
ND-1979	—	—	—	5.00	9.00	12.00

KM# 30a 10 SHILLINGS
28.28 g., 0.925 Silver 0.841 oz. ASW **Subject:** 10th Anniversary of Republic **Obv:** Crowned arms with supporters **Rev:** Lab workers

Date	Mintage	VF20	XF40	MS60	MS63	MS65
ND-1979	Est. 5000	PF63 35.00	PF65 45.00			

KM# 31 10 SHILLINGS
Copper-Nickel **Subject:** 10th Anniversary of Republic **Obv:** Crowned arms with supporters **Rev:** Dancers

Date	Mintage	VF20	XF40	MS60	MS63	MS65
ND-1979	—	—	—	5.00	9.00	12.00

KM# 31a 10 SHILLINGS
28.28 g., 0.925 Silver 0.841 oz. ASW **Subject:** 10th Anniversary of Republic **Obv:** Crowned arms with supporters **Rev:** Dancers

Date	Mintage	VF20	XF40	MS60	MS63	MS65
ND-1979	Est. 5000	PF63 35.00	PF65 45.00			

KM# 32 10 SHILLINGS
Copper-Nickel **Subject:** 10th Anniversary of Republic **Obv:** Crowned arms with supporters **Rev:** Man and woman

Date	Mintage	VF20	XF40	MS60	MS63	MS65
ND-1979	—	—	—	5.00	9.00	12.00

KM# 32a 10 SHILLINGS
28.28 g., 0.925 Silver 0.841 oz. ASW **Subject:** 10th Anniversary of Republic **Obv:** Crowned arms with supporters **Rev:** Man and woman

Date	Mintage	VF20	XF40	MS60	MS63	MS65
ND-1979	Est. 5000	PF63 35.00	PF65 45.00			

KM# 40 25 SHILLINGS
Copper-Nickel **Subject:** World Fisheries Conference **Obv:** Crowned arms with supporters **Rev:** Green sea turtle

Date	Mintage	VF20	XF40	MS60	MS63	MS65
ND-1984	2,600	—	—	—	30.00	35.00

KM# 40a 25 SHILLINGS
28.28 g., 0.925 Silver 0.841 oz. ASW **Subject:** World Fisheries Conference **Obv:** Crowned arms with supporters **Rev:** Green sea turtle

Date	Mintage	VF20	XF40	MS60	MS63	MS65
ND-1984	20,000	PF63 25.00	PF65 35.00			

KM# 40b 25 SHILLINGS
47.54 g., 0.917 Gold 1.4016 oz. AGW **Subject:** World Fisheries Conference **Obv:** Crowned arms with supporters **Rev:** Green sea turtle

Date	Mintage	VF20	XF40	MS60	MS63	MS65
ND-1984	200	PF65 2,500				

KM# 38 150 SHILLINGS
28.28 g., 0.925 Silver 0.841 oz. ASW **Series:** International Year of Disabled Persons **Obv:** Crowned arms with supporters **Rev:** Head left, emblem at lower left

Date	Mintage	VF20	XF40	MS60	MS63	MS65
1983	5,500	—	—	—	30.00	35.00
1983	5,500	PF65 50.00				

KM# 33 1500 SHILLINGS
15.98 g., 0.917 Gold 0.4711 oz. AGW **Subject:** 10th Anniversary of Republic **Obv:** Crowned arms with supporters **Rev:** Workers facing

Date	Mintage	VF20	XF40	MS60	MS63	MS65
ND-1979	500	—	—	—	—	875
ND-1979	500	PF65 875				

KM# 34 1500 SHILLINGS
15.98 g., 0.917 Gold 0.4711 oz. AGW **Subject:** 10th Anniversary of Republic **Obv:** Crowned arms with supporters **Rev:** Seated figures in front of tents

Date	Mintage	VF20	XF40	MS60	MS63	MS65
ND-1979	500	—	—	—	—	875
ND-1979	500	PF65 875				

KM# 35 1500 SHILLINGS
15.98 g., 0.917 Gold 0.4711 oz. AGW **Subject:** 10th Anniversary of Republic **Obv:** Crowned arms with supporters **Rev:** Lab workers

Date	Mintage	VF20	XF40	MS60	MS63	MS65
ND-1979	500	—	—	—	—	875
ND-1979	500	PF65 875				

KM# 36 1500 SHILLINGS
15.98 g., 0.917 Gold 0.4711 oz. AGW **Subject:** 10th Anniversary of Republic **Obv:** Crowned arms with supporters **Rev:** Dancers

Date	Mintage	VF20	XF40	MS60	MS63	MS65
ND-1979	500	—	—	—	—	875
ND-1979	500	PF65 875				

KM# 37 1500 SHILLINGS
15.98 g., 0.917 Gold 0.4711 oz. AGW **Subject:** 10th Anniversary of Republic **Obv:** Crowned arms with supporters **Rev:** Man and woman

Date	Mintage	VF20	XF40	MS60	MS63	MS65
1979	500	—	—	—	—	875
1979	500	PF65 875				

KM# 39 1500 SHILLINGS
15.98 g., 0.917 Gold 0.4711 oz. AGW **Series:** International Year of Disabled Persons **Obv:** Crowned arms with supporters **Rev:** Emblem above busts facing

Date	Mintage	VF20	XF40	MS60	MS63	MS65
1983	—	—	—	—	—	875
1983	—	PF65 875				

REPUBLIC OF SOMALIA

STANDARD COINAGE

KM# 45 5 SHILLING / SCELLINI
1.29 g., Aluminum, 21 mm. **Series:** F.A.O. **Obv:** Crowned arms with supporters **Rev:** Elephant **Edge:** Plain

Date	Mintage	VF20	XF40	MS60	MS63	MS65
1999	—	—	—	0.75	1.50	1.75
2000	—	—	—	0.75	1.50	1.75

KM# 46 10 SHILLINGS / SCELLINI
1.29 g., Aluminum, 21.9 mm. **Series:** F.A.O. **Obv:** Crowned arms with supporters **Rev:** Camel **Edge:** Plain

Date	Mintage	VF20	XF40	MS60	MS63	MS65
1999	—	—	—	1.00	2.00	2.25
2000	—	—	—	1.00	2.00	2.25

KM# 90 10 SHILLINGS / SCELLINI
4.82 g., Nickel Clad Steel, 24.9 mm. **Series:** Asian Astrology **Obv:** National arms **Rev:** Rat **Edge:** Plain

Date	Mintage	VF20	XF40	MS60	MS63	MS65
2000	—	—	—	0.50	1.00	1.25

KM# 91 10 SHILLINGS / SCELLINI
4.82 g., Nickel Clad Steel, 25 mm. **Series:** Asian Astrology **Obv:** National arms **Rev:** Ox **Edge:** Plain

Date	Mintage	VF20	XF40	MS60	MS63	MS65
2000	—	—	—	0.50	1.00	1.25

KM# 92 10 SHILLINGS / SCELLINI
4.82 g., Nickel Clad Steel, 25 mm. **Series:** Asian Astrology **Obv:** National arms **Rev:** Tiger **Edge:** plain

Date	Mintage	VF20	XF40	MS60	MS63	MS65
2000	—	—	—	0.50	1.00	1.25

KM# 93 10 SHILLINGS / SCELLINI
4.82 g., Nickel Clad Steel, 25 mm. **Series:** Asian Astrology **Obv:** National arms **Rev:** Rabbit **Edge:** Plain

Date	Mintage	VF20	XF40	MS60	MS63	MS65
2000	—	—	—	0.50	1.00	1.25

KM# 94 10 SHILLINGS / SCELLINI
4.82 g., Nickel Clad Steel, 25 mm. **Series:** Asian Astrology **Obv:** National arms **Rev:** Dragon **Edge:** Plain

Date	Mintage	VF20	XF40	MS60	MS63	MS65
2000	—	—	—	0.65	1.25	1.50

KM# 95 10 SHILLINGS / SCELLINI
4.82 g., Nickel Clad Steel, 25 mm. **Series:** Asian Astrology **Obv:** National arms **Rev:** Snake **Edge:** Plain

Date	Mintage	VF20	XF40	MS60	MS63	MS65
2000	—	—	—	0.50	1.00	1.25

KM# 96 10 SHILLINGS / SCELLINI
4.82 g., Nickel Clad Steel, 25 mm. **Series:** Asian Astrology **Obv:** National arms **Rev:** Horse **Edge:** Plain

Date	Mintage	VF20	XF40	MS60	MS63	MS65
2000	—	—	—	0.65	1.25	1.50

KM# 97 10 SHILLINGS / SCELLINI
4.82 g., Nickel Clad Steel, 25 mm. **Series:** Asian Astrology **Obv:** National arms **Rev:** Goat **Edge:** Plain

Date	Mintage	VF20	XF40	MS60	MS63	MS65
2000	—	—	—	0.50	1.00	1.25

KM# 98 10 SHILLINGS / SCELLINI
4.82 g., Nickel Clad Steel, 25 mm. **Series:** Asian Astrology **Obv:** National arms **Rev:** Monkey **Edge:** Plain

Date	Mintage	VF20	XF40	MS60	MS63	MS65
2000	—	—	—	0.50	1.00	1.25

KM# 99 10 SHILLINGS / SCELLINI
4.82 g., Nickel Clad Steel, 25 mm. **Series:** Asian Astrology **Obv:** National arms **Rev:** Rooster **Edge:** Plain

Date	Mintage	VF20	XF40	MS60	MS63	MS65
2000	—	—	—	0.50	1.00	1.25

KM# 100 10 SHILLINGS / SCELLINI
4.82 g., Nickel Clad Steel, 25 mm. **Series:** Asian Astrology **Obv:** National arms **Rev:** Dog **Edge:** Plain

Date	Mintage	VF20	XF40	MS60	MS63	MS65
2000	—	—	—	0.50	1.00	1.25

KM# 101 10 SHILLINGS / SCELLINI
4.82 g., Nickel Clad Steel, 25 mm. **Series:** Asian Astrology **Obv:** National arms **Rev:** Pig **Edge:** Plain

Date	Mintage	VF20	XF40	MS60	MS63	MS65
2000	—	—	—	0.50	1.00	1.25

KM# 107 10 SHILLINGS / SCELLINI
Silver **Obv:** Crowned arms with supporters **Rev:** Multicolored dragon

Date	Mintage	VF20	XF40	MS60	MS63	MS65
2000	—	PF65 35.00				

KM# 41 25 SHILLINGS
Copper-Nickel **Subject:** History of World Shipping - Sinking of Titanic **Obv:** Crowned arms with supporters **Rev:** Multicolor inner circle design with partially submerged ship **Rev. Legend:** Inner legend reads "THE TITANIC SINKS - APRIL 15, 1912"

Date	Mintage	VF20	XF40	MS60	MS63	MS65
1998	—	PF63 8.00	PF65 10.00			

KM# 47 25 SHILLINGS
Copper-Nickel, 37.9 mm. **Subject:** Wildlife of Somalia **Obv:** Crowned arms with supporters **Rev:** Multicolored hippopotamus **Edge:** Plain

Date	Mintage	VF20	XF40	MS60	MS63	MS65
1998	—	—	—	—	8.00	10.00

KM# 50 25 SHILLINGS
Copper-Nickel **Subject:** History of World Shipping - Cutty Sark **Obv:** Crowned arms with supporters **Rev:** Multicolored Ship **Edge:** Plain **Note:** Weight varies 18.42-20.2g.

Date	Mintage	VF20	XF40	MS60	MS63	MS65
1998	—	PF63 8.00	PF65 10.00			

KM# 51 25 SHILLINGS
Copper-Nickel **Subject:** History of World Shipping - Caravel Nina **Obv:** Crowned arms with supporters **Rev:** Multicolored ship

Date	Mintage	VF20	XF40	MS60	MS63	MS65
1998	—	PF63 8.00	PF65 10.00			

KM# 52 25 SHILLINGS
Copper-Nickel **Subject:** History of World Shipping **Obv:** Crowned arms with supporters **Rev:** Multicolored Greek Trireme **Note:** Weight varies 18.42-20.2g.

Date	Mintage	VF20	XF40	MS60	MS63	MS65
1998	—	PF63 8.00	PF65 10.00			

KM# 53 25 SHILLINGS
Copper-Nickel **Subject:** History of World Shipping **Obv:** Crowned arms with supporters **Rev:** Multicolored Roman merchant ship **Note:** Weight varies 18.42-20.2g.

Date	Mintage	VF20	XF40	MS60	MS63	MS65
1998	—	PF63 8.00	PF65 10.00			

KM# 54 25 SHILLINGS
Copper-Nickel **Subject:** History of World Shipping **Obv:** Crowned arms with supporters **Rev:** Multicolored Hansa Trading Cog **Note:** Weight varies 18.42-20.2g.

Date	Mintage	VF20	XF40	MS60	MS63	MS65
1998	—	PF63 8.00	PF65 10.00			

KM# 55 25 SHILLINGS

Copper-Nickel . **Subject:** History of World Shipping **Obv:** Crowned arms with supporters **Rev:** Multicolored Titanic **Note:** Weight varies 18.42-20.2g.

Date	Mintage	VF20	XF40	MS60	MS63	MS65
1998	—	PF63 8.00	PF65 10.00			

KM# 56 25 SHILLINGS

Copper-Nickel **Subject:** Wildlife of Somalia **Obv:** Crowned arms with supporters **Rev:** Multicolored Ostrich **Note:** Weight varies 18.42-20.2g.

Date	Mintage	VF20	XF40	MS60	MS63	MS65
1998	—	—	—	—	6.00	8.00

KM# 57 25 SHILLINGS

Copper-Nickel **Subject:** Wildlife of Somalia **Obv:** Crowned arms with supporters **Rev:** Multicolored running Eland **Note:** Weight varies 18.42-20.2g.

Date	Mintage	VF20	XF40	MS60	MS63	MS65
1998	—	—	—	—	6.00	8.00

KM# 58 25 SHILLINGS

Copper-Nickel **Subject:** Wildlife of Somalia **Obv:** Crowned arms with supporters **Rev:** Multicolored Spurfowl in grass **Note:** Weight varies 18.42-20.2g.

Date	Mintage	VF20	XF40	MS60	MS63	MS65
1998	—	—	—	—	6.00	8.00

KM# 59 25 SHILLINGS

Copper-Nickel **Subject:** Wildlife of Somalia **Obv:** Crowned arms with supporters **Rev:** Multicolored Leopard **Note:** Weight varies 18.42-20.2g.

Date	Mintage	VF20	XF40	MS60	MS63	MS65
1998	—	—	—	—	6.00	8.00

KM# 60 25 SHILLINGS

Copper-Nickel **Subject:** Wildlife of Somalia **Obv:** Crowned arms with supporters **Rev:** Multicolored bird on branch **Note:** Weight varies 18.42-20.2g.

Date	Mintage	VF20	XF40	MS60	MS63	MS65
1998	—	—	—	—	6.00	8.00

KM# 61 25 SHILLINGS

Copper-Nickel **Subject:** Wildlife of Somalia **Obv:** Crowned arms with supporters **Rev:** Multicolored variable sunbird on branch **Note:** Weight varies 18.42-20.2g.

Date	Mintage	VF20	XF40	MS60	MS63	MS65
1998	—	—	—	—	6.00	8.00

KM# 62 25 SHILLINGS

Copper-Nickel **Subject:** Wildlife of Somalia **Obv:** Crowned arms with supporters **Rev:** Multicolored starling on broken branch **Note:** Weight varies 18.42-20.2g.

Date	Mintage	VF20	XF40	MS60	MS63	MS65
1998	—	—	—	—	6.00	8.00

KM# 106 25 SHILLINGS

Copper-Nickel **Subject:** Fall of Berlin Wall **Obv:** Crowned arms with supporters **Rev:** Berlin wall destruction scene

Date	Mintage	VF20	XF40	MS60	MS63	MS65
1999	—	—	—	—	4.00	6.00

KM# 141 25 SHILLINGS

20.00 g., Copper-Nickel, 38 mm. **Subject:** 100th Birthday - British Queen Mother **Obv:** Crowned arms with supporters above value **Rev:** Queen Mother **Edge:** Plain

Date	Mintage	VF20	XF40	MS60	MS63	MS65
ND (1999)	—	—	—	—	6.00	8.00

KM# 70 25 SHILLINGS

Copper-Nickel, 38 mm. **Subject:** Winston Churchill **Obv:** Crowned arms with supporters **Rev:** Bust facing **Edge:** Plain

Date	Mintage	VF20	XF40	MS60	MS63	MS65
2000	—	—	—	—	5.00	7.00

KM# 71 25 SHILLINGS

Copper-Nickel, 38 mm. **Subject:** Pope John Paul II **Obv:** Crowned arms with supporters **Rev:** Bust facing **Edge:** Plain

Date	Mintage	VF20	XF40	MS60	MS63	MS65
2000	—	—	—	—	4.00	6.00

KM# 72 25 SHILLINGS

20.00 g., Copper-Nickel, 38 mm. **Subject:** Nelson Mandela **Obv:** Crowned arms with supporters **Rev:** Bust facing **Edge:** Reeded

Date	Mintage	VF20	XF40	MS60	MS63	MS65
2000	—	—	—	—	4.00	6.00

KM# 73 25 SHILLINGS

Copper-Nickel **Subject:** Che Guevara **Obv:** Crowned arms with supporters **Rev:** Bust with hat facing

Date	Mintage	VF20	XF40	MS60	MS63	MS65
2000	—	—	—	—	10.00	15.00

KM# 74 25 SHILLINGS
Copper-Nickel, 37.9 mm. **Subject:** Emperor Hirohito **Obv:** Crowned arms with supporters **Rev:** Bust facing **Edge:** Plain

Date	Mintage	VF20	XF40	MS60	MS63	MS65
2000 Prooflike	—	—	—	—	3.00	5.00

KM# 75 25 SHILLINGS
Copper-Nickel **Subject:** Mao Tse-Tung **Obv:** Crowned arms with supporters **Rev:** Bust facing

Date	Mintage	VF20	XF40	MS60	MS63	MS65
2000 Prooflike	—	—	—	—	5.00	7.00

KM# 76 25 SHILLINGS
Copper-Nickel **Subject:** Berlin **Obv:** Crowned arms with supporters **Rev:** Berlin wall destruction scene

Date	Mintage	VF20	XF40	MS60	MS63	MS65
ND-2000 Prooflike	—	—	—	—	4.00	6.00

KM# 108 25 SHILLINGS
Copper-Nickel , **Obv:** Crowned arms with supporters **Rev:** Multicolored penguins

Date	Mintage	VF20	XF40	MS60	MS63	MS65
2000	—	PF65 20.00				

KM# 77 150 SHILLINGS
14.81 g., 0.999 Silver 0.4757 oz. ASW, 34.25 mm. **Subject:** Christopher Columbus **Obv:** Crowned arms with supporters **Rev:** Cameo above 3 ships **Edge:** Reeded

Date	Mintage	VF20	XF40	MS60	MS63	MS65
2000	—	PF65 13.50				

KM# 113 150 SHILLINGS
15.00 g., 0.999 Silver 0.4818 oz. ASW, 34.25 mm. **Subject:** Millennium **Obv:** Crowned arms with supporters **Rev:** World globe **Edge:** Reeded

Date	Mintage	VF20	XF40	MS60	MS63	MS65
2000	—	PF65 13.50				

KM# 42 250 SHILLINGS
23.50 g., 0.925 Silver 0.6989 oz. ASW **Subject:** History of World Shipping - Sinking of Titanic **Obv:** Crowned arms with supporters **Rev:** Multicolored sinking ship

Date	Mintage	VF20	XF40	MS60	MS63	MS65
1998	20,000	PF65 32.00				

KM# 42a 250 SHILLINGS
Bi-Metallic Brass center in Copper-Nickel ring. **Subject:** Historic Ships **Obv:** Crowned arms with supporters **Rev:** Multicolor sinking ship

Date	Mintage	VF20	XF40	MS60	MS63	MS65
1998	—	—	—	—	—	27.00

KM# 48 250 SHILLINGS
23.70 g., 0.925 Silver 0.7048 oz. ASW, 38.1 mm. **Subject:** Wildlife of Somalia **Obv:** Crowned arms with supporters **Rev:** Multicolored Hippopotamus **Edge:** Reeded

Date	Mintage	VF20	XF40	MS60	MS63	MS65
1998	—	PF65 20.00				

KM# 48a 250 SHILLINGS
Bi-Metallic Copper-Nickel center in Brass ring, 38 mm. **Subject:** Wildlife of Somalia **Obv:** Crowned arms with supporters **Rev:** Multicolored Hippopotamus **Edge:** Reeded

Date	Mintage	VF20	XF40	MS60	MS63	MS65
1998	—	—	—	—	—	15.00

KM# 49 250 SHILLINGS
23.70 g., 0.925 Silver 0.7048 oz. ASW **Subject:** Wildlife of Somalia **Obv:** Crowned arms with supporters **Rev:** Multicolored Ostrich

Date	Mintage	VF20	XF40	MS60	MS63	MS65
1998	—	PF65 25.00				

KM# 49a 250 SHILLINGS
Bi-Metallic Brass center in Copper-nickel ring, 38 mm. **Subject:** Wildlife of Somalia **Obv:** Crowned arms with supporters **Rev:** Multicolored Ostrich

Date	Mintage	VF20	XF40	MS60	MS63	MS65
1998	—	—	—	—	—	20.00

KM# 64 250 SHILLINGS
24.83 g., 0.900 Silver 0.7185 oz. ASW, 37.2 mm. **Subject:** Wildlife of Somalia **Obv:** Crowned arms with supporters **Rev:** Multicolored Yellow-necked Spurfowl in grass **Edge:** Reeded

Date	Mintage	VF20	XF40	MS60	MS63	MS65
1998	—	PF65 22.50				

KM# 64a 250 SHILLINGS
Bi-Metallic Brass center in Copper-nickel ring, 38 mm. **Subject:** Wildlife of Somalia **Obv:** Crowned arms with supporters **Rev:** Multicolored Yellow-necked Spurfowl in grass

Date	Mintage	VF20	XF40	MS60	MS63	MS65
1998	—	—	—	—	—	20.00

KM# 65 250 SHILLINGS
24.83 g., 0.900 Silver 0.7185 oz. ASW **Subject:** Wildlife of Somalia **Obv:** Crowned arms with supporters **Rev:** Multicolored running Eland

Date	Mintage	VF20	XF40	MS60	MS63	MS65
1998	—	PF65 25.00				

KM# 66 250 SHILLINGS
24.83 g., 0.900 Silver 0.7185 oz. ASW **Subject:** Wildlife of Somalia **Obv:** Crowned arms with supporters **Rev:** Multicolored Leopard

Date	Mintage	VF20	XF40	MS60	MS63	MS65
1998	—	PF65 25.00				

KM# 66a 250 SHILLINGS
Bi-Metallic Brass center in Copper-nickel ring, 38 mm. **Subject:** Wildlife of Somalia **Obv:** Crowned arms with supporters **Rev:** Multicolored Leopard

Date	Mintage	VF20	XF40	MS60	MS63	MS65
1998	—	—	—	—	—	15.00

KM# 67 250 SHILLINGS
24.83 g., 0.900 Silver 0.7185 oz. ASW **Subject:** Wildlife of Somalia **Obv:** Crowned arms with supporters **Rev:** Multicolored Golden Palm Weaver on branch

Date	Mintage	VF20	XF40	MS60	MS63	MS65
1998	—	PF65 25.00				

KM# 67a 250 SHILLINGS
Bi-Metallic Brass center in Copper-nickel ring, 38 mm. **Subject:** Wildlife of Somalia **Obv:** Crowned arms with supporters **Rev:** Multicolored Golden Palm Weaver on branch

Date	Mintage	VF20	XF40	MS60	MS63	MS65
1998	—	—	—	—	—	20.00

KM# 68 250 SHILLINGS
24.83 g., 0.900 Silver 0.7185 oz. ASW **Subject:** Wildlife of Somalia **Obv:** Crowned arms with supporters **Rev:** Multicolored variable sunbird on branch

Date	Mintage	VF20	XF40	MS60	MS63	MS65
1998	—	PF65 25.00				

KM# 68a 250 SHILLINGS
Bi-Metallic Brass center in Copper-nickel ring, 38 mm. **Subject:** Wildlife of Somalia **Obv:** Crowned arms with supporters **Rev:** Multicolored variable sunbird on branch

Date	Mintage	VF20	XF40	MS60	MS63	MS65
1998	—	—	—	—	—	22.50

KM# 69 250 SHILLINGS
24.83 g., 0.900 Silver 0.7185 oz. ASW **Subject:** Wildlife of Somalia **Obv:** Crowned arms with supporters **Rev:** Multicolored starling on broken branch

Date	Mintage	VF20	XF40	MS60	MS63	MS65
1998	—	PF65 25.00				

KM# 69a 250 SHILLINGS
Bi-Metallic Copper-Nickel center in Brass ring, 38 mm. **Subject:** Wildlife of Somalia **Obv:** Crowned arms with supporters **Rev:** Multicolored starling on broken branch

Date	Mintage	VF20	XF40	MS60	MS63	MS65
1998	—	—	—	—	—	12.50

KM# 78 250 SHILLINGS
Bi-Metallic Brass center in Copper-nickel ring, 38 mm. **Subject:** History of World Shipping **Obv:** Crowned arms with supporters **Rev:** Multicolored Titanic

Date	Mintage	VF20	XF40	MS60	MS63	MS65
1998	—	—	—	—	—	12.50

KM# 79 250 SHILLINGS
Bi-Metallic Brass center in Copper-nickel ring, 38 mm. **Subject:** History of World Shipping **Obv:** Crowned arms with supporters **Rev:** Multicolored Greek trirema

Date	Mintage	VF20	XF40	MS60	MS63	MS65
1998	—	—	—	—	—	12.50

KM# 80 250 SHILLINGS
Bi-Metallic Brass center in Copper-nickel ring, 38 mm. **Subject:** History of World Shipping **Obv:** Crowned arms with supporters **Rev:** Multicolored Roman merchant ship

Date	Mintage	VF20	XF40	MS60	MS63	MS65
1998	—	—	—	—	—	12.50

KM# 81 250 SHILLINGS
Bi-Metallic Brass center in Copper-nickel ring, 38 mm. **Subject:** History of World Shipping **Obv:** Crowned arms with supporters **Rev:** Multicolored Hanseatic Trading Cog

Date	Mintage	VF20	XF40	MS60	MS63	MS65
1998	—	—	—	—	—	12.50

KM# 82 250 SHILLINGS
Bi-Metallic Brass center in Copper-nickel ring, 38 mm. **Subject:** History of World Shipping **Obv:** Crowned arms with supporters **Rev:** Multicolored Caravel "Nina" **Edge:** Reeded

Date	Mintage	VF20	XF40	MS60	MS63	MS65
1998	—	—	—	—	—	12.50

KM# 83 250 SHILLINGS
Bi-Metallic Brass center in Copper-nickel ring, 38 mm. **Subject:** History of World Shipping **Obv:** Crowned arms with supporters **Rev:** Multicolored Clipper "Cutty Sark"

Date	Mintage	VF20	XF40	MS60	MS63	MS65
1998	—	—	—	—	—	12.50

KM# 102 250 SHILLINGS
24.00 g., 0.900 Silver 0.6945 oz. ASW, 38.1 mm. **Subject:** Olympics **Obv:** Crowned arms with supporters **Rev:** Multicolor skier **Edge:** Reeded

Date	Mintage	VF20	XF40	MS60	MS63	MS65
1998	—	PF65 35.00				

KM# 105 250 SHILLINGS
23.10 g., 0.925 Silver 0.687 oz. ASW, 38.6 mm. **Obv:** Crowned arms with supporters **Rev:** Two giraffes **Edge:** Reeded

Date	Mintage	VF20	XF40	MS60	MS63	MS65
1999	—	PF65 25.00				

KM# 142 250 SHILLINGS
22.00 g., Tri-Metallic Gold Plated Brass center in Silver Plated Brass inner ring within a Gold Plated Brass outer ring, 38 mm. **Subject:** 100th Birthday - British Queen Mother **Obv:** Crowned arms with supporters above value **Rev:** Queen Mother **Edge:** Reeded

Date	Mintage	VF20	XF40	MS60	MS63	MS65
ND (1999)	—	—	—	—	25.00	30.00

KM# 63 250 SHILLINGS
24.83 g., 0.900 Silver 0.7185 oz. ASW, 37.2 mm. **Subject:** Marine Life Protection **Obv:** Crowned arms with supporters **Rev:** Multicolor penguins **Edge:** Reeded

Date	Mintage	VF20	XF40	MS60	MS63	MS65
2000	—	PF65 40.00				

KM# 114 250 SHILLINGS
23.00 g., 0.925 Silver 0.684 oz. ASW, 38 mm. **Subject:** Winston Churchill **Obv:** Crowned arms with supporters **Rev:** Bust facing **Edge:** Reeded

Date	Mintage	VF20	XF40	MS60	MS63	MS65
2000	—	—	—	—	27.00	30.00

KM# 115 250 SHILLINGS
23.00 g., 0.925 Silver 0.684 oz. ASW, 38 mm. **Subject:** Pope John Paul II **Obv:** Crowned arms with supporters **Rev:** Bust facing **Edge:** Reeded

Date	Mintage	VF20	XF40	MS60	MS63	MS65
2000	—	—	—	—	27.00	30.00

KM# 116 250 SHILLINGS
21.90 g., Tri-Metallic Brass center, Copper-Nickel inner ring, brass outer ring **Subject:** Millennium Icons - Nelson Mandela **Obv:** Crowned arms with supporters **Obv. Legend:** REPUBLIC OF SOMALIA **Rev:** Bust facing

Date	Mintage	VF20	XF40	MS60	MS63	MS65
2000	—	—	—	—	—	15.00

KM# 116a 250 SHILLINGS
23.00 g., 0.925 Silver 0.684 oz. ASW, 38 mm. **Subject:** Millennium Icons - Nelson Mandela **Obv:** Crowned arms with supporters **Obv. Legend:** REPUBLIC OF SOMALIA **Rev:** Bust facing **Edge:** Reeded

Date	Mintage	VF20	XF40	MS60	MS63	MS65
2000	—	PF65 30.00				

KM# 117 250 SHILLINGS
21.90 g., Tri-Metallic Brass center, Copper-Nickel inner ring, Brass outer ring **Subject:** Millennium Icons - Emperor Hirohito **Obv:** Crowned arms with supporters **Obv. Legend:** REPUBLIC OF SOMALIA **Rev:** Bust facing

Date	Mintage	VF20	XF40	MS60	MS63	MS65
2000	—	—	—	—	—	15.00

KM# 117a 250 SHILLINGS
23.00 g., 0.925 Silver 0.684 oz. ASW, 38 mm. **Subject:** Millennium Icons - Emperor Hirohito **Obv:** Crowned arms with supporters **Obv. Legend:** REPUBLIC OF SOMALIA **Rev:** Bust facing **Edge:** Reeded

Date	Mintage	VF20	XF40	MS60	MS63	MS65
2000	—	PF65 30.00				

KM# 118 250 SHILLINGS
21.90 g., Tri-Metallic Brass center, Copper-Nickel inner ring, Brass outer ring, 38 mm. **Subject:** Millennium Icons - Mao Tse-tung **Obv:** Crowned arms with supporters **Obv. Legend:** REPUBLIC OF SOMALIA **Rev:** Head right **Edge:** Reeded

Date	Mintage	VF20	XF40	MS60	MS63	MS65
2000	—	—	—	—	—	15.00

KM# 119 250 SHILLINGS
21.90 g., Tri-Metallic Brass center in Copper-Nickel inner ring, Brass outer ring, 38 mm. **Subject:** Millennium Icons - Che Guevara **Obv:** Crowned arms with supporters **Obv. Legend:** REPUBLIC OF SOMALIA **Rev:** Bust facing **Edge:** Reeded

Date	Mintage	VF20	XF40	MS60	MS63	MS65
2000	—	—	—	—	—	20.00

KM# 119a 250 SHILLINGS
23.00 g., 0.925 Silver 0.684 oz. ASW, 38 mm. **Subject:** Millennium Icons - Che Guevara **Obv:** Crowned arms with supporters **Obv. Legend:** REPUBLIC OF SOMALIA **Rev:** Bust facing **Edge:** Reeded

Date	Mintage	VF20	XF40	MS60	MS63	MS65
2000	—	PF65 40.00				

KM# 84 5000 SHILLINGS / SCELLINI
7.06 g., 0.999 Silver 0.2268 oz. ASW, 29.7 mm. **Subject:** Tall Ship Series: Amerigo Vespucci **Obv:** Crowned arms with supporters **Rev:** Sailing ship **Edge:** Plain

Date	Mintage	VF20	XF40	MS60	MS63	MS65
1998	—	PF65 15.00				

KM# 85 5000 SHILLINGS / SCELLINI
7.06 g., 0.999 Silver 0.2268 oz. ASW **Subject:** Tall Ships Series: Sedov **Obv:** Crowned arms with supporters **Rev:** Sailing ship

Date	Mintage	VF20	XF40	MS60	MS63	MS65
1998	—	PF65 15.00				

KM# 86 5000 SHILLINGS / SCELLINI
7.06 g., 0.999 Silver 0.2268 oz. ASW **Subject:** Tall Ships Series: Gorch Fock **Obv:** Crowned arms with supporters **Rev:** Sailing ship

Date	Mintage	VF20	XF40	MS60	MS63	MS65
1998	—	PF65 15.00				

KM# 87 5000 SHILLINGS / SCELLINI
7.06 g., 0.999 Silver 0.2268 oz. ASW **Subject:** Tall Ships Series: Libertad **Obv:** Crowned arms with supporters **Rev:** Sailing ship

Date	Mintage	VF20	XF40	MS60	MS63	MS65
1998	—	PF65 15.00				

KM# 88 5000 SHILLINGS / SCELLINI
7.06 g., 0.999 Silver 0.2268 oz. ASW **Subject:** Tall Ships Series: Alexander von Humboldt **Obv:** Crowned arms with supporters **Rev:** Sailing ship

Date	Mintage	VF20	XF40	MS60	MS63	MS65
1998	—	PF65 15.00				

KM# 89 5000 SHILLINGS / SCELLINI
7.06 g., 0.999 Silver 0.2268 oz. ASW **Subject:** Tall Ship Series: Eagle **Obv:** Crowned arms with supporters **Rev:** Sailing ship

Date	Mintage	VF20	XF40	MS60	MS63	MS65
1998	—	PF65 15.00				

KM# 43 10000 SHILLINGS / SCELLINI
15.00 g., 0.999 Silver 0.4818 oz. ASW **Subject:** Fauna of Africa **Obv:** Crowned arms with supporters **Rev:** Ostriches

Date	Mintage	VF20	XF40	MS60	MS63	MS65
1998	—	PF65 32.00				

KM# 44 10000 SHILLINGS / SCELLINI
15.00 g., 0.999 Silver 0.4818 oz. ASW **Subject:** Fauna of Africa **Obv:** Crowned arms with supporters **Rev:** Three Dammah Oryx

Date	Mintage	VF20	XF40	MS60	MS63	MS65
1998	—	PF65 32.00				

PIEDFORT

KM#	Date	Mintage	Identification	Mkt Val
P1	1983	500	150 Shillings. 0.925. Silver.	125
P2	1983	—	1500 Shillings. Gold. KM39.	1,100
P3	ND-1984	500	25 Shillings. 0.925. Silver.	110
P4	1998	2,500	250 Shillings. 0.925. Silver. Skier.	145
P5	1998	—	250 Shillings. Silver. Titanic. KM42.	85.00
P6	1998	—	250 Shillings. 0.925. Silver. Ostrich. KM49.	55.00

PROVAS

KM#	Date	Mintage	Identification	Mkt Val
Pr1	1950	—	Centesimo.	70.00
Pr2	1950	—	5 Centesimi.	70.00
Pr3	1950	—	10 Centesimi.	70.00
Pr4	1950	—	50 Centesimi.	95.00
Pr5	1950	—	Somalo.	125

MINT SETS

KM#	Date	Mintage	Identification	Issue Price	Mkt Val
MS1	1979 (5)	—	KM33-37	—	4,400

PROOF SETS

KM#	Date	Mintage	Identification	Issue Price	Mkt Val
PS1	1965 (5)	6,325	KM10-14	—	5,300
PS2	1965 (5)	—	KM10-14. Gilt Copper-Nickel.	—	500
PS3	1970 (5)	8,000	KM16, 17, 19, 21, 23	334	5,300
PS4	1970 (3)	14,500	KM18, 20, 22	—	2,200
PS5	1979 (5)	5,000	KM28a-32a	325	225
PS6	1979 (5)	—	KM33-37	—	4,400

SOMALILAND

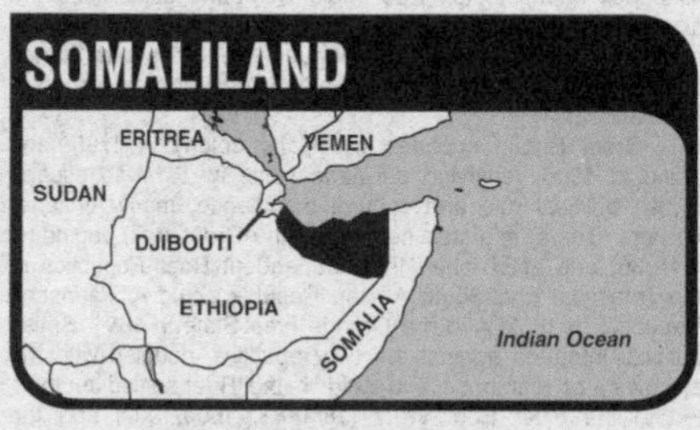

The Somaliland Republic, comprised of the former British Somaliland Protectorate is located on the coast of the northeastern projection of the African continent commonly referred to as the "Horn" on the southwestern end of the Gulf of Aden.

Bordered by Ethiopia to west and south and Somalia to the east. It has an area of 68,000* sq. mi. (176,000* sq. km). Capital: Hargeysa. It is mostly arid and mountainous except for the gulf shoreline.

The Protectorate of British Somaliland was established in 1888 and from 1905 a commissioner under the British Colonial Office administered the territory. Italian Somaliland was administered as a colony from 1893 to 1941, when British forces occupied the territory. In 1950 the United Nations allowed Italy to resume control of Italian Somaliland under a trusteeship. In 1960 British and Italian Somaliland were united as Somalia, an independent republic outside the Commonwealth.

Civil war erupted in the late 1970s and continued until the capital of Somalia was taken in 1990. The United Nations provided aid and peacekeeping. A UN sponsored truce was signed in March 1992 and a peace plan and pact was signed Jan. 15, 1993. The northern Somali National Movement (SNM) declared a secession of the Somaliland Republic on May 17, 1991, which is not recognized by the Somali Democratic Republic.

The currency issued by the East African Currency Board was used in British Somaliland from 1945 to 1961; Somali currency was used later until 1995.

REPUBLIC

SHILLING COINAGE

KM# 1 SHILLING
1.07 g., Aluminum, 20.5 mm. **Issuer:** Bank of Somaliland **Obv:** Bird **Obv. Legend:** REPUBLIC OF SOMALILAND **Rev:** Value **Rev. Legend:** • BAANKA SOMALILAND • **Edge:** Reeded

Date	Mintage	VF20	XF40	MS60	MS63	MS65
1994 PM	—	—	0.50	0.75	1.50	2.50

SOUTH AFRICA

The Republic of South Africa, located at the southern tip of Africa, has an area of 471,445 sq. mi. (1,221,043 sq. km.) and a population of *30.2 million. Capitals: Administrative, Pretoria; Legislative, Cape Town; Judicial, Bloemfontein. Manufacturing, mining and agriculture are the principal industries. Exports include wool, diamonds, gold, and metallic ores.

Portuguese navigator Bartholomew Diaz became the first European to sight the region of South Africa when he rounded the Cape of Good Hope in 1488, but throughout the 16th century the only white men to come ashore were the survivors of ships wrecked while attempting the stormy Cape passage. Jan van Riebeeck of the Dutch East India Company established the first permanent settlement in 1652. In subsequent decades additional Dutch, German and Huguenot refugees from France settled in the Cape area to form the Afrikaner segment of today's population.

Great Britain captured the Cape colony in 1795, and again in 1806, receiving permanent title in 1814. To escape British political rule and cultural dominance, many Afrikaner farmers (Boers) migrated northward (the Great Trek) beginning in 1836, and established the independent Boer Republics of the Transvaal (the South African Republic, Zuid Afrikaansche Republic) in 1852, and the Orange Free State in 1854. British political intrigues against the two republics, coupled with the discovery of diamonds and gold in the Boer-settled regions, led to the bitter Boer Wars (1880-81, 1899-1902) and the incorporation of the Boer republics into the British Empire.

On May 31, 1910, the two former Boer Republics (Transvaal and Orange Free State) were joined with the British colonies of Cape of Good Hope and Natal to form the Union of South Africa, a dominion of the British Empire. In 1934 the Union achieved status as a sovereign state within the British Empire.

Political integration of the various colonies did not still the conflict between the Afrikaners and the English-speaking groups, which continued to have a significant impact on political developments. A resurgence of Afrikaner nationalism in the 1940s and 1950s led to a referendum in the white community authorizing the relinquishment of dominion status and the establishment of a republic. The decision took effect on May 31, 1961. The Republic of South Africa withdrew from the British Commonwealth in Oct. 1961.

The apartheid era ended April 27, 1994 with the first democratic election for all people of South Africa. Nelson Mandela was inaugurated President May 10, 1994, and South Africa was readmitted into the Commonwealth of Nations. Walvis Bay, former enclave of Cape Province, transferred to Namibia.

South African coins and currency bear inscriptions in tribal languages, Afrikaans and English.

RULERS
British, until 1961

REPUBLIK

Zuid-Afrikaansche Republiek

STANDARD COINAGE

12 Pence = 1 Shilling; 20 Shillings = 1 Pond

KM# 11 POND (Een)
0.999 Gold **Subject:** Veld-Boer War Siege Issue **Obv:** ZAR monogram, date below **Rev:** Inscription **Rev. Inscription:** EEN / POND

Date	Mintage	F12	VF20	XF40	MS60	MS63
1902	986	1,150	2,750	6,500	22,500	27,500

UNION OF SOUTH AFRICA

Dominion under Great Britain

STANDARD COINAGE

12 Pence = 1 Shilling; 2 Shillings = 1 Florin; 20 Shillings 1 Pound

KM# 12.1 1/4 PENNY (Farthing)
Bronze, 20.2 mm. **Ruler:** George V **Obv:** Crowned bust left **Rev:** Wheat sprig and berries divide birds within circle **Edge:** Plain

Date	Mintage	F12	VF20	XF40	MS60	MS63
1923	33,000	2.00	5.00	12.00	25.00	40.00
1923	1,402	PF63 285	PF65 575			
1924	95,000	1.50	3.50	11.00	25.00	40.00

KM# 12.2 1/4 PENNY (Farthing)
Bronze **Ruler:** George V **Obv:** Crowned bust left **Rev:** Oat sprigs and berries divide birds within circle

Date	Mintage	F12	VF20	XF40	MS60	MS63
1926	16	PF63 20,500				
Note: Only 5 examples currently known						
1928	64,000	1.50	3.00	6.00	15.00	35.00
1930	6,560	30.00	60.00	100	150	250
1930	14	PF63 1,500	PF65 2,500			
1931	154,000	1.00	1.50	5.00	7.00	20.00

KM# 12.3 1/4 PENNY (Farthing)
Bronze **Ruler:** George V **Obv:** Crowned bust left **Rev:** Oat sprig and berries divide birds within circle

Date	Mintage	F12	VF20	XF40	MS60	MS63
1931	Inc. above	5.00	10.00	18.00	25.00	45.00
1931	62	PF63 200	PF65 450			
1932	105,000	1.00	1.50	4.00	8.00	20.00
1932	12	PF63 375	PF65 850			
1933	76	—	—	750	1,500	2,500
1933	20	PF63 4,000				
1934	52	—	—	750	1,500	2,500
1934	24	PF63 3,750				
1935	61,000	1.00	1.50	4.00	10.00	35.00
1935	20	PF63 3,000				
1936	43	—	—	750	1,500	2,500
1936	40	PF63 3,000				

KM# 23 1/4 PENNY (Farthing)
2.84 g., Bronze, 20 mm. **Ruler:** George VI **Obv:** Head left **Rev:** Oat sprig and berries divide birds within circle

Date	Mintage	VF20	XF40	MS60	MS63	MS65
1937	38,000	1.50	3.00	6.00	15.00	—
1937	116	PF63 200	PF65 400			
1938	51,000	1.00	2.00	4.00	10.00	—
1938	44	PF63 550	PF65 1,000			
1939	102,000	0.50	1.50	3.00	9.00	—
1939	30	PF63 650	PF65 1,250			
1941	91,000	0.50	1.50	3.00	9.00	—
1942	3,756,000	0.25	0.50	1.00	2.50	—
1943	9,918,000	0.25	0.50	0.75	1.75	—
1943	104	PF63 200	PF65 400			
1944	4,468,000	0.25	0.50	0.75	2.50	—
1944	150	PF63 175	PF65 350			
1945	5,297,000	0.25	0.50	1.50	4.00	—
1945	150	PF63 175	PF65 350			
1946	4,378,000	0.25	0.50	1.50	5.00	—
1946	150	PF63 175	PF65 350			
1947	3,895,000	0.25	0.50	1.50	5.00	—
1947	2,600	PF63 12.00	PF65 25.00			

KM# 32.1 1/4 PENNY (Farthing)
Bronze **Ruler:** George VI **Obv:** Head left **Rev:** Oat sprig and berries divide birds within circle

Date	Mintage	VF20	XF40	MS60	MS63	MS65
1948	2,415,000	0.25	0.50	1.00	2.50	10.00
1948	1,120	PF63 12.00	PF65 25.00			
1949	3,568,000	0.25	0.50	1.00	3.00	10.00
1949	800	PF63 20.00	PF65 45.00			
1950	8,694,000	0.25	0.50	0.75	1.75	7.00
1950	500	PF63 35.00	PF65 75.00			

KM# 32.2 1/4 PENNY (Farthing)
2.70 g., Bronze, 20.5 mm. **Ruler:** Edward VIII **Obv:** Head left **Rev:** Oat sprig and berries divide birds within circle **Rev. Legend:** SUID AFRIKA-SOUTH AFRICA

Date	Mintage	VF20	XF40	MS60	MS63	MS65
1951	3,511,000	0.15	0.35	0.75	3.00	7.50
1951	2,000	PF63 10.00	PF65 20.00			
1952	2,805,000	0.15	0.35	0.75	2.50	7.50
1952	16,000	PF63 4.00	PF65 10.00			

KM# 44 1/4 PENNY (Farthing)
2.80 g., Bronze **Ruler:** Elizabeth II **Obv:** Laureate head right **Rev:** Oat sprig and berries divide birds within circle

Date	Mintage	VF20	XF40	MS60	MS63	MS65
1953	7,193,000	0.15	0.25	0.50	1.75	3.00
1953	5,000	PF63 4.00	PF65 10.00			
1954	6,568,000	0.15	0.25	0.50	1.75	3.00
1954	3,150	PF63 4.00	PF65 10.00			
1955	11,798,000	0.15	0.25	0.50	1.75	3.00
1955	2,850	PF63 4.00	PF65 10.00			
1956	1,287,000	0.15	0.25	0.50	3.00	5.00
1956	1,700	PF63 6.00	PF65 15.00			
1957	3,065,000	0.15	0.25	0.50	1.75	3.00
1957	1,130	PF63 8.00	PF65 20.00			
1958	5,452,000	0.15	0.25	0.50	1.75	3.00
1958	985	PF63 10.00	PF65 25.00			
1959	1,567,000	0.15	0.25	0.50	1.75	3.00
1959	900	PF63 12.00	PF65 30.00			
1960	1,022,999	0.15	0.25	0.50	2.50	5.00
1960	3,360	PF63 3.00	PF65 8.00			

KM# 13.1 1/2 PENNY
Bronze **Ruler:** George V **Subject:** Dromedaris (ship) **Obv:** Crowned bust left **Rev:** Sailing ship

Date	Mintage	F12	VF20	XF40	MS60	MS63
1923	12,000	15.00	25.00	50.00	75.00	120
1923	1,402	PF60 100	PF63 250	PF65 500		
1924	64,000	5.00	10.00	25.00	50.00	90.00
1925	69,000	5.00	10.00	25.00	50.00	90.00
1926	65,000	7.50	15.00	35.00	65.00	100

KM# 13.2 1/2 PENNY
Bronze **Ruler:** George V **Subject:** Dromedaris (ship) **Obv:** Crowned bust left **Rev:** Sailing ship

Date	Mintage	F12	VF20	XF40	MS60	MS63
1928	105,000	5.00	12.50	30.00	75.00	120
1929	272,000	2.50	5.00	20.00	40.00	75.00
1930	147,000	3.50	7.00	25.00	50.00	90.00
1930	14	**PF63** 900	**PF65** 1,850			
1930	Inc. above	4.00	8.00	25.00	50.00	90.00
Note: Without star after date						
1931	145,000	3.50	7.00	25.00	50.00	90.00

KM# 13.3 1/2 PENNY

Bronze **Ruler:** George V **Subject:** Dromedaris (ship) **Obv:** Crowned bust left **Rev:** Sailing ship

Date	Mintage	F12	VF20	XF40	MS60	MS63
1931	62	**PF60** 1,000	**PF63** 1,250	**PF65** 2,500		
1932	106,000	5.00	10.00	27.00	55.00	95.00
1932	12	**PF60** 1,000	**PF63** 1,250	**PF65** 2,500		
1933	63,000	8.00	15.00	40.00	75.00	120
1933	20	**PF60** 500	**PF63** 650	**PF65** 1,250		
1934	326,000	1.50	5.00	20.00	40.00	75.00
1934	24	**PF60** 500	**PF63** 600	**PF65** 1,250		
1935	405,000	1.50	5.00	20.00	40.00	75.00
1935	20	**PF60** 500	**PF63** 600	**PF65** 1,250		
1936	407,000	1.50	5.00	20.00	40.00	75.00
1936	40	**PF60** 200	**PF63** 300	**PF65** 650		

KM# 24 1/2 PENNY

Bronze **Ruler:** George VI **Subject:** Dromedaris (ship) **Obv:** Head left **Rev:** Sailing ship

Date	Mintage	VF20	XF40	MS60	MS63	MS65
1937	638,000	1.00	2.00	11.00	20.00	—
1937	116	**PF63** 500	**PF65** 750			
1938	560,000	1.00	2.00	8.00	19.00	—
1938	44	**PF63** 1,250	**PF65** 2,500			
1939	271,000	2.50	5.00	13.00	25.00	—
1939	30	**PF63** 1,750	**PF65** 3,250			
1940	1,535,000	0.30	0.75	4.00	10.00	—
1941	2,053,000	0.30	0.75	4.00	10.00	—
1942	8,382,000	0.25	0.60	2.50	8.00	—
1943	5,135,000	0.25	0.60	2.50	8.00	—
1943	104	**PF63** 450	**PF65** 750			
1944	3,920,000	0.25	0.75	4.00	10.00	—
1944	150	**PF63** 350	**PF65** 650			
1945	2,357,000	0.25	0.60	3.00	9.00	—
1945	150	**PF63** 350	**PF65** 650			
1946	1,022,000	0.25	0.75	4.00	11.00	—
1946	150	**PF63** 350	**PF65** 650			
1947	258,000	1.00	3.00	8.00	22.50	—
1947	2,600	**PF63** 50.00	**PF65** 100			

KM# 33 1/2 PENNY

Bronze, 25 mm. **Ruler:** George VI **Subject:** Dromedaris (ship) **Obv:** Head left **Rev:** Sailing ship

Date	Mintage	VF20	XF40	MS60	MS63	MS65
1948	685,000	0.50	1.00	5.00	11.00	25.00
1948	1,120	**PF63** 70.00	**PF65** 150			
1949	1,850,000	0.25	0.50	2.25	5.00	15.00
1949	800	**PF63** 80.00	**PF65** 175			
1950	2,186,000	0.25	0.50	2.00	4.00	15.00
1950	500	**PF63** 100	**PF65** 200			
1951	3,746,000	0.25	0.50	1.50	4.00	15.00
1951	2,000	**PF63** 50.00	**PF65** 120			
1952	4,174,000	0.25	0.50	1.25	3.00	15.00
1952	1,550	**PF63** 50.00	**PF65** 120			

KM# 45 1/2 PENNY

5.60 g., Bronze **Ruler:** Elizabeth II **Subject:** Dromedaris (ship) **Obv:** Laureate head right **Rev:** Sailing ship

Date	Mintage	VF20	XF40	MS60	MS63	MS65
1953	5,572,000	0.15	0.35	1.00	4.00	15.00
1953	5,000	**PF63** 6.00	**PF65** 15.00			
1954	101,000	2.00	4.00	7.50	15.00	25.00
1954	3,150	**PF63** 15.00	**PF65** 35.00			
1955	3,774,000	0.15	0.35	1.00	4.00	15.00
1955	2,850	**PF63** 15.00	**PF65** 35.00			
1956	1,305,000	0.15	0.35	1.00	4.00	15.00
1956	1,700	**PF63** 15.00	**PF65** 35.00			
1957	2,025,000	0.15	0.35	1.00	4.00	15.00
1957	1,130	**PF63** 15.00	**PF65** 35.00			
1958	2,171,000	0.15	0.35	1.00	3.00	15.00
1958	985	**PF63** 20.00	**PF65** 45.00			
1959	2,397,000	0.15	0.25	0.75	2.50	15.00
1959	900	**PF63** 25.00	**PF65** 60.00			
1960	2,552,000	0.15	0.25	0.75	2.50	15.00
1960	3,360	**PF63** 6.00	**PF65** 15.00			

KM# 14.1 PENNY

Bronze, 30.8 mm. **Ruler:** George V **Subject:** Dromedaris (ship) **Obv:** Crowned bust left **Rev:** Sailing ship

Date	Mintage	F12	VF20	XF40	MS60	MS63
1923	91,000	3.00	7.00	20.00	42.00	75.00
1923	1,402	**PF60** 100	**PF63** 250	**PF65** 450		
1924	134,000	4.00	10.00	30.00	60.00	100

KM# 14.2 PENNY

Bronze, 30.8 mm. **Ruler:** George V **Subject:** Dromedaris (ship) **Obv:** Crowned bust left **Rev:** Sailing ship

Date	Mintage	F12	VF20	XF40	MS60	MS63
1926	393,000	3.00	10.00	30.00	75.00	120
1926	16	**PF63** 3,500	**PF65** 5,500			
1927	285,000	3.00	10.00	30.00	75.00	120
1928	386,000	3.00	10.00	30.00	75.00	120
1929	1,093,000	1.00	5.00	18.00	45.00	75.00
1930	754,000	1.00	5.00	20.00	47.00	80.00
1930	14	**PF63** 3,500	**PF65** 5,500			

KM# 14.3 PENNY

9.50 g., Bronze, 30.8 mm. **Ruler:** George V **Subject:** Dromedaris (ship) **Obv:** Crowned bust left **Rev:** Sailing ship

Date	Mintage	F12	VF20	XF40	MS60	MS63
1931	284,000	1.00	5.00	15.00	45.00	90.00
1931	62	**PF63** 1,600	**PF65** 3,000			
1932	260,000	1.00	5.00	20.00	60.00	100
1932	12	**PF63** 3,500	**PF65** 5,500			
1933	225,000	2.00	5.00	25.00	65.00	110
1933	20	**PF63** 2,500	**PF65** 4,500			
1933	Inc. above	3.00	6.00	25.00	65.00	110
Note: Without star after date						
1934	2,089,999	0.70	1.75	6.00	35.00	75.00
1934	24	**PF63** 2,700	**PF65** 5,000			
1935	2,295,000	0.70	1.75	6.00	35.00	75.00
1935	20	**PF63** 2,700	**PF65** 5,000			
1936	1,819,000	0.60	1.25	6.00	35.00	75.00
1936	40	**PF63** 1,400	**PF65** 3,000			

KM# 25 PENNY

9.30 g., Bronze, 30.8 mm. **Ruler:** George VI **Subject:** Dromedaris (ship) **Obv:** Head left **Rev:** Sailing ship

Date	Mintage	VF20	XF40	MS60	MS63	MS65
1937	3,281,000	0.50	1.50	12.00	30.00	75.00
1937	116	**PF63** 275	**PF65** 550			
1938	1,840,000	0.50	1.50	10.00	36.00	80.00
1938	44	**PF63** 300	**PF65** 600			
1939	1,506,000	0.50	1.50	12.00	30.00	75.00
1939	30	**PF63** 350	**PF65** 700			
1940	3,592,000	0.35	1.00	5.00	12.00	35.00
1940	Inc. above	1.50	3.00	7.00	18.00	40.00
Note: Without star after date						
1941	7,871,000	0.50	1.00	3.00	8.00	25.00
1942	14,428,000	0.50	1.00	2.50	7.00	25.00
1942	Inc. above	3.00	6.00	15.00	36.00	75.00
Note: Without star after date						
1943	4,010,000	0.50	1.00	3.00	7.00	25.00
1943	104	**PF63** 150	**PF65** 300			
1944	6,425,000	0.50	1.00	3.00	8.00	25.00
1944	150	**PF63** 120	**PF65** 250			
1945	4,810,000	0.50	1.00	3.00	8.00	25.00
1945	150	**PF63** 120	**PF65** 250			
1946	2,605,000	0.50	1.00	4.00	10.00	35.00
1946	150	**PF63** 120	**PF65** 250			
1947	135,000	2.50	4.00	9.00	20.00	50.00
1947	2,600	**PF63** 15.00	**PF65** 35.00			

KM# 34.1 PENNY

Bronze, 30.8 mm. **Ruler:** George VI **Subject:** Dromedaris (ship) **Obv:** Head left **Rev:** Sailing ship

Date	Mintage	VF20	XF40	MS60	MS63	MS65
1948	2,398,000	0.50	1.00	2.50	7.00	12.00
1948	1,120	**PF63** 10.00	**PF65** 25.00			
1948	Inc. above	1.00	2.00	5.00	12.00	20.00
Note: Without star after date						
1949	3,634,000	0.50	1.00	2.00	7.00	12.00
1949	800	**PF63** 25.00	**PF65** 60.00			
1950	4,890,000	0.50	1.00	2.00	6.00	12.00
1950	500	**PF63** 20.00	**PF65** 50.00			

KM# 34.2 PENNY

Bronze, 30.8 mm. **Ruler:** George VI **Subject:** Dromedaris (ship) **Obv:** Head left **Rev:** Sailing ship **Rev. Legend:** SUID AFRIKA-SOUTH AFRICA

Date	Mintage	VF20	XF40	MS60	MS63	MS65
1951	3,787,000	0.50	1.00	1.75	4.50	10.00
1951	2,000	**PF63** 12.00	**PF65** 30.00			
1952	12,674,000	0.50	0.75	1.25	3.00	8.00
1952	16,000	**PF63** 7.00	**PF65** 15.00			

KM# 46 PENNY
9.60 g., Bronze, 30.8 mm. **Ruler:** Elizabeth II **Subject:** Dromedaris (ship) **Obv:** Laureate head right **Rev:** Sailing ship

Date	Mintage	VF20	XF40	MS60	MS63	MS65
1953	5,491,000	0.20	0.35	1.00	2.50	7.50
1953	5,000	PF63 6.00	PF65 12.00			
1954	6,665,000	1.00	2.00	5.00	10.00	15.00
1954	3,150	PF63 30.00	PF65 50.00			
1955	6,508,000	0.20	0.35	1.00	3.50	8.50
1955	2,850	PF63 25.00	PF65 50.00			
1956	4,390,000	0.20	0.35	1.00	5.00	10.00
1956	1,700	PF63 25.00	PF65 50.00			
1957	3,973,000	0.20	0.35	1.00	3.50	8.50
1957	1,130	PF63 25.00	PF65 50.00			
1958	5,311,000	0.20	0.35	1.00	3.50	8.50
1958	985	PF63 30.00	PF65 60.00			
1959	5,066,000	0.20	0.35	1.00	2.50	7.50
1959	900	PF63 30.00	PF65 60.00			
1960	5,106,000	0.20	0.35	1.00	2.50	7.50
1960	3,360	PF63 8.00	PF65 15.00			

KM# A15 3 PENCE
1.41 g., 0.800 Silver 0.0363 oz. ASW, 16 mm. **Ruler:** George V **Obv:** Crowned bust left **Rev:** Value within wreath

Date	Mintage	F12	VF20	XF40	MS60	MS63
1923	302,000	4.00	8.00	25.00	55.00	100
1923	1,402	PF63 125	PF65 200			
1924	501,000	4.00	10.00	32.00	65.00	120
1925	—	10.00	35.00	150	350	500

KM# 15.1 3 PENCE
1.41 g., 0.800 Silver 0.0363 oz. ASW, 16 mm. **Ruler:** George V **Obv:** Crowned bust left **Rev:** Protea flower in center, value as 3 PENCE

Date	Mintage	F12	VF20	XF40	MS60	MS63
1925	358,000	5.00	25.00	50.00	150	275
1926	1,572,000	1.25	3.50	15.00	50.00	90.00
1926	16	PF63 2,000	PF65 3,000			
1927	2,285,000	1.25	2.50	12.00	50.00	90.00
1928	919,000	1.50	3.50	15.00	50.00	90.00
1929	1,948,000	1.25	2.50	12.00	50.00	90.00
1930	981,000	1.25	3.50	15.00	50.00	90.00
1930	14	PF63 1,000	PF65 1,500			

KM# 15.2 3 PENCE
1.41 g., 0.800 Silver 0.0363 oz. ASW, 16 mm. **Ruler:** George V **Obv:** Crowned bust left **Rev:** Protea flower in center, value as 3D

Date	Mintage	F12	VF20	XF40	MS60	MS63
1931	66	—	—	750	1,500	3,500
1931	62	PF63 3,250	PF65 3,750			
1932	2,622,000	1.25	2.50	10.00	25.00	50.00
1932	12	PF63 1,000	PF65 1,250			
1933	5,135,000	1.25	2.50	10.00	25.00	50.00
1933	20	PF63 1,000	PF65 1,250			
1934	2,357,000	1.25	2.50	10.00	25.00	50.00
1934	24	PF63 1,000	PF65 1,250			
1935	1,655,000	1.25	2.50	10.00	25.00	50.00
1935	20	PF63 1,000	PF65 1,250			
1936	1,095,000	1.25	2.50	10.00	25.00	50.00
1936	40	PF63 350	PF65 500			

KM# 26 3 PENCE
1.41 g., 0.800 Silver 0.0363 oz. ASW, 16 mm. **Ruler:** George VI **Obv:** Head left **Rev:** Protea flower in center of designed bars shaped as a triangle

Date	Mintage	VF20	XF40	MS60	MS63	MS65
1937	3,576,000	0.70	1.25	3.00	12.00	25.00
1937	116	PF63 400	PF65 600			
1938	2,394,000	0.70	1.50	7.00	25.00	45.00
1938	44	PF63 450	PF65 700			
1939	3,224,000	0.70	1.50	5.00	15.00	30.00
1939	30	PF63 500	PF65 800			
1940	4,887,000	0.70	1.25	3.00	15.00	30.00
1941	8,968,000	0.70	1.25	3.00	11.00	25.00
1942	8,055,999	0.70	1.25	3.00	11.00	25.00
1943	14,827,000	0.70	1.25	2.50	7.00	25.00
1943	104	PF63 375	PF65 550			
1944	3,331,000	0.70	1.25	3.00	11.00	25.00
1944	150	PF63 350	PF65 500			
1945/3	4,094,000	1.25	3.00	10.00	25.00	45.00
1945	Inc. above	0.70	1.25	3.00	11.00	25.00
1945	150	PF63 350	PF65 500			
1946	2,219,000	0.70	1.25	3.00	12.00	25.00
1946	150	PF63 350	PF65 500			
1947	1,127,000	0.70	1.25	2.50	10.00	25.00
1947	2,600	PF63 15.00	PF65 25.00			

KM# 35.1 3 PENCE
1.41 g., 0.800 Silver 0.0363 oz. ASW, 16 mm. **Ruler:** George VI **Obv:** Head left **Rev:** Protea flower in center of designed bars shaped as a triangle

Date	Mintage	VF20	XF40	MS60	MS63	MS65
1948	2,720,000	0.70	1.25	3.00	8.00	15.00
1948	1,120	PF63 15.00	PF65 25.00			
1949	1,904,000	0.70	1.25	3.00	8.00	15.00
1949	800	PF63 20.00	PF65 35.00			
1950	4,096,000	0.70	1.25	2.50	6.00	15.00
1950	500	PF63 35.00	PF65 60.00			

KM# 35.2 3 PENCE
1.41 g., 0.500 Silver 0.0227 oz. ASW, 16 mm. **Ruler:** George VI **Obv:** Head left **Rev:** Protea flower in center of designed bars shaped as a triangle **Note:** Many varieties exist of George VI 3 Pence.

Date	Mintage	VF20	XF40	MS60	MS63	MS65
1951	6,323,000	0.40	0.75	1.50	3.50	10.00
1951	2,000	PF63 10.00	PF65 15.00			
1952	13,057,000	0.40	0.75	1.25	2.50	10.00
1952	16,000	PF63 5.00	PF65 10.00			

KM# 47 3 PENCE
1.41 g., 0.500 Silver 0.0227 oz. ASW, 16 mm. **Ruler:** Elizabeth II **Obv:** Laureate head right **Rev:** Protea flower in center of designed bars shaped as a triangle

Date	Mintage	VF20	XF40	MS60	MS63	MS65
1953	5,483,000	0.40	0.75	1.25	3.00	7.50
1953	5,000	PF63 6.00	PF65 10.00			
1954	3,898,000	0.40	0.75	1.25	3.50	8.00
1954	3,150	PF63 8.00	PF65 15.00			
1955	4,720,000	0.40	0.75	1.25	3.00	7.50
1955	2,850	PF63 6.00	PF65 10.00			
1956	6,189,000	0.40	0.75	1.25	3.00	7.50
1956	1,700	PF63 8.00	PF65 15.00			
1957	1,893,000	0.40	0.75	1.25	3.00	7.50
1957	1,130	PF63 10.00	PF65 20.00			
1958	3,227,000	0.40	0.75	1.25	3.00	7.50
1958	985	PF63 10.00	PF65 20.00			
1959	2,552,000	0.40	0.75	1.25	2.25	7.50
1959	900	PF63 12.00	PF65 25.00			
1959	Inc. above	2.00	3.00	5.00	10.00	15.00
Note: No K-G on reverse						
1960	18,000	1.25	2.50	4.00	8.00	15.00
1960	3,360	PF63 6.00	PF65 10.00			

KM# A16 6 PENCE
2.83 g., 0.800 Silver 0.0728 oz. ASW, 19.41 mm. **Ruler:** George V **Obv:** Crowned bust left **Rev:** Value within wreath **Edge:** Reeded

Date	Mintage	F12	VF20	XF40	MS60	MS63
1923	208,000	5.00	10.00	20.00	75.00	120
1923	1,402	PF63 125	PF65 200			
1924	326,000	4.50	10.00	20.00	60.00	100

KM# 16.1 6 PENCE
2.83 g., 0.800 Silver 0.0728 oz. ASW, 19.41 mm. **Ruler:** George V **Obv:** Crowned bust left **Rev:** Protea flower in center, value as 6 PENCE **Edge:** Reeded

Date	Mintage	F12	VF20	XF40	MS60	MS63
1925	79,000	6.00	15.00	55.00	100	200
1926	722,000	3.00	10.00	45.00	90.00	175
1926	16	PF63 3,250	PF65 3,750			
1927	1,548,000	3.00	5.00	25.00	60.00	125
1928 Rare	—	—	—	—	—	—
Note: Heritage ANA sale 8-10, SP63 realized $135,000						
1929	784,000	3.00	9.00	30.00	70.00	150
1930	448,000	3.00	9.00	35.00	85.00	175
1930	14	PF63 1,650	PF65 2,000			

KM# 16.2 6 PENCE
2.83 g., 0.800 Silver 0.0728 oz. ASW, 19.41 mm. **Ruler:** George V **Obv:** Crowned bust left **Rev:** Protea flower in center, value as 6D **Edge:** Reeded

Date	Mintage	F12	VF20	XF40	MS60	MS63
1931	4,743	50.00	75.00	150	500	900
1931	62	PF63 1,000	PF65 1,250			
1932	1,525,000	3.00	6.00	15.00	35.00	75.00
1932	12	PF63 2,000	PF65 3,000			
1933	2,819,000	3.00	6.00	15.00	35.00	75.00
1933	20	PF63 1,850	PF65 2,850			
1934	1,519,000	3.00	8.00	20.00	45.00	90.00
1934	24	PF63 1,750	PF65 2,750			
1935	573,000	3.00	9.00	30.00	75.00	120
1935	20	PF63 1,850	PF65 2,850			
1936	627,000	3.00	8.00	20.00	45.00	90.00
1936	40	PF63 1,250	PF65 1,750			

KM# 27 6 PENCE
2.83 g., 0.800 Silver 0.0728 oz. ASW, 19.41 mm. **Ruler:** George VI **Obv:** Head left **Rev:** Protea flower in center of designed bars **Edge:** Reeded

Date	Mintage	VF20	XF40	MS60	MS63	MS65
1937	1,696,000	1.30	3.00	8.00	20.00	50.00
1937	116	PF63 800	PF65 1,200			
1938	1,725,000	1.30	3.00	8.00	20.00	50.00
1938	44	PF63 1,250	PF65 1,850			
1939	30	PF63 3,750	PF65 4,500			
1940	1,629,000	1.30	3.00	6.00	12.00	35.00
1941	2,263,000	1.30	3.00	6.00	12.00	35.00
1942	4,936,000	1.30	3.00	4.00	10.00	35.00
1943	3,776,000	1.30	3.00	4.00	10.00	35.00
1943	104	PF63 500	PF65 700			
1944	228,000	1.30	8.00	15.00	35.00	75.00
1944	150	PF63 450	PF65 600			
1945	420,000	1.30	6.00	15.00	35.00	75.00
1945	150	PF63 450	PF65 600			
1946	290,000	1.30	7.00	15.00	35.00	90.00
1946	150	PF63 450	PF65 600			
1947	577,000	1.30	3.00	6.00	12.00	35.00
1947	2,600	PF63 15.00	PF65 30.00			

KM# 36.1 6 PENCE
2.83 g., 0.800 Silver 0.0728 oz. ASW, 19.41 mm. **Ruler:** George VI **Obv:** Head left **Rev:** Protea flower in center of designed bars **Edge:** Reeded

Date	Mintage	VF20	XF40	MS60	MS63	MS65
1948	2,266,000	1.30	3.00	4.00	8.00	20.00
1948	1,120	PF63 15.00	PF65 25.00			
1949	196,000	3.00	5.00	10.00	25.00	45.00
1949	800	PF63 25.00	PF65 40.00			
1950	2,122,000	1.30	3.00	3.50	7.00	20.00
1950	500	PF63 35.00	PF65 60.00			

KM# 36.2 6 PENCE

2.83 g., 0.500 Silver 0.0455 oz. ASW, 19.41 mm. **Ruler:** George VI **Obv:** Head left **Rev:** Protea flower in center of designed bars **Edge:** Reeded

Date	Mintage	VF20	XF40	MS60	MS63	MS65
1951	2,602,000	0.80	2.00	2.75	5.00	10.00
1951	2,000	PF63 10.00	PF65 15.00			
1952	4,265,000	0.80	2.00	2.50	4.00	10.00
1952	16,000	PF63 5.00	PF65 10.00			

KM# 48 6 PENCE

2.83 g., 0.500 Silver 0.0455 oz. ASW, 19.41 mm. **Ruler:** Elizabeth II **Obv:** Laureate head right **Rev:** Protea flower in center of designed bars **Edge:** Reeded

Date	Mintage	VF20	XF40	MS60	MS63	MS65
1953	2,496,000	0.80	2.00	2.25	5.00	9.00
1953	5,000	PF63 6.00	PF65 10.00			
1954	2,196,000	0.80	2.00	2.50	5.00	9.00
1954	3,150	PF63 8.00	PF65 15.00			
1955	1,969,000	0.80	2.00	2.50	5.00	9.00
1955	2,850	PF63 6.00	PF65 10.00			
1956	1,772,000	0.80	2.00	3.00	6.00	10.00
1956	1,700	PF63 8.00	PF65 15.00			
1957	3,288,000	0.80	2.00	2.50	5.50	9.50
1957	1,130	PF63 12.00	PF65 20.00			
1958	1,172,000	0.80	2.00	2.50	5.50	9.50
1958	985	PF63 12.00	PF65 20.00			
1959	261,000	0.80	2.50	5.00	9.00	15.00
1959	900	PF63 15.00	PF65 30.00			
1960	1,587,000	0.80	2.00	2.25	3.00	7.50
1960	3,360	PF63 5.00	PF65 10.00			

KM# 17.1 SHILLING

5.66 g., 0.800 Silver 0.1456 oz. ASW, 23.6 mm. **Ruler:** George V **Obv:** Crowned bust left **Rev:** Value as 1 SHILLING 1

Date	Mintage	F12	VF20	XF40	MS60	MS63
1923	808,000	5.50	15.00	35.00	85.00	175
1923	1,402	PF63 125	PF65 200			
1924	1,269,000	5.50	12.50	30.00	80.00	175

KM# 17.2 SHILLING

5.66 g., 0.800 Silver 0.1456 oz. ASW, 23.6 mm. **Ruler:** George V **Obv:** Crowned bust left **Rev:** Value as SHILLING

Date	Mintage	F12	VF20	XF40	MS60	MS63
1926	238,000	15.00	50.00	200	750	1,000
1926	16	PF63 3,250	PF65 3,750			
1927	488,000	10.00	25.00	100	250	450
1928	889,000	8.00	20.00	60.00	250	450
1929	926,000	5.50	10.00	30.00	175	375
1930	422,000	6.00	15.00	45.00	150	375
1930	14	PF63 1,650	PF65 2,000			

KM# 17.3 SHILLING

5.66 g., 0.800 Silver 0.1456 oz. ASW, 23.6 mm. **Ruler:** George V **Obv:** Crowned bust left **Rev:** Standing female figure leaning on large anchor

Date	Mintage	F12	VF20	XF40	MS60	MS63
1931	6,541	50.00	90.00	200	500	1,000
1931	62	PF63 1,200	PF65 1,500			
1932	2,537,000	5.50	7.00	12.00	50.00	90.00
1932	12	PF63 2,000	PF65 3,500			
1933	1,463,000	5.50	9.00	20.00	75.00	120
1933	20	PF63 1,850	PF65 3,000			
1934	821,000	5.50	10.00	22.00	85.00	150
1934	24	PF63 1,850	PF65 3,000			
1935	685,000	6.00	12.00	25.00	95.00	150
1935	20	PF63 1,850	PF65 3,000			
1936	693,000	5.50	8.00	15.00	65.00	150
1936	40	PF63 1,250	PF65 1,750			

KM# 28 SHILLING

5.66 g., 0.800 Silver 0.1456 oz. ASW, 23.6 mm. **Ruler:** George VI **Obv:** Head left **Rev:** Standing female figure leaning on large anchor

Date	Mintage	VF20	XF40	MS60	MS63	MS65
1937	1,194,000	2.75	5.50	10.00	35.00	75.00
1937	116	PF63 1,000	PF65 1,500			
1938	1,160,000	2.75	5.50	10.00	35.00	75.00
1938	44	PF63 2,500	PF65 3,750			
1939	30	PF63 4,000	PF65 5,000			
1940	1,365,000	2.75	5.50	9.00	25.00	60.00
1941	1,826,000	2.75	5.50	9.00	25.00	60.00
1942	3,867,000	2.75	5.50	9.00	25.00	60.00
1943	4,187,999	2.75	5.50	6.50	22.00	60.00
1943	104	PF63 1,000	PF65 1,600			
1944	48,000	8.00	20.00	40.00	100	175
1944	160	PF63 850	PF65 1,250			
1945	54,000	8.00	20.00	40.00	100	175
1945	150	PF63 850	PF65 1,200			
1946	27,000	10.00	30.00	60.00	125	200
1946	150	PF63 850	PF65 1,200			
1947	7,184	10.00	20.00	30.00	75.00	125
1947	2,600	PF63 35.00	PF65 70.00			

KM# 37.1 SHILLING

5.66 g., 0.800 Silver 0.1456 oz. ASW, 23.6 mm. **Ruler:** George VI **Obv:** Head left **Rev:** Standing female figure leaning on large anchor

Date	Mintage	VF20	XF40	MS60	MS63	MS65
1948	4,974	10.00	20.00	35.00	65.00	100
1948	1,120	PF63 70.00	PF65 150			
1949	800	PF63 120	PF65 225			
1950	1,704,000	2.75	5.50	6.00	10.00	25.00
1950	500	PF63 150	PF65 300			

KM# 37.2 SHILLING

5.66 g., 0.500 Silver 0.091 oz. ASW, 23.6 mm. **Ruler:** George VI **Obv:** Head left **Rev:** Standing female figure, value as 1S

Date	Mintage	VF20	XF40	MS60	MS63	MS65
1951	2,405,000	1.70	3.25	5.00	9.00	15.00
1951	2,000	PF63 12.00	PF65 20.00			
1952	1,934,000	1.70	3.25	4.00	8.00	14.00
1952	1,550	PF63 6.00	PF65 12.00			

KM# 49 SHILLING

5.66 g., 0.500 Silver 0.091 oz. ASW, 23.6 mm. **Ruler:** Elizabeth II **Obv:** Laureate head right **Rev:** Standing female figure leaning on large anchor

Date	Mintage	VF20	XF40	MS60	MS63	MS65
1953	2,672,000	1.70	3.25	3.50	5.50	9.00
1953	5,000	PF63 12.00	PF65 20.00			
1954	3,576,000	1.70	3.25	3.50	5.50	9.00
1954	3,150	PF63 12.00	PF65 20.00			
1955	2,206,000	1.70	3.25	3.50	5.50	9.00
1955	2,850	PF63 15.00	PF65 25.00			
1956	2,142,000	1.70	3.25	3.50	6.00	10.00
1956	1,700	PF63 15.00	PF65 25.00			
1957	791,000	1.70	3.25	5.00	10.00	13.50
1957	1,130	PF63 15.00	PF65 25.00			
1958	4,067,000	1.70	3.25	3.50	5.50	9.00
1958	985	PF63 20.00	PF65 35.00			
1959	205,000	1.70	3.25	5.00	10.00	13.50
1959	900	PF63 25.00	PF65 45.00			
1960	2,187,000	1.70	3.25	3.50	5.50	9.00
1960	3,360	PF63 10.00	PF65 18.00			

KM# 18 FLORIN

11.31 g., 0.800 Silver 0.2909 oz. ASW, 28.52 mm. **Ruler:** George V **Obv:** Crowned bust left **Rev:** Shield divides date

Date	Mintage	F12	VF20	XF40	MS60	MS63
1923	695,000	10.50	20.00	45.00	100	175
1923	1,402	PF63 150	PF65 275			
1924	1,513,000	10.50	18.00	40.00	125	250
1925	50,000	75.00	125	500	1,000	2,500
1926	324,000	12.50	40.00	150	450	650
1927	399,000	12.50	40.00	150	450	650
1928	1,092,000	10.50	20.00	100	225	450
1929	648,000	10.50	20.00	100	250	475
1930	267,000	10.50	15.00	75.00	165	375
1930	14	PF63 1,750	PF65 2,850			

KM# 22 2 SHILLINGS

11.31 g., 0.800 Silver 0.2909 oz. ASW, 28.52 mm. **Ruler:** George V **Obv:** Crowned bust left **Rev:** Shield divides date

Date	Mintage	F12	VF20	XF40	MS60	MS63
1931	383	250	450	700	1,200	2,500
1931	62	PF63 2,000	PF65 3,500			
1932	1,315,000	5.50	11.00	20.00	75.00	175
1932	12	PF63 4,500	PF65 18,000			
1933	891,000	5.50	12.00	25.00	85.00	200
1933	20	PF63 4,000	PF65 7,500			
1934	559,000	5.50	12.00	25.00	60.00	150
1934	24	PF63 3,250	PF65 6,500			
1935	554,000	5.50	12.00	25.00	90.00	225
1935	20	PF63 3,250	PF65 6,500			
1936	669,000	5.50	12.00	25.00	70.00	175
1936	40	PF63 1,750	PF65 2,250			

KM# 29 2 SHILLINGS

11.31 g., 0.800 Silver 0.2909 oz. ASW, 28.52 mm. **Ruler:**

George VI **Obv:** Head left **Rev:** Shield divides date

Date	Mintage	VF20	XF40	MS60	MS63	MS65
1937	1,495,000	—	5.50	12.00	35.00	90.00
1937	116	PF63 1,200	PF65 1,700			
1938	214,000	5.50	11.00	20.00	55.00	150
1938	44	PF63 2,750	PF65 4,000			
1939	279,000	5.50	11.00	20.00	55.00	150
1939	30	PF63 4,500	PF65 6,000			
1940	2,600,000	5.50	11.00	12.00	25.00	75.00
1941	1,764,000	5.50	11.00	12.00	25.00	75.00
1942	2,847,000	—	5.50	11.00	16.00	75.00
1943	3,125,000	—	5.50	11.00	16.00	75.00
1943	104	PF63 1,000	PF65 1,600			
1944	225,000	5.50	11.00	17.50	45.00	125
1944	150	PF63 900	PF65 1,250			
1945	473,000	5.50	11.00	15.00	40.00	125
1945	150	PF63 900	PF65 1,250			
1946	14,000	11.00	20.00	40.00	95.00	150
1946	150	PF63 900	PF65 1,250			
1947	2,892	15.00	25.00	45.00	90.00	150
1947	2,600	PF63 35.00	PF65 70.00			

KM# 38.1 2 SHILLINGS

11.31 g., 0.800 Silver 0.2909 oz. ASW, 28.52 mm. **Ruler:** George VI **Obv:** Head left **Rev:** Shield divides date

Date	Mintage	VF20	XF40	MS60	MS63	MS65
1948	6,773	11.00	15.00	30.00	70.00	150
1948	1,120	PF63 80.00	PF65 175			
1949	203,000	5.50	11.00	25.00	35.00	75.00
1949	800	PF63 125	PF65 275			
1950	4,945	20.00	40.00	80.00	140	225
1950	500	PF63 200	PF65 450			

KM# 38.2 2 SHILLINGS

11.31 g., 0.500 Silver 0.1818 oz. ASW, 28.52 mm. **Ruler:** George VI **Obv:** Head left **Rev:** Shield, value as 2S

Date	Mintage	VF20	XF40	MS60	MS63	MS65
1951	730,000	3.25	6.50	8.00	12.00	20.00
1951	2,000	PF63 15.00	PF65 30.00			
1952	3,570,000	—	3.25	6.50	8.00	25.00
1952	16,000	PF63 10.00	PF65 20.00			

KM# 50 2 SHILLINGS

11.31 g., 0.500 Silver 0.1818 oz. ASW, 28.52 mm. **Ruler:** Elizabeth II **Obv:** Laureate head right **Rev:** Shield

Date	Mintage	VF20	XF40	MS60	MS63	MS65
1953	3,274,000	—	3.25	6.50	10.00	15.00
1953	5,000	PF63 13.50	PF65 22.50			
1954	5,866,000	—	3.25	6.50	9.00	15.00
1954	3,150	PF63 13.50	PF65 22.50			
1955	3,745,000	—	3.25	6.50	9.00	15.00
1955	2,850	PF63 13.50	PF65 22.50			
1956	2,549,000	—	3.25	6.50	10.00	15.00
1956	1,700	PF63 15.00	PF65 25.00			
1957	2,507,000	—	3.25	6.50	10.00	15.00
1957	1,130	PF63 15.00	PF65 25.00			
1958	2,821,000	—	3.25	6.50	10.00	15.00
1958	985	PF63 30.00	PF65 50.00			
1959	1,219,000	—	3.25	6.50	10.00	15.00
1959	900	PF63 40.00	PF65 65.00			
1960	1,951,000	—	3.25	6.50	9.00	15.00
1960	3,360	PF63 13.50	PF65 22.50			

KM# 19.1 2-1/2 SHILLINGS

14.14 g., 0.800 Silver 0.3637 oz. ASW, 32.3 mm. **Ruler:** George V **Obv:** Crowned bust left **Rev:** Value as 2-1/2 SHILLINGS 2-1/2 **Rev. Legend:** ZUID-AFRIKA

Date	Mintage	F12	VF20	XF40	MS60	MS63
1923	1,227,000	13.00	17.00	35.00	70.00	150
1923	1,402	PF63 175	PF65 300			
1924	2,556,000	6.75	15.00	50.00	120	250
1925	460,000	15.00	35.00	180	450	750

KM# 19.2 2-1/2 SHILLINGS

14.14 g., 0.800 Silver 0.3637 oz. ASW, 32.3 mm. **Ruler:** George V **Obv:** Crowned bust left **Rev:** Value as 2-1/2 SHILLINGS

Date	Mintage	F12	VF20	XF40	MS60	MS63
1926	205,000	16.50	40.00	250	450	750
1926	16	PF63 4,000	PF65 5,000			
1927	194,000	16.50	40.00	350	600	1,000
1928	984,000	13.00	25.00	125	200	450
1929	617,000	13.00	28.00	175	225	500
1930	324,000	13.00	20.00	75.00	150	375
1930	14	PF63 4,250	PF65 5,500			

KM# 19.3 2-1/2 SHILLINGS

14.14 g., 0.800 Silver 0.3637 oz. ASW, 32.3 mm. **Ruler:** George V **Obv:** Crowned bust left **Rev:** Crowned shield divides date **Rev. Legend:** SUID. AFRIKA

Date	Mintage	F12	VF20	XF40	MS60	MS63
1931	790	—	250	500	1,000	2,500
1931	62	PF63 1,800	PF65 2,200			
1932	1,028,999	13.00	18.00	35.00	90.00	175
1932	12	PF63 4,500	PF65 6,000			
1933	136,000	15.00	25.00	75.00	200	450
1933	20	PF63 3,750	PF65 5,750			
1934	416,000	13.00	20.00	40.00	100	200
1934	24	PF63 3,250	PF65 5,000			
1935	345,000	13.00	20.00	45.00	125	250
1935	20	PF63 3,250	PF65 5,000			
1936	553,000	13.00	20.00	35.00	90.00	175
1936	40	PF63 1,850	PF65 2,500			

KM# 30 2-1/2 SHILLINGS

14.14 g., 0.800 Silver 0.3637 oz. ASW, 32.3 mm. **Ruler:** George VI **Obv:** Head left **Rev:** Crowned shield divides date

Date	Mintage	VF20	XF40	MS60	MS63	MS65
1937	1,154,000	6.75	13.00	20.00	35.00	75.00
1937	116	PF63 1,250	PF65 1,800			
1938	534,000	13.00	15.00	25.00	60.00	90.00
1938	44	PF63 2,850	PF65 4,500			
1939	133,000	7.50	20.00	40.00	80.00	125
1939	30	PF63 4,500	PF65 6,000			
1940	2,976,000	6.75	13.00	14.00	25.00	75.00
1941	1,988,000	6.75	13.00	14.00	25.00	75.00
1942	3,180,000	6.75	13.00	14.00	25.00	75.00
1943	2,098,000	6.75	13.00	14.00	25.00	75.00
1943	104	PF63 1,000	PF65 1,600			
1944	1,360,000	6.75	13.00	16.00	30.00	80.00
1944	150	PF63 850	PF65 1,200			
1945	183,000	6.75	15.00	25.00	65.00	125
1945	150	PF63 850	PF65 1,200			
1946	11,000	15.00	20.00	40.00	90.00	175
1946	150	PF63 850	PF65 1,200			
1947	3,582	20.00	35.00	50.00	100	185
1947	2,600	PF63 65.00	PF65 120			

KM# 39.1 2-1/2 SHILLINGS

14.14 g., 0.800 Silver 0.3637 oz. ASW, 32.3 mm. **Ruler:** George VI **Obv:** Head left **Rev:** Crowned shield divides date

Date	Mintage	VF20	XF40	MS60	MS63	MS65
1948	1,600	15.00	35.00	60.00	90.00	150
1948	1,120	PF63 120	PF65 200			
1949	1,891	15.00	35.00	60.00	90.00	150
1949	800	PF63 150	PF65 300			
1950	5,076	15.00	35.00	60.00	125	175
1950	500	PF63 225	PF65 475			

KM# 39.2 2-1/2 SHILLINGS

14.14 g., 0.500 Silver 0.2273 oz. ASW, 32.3 mm. **Ruler:** George VI **Obv:** Head left **Rev:** Crowned shield, value as 2-1/2 S

Date	Mintage	VF20	XF40	MS60	MS63	MS65
1951	783,000	4.25	8.00	10.00	20.00	35.00
1951	2,000	PF63 17.00	PF65 35.00			
1952	1,996,000	4.25	8.00	10.00	20.00	35.00
1952	16,000	PF63 12.00	PF65 25.00			

KM# 51 2-1/2 SHILLINGS

14.14 g., 0.500 Silver 0.2273 oz. ASW, 32.3 mm. **Ruler:** Elizabeth II **Obv:** Laureate head right **Rev:** Crowned shield

Date	Mintage	VF20	XF40	MS60	MS63	MS65
1953	2,513,000	—	4.25	8.00	9.00	12.50
1953	6,000	PF63 16.00	PF65 27.00			
1954	4,249,000	—	4.25	8.00	9.00	12.50
1954	3,150	PF63 20.00	PF65 32.50			
1955	3,863,000	—	4.25	8.00	9.00	12.50
1955	2,850	PF63 20.00	PF65 32.50			
1956	2,437,000	—	4.25	8.00	9.00	12.50
1956	1,700	PF63 22.00	PF65 37.00			
1957	2,137,000	—	4.25	8.00	9.00	12.50
1957	1,130	PF63 22.00	PF65 37.00			
1958	2,260,000	—	4.25	8.00	10.00	13.50
1958	985	PF63 27.00	PF65 45.00			
1959	46,000	4.25	8.00	9.00	12.50	15.00
1959	900	PF63 40.00	PF65 65.00			
1960	12,000	4.25	8.00	9.00	12.50	15.00
1960	3,360					

KM# 31 5 SHILLINGS
28.28 g., 0.800 Silver 0.7274 oz. ASW, 38.8 mm. **Ruler:** George VI **Subject:** Royal Visit **Obv:** Head left **Rev:** Springbok

Date	Mintage	VF20	XF40	MS60	MS63	MS65
1947	300,000	13.50	20.00	25.00	35.00	45.00
1947	5,600	PF63 200	PF65 325			

KM# 40.1 5 SHILLINGS
28.28 g., 0.800 Silver 0.7274 oz. ASW, 38.8 mm. **Ruler:** George VI **Obv:** Head left **Rev:** Springbok

Date	Mintage	VF20	XF40	MS60	MS63	MS65
1948	780,000	—	13.50	26.00	30.00	45.00
1948 Prooflike	1,000	—	—	—	35.00	60.00
1948	1,120	PF63 180	PF65 300			
1949	535,000	—	13.50	26.00	30.00	45.00
1949 Prooflike	2,000	—	—	—	40.00	60.00
1949	800	PF63 250	PF65 500			
1950	83,000	13.50	26.00	27.50	35.00	45.00
1950 Prooflike	1,200	—	—	—	60.00	75.00
1950	500	PF63 350	PF65 650			

KM# 40.2 5 SHILLINGS
28.28 g., 0.500 Silver 0.4546 oz. ASW, 38.8 mm. **Ruler:** George VI **Obv:** Head left **Rev:** Springbok

Date	Mintage	VF20	XF40	MS60	MS63	MS65
1951	363,000	8.50	16.00	20.00	25.00	45.00
1951 Prooflike	1,483	—	—	—	30.00	60.00
1951	2,000	PF63 150	PF65 300			

KM# 41 5 SHILLINGS
28.28 g., 0.500 Silver 0.4546 oz. ASW, 38.8 mm. **Ruler:** George VI **Subject:** 300th Anniversary - Founding of Capetown **Obv:** Head left **Rev:** Schooner in harbor **Edge:** Reeded

Date	Mintage	VF20	XF40	MS60	MS63	MS65
ND-1952	1,698,000	8.50	16.00	18.50	22.50	40.00
ND-1952 Prooflike	12,000	—	—	—	27.50	60.00
ND-1952	16,000	PF63 55.00	PF65 90.00			

KM# 52 5 SHILLINGS
28.28 g., 0.500 Silver 0.4546 oz. ASW, 38.8 mm. **Ruler:** Elizabeth II **Obv:** Laureate head right **Rev:** Springbok

Date	Mintage	VF20	XF40	MS60	MS63	MS65
1953	250,000	8.50	16.00	16.50	20.00	22.50
1953 Prooflike	8,000	—	—	—	25.00	27.50
1953	5,000	PF63 45.00	PF65 75.00			
1953 Matte Proof	—	PF63 1,150				
1954	10,000	8.50	16.00	18.50	25.00	30.00
1954 Prooflike	3,890	—	—	—	27.50	32.50
1954	3,150	PF63 50.00	PF65 80.00			
1955	40,000	8.50	16.00	16.50	20.00	22.50
1955 Prooflike	2,230	—	—	—	25.00	27.50
1955	2,850	PF63 45.00	PF65 75.00			
1956	100,000	8.50	16.00	16.50	18.50	22.50
1956 Prooflike	2,200	—	—	—	25.00	27.50
1956	1,700	PF63 50.00	PF65 80.00			
1957	154,000	8.50	16.00	16.50	18.50	22.50
1957 Prooflike	1,600	—	—	—	27.50	30.00
1957	1,130	PF63 55.00	PF65 90.00			
1958	233,000	8.50	16.00	16.50	18.50	22.50
1958 Prooflike	1,500	—	—	—	27.50	30.00
1958	985	PF63 55.00	PF65 90.00			
1959	2,989	20.00	35.00	55.00	75.00	120
1959 Prooflike	2,200	—	—	—	90.00	150
1959	950	PF63 200	PF65 320			

KM# 55 5 SHILLINGS
28.28 g., 0.500 Silver 0.4546 oz. ASW, 38.8 mm. **Ruler:** Elizabeth II **Subject:** 50th Anniversary - South African Union **Obv:** Shield **Rev:** Building and ship divides dates **Edge:** Reeded **Note:** Many varieties exist of letters HM below building.

Date	Mintage	VF20	XF40	MS60	MS63	MS65
1960	396,000	8.75	16.00	17.00	20.00	22.50
1960 Prooflike	22,000	—	—	—	22.50	25.00
1960	3,360	PF63 45.00	PF65 75.00			

KM# 20 1/2 SOVEREIGN
3.99 g., 0.917 Gold 0.1178 oz. AGW **Ruler:** George V **Obv:** Head left **Rev:** St. George slaying dragon **Note:** British type with Pretoria mint mark: SA.

Date	Mintage	VF20	XF40	MS60	MS63	MS65
1923	655	PF63 1,750				
1925	947,000	—	—	157	210	280
1926	809,000	—	—	157	210	280

KM# 42 1/2 POUND
3.99 g., 0.917 Gold 0.1178 oz. AGW **Ruler:** George V **Obv:** Head left **Rev:** Springbok

Date	Mintage	VF20	XF40	MS60	MS63	MS65
1952	4,002	—	—	157	225	300
1952	12,000	PF63 210	PF65 280			

KM# 53 1/2 POUND
3.99 g., 0.917 Gold 0.1178 oz. AGW **Ruler:** Elizabeth II **Obv:** Laureate head right

Date	Mintage	VF20	XF40	MS60	MS63	MS65
1953	4,000	PF63 225	PF65 300			
1954	1,275	PF63 225	PF65 300			
1955	900	PF63 225	PF65 300			
1956	508	PF63 240	PF65 330			
1957	560	PF63 225	PF65 300			
1958	515	PF63 225	PF65 300			
1959	500	—	—	157	225	300
1959	630	PF63 225	PF65 300			
1960	1,052	—	—	157	225	300
1960	1,950	PF63 225	PF65 300			

KM# 21 SOVEREIGN
7.99 g., 0.917 Gold 0.2355 oz. AGW **Ruler:** George V **Obv:** Head left **Rev:** St. George slaying dragon **Note:** British type with Pretoria mint mark: SA.

Date	Mintage	VF20	XF40	MS60	MS63	MS65
1923	64	330	475	775	—	—
1923	655	PF63 2,800				
1924	3,184	2,000	3,500	7,000	—	—
1925	6,086,000	—	—	315	375	450
1926	11,108,000	—	—	315	375	450
1927	16,379,999	—	—	315	375	450
1928	18,235,000	—	—	315	375	450

KM# A22 SOVEREIGN
7.99 g., 0.917 Gold 0.2355 oz. AGW **Ruler:** George V **Obv:** Modified effigy, slightly smaller bust **Rev:** St. George slaying dragon

Date	Mintage	VF20	XF40	MS60	MS63	MS65
1929	12,024,000	—	—	315	375	450
1930	10,028,000	—	—	315	375	450
1931	8,512,000	—	—	315	375	450
1932	1,067,000	—	—	315	375	450

KM# 43 POUND
7.99 g., 0.917 Gold 0.2355 oz. AGW **Ruler:** George VI **Obv:** Head left **Rev:** Springbok

Date	Mintage	VF20	XF40	MS60	MS63	MS65
1952	4,508	—	—	330	435	530
1952	12,000	PF63 420	PF65 510			

KM# 54 POUND
7.99 g., 0.917 Gold 0.2355 oz. AGW **Ruler:** Elizabeth II **Obv:** Laureate head right **Rev:** Springbok

Date	Mintage	VF20	XF40	MS60	MS63	MS65
1953	4,000	PF63 435	PF65 530			
1954	1,275	PF63 435	PF65 530			
1955	900	PF63 435	PF65 530			
1956	508	PF63 435	PF65 530			
1957	560	PF63 435	PF65 530			
1958	515	PF63 435	PF65 530			
1959	502	—	—	315	375	450
1959	630	PF63 435	PF65 530			
1960	1,161	—	—	315	375	450
1960	1,950	PF63 435	PF65 530			

REPUBLIC

STANDARD COINAGE

100 Cents = 1 Rand

KM# 56 1/2 CENT

5.60 g., Brass **Obv:** Oat sprig and berries divide birds **Rev:** Bust facing 1/4 right

Date	Mintage	VF20	XF40	MS60	MS63	MS65
1961	39,189,000	0.15	0.25	1.25	2.00	2.50
1961	7,530	PF65 1.00				
1962	17,895,000	0.15	0.25	1.25	2.00	2.50
1962	3,844	PF65 1.00				
1963	11,611,000	0.15	0.25	2.00	2.50	3.00
1963	4,025	PF65 1.00				
1964	9,258,000	0.15	0.25	1.25	2.00	2.50
1964	16,000	PF65 1.00				

KM# 81 1/2 CENT

Bronze **Obv:** Arms with supporters **Rev:** Sparrows below value **Note:** Bilingual.

Date	Mintage	VF20	XF40	MS60	MS63	MS65
1970	Est. 57721000	0.10	0.25	0.50	0.75	1.00

Note: Coins dated 1970 were also struck for circulation in 1971, 1972 and 1973

Date	Mintage	VF20	XF40	MS60	MS63	MS65
1970	10,000	PF65 2.50				
1971	8,000	—	—	1.00	1.50	2.50
1971	12,000	PF65 2.50				
1972	8,000	—	—	1.00	1.50	2.50
1972	12,000	PF65 2.50				
1973	20,000	0.10	0.20	1.00	1.50	2.50
1973	11,000	PF65 2.50				
1974	20,000	0.20	0.40	1.00	1.50	2.50
1974	15,000	PF65 2.50				
1975	20,000	0.10	0.20	1.00	1.50	2.50
1975	18,000	PF65 2.50				
1977	20,000	0.10	0.20	1.00	1.50	2.50
1977	19,000	PF65 2.50				
1978	18,000	0.10	0.20	1.00	1.50	2.50
1978	19,000	PF65 2.50				
1980	15,000	PF65 2.50				
1981	10,000	PF65 2.50				
1983	14,000	PF65 2.50				

KM# 90 1/2 CENT

Bronze **Obv:** President Fouche left **Rev:** Birds on branches **Note:** Similar to 1 Cent, KM#91.

Date	Mintage	VF20	XF40	MS60	MS63	MS65
1976	20,000	—	—	0.50	0.75	1.00
1976	21,000	PF65 1.50				

KM# 97 1/2 CENT

Bronze **Obv:** Head of President Diederichs left **Rev:** Sparrows below value

Date	Mintage	VF20	XF40	MS60	MS63	MS65
1979	18,000	—	—	0.50	0.75	1.00
1979	17,000	PF65 1.50				

KM# 108 1/2 CENT

Bronze **Obv:** Head of President Vorster 1/4 right **Rev:** Sparrows below value

Date	Mintage	VF20	XF40	MS60	MS63	MS65
1982	12,000	PF65 1.50				

KM# 57 CENT

9.42 g., Brass **Obv:** Covered wagon **Rev:** Bust 1/4 right

Date	Mintage	VF20	XF40	MS60	MS63	MS65
1961	52,266,000	0.15	0.40	0.75	1.00	1.50
1961	7,530	PF65 0.75				
1962	21,929,000	0.15	0.40	0.75	1.00	1.50
1962	3,844	PF65 1.00				
1963	9,081,000	0.15	0.50	1.00	2.00	3.00
1963	4,025	PF65 1.00				
1964	14,265,000	0.15	0.40	0.50	1.00	1.50
1964	16,000	PF65 2.00				

KM# 65.1 CENT

3.00 g., Bronze, 19 mm. **Obv:** Head of Jan van Riebeeck right **Obv. Legend:** SOUTH AFRICA **Rev:** Sparrows below value **Edge:** Reeded

Date	Mintage	VF20	XF40	MS60	MS63	MS65
1965	26,000	—	—	0.75	1.25	2.00
1965	25,000	PF65 2.50				
1966	50,157,000	—	0.10	0.20	0.35	0.50
1967	21,114,000	—	0.10	0.20	0.35	0.50
1969	10,196,000	—	0.10	0.20	0.35	0.50

KM# 65.2 CENT

3.00 g., Bronze, 19 mm. **Obv:** Head of Jan van Riebeeck right **Obv. Legend:** SUID-AFRIKA **Rev:** Sparrows below value **Edge:** Reeded

Date	Mintage	VF20	XF40	MS60	MS63	MS65
1965	846	—	50.00	100	200	300
1965	185	PF65 350				
1966	50,157,000	—	0.10	0.20	0.35	0.50
1966	25,000	PF65 1.00				
1967	21,114,000	—	0.10	0.20	0.35	0.50
1967	25,000	PF65 1.00				
1969	10,196,000	—	0.10	0.20	0.35	0.50
1969	12,000	PF65 1.50				

KM# 74.1 CENT

3.00 g., Bronze, 19 mm. **Subject:** President Charles Swart **Obv:** Head left **Obv. Legend:** SOUTH AFRICA **Rev:** Sparrows below value **Edge:** Reeded

Date	Mintage	VF20	XF40	MS60	MS63	MS65
1968	6,000,000	—	0.10	0.20	0.35	0.50
1968	25,000	PF65 1.00				

KM# 74.2 CENT

3.00 g., Bronze, 19 mm. **Subject:** President Charles Swart **Obv:** Head left **Obv. Legend:** SUID-AFRIKA **Rev:** Sparrows below value **Edge:** Reeded

Date	Mintage	VF20	XF40	MS60	MS63	MS65
1968	6,000,000	—	0.10	0.20	0.35	0.50

KM# 82 CENT

3.00 g., Bronze, 19 mm. **Obv:** Arms with supporters **Obv. Legend:** Bilingual legend **Rev:** Sparrows below value **Edge:** Reeded

Date	Mintage	VF20	XF40	MS60	MS63	MS65
1970	37,072,000	—	—	0.15	0.30	0.50
1970	10,000	PF65 1.00				
1971	34,053,000	—	—	0.15	0.30	0.50
1971	12,000	PF65 1.00				
1972	35,662,000	—	—	0.15	0.30	0.50
1972	10,000	PF65 1.00				
1973	35,898,000	0.10	0.20	0.30	0.40	0.60
1973	11,000	PF65 1.00				
1974	54,940,000	—	—	0.15	0.25	0.50
1974	15,000	PF65 1.00				
1975	62,982,000	—	—	0.15	0.25	0.50
1975	18,000	PF65 1.00				
1977	72,444,000	—	—	0.15	0.25	0.50
1977	19,000	PF65 1.00				
1978	70,152,000	—	—	0.15	0.25	0.50
1978	17,000	PF65 0.50				
1980	63,432,000	—	—	0.15	0.25	0.50
1980	15,000	PF65 0.50				
1981	63,444,000	—	—	0.15	0.25	0.50
1981	10,000	PF65 0.50				
1983	182,131,000	—	—	0.15	0.25	0.50
1983	14,000	PF65 0.50				
1984	107,155,000	—	—	0.15	0.25	0.50
1984	11,000	PF65 0.50				
1985	186,042,000	—	—	0.15	0.25	0.50
1985	9,859	PF65 0.50				
1986	169,734,000	—	—	0.15	0.25	0.50
1986	7,000	PF65 0.50				
1987	120,674,000	—	—	0.15	0.25	0.50
1987	6,781	PF65 0.50				
1988	240,272,000	—	—	0.15	0.25	0.50
1988	7,250	PF65 0.50				
1989	—	—	—	0.50		
1989	—	PF65 0.50				

KM# 91 CENT

3.00 g., Bronze, 19 mm. **Obv:** Head of President Fouche right **Rev:** Sparrows below value **Edge:** Reeded

Date	Mintage	VF20	XF40	MS60	MS63	MS65
1976	91,860,000	—	—	0.15	0.25	0.50
1976	21,000	PF65 0.75				

KM# 98 CENT

3.00 g., Bronze, 19 mm. **Obv:** Head of President Diederichs left **Rev:** Sparrows below value **Edge:** Reeded

Date	Mintage	VF20	XF40	MS60	MS63	MS65
1979	63,432,000	—	—	0.15	0.25	0.50
1979	15,000	PF65 0.75				

KM# 109 CENT

3.00 g., Bronze, 19 mm. **Obv:** Head of President Vorster 1/4 right **Rev:** Sparrows below value **Edge:** Reeded

Date	Mintage	VF20	XF40	MS60	MS63	MS65
1982	145,954,000	—	—	0.15	0.25	0.50
1982	12,000	PF65 0.75				

KM# 132 CENT

1.50 g., Copper Plated Steel, 15 mm. **Obv:** Arms with supporters **Obv. Legend:** SOUTH AFRICA - SUD AFRIKA **Rev:** Value divides sparrows

Date	Mintage	VF20	XF40	MS60	MS63	MS65
1990	—	—	—	0.15	0.25	0.50
1990	—	PF65 0.50				
1991	—	—	—	0.15	0.25	0.50
1991	—	PF65 0.50				
1992	—	—	—	0.15	0.25	0.50
1992	—	PF65 0.50				
1993	—	—	—	0.15	0.25	0.50
1993	7,790	PF65 0.50				
1994	—	—	—	0.15	0.25	0.50
1994	5,804	PF65 0.50				
1995	—	—	—	0.15	0.25	0.50
1995	—	PF65 0.50				

KM# 158 CENT

1.50 g., Copper Plated Steel, 15 mm. **Obv:** Arms with supporters **Obv. Legend:** INGIZUMA AFRIKA **Rev:** Value divides sparrows **Edge:** Plain

Date	Mintage	VF20	XF40	MS60	MS63	MS65
1996	—	—	—	0.15	0.25	0.50
1996	10,000	PF65 0.50				

KM# 170 CENT
1.50 g., Copper Plated Steel, 15 mm. **Obv:** Arms with supporters **Obv. Legend:** ISEWULA AFRIKA **Rev:** Value divides sparrows

Date	Mintage	VF20	XF40	MS60	MS63	MS65
1997	—	—	—	0.15	0.25	0.50
1997	3,596	PF65 0.50				
1998	—	—	—	0.15	0.25	0.50
1998	—	PF65 0.50				
1999	—	—	—	0.15	0.25	0.50
1999	—	PF65 0.50				
2000	—	PF65 0.25				

KM# 221 CENT
1.50 g., Copper Plated Steel, 15 mm. **Obv:** New national arms **Obv. Legend:** ISEWULA AFRIKA **Rev:** Value divides two sparrows **Edge:** Plain

Date	Mintage	VF20	XF40	MS60	MS63	MS65
2000	—	—	0.15	0.25	0.35	0.50

KM# 66.1 2 CENTS
4.00 g., Bronze, 22.45 mm. **Obv:** Bust right **Obv. Legend:** SOUTH AFRICA **Rev:** Black wildebeest above value **Edge:** Reeded

Date	Mintage	VF20	XF40	MS60	MS63	MS65
1965	29,887,000	—	0.10	0.25	0.35	1.00
1966	9,267,000	—	0.10	0.25	0.40	1.00
1966	25,000	PF65 0.50				
1967	11,862,000	—	0.10	0.25	0.35	1.00
1967	25,000	PF65 0.50				
1969	5,817,000	—	0.10	0.25	0.40	1.00
1969	12,000	PF65 0.50				

KM# 66.2 2 CENTS
4.00 g., Bronze, 22.45 mm. **Obv:** Head right **Obv. Legend:** SUID-AFRIKA **Rev:** Black wildebeest above value **Edge:** Reeded

Date	Mintage	VF20	XF40	MS60	MS63	MS65
1965	29,887,000	—	0.10	0.25	0.35	1.00
1965	25,000	PF65 0.50				
1966	9,267,000	—	0.10	0.25	0.35	1.00
1967	11,862,000	—	0.10	0.25	0.35	1.00
1969	5,817,000	—	0.10	0.25	0.40	1.00

KM# 75.1 2 CENTS
4.00 g., Bronze, 22.5 mm. **Obv:** Head of President Charles Swart left **Obv. Legend:** SOUTH AFRICA **Rev:** Black wildebeest above value **Edge:** Reeded

Date	Mintage	VF20	XF40	MS60	MS63	MS65
1968	5,500,000	—	0.20	0.30	0.50	1.00

KM# 75.2 2 CENTS
4.00 g., Bronze, 22.45 mm. **Obv:** Head of President Charles Swart left **Obv. Legend:** SUID-AFRIKA **Rev:** Black wildebeest above value **Edge:** Reeded

Date	Mintage	VF20	XF40	MS60	MS63	MS65
1968	5,525,000	—	0.20	0.30	0.50	1.00
1968	25,000	PF65 1.00				

KM# 83 2 CENTS
4.00 g., Bronze, 22.45 mm. **Obv:** Arms with supporters **Obv. Legend:** Bilingual legend **Rev:** Black wildebeest above value **Edge:** Reeded

Date	Mintage	VF20	XF40	MS60	MS63	MS65
1970	35,217,000	—	0.15	0.30	0.50	1.00
1970	10,000	PF65 0.75				
1971	24,093,000	—	0.15	0.30	0.50	1.00
1971	12,000	PF65 0.75				
1972	7,304,000	—	0.15	0.30	0.50	1.00
1972	10,000	PF65 0.75				
1973	18,685,000	—	0.15	0.30	0.50	1.00
1973	11,000	PF65 0.75				
1974	25,301,000	—	0.15	0.30	0.50	1.00
1974	15,000	PF65 0.75				
1975	24,982,000	—	0.15	0.30	0.50	1.00
1975	18,000	PF65 0.75				
1977	45,116,000	—	0.15	0.30	0.50	1.00
1977	19,000	PF65 0.75				
1978	50,527,000	—	0.15	0.30	0.50	1.00
1978	17,000	PF65 0.75				
1980	37,795,000	—	0.15	0.30	0.50	1.00
1980	15,000	PF65 0.75				
1981	79,350,000	—	0.15	0.30	0.50	1.00
1981	10,000	PF65 0.75				
1983	112,575,000	—	0.15	0.30	0.50	1.00
1983	14,000	PF65 0.75				
1984	101,497,000	—	0.15	0.30	0.50	1.00
1984	11,000	PF65 0.75				
1985	102,708,000	—	0.15	0.30	0.50	1.00
1985	9,859	PF65 0.75				
1986	683,294,000	—	0.15	0.30	0.50	1.00
1986	7,100	PF65 0.75				
1987	104,981,000	—	0.15	0.30	0.50	1.00
1987	6,781	PF65 0.75				
1988	182,036,000	—	0.15	0.30	0.50	1.00
1988	7,250	PF65 0.75				
1989	—	—	0.15	0.30	0.50	1.00
1989	—	PF65 0.75				
1990	215,192,000	—	0.15	0.30	0.50	1.00

KM# 92 2 CENTS
4.00 g., Bronze, 22.45 mm. **Obv:** Head of President Fouche right **Rev:** Black wildebeest above value **Edge:** Reeded

Date	Mintage	VF20	XF40	MS60	MS63	MS65
1976	51,474,000	—	0.25	0.30	0.50	1.00
1976	21,000	PF65 0.75				

KM# 99 2 CENTS
4.00 g., Bronze, 22.45 mm. **Obv:** Head of President Diederichs left **Rev:** Black wildebeest above value **Edge:** Reeded

Date	Mintage	VF20	XF40	MS60	MS63	MS65
1979	40,043,000	—	0.25	0.35	0.50	1.00
1979	15,000	PF65 0.75				

KM# 110 2 CENTS
4.00 g., Bronze, 22.45 mm. **Obv:** Head of President Vorster 1/4 right **Rev:** Black wildebeest above value **Edge:** Reeded

Date	Mintage	VF20	XF40	MS60	MS63	MS65
1982	53,962,000	—	0.25	0.35	0.50	1.00
1982	12,000	PF65 0.75				

KM# 133 2 CENTS
3.00 g., Copper Plated Steel, 18 mm. **Obv:** Arms with supporters **Obv. Legend:** SOUTH AFRICA - SUD AFRIKA **Rev:** Eagle with fish in talons divides value

Date	Mintage	VF20	XF40	MS60	MS63	MS65
1990	—	—	—	0.75	1.50	1.75
1990	—	PF65 2.00				
1991	—	—	—	0.75	1.50	1.75
1991	12,000	PF65 2.00				
1992	—	—	—	0.25	0.50	0.75
1992	—	PF65 2.00				
1993	—	—	—	0.25	0.50	0.75
1993	7,790	PF65 2.00				
1994	—	—	—	0.25	0.50	0.75
1994	5,804	PF65 2.00				
1995	—	—	—	0.25	0.50	0.75
1995	—	PF65 2.00				

KM# 159 2 CENTS
3.00 g., Copper Plated Steel, 18 mm. **Obv:** Arms with supporters **Obv. Legend:** AFURIKA TSHIPEMBE **Rev:** Eagle with fish in talons divides value

Date	Mintage	VF20	XF40	MS60	MS63	MS65
1996	—	—	—	0.25	0.50	0.75
1996	—	PF65 1.00				
1997	—	—	—	0.25	0.50	0.75
1997	3,596	PF65 1.00				
1998	—	—	—	0.25	0.50	0.75
1998	—	PF65 1.00				
1999	—	—	—	25.00	0.50	0.75
1999	—	PF65 1.00				
2000	—	—	—	0.25	0.50	0.75

KM# 222 2 CENTS
3.00 g., Copper Plated Steel, 18 mm. **Obv:** New national arms **Obv. Legend:** AFURIKA TSHIPEMBE **Rev:** Eagle with fish in talons divides value **Edge:** Plain

Date	Mintage	VF20	XF40	MS60	MS63	MS65
2000	—	—	—	0.25	0.50	0.75

KM# 58 2-1/2 CENTS
1.41 g., 0.500 Silver 0.0227 oz. ASW **Obv:** Protea flower **Rev:** Bust facing

Date	Mintage	VF20	XF40	MS60	MS63	MS65
1961	292,000	0.75	1.25	1.50	2.00	3.00
1961	7,530	PF65 4.00				
1962	8,745	1.50	2.50	4.00	6.00	8.00
1962	3,844	PF65 8.00				
1963	33,000	1.00	1.50	2.00	3.00	5.00
1963	4,025	PF65 6.00				
1964	14,000	1.00	2.00	3.00	5.00	7.00
1964	16,000	PF65 4.00				

KM# 174 2-1/2 CENTS
1.41 g., 0.925 Silver 0.0421 oz. ASW **Obv:** Protea flower **Rev:** Knysna seahorse below value

Date	Mintage	VF20	XF40	MS60	MS63	MS65
1997	Est. 2627	PF65 25.00				

KM# 176 2-1/2 CENTS
1.41 g., 0.925 Silver 0.0421 oz. ASW **Obv:** Protea flower **Rev:** Jackass Penguin

Date	Mintage	VF20	XF40	MS60	MS63	MS65
1998	Est. 5000	PF65 30.00				

KM# 217 2-1/2 CENTS

1.41 g., 0.925 Silver 0.0421 oz. ASW **Obv:** Protea flower **Rev:** Great White Shark

Date	Mintage	VF20	XF40	MS60	MS63	MS65
1999	5,000	PF65 25.00				

KM# 233 2-1/2 CENTS

1.41 g.,, 0.925 Silver 0.0421 oz. ASW, 16.3 mm. **Obv:** Protea flower **Rev:** Octopus **Edge:** Reeded

Date	Mintage	VF20	XF40	MS60	MS63	MS65
2000	—	PF65 30.00				

KM# 59 5 CENTS

2.83 g., 0.500 Silver 0.0455 oz. ASW, 17.35 mm. **Obv:** Protea flower in center of designed bars **Rev:** Bust 1/4 right

Date	Mintage	VF20	XF40	MS60	MS63	MS65
1961	1,479,000	0.80	2.00	2.50	3.50	4.00
1961	7,530	PF65 3.50				
1962	4,187,999	0.80	1.75	2.25	2.50	3.00
1962	3,844	PF65 4.00				
1963	8,054,000	0.80	1.50	2.00	2.25	2.50
1963	4,025	PF65 4.00				
1964	3,567,000	0.80	1.50	2.00	2.25	2.50
1964	16,000	PF65 2.50				

KM# 67.1 5 CENTS

2.50 g., Nickel, 17.35 mm. **Obv:** English legend **Rev:** Blue Crane

Date	Mintage	VF20	XF40	MS60	MS63	MS65
1965	32,689,999	—	0.15	0.35	0.75	1.25
1965	25,000	PF65 0.80				
1966	4,101,000	—	0.15	0.35	0.75	1.25
1967	4,590,000	—	0.15	0.35	0.75	1.25
1969	5,020,000	—	0.15	0.35	0.75	1.25

KM# 67.2 5 CENTS

2.50 g., Nickel, 17.35 mm. **Obv:** Afrikaans legend **Rev:** Blue Crane

Date	Mintage	VF20	XF40	MS60	MS63	MS65
1965	32,689,999	—	0.15	0.35	0.75	1.25
1966	4,101,000	—	0.15	0.35	0.75	1.25
1966	25,000	PF65 0.80				
1967	4,590,000	—	0.15	0.35	0.75	1.25
1967	25,000	PF65 0.80				
1969	5,020,000	—	0.15	0.35	0.75	1.25
1969	12,000	PF65 0.80				

KM# 76.1 5 CENTS

2.50 g., Nickel, 17.35 mm. **Subject:** President Charles Swart **Obv:** Head left **Obv. Legend:** English legend **Rev:** Blue Crane

Date	Mintage	VF20	XF40	MS60	MS63	MS65
1968	6,000,000	—	0.15	0.35	0.75	1.00
1968	25,000	PF65 0.80				

KM# 76.2 5 CENTS

2.50 g., Nickel, 17.35 mm. **Subject:** President Charles Swart **Obv:** Afrikaans legend **Rev:** Blue Crane

Date	Mintage	VF20	XF40	MS60	MS63	MS65
1968	6,000,000	—	0.15	0.35	0.75	1.00

KM# 84 5 CENTS

2.50 g., Nickel, 17.35 mm. **Obv:** Arms with supporters **Obv. Legend:** Bilingual legend **Rev:** Blue Crane

Date	Mintage	VF20	XF40	MS60	MS63	MS65
1970	6,652,000	—	0.15	0.35	0.75	1.00
1970	10,000	PF65 0.80				
1971	20,329,000	—	0.15	0.35	0.75	1.00
1971	12,000	PF65 0.80				
1972	3,117,000	—	0.15	0.35	0.75	1.00
1972	9,000	PF65 0.80				
1973	17,092,000	—	0.15	0.35	0.75	1.00
1973	11,000	PF65 0.80				
1974	19,978,000	—	0.15	0.35	0.75	1.00
1974	15,000	PF65 0.80				
1975	21,982,000	—	0.15	0.35	0.75	1.00
1975	18,000	PF65 0.80				
1977	51,729,000	—	0.15	0.35	0.75	1.00
1977	19,000	PF65 0.80				
1978	30,050,000	—	0.15	0.35	0.75	1.00
1978	19,000	PF65 0.80				
1980	46,665,000	—	0.15	0.35	0.75	1.00
1980	15,000	PF65 0.80				
1981	40,351,000	—	0.15	0.35	0.75	1.00
1981	10,000	PF65 0.80				
1983	57,487,000	—	0.15	0.35	0.75	1.00
1983	14,000	PF65 0.80				
1984	67,345,000	—	0.15	0.35	0.75	1.00
1984	11,000	PF65 0.80				
1985	57,167,000	—	0.15	0.35	0.75	1.00
1985	9,859	PF65 0.80				
1986	54,226,000	—	0.15	0.35	0.75	1.00
1986	7,100	PF65 0.80				
1987	42,786,000	—	0.15	0.35	0.75	1.00
1987	5,297	PF65 0.80				
1988	110,164,000	—	0.15	0.35	0.75	1.00
1988	7,250	PF65 0.80				
1989	35,540,000	—	0.15	0.35	0.75	1.00
1989	Inc. above	PF65 1.50				

KM# 93 5 CENTS

2.50 g., Nickel, 17.35 mm. **Obv:** Head of President Fouche right **Rev:** Blue Crane

Date	Mintage	VF20	XF40	MS60	MS63	MS65
1976	48,972,000	—	0.25	0.35	0.75	1.00
1976	19,000	PF65 1.50				

KM# 100 5 CENTS

2.50 g., Nickel, 17.35 mm. **Obv:** Head of President Diederichs left **Rev:** Blue Crane

Date	Mintage	VF20	XF40	MS60	MS63	MS65
1979	17,533,000	—	0.25	0.35	0.75	1.00
1979	17,000	PF65 1.50				

KM# 111 5 CENTS

2.50 g., Nickel, 17.35 mm. **Obv:** Head of President Vorster 1/4 right **Rev:** Blue Crane

Date	Mintage	VF20	XF40	MS60	MS63	MS65
1982	47,236,000	—	0.25	0.35	0.75	1.00
1982	12,000	PF65 1.50				

KM# 134 5 CENTS

4.50 g., Copper Plated Steel, 21 mm. **Obv:** Arms with supporters **Obv. Legend:** SOUTH AFRICA - SUD AFRIKA **Rev:** Blue crane

Date	Mintage	VF20	XF40	MS60	MS63	MS65
1990	—	—	0.15	0.35	0.75	1.00
1990	—	PF65 1.25				
1991	—	—	0.15	0.35	0.75	1.00
1991	12,000	PF65 1.25				
1992	—	—	0.15	0.35	0.75	1.00
1992	—	PF65 1.26				
1993	—	—	0.15	0.35	0.75	1.00
1993	7,790	PF65 1.25				
1994	—	—	0.15	0.35	0.75	1.00
1994	5,804	PF65 1.25				
1995	—	—	0.15	0.35	0.75	1.00
1995	—	PF65 1.25				

KM# 160 5 CENTS

4.50 g., Copper Plated Steel, 21 mm. **Obv:** Arms with supporters **Obv. Legend:** AFRIKA DZONGA **Rev:** Blue crane

Date	Mintage	VF20	XF40	MS60	MS63	MS65
1996	—	—	0.15	0.35	0.75	1.00
1996	—	PF65 1.25				
1997	—	—	0.15	0.35	0.75	1.00
1997	3,596	PF65 1.25				
1998	—	—	0.15	0.35	0.75	1.00
1998	—	PF65 1.50				
1999	—	—	0.15	0.35	0.75	1.00
1999	—	PF65 1.50				
2000	—	—	0.15	0.35	0.75	1.00

KM# 223 5 CENTS

4.42 g., Copper Plated Steel, 21 mm. **Obv:** New national arms **Obv. Legend:** AFRIKA DZONGA **Rev:** Value and Blue crane **Edge:** Plain

Date	Mintage	VF20	XF40	MS60	MS63	MS65
2000	—	0.10	0.25	0.40	0.65	1.00
2000	—	PF65 5.00				

KM# 60 10 CENTS

5.66 g., 0.500 Silver 0.091 oz. ASW **Obv:** Standing female figure leaning on large anchor **Rev:** Bust 1/4 right

Date	Mintage	VF20	XF40	MS60	MS63	MS65
1961	1,136,000	1.70	3.00	3.50	4.00	4.50
1961	7,530	PF65 4.00				
1962	2,447,000	1.70	3.00	3.50	4.00	4.50
1962	3,844	PF65 5.00				
1963	3,327,000	1.70	3.00	3.50	4.00	4.50
1963	4,025	PF65 5.00				
1964	4,152,999	1.70	3.00	3.50	4.00	4.50
1964	16,000	PF65 4.00				

KM# 68.1 10 CENTS

4.00 g., Nickel, 20.7 mm. **Obv:** Head of Jan van Riebeeck right **Rev:** Aloe plant and value

Date	Mintage	VF20	XF40	MS60	MS63	MS65
1965	29,210,000	—	0.10	0.20	0.35	0.50
1966	3,685,000	—	0.10	0.25	0.45	0.60
1966	25,000	PF65 0.60				
1967	50,000	—	—	0.50	1.00	1.25
1967	25,000	PF65 0.60				
1969	558,000	—	0.10	0.30	0.50	0.75
1969	12,000	PF65 1.00				

KM# 68.2 10 CENTS

4.00 g., Nickel, 20.7 mm. **Obv:** Head of Jan van Riebeeck right **Rev:** Aloe plant and value

Date	Mintage	VF20	XF40	MS60	MS63	MS65
1965	29,210,000	—	0.10	0.20	0.35	0.50
1965	25,000	PF65 0.60				

Date	Mintage	VF20	XF40	MS60	MS63	MS65
1966	3,685,000	—	0.10	0.25	0.45	0.60
1967	50,000	—	—	—	1.00	1.50
1969	558,000	0.10	0.20	1.00	2.25	2.75

KM# 77.1 10 CENTS

4.00 g., Nickel, 20.7 mm. **Obv:** Head of President Charles Swart left **Rev:** Aloe plant and value

Date	Mintage	VF20	XF40	MS60	MS63	MS65
1968	50,000	—	—	1.00	2.00	2.50

KM# 77.2 10 CENTS

4.00 g., Nickel, 20.7 mm. **Obv:** Afrikaans legend **Rev:** Aloe plant and value

Date	Mintage	VF20	XF40	MS60	MS63	MS65
1968	50,000	—	—	0.75	1.50	2.00
1968	25,000	PF65 0.60				

KM# 85 10 CENTS

4.00 g., Nickel, 20.7 mm. **Obv:** Arms with supporters **Rev:** Aloe plant and value

Date	Mintage	VF20	XF40	MS60	MS63	MS65
1970	7,598,000	—	0.10	0.20	0.35	0.50
1970	10,000	PF65 0.60				
1971	6,440,000	—	0.10	0.20	0.35	0.50
1971	12,000	PF65 0.60				
1972	10,028,000	—	0.10	0.20	0.35	0.50
1972	10,000	PF65 0.60				
1973	1,760,000	—	0.10	0.20	0.35	0.50
1973	11,000	PF65 0.60				
1974	9,897,000	—	0.10	0.20	0.35	0.50
1974	15,000	PF65 0.60				
1975	12,982,000	—	0.10	0.20	0.35	0.50
1975	18,000	PF65 0.60				
1977	28,851,000	—	0.10	0.20	0.35	0.50
1977	19,000	PF65 0.60				
1978	25,008,000	—	0.10	0.20	0.35	0.50
1978	19,000	PF65 0.60				
1980	5,040,000	—	0.10	0.20	0.35	0.50
1980	15,000	PF65 0.60				
1981	9,604,000	—	0.10	0.20	0.35	0.50
1981	10,000	PF65 0.60				
1983	26,495,000	—	0.10	0.20	0.35	0.50
1983	14,000	PF65 0.60				
1984	35,465,000	—	0.10	0.20	0.35	0.50
1984	11,000	PF65 0.60				
1985	29,270,000	—	0.10	0.20	0.35	0.50
1985	9,859	PF65 0.60				
1986	24,480,000	—	0.10	0.20	0.35	0.50
1986	7,100	PF65 0.60				
1987	43,234,000	—	0.10	0.20	0.35	0.50
1987	6,781	PF65 0.60				
1988	48,267,000	—	0.10	0.20	0.35	0.50
1988	7,250	PF65 0.60				
1989	—	—	0.10	0.20	0.35	0.50
1989	—	PF65 0.60				

KM# 94 10 CENTS

4.00 g., Nickel, 20.7 mm. **Obv:** Head of President Fouche right **Rev:** Aloe plant and value

Date	Mintage	VF20	XF40	MS60	MS63	MS65
1976	30,986,000	—	0.40	0.60	1.00	1.25
1976	21,000	PF65 1.50				

KM# 101 10 CENTS

4.00 g., Nickel, 20.7 mm. **Obv:** Head of President Diederichs left **Rev:** Aloe plant and value

Date	Mintage	VF20	XF40	MS60	MS63	MS65
1979	5,042,000	—	0.40	0.60	1.00	1.25
1979	17,000	PF65 1.50				

KM# 112 10 CENTS

4.00 g., Nickel, 20.7 mm. **Obv:** Head of President Vorster 1/4 right **Rev:** Aloe plant and value

Date	Mintage	VF20	XF40	MS60	MS63	MS65
1982	15,806,000	—	0.40	0.60	1.00	1.25
1982	12,000	PF65 1.50				

KM# 135 10 CENTS

2.00 g., Bronze Plated Steel, 16 mm. **Obv:** Arms with supporters **Obv. Legend:** SOUTH AFRICA - SUD AFRIKA **Rev:** Arum lily and value **Edge:** Reeded

Date	Mintage	VF20	XF40	MS60	MS63	MS65
1990	—	—	—	0.20	0.40	0.60
1990	—	PF65 0.60				
1991	—	—	—	0.20	0.40	0.60
1991	12,000	PF65 0.60				
1992	—	—	—	0.20	0.40	0.60
1992	—	PF65 0.60				
1993	—	—	—	0.20	0.40	0.60
1993	7,790	PF65 0.60				
1994	—	—	—	0.20	0.40	0.60
1994	5,804	PF65 0.60				
1995	—	—	—	0.20	0.40	0.60
1995	—	PF65 0.60				

KM# 161 10 CENTS

2.00 g., Bronze Plated Steel, 16 mm. **Obv:** Arms **Obv. Legend:** SOUTH AFRICA **Rev:** Arum lily and value **Edge:** Reeded

Date	Mintage	VF20	XF40	MS60	MS63	MS65
1996	—	—	—	0.20	0.40	0.60
1996	—	PF65 0.75				
1997	—	—	—	0.20	0.40	0.60
1997	3,596	PF65 0.75				
1998	—	—	—	0.20	0.40	0.60
1998	—	PF65 1.75				
1999	—	—	—	0.20	0.40	0.60
1999	—	PF65 1.75				
2000	—	—	—	0.20	0.40	0.60

KM# 224 10 CENTS

2.00 g., Bronze Plated Steel, 16 mm. **Obv:** New national arms **Obv. Legend:** AFRIKA DZONGA **Rev:** Arum Lily and value **Edge:** Reeded

Date	Mintage	VF20	XF40	MS60	MS63	MS65
2000	—	—	0.30	0.50	0.75	1.00

KM# 61 20 CENTS

11.31 g., 0.500 Silver 0.1818 oz. ASW **Obv:** Shield **Rev:** Bust of Jan van Riebeeck 1/4 right

Date	Mintage	VF20	XF40	MS60	MS63	MS65
1961	2,954,000	3.25	5.00	6.00	7.00	7.50
1961	7,530	PF65 7.00				
1962 Small 2	3,568,000	3.25	5.00	6.00	7.00	7.50
1962 Large 2	Inc. above	—	—	—	—	—
1962 Small 2; Proof	3,844	PF65 8.00				
1963	4,380,000	3.25	5.00	6.00	7.00	7.50
1963	4,025	PF65 8.00				
1964	4,335,000	3.25	5.00	6.00	7.00	7.50
1964	16,000	PF65 7.00				

KM# 69.1 20 CENTS

6.00 g., Nickel, 24.2 mm. **Obv:** Head of Jan van Riebeeck, English legend **Obv. Legend:** English legend **Rev:** Protea flower within sprigs, value at left

Date	Mintage	VF20	XF40	MS60	MS63	MS65
1965	29,210,000	0.15	0.20	0.30	0.40	0.50
1965	25,000	PF65 0.60				
1966	4,049,000	0.15	0.20	0.30	0.50	0.70
1967	58,000	—	—	—	1.00	1.50
1969	9,952	—	—	—	10.00	12.00

KM# 69.2 20 CENTS

6.00 g., Nickel, 24.2 mm. **Obv:** Head of Jan van Riebeeck, Africaans legend **Obv. Legend:** Afrikaans legend **Rev:** Protea flower within sprigs, value at left

Date	Mintage	VF20	XF40	MS60	MS63	MS65
1965	29,210,000	0.15	0.20	0.30	0.40	0.50
1966	4,049,000	0.15	0.20	0.30	0.50	0.70
1966	25,000	PF65 0.60				
1967	58,000	—	—	—	1.00	1.50
1967	25,000	PF65 0.60				
1969	9,952	—	—	—	6.00	8.00
1969	12,000	PF65 4.00				

KM# 78.1 20 CENTS

6.00 g., Nickel, 24.2 mm. **Obv:** Head of President Charles Swart left, English legend **Rev:** Protea flower within sprigs, value at left

Date	Mintage	VF20	XF40	MS60	MS63	MS65
1968	50,000	—	—	—	3.00	5.00
1968	25,000	PF65 0.60				

KM# 78.2 20 CENTS

6.00 g., Nickel, 24.2 mm. **Obv:** Africaans legend **Rev:** Protea flower within sprigs, value at left

Date	Mintage	VF20	XF40	MS60	MS63	MS65
1968	50,000	—	—	—	3.50	5.00

KM# 86 20 CENTS

6.00 g., Nickel, 24.2 mm. **Obv:** Arms with supporters, bilingual legend **Obv. Legend:** Bilingual legend **Rev:** Protea flower within sprigs, value at left **Note:** Varieties exist.

Date	Mintage	VF20	XF40	MS60	MS63	MS65
1970	14,000	—	—	—	10.00	12.00
1970	10,000	PF65 1.50				
1971	5,893,000	0.15	0.25	0.40	0.60	0.75
1971	12,000	PF65 1.50				
1972	9,069,000	0.15	0.25	0.40	0.60	0.75
1972	10,000	PF65 1.50				
1973	20,000	—	—	—	5.00	7.00
1973	11,000	PF65 1.50				
1974	2,436,000	0.15	0.35	0.50	0.75	1.50
1974	15,000	PF65 1.50				
1975	12,982,000	—	0.20	0.40	0.60	0.75
1975	18,000	PF65 1.00				
1977	30,650,000	—	0.20	0.40	0.60	0.75
1977	19,000	PF65 0.75				
1978	10,049,000	—	0.20	0.40	0.60	0.75
1978	19,000	PF65 0.75				
1980	13,335,000	—	0.20	0.40	0.60	0.75
1980	15,000	PF65 0.75				
1981	8,534,000	—	0.20	0.40	0.60	0.75
1981	10,000	PF65 0.75				
1983	25,667,000	—	0.20	0.40	0.60	0.75
1983	14,000	PF65 0.75				
1984	31,607,000	—	0.20	0.40	0.60	0.75
1984	11,000	PF65 0.75				
1985	29,329,000	—	0.20	0.40	0.60	0.75
1985	9,859	PF65 0.75				
1986	11,408,000	—	0.20	0.40	0.60	0.75
1986	7,100	PF65 0.75				
1987	36,904,000	—	0.20	0.40	0.60	0.75
1987	6,781	PF65 0.75				
1988	43,115,000	—	0.20	0.40	0.60	0.75
1988	7,250	PF65 0.75				
1989	—	—	0.20	0.40	0.60	0.75
1989	—	PF65 0.75				
1990	98,512,000	—	0.20	0.40	0.60	0.75
1990	—	PF65 8.00				
1991	—	—	—	—	4.00	6.00
1991	11,800	PF65 8.00				
1992	—	—	—	0.40	0.60	0.75
1992	—	PF65 8.00				
1993	—	—	—	0.40	0.60	0.75
1993	7,790	PF65 8.00				
1994	—	—	—	0.40	0.60	0.75
1994	5,804	PF65 8.00				
1995	—	—	—	0.40	0.60	0.75
1995	—	PF65 8.00				

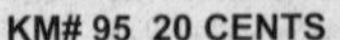

KM# 95 20 CENTS

6.00 g., Nickel, 24.2 mm. **Obv:** Head of President Fouche right **Rev:** Protea flower within sprigs, value at left

Date	Mintage	VF20	XF40	MS60	MS63	MS65
1976	18,826,000	—	0.70	1.00	1.50	2.00
1976	21,000	PF65 2.50				

KM# 102 20 CENTS

6.00 g., Nickel, 24.2 mm. **Obv:** Head of President Diederichs left **Rev:** Protea flower within sprigs, value at left

Date	Mintage	VF20	XF40	MS60	MS63	MS65
1979	5,032,000	—	0.70	1.00	1.50	2.00
1979	15,000	PF65 2.50				

KM# 113 20 CENTS

6.00 g., Nickel, 24.2 mm. **Obv:** Head of President Vorster 1/4 right **Rev:** Protea flower within sprigs, value at left

Date	Mintage	VF20	XF40	MS60	MS63	MS65
1982	18,083,000	—	0.70	1.00	1.50	2.00
1982	12,000	PF65 2.50				

KM# 136 20 CENTS

3.50 g., Bronze Plated Steel, 19 mm. **Obv:** Arms with supporters **Obv. Legend:** SOUTH AFRICA - SUID AFRIKA **Rev:** Protea flower within sprigs, value at upper right **Edge:** Reeded

Date	Mintage	VF20	XF40	MS60	MS63	MS65
1990	—	—	—	—	4.00	6.00

KM# 162 20 CENTS

3.50 g., Bronze Plated Steel, 19 mm. **Obv:** Arms with supporters **Obv. Legend:** AFERIKA BORWA **Rev:** Protea flower within sprigs, value at upper right **Edge:** Reeded

Date	Mintage	VF20	XF40	MS60	MS63	MS65
1996	—	—	—	0.40	0.60	0.75
1996	—	PF65 4.00				
1997	—	—	—	0.40	0.60	0.75
1997	3,596	PF65 4.00				
1998	—	—	—	0.40	0.60	0.75
1998	—	PF65 4.00				
1999	—	—	—	0.40	0.60	0.75
1999	—	PF65 4.00				
2000	—	—	—	0.40	0.60	0.75

KM# 225 20 CENTS

3.50 g., Bronze Plated Steel, 19 mm. **Obv:** New national arms **Obv. Legend:** AFERIKA BORWA **Rev:** Protea flower and value **Edge:** Reeded

Date	Mintage	VF20	XF40	MS60	MS63	MS65
2000	—	—	0.35	0.50	0.90	1.20

KM# 62 50 CENTS

28.28 g., 0.500 Silver 0.4546 oz. ASW **Obv:** Springbok **Rev:** Bust of Jan van Riebeeck 1/4 right **Note:** Varieties exist with narrow, high relief and wide, low letters.

Date	Mintage	VF20	XF40	MS60	MS63	MS65
1961	26,000	8.50	14.00	15.00	16.00	18.00
1961 Prooflike	20,000	—	—	—	—	20.00
1961	8,530	PF65 22.00				
1962	15,000	8.50	14.00	15.00	16.00	18.00
1962 Prooflike	6,024	—	—	—	—	20.00
1962	3,844	PF65 22.00				
1963	143,000	8.50	14.00	15.00	16.00	18.00
1963 Prooflike	10,000	—	—	—	—	20.00
1963	4,025	PF65 22.00				
1964	86,000	8.50	14.00	15.00	16.00	18.00
1964 Prooflike	25,000	—	—	—	—	20.00
1964	16,000	PF65 22.00				

KM# 70.1 50 CENTS

9.50 g., Nickel, 27.8 mm. **Obv:** Head of Jan van Riebeeck right, English legend **Rev:** Flower and value

Date	Mintage	VF20	XF40	MS60	MS63	MS65
1965	—	PF65 3,500				
1966	8,055,999	—	0.50	1.25	2.50	3.00
1966	25,000	PF65 4.00				
1967 Sets only	52,000	—	—	—	—	2.00
1967	25,000	PF65 4.00				
1969 Sets only	7,968	—	—	—	—	10.00
1969	12,000	PF65 10.00				

KM# 70.2 50 CENTS

9.50 g., Nickel, 27.8 mm. **Obv:** Head of Jan van Riebeeck right, Afrikaans legend **Rev:** Flower and value

Date	Mintage	VF20	XF40	MS60	MS63	MS65
1965	28,000	—	—	—	4.00	6.00
1965	25,000	PF65 6.00				
1966	8,055,999	—	0.50	1.25	2.50	3.00
1967 Sets only	52,000	—	—	—	—	4.00
1969 Sets only	7,968	—	—	—	—	15.00

KM# 79.1 50 CENTS

9.50 g., Nickel, 27.8 mm. **Obv:** Head of President Charles Swart left, English legend **Rev:** Flowers and value

Date	Mintage	VF20	XF40	MS60	MS63	MS65
1968	750,000	—	0.50	0.75	1.50	1.75

KM# 79.2 50 CENTS

9.50 g., Nickel, 27.8 mm. **Obv:** Head of President Charles Swart left, Afrikaans legend **Rev:** Flowers and value

Date	Mintage	VF20	XF40	MS60	MS63	MS65
1968	750,000	—	0.50	1.00	2.00	2.50
1968	25,000	PF65 3.50				

KM# 87 50 CENTS

9.50 g., Nickel, 27.9 mm. **Obv:** Arms with supporters, bilingual legend **Rev:** Flowers and value **Note:** Varieties exist.

Date	Mintage	VF20	XF40	MS60	MS63	MS65
1970	4,098,000	—	0.50	0.75	1.50	1.75
1970	10,000	PF65 2.00				
1971	5,062,000	—	0.50	0.75	1.50	1.75
1971	12,000	PF65 2.00				
1972	771,000	—	0.50	0.75	1.50	1.75
1972	10,000	PF65 2.00				
1973	1,042,999	—	0.50	0.75	1.50	1.75
1973	11,000	PF65 2.00				
1974	1,942,000	—	0.50	0.75	1.50	1.75
1974	15,000	PF65 2.00				
1975	4,888,000	—	0.50	0.75	1.50	1.75
1975	18,000	PF65 2.00				
1977	10,196,000	—	0.50	0.75	1.50	1.75
1977	19,000	PF65 2.00				
1978	5,071,000	—	0.50	0.75	1.50	1.75
1978	17,000	PF65 2.00				
1980	4,268,000	—	0.50	0.75	1.50	1.75
1980	15,000	PF65 2.00				
1981	5,681,000	—	0.50	0.75	1.50	1.75
1981	10,000	PF65 2.00				
1983	5,150,000	—	0.40	0.60	1.00	1.25
1983	14,000	PF65 1.50				
1984	9,687,000	—	0.40	0.60	1.00	1.25
1984	11,000	PF65 1.50				
1985	13,339,000	—	0.40	0.60	1.00	1.25

Date	Mintage	VF20	XF40	MS60	MS63	MS65
1985	9,859	PF65 1.50				
1986	2,294,000	—	0.40	0.60	1.00	1.25
1986	7,100	PF65 1.50				
1987	19,071,000	—	0.40	0.60	1.00	1.25
1987	6,781	PF65 1.50				
1988	27,698,000	—	0.40	0.60	1.00	1.25
1988	7,250	PF65 1.50				
1989	—	—	0.40	0.60	1.00	1.25
1989	—	PF65 1.50				
1990	29,442,000	—	0.40	0.60	1.00	1.25

KM# 96 50 CENTS

9.50 g., Nickel, 27.8 mm. **Obv:** Head of President Fouche right **Rev:** Flowers and value

Date	Mintage	VF20	XF40	MS60	MS63	MS65
1976	9,632,000	0.75	1.50	2.00	3.00	3.50
1976	21,000	PF65 5.00				

KM# 103 50 CENTS

9.50 g., Nickel, 27.8 mm. **Obv:** Head of President Diederichs left **Rev:** Flowers and value

Date	Mintage	VF20	XF40	MS60	MS63	MS65
1979	5,051,000	0.75	1.50	2.00	3.00	3.50
1979	15,000	PF65 5.00				

KM# 114 50 CENTS

9.50 g., Nickel, 27.8 mm. **Obv:** Head of President Vorster 1/4 right **Rev:** Flowers and value

Date	Mintage	VF20	XF40	MS60	MS63	MS65
1982	2,069,999	0.75	1.50	2.00	3.00	3.50
1982	12,000	PF65 5.00				

KM# 137 50 CENTS

5.00 g., Bronze Plated Steel, 22 mm. **Obv:** Arms with supporters **Obv. Legend:** SUID AFRIKA - SOUTH AFRICA **Rev:** Plant and value **Edge:** Reeded

Date	Mintage	VF20	XF40	MS60	MS63	MS65
1990	—	—	—	3.00	5.00	6.00
1990	—	PF65 10.00				
1991	—	—	—	3.00	5.00	6.00
1991	12,000	PF65 10.00				
1992	—	—	—	0.60	1.00	1.25
1992	—	PF65 10.00				
1993	—	—	—	0.60	1.00	1.25
1993	7,790	PF65 10.00				
1994	—	—	—	0.60	1.00	1.25
1994	5,804	PF65 10.00				
1995	—	—	—	0.60	1.00	1.25
1995	—	PF65 10.00				

KM# 163 50 CENTS

5.00 g., Bronze Plated Steel, 22 mm. **Obv:** Arms with supporters **Obv. Legend:** AFRIKA BORWA **Rev:** Plant and value **Edge:** Reeded

Date	Mintage	VF20	XF40	MS60	MS63	MS65
1996	—	—	—	0.60	1.00	1.25
1996	—	PF65 5.00				
1997	—	—	—	0.60	1.00	1.25
1997	—	PF65 5.00				
1998	—	—	—	0.60	1.00	1.25
1998	—	PF65 5.00				
1999	—	—	—	0.60	1.00	1.25
1999	—	PF65 5.00				
2000	—	—	—	0.60	1.00	1.25

KM# 226 50 CENTS

5.00 g., Bronze Plated Steel, 22 mm. **Obv:** New national arms **Obv. Legend:** AFERIKA BORWA **Rev:** Strelitzia plant, value **Edge:** Reeded

Date	Mintage	VF20	XF40	MS60	MS63	MS65
2000	—	—	0.50	0.75	1.20	1.60

KM# 63 RAND

3.99 g., 0.917 Gold 0.1178 oz. AGW **Obv:** Springbok **Rev:** Bust of Jan van Riebeeck 1/4 right

Date	Mintage	VF20	XF40	MS60	MS63	MS65
1961	4,246	—	—	—	170	180
1961	4,932	PF63 187	PF65 225			
1962	3,955	—	—	—	170	180
1962	2,344	PF63 187	PF65 225			
1963	4,023	—	—	—	170	180
1963	2,508	PF63 187	PF65 225			
1964	5,866	—	—	—	170	180
1964	4,000	PF63 187	PF65 225			
1965	10,000	—	—	—	170	180
1965	6,024	PF63 187	PF65 225			
1966	10,000	—	—	—	170	180
1966	11,000	PF63 187	PF65 225			
1967	10,000	—	—	—	170	180
1967	11,000	PF63 187	PF65 225			
1968	10,000	—	—	—	170	180
1968	11,000	PF63 187	PF65 225			
1969	10,000	—	—	—	170	180
1969	8,000	PF63 187	PF65 225			
1970	10,000	—	—	—	170	180
1970	7,000	PF63 187	PF65 225			
1971	10,000	—	—	—	170	180
1971	7,650	PF63 187	PF65 225			
1972	12,000	—	—	—	170	180
1972	7,500	PF63 187	PF65 225			
1973	15,000	—	—	—	170	180
1973	12,000	PF63 187	PF65 225			
1974	23,000	—	—	—	170	180
1974	17,000	PF63 187	PF65 225			
1975	12,000	—	—	—	170	180
1975	18,000	PF63 187	PF65 225			
1976	12,000	—	—	—	170	180
1976	21,000	PF63 187	PF65 225			
1977	27,000	—	—	—	170	180
1977	20,000	PF63 187	PF65 225			
1978	13,000	—	—	—	170	180
1978	19,000	PF63 187	PF65 225			
1979	17,000	—	—	—	170	180
1979	17,000	PF63 187	PF65 225			
1980	14,000	—	—	—	170	180
1980	18,000	PF63 187	PF65 225			
1981	9,274	—	—	—	170	180
1981	10,000	PF63 187	PF65 225			
1982	14,000	—	—	—	170	180
1983	15,000	—	—	—	170	180

KM# 71.1 RAND

15.00 g., 0.800 Silver 0.3858 oz. ASW **Obv:** Head of Jan van Riebeeck right **Rev:** Springbok above value

Date	Mintage	VF20	XF40	MS60	MS63	MS65
1965	—	—	7.50	8.25	14.00	—
1965	25,000	PF63 20.00				
1966	1,434,000	—	7.50	8.25	14.00	—
1966	20	PF63 1,250				
1968 Sets only	50,000	—	7.50	8.25	14.00	—
1968	25,000	PF63 14.00				

KM# 71.2 RAND

15.00 g., 0.800 Silver 0.3858 oz. ASW **Obv:** Head of Jan van Riebeeck right, Afrikaans legend **Rev:** Springbok above value

Date	Mintage	VF20	XF40	MS60	MS63	MS65
1965 V.I.P. Proof	—	PF63 1,000				
1966	1,434,000	—	7.50	8.25	14.00	—
1966	25,000	PF63 14.00				
1968 Sets only	50,000	—	—	—	14.00	—
1968	Est. 20	PF63 1,250				

KM# 72.1 RAND

15.00 g., 0.800 Silver 0.3858 oz. ASW **Subject:** 1st Anniversary - Death of Dr. Verwoerd **Obv:** Bust right, English legend **Rev:** Springbok above value

Date	Mintage	VF20	XF40	MS60	MS63	MS65
1967	1,544,000	—	7.50	8.25	14.00	—
1967	Est. 20	PF63 1,250				

KM# 72.2 RAND

15.00 g., 0.800 Silver 0.3858 oz. ASW **Subject:** 1st Anniversary - Death of Dr. Verwoerd **Obv:** Bust right, Afrikaans legend **Rev:** Springbok above value

Date	Mintage	VF20	XF40	MS60	MS63	MS65
1967	1,544,000	—	7.50	8.25	14.00	—
1967	25,000	PF63 14.50				

KM# 80.1 RAND

15.00 g., 0.800 Silver 0.3858 oz. ASW, 32.6 mm. **Subject:** Dr. T.E. Donges **Obv:** Bust right, English legend **Rev:** Springbok above value **Note:** The South African mint does not acknowledge the existence of these 1 Rand pieces struck in proof.

Date	Mintage	VF20	XF40	MS60	MS63	MS65
1969	506,000	—	7.50	8.25	14.00	—
1969	Est. 20	PF63 1,250				

KM# 80.2 RAND
15.00 g., 0.800 Silver 0.3858 oz. ASW, 32.6 mm. **Subject:** Dr. T.E. Donges **Obv:** Bust right, Afrikaans legend **Rev:** Springbok above value

Date	Mintage	VF20	XF40	MS60	MS63	MS65
1969	506,000	—	7.50	8.25	14.00	—
1969	12,000	PF63 15.00				

KM# 89 RAND
15.00 g., 0.800 Silver 0.3858 oz. ASW **Subject:** 50th Anniversary of Pretoria Mint **Obv:** Arms with supporters **Rev:** 4 Coin designs surround brick door at center

Date	Mintage	VF20	XF40	MS60	MS63	MS65
1974	20,000	—	—	—	15.00	—
1974	15,000	PF63 25.00				

KM# 88 RAND
15.00 g., 0.800 Silver 0.3858 oz. ASW **Obv:** Arms with supporters, bilingual legend **Rev:** Springbok

Date	Mintage	VF20	XF40	MS60	MS63	MS65
1970	14,000	—	7.50	8.25	14.00	—
1970	10,000	PF63 14.50				
1971	20,000	—	7.50	8.25	14.00	—
1971	12,000	PF63 14.50				
1972	20,000	—	7.50	8.25	14.00	—
1972	10,000	PF63 14.50				
1973	20,000	—	7.50	8.25	14.00	—
1973	11,000	PF63 14.50				
1975	20,000	—	7.50	8.25	14.00	—
1975	18,000	PF63 14.50				
1976	20,000	—	7.50	8.25	14.00	—
1976	21,000	PF63 14.50				
1977	19,000	PF63 15.00				
1978	17,000	PF63 15.00				
1979	15,000	PF63 15.00				
1980	15,000	PF63 15.00				
1981	12,000	PF63 17.50				
1982	10,000	PF63 17.50				
1983	14,000	PF63 17.50				
1984	11,000	PF63 17.50				
1987	4,526	—	7.50	8.25	20.00	—
1987	13,000	PF63 17.50				
1988	21	—	—	—	—	—
1988	7,250	PF63 20.00				
1989	3,684	—	7.50	8.25	20.00	—
1989	15,000	PF63 17.50				
1990	—	PF63 25.00				

KM# 88a RAND
12.00 g., Nickel, 31 mm. **Obv:** Arms with supporters, bilingual legend **Rev:** Springbok above value **Edge:** Reeded

Date	Mintage	VF20	XF40	MS60	MS63	MS65
1977	29,871,000	—	0.75	1.25	2.00	—
1977	10	PF63 1,500				
1978	12,021,000	—	0.75	1.25	2.00	—
1978	10	PF63 1,500				
1980	2,690,000	—	0.75	1.25	2.00	—
1981	2,035,000	—	0.75	1.25	2.00	—
1983	7,182,000	—	0.75	1.25	2.00	—
1983	10	PF63 1,500				
1984	5,736,000	—	0.75	1.25	2.00	—
1984	11,000	PF63 5.00				
1986	1,570,000	—	0.75	1.25	2.00	—
1986	7,000	PF63 5.00				
1987	12,152,000	—	0.75	1.25	2.00	—
1987	6,781	PF63 5.00				
1988	21,335,000	—	0.75	1.25	2.00	—
1988	7,250	PF63 5.00				
1989	—	—	—	1.25	2.00	—
1989	—	PF63 5.00				

KM# 104 RAND
12.00 g., Nickel, 31 mm. **Obv:** Head of President Diederichs left **Rev:** Springbok above value **Edge:** Reeded

Date	Mintage	VF20	XF40	MS60	MS63	MS65
1979	13,466,000	2.00	4.00	6.00	10.00	—
1979	5	PF63 2,000				

KM# 115 RAND
12.00 g., Nickel, 31 mm. **Obv:** Head of President Vorster 1/4 right **Rev:** Springbok above value **Edge:** Reeded

Date	Mintage	VF20	XF40	MS60	MS63	MS65
1982	7,685,000	2.50	5.00	7.00	11.00	—
1982	15	PF63 1,500				

KM# 116 RAND
15.00 g., 0.800 Silver 0.3858 oz. ASW **Subject:** 75th Anniversary of Parliament **Obv:** Crossed scepters divides shield and lion **Rev:** Parliament building

Date	Mintage	VF20	XF40	MS60	MS63	MS65
1985	8,731	—	—	—	17.50	—
1985	26,000	PF63 32.50				

KM# 117 RAND
12.00 g., Nickel, 31 mm. **Obv:** Head of President Marais Viljoen left **Rev:** Springbok above value **Edge:** Reeded

Date	Mintage	VF20	XF40	MS60	MS63	MS65
1985	3,983,000	2.50	5.00	7.00	11.00	—
1985	9,859	PF63 5.00				

KM# 119 RAND
15.00 g., 0.800 Silver 0.3858 oz. ASW **Subject:** 100th Anniversary of Johannesburg **Obv:** Arms with supporters **Rev:** View of city

Date	Mintage	VF20	XF40	MS60	MS63	MS65
1986	7,501	—	—	—	16.50	—
1986	5,683	PF63 35.00				

KM# 120 RAND
15.00 g., 0.800 Silver 0.3858 oz. ASW **Series:** Year of the Disabled **Obv:** Arms with supporters **Rev:** Stylized standing figure and figure in wheelchair, value at left

Date	Mintage	VF20	XF40	MS60	MS63	MS65
1986	1,005	—	—	—	50.00	—
1986	5,150	PF63 35.00				

KM# 122 RAND
15.00 g., 0.800 Silver 0.3858 oz. ASW **Subject:** Bartolomeu Dias **Obv:** Arms with supporters **Rev:** Crown above point of star design to left of map

Date	Mintage	VF20	XF40	MS60	MS63	MS65
1988	7,091	—	—	—	15.00	—
1988	9,640	PF63 20.00				

KM# 125 RAND
15.00 g., 0.800 Silver 0.3858 oz. ASW **Subject:** Huguenots **Obv:** Arms with supporters **Rev:** Descending dove and design divide dates below small cross, all within circle

Date	Mintage	VF20	XF40	MS60	MS63	MS65
1988	5,497	—	—	—	15.00	—
1988	9,028	PF63 20.00				

KM# 128 RAND
15.00 g., 0.800 Silver 0.3858 oz. ASW **Subject:** The Great Trek **Obv:** Arms with supporters **Rev:** Stylized wheel and arrow design

Date	Mintage	VF20	XF40	MS60	MS63	MS65
1988	6,555	—	—	—	15.00	—
1988	7,941	PF63 20.00				

KM# 141 RAND
12.00 g., Nickel, 31 mm. **Obv:** Head of President Botha facing **Rev:** Springbok above value **Edge:** Reeded

Date	Mintage	VF20	XF40	MS60	MS63	MS65
1990	25,323,000	—	1.75	2.50	3.50	—
1990	15,000	PF63 10.00				

KM# 148 RAND
4.00 g., Nickel Plated Copper, 20 mm. **Obv:** Head of President Botha facing **Obv. Legend:** SOUTH AFRICA - SUD AFRIKA **Rev:** Springbok below value

Date	Mintage	VF20	XF40	MS60	MS63	MS65
1990	12,000	—	—	—	10.00	—
1990	10,000	PF63 15.00				

KM# 138 RAND
4.00 g., Nickel Plated Copper, 20 mm. **Obv:** Arms with supporters **Obv. Legend:** SOUTH AFRICA - SUD AFRIKA **Rev:** Springbok below value **Edge:** Segmented reeding

Date	Mintage	VF20	XF40	MS60	MS63	MS65
1991	20,765,000	—	—	—	2.50	—
1991	12,000	PF63 15.00				
1992	59,571,000	—	—	—	2.50	—
1992	10,000	PF63 15.00				
1993	37,977,000	—	—	—	2.50	—
1993	7,790	PF63 20.00				
1994	54,633,000	—	—	—	2.50	—
1994	5,804	PF63 20.00				
1995	28,012,000	—	—	—	2.50	—
1995	5,816	PF63 20.00				

KM# 142 RAND
14.97 g., 0.925 Silver 0.4452 oz. ASW, 32.7 mm. **Subject:** South African Nursing Schools **Obv:** Protea flower **Rev:** Aladdin lamp divides dates within cross design **Edge:** Reeded

Date	Mintage	VF20	XF40	MS60	MS63	MS65
1991	13,576	—	—	—	16.50	—
1991	8,675	PF63 22.50				

KM# 143 RAND
14.97 g., 0.925 Silver 0.4452 oz. ASW, 32.7 mm. **Subject:** Coinage Centennial **Obv:** Protea flower **Rev:** Assorted coin designs **Edge:** Reeded

Date	Mintage	VF20	XF40	MS60	MS63	MS65
1992	13,920	—	—	—	16.50	—
1992	8,094	PF63 22.50				

KM# 168 RAND
14.97 g., 0.925 Silver 0.4452 oz. ASW, 32.7 mm. **Subject:** 200 Years of Banking **Obv:** Protea flower **Rev:** Tower divides lion head and coin designs **Edge:** Reeded

Date	Mintage	VF20	XF40	MS60	MS63	MS65
1993	7,584	—	—	—	18.50	—
1993	3,907	PF63 27.50				

KM# 149 RAND
15.00 g., 0.925 Silver 0.4461 oz. ASW, 32.7 mm. **Subject:** Presidential Inauguration **Obv:** National arms **Rev:** Building below value **Edge:** Reeded

Date	Mintage	VF20	XF40	MS60	MS63	MS65
1994	6,269	PF63 100				

KM# 167 RAND
15.00 g., 0.925 Silver 0.4461 oz. ASW, 32.7 mm. **Subject:** Conservation **Obv:** Protea flower **Rev:** Assorted animals within stylized design **Edge:** Reeded

Date	Mintage	VF20	XF40	MS60	MS63	MS65
1994	11,190	—	—	—	18.50	—
1994	4,706	PF63 27.50				

KM# 152 RAND
15.00 g., 0.925 Silver 0.4461 oz. ASW, 32.7 mm. **Subject:** Railway Centennial **Obv:** Protea flower **Rev:** Train and value **Edge:** Reeded

Date	Mintage	VF20	XF40	MS60	MS63	MS65
1995	8,006	—	—	—	18.50	—
1995	4,491	PF63 27.50				

KM# 164 RAND
4.00 g., Nickel Plated Copper, 20 mm. **Obv:** Arms with supporters **Obv. Legend:** SUID-AFRIKA **Rev:** Springbok and value **Edge:** Segmented reeding

Date	Mintage	VF20	XF40	MS60	MS63	MS65
1996	12,199,000	—	—	—	1.75	—
1996	4,827	PF63 6.00				
1997	38,876,000	—	—	—	1.75	—
1997	3,596	PF63 6.00				
1998	—	—	—	—	1.75	—
1998	—	PF63 6.00				
1999	—	—	—	—	1.75	—
1999	—	PF63 6.00				
2000	—	—	—	—	1.75	—

KM# 169 RAND
15.00 g., 0.925 Silver 0.4461 oz. ASW, 32.7 mm. **Subject:** Constitution **Obv:** Protea flower **Rev:** Hand writing in book **Edge:** Reeded

Date	Mintage	VF20	XF40	MS60	MS63	MS65
1996	5,059	—	—	—	20.00	—
1996	2,931	PF63 30.00				

KM# 181 RAND
15.00 g., 0.925 Silver 0.4461 oz. ASW, 32.7 mm. **Subject:** Women of South Africa **Obv:** Protea flower **Rev:** Stylized 1/2 head facing within map **Edge:** Reeded

Date	Mintage	VF20	XF40	MS60	MS63	MS65
1997	3,312	—	—	—	25.00	30.00
1997	2,329	PF63 35.00	PF65 40.00			

KM# 177 RAND
15.00 g., 0.925 Silver 0.4461 oz. ASW, 32.7 mm. **Obv:** Protea flower **Rev:** Assorted designs divided into 16 sections **Edge:** Reeded

Date	Mintage	VF20	XF40	MS60	MS63	MS65
1998	2,673	—	—	—	22.50	—
1998	1,999	PF63 35.00				

KM# 232 RAND
15.00 g., 0.925 Silver 0.4461 oz. ASW, 32.7 mm. **Obv:** Protea flower **Rev:** Mine tower outline **Edge:** Reeded

Date	Mintage	VF20	XF40	MS60	MS63	MS65
1999	6,277	—	—	—	30.00	—
1999	2,617	PF65 40.00				

KM# 227 RAND
4.00 g., Nickel Plated Copper, 20 mm. **Obv:** New national arms **Obv. Legend:** SUID-AFRIKA **Rev:** Springbok, value **Edge:** Segmented reeding

Date	Mintage	VF20	XF40	MS60	MS63	MS65
2000	—	—	0.60	1.50	2.00	—

KM# 238 RAND
15.00 g., 0.925 Silver 0.4461 oz. ASW, 32.7 mm. **Obv:** Protea flower **Rev:** Wine barrels, grapes and leaves **Edge:** Reeded

Date	Mintage	VF20	XF40	MS60	MS63	MS65
2000	2,131	—	—	—	30.00	—
2000	1,519	PF65 40.00				

KM# 64 2 RAND
7.99 g., 0.917 Gold 0.2355 oz. AGW **Obv:** Springbok **Rev:** Bust of Jan van Riebeeck 1/4 right

Date	Mintage	VF20	XF40	MS60	MS63	MS65
1961	3,014	—	—	—	345	390
1961	3,932	PF63 375	PF65 450			
1962	10,000	—	—	—	345	390
1962	2,344	PF63 375	PF65 450			
1963	3,179	—	—	—	345	390
1963	2,508	PF63 375	PF65 450			
1964	3,994	—	—	—	345	390
1964	4,000	PF63 375	PF65 450			
1965	10,000	—	—	—	335	360
1965	6,024	PF63 375	PF65 450			
1966	10,000	—	—	—	335	360
1966	11,000	PF63 345	PF65 390			
1967	10,000	—	—	—	335	360
1967	11,000	PF63 345	PF65 390			
1968	10,000	—	—	—	335	360
1968	11,000	PF63 345	PF65 390			
1969	10,000	—	—	—	335	360
1969	8,000	PF63 360	PF65 420			
1970	10,000	—	—	—	335	360
1970	7,000	PF63 360	PF65 420			
1971	10,000	—	—	—	335	360
1971	7,650	PF63 360	PF65 420			
1972	18,000	—	—	—	335	360
1972	7,500	PF63 360	PF65 420			
1973	14,000	—	—	—	335	360
1973	13,000	PF63 345	PF65 390			
1974	13,000	—	—	—	335	360
1974	17,000	PF63 345	PF65 390			
1975	12,000	—	—	—	335	360
1975	18,000	PF63 345	PF65 390			
1976	12,000	—	—	—	335	360
1976	21,000	PF63 345	PF65 390			
1977	12,000	—	—	—	335	360
1977	20,000	PF63 345	PF65 390			
1978	11,000	—	—	—	335	360
1978	19,000	PF63 345	PF65 390			
1979	12,000	—	—	—	335	360
1979	20,000	PF63 345	PF65 390			
1980	12,000	—	—	—	335	360
1980	18,000	PF63 345	PF65 390			
1981	8,538	—	—	—	335	360
1981	10,000	PF63 345	PF65 390			
1982	2,030	—	—	—	335	360
1982	12,000	PF63 345	PF65 390			
1983	15,000	—	—	—	335	360

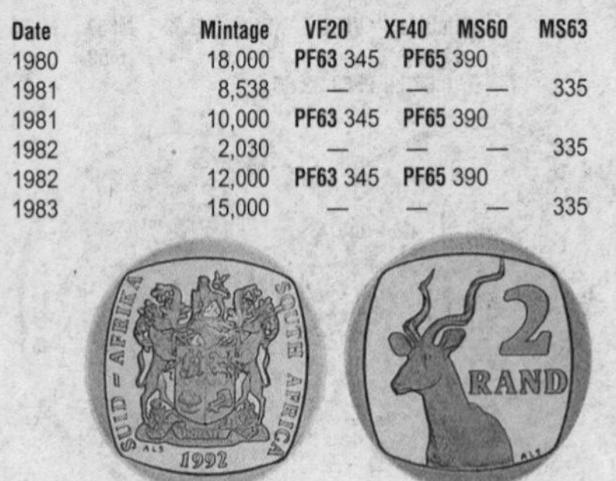

KM# 139 2 RAND
5.50 g., Nickel Plated Copper, 23 mm. **Obv:** Arms with supporters **Obv. Legend:** SUID AFRIKA - SOUTH AFRICA **Rev:** Greater Kudu and value **Edge:** Segmented reeding

Date	Mintage	VF20	XF40	MS60	MS63	MS65
1989	65,233,000	—	—	—	2.00	—
1989	13,000	PF63 10.00				
1990	70,655,000	—	—	—	2.00	—
1990	10,000	PF63 7.50				
1991	39,243,000	—	—	—	2.00	—
1991	12,000	PF63 7.50				
1992	2,115,000	—	—	—	2.00	—
1992	10,000	PF63 7.50				
1993	92,000	—	—	—	2.00	—
1993	7,790	PF63 7.50				
1994	994,000	—	—	—	2.00	—
1994	5,804	PF63 7.50				
1995	13,213,000	—	—	—	2.00	—
1995	5,816	PF63 7.50				

KM# 145 2 RAND
33.63 g., 0.925 Silver 1.000 oz. ASW, 38.7 mm. **Subject:** Coin Minting **Obv:** National arms **Rev:** Assorted coins and design above value **Edge:** Reeded **Note:** 50 pieces used in jewelry mountings.

Date	Mintage	VF20	XF40	MS60	MS63	MS65
1992	6,738	PF63 55.00	PF65 65.00			

KM# 147 2 RAND
33.63 g., 0.925 Silver 1.000 oz. ASW, 38.7 mm. **Series:** Barcelona Olympics **Obv:** Arms holding torch with outlined map behind **Rev:** Three event athletes **Edge:** Reeded **Note:** 1,670 used in jewelry mountings.

Date	Mintage	VF20	XF40	MS60	MS63	MS65
1992	16,523	PF63 40.00	PF65 45.00			

KM# 151 2 RAND
33.63 g., 0.925 Silver 1.000 oz. ASW, 38.7 mm. **Subject:** Peace **Obv:** National arms **Rev:** Stylized doves and figures within globe design **Edge:** Reeded **Note:** 828 pieces used in jewelry.

Date	Mintage	VF20	XF40	MS60	MS63	MS65
1993	5,628	PF63 57.00	PF65 65.00			

KM# 156 2 RAND
33.63 g., 0.925 Silver 1.000 oz. ASW, 38.7 mm. **Subject:** World Cup Soccer **Obv:** Stylized figure and soccer ball **Rev:** Soccer ball and North American map **Edge:** Reeded **Note:** 288 pieces used in jewelry.

Date	Mintage	VF20	XF40	MS60	MS63	MS65
1994	3,498	PF63 65.00	PF65 70.00			

KM# 153 2 RAND
33.63 g., 0.925 Silver 1.000 oz. ASW, 38.7 mm. **Subject:** Rugby World Cup **Obv:** National arms **Rev:** Three players running **Edge:** Reeded **Note:** 215 pieces used in jewelry.

Date	Mintage	VF20	XF40	MS60	MS63	MS65
1995	4,196	PF63 60.00	PF65 70.00			

KM# 154 2 RAND
33.63 g., 0.925 Silver 1.000 oz. ASW **Subject:** 50th Anniversary F. A. O. **Obv:** National arms **Rev:** Man with child in bird nest, sparrow and F.A.O. logo

Date	Mintage	VF20	XF40	MS60	MS63	MS65
1995	1,743	PF63 67.00	PF65 75.00			

KM# 155 2 RAND

33.63 g., 0.925 Silver 1.000 oz. ASW, 38.7 mm. **Subject:** 50th Anniversary United Nations **Obv:** National arms **Rev:** Numeral 50 and UN emblem above world globe and map **Edge:** Reeded

Date	Mintage	VF20	XF40	MS60	MS63	MS65
1995	1,412	PF63 70.00	PF65 80.00			

KM# 157 2 RAND

33.63 g., 0.925 Silver 1.000 oz. ASW, 38.7 mm. **Subject:** African Cup **Obv:** Arms with supporters **Rev:** Soccer player within soccerball design **Edge:** Reeded

Date	Mintage	VF20	XF40	MS60	MS63	MS65
1996	2,690	PF63 65.00	PF65 70.00			

KM# 165 2 RAND

5.50 g., Nickel Plated Copper, 23 mm. **Obv:** Arms with supporters **Obv. Legend:** UMZANTSI AFRIKA **Rev:** Greater Kudu and value **Edge:** Segmented reeding

Date	Mintage	VF20	XF40	MS60	MS63	MS65
1996	123,000	—	—	—	2.50	—
1996	4,827	PF63 8.00				
1997	1,804,000	—	—	—	2.50	—
1997	3,596	PF63 8.00				
1998	—	—	—	—	2.50	—
1998	—	PF63 8.00				
1999	—	—	—	—	2.50	—
1999	—	PF63 8.00				
2000	—	—	—	—	2.50	—

KM# 175 2 RAND

33.63 g., 0.925 Silver 1.000 oz. ASW, 38.7 mm. **Obv:** National arms **Rev:** Knysna Seahorse **Edge:** Reeded

Date	Mintage	VF20	XF40	MS60	MS63	MS65
1997	3,000	PF63 62.00	PF65 67.00			

KM# 179 2 RAND

33.63 g., 0.925 Silver 1.000 oz. ASW, 38.7 mm. **Obv:** National arms **Rev:** Jackass Penguin **Edge:** Reeded

Date	Mintage	VF20	XF40	MS60	MS63	MS65
1998	Est. 2053	PF63 67.00	PF65 75.00			

KM# 218 2 RAND

33.63 g., 0.925 Silver 1.000 oz. ASW, 38.7 mm. **Obv:** National arms **Rev:** Great white shark **Edge:** Reeded

Date	Mintage	VF20	XF40	MS60	MS63	MS65
1999	1,982	PF63 67.00	PF65 75.00			

KM# 228 2 RAND

5.50 g., Nickel Plated Copper, 23 mm. **Obv:** New national arms **Obv. Legend:** UMZANSTI AFRIKA **Rev:** Greater Kudu, value **Edge:** Segmented reeding

Date	Mintage	VF20	XF40	MS60	MS63	MS65
2000	—	—	0.80	2.00	3.00	—

KM# 240 2 RAND

33.63 g., 0.925 Silver 1.000 oz. ASW, 38.7 mm. **Obv:** National arms **Rev:** Octopus **Edge:** Reeded

Date	Mintage	VF20	XF40	MS60	MS63	MS65
2000	3,344	PF63 70.00	PF65 75.00			

KM# 140 5 RAND

7.00 g., Nickel Plated Copper, 26 mm. **Obv:** Arms with supporters **Obv. Legend:** SOUTH AFRICA - SUD AFRIKA **Rev:** Wildebeest

Date	Mintage	VF20	XF40	MS60	MS63	MS65
1994	45,212,000	—	—	4.50	5.50	—
1994	5,804	PF63 10.00				
1995	41,238,000	—	—	4.50	5.50	—
1995	5,816	PF63 10.00				

KM# 150 5 RAND

7.00 g., Nickel Plated Copper, 26 mm. **Subject:** Presidential Inauguration **Obv:** Arms with supporters **Rev:** Building below value

Date	Mintage	VF20	XF40	MS60	MS63	MS65
1994	10,095,000	—	4.00	6.50	8.00	—
1994	10,000	PF63 12.50				

KM# 166 5 RAND

7.00 g., Nickel Plated Copper, 26 mm. **Obv:** Arms with supporters **Obv. Legend:** ININGIZUMA AFRIKA **Rev:** Wildebeest

Date	Mintage	VF20	XF40	MS60	MS63	MS65
1996	15,435,000	—	—	4.50	—	—
1996	4,827	PF63 10.00				
1997	1,276,000	—	—	4.50	—	—
1997	3,596	PF63 10.00				
1998	—	—	—	4.50	—	—
1998	—	PF63 10.00				
1999	—	—	—	4.50	—	—
1999	—	PF63 10.00				
2000	—	—	—	4.50	—	—

KM# 229 5 RAND

7.00 g., Nickel Plated Copper, 26 mm. **Obv:** New national arms **Obv. Legend:** ININGIZIMU AFRIKA **Rev:** Wildebeest, value **Edge:** Segmented reeding

Date	Mintage	VF20	XF40	MS60	MS63	MS65
2000	—	—	1.20	3.75	5.00	—

KM# 230 5 RAND

7.00 g., Nickel Plated Steel, 26 mm. **Obv:** Head of Nelson Mandela 1/4 right **Obv. Legend:** ININGIZIMU AFRIKA, Zulu legend **Rev:** Wildebeest **Edge:** Reeded and plain sections

Date	Mintage	VF20	XF40	MS60	MS63	MS65
2000	—	7.00	13.00	27.50	49.50	—
2000	—	PF65 150				

GOLD BULLION COINAGE

KM# 105 1/10 KRUGERRAND

3.39 g., 0.917 Gold 0.100 oz. AGW, 16.5 mm. **Obv:** Bust of Paul Kruger left **Obv. Legend:** SUID-AFRIKA - SOUTH AFRICA **Rev:** Springbok walking right divides date **Edge:** Reeded **Note:** 180 edge serrations for uncirculated, 220 serrations for proof

Date	Mintage	VF20	XF40	MS60	MS63	MS65
1980	856,915	—	—	—	147	172
1980	60	PF67 2,500				
1981	1,313,522	—	—	—	147	172
1981	7,500	PF65 185	PF67 210			
1982	1,053,539	—	—	—	147	172
1982	11,270	PF65 185	PF67 210			
1983	495,445	—	—	—	147	172
1983	12,075	PF65 185	PF67 210			
1984	885,250	—	—	—	147	172
1984	13,020	PF65 185	PF67 210			
1985	275,548	—	—	—	147	172
1985	6,700	PF65 185	PF67 210			
1986	87,000	—	—	—	147	172
1986	8,612	PF65 185	PF67 210			
1987	53,400	—	—	—	147	172
1987	4,939	PF65 185	PF67 210			
1987 GRC	1,126	PF67 400				
1988	87,433	—	—	—	147	172
1988	1,913	PF65 185	PF67 210			
1988 GRC	949	PF67 400				
1989	—	—	—	—	147	172
1989	2,939	PF65 185	PF67 210			
1989 GRC	377	PF67 1,000				
1990	9,500	—	—	—	147	172
1990	2,363	PF65 185	PF67 210			
1990 GRC	1,096	PF67 285				
1991	82,273	—	—	—	147	172
1991	3,098	PF65 185	PF67 210			
1991 GRC	426	PF67 285				
1992	1,789	PF65 185	PF67 210			
1993	53,535	—	—	—	147	172
1993	3,811	PF65 185	PF67 210			
1994	85,753	—	—	—	147	172
1994	2,215	PF65 185	PF67 210			
1995	24,788	—	—	—	147	172
1995	1,612	PF65 185	PF67 210			
1996	8,945	—	—	—	147	172
1996	2,891	PF65 185	PF67 210			
1997	19,496	—	—	—	147	172
1997	2,440	PF65 185	PF67 210			
1997	30	PF67 350				
Note: 30th Anniversary of Krugerrand privy mark						
1998	15,452	—	—	—	147	172
1998	1,799	PF65 185	PF67 210			
1999	28,643	—	—	—	147	172
1999	—	PF65 185	PF67 210			
2000	64,759	—	—	—	147	172
2000	4,603	PF65 185	PF67 210			

KM# 106 1/4 KRUGERRAND

8.48 g., 0.917 Gold 0.2501 oz. AGW, 22 mm. **Obv:** Bust of Paul Kruger left **Obv. Legend:** SUID-AFRIKA - SOUTH AFRICA **Rev:** Springbok bounding right divides date **Edge:** Reeded **Note:** 180 edge serrations for uncirculated, 220 serrations for proof

Date	Mintage	VF20	XF40	MS60	MS63	MS65
1980	533,818	—	—	—	350	—
1980	60	PF67 3,000				
1981	718,928	—	—	—	350	400
1981	7,500	PF65 430	PF67 495			
1982	1,259,898	—	—	—	350	400
1982	11,270	PF65 430	PF67 495			
1983	51,612	—	—	—	350	400
1983	12,075	PF65 430	PF67 495			
1984	489,351	—	—	—	350	400
1984	13,020	PF65 430	PF67 495			
1985	587,193	—	—	—	350	400
1985	6,700	PF65 430	PF67 495			
1986	8,613	PF65 430	PF67 495			

Date	Mintage	VF20	XF40	MS60	MS63	MS65
1987	4,929	PF65 430	PF67 495			
1987 GRC	1,121	PF67 550				
1988	5,946	—	—	—	350	400
1988	2,027	PF65 430	PF67 495			
1988 GRC	835	PF67 550				
1989	5,943	—	—	—	350	400
1989	2,998	PF65 430	PF67 495			
1989 GRC	318	PF67 1,400				
1990	1,084	PF65 430	PF67 495			
1990 GRC	1,066	PF65 430	PF67 495			
1991	1,200	PF65 430	PF67 495			
1991 GRC	426	PF67 550				
1992	1,629	PF65 430	PF67 495			
1993	3,061	PF65 430	PF67 495			
1994	38,747	—	—	—	350	400
1994	1,874	PF65 430	PF67 495			
1995	12,865	—	—	—	350	400
1995	1,095	PF65 430	PF67 495			
1996	1,853	PF65 430	PF67 495			
1997	1,440	PF67 3,250				
1997	30	PF67 650				
Note: 30th Anniversary of Krugerrand privy mark						
1998	3,937	—	—	—	350	400
1998	1,701	PF65 430	PF67 495			
1999	34,844	—	—	—	350	400
1999	1,990	PF65 430	PF67 495			
2000	30,282	—	—	—	350	400
2000	3,600	PF65 430	PF67 495			

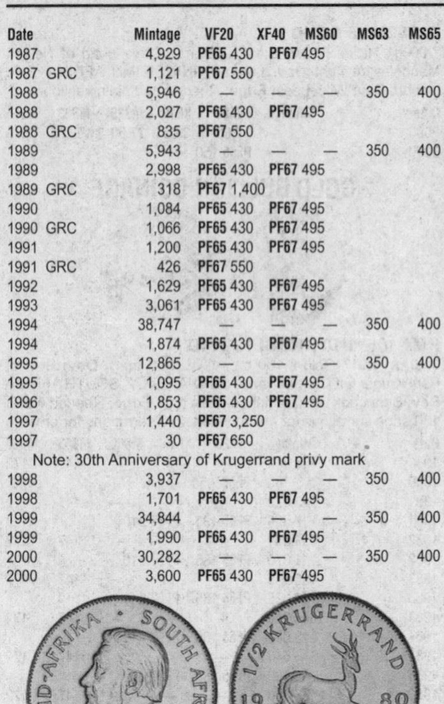

KM# 107 1/2 KRUGERRAND

16.97 g., 0.917 Gold 0.5002 oz. AGW, 27 mm. **Obv:** Bust of Paul Kruger left **Obv. Legend:** SUID-AFRIKA • SOUTH AFRICA **Rev:** Springbok walking right divides date **Edge:** Reeded **Note:** 180 edge serrations for uncirculated, 220 serrations for proof

Date	Mintage	VF20	XF40	MS60	MS63	MS65
1980	374,313	—	—	—	680	770
1980	60	PF67 3,500				
1981	169,014	—	—	—	680	770
1981	9,000	PF65 830	PF67 960			
1982	416,390	—	—	—	680	770
1982	13,000	PF65 830	PF67 960			
1983	46,805	—	—	—	680	770
1983	13,600	PF65 830	PF67 960			
1984	176,760	—	—	—	680	770
1984	9,900	PF65 830	PF67 960			
1985	97,689	—	—	—	680	770
1985	5,945	PF65 830	PF67 960			
1986	8,002	PF65 830	PF67 960			
1987	4,203	PF65 830	PF67 960			
1987 GRC	1,186	PF65 830	PF67 960			
1988	5,454	—	—	—	680	770
1988	2,062	PF65 830	PF67 960			
1988 GRC	1,026	PF65 830	PF67 960			
1989	4,980	—	—	—	680	770
1989	3,328	PF65 830	PF67 960			
1989 GRC	399	PF67 1,500				
1990	1,784	PF65 830	PF67 960			
1990 GRC	1,066	PF65 830	PF67 960			
1991	3,033	PF65 830	PF67 960			
1991 GRC	426	PF65 830	PF67 960			
1992	1,501	PF65 830	PF67 960			
1993	10,800	—	—	—	680	770
1993	2,439	PF65 830	PF67 960			
1994	15,910	—	—	—	680	770
1994	2,146	PF65 830	PF67 960			
1995	10,417	—	—	—	680	770
1995	1,012	PF65 830	PF67 960			
1996	3,311	—	—	—	680	770
1996	1,788	PF65 830	PF67 960			
1997	10,598	—	—	—	680	770
1997	2,030	PF65 830	PF67 960			
1997	30	PF65 830	PF67 960			
Note: 30th Anniversary of Krugerrand privy mark						
1998	1,303	PF65 830	PF67 960			
1999	23,971	—	—	—	680	770
1999	1,924	PF65 830	PF67 960			
2000	23,851	—	—	—	680	770
2000	3,453	PF65 830	PF67 960			

KM# 73 KRUGERRAND

33.93 g., 0.917 Gold 1.0003 oz. AGW, 32.7 mm. **Obv:** Bust of Paul Kruger left **Obv. Legend:** SUID — AFRIKA • SOUTH AFRICA **Rev:** Springbok walking right divides date **Edge:** Reeded **Note:** 180 edge serrations for uncirculated, 220 serrations for proof

Date	Mintage	VF20	XF40	MS60	MS63	MS65
1967	40,000	—	—	—	1,350	1,475
1967	10,000	PF65 1,600	PF67 1,850			
1968	20,000	—	—	—	1,350	1,475
1968	8,956	PF65 1,600	PF67 1,850			
1968	1,044	PF65 1,600	PF67 1,850			
Note: Frosted bust and frosted reverse						
1969	20,000	—	—	—	1,350	1,475
1969	10,000	PF65 1,600	PF67 1,850			
1970	211,018	—	—	—	1,350	1,475
1970	10,000	PF65 1,600	PF67 1,850			
1971	550,200	—	—	—	1,350	1,475
1971	6,000	PF65 1,600	PF67 1,850			
1972	553,700	—	—	—	1,350	1,475
1972	6,625	PF65 1,600	PF67 1,850			
1973	859,300	—	—	—	1,350	1,475
1973	10,000	PF65 1,600	PF67 1,850			
1974	3,203,000	—	—	—	1,350	1,475
1974	6,352	PF65 1,600	PF67 1,850			
1975	4,803,925	—	—	—	1,350	1,475
1975	5,600	PF65 1,600	PF67 1,850			
1976	3,004,945	—	—	—	1,350	1,475
1976	6,600	PF65 1,600	PF67 1,850			
1977	3,331,344	—	—	—	1,350	1,475
Note: 188 serrations on edge						
1977	Inc. above	—	—	—	1,350	1,475
Note: 220 serrations on edge						
1977	8,500	PF65 1,600	PF67 1,850			
Note: 188 serrations on edge						
1977	Inc. above	PF65 1,600	PF67 1,850			
Note: 220 serrations on edge						
1978	6,012,293	—	—	—	1,350	1,475
1978	10,000	PF65 1,600	PF67 1,850			
1979	4,940,755	—	—	—	1,350	1,475
1979	11,800	PF65 1,600	PF67 1,850			
1980	3,049,396	—	—	—	1,350	1,475
1980	12,000	PF65 1,600	PF67 1,850			
1981	3,185,827	—	—	—	1,350	1,475
1981	12,900	PF65 1,600	PF67 1,850			
1982	2,668,506	—	—	—	1,350	1,475
1982	16,960	PF65 1,600	PF67 1,850			
1983	3,349,061	—	—	—	1,350	1,475
1983	19,100	PF65 1,600	PF67 1,850			
1984	2,055,689	—	—	—	1,350	1,475
1984	14,000	PF65 1,600	PF67 1,850			
1985	864,995	—	—	—	1,350	1,475
1985	10,224	PF65 1,600	PF67 1,850			
1986	21,040	PF65 1,600	PF67 1,850			
1987	19,798	—	—	—	1,350	1,475
1987	10,196	PF65 1,600	PF67 1,850			
1987 GRC	1,160	PF65 1,600	PF67 1,850			
1988	614,673	—	—	—	1,350	1,475
1988	3,854	PF65 1,600	PF67 1,850			
1988 GRC	1,220	PF65 1,600	PF67 1,850			
1989	194,319	—	—	—	1,350	1,475
1989	4,083	PF65 1,600	PF67 1,850			
1989 GRC	987	PF65 1,600	PF67 1,850			
1990	391,393	—	—	—	1,350	1,475
1990	1,966	PF65 1,600	PF67 1,850			
1990 GRC	1,066	PF65 1,600	PF67 1,850			
1991	283,184	—	—	—	1,350	1,475
1991	1,755	PF65 1,600	PF67 1,850			
1991 GRC	426	PF65 1,600	PF67 1,850			
1992	1,803	—	—	—	1,350	1,475
1992	2,067	PF65 1,600	PF67 1,850			
1993	162,340	—	—	—	1,350	1,475
1993	3,963	PF65 1,600	PF67 1,850			
1994	129,530	—	—	—	1,350	1,475
1994	1,761	PF65 1,600	PF67 1,850			
1995	58,630	—	—	—	1,350	1,475
1995	1,678	PF65 1,600	PF67 1,850			
1996	9,874	—	—	—	1,350	1,475
1996	2,188	PF65 1,600	PF67 1,850			
1997	1,663	PF65 1,600	PF67 1,850			
1997 SS	72	PF67 2,000				
1997	30	PF67 2,250				
Note: 30th Anniversary of Krugerrand privy mark						
1998	7,097	—	—	—	1,350	1,475
1998	1,179	PF65 1,600	PF67 1,850			
1999	17,051	—	—	—	1,350	1,475

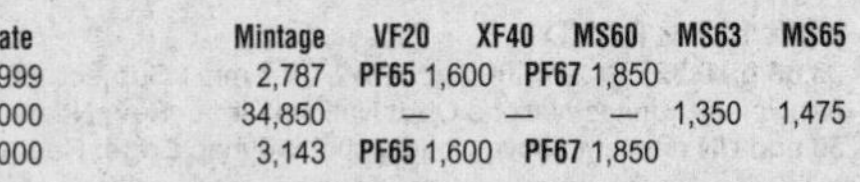

Date	Mintage	VF20	XF40	MS60	MS63	MS65
1999	2,787	PF65 1,600	PF67 1,850			
2000	34,850	—	—	—	1,350	1,475
2000	3,143	PF65 1,600	PF67 1,850			

KM# 118 OUNCE

33.93 g., 0.917 Gold 1.0003 oz. AGW, 32.7 mm. **Subject:** 75th Anniversary of Parliament **Obv:** Crossed Parliamentary maces divide lion and shield **Rev:** Parliament building **Edge:** Reeded

Date	Mintage	VF20	XF40	MS60	MS63	MS65
1985	3,019	PF65 1,600	PF67 1,850			

SILVER BULLION NATURA COINAGE

KM# 234 5 CENTS

8.46 g., 0.925 Silver 0.2515 oz. ASW, 26.7 mm. **Series:** Wildlife - Predator **Obv:** Lion's head 3/4 right **Rev:** Lions, value **Edge:** Reeded

Date	Mintage	VF20	XF40	MS60	MS63	MS65
2000	2,158	PF65 40.00				

KM# 235 10 CENTS

16.86 g., 0.925 Silver 0.5015 oz. ASW, 32.7 mm. **Series:** Wildlife - Predator **Obv:** Lion's head 3/4 right **Rev:** Lions, value **Edge:** Reeded

Date	Mintage	VF20	XF40	MS60	MS63	MS65
2000	2,139	PF65 65.00				

KM# 236 20 CENTS

33.73 g., 0.925 Silver 1.003 oz. ASW, 38.3 mm. **Series:** Wildlife - Predator **Obv:** Lion's head 3/4 right **Rev:** Lions, value **Edge:** Reeded

Date	Mintage	VF20	XF40	MS60	MS63	MS65
2000	2,270	PF65 85.00				

KM# 237 50 CENTS

76.40 g., 0.925 Silver 2.2722 oz. ASW, 50 mm. **Series:** Wildlife - Predator **Obv:** Lion's head 3/4 right **Rev:** Lion, value **Edge:** Reeded

Date	Mintage	VF20	XF40	MS60	MS63	MS65
2000	2,122	PF65 115				

GOLD BULLION NATURA COINAGE

KM# 189 1/10 OUNCE

3.11 g., 0.999 Gold 0.0999 oz. AGW, 16.5 mm. **Series:** Natura **Obv:** Lion's head right **Rev:** Male and female lions drinking **Edge:** Reeded **Note:** Matte finish restrikes exist used in jewelry.

Date	Mintage	VF20	XF40	MS60	MS63	MS65
1994	6,660	PF67 200				

KM# 195 1/10 OUNCE

3.11 g., 0.999 Gold 0.0999 oz. AGW, 16.5 mm. **Series:** Natura **Obv:** Rhinoceros walking facing **Rev:** Rhinocerous drinking **Edge:** Reeded **Note:** 222 pieces used in jewelry and matte finish restrikes exist also used in jewelry.

Date	Mintage	VF20	XF40	MS60	MS63	MS65
1995	2,834	PF67 200				

KM# 201 1/10 OUNCE

3.11 g., 0.999 Gold 0.0999 oz. AGW, 16.5 mm. **Series:** Natura **Obv:** Elephant's head **Rev:** Elephant walking carrying uprooted tree **Edge:** Reeded

Date	Mintage	VF20	XF40	MS60	MS63	MS65
1996	9,014	PF67 200				

KM# 207 1/10 OUNCE

3.11 g., 0.999 Gold 0.0999 oz. AGW, 16.5 mm. **Series:** Natura **Obv:** Buffalo's head **Rev:** Buffalo drinking water **Edge:** Reeded **Note:** Matte finish restrikes exist used in jewelry.

Date	Mintage	VF20	XF40	MS60	MS63	MS65
1997	3,590	PF67 200				

KM# 213 1/10 OUNCE

3.11 g., 0.999 Gold 0.0999 oz. AGW, 16.5 mm. **Series:** Natura **Obv:** Leopard's head **Rev:** Leopard drinking water **Edge:** Reeded

Date	Mintage	VF20	XF40	MS60	MS63	MS65
1998	4,405	PF67 200				

KM# 252.1 1/10 OUNCE

3.11 g., 0.9999 Gold 0.100 oz. AGW, 16.5 mm. **Series:** Natura **Obv:** Greater Kudu's head **Rev:** Kudu herd drinking **Edge:** Reeded

Date	Mintage	VF20	XF40	MS60	MS63	MS65
1999	4,930	PF67 200				

KM# 252.2 1/10 OUNCE
3.11 g., 0.9999 Gold 0.100 oz. AGW, 16.5 mm. **Series:** Natura **Subject:** President Mbeki's Inauguration **Obv:** Greater Kudu's head **Rev:** Kudu herd drinking **Rev. Inscription:** INAUGURATION 1999 **Edge:** Reeded

Date	Mintage	VF20	XF40	MS60	MS63	MS65
1999	600	PF67 275				

KM# 258 1/10 OUNCE
3.11 g., 0.9999 Gold 0.100 oz. AGW, 16.5 mm. **Series:** Natura **Obv:** Sable bull's head **Rev:** Sable drinking **Edge:** Reeded

Date	Mintage	VF20	XF40	MS60	MS63	MS65
2000	3,782	PF67 200				

KM# 190 1/4 OUNCE
7.78 g., 0.9999 Gold 0.250 oz. AGW, 22 mm. **Series:** Natura **Obv:** Lion's head right **Rev:** Family of lions at a kill **Edge:** Reeded

Date	Mintage	VF20	XF40	MS60	MS63	MS65
1994	4,159	PF67 450				

KM# 196 1/4 OUNCE
7.78 g., 0.9999 Gold 0.250 oz. AGW, 22 mm. **Series:** Natura **Obv:** Rhinoceros walking facing **Rev:** Rhinoceros standing in bush field **Edge:** Reeded

Date	Mintage	VF20	XF40	MS60	MS63	MS65
1995	1,752	PF67 450				

KM# 202 1/4 OUNCE
7.78 g., 0.9999 Gold 0.250 oz. AGW, 22 mm. **Series:** Natura **Obv:** Elephant's head **Rev:** Mother and baby elephants walking 3/4 right **Edge:** Reeded

Date	Mintage	VF20	XF40	MS60	MS63	MS65
1996	3,740	PF67 450				

KM# 208 1/4 OUNCE
7.78 g., 0.9999 Gold 0.250 oz. AGW, 22 mm. **Series:** Natura **Obv:** Buffalo's head **Rev:** Buffalo family resting **Edge:** Reeded

Date	Mintage	VF20	XF40	MS60	MS63	MS65
1997	2,164	PF67 450				

KM# 214 1/4 OUNCE
7.78 g., 0.9999 Gold 0.250 oz. AGW, 22 mm. **Series:** Natura **Obv:** Leopard's head **Rev:** Leopard mother and cub playing **Edge:** Reeded

Date	Mintage	VF20	XF40	MS60	MS63	MS65
1998	2,752	PF67 450				

KM# 253 1/4 OUNCE
7.78 g., 0.9999 Gold 0.250 oz. AGW, 22 mm. **Series:** Natura **Obv:** Kudu's head **Rev:** Two Kudu jousting **Edge:** Reeded

Date	Mintage	VF20	XF40	MS60	MS63	MS65
1999	3,019	PF67 450				

KM# 259 1/4 OUNCE
7.78 g., 0.9999 Gold 0.250 oz. AGW, 22 mm. **Series:** Natura **Obv:** Sable bull's head **Rev:** Two Sable bulls facing off **Edge:** Reeded

Date	Mintage	VF20	XF40	MS60	MS63	MS65
2000	2,128	PF67 450				

KM# 191 1/2 OUNCE
15.55 g., 0.9999 Gold 0.500 oz. AGW, 27 mm. **Series:** Natura **Obv:** Lion's head right **Rev:** Two lionesses attacking a bull Kudu **Edge:** Reeded

Date	Mintage	VF20	XF40	MS60	MS63	MS65
1994	3,999	PF67 850				

KM# 197 1/2 OUNCE
15.55 g., 0.9999 Gold 0.500 oz. AGW, 27 mm. **Series:** Natura **Obv:** Rhinoceros walking facing **Rev:** Mother rhinocerous and offspring grazing in the veld **Edge:** Reeded

Date	Mintage	VF20	XF40	MS60	MS63	MS65
1995	1,551	PF67 850				

KM# 203 1/2 OUNCE
15.55 g., 0.9999 Gold 0.500 oz. AGW, 27 mm. **Series:** Natura **Obv:** Elephant' head **Rev:** Two elephants drinking water **Edge:** Reeded

Date	Mintage	VF20	XF40	MS60	MS63	MS65
1996	3,457	PF67 850				

KM# 209 1/2 OUNCE
15.55 g., 0.9999 Gold 0.500 oz. AGW, 27 mm. **Series:** Natura **Obv:** Buffalo's head **Rev:** Herd of buffalo moving through veld **Edge:** Reeded

Date	Mintage	VF20	XF40	MS60	MS63	MS65
1997	1,912	PF67 850				

KM# 215 1/2 OUNCE
15.55 g., 0.9999 Gold 0.500 oz. AGW, 27 mm. **Series:** Natura **Obv:** Leopard's head **Rev:** Leopard in tree eating it's prey **Edge:** Reeded

Date	Mintage	VF20	XF40	MS60	MS63	MS65
1998	2,257	PF67 850				

KM# 254 1/2 OUNCE
15.55 g., 0.999 Gold 0.4995 oz. AGW, 27 mm. **Series:** Natura **Obv:** Greater Kudu's head **Rev:** Kudu attacked by lioness **Edge:** Reeded

Date	Mintage	VF20	XF40	MS60	MS63	MS65
1999	2,787	PF67 850				

KM# 260 1/2 OUNCE
15.55 g., 0.9999 Gold 0.500 oz. AGW, 27 mm. **Series:** Natura **Obv:** Sable bull's head **Rev:** Sable family resting **Edge:** Reeded

Date	Mintage	VF20	XF40	MS60	MS63	MS65
2000	1,964	PF67 850				

KM# 192 OUNCE
31.11 g., 0.9999 Gold 1.000 oz. AGW, 32.69 mm. **Series:** Natura **Obv:** Lion's head right **Rev:** Family of lions **Edge:** Reeded

Date	Mintage	VF20	XF40	MS60	MS63	MS65
1994	2,902	PF67 1,650				
1994 PTA ZOO	775	PF67 2,500				

KM# 198 OUNCE
31.11 g., 0.9999 Gold 1.000 oz. AGW, 32.69 mm. **Series:** Natura **Obv:** Rhinoceros walking facing **Rev:** Two rhinoceros grazing in the veld **Edge:** Reeded

Date	Mintage	VF20	XF40	MS60	MS63	MS65
1995	1,800	PF67 1,650				
1995 Hluhuwe	350	PF67 3,000				

KM# 204 OUNCE
31.11 g., 0.9999 Gold 1.000 oz. AGW, 32.69 mm. **Series:** Natura **Obv:** Elephant's head **Rev:** Four elephants drinking at river **Edge:** Reeded **Note:** CW/e logo - CW monogram on elephant.

Date	Mintage	VF20	XF40	MS60	MS63	MS65
1996	4,472	PF67 1,650				
1996 CW/e logo	300	PF67 3,250				

KM# 210 OUNCE
31.11 g., 0.9999 Gold 1.000 oz. AGW, 32.69 mm. **Series:** Natura **Obv:** Buffalo's head **Rev:** Buffalo defending itself from attacking lioness **Edge:** Reeded **Note:** SS - Sabi Sabi

Date	Mintage	VF20	XF40	MS60	MS63	MS65
1997	2,472	PF67 1,650				
1997 SS	220	PF67 3,500				

KM# 216 OUNCE
31.11 g., 0.9999 Gold 1.000 oz. AGW, 32.69 mm. **Series:** Natura **Obv:** Leopard's head **Rev:** Leopard resting on tree branch **Edge:** Reeded **Note:** "L" - Londo Lozi

Date	Mintage	VF20	XF40	MS60	MS63	MS65
1998	2,645	PF67 1,650				
1998 L	300	PF67 3,000				

KM# 255 OUNCE
31.11 g., 0.9999 Gold 1.000 oz. AGW, 32.69 mm. **Series:** Natura **Obv:** Greater Kudu's head **Rev:** Kudu eating tree leaves **Edge:** Reeded **Note:** SS - Sabi Sabi

Date	Mintage	VF20	XF40	MS60	MS63	MS65
1999	2,682	PF67 1,650				
1999 SS	247	PF67 3,500				

KM# 261 OUNCE
31.11 g., 0.9999 Gold 1.000 oz. AGW, 32.69 mm. **Series:** Natura **Obv:** Sable bull's head Left **Rev:** Sable bull's head 3/4 right **Edge:** Reeded

Date	Mintage	VF20	XF40	MS60	MS63	MS65
2000	1,514	PF67 1,650				
2000 PTA ZOO	591	PF67 3,000				

GOLD BULLION CULTURE COINAGE

KM# 182 RAND
3.11 g., 0.9999 Gold 0.100 oz. AGW, 16.5 mm. **Subject:** 30th Anniversary - First Heart Transplant **Obv:** National arms **Obv. Legend:** SOUTH AFRICA **Rev:** Doctor working on stylized heart **Edge:** Reeded

Date	Mintage	VF20	XF40	MS60	MS63	MS65
1997	1,000	PF65 175	PF67 200			

KM# 178 RAND
3.11 g., 0.9999 Gold 0.100 oz. AGW, 16.5 mm. **Series:** Cultural **Subject:** San Tribe **Obv:** National arms **Obv. Legend:** SOUTH AFRICA **Rev:** Tribesman hunting in Kalahari desert **Edge:** Reeded

Date	Mintage	VF20	XF40	MS60	MS63	MS65
1998	559	PF67 275				

KM# 219 RAND
3.11 g., 0.9999 Gold 0.100 oz. AGW, 16.5 mm. **Series:** Cultural **Obv:** National arms **Obv. Legend:** ININGIZIMU AFRIKA / SOUTH AFRICA **Rev:** Zulu warrior **Edge:** Reeded

Date	Mintage	VF20	XF40	MS60	MS63	MS65
1999	664	PF67 265				

KM# 239 RAND
3.11 g., 0.9999 Gold 0.100 oz. AGW, 16.5 mm. **Series:** Cultural **Obv:** National arms **Obv. Legend:** UMZANTSI AFRIKA / SOUTH AFRICA **Rev:** Three Xhosa tribe members **Edge:** Reeded

Date	Mintage	VF20	XF40	MS60	MS63	MS65
2000	564	PF67 275				

KM# 378 RAND
3.11 g., 0.9999 Gold 0.100 oz. AGW, 16.5 mm. **Series:** Cultural **Obv:** New national arms **Obv. Legend:** UMZANTSI AFRIKA - SOUTH AFRICA **Rev:** Three Xhosa tribe members **Edge:** Reeded

Date	Mintage	VF20	XF40	MS60	MS63	MS65
2000	395	PF67 285				

KM# 183 2 RAND
7.00 g., 0.9999 Gold 0.225 oz. AGW, 22 mm. **Subject:** Early Man **Obv:** Natinal arms **Rev:** Australopithecus Africanus - walking at left, skull at lower right **Edge:** Reeded

Date	Mintage	VF20	XF40	MS60	MS63	MS65
1997	1,000	PF67 450				

KM# 180 2 RAND
7.78 g., 0.9999 Gold 0.250 oz. AGW, 22 mm. **Obv:** National arms **Rev:** Coelacanth fish and fossil **Edge:** Reeded

Date	Mintage	VF20	XF40	MS60	MS63	MS65
1998	386	PF67 500				

KM# 220 2 RAND
7.78 g., 0.9999 Gold 0.250 oz. AGW, 22 mm. **Obv:** National arms **Rev:** Thrinaxodon dinosaur **Edge:** Reeded

Date	Mintage	VF20	XF40	MS60	MS63	MS65
1999	292	PF67 550				

KM# 241 2 RAND
7.78 g., 0.9999 Gold 0.250 oz. AGW, 22 mm. **Obv:** National arms **Rev:** "Little Foot" skeleton find **Edge:** Reeded

Date	Mintage	VF20	XF40	MS60	MS63	MS65
2000	394	PF67 500				

GOLD BULLION PROTEA COINAGE

KM# 184 OUNCE
31.11 g., 0.9999 Gold 1.000 oz. AGW, 32.7 mm. **Subject:** Presidential Inauguration **Obv:** National arms **Rev:** Union buildings in Pretoria **Edge:** Reeded

Date	Mintage	VF20	XF40	MS60	MS63	MS65
1994	1,742	PF67 1,850				

KM# 185 OUNCE
31.11 g., 0.9999 Gold 1.000 oz. AGW, 32.69 mm. **Subject:** Rugby World Cup **Obv:** National arms **Rev:** Three players running **Edge:** Reeded

Date	Mintage	VF20	XF40	MS60	MS63	MS65
1995	406	PF67 1,850				

KM# 131 1/10 PROTEA
3.39 g., 0.917 Gold 0.0999 oz. AGW, 16.5 mm. **Subject:** 100th Anniversary of Johannesburg **Obv:** Protea flower **Rev:** Miner, mine shaft tower with modern skyline in background **Edge:** Reeded

Date	Mintage	VF20	XF40	MS60	MS63	MS65
1986	5,212	PF67 200				

KM# 123 1/10 PROTEA
3.39 g., 0.917 Gold 0.0999 oz. AGW, 16.5 mm. **Subject:** 400th

Anniversary Bartolomeu Dias Discovery of Cape **Obv:** Protea plant **Rev:** Compass at left, caravel and map of Africa and southern Europe at right **Edge:** Reeded

Date	Mintage	VF20	XF40	MS60	MS63	MS65
1988	134	—	—	—	—	—
1988	2,199	PF67 200				

KM# 126 1/10 PROTEA

3.39 g., 0.917 Gold 0.0999 oz. AGW, 16.5 mm. **Subject:** 300th Anniversary of Huguenots **Obv:** Protea flowers **Rev:** Descending dove and design divide dates below small cross, all within circle **Edge:** Reeded

Date	Mintage	VF20	XF40	MS60	MS63	MS65
1988	90	—	—	—	—	—
1988	2,060	PF67 200				

KM# 129 1/10 PROTEA

3.39 g., 0.917 Gold 0.0999 oz. AGW, 16.5 mm. **Subject:** The Great Trek **Obv:** Protea flower **Rev:** Stylized wheel and arrow design **Edge:** Reeded

Date	Mintage	VF20	XF40	MS60	MS63	MS65
1988	—	—	—	—	—	—
1988	2,999	PF67 200				

KM# 171 1/10 PROTEA

3.39 g., 0.917 Gold 0.0999 oz. AGW, 16.5 mm. **Subject:** South African Nursing Schools **Obv:** Protea Flower **Rev:** Aladdin lamp divides dates within cross **Rev. Legend:** VERPLEGING PROTEA NURSING **Edge:** Reeded

Date	Mintage	VF20	XF40	MS60	MS63	MS65
1991	3,950	PF67 200				

KM# 144 1/10 PROTEA

3.39 g., 0.917 Gold 0.0999 oz. AGW, 16.5 mm. **Subject:** Coinage Centennial **Obv:** Protea flower **Rev:** 4 assorted coin designs **Rev. Legend:** SOLI DEO GLORIA **Edge:** Reeded

Date	Mintage	VF20	XF40	MS60	MS63	MS65
1992	2,503	PF67 200				

KM# 172 1/10 PROTEA

3.39 g., 0.917 Gold 0.0999 oz. AGW, 16.5 mm. **Subject:** 200 Years of Banking **Obv:** Protea flower **Rev:** 2 coins, stack of coins, Reserve Bank building, lion's head **Rev. Legend:** BANKWESE BANKING **Edge:** Reeded **Note:** 828 pieces used in jewelry.

Date	Mintage	VF20	XF40	MS60	MS63	MS65
1993	5,064	PF67 200				

KM# 187 1/10 PROTEA

3.39 g., 0.917 Gold 0,0999 oz. AGW, 16.5 mm. **Subject:** Conservation **Obv:** Protea flower **Rev:** Outlined map with big 5 animal heads **Rev. Legend:** BEWARING PROTEA CONSERVATION **Edge:** Reeded **Note:** 342 pieces used in jewelry.

Date	Mintage	VF20	XF40	MS60	MS63	MS65
1994	1,905	PF67 200				

KM# 193.1 1/10 PROTEA

3.39 g., 0.917 Gold 0.0999 oz. AGW, 16.5 mm. **Subject:** Centennial Delagoabay Railways **Obv:** Protea flower **Rev:** Train passing through NZASM tunnel, filled window and door in cab of locomotive **Edge:** Reeded

Date	Mintage	VF20	XF40	MS60	MS63	MS65
1995	Inc. below	PF67 200				

KM# 199 1/10 PROTEA

3.39 g., 0.917 Gold 0.0999 oz. AGW, 16.5 mm. **Subject:** Constitution **Obv:** Protea flower **Rev:** Hand writing in open book **Edge:** Reeded

Date	Mintage	VF20	XF40	MS60	MS63	MS65
1996	1,292	PF67 200				

KM# 205 1/10 PROTEA

3.39 g., 0.917 Gold 0.0999 oz. AGW, 16.5 mm. **Subject:** Women of South Africa **Obv:** Protea flower **Rev:** Partial woman's head at left, South African countryside, Mother Earth flowing into Sister Moon at right **Edge:** Reeded

Date	Mintage	VF20	XF40	MS60	MS63	MS65
1997	792	PF67 225				

KM# 193.2 1/10 PROTEA

3.39 g., 0.917 Gold 0.0999 oz. AGW, 16.5 mm. **Subject:** Centennial Delagoabay Railways **Obv:** Protea flower **Rev:** Train passing through NZASM tunnel. open window and door in locomotive cab **Edge:** Reeded **Note:** 222 pieces used in jewelry

Date	Mintage	VF20	XF40	MS60	MS63	MS65
1998	1,217	PF67 200				

KM# 211 1/10 PROTEA

3.39 g., 0.917 Gold 0.0999 oz. AGW, 16.5 mm. **Subject:** Year of the Child **Obv:** Protea flower **Rev:** Life's puzzle **Edge:** Reeded

Date	Mintage	VF20	XF40	MS60	MS63	MS65
1998	568	PF67 225				

KM# 250.1 1/10 PROTEA

3.11 g., 0.9999 Gold 0.100 oz. AGW, 16.5 mm. **Obv:** Protea flower **Rev:** Gold miner horizontal drilling **Edge:** Reeded **Note:** With initials "P B" above drill at lower right.

Date	Mintage	VF20	XF40	MS60	MS63	MS65
1999	461	PF67 225				

KM# 250.2 1/10 PROTEA

3.11 g., 0.9999 Gold 0.100 oz. AGW, 16.5 mm. **Obv:** Protea flower **Rev:** Gold miner horizontal drilling **Edge:** Reeded **Note:** Without initials "P B" above drill at lower right.

Date	Mintage	VF20	XF40	MS60	MS63	MS65
1999	Inc. above	PF67 225				

KM# 256 1/10 PROTEA

3.11 g., 0.9999 Gold 0.100 oz. AGW, 16.5 mm. **Subject:** Wine Industry **Obv:** Protea flower **Rev:** Cape Dutch farmstead **Rev. Legend:** PROTEA **Edge:** Reeded

Date	Mintage	VF20	XF40	MS60	MS63	MS65
2000	444	PF67 225				

KM# 121 PROTEA

33.93 g., 0.917 Gold 1.0003 oz. AGW, 32.69 mm. **Subject:** 100th Anniversary of Johannesburg **Obv:** Protea flower **Rev:** Miner, mine shaft tower with modern skyline in background **Edge:** Reeded

Date	Mintage	VF20	XF40	MS60	MS63	MS65
1986	4,701	PF67 1,650				

KM# 124.1 PROTEA

33.93 g., 0.917 Gold 1.0004 oz. AGW, 32.69 mm. **Subject:** 400th Anniversary Bartolomeu Discovery of Cape **Obv:** Protea plant **Rev:** Compass at left, caravel and map of Africa and southern Europe at right **Edge:** Reeded **Note:** ID Protea struck for Mossel Bat festival.

Date	Mintage	VF20	XF40	MS60	MS63	MS65
1988	Est. 160	PF67 1,650				

KM# 124.2 PROTEA

33.93 g., 0.917 Gold 1.0003 oz. AGW, 32.69 mm. **Subject:** 400th Anniversary Bartolomeu Dias Discovery of Cape **Obv:** Protea plant **Rev:** Compass at left, caravel and map of Africa and modified southern Europe at right **Edge:** Reeded

Date	Mintage	VF20	XF40	MS60	MS63	MS65
1988	26	—	—	—	—	—
1988	3,776	PF67 1,650				

KM# 127 PROTEA

33.93 g., 0.917 Gold 1.0003 oz. AGW, 32.69 mm. **Subject:** 300th Anniversary of Huguenots **Obv:** Protea flowers **Rev:** Descending dove and design divide dates below small cross, all within circle **Edge:** Reeded

Date	Mintage	VF20	XF40	MS60	MS63	MS65
1988	20	—	—	—	—	—
1988	3,391	PF67 1,650				

KM# 130 PROTEA

33.93 g., 0.917 Gold 1.0003 oz. AGW, 32.69 mm. **Subject:** The Great Trek **Obv:** Protea flower **Rev:** Wheel and arrow design **Edge:** Reeded

Date	Mintage	VF20	XF40	MS60	MS63	MS65
1988	—	—	—	—	—	—
1988	2,956	PF67 1,650				

KM# 186 PROTEA

33.93 g., 0.917 Gold 1.0003 oz. AGW, 32.69 mm. **Subject:** South Africa Nursing Schools **Obv:** Protea flower **Rev:** Alladin lamp divides dates within cross **Rev. Legend:** VERPLEGING PROTEA NURSING **Edge:** Reeded

Date	Mintage	VF20	XF40	MS60	MS63	MS65
1991	3,004	PF67 1,650				

KM# 146 PROTEA

33.93 g., 0.917 Gold 1.0003 oz. AGW, 32.69 mm. **Subject:** Coinage Centennial **Obv:** Protea flower **Rev:** 4 assorted coin designs **Rev. Legend:** SOLI DEO GLORIA **Edge:** Reeded

Date	Mintage	VF20	XF40	MS60	MS63	MS65
1992	1,752	PF67 1,650				

KM# 173 PROTEA

33.93 g., 0.917 Gold 1.0003 oz. AGW, 32.69 mm. **Subject:** 200 Years of Banking **Obv:** Protea flower **Rev:** 2 coins, stack of coins, Reserve Bank building, lion's head **Rev. Legend:** BANKWESE BANKING **Edge:** Reeded

Date	Mintage	VF20	XF40	MS60	MS63	MS65
1993	2,032	PF67 1,650				
1993 GRC	500	PF67 1,750				

KM# 188 PROTEA

33.93 g., 0.917 Gold 1.0003 oz. AGW, 32.69 mm. **Subject:** Conservation **Obv:** Protea flower **Rev:** Outlined map with big 5 animal heads **Rev. Legend:** BEWARING PROTEA CONSERVATION **Edge:** Reeded

Date	Mintage	VF20	XF40	MS60	MS63	MS65
1994	1,187	PF67 1,750				
1994 PTA ZOO	660	PF67 1,750				

KM# 194.1 PROTEA

33.93 g., 0.917 Gold 1.0003 oz. AGW, 32.69 mm. **Subject:** Centennial Delagoabay Railways **Obv:** Protea flower **Rev:** Train passing through NZASM tunnel, filled window and door in locomotive cab **Edge:** Reeded

Date	Mintage	VF20	XF40	MS60	MS63	MS65
1995	Inc. below	PF67 1,750				

KM# 194.2 PROTEA

33.93 g., 0.917 Gold 1.0003 oz. AGW, 32.69 mm. **Subject:** Centennial Delagoabay Railways **Obv:** Protea flower **Rev:** Train passing through NZASM tunnel, open window and door in locomotive cab **Edge:** Reeded

Date	Mintage	VF20	XF40	MS60	MS63	MS65
1995	694	PF67 1,750				

KM# 200 PROTEA

33.93 g., 0.917 Gold 1.0003 oz. AGW, 32.69 mm. **Subject:** Constitution **Obv:** Protea flower **Rev:** Hand writing in open book **Edge:** Reeded

Date	Mintage	VF20	XF40	MS60	MS63	MS65
1996	987	PF67 1,750				

KM# 206 PROTEA

33.93 g., 0.917 Gold 1.0003 oz. AGW, 32.69 mm. **Subject:** Women of South Africa **Obv:** Protea flower **Rev:** Partial woman's head at left, South Africa countryside, Mother Earth, Flowing into Sister Moon at right **Edge:** Reeded

Date	Mintage	VF20	XF40	MS60	MS63	MS65
1997	351	PF67 1,750				

KM# 212 PROTEA

33.93 g., 0.917 Gold 1.0003 oz. AGW, 32.69 mm. **Subject:** Year of the Child **Obv:** Protea flower **Rev:** Life's puzzle **Edge:** Reeded

Date	Mintage	VF20	XF40	MS60	MS63	MS65
1998	298	PF67 1,750				

KM# 251 PROTEA

31.11 g., 0.9999 Gold 1.000 oz. AGW, 32.69 mm. **Obv:** Protea flower **Rev:** Gold miner horizontal drilling **Edge:** Reeded

Date	Mintage	VF20	XF40	MS60	MS63	MS65
1999	253	**PF67** 1,750				
1999 GRC	198	**PF67** 1,750				

KM# 257 PROTEA

31.11 g., 0.9999 Gold 1.000 oz. AGW, 32.69 mm. **Subject:** Wine Industry **Obv:** Protea flower **Rev:** Woman carrying basket of grapes at right, Table Mountain in background **Rev. Legend:** PROTEA **Edge:** Reeded

Date	Mintage	VF20	XF40	MS60	MS63	MS65
2000	330	**PF67** 1,750				
2000 CW	52	**PF67** 3,000				
2000 WM	100	**PF67** 2,000				

PATTERNS

Including off metal strikes

KM#	Date	Mintage	Identification	Mkt Val
Pn1	1925	—	1/4 Penny. Lead.	—
Pn3	1942	—	1/4 Penny. Bronze. Smaller head of George VI.	—

TRIAL STRIKES

KM#	Date	Mintage	Identification	Mkt Val
TS1	1925	—	2 Shilling 6 Pence. Lead. Uniface. 2s6d.	—

MINT SETS

KM#	Date	Mintage	Identification	Issue Price	Mkt Val
MS1	1967 (7)	50,000	KM#65.1-70.1, 72.1	7.50	20.00
MS2	1967 (7)	50,000	KM#65.2-70.2, 72.2	7.50	20.00
MS3	1968 (7)	50,000	KM#71.1, 74.1-79.1	7.50	22.50
MS4	1968 (7)	50,000	KM#71.2, 74.2-79.2	7.50	25.00
MS5	1969 (7)	7,500	KM#65.1-70.1, 80.1	7.50	50.00
MS6	1969 (7)	7,500	KM#65.2-70.2, 80.2	7.50	50.00
MS7	1970 (8)	16,000	KM#81-88	7.50	30.00
MS8	1971 (8)	20,000	KM#81-88	7.50	22.50
MS9	1972 (8)	20,000	KM#81-88	7.50	22.50
MS10	1973 (8)	20,000	KM#81-88	7.50	25.00
MS11	1974 (8)	20,000	KM#81-87, 89	7.50	22.50
MS12	1975 (8)	20,000	KM#81-88	7.50	20.00
MS13	1976 (8)	20,000	KM#88, 90-96	5.65	22.50
MS14	1977 (8)	20,000	KM#81-87, 88a	—	12.50
MS15	1978 (8)	20,000	KM#81-87, 88a	—	12.50
MS16	1979 (8)	20,000	KM#97-104	—	25.00
MS17	1980 (7)	20,000	KM#82-87, 88a	—	12.50
MS18	1981 (7)	10,000	KM#82-87, 88a	—	12.50
MS19	1982 (7)	10,000	KM#109-115	—	25.00
MS20	1983 (7)	23,000	KM#82-87, 88a	—	8.00
MS21	1984 (7)	13,875	KM#82-87, 88a	—	10.00
MS22	1985 (7)	10,200	KM#82-87, 117	—	17.50
MS23	1986 (7)	9,100	KM#82-87, 88a	—	12.00
MS24	1987 (7)	7,642	KM#82-87, 88a	—	12.00
MS25	1988 (7)	6,250	KM#82-87, 88a	—	25.00
MS26	1989 (7)	13,000	KM#82-87, 88a	—	15.00
MS27	1990 (8)	12,000	KM#132-137, 139, 148	—	30.00
MS28	1991 (8)	15,000	KM#132-139	—	30.00
MSA29	1992 (8)	15,000	KM#132-139	—	30.00
MS29	1993 (8)	11,000	KM#132-139	—	30.00
MS30	1994 (9)	6,786	KM#132-140	—	35.00
MS31	1995 (9)	8,477	KM#132-140 Plastic holder	—	35.00
MS32	1995 (9)	—	KM#132-140 Card-board holder	—	30.00
MS33	1996 (9)	12,000	KM#158-166	12.50	15.00
MS34	1997 (9)	7,515	KM#159-166, 170	—	30.00
MS35	1998 (9)	—	KM#159-166, 170	—	30.00
MS36	1999 (9)	10,000	KM#159-166, 170	19.50	30.00
MS37	2000 (9)	—	KM#159-166, 170	—	30.00

PROOF SETS

KM#	Date	Mintage	Identification	Issue Price	Mkt Val
PS1	1923 (10)	655	KM#12.1-17.1, 18, 19.1, 20-21	—	4,900
PS2	1923 (8)	747	KM#12.1-17.1, 18, 19.1	—	1,000
PS3	1926 (6)	3	KM#12.2, 14-2-17.2, 19.2	—	33,500
PS4	1930 (8)	14	KM#12.2-17.2, 18, 19.2	—	8,000
PS5	1930 (8)	—	KM#12.2 (dated 1928), 13.2-17.2, 18, 19.2	—	15,000
PS6	1931 (8)	62	KM#12.3-17.3, 19.3, 22	—	10,600
PS7	1932 (8)	12	KM#12.3-17.3, 19.3, 22	—	10,250
PS8	1933 (8)	20	KM#12.3-17.3, 19.3, 22	—	13,000
PS9	1934 (8)	24	KM#12.3-17.3, 19.3, 22	—	11,750
PS10	1935 (8)	20	KM#12.3-17.3, 19.3, 22	—	11,000
PS11	1936 (8)	40	KM#12.3-17.3, 19.3, 22	—	6,000
PS12	1937 (8)	116	KM#23-30	—	800
PS13	1938 (8)	44	KM#23-30	—	4,500
PS14	1939 (8)	30	KM#23-30	—	11,300
PS15	1943 (8)	104	KM#23-30	—	750
PS16	1944 (8)	150	KM#23-30	—	675
PS17	1945 (8)	150	KM#23-30	—	650
PS18	1946 (8)	150	KM#23-30	—	725
PS19	1947 (8)	2,600	KM#23-31	—	300
PS20	1948 (9)	1,120	KM#32.1, 33, 34.1-40.1	—	330
PS21	1949 (9)	800	KM#32.1, 33, 34.1-40.1	—	525
PS22	1950 (9)	500	KM#32.1, 33, 34.1-40.1	—	525
PS23	1951 (9)	2,000	KM#32.2, 33, 34.2-40.2	—	210
PS24	1952 (11)	12,000	KM#32.2, 33, 34.2-39.2, 41-43	—	600
PS25	1952 (9)	3,500	KM#32.2, 33, 34.2-39.2, 41	—	70.00
PS26	1953 (11)	3,000	KM#44-54	29.40	600
PS27	1953 (9)	2,000	KM#44-52	4.35	65.00
PS28	1953 (2)	1,000	KM#53-54	25.20	525
PS29	1954 (11)	875	KM#44-54	29.40	620
PS30	1954 (9)	2,275	KM#44-52	4.35	95.00
PS31	1954 (2)	350	KM#53-54	25.20	525
PS32	1955 (11)	600	KM#44-54	29.40	600
PS33	1955 (9)	2,250	KM#44-52	4.35	67.50
PS34	1955 (2)	300	KM#53-54	25.20	530
PS35	1956 (11)	350	KM#44-54	29.40	675
PS36	1956 (9)	1,350	KM#44-52	4.35	75.00
PS37	1956 (2)	158	KM#53-54	25.20	600
PS38	1957 (11)	380	KM#44-54	29.40	650
PS39	1957 (9)	750	KM#44-52	4.35	90.00
PS40	1957 (2)	180	KM#53-54	25.20	575
PS41	1958 (11)	360	KM#44-54	29.40	680
PS42	1958 (9)	625	KM#44-52	4.35	105
PS43	1958 (2)	155	KM#53-54	25.20	575
PS44	1959 (11)	390	KM#44-54	29.40	775
PS45	1959 (9)	560	KM#44-52	4.35	225
PS46	1959 (2)	240	KM#53-54	25.20	550
PS47	1960 (11)	1,500	KM#44-51, 53-55	29.40	580
PS48	1960 (9)	1,860	KM#44-51, 55	4.35	20.00
PS49	1960 (2)	450	KM#53-54	25.20	275
PS50	1961 (9)	3,139	KM#56-64	—	200
PS51	1961 (7)	4,391	KM#56-62	—	20.00
PS52	1961 (2)	793	KM#63-64 BV + 20%	—	—
PS53	1962 (9)	1,544	KM#56-64	—	210
PS54	1962 (7)	2,300	KM#56-62	—	15.00
PS55	1962 (2)	800	KM#63-64 BV+20%	—	—
PS56	1963 (9)	1,500	KM#56-64	—	200
PS57	1963 (7)	2,525	KM#56-62	—	12.00
PS58	1963 (2)	1,008	KM#63-64 BV+20%	—	—
PS59	1964 (9)	3,000	KM#56-64	—	190
PS60	1964 (7)	13,000	KM#56-62	—	10.00
PS61	1964 (2)	1,000	KM#63-64 BV+20%	—	—
PS62	1965 (9)	5,099	KM#63-64, 65.1, 66.2, 67.1, 68.2, 69.1, 70.2, 71.1	23.50	185
PS63	1965 (9)	85	KM#63-64, 65.1-66.2, 67.1, 68.2, 69.1, 70.2, 71.2 V.I.P.	—	1,200
PS64	1965 (7)	19,889	KM#65.1, 66.2, 67.1, 68.2, 69.1, 70.2, 71.1	5.00	12.00
PS65	1965 (2)	925	KM#63-64 BV+20%	18.15	—
PS66	1966 (9)	10,000	KM#63-64, 65.2, 66.1, 67.2, 68.1, 69.2, 70.1, 71.2	24.10	185
PS67	1966 (7)	15,000	KM#65.2, 66.1, 67.2, 68.1, 69.2, 70.1, 71.2	5.00	8.00
PS68	1966 (2)	1,000	KM#63-64 BV+20%	18.15	—
PS69	1967 (9)	10,000	KM#63-64, 65.2, 66.1, 67.2, 68.1, 69.2, 70.1, 72.2	24.10	185
PS70	1967 (7)	15,000	KM#65.2, 66.1, 67.2, 68.1, 69.2, 70.1, 72.2	5.00	8.00
PS71	1967 (2)	1,000	KM#63-64 BV+20%	18.15	—
PS72	1968 (9)	10,000	KM#63-64, 71.1, 74.1, 75.2, 76.1, 77.2, 78.1, 79.2	35.00	185
PS73	1968 (7)	15,000	KM#71.1, 74.1, 75.2, 76.1, 77.2, 78.1, 79.2	16.00	8.00
PS74	1968 (2)	1,000	KM#63-64 BV+20%	28.00	—
PS75	1969 (9)	7,000	KM#63-64, 65.2, 66.1, 67.2, 68.1, 69.2, 70.1, 80.2	34.85	185
PS76	1969 (7)	5,000	KM#65.2, 66.1, 67.2, 68.1, 69.2, 70.1, 80.2	13.95	8.00
PS77	1969 (2)	1,000	KM#63-64 BV+20%	27.85	—
PS78	1970 (10)	6,000	KM#63-64, 81-88	35.05	185
PS79	1970 (8)	4,000	KM#81-88	14.00	9.00
PS80	1970 (2)	1,000	KM#63-64 BV+20%	28.05	—
PS81	1971 (10)	7,000	KM#63-64, 81-88	35.00	185
PS82	1971 (8)	5,000	KM#81-88	14.00	9.00
PS83	1971 (2)	650	KM#63-64 BV+20%	28.00	—
PS84	1972 (10)	6,000	KM#63-64, 81-88	32.80	185
PS85	1972 (8)	4,000	KM#81-88	13.10	9.00
PS86	1972 (2)	1,500	KM#63-64 BV+20%	26.25	—
PS87	1973 (10)	6,850	KM#63-64, 81-88	32.00	185
PS88	1973 (8)	4,000	KM#81-88	12.80	9.00
PS89	1973 (2)	6,088	KM#63-64 BV+20%	25.60	—
PS90	1974 (10)	11,000	KM#63-64, 81-87, 89	52.50	185
PS91	1974 (8)	4,000	KM#81-87, 89	15.00	9.00
PS92	1974 (2)	5,600	KM#63-64 BV+20%	45.00	—
PS93	1975 (10)	12,500	KM#63-64, 81-87, 88	116	185
PS94	1975 (8)	5,500	KM#81-88	14.55	9.00
PS95	1975 (2)	7,000	KM#63-64 BV+20%	101	—
PS96	1976 (10)	14,000	KM#63-64, 88, 90-96	92.00	185
PS97	1976 (8)	7,000	KM#88, 90-96	11.50	9.00
PS98	1976 (2)	8,000	KM#63-64 BV+20%	80.50	—
PS99	1977 (10)	12,000	KM#63-64, 81-88	92.00	185
PS100	1977 (8)	7,000	KM#81-88	11.50	12.00
PS101	1977 (2)	8,000	KM#63-64 BV+20%	80.50	—
PS102	1978 (10)	10,000	KM#63-64, 81-88	—	185
PS103	1978 (8)	7,000	KM#81-88	—	12.00
PS104	1978 (2)	9,000	KM#63-64 BV+20%	—	—
PS105	1979 (10)	10,000	KM#63-64, 97-103, 104a	—	185
PS106	1979 (8)	5,000	KM#88, 97-103	—	22.00
PS107	1979 (2)	10,000	KM#63-64 BV+20%	—	—
PS108	1980 (10)	10,000	KM#63-64, 81-88	—	185
PS109	1980 (8)	5,000	KM#81-88	—	22.00
PS110	1980 (2)	8,000	kM#63-64 BV+20%	—	—
PS111	1980 (2)	8,000	KM#63-64	—	—
PS112	1980 (3)	60	KM#105-107	—	9,000
PS113	1981 (10)	6,000	KM#63-64, 81-88	—	185
PS114	1981 (8)	4,900	KM#81-88	—	22.00
PS115	1981 (2)	6,238	KM#63-64 BV+20%	—	—
PS116	1982 (10)	7,100	KM#63-64, 108-115	—	190
PS117	1982 (8)	4,900	KM#88, 108-114	—	22.00
PS118	1982 (2)	6,930	KM#63-64 BV+20%	—	—
PS119	1983 (10)	7,300	KM#63-64, 81-88	—	185
PS120	1983 (8)	6,835	KM#81-88	—	22.00
PS121	1983 (2)	7,300	KM#63-64 BV+20%	—	—
PS122	1984 (8)	11,250	KM#82-88, 88a	—	15.00
PS123	1985 (8)	9,859	KM#82-87, 116, 117	—	25.00
PS124	1986 (8)	7,000	KM#82-87, 88a, 119	—	25.00
PS125	1986 (2)	428	KM#73, 121 Plus large gold plated Silver #1	—	1,400
PS126	1986 (2)	750	KM#121, 131	—	700
PS127	1986 (3)	500	KM#119, 121, 131	—	725
PS128	1987 (8)	6,781	KM#82-88, 88a	—	25.00
PS129	1987 (4)	750	KM#73, 105-107	—	3,750
PS130	1987 GRC (4)	1,121	KM#73, 105-107	—	3,750
PS131	1988 (8)	7,250	KM#82-88, 88a	—	50.00
PS132	1988 (4)	806	KM#73, 105-107	—	3,500
PS133	1988 GRC (4)	835	KM#73, 105-107	—	3,750
PS134	1988 (3)	3,388	KM#122, 125, 128	—	70.00
PS135	1988 (3)	600	KM#124, 127, 130	—	5,550
PS136	1989 (8)	9,571	KM#82-88, 88a	—	50.00
PS137	1989 (4)	—	KM#73, 105-107	—	3,500
PS138	1989 GRC (4)	318	KM#73, 105-107	—	5,750
PS139	1990 (8)	10,000	KM#132-137, 139, 148	—	70.00
PS140	1990 (4)	—	KM#73, 105-107	—	3,500
PS141	1990 GRC (4)	1,066	KM#73, 105-107	—	3,550
PS142	1991 (8)	12,000	KM#132-139	—	70.00
PSA143	1991 GRC (4)	426	KM#73, 105-107	—	3,600
PS143	1992 (8)	10,000	KM#132-139	—	50.00
PS144	1993 (8)	—	KM#132-139	—	50.00
PS145	1994 (9)	5,804	KM#132-140	—	60.00
PS146	1994 (4)	166	KM#189-192 Wood case	—	4,150
PS147	1994 (4)	1,750	KM#189-192 Velvet case	—	4,150
PS148	1994 (3)	420	KM#167, 187-188	—	2,100
PS149	1995 (9)	5,816	KM#132-140	—	65.00
PS150	1995 (4)	750	KM#73, 105-107	—	3,500
PS151	1995 (4)	—	KM#73, 105-107 Wooden box	—	3,500
PS152	1995 (4)	89	KM#195-198 Wood case	—	4,650
PS153	1995 (4)	926	KM#195-198 Velvet case	—	4,650
PS154	1995 (3)	210	KM#152, 193-194	—	2,100
PS155	1996 (9)	4,827	KM#158-166	30.00	38.00
PS156	1996 (4)	368	KM#201-204, Wood case	—	5,000
PS157	1996 (4)	1,677	KM#201-204 Velvet case	—	5,000
PS158	1996 (3)	346	KM#169, 199-200	—	2,100
PS159	1997 (4)	500	KM#73, 105-107	—	3,700
PS160	1997 (4)	500	KM#207-210 Wood case	—	5,150
PS161	1997 (4)	1,015	KM#207-210 Velvet case	—	5,150
PS162	1997 (3)	144	KM#181, 205-206	—	2,150
PS163	1997 (4)	30	KM#73, 105-107, 30 Year Wine set with privy marks	—	3,700
PS164	1997 (9)	3,596	KM#159-166, 170	—	40.00
PS165	1998 (9)	—	KM#159-166, 170	—	40.00

PS166	1998 (4)	—	KM#213-216 Wood case	—	3,500
PS167	1998 (4)	—	KM#213-216 Velvet case	—	3,500
PS168	1998 (3)	—	KM#177, 211-212	—	2,150
PS169	1999 (9)	6,000	KM#159-166, 170	39.50	40.00
PS191	2000 (4)	236	KM#234-237, wood case	—	325
PS192	2000 (4)	1,140	KM#234-237, velvet lined case	—	310
PS220	1999 (4)	509	KM#252.1, 253-255, prestige	—	1,325
PS221	1999 (4)	1,046	KM#252.1, 253-255, leatherette	—	3,500
PS222	1999 (4)	537	KM#252.1, 253-255, special	—	3,500
PS223	2000 (4)	483	KM#258-261, prestige	—	3,500
PS224	2000 (4)	334	KM#258-261, leatherette	—	3,500

SPECIMEN SETS (SS)

KM#	Date	Mintage	Identification	Issue Price	Mkt Val
SS1	1994 (9)	5,508	KM#132-140	—	25.00
SS2	1995 (9)	4,956	KM#132-140	—	25.00
SS3	1996 (9)	5,766	KM#158-166	19.50	25.00
SS4	1997 (9)	4,236	KM#159-166, 170	—	25.00
SS5	1998 (9)	—	KM#159-166, 170	—	25.00
SS6	1999 (9)	—	KM#159-166, 170	—	25.00

SOUTH ARABIA

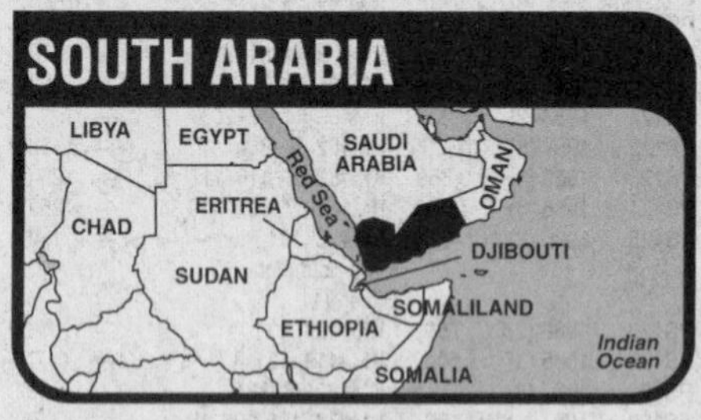

Fifteen of the sixteen Western Protectorate States, the Wahidi State of the Eastern Protectorate, and Aden Colony joined to form the Federation of South Arabia.

In 1959, Britain agreed to prepare South Arabia for full independence, which was achieved on Nov. 30, 1967, at which time South Arabia, including Aden, changed its name to the Peoples Republic of Southern Yemen. On Dec. 1, 1970, following the overthrow of the new government by the National Liberation Front, Southern Yemen changed its name to the Peoples Democratic Republic of Yemen.

TITLE

Al-Junubiya(t) al-Arabiya(t)

MONETARY SYSTEM

1000 Fils = 1 Dinar

FEDERATION

STANDARD COINAGE

KM# 1 FILS

0.60 g., Aluminum, 20 mm. **Obv:** Snowflake design **Rev:** Crossed swords

Date	Mintage	VF20	XF40	MS60	MS63	MS65
1964	10,000,000	0.25	0.35	0.50	0.75	1.00
1964	—	PF65 3.00				

KM# 2 5 FILS

4.50 g., Bronze, 23.1 mm. **Obv:** Snowflake design **Rev:** Crossed swords

Date	Mintage	VF20	XF40	MS60	MS63	MS65
1964	10,000,000	0.25	0.45	0.65	1.00	1.50
1964	—	PF65 4.00				

KM# 3 25 FILS

4.50 g., Copper-Nickel, 21 mm. **Obv:** Snowflake design **Rev:** Sailboat **Edge:** Reeded

Date	Mintage	VF20	XF40	MS60	MS63	MS65
1964	4,000,000	0.35	0.75	1.25	1.50	2.00
1964	—	PF65 5.50				

KM# 4 50 FILS

9.00 g., Copper-Nickel, 27.8 mm. **Obv:** Snowflake design **Rev:** Sailboat **Edge:** Reeded

Date	Mintage	VF20	XF40	MS60	MS63	MS65
1964	6,000,000	0.50	1.00	1.50	2.00	2.50
1964	—	PF65 7.50				

PROOF SETS

KM#	Date	Mintage	Identification	Issue Price	Mkt Val
PS1	1964 (4)	10,500	KM1-4	9.90	20.00

S. GEORGIA & THE S. SANDWICH IS.

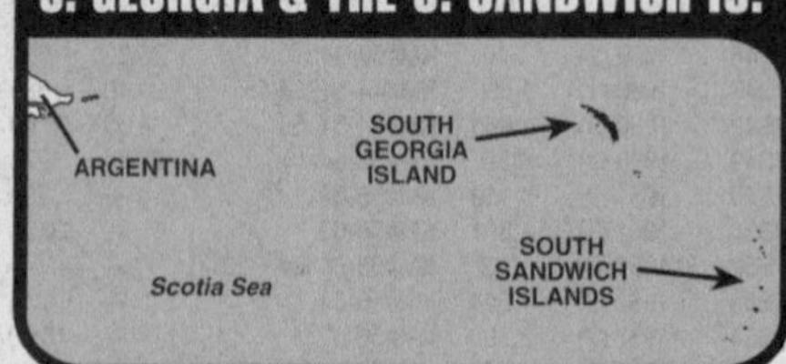

South Georgia and the South Sandwich Islands are a dependency of the Falkland Islands, and located about 800 miles east of them. South Georgia is 1,450 sq. mi. (1,770 sq. km.), and the South Sandwich Islands are 120 sq. mi. (311 sq. km.) Fishing and Antarctic research are the main industries. The islands were claimed for Great Britain in 1775 by Captain James Cook.

RULER

British since 1775

BRITISH OVERSEAS TERRITORY

STANDARD COINAGE

KM# 1 2 POUNDS

28.28 g., Copper-Nickel, 38.61 mm. **Ruler:** Elizabeth II **Subject:** 100th Birthday - Queen Mother **Obv:** Crowned bust of Queen Elizabeth II right **Rev:** Crowned arms with supporters **Edge:** Reeded **Mint:** Pobjoy Mint

Date	Mintage	VF20	XF40	MS60	MS63	MS65
2000 PM	—	—	—	—	7.00	9.00

KM# 1a 2 POUNDS

28.28 g., 0.925 Silver 0.841 oz. ASW, 38.61 mm. **Ruler:** Elizabeth II **Subject:** 100th Birthday - Queen Mother **Obv:** Crowned bust of Queen Elizabeth II right **Rev:** Crowned arms with supporters **Edge:** Reeded **Mint:** Pobjoy Mint

Date	Mintage	VF20	XF40	MS60	MS63	MS65
2000 PM	—	PF65 50.00				

KM# 1a.1 2 POUNDS

28.28 g., 0.925 Silver 0.841 oz. ASW, 38.6 mm. **Ruler:** Elizabeth II **Subject:** Queen Mother **Obv:** Bust with tiara right **Rev:** Crowned arms with supporters with a tiny black sapphire mounted below **Edge:** Reeded **Mint:** Pobjoy Mint

Date	Mintage	VF20	XF40	MS60	MS63	MS65
2000 PM	1,000	PF65 55.00				

KM# 3 2 POUNDS

28.28 g., Copper-Nickel, 38.61 mm. **Ruler:** Elizabeth II **Obv:** Crowned bust of Queen Elizabeth II right **Rev:** Standing figure on deck of ship within inner circle **Edge:** Reeded **Mint:** Pobjoy Mint

Date	Mintage	VF20	XF40	MS60	MS63	MS65
2000 PM	—	—	—	—	7.00	9.00

KM# 3a 2 POUNDS

28.28 g., 0.925 Silver 0.841 oz. ASW, 38.61 mm. **Ruler:** Elizabeth II **Obv:** Crowned bust of Queen Elizabeth II right **Rev:** Standing figure on the deck of the ship within inner circle **Edge:** Reeded **Mint:** Pobjoy Mint

Date	Mintage	VF20	XF40	MS60	MS63	MS65
2000 PM	—	PF65 45.00				

KM# 4 2 POUNDS

28.28 g., Copper-Nickel, 38.61 mm. **Ruler:** Elizabeth II **Subject:** 225th Anniversary - Possession by Captain Cook **Obv:** Crowned bust of Queen Elizabeth II right **Rev:** Bust right **Mint:** Pobjoy Mint

Date	Mintage	VF20	XF40	MS60	MS63	MS65
2000 PM	—	—	—	—	7.00	9.00

KM# 4a 2 POUNDS

28.28 g., 0.925 Silver 0.841 oz. ASW, 38.61 mm. **Ruler:** Elizabeth II **Subject:** 225th Anniversary - Possession by Captain Cook **Obv:** Crowned bust of Queen Elizabeth II right **Rev:** Bust right **Mint:** Pobjoy Mint

Date	Mintage	VF20	XF40	MS60	MS63	MS65
2000 PM	—	PF65 45.00				

KM# 2.1 20 POUNDS

6.22 g., 0.9999 Gold 0.200 oz. AGW, 22 mm. **Ruler:** Elizabeth II **Subject:** 100th Birthday - Queen Mother **Obv:** Crowned bust of Queen Elizabeth II right **Rev:** Crowned arms with supporters **Edge:** Reeded **Mint:** Pobjoy Mint

Date	Mintage	VF20	XF40	MS60	MS63	MS65
2000 PM	—	PF65 345	PF67 375			

KM# 2.2 20 POUNDS

6.22 g., 0.999 Gold 0.1998 oz. AGW, 22 mm. **Ruler:** Elizabeth II **Subject:** Queen Mother, 100th Birthday **Obv:** Crowned bust of Queen Elizabeth II right **Rev:** Crowned arms with supporters with a tiny black sapphire mounted below **Edge:** Reeded **Mint:** Pobjoy Mint

Date	Mintage	VF20	XF40	MS60	MS63	MS65
2000 PM	1,000	PF65 375	PF67 400			

KM# 5 20 POUNDS
6.22 g., 0.9999 Gold 0.200 oz. AGW, 22 mm. **Ruler:** Elizabeth II **Obv:** Crowned bust of Queen Elizabeth II right **Rev:** Standing figure on the deck of the ship within circle **Edge:** Reeded **Mint:** Pobjoy Mint

Date	Mintage	VF20	XF40	MS60	MS63	MS65
2000 PM	—	PF65 345	PF67 375			

KM# 6 20 POUNDS
6.22 g., 0.9999 Gold 0.200 oz. AGW, 22 mm. **Ruler:** Elizabeth II **Subject:** 225th Anniversary - Possession by Captain Cook **Obv:** Crowned bust of Queen Elizabeth II right **Rev:** Bust right **Mint:** Pobjoy Mint

Date	Mintage	VF20	XF40	MS60	MS63	MS65
2000 PM	—	PF65 345	PF67 375			

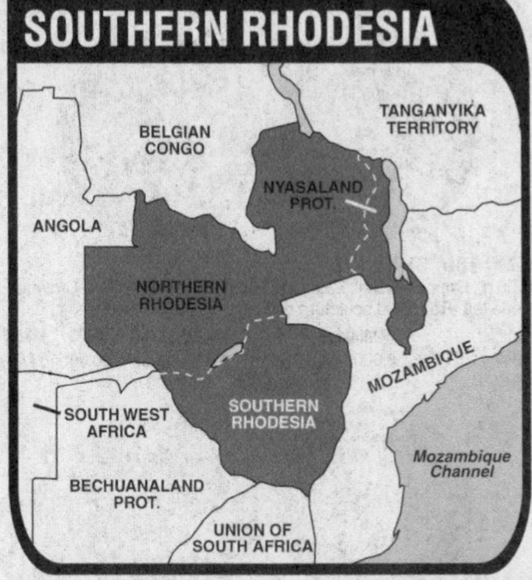

Colonization of Rhodesia began in 1890 when settlers forcibly acquired Shona lands and then Ndebele lands in 1893. It was named as Rhodesia, after Cecil Rhodes who led the build-up of the Colony.

Rhodesia became a self-governing colony under the name of Southern Rhodesia in 1923. Consequent upon later political difficulties and disagreement with the British authorities over common emancipation of the people, a unilateral declaration of independence (UDI) was declared on November 11, 1965.

Following United Nations sanctions against the country, various renamings as Rhodesia and Rhodesia-Zimbabwe, and elections in February 1980, the country became independent on April 18, 1980, as the Republic of Zimbabwe as a member of the Commonwealth of Nations.

RULER
British, until 1966

MONETARY SYSTEM
12 Pence = 1 Shilling
2 Shillings = 1 Florin
5 Shillings = 1 Crown
20 Shillings = 1 Pound

BRITISH COLONY

POUND COINAGE

KM# 6 1/2 PENNY
Copper-Nickel **Ruler:** George V **Obv:** Crowned flower design within circle, hole in center **Rev:** Value written within sprigs, hole in center

Date	Mintage	F12	VF20	XF40	MS60	MS63
1934	240,000	1.00	3.50	15.00	40.00	70.00
1934	—	PF63 300	PF65 500			
1936	240,000	5.00	25.00	60.00	100	150
1936 Proof	—	—	—	—	—	—

KM# 14 1/2 PENNY
Copper-Nickel **Ruler:** George VI **Obv:** Crowned flower design within circle, hole in center **Rev:** Value written within sprigs, hole in center

Date	Mintage	F12	VF20	XF40	MS60	MS63
1938	240,000	0.75	1.75	7.00	20.00	30.00
1938	—	PF63 750	PF65 1,000			
1939	480,000	1.00	2.00	20.00	60.00	85.00
1939 Proof	—	—	—	—	—	—

KM# 14a 1/2 PENNY
Bronze **Ruler:** George VI **Obv:** Crowned flower design within circle, hole in center **Rev:** Value within sprigs, hole in center

Date	Mintage	F12	VF20	XF40	MS60	MS63
1942	480,000	0.60	1.50	9.50	25.00	45.00
1942	—	PF63 700	PF65 900			
1943	960,000	0.35	0.75	1.50	6.50	18.00
1944	960,000	0.35	0.75	1.75	8.00	20.00
1944 Proof	—	—	—	—	—	—

KM# 26 1/2 PENNY
Bronze **Ruler:** George VI **Obv:** Crowned flower design within circle, hole in center **Obv. Legend:** KING GEORGE THE SIXTH **Rev:** Value witten within sprigs, hole in center

Date	Mintage	F12	VF20	XF40	MS60	MS63
1951	480,000	0.75	1.25	2.25	6.50	18.00
1951	—	PF63 850	PF65 1,250			
1952	480,000	0.75	1.25	5.00	10.00	22.00
1952 Proof	—	—	—	—	—	—

KM# 28 1/2 PENNY
Bronze **Ruler:** Elizabeth II **Obv:** Crowned flower design within circle, hole in center **Rev:** Value written within sprigs, hole in center

Date	Mintage	F12	VF20	XF40	MS60	MS63
1954	960,000	0.75	2.00	25.00	65.00	90.00
1954	20	PF63 550	PF65 850			

KM# 7 PENNY
Copper-Nickel **Ruler:** George V **Obv:** Crowned flower design within circle, hole in center **Rev:** Value written within sprigs, hole in center

Date	Mintage	F12	VF20	XF40	MS60	MS63
1934	360,000	0.75	1.50	9.50	25.00	50.00
1934	—	PF63 700	PF65 1,150			
1935	492,000	1.50	15.00	55.00	125	250
1935 Proof	—	—	—	—	—	—
1936	1,044,000	0.60	1.25	10.00	30.00	60.00
1936 Proof	—	—	—	—	—	—

KM# 8 PENNY
6.50 g., Copper-Nickel, 27 mm. **Ruler:** George VI **Obv:** Crowned flower design within circle, hole in center **Rev:** Value written within sprigs, hole in center

Date	Mintage	F12	VF20	XF40	MS60	MS63
1937	908,000	0.60	1.25	9.50	15.00	30.00
1937	—	PF63 500	PF65 800			
1938	240,000	1.50	3.00	20.00	30.00	50.00
1938 Proof	—	—	—	—	—	—
1939	1,284,000	0.45	1.00	16.50	25.00	45.00
1939 Proof	—	—	—	—	—	—
1940	1,080,000	0.45	1.00	16.50	25.00	45.00
1940 Proof	—	—	—	—	—	—
1941	720,000	0.50	1.25	17.50	27.00	48.00
1941 Proof	—	—	—	—	—	—
1942	960,000	0.50	1.25	27.50	40.00	75.00
1942 Proof	—	—	—	—	—	—

KM# 8a PENNY
Bronze **Ruler:** George VI **Obv:** Crowned flower design within circle, hole in center **Rev:** Written value within sprigs, hole in center

Date	Mintage	F12	VF20	XF40	MS60	MS63
1942	480,000	4.00	6.50	30.00	100	200
1942	—	PF63 400	PF65 650			
1943	3,120,000	0.50	0.80	4.50	15.00	30.00
1944	2,400,000	0.50	0.80	6.00	20.00	40.00
1944 Proof	—	—	—	—	—	—
1947	3,600,000	0.75	1.25	6.00	20.00	40.00
1947 Proof	—	—	—	—	—	—

KM# 25 PENNY
Bronze **Ruler:** George VI **Obv:** Crowned flower design within circle, hole in center **Rev:** Value written within sprigs, hole in center

Date	Mintage	F12	VF20	XF40	MS60	MS63
1949	1,440,000	0.50	1.00	8.50	25.00	50.00
1949	—	PF63 400	PF65 650			
1950	720,000	1.00	1.75	17.50	40.00	80.00
1950	—	PF63 400	PF65 650			
1951	4,896,000	0.50	0.75	2.25	10.00	18.00
1951	—	PF63 300	PF65 550			
1952	2,400,000	0.50	0.75	1.50	12.50	25.00
1952 Proof	—	—	—	—	—	—

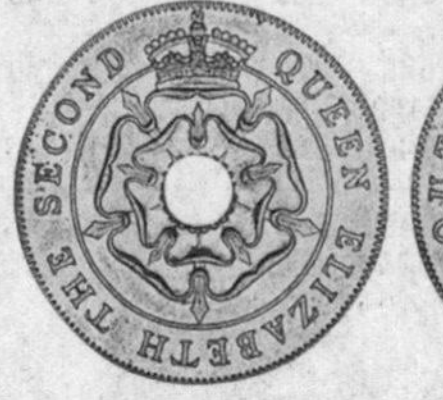

KM# 29 PENNY
Bronze **Ruler:** Elizabeth II **Obv:** Crowned flower design within circle, hole in center **Rev:** Value written within sprigs, hole in center

Date	Mintage	F12	VF20	XF40	MS60	MS63
1954	960,000	4.00	16.50	85.00	250	350
1954	20	PF63 750	PF65 1,000			

KM# 1 3 PENCE
1.41 g., 0.925 Silver 0.0419 oz. ASW, 16 mm. **Ruler:** George V **Obv:** Crowned bust left **Rev:** Three spearheads divide date

Date	Mintage	F12	VF20	XF40	MS60	MS63
1932	688,000	1.75	2.00	12.00	25.00	40.00
1932	—	PF63 200	PF65 325			
1934	628,000	1.75	2.50	25.00	40.00	75.00
1934	—	PF63 300	PF65 500			
1935	840,000	1.75	2.50	20.00	30.00	45.00
1935	—	PF63 200	PF65 325			
1936	1,052,000	1.75	2.50	20.00	30.00	45.00
1936	—	PF63 200	PF65 325			

KM# 9 3 PENCE
1.41 g., 0.925 Silver 0.0419 oz. ASW, 16 mm. **Ruler:** George VI **Obv:** Crowned head left **Rev:** Three spearheads divide date

Date	Mintage	F12	VF20	XF40	MS60	MS63
1937	1,228,000	1.75	2.00	15.00	40.00	60.00
1937	—	PF63 350	PF65 500			

KM# 16 3 PENCE

1.41 g., 0.925 Silver 0.0419 oz. ASW, 16 mm. **Ruler:** George VI **Obv:** Crowned head left **Rev:** Three spearheads divide date

Date	Mintage	F12	VF20	XF40	MS60	MS63
1939	160,000	6.00	10.00	55.00	100	150
1939	—	PF63 500	PF65 800			
1940	1,200,000	1.75	2.50	20.00	35.00	65.00
1940 Proof	—	—	—	—	—	—
1941	600,000	2.50	5.00	22.50	30.00	50.00
1941 Proof	—	—	—	—	—	—
1942	2,000,000	1.75	2.00	12.50	20.00	30.00
1942	—	PF63 450	PF65 750			

KM# 16a 3 PENCE

1.41 g., 0.500 Silver 0.0227 oz. ASW, 16 mm. **Ruler:** George VI **Obv:** Crowned head left **Rev:** Three spearheads divide date **Edge:** Plain

Date	Mintage	F12	VF20	XF40	MS60	MS63
1944	1,600,000	1.00	1.50	22.50	40.00	60.00
1945	800,000	1.00	3.00	25.00	42.00	65.00
1945 Proof	—	—	—	—	—	—
1946	2,400,000	1.00	1.50	12.50	20.00	35.00
1946 Proof	—	—	—	—	—	—

KM# 16b 3 PENCE

1.41 g., Copper-Nickel, 16 mm. **Ruler:** George VI **Obv:** Crowned head left **Rev:** Three spearheads divide date

Date	Mintage	F12	VF20	XF40	MS60	MS63
1947	8,000,000	0.40	0.80	8.00	20.00	—
1947	—	PF63 400	PF65 600			

KM# 20 3 PENCE

1.41 g., Copper-Nickel, 16 mm. **Ruler:** George VI **Obv:** Crowned head left **Rev:** Three spearheads divide date

Date	Mintage	F12	VF20	XF40	MS60	MS63
1948	2,000,000	0.40	2.00	9.50	30.00	45.00
1948 Proof	—	—	—	—	—	—
1949	4,000,000	0.40	2.00	9.00	25.00	40.00
1949	—	PF63 250	PF65 400			
1951	5,600,000	0.40	5.00	25.00	75.00	125
1951 Proof	—	—	—	—	—	—
1952	4,800,000	0.40	5.00	22.50	60.00	110
1952	—	PF63 250	PF65 400			

KM# 2 6 PENCE

2.83 g., 0.925 Silver 0.0842 oz. ASW, 19.41 mm. **Ruler:** George V **Obv:** Crowned bust left **Rev:** Crossed axes divide date and value **Edge:** Reeded

Date	Mintage	F12	VF20	XF40	MS60	MS63
1932	544,000	3.00	8.00	20.00	40.00	75.00
1932	—	PF63 200	PF65 325			
1934	214,000	3.00	10.00	38.00	75.00	125
1935	380,000	3.00	9.50	32.50	45.00	90.00
1935 Proof	—	—	—	—	—	—
1936	675,000	3.00	8.00	25.00	50.00	100
1936 Proof	—	—	—	—	—	—

KM# 10 6 PENCE

2.83 g., 0.925 Silver 0.0842 oz. ASW, 19.41 mm. **Ruler:** George VI **Obv:** Crowned head left **Rev:** Crossed axes divide date and value **Edge:** Reeded

Date	Mintage	F12	VF20	XF40	MS60	MS63
1937	823,000	3.00	9.00	22.50	45.00	75.00
1937	—	PF63 500	PF65 800			

KM# 17 6 PENCE

2.83 g., 0.925 Silver 0.0842 oz. ASW, 19.41 mm. **Ruler:** George VI **Obv:** Crowned head left **Rev:** Crossed axes divide date and value **Edge:** Reeded

Date	Mintage	F12	VF20	XF40	MS60	MS63
1939	200,000	4.00	16.50	90.00	200	300
1939	—	PF63 750	PF65 1,000			
1940	600,000	3.00	9.00	32.50	75.00	150
1940 Proof	—	—	—	—	—	—
1941	300,000	3.00	8.50	25.00	65.00	125
1941 Proof	—	—	—	—	—	—
1942	1,200,000	3.00	7.50	20.00	55.00	120
1942	—	PF63 400	PF65 650			

KM# 17a 6 PENCE

2.83 g., 0.500 Silver 0.0455 oz. ASW, 19.41 mm. **Ruler:** George VI **Obv:** Crowned head left **Rev:** Crossed axes divide date and value **Edge:** Reeded

Date	Mintage	F12	VF20	XF40	MS60	MS63
1944	800,000	1.75	3.50	38.00	90.00	150
1945	400,000	10.00	20.00	60.00	150	300
1945 Proof	—	—	—	—	—	—
1946	1,600,000	1.75	2.50	25.00	60.00	135
1946 Proof	—	—	—	—	—	—

KM# 17b 6 PENCE

2.83 g., Copper-Nickel, 19.41 mm. **Ruler:** George VI **Obv:** Crowned head left **Rev:** Crossed axes divide date and value **Edge:** Reeded

Date	Mintage	F12	VF20	XF40	MS60	MS63
1947	5,000,000	0.50	1.00	10.00	20.00	50.00
1947	—	PF63 400	PF65 600			

KM# 21 6 PENCE

2.83 g., Copper-Nickel, 19.41 mm. **Ruler:** George VI **Obv:** Crowned head left **Rev:** Crossed axes divide date and value **Edge:** Reeded

Date	Mintage	F12	VF20	XF40	MS60	MS63
1948	1,000,000	0.50	1.25	10.00	27.50	50.00
1948 Proof	—	—	—	—	—	—
1949	2,000,000	0.50	5.00	12.50	30.00	60.00
1949	—	PF63 400	PF65 650			
1950	2,000,000	0.50	6.00	16.50	55.00	95.00
1950	—	PF63 400	PF65 650			
1951	2,800,000	0.50	1.00	6.00	27.50	50.00
1951 Proof	—	—	—	—	—	—
1952	1,200,000	0.50	1.50	15.00	45.00	80.00
1952 Proof	—	—	—	—	—	—

KM# 3 SHILLING

5.65 g., 0.925 Silver 0.168 oz. ASW, 23.6 mm. **Ruler:** George V **Obv:** Crowned bust left **Rev:** Bird headdress divides date **Edge:** Reeded

Date	Mintage	F12	VF20	XF40	MS60	MS63
1932	896,000	6.00	12.00	30.00	90.00	175
1932	—	PF63 200	PF65 325			
1934	333,000	6.00	25.00	70.00	175	350
1935	830,000	6.00	15.00	50.00	120	225
1935	—	PF63 350	PF65 500			
1936	1,663,000	6.00	18.50	42.50	115	200
1936 Proof	—	—	—	—	—	—

KM# 11 SHILLING

5.65 g., 0.925 Silver 0.168 oz. ASW, 23.6 mm. **Ruler:** George VI **Obv:** Crowned head left **Rev:** Bird sculpture divides date **Edge:** Reeded

Date	Mintage	F12	VF20	XF40	MS60	MS63
1937	1,700,000	6.00	15.00	38.00	65.00	90.00
1937	—	PF63 500	PF65 800			

KM# 18 SHILLING

5.65 g., 0.925 Silver 0.168 oz. ASW, 23.6 mm. **Ruler:** George VI **Obv:** Crowned head left **Rev:** Bird sculpture divides date **Edge:** Reeded

Date	Mintage	F12	VF20	XF40	MS60	MS63
1939	420,000	7.50	27.50	110	150	275
1939	—	PF63 800	PF65 1,200			
1940	750,000	6.50	22.00	65.00	100	175
1940 Proof	—	—	—	—	—	—
1941	800,000	6.50	20.00	55.00	100	150
1941 Proof	—	—	—	—	—	—
1942	2,100,000	6.00	8.00	18.50	55.00	100
1942	—	PF63 600	PF65 950			

KM# 18a SHILLING

5.65 g., 0.500 Silver 0.0908 oz. ASW, 23.6 mm. **Ruler:** George VI **Obv:** Crowned head left **Rev:** Bird sculpture divides date **Edge:** Reeded

Date	Mintage	F12	VF20	XF40	MS60	MS63
1944	1,600,000	3.50	15.00	45.00	80.00	125
1946	1,700,000	4.50	20.00	60.00	100	150
1946 Proof	—	—	—	—	—	—

KM# 18b SHILLING

5.65 g., Copper-Nickel, 23.6 mm. **Ruler:** George VI **Obv:** Crowned head left **Rev:** Bird sculpture divides date **Edge:** Reeded

Date	Mintage	F12	VF20	XF40	MS60	MS63
1947	8,000,000	0.75	1.50	16.50	40.00	80.00
1947	—	PF63 500	PF65 800			

KM# 22 SHILLING

5.65 g., Copper-Nickel, 23.6 mm. **Ruler:** George VI **Obv:** Crowned head left **Rev:** Bird sculpture divides date **Edge:** Reeded

Date	Mintage	F12	VF20	XF40	MS60	MS63
1948	1,500,000	0.75	1.50	12.00	30.00	60.00
1948 Proof	—	—	—	—	—	—
1949	4,000,000	0.75	5.00	12.50	35.00	65.00
1949	—	PF63 400	PF65 700			
1950	2,000,000	1.00	8.00	22.00	55.00	90.00
1950	—	PF63 600	PF65 900			
1951	3,000,000	0.75	2.50	10.00	20.00	40.00
1951 Proof	—	—	—	—	—	—
1952	2,600,000	0.75	5.00	22.00	55.00	90.00
1952 Proof	—	—	—	—	—	—

KM# 4 2 SHILLINGS

11.31 g., 0.925 Silver 0.3364 oz. ASW, 28.52 mm. **Ruler:** George V **Obv:** Crowned bust left **Rev:** Sable antelope **Edge:** Reeded

Date	Mintage	F12	VF20	XF40	MS60	MS63
1932	498,000	12.50	13.50	37.50	110	200
1932	—	PF63 450	PF65 750			
1934	154,000	12.50	25.00	100	225	425
1935	365,000	12.50	17.00	50.00	120	200
1935 Proof	—	—	—	—	—	—
1936	683,000	12.50	15.00	45.00	120	200
1936 Proof	—	—	—	—	—	—

KM# 12 2 SHILLINGS

11.31 g., 0.925 Silver 0.3364 oz. ASW, 28.52 mm. **Ruler:** George VI **Obv:** Crowned head left **Rev:** Sable antelope **Edge:** Reeded

Date	Mintage	F12	VF20	XF40	MS60	MS63
1937	552,000	12.50	20.00	55.00	100	150
1937	—	PF63 650	PF65 950			

KM# 19 2 SHILLINGS

11.31 g., 0.925 Silver 0.3364 oz. ASW, 28.52 mm. **Ruler:** George VI **Obv:** Crowned head left **Rev:** Sable antelope **Edge:** Reeded

Date	Mintage	F12	VF20	XF40	MS60	MS63
1939	120,000	50.00	135	325	500	750
1939	—	PF63 550	PF65 750			
1940	525,000	12.50	32.50	110	200	300
1940 Proof	—	—	—	—	—	—
1941	400,000	12.50	20.00	125	200	350
1941 Proof	—	—	—	—	—	—
1942	850,000	12.50	13.50	32.50	65.00	100

KM# 19a 2 SHILLINGS

11.31 g., 0.500 Silver 0.1818 oz. ASW, 28.52 mm. **Ruler:** George VI **Obv:** Crowned head left **Rev:** Sable antelope **Edge:** Reeded

Date	Mintage	F12	VF20	XF40	MS60	MS63
1944	1,300,000	7.00	15.00	50.00	100	150
1946	700,000	100	180	280	400	650
1946 Proof	—	—	—	—	—	—

KM# 19b 2 SHILLINGS

11.31 g., Copper-Nickel, 28.52 mm. **Ruler:** George VI **Obv:** Crowned head left **Rev:** Sable antelope **Edge:** Reeded

Date	Mintage	F12	VF20	XF40	MS60	MS63
1947	3,750,000	1.75	4.00	22.50	45.00	90.00
1947	—	PF63 500	PF65 800			

KM# 23 2 SHILLINGS

11.31 g., Copper-Nickel, 28.52 mm. **Ruler:** George VI **Obv:** Crowned head left **Rev:** Sable antelope **Edge:** Reeded

Date	Mintage	F12	VF20	XF40	MS60	MS63
1948	750,000	1.00	3.00	22.50	60.00	110
1948 Proof	—	—	—	—	—	—
1949	2,000,000	1.00	3.00	22.50	80.00	180
1949	—	PF63 450	PF65 700			
1950	1,000,000	1.00	4.00	25.00	115	225
1950	—	PF63 600	PF65 950			
1951	2,600,000	1.00	3.00	12.00	47.00	90.00
1951	—	PF63 700	PF65 1,000			
1952	1,800,000	1.00	3.00	28.00	75.00	175
1952 Proof	—	—	—	—	—	—

KM# 30 2 SHILLINGS

11.31 g., Copper-Nickel, 28.52 mm. **Ruler:** Elizabeth II **Obv:** Laureate bust right **Rev:** Sable antelope **Edge:** Reeded

Date	Mintage	F12	VF20	XF40	MS60	MS63
1954	300,000	25.00	35.00	275	500	900
1954	20	PF63 950	PF65 1,250			

KM# 5 1/2 CROWN

14.14 g., 0.925 Silver 0.4205 oz. ASW, 32.3 mm. **Ruler:** George V **Obv:** Crowned bust left **Rev:** Crowned shield **Edge:** Reeded

Date	Mintage	F12	VF20	XF40	MS60	MS63
1932	634,000	15.50	17.00	35.00	125	200
1932	—	PF63 250	PF65 375			
1934	419,000	15.50	25.00	110	275	450
1934 Proof	—	—	—	—	—	—
1935	512,000	15.50	20.00	60.00	200	300
1935 Proof	—	—	—	—	—	—
1936	518,000	15.50	18.00	50.00	175	260
1936 Proof	—	—	—	—	—	—

KM# 13 1/2 CROWN

14.14 g., 0.925 Silver 0.4205 oz. ASW, 32.3 mm. **Ruler:** George VI **Obv:** Crowned head left **Rev:** Crowned shield **Edge:** Reeded

Date	Mintage	F12	VF20	XF40	MS60	MS63
1937	1,174,000	15.50	20.00	50.00	130	200
1937	—	PF63 550	PF65 850			

KM# 15 1/2 CROWN

14.14 g., 0.925 Silver 0.4205 oz. ASW, 32.3 mm. **Ruler:** George VI **Obv:** Crowned head left **Rev:** Crowned shield **Edge:** Reeded

Date	Mintage	F12	VF20	XF40	MS60	MS63
1938	400,000	15.50	20.00	55.00	150	260
1938 Proof	—	—	—	—	—	—
1939	224,000	15.50	20.00	115	300	550
1939	—	PF63 800	PF65 1,200			
1940	800,000	—	15.50	27.50	80.00	160
1940 Proof	—	—	—	—	—	—
1941	1,240,000	7.75	15.50	25.00	65.00	125
1941 Proof	—	—	—	—	—	—
1942	2,008,000	7.75	15.50	25.00	70.00	140
1942	—	PF63 2,500				

KM# 15a 1/2 CROWN

14.14 g., 0.500 Silver 0.2273 oz. ASW, 32.3 mm. **Ruler:** George VI **Obv:** Crowned head left **Rev:** Crowned shield **Edge:** Reeded

Date	Mintage	F12	VF20	XF40	MS60	MS63
1944	800,000	8.50	9.00	25.00	90.00	165
1946	1,400,000	8.50	10.00	55.00	135	200
1946 Proof	—	—	—	—	—	—

KM# 15b 1/2 CROWN

14.14 g., Copper-Nickel, 32.3 mm. **Ruler:** George VI **Obv:** Crowned head left **Rev:** Crowned shield **Edge:** Reeded

Date	Mintage	F12	VF20	XF40	MS60	MS63
1947	6,000,000	1.25	2.50	5.00	30.00	50.00
1947	—	PF63 850	PF65 1,250			

KM# 24 1/2 CROWN

14.14 g., Copper-Nickel, 32.3 mm. **Ruler:** George VI **Obv:** Crowned head left **Rev:** Crowned shield **Edge:** Reeded

Date	Mintage	F12	VF20	XF40	MS60	MS63
1948	800,000	1.25	2.50	22.00	60.00	100
1948 Proof	—	—	—	—	—	—
1949	1,600,000	1.25	2.50	18.00	65.00	110
1949	—	PF63 550	PF65 950			
1950	1,200,000	1.25	2.50	25.00	75.00	125
1950	—	PF63 550	PF65 950			
1951	3,200,000	1.25	2.50	20.00	50.00	90.00
1951	—	PF63 450	PF65 850			
1952	2,800,000	1.25	2.50	22.50	70.00	100
1952	—	PF63 450	PF65 850			

KM# 31 1/2 CROWN

14.14 g., Copper-Nickel, 32.3 mm. **Ruler:** Elizabeth II **Obv:** Laureate bust right **Rev:** Crowned shield **Edge:** Reeded

Date	Mintage	F12	VF20	XF40	MS60	MS63
1954	1,200,000	8.00	12.50	35.00	95.00	130
1954	20	PF63 750	PF65 1,000			

KM# 27 CROWN

28.28 g., 0.500 Silver 0.4546 oz. ASW, 38.5 mm. **Ruler:** Elizabeth II **Subject:** Birth of Cecil Rhodes Centennial **Obv:** Larueate bust right **Rev:** Cameo flanked by sprigs with ribbon above assorted shields **Edge Lettering:** 1853 OUT OF VISION CAME REALITY 1953 **Note:** Both upright and inverted edge varieties exist.

Date	Mintage	F12	VF20	XF40	MS60	MS63
1953	124,000	16.50	18.00	22.00	50.00	65.00
1953	Inc. above	—	—	—	150	225
Note: No space between CAME and REALITY on edge legend						
1953	1,500	PF63 225	PF65 350			
1953 Matte Proof	—	PF63 550	PF65 850			

TRIAL STRIKES

KM#	Date	Mintage	Identification	Mkt Val
TS1	1932	—	3 Pence. White Metal. Plain. Rev. KM#1.	550
TS2	1932	—	6 Pence. White Metal. Plain. Rev. KM#2.	550
TS3	1932	—	Shilling. White Metal. Plain. Rev. KM#3.	650
TS4	1932	—	Florin. White Metal. Plain. Rev. KM#4.	850
TS5	1932	—	1/2 Crown. White Metal. Plain. Rev. KM#5.	1,150
TS6	1934	—	3 Pence. White Metal. Plain. Rev. KM#1. Thick flan.	550
TS7	1934	—	1/2 Crown. White Metal. Plain. Rev. KM#5. Thick flan.	1,150

PROOF SETS

KM#	Date	Mintage	Identification	Issue Price	Mkt Val
PS1	1932 (5)	496	KM#1-5	—	2,000
PS2	1937 (6)	40	KM#8-13	—	4,000
PS3	1939 (5)	10	KM#15-19	—	9,750
PS4	1953 (2)	3	KM#27 Double set; Rare	—	—
PS5	1954 (4)	20	KM#28-31	—	3,500
PS6	1947 (5)	10	KM#15b-19b	—	5,000

The Spanish State, forming the greater part of the Iberian Peninsula of southwest Europe, has an area of 195,988 sq. mi. (504,714 sq. km.) and a population of 39.4 million including the Balearic and the Canary Islands. Capital: Madrid. The economy is based on agriculture, industry and tourism. Machinery, fruit, vegetables and chemicals are exported.

Discontent against the mother country increased after 1808 as colonists faced new imperialist policies from Napoleon or Spanish liberals. The revolutionary movement was established which resulted in the eventual independence of the Vice-royalties of New Spain, New Granada and Rio de la Plata within 2 decades.

The doomed republic was trapped in a tug-of-war between the right and left wing forces inevitably resulting in the Spanish Civil War of 1936-38. The leftist Republicans were supported by the U.S.S.R. and the International Brigade, which consisted of mainly communist volunteers from all over the western world. The right wing Nationalists were supported by the Fascist governments of Italy and Germany. Under the leadership of Gen. Francisco Franco, the Nationalists emerged victorious and immediately embarked on a program of reconstruction and neutrality as dictated by the new "Caudillo"(leader) Franco.

The monarchy was reconstituted in 1947 under the regency of General Francisco Franco; the king designate to be crowned after Franco's death. Franco died on Nov. 20, 1975. Two days after his passing, Juan Carlos de Borbon, the grandson of Alfonso XIII, was proclaimed King of Spain.

RULERS

Alfonso XIII, 1886-1931
2nd Republic and Civil War, 1931-1939
Francisco Franco, 1939-1947
as Caudillo and regent, 1947-1975
Juan Carlos I, 1975-

NOTE: From 1868 to 1982, two dates may be found on most Spanish coinage. The larger date is the year of authorization and the smaller date incused on the two 6-pointed-stars found on most types is the year of issue. The latter appears in parentheses in these listings.

MINT MARKS

Until 1980

6-pointed star - Madrid
NOTE: Letters after date are initials of mint officials.

After 1982

Crowned M – Madrid

KINGDOM

DECIMAL COINAGE

Peseta System
100 Centimos = 1 Peseta

KM# 726 CENTIMO

Bronze, 15 mm. **Ruler:** Alfonso XIII **Obv:** Head right **Rev:** Crowned shield divides value within beaded circle **Note:** Mint mark: 6-pointed star.

Date	Mintage	F12	VF20	XF40	MS60	MS63
1906 (6) SL-V	7,500,000	0.35	1.00	4.00	7.00	10.00
1906 (6) SM-V	Inc. above	300	500	900	1,200	1,500

KM# 731 CENTIMO

Bronze, 15 mm. **Ruler:** Alfonso XIII **Obv:** Head left **Rev:** Crowned shield divides value within beaded circle **Note:** Mint mark: 6-pointed star.

Date	Mintage	F12	VF20	XF40	MS60	MS63
1911 (1) PC-V	1,462,000	30.00	75.00	125	175	200
1912 (2) PC-V	2,109,000	2.50	4.00	8.00	18.00	25.00
1913 (3) PC-V	1,429,000	5.00	8.00	15.00	25.00	40.00

KM# 722 2 CENTIMOS

Copper, 20 mm. **Ruler:** Alfonso XIII **Obv:** Head right **Rev:** Crowned shield divides value within beaded circle **Note:** Mint mark: 6-pointed star.

Date	Mintage	F12	VF20	XF40	MS60	MS63
1904 (04) SM-V	10,000,000	0.75	2.50	8.00	15.00	20.00
1905 (05) SM-V	5,000,000	0.75	3.50	10.00	25.00	30.00

KM# 732 2 CENTIMOS

Copper, 20 mm. **Ruler:** Alfonso XIII **Obv:** Head left **Rev:** Crowned shield divides value within beaded circle **Note:** Mint mark: 6-pointed star.

Date	Mintage	F12	VF20	XF40	MS60	MS63
1911 (11) PC-V	2,284,000	0.75	2.00	5.00	15.00	20.00
1912 (12) PC-V	5,216,000	0.75	2.00	5.00	17.00	25.00

KM# 740 25 CENTIMOS

7.00 g., Copper-Nickel, 25 mm. **Ruler:** Alfonso XIII **Obv:** Sailing ship **Obv. Legend:** ESPAÑA 1927 **Rev:** Crowned value flanked by sprigs **Edge:** plain

Date	Mintage	F12	VF20	XF40	MS60	MS63
1925 PC-S	8,001,000	2.00	4.00	20.00	60.00	100

KM# 742 25 CENTIMOS

7.00 g., Copper-Nickel, 25.2 mm. **Ruler:** Alfonso XIII **Obv:** Vine entwined on cross, crown and date, hole in center **Rev:** Value above oat sprigs, hole in center

Date	Mintage	F12	VF20	XF40	MS60	MS63
1927 PC-S	12,000,000	0.75	1.00	20.00	60.00	100

KM# 723 50 CENTIMOS

2.50 g., 0.835 Silver 0.0671 oz. ASW **Ruler:** Alfonso XIII **Obv:** Head left **Rev:** Crowned shield flanked by pillars with banner **Note:** Mint mark: 6-pointed star.

Date	Mintage	F12	VF20	XF40	MS60	MS63
1904 (04) SM-V	4,851,000	3.50	6.00	8.00	20.00	30.00
1904 (10) PC-V	1,303,000	3.50	6.00	12.00	27.00	40.00

KM# 730 50 CENTIMOS

2.50 g., 0.835 Silver 0.0671 oz. ASW **Ruler:** Alfonso XIII **Obv:** Head left **Rev:** Crowned shield flanked by pillars with banner **Note:** Mint mark: 6-pointed star.

Date	Mintage	F12	VF20	XF40	MS60	MS63
1910 (10) PC-V	4,526,000	3.00	5.00	10.00	25.00	40.00

KM# 741 50 CENTIMOS

2.50 g., 0.835 Silver 0.0671 oz. ASW **Ruler:** Alfonso XIII **Obv:** Head left **Rev:** Crowned shield within wreath

Date	Mintage	F12	VF20	XF40	MS60	MS63
1926 PC-S	4,000,000	3.00	4.50	7.00	13.50	20.00

KM# 706 PESETA

5.00 g., 0.835 Silver 0.1342 oz. ASW **Ruler:** Alfonso XIII **Obv:** Child's head left **Obv. Legend:** ALFONSO XIII. **Rev:** Crowned arms, pillars, value below **Rev. Legend:** REYCONST. **Note:** Mint mark: 6-pointed star. Prices are for coins with full right star dates. Partial right star dates sell for less. Examples with no visable right star date have limited collector appeal.

Date	Mintage	F12	VF20	XF40	MS60	MS63
1901 (01) SM-V	8,449,000	6.00	16.00	55.00	125	175
1902 (02) SM-V	2,599,000	25.00	50.00	100	250	350

KM# 721 PESETA

5.00 g., 0.835 Silver 0.1342 oz. ASW **Ruler:** Alfonso XIII **Obv:** Head left **Rev:** Crowned shield flanked by pillars with banner **Note:** Mint mark 6-pointed star.

Date	Mintage	F12	VF20	XF40	MS60	MS63
1903 (03) SM-V	10,602,000	5.00	14.00	45.00	100	125
1904 (04) SM-V	5,294,000	6.00	15.00	50.00	125	150
1905 (05) SM-V	492,000	75.00	175	700	1,100	1,500

KM# 725 2 PESETAS

10.00 g., 0.835 Silver 0.2685 oz. ASW **Ruler:** Alfonso XIII **Obv:** Head left **Rev:** Crowned shield flanked by pillars with banner **Note:** Mint mark: 6-pointed star.

Date	Mintage	F12	VF20	XF40	MS60	MS63
1905 (05) SM-V	3,589,000	10.00	18.00	30.00	50.00	65.00

KM# 724 20 PESETAS
6.45 g., 0.900 Gold 0.1867 oz. AGW **Obv:** Head right **Rev:** Crowned and mantled shield **Note:** Mint mark: 6-pointed star.

Date	Mintage	F12	VF20	XF40	MS60	MS63
1904 (04) SM-V	3,814	1,500	2,500	3,200	5,000	—

REPUBLIC

1931 - 1939

KM# 752 5 CENTIMOS
Iron, 20 mm. **Obv:** Head left **Rev:** Value and date within wreath

Date	Mintage	F12	VF20	XF40	MS60	MS63
1937	10,000,000	0.35	1.00	2.00	10.00	15.00

Note: Prices given are for rust-free examples

KM# 756 10 CENTIMOS
Iron, 20 mm. **Obv:** Crowned shield **Rev:** Value and date within wreath

Date	Mintage	F12	VF20	XF40	MS60	MS63
1938	1,000	—	—	—	3,000	—

Note: This coin was never released into circulation. Known only in mint condition

KM# 751 25 CENTIMOS
Copper-Nickel **Obv:** Bust right holding sprig, hole in center **Rev:** Value above oat sprig and gear, hole in center

Date	Mintage	F12	VF20	XF40	MS60	MS63
1934	12,272,000	0.30	1.00	3.50	25.00	40.00

KM# 753 25 CENTIMOS
7.11 g., Copper-Nickel, 25 mm. **Obv:** Inscription, date and arrow design, hole in center **Rev:** Crowned shield, value and sprig, hole in center

Date	Mintage	F12	VF20	XF40	MS60	MS63
1937	42,000,000	0.35	0.75	1.50	5.00	8.00

Note: This coin was issued by way of decree April 5, 1938, by the Governmant in Burgos. Franco and the Nationalist forces controlled the majority of Spain by this point in time

Date	Mintage	
1937	—	PF63 500

KM# 757 25 CENTIMOS
Copper, 22 mm. **Obv:** Chain links around center hole **Rev:** Value and center hole divide sprigs

Date	Mintage	F12	VF20	XF40	MS60	MS63
1938	45,500,000	0.75	1.50	10.00	20.00	25.00

KM# 754.1 50 CENTIMOS
5.80 g., Copper, 23 mm. **Obv:** Seated figure holding sprig **Rev:** Value within beaded circle **Note:** Mint mark: 6-pointed star. Several varieties exist. Coins without star dates are considered dateless.

Date	Mintage	F12	VF20	XF40	MS60	MS63
1937 (34)	50,000,000	0.50	1.00	5.00	30.00	50.00
1937 (36)	1,000,000	0.65	1.50	7.00	20.00	35.00

KM# 754.2 50 CENTIMOS
Copper, 23 mm. **Obv:** Seated allegorical figure left **Rev:** Border of rectangles **Note:** Mint mark: 6-pointed star.

Date	Mintage	F12	VF20	XF40	MS60	MS63
1937 (36)	Inc. above	3.00	5.00	10.00	30.00	50.00

KM# 750 PESETA
5.00 g., 0.835 Silver 0.1342 oz. ASW, 23 mm. **Obv:** Seated figure holding sprig **Rev:** Crowned shield flanked by pillars with banner **Note:** Mint mark: 6-pointed star.

Date	Mintage	F12	VF20	XF40	MS60	MS63
1933 (3-4)	2,000,000	5.50	16.00	25.00	35.00	45.00

Note: Rotated reverse varieties exist, with values greatly increasing by the degree of rotation.

KM# 755 PESETA
Brass, 22 mm. **Obv:** Head left **Rev:** Value and grapes on vine

Date	Mintage	F12	VF20	XF40	MS60	MS63
1937	50,000,000	0.50	1.00	2.50	7.50	10.00

NATIONALIST GOVERNMENT

1939 - 1947

KM# 765 5 CENTIMOS
Aluminum, 20 mm. **Obv:** Armored figure on rearing horse **Rev:** Crowned shield within eagle flanked by pillars with banner **Note:** Mint mark: 6-pointed star. To realize the values below all Unc. and BU coins must have full strike including letters.

Date	Mintage	F12	VF20	XF40	MS60	MS63
1940	175,000,000	1.50	5.00	15.00	60.00	75.00
1941	202,107,000	1.00	2.50	5.00	15.00	25.00
1945	221,500,000	—	1.00	3.00	9.00	15.00
1953	31,573,000	15.00	30.00	45.00	70.00	90.00

KM# 766 10 CENTIMOS
1.84 g., Aluminum, 23 mm. **Obv:** Armored figure on rearing horse **Rev:** Crowned shield within eagle flanked by pillars with banner **Edge:** Coarse reeding **Note:** Varieties exist. To realize the values below all Unc. and BU coins must have full strike including letters.

Date	Mintage	F12	VF20	XF40	MS60	MS63
1940 PLUS	225,000,000	1.00	3.50	15.00	50.00	75.00
1940 PLVS	Inc. above	20.00	40.00	80.00	200	300
1941 PLUS	247,981,000	0.50	2.00	5.00	20.00	25.00
1941 PLVS	Inc. above	10.00	20.00	45.00	100	150
1945	250,000,000	—	0.60	3.00	10.00	20.00
1953	865,850,000	—	0.35	2.50	5.00	10.00

KM# 767 PESETA
3.50 g., Aluminum-Bronze, 21 mm. **Obv:** Crowned shield within eagle flanked by pillars with banner **Rev:** Value in center of design **Edge:** Reeded **Note:** To realize the values below all Unc. and BU coins must have full strike including letters.

Date	Mintage	F12	VF20	XF40	MS60	MS63
1944	150,000,000	—	0.45	5.00	35.00	45.00

KINGDOM

1949 - Present

KM# 790 10 CENTIMOS
0.70 g., Aluminum, 18 mm. **Ruler:** Francisco Franco, caudillo **Obv:** Head right **Rev:** Value within designed wreath **Edge:** Reeded

Date	Mintage	F12	VF20	XF40	MS60	MS63
1959	900,000,000	—	—	—	0.75	1.00
1959	101,000	PF63 3.00				

KM# 776 50 CENTIMOS
4.10 g., Copper-Nickel, 21 mm. **Ruler:** Caudillo and regent **Obv:** Anchor, date and part of ship's wheel, center hole **Rev:** Value, five shields around center hole, arrows pointing downward below **Edge:** Plain **Note:** Mint mark: 6-pointed star.

Date	Mintage	F12	VF20	XF40	MS60	MS63
1949 (51)	990,000	5.00	10.00	15.00	30.00	50.00

Note: Minting date "51" in incused star

KM# 777 50 CENTIMOS
4.10 g., Copper-Nickel, 21 mm. **Ruler:** Francisco Franco, caudillo **Obv:** Anchor, date and part of ship's wheel, center hole **Rev:** Value, five shields around center hole, arrows pointing upward below **Edge:** Plain **Note:** Mint mark: 6-pointed star.

Date	Mintage	F12	VF20	XF40	MS60	MS63
1949 (51)	8,010,000	—	4.00	6.00	20.00	30.00
1949 (E51)	—	—	—	—	600	700

Note: Issued to commemorate the 1st Ibero-American Numismatic Exposition December 2, 1951; An "E" replaces the "19" on the lower star

Date	Mintage	F12	VF20	XF40	MS60	MS63
1949 (52)	18,567,000	—	0.50	4.00	20.00	30.00
1949 (53)	17,500,000	—	1.00	10.00	32.00	50.00
1949 (54)	37,000,000	—	2.00	8.00	27.00	35.00
1949 (56)	38,000,000	—	0.50	4.00	16.00	22.00
1949 (62)	31,000,000	—	0.40	3.00	7.50	11.50
1963 (63)	4,000,000	6.00	14.00	20.00	27.00	40.00
1963 (64)	20,000,000	—	0.20	0.50	3.00	4.00
1963 (65)	14,000,000	—	0.20	0.40	2.00	3.00

KM# 795 50 CENTIMOS
1.10 g., Aluminum, 20 mm. **Ruler:** Francisco Franco, caudillo **Obv:** Head right **Rev:** Sprig divides value **Edge:** Reeded **Note:** Mint mark: 6-pointed star. These coins generally suffer from oxidation and the values given are for perfect proof specimens.

Date	Mintage	F12	VF20	XF40	MS60	MS63
1966 (67)	80,000,000	—	—	0.15	0.75	1.00
1966 (68)	100,000,000	—	—	0.15	0.25	0.50
1966 (69)	50,000,000	—	—	0.25	2.50	3.00
1966 (70) Prooflike, in sets only	—	—	—	—	150	250

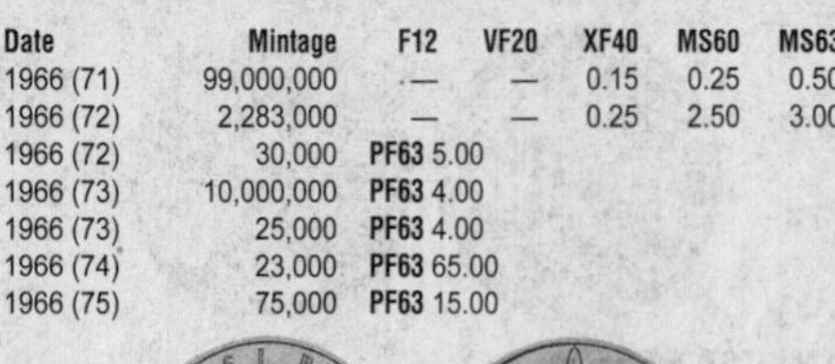

Date	Mintage	F12	VF20	XF40	MS60	MS63
1966 (71)	99,000,000	—	—	0.15	0.25	0.50
1966 (72)	2,283,000	—	—	0.25	2.50	3.00
1966 (72)	30,000	PF63 5.00				
1966 (73)	10,000,000	PF63 4.00				
1966 (73)	25,000	PF63 4.00				
1966 (74)	23,000	PF63 65.00				
1966 (75)	75,000	PF63 15.00				

KM# 805 50 CENTIMOS

Copper-Nickel **Ruler:** Juan Carlos I **Obv:** Head left **Rev:** Sprig divides value **Note:** Mint mark: 6-pointed star.

Date	Mintage	VF20	XF40	MS60	MS63	MS65
1975 (76)	4,060,000	—	0.10	0.20	0.50	—
1975 (76)	—	PF63 1.00				

KM# 815 50 CENTIMOS

1.10 g., Aluminum, 20 mm. **Ruler:** Juan Carlos I **Subject:** World Cup Soccer Games **Obv:** Head left **Rev:** Soccer ball and globe above value **Edge:** Reeded **Note:** Mint mark: 6-pointed star.

Date	Mintage	VF20	XF40	MS60	MS63	MS65
1980 (80)	15,000,000	—	0.10	0.20	0.35	—
1980 (80)	—	PF63 1.00				

KM# 775 PESETA

3.50 g., Aluminum-Bronze, 21 mm. **Ruler:** Francisco Franco, caudillo **Obv:** Head right **Rev:** Crowned shield within eagle flanked by pillars with banner **Edge:** Reeded **Note:** Mint mark: 6-pointed star. Values in uncirculated drop by 50% or more when the "PLUS" in legend is not readable. This defect is most often seen on coins struck before 1968.

Date	Mintage	F12	VF20	XF40	MS60	MS63
1946 (48)	Est. 5000	1,250	2,000	3,000	5,000	—
1947 (48)	15,000,000	—	2.00	20.00	125	300
1947 (49)	27,600,000	—	2.00	20.00	125	300
1947 (50)	4,000,000	4.00	20.00	50.00	900	1,200
1947 (51)	9,185,000	4.00	10.00	40.00	750	1,000
1947 (E51)	Est. 5000	—	—	—	700	900
Note: Issued to commemorate the 2nd National Numismatic Exposition December 2, 1951; An "E" replaces the "19" on the lower star						
1947 (52)	19,195,000	—	2.00	20.00	100	150
1947 (53)	34,000,000	—	1.50	20.00	100	150
1947 (54)	50,000,000	—	2.00	30.00	150	225
1947 (56)	—	30.00	70.00	200	1,000	1,300
1953 (54)	40,272,000	—	6.00	60.00	350	450
1953 (56)	118,000,000	—	0.20	2.00	5.00	10.00
1953 (60)	45,160,000	—	1.40	20.00	100	175
1953 (61)	25,830,000	—	1.20	20.00	50.00	100
1953 (62)	66,252,000	—	0.20	2.00	3.00	5.00
1953 (63)	37,000,000	—	0.50	3.00	20.00	35.00
1963 (63)	36,000,000	—	0.70	4.50	15.00	30.00
1963 (64)	80,000,000	—	0.20	2.00	3.00	5.00
1963 (65)	70,000,000	—	0.20	2.00	3.00	5.00
1963 (66)	63,000,000	—	0.20	2.00	5.00	8.00
1963 (67)	11,300,000	—	4.00	20.00	50.00	100

KM# 796 PESETA

3.50 g., Aluminum-Bronze, 21 mm. **Ruler:** Francisco Franco, caudillo **Obv:** Head right **Rev:** Crowned shield within eagle flanked by pillars with banner **Edge:** Reeded **Note:** Mint mark: 6-pointed star.

Date	Mintage	F12	VF20	XF40	MS60	MS63
1966 (67)	59,000,000	—	0.15	0.30	2.00	3.00
1966 (68)	120,000,000	—	0.10	0.20	1.00	2.00
1966 (69)	120,000,000	—	0.10	0.20	1.00	2.00
1966 (70)	75,000,000	—	0.10	0.20	2.00	3.00
1966 (71)	115,270,000	—	0.10	0.15	0.75	1.50

Date	Mintage	F12	VF20	XF40	MS60	MS63
1966 (72)	106,000,000	—	—	0.10	0.50	1.00
1966 (72)	30,000	PF63 3.00				
1966 (73)	25,000	PF63 3.00				
1966 (73)	152,000,000	—	—	0.10	0.35	0.65
1966 (74)	181,000,000	—	—	0.10	0.35	0.65
1966 (74)	23,000	PF63 3.00				
1966 (75)	227,580,000	—	—	0.10	0.25	0.35
1966 (75)	75,000	PF63 2.00				

KM# 806 PESETA

3.50 g., Aluminum-Bronze, 21 mm. **Ruler:** Juan Carlos I **Obv:** Head left **Rev:** Crowned shield within eagle flanked by pillars with banner **Edge:** Reeded

Date	Mintage	VF20	XF40	MS60	MS63	MS65
1975 (76)	170,380,000	—	0.10	0.25	0.35	—
1975 (76)	—	PF63 1.00				
1975 (77)	—	PF63 1.00				
1975 (77)	243,380,000	—	0.10	0.25	0.35	—
1975 (78)	Est. 603320000	—	0.10	0.25	0.35	—
1975 (79)	—	PF63 1.00				
1975 (79)	507,000,000	—	0.10	0.25	0.35	—
Note: Two varieties of tilde size for the n in España exist of this date; Large is Madrid mint, small is Santiago de Chile						
1975 (80)	590,000,000	—	0.10	0.25	0.50	—

KM# 816 PESETA

3.50 g., Aluminum-Bronze, 21 mm. **Ruler:** Juan Carlos I **Subject:** World Cup Soccer Games **Obv:** Head left **Rev:** Small crowned shield within eagle at left of value **Edge:** Reeded

Date	Mintage	VF20	XF40	MS60	MS63	MS65
1980 (80)	—	—	0.10	0.15	0.30	—
1980 (80)	—	PF63 1.00				
1980 (81)	385,000,000	—	0.10	0.25	0.35	—
1980 (82)	333,000,000	—	0.10	0.25	0.35	—

KM# 821 PESETA

1.20 g., Aluminum, 21 mm. **Ruler:** Juan Carlos I **Obv:** Head left **Rev:** Crowned shield flanked by pillars with banner to right of value

Date	Mintage	VF20	XF40	MS60	MS63	MS65
1982	—	—	0.20	0.40	0.70	—
Note: Mintage included in KM#816, 1980 (82)						
1983	52,000,000	—	0.20	1.00	1.50	—
1984	131,000,000	—	0.20	0.40	0.70	—
1985	220,065,000	—	0.20	0.40	0.70	—
1986	299,960,000	—	0.20	0.40	0.70	—
1987	299,550,000	—	0.20	0.40	0.70	—
1988	223,460,000	—	0.20	0.40	0.70	—
1989	—	—	0.20	1.20	2.00	—
Note: Mintage included in KM#832, 1989						

KM# 828 PESETA

Aluminum, 21 mm. **Ruler:** Juan Carlos I **Subject:** 3rd National Numismatic Exposition - Madrid **Obv:** Head left **Rev:** Crowned shield flanked by pillars with banner at right of value

Date	Mintage	VF20	XF40	MS60	MS63	MS65
1987/E-87	—	PF63 70.00	PF65 80.00			

KM# 832 PESETA

0.55 g., Aluminum, 14 mm. **Ruler:** Juan Carlos I **Obv:** Vertical line divides head left from value **Rev:** Crowned shield flanked by pillars with banner **Edge:** Plain

Date	Mintage	VF20	XF40	MS60	MS63	MS65
1989	198,415,000	—	0.10	0.25	0.50	0.75
1990	197,700,000	—	0.10	0.25	0.50	0.75
1991	173,780,000	—	0.10	0.25	0.50	0.75
1992	168,870,000	—	0.10	0.20	0.25	0.45
1993	300,013,000	—	0.10	0.20	0.25	0.45
1994	162,860,000	—	0.10	0.20	0.25	0.45
1995	183,175,000	—	0.10	0.20	0.25	0.45
1996	101,885,000	—	0.10	0.20	0.25	0.45
1997	342,620,000	—	0.10	0.20	0.25	0.45
1998	411,614,000	—	0.10	0.20	0.25	0.45
1999	84,946,000	—	0.10	0.20	0.25	0.45
2000	90,200,000	—	0.10	0.20	0.25	0.45

KM# 822 2 PESETAS

2.00 g., Aluminum, 24 mm. **Ruler:** Juan Carlos I **Obv:** Head left **Rev:** Value within map

Date	Mintage	VF20	XF40	MS60	MS63	MS65
1982	21,500,000	—	0.20	0.50	0.75	—
1984	47,650,000	—	0.20	1.00	1.50	—

KM# 785 2-1/2 PESETAS

7.00 g., Aluminum-Bronze, 25 mm. **Ruler:** Caudillo and regent **Obv:** Head right **Rev:** Crowned shield within eagle flanked by pillars with banner **Edge:** Reeded

Date	Mintage	F12	VF20	XF40	MS60	MS63
1953 (54)	22,729,000	—	0.50	2.00	12.00	20.00
1953 (56)	30,322,000	—	0.50	2.00	12.00	20.00
1953 (56)	—	PF63 100				
1953 (68)	1,000	—	—	—	—	1,500
Note: In sets only						
1953 (69)	2,000	—	—	—	—	1,250
Note: In sets only						
1953 (70)	6,000	—	—	—	—	200
Note: In sets only						
1953 (71)	10,000	—	—	—	—	200
Note: In sets only						

KM# 778 5 PESETAS

15.00 g., Nickel, 32 mm. **Ruler:** Caudillo and regent **Obv:** Head right **Rev:** Crowned shield within eagle flanked by pillars with banner **Edge:** Reeded

Date	Mintage	F12	VF20	XF40	MS60	MS63
1949 (49)	612,000	—	3.50	12.00	25.00	50.00
1949 (50)	21,000,000	—	1.00	2.25	6.00	20.00
1949 (E51)	Est. 6000	—	—	—	2,500	3,000
Note: Issued to commemorate the Second National Numismatic Exposition December 2, 1951; An "E" replaces the "19" on the lower star						
1949 (52) Rare	Est. 200000	—	—	—	50,000	—
1949 (51) Rare	145,000	—	—	—	18,000	—

KM# 786 5 PESETAS

5.75 g., Copper-Nickel, 23 mm. **Ruler:** Caudillo and regent **Obv:** Head right **Rev:** Crowned shield within flying bird **Edge:** Reeded **Note:** Values in uncirculated drop by 50% or more when the PLUS in legend is not readable. This defect is most often seen on coins struck before 1968.

Date	Mintage	F12	VF20	XF40	MS60	MS63
1957 BA	Est. 43000	—	100	150	200	250

Note: Issued to commemorate the 1958 2nd Ibero-American Numismatic Exposition in Barcelona with "BA" replacing the star on left side of reverse

Date	Mintage	F12	VF20	XF40	MS60	MS63
1957 (58)	13,000,000	—	0.90	6.00	100	150
1957 (59)	107,000,000	—	0.20	2.00	30.00	40.00
1957 (60)	26,000,000	—	0.20	2.00	25.00	30.00
1957 (61)	78,992,000	—	0.30	7.00	35.00	45.00
1957 (62)	40,963,000	—	0.20	2.00	10.00	15.00
1957 (63)	50,000,000	—	4.00	30.00	200	250
1957 (64)	51,000,000	—	0.20	2.00	20.00	30.00
1957 (65)	25,000,000	—	0.30	1.50	6.00	8.00
1957 (66)	28,000,000	—	0.30	6.00	30.00	40.00
1957 (67)	30,000,000	—	0.30	1.50	4.00	5.00
1957 (68)	60,000,000	—	0.40	1.20	4.00	5.00
1957 (69)	40,000,000	—	0.40	1.20	5.00	8.00
1957 (70)	43,000,000	—	0.40	1.20	8.00	10.00
1957 (71)	77,000,000	—	0.40	1.20	2.00	4.00
1957 (72)	30,000	PF63 10.00				
1957 (72)	70,000,000	—	—	1.25	5.00	8.00
1957 (73)	25,000	PF63 10.00				
1957 (73)	78,000,000	—	—	0.20	0.40	1.00
1957 (74)	100,000,000	—	—	0.20	0.35	0.75
1957 (74)	23,000	PF63 10.00				
1957 (75)	75,000	PF63 5.00				
1957 (75)	139,047,000	—	—	0.20	0.30	0.45

KM# 807 5 PESETAS

5.75 g., Copper-Nickel, 23 mm. **Ruler:** Juan Carlos I **Obv:** Head left **Rev:** Crossed scepters and shield within wreath divides value, crown on top **Edge:** Reeded

Date	Mintage	VF20	XF40	MS60	MS63	MS65
1975 (76)	150,560,000	—	0.10	0.25	0.35	—
1975 (76)	—	PF63 1.00				
1975 (77)	154,982,000	—	0.10	0.25	0.35	—
1975 (77)	—	PF63 1.00				
1975 (78)	412,610,000	—	0.20	1.00	3.00	—
1975 (79)	436,000,000	—	0.10	0.25	0.35	—
1975 (79)	—	PF63 1.00				
1975 (80)	322,000,000	—	0.10	1.50	4.00	—

KM# 811 5 PESETAS

Copper-Nickel **Ruler:** Juan Carlos I **Obv:** Head left **Rev:** World globe, soccerball, value and star with numeral 80 **Note:** Mule.

Date	Mintage	VF20	XF40	MS60	MS63	MS65
1975 (80)	Est. 30000	—	200	350	400	—

KM# 817 5 PESETAS

5.75 g., Copper-Nickel, 23 mm. **Ruler:** Juan Carlos I **Subject:** World Cup Soccer Games **Obv:** Head left **Rev:** Numeral 82 on world globe, soccer ball above value

Date	Mintage	VF20	XF40	MS60	MS63	MS65
1980 (80)	75,000,000	—	0.20	0.50	0.70	—
1980 (80)	—	PF63 2.00				
1980 (81)	294,000,000	—	0.20	0.50	1.00	—
1980 (82)	291,000,000	—	0.20	0.50	1.00	—

KM# 823 5 PESETAS

5.75 g., Copper-Nickel, 23 mm. **Ruler:** Juan Carlos I **Obv:** Head left **Rev:** Crossed scepters and shield within wreath divide value, crown on top **Note:** Mint mark: Crowned M.

Date	Mintage	VF20	XF40	MS60	MS63	MS65
1982	—	—	0.10	1.00	1.50	—

Note: Mintage included in KM#817, 1980 (82)

Date	Mintage	VF20	XF40	MS60	MS63	MS65
1983	200,000,000	—	0.10	0.50	0.65	—
1984	169,000,000	—	0.10	0.60	0.80	—
1989	—	—	0.10	0.75	1.00	—

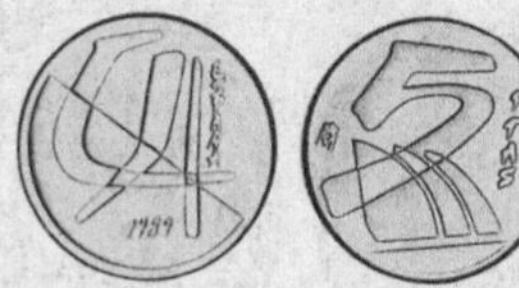

KM# 833 5 PESETAS

3.00 g., Aluminum-Bronze, 17.5 mm. **Ruler:** Juan Carlos I **Obv:** Stylized JC I and date **Rev:** Value above stylized sailboats **Edge:** Plain

Date	Mintage	VF20	XF40	MS60	MS63	MS65
1989	109,270,000	—	0.10	0.30	0.50	0.75
1990	191,740,000	—	0.10	0.50	1.00	1.50
1991	313,820,000	—	0.10	0.45	0.85	1.25
1992	493,224,000	—	0.10	0.35	0.50	0.75
1998	923,978,000	—	0.10	0.25	0.35	0.50
2000	4,900,000	—	0.10	0.25	0.75	1.00

KM# 919 5 PESETAS

3.00 g., Aluminum-Bronze, 17.5 mm. **Ruler:** Juan Carlos I **Subject:** Jacobeo **Obv:** Standing figure with staff at left of design **Rev:** Value, dates and design **Edge:** Plain **Note:** Coins with extra metal in the denomination 5 sell for a premium.

Date	Mintage	VF20	XF40	MS60	MS63	MS65
1993	372,746,000	—	—	0.25	0.40	0.65

KM# 931 5 PESETAS

3.00 g., Aluminum-Bronze, 17.5 mm. **Ruler:** Juan Carlos I **Subject:** Aragon **Obv:** Front view of building **Rev:** Ballerina **Edge:** Plain **Note:** Wide rim variety exists.

Date	Mintage	VF20	XF40	MS60	MS63	MS65
1994	199,678,000	—	—	0.25	0.40	0.65

KM# 946 5 PESETAS

3.00 g., Aluminum-Bronze, 17.5 mm. **Ruler:** Juan Carlos I **Subject:** Asturias **Obv:** Cross and date **Rev:** Value and design **Edge:** Plain

Date	Mintage	VF20	XF40	MS60	MS63	MS65
1995	301,756,000	—	—	0.25	0.40	0.65

KM# 960 5 PESETAS

3.00 g., Aluminum-Bronze, 17.5 mm. **Ruler:** Juan Carlos I **Subject:** La Rioja **Obv:** Front view of building **Rev:** Figure on stilts, value and grapes **Edge:** Plain

Date	Mintage	VF20	XF40	MS60	MS63	MS65
1996	674,168,000	—	—	0.15	0.25	0.45

KM# 981 5 PESETAS

3.00 g., Aluminum-Bronze, 17.5 mm. **Ruler:** Juan Carlos I **Subject:** Balearic Islands **Obv:** Stone monument **Rev:** Figure on rearing horse **Edge:** Plain

Date	Mintage	VF20	XF40	MS60	MS63	MS65
1997	709,006,000	—	—	0.15	0.25	0.45

KM# 1008 5 PESETAS

3.00 g., Aluminum-Bronze, 17.5 mm. **Ruler:** Juan Carlos I **Obv:** Crowned shield with supporters on arch **Rev:** Murcia waterwheel **Edge:** Plain

Date	Mintage	VF20	XF40	MS60	MS63	MS65
1999	216,230,000	—	—	0.15	0.25	0.45

KM# 827 10 PESETAS

4.00 g., Copper-Nickel, 18.5 mm. **Ruler:** Juan Carlos I **Obv:** Head left **Rev:** Crowned shield flanked by pillars with banner **Edge:** Reeded **Note:** Denomination "DIEZ".

Date	Mintage	VF20	XF40	MS60	MS63	MS65
1983	149,000,000	—	—	0.35	0.40	0.75
1984	66,000,000	—	—	1.00	2.00	3.00
1985	45,706,000	—	—	0.50	0.60	1.00

KM# 903 10 PESETAS

4.00 g., Copper-Nickel, 18.5 mm. **Ruler:** Juan Carlos I **Obv:** Head left **Rev:** Crowned shield flanked by pillars with banner **Edge:** Reeded

Date	Mintage	VF20	XF40	MS60	MS63	MS65
1992	51,820,000	—	—	0.75	1.00	1.50

KM# 918 10 PESETAS

4.00 g., Copper-Nickel, 18.5 mm. **Ruler:** Juan Carlos I **Subject:** Juan Miro **Obv:** Value, dates and inscription **Rev:** Head 3/4 right **Edge:** Reeded

Date	Mintage	VF20	XF40	MS60	MS63	MS65
1993	53,845,000	—	0.45	2.50	3.50	5.00

KM# 932 10 PESETAS

4.00 g., Copper-Nickel, 18.5 mm. **Ruler:** Juan Carlos I **Subject:** Musician P. Sarasate **Obv:** Head right **Rev:** Violin **Edge:** Reeded

Date	Mintage	VF20	XF40	MS60	MS63	MS65
1994	3,050,000	—	0.75	3.50	5.50	7.00

KM# 947 10 PESETAS

4.00 g., Copper-Nickel, 18.5 mm. **Ruler:** Juan Carlos I **Subject:** Don Francisco de Quevedo **Obv:** Bust 1/4 left **Rev:** Quill in ink, book, glasses and value **Edge:** Reeded

Date	Mintage	VF20	XF40	MS60	MS63	MS65
1995	1,050,000	—	1.25	4.50	7.00	9.00

KM# 961 10 PESETAS

4.00 g., Copper-Nickel, 18.5 mm. **Ruler:** Juan Carlos I **Subject:** Emilia Pardo Bazan **Obv:** Monument and value **Rev:** Half length figure facing **Edge:** Reeded

Date	Mintage	VF20	XF40	MS60	MS63	MS65
1996	1,060,000	—	0.45	3.75	6.00	7.50

KM# 982 10 PESETAS

4.00 g., Copper-Nickel, 18.5 mm. **Ruler:** Juan Carlos I **Subject:** Seneca **Obv:** Head facing **Rev:** Castle gate **Edge:** Reeded

Date	Mintage	VF20	XF40	MS60	MS63	MS65
1997	6,800,000	—	0.50	1.50	2.00	3.00

KM# 1012 10 PESETAS

4.00 g., Copper-Nickel, 18.5 mm. **Ruler:** Juan Carlos I **Obv:** Head left **Rev:** Value above national arms **Edge:** Reeded **Note:** Older portrait.

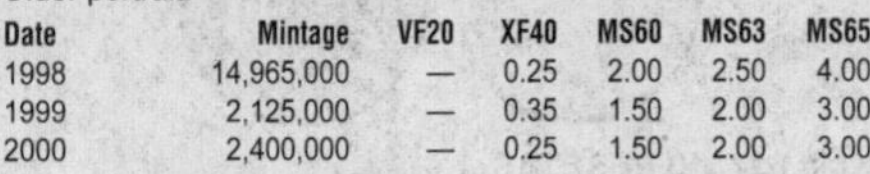

Date	Mintage	VF20	XF40	MS60	MS63	MS65
1998	14,965,000	—	0.25	2.00	2.50	4.00
1999	2,125,000	—	0.35	1.50	2.00	3.00
2000	2,400,000	—	0.25	1.50	2.00	3.00

KM# 787 25 PESETAS

8.50 g., Copper-Nickel, 26.5 mm. **Ruler:** Caudillo and regent **Obv:** Head right **Rev:** Crowned shield within flying bird **Edge Lettering:** UNA GRANDE LIBRE **Note:** Values in uncirculated drop by 50% or more when the "PLUS" in legend is not readable. This defect is most often seen on coins struck before 1968.

Date	Mintage	F12	VF20	XF40	MS60	MS63
1957 (58)	8,635,000	—	1.50	14.00	70.00	100
1957(BA)	43,000	—	35.00	60.00	90.00	125

Note: Issued to commemorate the 1958 Barcelona Exposition with "BA" replacing the star on left side of the reverse

Date	Mintage	F12	VF20	XF40	MS60	MS63
1957 (59)	42,185,000	—	0.45	2.00	35.00	50.00
1957 (61)	24,120,000	—	2.75	35.00	150	200
1957 (64)	42,200,000	—	0.25	2.00	25.00	40.00
1957 (65)	20,000,000	—	0.30	1.50	8.00	10.00
1957 (66)	15,000,000	—	0.30	1.50	12.00	15.00
1957 (67)	20,000,000	—	0.25	2.00	20.00	40.00
1957 (68)	30,000,000	—	0.30	1.50	5.00	7.00
1957 (69)	24,000,000	—	0.45	1.00	2.50	4.00
1957 (70)	25,000,000	—	0.30	1.50	5.00	8.00
1957 (71)	7,800,000	—	1.50	7.00	75.00	100
1957 (72)	4,733,000	—	0.28	1.00	4.00	10.00
1957 (72)	—	PF63 15.00				
1957 (73)	—	PF63 100				
1957 (74)	5,000,000	—	0.45	1.00	5.00	10.00
1957 (74)	—	PF63 15.00				
1957 (75)	10,270,000	—	0.45	1.00	2.25	3.00
1957 (75)	—	PF63 5.00				

KM# 808 25 PESETAS

8.50 g., Copper-Nickel, 26.5 mm. **Ruler:** Juan Carlos I **Obv:** Head left **Rev:** Crown above value **Edge Lettering:** UNA GRANDE LIBRE

Date	Mintage	VF20	XF40	MS60	MS63	MS65
1975 (76)	35,707,000	0.35	0.45	0.75	1.00	—
1975 (76)	—	PF63 1.00				
1975 (77)	46,690,000	0.35	0.45	0.75	1.00	—
1975 (77)	—	PF63 1.00				
1975 (78)	97,555,000	0.35	0.45	2.00	3.00	—
1975 (79)	172,000,000	0.35	0.45	0.75	1.00	—
1975 (79)	—	PF63 1.00				
1975 (80)	136,000,000	0.35	0.45	3.00	5.00	—

KM# 818 25 PESETAS

8.50 g., Copper-Nickel, 26.5 mm. **Ruler:** Juan Carlos I **Subject:** World Cup Soccer Games **Obv:** Head left **Rev:** Soccer ball on net above value **Edge Lettering:** UNA GRANDE LIBRE

Date	Mintage	VF20	XF40	MS60	MS63	MS65
1980 (80)	35,000,000	0.25	0.45	0.75	1.25	—
1980 (80)	—	PF63 2.00				
1980 (81)	117,000,000	0.25	0.45	1.00	1.50	—
1980 (82)	100,000,000	0.25	0.45	1.25	2.75	—

KM# 824 25 PESETAS

8.50 g., Copper-Nickel, 26.5 mm. **Ruler:** Juan Carlos I **Obv:** Head left **Rev:** Crown above value **Edge:** Reeded **Note:** Mint mark: Crowned M; Similar to KM#808.

Date	Mintage	VF20	XF40	MS60	MS63	MS65
1982	146,000,000	0.20	0.30	2.00	3.00	—
1983	248,000,000	0.30	0.45	1.50	2.00	—
1984	242,000,000	0.20	0.30	3.50	6.00	—

KM# 850 25 PESETAS

4.25 g., Aluminum-Bronze, 19.5 mm. **Ruler:** Juan Carlos I **Subject:** 1992 Olympics **Obv:** Discus thrower to right of center hole **Rev:** Center hole divides value, Olympic rings below

Date	Mintage	VF20	XF40	MS60	MS63	MS65
1990	150,000,000	0.25	0.30	1.50	2.00	3.00
1991	Inc. above	0.20	0.25	4.50	7.00	9.00

KM# 851 25 PESETAS

4.25 g., Aluminum-Bronze, 19.5 mm. **Ruler:** Juan Carlos I **Subject:** 1992 Olympics **Obv:** Center hole divides letters and bust left **Rev:** High jumper to upper right of center hole **Edge:** Plain

Date	Mintage	VF20	XF40	MS60	MS63	MS65
1990	Inc. above	—	—	2.00	2.50	4.00
1991	87,000,000	—	—	2.50	3.00	5.00

KM# 904 25 PESETAS

4.25 g., Aluminum-Bronze, 19.5 mm. **Ruler:** Juan Carlos I **Subject:** Giralda Tower of Sevilla **Obv:** Center hole divides letters and bust left **Rev:** Center hole divides tower and value

Date	Mintage	VF20	XF40	MS60	MS63	MS65
1992	179,833,000	—	—	2.50	3.50	5.00

KM# 905 25 PESETAS

4.25 g., Aluminum-Bronze, 19.5 mm. **Ruler:** Juan Carlos I **Subject:** Tower of Gold in Seville **Obv:** Globe design around center hole **Rev:** Center hole divides tower and vertical letters **Edge:** Plain

Date	Mintage	VF20	XF40	MS60	MS63	MS65
1992	Inc. above	—	—	1.25	2.00	3.00

KM# 920 25 PESETAS

4.25 g., Aluminum-Bronze, 19.5 mm. **Ruler:** Juan Carlos I **Subject:** Vasc Country **Obv:** Center hole divides inscription, date and design **Rev:** Center hole divides value and buildings

Date	Mintage	VF20	XF40	MS60	MS63	MS65
1993	150,012,000	—	—	1.25	2.00	3.00

KM# 933 25 PESETAS

4.25 g., Aluminum-Bronze, 19.5 mm. **Ruler:** Juan Carlos I **Subject:** Canary Islands **Obv:** Center hole divides inscription, date and flowers **Rev:** Center hole divides value, design and inscription **Edge:** Plain

Date	Mintage	VF20	XF40	MS60	MS63	MS65
1994	242,566,000	—	—	0.75	1.00	2.00

KM# 948 25 PESETAS

4.25 g., Aluminum-Bronze, 19.5 mm. **Ruler:** Juan Carlos I **Subject:** Castilla and Leon **Obv:** Center hole divides tower and inscription **Rev:** Center hole divides stylized animal figures, value and inscription **Edge:** Plain

Date	Mintage	VF20	XF40	MS60	MS63	MS65
1995	221,963,000	—	—	0.75	1.00	2.00
1995 without Y	Inc. above	—	45.00	75.00	100	—

KM# 962 25 PESETAS

4.25 g., Aluminum-Bronze, 19.5 mm. **Ruler:** Juan Carlos I **Subject:** Don Quixote **Obv:** Center hole divides figure on horse, design and inscription **Rev:** Center hole divides design, inscription and value **Edge:** Plain

Date	Mintage	VF20	XF40	MS60	MS63	MS65
1996	37,403,000	—	—	1.25	2.00	3.00

KM# 983 25 PESETAS

4.25 g., Aluminum-Bronze, 19.5 mm. **Ruler:** Juan Carlos I **Subject:** Melilla **Obv:** Center hole divides towered buildings **Rev:** Center hole divides ancient amphora and dates **Edge:** Plain

Date	Mintage	VF20	XF40	MS60	MS63	MS65
1997	461,688,000	—	—	0.75	1.00	2.00

KM# 990 25 PESETAS

4.25 g., Aluminum-Bronze, 19.5 mm. **Ruler:** Juan Carlos I **Subject:** Ceuta **Obv:** Center hole right of ornamented building corner **Rev:** Center hole divides statue on wall shelf and value **Edge:** Plain

Date	Mintage	VF20	XF40	MS60	MS63	MS65
1998	184,360,000	—	—	1.25	2.00	3.00

KM# 1007 25 PESETAS

4.25 g., Aluminum-Bronze, 19.5 mm. **Ruler:** Juan Carlos I **Subject:** Navarra **Obv:** Center hole between castle towers **Rev:** Man running from bull, value and shield, all around center hole **Edge:** Plain

Date	Mintage	VF20	XF40	MS60	MS63	MS65
1999	2,130,000	—	—	1.75	2.75	3.50

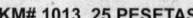

KM# 1013 25 PESETAS
4.25 g., Aluminum-Bronze, 19.5 mm. **Ruler:** Juan Carlos I **Obv:** Center hole divides bust left and vertical letters **Rev:** Crowned above center hole, order collar at right, value at left **Edge:** Plain

Date	Mintage	VF20	XF40	MS60	MS63	MS65
2000	19,900,000	—	—	1.50	2.00	3.00

KM# 788 50 PESETAS
12.35 g., Copper-Nickel, 30 mm. **Ruler:** Caudillo and regent **Obv:** Head right **Rev:** Crowned shield within flying bird **Edge Lettering:** UNA GRANDE LIBRE

Date	Mintage	F12	VF20	XF40	MS60	MS63
1957 (BA)	Est. 43000	—	30.00	60.00	90.00	125
Note: Issued to commemorate the 1958 Barcelona Exposition with "BA" replacing the star on left side of reverse						
1957 (58)	21,471,000	—	0.75	1.25	4.75	6.50
1957 (58)	Inc. above	150	275	400	700	1,000
Note: Edge variety with UNA - LIBRE - GRANDE						
1957 (59)	28,000,000	—	0.75	1.25	4.50	6.50
1957 (60)	24,800,000	—	0.75	1.25	5.50	7.00
1957 (67)	850,000	—	0.75	3.00	12.50	16.00
1957 (68)	1,000	—	—	—	—	1,750
Note: In sets only						
1957 (69)	1,200	—	—	—	—	1,250
Note: In sets only						
1957 (70)	19,000	—	—	—	—	275
Note: In sets only						
1957(71)	4,400,000	—	1.00	4.00	25.00	40.00
1957 (72)	23,000	PF63 50.00				
1957 (73)	28,000	PF63 60.00				
1957 (74)	25,000	PF63 60.00				
1957 (75)	75,000	PF63 15.00				

KM# 809 50 PESETAS
12.35 g., Copper-Nickel, 30 mm. **Ruler:** Juan Carlos I **Obv:** Head left **Rev:** Crossed scepters and shield within order collar, crown above

Date	Mintage	VF20	XF40	MS60	MS63	MS65
1975 (79)	—	PF63 2.00				
1975 (76)	4,400,000	0.75	1.00	1.25	1.75	—
1975 (76)	—	PF63 2.00				
1975 (78)	17,555,000	0.75	1.25	2.00	3.00	—
1975 (79)	33,000,000	0.75	1.00	1.25	1.75	—
1975 (80)	34,000,000	0.75	1.00	3.00	4.00	—

KM# 819 50 PESETAS
12.35 g., Copper-Nickel, 30 mm. **Ruler:** Juan Carlos I **Subject:** World Cup Soccer Games **Obv:** Head left **Rev:** Soccer ball above value **Edge Lettering:** UNA GRANDE LIBRE

Date	Mintage	VF20	XF40	MS60	MS63	MS65
1980 (80)	15,000,000	0.50	0.60	0.75	0.85	—
1980 (80)	—	PF63 2.00				
1980 (81)	38,300,000	0.50	0.60	1.35	1.50	—
1980 (82)	30,950,000	0.50	0.60	2.00	2.50	—

KM# 825 50 PESETAS
12.35 g., Copper-Nickel, 30 mm. **Ruler:** Juan Carlos I **Obv:** Head left **Rev:** Crossed scepters and shield within order collar, crown above **Note:** Mint mark: Crowned M.

Date	Mintage	VF20	XF40	MS60	MS63	MS65
1982	27,000,000	0.50	1.00	5.00	8.00	—
1983	93,000,000	0.50	1.00	4.00	6.00	—
1984	17,500,000	12.00	20.00	40.00	50.00	—

KM# 852 50 PESETAS
5.60 g., Copper-Nickel, 20.5 mm. **Ruler:** Juan Carlos I **Subject:** Expo '92 **Obv:** Bust left **Rev:** Globe and value **Edge:** Notched

Date	Mintage	VF20	XF40	MS60	MS63	MS65
1990	25,234,000	—	—	2.00	3.00	4.00

KM# 853 50 PESETAS
5.60 g., Copper-Nickel, 20.5 mm. **Ruler:** Juan Carlos I **Subject:** Expo '92 **Obv:** City view **Rev:** Globe and value **Edge:** Notched

Date	Mintage	VF20	XF40	MS60	MS63	MS65
1990	7,916,000	—	—	1.25	1.50	2.50

KM# 906 50 PESETAS
5.60 g., Copper-Nickel, 20.5 mm. **Ruler:** Juan Carlos I **Subject:** 1992 Olympics **Obv:** "La Pedrera" building **Rev:** Pointed designs above Olympic rings, value at left **Edge:** Notched

Date	Mintage	VF20	XF40	MS60	MS63	MS65
1992	40,370,000	—	—	1.50	2.00	3.00

KM# 907 50 PESETAS
5.60 g., Copper-Nickel, 20.5 mm. **Ruler:** Juan Carlos I **Subject:** 1992 Olympics **Obv:** Bust left **Rev:** Cathedral Sagrada Famillia (Gaudi) **Edge:** Notched

Date	Mintage	VF20	XF40	MS60	MS63	MS65
1992	Inc. above	—	—	3.00	4.00	6.00

KM# 921 50 PESETAS
5.60 g., Copper-Nickel, 20.5 mm. **Ruler:** Juan Carlos I **Subject:** Extremadura **Obv:** Bridge **Rev:** Tower **Edge:** Notched

Date	Mintage	VF20	XF40	MS60	MS63	MS65
1993	24,314,000	—	—	2.50	3.00	5.00

KM# 934 50 PESETAS
5.60 g., Copper-Nickel, 20.5 mm. **Ruler:** Juan Carlos I **Subject:** Altamira Cave Paintings **Obv:** Building **Rev:** Stylized design above value **Edge:** Notched

Date	Mintage	VF20	XF40	MS60	MS63	MS65
1994	3,002,000	—	—	2.50	4.00	6.50

KM# 949 50 PESETAS
5.60 g., Copper-Nickel, 20.5 mm. **Ruler:** Juan Carlos I **Subject:** Alcala Gate **Obv:** Partial building and date **Rev:** Steepled buildings **Edge:** Notched

Date	Mintage	VF20	XF40	MS60	MS63	MS65
1995	1,001,000	—	—	5.00	8.00	10.00

KM# 963 50 PESETAS
5.60 g., Copper-Nickel, 20.5 mm. **Ruler:** Juan Carlos I **Subject:** Philip V **Obv:** Head facing **Rev:** Shield divides value and letters, crown above divides date **Edge:** Notched

Date	Mintage	VF20	XF40	MS60	MS63	MS65
1996	11,047,000	—	—	4.00	5.50	8.00

KM# 985 50 PESETAS
5.60 g., Copper-Nickel, 20.5 mm. **Ruler:** Juan Carlos I **Subject:** Juan De Herrera **Obv:** Head left **Rev:** Escorial Monastery **Edge:** Notched

Date	Mintage	VF20	XF40	MS60	MS63	MS65
1997	17,496,000	—	—	1.25	2.00	3.00

KM# 991 50 PESETAS
5.60 g., Copper-Nickel, 20.5 mm. **Ruler:** Juan Carlos I **Obv:** Bust left **Rev:** Crossed scepters and shield within order chain, crown above, value at left **Edge:** Notched

Date	Mintage	VF20	XF40	MS60	MS63	MS65
1998	17,496,000	—	—	2.00	2.50	4.00
1999	2,100,000	—	—	2.25	3.50	5.00
2000	2,000,000	—	—	2.25	3.50	5.00

KM# 797 100 PESETAS
19.00 g., 0.800 Silver 0.4887 oz. ASW, 34 mm. **Ruler:** Caudillo and regent **Obv:** Head right **Rev:** Assorted emblems within flower design, crown on top **Edge Lettering:** UNA GRANDE LIBRE

Date	Mintage	F12	VF20	XF40	MS60	MS63
1966 (66)	15,045,000	—	—	9.50	21.50	22.50
1966 (67)	15,000,000	—	—	9.50	21.50	22.50
1966 (68)	24,000,000	—	—	9.50	21.50	22.50

Date	Mintage	F12	VF20	XF40	MS60	MS63
1966 (69)	1,000,000	—	—	—	600	700
Note: 69 with straight 9 in star						
1966 (69)	Inc. above	—	—	—	200	250
Note: 69 with curved 9 in star						
1966 (70)	995,000	9.50	21.50	22.50	30.00	35.00

Note: 1966(69) coins heavily altered; authentication recommended

KM# 810 100 PESETAS
17.10 g., Copper-Nickel, 34.2 mm. **Ruler:** Juan Carlos I **Obv:** Head left **Rev:** Crowned shield flanked by pillars with banner

Date	Mintage	VF20	XF40	MS60	MS63	MS65
1975 (76)	4,400,000	0.75	1.00	2.00	3.00	—
1975 (76)	—	PF63 4.00				

KM# 820 100 PESETAS
Copper-Nickel **Ruler:** Juan Carlos I **Subject:** World Cup Soccer Games - Spain '82 **Obv:** Head left **Rev:** Value in center of assorted emblems

Date	Mintage	VF20	XF40	MS60	MS63	MS65
1980 (80)	20,000,000	—	0.75	1.00	1.50	—
1980 (80)	—	PF63 3.00				

KM# 826 100 PESETAS
9.25 g., Aluminum-Bronze, 24.5 mm. **Ruler:** Juan Carlos I **Obv:** Head left **Rev:** Crowned shield flanked by pillars with banner **Edge:** Fleur-de-lis repeated

Date	Mintage	VF20	XF40	MS60	MS63	MS65
1982	117,600,000	1.15	1.75	4.00	6.00	—
1982	—	PF63 7.00				
1983	—	1.15	1.75	25.00	35.00	—
1984	208,000,000	1.15	1.75	7.00	15.00	—
1985	118,000,000	1.15	1.75	15.00	20.00	—
1986	160,000,000	1.15	1.75	4.00	6.00	—
1988	125,674,000	1.15	1.75	5.00	10.00	—
1989	80,877,000	1.15	1.75	3.50	4.50	—
1990	25,636,000	1.15	1.75	6.00	10.00	—

Note: Varieties exist

KM# 834 100 PESETAS
1.68 g., 0.925 Silver 0.050 oz. ASW **Ruler:** Juan Carlos I **Subject:** Discovery of America **Obv:** Crown within beaded circle **Rev:** Mayan pyramid within beaded circle

Date	Mintage	VF20	XF40	MS60	MS63	MS65
1989	43,045	—	—	—	8.00	9.00
1989	57,086	PF63 8.00	PF65 9.00			

KM# 854 100 PESETAS
1.68 g., 0.925 Silver 0.050 oz. ASW **Ruler:** Juan Carlos I **Obv:** Bust of Brother Juniper Serra 3/4 right **Rev:** Mission ruins within legend

Date	Mintage	VF20	XF40	MS60	MS63	MS65
1990	26,943	—	—	—	9.00	10.00
1990	26,972	PF63 9.00	PF65 10.00			

KM# 882 100 PESETAS
1.68 g., 0.925 Silver 0.050 oz. ASW **Ruler:** Juan Carlos I **Obv:** bust of Celestino Mutis 1/4 right **Rev:** Flower plant within beaded circle

Date	Mintage	VF20	XF40	MS60	MS63	MS65
1991	14,249	—	—	—	10.00	12.00
1991	14,383	PF63 10.00	PF65 12.00			

KM# 908 100 PESETAS
9.25 g., Aluminum-Bronze, 24.5 mm. **Ruler:** Juan Carlos I **Rev:** Crowned shield flanked by pillars with banner **Edge Lettering:** Fleur-dis-lis (repeated)

Date	Mintage	VF20	XF40	MS60	MS63	MS65
1992	22,661,000	—	—	4.00	5.00	7.00

Note: Edge varieties exist with positioning of fleur-de-lis

KM# 993 100 PESETAS
1.68 g., 0.925 Silver 0.050 oz. ASW **Ruler:** Juan Carlos I **Subject:** Seville Expo '92 **Obv:** Arched bridge **Rev:** Bridge

Date	Mintage	VF20	XF40	MS60	MS63	MS65
1992	16,000	—	—	—	10.00	12.00
1992	16,000	PF63 10.00	PF65 12.00			

KM# 922 100 PESETAS
9.25 g., Aluminum-Bronze, 24.5 mm. **Ruler:** Juan Carlos I **Subject:** European Union **Obv:** Value within map **Rev:** Radiant sun within star circle **Edge:** Fleur-de-lis repeated

Date	Mintage	VF20	XF40	MS60	MS63	MS65
1993 (M)	39,723,000	—	—	3.00	5.00	7.00

KM# 935 100 PESETAS
9.25 g., Aluminum-Bronze, 24.5 mm. **Ruler:** Juan Carlos I **Subject:** Museo del Prado **Obv:** Head left **Rev:** Statue in front of museum **Edge:** Fleur-de-lis repeated

Date	Mintage	VF20	XF40	MS60	MS63	MS65
1994 (M)	24,853,000	—	—	3.00	4.00	6.00

KM# 950 100 PESETAS
9.25 g., Aluminum-Bronze, 24.5 mm. **Ruler:** Juan Carlos I **Series:** F.A.O. **Obv:** Head left **Rev:** Oat sprig, value and F.A.O. logo **Edge:** Fleur-de-lis repeated

Date	Mintage	VF20	XF40	MS60	MS63	MS65
1995 (M)	71,957,000	—	—	2.00	3.00	5.00

KM# 964 100 PESETAS
9.25 g., Aluminum-Bronze, 24.5 mm. **Ruler:** Juan Carlos I **Obv:** Head left **Rev:** National Library **Edge:** Fleur-de-lis repeated

Date	Mintage	VF20	XF40	MS60	MS63	MS65
1996 (M)	21,466,000	—	—	3.00	4.00	6.00

KM# 984 100 PESETAS
9.25 g., Aluminum-Bronze, 24.5 mm. **Ruler:** Juan Carlos I **Subject:** Royal Theatre **Obv:** Head left **Rev:** Building **Edge:** Fleur-de-lis repeated

Date	Mintage	VF20	XF40	MS60	MS63	MS65
1997 (M)	29,480,000	—	—	2.00	3.00	5.00

KM# 989 100 PESETAS
9.25 g., Aluminum-Bronze, 24.5 mm. **Ruler:** Juan Carlos I **Obv:** Head left **Rev:** Crowned shield flanked by pillars with banner **Edge:** Fleur-de-lis repeated

Date	Mintage	VF20	XF40	MS60	MS63	MS65
1998 (M)	—	—	—	2.00	3.00	5.00
2000 (M)	—	—	—	2.50	3.50	6.00

KM# 1006 100 PESETAS
9.25 g., Aluminum-Bronze, 24.5 mm. **Ruler:** Juan Carlos I **Obv:** Head left **Rev:** Design above sprig and value **Edge:** Fleur-de-lis repeated

Date	Mintage	VF20	XF40	MS60	MS63	MS65
1999 M	60,332,000	—	—	2.50	3.00	5.00

KM# 829 200 PESETAS
Copper-Nickel, 21.7 mm. **Ruler:** Juan Carlos I **Obv:** Head left **Rev:** Value divides sprigs

Date	Mintage	VF20	XF40	MS60	MS63	MS65
1986	43,576,000	—	4.00	6.00	8.00	10.00
1987	66,718,000	—	4.00	14.00	16.00	18.00
1988	37,190,000	—	4.00	14.00	16.00	18.00

KM# 830 200 PESETAS
Copper-Nickel, 21.7 mm. **Ruler:** Juan Carlos I **Subject:** Madrid Numismatic Exposition **Obv:** Head left **Rev:** Value divides sprigs

Date	Mintage	VF20	XF40	MS60	MS63	MS65
1987 (E87)	60,000	PF63 50.00	PF65 60.00			

KM# 835 200 PESETAS
3.37 g., 0.925 Silver 0.1002 oz. ASW **Ruler:** Juan Carlos I

Subject: Discovery of America **Obv:** Crown above monogram within beaded circle **Rev:** Astrolobe within beaded circle

Date	Mintage	VF20	XF40	MS60	MS63	MS65
1989	43,045	—	—	—	9.00	10.00
1989	57,086	PF63 9.00	PF65 10.00			

KM# 855 200 PESETAS

Copper-Nickel, 25.5 mm. **Ruler:** Juan Carlos I **Obv:** Conjoined busts of King and Crown Prince right **Rev:** Pair of lions pulling Cibeles seated on Chariot within circle

Date	Mintage	VF20	XF40	MS60	MS63	MS65
1990	8,000,000	—	—	13.00	20.00	25.00

KM# 856 200 PESETAS

3.37 g., 0.925 Silver 0.1002 oz. ASW **Ruler:** Juan Carlos I **Subject:** History in Common-Alonso de Frcilla **Obv:** Bust left **Rev:** Hand writing in a book within inner circle

Date	Mintage	VF20	XF40	MS60	MS63	MS65
1990	26,973	—	—	—	10.00	12.00
1990	26,972	PF63 10.00	PF65 12.00			

KM# 883 200 PESETAS

3.37 g., 0.925 Silver 0.1002 oz. ASW **Ruler:** Juan Carlos I **Subject:** Las Casas **Obv:** Bust left within beaded circle **Rev:** 3 Indian figures within beaded circle

Date	Mintage	VF20	XF40	MS60	MS63	MS65
1991	14,249	—	—	—	11.00	13.00
1991	14,383	PF63 11.00	PF65 13.00			

KM# 884 200 PESETAS

Copper-Nickel, 25.5 mm. **Ruler:** Juan Carlos I **Subject:** Madrid - European Culture Capital **Obv:** Conjoined busts of King and Crown Prince right **Rev:** Pair of lions pulling Cibeles seated on chariot within circle

Date	Mintage	VF20	XF40	MS60	MS63	MS65
1991	11,404,000	—	—	4.00	5.00	7.00

KM# 884a 200 PESETAS

12.25 g., 0.925 Silver 0.3643 oz. ASW **Ruler:** Juan Carlos I **Subject:** Madrid - European Culture Capital **Obv:** Conjoined busts of King and Crown Prince right **Rev:** Pair of lions pulling Cibeles seated on chariot within circle

Date	Mintage	VF20	XF40	MS60	MS63	MS65
1992	38,000	PF65 150				

KM# 909 200 PESETAS

Copper-Nickel, 25.5 mm. **Ruler:** Juan Carlos I **Subject:** Madrid - European Culture Capital **Obv:** Conjoined busts of King and Crown Prince right **Rev:** Equestrian sculpture within circle

Date	Mintage	VF20	XF40	MS60	MS63	MS65
1992	38,063,000	—	—	5.00	7.00	9.00

KM# 910 200 PESETAS

Copper-Nickel, 25.5 mm. **Ruler:** Juan Carlos I **Subject:** Madrid - European Culture Capital **Obv:** Conjoined busts of King and Crown Prince right **Rev:** Upright bear by tree within circle

Date	Mintage	VF20	XF40	MS60	MS63	MS65
1992	Inc. above	—	—	5.00	7.00	9.00

KM# 994 200 PESETAS

3.37 g., 0.925 Silver 0.1002 oz. ASW **Ruler:** Juan Carlos I **Subject:** Seville Expo '92 **Obv:** Hydro-electric dam within beaded circle **Rev:** Tower of Seville within beaded circle

Date	Mintage	VF20	XF40	MS60	MS63	MS65
1992	16,430	PF63 12.00	PF65 14.00			
1992	16,610	—	—	—	12.00	14.00

KM# 923 200 PESETAS

Copper-Nickel, 25.5 mm. **Ruler:** Juan Carlos I **Subject:** Juan Luis Vives **Obv:** Feather and designs within circle **Rev:** Bust facing and crowned design within circle

Date	Mintage	VF20	XF40	MS60	MS63	MS65
1993	2,811,000	—	—	6.00	8.00	10.00

KM# 936 200 PESETAS

Copper-Nickel, 25.5 mm. **Ruler:** Juan Carlos I **Subject:** Velasquez and Goya Paintings **Obv:** Three figures within circle **Rev:** Kneeling figures with umbrella within circle

Date	Mintage	VF20	XF40	MS60	MS63	MS65
1994	2,997,000	—	—	6.00	8.00	10.00

KM# 951 200 PESETAS

Copper-Nickel, 25.5 mm. **Ruler:** Juan Carlos I **Subject:** Murillo and El Greco paintings **Obv:** Standing figures within circle **Rev:** Child and lamb within circle

Date	Mintage	VF20	XF40	MS60	MS63	MS65
1995	1,022,000	—	—	30.00	40.00	50.00

KM# 965 200 PESETAS

Copper-Nickel, 25.5 mm. **Ruler:** Juan Carlos I **Subject:** Fortuny and Balleau paintings **Obv:** Seated figure blowing on instrument within circle **Rev:** Seated figure playing guitar within circle

Date	Mintage	VF20	XF40	MS60	MS63	MS65
1996	9,206,000	—	—	3.00	4.00	6.00

KM# 986 200 PESETAS

Copper-Nickel, 25.5 mm. **Ruler:** Juan Carlos I **Subject:** Jacinto Benavente **Obv:** Stylized books within circle **Rev:** Bust left within circle

Date	Mintage	VF20	XF40	MS60	MS63	MS65
1997	6,845,000	—	—	3.50	5.00	7.00

KM# 992 200 PESETAS

Copper-Nickel, 25.5 mm. **Ruler:** Juan Carlos I **Obv:** Conjoined busts of King and Crown Prince right **Rev:** Value within circle

Date	Mintage	VF20	XF40	MS60	MS63	MS65
1998	5,008,000	—	—	5.00	6.00	8.00
1999	2,170,000	—	—	5.00	6.00	8.00
2000	1,900,000	—	—	6.00	8.00	10.00

KM# 831 500 PESETAS

12.00 g., Aluminum-Bronze, 28 mm. **Ruler:** Juan Carlos I **Obv:** Conjoined heads of Juan Carlos and Sofia left **Rev:** Crowned shield flanked by pillars with banner, vertical value at right

Date	Mintage	VF20	XF40	MS60	MS63	MS65
1987	400,000,000	—	—	9.00	11.00	13.00
1987	Inc. above	PF63 12.00	PF65 14.00			
1988	81,309,000	—	—	9.00	11.00	13.00
1989	103,861,000	—	—	5.00	6.00	8.00
1990	28,372,000	—	—	14.00	16.00	18.00

KM# 836 500 PESETAS

6.75 g., 0.925 Silver 0.2007 oz. ASW **Ruler:** Juan Carlos I **Subject:** Discovery of America - Juego De Pelota Game **Obv:** Head facing within beaded circle **Rev:** Kneeling masked figure within beaded circle

Date	Mintage	VF20	XF40	MS60	MS63	MS65
1989	43,045	—	—	—	12.00	14.00
1989	57,086	PF63 12.00	PF65 14.00			

KM# 857 500 PESETAS

6.75 g., 0.925 Silver 0.2007 oz. ASW **Ruler:** Juan Carlos I **Subject:** Juan de la Cosa **Obv:** Bust with hat facing within beaded circle **Rev:** Ocean navigation map within legend

Date	Mintage	VF20	XF40	MS60	MS63	MS65
1990	11,483	—	—	—	12.00	14.00
1990	12,596	PF63 12.00	PF65 14.00			

KM# 885 500 PESETAS
6.75 g., 0.925 Silver 0.2007 oz. ASW **Ruler:** Juan Carlos I **Obv:** Bust of Jorge Juan 1/4 left within beaded circle **Rev:** World globe map within beaded circle

Date	Mintage	VF20	XF40	MS60	MS63	MS65
1991	14,249	—	—	—	16.00	18.00
1991	14,383	PF63 16.00	PF65 18.00			

KM# 995 500 PESETAS
6.75 g., 0.925 Silver 0.2007 oz. ASW **Ruler:** Juan Carlos I **Subject:** Seville Expo '92 **Obv:** Church within beaded circle **Rev:** Palace portal within beaded circle

Date	Mintage	VF20	XF40	MS60	MS63	MS65
1992	16,610	—	—	—	18.00	20.00
1992	16,430	PF63 18.00	PF65 20.00			

KM# 924 500 PESETAS
12.00 g., Aluminum-Bronze, 28 mm. **Ruler:** Juan Carlos I **Obv:** Conjoined heads of Juan Carlos and Sofia left **Rev:** Crowned shield flanked by pillars with banner, vertical value at right

Date	Mintage	VF20	XF40	MS60	MS63	MS65
1993	3,059,000	—	—	40.00	50.00	60.00
1994	3,041,000	—	—	50.00	60.00	70.00
1995	1,015,000	—	—	35.00	40.00	50.00
1996	1,031,000	—	—	18.00	20.00	25.00
1997	4,881,000	—	—	7.00	9.00	11.00
1998	5,161,000	—	—	8.00	10.00	12.00
1999	2,030,000	—	—	9.00	11.00	13.00
2000	4,500,000	—	—	8.00	10.00	12.00

KM# 837 1000 PESETAS
13.50 g., 0.925 Silver 0.4015 oz. ASW **Ruler:** Juan Carlos I **Subject:** Discovery of America - Capture of Granada **Obv:** Standing figure divides date and beaded circle **Rev:** Armored figures on horses within beaded circle

Date	Mintage	VF20	XF40	MS60	MS63	MS65
1989	43,045	—	—	—	18.00	20.00
1989	57,086	PF63 18.00	PF65 20.00			

KM# 858 1000 PESETAS
13.50 g., 0.925 Silver 0.4015 oz. ASW **Ruler:** Juan Carlos I **Subject:** Magallanes and Elcano **Obv:** Busts facing above ships wheel **Rev:** Primitive global world map within legend

Date	Mintage	VF20	XF40	MS60	MS63	MS65
1990	23,943	—	—	—	18.00	20.00
1990	26,972	PF63 19.00	PF65 20.00			

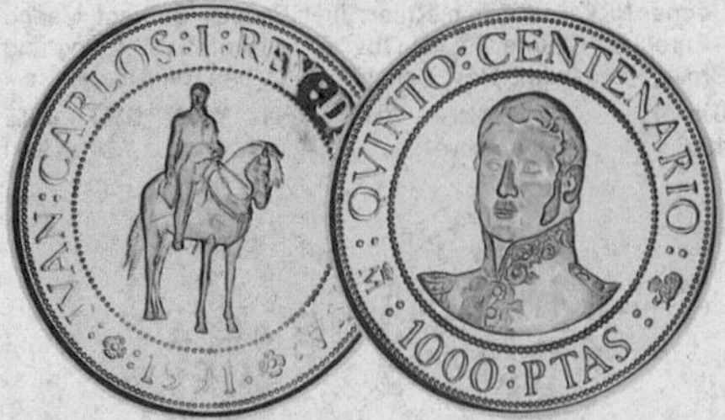

KM# 886 1000 PESETAS
13.50 g., 0.925 Silver 0.4015 oz. ASW **Ruler:** Juan Carlos I **Subject:** Simon Bolivar and San Martin **Obv:** Figure on horse within beaded circle **Rev:** Bust facing within beaded circle

Date	Mintage	VF20	XF40	MS60	MS63	MS65
1991	8,468	—	—	—	22.00	24.00
1991	8,145	PF63 22.00	PF65 24.00			

KM# 996 1000 PESETAS
13.50 g., 0.925 Silver 0.4015 oz. ASW **Ruler:** Juan Carlos I **Subject:** Seville Expo '92 **Obv:** Expo buildings within beaded circle **Rev:** India's archives building within beaded circle

Date	Mintage	VF20	XF40	MS60	MS63	MS65
1992	16,610	—	—	—	28.00	30.00
1992	16,430	PF63 28.00	PF65 30.00			

KM# 952 1000 PESETAS
13.66 g., 0.925 Silver 0.4062 oz. ASW **Ruler:** Juan Carlos I **Subject:** 1996 Olympics **Obv:** Head left **Rev:** Stylized figure, torch and value

Date	Mintage	VF20	XF40	MS60	MS63	MS65
1995	67,743	PF65 28.00				

KM# 973 1000 PESETAS
13.66 g., 0.925 Silver 0.4062 oz. ASW **Ruler:** Juan Carlos I **Subject:** Olympics **Obv:** Head left **Rev:** Three divers

Date	Mintage	VF20	XF40	MS60	MS63	MS65
1996	30,000	PF65 28.00				

KM# 988 1000 PESETAS
13.50 g., 0.925 Silver 0.4015 oz. ASW **Ruler:** Juan Carlos I **Subject:** Soccer World Championship - France '98 **Obv:** Head left **Rev:** Two soccer players

Date	Mintage	VF20	XF40	MS60	MS63	MS65
1998	30,000	PF65 35.00				

KM# 1000 1000 PESETAS
13.50 g., 0.925 Silver 0.4015 oz. ASW **Ruler:** Juan Carlos I **Subject:** Expo '98 Lisbon **Obv:** Head left **Rev:** El Cano

Date	Mintage	VF20	XF40	MS60	MS63	MS65
1998	50,000	PF65 26.00				

KM# 1034 1000 PESETAS
13.50 g., 0.925 Silver 0.4015 oz. ASW, 32.9 mm. **Ruler:** Juan Carlos I **Subject:** Constitution **Obv:** Head left **Rev:** Building **Edge:** Reeded

Date	Mintage	VF20	XF40	MS60	MS63	MS65
1998	75,000	PF65 28.00				

KM# 1009 1000 PESETAS
13.50 g., 0.925 Silver 0.4015 oz. ASW **Ruler:** Juan Carlos I **Subject:** Olympics - Sidney 2000 **Obv:** Head left **Rev:** Water polo players **Edge:** Plain

Date	Mintage	VF20	XF40	MS60	MS63	MS65
1999	27,103	PF65 26.00				

KM# 1010 1500 PESETAS
19.83 g., 0.925 Silver 0.5897 oz. ASW **Ruler:** Juan Carlos I **Subject:** Millennium **Obv:** Head left within beaded border **Rev:** Space walking astronaut above Columbus's ships **Edge:** Plain **Shape:** Octagon

Date	Mintage	VF20	XF40	MS60	MS63	MS65
1999	50,000	PF65 35.00				

KM# 1035 1500 PESETAS
20.00 g., 0.925 Silver 0.5948 oz. ASW, 33 mm. **Ruler:** Juan Carlos I **Subject:** Printing **Obv:** Head left **Rev:** Antique printing press **Edge:** Plain **Shape:** Octagon

Date	Mintage	VF20	XF40	MS60	MS63	MS65
2000	19,504	PF65 40.00				

KM# 1039 1500 PESETAS
20.00 g., 0.925 Silver 0.5948 oz. ASW, 33 mm. **Ruler:** Juan Carlos I **Subject:** Millennium **Obv:** Head left **Rev:** Dove above Atlantic Ocean **Edge:** Plain **Shape:** Octagon

Date	Mintage	VF20	XF40	MS60	MS63	MS65
2000	21,663	PF65 40.00				

KM# 838 2000 PESETAS
27.00 g., 0.925 Silver 0.803 oz. ASW **Ruler:** Juan Carlos I **Subject:** Discovery of America **Obv:** Busts facing each other within beaded circle **Rev:** Head of Columbus 1/4 left within beaded circle

Date	Mintage	VF20	XF40	MS60	MS63	MS65
1989	23,610	—	—	—	—	45.00
1989	32,799	PF65 45.00				

KM# 859 2000 PESETAS
27.00 g., 0.925 Silver 0.803 oz. ASW **Ruler:** Juan Carlos I **Subject:** 1992 Olympics **Obv:** Conjoined busts of King and Crown Prince right **Rev:** Symbols

Date	Mintage	VF20	XF40	MS60	MS63	MS65
1990	52,524	—	—	—	—	45.00
1990	130,993	PF65 40.00				

Note: See note below KM#914

KM# 860 2000 PESETAS
26.70 g., 0.925 Silver 0.794 oz. ASW **Ruler:** Juan Carlos I **Obv:** Conjoined busts of King and Crown Prince right **Rev:** Symbols and Olympic rings **Note:** Counterstamp on reverse below Olympic rings

Date	Mintage	VF20	XF40	MS60	MS63	MS65
1990 "1992"; Proof	—	PF65 100				

Note: Uncirculated strikes have medallic die alignment and edges with reeded and plain sections; Proof strikes have coin die alignment and reeded edges

KM# 861 2000 PESETAS
27.00 g., 0.925 Silver 0.803 oz. ASW **Ruler:** Juan Carlos I **Subject:** 1992 Olympics **Obv:** Conjoined busts of King and Crown Prince right **Rev:** Archer

Date	Mintage	VF20	XF40	MS60	MS63	MS65
1990	26,843	—	—	—	—	50.00
1990	87,655	PF65 45.00				

Note: Uncirculated strikes have medallic die alignment and edges with reeded and plain sections; Proof strikes have coin die alignment and reeded edges

KM# 862 2000 PESETAS
26.70 g., 0.925 Silver 0.794 oz. ASW **Ruler:** Juan Carlos I **Subject:** 1992 Olympics **Obv:** Conjoined busts of King and Crown Prince right **Rev:** Soccer player

Date	Mintage	VF20	XF40	MS60	MS63	MS65
1990	Est. 19638	—	—	—	—	50.00
1990	Est. 104351	PF65 30.00				

Note: Uncirculated strikes have medallic die alignment and edges with reeded and plain sections; Proof strikes have coin die alignment and reeded edges

KM# 863 2000 PESETAS
26.70 g., 0.925 Silver 0.794 oz. ASW **Ruler:** Juan Carlos I **Subject:** 1992 Olympics **Obv:** Conjoined busts of King and Crown Prince right **Rev:** Human pyramid

Date	Mintage	VF20	XF40	MS60	MS63	MS65
1990	Est. 16332	—	—	—	—	45.00
1990	Est. 73510	PF65 35.00				

Note: Uncirculated strikes have medallic die alignment and edges with reeded and plain sections; Proof strikes have coin die alignment and reeded edges

KM# 864 2000 PESETAS
26.70 g., 0.925 Silver 0.794 oz. ASW **Ruler:** Juan Carlos I **Subject:** 1992 Olympics **Obv:** Conjoined busts of King and Crown Prince right **Rev:** Greek runner

Date	Mintage	VF20	XF40	MS60	MS63	MS65
1990	Est. 15407	—	—	—	—	45.00
1990	Est. 73469	PF65 35.00				

Note: Uncirculated strikes have medallic die alignment and edges with reeded and plain sections; Proof strikes have coin die alignment and reeded edges

KM# 865 2000 PESETAS
26.70 g., 0.925 Silver 0.794 oz. ASW **Ruler:** Juan Carlos I **Subject:** 1992 Olympics **Obv:** Conjoined busts of King and Crown Prince right **Rev:** Ancient boat

Date	Mintage	VF20	XF40	MS60	MS63	MS65
1990	Est. 14223	—	—	—	—	45.00
1990	Est. 53835	PF65 35.00				

Note: Uncirculated strikes have medallic die alignment and edges with reeded and plain sections; Proof strikes have coin die alignment and reeded edges

KM# 866 2000 PESETAS
26.70 g., 0.925 Silver 0.794 oz. ASW **Ruler:** Juan Carlos I **Subject:** 1992 Olympics **Obv:** Conjoined busts of King and Crown Prince right **Rev:** Basketball players

Date	Mintage	VF20	XF40	MS60	MS63	MS65
1990	14,295	—	—	—	—	45.00
1990	Est. 56356	PF65 35.00				

Note: Uncirculated strikes have medallic die alignment and edges with reeded and plain sections; Proof strikes have coin die alignment and reeded edges

KM# 867 2000 PESETAS
26.70 g., 0.925 Silver 0.794 oz. ASW **Ruler:** Juan Carlos I **Subject:** 1992 Olympics **Obv:** Conjoined busts of King and Crown Prince right **Rev:** Pelota player

Date	Mintage	VF20	XF40	MS60	MS63	MS65
1990	15,407	—	—	—	—	55.00
1990	73,469	PF65 35.00				

Note: Uncirculated strikes have medallic die alignment and edges with reeded and plain sections; Proof strikes have coin die alignment and reeded edges

KM# 868 2000 PESETAS
26.70 g., 0.925 Silver 0.794 oz. ASW **Ruler:** Juan Carlos I

Subject: Hidalgo, Morelos and Juarez **Obv:** Three busts facing **Rev:** Aztec pictorial design within legend

Date	Mintage	VF20	XF40	MS60	MS63	MS65
1990	23,943	—	—	—	50.00	60.00
1990	26,972	PF63 50.00	PF65 60.00			

KM# 887 2000 PESETAS

26.70 g., 0.925 Silver 0.794 oz. ASW **Ruler:** Juan Carlos I **Subject:** Olympics **Obv:** Conjoined busts of King and Crown Prince right **Rev:** Torch, flag and Olympic rings

Date	Mintage	VF20	XF40	MS60	MS63	MS65
1991	18,545	—	—	—	50.00	60.00
1991	78,192	PF63 50.00	PF65 60.00			

KM# 888 2000 PESETAS

26.70 g., 0.925 Silver 0.794 oz. ASW **Ruler:** Juan Carlos I **Subject:** Olympics **Obv:** Conjoined busts of King and Crown Prince right **Rev:** Tennis player

Date	Mintage	VF20	XF40	MS60	MS63	MS65
1991	12,350	—	—	—	50.00	60.00
Note: Coin rotation, segmented reeded edge						
1991	38,905	PF63 50.00	PF65 60.00			
Note: Medal rotation, reeded edge						

KM# 889 2000 PESETAS

26.70 g., 0.925 Silver 0.794 oz. ASW **Ruler:** Juan Carlos I **Subject:** Olympics **Obv:** Conjoined busts of King and Crown Prince right **Rev:** Iberian rider

Date	Mintage	VF20	XF40	MS60	MS63	MS65
1991	15,056	—	—	—	50.00	60.00
1991	31,317	PF63 50.00	PF65 60.00			

Note: Medal rotation

KM# 890 2000 PESETAS

26.70 g., 0.925 Silver 0.794 oz. ASW **Ruler:** Juan Carlos I **Subject:** Olympics **Obv:** Conjoined busts of King and Crown Prince right **Rev:** Bowling

Date	Mintage	VF20	XF40	MS60	MS63	MS65
1991	10,561	—	—	—	70.00	80.00
1991	35,447	PF63 60.00	PF65 70.00			

Note: Medal rotation

KM# 891 2000 PESETAS

26.70 g., 0.925 Silver 0.794 oz. ASW **Ruler:** Juan Carlos I **Subject:** Ibero - American Series **Obv:** Crowned shield flanked by pillars with banner in center of assorted shields **Rev:** Crown divides beaded circle with assorted designs in center

Date	Mintage	VF20	XF40	MS60	MS63	MS65
(19)91	50,000	PF65 120				

KM# 892 2000 PESETAS

26.70 g., 0.925 Silver 0.794 oz. ASW **Ruler:** Juan Carlos I **Subject:** Federman, Quesada and Benalcazar **Obv:** Armored busts left within beaded circle **Rev:** Standing figures around armored figure on horse within beaded circle

Date	Mintage	VF20	XF40	MS60	MS63	MS65
1991	14,249	—	—	—	80.00	90.00
1991	14,383	PF63 80.00	PF65 90.00			

KM# 911 2000 PESETAS

26.70 g., 0.925 Silver 0.794 oz. ASW **Ruler:** Juan Carlos I **Subject:** Olympics **Obv:** Conjoined busts of King and Crown Prince right **Rev:** Tug-of-war

Date	Mintage	VF20	XF40	MS60	MS63	MS65
1992	9,043	—	—	—	65.00	75.00
1992	33,980	PF63 60.00	PF65 70.00			

Note: Uncirculated strikes have medallic die alignment and edges with reeded and plain sections; Proof strikes have coin die alignment and reeded edges

KM# 912 2000 PESETAS

26.70 g., 0.925 Silver 0.794 oz. ASW **Ruler:** Juan Carlos I **Subject:** Olympics **Obv:** Conjoined busts of King and Crown Prince right **Rev:** Wheelchair basketball

Date	Mintage	VF20	XF40	MS60	MS63	MS65
1992	8,997	—	—	—	70.00	80.00
1992	27,886	PF63 60.00	PF65 70.00			

Note: Uncirculated strikes have medallic die alignment and edges with reeded and plain sections; Proof strikes have coin die alignment and reeded edges

KM# 913 2000 PESETAS

26.70 g., 0.925 Silver 0.794 oz. ASW **Ruler:** Juan Carlos I **Subject:** Olympics **Obv:** Conjoined busts of King and Crown Prince right **Rev:** Sprinters

Date	Mintage	VF20	XF40	MS60	MS63	MS65
1992	15,633	—	—	—	80.00	90.00
1992	41,651	PF63 70.00	PF65 80.00			

Note: Uncirculated strikes have medallic die alignment and edges with reeded and plain sections; Proof strikes have coin die alignment and reeded edges

KM# 914 2000 PESETAS

26.70 g., 0.925 Silver 0.794 oz. ASW **Ruler:** Juan Carlos I **Subject:** Olympics **Obv:** Conjoined busts of King and Crown Prince right **Rev:** Chariot racing

Date	Mintage	VF20	XF40	MS60	MS63	MS65
1992	36,538	PF63 70.00	PF65 80.00			
Note: Uncirculated strikes have medallic die alignment and edges with reeded and plain sections; Proof strikes have coin die alignment and reeded edges						
1992	13,037	—	—	—	80.00	90.00

KM# 980 2000 PESETAS
26.70 g., 0.925 Silver 0.794 oz. ASW **Ruler:** Juan Carlos I **Subject:** Seville Expo '92 **Obv:** Exposition building and date within beaded circle **Rev:** Tower of Seville within beaded circle

Date	Mintage	VF20	XF40	MS60	MS63	MS65
1992	16,610	—	—	—	80.00	90.00
1992	16,430	PF63 80.00	PF65 90.00			

KM# 925 2000 PESETAS
26.70 g., 0.925 Silver 0.794 oz. ASW **Ruler:** Juan Carlos I **Subject:** Holy Jacobean Year **Obv:** Head left **Rev:** German Jacobean Pilgrims within square and beaded circle

Date	Mintage	VF20	XF40	MS60	MS63	MS65
1993	10,786	PF65 100				

KM# 926 2000 PESETAS
26.70 g., 0.925 Silver 0.794 oz. ASW **Ruler:** Juan Carlos I **Subject:** Holy Jacobean Year **Obv:** Head left **Rev:** Santiago cross and scallop shell within beaded circle

Date	Mintage	VF20	XF40	MS60	MS63	MS65
1993	17,236	PF65 100				

KM# 937 2000 PESETAS
18.00 g., 0.925 Silver 0.5353 oz. ASW **Ruler:** Juan Carlos I **Subject:** International Monetary Fund and Bank **Obv:** Head left **Rev:** Designs above building

Date	Mintage	VF20	XF40	MS60	MS63	MS65
1994	8,669,000	—	—	—	22.00	24.00

KM# 938 2000 PESETAS
27.00 g., 0.925 Silver 0.803 oz. ASW **Ruler:** Juan Carlos I **Subject:** Courtyard of the Lions **Rev:** Courtyard scene

Date	Mintage	VF20	XF40	MS60	MS63	MS65
1994	7,131	PF65 60.00				

KM# 939 2000 PESETAS
27.00 g., 0.925 Silver 0.803 oz. ASW **Ruler:** Juan Carlos I **Subject:** Ibero-American series **Rev:** Spanish lynx within circle

Date	Mintage	VF20	XF40	MS60	MS63	MS65
1994	20,000	PF65 150				

KM# 940 2000 PESETAS
27.00 g., 0.925 Silver 0.803 oz. ASW **Ruler:** Juan Carlos I **Obv:** Head left **Rev:** Purple herons in swamp

Date	Mintage	VF20	XF40	MS60	MS63	MS65
1994	6,555	PF65 60.00				

KM# 941 2000 PESETAS
27.00 g., 0.925 Silver 0.803 oz. ASW **Ruler:** Juan Carlos I **Obv:** Head left **Rev:** Two bulls fighting

Date	Mintage	VF20	XF40	MS60	MS63	MS65
1994	10,388	PF65 60.00				

KM# 953 2000 PESETAS
27.00 g., 0.925 Silver 0.803 oz. ASW **Ruler:** Juan Carlos I **Obv:** Head left **Rev:** Capercaillie bird

Date	Mintage	VF20	XF40	MS60	MS63	MS65
1995	18,359	PF65 60.00				

KM# 954 2000 PESETAS
18.00 g., 0.925 Silver 0.5353 oz. ASW **Ruler:** Juan Carlos I **Subject:** Presidential Council - V.E **Obv:** Head left **Rev:** Designs above building

Date	Mintage	VF20	XF40	MS60	MS63	MS65
1995	—	—	—	—	22.00	24.00

KM# 955 2000 PESETAS
27.00 g., 0.925 Silver 0.803 oz. ASW **Ruler:** Juan Carlos I **Subject:** 50th Anniversary - United Nations **Obv:** Head left **Rev:** Numeral 50 and UN logo above design

Date	Mintage	VF20	XF40	MS60	MS63	MS65
1995	26,049	PF65 100				

KM# 966 2000 PESETAS
27.00 g., 0.925 Silver 0.803 oz. ASW **Ruler:** Juan Carlos I **Obv:** Head left **Rev:** Gray wolves

Date	Mintage	VF20	XF40	MS60	MS63	MS65
1996	35,000	PF65 100				

KM# 967 2000 PESETAS
27.00 g., 0.925 Silver 0.803 oz. ASW **Ruler:** Juan Carlos I **Obv:** Head left **Rev:** Brown bears

Date	Mintage	VF20	XF40	MS60	MS63	MS65
1996	35,000	PF65 60.00				

KM# 968 2000 PESETAS
18.00 g., 0.925 Silver 0.5353 oz. ASW **Ruler:** Juan Carlos I **Subject:** Francisco de Goya **Obv:** Head left **Rev:** Reclining female figure

Date	Mintage	VF20	XF40	MS60	MS63	MS65
1996	—	—	—	—	22.00	24.00

KM# 974 2000 PESETAS
27.00 g., 0.925 Silver 0.803 oz. ASW **Ruler:** Juan Carlos I **Series:** Patrimonio de la Humanidad **Obv:** UNESCO logo **Rev:** Taj Mahal, India

Date	Mintage	VF20	XF40	MS60	MS63	MS65
1996	30,000	PF65 45.00				

KM# 975 2000 PESETAS
27.00 g., 0.925 Silver 0.803 oz. ASW **Ruler:** Juan Carlos I **Series:** Patrimonio de la Humanidad **Obv:** Crowned shield with value as II **Rev:** Djenne, Mali

Date	Mintage	VF20	XF40	MS60	MS63	MS65
1996	30,000	PF65 45.00				

KM# 976 2000 PESETAS
27.00 g., 0.925 Silver 0.803 oz. ASW **Ruler:** Juan Carlos I **Series:** Patrimonio de la Humanidad **Obv:** Crowned shield with value as II **Rev:** Abu Simbel, Egypt

Date	Mintage	VF20	XF40	MS60	MS63	MS65
1996	30,000	PF65 45.00				

KM# 977 2000 PESETAS
27.00 g., 0.925 Silver 0.803 oz. ASW **Ruler:** Juan Carlos I **Series:** Patrimonio de la Humanidad **Obv:** Crowned shield with value as II **Rev:** Palenque, Mexico

Date	Mintage	VF20	XF40	MS60	MS63	MS65
1996	30,000	PF65 45.00				

KM# 978 2000 PESETAS
27.00 g., 0.925 Silver 0.803 oz. ASW **Ruler:** Juan Carlos I **Series:** Patrimonio de la Humanidad **Obv:** Crowned shield with value as II **Rev:** Merida, Spain

Date	Mintage	VF20	XF40	MS60	MS63	MS65
1996	30,000	PF65 45.00				

KM# 999 2000 PESETAS
18.00 g., 0.925 Silver 0.5353 oz. ASW **Ruler:** Juan Carlos I **Subject:** Don Quixote **Obv:** Head left **Rev:** Quixote and friend plus cameo of Cervantes

Date	Mintage	VF20	XF40	MS60	MS63	MS65
1997	2,587,750	—	—	—	22.00	24.00

KM# 1018 2000 PESETAS
27.00 g., 0.925 Silver 0.803 oz. ASW, 40 mm. **Ruler:** Juan Carlos I **Series:** "Patrimono de la Humanidad" UNESCO **Obv:** UNESCO logo **Rev:** Abomey lion **Edge:** Reeded

Date	Mintage	VF20	XF40	MS60	MS63	MS65
1997	30,000	PF65 45.00				

KM# 1019 2000 PESETAS
27.00 g., 0.925 Silver 0.803 oz. ASW **Ruler:** Juan Carlos I **Series:** "Patrimono de la Humanidad" UNESCO **Obv:** UNESCO logo **Rev:** Easter Island statues

Date	Mintage	VF20	XF40	MS60	MS63	MS65
1997	30,000	PF65 45.00				

KM# 1020 2000 PESETAS
27.00 g., 0.925 Silver 0.803 oz. ASW **Ruler:** Juan Carlos I **Series:** "Patrimono de la Humanidad" UNESCO **Obv:** UNESCO logo **Rev:** Temple at Petra

Date	Mintage	VF20	XF40	MS60	MS63	MS65
1997	30,000	PF65 45.00				

KM# 1021 2000 PESETAS
27.00 g., 0.925 Silver 0.803 oz. ASW **Ruler:** Juan Carlos I **Series:** "Patrimono de la Humanidad" UNESCO **Obv:** UNESCO logo **Rev:** Acropolis

Date	Mintage	VF20	XF40	MS60	MS63	MS65
1997	30,000	PF65 45.00				

KM# 1022 2000 PESETAS
27.00 g., 0.925 Silver 0.803 oz. ASW **Ruler:** Juan Carlos I **Series:** "Patrimono de la Humanidad" UNESCO **Obv:** UNESCO logo **Rev:** Horyu-Ji pagoda

Date	Mintage	VF20	XF40	MS60	MS63	MS65
1997	30,000	PF65 45.00				

KM# 1024 2000 PESETAS

27.00 g., 0.925 Silver 0.803 oz. ASW, 40 mm. **Ruler:** Juan Carlos I **Subject:** House of Borbon **Obv:** Bust of Philip V facing within beaded border **Rev:** Figural sculpture within beaded border **Edge:** Reeded

Date	Mintage	VF20	XF40	MS60	MS63	MS65
1997	5,894	PF65 55.00				

KM# 1025 2000 PESETAS

27.00 g., 0.925 Silver 0.803 oz. ASW **Ruler:** Juan Carlos I **Subject:** House of Borbon **Obv:** Bust of Louis I left within beaded border **Rev:** Crowned arms in order chain within beaded border

Date	Mintage	VF20	XF40	MS60	MS63	MS65
1997	5,889	PF65 55.00				

KM# 1026 2000 PESETAS

27.00 g., 0.925 Silver 0.803 oz. ASW **Ruler:** Juan Carlos I **Subject:** House of Borbon **Obv:** Bust of Ferdinand VI 1/4 right within beaded circle **Rev:** Spanish galleon within beaded circle

Date	Mintage	VF20	XF40	MS60	MS63	MS65
1997	6,072	PF65 55.00				

KM# 987 2000 PESETAS

18.00 g., 0.925 Silver 0.5353 oz. ASW **Ruler:** Juan Carlos I **Subject:** Philip II **Obv:** Head left within beaded circle **Rev:** Head left, design above steepled building within beaded circle

Date	Mintage	VF20	XF40	MS60	MS63	MS65
1998	2,324,000	—	—	—	22.00	24.00

KM# 1036 2000 PESETAS

27.30 g., 0.925 Silver 0.8119 oz. ASW, 39.9 mm. **Ruler:** Juan Carlos I **Subject:** House of Borbon **Obv:** Bust of Ferdinand VII 1/4 right **Rev:** Prado Museum **Edge:** Reeded

Date	Mintage	VF20	XF40	MS60	MS63	MS65
1998	30,000	PF65 50.00				

KM# 1011 2000 PESETAS

18.00 g., 0.925 Silver 0.5353 oz. ASW **Ruler:** Juan Carlos I **Subject:** St. Jacob **Obv:** Head left within beaded circle **Rev:** St. Jacob, value and dagger

Date	Mintage	VF20	XF40	MS60	MS63	MS65
1999	2,043,800	—	—	—	30.00	35.00

KM# 1029 2000 PESETAS

27.00 g., 0.925 Silver 0.803 oz. ASW **Ruler:** Juan Carlos I **Subject:** Barcelona City Government 750 Years **Obv:** Head left **Rev:** Stylized city arms

Date	Mintage	VF20	XF40	MS60	MS63	MS65
1999	22,498	PF65 55.00				

KM# 1030 2000 PESETAS

27.00 g., 0.925 Silver 0.803 oz. ASW **Ruler:** Juan Carlos I **Subject:** House of Borbon **Obv:** Bust of Isabel II 1/4 right within beaded circle

Date	Mintage	VF20	XF40	MS60	MS63	MS65
1999	5,081	PF65 60.00				

KM# 1031 2000 PESETAS

27.00 g., 0.925 Silver 0.803 oz. ASW **Ruler:** Juan Carlos I **Subject:** House of Borbon **Obv:** Head of Alfonso XII 1/4 right within beaded circle **Rev:** Train within beaded circle

Date	Mintage	VF20	XF40	MS60	MS63	MS65
1999	5,690	PF65 55.00				

KM# 1032 2000 PESETAS

27.00 g., 0.925 Silver 0.803 oz. ASW **Ruler:** Juan Carlos I **Subject:** House of Borbon - Alfonso XIII **Obv:** Childhood portrait of Alfonso XIII within circle and beaded border

Date	Mintage	VF20	XF40	MS60	MS63	MS65
1999	—	PF65 35.00				

KM# 1033 2000 PESETAS

27.00 g., 0.925 Silver 0.803 oz. ASW **Ruler:** Juan Carlos I **Subject:** House of Borbon - Alfonso XIII **Obv:** Adult portrait of Alfonso XIIII within beaded border

Date	Mintage	VF20	XF40	MS60	MS63	MS65
1999	5,603	PF65 55.00				

KM# 1015 2000 PESETAS

18.00 g., 0.925 Silver 0.5353 oz. ASW, 33 mm. **Ruler:** Juan Carlos I **Subject:** Charles V **Obv:** Head left within beaded border **Rev:** Laureate Head right within beaded border **Edge:** Plain

Date	Mintage	VF20	XF40	MS60	MS63	MS65
2000	1,565,400	—	—	—	26.00	28.00

KM# 1037 2000 PESETAS

27.00 g., 0.925 Silver 0.803 oz. ASW, 40 mm. **Ruler:** Juan Carlos I **Obv:** Head left **Rev:** Bilbao city arms **Edge:** Reeded

Date	Mintage	VF20	XF40	MS60	MS63	MS65
2000	12,100	PF65 60.00				

KM# 839 5000 PESETAS

54.00 g., 0.925 Silver 1.6059 oz. ASW **Ruler:** Juan Carlos I **Subject:** Discovery of America **Obv:** Crowned shield flanked by pillars with banner within beaded circle **Rev:** Santa Maria

Date	Mintage	VF20	XF40	MS60	MS63	MS65
1989	23,630	—	—	—	—	60.00
1989	32,799	PF65 75.00				

KM# 840 5000 PESETAS

1.68 g., 0.999 Gold 0.054 oz. AGW **Ruler:** Juan Carlos I **Subject:** Discovery of America **Obv:** Crown within beaded circle **Rev:** Crown above compass face within beaded circle

Date	Mintage	VF20	XF40	MS60	MS63	MS65
1989	6,218	—	—	—	—	125
1989	8,143	PF65 125				

KM# 869 5000 PESETAS
54.00 g., 0.925 Silver 1.6059 oz. ASW **Ruler:** Juan Carlos I **Subject:** Cortes, Montezuma and Marina **Obv:** Three busts facing within beaded circle **Rev:** Scene from Aztec mythology within legend

Date	Mintage	VF20	XF40	MS60	MS63	MS65
1990	11,483	—	—	—	—	75.00
1990	12,586	PF65 75.00				

KM# 870 5000 PESETAS
1.68 g., 0.999 Gold 0.054 oz. AGW **Ruler:** Juan Carlos I **Obv:** Bust of Philip V facing **Rev:** Compass face

Date	Mintage	VF20	XF40	MS60	MS63	MS65
1990	3,103	—	—	—	—	125
1990	4,089	PF65 125				

KM# 893 5000 PESETAS
54.00 g., 0.925 Silver 1.6059 oz. ASW **Ruler:** Juan Carlos I **Obv:** Pizarro and Atahualpa facing right within circle **Rev:** Incan ruins in mountains within beaded circle

Date	Mintage	VF20	XF40	MS60	MS63	MS65
1991	8,468	—	—	—	—	95.00
1991	8,145	PF65 95.00				

KM# 894 5000 PESETAS
1.68 g., 0.999 Gold 0.054 oz. AGW **Ruler:** Juan Carlos I **Obv:** Bust of Fernando VI 1/4 right **Rev:** Crown above compass face within beaded circle

Date	Mintage	VF20	XF40	MS60	MS63	MS65
1991	2,260	—	—	—	—	125
1991	2,037	PF65 125				

KM# 997 5000 PESETAS
54.00 g., 0.925 Silver 1.6059 oz. ASW **Ruler:** Juan Carlos I **Subject:** Seville Expo '92 **Obv:** Mint building within beaded circle **Rev:** Old coin press within beaded circle

Date	Mintage	VF20	XF40	MS60	MS63	MS65
1992	16,610	—	—	—	—	125
1992	16,430	PF65 120				

KM# 1001 5000 PESETAS
1.68 g., 0.999 Gold 0.054 oz. AGW **Ruler:** Juan Carlos I **Obv:** Crown within beaded circle **Rev:** Screw press

Date	Mintage	VF20	XF40	MS60	MS63	MS65
1992	1,258	—	—	—	—	125
1992	1,227	PF65 150				

KM# 942 5000 PESETAS
54.00 g., 0.925 Silver 1.6059 oz. ASW **Ruler:** Juan Carlos I **Rev:** Imperial Eagle

Date	Mintage	VF20	XF40	MS60	MS63	MS65
1994	7,436	PF65 125				

KM# 956 5000 PESETAS
54.00 g., 0.925 Silver 1.6059 oz. ASW **Ruler:** Juan Carlos I **Rev:** Spanish Ibex

Date	Mintage	VF20	XF40	MS60	MS63	MS65
1995	5,973	PF65 120				

KM# 969 5000 PESETAS
54.00 g., 0.925 Silver 1.6059 oz. ASW **Ruler:** Juan Carlos I **Rev:** Gaudi sculpture

Date	Mintage	VF20	XF40	MS60	MS63	MS65
1996	Est. 20000	PF65 70.00				

KM# 841 10000 PESETAS
168.75 g., 0.925 Silver 5.0185 oz. ASW, 73 mm. **Ruler:** Juan Carlos I **Subject:** Regional Autonomy **Obv:** Royal family depicted in circular frames **Rev:** Crowned arms at center of crowned provincial arms **Note:** Illustration reduced.

Date	Mintage	VF20	XF40	MS60	MS63	MS65
1989	47,041	—	—	—	—	175

KM# 842 10000 PESETAS
3.37 g., 0.999 Gold 0.1082 oz. AGW **Ruler:** Juan Carlos I **Subject:** Discovery of America **Obv:** Crown above monogram within beaded circle **Rev:** Armillary sphere within beaded circle

Date	Mintage	VF20	XF40	MS60	MS63	MS65
1989	5,130	—	—	—	—	225
1989	6,818	PF65 225				

KM# 871 10000 PESETAS
3.37 g., 0.999 Gold 0.1082 oz. AGW **Ruler:** Juan Carlos I **Series:** 1992 Olympics **Obv:** Bust right **Rev:** Stylized field hockey player

Date	Mintage	VF20	XF40	MS60	MS63	MS65
1990	3,101	—	—	—	—	225
1990	5,382	PF65 225				

Note: Uncirculated strikes have medallic die alignment and edges with reeded and plain sections; Proof strikes have coin die alignment and reeded edges

KM# 872 10000 PESETAS
3.37 g., 0.999 Gold 0.1082 oz. AGW **Ruler:** Juan Carlos I **Series:** 1992 Olympics **Obv:** Bust right **Rev:** Stylized gymnast

Date	Mintage	VF20	XF40	MS60	MS63	MS65
1990	3,339	—	—	—	—	225
1990	3,305	PF65 225				

Note: Uncirculated strikes have medallic die alignment and edges with reeded and plain sections; Proof strikes have coin die alignment and reeded edges

KM# 873 10000 PESETAS
168.75 g., 0.925 Silver 5.0185 oz. ASW, 73 mm. **Ruler:** Juan Carlos I **Subject:** Spanish Royal Family **Obv:** Royal family depicted in circular frames within beaded circle **Rev:** Center circle depicts men holding up world within beaded circle, busts of discoverers and liberators surround **Note:** Illustration reduced.

Date	Mintage	VF20	XF40	MS60	MS63	MS65
1990	29,625	—	—	—	—	175

KM# 874 10000 PESETAS
3.37 g., 0.999 Gold 0.1082 oz. AGW **Ruler:** Juan Carlos I **Obv:** Quauchtemoc within beaded circle **Rev:** Crown above compass face within beaded circle

Date	Mintage	VF20	XF40	MS60	MS63	MS65
1990	2,500	—	—	—	—	225
1990	2,113	PF65 225				

KM# 895 10000 PESETAS
3.37 g., 0.999 Gold 0.1082 oz. AGW **Ruler:** Juan Carlos I **Series:** Olympics **Obv:** Bust 3/4 right within circle **Rev:** Tae Kwon Do participant within circle

Date	Mintage	VF20	XF40	MS60	MS63	MS65
1991	2,679	—	—	—	—	225
1991	2,423	PF65 225				

Note: Uncirculated strikes have medallic die alignment and edges with reeded and plain sections; Proof strikes have coin die alignment and reeded edges.

KM# 896 10000 PESETAS
168.75 g., 0.925 Silver 5.0185 oz. ASW, 73 mm. **Ruler:** Juan Carlos I **Subject:** Discoverers and Liberators **Obv:** Royal family depicted in circular frames within beaded circle **Rev:** Center circle depicts men holding up world within beaded circle, busts of discoverers and liberators surround **Note:** Illustration reduced.

Date	Mintage	VF20	XF40	MS60	MS63	MS65
1991	17,024	—	—	—	—	200

KM# 897 10000 PESETAS
3.37 g., 0.999 Gold 0.1082 oz. AGW **Ruler:** Juan Carlos I **Obv:** Tupac Amaru II within beaded circle **Rev:** Armillary sphere within beaded circle

Date	Mintage	VF20	XF40	MS60	MS63	MS65
1991	1,577	—	—	—	—	250
1991	1,759	PF65 250				

KM# 915 10000 PESETAS

3.37 g., 0.999 Gold 0.1082 oz. AGW **Ruler:** Juan Carlos I **Series:** Olympics **Obv:** Bust 1/4 right within circle **Rev:** Baseball player within circle

Date	Mintage	VF20	XF40	MS60	MS63	MS65
1992	1,496	—	—	—	—	250
1992	5,714	PF65 225				

Note: Uncirculated strikes have medallic die alignment and edges with reeded and plain sections; Proof strikes have coin die alignment and reeded edges

KM# 998 10000 PESETAS

168.75 g., 0.925 Silver 5.0185 oz. ASW **Ruler:** Juan Carlos I **Series:** Seville Expo '92 - Nobel Prize winners **Obv:** Royal family depicted in circular frames **Rev:** Nobel winners depicted in oval frames, hand with quill encircled below

Date	Mintage	VF20	XF40	MS60	MS63	MS65
1992	13,511	PF65 300				

KM# 1002 10000 PESETAS

3.37 g., 0.999 Gold 0.1082 oz. AGW **Ruler:** Juan Carlos I **Obv:** Crowned monogram **Rev:** Worker operating screw press

Date	Mintage	VF20	XF40	MS60	MS63	MS65
1992	1,227	PF65 250				
1992	1,258	—	—	—	—	250

KM# 928 10000 PESETAS

168.75 g., 0.925 Silver 5.0185 oz. ASW, 75 mm. **Ruler:** Juan Carlos I **Subject:** Holy Jacobean Year **Obv:** Crowned cameo above cathedral within beaded circle **Rev:** Pilgrims within beaded circle, crown at top **Note:** Illustration reduced.

Date	Mintage	VF20	XF40	MS60	MS63	MS65
1993	7,818	PF63 350	PF65 425			

KM# 943 10000 PESETAS

167.75 g., 0.925 Silver 4.9888 oz. ASW, 73 mm. **Ruler:** Juan Carlos I **Subject:** Goya's paintings **Obv:** The Parasol **Rev:** Bull fighting scene **Note:** Illustration reduced.

Date	Mintage	VF20	XF40	MS60	MS63	MS65
1994	15,000	PF65 250				

KM# 957 10000 PESETAS

168.75 g., 0.925 Silver 5.0185 oz. ASW, 73 mm. **Ruler:** Juan Carlos I **Subject:** Velazguez's paintings **Obv:** Cameo to right of figure on horse **Rev:** Radiant sun and three standing figures **Note:** Illustration reduced.

Date	Mintage	VF20	XF40	MS60	MS63	MS65
1995	5,368	PF65 250				

KM# 970 10000 PESETAS

168.75 g., 0.925 Silver 5.0185 oz. ASW **Ruler:** Juan Carlos I **Subject:** Goya's paintings **Obv:** The Naked Maja **Rev:** Family picking flowers

Date	Mintage	VF20	XF40	MS60	MS63	MS65
1996	5,950	PF63 275	PF65 300			

KM# 1027 10000 PESETAS

168.75 g., 0.925 Silver 5.0185 oz. ASW, 73 mm. **Ruler:** Juan Carlos I **Subject:** House of Borbon - Juan Carlos I **Obv:** King standing and Queen seated **Rev:** Crowned provincial arms within circle at center of family heads separated by fleur-de-lis **Edge:** Reeded **Note:** Illustration reduced.

Date	Mintage	VF20	XF40	MS60	MS63	MS65
1997	5,573	PF63 225	PF65 250			

KM# 1068 10000 PESETAS
169.10 g., 0.925 Silver 5.0289 oz. ASW, 73 mm. **Ruler:** Juan Carlos I **Subject:** 500th Birthday of Charles I **Obv:** Uniformed half-figure facing **Rev:** Uniformed figure seated on an eagle with pillars in background **Edge:** Plain

Date	Mintage	VF20	XF40	MS60	MS63	MS65
ND (2000)	9,000	PF63 275	PF65 300			

KM# 843 20000 PESETAS
6.75 g., 0.999 Gold 0.2168 oz. AGW **Ruler:** Juan Carlos I **Subject:** Discovery of America **Obv:** Head facing within beaded circle **Rev:** Pinzon Brother within beaded circle

Date	Mintage	VF20	XF40	MS60	MS63	MS65
1989	4,750	—	—	—	—	450
1989	6,427	PF65 450				

KM# 875 20000 PESETAS
6.75 g., 0.999 Gold 0.2168 oz. AGW **Ruler:** Juan Carlos I **Subject:** 1992 Olympics - La Sagrada Familia **Obv:** Bust 1/4 right within beaded circle **Rev:** Cathedral towers within beaded circle

Date	Mintage	VF20	XF40	MS60	MS63	MS65
1990	3,101	—	—	—	—	450
1990	5,382	PF65 450				

Note: Uncirculated strikes have medallic die alignment and edges with reeded and plain sections; Proof strikes have coin die alignment and reeded edges

KM# 876 20000 PESETAS
6.75 g., 0.999 Gold 0.2168 oz. AGW **Ruler:** Juan Carlos I **Series:** 1992 Olympics **Obv:** Bust 1/4 right within beaded circle **Rev:** Ruins of Empuries within beaded circle

Date	Mintage	VF20	XF40	MS60	MS63	MS65
1990	2,246	—	—	—	—	500
1990	3,785	PF65 400				

Note: Uncirculated strikes have medallic die alignment and edges with reeded and plain sections; Proof strikes have coin die alignment and reeded edges

KM# 877 20000 PESETAS
6.75 g., 0.999 Gold 0.2168 oz. AGW **Ruler:** Juan Carlos I **Subject:** Tupac Amaru I **Obv:** Bust 1/4 right within beaded circle **Rev:** Stylized standing figure with hat and scepter within beaded circle

Date	Mintage	VF20	XF40	MS60	MS63	MS65
1990	1,910	—	—	—	—	500
1990	2,750	PF65 450				

KM# 898 20000 PESETAS
6.75 g., 0.999 Gold 0.2168 oz. AGW **Ruler:** Juan Carlos I **Series:** Olympics **Obv:** Bust 1/4 right within circle **Rev:** Montjuic Stadium within circle

Date	Mintage	VF20	XF40	MS60	MS63	MS65
1991	1,965	—	—	—	—	500
1991	3,329	PF65 400				

Note: Uncirculated strikes have medallic die alignment and edges with reeded and plain sections; Proof strikes have coin die alignment and reeded edges

KM# 899 20000 PESETAS
6.75 g., 0.999 Gold 0.2168 oz. AGW **Ruler:** Juan Carlos I **Subject:** Huascar **Obv:** Bust facing within beaded circle **Rev:** Armored bust with spear within beaded circle

Date	Mintage	VF20	XF40	MS60	MS63	MS65
1991	1,292	—	—	—	—	500
1991	1,656	PF65 450				

KM# 916 20000 PESETAS
6.75 g., 0.999 Gold 0.2168 oz. AGW **Ruler:** Juan Carlos I **Series:** Olympics **Obv:** Bust 1/4 right within circle **Rev:** Dome building within circle

Date	Mintage	VF20	XF40	MS60	MS63	MS65
1992	1,475	—	—	—	—	500
1992	3,235	PF65 450				

Note: Uncirculated strikes have medallic die alignment and edges with reeded and plain sections; Proof strikes have coin die alignment and reeded edges

KM# 1003 20000 PESETAS
6.75 g., 0.999 Gold 0.2168 oz. AGW **Ruler:** Juan Carlos I **Obv:** Bust facing within beaded circle **Rev:** Worker feeding screw press

Date	Mintage	VF20	XF40	MS60	MS63	MS65
1992	1,045	—	—	—	—	550
1992	1,147	PF65 550				

KM# 929 20000 PESETAS
6.75 g., 0.999 Gold 0.2168 oz. AGW **Ruler:** Juan Carlos I **Subject:** Holy Jacobean Year **Rev:** Conveyance of Santiago's body

Date	Mintage	VF20	XF40	MS60	MS63	MS65
1993	1,867	PF65 400				

KM# 944 20000 PESETAS
6.75 g., 0.999 Gold 0.2168 oz. AGW **Ruler:** Juan Carlos I **Subject:** Paleolithic Cave Painting **Rev:** Stylized animal cave paintings

Date	Mintage	VF20	XF40	MS60	MS63	MS65
1994	2,097	PF65 450				

KM# 958 20000 PESETAS
6.75 g., 0.999 Gold 0.2168 oz. AGW, 20 mm. **Ruler:** Juan Carlos I **Subject:** Ancient Sculpture - Dama de Elche **Rev:** Hooded bust left

Date	Mintage	VF20	XF40	MS60	MS63	MS65
1995	2,089	PF65 450				

KM# 971 20000 PESETAS
6.75 g., 0.999 Gold 0.2168 oz. AGW **Ruler:** Juan Carlos I **Rev:** Pillars and arches

Date	Mintage	VF20	XF40	MS60	MS63	MS65
1996	—	PF65 400				

KM# 844 40000 PESETAS
13.50 g., 0.999 Gold 0.4336 oz. AGW **Ruler:** Juan Carlos I **Subject:** Discovery of America **Obv:** Standing figure divides date and beaded circle **Rev:** Sea monster attacking ship within beaded circle

Date	Mintage	VF20	XF40	MS60	MS63	MS65
1989	4,476	—	—	—	—	800
1989	6,380	PF65 800				

KM# 878 40000 PESETAS
13.50 g., 0.999 Gold 0.4336 oz. AGW **Ruler:** Juan Carlos I **Subject:** Felipe II **Obv:** Standing figure divides date and beaded circle **Rev:** King seated on throne within beaded circle

Date	Mintage	VF20	XF40	MS60	MS63	MS65
1990	1,910	—	—	—	—	1,000
1990	2,812	PF65 900				

KM# 900 40000 PESETAS
13.50 g., 0.999 Gold 0.4336 oz. AGW **Ruler:** Juan Carlos I **Obv:** Standing figure divides beaded circle and dates **Rev:** Imperial double eagle

Date	Mintage	VF20	XF40	MS60	MS63	MS65
1991	1,251	—	—	—	—	1,100
1991	1,702	PF65 1,000				

KM# 1004 40000 PESETAS

13.50 g., 0.999 Gold 0.4336 oz. AGW **Ruler:** Juan Carlos I **Obv:** Standing figure divides beaded circle and dates **Rev:** Horse-powered coin press

Date	Mintage	VF20	XF40	MS60	MS63	MS65
1992	1,018	—	—	—	—	1,100
1992	1,199	PF65 1,100				

KM# 979 40000 PESETAS

13.50 g., 0.999 Gold 0.4336 oz. AGW **Ruler:** Juan Carlos I **Subject:** Patrimonio de la Humanidad **Obv:** UNESCO logo **Rev:** Statues at Abu Simbel

Date	Mintage	VF20	XF40	MS60	MS63	MS65
1996	4,000	PF65 900				

KM# 1023 40000 PESETAS

13.50 g., 0.999 Gold 0.4336 oz. AGW, 30 mm. **Ruler:** Juan Carlos I **Series:** Patrimonio de la Humanidad - UNESCO **Obv:** UNESCO logo **Rev:** Horyu-Ji pagoda **Edge:** Reeded

Date	Mintage	VF20	XF40	MS60	MS63	MS65
1997	4,000	PF65 900				

KM# 845 80000 PESETAS

27.00 g., 0.999 Gold 0.8672 oz. AGW **Ruler:** Juan Carlos I **Subject:** Discovery of America **Obv:** Crowned busts of Juan Carlos and Sofia facing each other within beaded circle **Rev:** Crowned busts of Ferdinand and Isabella facing each other within beaded circle

Date	Mintage	VF20	XF40	MS60	MS63	MS65
1989	5,583	—	—	—	—	1,500
1989	6,994	PF65 1,500				

KM# 879 80000 PESETAS

27.00 g., 0.999 Gold 0.8672 oz. AGW **Ruler:** Juan Carlos I **Series:** 1992 Olympics **Obv:** Royal family facing within circle **Rev:** Discus thrower within circle

Date	Mintage	VF20	XF40	MS60	MS63	MS65
1990	2,894	—	—	—	—	1,500
1990	1,128	PF65 1,850				

Note: Uncirculated strikes have medallic die alignment and edges with reeded and plain sections; Proof strikes have coin die alignment and reeded edges

KM# 880 80000 PESETAS

27.00 g., 0.999 Gold 0.8672 oz. AGW **Ruler:** Juan Carlos I **Series:** 1992 Olympics **Obv:** Royal family facing **Rev:** Prince Balthasar Carlos on horseback

Date	Mintage	VF20	XF40	MS60	MS63	MS65
1990	1,093	—	—	—	—	1,700
1990	3,729	PF65 1,500				

Note: Uncirculated strikes have medallic die alignment and edges with reeded and plain sections; Proof strikes have coin die alignment and reeded edges

KM# 881 80000 PESETAS

27.00 g., 0.999 Gold 0.8672 oz. AGW **Ruler:** Juan Carlos I **Subject:** Carlos V **Obv:** Crowned heads of Juan Carlos and Sofia facing each other within beaded circle **Rev:** Armored half-figure facing within beaded circle

Date	Mintage	VF20	XF40	MS60	MS63	MS65
1990	2,002	—	—	—	—	1,500
1990	2,688	PF65 1,350				

KM# 901 80000 PESETAS

27.00 g., 0.999 Gold 0.8672 oz. AGW **Ruler:** Juan Carlos I **Series:** Olympics **Obv:** Royal family facing **Rev:** Women tossing man on blanket within circle

Date	Mintage	VF20	XF40	MS60	MS63	MS65
1991	869	—	—	—	—	2,400
1991	2,388	PF65 1,400				

Note: Uncirculated strikes have medallic die alignment and edges with reeded and plain sections; Proof strikes have coin die alignment and reeded edges

KM# 902 80000 PESETAS

27.00 g., 0.999 Gold 0.8672 oz. AGW **Ruler:** Juan Carlos I **Subject:** Carlos III **Obv:** Crowned busts of Juan Carlos and Sofia facing each other within beaded circle **Rev:** Armored bust right within beaded circle

Date	Mintage	VF20	XF40	MS60	MS63	MS65
1991	1,267	—	—	—	—	1,550
1991	1,595	PF65 1,500				

KM# 917 80000 PESETAS

27.00 g., 0.999 Gold 0.8672 oz. AGW **Ruler:** Juan Carlos I **Series:** Olympics **Rev:** Two children playing within circle

Date	Mintage	VF20	XF40	MS60	MS63	MS65
1992	745	—	—	—	—	2,400
1992	2,157	PF65 1,500				

Note: Uncirculated strikes have medallic die alignment and edges with reeded and plain sections; Proof strikes have coin die alignment and reeded edges

KM# 1005 80000 PESETAS

27.00 g., 0.999 Gold 0.8672 oz. AGW **Ruler:** Juan Carlos I **Obv:** Crowned busts of Juan Carlos and Sofia facing each other within beaded circle **Rev:** Hammer minting scene

Date	Mintage	VF20	XF40	MS60	MS63	MS65
1992	1,015	—	—	—	—	2,000
1992	1,101	PF65 2,000				

KM# 930 80000 PESETAS

27.00 g., 0.999 Gold 0.8672 oz. AGW **Ruler:** Juan Carlos I **Subject:** Holy Jacobean Year **Obv:** Head left **Rev:** French Fraternity of Santiago Medallion within beaded circle

Date	Mintage	VF20	XF40	MS60	MS63	MS65
1993	1,500	PF65 1,500				

KM# 945 80000 PESETAS

27.00 g., 0.999 Gold 0.8672 oz. AGW **Ruler:** Juan Carlos I **Rev:** Iberian Lynx

Date	Mintage	VF20	XF40	MS60	MS63	MS65
1994	1,639	PF65 1,600				

KM# 959 80000 PESETAS

27.00 g., 0.999 Gold 0.8672 oz. AGW **Ruler:** Juan Carlos I **Rev:** Leda and the Swan

Date	Mintage	VF20	XF40	MS60	MS63	MS65
1995	1,914	PF65 1,500				

KM# 972 80000 PESETAS
27.00 g., 0.999 Gold 0.8672 oz. AGW **Ruler:** Juan Carlos I **Rev:** Folk dancers

Date	Mintage	VF20	XF40	MS60	MS63	MS65
1996	Est. 3500	PF65 1,500				

KM# 1028 80000 PESETAS
27.00 g., 0.999 Gold 0.8672 oz. AGW, 38 mm. **Ruler:** Juan Carlos I **Subject:** House of Borbon **Obv:** Head of Ferdinand VI right within circle and beaded border **Rev:** Crowned shield within circle and beaded border **Edge:** Reeded

Date	Mintage	VF20	XF40	MS60	MS63	MS65
1997	1,248	PF65 1,600				

EURO COINAGE

European Union Issues

KM# 1040 EURO CENT
2.30 g., Copper Plated Steel, 16.25 mm. **Ruler:** Juan Carlos I **Obv:** Cathedral of Santiago de Compostela **Rev:** Value and globe **Edge:** Plain

Date	Mintage	VF20	XF40	MS60	MS63	MS65
1999 (M)	721,000,000	—	—	0.15	0.25	0.35
2000 (M)	83,400,000	—	—	0.50	1.00	1.25

KM# 1041 2 EURO CENT
3.06 g., Copper Plated Steel, 18.75 mm. **Ruler:** Juan Carlos I **Obv:** Cathedral of Santiago de Compostela **Rev:** Value and globe **Edge:** Grooved

Date	Mintage	VF20	XF40	MS60	MS63	MS65
1999 (M)	291,700,000	—	—	0.45	0.75	1.00
2000 (M)	711,300,000	—	—	0.15	0.25	0.35

KM# 1042 5 EURO CENT
3.92 g., Copper Plated Steel, 21.25 mm. **Ruler:** Juan Carlos I **Obv:** Cathedral of Santiago de Compostela **Rev:** Value and globe **Edge:** Plain

Date	Mintage	VF20	XF40	MS60	MS63	MS65
1999 (M)	483,500,000	—	—	0.30	0.60	0.75
2000 (M)	399,900,000	—	—	0.30	0.60	0.75

KM# 1043 10 EURO CENT
4.10 g., Brass, 19.75 mm. **Ruler:** Juan Carlos I **Obv:** Head of Cervantes with ruffed collar 1/4 left within star border **Rev:** Value and map **Edge:** Reeded

Date	Mintage	VF20	XF40	MS60	MS63	MS65
1999 (M)	588,100,000	—	—	0.30	0.60	0.75
2000 (M)	243,900,000	—	—	0.30	0.60	0.75

KM# 1044 20 EURO CENT
5.74 g., Brass, 22.25 mm. **Ruler:** Juan Carlos I **Obv:** Head of Cervantes with ruffed collar 1/4 left within star border **Rev:** Value and map **Edge:** Notched

Date	Mintage	VF20	XF40	MS60	MS63	MS65
1999 (M)	762,300,000	—	—	0.40	0.75	1.00
2000 (M)	29,300,000	—	—	1.25	2.75	3.50

KM# 1045 50 EURO CENT
7.80 g., Brass, 24.25 mm. **Ruler:** Juan Carlos I **Obv:** Head of Cervantes with ruffed collar 1/4 left within star border **Rev:** Value and map **Edge:** Reeded

Date	Mintage	VF20	XF40	MS60	MS63	MS65
1999 (M)	371,000,000	—	—	0.75	1.50	1.75
2000 (M)	519,600,000	—	—	0.65	1.25	1.50

KM# 1046 EURO
7.50 g., Bi-Metallic Copper-Nickel center in Nickel-Brass ring, 23.25 mm. **Ruler:** Juan Carlos I **Obv:** Head 1/4 left within circle and star border **Rev:** Value and map within circle **Edge:** Segmented reeding

Date	Mintage	VF20	XF40	MS60	MS63	MS65
1999 (M)	100,200,000	—	—	1.50	3.00	3.50
2000 (M)	89,300,000	—	—	2.00	4.00	4.50

KM# 1047 2 EURO
8.50 g., Bi-Metallic Nickel-Brass center in Copper-Nickel ring, 25.75 mm. **Ruler:** Juan Carlos I **Obv:** Head 1/4 left within circle and star border **Rev:** Value and map within circle **Edge:** Reeding over stars and 2s

Date	Mintage	VF20	XF40	MS60	MS63	MS65
1999 (M)	60,500,000	—	—	3.50	5.00	6.00
2000 (M)	36,600,000	—	—	3.50	5.00	6.00

TRIAL STRIKES

KM#	Date	Mintage	Identification	Mkt Val
TS1	1987	Est. 200000	500 Pesetas. Silver. Conjoined heads left. Inscription divides crown, letter and star. KM#831.	75.00
TS2	1987	—	500 Pesetas. Stainless Steel.	70.00
TS3	1987	Est. 200000	500 Pesetas. Silver. Inscription divides crown, letter and star. Crown above monogram within banner.	75.00
TS4	1987	—	500 Pesetas. Stainless Steel. Inscription divides crown, letter and star. Value above design and crown.	70.00
TS5	ND (1990)	—	2000 Pesetas. Silver. KM#859.	175

PATTERNS

Including off metal strikes

KM#	Date	Mintage	Identification	Mkt Val
Pn16	1937	—	10 Centimos. Zinc. Denomination. Crowned arms on eagle.	1,200
Pn17	ND (2000)	—	5 Euro Cent. Bronze. Sumpol, mint mark and denomination. Denomination. Plain.	—
Pn18	ND (2000)	—	10 Euro Cent. Brass. Symbol, mint mark and denomination. Denomination. Plain.	—

MINT SETS

KM#	Date	Mintage	Identification	Issue Price	Mkt Val
MSA2	1962 (7)	—	KM785-788, 790, 795-796, in Carton	—	100
MSB2	1963 (7)	—	KM785-788, 790, 795-796, in carton, 2.5 peseta struck from rusty dies with new alloy onlu found in this set.	—	100
MS2	1958Ba (3)	—	KM#786-788	—	250
MS3	1964 (7)	—	KM#785-788, 790, 795-796; Set contains KM#790, dated 1959. Mixed dates, 1964 latest date, 1 peseta proof. In cardboard holder.	3.60	100
MS4	1965 (7)	—	KM#785-788, 790, 795-796; Set contains KM#790, dated 1959. 1965 1 peseta proof. Mixed dates, 1965 latest date. In cardboard holder.	3.60	65.00
MSA5	1966 (7)	—	KM775, 777, 785-788, 790, 1 peseta & 2.5 peseta proofs	—	150
MS5	1966 (8)	—	KM#775, 777, 785-788, 790, 797; Set contains KM#790, dated 1959. Mixed date, 1966 1 peseta & 1956 2.5 peseta proof, 1966 latest date. In cardboard holder.	—	150
MS6	1966 (8)	—	KM#775, 777, 785-788, 790, 797; Set contains KM#790, dated 1959. Mixed dates, 1peseta & 2.5 peseta proof, 1966 latest date. In plastic sleeve.	—	200
MSA7	1967 (7)	—	KM786-788, 790, 795-797; Prooflike in plastic sleeve, all * 67, except 25 pesetas * 66.	—	250
MS7	1968 (8)	1,000	KM#785-788, 790, 795-797; Set contains KM#790, dated 1959 with added 'strike date' to match the set	3.60	3,350
MS8	1969 (8)	1,200	KM#785-788, 790, 795-797; Set contains KM#790, dated 1959 with added 'strike date' to match the set	3.60	3,200
MS9	1970 (8)	6,000	KM#785-788, 790, 795-797; Set contains KM#790, dated 1959 with added 'strike date' to match the set	3.60	625
MS10	1971 (8)	10,000	KM#785-788, 790, 795-797; Set contains KM#790, dated 1959 with added 'strike date' to match the set. KM797 is *70.	3.60	300
MS12	1982 (4)	—	KM#823, 824, 825, 826. Unofficial Tourist set.	—	15.00
MS13	1990 (U) (5)	—	KM#854, 856-858, 868	—	90.00
MS15	1991 (U) (5)	—	KM#882-883, 885-886, 892	—	100
MS18	1992 (10)	—	KM#832-833, 903-910	12.00	40.00

KM#	Date	Mintage	Identification	Issue Price	Mkt Val
MS19	1993 (8)	—	KM#832, 918-919, 920-924, labeled as proof	15.00	60.00
MS20	1994 (8)	—	KM#832, 924, 931-936	12.00	70.00
MS21	1995 (8)	—	KM#832, 924, 946-951	13.50	100
MS23	1997 (8)	—	KM#832, 924, 981-986	15.50	30.00
MS24	1998 (8)	—	KM#832-833, 924, 989-992, 1012	15.50	32.50
MS25	1999 (8)	49,030	KM#832, 924, 991-992, 1006-1008, 1012	15.50	32.50
MS26	2000 (8)	49,600	KM#832-833, 924, 989, 991-992, 1012-1013	15.50	45.00
MS27	2000-2001 (8)	49,426	KM#832-833, 924, 991-992 (both dated 2000), 1012-1013, 1016	15.50	35.00

PROOF SETS

KM#	Date	Mintage	Identification	Issue Price	Mkt Val
PS1	1972 (6)	30,000	KM#786-788, 790, 795-796	5.00	60.00
PS2	1973 (6)	25,000	KM#786-788, 790, 795-796	5.00	160
PS3	1974 (6)	23,000	KM#786-788, 790, 795-796	5.00	130
PS4	1975 (6)	75,000	KM#786-788, 790, 795-796	5.00	35.00
PS5	1976 (6)	400,000	KM#805-810	5.00	9.00
PS6	1977 (3)	300,000	KM#806-808	0.35	3.00
PS7	1979 (4)	300,000	KM#806-809	0.90	5.00
PS8	1987 (4)	—	KM#831, Pn4, Pn4a, Pn5-6	25.00	—
PS9	1987 (2)	—	KM#828, 830	—	110
PS10	1989 (7)	—	KM#834-839, 841	—	300
PS11	1989 (5)	—	KM#M23-M27	—	1,825
PS12	1989 (5)	—	KM#840, 842-845	3,177	3,250
PS13	1990 (7)	—	KM#854, 856-858, 868-869, 873	—	330
PS14	1991 (7)	—	KM#882-883, 885-886, 892-893, 896	—	400
PS15	1992 (7)	—	KM#980, 993-998	—	475
PS16	1995 (6)	Inc. above	KM#938, 953, 956-959	—	2,000
PS17	1995 (4)	25,000	KM#938, 953, 956-957	—	360
PS18	1996 (6)	—	KM#966-967, 969-972	1,675	2,400
PS19	1996 (6)	—	KM#966-967, 969-972	1,650	2,400
PS20	1996 (4)	—	KM#966-967, 969-970	—	400
PS21	1996 (4)	—	KM#966-967, 969-970	—	400
PS22	1996 (6)	—	KM#973-978	198	225
PS23	1996 (7)	—	KM#973-979	702	1,000

With the loss of her American empire, Spain drifted into chaotic times. Stung by their defeats in Cuba, the army blamed the Socialists for what they considered to be mismanagement at home. Additional political complications were derived from the successful Russian Revolution which gave impetus to an already thriving Socialist party and trade union movement. Finally, King Alphonso XIII committed the fatal mistake of encouraging a reckless general to start a campaign in Morocco that ended in the virtual extermination of the Spanish army. Fearing that the inevitable parliamentary investigation would incriminate the crown, he offered no objection when General Primo de Rivera seized the government and established himself as dictator in 1926. Rivera fell from power in 1930, and the government was taken over by an alliance of Liberals and Socialists who tried to separate the Church and State, take the army out of politics, and introduce effective labor and agrarian reforms despite numerous strikes and street riots. The election of 1936 brought to power a coalition of Socialists, Liberals and Communists, to the dismay of the traditionalists and landowners.

A number of right-wing generals, including the young and clever Francisco Franco, began preparations for a military coup which erupted into a civil war in July of 1936.The destructive conflict, in which more than a million died, lasted three years. During the struggle, areas under control of both the Nationalists (rebels) and the Republicans (Loyalists) issued coinages that circulated to whatever extent the political and military situation permitted. The war ended defeat for the Loyalists when Madrid fell to Franco on March 28, 1939.

During the Spanish Civil War (1936-1939) a great many coins and tokens were minted in the provincial districts. The coins are grouped here under the heading of the district in which they most commonly circulated.

CAUTIONARY NOTE: Many counterfeits of the Civil War coinage exist. Authentication has been recommended by leading experts in this field.

AMETLLA DEL VALLES

A town in the province of Tarragona in northeastern Spain. The town adopted the name L'Ametlla del Valles in 1933. Before that the name was La Ametlla.

REPUBLICAN ZONE

DECIMAL COINAGE

KM# 1 25 CENTIMOS
Brass, 25 mm.

Date	Mintage	F12	VF20	XF40	MS60	MS63
ND (1937)	50,000	20.00	30.00	50.00	90.00	—

KM# 2.1 50 CENTIMOS
Aluminum, 20 mm.

Date	Mintage	F12	VF20	XF40	MS60	MS63
ND (1937)	3,000	200	250	300	400	—

KM# 2.2 50 CENTIMOS
Aluminum, 20 mm. **Obv:** Without legend

Date	Mintage	F12	VF20	XF40	MS60	MS63
ND (1937)	30,000	80.00	100	140	200	—

KM# 3.1 PESETA
Aluminum, 26 mm.

Date	Mintage	F12	VF20	XF40	MS60	MS63
ND (1937)	3,000	100	125	175	280	—

KM# 3.2 PESETA
Aluminum, 26 mm. **Obv:** Without legend

Date	Mintage	F12	VF20	XF40	MS60	MS63
ND (1937)	30,000	50.00	75.00	100	175	—

ARAHAL

A town 30 miles east of Seville. Issued 3 undated types of coins in 1936.

NATIONALIST ZONE

DECIMAL COINAGE

KM# 1 50 CENTIMOS
Brass, 19 mm. **Obv:** Value within legend **Note:** Uniface.

Date	Mintage	F12	VF20	XF40	MS60	MS63
ND (1936)	3,000	150	200	300	—	—

Note: Forgeries exist

KM# 2 PESETA
Brass, 25 mm. **Obv:** Value within legend **Note:** Uniface.

Date	Mintage	F12	VF20	XF40	MS60	MS63
ND (1936)	10,000	100	150	200	350	—

Note: Forgeries exist

KM# 3 2 PESETAS
Brass, 30 mm. **Obv:** Value within legend **Note:** Uniface.

Date	Mintage	F12	VF20	XF40	MS60	MS63
ND (1936)	10,000	100	150	200	350	—

Note: Forgeries exist

ARENYS DE MAR

A resort village on the Mediterranean shore that is 20 miles north of Barcelona. One of the villages in the area of operations of General Mola at the beginning of the war.

REPUBLICAN ZONE

DECIMAL COINAGE

KM# 1 50 CENTIMOS
Aluminum, 21 mm. **Obv:** Shield divides value **Note:** Uniface.

Date	Mintage	F12	VF20	XF40	MS60	MS63
ND (1937)	6,000	150	225	350	500	—

Note: Forgeries exist

KM# 2 PESETA
Aluminum, 29 mm. **Obv:** Shield divides value **Note:** Uniface.

Date	Mintage	F12	VF20	XF40	MS60	MS63
ND (1937)	3,500	150	250	375	550	—

Note: Forgeries exist

ASTURIAS AND LEON

Asturias is a province on the northern coast of Spain with the province of Leon just to its south. The councils of these adjoining provinces decided to mint coins in 1937 for use in the area due to lack of other circulating coins in the north.

REPUBLICAN ZONE

DECIMAL COINAGE

KM# 1 50 CENTIMOS
Copper-Nickel, 21 mm. **Obv:** Crossed tools and gear in back of upright design **Rev:** Value and date

Date	Mintage	F12	VF20	XF40	MS60	MS63
1937	200,000	20.00	30.00	40.00	65.00	80.00

KM# 2 PESETA
Copper, 23 mm. **Obv:** Standing figure with hat facing left **Rev:** Value and date

Date	Mintage	F12	VF20	XF40	MS60	MS63
1937	100,000	15.00	25.00	35.00	55.00	70.00

KM# 3 2 PESETAS
Copper-Nickel **Obv:** Standing figure with hand on gear **Rev:** Value and date **Note:** Varieties exist with differences in the leaves.

Date	Mintage	F12	VF20	XF40	MS60	MS63
1937	400,000	10.00	12.00	15.00	25.00	40.00

CAZALLA DE LA SIERRA

A town 43 miles north of Seville that issued a 10 Centimos in brass in 1936 (undated).

NATIONALIST ZONE

DECIMAL COINAGE

KM# 1 10 CENTIMOS
Brass, 23 mm. **Obv:** Crowned shield to right of legend **Rev:** Legend and value, single sprig at left

Date	Mintage	F12	VF20	XF40	MS60	MS63
ND (1936)	10,000	30.00	50.00	90.00	175	—

EUZKADI

Euzkadi or the Viscayan Republic was located in north central Spain adjoining the southeast corner of France. It was made up of 3 provinces - Guipuzcoa, Alava, and Viscaya. These Basque provinces declared autonomy on October 8, 1936. The 2 nickel coins were made in Brussels, Belgium and saw some circulation before the end of the Republic on June 18, 1937.

VISCAYAN REPUBLIC

DECIMAL COINAGE

KM# 1 PESETA
3.90 g., Nickel, 22 mm. **Obv:** Liberty head right **Rev:** Value and date within wreath

Date	Mintage	F12	VF20	XF40	MS60	MS63
1937	7,000,000	4.00	7.00	9.00	15.00	20.00

KM# 2 2 PESETAS
8.50 g., Nickel, 26 mm. **Obv:** Liberty head right **Rev:** Value and date within wreath

Date	Mintage	F12	VF20	XF40	MS60	MS63
1937	6,000,000	4.00	7.00	10.00	18.00	25.00

GRATALLOPS

Gratallops is an old municipality located in the province of Tarragona overhanging the Siurana River.

REPUBLICAN ZONE

DECIMAL COINAGE

KM# 1 5 CENTIMOS
Zinc **Ruler:** (no ruler) **Issuer:** Ayuntamiento de Gratallops **Shape:** Square with corners removed **Note:** Stamped 5-C/G. Size 21x21mm.

Date	Mintage	F12	VF20	XF40	MS60	MS63
ND(1937)	—	150	200	300	—	—

KM# 2 10 CENTIMOS
Zinc **Ruler:** (no ruler) **Issuer:** Ayuntamiento de Gratallops **Shape:** Square with corners removed **Note:** Stamped 10-C/G. Size 26x26mm.

Date	Mintage	F12	VF20	XF40	MS60	MS63
ND(1937)	—	150	200	300	—	—

KM# 3 25 CENTIMOS
Zinc **Ruler:** (no ruler) **Issuer:** Ayuntamiento de Gratallops **Shape:** Rectangular with corners removed **Note:** Stamped 25-C/G. Size 31x22mm.

Date	Mintage	F12	VF20	XF40	MS60	MS63
ND(1937)	—	150	200	300	—	—

KM# 4 50 CENTIMOS
Zinc, 23 mm. **Ruler:** (no ruler) **Issuer:** Ayuntamiento de Grattalops **Note:** Stamped 50/C.

Date	Mintage	F12	VF20	XF40	MS60	MS63
ND(1937)	—	150	225	350	—	—

KM# 5 PESO
Zinc, 25 mm. **Ruler:** (no ruler) **Issuer:** Ayuntamiento de Gratallops **Note:** Stamped 1-P/G.

Date	Mintage	F12	VF20	XF40	MS60	MS63
ND(1937)	—	150	225	350	—	—

IBI

A village north and west of Alicante on the east coast of Spain. The isolation of the area in comparison with other contending areas made the maintaining of this area during the war very difficult.

REPUBLICAN ZONE

DECIMAL COINAGE

KM# 1.1 25 CENTIMOS
Copper, 24 mm. **Obv:** Legend and value **Rev:** Liberty head left flanked by sprigs **Note:** Varieties exist.

Date	Mintage	F12	VF20	XF40	MS60	MS63
1937	30,000	35.00	50.00	80.00	120	—

KM# 1.2 25 CENTIMOS
Copper, 24 mm. **Obv:** Value and map of Spain in field **Rev:** Liberty head left flanked by sprigs

Date	Mintage	F12	VF20	XF40	MS60	MS63
1937	7,000	100	150	200	300	—

KM# 2 PESETA
Nickel-Brass, 24 mm. **Obv:** Legend and date **Rev:** Value

Date	Mintage	F12	VF20	XF40	MS60	MS63
1937	5,000	100	175	250	350	—

LORA DEL RIO

A town 35 miles northeast of Seville. Issued an undated 25 Centimos in 1936.

NATIONALIST ZONE

DECIMAL COINAGE

KM# 1 25 CENTIMOS
Brass, 23 mm. **Obv:** Crowned shield within cross **Rev:** Legend and value, wheat sprig at right

Date	Mintage	F12	VF20	XF40	MS60	MS63
ND (1936)	1,500	350	450	650	1,000	—

MARCHENA

A village 30 miles east of Seville. It was the last issuer in Seville province. Two varieties of undated coins were produced in 1936.

NATIONALIST ZONE

DECIMAL COINAGE

KM# 1.1 25 CENTIMOS
Brass, 40 mm. **Obv:** Value at center of Legend **Note:** Uniface; denomination: 25C.

Date	Mintage	F12	VF20	XF40	MS60	MS63
ND (1936)	5,000	150	200	300	550	—

KM# 1.2 25 CENTIMOS
Brass, 40 mm. **Obv:** Value at center of legend **Note:** Uniface; denomination: 025C.

Date	Mintage	F12	VF20	XF40	MS60	MS63
ND (1936)	500	500	700	1,100	1,800	—

Note: Forgeries exist

MENORCA

Menorca is the smaller of the 2 major islands in the Balearic Islands. A serious coin and supply shortage developed during the war because of the isolation of the island from the mainland.

REPUBLICAN ZONE

DECIMAL COINAGE

KM# 1 5 CENTIMOS
Brass, 13 mm. **Obv:** Emblem within beaded circle **Rev:** Value above star, single sprig at left **Note:** Varieties exist.

Date	Mintage	F12	VF20	XF40	MS60	MS63
1937	42,000	—	50.00	75.00	95.00	—

KM# 2 10 CENTIMOS
Brass, 16 mm. **Obv:** Emblem within beaded circle **Rev:** Value above star, single sprig at left **Note:** Varieties exist.

Date	Mintage	F12	VF20	XF40	MS60	MS63
1937	32,000	—	35.00	45.00	70.00	—

KM# 3 25 CENTIMOS
Brass, 18 mm. **Obv:** Emblem within beaded circle **Rev:** Value above star, single sprig at left

Date	Mintage	F12	VF20	XF40	MS60	MS63
1937	38,000	—	30.00	40.00	65.00	—

KM# 4 PESETA
Brass, 20 mm. **Obv:** Emblem within beaded circle **Rev:** Value above star, single sprig at left

Date	Mintage	F12	VF20	XF40	MS60	MS63
1937	37,000	—	30.00	40.00	65.00	—

KM# 5 2-1/2 PESETAS
Brass, 22 mm. **Obv:** Emblem within beaded circle **Rev:** Value above star, single sprig at left

Date	Mintage	F12	VF20	XF40	MS60	MS63
1937	24,000	—	75.00	100	125	—

NULLES

Nulles is a mountain village in the province of Tarragona. The mountainous terrain of the area isolated the village from friendly forces and normal commerce. Therefore, in 1937, an undated series of 5 denominations were issued.

REPUBLICAN ZONE

DECIMAL COINAGE

KM# 1 5 CENTIMOS
Zinc, 23 mm. **Obv:** Value at center of legend **Shape:** Octagonal **Note:** Uniface, legends similar to 10 Centimos, KM#2.

Date	Mintage	F12	VF20	XF40	MS60	MS63
ND (1937)	5,000	350	500	600	750	—

KM# 2 10 CENTIMOS
Zinc, 21 mm. **Obv:** Value at center of legend **Note:** Uniface.

Date	Mintage	F12	VF20	XF40	MS60	MS63
ND (1937)	3,000	400	600	700	900	—

KM# 3 25 CENTIMOS
Brass, 20 mm. **Obv:** Value at center of legend **Shape:** Square **Note:** Uniface. Legends similar to 10 Centimos, KM#2.

Date	Mintage	F12	VF20	XF40	MS60	MS63
ND (1937)	5,000	350	500	600	750	—

KM# 4 50 CENTIMOS
Brass, 22 mm. **Obv:** Value at center of legend **Shape:** Octagonal **Note:** Uniface, legends similar to 10 Centimos, KM#2.

Date	Mintage	F12	VF20	XF40	MS60	MS63
ND (1937)	1,000	350	500	650	850	—

KM# 5 PESETA
Brass, 22 mm. **Obv:** Value at center of legend **Note:** Uniface.

Date	Mintage	F12	VF20	XF40	MS60	MS63
ND (1937)	5,000	200	300	400	550	—

OLOT

A village in the province of Gerona in northeastern Spain near the French border. The village council authorized 2 denominations of coins on September 24, 1937.

REPUBLICAN ZONE

DECIMAL COINAGE

KM# 1 10 CENTIMOS
Iron, 24 mm. **Obv:** Vertical lines and eagle wing within design **Rev:** Caduceus divides value

Date	Mintage	F12	VF20	XF40	MS60	MS63
1937	25,000	70.00	100	200	350	—

KM# 2 15 CENTIMOS
Iron, 30 mm. **Obv:** Vertical lines and eagle wing within design **Rev:** Stylized factory scene and value

Date	Mintage	F12	VF20	XF40	MS60	MS63
1937	100	1,600	1,850	3,750	7,500	—

Note: Forgeries exist

PUEBLA DE CAZALLA

A village only a few miles east of El Arahal and some 40 miles from Sevilla. Undated coins of 2 values were issued in 1936.

NATIONALIST ZONE

DECIMAL COINAGE

KM# 1 10 CENTIMOS
Brass, 23 mm. **Obv:** Tied arrows with banner to left of legend **Rev:** Value **Note:** Counterstamped varieties exist.

Date	Mintage	F12	VF20	XF40	MS60	MS63
ND (1936)	1,500	300	400	530	800	—

KM# 2 25 CENTIMOS
Brass, 25 mm. **Obv:** Tied arrows with banner to left of legend **Rev:** Value **Note:** Counterstamped varieties exist.

Date	Mintage	F12	VF20	XF40	MS60	MS63
ND (1936)	5,000	250	350	500	750	—

SANTANDER, PALENCIA & BURGOS

Three provinces in northern Spain with Santander being the northern-most on the Spanish coast. The three provinces met in council and issued two denominations of coins for use in the provinces.

REPUBLICAN ZONE

DECIMAL COINAGE

KM# 1.1 50 CENTIMOS
Copper-Nickel, 20 mm. **Obv:** Standing 1/2 length figure with hammer **Rev:** Value above crossed sprigs

Date	Mintage	F12	VF20	XF40	MS60	MS63
1937	100,000	—	25.00	35.00	50.00	60.00

KM# 1.2 50 CENTIMOS
Copper-Nickel, 20 mm. **Obv:** Blacksmith with factory in background **Rev:** Letters PR or PJR below CTS

Date	Mintage	F12	VF20	XF40	MS60	MS63
1937	10,000	—	30.00	40.00	55.00	65.00

KM# 2 PESETA
Copper-Nickel, 23 mm. **Obv:** Crowned shield to left of legend **Rev:** Value within 1/2 wreath

Date	Mintage	F12	VF20	XF40	MS60	MS63
1937	300,000	—	15.00	20.00	35.00	—

SEGARRA DE GAIA

A village in the southern part of the province of Tarragona. A single denomination of coin was authorized in 1937.

REPUBLICAN ZONE

DECIMAL COINAGE

KM# 1 PESETA
Copper-Nickel, 23 mm. **Obv:** Value over bars of Aragon in circle

Date	Mintage	F12	VF20	XF40	MS60	MS63
ND(1937)	30,000	15.00	25.00	40.00	75.00	—

KM# 1a PESETA
Copper, 23 mm. **Obv:** Value over bars of Aragon in circle **Note:** Uniface. Value over bars of Aragon in circle.

Date	Mintage	F12	VF20	XF40	MS60	MS63
ND(1937)	20,000	75.00	125	200	300	—

KM# 2 PESETA
Aluminum, 24 mm. **Obv:** C.M. SEGARRA = DE GAIA = above, 1pta. below, numerals stamped at center **Note:** Uniface

Date	Mintage	F12	VF20	XF40	MS60	MS63
ND(1937)	5,000	150	250	400	—	—

SPITZBERGEN

Spitzbergen (Svalbard), a Norwegian territory, is a group of mountainous islands in the Arctic Ocean 360 miles (579 km.) north of Norway. The islands have an area of 23,957 sq. mi. (62,050 sq. km.) and a population of about 4,000. West Spitzbergen, the largest island, is the seat of administration. Sealing and fishing are economically important. Despite rich carboniferous and tertiary coal deposits, coal mining, which was started on a commercial scale by the Arctic Coal Co. of Boston, Mass. in 1904, produces only small quantities.

Spitzbergen was probably discovered in 1194, but modern knowledge of it dates from its discovery by William Barents in 1596. Quarrels among the various nationalities involved in the whaling industry, which was set up in 1611, resulted in a de facto division of the coast, but despite diverse interests in, and claims to the islands by British, Dutch, Norwegians, Swedes, Danes, Russians and Americans, the question of sovereignty was not resolved until 1920, when a treaty agreed to by the claimants awarded the islands to Norway.

In 1932, the Russian mining company Arktikugol began operations in the islands. The tokens listed here were minted in Leningrad for use by the company in Spitzbergen.

RULER
Norwegian, 1920-

LEGENDS
ШПИЦБЕРГЕН = Spitzbergen
АРКТИКУГОЛЬ = Artikugol = Arctic Coal Co.
РАЗМЂННЫЙ ЗНАК = Exchange Tokens

NORWEGIAN TERRITORY

TOKEN COINAGE

Artic Coal Issues

KM# Tn1 10 KOPEKS
Aluminum-Bronze **Obv:** Star below date, legend around **Rev:** Value, legend

Date	Mintage	F12	VF20	XF40	MS60	MS63
1946	—	25.00	45.00	95.00	185	—

KM# Tn2 15 KOPEKS
Aluminum-Bronze **Obv:** Star below date, legend around **Rev:** Value, legend

Date	Mintage	F12	VF20	XF40	MS60	MS63
1946	—	30.00	50.00	100	200	—

KM# Tn3 20 KOPEKS
Copper-Nickel **Obv:** Star below date, legend around **Rev:** Value, legend

Date	Mintage	F12	VF20	XF40	MS60	MS63
1946	—	35.00	65.00	115	225	—

KM# Tn4.1 50 KOPEKS
Copper-Nickel **Obv:** Larger star below date, legend around **Rev:** Value, legend

Date	Mintage	F12	VF20	XF40	MS60	MS63
1946	—	45.00	75.00	125	250	—

KM# Tn4.2 50 KOPEKS
Copper-Nickel **Obv:** Smaller star below date, legend around **Rev:** Value, legend

Date	Mintage	F12	VF20	XF40	MS60	MS63
1946	—	45.00	75.00	125	250	—

KM# Tn5 10 ROUBLES
Copper-Nickel Clad Steel, 20 mm. **Obv:** Polar bear seated on 1/2 world globe **Rev:** Value within circle, legend around with date below **Edge:** Plain

Date	Mintage	VF20	XF40	MS60	MS63	MS65
1993	—	—	—	3.00	5.00	9.00

KM# Tn6 25 ROUBLES
Copper-Nickel Clad Steel, 22 mm. **Obv:** Polar bear seated on 1/2 world globe **Rev:** Value within circle, legend around with date below **Edge:** Plain

Date	Mintage	VF20	XF40	MS60	MS63	MS65
1993	—	—	—	3.00	5.00	9.00

KM# Tn7 50 ROUBLES
Copper-Nickel Clad Steel, 24 mm. **Obv:** Polar bear seated on 1/2 world globe **Rev:** Value within circle, legend around with date below **Edge:** Plain

Date	Mintage	VF20	XF40	MS60	MS63	MS65
1993	—	—	—	4.00	6.00	10.00

KM# Tn8 100 ROUBLES
Aluminum-Bronze, 25 mm. **Obv:** Polar bear seated on 1/2 world globe **Rev:** Value within circle, legend around with date below **Edge:** Reeded

Date	Mintage	VF20	XF40	MS60	MS63	MS65
1993	—	—	—	7.00	9.00	12.00

SRI (SHRI) LANKA

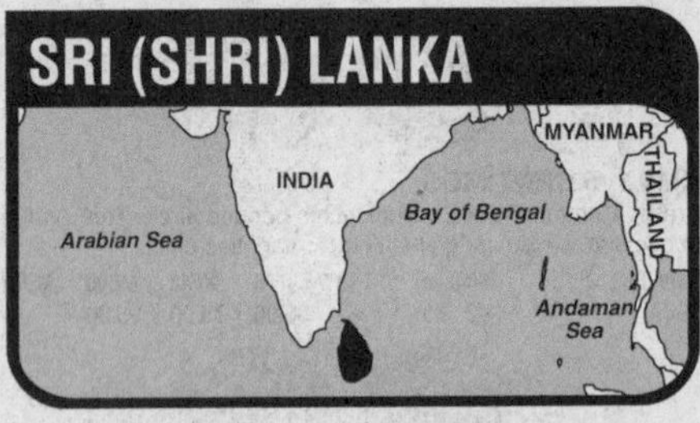

The Democratic Socialist Republic of Sri Lanka (formerly Ceylon) situated in the Indian Ocean 18 miles (29 km.) southeast of India, has an area of 25,332 sq. mi. (65,610 sq. km.) and a population of *16.9 million. Capital: Colombo. The economy is chiefly agricultural. Tea, coconut products and rubber are exported.

Sri Lanka is a member of the Commonwealth of Nations. The president is Chief of State. The prime minister is Head of Government. The present leaders of the country have reverted the country name back to Sri Lanka.

DEMOCRATIC SOCIALIST REPUBLIC

DECIMAL COINAGE

100 Cents = 1 Rupee

KM# 137 CENT
0.50 g., Aluminum, 25 mm. **Obv:** Value above designs within wreath **Rev:** National arms

Date	Mintage	VF20	XF40	MS60	MS63	MS65
1975	52,778,000	—	0.10	0.15	0.25	0.45
1978	34,006,000	—	0.10	0.15	0.25	0.45
1978	—	PF65 2.50				
1989	6,000,000	—	0.10	0.15	0.25	0.45
1994	5,000,000	—	0.10	0.15	0.25	0.45

KM# 138 2 CENTS
0.76 g., Aluminum, 18.5 mm. **Obv:** Value above designs within wreath **Rev:** National arms **Shape:** Scalloped

Date	Mintage	VF20	XF40	MS60	MS63	MS65
1975	62,503,000	—	0.10	0.15	0.25	0.45
1978	—	PF65 3.00				
1978	23,425,000	—	0.10	0.15	0.25	0.45

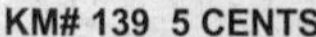

KM# 139 5 CENTS

3.30 g., Nickel-Brass **Obv:** Value above designs within wreath **Rev:** National arms **Shape:** Round-edged square

Date	Mintage	VF20	XF40	MS60	MS63	MS65
1975	19,584,000	—	0.10	0.15	0.25	0.75

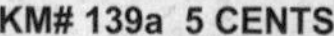

KM# 139a 5 CENTS

1.00 g., Aluminum **Obv:** Value above designs within wreath **Rev:** National arms **Shape:** Round-edged square

Date	Mintage	VF20	XF40	MS60	MS63	MS65
1978	272,308,000	—	0.10	0.15	0.25	0.45
1978	—	PF65 3.00				
1988	40,000,000	—	0.10	0.15	0.25	0.45
1991	50,000,000	—	0.10	0.15	0.25	0.45

KM# 140 10 CENTS

4.10 g., Nickel-Brass **Obv:** Value above designs within wreath **Rev:** National arms **Shape:** Scalloped

Date	Mintage	VF20	XF40	MS60	MS63	MS65
1975	10,800,000	—	0.10	0.15	0.25	0.75

KM# 140a 10 CENTS

1.27 g., Aluminum, 23 mm. **Obv:** Value above designs within wreath **Rev:** National arms **Shape:** Scalloped

Date	Mintage	VF20	XF40	MS60	MS63	MS65
1978	188,820,000	—	0.10	0.15	0.25	0.45
1978	—	PF65 3.50				
1988	40,000,000	—	0.10	0.15	0.25	0.45
1991	50,000,000	—	0.10	0.15	0.25	0.45

KM# 141.1 25 CENTS

Copper-Nickel **Obv:** National Arms **Rev:** Denomination **Edge:** Security

Date	Mintage	VF20	XF40	MS60	MS63	MS65
1975	39,600,000	—	0.10	0.15	0.25	0.45
1978	65,009,000	—	0.10	0.15	0.25	0.45
1978	—	PF65 3.50				

KM# 141.2 25 CENTS

Copper-Nickel **Obv:** National Arms **Rev:** Denomination **Edge:** Reeded

Date	Mintage	VF20	XF40	MS60	MS63	MS65
1982	90,000,000	—	0.10	0.15	0.25	0.45
1989	45,000,000	—	0.10	0.15	0.25	0.45
1991	50,000,000	—	0.10	0.15	0.25	0.45
1994	50,000,000	—	0.10	0.15	0.25	0.45

KM# 141a 25 CENTS

Nickel Clad Steel **Obv:** National arms **Rev:** Denomination **Edge:** Reeded

Date	Mintage	VF20	XF40	MS60	MS63	MS65
1996	50,000,000	—	0.10	0.15	0.25	0.45

KM# 135.1 50 CENTS

Copper-Nickel **Obv:** National arms **Rev:** Value above designs within wreath **Edge:** Security

Date	Mintage	VF20	XF40	MS60	MS63	MS65
1972	11,000,000	0.15	0.30	0.50	0.75	1.25
1975	34,000,000	0.15	0.30	0.50	0.75	1.25
1978	66,010,000	0.15	0.30	0.50	0.75	1.25
1978	—	PF65 4.50				

KM# 135.2 50 CENTS

5.50 g., Copper-Nickel **Obv:** National arms **Rev:** Value above designs within wreath **Edge:** Reeded

Date	Mintage	VF20	XF40	MS60	MS63	MS65
1982	65,000,000	0.10	0.25	0.40	0.65	1.00
1991	40,000,000	0.10	0.25	0.40	0.65	1.00
1994	40,000,000	0.10	0.25	0.40	0.65	1.00

KM# 135.2a 50 CENTS

Nickel Plated Steel, 21.5 mm. **Obv:** National arms **Rev:** Value above designs within wreath **Edge:** Reeded

Date	Mintage	VF20	XF40	MS60	MS63	MS65
1996	50,000,000	0.10	0.25	0.40	0.65	1.00

KM# 136.1 RUPEE

Copper-Nickel **Obv:** National arms **Rev:** Inscription below designs within wreath **Edge:** Security

Date	Mintage	VF20	XF40	MS60	MS63	MS65
1972	7,000,000	0.30	0.60	0.80	1.25	1.75
1975	31,500,000	0.25	0.50	0.70	1.00	1.50
1978	37,018,000	0.25	0.50	0.70	1.00	1.50
1978	—	PF65 6.50				

KM# 136.2 RUPEE

Copper-Nickel **Obv:** National arms **Rev:** Inscription below designs within wreath **Edge:** Reeded

Date	Mintage	VF20	XF40	MS60	MS63	MS65
1982	75,000,000	0.25	0.50	0.70	1.00	1.50
1994	50,000,000	0.25	0.50	0.70	1.00	1.50

KM# 136a RUPEE

Nickel Clad Steel **Obv:** National arms **Rev:** Inscription below designs within wreath **Edge:** Reeded

Date	Mintage	VF20	XF40	MS60	MS63	MS65
1996	50,000,000	—	0.50	0.70	1.00	1.50
2000	30,000,000	—	0.50	0.70	1.00	1.50

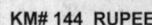

KM# 144 RUPEE

Copper-Nickel **Subject:** Inauguration of President Jayewardene **Obv:** National arms **Rev:** Head left

Date	Mintage	VF20	XF40	MS60	MS63	MS65
1978	1,997,400	0.30	0.60	1.00	2.00	3.50
1978	2,600	—	—	—	20.00	50.00

Note: Right shoulder straight

Date	Mintage	VF20	XF40	MS60	MS63	MS65
1978	—	PF65 6.50				

KM# 144a RUPEE

Gold **Subject:** Inauguration of President Jayawardene **Obv:** National arms **Rev:** Head left

Date	Mintage	VF20	XF40	MS60	MS63	MS65
1978 Proof	—	—	—	—	—	—

KM# 151 RUPEE

7.13 g., Copper-Nickel, 25.4 mm. **Subject:** 3rd Anniversary of 2nd Executive President Premadusa **Obv:** Facing lions with swords above rectangular design **Rev:** Bust facing within wreath

Date	Mintage	VF20	XF40	MS60	MS63	MS65
1992	25,000,000	0.30	0.65	1.25	2.50	4.00
1992	2,500	PF65 10.00				

KM# 151a RUPEE

7.13 g., 0.925 Silver 0.212 oz. ASW, 25.4 mm. **Subject:** 3rd Anniversary of 2nd Executive President Premadusa **Obv:** Facing lions with swords above rectangular design **Rev:** Bust facing within wreath

Date	Mintage	VF20	XF40	MS60	MS63	MS65
1992 Frosted Proof	2,000	PF65 45.00				

KM# 151b RUPEE

12.82 g., 0.9167 Gold 0.3778 oz. AGW, 25.4 mm. **Subject:** 3rd Anniversary of 2nd Executive President Premadusa **Obv:** Lions with swords above rectangular design **Rev:** Bust facing within wreath

Date	Mintage	VF20	XF40	MS60	MS63	MS65
1992 Proof	100	—	—	—	—	—

KM# 157 RUPEE

Copper-Nickel **Subject:** UNICEF 50th Anniversary **Obv:** Inscription and value below designs within wreath **Rev:** Numeral 50 and UNICEF logo within circle

Date	Mintage	VF20	XF40	MS60	MS63	MS65
1996	5,000,000	—	—	1.25	2.50	3.50

KM# 162 RUPEE

7.13 g., Nickel Plated Steel, 25.4 mm. **Subject:** Army's 50th Anniversary **Obv:** National arms above crossed swords above dates within beaded circle **Rev:** Soldier giving dove to boy **Edge:** Reeded

Date	Mintage	VF20	XF40	MS60	MS63	MS65
1999 Prooflike	127,000	—	—	—	7.00	10.00
1999	—	PF65 25.00				

KM# 164 RUPEE

7.13 g., Nickel Plated Steel, 25.4 mm. **Subject:** Sri Lankan Navy 50 Years **Obv:** National arms within circle **Rev:** Patrol boat within circle **Edge:** Reeded

Date	Mintage	VF20	XF40	MS60	MS63	MS65
2000	20,000	—	—	—	10.00	12.00

KM# 164a RUPEE

7.13 g., Copper-Nickel, 25.4 mm. **Subject:** Sri Lankan Navy 50 Years **Obv:** National arms within circle **Rev:** Patrol boat within circle **Edge:** Reeded

Date	Mintage	VF20	XF40	MS60	MS63	MS65
2000	2,000	PF65 30.00				

KM# 142 2 RUPEES
Copper-Nickel, 30 mm. **Subject:** Non-Aligned Nations Conference **Obv:** Value within inscription, legend around border **Rev:** Conference building **Edge:** Plain **Shape:** 7-sided

Date	Mintage	VF20	XF40	MS60	MS63	MS65
1976	2,000,000	0.50	1.50	2.50	3.50	6.00
1976	—	PF65 12.00				

KM# 145 2 RUPEES
Copper-Nickel **Subject:** Mahaweli Dam **Obv:** Numeral value within inscription, legend around border **Rev:** Dam within circle

Date	Mintage	VF20	XF40	MS60	MS63	MS65
1981	45,000,000	0.35	0.50	1.00	2.00	3.50

KM# 147 2 RUPEES
8.25 g., Copper-Nickel, 28.5 mm. **Obv:** National arms **Rev:** Value

Date	Mintage	VF20	XF40	MS60	MS63	MS65
1984	25,000,000	0.25	0.50	0.70	1.00	1.50
1993	40,000,000	0.30	0.60	0.85	1.35	1.75
1996	50,000,000	0.30	0.60	0.85	1.35	1.75

KM# 155 2 RUPEES
Copper-Nickel **Series:** F.A.O. **Subject:** F.A.O. 50th Anniversary **Obv:** Value within inscription, legend around border **Rev:** F.A.O. logo and dates within circle

Date	Mintage	VF20	XF40	MS60	MS63	MS65
1995	40,000,000	—	—	1.00	2.00	3.50

KM# 143 5 RUPEES
13.70 g., Nickel **Subject:** Non-Aligned Nations Conference **Obv:** Value within inscription, legend around border **Rev:** Conference building **Shape:** 10-sided

Date	Mintage	VF20	XF40	MS60	MS63	MS65
1976	1,000,000	0.75	1.50	2.00	3.00	4.50
1976	—	PF65 15.00				

KM# 146 5 RUPEES
Copper-Nickel **Subject:** 50th Anniversary - Universal Adult Franchise **Obv:** Value within inscription, legend around border **Rev:** Building with flag **Shape:** 10-sided

Date	Mintage	VF20	XF40	MS60	MS63	MS65
1981	2,000,000	0.75	1.50	2.00	3.00	4.50

KM# 148.1 5 RUPEES
9.50 g., Nickel-Brass **Obv:** National arms **Rev:** Value within inscription, legend around border **Edge Lettering:** C.B.C.

Date	Mintage	VF20	XF40	MS60	MS63	MS65
1984	25,000,000	0.35	0.75	1.25	2.25	3.00

KM# 148.2 5 RUPEES
9.50 g., Nickel-Brass, 23.5 mm. **Obv:** National arms **Rev:** Value **Edge Lettering:** C.B.S.L.

Date	Mintage	VF20	XF40	MS60	MS63	MS65
1986	60,000,000	0.35	0.75	1.25	2.25	3.00
1991	40,000,000	0.35	0.75	1.25	2.25	3.00
1994	50,000,000	0.35	0.65	1.00	2.00	2.75

KM# 156 5 RUPEES
Aluminum-Bronze **Subject:** 50th Anniversary - United Nations **Obv:** Value within inscription, legend around border **Rev:** Numeral 50 and UN logo within circle

Date	Mintage	VF20	XF40	MS60	MS63	MS65
1995	50,000,000	—	—	1.00	2.00	3.50
1995	—	PF65 8.00				

KM# 161 5 RUPEES
Aluminum-Bronze **Subject:** World Cricket Champions **Obv:** Trophy **Rev:** Batsman within circle

Date	Mintage	VF20	XF40	MS60	MS63	MS65
1999	50,000,000	—	—	1.00	2.00	3.50

KM# 149 10 RUPEES
Copper-Nickel, 24x24 mm. **Subject:** International Year of Shelter for Homeless **Obv:** Value within inscription, legend around border **Rev:** Logo, legend around border **Edge:** Segmented reeding **Shape:** 4-sided

Date	Mintage	VF20	XF40	MS60	MS63	MS65
1987	2,000,000	—	—	—	2.50	4.00
1987	—	PF65 12.50				

KM# 158 10 RUPEES
9.00 g., Bi-Metallic Brass center in Copper-Nickel ring, 27 mm. **Subject:** 50th Anniversary of Independence **Obv:** Value and dates within designed wreath **Rev:** Building within and outside of circle **Edge:** CBSL, (4 times) reeded

Date	Mintage	VF20	XF40	MS60	MS63	MS65
1998	50,000,000	—	—	2.00	3.00	5.00

KM# 152 100 RUPEES
10.20 g., 0.925 Silver 0.3033 oz. ASW **Subject:** 5th South Asian Federation Games **Obv:** Sunface above lion, elephant and rabbit, crescent below **Rev:** Logo above inscription, date and value **Shape:** Square

Date	Mintage	VF20	XF40	MS60	MS63	MS65
1991	20,000	PF63 20.00	PF65 25.00			

KM# 150 500 RUPEES
28.28 g., 0.925 Silver 0.841 oz. ASW, 38.6 mm. **Subject:** 40th Anniversary of Central Bank **Obv:** Logo of the Central Bank of Sri Lanka **Rev:** Central Bank building within circle **Edge:** Reeded

Date	Mintage	VF20	XF40	MS60	MS63	MS65
1990	10,000	—	—	—	45.00	55.00
1990	—	PF63 65.00	PF65 75.00			

KM# 153 500 RUPEES
1.60 g., 0.500 Gold 0.0257 oz. AGW, 14 mm. **Subject:** 5th South Asian Federation Games **Obv:** Figure of Kuvera **Rev:** Value above logo and inscription

Date	Mintage	VF20	XF40	MS60	MS63	MS65
1991	8,000	PF65 65.00				

KM# 154 500 RUPEES
28.28 g., 0.925 Silver 0.841 oz. ASW, 38.6 mm. **Subject:** 2,300th Anniversary - Buddha's Teachings in Sri Lanka **Obv:** Large stylized leaf within circle **Rev:** Kneeling figure praying within forest, design above, all within circle **Note:** This is the only coin on which the country name SHRI LANKA appears. Shri Lanka was used only from June 1992 to December 1993, without constitutional authority, by decision of President Premadasa.

Date	Mintage	VF20	XF40	MS60	MS63	MS65
1993	30,000	PF63 65.00	PF65 75.00			

KM# 159 1000 RUPEES
28.28 g., 0.925 Silver 0.841 oz. ASW, 38.6 mm. **Subject:** 50 Years of Independence **Obv:** Flag and value within wreath **Rev:** Lion statue within circle

Date	Mintage	VF20	XF40	MS60	MS63	MS65
1998	25,000	PF63 60.00	PF65 70.00			

KM# 163 1000 RUPEES
28.28 g., 0.925 Silver 0.841 oz. ASW, 38.6 mm. **Subject:** 1996 Cricket Champions **Obv:** Trophy **Rev:** Two players **Edge:** Reeded **Note:** Struck at British Royal Mint.

Date	Mintage	VF20	XF40	MS60	MS63	MS65
1999	25,000	PF63 60.00	PF65 70.00			

KM# 165 1000 RUPEES
28.28 g., 0.925 Silver 0.841 oz. ASW, 38.6 mm. **Subject:** Central Bank 50 Years **Obv:** Sunface in center circle of designs **Rev:** Building and value within circle **Edge:** Milled

Date	Mintage	VF20	XF40	MS60	MS63	MS65
2000	10,000	PF63 55.00	PF65 65.00			

KM# 160 5000 RUPEES
7.98 g., 0.9167 Gold 0.2352 oz. AGW **Subject:** 50 Years of Independence **Obv:** Flag and value within wreath **Rev:** Avalokitheshvara, an aspirant Buddha, seated in a graceful stance within circle

Date	Mintage	VF20	XF40	MS60	MS63	MS65
1998	5,000	PF63 425	PF65 450			

PATTERNS

Including off metal strikes

KM#	Date	Mintage	Identification	Mkt Val
Pn1	1971	—	5 Cents. Nickel-Brass Plated Steel. Similar to KM#129, with TRIAL in raised letters on obverse.	—
Pn2	1971	—	5 Cents. Steel. Similar to KM#129, with TRIAL in raised letters on obverse.	—
Pn3	1971	—	5 Cents. Aluminum. Similar to #KM129, with TRIAL in raised letters on obverse.	—
Pn4	1971	—	10 Cents. Nickel-Brass Plated Steel. Similar to KM#130, with TRIAL in raised letters on obverse.	—
Pn5	1971	—	10 Cents. Steel. Similar to KM#130, with TRIAL in raised letters on obverse.	—
Pn6	1971	—	10 Cents. Aluminum. Similar to KM#130, with TRIAL in raised letters on obverse.	—
Pn7	1975	—	5 Cents. Aluminum. KM#139a.	—
Pn8	1975	—	10 Cents. Aluminum. KM#140a.	—

PROOF SETS

KM#	Date	Mintage	Identification	Issue Price	Mkt Val
PS1	1978 (8)	20,000	KM135.1, 136.1, 137, 138, 139a, 140a, 141.1, 144	26.00	35.00

STRAITS SETTLEMENTS

Straits Settlements, a former British crown colony situated on the Malay Peninsula of Asia, was formed in 1826 by combining the territories of Singapore, Penang and Malacca. The colony was administered by the East India Company until its abolition in 1858. Straits Settlements was a part of British India from 1858 to 1867 at which time it became a Crown Colony.

The Straits Settlements coinage gradually became acceptable legal tender in the neighboring Federated as well as the Un-federated Malay States. The Straits Settlements were dissolved in 1946, while the coinage continued to circulate until demonetized at the end of 1952.

RULER
British

MINT MARKS
H - Heaton, Birmingham
W - Soho Mint
B - Bombay

MONETARY SYSTEM
100 Cents = 1 Dollar

BRITISH CROWN COLONY

1867-1942

STANDARD COINAGE

KM# 14 1/4 CENT
Bronze, 18 mm. **Ruler:** Victoria **Obv:** Crowned head left **Obv. Legend:** VICTORIA QUEEN **Rev:** Value within beaded circle **Rev. Legend:** STRAITS SETTLEMENTS **Edge:** Reeded

Date	Mintage	F12	VF20	XF40	MS60	MS63
1901	2,000,000	13.50	27.00	75.00	185	365

KM# 17 1/4 CENT
Bronze, 18 mm. **Ruler:** Edward VII **Obv:** Crowned bust right **Rev:** Value within beaded circle

Date	Mintage	F12	VF20	XF40	MS60	MS63
1904	—	PF63 2,600				
Note: Plain edge						
1905	2,008,000	15.00	30.00	75.00	150	350
1905	—	PF63 2,400				
1908	1,200,000	15.00	30.00	75.00	150	350

KM# 27 1/4 CENT
Bronze, 18 mm. **Ruler:** George V **Obv:** Crowned bust left **Rev:** Value within beaded circle

Date	Mintage	F12	VF20	XF40	MS60	MS63
1916	4,000,000	6.00	10.00	20.00	35.00	75.00
1916	—	PF63 800				

KM# 18 1/2 CENT
Bronze, 22.5 mm. **Ruler:** Edward VII **Obv:** Crowned bust right **Rev:** Value within beaded circle

Date	Mintage	F12	VF20	XF40	MS60	MS63
1904	—	PF63 4,600				
1908	2,000,000	18.00	35.00	75.00	175	400

KM# 28 1/2 CENT
Bronze, 23 mm. **Ruler:** George V **Obv:** Crowned bust left **Rev:** Value within beaded circle

Date	Mintage	F12	VF20	XF40	MS60	MS63
1916	3,000,000	6.00	10.00	20.00	35.00	65.00
1916	—	PF63 850				

KM# 37 1/2 CENT
Bronze, 18.5 mm. **Ruler:** George V **Rev:** Value within beaded circle **Edge:** Crowned bust left **Shape:** 4-sided

Date	Mintage	F12	VF20	XF40	MS60	MS63
1932	5,000,000	3.00	5.00	10.00	25.00	40.00
1932	—	PF63 650				

KM# 16 CENT
Bronze, 29 mm. **Ruler:** Victoria **Obv:** Crowned head left **Obv. Legend:** VICTORIA QUEEN **Rev:** Value within beaded circle **Rev. Legend:** STRAITS SETTLEMENTS **Edge:** Reeded

Date	Mintage	F12	VF20	XF40	MS60	MS63
1901	15,230,000	4.00	10.00	25.00	100	200

KM# 19 CENT
Bronze, 28.5 mm. **Ruler:** Edward VII **Obv:** Crowned bust right **Rev:** Value within beaded circle

Date	Mintage	F12	VF20	XF40	MS60	MS63
1903	7,053,000	4.00	10.00	50.00	100	200
1903 Proof, Rare	—	—	—	—	—	—
1904	6,647,000	4.00	10.00	50.00	100	200
1904 Proof, Rare	—	—	—	—	—	—
1906	7,504,000	20.00	35.00	75.00	250	450
1907	5,015,000	6.00	12.00	50.00	100	200
1908 Proof, Rare	—	—	—	—	—	—
1908	Inc. above	5.00	10.00	35.00	75.00	100

KM# 32 CENT
5.80 g., Bronze, 21 mm. **Ruler:** George V **Obv:** Crowned bust left **Rev:** Value within beaded circle **Edge:** Plain **Shape:** 4-sided

Date	Mintage	F12	VF20	XF40	MS60	MS63
1919	20,165,000	1.00	2.00	5.00	20.00	35.00
1919	—	**PF63** 650				
1920	55,000,000	1.00	2.00	5.00	20.00	35.00
1920	—	**PF63** 650				
1926	5,000,000	1.00	2.00	7.00	35.00	50.00

KM# 10 5 CENTS
1.36 g., 0.800 Silver 0.035 oz. ASW, 15 mm. **Ruler:** Victoria **Obv:** Crowned head left **Obv. Legend:** VICTORIA QUEEN **Rev:** Value within beaded circle **Rev. Legend:** STRAITS SETTLEMENTS

Date	Mintage	F12	VF20	XF40	MS60	MS63
1901	3,000,000	12.00	18.00	50.00	150	300
1901	—	**PF63** 1,800				

KM# 20 5 CENTS
1.36 g., 0.800 Silver 0.035 oz. ASW **Ruler:** Edward VII **Obv:** Crowned bust right **Rev:** Value within beaded circle

Date	Mintage	F12	VF20	XF40	MS60	MS63
1902	1,920,000	12.00	28.00	75.00	150	300
1902	—	**PF63** 1,600				
1903	2,270,000	12.00	28.00	75.00	150	300
1903	—	**PF63** 1,600				

KM# 20a 5 CENTS
1.36 g., 0.600 Silver 0.0262 oz. ASW, 15.4 mm. **Ruler:** Edward VII **Obv:** Crowned bust right **Rev:** Value within beaded circle

Date	Mintage	F12	VF20	XF40	MS60	MS63
1910 B	13,012,000	3.00	9.00	16.00	45.00	75.00
1910 B	—	**PF63** 1,500				

KM# 31 5 CENTS
1.36 g., 0.400 Silver 0.0175 oz. ASW **Ruler:** George V **Obv:** Crowned bust left **Rev:** Value within beaded circle

Date	Mintage	F12	VF20	XF40	MS60	MS63
1918	3,100,000	2.00	4.00	15.00	30.00	50.00
1919	6,900,000	2.00	4.00	15.00	30.00	50.00
1920	4,000,000	450	750	1,500	3,000	8,000

KM# 34 5 CENTS
Copper-Nickel, 20 mm. **Ruler:** George V **Obv:** Crowned bust left **Rev:** Value within beaded circle

Date	Mintage	F12	VF20	XF40	MS60	MS63
1920	20,000,000	2.00	15.00	50.00	100	225
1920 Proof, Rare	—	—	—	—	—	—

KM# 36 5 CENTS
1.36 g., 0.600 Silver 0.0262 oz. ASW **Ruler:** George V **Obv:** Smaller bust, broader rim **Rev:** Value within beaded circle

Date	Mintage	F12	VF20	XF40	MS60	MS63
1926	10,000,000	1.50	3.00	7.00	15.00	25.00
1926	—	**PF63** 2,800				
1935	3,000,000	1.50	3.00	5.00	12.00	20.00
1935	—	**PF63** 2,800				

KM# 11 10 CENTS
2.71 g., 0.800 Silver 0.0697 oz. ASW, 18 mm. **Ruler:** Victoria **Obv:** Crowned head left **Obv. Legend:** VICTORIA QUEEN **Rev:** Value within beaded circle **Rev. Legend:** STRAITS SETTLEMENTS

Date	Mintage	F12	VF20	XF40	MS60	MS63
1901	2,700,000	15.00	22.00	75.00	175	350

KM# 21 10 CENTS
2.71 g., 0.800 Silver 0.0697 oz. ASW, 18 mm. **Ruler:** Edward VII **Obv:** Crowned bust right **Rev:** Value within beaded circle

Date	Mintage	F12	VF20	XF40	MS60	MS63
1902	6,118,000	5.00	10.00	50.00	150	350
1902 Proof, Rare	—	—	—	—	—	—
1903	1,401,000	5.00	10.00	50.00	150	350
1903 Proof, Rare	—	—	—	—	—	—

KM# 21a 10 CENTS
2.71 g., 0.600 Silver 0.0523 oz. ASW, 18 mm. **Ruler:** Edward VII **Obv:** Crowned bust right **Rev:** Value within beaded circle

Date	Mintage	F12	VF20	XF40	MS60	MS63
1909 B	11,088,000	5.00	20.00	75.00	150	225
1910 B Proof, Rare	—	—	—	—	—	—
1910 B	1,657,000	3.00	6.00	15.00	35.00	50.00

KM# 29 10 CENTS
2.71 g., 0.600 Silver 0.0523 oz. ASW, 18 mm. **Ruler:** George V **Obv:** Crowned bust left **Rev:** Value within beaded circle

Date	Mintage	F12	VF20	XF40	MS60	MS63
1916	600,000	3.00	8.00	35.00	75.00	150
1917	5,600,000	2.00	3.00	12.00	35.00	75.00

KM# 29a 10 CENTS
2.71 g., 0.400 Silver 0.0349 oz. ASW, 18 mm. **Ruler:** George V **Obv:** Crowned bust left **Rev:** Value within beaded circle

Date	Mintage	F12	VF20	XF40	MS60	MS63
1918	7,500,000	1.50	3.00	15.00	75.00	150
1919	11,500,000	1.50	3.00	15.00	75.00	150
1920	4,000,000	18.00	60.00	200	500	750

KM# 29b 10 CENTS
2.71 g., 0.600 Silver 0.0523 oz. ASW, 18 mm. **Ruler:** George V **Obv:** Crowned bust left **Rev:** Value within beaded circle

Date	Mintage	F12	VF20	XF40	MS60	MS63
1926	20,000,000	2.00	4.00	9.00	18.00	35.00
1926	—	**PF63** 900				
1927	23,000,000	2.00	4.00	6.00	10.00	20.00
1927	—	**PF63** 900				

KM# 12 20 CENTS
5.43 g., 0.800 Silver 0.1397 oz. ASW, 23 mm. **Ruler:** Victoria **Obv:** Crowned head left **Obv. Legend:** VICTORIA QUEEN **Rev:** Value within beaded circle **Rev. Legend:** STRAITS SETTLEMENTS

Date	Mintage	F12	VF20	XF40	MS60	MS63
1901	600,000	9.00	18.00	50.00	175	350

KM# 22 20 CENTS
5.43 g., 0.800 Silver 0.1397 oz. ASW, 23 mm. **Ruler:** Edward VII **Obv:** Crowned bust right **Rev:** Value within beaded circle

Date	Mintage	F12	VF20	XF40	MS60	MS63
1902	1,105,000	10.00	20.00	75.00	225	500
1902 Proof, Rare	—	—	—	—	—	—
1903	1,150,000	10.00	20.00	75.00	225	500
1903 Proof, Rare	—	—	—	—	—	—

KM# 22a 20 CENTS
5.43 g., 0.600 Silver 0.1047 oz. ASW, 23 mm. **Ruler:** Edward VII **Obv:** Crowned bust right **Rev:** Value within beaded circle

Date	Mintage	F12	VF20	XF40	MS60	MS63
1910 B	3,276,000	8.00	15.00	50.00	150	250
1910 B Proof, Rare	—	—	—	—	—	—

KM# 30 20 CENTS
5.43 g., 0.600 Silver 0.1047 oz. ASW, 23 mm. **Ruler:** George V **Obv:** Crowned bust left **Rev:** Value within beaded circle

Date	Mintage	F12	VF20	XF40	MS60	MS63
1916 B	545,000	12.00	25.00	100	225	450
1916 B Proof, Rare	—	—	—	—	—	—
1917 B	652,000	5.00	15.00	50.00	150	250

KM# 30a 20 CENTS
5.43 g., 0.400 Silver 0.0698 oz. ASW, 23 mm. **Ruler:** George V **Obv:** Crowned bust left **Rev:** Value within beaded circle

Date	Mintage	F12	VF20	XF40	MS60	MS63
1919 B	2,500,000	4.00	9.00	50.00	150	250
1919 B Proof, Rare	—	—	—	—	—	—

KM# 30b 20 CENTS

5.30 g., 0.600 Silver 0.1022 oz. ASW, 23.3 mm. **Ruler:** George V **Obv:** Crowned bust left **Rev:** Value within beaded circle

Date	Mintage	F12	VF20	XF40	MS60	MS63
1926	2,500,000	3.50	5.00	15.00	35.00	75.00
1926 Proof, Rare	—	—	—	—	—	—
1927	3,000,000	3.50	5.00	10.00	20.00	35.00
1927 Proof, Rare	—	—	—	—	—	—
1935 Round-top 3	1,000,000	3.50	5.00	10.00	20.00	35.00
1935 Flat-top 3	Inc. above	3.50	5.00	10.00	20.00	35.00

KM# 13 50 CENTS

13.58 g., 0.800 Silver 0.3492 oz. ASW, 31 mm. **Ruler:** Victoria **Obv:** Crowned head left **Obv. Legend:** VICTORIA QUEEN **Rev:** Value within beaded circle **Rev. Legend:** STRAITS SETTLEMENTS

Date	Mintage	F12	VF20	XF40	MS60	MS63
1901	120,000	35.00	50.00	125	375	750

KM# 23 50 CENTS

13.58 g., 0.800 Silver 0.3492 oz. ASW, 31 mm. **Ruler:** Edward VII **Obv:** Crowned bust right **Rev:** Value within beaded circle

Date	Mintage	F12	VF20	XF40	MS60	MS63
1902	148,000	50.00	100	200	500	1,000
1902 Proof, Rare	—	—	—	—	—	—
1903	193,000	50.00	100	200	500	1,000
1903 Proof, Rare	—	—	—	—	—	—
1905 B Raised	498,000	50.00	100	200	450	750
1905 B Proof, raised, Rare	—	—	—	—	—	—
1905 B Proof, incuse, Rare	—	—	—	—	—	—

KM# 24 50 CENTS

10.10 g., 0.900 Silver 0.2923 oz. ASW, 28 mm. **Ruler:** Edward VII **Obv:** Crowned bust right **Rev:** Value within beaded circle

Date	Mintage	F12	VF20	XF40	MS60	MS63
1907	464,000	10.00	20.00	75.00	150	300
1907 H	2,667,000	10.00	20.00	75.00	150	300
1908	2,869,000	10.00	20.00	75.00	150	300
1908 H	Inc. above	10.00	20.00	75.00	160	320

Note: Mintage included with 1907H

KM# 35.1 50 CENTS

8.42 g., 0.500 Silver 0.1354 oz. ASW **Ruler:** George V **Obv:** Crowned bust left **Rev:** Value within beaded circle

Date	Mintage	F12	VF20	XF40	MS60	MS63
1920	3,900,000	3.00	5.00	10.00	25.00	40.00
1920 Proof, Rare	—	—	—	—	—	—
1921	2,579,000	3.00	5.00	12.00	28.00	50.00
1921 Proof, Rare	—	—	—	—	—	—

KM# 35.2 50 CENTS

8.42 g., 0.500 Silver 0.1354 oz. ASW **Ruler:** George V **Obv:** Crowned bust left with dot below bust **Rev:** Value within beaded circle

Date	Mintage	F12	VF20	XF40	MS60	MS63
1920	Inc. above	100	250	500	1,000	1,500

KM# 25 DOLLAR

26.95 g., 0.900 Silver 0.7798 oz. ASW, 36.5 mm. **Ruler:** Edward VII **Obv:** Crowned bust right **Rev:** Artistic design within circle

Date	Mintage	F12	VF20	XF40	MS60	MS63
1903 Proof, Rare	—	—	—	—	—	—
1903 B Incuse	15,010,000	20.00	50.00	100	200	450
1903 B Raised	Inc. above	50.00	100	300	750	1,250
1903 B Proof, raised, Rare	—	—	—	—	—	—
1904 B	20,365,000	20.00	30.00	75.00	125	250
1904 B Proof, Rare	—	—	—	—	—	—

KM# 26 DOLLAR

20.21 g., 0.900 Silver 0.5848 oz. ASW, 34.5 mm. **Ruler:** Edward VII **Obv:** Crowned bust right **Rev:** Artistic design within circle **Note:** Reduced size.

Date	Mintage	F12	VF20	XF40	MS60	MS63
1907	6,842,000	20.00	30.00	75.00	125	200
1907 H	4,000,000	20.00	30.00	75.00	125	200
1907 H Proof, Rare	—	—	—	—	—	—
1908	4,152,000	20.00	30.00	75.00	125	200
1908 Proof, Rare	—	—	—	—	—	—
1909	1,014,000	22.00	40.00	120	175	300
1909 Proof, Rare	—	—	—	—	—	—

KM# 33 DOLLAR

16.85 g., 0.500 Silver 0.2709 oz. ASW, 36.5 mm. **Ruler:** George V **Obv:** Crowned bust left **Rev:** Artistic design within circle **Edge:** Reeded

Date	Mintage	F12	VF20	XF40	MS60	MS63
1919	6,000,000	25.00	50.00	100	250	450
1919	—	**PF63** 400				
Note: Restrike						
1920	8,164,000	25.00	35.00	75.00	150	275
1920	—	**PF63** 400				
Note: Restrike						
1925	—	—	—	15,000	—	—
1925 Proof, Rare	—	—	—	—	—	—
1925 Proof, Rare	—	—	—	—	—	—
Note: Restrike						
1926	—	—	—	12,000	—	—
1926	—	**PF63** 15,000				
1926 Proof, Rare	—	—	—	—	—	—
Note: Restrike						

SUDAN

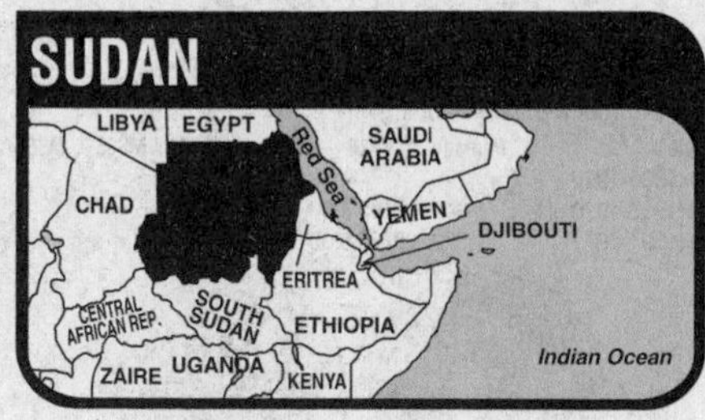

The Democratic Republic of the Sudan, located in northeast Africa on the Red Sea between Egypt and Ethiopia, has an area of 967,500 sq. mi. (2,505,810 sq. km.) and a population of *24.5 million. Capital: Khartoum. Agriculture and livestock raising are the chief occupations. Cotton, gum arabic and peanuts are exported.

The Sudan, site of the powerful Nubian kingdom of Roman times, was a collection of small independent states from the 14th century until 1820-22 when it was conquered and united by Mohammed Ali, Pasha of Egypt. Egyptian forces were driven from the area during the Mahdist revolt, 1881-98, but the Sudan was retaken by Anglo-Egyptian expeditions, 1896-98, and established as an Anglo-Egyptian condominium in 1899. Britain supplied the administrative apparatus and personnel, but the appearance of joint Anglo-Egyptian administration was continued until Jan. 9, 1954, when the first Sudanese self-government parliament was inaugurated. The Sudan achieved independence on Jan. 1, 1956 with the consent of the British and Egyptian government.

TITLES

جمهورية السودان

Jumhuriya(t) as-Sudan

الجمهورية السودان
الديمقراطية

al-Jumhuriya(t) as-Sudan ad-Dimiqratiya(t)

MINT NAME

مالناپور

Omdurman

REPUBLIC

STANDARD COINAGE

KM# 29.1 MILLIM

1.78 g., Bronze **Obv:** Large legend and value above flower sprigs **Rev:** Camel with rider running left

Date	Mintage	VF20	XF40	MS60	MS63	MS65
AH1376-1956	5,000,000	—	0.20	0.50	1.00	1.50
AH1379-1960	1,300,000	—	0.20	0.50	1.00	1.50
AH1386-1966 Proof	—	—	—	—	—	—
AH1387-1967	—	—	0.20	0.50	1.00	1.50
AH1388-1968	—	—	0.20	0.50	1.00	1.50
AH1389-1969	—	—	0.20	0.50	1.00	1.50

KM# 29.2 MILLIM
Bronze **Obv:** Small legend and value above flower sprigs **Rev:** Camel with rider running left **Note:** Except for proof sets, mintage figures have generally not been released since 1967.

Date	Mintage	VF20	XF40	MS60	MS63	MS65
AH1387-1967	7,834	PF65 1.25				
AH1388-1968	5,251	PF65 1.50				
AH1389-1969	2,149	PF65 2.00				

KM# 39 MILLIM
Bronze **Obv:** New Arabic legend and value above flower sprigs **Rev:** Camel with rider running left

Date	Mintage	VF20	XF40	MS60	MS63	MS65
AH1390-1970	—	—	—	—	—	—
AH1390-1970	1,646	PF65 5.00				
AH1391-1971	1,772	PF65 5.00				

KM# 30.1 2 MILLIM
Bronze **Obv:** Large written value with legend above flower sprigs **Rev:** Camel with rider running left **Edge:** Plain **Shape:** Scalloped

Date	Mintage	VF20	XF40	MS60	MS63	MS65
AH1376-1956	5,000,000	—	0.20	0.65	1.25	1.75
AH1386-1966	—	PF65 1.50				
AH1387-1967	—	—	0.20	0.65	1.25	1.75
AH1388-1968	—	—	0.20	0.65	1.25	1.75
AH1389-1969	—	—	0.20	0.65	1.25	1.75

KM# 30.2 2 MILLIM
Bronze, 20.5 mm. **Obv:** Small written value with legend above flower sprigs **Rev:** Camel with rider running left **Edge:** Plain **Shape:** Scalloped

Date	Mintage	VF20	XF40	MS60	MS63	MS65
AH1387-1967	7,834	PF65 1.25				
AH1388-1968	5,251	PF65 1.50				
AH1389-1969	2,149	PF65 2.00				

KM# 40 2 MILLIM
Bronze **Obv:** New Arabic legend and value above flower sprigs **Rev:** Camel with rider running left **Shape:** Scalloped

Date	Mintage	VF20	XF40	MS60	MS63	MS65
AH1390-1970	1,646	PF65 5.00				
AH1391-1971	1,772	PF65 5.00				

KM# 31.1 5 MILLIM
3.95 g., Bronze **Obv:** Thin legend and narrow 5 **Rev:** Camel with rider running left **Shape:** Scalloped **Note:** Camel and rider, date size varieties exist, and with or without outlined bare line.

Date	Mintage	VF20	XF40	MS60	MS63	MS65
AH1376-1956	30,000,000	0.10	0.20	0.65	1.25	1.75
AH1382-1962	6,000,000	0.10	0.20	0.65	1.25	1.75
AH1386-1966	4,000,000	0.10	0.15	0.65	1.25	1.75
AH1386-1966 Proof	—	—	—	—	—	—
AH1387-1967	4,000,000	0.10	0.15	0.45	1.25	1.75
AH1388-1968	—	0.10	0.15	0.45	1.25	1.75
AH1389-1969	—	0.10	0.15	0.45	1.25	1.75

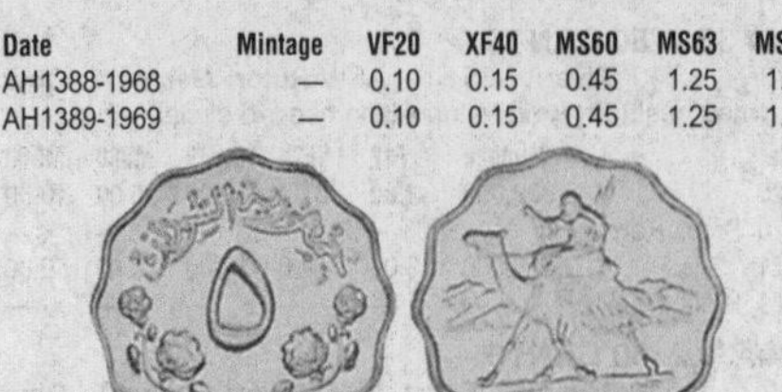

KM# 31.2 5 MILLIM
Bronze **Obv:** Thick legend and small value **Rev:** Camel with rider running left **Shape:** Scalloped

Date	Mintage	VF20	XF40	MS60	MS63	MS65
AH1387-1967	7,834	PF65 1.25				
AH1388-1968	5,251	PF65 1.75				
AH1389-1969	2,149	PF65 2.50				

KM# 41.1 5 MILLIM
Bronze **Obv:** New large Arabic legend narrow 5 **Rev:** Camel with rider running left **Shape:** Scalloped **Note:** Date height and size varieties exist

Date	Mintage	VF20	XF40	MS60	MS63	MS65
AH1390-1970	—	0.20	0.45	1.25	1.75	3.00
AH1391-1971	3,000,000	0.20	0.45	1.25	1.75	3.00

KM# 41.2 5 MILLIM
Bronze **Obv:** Small legend and wide 5 **Rev:** Camel with rider running left **Shape:** Scalloped

Date	Mintage	VF20	XF40	MS60	MS63	MS65
AH1390-1970	1,646	PF65 5.00				
AH1391-1971	1,772	PF65 5.00				

KM# 47 5 MILLIM
Bronze **Subject:** 2nd Anniversary of Revolution **Obv:** Legend and value above flower sprigs **Rev:** Eagle divides dates below legend

Date	Mintage	VF20	XF40	MS60	MS63	MS65
AH1391-1971	500,000	0.15	0.25	0.50	1.00	3.00

KM# 53 5 MILLIM
3.32 g., Bronze, 21.5 mm. **Series:** F.A.O. **Obv:** Legend and value above flower sprigs **Rev:** Eagle divides dates below legend **Edge:** Plain

Date	Mintage	VF20	XF40	MS60	MS63	MS65
AH1392-1972	6,000,000	—	0.20	0.60	1.00	3.00
AH1393-1973	9,000,000	—	0.20	0.60	1.00	3.00

KM# 54 5 MILLIM
Bronze **Obv:** Legend and value **Rev:** Eagle divides AH and CE dates **Note:** Similar to 10 Millim, KM#55, but round.

Date	Mintage	VF20	XF40	MS60	MS63	MS65
AH1392-1972	—	—	0.25	0.75	1.50	3.50

KM# 54a.1 5 MILLIM
Brass **Obv:** Thick legend and written value **Rev:** Ribbon with 3 equal sections

Date	Mintage	VF20	XF40	MS60	MS63	MS65
AH1395-1975	4,132,000	—	0.25	0.65	1.25	3.00
AH1398-1978	—	—	0.25	0.65	1.25	3.00

KM# 60 5 MILLIM
Brass **Series:** F.A.O. **Obv:** Legend and value above flower sprigs **Rev:** Eagle within sprigs divide legend and dates **Note:** Size varies 21.4 - 22.5 mm.

Date	Mintage	VF20	XF40	MS60	MS63	MS65
AH1396-1976	7,868,000	—	0.15	0.35	1.00	1.50
AH1398-1978	7,000,000	—	0.15	0.35	1.00	1.50

KM# 94 5 MILLIM
Brass **Subject:** 20th Anniversary of Independence **Obv:** Legend and value above flower sprigs **Rev:** Eagle divides dates below legend

Date	Mintage	VF20	XF40	MS60	MS63	MS65
AH1396-1976	—	0.25	0.50	1.00	1.50	3.50

KM# 54a.2 5 MILLIM
Brass **Obv:** Large legend and large 5 **Rev:** Eagle divides dates, ribbon with long center section

Date	Mintage	VF20	XF40	MS60	MS63	MS65
AH1398-1978	—	0.15	0.25	0.65	1.25	3.00

KM# 54a.3 5 MILLIM
Brass **Obv:** Thin legend and narrow 5, different style **Rev:** Eagle divides dates, ribbon with 3 equal sections

Date	Mintage	VF20	XF40	MS60	MS63	MS65
AH1400-1980	—	PF65 1.50				

KM# 32.1 10 MILLIM
Bronze **Obv:** Large written value **Rev:** Camel with rider running left **Shape:** Scalloped **Note:** Camel, rider and date size varieties exist.

Date	Mintage	VF20	XF40	MS60	MS63	MS65
AH1376-1956	15,000,000	0.15	0.25	1.00	1.50	3.50
AH1380-1960	12,250,000	0.15	0.20	0.85	1.50	3.50
AH1381-1962 High date	—	0.15	0.20	0.85	1.25	3.00
AH1381-1962 Low date	—	0.15	0.20	0.85	1.25	3.00
AH1386-1966	1,000,000	0.15	0.25	1.00	1.50	3.50
AH1386-1966 Proof	—	—	—	—	—	—
AH1387-1967	1,000,000	0.15	0.20	0.85	1.25	3.00
AH1388-1968	—	0.15	0.20	0.85	1.50	3.50
AH1389-1969	—	0.15	0.20	0.85	1.50	3.50

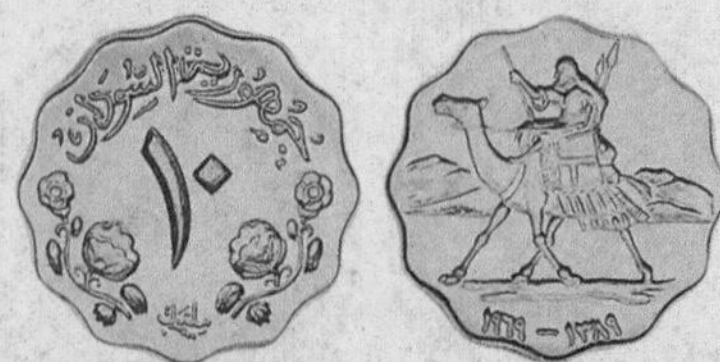

KM# 32.2 10 MILLIM
Bronze **Obv:** Small written value **Rev:** Camel with rider running

left **Shape:** Scalloped

Date	Mintage	VF20	XF40	MS60	MS63	MS65
AH1387-1967	7,834	**PF65** 1.75				
AH1388-1968	5,251	**PF65** 3.00				
AH1389-1969	2,149	**PF65** 3.50				

KM# 42.1 10 MILLIM

Bronze **Obv:** New large Arabic legend and written value **Rev:** Camel with rider running left **Shape:** Scalloped

Date	Mintage	VF20	XF40	MS60	MS63	MS65
AH1390-1970	—	0.20	0.40	1.00	1.75	3.50
AH1391-1971	3,000,000	0.20	0.40	1.00	1.75	3.50

KM# 42.2 10 MILLIM

Bronze **Obv:** Small legend and written value **Rev:** Camel with rider running left **Shape:** Scalloped

Date	Mintage	VF20	XF40	MS60	MS63	MS65
AH1390-1970	1,646	**PF65** 5.00				
AH1391-1971	1,772	**PF65** 5.00				

KM# 48 10 MILLIM

Bronze **Subject:** 2nd Anniversary of the Revolution **Obv:** Legend and value above flower sprigs **Rev:** Eagle divides dates below legend

Date	Mintage	VF20	XF40	MS60	MS63	MS65
AH1391-1971	500,000	3.00	5.00	10.00	15.00	25.00

KM# 55 10 MILLIM

Bronze **Obv:** Legend and value above flower sprigs **Rev:** Eagle divides dates **Shape:** Scalloped

Date	Mintage	VF20	XF40	MS60	MS63	MS65
AH1392-1972	6,500,000	0.15	0.25	0.50	1.50	3.50

KM# 55a.1 10 MILLIM

Brass **Obv:** Large legend and written value **Rev:** Ribbon with three equal sections **Shape:** Scalloped

Date	Mintage	VF20	XF40	MS60	MS63	MS65
AH1395-1975	12,000,000	0.25	0.35	0.75	1.25	3.00
AH1398-1978	9,410,000	0.25	0.45	1.00	1.50	3.50

KM# 55a.2 10 MILLIM

Brass, 25.5 mm. **Obv:** Large legend **Rev:** Ribbon with long center section, eagle divides AH and CE dates **Edge:** Plain **Shape:** Scalloped

Date	Mintage	VF20	XF40	MS60	MS63	MS65
AH1398-1978	—	0.75	1.00	1.50	3.00	5.00

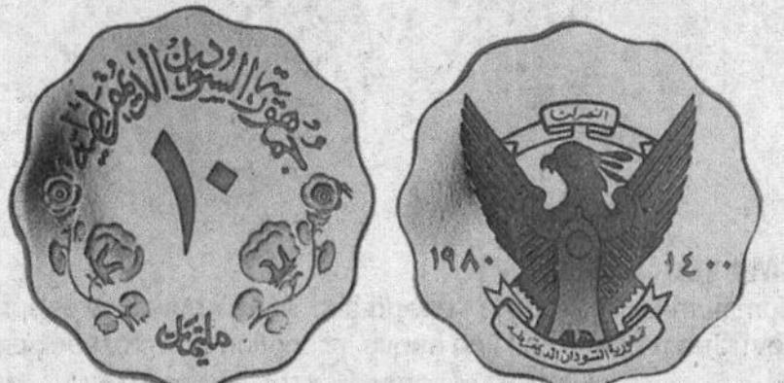

KM# 55a.3 10 MILLIM

Brass **Obv:** Small legend and written value **Rev:** Eagle divides dates, ribbon with 3 equal sections **Shape:** Scalloped

Date	Mintage	VF20	XF40	MS60	MS63	MS65
AH1400-1980	—	**PF65** 2.50				
AH1400-1980	2,490,000	0.25	0.45	1.00	1.50	3.50

KM# 61 10 MILLIM

Brass **Series:** F.A.O. **Obv:** Legend and value above flower sprigs **Rev:** Eagle within sprigs divides date and legend **Shape:** Scalloped

Date	Mintage	VF20	XF40	MS60	MS63	MS65
AH1396-1976	3,000,000	0.10	0.15	0.25	1.00	3.00
AH1398-1978	—	0.10	0.15	0.25	1.00	3.00

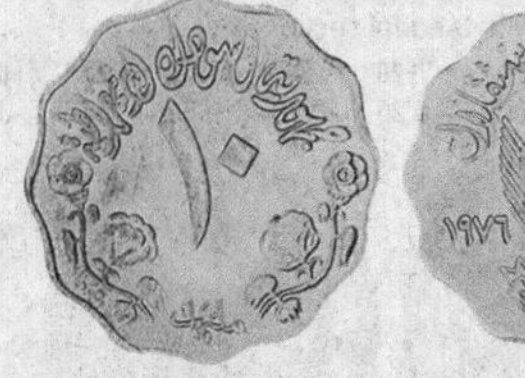

KM# 62 10 MILLIM

Brass **Subject:** 20th Anniversary of Independence **Obv:** Legend and value above flower sprigs **Rev:** Eagle divides dates below legend **Shape:** Scalloped

Date	Mintage	VF20	XF40	MS60	MS63	MS65
AH1396-1976	3,610,000	0.10	0.20	0.40	1.00	3.00

KM# 111 10 MILLIM

Brass, 24.5 mm. **Obv:** Legend and value above flower sprigs **Rev:** Eagle divides dates **Shape:** Round

Date	Mintage	VF20	XF40	MS60	MS63	MS65
AH1400-1980	—	0.50	0.75	1.50	3.00	5.00

KM# 97 GHIRSH

Brass **Obv:** Legend and value above flower sprigs **Rev:** Eagle divides dates, ribbon with 3 equal sections

Date	Mintage	VF20	XF40	MS60	MS63	MS65
AH1403-1983	1,140,000	0.25	0.65	1.00	3.00	5.00

KM# 99 GHIRSH

Aluminum-Bronze **Obv:** Legend and value above flower sprigs **Rev:** Building above inscription and crossed sprigs

Date	Mintage	VF20	XF40	MS60	MS63	MS65
AH1408-1987	—	0.30	0.80	1.00	3.00	5.00

KM# 33 2 GHIRSH

3.00 g., Copper-Nickel, 17.5 mm. **Obv:** Legend and value above flower sprigs **Rev:** Camel with rider running left **Edge:** Reeded

Date	Mintage	VF20	XF40	MS60	MS63	MS65
AH1376-1956	5,000,000	0.15	0.35	0.75	1.50	3.50
AH1381-1962	—	0.15	0.35	0.75	1.50	3.50

KM# 36 2 GHIRSH

Copper-Nickel, 20 mm. **Obv:** Legend and value above flower sprigs **Rev:** Camel with rider running left

Date	Mintage	VF20	XF40	MS60	MS63	MS65
AH1382-1963	1,250,000	0.15	0.35	0.85	1.75	3.50
AH1386-1966 Proof	7,834	—	—	—	—	—
AH1387-1967	—	0.15	0.35	0.85	1.75	3.50
AH1387-1967	5,251	**PF65** 1.75				

Date	Mintage	VF20	XF40	MS60	MS63	MS65
AH1388-1968	—	0.15	0.35	0.85	1.75	3.50
AH1388-1968	2,149	**PF65** 3.00				
AH1389-1969	—	0.15	0.35	0.85	1.75	3.50
AH1389-1969	—	**PF65** 3.50				

KM# 43.1 2 GHIRSH

Copper-Nickel **Obv:** New large Arabic legend and written value **Rev:** Camel with rider running left

Date	Mintage	VF20	XF40	MS60	MS63	MS65
AH1390-1970	—	0.30	0.60	1.25	2.00	4.00

KM# 43.2 2 GHIRSH

Copper-Nickel **Obv:** New small legend and written value **Rev:** Camel with rider running left

Date	Mintage	VF20	XF40	MS60	MS63	MS65
AH1390-1970	1,646	**PF65** 7.50				
AH1391-1971	1,772	**PF65** 7.50				

KM# 49 2 GHIRSH

Copper-Nickel **Subject:** 2nd Anniversary of Revolution **Obv:** Legend and value above flower sprigs **Rev:** Eagle divides dates below legend

Date	Mintage	VF20	XF40	MS60	MS63	MS65
AH1391-1971	500,000	0.25	0.50	1.50	3.00	5.00

KM# 57.1 2 GHIRSH

Copper-Nickel **Obv:** Thick legend and value above flower sprigs **Rev:** Eagle divides dates, ribbon with 3 equal sections

Date	Mintage	VF20	XF40	MS60	MS63	MS65
AH1395-1975	1,000,000	0.20	0.35	0.75	1.50	3.50
AH1398-1978	1,250,000	0.20	0.35	0.75	1.50	3.50

KM# 57.2 2 GHIRSH

Copper-Nickel **Obv:** Large legend **Rev:** Ribbon with long center section, eagle divides AH and AD dates

Date	Mintage	VF20	XF40	MS60	MS63	MS65
AH1398-1978	—	0.20	0.35	0.75	1.50	3.50
AH1400-1980	—	0.20	0.35	0.75	1.50	3.50

KM# 57.2a 2 GHIRSH

Brass **Obv:** Legend with different style and value above flower sprigs **Rev:** Eagle divides dates

Date	Mintage	VF20	XF40	MS60	MS63	MS65
AH1403-1983	100,000	0.50	1.00	1.75	3.00	5.00

KM# 57.3 2 GHIRSH

Copper-Nickel, 20 mm. **Obv:** Thin legend and value above flower sprig **Rev:** Eagle divides dates, ribbon with 3 equal sections **Edge:** Reeded

Date	Mintage	VF20	XF40	MS60	MS63	MS65
AH1399-1979	2,000,000	0.20	0.35	0.75	1.50	3.50
AH1400-1980	6,825,000	0.20	0.35	0.75	1.50	3.50
AH1400-1980	Inc. above	**PF65** 2.00				

KM# 63.1 2 GHIRSH
Copper-Nickel **Series:** F.A.O. **Obv:** Thick value **Rev:** Eagle within sprigs divides dates and legend

Date	Mintage	VF20	XF40	MS60	MS63	MS65
AH1396-1976	500,000	0.20	0.35	0.75	1.50	3.50
AH1398-1978	Inc. above	0.20	0.35	0.75	1.50	3.50

KM# 64 2 GHIRSH
Copper-Nickel **Subject:** 20th Anniversary of Independence **Obv:** Legend and value above flower sprigs **Rev:** Eagle divides dates below legend

Date	Mintage	VF20	XF40	MS60	MS63	MS65
AH1396-1976	1,750,000	0.20	0.30	0.60	1.50	3.50

KM# 63.2 2 GHIRSH
Copper-Nickel **Series:** F.A.O. **Obv:** Thin value **Rev:** Eagle divides AH and AD dates **Note:** Like KM#63.1.

Date	Mintage	VF20	XF40	MS60	MS63	MS65
AH1398-1978	Inc. above	1.50	3.00	5.00	7.50	10.00

KM# 34.1 5 GHIRSH
5.00 g., Copper-Nickel, 24 mm. **Obv:** Large written value **Rev:** Camel with rider running left **Edge:** Reeded

Date	Mintage	VF20	XF40	MS60	MS63	MS65
AH1376-1956	40,000,000	0.20	0.35	1.00	1.50	3.50
AH1386-1966	—	**PF65** 2.00				
AH1387-1967	—	0.20	0.35	1.00	1.50	3.50
AH1388-1968	—	0.20	0.35	1.00	1.50	3.50
AH1389-1969	—	0.20	0.35	1.00	1.50	3.50

KM# 34.2 5 GHIRSH
Copper-Nickel **Obv:** Small written value **Rev:** Camel with rider running left

Date	Mintage	VF20	XF40	MS60	MS63	MS65
AH1387-1967	7,834	**PF65** 2.00				
AH1388-1968	5,251	**PF65** 3.00				
AH1389-1969	2,149	**PF65** 3.50				

KM# 44 5 GHIRSH
Copper-Nickel **Obv:** New Arabic legend, value above flower sprigs **Rev:** Camel with rider running left

Date	Mintage	VF20	XF40	MS60	MS63	MS65
AH1390-1970	1,646	**PF65** 7.50				
AH1391-1971	1,772	**PF65** 7.50				

KM# 51 5 GHIRSH
Copper-Nickel **Subject:** 2nd Anniversary of Revolution **Obv:** Legend and value above flower sprigs **Rev:** Eagle divides dates below legend

Date	Mintage	VF20	XF40	MS60	MS63	MS65
AH1391-1971	500,000	0.30	0.60	1.20	2.50	5.00

KM# 58.1 5 GHIRSH
Copper-Nickel **Obv:** Large legend and value **Rev:** Eagle divides dates, ribbon with 3 equal sections

Date	Mintage	VF20	XF40	MS60	MS63	MS65
AH1395-1975	1,600,000	0.25	0.45	0.85	1.75	3.50

KM# 58.2 5 GHIRSH
Copper-Nickel **Obv:** Large legend style change, small value **Rev:** Eagle divides dates, ribbon with long center section **Note:** Edge varieties exist.

Date	Mintage	VF20	XF40	MS60	MS63	MS65
AH1400-1980	—	0.25	0.45	0.85	1.75	3.50

Note: Mintage included with KM#58.1.

KM# 58.3 5 GHIRSH
Copper-Nickel, 23.5 mm. **Obv:** Small legend with different style and value above flower sprigs **Rev:** Ribbon with 3 equal sections, eagle divides dates **Edge:** Reeded

Date	Mintage	VF20	XF40	MS60	MS63	MS65
AH1397-1977	2,000,000	0.25	0.45	0.85	1.50	3.50
AH1398-1978	1,000,000	0.25	0.45	0.85	1.50	3.50
AH1400-1980	1,000,000	0.25	0.45	0.85	1.50	3.50
AH1400-1980	Inc. above	**PF65** 3.00				

KM# 58.4 5 GHIRSH
Copper-Nickel **Obv:** Large legend in different style **Rev:** Ribbon with long center section, eagle divides AH and AD dates **Note:** Edge varieties exist.

Date	Mintage	VF20	XF40	MS60	MS63	MS65
AH1400-1980	—	0.25	0.45	0.85	1.50	3.50

Note: Mintage included with KM#58.1.

KM# 65 5 GHIRSH
Copper-Nickel **Series:** F.A.O. **Obv:** Legend and value above flower sprigs **Rev:** Eagle within sprigs divides dates and legend

Date	Mintage	VF20	XF40	MS60	MS63	MS65
AH1396-1976	500,000	0.20	0.30	1.00	3.00	5.00
AH1398-1978	—	0.20	0.30	1.00	3.00	5.00

KM# 66 5 GHIRSH
Copper-Nickel **Subject:** 20th Anniversary of Independence **Obv:** Legend and value above flower sprigs **Rev:** Eagle divides dates below legend

Date	Mintage	VF20	XF40	MS60	MS63	MS65
AH1396-1976	3,940,000	0.25	0.50	1.00	1.50	3.50

KM# 74 5 GHIRSH
Copper-Nickel **Subject:** Council of Arab Economic Unity **Obv:** Clasped hands and legend within wreath **Rev:** Eagle divides dates **Note:** Edge varieties exist.

Date	Mintage	VF20	XF40	MS60	MS63	MS65
AH1398-1978	5,040,000	0.15	0.25	0.50	1.50	3.50

KM# 84 5 GHIRSH
Copper-Nickel **Series:** F.A.O. **Obv:** Cow and calf flanked by designs **Rev:** Eagle divides dates **Note:** Edge varieties exist.

Date	Mintage	VF20	XF40	MS60	MS63	MS65
AH1401-1981	1,000,000	0.20	0.40	0.75	1.50	3.50

KM# 110.1 5 GHIRSH
Brass **Obv:** Large value **Rev:** Ribbon with three equal sections, eagle divides AH and AD dates

Date	Mintage	VF20	XF40	MS60	MS63	MS65
AH1403-1983	—	0.25	0.60	1.00	3.00	5.00

KM# 110.2 5 GHIRSH
Brass **Obv:** Legend and value above flower sprigs **Rev:** Eagle divides dates, ribbon with long center section

Date	Mintage	VF20	XF40	MS60	MS63	MS65
AH1403-1983	—	0.50	1.25	2.25	3.50	7.50

KM# 110.3 5 GHIRSH
Brass **Obv:** Small value, legend in different style **Rev:** Ribbon with three equal sections, eagle divides AH and AD dates

Date	Mintage	VF20	XF40	MS60	MS63	MS65
AH1403-1983	—	1.50	3.00	5.00	7.50	10.00

KM# 110.4 5 GHIRSH
Brass **Obv:** Large value and legend **Rev:** Ribbon with long center section, eagle divides AH and AD dates

Date	Mintage	VF20	XF40	MS60	MS63	MS65
AH1403-1983	—	1.50	3.00	5.00	7.50	10.00

KM# 100 5 GHIRSH
Aluminum-Bronze **Obv:** Legend and value above flower sprigs **Rev:** Central bank building above inscription and crossed sprigs

Date	Mintage	VF20	XF40	MS60	MS63	MS65
AH1408-1987	—	0.40	0.75	1.00	1.50	3.50

KM# 35.1 10 GHIRSH

10.00 g., Copper-Nickel, 28 mm. **Obv:** Large written value **Rev:** Camel with rider running left **Edge:** Reeded

Date	Mintage	VF20	XF40	MS60	MS63	MS65
AH1376-1956	15,000,000	0.35	1.00	3.00	4.50	7.50
AH1386-1966 Proof	—	—	—	—	—	—
AH1387-1967	—	0.30	0.75	2.00	3.00	5.00
AH1388-1968	—	0.30	0.75	2.00	3.00	5.00
AH1389-1969	—	0.30	0.75	2.00	3.00	5.00

KM# 35.2 10 GHIRSH

10.00 g., Copper-Nickel, 28 mm. **Obv:** Small written value **Rev:** Camel with rider running left **Edge:** Reeded

Date	Mintage	VF20	XF40	MS60	MS63	MS65
AH1387-1967	7,834	**PF65** 3.00				
AH1388-1968	5,251	**PF65** 3.50				
AH1389-1969	2,149	**PF65** 4.00				

KM# 45.1 10 GHIRSH

10.00 g., Copper-Nickel, 28 mm. **Obv:** New large Arabic legend and written value **Rev:** Camel with rider running left **Edge:** Reeded

Date	Mintage	VF20	XF40	MS60	MS63	MS65
AH1390-1970	—	0.60	1.25	3.00	5.00	10.00
AH1391-1971	385,000	0.60	1.25	3.00	5.00	10.00

KM# 45.2 10 GHIRSH

10.00 g., Copper-Nickel, 28 mm. **Obv:** New small Arabic legend and written value **Rev:** Camel with rider running left **Edge:** Reeded

Date	Mintage	VF20	XF40	MS60	MS63	MS65
AH1390-1970	1,646	**PF65** 7.50				
AH1391-1971	1,772	**PF65** 7.50				

KM# 52 10 GHIRSH

10.00 g., Copper-Nickel, 28 mm. **Subject:** 2nd Anniversary of Revolution **Obv:** Legend and value above flower sprigs **Rev:** Eagle divides dates below legend **Edge:** Reeded

Date	Mintage	VF20	XF40	MS60	MS63	MS65
AH1391-1971	500,000	0.60	1.25	3.00	5.00	10.00

KM# 59.1 10 GHIRSH

Copper-Nickel, 28 mm. **Obv:** Legend and value above flower sprigs **Rev:** Eagle divides dates, ribbon with 3 equal sections **Edge:** Reeded

Date	Mintage	VF20	XF40	MS60	MS63	MS65
AH1395-1975	1,000,000	0.50	1.00	2.50	5.00	10.00

KM# 59.2 10 GHIRSH

Copper-Nickel, 28 mm. **Obv:** Legend and value above flower sprigs **Rev:** Eagle divides dates, ribbon with long center section **Note:** Edge varieties exist.

Date	Mintage	VF20	XF40	MS60	MS63	MS65
AH1400-1980	—	0.50	1.00	2.50	5.00	10.00

KM# 59.3 10 GHIRSH

Copper-Nickel **Obv:** Legend and value above flower sprigs **Rev:** Eagle divides dates **Note:** Reduced size. Edge varieties exist.

Date	Mintage	VF20	XF40	MS60	MS63	MS65
AH1403-1983	—	0.50	1.00	2.50	5.00	10.00

KM# 59.4 10 GHIRSH

Copper-Nickel **Obv:** Value within flower sprigs below legend **Rev:** Ribbon with three equal sections, eagle divides AH and AD dates

Date	Mintage	VF20	XF40	MS60	MS63	MS65
AH1403-1983	1,100,000	1.50	3.00	7.50	10.00	15.00

KM# 59.5 10 GHIRSH

9.90 g., Copper-Nickel, 28 mm. **Obv:** Thin legend, different style and value above flower sprigs **Rev:** Eagle divides dates **Edge:** Reeded

Date	Mintage	VF20	XF40	MS60	MS63	MS65
AH1397-1977	1,000,000	0.50	1.00	1.50	3.00	5.00
AH1400-1980	2,965,000	0.50	1.00	1.50	3.00	5.00
AH1400-1980	—	**PF65** 7.50				

KM# 67 10 GHIRSH

Copper-Nickel, 28 mm. **Series:** F.A.O. **Obv:** Legend and value above flower sprigs **Rev:** Eagle within sprigs divides dates and legend

Date	Mintage	VF20	XF40	MS60	MS63	MS65
AH1396-1976	500,000	0.30	0.65	1.50	3.50	5.50
AH1398-1978	—	0.30	0.65	1.50	3.50	5.50

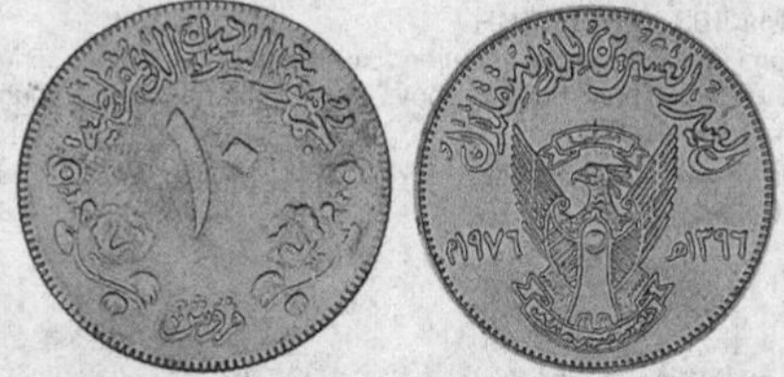

KM# 68 10 GHIRSH

Copper-Nickel, 28 mm. **Subject:** 20th Anniversary of Independence **Obv:** Legend and value above flower sprigs **Rev:** Eagle divides dates below legend **Edge:** Reeded **Note:** Edge varieties exist.

Date	Mintage	VF20	XF40	MS60	MS63	MS65
AH1396-1976	5,540,000	0.25	0.60	1.25	2.50	5.00

KM# 95 10 GHIRSH

Copper-Nickel, 28 mm. **Subject:** Council of Arab Economic Unity **Obv:** Clasped hands below inscription within wreath **Rev:** Eagle divides dates **Note:** Edge varieties exist.

Date	Mintage	VF20	XF40	MS60	MS63	MS65
AH1398-1978	1,000,000	0.60	1.25	2.50	3.50	5.50

KM# 85 10 GHIRSH

Copper-Nickel, 28 mm. **Series:** F.A.O. **Obv:** Cow and calf flanked by designs **Rev:** Eagle divides dates **Edge:** Reeded **Note:** Edge varieties exist.

Date	Mintage	VF20	XF40	MS60	MS63	MS65
AH1401-1981	1,000,000	0.60	1.00	2.00	3.50	5.50

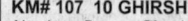

KM# 107 10 GHIRSH

Aluminum-Bronze **Obv:** Legend and value above flower sprigs **Rev:** Central bank building above inscription and crossed sprigs

Date	Mintage	VF20	XF40	MS60	MS63	MS65
AH1408-1987	—	—	0.50	1.00	1.50	3.00

KM# 37 20 GHIRSH

Copper-Nickel, 37 mm. **Obv:** Legend and value above flower sprigs **Rev:** Camel with rider running left

Date	Mintage	VF20	XF40	MS60	MS63	MS65
AH1387-1967	7,834	**PF65** 5.00				
AH1388-1968	5,251	**PF65** 6.00				
AH1389-1969	2,149	**PF65** 7.50				

KM# 46 20 GHIRSH

Copper-Nickel, 35 mm. **Obv:** New Arabic legend and value above flower sprigs **Rev:** Camel with rider running left

Date	Mintage	VF20	XF40	MS60	MS63	MS65
AH1390-1970	1,646	**PF65** 25.00				
AH1391-1971	1,772	**PF65** 25.00				

KM# 98 20 GHIRSH
Copper-Nickel, 26.5 mm. **Obv:** Legend and value above flower sprigs **Rev:** Eagle divides dates

Date	Mintage	VF20	XF40	MS60	MS63	MS65
AH1403-1983	72,000	—	3.00	5.00	9.00	15.00

KM# 96 20 GHIRSH
Copper-Nickel **Series:** F.A.O. **Obv:** Designs, value and F.A.O. letters **Rev:** Eagle divides dates

Date	Mintage	VF20	XF40	MS60	MS63	MS65
AH1405-1985	—	—	1.00	1.50	3.00	5.00

KM# 101.1 20 GHIRSH
Aluminum-Bronze **Obv:** Small value **Rev:** Central bank building above inscription and crossed sprigs **Note:** Denomination is 8 mm high.

Date	Mintage	VF20	XF40	MS60	MS63	MS65
AH1408-1987	—	—	0.50	1.00	3.00	7.50

KM# 101.2 20 GHIRSH
Aluminum-Bronze **Obv:** Large value **Rev:** Central bank building **Note:** Denomination is 9.5 mm high.

Date	Mintage	VF20	XF40	MS60	MS63	MS65
AH1408-1987	—	—	0.50	1.00	3.00	7.50

KM# 38 25 GHIRSH
Copper-Nickel **Series:** F.A.O. **Obv:** Legend and value above flower sprigs **Rev:** Camel with rider running left

Date	Mintage	VF20	XF40	MS60	MS63	MS65
AH1388-1968	Inc. below	—	1.50	4.50	7.50	12.00
AH1388-1968 Prooflike	224,000	—	2.00	5.00	8.00	14.00

KM# 102.1 25 GHIRSH
Aluminum-Bronze **Obv:** Legend and value above flower sprigs **Rev:** Central bank building, inner ring of dashes only visible on the corners **Shape:** Square

Date	Mintage	VF20	XF40	MS60	MS63	MS65
AH1408-1987	—	—	0.50	1.50	3.00	7.50

KM# 102.2 25 GHIRSH
Aluminum-Bronze **Obv:** Value **Rev:** Inner ring of dashes completely visible **Shape:** Square

Date	Mintage	VF20	XF40	MS60	MS63	MS65
AH1408-1987	—	—	0.50	1.50	3.00	7.50

KM# 108 25 GHIRSH
Copper-Nickel Plated Steel **Obv:** Legend, value and dates **Rev:** Central bank building

Date	Mintage	VF20	XF40	MS60	MS63	MS65
AH1409-1989	—	—	0.50	1.00	1.50	3.00

KM# 56.1 50 GHIRSH
Copper-Nickel, 40 mm. **Series:** F.A.O. **Obv:** Eagle divides dates **Rev:** Large design

Date	Mintage	VF20	XF40	MS60	MS63	MS65
AH1392-1972	1,000,000	1.00	1.50	3.00	5.00	7.50

KM# 56.2 50 GHIRSH
Copper-Nickel, 40 mm. **Series:** F.A.O. **Obv:** Eagle divides dates **Rev:** Small design **Note:** Struck in 1976.

Date	Mintage	VF20	XF40	MS60	MS63	MS65
AH1392-1972	30,000	1.00	1.50	3.50	6.50	10.00

KM# 69 50 GHIRSH
Copper-Nickel **Subject:** Establishment of Arab Cooperative **Obv:** Shield and value **Rev:** Legend above eagle and dates

Date	Mintage	VF20	XF40	MS60	MS63	MS65
AH1396-1976	—	0.75	1.25	2.50	5.00	9.00

KM# 73 50 GHIRSH
Copper-Nickel **Subject:** 8th Anniversary of 1969 Revolt **Obv:** Eagle divides dates **Rev:** Cogwheel design with inscription on circular design at bottom

Date	Mintage	VF20	XF40	MS60	MS63	MS65
AH1397-1977	100,000	0.75	1.25	2.50	5.00	9.00

KM# 103 50 GHIRSH
Aluminum-Bronze **Obv:** Legend and value above flower sprigs **Rev:** Central bank building above inscription and crossed sprigs **Shape:** 8-sided

Date	Mintage	VF20	XF40	MS60	MS63	MS65
AH1408-1987	—	—	0.75	1.00	1.50	5.00

KM# 105 50 GHIRSH
Aluminum-Bronze **Subject:** 33rd Anniversary of Independence **Obv:** Legend and value above flower sprigs **Rev:** Inscription within map flanked by dates, designs below and legend above **Shape:** 8-sided

Date	Mintage	VF20	XF40	MS60	MS63	MS65
AH1409-1989	—	0.75	0.75	1.00	1.50	5.00

KM# 109 50 GHIRSH
Copper-Nickel Plated Steel **Obv:** Value **Rev:** Central Bank building

Date	Mintage	VF20	XF40	MS60	MS63	MS65
AH1409-1989	—	—	0.75	1.00	1.50	3.00

KM# 75 POUND
Copper-Nickel **Series:** F.A.O. **Subject:** Rural women **Obv:** Eagle divides dates **Rev:** Stylized designs **Shape:** 10-sided

Date	Mintage	VF20	XF40	MS60	MS63	MS65
AH1398-1978	456,000	1.00	2.00	4.50	7.50	10.00

KM# 104 POUND
Aluminum-Bronze **Obv:** Legend and value above flower sprigs **Rev:** Central bank building

Date	Mintage	VF20	XF40	MS60	MS63	MS65
AH1408-1987	—	—	1.00	3.00	5.00	9.00

KM# 106 POUND
Copper-Nickel Plated Steel **Obv:** Value **Rev:** Central Bank building

Date	Mintage	VF20	XF40	MS60	MS63	MS65
AH1409-1989	—	—	0.75	1.00	1.50	3.00

KM# 70 2-1/2 POUNDS
28.28 g., 0.925 Silver 0.841 oz. ASW **Subject:** Conservation **Obv:** Eagle divides date **Rev:** Shoebill Stork

Date	Mintage	VF20	XF40	MS60	MS63	MS65
AH1396-1976	5,183	—	—	27.50	30.00	32.50
AH1396-1976	5,590	PF63 45.00	PF65 50.00			

KM# 71 5 POUNDS
35.00 g., 0.925 Silver 1.0409 oz. ASW **Subject:** Conservation **Obv:** Eagle divides dates **Rev:** Hippopotamus with calf

Date	Mintage	VF20	XF40	MS60	MS63	MS65
AH1396-1976	5,087	—	—	37.50	42.50	47.50
AH1396-1976	5,393	PF63 55.00	PF65 60.00			

KM# 76 5 POUNDS
17.50 g., 0.925 Silver 0.5204 oz. ASW **Subject:** Khartoum meeting of O.A.U. **Obv:** Eagle divides value **Rev:** African map within circle

Date	Mintage	VF20	XF40	MS60	MS63	MS65
AH1398-1978	21	—	—	—	—	—
AH1398-1978	1,423	PF63 42.00	PF65 47.00			
Note: Without countermarks						
AH1398-1978	2,000	PF63 35.00	PF65 40.00			
Note: AH1398 with countermarks of B23 in hexagon and bell between dates						

KM# 80 5 POUNDS
17.50 g., 0.925 Silver 0.5204 oz. ASW **Subject:** 1,400th Anniversary of Islam **Obv:** Eagle divides value below legend **Rev:** Monument

Date	Mintage	VF20	XF40	MS60	MS63	MS65
AH1400-1980	7,500	—	—	17.50	20.00	22.50
AH1400-1980	5,500	PF63 30.00	PF65 35.00			

KM# 86 5 POUNDS
28.28 g., 0.925 Silver 0.841 oz. ASW **Subject:** 25th Anniversary of Independence **Obv:** Bust 3/4 right **Rev:** Monument **Shape:** Hexagonal

Date	Mintage	VF20	XF40	MS60	MS63	MS65
AH1401-1981	20,000	—	—	40.00	45.00	55.00
AH1401-1981	—	PF63 60.00	PF65 70.00			

KM# 87 5 POUNDS
19.44 g., 0.925 Silver 0.5781 oz. ASW **Series:** UNICEF, International Year of the Child **Obv:** Eagle divides value **Rev:** Children playing in front of building with logos below

Date	Mintage	VF20	XF40	MS60	MS63	MS65
AH1401-1981	35,000	PF63 25.00	PF65 30.00			

KM# 92 5 POUNDS
19.44 g., 0.925 Silver 0.5781 oz. ASW **Series:** Decade for Women **Obv:** Eagle divides value **Rev:** Dancing female within map

Date	Mintage	VF20	XF40	MS60	MS63	MS65
AH1404-1984	20,000	PF63 30.00	PF65 35.00			

KM# 77 10 POUNDS
35.00 g., 0.925 Silver 1.0409 oz. ASW **Subject:** Khartoum Meeting of O.A.U. **Obv:** Eagle divides value **Rev:** African map within circle

Date	Mintage	VF20	XF40	MS60	MS63	MS65
AH1398-1978	21	—	—	—	350	—
AH1398-1978	1,417	PF63 60.00	PF65 75.00			
Note: Without countermarks						
AH1398-1978	2,000	PF63 40.00	PF65 55.00			
Note: AH1398 with countermarks of B23 in hexagon and bell between dates						

KM# 81 10 POUNDS
35.00 g., 0.925 Silver 1.0409 oz. ASW **Subject:** 1,400th Anniversary of Islam **Obv:** Eagle divides value **Rev:** Buildings and upright design

Date	Mintage	VF20	XF40	MS60	MS63	MS65
AH1400-1980	3,000	—	—	45.00	50.00	55.00
AH1400-1980	2,000	PF63 60.00	PF65 65.00			

KM# 88 10 POUNDS
28.28 g., 0.925 Silver 0.841 oz. ASW **Series:** Year of the Disabled Person **Obv:** Eagle divides legend and dates **Rev:** Rope entwined on post and tree trunk

Date	Mintage	VF20	XF40	MS60	MS63	MS65
AH1401-1981	Est. 10000	—	—	30.00	35.00	40.00
AH1401-1981	10,000	PF63 55.00	PF65 60.00			

KM# 78 25 POUNDS
8.25 g., 0.917 Gold 0.2432 oz. AGW **Subject:** Khartoum Meeting of O.A.U. **Obv:** Eagle divides value **Rev:** African map within circle

Date	Mintage	VF20	XF40	MS60	MS63	MS65
AH1398-1978	15	—	—	—	750	850
AH1398-1978	467	PF63 450	PF65 525			
Note: Without countermarks						
AH1398-1978	350	PF63 475	PF65 525			
Note: With countermarks of B23 in hexagon and bell between dates						

KM# 82 25 POUNDS
8.25 g., 0.917 Gold 0.2432 oz. AGW **Subject:** 1,400th Anniversary of Islam **Obv:** Eagle divides value **Rev:** Buildings and upright design

Date	Mintage	VF20	XF40	MS60	MS63	MS65
AH1400-1980	7,500	—	—	380	420	450
AH1400-1980	5,500	PF63 450	PF65 500			

KM# 79 50 POUNDS
17.50 g., 0.917 Gold 0.5159 oz. AGW **Subject:** Khartoum Meeting of O.A.U. **Obv:** Eagle divides value **Rev:** African map within circle

Date	Mintage	VF20	XF40	MS60	MS63	MS65
AH1398-1978	11	—	—	1,650	1,850	—
AH1398-1978	211	PF63 950	PF65 1,050			
Note: Without countermarks						
AH1398-1978	350	PF63 950	PF65 1,050			
Note: With countermarks of B23 in hexagon and bell between dates						

KM# 83 50 POUNDS
17.50 g., 0.917 Gold 0.5159 oz. AGW **Subject:** 1,400th Anniversary of Islam **Obv:** Eagle divides value **Rev:** Buildings and upright design

Date	Mintage	VF20	XF40	MS60	MS63	MS65
AH1400-1979	3,000	—	—	875	925	950
AH1400-1979	2,000	PF63 950	PF65 975			

KM# 89 50 POUNDS
7.99 g., 0.917 Gold 0.2356 oz. AGW **Subject:** 25th Anniversary of Independence

Date	Mintage	VF20	XF40	MS60	MS63	MS65
AH1401-1981	5,000	—	—	375	425	475
AH1401-1981	—	PF63 475	PF65 550			

KM# 72 100 POUNDS
33.44 g., 0.900 Gold 0.9675 oz. AGW **Subject:** Conservation **Obv:** Eagle divides dates **Rev:** Scimitar-horned oryx

Date	Mintage	VF20	XF40	MS60	MS63	MS65
AH1396-1976	872	—	—	1,700	1,750	1,850
AH1396-1976	251	PF63 1,900	PF65 2,000			

KM# 90 100 POUNDS
15.98 g., 0.917 Gold 0.4711 oz. AGW **Subject:** 25th Anniversary of Independence

Date	Mintage	VF20	XF40	MS60	MS63	MS65
AH1401-1981	2,500	—	—	800	850	900
AH1401-1981	—	PF63 900	PF65 950			

KM# 91 100 POUNDS
15.98 g., 0.917 Gold 0.4711 oz. AGW **Series:** Year of the Disabled Person **Obv:** Eagle **Rev:** Stylized arrowhead within wreath

Date	Mintage	VF20	XF40	MS60	MS63	MS65
AH1401-1981	2,000	—	—	800	850	900
AH1401-1981	—	PF63 900	PF65 950			

KM# 93 100 POUNDS
8.10 g., 0.917 Gold 0.2388 oz. AGW **Series:** Decade for Women **Obv:** Eagle divides value **Rev:** Half female figure facing right

Date	Mintage	VF20	XF40	MS60	MS63	MS65
AH1404-1984	513	PF63 475	PF65 550			

REFORM COINAGE

100 Qurush (Piastres) = 1 Dinar
10 Pounds = 1 Dinar

KM# 117 1/4 DINAR
3.00 g., Brass Plated Steel, 18 mm. **Obv:** Value **Rev:** Central Bank building **Edge:** Plain

Date	Mintage	VF20	XF40	MS60	MS63	MS65
AH1415-1994 Rare	—	—	—	—	—	—

KM# 118 1/2 DINAR
4.00 g., Brass Plated Steel, 20 mm. **Obv:** Value **Rev:** Central Bank building **Edge:** Plain

Date	Mintage	VF20	XF40	MS60	MS63	MS65
AH1415-1994 Rare	—	—	—	—	—	—

KM# 112 DINAR
5.14 g., Brass, 22.2 mm. **Obv:** Value **Rev:** Central Bank building **Edge:** Plain

Date	Mintage	VF20	XF40	MS60	MS63	MS65
AH1415-1994	—	—	0.25	0.50	0.75	1.50

KM# 113 2 DINAR
Brass Plated Steel **Obv:** Value **Rev:** Central Bank building **Edge:** Plain **Note:** Varieties exist with finely spaced and widely spaced shading to the number "2" in the denomination.

Date	Mintage	VF20	XF40	MS60	MS63	MS65
AH1415-1994	—	—	0.45	0.75	1.00	2.00

KM# 114 5 DINARS
8.20 g., Brass, 22.24 mm. **Obv:** Value **Rev:** Central Bank building **Edge:** Plain

Date	Mintage	VF20	XF40	MS60	MS63	MS65
AH1417-1996	—	—	0.50	1.00	1.50	3.00

KM# 115.1 10 DINARS
Brass **Obv:** Legend and value above designs **Rev:** Central Bank building, thin inscription below **Edge:** Plain

Date	Mintage	VF20	XF40	MS60	MS63	MS65
AH1417-1996	—	—	0.50	0.75	1.50	3.00

KM# 115.2 10 DINARS
Brass **Obv:** Legend and value **Rev:** Central Bank building, thick inscription below **Edge:** Plain

Date	Mintage	VF20	XF40	MS60	MS63	MS65
AH1417-1996	—	—	0.50	0.75	1.50	3.00

KM# 116.1 20 DINARS
Copper-Nickel, 22 mm. **Obv:** Value **Rev:** Central Bank building, "a" to right of "n" at the left end of the Arabic inscription, 72 border beads **Edge:** Plain

Date	Mintage	VF20	XF40	MS60	MS63	MS65
AH1417-1996	—	—	0.75	1.00	2.00	4.00

KM# 116.2 20 DINARS
4.61 g., Copper-Nickel, 22.17 mm. **Obv:** Legend and value **Rev:** Smaller Central Bank building, "a" above "n" at the left end of the Arabic inscription, 64 border beads **Edge:** Plain

Date	Mintage	VF20	XF40	MS60	MS63	MS65
AH1419-1999	—	—	0.75	1.00	2.00	4.00

PATTERNS

Including off metal strikes

KM#	Date	Mintage	Identification	Mkt Val
Pn1	1956AD-1375AH (1956)	—	Millim. Copper. HAKUMAT AS-SUDAN.	200
Pn2	1956AD-1375AH (1956)	—	5 Millim. Copper. HAKUMAT AS-SUDAN.	200
Pn3	1956AD-1375AH (1956)	—	5 Ghirsh. Copper-Nickel. HAKUMAT AS-SUDAN.	225
Pn4	1956AD-1375AH (1956)	—	10 Ghirsh. Copper-Nickel. HAKUMAT AS-SUDAN.	275

ESSAIS

KM#	Date	Mintage	Identification	Mkt Val
E1	1978	25	5 Pounds. Aluminum.	50.00
E2	1978	15	5 Pounds. Copper.	95.00
E3	1978	25	10 Pounds. Aluminum.	50.00
E4	1978	21	10 Pounds. Copper. KM77.	135
E5	1978	25	25 Pounds. Aluminum.	50.00
E6	1978	21	25 Pounds. Copper.	85.00
E7	1978	25	50 Pounds. Aluminum.	50.00
E8	1978	21	50 Pounds. Copper.	95.00
E9	1979	15	5 Pounds. Copper. KM817.	95.00
E10	1979	40	10 Pounds. Aluminum. KM81.	50.00
E11	1979	21	10 Pounds. Copper. KM81.	135
E12	1979	21	50 Pounds. Copper. KM83.	95.00
E13	1980	25	5 Pounds. Aluminum.	50.00
E14	1980	15	5 Pounds. Copper.	95.00
E15	1980	25	10 Pounds. Aluminum.	50.00
E16	1980	21	10 Pounds. Copper.	135
E17	1980	25	25 Pounds. Aluminum.	50.00
E18	1980	20	25 Pounds. Copper.	85.00
E19	1980	25	50 Pounds. Aluminum.	50.00
E20	1980	21	50 Pounds. Copper.	85.00

PIEDFORT

KM#	Date	Mintage	Identification	Mkt Val
P1	1978	5	5 Pounds. Copper. KM76.	195
P2	1978	10	5 Pounds. 0.925. Silver. KM76.	335
P3	1978	5	10 Pounds. Copper.	235
P4	1978	10	10 Pounds. 0.925. Silver. KM77.	—
P5	1978	5	25 Pounds. Copper.	195
P6	1979	5	5 Pounds. Copper. KM80.	195
P7	1979	10	5 Pounds. 0.925. Silver. KM80.	—
P8	1979	5	10 Pounds. Copper. KM81.	235
P9	1979	10	10 Pounds. 0.925. Silver. KM81.	—
P10	1979	—	25 Pounds. Brass. KM83.	195
P11	1979	10	25 Pounds. Silver. KM83.	195
PA12	1979	—	50 Pounds. Silver. KM#83.	—
P12	1979	—	50 Pounds. Copper. KM83. Gold plated.	—
P16	1979	—	50 Pounds. Gold. KM83.	1,350
P13	1980	5	5 Pounds. Copper.	195
P14	1980	5	10 Pounds. Copper.	235
P15	1980	5	25 Pounds. Copper.	195
P17	1981	2,587	5 Pounds. Silver. KM87.	50.00
P18	1981	1,000	10 Pounds. Silver. KM88.	85.00
P19	1981	Est. 500	100 Pounds. Gold. KM91.	1,500

MINT SETS

KM#	Date	Mintage	Identification	Issue Price	Mkt Val
MS1	1976 (2)	—	KM70-71	—	70.00

PROOF SETS

KM#	Date	Mintage	Identification	Issue Price	Mkt Val
PS1	1967 (8)	7,834	KM29-32, 34-37	12.25	17.50
PS2	1968 (8)	5,251	KM29-32, 34-37	15.25	24.00
PS3	1969 (8)	2,149	KM29-32, 34-37	15.25	28.50
PS4	1970 (8)	1,646	KM39-46	15.25	33.00
PS5	1971 (8)	1,772	KM39-46	15.25	33.00
PS6	1976 (2)	—	KM70-71	—	90.00
PS7	1978 (4)	—	KM76-79	—	1,600
PS8	1980 (5)	—	KM54, 55a, 57-59	12.00	13.50
PS9	1980 (4)	—	KM80-83	—	1,550

DARFUR

Darfur had been an independent Sultanate until taken over by Egypt in 1874, and subsequently by the Mahdists. After the latter's defeat in 1898 by the British, 'Ali Dinar re-established the Sultanate which ended in 1916 with his demise. His coins copied the Ottoman coins of Egypt. The mint was located at El Fasher, the Sultanate capital, and was active from 1909 to 1914.

MINT

الفشير

al-Fasher

RULER
Ali Dinar, AH1316-1335/1898-1916AD

SULTANATE

HAMMERED COINAGE

KM# 1 PIASTRE
Copper-Nickel-Zinc **Obv:** Toughra within circle **Rev:** Inscription, date and value within circle

Date	Mintage	G4	VG8	F12	VF20	XF40
AH1223 (sic)/23 Rare	—	—	—	—	—	—
AH1223 (sic)/13 Rare	—	—	—	—	—	—

Note: Due to a shortage of small change, debased, unmilled imitations of Egyptian Qirsh (Piastre) KM#181, which had been produced outside of Sudan were brought into circulation in Darfur from AH1323-1325/1905-1907AD, privately struck in agreement with the Sultan

KM# 2 PIASTRE
Billon **Obv:** Toughra within circle **Rev:** Inscription, date and value within circle **Note:** Struck at al-Fasher mint from 1909-1914. Flan size varies and most appear crude due to thinness of flan. Off center and double strikes exist. Those bearing the date AH1327, regnal year 17 are probably the sultan's approved type. Other hejira and regnal years are engraving errors of filled dies.

Date	Mintage	G4	VG8	F12	VF20	XF40
AH1227(sic)/5	—	—	—	—	—	—
AH1237(sic)/71	—	—	—	—	—	—
Note: With retrograde 3						
AH1321(sic)/71	—	—	—	—	—	—
AH1323(sic)/65	—	—	—	—	—	—
AH1327/7	—	—	—	—	—	—
AH1327/17	—	30.00	80.00	160	190	—
AH1327/26	—	—	—	—	—	—
AH3127/71	—	—	—	—	—	—
AH1327/71	—	15.00	30.00	45.00	60.00	—
AH1327/71	—	—	—	—	—	—
Note: Retrograde 3						
AH1327/76	—	—	—	—	—	—
AH1327/77	—	—	—	—	—	—
AHx321(sic)/17	—	—	—	—	—	—
AH3167/7x	—	—	—	—	—	—
AH1387(sic)/17	—	—	—	—	—	—
AH7132(sic)/x	—	—	—	—	—	—

COUNTERMARKED COINAGE

KM# 3 PIASTRE
Copper-Nickel-Zinc **Obv:** Inscription, date and value within circle **Rev:** Toughra within circle **Countermark:** "Ali" 1312 **Note:** Countermark on KM#1.

CM Date	Host Date	G4	VG8	F12	VF20	XF40
ND	1223/13 Rare	—	—	—	—	—

Note: In a move to control import and circulation of KM#1, the Sultan ordered the countermarking; AH1312 is the year 'Ali Dinar used as the official beginning of his Sultanate. The countermark can be on the obverse or reverse. Counterfeit (contemporary) may exist. AH1327/17 approximates 1312, the year 'Ali Dinar officially used as the beginning of his dynasty as per noted historian O'Fahey.

CM Date	Host Date	G4	VG8	F12	VF20	XF40
ND	1223/23 Rare	—	—	—	—	—

Ali Dinar
AH1316-35/1898-1916AD

HAMMERED COINAGE

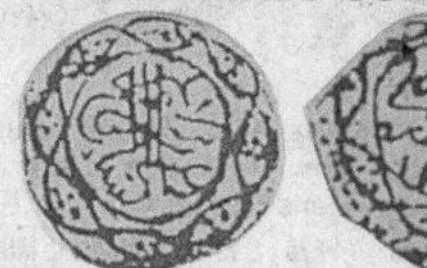

KM# 4 1/2 PIASTRE
Billon **Ruler:** Ali Dinar **Obv:** Toughra within circle **Rev:** Value and date within circle

Date	Mintage	G4	VG8	F12	VF20	XF40
AH1328/8 Rare	—	—	—	—	—	—

Note: Due to the low denomination and little demand, this coin was only struck for a very short time, though varieties do exist

KM# 5 5 PIASTRES
Copper-Nickel-Zinc **Ruler:** Ali Dinar **Obv:** Toughra within design **Rev:** Inscription, value and date within design **Note:** Size varies: 21.6-24.4 mm.

Date	Mintage	G4	VG8	F12	VF20	XF40
AH1328 Rare	—	—	—	—	—	—

Note: Copied from Ottoman Mejidiye coinage; about 800 are reported having been put into circulation; further striking was discontinued as the coin was unpopular due to low silver content. Specimens dated 8231 are contemporary forgeries.

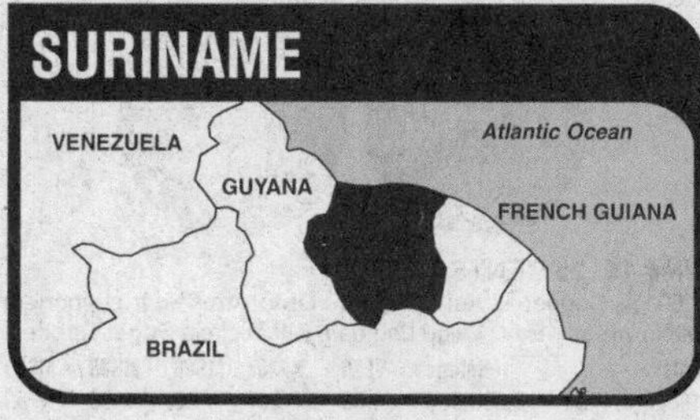

The Republic of Suriname also known as Dutch Guiana, located on the north central coast of South America between Guyana and French Guiana has an area of 63,037 sq. mi. (163,270 sq. km.) and a population of *485,000. Capital: Paramaribo. The country is rich in minerals and forests, and self-sufficient in rice, the staple food crop. The mining, processing and exporting of bauxite is the principal economic activity.

Lieutenants of Amerigo Vespucci sighted the Guiana coast in 1499. Spanish explorers of the 16th century, disappointed at finding no gold, departed leaving the area to be settled by the British in 1652. The colony prospered and the Netherlands acquired it in 1667 in exchange for the Dutch rights in Nieuw Nederland (state of New York). During the European wars of the 18th and 19th centuries, which were fought in part in the new world, Suriname was occupied by the British from 1781-1784 and 1796-1814.Suriname became an autonomous part of the Kingdom of the Netherlands on Dec. 15, 1954. Full independence was achieved on Nov. 25, 1975. In 1980, a coup installed a military government, which has since been dissolved.

RULER
Dutch, until 1975

MINT MARKS
(B) - British Royal Mint, no mint mark
FM - Franklin Mint, U.S.A.**
P - Philadelphia, U.S.A.
S - J. Sedney, Finance Minister
(u) - Utrecht (privy marks only)

**NOTE: From 1975-1985 the Franklin Mint produced coinage in up to 3 different qualities. Qualities of issue are designated in ( ) after each date and are defined as follows:

(M) MATTE - Normal circulation strike or a dull finish produced by sandblasting special uncirculated (polish finish) or proof quality dies.

(U) SPECIAL UNCIRCULATED - Polished or prooflike in appearance without any frosted features.

(P) PROOF - The highest quality obtainable having mirror-like fields and frosted features.

MONETARY SYSTEM
100 Cents = 1 Gulden (Guilders)
After January, 2004
1 Dollar = 100 Cents

DUTCH ADMINISTRATION

WORLD WAR II COINAGE

The 1942-1943 issues that follow are homeland coinage types of the Netherlands. KM#152, KM#163 and KM#164 were executed expressly for use in Suriname. Related issues produced for use in Curacao and Suriname are listed under Curacao. They are distinguished by a palm tree (acorn on homeland issues) and a mint mark (P-Philadelphia, D-Denver, S-San Francisco) flanking the date. See the Netherlands for similar issues. See Curacao for similar coins dated 1941-P, 1942-P and 1943-P.

KM# 10 CENT
2.50 g., Brass, 19 mm. **Obv:** Upright lion with sword within beaded circle **Rev:** Value within orange wreath **Edge:** Reeded

Date	Mintage	F12	VF20	XF40	MS60	MS63
1942 P Palm, see under Curacao	—	—	—	—	—	—
1943 P Palm	4,000,000	0.85	3.75	7.50	25.00	40.00

KM# 10a CENT
2.50 g., Bronze, 19 mm. **Obv:** Upright lion with sword within beaded circle **Rev:** Value within orange wreath **Edge:** Reeded

Date	Mintage	F12	VF20	XF40	MS60	MS63
1943 P	—	25.00	50.00	100	150	200
1957 (u)	1,200,000	—	1.00	2.00	4.50	10.00
1957 (u)	—	PF63 35.00				
1959 (u)	1,800,000	—	1.00	2.00	4.50	10.00
1959 (u)	—	PF63 35.00				
1960 (u)	1,200,000	—	1.00	2.00	4.50	10.00
1960 (u)	—	PF63 35.00				

KM# A9 5 CENTS
4.35 g., Copper-Nickel-Zinc, 18x18 mm. **Shape:** Square

Date	Mintage	F12	VF20	XF40	MS60	MS63
1943	2,850,000	1.25	2.50	6.00	12.00	20.00

Note: Struck at Philadelphia Mint for use in Suriname. An addition 1,415,000 were struck for use in Curacao

KM# 9 10 CENTS
1.40 g., 0.640 Silver 0.0288 oz. ASW **Obv:** Head of Queen Wilhelmina left **Rev:** Value and date within orange wreath **Edge:** Reeded

Date	Mintage	F12	VF20	XF40	MS60	MS63
1942 P Palm	1,500,000	6.00	12.50	15.00	30.00	40.00
1943 P Palmtree	4,000,000	3.00	6.00	10.00	20.00	30.00

Note: An addition 500,000 mintage was struck for Curacao

REPUBLIC

MODERN COINAGE

KM# 11 CENT
2.55 g., Bronze, 18 mm. **Obv:** Arms with supporters within wreath **Rev:** Value divides date within circle **Edge:** Plain

Date	Mintage	VF20	XF40	MS60	MS63	MS65
1962 (u) Fish	6,000,000	0.25	0.50	0.75	1.50	3.00
1962 (u) S	650	PF65 28.00				
1966 (u)	6,500,000	0.25	0.50	0.75	1.50	3.00
1966 (u)	—	PF65 42.00				
1970 (u) Cock	5,000,000	0.25	0.50	0.65	1.00	2.50
1972 (u)	6,000,000	0.25	0.50	0.65	1.00	2.50
1972	—	PF65 45.00				

KM# 11a CENT
0.80 g., Aluminum, 18 mm. **Obv:** Arms with supporters within wreath **Rev:** Value divides date within circle **Edge:** Plain

Date	Mintage	VF20	XF40	MS60	MS63	MS65
1974 (u)	1,000,000	0.10	0.25	0.35	0.50	1.00
1975 (u)	1,000,000	0.10	0.25	0.35	0.50	1.00
1976	Est. 10	PF65 55.00				
1976 (u)	3,000,000	0.10	0.25	0.35	0.50	1.00
1977 (u)	10,000,000	—	0.25	0.35	0.50	1.00
1978 (u)	6,000,000	—	0.25	0.35	0.50	1.00
1979 (u)	10,000,000	—	0.25	0.35	0.50	1.00
1980 (u)	8,000,000	—	0.25	0.35	0.50	1.00

Note: Cock and star privy marks

Date	Mintage	VF20	XF40	MS60	MS63	MS65
1982 (u) Anvil	8,000,000	—	0.25	0.35	0.50	1.00
1984 (u)	5,000,000	—	0.25	0.35	0.50	1.00
1985 (u)	2,000,000	—	0.25	0.35	0.50	1.00
1986 (u)	3,000,000	—	0.25	0.35	0.50	1.00

KM# 11b CENT

2.50 g., Copper Plated Steel, 18 mm. **Obv:** Arms with supporters within wreath **Rev:** Value divides date within circle **Edge:** Plain

Date	Mintage	VF20	XF40	MS60	MS63	MS65
1987 (B)	—	—	0.20	0.40	0.80	1.25
1988 (B)	—	—	0.20	0.40	0.80	1.25
1988 (B)	1,500	PF65 4.00				
1989 (B)	—	—	0.20	0.40	0.80	1.25

KM# 12.1 5 CENTS

4.00 g., Nickel-Brass, 22 mm. **Obv:** Arms with supporters within circle **Rev:** Value divides date within circle **Shape:** 4-sided

Date	Mintage	VF20	XF40	MS60	MS63	MS65
1962 (u) fish	2,200,000	0.50	0.75	1.25	2.00	4.00
1962 (u) S	650	PF65 25.00				
1966 (u) Short "66" and mintmaster's markt straight	2,300,000	0.50	1.00	1.50	3.00	6.00
Note: With mint mark and mintmaster's mark						
1966 (u) Short "66" and mintmaster's mark slanting	Inc. above	0.50	0.75	1.25	2.00	4.00
1966 (u) Long "66	Inc. above	0.75	1.50	2.50	4.00	6.00
1966 (u)	Inc. above	PF65 50.00				
1966 (u)	400,000	1.75	2.75	4.00	7.00	10.00
Note: Without mint mark and mint master's mark						
1971 (u) Cock	500,000	0.75	1.25	2.00	3.00	5.00
1972 (u)	1,500,000	0.50	0.75	1.25	2.00	4.00

KM# 12.2 5 CENTS

4.00 g., Nickel-Brass, 22 mm. **Obv:** Arms with supporters within circle **Rev:** Value divides date within circle **Shape:** Square **Note:** Medal turn.

Date	Mintage	VF20	XF40	MS60	MS63	MS65
1966 (u)	Inc. above	8.00	15.00	20.00	40.00	85.00
1966 (u)	—	PF65 450				

KM# 12.1a 5 CENTS

1.24 g., Aluminum, 20 mm. **Obv:** Arms with supporters within circle **Rev:** Value divides date within circle **Shape:** Square

Date	Mintage	VF20	XF40	MS60	MS63	MS65
1976 (u)	5,500,000	0.10	0.25	0.45	0.80	1.50
1976	Est. 10	PF65 75.00				
1978 (u)	3,000,000	0.10	0.25	0.45	0.80	1.50
1979 (u)	2,000,000	0.10	0.25	0.45	0.80	1.50
1980 (u)	1,000,000	0.10	0.25	0.45	0.80	1.50
Note: Cock and star privy marks						
1982 (u) Anvil	1,000,000	0.10	0.25	0.45	0.80	1.50
1985 (u)	1,000,000	0.10	0.25	0.45	0.80	1.50
1986 (u)	1,500,000	0.10	0.25	0.45	0.80	1.50

KM# 12.1b 5 CENTS

3.00 g., Copper Plated Steel, 18 mm. **Obv:** Arms with supporters within circle **Rev:** Value divides date within circle **Edge:** Plain **Shape:** Square

Date	Mintage	VF20	XF40	MS60	MS63	MS65
1987 (B)	—	—	0.30	0.50	0.80	1.00
1988 (B)	—	—	0.30	0.50	0.80	1.00
1988 (B)	Est. 1500	PF65 25.00				
1989 (B)	—	—	0.30	0.50	0.80	1.50

KM# 13 10 CENTS

2.00 g., Copper-Nickel, 16 mm. **Obv:** Arms with supporters within wreath **Rev:** Value and date within circle **Edge:** Reeded

Date	Mintage	VF20	XF40	MS60	MS63	MS65
1962 (u) Fish	3,000,000	0.25	0.50	0.75	1.50	2.50
1962 (u) S	650	PF65 25.00				
1966 (u)	2,500,000	0.25	0.50	0.75	1.50	2.50
1966 (u)	—	PF65 50.00				
1971 (u) Cock	500,000	0.75	1.50	2.50	4.00	7.00
1972 (u)	1,500,000	0.25	0.50	0.75	1.50	2.50
1974 (u)	1,500,000	0.25	0.50	0.75	1.50	2.50
1976 (u)	5,000,000	0.15	0.30	0.50	0.75	1.50
1976	Est. 10	PF65 100				
1978 (u)	2,000,000	0.15	0.30	0.50	0.75	1.50
1979 (u)	2,000,000	0.15	0.30	0.50	0.75	1.50
1982 (u) Anvil	1,000,000	0.15	0.30	0.50	0.75	1.50
1985 (u)	1,000,000	0.15	0.30	0.50	0.75	1.50
1986 (u)	1,500,000	0.15	0.30	0.50	0.75	1.50

KM# 13a 10 CENTS

2.00 g., Nickel Plated Steel, 16 mm. **Obv:** Arms with supporters within wreath **Rev:** Value and date within circle **Edge:** Reeded

Date	Mintage	VF20	XF40	MS60	MS63	MS65
1987 (B)	—	0.15	0.30	0.50	0.75	1.50
1988 (B)	—	0.15	0.30	0.50	0.75	1.50
1988 (B)	Est. 1500	PF65 25.00				
1989 (B)	—	0.10	0.30	0.50	0.75	1.50

KM# 14 25 CENTS

3.50 g., Copper-Nickel, 20 mm. **Obv:** Arms with supporters within wreath **Rev:** Value and date within circle **Edge:** Reeded

Date	Mintage	VF20	XF40	MS60	MS63	MS65
1962 (u) Fish	2,300,000	0.30	0.50	1.00	2.00	3.50
1962 (u) S	650	PF65 20.00				
1966 (u)	2,300,000	0.30	0.50	1.00	2.00	3.50
1966 (u)	—	PF65 50.00				
1972 (u) Cock	1,800,000	0.30	0.50	1.00	2.00	3.50
1974 (u)	1,500,000	0.30	0.50	1.00	2.00	3.50
1976 (u)	5,000,000	0.30	0.50	1.00	2.00	3.50
1976	Est. 10	PF65 125				
1979 (u)	2,000,000	0.30	0.50	0.75	1.25	2.50
1982 (u) Anvil	2,000,000	0.30	0.50	0.75	1.25	2.50
1985 (u)	1,000,000	0.30	0.50	0.75	1.25	2.50
1986 (u)	1,500,000	0.30	0.50	0.75	1.25	2.50

KM# 14a 25 CENTS

3.50 g., Nickel Plated Steel, 20 mm. **Obv:** Arms with supporters within wreath **Rev:** Value and date within circle **Edge:** Reeded

Date	Mintage	VF20	XF40	MS60	MS63	MS65
1987 (B)	—	0.30	0.50	0.75	1.25	2.50
1988 (B)	—	0.30	0.50	0.75	1.25	2.50
1988 (B)	Est. 1500	PF65 30.00				
1989 (B)	—	0.30	0.50	0.75	1.25	2.50

KM# 15 GULDEN

10.00 g., 0.720 Silver 0.2315 oz. ASW, 28 mm. **Obv:** Head of Queen Juliana right **Rev:** Arms with supporters within wreath **Edge Lettering:** JUSTITIA * PIETAS * FIDES *

Date	Mintage	VF20	XF40	MS60	MS63	MS65
1962 (u)	150,000	8.50	12.50	15.00	20.00	30.00
1962 (u) S	650	PF65 70.00				
1966 (u)	100,000	40.00	70.00	100	150	230
Note: Never officially released to circulation						
1966 (u)	—	PF65 300				

KM# 23 100 CENTS

5.65 g., Copper-Nickel, 23 mm. **Obv:** Arms with supporters within wreath **Rev:** Value and date within circle **Edge:** Reeded

Date	Mintage	VF20	XF40	MS60	MS63	MS65
1987 (B)	—	0.40	0.75	1.25	1.75	3.00
1988 (B)	—	0.40	0.75	1.25	1.75	3.00
1988 (B)	Est. 1500	PF65 50.00				
1989 (B)	—	0.40	0.75	1.25	1.75	3.00

KM# 24 250 CENTS

9.57 g., Copper-Nickel, 28 mm. **Obv:** Arms with supporters within wreath **Rev:** Value and date within circle

Date	Mintage	VF20	XF40	MS60	MS63	MS65
1987 (B)	—	0.80	1.50	2.00	3.50	5.00
1988 (B) Proof only	Est. 1500	PF65 17.50				
1989 (B)	—	0.80	1.50	2.00	3.50	5.00

KM# 16 10 GULDEN

15.95 g., 0.925 Silver 0.4743 oz. ASW, 33 mm. **Subject:** 1st Anniversary of Independence **Obv:** Flag, Surinam map, rising sun **Rev:** Arms with supporters divide date **Edge Lettering:** JUSTITIA * PIETAS * FIDES *

Date	Mintage	VF20	XF40	MS60	MS63	MS65
1976 (u)	100,000	—	—	9.00	12.00	16.00
1976 (u)	5,711	PF65 22.50				

KM# 17 25 GULDEN

26.20 g., 0.925 Silver 0.7792 oz. ASW, 38 mm. **Subject:** 1st Anniversary of Independence **Obv:** Flag, Surinam map, rising sun **Rev:** Arms with supporters divide date

Date	Mintage	VF20	XF40	MS60	MS63	MS65
1976 (u)	75,000	—	—	17.00	22.00	27.00
1976 (u) F	5,503	PF65 32.50				

KM# 19 25 GULDEN

15.50 g., 0.925 Silver 0.461 oz. ASW, 32 mm. **Subject:** 1st Anniversary of Revolution **Obv:** Revolution monument **Rev:** Allegorical group of revolutionaries **Edge:** Reeded

Date	Mintage	VF20	XF40	MS60	MS63	MS65
1981 FM (U)	10,000	—	—	—	25.00	30.00
1981 FM (P)	800	PF65 95.00				

KM# 21 25 GULDEN
25.10 g., 0.925 Silver 0.7465 oz. ASW, 38 mm. **Subject:** 5th Anniversary of Revolution **Obv:** Peace dove, flag superimposed on Surinam map **Rev:** Stylized fist and 5 on star within designed circle **Edge Lettering:** JUSTITIA * PIETAS * FIDES *

Date	Mintage	VF20	XF40	MS60	MS63	MS65
ND-1985 (u)	4,800	—	—	—	55.00	60.00
ND-1985 (u)	200	PF65 120				

KM# 32 25 GUILDER
28.28 g., 0.925 Silver 0.841 oz. ASW, 39 mm. **Subject:** World Cup Soccer **Obv:** Arms with supporters within wreath **Rev:** Player R. Gullit, stadium and half globe

Date	Mintage	VF20	XF40	MS60	MS63	MS65
1990 (B)	50,000	PF65 50.00				

KM# 36 25 GUILDER
28.28 g., 0.925 Silver 0.841 oz. ASW, 38.61 mm. **Series:** Save the Children **Obv:** Arms with supporters **Rev:** Children **Edge:** Reeded

Date	Mintage	VF20	XF40	MS60	MS63	MS65
1991	30,000	PF65 65.00				
1992	—	—	—	—	—	—

Requires confirmation

KM# 27 30 GULDEN
14.30 g., 0.925 Silver 0.4253 oz. ASW, 30 mm. **Subject:** 30th Anniversary of Central Bank **Obv:** Arms with supporters divide date **Rev:** Central Bank building

Date	Mintage	VF20	XF40	MS60	MS63	MS65
1987 (u)	7,000	—	—	17.00	22.00	35.00

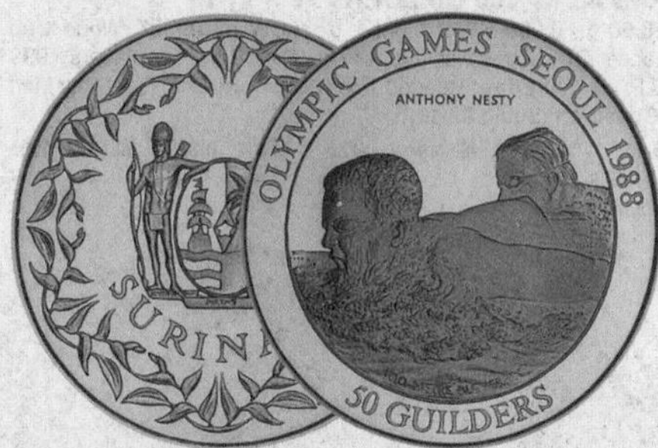

KM# 28.1 50 GUILDER
28.28 g., 0.925 Silver 0.841 oz. ASW, 39 mm. **Subject:** Anthony Nesty, Butterfly gold medalist, Seoul Olympics **Obv:** Arms with supporters within wreath **Rev:** Conjoined swimmers left within circle **Edge:** Reeded **Note:** Coin alignment

Date	Mintage	VF20	XF40	MS60	MS63	MS65
1988 (B)	Est. 25000	PF65 55.00				

KM# 28.2 50 GUILDER
28.28 g., 0.925 Silver 0.841 oz. ASW, 39 mm. **Subject:** Anthony Nesty, Butterfly gold medalist, Seoul Olympics **Obv:** Arms with supporters within wreath **Rev:** Conjoined swimmers left within circle **Edge:** Reeded **Note:** Medal alignment

Date	Mintage	VF20	XF40	MS60	MS63	MS65
1988 (B)	—	PF65 50.00				

KM# 30 50 GUILDER
28.28 g., 0.925 Silver 0.841 oz. ASW, 30 mm. **Subject:** 125th Anniversary of De Surinaamsche Bank **Obv:** Arms with supporters within wreath **Rev:** Designs and horizontal lines within circle **Edge:** Reeded

Date	Mintage	VF20	XF40	MS60	MS63	MS65
ND-1990 (B)	Est. 7500	PF65 55.00				

KM# 34 50 GUILDER
26.00 g., 0.925 Silver 0.7732 oz. ASW, 35 mm. **Subject:** 15th Anniversary of Independence **Obv:** Arms with supporters **Rev:** Stylized design **Edge:** Reeded **Note:** Similar to 500 Guilders, KM#35.

Date	Mintage	VF20	XF40	MS60	MS63	MS65
ND-1990 (B)	—	PF65 50.00				

KM# 38 50 GUILDER
26.00 g., 0.925 Silver 0.7732 oz. ASW, 35 mm. **Subject:** 35th Anniversary of Central Bank **Obv:** Arms with supporters within wreath **Rev:** Geometric arrow design divides date at top and bottom within circle **Edge:** Reeded

Date	Mintage	VF20	XF40	MS60	MS63	MS65
ND-1992 (B)	Est. 1500	PF65 65.00				

KM# 18a 100 GULDEN
6.72 g., 0.900 Yellow Gold 0.1944 oz., 22 mm. **Subject:** 1st Anniversary of Independence **Obv:** Flag, Surinam map, rising sun within circle **Rev:** Arms with supporters divide date

Date	Mintage	VF20	XF40	MS60	MS63	MS65
1976 (u)	19,100	—	—	—	—	325
1976 (u)	4,749	PF65 350				

KM# 18b 100 GULDEN
6.72 g., 0.900 Red Gold 0.1944 oz., 22 mm. **Subject:** 1st Anniversary of Independence **Obv:** Flag, Surinam map, rising sun within circle **Rev:** Arms with supporters divide date

Date	Mintage	VF20	XF40	MS60	MS63	MS65
1976 (u)	900	—	—	—	375	400

KM# 52.1 100 GULDEN
20.00 g., 0.999 Silver 0.6424 oz. ASW, 38 mm. **Subject:** 700th Anniversary of the Helvetic Confederation and 125th Anniversary of the Red Cross **Obv:** Arms with supporters **Rev:** Wilhelm Tell, maps, flags and arms of Suriname and Switzerland above "999". **Edge:** Reeded **Note:** Struck at Gold Reef City Mint (Capetown, South Africa)

Date	Mintage	VF20	XF40	MS60	MS63	MS65
ND(1991)	2,250	PF65 100				

KM# 52.2 100 GULDEN
26.00 g., 0.999 Silver 0.8351 oz. ASW, 38 mm. **Subject:** 700th Anniversary of the Helvetic Confederation and 125th Anniversary of the Red Cross **Obv:** Arms with supporters **Rev:** Wilhelm Tell, maps, flags and arms of Suriname and Switzerland above "999". **Edge:** Partially lettered **Edge Lettering:** CM AG 999 M5 **Note:** Struck at Gold Reef City Mint (Capetown, South Aftrica)

Date	Mintage	VF20	XF40	MS60	MS63	MS65
ND(1991)	—	PF65 110				

KM# 40.1 100 GUILDER
20.00 g., 0.999 Silver 0.6424 oz. ASW, 38 mm. **Series:** Barcelona Olympics **Subject:** Basketball **Obv:** Arms with supporters within wreath **Rev:** Four basketball players within circle **Edge:** Reeded **Note:** Medal alignment

Date	Mintage	VF20	XF40	MS60	MS63	MS65
1992	Inc. below	PF65 60.00				

KM# 40.2 100 GUILDER
20.00 g., 0.999 Silver 0.6424 oz. ASW, 38 mm. **Series:** Barcelona Olympics **Subject:** Basketball **Obv:** Arms with supporters within wreath **Rev:** Four basketball players within circle, with .999 **Edge:** Reeded

Date	Mintage	VF20	XF40	MS60	MS63	MS65
1992	15,000	PF65 65.00				

KM# 41.1 100 GUILDER
20.00 g., 0.999 Silver 0.6424 oz. ASW, 28.5 mm. **Series:** Barcelona Olympics **Subject:** Cyclists **Obv:** Arms with supporters with .999 (left above "S"). **Rev:** Three cyclists **Edge:** Reeded

Date	Mintage	VF20	XF40	MS60	MS63	MS65
1992	Est. 15000	PF65 65.00				

KM# 41.2 100 GUILDER
20.00 g., 0.999 Silver 0.6424 oz. ASW, 38.5 mm. **Series:** Barcelona Olympics **Subject:** Cyclists **Obv:** Arms with supporters **Rev:** Three cyclists **Edge:** Reeded **Note:** Medal alignment

Date	Mintage	VF20	XF40	MS60	MS63	MS65
1992	Inc. above	PF65 70.00				

KM# 42.1 100 GUILDER
20.00 g., 0.999 Silver 0.6424 oz. ASW, 38 mm. **Series:** Barcelona Olympics **Subject:** Anthony Nesty **Obv:** Arms with supporters **Rev:** Swimmer within circle 100m above swimmer **Edge:** Reeded **Note:** Struck at Kaapstad (Capetown, South Africa).

Date	Mintage	VF20	XF40	MS60	MS63	MS65
ND-1992	2,500	PF65 70.00				

KM# 42.1a 100 GUILDER
26.00 g., 0.7732 Silver 0.6463 oz. ASW, 38 mm. **Series:** Barcelona Olympics **Subject:** Anthony Nesty **Obv:** Arms with supporters **Rev:** Swimer within circle with 100m **Edge:** Reeded **Note:** Struck at Kaapstad (Capetown, South Africa)

Date	Mintage	VF20	XF40	MS60	MS63	MS65
ND (1992)	Inc. above	PF65 65.00				

KM# 42.1b 100 GUILDER
30.00 g., Copper-Nickel, 38 mm. **Series:** Barcelona Olympics **Subject:** Anthony Nesty **Obv:** Arms with supporters **Rev:** Swimmer Antony Nesty, "100M" above swimmer **Edge:** Reeded **Note:** Struck at Kaapstad (Capetown, South Africa).

Date	Mintage	VF20	XF40	MS60	MS63	MS65
ND-1992 Proof	Inc. above	—	—	—	—	—

KM# 42.2 100 GUILDER
20.00 g., 0.999 Silver 0.6424 oz. ASW, 38 mm. **Series:** Barcelona Olympics **Obv:** Arms with supporters **Rev:** Swimmer Antony Nesty, "200 M" above swimmer **Edge:** Reeded **Note:** Struck at Kaapstad (Capetown, South Africa)

Date	Mintage	VF20	XF40	MS60	MS63	MS65
ND-1992	2,500	PF65 65.00				

KM# 42.2a 100 GUILDER
26.00 g., 0.7732 Silver 0.6463 oz. ASW, 38 mm. **Series:** Barcelona Olympics **Obv:** Arms with supporters **Rev:** Swimmer Antony Nesty, "200 M" above swimmer **Edge:** Reeded **Note:** Struck at Kaapstad (Capetown, South Africa)

Date	Mintage	VF20	XF40	MS60	MS63	MS65
ND (1992)	Inc. above	PF65 70.00				

KM# 42.2b 100 GUILDER
30.00 g., 0.7732 Copper-Nickel 0.7458 oz., 38 mm. **Series:** Barcelona Olympics **Subject:** Anthony Nesty **Obv:** Arms with supporters **Rev:** Swimmer Antony Nesty, "200M" above swimmer **Edge:** Reeded **Note:** Struck at Kaapstad (Capetown, South Africa)

Date	Mintage	VF20	XF40	MS60	MS63	MS65
ND-1992	Inc. above	PF65 75.00				

KM# 43.1 100 GUILDER
20.00 g., Silver Plated Brass, 38 mm. **Subject:** World Cup soccer **Obv:** Arms with supporters **Rev:** 2 soccer players, "999 E.P." at right **Edge:** Reeded **Note:** Struck at Gold Reef City Mint (Capetown, South Africa)

Date	Mintage	VF20	XF40	MS60	MS63	MS65
ND-1994 Proof, shiney figures	—	PF65 55.00				

KM# 43.1a 100 GUILDER
26.00 g., 0.999 Silver 0.8351 oz. ASW **Subject:** World Cup soccer **Obv:** Arms with supporters **Rev:** 2 soccer players, "999 E.P." at right **Edge:** Reeded **Note:** Struck at Gold Reef City Mint (Capetown, South Africa)

Date	Mintage	VF20	XF40	MS60	MS63	MS65
ND-1994 Proof, frosted figures	—	—	—	—	—	—

KM# 43.2 100 GUILDER
20.00 g., 0.999 Silver Plated Brass 0.6424 oz., 38 mm. **Subject:** World Cup soccer **Obv:** Arms with supporters **Rev:** 2 soccer players, "999 E.P." at left **Edge:** Reeded **Note:** Struck at Gold Reef City Mint (Capetown, South Africa)

Date	Mintage	VF20	XF40	MS60	MS63	MS65
ND-1994 Proof, shiney figures	—	PF65 55.00				

KM# 43.2a 100 GUILDER
26.00 g., 0.999 Silver Plated Brass 0.8351 oz., 38 mm. **Subject:** World Cup soccer **Obv:** Arms with supporters **Rev:** 2 soccer players, "999 E.P." at left **Edge:** Reeded **Note:** Struck at Gold Reef City Mint (Capetown, South Africa)

Date	Mintage	VF20	XF40	MS60	MS63	MS65
ND-1994	—	PF65 65.00				

KM# 44.1a 100 GUILDER
0.999 Silver **Subject:** World Cup soccer **Obv:** Arms with supporters within wreath **Obv. Legend:** Football World Cup USA '94. 100 Guilders **Rev:** Soccer player in stadium, "999" right **Edge:** Reeded **Note:** Struck at Capetown.

Date	Mintage	VF20	XF40	MS60	MS63	MS65
ND-1994	—	PF65 65.00				

KM# 44.1b 100 GUILDER
21.00 g., 0.500 Silver 0.3376 oz. ASW **Subject:** World Cup soccer **Obv:** Arms with supporters within wreath **Obv. Legend:** Football World Cup USA '94. 100 Guilders **Rev:** Soccer player in stadium, "CuNi" left and "999" right **Edge:** Reeded **Note:** Struck at Capetown

Date	Mintage	VF20	XF40	MS60	MS63	MS65
ND-1994 Proof	—	—	—	—	—	—

KM# 44.1c 100 GUILDER
22.00 g., Copper-Nickel **Subject:** World Cup soccer **Obv:** Arms with supporters within wreath **Obv. Legend:** Football World Cup USA '94. 100 Guilders **Rev:** Soccer player in stadium, "CuNi" left and "999" right **Edge:** Reeded **Note:** Medal rotation

Date	Mintage	VF20	XF40	MS60	MS63	MS65
ND-1994	—	PF65 65.00				

KM# 44 100 GUILDER
20.00 g., 0.999 Silver 0.6424 oz. ASW, 38.5 mm. **Subject:** World Cup soccer **Obv:** Arms with supporters within wreath **Rev:** Soccer player in stadium, Brazil winner **Edge:** Reeded **Note:** Struck at Capetown.

Date	Mintage	VF20	XF40	MS60	MS63	MS65
ND-1994	—	PF65 50.00				

KM# 44a 100 GUILDER
0.500 Silver **Subject:** World Cup soccer **Obv:** Arms with supporters within wreath **Obv. Legend:** Football World Cup USA '94. 100 Guilders **Rev:** Soccer player in stadium, Brazil winner **Edge:** Reeded **Note:** Struck at Capetown

Date	Mintage	VF20	XF40	MS60	MS63	MS65
ND-1994	—	PF65 40.00				

KM# 44b 100 GUILDER
0.999 Copper-Nickel, 30 mm. **Subject:** World Cup soccer **Obv:** Arms with supporters within wreath **Obv. Legend:** Football World Cup USA '94. 100 Guilders **Rev:** Soccer player in stadium, Brazil winner **Edge:** Reeded **Note:** Medal rotation, Struck at Capetown

Date	Mintage	VF20	XF40	MS60	MS63	MS65
ND-1994	—	PF65 40.00				

KM# 67 100 GUILDER
26.00 g., Copper-Nickel, 38 mm. **Subject:** World Cup soccer **Obv:** 2000 kwacha under arms Zambia with supporters **Rev:** 2 soccer players, "999 E.P." at right **Edge:** Reeded **Note:** See also under Zambia KM#146. Struck: Not known

Date	Mintage	VF20	XF40	MS60	MS63	MS65
1994 Proof, frosted figures	—	PF65 150				

KM# 46 100 GUILDER
28.50 g., Copper-Nickel, 38 mm. **Obv:** Arms with supporters **Rev:** 1956 Ford Thunderbird **Edge:** Reeded **Note:** Struck at Gold Reef City Mint, South Africa

Date	Mintage	VF20	XF40	MS60	MS63	MS65
1996	500	PF63 75.00	PF65 95.00			

KM# 47 100 GUILDER
28.50 g., Copper-Nickel, 38 mm. **Obv:** Arms with supporters **Rev:** 1957 Ford Thunderbird **Edge:** Reeded **Note:** Struck at Gold Reef City Mint, South Africa

Date	Mintage	VF20	XF40	MS60	MS63	MS65
1996	500	PF63 75.00	PF65 95.00			

KM# 49.1 100 GUILDER
20.00 g., 0.999 Silver 0.6424 oz. ASW **Series:** Olympics **Obv:** Arms with supporters within wreath **Rev:** Discus thrower flanked by sprigs within pillars **Edge:** Reeded

Date	Mintage	VF20	XF40	MS60	MS63	MS65
1996	—	PF65 125				

KM# 49 100 GUILDER
28.30 g., 0.999 Silver 0.909 oz. ASW, 38 mm. **Series:** Olympics **Obv:** Arms with supporters within wreath **Rev:** Discus thrower flanked by sprigs within pillars **Edge:** Reeded

Date	Mintage	VF20	XF40	MS60	MS63	MS65
1996	—	PF65 45.00				

KM# 68 100 GUILDER
Copper-Nickel, 38 mm. **Obv:** Arms with supporters **Rev:** Athlete with flag **Edge:** Reeded

Date	Mintage	VF20	XF40	MS60	MS63	MS65
1996	—	PF65 600				

KM# 20 200 GULDEN
7.12 g., 0.500 Gold 0.1145 oz. AGW, 26 mm. **Subject:** 1st Anniversary of Revolution **Obv:** Revolution monument **Rev:** Allegorical group of revolutionaries **Edge:** Reeded

Date	Mintage	VF20	XF40	MS60	MS63	MS65
1981 FM (U)	11,000	—	—	—	200	225
1981 FM (P)	1,363	PF65 375				

KM# 22 250 GUILDER
6.72 g., 0.900 Gold 0.1944 oz. AGW, 22.5 mm. **Subject:** 5th Anniversary of Revolution **Obv:** Dove and "10" on map-shaped flag **Rev:** Stylized fist on star design **Edge:** Reeded

Date	Mintage	VF20	XF40	MS60	MS63	MS65
1985 (u)	5,000	—	—	—	350	375
1985 (u)	200	PF65 500				

KM# 33 250 GUILDER
7.98 g., 0.917 Gold 0.2353 oz. AGW, 22 mm. **Subject:** World Cup Soccer **Obv:** Arms with supporters within wreath **Rev:** Soccer player R. Gullit, stadium and half-globe **Edge:** Reeded

Date	Mintage	VF20	XF40	MS60	MS63	MS65
1990 (B)	1,000	PF65 450				

KM# 37 250 GUILDER
7.98 g., 0.917 Gold 0.2353 oz. AGW, 22 mm. **Series:** Save the Children **Obv:** Arms with supporters within wreath **Rev:** Children looking at spider web **Edge:** Reeded

Date	Mintage	VF20	XF40	MS60	MS63	MS65
1991	3,000	PF65 425				
1992	—	PF65 425				

KM# 25 500 GUILDER
7.98 g., 0.917 Gold 0.2353 oz. AGW, 22 mm. **Subject:** 43rd General Assembly, Military Sports Organization CISM **Obv:** Arms with supporters **Rev:** Globe, laurel wreath, rings and sword within flower design **Edge:** Reeded

Date	Mintage	VF20	XF40	MS60	MS63	MS65
ND-1988 (B)	2,500	PF65 425				

KM# 29 500 GUILDER
7.98 g., 0.917 Gold 0.2353 oz. AGW, 22 mm. **Series:** Seoul Olympics **Subject:** Anthony Nesty, butterfly gold medalist **Obv:** Arms with supporters within wreath **Rev:** Swimmer within circle **Edge:** Reeded

Date	Mintage	VF20	XF40	MS60	MS63	MS65
1988 (B)	Est. 2000	PF65 425				

KM# 31 500 GUILDER
7.98 g., 0.917 Gold 0.2353 oz. AGW, 22 mm. **Subject:** 125th Anniversary - De Surinaamsche Bank **Obv:** Arms with supporters **Rev:** Abstract design **Edge:** Reeded

Date	Mintage	VF20	XF40	MS60	MS63	MS65
1990 (B)	Est. 2000	PF65 425				

KM# 35 500 GUILDER
7.98 g., 0.917 Gold 0.2353 oz. AGW, 22 mm. **Subject:** 15th Anniversary of Independence **Obv:** Arms with supporters within wreath **Rev:** Floral design **Edge:** Reeded

Date	Mintage	VF20	XF40	MS60	MS63	MS65
ND-1990 (B)	Est. 1250	PF65 475				

KM# 39 500 GUILDER
7.98 g., 0.917 Gold 0.2353 oz. AGW, 22 mm. **Subject:** 35th Anniversary of Central Bank **Obv:** Arms with supporters **Rev:** Symetric arrow design and dates within circle and legend **Edge:** Reeded

Date	Mintage	VF20	XF40	MS60	MS63	MS65
1992 (B)	Est. 300	PF65 575				

KM# 26 1000 GUILDER
15.98 g., 0.917 Gold 0.4711 oz. AGW, 28.5 mm. **Subject:** 40th Anniversary - Military Sports Organization CISM **Obv:** Arms with supporters **Rev:** Globe, laurel wreath, rings and sword within flower design **Edge:** Reeded

Date	Mintage	VF20	XF40	MS60	MS63	MS65
ND-1988 (B)	1,250	PF65 850				

KM# 48 1000 GUILDER
Brass **Series:** Olympics **Obv:** Arms with supporters **Rev:** Three cyclists **Edge:** Reeded **Note:** Struck at Capetown.

Date	Mintage	VF20	XF40	MS60	MS63	MS65
1992	—	—	—	—	—	—

KM# 48a 1000 GUILDER
Silver **Series:** Olympics **Obv:** Arms with supporters **Rev:** Three cyclists **Edge:** Reeded **Note:** Struck at Capetown

Date	Mintage	VF20	XF40	MS60	MS63	MS65
1992	—	—	—	—	—	—

KM# 48b 1000 GUILDER
4.80 g., Brass Gilt **Series:** Olympics **Obv:** Arms with supporters **Rev:** Three cyclists **Edge:** Reeded **Note:** Struck at Capetown.

Date	Mintage	VF20	XF40	MS60	MS63	MS65
1992	—	—	—	—	—	—

KM# 48c 1000 GUILDER
7.98 g., 0.917 Gold 0.2353 oz. AGW, 22 mm. **Series:** Olympics **Obv:** Arms with supporters **Rev:** Three cyclists **Edge:** Reeded **Note:** Struck at Capetown.

Date	Mintage	VF20	XF40	MS60	MS63	MS65
1992	30	PF65 4,000				

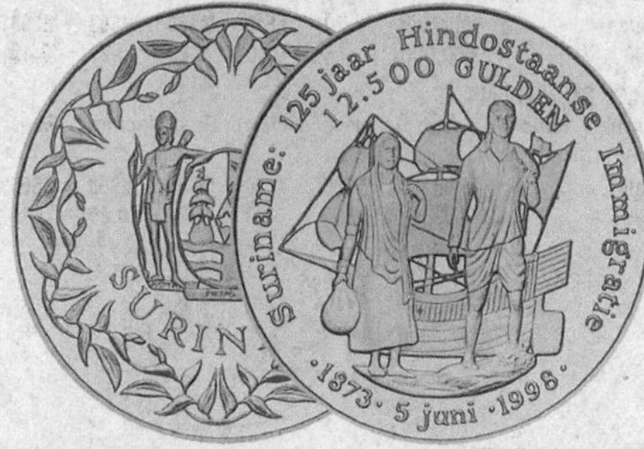

KM# 50 12500 GULDEN
28.28 g., 0.925 Silver 0.841 oz. ASW, 38 mm. **Subject:** Hindu Immigration **Obv:** Arms with supporters within wreath **Rev:** Standing figures in front of ship **Edge:** Reeded

Date	Mintage	VF20	XF40	MS60	MS63	MS65
ND-1999 (B)	Est. 1000	PF65 120				

KM# 51 50000 GULDEN
7.98 g., 0.917 Gold 0.2353 oz. AGW, 22 mm. **Subject:** Hindu Immigration **Obv:** Arms with supporters **Rev:** Hindu couple with ship in background **Edge:** Reeded

Date	Mintage	VF20	XF40	MS60	MS63	MS65
ND-1998 (B)	2,500	PF65 425				

KM# 53 75000 GULDEN
7.98 g., 0.917 Gold 0.2353 oz. AGW, 22 mm. **Subject:** Coppename Bridge **Obv:** Arms with supporters **Rev:** Bridge **Edge:** Reeded

Date	Mintage	VF20	XF40	MS60	MS63	MS65
1999 (B)	750	PF65 575				

KM# 54 100000 GULDEN
7.98 g., 0.917 Gold 0.2353 oz. AGW, 22 mm. **Subject:** 25th Anniversary of Independence **Obv:** Arms with supporters **Rev:** Flag **Edge:** Reeded

Date	Mintage	VF20	XF40	MS60	MS63	MS65
2000 (B)	1,000	PF65 550				

KM# 55 100000 GULDEN
7.98 g., 0.917 Gold 0.2353 oz. AGW, 22 mm. **Subject:** Surinam River Bridge **Obv:** Arms with supporters **Rev:** Bridge over Suriam River **Edge:** Reeded

Date	Mintage	VF20	XF40	MS60	MS63	MS65
2000 (B)	1,000	PF65 550				

KM# 56 100000 GULDEN
7.98 g., 0.917 Gold 0.2353 oz. AGW, 22 mm. **Subject:** Millennium 2000-2001 **Obv:** Arms with supporters **Rev:** Circles **Edge:** Reeded

Date	Mintage	VF20	XF40	MS60	MS63	MS65
2000 (B)	1,500	PF65 550				

KM# 57 125000 GULDEN
15.00 g., 0.585 Gold 0.2821 oz. AGW, 30 mm. **Subject:** Millennium 2000-2001 **Obv:** Arms with supporters **Rev:** Circles **Edge:** Reeded

Date	Mintage	VF20	XF40	MS60	MS63	MS65
2000 (B)	2,500	PF65 525				

PATTERNS

Including off metal strikes

KM#	Date	Mintage	Identification	Mkt Val
Pn1	1962	—	Gulden. Bronze. KM#15. Nickel coated.	70.00
Pn2	1970	—	Cent. Nickel. KM#11.	300
Pn3	ND-1994	—	100 Guilder. Copper-Nickel. Reeded. KM#44b.	—
Pn4	ND-1994	—	100 Guilder. Silver. KM#44a.	—

TRIAL STRIKES

KM#	Date	Mintage	Identification	Mkt Val
TS1	1984	—	10 Guilders. Silver. Arms with supporters. Shot put thrower and torch.	—
TS2	1990	—	25 Guilder. Nickel. MODEL. Player, stadium and half globe. KM#32.	650
TS3	1990	—	25 Guilder. Nickel. MODEL. Player, stadium and half globe. KM#32.	650

PROOF SETS

KM#	Date	Mintage	Identification	Issue Price	Mkt Val
PS1	1962 (5)	650	KM11-15	—	250
PS2	1966 (5)	—	KM11-15	—	600
PS3	1976 (4)	10	KM11a, 12.1a, 13, 14	—	750
PS4	1976 (3)	—	KM16-18	145	450
PS5	1976 (2)	—	KM16-17	50.00	65.00
PS6	1988 (6)	1,500	KM11b, 12.1b, 13a, 14a, 23, 24	42.00	500

SWAZILAND

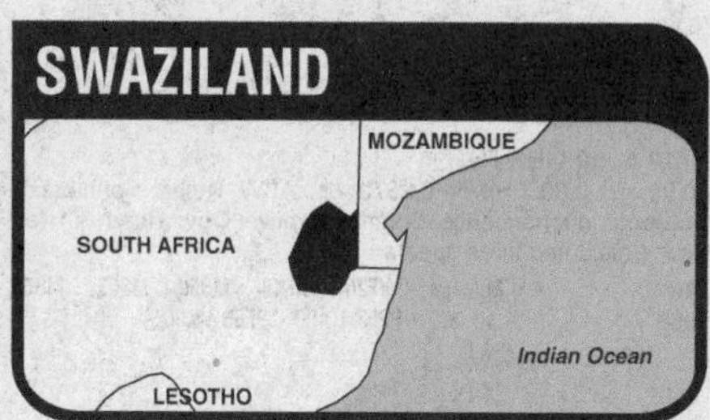

The Kingdom of Swaziland, located in southeastern Africa, has an area of 6,704 sq. mi. (17,360 sq. km.) and a population of *756,000. Capital: Mbabane (administrative); Lobamba (legislative). The diversified economy includes mining, agriculture, and light industry. Asbestos, iron ore, wood pulp, and sugar are exported.

The people of the present Swazi nation established themselves in an area including what is now Swaziland in the early 1800s. The first Swazi contact with the British came early in the reign of the extremely able Swazi leader Mswati when he asked the British for aid against Zulu raids into Swaziland. The British and Transvaal responded by guaranteeing the independence of Swaziland, 1881. South Africa assumed the power of protection and administration in 1894 and Swaziland continued under this administration until the conquest of the Transvaal during the Anglo-Boer War, when administration was transferred to the British government. After World War II, Britain began to prepare Swaziland for independence, which was achieved on Sept. 6, 1968. The Kingdom is a member of the Commonwealth of Nations. King Mswati III is Head of State. The prime minister is Head of Government.

RULERS
Sobhuza II, 1968-1982
Queen Dzeliwe, Regent for
Prince Makhosetive, 1982-1986
King Mswati III, 1986-

MONETARY SYSTEM
100 Cents = 1 Luhlanga
25 Luhlanga = 1 Lilangeni
(plural - Emalangeni)

KINGDOM

STANDARD COINAGE

KM# 1 5 CENTS

2.75 g., 0.800 Silver 0.0707 oz. ASW **Ruler:** Sobhuza II **Subject:** Independence Commemorative **Obv:** Head 3/4 left **Rev:** Shield and three spears

Date	Mintage	VF20	XF40	MS60	MS63	MS65
1968	10,000	PF63 4.00	PF65 6.00			

KM# 2 10 CENTS

4.38 g., 0.800 Silver 0.1127 oz. ASW **Ruler:** Sobhuza II **Subject:** Independence Commemorative **Obv:** Head 3/4 left **Rev:** Shield and three spears

Date	Mintage	VF20	XF40	MS60	MS63	MS65
1968	10,000	PF63 6.00	PF65 8.00			

KM# 3 20 CENTS

6.63 g., 0.800 Silver 0.1705 oz. ASW **Ruler:** Sobhuza II **Subject:** Independence Commemorative **Obv:** Head 3/4 left **Rev:** Shield and three spears

Date	Mintage	VF20	XF40	MS60	MS63	MS65
1968	10,000	PF63 8.00	PF65 10.00			

KM# 4 50 CENTS

10.39 g., 0.800 Silver 0.2672 oz. ASW **Ruler:** Sobhuza II **Subject:** Independence Commemorative **Obv:** Head 3/4 left **Rev:** Shield and three spears

Date	Mintage	VF20	XF40	MS60	MS63	MS65
1968	10,000	PF63 10.00	PF65 14.00			

KM# 5 LUHLANGA

15.00 g., 0.800 Silver 0.3858 oz. ASW **Ruler:** Sobhuza II **Subject:** Independence Commemorative **Obv:** Head 3/4 left **Rev:** Shield with three spears divides date

Date	Mintage	VF20	XF40	MS60	MS63	MS65
1968	10,000	PF63 17.00	PF65 22.00			

KM# 6 LILANGENI

33.93 g., 0.917 Gold 1.0003 oz. AGW **Ruler:** Sobhuza II **Subject:** Independence Commemorative **Obv:** Head 3/4 left **Rev:** Arms with supporters **Note:** Approximately 1,450 melted.

Date	Mintage	VF20	XF40	MS60	MS63	MS65
1968	2,000	PF63 1,550	PF65 1,650		PF67 1,850	

DECIMAL COINAGE

100 Cents = 1 Lilangeni (plural emelangeni)

KM# 7 CENT

2.00 g., Bronze, 18.3 mm. **Ruler:** Sobhuza II **Obv:** Head 1/4 right **Rev:** Pineapple and value

Date	Mintage	VF20	XF40	MS60	MS63	MS65
1974	6,002,000	—	0.10	0.15	0.20	0.40
1974	13,000	PF65 0.75				
1979	500,000	—	0.10	0.20	0.25	0.45
1979	10,000	PF65 0.75				
1982	—	—	0.10	0.20	0.25	0.45
1983	1,100,000	—	0.10	0.20	0.25	0.45

KM# 21 CENT

2.00 g., Bronze, 18.3 mm. **Ruler:** Sobhuza II **Series:** F.A.O. **Obv:** Head 1/4 right **Rev:** Pineapple and value **Shape:** 12-sided

Date	Mintage	VF20	XF40	MS60	MS63	MS65
1975	2,500,000	—	0.10	0.20	0.25	0.45

KM# 39 CENT

Copper Plated Steel **Ruler:** Queen Dzeliwe **Obv:** Bust facing **Rev:** Pineapple

Date	Mintage	VF20	XF40	MS60	MS63	MS65
1986	12,000,000	—	0.10	0.20	0.25	0.45

KM# 39a CENT

Bronze **Ruler:** Queen Dzeliwe **Obv:** Bust facing **Rev:** Pineapple

Date	Mintage	VF20	XF40	MS60	MS63	MS65
1986	—	—	0.10	0.20	0.25	0.45

KM# 51 CENT

Bronze **Ruler:** Mswati III **Obv:** Head 1/4 right **Rev:** Pineapple and value

Date	Mintage	VF20	XF40	MS60	MS63	MS65
1995	—	—	0.10	0.20	0.25	0.45

KM# 8 2 CENTS

2.80 g., Bronze, 18.6 mm. **Ruler:** Sobhuza II **Obv:** Head 1/4 right **Rev:** Trees and value **Shape:** Square

Date	Mintage	VF20	XF40	MS60	MS63	MS65
1974	2,252,000	—	0.15	0.25	0.30	0.50
1974	13,000	PF65 0.75				
1979	1,000,000	—	0.15	0.25	0.30	0.50
1979	10,000	PF65 1.00				
1982	500,000	—	0.15	0.25	0.30	0.50

KM# 22 2 CENTS

2.80 g., Bronze, 18.6 mm. **Ruler:** Sobhuza II **Series:** F.A.O. **Obv:** Head 1/4 right **Rev:** Trees and value **Edge:** Plain **Shape:** 4-sided

Date	Mintage	VF20	XF40	MS60	MS63	MS65
1975	1,500,000	—	0.15	0.25	0.30	0.50

KM# 9 5 CENTS

2.15 g., Copper-Nickel, 18.5 mm. **Ruler:** Sobhuza II **Obv:** Head 1/4 right **Rev:** Arum lily and value **Shape:** Scalloped

Date	Mintage	VF20	XF40	MS60	MS63	MS65
1974	1,252,000	0.10	0.20	0.30	0.40	0.65
1974	13,000	PF65 1.00				
1975	1,500,000	0.10	0.20	0.30	0.40	0.65
1979	1,680,000	0.10	0.20	0.30	0.40	0.65
1979	10,000	PF65 1.75				

KM# 40.1 5 CENTS

2.15 g., Copper-Nickel, 18.5 mm. **Ruler:** Queen Dzeliwe **Obv:** Bust facing **Rev:** Arum lily and value **Edge:** Plain **Shape:** Scalloped

Date	Mintage	VF20	XF40	MS60	MS63	MS65
1986	—	0.15	0.25	0.35	0.50	0.75

KM# 40.2 5 CENTS

Nickel Plated Steel, 18.5 mm. **Ruler:** Mswati III **Obv:** Bust facing **Rev:** Arum lily **Edge:** Plain **Shape:** Scalloped

Date	Mintage	VF20	XF40	MS60	MS63	MS65
1992	—	0.15	0.25	0.35	0.50	0.75

KM# 48 5 CENTS

2.10 g., Copper-Nickel, 18.5 mm. **Ruler:** Mswati III **Obv:** Bust 3/4 right **Rev:** Arum lily and value **Edge:** Plain **Shape:** Scalloped

Date	Mintage	VF20	XF40	MS60	MS63	MS65
1995	—	—	0.20	0.30	0.50	0.75
1996	—	—	0.20	0.30	0.50	0.75
1998	—	—	0.20	0.30	0.50	0.75
1999	—	—	0.20	0.30	0.50	0.75
2000	—	—	0.20	0.30	0.50	0.75
Note: Thick inscription						
2000	—	—	0.20	0.30	0.50	0.75
Note: Thin inscription						

KM# 48a 5 CENTS

Copper-Nickel, 18.5 mm. **Ruler:** Mswati III **Obv:** Bust 1/4 right **Rev:** Arum lily and value

Date	Mintage	VF20	XF40	MS60	MS63	MS65
1999	—	—	—	0.30	0.50	0.75

KM# 10 10 CENTS

Copper-Nickel, 22 mm. **Ruler:** Sobhuza II **Obv:** Head 1/4 right **Rev:** Sugar cane and value **Shape:** Scalloped

Date	Mintage	VF20	XF40	MS60	MS63	MS65
1974	752,000	0.15	0.25	0.35	0.50	0.75
1974	13,000	PF65 1.00				
1979	500,000	0.15	0.25	0.35	0.50	0.75
1979	4,231	PF65 2.50				

KM# 23 10 CENTS
Copper-Nickel, 22 mm. **Ruler:** Sobhuza II **Series:** F.A.O. **Obv:** Head 1/4 right **Rev:** Sugar cane and value **Shape:** Scalloped

Date	Mintage	VF20	XF40	MS60	MS63	MS65
1975	1,500,000	0.15	0.25	0.35	0.50	0.75

KM# 41 10 CENTS
3.60 g., Copper-Nickel, 22 mm. **Ruler:** Mswati III **Obv:** Head facing **Rev:** Sugar cane and value **Edge:** Plain **Shape:** Scalloped

Date	Mintage	VF20	XF40	MS60	MS63	MS65
1986	—	0.15	0.25	0.35	0.50	0.75
1992	—	0.15	0.25	0.35	0.50	0.75

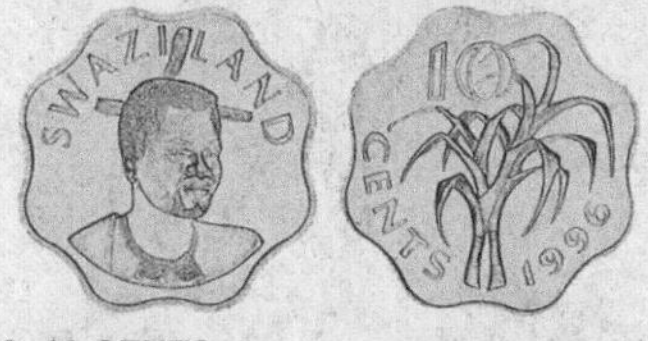

KM# 49 10 CENTS
3.60 g., Copper-Nickel, 22 mm. **Ruler:** Mswati III **Obv:** Bust 3/4 right **Rev:** Sugar cane and value **Edge:** Plain **Shape:** Scalloped

Date	Mintage	VF20	XF40	MS60	MS63	MS65
1995	—	—	0.30	0.50	0.75	1.00
1996	—	—	0.30	0.50	0.75	1.00
1998	—	—	0.30	0.50	0.75	1.00
2000	—	—	0.30	0.50	0.75	1.00

KM# 11 20 CENTS
5.60 g., Copper-Nickel, 25.2 mm. **Ruler:** Sobhuza II **Obv:** Head 1/4 right **Rev:** Elephant head and value **Shape:** Scalloped

Date	Mintage	VF20	XF40	MS60	MS63	MS65
1974	502,000	0.35	0.75	1.25	2.50	4.00
1974	13,000	PF65 5.00				
1975	1,000,000	0.35	0.75	1.25	2.50	4.00
1979	—	0.35	0.75	1.25	2.50	4.00
1979	—	PF65 4.00				

KM# 31 20 CENTS
5.60 g., Copper-Nickel, 25.2 mm. **Ruler:** Sobhuza II **Series:** F.A.O. **Obv:** Head 1/4 right **Rev:** Sprigs and logo **Shape:** Scalloped

Date	Mintage	VF20	XF40	MS60	MS63	MS65
1981	150,000	0.40	0.75	1.00	1.50	2.00

KM# 42 20 CENTS
5.50 g., Copper-Nickel, 25.2 mm. **Ruler:** Queen Dzeliwe **Obv:** Head facing **Rev:** Elephant head and value **Edge:** Plain **Shape:** Scalloped

Date	Mintage	VF20	XF40	MS60	MS63	MS65
1986	—	0.40	0.75	1.50	2.00	3.50

KM# 50.1 20 CENTS
5.60 g., Copper-Nickel, 25.2 mm. **Ruler:** Mswati III **Obv:** Large bust 3/4 right **Rev:** Elephant head and value **Edge:** Plain **Shape:** Scalloped

Date	Mintage	VF20	XF40	MS60	MS63	MS65
1996	—	0.40	0.90	1.25	1.75	2.50
2000	—	0.40	0.90	1.25	1.75	2.50

KM# 50.2 20 CENTS
5.52 g., Copper-Nickel, 25.2 mm. **Ruler:** Mswati III **Obv:** Small bust 3/4 right **Rev:** Elephant head, value **Edge:** Plain **Shape:** Scalloped

Date	Mintage	VF20	XF40	MS60	MS63	MS65
1998	—	—	0.45	0.75	1.10	1.50

KM# 12 50 CENTS
8.90 g., Copper-Nickel, 29.45 mm. **Ruler:** Sobhuza II **Obv:** Head 1/4 right **Rev:** Arms with supporters **Shape:** 12-sided

Date	Mintage	VF20	XF40	MS60	MS63	MS65
1974	252,000	1.00	1.50	2.00	2.75	3.75
1974	13,000	PF65 3.00				
1975	500,000	1.00	1.50	2.00	2.75	3.75
1979	—	0.50	1.00	1.25	2.50	3.50
1979	10,000	PF65 5.00				
1981	1,150,000	0.50	0.75	1.00	2.00	3.00

KM# 43 50 CENTS
8.90 g., Copper-Nickel, 29.45 mm. **Ruler:** Mswati III **Obv:** Head facing **Rev:** Arms with supporters **Edge:** Plain

Date	Mintage	VF20	XF40	MS60	MS63	MS65
1986	1,000,000	0.50	0.75	1.00	2.00	3.50
1993	—	0.50	0.75	1.00	2.00	3.50

KM# 52 50 CENTS
8.90 g., Copper-Nickel, 29.45 mm. **Ruler:** Mswati III **Obv:** Head 1/4 right **Rev:** Arms with supporters

Date	Mintage	VF20	XF40	MS60	MS63	MS65
1996	—	—	0.75	1.25	2.50	4.00
1998	—	—	0.75	1.25	2.50	4.00

KM# 13 LILANGENI
11.65 g., Copper-Nickel, 30 mm. **Ruler:** Sobhuza II **Obv:** Head 1/4 right **Rev:** Female and child facing

Date	Mintage	VF20	XF40	MS60	MS63	MS65
1974	127,000	0.75	1.25	2.50	3.50	5.00
1974	13,000	PF65 6.00				
1979	—	0.75	1.25	2.50	3.50	5.00
1979	110,000	PF65 7.50				

KM# 24 LILANGENI
Copper-Nickel, 30.5 mm. **Ruler:** Sobhuza II **Series:** F.A.O., International Women's Year **Obv:** Head 1/4 right **Rev:** Female and child facing

Date	Mintage	VF20	XF40	MS60	MS63	MS65
1975	100,000	0.75	1.50	2.75	3.75	6.00

KM# 28 LILANGENI
11.65 g., Copper-Nickel, 30 mm. **Ruler:** Sobhuza II **Series:** F.A.O. **Obv:** Head 1/4 right **Rev:** Female and child facing

Date	Mintage	VF20	XF40	MS60	MS63	MS65
1976	100,000	0.75	1.50	2.75	3.75	6.00

KM# 29.1 LILANGENI
15.55 g., 0.999 Gold 0.4994 oz. AGW **Ruler:** Sobhuza II **Subject:** 80th Anniversary - Birth of King Sobhuza II **Obv:** Head 1/4 right **Rev:** Arms with supporters

Date	Mintage	XF40	MS60	MS63	MS65	MS66
ND-1979	1,250	—	—	825	850	900
ND-1979	Inc. above	PF65 900	PF67 950			

KM# 29.2 LILANGENI
15.55 g., 0.999 Gold 0.4994 oz. AGW **Ruler:** Sobhuza II **Subject:** 80th Anniversary - Birth of King Sobhuza II **Obv:** Head 1/4 right **Rev:** Dates 1923-1979 above arms with supporters

Date	Mintage	XF40	MS60	MS63	MS65	MS66
ND-1979	—	—	—	850	900	950

KM# 32 LILANGENI
11.65 g., Copper-Nickel, 30 mm. **Ruler:** Sobhuza II **Series:** F.A.O. **Obv:** Head 1/4 right **Rev:** Half length figure husking corn

Date	Mintage	VF20	XF40	MS60	MS63	MS65
1981	871,000	1.00	2.00	3.00	5.00	8.00

KM# 32a LILANGENI
11.66 g., 0.925 Silver 0.3468 oz. ASW **Ruler:** Sobhuza II **Series:** F.A.O. **Obv:** Head 1/4 right **Rev:** Half length figure husking corn

Date	Mintage	VF20	XF40	MS60	MS63	MS65
1981	5,000	—	—	22.50	25.00	27.00
1981	5,000	PF63 35.00	PF65 38.00			

KM# 44.1 LILANGENI
9.50 g., Nickel-Brass, 22.5 mm. **Ruler:** Queen Dzeliwe **Obv:** Head facing **Rev:** Bust facing **Edge:** Reeded

Date	Mintage	VF20	XF40	MS60	MS63	MS65
1986	1,025,000	—	0.75	1.25	2.25	3.50

KM# 44.2 LILANGENI
Nickel-Brass Plated Steel, 22.5 mm. **Ruler:** Mswati III **Obv:** Head facing **Rev:** Bust facing **Edge:** Reeded

Date	Mintage	VF20	XF40	MS60	MS63	MS65
1992	—	—	0.75	1.25	2.25	3.50

KM# 45 LILANGENI
9.50 g., Brass, 22.5 mm. **Ruler:** Mswati III **Obv:** Head 1/4 right **Rev:** Bust facing

Date	Mintage	VF20	XF40	MS60	MS63	MS65
1995	—	—	0.75	1.25	2.25	3.50
1996	—	—	0.75	1.25	2.25	3.50
1998	—	—	0.75	1.25	2.25	3.50

KM# 33 2 EMALANGENI
17.00 g., 0.925 Silver 0.5056 oz. ASW, 34 mm. **Ruler:** Sobhuza II **Subject:** Diamond Jubilee of King Sobhuza II **Obv:** Head 1/4 right **Rev:** Lilies and value

Date	Mintage	VF20	XF40	MS60	MS63	MS65
1981	—	PF63 35.00	PF65 40.00			

KM# 33a 2 EMALANGENI
Copper-Nickel **Ruler:** Sobhuza II **Subject:** Diamond Jubilee of King Sobhuza II **Obv:** Head 1/4 right **Rev:** Lilies and value

Date	Mintage	VF20	XF40	MS60	MS63	MS65
1981	50,000	2.00	3.50	5.00	7.00	9.00

KM# 46 2 EMALANGENI
5.00 g., Brass **Ruler:** Mswati III **Obv:** Head 1/4 right **Rev:** Lilies and value

Date	Mintage	VF20	XF40	MS60	MS63	MS65
1995 lg. bust	—	—	—	1.50	2.50	4.00
1996 sm. bust	—	—	—	1.50	2.50	4.00
1998 lg. bust	—	—	—	1.50	2.50	4.00

KM# 14 5 EMALANGENI
10.30 g., 0.925 Silver 0.3063 oz. ASW **Ruler:** Sobhuza II **Subject:** 75th Anniversary - Birth of King Sobhuza II **Obv:** Head 1/4 right **Rev:** Building and emblem **Shape:** Scalloped

Date	Mintage	VF20	XF40	MS60	MS63	MS65
1974	—	PF63 50.00	PF65 55.00			

KM# 15 5 EMALANGENI
5.56 g., 0.900 Gold 0.1609 oz. AGW **Ruler:** Sobhuza II **Subject:** 75th Anniversary - Birth of King Sobhuza II **Obv:** Head 1/4 right **Rev:** Arms with supporters within circle

Date	Mintage	VF20	XF40	MS60	MS63	MS65
1974	60,000	PF63 285	PF65 325			

KM# 47 5 EMALANGENI
7.60 g., Brass **Ruler:** Mswati III **Obv:** Head 1/4 right **Rev:** Arms with supporters above value that divides date

Date	Mintage	VF20	XF40	MS60	MS63	MS65
1995 sm. bust	—	—	—	1.75	2.75	4.50
1996 sm. bust	—	—	—	1.75	2.75	4.50
1998 lg. bust	—	—	—	1.75	2.75	4.50
1999	—	—	—	1.75	2.75	4.50

KM# 53 5 EMALANGENI
Brass **Ruler:** Mswati III **Subject:** Central Bank's 25th Anniversary **Obv:** Head 1/4 right **Rev:** Bank seal within circle

Date	Mintage	VF20	XF40	MS60	MS63	MS65
ND-1999	—	—	—	1.75	2.75	4.50

KM# 16 7-1/2 EMALANGENI
16.20 g., 0.925 Silver 0.4818 oz. ASW **Ruler:** Sobhuza II **Subject:** 75th Anniversary - Birth of King Sobhuza II **Obv:** Head 1/4 right **Rev:** Bird **Shape:** 10-sided

Date	Mintage	VF20	XF40	MS60	MS63	MS65
1974	—	PF63 125	PF65 150			

KM# 17 10 EMALANGENI
11.12 g., 0.900 Gold 0.3218 oz. AGW **Ruler:** Sobhuza II **Subject:** 75th Anniversary - Birth of King Sobhuza II **Obv:** Head 1/4 right **Rev:** Standing figure divides date and value within circle **Shape:** Scalloped

Date	Mintage	VF20	XF40	MS60	MS63	MS65
1974	Est. 40000	PF63 525	PF65 575	PF67 675		

KM# 25 10 EMALANGENI
25.50 g., 0.925 Silver 0.7584 oz. ASW **Ruler:** Sobhuza II **Subject:** 75th Anniversary - Birth of King Sobhuza II **Obv:** Head 1/4 right **Rev:** Heron

Date	Mintage	VF20	XF40	MS60	MS63	MS65
1975	Est. 1000	—	—	—	50.00	60.00
1975	Est. 1500	PF63 55.00	PF65 65.00			

KM# 18 15 EMALANGENI
32.60 g., 0.925 Silver 0.9695 oz. ASW **Ruler:** Sobhuza II **Subject:** 75th Anniversary - Birth of King Sobhuza II **Obv:** Head 1/4 right **Rev:** Uniformed bust right saluting army with flags

Date	Mintage	VF20	XF40	MS60	MS63	MS65
1974	—	PF63 85.00	PF65 95.00			

KM# 19 20 EMALANGENI
22.23 g., 0.900 Gold 0.6432 oz. AGW **Ruler:** Sobhuza II **Subject:** 75th Anniversary - Birth of King Sobhuza II **Obv:** Head 1/4 right **Rev:** Child facing and UNICEF emblem **Shape:** 10-sided

Date	Mintage	XF40	MS60	MS63	MS65	MS66
1974	Est. 25000	PF65 1,000	PF67 1,250	PF69 1,400		

KM# 20 25 EMALANGENI
27.78 g., 0.900 Gold 0.8038 oz. AGW **Ruler:** Sobhuza II **Subject:** 75th Anniversary - Birth of King Sobhuza II **Obv:** Head 1/4 right **Rev:** Conjoined busts facing within circle

Date	Mintage	XF40	MS60	MS63	MS65	MS66
1974	Est. 15000	PF65 1,200	PF67 1,350	PF69 1,500		

KM# 34 25 EMALANGENI
28.28 g., 0.925 Silver 0.841 oz. ASW, 38.61 mm. **Ruler:** Sobhuza II **Subject:** Diamond Jubilee of King Sobhuza II **Obv:** Head 1/4 right **Rev:** Bird and value

Date	Mintage	VF20	XF40	MS60	MS63	MS65
1981	Est. 10000	—	—	35.00	40.00	45.00
1981	Est. 10000	PF63 55.00	PF65 60.00			

KM# 37 25 EMALANGENI
28.28 g., 0.925 Silver 0.841 oz. ASW **Ruler:** Mswati III **Subject:** Accession of King Makhosetive **Obv:** Bust facing **Rev:** Bust facing

Date	Mintage	VF20	XF40	MS60	MS63	MS65
ND-1986	Est. 2500	PF63 45.00	PF65 55.00			

KM# 26 50 EMALANGENI
4.31 g., 0.900 Gold 0.1247 oz. AGW **Ruler:** Sobhuza II **Subject:** 75th Anniversary - Birth of King Sobhuza II **Obv:** Head 1/4 right **Rev:** Antelope

Date	Mintage	XF40	MS60	MS63	MS65	MS66
1975	3,510	—	—	225	245	300
1975	3,262	PF65 235	PF67 265	PF69 375		

KM# 27 100 EMALANGENI
8.64 g., 0.900 Gold 0.250 oz. AGW **Ruler:** Sobhuza II **Subject:** 75th Anniversary - Birth of King Sobhuza II **Obv:** Head 1/4 right **Rev:** Bust 1/4 left

Date	Mintage	XF40	MS60	MS63	MS65	MS66
ND-1975	1,000	—	—	425	450	575
ND-1975	1,000	PF65 450	PF67 475	PF69 625		

KM# 35 250 EMALANGENI
15.98 g., 0.917 Gold 0.4711 oz. AGW **Ruler:** Sobhuza II **Subject:** Diamond Jubilee of King Sobhuza II **Obv:** Head 1/4 right **Rev:** Elephant

Date	Mintage	XF40	MS60	MS63	MS65	MS66
1981	2,000	—	—	775	825	900
1981	2,000	PF65 800	PF67 850	PF69 950		

KM# 38 250 EMALANGENI
15.98 g., 0.917 Gold 0.4711 oz. AGW **Ruler:** Mswati III **Subject:** Accession of King Makhosetive **Obv:** Bust facing **Rev:** Bust facing

Date	Mintage	XF40	MS60	MS63	MS65	MS66
ND-1986	250	—	—	825	875	950
ND-1986	250	PF65 875	PF67 925	PF69 1,000		

GOLD BULLION COINAGE

KM# 30 2 EMALANGENI
31.10 g., 0.999 Gold 0.9989 oz. AGW **Ruler:** Sobhuza II **Subject:** 80th Anniversary - Birth of King Sobhuza II **Obv:** Head 1/4 right **Rev:** Young bust of Queen Elizabeth II right

Date	Mintage	VF20	XF40	MS60	MS63	MS65
ND-1979	1,250	—	—	1,600	1,650	1,700
ND-1979	Inc. above	PF63 1,650	PF65 1,750	PF67 1,800		

KM# 36 5 EMALANGENI
31.10 g., 0.999 Gold 0.9989 oz. AGW **Ruler:** Sobhuza II **Subject:** Queen Elizabeth II's Silver Jubilee **Obv:** Head 1/4 right within circle **Rev:** Crowned bust of Queen Elizabeth II facing divides dates within circle

Date	Mintage	VF20	XF40	MS60	MS63	MS65
ND-1978	—	PF63 1,650	PF65 1,750	PF67 1,800		

MINT SETS

KM#	Date	Mintage	Identification	Issue Price	Mkt Val
MS1	1974 (7)	—	KM7-13	10.00	18.50
MS2	1975 (3)	1,000	KM25-27	—	800
MS3	1986 (6)	—	KM39, 40.1, 41-43, 44.1	—	19.00

PROOF SETS

KM#	Date	Mintage	Identification	Issue Price	Mkt Val
PS1	1968 (5)	10,000	KM1-5	25.80	52.50
PS2	1974 (7)	20,000	KM7-13	18.00	17.50
PS3	1974 (4)	—	KM15, 17, 19, 20	745	3,700
PS4	1974 (3)	—	KM14, 16, 17	70.00	850
PS5	1975 (3)	—	KM25-27	—	800
PS6	1975 (2)	—	KM26-27	252	725
PS7	1979 (7)	3,231	KM7-13	34.00	22.50
PS8	1979 (2)	—	KM29.1, 30	1,172	2,800

SWEDEN

The Kingdom of Sweden, a limited constitutional monarchy located in northern Europe between Norway and Finland, has an area of 173,732 sq. mi. (449,960 sq. km.) and a population of *8.5 million. Capital: Stockholm. Mining, lumbering and a specialized machine industry dominate the economy. Machinery, paper, iron and steel, motor vehicles and wood pulp are exported.

Olaf Skottkonung founded Sweden as a Christian stronghold late in the 10th century. After conquering Finland late in the 13th century, Sweden, together with Norway, came under the rule of Denmark, 1397-1523, in an association known as the Union of Kalmar. Modern Sweden had its beginning in 1523 when Gustaf Vasa drove the Danes out of Sweden and was himself chosen king. Under Gustaf Adolphus II and Charles XII, Sweden was one of the great powers of 17th century Europe – until Charles invaded Russia in 1708, and was defeated at the Battle of Pultowa in June, 1709. Early in the 18th century, a coalition of Russia, Poland and Denmark took away Sweden's Baltic empire and in 1809 Sweden was forced to cede Finland to Russia. The Treaty of Kiel ceded Norway to Sweden in January 1814. The Norwegians resisted for a time but later signed the Act of Union at the Convention of Moss in August 1814,The Union was dissolved in 1905 and Norway became independent. A new constitution that took effect on Jan. 1, 1975, restricts the function of the king largely to a ceremonial role.

RULERS
Oscar II, 1872-1907
Gustaf V, 1907-1950
Gustaf VI, 1950-1973
Carl XVI Gustaf, 1973-

MINT OFFICIALS' INITIALS

Letter	Date	Name
AL	1898-1916	Adolf Lindberg, engraver
B	1992-2005	Stefan Ingves
D	1986-1992	Bengt Dennis
EB	1876-1908	Emil Brusewitz
EL	1916-1944	Erik Lindberg, engraver
G	1927-1945	Alf Grabe
LH	1944-1974	Leo Holmberg, engraver
SI	2005-	Stefan Ingves
TS	1945-1961	Torsten Swensson
U	1961-1986	Benkt Ulvfot
W	1908-1927	Karl-August Wallroth

MONETARY SYSTEM
100 Ore = 1 Krona

KINGDOM

REFORM COINAGE

1873 - present

KM# 750 ÖRE
2.00 g., Bronze, 16 mm. **Ruler:** Oscar II **Obv:** Monogram within crowned shield, legend lengthened **Rev:** Value and date flanked by 3 crowns

Date	Mintage	F12	VF20	XF40	MS60	MS63
1901	3,074,700	—	1.00	2.50	7.50	15.00
1902	2,685,400	—	1.00	2.50	7.50	15.00
1903	2,695,600	—	1.00	2.50	7.50	15.00
1904	2,032,700	—	1.00	2.50	7.50	15.00
1905	3,556,000	—	1.00	2.25	7.50	12.00

KM# 768 ÖRE
2.00 g., Bronze, 16 mm. **Ruler:** Oscar II **Obv:** Crowned shield **Rev:** Value and date flanked by crowns

Date	Mintage	F12	VF20	XF40	MS60	MS63
1906	1,783,300	—	1.50	5.00	20.00	45.00
1907	8,250,500	—	0.75	2.00	7.50	12.00

KM# 777.1 ÖRE
2.00 g., Bronze, 16 mm. **Ruler:** Gustaf V **Obv:** Crowned monogram with small cross on crown **Rev:** Value and crowns

Date	Mintage	F12	VF20	XF40	MS60	MS63
1909	3,805,600	1.00	3.00	10.00	35.00	75.00

KM# 777.2 ÖRE

2.00 g., Bronze, 16 mm. **Ruler:** Gustaf V **Obv:** Large cross **Rev:** Value and crowns **Edge:** Plain

Date	Mintage	F12	VF20	XF40	MS60	MS63
1909	Inc. above	1.00	2.00	5.00	15.00	25.00
1910	1,582,600	1.50	3.00	5.00	25.00	45.00
1911	3,149,000	—	0.75	1.00	5.00	10.00
1912/1	3,170,000	8.50	10.00	25.00	75.00	125
1912	Inc. above	—	0.75	1.00	5.00	10.00
1913/12	3,197,300	3.00	4.00	10.00	45.00	90.00
1913	Inc. above	—	0.75	1.00	5.00	10.00
Note: Long and short-tailed 9						
1914 Open 4	2,214,050	25.00	35.00	60.00	125	225
1914 Closed 4	Inc. above	—	0.75	3.00	15.00	25.00
1915/3	4,471,300	2.25	3.00	5.00	20.00	35.00
1915	Inc. above	—	0.25	1.00	3.00	5.00
1916 Short 6	7,615,500	—	0.25	1.00	3.00	5.00
1916 Long 6	Inc. above	—	0.30	1.00	6.00	9.00
1919 Unique	—	—	—	—	—	—
1920	5,547,600	—	0.25	1.00	3.00	5.00
1921	7,441,510	—	0.25	1.00	3.00	5.00
1922	1,165,700	1.00	2.00	3.00	15.00	25.00
1923	4,511,800	—	0.35	1.00	3.00	5.00
1924	2,578,900	—	0.25	1.00	4.00	7.50
1925	4,714,900	—	0.20	0.50	1.50	3.00
1926	7,739,300	—	0.20	0.50	1.50	3.00
1927	3,601,600	—	0.20	0.50	1.50	3.00
1928	2,380,800	—	0.25	1.00	6.00	9.00
1929 Curved 2	6,090,500	—	0.20	0.50	2.00	5.00
1929 Straight 2	Inc. above	—	0.40	1.00	6.00	9.00
1930	5,477,300	—	0.20	0.50	2.00	5.00
1931	5,678,500	—	0.20	0.50	2.00	5.00
1932	3,339,000	—	0.25	1.00	2.00	5.00
1933	3,426,800	—	0.25	0.50	2.00	5.00
1934	6,120,500	—	0.20	0.50	1.50	3.00
1935	4,599,800	—	0.20	0.50	1.50	3.00
1936 Long 6	6,166,100	—	0.20	1.25	1.50	3.00
1936 Short 6	Inc. above	—	0.10	0.50	1.50	3.00
1937	7,738,200	—	0.10	0.50	1.50	3.00
1938	6,992,900	—	0.10	0.50	1.50	3.00
1939	6,562,300	—	0.10	0.50	1.50	3.00
1940	4,059,900	—	0.10	0.50	1.50	3.00
1941	11,599,090	—	0.10	0.50	1.50	3.00
1942	3,992,000	—	0.20	0.60	1.50	3.00
1950	22,421,200	—	0.10	0.50	1.50	3.00

KM# 789 ÖRE

1.75 g., Iron, 16 mm. **Ruler:** Gustaf V **Obv:** Crowned monogram divides date **Rev:** Value and crowns **Note:** World War I issues.

Date	Mintage	F12	VF20	XF40	MS60	MS63
1917	8,127,700	0.50	1.50	4.00	10.00	25.00
1918	9,706,100	1.00	2.25	6.50	12.00	30.00
1919	7,169,500	1.50	3.00	8.00	20.00	45.00

KM# 810 ÖRE

1.75 g., Iron, 16 mm. **Ruler:** Gustaf V **Obv:** Crowned monogram divides date **Rev:** Value and crowns **Note:** World War II issues. Similar to KM#777.

Date	Mintage	F12	VF20	XF40	MS60	MS63
1942	10,053,000	—	—	0.50	1.50	3.00
1943	10,714,000	—	—	0.50	1.50	3.00
1944	8,648,500	—	—	0.50	1.50	3.00
1945	9,527,000	—	—	0.50	1.50	3.00
1945 Serif 4	Inc. above	—	1.50	5.00	15.00	25.00
1946	6,611,000	—	—	0.50	1.50	3.00
1947	14,244,500	—	—	0.25	0.50	3.00
1948	15,442,000	—	—	0.25	0.50	3.00
1949	11,778,900	—	—	0.25	0.50	3.00
1950	14,431,500	—	—	0.25	0.50	3.00

KM# 820 ÖRE

2.00 g., Bronze, 16 mm. **Ruler:** Gustaf VI **Obv:** Crown above inscription **Rev:** Value within circle divides date below crown **Edge:** Plain **Note:** Varieties exist.

Date	Mintage	VF20	XF40	MS60	MS63	MS65
1952 TS	3,819,000	—	0.50	1.00	1.50	2.50
1953 TS	22,635,800	—	—	0.50	0.75	1.50
1954 TS	15,492,000	—	—	0.75	1.50	3.00
1955 TS	24,008,000	—	—	0.75	1.50	3.00
1956 TS	20,792,000	—	—	0.75	1.50	3.00
1957 TS	21,018,500	—	—	0.75	1.50	3.00
1958 TS	20,220,000	—	—	0.75	1.50	3.00
1959 TS	14,027,500	—	—	0.75	1.50	3.00
1960 TS	21,840,000	—	—	0.75	1.50	3.00
1961 TS	11,457,500	—	—	0.75	1.50	3.00
1961 U	4,927,500	—	0.50	1.00	2.00	3.50
1962 U	19,692,500	—	—	0.50	0.75	1.00
1963 U	26,070,000	—	—	0.50	0.75	1.00
1964 U	19,290,000	—	—	0.50	0.75	1.00
1965 U	22,335,000	—	—	0.50	0.75	1.00
1966 U	24,092,500	—	—	0.30	0.40	0.50
1967 U	30,420,000	—	—	0.30	0.40	0.50
1968 U	20,760,000	—	—	0.30	0.40	0.50
1969 U	20,197,500	—	—	0.30	0.40	0.50
1970 U	44,400,000	—	—	0.30	0.40	0.50
1971 U	16,490,000	—	—	0.30	0.40	0.50

KM# 746 2 ÖRE

4.00 g., Bronze, 21 mm. **Ruler:** Oscar II **Obv:** Large lettering **Rev:** Value, date and crowns within circle

Date	Mintage	F12	VF20	XF40	MS60	MS63
1901	1,415,200	0.50	1.25	3.50	10.00	15.00
1902	2,035,550	0.50	1.25	3.50	10.00	15.00
1904	698,050	0.50	1.25	4.50	15.00	20.00
1905	1,429,900	0.50	1.25	3.50	10.00	15.00

KM# 769 2 ÖRE

4.00 g., Bronze, 21 mm. **Ruler:** Oscar II **Obv:** Crowned shield **Rev:** Value, date and crowns within circle

Date	Mintage	F12	VF20	XF40	MS60	MS63
1906/5	994,250	50.00	75.00	125	225	500
1906	Inc. above	1.00	3.00	12.00	25.00	50.00
1907	3,807,350	—	1.00	2.50	7.50	12.00

KM# 778 2 ÖRE

4.00 g., Bronze, 21 mm. **Ruler:** Gustaf V **Obv:** Crowned monogram divides date **Rev:** Value and crowns

Date	Mintage	F12	VF20	XF40	MS60	MS63
1909	1,584,550	—	1.00	5.00	30.00	45.00
1910	809,400	1.00	3.00	15.00	50.00	75.00
1912	445,750	2.00	5.00	18.00	60.00	90.00
1913	805,650	—	1.00	7.50	30.00	45.00
1914	1,196,900	—	1.00	7.50	30.00	45.00
1915/4	813,850	2.00	5.00	18.00	45.00	75.00
1915	Inc. above	—	1.00	7.50	30.00	45.00
1916/5	2,815,450	1.00	3.00	15.00	45.00	35.00
1916 Short 6	Inc. above	—	—	3.00	20.00	35.00
1916 Long 6	Inc. above	—	—	3.00	20.00	35.00
1919	1,202,700	—	1.00	1.50	12.00	20.00
1920	3,464,750	—	1.00	1.00	6.00	10.00
1921	2,958,250	—	0.75	1.00	6.00	10.00
1922	521,600	0.50	1.00	3.00	20.00	35.00
1923	769,200	0.75	1.50	3.00	30.00	45.00
1924	1,283,000	—	0.75	1.50	15.00	25.00
1925	3,903,350	—	—	1.00	9.00	15.00
1926	3,573,950	—	—	1.00	9.00	15.00
1927	2,190,250	—	—	1.00	9.00	15.00
1928	832,250	—	0.75	1.50	20.00	35.00
1929	2,384,350	—	—	1.00	5.00	9.00
1930	2,589,850	—	—	1.00	5.00	9.00
1931	2,295,200	—	—	1.00	5.00	9.00
1932	1,179,150	—	0.70	1.50	20.00	35.00
1933	1,721,300	—	—	1.00	5.00	9.00
1934	1,794,950	—	—	1.00	5.00	9.00
1935	3,677,750	—	—	0.50	3.00	6.00
1936 Short 6	2,244,100	—	—	0.50	3.00	6.00
1936 Long 6	Inc. above	—	0.75	1.50	10.00	18.00
1937	2,980,950	—	—	0.50	3.00	6.00
1938	3,224,800	—	—	0.50	3.00	6.00
1939	4,014,200	—	—	0.50	1.50	5.00
1940	3,304,750	—	—	0.50	1.50	5.00
1941	7,337,198	—	—	0.50	1.50	5.00
1942	1,614,000	—	—	1.00	5.00	7.50
1950	5,823,000	—	—	0.50	1.50	3.00

KM# 790 2 ÖRE

3.50 g., Iron, 21 mm. **Ruler:** Gustaf V **Obv:** Crowned monogram divides date **Rev:** Value and crowns **Note:** World War I issues. Similar to KM#553.

Date	Mintage	F12	VF20	XF40	MS60	MS63
1917	4,576,200	2.00	3.00	8.50	20.00	45.00
1918	4,981,750	2.50	5.00	12.50	30.00	60.00
1919	2,923,100	4.00	7.50	20.00	45.00	100
1920	1	—	—	—	—	—

KM# 811 2 ÖRE

3.50 g., Iron, 21 mm. **Ruler:** Gustaf V **Obv:** Crowned monogram divides date **Rev:** Value and crowns **Note:** World War II issues.

Date	Mintage	F12	VF20	XF40	MS60	MS63
1942	9,343,350	—	0.30	1.50	5.00	15.00
1943	6,999,300	—	0.30	1.50	5.00	15.00
1944	6,125,900	—	0.30	1.50	5.00	15.00
1945	4,773,400	—	0.30	1.50	5.00	15.00
1946	5,854,000	—	0.30	1.50	5.00	10.00
1947	9,535,750	—	0.30	0.75	3.00	5.00
1948	11,424,250	—	0.30	0.75	3.00	5.00
1949 Long 9	10,599,750	—	0.30	0.75	3.00	5.00
1949 Short 9	Inc. above	—	0.30	0.75	3.00	5.00
1950	13,323,000	—	0.30	0.75	3.00	5.00

KM# 821 2 ÖRE

4.00 g., Bronze, 21 mm. **Ruler:** Gustaf VI **Obv:** Crown above inscription **Rev:** Value within circle divides date below crown **Edge:** Plain **Note:** Varieties exist.

Date	Mintage	VF20	XF40	MS60	MS63	MS65
1952 TS	3,011,000	—	0.75	1.50	3.00	5.00
1953 TS	15,619,900	—	0.75	1.50	3.00	5.00
1954 TS	10,086,000	—	0.75	1.50	3.00	5.00
1955 TS	12,963,400	—	0.75	1.50	3.00	5.00
1956 TS	13,890,250	—	0.75	1.50	3.00	5.00
1957 TS	9,991,300	—	0.75	1.50	3.00	5.00
1958 TS	10,105,500	—	0.75	1.50	3.00	5.00
1959 TS	11,571,750	—	0.75	1.50	3.00	5.00
1960 TS	11,092,500	—	0.75	1.50	3.00	5.00
1961 TS	9,672,500	—	0.75	1.50	3.00	5.00
1961 U	1,075,000	0.50	1.50	5.00	7.50	11.50
1962 U	9,568,750	—	0.25	1.50	3.00	5.00
1963 U	13,337,500	—	0.25	1.50	3.00	5.00
1964 U	19,346,250	—	0.25	1.50	3.00	5.00
1964 U	Inc. above	0.50	1.00	3.00	5.00	7.00
Note: O in crown: first dot in crown on left with hollow center						
1965 U	23,356,000	—	—	0.25	0.50	1.00
1966 U	18,278,000	—	—	0.25	0.50	1.00
1967 U	23,931,000	—	—	0.25	0.50	1.00
1968 U	26,238,000	—	—	0.25	0.50	1.00
1969 U	16,843,000	—	—	0.25	0.50	1.00
1970 U	31,254,000	—	—	0.25	0.50	1.00
1971 U	19,179,000	—	—	0.25	0.50	1.00

KM# 757 5 ÖRE

8.00 g., Bronze, 27 mm. **Ruler:** Oscar II **Obv:** Large lettering **Rev:** Value, date and crowns within beaded circle

Date	Mintage	F12	VF20	XF40	MS60	MS63
1901	441,660	0.50	1.50	7.50	25.00	40.00
1902	652,420	0.50	1.50	7.50	25.00	40.00
1903	243,000	0.50	1.50	7.50	30.00	45.00
1904	414,240	0.50	1.50	7.50	20.00	35.00
1905	545,080	0.50	1.50	7.50	20.00	35.00

KM# 770 5 ÖRE

8.00 g., Bronze, 27 mm. **Ruler:** Oscar II **Obv:** Crowned shield **Rev:** Value, date and crowns within beaded circle

Date	Mintage	F12	VF20	XF40	MS60	MS63
1906	565,280	0.50	1.50	7.50	20.00	35.00
1907	1,953,260	0.50	1.50	3.00	12.00	18.00

KM# 779.1 5 ÖRE

8.00 g., Bronze, 27 mm. **Ruler:** Gustaf V **Obv:** Small cross above crowned monograms **Rev:** Value above crowns

Date	Mintage	F12	VF20	XF40	MS60	MS63
1909	917,230	0.50	1.50	20.00	50.00	125

KM# 779.2 5 ÖRE

8.00 g., Bronze, 27 mm. **Ruler:** Gustaf V **Obv:** Large cross above crowned monogram **Rev:** Value above crowns **Note:** Varieties exist.

Date	Mintage	F12	VF20	XF40	MS60	MS63
1909	Inc. above	5.00	15.00	100	300	600
1910	30,630	50.00	100	250	500	900
1911	778,000	0.50	1.50	15.00	60.00	100
Note: Narrow base mint mark						
1911	Inc. above	1.00	5.00	30.00	75.00	150
Note: Wide base mint mark						
1912	547,480	0.50	1.50	20.00	75.00	150
1913	761,780	0.50	1.00	15.00	60.00	100
1914	400,100	1.00	3.00	30.00	100	150
1915	1,122,820	0.50	1.50	10.00	35.00	50.00
1916/5	955,440	2.00	5.00	7.50	75.00	125
1916 Short 6	Inc. above	0.50	1.00	7.50	40.00	65.00
1916 Long 6	Inc. above	0.50	1.00	20.00	40.00	65.00
1917	1	—	—	—	—	—
1919	1,129,380	0.50	1.00	7.50	35.00	75.00
1920	2,360,920	—	1.00	5.00	20.00	35.00
1921	1,878,500	1.00	3.00	7.50	30.00	50.00
1922	763,420	0.50	1.50	20.00	60.00	100
1923	505,580	1.00	2.50	35.00	125	200
1924	899,500	0.50	1.00	9.00	45.00	90.00
1925	1,943,500	1.00	2.50	5.00	30.00	50.00
1926	1,742,100	1.00	2.50	5.00	30.00	50.00
1927	36,380	25.00	75.00	200	400	800
1928	987,900	0.50	1.00	7.50	35.00	65.00
1929	1,668,560	1.00	2.50	5.00	30.00	50.00
1930	1,716,040	1.00	2.50	5.00	30.00	50.00
1931	1,130,960	1.00	2.50	5.00	30.00	50.00
1932	1,165,220	1.00	2.50	5.00	30.00	50.00
1933	574,340	0.50	1.00	15.00	60.00	120
1934	1,710,260	—	—	3.00	20.00	35.00
1935	1,682,020	—	—	3.00	20.00	35.00
1936 Short 6	1,625,700	—	—	3.00	20.00	35.00
1936	Inc. above	—	—	3.00	25.00	45.00
1937	2,637,260	—	—	3.00	12.00	18.00
1938	2,354,240	—	—	3.00	12.00	18.00
1939	2,591,500	—	—	3.00	12.00	18.00
1940	2,729,580	—	—	1.50	10.00	15.00
1940 Serif 4	Inc. above	—	—	2.00	12.00	20.00
1941	2,054,540	—	—	1.50	9.00	15.00
1942	395,400	0.50	1.00	12.00	45.00	75.00
1950	12,559,100	—	—	0.25	1.50	5.00

KM# 791 5 ÖRE

7.00 g., Iron, 27 mm. **Ruler:** Gustaf V **Obv:** Crowned monogram divides date **Rev:** Value above crowns **Note:** World War I issues

Date	Mintage	F12	VF20	XF40	MS60	MS63
1917	2,953,320	1.50	3.00	15.00	45.00	75.00
1918	2,457,840	3.00	10.00	25.00	75.00	150
1919	2,302,480	3.00	10.00	25.00	75.00	150

KM# 812 5 ÖRE

7.00 g., Iron, 27 mm. **Ruler:** Gustaf V **Obv:** Crowned monogram divides date **Rev:** Value above crowns **Note:** World War II issues.

Date	Mintage	F12	VF20	XF40	MS60	MS63
1942	4,343,420	—	0.75	4.00	12.00	20.00
1943	5,570,180	—	0.75	4.00	12.00	20.00
1944	4,561,980	—	0.75	4.00	12.00	20.00
1945	3,771,100	—	0.75	4.00	12.00	20.00
1946	2,375,080	—	0.50	3.00	7.00	12.00
1947	6,034,840	—	0.50	3.00	7.00	12.00
1948	6,246,000	—	0.50	3.00	7.00	12.00
1949	7,839,640	—	0.50	2.00	5.00	10.00
1950	5,289,500	—	0.50	2.00	5.00	10.00

KM# 822 5 ÖRE

8.00 g., Bronze, 27 mm. **Ruler:** Gustaf VI **Obv:** Crown above inscription **Rev:** Value within circle divides date below crown **Edge:** Plain

Date	Mintage	VF20	XF40	MS60	MS63	MS65
1952 TS	3,065,400	—	1.00	3.00	5.00	7.00
1953 TS	12,329,320	—	1.00	3.00	5.00	7.00
1954 TS	7,232,100	—	1.00	3.00	5.00	7.00
1955 TS	8,464,620	—	1.00	3.00	5.00	7.00
1956 TS	7,997,120	—	1.00	3.00	5.00	7.00
1957 TS	6,275,600	—	1.00	3.00	5.00	7.00
1958 TS	9,498,400	—	1.00	3.00	5.00	7.00
1959 TS	8,370,500	—	1.00	3.00	5.00	7.00
1960 TS	10,542,300	—	0.50	2.00	3.00	5.00
1961 TS	3,909,000	—	0.50	2.00	3.00	5.00
1961 U	2,451,500	—	0.50	2.00	3.00	5.00
1962 U	22,305,500	—	0.50	2.00	3.00	5.00
1963 U	17,156,500	—	0.50	2.00	3.00	5.00
1964 U	10,922,500	—	0.75	2.00	3.00	5.00
1964 U	Inc. above	1.50	3.00	10.00	25.00	—
Note: O in crown: first dot in crown on left with hollow center						
1965 U	22,635,000	—	0.20	0.50	0.75	1.25
1966 U	18,213,000	—	0.20	0.50	0.75	1.25
1967 U	20,776,000	—	0.20	0.50	0.75	1.25
1968 U	27,093,500	—	0.20	0.50	0.75	1.25
1969 U	26,886,500	—	0.20	0.50	0.75	1.25
1970 U	29,419,500	—	0.20	0.50	0.75	1.25
1971 U	15,749,000	—	0.20	0.50	0.75	1.25

KM# 845 5 ÖRE

2.70 g., Bronze, 18 mm. **Ruler:** Gustaf VI **Obv:** Large crown above smaller crown **Rev:** Value divides date

Date	Mintage	VF20	XF40	MS60	MS63	MS65
1972 U	107,894,000	—	—	0.25	0.60	1.00
1973 U	193,037,580	—	—	0.25	0.60	1.00

KM# 849 5 ÖRE

2.70 g., Bronze, 18 mm. **Ruler:** Carl XVI Gustaf **Obv:** Value **Rev:** Crowned monogram divides date **Edge:** Plain

Date	Mintage	VF20	XF40	MS60	MS63	MS65
1976 U	4,672,350	—	—	0.25	0.60	1.00
1977 U	31,037,129	—	—	0.25	0.60	1.00
1978 U	46,021,707	—	—	0.25	0.60	1.00
1979 U	65,833,193	—	—	0.25	0.60	1.00
1980 U	60,996,699	—	—	0.25	0.60	1.00
1981 U	19,791,000	—	—	0.25	0.60	1.00

KM# 849a 5 ÖRE

2.70 g., Brass, 18 mm. **Ruler:** Carl XVI Gustaf **Obv:** Value **Rev:** Crowned monogram divides date

Date	Mintage	VF20	XF40	MS60	MS63	MS65
1981 U	34,960,593	—	—	0.25	0.60	1.00
1982 U	40,471,115	—	—	0.25	0.60	1.00
1983 U	36,304,042	—	—	0.25	0.60	1.00
1984 U	13,449,245	—	—	0.25	0.60	1.00

KM# 755 10 ÖRE

1.45 g., 0.400 Silver 0.0186 oz. ASW, 15 mm. **Ruler:** Oscar II **Obv:** Large lettering **Rev:** Value, date **Note:** Varieties exist.

Date	Mintage	F12	VF20	XF40	MS60	MS63
1902 EB	1,945,600	0.40	1.50	7.50	15.00	25.00
1903 EB	1,508,930	0.40	1.50	7.50	15.00	25.00
1904 EB	3,279,520	0.40	0.75	3.00	10.00	15.00

KM# 774 10 ÖRE

1.45 g., 0.400 Silver 0.0186 oz. ASW, 15 mm. **Ruler:** Oscar II **Obv:** Crowned shield flanked by crowns **Rev:** Value and date

Date	Mintage	F12	VF20	XF40	MS60	MS63
1907 EB	7,319,040	0.40	1.00	3.00	12.00	18.00

KM# 780 10 ÖRE

1.45 g., 0.400 Silver 0.0186 oz. ASW, 15 mm. **Ruler:** Gustaf V **Obv:** Three small crowns within crowned shield divides date **Rev:** Value

Date	Mintage	F12	VF20	XF40	MS60	MS63
1909 W	1,610,400	1.00	3.00	10.00	50.00	75.00
1911 W	3,180,650	0.75	1.50	7.50	20.00	35.00
1913 W	1,580,910	0.75	1.50	9.00	35.00	50.00
1914 W	1,571,330	0.75	1.50	7.50	20.00	35.00
1914 Serif 4	Inc. above	0.75	1.50	7.50	35.00	50.00
1915 W	1,546,950	—	1.50	7.50	35.00	50.00
1916/5 W	3,034,880	2.00	5.00	15.00	50.00	75.00
1916 W	Inc. above	0.75	1.50	5.00	20.00	35.00
1917 W	4,996,139	—	0.40	1.50	15.00	25.00
1918 W	4,114,180	—	0.40	1.50	15.00	25.00
1919 W	5,737,020	—	0.40	1.50	15.00	25.00
1927 W	2,509,590	—	0.40	1.50	15.00	25.00
1928 G	2,901,150	—	0.40	1.50	15.00	25.00
1929 G	5,505,200	—	0.40	1.50	7.50	10.00
1930 G	3,222,710	—	0.40	1.50	7.50	10.00
1931 G	4,272,073	—	0.40	1.50	7.50	10.00
1933 G	1,948,090	0.75	1.50	3.00	40.00	—
1934 G	4,059,293	—	0.40	1.00	3.00	5.00
1935 G	2,426,283	—	0.40	1.00	3.00	5.00
1936 G Short 6	5,099,270	1.00	3.00	15.00	35.00	50.00
1936 G Long 6	Inc. above	—	0.40	1.00	4.50	7.50
1937 G	5,116,920	—	0.40	1.00	3.00	5.00
1938 G	7,428,140	—	0.40	1.00	3.00	5.00
1938 G	—	PF60 12.50				
1939/29 G	2,020,670	2.00	5.00	15.00	25.00	45.00
1939 G	Inc. above	—	0.40	1.00	9.00	15.00
1939 G	—	PF60 17.50				
1940 G	3,017,320	—	0.40	1.00	3.00	5.00
1941 G	9,106,380	—	0.40	1.00	3.00	5.00
1942 G	3,691,640	—	0.40	1.00	3.00	5.00

KM# 795 10 ÖRE

1.50 g., Nickel-Bronze, 15 mm. **Ruler:** Gustaf V **Obv:** Crowned monogram divides date **Rev:** Value **Edge:** Reeded

Date	Mintage	F12	VF20	XF40	MS60	MS63
1920 W	3,612,250	0.50	1.00	5.00	20.00	30.00
1920 W Large W	Inc. above	5.00	12.00	35.00	125	200
1921 W	2,269,950	0.50	1.00	5.00	20.00	30.00
1923 W	2,143,560	0.50	1.00	5.00	25.00	40.00
1924 W	1,600,000	0.50	1.00	5.00	35.00	50.00

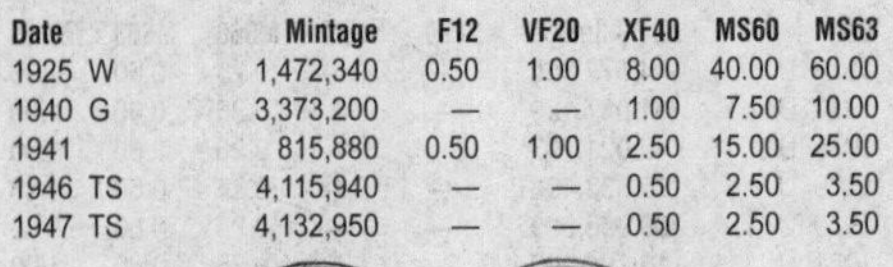

Date	Mintage	F12	VF20	XF40	MS60	MS63
1925 W	1,472,340	0.50	1.00	8.00	40.00	60.00
1940 G	3,373,200	—	—	1.00	7.50	10.00
1941	815,880	0.50	1.00	2.50	15.00	25.00
1946 TS	4,115,940	—	—	0.50	2.50	3.50
1947 TS	4,132,950	—	—	0.50	2.50	3.50

KM# 813 10 ÖRE

1.44 g., 0.400 Silver 0.0185 oz. ASW, 15 mm. **Ruler:** Gustaf V **Obv:** Crown **Rev:** Value **Note:** Varieties exist.

Date	Mintage	VF20	XF40	MS60	MS63	MS65
1942 G	1,600,000	0.40	1.00	4.00	6.00	9.00
1942 G	—	PF63 35.00				
1943 G	7,661,100	0.40	1.00	4.00	6.00	9.00
1944 G	12,276,900	0.40	1.00	3.00	5.00	7.00
1945 G	11,702,510	0.40	1.00	3.00	5.00	7.00
1945 TS	Inc. above	0.40	1.00	3.00	5.00	7.00
1945 TS/G	Inc. above	0.40	1.00	4.00	6.00	9.00
1946/5 TS Open 6	3,575,500	5.00	10.00	25.00	50.00	—
1946 TS Open 6	Inc. above	0.40	2.50	15.00	25.00	—
1946 TS Closed 6	Inc. above	0.40	1.50	8.00	12.00	—
1947 TS	7,293,250	0.40	1.00	3.00	5.00	7.00
1948 TS	10,418,650	0.40	1.00	3.00	5.00	7.00
1949 TS	12,044,000	0.40	1.00	3.00	5.00	7.00
1950 TS	31,823,870	0.40	1.00	3.00	5.00	7.00

KM# 823 10 ÖRE

1.44 g., 0.400 Silver 0.0185 oz. ASW, 15 mm. **Ruler:** Gustaf VI **Obv:** Crown **Rev:** Value

Date	Mintage	VF20	XF40	MS60	MS63	MS65
1952 TS	4,659,700	—	0.40	1.25	3.00	5.00
1953 TS	28,484,040	—	0.40	1.25	3.00	5.00
1954 TS	15,913,250	—	0.40	1.25	3.00	5.00
1955 TS	16,687,200	—	0.40	1.25	3.00	5.00
1956 TS	21,985,600	—	0.40	1.00	1.50	2.00
1957 TS	21,294,400	—	0.40	1.00	1.50	2.00
1958 TS	19,605,400	—	0.40	1.00	1.50	2.00
1959 TS	18,523,000	—	0.40	1.00	1.50	2.00
1960 TS	16,605,000	—	0.40	1.00	1.50	2.00
1961 TS	8,283,000	—	0.40	1.00	1.50	2.00
1961 U	7,843,000	—	0.40	1.00	1.50	2.00
1962 U	8,619,000	—	0.40	1.00	1.50	2.00

KM# 835 10 ÖRE

1.40 g., Copper-Nickel, 15 mm. **Ruler:** Gustaf VI **Obv:** Crowned monogram divides date **Rev:** Value

Date	Mintage	VF20	XF40	MS60	MS63	MS65
1962 U	8,814,000	—	0.50	1.20	3.00	5.00
1963 U	28,170,000	—	—	0.25	0.50	0.75
1964 U	36,895,000	—	—	0.25	0.50	0.75
1965 U	29,870,000	—	—	0.25	0.50	0.75
1966 U	20,435,000	—	—	0.25	0.50	0.75
1967 U	18,245,000	—	—	0.25	0.50	0.75
1968 U	51,490,000	—	—	0.25	0.50	0.75
1969 U	55,880,000	—	—	0.25	0.50	0.75
1970 U	60,910,000	—	—	0.25	0.50	0.75
1971 U	27,075,000	—	—	0.25	0.50	0.75
1972 U	36,766,500	—	—	0.25	0.50	0.75
1973 U	160,740,000	—	—	0.25	0.50	0.75

KM# 850 10 ÖRE

1.45 g., Copper-Nickel, 14.54 mm. **Ruler:** Carl XVI Gustaf **Obv:** Crowned monogram divides date **Rev:** Value **Edge:** Plain

Date	Mintage	VF20	XF40	MS60	MS63	MS65
1976 U	4,172,790	—	—	0.15	0.50	0.75
1977 U	44,517,287	—	—	0.15	0.30	0.50
1978 U	74,341,720	—	—	0.15	0.30	0.50
1979 U	75,305,608	—	—	0.15	0.30	0.50
1980 U	108,293,811	—	—	0.15	0.30	0.50
1981 U	102,453,931	—	—	0.15	0.30	0.50
1982 U	103,905,592	—	—	0.15	0.30	0.50
1983 U	773,149,400	—	—	0.15	0.30	0.50
1984 U	122,128,092	—	—	0.15	0.30	0.50

Date	Mintage	VF20	XF40	MS60	MS63	MS65
1985 U	79,154,951	—	—	0.15	0.30	0.50
1986 U	48,945,396	—	—	0.15	0.30	0.50
1986 D	48,945,220	—	—	0.15	0.30	0.50
1987 D	146,877,318	—	—	0.15	0.30	0.50
1988 D	194,986,479	—	—	0.15	0.30	0.50
1989 D	245,180,644	—	—	0.15	0.30	0.50
1990 D	139,298,404	—	—	0.15	0.30	0.50
1991 D	5,176,842	—	—	0.15	0.30	0.50

KM# 739 25 ÖRE

2.42 g., 0.600 Silver 0.0467 oz. ASW, 17 mm. **Ruler:** Oscar II **Obv:** Large lettering **Rev:** Value within wreath, date below

Date	Mintage	F12	VF20	XF40	MS60	MS63
1902 EB	1,259,039	0.90	2.50	12.00	35.00	60.00
1904 EB	691,888	0.90	2.50	12.00	35.00	60.00
1905 EB	732,000	0.90	2.00	10.00	25.00	45.00

KM# 775 25 ÖRE

2.42 g., 0.600 Silver 0.0467 oz. ASW, 17 mm. **Ruler:** Oscar II **Obv:** Crowned shield flanked by crowns **Rev:** Value within wreath

Date	Mintage	F12	VF20	XF40	MS60	MS63
1907 EB	3,222,580	0.90	2.50	7.00	20.00	35.00

KM# 785 25 ÖRE

2.42 g., 0.600 Silver 0.0467 oz. ASW, 17 mm. **Ruler:** Gustaf V **Obv:** Small crowns within crowned shield divides date **Rev:** Value above sprigs

Date	Mintage	F12	VF20	XF40	MS60	MS63
1910 W Large cross	2,043,936	0.90	2.00	6.00	35.00	50.00
1910 W Small cross	Inc. above	3.00	20.00	75.00	125	300
1912 W	1,013,740	0.90	3.00	15.00	40.00	75.00
1914 W	3,719,232	0.90	3.00	15.00	25.00	40.00
1916 W	1,269,120	0.90	3.00	15.00	40.00	75.00
1917 W	1,657,312	0.90	2.00	5.00	20.00	30.00
1918 W Small 8	2,364,784	0.90	2.00	6.00	30.00	45.00
1918 W Wide 8	Inc. above	0.90	2.00	7.50	30.00	45.00
1919 W	3,205,164	0.90	1.50	5.00	20.00	30.00
1927 W	1,687,984	0.90	1.50	5.00	20.00	30.00
1928 G	836,899	0.90	1.50	7.50	30.00	45.00
1929 G	1,124,932	0.90	1.50	5.00	20.00	30.00
1930 G	3,489,628	0.90	1.50	3.00	9.00	15.00
1931 G	1,391,938	0.90	1.50	3.00	9.00	15.00
1932 G	1,133,344	0.90	1.50	3.00	9.00	15.00
1933 G	964,340	0.90	1.50	6.00	20.00	30.00
1934 G	1,403,648	0.90	1.50	3.00	5.00	9.00
1936 G	1,852,000	0.90	1.50	3.00	5.00	9.00
1937 G	Inc. above	PF60 20.00				
1937 G Large G	Inc. above	0.90	1.50	3.00	9.00	15.00
1937 G Small G	3,258,956	0.90	1.50	3.00	5.00	9.00
1938	3,678,876	0.90	1.00	1.50	3.00	5.00
1939	2,136,600	—	0.90	1.50	3.00	5.00
1940	2,301,788	—	0.90	1.50	3.00	5.00
1941	1,995,200	—	0.90	1.50	3.00	5.00

KM# 798 25 ÖRE

2.40 g., Nickel-Bronze, 17 mm. **Ruler:** Gustaf V **Obv:** Crowned monogram divides date **Rev:** Value within oat sprigs

Date	Mintage	F12	VF20	XF40	MS60	MS63
1921 W	1,354,656	1.50	3.00	9.00	30.00	65.00
1940 G	2,333,040	—	0.50	2.00	10.00	15.00
1941 G	1,056,680	—	0.50	2.00	15.00	20.00
1946 TS	2,066,048	—	0.30	1.00	5.00	7.50
1947 TS	1,594,200	—	0.30	1.00	5.00	7.50

KM# 816 25 ÖRE

2.32 g., 0.400 Silver 0.0298 oz. ASW, 17 mm. **Ruler:** Gustaf V **Obv:** Crown **Rev:** Value and date

Date	Mintage	F20	XF40	MS60	MS63	MS65
1943 G	9,854,640	0.60	1.00	3.00	5.00	7.00
1944 G	9,532,148	0.60	1.00	3.00	5.00	7.00
1945 G	5,362,800	0.60	1.00	3.00	5.00	7.00
1945 TS	Inc. above	0.60	2.00	5.00	10.00	12.00
1945 G/TS	Inc. above	0.60	2.00	8.00	15.00	18.00
1946 TS	2,249,600	0.60	2.00	5.00	10.00	12.00
1946 TS serif 6	Inc. above	2.50	7.50	15.00	30.00	40.00
1947 TS	5,332,800	0.60	1.00	2.50	4.00	6.00
1948 TS	3,191,000	0.60	1.00	2.50	4.00	6.00
1949 TS	5,812,180	0.60	1.00	2.50	4.00	6.00
1950 TS	12,059,144	0.60	1.00	2.50	4.00	6.00

KM# 824 25 ÖRE

2.32 g., 0.400 Silver 0.0298 oz. ASW, 17 mm. **Ruler:** Gustaf VI **Obv:** Value and date **Rev:** Crown

Date	Mintage	VF20	XF40	MS60	MS63	MS65
1952 TS	2,113,890	—	0.60	1.50	3.00	5.00
1953 TS	18,177,420	—	0.60	1.00	1.50	2.00
1954 TS	9,491,740	—	0.60	1.00	1.50	2.00
1955 TS	7,663,100	—	0.60	1.00	1.50	2.00
1956 TS	10,930,800	—	0.60	1.00	1.50	2.00
1957 TS	12,497,200	—	0.60	1.00	1.50	2.00
1958 TS	6,883,940	—	0.60	1.00	1.50	2.00
1959 TS	4,772,000	—	0.60	1.00	1.50	2.00
1960 TS	4,374,000	0.60	0.70	3.00	5.00	7.00
1961 TS	8,380,800	—	0.60	1.00	1.50	2.00

KM# 836 25 ÖRE

2.29 g., Copper-Nickel, 16.94 mm. **Ruler:** Gustaf VI **Obv:** Crowned monogram divides date **Rev:** Value **Edge:** Plain

Date	Mintage	VF20	XF40	MS60	MS63	MS65
1962 U	4,426,000	—	0.50	1.50	2.00	3.00
1963 U	26,710,000	—	0.50	1.00	1.50	2.00
1964 U	17,300,000	—	0.50	1.00	1.50	2.00
1965 U	6,884,000	—	0.50	1.00	1.50	2.00
1966 U	12,932,000	—	—	0.25	0.50	0.75
1967 U	28,038,000	—	—	0.25	0.50	0.75
1968 U	14,366,000	—	—	0.25	0.50	0.75
1969 U	20,214,000	—	—	0.25	0.50	0.75
1970 U	23,780,000	—	—	0.25	0.50	0.75
1971 U	8,606,000	—	—	0.25	0.50	0.75
1972 U	1,323,200	—	—	0.25	0.50	0.75
1973 U	76,993,000	—	—	0.25	0.50	0.75

KM# 851 25 ÖRE

2.20 g., Copper-Nickel, 17 mm. **Ruler:** Carl XVI Gustaf **Obv:** Crowned monogram divides date **Rev:** Value

Date	Mintage	VF20	XF40	MS60	MS63	MS65
1976 U	2,515,285	—	0.15	0.65	1.25	1.75
1977 U	5,509,491	—	0.15	0.50	0.75	1.25
1978 U	54,593,293	—	0.10	0.30	0.50	0.75
1979 U	48,423,422	—	0.10	0.30	0.50	0.75
1980 U	38,889,325	—	0.10	0.30	0.50	0.75
1981 U	46,371,204	—	0.10	0.30	0.50	0.75
1982 U	43,212,638	—	0.10	0.30	0.50	0.75
1983 U	28,954,257	—	0.10	0.30	0.50	0.75
1984 U	7,293,722	—	0.10	0.30	0.50	0.75

KM# 771 50 ÖRE
5.00 g., 0.600 Silver 0.0965 oz. ASW, 22 mm. **Ruler:** Oscar II **Obv:** Crowned shield flanked by crowns **Rev:** Value and date within wreath

Date	Mintage	F12	VF20	XF40	MS60	MS63
1906 EB	319,452	2.00	5.00	15.00	75.00	100
1907 EB	803,340	1.90	3.00	12,00	35.00	75.00

KM# 788 50 ÖRE
5.00 g., 0.600 Silver 0.0965 oz. ASW, 22 mm. **Ruler:** Gustaf V **Obv:** Three small crowns within crowned shield divides date **Rev:** Value above sprigs

Date	Mintage	F12	VF20	XF40	MS60	MS63
1911 W	472,534	1.90	3.00	15.00	50.00	75.00
1912 W	483,062	1.90	5.00	15.00	60.00	90.00
1914 W	378,448	1.90	5.00	15.00	60.00	90.00
1916 W	536,718	1.90	3.00	15.00	50.00	75.00
1919 W	458,296	1.90	3.00	15.00	40.00	60.00
1927 W	671,596	1.90	3.00	7.50	30.00	45.00
1928 G	1,135,054	1.90	2.00	5.00	20.00	30.00
1929 G	470,990	1.90	3.00	7.50	30.00	45.00
1930 G	547,920	1.90	3.00	7.50	30.00	45.00
1931 G	671,457	1.90	2.00	7.50	20.00	30.00
1933 G	547,606	1.90	2.00	7.50	20.00	30.00
1934 G	613,124	1.90	2.00	5.00	15.00	20.00
1935 G	690,792	1.90	2.00	5.00	15.00	20.00
1936 G Short 6	823,176	1.90	2.00	5.00	15.00	20.00
1936 G Long 6	Inc. above	1.90	3.00	7.50	25.00	35.00
1938 G	441,546	1.90	2.00	3.50	12.00	15.00
1939 G	921,750	—	1.90	2.50	10.00	12.00
1939 G	—	PF60 35.00				

KM# 796 50 ÖRE
4.80 g., Nickel-Bronze, 22 mm. **Ruler:** Gustaf V **Obv:** Crowned monogram divides date **Rev:** Value within oat sprigs **Note:** Varieties exist.

Date	Mintage	F12	VF20	XF40	MS60	MS63
1920 W Oval 0	479,500	1.00	3.00	10.00	50.00	75.00
1920 W Round 0	Inc. above	10.00	25.00	75.00	200	350
1921 W	214,922	1.50	5.00	50.00	100	175
1924 W	645,368	1.00	3.00	12.00	65.00	125
1940 G	1,340,750	0.50	1.00	3.00	12.00	20.00
1940 G large G	Inc. above	1.50	5.00	10.00	25.00	45.00
1946 TS	1,425,990	—	0.25	2.50	8.00	12.50
1947 TS	1,031,800	—	0.25	2.50	8.00	12.50

KM# 817 50 ÖRE
4.80 g., 0.400 Silver 0.0617 oz. ASW, 22 mm. **Ruler:** Gustaf V **Obv:** Crown **Rev:** Value and date

Date	Mintage	VF20	XF40	MS60	MS63	MS65
1943 G	784,700	3.00	5.00	20.00	35.00	—
1944 G	1,540,296	1.20	2.00	5.00	8.00	10.00
1945 G	2,584,800	1.20	2.00	5.00	8.00	10.00
1946 TS	1,091,000	1.20	2.00	5.00	8.00	10.00
1947 TS	1,770,500	1.20	2.00	5.00	8.00	10.00
1948 TS	1,731,400	1.20	2.00	5.00	8.00	10.00
1949 TS	1,883,100	1.20	2.00	5.00	8.00	10.00
1950 TS	3,353,620	1.20	2.00	5.00	8.00	10.00

KM# 825 50 ÖRE
4.80 g., 0.400 Silver 0.0617 oz. ASW, 22 mm. **Ruler:** Gustaf VI **Obv:** Value and date **Rev:** Crown

Date	Mintage	VF20	XF40	MS60	MS63	MS65
1952 TS	1,197,760	1.20	1.50	7.50	15.00	18.00
1953 TS	4,395,620	1.20	1.50	7.50	15.00	18.00
1954 TS	5,778,850	1.20	1.50	7.50	15.00	18.00
1955 TS	2,699,700	1.20	1.50	6.00	12.00	15.00
1956 TS	7,056,670	1.20	1.50	5.00	7.50	9.50
1957 TS	2,404,700	1.20	1.50	6.00	12.00	15.00
1958 TS	1,659,800	1.20	1.50	6.00	12.00	15.00
1961 TS	2,775,000	1.20	1.50	5.00	8.00	10.00

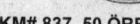

KM# 837 50 ÖRE
4.50 g., Copper-Nickel, 22 mm. **Ruler:** Gustaf VI **Obv:** Crowned monogram divides date **Rev:** Value

Date	Mintage	VF20	XF40	MS60	MS63	MS65
1962 U	1,400,000	0.50	1.50	7.50	9.50	12.00
1963 U	5,808,000	—	0.50	5.00	7.50	9.50
1964 U	5,325,000	—	0.50	5.00	7.50	9.50
1965 U	6,453,000	—	0.25	3.00	5.00	7.00
1966 U	6,309,000	—	0.25	1.00	1.50	2.00
1967 U	7,890,000	—	0.25	1.00	1.50	2.00
1968 U	9,198,000	—	0.25	0.50	1.00	1.25
1969 U	7,265,000	—	0.25	0.50	1.00	1.25
1970 U	9,426,000	—	0.25	0.50	1.00	1.25
1971 U	7,218,000	—	0.25	0.50	1.00	1.25
1972 U	7,388,000	—	0.25	0.50	1.00	1.25
1973 U	52,467,000	—	—	0.25	0.50	0.75

KM# 855 50 ÖRE
4.50 g., Copper-Nickel, 22 mm. **Ruler:** Carl XVI Gustaf **Obv:** Crowned monogram divides date **Rev:** Value **Edge:** Plain

Date	Mintage	VF20	XF40	MS60	MS63	MS65
1976 U	2,588,575	—	—	0.25	0.50	0.75
1977 U	10,359,708	—	—	0.25	0.50	0.75
1978 U	33,282,476	—	—	0.25	0.50	0.75
1979 U	30,723,730	—	—	0.25	0.50	0.75
1980 U	28,665,662	—	—	0.25	0.50	0.75
1981 U	15,516,559	—	—	0.25	0.50	0.75
1982 U	14,778,358	—	—	0.25	0.50	0.75
1983 U	17,528,777	—	—	0.25	0.50	0.75
1984 U	27,527,534	—	—	0.25	0.50	0.75
1985 U	14,078,477	—	—	0.25	0.50	0.75
1986 U	937,214	—	—	0.25	0.50	0.75
1987 D	1,077,317	—	—	0.25	0.50	0.75
1988 D	531,669	—	—	0.25	0.50	0.75
1989 D	605,780	—	—	0.25	0.50	0.75
1990 D	31,934,675	—	—	0.15	0.25	0.35
1991 D	16,315,160	—	—	0.15	0.25	0.35

KM# 878 50 ÖRE
3.70 g., Bronze, 18.7 mm. **Ruler:** Carl XVI Gustaf **Obv:** Value **Rev:** Three crowns and date **Edge:** Reeded

Date	Mintage	VF20	XF40	MS60	MS63	MS65
1992 B	39,530,810	—	—	0.15	0.25	0.35
1992 D	39,531,000	—	—	0.15	0.25	0.35
1993 B	643,520	—	—	0.30	0.50	0.65
1993 D	—	—	—	0.15	0.25	0.35
1994 B	517,575	—	—	0.40	0.50	0.65
1995 B	486,538	—	—	0.40	0.50	0.65
1996 B	247,620	—	—	0.50	0.75	1.00
1997 B	69,995	—	0.50	1.00	1.50	2.00
1998 B	5,064,956	—	—	0.15	0.25	0.35
1999 B	22,076,128	—	—	0.15	0.25	0.35
2000 B	33,060,252	—	—	0.15	0.25	0.35

KM# 760 KRONA
7.50 g., 0.800 Silver 0.1929 oz. ASW, 25 mm. **Ruler:** Oscar II **Obv:** Head left **Obv. Legend:** OSCAR II SVERIGES. **Rev:** Crowned arms with supporters **Edge:** Reeded

Date	Mintage	F12	VF20	XF40	MS60	MS63
1901/898 EB	270,960	7.00	18.00	100	250	350
1901 EB	Inc. above	6.00	15.00	75.00	200	275
1903 EB	473,386	5.00	12.00	50.00	125	250
1904 EB	563,586	5.00	9.00	50.00	125	250

KM# 772 KRONA
7.50 g., 0.800 Silver 0.1929 oz. ASW, 25 mm. **Ruler:** Oscar II **Obv:** Head left **Rev:** Crowned arms with supporters **Edge:** Reeded

Date	Mintage	F12	VF20	XF40	MS60	MS63
1906 EB	426,939	5.00	10.00	125	225	—
1907 EB	1,058,286	5.00	9.00	100	200	—

KM# 786.1 KRONA
7.50 g., 0.800 Silver 0.1929 oz. ASW, 25 mm. **Ruler:** Gustaf V **Obv:** Head left **Rev:** Crowned arms within order chain **Edge:** Reeded

Date	Mintage	F12	VF20	XF40	MS60	MS63
1.9.1.0 W	643,065	3.75	6.00	18.00	50.00	80.00
1.9.1.2 W	303,420	3.75	8.00	35.00	90.00	150
1.9.1.3 W	353,051	3.75	6.00	18.00	60.00	90.00
1.9.1.4 W	622,217	3.75	6.00	18.00	50.00	80.00
1.9.1.5 W	1,415,956	3.75	5.00	12.00	35.00	75.00
1.9.1.6/5 W	1,139,245	3.75	6.00	20.00	75.00	100
1.9.1.6 W	Inc. above	3.75	6.00	15.00	30.00	65.00
1.9.1.8 W	258,091	3.75	5.00	15.00	50.00	80.00
1.9.2.3 W	746,277	3.75	5.00	12.00	30.00	65.00
1.9.2.4 W	2,066,155	3.75	5.00	10.00	25.00	40.00

KM# 786.2 KRONA
7.50 g., 0.800 Silver 0.1929 oz. ASW, 25 mm. **Ruler:** Gustaf V **Obv:** Head left **Rev:** Crowned arms within order chain **Edge:** Reeded

Date	Mintage	F12	VF20	XF40	MS60	MS63
1924 W	Inc. above	—	4.00	12.00	25.00	45.00
1925 W	369,919	—	4.00	20.00	65.00	90.00
1926 W	465,467	—	4.00	13.00	30.00	65.00
1927 G	401,167	—	4.00	18.00	60.00	90.00
1928 G	739,189	—	4.00	12.00	25.00	40.00
1929 G	1,345,647	—	3.75	5.00	15.00	25.00
1930 G	1,743,783	—	3.75	5.00	10.00	20.00
1931 G	1,007,523	—	3.75	5.00	10.00	20.00
1932 G	1,035,877	—	3.75	5.00	10.00	20.00
1933 G	1,044,634	—	3.75	5.00	10.00	20.00
1934 G	585,673	—	3.75	7.00	60.00	80.00
1935 G	1,604,343	—	3.75	5.00	7.00	8.00
1936 G	3,222,312	—	3.75	5.00	7.00	8.00
1937 G	2,666,998	—	3.75	5.00	7.00	8.00
1938 G	—	PF60 25.00				
1938 G	1,911,464	—	3.75	5.00	7.00	8.00
1939 G	7,589,316	—	3.75	5.00	7.00	8.00
1940 G	6,917,460	—	3.75	5.00	7.00	8.00
1941 G	Inc. below	—	3.75	5.00	7.00	8.00
1941/4 G	2,183,338	—	3.75	7.00	10.00	20.00
1942 G	240,000	30.00	80.00	160	475	500

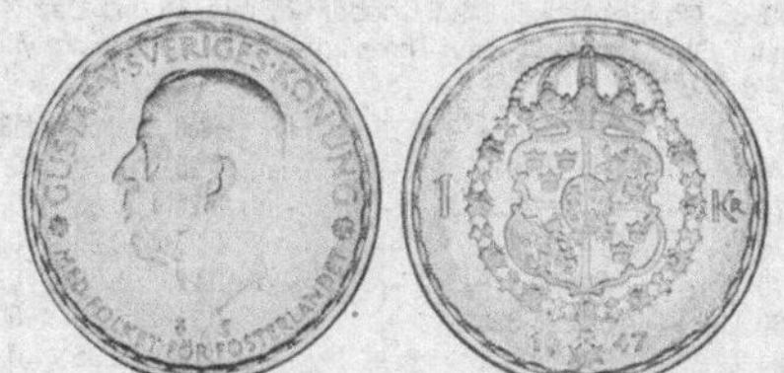

KM# 814 KRONA
7.00 g., 0.400 Silver 0.090 oz. ASW, 25 mm. **Ruler:** Gustaf V **Obv:** Head left **Rev:** Crowned arms within order chain divide value **Edge:** Reeded

Date	Mintage	VF20	XF40	MS60	MS63	MS65
1942 G	5,644,990	1.70	2.50	7.50	10.00	12.00
1943 G Plain 4	7,915,850	1.70	2.50	7.50	10.00	12.00
1943 G Crosslet 4	Inc. above	1.70	2.50	7.50	10.00	12.00
1944 G	7,423,463	1.70	2.50	3.25	4.50	6.00

Date	Mintage	VF20	XF40	MS60	MS63	MS65
1945 G	7,359,360	1.70	2.50	3.25	4.50	6.00
1945 TS	Inc. above	1.70	2.50	7.50	15.00	18.00
1945 TS/G	Inc. above	1.70	2.50	9.00	12.00	15.00
1946 TS	19,170,454	1.70	2.50	3.25	4.50	6.00
1947 TS	9,124,335	1.70	2.50	3.25	4.50	6.00
1948 TS	10,430,588	1.70	2.50	3.25	4.50	6.00
1949 TS	7,981,162	1.70	2.50	3.25	4.50	6.00
1950 TS	5,310,141	1.70	2.50	3.25	4.50	6.00

KM# 826 KRONA

7.00 g., 0.400 Silver 0.090 oz. ASW, 25 mm. **Ruler:** Gustaf VI **Obv:** Head left **Rev:** Crowned shield divides value **Edge:** Reeded

Date	Mintage	VF20	XF40	MS60	MS63	MS65
1952 TS	1,101,625	1.70	3.00	10.00	15.00	18.00
1953/2 TS	Inc. above	1.70	3.00	10.00	15.00	18.00
1953 TS	3,305,843	1.70	3.00	10.00	15.00	18.00
1954 TS	6,460,770	1.70	3.00	5.00	6.00	7.50
1955 TS	4,140,904	1.70	3.00	5.00	6.00	7.50
1956 TS	6,226,705	1.70	3.00	4.00	5.00	7.00
1957 TS	3,544,268	1.70	3.00	4.00	5.00	7.00
1958 TS	1,438,940	1.70	3.00	5.00	9.00	11.00
1959 TS	1,187,000	1.70	3.00	10.00	15.00	18.00
1960 TS	4,085,250	1.70	3.00	4.00	5.00	7.00
1961 TS	4,283,000	1.70	3.00	4.00	5.00	7.00
1961 U	2,973,275	1.70	3.00	5.00	9.00	11.00
1962 U	6,838,550	1.70	2.25	3.25	4.00	5.50
1963 U	14,227,500	1.70	2.25	3.25	4.00	5.50
1964 U	15,972,500	1.70	2.25	3.25	4.00	5.50
1965 U	18,638,500	1.70	2.25	3.25	4.00	5.50
1966 U	22,396,500	1.70	2.25	3.25	4.00	5.50
1967 U	17,234,500	1.70	2.25	3.25	4.00	5.50
1968 U	12,325,500	1.70	2.25	3.25	4.00	5.50

KM# 826a KRONA

7.00 g., Copper-Nickel Clad Copper, 25 mm. **Ruler:** Gustaf VI **Obv:** Head left **Rev:** Crowned shield divides value **Edge:** Reeded

Date	Mintage	VF20	XF40	MS60	MS63	MS65
1968 U	5,177,000	—	0.25	0.75	1.50	2.00
1969 U	30,855,500	—	0.25	0.50	1.00	1.25
1970 U	25,314,500	—	0.25	0.50	1.00	1.25
1971 U	18,342,000	—	0.25	0.50	1.00	1.25
1972 U	21,941,000	—	0.25	0.50	1.00	1.25
1973 U	142,000,000	—	0.25	0.50	1.00	1.50

KM# 852 KRONA

7.00 g., Copper-Nickel Clad Copper, 25 mm. **Ruler:** Carl XVI Gustaf **Obv:** Head left **Rev:** Three small crowns within crowned shield

Date	Mintage	VF20	XF40	MS60	MS63	MS65
1976 U	4,320,811	—	—	0.25	0.50	0.75
1977 U	80,477,822	—	—	0.25	0.35	0.50
1978 U	81,407,892	—	—	0.25	0.35	0.50
1979 U	47,450,148	—	—	0.25	0.35	0.50
1980 U	51,694,323	—	—	0.25	0.35	0.50
1981 U	62,078,991	—	—	0.25	0.35	0.50

KM# 852a KRONA

7.00 g., Copper-Nickel, 25 mm. **Ruler:** Carl XVI Gustaf **Obv:** Head left **Rev:** Three small crowns within crowned shield **Edge:** Reeded

Date	Mintage	VF20	XF40	MS60	MS63	MS65
1982 U	24,836,789	—	—	0.25	0.35	0.50
1983 U	23,530,222	—	—	0.25	0.35	0.50
1984 U	37,811,592	—	—	0.25	0.35	0.50
1985 U	4,909,279	—	—	0.25	0.35	0.50
1986 U	901,095	—	0.25	0.75	1.00	1.50
1987 D	21,543,317	—	—	0.25	0.35	0.50
1988 D	30,341,842	—	—	0.25	0.35	0.50
1989 D	55,963,148	—	—	0.25	0.35	0.50
1990 D	54,469,545	—	—	0.25	0.35	0.50
1991 D	34,249,994	—	—	0.25	0.35	0.50
1992 D	16,770,810	—	—	0.25	0.35	0.50
1993 B	407,208	—	0.25	0.75	1.00	1.50
1994 B	567,137	—	0.25	0.75	1.00	1.50
1995 B	499,758	—	0.25	0.75	1.00	1.50
1996 B	323,656	—	0.25	0.75	1.00	1.50
1997 B	25,042,398	—	—	0.25	0.35	0.50
1998 B	39,747,941	—	—	0.25	0.35	0.50
1999 B	55,018,508	—	—	0.25	0.35	0.50
2000 B	104,213,074	—	—	0.25	0.35	0.50

KM# 897 KRONA

6.98 g., Copper-Nickel, 24.9 mm. **Ruler:** Carl XVI Gustaf **Subject:** Millennium **Obv:** Head left **Rev:** Crowned monogram **Edge:** Reeded

Date	Mintage	VF20	XF40	MS60	MS63	MS65
2000	2,978,113	—	—	0.25	0.35	0.50

KM# 761 2 KRONOR

15.00 g., 0.800 Silver 0.3858 oz. ASW, 31 mm. **Ruler:** Oscar II **Obv:** Head left **Obv. Legend:** OSCAR II SVERIGES. **Rev:** Crowned arms with supporters **Edge:** Reeded

Date	Mintage	F12	VF20	XF40	MS60	MS63
1903 EB	64,308	12.00	35.00	125	275	500
1904 EB	175,029	10.00	20.00	85.00	175	350

KM# 773 2 KRONOR

15.00 g., 0.800 Silver 0.3858 oz. ASW, 31 mm. **Ruler:** Oscar II **Obv:** Head left **Rev:** Crowned arms with supporters **Edge:** Reeded

Date	Mintage	F12	VF20	XF40	MS60	MS63
1906 EB	112,468	9.00	15.00	60.00	125	225
1907 EB	300,573	8.50	12.00	50.00	125	225

KM# 776 2 KRONOR

15.00 g., 0.800 Silver 0.3858 oz. ASW, 31 mm. **Ruler:** Oscar II **Subject:** Golden Wedding Anniversary **Obv:** Busts of King Oscar II and Queen Sofia right **Rev:** Crowned arms within order chain **Edge:** Reeded

Date	Mintage	VF20	XF40	MS60	MS63	MS65
1907	250,700	7.50	9.00	12.00	16.00	20.00

KM# 787 2 KRONOR

15.00 g., 0.800 Silver 0.3858 oz. ASW, 31 mm. **Ruler:** Gustaf V **Obv:** Head left **Rev:** Crowned arms within order chain **Edge:** Reeded

Date	Mintage	F12	VF20	XF40	MS60	MS63
1910 W Initial close to date	374,725	7.50	10.00	35.00	75.00	—
1910 W Initial far from date	Inc. above	15.00	45.00	100	250	—
1912 W	156,912	7.50	12.00	40.00	100	—
1913 W	304,616	7.50	10.00	20.00	75.00	—
1914 W	191,905	7.50	12.00	30.00	75.00	—
1915 W	155,965	7.50	10.00	15.00	75.00	—
1922 W	201,821	—	7.50	15.00	25.00	—
1924 W	199,314	—	7.50	13.00	30.00	—
1926 W	221,577	—	7.50	15.00	25.00	—
1928 G	160,319	—	7.50	13.00	35.00	—
1929 G	184,458	—	7.50	12.00	25.00	—
1930 G	178,387	—	7.50	9.00	25.00	—
1931 G	210,576	—	7.50	9.00	12.00	—
1934 G	273,419	—	7.50	9.00	12.00	—
1935 G	211,059	—	7.50	9.00	15.00	—
1936 G	491,296	—	7.50	10.00	12.00	—
1937 G	—	**PF60** 200				
1937 G	129,760	—	7.50	9.00	11.00	—
1938 G	638,970	—	7.50	9.00	11.00	—
1938 G	—	**PF60** 30.00				
1939 G	1,200,329	—	7.50	9.00	11.00	—
1939 G	—	**PF60** 30.00				
1940 G	517,740	—	7.50	9.00	15.00	—
1940 G Serif 4	Inc. above	—	7.50	9.00	11.00	—

KM# 799 2 KRONOR

15.00 g., 0.800 Silver 0.3858 oz. ASW, 31 mm. **Ruler:** Gustaf V **Subject:** 400th Anniversary of Political Liberty **Obv:** Head right within decorative inner circle **Rev:** Crowned shield divides date within decorative inner circle **Edge:** Reeded

Date	Mintage	VF20	XF40	MS60	MS63	MS65
1921 W	264,943	7.50	9.00	12.00	14.00	17.00

KM# 805 2 KRONOR

15.00 g., 0.800 Silver 0.3858 oz. ASW, 31 mm. **Ruler:** Gustaf V **Subject:** 300th Anniversary - Death of Gustaf II Adolf **Obv:** Inscription within square with three small crowns within shield below **Rev:** Laureate bust right **Edge:** Reeded

Date	Mintage	VF20	XF40	MS60	MS63	MS65
1932 G	253,770	7.50	9.00	12.00	14.00	17.00

KM# 807 2 KRONOR

15.00 g., 0.800 Silver 0.3858 oz. ASW, 31 mm. **Ruler:** Gustaf V

Subject: 300th Anniversary - Settlement of Delaware **Obv:** Head left **Rev:** The ship "Calmare Nyckel **Edge:** Reeded

Date	Mintage	VF20	XF40	MS60	MS63	MS65
ND-1938 G	508,815	7.50	9.00	12.00	14.00	17.00

KM# 815 2 KRONOR

14.00 g., 0.400 Silver 0.180 oz. ASW, 31 mm. **Ruler:** Gustaf V **Obv:** Head left **Rev:** Crowned arms divides value **Edge:** Reeded

Date	Mintage	VF20	XF40	MS60	MS63	MS65
1942 G	200,000	5.00	8.00	15.00	25.00	35.00
1943 G	271,824	9.00	10.00	35.00	50.00	65.00
1944 G	627,200	4.50	6.50	10.00	15.00	20.00
1945 G	969,675	4.50	6.00	8.00	12.00	16.00
1945 G	Inc. above	19.00	15.00	50.00	75.00	100
Note: Without dots in motto						
1945 TS	Inc. above	4.50	6.00	8.00	12.00	16.00
1945 TS/G	Inc. above	5.00	8.00	15.00	20.00	25.00
1946 TS	978,000	—	3.50	5.00	7.50	9.00
1947 TS	1,465,975	—	3.50	5.00	7.50	9.00
1948 TS	281,660	4.50	6.50	10.00	12.00	14.00
1949 TS	331,715	4.50	6.50	10.00	12.00	14.00
1950/1 TS	3,727,465	—	3.50	5.00	7.50	9.00
1950 TS	Inc. above	—	3.50	5.00	7.50	9.00

KM# 827 2 KRONOR

14.00 g., 0.400 Silver 0.180 oz. ASW, 31 mm. **Ruler:** Gustaf VI **Obv:** Head left **Rev:** Crowned shield divides value **Edge:** Reeded

Date	Mintage	VF20	XF40	MS60	MS63	MS65
1952 TS	315,325	3.50	6.00	12.00	15.00	18.00
1953 TS	1,009,380	3.50	4.50	7.50	9.00	11.50
1954 TS	2,300,835	3.50	4.50	7.50	9.00	11.50
1955 TS	1,137,734	3.50	4.50	7.50	9.00	11.50
1956 TS	1,709,468	3.50	4.50	7.50	9.00	11.50
1957 TS	688,900	3.50	5.00	10.00	12.00	14.00
1958 TS	1,104,555	3.50	4.50	7.50	9.00	11.50
1959 TS	581,330	3.50	5.00	10.00	12.00	14.00
1961 TS	533,220	3.50	4.50	7.50	9.00	11.50
1963 U	1,468,750	—	3.50	5.00	6.00	7.50
1964 U	1,212,750	—	3.50	5.00	6.00	7.50
1965 U	1,189,500	—	3.50	5.00	6.00	7.50
1966 U	989,250	—	3.50	5.00	6.00	7.50

KM# 827a 2 KRONOR

14.00 g., Copper-Nickel, 31 mm. **Ruler:** Gustaf VI **Obv:** Head left **Rev:** Crowned shield divides value **Edge:** Reeded

Date	Mintage	VF20	XF40	MS60	MS63	MS65
1968 U	1,170,750	—	0.50	1.00	2.50	3.50
1969 U	1,148,250	—	0.50	1.00	2.00	3.00
1970 U	1,159,000	—	0.50	1.00	2.00	3.00
1971 U	1,213,250	—	0.50	1.00	2.00	3.00

KM# 766 5 KRONOR

2.24 g., 0.900 Gold 0.0648 oz. AGW, 16 mm. **Ruler:** Oscar II **Obv:** Head right **Rev:** Value and crowns within wreath

Date	Mintage	F12	VF20	XF40	MS60	MS63
1901 EB	109,186	—	87.00	120	135	200

KM# 797 5 KRONOR

2.24 g., 0.900 Gold 0.0648 oz. AGW, 16 mm. **Ruler:** Gustaf V **Obv:** Head right **Rev:** Value and crowns above sprigs

Date	Mintage	F12	VF20	XF40	MS60	MS63
1920 W	103,000	—	87.00	120	135	200

KM# 806 5 KRONOR

25.10 g., 0.900 Silver 0.7263 oz. ASW, 36 mm. **Ruler:** Gustaf V **Subject:** 500th Anniversary of Riksdag **Obv:** Head left **Rev:** Three small crowns within shield in center of cross design

Date	Mintage	VF20	XF40	MS60	MS63	MS65
ND-1935 G	663,815	14.00	16.00	18.00	22.00	37.00

KM# 828 5 KRONOR

22.88 g., 0.400 Silver 0.2942 oz. ASW, 36 mm. **Ruler:** Gustaf VI **Subject:** 70th Birthday of Gustaf VI Adolf **Obv:** Head left **Rev:** Crowned monogram divides value **Edge:** Plain

Date	Mintage	VF20	XF40	MS60	MS63	MS65
ND-1952 TS	242,241	5.75	7.50	10.00	18.00	32.00

KM# 829 5 KRONOR

18.00 g., 0.400 Silver 0.2315 oz. ASW, 34 mm. **Ruler:** Gustaf VI **Obv:** Head left **Rev:** Crowned shield divides value **Edge Lettering:** PLIKTEN FRAMFOR ALLT **Note:** Regular issue.

Date	Mintage	VF20	XF40	MS60	MS63	MS65
1954 TS	1,510,316	4.50	5.50	7.50	9.00	12.00
1955 TS	3,568,985	4.50	5.50	7.50	9.00	12.00
1971 U	712,500	4.50	5.50	7.50	9.00	12.00

KM# 830 5 KRONOR

18.00 g., 0.400 Silver 0.2315 oz. ASW, 34 mm. **Ruler:** Gustaf VI **Subject:** Constitution Sesquicentennial **Obv:** Head left **Rev:** Standing figures with hats facing

Date	Mintage	VF20	XF40	MS60	MS63	MS65
1959 TS	504,150	4.50	5.50	7.50	9.00	12.00

KM# 838 5 KRONOR

18.00 g., 0.400 Silver 0.2315 oz. ASW, 34 mm. **Ruler:** Gustaf VI **Subject:** 80th Birthday of Gustaf VI Adolf **Obv:** Head left **Rev:** Pallas Athena left holding shield and owl

Date	Mintage	VF20	XF40	MS60	MS63	MS65
ND-1962 U	256,000	4.50	7.50	12.00	17.00	28.00

Note: 96,525 were melted

KM# 839 5 KRONOR

18.00 g., 0.400 Silver 0.2315 oz. ASW, 34 mm. **Ruler:** Gustaf VI **Subject:** 100th Anniversary of Constitution Reform **Obv:** Head left **Rev:** Inscription within square flanked by sprigs **Edge:** Horizontal wavy lines

Date	Mintage	VF20	XF40	MS60	MS63	MS65
1966 U	1,023,500	—	4.50	5.50	7.00	9.00

KM# 846 5 KRONOR

9.50 g., Copper-Nickel Clad Nickel, 28.5 mm. **Ruler:** Gustaf VI **Obv:** Head left **Rev:** Crowned shield divides value

Date	Mintage	VF20	XF40	MS60	MS63	MS65
1972 U	21,736,000	—	0.85	1.00	1.25	1.75
1973 U	1,139,000	—	1.00	2.00	2.50	3.00

KM# 853 5 KRONOR

9.50 g., Copper-Nickel, 28.5 mm. **Ruler:** Carl XVI Gustaf **Obv:** Crowned monogram **Rev:** Value

Date	Mintage	VF20	XF40	MS60	MS63	MS65
1976 U	2,252,923	—	0.85	1.00	1.25	1.75
1977 U	3,985,381	—	0.85	1.00	1.25	1.75
1978 U	3,952,352	—	0.85	1.00	1.25	1.75
1979 U	3,164,051	—	0.85	1.00	1.25	1.75
1980 U	2,221,846	—	0.85	1.00	1.25	1.75
1981 U	5,507,222	—	0.85	1.00	1.25	1.75
1982 U	36,603,696	—	0.85	1.00	1.25	1.75
1983 U	31,364,320	—	0.85	1.00	1.25	1.75
1984 U	27,689,251	—	0.85	1.00	1.25	1.75
1985 U	10,603,060	—	0.85	1.00	1.25	1.75
1986 U	714,132	—	1.00	1.50	2.00	2.50
1987 D	15,117,317	—	0.85	1.00	1.25	1.75
1988 D	18,643,957	—	0.85	1.00	1.25	1.75
1989 D	960,667	—	1.00	1.50	2.00	2.50
1990 D	10,557,882	—	0.85	1.00	1.25	1.75
1991 D	15,792,139	—	0.85	1.00	1.25	1.75
1991 U	Est. 25000	5.00	20.00	35.00	50.00	65.00
1992 D	5,350,810	—	0.85	1.00	1.25	1.75

KM# 853a 5 KRONOR

9.60 g., Copper-Nickel Clad Nickel, 28.5 mm. **Ruler:** Carl XVI Gustaf **Obv:** Crowned monogram **Rev:** Value

Date	Mintage	VF20	XF40	MS60	MS63	MS65
1993 B	274,932	—	1.00	1.25	1.50	2.00

Date	Mintage	VF20	XF40	MS60	MS63	MS65
1994 B	173,438	—	1.00	1.25	1.50	2.00
1995 B	186,687	—	1.00	2.00	2.50	3.00
1996 B	180,405	—	1.00	2.00	2.50	3.00
1997 B	174,455	—	1.00	2.00	2.50	3.00
1998 B	84,991	—	1.50	2.50	3.50	5.00
1999 B	96,035	—	1.50	2.50	3.50	5.00
2000 B	3,851,326	—	—	1.00	1.25	1.50

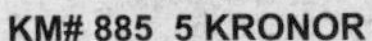

KM# 885 5 KRONOR
9.50 g., Copper-Nickel Clad Nickel, 28.5 mm. **Ruler:** Carl XVI Gustaf **Subject:** 50th Anniversary - United Nations **Obv:** Crowned monogram **Rev:** Numeral 50 and UN emblem

Date	Mintage	VF20	XF40	MS60	MS63	MS65
ND(1995) B	300,000	—	—	1.50	2.25	3.50

KM# 767 10 KRONOR
4.48 g., 0.900 Gold 0.1296 oz. AGW **Ruler:** Oscar II **Obv:** Large head right **Rev:** Crowned and mantled arms

Date	Mintage	F12	VF20	XF40	MS60	MS63
1901 EB	213,286	—	172	200	225	250
1901 EB	Inc. above	PF60 525				

KM# 847 10 KRONOR
18.00 g., 0.830 Silver 0.4803 oz. ASW, 32 mm. **Ruler:** Gustaf VI **Subject:** 90th Birthday of Gustaf VI Adolf **Obv:** Head left **Rev:** Inscription and value

Date	Mintage	VF20	XF40	MS60	MS63	MS65
1972 U	2,000,000	—	9.25	11.00	13.00	15.00

Note: 652,907 were returned to the mint.

KM# 877 10 KRONOR
6.60 g., Copper-Aluminum-Zinc-Tin, 20.5 mm. **Ruler:** Carl XVI Gustaf **Obv:** Head left **Rev:** Three crowns within value **Edge:** Segmented reeding

Date	Mintage	VF20	XF40	MS60	MS63	MS65
1991 D Medal	106,548,000	—	—	1.75	2.00	2.50
1991 D Coin	Inc. above	10.00	15.00	25.00	35.00	45.00
1992 D	42,506,792	—	—	1.75	2.00	2.50
1993 D	20,107,110	—	—	1.75	2.00	2.50
1994 B	573,243	—	1.75	2.50	3.00	3.50
1995 B	523,685	—	1.75	2.50	3.00	3.50
1996 B	295,053	—	1.75	2.50	3.00	3.50
1997 B	332,450	—	1.75	2.50	3.00	3.50
1998 B	332,000	—	1.75	2.50	3.00	3.50
1999 B	81,430	—	2.50	3.00	4.00	5.00
2000 B	8,520,983	—	—	1.75	2.00	2.50

KM# 765 20 KRONOR
8.96 g., 0.900 Gold 0.2593 oz. AGW **Ruler:** Oscar II **Obv:** Head right **Obv. Legend:** OSCAR II SVERIGES. **Rev:** Crowned and mantled arms

Date	Mintage	F12	VF20	XF40	MS60	MS63
1901 EB	226,679	—	—	345	450	500
1902 EB	113,810	—	—	345	450	500

KM# 800 20 KRONOR
8.96 g., 0.900 Gold 0.2593 oz. AGW **Ruler:** Gustaf V **Obv:** Head right **Rev:** Crowned arms within order chain divide value

Date	Mintage	F12	VF20	XF40	MS60	MS63
1925 W	387,257	—	345	450	750	800

KM# 848 50 KRONOR
27.03 g., 0.925 Silver 0.8039 oz. ASW, 36 mm. **Ruler:** Carl XVI Gustaf **Subject:** Constitutional Reform **Obv:** Three crowns above value **Rev:** Flaming torch divides date within cluster of reaching hands, all within inner circle

Date	Mintage	VF20	XF40	MS60	MS63	MS65
1975 U	500,000	—	—	16.00	18.00	20.00

KM# 854 50 KRONOR
27.03 g., 0.925 Silver 0.8039 oz. ASW, 36 mm. **Ruler:** Carl XVI Gustaf **Subject:** Wedding of King Carl XVI Gustaf and Queen Silvia **Obv:** Heads facing **Rev:** Crowned arms with supporters

Date	Mintage	VF20	XF40	MS60	MS63	MS65
ND-1976 U	2,000,000	—	—	16.00	18.00	20.00

KM# 861 100 KRONOR
16.00 g., 0.925 Silver 0.4758 oz. ASW, 32 mm. **Ruler:** Carl XVI Gustaf **Subject:** Parliament **Obv:** Front view of radiant arched building **Rev:** Three crowns within brick designed circle

Date	Mintage	VF20	XF40	MS60	MS63	MS65
1983	400,000	—	—	9.75	14.00	17.00

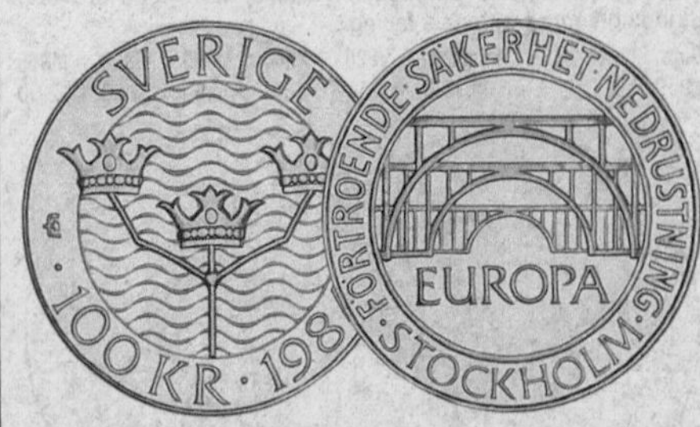

KM# 863 100 KRONOR
16.00 g., 0.925 Silver 0.4758 oz. ASW, 32 mm. **Ruler:** Carl XVI Gustaf **Subject:** Stockholm Conference **Obv:** Three crowns on thin upright branch within waved circle **Rev:** Design and arch within circle

Date	Mintage	VF20	XF40	MS60	MS63	MS65
1984	300,000	—	—	9.75	14.00	17.00

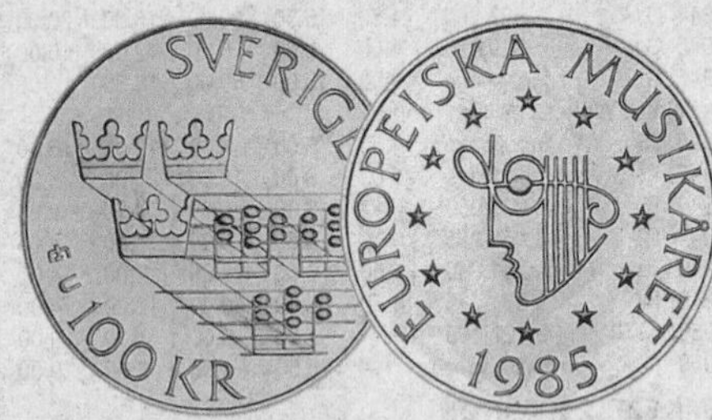

KM# 864 100 KRONOR
16.00 g., 0.925 Silver 0.4758 oz. ASW, 32 mm. **Ruler:** Carl XVI Gustaf **Subject:** International Youth Year **Obv:** Three small crowns within crowned shield **Rev:** Three conjoined lined profiles left within wreath, inner circle surrounds

Date	Mintage	VF20	XF40	MS60	MS63	MS65
1985	120,000	—	—	9.75	14.00	17.00

KM# 865 100 KRONOR
16.00 g., 0.925 Silver 0.4758 oz. ASW, 32 mm. **Ruler:** Carl XVI Gustaf **Subject:** European Music Year **Obv:** Three crowns at upper left of music notes **Rev:** Stylized profile left within circle of stars

Date	Mintage	VF20	XF40	MS60	MS63	MS65
1985	120,000	—	—	9.75	14.00	17.00

KM# 866 100 KRONOR
16.00 g., 0.925 Silver 0.4758 oz. ASW, 32 mm. **Ruler:** Carl XVI Gustaf **Subject:** International Year of the Forest **Obv:** Three crowns on tree ring design **Rev:** Standing figures under tree within circle flanked by small trees

Date	Mintage	VF20	XF40	MS60	MS63	MS65
1985	120,000	—	—	9.75	14.00	17.00

KM# 867.1 100 KRONOR
16.00 g., 0.925 Silver 0.4758 oz. ASW, 32 mm. **Ruler:** Carl XVI Gustaf **Subject:** 350th Anniversary of Swedish Colony in Delaware **Obv:** Large head left **Rev:** Three small crowns, map and ship

Date	Mintage	VF20	XF40	MS60	MS63	MS65
ND-1988	32,000	—	—	9.75	14.00	17.00

KM# 867.2 100 KRONOR
16.00 g., 0.925 Silver 0.4758 oz. ASW, 32 mm. **Ruler:** Carl XVI Gustaf **Subject:** 350th Anniversary of Swedish Colony in Delaware **Obv:** Small head left **Rev:** Three small crowns, map and ship

Date	Mintage	VF20	XF40	MS60	MS63	MS65
ND-1988	118,000	—	—	9.75	14.00	17.00

KM# 860 200 KRONOR
27.03 g., 0.925 Silver 0.8039 oz. ASW, 36 mm. **Ruler:** Carl XVI Gustaf **Subject:** Swedish Royal Succession Law **Obv:** Head left **Rev:** Inscription, date and value

Date	Mintage	VF20	XF40	MS60	MS63	MS65
1980 U Prooflike	500,000	—	—	17.50	28.00	32.00

KM# 862 200 KRONOR
27.03 g., 0.925 Silver 0.8039 oz. ASW, 36 mm. **Ruler:** Carl XVI Gustaf **Subject:** 10th Anniversary of Reign **Obv:** Head left **Rev:** Crowned arms with supporters

Date	Mintage	VF20	XF40	MS60	MS63	MS65
1983	100,000	—	—	17.50	28.00	32.00

KM# 869 200 KRONOR
27.03 g., 0.925 Silver 0.8039 oz. ASW, 36 mm. **Ruler:** Carl XVI Gustaf **Subject:** Ice Hockey **Obv:** Three small crowns within patterned circle **Rev:** Hockey goalie within circle

Date	Mintage	VF20	XF40	MS60	MS63	MS65
1989	80,000	—	—	17.50	28.00	32.00

KM# 875 200 KRONOR
27.03 g., 0.925 Silver 0.8039 oz. ASW, 36 mm. **Ruler:** Carl XVI Gustaf **Subject:** Warship - Vasa **Obv:** Head left **Rev:** Ship

Date	Mintage	VF20	XF40	MS60	MS63	MS65
1990	50,000	—	—	17.50	28.00	32.00

KM# 879 200 KRONOR
27.03 g., 0.925 Silver 0.8039 oz. ASW, 36 mm. **Ruler:** Carl XVI Gustaf **Subject:** 200th Anniversary - Death of Gustaf III **Obv:** Three small crowns within mantle **Rev:** Head right

Date	Mintage	VF20	XF40	MS60	MS63	MS65
ND-1992	50,000	—	—	17.50	28.00	32.00

KM# 881 200 KRONOR
27.03 g., 0.925 Silver 0.8039 oz. ASW, 36 mm. **Ruler:** Carl XVI Gustaf **Subject:** 20th Anniversary of Reign **Obv:** Head left **Rev:** Crown

Date	Mintage	VF20	XF40	MS60	MS63	MS65
1993	50,000	—	—	17.50	28.00	32.00

KM# 882 200 KRONOR
27.03 g., 0.925 Silver 0.8039 oz. ASW, 36 mm. **Ruler:** Carl XVI Gustaf **Subject:** 50th Birthday of Queen Silvia **Obv:** Crowned head right **Rev:** Crowned arms with supporters

Date	Mintage	VF20	XF40	MS60	MS63	MS65
ND-1993	49,000	—	—	17.50	28.00	32.00
ND-1993 Prooflike	1,000	—	—	—	—	45.00

KM# 886 200 KRONOR
27.03 g., 0.925 Silver 0.8039 oz. ASW, 36 mm. **Ruler:** Carl XVI Gustaf **Subject:** 1000th Anniversary - Swedish Coinage **Obv:** Head left **Rev:** Coin designs within circle

Date	Mintage	VF20	XF40	MS60	MS63	MS65
ND-1995	49,000	—	—	18.00	28.00	32.00
ND-1995 Prooflike	1,000	—	—	—	—	75.00

KM# 888 200 KRONOR
27.03 g., 0.925 Silver 0.8039 oz. ASW, 36 mm. **Ruler:** Carl XVI Gustaf **Subject:** 50th Birthday - King Carl XVI Gustaf **Obv:** Head left **Rev:** Crowned arms with supporters

Date	Mintage	VF20	XF40	MS60	MS63	MS65
ND-1996	49,000	—	—	17.50	28.00	32.00
ND-1996 Prooflike	1,000	—	—	—	—	45.00

KM# 890 200 KRONOR
27.03 g., 0.925 Silver 0.8039 oz. ASW **Ruler:** Carl XVI Gustaf **Subject:** Kalmar Union **Obv:** Head left **Rev:** Queen Margareta's head left and castle

Date	Mintage	VF20	XF40	MS60	MS63	MS65
1997	50,000	—	—	17.50	28.00	32.00

KM# 892 200 KRONOR
27.03 g., 0.925 Silver 0.8039 oz. ASW, 36 mm. **Ruler:** Carl XVI Gustaf **Subject:** 25th Anniversary - Reign of Carl XVI Gustaf **Obv:** Head 1/4 left **Rev:** Crown above sceptre, crowned monogram and orb

Date	Mintage	VF20	XF40	MS60	MS63	MS65
1998 B-E	49,000	—	—	17.50	28.00	32.00
1998 B-E Prooflike	1,000	—	—	—	—	45.00

KM# 898 200 KRONOR
27.03 g., 0.925 Silver 0.8039 oz. ASW, 36 mm. **Ruler:** Carl XVI Gustaf **Subject:** Millennium **Obv:** Conjoined heads of King Carl XVI Gustaf and Crown Princess Victoria left **Rev:** Crowned and mantled arms **Edge:** Plain

Date	Mintage	VF20	XF40	MS60	MS63	MS65
1999 B-E	68,000	—	—	17.50	28.00	32.00
1999 B-E Prooflike	2,000	—	—	—	—	45.00

KM# 868 1000 KRONOR
5.80 g., 0.900 Gold 0.1678 oz. AGW, 21 mm. **Ruler:** Carl XVI Gustaf **Subject:** 350th Anniversary of Swedish Colony in Delaware **Obv:** Head left **Rev:** Ship at sea

Date	Mintage	VF20	XF40	MS60	MS63	MS65
ND-1988 D-E	10,000	—	225	300	350	375

KM# 870 1000 KRONOR
5.80 g., 0.900 Gold 0.1678 oz. AGW, 21 mm. **Ruler:** Carl XVI Gustaf **Subject:** Ice Hockey **Obv:** Three small crowns within designed circle **Rev:** Hockey goalie within circle

Date	Mintage	VF20	XF40	MS60	MS63	MS65
1989 D-E	20,000	—	225	300	340	350

KM# 876 1000 KRONOR
5.80 g., 0.900 Gold 0.1678 oz. AGW, 21 mm. **Ruler:** Carl XVI Gustaf **Subject:** The Vasa - Arms **Obv:** Head left **Rev:** The Vasa - Arms

Date	Mintage	VF20	XF40	MS60	MS63	MS65
1990 D-E	15,000	—	225	300	350	375

KM# 880 1000 KRONOR
5.80 g., 0.900 Gold 0.1678 oz. AGW, 21 mm. **Ruler:** Carl XVI Gustaf **Subject:** 200th Anniversary - Death of Gustaf III **Obv:** Crowned arms within order chain **Rev:** Head right

Date	Mintage	VF20	XF40	MS60	MS63	MS65
ND-1992	15,000	—	225	300	350	375

KM# 883 1000 KRONOR
5.80 g., 0.900 Gold 0.1678 oz. AGW, 21 mm. **Ruler:** Carl XVI Gustaf **Subject:** 20th Anniversary of Reign **Obv:** Head left **Rev:** Crown

Date	Mintage	VF20	XF40	MS60	MS63	MS65
1993	15,000	—	225	300	350	375

KM# 884 1000 KRONOR
5.80 g., 0.900 Gold 0.1678 oz. AGW, 21 mm. **Ruler:** Carl XVI Gustaf **Subject:** 50th Birthday of Queen Silvia **Obv:** Crowned head right **Rev:** Crowned arms with supporters

Date	Mintage	VF20	XF40	MS60	MS63	MS65
ND-1993	14,000	—	225	300	350	375
ND-1993 Prooflike	1,000	—	—	—	—	400

KM# 887 1000 KRONOR
5.80 g., 0.900 Gold 0.1678 oz. AGW, 21 mm. **Ruler:** Carl XVI Gustaf **Subject:** 100th Anniversary - Swedish Coinage **Obv:** Head left **Rev:** Coin designs within circle

Date	Mintage	VF20	XF40	MS60	MS63	MS65
ND-1995	14,000	—	225	300	350	375
ND-1995 Prooflike	1,000	—	—	—	—	400

KM# 889 1000 KRONOR
5.80 g., 0.900 Gold 0.1678 oz. AGW, 21 mm. **Ruler:** Carl XVI Gustaf **Subject:** 50th Birthday - King Carl XVI Gustaf **Obv:** Head left **Rev:** Crowned arms with supporters

Date	Mintage	VF20	XF40	MS60	MS63	MS65
ND-1996	14,000	—	225	300	350	375
ND-1996 Prooflike	1,000	—	—	—	—	400

KM# 891 1000 KRONOR
5.80 g., 0.900 Gold 0.1678 oz. AGW, 21 mm. **Ruler:** Carl XVI Gustaf **Subject:** Kalmar Union - Queen Margareta **Obv:** Head left **Rev:** Crowned head left and shield

Date	Mintage	VF20	XF40	MS60	MS63	MS65
1997	15,000	—	225	300	350	375

KM# 893 1000 KRONOR
5.80 g., 0.900 Gold 0.1678 oz. AGW, 21 mm. **Ruler:** Carl XVI Gustaf **Subject:** 25th Anniversary - Reign of King Carl XVI Gustaf **Obv:** Head 1/4 left **Rev:** Crown above sceptre, crowned monogram and orb

Date	Mintage	VF20	XF40	MS60	MS63	MS65
1998	14,000	—	225	300	350	375
1998 Prooflike	1,000	—	—	—	—	385

KM# 899 2000 KRONOR
13.00 g., 0.900 Gold 0.3762 oz. AGW, 26 mm. **Ruler:** Carl XVI Gustaf **Subject:** Millennium **Obv:** Conjoined heads of King Carl XVI Gustaf and Crown Princess Victoria left **Rev:** Crowned mantled arms **Edge:** Plain

Date	Mintage	VF20	XF40	MS60	MS63	MS65
1999	7,820	—	530	625	675	725
1999 Prooflike	2,000	—	—	—	—	750

PATTERNS

Including off metal strikes

KM#	Date	Mintage	Identification	Mkt Val
Pn99	1901	—	2 Öre. Iron. KM#716.	—
Pn100	1901	—	5 Kronor. Bronze. KM#766.	—
Pn101	1909	—	2 Öre. Bronze. Flat-based 2.	—
Pn102	1909	—	5 Öre. Bronze. Flat-based 5.	—
Pn103	1913	—	2 Kronor. Bronze. KM#787.	—
Pn104	1916	—	Öre. Iron. KM#777.2.	—
Pn105	1916	—	2 Öre. Iron. KM#778.	—
Pn106	1916	—	5 Öre. Iron. KM#779.2.	—
Pn107	1918 W	—	10 Öre. Iron. Center hole.	650
Pn108	1918 W	—	25 Öre. Iron. Center hole.	—
Pn109	1918 W	—	25 Öre. Silver. Center hole.	—
Pn110	1918 W	—	50 Öre. Iron. Center hole.	—
Pn111	1918 W	—	50 Öre. Silver. Center hole.	—
Pn112	1918 W	—	Krona. Iron. Center hole.	—
Pn113	1918 W	—	Krona. Nickel. Center hole.	—
Pn114	1918 W	—	Krona. Silver. Center hole.	—
Pn115	1918	—	5 Kronor. Nickel. KM#797.	—
Pn116	1919	—	Öre. Bronze. Center hole.	—
Pn117	1919	—	5 Öre. Iron. Center hole.	—
Pn118	1919	—	5 Öre. Bronze. Center hole.	—
Pn119	1919	—	10 Öre. Nickel. KM#780.	—
Pn120	1919	—	2 Kronor. Bronze. KM#787.	—
Pn121	1920	—	2 Öre. Bronze. Copper hole.	—
Pn122	1920	—	5 Öre. Bronze. Center hole.	—
Pn123	1920 W	—	50 Öre. Silver.	—
Pn124	1921	—	2 Kronor. Bronze. KM#787.	—
Pn125	1949	—	5 Öre. Bronze. PROV.	—
PnA126	1949	—	50 Öre. Aluminum. PROV.	—
Pn126	1950	—	Öre. Copper Plated Iron. KM#810.	—
Pn127	1950	—	Öre. Copper Plated Iron. PROV.	—
Pn128	1950	—	2 Öre. Copper Plated Iron. KM#811.	—
Pn129	1950	—	2 Öre. Copper Plated Iron. PROV.	—
Pn130	1950	—	5 Öre. Tombac Plated Iron. KM#812.	—
Pn131	1950	—	5 Öre. Copper Plated Iron. PROV.	—
Pn132	1950	—	10 Öre. Nickel Plated Iron. PROV.	—
Pn133	1950	—	25 Öre. Nickel Plated Iron. PROV.	—
Pn134	1951	—	2 Öre. Bronze. PROV.	—
Pn135	1951	—	2 Öre. Iron. PROV.	—
Pn136	1951	—	50 Öre. Silver. PROV.	—
Pn137	1951	—	Krona. Silver. Plain. PROV.	—
Pn138	1951	—	Krona. Silver. Reeded. PROV.	—
Pn139	1951 TS	—	Krona. Silver. PROV.	—
Pn140	1951 TS	—	5 Kronor. Silver. PROV.	—
Pn141	1952 TS	—	5 Öre. Bronze. PROV.	—
Pn142	1952 TS	—	10 Öre. Silver. PROV.	—
Pn143	1952 TS	—	10 Öre. Copper-Nickel. PROV.	—
Pn144	1952 TS	—	10 Öre. Silver. PROV.	—
Pn145	1952 TS	—	25 Öre. Silver. PROV.	—
Pn146	1952 TS	—	50 Öre. Silver. "PROV", high relief.	—
Pn147	1952 TS	—	50 Öre. Silver. "PROV", low relief.	950
Pn148	1952 TS	—	Krona. Silver. PROV.	—
Pn149	1952 TS	—	Krona. Silver. PROV"; different head.	—
Pn150	1952 TS	—	5 Kronor. Silver. Plain. PROV.	—
Pn151	1952 TS	—	5 Kronor. Silver. Reeded. PROV.	—
Pn152	1953 TS	—	5 Kronor. Silver. Plain. PROV.	—
Pn153	1953 TS	—	5 Kronor. Silver. Reeded. PROV.	—
Pn154	1953 TS	—	5 Kronor. Silver. "PROV"; small value.	—
Pn155	1953 TS	—	5 Kronor. Silver. "PROV"; large value.	—
Pn156	1954 TS	—	5 Kronor. Silver. PROV.	—
Pn157	1970 U	—	Öre. Iron. KM#820.	200

MINT SETS

KM#	Date	Mintage	Identification	Issue Price	Mkt Val
MS1	1973 (6)	20,000	KM#826a, 835-837, 845, 846	5.00	22.50
MS2	1976 (6)	61,234	KM#849-853, 855 Swedish - soft plastic case	5.00	11.00
MS3	1976 (6)	10,000	KM#849-853, 855 English - soft plastic case	5.00	11.00
MS4	1977 (6)	43,346	KM#849-853, 855 Swedish - soft plastic case	5.00	12.00
MS5	1977 (6)	5,800	KM#849-853, 855 English - soft plastic case	5.00	13.50
MS6	1978 (6)	20,115	KM#849-853, 855 Swedish - soft plastic case	5.00	20.00
MS7	1978 (6)	1,500	KM#849-853, 855 English - soft plastic case	5.00	22.50
MS8	1978 (6)	31,245	KM#849-853, 855 Swedish - soft plastic case	5.00	27.50
MS9	1979 (6)	10,200	KM#849-853, 855 Swedish - soft plastic case	5.00	12.00
MS10	1979 (6)	1,900	KM#849-853, 855 English - soft plastic case	5.00	17.50
MS11	1979 (6)	38,957	KM#849-853, 855 Swedish - soft plastic case	5.00	16.50
MS12	1979 (6)	9,871	KM#849-853, 855 English - soft plastic case	5.00	25.00
MS13	1980 (6)	10,140	KM#849-853, 855 Swedish - soft plastic case	5.00	12.00
MS14	1980 (6)	2,000	KM#849-853, 855 English - soft plastic case	5.00	17.50
MS15	1980 (6)	45,495	KM#849-853, 855 Swedish - soft plastic case	5.50	15.00
MS16	1980 (6)	9,880	KM#849-853, 855 English - soft plastic case	5.50	25.00
MS17	1981 (6)	11,927	KM#849a, 850-853, 855 Swedish - soft plastic case	5.50	12.00
MS18	1981 (6)	2,000	KM#849a, 850-853, 855 English - soft plastic case	5.50	17.50
MS19	1981 (6)	65,338	KM#849a, 850-853, 855 Swedish - hard plastic case	5.50	10.00
MS20	1981 (6)	5,000	KM#849a, 850-853, 855 English - hard plastic case	5.50	30.00
MS21	1982 (5)	9,463	KM#849a, 850-851, 852a, 853 Swedish - soft plastic case	5.50	12.00
MS22	1982 (5)	2,300	KM#849a, 850-851, 852a, 853 English - soft plastic case	5.50	13.50
MS23	1982 (5)	58,772	KM#849a, 850-851, 852a, 853 Swedish - hard plastic case	5.50	10.00
MS24	1982 (5)	4,978	KM#849a, 850-851, 852a, 853 Swedish - hard plastic case	5.50	30.00

MS25	1983 (5)	10,300	KM#849a, 850-851, 852a, 853 Swedish - soft plastic case	6.00	12.00
MS26	1983 (6)	2,750	KM#849a, 850-851, 852a, 853 English - soft plastic case	6.00	13.50
MS27	1983 (6)	57,205	KM#849a, 850-851, 852a, 853 Swedish - hard plastic case	6.00	10.00
MS28	1983 (6)	5,017	KM#849a, 850-851, 852a, 853 English - hard plastic case	6.00	30.00
MS29	1984 (6)	10,100	KM#849a, 850-851, 852a, 853, 855 Swedish - soft plastic case	6.00	10.00
MS30	1984 (6)	1,600	KM#849a, 850-851, 852a, 853, 855 English - soft plastic case	6.00	22.50
MS31	1984 (6)	70,849	KM#849a, 850-851, 852a, 853, 855 Swedish - hard plastic case	6.00	10.00
MS32	1984 (6)	4,271	KM#849a, 850-851, 852a, 853, 855 English - hard plastic case	6.00	35.00
MS33	1985 (4)	8,000	KM#850, 852a, 853, 855 Swedish - soft plastic case	6.50	11.50
MS34	1985 (4)	1,445	KM#850, 852a, 853, 855 English - soft plastic case	6.50	22.50
MS35	1985 (4)	52,462	KM#850, 852a, 853, 855 Swedish - hard plastic case	6.50	10.00
MS36	1985 (4)	2,717	KM#850, 852a, 853, 855 English - hard plastic case	6.50	45.00
MS37	1986 (4)	16,265	KM#850, 852a, 853, 855 Swedish - soft plastic case	6.50	16.50
MS38	1986 (4)	1,880	KM#850, 852a, 853, 855 English - soft plastic case	6.50	22.50
MS39	1986 (4)	54,890	KM#850, 852a, 853, 855 Swedish - hard plastic case	6.50	20.00
MS40	1986 (4)	967	KM#850, 852a, 853, 855 English - hard plastic case	6.50	100
MS41	1987 (4)	5,600	KM#850, 852a, 853, 855 Swedish - soft plastic case	6.50	10.00
MS42	1987 (4)	1,100	KM#850, 852a, 853, 855 English - soft plastic case	6.55	25.00
MS43	1987 (4)	70,060	KM#850, 852a, 853, 855 Swedish - hard plastic case	6.50	10.00
MS44	1987 (4)	557	KM#850, 852a, 853, 855 Swedish and English - hard plastic case	6.50	200
MS45	1988 (4)	4,815	KM#850, 852a, 853, 855 Swedish - soft plastic case	6.50	15.00
MS46	1988 (4)	2,456	KM#850, 852a, 853, 855 English - soft plastic case	6.50	16.50
MS47	1988 (4)	56,753	KM#850, 852a, 853, 855 Swedish - hard plastic case	6.50	15.00
MS48	1988 (4)	1,777	KM#850, 852a, 853, 855 English - hard plastic case	6.50	47.50
MS49	1989 (4)	7,170	KM#850, 852a, 853, 855 Swedish - soft plastic case	6.50	16.00
MS50	1989 (4)	56,895	KM#850, 852a, 853, 855 Swedish - hard plastic case	6.50	15.00
MS51	1989 (4)	2,780	KM#850, 852a, 853, 855 English - hard plastic case	—	17.50
MS52	1989 (4)	1,000	KM#850, 852a, 853, 855 English - hard plastic case	—	32.50
MS53	1990 (4)	6,503	KM#850, 852a, 853, 855 Swedish - soft plastic case	6.50	12.50
MS54	1990 (4)	55,265	KM#850, 852a, 853, 855 Swedish - hard plastic case	6.50	13.50
MS55	1990 (4)	2,440	KM#850, 852a, 853, 855 English - hard plastic case	—	13.50
MS56	1990 (4)	2,492	KM#850, 852a, 853, 855 English - hard plastic case	—	11.50
MS57	1991 (5)	8,079	KM#850, 852a, 853, 855, 877 Swedish - soft plastic case	—	17.50
MS58	1991 (5)	1,680	KM#850, 852a, 853, 855, 877 English - soft plastic case	—	17.50
MS59	1991 (5)	62,517	KM#850, 852a, 853, 855, 877 Swedish - hard plastic case	—	18.50
MS60	1991 (5)	2,884	KM#850, 852a, 853, 855, 877 English - hard plastic case	—	20.00
MS61	1991 (5)	5,000	KM#850 (3), 855 (2), medal	—	12.00
MS62	1992 (4)	5,600	KM#852a, 853, 877-878 Swedish - soft plastic case	6.50	11.50
MS63	1992 (4)	1,840	KM#852a, 853, 877-878 English - soft plastic case	6.50	11.50
MS64	1992 (4)	61,183	KM#852a, 853, 877-878 Swedish - hard plastic case	6.50	11.00
MS65	1992 (4)	2,187	KM#852a, 853, 877-878 English - hard plastic case	6.50	13.50
MS66	1993 (4)	4,784	KM#852a, 853a, 877, 878 Swedish - soft plastic case	6.50	16.50
MS67	1993 (4)	2,016	KM#852a, 853a, 877, 878 English - soft plastic case	6.50	11.00
MS68	1993 (4)	57,700	KM#852a, 853a, 877, 878 Swedish - hard plastic case	6.50	16.50
MS69	1993 (4)	2,164	KM#852a, 853a, 877, 878 English - hard plastic case	6.50	17.50
MS70	1993 (4)	4,956	KM#852a, 853a, 877, 878 Souvenir folder	—	22.50
MS71	1994 (4)	5,360	KM#852a, 853a, 877, 878 Swedish - soft plastic case	—	16.50
MS72	1994 (4)	2,240	KM#852a, 853a, 877, 878 English - soft plastic case	—	15.00
MS73	1994 (4)	48,881	KM#852a, 853a, 877, 878, mint medal Swedish - hard plastic case	—	16.50
MS74	1994 (4)	1,966	KM#852a, 853a, 877, 878, mint medal English - hard plastic case	—	17.50
MS75	1994 (4)	9,950	KM#852a, 853a, 877, 878, mint medal Souvenir folder	—	13.50
MS76	1995 (5)	10,000	KM#852a, 853a, 877, 878, 885 Swedish - soft plastic case	14.00	32.50
MS77	1995 (4)	45,836	KM#852a, 877, 878, 885, medal Swedish - hard plastic case	20.00	16.50
MS78	1995 (5)	4,650	KM#852a, 853a, 877, 878, 885 English - soft plastic case	—	15.00
MS79	1995 (4)	2,479	KM#852a, 853a, 877, 878, 885, medal English - hard plastic case	—	18.50
MS80	1995 (4)	5,000	KM#852a, 877, 878, 885, medal Souvenir folder	—	32.50
MS81	1996 (4)	42,729	KM#852a, 853a, 877, 878 Swedish - hard plastic case	11.05	13.50
MS82	1996 (4)	2,000	KM#852a, 853a, 877, 878 English - hard plastic case	11.05	16.50
MS83	1996 (4)	7,100	KM#852a, 853a, 877, 878 Swedish - soft plastic case	7.55	11.50
MS84	1996 (4)	2,500	KM#852a, 853a, 877, 878 English - soft plastic case	7.55	12.50
MS85	1996 (4)	5,481	KM#852a, 853a, 877, 878 Souvenir folder	11.05	14.50
MS86	1997 (4)	39,470	KM#852a, 853a, 877, 878 Swedish - hard plastic case	11.05	18.50
MS87	1997 (4)	1,997	KM#852a, 853a, 877, 878 English - hard plastic case	11.05	22.50
MS88	1997 (4)	5,100	KM#852a, 853a, 877, 878 Swedish - soft plastic case	7.55	15.00
MS89	1997 (4)	2,200	KM#852a, 853a, 877, 878 English - soft plastic case	7.55	16.50
MS90	1997 (4)	4,954	KM#852a, 853a, 877, 878 Souvenir folder	11.05	16.50
MS91	1998 (4)	7,067	KM#852a, 853a, 877, 878 Souvenir folder	13.34	13.50
MS92	1998 (4)	5,170	KM#852a, 853a, 877, 878 Swedish - soft plastic case	—	15.00
MS93	1998 (4)	2,000	KM#852a, 853a, 877, 878 English - soft plastic case	—	16.50
MS94	1998 (4)	34,750	KM#852a, 853a, 877, 878 Swedish - hard plastic case	—	18.50
MS95	1998 (4)	1,980	KM#852a, 853a, 877, 878 English - hard plastic case	—	20.00
MS96	1999 (4)	4,480	KM#852a, 853a, 877, 878 Swedish - hard plastic case	—	11.50
MS97	1999 (4)	2,080	KM#852a, 853a, 877, 878 English - soft plastic case	—	12.50
MS98	1999 (4)	33,334	KM#852a, 853a, 877, 878 Swedish - hard plastic case	—	16.50
MS99	1999 (4)	1,970	KM#852a, 853a, 877, 878 English - hard plastic case	—	17.50
MS100	1999 (4)	8,045	KM#852a, 853a, 877, 878 Souvenir folder	—	13.50
MS101	2000 (4)	5,000	KM#852a, 853a, 877, 878 Swedish - hard plastic case	—	8.00
MS102	2000 (4)	1,000	KM#852a, 853a, 877, 878 English - soft plastic case	—	8.00
MS103	2000 (4)	30,912	KM#852a, 853a, 877, 878 Swedish - hard plastic case	—	13.50
MS104	2000 (4)	1,801	KM#852a, 853a, 877, 878 English - hard plastic case	—	13.50
MS105	2000 (4)	7,209	KM#852a, 853a, 877, 878 Souvenir folder	—	13.50
MS106	2000 (4)	14,300	KM#852a, 853a, 877, 878 Special Millennium set	—	20.00

PROOF-LIKE SETS (PL)

KM#	Date	Mintage	Identification	Issue Price	Mkt Val
PL1	1993 (2)	1,000	KM#882, 884	—	475
PL2	1995 (2)	1,000	KM#886, 887	—	450
PL3	ND(1996) (2)	1,000	KM#888, 889	—	450
PL4	1999 (2)	2,000	KM#898-899	—	795

The Swiss Confederation, located in central Europe north of Italy and south of Germany, has an area of 15,941 sq. mi. (41,290 sq. km.) and a population of *6.6 million. Capital: Bern. The economy centers about a well developed manufacturing industry. Machinery, chemicals, watches and clocks, and textiles are exported.

Switzerland, the habitat of lake dwellers in prehistoric times, was peopled by the Celtic Helvetians when Julius Caesar made it a part of the Roman Empire in 58 B.C. After the decline of Rome, Switzerland was invaded by Teutonic tribes, who established small temporal holdings which in the Middle Ages, became a federation of fiefs of the Holy Roman Empire. As a nation, Switzerland originated in 1291 when the districts of Nidwalden, Schwyz and Uri united to defeat Austria and attain independence as the Swiss Confederation. After acquiring new cantons in the 14th century, Switzerland was made independent from the Holy Roman Empire by the 1648 Treaty of Westphalia. The revolutionary armies of Napoleonic France occupied Switzerland and set up the Helvetian Republic, 1798-1803. After the fall of Napoleon, the Congress of Vienna, 1815, recognized the independence of Switzerland and guaranteed its neutrality. The Swiss Constitutions of 1848 and 1874 established a union modeled upon that of the United States.

MINT MARKS

B - Bern
BA - Basel
BB - Strasbourg
S – Solothurn

NOTE: The coinage of Switzerland has been struck at the Bern Mint since 1853 with a few exceptions. All coins minted there carry a B mint mark through 1969, and from 1986 to date. All Swiss coins minted from 1970 through 1985 were also struck by the Bern Mint but without the B mint mark. The 1968 and 1969 coins without the B mint mark were struck by the British Royal Mint in London. The two exceptions to the foregoing are: Some of the 1969 1 Franc coins with the B mint mark and some of the 1970 ½ Franc coins without the B mint mark were struck by the British Royal Mint in London.

NOTE: The Swiss Shooting Fest coins, KM#S18-S68 previously listed here are actually medallic issues without legal tender status and as such are now listed in *Unusual World Coins, 6th Edition*, by Krause Publications.

CONFEDERATION

DECIMAL COINAGE

KM# 3.2 RAPPEN

1.50 g., Bronze, 16 mm. **Obv:** Thin cross in shield within sprigs **Rev:** Value within wreath

Date	Mintage	VF20	XF40	MS60	MS63	MS65
1902 B	950,000	65.00	125	150	225	350
1903 B	1,000,000	35.00	55.00	85.00	115	160
1904 B	1,000,000	35.00	55.00	75.00	100	145

Date	Mintage	VF20	XF40	MS60	MS63	MS65
1905 B	2,000,000	12.00	18.00	24.00	30.00	45.00
1906 B	1,000,000	30.00	45.00	65.00	90.00	145
1907 B	2,000,000	9.00	12.50	24.00	32.00	45.00
1908 B	3,000,000	7.50	10.00	15.00	20.00	32.00
1909 B	1,000,000	20.00	27.00	36.00	48.00	70.00
1910 B	1,500,000	15.00	20.00	27.00	36.00	56.00
1911 B	1,500,000	15.00	20.00	27.00	36.00	56.00
1912 B	2,000,000	8.50	10.00	15.00	20.00	36.00
1913 B	3,000,000	3.00	5.00	6.00	9.00	20.00
1914 B	3,500,000	4.50	9.50	18.00	24.00	48.00
1915 B	3,000,000	6.00	11.00	27.00	36.00	60.00
1917 B	2,000,000	8.50	16.00	21.00	28.00	52.00
1918 B	3,000,000	3.00	5.00	12.00	16.00	44.00
1919 B	3,000,000	3.50	6.00	12.00	16.00	36.00
1920 B	1,000,000	8.00	12.00	15.00	20.00	32.00
1921 B	3,000,000	4.00	5.50	15.00	20.00	36.00
1924 B	2,000,000	8.00	15.00	21.00	28.00	44.00
1925/4 B	incl below	8.00	20.00	30.00	45.00	60.00
1925 B	2,500,000	4.50	9.00	12.00	16.00	28.00
1926 B	2,000,000	4.50	9.00	18.00	24.00	32.00
1927 B	1,500,000	9.00	13.00	18.00	24.00	36.00
1928 B	2,000,000	5.00	7.50	13.00	20.00	36.00
1929 B	4,000,000	1.25	2.00	6.00	8.00	16.00
1930 B	2,500,000	3.50	6.50	18.00	24.00	32.00
1931 B	5,000,000	1.00	1.50	6.00	8.00	16.00
1932 B	5,000,000	1.00	1.50	6.00	8.00	16.00
1933 B	3,000,000	1.50	3.00	9.00	12.00	24.00
1934 B	3,000,000	1.50	2.50	9.00	12.00	24.00
1936 B	2,000,000	3.50	8.00	12.00	16.00	28.00
1937 B	2,400,000	1.50	2.50	6.00	8.00	12.00
1938 B	5,300,000	1.50	2.50	6.00	8.00	12.00
1939 B	10,000	40.00	45.00	50.00	70.00	105
1940 B	3,027,000	4.00	5.00	9.00	12.00	28.00
1941 B	12,794,000	0.50	1.00	3.00	5.00	8.00

KM# 3a RAPPEN

1.20 g., Zinc, 16 mm. **Obv:** Cross in shield **Rev:** Value within wreath

Date	Mintage	VF20	XF40	MS60	MS63	MS65
1942 B	17,969,000	0.75	2.50	7.00	9.50	20.00
1943 B	8,647,000	2.00	5.00	9.00	12.00	28.00
1944 B	11,825,000	0.75	3.00	7.00	9.50	20.00
1945 B	2,800,000	10.00	18.00	24.00	32.00	65.00
1946 B	12,063,000	0.75	2.50	6.00	8.00	20.00

KM# 46 RAPPEN

1.50 g., Bronze, 16 mm. **Obv:** Cross **Rev:** Value and oat sprig **Edge:** Plain

Date	Mintage	VF20	XF40	MS60	MS63	MS65
1948 B	10,500,000	0.25	0.35	2.00	4.00	20.00
1949 B	11,100,000	0.25	0.35	2.00	4.00	20.00
1950 B	3,610,000	1.25	2.50	4.00	8.00	24.00
1951 B	22,624,000	0.20	0.30	2.00	4.00	16.00
1952 B	11,520,000	0.20	0.30	3.00	5.50	20.00
1953 B	5,947,000	0.25	0.60	6.00	12.00	40.00
1954 B	5,175,000	0.25	0.60	2.00	4.00	16.00
1955 B	5,282,000	0.55	1.00	2.00	4.00	16.00
1956 B	4,960,000	0.25	0.60	2.00	4.00	14.00
1957 B	15,226,000	0.10	0.25	1.00	2.00	8.00
1958 B	20,142,000	0.10	0.25	1.00	2.00	6.50
1959 B	5,582,000	0.20	0.35	1.00	2.00	6.50
1962 B	5,010,000	0.20	0.35	1.00	2.00	6.50
1963 B	15,920,000	—	0.15	0.50	1.00	2.00
1966 B	5,030,000	—	0.20	0.50	1.00	2.00
1967 B	3,020,000	—	0.30	0.50	1.00	2.00
1968 B	4,920,000	—	0.20	0.50	1.00	2.00
1969 B	4,810,000	—	0.15	0.25	0.50	1.00
1970	7,810,000	—	0.10	0.25	0.50	1.00
1971	5,030,000	—	0.10	0.25	0.50	1.00
1973	3,000,000	—	0.10	0.25	0.50	1.00
1974	3,005,000	—	0.10	0.25	0.50	1.00
1974	2,400	PF65 35.00				
1975	3,000,000	—	0.10	0.25	0.50	1.00
1975	10,000	PF65 2.50				
1976	3,000,000	—	0.10	0.25	0.50	1.00
1976	5,130	PF65 3.00				
1977	2,000,000	—	0.10	0.25	0.50	1.00
1977	7,030	PF65 3.00				
1978	2,000,000	—	0.10	0.25	0.50	1.00
1978	10,000	PF65 2.50				
1979	1,015,000	—	0.10	0.25	0.50	1.00
1979	10,000	PF65 2.50				
1980	1,030,000	—	0.10	0.25	0.50	1.00
1980	10,000	PF65 2.50				
1981	4,935,000	—	0.10	0.25	0.50	1.00
1981	10,000	PF65 2.50				
1982	6,655,000	—	0.10	0.25	0.50	1.00
1982	10,000	PF65 2.50				
1983	4,031,000	—	0.10	0.25	0.50	1.00
1983	11,000	PF65 2.50				
1984	3,995,000	—	0.10	0.25	0.50	1.00
1984	14,000	PF65 2.50				
1985	3,027,000	—	0.10	0.25	0.50	1.00
1985	12,000	PF65 2.50				
1986 B	2,021,400	—	0.10	0.25	0.50	1.00
1986 B	10,000	PF65 2.50				
1987 B	1,019,100	—	0.10	0.25	0.50	1.00
1987 B	8,800	PF65 3.00				
1988 B	2,020,700	—	0.10	0.25	0.50	1.00
1988 B	9,050	PF65 3.00				
1989 B	2,022,700	—	0.10	0.25	0.50	1.00
1989 B	8,800	PF65 3.00				
1990 B	1,023,100	—	—	0.25	0.50	1.00
1990 B	8,900	PF65 3.00				
1991 B	526,100	—	—	1.00	1.50	2.50
1991 B	9,900	PF65 5.00				
1992 B	520,300	—	—	1.00	1.50	2.50
1992 B	7,450	PF65 5.00				
1993 B	516,400	—	—	1.00	2.00	3.00
1993 B	6,300	PF65 5.00				
1994 B	2,017,300	—	—	0.25	0.50	1.00
1994 B	6,100	PF65 3.00				
1995 B	6,018,000	—	—	0.25	0.50	1.00
1995 B	6,100	PF65 3.00				
1996 B	1,017,300	—	—	0.25	0.50	1.00
1996 B	6,100	PF65 3.00				
1997 B	1,016,500	—	—	0.25	0.50	1.00
1997 B	5,500	PF65 3.00				
1998 B	1,016,000	—	—	0.25	0.50	1.00
1998 B	4,800	PF65 3.00				
1999 B	1,016,000	—	—	0.25	0.50	1.00
1999 B	5,000	PF65 3.00				
2000 B	1,020,000	—	—	0.25	0.50	1.00
2000 B	5,500	PF65 3.00				

KM# 4.2 2 RAPPEN

2.50 g., Bronze, 20 mm. **Obv:** Cross in shield within sprigs **Rev:** Value within wreath

Date	Mintage	VF20	XF40	MS60	MS63	MS65
1902 B	500,000	45.00	85.00	135	180	400
1903 B	500,000	35.00	60.00	75.00	90.00	120
1904 B	500,000	35.00	45.00	50.00	60.00	80.00
1906 B	500,000	35.00	45.00	80.00	110	180
1907 B	1,000,000	12.00	16.00	19.00	24.00	32.00
1908 B	1,000,000	9.50	15.00	21.00	28.00	50.00
1909 B	1,000,000	6.00	13.00	15.00	18.00	24.00
1910 B	500,000	35.00	45.00	50.00	55.00	75.00
1912 B	1,000,000	11.00	17.00	19.00	21.00	28.00
1913 B	1,000,000	16.00	21.00	40.00	52.00	90.00
1914 B	1,000,000	16.00	21.00	36.00	48.00	90.00
1915 B	1,000,000	12.50	19.00	30.00	40.00	72.00
1918 B	1,000,000	9.50	12.00	18.00	24.00	40.00
1919 B	2,000,000	3.50	5.00	18.00	24.00	28.00
1920 B	500,000	45.00	65.00	90.00	120	190
1925 B	1,250,000	2.50	4.00	9.00	12.00	28.00
1926 B	750,000	28.00	42.00	55.00	75.00	125
1927 B	500,000	35.00	50.00	70.00	90.00	145
1928 B	500,000	30.00	45.00	50.00	60.00	80.00
1929 B	750,000	11.00	16.00	24.00	32.00	48.00
1930 B	1,000,000	11.00	16.00	19.00	24.00	32.00
1931 B	1,288,000	9.00	13.00	24.00	32.00	48.00

KM# 4.2a 2 RAPPEN

3.00 g., Bronze, 20 mm. **Obv:** Cross in shield within sprigs **Rev:** Value within wreath

Date	Mintage	VF20	XF40	MS60	MS63	MS65
1932 B	1,500,000	3.00	4.50	9.00	12.00	25.00
1933 B	1,000,000	6.00	9.50	18.00	24.00	36.00
1934 B	500,000	19.00	25.00	36.00	48.00	72.00
1936 B	500,000	9.00	12.00	15.00	25.00	40.00
1937 B	1,200,000	4.50	6.00	9.00	12.00	20.00
1938 B	1,369,000	6.50	11.00	16.00	20.00	36.00
1941 B	3,448,000	1.00	1.50	3.00	4.00	20.00

KM# 4.2b 2 RAPPEN

2.40 g., Zinc, 20 mm. **Obv:** Cross on shield within sprigs **Rev:** Value within wreath

Date	Mintage	VF20	XF40	MS60	MS63	MS65
1942 B	8,954,000	0.75	2.50	8.00	12.00	24.00
1943 B	4,499,000	1.00	8.00	16.00	20.00	45.00
1944 B	8,086,000	0.75	2.50	9.00	12.00	24.00
1945 B	3,640,000	7.00	16.00	24.00	35.00	60.00
1946 B	1,393,000	28.00	37.00	42.00	55.00	85.00

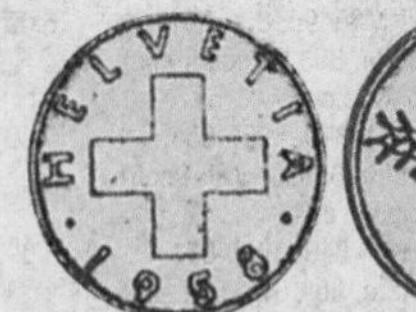

KM# 47 2 RAPPEN

3.00 g., Bronze, 20 mm. **Obv:** Cross **Rev:** Value and oat sprig **Edge:** Plain

Date	Mintage	VF20	XF40	MS60	MS63	MS65
1948 B	10,197,000	0.25	0.50	3.50	6.50	20.00
1951 B	9,622,000	0.25	0.50	3.50	6.50	24.00
1952 B	1,916,000	0.50	1.75	6.00	12.00	40.00
1953 B	2,007,000	0.50	1.75	3.50	6.50	24.00
1954 B	2,539,000	0.50	1.00	3.00	5.00	12.00
1955 B	2,493,000	0.25	1.00	3.00	5.00	14.00
1957 B	8,099,000	0.10	0.25	1.50	3.00	8.00
1958 B	6,078,000	0.10	0.25	1.50	3.00	8.00
1963 B	10,065,000	0.10	0.25	1.00	2.00	4.00
1966 B	2,510,000	0.10	0.25	1.00	2.00	4.00
1967 B	1,510,000	0.20	0.95	1.00	2.00	4.00
1968 B	2,865,000	0.10	0.25	0.75	1.50	2.50
1969	6,200,000	0.10	0.20	0.50	1.00	2.00
1970	3,115,000	0.10	0.20	0.50	1.00	2.00
1974	3,538,000	0.10	0.20	0.50	1.00	2.00
1974	2,400	PF65 60.00				

KM# 26 5 RAPPEN

2.00 g., Copper-Nickel, 17.15 mm. **Obv:** Crowned head right **Obv. Legend:** CONFOEDERATIO HELVETICA **Rev:** Value within wreath **Edge:** Plain

Date	Mintage	VF20	XF40	MS60	MS63	MS65
1901 B	3,000,000	3.00	5.00	25.00	40.00	60.00
1902 B	1,000,000	10.00	40.00	105	140	260
1902 B	Inc. above	15.00	60.00	125	185	300
Note: "T" over "L" in HELVETICA						
1902 B	Inc. above	10.00	45.00	110	175	275
Note: "I" over tilted "I" in Helvetica						
1903 B	2,000,000	2.50	12.00	60.00	80.00	180
1904 B	1,000,000	10.00	30.00	135	180	365
1905 B	1,000,000	7.00	12.00	85.00	115	245
1906 B	3,000,000	2.50	9.50	24.00	35.00	75.00
1907 B	5,000,000	2.50	6.00	12.00	16.00	30.00
1908 B	3,000,000	2.50	6.00	15.00	20.00	48.00
1909 B	2,000,000	2.50	6.00	15.00	24.00	48.00
1910 B	1,000,000	5.00	10.00	35.00	50.00	115
1911 B	2,000,000	1.00	3.00	12.00	20.00	45.00
1912 B	3,000,000	1.00	3.00	10.00	16.00	40.00
1913 B	3,000,000	1.00	3.00	12.00	20.00	45.00
1914 B	3,000,000	1.00	7.00	70.00	100	200
1915 B	3,000,000	1.00	12.50	135	200	450
1917 B	1,000,000	2.50	10.00	120	165	365
1919 B	6,000,000	0.50	2.50	16.00	24.00	45.00
1920 B	5,000,000	0.50	2.50	12.00	20.00	45.00
1921 B	3,000,000	0.50	2.50	12.00	20.00	40.00
1922 B	4,000,000	0.50	1.75	10.00	16.00	30.00
1925 B	3,000,000	0.50	2.00	12.00	20.00	32.00
1926 B	3,000,000	0.50	2.00	12.00	20.00	35.00
1927 B	2,000,000	0.50	4.50	22.00	32.00	65.00
1928 B	2,000,000	0.50	2.50	12.00	20.00	35.00
1929 B	2,000,000	0.50	1.75	12.00	20.00	35.00
1930 B	3,000,000	0.50	1.75	12.00	20.00	35.00
1931 B	5,037,000	0.50	1.75	10.00	16.00	30.00
1940 B	1,416,000	0.50	7.00	60.00	80.00	285
1942 B	5,078,000	0.25	0.50	13.00	20.00	36.00
1943 B	6,591,000	0.25	0.50	13.00	20.00	36.00
1944 B	9,981,000	0.25	0.50	10.00	16.00	32.00
1945 B	985,000	1.00	12.00	125	165	365
1946 B	6,179,000	0.25	0.50	10.00	20.00	32.00
1947 B	5,125,000	0.25	0.50	10.00	20.00	32.00
1948 B	4,710,000	0.25	0.50	4.00	8.00	12.00
1949 B	4,589,000	0.25	0.50	3.50	6.50	8.00
1950 B	920,000	0.50	1.50	2.50	3.50	6.50
1951 B	2,141,000	0.50	2.50	20.00	30.00	65.00
1952 B	4,690,000	0.20	0.35	4.00	6.00	16.00
1953 B	9,131,000	0.20	0.35	3.50	5.50	10.00
1954 B	8,038,000	0.20	0.35	5.00	7.50	25.00
1955 B	19,943,000	0.20	0.30	4.50	7.00	20.00
1957 B	10,147,000	0.20	0.30	4.50	7.00	20.00
1958 B	10,217,000	0.20	0.30	4.50	7.00	20.00
1959 B	11,085,000	0.20	0.30	4.50	7.00	16.00
1962 B	23,840,000	0.10	0.20	0.50	1.25	12.00
1963 B	29,730,000	0.10	0.20	0.50	1.00	8.00
1964 B	17,080,000	0.10	0.20	0.50	1.00	8.00
1965 B	1,430,000	0.25	1.00	1.50	2.50	6.50
1966 B	10,010,000	—	0.15	0.50	1.00	4.00
1967 B	13,010,000	—	0.55	1.00	2.00	4.00
1968 B	10,020,000	—	0.15	0.50	1.00	4.00
1969 B	32,990,000	—	0.10	0.50	1.00	4.00

Date	Mintage	VF20	XF40	MS60	MS63	MS65
1970	34,800,000	—	0.10	0.50	1.00	4.00
1971	40,020,000	—	0.10	0.50	1.00	4.00
1974	30,000,000	—	0.10	0.50	1.00	4.00
1974	2,400	PF65 35.00				
1975	10,000	PF65 3.00				
1975	33,995,000	—	0.10	0.25	0.50	2.00
1976	12,000,000	—	0.10	0.25	0.50	2.00
1976	5,130	PF65 4.00				
1977	7,030	PF65 4.00				
1977	14,005,000	—	0.10	0.25	0.50	2.00
1978	16,405,000	—	0.10	0.25	0.50	2.00
1978	10,000	PF65 3.00				
1979	10,000	PF65 3.00				
1979	27,000,000	—	0.10	0.25	0.50	2.00
1980	15,500,000	—	0.10	0.25	0.50	2.00
1980	10,000	PF65 3.00				

KM# 26a 5 RAPPEN

2.00 g., Brass, 17.15 mm. **Obv:** Crowned head right **Rev:** Value within wreath

Date	Mintage	VF20	XF40	MS60	MS63	MS65
1918 B	6,000,000	7.00	15.00	25.00	35.00	45.00

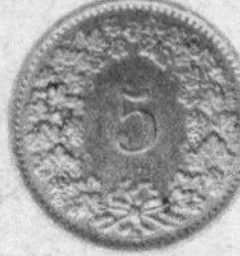

KM# 26b 5 RAPPEN

2.00 g., Nickel, 17.15 mm. **Obv:** Crowned head right **Rev:** Value within wreath **Edge:** Plain **Note:** Retired legal tender status as of January 1, 2004, removed from circulation.

Date	Mintage	VF20	XF40	MS60	MS63	MS65
1932 B	6,000,000	0.50	1.50	6.00	12.00	20.00
1933 B	3,000,000	0.50	1.50	6.00	12.00	48.00
1934 B	4,000,000	0.50	1.50	6.00	12.00	70.00
1936 B	1,000,000	0.75	2.50	6.00	12.00	48.00
1937 B	2,000,000	0.50	1.00	8.00	16.00	36.00
1938 B	1,000,000	0.50	1.50	8.00	15.00	45.00
1939 B	10,048,000	0.50	1.00	6.00	12.00	24.00
1941 B	3,087,000	1.75	5.00	40.00	65.00	185

KM# 26c 5 RAPPEN

1.80 g., Aluminum-Bronze, 17.15 mm. **Obv:** Crowned head right **Rev:** Value within wreath **Edge:** Plain

Date	Mintage	VF20	XF40	MS60	MS63	MS65
1981	79,020,000	—	—	0.25	0.50	1.00
1981	10,000	PF65 3.00				
1982	75,340,000	—	—	0.25	0.50	1.00
1982	10,000	PF65 3.00				
1983	92,746,000	—	—	0.25	0.50	1.00
1983	11,000	PF65 3.00				
1984	69,960,000	—	—	0.25	0.50	1.00
1984	14,000	PF65 3.00				
1985	60,032,000	—	—	0.25	0.50	1.00
1985	12,000	PF65 3.00				
1986 B	55,031,000	—	—	0.25	0.50	1.00
1986 B	10,000	PF65 3.00				
1987 B	39,819,100	—	—	0.25	0.50	1.00
1987 B	8,800	PF65 4.00				
1988 B	55,035,000	—	—	0.25	0.50	1.00
1988 B	9,050	PF65 4.00				
1989 B	45,022,700	—	—	0.25	0.50	1.00
1989 B	8,800	PF65 4.00				
1990 B	16,033,000	—	—	0.25	0.50	1.00
1990 B	8,900	PF65 4.00				
1991 B	35,026,100	—	—	0.25	0.50	1.00
1991 B	9,900	PF65 3.00				
1992 B	35,020,300	—	—	0.25	0.50	1.00
1992 B	7,450	PF65 4.00				
1993 B	38,017,000	—	—	0.25	0.50	1.00
1993 B	6,300	PF65 4.00				
1994 B	35,016,400	—	—	0.25	0.50	1.00
1994 B	6,100	PF65 4.00				
1995 B	20,018,000	—	—	0.25	0.50	1.00
1995 B	6,100	PF65 4.00				
1996 B	25,017,300	—	—	0.25	0.50	1.00
1996 B	6,100	PF65 4.00				
1997 B	25,016,500	—	—	0.25	0.50	1.00
1997 B	5,500	PF65 4.00				
1998 B	10,016,000	—	—	0.25	0.50	1.00
1998 B	4,800	PF65 4.00				
1999 B	8,016,000	—	—	0.25	0.50	1.00
1999 B	5,000	PF65 4.00				
2000 B	5,020,000	—	—	0.25	0.50	1.00
2000 B	5,500	PF65 4.00				

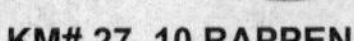

KM# 27 10 RAPPEN

3.00 g., Copper-Nickel, 19.15 mm. **Obv:** Crowned head right **Obv. Legend:** CONFOEDERATIO HELVETICA **Rev:** Value within wreath **Edge:** Plain

Date	Mintage	VF20	XF40	MS60	MS63	MS65
1901 B	1,000,000	6.50	19.00	70.00	100	245
1902 B	1,000,000	6.50	12.00	55.00	80.00	185
1903 B	1,000,000	6.50	10.00	100	145	265
1904 B	1,000,000	5.00	26.00	160	225	575
1906 B	1,000,000	5.00	10.00	50.00	75.00	200
1907 B	2,000,000	2.00	5.00	30.00	50.00	90.00
1908 B	2,000,000	2.00	5.00	25.00	40.00	75.00
1909 B	2,000,000	2.00	5.00	25.00	40.00	85.00
1911 B	1,000,000	3.00	8.00	30.00	50.00	90.00
1912 B	1,500,000	1.50	5.00	35.00	50.00	105
1913 B	2,000,000	1.00	5.00	50.00	75.00	180
1914 B	2,000,000	1.50	8.00	70.00	100	230
1915 B	1,200,000	2.00	30.00	240	325	685
1919 B	3,000,000	0.50	3.00	25.00	40.00	100
1920 B	3,500,000	0.50	3.00	18.00	30.00	100
1921 B	3,000,000	0.50	3.00	18.00	30.00	70.00
1922 B	2,000,000	0.50	3.00	18.00	30.00	80.00
1924 B	2,000,000	0.50	3.00	25.00	40.00	90.00
1925 B	3,000,000	0.50	3.00	16.00	30.00	50.00
1926 B	3,000,000	0.50	3.00	16.00	30.00	50.00
1927 B	2,000,000	0.50	3.00	16.00	28.00	55.00
1928 B	2,000,000	0.50	3.00	15.00	25.00	40.00
1929 B	2,000,000	0.50	3.00	22.00	35.00	100
1930 B	2,000,000	0.50	3.00	22.00	35.00	80.00
1931 B	2,244,000	0.50	3.00	22.00	35.00	72.00

Note: The 1932-39 dated coins are made of Nickel, and are listed as KM#27b following this type listing.

Date	Mintage	VF20	XF40	MS60	MS63	MS65
1940 B	2,000,000	0.75	15.00	100	165	485
1942 B	2,110,000	0.75	10.00	40.00	65.00	165
1943 B	3,176,000	0.50	5.00	30.00	50.00	100
1944 B	6,133,000	0.50	2.50	10.00	16.00	40.00
1945 B	993,000	1.00	15.00	100	165	425
1946 B	4,010,000	0.50	2.50	20.00	35.00	95.00
1947 B	3,152,000	0.50	2.50	35.00	60.00	145
1948 B	1,000,000	1.00	18.00	190	285	725
1949 B	2,269,000	0.50	1.00	30.00	50.00	105
1950 B	3,200,000	0.35	0.70	2.00	4.00	8.00
1951 B	3,430,000	0.35	0.70	5.00	10.00	36.00
1952 B	4,451,000	0.35	0.70	4.00	10.00	36.00
1953 B	6,149,000	0.35	0.70	4.00	10.00	32.00
1954 B	3,200,000	0.35	0.70	15.00	24.00	80.00
1955 B	11,795,000	0.35	0.70	4.00	8.00	35.00
1957 B	10,092,000	0.35	0.70	6.00	12.00	40.00
1958 B	10,040,000	0.35	0.70	4.00	8.00	32.00
1959 B	13,053,000	0.35	0.70	4.00	8.00	24.00
1960 B	4,040,000	0.35	0.70	2.00	4.00	12.00
1961 B	7,949,000	—	0.50	2.00	4.00	16.00
1962 B	34,965,000	—	0.20	0.50	1.50	6.50
1964 B	16,340,000	—	0.20	0.50	1.50	6.50
1965 B	14,190,000	—	0.20	0.50	1.50	6.50
1966 B	4,025,000	—	0.50	0.50	1.50	4.00
1967 B	10,000,000	—	0.50	1.00	2.00	4.00
1968 B	14,065,000	—	0.25	0.50	1.00	4.00
1969 B	28,855,000	—	0.25	0.50	1.00	4.00
1970	40,020,000	—	0.25	0.50	1.00	4.00
1972	7,877,000	—	0.25	0.50	1.00	4.00
1973	30,350,000	—	—	0.50	1.00	4.00
1974	30,005,000	—	—	0.50	1.00	4.00
1974	2,400	PF65 60.00				
1975	24,992,000	—	—	0.50	1.00	2.00
1975	10,000	PF65 4.00				
1976	19,007,000	—	—	0.50	1.00	2.00
1976	5,130	PF65 5.00				
1977	10,000,000	—	—	0.50	1.00	2.00
1977	7,030	PF65 5.00				
1978	19,947,000	—	—	0.50	1.00	2.00
1978	10,000	PF65 4.00				
1979	18,000,000	—	—	0.50	1.00	2.00
1979	10,000	PF65 4.00				
1980	18,005,000	—	—	0.50	1.00	2.00
1980	10,000	PF65 4.00				
1981	30,140,000	—	—	0.25	0.50	1.00
1981	10,000	PF65 4.00				
1982	50,110,000	—	—	0.25	0.50	1.00
1982	10,000	PF65 4.00				
1983	40,033,000	—	—	0.25	0.50	1.00
1983	11,000	PF65 4.00				
1984	22,022,000	—	—	0.25	0.50	1.00

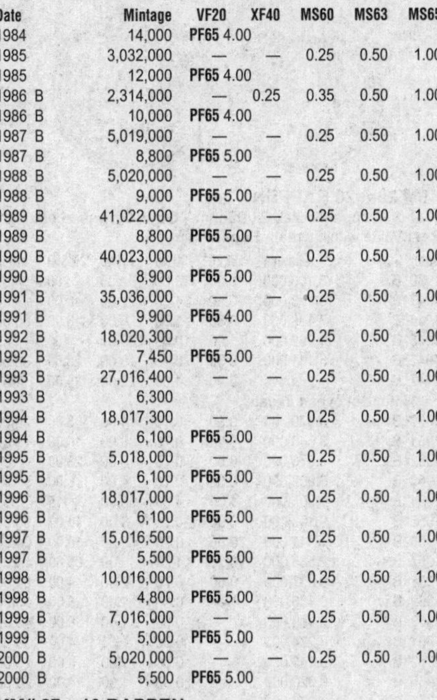

Date	Mintage	VF20	XF40	MS60	MS63	MS65
1984	14,000	PF65 4.00				
1985	3,032,000	—	—	0.25	0.50	1.00
1985	12,000	PF65 4.00				
1986 B	2,314,000	—	0.25	0.35	0.50	1.00
1986 B	10,000	PF65 4.00				
1987 B	5,019,000	—	—	0.25	0.50	1.00
1987 B	8,800	PF65 5.00				
1988 B	5,020,000	—	—	0.25	0.50	1.00
1988 B	9,000	PF65 5.00				
1989 B	41,022,000	—	—	0.25	0.50	1.00
1989 B	8,800	PF65 5.00				
1990 B	40,023,000	—	—	0.25	0.50	1.00
1990 B	8,900	PF65 5.00				
1991 B	35,036,000	—	—	0.25	0.50	1.00
1991 B	9,900	PF65 4.00				
1992 B	18,020,300	—	—	0.25	0.50	1.00
1992 B	7,450	PF65 5.00				
1993 B	27,016,400	—	—	0.25	0.50	1.00
1993 B	6,300					
1994 B	18,017,300	—	—	0.25	0.50	1.00
1994 B	6,100	PF65 5.00				
1995 B	5,018,000	—	—	0.25	0.50	1.00
1995 B	6,100	PF65 5.00				
1996 B	18,017,000	—	—	0.25	0.50	1.00
1996 B	6,100	PF65 5.00				
1997 B	15,016,500	—	—	0.25	0.50	1.00
1997 B	5,500	PF65 5.00				
1998 B	10,016,000	—	—	0.25	0.50	1.00
1998 B	4,800	PF65 5.00				
1999 B	7,016,000	—	—	0.25	0.50	1.00
1999 B	5,000	PF65 5.00				
2000 B	5,020,000	—	—	0.25	0.50	1.00
2000 B	5,500	PF65 5.00				

KM# 27a 10 RAPPEN

3.00 g., Brass, 19.15 mm. **Obv:** Crowned head right **Rev:** Value within wreath

Date	Mintage	VF20	XF40	MS60	MS63	MS65
1918 B	6,000,000	15.00	22.00	35.00	65.00	—
1919 B	3,000,000	60.00	75.00	120	200	—

KM# 27b 10 RAPPEN

3.00 g., Nickel, 19.15 mm. **Obv:** Crowned head right **Rev:** Value within wreath **Edge:** Plain **Note:** Retired legal tender status as of January 1, 2004, removed from circulation but still redeemable.

Date	Mintage	VF20	XF40	MS60	MS63	MS65
1932 B	3,500,000	0.50	1.00	10.00	16.00	35.00
1933 B	2,000,000	0.50	1.00	12.00	20.00	70.00
1934 B	3,000,000	0.50	1.00	15.00	30.00	90.00
1936 B	1,500,000	0.50	1.00	12.00	24.00	100
1937 B	1,000,000	0.75	1.50	15.00	32.00	140
1938 B	1,000,000	0.75	1.50	10.00	16.00	60.00
1939 B	10,022,000	0.50	1.00	10.00	16.00	60.00

KM# 29 20 RAPPEN

4.00 g., Nickel, 21.05 mm. **Obv:** Crowned head right **Obv. Legend:** CONFOEDERATIO HELVETICA **Rev:** Value within wreath **Note:** Retired legal tender status as of January 1, 2004, removed from circulation but still redeemable.

Date	Mintage	VF20	XF40	MS60	MS63	MS65
1901 B	1,000,000	1.00	8.00	125	185	365
1902 B	1,000,000	1.00	8.00	60.00	100	200
1903 B	1,000,000	1.00	8.00	55.00	90.00	185
1906 B	1,000,000	1.00	8.00	65.00	105	185
1907 B	1,000,000	1.00	7.00	30.00	50.00	105
1908 B	1,500,000	1.00	5.00	30.00	50.00	105
1909 B	2,000,000	1.00	5.00	30.00	50.00	90.00
1911 B	1,000,000	1.00	6.00	60.00	100	225
1912 B	2,000,000	0.75	5.00	55.00	100	250
1913 B	1,500,000	0.75	5.00	85.00	135	325
1919 B	1,500,000	0.75	5.00	30.00	48.00	105
1920 B	3,100,000	0.50	2.00	25.00	40.00	115
1921 B	2,500,000	0.50	2.00	22.00	36.00	105
1924 B	1,100,000	0.50	2.00	50.00	80.00	185
1925 B	1,500,000	0.50	2.00	24.00	40.00	120
1926 B	1,500,000	0.50	2.00	30.00	50.00	145
1927 B	500,000	2.50	12.00	100	160	400
1929 B	2,000,000	0.50	1.00	22.00	36.00	80.00
1930 B	2,000,000	0.50	1.00	18.00	32.00	120
1931 B	2,250,000	0.50	1.00	18.00	32.00	120
1932 B	2,000,000	0.50	1.00	35.00	60.00	160
1933 B	1,500,000	0.50	1.00	42.00	72.00	200
1934 B	2,000,000	0.50	1.00	18.00	32.00	140
1936 B	1,000,000	1.00	2.00	20.00	36.00	120
1938 B	2,805,000	0.50	1.50	35.00	60.00	160

KM# 29a 20 RAPPEN

4.00 g., Copper-Nickel, 21.05 mm. **Obv:** Crowned head right **Rev:** Value within wreath **Edge:** Plain

Date	Mintage	VF20	XF40	MS60	MS63	MS65
1939 B	8,100,000	0.50	18.00	135	200	485
1943 B	10,173,000	0.50	1.00	22.00	40.00	100
1944 B	7,139,000	0.50	1.00	8.00	16.00	60.00
1945 B	1,992,000	1.00	10.00	65.00	100	365
1947 B	5,131,000	0.50	0.75	18.00	28.00	80.00
1947 B	Inc. above	2.00	4.00	22.00	35.00	100
Note: Dot over 4 in date						
1950 B	5,970,000	0.50	0.75	4.00	8.00	20.00
1951 B	3,640,000	0.50	0.75	8.00	16.00	70.00
1952 B	3,075,000	0.50	0.75	16.00	28.00	100
1953 B	6,958,000	0.50	0.75	4.00	8.00	55.00
1954 B	1,504,000	1.00	4.00	65.00	115	385
1955 B	9,103,000	0.50	0.75	8.00	16.00	95.00
1956 B	5,111,000	0.50	0.75	5.00	10.00	60.00
1957 B	2,535,000	0.50	1.25	40.00	65.00	285
1958 B	5,037,000	0.50	0.75	2.00	4.00	50.00
1959 B	10,136,000	—	0.50	1.00	8.00	65.00
1960 B	15,469,000	—	0.50	1.00	6.00	45.00
1961 B	8,234,000	—	0.50	1.00	4.00	35.00
1962 B	30,145,000	—	0.50	1.00	4.00	25.00
1963 B	9,020,000	—	0.50	1.00	4.00	20.00
1964 B	14,370,000	—	0.50	1.00	3.00	15.00
1965 B	15,005,000	—	0.50	1.00	3.00	15.00
1966 B	10,785,000	—	—	0.50	1.00	7.00
1967 B	8,995,000	—	—	1.00	2.00	8.00
1968 B	10,540,000	—	—	0.50	1.00	3.00
1969 B	39,875,000	—	—	0.50	1.00	3.00
1970	45,605,000	—	—	0.50	1.00	3.00
1971	25,160,000	—	—	0.50	1.00	3.00
1974	30,023,000	—	—	0.50	1.00	3.00
1974	2,400	PF65 75.00				
1975	50,050,000	—	—	0.50	1.00	2.00
1975	10,000	PF65 5.00				
1976	23,145,000	—	—	0.50	1.00	2.00
1976	5,130	PF65 6.00				
1977	14,005,000	—	—	0.50	1.00	2.00
1977	7,030	PF65 6.00				
1978	14,805,000	—	—	0.50	1.00	2.00
1978	10,000	PF65 5.00				
1979	18,368,000	—	—	0.50	1.00	2.00
1979	10,000	PF65 5.00				
1980	24,560,000	—	—	0.50	1.00	2.00
1980	10,000	PF65 5.00				
1981	22,020,000	—	—	0.50	1.00	2.00
1981	10,000	PF65 5.00				
1982	25,035,000	—	—	0.50	1.00	2.00
1982	10,000	PF65 5.00				
1983	10,026,000	—	—	0.50	1.00	2.00
1983	11,000	PF65 5.00				
1984	22,055,000	—	—	0.50	1.00	2.00
1984	14,000	PF65 5.00				
1985	40,027,000	—	—	0.50	1.00	2.00
1985	12,000	PF65 5.00				
1986 B	10,289,000	—	—	0.50	1.00	2.00
1986 B	10,000	PF65 5.00				
1987 B	10,019,100	—	—	0.50	1.00	2.00
1987 B	8,800	PF65 6.00				
1988 B	25,020,700	—	—	0.50	1.00	2.00
1988 B	9,050	PF65 6.00				
1989 B	20,022,700	—	—	0.50	1.00	2.00
1989 B	8,800	PF65 6.00				
1990 B	6,525,000	—	—	0.50	1.00	2.00
1990 B	8,900	PF65 6.00				
1991 B	48,066,100	—	—	0.50	1.00	2.00
1991 B	9,900	PF65 6.00				
1992 B	12,620,300	—	—	0.50	1.00	2.00
1992 B	7,450	PF65 6.00				
1993 B	32,516,400	—	—	0.50	1.00	2.00
1993 B	6,300	PF65 6.00				
1994 B	20,017,300	—	—	0.50	1.00	2.00
1994 B	6,100	PF65 6.00				
1995 B	8,018,000	—	—	0.50	1.00	2.00
1995 B	6,100	PF65 6.00				
1996 B	4,017,300	—	—	0.50	1.00	2.00
1996 B	6,100	PF65 6.00				
1997 B	6,016,500	—	—	0.50	1.00	2.00
1997 B	5,500	PF65 6.00				
1998 B	7,016,000	—	—	0.50	1.00	2.00
1998 B	4,800	PF65 6.00				
1999 B	4,016,000	—	—	0.50	1.00	2.00
1999 B	5,000	PF65 6.00				
2000 B	3,020,000	—	—	0.50	1.00	2.00
2000 B	5,500	PF65 6.00				

KM# 23 1/2 FRANC

2.50 g., 0.835 Silver 0.0671 oz. ASW, 18.2 mm. **Obv:** Standing Helvetia with lance and shield within star border **Rev:** Value, date within wreath **Edge:** Reeded

Date	Mintage	VF20	XF40	MS60	MS63	MS65
1901 B	200,000	60.00	225	1,000	1,400	2,125
1901 B Specimen	—	—	—	—	—	5,000
1903 B	800,000	4.00	15.00	100	185	275
1903 B Specimen	—	—	—	—	—	2,000
1904 B	400,000	8.00	100	1,000	1,500	2,300
1904 B Specimen	—	—	—	—	—	5,000
1905 B	600,000	4.00	23.00	200	300	450
1905 B Specimen	—	—	—	—	—	2,000
1906 B	1,000,000	4.00	23.00	175	275	375
1906 B Specimen	—	—	—	—	—	2,000
1907 B	1,200,000	4.00	15.00	140	215	300
1907 B Specimen	—	—	—	—	—	1,800
1908 B	800,000	4.00	18.00	160	240	350
1908 B Specimen	—	—	—	—	—	1,600
1909 B	1,000,000	4.00	12.00	110	150	200
1909 B Specimen	—	—	—	—	—	1,500
1910 B	1,000,000	4.00	12.00	95.00	135	185
1910 B Specimen	—	—	—	—	—	1,500
1913 B	800,000	4.00	7.50	90.00	130	185
1913 B Specimen	—	—	—	—	—	1,000
1914 B	2,000,000	4.00	6.00	45.00	70.00	100
1914 B Specimen	—	—	—	—	—	600
1916 B	800,000	4.00	5.00	100	160	230
1916 B Specimen	—	—	—	—	—	1,200
1920 B	5,400,000	4.00	5.00	20.00	35.00	55.00
1920 B Specimen	—	—	—	—	—	450
1921 B	6,000,000	4.00	6.00	20.00	35.00	55.00
1921 B Specimen	—	—	—	—	—	450
1928 B	1,000,000	4.00	9.50	95.00	145	210
1928 B Specimen	—	—	—	—	—	600
1929 B	2,000,000	4.00	6.00	20.00	32.00	50.00
1929 B Specimen	—	—	—	—	—	300
1931 B	1,000,000	3.00	9.50	55.00	85.00	125
1931 B Specimen	—	—	—	—	—	500
1932 B	1,000,000	3.00	6.50	40.00	65.00	90.00
1932 B Specimen	—	—	—	—	—	400
1934 B	2,000,000	3.00	6.50	20.00	32.00	45.00
1934 B Specimen	—	—	—	—	—	250
1936 B	400,000	4.00	9.50	50.00	85.00	125
1936 B Specimen	—	—	—	—	—	450
1937 B	1,000,000	4.00	6.00	22.00	40.00	60.00
1937 B Specimen	—	—	—	—	—	275
1939 B	1,001,000	3.00	6.00	22.00	40.00	65.00
1939 B Specimen	—	—	—	—	—	200
1940 B	2,002,000	3.00	5.00	16.00	27.00	42.00
1940 B Specimen	—	—	—	—	—	120
1941 B	200,000	4.00	8.00	28.00	42.00	60.00
1941 B Specimen	—	—	—	—	—	90.00
1942 B	2,969,000	2.50	3.50	8.00	14.00	25.00
1942 B Specimen	—	—	—	—	—	90.00
1943 B	4,573,000	2.50	3.50	8.00	14.00	25.00
1943 B Specimen	—	—	—	—	—	90.00
1944 B	7,455,000	2.50	3.50	7.00	10.00	17.00
1944 B Specimen	—	—	—	—	—	90.00
1945 B	4,928,000	2.50	3.50	6.00	12.00	21.00
1945 B Specimen	—	—	—	—	—	90.00
1946 B	Inc. above	165	280	635	900	1,275
Note: Medal alignment						
1946 B	6,817,000	2.50	3.50	6.00	9.00	12.50
1946 B Specimen	—	—	—	—	—	90.00
1948 B	6,113,000	2.50	3.50	6.00	8.00	11.00
1948 B Specimen	—	—	—	—	—	90.00
1950 B	7,148,000	2.50	3.00	6.00	8.00	11.00
1950 B Specimen	—	—	—	—	—	90.00
1951 B	8,530,000	2.50	3.00	5.00	6.50	8.50
1951 B Specimen	—	—	—	—	—	90.00
1952 B	14,023,000	2.50	3.00	5.00	6.50	8.50
1952 B Specimen	—	—	—	—	—	75.00
1953 B	3,567,000	2.50	3.00	6.50	9.00	13.00
1953 B Specimen	—	—	—	—	—	90.00
1955 B	1,320,000	2.50	4.00	10.00	13.50	17.00
1955 B Specimen	—	—	—	—	—	110
1956 B	4,250,000	2.50	3.50	6.00	9.00	12.50
1956 B Specimen	—	—	—	—	—	60.00
1957 B	12,085,000	2.50	3.00	5.00	6.50	8.50
1957 B Specimen	—	—	—	—	—	30.00
1958 B	11,558,000	2.50	3.50	5.00	6.50	8.50
1958 B Specimen	—	—	—	—	—	30.00
1959 B	12,581,000	2.50	3.00	5.00	6.50	8.50
1959 B Specimen	—	—	—	—	—	30.00
1960 B	14,528,000	2.50	3.00	5.00	6.50	8.50
1960 B Specimen	—	—	—	—	—	30.00
1961 B	6,906,000	2.50	3.00	5.00	6.50	8.50
1961 B Specimen	—	—	—	—	—	30.00
1962 B	18,272,000	2.50	3.00	5.00	6.50	8.50
1962 B Specimen	—	—	—	—	—	30.00
1963 B	25,168,000	2.50	3.00	5.00	6.50	8.50
1963 B Specimen	—	—	—	—	—	30.00
1964 B	22,720,000	2.50	3.00	5.00	6.50	8.50
1964 B Specimen	—	—	—	—	—	30.00
1965 B	17,920,000	2.50	3.00	5.00	6.50	8.50
1965 B Specimen	—	—	—	—	—	30.00
1966 B	10,008,000	2.50	3.00	5.00	6.50	8.50
1966 B Specimen	—	—	—	—	—	30.00
1967 B	16,096,000	2.50	3.00	5.00	6.50	8.50
1967 B Specimen	—	—	—	—	—	30.00

KM# 23a.1 1/2 FRANC

2.20 g., Copper-Nickel, 18.2 mm. **Obv:** Standing Helvetia with lance and shield within star border **Rev:** Value within wreath **Edge:** Reeded

Date	Mintage	VF20	XF40	MS60	MS63	MS65
1968	20,000,000	—	—	1.00	2.00	8.00
1968 B	44,920,000	—	—	1.00	2.00	7.00
1969	31,400,000	—	—	1.00	2.00	9.00
1969 B	51,704,000	—	—	1.00	2.00	7.00
1970	52,620,000	—	—	1.00	2.00	7.00
Note: 28,608,000 struck in Bern and 24,012,000 struck in London						
1971	34,472,000	—	—	1.00	2.00	7.00
1972	9,996,000	—	—	1.00	2.00	8.00
1973	5,000,000	—	—	1.50	3.00	16.00
1974	45,004,000	—	—	1.00	2.00	7.00
1974	2,400	PF65 85.00				
1975	27,224,000	—	—	1.00	2.00	6.00
1975	10,000	PF65 8.00				
1976	10,004,000	—	—	1.00	2.00	6.00
1976	5,130	PF65 8.00				
1977	19,004,000	—	—	1.00	2.00	4.00
1977	7,030	PF65 6.00				
1978	20,808,000	—	—	1.00	2.00	4.00
1978	10,000	PF65 6.00				
1979	27,004,000	—	—	1.00	2.00	4.00
1979	10,000	PF65 6.00				
1980	31,064,000	—	—	1.00	2.00	4.00
1980	10,000	PF65 6.00				
1981	30,155,000	—	—	1.00	2.00	3.00
1981	10,000	PF65 5.00				

KM# 23a.2 1/2 FRANC

2.20 g., Copper-Nickel, 18.2 mm. **Obv:** 22 Stars around figure **Rev:** Value within wreath **Edge:** Reeded **Note:** Medal alignment.

Date	Mintage	VF20	XF40	MS60	MS63	MS65
1982	30,151,000	—	—	1.00	2.00	3.00
1982	10,000	PF65 8.00				

KM# 23a.3 1/2 FRANC

2.20 g., Copper-Nickel, 18.2 mm. **Obv:** 23 Stars around figure **Rev:** Value within wreath **Edge:** Reeded

Date	Mintage	VF20	XF40	MS60	MS63	MS65
1983	22,020,000	—	—	1.00	2.00	3.00
1983	11,000	PF65 6.00				
1984	22,036,000	—	—	1.00	2.00	3.00
1984	14,000	PF65 6.00				
1985	6,026,000	—	—	1.00	2.00	3.00
1985	12,000	PF65 6.00				
1986 B	5,021,400	—	—	1.00	2.00	3.00
1986 B	10,000	PF65 6.00				
1987 B	10,019,100	—	—	1.00	2.00	3.00
1987 B	8,800	PF65 6.00				
1988 B	5,020,700	—	—	1.00	2.00	3.00
1988 B	9,050	PF65 6.00				
1989 B	10,022,700	—	—	1.00	2.00	3.00
1989 B	8,800	PF65 6.00				
1990 B	20,023,100	—	—	1.00	2.00	3.00
1990 B	8,900	PF65 6.00				
1991 B	10,026,100	—	—	1.00	2.00	3.00
1991 B	9,900	PF65 6.00				
1992 B	30,020,300	—	—	1.00	2.00	3.00
1992 B	7,450	PF65 7.00				
1993 B	13,016,400	—	—	1.00	2.00	3.00
1993 B	6,300	PF65 7.00				
1994 B	15,017,300	—	—	1.00	2.00	3.00
1994 B	6,100	PF65 7.00				
1995 B	10,018,000	—	—	1.00	2.00	3.00
1995 B	6,000	PF65 7.00				
1996 B	8,017,300	—	—	1.00	2.50	3.50
1996 B	6,100	PF65 7.00				
1997 B	6,016,500	—	—	1.00	2.50	3.50
1997 B	5,500	PF65 8.00				

Date	Mintage	VF20	XF40	MS60	MS63	MS65
1998 B	6,016,000	—	—	1.00	2.50	3.50
1998 B	4,800	PF65 8.00				
1999 B	5,016,000	—	—	1.00	2.50	3.50
1999 B	5,000	PF65 8.00				
2000 B	4,020,000	—	—	1.00	2.50	3.50
2000 B	5,500	PF65 8.00				

KM# 24 FRANC

5.00 g., 0.835 Silver 0.1342 oz. ASW, 23.2 mm. **Obv:** Standing Helvetia with lance and shield within star border **Rev:** Value, date within wreath **Edge:** Reeded

Date	Mintage	VF20	XF40	MS60	MS63	MS65
1901 B	400,000	12.00	100	600	950	1,350
1901 B Specimen	—	—	—	—	—	4,500
1903 B	1,000,000	7.00	20.00	200	275	375
1903 B Specimen	—	—	—	—	—	2,000
1904 B	400,000	12.00	200	1,600	2,500	3,400
1904 B Specimen	—	—	—	—	—	5,500
1905 B	700,000	8.00	30.00	275	375	500
1905 B Specimen	—	—	—	—	—	2,000
1906 B	700,000	8.00	50.00	475	625	850
1906 B Specimen	—	—	—	—	—	2,500
1907 B	800,000	7.50	40.00	425	550	750
1907 B Specimen	—	—	—	—	—	2,250
1908 B	1,200,000	7.50	14.00	175	250	350
1908 B Specimen	—	—	—	—	—	1,750
1909 B	900,000	7.50	14.00	165	225	300
1909 B Specimen	—	—	—	—	—	1,750
1910 B	1,000,000	7.50	12.00	95.00	160	235
1910 B Specimen	—	—	—	—	—	1,500
1911 B	1,200,000	7.50	12.00	95.00	150	215
1911 B Specimen	—	—	—	—	—	1,500
1912 B	1,200,000	7.50	9.00	90.00	135	195
1912 B Specimen	—	—	—	—	—	1,250
1913 B	1,200,000	7.50	9.00	70.00	120	160
1913 B Specimen	—	—	—	—	—	1,250
1914 B	4,200,000	7.50	9.00	35.00	60.00	95.00
1914 B Specimen	—	—	—	—	—	750
1916 B	1,000,000	7.50	9.00	120	180	250
1916 B Specimen	—	—	—	—	—	1,500
1920 B	3,300,000	7.00	8.00	30.00	45.00	70.00
1920 B Specimen	—	—	—	—	—	450
1921 B	3,800,000	7.00	8.00	30.00	45.00	70.00
1921 B Specimen	—	—	—	—	—	450
1928 B	1,500,000	7.00	8.00	22.00	38.00	55.00
1928 B Specimen	—	—	—	—	—	400
1931 B	1,000,000	7.00	8.00	40.00	65.00	95.00
1931 B Specimen	—	—	—	—	—	350
1932 B	500,000	7.00	9.00	100	160	225
1932 B Specimen	—	—	—	—	—	750
1934 B	500,000	7.00	10.00	100	160	225
1934 B Specimen	—	—	—	—	—	700
1936 B	500,000	7.00	10.00	85.00	135	200
1936 B Specimen	—	—	—	—	—	650
1937 B	1,000,000	7.00	8.00	25.00	45.00	70.00
1937 B Specimen	—	—	—	—	—	300
1939 B	2,106,000	7.00	8.00	16.00	22.00	30.00
1939 B Specimen	—	—	—	—	—	175
1940 B	2,003,000	7.00	8.00	16.00	22.00	30.00
1940 B Specimen	—	—	—	—	—	150
1943 B	3,526,000	7.00	8.00	10.00	17.00	26.00
1943 B Specimen	—	—	—	—	—	150
1944 B	6,225,000	7.00	8.00	10.00	14.00	22.00
1944 B Specimen	—	—	—	—	—	150
1945 B	7,794,000	7.00	8.00	10.00	14.00	22.00
1945 B Specimen	—	—	—	—	—	150
1946 B	2,539,000	7.00	8.00	14.00	20.00	30.00
1946 B Specimen	—	—	—	—	—	150
1947 B	624,000	7.50	9.00	14.00	20.00	28.00
1947 B Specimen	—	—	—	—	—	150
1952 B	2,853,000	7.00	8.00	9.00	11.00	14.00
1952 B Specimen	—	—	—	—	—	120
1953 B	786,000	7.50	8.00	20.00	25.00	33.00
1953 B Specimen	—	—	—	—	—	120
1955 B	194,000	7.50	14.00	20.00	30.00	42.00
1955 B Specimen	—	—	—	—	—	150
1956 B	2,500,000	2.50	6.00	8.00	10.00	13.00
1956 B Specimen	—	—	—	—	—	90.00
1957 B	6,421,000	2.50	6.00	8.00	10.00	13.00
1957 B Specimen	—	—	—	—	—	45.00
1958 B	3,580,000	2.50	6.00	8.00	10.00	13.00
1958 B Specimen	—	—	—	—	—	45.00
1959 B	1,859,000	2.50	6.00	9.00	11.00	16.00
1959 B Specimen	—	—	—	—	—	45.00
1960 B	3,523,000	2.50	6.00	9.00	12.00	17.00
1960 B Specimen	—	—	—	—	—	45.00
1961 B	6,549,000	2.50	6.00	8.00	10.00	13.00
1961 B Specimen	—	—	—	—	—	45.00
1962 B	6,220,000	2.50	6.00	8.00	10.00	13.00
1962 B Specimen	—	—	—	—	—	45.00
1963 B	13,476,000	2.50	6.00	8.00	10.00	13.00
1963 B Specimen	—	—	—	—	—	45.00
1964 B	12,560,000	2.50	6.00	8.00	10.00	13.00
1964 B Specimen	—	—	—	—	—	45.00
1965 B	5,032,000	2.50	6.00	8.00	10.00	13.00
1965 B Specimen	—	—	—	—	—	45.00
1966 B	3,032,000	2.50	6.00	8.00	10.00	13.00
1966 B Specimen	—	—	—	—	—	45.00
1967 B	2,088,000	2.50	6.00	8.00	10.00	13.00
1967 B Specimen	—	—	—	—	—	45.00

KM# 24a.1 FRANC

4.40 g., Copper-Nickel, 23.2 mm. **Obv:** Standing Helvetia with lance and shield within star border **Rev:** Value within wreath **Edge:** Reeded

Date	Mintage	VF20	XF40	MS60	MS63	MS65
1968	15,000,000	—	1.25	2.00	3.00	16.00
1968 B	40,864,000	—	—	2.00	3.00	16.00
1969 B	37,598,000	—	—	2.00	3.00	16.00
Note: 17,688,000 struck in Bern and 19,910,000 struck in London						
1970	24,240,000	—	—	2.00	3.00	17.00
1971	11,496,000	—	—	2.00	3.00	17.00
1973	5,000,000	—	—	2.00	3.00	20.00
1974	15,010,000	—	—	2.00	3.00	16.00
1974	2,400	PF65 85.00				
1975	13,002,000	—	—	2.00	3.00	15.00
1975	10,000	PF65 10.00				
1976	5,004,000	—	—	2.00	3.00	15.00
1976	5,130	PF65 10.00				
1977	6,012,000	—	—	2.00	3.00	15.00
1977	7,030	PF65 10.00				
1978	13,538,000	—	—	2.00	3.00	10.00
1978	10,000	PF65 9.00				
1979	10,800,000	—	—	2.00	3.00	10.00
1979	10,000	PF65 9.00				
1980	11,002,000	—	—	2.00	3.00	10.00
1980	10,000	PF65 9.00				
1981	18,013,000	—	—	2.00	3.00	10.00
1981	10,000	PF65 9.00				

KM# 24a.2 FRANC

4.40 g., Copper-Nickel, 23.2 mm. **Obv:** 22 Stars around figure **Rev:** Value and date within wreath **Edge:** Reeded **Note:** Medal alignment.

Date	Mintage	VF20	XF40	MS60	MS63	MS65
1982	15,039,000	—	—	2.00	3.00	10.00
1982	10,000	PF65 12.00				

KM# 24a.3 FRANC

4.40 g., Copper-Nickel, 23.2 mm. **Obv:** 23 Stars around figure **Rev:** Value and date within wreath **Edge:** Reeded

Date	Mintage	VF20	XF40	MS60	MS63	MS65
1983	7,018,000	—	—	2.00	3.00	7.00
1983	11,000	PF65 8.00				
1984	3,028,000	—	—	2.00	3.00	7.00
1984	14,000	PF65 8.00				
1985	20,042,000	—	—	2.00	3.00	5.00
1985	12,000	PF65 7.00				
1986 B	17,987,000	—	—	2.00	3.00	5.00
1986 B	10,000	PF65 7.00				
1987 B	17,019,100	—	—	2.00	3.00	5.00
1987 B	8,800	PF65 7.00				
1988 B	18,020,000	—	—	2.00	3.00	5.00
1988 B	9,050	PF65 7.00				
1989 B	15,022,700	—	—	2.00	3.00	5.00
1989 B	8,800	PF65 7.00				
1990 B	2,023,100	—	1.50	1.75	2.50	4.00
1990 B	8,900	PF65 7.00				
1991 B	9,026,100	—	—	1.75	2.50	4.00
1991 B	9,900	PF65 7.00				
1992 B	12,020,300	—	—	1.75	2.50	4.00
1992 B	7,450	PF65 7.00				
1993 B	12,016,400	—	—	1.75	2.50	4.00
1993 B	6,300	PF65 7.00				
1994 B	10,017,300	—	—	1.75	2.50	4.00
1994 B	6,100	PF65 7.00				
1995 B	13,018,000	—	—	1.75	2.50	4.00
1995 B	6,100	PF65 7.00				
1996 B	3,017,300	—	—	1.75	2.50	4.00
1996 B	6,100	PF65 7.00				
1997 B	3,016,500	—	—	1.75	2.50	4.00
1997 B	5,500	PF65 7.00				
1998 B	3,016,000	—	—	1.75	2.50	4.00
1998 B	4,800	PF65 7.00				
1999 B	3,016,000	—	—	1.75	2.50	4.00
1999 B	5,000	PF65 7.00				
2000 B	4,020,000	—	—	1.75	2.50	4.00
2000 B	5,500	PF65 7.00				

KM# 21 2 FRANCS

10.00 g., 0.835 Silver 0.2685 oz. ASW, 27.4 mm. **Obv:** Standing Helvetia with lance and shield within star border **Rev:** Value, date within wreath **Edge:** Reeded

Date	Mintage	VF20	XF40	MS60	MS63	MS65
1901 B	50,000	150	1,750	9,000	15,000	21,500
1901 B Specimen	—	—	—	—	—	50,000
1903 B	300,000	14.00	100	700	1,050	1,500
1903 B Specimen	—	—	—	—	—	4,500
1904 B	200,000	20.00	300	1,450	2,600	3,800
1904 B Specimen	—	—	—	—	—	7,500
1905 B	300,000	14.00	85.00	875	1,400	1,950
1905 B Specimen	—	—	—	—	—	5,000
1906 B	400,000	14.00	125	800	1,150	1,550
1906 B Specimen	—	—	—	—	—	4,500
1907 B	300,000	14.00	225	1,600	2,900	4,250
1907 B Specimen	—	—	—	—	—	6,000
1908 B	200,000	15.00	450	1,800	3,000	4,250
1908 B Specimen	—	—	—	—	—	8,000
1909 B	300,000	14.00	85.00	700	1,200	1,700
1909 B Specimen	—	—	—	—	—	5,000
1910 B	250,000	15.00	175	800	1,300	1,900
1910 B Specimen	—	—	—	—	—	6,000
1911 B	400,000	14.00	60.00	240	425	600
1911 B Specimen	—	—	—	—	—	2,500
1912 B	400,000	14.00	60.00	190	285	380
1912 B Specimen	—	—	—	—	—	2,000
1913 B	300,000	14.00	70.00	240	350	465
1913 B Specimen	—	—	—	—	—	2,500
1914 B	1,000,000	12.00	25.00	140	215	300
1914 B Specimen	—	—	—	—	—	2,000
1916 B	250,000	14.00	165	600	900	1,500
1916 B Specimen	—	—	—	—	—	3,000
1920 B	2,300,000	12.00	15.00	45.00	70.00	95.00
1920 B Specimen	—	—	—	—	—	750
1921 B	2,000,000	12.00	15.00	45.00	70.00	95.00
1921 B Specimen	—	—	—	—	—	750
1922 B	400,000	15.00	35.00	220	360	500
1922 B Specimen	—	—	—	—	—	2,000
1928 B	750,000	12.00	15.00	45.00	85.00	130
1928 B Specimen	—	—	—	—	—	750
1931 B	500,000	12.00	15.00	45.00	85.00	120
1931 B Specimen	—	—	—	—	—	700
1932 B	250,000	14.00	35.00	220	375	550
1932 B Specimen	—	—	—	—	—	1,200
1936 B	250,000	14.00	24.00	120	185	260
1936 B Specimen	—	—	—	—	—	750
1937 B	250,000	12.00	18.00	90.00	130	175
1937 B Specimen	—	—	—	—	—	600
1939 B	1,455,000	11.00	12.00	15.00	24.00	35.00
1939 B Specimen	—	—	—	—	—	500
1940 B	2,503,000	11.00	12.00	15.00	24.00	40.00
1940 B Specimen	—	—	—	—	—	180
1941 B	1,192,000	11.00	12.00	20.00	32.00	42.00
1941 B Specimen	—	—	—	—	—	180
1943 B	2,089,000	11.00	12.00	20.00	26.00	32.00
1943 B Specimen	—	—	—	—	—	180
1944 B	6,276,000	11.00	12.00	15.00	20.00	26.00
1944 B Specimen	—	—	—	—	—	180
1945 B	1,134,000	11.00	15.00	28.00	40.00	52.50
1945 B Specimen	—	—	—	—	—	180
1946 B	1,629,000	11.00	15.00	24.00	33.00	42.50
1946 B Specimen	—	—	—	—	—	180
1947 B	500,000	11.00	15.00	32.00	50.00	65.00
1947 B Specimen	—	—	—	—	—	250
1948 B	920,000	11.00	14.00	21.00	30.00	42.50
1948 B Specimen	—	—	—	—	—	180
1953 B	438,000	11.00	14.00	30.00	45.00	65.00
1953 B Specimen	—	—	—	—	—	200
1955 B	1,032,000	11.00	12.00	15.00	25.00	35.00
1955 B Specimen	—	—	—	—	—	150
1957 B	2,298,000	8.00	10.00	12.00	18.00	27.50
1957 B Specimen	—	—	—	—	—	60.00
1958 B	650,000	8.00	10.00	12.00	18.00	27.50
1958 B Specimen	—	—	—	—	—	60.00
1959 B	2,905,000	8.00	10.00	12.00	21.00	30.00
1959 B Specimen	—	—	—	—	—	60.00
1960 B	1,980,000	8.00	10.00	12.00	25.00	35.00

Date	Mintage	VF20	XF40	MS60	MS63	MS65
1960 B Specimen	—	—	—	—	—	60.00
1961 B	4,653,000	—	5.25	8.00	12.50	17.00
1961 B Specimen	—	—	—	—	—	60.00
1963 B	8,030,000	—	5.25	8.00	12.50	17.00
1963 B Specimen	—	—	—	—	—	60.00
1964 B	4,558,000	—	5.25	8.00	12.50	17.00
1964 B Specimen	—	—	—	—	—	60.00
1965 B	8,526,000	—	5.25	8.00	12.50	17.00
1965 B Specimen	—	—	—	—	—	60.00
1967 B	4,132,000	—	5.25	8.00	12.50	17.00
1967 B Specimen	—	—	—	—	—	60.00

KM# 21a.1 2 FRANCS

8.80 g., Copper-Nickel, 27.4 mm. **Obv:** Standing Helvetia with lance and shield within star border **Rev:** Value within wreath **Edge:** Reeded

Date	Mintage	VF20	XF40	MS60	MS63	MS65
1968	10,000,000	—	—	4.00	7.00	20.00
1968 B	31,588,000	—	—	4.00	6.00	16.00
1969 B	17,296,000	—	—	3.00	5.00	20.00
1970	10,350,000	—	—	3.00	5.00	30.00
1972	5,003,000	—	—	3.00	5.00	22.00
1973	5,996,000	—	—	3.00	5.00	25.00
1974	15,007,000	—	—	3.00	5.00	24.00
1974	2,400	PF65 85.00				
1975	7,051,000	—	—	3.00	5.00	16.00
1975	10,000	PF65 12.00				
1976	5,006,000	—	—	3.00	5.00	12.00
1976	5,130	PF65 15.00				
1977	2,003,000	—	—	3.00	5.00	12.00
1977	7,030	PF65 15.00				
1978	12,802,000	—	—	3.00	5.00	10.00
1978	10,000	PF65 12.00				
1979	10,985,000	—	—	3.00	5.00	10.00
1979	10,000	PF65 12.00				
1980	10,001,000	—	—	3.00	5.00	10.00
1980	10,000	PF65 12.00				
1981	13,852,000	—	—	3.00	5.00	9.00
1981	10,000	PF65 12.00				

KM# 21a.2 2 FRANCS

8.80 g., Copper-Nickel, 27.4 mm. **Obv:** 22 Stars around figure **Rev:** Value within wreath **Edge:** Reeded **Note:** Medal alignment.

Date	Mintage	VF20	XF40	MS60	MS63	MS65
1982	5,912,000	—	—	3.00	5.00	8.00
1982	10,000	PF65 20.00				

KM# 21a.3 2 FRANCS

8.80 g., Copper-Nickel, 27.4 mm. **Obv:** 23 Stars around figure **Rev:** Value within wreath **Edge:** Reeded

Date	Mintage	VF20	XF40	MS60	MS63	MS65
1983	3,023,000	—	—	3.00	5.00	8.00
1983	11,000	PF65 12.00				
1984	2,029,000	—	—	3.00	5.00	8.00
1984	14,000	PF65 12.00				
1985	2,022,000	—	—	3.00	5.00	8.00
1985	12,000	PF65 12.00				
1986 B	3,021,400	—	—	3.00	5.00	8.00
1986 B	10,000	PF65 12.00				
1987 B	8,019,100	—	—	3.00	5.00	8.00
1987 B	8,800	PF65 15.00				
1988 B	10,020,700	—	—	3.00	5.00	8.00
1988 B	9,050	PF65 12.00				
1989 B	8,022,700	—	—	3.00	5.00	8.00
1989 B	8,800	PF65 12.00				
1990 B	5,036,000	—	—	3.00	5.00	8.00
1990 B	8,900	PF65 12.00				
1991 B	12,026,100	—	—	3.00	5.00	7.00
1991 B	9,900	PF65 12.00				
1992 B	10,020,300	—	—	3.00	5.00	7.00
1992 B	7,450	PF65 15.00				
1993 B	13,043,400	—	—	3.00	5.00	7.00
1993 B	6,300	PF65 15.00				
1994 B	16,017,300	—	—	3.00	5.00	7.00
1994 B	6,100	PF65 15.00				
1995 B	7,018,000	—	—	3.00	5.00	7.00
1995 B	6,100	PF65 15.00				
1996 B	5,017,300	—	—	3.00	5.00	7.00
1996 B	6,100	PF65 15.00				
1997 B	5,016,500	—	—	3.00	5.00	7.00
1997 B	5,500	PF65 15.00				
1998 B	4,016,000	—	—	3.00	5.00	7.00
1998 B	4,800	PF65 15.00				
1999 B	3,016,000	—	—	3.00	5.00	7.00
1999 B	5,000	PF65 15.00				
2000 B	3,020,000	—	—	3.00	5.00	7.00
2000 B	5,500	PF65 15.00				

KM# 34 5 FRANCS

25.00 g., 0.900 Silver 0.7234 oz. ASW, 37 mm. **Obv:** Laureate head left **Obv. Legend:** CONFOEDERATIO HELVETICA **Rev:** Shield divides value within wreath, star above

Date	Mintage	VF20	XF40	MS60	MS63	MS65
1904 B	40,000	900	1,500	3,800	5,100	7,000
1904 B Specimen	—	—	—	—	—	10,000
1907 B	277,000	175	325	925	1,525	2,100
1907 B Specimen	—	—	—	—	—	5,000
1908 B	200,000	175	400	1,100	1,600	2,150
1908 B Specimen	—	—	—	—	—	5,000
1909 B	120,000	250	450	1,325	1,850	2,400
1909 B Specimen	—	—	—	—	—	5,000
1912 B	11,000	4,200	5,000	6,500	9,000	12,500
1912 B Specimen	—	—	—	—	—	17,500
1916 B	22,000	1,500	2,000	2,800	3,500	4,300
1916 B Specimen	—	—	—	—	—	8,000

KM# 37 5 FRANCS

25.00 g., 0.900 Silver 0.7234 oz. ASW, 37 mm. **Obv:** William Tell right **Rev:** Shield flanked by sprigs

Date	Mintage	VF20	XF40	MS60	MS63	MS65
1922 B	2,400,000	85.00	110	200	310	425
1922 B	Inc. above	800	1,500	2,500	3,500	4,500
Note: Dot between Confoederatio and Helvetica						
1922 B Specimen	—	—	—	—	—	3,000
1923 B	11,300,000	50.00	95.00	175	265	350
1923 B Specimen	—	—	—	—	—	3,000

KM# 38 5 FRANCS

25.00 g., 0.900 Silver 0.7234 oz. ASW, 37 mm. **Obv:** William Tell right **Rev:** Shield flanked by sprigs

Date	Mintage	VF20	XF40	MS60	MS63	MS65
1924 B	182,000	450	700	1,000	1,550	2,100
1924 B Specimen	—	—	—	—	—	3,500
1925 B	2,830,000	110	140	250	375	500
1925 B Specimen	—	—	—	—	—	1,500
1926 B	2,000,000	140	180	285	400	550
1926 B Specimen	—	—	—	—	—	1,500
1928 B	24,000	9,000	12,000	15,000	17,500	22,000
1928 B	—	—	—	—	—	30,000
Specimen; Rare						

KM# 40 5 FRANCS

15.00 g., 0.835 Silver 0.4027 oz. ASW, 31.45 mm. **Obv:** William Tell right **Rev:** Shield flanked by sprigs **Edge:** Lettered; two variations **Edge Lettering:** Lettering starts with vertical dividing line and group of three stars. Type I; "3 stars/DOMINUS/PROVIDEBIT/10 stars" Type II; "3 stars/DOMINUS/10 stars/PROVIDEBIT" **Note:** Raised edge lettering.

Date	Mintage	VF20	XF40	MS60	MS63	MS65
1931 B	3,520,000	16.00	28.00	80.00	110	140
Note: Edge lettering type I starts at 6 o'clock						
1931 B	Inc. above	50.00	90.00	300	425	550
Note: Edge lettering type II starts at 6 o'clock						
1931 B Specimen	Inc. above	—	—	—	—	2,000
Note: Edge lettering type I starts at 6 o'clock						
1931 B	Inc. above	20.00	50.00	95.00	150	210
Note: Edge lettering type I starts at 2 o'clock						
1931 B	Inc. above	1,350	1,600	2,250	3,000	4,000
Note: Edge lettering type II starts at 10 o'clock						
1932 B	10,580,000	7.75	16.00	24.00	37.00	51.00
1932 B Specimen	—	—	—	—	—	600
1933 B	5,900,000	7.75	16.00	24.00	45.00	68.00
1933 B Specimen	—	—	—	—	—	600
1935 B	3,000,000	7.75	20.00	36.00	60.00	85.00
1935 B Specimen	—	—	—	—	—	650
1937 B	645,000	7.75	20.00	48.00	80.00	115
1937 B Specimen	—	—	—	—	—	900
1939 B	2,197,000	7.75	20.00	24.00	37.00	51.00
1939 B Specimen	—	—	—	—	—	500
1940 B	1,601,000	7.75	22.00	40.00	72.00	105
1940 B Specimen	—	—	—	—	—	750
1948 B	416,000	7.75	22.00	48.00	75.00	105
1948 B Specimen	—	—	—	—	—	700
1949 B	407,000	7.75	22.00	55.00	92.00	130
1949 B Specimen	—	—	—	—	—	700
1950 B	482,000	7.75	22.00	45.00	65.00	90.00
1950 B Specimen	—	—	—	—	—	600
1951 B	1,096,000	7.75	20.00	28.00	45.00	60.00
1951 B Specimen	—	—	—	—	—	350
1952 B	155,000	40.00	80.00	100	170	245
1952 B Specimen	—	—	—	—	—	800
1953 B	3,403,000	7.75	16.00	16.00	25.00	35.00
1953 B Specimen	—	—	—	—	—	150
1954 B	6,600,000	7.75	16.00	16.00	20.00	27.00
1954 B Specimen	—	—	—	—	—	150
1965 B	5,021,000	—	7.75	16.00	18.00	22.00
1965 B Specimen	—	—	—	—	—	120
1966 B	9,016,000	—	7.75	16.00	18.00	22.00
1966 B Specimen	—	—	—	—	—	120
1967 B	13,817,000	—	7.75	16.00	18.00	22.00
Note: Edge lettering type I starts at 6 o'clock						
1967 B Specimen	—	—	—	—	—	120
Note: Edge lettering type I starting at 6 o'clock						
1967 B	Inc. above	70.00	100	125	200	275
Note: Edge lettering type II starts at 2 o'clock						
1969 B	8,637,000	7.75	15.00	16.00	18.00	22.00
1969 B Specimen	—	—	—	—	—	120

KM# A48 5 FRANCS

Gold **Edge Lettering:** DOMINUS PROVIDEBIT (13 stars)

Date	Mintage	VF20	XF40	MS60	MS63	MS65
1948 B	Est. 50	—	—	—	—	15,000

KM# 40a.1 5 FRANCS

13.20 g., Copper-Nickel, 31.45 mm. **Obv:** William Tell right **Rev:** Shield flanked by sprigs **Edge Lettering:** DOMINUS PROVIDEBIT

Date	Mintage	VF20	XF40	MS60	MS63	MS65
1968 B	33,871,000	—	—	8.00	10.00	28.00
1970	6,306,000	—	—	8.00	10.00	28.00
1973	5,002,000	—	—	8.00	10.00	28.00
1974	6,005,000	—	—	8.00	10.00	32.00
1974	2,400	PF65 125				
1975	4,005,000	—	—	8.00	10.00	24.00
1975	10,000	PF65 26.00				
1976	3,002,000	—	—	8.00	10.00	16.00
1976	5,130	PF65 22.00				
1977	2,002,000	—	—	8.00	10.00	16.00
1977	7,030	PF65 20.00				
1978	4,401,000	—	—	8.00	10.00	14.00
1978	10,000	PF65 16.00				
1979	4,001,000	—	—	8.00	10.00	14.00
1979	10,000	PF65 16.00				
1980	4,016,000	—	—	8.00	10.00	14.00
1980	10,000	PF65 16.00				
1981	6,008,000	—	—	8.00	10.00	14.00
1981	10,000	PF65 16.00				

KM# 40a.2 5 FRANCS

13.20 g., Copper-Nickel, 31.45 mm. **Obv:** William Tell right **Rev:** Cross on shield flanked by sprigs **Edge:** Raised lettering **Edge Lettering:** DOMINUS PROVIDEBIT and 13 stars **Note:** Medal alignment.

Date	Mintage	VF20	XF40	MS60	MS63	MS65
1982	5,040,000	—	—	7.50	9.00	12.00
1982	10,000	PF65 18.00				
1983	4,022,000	—	—	7.50	9.00	12.00
1983	11,000	PF65 18.00				
1984	3,939,000	—	—	7.50	9.00	12.00
1984	14,000	PF65 16.00				

KM# 40a.3 5 FRANCS

13.20 g., Copper-Nickel, 31.45 mm. **Obv:** William Tell right **Rev:** Shield flanked by sprigs **Note:** Incuse edge lettering. Retired legal tender status as of January 1, 2004, 1985-1993 removed from circulation.

Date	Mintage	VF20	XF40	MS60	MS63	MS65
1985	4,038,000	—	—	7.50	9.00	12.00
1985	12,000	PF65 16.00				
1986 B	7,073,000	—	—	7.50	9.00	12.00
1986 B	10,000	PF65 16.00				
1987 B	7,019,100	—	—	7.50	9.00	12.00
1987 B	8,800	PF65 20.00				
1988 B	7,020,700	—	—	7.50	9.00	12.00
1988 B	9,050	PF65 18.00				
1989 B	5,022,700	—	—	7.50	9.00	12.00
1989 B	8,800	PF65 18.00				
1990 B	1,040,000	—	—	7.50	9.00	12.00
1990 B	8,900	PF65 16.00				
1991 B	26,100	—	—	—	150	175
Note: In sets only; 508,000 were minted and destroyed						
1991 B	9,900	PF65 185				
1992 B	5,028,000	—	—	7.50	9.00	12.00
1992 B	7,450	PF65 16.00				
1993 B Variety 1 closed shirt	16,400	—	—	—	150	175
Note: In sets only; 5,000,300 were minted and destroyed						
1993 B Variety 2 open shirt	Inc. above	—	—	—	150	175
1993 B	6,300	PF65 185				

KM# 40a.4 5 FRANCS

13.20 g., Copper-Nickel, 31.45 mm. **Obv:** William Tell right **Rev:** Shield flanked by sprigs **Edge:** DOMINUS PROVIDEBIT and 13 stars raised

Date	Mintage	VF20	XF40	MS60	MS63	MS65
1994 B	12,017,300	—	—	7.50	9.00	12.00
1994 B	6,100	PF65 16.00				
1995 B	12,018,000	—	—	7.50	10.00	15.00
1995 B	6,100	PF65 18.00				
1996 B	12,017,300	—	—	7.50	10.00	15.00
1996 B	6,100	PF65 20.00				
1997 B	9,016,500	—	—	7.50	10.00	15.00
1997 B	5,500	PF65 20.00				
1998 B	9,016,000	—	—	7.50	10.00	15.00
1998 B	4,800	PF65 22.50				
1999 B	9,016,000	—	—	7.50	10.00	15.00
1999 B	5,000	PF65 22.50				
2000 B	7,020,000	—	—	7.50	9.00	12.00
2000 B	5,500	PF65 18.00				

KM# 36 10 FRANCS

3.23 g., 0.900 Gold 0.0933 oz. AGW **Obv:** Young bust left **Rev:** Radiant cross above date and sprigs

Date	Mintage	VF20	XF40	MS60	MS63	MS65
1911 B	100,000	325	425	525	700	800
1912 B	200,000	180	200	230	280	285
1913 B	600,000	175	180	200	225	230
1914 B	200,000	175	185	200	230	235
1915 B	400,000	175	185	200	225	235
1916 B	130,000	145	200	250	275	280
1922 B	1,020,000	125	145	165	185	200

KM# 35.1 20 FRANCS

6.45 g., 0.900 Gold 0.1867 oz. AGW **Obv:** Young head left **Obv. Legend:** HELVETIA **Rev:** Shield within oak branches divides value

Date	Mintage	VF20	XF40	MS60	MS63	MS65
1901 B	500,000	250	250	300	330	350
1902 B	600,000	250	250	310	330	350
1903 B	200,000	250	270	285	300	325
1904 B	100,000	250	300	325	375	500
1905 B	100,000	250	285	310	350	450
1906 B	100,000	250	275	295	315	345
1907 B	150,000	—	250	285	300	325
1908 B	355,000	—	250	260	275	300
1909 B	400,000	—	250	260	275	300
1910 B	375,000	—	250	260	275	300
1911 B	350,000	—	250	260	275	300
1912 B	450,000	—	250	260	275	300
1913 B	700,000	—	250	260	275	300
1914 B	700,000	—	250	260	275	300
1915 B	750,000	—	250	260	275	300
1916 B	300,000	—	250	260	275	300
1922 B	2,783,678	—	250	300	320	340
1925 B	400,000	—	250	260	275	285
1926 B	50,000	250	275	300	325	365
1927 B	5,015,000	—	250	260	300	320
1930 B	3,371,764	—	250	260	300	320
1935 B	175,000	—	250	260	275	300
1935 L-B	20,008,813	—	250	275	320	340

Note: The 1935L-B issue was struck in 1945, 1946 and 1947

KM# 35.2 20 FRANCS

6.45 g., 0.900 Gold 0.1867 oz. AGW **Obv:** Bust left **Rev:** Shield within oak branches divides value **Edge Lettering:** AD LEGEM ANNI MCMXXXI

Date	Mintage	VF20	XF40	MS60	MS63	MS65
1947 B	9,200,000	—	250	275	300	325
1949 B	10,000,000	—	250	275	300	325

KM# 49 25 FRANCS

5.65 g., 0.900 Gold 0.1633 oz. AGW **Obv:** Value above small cross **Rev:** William Tell with bow **Note:** Not available in commercial channels.

Date	Mintage	VF20	XF40	MS60	MS63	MS65
1955 B	5,000,000	—	—	—	—	—
1958 B	5,000,000	—	—	—	—	—
1959 B	5,000,000	—	—	—	—	—

KM# 50 50 FRANCS

11.29 g., 0.900 Gold 0.3267 oz. AGW **Obv:** Value above small cross **Rev:** Three standing figures facing **Note:** Not available in commercial channels.

Date	Mintage	VF20	XF40	MS60	MS63	MS65
1955 B	2,000,000	—	—	—	—	—
1958 B	2,000,000	—	—	—	—	—
1959 B	2,000,000	—	—	—	—	—

KM# 39 100 FRANCS

32.26 g., 0.900 Gold 0.9334 oz. AGW **Obv:** Young bust left **Rev:** Radiant cross above value, date and sprigs

Date	Mintage	VF20	XF40	MS60	MS63	MS65
1925 B	5,000	8,000	9,000	12,500	15,000	20,000

COMMEMORATIVE COINAGE

KM# 41 5 FRANCS

15.00 g., 0.835 Silver 0.4027 oz. ASW, 31 mm. **Subject:** Confederation Armament Fund **Obv:** Kneeling female figure holding sword and dove right **Rev:** Inscription within square flanked by oak leaves **Edge:** DOMINUS PROVIDEBIT (13 stars)

Date	Mintage	VF20	XF40	MS60	MS63	MS65
1936 B	130,000	15.00	20.00	30.00	40.00	75.00
1936 B Specimen	—	—	—	—	—	300

KM# 42 5 FRANCS

15.00 g., 0.835 Silver 0.4027 oz. ASW, 31 mm. **Subject:** 600th Anniversary - Battle of Laupen **Obv:** Seated hooded figure facing right **Rev:** Cross, date and value **Edge Lettering:** DOMINUS PROVIDEBIT (13 stars)

Date	Mintage	VF20	XF40	MS60	MS63	MS65
1939 B	30,600	200	300	400	450	550

KM# 43 5 FRANCS

15.00 g., 0.835 Silver 0.4027 oz. ASW, 31 mm. **Subject:** Zurich Exposition **Obv:** Small cross on shield above inscription **Rev:** Shaking hands below standing figures with horse **Edge:** Reeded

Date	Mintage	VF20	XF40	MS60	MS63	MS65
1939 B	60,000	40.00	50.00	70.00	95.00	150
Note: Minted at Huguenin, Le Locle						
1939 Specimen	—	—	—	—	—	900
1939 B Matte	—	1,000	1,200	1,750	1,900	2,200

KM# 44 5 FRANCS
15.00 g., 0.835 Silver 0.4027 oz. ASW, 31 mm. **Subject:** 650th Anniversary of Confederation **Obv:** Three standing figures representing the original cantons of Uri, Schwyz and Unterwalden **Rev:** Small cross divides dates above inscription **Edge Lettering:** DOMINUS PROVIDEBIT (13 stars)

Date	Mintage	VF20	XF40	MS60	MS63	MS65
ND-1941 B	100,150	20.00	35.00	45.00	60.00	90.00
ND-1941 B Specimen	—	—	—	—	—	360

KM# 45 5 FRANCS
15.00 g., 0.835 Silver 0.4027 oz. ASW, 31 mm. **Subject:** 500th Anniversary - Battle of St. Jakob An Der Birs **Obv:** Kneeling figure looking right **Rev:** Small cross above inscription **Edge Lettering:** DOMINUS PROVIDEBIT (13 stars)

Date	Mintage	VF20	XF40	MS60	MS63	MS65
1944 B	101,680	20.00	30.00	45.00	55.00	70.00
1944 B Specimen	—	—	—	—	—	360

KM# 48 5 FRANCS
15.00 g., 0.835 Silver 0.4027 oz. ASW, 31 mm. **Subject:** Swiss Constitution Centennial **Obv:** Seated woman and child facing left **Rev:** Small cross divides date below inscription **Edge Lettering:** DOMINUS PROVIDEBIT (13 stars)

Date	Mintage	VF20	XF40	MS60	MS63	MS65
1948 B	500,400	7.75	15.00	18.00	25.00	30.00
1948 B Specimen	—	—	—	—	—	150

KM# 51 5 FRANCS
15.00 g., 0.835 Silver 0.4027 oz. ASW, 31 mm. **Subject:** Red Cross Centennial **Obv:** Value **Rev:** Nurse standing, patient on stretcher, motif forming a cross **Edge Lettering:** DOMINUS PROVIDEBIT (13 stars)

Date	Mintage	VF20	XF40	MS60	MS63	MS65
ND-1963 B	623,000	7.75	15.00	18.00	22.00	28.00
ND-1963 B Specimen	—	—	—	—	—	120

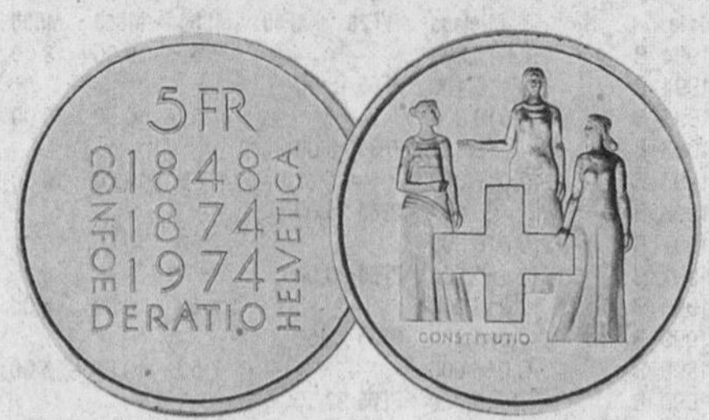

KM# 52 5 FRANCS
13.20 g., Copper-Nickel, 31.45 mm. **Subject:** 100th Anniversary - Revision of Constitution **Obv:** Dates flanked by vertical inscriptions **Rev:** Three standing female figures and cross **Edge Lettering:** DOMINUS PROVIDEBIT (13 stars)

Date	Mintage	VF20	XF40	MS60	MS63	MS65
ND-1974	3,709,000	—	—	8.00	10.00	12.00
ND-1974	130,000	PF65 20.00				

KM# 53 5 FRANCS
13.20 g., Copper-Nickel, 31.45 mm. **Subject:** European Monument Protection Year **Obv:** Value and inscription **Rev:** Date above inscription flanked by hands **Edge Lettering:** DOMINUS PROVIDEBIT (13 stars)

Date	Mintage	VF20	XF40	MS60	MS63	MS65
1975	2,500,000	—	—	8.00	10.00	12.00
1975	60,000	PF65 30.00				

KM# 54 5 FRANCS
13.20 g., Copper-Nickel, 31.45 mm. **Subject:** 500th Anniversary - Battle of Murten **Obv:** Value **Rev:** Stylized figures **Edge Lettering:** DOMINUS PROVIDEBIT (13 stars)

Date	Mintage	VF20	XF40	MS60	MS63	MS65
1976	1,506,000	—	—	8.00	10.00	12.00
1976	100,900	PF65 25.00				

KM# 55 5 FRANCS
13.20 g., Copper-Nickel, 31.45 mm. **Subject:** 150th Anniversary - Death of Johann Pestalozzi **Obv:** Value and cross at center **Rev:** Hooded head left **Edge Lettering:** DOMINUS PROVIDEBIT (13 stars)

Date	Mintage	VF20	XF40	MS60	MS63	MS65
1977	802,000	—	—	8.00	10.00	12.00
1977	50,260	PF65 25.00				

KM# 56 5 FRANCS
13.20 g., Copper-Nickel, 31.45 mm. **Subject:** 150th Anniversary - Birth of Henry Dunant, founder of the International Red Cross **Obv:** Value and date **Rev:** Head facing **Edge Lettering:** DOMINUS PROVIDEBIT (13 stars)

Date	Mintage	VF20	XF40	MS60	MS63	MS65
1978	903,000	—	—	8.00	10.00	12.00
1978	60,000	PF65 25.00				

KM# 57 5 FRANCS
13.20 g., Copper-Nickel, 31.45 mm. **Subject:** Centennial - Birth of Albert Einstein (Portrait) **Obv:** Inscription, value and date **Rev:** Head facing **Edge Lettering:** DOMINUS PROVIDEBIT (13 stars)

Date	Mintage	VF20	XF40	MS60	MS63	MS65
1979	900,000	—	—	10.00	12.00	14.00
1979	35,000	PF65 50.00				

KM# 58 5 FRANCS
13.20 g., Copper-Nickel, 31.45 mm. **Subject:** Centennial - Birth of Albert Einstein (Formula) **Obv:** Inscription above value **Rev:** Formulas

Date	Mintage	VF20	XF40	MS60	MS63	MS65
1979	902,000	—	—	10.00	12.00	14.00
1979	35,000	PF65 50.00				

KM# 59 5 FRANCS
13.20 g., Copper-Nickel, 31.45 mm. **Subject:** Ferdinand Hodler - Painter **Obv:** Value above legend and date **Rev:** Head facing **Edge Lettering:** DOMINUS PROVIDEBIT (13 stars)

Date	Mintage	VF20	XF40	MS60	MS63	MS65
1980	951,000	—	—	10.00	12.00	14.00
1980	50,200	PF65 25.00				

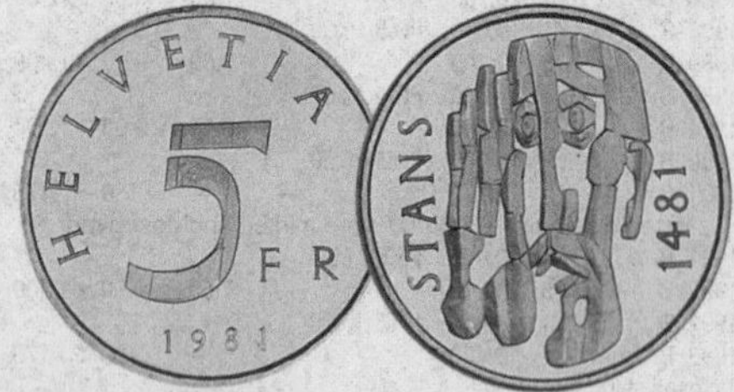

KM# 60 5 FRANCS
13.20 g., Copper-Nickel, 31.45 mm. **Subject:** 500th Anniversary - Stans Convention of 1481 **Obv:** Value and date **Rev:** Stylized design **Edge Lettering:** DOMINUS PROVIDEBIT (13 stars)

Date	Mintage	VF20	XF40	MS60	MS63	MS65
1981	951,000	—	—	8.00	10.00	12.00
1981	50,200	PF65 20.00				

KM# 61 5 FRANCS

13.20 g., Copper-Nickel, 31.45 mm. **Subject:** 100th Anniversary - Gotthard Railway **Obv:** Value and date above sprigs **Rev:** Stylized design **Edge:** Lettering in relief **Edge Lettering:** DOMINUS PROVIDEBIT (stars)

Date	Mintage	VF20	XF40	MS60	MS63	MS65
1982	902,000	—	—	8.00	10.00	12.00
1982	35,100	PF65 20.00				

KM# 62 5 FRANCS

13.20 g., Copper-Nickel, 31.45 mm. **Subject:** 100th Anniversary - Birth of Ernest Ansermet **Obv:** Value and date **Rev:** Music notes within head right **Edge Lettering:** DOMINUS PROVIDEBIT (13 stars)

Date	Mintage	VF20	XF40	MS60	MS63	MS65
1983	951,000	—	—	8.00	10.00	12.00
1983	60,160	PF65 20.00				

KM# 63 5 FRANCS

13.20 g., Copper-Nickel, 31.45 mm. **Subject:** Centennial - Birth of Auguste Piccard **Obv:** Value and date **Rev:** Stylized designs **Edge Lettering:** DOMINUS PROVIDEBIT (13 stars)

Date	Mintage	VF20	XF40	MS60	MS63	MS65
1984	1,012,000	—	—	8.00	10.00	12.00
1984	75,990	PF65 20.00				

KM# 64 5 FRANCS

13.20 g., Copper-Nickel, 31.45 mm. **Subject:** European Year of Music **Obv:** Value and vertical inscription **Rev:** Sphere design **Edge Lettering:** DOMINUS PROVIDEBIT (13 stars)

Date	Mintage	VF20	XF40	MS60	MS63	MS65
1985	1,156,000	—	—	7.00	8.00	10.00
1985	84,400	PF65 15.00				

KM# 65 5 FRANCS

13.20 g., Copper-Nickel, 31.45 mm. **Subject:** 500th Anniversary - Battle of Sempach **Obv:** Cross above inscription and date **Rev:** Stylized design **Edge Lettering:** DOMINUS PROVIDEBIT (13 stars)

Date	Mintage	VF20	XF40	MS60	MS63	MS65
1986 B	1,082,000	—	—	7.00	8.00	10.00
1986 B	75,800	PF65 15.00				

KM# 66 5 FRANCS

13.20 g., Copper-Nickel, 31.45 mm. **Subject:** 100th Anniversary - Birth of Le Corbusier **Obv:** Value within diamond shape **Rev:** Standing figure within squared design **Edge Lettering:** DOMINUS PROVIDEBIT (13 stars)

Date	Mintage	VF20	XF40	MS60	MS63	MS65
1987 B	960,000	—	—	7.00	8.00	10.00
1987 B	62,515	PF65 20.00				

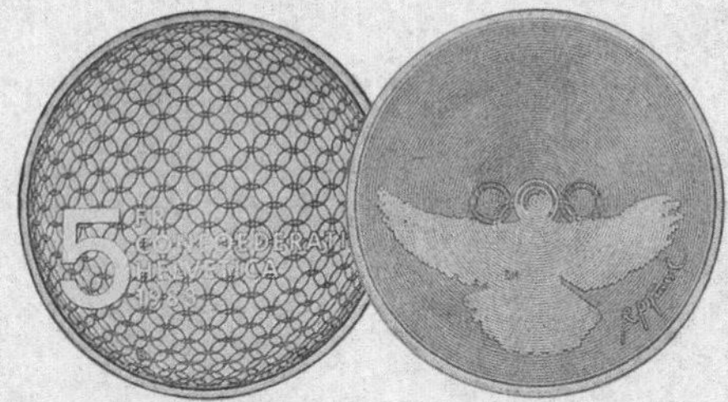

KM# 67 5 FRANCS

13.20 g., Copper-Nickel, 31.45 mm. **Subject:** Olympics - Dove and Rings **Obv:** Value within entwined circles **Rev:** Stylized dove and circles **Edge Lettering:** DOMINUS PROVIDEBIT (13 stars)

Date	Mintage	VF20	XF40	MS60	MS63	MS65
1988 B	1,026,000	—	—	7.00	8.00	10.00
1988 B	68,527	PF65 20.00				

KM# 68 5 FRANCS

13.20 g., Copper-Nickel, 31.45 mm. **Subject:** General Guisan - 1939 Mobilization **Obv:** Value within cluster of small crosses **Rev:** Stylized head with cap facing 1/4 left **Edge Lettering:** DOMINUS PROVIDEBIT (13 stars)

Date	Mintage	VF20	XF40	MS60	MS63	MS65
1989 B	1,270,000	—	—	7.00	8.00	10.00
1989 B	69,012	PF65 20.00				

KM# 69 5 FRANCS

13.20 g., Copper-Nickel, 31.45 mm. **Subject:** Gottfried Keller **Obv:** Value, inscription and date **Rev:** Bust left **Edge Lettering:** DOMINUS PROVIDEBIT (13 stars)

Date	Mintage	VF20	XF40	MS60	MS63	MS65
1990 B	1,100,000	—	—	7.00	8.00	10.00
1990 B	69,412	PF65 15.00				

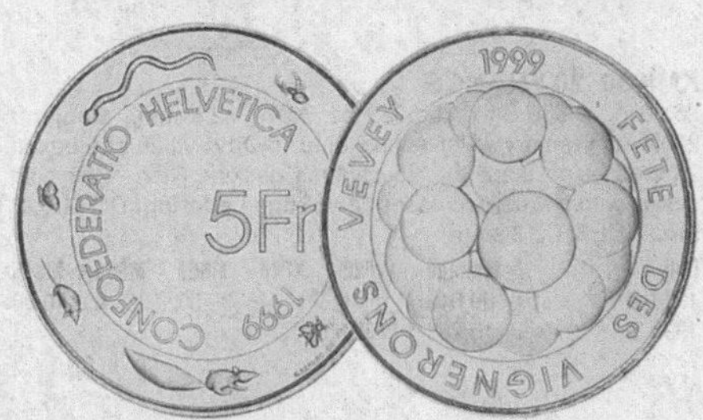

KM# 86 5 FRANCS

15.00 g., Bi-Metallic Nordic gold center in Copper-Nickel ring, 32.85 mm. **Subject:** Wine Festival **Obv:** Value and inscription within circle, assorted rodents around border **Rev:** Grapes within circle **Edge:** Reeded **Edge Lettering:** DOMINUS PROVIDEBIT (13 stars)

Date	Mintage	VF20	XF40	MS60	MS63	MS65
1999 B	160,000	—	—	7.00	9.00	12.00
1999 B	16,000	PF65 30.00				

KM# 89 5 FRANCS

15.00 g., Bi-Metallic Nordic gold center in Copper-Nickel ring, 32.85 mm. **Subject:** Basler Fasnacht **Obv:** Value within circle **Rev:** Costumed flutists within circle **Edge:** Reeded **Edge Lettering:** DOMINUS PROVIDEBIT (13 stars)

Date	Mintage	VF20	XF40	MS60	MS63	MS65
2000 B	170,000	—	—	7.00	9.00	12.00
2000 B	20,000	PF65 30.00				

KM# 91 5 FRANCS

15.00 g., Bi-Metallic Nordic Gold center in Copper-Nickel ring, 32.85 mm. **Subject:** Swiss National Coinage, 150 Years **Obv:** Value within detailed leaf surface showing vein structure **Rev:** Honeycomb design within circle **Edge:** Reeded **Edge Lettering:** DOMINUS PROVIDEBIT (13 stars)

Date	Mintage	VF20	XF40	MS60	MS63	MS65
2000 B	150,000	—	—	7.00	9.00	12.00
2000 B	15,000	PF65 30.00				

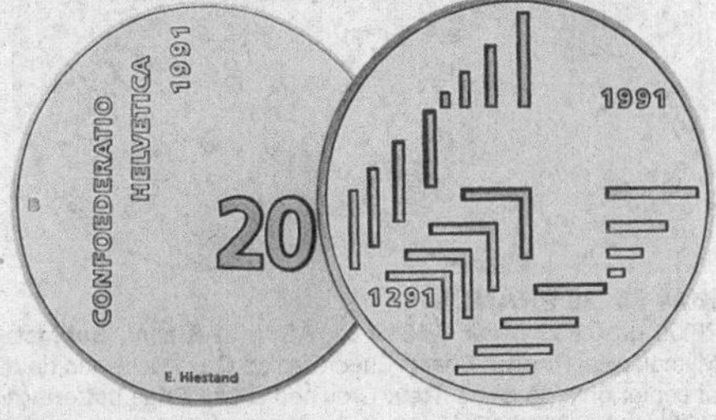

KM# 70 20 FRANCS

20.00 g., 0.835 Silver 0.5369 oz. ASW, 32.8 mm. **Subject:** 700 Years of Confederation **Obv:** Value **Rev:** Dates and designs **Edge Lettering:** CONFOEDERATIO HELVETICA ++ 1291-- 1991 ++

Date	Mintage	VF20	XF40	MS60	MS63	MS65
1991 B	641,553	—	—	26.00	28.00	32.00
1991 B	8,340	PF65 40.00				

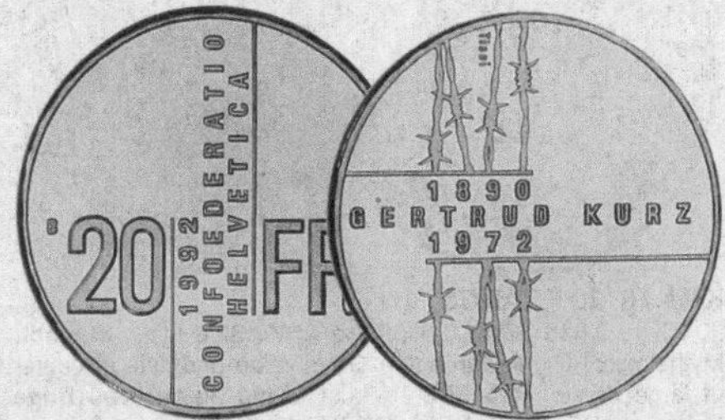

KM# 72 20 FRANCS

20.00 g., 0.835 Silver 0.5369 oz. ASW, 32.8 mm. **Subject:** Gertrud Kurz **Obv:** Vertical inscription and date divides value **Rev:** Horizontal dates and inscription divides barbed wire **Edge Lettering:** DOMINUS PROVIDEBIT (13 stars)

Date	Mintage	VF20	XF40	MS60	MS63	MS65
1992 B	179,203	—	—	26.00	28.00	32.00
1992 B	36,000	PF65 40.00				

KM# 73 20 FRANCS
20.00 g., 0.835 Silver 0.5369 oz. ASW, 32.8 mm. **Subject:** 500th Anniversary - Birth of Paracelsus **Obv:** Value and date **Rev:** Head 1/4 left **Edge Lettering:** DOMINUS PROVIDEBIT (13 stars)

Date	Mintage	VF20	XF40	MS60	MS63	MS65
1993 B	176,574	—	—	26.00	30.00	34.00
1993 B	29,530	PF65 42.00				

KM# 74 20 FRANCS
20.00 g., 0.835 Silver 0.5369 oz. ASW, 32.8 mm. **Subject:** Devil's Bridge - Teufelsbrucke raised **Obv:** Value and date at center of large cross **Rev:** Stylized devil within trees **Edge Lettering:** DOMINUS PROVIDEBIT (13 stars)

Date	Mintage	VF20	XF40	MS60	MS63	MS65
1994 B	175,897	—	—	26.00	30.00	34.00
1994 B	32,195	PF65 42.00				

KM# 75 20 FRANCS
20.00 g., 0.835 Silver 0.5369 oz. ASW, 32.8 mm. **Subject:** Mythological Raetian Snake Queen raised **Obv:** Value and date at center of large cross **Rev:** Crowned snake **Edge Lettering:** DOMINUS PROVIDEBIT (13 stars)

Date	Mintage	VF20	XF40	MS60	MS63	MS65
1995 B	143,068	—	—	26.00	30.00	34.00
1995 B	30,381	PF65 42.00				

KM# 76 20 FRANCS
20.00 g., 0.835 Silver 0.5369 oz. ASW, 32.8 mm. **Subject:** Mythological Giant Gargantua **Obv:** Value and date at center of large cross **Rev:** Giant's bust facing above trees **Edge Lettering:** DOMINUS PROVIDEBIT (13 stars)

Date	Mintage	VF20	XF40	MS60	MS63	MS65
1996 B	112,103	—	—	26.00	30.00	34.00
1996 B	29,424	PF65 42.00				

KM# 77 20 FRANCS
20.00 g., 0.835 Silver 0.5369 oz. ASW, 32.8 mm. **Subject:** Mythological Dragon of Breno **Obv:** Value and date at center of large cross **Rev:** Dragon above mountains and water **Edge Lettering:** DOMINUS PROVIDEBIT (13 stars)

Date	Mintage	VF20	XF40	MS60	MS63	MS65
1996 B	98,038	—	—	26.00	30.00	34.00
1996 B	26,367	PF65 42.00				

KM# 78 20 FRANCS
20.00 g., 0.835 Silver 0.5369 oz. ASW, 32.8 mm. **Subject:** 150th Anniversary - Swiss Railway **Obv:** Modern train wheel **Rev:** Ancient train wheel **Edge Lettering:** DOMINUS PROVIDEBIT (13 stars)

Date	Mintage	VF20	XF40	MS60	MS63	MS65
1997 B	160,172	—	—	26.00	30.00	34.00
1997 B	18,997	PF65 50.00				

KM# 79 20 FRANCS
20.00 g., 0.835 Silver 0.5369 oz. ASW, 32.8 mm. **Subject:** 200th Anniversary - Birth of Jeremias Gotthelf **Obv:** Stylized numeral value and date **Rev:** Bust facing **Edge Lettering:** DOMINUS PROVIDEBIT (13 stars)

Date	Mintage	VF20	XF40	MS60	MS63	MS65
1997 B	99,512	—	—	26.00	30.00	34.00
1997 B	19,494	PF65 50.00				

KM# 80 20 FRANCS
20.00 g., 0.835 Silver 0.5369 oz. ASW, 32.8 mm. **Subject:** 200th Anniversary - Helvetian Republic **Obv:** Value and boxed 25 crosses to mark the 25 cantons design **Rev:** 1798 coin design within square, crosses flank **Edge Lettering:** DOMINUS PROVIDEBIT (13 stars)

Date	Mintage	VF20	XF40	MS60	MS63	MS65
1998 B	69,013	—	—	30.00	35.00	40.00
1998 B	15,284	PF65 55.00				

KM# 82 20 FRANCS
20.00 g., 0.835 Silver 0.5369 oz. ASW, 32.8 mm. **Subject:** 150th Anniversary - Confederation **Obv:** Boxed crosses design and value **Rev:** 1848 coin design within square flanked by crosses **Edge Lettering:** DOMINUS PROVIDEBIT (13 stars)

Date	Mintage	VF20	XF40	MS60	MS63	MS65
1998 B	72,187	—	—	30.00	35.00	40.00
1998 B	15,500	PF65 55.00				

KM# 84 20 FRANCS
20.00 g., 0.835 Silver 0.5369 oz. ASW, 32.8 mm. **Subject:** Death of C.F. Meyer **Obv:** Value and date **Rev:** Large head 3/4 right with signature across face **Edge Lettering:** DOMINUS PROVIDEBIT (13 stars)

Date	Mintage	VF20	XF40	MS60	MS63	MS65
1998 B	67,995	—	—	30.00	38.00	45.00
1998 B	14,411	PF65 60.00				

KM# 85 20 FRANCS
20.00 g., 0.835 Silver 0.5369 oz. ASW, 32.8 mm. **Subject:** 150th Anniversary Swiss Postal Service **Obv:** Value, country name and date within wreath **Rev:** Cartoon-like postal carrier above globe **Edge Lettering:** DOMINUS PROVIDEBIT (13 stars)

Date	Mintage	VF20	XF40	MS60	MS63	MS65
1999 B	135,160	—	—	26.00	30.00	35.00
1999 B	10,325	PF65 55.00				

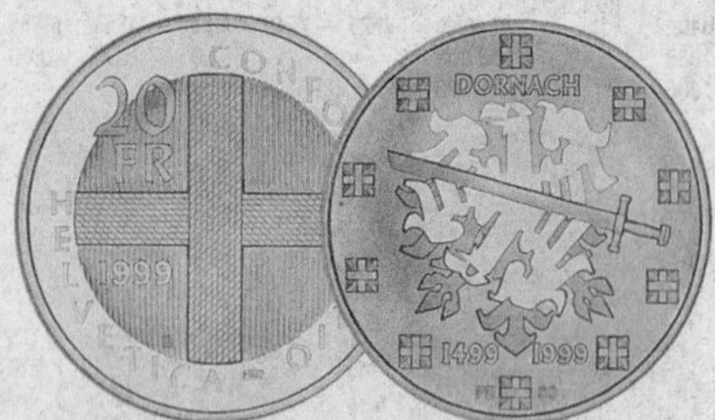

KM# 87 20 FRANCS
20.00 g., 0.835 Silver 0.5369 oz. ASW, 32.8 mm. **Subject:** Battle of Dornach **Obv:** Value and cross design **Rev:** Sword splitting an eagle, boxed crosses around border **Edge Lettering:** DOMINUS PROVIDEBIT (13 stars)

Date	Mintage	VF20	XF40	MS60	MS63	MS65
1999 B	61,828	—	—	26.00	30.00	35.00
1999 B	11,000	PF65 55.00				

KM# 90 20 FRANCS
20.00 g., 0.835 Silver 0.5369 oz. ASW, 32.8 mm. **Subject:** Year 2000 - Peace on Earth **Obv:** Olive branch **Rev:** Angel floating above people **Edge Lettering:** DOMINUS PROVIDEBIT (13 stars)

Date	Mintage	VF20	XF40	MS60	MS63	MS65
2000 B	56,469	—	—	26.00	30.00	35.00
2000 B	9,635	PF65 55.00				

KM# 97 20 FRANCS
20.00 g., 0.835 Silver 0.5369 oz. ASW, 32.8 mm. **Subject:** Lumen Christi **Obv:** Inscription above value **Rev:** Jesus preaching within design **Edge Lettering:** DOMINUS PROVIDEBIT (13 stars)

Date	Mintage	VF20	XF40	MS60	MS63	MS65
2000 B	43,787	—	—	26.00	30.00	35.00
2000 B	8,111	PF65 55.00				

KM# 81 100 FRANCS
22.58 g., 0.900 Gold 0.6534 oz. AGW, 27.8 mm. **Subject:** 200th Anniversary of Helvetian Republic **Obv:** Value and boxed crosses design **Rev:** 1798 coin design within square flanked by crosses **Edge Lettering:** DOMINUS PROVIDEBIT (13 stars)

Date	Mintage	VF20	XF40	MS60	MS63	MS65
1998 B	2,500	PF65 1,900				

KM# 83 100 FRANCS
22.58 g., 0.900 Gold 0.6534 oz. AGW, 27.8 mm. **Subject:** 150th Anniversary of Swiss Confederation **Obv:** Value and boxed crosses design **Rev:** 1848 coin design within square flanked by crosses **Edge Lettering:** DOMINUS PROVIDEBIT (13 stars)

Date	Mintage	VF20	XF40	MS60	MS63	MS65
1998 B	2,500	PF65 1,800				

KM# 88 100 FRANCS
22.58 g., 0.900 Gold 0.6534 oz. AGW, 27.8 mm. **Subject:** Wine Festival **Obv:** Value and small fox looking up at grapes **Rev:** Small fox eating grapes and cresent **Edge Lettering:** DOMINUS PROVIDEBIT (13 stars)

Date	Mintage	VF20	XF40	MS60	MS63	MS65
1999 B	3,000	PF65 1,500				

KM# 96 100 FRANCS
22.58 g., 0.900 Gold 0.6534 oz. AGW, 27.8 mm. **Subject:** 2000 Years of Christianity **Obv:** Inscription and date divides value **Rev:** Stylized baby **Edge:** Lettered

Date	Mintage	VF20	XF40	MS60	MS63	MS65
2000 B	2,130	PF65 1,500				

KM# 71.1 250 FRANCS
8.00 g., 0.900 Gold 0.2315 oz. AGW, 22.85 mm. **Subject:** 700 Years of Confederation **Obv:** Diagonal and horizontal inscription to right of value **Rev:** Dates **Edge Lettering:** DOMINUS PROVIDEBIT (13 stars)

Date	Mintage	VF20	XF40	MS60	MS63	MS65
1991 B	296,741	—	310	400	425	450

Note: 200,000 recalled and melted due to poor quality

KM# 71.2 250 FRANCS
8.00 g., 0.900 Gold 0.2315 oz. AGW, 22.85 mm. **Subject:** 700 Years of Confederation **Edge Lettering:** DOMINUS PROVIDEBIT (13 stars)

Date	Mintage	VF20	XF40	MS60	MS63	MS65
1991 B	193,259	—	310	400	425	450

ESSAIS

KM#	Date	Mintage	Identification	Mkt Val
EA4	1910B	56	10 Francs. Gold.	35,000
E4	1911	Inc. above	10 Francs. Gold.	50,000
E5	1925B	—	100 Francs. Bronze. Young head left. Radiant cross above value, date and sprigs.	4,000
E6	1925B	—	100 Francs. Bronze. Head left.	3,500
E17	1928B	—	100 Francs. Brass. Plain. Prev. KM#E5.	5,000
EA8	1930B	—	5 Francs. Silver. Hooded bust right. Cross on shield flanked by sprigs. Formerly Pn63.	20,000
E8	1930	—	Franc. Nickel.	20,000
E18	1930B	—	100 Francs. Brass. Lettered. Prev. KM#E6.	7,500
E9	1998B	250	20 Francs. 0.835. Silver. KM#80.	650
E10	1998B	250	20 Francs. 0.835. Silver. KM#82.	650
E11	1998B	500	20 Francs. 0.835. Silver. KM#84.	400
EA12	1999B	765	5 Francs. Bi-Metallic. KM#86.	210
E12	2000B	750	20 Francs. 0.835. Silver. KM#97.	300

PATTERNS

Including off metal strikes

KM#	Date	Mintage	Identification	Mkt Val
Pn40	1910	56	10 Francs. Gold. Reeded.	75,000
Pn41	1910	Inc. above	10 Francs. Gold. Plain.	80,000
Pn42	1917	6	5 Rappen. Brass.	6,000
Pn43	1918	—	10 Rappen. Nickel.	—
Pn44	1922B	—	5 Francs. Silver.	3,500
Pn45	1924B	—	5 Francs.	20,000
Pn46	1925B	—	10 Francs. Silver.	6,000
Pn47	1925B	—	100 Francs. Copper.	5,000
Pn48	1927B	—	20 Rappen. Nickel.	5,000
Pn49	1928B	—	20 Rappen. Nickel.	5,000
Pn50	1928B	—	Franc. Nickel.	8,000
Pn51	1928B	—	2 Francs. Nickel.	8,500
Pn52	1928B	—	5 Francs. Silver.	25,000
Pn53	1928B	—	5 Francs. Nickel.	20,000
Pn54	1929B	—	5 Rappen. Bronze.	—
Pn55	1929B	—	50 Rappen. Nickel.	8,000
Pn56	1929	—	5 Francs. Silver.	35,000
Pn57	1930B	—	10 Rappen. Nickel.	3,000
Pn58	1930B	—	20 Rappen. Nickel.	3,000
Pn59	1930B	—	50 Rappen. Nickel.	6,000
Pn60	1930	—	50 Rappen. Nickel. Triangle.	5,500
Pn61	19xx (1930)B	—	Franc. Nickel.	—
Pn62	19xx (1930)B	—	5 Francs. Silver.	30,000
Pn64	1931	—	5 Rappen. Copper-Nickel.	—
Pn65	1931	—	50 Rappen. Nickel.	4,000
Pn66	1935	—	20 Francs. Copper.	—
Pn67	1937B	—	Franc. Copper-Nickel.	8,000
Pn68	1937B	—	2 Francs. Copper-Nickel.	8,000
Pn69	1937	—	5 Francs. Aluminum.	5,000
Pn70	1938B	—	20 Rappen. Zinc.	2,500
Pn71	1938B	—	Franc. Copper-Nickel.	4,500
Pn72	1938B	—	2 Francs. Copper-Nickel.	5,000
Pn73	1939B	—	5 Rappen. Zinc. KM#26.	1,600
Pn74	1939	—	5 Francs. Silver.	6,000
Pn75	1940B	—	5 Rappen. Aluminum. KM#26.	3,500
PnA76	1940B	—	20 Rappen. Copper-Nickel. KM#29a.	2,850
Pn76	1940B	—	10 Rappen. Zinc. KM#27.	2,000
Pn77	1940B	—	10 Rappen. Aluminum. KM#27.	4,200
Pn78	1941B	—	2 Francs. Silver-Zinc.	2,500
Pn79	1941B	—	Rappen. Aluminum. KM#3.	2,500
Pn80	1941B	—	2 Rappen. Aluminum. KM#4.	3,000
Pn81	1947	—	20 Francs, Gold.	—
Pn82	1948B	—	5 Francs. Copper Gilt.	3,500
Pn83	1955B	—	25 Francs. Silver. KM#49.	17,500
Pn84	1955B	—	50 Francs. Silver. KM#50.	17,500
Pn85	1959B	—	50 Francs. Aluminum. KM#50.	9,000
Pn86	1979	—	5 Rappen. Aluminum-Bronze. Prev. Pn.#85.	2,000

TRIAL STRIKES

KM#	Date	Mintage	Identification	Mkt Val
TS3	1935	—	20 Francs. Copper.	3,250

MINT SETS

KM#	Date	Mintage	Identification	Issue Price	Mkt Val
MS2	1970 (9)	10,000	KM#21a.1, 23a.1-24a.1, 26-27, 29a, 40a.1, 46-47	6.40	60.00
MS3	1971 (5)	5,000	KM#23a.1-24a.1, 26, 29a, 46	2.40	45.00
MS4	1972 (3)	5,000	KM#21a.1, 23a.1, 27	2.40	45.00
MS5	1973 (6)	10,000	KM#21a.1, 23a.1-24a.1, 27, 40a.1, 46	6.40	55.00
MS6	1974 (9)	10,000	KM#21a.1, 23a.1-24a.1, 26-27, 29a, 40a.1, 46-47	6.40	75.00
MS7	1975 (8)	10,000	KM#21a.1, 23a.1-24a.1, 26-27, 29a, 40a.1, 46	6.40	45.00
MS8	1976 (8)	10,000	KM#21a.1, 23a.1-24a.1, 26-27, 29a, 40a.1, 46	9.00	45.00
MS9	1977 (8)	10,000	KM#21a.1, 23a.1-24a.1, 26-27, 29a, 40a.1, 46	9.00	40.00
MS10	1978 (8)	10,000	KM#21a.1, 23a.1-24a.1, 26-27, 29a, 40a.1, 46	9.00	35.00
MS11	1979 (8)	10,000	KM#21a.1, 23a.1-24a.1, 26-27, 29a, 40a.1, 46	9.00	35.00
MS12	1980 (8)	15,000	KM#21a.1, 23a.1-24a.1, 26-27, 29a, 40a.1, 46	9.00	40.00
MS13	1981 (8)	15,000	KM#21a.1, 23a.1-24a.1, 26c, 27, 29a, 40a.1, 46	9.00	35.00
MS14	1982 (8)	15,000	KM#21a.2, 23a.2-24a.2, 26c, 27, 29a, 40a.2, 46	9.00	35.00
MS15	1983 (8)	15,740	KM#21a.3, 23a.3-24a.3, 26c, 27, 29a, 40a.2, 46	9.00	35.00
MS16	1984 (8)	20,000	KM#21a.3, 23a.3-24a.3, 26c, 27, 29a, 40a.2, 46	9.00	35.00
MS17	1985 (8)	22,250	KM#21a.3, 23a.3-24a.3, 26c, 27, 29a, 40a.3, 46	9.00	35.00
MS18	1986 (8)	21,400	KM#21a.3, 23a.3-24a.3, 26c, 27, 29a, 40a.3, 46	9.00	35.00
MS19	1987 (8)	19,100	KM#21a.3, 23a.3-24a.3, 26c, 27, 29a, 40a.3, 46	9.00	45.00
MS20	1988 (8)	20,700	KM#21a.3, 23a.3-24a.3, 26c, 27, 29a, 40a.3, 46	—	35.00
MS21	1989 (8)	22,700	KM#21a.3, 23a.3-24a.3, 26c, 27, 29a, 40a.3, 46	11.00	35.00
MS22	1990 (8)	23,100	KM#21a.3, 23a.3-24a.3, 26c, 27, 29a, 40a.3, 46	—	35.00
MS23	1991 (8)	26,100	KM#21a.3, 23a.3-24a.3, 26c, 27, 29a, 40a.3, 46	—	200
MS24	1991 (2)	110,000	KM#70-71	210	500
MS25	1992 (8)	20,300	KM#21a.3, 23a.3-24a.3, 26c, 27, 29a, 40a.3, 46	—	35.00
MS26	1993 (8)	16,200	KM#21a.3, 23a.3-24a.3, 26c, 27, 29a, 40a.3, 46	—	200
MS27	1994 (8)	17,300	KM#21a.3, 23a.3-24a.3, 26c, 27, 29a, 40a.4, 46	—	30.00
MS28	1995 (8)	18,000	KM#21a.3, 23a.3-24a.3, 26c, 27, 29a, 40a.4, 46	—	30.00
MS29	1996 (8)	17,300	KM#21a.3, 23a.3-24a.3, 26c, 27, 29a, 40a.3, 46	—	30.00
MS30	1997 (8)	16,500	KM#21a.3, 23a.3, 24a.3, 26c, 27, 29a, 40a.4, 46	—	30.00
MS31	1998 (8)	16,000	KM#21a.3, 23a.3, 24a.3, 26c, 27, 29a, 40a.4, 46	—	30.00

KM#	Date	Mintage	Identification	Issue Price	Mkt Val
MS32	1999 (8)	16,000	KM#21a.3, 23a.3, 24a.3, 26c, 27, 29a, 40a.4, 46	—	65.00
MS33	2000 (9)	18,000	KM#21a.3, 23a.3, 24a.3, 26c, 27, 29a, 40a.4, 46, 89 Fasnacht	—	70.00
MS34	2000 (9)	2,000	KM#21a.3, 23a.3, 24a.3, 26c, 27, 29a, 40a.4, 46, 91 150 Years of the Swiss Franken	—	325

PROOF SETS

KM#	Date	Mintage	Identification	Issue Price	Mkt Val
PS1	1974 (9)	2,400	KM#21a.1, 23a.1, 24a.1, 26, 27, 29a, 40a.1, 46-47	12.80	650
PS2	1975 (8)	10,000	KM#21a.1, 23a.1, 24a.1, 26, 27, 29a, 40a.1, 46	16.75	60.00
PS3	1976 (8)	5,130	KM#21a.1, 23a.1, 24a.1, 26, 27, 29a, 40a.1, 46	16.75	70.00
PS4	1977 (8)	7,030	KM#21a.1, 23a.1, 24a.1, 26, 27, 29a, 40a.1, 46	16.75	70.00
PS5	1978 (8)	10,090	KM#21a.1, 23a.1, 24a.1, 26, 27, 29a, 40a.1, 46	28.00	60.00
PS6	1979 (8)	10,150	KM#21a.1, 23a.1, 24a.1, 26, 27, 29a, 40a.1, 46	28.00	60.00
PS7	1980 (8)	10,010	KM#21a.1, 23a.1, 24a.1, 26, 27, 29a, 40a.1, 46	30.00	60.00
PS8	1981 (8)	10,280	KM#21a.1, 23a.1, 24a.1, 26c, 27, 29a, 40a.1, 46	30.00	60.00
PS9	1982 (8)	10,090	KM#21a.2, 23a.2, 24a.2, 26c, 27, 29a, 40a.2, 46	30.00	65.00
PS10	1983 (8)	11,390	KM#21a.3, 23a.3, 24a.3, 26c, 27, 29a, 40a.2, 46	30.00	60.00
PS11	1984 (8)	14,100	KM#21a.3, 23a.3, 24a.3, 26c, 27, 29a, 40a.2, 46	30.00	60.00
PS12	1985 (8)	12,000	KM#21a.3, 23a.3-24a.3, 26c, 27, 29a, 40a.3, 46	30.00	60.00
PS13	1986 (8)	10,000	KM#21a.3, 23a.3, 24a.3, 26c, 27, 29a, 40a.3, 46	30.00	60.00
PS14	1987 (8)	8,800	KM#21a.3, 23a.3, 24a.3, 26c, 27, 29a, 40a.3, 46	30.00	70.00
PS15	1988 (8)	9,050	KM#21a.3, 23a.3, 24a.3, 26c, 27, 29a, 40a.3, 46	—	65.00
PS16	1989 (8)	8,800	KM#21a.3, 23a.3, 24a.3, 26c, 27, 29a, 40a.3, 46	36.50	65.00
PS17	1990 (8)	8,900	KM#21a.3, 23a.3, 24a.3, 26c, 27, 29a, 40a.3, 46	—	65.00
PS18	1991 (8)	9,900	KM#21a.3, 23a.3, 24a.3, 26c, 27, 29a, 40a.3, 46	—	225
PS19	1992 (8)	7,450	KM#21a.3, 23a.3, 24a.3, 26c, 27, 29a, 40a.3, 46	—	70.00
PS20	1993 (8)	6,300	KM#21a.3, 23a.3, 24a.3, 26c, 27, 29a, 40a.3, 46	—	230
PS21	1994 (8)	6,100	KM#21a.3, 23a.3, 24a.3, 26c, 27, 29a, 40a.4, 46	—	70.00
PS22	1995 (8)	6,100	KM#21a.3, 23a.3, 24a.3, 26c, 27, 29a, 40a.4, 46	42.50	70.00
PS24	1996 (8)	6,100	KM#21a.3, 23a.3, 24a.3, 26c, 27, 29a, 40a.4, 46	—	70.00
PS25	1997 (8)	5,500	KM#21a.3, 23a.3, 24a.3, 26c, 27, 29a, 40a.4, 46	—	70.00
PS26	1998 (8)	4,800	KM#21a.3, 23a.3, 24a.3, 26c, 27, 29a, 40a.4, 46	—	75.00
PS27	1999 (9)	5,000	KM#21a.3, 23a.3, 24a.3, 26c, 27, 29a, 40a.4, 46, 86	—	110
PS28	2000 (9)	5,500	KM#21a.3, 23a.3, 24a.3, 26c, 27, 29a, 40a.4, 46, 89 Fasnacht	—	100
PS29	2000 (9)	500	KM#21a.3, 23a.3, 24a.3, 26c, 27, 29a, 40a.4, 46, 91 150 Years of the Swiss Franken	—	120

SYRIA

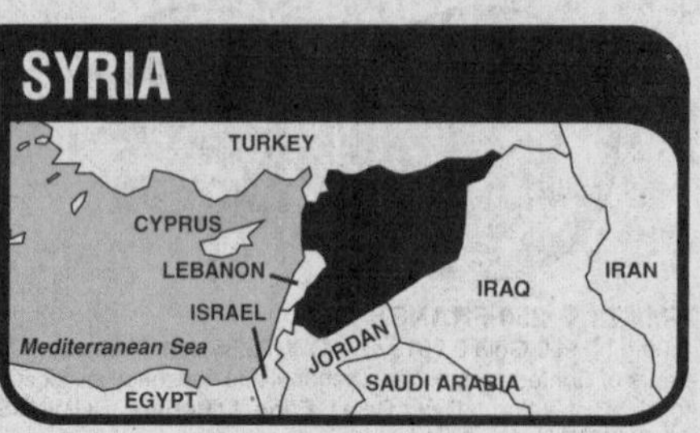

The Syrian Arab Republic, located in the Near East at the eastern end of the Mediterranean Sea, has an area of 71,498 sq. mi. (185,180 sq. km.) and a population of *12 million. Capital: Greater Damascus. Agriculture and animal breeding are the chief industries. Cotton, crude oil and livestock are exported.

Ancient Syria, a land bridge connecting Europe, Africa and Asia, has spent much of its history in thrall to the conqueror's whim. Its subjection by Egypt about 1500 B.C. was followed by successive conquests by the Hebrews, Phoenicians, Babylonians, Assyrians, Persians, Macedonians, Romans, Byzantines and finally, in 636 A.D., by the Moslems. The Arabs made Damascus, one of the oldest continuously inhabited cities of the world, the trade center and capital of an empire stretching from India to Spain. In 1516, following the total destruction of Damascus by the Mongols of Tamerlane, Syria fell to the Ottoman Turks and remained a part of Turkey until the end of World War I. The League of Nations gave France a mandate to the Levant states of Syria and Lebanon in 1920. In 1930, following a series of uprisings, France recognized Syria as an independent republic, but still subject to the mandate. Lebanon became fully independent on Nov. 22, 1943, and Syria on Jan. 1,1944.

TITLES

الجمهورية السورية

al-Jumhuriya(t) al-Suriya(t)

الجمهورية لعربية السورية

al-Jumhuriya(t) al-Arabiya(t) as-Suriya(t)

RULERS

Ottoman, until 1918
Faysal, 1918-1920

MINT MARK

(a)- Paris, privy marks only

MINT NAME

دمشق

Damascus (Dimask)

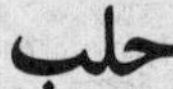

Haleb (Aleppo)

KINGDOM

STANDARD COINAGE

KM# 67 DINAR

6.70 g., Gold **Obv:** Crowned shield within sprigs **Rev:** Design within wreath

Date	Mintage	F12	VF20	XF40	MS60	MS63
AH1338 Rare	Est. 12	—	—	—	—	—

Note: Morton & Eden Auction 82, 10-16, about XF, realized approximately $22,040

FRENCH PROTECTORATE

KM# 68 1/2 PIASTRE

4.00 g., Copper-Nickel **Obv:** Value within roped wreath flanked by oat sprigs **Rev:** Value within wreath

Date	Mintage	F12	VF20	XF40	MS60	MS63
1921 (a)	4,000,000	3.00	8.00	30.00	60.00	90.00

KM# 75 1/2 PIASTRE

4.00 g., Nickel-Brass, 21 mm. **Obv:** Value within roped circle **Rev:** Value within oat sprigs

Date	Mintage	F12	VF20	XF40	MS60	MS63
1935 (a)	600,000	6.00	15.00	50.00	125	200
1936 (a)	800,000	5.00	12.00	45.00	100	175

KM# 71 PIASTRE

5.00 g., Nickel-Brass, 24 mm. **Obv:** Hole in center of wreath flanked by stars **Rev:** Hole in center of sprigs flanked by lion heads

Date	Mintage	F12	VF20	XF40	MS60	MS63
1929 (a)	750,000	5.00	15.00	60.00	90.00	200
1933 (a)	600,000	6.00	20.00	75.00	125	250
1935 (a)	1,900,000	3.00	8.00	30.00	75.00	125
1936 (a)	1,400,000	3.00	8.00	30.00	75.00	125

KM# 71a PIASTRE

3.50 g., Zinc **Obv:** Hole in center of wreath flanked by stars **Rev:** Hole in center flanked by lion heads

Date	Mintage	VF20	XF40	MS60	MS63	MS65
1940 (a)	2,000,000	20.00	45.00	75.00	150	—

KM# 69 2 PIASTRES

Aluminum-Bronze **Obv:** Inscription divides dates within design **Rev:** Crossed oat sprigs divide value

Date	Mintage	F12	VF20	XF40	MS60	MS63
1926	600,000	10.00	30.00	90.00	150	250

Note: Without privy marks by date

KM# 76 2-1/2 PIASTRES

Aluminum-Bronze **Obv:** Hole in center of wreath flanked by stars **Rev:** Hole in center of sprigs flanked by lion heads

Date	Mintage	F12	VF20	XF40	MS60	MS63
1940 (a)	2,000,000	2.00	5.00	10.00	30.00	45.00

KM# 70 5 PIASTRES

3.90 g., Aluminum-Bronze **Obv:** Inscription divides dates within design **Rev:** Crossed oat sprigs divide value

Date	Mintage	F12	VF20	XF40	MS60	MS63
1926 (a)	300,000	3.00	10.00	30.00	75.00	150
1926	600,000	3.00	10.00	30.00	75.00	150
1933 (a) (1933)	1,200,000	2.00	8.00	30.00	75.00	150
1935 (a)	2,000,000	1.50	6.00	20.00	50.00	100
1936 (a)	900,000	2.00	8.00	25.00	60.00	125
1940 (a)	500,000	1.50	6.00	20.00	50.00	100

KM# 72 10 PIASTRES

2.00 g., 0.680 Silver 0.0437 oz. ASW, 17 mm. **Obv:** Star in center of flower design **Rev:** Value within circle

Date	Mintage	F12	VF20	XF40	MS60	MS63
1929	1,000,000	5.00	15.00	50.00	120	225

KM# 73 25 PIASTRES
5.00 g., 0.680 Silver 0.1093 oz. ASW **Obv:** Value within circle **Rev:** Star in center of flower design

Date	Mintage	F12	VF20	XF40	MS60	MS63
1929	1,000,000	8.00	25.00	75.00	150	275
1933 (a)	500,000	12.00	35.00	100	200	350
1936 (a)	897,000	8.00	30.00	90.00	175	300
1937 (a)	393,000	12.00	35.00	100	200	350

KM# 74 50 PIASTRES
10.00 g., 0.680 Silver 0.2186 oz. ASW **Obv:** Value within circle **Rev:** Star in center of flower design

Date	Mintage	F12	VF20	XF40	MS60	MS63
1929	880,000	20.00	50.00	100	200	375
1933 (a)	250,000	30.00	75.00	150	275	500
1936 (a)	400,000	30.00	60.00	125	250	400
1937 (a)	Inc. above	30.00	75.00	150	275	500

WORLD WAR II EMERGENCY COINAGE

KM# 77 PIASTRE
Brass **Obv:** English value **Rev:** Arabic value

Date	Mintage	F12	VF20	XF40	MS60	MS63
ND (1941)	—	4.00	8.00	15.00	35.00	75.00

KM# 78 2-1/2 PIASTRES
Aluminum **Obv:** English value **Rev:** Arabic value

Date	Mintage	F12	VF20	XF40	MS60	MS63
ND (1941)	—	20.00	35.00	60.00	90.00	150

REPUBLIC

STANDARD COINAGE

KM# 81 2-1/2 PIASTRES
Copper-Nickel **Obv:** Falcon of Qureish **Rev:** Inscription within rectangle below value

Date	Mintage	VF20	XF40	MS60	MS63	MS65
AH1367-1948	2,500,000	0.50	1.00	2.00	3.00	5.00
AH1375-1956	5,000,000	0.50	1.00	2.00	3.00	5.00

KM# 82 5 PIASTRES
3.00 g., Copper-Nickel **Obv:** Falcon of Qureish **Rev:** Value within diamond shape above design flanked by stars

Date	Mintage	VF20	XF40	MS60	MS63	MS65
AH1367-1948	8,000,000	0.50	1.00	2.00	3.00	5.00
AH1375-1956	4,000,000	0.50	1.00	2.00	3.00	5.00

KM# 83 10 PIASTRES
4.00 g., Copper-Nickel, 21 mm. **Obv:** Falcon of Qureish **Rev:** Value above 1/2 designed wreath

Date	Mintage	VF20	XF40	MS60	MS63	MS65
AH1367-1948	—	0.50	1.00	2.00	3.00	5.00
AH1375-1956	4,000,000	0.50	1.00	2.00	3.00	5.00

KM# 79 25 PIASTRES
2.50 g., 0.600 Silver 0.0482 oz. ASW **Obv:** Falcon of Qureish **Rev:** Value within circle of design flanked by oat sprigs

Date	Mintage	F12	VF20	XF40	MS60	MS63
AH1366-1947	6,300,000	1.00	1.50	3.00	6.00	10.00

KM# 80 50 PIASTRES
5.00 g., 0.600 Silver 0.0965 oz. ASW **Obv:** Falcon of Qureish **Rev:** Value in center circle of design

Date	Mintage	F12	VF20	XF40	MS60	MS63
AH1366-1947	4,500,000	2.00	3.00	5.00	9.00	15.00

KM# 84 1/2 POUND
3.38 g., 0.900 Gold 0,0978 oz. AGW **Obv:** Falcon of Qureish **Rev:** Inscription within rectangle above sprigs

Date	Mintage	VF20	XF40	MS60	MS63	MS65
AH1369-1950	100,000	125	150	160	180	200

KM# 85 LIRA
9.90 g., 0.680 Silver 0.2164 oz. ASW, 27.8 mm. **Obv:** Falcon of Qureish **Rev:** Inscription and value within center of rectangle and sprigs

Date	Mintage	VF20	XF40	MS60	MS63	MS65
AH1369-1950	7,000,000	7.00	10.00	15.00	20.00	30.00

KM# 86 POUND
6.76 g., 0.900 Gold 0.1956 oz. AGW **Obv:** Falcon of Qureish **Rev:** Inscription and value within rectangle above sprigs

Date	Mintage	VF20	XF40	MS60	MS63	MS65
AH1369-1950	250,000	250	265	300	350	375

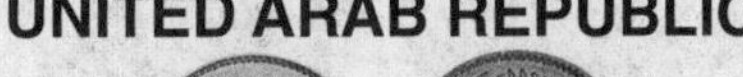

UNITED ARAB REPUBLIC

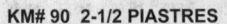

KM# 90 2-1/2 PIASTRES
2.00 g., Aluminum-Bronze, 17 mm. **Obv:** Falcon of Qureish flanked by dates **Rev:** Inscription within rectangle below value

Date	Mintage	VF20	XF40	MS60	MS63	MS65
AH1380-1960	1,100,000	0.25	0.35	0.50	0.75	1.00

KM# 91 5 PIASTRES
3.00 g., Aluminum-Bronze, 19 mm. **Obv:** Falcon of Qureish **Rev:** Value, inscription

Date	Mintage	VF20	XF40	MS60	MS63	MS65
AH1380-1960	4,240,000	0.25	0.35	0.50	0.75	1.00

KM# 92 10 PIASTRES
4.00 g., Aluminum-Bronze, 21 mm. **Obv:** Falcon of Qureish flanked by dates **Rev:** Value in center of 1/2 wreath

Date	Mintage	VF20	XF40	MS60	MS63	MS65
AH1380-1960	2,800,000	0.25	0.40	0.60	0.75	1.00

KM# 87 25 PIASTRES
0.35 g., 0.600 Silver 0.0068 oz. ASW, 20.3 mm. **Obv:** Falcon of Qureish **Rev:** Value flanked by oat sprigs in center of gear

Date	Mintage	VF20	XF40	MS60	MS63	MS65
AH1377-1958	2,300,000	1.50	2.50	4.00	5.00	9.00

KM# 88 50 PIASTRES
5.00 g., 0.600 Silver 0.0965 oz. ASW, 23.4 mm. **Obv:** Falcon of Qureish **Rev:** Sword divides value within wreath

Date	Mintage	VF20	XF40	MS60	MS63	MS65
AH1377-1958	120,000	3.00	4.50	7.00	10.00	20.00

KM# 89 50 PIASTRES
5.00 g., 0.600 Silver 0.0965 oz. ASW **Subject:** 1st Anniversary - Founding of United Arab Republic **Obv:** Falcon of Qureish **Rev:** Value

Date	Mintage	VF20	XF40	MS60	MS63	MS65
AH1378-1959	1,500,000	3.00	4.50	7.00	10.00	20.00

SYRIAN ARAB REPUBLIC

KM# 93 2-1/2 PIASTRES
2.00 g., Aluminum-Bronze, 17 mm. **Obv:** Falcon of Qureish **Rev:** Inscription within rectangle below value

Date	Mintage	VF20	XF40	MS60	MS63	MS65
AH1382-1962	8,000,000	0.15	0.30	0.50	1.00	1.25
AH1385-1965	8,000,000	0.15	0.30	0.50	1.00	1.25

KM# 104 2-1/2 PIASTRES
2.00 g., Aluminum-Bronze, 17 mm. **Obv:** Falcon of Qureish **Rev:** Inscription within rectangle below value

Date	Mintage	VF20	XF40	MS60	MS63	MS65
AH1393-1973	10,000,000	0.15	0.25	0.45	0.75	1.00

KM# 94 5 PIASTRES
3.00 g., Aluminum-Bronze, 19 mm. **Obv:** Falcon of Qureish **Rev:** Value within diamond shape above design flanked by stars

Date	Mintage	VF20	XF40	MS60	MS63	MS65
AH1382-1962	7,000,000	0.15	0.25	0.45	0.75	1.00
AH1385-1965	18,000,000	0.15	0.25	0.45	0.75	1.00

KM# 100 5 PIASTRES

3.00 g., Aluminum-Bronze, 19 mm. **Series:** F.A.O. **Obv:** Falcon of Qureish **Rev:** Upright oat sprig within sprigs

Date	Mintage	VF20	XF40	MS60	MS63	MS65
AH1391-1971	15,000,000	0.15	0.25	0.45	0.75	1.00

KM# 105 5 PIASTRES

3.00 g., Aluminum-Bronze, 19 mm. **Obv:** Falcon of Qureish **Rev:** Value within diamond shape above design flanked by stars

Date	Mintage	VF20	XF40	MS60	MS63	MS65
AH1394-1974	—	0.15	0.25	0.45	0.75	1.00

KM# 110 5 PIASTRES

3.00 g., Aluminum-Bronze, 19 mm. **Series:** F.A.O. **Obv:** Falcon of Qureish **Rev:** Euphrates dam within 1/2 gear and 1/2 oat sprig

Date	Mintage	VF20	XF40	MS60	MS63	MS65
AH1396-1976	2,000,000	0.15	0.25	0.45	0.75	1.00

KM# 116 5 PIASTRES

3.00 g., Aluminum-Bronze, 19 mm. **Obv:** Falcon of Qureish with heavy neck feathers **Rev:** Value within diamond shape above design flanked by stars **Note:** Similar to KM#94 but heavier neck feathers

Date	Mintage	VF20	XF40	MS60	MS63	MS65
AH1399-1979	—	0.15	0.25	0.45	0.75	1.00

KM# 95 10 PIASTRES

4.00 g., Aluminum-Bronze, 21 mm. **Obv:** Falcon of Qureish **Rev:** Value within 1/2 designed wreath **Note:** Varieties exist with fine (narrow) and course (widely spaced) reeding.

Date	Mintage	VF20	XF40	MS60	MS63	MS65
AH1382-1962	6,000,000	0.15	0.30	0.45	0.75	1.00
AH1385-1965	22,000,000	0.15	0.30	0.45	0.75	1.00

Note: Reeding varieties exist

KM# 106 10 PIASTRES

4.00 g., Aluminum-Bronze, 21 mm. **Obv:** Falcon of Qureish **Rev:** Value within 1/2 designed wreath

Date	Mintage	VF20	XF40	MS60	MS63	MS65
AH1394-1974	—	0.15	0.30	0.45	0.75	1.00

KM# 111 10 PIASTRES

4.00 g., Brass, 21 mm. **Series:** F.A.O. **Obv:** Falcon of Qureish with heavy neck feathers **Rev:** Euphrates dam within 1/2 gear and 1/2 oat sprig **Note:** Similar to 5 Piastres, KM#110.

Date	Mintage	VF20	XF40	MS60	MS63	MS65
AH1396-1976	500,000	0.15	0.30	0.45	0.75	1.00

KM# 117 10 PIASTRES

4.00 g., Copper-Nickel, 21 mm. **Obv:** Falcon of Qureish **Rev:** Value within 1/2 designed wreath

Date	Mintage	VF20	XF40	MS60	MS63	MS65
AH1399-1979	—	0.10	0.15	0.20	0.30	0.75

KM# 96 25 PIASTRES

3.50 g., Nickel, 20.3 mm. **Obv:** Falcon of Qureish **Rev:** Inscription within rectangle flanked by dates below value

Date	Mintage	VF20	XF40	MS60	MS63	MS65
AH1387-1968	15,000,000	0.20	0.35	—	0.85	1.50

KM# 101 25 PIASTRES

3.50 g., Nickel, 20.3 mm. **Subject:** 25th Anniversary - Al-Ba'ath Party **Obv:** Falcon of Qureish **Rev:** Flaming torch divides value within oat sprigs

Date	Mintage	VF20	XF40	MS60	MS63	MS65
AH1392-1972	—	0.15	0.30	0.45	0.75	1.00

KM# 107 25 PIASTRES

3.50 g., Nickel, 20.3 mm. **Obv:** Falcon of Qureish **Rev:** Inscription within rectangle below value

Date	Mintage	VF20	XF40	MS60	MS63	MS65
AH1394-1974	—	0.15	0.30	0.45	0.75	1.00

KM# 112 25 PIASTRES

3.50 g., Nickel, 20.5 mm. **Series:** F.A.O. **Obv:** Falcon of Qureish **Rev:** Euphrates dam within 1/2 gear and 1/2 oat sprig

Date	Mintage	VF20	XF40	MS60	MS63	MS65
AH1396-1976	1,000,000	0.15	0.30	0.45	0.75	1.00

KM# 118 25 PIASTRES

3.50 g., Copper-Nickel, 20.3 mm. **Obv:** Falcon of Qureish **Rev:** Inscription within rectangle below value

Date	Mintage	VF20	XF40	MS60	MS63	MS65
AH1399-1979	—	0.15	0.25	0.35	0.50	0.80

KM# 97 50 PIASTRES

5.00 g., Nickel, 23.4 mm. **Obv:** Falcon of Qureish **Rev:** Value in center square of design above dates and oat sprigs

Date	Mintage	VF20	XF40	MS60	MS63	MS65
AH1387-1968	10,000,000	0.25	0.35	0.50	0.85	1.25

KM# 102 50 PIASTRES

5.00 g., Nickel, 23.4 mm. **Subject:** 25th Anniversary - Al-Ba'ath Party **Obv:** Falcon of Qureish **Rev:** Inscription, dates, value and flames

Date	Mintage	VF20	XF40	MS60	MS63	MS65
AH1392-1972	—	0.50	0.75	1.25	2.00	2.50

KM# 108 50 PIASTRES

5.00 g., Nickel, 23.4 mm. **Obv:** Falcon of Qureish **Rev:** Value within center square of design above sprigs

Date	Mintage	VF20	XF40	MS60	MS63	MS65
AH1394-1974	—	0.25	0.35	0.50	0.75	1.00

KM# 113 50 PIASTRES

5.00 g., Nickel, 23.4 mm. **Series:** F.A.O. **Obv:** Falcon of Qureish **Rev:** Euphrates dam within 1/2 gear and 1/2 oat sprig

Date	Mintage	VF20	XF40	MS60	MS63	MS65
AH1396-1976	1,000,000	0.25	0.50	1.00	1.25	1.50

KM# 119 50 PIASTRES

5.00 g., Copper-Nickel, 23.4 mm. **Obv:** Falcon of Qureish **Rev:** Value in center square of design above sprigs

Date	Mintage	VF20	XF40	MS60	MS63	MS65
AH1399-1979	—	0.25	0.35	0.75	1.00	1.25

KM# 98 POUND

7.50 g., Nickel, 27 mm. **Obv:** Falcon of Qureish **Rev:** Value in diamond shape within rectangle **Edge:** Reeded

Date	Mintage	VF20	XF40	MS60	MS63	MS65
AH1387-1968	10,000,000	0.35	0.50	0.75	1.25	1.75
AH1391-1971	10,000,000	0.35	0.50	0.75	1.25	1.75

KM# 99 POUND

7.50 g., Nickel, 27 mm. **Series:** F.A.O. **Obv:** Falcon of Qureish **Rev:** Hands holding rectangle, oat sprig bouquet above

Date	Mintage	VF20	XF40	MS60	MS63	MS65
AH1388-1968	500,000	0.50	0.75	1.50	2.00	3.00

KM# 103 POUND
7.50 g., Nickel, 27 mm. **Subject:** 25th Anniversary - Al-Ba'ath Party **Obv:** Falcon of Qureish **Rev:** Stylized map and flaming torch

Date	Mintage	VF20	XF40	MS60	MS63	MS65
AH1392-1972	10,000,000	0.50	1.00	2.25	2.50	3.00

KM# 109 POUND
7.50 g., Nickel, 27 mm. **Obv:** Falcon of Qureish **Rev:** Value in diamond shape at center of rectangle

Date	Mintage	VF20	XF40	MS60	MS63	MS65
AH1394-1974	—	0.35	0.50	1.25	2.00	2.50

KM# 114 POUND
7.50 g., Nickel, 27 mm. **Series:** F.A.O. **Obv:** Falcon of Qureish **Rev:** Euphrates dam within 1/2 gear and 1/2 oat sprig

Date	Mintage	VF20	XF40	MS60	MS63	MS65
AH1396-1976	500,000	0.50	0.75	2.25	2.50	3.00

KM# 115 POUND
7.50 g., Nickel, 27 mm. **Subject:** Re-election of President **Obv:** Falcon of Qureish within circle **Rev:** Head left within circle

Date	Mintage	VF20	XF40	MS60	MS63	MS65
AH1398-1978	—	0.50	0.75	2.00	3.00	5.00

KM# 120.1 POUND
7.50 g., Copper-Nickel, 27 mm. **Obv:** Falcon of Qureish **Rev:** Value in diamond shape at center of rectangle **Edge:** Reeded

Date	Mintage	VF20	XF40	MS60	MS63	MS65
AH1399-1979	—	0.35	0.50	1.00	1.50	2.00

KM# 120.2 POUND
4.94 g., Stainless Steel, 21 mm. **Obv:** Falcon of Qureish **Rev:** Value in diamond shape at center of rectangle **Note:** Reduced size and weight.

Date	Mintage	VF20	XF40	MS60	MS63	MS65
AH1412-1991	—	0.35	0.50	1.00	1.50	2.00

KM# 121 POUND
5.00 g., Stainless Steel **Obv:** Falcon of Qureish **Rev:** Value in diamond shape at center of rectangle

Date	Mintage	VF20	XF40	MS60	MS63	MS65
AH1414-1994	—	0.30	0.50	1.00	1.50	2.00
AH1416 1996	—	0.30	0.50	1.00	1.50	2.00

KM# 132 POUND
5.00 g., Stainless Steel, 25.5 mm. **Obv:** Flowers to left of dates below heraldic bird **Rev:** Value and ornamentation **Edge:** Reeded

Date	Mintage	VF20	XF40	MS60	MS63	MS65
AH1416-1996	—	—	0.50	1.00	1.50	2.00

KM# 125 2 POUNDS
6.00 g., Stainless Steel, 23 mm. **Obv:** Falcon of Qureish flanked by dates **Rev:** Ancient ruins and value

Date	Mintage	VF20	XF40	MS60	MS63	MS65
AH1416-1996	—	—	0.85	1.25	1.75	2.50

KM# 123 5 POUNDS
5.01 g., Copper-Nickel, 24.4 mm. **Obv:** Falcon of Qureish within pentagon design **Rev:** Palace above value within pentagon design

Date	Mintage	VF20	XF40	MS60	MS63	MS65
AH1416-1996	—	—	1.00	1.50	2.00	3.00

KM# 124 10 POUNDS
7.00 g., Copper-Nickel, 26.40 mm. **Obv:** Falcon of Qureish within circle **Rev:** Ancient ruins above value within circle

Date	Mintage	VF20	XF40	MS60	MS63	MS65
AH1416-1996	—	—	1.25	2.00	2.50	3.50

KM# 128 10 POUNDS
7.00 g., Copper-Nickel, 26.5 mm. **Subject:** 50th Anniversary of Al Ba'ath Party **Obv:** Falcon of Qureish within circle **Rev:** Map and flag above sprigs within circle **Edge:** Reeded

Date	Mintage	VF20	XF40	MS60	MS63	MS65
AH1417-1997	100,000	—	1.25	2.00	2.50	3.50

KM# 122 25 POUNDS
Bi-Metallic Stainless Steel center in Aluminum-Bronze ring **Obv:** Falcon of Qureish within circle **Rev:** Head of President Hafez al-Assad left within circle

Date	Mintage	VF20	XF40	MS60	MS63	MS65
ND-1995	—	—	1.00	2.25	3.00	5.00

KM# 126 25 POUNDS
6.45 g., Bi-Metallic Stainless Steel center in Aluminum-Bronze ring, 25 mm. **Obv:** Falcon of Qureish within designed wreath **Rev:** Central Bank building within circle

Date	Mintage	VF20	XF40	MS60	MS63	MS65
AH1416-1996	—	—	1.00	2.25	3.00	5.00

ESSAIS

KM#	Date	Mintage	Identification	Mkt Val
E1	1926(a)	—	2 Piastres. Aluminum-Bronze. KM69.	600
E2	1926(a)	—	5 Piastres. Aluminum-Bronze. KM70.	400
E3	1929(a)	Est. 64	Piastre. Nickel-Brass. Hole in center of wreath. Value and dates below hole in center flanked by lion heads. KM71.	400
E4	1929(a)	Est. 64	10 Piastres. Silver. KM72.	600
E5	1929(a)	Est. 64	25 Piastres. Silver. KM73.	750
E6	1929(a)	Est. 64	50 Piastres. Silver. Value within circle. Star in center of flower design. KM74.	900
E8	1935(a)	—	1/2 Piastre. Nickel-Brass. KM75.	350

MINT SETS

KM#	Date	Mintage	Identification	Issue Price	Mkt Val
MS1	1968 (3)	—	KM96-98	—	5.50
MS2	1978-79 (6)	—	KM115 (1978), 116-120.1 (1979)	—	12.50

The Republic of Tajikistan (Tadjiquistan), was formed from those regions of Bukhara and Turkestan where the population consisted mainly of Tajiks. Is bordered in the north and west by Uzbekistan and Kyrgyzstan, in the east by China and in the south by Afghanistan. It has an area of 55,240 sq. miles (143,100 sq. km.) and a population of 5.95 million. It includes 2 provinces of Khudzand and Khatlon together with the Gorno-Badakhshan Autonomous Region with a population of 5,092,603. Capital: Dushanbe. Tajikistan was admitted as a constituent republic of the Soviet Union on Dec. 5, 1929. In August 1990 the Tajik Supreme Soviet adopted a declaration of republican sovereignty, and in Dec. 1991 the republic became a member of the CIS.

After demonstrations and fighting, the Communist government was replaced by a Revolutionary Coalition Council on May 7, 1992. Following further demonstrations President Nabiev was ousted on Sept. 7, 1992. Civil war broke out, and the government resigned on Nov. 10, 1992. On Nov. 30, 1992 it was announced that a CIS peacekeeping force would be sent to Tajikistan. A state of emergency was imposed in Jan. 1993. A ceasefire was signed in 1996 and a peace agreement signed in June 1997.

MONETARY SYSTEM
1 Ruble = 100 Tanga

REPUBLIC

DECIMAL COINAGE

KM# 1 20 ROUBLES
20.00 g., 0.925 Silver 0.5948 oz. ASW, 35.1 mm. **Subject:** Medal without denomination **Obv:** Radiant Royal device within circle **Rev:** Crowned bust 1/4 right **Edge:** Reeded **Note:** Medallic.

Date	Mintage	VF20	XF40	MS60	MS63	MS65
1999	—	PF63 70.00	PF65 80.00			

TANNU TUVA

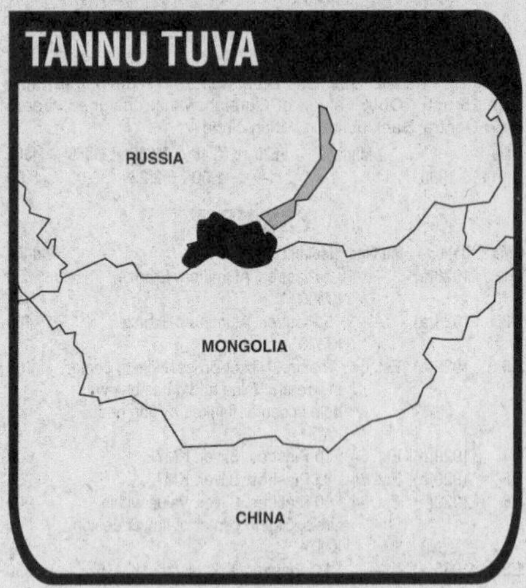

The Tannu-Tuva Peoples Republic (Tuva), an autonomous part of Russia located in central Asia on the northwest border of Outer Mongolia, has an area of 64,000 sq. mi. (165,760 sq. km.) and a population of about 175,000. Capital: Kyzyl. The economy is based on herding, forestry and mining.

As Urianghi, Tuva was part of Outer Mongolia of the Chinese Empire when tsarist Russia, after fomenting a separatist movement, extended its protection to the mountainous country in 1914. Tuva declared its independence as the Tannu-Tuva Peoples Republic in 1921 under the auspices of the Tuva Peoples Revolutionary Party. In 1926, following Russia's successful mediation of the resultant Tuvinian-Mongolian territorial dispute, Tannu-Tuva and Outer Mongolia formally recognized each other's independence. The Tannu-Tuva Peoples Republic became an autonomous region of the U.S.S.R. on Oct. 13, 1944.

MONETARY SYSTEM
100 Kopejek (Kopeks) = 1 Aksha

REPUBLIC

STANDARD COINAGE

KM# 1 KOPEJEK
Aluminum-Bronze **Obv:** Inscription within circle **Rev:** Value and date

Date	Mintage	VG8	F12	VF20	XF40	MS60
1934	—	45.00	75.00	150	250	—

KM# 2 2 KOPEJEK
Aluminum-Bronze **Obv:** Inscription within circle **Rev:** Value and date

Date	Mintage	VG8	F12	VF20	XF40	MS60
1933	—	—	—	—	—	—
1934	—	50.00	80.00	175	300	—

KM# 3 3 KOPEJEK
Aluminum-Bronze **Obv:** Inscription within circle **Rev:** Value and date

Date	Mintage	VG8	F12	VF20	XF40	MS60
1933	—	—	—	—	—	—
1934	—	45.00	75.00	150	250	—

KM# 4 5 KOPEJEK
Aluminum-Bronze **Obv:** Inscription within circle **Rev:** Value and date

Date	Mintage	VG8	F12	VF20	XF40	MS60
1934	—	50.00	80.00	175	300	—

KM# 5 10 KOPEJEK
Copper-Nickel **Obv:** Inscription within circle **Rev:** Value and date

Date	Mintage	VG8	F12	VF20	XF40	MS60
1934	—	50.00	80.00	175	300	—

KM# 6 15 KOPEJEK
Copper-Nickel **Obv:** Inscription within circle **Rev:** Value and date

Date	Mintage	VG8	F12	VF20	XF40	MS60
1934	—	50.00	80.00	175	300	—

KM# 7 20 KOPEJEK
Copper-Nickel **Obv:** Inscription within circle **Rev:** Value and date

Date	Mintage	VG8	F12	VF20	XF40	MS60
1934	—	60.00	100	220	350	—

TANZANIA

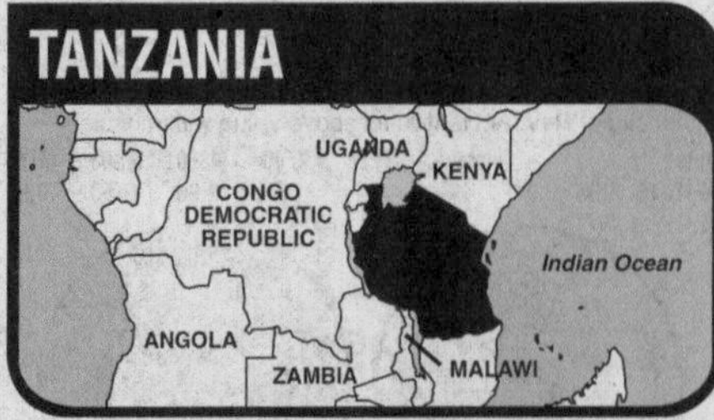

The United Republic of Tanzania, located on the east coast of Africa between Kenya and Mozambique, consists of Tanganyika and the islands of Zanzibar and Pemba. It has an area of 364,900 sq. mi. (945,090 sq. km.) and a population of *25.2 million. Capital: Dar es Salaam (Haven of Peace). The chief exports are cotton, coffee, diamonds, sisal, cloves, petroleum products, and cashew nuts.

Tanzania is a member of the Commonwealth of Nations. The President is Chief of State.

NOTE: For earlier coinage see East Africa.

REPUBLIC

STANDARD COINAGE

100 Senti = 1 Shilingi

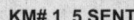

KM# 1 5 SENTI
4.00 g., Bronze, 22.5 mm. **Obv:** Head of President J.K. Nyerere left **Rev:** Sailfish above value **Shape:** 12-sided

Date	Mintage	VF20	XF40	MS60	MS63	MS65
1966	55,250,000	0.10	0.20	0.50	1.00	1.75
1966	5,500	PF63 4.00	PF65 8.00			
1971	5,000,000	0.10	0.20	0.50	1.00	1.75
1972	—	0.10	0.20	0.50	1.00	1.75
1973	20,000,000	0.10	0.20	0.50	1.00	1.75
1974	12,500,000	0.10	0.20	0.50	1.00	1.75
1975	—	0.10	0.20	0.50	1.00	1.75
1976	37,500,000	0.10	0.20	0.50	1.00	1.75
1977	10,000,000	0.10	0.20	0.50	1.00	1.75
1979	7,200,000	0.10	0.20	0.50	1.00	1.75
1980	10,000,000	0.10	0.20	0.50	1.00	1.75
1981	13,650,000	0.10	0.20	0.50	1.00	1.75
1982	—	0.10	0.20	0.50	1.00	1.75
1983	18,000	0.10	0.20	0.50	1.00	1.75
1984	—	0.10	0.20	0.50	1.00	1.75

KM# 11 10 SENTI
4.80 g., Nickel-Brass, 25 mm. **Obv:** Head of President J.K. Nyerere left **Rev:** Zebra running right **Shape:** Scalloped

Date	Mintage	VF20	XF40	MS60	MS63	MS65
1977	19,505,000	0.75	1.25	2.00	3.00	5.00
1979	8,000,000	0.75	1.25	2.00	3.00	5.00
1980	10,000,000	0.75	1.25	2.00	3.00	5.00
1981	10,000,000	0.75	1.25	2.00	3.00	5.00
1984	—	0.75	1.25	2.00	3.00	5.00

KM# 2 20 SENTI
5.00 g., Nickel-Brass, 24 mm. **Obv:** Head of President J.K. Nyerere left **Rev:** Ostrich running left **Edge:** Plain

Date	Mintage	VF20	XF40	MS60	MS63	MS65
1966	26,500,000	0.20	0.40	1.00	1.50	3.00
1966	5,500	PF63 6.00	PF65 12.00			
1970	5,000,000	0.20	0.40	1.00	1.50	3.00
1973	20,100,000	0.20	0.40	1.00	1.50	3.00
1975	—	0.20	0.40	1.00	1.50	3.00
1976	10,000,000	0.20	0.40	1.00	1.50	3.00
1977	10,000,000	0.20	0.40	1.00	1.50	3.00
1979	10,000,000	0.20	0.40	1.00	1.50	3.00
1980	10,000,000	0.20	0.40	1.00	1.50	3.00
1981	10,000,000	0.20	0.40	1.00	1.50	3.00
1982	—	0.20	0.40	1.00	1.50	3.00
1983	50,000	0.20	0.40	1.00	1.50	3.00
1984	—	0.20	0.40	1.00	1.50	3.00

KM# 3 50 SENTI
4.00 g., Copper-Nickel, 21 mm. **Obv:** Head of President J.K. Nyerere left **Rev:** Rabbit left **Edge:** Reeded

Date	Mintage	VF20	XF40	MS60	MS63	MS65
1966	6,250,000	0.20	0.40	1.00	2.00	2.50
1966	5,500	PF63 8.00	PF65 16.00			
1970	10,000,000	0.20	0.40	1.00	2.00	2.50
1973	10,000,000	0.25	0.50	1.00	2.00	2.50
1980	10,000,000	0.25	0.50	1.00	2.00	2.50
1981	—	0.25	0.50	1.00	2.00	2.50

Date	Mintage	VF20	XF40	MS60	MS63	MS65
1982	10,000,000	0.25	0.50	1.00	2.00	2.50
1983	—	0.25	0.50	1.00	2.00	2.50
1984	10,000,000	0.25	0.50	1.00	2.00	2.50

KM# 26 50 SENTI

4.00 g., Nickel Clad Steel, 20.7 mm. **Obv:** President Mwinyi right flanked by flowers **Rev:** Rabbit left **Edge:** Reeded

Date	Mintage	VF20	XF40	MS60	MS63	MS65
1988	10,000,000	0.25	0.50	0.75	1.50	2.00
1989	—	0.25	0.50	0.75	1.50	2.00
1990	—	0.25	0.50	0.75	1.50	2.00

KM# 4 SHILINGI

8.00 g., Copper-Nickel, 27.5 mm. **Obv:** Head of President J.K. Nyerere left **Rev:** Hand holding torch **Edge:** Reeded

Date	Mintage	VF20	XF40	MS60	MS63	MS65
1966	48,000,000	0.25	0.50	0.75	1.50	2.00
1966	5,500	PF63 12.00	PF65 25.00			
1972	10,000,000	0.25	0.50	0.75	1.50	2.00
1974	15,000,000	0.30	0.60	0.90	1.75	2.25
1975	—	0.30	0.60	0.90	1.75	2.25
1977	5,000,000	0.30	0.60	0.90	1.75	2.25
1980	10,000,000	0.25	0.50	0.75	1.50	2.00
1981	—	0.30	0.60	0.90	1.75	2.25
1982	10,000,000	0.30	0.60	0.90	1.75	2.25
1983	10,000,000	0.30	0.60	0.90	1.75	2.25
1984	10,000,000	0.30	0.60	0.90	1.75	2.25

KM# 22 SHILINGI

6.50 g., Nickel Clad Steel, 23.5 mm. **Obv:** President Mwinyi right flanked by flowers **Rev:** Hand holding torch **Edge:** Reeded

Date	Mintage	VF20	XF40	MS60	MS63	MS65
1987	5,000,000	0.40	0.80	1.25	2.00	2.50
1988	10,000,000	0.40	0.80	1.25	2.00	2.50
1989	—	0.40	0.80	1.25	2.00	2.50
1990	—	0.20	0.40	0.75	1.25	1.75
1991	—	0.20	0.40	0.75	1.25	1.75
1992	—	0.20	0.40	0.75	1.25	1.75

KM# 5 5 SHILINGI

Copper-Nickel, 31.5 mm. **Series:** F.A.O. **Subject:** 10th Anniversary of Independence **Obv:** Head of President J.K. Nyerere left **Rev:** Value in center circle, food sources in frames surround **Shape:** 10-sided

Date	Mintage	VF20	XF40	MS60	MS63	MS65
ND-1971	1,000,000	0.75	1.25	1.50	2.50	4.00

KM# 6 5 SHILINGI

13.80 g., Copper-Nickel, 31.5 mm. **Series:** F.A.O. **Obv:** Head of President J.K. Nyerere left **Rev:** Value in center circle, food sources in frames surround **Shape:** 10-sided

Date	Mintage	VF20	XF40	MS60	MS63	MS65
1972	8,000,000	0.75	1.25	1.50	2.50	4.00
1973	5,000,000	0.75	1.25	1.75	3.00	4.50
1980	5,000,000	0.75	1.25	1.75	3.00	4.50

KM# 10 5 SHILINGI

Copper-Nickel, 31.5 mm. **Subject:** 10th Anniversary - Bank of Tanzania **Obv:** Head of President J.K. Nyerere left **Rev:** Bank building above sprigs and value **Shape:** 10-sided

Date	Mintage	VF20	XF40	MS60	MS63	MS65
ND-1976	1,000,000	0.75	1.25	1.75	3.00	4.50
ND-1976	200	PF63 45.00	PF65 60.00			

KM# 12 5 SHILINGI

Copper-Nickel, 31.5 mm. **Series:** F.A.O. **Subject:** Regional Conference for Africa **Obv:** President J.K. Nyerere left flanked by oat sprigs **Rev:** Farmer working with tractor **Shape:** 10-sided

Date	Mintage	VF20	XF40	MS60	MS63	MS65
1978	50,000	0.75	1.25	1.75	2.75	3.75
1978	2,000	PF63 15.00	PF65 30.00			

KM# 23 5 SHILINGI

Copper-Nickel **Obv:** Large (18mm) bust of President Mwinyi right flanked by flowers **Rev:** Value within center circle, food sources in frames surround **Shape:** 10-sided

Date	Mintage	VF20	XF40	MS60	MS63	MS65
1987	5,000,000	0.75	1.50	1.75	2.75	3.50
1988	10,000,000	0.75	1.50	1.75	2.75	3.50
1989	—	0.75	1.50	1.75	2.75	3.50

KM# 23a.1 5 SHILINGI

8.50 g., Nickel Clad Steel, 26.5 mm. **Obv:** Small (17mm) head right flanked by flowers **Rev:** Value within center circle, food sources in frames surround **Edge:** Reeded

Date	Mintage	VF20	XF40	MS60	MS63	MS65
1990	—	0.60	1.00	1.25	1.85	2.25

KM# 23a.2 5 SHILINGI

8.50 g., Nickel Clad Steel, 26.5 mm. **Obv:** Large (18mm) head right flanked by flowers **Rev:** Value within center circle, food sources in frames surround

Date	Mintage	VF20	XF40	MS60	MS63	MS65
1991	—	0.60	1.00	1.25	1.85	2.25
1992	—	0.50	0.75	1.00	1.50	2.00
1993	—	0.50	0.75	1.00	1.50	2.00

KM# 20 10 SHILINGI

9.70 g., Copper-Nickel, 29 mm. **Obv:** President J.K. Nyerere 1/4 left within circle **Rev:** National arms

Date	Mintage	VF20	XF40	MS60	MS63	MS65
1987	10,000,000	0.50	1.00	1.50	2.25	3.50
1988	10,000,000	0.50	1.00	1.50	2.25	3.50
1989	—	0.50	1.00	1.50	2.25	3.50

KM# 20a.1 10 SHILINGI

10.00 g., Nickel Clad Steel, 29 mm. **Obv:** Bust of President J.K. Nyerere 1/4 left within circle **Rev:** 4 mm "10"; inscription near edge

Date	Mintage	VF20	XF40	MS60	MS63	MS65
1990	—	5.00	1.00	1.25	1.85	2.25

KM# 20a.2 10 SHILINGI

10.00 g., Nickel Clad Steel, 29 mm. **Obv:** Bust of President J.K. Nyerere 1/4 left within circle **Rev:** 3 mm "10"; inscription away from edge

Date	Mintage	VF20	XF40	MS60	MS63	MS65
1991	—	0.50	1.00	1.25	1.85	2.25
1992	—	0.50	1.00	1.25	1.85	2.25
1993	—	0.50	1.00	1.25	1.85	2.25

KM# 13 20 SHILINGI

Copper-Nickel **Subject:** 20th Anniversary of Independence **Obv:** President J.K. Nyerere 1/4 left within circle **Rev:** National arms

Date	Mintage	VF20	XF40	MS60	MS63	MS65
ND-1981	997,000	1.00	2.00	4.00	6.50	9.50

KM# 13a 20 SHILINGI
16.00 g., 0.925 Silver 0.4758 oz. ASW **Obv:** Bust of President J.K. Nyerere 1/4 left within circle **Rev:** National arms

Date	Mintage	VF20	XF40	MS60	MS63	MS65
ND-1981	20,000	PF63 35.00	PF65 40.00			

KM# 21 20 SHILINGI
Copper-Nickel **Subject:** 20th Anniversary of Central Bank **Obv:** President Mwinyi right **Rev:** Torch within sprigs

Date	Mintage	VF20	XF40	MS60	MS63	MS65
ND-1986	—	—	—	—	40.00	55.00

KM# 21a 20 SHILINGI
16.00 g., 0.925 Silver 0.4758 oz. ASW **Obv:** Head of President Mwinyi right **Rev:** Torch within sprigs

Date	Mintage	VF20	XF40	MS60	MS63	MS65
ND-1986	5,000	PF63 95.00	PF65 125			

KM# 27.1 20 SHILINGI
Nickel Bonded Steel **Obv:** President Mwinyi right flanked by flowers **Rev:** Elephants **Shape:** 7-sided

Date	Mintage	VF20	XF40	MS60	MS63	MS65
1990	—	0.75	1.25	1.75	2.50	3.75
1991	—	0.75	1.25	1.75	2.50	3.75

KM# 27.2 20 SHILINGI
13.00 g., Nickel Bonded Steel, 31 mm. **Obv:** President Mwinyi right flanked by flowers **Rev:** Elephant with calf **Shape:** 7-sided **Note:** Reduced size.

Date	Mintage	VF20	XF40	MS60	MS63	MS65
1992	—	0.75	1.25	1.75	2.75	4.00

KM# 7 25 SHILINGI
25.40 g., 0.500 Silver 0.4083 oz. ASW, 38.6 mm. **Subject:** Conservation **Obv:** Head of President J.K. Nyerere left **Rev:** Giraffes running right

Date	Mintage	VF20	XF40	MS60	MS63	MS65
1974	8,848	—	—	—	18.00	22.00

KM# 7a 25 SHILINGI
28.28 g., 0.925 Silver 0.841 oz. ASW, 38.6 mm. **Obv:** Head of President J.K. Nyerere left **Rev:** Giraffes running right

Date	Mintage	VF20	XF40	MS60	MS63	MS65
1974	13,000	PF63 30.00	PF65 35.00			

KM# 30 25 SHILINGI
Copper-Nickel **Subject:** 25 Years of Independence **Obv:** President J.K. Nyerere 1/4 left within circle **Rev:** National arms

Date	Mintage	VF20	XF40	MS60	MS63	MS65
ND-1985	—	PF63 275	PF65 300			

KM# 28 25 SHILINGI
Nickel Bonded Steel **Subject:** 25th Anniversary of Central Bank **Obv:** President Mwinyi right **Rev:** Building within sprigs

Date	Mintage	VF20	XF40	MS60	MS63	MS65
ND-1991	—	—	—	—	2.50	3.50

KM# 28a 25 SHILINGI
13.04 g., 0.925 Silver 0.3878 oz. ASW **Obv:** Head of President Mwinyi right **Rev:** Building within sprigs

Date	Mintage	VF20	XF40	MS60	MS63	MS65
ND-1991	Est. 2000	PF63 50.00	PF65 60.00			

KM# 8 50 SHILINGI
31.85 g., 0.500 Silver 0.512 oz. ASW, 42 mm. **Subject:** Conservation **Obv:** Head of President J.K. Nyerere left **Rev:** Black Rhinoceros facing

Date	Mintage	VF20	XF40	MS60	MS63	MS65
1974	8,826	—	—	—	20.00	25.00

KM# 8a 50 SHILINGI
35.00 g., 0.925 Silver 1.0409 oz. ASW, 42 mm. **Obv:** Head of President J.K. Nyerere left **Rev:** Black Rhinoceros facing

Date	Mintage	VF20	XF40	MS60	MS63	MS65
1974	12,000	PF63 35.00	PF65 40.00			

KM# 33 50 SHILINGI
7.91 g., Brass Plated Steel, 22 mm. **Subject:** Conservation **Obv:** Head of Ali Nassan Mwinyi right within circle **Rev:** Mother rhinoceros and calf **Shape:** 7-sided

Date	Mintage	VF20	XF40	MS60	MS63	MS65
1996	—	—	—	1.25	2.50	4.00

KM# 16 100 SHILINGI
23.33 g., 0.925 Silver 0.6938 oz. ASW **Series:** Decade for Women **Obv:** Head of President J.K. Nyerere left **Rev:** Kneeling nurse holding baby in air

Date	Mintage	VF20	XF40	MS60	MS63	MS65
1984	1,000	PF63 45.00	PF65 55.00			

KM# 18 100 SHILINGI
Copper-Nickel **Subject:** Conservation **Obv:** President J.K. Nyerere left flanked by flowers **Rev:** Elephant mother and calf

Date	Mintage	VF20	XF40	MS60	MS63	MS65
1986	—	—	—	3.00	5.00	7.50

KM# 18a 100 SHILINGI
19.44 g., 0.925 Silver 0.5781 oz. ASW **Obv:** Head of President J.K. Nyerere left **Rev:** Elephant mother and calf

Date	Mintage	VF20	XF40	MS60	MS63	MS65
1986	25,000	PF63 28.00	PF65 32.00			

KM# 24 100 SHILINGI

19.44 g., 0.925 Silver 0.5781 oz. ASW **Series:** Save the Children Fund **Rev:** Two girls with clubs mashing grain in pail within circle

Date	Mintage	VF20	XF40	MS60	MS63	MS65
1990	Est. 20000	PF63 22.00	PF65 25.00			

KM# 32 100 SHILINGI

9.00 g., Brass Plated Steel, 24.5 mm. **Subject:** Conservation **Obv:** Bust of President J.K. Nyerere left **Rev:** Four Impalas running right **Edge:** Reeded

Date	Mintage	VF20	XF40	MS60	MS63	MS65
1993	—	—	—	1.25	2.50	4.00
1994	—	—	—	1.25	2.50	4.00

KM# 14 200 SHILINGI

28.28 g., 0.925 Silver 0.841 oz. ASW **Subject:** 20th Anniversary of Independence **Obv:** Bust of President J.K. Nyerere left **Rev:** National arms

Date	Mintage	VF20	XF40	MS60	MS63	MS65
ND-1981	110	—	—	125	150	175
ND-1981	Inc. above	PF63 200	PF65 250			

KM# 41 200 SHILINGI

20.00 g., 0.500 Silver 0.3215 oz. ASW, 34 mm. **Subject:** Wildlife of Africa **Obv:** National arms **Rev:** Adult and baby rhino **Edge:** Reeded

Date	Mintage	VF20	XF40	MS60	MS63	MS65
1997	—	PF63 22.00	PF65 27.00			

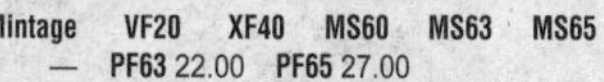

KM# 34 200 SHILINGI

8.00 g., Copper-Nickel-Zinc **Obv:** Head of Sheikh Karume 1/4 left within circle **Rev:** Two lions **Edge:** Segmented reeding

Date	Mintage	VF20	XF40	MS60	MS63	MS65
1998	—	—	—	2.50	4.00	6.00

KM# 40 200 SHILINGI

15.40 g., 0.925 Silver 0.458 oz. ASW, 33.9 mm. **Subject:** Pan Troglodytes **Obv:** National arms **Rev:** Chimpanzee family **Edge:** Reeded

Date	Mintage	VF20	XF40	MS60	MS63	MS65
1999	—	PF63 30.00	PF65 35.00			

KM# 59 200 SHILINGI

15.40 g., 0.925 Silver 0.458 oz. ASW, 33.9 mm. **Obv:** National arms **Rev:** Water Buffalo **Edge:** Reeded

Date	Mintage	VF20	XF40	MS60	MS63	MS65
1999	—	PF63 30.00	PF65 35.00			

KM# 29 250 SHILINGI

28.16 g., 0.925 Silver 0.8375 oz. ASW **Subject:** 25th Anniversary of Independence **Obv:** Bust of President J.K. Nyerere left **Rev:** National arms

Date	Mintage	VF20	XF40	MS60	MS63	MS65
ND-1985	—	PF63 225	PF65 250	PF67 300		

KM# 57 250 SHILINGI

19.34 g., 0.925 Silver 0.5752 oz. ASW, 26.9 mm. **Subject:** Serengeti Wildlife **Obv:** National arms **Rev:** Lion, Cheetah and Zebra **Edge:** Reeded

Date	Mintage	VF20	XF40	MS60	MS63	MS65
1998	—	PF63 32.00	PF65 37.00			

KM# 47 500 SHILLINGS

31.22 g., 0.925 Silver 0.9285 oz. ASW, 38.5 mm. **Subject:** British Queen Mother **Obv:** National arms **Rev:** Scene from Queen Mother's African tour **Edge:** Reeded

Date	Mintage	VF20	XF40	MS60	MS63	MS65
1997	—	PF63 45.00	PF65 60.00			

KM# 44 500 SHILINGI

20.00 g., 0.999 Silver 0.6424 oz. ASW **Subject:** Visit of Richard von Weizsacker **Obv:** National arms **Rev:** Weizsacker and elephant

Date	Mintage	VF20	XF40	MS60	MS63	MS65
1992	—	PF63 35.00	PF65 50.00			

KM# 43 500 SHILINGI

33.80 g., 0.925 Silver 1.0052 oz. ASW, 38.5 mm. **Subject:** Serengeti Wildlife **Obv:** National arms **Rev:** Lions **Edge:** Reeded

Date	Mintage	VF20	XF40	MS60	MS63	MS65
1998	—	PF63 45.00	PF65 60.00			

KM# 48 500 SHILINGI

33.63 g., 0.925 Silver 1.0001 oz. ASW, 38.4 mm. **Subject:** Serengeti Wildlife **Obv:** National arms **Rev:** Leopard head and full body portraits **Edge:** Reeded

Date	Mintage	VF20	XF40	MS60	MS63	MS65
1998	—	PF63 45.00	PF65 60.00			

KM# 49 500 SHILINGI

33.63 g., 0.925 Silver 1.0001 oz. ASW, 38.4 mm. **Subject:** Serengeti Wildlife **Obv:** National arms **Rev:** Cheetah head and full body portraits **Edge:** Reeded

Date	Mintage	VF20	XF40	MS60	MS63	MS65
1998	—	PF63 45.00	PF65 60.00			

KM# 50 500 SHILINGI

33.63 g., 0.925 Silver 1.0001 oz. ASW, 38.4 mm. **Subject:** Serengeti Wildlife **Obv:** National arms **Rev:** Hyena head and full body portraits **Edge:** Reeded

Date	Mintage	VF20	XF40	MS60	MS63	MS65
1998	—	PF63 45.00	PF65 60.00			

KM# 51 500 SHILINGI

33.63 g., 0.925 Silver 1.0001 oz. ASW, 38.4 mm. **Subject:** Serengeti Wildlife **Obv:** National arms **Rev:** Crocodile head and full body portraits **Edge:** Reeded

Date	Mintage	VF20	XF40	MS60	MS63	MS65
1998	—	PF63 50.00	PF65 65.00			

KM# 17 1000 SHILINGI

8.10 g., 0.900 Gold 0.2344 oz. AGW **Series:** Decade for Women **Obv:** President J.K. Nyerere left flanked by flowers **Rev:** Half figure separating grain

Date	Mintage	VF20	XF40	MS60	MS63	MS65
1984	500	PF63 400	PF65 450	PF67 500		

KM# 45 1000 SHILINGI

6.00 g., 0.999 Gold 0.1927 oz. AGW **Subject:** Visit of Richard von Weizsacker **Obv:** National arms **Rev:** Weizsacker and elephant

Date	Mintage	VF20	XF40	MS60	MS63	MS65
1992	Est. 8000	PF63 300	PF65 350	PF67 400		

KM# 60 1000 SHILINGI

1.24 g., 0.999 Gold 0.040 oz. AGW, 13.92 mm. **Obv:** National arms **Rev:** Primitive gold refining scene **Edge:** Reeded

Date	Mintage	VF20	XF40	MS60	MS63	MS65
1998	—	PF63 65.00	PF65 75.00			

KM# 9 1500 SHILINGI

33.44 g., 0.900 Gold 0.9675 oz. AGW **Subject:** Conservation **Obv:** President J.K. Nyerere left flanked by flowers **Rev:** Cheetahs

Date	Mintage	XF40	MS60	MS63	MS65	MS66
1974	2,779	—	—	1,450	1,550	1,650
1974	866	PF65 1,650	PF67 1,750	PF69 1,900		

KM# 15 2000 SHILINGI
15.98 g., 0.917 Gold 0.4711 oz. AGW **Subject:** 20th Anniversary of Independence **Obv:** President J.K. Nyerere **Rev:** National arms

Date	Mintage	XF40	MS60	MS63	MS65	MS66
ND-1981	110	—	—	875	925	975
ND-1981	Inc. above	PF65 950	PF67 1,000			

KM# 19 2000 SHILINGI
15.98 g., 0.917 Gold 0.4711 oz. AGW **Subject:** Conservation **Obv:** President J.K. Nyerere left flanked by flowers **Rev:** Banded Green Sunbird

Date	Mintage	VF20	XF40	MS60	MS63	MS65
1986	5,000	PF63 850	PF65 900	PF67 950		

KM# 25 2000 SHILINGI
10.00 g., 0.917 Gold 0.2948 oz. AGW **Series:** Save the Children Fund **Obv:** President Mwinyi right flanked by small sprigs **Rev:** Child and calf within circle

Date	Mintage	VF20	XF40	MS60	MS63	MS65
1990	Est. 3000	PF63 500	PF65 550	PF67 600		

KM# 46 2000 SHILINGI
10.00 g., 0.999 Gold 0.3212 oz. AGW **Subject:** Visit of Richard von Weizsacker **Obv:** National arms **Rev:** Weizsacker and elephant

Date	Mintage	VF20	XF40	MS60	MS63	MS65
1992	Est. 5000	PF63 550	PF65 575	PF67 650		

KM# 31 2500 SHILINGI
46.85 g., 0.917 Gold 1.3812 oz. AGW **Subject:** 25 Years of Independence **Obv:** President J.K. Nyerere 1/4 left within circle **Rev:** National arms

Date	Mintage	VF20	XF40	MS60	MS63	MS65
ND-1985	—	PF63 2,250	PF65 2,750	PF67 3,000		

KM# 35 2500 SHILINGI
155.36 g., 0.999 Silver 4.9899 oz. ASW, 65 mm. **Subject:** Serengeti Wildlife **Obv:** National arms **Rev:** Zebra head and full body zebra **Edge:** Reeded **Note:** Illustration reduced.

Date	Mintage	VF20	XF40	MS60	MS63	MS65
1998	—	PF63 125	PF65 145	PF67 175		

KM# 36 2500 SHILINGI
155.36 g., 0.999 Silver 4.9899 oz. ASW, 65 mm. **Subject:** Serengeti Wildlife **Obv:** National arms **Rev:** Giraffe head and full body giraffe **Note:** Illustration reduced.

Date	Mintage	VF20	XF40	MS60	MS63	MS65
1998	—	PF63 125	PF65 145	PF67 175		

KM# 37 2500 SHILINGI
155.36 g., 0.999 Silver 4.9899 oz. ASW, 65 mm. **Subject:** Serengeti Wildlife **Obv:** National arms **Rev:** Cheetah head and full body portrait **Note:** Illustration reduced.

Date	Mintage	VF20	XF40	MS60	MS63	MS65
1998	—	PF63 135	PF65 155	PF67 185		

KM# 38 2500 SHILINGI
155.36 g., 0.999 Silver 4.9899 oz. ASW, 65 mm. **Subject:** Serengeti Wildlife **Obv:** National arms **Rev:** Wildebeast herd **Note:** Illustration reduced.

Date	Mintage	VF20	XF40	MS60	MS63	MS65
1998	—	PF63 135	PF65 155	PF67 185		

KM# 39 2500 SHILINGI
155.36 g., 0.999 Silver 4.9899 oz. ASW, 65 mm. **Subject:** Serengeti Wildlife **Obv:** National arms **Rev:** Gazelle head and full body portrait **Note:** Illustration reduced.

Date	Mintage	VF20	XF40	MS60	MS63	MS65
1998	—	PF63 125	PF65 145	PF67 175		

KM# 52 2500 SHILINGI
155.36 g., 0.999 Silver 4.9899 oz. ASW, 65 mm. **Subject:** Serengeti Wildlife **Obv:** National arms **Rev:** Lion head and full body lion **Edge:** Reeded **Note:** Illustration reduced.

Date	Mintage	VF20	XF40	MS60	MS63	MS65
1998	—	PF63 125	PF65 145	PF67 175		

KM# 53 2500 SHILINGI
155.36 g., 0.999 Silver 4.9899 oz. ASW, 65 mm. **Subject:** Serengeti Wildlife **Obv:** National arms **Rev:** Leopard head and full body portraits **Edge:** Reeded **Note:** Illustration reduced.

Date	Mintage	VF20	XF40	MS60	MS63	MS65
1998	—	PF63 125	PF65 145	PF67 175		

KM# 54 2500 SHILINGI
155.36 g., 0.999 Silver 4.9899 oz. ASW, 65 mm. **Subject:** Serengeti Wildlife **Obv:** National arms **Rev:** Hyena head and full body portraits **Edge:** Reeded **Note:** Illustration reduced.

Date	Mintage	VF20	XF40	MS60	MS63	MS65
1998	—	PF63 125	PF65 145	PF67 175		

KM# 55 2500 SHILINGI
155.36 g., 0.999 Silver 4.9899 oz. ASW, 65 mm. **Subject:** Serengeti Wildlife **Obv:** National arms **Rev:** Crocodile head and full body portraits **Edge:** Reeded **Note:** Illustration reduced.

Date	Mintage	VF20	XF40	MS60	MS63	MS65
1998	—	PF63 125	PF65 145	PF67 175		

KM# 42 10000 SHILINGI
31.10 g., 0.9999 Gold 0.9999 oz. AGW, 32.5 mm. **Subject:** Serengeti Wildlife **Obv:** National arms **Rev:** Lion, Cheetah and Zebra **Edge:** Reeded

Date	Mintage	VF20	XF40	MS60	MS63	MS65
1998	Est. 1000	PF65 1,600	PF67 1,800			

KM# A58 25000 SHILINGI
1001.00 g., 0.999 Silver 32.1507 oz. ASW **Subject:** Serengeti Wildlife **Obv:** National arms **Rev:** Lion, Cheetah and Zebra

Date	Mintage	VF20	XF40	MS60	MS63	MS65
1998	—	PF65 750	PF67 850			

KM# 58 50000 SHILINGI
155.51 g., 0.999 Gold 4.9948 oz. AGW **Subject:** Serengeti Wildlife **Obv:** National arms **Rev:** Lion, Cheetah and Zebra

Date	Mintage	VF20	XF40	MS60	MS63	MS65
1998	—	PF65 7,500	PF67 8,500			

TRIAL STRIKES

KM#	Date	Mintage	Identification	Mkt Val
TS1	1980	—	5 Senti. Copper-Nickel. KM#6.	150
TS2	1980	—	Shilingi. Copper-Nickel. KM#4.	125
TS3	1981	—	50 Senti. Copper-Nickel. KM#3.	95.00

PATTERNS

Including off metal strikes

KM#	Date	Mintage	Identification	Mkt Val
Pn1	1973	—	50 Senti. Nickel-Bronze. KM#3.	100

PROOF SETS

KM#	Date	Mintage	Identification	Issue Price	Mkt Val
PS1	1966 (4)	5,500	KM#1-4	10.20	35.00
PS2	1974 (2)	30,000	KM#7a-8a	50.00	75.00
PS3	1985 (3)	—	KM#29-31	—	3,250

TATARSTAN

Tatarstan, an autonomous republic in the Russian Federation, is situated between the middle of the Volga river and its tributary Kama, extends east to the Ural mountains, covering 26,500 sq. mi. (68,000 sq. km.) and as of the 1970 census, has a population of 3,743,600. Capital: Kazan. Tatarstan's economy combines its ancient traditions in the craftmanship of wood, leather, cloth, and ceramics with modern engineering, chemical, and food industries.

Colonized by the Bulgars in the 5th century, the territory of the Volga-Kama Bulgar State was inhabited by Turks. In the 13th century, Ghengis Khan conquered the area and established control until the 15th century, when residual Mongol influence left Tatarstan as the Tatar Khanate, seat of the Kazan (Tatar) Khans. In 1552, under Ivan IV (The Terrible), Russia conquered, absorbed and controlled Tatarstan until the dissolution of the U.S.S.R. in the late 20th century.

Constituted as an autonomous republic on May 27,1990, and as a sovereign state equal with Russia April, 1992, Tatarstan, with Russia's president, signed a treaty in Feb. 1994 defining Tatarstan as a state united with Russia (Commonwealth of Independent States).

RULER
President Mintimir Shaimiev

RUSSIAN STATE

TOKEN COINAGE

KM# Tn1 KILO (Bread)
Bronze **Ruler:** President Mintimir Shaimiev **Obv:** Arms **Rev:** Wheat stalks **Edge:** Reeded

Date	Mintage	F12	VF20	XF40	MS60	MS63
ND (1993)	—	1.50	3.00	6.00	12.00	25.00

KM# Tn2 10 LITRES (Petrol)
Bronze **Ruler:** President Mintimir Shaimiev **Obv:** Arms **Rev:** Oil derrick **Edge:** Reeded **Note:** The bronze 10 Litres token was withdrawn from circulation because it was nickel plated in large numbers and passed off as the higher valued copper-nickel version KM-Tn3.

Date	Mintage	F12	VF20	XF40	MS60	MS63
ND (1993)	—	2.00	4.00	8.00	18.00	35.00

KM# Tn3 20 LITRES (Petrol)
5.25 g., Copper-Nickel, 24.86 mm. **Ruler:** President Mintimir Shaimiev **Obv:** Arms **Rev:** Oil derrick **Edge:** Reeded **Note:** The copper-nickel Tn3 are often found with test file notches, because of the nickel plating problems of the bronze Tn2.

Date	Mintage	F12	VF20	XF40	MS60	MS63
ND (1993)	—	2.50	5.00	10.00	20.00	40.00

The Kingdom of Thailand (formerly Siam), a constitutional monarchy located in the center of mainland Southeast Asia between Burma and Laos, has an area of 198,457 sq. mi. (514,000 sq. km.) and a population of *55.5 million. Capital: Bangkok. The economy is based on agriculture and mining. Rubber, rice, teakwood, tin and tungsten are exported.

The history of The Kingdom of Siam, the only country in south and Southeast Asia that was never colonized by a European power, dates from the 6th century A.D. when Thai people started to migrate into the area, a process that accelerated with the Mongol invasion of China in the 13th century. After 400 years of sporadic warfare with the neighboring Burmese, King Taskin won the last battle in 1767. He founded a new capital, Dhonburi, on the west bank of the Chao Praya River. King Rama I moved the capital to Bangkok in 1782, thus initiating the so-called Bangkok Period of Siamese coinage characterized by Pot Duang money (bullet coins) stamped with regal symbols.

The Portuguese, who were followed by the Dutch, British and French, introduced the Thai to the Western world. Rama III of the present ruling dynasty negotiated a treaty of friendship and commerce with Britain in 1826, and in 1896 the independence of the kingdom was guaranteed by an Anglo-French accord.

In 1909 Siam ceded to Great Britain its suzerain rights over the dependencies of Kedah, Kelantan, Trengganu and Perlis, Malay states situated in southern Siam just north of British Malaya, which eliminated any British jurisdiction in Siam proper.

The absolute monarchy was changed into a constitutional monarchy in 1932.

On Dec. 8, 1941, after five hours of fighting, Thailand agreed to permit Japanese troops passage through the country to invade Northern British Malaysia. This eventually led to increased Japanese intervention and finally occupation of the country. On Jan. 25, 1942, Thailand declared war on Great Britain and the United States. A free Thai guerilla movement was soon organized to counteract the Japanese. In July 1943 Japan transferred the four northern Malay States back to Thailand. These were returned to Great Britain after peace treaties were signed in 1946.

RULERS

Rama V (Phra Maha Chulalongkorn), 1868-1910
Rama VI (Phra Maha Vajiravudh), 1910-1925
Rama VII (Phra Maha Prajadhipok), 1925-1935
Rama VIII (Phra Maha Ananda Mahidol), 1935-1946
Rama IX (Phra Maha Bhumibol Adulyadej), 1946-

MONETARY SYSTEM

OLD CURRENCY SYSTEM

2 Solos = 1 Att
2 Att = 1 Sio (Pai)
2 Sio = 1 Sik
2 Sik = 1 Fuang
2 Fuang = 1 Salung (not Sal'ung)
4 Salung = 1 Baht
4 Baht = 1 Tamlung
20 Tamlung = 1 Chang

UNITS OF OLD THAI CURRENCY

Chang -	ชั่ง	Sik -	ซีก
Tamlung -	ตำลึง	Sio (Pai) -	เสี้ยว
Baht -	บาท	Att -	อัฐ
Salung -	สลึง	Solos -	โสฬส
Fuang -	เฟื้อง		

MINT MARK

H-Heaton Birmingham

Typical BE Dating

Typical CS Dating

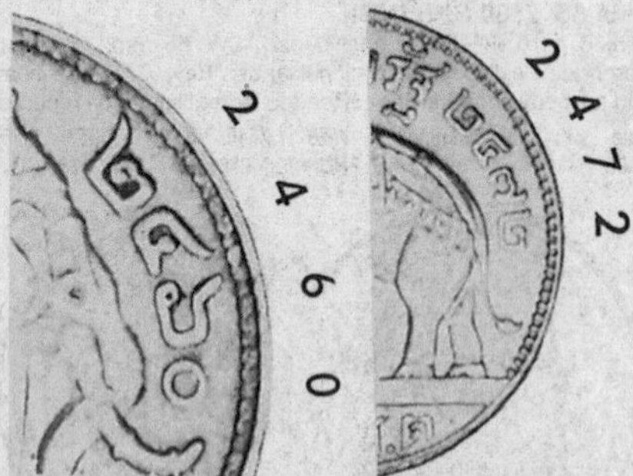

NOTE: Sometimes the era designator *BE* or *CS* will actually appear on the coin itself.

DENOMINATION

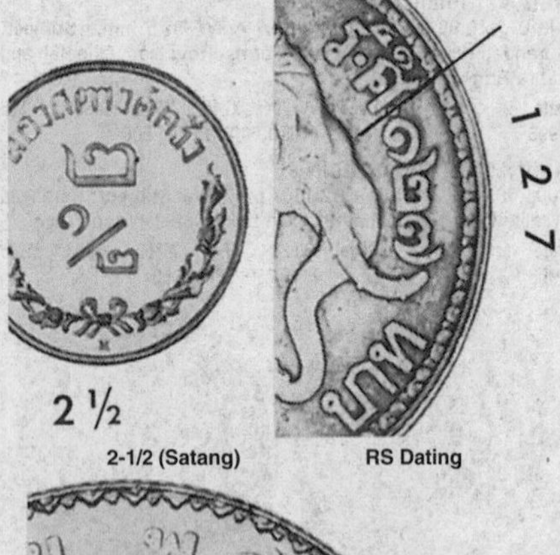

2-1/2 (Satang) RS Dating

DATE CONVERSION TABLES

B.E. date - 543 = A.D. date
Ex: 2516 - 543 = 1973
R.S. date + 1781 = A.D. date
Ex: 127 + 1781 = 1908
C.S. date + 638 = A.D. date
Ex 1238 + 638 = 1876

Primary denominations used were 1 Baht, 1/4 and 1/8 Baht up to the reign of Rama IV. Other denominations are much scarcer.

KINGDOM OF SIAM

until 1939

STANDARD COINAGE

Y# 21 1/2 ATT (1 Solot)

Bronze **Ruler:** Rama V **Obv:** Uniformed bust left **Rev:** Crowned seated figure right

Date	Mintage	F12	VF20	XF40	MS60	MS63
RS124	—	1.50	2.50	30.00	140	—

Note: These coins were also minted in RS114, RS115, RS121 and RS122. The last year had a mintage of 5,120,000. Coins with these dates have not been observed and were probably additional mintings of coins dated RS109 and RS118. A nickel pattern dated RS114 does exist. Varieties in numeral size and rotated dies exist

Y# 22 ATT

Bronze **Ruler:** Rama V **Obv:** Uniformed bust left **Rev:** Crowned seated figure right **Note:** Full red uncirculated coins of this type carry a substantial premium.

Date	Mintage	F12	VF20	XF40	MS60	MS63
RS121	11,251,000	3.50	5.00	40.00	220	450
RS122	4,109,000	4.50	10.00	55.00	235	475

Note: Exists with large (greater than 1mm) and small (less than 1mm) numerals

Date	Mintage	F12	VF20	XF40	MS60	MS63
RS124	—	3.50	5.00	40.00	220	450

Y# 23 2 ATT (1/32 Baht = 1 Sio)

Bronze **Ruler:** Rama V **Obv:** Uniformed bust left **Rev:** Crowned seated figure right **Note:** Varieties in numeral size and rotated dies exist. Full red uncirculated coins of this type carry a substantial premium.

Date	Mintage	F12	VF20	XF40	MS60	MS63
RS121	2,797,000	1.50	3.00	40.00	250	—
RS122	2,323,000	1.50	3.00	40.00	250	—
RS124	—	1.50	3.00	40.00	250	—

Y# 32a FUANG (1/8 Baht)

Silver **Ruler:** Rama V **Obv:** Bust left **Rev:** National arms **Note:** Weight range: 1.7-2.01 g.

Date	Mintage	F12	VF20	XF40	MS60	MS63
RS121	380,000	6.00	25.00	78.00	160	—
RS122	460,000	10.00	30.00	80.00	170	—
RS123	310,000	6.00	25.00	70.00	160	—
RS124	410,000	6.00	25.00	70.00	160	—
RS125	—	6.00	25.00	70.00	160	—
RS126	—	10.00	30.00	80.00	170	—
RS127	480,000	3.00	15.00	90.00	200	—

Y# 32c FUANG (1/8 Baht)

Gold **Ruler:** Rama V **Obv:** Bust left **Rev:** National arms

Date	Mintage	F12	VF20	XF40	MS60	MS63
RS122	—	—	—	—	—	—
RS123	—	1,500	3,000	5,000	7,000	—
RS124	—	1,500	3,000	5,000	7,000	—
RS125	—	1,500	3,000	5,000	7,000	—
RS126	—	1,500	3,000	5,000	7,000	—
RS127	—	1,500	3,000	5,000	7,000	—
RS128	—	1,500	3,000	5,000	7,000	—
RS129	—	1,500	3,000	5,000	7,000	—

Y# 33a SALUNG = 1/4 BAHT
Silver **Ruler:** Rama V **Obv:** Bust left **Rev:** National arms **Note:** Weight range: 3.60-4.02g.

Date	Mintage	F12	VF20	XF40	MS60	MS63
RS120	—	100	200	300	4,000	—
RS121	560,000	20.00	40.00	80.00	250	—
RS122	340,000	30.00	60.00	120	500	—
RS123	190,000	30.00	40.00	70.00	200	—
RS125	—	20.00	40.00	70.00	200	—
RS126	—	20.00	40.00	70.00	200	—
RS127	270,000	20.00	60.00	90.00	220	—

Y# 43 SALUNG = 1/4 BAHT
3.75 g., 0.800 Silver 0.0965 oz. ASW **Ruler:** Rama VI **Obv:** Bust right **Rev:** Elephant heads flank facing elephant

Date	Mintage	F12	VF20	XF40	MS60	MS63
BE2458	2,040,000	—	5.00	10.00	20.00	—

Y# 43a SALUNG = 1/4 BAHT
3.75 g., 0.650 Silver 0.0784 oz. ASW **Ruler:** Rama VI **Obv:** Bust right **Rev:** Elephant heads flank facing elephant

Date	Mintage	F12	VF20	XF40	MS60	MS63
BE2460	1,100,000	—	4.00	8.00	18.50	—
BE2461	2,170,000	—	4.00	8.00	18.50	—
BE2462	7,860,000	—	3.00	6.50	15.00	—
BE2467	2,100,000	—	4.00	8.00	18.50	—
BE2468	—	—	4.00	8.00	18.50	—

Y# 43b SALUNG = 1/4 BAHT
3.75 g., 0.500 Silver 0.0603 oz. ASW **Ruler:** Rama VI **Obv:** Bust right **Rev:** Elephant heads flank facing elephant

Date	Mintage	F12	VF20	XF40	MS60	MS63
BE2462 Dot after legend	Inc. above	—	40.00	65.00	120	—

Y# 34a BAHT
Silver, 31.5 mm. **Ruler:** Rama V **Obv:** Bust left **Rev:** National arms, flags flanking **Edge:** Plain

Date	Mintage	F12	VF20	XF40	MS60	MS63
RS120	—	200	300	700	2,200	—
RS121	4,070,000	20.00	40.00	100	400	—
Note: There are two varieties, large and small date						
RS122	19,150,000	30.00	50.00	90.00	250	—
RS123	4,790,000	20.00	40.00	70.00	200	—
RS124	6,770,000	20.00	40.00	70.00	200	—
RS125	—	20.00	40.00	70.00	200	—
RS126	—	40.00	60.00	170	400	—

DECIMAL COINAGE

25 Satang = 1 Salung; 100 Satang = 1 Baht

Y# 50 1/2 SATANG
Bronze **Ruler:** Rama VIII **Obv:** Hole in center divides inscription **Rev:** Hole in center of design

Date	Mintage	F12	VF20	XF40	MS60	MS63
BE2480	—	—	0.75	1.75	3.50	—

Y# 35 SATANG
Bronze **Ruler:** Rama VI **Obv:** Hole in center divides inscription **Rev:** Hole in center of design **Edge:** Plain **Note:** Variations in lettering exist.

Date	Mintage	F12	VF20	XF40	MS60	MS63
RS127	17,000,000	—	2.50	35.00	120	—
RS128	150,000	—	3.50	35.00	120	—
RS129	9,000,000	—	1.50	35.00	100	—
RS130	30,000,000	—	1.50	25.00	50.00	—
BE2456	10,000,000	—	1.00	1.50	4.00	—
RS132 Rare	—	—	—	—	—	—
BE2457	1,000,000	—	2.00	4.00	12.50	—
BE2458	5,000,000	—	0.75	1.00	2.75	—
BE2461	18,880,000	—	0.65	1.25	3.00	—
BE2462	6,400,000	—	0.65	1.00	2.75	—
BE2463	17,240,000	—	1.00	1.50	3.50	—
BE2464	6,360,000	—	15.00	25.00	100	—
BE2466	14,000,000	—	0.75	1.00	2.75	—
BE2467	Inc. above	—	1.00	1.50	3.50	—
BE2469	20,000,000	—	0.50	0.75	2.50	—
BE2470	—	—	0.50	0.75	2.50	—
BE2472	—	—	0.50	1.00	2.75	—
BE2478	—	—	0.50	0.70	2.00	—
BE2480	—	—	0.50	0.70	2.00	—

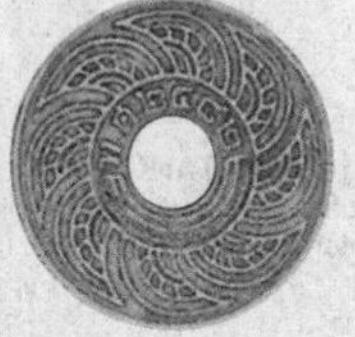

Y# 51 SATANG
Bronze **Ruler:** Rama VIII **Obv:** Hole in center divides inscription **Rev:** Hole in center of design **Edge:** Plain

Date	Mintage	F12	VF20	XF40	MS60	MS63
BE2482	24,400,000	—	1.50	3.00	6.00	—

Y# 36 5 SATANG
Nickel, 18 mm. **Ruler:** Rama VI **Obv:** Hole in center divides inscription **Rev:** Center hole within design

Date	Mintage	F12	VF20	XF40	MS60	MS63
RS127	7,000,000	—	3.00	35.00	120	—
RS128	4,000,000	—	3.50	35.00	100	—
RS129	4,000,000	—	1.50	35.00	100	—
RS131	2,000,000	—	1.50	25.00	50.00	—
BE2456	2,000,000	—	1.50	2.50	6.00	—
RS132 Rare	—	—	—	—	—	—
BE2457	2,000,000	—	1.50	2.50	6.00	—
BE2461	2,000,000	—	1.50	2.50	6.00	—
BE2462	2,000,000	—	1.00	2.00	6.00	—
BE2463	9,900,000	—	1.00	1.50	4.50	—
BE2464	13,000,000	—	0.60	1.25	3.00	—
BE2469	20,000,000	—	0.60	1.25	3.00	—
BE2478	10,000,000	—	0.60	1.25	3.00	—
BE2480	20,000,000	—	0.60	1.25	3.00	—

Y# 37 10 SATANG
3.30 g., Nickel **Ruler:** Rama VI **Obv:** Hole in center divides inscription **Rev:** Hole in center of design **Edge:** Plain **Note:** Variations in lettering exist.

Date	Mintage	F12	VF20	XF40	MS60	MS63
RS127	7,000,000	—	1.50	35.00	130	—
RS129	5,000,000	—	1.50	35.00	120	—
RS130	500,000	—	2.00	5.00	12.00	—
RS131	1,500,000	—	1.50	3.00	10.00	—
BE2456	1,000,000	—	1.25	2.00	6.00	—
BE2457	1,000,000	—	1.25	2.00	6.00	—
BE2461	770,000	—	2.50	3.50	9.00	—
BE2462	774,000	—	1.25	1.50	3.50	—
BE2463	Inc. above	—	1.25	1.50	3.50	—
BE2464	21,727,000	—	1.00	1.25	3.00	—
BE2478	5,000,000	—	1.00	1.25	3.00	—
BE2480	5,000,000	—	0.75	1.00	2.50	—

Y# 48 25 SATANG = 1/4 BAHT
3.75 g., 0.650 Silver 0.0784 oz. ASW **Ruler:** Rama VII **Obv:** Uniformed bust left **Rev:** Elephant

Date	Mintage	F12	VF20	XF40	MS60	MS63
BE2472 (1929)	—	—	4.50	9.00	22.50	—

Y# 49 50 SATANG = 1/2 BAHT
7.50 g., 0.650 Silver 0.1567 oz. ASW **Ruler:** Rama VII **Obv:** Uniformed bust left **Rev:** Elephant

Date	Mintage	F12	VF20	XF40	MS60	MS63
BE2472	17,008,000	—	7.00	16.50	35.00	45.00

Y# 44 2 SALUNG = 1/2 BAHT
7.50 g., 0.800 Silver 0.1929 oz. ASW, 30.4 mm. **Ruler:** Rama VI **Obv:** Uniformed bust right **Rev:** Elephant heads flank facing elephant

Date	Mintage	F12	VF20	XF40	MS60	MS63
BE2458	2,740,000	—	7.50	18.50	40.00	—

Y# 44a 2 SALUNG = 1/2 BAHT
7.50 g., 0.650 Silver 0.1567 oz. ASW **Ruler:** Rama VI **Obv:** Uniformed bust right **Rev:** Elephant heads flank facing elephant **Note:** Date varieties exist.

Date	Mintage	F12	VF20	XF40	MS60	MS63
BE2462	3,230,000	—	6.00	14.00	30.00	—
BE2463	4,970,000	—	6.00	14.00	30.00	—
BE2464	—	—	6.00	14.00	30.00	—

Y# 44b 2 SALUNG = 1/2 BAHT
7.50 g., 0.500 Silver 0.1206 oz. ASW **Ruler:** Rama VI **Obv:** Uniformed bust right **Rev:** Elephant heads flank facing elephant

Date	Mintage	F12	VF20	XF40	MS60	MS63
BE2462	Inc. above	—	7.50	16.50	32.50	—
Note: Large dot after legend						
BE2462	Inc. above	—	7.50	16.50	32.50	—
Note: Small dot after legend						

Y# 39 BAHT
15.00 g., 0.900 Silver 0.434 oz. ASW **Ruler:** Rama V **Obv:** Uniformed bust left **Rev:** Elephant heads flank facing elephant

Date	Mintage	F12	VF20	XF40	MS60	MS63
RS127	1,037,000	—	2,200	3,500	6,500	—

Y# 45 BAHT
15.00 g., 0.900 Silver 0.434 oz. ASW **Ruler:** Rama VI **Obv:** Uniformed bust right **Rev:** Elephant heads flank facing elephant

Date	Mintage	F12	VF20	XF40	MS60	MS63
BE2456	2,690,000	—	14.50	18.50	40.00	150
Note: BE2456 is often found weakly struck so it does appear similar to a counterfeit						
BE2457	490,000	—	16.50	25.00	50.00	175
BE2458	5,000,000	—	14.50	18.50	40.00	150
BE2459	9,080,000	—	14.50	18.50	32.00	125
BE2460	14,340,000	—	14.50	18.50	32.00	125
BE2461	3,840,000	—	14.50	18.50	45.00	160

KINGDOM OF THAILAND

1939-

Y# 54 SATANG

Bronze **Ruler:** Rama VIII **Obv:** Hole in center of design **Rev:** Hole in center of design **Edge:** Plain

Date	Mintage	VF20	XF40	MS60	MS63	MS65
BE2484	—	0.50	1.50	3.00	—	—

Y# 57 SATANG

1.50 g., Tin **Ruler:** Rama VIII **Obv:** Center circle within design **Rev:** Center circle within design **Edge:** Plain **Note:** BE date and denomination in Thai numerals, without hole.

Date	Mintage	VF20	XF40	MS60	MS63	MS65
BE2485	20,700,000	0.30	0.50	1.00	—	—

Note: Approximately 790,000 coins were struck for circulation 1967-73

Y# 60 SATANG

Tin **Ruler:** Rama VIII **Obv:** Hole in center of design **Rev:** Hole in center of design **Edge:** Plain **Note:** BE date and denomination in Western numerals. No hole.

Date	Mintage	VF20	XF40	MS60	MS63	MS65
BE2487	500,000	0.10	0.20	0.50	—	—

Y# 186 SATANG

0.50 g., Aluminum, 14.58 mm. **Ruler:** Rama IX **Obv:** Head left **Rev:** Haripunchai Temple, Lumpoon province **Edge:** Plain

Date	Mintage	VF20	XF40	MS60	MS63	MS65
BE2530	93,000	—	—	0.15	0.20	—
BE2531	200,000	—	—	0.15	0.20	—
BE2532	109,000	—	—	0.15	0.20	—
BE2533	191,050	—	—	0.15	0.20	—
BE2534	25,000	—	0.25	1.00	1.25	—
BE2535	61,000	—	0.25	0.75	1.00	—
BE2536	126,000	—	—	0.15	0.20	—
BE2537	500,000	—	—	0.15	0.20	—
BE2538	500,000	—	—	0.15	0.20	—
BE2540	10,000	—	0.50	1.50	2.00	—
BE2541	10,000	—	—	1.50	2.00	—
BE2542	20,000	—	—	1.25	1.75	—
BE2543	10,000	—	—	1.50	2.00	—

Y# 342 SATANG

0.50 g., Aluminum **Ruler:** Rama IX **Subject:** 50th Anniversary - Reign of King Rama IX **Obv:** Uniformed bust facing **Rev:** Arms

Date	Mintage	VF20	XF40	MS60	MS63	MS65
BE2539	3,250,000	—	—	0.15	0.20	—

Y# 55 5 SATANG

1.50 g., 0.650 Silver 0.0313 oz. ASW **Ruler:** Rama VIII **Obv:** Center hole within design **Rev:** Center hole within design

Date	Mintage	VF20	XF40	MS60	MS63	MS65
BE2484	—	1.50	3.00	4.50	—	—

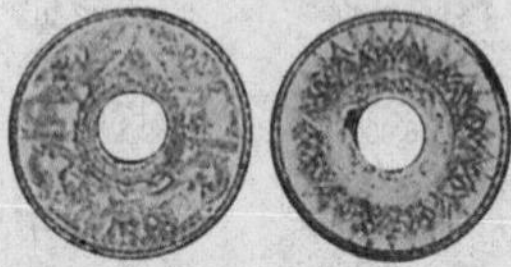

Y# 58 5 SATANG

Tin **Ruler:** Rama VIII **Obv:** Hole in center of design **Rev:** Hole in center of design **Note:** BE date and denomination in Thai numerals.

Date	Mintage	VF20	XF40	MS60	MS63	MS65
BE2485	—	0.50	1.50	3.00	—	—

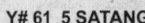

Y# 61 5 SATANG

Tin **Ruler:** Rama VIII **Obv:** Hole in center of design **Rev:** Hole in center of design **Note:** Thick (2.2mm) planchet. BE date and denomination in Western numerals.

Date	Mintage	VF20	XF40	MS60	MS63	MS65
BE2487	—	0.50	1.25	3.00	—	—
BE2488	—	0.50	1.25	3.00	—	—

Y# 61a 5 SATANG

Tin **Ruler:** Rama VIII **Obv:** Hole in center of design **Rev:** Hole in center of design **Note:** Thin (2mm) planchet.

Date	Mintage	VF20	XF40	MS60	MS63	MS65
BE2488	—	0.50	1.25	3.00	—	—

Y# 61b 5 SATANG

Tin **Ruler:** Rama VIII **Obv:** Hole in center of design **Rev:** Hole in center of design **Note:** Medium planchet.

Date	Mintage	VF20	XF40	MS60	MS63	MS65
BE2488	—	0.50	1.25	3.00	—	—

Y# 64 5 SATANG

Tin **Ruler:** Rama VIII **Obv:** King Ananda, youth head left **Rev:** Mythical creature "Garuda"

Date	Mintage	VF20	XF40	MS60	MS63	MS65
BE2489	—	0.50	1.00	2.00	—	—

Y# 68 5 SATANG

1.10 g., Tin **Ruler:** Rama VIII **Obv:** King Ananda, youth head left **Rev:** Mythical creature "Garuda"

Date	Mintage	VF20	XF40	MS60	MS63	MS65
BE2489 (1946)	24,480,000	0.15	0.50	1.00	—	—

Y# 72 5 SATANG

1.25 g., Tin (92 copper), 15 mm. **Ruler:** Rama IX **Obv:** Uniformed bust left with one medal **Rev:** Mantled arms **Edge:** Plain

Date	Mintage	VF20	XF40	MS60	MS63	MS65
BE2493	Est. 6480000	0.50	0.75	1.25	—	—

Note: Coins bearing this date were also struck in 1954, 58, 59, and 73. Mintages are included here

Y# 72a 5 SATANG

1.25 g., Aluminum-Bronze, 15 mm. **Ruler:** Rama IX **Obv:** Uniformed bust left **Rev:** Mantled arms **Edge:** Plain

Date	Mintage	VF20	XF40	MS60	MS63	MS65
BE2493	15,500,000	0.25	1.00	2.00	—	—

Y# 78 5 SATANG

1.25 g., Aluminum-Bronze, 15 mm. **Ruler:** Rama IX **Obv:** Smaller head, 3 medals on uniform **Rev:** Mantled arms **Edge:** Plain

Date	Mintage	VF20	XF40	MS60	MS63	MS65
BE2500	Est. 46440000	—	0.10	0.25	—	—

Note: Minted without date change until 1987

Y# 78a 5 SATANG

1.25 g., Bronze, 15 mm. **Ruler:** Rama IX **Obv:** Uniformed bust left **Rev:** Mantled arms **Edge:** Plain

Date	Mintage	VF20	XF40	MS60	MS63	MS65
BE2500	Est. 6240000	0.50	1.50	2.00	—	—

Y# 78b 5 SATANG

1.25 g., Tin, 15 mm. **Ruler:** Rama IX **Obv:** Uniformed bust left **Rev:** Mantled arms

Date	Mintage	VF20	XF40	MS60	MS63	MS65
BE2500	—	1.75	3.00	5.00	—	—

Note: The above coins were struck to replace Y#72 in mint sets

Y# 208 5 SATANG

0.60 g., Aluminum, 16 mm. **Ruler:** Rama IX **Obv:** Bust left **Rev:** Phra Patom Temple, Nakhon Pathom province **Edge:** Plain

Date	Mintage	VF20	XF40	MS60	MS63	MS65
BE2530	10,000	—	—	30.00	40.00	—
BE2531	694,000	—	—	0.15	0.20	—
BE2532	462,000	—	—	0.15	0.20	—
BE2533	368,050	—	—	0.15	0.20	—
BE2534	25,000	—	0.60	1.25	1.50	—
BE2535	61,000	—	0.40	0.80	1.10	—
BE2536	100,000	—	—	0.20	0.25	—
BE2537	500,000	—	—	0.15	0.20	—
BE2538	500,000	—	—	0.15	0.20	—
BE2540	10,000	—	0.60	2.00	2.50	—
BE2541	10,000	—	—	2.00	2.50	—
BE2542	20,000	—	0.60	1.25	1.50	—
BE2543	10,000	—	—	2.00	2.50	—

Y# 343 5 SATANG

0.60 g., Aluminum, 16 mm. **Ruler:** Rama IX **Subject:** 50th Anniversary - Reign of King Rama IX **Obv:** Bust facing **Rev:** Arms **Edge:** Reeded

Date	Mintage	VF20	XF40	MS60	MS63	MS65
BE2539	3,250,000	—	—	0.25	0.40	—

Y# 56 10 SATANG

2.50 g., 0.650 Silver 0.0522 oz. ASW **Ruler:** Rama VIII **Obv:** Hole in center of design **Rev:** Hole in center of design **Edge:** Plain

Date	Mintage	VF20	XF40	MS60	MS63	MS65
BE2484	—	2.00	4.00	8.00	—	—

Y# 59 10 SATANG

Tin **Ruler:** Rama VIII **Obv:** Hole in center of design **Rev:** Hole in center of design **Note:** BE date and denomination in Thai numerals.

Date	Mintage	VF20	XF40	MS60	MS63	MS65
BE2485	230,000	1.00	2.00	5.00	—	—

Y# 62 10 SATANG

Tin **Ruler:** Rama VIII **Obv:** Hole in center of design **Rev:** Hole in center of design **Note:** Thick (2.5mm) planchet. BE date and denomination in Western numerals.

Date	Mintage	VF20	XF40	MS60	MS63	MS65
BE2487	—	1.00	2.00	3.50	—	—
BE2488	—	3.50	7.00	15.00	—	—

Y# 62a 10 SATANG

Tin **Ruler:** Rama IX **Obv:** Hole in center of design **Rev:** Hole in center of design **Note:** Thin (2mm) planchet.

Date	Mintage	VF20	XF40	MS60	MS63	MS65
BE2488	—	1.00	2.50	4.00	—	—

Y# 65 10 SATANG
Tin **Ruler:** Rama IX **Obv:** King Ananda, child head **Rev:** Mythical creature "Garuda-"

Date	Mintage	VF20	XF40	MS60	MS63	MS65
BE2489	—	0.50	1.25	2.25	—	—

Y# 69 10 SATANG
Tin **Ruler:** Rama IX **Obv:** Youth head **Rev:** Mythical creature "Garuda" **Edge:** Plain

Date	Mintage	VF20	XF40	MS60	MS63	MS65
BE2489	40,470,000	0.50	1.25	2.00	—	—

Y# 73 10 SATANG
1.75 g., Tin, 17.5 mm. **Ruler:** Rama IX **Obv:** King Bhumiphol, one medal on uniform **Rev:** Arms **Edge:** Plain

Date	Mintage	VF20	XF40	MS60	MS63	MS65
BE2493	139,695,000	0.40	1.00	1.50	—	—

Note: These coins were also struck in 1954-1973 and the mintages are also included here

Y# 73a 10 SATANG
1.75 g., Aluminum-Bronze, 17.5 mm. **Ruler:** Rama IX **Obv:** King Bhumiphol left **Rev:** Arms

Date	Mintage	VF20	XF40	MS60	MS63	MS65
BE2493	4,060,000	0.75	1.50	2.50	—	—

Y# 79 10 SATANG
1.75 g., Aluminum-Bronze, 17.5 mm. **Ruler:** Rama IX **Obv:** Smaller head, 3 medals on uniform **Rev:** Mantled arms with thin-style legend

Date	Mintage	VF20	XF40	MS60	MS63	MS65
BE2500	Est. 55410000	0.10	0.25	0.50	—	—

Note: Minted without date change until 1987

Y# 79a 10 SATANG
1.75 g., Bronze, 17.5 mm. **Ruler:** Rama IX **Obv:** Uniformed bust left **Rev:** Mantled arms with thick-style legend **Edge:** Plain

Date	Mintage	VF20	XF40	MS60	MS63	MS65
BE2500	13,365,000	0.25	0.75	1.25	—	—
BE2501	—	0.25	0.75	1.25	—	—

Y# 79b 10 SATANG
Tin **Ruler:** Rama IX **Obv:** Uniformed bust left **Rev:** Mantled arms with thick-style legend

Date	Mintage	VF20	XF40	MS60	MS63	MS65
BE2500	—	—	—	20.00	—	—

Y# 79c 10 SATANG
1.75 g., Bronze, 17.5 mm. **Ruler:** Rama IX **Obv:** Uniformed bust left **Rev:** Mantled arms with thin-style legend

Date	Mintage	VF20	XF40	MS60	MS63	MS65
BE2500	Inc. above	100	200	400	—	—

Y# 79d 10 SATANG
Aluminum-Bronze **Ruler:** Rama IX **Obv:** Uniformed bust left **Rev:** Mantled arms with thick-style legend **Edge:** Plain

Date	Mintage	VF20	XF40	MS60	MS63	MS65
BE2500	—	0.10	0.25	0.50	—	—

Y# 209 10 SATANG
0.80 g., Aluminum, 17.5 mm. **Ruler:** Rama IX **Obv:** Young bust left **Rev:** Phra Tat Chungchum Temple, Sakon Nakhon province **Edge:** Plain

Date	Mintage	VF20	XF40	MS60	MS63	MS65
BE2530	5,000	—	—	25.00	—	—
BE2531	895,000	—	—	0.10	—	—
BE2532	80,000	—	—	1.00	—	—
BE2533	100,050	—	—	0.10	—	—
BE2534	25,000	—	—	1.00	—	—
BE2535	61,000	—	—	1.00	—	—
BE2536	100,000	—	—	0.10	—	—
BE2537	500,000	—	—	0.10	—	—
BE2538	500,000	—	—	0.10	—	—
BE2540	10,000	—	1.00	2.00	2.50	—
BE2541	10,000	—	1.00	2.00	2.50	—
BE2542	20,000	—	0.75	1.50	1.75	—
BE2543	10,000	—	1.00	2.00	2.50	—

Y# 344 10 SATANG
0.80 g., Aluminum, 17.5 mm. **Ruler:** Rama IX **Subject:** 50th Anniversary - Reign of King Rama IX **Obv:** Bust facing **Rev:** Arms **Edge:** Reeded

Date	Mintage	VF20	XF40	MS60	MS63	MS65
BE2539	3,250,000	—	—	0.35	—	—

Y# A56 20 SATANG
3.00 g., 0.650 Silver 0.0627 oz. ASW **Ruler:** Rama VIII **Obv:** Hole in center of design **Rev:** Hole in center of design **Note:** BE date and denomination in Thai numerals

Date	Mintage	VF20	XF40	MS60	MS63	MS65
BE2485	—	3.00	6.00	12.00	—	—

Y# 63 20 SATANG
Tin **Ruler:** Rama VIII **Obv:** Hole in center of design **Rev:** Hole in center of design **Edge:** Plain **Note:** BE date and denomination in Western numerals.

Date	Mintage	VF20	XF40	MS60	MS63	MS65
BE2488	—	1.00	2.50	5.00	—	—

Y# 66 25 SATANG = 1/4 BAHT
Tin **Ruler:** Rama VIII **Obv:** King Ananda, childs head **Rev:** Mythical creature "Garuda"

Date	Mintage	VF20	XF40	MS60	MS63	MS65
BE2489	—	2.50	4.50	12.50	—	—

Y# 70 25 SATANG = 1/4 BAHT
Tin **Ruler:** Rama VIII **Obv:** Youth's head left **Rev:** Mythical creature "Garuda" **Edge:** Reeded

Date	Mintage	VF20	XF40	MS60	MS63	MS65
BE2489	—	0.20	0.40	0.75	—	—

Note: These coins were also struck 1954-64 and mintage figure is a total

Y# 76 25 SATANG = 1/4 BAHT
2.50 g., Aluminum-Bronze, 20.5 mm. **Ruler:** Rama IX **Obv:** Young bust left, one medal on uniform **Rev:** Mantled arms **Edge:** Reeded

Date	Mintage	VF20	XF40	MS60	MS63	MS65
BE2493	23,170,000	0.75	1.75	4.00	—	—

Y# 80 25 SATANG = 1/4 BAHT
2.50 g., Aluminum-Bronze, 20.5 mm. **Ruler:** Rama IX **Obv:** Smaller head, 3 medals on uniform **Rev:** Mantled arms **Edge:** Reeded **Note:** Dot after the letters for "Satang" are found with raised and incuse varieties.

Date	Mintage	VF20	XF40	MS60	MS63	MS65
BE2500	620,480,000	0.10	0.15	0.25	—	—

Note: Minted without date change and with and without reeded edges until 1987

Y# 109 25 SATANG = 1/4 BAHT
2.80 g., Brass, 20.5 mm. **Ruler:** Rama IX **Obv:** Bust left **Rev:** Value and inscription **Edge:** Plain **Note:** Date varieties exist.

Date	Mintage	VF20	XF40	MS60	MS63	MS65
BE2520	183,356,000	—	0.10	0.15	—	—

Y# 187 25 SATANG = 1/4 BAHT
1.90 g., Aluminum-Bronze, 16 mm. **Ruler:** Rama IX **Obv:** Head left **Rev:** Mahathat Temple, Nakhon Si Thammarat province **Edge:** Reeded

Date	Mintage	VF20	XF40	MS60	MS63	MS65
BE2530	5,108,000	—	—	0.50	0.75	—
BE2531	42,096,000	—	—	0.10	0.15	—
BE2532 dj	58,940,000	—	—	0.10	0.15	—
BE2533	81,384,000	—	—	0.10	0.15	—
BE2534	45,496,380	—	—	0.10	0.15	—
BE2535	71,311,000	—	—	0.10	0.15	—
BE2536	236,130,000	—	—	0.10	0.15	—
BE2537 r	102,856,000	—	—	0.10	0.15	—
BE2538 r	17,000,000	—	—	0.20	0.25	—
BE2539 v	185,012,523	—	—	0.10	0.15	—
BE2540 v	85,000,000	—	—	0.10	0.15	—
BE2541 v	20,000	—	—	0.10	0.15	—
BE2542 v	10,000	2.00	3.00	5.00	6.00	—
BE2543 so	200,098,000	—	—	0.10	0.15	—

Y# 345 25 SATANG = 1/4 BAHT
1.90 g., Aluminum-Bronze, 16 mm. **Ruler:** Rama IX **Subject:** Golden Jubilee - Reign of King Rama IX **Obv:** Bust facing **Rev:** Arms with supporters

Date	Mintage	VF20	XF40	MS60	MS63	MS65
BE2539	41,800,000	—	—	0.50	—	—

Y# 67 50 SATANG = 1/2 BAHT
Tin **Ruler:** Rama VIII **Obv:** King Ananda, child's head left **Rev:** Mythical creature "Garuda"

Date	Mintage	VF20	XF40	MS60	MS63	MS65
BE2489	—	40.00	75.00	180	—	—

Y# 71 50 SATANG = 1/2 BAHT
Tin **Ruler:** Rama VIII **Obv:** Youth's head left **Rev:** Mythical creature "Garuda" **Edge:** Reeded

Date	Mintage	VF20	XF40	MS60	MS63	MS65
BE2489	17,008,000	0.75	1.50	4.00	—	—

Note: These coins were minted from 1954-1957 and mintage figure is a total

Y# 77 50 SATANG = 1/2 BAHT
4.50 g., Aluminum-Bronze, 23 mm. **Ruler:** Rama IX **Obv:** Young bust left, 1 medal on uniform **Rev:** Mantled arms **Edge:** Reeded

Date	Mintage	VF20	XF40	MS60	MS63	MS65
BE2493	20,710,000	—	—	20.00	—	—

Y# 81 50 SATANG = 1/2 BAHT
4.50 g., Aluminum-Bronze, 23 mm. **Ruler:** Rama IX **Obv:** Smaller head, 3 medals on uniform **Rev:** Mantled arms **Edge:** Reeded

Date	Mintage	VF20	XF40	MS60	MS63	MS65
BE2500	439,874,000	0.10	0.15	0.25	—	—

Note: Minted without date change until 1987

Y# 168 50 SATANG = 1/2 BAHT
4.90 g., Brass, 23 mm. **Ruler:** Rama IX **Obv:** Bust left **Rev:** Value and inscription **Edge:** Plain

Date	Mintage	VF20	XF40	MS60	MS63	MS65
BE2523	122,260,000	0.10	0.15	0.25	—	—

Y# 203 50 SATANG = 1/2 BAHT
2.40 g., Aluminum-Bronze, 18 mm. **Ruler:** Rama IX **Obv:** Head left **Rev:** Soi Suthep Temple, Chiang Mai province

Date	Mintage	VF20	XF40	MS60	MS63	MS65
BE2530	1,000	10.00	15.00	20.00	25.00	—
BE2531	23,775,000	—	—	0.10	0.15	—
BE2532	57,969,000	0.20	0.30	1.00	1.50	—
BE2533	92,960,000	—	—	0.10	0.15	—
BE2534	4,660,380	—	—	0.50	0.75	—
BE2535	105,451,000	—	—	0.10	0.15	—
BE2536	36,296,000	—	—	0.10	0.15	—
BE2537	161,172,000	—	—	0.10	0.15	—
BE2538	147,670,000	—	—	0.10	0.15	—
BE2539	30,840,000	—	—	0.10	0.15	—
BE2540	58,336,000	—	—	0.10	0.15	—
BE2541	23,834,000	—	—	0.10	0.15	—
BE2542	73,379,700	—	—	0.10	0.15	—
BE2543	115,332,000	—	—	0.10	0.15	—

Y# 329 50 SATANG = 1/2 BAHT
2.50 g., Aluminum-Bronze, 18 mm. **Ruler:** Rama IX **Subject:** 50th Year of Reign - King Rama IX **Obv:** Bust facing **Rev:** Arms

Date	Mintage	VF20	XF40	MS60	MS63	MS65
BE2539	105,434,000	—	—	0.35	—	—

Y# 82.1 BAHT
7.50 g., Copper-Nickel-Silver-Zinc, 26.9 mm. **Ruler:** Rama IX **Obv:** Bust left, three medals on uniform **Rev:** Mantled arms **Edge:** Reeded

Date	Mintage	VF20	XF40	MS60	MS63	MS65
BE2500	3,143,000	0.75	1.50	6.00	—	—

Note: These coins were minted from 1958-60 and mintage figure is a total

Y# 82.2 BAHT
Copper-Nickel, 26.9 mm. **Ruler:** Rama IX **Obv:** Bust left, one medal on uniform **Rev:** Mantled arms

Date	Mintage	VF20	XF40	MS60	MS63	MS65
BE2500	—	0.75	1.50	6.00	—	—

Y# 82a BAHT
Silver, 26.9 mm. **Ruler:** Rama IX **Obv:** Bust left **Rev:** National arms

Date	Mintage	VF20	XF40	MS60	MS63	MS65
BE2500 Rare	—	—	—	—	—	—

Y# 83 BAHT
9.00 g., Copper-Nickel, 26.9 mm. **Ruler:** Rama IX **Subject:** King Rama IX and Queen Sirikit return from abroad **Obv:** Conjoined busts left flanked by diamonds **Rev:** Mantled arms **Edge:** Reeded

Date	Mintage	VF20	XF40	MS60	MS63	MS65
BE2504	4,430,000	0.40	0.75	2.00	—	—

Y# 84 BAHT
7.50 g., Copper-Nickel, 26.9 mm. **Ruler:** Rama IX **Obv:** Young bust left **Rev:** Mantled arms **Edge:** Reeded

Date	Mintage	VF20	XF40	MS60	MS63	MS65
BE2505	883,086,000	0.10	0.15	0.50	—	—

Note: These coins were minted from 1962-82 and mintage figure is a total

Y# 85 BAHT
9.00 g., Copper-Nickel, 26.9 mm. **Ruler:** Rama IX **Subject:** 36th Birthday - King Rama IX **Obv:** Uniformed bust left **Rev:** Design in center circle of design **Edge:** Reeded

Date	Mintage	VF20	XF40	MS60	MS63	MS65
ND (1963)	3,000,000	0.25	0.75	2.00	—	—

Y# 87 BAHT
7.50 g., Copper-Nickel, 26.9 mm. **Ruler:** Rama IX **Subject:** 5th Asian Games Bangkok **Obv:** Conjoined busts right **Rev:** Star design **Edge:** Reeded

Date	Mintage	VF20	XF40	MS60	MS63	MS65
BE2509	9,000,000	0.25	0.75	3.00	—	—

Y# 91 BAHT
7.50 g., Copper-Nickel, 26.9 mm. **Ruler:** Rama IX **Subject:** 6th Asian Games Bangkok **Obv:** Conjoined busts right **Rev:** Star design **Edge:** Reeded

Date	Mintage	VF20	XF40	MS60	MS63	MS65
BE2513	9,000,000	0.25	0.75	1.50	—	—

Y# 96 BAHT
7.50 g., Copper-Nickel, 26.9 mm. **Ruler:** Rama IX **Series:** F.A.O. **Obv:** Head left **Rev:** State ploughing ceremony **Edge:** Reeded **Note:** Released on May 7, 1973.

Date	Mintage	VF20	XF40	MS60	MS63	MS65
BE2515	9,000,000	0.10	0.25	0.75	—	—

Y# 97 BAHT
7.50 g., Copper-Nickel, 26.9 mm. **Ruler:** Rama IX **Subject:** Prince Vajiralongkorn Investiture **Obv:** Young head left **Rev:** Crowned monogram **Edge:** Reeded

Date	Mintage	VF20	XF40	MS60	MS63	MS65
BE2515	9,000,000	0.15	0.40	1.00	—	—

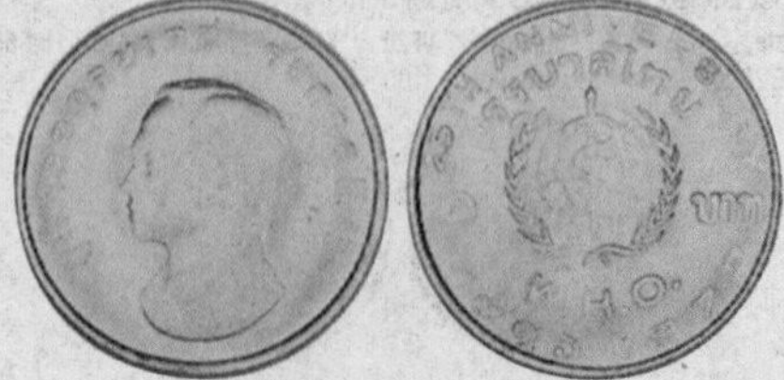

Y# 99 BAHT

7.50 g., Copper-Nickel, 26.9 mm. **Ruler:** Rama IX **Subject:** 25th Anniversary - World Health Organization **Obv:** Head left **Rev:** Arms within wreath **Edge:** Reeded

Date	Mintage	VF20	XF40	MS60	MS63	MS65
BE2516	1,000,000	0.25	0.65	1.25	—	—

Y# 100 BAHT

7.00 g., Copper-Nickel, 25 mm. **Ruler:** Rama IX **Obv:** Head left **Rev:** Mythical creature "Garuda" **Edge:** Reeded

Date	Mintage	VF20	XF40	MS60	MS63	MS65
BE2517	248,978,000	0.15	0.40	1.00	—	—

Y# 105 BAHT

7.00 g., Copper-Nickel, 25 mm. **Ruler:** Rama IX **Subject:** 8th SEAP Games **Obv:** Conjoined heads right **Rev:** Flower design within center circle of poinsettia design **Edge:** Reeded

Date	Mintage	VF20	XF40	MS60	MS63	MS65
BE2518	3,000,000	0.25	0.65	1.25	—	—

Y# 107 BAHT

7.00 g., Copper-Nickel, 25 mm. **Ruler:** Rama IX **Subject:** 75th Birthday of Princess Mother October 21st **Obv:** Bust facing **Rev:** Monogram **Edge:** Reeded

Date	Mintage	VF20	XF40	MS60	MS63	MS65
BE2518	9,000,000	0.15	0.40	1.00	—	—

Y# 110 BAHT

7.00 g., Copper-Nickel, 25 mm. **Ruler:** Rama IX **Obv:** Head left **Rev:** Suphannahong, with Wat Aran Temple **Edge:** Reeded **Note:** Varieties exist.

Date	Mintage	VF20	XF40	MS60	MS63	MS65
BE2520	506,460,000	0.10	0.20	0.50	—	—

Y# 112 BAHT

7.00 g., Copper-Nickel, 25 mm. **Ruler:** Rama IX **Series:** F.A.O. **Obv:** Figures scattering rice **Rev:** Seated female figure left **Edge:** Reeded

Date	Mintage	VF20	XF40	MS60	MS63	MS65
BE2520	2,000,000	0.15	0.40	1.00	—	—

Y# 114 BAHT

7.00 g., Copper-Nickel, 25 mm. **Ruler:** Rama IX **Subject:** Princess Sirindhorn, 1st Thai Royal graduate of a great university **Obv:** Bust left **Rev:** Radiant crown **Edge:** Reeded

Date	Mintage	VF20	XF40	MS60	MS63	MS65
BE2520	9,000,000	0.15	0.40	1.00	—	—

Y# 114a BAHT

Bronze, 25 mm. **Ruler:** Rama IX **Subject:** Princess Sirindhorn, 1st Thai Royal graduate of a great university **Obv:** Bust left **Rev:** Radiant crown

Date	Mintage	VF20	XF40	MS60	MS63	MS65
BE2520	—	—	—	—	—	—

Y# 124 BAHT

7.00 g., Copper-Nickel, 25 mm. **Ruler:** Rama IX **Subject:** Investiture of Princess Sirindhorn, May 12, female counterpart to the crown prince **Obv:** Bust right **Rev:** Crowned monogram

Date	Mintage	VF20	XF40	MS60	MS63	MS65
BE2520	5,000,000	0.15	0.40	1.00	—	—

Y# 127 BAHT

7.00 g., Copper-Nickel, 25 mm. **Ruler:** Rama IX **Subject:** Graduation of Crown Prince Vajiralongkorn September 15, with the rank of "Panturi" **Obv:** Bust left **Rev:** Crown within oval design **Edge:** Reeded

Date	Mintage	VF20	XF40	MS60	MS63	MS65
BE2521	5,000,000	0.10	0.20	0.50	—	—

Y# 130 BAHT

7.00 g., Copper-Nickel, 25 mm. **Ruler:** Rama IX **Subject:** 8th Asian Games **Obv:** Conjoined busts right **Rev:** Small radiant sun within design **Edge:** Reeded

Date	Mintage	VF20	XF40	MS60	MS63	MS65
BE2521	5,000,000	0.10	0.20	0.50	—	—

Y# 157 BAHT

7.00 g., Copper-Nickel, 25 mm. **Ruler:** Rama IX **Series:** World Food Day October 16 **Obv:** Bust left **Rev:** F.A.O. logo above wheat sprigs **Edge:** Reeded

Date	Mintage	VF20	XF40	MS60	MS63	MS65
BE2525	5,000,000	0.10	0.20	0.50	—	—

Y# 159.1 BAHT

7.00 g., Copper-Nickel, 25 mm. **Ruler:** Rama IX **Obv:** Large bust with collar touching hairline **Rev:** The Grand Palace **Edge:** Reeded **Note:** 2527 and 2528 are frozen dates, with the Thai numerals for 27 and 28 in the Finance Ministry decal at the bottom of the reverse.

Date	Mintage	VF20	XF40	MS60	MS63	MS65
BE2525	4,150,000	0.50	0.75	1.00	—	—
BE2526	38,735,000	0.20	0.30	0.60	—	—
BE2527	108,995,000	0.15	0.25	0.50	—	—
BE2528	105,465,000	0.15	0.25	0.50	—	—

Y# 159.2 BAHT

7.00 g., Copper-Nickel **Ruler:** Rama IX **Obv:** Small bust with space between collar and lower hairline **Rev:** The Grand Palace **Edge:** Reeded

Date	Mintage	VF20	XF40	MS60	MS63	MS65
BE2525	Inc. above	2.50	5.00	10.00	—	—

Y# 183 BAHT

3.45 g., Copper-Nickel, 20 mm. **Ruler:** Rama IX **Obv:** Head left **Rev:** Phra Kaew Temple, Bangkok **Edge:** Reeded **Note:** Varieties exist.

Date	Mintage	VF20	XF40	MS60	MS63	MS65
BE2529	4,200,000	0.20	0.30	1.00	1.50	—
BE2530	329,471,000	—	—	0.10	0.20	—
BE2531	391,442,000	—	—	0.10	0.20	—
BE2532	466,684,000	—	—	0.10	0.20	—
BE2533	409,924,000	—	—	0.10	0.20	—
BE2534	329,946,380	—	—	0.10	0.20	—
BE2535	426,230,000	—	—	0.10	0.20	—
BE2536	235,623,000	—	—	0.10	0.20	—
BE2537	475,200,000	—	—	0.10	0.20	—
BE2538	589,394,650	—	—	0.10	0.20	—
BE2539	98,487,000	—	—	0.10	0.20	—
BE2540	350,660,600	—	—	0.10	0.20	—
BE2541	25,252,000	—	—	0.25	0.35	—
BE2542	224,389,000	—	—	0.10	0.15	—
BE2543	468,610,000	—	—	0.10	0.15	—

Y# 330 BAHT

3.40 g., Copper-Nickel, 20 mm. **Ruler:** Rama IX **Subject:** 50th Anniversary - Reign of King Rama IX June 8 **Obv:** Bust facing **Rev:** Arms with supporters **Edge:** Reeded

Date	Mintage	VF20	XF40	MS60	MS63	MS65
BE2539	272,512,000	—	—	0.35	—	—

Y# 134 2 BAHT

9.00 g., Copper-Nickel, 27 mm. **Ruler:** Rama IX **Subject:** Graduation of Princess Chulabhorn from Gusaehit University July 19 **Obv:** Bust 1/4 left **Rev:** Design within circle **Edge:** Plain **Note:** Science of Agriculture University.

Date	Mintage	VF20	XF40	MS60	MS63	MS65
BE2522	5,000,000	0.25	0.50	1.00	1.50	—

Y# 176 2 BAHT

9.30 g., Copper-Nickel Clad Copper, 22 mm. **Ruler:** Rama IX **Subject:** International Youth Year **Obv:** Bust left **Rev:** Conjoined profiles right within wreath **Edge:** Reeded

Date	Mintage	VF20	XF40	MS60	MS63	MS65
BE2528	5,000,000	0.25	0.50	1.25	2.00	—

Y# 177 2 BAHT
7.30 g., Copper-Nickel Clad Copper, 22 mm. **Ruler:** Rama IX **Subject:** XII SEAP Games Bangkok December 8-17 **Obv:** Half length bust facing **Rev:** Games logo flanked by value **Edge:** Reeded

Date	Mintage	VF20	XF40	MS60	MS63	MS65
BE2528	5,000,000	0.25	0.50	1.25	2.00	—

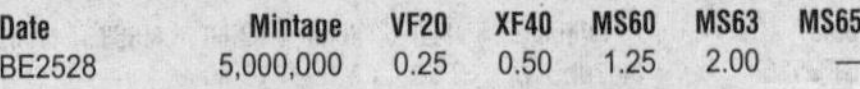

Y# 178 2 BAHT
7.30 g., Copper-Nickel Clad Copper, 22 mm. **Ruler:** Rama IX **Subject:** National Years of the Trees 2528-2531 **Obv:** Bust left **Rev:** Inscription within tree flanked by emblems below **Edge:** Reeded

Date	Mintage	VF20	XF40	MS60	MS63	MS65
ND (1986)	3,000,000	0.50	1.00	3.50	4.00	—

Y# 180 2 BAHT
7.30 g., Copper-Nickel Clad Copper, 22 mm. **Ruler:** Rama IX **Subject:** Year of Peace **Obv:** Bust left **Rev:** Dove divides wreath below inscription **Edge:** Reeded **Note:** Australia, Russia and Mongolia issued coins with identical motif.

Date	Mintage	VF20	XF40	MS60	MS63	MS65
BE2529	5,000,000	—	0.40	0.75	1.00	—

Y# 191 2 BAHT
7.30 g., Copper-Nickel Clad Copper, 22 mm. **Ruler:** Rama IX **Subject:** Princess Chulabhorn Awarded Einstein Medal for research October 24 **Obv:** Bust in cap and gown 1/4 left **Rev:** Head left within center circle of hexagon design **Edge:** Reeded

Date	Mintage	VF20	XF40	MS60	MS63	MS65
BE2529	3,000,000	—	0.40	0.75	1.00	—

Y# 188 2 BAHT
7.30 g., Copper-Nickel Clad Copper, 22 mm. **Ruler:** Rama IX **Subject:** 100th Year of "Nairoi" Chulalongkorn Military Academy **Obv:** Conjoined busts left **Rev:** Flagged arms **Edge:** Reeded

Date	Mintage	VF20	XF40	MS60	MS63	MS65
BE2530	3,000,000	—	0.40	0.75	1.00	—

Y# 194 2 BAHT
7.30 g., Copper-Nickel Clad Copper, 22 mm. **Ruler:** Rama IX **Subject:** 60th Birthday - King Rama IX, December 5 **Obv:** Bust facing **Rev:** Radiant crown **Edge:** Reeded **Note:** Minted and released in 1986

Date	Mintage	VF20	XF40	MS60	MS63	MS65
BE2530	10,000,000	—	—	0.50	0.75	—

Y# 204 2 BAHT
7.30 g., Copper-Nickel Clad Copper, 22 mm. **Ruler:** Rama IX **Subject:** 72nd Anniversary of Thai Cooperatives February 26 **Obv:** Conjoined busts left **Rev:** Inscription **Edge:** Reeded

Date	Mintage	VF20	XF40	MS60	MS63	MS65
BE2531	3,000,000	—	0.40	0.75	1.00	—

Y# 210 2 BAHT
7.30 g., Copper-Nickel Clad Copper, 22 mm. **Ruler:** Rama IX **Subject:** 42nd Anniversary - Reign of King Rama IX July 2 **Obv:** Bust facing **Rev:** Crowned monogram **Edge:** Reeded

Date	Mintage	VF20	XF40	MS60	MS63	MS65
BE2531	5,000,000	—	0.40	0.75	1.00	—

Y# 220 2 BAHT
7.30 g., Copper-Nickel Clad Copper, 22 mm. **Ruler:** Rama IX **Subject:** 100th Anniversary of Siriraj Hospital April 26 **Obv:** Conjoined busts left **Rev:** Radiant crown above design

Date	Mintage	VF20	XF40	MS60	MS63	MS65
BE2531	3,412,022	—	0.40	0.75	1.00	—

Y# 222 2 BAHT
7.30 g., Copper-Nickel Clad Copper, 22 mm. **Ruler:** Rama IX **Subject:** Crown Prince's 36th birthday **Obv:** Head 1/4 left **Rev:** Crowned monogram within lightning bolts **Edge:** Reeded

Date	Mintage	VF20	XF40	MS60	MS63	MS65
BE2531	2,000,011	—	0.50	0.85	1.25	—

Y# 225 2 BAHT
7.30 g., Copper-Nickel Clad Copper, 22 mm. **Ruler:** Rama IX **Subject:** 72nd Anniversary of Chulalongkorn University March 26 **Obv:** Conjoined busts left **Rev:** Radiant crown **Edge:** Reeded

Date	Mintage	VF20	XF40	MS60	MS63	MS65
BE2532	3,000,011	—	0.40	0.75	1.00	—

Y# 230 2 BAHT
7.30 g., Copper-Nickel Clad Copper, 22 mm. **Ruler:** Rama IX **Subject:** Centennial of First Medical College, Siriraj, September 5 2433-2533 **Obv:** Conjoined uniformed busts facing **Rev:** First medical college **Edge:** Reeded

Date	Mintage	VF20	XF40	MS60	MS63	MS65
BE2533	1,003,600	—	0.75	1.25	1.50	—

Y# 232 2 BAHT
7.30 g., Copper-Nickel Clad Copper, 22 mm. **Ruler:** Rama IX **Subject:** 90th Birthday of Queen Mother October 21 **Obv:** Crown on stand flanked by others **Rev:** Bust 1/4 left **Edge:** Reeded

Date	Mintage	VF20	XF40	MS60	MS63	MS65
BE2533	2,000,011	—	0.50	0.85	1.25	—

Y# 235 2 BAHT
7.30 g., Copper-Nickel Clad Copper, 22 mm. **Ruler:** Rama IX **Subject:** 100th Anniversary - Office of the Comptroller General 2433-2533 **Obv:** Conjoined uniformed busts 1/4 left **Rev:** Building above computer, typewriter and phone **Edge:** Reeded

Date	Mintage	VF20	XF40	MS60	MS63	MS65
BE2533	1,000,000	—	0.75	1.25	1.50	—

Y# 243 2 BAHT
7.30 g., Copper-Nickel Clad Copper, 22 mm. **Ruler:** Rama IX **Subject:** World Health Organization **Obv:** Bust of Queen Mother 1/4 left **Rev:** Gold medal for good health, December 17 **Edge:** Reeded **Note:** Minted and released in 1991.

Date	Mintage	VF20	XF40	MS60	MS63	MS65
BE2533	2,000,000	—	0.50	1.00	1.25	—

Y# 237 2 BAHT
7.30 g., Copper-Nickel Clad Copper, 22 mm. **Ruler:** Rama IX **Subject:** 36th Birthday of Princess Sirindhorn April 2 **Obv:** Uniformed bust 1/4 left **Rev:** Crowned monogram flanked by stars above sprigs **Edge:** Reeded

Date	Mintage	VF20	XF40	MS60	MS63	MS65
BE2534	2,000,011	—	0.50	0.85	1.25	—

Y# 240 2 BAHT
7.30 g., Copper-Nickel Clad Copper, 22 mm. **Ruler:** Rama IX **Subject:** 80th Anniversary of Thai Boy Scouts July 1 2454-2534 **Obv:** Conjoined young busts 1/4 left in scout uniforms **Rev:** Scouting emblem and phrase "Better to die than to lie" **Edge:** Reeded

Date	Mintage	VF20	XF40	MS60	MS63	MS65
BE2534	2,000,000	—	0.75	1.50	1.75	—

Y# 255 2 BAHT
7.30 g., Copper-Nickel Clad Copper, 22 mm. **Ruler:** Rama IX **Subject:** Princess Sirindhorn's Magsaysay Foundation Award for public administration August 31 **Obv:** Seated figures within circle **Rev:** Shield within sprig and circle below cameo **Edge:** Reeded **Note:** Minted and released in 1992

Date	Mintage	VF20	XF40	MS60	MS63	MS65
BE2534	1,200,011	—	0.75	1.25	1.50	—

Y# 248 2 BAHT

7.30 g., Copper-Nickel Clad Copper, 22 mm. **Ruler:** Rama IX **Subject:** Centenary Celebration of Mahitorn - Father of King Rama IX, January 1 **Obv:** Head facing **Rev:** Crown on stand flanked by others **Edge:** Reeded

Date	Mintage	VF20	XF40	MS60	MS63	MS65
BE2535	2,308,003	—	0.50	0.85	1.25	—

Y# 251 2 BAHT

7.30 g., Copper-Nickel Clad Copper, 22 mm. **Ruler:** Rama IX **Subject:** Ministry of Justice Centennial March 25 **Obv:** Conjoined busts left **Rev:** Balance scales within design **Edge:** Reeded

Date	Mintage	VF20	XF40	MS60	MS63	MS65
BE2535	1,500,000	—	0.50	0.85	1.25	—

Y# 253 2 BAHT

7.30 g., Copper-Nickel Clad Copper, 22 mm. **Ruler:** Rama IX **Subject:** Ministry of Interior Centennial April 1 2435-2535 **Obv:** Conjoined busts facing **Rev:** Mythical animal within circle **Edge:** Reeded

Date	Mintage	VF20	XF40	MS60	MS63	MS65
BE2535	1,500,000	—	0.50	0.85	1.25	—

Y# 259 2 BAHT

7.30 g., Copper-Nickel Clad Copper, 22 mm. **Ruler:** Rama IX **Subject:** Queen's 60th Birthday August 12 (Thai Mother's Day) **Obv:** Crowned bust facing **Rev:** Crowned monogram **Edge:** Reeded

Date	Mintage	VF20	XF40	MS60	MS63	MS65
BE2535	1,700,000	—	0.50	1.00	1.25	—

Y# 268 2 BAHT

7.30 g., Copper-Nickel Clad Copper, 22 mm. **Ruler:** Rama IX **Subject:** 60th Anniversary of the National Assembly - June 28 **Obv:** Conjoined busts left **Rev:** Anatasamakhom Throne Hall **Edge:** Reeded

Date	Mintage	VF20	XF40	MS60	MS63	MS65
BE2535	1,000,000	—	0.75	1.25	1.50	—

Y# 270 2 BAHT

7.30 g., Copper-Nickel Clad Copper, 22 mm. **Ruler:** Rama IX **Subject:** 100th Anniversary Ministry of Agriculture April 1 2435-2535 **Obv:** Conjoined busts 1/4 left **Rev:** Emblem within sprigs **Edge:** Reeded

Date	Mintage	VF20	XF40	MS60	MS63	MS65
BE2535	1,000,000	—	0.75	1.25	1.50	—

Y# 272 2 BAHT

7.30 g., Copper-Nickel Clad Copper, 22 mm. **Ruler:** Rama IX **Subject:** King's 64th Birthday November 18 **Obv:** Conjoined busts 1/4 left **Rev:** Crowned monograms **Edge:** Reeded **Note:** In honor of the King reaching the lifespan of his great-grandfather.

Date	Mintage	VF20	XF40	MS60	MS63	MS65
BE2535	1,000,000	—	0.75	1.25	1.50	—

Y# 276 2 BAHT

7.30 g., Copper-Nickel Clad Copper, 22 mm. **Ruler:** Rama IX **Subject:** Centennial of Thai Teacher Training October 12 **Obv:** Conjoined busts left **Rev:** Emblem **Edge:** Reeded

Date	Mintage	VF20	XF40	MS60	MS63	MS65
BE2535	1,200,000	—	0.75	1.25	1.50	—

Y# 277 2 BAHT

7.30 g., Copper-Nickel Clad Copper, 22 mm. **Ruler:** Rama IX **Subject:** 50th Year of Thai National Bank December 10 **Obv:** Conjoined busts facing **Rev:** Seated figure **Edge:** Reeded

Date	Mintage	VF20	XF40	MS60	MS63	MS65
BE2535	1,000,011	—	0.75	1.25	1.50	—

Y# 278 2 BAHT

7.30 g., Copper-Nickel Clad Copper, 22 mm. **Ruler:** Rama IX **Subject:** Centennial of Attorney General's Office April 1 2436-2536 **Obv:** Conjoined busts facing **Rev:** Crowned balance scale **Edge:** Reeded

Date	Mintage	VF20	XF40	MS60	MS63	MS65
BE2536	1,000,000	—	0.75	1.25	1.50	—

Y# 279 2 BAHT

7.30 g., Copper-Nickel Clad Copper, 22 mm. **Ruler:** Rama IX **Subject:** Centennial of Thai Red Cross 2436-2536 **Obv:** Conjoined busts 1/4 left **Rev:** Symbols **Edge:** Reeded

Date	Mintage	VF20	XF40	MS60	MS63	MS65
BE2536	1,200,000	—	0.75	1.25	1.50	—

Y# 282 2 BAHT

7.30 g., Copper-Nickel Clad Copper, 22 mm. **Ruler:** Rama IX **Subject:** 60th Year of the Treasury Department May 23 **Obv:** Conjoined busts left **Rev:** Emblem within circle **Edge:** Reeded

Date	Mintage	VF20	XF40	MS60	MS63	MS65
BE2536	1,000,000	—	0.75	1.25	1.50	—

Y# 288 2 BAHT

7.30 g., Copper-Nickel Clad Copper, 22 mm. **Ruler:** Rama IX **Subject:** 100th Anniversary of Rama VII November 8 **Obv:** Bust left **Rev:** Crown and designs within oval circle **Edge:** Reeded

Date	Mintage	VF20	XF40	MS60	MS63	MS65
BE2536	1,500,000	—	0.50	0.85	1.25	—

Y# 292 2 BAHT

7.30 g., Copper-Nickel Clad Copper, 22 mm. **Ruler:** Rama IX **Subject:** 60th Anniversary - Royal Thai Language Academy March 31 **Obv:** Conjoined busts left **Rev:** Crowned emblem **Edge:** Reeded

Date	Mintage	VF20	XF40	MS60	MS63	MS65
BE2537	1,200,000	—	0.25	1.25	1.50	—

Y# 294 2 BAHT

7.30 g., Copper-Nickel Clad Copper, 22 mm. **Ruler:** Rama IX **Subject:** 120th Anniversary - Council of Advisors to the King - Royal decree 2417-2537 **Obv:** Conjoined busts facing **Rev:** Building **Edge:** Reeded

Date	Mintage	VF20	XF40	MS60	MS63	MS65
BE2537	1,250,011	—	0.75	1.25	1.50	—

Y# 296 2 BAHT

7.30 g., Copper-Nickel Clad Copper, 22 mm. **Ruler:** Rama IX **Subject:** 60th Anniversary - Thammasat University June 27 **Obv:** Conjoined busts left **Rev:** University emblem within circle **Edge:** Reeded

Date	Mintage	VF20	XF40	MS60	MS63	MS65
BE2537	1,250,011	—	0.75	1.25	1.50	—

Y# 307 2 BAHT

7.30 g., Copper-Nickel Clad Copper, 22 mm. **Ruler:** Rama IX **Series:** F.A.O. 50th Year, 1945-1995 **Obv:** Bust left **Rev:** Emblem and dates **Edge:** Reeded

Date	Mintage	VF20	XF40	MS60	MS63	MS65
BE2538	1,400,000	—	0.50	0.85	1.25	—

Y# 313 2 BAHT

7.30 g., Copper-Nickel Clad Copper, 22 mm. **Ruler:** Rama IX **Subject:** Information Technology Year **Obv:** Bust 3/4 left **Rev:** Symbols on globe background **Edge:** Reeded

Date	Mintage	VF20	XF40	MS60	MS63	MS65
BE2538	1,500,011	—	0.50	0.85	1.25	—

Y# 315 2 BAHT
7.30 g., Copper-Nickel Clad Copper, 22 mm. **Ruler:** Rama IX **Subject:** ASEAN Environment Year "Greenland Clean" **Obv:** Conjoined busts left **Rev:** Design within circle flanked by sprig and arrow **Edge:** Reeded

Date	Mintage	VF20	XF40	MS60	MS63	MS65
BE2538	1,200,011	—	0.75	1.25	1.50	—

Y# 317 2 BAHT
7.30 g., Copper-Nickel Clad Copper, 22 mm. **Ruler:** Rama IX **Subject:** Siriraj Nursing and Midwife School Centennial January 12 **Obv:** Bust facing **Rev:** Crowned monogram **Edge:** Reeded

Date	Mintage	VF20	XF40	MS60	MS63	MS65
BE2539	1,000,011	—	0.75	1.25	1.50	—

Y# 319 2 BAHT
7.30 g., Copper-Nickel Clad Copper, 22 mm. **Ruler:** Rama IX **Subject:** King's 50th Year of Reign June 9 **Obv:** Bust facing **Rev:** National arms **Edge:** Reeded

Date	Mintage	VF20	XF40	MS60	MS63	MS65
BE2539	5,500,000	—	—	1.25	1.50	—

Y# 98 5 BAHT
9.00 g., Copper-Nickel, 27 mm. **Ruler:** Rama IX **Obv:** Head left **Rev:** Mythical creature "Garuda" **Edge:** Plain **Shape:** 9-sided

Date	Mintage	VF20	XF40	MS60	MS63	MS65
BE2515	30,016,000	0.30	0.60	1.20	—	—

Y# 111 5 BAHT
12.00 g., Copper-Nickel Clad Copper, 29.5 mm. **Ruler:** Rama IX **Obv:** Head left **Rev:** Mythical creature "Garuda" **Edge:** Lettered

Date	Mintage	VF20	XF40	MS60	MS63	MS65
BE2520	27,257,000	0.30	0.60	1.20	—	—
BE2522	72,740,000	0.30	0.60	1.20	—	—

Y# 120 5 BAHT
12.00 g., Copper-Nickel Clad Copper, 30 mm. **Ruler:** Rama IX **Subject:** 50th Birthday - Rama IX December 5 **Obv:** Head left **Obv. Legend:** PRATHET THAI **Rev:** Crowned monogram **Edge:** Reeded

Date	Mintage	VF20	XF40	MS60	MS63	MS65
BE2520	5,000,000	0.35	0.75	1.50	—	—

Y# 121 5 BAHT
12.00 g., Copper-Nickel Clad Copper, 29.5 mm. **Ruler:** Rama IX **Subject:** 50th Birthday - Rama IX December 5 **Obv:** Bust left **Obv. Legend:** SIAM MINTA **Rev:** Crowned monogram **Edge:** Reeded **Note:** Error legend

Date	Mintage	VF20	XF40	MS60	MS63	MS65
BE2520	—	7.00	15.00	30.00	—	—

Y# 131 5 BAHT
12.00 g., Copper-Nickel Clad Copper, 29.5 mm. **Ruler:** Rama IX **Subject:** 8th ASEAN Games Bangkok **Obv:** Conjoined busts right **Rev:** Small radiant sun within designs **Edge:** Reeded

Date	Mintage	VF20	XF40	MS60	MS63	MS65
BE2521	500,000	1.50	3.50	5.50	7.00	—

Y# 132 5 BAHT
12.00 g., Copper-Nickel Clad Copper, 30 mm. **Ruler:** Rama IX **Subject:** Royal Cradle Ceremony January 11 **Obv:** Small child head right **Rev:** Inscription within designed wreath **Edge:** Reeded

Date	Mintage	VF20	XF40	MS60	MS63	MS65
BE2522	1,000,000	0.75	1.50	3.00	3.50	—

Y# 137 5 BAHT
12.00 g., Copper-Nickel Clad Copper, 30 mm. **Ruler:** Rama IX **Subject:** Queen's Birthday August 12 and F.A.O. Ceres Medal **Obv:** Crowned head 1/4 left **Rev:** Figures working within football-like designs **Edge:** Reeded

Date	Mintage	VF20	XF40	MS60	MS63	MS65
BE2523	9,000,000	0.25	0.50	1.50	1.75	—

Y# 140 5 BAHT
12.00 g., Copper-Nickel Clad Copper, 30 mm. **Ruler:** Rama IX **Subject:** 80th Birthday of King's Mother October 21 **Obv:** Bust with hat left **Rev:** Crown on stand flanked by others **Edge:** Reeded

Date	Mintage	VF20	XF40	MS60	MS63	MS65
BE2523	3,504,000	0.30	0.60	1.75	2.00	—

Y# 144 5 BAHT
12.00 g., Copper-Nickel Clad Copper, 30 mm. **Ruler:** Rama IX **Subject:** Rama VII Constitutional Monarchy December 10 2475-2523 **Obv:** Head left **Rev:** Crowned monogram **Edge:** Reeded

Date	Mintage	VF20	XF40	MS60	MS63	MS65
BE2523	2,113,000	0.30	0.60	1.75	2.00	—

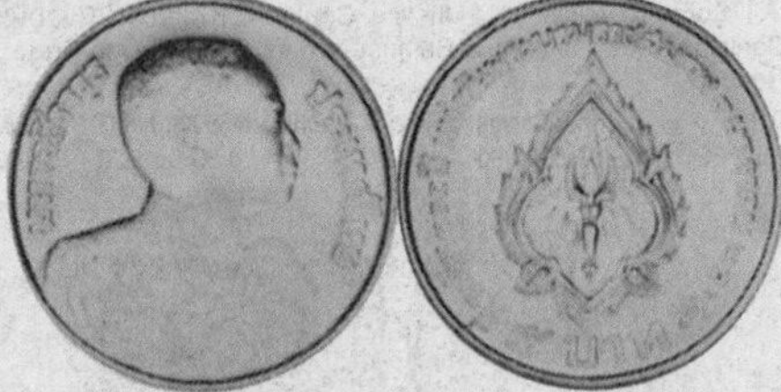

Y# 142 5 BAHT
12.00 g., Copper-Nickel Clad Copper, 30 mm. **Ruler:** Rama IX **Subject:** Centennial - Birth of King Rama VI January 3 **Obv:** Bust right **Rev:** Design **Edge:** Reeded **Note:** Minted and released in 1980.

Date	Mintage	VF20	XF40	MS60	MS63	MS65
BE2524	2,222,000	0.30	0.60	1.75	2.00	—

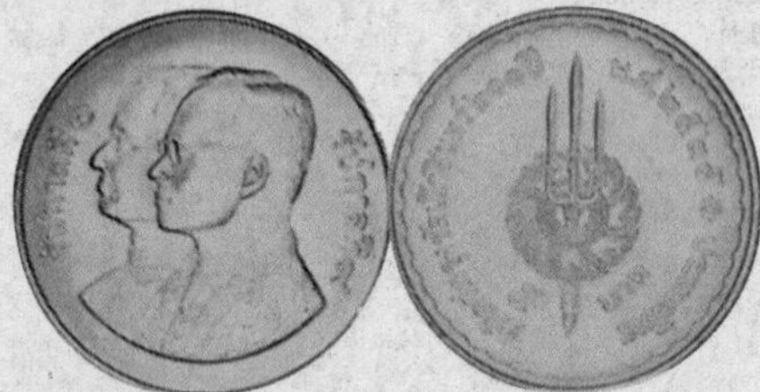

Y# 149 5 BAHT
12.00 g., Copper-Nickel Clad Copper, 30 mm. **Ruler:** Rama IX **Subject:** Bicentennial of the Chakri Dynasty **Obv:** Conjoined busts left **Rev:** Emblem **Edge:** Reeded **Note:** Minted and released in 1981.

Date	Mintage	VF20	XF40	MS60	MS63	MS65
BE2525	5,000,000	0.30	0.60	1.75	2.00	—

Y# 158 5 BAHT
12.00 g., Copper-Nickel Clad Copper, 30 mm. **Ruler:** Rama IX **Series:** World Food Day **Obv:** Uniformed bust left **Rev:** Emblem above wheat sprigs **Edge:** Reeded

Date	Mintage	VF20	XF40	MS60	MS63	MS65
BE2525	1,000,000	0.40	0.80	1.75	2.00	—

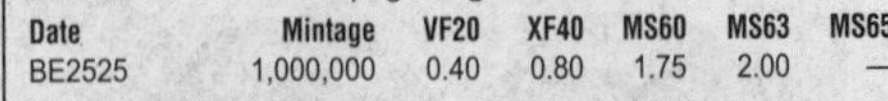

Y# 160 5 BAHT
12.00 g., Copper-Nickel Clad Copper, 30 mm. **Ruler:** Rama IX **Obv:** Bust left **Rev:** Mythical creature "Garuda" **Edge:** Reeded

Note: 2525 is a frozen date, with the Thai numerals for the first 2 digits of the actual year (25, 28, 29) in the Finance Ministry decal at the bottom of the reverse

Date	Mintage	VF20	XF40	MS60	MS63	MS65
BE2525	500,000	1.50	3.00	6.00	—	—
BE2526	100,000	2.00	5.00	10.00	—	—
BE2527	700,000	1.50	3.00	6.00	—	—
BE2528	17,911,000	0.20	0.50	1.00	—	—
BE2529	7,201,000	0.20	0.50	1.00	—	—

Y# 161 5 BAHT

12.00 g., Copper-Nickel Clad Copper, 30 mm. **Ruler:** Rama IX **Subject:** 75th Anniversary of Boy Scouts **Obv:** Bust left in scout uniform **Rev:** Stylized banner and flag **Edge:** Reeded

Date	Mintage	VF20	XF40	MS60	MS63	MS65
BE2525	206,000	1.75	4.00	7.00	8.00	—

Y# 171 5 BAHT

12.00 g., Copper-Nickel Clad Copper, 30 mm. **Ruler:** Rama IX **Subject:** 84th Birthday of King's Mother October 21 **Obv:** Crown on stand flanked by others **Rev:** Bust 3/4 left **Edge:** Reeded

Date	Mintage	VF20	XF40	MS60	MS63	MS65
BE2527	600,000	1.00	2.00	4.50	5.00	—

Y# 184 5 BAHT

7.50 g., Copper-Nickel Clad Copper, 24 mm. **Ruler:** Rama IX **Subject:** 200th Anniversary - Birth of Rama III 2330-2530 **Obv:** Bust facing **Rev:** Design within circle **Edge:** Reeded

Date	Mintage	VF20	XF40	MS60	MS63	MS65
BE2530	2,000,000	—	0.75	1.25	1.50	—

Y# 185 5 BAHT

7.50 g., Copper-Nickel Clad Copper, 24 mm. **Ruler:** Rama IX **Obv:** Head left **Rev:** Suphannahong, royal grand palace **Note:** Circulation coinage.

Date	Mintage	VF20	XF40	MS60	MS63	MS65
BE2530	41,514,000	—	—	0.75	1.00	—
BE2531	2,400,000	—	0.75	2.00	2.50	—

Y# 195 5 BAHT

12.00 g., Copper-Nickel Clad Copper, 30 mm. **Ruler:** Rama IX **Subject:** 60th Birthday - King Rama IX December 5 **Obv:** Uniformed bust facing **Rev:** Crowned emblem within lightning bolts **Edge:** Reeded **Note:** Minted and released in 1986.

Date	Mintage	VF20	XF40	MS60	MS63	MS65
BE2530	1,500,000	—	0.75	2.00	2.50	—

Y# 211 5 BAHT

12.00 g., Copper-Nickel Clad Copper, 30 mm. **Ruler:** Rama IX **Subject:** 42nd Anniversary - Reign of King Rama IX July 2 **Obv:** Uniformed bust facing **Rev:** Crowned monogram **Edge:** Reeded

Date	Mintage	VF20	XF40	MS60	MS63	MS65
BE2531	1,500,000	—	0.75	2.00	2.50	—

Y# 219 5 BAHT

7.50 g., Copper-Nickel Clad Copper, 24 mm. **Ruler:** Rama IX **Obv:** Head left **Rev:** Benchamabophit Temple, Bangkok **Edge:** Coarse reeding

Date	Mintage	VF20	XF40	MS60	MS63	MS65
BE2531	44,503,000	—	—	0.75	1.00	—
BE2532	86,339,000	—	—	0.50	0.75	—
BE2533	38,005,000	—	—	0.75	1.00	—
BE2534	68,520,380	—	—	0.50	0.75	—
BE2535	48,939,620	—	—	0.75	1.00	—
BE2536	46,992,000	—	—	0.75	1.00	—
BE2537	123,443,000	—	—	0.50	0.75	—
BE2538	105,100,000	—	—	0.50	0.75	—
BE2539	28,485,000	—	—	0.75	1.00	—
BE2540	10,600	9.00	12.50	25.00	30.00	—
BE2541	7,863,000	—	—	1.00	1.25	—
BE2542	50,760,000	—	—	0.50	0.75	—
BE2543	146,920,000	—	—	0.50	0.75	—

Y# 260 5 BAHT

7.50 g., Copper-Nickel Clad Copper, 24 mm. **Ruler:** Rama IX **Subject:** Queen's 60th Birthday August 12 **Obv:** Crowned bust facing **Rev:** Crowned monogram **Edge:** Reeded

Date	Mintage	VF20	XF40	MS60	MS63	MS65
BE2535	1,000,000	—	0.80	1.75	2.00	—

Y# 306 5 BAHT

Copper-Nickel Clad Copper, 24 mm. **Ruler:** Rama IX **Subject:** 18th SEA Games December 9-17 held at Ching My **Obv:** Half length bust facing **Rev:** Designs and inscription within circle above designed sprigs **Edge:** Reeded

Date	Mintage	VF20	XF40	MS60	MS63	MS65
BE2538	5,000,000	—	0.50	1.25	1.50	—

Y# 320 5 BAHT

7.50 g., Copper-Nickel Clad Copper, 24 mm. **Ruler:** Rama IX **Subject:** King's 50th Year of Reign June 9 **Obv:** Bust facing **Rev:** National arms **Edge:** Reeded

Date	Mintage	VF20	XF40	MS60	MS63	MS65
BE2539	2,500,000	—	0.50	1.50	1.75	—

Y# 92 10 BAHT

5.00 g., 0.800 Silver 0.1286 oz. ASW, 20.5 mm. **Ruler:** Rama IX **Subject:** 25th Anniversary - Reign of King Rama IX June 9 **Obv:** Head right **Rev:** Radiant crowned monogram **Edge:** Reeded

Date	Mintage	VF20	XF40	MS60	MS63	MS65
BE2514	2,000,000	—	5.00	7.00	9.00	12.00

Y# 115 10 BAHT

15.00 g., Nickel, 32 mm. **Ruler:** Rama IX **Subject:** Graduation of Princess Sirindhorn 1st royal graduate **Obv:** Bust left **Rev:** Radiant crown **Edge:** Reeded

Date	Mintage	VF20	XF40	MS60	MS63	MS65
BE2520	2,097,000	—	0.75	1.25	2.00	3.00

Y# 115a 10 BAHT

Bronze, 32 mm. **Ruler:** Rama IX **Subject:** Graduation of Princess Sirindhorn 1st royal graduate **Obv:** Bust left **Rev:** Radiant crown

Date	Mintage	VF20	XF40	MS60	MS63	MS65
BE2520	—	—	—	7.00	12.00	20.00

Y# 117 10 BAHT

15.00 g., Nickel, 32 mm. **Ruler:** Rama IX **Subject:** Crown Prince Vajiralongkorn and Princess Soamsawali Wedding January 3 **Obv:** Conjoined busts right **Rev:** Crowned monogram **Edge:** Reeded

Date	Mintage	VF20	XF40	MS60	MS63	MS65
BE2520	1,890,500	—	0.75	1.25	2.00	3.00

Y# 135 10 BAHT

15.00 g., Nickel, 32 mm. **Ruler:** Rama IX **Subject:** Graduation of Princess Chulabhorn **Obv:** Bust 3/4 left **Rev:** Graduation emblem within circle

Date	Mintage	VF20	XF40	MS60	MS63	MS65
BE2522	1,196,000	—	0.75	1.25	2.00	3.00

Y# 141 10 BAHT

15.00 g., Nickel, 32 mm. **Ruler:** Rama IX **Subject:** 80th Birthday of King's Mother October 21 **Obv:** Bust with hat left **Rev:** Crown on stand flanked by others **Edge:** Reeded

Date	Mintage	VF20	XF40	MS60	MS63	MS65
BE2523	1,288,000	—	0.75	1.25	2.00	3.00

Y# 145 10 BAHT
15.00 g., Nickel, 32 mm. **Ruler:** Rama IX **Subject:** 30th Anniversary of Buddhist Fellowship **Obv:** Bust left **Rev:** Design within circle and wreath **Edge:** Reeded

Date	Mintage	VF20	XF40	MS60	MS63	MS65
BE2523	1,035,000	—	0.75	1.25	2.00	3.00

Y# 146 10 BAHT
15.00 g., Nickel, 32 mm. **Ruler:** Rama IX **Subject:** King Rama IX Anniversary of Reign, twice as long on the throne - June 19 **Obv:** Conjoined busts left **Rev:** Crowns and emblems **Edge:** Reeded

Date	Mintage	VF20	XF40	MS60	MS63	MS65
BE2524	2,039,000	—	0.75	1.25	2.00	3.00

Y# 154 10 BAHT
15.00 g., Nickel, 32 mm. **Ruler:** Rama IX **Subject:** 50th Birthday of Queen Sirikit August 12 **Obv:** Crowned head 1/4 left **Rev:** Crowned monogram **Edge:** Reeded

Date	Mintage	VF20	XF40	MS60	MS63	MS65
BE2525	500,000	—	1.25	2.00	3.50	5.00
BE2525	7,210	PF63 17.50	PF65 22.50			

Y# 162 10 BAHT
15.00 g., Nickel, 32 mm. **Ruler:** Rama IX **Subject:** 75th Anniversary of Boy Scouts **Obv:** Bust left in scouting uniform **Rev:** Stylized banner and flag **Edge:** Reeded **Note:** Similar to 5 Baht, Y#161.

Date	Mintage	VF20	XF40	MS60	MS63	MS65
BE2525	100,000	—	1.50	3.00	5.00	7.50
BE2525	1,500	PF63 40.00	PF65 45.00			

Y# 163 10 BAHT
15.00 g., Nickel, 32 mm. **Ruler:** Rama IX **Subject:** Thai Post, 100th Anniversary **Obv:** Bust left **Rev:** Radiant crown above inscription **Edge:** Reeded

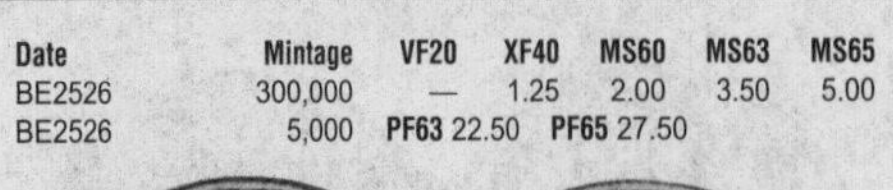

Date	Mintage	VF20	XF40	MS60	MS63	MS65
BE2526	300,000	—	1.25	2.00	3.50	5.00
BE2526	5,000	PF63 22.50	PF65 27.50			

Y# 165 10 BAHT
15.00 g., Nickel, 32 mm. **Ruler:** Rama IX **Subject:** 700th Anniversary of Thai Alphabet **Obv:** Seated figure, Ramkamhaeng the Great, pre-Bangkok era **Rev:** Six-line inscription **Edge:** Reeded

Date	Mintage	VF20	XF40	MS60	MS63	MS65
BE2526	500,000	—	1.25	2.00	3.50	5.00
BE2526	5,167	PF63 20.00	PF65 25.00			

Y# 172 10 BAHT
15.00 g., Nickel, 32 mm. **Ruler:** Rama IX **Subject:** 84th Birthday of King's Mother October 21 **Obv:** Three crowns on stands **Rev:** Bust left **Edge:** Reeded **Note:** Similar to 5 Baht, Y#171.

Date	Mintage	VF20	XF40	MS60	MS63	MS65
BE2527	200,000	1.25	2.00	3.50	5.00	7.00
BE2527	3,492	PF63 32.50	PF65 37.50			

Y# 175 10 BAHT
15.00 g., Nickel, 32 mm. **Ruler:** Rama IX **Subject:** 72nd Anniversary of Government Savings Bank April 1 **Obv:** Conjoined uniformed busts 1/4 left **Rev:** Designs within sectioned circle **Edge:** Reeded

Date	Mintage	VF20	XF40	MS60	MS63	MS65
BE2528	500,000	—	1.25	2.50	2.50	4.00
BE2528	3,000	PF63 32.50	PF65 37.50			

Y# 179 10 BAHT
15.00 g., Nickel, 32 mm. **Ruler:** Rama IX **Subject:** National Years of the Trees 2528-2531 **Obv:** Bust left **Rev:** Circular design below inscription within tree, emblems flank tree below **Edge:** Reeded

Date	Mintage	VF20	XF40	MS60	MS63	MS65
ND (1986)	100,000	1.50	3.50	7.50	12.00	20.00
ND (1986)	2,100	PF63 40.00	PF65 45.00			

Y# 181 10 BAHT
15.00 g., Nickel, 32 mm. **Ruler:** Rama IX **Subject:** 6th ASEAN Orchid Congress November 7-14 **Obv:** Bust left **Rev:** Symbols of congress meeting **Edge:** Reeded

Date	Mintage	VF20	XF40	MS60	MS63	MS65
BE2529	200,000	—	1.25	2.00	3.50	5.00
BE2529	3,000	PF63 32.50	PF65 37.50			

Y# 192 10 BAHT
15.00 g., Nickel, 32 mm. **Ruler:** Rama IX **Subject:** Princess Chulabhorn Awarded Einstein Medal October 24 **Obv:** Graduate's bust 1/4 left **Rev:** Head left within center circle of hexagon design **Edge:** Reeded **Note:** Minted and released in 1987.

Date	Mintage	VF20	XF40	MS60	MS63	MS65
BE2529	200,000	—	1.25	2.00	3.50	5.00
BE2529	1,080	PF63 45.00	PF65 50.00			

Y# 189 10 BAHT
15.00 g., Nickel, 32 mm. **Ruler:** Rama IX **Subject:** Chulachomklao Royal Military Academy, 100th Anniversary **Obv:** Conjoined busts left **Rev:** Flagged arms **Edge:** Reeded

Date	Mintage	VF20	XF40	MS60	MS63	MS65
BE2530	300,000	—	1.25	2.00	3.50	5.00
BE2530	2,060	PF63 40.00	PF65 45.00			

Y# 190 10 BAHT
15.00 g., Nickel, 32 mm. **Ruler:** Rama IX **Subject:** Rural Development Leadership July 21 **Obv:** Kneeling figure facing left talking to seated figures **Rev:** Emblem above inscription **Edge:** Reeded

Date	Mintage	VF20	XF40	MS60	MS63	MS65
BE2530	300,000	—	1.25	2.00	3.50	5.00
BE2530	2,100	PF63 40.00	PF65 45.00			

Y# 196 10 BAHT
15.00 g., Nickel, 32 mm. **Ruler:** Rama IX **Subject:** 60th Birthday of King Rama IX December 5 **Obv:** Uniformed bust facing **Rev:** Crowned emblem within lightning bolts **Edge:** Reeded **Note:** Minted and released in 1986.

Date	Mintage	VF20	XF40	MS60	MS63	MS65
BE2530	500,000	—	0.40	1.00	2.00	3.50
BE2530	5,000	PF63 27.50	PF65 32.50			

Y# 205 10 BAHT

15.00 g., Nickel, 32 mm. **Ruler:** Rama IX **Subject:** 72nd Anniversary of Thai Cooperatives February 26 **Obv:** Conjoined busts left **Rev:** Inscription **Edge:** Reeded

Date	Mintage	VF20	XF40	MS60	MS63	MS65
BE2531	143,000	—	1.50	3.00	5.00	7.50
BE2530	3,000	PF63 27.50		PF65 32.50		

Y# 212 10 BAHT

15.00 g., Nickel, 32 mm. **Ruler:** Rama IX **Subject:** 42nd Anniversary - Reign of King Rama IX July 2 **Obv:** Bust facing **Rev:** Crowned monogram **Edge:** Reeded

Date	Mintage	VF20	XF40	MS60	MS63	MS65
BE2531	500,000	—	0.50	1.00	2.00	3.50
BE2531	8,110	PF63 20.00		PF65 25.00		

Y# 221 10 BAHT

15.00 g., Nickel, 32 mm. **Ruler:** Rama IX **Subject:** Siriraj Hospital, 100th Anniversary **Obv:** Crowned busts left **Rev:** Crown above design **Edge:** Reeded

Date	Mintage	VF20	XF40	MS60	MS63	MS65
BE2531	290,000	—	1.00	1.50	2.50	4.00
BE2531	5,000	PF63 22.50		PF65 27.50		

Y# 223 10 BAHT

15.00 g., Nickel, 32 mm. **Ruler:** Rama IX **Subject:** Crown Prince's Birthday **Obv:** Head 1/4 left **Rev:** Crowned monogram within lightning bolts **Edge:** Reeded

Date	Mintage	VF20	XF40	MS60	MS63	MS65
BE2531	200,000	—	0.50	1.00	2.00	3.50
BE2531	3,000	PF63 27.50		PF65 32.50		

Y# 227 10 BAHT

8.50 g., Bi-Metallic Aluminum-Bronze center in Copper-Nickel ring, 26 mm. **Ruler:** Rama IX **Obv:** Head left within circle **Rev:** Arun Temple (Temple of the Dawn), Bankok **Edge:** Segmented reeding **Note:** Varieties exist.

Date	Mintage	VF20	XF40	MS60	MS63	MS65
BE2531	60,200	—	—	—	—	—
Prooflike; Rare						
Note: The BE2531 (1988) pieces were not released to general circulation and are very scarce in the numismatic community						
BE2532 r	100,000,000	—	—	1.25	2.50	3.50
BE2533	100	500	1,000	1,500	2,500	2,700
BE2534	1,380,650	—	—	1.50	5.00	7.00
BE2535	13,805,000	—	—	1.25	2.50	3.50
BE2536	10,556,000	—	—	1.25	2.50	3.50
BE2537 v	150,598,831	—	—	1.25	2.50	4.00
BE2538	53,700,000	—	—	1.25	2.50	4.00
BE2539	17,086,000	—	—	1.25	2.50	4.00
BE2540	9,310,600	—	—	1.00	6.00	8.00
BE2541	980,000	—	0.75	1.50	4.00	7.00
BE2542	1,030,000	—	0.75	2.00	5.00	7.00
BE2543	1,666,000	—	0.75	2.00	5.00	7.00

Y# 228 10 BAHT

15.00 g., Nickel, 32 mm. **Ruler:** Rama IX **Subject:** 72nd Anniversary Chulalongkorn University March 26 **Obv:** 3 Conjoined busts left **Rev:** Radiant crown **Edge:** Reeded

Date	Mintage	VF20	XF40	MS60	MS63	MS65
BE2532	500,000	—	0.50	1.00	2.00	3.50

Y# 231 10 BAHT

15.00 g., Nickel, 32 mm. **Ruler:** Rama IX **Subject:** Centennial of First Medical College September 5 2433 to September 5 2533 **Obv:** Conjoined busts facing **Rev:** Building **Edge:** Reeded

Date	Mintage	VF20	XF40	MS60	MS63	MS65
BE2533	300,000	—	0.50	1.00	2.00	3.50
BE2533	3,700	PF63 27.50		PF65 32.50		

Y# 233 10 BAHT

15.00 g., Nickel, 32 mm. **Ruler:** Rama IX **Subject:** 90th Birthday of the King's Mother October 21 **Obv:** Crown on stand flanked by others **Rev:** Bust 1/4 left **Edge:** Reeded

Date	Mintage	VF20	XF40	MS60	MS63	MS65
BE2533	500,000	—	0.50	1.00	2.00	3.50
BE2533	6,076	PF63 27.50		PF65 32.50		

Y# 236 10 BAHT

15.00 g., Copper-Nickel, 32 mm. **Ruler:** Rama IX **Subject:** 100th Anniversary - Office of Comptroller General **Obv:** Conjoined busts 1/4 left **Rev:** Building above computer, typewriter and phone

Date	Mintage	VF20	XF40	MS60	MS63	MS65
BE2533	300,022	—	0.50	1.00	2.00	3.50

Y# 244 10 BAHT

Copper-Nickel, 32 mm. **Ruler:** Rama IX **Subject:** World Health Organization December 17 **Obv:** Bust 1/4 left **Rev:** Gold medal for good health **Edge:** Reeded **Note:** Minted and released in 1991.

Date	Mintage	VF20	XF40	MS60	MS63	MS65
BE2533	800,000	—	0.50	1.00	2.00	3.50
BE2533	4,011	PF63 40.00		PF65 45.00		

Y# 238 10 BAHT

15.00 g., Copper-Nickel, 32 mm. **Ruler:** Rama IX **Subject:** 36th Birthday of Princess Sirindhorn April 2 **Obv:** Uniformed bust 1/4 left **Rev:** Crowned monogram flanked by stars above sprigs **Edge:** Reeded

Date	Mintage	VF20	XF40	MS60	MS63	MS65
BE2534	800,000	—	0.50	1.00	2.00	3.50
BE2534	4,300	PF63 30.00		PF65 35.00		

Y# 241 10 BAHT

15.00 g., Copper-Nickel, 32 mm. **Ruler:** Rama IX **Subject:** 80th Anniversary of Thai Boy Scouts July 1 2454-2534 **Obv:** Conjoined busts 1/4 left in scouting uniform **Rev:** Scout emblem and motto "Better to die than to lie" **Edge:** Reeded

Date	Mintage	VF20	XF40	MS60	MS63	MS65
BE2534	650,022	—	0.50	1.00	2.00	3.50
BE2534	3,237	PF63 30.00		PF65 35.00		

Y# 256 10 BAHT

15.00 g., Copper-Nickel, 32 mm. **Ruler:** Rama IX **Subject:** Princess Sirindhorn's Magsaysay Foundation Award August 31 **Obv:** Seated and kneeling figures within circle **Rev:** Foundation Award medal below cameo **Edge:** Reeded

Date	Mintage	VF20	XF40	MS60	MS63	MS65
BE2534	800,000	—	0.50	1.00	2.00	3.50
BE2534	2,111	PF63 32.50		PF65 37.50		

Y# 249 10 BAHT

15.00 g., Copper-Nickel, 32 mm. **Ruler:** Rama IX **Subject:** Centenary Celebration - Father of King Rama IX Mahidon - January 1 **Obv:** Crown on stand flanked by others **Rev:** Bust facing **Edge:** Reeded **Note:** Minted and released in 1991.

Date	Mintage	VF20	XF40	MS60	MS63	MS65
BE2535	800,000	—	0.50	1.00	2.00	3.50
BE2535	5,044	PF63 20.00		PF65 25.00		

Y# 252 10 BAHT

15.00 g., Copper-Nickel, 32 mm. **Ruler:** Rama IX **Subject:** Ministry of Justice Centennial March 25 **Obv:** Conjoined busts left **Rev:** Balance scales within design **Edge:** Reeded

Date	Mintage	VF20	XF40	MS60	MS63	MS65
BE2535	800,000	—	0.50	1.00	2.00	3.50
BE2535	—	PF63 17.50	PF65 22.50			

Y# 254 10 BAHT

15.00 g., Copper-Nickel, 32 mm. **Ruler:** Rama IX **Subject:** Ministry of Interior Centennial April 1 2435 to 2535 **Obv:** Conjoined uniformed busts facing **Rev:** Mythical animal within circle **Edge:** Reeded

Date	Mintage	VF20	XF40	MS60	MS63	MS65
BE2535	800,000	—	0.50	1.00	2.00	3.50
BE2535	10,000	PF63 12.50	PF65 17.50			

Y# 261 10 BAHT

15.00 g., Copper-Nickel, 32 mm. **Ruler:** Rama IX **Subject:** Queen's 60th Birthday August 12 (Thai Mother's Day) **Obv:** Crowned bust facing **Rev:** Crowned monogram **Edge:** Reeded

Date	Mintage	VF20	XF40	MS60	MS63	MS65
BE2535	1,100,000	—	0.50	1.00	2.00	3.50
BE2535	20,000	PF63 12.50	PF65 17.50			

Y# 269 10 BAHT

15.00 g., Copper-Nickel, 32 mm. **Ruler:** Rama IX **Subject:** 60th Anniversary of National Assembly June 28 **Obv:** Conjoined busts left **Rev:** Ratasapa - Paraliment building **Edge:** Reeded

Date	Mintage	VF20	XF40	MS60	MS63	MS65
BE2535	600,000	—	0.50	1.00	2.00	3.50

Y# 271 10 BAHT

15.00 g., Copper-Nickel, 32 mm. **Ruler:** Rama IX **Subject:** Ministry of Agriculture, 100th Anniversary **Obv:** Conjoined busts 1/4 left **Rev:** Emblem above designed sprigs **Edge:** Reeded

Date	Mintage	VF20	XF40	MS60	MS63	MS65
BE2535	550,000	—	0.50	1.00	2.00	3.50
BE2535	—	PF63 20.00	PF65 25.00			

Y# 273 10 BAHT

15.00 g., Copper-Nickel, 32 mm. **Ruler:** Rama IX **Subject:** King's 64th Birthday November 18 **Obv:** Conjoined busts 1/4 left **Rev:** Crowned monograms **Edge:** Reeded **Note:** In honor of the King reaching the life span of his great grandfather.

Date	Mintage	VF20	XF40	MS60	MS63	MS65
BE2535	550,000	—	0.50	1.00	2.00	3.50
BE2535	3,711	PF63 20.00	PF65 25.00			

Y# 284 10 BAHT

15.00 g., Copper-Nickel, 32 mm. **Ruler:** Rama IX **Subject:** Centennial of Thai Teacher Training October 12 **Obv:** Conjoined busts left **Rev:** Emblem **Edge:** Reeded

Date	Mintage	VF20	XF40	MS60	MS63	MS65
BE2535	700,000	—	0.50	1.00	2.00	3.50

Y# 285 10 BAHT

15.00 g., Copper-Nickel, 32 mm. **Ruler:** Rama IX **Subject:** Centennial of Thai National Bank December 10 **Obv:** Conjoined busts facing **Rev:** Seated figure **Edge:** Reeded **Note:** Minted and released in 1993.

Date	Mintage	VF20	XF40	MS60	MS63	MS65
BE2535	700,000	—	0.50	1.00	2.00	3.50
BE2535	36,527	PF63 15.00	PF65 20.00			

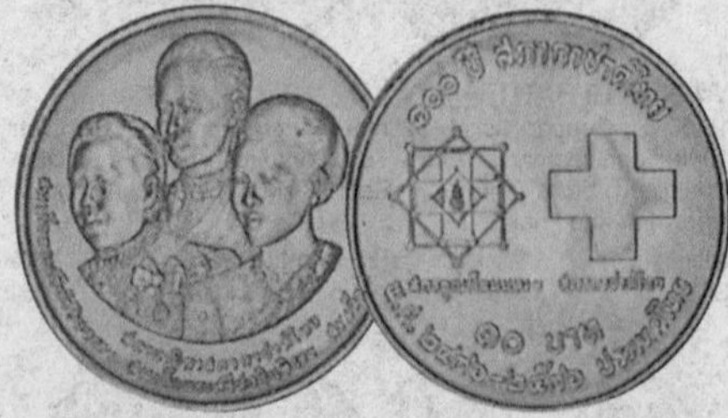

Y# 280 10 BAHT

15.00 g., Copper-Nickel, 32 mm. **Ruler:** Rama IX **Subject:** Centennial of Thai Red Cross 2436-2536 **Obv:** Conjoined busts 1/4 left **Rev:** Symbols **Edge:** Reeded

Date	Mintage	VF20	XF40	MS60	MS63	MS65
BE2536	700,000	—	0.50	1.00	2.00	3.50
BE2536	20,000	PF63 13.50	PF65 18.50			

Y# 283 10 BAHT

15.00 g., Copper-Nickel, 32 mm. **Ruler:** Rama IX **Subject:** 60th Anniversary Treasury Department May 23 **Obv:** Conjoined busts left **Rev:** Emblem within circle **Edge:** Reeded

Date	Mintage	VF20	XF40	MS60	MS63	MS65
BE2536	600,000	—	0.50	1.00	2.00	3.50
BE2536	9,900	PF63 17.50	PF65 22.50			

Y# 286 10 BAHT

15.00 g., Copper-Nickel, 32 mm. **Ruler:** Rama IX **Subject:** Centennial of Attorney General's Office April 1 2436-2536 **Obv:** Conjoined busts facing **Rev:** Crowned balance scales above sprigs **Edge:** Reeded

Date	Mintage	VF20	XF40	MS60	MS63	MS65
BE2536	700,000	—	0.50	1.00	2.00	3.50

Y# 289 10 BAHT

15.00 g., Copper-Nickel, 32 mm. **Ruler:** Rama IX **Subject:** 100th Anniversary of Rama VII November 8 **Obv:** Bust left **Rev:** Crown and designs within oval circle **Edge:** Reeded

Date	Mintage	VF20	XF40	MS60	MS63	MS65
BE2536	800,000	—	0.50	1.00	2.00	3.50
BE2536	10,000	PF63 17.50	PF65 22.50			

Y# 293 10 BAHT

15.00 g., Copper-Nickel, 32 mm. **Ruler:** Rama IX **Subject:** 60th Anniversary - Royal Thai Language Academy March 31 **Obv:** Conjoined busts left **Rev:** Crowned emblem **Edge:** Reeded

Date	Mintage	VF20	XF40	MS60	MS63	MS65
BE2537	700,000	—	0.50	1.00	2.00	3.50
BE2537	10,000	PF63 17.50	PF65 22.50			

Y# 295 10 BAHT

15.00 g., Copper-Nickel, 32 mm. **Ruler:** Rama IX **Subject:** 120th Anniversary Council of Advisors to the King - Royal decree 2417-2537 **Obv:** Conjoined busts facing **Rev:** Building **Edge:** Reeded

Date	Mintage	VF20	XF40	MS60	MS63	MS65
BE2537	800,011	—	0.50	1.00	2.00	3.50
BE2537	12,011	**PF63** 17.50	**PF65** 22.50			

Y# 297 10 BAHT

15.00 g., Copper-Nickel, 32 mm. **Ruler:** Rama IX **Subject:** 60th Anniversary - Thammasat University June 27 **Obv:** Conjoined busts left **Rev:** Emblem within circle and wreath **Edge:** Reeded

Date	Mintage	VF20	XF40	MS60	MS63	MS65
BE2537	800,011	—	0.50	1.00	2.00	3.50
BE2537	12,011	**PF63** 17.50	**PF65** 22.50			

Y# 334 10 BAHT

Bi-Metallic Aluminum-Bronze center in Copper-Nickel ring, 26 mm. **Ruler:** Rama IX **Subject:** F.A.O. World Summit December 2, King's Agricola Award **Obv:** Bust left within circle **Rev:** Seated and kneeling figures within circle **Edge:** Segmented reeding

Date	Mintage	VF20	XF40	MS60	MS63	MS65
BE2538	5,006,001	—	0.50	0.75	1.25	2.50

Y# 339 10 BAHT

8.50 g., Bi-Metallic Aluminum-Bronze center in Copper-Nickel ring, 26 mm. **Ruler:** Rama IX **Subject:** F.A.O. King's International Rice Award June 5 **Obv:** Half length figure with camera left within circle **Rev:** Rice plant within circle **Edge:** Segmented reeding

Date	Mintage	VF20	XF40	MS60	MS63	MS65
BE2538	5,000,011	—	0.50	0.75	1.25	2.50

Y# 328.1 10 BAHT

8.50 g., Bi-Metallic Aluminum-Bronze center in Copper-Nickel ring, 26 mm. **Ruler:** Rama IX **Subject:** Reign of King Rama IX, June 9th, 50th Anniversary **Obv:** Bust facing within circle **Rev:** National arms within circle **Edge:** Segmented reeding

Date	Mintage	VF20	XF40	MS60	MS63	MS65
BE2539	—	—	0.50	0.75	1.25	2.50

Y# 328.2 10 BAHT

8.50 g., Bi-Metallic Aluminum-Bronze center in Copper-Nickel ring, 26 mm. **Ruler:** Rama IX **Subject:** 50th Anniversary - Reign of King Rama IX June 9 **Obv:** Bust facing within circle **Rev:** National arms within circle **Edge:** Segmented reeding

Date	Mintage	VF20	XF40	MS60	MS63	MS65
BE2539	2,800,000	—	0.50	0.75	1.25	2.50

Y# 347 10 BAHT

8.50 g., Bi-Metallic Aluminum-Bronze center in Copper-Nickel ring., 26 mm. **Ruler:** Rama IX **Subject:** Chulalongkorn's (Rama V) European Tour, 100th anniversary **Obv:** Bust right within circle **Rev:** Design and inscription divides circle **Edge:** Segmented reeding **Note:** Minted and released in 1998.

Date	Mintage	VF20	XF40	MS60	MS63	MS65
BE2540	5,000,000	—	0.50	1.00	1.75	3.00

Y# 346 10 BAHT

8.50 g., Bi-Metallic Aluminum-Bronze center in Copper-Nickel ring, 26 mm. **Ruler:** Rama IX **Subject:** Central General Hospital - Medication Office 2441-2541, 100th Anniversary **Obv:** Conjoined busts facing within circle **Rev:** Figure seated on facing elephant within circle **Edge:** Segmented reeding

Date	Mintage	VF20	XF40	MS60	MS63	MS65
BE2541	2,000,000	—	0.50	1.00	1.75	3.00

Y# 348 10 BAHT

8.50 g., Bi-Metallic Aluminum-Bronze center in Copper-Nickel ring, 26 mm. **Ruler:** Rama IX **Subject:** 13th Asian Games, Bangkok, December 6-20 **Obv:** Bust left within circle **Rev:** Symbols within circle **Edge:** Segmented reeding

Date	Mintage	VF20	XF40	MS60	MS63	MS65
BE2541	8,000,022	—	0.50	1.00	1.75	3.00

Y# 352 10 BAHT

8.50 g., Bi-Metallic Aluminum-Bronze center in Copper-Nickel ring, 26 mm. **Ruler:** Rama IX **Subject:** Rama III honored with the title "Great" March 31 **Obv:** Head facing within circle **Rev:** Crowned arms within circle **Edge:** Segmented reeding

Date	Mintage	VF20	XF40	MS60	MS63	MS65
BE2541	3,000,028	—	0.50	1.00	1.75	3.00

Y# 349 10 BAHT

8.50 g., Bi-Metallic Aluminum-Bronze center in Copper-Nickel ring, 26 mm. **Ruler:** Rama IX **Subject:** Customs Department, July 4, 125th Anniversary **Obv:** Conjoined busts 1/4 right **Rev:** Buildings below emblem **Edge:** Segmented reeding

Date	Mintage	VF20	XF40	MS60	MS63	MS65
BE2542	300,030	—	0.50	1.00	1.75	3.00

Y# 350 10 BAHT

8.50 g., Bi-Metallic Aluminum-Bronze center in Copper-Nickel ring, 26 mm. **Ruler:** Rama IX **Subject:** King's 6th cycle, 72nd Birthday, December 5 **Obv:** Head left within circle **Rev:** Crowned emblem within circle **Edge:** Segmented reeding

Date	Mintage	VF20	XF40	MS60	MS63	MS65
BE2542	6,300,011	—	0.50	1.00	1.75	3.00

Y# 354 10 BAHT

8.50 g., Bi-Metallic Aluminum-Bronze center in Copper-Nickel ring, 26 mm. **Ruler:** Rama IX **Subject:** Army Medical Department, January 7, 2443-2543, 100th Anniversary **Obv:** Conjoined busts facing **Rev:** Emblem within circle **Edge:** Segmented reeding

Date	Mintage	VF20	XF40	MS60	MS63	MS65
BE2543	3,000,017	—	0.50	1.00	1.75	3.00

Y# 358 10 BAHT

8.50 g., Bi-Metallic Aluminum-Bronze center in Copper-Nickel ring, 26 mm. **Ruler:** Rama IX **Subject:** Ministry of Commerce, August 20, 80th Anniversary **Obv:** Head facing within circle **Rev:** Ministry logo within square and circle **Edge:** Segmented reeding

Date	Mintage	VF20	XF40	MS60	MS63	MS65
BE2543	30,001,040	—	0.50	0.75	1.25	2.50

Y# 361 10 BAHT

8.50 g., Bi-Metallic Aluminum-Bronze center in Copper-Nickel ring, 26 mm. **Ruler:** Rama IX **Subject:** Princess Mother (King's mother) 100th Birthday, October 21 **Obv:** Bust left within circle **Rev:** Emblem within circle **Edge:** Segmented reeding

Date	Mintage	VF20	XF40	MS60	MS63	MS65
BE2543	5,000,000	—	0.50	1.00	1.75	3.00

Y# 371 10 BAHT

8.50 g., Bi-Metallic Aluminum-Bronze center in Copper-Nickel ring, 26 mm. **Ruler:** Rama IX **Subject:** National Economic and Social Development Board, February 15, 50th Anniversary **Obv:** Bust 3/4 left **Rev:** Three seated figures within circle **Edge:** Segmented reeding

Date	Mintage	VF20	XF40	MS60	MS63	MS65
BE2543 (2000)	1,900,040	—	0.50	1.00	1.75	3.00

Y# 86 20 BAHT

20.00 g., 0.750 Silver 0.4823 oz. ASW, 34.5 mm. **Ruler:** Rama IX **Subject:** 36th Birthday - Rama IX **Obv:** Uniformed bust left **Rev:** Crown and emblem divided by crossed scepter and spear

Date	Mintage	VF20	XF40	MS60	MS63	MS65
ND (1963)	1,000,000	—	12.00	15.00	20.00	25.00

Y# 298 20 BAHT

15.00 g., Copper-Nickel, 32 mm. **Ruler:** Rama IX **Subject:** 120th Anniversary - Ministry of Finance 2418-2538 **Obv:** Conjoined busts right **Rev:** Stylized eagle **Edge:** Reeded

Date	Mintage	VF20	XF40	MS60	MS63	MS65
BE2538	800,000	—	—	1.50	2.50	4.00
BE2538	11,850	PF63 25.00	PF65 30.00			

Y# 300 20 BAHT

15.00 g., Copper-Nickel, 32 mm. **Ruler:** Rama IX **Subject:** 108th Anniversary - Ministry of Defense April 8 **Obv:** Conjoined uniformed busts facing **Rev:** Mythical animal within circle **Edge:** Reeded

Date	Mintage	VF20	XF40	MS60	MS63	MS65
BE2538	800,000	—	—	1.50	2.50	4.00
BE2538	10,821	PF63 25.00	PF65 30.00			

Y# 302 20 BAHT

15.00 g., Copper-Nickel, 32 mm. **Ruler:** Rama IX **Subject:** 120th Anniversary - Ministry of Foreign Affairs April 14 **Obv:** Conjoined busts facing **Rev:** Seated figure within designed circle and wreath **Edge:** Reeded

Date	Mintage	VF20	XF40	MS60	MS63	MS65
BE2538	800,000	—	—	1.50	2.50	4.00
BE2538	10,278	PF63 40.00	PF65 45.00			

Y# 304 20 BAHT

15.00 g., Copper-Nickel, 32 mm. **Ruler:** Rama IX **Subject:** 72nd Birthday of Princess Galyani Vedhana **Obv:** Uniformed bust 3/4 facing right **Rev:** Crowned arms **Edge:** Reeded

Date	Mintage	VF20	XF40	MS60	MS63	MS65
BE2538	800,000	—	—	1.50	2.50	4.00
BE2538	13,330	PF63 17.50	PF65 22.50			

Y# 308 20 BAHT

15.00 g., Copper-Nickel, 32 mm. **Ruler:** Rama IX **Series:** F.A.O. 1945-1995 **Obv:** Bust left **Rev:** F.A.O. logo and dates **Edge:** Reeded

Date	Mintage	VF20	XF40	MS60	MS63	MS65
BE2538	800,000	—	—	1.50	2.50	4.00
BE2538	12,000	PF63 15.00	PF65 20.00			

Y# 309 20 BAHT

15.00 g., Copper-Nickel, 32 mm. **Ruler:** Rama IX **Subject:** 80th Anniversary - Department of Revenue September 2 **Obv:** Conjoined busts 1/4 left **Rev:** Seated figure within circle **Edge:** Reeded

Date	Mintage	VF20	XF40	MS60	MS63	MS65
BE2538	800,000	—	—	1.50	2.50	4.00
BE2538	10,000	PF63 12.50	PF65 17.50			

Y# 311 20 BAHT

15.00 g., Copper-Nickel, 32 mm. **Ruler:** Rama IX **Subject:** 120th Anniversary - Audit Council 2418-2538 **Obv:** Conjoined uniformed busts facing **Rev:** Balance scales **Edge:** Reeded

Date	Mintage	VF20	XF40	MS60	MS63	MS65
BE2538	800,000	—	—	1.50	2.50	4.00
BE2538	10,000	PF63 12.50	PF65 17.50			

Y# 314 20 BAHT

15.00 g., Copper-Nickel, 32 mm. **Ruler:** Rama IX **Subject:** Information Technology Year **Obv:** Bust left **Rev:** Design and inscription within world globe **Edge:** Reeded

Date	Mintage	VF20	XF40	MS60	MS63	MS65
BE2538	850,000	—	—	1.50	2.50	4.00
BE2538	12,000	PF63 12.50	PF65 17.50			

Y# 316 20 BAHT

15.00 g., Copper-Nickel, 32 mm. **Ruler:** Rama IX **Subject:** Asean Environment Year **Obv:** Conjoined busts right **Rev:** Symbol within center circle, grain sprig and arrow surround **Edge:** Reeded

Date	Mintage	VF20	XF40	MS60	MS63	MS65
BE2538	1,000,011	—	—	1.50	2.50	4.00
BE2538	12,000	PF63 12.50	PF65 17.50			

Y# 331 20 BAHT

15.00 g., Copper-Nickel, 32 mm. **Ruler:** Rama IX **Subject:** Ministry of Commerce, 75th Anniversary **Obv:** Conjoined uniformed busts facing **Rev:** Seal within circle **Edge:** Reeded **Note:** Minted and released in 1996.

Date	Mintage	VF20	XF40	MS60	MS63	MS65
BE2538	1,200,011	—	—	2.00	3.00	4.50
BE2538	10,773	PF63 12.50	PF65 17.50			

Y# 338 20 BAHT

15.00 g., Copper-Nickel, 32 mm. **Ruler:** Rama IX **Subject:** 50 Years of Peace August 16 **Obv:** Uniformed busts of Rama VIII and Rama IX facing **Rev:** Busts left with flag and doves within center circle **Edge:** Reeded **Note:** Minted and released in 1997.

Date	Mintage	VF20	XF40	MS60	MS63	MS65
BE2538	1,002,511	—	—	2.00	3.00	4.50
BE2538	11,288	PF63 12.50	PF65 17.50			

Y# 318 20 BAHT

15.00 g., Copper-Nickel, 32 mm. **Ruler:** Rama IX **Subject:** Siriraj Nursing and Midwife School Centennial **Obv:** Uniformed bust facing **Rev:** Crowned monogram flanked by sprigs **Edge:** Reeded

Date	Mintage	VF20	XF40	MS60	MS63	MS65
BE2539	800,000	—	—	1.50	2.50	4.00
BE2539	10,000	PF63 12.50	PF65 17.50			

Y# 321.1 20 BAHT

15.00 g., Copper-Nickel, 32 mm. **Ruler:** Rama IX **Subject:** 50th Anniversary - Reign of King Rama IX June 9 **Obv:** Bust facing **Rev:** National arms **Edge:** Reeded

Date	Mintage	VF20	XF40	MS60	MS63	MS65
BE2539	5,010,000	—	—	2.00	3.00	4.50
BE2539	164,995	PF63 20.00	PF65 25.00			

Y# 321.2 20 BAHT

15.00 g., Copper-Nickel, 32 mm. **Ruler:** Rama IX **Subject:** 50th Anniversary - Reign of King Rama IX June 9 **Obv:** Bust facing **Rev:** Crowned arms with supporters **Edge:** Plain

Date	Mintage	VF20	XF40	MS60	MS63	MS65
BE2539	—	—	—	2.00	3.00	4.50
Note: Mintage included with 321.1 totals						
BE2539	—	PF63 22.50	PF65 27.50			

Y# 335 20 BAHT

15.00 g., Copper-Nickel, 32 mm. **Ruler:** Rama IX **Subject:** F.A.O. World Food Summit **Obv:** Bust left within circle **Rev:** Seated and kneeling figures within circle **Edge:** Reeded

Date	Mintage	VF20	XF40	MS60	MS63	MS65
BE2539	1,500,000	—	—	2.00	3.00	4.50
BE2539	12,722	PF63 15.00	PF65 20.00			

Y# 340 20 BAHT
15.00 g., Copper-Nickel, 32 mm. **Ruler:** Rama IX **Subject:** International Rice Award June 5 **Obv:** Half length bust left within circle **Rev:** Inscription and sprigs within circle **Edge:** Reeded **Note:** Minted and released in 1997.

Date	Mintage	VF20	XF40	MS60	MS63	MS65
BE2539	788,511	—	—	2.00	3.00	4.50
BE2539	10,374	PF63 15.00	PF65 20.00			

Y# 332 20 BAHT
15.00 g., Copper-Nickel, 32 mm. **Ruler:** Rama IX **Subject:** 100th Anniversary - Thai Railway March 26 **Obv:** Conjoined busts 1/4 left **Rev:** Radiant crown above stylized eagle **Edge:** Reeded

Date	Mintage	VF20	XF40	MS60	MS63	MS65
BE2540	1,202,011	—	—	2.00	3.00	4.50
BE2540	11,277	PF63 15.00	PF65 20.00			

Y# 333 20 BAHT
15.00 g., Copper-Nickel, 32 mm. **Ruler:** Rama IX **Subject:** 84th Anniversary - Thai Savings Bank April 1 **Obv:** Uniformed bust facing **Rev:** Designs within sectioned circle **Edge:** Reeded

Date	Mintage	VF20	XF40	MS60	MS63	MS65
BE2540	1,350,001	—	—	2.00	3.00	4.50
BE2540	21,000	PF63 17.00	PF65 22.00			

Y# 341 20 BAHT
15.00 g., Copper-Nickel, 32 mm. **Ruler:** Rama IX **Subject:** 50th Anniversary - Thai Veterans Organization; Veteran's Day February 3 **Obv:** Uniformed bust facing **Rev:** Armored figures within circle **Edge:** Reeded

Date	Mintage	VF20	XF40	MS60	MS63	MS65
BE2541	1,000,011	—	—	2.00	3.00	4.50
BE2541	5,011	PF63 15.00	PF65 20.00			

Y# 351 20 BAHT
15.00 g., Copper-Nickel, 32 mm. **Ruler:** Rama IX **Subject:** 72nd Birthday of the King December 5 **Obv:** Bust left **Rev:** Crowned emblem **Edge:** Reeded

Date	Mintage	VF20	XF40	MS60	MS63	MS65
BE2542	2,507,011	—	—	1.50	2.50	3.00
BE2542	30,011	PF63 12.50	PF65 17.50			

Y# 355 20 BAHT
15.00 g., Copper-Nickel, 32 mm. **Ruler:** Rama IX **Subject:** 84th Anniversary - Audit Council Bureau September 18 **Obv:** Uniformed bust facing **Rev:** Balance scale **Edge:** Reeded **Note:** Minted and released in 2000.

Date	Mintage	VF20	XF40	MS60	MS63	MS65
BE2542	801,040	—	—	2.00	3.00	4.50

Y# 357 20 BAHT
15.00 g., Copper-Nickel, 32 mm. **Ruler:** Rama IX **Subject:** Asian Development Bank Board Meeting **Obv:** Bust 1/4 right **Rev:** Chieng money illustration **Edge:** Reeded

Date	Mintage	VF20	XF40	MS60	MS63	MS65
ND (2000)	800,000	—	—	2.00	3.00	4.50
ND (2000)	5,000	PF63 15.00	PF65 20.00			

Y# 362 20 BAHT
Copper-Nickel, 32 mm. **Ruler:** Rama IX **Subject:** 100th Birthday - King's Mother **Obv:** Bust left **Rev:** Emblem divides date **Edge:** Reeded

Date	Mintage	VF20	XF40	MS60	MS63	MS65
BE2543	1,000,040	—	—	2.00	3.00	4.50
BE2543	10,040	PF63 12.50	PF65 17.50			

Y# 376 20 BAHT
15.00 g., Copper-Nickel, 32 mm. **Ruler:** Rama IX **Subject:** The 9th King reaches the age of the 1st King May 23 **Obv:** Conjoined busts facing **Rev:** Two royal symbols **Edge:** Reeded **Note:** Minted and released in 2001.

Date	Mintage	VF20	XF40	MS60	MS63	MS65
BE2543 (2000)	500,000	—	—	2.00	3.50	5.00
BE2543 (2000)	5,000	PF63 22.00	PF65 27.00			

Y# 95 50 BAHT
24.70 g., 0.900 Silver 0.7147 oz. ASW, 40 mm. **Ruler:** Rama IX **Subject:** 20th Year Buddhist Fellowship **Obv:** Bust 1/4 left **Rev:** The Buddhist wheel of law, Dhamachakr **Edge:** Reeded

Date	Mintage	VF20	XF40	MS60	MS63	MS65
BE2514	200,000	—	14.00	18.00	22.00	25.00
BE2514 Prooflike	60,000	PF63 28.00	PF65 32.00			

Y# 101 50 BAHT
24.85 g., 0.400 Silver 0.3196 oz. ASW, 38 mm. **Ruler:** Rama IX **Subject:** National Museum Centennial **Obv:** Conjoined busts left **Rev:** Crowns within designed wreath

Date	Mintage	VF20	XF40	MS60	MS63	MS65
BE2517	200,000	—	—	9.00	12.00	16.00

Y# 102 50 BAHT
28.28 g., 0.500 Silver 0.4546 oz. ASW, 38.6 mm. **Ruler:** Rama IX **Subject:** Wildlife Conservation **Obv:** Bust 1/4 left **Rev:** Sumatran Rhinoceros **Edge:** Reeded

Date	Mintage	VF20	XF40	MS60	MS63	MS65
BE2517	20,339	—	—	16.00	22.00	28.00

Y# 102a 50 BAHT
28.28 g., 0.925 Silver 0.841 oz. ASW, 38.6 mm. **Ruler:** Rama IX **Series:** Wildlife Conservation **Obv:** Bust 1/4 left **Rev:** Rhinoceros

Date	Mintage	VF20	XF40	MS60	MS63	MS65
BE2517	9,885	PF63 42.00	PF65 47.00			

Y# 336 50 BAHT
21.00 g., Copper-Nickel, 36 mm. **Ruler:** Rama IX **Subject:** F.A.O. World Food Summit December 2 **Obv:** Bust left within circle **Rev:** Seated and kneeling figures within circle **Edge:** Reeded **Note:** Similar to 20 Baht, Y#335.

Date	Mintage	VF20	XF40	MS60	MS63	MS65
BE2539	238,900	—	—	3.00	7.00	10.00
BE2539	5,026	PF63 18.00	PF65 22.00			

Y# 363 50 BAHT
20.00 g., 0.925 Silver 0.5948 oz. ASW, 38.7 mm. **Ruler:** Rama IX **Subject:** Year of the Dragon **Obv:** Bust 1/4 left **Rev:** Dragon and latent image date pearl **Edge:** Reeded

Date	Mintage	VF20	XF40	MS60	MS63	MS65
BE2543	8,500	PF63 150	PF65 175			

Y# 364 50 BAHT
20.00 g., 0.925 Silver 0.5948 oz. ASW **Ruler:** Rama IX **Subject:** Year of the Dragon **Obv:** Bust 1/4 left **Rev:** Two dragons with pearl hologram

Date	Mintage	VF20	XF40	MS60	MS63	MS65
BE2543	8,500	PF63 225	PF65 250			

Y# 365 50 BAHT
20.00 g., 0.925 Silver 0.5948 oz. ASW **Ruler:** Rama IX **Subject:** Year of the Dragon **Obv:** Bust 1/4 left **Rev:** Dragon with gold-plated pearl

Date	Mintage	VF20	XF40	MS60	MS63	MS65
BE2543	8,500	PF63 175	PF65 200			

Y# 103 100 BAHT
31.65 g., 0.500 Silver 0.5088 oz. ASW, 42 mm. **Ruler:** Rama IX **Subject:** Wildlife Conservation **Obv:** Bust 1/4 left **Rev:** Brown-antlered deer **Edge:** Reeded

Date	Mintage	VF20	XF40	MS60	MS63	MS65
BE2517	20,351	—	—	16.00	28.00	32.00

Y# 103a 100 BAHT
35.00 g., 0.925 Silver 1.0409 oz. ASW, 42 mm. **Ruler:** Rama IX **Series:** Conservation **Obv:** Bust 1/4 left **Rev:** Brown-antlered deer

Date	Mintage	VF20	XF40	MS60	MS63	MS65
BE2517	9,294	PF63 50.00	PF65 55.00			

Y# 106 100 BAHT
25.00 g., 0.900 Silver 0.7234 oz. ASW, 38 mm. **Ruler:** Rama IX **Subject:** 100th Anniversary - Ministry of Finance **Obv:** Conjoined busts facing **Rev:** Building within circle

Date	Mintage	VF20	XF40	MS60	MS63	MS65
BE2518	30,020	—	—	20.00	25.00	30.00

Y# 242 100 BAHT
25.00 g., Copper-Nickel, 38 mm. **Ruler:** Rama IX **Subject:** World Bank - International Monetary Fund **Obv:** Conjoined busts right **Rev:** Emblem **Edge:** Reeded

Date	Mintage	VF20	XF40	MS60	MS63	MS65
BE2534	500,000	—	—	5.00	7.00	12.00
BE2534	60,000	PF63 15.00	PF65 20.00			

Y# 287 100 BAHT
25.00 g., Copper-Nickel, 38 mm. **Ruler:** Rama IX **Subject:** 33rd World Scout Conference **Obv:** Conjoined busts right **Rev:** Crowned emblem

Date	Mintage	VF20	XF40	MS60	MS63	MS65
BE2536	200,000	—	—	6.00	9.00	15.00
BE2536	30,000	PF63 20.00	PF65 25.00			

Y# 359 100 BAHT
15.00 g., 0.925 Silver 0.4461 oz. ASW, 30 mm. **Ruler:** Rama IX **Series:** World Wildlife Fund **Obv:** Bust left **Rev:** Tiger head and value **Edge:** Reeded **Note:** Thickness of coin is 3mm.

Date	Mintage	VF20	XF40	MS60	MS63	MS65
BE2540	50,000	PF63 22.00	PF65 28.00			

Y# 366 100 BAHT
7.75 g., 0.9999 Gold 0.2491 oz. AGW, 22 mm. **Ruler:** Rama IX **Subject:** Year of the Dragon **Obv:** Bust 1/4 left **Rev:** Dragon with golden plated pearl **Edge:** Reeded

Date	Mintage	VF20	XF40	MS60	MS63	MS65
BE2543 sg	1,800	PF63 420	PF65 450			

Y# 88 150 BAHT
3.75 g., 0.900 Gold 0.1085 oz. AGW, 17 mm. **Ruler:** Rama IX **Subject:** Queen Sirikit 36th Birthday **Obv:** Bust right **Rev:** Crowned monogram **Edge:** Reeded

Date	Mintage	VF20	XF40	MS60	MS63	MS65
BE2511	202,316	—	—	—	180	220

Y# 108 150 BAHT
22.00 g., 0.925 Silver 0.6543 oz. ASW, 35 mm. **Ruler:** Rama IX **Subject:** 75th Birthday of King's Mother October 21 **Obv:** Bust with hat facing **Rev:** Emblem

Date	Mintage	VF20	XF40	MS60	MS63	MS65
BE2518	200,000	—	—	17.00	20.00	22.50

Y# 113 150 BAHT
22.00 g., 0.925 Silver 0.6543 oz. ASW, 35 mm. **Ruler:** Rama IX **Subject:** F.A.O. **Obv:** Standing half length figures scattering rice **Rev:** Elephants within circle **Edge:** Reeded

Date	Mintage	VF20	XF40	MS60	MS63	MS65
BE2520	50,000	—	—	17.50	21.50	25.00

Y# 116 150 BAHT
22.00 g., 0.925 Silver 0.6543 oz. ASW, 35 mm. **Ruler:** Rama IX **Subject:** Graduation of Princess Sirindhorn; 1st royal graduate of a Thai University **Obv:** Bust left **Rev:** Radiant crown **Edge:** Reeded

Date	Mintage	VF20	XF40	MS60	MS63	MS65
BE2520	100,000	—	—	17.50	21.50	25.00

Y# 118 150 BAHT
22.00 g., 0.925 Silver 0.6543 oz. ASW, 35 mm. **Ruler:** Rama IX **Subject:** Crown Prince Vajiralongkorn and Princess Soamsawali Wedding January 3 **Obv:** Conjoined busts right **Rev:** Crowned monogram within designs **Edge:** Reeded

Date	Mintage	VF20	XF40	MS60	MS63	MS65
BE2520	200,000	—	—	17.50	21.50	25.00

Y# 125 150 BAHT
22.00 g., 0.925 Silver 0.6543 oz. ASW, 35 mm. **Ruler:** Rama IX **Subject:** Investiture of Princess Sirindhorn May 12 **Obv:** Bust right **Rev:** Crowned monogram **Edge:** Plain

Date	Mintage	VF20	XF40	MS60	MS63	MS65
BE2520	50,000	—	—	18.50	22.50	27.00

Y# 123 150 BAHT
22.00 g., 0.925 Silver 0.6543 oz. ASW, 35 mm. **Ruler:** Rama IX **Subject:** 9th World Orchid Conference **Obv:** Uniformed bust 1/4 left **Rev:** Orchids **Edge:** Plain

Date	Mintage	VF20	XF40	MS60	MS63	MS65
BE2521	30,000	—	—	18.50	21.50	25.00

Y# 128 150 BAHT
22.00 g., 0.925 Silver 0.6543 oz. ASW, 35 mm. **Ruler:** Rama IX **Subject:** Graduation of Crown Prince Vajiralongkorn **Obv:** Bust left **Rev:** Crowned elephant head facing within frame **Edge:** Reeded

Date	Mintage	VF20	XF40	MS60	MS63	MS65
BE2521	50,000	—	—	18.50	21.50	25.00

Y# 197 150 BAHT
7.50 g., 0.925 Silver 0.223 oz. ASW, 27 mm. **Ruler:** Rama IX **Subject:** 60th Birthday - King Rama IX **Obv:** Uniformed bust facing **Rev:** Crowned radiant emblem **Note:** Similar to 6000 Baht, Y#202. Minted and struck in 1986.

Date	Mintage	VF20	XF40	MS60	MS63	MS65
BE2530	11,500	—	—	14.00	24.00	28.00
BE2530	1,100	PF63 100	PF65 120			

Y# 213 150 BAHT
7.50 g., 0.925 Silver 0.223 oz. ASW, 27 mm. **Ruler:** Rama IX **Subject:** 42nd Anniversary - Reign of King Rama IX **Obv:** Uniformed bust facing **Rev:** Crowned monogram **Edge:** Reeded **Note:** Similar to 10 Baht, Y#212.

Date	Mintage	VF20	XF40	MS60	MS63	MS65
BE2531	20,000	—	—	12.00	20.00	24.00
BE2531	2,454	PF63 90.00	PF65 110			

Y# 262 150 BAHT
7.50 g., 0.925 Silver 0.223 oz. ASW, 27 mm. **Ruler:** Rama IX **Subject:** Queen's 60th Birthday **Obv:** Crowned bust facing **Rev:** Crowned monogram **Edge:** Reeded **Note:** Similar to 10 Baht, Y#261.

Date	Mintage	VF20	XF40	MS60	MS63	MS65
BE2535	25,000	—	—	12.00	20.00	24.00
BE2535	5,600	PF63 35.00	PF65 45.00			

Y# 322 150 BAHT
7.50 g., 0.925 Silver 0.223 oz. ASW, 27 mm. **Ruler:** Rama IX **Subject:** 50th Anniversary - Reign of King Rama IX **Obv:** Bust facing **Rev:** National arms **Edge:** Reeded **Note:** Similar to 20 Baht, Y#321.1.

Date	Mintage	VF20	XF40	MS60	MS63	MS65
BE2539	203,834	—	—	10.00	14.00	18.00
BE2539	64,198	PF63 25.00	PF65 35.00			

Y# 133 200 BAHT
22.00 g., 0.925 Silver 0.6543 oz. ASW, 35 mm. **Ruler:** Rama IX **Subject:** Royal Cradle Ceremony **Obv:** Infant head 1/4 right **Rev:** Inscription within designed wreath **Edge:** Reeded

Date	Mintage	VF20	XF40	MS60	MS63	MS65
BE2522	50,000	—	—	18.50	21.50	25.00

Y# 152 200 BAHT
23.32 g., 0.925 Silver 0.6935 oz. ASW **Ruler:** Rama IX **Series:** International Year of the Child **Obv:** Bust left **Rev:** Dancing figure flanked by emblems below

Date	Mintage	VF20	XF40	MS60	MS63	MS65
BE2524	9,525	PF63 45.00	PF65 50.00			

Y# 206 200 BAHT
23.18 g., 0.925 Silver 0.6894 oz. ASW **Ruler:** Rama IX **Series:** 25th Anniversary of World Wildlife Fund **Obv:** Bust left **Rev:** Siamese Fireback pheasant **Edge:** Reeded **Shape:** 38.6

Date	Mintage	VF20	XF40	MS60	MS63	MS65
BE2530-1987	22,280	PF63 27.00	PF65 32.00			

Y# 379 200 BAHT
23.33 g., 0.925 Silver 0.6938 oz. ASW, 38.6 mm. **Ruler:** Rama IX **Subject:** UNICEF **Obv:** Bust left **Rev:** Three seated children **Edge:** Reeded

Date	Mintage	VF20	XF40	MS60	MS63	MS65
BE2540-1997	2,123	PF63 35.00	PF65 45.00			

Y# 360 200 BAHT
23.18 g., 0.925 Silver 0.6894 oz. ASW, 38.6 mm. **Ruler:** Rama IX **Subject:** World Wildlife Fund **Obv:** Bust left **Rev:** Two tigers above value **Edge:** Reeded **Note:** Thickness of coin is 4.7mm.

Date	Mintage	VF20	XF40	MS60	MS63	MS65
BE2541-1998	3,250	PF63 55.00	PF65 65.00			

Y# 372 200 BAHT
23.18 g., 0.925 Silver 0.6894 oz. ASW, 38.6 mm. **Ruler:** Rama IX **Series:** World Wildlife Fund **Obv:** Bust left **Rev:** Elephants

Date	Mintage	VF20	XF40	MS60	MS63	MS65
BE2541-1998	—	PF63 50.00	PF65 60.00			

Y# 399 200 BAHT
23.18 g., 0.925 Silver 0.6894 oz. ASW, 38.6 mm. **Ruler:** Rama IX **Subject:** World Wildlife Fund **Obv:** Bust left **Rev:** Elephants right **Edge:** Reeded

Date	Mintage	VF20	XF40	MS60	MS63	MS65
BE2541-1998	3,250	PF63 90.00	PF65 110			

Y# 367 200 BAHT
155.52 g., 0.925 Silver 4.625 oz. ASW, 65 mm. **Ruler:** Rama IX **Subject:** Year of the Dragon **Obv:** Bust left **Rev:** Two dragons around silver pearl within orange circle **Edge:** Reeded

Date	Mintage	VF20	XF40	MS60	MS63	MS65
BE2543-2000 sg	2,000	PF65 300				

Y# 169 250 BAHT

28.28 g., 0.925 Silver 0.841 oz. ASW, 38.61 mm. **Ruler:** Rama IX **Subject:** International Year of Disabled Persons **Obv:** Bust left **Rev:** Emblem within sprigs

Date	Mintage	VF20	XF40	MS60	MS63	MS65
BE2526	307	—	200	250	300	350
BE2526	353	PF63 550	PF65 575			

Y# 368 250 BAHT

15.55 g., 0.9999 Gold 0.4999 oz. AGW, 27 mm. **Ruler:** Rama IX **Subject:** Year of the Dragon **Obv:** Bust left **Rev:** Dragon with latent image pearl **Edge:** Reeded

Date	Mintage	VF20	XF40	MS60	MS63	MS65
BE2543-2000 sg	2,800	PF65 950				

Y# 89 300 BAHT

7.50 g., 0.900 Gold 0.217 oz. AGW, 21 mm. **Ruler:** Rama IX **Subject:** Queen Sirikit 36th Birthday **Obv:** Bust right **Rev:** Crowned monogram **Edge:** Reeded

Date	Mintage	VF20	XF40	MS60	MS63	MS65
BE2511	101,362	—	290	375	425	—

Y# 136 300 BAHT

22.00 g., 0.925 Silver 0.6543 oz. ASW, 35 mm. **Ruler:** Rama IX **Subject:** Graduation of Princess Chulabhorn **Obv:** Bust 1/4 left **Rev:** Graduation emblem within circle **Note:** Similar to 10 Baht, Y#135.

Date	Mintage	VF20	XF40	MS60	MS63	MS65
BE2522	20,000	—	—	18.50	21.50	24.00

Y# 198 300 BAHT

15.00 g., 0.925 Silver 0.4461 oz. ASW, 31 mm. **Ruler:** Rama IX **Subject:** 60th Birthday - King Rama IX **Obv:** Uniformed bust facing **Rev:** Radiant crowned emblem **Edge:** Reeded **Note:** Minted and released in 1986.

Date	Mintage	VF20	XF40	MS60	MS63	MS65
BE2530	6,680	—	—	15.00	20.00	22.50
BE2530	800	PF63 40.00	PF65 50.00			

Y# 214 300 BAHT

15.00 g., 0.925 Silver 0.4461 oz. ASW, 31 mm. **Ruler:** Rama IX **Subject:** 42nd Anniversary - Reign of King Rama IX **Obv:** Uniformed bust 1/4 facing left **Rev:** Crowned monogram **Edge:** Reeded

Date	Mintage	VF20	XF40	MS60	MS63	MS65
BE2531	10,793	—	—	16.00	18.00	20.00
BE2531	2,391	PF63 37.00	PF65 48.00			

Y# 263 300 BAHT

15.00 g., 0.925 Silver 0.4461 oz. ASW, 31 mm. **Ruler:** Rama IX **Subject:** Queen's 60th Birthday **Obv:** Crowned bust facing **Rev:** Crowned monogram **Edge:** Reeded

Date	Mintage	VF20	XF40	MS60	MS63	MS65
BE2535	25,000	—	—	22.00	25.00	30.00
BE2535	4,000	PF63 35.00	PF65 45.00			

Y# 323 300 BAHT

15.00 g., 0.925 Silver 0.4461 oz. ASW, 31 mm. **Ruler:** Rama IX **Subject:** 50th Anniversary - Reign of King Rama IX **Obv:** Bust facing **Rev:** National arms **Edge:** Reeded

Date	Mintage	VF20	XF40	MS60	MS63	MS65
BE2539	115,716	—	—	15.00	20.00	22.50
BE2539	30,698	PF63 32.00	PF65 42.00			

Y# 93 400 BAHT

10.00 g., 0.900 Gold 0.2894 oz. AGW, 23 mm. **Ruler:** Rama IX **Subject:** 25th Anniversary - Reign of King Rama IX **Obv:** Head right **Rev:** Radiant crowned monogram **Edge:** Reeded

Date	Mintage	VF20	XF40	MS60	MS63	MS65
BE2514	46,584	—	—	385	500	550

Y# 90 600 BAHT

15.04 g., 0.900 Gold 0.4352 oz. AGW, 27 mm. **Ruler:** Rama IX **Subject:** Queen Sirikit 36th Birthday **Obv:** Crowned bust right **Rev:** Crowned monogram within wreath **Edge:** Reeded

Date	Mintage	VF20	XF40	MS60	MS63	MS65
BE2511	45,829	—	—	580	775	825

Y# 138 600 BAHT

12.00 g., 0.800 Silver 0.3086 oz. ASW, 30 mm. **Ruler:** Rama IX **Subject:** Queen's Anniversary and F.A.O. Ceres Medal **Obv:** Crowned bust 1/4 left **Rev:** Figures working within football-like frames **Edge:** Plain

Date	Mintage	VF20	XF40	MS60	MS63	MS65
BE2523	23,000	—	—	14.00	22.00	25.00

Y# 143 600 BAHT

15.00 g., 0.925 Silver 0.4461 oz. ASW, 31 mm. **Ruler:** Rama IX **Subject:** Centennial - Birth of Rama VI **Obv:** Bust right **Rev:** Emblem **Edge:** Reeded

Date	Mintage	VF20	XF40	MS60	MS63	MS65
BE2524	19,000	—	—	12.50	18.50	22.50

Y# 147 600 BAHT

22.00 g., 0.925 Silver 0.6543 oz. ASW, 35 mm. **Ruler:** Rama IX **Subject:** 35th Anniversary - Reign of King Rama IX **Obv:** Conjoined busts left **Rev:** Crowns and emblem **Edge:** Reeded

Date	Mintage	VF20	XF40	MS60	MS63	MS65
BE2524	15,000	—	—	20.00	25.00	28.00

Y# 150 600 BAHT

22.00 g., 0.925 Silver 0.6543 oz. ASW, 35 mm. **Ruler:** Rama IX **Subject:** Bicentennial of Bangkok **Obv:** Conjoined busts left **Rev:** Emblem **Edge:** Reeded

Date	Mintage	VF20	XF40	MS60	MS63	MS65
BE2525	15,000	—	—	20.00	25.00	28.00

Y# 155 600 BAHT

22.00 g., 0.925 Silver 0.6543 oz. ASW, 35 mm. **Ruler:** Rama IX **Subject:** 50th Birthday of Queen Sirikit **Obv:** Crowned bust 1/4 left **Rev:** Crowned monogram **Edge:** Reeded

Date	Mintage	VF20	XF40	MS60	MS63	MS65
BE2525	3,735	—	—	42.00	48.00	55.00
BE2525	991	PF63 175	PF65 200			

Y# 164 600 BAHT

22.00 g., 0.925 Silver 0.6543 oz. ASW, 35 mm. **Ruler:** Rama IX **Subject:** 100th Anniversary of Thai Post **Obv:** Conjoined busts left **Rev:** Stamps **Edge:** Reeded

Date	Mintage	VF20	XF40	MS60	MS63	MS65
BE2526	5,000	—	—	42.00	48.00	55.00
BE2526	1,400	PF63 120	PF65 140			

Y# 166 600 BAHT

22.00 g., 0.925 Silver 0.6543 oz. ASW, 35 mm. **Ruler:** Rama IX **Subject:** 700th Anniversary of Thai Alphabet **Obv:** Seated figure left **Rev:** Inscription **Edge:** Reeded

Date	Mintage	VF20	XF40	MS60	MS63	MS65
BE2526	4,300	—	—	42.00	48.00	55.00
BE2526	1,000	PF63 160	PF65 185			

Y# 173 600 BAHT

22.00 g., 0.925 Silver 0.6543 oz. ASW, 35 mm. **Ruler:** Rama IX **Subject:** 84th Birthday of Princess Mother **Obv:** Bust 1/4 left **Rev:** Crown on stand flanked by others **Edge:** Reeded

Date	Mintage	VF20	XF40	MS60	MS63	MS65
BE2527	3,530	—	—	35.00	40.00	45.00
BE2527	520	PF63 225	PF65 250			

Y# 182 600 BAHT

22.00 g., 0.925 Silver 0.6543 oz. ASW, 35 mm. **Ruler:** Rama IX **Subject:** 6th ASEAN Orchid Congress **Obv:** Uniformed bust left **Rev:** Symbols of congress **Edge:** Reeded **Note:** Similar to 10 Baht, Y#181.

Date	Mintage	VF20	XF40	MS60	MS63	MS65
BE2529	5,000	—	—	40.00	45.00	50.00
BE2529	800	PF63 160	PF65 180			

Y# 193 600 BAHT

22.00 g., 0.925 Silver 0.6543 oz. ASW, 35 mm. **Ruler:** Rama IX **Subject:** Princess Chulabhorn Awarded Einstein Medal **Obv:** Head of Albert Einstein left within circle at center of hexagon **Rev:** Graduate's bust left **Edge:** Reeded **Note:** Similar to 10 Baht, Y#192. Minted and released in 1987.

Date	Mintage	VF20	XF40	MS60	MS63	MS65
BE2529	2,400	—	—	42.00	48.00	55.00
BE2529	212	PF63 300	PF65 375			

Y# 199 600 BAHT

30.00 g., 0.925 Silver 0.8922 oz. ASW, 37 mm. **Ruler:** Rama IX **Subject:** 60th Birthday - King Rama IX **Obv:** Uniformed bust facing **Rev:** Radiant crowned emblem **Note:** Similar to 6000 Baht, Y#202. Minted and released in 1986.

Date	Mintage	VF20	XF40	MS60	MS63	MS65
BE2530	5,000	—	—	75.00	95.00	115
BE2530	750	PF63 265	PF65 295			

Y# 229 600 BAHT

22.00 g., 0.925 Silver 0.6543 oz. ASW, 35 mm. **Ruler:** Rama IX **Subject:** Rural Development Leadership **Obv:** Kneeling figure left with students **Rev:** Symbol above inscription **Edge:** Reeded **Note:** Similar to 10 Baht, Y#190.

Date	Mintage	VF20	XF40	MS60	MS63	MS65
BE2530	2,700	—	—	30.00	35.00	40.00
BE2530	400	PF63 175	PF65 200			

Y# 215 600 BAHT

30.00 g., 0.925 Silver 0.8922 oz. ASW, 37 mm. **Ruler:** Rama IX **Subject:** 42nd Anniversary - Reign of King Rama IX **Obv:** Uniformed bust facing left **Rev:** Crowned monogram **Note:** Similar to 10 Baht, Y#212.

Date	Mintage	VF20	XF40	MS60	MS63	MS65
BE2531 Plain edge	8,840	—	—	35.00	40.00	45.00
BE2531 Proof, reeded edge	1,110	PF63 110	PF65 125			

Y# 224 600 BAHT

22.00 g., 0.925 Silver 0.6543 oz. ASW, 35 mm. **Ruler:** Rama IX **Subject:** Crown Prince's 36th Birthday **Obv:** Head 1/4 left **Rev:** Crowned monogram within lightning bolts **Edge:** Reeded

Date	Mintage	VF20	XF40	MS60	MS63	MS65
BE2531	5,000	—	—	35.00	40.00	45.00
BE2531	1,000	PF63 115	PF65 130			

Y# 226 600 BAHT

22.00 g., 0.925 Silver 0.6543 oz. ASW, 35 mm. **Ruler:** Rama IX **Subject:** 72nd Anniversary of Chulalongkorn University **Obv:** Conjoined busts left **Rev:** Radiant crown **Edge:** Reeded

Date	Mintage	VF20	XF40	MS60	MS63	MS65
BE2532	10,000	—	—	42.00	48.00	55.00

Y# 234 600 BAHT

22.00 g., 0.925 Silver 0.6543 oz. ASW, 35 mm. **Ruler:** Rama IX **Subject:** 90th Birthday of Princess Mother **Obv:** Bust 1/4 left **Rev:** Crown on stand flanked by others **Edge:** Plain

Date	Mintage	VF20	XF40	MS60	MS63	MS65
BE2533	20,000	—	—	25.00	30.00	35.00
BE2533	2,811	PF63 70.00	PF65 90.00			

Y# 245 600 BAHT

22.00 g., 0.925 Silver 0.6543 oz. ASW, 35 mm. **Ruler:** Rama IX **Subject:** World Health Organization **Obv:** Bust facing **Rev:** Medal with small emblem above **Edge:** Reeded **Note:** Similar to 10 Baht, Y#244. Minted and released in 1991.

Date	Mintage	VF20	XF40	MS60	MS63	MS65
BE2533	25,000	—	—	25.00	30.00	35.00
BE2533	596	PF63 225	PF65 275			

Y# 239 600 BAHT

22.00 g., 0.925 Silver 0.6543 oz. ASW, 35 mm. **Ruler:** Rama IX **Subject:** 36th Birthday of Princess Sirindhorn **Obv:** Uniformed bust 1/4 left **Rev:** Crowned monogram flanked by stars above sprigs **Edge:** Plain

Date	Mintage	VF20	XF40	MS60	MS63	MS65
BE2534	27,000	—	—	25.00	30.00	35.00
BE2534	2,583	PF63 65.00	PF65 80.00			

Y# 257 600 BAHT

22.00 g., 0.925 Silver 0.6543 oz. ASW, 35 mm. **Ruler:** Rama IX **Subject:** Princess Sirindhorn's Magsaysay Foundation Award **Obv:** Seated and kneeling figures within circle **Rev:** Inscription within sprigs and circle below cameo **Note:** Minted and released in 1992.

Date	Mintage	VF20	XF40	MS60	MS63	MS65
BE2534	15,000	—	—	25.00	30.00	35.00
BE2534	1,000	PF63 70.00	PF65 90.00			

Y# 250 600 BAHT

22.00 g., 0.925 Silver 0.6543 oz. ASW, 35 mm. **Ruler:** Rama IX **Subject:** Centenary Celebration - Father of King Rama IX **Obv:** Three crowns on stands **Rev:** Bust facing **Edge:** Plain

Date	Mintage	VF20	XF40	MS60	MS63	MS65
BE2535	18,900	—	—	25.00	30.00	35.00
BE2535	2,169	PF63 60.00	PF65 75.00			

Y# 264 600 BAHT

30.00 g., 0.925 Silver 0.8922 oz. ASW, 37 mm. **Ruler:** Rama IX **Subject:** Queen's 60th Birthday **Obv:** Crowned bust facing **Rev:** Crowned monogram **Edge:** Reeded

Date	Mintage	VF20	XF40	MS60	MS63	MS65
BE2535	25,000	—	—	25.00	30.00	35.00
BE2535	3,500	PF63 65.00	PF65 80.00			

Y# 274 600 BAHT

22.00 g., 0.925 Silver 0.6543 oz. ASW, 35 mm. **Ruler:** Rama IX **Subject:** 64th Birthday - King Rama IX **Obv:** Conjoined busts 1/4 left **Rev:** Crowned monograms **Edge:** Reeded

Date	Mintage	VF20	XF40	MS60	MS63	MS65
BE2535	10,000	—	—	25.00	30.00	35.00
BE2535	542	PF63 250	PF65 280			

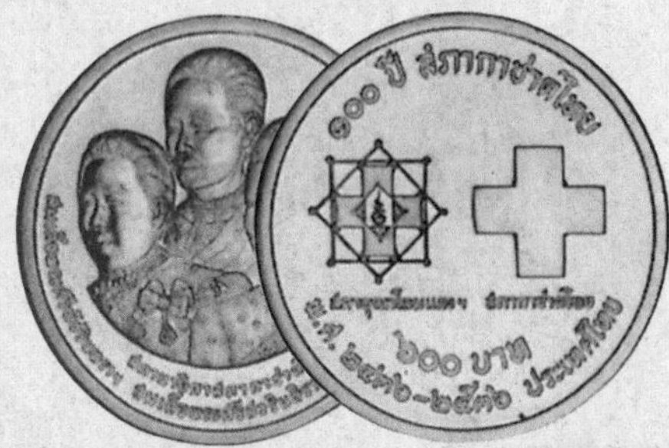

Y# 281 600 BAHT

22.00 g., 0.925 Silver 0.6543 oz. ASW, 35 mm. **Ruler:** Rama IX **Subject:** Centennial of Thai Red Cross **Obv:** Conjoined busts 1/4 left **Rev:** Emblems **Edge:** Reeded

Date	Mintage	VF20	XF40	MS60	MS63	MS65
BE2536	12,500	—	—	25.00	30.00	35.00

Y# 290 600 BAHT

22.00 g., 0.925 Silver 0.6543 oz. ASW, 35 mm. **Ruler:** Rama IX **Subject:** 100th Anniversary of Birth, Rama VII **Obv:** Uniformed bust left **Rev:** Crown and designs within oval **Edge:** Reeded

Date	Mintage	VF20	XF40	MS60	MS63	MS65
BE2536	12,000	—	—	25.00	30.00	35.00
BE2536	1,000	PF63 95.00	PF65 115			

Y# 299 600 BAHT

22.00 g., 0.925 Silver 0.6543 oz. ASW, 35 mm. **Ruler:** Rama IX **Subject:** 120th Anniversary - Ministry of Finance **Obv:** Conjoined busts right **Rev:** Stylized eagle within circle **Edge:** Reeded

Date	Mintage	VF20	XF40	MS60	MS63	MS65
BE2538	17,000	—	—	25.00	30.00	35.00
BE2538	648	PF63 100	PF65 120			

Y# 301 600 BAHT

22.00 g., 0.925 Silver 0.6543 oz. ASW, 35 mm. **Ruler:** Rama IX **Subject:** Ministry of Defense, 108th Anniversary **Obv:** Conjoined uniformed busts facing **Rev:** Mythical animal within circle **Edge:** Reeded

Date	Mintage	VF20	XF40	MS60	MS63	MS65
BE2538	18,000	—	—	25.00	30.00	35.00
BE2538	3,008	PF63 55.00	PF65 65.00			

Y# 303 600 BAHT
22.00 g., 0.925 Silver 0.6543 oz. ASW, 35 mm. **Ruler:** Rama IX **Subject:** Ministry of Foreign Affairs, 120th Anniversary **Obv:** Conjoined busts facing **Rev:** Seated figure within designed circle and wreath **Edge:** Reeded

Date	Mintage	VF20	XF40	MS60	MS63	MS65
BE2538	14,000	—	—	25.00	30.00	35.00
BE2538	997	PF63 75.00	PF65 90.00			

Y# 305 600 BAHT
22.00 g., 0.925 Silver 0.6543 oz. ASW, 35 mm. **Ruler:** Rama IX **Subject:** 72nd Birthday of Princess Calyani Vedhani **Obv:** Uniformed bust 3/4 facing **Rev:** Crowned arms **Edge:** Reeded

Date	Mintage	VF20	XF40	MS60	MS63	MS65
BE2538	15,697	—	—	25.00	30.00	35.00
BE2538	1,216	PF63 60.00	PF65 70.00			

Y# 310 600 BAHT
22.00 g., 0.925 Silver 0.6543 oz. ASW, 35 mm. **Ruler:** Rama IX **Subject:** 80th Anniversary - Department of Revenue **Obv:** Conjoined busts 1/4 left **Rev:** Seated figure within circle **Edge:** Reeded

Date	Mintage	VF20	XF40	MS60	MS63	MS65
BE2538	12,000	—	—	25.00	30.00	35.00
BE2538	2,000	PF63 50.00	PF65 65.00			

Y# 312 600 BAHT
22.00 g., 0.925 Silver 0.6543 oz. ASW, 35 mm. **Ruler:** Rama IX **Subject:** 120th Anniversary - Audit Council **Obv:** Conjoined busts facing **Rev:** Balance scale **Edge:** Reeded

Date	Mintage	VF20	XF40	MS60	MS63	MS65
BE2538	16,305	—	—	25.00	30.00	35.00
BE2538	2,000	PF63 60.00	PF65 70.00			

Y# 324 600 BAHT
30.00 g., 0.925 Silver 0.8922 oz. ASW, 37 mm. **Ruler:** Rama IX **Subject:** 50th Anniversary - Reign of King Rama IX **Obv:** Bust facing **Rev:** National arms **Edge:** Reeded **Note:** Similar to 20 Baht, Y#321.1.

Date	Mintage	VF20	XF40	MS60	MS63	MS65
BE2539	100,814	—	—	25.00	30.00	35.00
BE2539	24,003	PF63 60.00	PF65 70.00			

Y# 356 600 BAHT
22.00 g., 0.925 Silver 0.6543 oz. ASW, 35 mm. **Ruler:** Rama IX **Subject:** King's 6th Cycle Birthday (72nd) **Obv:** Bust facing **Rev:** Radiant arms **Edge:** Reeded

Date	Mintage	VF20	XF40	MS60	MS63	MS65
BE2542	47,811	—	—	20.00	24.00	28.00
BE2542	10,011	PF63 35.00	PF65 40.00			

Y# 377 600 BAHT
22.00 g., 0.925 Silver 0.6543 oz. ASW, 35 mm. **Ruler:** Rama IX **Subject:** Rama IX reaches age of Rama I at his death **Obv:** King and Rama I portraits **Rev:** Two royal symbols **Edge:** Reeded **Note:** Minted and released in 2001.

Date	Mintage	VF20	XF40	MS60	MS63	MS65
BE2543 (2000)	5,000	—	—	35.00	55.00	75.00
BE2543 (2000)	1,400	PF63 95.00	PF65 115			

Y# 94 800 BAHT
20.00 g., 0.900 Gold 0.5787 oz. AGW, 30 mm. **Ruler:** Rama IX **Subject:** 25th Anniversary - Reign of King Rama IX **Obv:** Head right **Rev:** Radiant crowned monogram flanked by sprigs **Edge:** Reeded

Date	Mintage	VF20	XF40	MS60	MS63	MS65
BE2514	22,243	—	—	770	950	1,100

Y# 200 1500 BAHT
3.75 g., 0.900 Gold 0.1085 oz. AGW, 17 mm. **Ruler:** Rama IX **Subject:** 60th Birthday - King Rama IX **Obv:** Bust facing **Rev:** Radiant crowned emblem **Edge:** Reeded **Note:** Minted and released in 1986.

Date	Mintage	VF20	XF40	MS60	MS63	MS65
BE2530	400	—	145	200	235	270
BE2530	5,000	PF63 250	PF65 275			

Y# 216 1500 BAHT
3.75 g., 0.900 Gold 0.1085 oz. AGW, 17 mm. **Ruler:** Rama IX **Subject:** 42nd Anniversary - Reign of King Rama IX **Obv:** Bust facing **Rev:** Crowned monogram **Edge:** Reeded

Date	Mintage	VF20	XF40	MS60	MS63	MS65
BE2531	11,373	—	145	200	225	260
BE2531	995	PF63 260	PF65 285			

Y# 265 1500 BAHT
3.75 g., 0.900 Gold 0.1085 oz. AGW, 17 mm. **Ruler:** Rama IX **Subject:** Queen's 60th Birthday **Obv:** Crowned bust facing **Rev:** Crowned monogram **Edge:** Reeded **Note:** Similar to 10 Baht, Y#261.

Date	Mintage	VF20	XF40	MS60	MS63	MS65
BE2535	10,000	—	145	200	225	260
BE2535	1,500	PF63 260	PF65 285			

Y# 487 1500 BAHT
3.75 g., 0.900 Gold 0.1085 oz. AGW, 17 mm. **Ruler:** Rama IX **Subject:** Rama IX, 50th Anniversary of Reign **Obv:** Bust facing **Edge:** Reeded

Date	Mintage	VF20	XF40	MS60	MS63	MS65
BE2539 (1996)	63,068	—	145	200	225	260
BE2539 (1996)	12,940	PF63 250	PF65 270			

Y# 380 2000 BAHT
6.22 g., 0.999 Gold 0.1998 oz. AGW, 22 mm. **Ruler:** Rama IX **Subject:** 50th Anniversary of UNICEF **Obv:** Bust 3/4 left **Rev:** Girl with Thai desk **Edge:** Reeded **Note:** Minted and released in 1998.

Date	Mintage	VF20	XF40	MS60	MS63	MS65
BE2540-1997	1,290	PF63 425	PF65 450			

Y# 119 2500 BAHT
15.00 g., 0.900 Gold 0.434 oz. AGW, 27 mm. **Ruler:** Rama IX **Subject:** Crown Prince Vajiralongkorn and Princess Soamsawali Wedding **Obv:** Conjoined busts right **Rev:** Crowned monogram within lightning bolts **Edge:** Reeded

Date	Mintage	VF20	XF40	MS60	MS63	MS65
BE2520	20,000	—	—	675	750	800

Y# 126 2500 BAHT
15.00 g., 0.900 Gold 0.434 oz. AGW, 25 mm. **Ruler:** Rama IX **Subject:** Investiture of Princess Sirindhorn **Obv:** Bust 1/4 right **Rev:** Crowned monogram **Edge:** Plain

Date	Mintage	VF20	XF40	MS60	MS63	MS65
BE2520	5,000	—	—	700	775	825

Y# 170 2500 BAHT
15.98 g., 0.9166 Gold 0.4709 oz. AGW, 28.4 mm. **Ruler:** Rama IX **Series:** International Year of Disabled Persons **Obv:** Bust left **Rev:** Emblem within sprigs **Edge:** Reeded

Date	Mintage	VF20	XF40	MS60	MS63	MS65
BE2526	92	—	—	—	2,500	3,000
BE2526	105	PF63 3,000	PF65 3,500			

Y# 207 2500 BAHT
15.98 g., 0.900 Gold 0.4624 oz. AGW, 28.4 mm. **Ruler:** Rama IX **Series:** 25th Anniversary of World Wildlife Fund **Obv:** Bust left **Rev:** Elephant left within circle **Edge:** Reeded

Date	Mintage	VF20	XF40	MS60	MS63	MS65
BE2530-1987	3,218	PF63 800	PF65 850			

Y# 369 2500 BAHT
155.52 g., 0.9999 Gold 4.9995 oz. AGW, 55 mm. **Ruler:** Rama IX **Subject:** Year of the Dragon **Obv:** Bust left **Rev:** Two dragons with pearl hologram **Edge:** Reeded

Date	Mintage	VF20	XF40	MS60	MS63	MS65
BE2543 sg	1,500	PF65 9,000				

Note: Sets only

Y# 129 3000 BAHT
15.00 g., 0.900 Gold 0.434 oz. AGW, 26 mm. **Ruler:** Rama IX **Subject:** Graduation of Crown Prince Vijiralongkorn **Obv:** Bust left **Rev:** Crowned elephant head facing within frame **Edge:** Reeded

Date	Mintage	VF20	XF40	MS60	MS63	MS65
BE2521	10,000	—	—	—	775	825

Y# 201 3000 BAHT
7.50 g., 0.900 Gold 0.217 oz. AGW, 21 mm. **Ruler:** Rama IX **Subject:** 60th Birthday - King Rama IX **Obv:** Uniformed bust facing **Rev:** Radiant crowned emblem **Edge:** Reeded **Note:** Minted and released in 1986.

Date	Mintage	VF20	XF40	MS60	MS63	MS65
BE2530	3,000	—	—	350	400	435
BE2530	400	PF63 500	PF65 550			

Y# 217 3000 BAHT
7.50 g., 0.900 Gold 0.217 oz. AGW, 21 mm. **Ruler:** Rama IX **Subject:** 42nd Anniversary - Reign of King Rama IX **Obv:** Uniformed bust facing **Rev:** Radiant crowned monogram **Edge:** Reeded

Date	Mintage	VF20	XF40	MS60	MS63	MS65
BE2531	7,904	—	—	325	375	435
BE2531	780	PF63 650	PF65 750			

Y# 266 3000 BAHT
7.50 g., 0.900 Gold 0.217 oz. AGW, 21 mm. **Ruler:** Rama IX **Subject:** Queen's 60th Birthday **Obv:** Crowned bust facing **Rev:** Crowned monogram **Edge:** Reeded

Date	Mintage	VF20	XF40	MS60	MS63	MS65
BE2535	7,000	—	—	325	375	435
BE2535	1,100	PF63 475	PF65 500			

Y# 326 3000 BAHT
7.50 g., 0.900 Gold 0.217 oz. AGW, 21 mm. **Ruler:** Rama IX **Subject:** 50th Anniversary - Reign of King Rama IX **Obv:** Uniformed bust facing **Rev:** National arms **Edge:** Reeded

Date	Mintage	VF20	XF40	MS60	MS63	MS65
BE2539	35,057	—	—	300	350	425
BE2539	9,408	PF63 450	PF65 475			

Y# 153 4000 BAHT
17.17 g., 0.900 Gold 0.4968 oz. AGW **Ruler:** Rama IX **Series:** International Year of the Child **Obv:** Bust left **Rev:** Two children playing

Date	Mintage	XF40	MS60	MS63	MS65	MS66
BE2524	3,963	PF67 1,750	PF69 2,150			

Y# 104 5000 BAHT
33.44 g., 0.900 Gold 0.9675 oz. AGW, 34 mm. **Ruler:** Rama IX **Series:** Conservation **Obv:** Bust 1/4 left **Rev:** White-eyed River Martin **Edge:** Reeded

Date	Mintage	XF40	MS60	MS63	MS65	MS66
BE2517	2,602	—	1,850	1,950	2,000	—
BE2517	623	PF67 2,250	PF69 2,750			

Y# 122 5000 BAHT
30.00 g., 0.900 Gold 0.8681 oz. AGW, 30 mm. **Ruler:** Rama IX **Subject:** 50th Birthday - King Rama IX **Obv:** Bust left **Rev:** Radiant crowned monogram **Edge:** Reeded

Date	Mintage	VF20	XF40	MS60	MS63	MS65
BE2520	6,400	—	—	1,650	1,750	1,950

Y# 156 6000 BAHT
15.00 g., 0.900 Gold 0.434 oz. AGW, 26 mm. **Ruler:** Rama IX **Subject:** 50th Birthday - Queen Sirikit **Obv:** Crowned bust 1/4 left **Rev:** Crowned monogram **Edge:** Reeded

Date	Mintage	VF20	XF40	MS60	MS63	MS65
BE2525	1,431	—	—	750	850	900
BE2525	99	PF63 4,250	PF65 4,500			

Y# 167 6000 BAHT
15.00 g., 0.900 Gold 0.434 oz. AGW, 26 mm. **Ruler:** Rama IX **Subject:** 700th Anniversary - Thai Alphabet **Obv:** Seated figure left **Rev:** Inscription **Edge:** Reeded

Date	Mintage	VF20	XF40	MS60	MS63	MS65
BE2526	700	—	—	775	875	950
BE2526	235	PF63 1,650	PF65 1,800			

Y# 174 6000 BAHT
15.00 g., 0.900 Gold 0.434 oz. AGW, 26 mm. **Ruler:** Rama IX **Subject:** 84th Birthday - Princess Mother **Obv:** Bust left **Rev:** Crown on stand flanked by others **Edge:** Reeded

Date	Mintage	VF20	XF40	MS60	MS63	MS65
BE2527	835	—	—	775	875	950
BE2527	246	PF63 1,650	PF65 1,800			

Y# 202 6000 BAHT
15.00 g., 0.900 Gold 0.434 oz. AGW, 27 mm. **Ruler:** Rama IX **Subject:** 60th Birthday - King Rama IX **Obv:** Uniformed bust facing **Rev:** Radiant crowned emblem **Edge:** Reeded **Note:** Minted and issued in BE2529

Date	Mintage	VF20	XF40	MS60	MS63	MS65
BE2530	2,000	—	—	725	825	850
BE2530	350	PF63 850	PF65 900			

Y# 247 6000 BAHT
15.00 g., 0.900 Gold 0.434 oz. AGW, 26 mm. **Ruler:** Rama IX **Subject:** Asian Institute of Technology **Obv:** Kneeling and seated figures within circle **Rev:** Emblem **Edge:** Reeded

Date	Mintage	VF20	XF40	MS60	MS63	MS65
BE2530	700	—	—	750	850	875
BE2530	100	PF63 900	PF65 1,000			

Y# 218 6000 BAHT
15.00 g., 0.900 Gold 0.434 oz. AGW, 27 mm. **Ruler:** Rama IX **Subject:** 42nd Anniversary - Reign of King Rama IX **Obv:** Uniformed bust facing **Rev:** Radiant crowned monogram **Edge:** Reeded

Date	Mintage	VF20	XF40	MS60	MS63	MS65
BE2531	6,067	—	—	725	825	850
BE2531	670	PF63 1,250	PF65 1,300			

Y# 246 6000 BAHT
15.00 g., 0.900 Gold 0.434 oz. AGW, 26 mm. **Ruler:** Rama IX **Subject:** Queen Mother's role in World Health Organization **Obv:** Queen Mother facing 1/4 left **Rev:** Medal with inscription "HEALTH FOR ALL" and value **Note:** Minted and issued in BE2534

Date	Mintage	VF20	XF40	MS60	MS63	MS65
BE2533 (1990)	5,000	—	—	725	825	850
BE2534 (1990)	604	PF63 900	PF65 1,000			

Y# 258 6000 BAHT
15.00 g., 0.900 Gold 0.434 oz. AGW, 26 mm. **Ruler:** Rama IX **Subject:** Princess Sirindhorn's Magsaysay Foundation Award **Obv:** Princess seated with children **Rev:** Obverse of medal above larger reverse with inscription **Edge:** Reeded

Date	Mintage	VF20	XF40	MS60	MS63	MS65
BE2535	1,636	—	—	750	850	875
BE2535	500	PF63 950	PF65 1,100			

Y# 267 6000 BAHT
15.00 g., 0.900 Gold 0.434 oz. AGW, 27 mm. **Ruler:** Rama IX **Subject:** Queen's 60th Birthday **Obv:** Crowned bust facing **Rev:** Crowned monogram **Edge:** Reeded

Date	Mintage	VF20	XF40	MS60	MS63	MS65
BE2535	7,000	—	—	675	775	800
BE2535	1,200	PF63 850	PF65 900			

Y# 275 6000 BAHT
15.00 g., 0.900 Gold 0.434 oz. AGW, 27 mm. **Ruler:** Rama IX **Subject:** 64th Birthday - King Rama IX **Obv:** Conjoined busts left **Rev:** Crowned monograms **Edge:** Reeded **Note:** Minted and issues in BE 2535

Date	Mintage	VF20	XF40	MS60	MS63	MS65
BE2534 (1991)	3,000	—	—	700	800	825
BE2534 (1991)	500	PF63 875	PF65 950			

Y# 291 6000 BAHT
15.00 g., 0.900 Gold 0.434 oz. AGW, 26 mm. **Ruler:** Rama IX **Subject:** 100th Anniversary of Rama VII **Obv:** Bust left **Rev:** Royal crown and accoutrements **Edge:** Reeded

Date	Mintage	VF20	XF40	MS60	MS63	MS65
BE2536	2,484	—	—	700	800	825
BE2536	300	PF63 875	PF65 950			

Y# 327 6000 BAHT

15.00 g., 0.900 Gold 0.434 oz. AGW, 27 mm. **Ruler:** Rama IX **Subject:** King's 50th Year of Reign **Obv:** Uniformed bust facing **Rev:** National arms **Edge:** Reeded

Date	Mintage	VF20	XF40	MS60	MS63	MS65
BE2539	35,331	—	—	675	775	800
BE2539	9,044	PF63 850	PF65 900			

Y# 337 6000 BAHT

15.00 g., 0.900 Gold 0.434 oz. AGW, 26 mm. **Ruler:** Rama IX **Series:** F.A.O. **Subject:** 50th Anniversary - Reign of King Rama IX and World Food Summit **Obv:** Bust left within circle **Rev:** King planting seedlings before adoring crowd **Edge:** Reeded

Date	Mintage	VF20	XF40	MS60	MS63	MS65
BE2539	2,562	—	—	700	800	825
BE2539	2,562	PF63 875	PF65 950			

Y# 370 6000 BAHT

15.00 g., 0.900 Gold 0.434 oz. AGW, 26 mm. **Ruler:** Rama IX **Subject:** King's 72nd Birthday **Obv:** King's portrait **Rev:** Crowned emblem **Edge:** Reeded

Date	Mintage	VF20	XF40	MS60	MS63	MS65
BE2542	15,011	—	—	675	775	800
BE2542	1,211	PF63 850	PF65 900			

Y# 378 6000 BAHT

15.00 g., 0.900 Gold 0.434 oz. AGW, 26 mm. **Ruler:** Rama IX **Subject:** King's 73rd Birthday, Ag King Rama I **Obv:** King and Rama I portraits **Rev:** Two royal symbols **Edge:** Reeded

Date	Mintage	VF20	XF40	MS60	MS63	MS65
BE2534 (2000)	2,500	—	—	700	800	825
BE2543(2000)	531	PF63 875	PF65 950			

Y# 139 9000 BAHT

12.00 g., 0.900 Gold 0.3472 oz. AGW, 24 mm. **Ruler:** Rama IX **Series:** F.A.O. Ceres Medal **Subject:** Queen's Anniversary **Obv:** Crowned bust 3/4 facing left **Rev:** Medal design

Date	Mintage	VF20	XF40	MS60	MS63	MS65
BE2523	3,900	—	—	550	650	700

Y# A143 9000 BAHT

12.00 g., 0.900 Gold 0.3472 oz. AGW, 24 mm. **Ruler:** Rama IX **Subject:** Centennial - Birth of King Rama VI **Obv:** Uniformed bust right **Rev:** Radiant crown on stand flanked by others **Edge:** Reeded

Date	Mintage	VF20	XF40	MS60	MS63	MS65
BE2524	2,600	—	—	550	650	700

Y# 148 9000 BAHT

15.00 g., 0.900 Gold 0.434 oz. AGW, 26 mm. **Ruler:** Rama IX **Subject:** King Rama IX Anniversary of Reign twice the length of King Rama IV **Obv:** Conjoined busts left and inscription **Rev:** Two symbols, inscription, value and date **Edge:** Reeded

Date	Mintage	VF20	XF40	MS60	MS63	MS65
BE2524	4,000	—	—	725	825	850

Y# 151 9000 BAHT

15.00 g., 0.900 Gold 0.434 oz. AGW, 26 mm. **Ruler:** Rama IX **Subject:** Bicentennial of Bangkok **Obv:** Uniformed conjoined busts left and inscription **Rev:** Emblem, inscriptions, value and date

Date	Mintage	VF20	XF40	MS60	MS63	MS65
BE2525	3,290	—	—	725	825	850

OCCUPATION COINAGE

These coins were to be circulated in the four occupied provinces of Malaya during World War II. They were not put into circulation there but were later used in Japanese military service clubs in Bangkok before Japan's surrender in 1945.

KM# 5 SEN

Tin **Ruler:** Rama VIII **Obv:** Mythical creature "Garuda" **Rev:** Value

Date	Mintage	F12	VF20	XF40	MS60	MS63
BE2486	—	—	—	7,000	—	—

KM# 10 5 SEN

Tin **Ruler:** Rama VIII **Obv:** Mythical creature "Garuda" **Rev:** Value within beaded circle

Date	Mintage	F12	VF20	XF40	MS60	MS63
BE2486	—	—	—	5,000	—	—

KM# 15 10 SEN

Tin **Ruler:** Rama VIII **Obv:** Mythical creature "Garuda" **Rev:** Value within beaded circle

Date	Mintage	F12	VF20	XF40	MS60	MS63
BE2486	—	—	—	4,000	—	—

BULLION COINAGE

In 1943, the government of Thailand made an internal loan by virtue of the Royal Act of Internal Loan related regulation of the Ministry of Finance, both dated 17th May, 1943.

Eight years later another Regulation of the Ministry of Finance dated 11th June, 1951 related to the actual redemption of the loan above mentioned was proclaimed with the following effect: Bond holders have the choice to be paid either in gold coins or gold bars or in other forms, all of which should bear the Garuda emblem and the specific inscription as to its weight and gold purity.

KM# 1 50 BAHT

8.69 g., 0.995 Gold 0.2781 oz. AGW **Ruler:** Rama IX **Obv:** Mythical creature "Garuda" flanked by sprigs **Rev:** Inscription

Date	Mintage	F12	VF20	XF40	MS60	MS63
ND-1951	—	—	750	1,500	2,500	—

KM# 2 100 BAHT

17.39 g., 0.995 Gold 0.5562 oz. AGW **Ruler:** Rama IX **Obv:** Mythical creature "Garuda" flanked by sprigs **Rev:** Inscription

Date	Mintage	F12	VF20	XF40	MS60	MS63
ND-1951	—	—	1,250	2,500	3,750	—

KM# 3 1000 BAHT

173.88 g., 0.995 Gold 5.5624 oz. AGW **Ruler:** Rama IX **Obv:** Mythical creature "Garuda" flanked by sprigs **Rev:** Inscription

Date	Mintage	F12	VF20	XF40	MS60	MS63
ND-1951	—	9,500	10,500	11,500	14,500	—

TRIAL STRIKES

KM#	Date	Mintage	Identification	Mkt Val
TS1	ND (1963)	—	20 Baht. Copper. Trial strike in copper of 20 Baht, Y#86.	—

ESSAIS

KM#	Date	Mintage	Identification	Mkt Val
E1	RS127 (1908)	—	Baht. Silver. Y#39.	23,000
E2	RS128 (1909)	—	1/4 Baht. Silver.	10,000
E3	RS129 (1910)	—	1/2 Baht. Silver.	—

Note: Struck at the Paris Mint. Taisei-Baldwin-Gillio Hong Kong sale 25 9-97 BU realized $23,000. Spink-Taisei Singapore Auction 14 3-93 Unc set of E 1, 2 and 2 realized $190,000

PATTERNS

Including off metal strikes

KM#	Date	Mintage	Identification	Mkt Val
Pn47	RS124 (1905)	—	2 Att. Copper. Facing bust.	10,000
Pn48	RS126 (1907)	—	Baht. Silver. Y#39. Vishnu and Garuda.	40,000
Pn49	RS127 (1908)	—	Satang. Nickel. Y#35.	3,000
Pn50	RS127 (1908)	—	Satang. Gold. Y#35a.	9,000
Pn51	RS127 (1908)	—	5 Satang. Gold. Y#36a.	7,000
Pn52	RS127 (1908)	—	10 Satang. Gold. Y#37a.	8,000
Pn53	RS129 (1910)	—	Baht. Silver. Y#39.	—
PnA54	BE2488 (1945)	—	Baht. Tin. Child's head of King Rama VIII (Ananda Mahidol) facing left. National arms.	—
Pn54	BE2489 (1946)	—	Baht. Tin. Y#67.	—
Pn55	BE2505 (1962)	—	Baht. Copper-Nickel. Y#84.	—
Pn56	BE2515 (1972)	—	5 Baht. Copper-Nickel. Small bust, Y#28.	—
Pn57	BE2515 (1972)	—	5 Baht. Copper-Nickel. Royal parasol.	—
Pn58	BE2515 (1972)	—	5 Baht. Copper-Nickel. Different bust.	125

PIEDFORT

KM#	Date	Mintage	Identification	Mkt Val
P1	BE2524 (1981)	126	200 Baht. I.Y.O.C.	2,000
P2	BE2524 (1981)	61	4000 Baht. Gold. I.Y.O.C.	4,000
P3	BE2526 (1983)	500	250 Baht. 0.925. Silver. I.Y.D.P.	2,000
P4	BE2526 (1983)	Est. 100	2500 Baht. Gold. I.Y.D.P.	7,000
P5	BE2540 (1997)	—	100 Baht. 0.925. Silver. WWF Tiger.	75.00
P6	BE2541 (1998)	—	200 Baht. 0.925. Silver. WWF Tigers.	120
P7	BE2541 (1998)	—	200 Baht. 0.925. Silver. WWF Elephants.	140

MINT SETS

KM#	Date	Mintage	Identification	Issue Price	Mkt Val
MS2	Mixed (16)	—	Two each Y#57, 70, 72, 73, 78a, 78-87, 91	22.00	90.00
MS3	Mixed (15)	100,000	Two each Y#60, 70, 72, 73, 78, 78a, 79, 79a, 80-86	20.00	80.00
MS4	Mixed (10)	—	Y#70, 72, 73, 78, 78a, 79, 79a, 80-82	—	15.00
MS5	Mixed (10)	—	Y#70, 78, 78a, 78b, 79a, 79b, 79d, 80, 81, 82	—	37.50
MS6	Mixed (8)	—	Y#83, 85-87, 91, 92, 95, 97	11.00	70.00
MS7	1975 (2)	—	Y#102-103	32.50	75.00
MS8	1988 (7)	—	Y#183, 185-187, 203, 208-209	—	4.00
MS9	1991 (8)	—	Y#183, 186-187, 203, 208-209, 219, 227	4.00	12.50
MS10	1992 (8)	—	Y#183, 186-187, 203, 208-209, 219, 227	—	10.00
MS11	1993 (8)	—	Y#183, 186-187, 203, 208-209, 219, 227	—	10.00
MS12	1994 (8)	—	Y#183, 186-187, 203, 208-209, 219, 227	—	10.00

MS13	Mixed (17)	—	Two each Y#57, 70, 72-73, 78, 78a, 79, 79a, 80-87, 91	—	90.00
MS14	Mixed (15)	—	Y#86 plus two each Y#57, 68, 73, 78, 78a, 79, 79a, 80-85, 87	—	85.00

PROOF SETS

KM#	Date	Mintage	Identification	Issue Price	Mkt Val
PS1	1974 (2)	—	Y#102a-103a	50.00	140
PS2	2000 (3)	3,500	Y#363-365	115	700
PS3	2000 (5)	500	Y#363-365, 367, 369	3,480	10,000
PS4	2000 (2)	1,800	Y#366, 368	446	1,450

TIBET

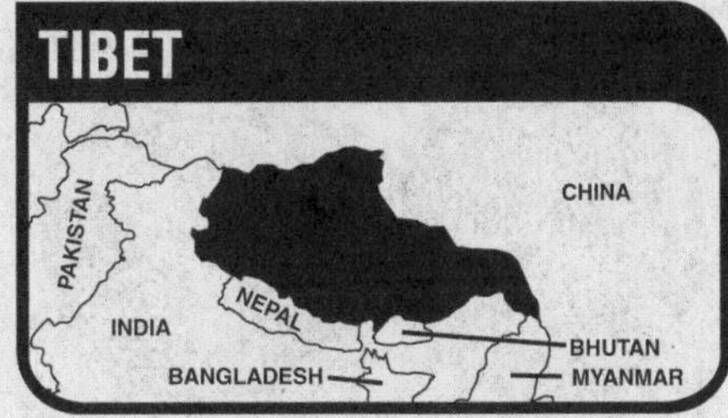

Tibet, an autonomous region of China located in central Asia between the Himalayan and Kunlun Mountains. has an area of 471,660 sq. mi. (1,221,599 sq. km.) and a population of *1.9 million. Capital: Lhasa. The economy is based on agriculture and livestock. Wool, livestock, salt and hides are exported.

Lamaism, a form of Buddhism, developed in Tibet in the 8th century. From that time until the 1900s, the Tibetan rulers virtually isolated the country from the outside world. The British in India achieved some influence in the early 20th century. British troops were sent with the F. E. Younghusband mission to extend trade in the north of India in December 1903; leaving during September 1904. The 13th Dalai Lama had fled to Urga where he remained until 1907. In April 1905 a revolt broke out and spread through southwestern Szechuan and northwestern Yunnan. Chao Erh-feng was appointed to subdue this rebellion and entered Lhasa in January 1910 with 2,000 troops. The Dalai Lama fled to India until he returned in June 1912. The British encouraged Tibet to declare its independence from China in 1913. The Communist revolution in China marked a new era in Tibetan history. Chinese Communist troops invaded Tibet in October 1950. After a token resistance, Tibet signed an agreement with China in which China recognized the spiritual and temporal leadership of the Dalai Lama, and Tibet recognized the suzerainty of China. In 1959, a nationwide revolt triggered by Communist-initiated land reform broke out. The revolt was ruthlessly crushed. The Dalai Lama fled to India, and on Sept. 1,1965, the Chinese made Tibet an autonomous region of China.

The first coins to circulate in Tibet were those of neighboring Nepal from about 1570. Shortly after 1720, the Nepalese government began striking specific issues for use in Tibet. These coins had a lower silver content than those struck for use in Nepal and were exchanged with the Tibetans for an equal weight in silver bullion. Around 1763 the Tibetans struck their own coins for the first time in history. The number of coins struck at that time must have been very small. Larger quantities of coins were struck by the Tibetan government mint, which opened in 1791 with the permission of the Chinese. Operations of this mint however were suspended two years later. The Chinese opened a second mint in Lhasa in 1792. It produced a coinage until 1836. Shortly thereafter, the Tibetan mint was reopened and the government of Tibet continued to strike coins until 1953.

DATING

Based on the Tibetan calendar, Tibetan coins are dated by the cycle, which contains 60 years. To calculate the western date use the following formula: Number of cycles -1, x 60 + number of years + 1026. Example 15th cycle 25th year = 1891 AD. Example: 15th cycle, 25th year 15 - 1 x 60 + 25 + 1026 = 1891AD.

13/30 = 1776	14/30 = 1836	15/30 = 1896
13/40 = 1786	14/40 = 1846	15/40 = 1906
13/50 = 1796	14/50 = 1856	15/50 = 1916
13/60 = 1806	14/60 = 1866	15/60 = 1926
14/10 = 1816	15/10 = 1876	16/10 = 1936
14/20 = 1826	15/20 = 1886	16/20 = 1946

Certain Sino-Tibetan issues are dated in the year of reign of the Emperor of China.

TIBETAN CURRENCY UNITS

Tibet had a dual and therefore complicated system of currency units. One was imported from Nepal and its basic unit is the "tangka" (also called 'trangks', 'tam' or 'tamga', equivalent to about 5.4 to 5.6 grams of alloyed silver) and the other was imported from China and its basic unit is the "srang" (Chinese *liang*, , equivalent to 37.3 grams of silver). These two systems were used in Tibet concurrently from about 1640 until 1959. The respective value was calculated as follows:

1 Srang = 6-2/3 Tangkas
1 Tangka = 1-1/2 Sho = 15 Skar
½ Tangka = 7-1/2 Skar
1 Sho = 2/3 Tangka = 10 Skar

The subdivisions of the Srang were as follows:

1 Srang = 10 Zho = 100 Skar
1 Sho = 10 Skar
1 srang was called *Srang Gang*
1 Sho was called *Zho Gang*
2 Sho were called *Zho Do*
1 Skar was called *Skar Gang*

In the 20th century the following units were struck:

Copper
½ Skar (Skar Che)
1 Skar (Skar Gang)
1/8 Sho
¼ Sho
2-1/2 Skar (Skar Phyed Gsum or Kha Gang)
5 Skar (Skar Inga)
7-1/2 Skar (Skar Phyed Brgyad)
1 Sho
3 Sho
5 Sho

Silver or Billon
1 Tangka
1 Sho (Zho Gang)
2 Sho (Zho Do)
5 Sho (Zho Inga)
1 Srang (Srang Gang)
1-1/2 Srang (Srang Gang Zho Inga)
3 Srang (Srang Sum)
5 Srang (in limited numbers; this coin was also struck in copper)
10 Srang (Srang Bcu)

Gold
20 Srang (Gser Tam)

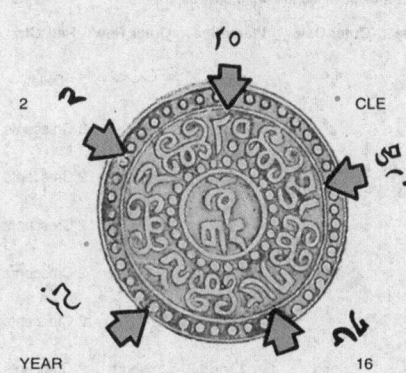

TANGKA
CY
2 CLE
YEAR 16

16(th)CYCLE 2(nd)YEAR = 1928AD

"CYCLE"

7 (YEAR) 16 (CYCLE)

16(th) CYCLE 7(th) YEAR = 1933AD

NUMERALS

1	༡	གཅིག
2	༢	གཉིས
3	༣	གསུམ
4	༤	བཞི
5	༥	ལྔ
6	༦	དྲུག
7	༧	བདུན
8	༨	བརྒྱད
9	༩	དགུ
10	༡༠	བཅུ or བཅུ་ཐམ་པ
11	༡༡	བཅུག or བཅུ་གཅིག
12	༡༢	བཅུས or བཅུ་གཉིས
13	༡༣	བཅུ་མ or བཅུ་གསུམ
14	༡༤	བཅུ་བཞི
15	༡༥	བཅོ་ལྔ
16	༡༦	བཅུ་དྲུག
17	༡༧	བཅུ་བདུན
18	༡༨	བཅོ་བརྒྱད
19	༡༩	བཅུ་དགུ
20	༢༠	ཉི་ཤུ
21	༢༡	ཉི་ཤུ་རྩ་གཅིག or ཉེར་གཅིག
22	༢༢	ཉེར་གཉིས
23	༢༣	ཉེར་གསུམ
24	༢༤	ཉེར་བཞི
25	༢༥	ཉེར་ལྔ
26	༢༦	ཉེར་དྲུག
27	༢༧	ཉེར་བདུན
28	༢༨	ཉེར་བརྒྱད

TIBETAN AUTHORITY

TIBETAN TANGKA COINAGE

The legend of this Tangka appears to be in ornamental Lantsa (Ranjana)script and has yet to be deciphered. The type is a copy of the Nepalese debased Tangka of Pratap Simha. Struck unofficially by Nepalese traders in Tibet between 1880 and 1912, it was legal tender, due to an edict issued in 1881 ordering that no distinction be made between false and genuine coins. The Tangka, C#27 was cut in parts of 3, 4, and 5 petals to make change and the resulting fractions are occasionally encountered.

C# 27.1 RANJANA TANGKA

Silver **Obv:** Crescent and sun at top **Mint:** (no Mint Information) **Note:** Weight varies: 3.60-5.40 grams. Diameter varies: 28.2-28.8mm. 2 varieties exist with large or small circle around lotus. Varieties of ornamentation as well as style of inscription exist. Prev. #C27.

Date	Mintage	G4	VG8	F12	VF20	XF40
BE15-40 (1906)	—	8.00	15.00	25.00	40.00	70.00

Note: In addition to the meaningful dates, the following meaningless ones exist: 13-16, 13-31, 13-92, 15-40, 16-16, 16-61, 16-64, 16-69, 16-92, 16-93, 92-34, 92-39, 96-61 (sixes may be reversed threes and nines reversed ones).

C# 27.2 RANJANA TANGKA
4.50 g., Silver **Obv:** Crescent and swastika at top **Mint:** (no Mint Information) **Note:** See note for C#27.1.

Date	Mintage	G4	VG8	F12	VF20	XF40
BE15-46 (1912)	—	60.00	80.00	125	175	350

GA-DEN TANGKA COINAGE

Hammered

The Ga-den Tangkas are among the most common and perhaps most beautiful of all Tibetan silver coins. The obverse shows a stylized Lotus flower within a circle surrounded by the 8 Buddhist lucky symbols in radiating petals. The reverse shows an 8-petalled wheel (flower) within a star surrounded by a Tibetan inscription (reading Ga-den Palace, victorious in all directions), which is broken up into 8 oval frames. The Ga-den Palace is the former residence of the Dala Lamas, located in Drepung Monastery near Lhasa. On Tibetan coins the name "Ga-den Palace" is used as epithet for "Tibetan Government". Compass directions indicate the location of the Buddhist emblems.

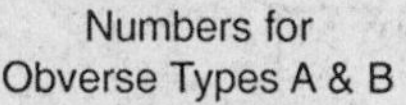
Numbers for Obverse Types A & B

Numbers for Obverse Types C thru H

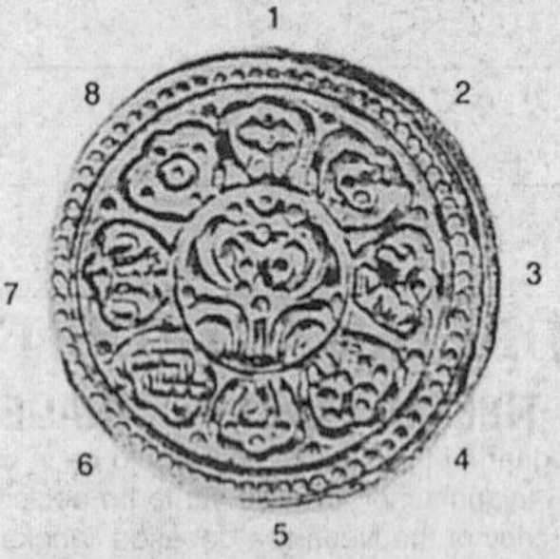

1. Umbrella of sovereignty.
2. Two golden fish of good fortune.
3. Amphora of ambrosia.
4. Lotus.
5. Conch shell.
6. Emblem of endless birth.
7. Banner of victory.
8. Wheel of empire.

Reverse - All Types

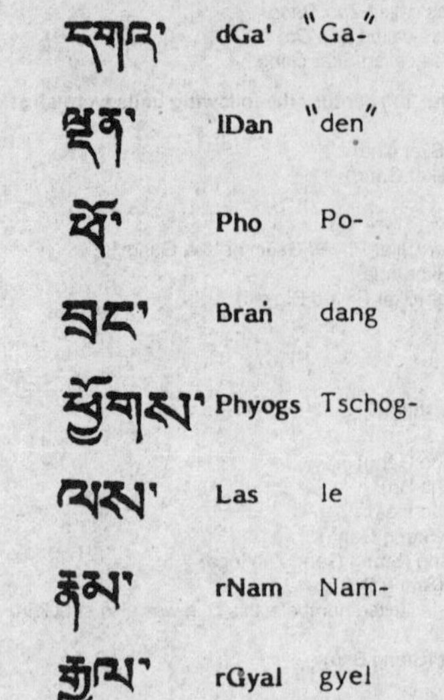

Based on the ornamentation in the outer angles between the petals on both sides of the coin, the Ga-Den Tangkas can be differentiated in the following 8 types, A-H.

Type	Outer Obv.	Water-line	Outer Rev.	Rev. Ctr.
A	⁖	None	~~~	Pellet
B	⁖	2 lines	~~~	3 Crescents
C	⁖	1 line	~~~	2 Crescents
D	⁖	1 line	⁖	2 Crescents
E	~~~	1 line	⁖	2 Crescents
F	•	1 line	⁖	2 Crescents
G	None	1 line	None	2 Crescents
H	•	1 line	•	3 Crescents

Within these types, changes in the order, design, and style of the 8 lucky signs or significant errors constitute subtypes. The subtypes appearing in this catalog are not the only ones. Some subtypes show a wide range of styles and die varieties. Weights given include 95 percent of the indicated types.

Error strikes with muled reverses exist. Specimens of Types D, E, and F with lumps are known, reportedly containing gold, probably used by high lamas in their offerings.

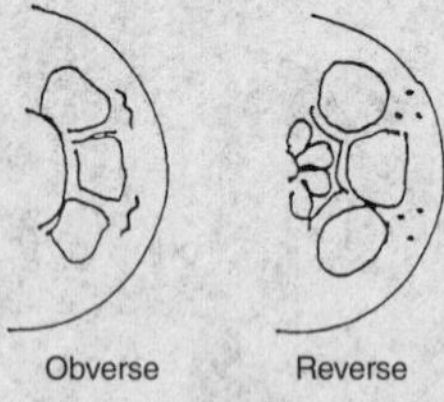

Obverse has wavy water line in outer angles. New style lotus without three small leaves to left and right. Reverse has three dots in outer angles, wheel with spokes.

Hammered

Y# C13.1 TANGKA (1-1/2 Sho)
Silver **Rev:** Central wheel spokes extend to octagon **Mint:** (no Mint Information) **Note:** Weight varies: 4.40-4.60 grams.

Date	Mintage	VG8	F12	VF20	XF40	MS60
ND(ca.1895-96)	—	4.00	6.00	9.00	13.50	—

Obverse has wavy water line in outer angles. New style lotus without 3 small leaves to left and right. Reverse has 3 dots in outer angles, wheel with spokes.

Obverse Reverse

Y# E13.1 TANGKA (1-1/2 Sho)
Silver **Obv:** Dot to left and right of lotus **Edge:** Plain **Mint:** (no Mint Information) **Note:** Weight varies: 4.60-4.80 grams. Prev. Y#13.4.

Date	Mintage	VG8	F12	VF20	XF40	MS60
ND(ca.1899-1907)	—	3.00	4.00	7.00	12.00	35.00

Y# E13.4 TANGKA (1-1/2 Sho)
3.80 g., Silver **Obv:** 7.5-8.0mm lotus circle, no dot at left and right of lotus **Edge:** Plain **Mint:** (no Mint Information) **Note:** Prev. Y#E13.8 (Y#13.5).

Date	Mintage	VG8	F12	VF20	XF40	MS60
ND(ca.1904)	—	60.00	85.00	120	180	250

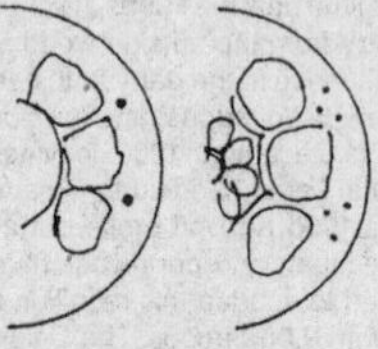

Y# F13.1 TANGKA (1-1/2 Sho)
Billon **Obv:** Nine dots within lotus circle **Rev:** Flower buds full or outlined **Edge:** Plain **Mint:** Dode **Note:** Six varieties exist. Weight varies: 4.10-4.70 grams. Prev. Y#13.6.

Date	Mintage	VG8	F12	VF20	XF40	MS60
ND(ca.1907-09)	—	4.00	6.00	10.00	16.00	40.00

Y# F13.2 TANGKA (1-1/2 Sho)
Billon **Obv:** Northwest symbol circle with dots; no dot at left and right of lotus; lotus circle varies 10-12mm **Rev:** Central lotus buds hollow **Edge:** Plain **Mint:** Dode **Note:** Weight varies: 4.10-4.70. Four varieties exist.

Date	Mintage	G4	VG8	F12	VF20	XF40
ND(1910-15)	—	15.00	25.00	50.00	80.00	150

Y# F13.3 TANGKA (1-1/2 Sho)
Billon **Obv:** 11mm lotus circle **Rev:** Solid lotus buds **Edge:** Plain **Mint:** (no Mint Information) **Note:** Machine struck. Similar to Y#F13.2 and 2 Tangka, Y#15. Weight varies: 5.20-5.60 grams.

Date	Mintage	G4	VG8	F12	VF20	XF40
ND(ca.1912)	—	100	150	200	275	500

Y# F13.5 TANGKA (1-1/2 Sho)
Billon **Obv:** Dot to left and right of lotus; northeast symbol double hook between two fish and dots; northwest symbol circle with two hooks, dots south symbol has three dots **Edge:** Plain **Mint:** (no Mint Information) **Note:** Weight varies: 4.10-4.70 grams. Varieties exist including 34-78 dots for outer circle. Prev. Y#13.8.

Date	Mintage	G4	VG8	F12	VF20	XF40
ND(1912-22)	—	8.00	12.00	20.00	32.00	60.00

Y# F13.6 TANGKA (1-1/2 Sho)

Billon, 27 mm. **Obv:** Dots to left and right of base of lotus in the water line; northwest symbol a circle with dots; northeast symbol two fish with dots; south symbol very ornate with two side hooks and a dot **Edge:** Plain **Mint:** (no Mint Information) **Note:** Weight varies: 4.10-4.70 grams.

Date	Mintage	G4	VG8	F12	VF20	XF40
ND(ca.1909)	—	8.00	12.00	18.00	30.00	50.00

Y# F13.4 TANGKA (1-1/2 Sho)

Billon **Obv:** Dot to left and right of lotus; northeast symbol two fish with dots; south symbol with 3 dots; northwest symbol circle with 4 dots around center dot **Edge:** Plain **Mint:** (no Mint Information) **Note:** Weight varies: 4.10-4.70 grams. Varieties exist including 34-78 dots for outer circles. Prev. Y#13.7.

Date	Mintage	VG8	F12	VF20	XF40	MS60
ND(ca.1912-22)	—	8.00	12.00	20.00	32.00	60.00

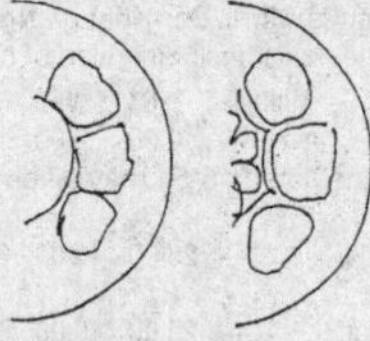

Y# G13 TANGKA (1-1/2 Sho)

Billon **Rev:** No outer angles at inner circle **Edge:** Plain **Mint:** Ser-Khang **Note:** Weight varies: 3.30-4.60 grams. Prev. Y#13.9.

Date	Mintage	VG8	F12	VF20	XF40	MS60
ND(ca.1921)	—	4.00	6.00	9.00	15.00	45.00

Y# F13.7 TANGKA (1-1/2 Sho)

Billon, 31 mm. **Edge:** Plain **Mint:** (no Mint Information) **Note:** Similar to Y#F13.6.

Date	Mintage	G4	VG8	F12	VF20	XF40
ND(ca.1924-25) Rare	—	8.00	12.00	20.00	32.00	60.00

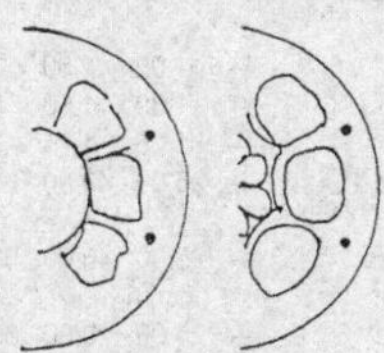

Y# H13.1 TANGKA (1-1/2 Sho)

Billon **Obv:** Dot between symbols at inner circle, lotus petals joined **Rev:** Dot between characters at inner circle **Edge:** Plain **Mint:** Dode **Note:** Weight varies: 4.00-4.20 grams. Two minor die varieties exist. Prev. Y#13.10.

Date	Mintage	VG8	F12	VF20	XF40	MS60
ND(1929)	—	10.00	14.00	20.00	30.00	50.00

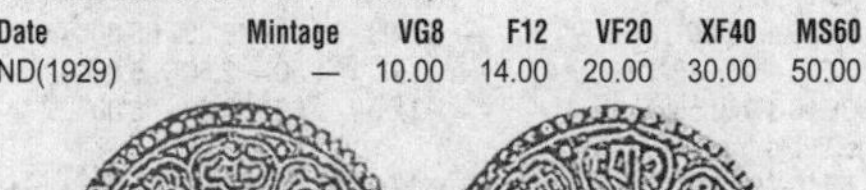

Y# H13.2 TANGKA (1-1/2 Sho)

Billon **Obv:** Similar to Y#H13.1 **Rev:** Similar to Y#H13.1 but Northeast character in retrograde **Edge:** Plain **Mint:** (no Mint Information) **Note:** Weight varies: 4.00-4.20 grams. Machine struck.

Date	Mintage	VG8	F12	VF20	XF40	MS60
ND(ca.1929-30)	—	60.00	90.00	120	150	—

Y# 15 2 TANGKA

Billon **Mint:** Dode **Note:** Weight varies: 7.80-10.50 grams. Varieties exist.

Date	Mintage	VG8	F12	VF20	XF40	MS60
ND(ca.1912)	—	100	350	600	1,000	—

PRESENTATION TANGKA COINAGE

Y# 14 TANGKA (1-1/2 Sho)

Silver **Obv:** Fifteen obverse varieties exist with combinations of none or up to two dots inside trapezoids enclosing the legend **Rev:** 2 crescents in center point clock or counter-clockwise **Edge:** Plain **Mint:** (no Mint Information) **Note:** Weight varies: 2.70-5.00 grams. Struck for presentation to monks.

Date	Mintage	VG8	F12	VF20	XF40	MS60
ND(1930)	600,000	15.00	20.00	40.00	60.00	100

Note: Cut pieces in 4 and 5 petals exist but are considered dubious since cut pieces usually were done in the 19th century before Y14 was struck

Y# 31 TANGKA (1-1/2 Sho)

0.900 Silver **Edge:** Reeded **Mint:** Tapchi **Note:** Weight varies: 3.10-5.30 grams. Varieties exist, the two "commas" in central circle are in either vertical or horizontal alignment.

Date	Mintage	VG8	F12	VF20	XF40	MS60
ND(1953)	331,292	7.00	10.00	15.00	22.00	40.00

Note: Struck for presentation to Monks; Circulated later but briefly with value of 5 and then 10 Srang

SHO-SRANG COINAGE

Y# A7 1/8 SHO

4.00 g., Copper, 22 mm. **Ruler:** Hsüan-t'ung **Mint:** Dode **Note:** Two reverse varieties exist, one with a dot between the upper two syllables of the legend, the other is without a dot.

Date	Mintage	G4	VG8	F12	VF20	XF40
CD1(1901)	—	100	175	250	450	—

Note: A silver striking of this type exists (rare), probably a pattern

Y# B7 1/4 SHO

Copper, 26 mm. **Ruler:** Hsüan-t'ung **Mint:** Dode

Date	Mintage	G4	VG8	F12	VF20	XF40
CD1(1909)	—	50.00	100	150	250	—

Note: This coin struck in silver is a forgery; Modern forgeries struck in copper and copper-nickel exist.

Y# 10 2-1/2 SKAR

Copper, 22 mm. **Obv:** Lion standing left, looking backwards **Edge:** Plain **Mint:** Dode **Note:** Lion varieties exist as do counterfeits.

Date	Mintage	G4	VG8	F12	VF20	XF40
BE15-43	—	150	250	400	600	—

Y# 16.1 2-1/2 SKAR

Copper **Obv:** Lion crouching and looking upwards **Edge:** Plain **Mint:** Dode **Note:** Weight varies: 3.70-6.00 grams. Varieties and overstrikes exist.

Date	Mintage	G4	VG8	F12	VF20	XF40
BE15-47	—	5.00	12.00	20.00	50.00	—
BE15-48	—	5.00	12.00	20.00	50.00	—
BE15-49	—	15.00	30.00	60.00	120	—
BE15-50	—	8.00	16.00	30.00	70.00	—
BE15-51	—	50.00	100	200	300	—
BE15-52	—	6.50	14.00	25.00	60.00	—

Y# 16.2 2-1/2 SKAR

Copper **Obv:** Lion standing left looking backwards with and without rays from sun **Edge:** Plain **Mint:** Mekyi **Note:** Weight varies: 3.70-6.00 grams. Varieties exist, one with retrograde u-sign on reverse top in the word "gsum" (three)(error); the other variety has the letter corrected. With and without rays from sun.

Date	Mintage	G4	VG8	F12	VF20	XF40
BE15-48	—	8.00	16.00	30.00	70.00	—

Y# 16.3 2-1/2 SKAR

Copper **Obv:** Lion crouching looking back **Mint:** Mekyi

Date	Mintage	G4	VG8	F12	VF20	XF40
BE15-48(1914)	—	10.00	15.00	35.00	60.00	—

Y# A19 2-1/2 SKAR

Copper **Obv:** Lion standing left, looking back and upwards **Shape:** Scalloped **Mint:** Dode **Note:** Forgeries exist.

Date	Mintage	G4	VG8	F12	VF20	XF40
BE15-52	—	50.00	85.00	110	200	—
BE15-53	—	50.00	90.00	120	225	—
BE15-55	—	150	250	350	600	—

Y# A10 5 SKAR

Copper, 25 mm. **Obv:** Lion standing left, looking back and upwards **Edge:** Plain **Mint:** Dode **Note:** Counterfeits exist.

Date	Mintage	G4	VG8	F12	VF20	XF40
BE15-43	—	200	300	500	800	—

Y# 17 5 SKAR

Copper **Obv:** Lion standing left and looking upward **Edge:** Plain **Mint:** Dode **Note:** Overstrikes exist.

Date	Mintage	G4	VG8	F12	VF20	XF40
BE15-47	—	6.00	10.00	25.00	55.00	—

Date	Mintage	G4	VG8	F12	VF20	XF40
BE15-48	—	4.00	7.00	15.00	35.00	—
BE15-49	—	5.00	8.00	25.00	50.00	—
BE15-50	—	5.00	8.00	25.00	50.00	—
BE15-51	—	3.50	6.00	15.00	30.00	—
BE15-52	—	25.00	55.00	120	250	—

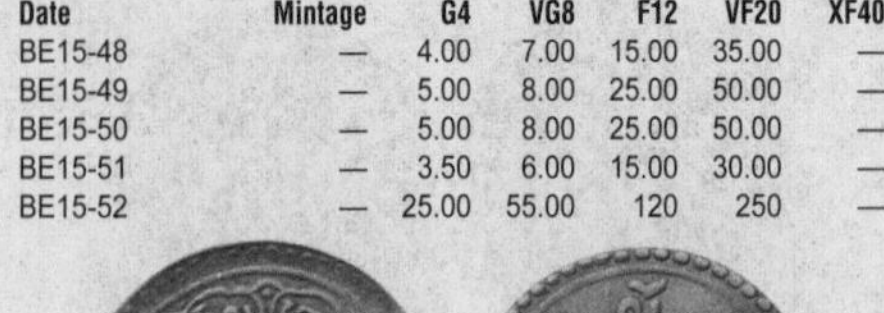

Y# 17.1 5 SKAR

Copper **Obv:** Lion standing left, looking back **Edge:** Plain **Mint:** Mekyi **Note:** Size of obverse circle and weight of coin vary considerably. Inscription varieties exist plus in dots.

Date	Mintage	G4	VG8	F12	VF20	XF40
BE15-48	—	4.00	7.00	15.00	32.00	—
BE15-48	—	4.00	7.00	15.00	32.00	—
Note: Inscription varieties exist.						
BE15-49	—	4.00	7.00	15.00	32.00	—
Note: Obverse varieties (lion) exist						
BE15-50	—	4.00	7.00	15.00	32.00	—
BE15-51	—	4.00	7.00	15.00	32.00	—
BE15-52	—	5.00	8.00	18.00	40.00	—

Y# 17.2 5 SKAR

Copper **Obv:** Lion standing left looking back and upwards **Edge:** Plain **Mint:** Mekyi

Date	Mintage	G4	VG8	F12	VF20	XF40
BE15-48	—	5.00	9.00	20.00	45.00	—
Note: 2-line varieties exist of 15-48.						
BE15-49	—	8.00	14.00	35.00	70.00	—

Y# 17.3 5 SKAR

Copper **Obv:** Lion standing left looking back and sideways **Rev:** Flower with eight petals rather than wheel with eight spokes **Edge:** Plain **Mint:** Mekyi

Date	Mintage	G4	VG8	F12	VF20	XF40
BE15-48	—	6.00	10.00	25.00	55.00	—

Y# 19 5 SKAR

2.80 g., Copper, 20.7 mm. **Obv:** Lion standing left **Edge:** Reeded **Mint:** Lower Dode **Note:** Varieties exist.

Date	Mintage	G4	VG8	F12	VF20	XF40
BE15-52	—	2.25	3.50	6.00	12.00	—
BE15-53	—	2.00	3.00	5.50	11.00	—
BE15-54	—	1.50	2.50	5.00	10.00	—
Note: 2 varieties of 4 in 54 exist						
BE15-55	—	5.00	10.00	20.00	40.00	—
BE15-56	—	1.50	2.50	5.00	10.00	—
BE56-15 Error	—	35.00	50.00	90.00	130	—
Note: Reverse inscription reads counterclockwise on error date coin						

Y# 19.1 5 SKAR

Copper **Obv:** Lion standing left **Rev:** Dot added above center **Edge:** Reeded **Mint:** Upper Dode

Date	Mintage	G4	VG8	F12	VF20	XF40
BE15-55	—	10.00	25.00	45.00	80.00	—
BE15-56	—	5.00	8.00	20.00	35.00	—

Y# 11 7-1/2 SKAR

Copper, 28 mm. **Obv:** Lion standing left, looking back and upwards **Edge:** Plain **Mint:** Dode **Note:** Modern counterfeits exist.

Date	Mintage	G4	VG8	F12	VF20	XF40
BE15-43	—	150	250	350	500	—

Y# 20 7-1/2 SKAR

3.60 g., Copper, 22 mm. **Edge:** Plain **Mint:** Dode **Note:** Some 15-52, 15-53, 15-54, and 15-55 specimens have the reverse central pinwheel fishes in a counterclockwise direction. Many varieties exist with size of inner circle on reverse.

Date	Mintage	G4	VG8	F12	VF20	XF40
BE15-52	—	2.00	3.00	5.00	8.50	—
BE15-53	—	1.50	2.50	4.00	7.00	—
BE15-54	—	1.50	2.50	4.00	7.00	—
BE15-55	—	1.50	2.50	4.00	7.00	—
BE15-56	—	1.50	2.50	4.00	7.00	—
BE15-60	—	20.00	30.00	50.00	100	—
Note: 5 varieties exist						

Y# 21.1a SHO

Copper, 24 mm. **Obv:** Lion standing left, looking backwards, with dots in obverse angles **Rev:** Without dots in reverse arabesques **Mint:** Mekyi **Note:** Weight varies: 3.95-7.13 grams. Varieties exist and also in planchet thickness and size of circles

Date	Mintage	G4	VG8	F12	VF20	XF40
BE15-52	—	1.50	2.00	3.25	7.00	—
BE15-53/52	—	1.50	2.00	3.25	7.00	—
BE15-53	—	1.00	1.50	2.50	5.00	—
BE15-54	—	1.00	1.50	2.50	5.00	—
BE15-55	—	1.00	1.50	2.50	5.00	—
BE15-56	—	1.00	1.50	2.50	5.00	—
BE15-57	—	1.50	2.00	3.25	7.00	—
BE15-58	—	1.00	1.50	2.50	5.00	—
BE15-59	—	1.00	1.50	2.50	5.00	—
BE15-60	—	1.00	1.50	2.50	5.00	—
BE16-1	—	1.00	1.50	2.50	5.00	—
BE16-2 w/ retrograde 2 (error)	—	1.00	1.50	2.50	5.00	—
BE16-2	—	1.00	1.50	2.50	5.00	—

Y# 21 SHO

Copper **Obv:** Lion standing left, looking upwards **Rev:** Central legend horizontal **Mint:** Dode **Note:** Large size 25.6 mm.

Date	Mintage	G4	VG8	F12	VF20	XF40
BE15-52	—	30.00	45.00	75.00	120	—

Y# 21b SHO

Copper **Obv:** Lion standing left looking backwards **Rev:** Central legend horizontal **Mint:** Dode **Note:** Large size 25.6 mm.

Date	Mintage	G4	VG8	F12	VF20	XF40
BE15-52	—	50.00	80.00	100	150	—

Y# 21.1b SHO

Copper, 24 mm. **Obv:** W/o dots in obverse angles **Rev:** W/o dots in reverse arabesques **Mint:** Mekyi **Note:** Weight varies: 3.95-7.13 grams. Varieties exist.

Date	Mintage	G4	VG8	F12	VF20	XF40
BE15-53	—	5.00	10.00	20.00	30.00	—
BE15-57	—	5.00	10.00	20.00	30.00	—
BE15-58	—	20.00	30.00	50.00	80.00	—
BE15-59	—	5.00	10.00	20.00	30.00	—

Y# 21.2 SHO

Copper **Obv:** Lion standing left looking upwards, **Rev:** Dots in reverse arabesques **Mint:** Ser-Khang **Note:** Weight varies: 3.31-7.27 g. Varieties exist including size of circles.

Date	Mintage	G4	VG8	F12	VF20	XF40
BE15-54	—	2.00	3.00	5.00	9.00	—
Note: Specimens dated 15-54 may all be contemporary forgeries						
BE51-15 (error) cycle and 15 transposed	—	25.00	40.00	65.00	100	—
BE15-54 (error) "year" and 15 transposed	—	25.00	40.00	65.00	100	—
Note: 2 lion varieties exist of 15-54.						
BE51-54 (error) 51 instead of 15	—	2.00	3.00	5.00	9.00	—
BE54-15 (error) cycle and 15 transposed	—	25.00	40.00	65.00	100	—
BE15-54 "year" retrograde	—	25.00	40.00	65.00	100	—
BE15-55	—	1.50	2.50	4.50	7.00	—
BE15-55 (error) "year" and 15 transposed	—	25.00	40.00	65.00	100	—
BE55-15 (error) cycle and 15 transposed	—	25.00	40.00	65.00	100	—
BE15-56/5	—	1.00	1.50	2.50	5.00	—
BE15-56	—	1.00	1.50	2.50	5.00	—
BE15-57	—	1.25	1.75	3.25	7.00	—
BE15-57 "year" and 15 transposed	—	25.00	40.00	65.00	100	—
BE15-57 (error) "year" and 15 transposed	—	25.00	40.00	65.00	100	—
BE15-58 "year" and 15 transposed	—	25.00	40.00	65.00	100	—
BE15-58	—	1.00	1.50	2.50	5.00	—
BE15-59	—	1.00	1.50	2.50	5.00	—
BE15-60	—	1.00	1.50	2.50	5.00	—
BE15-6 (error) for 15-60	—	25.00	40.00	65.00	100	—
BE16-1/15-60	—	15.00	25.00	40.00	65.00	—
BE16-1	—	1.00	1.50	2.50	5.00	—
BE16-1 dot below syllable "rab"	—	1.00	1.50	2.50	5.00	—
BE16-2/1	—	1.00	1.50	2.50	5.00	—
BE16-2	—	1.00	1.50	2.50	5.00	—

Y# 21a SHO

Copper **Rev:** Central legend vertical **Mint:** Dode **Note:** Two varieties (lion) exist for each of the following dates: 15-56, 15-57, 15-58, and 16-2. Overstrikes on 5 Skar, Y#17 exist. Varieties exist. Weight varies: 3.48-4.78 g.

Date	Mintage	VG8	F12	VF20	XF40	MS60
BE15-56	—	8.00	13.50	20.00	30.00	—
BE15-57	—	2.00	3.50	6.00	10.00	—
BE15-57 Error; "year" and 15 transposed	—	25.00	40.00	65.00	100	—
BE15-58	—	2.00	3.50	6.00	10.00	—
BE15-59/8	—	1.25	2.25	4.00	8.00	—
BE15-59	—	1.25	2.25	4.00	8.00	—
BE15-60	—	1.25	2.25	4.00	8.00	—
BE15-60/59	—	1.25	2.25	4.00	8.00	—
BE16-1	—	1.25	2.25	4.00	8.00	—
BE16-1 Dot below syllable rab	—	1.25	2.25	4.00	8.00	—

Date	Mintage	VG8	F12	VF20	XF40	MS60
BE16-2	—	2.00	3.50	6.00	10.00	—

Note: A scarce 16-2 variety features a reversed 2

The following marks are located in the position indicated by the arrow:

a: ● b: ● c: ✚ d: ↓ e: ⌄ f: ⌄ g: ❙

Y# 23 SHO

4.83 g., Copper, 24 mm. **Edge:** Reeded **Mint:** Tapchi **Note:** Weight varies: 4.02-6.09 grams. Dates 16-10, 16-11, 16-12, and 16-16 exist struck on thin planchets, many lion obverse varieties.

Date	Mintage	VG8	F12	VF20	XF40	MS60
BE16-6 (a)	6,000,000	3.00	5.00	9.00	15.00	—
BE16-7 (a)	Inc. above	3.00	5.00	9.00	15.00	—
BE16-8 (a)	Inc. above	3.00	5.00	9.00	15.00	—
Note: Two varieties exist						
BE16-9 (a)	Inc. above	2.00	3.50	6.00	11.00	—
Note: Two varieties exist						
BE16-9 (b)	Inc. above	1.50	3.00	5.00	10.00	—
Note: A scarce 16-9 variety features a hook ("bird") on the Sengi's (lion's) back						
BE16-10 (a)	Inc. above	5.00	10.00	15.00	25.00	—
BE16-10 (b)	Inc. above	5.00	10.00	15.00	25.00	—
BE16-10 (c)	Inc. above	1.50	3.00	5.00	10.00	—
BE16-11 (a)	Inc. above	2.50	4.00	9.00	15.00	—
BE16-11 (b)	Inc. above	5.00	10.00	15.00	25.00	—
BE16-11 (c)	Inc. above	2.50	4.00	9.00	15.00	—
Note: A variety exists with stars at 4:00 and 8:00 close to inner reverse circle						
BE16-11 (d)	Inc. above	2.50	4.00	9.00	15.00	—
BE16-11 (e)	Inc. above	1.50	3.00	5.00	10.00	—
BE16-11 (f)	Inc. above	5.00	10.00	15.00	25.00	—
BE16-11 (g)	Inc. above	5.00	10.00	15.00	25.00	—
BE16-12 (c)	Inc. above	5.00	10.00	15.00	25.00	—
BE16-12 (d)	Inc. above	5.00	10.00	15.00	25.00	—
BE16-12 (f)	Inc. above	4.00	8.00	12.00	20.00	—
BE16-12 (g)	Inc. above	4.00	8.00	12.00	20.00	—
BE16-16 (f) Rare	Inc. above	—	—	—	—	—

Y# 27.1 3 SHO

Copper **Obv:** Single cloud line **Rev:** Four varieties of conch shell on reverse **Mint:** Tapchi **Note:** Variety with line or cloud (scarcer) right of right obverse mountain.

Date	Mintage	VG8	F12	VF20	XF40	MS60
BE16-20	—	15.00	30.00	100	200	—

Y# 27.2 3 SHO

Copper **Obv:** Double cloud line **Mint:** Tapchi

Date	Mintage	VG8	F12	VF20	XF40	MS60
BE16-20	—	30.00	60.00	150	300	—

Y# 8 5 SHO

Silver **Ruler:** Hsüan-t'ung **Edge:** Reeded **Mint:** Dode **Note:** Weight varies: 9.4-9.7 grams.

Date	Mintage	VG8	F12	VF20	XF40	MS60
CD1(1909)	—	800	1,500	3,000	5,000	—

Note: Forgeries exist: some of the stars blundered and letters inaccurate, modern ones of larger size struck in base metals.

Y# 18 5 SHO

Silver **Obv:** Lion looking upwards **Edge:** Reeded **Mint:** Dode **Note:** Weight varies: 8.4-11.4 grams.

Date	Mintage	VG8	F12	VF20	XF40	MS60
BE15-47	—	50.00	70.00	100	150	—
BE15-48	—	35.00	50.00	80.00	125	—
BE15-49	—	35.00	50.00	80.00	125	—
BE15-50	—	35.00	50.00	80.00	125	—
Note: Two BE15-50 varieties exist; small and large lions, or 13.5mm vs. 14.5mm obverse circle, short or long flowers on reverse						
BE15-58 Rare	—	—	—	—	—	—
BE15-59	—	200	400	600	1,000	—
BE15-60	—	250	500	800	1,200	—

Y# 18.1 5 SHO

Silver **Obv:** Lion looking backwards **Edge:** Reeded **Mint:** Mekyi **Note:** Weight varies: 7.40-9.80 grams. Varieties exist.

Date	Mintage	VG8	F12	VF20	XF40	MS60
BE15-49	—	35.00	50.00	80.00	125	—
BE15-50	—	35.00	50.00	80.00	125	—
BE15-51	—	35.00	50.00	80.00	125	—
BE15-52	—	35.00	50.00	80.00	125	—
BE15-53	—	150	250	600	600	—
BE15-56	—	200	350	500	700	—
BE15-59	—	600	800	1,200	2,750	—
BE15-60	—	600	800	1,200	2,750	—
BE16-1	—	150	250	450	600	—

Y# 18.2 5 SHO

Silver **Edge:** Reeded **Mint:** Dode **Note:** Weight varies: 8.00-9.70 grams.

Date	Mintage	VG8	F12	VF20	XF40	MS60
BE15-52	—	150	250	500	800	—

Y# 18.1a 5 SHO

Copper **Mint:** (no Mint Information) **Note:** Some specimens are silver plated or silver washed.

Date	Mintage	VG8	F12	VF20	XF40	MS60
BE15-53	—	300	500	600	900	—
BE15-56	—	400	600	800	1,200	—

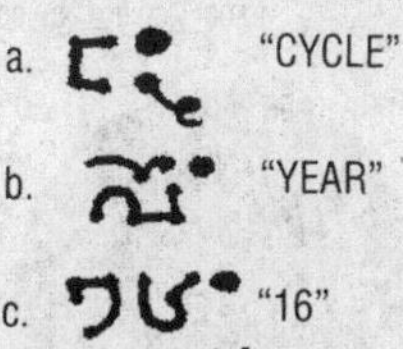

a. "CYCLE"

b. "YEAR"

c. "16"

Y# 28 5 SHO

Copper **Obv:** Two mountains with two suns **Edge:** Reeded **Mint:** Tapchi **Note:** Three lion die varieties exist. Modern counterfiets made of yellowish copper exist.

Date	Mintage	VG8	F12	VF20	XF40	MS60
BE16-21	—	4.00	7.50	10.00	20.00	—

Y# 28a 5 SHO

8.50 g., Copper, 29 mm. **Obv:** Moon and sun above 3 mountains **Edge:** Reeded **Mint:** Tapchi **Note:** Lion and edge varieties exist.

Date	Mintage	VG8	F12	VF20	XF40	MS60
BE16-23 dots a and b	—	20.00	28.00	38.00	50.00	—
BE16-24/3 dots a and b	—	40.00	60.00	80.00	100	—
BE16-24 dot b	—	2.00	3.50	6.50	11.00	—
BE16-24 dots a and b	—	2.00	3.50	6.50	11.00	—
Note: Unclear overdates of 15-24 exist						
BE16-24 dots a and b	—	10.00	15.00	22.00	30.00	—
Note: Cloud merged with mountain as in illustration						
BE16-24 dots a and b	—	15.00	22.00	30.00	40.00	—
Note: Moon engraved over sun						
BE16-25/24 dot a and b	—	4.00	7.00	12.50	20.00	—
BE16-25 dot a and b (tiny)	—	4.00	7.00	12.00	20.00	—
BE16-25 dot a	—	2.00	3.50	6.50	11.00	—
BE16-25 dot a and b	—	6.00	10.00	16.00	25.00	—
Note: Moon engraved over sun; Unclear overdates exist for BE16-25						
BE16-26 dot a	—	4.00	7.00	12.00	20.00	—
Note: Without dot after "26"						
BE16-26 dots a and b	—	4.00	7.00	12.00	20.00	—
BE16-27 without dots	—	6.00	10.00	18.00	30.00	—
BE16-27 dot a	—	23.00	30.00	40.00	50.00	—
BE16-27 dots a and b	—	6.00	7.00	12.00	20.00	—

Y# 28.1 5 SHO

8.90 g., Copper, 29.4 mm. **Obv:** Three mountains with two suns **Edge:** Reeded **Mint:** Tapchi **Note:** Die varieties involving lion's tail hairs (5-8), leg hairs (2-5) and yin-yang features (S, reversed S or the incuse of either) include 5 of 16-21, 38 of 16-22 and 30 of 16-23.

Date	Mintage	VG8	F12	VF20	XF40	MS60
BE16-21	—	2.00	3.50	6.00	10.00	—

Date	Mintage	VG8	F12	VF20	XF40	MS60
Note: A modern medallic series dated 16-21 (1947) exists struck in copper, silver, and gold which were authorized by the Dalai Lama while in exile; Refer to Unusual World Coins, 5th edition, KP Books, 2007						
BE16-21 dots a and b	—	—	—	—	—	—
BE16-22 dots a and b	—	2.50	4.00	7.50	12.50	—
BE16-22 dots a, b, and c	—	23.00	30.00	40.00	50.00	—
BE16-23 dots a and b	—	5.00	8.00	14.00	25.00	—
Note: With 8, 9, 10 or 12 sunrays						
BE16-23 dots a, b, and c	—	1.50	3.00	5.00	8.50	—
Note: Unclear overdates and varieties of BE16-23 exist						
BE16-24 dots a and b	—	30.00	40.00	50.00	65.00	—
BE16-24/3 dots a and b	—	40.00	60.00	80.00	100	—

Y# 28.2 5 SHO
Copper **Obv:** Cloud above middle mountain missing **Edge:** Reeded **Mint:** Tapchi

Date	Mintage	VG8	F12	VF20	XF40	MS60
BE16-22	—	35.00	60.00	95.00	150	—

Y# 9 SRANG
Silver **Ruler:** Hsüan-t'ung **Edge:** Reeded **Mint:** Dode **Note:** 17.2-19.9 g. Seven reverse varieties exist.

Date	Mintage	VG8	F12	VF20	XF40	MS60
CD1(1909)	—	200	400	1,000	3,000	—

Y# 12 SRANG
Silver, 35 mm. **Obv:** Lion standing left, looking backwards **Edge:** Plain **Mint:** Dode **Note:** Weight varies: 18.00-18.30 grams. Varieties exist.

Date	Mintage	VG8	F12	VF20	XF40	MS60
BE15-43	—	150	225	500	3,500	—

Y# A18 SRANG
18.10 g., Silver **Obv:** Lion standing left looking back and upwards **Edge:** Reeded **Mint:** Dode

Date	Mintage	VG8	F12	VF20	XF40	MS60
BE15-48	—	1,000	2,000	5,000	8,000	—

Y# A18.1 SRANG
Silver **Obv:** Lion standing left looking backwards **Edge:** Reeded **Mint:** Mekyi **Note:** Weight varies: 17.80-18.30 grams

Date	Mintage	VG8	F12	VF20	XF40	MS60
BE15-52	—	450	800	2,000	5,000	—
BE15-53	—	300	600	1,500	4,000	—

Y# 24 1-1/2 SRANG
5.00 g., Silver **Edge:** Reeded **Mint:** Tapchi **Note:** Dates are written in words, not numerals. Obverse and reverse varieties exist.

Date	Mintage	F12	VF20	XF40	MS60	MS63
BE16-10 coin rotation	—	3.50	6.00	10.00	20.00	—
BE16-10 medal rotation	—	3.50	6.00	10.00	20.00	—
BE16-11	—	3.00	5.00	9.00	17.00	—
BE16-12	—	3.50	6.00	10.00	20.00	—
BE16-20	—	30.00	50.00	100	200	—

Y# 25 3 SRANG
11.30 g., Silver **Edge:** Reeded **Mint:** Tapchi **Note:** Dates are written in words, not numerals. Varieties exist in lion.

Date	Mintage	F12	VF20	XF40	MS60	MS63
BE16-7	—	20.00	40.00	80.00	150	—
Note: 7 or 8-tail plume variety						
BE16-8	—	20.00	40.00	80.00	150	—

Y# 26 3 SRANG
Silver **Edge:** Reeded **Mint:** Tapchi **Note:** Dates are written in words, not numerals. Obverse and reverse varieties exist.

Date	Mintage	F12	VF20	XF40	MS60	MS63
BE16-9	—	7.00	10.00	18.00	30.00	—
BE16-10/9	—	7.00	10.00	18.00	30.00	—
BE16-10	—	6.00	9.00	15.00	25.00	—
BE16-11	—	6.00	9.00	15.00	25.00	—
BE16-12	—	6.00	9.00	15.00	25.00	—
BE16-20	—	30.00	50.00	100	250	—
BE16-20 dot after date	—	30.00	50.00	100	250	—

Y# 29 10 SRANG
Billon **Obv:** Two suns **Rev:** Numerals for denomination at center right **Edge:** Reeded **Mint:** Tapchi

Date	Mintage	F12	VF20	XF40	MS60	MS63
BE(16)-22	—	4.50	9.00	18.00	40.00	—

Y# 29a 10 SRANG
Billon **Obv:** Moon and sun **Rev:** Value written in words at center right **Edge:** Reeded **Mint:** Tapchi **Note:** The "dot" is after the denomination. No cycle written. Refer to *Unusual World Coins*, 5th edition, KP Books, 2007.

Date	Mintage	F12	VF20	XF40	MS60	MS63
BE(16)-23	—	30.00	50.00	150	200	—
Note: With dot						
BE(16)-24/23	—	7.00	15.00	30.00	60.00	—
Note: With dot						
BE(16)-24/23	—	20.00	40.00	80.00	140	—
Note: With dot and moon cut over sun						
BE(16)-24/22 with dot	—	9.00	18.00	35.00	70.00	—
Note: A modern medallic series dated 16-24 (1950) exists struck in copper-nickel, silver, and gold which were authorized by the Dalai Lama while in exile.						
BE(16)-24	—	10.00	20.00	40.00	70.00	—
Note: With dot and moon cut over sun						
BE(16)-24	—	12.00	22.00	50.00	90.00	—
Note: With dot						
BE(16)-25/24	—	7.00	15.00	30.00	60.00	—
Note: With dot						
BE(16)-25 w/o dot	—	7.00	15.00	30.00	60.00	—
BE(16)-25/24	—	10.00	20.00	40.00	70.00	—
Note: Without dot						
BE(16)-25	—	7.00	15.00	30.00	60.00	—
Note: With dot						
BE(16)-26/25	—	7.00	15.00	30.00	60.00	—
Note: Without dot						
BE(16)-26	—	7.00	15.00	30.00	60.00	—
Note: With dot						

Y# 29.1 10 SRANG
Billon **Obv:** 2 suns **Rev:** Words for denomination at center right **Mint:** Tapchi **Note:** No cycle written.

Date	Mintage	F12	VF20	XF40	MS60	MS63
BE(16)-23	—	6.00	10.00	20.00	40.00	—
Note: With dot before and after ten						
BE(16)-23/22	—	12.00	20.00	35.00	70.00	—
BE(16)-23	—	6.00	10.00	20.00	40.00	—
Note: Without dot after ten						

Y# 30 10 SRANG

Billon **Rev:** Cycle and year in words **Edge:** Reeded **Mint:** Dogu **Note:** Said to be struck for payment of Tibetan Army members

Date	Mintage	F12	VF20	XF40	MS60	MS63
BE16-24	—	6.00	12.00	25.00	55.00	—
Note: Without dot after year						
BE16-24	—	7.00	15.00	30.00	65.00	—
Note: With dot						
BE16-25/4	—	5.00	10.00	20.00	45.00	—
Note: With dot						
BE16-25	—	5.00	10.00	20.00	45.00	—
Note: With dot						

Y# 22 20 SRANG

Gold **Obv:** Eight Buddhist lucky symbols in outer circle **Rev:** Varieties with 2.8mm, 2.5 mm, and 2.2 mm central reverse circle **Edge:** Reeded **Mint:** Ser-Khang

Date	Mintage	F12	VF20	XF40	MS60	MS63
BE15-52	—	800	1,100	2,000	3,000	—
Note: With dot in reverse center						
BE15-52	—	800	1,100	2,000	3,000	—
Note: w/o dot in rev. center						
BE15-53	—	800	1,100	2,000	3,000	—
Note: With small circle in reverse center; Silver strikings for 15-53 exist and are forgeries						
BE15-53	—	800	1,100	2,000	3,000	—
Note: With small circle in reverse center						
BE15-54	—	700	1,100	2,000	3,000	—
Note: Silver strikings for 15-54 exist and are believed to be forgeries; Deceptive forgeries struck in high grade gold also exist; without dot in reverse center						
BE15-54	—	700	1,100	2,000	3,000	—
Note: With dot in reverse center						
BE15-55	—	2,000	4,000	8,000	12,000	—
Note: w/o dot in rev. center						

TRADE COINAGE

Rupees (Y#3) due to their inscription and first mint also called Szechuan Rupees. Total mintage of the 1 Rupee between 1902 and 1942 (with decreasing fineness) was between 25.5 and 27.5 million according to Chinese sources. In addition to the types illustrated above, large quantities of the following coins also circulated in Tibet: China Dollars, Y#318a, 329, and 345 plus Szechuan issues Y#449 and 459, and Indian Rupees, KM#473, 492, and 508.

Rupees exist with local merchant countermarks in Chinese, Tibetan, and other scripts. Examples of crown-size rupees struck in silver (26.30-27.90 grams) and gold (36.30 grams) are considered fantasies and are listed in Unusual World Coins, 5th edition, Krause Publications, 2007.

1 Rupee = 3 Tangka

Y# 1 1/4 RUPEE

2.80 g., 0.935 Silver 0.0842 oz. ASW, 19 mm. **Edge:** Reeded **Mint:** Chengdu **Note:** Varieties exist as do modern forgeries.

Date	Mintage	F12	VF20	XF40	MS60	MS63
ND(1904-05 1912)	120,000	60.00	100	200	500	—

Y# 1a 1/4 RUPEE

5.45 g., Gold **Mint:** Chengdu **Note:** Deceptive forgeries exist.

Date	Mintage	F12	VF20	XF40	MS60	MS63
ND (1905)	—	1,500	2,500	4,000	6,000	—

Y# 2 1/2 RUPEE

5.60 g., 0.935 Silver 0.1683 oz. ASW, 24 mm. **Edge:** Reeded **Mint:** Chengdu **Note:** Varieties exist

Date	Mintage	F12	VF20	XF40	MS60	MS63
ND(1904-05 1907 1912)	130,000	60.00	100	200	500	—

Y# 2a 1/2 RUPEE

9.38 g., Gold **Mint:** Chengdu

Date	Mintage	F12	VF20	XF40	MS60	MS63
ND (1905)	—	1,500	2,500	4,000	6,000	—

Y# A1.1 RUPEE

11.50 g., Silver **Ruler:** Hsüan-t'ung **Edge:** Plain **Mint:** (no Mint Information) **Note:** Prev. #C20.

Date	Mintage	G4	VG8	F12	VF20	XF40
ND(1902-03)	—	750	2,000	4,500	8,000	—
Note: Struck in or near Kangding (Tachienlu) and known as Lu Kuan Rupee. It was meant to replace the Indian Rupee which was used in eastern Tibet and western Szechuan (Sichuan) in the 19th century and is considered the forerunner of the Szechuan Rupee (Y#3).						

Y# A1.2 RUPEE

Silver **Ruler:** Hsüan-t'ung **Obv:** Similar to Y#A1.1. **Rev:** Different inscription w/o inner beaded circle **Mint:** Kangding **Note:** Kann#1285

Date	Mintage	G4	VG8	F12	VF20	XF40
ND(1902-03)	—	750	2,000	4,500	8,000	—

Y# A1.3 RUPEE

11.67 g., Silver **Ruler:** Hsüan-t'ung **Obv:** Similar to Y#A1.1. **Rev:** Tibetan legend in the inner circle engraved in revers, legends between the inner and outer circle are engraved inverted (upside down). The inner circle consists of 38 beads **Mint:** Kangding

Date	Mintage	G4	VG8	F12	VF20	XF40
ND(1902-02)	—	—	—	—	—	—

Y# 3.1 RUPEE

11.40 g., Silver **Obv:** Small bust w/o collar **Rev:** Horizontal rosette **Edge:** Reeded **Mint:** Chengdu **Note:** Two reverse varieties exist. Finenesses vary: .880-.835.

Date	Mintage	F12	VF20	XF40	MS60	MS63
ND(1902-11)	—	20.00	40.00	60.00	100	—

Y# 3 RUPEE

11.40 g., Silver **Obv:** Small bust without collar **Rev:** Vertical rosette **Edge:** Reeded **Mint:** Chengdu **Note:** Two reverse varieties exist. Finenesses vary: .880-.935.

Date	Mintage	F12	VF20	XF40	MS60	MS63
ND(1902-11)	—	30.00	50.00	80.00	125	—

Y# 3.2a RUPEE

20.67 g., Gold **Obv:** Small bust with collar **Rev:** Vertical rosette **Mint:** Chengdu

Date	Mintage	F12	VF20	XF40	MS60	MS63
ND(ca. 1903-05)	—	1,200	2,000	3,500	5,000	—
Note: An example with two obverses exists (20.40 grams)						

Y# 3.2 RUPEE

0.700 Silver **Obv:** Small bust with collar, varieties with missing base of bust exist **Rev:** Vertical rosette **Mint:** Chengdu **Note:** Two reverse varieties exist. Weight varies .700-.740 g.

Date	Mintage	F12	VF20	XF40	MS60	MS63
ND(1911-16 1930-33)	—	15.00	25.00	45.00	75.00	—
Note: An example with two obverses exists						

Y# 3.3 RUPEE

Silver **Obv:** Large bust with collar **Rev:** Vertical rosette **Mint:** Kangding **Note:** Finenesses vary .420-.500. Varieties exist.

Date	Mintage	F12	VF20	XF40	MS60	MS63
ND(1939-42)	—	20.00	35.00	65.00	110	—

Y# 3b RUPEE

23.15 g., Gold **Obv:** Large bust with collar **Rev:** Vertical rosette **Mint:** Kangding

Date	Mintage	F12	VF20	XF40	MS60	MS63
ND(ca.193)	—	1,200	2,000	3,500	5,000	—

Y# 3.4 RUPEE

Silver **Obv:** Small bust with flat nose and collar, revised non-floral gown and solid line separating nose and lips sections from face **Rev:** Vertical rosette **Mint:** Kangding **Note:** Weight varies: .500-.650

Date	Mintage	F12	VF20	XF40	MS60	MS63
ND(1933-39)	—	20.00	35.00	65.00	110	—

Y# 3.5 RUPEE
Silver **Obv:** Small bust with collar **Rev:** Horizontal rosette **Mint:** Kangding **Note:** Weight varies .420-.500. Varieties exist.

Date	Mintage	F12	VF20	XF40	MS60	MS63
ND(1933-39)	—	30.00	50.00	90.00	160	—

Y# 3a RUPEE
Billon **Obv:** Large bust with collar **Rev:** Vertical rosette **Mint:** Kangding **Note:** Fineness .220 or less.

Date	Mintage	F12	VF20	XF40	MS60	MS63
ND(1939-42)	—	10.00	20.00	40.00	70.00	—

Note: Coins with copper base and silver wash exist

CUT COINAGE

The Tangka C#27 was cut in parts of 3, 4, and 5 petals to make change and the resulting fraactions are occasionally encountered. Cut pieces of the presentation Tangka Y#14 in 4 and 5 petals exist but are considered dubious. Tibetan Rupees (Y3) due to their inscriptions also called Szechuan Rupees, have been cut in half and quarter for use as small change. The process of cutting the rupee frequently allowed customers to chip away from the coin's middle. In 1934 the treasury made cutting of the rupee illegal. To enforce this decree, all official payments had to be made with uncut coins; payment of smaller values was to be made with copper coins. However, the shortage of coinage made this decree impractical.

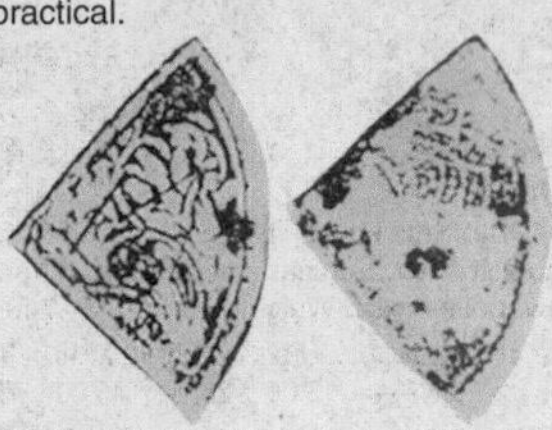

Y# A5 1/4 RUPEE
Silver **Mint:** (no Mint Information) **Note:** 1/4 segment of 1 Rupee, Y#3.

Date	Mintage	VG8	F12	VF20	XF40	MS60
ND (1902-42)	—	25.00	30.00	50.00	80.00	—

Y# B5 1/2 RUPEE
Silver **Mint:** (no Mint Information) **Note:** 1/2 segment of 1 Rupee, of all types Y#3.

Date	Mintage	VG8	F12	VF20	XF40	MS60
ND (1902-42)	—	15.00	20.00	35.00	60.00	—

TOKEN COINAGE

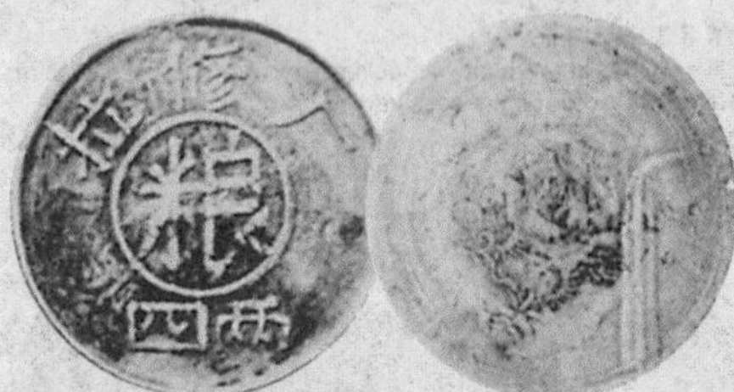

KM# Tn1 TAEL / (SRANG)
Copper **Mint:** (no Mint Information) **Note:** 8.23-8.98 grams. Struck over 3 Sho, Y#27 and 5 Sho, Y#28a and Y#28.1. This token was issued by the Llhasa Motor Car Repair Factory and was good for 4 Taels of grain (=200 g).

Date	Mintage	G4	VG8	F12	VF20	XF40
ND(1959-60) Rare	—	75.00	100	200	400	600

JOINT CHINESE AND TIBETAN AUTHORITY

SINO-TIBETAN COINAGE

Struck in the name of the Chinese Emperor

Y# A4 1/2 SKAR
Copper **Ruler:** Hsüan-t'ung **Edge:** Plain **Mint:** (no Mint Information) **Note:** Weight varies: 3.10-3.60 grams.

Date	Mintage	G4	VG8	F12	VF20	XF40
ND (1910)	—	300	500	1,000	2,000	—

Y# 4 SKAR
Copper, 27 mm. **Ruler:** Hsüan-t'ung **Rev. Inscription:** Hsüan-t'ung. **Edge:** Plain **Mint:** (no Mint Information) **Note:** Weight varies: 5.40-6.60 grams. Varieties in dragon and spacing of inscription exist. Modern counterfeits exist.

Date	Mintage	G4	VG8	F12	VF20	XF40
ND (1910)	—	90.00	150	250	500	—

Y# 5 SHO
Silver, 22 mm. **Ruler:** Hsüan-t'ung **Rev. Inscription:** Hsüan-t'ung. **Edge:** Reeded **Mint:** (no Mint Information) **Note:** Weight varies: 3.30-4.10 grams. Varieties exist, one having the inner circle of dots, on the Chinese side, connected by lines. Modern counterfeits in copper and base metal exist.

Date	Mintage	G4	VG8	F12	VF20	XF40
ND (1910)	—	30.00	50.00	100	250	500

Y# 6 2 SHO
Silver, 25 mm. **Ruler:** Hsüan-t'ung **Rev. Inscription:** Hsüan-t'ung. **Edge:** Reeded **Mint:** (no Mint Information) **Note:** Weight varies: 5.20-8.40 grams. Varieties with different dragon claws and lotus exist. Modern counterfeits exist.

Date	Mintage	G4	VG8	F12	VF20	XF40
ND (1910)	—	30.00	50.00	100	250	500

PATTERNS

Including off metal strikes

KM#	Date	Mintage	Identification	Mkt Val
Pn3	ND (1909)	—	10 Tam. Silver.	—
Pn4	ND (1910)	—	Shokang. Silver. Y5.	—
Pn5	BE15-57 (1923)	—	Sho. Copper.	—
Pn6	BE15-57 (1923)	—	Sho. Brass.	—
Pn8	BE15-57 (1923)	—	20 Srang. Brass.	—
Pn9	BE16-1 (1928)	—	Sho. Brass.	—
Pn10	ND (1928)	—	Srang. Silver.	—
Pn11	ND (1928)	—	10 Tam. Silver.	—
PnA12	ND(1928-29)	—	5 Sho. Silver. Reeded. Weight varies: 5.43-6.55 grams. Two obverse varieties exist.	—
Pn12	ND ND (1929-30)	—	10 Tam. Silver.	—
Pn13	BE16-4 (1931)	—	5 Sho. Silver.	—
Pn14	Yr.925 (1951)	—	25 Srang. Silver.	—
Pn15	Yr.925 (1951)	—	50 Srang. Copper.	—
Pn16	Yr.925 (1951)	—	50 Srang. Silver.	—
Pn17	Yr.925 (1951)	—	50 Srang. Silver.	—
Pn18	ND (1951)	—	50 Srang. Silver.	—
Pn20	Yr.927 (1953)	—	5 Srang. Copper.	600

Note: Some specimens of Pn20 seem to have entered circulation.

KM#	Date	Mintage	Identification	Mkt Val
Pn21	Yr. 927 (1953)	—	5 Srang. Silver.	—

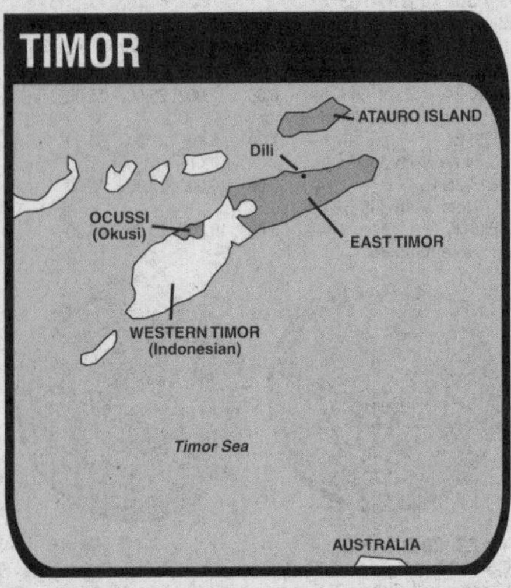

(East Timor)

Timor is an island between the Savu and Timor Seas. It has an area, including the former colony of Portuguese Timor, of 11,883 sq. mi. (30,775 sq. km.) and a population of 1.5 million. Western Timor is administered as part of Nusa Tenggara Timur (East Nusa Tenggara) province. Capital: Kupang. The eastern half of the island, the former Portuguese colony, forms a single province, Timor Timur (East Timor). Originally the Portuguese colony also included the area around Ocussi-Ambeno and the small island of Atauro (Pulau Kambing) located north of Dili. Capital: Dili. Timor exports sandalwood, coffee, tea, hides, rubber and copra.

Portuguese traders reached Timor about 1520, and moved to the north and east when the Dutch established themselves in Kupang, a sheltered bay at the southwestern tip in 1613. Treaties effective in 1860 and 1914 established the boundaries between the two colonies. Japan occupied the entire island during World War II. The former Dutch colony in the western part of the island became part of Indonesia in 1950.

For later coinage see East Timor.

MONETARY SYSTEM

100 Avos = 1 Pataca

PORTUGUESE COLONY

MILLED COINAGE

100 Avos = 1 Pataca

KM# 5 10 AVOS
Bronze, 20 mm. **Obv:** Small circles within cross design **Obv. Legend:** REPUBLICA PORTUGUESA **Rev:** Value above sprigs **Rev. Legend:** COLONIA DE TIMOR

Date	Mintage	VF20	XF40	MS60	MS63	MS65
1945	50,000	220	400	700	1,200	—
1948	500,000	5.00	10.00	25.00	40.00	75.00
1951	6,250,000	2.50	6.00	9.00	15.00	25.00

KM# 6 20 AVOS
Nickel-Bronze, 26 mm. **Obv:** Laureate liberty head right **Obv. Legend:** REPUBLICA PORTUGUESA **Rev:** Shield within globe and wreath **Rev. Legend:** COLONIA DE TIMOR

Date	Mintage	VF20	XF40	MS60	MS63	MS65
1945	50,000	35.00	85.00	150	250	350

KM# 7 50 AVOS
3.50 g., 0.650 Silver 0.0731 oz. ASW, 20.5 mm. **Obv:** Shield within globe on maltese cross **Obv. Legend:** REPUBLICA

PORTUGUESA **Rev:** Value above sprigs **Rev. Legend:** COLONIA DE TIMOR

Date	Mintage	VF20	XF40	MS60	MS63	MS65
1945	100,000	25.00	75.00	150	300	—
1948	500,000	5.50	12.00	20.00	30.00	45.00
1951	6,250,000	4.50	7.50	10.00	17.00	27.00

1958 REFORM COINAGE

100 Centavos = 1 Escudo

KM# 10 10 CENTAVOS
Bronze, 18 mm. **Obv:** Value **Obv. Legend:** REPUBLICA PORTUGUESA **Rev:** Shield within crowned globe, flowers in legend, date below **Rev. Legend:** TIMOR

Date	Mintage	VF20	XF40	MS60	MS63	MS65
1958	1,000,000	3.00	7.00	12.00	20.00	35.00

KM# 17 20 CENTAVOS
Bronze **Obv:** Value **Obv. Legend:** REPUBLICA PORTUGUESA **Rev:** Shield within crowned globe, flowers in legend, date below **Rev. Legend:** TIMOR

Date	Mintage	VF20	XF40	MS60	MS63	MS65
1970	1,000,000	0.75	1.50	3.00	5.00	9.00

KM# 11 30 CENTAVOS
Bronze, 22 mm. **Obv:** Value **Obv. Legend:** REPUBLICA PORTUGUESA **Rev:** Shield within crowned globe, flowers in legend, date below **Rev. Legend:** TIMOR

Date	Mintage	VF20	XF40	MS60	MS63	MS65
1958	2,000,000	1.50	5.00	15.00	25.00	40.00

KM# 18 50 CENTAVOS
4.00 g., Bronze, 19.8 mm. **Obv:** Value **Obv. Legend:** REPUBLICA PORTUGUESA **Rev:** Shield within crowned globe, flowers in legend, date below **Rev. Legend:** TIMOR

Date	Mintage	VF20	XF40	MS60	MS63	MS65
1970	1,000,000	0.75	1.50	3.50	6.00	10.00

KM# 12 60 CENTAVOS
Copper-Nickel-Zinc, 23 mm. **Obv:** Shield within globe on maltese cross, date below **Obv. Legend:** REPUBLICA PORTUGUESA **Rev:** Shield within crowned globe, flowers in legend, value below **Rev. Legend:** TIMOR

Date	Mintage	VF20	XF40	MS60	MS63	MS65
1958	1,000,000	2.75	6.00	12.00	20.00	35.00

KM# 13 ESCUDO
Copper-Nickel-Zinc, 26.5 mm. **Obv:** Shield within globe on maltese cross, date below **Obv. Legend:** REPUBLICA PORTUGUESA **Rev:** Shield within crowned globe, flowers in legend, value below **Rev. Legend:** TIMOR

Date	Mintage	VF20	XF40	MS60	MS63	MS65
1958	1,200,000	4.00	15.00	25.00	45.00	75.00

KM# 19 ESCUDO
7.87 g., Bronze, 25.7 mm. **Obv:** Value **Obv. Legend:** REPUBLICA PORTUGUESA **Rev:** Shield within crowned globe, flowers in legend, date below **Rev. Legend:** TIMOR

Date	Mintage	VF20	XF40	MS60	MS63	MS65
1970	1,200,000	3.00	5.00	10.00	15.00	35.00

KM# 20 2-1/2 ESCUDOS
Copper-Nickel **Obv:** Shield within globe on maltese cross, date below **Obv. Legend:** REPUBLICA PORTUGUESA **Rev:** Shield within crowned globe, flowers in legend, value below **Rev. Legend:** TIMOR

Date	Mintage	VF20	XF40	MS60	MS63	MS65
1970	1,000,000	1.50	3.50	7.50	15.00	25.00

KM# 14 3 ESCUDOS
3.50 g., 0.650 Silver 0.0731 oz. ASW, 20 mm. **Obv:** Shield within globe on maltese cross, date below **Obv. Legend:** REPUBLICA PORTUGUESA **Rev:** Shield within crowned globe, flowers in legend, value below **Rev. Legend:** TIMOR

Date	Mintage	VF20	XF40	MS60	MS63	MS65
1958	1,000,000	5.00	9.00	12.00	20.00	35.00

KM# 21 5 ESCUDOS
6.93 g., Copper-Nickel, 24 mm. **Obv:** Shield within globe on maltese cross, date below **Obv. Legend:** REPUBLICA PORTUGUESA **Rev:** Shield within crowned globe, flowers in legend, value below **Rev. Legend:** TIMOR

Date	Mintage	VF20	XF40	MS60	MS63	MS65
1970	1,200,000	3.00	6.50	9.00	14.00	25.00

KM# 15 6 ESCUDOS
7.00 g., 0.650 Silver 0.1463 oz. ASW, 25 mm. **Obv:** Shield within globe on maltese cross, date below **Obv. Legend:** REPUBLICA PORTUGUESA **Rev:** Shield within crowned globe, flowers in legend, value below **Rev. Legend:** TIMOR

Date	Mintage	VF20	XF40	MS60	MS63	MS65
1958	1,000,000	5.00	7.50	12.00	20.00	35.00

KM# 16 10 ESCUDOS
7.00 g., 0.650 Silver 0.1463 oz. ASW **Obv:** Shield within globe on maltese cross, date below **Obv. Legend:** REPUBLICA PORTUGUESA **Rev:** Shield within crowned globe, flowers in legend, value below **Rev. Legend:** TIMOR

Date	Mintage	VF20	XF40	MS60	MS63	MS65
1964	600,000	6.00	9.00	15.00	25.00	40.00

KM# 22 10 ESCUDOS
9.00 g., Copper-Nickel, 28 mm. **Obv:** Shield within globe on maltese cross, date below **Obv. Legend:** REPUBLICA PORTUGUESA **Rev:** Shield within crowned globe, flowers in legend, value below **Rev. Legend:** TIMOR

Date	Mintage	VF20	XF40	MS60	MS63	MS65
1970	700,000	3.00	6.00	10.00	20.00	35.00

PROVAS

Raised or stamped "PROVA" in field

KM#	Date	Mintage	Identification	Mkt Val
Pr1	1948	—	10 Avos. Bronze. KM#5.	—
Pr2	1948	—	50 Avos. Silver. KM#7.	—

TOGO

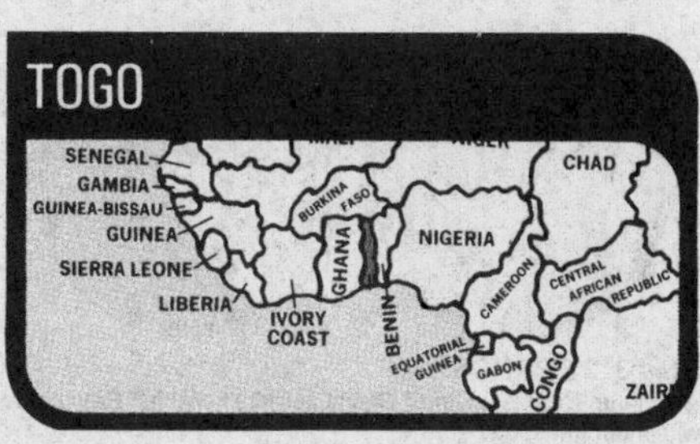

The Republic of Togo (formerly part of German Togoland), situated on the Gulf of Guinea in West Africa between Ghana and Dahomey, has an area of 21,622 sq.mi. (56,790 sq. km.) and a population of *3.4 million. Capital: Lome. Agriculture and herding, the production of dyewoods, and the mining of phosphates and iron ore are the chief industries. Copra, phosphates and coffee are exported.

Although Brazilians were the first traders to settle in Togo, Germany achieved possession, in 1884, by inducing coastal chiefs to place their territories under German protection. The German protectorate was extended international recognition at the Berlin conference of 1885 and its ultimate boundaries delimited by treaties with France in 1897 and with Britain in 1904. Anglo-French forces occupied Togoland in 1914, subsequently becoming a League of Nations mandate and a U.N. trusteeship divided, for administrative purpose, between Great Britain and France. The British portion voted in 1957 for incorporation with Ghana. The French portion became the independent Republic of Togo on April 27, 1960.

RULERS
German, 1884-1914
Anglo - French, 1914-1957
French, 1957-1960

MINT MARK
(a) - Paris, privy marks only

MONETARY SYSTEM
100 Centimes = 1 Franc

FRENCH MANDATE

U.N. Trusteeship

STANDARD COINAGE

100 Centimes = 1 Franc

KM# 1 50 CENTIMES
Aluminum-Bronze, 17.5 mm. **Obv:** Laureate head left **Rev:** Value within upright sprigs

Date	Mintage	F12	VF20	XF40	MS60	MS63
1924 (a)	3,691,000	4.00	25.00	50.00	80.00	125
1925 (a)	2,064,000	5.00	27.50	55.00	100	150
1926 (a)	445,000	20.00	60.00	100	300	375

KM# 2 FRANC

5.00 g., Aluminum-Bronze, 22 mm. **Obv:** Laureat head left **Rev:** Value within upright sprigs

Date	Mintage	F12	VF20	XF40	MS60	MS63
1924 (a)	3,472,000	3.50	33.00	60.00	125	175
1925 (a)	2,768,000	4.00	22.50	65.00	140	200

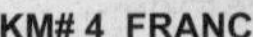

KM# 4 FRANC

Aluminum, 23 mm. **Obv:** Winged head left **Rev:** Slender-horned gazelle head divides value within sprigs

Date	Mintage	VF20	XF40	MS60	MS63	MS65
1948 (a)	5,000,000	5.00	12.00	35.00	50.00	90.00

KM# 3 2 FRANCS

Aluminum-Bronze, 27 mm. **Obv:** Laureate head left **Rev:** Value within upright sprigs

Date	Mintage	F12	VF20	XF40	MS60	MS63
1924 (a)	750,000	6.00	42.00	110	175	250
1925 (a)	580,000	7.00	45.50	120	200	350

KM# 5 2 FRANCS

2.10 g., Aluminum, 27 mm. **Obv:** Winged head left **Rev:** Slender-horned gazelle head divides value within sprigs **Note:** Similar to 1 Franc, KM#4.

Date	Mintage	VF20	XF40	MS60	MS63	MS65
1948 (a)	5,000,000	6.00	15.00	45.00	75.00	150

KM# 6 5 FRANCS

Aluminum-Bronze, 20 mm. **Obv:** Head left **Rev:** Slender-horned gazelle head divides value within sprigs

Date	Mintage	VF20	XF40	MS60	MS63	MS65
1956 (a)	10,000,000	3.00	5.00	8.00	15.00	25.00

REPUBLIC

KM# 13 500 FRANCS

7.00 g., 0.999 Silver 0.2248 oz. ASW, 30 mm. **Obv:** Arms with supporters **Rev:** Apollo 11 launch scene **Edge:** Plain

Date	Mintage	VF20	XF40	MS60	MS63	MS65
ND-1999	—	PF65 25.00				

KM# 14 500 FRANCS

7.00 g., 0.999 Silver 0.2248 oz. ASW **Obv:** Arms with supporters **Rev:** Three astronauts, moon and space capsule

Date	Mintage	VF20	XF40	MS60	MS63	MS65
ND-1999	—	PF65 25.00				

KM# 15 500 FRANCS

7.00 g., 0.999 Silver 0.2248 oz. ASW **Obv:** Arms with supporters **Rev:** Moon-walking astronaut

Date	Mintage	VF20	XF40	MS60	MS63	MS65
ND-1999	—	PF65 25.00				

KM# 18 500 FRANCS

6.93 g., 0.999 Silver 0.2226 oz. ASW, 29.7 mm. **Obv:** National arms **Obv. Legend:** REPUBLIQUE TOGOLAISE **Rev:** German Naval sailing ship **Rev. Legend:** GORCH FOCK **Edge:** Plain

Date	Mintage	VF20	XF40	MS60	MS63	MS65
ND-2000	5,000	PF65 25.00				

KM# 19 500 FRANCS

6.93 g., 0.999 Silver 0.2226 oz. ASW, 27.9 mm. **Obv:** Arms with supporters **Rev:** Head of Albert Einstein facing **Edge:** Plain

Date	Mintage	VF20	XF40	MS60	MS63	MS65
ND	—	PF65 25.00				

KM# 16 1000 FRANCS

14.97 g., 0.999 Silver 0.4808 oz. ASW, 35 mm. **Obv:** Arms with supporters **Rev:** Bust of Martin Luther 3/4 right **Edge:** Plain

Date	Mintage	VF20	XF40	MS60	MS63	MS65
1999	—	PF65 30.00				

KM# 42 1000 FRANCS

0.999 Silver, 42x24 mm. **Shape:** Rectangle

Date	Mintage	VF20	XF40	MS60	MS63	MS65
1999	—	PF65 60.00				

KM# 28 1000 FRANCS

14.95 g., 0.999 Silver 0.4802 oz. ASW, 35 mm. **Obv:** Arms with supporters **Rev:** Lion **Edge:** Plain

Date	Mintage	VF20	XF40	MS60	MS63	MS65
2000	5,000	PF65 42.00				

KM# 67 1000 FRANCS

15.00 g., Silver, 35 mm. **Rev:** Flying "P" Liner PAMIR in color

Date	Mintage	VF20	XF40	MS60	MS63	MS65
2000	5,000	PF65 32.00				

KM# 8 5000 FRANCS

24.36 g., 0.925 Silver 0.7245 oz. ASW **Subject:** 10th Year of General Gnassingbe Eyadema as President **Obv:** Arms with supporters **Rev:** Head left

Date	Mintage	VF20	XF40	MS60	MS63	MS65
1977	150	PF63 175	PF65 225			

KM# 9 10000 FRANCS

49.32 g., 0.925 Silver 1.4667 oz. ASW **Subject:** 10th Year of General Gnassingbe Eyadema as President **Obv:** Arms with supporters **Rev:** Head left

Date	Mintage	VF20	XF40	MS60	MS63	MS65
1977	150	PF63 250	PF65 300			

KM# 10 15000 FRANCS

4.48 g., 0.917 Gold 0.1321 oz. AGW **Subject:** 10th Year of General Gnassingbe Eyadema as President **Obv:** Arms with supporters **Rev:** Head facing

Date	Mintage	VF20	XF40	MS60	MS63	MS65
1977	75	PF65 1,200				

KM# 11 25000 FRANCS

9.00 g., 0.917 Gold 0.2653 oz. AGW **Subject:** 10th Year of General Gnassingbe Eyadema as President **Obv:** Arms with supporters **Rev:** Head facing

Date	Mintage	VF20	XF40	MS60	MS63	MS65
1977	75	PF65 1,400				

KM# 12 50000 FRANCS

18.00 g., 0.917 Gold 0.5307 oz. AGW **Subject:** 10th Year of General Gnassingbe Eyadema as President **Obv:** Arms with supporters **Rev:** Head facing **Note:** Similar to 25,000 Francs, KM#11.

Date	Mintage	VF20	XF40	MS60	MS63	MS65
1977	50	PF65 2,200				

ESSAIS

KM#	Date	Mintage	Identification	Mkt Val
E1	1924(a)	—	50 Centimes. Aluminum-Bronze. KM#1.	275
E2	1924(a)	—	Franc. Aluminum-Bronze. Head laureate left. Value within upright sprigs. KM#2.	325
E3	1924(a)	—	2 Francs. Aluminum-Bronze. KM#3.	300
E4	1948(a)	2,000	Franc. Copper-Nickel. KM#4.	120
E5	1948(a)	2,000	2 Francs. Copper-Nickel. KM#5.	120
E6	1956(a)	2,300	5 Francs. Aluminum-Bronze. KM#6.	75.00
E7	1956(a)	2,300	10 Francs. KM#7.	95.00
E8	1956(a)	2,300	25 Francs.	120
E9	1977	25	5000 Francs. Aluminum. KM#8.	375
E10	1977	20	5000 Francs. Copper. KM#8.	375
E11	1977	25	10000 Francs. Aluminum. KM#9.	475
E12	1977	20	10000 Francs. Copper. KM#9.	475
E13	1977	25	15000 Francs. Aluminum. KM#10.	175
E14	1977	20	15000 Francs. Copper. KM#10.	175
E15	1977	25	25000 Francs. Aluminum. KM#11.	250
E16	1977	20	25000 Francs. Copper. KM#11.	250

PIEDFORT

KM#	Date	Mintage	Identification	Mkt Val
P1	1977	5	5000 Francs. Copper. KM#8.	900
P2	1977	10	5000 Francs. Silver. KM#8.	800
P3	1977	5	10000 Francs. Copper. KM#9.	900
P3a	1977	10	10000 Francs. Silver. KM#9.	900
P4	1977	5	15000 Francs. Copper. KM#10.	700
P4a	1977	10	15000 Francs. Silver. KM#10.	700
P4b	1977	2	15000 Francs. Gold. KM#10.	1,200
P5	1977	5	25000 Francs. Copper. KM#11.	700
P5a	1977	10	25000 Francs. Silver. KM#11.	700
P5b	1977	2	25000 Francs. Gold. KM#11.	1,500

PIEDFORT WITH ESSAI

KM#	Date	Mintage	Identification	Mkt Val
PE1	1948(a)	104	Franc. Aluminum. KM#4.	200
PE2	1948(a)	104	2 Francs. Aluminum. KM#5.	220

TRIAL STRIKES

KM#	Date	Mintage	Identification	Mkt Val
TS1	1977	10	5000 Francs. Copper. Obverse of KM#8. PRUEBA.	225
TS2	1977	10	5000 Francs. Copper. Reverse of KM#8. PRUEBA.	225
TS3	1977	10	5000 Francs. Silver. Obverse of KM#8. PRUEBA.	275
TS4	1977	10	5000 Francs. Silver. Reverse of KM#8. PRUEBA.	275
TS5	1977	10	10000 Francs. Copper. Obverse of KM#9. PRUEBA.	275
TS6	1977	10	10000 Francs. Copper. Reverse of KM#9. PRUEBA.	275
TS7	1977	10	10000 Francs. Silver. Obverse of KM#9. PRUEBA.	325
TS8	1977	10	10000 Francs. Silver. Obverse of KM#9. PRUEBA.	325
TS9	1977	10	15000 Francs. Copper. Obverse of KM#10. PRUEBA.	125
TS10	1977	10	15000 Francs. Copper. Reverse of KM#10. PRUEBA.	125
TS11	1977	10	15000 Francs. Silver. Obverse of KM#10. PRUEBA.	150
TS12	1977	10	15000 Francs. Silver. Reverse of KM#10. PRUEBA.	150
TS13	1977	10	25000 Francs. Copper. Obverse of KM#11. PRUEBA.	175
TS14	1977	10	25000 Francs. Copper. Reverse of KM11. PRUEBA.	175
TS15	1977	10	25000 Francs. Silver. Obverse of KM#11. PRUEBA.	200
TS16	1977	10	25000 Francs. Silver. Reverse of KM#11. PRUEBA.	200

TOKELAU ISLANDS

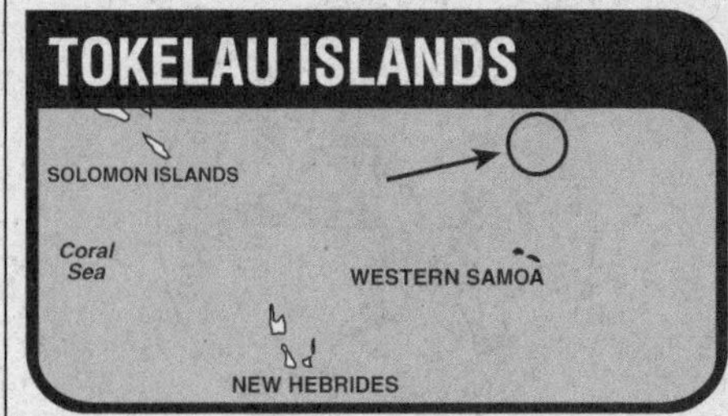

Tokelau or Union Islands, a New Zealand Territory located in the South Pacific 2,100 miles (3,379 km.) northeast of New Zealand and 300 miles (483 km.) north of Samoa, has an area of 4 sq. mi. (10 sq. km.) and a population of *2,000. Geographically, the group consists of four atolls - Atafu, Nukunono, Fakaofo and Swains – but the last belongs to American Samoa (and the United States claims the other three). The people are of Polynesian origin; Samoan is the official language. The New Zealand Minister for Foreign Affairs governs the islands; councils of family elders handle local government at the village level. The chief settlement is Fenuafala, on Fakaofo. It is connected by wireless with the offices of the New Zealand Administrative Center, located at Apia, Western Samoa. Subsistence farming and the production of copra for export are the main occupations. Revenue is also derived from the sale of postage stamps and, since 1978,coins.

Great Britain annexed the group of islands in 1889. They were added to the Gilbert and Ellice Islands colony in 1916. In 1926, they were brought under the jurisdiction of Western Samoa, which was held as a mandate of the League of Nations by New Zealand. They were declared a part of New Zealand in 1948.

Tokelau Islands issued its first coin in 1978, a "$1 TahiTala," Tokelauan for "One Dollar."

RULER
British

MINT MARK
PM - Pobjoy

NEW ZEALAND TERRITORY

STANDARD COINAGE

KM# 1 TALA

Copper-Nickel, 38.5 mm. **Ruler:** Elizabeth II **Obv:** Young bust right **Rev:** Coconut and value **Edge:** Reeded

Date	Mintage	VF20	XF40	MS60	MS63	MS65
1978	10,000	—	3.00	5.00	7.00	12.00

KM# 1a TALA

27.25 g., 0.925 Silver 0.8104 oz. ASW, 38.5 mm. **Ruler:** Elizabeth II **Obv:** Young bust right **Rev:** Coconut and value

Date	Mintage	VF20	XF40	MS60	MS63	MS65
1978	5,000	PF63 29.00	PF65 32.00			

KM# 2 TALA

Copper-Nickel, 38.5 mm. **Ruler:** Elizabeth II **Obv:** Young bust right **Rev:** V-shaped tool, bucket, rope and value

Date	Mintage	VF20	XF40	MS60	MS63	MS65
1979	—	—	2.50	4.00	6.00	12.00

KM# 2a TALA

27.25 g., 0.925 Silver 0.8104 oz. ASW, 38.5 mm. **Ruler:** Elizabeth II **Obv:** Young bust right **Rev:** V-shaped tool, bucket, rope and value

Date	Mintage	VF20	XF40	MS60	MS63	MS65
1979	—	PF63 29.00	PF65 32.00			

KM# 3 TALA

Copper-Nickel **Ruler:** Elizabeth II **Obv:** Young bust right **Rev:** Coconut crab and value **Edge:** Reeded

Date	Mintage	VF20	XF40	MS60	MS63	MS65
1980	10,000	—	4.00	6.00	9.00	17.00

KM# 3a TALA

27.25 g., 0.925 Silver 0.8104 oz. ASW, 38.5 mm. **Ruler:** Elizabeth II **Obv:** Young bust right **Rev:** Coconut Crab and value

Date	Mintage	VF20	XF40	MS60	MS63	MS65
1980	6,004	PF63 32.00	PF65 35.00			

KM# 4 TALA

Copper-Nickel **Ruler:** Elizabeth II **Obv:** Young bust right **Rev:** Frigate bird and value

Date	Mintage	VF20	XF40	MS60	MS63	MS65
1981	6,500	—	4.00	6.00	9.00	17.00

KM# 4a TALA

27.25 g., 0.925 Silver 0.8104 oz. ASW, 38.5 mm. **Ruler:** Elizabeth II **Obv:** Arnold Machin **Rev:** Frigate bird and value

Date	Mintage	VF20	XF40	MS60	MS63	MS65
1981	6,500	PF63 32.00	PF65 35.00			

KM# 5 TALA

Copper-Nickel, 38.5 mm. **Ruler:** Elizabeth II **Obv:** Young bust right **Rev:** Outrigger canoe **Edge:** Reeded

Date	Mintage	VF20	XF40	MS60	MS63	MS65
1982	10,000	—	5.00	7.00	10.00	18.00

KM# 5a TALA

27.25 g., 0.925 Silver 0.8104 oz. ASW, 38.5 mm. **Ruler:** Elizabeth II **Obv:** Young bust right **Rev:** Outrigger canoe

Date	Mintage	VF20	XF40	MS60	MS63	MS65
1982	5,000	PF63 29.00	PF65 32.00			

KM# 6 TALA

Copper-Nickel, 38.5 mm. **Ruler:** Elizabeth II **Subject:** Water Conservation **Obv:** Young bust right **Rev:** Seated and standing figure next to ancient water barrel

Date	Mintage	VF20	XF40	MS60	MS63	MS65
1983	2,000	—	—	—	25.00	45.00

KM# 7 5 TALA

28.28 g., 0.925 Silver 0.841 oz. ASW **Ruler:** Elizabeth II **Subject:** Water Conservation **Obv:** Young bust right **Rev:** Seated and standing figure next to ancient water barrel **Note:** Similar to 1 Tala, KM#6.

Date	Mintage	VF20	XF40	MS60	MS63	MS65
1983	1,000	PF63 60.00	PF65 70.00			

KM# 8.1 5 TALA

27.05 g., 0.925 Silver 0.8045 oz. ASW **Ruler:** Elizabeth II **Obv:** Young bust right **Rev:** Fishermen in sailboat **Edge:** Plain

Date	Mintage	VF20	XF40	MS60	MS63	MS65
1984	1,500	—	—	25.00	30.00	40.00

KM# 8.2 5 TALA

27.05 g., 0.925 Silver 0.8045 oz. ASW **Ruler:** Elizabeth II **Obv:** Young bust right **Rev:** Fishermen in sailboat **Edge:** Reeded

Date	Mintage	VF20	XF40	MS60	MS63	MS65
1984	500	PF63 75.00	PF65 85.00			

KM# 10 5 TALA

27.05 g., 0.925 Silver 0.8045 oz. ASW **Ruler:** Elizabeth II **Series:** Olympics **Obv:** Young bust right **Rev:** Javelin thrower

Date	Mintage	VF20	XF40	MS60	MS63	MS65
1988	20,000	—	—	—	18.00	20.00

KM# 9 5 TALA

27.21 g., 0.925 Silver 0.8092 oz. ASW **Ruler:** Elizabeth II **Obv:** Crowned head right **Rev:** Captain John Byron and HMS Dolphin **Edge:** Reeded

Date	Mintage	VF20	XF40	MS60	MS63	MS65
1989	500	PF63 45.00	PF65 55.00			

KM# 11 5 TALA

Copper-Nickel **Ruler:** Elizabeth II **Subject:** 50th Anniversary of Attack on Pearl Harbor **Obv:** Crowned bust right **Rev:** Pearl Harbor scene within circle

Date	Mintage	VF20	XF40	MS60	MS63	MS65
1991 Prooflike	—	—	—	3.00	5.00	7.00

KM# 13 5 TALA

Copper-Nickel **Ruler:** Elizabeth II **Obv:** Crowned bust right **Rev:** Battle of Guadal canal scene within circle

Date	Mintage	VF20	XF40	MS60	MS63	MS65
1991 Proof-like	—	—	—	3.00	5.00	7.00

KM# 14 5 TALA

Copper-Nickel **Ruler:** Elizabeth II **Obv:** Crowned bust right **Rev:** General Dwight Eisenhower saluting left

Date	Mintage	VF20	XF40	MS60	MS63	MS65
1991 Proof-like	—	—	—	3.00	5.00	7.00

KM# 15 5 TALA

Copper-Nickel **Ruler:** Elizabeth II **Obv:** Crowned bust right **Rev:** Raising the flag on Iwo Jima scene

Date	Mintage	VF20	XF40	MS60	MS63	MS65
1991 Proof-like	—	—	—	3.00	5.00	7.00

KM# 16 5 TALA

31.47 g., 0.925 Silver 0.9359 oz. ASW **Ruler:** Elizabeth II **Obv:** Crowned head right **Rev:** Scene of first lunar orbit

Date	Mintage	VF20	XF40	MS60	MS63	MS65
1993	10,000	PF63 21.50	PF65 24.00			

KM# 17 5 TALA

31.47 g., 0.925 Silver 0.9359 oz. ASW **Ruler:** Elizabeth II **Series:** Endangered Wildlife **Obv:** Crowned head right **Rev:** Steindachner's Emo Skink

Date	Mintage	VF20	XF40	MS60	MS63	MS65
1993	15,000	PF63 23.50	PF65 26.00			

KM# 18 5 TALA
31.47 g., 0.925 Silver 0.9359 oz. ASW **Ruler:** Elizabeth II **Obv:** Crowned head right **Rev:** H.M.S. Pandora

Date	Mintage	VF20	XF40	MS60	MS63	MS65
1993	15,000	PF63 21.50	PF65 24.00			

KM# 19 5 TALA
31.47 g., 0.925 Silver 0.9359 oz. ASW **Ruler:** Elizabeth II **Series:** Olympics **Obv:** Crowned head right **Rev:** Swimmers

Date	Mintage	VF20	XF40	MS60	MS63	MS65
1994	40,000	PF63 21.50	PF65 24.00			

KM# 20 5 TALA
31.47 g., 0.925 Silver 0.9359 oz. ASW **Ruler:** Elizabeth II **Subject:** World Cup Soccer **Obv:** Crowned head right **Rev:** Soccer player and flying bird within globe design

Date	Mintage	VF20	XF40	MS60	MS63	MS65
1994	25,000	PF63 21.50	PF65 24.00			

KM# 21 5 TALA
31.47 g., 0.925 Silver 0.9359 oz. ASW **Ruler:** Elizabeth II **Series:** Protect Our World **Obv:** Crowned head right **Rev:** Swamp scene

Date	Mintage	VF20	XF40	MS60	MS63	MS65
1994	10,000	PF63 21.50	PF65 24.00			

KM# 22 5 TALA
31.47 g., 0.925 Silver 0.9359 oz. ASW **Ruler:** Elizabeth II **Series:** Olympics **Obv:** Crowned head right **Rev:** Sailboarding

Date	Mintage	VF20	XF40	MS60	MS63	MS65
1994	50,000	PF63 21.50	PF65 24.00			

KM# 23 5 TALA
31.47 g., 0.925 Silver 0.9359 oz. ASW **Ruler:** Elizabeth II **Series:** Queen Elizabeth The Queen Mother **Obv:** Crowned head right **Rev:** Queen Mother, daughter and son

Date	Mintage	VF20	XF40	MS60	MS63	MS65
1995	30,000	PF63 21.50	PF65 24.00			

KM# 27 5 TALA
31.55 g., 0.925 Silver 0.9383 oz. ASW, 38.5 mm. **Ruler:** Elizabeth II **Series:** Queen Elizabeth The Queen Mother **Subject:** VE Day Celebrations, 8th of May **Obv:** Crowned head right **Rev:** 1/2 Figures of royal couple facing within beaded circle **Edge:** Reeded

Date	Mintage	VF20	XF40	MS60	MS63	MS65
1997	—	PF63 21.50	PF65 24.00			

KM# 25 5 TALA
31.47 g., 0.925 Silver 0.9359 oz. ASW, 38.5 mm. **Ruler:** Elizabeth II **Obv:** Crowned head right **Rev:** H.M.S. Dolphin **Edge:** Reeded

Date	Mintage	VF20	XF40	MS60	MS63	MS65
1998	—	PF63 21.50	PF65 24.00			

KM# 29 5 TALA
31.52 g., 0.925 Silver 0.9374 oz. ASW, 38.6 mm. **Ruler:** Elizabeth II **Subject:** Diana Princess Of Wales **Obv:** Crowned head right **Rev:** Diana and young dancers **Edge:** Reeded

Date	Mintage	VF20	XF40	MS60	MS63	MS65
1999	—	PF63 21.50	PF65 24.00			

KM# 26 5 TALA
28.12 g., 0.925 Silver 0.8363 oz. ASW, 38.4 mm. **Ruler:** Elizabeth II **Subject:** Queen Mother **Obv:** Crowned head right **Rev:** Queen Mother celebrating "VE" day **Edge:** Reeded

Date	Mintage	VF20	XF40	MS60	MS63	MS65
2000	10,000	PF63 19.50	PF65 22.00			

Note: With gold gilt outer ring

KM# 31 10 TALA
1.24 g., 0.999 Gold 0.040 oz. AGW, 13.92 mm. **Ruler:** Elizabeth II **Obv:** Elizabeth II **Rev:** Ship, the Golden Hind above value **Edge:** Reeded

Date	Mintage	VF20	XF40	MS60	MS63	MS65
1997	—	PF65 65.00	PF67 75.00			

KM# 45 10 TALA
1.24 g., 0.999 Gold 0.0398 oz. AGW **Ruler:** Elizabeth II **Obv:** Crowned head right **Obv. Legend:** TOKELAU **Rev:** Sea maiden and turtle **Edge:** Reeded

Date	Mintage	VF20	XF40	MS60	MS63	MS65
1999	25,000	PF65 65.00	PF67 75.00			

KM# 12 50 TALA
31.10 g., 0.999 Silver 0.999 oz. ASW **Ruler:** Elizabeth II **Subject:** 50th Anniversary of **Obv:** Crowned bust right **Rev:** Pearl Harbor scene

Date	Mintage	VF20	XF40	MS60	MS63	MS65
1991	50,000	PF63 23.00	PF65 25.50			

KM# 34 50 TALA
31.10 g., 0.999 Silver 0.9989 oz. ASW **Ruler:** Elizabeth II **Obv:** Crowned bust right **Obv. Legend:** TOKELAU **Rev:** Battle of Guadalcanal

Date	Mintage	VF20	XF40	MS60	MS63	MS65
1991	50,000	PF63 23.00	PF65 25.50			

KM# 35 50 TALA
31.10 g., 0.999 Silver 0.9989 oz. ASW **Ruler:** Elizabeth II **Obv:** Crowned bust right **Obv. Legend:** TOKELAU **Rev:** Mount Sirubachi and Iwo Jima battle scene

Date	Mintage	VF20	XF40	MS60	MS63	MS65
1991	50,000	PF63 23.00	PF65 25.50			

KM# 36 50 TALA
31.10 g., 0.999 Silver 0.9989 oz. ASW **Ruler:** Elizabeth II **Obv:** Crowned bust right **Obv. Legend:** TOKELAU **Rev:** General Dwight D. Eisenhower and troups

Date	Mintage	VF20	XF40	MS60	MS63	MS65
1991	50,000	PF63 23.00	PF65 25.50			

KM# 28 50 TALA
31.25 g., 0.999 Silver 1.0037 oz. ASW, 38.6 mm. **Ruler:** Elizabeth II **Subject:** Anne Frank **Obv:** Crowned bust right **Rev:** Building arch and head facing within circle **Edge:** Reeded

Date	Mintage	VF20	XF40	MS60	MS63	MS65
1993	—	PF63 23.00	PF65 25.50			

KM# 37 50 TALA
31.10 g., 0.999 Silver 0.9989 oz. ASW **Ruler:** Elizabeth II **Series:** World War II **Obv:** Crowned bust right **Obv. Legend:** TOKELAU **Rev:** Three airplanes and carrier **Rev. Legend:** • CARRIERS • THE STRIKE FORCE • **Edge:** Reeded

Date	Mintage	VF20	XF40	MS60	MS63	MS65
1993	—	PF63 23.00	PF65 25.50			

KM# 38 50 TALA
31.10 g., 0.999 Silver 0.9989 oz. ASW **Ruler:** Elizabeth II **Series:** World War II **Obv:** Crowned bust right **Obv. Legend:** TOKELAU **Rev:** Bust of pilot 3/4 right, three planes at right in background **Rev. Legend:** • TUSKEGEE AIRMEN • **Edge:** Reeded

Date	Mintage	VF20	XF40	MS60	MS63	MS65
1993	—	PF63 23.00	PF65 25.50			

KM# 39 50 TALA
31.10 g., 0.999 Silver 0.9989 oz. ASW **Ruler:** Elizabeth II **Series:** World War II **Obv:** Crowned bust right **Obv. Legend:** TOKELAU **Rev:** Headdress at left, bust of Navajo soldier at right on radio **Rev. Legend:** NATIVE AMERICAN CODE TALKERS **Edge:** Reeded

Date	Mintage	VF20	XF40	MS60	MS63	MS65
1993	—	PF63 23.00	PF65 25.50			

KM# 40 50 TALA
31.10 g., 0.999 Silver 0.9989 oz. ASW **Ruler:** Elizabeth II **Series:** World War II **Obv:** Crowned bust right **Obv. Legend:** TOKELAU **Rev:** Bust of WAC facing saluting **Rev. Legend:** WOMEN IN THE ARMED FORCES **Edge:** Reeded

Date	Mintage	VF20	XF40	MS60	MS63	MS65
1993	—	PF63 23.00	PF65 25.50			

KM# 41 50 TALA
31.10 g., 0.999 Silver 0.9989 oz. ASW **Ruler:** Elizabeth II **Series:** World War II **Obv:** Crowned bust right **Obv. Legend:** TOKELAU **Rev:** 1/2 length bust of Polish soldier at left, patroling soldiers in background **Rev. Legend:** POLISH FREEDOM FIGHTERS **Edge:** Reeded

Date	Mintage	VF20	XF40	MS60	MS63	MS65
1993	—	PF63 23.00	PF65 25.50			

KM# 42 50 TALA
31.10 g., 0.999 Silver 0.9989 oz. ASW **Ruler:** Elizabeth II **Series:** World War II **Obv:** Crowned bust right **Obv. Legend:** TOKELAU **Rev:** P. O. W. camp, guard tower **Rev. Legend:** M. I. A.s + P. O. W.s **Edge:** Reeded

Date	Mintage	VF20	XF40	MS60	MS63	MS65
1993	—	PF63 23.00	PF65 25.50			

KM# 44 50 TALA
7.78 g., 0.5833 Gold 0.1459 oz. AGW, 24.5 mm. **Ruler:** Elizabeth II **Subject:** 50th Anniversary Birth of Prince Charles **Obv:** Crowned head right **Obv. Legend:** TOKELAU **Rev:** Queen Mother and Princess Elizabeth seated holding Prince Charles **Rev. Legend:** QUEEN ELIZABETH THE QUEEN MOTHER **Edge:** Reeded

Date	Mintage	VF20	XF40	MS60	MS63	MS65
1998	—	PF65 220	PF67 240			

KM# 24 100 TALA
1000.00 g., 0.999 Silver 32.1186 oz. ASW, 100 mm. **Ruler:** Elizabeth II **Subject:** Warships; H.M.S. Dolphin, Pandora and General Jackson **Obv:** Crowned head right **Rev:** Three sailing warships and compass face **Note:** Illustration reduced.

Date	Mintage	VF20	XF40	MS60	MS63	MS65
1996	1,500	PF67 750				

TONGA

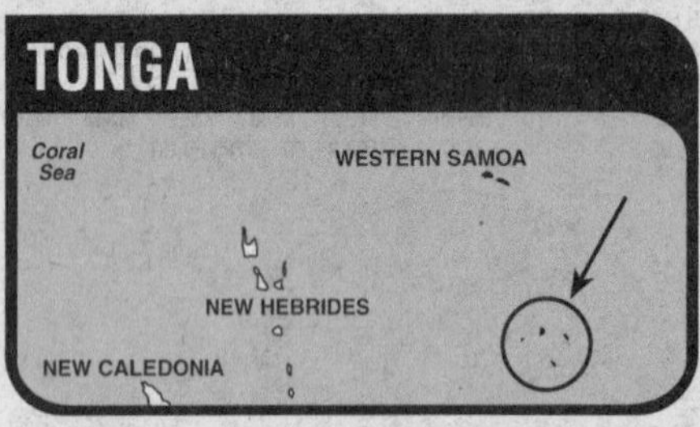

The Kingdom of Tonga (or Friendly Islands) is an archipelago situated in the southern Pacific Ocean south of Western Samoa and east of Fiji comprised of 150 islands. Tonga has an area of 270 sq. mi. (748 sq. km.) and a population of *100,000. Capital: Nuku'alofa. Primarily agricultural, the kingdom exports bananas and copra.

Dutch navigators Willem Schouten and Jacob Lemaire were the first Europeans to visit Tonga in 1616. The noted Dutch explorer Abel Tasman who visited the Tongatapu group in 1643 followed them. No further European contact was made until 1773 when British navigator Capt. James Cook arrived and, impressed by the peaceful deportment of the natives, named the islands the Friendly Islands. Within a few years of Cook's visit, Tonga was embroiled in a civil war that lasted until the great chief Taufa'ahau, who reigned as Siasoi Tupou I (1845-93), was converted to Christianity and brought unity and peace to the islands. Tonga became a self-governing protectorate of Great Britain in 1900 and a fully independent state on June 4, 1970. The monarchy is a member of the Commonwealth of Nations. King Taufa'ahau is Head of State and Government.

RULERS
Queen Salote, 1918-1965
King Taufa'ahau IV, 1967—2006

MONETARY SYSTEM
12 Pence = 1 Shilling
20 Shillings = 1 Pound

KINGDOM

STANDARD COINAGE

16 Pounds = 1 Koula

KM# 1 1/4 KOULA
8.13 g., 0.916 Gold 0.2393 oz. AGW **Ruler:** Salote **Obv:** Head right **Rev:** Crowned arms

Date	Mintage	VF20	XF40	MS60	MS63	MS65
1962	—	—	—	—	425	450
1962	6,300	PF63 475	PF65 500			

KM# 1a 1/4 KOULA
Platinum APW **Ruler:** Salote **Obv:** Head right **Rev:** Crowned arms

Date	Mintage	VF20	XF40	MS60	MS63	MS65
1962	—	PF63 650	PF65 700			

KM# 2 1/2 KOULA
16.25 g., 0.916 Gold 0.4786 oz. AGW **Ruler:** Salote **Obv:** Crowned arms **Rev:** Standing female half left

Date	Mintage	VF20	XF40	MS60	MS63	MS65
1962	—	—	—	—	825	875
1962	3,000	PF63 925	PF65 975			

KM# 2a 1/2 KOULA
Platinum APW **Ruler:** Salote **Obv:** Crowned arms **Rev:** Standing female half left

Date	Mintage	VF20	XF40	MS60	MS63	MS65
1962	—	PF63 1,100	PF65 1,200			

KM# 3 KOULA
32.50 g., 0.916 Gold 0.9571 oz. AGW **Ruler:** Salote **Obv:** Crowned arms below value **Rev:** Standing figure half left

Date	Mintage	VF20	XF40	MS60	MS63	MS65
1962	1,500	—	—	—	1,650	1,750
1962	—	PF63 1,800	PF65 1,900			

KM# 3a KOULA
Platinum APW **Ruler:** Salote **Obv:** Crowned arms below value **Rev:** Standing figure half left

Date	Mintage	VF20	XF40	MS60	MS63	MS65
1962	—	PF63 2,000	PF65 2,200			

DECIMAL COINAGE

100 Senti = 1 Pa'anga; 100 Pa'anga = 1 Hau

KM# 4 SENITI
1.85 g., Bronze, 17.5 mm. **Ruler:** Taufa'ahau Tupou IV **Obv:** Head right **Rev:** Giant Tortoise **Edge:** Plain

Date	Mintage	VF20	XF40	MS60	MS63	MS65
1967	500,000	0.10	0.15	0.75	1.50	3.00
1967	—	PF65 3.00				

KM# 27 SENITI
1.85 g., Bronze, 17.5 mm. **Ruler:** Taufa'ahau Tupou IV **Obv:** Head right **Rev:** Giant tortoise **Edge:** Plain

Date	Mintage	VF20	XF40	MS60	MS63	MS65
1968	500,000	0.10	0.15	0.75	1.50	3.00
1968	—	PF65 3.00				

KM# 27a SENITI
1.69 g., Brass, 17.5 mm. **Ruler:** Taufa'ahau Tupou IV **Obv:** Head right **Rev:** Giant tortoise **Edge:** Plain

Date	Mintage	VF20	XF40	MS60	MS63	MS65
1974	500,000	0.10	0.15	0.35	0.75	1.50

KM# 42 SENITI
1.85 g., Bronze, 17.5 mm. **Ruler:** Taufa'ahau Tupou IV **Series:** F.A.O. **Obv:** Ear of corn **Rev:** Sow right **Edge:** Plain

Date	Mintage	VF20	XF40	MS60	MS63	MS65
1975	1,000,000	—	0.10	0.25	0.45	1.50
1979	1,000,000	—	0.10	0.25	0.45	1.50

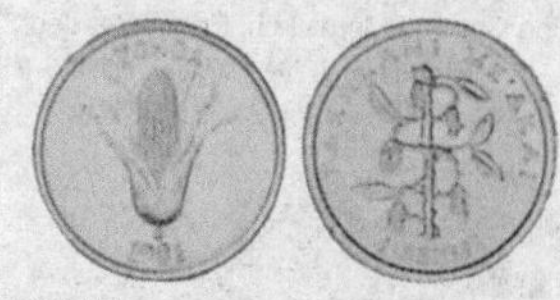

KM# 66 SENITI
1.80 g., Bronze, 16.51 mm. **Ruler:** Taufa'ahau Tupou IV **Series:** World Food Day **Obv:** Ear of corn **Rev:** Vanilla plant **Edge:** Plain

Date	Mintage	VF20	XF40	MS60	MS63	MS65
1981	1,544,000	—	0.10	0.25	0.45	0.80
1990	—	—	0.10	0.20	0.35	0.75
1991	—	—	0.10	0.20	0.35	0.75
1994	500,000	—	0.10	0.20	0.35	0.75
1996	—	—	0.10	0.20	0.35	0.75

KM# 5 2 SENITI
3.90 g., Bronze, 21 mm. **Ruler:** Taufa'ahau Tupou IV **Obv:** Head right **Rev:** Giant Tortoise **Edge:** Plain

Date	Mintage	VF20	XF40	MS60	MS63	MS65
1967	500,000	0.10	0.20	1.00	2.00	4.00
1967	—	PF65 3.00				

KM# 28 2 SENITI
3.90 g., Bronze, 21 mm. **Ruler:** Taufa'ahau Tupou IV **Obv:** Head right **Rev:** Giant tortoise **Edge:** Plain

Date	Mintage	VF20	XF40	MS60	MS63	MS65
1968	200,000	0.10	0.20	1.00	2.00	4.00
1968	—	PF65 4.50				
1974	25,000	0.10	0.20	1.00	2.00	4.00

KM# 43 2 SENITI
3.90 g., Bronze, 21 mm. **Ruler:** Taufa'ahau Tupou IV **Series:** F.A.O. **Obv:** Two watermelons **Rev:** Paper doll cutouts form design in center circle of wreath **Edge:** Plain

Date	Mintage	VF20	XF40	MS60	MS63	MS65
1975	400,000	—	0.15	0.30	0.65	1.50
1979	500,000	—	0.15	0.30	0.65	1.50

KM# 67 2 SENITI
3.87 g., Bronze, 19.46 mm. **Ruler:** Taufa'ahau Tupou IV **Series:** World Food Day **Obv:** Taro Plants **Rev:** Paper doll cutouts form design in center circle of wreath **Edge:** Plain

Date	Mintage	VF20	XF40	MS60	MS63	MS65
1981	1,102,000	—	0.15	0.30	0.65	1.35
1990	—	—	0.15	0.25	0.50	1.25
1991	—	—	0.15	0.25	0.50	1.25
1994	250,000	—	0.15	0.25	0.50	1.25
1996	—	—	0.15	0.25	0.50	1.25

KM# 6 5 SENITI
2.80 g., Copper-Nickel, 19.5 mm. **Ruler:** Taufa'ahau Tupou IV **Obv:** Head right **Rev:** Value and stars flanked by sprigs **Edge:** Plain

Date	Mintage	VF20	XF40	MS60	MS63	MS65
1967	300,000	0.10	0.25	0.85	1.75	2.50
1967	—	PF65 3.50				

KM# 29 5 SENITI
2.80 g., Copper-Nickel, 19.5 mm. **Ruler:** Taufa'ahau Tupou IV **Obv:** Head right **Rev:** Value and stars flanked by sprigs

Date	Mintage	VF20	XF40	MS60	MS63	MS65
1968	100,000	0.10	0.25	0.75	1.50	2.25
1968	—	PF65 2.50				
1974	75,000	0.10	0.25	0.75	1.50	2.25

KM# 44 5 SENITI
2.80 g., Copper-Nickel, 19.5 mm. **Ruler:** Taufa'ahau Tupou IV **Series:** F.A.O. **Obv:** Hen with chicks **Rev:** Banana bunch

Date	Mintage	VF20	XF40	MS60	MS63	MS65
1975	100,000	0.10	0.25	0.50	1.00	1.75
1977	110,000	0.10	0.25	0.50	1.00	1.75
1979	100,000	0.10	0.25	0.50	1.00	1.75

KM# 68 5 SENITI
2.80 g., Copper-Nickel, 19.5 mm. **Ruler:** Taufa'ahau Tupou IV **Series:** World Food Day **Obv:** Hen with chicks **Rev:** Coconuts above sprig **Edge:** Reeded

Date	Mintage	VF20	XF40	MS60	MS63	MS65
1981	941,000	0.10	0.25	0.45	0.85	1.50
1990	—	0.10	0.25	0.45	0.85	1.50
1991	—	—	0.25	0.45	0.85	1.50
1994	200,000	0.10	0.25	0.45	0.85	1.50
1996	—	0.10	0.25	0.35	0.75	1.25

KM# 7 10 SENITI
5.65 g., Copper-Nickel, 23.5 mm. **Ruler:** Taufa'ahau Tupou IV **Obv:** Head right **Rev:** Value and stars flanked by sprigs

Date	Mintage	VF20	XF40	MS60	MS63	MS65
1967	300,000	0.20	0.35	0.90	1.85	2.50
1967	—	PF65 3.50				

KM# 30 10 SENITI
5.65 g., Copper-Nickel, 23.5 mm. **Ruler:** Taufa'ahau Tupou IV **Obv:** Head right **Rev:** Value and stars flanked by sprigs

Date	Mintage	VF20	XF40	MS60	MS63	MS65
1968	100,000	0.20	0.40	0.85	1.75	2.25
1968	—	PF65 3.00				
1974	50,000	0.25	0.50	0.85	1.75	2.25

KM# 45 10 SENITI
5.65 g., Copper-Nickel, 23.5 mm. **Ruler:** Taufa'ahau Tupou IV **Series:** F.A.O. **Obv:** Uniformed bust facing **Rev:** Cows in pasture

Date	Mintage	VF20	XF40	MS60	MS63	MS65
1975	75,000	0.20	0.30	0.65	1.25	2.00

Date	Mintage	VF20	XF40	MS60	MS63	MS65
1977	25,000	0.20	0.30	0.65	1.25	2.00
1979	100,000	0.20	0.30	0.65	1.25	2.00

KM# 69 10 SENITI
5.65 g., Copper-Nickel, 23.5 mm. **Ruler:** Taufa'ahau Tupou IV **Series:** World Food Day **Obv:** Uniformed bust facing **Rev:** Banana tree **Edge:** Reeded

Date	Mintage	VF20	XF40	MS60	MS63	MS65
1981	712,000	0.20	0.30	0.65	1.25	2.00
1990	—	0.20	0.30	0.50	1.00	1.75
1991	—	0.20	0.30	0.50	1.00	1.75
1994	140,000	0.20	0.30	0.50	1.00	1.75
1996	—	0.20	0.30	0.50	1.00	1.75

KM# 8 20 SENITI
11.30 g., Copper-Nickel, 28.5 mm. **Ruler:** Taufa'ahau Tupou IV **Obv:** Head right **Rev:** Crowned arms

Date	Mintage	VF20	XF40	MS60	MS63	MS65
1967	150,000	0.25	0.50	1.00	2.25	3.50
1967	—	PF65 4.50				

KM# 13 20 SENITI
11.30 g., Copper-Nickel, 28.5 mm. **Ruler:** Taufa'ahau Tupou IV **Subject:** Coronation of Taufa'ahau Tupou IV **Obv:** Head right, small crowns around border **Rev:** Crowned arms **Edge:** Reeded

Date	Mintage	VF20	XF40	MS60	MS63	MS65
ND-1967	15,000	0.50	1.00	1.25	2.25	3.50
ND-1967	—	PF65 3.50				

KM# 31 20 SENITI
11.30 g., Copper-Nickel, 28.5 mm. **Ruler:** Taufa'ahau Tupou IV **Obv:** Head right **Rev:** Crowned arms

Date	Mintage	VF20	XF40	MS60	MS63	MS65
1968	35,000	0.25	0.50	1.00	2.00	2.75
1968	—	PF65 3.00				
1974	50,000	0.25	0.50	1.00	2.00	2.75

KM# 46 20 SENITI
11.30 g., Copper-Nickel, 28.5 mm. **Ruler:** Taufa'ahau Tupou IV **Series:** F.A.O. **Obv:** Uniformed bust facing **Rev:** Box hive and 20 bees

Date	Mintage	VF20	XF40	MS60	MS63	MS65
1975	75,000	0.25	0.60	1.25	3.00	5.00
1977	25,000	0.25	0.60	1.25	3.00	5.00
1979	50,000	0.25	0.60	1.25	3.00	5.00

KM# 70 20 SENITI
11.30 g., Copper-Nickel, 28.5 mm. **Ruler:** Taufa'ahau Tupou IV **Series:** World Food Day - FAO **Obv:** Uniformed bust facing **Obv. Legend:** TONGA **Rev:** Yams **Rev. Legend:** FAKALAHI ME'AKAI **Edge:** Reeded

Date	Mintage	VF20	XF40	MS60	MS63	MS65
1981	610,000	0.25	0.50	0.75	1.50	2.50
1990	610,000	0.25	0.50	0.65	1.25	2.25
1991	—	0.25	0.50	0.65	1.25	2.25
1994	680,000	0.25	0.50	0.65	1.25	2.00
1996	—	0.25	0.50	0.65	1.25	2.00

KM# 9 50 SENITI
18.00 g., Copper-Nickel, 34.5 mm. **Ruler:** Taufa'ahau Tupou IV **Obv:** Head right **Rev:** Crowned arms

Date	Mintage	VF20	XF40	MS60	MS63	MS65
1967	75,000	0.75	1.25	1.50	2.75	4.00
1967	—	PF65 5.00				

KM# 15 50 SENITI
18.00 g., Copper-Nickel, 34.5 mm. **Ruler:** Taufa'ahau Tupou IV **Subject:** Coronation of Taufa'ahau Tupou IV **Obv:** Head right **Rev:** Crowned arms

Date	Mintage	VF20	XF40	MS60	MS63	MS65
ND-1967	15,000	1.00	1.50	2.00	3.00	4.50
ND-1967	—	PF65 6.00				

KM# 32 50 SENITI
17.80 g., Copper-Nickel, 34.5 mm. **Ruler:** Taufa'ahau Tupou IV **Obv:** Head right **Rev:** Crowned arms

Date	Mintage	VF20	XF40	MS60	MS63	MS65
1968	25,000	0.75	1.25	1.75	2.25	3.50
1968	—	PF65 4.00				

KM# 41 50 SENITI
14.60 g., Copper-Nickel, 32.5 mm. **Ruler:** Taufa'ahau Tupou IV **Obv:** Head right **Rev:** Crowned arms **Edge:** Plain **Shape:** 12-sided

Date	Mintage	VF20	XF40	MS60	MS63	MS65
1974	50,000	0.75	1.25	1.50	2.00	3.50

KM# 47 50 SENITI
14.60 g., Copper-Nickel, 32.5 mm. **Ruler:** Taufa'ahau Tupou IV **Series:** F.A.O. **Obv:** Uniformed bust facing **Rev:** 50 Fish swimming in circle formation **Edge:** Plain **Shape:** 12-sided

Date	Mintage	VF20	XF40	MS60	MS63	MS65
1975	40,000	0.50	1.00	1.50	2.25	5.00
1977	20,000	0.75	1.25	1.75	2.75	6.00
1978	60,000	0.50	1.00	1.50	2.25	5.00

KM# 71 50 SENITI
14.60 g., Copper-Nickel, 32.5 mm. **Ruler:** Taufa'ahau Tupou IV **Series:** World Food Day **Obv:** Uniformed bust facing **Obv. Legend:** TONGA **Rev:** Tomato plants **Rev. Legend:** FAKALAHI ME'AKAI **Edge:** Plain **Shape:** 12-sided

Date	Mintage	VF20	XF40	MS60	MS63	MS65
1981	555,000	0.45	0.75	1.25	1.75	3.00
1990	—	0.45	0.75	1.00	1.50	3.00
1991	—	0.45	0.75	1.00	1.50	2.75
1994	41,000	0.45	0.75	1.00	1.50	2.75
1996	—	0.45	0.75	1.00	1.50	2.50

KM# 82 50 SENITI
Copper-Nickel, 38.5 mm. **Ruler:** Taufa'ahau Tupou IV **Subject:** 100th Anniversary of Automobile Industry **Obv:** Head right **Rev:** Silver Ghost and Camargue by Rolls-Royce **Edge:** Reeded

Date	Mintage	VF20	XF40	MS60	MS63	MS65
1985	Est. 20000	—	—	1.25	2.50	4.00

KM# 83 50 SENITI
Copper-Nickel, 38.5 mm. **Ruler:** Taufa'ahau Tupou IV **Subject:** 100th Anniversary of Automobile Industry **Obv:** Head right **Rev:** Range Rover and Land Rover **Edge:** Reeded

Date	Mintage	VF20	XF40	MS60	MS63	MS65
1985	Est. 20000	—	—	1.50	3.00	5.00

KM# 84 50 SENITI
Copper-Nickel, 38.5 mm. **Ruler:** Taufa'ahau Tupou IV **Subject:** 100th Anniversary of Automobile Industry **Obv:** Head right **Rev:** Cowley Touring Car and Morris Mini **Edge:** Reeded

Date	Mintage	VF20	XF40	MS60	MS63	MS65
1985	Est. 20000	—	—	1.50	3.00	5.00

KM# 85 50 SENITI
Copper-Nickel, 38.5 mm. **Ruler:** Taufa'ahau Tupou IV **Subject:** 100th Anniversary of Automobile Industry **Obv:** Head right **Rev:** MGB GT and MG TA **Edge:** Reeded

Date	Mintage	VF20	XF40	MS60	MS63	MS65
1985	Est. 20000	—	—	1.50	3.00	5.00

KM# 98 50 SENITI
Copper-Nickel, 38.5 mm. **Ruler:** Taufa'ahau Tupou IV **Subject:** 85th Birthday of Queen Mother **Obv:** Head right **Rev:** Queen Mother as a young girl **Edge:** Reeded

Date	Mintage	VF20	XF40	MS60	MS63	MS65
1985	Est. 20000	—	—	1.00	2.00	3.50

KM# 99 50 SENITI
Copper-Nickel, 38.5 mm. **Ruler:** Taufa'ahau Tupou IV **Subject:** 85th Birthday of Queen Mother **Obv:** Head right **Rev:** Wedding of King George VI and Elizabeth **Edge:** Reeded

Date	Mintage	VF20	XF40	MS60	MS63	MS65
1985	—	—	—	1.00	2.00	3.50

KM# 100 50 SENITI
Copper-Nickel, 38.5 mm. **Ruler:** Taufa'ahau Tupou IV **Subject:** 85th Birthday of Queen Mother **Obv:** Head right **Rev:** King George VI and Elizabeth **Edge:** Reeded

Date	Mintage	VF20	XF40	MS60	MS63	MS65
1985	Est. 20000	—	—	1.00	2.00	3.50

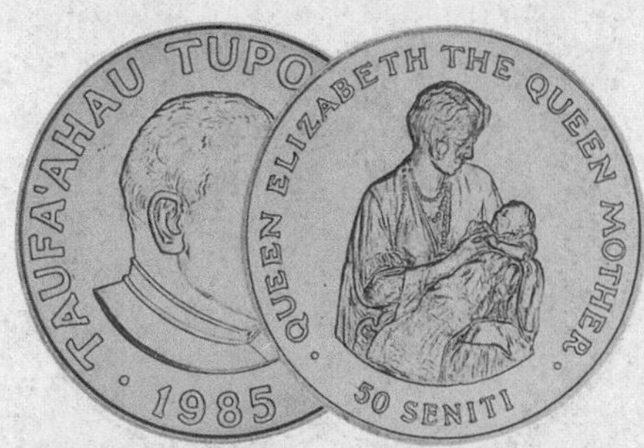

KM# 101 50 SENITI
Copper-Nickel, 38.5 mm. **Ruler:** Taufa'ahau Tupou IV **Subject:** 85th Birthday of Queen Mother **Obv:** Head right **Rev:** Queen Mother holding Queen Elizabeth II **Edge:** Reeded

Date	Mintage	VF20	XF40	MS60	MS63	MS65
1985	Est. 20000	—	—	1.00	2.00	3.50

KM# 102 50 SENITI
Copper-Nickel, 38.5 mm. **Ruler:** Taufa'ahau Tupou IV **Subject:** 85th Birthday of Queen Mother **Obv:** Head right **Rev:** Queen Mother facing **Edge:** Reeded

Date	Mintage	VF20	XF40	MS60	MS63	MS65
1985	Est. 20000	—	—	1.00	2.00	3.50

KM# 203 50 SENITI
28.28 g., Copper-Nickel, 38.61 mm. **Ruler:** Siaosi Tupou V **Subject:** Queen Mother, 96th Birthday

Date	Mintage	VF20	XF40	MS60	MS63	MS65
1996	—	PF65 32.00				

KM# 204 50 SENITI
15.98 g., 0.925 Silver 0.4752 oz. ASW, 28.4 mm. **Ruler:** Siaosi Tupou V **Subject:** Queen Mother, 97th Birthday

Date	Mintage	VF20	XF40	MS60	MS63	MS65
1997	—	PF65 30.00				

KM# 171 50 SENITI
20.00 g., 0.925 Silver 0.5948 oz. ASW, 34 mm. **Ruler:** Taufa'ahau Tupou IV **Subject:** Olympics **Obv:** Crowned arms within circle **Rev:** Boxer within circle **Edge:** Reeded

Date	Mintage	VF20	XF40	MS60	MS63	MS65
1998	50,000	PF63 25.00	PF65 35.00			

KM# 11 PA'ANGA
Copper-Nickel, 38.5 mm. **Ruler:** Taufa'ahau Tupou IV **Obv:** Head right **Rev:** Crowned arms **Edge:** Reeded

Date	Mintage	VF20	XF40	MS60	MS63	MS65
1967	78,000	—	1.50	2.50	4.50	6.00
1967	—	PF65 8.00				

KM# 17 PA'ANGA
Copper-Nickel, 38.5 mm. **Ruler:** Taufa'ahau Tupou IV **Subject:** Coronation of Taufa'ahau Tupou IV **Obv:** Head right, small crowns around border **Rev:** Crowned arms **Edge:** Reeded

Date	Mintage	VF20	XF40	MS60	MS63	MS65
ND-1967	13,000	—	1.50	2.50	4.50	6.00
ND-1967	1,923	PF65 8.00				

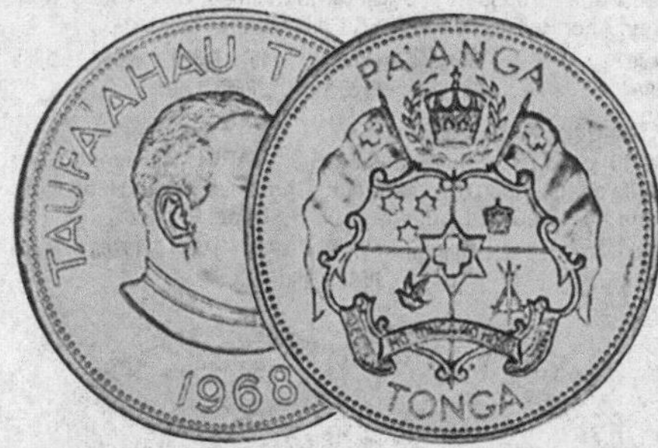

KM# 33 PA'ANGA
Copper-Nickel, 38.5 mm. **Ruler:** Taufa'ahau Tupou IV **Obv:** Head right **Rev:** Crowned arms **Edge:** Reeded

Date	Mintage	VF20	XF40	MS60	MS63	MS65
1968	14,000	—	1.50	2.50	4.50	6.00
1968	—	PF65 8.00				
1974	10,000	—	1.50	2.50	4.50	6.00

KM# 48 PA'ANGA
Copper-Nickel, 38.5 mm. **Ruler:** Taufa'ahau Tupou IV **Series:** F.A.O. **Obv:** Uniformed bust facing **Rev:** 100 Palm trees **Edge:** Reeded

Date	Mintage	VF20	XF40	MS60	MS63	MS65
1975	13,000	—	1.25	2.50	4.50	6.00

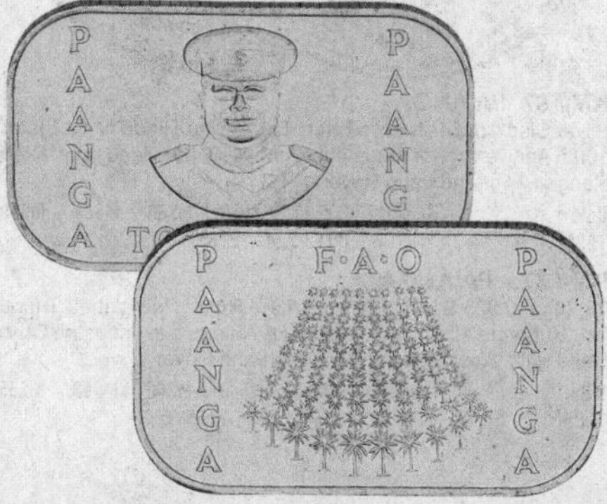

KM# 57 PA'ANGA
Copper-Nickel, 48x27 mm. **Ruler:** Taufa'ahau Tupou IV **Series:** F.A.O **Obv:** Uniformed bust facing **Rev:** 100 Palm trees **Edge:** Plain **Shape:** Rectangular

Date	Mintage	VF20	XF40	MS60	MS63	MS65
1977	25,000	—	—	4.50	8.50	16.50

KM# 58 PA'ANGA
Copper-Nickel, 48x27 mm. **Ruler:** Taufa'ahau Tupou IV **Series:** F.A.O. **Subject:** 60th Birthday **Obv:** Uniformed bust facing flanked by stars and dates **Rev:** 100 Palm trees **Edge:** Plain **Shape:** Rectangular

Date	Mintage	VF20	XF40	MS60	MS63	MS65
1978	10,000	—	—	4.50	8.50	16.50

KM# 58a PA'ANGA
24.50 g., 0.999 Silver 0.7869 oz. ASW, 48x27 mm. **Ruler:** Taufa'ahau Tupou IV **Obv:** Uniformed bust facing flanked by stars and dates **Rev:** 100 Palm trees **Shape:** Rectangular

Date	Mintage	VF20	XF40	MS60	MS63	MS65
1978	750	PF63 85.00	PF65 125			

KM# 60 PA'ANGA
Copper-Nickel, 48x27 mm. **Ruler:** Taufa'ahau Tupou IV **Series:** F.A.O. **Subject:** Technical Cooperation Program **Obv:** Uniformed bust facing divides circular inscriptions **Rev:** 100 Palm trees **Shape:** Rectangular

Date	Mintage	VF20	XF40	MS60	MS63	MS65
1979	26,000	—	—	2.50	5.50	8.50

KM# 60a PA'ANGA
24.50 g., 0.999 Silver 0.7869 oz. ASW, 48x27 mm. **Ruler:** Taufa'ahau Tupou IV **Obv:** Uniformed bust facing divides circular inscriptions **Rev:** 100 Palm trees **Shape:** Rectangular

Date	Mintage	VF20	XF40	MS60	MS63	MS65
1979	850	PF63 75.00	PF65 115			

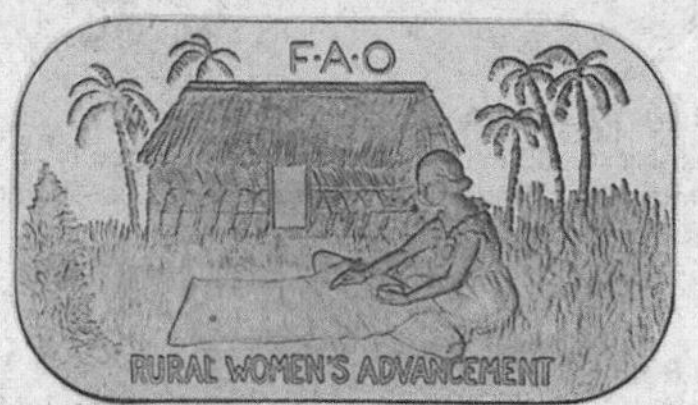

KM# 62 PA'ANGA
Copper-Nickel, 48x27 mm. **Ruler:** Taufa'ahau Tupou IV **Series:** F.A.O. **Subject:** Rural Women's Advancement **Obv:** Bust facing **Rev:** Kneeling figure in front of hut and palm trees **Edge:** Plain **Shape:** Rectangular

Date	Mintage	VF20	XF40	MS60	MS63	MS65
1980	8,000	—	—	2.50	5.50	8.50

KM# 62a PA'ANGA
24.50 g., 0.999 Silver 0.7869 oz. ASW, 48x27 mm. **Ruler:** Taufa'ahau Tupou IV **Subject:** Rural Women's Adnancement **Obv:** Bust facing **Rev:** Kneeling figure in front of hut and palm trees **Rev. Legend:** F.A.O. **Shape:** Rectangular

Date	Mintage	VF20	XF40	MS60	MS63	MS65
1980	2,200	PF63 35.00	PF65 45.00			

KM# 72 PA'ANGA

Copper-Nickel, 48x27 mm. **Ruler:** Taufa'ahau Tupou IV **Series:** World Food Day **Obv:** Uniformed bust facing **Rev:** Sailboat **Edge:** Plain **Shape:** Rectangular

Date	Mintage	VF20	XF40	MS60	MS63	MS65
1981	485,000	—	—	2.50	5.50	8.50

KM# 72a PA'ANGA

24.50 g., 0.999 Silver 0.7869 oz. ASW, 48x27 mm. **Ruler:** Taufa'ahau Tupou IV **Subject:** World Food Day **Obv:** Uniformed bust facing **Rev:** Sailboat **Shape:** Rectangular

Date	Mintage	VF20	XF40	MS60	MS63	MS65
1981	3,500	PF63 30.00	PF65 40.00			

KM# 77 PA'ANGA

Copper-Nickel, 30 mm. **Ruler:** Taufa'ahau Tupou IV **Subject:** Christmas **Obv:** Head right **Rev:** Praying hands **Edge:** Plain **Shape:** 7-sided

Date	Mintage	VF20	XF40	MS60	MS63	MS65
1982	5,000	—	—	1.50	3.50	5.00
1982	—	PF63 4.00	PF65 6.00			

KM# 77a PA'ANGA

15.50 g., 0.925 Silver 0.461 oz. ASW, 30 mm. **Ruler:** Taufa'ahau Tupou IV **Subject:** Christmas **Obv:** Head right **Rev:** Praying hands **Shape:** 7-sided

Date	Mintage	VF20	XF40	MS60	MS63	MS65
1982	2,500	PF63 22.00	PF65 27.00	PF67 30.00		

KM# 77b PA'ANGA

26.00 g., 0.917 Gold 0.7665 oz. AGW, 30 mm. **Ruler:** Taufa'ahau Tupou IV **Subject:** Christmas **Obv:** Head right **Rev:** Praying hands **Shape:** 7-sided

Date	Mintage	VF20	XF40	MS60	MS63	MS65
1982	250	PF65 1,350	PF67 1,500			

KM# 77c PA'ANGA

30.40 g., 0.950 Platinum 0.9285 oz. APW, 30 mm. **Ruler:** Taufa'ahau Tupou IV **Subject:** Christmas **Obv:** Head right **Rev:** Praying hands **Shape:** 7-sided

Date	Mintage	VF20	XF40	MS60	MS63	MS65
1982	25	PF67 2,250				

KM# 80 PA'ANGA

Copper-Nickel, 30 mm. **Ruler:** Taufa'ahau Tupou IV **Subject:** Christmas **Obv:** Head right **Rev:** Kneeling Joseph and Mary **Edge:** Plain **Shape:** 7-sided

Date	Mintage	VF20	XF40	MS60	MS63	MS65
1983	5,000	—	—	1.50	2.50	5.00

KM# 80a PA'ANGA

15.50 g., 0.925 Silver 0.461 oz. ASW, 30 mm. **Ruler:** Taufa'ahau Tupou IV **Subject:** Christmas **Obv:** Head right **Rev:** Kneeling Joseph and Mary **Shape:** 7-sided

Date	Mintage	VF20	XF40	MS60	MS63	MS65
1983	2,500	PF63 22.00	PF65 27.00	PF67 30.00		

KM# 80b PA'ANGA

26.00 g., 0.917 Gold 0.7665 oz. AGW, 30 mm. **Ruler:** Taufa'ahau Tupou IV **Subject:** Christmas **Obv:** Head right **Rev:** Kneeling Joseph and Mary **Shape:** 7-sided

Date	Mintage	VF20	XF40	MS60	MS63	MS65
1983	250	PF65 1,350	PF67 1,500			

KM# 80c PA'ANGA

30.40 g., 0.950 Platinum 0.9285 oz. APW, 30 mm. **Ruler:** Taufa'ahau Tupou IV **Subject:** Christmas **Obv:** Head right **Rev:** Kneeling Joseph and Mary **Shape:** 7-sided

Date	Mintage	VF20	XF40	MS60	MS63	MS65
1983	25	PF67 2,250				

KM# 81 PA'ANGA

Copper-Nickel, 30 mm. **Ruler:** Taufa'ahau Tupou IV **Subject:** Christmas **Obv:** Head right **Rev:** After Bellini's Madonna & Child **Edge:** Plain **Shape:** 7-sided

Date	Mintage	VF20	XF40	MS60	MS63	MS65
1984	5,000	—	—	1.50	3.50	5.00

KM# 81a PA'ANGA

15.50 g., 0.925 Silver 0.461 oz. ASW, 30 mm. **Ruler:** Taufa'ahau Tupou IV **Subject:** Christmas **Obv:** Head right **Rev:** After Bellini's Madonna & Child **Shape:** 7-sided

Date	Mintage	VF20	XF40	MS60	MS63	MS65
1984	2,500	PF63 22.00	PF65 27.00	PF67 30.00		

KM# 81b PA'ANGA

26.00 g., 0.917 Gold 0.7665 oz. AGW, 30 mm. **Ruler:** Taufa'ahau Tupou IV **Subject:** Christmas **Obv:** Head right **Rev:** After Bellini's Madonna & Child **Shape:** 7-sided

Date	Mintage	VF20	XF40	MS60	MS63	MS65
1984	250	PF65 1,350	PF67 1,500			

KM# 81c PA'ANGA

30.40 g., 0.950 Platinum 0.9285 oz. APW, 30 mm. **Ruler:** Taufa'ahau Tupou IV **Subject:** Christmas **Obv:** Head right **Rev:** After Bellini's Madonna & Child **Shape:** 7-sided

Date	Mintage	VF20	XF40	MS60	MS63	MS65
1984	25	PF67 2,250				

KM# 86 PA'ANGA

Silver Clad Copper-Nickel **Ruler:** Taufa'ahau Tupou IV **Subject:** 100th Anniversary of Automobile Industry **Obv:** Head right **Rev:** Rolls-Royce and Silver Ghost

Date	Mintage	VF20	XF40	MS60	MS63	MS65
1985	—	PF63 3.50	PF65 5.00			

KM# 86a PA'ANGA

28.28 g., 0.925 Silver 0.841 oz. ASW **Ruler:** Taufa'ahau Tupou IV **Subject:** 100th Anniversary of Automobile Industry **Obv:** Head right **Rev:** Rolls Royce and Silver Ghost

Date	Mintage	VF20	XF40	MS60	MS63	MS65
1985	5,000	PF63 32.00	PF65 35.00			

KM# 87 PA'ANGA

Silver Clad Copper-Nickel **Ruler:** Taufa'ahau Tupou IV **Subject:** 100th Anniversary of Automobile Industry **Obv:** Head right **Rev:** Range Rover and Land Rover

Date	Mintage	VF20	XF40	MS60	MS63	MS65
1985	—	PF63 3.50	PF65 5.00			

KM# 87a PA'ANGA

28.28 g., 0.925 Silver 0.841 oz. ASW **Ruler:** Taufa'ahau Tupou IV **Subject:** 100th Anniversary of Automobile Industry **Obv:** Head right **Rev:** Range Rover and Land Rover

Date	Mintage	VF20	XF40	MS60	MS63	MS65
1985	5,000	PF63 32.00	PF65 35.00			

KM# 88 PA'ANGA

Silver Clad Copper-Nickel **Ruler:** Taufa'ahau Tupou IV **Subject:** 100th Anniversary of Automobile Industry **Obv:** Head right **Rev:** Mini Morris Cowley and Touring Car

Date	Mintage	VF20	XF40	MS60	MS63	MS65
1985	—	PF63 3.50	PF65 5.00			

KM# 88a PA'ANGA

28.28 g., 0.925 Silver 0.841 oz. ASW **Ruler:** Taufa'ahau Tupou IV **Subject:** 100th Anniversary of Automobile Industry **Obv:** Head right **Rev:** Mini Morris Cowley and Touring Car

Date	Mintage	VF20	XF40	MS60	MS63	MS65
1985	5,000	PF63 32.00	PF65 35.00			

KM# 89 PA'ANGA

Silver Clad Copper-Nickel **Ruler:** Taufa'ahau Tupou IV **Subject:** 100th Anniversary of Automobile Industry **Obv:** Head right **Rev:** MGB GT and MG TA **Note:** Similar to 50 Seniti, KM#85.

Date	Mintage	VF20	XF40	MS60	MS63	MS65
1985	—	PF63 3.50	PF65 5.00			

KM# 89a PA'ANGA

28.28 g., 0.925 Silver 0.841 oz. ASW **Ruler:** Taufa'ahau Tupou IV **Subject:** 100th Anniversary of Automobile Industry **Obv:** Head right **Rev:** MGB GT and MG TA

Date	Mintage	VF20	XF40	MS60	MS63	MS65
1985	5,000	PF63 32.00	PF65 35.00			

KM# 103 PA'ANGA

Silver Clad Copper-Nickel **Ruler:** Taufa'ahau Tupou IV **Subject:** 85th Birthday of Queen Mother **Obv:** Head right **Rev:** Queen Mother as a young girl **Note:** Similar to 50 Seniti, KM#98.

Date	Mintage	VF20	XF40	MS60	MS63	MS65
1985	—	PF63 3.00	PF65 4.50			

KM# 103a PA'ANGA

28.28 g., 0.925 Silver 0.841 oz. ASW **Ruler:** Taufa'ahau Tupou IV **Subject:** 85th Birthday of Queen Mother **Obv:** Head right **Rev:** Queen Mother as a young girl

Date	Mintage	VF20	XF40	MS60	MS63	MS65
1985	5,000	PF63 30.00	PF65 32.00			

KM# 104 PA'ANGA

Silver Clad Copper-Nickel **Ruler:** Taufa'ahau Tupou IV **Subject:** 85th Birthday of Queen mother **Obv:** Head right **Rev:** Wedding of King George VI and Elizabeth **Note:** Similar to 50 Seniti, KM#99.

Date	Mintage	VF20	XF40	MS60	MS63	MS65
1985	—	PF63 3.00	PF65 4.50			

KM# 104a PA'ANGA

28.28 g., 0.925 Silver 0.841 oz. ASW **Ruler:** Taufa'ahau Tupou IV **Subject:** 85th Birthday of Queen Mother **Obv:** Head right **Rev:** Wedding of King George VI and Elizabeth

Date	Mintage	VF20	XF40	MS60	MS63	MS65
1985	5,000	PF63 30.00	PF65 32.00			

KM# 105 PA'ANGA

Silver Clad Copper-Nickel **Ruler:** Taufa'ahau Tupou IV **Subject:** 85th Birthday of Queen Mother **Obv:** Head right **Rev:** King George VI and Elizabeth **Note:** Similar to 50 Seniti, KM#100.

Date	Mintage	VF20	XF40	MS60	MS63	MS65
1985	—	PF63 3.00	PF65 4.50			

KM# 105a PA'ANGA

28.28 g., 0.925 Silver 0.841 oz. ASW **Ruler:** Taufa'ahau Tupou IV **Subject:** 85th Birthday of Queen mother **Obv:** Head right **Rev:** King George VI and Elizabeth

Date	Mintage	VF20	XF40	MS60	MS63	MS65
1985	5,000	PF63 30.00	PF65 32.00			

KM# 106 PA'ANGA

Silver Clad Copper-Nickel **Ruler:** Taufa'ahau Tupou IV **Subject:** 85th Birthday of Queen Mother **Obv:** Head right **Rev:** Queen Mother holding Queen Elizabeth II **Note:** Similar to 50 Seniti, KM#101.

Date	Mintage	VF20	XF40	MS60	MS63	MS65
1985	—	PF63 3.00	PF65 4.50			

KM# 106a PA'ANGA

28.28 g., 0.925 Silver 0.841 oz. ASW **Ruler:** Taufa'ahau Tupou IV **Subject:** 85th Birthday of Queen Mother **Obv:** Head right **Rev:** Queen Mother holding Queen Elizabeth II

Date	Mintage	VF20	XF40	MS60	MS63	MS65
1985	5,000	PF63 30.00	PF65 32.00			

KM# 107 PA'ANGA

Silver Clad Copper-Nickel **Ruler:** Taufa'ahau Tupou IV **Subject:** 85th Birthday of Queen Mother **Obv:** Head right **Rev:** Queen Mother facing **Note:** Similar to 50 Seniti, KM#102.

Date	Mintage	VF20	XF40	MS60	MS63	MS65
1985	—	PF63 3.00	PF65 4.50			

KM# 107a PA'ANGA

28.28 g., 0.925 Silver 0.841 oz. ASW **Ruler:** Taufa'ahau Tupou IV **Subject:** 85th Birthday of the Queen Mother **Obv:** Head right **Rev:** Queen Mother facing

Date	Mintage	VF20	XF40	MS60	MS63	MS65
1985	5,000	PF63 30.00	PF65 32.00			

KM# 118 PA'ANGA

Copper-Nickel, 30 mm. **Ruler:** Taufa'ahau Tupou IV **Subject:** Christmas **Obv:** Head right **Rev:** Dove with laurel branch **Edge:** Plain **Shape:** 7-sided

Date	Mintage	VF20	XF40	MS60	MS63	MS65
1985	—	—	—	1.50	3.50	5.00

KM# 118a PA'ANGA

15.50 g., 0.925 Silver 0.461 oz. ASW **Ruler:** Taufa'ahau Tupou IV **Subject:** Christmas **Obv:** Head right **Rev:** Dove with laurel branch

Date	Mintage	VF20	XF40	MS60	MS63	MS65
1985	250	PF63 25.00	PF65 30.00			

KM# 118b PA'ANGA

26.00 g., 0.917 Gold 0.7665 oz. AGW **Ruler:** Taufa'ahau Tupou IV **Subject:** Christmas **Obv:** Head right **Rev:** Dove with laurel branch

Date	Mintage	VF20	XF40	MS60	MS63	MS65
1985	250	PF63 1,350	PF65 1,500			

KM# 118c PA'ANGA

30.40 g., 0.950 Platinum 0.9285 oz. APW **Ruler:** Taufa'ahau Tupou IV **Subject:** Christmas **Obv:** Head right **Rev:** Dove with laurel branch

Date	Mintage	VF20	XF40	MS60	MS63	MS65
1985	—	PF65 2,250				

KM# 123 PA'ANGA

Copper-Nickel **Ruler:** Taufa'ahau Tupou IV **Subject:** Christmas **Obv:** Head right **Rev:** Three Wise Men

Date	Mintage	VF20	XF40	MS60	MS63	MS65
1986	—	—	—	1.50	3.50	5.00

KM# 123a PA'ANGA

15.50 g., 0.925 Silver 0.461 oz. ASW **Ruler:** Taufa'ahau Tupou IV **Subject:** Christmas **Obv:** Head right **Rev:** Three Wise Men

Date	Mintage	VF20	XF40	MS60	MS63	MS65
1986	—	PF63 22.00	PF65 27.00			

KM# 123b PA'ANGA

26.00 g., 0.917 Gold 0.7665 oz. AGW **Ruler:** Taufa'ahau Tupou IV **Subject:** Christmas **Obv:** Head right **Rev:** Three Wise Men

Date	Mintage	VF20	XF40	MS60	MS63	MS65
1986	—	PF63 1,250	PF65 1,400			

KM# 123c PA'ANGA

30.40 g., 0.950 Platinum 0.9285 oz. APW **Ruler:** Taufa'ahau Tupou IV **Subject:** Christmas **Obv:** Head right **Rev:** Three Wise Men

Date	Mintage	VF20	XF40	MS60	MS63	MS65
1986	—	PF65 2,200				

KM# 128 PA'ANGA

Copper-Nickel **Ruler:** Taufa'ahau Tupou IV **Series:** 25th Anniversary of World Wildlife Fund **Obv:** Head right **Rev:** Humpback whale cow and calf within circle **Edge:** Reeded

Date	Mintage	VF20	XF40	MS60	MS63	MS65
1986	—	—	—	5.00	8.00	12.00

KM# 139 PA'ANGA

Copper-Nickel **Ruler:** Taufa'ahau Tupou IV **Subject:** Christmas **Obv:** Head right **Rev:** Madonna and child

Date	Mintage	VF20	XF40	MS60	MS63	MS65
1987	—	—	—	1.50	3.50	5.00
1987	—	PF63 4.00	PF65 6.00			

KM# 127 PA'ANGA

Copper-Nickel, 30 mm. **Ruler:** Taufa'ahau Tupou IV **Subject:** Christmas **Obv:** Head right **Rev:** After Albrecht Durer, Madonna and child **Edge:** Plain **Shape:** 7-sided

Date	Mintage	VF20	XF40	MS60	MS63	MS65
1988	—	—	—	2.50	4.50	7.00
1988	—	PF63 10.00	PF65 15.00			

KM# 127a PA'ANGA

15.50 g., 0.925 Silver 0.461 oz. ASW **Ruler:** Taufa'ahau Tupou IV **Subject:** Christmas **Obv:** Head right **Rev:** After Albrecht Durer, Madonna and child

Date	Mintage	VF20	XF40	MS60	MS63	MS65
1988	—	PF63 25.00	PF65 30.00			

KM# 127b PA'ANGA

26.00 g., 0.917 Gold 0.7665 oz. AGW **Ruler:** Taufa'ahau Tupou IV **Subject:** Christmas **Obv:** Head right **Rev:** After Albrecht Durer, Madonna and child

Date	Mintage	VF20	XF40	MS60	MS63	MS65
1988	—	PF63 1,450	PF65 1,650			

KM# 127c PA'ANGA

30.40 g., 0.950 Platinum 0.9285 oz. APW **Ruler:** Taufa'ahau Tupou IV **Subject:** Christmas **Obv:** Head right **Rev:** After Albrecht Durer, Madonna and child

Date	Mintage	VF20	XF40	MS60	MS63	MS65
1988	—	PF65 2,500				

KM# 133 PA'ANGA

31.73 g., 0.925 Silver 0.9436 oz. ASW **Ruler:** Taufa'ahau Tupou IV **Series:** Olympics **Obv:** Head right **Rev:** Javelin thrower within circle

Date	Mintage	VF20	XF40	MS60	MS63	MS65
1988	—	PF63 20.00	PF65 22.50	PF67 26.00		

KM# 134 PA'ANGA

31.73 g., 0.925 Silver 0.9436 oz. ASW **Ruler:** Taufa'ahau Tupou IV **Series:** Olympics **Obv:** Head right **Rev:** Swimmers within circle

Date	Mintage	VF20	XF40	MS60	MS63	MS65
1988	—	PF63 20.00	PF65 22.50	PF67 26.00		

KM# 135 PA'ANGA

31.73 g., 0.925 Silver 0.9436 oz. ASW **Ruler:** Taufa'ahau Tupou IV **Series:** Olympics **Obv:** Head right **Rev:** Boxers

Date	Mintage	VF20	XF40	MS60	MS63	MS65
1988	—	PF63 20.00	PF65 22.50	PF67 26.00		

KM# 136 PA'ANGA

31.73 g., 0.925 Silver 0.9436 oz. ASW **Ruler:** Taufa'ahau Tupou IV **Series:** Olympics **Obv:** Head right **Rev:** Discus thrower within circle

Date	Mintage	VF20	XF40	MS60	MS63	MS65
1988	—	PF63 20.00	PF65 22.50	PF67 26.00		

KM# 137 PA'ANGA

31.73 g., 0.925 Silver 0.9436 oz. ASW **Ruler:** Taufa'ahau Tupou IV **Series:** Olympics **Obv:** Head right **Rev:** Shotput thrower

Date	Mintage	VF20	XF40	MS60	MS63	MS65
1988	—	PF63 20.00	PF65 22.50	PF67 26.00		

KM# 138 PA'ANGA

31.73 g., 0.925 Silver 0.9436 oz. ASW **Ruler:** Taufa'ahau Tupou IV **Series:** Olympics **Obv:** Head right **Rev:** Runners within circle

Date	Mintage	VF20	XF40	MS60	MS63	MS65
1988	—	PF63 20.00	PF65 22.50	PF67 26.00		

KM# 145 PA'ANGA
31.73 g., 0.925 Silver 0.9436 oz. ASW **Ruler:** Taufa'ahau Tupou IV **Series:** Olympics **Obv:** Head right **Rev:** Bicycling within circle

Date	Mintage	VF20	XF40	MS60	MS63	MS65
1988	—	PF63 20.00	PF65 22.50	PF67 26.00		

KM# 146 PA'ANGA
31.73 g., 0.925 Silver 0.9436 oz. ASW **Ruler:** Taufa'ahau Tupou IV **Series:** Olympics **Obv:** Head right **Rev:** Gymnast on rings within circle

Date	Mintage	VF20	XF40	MS60	MS63	MS65
1988	—	PF63 20.00	PF65 22.50	PF67 26.00		

KM# 147 PA'ANGA
31.73 g., 0.925 Silver 0.9436 oz. ASW **Ruler:** Taufa'ahau Tupou IV **Series:** Olympics **Obv:** Head right **Rev:** Diver

Date	Mintage	VF20	XF40	MS60	MS63	MS65
1988	—	PF63 20.00	PF65 22.50	PF67 26.00		

KM# 148 PA'ANGA
31.73 g., 0.925 Silver 0.9436 oz. ASW **Ruler:** Taufa'ahau Tupou IV **Series:** Olympics **Obv:** Head right **Rev:** Judo

Date	Mintage	VF20	XF40	MS60	MS63	MS65
1988	—	PF63 20.00	PF65 22.50	PF67 26.00		

KM# 149 PA'ANGA
31.73 g., 0.925 Silver 0.9436 oz. ASW **Ruler:** Taufa'ahau Tupou IV **Series:** Olympics **Obv:** Head right **Rev:** Broad jumper

Date	Mintage	VF20	XF40	MS60	MS63	MS65
1988	—	PF63 20.00	PF65 22.50	PF67 26.00		

KM# 150 PA'ANGA
31.73 g., 0.925 Silver 0.9436 oz. ASW **Ruler:** Taufa'ahau Tupou IV **Series:** Olympics **Obv:** Head right **Rev:** Weight lifter

Date	Mintage	VF20	XF40	MS60	MS63	MS65
1988	—	PF63 20.00	PF65 22.50	PF67 26.00		

KM# 175 PA'ANGA
31.80 g., 0.925 Silver 0.9457 oz. ASW **Ruler:** Taufa'ahau Tupou IV **Subject:** 25th Anniversary of Reign **Obv:** Crowned arms **Rev:** Radiant sun rising through stone structure

Date	Mintage	VF20	XF40	MS60	MS63	MS65
ND-1990	—	PF63 19.00	PF65 22.00			

KM# 140 PA'ANGA
31.60 g., 0.925 Silver 0.9398 oz. ASW **Ruler:** Taufa'ahau Tupou IV **Series:** Olympics **Obv:** National arms **Rev:** Diver

Date	Mintage	VF20	XF40	MS60	MS63	MS65
1991	Est. 40000	PF63 19.00	PF65 21.50			

KM# 141 PA'ANGA
31.60 g., 0.925 Silver 0.9398 oz. ASW **Ruler:** Taufa'ahau Tupou IV **Subject:** Explorers **Rev:** William Schouten and Jakob LeMaire and ship

Date	Mintage	VF20	XF40	MS60	MS63	MS65
1991	Est. 10000	PF63 19.00	PF65 21.50			

KM# 143 PA'ANGA
31.60 g., 0.925 Silver 0.9398 oz. ASW **Ruler:** Taufa'ahau Tupou IV **Subject:** Endangered Wildlife **Rev:** Pritchard's Megapode Birds

Date	Mintage	VF20	XF40	MS60	MS63	MS65
1991	—	PF63 19.00	PF65 21.50			

KM# 156 PA'ANGA
31.60 g., 0.925 Silver 0.9398 oz. ASW **Ruler:** Taufa'ahau Tupou IV **Series:** 1996 Olympics **Obv:** National arms **Rev:** Sailing

Date	Mintage	VF20	XF40	MS60	MS63	MS65
1992	40,000	PF63 19.00	PF65 21.50			

KM# 157 PA'ANGA
31.60 g., 0.925 Silver 0.9398 oz. ASW **Ruler:** Taufa'ahau Tupou IV **Subject:** Soccer **Rev:** Players

Date	Mintage	VF20	XF40	MS60	MS63	MS65
1992	10,000	PF63 20.00	PF65 22.50			

KM# 158 PA'ANGA
31.60 g., 0.925 Silver 0.9398 oz. ASW **Ruler:** Taufa'ahau Tupou IV **Subject:** Space Flight **Obv:** National arms within circle **Rev:** Saturn V on launchpad at right, US map at left

Date	Mintage	VF20	XF40	MS60	MS63	MS65
1992	10,000	PF63 19.00	PF65 21.50			

KM# 168 PA'ANGA
31.60 g., 0.925 Silver 0.9398 oz. ASW **Ruler:** Taufa'ahau Tupou IV **Subject:** 25th Anniversary - Coronation of Tupou IV **Obv:** National arms within circle **Rev:** Coronation scene

Date	Mintage	VF20	XF40	MS60	MS63	MS65
1992	Est. 5000	PF63 20.00	PF65 22.50			

KM# 144 PA'ANGA
31.47 g., 0.925 Silver 0.9359 oz. ASW **Ruler:** Taufa'ahau Tupou IV **Subject:** 40th Anniversary of Queen Elizabeth's Coronation **Obv:** National arms within circle **Rev:** Symbols of royalty

Date	Mintage	VF20	XF40	MS60	MS63	MS65
1993	Est. 10000	PF63 19.00	PF65 21.50			

KM# 151 PA'ANGA
31.47 g., 0.925 Silver 0.9359 oz. ASW **Ruler:** Taufa'ahau Tupou IV **Subject:** Hermann Oberth 1894-1989 **Obv:** Crowned arms within circle **Rev:** Bust facing left to right of standing figures and rockets

Date	Mintage	VF20	XF40	MS60	MS63	MS65
1993	Est. 10000	PF63 21.00	PF65 24.00			

KM# 152 PA'ANGA
31.47 g., 0.925 Silver 0.9359 oz. ASW **Ruler:** Taufa'ahau Tupou IV **Subject:** Johannes Gutenberg 1400-1468 **Obv:** Crowned arms within circle **Rev:** Half-length bust at left, stack of printed pages and press at right

Date	Mintage	VF20	XF40	MS60	MS63	MS65
1993	Est. 10000	PF63 21.00	PF65 24.00			

KM# 153 PA'ANGA
31.47 g., 0.925 Silver 0.9359 oz. ASW **Ruler:** Taufa'ahau Tupou IV **Subject:** Protect Our World **Obv:** Crowned arms within circle **Rev:** Alexander von Humboldt

Date	Mintage	VF20	XF40	MS60	MS63	MS65
1993	Est. 10000	PF63 21.00	PF65 24.00			

KM# 154 PA'ANGA
31.47 g., 0.925 Silver 0.9359 oz. ASW **Ruler:** Taufa'ahau Tupou IV **Obv:** Crowned arms within circle **Rev:** Sailing ship - "La Princesa"

Date	Mintage	VF20	XF40	MS60	MS63	MS65
1993	Est. 15000	PF63 20.00	PF65 22.50			
1994	—	PF63 20.00	PF65 22.50			

KM# 160 PA'ANGA
31.47 g., 0.925 Silver 0.9359 oz. ASW **Ruler:** Taufa'ahau Tupou IV **Subject:** Richard Wagner **Obv:** Crowned arms within circle **Rev:** Bust at right, dancers at upper left

Date	Mintage	VF20	XF40	MS60	MS63	MS65
1993	Est. 10000	PF63 21.00	PF65 24.00			

KM# 169 PA'ANGA
31.47 g., 0.925 Silver 0.9359 oz. ASW **Ruler:** Taufa'ahau Tupou IV **Subject:** 75th Birthday, July 4, 1993 **Obv:** Uniformed bust facing **Rev:** Siu'a'alo rowers

Date	Mintage	VF20	XF40	MS60	MS63	MS65
1993	Est. 2000	PF63 21.50	PF65 26.00			

KM# 159.1 PA'ANGA
31.55 g., 0.925 Silver 0.9383 oz. ASW **Ruler:** Taufa'ahau Tupou IV **Series:** 1996 Olympics **Obv:** Crowned arms within circle **Rev:** Javelin thrower within circle **Note:** Prev. KM#159.

Date	Mintage	VF20	XF40	MS60	MS63	MS65
1994	40,000	PF63 20.00	PF65 22.50			

KM# 159.2 PA'ANGA
31.47 g., 0.925 Silver 0.9359 oz. ASW, 38.7 mm. **Ruler:** Taufa'ahau Tupou IV **Subject:** Olympics **Obv:** Crowned arms within circle **Rev:** Javelin thrower within circle **Edge:** Reeded **Note:** Smaller letters in legend than the KM-159.1 version

Date	Mintage	VF20	XF40	MS60	MS63	MS65
1994	—	PF63 21.00	PF65 24.00			

KM# 161 PA'ANGA
31.47 g., 0.925 Silver 0.9359 oz. ASW **Ruler:** Taufa'ahau Tupou IV **Subject:** World Cup Soccer **Obv:** Crowned arms within circle **Rev:** Two soccer players

Date	Mintage	VF20	XF40	MS60	MS63	MS65
1994	Est. 10000	PF63 20.00	PF65 22.50			

KM# 162 PA'ANGA
31.47 g., 0.925 Silver 0.9359 oz. ASW **Ruler:** Taufa'ahau Tupou IV **Series:** Endangered Wildlife **Obv:** Crowned arms within circle **Rev:** Humpback whale cow and calf

Date	Mintage	VF20	XF40	MS60	MS63	MS65
1994	Est. 10000	PF63 21.50	PF65 26.00			

KM# 180 PA'ANGA
31.10 g., 0.925 Silver 0.9249 oz. ASW, 38.5 mm. **Ruler:** Taufa'ahau Tupou IV **Subject:** 50 Years - FAO **Obv:** Bust facing at left, TONGA at right **Rev:** FAO emblem, value above, date at right **Edge:** Reeded

Date	Mintage	VF20	XF40	MS60	MS63	MS65
1995	—	PF65 275				

KM# 181 PA'ANGA
Silver, 38 mm. **Ruler:** Taufa'ahau Tupou IV **Subject:** FAO **Obv:** Bust facing **Rev:** FAO anniversary logo **Edge:** Reeded

Date	Mintage	VF20	XF40	MS60	MS63	MS65
1995	2,000	PF63 65.00	PF65 75.00			

KM# 166 PA'ANGA
31.47 g., 0.925 Silver 0.9359 oz. ASW **Ruler:** Taufa'ahau Tupou IV **Series:** Queen Elizabeth The Queen Mother **Obv:** Crowned arms within circle **Rev:** Crown within beaded circle

Date	Mintage	VF20	XF40	MS60	MS63	MS65
1996	Est. 40000	—	—	—	21.00	24.00

KM# 170 PA'ANGA
31.47 g., 0.925 Silver 0.9359 oz. ASW **Ruler:** Taufa'ahau Tupou IV **Subject:** 70th Birthday - Queen Mata'aho, May 25, 1996 **Obv:** National arms within circle **Rev:** Crown above bust of Queen Mata'aho facing within wreath

Date	Mintage	VF20	XF40	MS60	MS63	MS65
1996	Est. 5000	PF63 20.00	PF65 22.50			

KM# 177 PA'ANGA
31.41 g., 0.925 Silver 0.9341 oz. ASW, 38.6 mm. **Ruler:** Taufa'ahau Tupou IV **Series:** Queen Elizabeth The Queen Mother **Subject:** The Coronation of Elizabeth **Obv:** Crowned arms within circle **Rev:** Queen seated on throne within beaded circle **Edge:** Reeded

Date	Mintage	VF20	XF40	MS60	MS63	MS65
1996	—	PF63 20.00	PF65 22.50			

KM# 207 PA'ANGA
23.00 g., 0.925 Silver 0.684 oz. ASW, 48 x 30 mm. **Ruler:** Siaosi Tupou V **Subject:** 1997 Rugby World Cup, Hong Kong - Skyline

Date	Mintage	VF20	XF40	MS60	MS63	MS65
1997	5,000	PF65 95.00				

KM# 208 PA'ANGA
28.28 g., 0.925 Silver 0.841 oz. ASW, 48 x 30 mm. **Ruler:** Siaosi Tupou V **Subject:** 1997 Rugby World Cup, Hong Kong - Touchdown

Date	Mintage	VF20	XF40	MS60	MS63	MS65
1997	5,000	PF65 95.00				

KM# 174 PA'ANGA
31.47 g., 0.925 Silver 0.9359 oz. ASW **Ruler:** Taufa'ahau Tupou IV **Obv:** National arms within circle **Rev:** Polynesian sailing catamaran

Date	Mintage	VF20	XF40	MS60	MS63	MS65
1998	20,000	PF63 20.00	PF65 22.50			

KM# 206 PA'ANGA
23.00 g., 0.925 Silver 0.684 oz. ASW, 48 x 30 mm. **Ruler:** Siaosi Tupou V **Subject:** 1997 Rugby World Cup, Hong Kong

Date	Mintage	VF20	XF40	MS60	MS63	MS65
1997	5,000	PF65 95.00				

KM# 176 PA'ANGA
31.11 g., 0.925 Silver 0.9252 oz. ASW, 35.5 mm. **Ruler:** Taufa'ahau Tupou IV **Subject:** Millennium 2000 **Obv:** Crowned arms within circle and beaded border **Rev:** Stone archway **Edge:** Reeded **Shape:** Scalloped

Date	Mintage	VF20	XF40	MS60	MS63	MS65
1999	—	PF63 22.50	PF65 27.50			

KM# 210 PA'ANGA
31.47 g., 0.925 Silver 0.9359 oz. ASW, 38.61 mm. **Subject:** The History of Seafaring - The Concord

Date	Mintage	VF20	XF40	MS60	MS63	MS65
1999	10,000	PF63 20.00	PF65 22.50			

KM# 19 2 PA'ANGA
Copper-Nickel, 44.5 mm. **Ruler:** Taufa'ahau Tupou IV **Subject:** Coronation of Taufa'ahau Tupou IV **Obv:** Head right **Rev:** National arms

Date	Mintage	VF20	XF40	MS60	MS63	MS65
ND-1967	10,000	—	1.50	2.75	5.50	7.00
ND-1967	—	PF65 10.00				

KM# 37 2 PA'ANGA
Copper-Nickel, 44.5 mm. **Ruler:** Taufa'ahau Tupou IV **Obv:** Head right **Rev:** National arms **Edge:** Reeded

Date	Mintage	VF20	XF40	MS60	MS63	MS65
1968	14,000	—	1.50	2.50	5.50	6.50
1968	—	PF65 8.00				
1974	10,000	—	1.50	3.00	6.00	7.00

KM# 49 2 PA'ANGA
Copper-Nickel, 44.5 mm. **Ruler:** Taufa'ahau Tupou IV **Series:** F.A.O. **Obv:** Uniformed bust facing **Rev:** Palm tree in center of assorted animals, grains and fruit **Edge:** Reeded

Date	Mintage	VF20	XF40	MS60	MS63	MS65
1975	13,000	—	—	6.00	10.00	12.00
1977	12,000	—	—	6.00	10.00	12.00

KM# 59 2 PA'ANGA

Copper-Nickel, 44.5 mm. **Ruler:** Taufa'ahau Tupou IV **Series:** F.A.O. **Subject:** 60th Birthday **Obv:** Uniformed bust facing **Rev:** Palm tree in center of assorted animals and grains **Edge:** Reeded

Date	Mintage	VF20	XF40	MS60	MS63	MS65
1978	10,000	—	3.00	7.00	12.00	15.00

KM# 59a 2 PA'ANGA

42.10 g., 0.999 Silver 1.3522 oz. ASW, 44.5 mm. **Ruler:** Taufa'ahau Tupou IV **Series:** F.A.O. **Subject:** 60th Birthday **Obv:** Uniformed bust facing **Rev:** Palm tree in center of assorted animals and grains

Date	Mintage	VF20	XF40	MS60	MS63	MS65
1978	750	PF63 75.00	PF65 100			

KM# 61 2 PA'ANGA

Copper-Nickel, 44.5 mm. **Ruler:** Taufa'ahau Tupou IV **Series:** F.A.O. **Subject:** SEA Resource Management **Obv:** Uniformed bust facing **Rev:** Humpback whale - bull in breach **Edge:** Reeded

Date	Mintage	VF20	XF40	MS60	MS63	MS65
1979	8,000	—	—	7.00	12.00	15.00

KM# 61a 2 PA'ANGA

42.10 g., 0.999 Silver 1.3522 oz. ASW, 44.5 mm. **Ruler:** Taufa'ahau Tupou IV **Series:** F.A.O. **Subject:** SEA Resource Management **Obv:** Uniformed bust facing **Rev:** Humpback whale - bull in breach

Date	Mintage	VF20	XF40	MS60	MS63	MS65
1979	850	PF63 75.00	PF65 100			

KM# 63 2 PA'ANGA

Copper-Nickel, 44.5 mm. **Ruler:** Taufa'ahau Tupou IV **Series:** F.A.O. **Subject:** SEA Resource Management **Obv:** Uniformed bust facing **Rev:** Humpback whale - bull in breach **Edge:** Reeded

Date	Mintage	VF20	XF40	MS60	MS63	MS65
1980	8,000	—	—	5.00	7.00	10.00

KM# 63a 2 PA'ANGA

42.10 g., 0.999 Silver 1.3522 oz. ASW, 44.5 mm. **Ruler:** Taufa'ahau Tupou IV **Series:** F.A.O. **Subject:** SEA Resource Management **Obv:** Uniformed bust facing **Rev:** Humpback whale - bull in breach

Date	Mintage	VF20	XF40	MS60	MS63	MS65
1980	2,200	PF63 45.00	PF65 55.00			

KM# 73 2 PA'ANGA

Copper-Nickel, 44.5 mm. **Ruler:** Taufa'ahau Tupou IV **Series:** World Food Day **Obv:** Uniformed bust facing **Rev:** Pigs, chickens and nursing calf, logo at top **Edge:** Reeded

Date	Mintage	VF20	XF40	MS60	MS63	MS65
1981	485,000	—	—	5.00	7.00	10.00

KM# 73a 2 PA'ANGA

42.10 g., 0.999 Silver 1.3522 oz. ASW, 44.5 mm. **Ruler:** Taufa'ahau Tupou IV **Series:** World Food Day **Obv:** Uniformed bust facing **Rev:** Chickens, pig and nursing calf, logo at top

Date	Mintage	VF20	XF40	MS60	MS63	MS65
1981	3,500	PF63 35.00	PF65 45.00			

KM# 120 2 PA'ANGA

28.28 g., 0.500 Silver 0.4546 oz. ASW, 38.61 mm. **Ruler:** Taufa'ahau Tupou IV **Subject:** Commonwealth Games **Obv:** Head right **Rev:** Boxing match

Date	Mintage	VF20	XF40	MS60	MS63	MS65
1986	50,000	—	—	—	9.25	10.50

KM# 120a 2 PA'ANGA

28.28 g., 0.925 Silver 0.841 oz. ASW, 38.61 mm. **Ruler:** Taufa'ahau Tupou IV **Subject:** Commonwealth Games **Obv:** Head right **Rev:** Boxing match

Date	Mintage	VF20	XF40	MS60	MS63	MS65
1986	20,000	PF63 19.50	PF65 21.00			

KM# 121 2 PA'ANGA

28.28 g., 0.925 Silver 0.841 oz. ASW, 38.61 mm. **Ruler:** Taufa'ahau Tupou IV **Subject:** Wildlife **Obv:** Uniformed bust facing **Rev:** Humpback whales - cow and calf within circle

Date	Mintage	VF20	XF40	MS60	MS63	MS65
1986	25,000	PF63 22.00	PF65 26.50			

KM# 124 2 PA'ANGA

155.52 g., 0.999 Silver 4.9951 oz. ASW, 65 mm. **Ruler:** Taufa'ahau Tupou IV **Subject:** America's Cup **Rev:** Sailing ship in front of map within circle **Note:** Illustration reduced.

Date	Mintage	VF20	XF40	MS60	MS63	MS65
1987	7,500	PF63 115	PF65 137			

KM# 129 2 PA'ANGA

155.52 g., 0.999 Silver 4.9951 oz. ASW, 65 mm. **Ruler:** Taufa'ahau Tupou IV **Series:** Olympics **Obv:** Head right **Rev:** Swimmers within circle **Note:** Illustration reduced.

Date	Mintage	VF20	XF40	MS60	MS63	MS65
1988	2,000	PF63 115	PF65 137			

KM# 205 2 PA'ANGA

28.28 g., 0.925 Silver 0.841 oz. ASW, 38.61 mm. **Ruler:** Siaosi Tupou V **Subject:** 50th Wedding Anniversary of Queen Elizabeth II and Prince Philip

Date	Mintage	VF20	XF40	MS60	MS63	MS65
1997	Est. 30000	PF65 60.00				

KM# 50 5 PA'ANGA

31.00 g., 0.999 Silver 0.9957 oz. ASW **Ruler:** Taufa'ahau Tupou IV **Subject:** Constitution Centennial **Obv:** Uniformed bust left above open scroll **Rev:** Crowned arms

Date	Mintage	VF20	XF40	MS60	MS63	MS65
ND-1975	2,118	—	—	—	30.00	35.00
ND-1975	418	PF63 40.00	PF65 50.00			

KM# 51 10 PA'ANGA
62.00 g., 0.999 Silver 1.9914 oz. ASW **Ruler:** Taufa'ahau Tupou IV **Subject:** Constitution Centennial **Obv:** Uniformed bust left above stone arch **Rev:** Crowned arms

Date	Mintage	VF20	XF40	MS60	MS63	MS65
ND-1975	1,116	—	—	—	55.00	70.00
ND-1975	420	PF63 75.00	PF65 90.00			

KM# 64 10 PA'ANGA
0.40 g., 0.917 Gold 0.0118 oz. AGW **Ruler:** Taufa'ahau Tupou IV **Series:** F.A.O. **Subject:** Rural Women's Advancement **Obv:** Queen Salote **Rev:** Female symbol on dove

Date	Mintage	VF20	XF40	MS60	MS63	MS65
1980	7,500	—	—	—	35.00	40.00
1980	2,000	PF63 45.00	PF65 55.00			

KM# 78 10 PA'ANGA
28.28 g., 0.925 Silver 0.841 oz. ASW, 38.61 mm. **Ruler:** Taufa'ahau Tupou IV **Subject:** Commonwealth Games **Obv:** Head right **Rev:** Two runners at finish line **Edge:** Reeded

Date	Mintage	VF20	XF40	MS60	MS63	MS65
1982	500	—	—	—	45.00	55.00
1982	1,000	PF63 45.00	PF65 55.00			

KM# 90 10 PA'ANGA
5.10 g., 0.375 Gold 0.0615 oz. AGW **Ruler:** Taufa'ahau Tupou IV **Subject:** 100th Anniversary of Automobile Industry **Obv:** Head right **Rev:** Rolls Royce and Silver Ghost **Note:** Similar to 50 Seniti, KM#82

Date	Mintage	XF40	MS60	MS63	MS65	MS66
1985	1,000	PF65 95.00	PF67 125	PF69 150		

KM# 90a 10 PA'ANGA
7.96 g., 0.917 Gold 0.2347 oz. AGW **Ruler:** Taufa'ahau Tupou IV **Subject:** 100th Anniversary of Automobile Industry **Obv:** Head right **Rev:** Rolls Royce and Silver Ghost

Date	Mintage	XF40	MS60	MS63	MS65	MS66
1985	500	PF65 375	PF67 425	PF69 475		

KM# 91 10 PA'ANGA
5.10 g., 0.375 Gold 0.0615 oz. AGW **Ruler:** Taufa'ahau Tupou IV **Subject:** 100th Anniversary of Automobile Industry **Obv:** Head right **Rev:** Range Rover and Land Rover **Note:** Similar to 50 Seniti, KM#83.2

Date	Mintage	XF40	MS60	MS63	MS65	MS66
1985	1,000	PF65 95.00	PF67 125	PF69 150		

KM# 91a 10 PA'ANGA
7.96 g., 0.917 Gold 0.2347 oz. AGW **Ruler:** Taufa'ahau Tupou IV **Subject:** 100th Anniversary of Automobile Industry **Obv:** Head right **Rev:** Range Rover and Land Rover

Date	Mintage	XF40	MS60	MS63	MS65	MS66
1985	500	PF65 375	PF67 425	PF69 475		

KM# 92 10 PA'ANGA
5.10 g., 0.375 Gold 0.0615 oz. AGW **Ruler:** Taufa'ahau Tupou IV **Subject:** 100th Anniversary of Automobile Industry **Obv:** Head right **Rev:** Mini Morris Cowley and Touring Car **Note:** Similar to 50 Seniti, KM#84.

Date	Mintage	XF40	MS60	MS63	MS65	MS66
1985	1,000	PF65 95.00	PF67 125	PF69 150		

KM# 92a 10 PA'ANGA
7.96 g., 0.917 Gold 0.2347 oz. AGW **Ruler:** Taufa'ahau Tupou IV **Subject:** 100th Anniversary of Automobile Industry **Obv:** Head right **Rev:** Mini Morris Cowley and Touring Car

Date	Mintage	XF40	MS60	MS63	MS65	MS66
1985	500	PF65 375	PF67 425	PF69 475		

KM# 93 10 PA'ANGA
5.10 g., 0.375 Gold 0.0615 oz. AGW **Ruler:** Taufa'ahau Tupou IV **Subject:** 100th Anniversary of Automobile Industry **Obv:** Head right **Rev:** MGB GT and MG TA **Note:** Similar to 50 Seniti, KM#85.

Date	Mintage	XF40	MS60	MS63	MS65	MS66
1985	1,000	PF65 95.00	PF67 125	PF69 150		

KM# 93a 10 PA'ANGA
7.96 g., 0.917 Gold 0.2347 oz. AGW **Ruler:** Taufa'ahau Tupou IV **Subject:** 100th Anniversary of Automobile Industry **Obv:** Head right **Rev:** MGB GT and MG TA

Date	Mintage	XF40	MS60	MS63	MS65	MS66
1985	500	PF65 375	PF67 425	PF69 475		

KM# 108 10 PA'ANGA
5.10 g., 0.375 Gold 0.0615 oz. AGW **Ruler:** Taufa'ahau Tupou IV **Subject:** 85th Birthday of Queen Mother **Obv:** Head right **Rev:** Queen Mother as a young girl **Note:** Similar to 50 Seniti, KM#98.

Date	Mintage	XF40	MS60	MS63	MS65	MS66
1985	1,000	PF65 95.00	PF67 125	PF69 150		

KM# 108a 10 PA'ANGA
7.96 g., 0.917 Gold 0.2347 oz. AGW **Ruler:** Taufa'ahau Tupou IV **Subject:** 85th Birthday of Queen Mother **Obv:** Head right **Rev:** Queen Mother as a young girl

Date	Mintage	XF40	MS60	MS63	MS65	MS66
1985	500	PF65 375	PF67 425	PF69 475		

KM# 109 10 PA'ANGA
5.10 g., 0.375 Gold 0.0615 oz. AGW **Ruler:** Taufa'ahau Tupou IV **Subject:** 85th Birthday of Queen Mother **Obv:** Head right **Rev:** Wedding of King George VI and Elizabeth **Note:** Similar to 50 Seniti, KM#99.

Date	Mintage	XF40	MS60	MS63	MS65	MS66
1985	1,000	PF65 95.00	PF67 125	PF69 150		

KM# 109a 10 PA'ANGA
7.96 g., 0.917 Gold 0.2347 oz. AGW **Ruler:** Taufa'ahau Tupou IV **Subject:** 85th Birthday of Queen Mother **Obv:** Head right **Rev:** Wedding of King George VI and Elizabeth

Date	Mintage	XF40	MS60	MS63	MS65	MS66
1985	500	PF65 375	PF67 425	PF69 475		

KM# 110 10 PA'ANGA
5.10 g., 0.375 Gold 0.0615 oz. AGW **Ruler:** Taufa'ahau Tupou IV **Subject:** 85th Birthday of Queen Mother **Obv:** Head right **Rev:** King George VI and Elizabeth **Note:** Similar to 50 Seniti, KM#100.

Date	Mintage	XF40	MS60	MS63	MS65	MS66
1985	1,000	PF65 95.00	PF67 125	PF69 150		

KM# 110a 10 PA'ANGA
7.96 g., 0.917 Gold 0.2347 oz. AGW **Ruler:** Taufa'ahau Tupou IV **Subject:** 85th Birthday of Queen Mother **Obv:** Head right **Rev:** King George VI and Elizabeth

Date	Mintage	XF40	MS60	MS63	MS65	MS66
1985	500	PF65 375	PF67 425	PF69 475		

KM# 111 10 PA'ANGA
5.10 g., 0.375 Gold 0.0615 oz. AGW **Ruler:** Taufa'ahau Tupou IV **Subject:** 85th Birthday of Queen Mother **Obv:** Head right **Rev:** Queen Mother holding Queen Elizabeth II **Note:** Similar to 50 Seniti, KM#101.

Date	Mintage	XF40	MS60	MS63	MS65	MS66
1985	1,000	PF65 95.00	PF67 125	PF69 150		

KM# 111a 10 PA'ANGA
7.96 g., 0.917 Gold 0.2347 oz. AGW **Ruler:** Taufa'ahau Tupou IV **Subject:** 85th Birthday of Queen Mother **Obv:** Head right **Rev:** Queen Mother holding Queen Elizabeth II

Date	Mintage	XF40	MS60	MS63	MS65	MS66
1985	500	PF65 375	PF67 425	PF69 475		

KM# 112 10 PA'ANGA
5.10 g., 0.375 Gold 0.0615 oz. AGW **Ruler:** Taufa'ahau Tupou IV **Subject:** 85th Birthday of Queen Mother **Obv:** Head right **Rev:** Queen Mother facing **Note:** Similar to 50 Seniti, KM#102.

Date	Mintage	XF40	MS60	MS63	MS65	MS66
1985	1,000	PF65 95.00	PF67 125	PF69 150		

KM# 112a 10 PA'ANGA
7.96 g., 0.917 Gold 0.2347 oz. AGW **Ruler:** Taufa'ahau Tupou IV **Subject:** 85th Birthday of Queen Mother **Obv:** Head right **Rev:** Queen Mother facing

Date	Mintage	XF40	MS60	MS63	MS65	MS66
1985	500	PF65 375	PF67 425	PF69 475		

KM# 125 10 PA'ANGA
311.04 g., 0.999 Silver 9.9902 oz. ASW, 75 mm. **Ruler:** Taufa'ahau Tupou IV **Subject:** America's Cup **Obv:** Head right **Rev:** Sailboat and map **Note:** Illustration reduced.

Date	Mintage	VF20	XF40	MS60	MS63	MS65
1987	5,000	PF63 275	PF65 325			

KM# 126 10 PA'ANGA
Copper-Nickel **Ruler:** Taufa'ahau Tupou IV **Subject:** America's Cup **Obv:** Head right **Rev:** National flags and sailboat

Date	Mintage	VF20	XF40	MS60	MS63	MS65
1987	—	—	—	3.00	5.00	7.00

KM# 126a 10 PA'ANGA
31.10 g., 0.999 Palladium 0.999 oz. APW **Ruler:** Taufa'ahau Tupou IV **Subject:** America's Cup **Obv:** Head right **Rev:** National flags and sailboat

Date	Mintage	VF20	XF40	MS60	MS63	MS65
1987	25,000	PF65 925	PF67 975			

KM# 130 10 PA'ANGA
15.55 g., 0.999 Gold 0.4994 oz. AGW **Ruler:** Taufa'ahau Tupou IV **Subject:** Summer Olympics **Obv:** Head right **Rev:** Boxing match within circle

Date	Mintage	XF40	MS60	MS63	MS65	MS66
1988	—	PF65 800	PF67 850	PF69 950		

KM# 131 10 PA'ANGA
31.10 g., 0.999 Palladium 0.9989 oz. APW **Ruler:** Taufa'ahau Tupou IV **Series:** Summer Olympics **Obv:** Head right **Rev:** Shot putter within circle

Date	Mintage	XF40	MS60	MS63	MS65	MS66
1988	Est. 2000	PF65 925	PF67 950	PF69 1,000		

KM# 132 10 PA'ANGA
15.63 g., 0.950 Platinum 0.4774 oz. APW **Ruler:** Taufa'ahau Tupou IV **Series:** Summer Olympics **Obv:** Head right **Rev:** Discus thrower within circle

Date	Mintage	XF40	MS60	MS63	MS65	MS66
1988	Est. 2000	PF65 650	PF67 700	PF69 750		

KM# 172 10 PA'ANGA
1.24 g., 0.9999 Gold 0.040 oz. AGW, 13.92 mm. **Ruler:** Taufa'ahau Tupou IV **Subject:** King's 80th Birthday July 3, 1998 **Obv:** National arms within circle **Rev:** Bust 3/4 left **Edge:** Reeded **Note:** Struck at Valcambi Mint.

Date	Mintage	VF20	XF40	MS60	MS63	MS65
1998	—	PF63 65.00	PF65 75.00			

KM# 173 10 PA'ANGA
1.24 g., 0.9999 Gold 0.040 oz. AGW, 13.92 mm. **Ruler:** Taufa'ahau Tupou IV **Subject:** Destruction of the English Privateer "Port-au-Prince" **Obv:** Crowned arms **Rev:** Looted shipwreck and native **Edge:** Reeded

Date	Mintage	VF20	XF40	MS60	MS63	MS65
1998	—	PF63 65.00	PF65 75.00			

KM# 209 10 PA'ANGA
1.24 g., 0.999 Gold 0.0398 oz. AGW, 13.92 mm. **Ruler:** Siaosi Tupou V **Subject:** The History of Seafaring

Date	Mintage	XF40	MS60	MS63	MS65
1998	15,000	PF65 70.00			

KM# 52 20 PA'ANGA
140.00 g., 0.999 Silver 4.4966 oz. ASW **Ruler:** Taufa'ahau Tupou IV **Subject:** Constitution Centennial **Obv:** Heads of various Monarchs **Rev:** National arms

Date	Mintage	VF20	XF40	MS60	MS63	MS65
1975	1,170	—	—	—	85.00	115
1975	800	PF63 150	PF65 180			

KM# 65 20 PA'ANGA
0.80 g., 0.917 Gold 0.0236 oz. AGW **Ruler:** Taufa'ahau Tupou IV **Series:** F.A.O. **Subject:** Rural Women's Advancement **Obv:** Head of Queen Salote right **Rev:** Female symbol on dove

Date	Mintage	VF20	XF40	MS60	MS63	MS65
1980	7,500	—	—	—	45.00	55.00
1980	2,000	PF63 60.00	PF65 70.00			

KM# 211 20 PA'ANGA
7.78 g., 0.583 Gold 0.1458 oz. AGW, 25 mm. **Ruler:** Siaosi Tupou V **Subject:** Birthday of Queen Elizabeth II

Date	Mintage	VF20	XF40	MS60	MS63	MS65
1999	5,000	PF65 245				

KM# 53 25 PA'ANGA
5.00 g., 0.917 Gold 0.1474 oz. AGW **Ruler:** Taufa'ahau Tupou IV **Subject:** Constitution Centennial **Obv:** Head facing **Rev:** National arms

Date	Mintage	VF20	XF40	MS60	MS63	MS65
1975	405	—	—	—	300	350
1975	105	PF63 325	PF65 375	PF67 425		

KM# 54 50 PA'ANGA
10.00 g., 0.917 Gold 0.2948 oz. AGW **Ruler:** Taufa'ahau Tupou IV **Subject:** Constitution Centennial **Obv:** Head facing **Rev:** National arms

Date	Mintage	VF20	XF40	MS60	MS63	MS65
1975	205	—	—	—	575	625
1975	105	PF63 625	PF65 675	PF67 725		

KM# 55 75 PA'ANGA
15.00 g., 0.917 Gold 0.4422 oz. AGW **Ruler:** Taufa'ahau Tupou IV **Subject:** Constitution Centennial **Obv:** Queen Salote Tupou III **Rev:** National arms

Date	Mintage	VF20	XF40	MS60	MS63	MS65
1975	204	—	—	—	800	825
1975	105	PF63 825	PF65 875	PF67 925		

KM# 56 100 PA'ANGA
20.00 g., 0.917 Gold 0.5896 oz. AGW **Ruler:** Taufa'ahau Tupou IV **Subject:** Constitution Centennial **Obv:** Uniformed bust left **Rev:** National arms

Date	Mintage	VF20	XF40	MS60	MS63	MS65
ND-1975	205	—	—	—	1,150	1,200
ND-1975	105	PF63 1,250	PF65 1,300	PF67 1,350		

KM# 167 100 PA'ANGA
7.65 g., 0.5833 Gold 0.1435 oz. AGW **Ruler:** Taufa'ahau Tupou IV **Subject:** 25th Jubilee of Accession **Obv:** Head left at center of circle with dove, crown and stars **Rev:** National arms within circle

Date	Mintage	XF40	MS60	MS63	MS65	MS66
ND-1990	Est. 5000	PF67 250	PF69 300			

KM# 155 100 PA'ANGA
7.65 g., 0.5833 Gold 0.1435 oz. AGW **Ruler:** Taufa'ahau Tupou IV **Series:** Olympics **Obv:** Crowned arms within circle **Rev:** Gymnast on rings

Date	Mintage	XF40	MS60	MS63	MS65	MS66
1993	3,000	PF67 250	PF69 300			

KM# 163 100 PA'ANGA
7.65 g., 0.5833 Gold 0.1435 oz. AGW **Ruler:** Taufa'ahau Tupou IV **Subject:** World Cup Soccer **Obv:** Crowned arms within circle **Rev:** Goalie

Date	Mintage	XF40	MS60	MS63	MS65	MS66
1994	Est. 3000	PF67 250	PF69 300			

KM# 164 100 PA'ANGA
7.65 g., 0.5833 Gold 0.1435 oz. AGW **Ruler:** Taufa'ahau Tupou IV **Series:** 1996 Olympic Games **Obv:** Crowned arms within circle **Rev:** High jumper

Date	Mintage	XF40	MS60	MS63	MS65	MS66
1994	Est. 3000	PF67 250	PF69 300			

KM# 165 100 PA'ANGA
7.65 g., 0.5833 Gold 0.1435 oz. AGW **Ruler:** Taufa'ahau Tupou IV **Series:** Endangered Wildlife **Obv:** Crowned arms within circle **Rev:** Banded iguana

Date	Mintage	XF40	MS60	MS63	MS65	MS66
1994	Est. 2000	PF67 250	PF69 300			

KM# 21 1/4 HAU
16.00 g., 0.980 Palladium 0.5041 oz. APW, 25 mm. **Ruler:** Taufa'ahau Tupou IV **Subject:** Coronation of Taufa'ahau Tupou IV **Obv:** Head right, small crowns around border **Rev:** Crowned arms **Edge Lettering:** HISTORICALLY THE FIRST PALLADIUM COINAGE

Date	Mintage	VF20	XF40	MS60	MS63	MS65
1967	1,700	—	—	—	485	—

KM# 23 1/2 HAU
32.00 g., 0.980 Palladium 1.0082 oz. APW **Ruler:** Taufa'ahau Tupou IV **Subject:** Coronation of Taufa'ahau Tupou IV **Rev:** National arms **Edge Lettering:** HISTORICALLY THE FIRST PALLADIUM COINAGE

Date	Mintage	VF20	XF40	MS60	MS63	MS65
1967	1,650	—	—	—	975	—

KM# 74 1/2 HAU
28.28 g., 0.925 Silver 0.841 oz. ASW **Ruler:** Taufa'ahau Tupou IV **Subject:** Wedding and Treaty of Friendship **Obv:** Head right **Rev:** Wedding of Prince Charles and Lady Diana

Date	Mintage	VF20	XF40	MS60	MS63	MS65
1981	1,000	—	—	—	35.00	—
1981	15,000	PF65 30.00				

KM# 122 1/2 HAU
10.00 g., 0.917 Gold 0.2948 oz. AGW **Ruler:** Taufa'ahau Tupou IV **Subject:** Wildlife **Obv:** Head right **Rev:** Ground dwelling birds

Date	Mintage	VF20	XF40	MS60	MS63	MS65
1986	5,000	PF63 475	PF65 550			

KM# 25 HAU
64.00 g., 0.980 Palladium 2.0165 oz. APW **Ruler:** Taufa'ahau Tupou IV **Subject:** Coronation of Taufa'ahau Tupou IV **Obv:** Head right, small crowns around border **Rev:** National arms **Edge Lettering:** HISTORICALLY THE FIRST PALLADIUM COINAGE

Date	Mintage	VF20	XF40	MS60	MS63	MS65
1967	1,500	—	—	—	1,850	—

KM# 75 HAU
7.99 g., 0.917 Gold 0.2356 oz. AGW **Ruler:** Taufa'ahau Tupou IV **Subject:** Wedding and Treaty of Friendship **Obv:** Head right **Rev:** Wedding of Prince Charles and Lady Diana

Date	Mintage	VF20	XF40	MS60	MS63	MS65
1981	500	—	—	—	475	525
1981	2,500	PF63 450	PF65 500			

KM# 79 HAU
7.99 g., 0.917 Gold 0.2356 oz. AGW **Ruler:** Taufa'ahau Tupou IV **Subject:** Commonwealth Games **Obv:** Head right **Rev:** Runners and emblem

Date	Mintage	VF20	XF40	MS60	MS63	MS65
1982	500	—	—	—	850	900
1982	500	PF63 900	PF65 950			

KM# 94 HAU
52.00 g., 0.950 Platinum 1.5882 oz. APW **Ruler:** Taufa'ahau Tupou IV **Subject:** 100th Anniversary of Automobile Industry **Obv:** Head right **Rev:** Rolls Royce and Silver Ghost **Note:** Similar to 50 Seniti, KM#82.

Date	Mintage	VF20	XF40	MS60	MS63	MS65
1985	—	PF65 2,250	PF67 2,500			

KM# 95 HAU
52.00 g., 0.950 Platinum 1.5882 oz. APW **Ruler:** Taufa'ahau Tupou IV **Subject:** 100th Anniversary of Automobile Industry **Obv:** Head right **Rev:** Range Rover and Land Rover **Note:** Similar to 50 Seniti, KM#83.

Date	Mintage	VF20	XF40	MS60	MS63	MS65
1985	—	PF65 2,250	PF67 2,500			

KM# 96 HAU
52.00 g., 0.950 Platinum 1.5882 oz. APW **Ruler:** Taufa'ahau Tupou IV **Subject:** 100th Anniversary of Automobile Industry **Obv:** Head right **Rev:** Mini Morris Cowley and Touring Car **Note:** Similar to 50 Seniti, KM#84.

Date	Mintage	VF20	XF40	MS60	MS63	MS65
1985	—	PF65 2,250	PF67 2,500			

KM# 97 HAU
52.00 g., 0.950 Platinum 1.5882 oz. APW **Ruler:** Taufa'ahau Tupou IV **Subject:** 100th Anniversary of Automobile Industry **Obv:** Head right **Rev:** MGB GT and MG TA **Note:** Similar to 50 Seniti, KM#85.

Date	Mintage	VF20	XF40	MS60	MS63	MS65
1985	—	PF65 2,250	PF67 2,500			

KM# 113 HAU
52.00 g., 0.950 Platinum 1.5882 oz. APW **Ruler:** Taufa'ahau Tupou IV **Subject:** 85th Birthday of Queen Mother **Obv:** Head right **Rev:** Queen Mother as a young girl **Note:** Similar to 50 Seniti, KM#98.

Date	Mintage	VF20	XF40	MS60	MS63	MS65
1985	—	PF65 2,250	PF67 2,500			

KM# 114 HAU
52.00 g., 0.950 Platinum 1.5882 oz. APW **Ruler:** Taufa'ahau Tupou IV **Subject:** 85th Birthday of Queen Mother **Obv:** Head right **Rev:** Wedding of King George VI and Elizabeth **Note:** Similar to 50 Seniti, KM#99.

Date	Mintage	VF20	XF40	MS60	MS63	MS65
1985	—	PF65 2,250	PF67 2,500			

KM# 115 HAU
52.00 g., 0.950 Platinum 1.5882 oz. APW **Ruler:** Taufa'ahau Tupou IV **Subject:** 85th Birthday of Queen Mother **Obv:** Head right **Rev:** King George VI and Elizabeth **Note:** Similar to 50 Seniti, KM#100.

Date	Mintage	VF20	XF40	MS60	MS63	MS65
1985	—	PF65 2,250	PF67 2,500			

KM# 116 HAU
52.00 g., 0.950 Platinum 1.5882 oz. APW **Ruler:** Taufa'ahau Tupou IV **Subject:** 85th Birthday of Queen Mother **Obv:** Head right **Rev:** Queen Mother holding Queen Elizabeth II **Note:** Similar to 50 Seniti, KM#101.

Date	Mintage	VF20	XF40	MS60	MS63	MS65
1985	—	PF65 2,250	PF67 2,500			

KM# 117 HAU
52.00 g., 0.950 Platinum 1.5882 oz. APW **Ruler:** Taufa'ahau Tupou IV **Subject:** 85th Birthday of Queen Mother **Obv:** Head right **Rev:** Queen Mother facing **Note:** Similar to 50 Seniti, KM#102.

Date	Mintage	VF20	XF40	MS60	MS63	MS65
1985	—	PF65 2,250	PF67 2,500			

KM# 76 5 HAU
15.98 g., 0.917 Gold 0.4711 oz. AGW **Ruler:** Taufa'ahau Tupou IV **Subject:** Wedding and Treaty of Friendship **Obv:** Head right **Rev:** Wedding of Prince Charles and Lady Diana

Date	Mintage	VF20	XF40	MS60	MS63	MS65
1981	250	—	—	—	875	925
1981	1,000	PF63 850	PF65 900			

COUNTERMARKED COMMEMORATIVE COINAGE

Commemorative coins which contain a countermark creating a new commemorative representation. The Date listed refers to the original date the coin was struck.

KM# 14 20 SENITI
Copper-Nickel, 28.5 mm. **Ruler:** Taufa'ahau Tupou IV **Obv:** Head right, small crowns around border **Countermark:** 1918/ TTIV/1968 **Note:** Countermark on KM#13.

Date	Mintage	VF20	XF40	MS60	MS63	MS65
ND-1967	1,577	PF65 9.00				

KM# 10 50 SENITI
Copper-Nickel Gilt, 34.5 mm. **Ruler:** Taufa'ahau Tupou IV **Obv:** Head right **Edge:** Reeded **Countermark:** IN MEMORIAM/1965 +1970 **Note:** Countermark on KM#10.

Date	Mintage	VF20	XF40	MS60	MS63	MS65
1967	Inc. above	—	—	1.50	3.00	5.00

KM# 16 50 SENITI
Copper-Nickel, 34.5 mm. **Ruler:** Taufa'ahau Tupou IV **Obv:** Head right, small crowns around border **Countermark:** 1918/ TTIV/1968 **Note:** Countermark on KM#15.

Date	Mintage	VF20	XF40	MS60	MS63	MS65
ND-1967	1,577	PF65 10.00				

KM# 12 PA'ANGA
Copper-Nickel Gilt, 38.5 mm. **Ruler:** Taufa'ahau Tupou IV **Obv:** Head right **Countermark:** IN MEMORIAM/1965 + 1970 **Note:** Countermark on KM#11.

Date	Mintage	VF20	XF40	MS60	MS63	MS65
1967	Inc. above	—	—	—	—	7.00

KM# 18 PA'ANGA
Copper-Nickel, 38.5 mm. **Ruler:** Taufa'ahau Tupou IV **Obv:** Head right, small crowns around border **Countermark:** 1918/ TTIV/1968 **Note:** Countermark on KM#17.

Date	Mintage	VF20	XF40	MS60	MS63	MS65
1967	1,577	PF65 10.00				

KM# 34 PA'ANGA
Copper-Nickel Gilt, 38.5 mm. **Ruler:** Taufa'ahau Tupou IV **Obv:** Head right **Edge:** Reeded **Countermark:** Oil rig 1969 OIL SEARCH **Note:** Countermark on KM#17.

Date	Mintage	VF20	XF40	MS60	MS63	MS65
1968	5,017	—	—	1.50	3.00	5.50

KM# 35 PA'ANGA
Copper-Nickel Gilt, 38.5 mm. **Obv:** Head right **Edge:** Reeded **Countermark:** COMMONWEALTH MEMBER/1970 **Note:** Countermark on KM#17.

Date	Mintage	VF20	XF40	MS60	MS63	MS65
1968	3,000	—	—	1.75	3.50	6.50

KM# 36 PA'ANGA
Copper-Nickel Gilt, 38.5 mm. **Ruler:** Taufa'ahau Tupou IV **Obv:** Head right **Edge:** Reeded **Countermark:** INVESTITURE/1971 **Note:** Countermark on KM#33.

Date	Mintage	VF20	XF40	MS60	MS63	MS65
1968	3,000	—	—	1.75	3.50	6.50
1968	1,000	PF65 12.00				

KM# 20 2 PA'ANGA
Copper-Nickel, 44.5 mm. **Ruler:** Taufa'ahau Tupou IV **Obv:** Head right, small crowns around border **Countermark:** 1918/ TTIV/1968 **Note:** Countermark on KM#19.

Date	Mintage	VF20	XF40	MS60	MS63	MS65
ND-1967	1,577	PF65 12.00				

KM# 38 2 PA'ANGA
Copper-Nickel Gilt, 44.5 mm. **Ruler:** Taufa'ahau Tupou IV **Obv:** Head right **Edge:** Reeded **Countermark:** Oil rig 1969 OIL SEARCH **Note:** Countermark on KM#37.

Date	Mintage	VF20	XF40	MS60	MS63	MS65
1968	5,039	—	—	2.50	4.50	7.50

KM# 39 2 PA'ANGA
Copper-Nickel Gilt, 44.5 mm. **Ruler:** Taufa'ahau Tupou IV **Obv:** Head right **Edge:** Reeded **Countermark:** COMMONWEALTH MEMBER/1970 **Note:** Countermark on KM#37.

Date	Mintage	VF20	XF40	MS60	MS63	MS65
1968	3,006	—	—	3.00	5.00	8.50

KM# 40 2 PA'ANGA
Copper-Nickel Gilt, 44.5 mm. **Ruler:** Taufa'ahau Tupou IV **Obv:** Head right **Countermark:** INVESTITURE/1971 **Note:** Countermark on KM#37.

Date	Mintage	VF20	XF40	MS60	MS63	MS65
1968	3,000	—	—	3.00	5.00	8.50
1968	1,000	PF65 15.00				

KM# 22 1/4 HAU
16.00 g., 0.980 Palladium 0.5041 oz. APW **Ruler:** Taufa'ahau Tupou IV **Edge Lettering:** HISTORICALLY THE FIRST PALLADIUM COINAGE **Countermark:** 1918/TTIV/1968 **Note:** Countermark on KM#21.

Date	Mintage	VF20	XF40	MS60	MS63	MS65
1967	400	—	—	—	—	500

KM# 24 1/2 HAU
32.00 g., 0.980 Palladium 1.0082 oz. APW **Ruler:** Taufa'ahau Tupou IV **Obv:** Head right, small crowns around border **Rev:** Crowned arms **Edge Lettering:** HISTORICALLY THE FIRST PALLADIUM COINAGE **Countermark:** 1918/TTIV/1968 **Note:** Countermark on KM#23.

Date	Mintage	VF20	XF40	MS60	MS63	MS65
ND-1967	513	—	—	—	—	900

KM# 26 HAU
64.00 g., 0.980 Palladium 2.0165 oz. APW **Ruler:** Taufa'ahau Tupou IV **Edge Lettering:** HISTORICALLY THE FIRST PALLADIUM COINAGE **Countermark:** 1918/TTIV/1968 **Note:** Countermark on KM#25.

Date	Mintage	VF20	XF40	MS60	MS63	MS65
ND-1967	400	—	—	—	—	1,800

MINT SETS

KM#	Date	Mintage	Identification	Issue Price	Mkt Val
MS1	1962 (3)	—	KM#1-3	—	2,450
MS2	1967 (3)	1,500	KM#21, 23, 25	207	3,100
MS3	1968 (3)	400	KM#22, 24, 26	—	3,200
MS4	1970 (2)	10,000	KM#10, 12	2.30	11.50
MS5	1969 (2)	10,000	KM#34, 38	13.68	13.50
MS6	1970 (2)	3,000	KM#35, 39	13.68	15.00
MS7	1971 (2)	3,000	KM#36, 40	4.80	15.00
MS8	1974 (6)	10,000	KM#27-33, 37	7.60	25.00
MS9	1975 (8)	—	KM#42-49	7.75	40.00
MS10	1975 (4)	—	KM#53-56	384	2,400
MS11	1975 (3)	—	KM#50-52	59.60	265
MS12	1977 (4)	—	KM#44-47	0.85	15.00
MS13	1977 (2)	—	KM#49, 57	3.00	27.50
MS14	1978 (2)	—	KM#58-59	3.00	30.00
MS15	1978 (5)	—	KM#42-46	—	5.50
MS16	1979 (2)	8,008	KM#60-61	3.00	27.50
MS17	1980 (2)	8,000	KM#62-63	3.00	24.00
MS18	1980 (2)	750	KM#64-65, Gold	30.00	125
MS19	1981 (8)	15,000	KM#66-73	5.38	35.00
MS20	1985 (5)	20,000	KM#98-102	25.25	17.50
MS21	1985 (4)	20,000	KM#82-85. Auto Industry.	21.00	16.00
MS22	1991 (6)	—	KM#66-71	—	11.00

PROOF SETS

KM#	Date	Mintage	Identification	Issue Price	Mkt Val
PS1	1962 (3)	250	KM#1-3	—	2,575
PS2	1962 (3)	25	KM#1a-3a. Platinum.	—	3,450
PS3	1967 (7)	5,000	KM#4-9, 11	15.00	32.50
PS4	1967 (4)	1,923	KM#13, 15, 17, 19	17.25	27.50
PS5	1968 (8)	2,500	KM#27-33, 37	22.50	36.00
PS6	1968 (4)	1,577	KM#14, 16, 18, 20	22.80	32.50
PS8	1971 (2)	1,000	KM#36, 40	13.40	25.00
PS9	1975 (3)	418	KM#50-52	82.00	300
PS10	1975 (4)	105	KM#53-56	538	2,000
PS11	1978 (2)	750	KM#58a-59a	—	250
PS12	1979 (2)	854	KM#60a-61a	45.00	250
PS13	1980 (2)	400	KM#62a-63a	80.00	95.00
PS14	1980 (2)	200	KM#64-65	60.00	135
PSA15	1981 (3)	—	KM#74-76	—	1,075
PS15	1981 (2)	3,500	KM#72a-73a	88.00	80.00
PS16	1985 (5)	20,000	KM#98-102, Copper-nickel	26.25	18.00
PS17	1985 (5)	10,000	KM#103-107, Silver clad copper-nickel	55.00	22.50
PS18	1985 (5)	5,000	KM#103a-107a, .925 Silver	180	140
PS19	1985 (5)	1,000	KM#108-112, .374 Gold	315	550
PS20	1985 (5)	500	KM#108a-112a, .917 Gold	775	1,750
PS21	1985 (5)	50	KM#113-117, .950 Platinum	5,850	15,000
PS22	1985 (4)	10,000	KM#86-89	44.00	20.00
PS23	1985 (4)	5,000	KM#86a-89a, .925 Silver	144	110
PS24	1985 (4)	1,000	KM#90-93, .374 Gold	252	450
PS25	1985 (4)	500	KM#90a-93a, .917 Gold	620	1,400
PS26	1985 (4)	50	KM#94-97, .950 Platinum	4,680	12,000
PS28	1988 (4)	2,000	KM#129-132	—	2,800

TONKIN

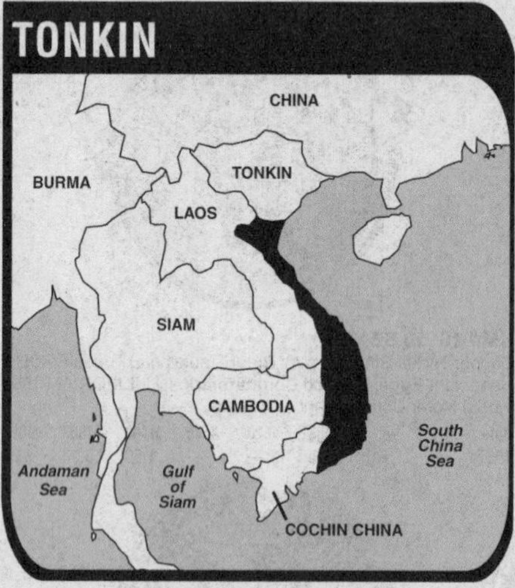

Tonkin (North Viet Nam), a former French protectorate in North Indo-China, comprises the greater part of present North Viet Nam. It had an area of 44,672 sq. mi. (75,700 sq. km.) and a population of about 4 million. Capital: Hanoi. The initial value of Tonkin to France was contained in the access it afforded to the trade of China's Yunnan province.

France established a protectorate over Annam and Tonkin by the treaties of Tientsin and Hue negotiated in1884. Tonkin was incorporated in the independent state of Viet Nam (within the French Union) and upon the defeat of France by the Viet Minh became the body of North Viet Nam.

MINT MARK
(a) - Paris, privy marks only

FRENCH PROTECTORATE

MILLED COINAGE

KM# 1 1/600 PIASTRE
2.10 g., Zinc, 25 mm. **Obv:** Legend around square center hole **Obv. Legend:** PROTECTORAT DU TONKIN **Rev:** Value above and below, "Thong-bao" at left and right **Note:** 0.9 mm thick planchet.

Date	Mintage	F12	VF20	XF40	MS60	MS63
1905 (a)	60,000,000	4.50	7.50	15.00	35.00	95.00

ESSAIS

KM#	Date	Mintage	Identification	Mkt Val
E1	1905(a)	—	1/600 Piastre. Zinc. Legend around center squared hole. Value above and below squared hole in center flanked by thong-bao. 0.9 mm thick planchet.	350

PIEDFORT

KM#	Date	Mintage	Identification	Mkt Val
P1	1905(a)	—	1/600 Piastre. Zinc. Value above and below, "Thong-bao" at left and right. 1.5 mm thick planchet.	750

TRANSNISTRIA

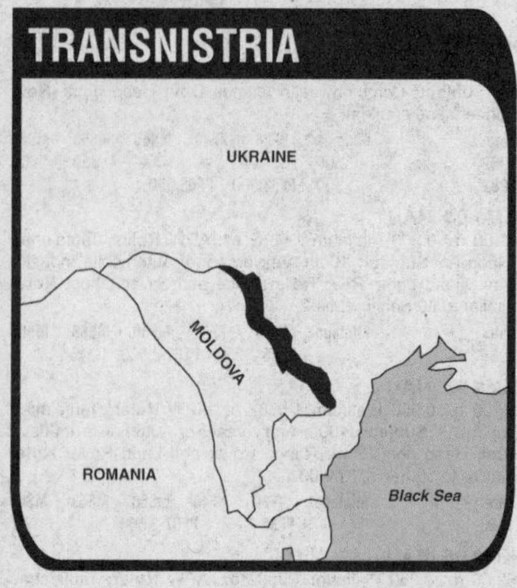

The Pridnestrovskaia Moldavskaia Respublica was formed in 1990, even before the separation of Moldavia from Russia. It has an area of 11,544 sq. mi. (29,900 sq. km.) and a population of 555,000. Capital: Tiraspol.

The area was conquered from the Turks in the last half of the 18th century, and in 1792 the capital city of Bessarabia (present Moldova and part of the Ukraine) became part of the Russian Empire. During the Russian Revolution, in 1918, the area was taken by Romanian troops, and in 1924 the Moldavian Autonomous SSR was formed on the left bank of the Dniester River. On June 22, 1941, Romania declared war on the U.S.S.R. and Romanian troops fought alongside the Germans up to Stalingrad. A Romanian occupation area between the Dniester and Bug Rivers called Transnistria was established in October 1941. Its center was the port of Odessa.

Once the Moldavian SSR declared independence in August 1991, Transnistria did not want to be part of Moldavia. In 1992, Moldova tried to solve the issue militarily with battles in Bendery and Doubossary. The conflict was ended with Russian mediation and Russian peacekeeping forces were stationed there.

Transnistria (or Transdniestra) has a president, parliament, army and police forces, but as yet it is lacking international recognition.

MOLDAVIAN REPUBLIC

STANDARD COINAGE

1 Rublei = 100 Kopeek

KM# 1 KOPEEK
0.62 g., Aluminum, 15.9 mm. **Obv:** National arms **Obv. Legend:** ПРИДНЕСТРОВСКАЯ МОЛДАВСКАЯ РЕСПУБЛИКА **Rev:** Value between wheat stalks **Edge:** Plain

Date	Mintage	VF20	XF40	MS60	MS63	MS65
2000	—	—	0.10	0.30	0.40	1.00

KM# 2 5 KOPEEK
0.70 g., Aluminum, 17.9 mm. **Obv:** National arms **Obv. Legend:** ПРИДНЕСТРОВСКАЯ МОЛДАВСКАЯ РЕСПУБЛИКА **Rev:** Value flanked by wheat stalks **Edge:** Plain

Date	Mintage	VF20	XF40	MS60	MS63	MS65
2000	—	—	0.20	0.50	0.65	1.25

KM# 3 10 KOPEEK
1.00 g., Aluminum, 20 mm. **Obv:** National arms **Obv. Legend:** ПРИДНЕСТРОВСКАЯ МОЛДАВСКАЯ РЕСПУБЛИКА **Rev:** Value flanked by wheat stalks **Edge:** Plain

Date	Mintage	VF20	XF40	MS60	MS63	MS65
2000	—	—	0.25	0.65	0.85	1.50

KM# 4 50 KOPEEK

2.60 g., Aluminum-Bronze, 18.86 mm. **Obv:** National arms **Obv. Legend:** ПРИДНЕСТРОВСКАЯ МОЛДАВСКАЯ РЕСПУБЛИКА **Rev:** Value within sprays **Edge:** Plain

Date	Mintage	VF20	XF40	MS60	MS63	MS65
2000	—	0.15	0.45	1.10	1.50	2.00

KM# 8 RUBLE

14.35 g., 0.925 Silver 0.4268 oz. ASW, 33 mm. **Subject:** 10th Anniversary **Obv:** National Arms **Rev:** Statue of mounted rider

Date	Mintage	VF20	XF40	MS60	MS63	MS65
2000	—	PF65 80.00				

KM# 7 25 RUBLEI

12.80 g., 0.925 Copper-Nickel 0.3807 oz., 31 mm. **Subject:** 10th Anniversary **Obv:** National Arms **Rev:** Parliament Building

Date	Mintage	VF20	XF40	MS60	MS63	MS65
2000	—	PF65 80.00				

KM# 6 50 RUBLEI

14.37 g., Copper-Nickel, 32.75 mm. **Subject:** 10th Anniversary **Obv:** State arms above value **Rev:** Statue **Edge:** Plain

Date	Mintage	VF20	XF40	MS60	MS63	MS65
(ND)2000	—	PF65 40.00				

TRINIDAD & TOBAGO

The Republic of Trinidad and Tobago is situated 7 miles (11 km.) off the coast of Venezuela, has an area of 1,981 sq. mi. (5,130 sq. km.) and a population of *1.2 million. Capital: Port-of-Spain. The island of Trinidad contains the world's largest natural asphalt bog. Birds of Paradise live on little Tobago, the only place outside of their native New Guinea where they can be found in a wild state. Petroleum and petroleum products are the mainstay of the economy. Petroleum products, crude oil and sugar are exported.

Columbus discovered Trinidad and Tobago in 1498. Trinidad remained under Spanish rule from the time of its settlement in 1592 until its capture by the British in 1797. It was ceded to the British in 1802. Tobago was occupied at various times by the French, Dutch and English before being ceded to Britain in 1814. Trinidad and Tobago were merged into a single colony in 1888. The colony was part of the Federation of the West Indies until Aug. 31, 1962, when it became independent. A new constitution establishing a republican form of government was adopted on Aug. 1, 1976. Trinidad and Tobago is a member of the Commonwealth of Nations. The President is Chief of State. The Prime Minister is Head of Government.

RULER

British, until 1976

MINT MARKS

FM - Franklin Mint, U.S.A.*

***NOTE**: From 1975-1985 the Franklin Mint produced coinage in up to 3 different qualities. Qualities of issue are designated in ( ) after each date and are defined as follows:

(M) MATTE - Normal circulation strike or a dull finish produced by sandblasting special uncirculated (polish finish) or proof quality dies.

(U) SPECIAL UNCIRCULATED - Polished or proof-like in appearance without any frosted features.

(P) PROOF - The highest quality obtainable having mirror-like fields and frosted features.

MONETARY SYSTEM

100 Cents = 1 Dollar

BRITISH COLONIAL

STANDARD COINAGE

KM# 1 CENT

1.95 g., Bronze, 17.8 mm. **Obv:** Value **Rev:** National arms **Edge:** Plain

Date	Mintage	VF20	XF40	MS60	MS63	MS65
1966	24,500,000	—	0.10	0.15	0.20	0.30
1966	8,000	PF65 1.00				
1967	4,000,000	—	0.10	0.25	0.35	0.50
1968	5,000,000	—	0.10	0.25	0.35	0.50
1970	5,000,000	—	0.10	0.25	0.35	0.50
1970	2,104	PF65 1.50				
1971	10,600,000	—	0.10	0.15	0.20	0.30
1971 FM (M)	286,000	—	0.10	0.20	0.30	0.40
1971 FM (P)	12,000	PF65 0.50				
1972	16,500,000	—	0.10	0.20	0.25	0.30
1973	10,000,000	—	0.10	0.20	0.25	0.30

KM# 9 CENT

1.95 g., Bronze, 17.8 mm. **Subject:** 10th Anniversary of Independence **Obv:** Value and date **Rev:** National arms **Edge:** Plain

Date	Mintage	VF20	XF40	MS60	MS63	MS65
1972	5,000,000	—	0.10	0.15	0.20	0.30
1972 FM (M)	125,000	—	0.10	0.25	0.35	0.50
1972 FM (P)	16,000	PF65 0.50				

KM# 17 CENT

1.95 g., Bronze, 17.8 mm. **Obv:** Value and date **Rev:** National arms **Edge:** Plain

Date	Mintage	VF20	XF40	MS60	MS63	MS65
1973 FM (M)	127,000	—	0.20	0.50	0.65	1.00
1973 FM (P)	20,000	PF65 1.50				

KM# 25 CENT

1.95 g., Bronze, 17.8 mm. **Obv:** National arms **Rev:** Hummingbird and value **Edge:** Plain

Date	Mintage	VF20	XF40	MS60	MS63	MS65
1974 FM (M)	128,000	—	0.20	0.50	0.65	1.00
1974 FM (P)	14,000	PF65 0.80				
1975	10,000,000	—	0.20	0.50	0.65	1.00
1975 FM (M)	125,000	—	0.20	0.50	0.65	1.00
1975 FM (U)	1,111	—	0.50	1.25	2.00	2.50
1975 FM (P)	24,000	PF65 0.80				
1976	15,050,000	—	0.20	0.50	0.65	1.00

KM# 2 5 CENTS

3.25 g., Bronze, 21.15 mm. **Obv:** Value **Rev:** National arms

Date	Mintage	VF20	XF40	MS60	MS63	MS65
1966	7,500,000	—	0.10	0.25	0.35	0.50
1966	—	PF65 1.25				
1967	3,000,000	—	0.10	0.50	0.65	1.00
1970	—	PF65 1.75				
1971	2,400,000	—	0.10	0.50	0.65	1.00
1971 FM (M)	57,000	—	—	0.15	0.20	0.30
1971 FM (P)	12,000	PF65 0.75				
1972	2,250,000	—	0.10	0.50	0.35	1.00

KM# 10 5 CENTS

3.25 g., Bronze, 21.15 mm. **Subject:** 10th Anniversary of Independence **Obv:** Value and date **Rev:** National arms

Date	Mintage	VF20	XF40	MS60	MS63	MS65
1972	15,000	—	0.15	0.35	0.50	0.70
1972 FM (M)	25,000	—	0.15	0.25	0.35	0.50
1972 FM (P)	16,000	PF65 0.75				

KM# 57 5 CENTS

3.25 g., Bronze, 21.15 mm. **Obv:** Value **Rev:** National arms

Date	Mintage	VF20	XF40	MS60	MS63	MS65
1973 FM (M)	27,000	—	0.20	0.50	0.65	1.00
1973 FM (P)	20,000	PF65 1.50				

KM# 26 5 CENTS

3.25 g., Bronze, 21.15 mm. **Obv:** National arms **Rev:** Bird of Paradise and value

Date	Mintage	VF20	XF40	MS60	MS63	MS65
1974 FM (M)	28,000	—	0.20	0.50	0.65	1.00
1974 FM (P)	14,000	PF65 0.75				
1975	1,500,000	—	0.10	0.45	0.60	0.90
1975 FM (M)	25,000	—	0.20	0.45	0.60	0.90
1975 FM (U)	1,111	—	1.00	2.50	3.50	5.00
1975 FM (P)	24,000	PF65 0.75				
1976	7,500,000	—	0.10	0.45	0.60	0.90

KM# 3 10 CENTS

1.40 g., Copper-Nickel, 16.3 mm. **Obv:** Value and date **Rev:** National arms **Edge:** Reeded

Date	Mintage	VF20	XF40	MS60	MS63	MS65
1966	7,800,000	—	0.10	0.30	0.40	0.60
1966	8,000	PF65 1.50				
1967	4,000,000	—	0.10	0.45	0.60	0.90
1970	2,104	PF65 2.00				
1971	—	—	0.10	0.45	0.60	0.90
1971 FM (M)	29,000	—	—	0.35	0.50	0.70
1971 FM (P)	12,000	PF65 1.00				
1972	4,000,000	—	0.10	0.30	0.40	0.60

KM# 11 10 CENTS

1.40 g., Copper-Nickel, 16.3 mm. **Subject:** 10th Anniversary of Independence **Obv:** Value **Rev:** National arms **Edge:** Reeded

Date	Mintage	VF20	XF40	MS60	MS63	MS65
1972	41,000	—	—	0.40	0.50	0.80
1972 FM (M)	13,000	—	—	0.60	0.75	1.25
1972 FM (P)	16,000	PF65 1.00				

KM# 58 10 CENTS

1.40 g., Copper-Nickel, 16.3 mm. **Obv:** Value **Rev:** National arms **Edge:** Reeded

Date	Mintage	VF20	XF40	MS60	MS63	MS65
1973 FM (M)	14,000	—	—	1.00	1.50	2.00
1973 FM (P)	20,000	PF65 2.50				

KM# 27 10 CENTS

1.40 g., Copper-Nickel, 16.3 mm. **Obv:** National arms **Rev:** Flaming Hibiscus and value **Edge:** Reeded

Date	Mintage	VF20	XF40	MS60	MS63	MS65
1974 FM (M)	16,000	—	0.50	1.00	1.50	2.00
1974 FM (P)	14,000	PF65 1.00				
1975	4,000,000	—	0.10	0.25	0.35	0.50
1975 FM (M)	13,000	—	0.25	0.50	0.65	1.00
1975 FM (U)	1,111	—	1.00	2.50	3.50	5.00
1975 FM (P)	24,000	PF65 1.00				
1976	14,720,000	—	0.10	0.20	0.30	0.40

KM# 4 25 CENTS
3.50 g., Copper-Nickel, 20 mm. **Obv:** Value **Rev:** National arms **Edge:** Reeded

Date	Mintage	VF20	XF40	MS60	MS63	MS65
1966	7,200,000	0.10	0.15	0.35	0.50	0.70
1966	8,000	PF65 1.75				
1967	1,800,000	0.10	0.15	0.50	0.65	1.00
1970	2,014	PF65 2.50				
1971	1,500,000	0.10	0.15	0.50	0.65	1.00
1971 FM (M)	11,000	—	0.30	0.65	0.85	1.35
1971 FM (P)	12,000	PF65 1.25				
1972	3,000,000	0.10	0.15	0.35	0.50	0.70

KM# 12 25 CENTS
3.50 g., Copper-Nickel, 20 mm. **Subject:** 10th Anniversary of Independence **Obv:** Value and date **Rev:** National arms **Edge:** Reeded

Date	Mintage	VF20	XF40	MS60	MS63	MS65
1972	14,000	0.20	0.65	1.00	1.50	2.00
1972 FM (M)	5,000	—	0.50	1.50	2.00	3.00
1972 FM (P)	16,000	PF65 1.25				

KM# 59 25 CENTS
3.50 g., Copper-Nickel, 20 mm. **Obv:** Value **Rev:** National arms **Edge:** Reeded

Date	Mintage	VF20	XF40	MS60	MS63	MS65
1973 FM (M)	6,575	—	0.50	2.25	3.25	4.50
1973 FM (P)	20,000	PF65 3.00				

KM# 28 25 CENTS
3.50 g., Copper-Nickel, 20 mm. **Obv:** National arms **Rev:** Chaconia and value **Edge:** Reeded

Date	Mintage	VF20	XF40	MS60	MS63	MS65
1974 FM (M)	8,258	—	0.50	1.75	2.50	3.50
1974 FM (P)	14,000	PF65 1.25				
1975	3,000,000	0.10	0.15	0.30	0.40	0.60
1975 FM (M)	5,000	—	0.50	1.50	2.25	3.00
1975 FM (U)	1,111	—	0.75	2.00	3.00	4.00
1975 FM (P)	24,000	PF65 1.25				
1976	9,000,000	0.10	0.15	0.30	0.40	0.60

KM# 5 50 CENTS
7.00 g., Copper-Nickel, 26 mm. **Obv:** Value **Rev:** National arms **Edge:** Reeded

Date	Mintage	VF20	XF40	MS60	MS63	MS65
1966	975,000	0.25	0.60	1.50	2.25	3.00
1966	8,000	PF65 2.50				
1967	750,000	0.25	0.50	1.25	2.00	2.50
1970	2,104	PF65 3.00				
1971 FM (M)	5,714	—	0.75	2.50	3.50	5.00
1971 FM (P)	12,000	PF65 1.75				

KM# 13 50 CENTS
7.00 g., Copper-Nickel, 26 mm. **Subject:** 10th Anniversary of Independence **Obv:** Value **Rev:** National arms **Edge:** Reeded

Date	Mintage	VF20	XF40	MS60	MS63	MS65
1972	375,000	0.50	0.75	1.50	2.25	3.00
1972 FM (M)	2,500	—	1.50	3.00	5.00	7.00
1972 FM (P)	16,000	PF65 1.75				

KM# 22 50 CENTS
7.00 g., Copper-Nickel, 26 mm. **Obv:** National arms **Rev:** Kettle drums and value **Edge:** Reeded

Date	Mintage	VF20	XF40	MS60	MS63	MS65
1973 FM (M)	4,075	—	1.00	2.50	3.50	5.00
1973 FM (P)	20,000	PF65 2.25				
1974 FM (M)	5,758	—	1.00	2.50	3.50	5.00
1974 FM (P)	14,000	PF65 2.25				
1975 FM (M)	2,500	—	1.25	3.25	5.50	8.00
1975 FM (U)	1,111	—	1.00	2.50	3.50	5.00
1975 FM (P)	24,000	PF65 2.00				
1976	750,000	0.50	0.75	1.50	2.25	3.00

KM# 6 DOLLAR
12.70 g., Nickel, 32 mm. **Series:** F.A.O. **Obv:** National arms **Rev:** Value in front of leaves

Date	Mintage	VF20	XF40	MS60	MS63	MS65
1969	250,000	0.75	1.50	2.00	3.00	5.00

KM# 7 DOLLAR
12.70 g., Copper-Nickel, 32 mm. **Obv:** Value **Rev:** National arms

Date	Mintage	VF20	XF40	MS60	MS63	MS65
1971 (M)	2,857	—	2.00	3.00	5.00	7.00
1971 (P)	12,000	PF65 3.00				

KM# 7a DOLLAR
Nickel, 36 mm. **Obv:** Value **Rev:** National arms

Date	Mintage	VF20	XF40	MS60	MS63	MS65
1970	2,014	PF65 6.00				

KM# 14 DOLLAR
Copper-Nickel, 36 mm. **Subject:** 10th Anniversary of Independence **Obv:** National arms **Rev:** Cocrico bird on branch and value

Date	Mintage	VF20	XF40	MS60	MS63	MS65
1972	9,700	—	2.00	3.00	5.00	7.00
1972 FM (M)	1,250	—	3.00	5.00	7.00	12.00
1972 FM (P)	16,000	PF65 4.00				

KM# 23 DOLLAR
Copper-Nickel, 36 mm. **Obv:** National arms **Rev:** Cocrico bird on branch and value

Date	Mintage	VF20	XF40	MS60	MS63	MS65
1973 FM (M)	2,825	—	2.00	3.00	4.50	7.00
1973 FM (P)	20,000	PF65 4.00				
1974 FM (M)	4,508	—	2.00	3.00	4.50	7.00
1974 FM (P)	14,000	PF65 4.00				
1975 FM (M)	1,250	—	2.50	3.50	5.50	8.00
1975 FM (U)	1,111	—	2.50	3.50	5.50	8.00
1975 FM (P)	24,000	PF65 4.00				

KM# 8 5 DOLLARS
29.70 g., 0.925 Silver 0.8833 oz. ASW, 40 mm. **Obv:** National arms **Rev:** Scarlet Ibis and value

Date	Mintage	VF20	XF40	MS60	MS63	MS65
1971 FM (M)	571	—	—	32.00	35.00	37.00
1971 FM (P)	11,000	PF65 19.50				
1973 FM (M)	1,825	—	—	30.00	32.00	35.00
1973 FM (P)	25,000	PF65 19.50				
1974 FM (P)	16,000	PF65 19.50				
1975 FM (P)	26,000	PF65 19.50				

KM# 8a 5 DOLLARS
Copper-Nickel, 40 mm. **Obv:** National arms **Rev:** Scarlet Ibis and value

Date	Mintage	VF20	XF40	MS60	MS63	MS65
1974 FM (M)	3,508	—	—	5.00	7.00	9.00
1975 FM (M)	250	—	—	10.00	20.00	22.00
1975 FM (U)	1,111	—	—	5.00	7.50	10.00

KM# 15 5 DOLLARS
29.70 g., 0.925 Silver 0.8833 oz. ASW, 40 mm. **Subject:** 10th Anniversary of Independence **Obv:** National arms **Rev:** Scarlet Ibis and value

Date	Mintage	VF20	XF40	MS60	MS63	MS65
1972	10,000	—	—	17.00	20.00	22.50
1972 FM	250	—	—	35.00	50.00	55.00
1972 FM	19,000	PF65 19.50				

KM# 16 10 DOLLARS
35.00 g., 0.925 Silver 1.0409 oz. ASW, 42 mm. **Subject:** 10th Anniversary of Independence **Obv:** National arms **Rev:** Fish, ship, map and value within waves

Date	Mintage	VF20	XF40	MS60	MS63	MS65
1972	—	—	—	20.00	22.00	25.00
1972 FM (M)	125	—	—	100	125	130
1972 FM (P)	26,000	PF65 23.00				

KM# 24a 10 DOLLARS
35.00 g., 0.925 Silver 1.0409 oz. ASW, 42 mm. **Obv:** National arms **Rev:** Fish, ship, map and value within waves

Date	Mintage	VF20	XF40	MS60	MS63	MS65
1973 FM (M)	1,700	—	—	20.00	23.00	26.00
1973 FM (U)	—	—	—	20.00	23.00	26.00
1973 FM (P)	24,000	PF65 23.00				
1974 FM (P)	21,000	PF65 23.00				
1975 FM (P)	28,000	PF65 23.00				

KM# 24 10 DOLLARS
Copper-Nickel, 42 mm. **Obv:** National arms **Rev:** Fish, ship, map and value within waves

Date	Mintage	VF20	XF40	MS60	MS63	MS65
1974 FM (M)	3,632	—	—	4.00	8.00	12.00
1975 FM (M)	125	—	—	30.00	50.00	60.00
1975 FM (U)	1,111	—	—	5.00	10.00	15.00

REPUBLIC

KM# 29 CENT
1.95 g., Bronze, 17.76 mm. **Obv:** National arms **Rev:** Hummingbird and value **Edge:** Plain

Date	Mintage	VF20	XF40	MS60	MS63	MS65
1976	—	—	0.20	0.35	0.50	1.00
1976 FM (M)	150,000	—	0.20	0.35	0.50	1.00
1976 FM (U)	582	—	0.75	1.50	2.50	3.50
1976 FM (P)	10,000	PF65 0.60				
1977	25,000,000	—	0.20	0.35	0.50	1.00
1977 FM (M)	150,000	—	0.20	0.35	0.50	1.00
1977 FM (U)	633	—	0.75	1.50	2.50	3.50
1977 FM (P)	5,337	PF65 0.60				
1978	12,500,000	—	0.20	0.35	0.50	1.00
1978 FM (M)	150,000	—	0.20	0.35	0.50	1.00
1978 FM (U)	472	—	0.75	1.50	2.50	3.50
1978 FM (P)	4,845	PF65 1.00				
1979	30,200,000	—	0.20	0.35	0.50	1.00
1979 FM (M)	150,000	—	0.20	0.35	0.50	1.00
1979 FM (U)	518	—	0.75	1.50	2.50	3.50
1979 FM (P)	3,270	PF65 1.00				
1980	12,500,000	—	0.20	0.35	0.50	1.00
1980 FM (M)	75,000	—	0.20	0.35	0.50	1.00
1980 FM (U)	796	—	0.75	1.50	2.50	3.50
1980 FM (P)	2,393	PF65 1.00				
1981	—	—	0.20	0.35	0.50	1.00
1981 FM (M)	—	—	0.20	0.35	0.50	1.00
1981 FM (U)	—	—	0.75	1.50	2.50	3.50
1981 FM (P)	—	PF65 1.00				
1982	—	—	0.20	0.35	0.50	1.00
1983	—	—	0.20	0.35	0.50	1.00
1984	—	—	0.20	0.35	0.50	1.00
1985	25,400,000	—	0.20	0.35	0.50	1.00
1986	10,000,000	—	0.20	0.35	0.50	1.00
1987	10,000,000	—	0.20	0.35	0.50	1.00
1988	5,000,000	—	0.20	0.35	0.50	1.00
1989	—	—	0.20	0.35	0.50	1.00
1990	—	—	0.20	0.35	0.50	1.00
1991	—	—	0.20	0.35	0.50	1.00
1993	—	—	0.20	0.35	0.50	1.00
1994	—	—	0.20	0.35	0.50	1.00
1995	—	—	0.20	0.35	0.50	1.00
1996	—	—	0.20	0.35	0.50	1.00
1997	—	—	0.20	0.35	0.50	1.00
1998	—	—	0.20	0.35	0.50	1.00
1999	—	PF65 0.60				
1999	—	—	0.20	0.35	0.50	1.00
2000	—	—	0.20	0.35	0.50	1.00

KM# 29a CENT
2.00 g., 0.925 Silver 0.0595 oz. ASW, 17.8 mm. **Obv:** National arms **Rev:** Hummingbird and value

Date	Mintage	VF20	XF40	MS60	MS63	MS65
1981 FM (P)	898	PF65 10.00				

KM# 42 CENT
1.95 g., Bronze, 17.8 mm. **Subject:** 20th Anniversary of Independence **Obv:** National arms **Rev:** Flaming hibiscus and value **Edge:** Plain

Date	Mintage	VF20	XF40	MS60	MS63	MS65
1982 FM (M)	—	—	0.10	0.15	0.20	0.30
1982 FM (U)	—	—	0.75	1.50	2.00	3.00
1982 FM (P)	—	PF65 1.00				

KM# 42a CENT
2.00 g., 0.925 Silver 0.0595 oz. ASW, 17.8 mm. **Obv:** National arms **Rev:** Flaming hibiscus and value

Date	Mintage	VF20	XF40	MS60	MS63	MS65
1982 FM (P)	699	PF65 10.00				

KM# 51 CENT
1.95 g., Bronze, 17.8 mm. **Obv:** National arms **Rev:** Flaming hibiscus and value **Edge:** Plain

Date	Mintage	VF20	XF40	MS60	MS63	MS65
1983 FM (M)	—	—	—	1.50	2.00	3.00
1983 FM (P)	—	PF65 1.00				
1984 FM (P)	—	PF65 1.00				

KM# 51a CENT
2.00 g., 0.925 Silver 0.0595 oz. ASW, 17.8 mm. **Obv:** National arms **Rev:** Flaming hibiscus and value

Date	Mintage	VF20	XF40	MS60	MS63	MS65
1983 FM (P)	1,344	PF65 10.00				
1984 FM (P)	—	PF65 10.00				

KM# 30 5 CENTS
3.31 g., Bronze, 21.2 mm. **Obv:** National arms **Rev:** Bird of paradise and value **Edge:** Plain

Date	Mintage	VF20	XF40	MS60	MS63	MS65
1976 FM (M)	30,000	—	0.10	0.25	0.50	1.00
1976 FM (U)	582	—	0.80	1.75	2.50	3.50
1976 FM (P)	10,000	PF65 0.75				
1977 FM	12,000,000	—	0.10	0.25	0.50	1.00
1977 FM (M)	30,000	—	0.10	0.25	0.50	1.00
1977 FM (U)	633	—	0.55	1.75	2.50	3.50
1977 FM (P)	5,337	PF65 0.75				
1978 FM	1,500,000	—	0.10	0.25	0.50	1.00
1978 FM (M)	30,000	—	0.10	0.25	0.50	1.00
1978 FM (U)	472	—	0.65	1.75	2.50	3.50
1978 FM (P)	4,845	PF65 1.25				
1979 FM	—	—	0.10	0.25	0.50	1.00
1979 FM (M)	30,000	—	0.10	0.25	0.50	1.00
1979 FM (U)	518	—	0.65	1.75	2.50	3.50
1979 FM (P)	3,270	PF65 1.25				
1980 FM	15,000,000	—	0.10	0.25	0.50	1.00
1980 FM (M)	15,000	—	0.10	0.25	0.50	1.00
1980 FM (U)	796	—	1.25	3.00	5.00	7.50
1980 FM (P)	2,393	PF65 1.25				
1981 FM	—	—	0.10	0.25	0.50	1.00
1981 FM (M)	—	—	0.10	0.25	0.50	1.00
1981 FM (U)	—	—	0.65	1.75	2.50	3.50
1981 FM (P)	—	PF65 1.25				
1983	—	—	0.10	0.25	0.50	1.00
1984	4,094,999	—	0.10	0.25	0.75	1.25
1988	20,000,000	—	0.10	0.25	0.50	1.00
1990	—	—	0.10	0.25	0.50	1.00
1992	—	—	0.10	0.25	0.50	1.00
1995	—	—	0.10	0.25	0.50	1.00
1996	—	—	0.10	0.25	0.50	1.00
1997	—	—	0.10	0.25	0.50	1.00
1998	—	—	0.10	0.25	0.50	1.00
1999	—	—	0.10	0.25	0.50	1.00
1999	—	PF65 1.00				
2000	—	—	0.10	0.25	0.50	1.00

KM# 30a 5 CENTS
3.50 g., 0.925 Silver 0.1041 oz. ASW, 21.15 mm. **Obv:** National arms **Rev:** Bird of paradise and value

Date	Mintage	VF20	XF40	MS60	MS63	MS65
1981 FM (P)	898	PF65 13.50				

KM# 43 5 CENTS
3.25 g., Bronze, 21.15 mm. **Subject:** 20th Anniversary of Independence **Obv:** National arms **Rev:** Butterfly and value

Date	Mintage	VF20	XF40	MS60	MS63	MS65
1982 FM (M)	—	—	—	1.50	2.50	5.00
1982 FM (U)	—	—	—	2.00	4.00	6.00
1982 FM (P)	—	PF65 5.00				

KM# 43a 5 CENTS
3.50 g., 0.925 Silver 0.1041 oz. ASW, 21.15 mm. **Obv:** National arms **Rev:** Butterfly and value

Date	Mintage	VF20	XF40	MS60	MS63	MS65
1982 FM (P)	699	PF65 15.00				

KM# 52 5 CENTS
3.25 g., Bronze, 21.15 mm. **Obv:** National arms **Rev:** Butterfly

Date	Mintage	VF20	XF40	MS60	MS63	MS65
1983 FM (M)	—	—	1.00	2.00	3.00	5.00
1983 FM (P)	—	PF65 6.00				
1984 FM (P)	—	PF65 6.00				

KM# 52a 5 CENTS
3.50 g., 0.925 Silver 0.1041 oz. ASW, 21.15 mm. **Obv:** National arms **Rev:** Butterfly and value

Date	Mintage	VF20	XF40	MS60	MS63	MS65
1983 FM (P)	1,324	PF65 17.50				
1984 FM (P)	—	PF65 17.50				

KM# 31 10 CENTS
1.40 g., Copper-Nickel, 16.2 mm. **Obv:** National arms **Rev:** Hibiscus and value **Edge:** Reeded

Date	Mintage	VF20	XF40	MS60	MS63	MS65
1976 FM (M)	15,000	—	—	0.50	0.75	1.00
1976 FM (U)	582	—	—	5.00	7.50	10.00
1976 FM (P)	10,000	PF65 1.00				
1977 FM	17,280,000	—	0.10	0.20	0.30	0.40
1977 FM (M)	15,000	—	—	0.50	0.75	1.00
1977 FM (U)	633	—	—	5.00	7.50	10.00
1977 FM (P)	5,337	PF65 1.00				
1978 FM	10,000,000	—	0.10	0.20	0.30	0.40
1978 FM (M)	15,000	—	—	0.50	0.75	1.00
1978 FM (U)	472	—	—	5.00	7.00	9.00
1978 FM (P)	4,845	PF65 1.50				
1979 FM	1,970,000	—	0.10	0.30	0.45	0.60
1979 FM (M)	15,000	—	—	0.50	0.75	1.00
1979 FM (U)	518	—	—	4.50	7.00	9.00
1979 FM (P)	3,270	PF65 1.50				

Date	Mintage	VF20	XF40	MS60	MS63	MS65
1980 FM	20,000,000	—	0.10	0.30	0.45	0.60
1980 FM (M)	7,500	—	—	0.50	0.75	1.00
1980 FM (U)	796	—	—	4.50	7.00	9.00
1980 FM (P)	2,393	PF65 1.50				
1981 FM	—	—	0.10	0.30	0.45	0.60
1981 FM (M)	—	—	—	0.50	0.75	1.00
1981 FM (U)	—	—	—	4.50	7.00	9.00
1981 FM (P)	—	PF65 1.50				
1990	—	—	0.10	0.30	0.45	0.60
1997	—	—	0.20	0.50	0.75	1.00
1998	—	—	0.20	0.50	0.75	1.00
1999	—	—	0.20	0.50	0.75	1.00
1999	—	PF65 2.00				
2000	—	—	0.20	0.50	0.75	1.00

KM# 31a 10 CENTS

1.50 g., 0.925 Silver 0.0446 oz. ASW, 16.3 mm. **Obv:** National arms **Rev:** Hibiscus and value

Date	Mintage	VF20	XF40	MS60	MS63	MS65
1981 FM (P)	898	PF65 15.00				

KM# 44 10 CENTS

1.40 g., Copper-Nickel, 16.3 mm. **Subject:** 20th Anniversary of Independence **Obv:** National arms **Rev:** Hummingbird and value **Edge:** Reeded

Date	Mintage	VF20	XF40	MS60	MS63	MS65
1982 FM (M)	—	—	1.00	3.00	5.00	7.00
1982 FM (U)	—	—	1.25	3.50	5.00	7.00
1982 FM (P)	—	PF65 2.50				

KM# 44a 10 CENTS

1.50 g., 0.925 Silver 0.0446 oz. ASW, 16.3 mm. **Obv:** National arms **Rev:** Hummingbird and value

Date	Mintage	VF20	XF40	MS60	MS63	MS65
1982 FM (P)	699	PF65 15.00				

KM# 53 10 CENTS

1.40 g., Copper-Nickel, 16.3 mm. **Obv:** National arms **Rev:** Hummingbird and value

Date	Mintage	VF20	XF40	MS60	MS63	MS65
1983 FM (M)	—	—	1.50	3.00	4.50	6.00
1983 FM (P)	—	PF65 2.00				
1984 FM (P)	—	PF65 2.00				

KM# 53a 10 CENTS

1.50 g., 0.925 Silver 0.0446 oz. ASW, 16.3 mm. **Obv:** National arms **Rev:** Hummingbird and value

Date	Mintage	VF20	XF40	MS60	MS63	MS65
1983 FM (P)	—	PF65 10.00				
1984 FM (P)	—	PF65 10.00				

KM# 32 25 CENTS

3.50 g., Copper-Nickel, 20 mm. **Obv:** National arms **Rev:** Chaconia and value **Edge:** Reeded

Date	Mintage	VF20	XF40	MS60	MS63	MS65
1976 FM (M)	6,000	—	0.50	1.00	1.50	2.00
1976 FM (U)	582	—	—	5.00	7.50	10.00
1976 FM (P)	10,000	PF65 1.25				
1977 FM	9,000,000	0.10	0.15	0.30	0.45	0.60
1977 FM (M)	6,000	—	0.50	1.00	1.50	2.00
1977 FM (U)	633	—	—	5.00	7.50	10.00
1977 FM (P)	5,337	PF65 1.25				
1978 FM	5,470,000	0.10	0.15	0.30	0.45	0.60
1978 FM (M)	6,000	—	0.50	1.00	1.50	2.00
1978 FM (U)	472	—	—	5.00	7.50	10.00
1978 FM (P)	4,845	PF65 1.75				
1979 FM	—	0.10	0.15	0.40	0.60	0.80
1979 FM (M)	6,000	—	0.90	1.00	1.50	2.00
1979 FM (U)	518	—	—	5.00	7.50	10.00
1979 FM (P)	3,270	PF65 2.00				
1980 FM	15,000,000	0.10	0.15	0.40	0.60	0.80
1980 FM (M)	3,000	—	0.50	1.00	1.50	2.00
1980 FM (U)	796	—	—	5.00	7.50	10.00
1980 FM (P)	2,393	PF65 2.00				
1981 FM	—	0.10	0.15	0.40	0.60	0.80
1981 FM (M)	—	—	0.50	1.00	1.50	2.00
1981 FM (U)	—	—	—	5.00	7.50	10.00
1981 FM (P)	—	PF65 2.00				
1983 FM	—	0.10	0.15	0.40	0.60	0.80
1983 FM (M)	—	—	0.60	2.00	3.00	4.00
1983 FM (P)	—	PF65 2.00				
1984	—	0.10	0.15	0.40	0.60	0.80
1984	—	PF65 2.00				
1993	—	—	0.15	0.40	0.60	0.80
1997	—	—	0.15	0.40	0.60	0.80
1998	—	—	0.15	0.40	0.60	0.80
1999	—	—	0.15	0.40	0.60	0.80
1999	—	PF65 3.00				
2000	—	—	0.30	0.50	0.75	1.00

KM# 32a 25 CENTS

3.60 g., 0.925 Silver 0.1071 oz. ASW, 20 mm. **Obv:** National arms **Rev:** Chaconia and value

Date	Mintage	VF20	XF40	MS60	MS63	MS65
1981 FM (P)	898	PF65 12.00				
1983 FM (P)	—	PF65 12.00				
1984 FM (P)	—	PF65 12.00				

KM# 45 25 CENTS

3.50 g., Copper-Nickel, 20 mm. **Subject:** 20th Anniversary of Independence **Obv:** National arms **Rev:** Chaconia and value **Edge:** Reeded

Date	Mintage	VF20	XF40	MS60	MS63	MS65
1982 FM (M)	—	—	0.50	1.00	1.50	2.00
1982 FM (U)	—	—	1.00	1.50	2.25	4.50
1982 FM (P)	—	PF65 2.00				

KM# 45a 25 CENTS

3.60 g., 0.925 Silver 0.1071 oz. ASW, 20 mm. **Obv:** National arms **Rev:** Chaconia and value

Date	Mintage	VF20	XF40	MS60	MS63	MS65
1982 FM (P)	699	PF65 15.00				

KM# 33 50 CENTS

7.00 g., Copper-Nickel, 26 mm. **Obv:** National arms **Rev:** Kettle drums and value **Edge:** Reeded

Date	Mintage	VF20	XF40	MS60	MS63	MS65
1976 FM (M)	3,000	—	1.00	2.00	3.50	5.00
1976 FM (U)	582	—	—	5.00	8.00	15.00
1976 FM (P)	10,000	PF65 1.50				
1977 FM	1,500,000	0.25	0.50	1.00	1.50	2.00
1977 FM (M)	3,000	—	1.50	3.00	4.50	6.00
1977 FM (U)	633	—	—	5.00	8.00	15.00
1977 FM (P)	5,337	PF65 1.50				
1978 FM	563,000	0.50	0.75	1.50	2.50	3.50
1978 FM (M)	3,000	—	1.50	3.00	4.50	6.00
1978 FM (U)	472	—	—	5.00	8.00	15.00
1978 FM (P)	4,845	PF65 2.00				
1979 FM	750,000	0.50	0.75	1.50	2.50	3.50
1979 FM (M)	3,000	—	1.50	3.25	4.75	6.00
1979 FM (U)	518	—	—	5.00	8.00	15.00
1979 FM (P)	3,270	PF65 2.00				
1980 FM	3,750,000	0.25	0.50	1.00	1.50	2.00
1980 FM (M)	1,500	—	1.50	3.00	4.50	6.00
1980 FM (U)	796	—	—	5.00	8.00	15.00
1980 FM (P)	2,393	PF65 2.00				
1981 FM (M)	—	—	1.50	3.00	4.50	6.00
1981 FM (U)	—	—	—	5.00	8.00	10.00
1981 FM (P)	—	PF65 2.00				
1999	—	—	1.00	2.00	3.00	4.00
1999	—	PF65 4.00				

KM# 33a 50 CENTS

7.25 g., 0.925 Silver 0.2156 oz. ASW, 26 mm. **Obv:** National arms **Rev:** Kettle drums and value

Date	Mintage	VF20	XF40	MS60	MS63	MS65
1981 FM (P)	898	PF65 18.00				

KM# 46 50 CENTS

7.00 g., Copper-Nickel, 26 mm. **Subject:** 20th Anniversary of Independence **Obv:** National arms **Rev:** Kettle drums and player **Edge:** Reeded

Date	Mintage	VF20	XF40	MS60	MS63	MS65
1982 FM (M)	—	—	1.50	3.00	4.50	6.00
1982 FM (U)	—	—	1.00	2.50	3.50	5.00
1982 FM (P)	—	PF65 2.00				

KM# 46a 50 CENTS

7.25 g., 0.925 Silver 0.2156 oz. ASW, 26 mm. **Obv:** National arms **Rev:** Kettle drums and player

Date	Mintage	VF20	XF40	MS60	MS63	MS65
1982 FM (P)	699	PF65 20.00				

KM# 54 50 CENTS

7.00 g., Copper-Nickel, 26 mm. **Obv:** National arms **Rev:** Kettle drums and player

Date	Mintage	VF20	XF40	MS60	MS63	MS65
1983 FM (M)	—	—	1.75	4.00	6.00	8.00
1983 FM (P)	—	PF65 2.00				
1984 FM (P)	—	PF65 2.00				

KM# 54a 50 CENTS

7.25 g., 0.925 Silver 0.2156 oz. ASW, 26 mm. **Obv:** National arms **Rev:** Kettle drums and player

Date	Mintage	VF20	XF40	MS60	MS63	MS65
1983 FM (P)	1,325	PF65 12.00				
1984 FM (P)	—	PF65 12.00				

KM# 34 DOLLAR

Copper-Nickel, 36 mm. **Obv:** National arms **Rev:** Cocrico bird on branch and value

Date	Mintage	VF20	XF40	MS60	MS63	MS65
1976 FM (M)	1,500	—	3.00	6.00	8.00	10.00
1976 FM (U)	582	—	8.00	10.00	12.00	15.00
1976 FM (P)	10,000	PF65 2.00				
1977 FM (M)	1,500	—	2.00	6.00	8.00	10.00
1977 FM (U)	633	—	8.00	10.00	12.00	15.00
1977 FM (P)	5,337	PF65 2.00				
1978 FM (M)	1,500	—	2.00	6.00	8.00	10.00
1978 FM (U)	472	—	8.00	10.00	12.00	15.00
1978 FM (P)	4,845	PF65 3.00				
1979 FM (M)	1,500	—	2.00	6.00	8.00	10.00
1979 FM (U)	518	—	8.00	10.00	12.00	15.00
1979 FM (P)	3,270	PF65 3.00				
1980 FM (M)	750	—	8.00	10.00	12.00	15.00
1980 FM (U)	796	—	8.00	10.00	12.00	15.00
1980 FM (P)	2,393	PF65 5.00				
1981 FM (M)	—	—	1.75	5.00	7.00	10.00
1981 FM (U)	—	—	1.00	3.00	4.50	6.00
1981 FM (P)	—	PF65 2.50				
1983 FM (M)	—	—	2.00	6.00	8.00	10.00
1983 FM (P)	—	PF65 2.50				
1984 FM (P)	—	PF65 2.50				

KM# 38 DOLLAR

12.70 g., Copper-Nickel, 32 mm. **Series:** F.A.O. **Obv:** National arms **Rev:** Value in front of leaves

Date	Mintage	VF20	XF40	MS60	MS63	MS65
1979	—	0.75	1.50	2.50	4.00	6.00

KM# 34a DOLLAR

18.60 g., 0.925 Silver 0.5532 oz. ASW, 36 mm. **Obv:** National arms **Rev:** Cocrico bird on branch and value

Date	Mintage	VF20	XF40	MS60	MS63	MS65
1981 FM (P)	898	PF65 22.50				
1983 FM (P)	2,544	PF65 15.00				
1984 FM (P)	—	PF65 15.00				

KM# 47 DOLLAR
Copper-Nickel, 36 mm. **Subject:** 20th Anniversary of Independence **Obv:** National arms **Rev:** Cocrico bird on branch and value within circle

Date	Mintage	VF20	XF40	MS60	MS63	MS65
1982 FM (M)	—	—	3.00	7.00	9.00	12.50
1982 FM (U)	—	—	2.00	4.00	6.00	9.00
1982 FM (P)	—	PF65 5.00				

KM# 47a DOLLAR
18.60 g., 0.925 Silver 0.5532 oz. ASW, 36 mm. **Obv:** National arms **Rev:** Cocrico bird on branch and value within circle

Date	Mintage	VF20	XF40	MS60	MS63	MS65
1982 FM (P)	699	PF65 22.50				

KM# 61 DOLLAR
8.40 g., Copper-Nickel **Subject:** 50th Anniversary - F.A.O. **Obv:** National arms **Rev:** Sprig, value and logo

Date	Mintage	VF20	XF40	MS60	MS63	MS65
1995	500,000	—	0.75	1.25	1.50	2.00
1999	—	—	0.75	1.25	1.50	2.00
1999	—	PF65 5.00				

KM# 61a DOLLAR
15.98 g., 0.925 Silver 0.4752 oz. ASW

Date	Mintage	VF20	XF40	MS60	MS63	MS65
1995	1,000	PF65 75.00				

KM# 35 5 DOLLARS
Copper-Nickel, 40 mm. **Obv:** National arms **Rev:** Scarlet Ibis and value

Date	Mintage	VF20	XF40	MS60	MS63	MS65
1976 FM (M)	300	—	7.00	12.00	20.00	25.00
1976 FM (U)	582	—	7.00	12.00	20.00	25.00
1977 FM (M)	300	—	7.00	12.00	20.00	25.00
1977 FM (U)	633	—	6.00	10.00	17.00	20.00
1978 FM (M)	300	—	7.00	12.00	20.00	25.00
1978 FM (U)	472	—	7.00	12.00	20.00	25.00
1979 FM (M)	300	—	7.00	12.00	20.00	25.00
1979 FM (U)	518	—	7.00	12.00	20.00	25.00
1980 FM (M)	150	—	8.00	15.00	25.00	30.00
1980 FM (U)	796	—	6.00	10.00	17.00	20.00
1981 FM (M)	—	—	7.00	12.00	20.00	25.00
1981 FM (U)	—	—	6.00	10.00	17.00	20.00
1981 FM (P)	—	PF65 18.00				
1983 FM (U)	—	—	7.00	12.00	20.00	25.00
1983 FM (P)	1,312	PF65 18.00				
1984 FM (P)	—	PF65 18.00				

KM# 35a 5 DOLLARS
29.70 g., 0.925 Silver 0.8833 oz. ASW, 40 mm. **Obv:** National arms **Rev:** Scarlet Ibis and value

Date	Mintage	VF20	XF40	MS60	MS63	MS65
1976 FM (P)	11,000	PF65 18.00				
1977 FM (P)	6,107	PF65 18.00				
1978 FM (P)	5,460	PF65 18.00				
1979 FM (P)	3,755	PF65 22.50				
1980 FM (P)	2,393	PF65 22.50				
1981 FM (P)	—	PF65 26.00				
1983 FM (P)	—	PF65 26.00				
1984 FM (P)	—	PF65 26.00				

KM# 35a.1 5 DOLLARS
11.00 g., Copper-Nickel, 30 mm. **Obv:** National arms **Rev:** Scarlet Ibis and value **Note:** Reduced size.

Date	Mintage	VF20	XF40	MS60	MS63	MS65
1999	—	PF65 12.00				

KM# 48 5 DOLLARS
Copper-Nickel, 40 mm. **Subject:** 20th Anniversary of Independence **Obv:** National arms **Rev:** Scarlet Ibis and value

Date	Mintage	VF20	XF40	MS60	MS63	MS65
1982 FM (M)	—	—	7.00	12.00	20.00	25.00
1982 FM (U)	—	—	5.00	8.00	12.50	15.00
1982 FM (P)	—	PF65 12.00				

KM# 48a 5 DOLLARS
30.00 g., 0.925 Silver 0.8922 oz. ASW, 40 mm. **Obv:** National arms **Rev:** Scarlet Ibis and value

Date	Mintage	VF20	XF40	MS60	MS63	MS65
1982 FM (P)	699	PF65 35.00				

KM# 36 10 DOLLARS
Copper-Nickel, 42 mm. **Obv:** National arms **Rev:** Fish, ship, value and map within waves

Date	Mintage	VF20	XF40	MS60	MS63	MS65
1976 FM (M)	150	—	—	20.00	40.00	45.00
1976 FM (U)	582	—	—	15.00	30.00	35.00
1977 FM (M)	150	—	—	20.00	40.00	45.00
1977 FM (U)	633	—	10.00	15.00	30.00	35.00
1978 FM (M)	150	—	12.00	20.00	40.00	45.00
1978 FM (U)	472	—	10.00	15.00	30.00	35.00
1979 FM (M)	150	—	12.00	20.00	40.00	45.00
1979 FM (U)	518	—	10.00	15.00	30.00	35.00
1980 FM (M)	—	—	12.00	20.00	40.00	45.00
1980 FM (U)	—	—	10.00	15.00	30.00	35.00

KM# 36a 10 DOLLARS
35.00 g., 0.925 Silver 1.0409 oz. ASW, 42 mm. **Obv:** National arms **Rev:** Fish, ship, map and value within waves

Date	Mintage	VF20	XF40	MS60	MS63	MS65
1976 FM (P)	13,000	PF65 23.00				
1977 FM (P)	6,643	PF65 23.00				
1978 FM (P)	7,449	PF65 23.00				
1979 FM (P)	4,994	PF65 26.00				
1980 FM (P)	3,726	PF65 26.00				

KM# 40 10 DOLLARS
Copper-Nickel, 42 mm. **Subject:** 5th Anniversary of the Republic **Obv:** National arms **Rev:** Fish, ship, map and value in waves within circle

Date	Mintage	VF20	XF40	MS60	MS63	MS65
1981 FM (U)	—	—	7.00	12.00	20.00	25.00

KM# 40a 10 DOLLARS
35.00 g., 0.925 Silver 1.0409 oz. ASW, 42 mm. **Obv:** National arms **Rev:** Fish, boat, map and value in waves within circle

Date	Mintage	VF20	XF40	MS60	MS63	MS65
1981 FM (P)	2,374	PF63 30.00	PF65 34.00			

KM# 49 10 DOLLARS
Copper-Nickel, 42 mm. **Subject:** 20th Anniversary of Independence **Obv:** National arms **Rev:** Flag and value

Date	Mintage	VF20	XF40	MS60	MS63	MS65
1982 FM (M)	—	—	7.00	12.00	20.00	25.00
1982 FM (U)	—	—	7.00	12.00	20.00	25.00
1982 FM (P)	—	PF65 20.00				

KM# 49a 10 DOLLARS
35.00 g., 0.925 Silver 1.0409 oz. ASW, 42 mm. **Obv:** National arms **Rev:** Flag and value

Date	Mintage	VF20	XF40	MS60	MS63	MS65
1982 FM (P)	1,682	PF63 34.00	PF65 39.00			

KM# 55 10 DOLLARS
Copper-Nickel, 42 mm. **Obv:** National arms **Rev:** Ships and value

Date	Mintage	VF20	XF40	MS60	MS63	MS65
1983 FM (U)	288	—	—	45.00	55.00	65.00

KM# 55a 10 DOLLARS
35.00 g., 0.925 Silver 1.0409 oz. ASW, 42 mm. **Obv:** National arms **Rev:** Ships and value

Date	Mintage	VF20	XF40	MS60	MS63	MS65
1983 FM (P)	1,565	PF63 34.00	PF65 39.00			
1984 FM (P)	—	PF63 34.00	PF65 39.00			

KM# 60 10 DOLLARS
28.28 g., 0.925 Silver 0.841 oz. ASW, 38.61 mm. **Subject:** 30th Anniversary - Central Bank **Obv:** National arms **Rev:** Bird and sprigs

Date	Mintage	VF20	XF40	MS60	MS63	MS65
1994	—	PF63 22.50	PF65 27.50			

KM# 62 10 DOLLARS

Bi-Metallic Silver center in Gold-plated ring, 28.4 mm. **Subject:** Central Bank 35 Years **Obv:** National arms within circle **Rev:** Bank building within circle **Edge:** Reeded **Shape:** Octagonal

Date	Mintage	VF20	XF40	MS60	MS63	MS65
1999	—	PF63 12.00	PF65 15.00			

KM# 39 25 DOLLARS

30.28 g., 0.500 Silver 0.4868 oz. ASW **Subject:** 10th Anniversary of Caribbean Development Bank **Obv:** National arms **Rev:** Map on globe above flag, beaded border

Date	Mintage	VF20	XF40	MS60	MS63	MS65
ND(1980) FM (P)	3,039	PF63 17.50	PF65 21.50			

KM# 37 100 DOLLARS

6.21 g., 0.500 Gold 0.0998 oz. AGW **Obv:** National arms **Rev:** Flying birds and value

Date	Mintage	XF40	MS60	MS63	MS65	MS66
1976 FM (M)	200	—	—	—	225	275
1976 FM (P)	29,000	PF65 160	PF67 180	PF69 200		

KM# 41 100 DOLLARS

6.21 g., 0.500 Gold 0.0998 oz. AGW **Subject:** 5th Anniversary of the Republic **Obv:** National arms **Rev:** Hummingbird and flower **Edge:** Reeded

Date	Mintage	XF40	MS60	MS63	MS65	MS66
1981 FM (U)	100	—	—	—	250	300
1981 FM (P)	400	PF65 225	PF67 275			

KM# 50 100 DOLLARS

6.21 g., 0.500 Gold 0.0998 oz. AGW **Subject:** 20th Anniversary of Independence **Obv:** National arms **Rev:** Building within circle

Date	Mintage	XF40	MS60	MS63	MS65	MS66
1982 FM (P)	1,380	PF65 200	PF67 250	PF69 300		

KM# 56 200 DOLLARS

11.17 g., 0.500 Gold 0.1796 oz. AGW **Subject:** 20th Anniversary of Central Bank **Obv:** National arms **Rev:** Building below value

Date	Mintage	XF40	MS60	MS63	MS65	MS66
1984 FM (P)	1,200	PF65 325	PF67 375	PF69 425		

MINT SETS

KM#	Date	Mintage	Identification	Issue Price	Mkt Val
MS1	1973 (8)	1,575	KM#8, 18-24	24.00	50.00
MS2	1974 (8)	3,258	KM#8a, 22-28	25.00	50.00
MS3	1975 (8)	1,111	KM#8a, 22-23, 24a, 25-28	27.50	105
MS4	1976 (8)	582	KM#29-34, 35a-36a	27.50	90.00
MS5	1977 (8)	632	KM#29-34, 35a-36a	27.50	85.00
MS6	1978 (8)	472	KM#29-34, 35a-36a	27.50	90.00
MS7	1979 (8)	518	KM#29-34, 35a-36a	28.50	90.00
MS8	1980 (8)	796	KM#29-34, 35a-36a	28.50	100
MS9	1981 (8)	—	KM#29-34, 35a, 40	28.50	70.00
MS10	1982 (8)	—	KM#42-49	28.50	85.00
MS11	1983 (8)	281	KM#32, 34, 35a, 51-55	37.00	125
MS12	1999 (6)	—	KM#29-33, 61	35.00	15.00

PROOF SETS

KM#	Date	Mintage	Identification	Issue Price	Mkt Val
PS1	1966 (5)	8,000	KM#1-5	12.50	7.00
PS2	1970 (6)	2,104	KM#1-5, 7	15.25	12.50
PS3	1971 (7)	11,039	KM#1-5, 7a, 8	21.00	20.00
PS4	1971 (5)	488	KM#1-6	15.00	12.50
PS5	1972 (8)	13,874	KM#9-16	35.00	35.00
PS6	1972 (7)	15,957	KM#9-15	22.00	20.00
PS7	1973 (8)	14,615	KM#8, 17, 22-23, 24a, 57-59	35.00	45.00
PS8	1973 (7)	5,050	KM#8,17,22-23, 57-59	22.00	25.00
PS9	1974 (8)	13,991	KM#8, 22-28	50.00	75.00
PS10	1975 (8)	24,472	KM#8, 22-28	55.00	72.50
PS11	1976 (8)	10,099	KM#29-36	55.00	40.00
PS12	1977 (8)	5,337	KM#29-36	55.00	50.00
PS13	1978 (8)	4,845	KM#29-36	55.00	50.00
PS14	1979 (8)	3,270	KM#29-36	57.00	50.00
PS15	1980 (8)	2,393	KM#29-36	66.00	60.00
PS16	1981 (8)	—	KM#29-34, 35a, 40a	87.00	70.00
PS17	1981 (8)	—	KM#29a-34a, 35, 40a	222	150
PS18	1982 (8)	—	KM#42-49	87.00	45.00
PS19	1982 (8)	—	KM#42a-49a	222	160
PS20	1983 (8)	461	KM#32, 34, 35a, 51-54, 55a	87.00	87.50
PS21	1983 (8)	753	KM#32a, 34a, 35, 51a-55a	197	165
PS22	1984 (8)	—	KM#32, 34, 35a, 51-54, 55a	87.00	85.00
PS23	1984 (8)	—	KM#32a, 34a, 35, 51a-55a	197	165
PS24	1999 (8)	3,000	KM#29-33, 35a.1, 61-62	90.00	60.00

TRISTAN DA CUNHA

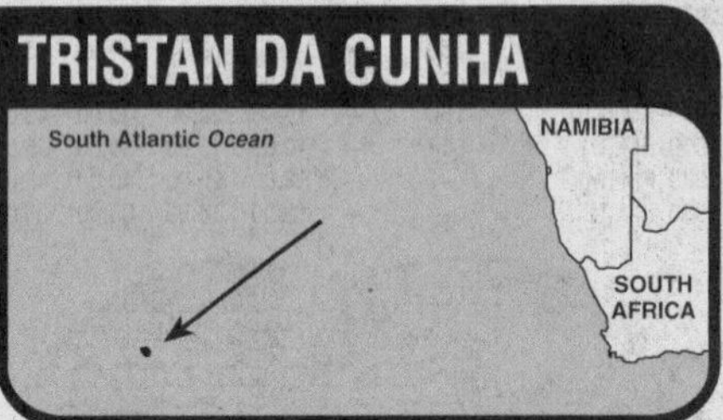

Tristan da Cunha is the principal island and group name of a small cluster of volcanic islands located in the South Atlantic midway between the Cape of Good Hope and South America, and 1,500 miles (2,414 km.) south-southwest of the British colony of St. Helena. The other islands are Inaccessible, Gough, and the three Nightingale Islands. The group, which comprises a dependency of St. Helena, has a total area of 40 sq. mi. (104 sq. km.) and a population of less than 300. There is a village of 60 houses called Edinburgh. Potatoes are the staple subsistence crop.

Portuguese admiral Tristao da Cunha discovered Tristan da Cunha in 1506. Unsuccessful attempts to colonize the islands were made by the Dutch in 1656, but the first permanent inhabitant didn't arrive until 1810. During the exile of Napoleon on St. Helena, Britain placed a temporary garrison on Tristan da Cunha to prevent any attempt to rescue Napoleon from his island prison. The islands were formally annexed to Britain in 1816 and became a dependency of St. Helena in 1938.

RULER
British

MINT MARK
PM - Pobjoy Mint

MONETARY SYSTEM
25 Pence = 1 Crown
100 Pence = 1 Pound

ST. HELENA DEPENDENCY

STANDARD COINAGE

KM# 1 25 PENCE

Copper-Nickel, 38.5 mm. **Ruler:** Elizabeth II **Subject:** Queen's Silver Jubilee **Obv:** Young bust right **Rev:** Boat and rock **Edge:** Reeded

Date	Mintage	VF20	XF40	MS60	MS63	MS65
ND-1977	50,000	—	1.00	2.00	3.00	5.00

KM# 1a 25 PENCE

28.28 g., 0.925 Silver 0.841 oz. ASW, 38.61 mm. **Ruler:** Elizabeth II **Subject:** Queen's Silver Jubilee **Obv:** Young bust right **Rev:** Boat and rock **Edge:** Reeded

Date	Mintage	VF20	XF40	MS60	MS63	MS65
ND-1977	25,000	PF63 17.00	PF65 20.50	PF67 25.00		

KM# 3 25 PENCE

Copper-Nickel, 38.5 mm. **Ruler:** Elizabeth II **Subject:** 80th Birthday of Queen Mother **Obv:** Young bust right **Rev:** Queen Mother 1/4 left above sprig **Edge:** Reeded

Date	Mintage	VF20	XF40	MS60	MS63	MS65
ND-1980	65,000	—	—	1.50	2.50	3.50

KM# 3a 25 PENCE

28.28 g., 0.925 Silver 0.841 oz. ASW, 38.5 mm. **Ruler:** Elizabeth II **Subject:** 80th Birthday of Queen Mother **Obv:** Young bust right **Rev:** Queen Mother 1/4 left above sprig

Date	Mintage	VF20	XF40	MS60	MS63	MS65
ND-1980	25,000	PF63 17.00	PF65 20.50	PF67 25.00		

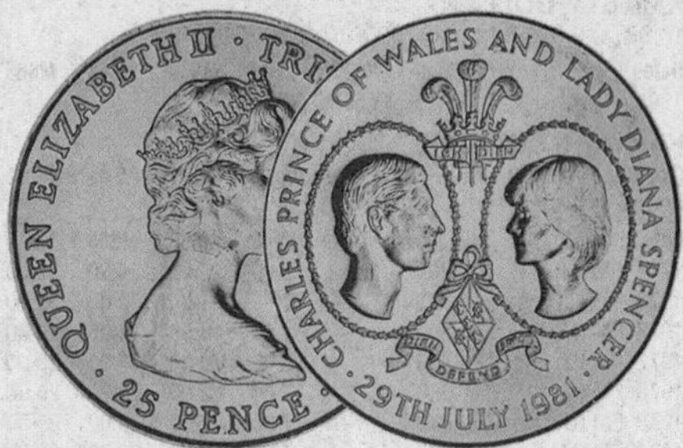

KM# 4 25 PENCE

Copper-Nickel, 38.5 mm. **Ruler:** Elizabeth II **Subject:** Wedding of Prince Charles and Lady Diana **Obv:** Young bust right **Rev:** Design in center divides cameo heads facing each other **Edge:** Reeded

Date	Mintage	VF20	XF40	MS60	MS63	MS65
ND-1981 PM	—	—	—	1.50	2.50	3.50

KM# 4a 25 PENCE

28.28 g., 0.925 Silver 0.841 oz. ASW, 38.5 mm. **Ruler:** Elizabeth II **Subject:** Wedding of Prince Charles and Lady Diana **Obv:** Young bust right **Rev:** Design in center divides cameo heads facing each other

Date	Mintage	VF20	XF40	MS60	MS63	MS65
ND-1981 PM	30,000	PF63 17.00	PF65 20.50	PF67 25.00		

KM# 5 25 PENCE

28.28 g., 0.925 Silver 0.841 oz. ASW, 38.5 mm. **Ruler:** Elizabeth II **Series:** International Year of the Scout **Obv:** Young bust right **Rev:** Scouting emblem within roped wreath

Date	Mintage	VF20	XF40	MS60	MS63	MS65
ND-1983	10,000	—	—	—	17.00	20.50
ND-1983	10,000	PF63 19.00	PF65 22.50	PF67 27.00		

KM# 7 50 PENCE

28.28 g., 0.925 Silver 0.841 oz. ASW, 38.5 mm. **Ruler:** Elizabeth II **Subject:** 40th Wedding Anniversary of Queen Elizabeth and Prince Philip **Obv:** Crowned bust right **Rev:** Crowned initials at center of flower design **Edge:** Reeded

Date	Mintage	VF20	XF40	MS60	MS63	MS65
ND-1987	2,000	PF65 28.00	PF67 35.00			

KM# 7a 50 PENCE

47.54 g., 0.917 Gold 1.4016 oz. AGW, 38.5 mm. **Ruler:** Elizabeth II **Subject:** 40th Wedding Anniversary of Queen Elizabeth and Prince Philip **Obv:** Crowned head right **Rev:** Crowned initials at center of flower design

Date	Mintage	XF40	MS60	MS63	MS65	MS66
ND-1987	75	PF67 2,350	PF69 2,600			

KM# 7b 50 PENCE

Copper-Nickel, 38.5 mm. **Ruler:** Elizabeth II **Subject:** 40th Wedding Anniversary of Queen Elizabeth and Prince Philip **Obv:** Crowned bust right **Rev:** Crowned initials at center of flower design

Date	Mintage	XF40	MS60	MS63	MS65	MS66
ND-1987	—	—	2.00	3.00	5.00	—

KM# 9 50 PENCE

28.28 g., Copper-Nickel, 38.6 mm. **Ruler:** Elizabeth II **Subject:** Winston Churchill **Obv:** Crowned bust right **Rev:** Uniformed bust 1/4 left and two fighter planes **Edge:** Reeded **Note:** Struck at British Royal Mint.

Date	Mintage	VF20	XF40	MS60	MS63	MS65
1999	—	—	—	4.00	6.00	9.00

KM# 9a 50 PENCE

28.28 g., 0.925 Silver 0.841 oz. ASW, 38.6 mm. **Ruler:** Elizabeth II **Subject:** Winston Churchill **Obv:** Crowned head right **Rev:** Uniformed bust 1/4 left and two fighter planes

Date	Mintage	VF20	XF40	MS60	MS63	MS65
1999	—	PF65 50.00	PF67 70.00			

KM# 9b 50 PENCE

47.54 g., 0.917 Gold 1.4016 oz. AGW, 38.6 mm. **Ruler:** Elizabeth II **Subject:** Winston Churchill **Obv:** Crowned bust right **Rev:** Uniformed bust 1/4 left and two fighter planes

Date	Mintage	XF40	MS60	MS63	MS65	MS66
1999	Est. 125	PF67 2,250	PF69 2,500			

KM# 10 50 PENCE

28.64 g., Copper-Nickel, 38.6 mm. **Ruler:** Elizabeth II **Subject:** Queen Mother's Centennial Birthday **Obv:** Crowned bust right **Rev:** Bust of Queen Mother right **Edge:** Reeded

Date	Mintage	VF20	XF40	MS60	MS63	MS65
ND-2000	—	—	—	2.00	4.00	7.00

KM# 10a 50 PENCE

28.40 g., 0.925 Silver 0.8446 oz. ASW, 38.6 mm. **Ruler:** Elizabeth II **Subject:** Queen Mother's Centennial Birthday **Obv:** Crowned bust right **Rev:** Bust of Queen Mother right

Date	Mintage	XF40	MS60	MS63	MS65	MS66
ND-2000	—	—	—	25.00	30.00	35.00
ND-2000	10,000	PF65 40.00	PF67 45.00			

KM# 10b 50 PENCE

47.54 g., 0.9166 Gold 1.401 oz. AGW, 38.6 mm. **Ruler:** Elizabeth II **Subject:** Queen Mother's 100th Birthday **Obv:** Crowned bust right **Rev:** Bust of Queen Mother right **Edge:** Reeded

Date	Mintage	XF40	MS60	MS63	MS65	MS66
ND(2000)	100	PF67 2,250	PF69 2,500			

KM# 11 50 PENCE

28.64 g., Copper-Nickel, 38.6 mm. **Ruler:** Elizabeth II **Subject:** Princess Anne's 50th Birthday **Obv:** Crowned bust right **Rev:** Bust of Princess Anne facing **Edge:** Reeded

Date	Mintage	VF20	XF40	MS60	MS63	MS65
ND-2000	—	—	—	2.00	4.00	7.00

KM# 11a 50 PENCE

28.28 g., 0.925 Silver 0.841 oz. ASW, 38.6 mm. **Ruler:** Elizabeth II **Subject:** Princess Anne's 50th Birthday **Obv:** Crowned bust right **Rev:** Bust of Princess Anne facing **Edge:** Reeded

Date	Mintage	VF20	XF40	MS60	MS63	MS65
ND(2000)	2,500	PF65 45.00	PF67 50.00			

KM# 11b 50 PENCE

47.54 g., 0.9166 Gold 1.401 oz. AGW, 38.6 mm. **Ruler:** Elizabeth II **Subject:** Princess Anne's 50th Birthday **Obv:** Crowned bust right **Rev:** Bust of Princess Anne facing **Edge:** Reeded

Date	Mintage	XF40	MS60	MS63	MS65	MS66
ND(2000)	50	PF67 2,450	PF69 2,700			

KM# 2 CROWN

Copper-Nickel, 38.5 mm. **Ruler:** Elizabeth II **Subject:** 25th Anniversary of Coronation **Obv:** Young bust right **Rev:** Tristan rock lobster on coat of arms **Edge:** Reeded

Date	Mintage	VF20	XF40	MS60	MS63	MS65
1978 PM	—	—	—	3.00	5.00	8.00

KM# 2a CROWN

28.28 g., 0.925 Silver 0.841 oz. ASW, 38.5 mm. **Ruler:** Elizabeth II **Obv:** Young bust right **Rev:** Tristan rock lobster on coat of arms

Date	Mintage	XF40	MS60	MS63	MS65	MS66
1978 PM	70,000	—	—	20.00	30.00	35.00
1978 PM	25,000	PF65 32.00	PF67 37.00			

KM# 6 2 POUNDS

15.98 g., 0.917 Gold 0.4711 oz. AGW **Ruler:** Elizabeth II **Series:** International Year of the Scout **Obv:** Young bust right **Rev:** Sailboat

Date	Mintage	XF40	MS60	MS63	MS65	MS66
1983	2,000	—	—	750	800	850
1983	2,000	PF65 850	PF67 900			

KM# 8 2 POUNDS

Copper-Nickel, 38.5 mm. **Ruler:** Elizabeth II **Subject:** 90th Anniversary of Queen Mother **Obv:** Crowned bust right **Rev:** Crowned monogram flanked by flower sprigs **Edge:** Reeded

Date	Mintage	VF20	XF40	MS60	MS63	MS65
ND-1990	—	—	—	4.00	7.00	9.00

KM# 8a 2 POUNDS

28.28 g., 0.925 Silver 0.841 oz. ASW, 38.5 mm. **Ruler:** Elizabeth II **Subject:** 90th Anniversary of Queen Mother **Obv:** Crowned bust right **Rev:** Crowned monogram flanked by flower sprigs

Date	Mintage	VF20	XF40	MS60	MS63	MS65
ND-1990	Est. 10000	PF65 25.00	PF67 30.00			

The Republic of Tunisia, located on the northern coast of Africa between Algeria and Libya, has an area of 63,170 sq. mi. (163,610 sq. km.) and a population of *7.9 million. Capital: Tunis. Agriculture is the backbone of the economy. Crude oil, phosphates, olive oil, and wine are exported.

Tunisia, settled by the Phoenicians in the 12th century B.C., was the center of the seafaring Carthaginian Empire. After the total destruction of Carthage, Tunisia became part of Rome's African province. It remained a part of the Roman Empire (except for the 439-533 interval of Vandal conquest) until taken by the Arabs, 648, who administered it until the Turkish invasion of 1570. Under Turkish control, the public revenue was heavily dependent upon the piracy of Mediterranean shipping, an endeavor that wasn't abandoned until 1819 when a coalition of powers threatened appropriate reprisal. Deprived of its major source of income, Tunisia underwent a financial regression that ended in bankruptcy, enabling France to establish a protectorate over the country in 1881. National agitation and guerrilla fighting forced France to grant Tunisia internal autonomy in 1955 and to recognize Tunisian independence on March 20, 1956. Tunisia abolished the monarchy and established a republic on July 25, 1957.

TITLES

المملكة التونسية

al-Mamlaka al-Tunisiya

الجمهورية العراقية

al-Jumhuriya al-Tunisiya

al-Amala al-Tunisiya
(Tunisian Protectorate)

MINT MARKS

A - Paris, AH1308/1891-AH1348/1928
(a) - Paris, privy marks, AH1349/1929-AH1376/1957
FM - Franklin Mint, Franklin Center, PA
Numismatic Italiana, Arezzo, Italy

FRENCH PROTECTORATE

Ali Bey

Struck in his name

DECIMAL COINAGE

The following coins all bear French inscriptions on one side, Arabic on the other, and usually have both AH and AD dates. Except for KM#246-48, they are struck in the name of the Tunisian Bey.

100 Centimes = 1 Franc

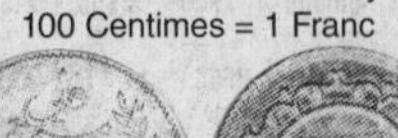

KM# 223 50 CENTIMES

2.50 g., 0.835 Silver 0.0671 oz. ASW **Obv:** Legend flanked by sprigs **Obv. Legend:** ALI **Rev:** Value, date in center circle of ornate design

Date	Mintage	F12	VF20	XF40	MS60	MS63
AH1319/1901 A	1,000	—	—	350	500	600
AH1320/1902 A	1,000	—	—	350	500	600

KM# 224 FRANC

5.00 g., 0.835 Silver 0.1342 oz. ASW **Obv:** Legend flanked by sprigs **Obv. Legend:** ALI **Rev:** Value, date in center circle of ornate design

Date	Mintage	F12	VF20	XF40	MS60	MS63
AH1319/1901 A	700	—	—	400	550	750
AH1320/1902 A	703	—	—	400	550	750

KM# 225 2 FRANCS

10.00 g., 0.835 Silver 0.2685 oz. ASW **Obv:** Legend flanked by sprigs **Obv. Legend:** ALI **Rev:** Value, date within center circle of ornate design

Date	Mintage	F12	VF20	XF40	MS60	MS63
AH1319/1901 A	300	—	—	450	650	900
AH1320/1902 A	300	—	—	450	650	900

KM# 226 10 FRANCS

3.23 g., 0.900 Gold 0.0933 oz. AGW **Obv:** Legend flanked by sprigs **Obv. Legend:** ALI **Rev:** Value, date in center circle of ornate design

Date	Mintage	F12	VF20	XF40	MS60	MS63
AH1319/1901 A	80	—	—	—	950	1,500
AH1319/1901 A	80	—	—	—	950	1,500
AH1320/1902 A	83	—	—	—	950	1,500

KM# 227 20 FRANCS

6.45 g., 0.900 Gold 0.1867 oz. AGW **Obv:** Legend flanked by sprigs **Obv. Legend:** ALI **Rev:** Value, date in center circle of ornate design

Date	Mintage	F12	VF20	XF40	MS60	MS63
AH1319/1901 A	150,000	—	237	325	345	400
AH1319/1901 A	150,000	—	237	325	345	400
AH1320/1902 A	20	—	—	—	950	2,200

Muhammad al-Hadi Bey

Struck in his name

KM# 228 5 CENTIMES

Bronze **Obv:** Inscription within sprigs **Obv. Legend:** MUHAMMAD AL-HADI **Rev:** Value and date within center circle

Date	Mintage	F12	VF20	XF40	MS60	MS63
AH1321/1903 A	500,000	—	3.00	8.00	15.00	30.00
AH1322/1904 A	1,000,000	—	3.00	8.00	15.00	30.00

KM# 229 10 CENTIMES

Bronze **Obv:** Inscription within sprigs **Obv. Legend:** MUHAMMAD AL-HADI **Rev:** Value and date within center circle

Date	Mintage	F12	VF20	XF40	MS60	MS63
AH1321/1903 A	250,000	—	3.00	8.00	15.00	30.00
AH1322/1904 A	500,000	—	3.00	8.00	15.00	30.00

KM# 230 50 CENTIMES

2.50 g., 0.835 Silver 0.0671 oz. ASW **Obv. Legend:** MUHAMMAD AL-HADI

Date	Mintage	F12	VF20	XF40	MS60	MS63
AH1321/1903 A	1,003	—	—	300	450	600
AH1322/1904 A	1,003	—	—	300	450	600
AH1323/1905 A	1,003	—	—	300	450	600
AH1324/1906 A	1,003	—	—	300	450	600

KM# 231 FRANC

5.00 g., 0.835 Silver 0.1342 oz. ASW **Obv. Legend:** MUHAMMAD AL-HADI

Date	Mintage	F12	VF20	XF40	MS60	MS63
AH1321/1903 A	703	—	—	400	550	750
AH1322/1904 A	300,000	—	50.00	90.00	150	250
AH1323/1905 A	703	—	—	400	550	750
AH1324/1906 A	703	—	—	400	550	750

KM# 232 2 FRANCS

10.00 g., 0.835 Silver 0.2685 oz. ASW **Obv. Legend:** MUHAMMAD AL-HADI

Date	Mintage	F12	VF20	XF40	MS60	MS63
AH1321/1903 A	303	—	—	475	650	850
AH1322/1904 A	150,000	—	60.00	90.00	175	300
AH1323/1905 A	303	—	—	475	650	850
AH1324/1906 A	303	—	—	472	650	850

KM# 233 10 FRANCS

3.23 g., 0.900 Gold 0.0933 oz. AGW **Obv. Legend:** MUHAMMAD AL-HADI

Date	Mintage	F12	VF20	XF40	MS60	MS63
AH1321/1903 A	83	—	—	—	950	1,950
AH1322/1904 A	83	—	—	—	950	1,950
AH1323/1905 A	83	—	—	—	950	1,950
AH1324/1906 A	83	—	—	—	950	1,950

KM# 234 20 FRANCS

6.45 g., 0.900 Gold 0.1867 oz. AGW **Obv:** Inscription within sprigs **Obv. Legend:** MUHAMMAD AL-HADI **Rev:** Value and date within center circle

Date	Mintage	F12	VF20	XF40	MS60	MS63
AH1321/1903 A	300,000	—	—	237	350	375
AH1321/1904 A	600,000	—	—	237	350	375
AH1322/1904 A	Inc. above	—	—	237	350	375
AH1323/1905 A	23	—	—	—	1,400	2,200
AH1324/1906 A	23	—	—	—	1,400	2,200

Muhammad al-Nasir Bey

Struck in his name

KM# 235 5 CENTIMES

Bronze, 26 mm. **Obv:** Inscription within sprigs **Obv. Legend:** MUHAMMAD AL-NASIR **Rev:** Value and date within center circle **Edge:** Plain

Date	Mintage	F12	VF20	XF40	MS60	MS63
AH1325/1907 A	1,000,000	—	1.00	3.00	10.00	20.00
AH1326/1908 A	1,000,000	—	1.00	3.00	10.00	20.00
AH1330/1912 A	1,000,000	—	1.00	3.00	10.00	20.00
AH1332/1914 A	1,000,000	—	1.00	3.00	10.00	20.00
AH1334/1916 A	2,000,000	—	1.00	3.00	10.00	15.00
AH1336/1917 A	2,021,000	—	1.00	3.00	10.00	15.00

KM# 242 5 CENTIMES

Nickel-Bronze, 19 mm. **Obv:** Hole in center of inscription **Obv. Legend:** MOHAMMED AL-NASIR **Rev:** Value above hole in center, date and sprigs

Date	Mintage	F12	VF20	XF40	MS60	MS63
AH1337/1918 (a)	1,549,000	—	1.00	3.00	10.00	25.00
AH1337/1919 (a)	4,451,000	—	1.00	3.00	10.00	25.00
AH1338/7/1920 (a)	Inc. above	—	1.00	3.00	10.00	25.00
AH1338/6/1920 (a)	2,206,000	—	1.00	3.00	10.00	25.00
AH1338/1920 (a)	Inc. above	—	1.00	3.00	10.00	25.00
AH1339/1920 (a)	Inc. above	—	1.00	3.00	10.00	25.00

KM# 245 5 CENTIMES
Nickel-Bronze, 17 mm. **Obv:** Hole in center of inscription **Rev:** Value above hole in center, date and sprigs **Note:** Reduced size.

Date	Mintage	F12	VF20	XF40	MS60	MS63
AH1339/1920 (a)	1,794,000	—	10.00	25.00	65.00	125

KM# 236 10 CENTIMES
9.40 g., Bronze **Obv:** Inscription within sprigs **Obv. Legend:** MUHAMMAD AL-NASIR **Rev:** Value and date within center circle

Date	Mintage	F12	VF20	XF40	MS60	MS63
AH1325/1907 A	500,000	—	1.00	5.00	10.00	20.00
AH1326/1908 A	500,000	—	1.00	5.00	10.00	20.00
AH1329/1911 A	500,000	—	1.00	5.00	10.00	20.00
AH1330/1912 A	500,000	—	1.00	5.00	10.00	20.00
AH1332/1914 A	500,000	—	1.00	5.00	10.00	20.00
AH1334/1916 A	1,000,000	—	1.00	5.00	10.00	20.00
AH1336/1917 A	1,050,000	—	1.00	5.00	10.00	20.00

KM# 243 10 CENTIMES
Nickel-Bronze **Obv:** Hole in center of inscription **Obv. Legend:** MUHAMMAD AL-NASIR **Rev:** Value above hole in center, date and sprigs

Date	Mintage	F12	VF20	XF40	MS60	MS63
AH1337/1918 (a)	1,288,000	—	1.00	5.00	10.00	25.00
AH1337/1919 (a)	2,712,000	—	1.00	5.00	10.00	25.00
AH1338/1920 (a)	3,000,000	—	1.00	5.00	10.00	25.00

KM# 244 25 CENTIMES
Nickel-Bronze **Obv:** Hole in center of inscription **Obv. Legend:** MUHAMMAD AL-NASIR **Rev:** Value above hole in center, date and sprigs

Date	Mintage	F12	VF20	XF40	MS60	MS63
AH1337/1918 (a)	2,000,000	—	1.00	5.00	20.00	35.00
AH1337/1919 (a)	Inc. above	—	1.00	5.00	20.00	35.00
AH1338/1920 (a)	2,000,000	—	1.00	5.00	20.00	35.00

KM# 237 50 CENTIMES
2.50 g., 0.835 Silver 0.0671 oz. ASW **Obv:** Inscription within sprigs **Obv. Legend:** MUHAMMAD AL-NASIR **Rev:** Value and date within center circle

Date	Mintage	F12	VF20	XF40	MS60	MS63
AH1325/1907 A	201,000	—	5.00	12.00	30.00	50.00
AH1326/1908 A	2,006	—	—	250	300	450
AH1327/1909 A	1,003	—	—	300	400	600
AH1328/1910 A	1,003	—	—	300	400	600
AH1329/1911 A	1,003	—	—	300	450	600
AH1330/1912 A	201,000	—	5.00	12.00	30.00	50.00
AH1331/1913 A	1,003	—	—	350	450	600
AH1332/1914 A	201,000	—	5.00	12.00	30.00	50.00
AH1334/1915 A	707,000	—	3.00	8.00	18.00	35.00
AH1334/1916 A	3,614,000	—	3.00	8.00	15.00	30.00
AH1335/1916 A	Inc. above	—	3.00	8.00	15.00	30.00
AH1336/1917 A	Inc. above	—	3.00	8.00	15.00	30.00
AH1335/1917 A	2,139,000	—	3.00	8.00	15.00	30.00
AH1337/1918 A	1,003	—	—	350	450	600
AH1338/1919 A	1,003	—	—	350	450	600
AH1339/1920 A	1,003	—	—	350	450	600
AH1340/1921 A	1,003	—	—	350	450	600

KM# 238 FRANC
5.00 g., 0.835 Silver 0.1342 oz. ASW **Obv:** Inscription within sprigs **Obv. Legend:** MUHAMMAD AL-NASIR **Rev:** Value and date within center circle

Date	Mintage	F12	VF20	XF40	MS60	MS63
AH1325/1907 A	301,000	—	5.00	15.00	25.00	40.00
AH1326/1908 A	401,000	—	5.00	10.00	25.00	40.00
AH1327/1909 A	703	—	—	450	550	750
AH1328/1910 A	703	—	—	450	550	750
AH1329/1911 A	1,051,000	—	5.00	8.00	30.00	45.00
AH1330/1912 A	501,000	—	5.00	8.00	30.00	45.00
AH1331/1913 A	703	—	—	450	550	750
AH1333/1914 A	Inc. above	—	5.00	10.00	30.00	45.00
AH1332/1914 A	201,000	—	5.00	10.00	30.00	45.00
AH1334/1915 A	1,060,000	—	5.00	10.00	30.00	—
AH1334/1916 A	3,270,000	—	5.00	8.00	20.00	35.00
AH1335/1916 A	Inc. above	—	5.00	8.00	20.00	35.00
AH1335/1917 A	1,628,000	—	5.00	8.00	20.00	35.00
AH1336/1918 A	804,000	—	5.00	8.00	20.00	35.00
AH1337/1918 A	Inc. above	—	5.00	8.00	20.00	35.00
AH1338/1919 A	703	—	—	450	550	750
AH1339/1920 A	703	—	—	450	550	750
AH1340/1921 A	703	—	—	450	550	750

KM# 239 2 FRANCS
10.00 g., 0.835 Silver 0.2685 oz. ASW **Obv:** Inscription within sprigs **Obv. Legend:** MUHAMMAD AL-NASIR **Rev:** Value and date within center circle

Date	Mintage	F12	VF20	XF40	MS60	MS63
AH1325/1907 A	306	—	—	500	600	900
AH1326/1908 A	101,000	—	20.00	40.00	100	150
AH1327/1909 A	303	—	—	500	600	900
AH1328/1910 A	303	—	—	500	600	900
AH1329/1911 A	475,000	—	20.00	30.00	50.00	75.00
AH1330/1912 A	200,000	—	20.00	30.00	50.00	75.00
AH1331/1913 A	303	—	—	500	600	900
AH1332/1914 A	100,000	—	20.00	30.00	50.00	75.00
AH1333/1914 A	Inc. above	—	20.00	30.00	50.00	75.00
AH1334/1915 A	408,000	—	15.00	30.00	50.00	75.00
AH1335/1916 A	Inc. above	—	15.00	30.00	50.00	75.00
AH1334/1916 A	1,000,000	—	15.00	30.00	50.00	75.00
AH1336/1917 A	303	—	—	500	600	900
AH1337/1918 A	303	—	—	500	600	900
AH1338/1919 A	303	—	—	500	600	900
AH1339/1920 A	303	—	—	500	600	900
AH1340/1921 A	303	—	—	500	600	900

KM# 240 10 FRANCS
3.23 g., 0.900 Gold 0.0933 oz. AGW **Obv. Legend:** MUHAMMAD AL-NASIR

Date	Mintage	F12	VF20	XF40	MS60	MS63
AH1325/1907 A	36	—	—	—	1,000	1,900
AH1326/1908 A	166	—	—	—	600	1,250
AH1327/1909 A	83	—	—	—	900	1,700
AH1328/1910 A	83	—	—	—	900	1,700
AH1329/1911 A	83	—	—	—	900	1,700
AH1330/1912 A	83	—	—	—	900	1,700
AH1331/1913 A	83	—	—	—	900	1,700
AH1332/1914 A	83	—	—	—	900	1,700
AH1334/1915 A	83	—	—	—	900	1,700
AH1334/1916 A	83	—	—	—	900	1,700
AH1336/1917 A	83	—	—	—	900	1,700
AH1337/1918 A	83	—	—	—	900	1,700
AH1338/1919 A	83	—	—	—	900	1,700
AH1339/1920 A	83	—	—	—	900	1,700
AH1340/1921 A	83	—	—	—	900	1,700

KM# 241 20 FRANCS
6.45 g., 0.900 Gold 0.1867 oz. AGW **Obv. Legend:** MUHAMMAD AL-NASIR

Date	Mintage	F12	VF20	XF40	MS60	MS63
AH1325/1907 A	26	—	—	—	1,100	1,900
AH1326/1908 A	46	—	—	—	900	1,700
AH1327/1909 A	23	—	—	—	1,100	1,900
AH1328/1910 A	23	—	—	—	1,100	1,900
AH1329/1911 A	23	—	—	—	1,100	1,900
AH1330/1912 A	23	—	—	—	1,100	1,900
AH1331/1913 A	23	—	—	—	1,100	1,900
AH1332/1914 A	23	—	—	—	1,100	1,900
AH1334/1915 A	23	—	—	—	1,100	1,900
AH1334/1916 A	23	—	—	—	1,100	1,900
AH1336/1917 A	23	—	—	—	1,100	1,900
AH1337/1918 A	23	—	—	—	1,100	1,900
AH1338/1919 A	23	—	—	—	1,100	1,900
AH1339/1920 A	23	—	—	—	1,100	1,900
AH1340/1921 A	23	—	—	—	1,100	1,900

Muhammad al-Habib Bey
Struck in his name

KM# 254 10 CENTIMES
4.00 g., Nickel-Bronze **Obv:** Hole in center of inscription **Obv. Legend:** MUHAMMAD AL-HABIB **Rev:** Value above hole in center, date and sprigs

Date	Mintage	F12	VF20	XF40	MS60	MS63
AH1345/1926 (a)	1,000,000	—	20.00	50.00	100	150

KM# 249 50 CENTIMES
2.50 g., 0.835 Silver 0.0671 oz. ASW **Obv:** Inscription within sprigs **Obv. Legend:** MUHAMMAD AL-HABIB **Rev:** Value and date within center circle

Date	Mintage	F12	VF20	XF40	MS60	MS63
AH1341/1922 A	1,003	—	—	300	400	500
AH1342/1923 A	2,009	—	—	300	400	500
AH1343/1924 A	1,003	—	—	300	400	500
AH1344/1925 A	1,003	—	—	300	400	500
AH1345/1926 A	1,003	—	—	300	400	500
AH1346/1927 A	1,003	—	—	300	400	500
AH1347/1928 A	1,003	—	—	300	400	500

KM# 250 FRANC
5.00 g., 0.835 Silver 0.1342 oz. ASW **Obv. Legend:** MUHAMMAD AL-HABIB

Date	Mintage	F12	VF20	XF40	MS60	MS63
AH1341/1922 A	703	—	—	400	600	750
AH1342/1923 A	1,409	—	—	300	450	600
AH1343/1924 A	703	—	—	400	600	750
AH1344/1925 A	703	—	—	400	600	750
AH1345/1926 A	703	—	—	400	600	750
AH1346/1927 A	703	—	—	400	600	750
AH1347/1928A	703	—	—	400	600	750

KM# 250a FRANC
5.50 g., 0.835 Silver 0.1477 oz. ASW

Date	Mintage	VF20	XF40	MS60	MS63	MS65
AH1347/1928 A	Inc. above	—	450	650	900	—

KM# 251 2 FRANCS
10.00 g., 0.835 Silver 0.2685 oz. ASW **Obv. Legend:** MUHAMMAD AL-HABIB

Date	Mintage	F12	VF20	XF40	MS60	MS63
AH1341/1922 A	303	—	—	450	600	750
AH1342/1923 A	690	—	—	350	450	600
AH1343/1924 A	303	—	—	450	600	750
AH1344/1925 A	303	—	—	450	600	750
AH1345/1926 A	303	—	—	450	600	750
AH1346/1927 A	303	—	—	450	600	750

KM# 251a 2 FRANCS
8.60 g., 0.835 Silver 0.2309 oz. ASW

Date	Mintage	VF20	XF40	MS60	MS63	MS65
AH1347/1928 A	303	—	750	900	1,250	—

KM# 252 10 FRANCS
3.23 g., 0.900 Gold 0.0933 oz. AGW **Obv. Legend:** MUHAMMAD AL-HABIB BEY

Date	Mintage	F12	VF20	XF40	MS60	MS63
AH1341/1922 A	83	—	—	—	900	1,700
AH1342/1923 A	169	—	—	—	600	1,250
AH1343/1924 A	83	—	—	—	900	1,700
AH1344/1925 A	83	—	—	—	900	1,700
AH1345/1926 A	83	—	—	—	900	1,700
AH1346/1927 A	83	—	—	—	900	1,700
AH1347/1928 A	83	—	—	—	900	1,700

KM# 253 20 FRANCS
6.45 g., 0.900 Gold 0.1867 oz. AGW **Obv. Legend:** MUHAMMAD AL-HABIB

Date	Mintage	F12	VF20	XF40	MS60	MS63
AH1341/1922 A	23	—	—	—	1,300	1,900

Date	Mintage	F12	VF20	XF40	MS60	MS63
AH1342/1923 A	49	—	—	—	900	1,700
AH1343/1924 A	23	—	—	—	1,100	1,900
AH1344/1925 A	23	—	—	—	1,100	1,900
AH1345/1926 A	23	—	—	—	1,100	1,900
AH1346/1927 A	23	—	—	—	1,100	1,900
AH1347/1928 A	23	—	—	—	1,100	1,900

Ahmad Pasha Bey

Struck in his name

KM# 258 5 CENTIMES

2.00 g., Nickel-Bronze **Obv:** Hole in center of inscription **Obv. Legend:** AHMAD **Rev:** Value above hole in center, date and sprigs

Date	Mintage	F12	VF20	XF40	MS60	MS63
AH1350/1931 (a)	2,000,000	—	1.00	5.00	12.00	25.00
AH1352/1933 (a)	1,000,000	—	1.00	5.00	12.00	25.00
AH1357/1938 (a)	1,200,000	—	1.00	5.00	12.00	25.00

KM# 259 10 CENTIMES

Nickel-Bronze **Obv:** Hole in center of inscription **Obv. Legend:** AHMAD **Rev:** Value above hole in center, date and sprigs

Date	Mintage	F12	VF20	XF40	MS60	MS63
AH1350/1931 (a)	750,000	—	2.00	8.00	18.00	35.00
AH1352/1933 (a)	1,000,000	—	2.00	8.00	18.00	35.00
Note: Wide and narrow dates						
AH1357/1938 (a)	1,200,000	—	2.00	8.00	18.00	35.00

KM# 267 10 CENTIMES

2.50 g., Zinc **Obv. Legend:** AHMAD

Date	Mintage	F12	VF20	XF40	MS60	MS63
AH1360/1941 (a)	5,000,000	—	1.00	3.00	15.00	35.00
AH1361/1942 (a)	10,000,000	—	1.00	3.00	15.00	35.00

KM# 268 20 CENTIMES

3.60 g., Zinc **Obv:** Hole in center of inscription **Obv. Legend:** AHMAD **Rev:** Value above hole in center, date and sprigs

Date	Mintage	F12	VF20	XF40	MS60	MS63
AH1361/1942 A	5,000,000	—	10.00	25.00	45.00	75.00

KM# 260 25 CENTIMES

5.00 g., Nickel-Aluminum-Bronze **Obv:** Hole in center of inscription **Obv. Legend:** AHMAD **Rev:** Value above hole in center, date and sprigs

Date	Mintage	F12	VF20	XF40	MS60	MS63
AH1350/1931 (a)	300,000	—	3.00	8.00	20.00	35.00
AH1352/1933 (a)	400,000	—	3.00	8.00	20.00	35.00
AH1357/1938 (a)	480,000	—	3.00	8.00	15.00	35.00

KM# 261 5 FRANCS

5.00 g., 0.680 Silver 0.1093 oz. ASW **Obv:** Inscription and date within sprigs **Obv. Legend:** AHMAD **Rev:** Value flanked by designs

Date	Mintage	F12	VF20	XF40	MS60	MS63
AH1353 (a)	2,000,000	—	5.00	15.00	25.00	45.00
AH1355 (a)	2,000,000	—	5.00	15.00	25.00	45.00

KM# 264 5 FRANCS

5.00 g., 0.680 Silver 0.1093 oz. ASW, 24 mm. **Obv:** Inscription and date within sprigs **Obv. Legend:** AHMAD **Rev:** Value in center of circular inscription and design **Edge:** Reeded

Date	Mintage	F12	VF20	XF40	MS60	MS63
AH1358/1939 (a)	1,600,000	—	15.00	25.00	40.00	75.00

KM# 255 10 FRANCS

10.00 g., 0.680 Silver 0.2186 oz. ASW **Obv:** Inscription within oblong design flanked by sprigs **Obv. Legend:** AHMAD **Rev:** Value and date within center circle of design

Date	Mintage	F12	VF20	XF40	MS60	MS63
AH1349/1930 (a)	60,000	—	30.00	75.00	100	150
AH1350/1931 (a)	1,103	—	150	350	450	600
AH1351/1932 (a)	60,000	—	45.00	100	200	295
AH1352/1933 (a)	1,103	—	150	350	450	600
AH1353/1934 (a)	30,000	—	30.00	75.00	100	150

KM# 262 10 FRANCS

10.00 g., 0.680 Silver 0.2186 oz. ASW **Obv:** Inscription and date within sprigs **Rev:** Value flanked by designs

Date	Mintage	F12	VF20	XF40	MS60	MS63
AH1353 (a)	1,501,000	—	8.00	15.00	30.00	50.00
AH1354 (a)	1,103	—	—	350	400	600
AH1355 (a)	2,006	—	—	300	400	600
AH1356 (a)	1,103	—	—	350	450	600
AH1357	—	—	—	600	800	1,000
AH1358	—	—	—	600	800	1,000

KM# 265 10 FRANCS

10.00 g., 0.680 Silver 0.2186 oz. ASW **Obv:** Inscription and date within sprigs **Rev:** Value and date within circular inscription and design

Date	Mintage	F12	VF20	XF40	MS60	MS63
AH1358/1939 (a)	501,000	—	8.00	15.00	30.00	50.00
AH1359/1940 (a)	—	—	—	450	600	750
AH1360/1941 (a)	1,103	—	—	350	450	600
AH1361/1942 (a)	1,103	—	—	350	450	600

KM# 256 20 FRANCS

20.00 g., 0.680 Silver 0.4372 oz. ASW, 35 mm. **Obv:** Inscription within oblong design flanked by sprigs **Obv. Legend:** AHMAD **Rev:** Value and date within center circle of design

Date	Mintage	F12	VF20	XF40	MS60	MS63
AH1349/1930 (a)	20,000	—	75.00	175	275	350
AH1350/1931 (a)	53	—	250	300	500	750
AH1351/1932 (a)	20,000	—	75.00	175	275	350
AH1352/1933 (a)	53	—	200	300	500	750
AH1353/1934 (a)	9,500	—	90.00	200	300	400

Note: It is believed that an additional number of coins dated AH1353/1934(a) were struck and included in mintage figures of KM#263 of the same date

KM# 263 20 FRANCS

20.00 g., 0.680 Silver 0.4372 oz. ASW, 35 mm. **Obv:** Inscription and date within sprigs **Rev:** Value flanked by designs

Date	Mintage	F12	VF20	XF40	MS60	MS63
AH1353 (a)	1,250,000	—	12.00	25.00	40.00	65.00
AH1354 (a)	53	—	—	600	750	900
AH1355 (a)	106	—	—	450	600	750
AH1356 (a)	53	—	—	600	750	900

KM# 266 20 FRANCS

20.00 g., 0.680 Silver 0.4372 oz. ASW, 35 mm. **Obv:** Inscription and date within sprigs **Rev:** Value and date within circular inscription and design

Date	Mintage	F12	VF20	XF40	MS60	MS63
AH1358/1939 (a)	100,000	—	18.00	35.00	65.00	110
AH1359/1940 (a)	—	—	—	—	—	—
Note: Requires Confirmation						
AH1360/1941 (a)	53	—	—	650	850	1,100
AH1361/1942 (a)	53	—	—	650	850	1,100

KM# 257 100 FRANCS

6.55 g., 0.900 Gold 0.1895 oz. AGW **Obv:** Inscription within oblong design flanked by sprigs **Obv. Legend:** AHMAD **Rev:** Value and date within center circle of design

Date	Mintage	F12	VF20	XF40	MS60	MS63
AH1349/1930 (a)	3,000	—	—	360	375	450
AH1350/1931 (a)	33	—	—	1,000	1,600	—
AH1351/1932 (a)	3,000	—	—	360	375	450
AH1352/1933 (a)	33	—	—	1,000	1,600	—
AH1353/1934 (a)	133	—	—	600	800	—
AH1354/1935 (a)	3,000	—	—	360	375	450
AH1355/1936 (a)	33	—	—	1,000	1,600	—
AH1356/1937 (a)	33	—	—	1,000	1,600	—

Muhammad al-Amin Bey

Struck in his name

KM# 271 10 CENTIMES

1.60 g., Zinc **Obv:** Hole in center of inscription **Obv. Legend:** MUHAMMAD AL AMIN **Rev:** Value above hole in center, date and sprigs

Date	Mintage	VF20	XF40	MS60	MS63	MS65
AH1364/1945 (a)	10,000,000	30.00	50.00	125	200	—

Note: Most were probably melted

KM# 272 20 CENTIMES
Zinc **Obv:** Hole in center of inscription **Obv. Legend:** MUHAMMAD AL-AMIN **Rev:** Value above hole in center, date and sprigs

Date	Mintage	VF20	XF40	MS60	MS63	MS65
AH1364/1945 (a)	5,205,000	45.00	75.00	150	250	—

Note: A large quantity was remelted

KM# 273 5 FRANCS
Aluminum-Bronze **Obv:** Inscription and date within sprigs **Obv. Legend:** MUHAMMAD AL-AMIN **Rev:** Value and date within circular inscription and design

Date	Mintage	VF20	XF40	MS60	MS63	MS65
AH1365/1946 (a)	10,000,000	—	2.00	5.00	10.00	—

KM# 277 5 FRANCS
Copper-Nickel **Obv:** Dates within crescent below design **Rev:** Value and date within upper circle

Date	Mintage	VF20	XF40	MS60	MS63	MS65
AH1373/1954 (a)	18,000,000	—	1.00	2.00	3.00	5.00
AH1376/1957 (a)	4,000,000	—	1.00	2.00	3.00	5.00

KM# 269 10 FRANCS
10.00 g., 0.680 Silver 0.2186 oz. ASW **Obv:** Inscription and date within sprigs **Rev:** Value and date within circular inscription and design

Date	Mintage	F12	VF20	XF40	MS60	MS63
AH1363/1943 (a)	1,503	—	—	250	375	500
AH1364/1944 (a)	2,206	—	—	250	375	500

KM# 270 20 FRANCS
20.00 g., 0.680 Silver 0.4372 oz. ASW **Obv. Legend:** MUHAMMAD AL-AMIN

Date	Mintage	F12	VF20	XF40	MS60	MS63
AH1363/1943 (a)	103	—	—	500	750	1,250
AH1364/1944 (a)	106	—	—	500	750	1,250

KM# 274 20 FRANCS
Copper-Nickel **Obv:** Dates within crescent below design **Rev:** Value and date within upper circle

Date	Mintage	VF20	XF40	MS60	MS63	MS65
AH1370/1950 (a)	10,000,000	—	1.00	2.00	3.00	5.00
AH1376/1957 (a)	4,000,000	—	1.00	2.00	3.00	5.00

KM# 275 50 FRANCS
Copper-Nickel **Obv:** Dates within crescent below design **Obv. Legend:** MUHAMMAD AL-AMIN **Rev:** Value and date within upper circle

Date	Mintage	VF20	XF40	MS60	MS63	MS65
AH1370/1950 (a)	5,000,000	1.00	1.50	2.50	4.00	7.00
AH1376/1957 (a)	600,000	1.00	1.50	2.50	4.00	7.00

KM# 276 100 FRANCS
Copper-Nickel **Obv:** Dates within crescent below design **Obv. Legend:** MUHAMMAD AL-AMIN **Rev:** Value and date within upper circle

Date	Mintage	VF20	XF40	MS60	MS63	MS65
AH1370/1950 (a)	8,000,000	1.00	3.00	5.00	8.00	15.00
AH1376/1957 (a)	1,000,000	1.00	3.00	5.00	8.00	15.00

Anonymous

TOKEN COINAGE

KM# 246 50 CENTIMES
2.00 g., Aluminum-Bronze, 18 mm. **Obv:** Date within wreath **Rev:** Value within wreath **Rev. Inscription:** BON POUR (Good For) 50 CENTIMES **Edge:** Reeded

Date	Mintage	VF20	XF40	MS60	MS63	MS65
AH1340/1921 (a)	4,000,000	2.00	4.00	7.00	20.00	30.00
AH1345/1926 (a)	1,000,000	3.00	5.00	10.00	25.00	35.00
AH1352/1933 (a)	500,000	6.00	9.00	17.00	35.00	50.00
AH1360/1941 (a)	4,646,000	1.00	2.00	3.00	10.00	15.00
AH1364/1945 (a)	11,180,000	1.00	1.50	2.00	10.00	15.00

KM# 246a 50 CENTIMES
1.95 g., Aluminum-Bronze Gold-plated, 18 mm. **Obv:** Date within wreath **Rev:** Value within wreath **Rev. Inscription:** BON POUR (Good For) 50 CENTIMES **Note:** Exists in gilt only.

Date	Mintage	VF20	XF40	MS60	MS63	MS65
AH1347/1928	—	—	—	—	—	—

KM# 247 FRANC
4.00 g., Aluminum-Bronze, 23 mm. **Obv:** Date within wreath **Rev:** Value within wreath **Rev. Inscription:** BON POUR (Good For) 1 FRANC **Edge:** Reeded

Date	Mintage	VF20	XF40	MS60	MS63	MS65
AH1340/1921 (a)	5,000,000	2.00	4.00	7.00	20.00	30.00
AH1345/1926 (a)	1,000,000	4.00	9.00	17.00	28.00	50.00
AH1344/1926 (a)	1,000,000	2.00	7.00	15.00	25.00	45.00
AH1360/1941 (a)	6,612,000	1.00	2.50	4.00	10.00	15.00
AH1364/1945 (a)	10,699,000	1.00	2.00	3.00	10.00	15.00

KM# 247a FRANC
Aluminum-Bronze Gold-plated, 23.5 mm. **Obv:** Date within wreath **Rev:** Value within wreath **Rev. Inscription:** BON POUR (Good For) 1 FRANC **Note:** Exists in gilt only.

Date	Mintage	VF20	XF40	MS60	MS63	MS65
AH1347/1928	—	—	—	—	—	—

KM# 248 2 FRANCS
8.00 g., Aluminum-Bronze, 27 mm. **Obv:** Date within wreath **Rev:** Value within wreath **Rev. Inscription:** BON POUR (Good For) 2 FRANCS **Edge:** Reeded

Date	Mintage	VF20	XF40	MS60	MS63	MS65
AH1340/1921 (a)	1,500,000	3.00	7.00	15.00	25.00	35.00
AH1343/1924 (a)	500,000	8.00	15.00	20.00	35.00	50.00
AH1345/1926 (a)	500,000	8.00	15.00	20.00	35.00	50.00
AH1360/1941 (a)	1,976,000	3.00	5.00	8.00	15.00	25.00
AH1364/1945 (a)	6,464,000	3.00	4.00	7.00	15.00	25.00

KM# 248a 2 FRANCS
8.10 g., Aluminum-Bronze Gold-plated. **Obv:** Date within wreath **Rev:** Value within wreath **Rev. Inscription:** BON POUR (Good For) 2 FRANCS **Note:** Exists in gilt only.

Date	Mintage	VF20	XF40	MS60	MS63	MS65
AH1347/1928	—	—	—	—	—	—

REPUBLIC

DECIMAL COINAGE

1000 Millim = 1 Dinar

KM# 280 MILLIM
0.65 g., Aluminum, 18 mm. **Obv:** Oak tree and date **Rev:** Value within sprigs

Date	Mintage	VF20	XF40	MS60	MS63	MS65
1960	—	—	—	0.10	0.25	1.00

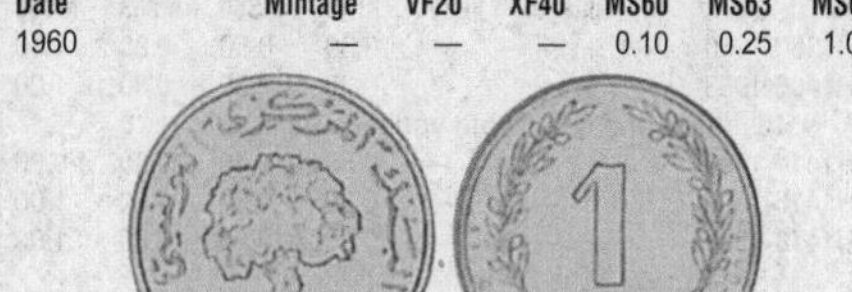

KM# 349 MILLIM
1.20 g., Aluminum **Series:** F.A.O. **Obv:** Oak tree and date **Rev:** Value within sprigs

Date	Mintage	VF20	XF40	MS60	MS63	MS65
1999	—	—	—	0.25	0.75	1.50
2000	—	—	—	0.25	0.75	1.50

KM# 281 2 MILLIM
1.00 g., Aluminum, 21 mm. **Obv:** Oak tree and date **Rev:** Value within sprigs

Date	Mintage	VF20	XF40	MS60	MS63	MS65
1960	—	—	—	0.10	0.25	1.00

KM# 282 5 MILLIM
1.50 g., Aluminum, 24 mm. **Obv:** Oak tree and date **Rev:** Value within sprigs

Date	Mintage	VF20	XF40	MS60	MS63	MS65
1960	—	—	—	0.10	0.25	1.00
1983	—	—	—	0.10	0.25	1.00
1993	—	—	—	0.10	0.25	1.00
1996	—	—	—	0.10	0.25	1.00

KM# 348 5 MILLIM
1.49 g., Aluminum, 24 mm. **Obv:** Oak tree and dates **Rev:** Value within sprigs

Date	Mintage	VF20	XF40	MS60	MS63	MS65
AH1418-1997	—	—	—	0.25	0.50	1.00

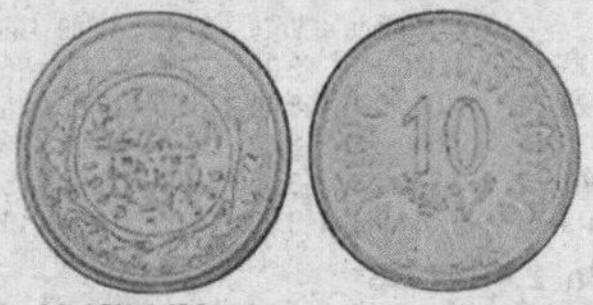

KM# 306 10 MILLIM
3.50 g., Brass, 19 mm. **Obv:** Inscription and dates within inner circle of design **Rev:** Value in center of design **Edge:** Reeded

Date	Mintage	VF20	XF40	MS60	MS63	MS65
AH1380-1960	—	—	0.15	0.25	0.50	1.00
AH1414-1993	—	—	0.15	0.25	0.50	1.00
AH1416-1996	—	—	0.15	0.25	0.50	1.00
AH1418-1997	—	—	0.15	0.25	0.50	1.00

KM# 307 20 MILLIM
4.50 g., Brass, 22 mm. **Obv:** Inscription and dates within center circle of design **Rev:** Value in center of design

Date	Mintage	VF20	XF40	MS60	MS63	MS65
AH1380-1960	—	—	0.30	0.50	0.80	1.00
AH1403-1983	—	—	0.30	0.50	0.80	1.00
Note: Large and small date varieties exist.						
AH1414-1993	—	—	0.30	0.50	0.80	1.00
AH1416-1996	—	—	0.30	0.50	0.80	1.00
AH1418-1997	—	—	0.30	0.50	0.80	1.00

KM# 308 50 MILLIM
6.00 g., Brass, 25 mm. **Obv:** Inscription and dates within center circle of design **Rev:** Value in center of design

Date	Mintage	VF20	XF40	MS60	MS63	MS65
AH1380-1960	—	—	0.65	0.85	1.25	1.50
AH1403-1983	—	—	0.65	0.85	1.25	1.50
Note: Large and small date varieties exist.						
AH1414-1993	—	—	0.65	0.85	1.25	1.50
AH1416-1996	—	—	0.65	0.85	1.25	1.50
AH1418-1997	—	—	0.65	0.85	1.25	1.50

KM# 414 100 MILLIM
9.00 g., 0.900 Silver 0.2604 oz. ASW, 26 mm. **Subject:** Banque Central, 1st Anniversary **Obv:** Head left **Rev:** Value

Date	Mintage	VF20	XF40	MS60	MS63	MS65
1959	250	—	—	—	—	—

KM# 309 100 MILLIM
7.50 g., Brass, 27 mm. **Obv:** Inscription and dates within center circle of design **Rev:** Value in center of design

Date	Mintage	VF20	XF40	MS60	MS63	MS65
AH1380-1960	—	—	—	1.25	1.50	2.00
AH1403-1983	—	—	—	1.25	1.50	2.00
Note: Large and small date varieties exist.						
AH1414-1993	—	—	—	1.25	1.50	2.00
AH1416-1996	—	—	—	1.25	1.50	2.00
AH1418-1997	—	—	—	1.25	1.50	2.00
AH1421-2000	—	—	—	1.25	1.50	2.00

KM# 415 1/4 DINAR
22.60 g., 0.900 Silver 0.6539 oz. ASW, 36 mm. **Subject:** banque Centrale, 1st Anniversary **Obv:** Head left **Rev:** Value and legend

Date	Mintage	VF20	XF40	MS60	MS63	MS65
1959	350	—	—	—	—	—

KM# 291 1/2 DINAR
Nickel **Obv:** Head left **Rev:** Value and date

Date	Mintage	VF20	XF40	MS60	MS63	MS65
1968 (a)	500,000	—	—	1.00	2.00	4.50

KM# 303 1/2 DINAR
Copper-Nickel **Series:** F.A.O. **Obv:** Head left **Rev:** 2 Hands with fruit and wheat sprig

Date	Mintage	VF20	XF40	MS60	MS63	MS65
1976	700,000	—	—	1.50	3.50	6.50
Note: Variations exist with large and small designer's name						
1983	400,000	—	—	1.50	3.50	6.50

KM# 318 1/2 DINAR
Copper-Nickel **Series:** F.A.O. **Obv:** Map and date **Rev:** 2 Hands with fruit and wheat sprig

Date	Mintage	VF20	XF40	MS60	MS63	MS65
1988	—	—	—	0.50	1.50	3.00
1990	300,000	—	—	0.50	1.50	3.00

KM# 346 1/2 DINAR
Copper-Nickel **Obv:** Shield within circle **Rev:** 2 hands with fruit and wheat sprig **Note:** Rim width varieties exist.

Date	Mintage	VF20	XF40	MS60	MS63	MS65
AH1416-1996	5,000,000	—	—	0.50	1.50	3.00
AH1418-1997	—	—	—	0.50	1.50	3.00

KM# 292 DINAR
20.00 g., 0.925 Silver 0.5948 oz. ASW, 40 mm. **Obv:** Head of Habib Bourguiba left **Rev:** Standing armored figure of Hannibal among elephant heads and designs

Date	Mintage	VF20	XF40	MS60	MS63	MS65
1969 NI	5,000	PF63 20.00	PF65 22.50			
1969 FM NI	15,000	PF63 15.00	PF65 17.50			

KM# 293 DINAR
20.00 g., 0.925 Silver 0.5948 oz. ASW, 40 mm. **Obv:** Head of Habib Bourguiba left **Rev:** Stylized armored figure on horse and head of Masinissa left

Date	Mintage	VF20	XF40	MS60	MS63	MS65
1969 FM NI	15,000	PF63 15.00	PF65 17.50			
1969 NI	5,000	PF63 20.00	PF65 22.50			

KM# 294 DINAR
20.00 g., 0.925 Silver 0.5948 oz. ASW, 40 mm. **Obv:** Head of Habib Bourguiba left **Rev:** Stylized head of Jugurtha left in center of balance scale

Date	Mintage	VF20	XF40	MS60	MS63	MS65
1969 FM NI	15,000	PF63 15.00	PF65 17.50			
1969 NI	5,000	PF63 20.00	PF65 22.50			

KM# 295 DINAR
20.00 g., 0.925 Silver 0.5948 oz. ASW, 40 mm. **Obv:** Head of Habib Bourguiba left **Rev:** Seated figure of Virgil flanked by standing figures

Date	Mintage	VF20	XF40	MS60	MS63	MS65
1969 FM NI	15,000	PF63 15.00	PF65 17.50			
1969 NI	5,000	PF63 20.00	PF65 22.50			

KM# 296 DINAR

20.00 g., 0.925 Silver 0.5948 oz. ASW, 40 mm. **Obv:** Head of Habib Bourguiba left **Rev:** Seated figure of St. Augustine at desk and bust facing

Date	Mintage	VF20	XF40	MS60	MS63	MS65
1969 FM NI	15,000	PF63 15.00	PF65 17.50			
1969 NI	5,000	PF63 20.00	PF65 22.50			

KM# 297 DINAR

20.00 g., 0.925 Silver 0.5948 oz. ASW, 40 mm. **Obv:** Head of Habib Bourguiba left **Rev:** Phoenician Ship

Date	Mintage	VF20	XF40	MS60	MS63	MS65
1969 FM NI	15,000	PF63 20.00	PF65 22.00			
1969 NI	5,000	PF63 28.00	PF65 32.00			

KM# 298 DINAR

20.00 g., 0.925 Silver 0.5948 oz. ASW, 40 mm. **Obv:** Head of Habib Bourguiba left **Rev:** Standing Neptune surrounded by mermaids and sea horses

Date	Mintage	VF20	XF40	MS60	MS63	MS65
1969 FM NI	15,000	PF63 15.00	PF65 17.50			
1969 NI	5,000	PF63 20.00	PF65 22.50			

KM# 299 DINAR

20.00 g., 0.925 Silver 0.5948 oz. ASW, 40 mm. **Obv:** Head of Habib Bourguiba left **Rev:** Venus, with the ribbon of love

Date	Mintage	VF20	XF40	MS60	MS63	MS65
1969 FM NI	15,000	PF63 17.00	PF65 20.00			
1969 NI	5,000	PF63 22.00	PF65 25.00			

KM# 300 DINAR

20.00 g., 0.925 Silver 0.5948 oz. ASW, 40 mm. **Obv:** Head of Habib Bourguiba left **Rev:** Thysdrus-El Djem, Africa's Colosseum

Date	Mintage	VF20	XF40	MS60	MS63	MS65
1969 FM NI	15,000	PF63 15.00	PF65 17.50			
1969 NI	5,000	PF63 20.00	PF65 22.50			

KM# 301 DINAR

20.00 g., 0.925 Silver 0.5948 oz. ASW, 40 mm. **Obv:** Head of Habib Bourguiba left **Rev:** Building - Sbeitla-Sufetula

Date	Mintage	VF20	XF40	MS60	MS63	MS65
1969 FM NI	15,000	PF63 15.00	PF65 17.50			
1969 NI	5,000	PF63 28.00	PF65 32.00			

KM# 302 DINAR

18.00 g., 0.680 Silver 0.3935 oz. ASW **Series:** F.A.O. **Obv:** Head of Habib Bourguiba left **Rev:** Date Palm, oxen and figure, tractor in background at left

Date	Mintage	VF20	XF40	MS60	MS63	MS65
1970 (a)	100,000	—	7.25	9.00	12.00	16.00
1970 (a)	1,250	PF65 45.00				

KM# 304 DINAR

Copper-Nickel **Series:** F.A.O. **Obv:** Head of Habib Bourguiba left **Rev:** Female half figure right **Note:** Varieties exist. Coins dated 1976 exist with or without dots (error) below iy of Tunisiya.

Date	Mintage	VF20	XF40	MS60	MS63	MS65
1976	12,000,000	—	0.75	1.25	2.00	3.50
1983	4,000,000	—	0.75	1.25	2.00	3.50

KM# 319 DINAR

Copper-Nickel **Series:** F.A.O. **Obv:** Map and date **Rev:** Female half figure right

Date	Mintage	VF20	XF40	MS60	MS63	MS65
1988	—	—	0.75	1.25	2.00	3.50
1989	—	—	0.75	1.25	2.00	3.50
1990	8,000,000	—	0.75	1.25	2.00	3.50

KM# 351 DINAR

18.00 g., 0.680 Silver 0.3935 oz. ASW, 32 mm. **Subject:** F.A.O. 50th Anniversary **Obv:** F.A.O. logo **Rev:** Orchard workers with ladder **Edge:** Reeded

Date	Mintage	VF20	XF40	MS60	MS63	MS65
ND (1995)	5,000	PF65 15.00				

KM# 347 DINAR

10.10 g., Copper-Nickel, 28 mm. **Series:** F.A.O. **Obv:** Shield within circle **Rev:** Female half figure right

Date	Mintage	VF20	XF40	MS60	MS63	MS65
AH1416-1996	—	—	0.75	1.25	2.00	3.50
AH1417-1997	—	—	0.75	1.25	2.00	3.50
AH1418-1998	—	—	0.75	1.25	2.00	3.50

KM# 286 2 DINARS

3.80 g., 0.900 Gold 0.110 oz. AGW **Subject:** 10th Anniversary of Republic **Obv:** Head of Habib Bourguiba left **Rev:** Towered building flanked by dates

Date	Mintage	VF20	XF40	MS60	MS63	MS65
ND-1967 NI	7,259	PF65 225				

KM# 283 5 DINARS

11.79 g., 0.900 Gold 0.3412 oz. AGW, 25 mm. **Obv:** Head of Habib Bourguiba left, French legend **Rev:** Coat of arms with flags above sprigs, value and banner, French legend

Date	Mintage	VF20	XF40	MS60	MS63	MS65
1959	—	PF65 900				
1960	—	PF65 900				
1962	—	PF65 900				

KM# 416 5 DINARS

11.75 g., 0.900 Gold 0.340 oz. AGW, 25 mm. **Subject:** Banque Centrale, 1st Anniversary **Obv:** Head left **Rev:** Value and legend

Date	Mintage	VF20	XF40	MS60	MS63	MS65
1959	200	—	—	—	—	850

KM# 320 5 DINARS

11.79 g., 0.900 Gold 0.3412 oz. AGW, 25 mm. **Obv:** Arabic legends **Rev:** Arabic legends, coat of arms with flags

Date	Mintage	VF20	XF40	MS60	MS63	MS65
1960-1380	—	PF65 900				
1962-1382	—	PF65 900				

KM# 284 5 DINARS

11.79 g., 0.900 Gold 0.3412 oz. AGW, 25 mm. **Obv:** Head of Habib Bourguiba left, French legends **Rev:** Coat of arms w/o flags above value, French legends

Date	Mintage	VF20	XF40	MS60	MS63	MS65
1963	—	PF65 900				
1964	—	PF65 900				
1965	—	PF65 1,750				

KM# 321 5 DINARS

11.79 g., 0.900 Gold 0.3412 oz. AGW, 25 mm. **Obv:** Arabic legends **Rev:** Arabic legends, coat of arms w/o flags

Date	Mintage	VF20	XF40	MS60	MS63	MS65
1963-1383	—	PF65 900				
1964-1384	—	PF65 900				
1966-1386	—	PF65 900				

KM# 287 5 DINARS

9.50 g., 0.900 Gold 0.2749 oz. AGW **Subject:** 10th Anniversary of Republic **Obv:** Head of Habib Bourguiba left **Rev:** Minaret

Date	Mintage	VF20	XF40	MS60	MS63	MS65
ND-1967 NI	7,259	PF65 525				

KM# 326 5 DINARS

9.41 g., 0.900 Gold 0.2722 oz. AGW, 22 mm. **Obv:** Coat of arms, Arabic legends **Rev:** Arabic legends

Date	Mintage	VF20	XF40	MS60	MS63	MS65
1967-1387	550	PF65 750				
1968-1388	550	PF65 750				
1969-1389	550	PF65 750				
1972-1392	550	PF65 750				
1974-1394	550	PF65 750				
1976-1396	550	PF65 750				
1978-1398	550	PF65 750				
1979-1399	550	PF65 750				
1980-1400	1,450	PF65 600				
1981-1401	1,450	PF65 600				
1982-1402	725	PF65 600				

KM# 325a 5 DINARS

9.41 g., 0.900 Gold 0.2722 oz. AGW, 22 mm. **Obv:** Head of Habib Bourguiba left, French legends **Rev:** Coat of arms above value, French legends

Date	Mintage	VF20	XF40	MS60	MS63	MS65
1972	—	PF65 800				
1973	—	PF65 800				
1974	—	PF65 800				
1975	—	PF65 800				
1976	—	PF65 800				
1978	—	PF65 800				
1979	—	PF65 800				
1980	1,450	PF65 650				
1981	1,450	PF65 650				
1982	725	PF65 650				

KM# 305 5 DINARS

24.00 g., 0.680 Silver 0.5247 oz. ASW **Subject:** 20th Anniversary of Independence **Obv:** Head of Habib Bourguiba left **Rev:** Design and value

Date	Mintage	VF20	XF40	MS60	MS63	MS65
ND-1976	200,000	—	—	14.50	20.00	26.50

KM# 313 5 DINARS

27.22 g., 0.925 Silver 0.8095 oz. ASW **Series:** International Year of the Child and UNICEF **Obv:** Head of Habib Bourguiba left **Rev:** Seated child playing

Date	Mintage	VF20	XF40	MS60	MS63	MS65
1982	1,129	PF63 30.00	PF65 40.00			

KM# 327 5 DINARS

9.41 g., 0.900 Gold 0.2722 oz. AGW **Subject:** 25th Anniversary of Republic **Obv:** French legends **Rev:** Coat of arms, French legends **Rev. Inscription:** President de la Republique

Date	Mintage	VF20	XF40	MS60	MS63	MS65
1983	—	PF65 750				
1984	—	PF65 750				
1985	—	PF65 750				
1986	—	PF65 750				

KM# 328 5 DINARS

9.41 g., 0.900 Gold 0.2722 oz. AGW **Subject:** 25th Anniversary of Republic **Obv:** Arabic legends **Rev:** Coat of arms, Arabic legends **Note:** Similar to 10 Dinars, KM#335.

Date	Mintage	VF20	XF40	MS60	MS63	MS65
1983-1403	—	PF65 750				
1984-1404	—	PF65 750				
1985-1406	—	PF65 750				
1985-1405	—	PF65 750				
1986-1406	—	PF65 750				

KM# 355 5 DINARS

9.41 g., 0.900 Gold 0.2722 oz. AGW **Obv:** Country map **Rev:** Coat of arms **Note:** Arabic legends.

Date	Mintage	VF20	XF40	MS60	MS63	MS65
1987-1407	—	—	—	—	750	800

KM# 423 5 DINARS

9.40 g., 0.900 Gold 0.272 oz. AGW, 22 mm. **Note:** French legends

Date	Mintage	VF20	XF40	MS60	MS63	MS65
AH1407(1987)	725	PF65 725				

KM# 329 5 DINARS

9.41 g., 0.900 Gold 0.2722 oz. AGW **Subject:** Anniversary of 7 Nov 1987 **Obv:** Shield **Rev:** Upstretched hand, flag **Note:** French legends vary by year.

Date	Mintage	VF20	XF40	MS60	MS63	MS65
1988-1409	250	—	—	—	750	800
1989-1410	125	—	—	—	750	800
1990-1411	125	—	—	—	750	800
1991-1412	165	—	—	—	750	800
1992-1413	40	—	—	—	800	850
1993-1414	40	—	—	—	800	850
1994-1415	40	—	—	—	800	850
1995-1416	40	—	—	—	800	850
1996-1417	40	—	—	—	800	850
1997-1418	40	—	—	—	800	850
1998-1419	40	—	—	—	800	850
1999-1420	40	—	—	—	800	850
2000-1421	40	—	—	—	800	850

KM# 330 5 DINARS

9.41 g., 0.900 Gold 0.2722 oz. AGW **Subject:** Anniversary of 7 Nov 1987 **Obv:** Shield **Rev:** Upstretched hand, flag **Note:** Arabic legends vary by year.

Date	Mintage	VF20	XF40	MS60	MS63	MS65
1988-1409	250	—	—	—	750	800
1989-1410	125	—	—	—	750	800
1990-1411	125	—	—	—	750	800
1991-1412	165	—	—	—	800	850
1992-1413	40	—	—	—	800	850
1993-1414	40	—	—	—	800	850
1994-1415	40	—	—	—	800	850
1995-1415	40	—	—	—	800	850
1996-1416	40	—	—	—	800	850
1997-1417	40	—	—	—	800	850
1998-1418	40	—	—	—	800	850
1999-1419	40	—	—	—	800	850
2000-1420	40	—	—	—	800	850

KM# 285 10 DINARS

23.48 g., 0.900 Gold 0.6794 oz. AGW, 31 mm. **Obv:** Head of Habib Bourguiba left, Arabic legends **Rev:** Coat of arms with flags above value, Arabic legends

Date	Mintage	VF20	XF40	MS60	MS63	MS65
1959-1379	—	PF65 1,400				
1960-1380	—	PF65 1,400				
1962-1382	—	PF65 1,400				

KM# 322 10 DINARS

23.48 g., 0.900 Gold 0.6794 oz. AGW, 31 mm. **Obv:** French legends **Rev:** Coat of arms with flags, French legends

Date	Mintage	VF20	XF40	MS60	MS63	MS65
1959	—	PF65 1,400				
1960	—	PF65 1,400				
1962	—	PF65 1,400				

KM# 417 10 DINARS

23.50 g., 0.900 Gold 0.680 oz. AGW, 31 mm. **Subject:** Banque Centrale, 1st Anniversary **Obv:** Bust right **Rev:** Value

Date	Mintage	VF20	XF40	MS60	MS63	MS65
1959	200	—	—	—	—	1,500

KM# 359 10 DINARS

23.98 g., 0.900 Gold 0.6939 oz. AGW, 31 mm. **Obv:** Head of Bourguiba left **Rev:** National arms without flags **Note:** French legends.

Date	Mintage	VF20	XF40	MS60	MS63	MS65
1963	—	PF65 1,400				

KM# 360 10 DINARS

23.48 g., 0.900 Gold 0.6794 oz. AGW, 31 mm. **Obv:** Head of Bourguiba left **Rev:** National arms without flags **Note:** Arabic legends.

Date	Mintage	VF20	XF40	MS60	MS63	MS65
1963-1383	—	PF65 1,400				
1964-1384	—	PF65 1,400				

KM# 418 10 DINARS

23.50 g., 0.900 Gold 0.680 oz. AGW, 31 mm. **Obv:** Head left **Rev:** Shield **Note:** Arabic legends

Date	Mintage	VF20	XF40	MS60	MS63	MS65
AH1383	1,000	PF65 1,400				
AH1384	1,000	PF65 1,400				

KM# 288 10 DINARS

19.00 g., 0.900 Gold 0.5498 oz. AGW **Subject:** 10th Anniversary of Republic **Obv:** Head of Habib Bourguiba left **Rev:** Towered building flanked by dates

Date	Mintage	VF20	XF40	MS60	MS63	MS65
ND-1967 NI	6,480	PF63 950	PF65 1,050			

KM# 331 10 DINARS
18.77 g., 0.900 Gold 0.5431 oz. AGW **Obv:** Head of President Bourguiba left, date below **Rev:** Coat of arms without flags, value below **Note:** French legends.

Date	Mintage	VF20	XF40	MS60	MS63	MS65
1971	—	**PF63** 1,150	**PF65** 1,250			
1972	—	**PF63** 1,150	**PF65** 1,250			
1973	—	**PF63** 1,150	**PF65** 1,250			
1974	—	**PF63** 1,150	**PF65** 1,250			
1975	—	**PF63** 1,150	**PF65** 1,250			
1977	—	**PF63** 1,150	**PF65** 1,250			
1979	—	**PF63** 1,150	**PF65** 1,250			
1980	—	**PF63** 1,150	**PF65** 1,250			
1981	2,000	**PF63** 1,000	**PF65** 1,100			
1982	700	**PF63** 1,000	**PF65** 1,100			

KM# 332 10 DINARS
18.77 g., 0.5431 Gold 0.3277 oz. AGW **Obv:** Head of President Bourguisa left **Rev:** Coat of arms without flags **Note:** Arabic legends.

Date	Mintage	VF20	XF40	MS60	MS63	MS65
1971-1391	—	**PF65** 900				
1973-1393	—	**PF65** 900				
1974-1394	—	**PF65** 900				
1976-1396	—	**PF65** 900				
1977-1397	—	**PF65** 900				
1979-1399	—	**PF65** 900				
1980-1400	—	**PF65** 900				
1981-1401	1,400	**PF65** 750				
1982-1402	700	**PF65** 750				

KM# 361 10 DINARS
18.77 g., 0.900 Gold 0.5431 oz. AGW **Subject:** 20th Anniversary - Victory and Return of Bourguiba **Obv:** Head of Bourguiba **Rev:** Boats in harbor

Date	Mintage	VF20	XF40	MS60	MS63	MS65
ND-1975	2,000	—	—	950	1,000	1,050

KM# 324 10 DINARS
18.77 g., 0.900 Gold 0.5431 oz. AGW **Subject:** 20th Anniversary of Independence - 20. March 1956 **Obv:** Head of Habib Bourguiba left **Rev:** Coat of arms without flags

Date	Mintage	VF20	XF40	MS60	MS63	MS65
ND-1976	2,000	—	—	950	1,000	1,050

KM# 343 10 DINARS
18.77 g., 0.900 Gold 0.5431 oz. AGW **Subject:** 20th Anniversary of Republic **Obv:** Head of President Habib Bourguiba left **Rev:** Dates in wreath

Date	Mintage	VF20	XF40	MS60	MS63	MS65
ND-1977	2,000	—	—	950	1,000	1,050

KM# 344 10 DINARS
38.00 g., 0.900 Silver 1.0996 oz. ASW, 40 mm. **Subject:** 20th Anniversary - Central Bank **Obv:** Head of Habib Bourguiba left **Rev:** Sadiki College building

Date	Mintage	VF20	XF40	MS60	MS63	MS65
ND-1978	—	—	—	—	285	300
ND-1978	—	**PF65** 350				

KM# 345 10 DINARS
38.00 g., 0.900 Silver 1.0996 oz. ASW, 40 mm. **Subject:** 20th Anniversary - Central Bank **Obv:** Head of President Habib Bourguiba left **Rev:** Tunis Central Bank building

Date	Mintage	VF20	XF40	MS60	MS63	MS65
ND-1978	—	—	—	—	285	300
ND-1978	—	**PF65** 350				

KM# 345a 10 DINARS
18.81 g., 0.900 Gold 0.5442 oz. AGW, 28 mm. **Subject:** 20th Anniversary - Central Bank

Date	Mintage	VF20	XF40	MS60	MS63	MS65
ND-1978	2,000	—	—	950	1,000	1,050

KM# 356 10 DINARS
38.00 g., 0.900 Silver 1.0996 oz. ASW, 40 mm. **Subject:** 20th Anniversary - Central Bank **Obv:** Head of President Bourguiba right **Rev:** Mosque of El Zituna

Date	Mintage	VF20	XF40	MS60	MS63	MS65
ND-1978	—	—	—	—	285	300
ND-1978	—	**PF65** 350				

KM# 311 10 DINARS
18.82 g., 0.900 Gold 0.5447 oz. AGW **Subject:** 25th Anniversary of President's Return **Obv:** Habib Bourguiba

Date	Mintage	VF20	XF40	MS60	MS63	MS65
1980	2,000	**PF63** 950	**PF65** 1,050			

KM# 312 10 DINARS
18.77 g., 0.900 Gold 0.5431 oz. AGW **Subject:** 25th Anniversary of Independence **Obv:** Head of Habib Bourguiba left **Rev:** Stylized silhouette of girl leaping with large veil overhead

Date	Mintage	VF20	XF40	MS60	MS63	MS65
ND-1981	2,000	**PF63** 950	**PF65** 1,050			

KM# 333 10 DINARS
18.77 g., 0.900 Gold 0.5431 oz. AGW **Subject:** 25th Anniversary of the Republic **Rev:** Tunisian girl

Date	Mintage	VF20	XF40	MS60	MS63	MS65
ND-1982	2,000	**PF63** 950	**PF65** 1,050			

KM# A314 10 DINARS
18.80 g., 0.900 Gold 0.544 oz. AGW, 28 mm. **Subject:** 25th Anniversary - Central Bank **Obv:** Head left **Rev:** Gabes branch bank building

Date	Mintage	VF20	XF40	MS60	MS63	MS65
ND-1983	2,000	**PF65** 850				

KM# 314 10 DINARS
38.00 g., 0.900 Silver 1.0996 oz. ASW, 40 mm. **Subject:** 25th Anniversary - Central Bank **Obv:** Head left **Rev:** Gabes branch bank building

Date	Mintage	VF20	XF40	MS60	MS63	MS65
ND-1983	—	—	—	125	175	—
ND-1983	2,500	**PF63** 225				

KM# 315 10 DINARS
38.00 g., 0.900 Silver 1.0996 oz. ASW **Subject:** 25th Anniversary - Central Bank **Obv:** Head left **Rev:** Nabeul branch bank building

Date	Mintage	VF20	XF40	MS60	MS63	MS65
ND-1983	—	—	—	125	175	—
ND-1983	1,000	**PF63** 225				

KM# 316 10 DINARS
38.00 g., 0.900 Silver 1.0996 oz. ASW **Subject:** 25th Anniversary - Central Bank **Obv:** Head left **Rev:** Sfax branch bank building

Date	Mintage	VF20	XF40	MS60	MS63	MS65
ND-1983	—	—	—	125	175	—
ND-1983	1,000	**PF63** 225				

KM# 334 10 DINARS
18.77 g., 0.900 Gold 0.5431 oz. AGW **Subject:** 25th Anniversary of Republic **Obv:** "President" added to inscription, head left **Obv. Inscription:** President de la Republique **Rev:** Coat of arms without flags, value below **Note:** French legends.

Date	Mintage	VF20	XF40	MS60	MS63	MS65
1983	—	**PF63** 1,150	**PF65** 1,250			
1984	—	**PF63** 1,150	**PF65** 1,250			
1985	—	**PF63** 1,150	**PF65** 1,250			
1986	—	**PF63** 1,150	**PF65** 1,250			

KM# 335 10 DINARS
18.77 g., 0.900 Gold 0.5431 oz. AGW **Subject:** 25th Anniversary of Republic **Obv:** Head of president left **Rev:** Coat of arms without flags **Note:** Arabic legends.

Date	Mintage	VF20	XF40	MS60	MS63	MS65
1983-1403	—	**PF63** 1,150	**PF65** 1,250			
1984-1404	—	**PF63** 1,150	**PF65** 1,250			
1985-1405	—	**PF63** 1,150	**PF65** 1,250			
1986-1406	—	**PF63** 1,150	**PF65** 1,250			

KM# 336 10 DINARS
18.77 g., 0.900 Gold 0.5431 oz. AGW **Subject:** 50th Anniversary of the Socialist Party (DESTUR)

Date	Mintage	VF20	XF40	MS60	MS63	MS65
ND-1984	—	**PF63** 1,000	**PF65** 1,100			

KM# 323 10 DINARS
18.77 g., 0.900 Gold 0.5431 oz. AGW **Subject:** 30th Anniversary

- Return of Bourguiba **Obv:** Head left **Rev:** Statue of Bourghiba

Date	Mintage	VF20	XF40	MS60	MS63	MS65
ND(1985-1405)	2,000	PF63 950	PF65 1,050			

KM# 337 10 DINARS
18.77 g., 0.900 Gold 0.5431 oz. AGW **Subject:** 30th Anniversary of Independence **Obv:** Head left **Rev:** Stylized horse and rider

Date	Mintage	VF20	XF40	MS60	MS63	MS65
ND-1986	—	PF63 1,000	PF65 1,100			

KM# 338 10 DINARS
18.77 g., 0.900 Gold 0.5431 oz. AGW **Subject:** 30th Anniversary of Republic

Date	Mintage	VF20	XF40	MS60	MS63	MS65
1987	2,000	PF63 1,000	PF65 1,100			

KM# 363 10 DINARS
18.77 g., 0.900 Gold 0.5431 oz. AGW **Obv:** Country map **Rev:** National arms without flags **Note:** Arabic legends.

Date	Mintage	VF20	XF40	MS60	MS63	MS65
AH1407-1987	—	—	—	—	950	1,050

KM# 422 10 DINARS
18.80 g., 0.900 Gold 0.544 oz. AGW, 28 mm. **Obv:** Shield **Rev:** Logo **Note:** French legends

Date	Mintage	VF20	XF40	MS60	MS63	MS65
AH1407(1987)	700	PF63 950	PF65 1,050			

KM# 339 10 DINARS
38.00 g., 0.900 Silver 1.0996 oz. ASW **Subject:** 30th Anniversary - Central Bank **Obv:** Map of country **Rev:** Kasserin branch bank building

Date	Mintage	VF20	XF40	MS60	MS63	MS65
ND-1988	4,000	PF65 150				
ND-1988	—	—	—	—	—	100

KM# 340 10 DINARS
18.77 g., 0.900 Gold 0.5431 oz. AGW **Subject:** Anniversary - 7 Nov 1987 **Obv:** Shield **Rev:** Upstretched hand, flag **Note:** French legends vary by year.

Date	Mintage	VF20	XF40	MS60	MS63	MS65
1988-1409	250	—	—	—	1,100	1,200
1989-1410	125	—	—	—	1,100	1,200
1990-1411	125	—	—	—	1,100	1,200
1991-1412	125	—	—	—	1,100	1,200
1992-1413	40	—	—	—	1,150	1,250
1993-1414	40	—	—	—	1,150	1,250
1994-1415	40	—	—	—	1,150	1,250
1995-1416	40	—	—	—	1,150	1,250
1996-1417	40	—	—	—	1,150	1,250
1997-1418	40	—	—	—	1,150	1,250
1998-1419	40	—	—	—	1,150	1,250
1999-1420	40	—	—	—	1,150	1,250
2000-1421	40	—	—	—	1,150	1,250

KM# 341 10 DINARS
18.77 g., 0.900 Gold 0.5431 oz. AGW **Subject:** Anniversary - 7 Nov 1987 **Obv:** Shield **Rev:** Upstretched hand, flag **Note:** Arabic legends vary by year.

Date	Mintage	VF20	XF40	MS60	MS63	MS65
1988-1409	250	—	—	—	1,100	1,200
1989-1410	125	—	—	—	1,100	1,200
1990-1411	125	—	—	—	1,100	1,200
1991-1412	165	—	—	—	1,100	1,200
1992-1413	40	—	—	—	1,150	1,250
1993-1414	40	—	—	—	1,150	1,250
1994-1415	40	—	—	—	1,150	1,250
1995-1416	40	—	—	—	1,150	1,250
1996-1417	40	—	—	—	1,150	1,250
1997-1418	40	—	—	—	1,150	1,250
1998-1419	40	—	—	—	1,150	1,250
1999-1420	40	—	—	—	1,150	1,250
2000-1421	40	—	—	—	1,150	1,250

KM# 364 10 DINARS
38.00 g., 0.900 Silver 1.0996 oz. ASW **Subject:** 30th Anniversary - Central Bank **Rev:** Gafsa branch bank building

Date	Mintage	VF20	XF40	MS60	MS63	MS65
ND-1988	—	PF65 150				
ND-1988	—	—	—	—	—	100

KM# 365 10 DINARS
38.00 g., 0.900 Silver 1.0996 oz. ASW **Subject:** 30th Anniversary - Central Bank **Obv:** Country map **Rev:** Kairuan branch bank building

Date	Mintage	VF20	XF40	MS60	MS63	MS65
ND-1988	—	—	—	—	—	100
ND-1988	—	PF65 150				

KM# 368 10 DINARS
38.00 g., 0.900 Silver 1.0996 oz. ASW **Subject:** 6th Anniversary - 7 Nov 1987 **Obv:** National arms **Rev:** Allegorical design over country map

Date	Mintage	VF20	XF40	MS60	MS63	MS65
AH1414-1993	—	—	—	—	—	250

KM# 369 10 DINARS
38.00 g., 0.900 Silver 1.0996 oz. ASW **Subject:** 7th Anniversary of 7 Nov 87

Date	Mintage	VF20	XF40	MS60	MS63	MS65
AH1415-1994	—	—	—	—	—	250

KM# 370 10 DINARS
38.00 g., 0.900 Silver 1.0996 oz. ASW **Subject:** 8th Anniversary - 7 Nov 87

Date	Mintage	VF20	XF40	MS60	MS63	MS65
AH1416-1995	—	—	—	—	—	250

KM# 371 10 DINARS
38.00 g., 0.900 Silver 1.0996 oz. ASW **Subject:** 9th Anniversary - 7 Nov 1987

Date	Mintage	VF20	XF40	MS60	MS63	MS65
AH1417-1996	—	—	—	—	—	250

KM# 424 10 DINARS
38.00 g., 0.900 Silver 1.0996 oz. ASW, 40 mm. **Subject:** 7 November 1987, 10th Anniversary **Obv:** Bust right of Zine ed Abidine Ben Ali **Rev:** Shield **Note:** Arabic legends

Date	Mintage	VF20	XF40	MS60	MS63	MS65
AH1418-1997	400	PF65 80.00				

KM# 425 10 DINARS
38.00 g., 0.900 Silver 1.0996 oz. ASW, 40 mm. **Subject:** 7 November 1987, 10th Anniversary **Obv:** Bust right of Zine ed Abidine ben Ali **Rev:** Shield **Note:** French legend

Date	Mintage	VF20	XF40	MS60	MS63	MS65
AH1418-1997	200	PF65 90.00				

KM# 372 10 DINARS
38.00 g., 0.900 Silver 1.0996 oz. ASW **Subject:** 40th Anniversary - Central Bank **Obv:** National arms **Rev:** Monastir branch bank building

Date	Mintage	VF20	XF40	MS60	MS63	MS65
ND-1998	—	PF65 150				

KM# 373 10 DINARS
38.00 g., 0.900 Silver 1.0996 oz. ASW **Subject:** 40th Anniversary - Central Bank **Obv:** National arms **Rev:** Sfax branch bank building **Note:** Arabic legend

Date	Mintage	VF20	XF40	MS60	MS63	MS65
ND-1998	—	PF65 150				

KM# 374 10 DINARS
38.00 g., 0.900 Silver 1.0996 oz. ASW **Subject:** 40th Anniversary - Central Bank **Obv:** National arms **Rev:** Sfax branch bank building **Note:** French legends.

Date	Mintage	VF20	XF40	MS60	MS63	MS65
ND-1998	—	PF65 150				

KM# 375 10 DINARS
38.00 g., 0.900 Silver 1.0996 oz. ASW **Subject:** 11th Anniversary 7 Nov 1987 **Note:** Arabic legends.

Date	Mintage	VF20	XF40	MS60	MS63	MS65
AH1419-1998	—	—	—	—	—	250

KM# 426 10 DINARS
38.00 g., 0.900 Silver 1.0996 oz. ASW, 40 mm. **Subject:** 7 November 1987, 11th Anniversary **Obv:** Shield **Note:** French legends

Date	Mintage	VF20	XF40	MS60	MS63	MS65
AH1419-1998	100	PF65 85.00				

KM# 427 10 DINARS
38.00 g., 0.900 Silver 1.0996 oz. ASW **Subject:** Banque Centrale, 40th Anniversary **Obv:** Shield **Rev:** Building **Shape:** 40 **Note:** Arabic legend

Date	Mintage	VF20	XF40	MS60	MS63	MS65
1998	850	PF65 65.00				

KM# 376 10 DINARS
38.00 g., 0.900 Silver 1.0996 oz. ASW, 40 mm. **Subject:** Millennium - 12th Anniversary 7 Nov 87 **Obv:** National arms **Rev:** Stylized 2000 design

Date	Mintage	VF20	XF40	MS60	MS63	MS65
AH1420-1999	450	—	—	—	—	250

KM# 428 10 DINARS
38.00 g., 0.900 Silver 1.0996 oz. ASW, 40 mm. **Subject:** 7 November 1987, 12th Anniversary **Obv:** Shield **Rev:** Year 2000 **Note:** French legends

Date	Mintage	VF20	XF40	MS60	MS63	MS65
AH1420-1999	50	PF65 150				

KM# 377 10 DINARS
38.00 g., 0.900 Silver 1.0996 oz. ASW **Subject:** 13th Anniversary of 7 Nov 1987 and 21st Century

Date	Mintage	VF20	XF40	MS60	MS63	MS65
AH1421-2000	—	—	—	—	—	250

KM# 429 10 DINARS
38.00 g., 0.900 Silver 1.0996 oz. ASW, 40 mm. **Subject:** 7 November 1987, 13th Anniversary **Obv:** Shield **Rev:** 21st Century

Date	Mintage	VF20	XF40	MS60	MS63	MS65
AH1421-2000	50	PF65 150				

KM# 289 20 DINARS
38.00 g., 0.900 Gold 1.0996 oz. AGW **Subject:** 10th Anniversary of Republic **Rev:** Minaret

Date	Mintage	VF20	XF40	MS60	MS63	MS65
ND-1967 NI	3,536	PF65 2,100				

KM# 290 40 DINARS
76.00 g., 0.900 Gold 2.1991 oz. AGW **Subject:** 10th Anniversary of Republic **Obv:** Head left **Rev:** Minaret **Note:** Similar to 20 Dinars, KM#289.

Date	Mintage	VF20	XF40	MS60	MS63	MS65
ND-1967 NI	3,031	PF65 4,000				

KM# 384 50 DINARS
21.00 g., 0.900 Gold 0.6076 oz. AGW, 34 mm. **Subject:** 5th Anniversary of 7 Nov 1987 **Edge:** Reeded

Date	Mintage	VF20	XF40	MS60	MS63	MS65
AH1413-1992	400	PF65 1,250				

KM# 385 50 DINARS
21.00 g., 0.900 Gold 0.6076 oz. AGW, 34 mm. **Subject:** 6th Anniversary 7 Nov 1987 **Edge:** Reeded

Date	Mintage	VF20	XF40	MS60	MS63	MS65
AH1414-1993	—	PF65 1,250				

KM# 386 50 DINARS
21.00 g., 0.900 Gold 0.6076 oz. AGW, 34 mm. **Subject:** 7th Anniversary of 7 Nov 87 **Edge:** Reeded

Date	Mintage	VF20	XF40	MS60	MS63	MS65
AH1415-1994	400	PF65 1,250				

KM# 387 50 DINARS
21.00 g., 0.900 Gold 0.6076 oz. AGW, 34 mm. **Subject:** 8th Anniversary of 7 Nov 1987 **Obv:** National arms **Rev:** Stylized 7 with dove in flight **Edge:** Reeded

Date	Mintage	VF20	XF40	MS60	MS63	MS65
AH1416-1995	400	PF65 1,250				

KM# 388 50 DINARS
21.00 g., 0.900 Gold 0.6076 oz. AGW, 34 mm. **Subject:** 20th Soccer Africa Cup plus 9th Anniversary of 7 Nov 87 **Edge:** Reeded

Date	Mintage	VF20	XF40	MS60	MS63	MS65
AH1417-1996	—	PF65 1,250				

KM# 389 50 DINARS
21.00 g., 0.900 Gold 0.6076 oz. AGW, 34 mm. **Subject:** 10th Anniversary of 7 Nov 1987 **Obv:** National arms **Rev:** Head of Zine El Abdine Ben Ali **Edge:** Reeded **Note:** French legends.

Date	Mintage	VF20	XF40	MS60	MS63	MS65
AH1418-1997	—	PF65 1,250				

KM# 390 50 DINARS
21.00 g., 0.900 Gold 0.6076 oz. AGW, 34 mm. **Subject:** 10th Anniversary of 7 Nov 1987 **Rev:** Head of Zine El Abdine Ben Ali **Edge:** Reeded **Note:** Arabic legends.

Date	Mintage	VF20	XF40	MS60	MS63	MS65
AH1418-1997	—	PF65 1,250				

KM# 391 50 DINARS
21.00 g., 0.900 Gold 0.6076 oz. AGW, 34 mm. **Subject:** 11th Anniversary of 7 Nov 1987 **Obv:** National arms **Edge:** Reeded **Note:** French legends.

Date	Mintage	VF20	XF40	MS60	MS63	MS65
AH1419-1998	—	PF65 1,250				

KM# 392 50 DINARS
21.00 g., 0.900 Gold 0.6076 oz. AGW, 34 mm. **Subject:** 11th Anniversary of 7 Nov 1987 **Obv:** National arms **Edge:** Reeded **Note:** Arabic legends.

Date	Mintage	VF20	XF40	MS60	MS63	MS65
AH1419-1998	550	**PF65** 1,250				

KM# 393 50 DINARS
21.00 g., 0.900 Gold 0.6076 oz. AGW, 34 mm. **Subject:** 12th Anniversary of 7 Nov 1987 plus the Millennium **Obv:** National arms **Edge:** Reeded **Note:** French legends.

Date	Mintage	VF20	XF40	MS60	MS63	MS65
AH1420-1999	—	**PF65** 1,250				

KM# 394 50 DINARS
21.00 g., 0.900 Gold 0.6076 oz. AGW, 34 mm. **Subject:** 12th Anniversary of 7 Nov 1987 plus The Millennium **Obv:** National arms **Edge:** Reeded **Note:** Arabic legends.

Date	Mintage	VF20	XF40	MS60	MS63	MS65
AH1420-1999	—	**PF65** 1,250				

KM# 353 50 DINARS
0.900 Gold, 34 mm. **Subject:** 13th Anniversary of 7 Nov 1987 plus 21st Century **Obv:** National arms **Rev:** Two interlocked currycombs, each with the number 21 **Note:** French legends.

Date	Mintage	VF20	XF40	MS60	MS63	MS65
2000-1421	—	**PF65** 1,250				

KM# 395 50 DINARS
21.00 g., 0.900 Gold 0.6076 oz. AGW, 34 mm. **Subject:** 13th Anniversary 7 Nov 1987 plus 21st Century **Obv:** National arms **Rev:** Two interlocked currycombs, each with the number 21 **Edge:** Reeded **Note:** Arabic legends.

Date	Mintage	VF20	XF40	MS60	MS63	MS65
AH1421-2000	—	**PF65** 1,250				

KM# 317 75 DINARS
15.55 g., 0.900 Gold 0.4499 oz. AGW **Series:** International Year of the Child and UNICEF **Obv:** Head of Habib Bourguiba left **Rev:** Standing figures facing left

Date	Mintage	VF20	XF40	MS60	MS63	MS65
1982	4,518	**PF65** 750				

KM# 399 100 DINARS
38.00 g., 0.900 Gold 1.0996 oz. AGW, 40 mm. **Subject:** 5th Anniversary of 7 Nov 1987

Date	Mintage	VF20	XF40	MS60	MS63	MS65
AH1413-1992	250	**PF65** 2,150				

KM# 400 100 DINARS
38.00 g., 0.900 Gold 1.0996 oz. AGW **Subject:** 6th Anniversary of 7 Nov 1987

Date	Mintage	VF20	XF40	MS60	MS63	MS65
AH1414-1993	250	**PF65** 2,150				

KM# A401 100 DINARS
38.00 g., 0.900 Gold 1.0996 oz. AGW **Subject:** 6th Anniversary of 7 Nov 1987 **Obv:** National arms **Note:** Arabic legends.

Date	Mintage	VF20	XF40	MS60	MS63	MS65
AH1414-1993	250	**PF65** 2,150				

KM# 401 100 DINARS
38.00 g., 0.900 Gold 1.0996 oz. AGW **Subject:** 7th Anniversary of 7 Nov 1987

Date	Mintage	VF20	XF40	MS60	MS63	MS65
AH1415-1994	250	**PF65** 2,150				

KM# 402 100 DINARS
38.00 g., 0.900 Gold 1.0996 oz. AGW **Subject:** 8th Anniversary of 7 Nov 1987

Date	Mintage	VF20	XF40	MS60	MS63	MS65
AH1416-1995	—	**PF65** 2,150				

KM# 403 100 DINARS
38.00 g., 0.900 Gold 1.0996 oz. AGW **Subject:** 9th Anniversary of 7 Nov 1987 and 20th Soccer Africa Cup

Date	Mintage	VF20	XF40	MS60	MS63	MS65
AH1417-1996	—	**PF65** 2,150				

KM# 404 100 DINARS
38.00 g., 0.900 Gold 1.0996 oz. AGW **Subject:** 10th Anniversary of 7 Nov 1987 **Obv:** National arms **Rev:** Bust of Zine El Abdine Ben Ali right **Note:** French legends.

Date	Mintage	VF20	XF40	MS60	MS63	MS65
AH1418-1997	—	**PF65** 2,150				

KM# 405 100 DINARS
38.00 g., 0.900 Gold 1.0996 oz. AGW **Subject:** 10th Anniversary of 7 Nov 1987 **Obv:** National arms **Rev:** Bust of Zine El Abdine Ben Ali **Note:** Arabic legends.

Date	Mintage	VF20	XF40	MS60	MS63	MS65
AH1418-1997	—	**PF65** 2,150				

KM# 406 100 DINARS
38.00 g., 0.900 Gold 1.0996 oz. AGW **Subject:** 11th Anniversary of 7 Nov 1987 **Note:** French legends.

Date	Mintage	VF20	XF40	MS60	MS63	MS65
AH1419-1998	—	**PF65** 2,150				

KM# 407 100 DINARS
38.00 g., 0.900 Gold 1.0996 oz. AGW **Subject:** 11th Anniversary of 7 Nov 1987 **Note:** Arabic legends.

Date	Mintage	VF20	XF40	MS60	MS63	MS65
AH1419-1998	—	**PF65** 2,150				

KM# 408 100 DINARS
38.00 g., 0.900 Gold 1.0996 oz. AGW **Subject:** 12th Anniversary of 7 Nov 1987 and The Millennium **Note:** French legends.

Date	Mintage	VF20	XF40	MS60	MS63	MS65
AH1420-1999	—	**PF65** 2,150				

KM# 409 100 DINARS
38.00 g., 0.900 Gold 1.0996 oz. AGW **Subject:** 12th Anniversary of 7 Nov 1987 and The Millennium **Obv:** National arms **Note:** Arabic legends.

Date	Mintage	VF20	XF40	MS60	MS63	MS65
AH1420-1999	—	**PF65** 2,150				

KM# 410 100 DINARS
38.00 g., 0.900 Gold 1.0996 oz. AGW **Subject:** 13th Anniversary of 7 Nov 1987 and 21st Century **Note:** French legends.

Date	Mintage	VF20	XF40	MS60	MS63	MS65
AH1421-2000	—	**PF65** 2,150				

KM# 411 100 DINARS

38.00 g., 0.900 Gold 1.0996 oz. AGW **Subject:** 13th Anniversary of 7 Nov 1987 and 21st Century **Obv:** National arms **Note:** Arabic legends.

Date	Mintage	VF20	XF40	MS60	MS63	MS65
AH1421-2000	—	PF65 2,150				

ESSAIS

Standard metals unless otherwise noted

KM#	Date	Mintage	Identification	Mkt Val
E1	1918(a)	—	5 Centimes. Nickel-Bronze. KM#242.	85.00
E2	1918(a)	—	10 Centimes. Nickel-Bronze. KM#243.	90.00
E3	1918(a)	—	25 Centimes. Nickel-Bronze. KM#244.	95.00
E4	1920(a)	—	5 Centimes. Nickel-Bronze. KM#245.	125
E5	1921(a)	—	50 Centimes. Aluminum-Bronze. KM#246.	95.00
E6	1921(a)	—	Franc. Aluminum-Bronze. KM#247.	120
E7	1921(a)	—	Franc. Aluminum. KM#247.	130
E8	1928A	—	Franc. Nickel-Bronze. KM#250a.	250
E9	1928	—	2 Francs. Silver-Bronze. KM#251.	260
E10	1930(a)	—	10 Francs. Silver. KM#255, uniface.	180
E11	1930(a)	—	20 Francs. Silver. KM#256, uniface.	360
E12	1930(a)	—	100 Francs. Gold. KM#257, uniface.	450
E13	1931(a)	—	5 Centimes. Nickel-Bronze. KM#258.	80.00
E14	1931(a)	—	10 Centimes. Nickel-Bronze. KM#259.	85.00
E15	1931(a)	—	25 Centimes. Nickel-Aluminum-Bronze. KM#260.	90.00
E16	AH1353 (1934)(a)	—	5 Francs. Silver. KM#261.	95.00
E17	AH1353 (1934)(a)	—	10 Francs. Silver. KM#255.	110
E17a	AH1353 (1934)(a)	—	10 Francs. Silver.	300
E18	AH1353 (1934)(a)	—	20 Francs. Silver. KM#256.	185
EA19	AH1354 (1935)(a)	—	100 Francs. Bronze Gilt. KM#257.	—
E19	1938(a)	—	100 Francs. Bronze Gilt. KM-M1.	120
E20	1938(a)	—	100 Francs. Gold. KM-M1.	1,000
E21	1939(a)	—	5 Francs. Silver. KM#264.	65.00
E22	1939(a)	—	10 Francs. Silver. KM#265.	85.00
E23	1939(a)	—	20 Francs. Silver. KM#266.	160
EA24	19--/ AH135-(1939)	—	5 Centimes. Zinc. Never issued as a regular coin.	170
E24	1942(a)	—	20 Centimes. Zinc. KM#268.	55.00
E25	1945(a)	1,100	10 Centimes. Nickel-Aluminum-Bronze. KM#271.	55.00
E26	1945(a)	1,100	20 Centimes. Zinc. KM#272.	65.00
E27	1946(a)	1,100	5 Francs. Aluminum-Bronze. Inscription and date within sprigs. Value and date within circular inscription and design. KM#273.	40.00
E28	1950(a)	1,100	20 Francs. Copper-Nickel. KM#274.	40.00
E29	1950(a)	1,100	50 Francs. Copper-Nickel. KM#275.	40.00
E30	1950(a)	1,100	100 Francs. Copper-Nickel. KM#276.	40.00
E31	1954(a)	1,100	5 Francs. Copper-Nickel. KM#277.	25.00
EA32	1967	—	2 Dinars. Aluminum. KM#286.	25.00
EB32	1967	—	5 Dinars. Aluminum. KM#287.	25.00
EC32	1967	—	10 Dinars. Aluminum. KM#288.	25.00
ED32	1967	—	20 Dinars. Aluminum. KM#289.	25.00
EE32	1967	—	40 Dinars. Aluminum. KM#290.	25.00
E32	1968(a)	1,260	1/2 Dinar. Nickel. KM#291.	40.00
E33	1968(a)	70	1/2 Dinar. Gold.	650
E34	1970(a)	1,250	Dinar. Silver. Head left. Coconut tree in center of oxen, tractor and figure. KM#302.	50.00
E35	1976	2,050	1/2 Dinar. Copper-Nickel. KM#303.	35.00
E36	1976	2,050	Dinar. Copper-Nickel. KM#304.	45.00

PIEDFORT WITH ESSAI

Double thickness

KM#	Date	Mintage	Identification	Mkt Val
PE1	1945(a)	104	20 Centimes. Zinc. KM#272.	250
PE2	1945(a)	104	50 Centimes. Aluminum-Bronze. KM#246.	250
PE3	1945(a)	104	Franc. Aluminum-Bronze. KM#247.	250
PE4	1945(a)	104	2 Francs. Aluminum-Bronze. Date within wreath. Value flanked by sprigs. KM#248.	250
PE5	1946(a)	104	5 Francs. Aluminum-Bronze. KM#273.	250
PE6	1954(a)	104	5 Francs. Copper-Nickel. KM#277.	250

PIEDFORT

Double thickness;
standard metals unless otherwise noted

KM#	Date	Mintage	Identification	Mkt Val
P1	1968(a)	500	1/2 Dinar. Nickel. KM#291.	125
P2	1982	96	5 Dinars. Silver. KM#313.	175
P3	1982	55	75 Dinars. Gold. KM#317.	2,000

MINT SETS

KM#	Date	Mintage	Identification	Issue Price	Mkt Val
MS1	1960 (7)	—	KM#280-282, 306-309	—	5.50
MS2	1996 (7)	—	KM#282, 306-309, 346-347	—	17.50

PROOF SETS

KM#	Date	Mintage	Identification	Issue Price	Mkt Val
PS2	1967 (5)	3,031	KM#286-290	—	7,900
PS3	1969FM-NI (10)	15,202	KM#292-301 Many sets were ruined while in storage.	77.00	BV+10%
PS4	1969NI (10)	5,000	KM#292-301	—	BV+15%

TURKEY

The Republic of Turkey, a parliamentary democracy of the Near East located partially in Europe and partially in Asia between the Black and the Mediterranean Seas, has an area of 301,382 sq. mi. (780,580 sq. km.) and a population of *55.4 million. Capital: Ankara. Turkey exports cotton, hazelnuts, and tobacco, and enjoys a virtual monopoly in meerschaum.

The Ottoman Turks, a tribe from Central Asia, first appeared in the early 13th century, and by the 17th century had established the Ottoman Empire which stretched from the Persian Gulf to the southern frontier of Poland, and from the Caspian Sea to the Algerian plateau. The defeat of the Turkish navy by the Holy League in 1571, and of the Turkish forces besieging Vienna in 1683, began the steady decline of the Ottoman Empire which, accelerated by the rise of nationalism, contracted its European border, and by the end of World War I deprived it of its Arab lands. The present Turkish boundaries were largely fixed by the Treaty of Lausanne in 1923. The sultanate and caliphate, the political and spiritual ruling institutions of the old empire, were separated and the sultanate abolished in 1922. On Oct. 29, 1923, Turkey formally became a republic.

RULERS

Abdul Hamid II, AH1293-1327/1876-1909AD
Muhammad V, AH1327-1336/1909-1918AD
Muhammad VI, AH1336-1341/1918-1923AD
Republic, AH1341/AD1923-

MINT NAMES

قسطنطنية

Constantinople
(Qustantiniyah)

مصر

Misr
See Egypt

MONETARY EQUIVALENTS

3 Akche = 1 Para
5 Para = Beshlik (Beshparalik)
10 Para = Onluk
20 Para = Yirmilik
30 Para = Zolota
40 Para = Kurush (Piastre)
1-1/2 Kurush (Piastres) = Altmishlik

MONETARY SYSTEM

Silver Coinage

40 Para = 1 Kurush (Piastre)
2 Kurush (Piastres) = 1 Ikilik
2-1/2 Kurush (Piastres) = Yuzluk
3 Kurush (Piastres) = Uechlik
5 Kurush (Piastres) = Beshlik
6 Kurush (Piastres) = Altilik

Gold Coinage

100 Kurush (Piastres) = 1 Turkish Pound (Lira)

This system has remained essentially unchanged since its introduction by Ahmad III in 1688, except that the Asper and Para have long since ceased to be coined. The Piastre, established as a crown-sized silver coin approximately equal to the French Ecu of Louis XIV, has shrunk to a tiny copper coin, worth about 1/15 of a U.S. cent. Since the establishment of the Republic in 1923, the Turkish terms, Kurus and Lira, have replaced the European names Piastres and Turkish Pounds.

MINT VISIT ISSUES

From time to time, certain cities of the Ottoman Empire,

such as Bursa, Edirne, Kosova, Manistir and Salonika were honored by having special coins struck at Istanbul, but with inscriptions stating that they were struck in the city of honor. These were produced on the occasion of the Sultan's visit to that city. The coins were struck in limited, but not small quantities, and were probably intended for distribution to the notables of the city and the Sultan's own followers. Because they were of the same size and type as the regular circulation issues struck at Istanbul, many specimens found their way into circulation and worn or mounted specimens are found today, although some have been preserved in XF or better condition. Mintage statistics are not known.

MONNAIE DE LUXE

In the 23rd year of the reign of Abdul Hamid II, two parallel series of gold coins were produced, regular mint issues and monnaies de luxe', which were intended primarily for presentation and jewelry purposes. The Monnaie de Luxe' were struck to a slightly less weight and the same fineness as regular issues, but were broader and thinner, and from more ornate dies.

Coins are listed by type, followed by a list of reported years. Most of the reported years have never been confirmed and other years may also exist. Mintage figures are known for the AH1293 and 1327 series, but are unreliable and of little utility.

Although some years are undoubtedly much rarer than others, there is at present no date collecting of Ottoman gold and therefore little justification for higher prices for rare dates.

There is no change in design in the regular series. Only the toughra, accessional date and regnal year vary. The deluxe series show ornamental changes. The standard coins generally do not bear the denomination.

HONORIFIC TITLES

El Ghazi

Reshat

The first coinage of Abdul Hamid II has a flower right of the toughra while the second coinage has *el Ghazi* (The Victorious). The first coinage of Mohammad Reshat Vhas *Reshat* right of the toughra while his second coinage has *el Ghazi*.

SULTANATE

Abdul Hamid II

AH1293-1327/1876-1909AD

STANDARD COINAGE

KM# 743 5 PARA
1.00 g., 0.100 Silver 0.0032 oz. ASW **Obv:** Toughra; "el-Ghazi" to right **Rev:** Text within crescent below value, date and star **Mint:** Qustantiniyah

Date	Mintage	VG8	F12	VF20	XF40	MS60
AH1293//26	—	0.25	0.50	1.25	4.00	—
AH1293//27	—	2.00	4.00	6.00	12.00	—
AH1293//28	—	3.00	4.00	9.00	25.00	—
AH1293//30	—	6.00	12.00	25.00	60.00	—

KM# 744 10 PARA
2.00 g., 0.100 Silver 0.0064 oz. ASW **Obv:** Toughra; "el-Ghazi" to right **Rev:** Text within crescent below date, value and star **Mint:** Qustantiniyah

Date	Mintage	VG8	F12	VF20	XF40	MS60
AH1293//26	—	1.00	2.00	3.00	6.00	—
AH1293//27	—	1.00	2.00	5.00	10.00	—
Note: Varieties exist in size of regnal year 27						
AH1293//28	—	1.00	3.00	5.00	15.00	—
AH1293//30	—	2.00	4.00	8.00	25.00	—

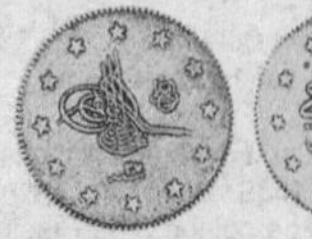

KM# 735 KURUSH
1.20 g., 0.830 Silver 0.0321 oz. ASW **Obv:** Toughra; "el-Ghazi" to right **Rev:** Text, value and date within circle of stars **Mint:** Qustantiniyah **Note:** Varieties exist in the size of year and inscription.

Date	Mintage	VG8	F12	VF20	XF40	MS60
AH1293//26	55,000	1.50	7.50	15.00	30.00	—
AH1293//27	9,945,000	0.60	2.00	3.00	5.00	—
AH1293//28	16,139,000	0.60	2.00	5.00	8.00	—
AH1293//29	7,076,000	0.60	2.00	5.00	8.00	—
AH1293//30	707,000	0.60	4.00	8.00	15.00	—
AH1293//31	1,366,000	0.60	2.00	5.00	8.00	—
AH1293//32	1,140,000	0.60	2.00	5.00	8.00	—
AH1293//33	1,700,000	0.60	2.00	5.00	8.00	—
AH1293//34	—	—	200	230	260	—

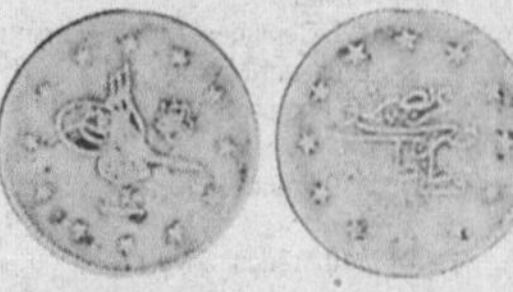

KM# 736 2 KURUSH
2.41 g., 0.830 Silver 0.0642 oz. ASW **Obv:** Toughra; "el-Ghazi" to right **Rev:** Text, value and date within circle of stars **Mint:** Qustantiniyah **Note:** Varieties exist in the size of toughra and year.

Date	Mintage	VG8	F12	VF20	XF40	MS60
AH1293//26	17,000	15.00	25.00	35.00	75.00	—
AH1293//27	4,689,000	1.20	2.50	4.00	7.00	—
AH1293//28	7,567,000	1.20	2.50	6.00	10.00	—
AH1293//29	7,775,000	1.20	2.50	6.00	10.00	—
AH1293//30	1,366,000	1.20	2.50	6.00	10.00	—
AH1293//31	3,014,000	1.20	2.50	6.00	10.00	—
AH1293//32	1,625,000	1.20	2.50	6.00	10.00	—
AH1293//33	2,173,000	1.20	2.50	6.00	10.00	—
AH1293//34	—	150	225	250	300	—

KM# 737 5 KURUSH
6.01 g., 0.830 Silver 0.1605 oz. ASW **Obv:** Toughra; "el-Ghazi" to right **Rev:** Text, value and date within circle of stars and crescent border **Mint:** Qustantiniyah **Note:** Varieties exist in the size of toughra, inscription, and date.

Date	Mintage	VG8	F12	VF20	XF40	MS60
AH1293//26	8,000	15.00	30.00	45.00	75.00	—
AH1293//27	16,000	15.00	30.00	45.00	75.00	—
AH1293//28	6,000	100	150	200	250	—
AH1293//29	7,000	100	150	200	250	—
AH1293//30	38,000	7.00	15.00	20.00	40.00	—
AH1293//31	Inc. above	3.00	8.00	12.00	20.00	—
AH1293//31/0	3,175,000	7.00	13.00	25.00	35.00	—
AH1293//32	3,334,000	3.00	7.00	10.00	18.00	—
AH1293//33	907,000	3.00	8.00	12.00	20.00	—
AH1293//34	—	200	225	275	350	—

KM# 738 10 KURUSH
12.03 g., 0.830 Silver 0.3209 oz. ASW **Obv:** Toughra; "el-Ghazi" to right **Rev:** Text, value and date within circle of stars and crescent border **Mint:** Istanbul

Date	Mintage	VG8	F12	VF20	XF40	MS60
AH1293//31	51,000	60.00	100	120	150	—
AH1293//32	575,000	6.25	20.00	30.00	45.00	—
AH1293//33	274,000	6.25	20.00	30.00	45.00	—

MILLED COINAGE

Gold Issues

KM# 745 12-1/2 KURUSH
0.88 g., 0.917 Gold 0.0259 oz. AGW **Series:** Monnaie de Luxe **Obv:** Toughra **Mint:** Qustantiniyah

Date	Mintage	VG8	F12	VF20	XF40	MS60
AH1293//26	720	—	—	—	—	—
AH1293//27	720	—	—	—	—	—
AH1293//28	800	50.00	150	280	400	—
AH1293//29	11,696	50.00	100	220	300	—
AH1293//30	13,208	50.00	100	220	300	—
AH1293//31	24,504	50.00	100	220	300	—
AH1293//32	14,392	50.00	100	220	300	—
AH1293//33	13,032	50.00	100	220	300	—
AH1293//34	—	50.00	180	280	400	—

KM# 729 25 KURUSH
1.80 g., 0.917 Gold 0.0532 oz. AGW **Obv:** Toughra; "el-Ghazi" to right **Rev:** Text, value and date within wreath, star above **Mint:** Qustantiniyah

Date	Mintage	VG8	F12	VF20	XF40	MS60
AH1293//26	47,800	—	71.00	95.00	110	130
AH1293//27	99,500	—	71.00	97.50	120	150
AH1293//28	77,300	—	71.00	97.50	120	150
AH1293//29	101,548	—	71.00	97.50	120	150
AH1293//30	156,280	—	71.00	97.50	120	150
AH1293//31	58,404	—	71.00	97.50	120	150
AH1293//32	112,000	—	71.00	97.50	120	150
AH1293//33	15,535	—	71.00	97.50	140	200
AH1293//34	115,484	—	71.00	97.50	120	150

KM# 739 25 KURUSH
1.75 g., 0.917 Gold 0.0517 oz. AGW **Series:** Monnaie de Luxe **Obv:** Toughra; "el-Ghazi" to right **Rev:** Text, value and date in beaded circle within circular text **Mint:** Qustantiniyah

Date	Mintage	VG8	F12	VF20	XF40	MS60
AH1293//26	7,620	95.00	100	200	300	—
AH1293//27	7,620	95.00	100	200	300	—
AH1293//28	9,268	95.00	100	200	300	—
AH1293//29	29,056	95.00	100	150	220	—
AH1293//30	27,964	95.00	100	150	220	—
AH1293//31	39,192	95.00	100	150	220	—
AH1293//32	41,696	95.00	100	150	220	—
AH1293//33	17,728	95.00	100	150	220	—
AH1293//34	—	95.00	200	250	350	—

KM# 731 50 KURUSH
3.61 g., 0.917 Gold 0.1064 oz. AGW **Obv:** Toughra; "el-Ghazi" to right **Rev:** Text, value and date within wreath, star above **Mint:** Qustantiniyah

Date	Mintage	VG8	F12	VF20	XF40	MS60
AH1293//26	13,956	—	142	200	250	300
AH1293//27	14,200	—	142	200	250	300
AH1293//28	33,450	—	142	200	250	300
AH1293//29	24,244	—	142	200	250	300
AH1293//30	66,000	—	142	200	250	300
AH1293//31	58,612	—	142	200	250	300
AH1293//32	48,000	—	142	200	250	300
AH1293//33	16,145	—	142	200	250	300
AH1293//34	6,276	—	142	300	500	800

KM# 740 50 KURUSH
3.51 g., 0.917 Gold 0.1034 oz. AGW **Series:** Monnaie de Luxe **Obv:** Toughra; "el-Ghazi" to right **Rev:** Text, value and date in beaded circle within circular text **Mint:** Qustantiniyah

Date	Mintage	VG8	F12	VF20	XF40	MS60
AH1293//26	5,436	—	137	250	350	—
AH1293//27	6,630	—	137	250	350	—
AH1293//28	8,660	—	137	250	350	—
AH1293//29	14,924	—	137	220	300	—
AH1293//30	18,812	—	137	220	300	—
AH1293//31	22,460	—	137	220	300	—
AH1293//32	27,542	—	137	220	300	—
AH1293//33	12,886	—	137	220	300	—
AH1293//34	—	—	200	600	800	—

KM# 730 100 KURUSH
7.22 g., 0.917 Gold 0.2127 oz. AGW **Obv:** Toughra; "el-Ghazi" to right **Rev:** Text, value and date within wreath, star above **Mint:** Qustantiniyah

Date	Mintage	VG8	F12	VF20	XF40	MS60
AH1293//26	2,000	—	—	285	450	500
AH1293//27	48,200	—	285	400	425	450
AH1293//28	865,011	—	—	285	400	425
AH1293//29	1,026,275	—	—	285	400	425
AH1293//30	1,643,795	—	—	285	400	425
AH1293//31	2,748,448	—	—	285	400	425
AH1293//32	1,951,611	—	—	285	400	425
AH1293//33	962,672	—	—	285	400	425
AH1293//34	1,715,274	—	—	285	400	450

Note: Combined mintage total, with 100 Kurush KM#754, AH1327//1

KM# 741 100 KURUSH
7.02 g., 0.917 Gold 0.2068 oz. AGW **Series:** Monnaie de Luxe **Obv:** Toughra; "el-Ghazi" to right **Rev:** Text, value and date in beaded circle within circular text **Mint:** Qustantiniyah

Date	Mintage	VG8	F12	VF20	XF40	MS60
AH1293//26	5,590	—	275	400	450	—
AH1293//27	9,580	—	275	400	600	—
AH1293//28	13,638	—	275	400	600	—
AH1293//29	18,129	—	275	400	600	—
AH1293//30	22,796	—	275	400	600	—
AH1293//31	31,126	—	275	400	600	—
AH1293//32	42,662	—	275	400	600	—
AH1293//33	18,716	—	275	400	700	—
AH1293//34	—	—	275	500	800	—

KM# 732 250 KURUSH
18.04 g., 0.917 Gold 0.5319 oz. AGW **Obv:** Toughra; "el-Ghazi" to right **Rev:** Text, value and date within wreath, star above **Mint:** Qustantiniyah

Date	Mintage	VG8	F12	VF20	XF40	MS60
AH1293//26	1,428	—	710	975	1,200	—
AH1293//27	1,450	—	710	1,100	1,500	—
AH1293//28	7,027	—	710	975	1,200	—
AH1293//29	7,522	—	710	975	1,200	—
AH1293//30	4,900	—	710	975	1,200	—
AH1293//31	8,552	—	710	975	1,200	—
AH1293//32	6,729	—	710	975	1,200	—
AH1293//33	2,669	—	710	975	1,200	—
AH1293//34	6,478	—	710	1,100	1,500	—

KM# 742 250 KURUSH
17.54 g., 0.917 Gold 0.5171 oz. AGW **Series:** Monnaie de Luxe **Obv:** Toughra; "el-Ghazi" to right **Rev:** Text, value and date within beaded circle, designed wreath **Mint:** Qustantiniyah

Date	Mintage	VG8	F12	VF20	XF40	MS60
AH1293//26	1,538	—	690	1,200	1,500	—
AH1293//27	1,770	—	690	1,200	1,500	—
AH1293//28	1,520	—	690	1,200	1,500	—
AH1293//29	1,631	—	690	1,200	1,500	—
AH1293//30	1,922	—	690	1,200	1,500	—
AH1293//31	1,778	—	690	1,200	1,500	—
AH1293//32	2,650	—	690	1,200	1,500	—
AH1293//33	931	690	965	1,500	1,800	—
AH1293//34 Rare	—	—	—	—	—	—

KM# 733 500 KURUSH
36.08 g., 0.917 Gold 1.0637 oz. AGW **Obv:** Toughra; "el-Ghazi" to right **Rev:** Text, value and date within wreath, star above **Mint:** Qustantiniyah

Date	Mintage	VG8	F12	VF20	XF40	MS60
AH1293//26	8,735	—	1,425	1,950	2,200	—
AH1293//27	22,450	—	1,425	1,950	2,200	—
AH1293//28	35,918	—	1,425	1,950	2,200	—
AH1293//29	16,621	—	1,425	1,950	2,200	—
AH1293//30	33,129	—	1,425	1,950	2,200	—
AH1293//31	40,953	—	1,425	1,950	2,200	—
AH1293//32	32,516	—	1,425	1,950	2,200	—
AH1293//33	16,403	—	1,425	1,950	2,200	—
AH1293//34	39,028	—	1,425	1,950	2,200	—

KM# 746 500 KURUSH
35.08 g., 0.917 Gold 1.0342 oz. AGW **Series:** Monnaie de Luxe **Obv:** Radiant Toughra above crossed flags, ornamental base **Rev:** Inscription and date within star and designed border **Mint:** Qustantiniyah

Date	Mintage	VG8	F12	VF20	XF40	MS60
AH1293//26	550	—	1,375	1,950	2,200	—
AH1293//27	1,428	—	1,375	1,950	2,200	—
AH1293//28	858	—	1,375	1,950	2,200	—
AH1293//29	804	—	1,375	1,950	2,200	—
AH1293//30	1,204	—	1,375	1,950	2,200	—
AH1293//31	1,021	—	1,375	1,950	2,200	—
AH1293//32	1,334	—	1,375	1,950	2,200	—
AH1293//33	812	—	1,375	1,950	2,200	—
AH1293//34	—	—	1,375	1,950	2,500	—

Muhammad V
AH1327-36/1909-18AD

STANDARD COINAGE

KM# 759 5 PARA
1.71 g., Nickel, 16.2 mm. **Obv:** Toughra; "Reshat" to right **Rev:** Value within beaded circle above sprigs **Mint:** Qustantiniyah

Date	Mintage	G4	VG8	F12	VF20	XF40
AH1327//2	1,664,000	—	2.00	4.00	6.00	9.00
AH1327//3	21,760,000	—	0.50	1.00	2.00	4.00
AH1327//4	21,392,000	—	0.50	1.00	2.00	4.00
AH1327//5	30,579,000	—	0.50	1.00	2.00	4.00
AH1327//6	15,751,000	—	0.50	1.00	2.00	4.00
AH1327//7	2,512,000	—	10.00	15.00	20.00	30.00

KM# 767 5 PARA
Nickel **Obv:** Toughra; "el-Ghazi" to right **Rev:** Value within beaded circle above sprigs **Mint:** Qustantiniyah

Date	Mintage	G4	VG8	F12	VF20	XF40
AH1327//7	740,000	—	15.00	30.00	65.00	125

KM# 760 10 PARA
2.60 g., Nickel **Obv:** Toughra; "Reshat" to right **Rev:** Value within beaded circle above sprigs **Mint:** Qustantiniyah

Date	Mintage	G4	VG8	F12	VF20	XF40
AH1327//2	2,576,000	—	0.25	0.50	2.00	5.00
AH1327//3	18,992,000	—	0.15	0.25	1.00	3.00
AH1327//4	18,576,000	—	0.15	0.25	1.00	3.00
AH1327//5	31,799,000	—	0.15	0.25	1.00	3.00
AH1327//6	17,024,000	—	0.15	0.25	1.00	3.00
AH1327//7	21,680,000	—	0.30	0.65	1.50	4.00

KM# 768 10 PARA
2.60 g., Nickel **Obv:** Toughra; "el-Ghazi" to right **Rev:** Value within beaded circle above sprigs **Mint:** Qustantiniyah

Date	Mintage	G4	VG8	F12	VF20	XF40
AH1327//7	—	—	0.30	0.60	1.50	4.00
Note: Mintage included in KM760						
AH1327//8	7,590,000	—	0.50	1.00	4.00	10.00

KM# 761 20 PARA
Nickel **Obv:** Toughra; "Reshat" to right **Rev:** Value within beaded circle above sprigs **Mint:** Qustantiniyah

Date	Mintage	G4	VG8	F12	VF20	XF40
AH1327 No regnal year	—	—	5.00	8.50	15.00	25.00
AH1327//2	1,524,000	—	0.25	0.50	2.00	8.00
AH1327//3	11,418,000	—	0.15	0.35	1.50	6.00
AH1327//4	10,848,000	—	0.15	0.25	1.00	5.00
AH1327//5	24,350,000	—	0.15	0.25	1.00	5.00
AH1327//6	20,663,000	—	0.15	0.25	1.00	5.00
AH1327//7	—	—	—	—	1,500	2,500

KM# 769 20 PARA

Nickel **Obv:** Toughra; "el-Ghazi" to right **Mint:** Qustantiniyah

Date	Mintage	G4	VG8	F12	VF20	XF40
AH1327//7	—	—	—	—	1,500	2,500

KM# 766 40 PARA

6.10 g., Nickel, 23.8 mm. **Obv:** Toughra; "Reshat" to right **Mint:** Qustantiniyah **Note:** Struck at Qustantiniyah.

Date	Mintage	G4	VG8	F12	VF20	XF40
AH1327//3	1,992,000	—	0.50	1.00	3.00	10.00
AH1327//4	8,716,000	—	0.15	0.30	2.00	5.00
AH1327//5	9,248,000	—	0.15	0.30	2.00	5.00

KM# 779 40 PARA

Copper-Nickel **Obv:** Toughra; "el-Ghazi" to right **Rev:** Value within beaded circle above sprigs **Mint:** Qustantiniyah

Date	Mintage	G4	VG8	F12	VF20	XF40
AH1327//8	16,339,000	—	0.15	0.30	2.00	5.00
AH1327//9	3,034,000	—	1.00	2.00	10.00	25.00

KM# 748 KURUSH

1.20 g., 0.830 Silver 0.0321 oz. ASW **Obv:** Toughra within star border **Rev:** Inscription and date within star border **Mint:** Qustantiniyah

Date	Mintage	G4	VG8	F12	VF20	XF40
AH1327//1	1,270,000	—	1.25	2.50	3.50	6.00
AH1327//2	8,770,000	—	1.25	2.00	3.00	5.00
AH1327//3	840,000	—	1.50	3.00	6.00	12.50

KM# 749 2 KURUSH

2.41 g., 0.830 Silver 0.0642 oz. ASW **Obv:** Toughra; "Reshat" to right **Rev:** Inscription and date within star border **Mint:** Qustantiniyah **Note:** Varieties exist in the size of date.

Date	Mintage	G4	VG8	F12	VF20	XF40
AH1327//1	5,157,000	—	2.25	2.75	4.00	7.50
AH1327//2	11,120,000	—	2.25	2.50	3.50	6.50
AH1327//3	6,110,000	—	2.25	2.50	3.50	6.50
AH1327//4	4,031,000	—	2.25	2.50	3.50	6.50
AH1327//5	301,000	—	2.25	5.00	10.00	20.00
AH1327//6	1,884,000	—	2.25	2.75	4.50	8.00
AH1327//6/2	Inc. above	—	2.25	2.75	4.50	8.00

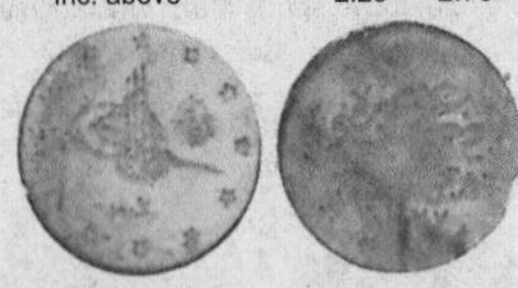

KM# 770 2 KURUSH

2.41 g., 0.830 Silver 0.0642 oz. ASW **Obv:** Toughra; "el-Ghazi" to right **Rev:** Inscription and date within star border **Mint:** Qustantiniyah **Note:** Varieties exist in the size of date.

Date	Mintage	G4	VG8	F12	VF20	XF40
AH1327//7	17,000	—	12.50	25.00	40.00	75.00
AH1327//8	398,000	—	20.00	30.00	50.00	100
AH1327//9	8,000	—	250	350	450	600

KM# 750 5 KURUSH

6.01 g., 0.830 Silver 0.1605 oz. ASW **Obv:** Toughra; "Reshat" to right **Rev:** Inscription and date within star border and design **Mint:** Qustantiniyah

Date	Mintage	G4	VG8	F12	VF20	XF40
AH1327//1	1,558,000	—	3.00	8.00	10.00	15.00
AH1327//2	1,886,000	—	3.00	8.00	10.00	15.00
AH1327//3	1,273,000	—	3.00	8.00	10.00	15.00
AH1327//4	1,635,000	—	3.00	8.00	10.00	15.00
AH1327//5	194,000	—	6.00	12.00	18.00	30.00
AH1327//6	664,000	—	3.00	8.00	10.00	15.00
AH1327//7	834,000	—	3.00	8.00	15.00	20.00

KM# 771 5 KURUSH

6.01 g., 0.830 Silver 0.1605 oz. ASW **Obv:** Toughra; "el-Ghazi" to right **Rev:** Inscription and date within star border and design **Mint:** Qustantiniyah

Date	Mintage	G4	VG8	F12	VF20	XF40
AH1327//7	—	—	3.00	8.00	15.00	25.00
Note: Mintage included in KM750						
AH1327//8	648,000	—	6.00	10.00	15.00	25.00
AH1327//9	3,938	—	100	200	250	350

KM# 751 10 KURUSH

12.03 g., 0.830 Silver 0.3209 oz. ASW **Obv:** Toughra; "Reshat" to right **Rev:** Inscription and date within star border and design **Mint:** Qustantiniyah

Date	Mintage	G4	VG8	F12	VF20	XF40
AH1327//1	110,000	—	13.50	25.00	50.00	100
AH1327//2	Inc. above	—	12.00	20.00	50.00	100
AH1327//3	8,000	—	70.00	125	1,000	1,600
AH1327//4	96,000	—	12.00	15.00	20.00	30.00
AH1327//5	34,000	—	12.00	20.00	50.00	100
AH1327//6	81,000	—	6.25	15.00	20.00	35.00
AH1327//7	582,000	—	6.25	12.00	18.00	32.00

KM# 772 10 KURUSH

12.03 g., 0.830 Silver 0.3209 oz. ASW **Obv:** Toughra; "el-Ghazi" to right **Rev:** Inscription and date within star border and design **Mint:** Qustantiniyah

Date	Mintage	G4	VG8	F12	VF20	XF40
AH1327//7	—	—	6.25	12.00	15.00	28.00
Note: Mintage included in KM751						
AH1327//8	408,000	—	6.25	12.00	18.00	32.00
AH1327//9	299,000	—	12.50	25.00	40.00	60.00
AH1327//10	666,000	—	15.00	30.00	60.00	85.00

KM# 780 20 KURUSH

24.06 g., 0.830 Silver 0.6419 oz. ASW, 37 mm. **Obv:** Toughra within star border and cresent wreath **Rev:** Inscription and date within star border and crescent wreath **Mint:** Qustantiniyah

Date	Mintage	G4	VG8	F12	VF20	XF40
AH1327//8	713,000	—	—	12.50	30.00	50.00
AH1327//9	5,962,000	—	—	12.50	30.00	50.00
AH1327//10	11,025,000	—	—	12.50	30.00	50.00

MILLED COINAGE

Gold Issues

KM# 762 12-1/2 KURUSH

0.90 g., 0.917 Gold 0.0266 oz. AGW **Series:** Monnaie de Luxe **Obv:** Toughra; "Reshat" to right **Rev:** Value and date within designed wreath **Mint:** Qustantiniyah

Date	Mintage	VG8	F12	VF20	XF40	MS60
AH1327//2	—	35.50	50.00	180	250	—
AH1327//3	50,368	35.50	50.00	180	250	—
AH1327//4	19,344	35.50	50.00	180	250	—
AH1327//5	9,160	35.50	50.00	180	250	—
AH1327//6	11,880	35.50	50.00	180	250	—

KM# 752 25 KURUSH

1.80 g., 0.917 Gold 0.0532 oz. AGW **Obv:** Toughra; "Reshat" to right **Rev:** Inscription and date within wreath, star on top **Mint:** Qustantiniyah

Date	Mintage	VG8	F12	VF20	XF40	MS60
AH1327//1	115,484	—	71.00	95.00	125	—
AH1327//2	194,740	—	71.00	95.00	125	—
AH1327//3	249,416	—	71.00	95.00	125	—
AH1327//4	338,172	—	71.00	95.00	125	—
AH1327//5	167,592	—	71.00	95.00	125	—
AH1327//6	72,872	—	71.00	95.00	125	—

KM# 763 25 KURUSH

1.75 g., 0.917 Gold 0.0517 oz. AGW **Series:** Monnaie de Luxe **Obv:** Toughra within designed wreath **Rev:** Inscription and date within designed wreath **Mint:** Qustantiniyah

Date	Mintage	VG8	F12	VF20	XF40	MS60
AH1327//2	47,788	69.00	100	125	150	—
AH1327//3	70,775	69.00	100	125	150	—
AH1327//4	47,088	69.00	100	125	150	—
AH1327//5	25,964	69.00	100	135	180	—
AH1327//6	23,348	69.00	100	135	180	—

KM# 773 25 KURUSH

1.80 g., 0.917 Gold 0.0532 oz. AGW **Obv:** Toughra; "el-Ghazi" to right **Rev:** Inscription and date within wreath, star on top **Mint:** Qustantiniyah

Date	Mintage	VG8	F12	VF20	XF40	MS60
AH1327//7	22,420	—	71.00	100	150	—
AH1327//8	5,926	—	71.00	150	200	—
AH1327//9	4,060	—	71.00	150	200	—
AH1327//10	53,524	1,000	1,500	2,000	2,500	—

KM# 774 25 KURUSH

1.75 g., 0.917 Gold 0.0517 oz. AGW **Series:** Monnaie de Luxe **Obv:** Toughra **Mint:** Qustantiniyah

Date	Mintage	VG8	F12	VF20	XF40	MS60
AH1327//8	10,612	1,750	2,500	3,500	5,000	—

KM# 753 50 KURUSH

3.61 g., 0.917 Gold 0.1064 oz. AGW **Obv:** Toughra; "Reshat" to right **Rev:** Inscription and date within wreath, star on top **Mint:** Qustantiniyah

Date	Mintage	VG8	F12	VF20	XF40	MS60
AH1327//1	6,276	1,000	1,500	2,000	3,000	—
AH1327//2	89,712	—	142	200	220	—
AH1327//3	75,442	—	142	200	220	—
AH1327//4	96,030	—	142	200	220	—
AH1327//5	40,618	—	142	200	220	—
AH1327//6	26,408	—	142	200	220	—

KM# 764 50 KURUSH
3.51 g., 0.917 Gold 0.1034 oz. AGW **Series:** Monnaie de Luxe **Obv:** Toughra within designed wreath **Rev:** Inscription and date within designed wreath **Mint:** Qustantiniyah

Date	Mintage	VG8	F12	VF20	XF40	MS60
AH1327//2	25,224	—	137	200	250	—
AH1327//3	23,971	—	137	200	250	—
AH1327//4	15,716	—	137	200	250	—
AH1327//5	17,118	—	137	200	250	—
AH1327//6	8,706	—	137	220	250	—

KM# 775 50 KURUSH
3.61 g., 0.917 Gold 0.1064 oz. AGW **Obv:** Toughra; "el-Ghazi" to right **Mint:** Qustantiniyah

Date	Mintage	VG8	F12	VF20	XF40	MS60
AH1327//7	9,175	—	142	225	280	—
AH1327//8	7,330	—	142	225	280	—
AH1327//9	2,000	—	142	225	280	—
AH1327//10	53,524	1,000	1,500	2,000	3,000	—

KM# 781 50 KURUSH
3.51 g., 0.917 Gold 0.1034 oz. AGW **Series:** Monnaie de Luxe **Obv:** Toughra **Mint:** Qustantiniyah

Date	Mintage	VG8	F12	VF20	XF40	MS60
AH1327//8	3,291	250	500	950	1,500	—

KM# 754 100 KURUSH
7.22 g., 0.917 Gold 0.2127 oz. AGW **Obv:** Toughra; "Reshat" to right **Rev:** Inscription and date within wreath, star on top **Mint:** Qustantiniyah

Date	Mintage	VG8	F12	VF20	XF40	MS60
AH1327//1	1,715,274	—	—	285	400	425
Note: Combined mintage total, with 100 Kurush KM#730, AH1293//34						
AH1327//2	3,376,679	—	—	285	400	425
AH1327//3	4,627,115	—	—	285	400	425
AH1327//4	3,591,676	—	—	285	400	425
AH1327//5	881,895	—	—	285	400	425
AH1327//6	3,769,100	—	—	285	400	425
AH1327//7	2,989,609	—	—	285	400	425

KM# 755 100 KURUSH
7.02 g., 0.917 Gold 0.2068 oz. AGW **Series:** Monnaie de Luxe **Obv:** Toughra within designed wreath **Rev:** Inscription and date within designed wreath **Mint:** Istanbul

Date	Mintage	VG8	F12	VF20	XF40	MS60
AH1327//1	—	—	275	400	420	—
AH1327//2	37,110	—	275	400	420	—
AH1327//3	53,738	—	275	400	420	—
AH1327//4	41,507	—	275	400	420	—
AH1327//5	58,819	—	275	400	420	—
AH1327//6	19,768	—	275	400	420	—

KM# 776 100 KURUSH
7.22 g., 0.917 Gold 0.2127 oz. AGW **Obv:** Toughra; "el-Ghazi" to right **Rev:** Inscription and date within wreath, star on top **Mint:** Qustantiniyah

Date	Mintage	VG8	F12	VF20	XF40	MS60
AH1327//7	1,232,090	—	—	285	420	—
AH1327//8	Inc. above	—	—	285	420	—
AH1327//9	3,582,005	—	—	285	420	—
AH1327//10	—	—	—	285	450	—

KM# 782 100 KURUSH
7.02 g., 0.917 Gold 0.2068 oz. AGW **Series:** Monnaie de Luxe **Obv:** Toughra **Mint:** Qustantiniyah

Date	Mintage	G4	VG8	F12	VF20	XF40
AH1327//8	13,250	275	400	450	650	1,000

KM# 756 250 KURUSH
18.04 g., 0.917 Gold 0.5319 oz. AGW **Obv:** Toughra; "Reshat" to right **Rev:** Inscription and date within wreath, star on top **Mint:** Qustantiniyah

Date	Mintage	VG8	F12	VF20	XF40	MS60
AH1327//1	6,878	—	710	1,100	1,400	—
AH1327//2	9,207	—	710	1,100	1,400	—
AH1327//3	9,990	—	710	1,100	1,400	—
AH1327//4	13,400	—	710	1,100	1,400	—
AH1327//5	18,143	—	710	1,100	1,400	—
AH1327//6	6,155	—	710	1,100	1,400	—

KM# 757 250 KURUSH
17.54 g., 0.917 Gold 0.5171 oz. AGW **Series:** Monnaie de Luxe **Obv:** Toughra within designed wreath **Rev:** Inscription and date within designed wreath **Mint:** Qustantiniyah

Date	Mintage	VG8	F12	VF20	XF40	MS60
AH1327//1	—	—	690	1,100	1,500	—
AH1327//2	6,995	—	690	1,100	1,500	—
AH1327//3	12,084	—	690	1,100	1,500	—
AH1327//4	10,250	—	690	1,100	1,500	—
AH1327//5	16,879	—	690	1,100	1,500	—
AH1327//6	9,039	—	690	1,100	1,500	—

KM# 777 250 KURUSH
18.04 g., 0.917 Gold 0.5319 oz. AGW **Obv:** Toughra; "el-Ghazi" to right **Rev:** Inscription and date within wreath, star on top **Mint:** Qustantiniyah

Date	Mintage	VG8	F12	VF20	XF40	MS60
AH1327//7	30	1,250	1,750	2,800	4,000	—
AH1327//8	21	1,750	2,500	3,500	5,000	—
AH1327//9	28	1,750	2,500	3,500	5,000	—

KM# 783 250 KURUSH
17.54 g., 0.917 Gold 0.5171 oz. AGW **Series:** Monnaie de Luxe **Obv:** Toughra within designed wreath **Rev:** Inscription and date within designed wreath **Mint:** Qustantiniyah

Date	Mintage	VG8	F12	VF20	XF40	MS60
AH1327//8 Rare	3,107	—	—	—	—	—

KM# 758 500 KURUSH
35.08 g., 0.917 Gold 1.0342 oz. AGW **Obv:** Toughra; "Reshat" to right **Rev:** Inscription and date within wreath, star on top **Mint:** Qustantiniyah

Date	Mintage	VG8	F12	VF20	XF40	MS60
AH1327//1	39,028	—	1,375	1,800	2,000	—
AH1327//2	37,474	—	1,375	1,800	2,000	—
AH1327//3	53,900	—	1,375	1,800	2,000	—
AH1327//4	41,863	—	1,375	1,800	2,000	—
AH1327//5	36,996	—	1,375	1,800	2,000	—
AH1327//6	17,792	—	1,375	1,800	2,000	—

KM# 765 500 KURUSH
35.08 g., 0.917 Gold 1.0342 oz. AGW **Series:** Monnaie de Luxe **Obv:** Radiant Toughra above crossed flags, ornamental base **Rev:** Inscription and date within designed wreath **Mint:** Qustantiniyah

Date	Mintage	VG8	F12	VF20	XF40	MS60
AH1327//2	1,718	—	1,375	1,900	2,200	—
AH1327//3	4,631	—	1,375	1,900	2,200	—
AH1327//4	3,887	—	1,375	1,900	2,200	—
AH1327//5	5,145	—	1,375	1,900	2,200	—
AH1327//6	2,401	—	1,375	1,900	2,200	—

KM# 778 500 KURUSH
35.08 g., 0.917 Gold 1.0342 oz. AGW **Series:** Monnaie de Luxe **Obv:** Radiant Toughra above crossed flags, ornamental base **Rev:** Inscription and date within designed wreath **Mint:** Qustantiniyah **Note:** Struck at Qustantiniyah.

Date	Mintage	VG8	F12	VF20	XF40	MS60
AH1327//7	295	1,375	2,100	2,500	3,500	—
AH1327//8	1,618	1,375	2,100	2,200	3,000	—

KM# 784 500 KURUSH
36.08 g., 0.917 Gold 1.0637 oz. AGW **Obv:** Toughra; "el-Ghazi" to right **Rev:** Inscription and date within wreath, star on top **Mint:** Qustantiniyah

Date	Mintage	VG8	F12	VF20	XF40	MS60
AH1327//7	484	2,000	2,500	3,500	5,000	—
AH1327//8	19	2,000	2,750	4,250	6,000	—
AH1327//9	22	2,000	2,750	4,250	6,000	—
AH1327//10	—	2,000	2,500	3,500	5,000	—

MILLED COINAGE

Muhammad V's visit to Bursa
Gold Mint Visit Issues

KM# 787 25 KURUSH
1.80 g., 0.917 Gold 0.0532 oz. AGW **Obv:** Toughra in center of sprigs and stars **Rev:** Inscription and date within wreath, star on top **Mint:** Bursa

Date	Mintage	F12	VF20	XF40	MS60	MS63
AH1327//1	—	225	450	750	1,250	—

KM# 788 50 KURUSH
3.61 g., 0.917 Gold 0.1064 oz. AGW **Obv:** Toughra in center of sprigs and stars **Rev:** Inscription and date within wreath, star on top **Mint:** Bursa

Date	Mintage	F12	VF20	XF40	MS60	MS63
AH1327//1	—	275	550	900	1,500	—

KM# 789 100 KURUSH
7.22 g., 0.917 Gold 0.2127 oz. AGW **Obv:** Toughra in center of sprigs and stars **Rev:** Inscription and date within wreath, star on top **Mint:** Bursa

Date	Mintage	F12	VF20	XF40	MS60	MS63
AH1327//1	—	375	400	475	750	—

MILLED COINAGE

Muhammad V's visit to Edirne
Gold Mint Visit Issues

KM# 793 50 KURUSH
3.61 g., 0.917 Gold 0.1064 oz. AGW **Obv:** Toughra in center of sprigs and stars **Rev:** Inscription and date within wreath, star on top **Mint:** Edirne

Date	Mintage	F12	VF20	XF40	MS60	MS63
AH1327//2	—	240	300	500	900	—

KM# 794 100 KURUSH
7.22 g., 0.917 Gold 0.2127 oz. AGW **Obv:** Toughra in center of sprigs and stars **Rev:** Inscription and date within wreath, star on top **Mint:** Edirne

Date	Mintage	F12	VF20	XF40	MS60	MS63
AH1327//2	—	450	500	650	1,000	—

KM# 795 500 KURUSH
36.08 g., 0.917 Gold 1.0637 oz. AGW **Obv:** Toughra in center of sprigs and stars **Rev:** Inscription and date within wreath, star on top **Mint:** Edirne

Date	Mintage	F12	VF20	XF40	MS60	MS63
AH1327//2	—	2,000	3,000	4,500	7,000	—

MILLED COINAGE

Muhammad V's visit to Kosova
Gold Mint Visit Issues

KM# 799 50 KURUSH
3.61 g., 0.917 Gold 0.1064 oz. AGW **Obv:** Toughra in center of sprigs and stars **Rev:** Inscription and date within wreath, star on top **Mint:** Kosova

Date	Mintage	F12	VF20	XF40	MS60	MS63
AH1327//3	1,200	225	450	750	1,250	—

KM# 800 100 KURUSH
7.22 g., 0.917 Gold 0.2127 oz. AGW **Obv:** Toughra in center of stars and sprigs **Rev:** Inscription and date within wreath, star on top **Mint:** Kosova

Date	Mintage	F12	VF20	XF40	MS60	MS63
AH1327//3	750	400	450	600	900	—

KM# 801 500 KURUSH
36.08 g., 0.917 Gold 1.0637 oz. AGW **Obv:** Toughra in center of stars and sprigs **Rev:** Inscription and date within wreath, star on top **Mint:** Kosova

Date	Mintage	F12	VF20	XF40	MS60	MS63
AH1327//3	20	3,250	4,500	7,500	12,500	—

MILLED COINAGE

Muhammad V's visit to Manastir
Gold Mint Visit Issues

KM# 805 50 KURUSH
3.61 g., 0.917 Gold 0.1064 oz. AGW **Obv:** Toughra in center of sprigs and stars **Rev:** Inscription and date within wreath, star on top **Mint:** Manastir

Date	Mintage	F12	VF20	XF40	MS60	MS63
AH1327//3	1,200	225	450	750	1,250	—

KM# 806 100 KURUSH
7.22 g., 0.917 Gold 0.2127 oz. AGW **Obv:** Toughra in center of sprigs and stars **Rev:** Inscription and date within wreath, star on top **Mint:** Manastir

Date	Mintage	F12	VF20	XF40	MS60	MS63
AH1327//3	750	400	450	650	1,000	—

KM# 807 500 KURUSH
36.08 g., 0.917 Gold 1.0637 oz. AGW **Obv:** Toughra in center of sprigs and stars **Rev:** Inscription and date within wreath, star on top **Mint:** Manastir

Date	Mintage	F12	VF20	XF40	MS60	MS63
AH1327//3	20	3,500	6,500	9,500	17,500	—

MILLED COINAGE

Muhammad V's visit to Salonika
Gold Mint Visit Issues

KM# 811 50 KURUSH
3.61 g., 0.917 Gold 0.1064 oz. AGW **Obv:** Toughra in center of sprigs and stars **Rev:** Inscription and date within wreath, star on top **Mint:** Salonika

Date	Mintage	F12	VF20	XF40	MS60	MS63
AH1327//3	1,200	225	450	750	1,250	—

KM# 812 100 KURUSH
7.22 g., 0.917 Gold 0.2127 oz. AGW **Obv:** Toughra in center of sprigs and stars **Rev:** Inscription and date within wreath, star on top **Mint:** Salonika

Date	Mintage	F12	VF20	XF40	MS60	MS63
AH1327//3	750	400	500	850	1,350	—

KM# 813 500 KURUSH
36.08 g., 0.917 Gold 1.0637 oz. AGW **Obv:** Toughra in center of sprigs and stars **Rev:** Inscription and date within wreath, star on top **Mint:** Salonika

Date	Mintage	F12	VF20	XF40	MS60	MS63
AH1327//3	20	3,500	6,500	9,500	17,500	—

MINT VISIT COINAGE

Silver Issues

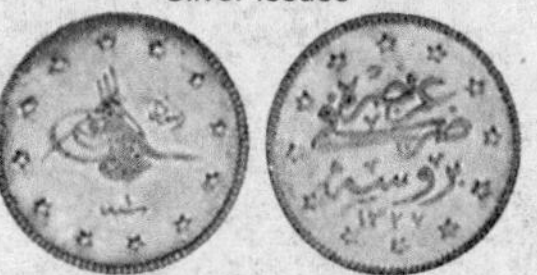

KM# 785 2 KURUSH
2.41 g., 0.830 Silver 0.0642 oz. ASW **Obv:** Toughra within star border **Rev:** Inscription and date within star border **Mint:** Bursa

Date	Mintage	F12	VF20	XF40	MS60	MS63
AH1327//1	—	15.00	25.00	45.00	75.00	125

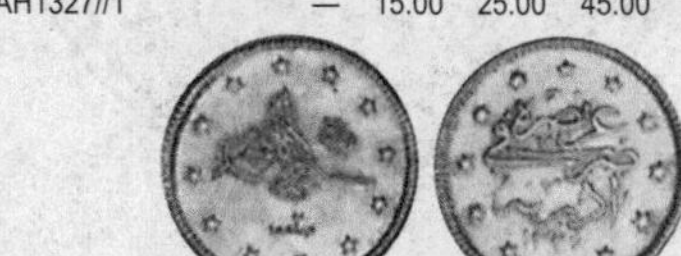

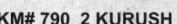

KM# 790 2 KURUSH
2.41 g., 0.830 Silver 0.0642 oz. ASW **Obv:** Toughra within star border **Rev:** Inscription and date within star border **Mint:** Edirne

Date	Mintage	F12	VF20	XF40	MS60	MS63
AH1327//2	—	15.00	25.00	45.00	75.00	125

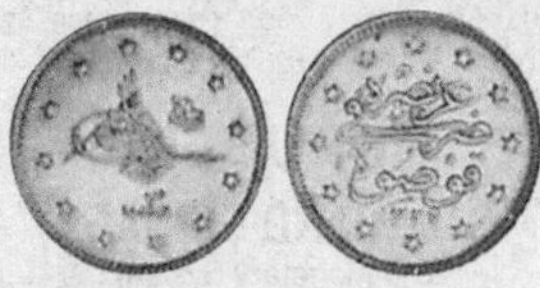

KM# 796 2 KURUSH
2.41 g., 0.830 Silver 0.0642 oz. ASW **Obv:** Toughra within star border **Rev:** Inscription and date within star border **Mint:** Kosova

Date	Mintage	F12	VF20	XF40	MS60	MS63
AH1327//3	13,000	15.00	30.00	50.00	100	150

KM# 802 2 KURUSH
2.41 g., 0.830 Silver 0.0642 oz. ASW **Obv:** Toughra within star border **Rev:** Inscription and date within star border **Mint:** Manastir

Date	Mintage	F12	VF20	XF40	MS60	MS63
AH1327//3	13,000	15.00	30.00	50.00	100	150

KM# 808 2 KURUSH
2.41 g., 0.830 Silver 0.0642 oz. ASW **Obv:** Toughra within star border **Rev:** Inscription and date within star border **Mint:** Salonika

Date	Mintage	F12	VF20	XF40	MS60	MS63
AH1327//3	13,000	15.00	30.00	50.00	100	150

KM# 786 5 KURUSH
6.01 g., 0.830 Silver 0.1605 oz. ASW **Obv:** Toughra within star border and design **Rev:** Inscription and date within star border and design **Mint:** Bursa

Date	Mintage	F12	VF20	XF40	MS60	MS63
AH1327//1	—	20.00	50.00	100	200	275

KM# 791 5 KURUSH
6.01 g., 0.830 Silver 0.1605 oz. ASW **Obv:** Toughra within star border and design **Rev:** Inscription and date within star border and design **Mint:** Edirne

Date	Mintage	F12	VF20	XF40	MS60	MS63
AH1327//2	—	20.00	50.00	100	200	275

KM# 797 5 KURUSH
6.01 g., 0.830 Silver 0.1605 oz. ASW **Obv:** Toughra within star border and design **Rev:** Inscription and date within star border and design **Mint:** Kosova

Date	Mintage	F12	VF20	XF40	MS60	MS63
AH1327//3	3,000	20.00	50.00	100	225	300

KM# 803 5 KURUSH
6.01 g., 0.830 Silver 0.1605 oz. ASW **Obv:** Toughra within star border and design **Rev:** Inscription and date within star border and design **Mint:** Manastir

Date	Mintage	F12	VF20	XF40	MS60	MS63
AH1327//3	3,000	20.00	50.00	100	225	300

KM# 809 5 KURUSH
6.01 g., 0.830 Silver 0.1605 oz. ASW **Obv:** Toughra within star border and design **Rev:** Inscription and date within star border and design **Mint:** Salonika

Date	Mintage	F12	VF20	XF40	MS60	MS63
AH1327//3	3,000	20.00	50.00	100	225	300

KM# 792 10 KURUSH
12.03 g., 0.830 Silver 0.3209 oz. ASW **Obv:** Toughra within star border and design **Rev:** Inscription and date within star border and design **Mint:** Edirne

Date	Mintage	F12	VF20	XF40	MS60	MS63
AH1327//2	—	90.00	150	225	375	500

KM# 798 10 KURUSH
12.03 g., 0.830 Silver 0.3209 oz. ASW **Obv:** Toughra within star border and crescent wreath **Rev:** Inscription and date within star border and crescent wreath **Mint:** Kosova

Date	Mintage	F12	VF20	XF40	MS60	MS63
AH1327//3	1,500	100	175	300	500	675

KM# 804 10 KURUSH
12.03 g., 0.830 Silver 0.3209 oz. ASW **Obv:** Toughra within star border and design **Rev:** Inscription and date within star border and design **Mint:** Manastir

Date	Mintage	F12	VF20	XF40	MS60	MS63
AH1327//3	1,500	100	200	350	550	750

KM# 810 10 KURUSH
12.03 g., 0.830 Silver 0.3209 oz. ASW **Obv:** Toughra within star border and design **Rev:** Inscription and date within star border and design **Mint:** Salonika

Date	Mintage	F12	VF20	XF40	MS60	MS63
AH1327//3	1,500	100	200	350	550	750

Muhammad VI
AH1336-41/1918-23AD

STANDARD COINAGE

KM# 828 40 PARA
5.90 g., Copper-Nickel, 23.7 mm. **Obv:** Toughra within beaded circle above sprigs **Rev:** Value within beaded circle above sprigs **Mint:** Qustantiniyah

Date	Mintage	G4	VG8	F12	VF20	XF40
AH1336//4	6,520,000	—	3.00	5.00	8.00	15.00

KM# 815 2 KURUSH
2.41 g., 0.830 Silver 0.0642 oz. ASW **Obv:** Toughra within star border **Rev:** Inscription and date within star border **Mint:** Qustantiniyah

Date	Mintage	G4	VG8	F12	VF20	XF40
AH1336//1	25,000	—	50.00	150	180	220
AH1336//2	3,000	—	75.00	180	250	400

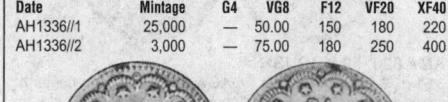

KM# 816 5 KURUSH

6.01 g., 0.830 Silver 0.1605 oz. ASW **Obv:** Toughra within star border and crescent wreath **Rev:** Inscription and date within star border and crescent wreath **Mint:** Qustantiniyah

Date	Mintage	G4	VG8	F12	VF20	XF40
AH1336//1	10,000	—	50.00	180	220	300
AH1336//2	2,000	—	75.00	250	280	450

KM# 817 10 KURUSH

12.03 g., 0.830 Silver 0.3209 oz. ASW **Obv:** Toughra within star border and crescent wreath **Rev:** Inscription and date within star border and crescent wreath **Mint:** Qustantiniyah

Date	Mintage	G4	VG8	F12	VF20	XF40
AH1336//1	10,000	—	120	350	450	800
AH1336//2	2,000	—	200	450	800	1,200

KM# 818 20 KURUSH

24.06 g., 0.830 Silver 0.6419 oz. ASW, 37 mm. **Obv:** Toughra within star border and crescent wreath **Rev:** Inscription and date within star border and crescent wreath **Mint:** Qustantiniyah

Date	Mintage	G4	VG8	F12	VF20	XF40
AH1336//1	—	—	35.00	65.00	125	185
AH1336//2	1,530	—	350	525	650	925

MILLED COINAGE

Gold Issues

KM# 819 25 KURUSH

1.80 g., 0.917 Gold 0.0532 oz. AGW **Obv:** Toughra in center of sprigs and stars **Rev:** Inscription and date within wreath, star on top **Mint:** Qustantiniyah

Date	Mintage	VG8	F12	VF20	XF40	MS60
AH1336//1	53,524	100	110	125	190	—
AH1336//2	62,253	100	110	125	190	—
AH1336//3	52,421	100	110	195	290	—
AH1336//4	400	125	195	295	475	—
AH1336//5	819	125	195	325	475	—

KM# 825 25 KURUSH

1.75 g., 0.917 Gold 0.0517 oz. AGW **Series:** Monnaie de Luxe **Obv:** Toughra **Mint:** Qustantiniyah

Date	Mintage	VG8	F12	VF20	XF40	MS60
AH1336//2	8,400	100	125	195	295	—
AH1336//3	11,179	100	125	195	295	—

KM# 820 50 KURUSH

3.61 g., 0.917 Gold 0.1064 oz. AGW **Obv:** Toughra in center of sprigs and stars **Rev:** Inscription and date within wreath, star on top **Mint:** Qustantiniyah

Date	Mintage	VG8	F12	VF20	XF40	MS60
AH1336//1	162,363	142	220	250	325	—
AH1336//2	346	142	220	250	325	—
AH1336//3	447	142	225	275	525	—
AH1336//4	200	275	475	775	1,500	—
AH1336//5	204	225	325	475	1,000	—

KM# 821 100 KURUSH

7.22 g., 0.917 Gold 0.2127 oz. AGW **Obv:** Toughra in center of sprigs and stars **Rev:** Inscription and date within wreath, star on top **Mint:** Qustantiniyah

Date	Mintage	VG8	F12	VF20	XF40	MS60
AH1336//1	5,036,830	—	285	425	450	—
AH1336//2	37,634	—	285	425	450	—
AH1336//3	30,313	—	285	425	525	—
AH1336/4	200	450	600	800	1,000	—
AH1336//5	—	450	600	800	1,000	—

KM# 826 100 KURUSH

7.02 g., 0.917 Gold 0.2068 oz. AGW **Series:** Monnaie de Luxe **Obv:** Toughra in center of legend **Rev:** Inscription and date in center of legend **Mint:** Qustantiniyah

Date	Mintage	VG8	F12	VF20	XF40	MS60
AH1336//2	33,077	400	450	475	550	—
AH1336//3	20,248	400	450	475	550	—

KM# 822 250 KURUSH

18.04 g., 0.917 Gold 0.5319 oz. AGW **Obv:** Toughra in center of sprigs and stars **Rev:** Inscription and date within wreath, star on top **Mint:** Qustantiniyah

Date	Mintage	VG8	F12	VF20	XF40	MS60
AH1336//1	39	1,750	3,000	4,500	6,500	—
AH1336//2	26	1,750	3,000	4,500	6,500	—
AH1336//3	31	1,750	3,000	4,500	6,500	—
AH1336/4	20	1,750	3,000	4,500	6,500	—
AH1336/5	21	1,750	3,000	4,500	6,500	—

KM# 827 250 KURUSH

17.54 g., 0.917 Gold 0.5171 oz. AGW **Series:** Monnaie de Luxe **Obv:** Toughra within beaded circle **Rev:** Inscription and date within beaded circle **Mint:** Qustantiniyah

Date	Mintage	VG8	F12	VF20	XF40	MS60
AH1336//2	5,995	690	1,000	1,150	1,350	—
AH1336//3	12,739	690	1,000	1,150	1,350	—

KM# 823 500 KURUSH

36.08 g., 0.917 Gold 1.0637 oz. AGW **Obv:** Toughra in center of sprigs and stars **Rev:** Inscription and date within wreath, star on top **Mint:** Qustantiniyah **Note:** Beware of counterfeits

Date	Mintage	VG8	F12	VF20	XF40	MS60
AH1336//1	26,984	1,950	2,000	2,100	2,400	—
AH1336//2	22,192	1,950	2,000	2,100	2,400	—
AH1336//3	16,424	1,950	2,000	2,100	2,400	—
AH1336//4	23	2,500	4,500	6,500	8,500	—
AH1336//5	22	2,500	4,500	6,500	8,500	—

KM# 824 500 KURUSH

35.08 g., 0.917 Gold 1.0342 oz. AGW **Series:** Monnaie de Luxe **Obv:** Radiant Toughra above crossed flags, ornamental base **Rev:** Inscription and date within designed wreath **Mint:** Qustantiniyah

Date	Mintage	VG8	F12	VF20	XF40	MS60
AH1336//1	—	1,375	1,900	2,000	2,650	—
AH1336//2	—	—	1,375	1,900	2,000	—
AH1336//3	5,207	—	1,375	1,900	2,000	—
AH1336//4	88	1,525	2,250	2,750	3,450	—

REPUBLIC

STANDARD COINAGE

Old Monetary System

KM# 830 100 PARA

2.00 g., Aluminum-Bronze **Obv:** Inscription and date to left of oat sprig **Rev:** Value to left of sprig, crescent and star at top **Mint:** Istanbul

Date	Mintage	F12	VF20	XF40	MS60	MS63
AH1340	1,798,026	3.00	5.00	10.00	60.00	100
AH1341	5,582,846	1.00	2.50	5.00	30.00	75.00

KM# 834 100 PARA

Aluminum-Bronze **Obv:** Inscription and date to left of oat sprig **Rev:** Value to left of sprig, crescent and star on top **Mint:** Istanbul

Date	Mintage	F12	VF20	XF40	MS60	MS63
1926	4,388,266	1.00	2.50	6.00	32.00	75.00
1928	4,000	150	225	300	600	750

KM# 831 5 KURUS

4.00 g., Aluminum-Bronze **Obv:** Inscription and date to left of oat sprig **Rev:** Value to left of sprig, crescent and star on top **Mint:** Istanbul

Date	Mintage	F12	VF20	XF40	MS60	MS63
AH1340	5,023,238	1.00	2.50	7.00	32.00	75.00
AH1341	23,544,591	1.00	2.50	7.00	32.00	75.00

KM# 835 5 KURUS

Aluminum-Bronze **Obv:** Inscription and date to left of oat sprig **Rev:** Value to left of sprig, crescent and star on top **Mint:** Istanbul

Date	Mintage	F12	VF20	XF40	MS60	MS63
1926	355,910	1.00	2.50	7.00	32.00	75.00
1928	2,000	175	250	500	700	900

KM# 832 10 KURUS

Aluminum-Bronze **Obv:** Inscription and date to left of oat sprig **Rev:** Value to left of sprig, crescent and star on top **Mint:** Istanbul **Note:** Varieties exist.

Date	Mintage	F12	VF20	XF40	MS60	MS63
AH1340	4,836,483	1.50	3.00	8.00	35.00	75.00
AH1341	14,223,098	1.50	3.00	8.00	35.00	75.00

KM# 836 10 KURUS

Aluminum-Bronze **Obv:** Inscription and date to left of oat sprig **Rev:** Value to left of sprigs, crescent and star on top **Mint:** Istanbul

Date	Mintage	F12	VF20	XF40	MS60	MS63
1926	855,982	1.50	3.00	8.00	35.00	75.00
1928	1,000	125	200	375	750	900

KM# 833 25 KURUS

9.87 g., Nickel, 30 mm. **Obv:** Inscription and date to left of oat sprig **Rev:** Value to left of sprigs, crescent and star on top **Mint:** Istanbul

Date	Mintage	F12	VF20	XF40	MS60	MS63
AH1341	4,972,686	2.00	4.00	10.00	30.00	75.00

KM# 837 25 KURUS

9.87 g., Nickel, 30 mm. **Obv:** Inscription and date to left of oat sprig **Rev:** Value to left of sprigs, crescent and star on top **Mint:** Istanbul **Note:** Varieties exist.

Date	Mintage	F12	VF20	XF40	MS60	MS63
1926	26,869	175	275	475	750	—
1928	5,794,000	1.50	3.00	8.00	75.00	—

KM# 840 25 KURUSH

1.80 g., 0.917 Gold 0.0532 oz. AGW **Obv:** Inscription and date within wreath **Rev:** Star divides inner circle above inscription and date **Mint:** Istanbul

Date	Mintage	F12	VF20	XF40	MS60	MS63
1926	4,539	71.00	100	140	175	235
1927	14,000	71.00	100	120	150	200
1928	8,424	71.00	100	130	165	220
1929	—	71.00	100	120	150	200

KM# 844 25 KURUSH

1.75 g., 0.917 Gold 0.0517 oz. AGW, 23 mm. **Series:** Monnaie de Luxe **Obv:** Radiant star and crescent above inscription within sprigs **Rev:** Value and date within designed wreath **Mint:** Istanbul

Date	Mintage	F12	VF20	XF40	MS60	MS63
1927	4,103	69.00	120	225	300	—
1928	4,549	69.00	120	225	300	—

KM# 841 50 KURUSH

3.61 g., 0.917 Gold 0.1064 oz. AGW **Obv:** Inscription and date within wreath **Rev:** Star divides circle above inscription and date **Mint:** Istanbul

Date	Mintage	F12	VF20	XF40	MS60	MS63
1926	2,168	155	200	225	275	325
1927	2,116	155	200	225	275	325
1928	2,431	155	200	225	275	325
1929	—	155	200	225	275	325

KM# 845 50 KURUSH

3.51 g., 0.917 Gold 0.1034 oz. AGW, 28 mm. **Series:** Monnaie de Luxe **Obv:** Radiant star and crescent above inscription within sprigs **Rev:** Inscription and date within designed wreath **Mint:** Istanbul

Date	Mintage	F12	VF20	XF40	MS60	MS63
1927	3,903	152	225	375	575	—
1928	3,620	152	225	375	575	—

KM# 842 100 KURUSH

7.22 g., 0.917 Gold 0.2127 oz. AGW **Obv:** Inscription and date within wreath **Rev:** Star divides circle above inscription and date **Mint:** Istanbul

Date	Mintage	F12	VF20	XF40	MS60	MS63
1926	1,073	—	285	450	475	550
1927	—	—	285	450	475	550
1928	920	—	285	450	475	550
1929	—	—	285	450	475	550

KM# 846 100 KURUSH

7.02 g., 0.917 Gold 0.2068 oz. AGW, 35 mm. **Series:** Monnaie de Luxe **Mint:** Istanbul

Date	Mintage	F12	VF20	XF40	MS60	MS63
1927	8,676	—	275	425	450	—
1928	6,092	—	275	425	450	—

KM# 843 250 KURUSH

18.04 g., 0.917 Gold 0.5319 oz. AGW **Obv:** Inscription and date within wreath **Rev:** Star divides circle above inscription and date **Mint:** Istanbul

Date	Mintage	F12	VF20	XF40	MS60	MS63
1926	604	—	710	1,000	1,050	1,150
1927	886	—	710	1,000	1,050	1,150
1928	110	—	710	1,000	1,050	1,200
1929	—	—	710	1,000	1,050	1,200

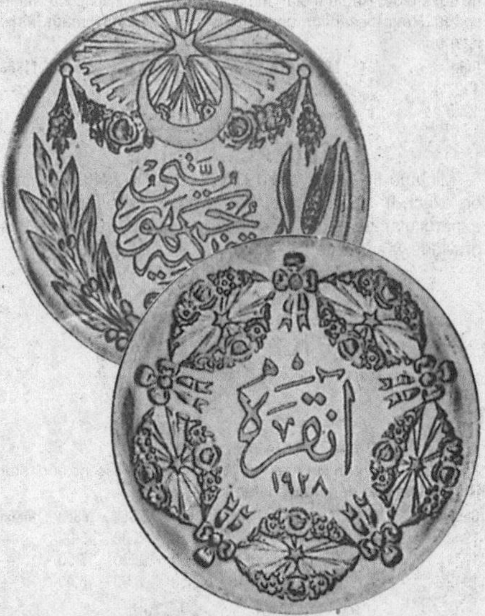

KM# 847 250 KURUSH

17.54 g., 0.917 Gold 0.5171 oz. AGW, 45 mm. **Series:** Monnaie de Luxe **Obv:** Radiant star and crescent above inscription within sprigs **Rev:** Inscription and date within designed wreath **Mint:** Istanbul

Date	Mintage	F12	VF20	XF40	MS60	MS63
1927	7,411	—	690	1,000	1,650	—
1928	5,045	—	690	1,000	1,650	—

KM# 839 500 KURUSH

36.08 g., 0.917 Gold 1.0637 oz. AGW **Obv:** Inscription and date within wreath **Rev:** Star divides circle above inscription and date **Mint:** Istanbul

Date	Mintage	F12	VF20	XF40	MS60	MS63
1925	226	—	1,425	1,950	2,100	—
1926	2,268	—	—	1,425	1,950	—
1927	4,011	—	—	1,425	1,950	—
1928	375	—	1,425	1,950	2,100	—
1929	—	—	1,425	1,950	2,100	—

KM# 848 500 KURUSH
35.08 g., 0.917 Gold 1.0342 oz. AGW, 49 mm. **Series:** Monnaie de Luxe **Obv:** Radiant star and crescent above inscription within sprigs **Rev:** Inscription and date within designed wreath **Mint:** Istanbul

Date	Mintage	F12	VF20	XF40	MS60	MS63
1927	5,097	—	1,375	1,950	3,400	—
1928	2,242	—	1,375	1,950	3,400	—

DECIMAL COINAGE

Mintage figures of the 1930s and early 1940s may not be exact. It is suspected that in some cases, figures for a particular year may include quantities struck with the previous year's date.

40 Para = 1 Kurus; 100 Kurus = 1 Lira

KM# 868 10 PARA (1/4 Kurus)
2.00 g., Aluminum-Bronze, 17 mm. **Obv:** Crescent and star **Rev:** Value and date **Mint:** Istanbul

Date	Mintage	VF20	XF40	MS60	MS63	MS65
1940	30,800,000	0.75	2.50	8.00	15.00	—
1941	22,400,000	0.75	2.50	8.00	15.00	—
1942	26,800,000	0.75	2.50	8.00	15.00	—

KM# 884 1/2 KURUS (20 Para)
Brass **Obv:** Center hole and date **Rev:** Center hole divides oat sprig and value **Mint:** Istanbul

Date	Mintage	VF20	XF40	MS60	MS63	MS65
1948	150	—	—	750	1,000	1,350

Note: Not released to circulation

KM# 884a 1/2 KURUS (20 Para)
3.90 g., 0.916 Gold 0.1149 oz. AGW, 16 mm. **Series:** Nostalgia **Obv:** Center hole and date **Rev:** Center hole divides value and sprig **Edge:** Plain **Mint:** Istanbul

Date	Mintage	VF20	XF40	MS60	MS63	MS65
1948	441	—	—	—	—	250

KM# 861 KURUS
Copper-Nickel, 18.5 mm. **Obv:** Star above crescent **Rev:** Value within designed sprigs **Mint:** Istanbul

Date	Mintage	VF20	XF40	MS60	MS63	MS65
1935	784,000	4.00	15.00	30.00	45.00	—
1936	5,300,000	4.00	10.00	25.00	35.00	—
1937	4,500,000	4.00	10.00	25.00	35.00	—

KM# 867 KURUS
2.40 g., Copper-Nickel, 18.5 mm. **Obv:** Star above crescent **Rev:** Value within designed sprigs **Mint:** Istanbul

Date	Mintage	VF20	XF40	MS60	MS63	MS65
1938	16,400,000	0.50	5.00	10.00	20.00	—
1939	21,600,000	0.50	5.00	10.00	20.00	—
1940	8,800,000	1.00	8.00	15.00	35.00	—
1941	6,700,000	0.75	6.00	12.00	25.00	—
1942	10,800,000	0.50	5.00	10.00	20.00	—
1943	4,000,000	0.75	6.00	12.00	25.00	—
1944	6,000,000	0.75	6.00	12.00	25.00	—

KM# 881 KURUS
2.10 g., Brass, 18.5 mm. **Obv:** Date below hole in center **Rev:** Hole in center flanked by oat sprig and value **Edge:** Plain **Mint:** Istanbul

Date	Mintage	VF20	XF40	MS60	MS63	MS65
1947	890,000	—	1.50	2.50	5.00	10.00
1948	35,470,000	—	0.25	0.50	1.50	5.00
1949	29,530,000	—	0.25	0.50	1.25	5.00
1950	32,800,000	—	0.25	0.50	1.25	5.00
1951	6,310,000	—	0.30	0.75	2.25	5.00

KM# 881a KURUS
4.90 g., 0.916 Gold 0.1443 oz. AGW, 18 mm. **Series:** Nostalgia **Obv:** Date below hole in center **Rev:** Hole in center flanked by oat sprig and value **Edge:** Plain **Mint:** Istanbul

Date	Mintage	VF20	XF40	MS60	MS63	MS65
1949	441	—	—	—	—	275

KM# 895 KURUS
1.00 g., Brass, 14 mm. **Obv:** Crescent and star **Rev:** Olive branch divides value and date **Mint:** Istanbul

Date	Mintage	VF20	XF40	MS60	MS63	MS65
1961	1,180,000	—	0.50	1.00	3.00	8.00
1962	3,620,000	—	0.50	1.00	3.00	8.00
1963	1,085,000	—	0.50	1.00	3.00	8.00

KM# 895a KURUS
1.00 g., Bronze, 14 mm. **Obv:** Crescent and star **Rev:** Olive branch divides value and date **Edge:** Plain **Mint:** Istanbul

Date	Mintage	VF20	XF40	MS60	MS63	MS65
1963	1,180,000	—	0.50	1.00	3.00	8.00
1964	2,520,000	—	0.50	1.00	3.00	8.00
1965	1,860,000	—	0.50	1.00	3.00	8.00
1966	1,820,000	—	0.50	1.00	3.00	8.00
1967	2,410,000	—	0.50	1.00	3.00	8.00
1968	1,040,000	—	0.50	1.00	3.00	8.00
1969	900,000	—	0.50	1.00	3.00	8.00
1970	1,960,000	—	0.50	1.00	3.00	8.00
1971	2,940,000	—	0.50	1.00	3.00	8.00
1972	720,000	—	0.50	1.00	3.00	8.00
1973	540,000	—	0.50	1.00	3.00	8.00
1974	510,000	—	0.50	1.00	3.00	8.00

KM# 895b KURUS
Aluminum, 14 mm. **Obv:** Crescent and star **Rev:** Olive branch divides date and value **Mint:** Istanbul

Date	Mintage	VF20	XF40	MS60	MS63	MS65
1975	690,000	—	0.50	1.00	3.00	8.00
1976	200,000	—	0.50	1.00	3.00	8.00
1977	110,000	—	0.50	1.00	3.00	8.00

KM# 924 KURUS
Bronze **Series:** F.A.O. **Obv:** Anatolic bride's head left **Rev:** Olive branch divides value and date **Mint:** Istanbul

Date	Mintage	VF20	XF40	MS60	MS63	MS65
1979	15,000	—	0.50	1.00	3.00	5.00

KM# 924a KURUS
Aluminum **Series:** F.A.O. **Obv:** Head left **Rev:** Olive branch divides date and value **Mint:** Istanbul

Date	Mintage	VF20	XF40	MS60	MS63	MS65
1979	15,000	—	0.50	1.00	3.00	5.00

KM# 885 2-1/2 KURUS
3.20 g., Brass, 21 mm. **Obv:** Date below center hole **Rev:** Center hole divides oat sprig and value **Mint:** Istanbul

Date	Mintage	VF20	XF40	MS60	MS63	MS65
1948	24,720,000	—	0.50	1.00	3.00	8.00
1949	23,720,000	—	0.50	1.00	3.00	8.00
1950	11,560,000	3.00	5.00	8.00	15.00	25.00
1951	2,000,000	10.00	20.00	35.00	50.00	100

KM# 885a 2-1/2 KURUS
6.90 g., 0.916 Gold 0.2032 oz. AGW, 21 mm. **Series:** Nostalgia **Obv:** Date below center hole **Rev:** Hole in center divides oat sprig and value **Edge:** Plain **Mint:** Istanbul

Date	Mintage	VF20	XF40	MS60	MS63	MS65
1950	441	—	—	—	—	375

KM# 862 5 KURUS
4.00 g., Copper-Nickel, 21.5 mm. **Obv:** Star within crescent **Rev:** Value within designed sprigs **Mint:** Istanbul

Date	Mintage	VF20	XF40	MS60	MS63	MS65
1935	100,000	5.00	10.00	50.00	100	—
1936	2,900,000	1.00	5.00	20.00	50.00	—
1937	4,060,000	1.00	5.00	20.00	50.00	—
1938	13,380,000	1.00	5.00	15.00	35.00	—
1939	12,520,000	1.00	5.00	15.00	35.00	—
1940	4,340,000	1.00	5.00	15.00	40.00	—
1942	10,160,000	1.00	5.00	15.00	35.00	—
1943	15,360,000	1.00	5.00	15.00	35.00	—

KM# 887 5 KURUS
2.20 g., Brass, 16.3 mm. **Obv:** Crescent, star and date **Rev:** Value within wreath **Edge Lettering:** TURMITE CUMHURITETI **Mint:** Istanbul

Date	Mintage	VF20	XF40	MS60	MS63	MS65
1949	4,500,000	0.50	1.00	3.00	7.00	12.00
1950	45,900,000	—	0.50	1.00	3.00	8.00
1951	29,600,000	—	0.50	1.00	3.00	8.00
1955	15,300,000	—	0.50	1.00	3.00	8.00
1956	21,380,000	—	0.50	1.00	3.00	8.00
1957	3,320,000	0.50	2.00	5.00	10.00	15.00

KM# 890.1 5 KURUS
2.50 g., Bronze, 17 mm. **Obv:** Crescent and star **Rev:** Oak branch divides value and date **Mint:** Istanbul

Date	Mintage	VF20	XF40	MS60	MS63	MS65
1958	25,870,000	0.25	0.50	7.00	15.00	30.00
1959	21,580,000	—	0.50	5.00	10.00	25.00
1960	17,150,000	—	0.50	3.00	8.00	20.00
1961	11,110,000	—	0.50	3.00	8.00	20.00
1962	15,280,000	—	0.50	2.50	6.00	10.00
1963	17,680,000	—	0.50	2.50	6.00	10.00
1964	18,190,000	—	0.50	2.00	5.00	10.00
1965	19,170,000	—	0.50	1.50	3.00	5.00
1966	19,840,000	—	0.50	1.50	3.00	5.00
1967	16,170,000	—	0.50	1.00	2.00	5.00
1968	26,050,000	—	0.50	1.00	2.00	5.00

KM# 890.2 5 KURUS
2.00 g., Bronze, 17 mm. **Obv:** Crescent and star **Rev:** Oak branch divides value and date **Mint:** Istanbul **Note:** Reduced weight.

Date	Mintage	VF20	XF40	MS60	MS63	MS65
1969	33,630,000	—	—	0.50	1.00	3.00
1970	29,360,000	—	—	0.50	1.00	3.00
1971	17,440,000	—	—	0.50	1.00	3.00
1972	22,670,000	—	—	0.50	1.00	3.00
1973	17,370,000	—	—	0.50	1.00	3.00

KM# 890.3 5 KURUS
1.35 g., Bronze, 17 mm. **Obv:** Crescent and star **Rev:** Oak branch divides value and date **Mint:** Istanbul **Note:** Varieties exist.

Date	Mintage	VF20	XF40	MS60	MS63	MS65
1974	13,540,000	—	—	0.50	1.00	5.00
1974 Without acorns	Inc. above	—	25.00	50.00	75.00	125

KM# 890a 5 KURUS
1.69 g., Aluminum, 21 mm. **Obv:** Crescent and star **Rev:** Oak branch divides value and date **Mint:** Istanbul

Date	Mintage	VF20	XF40	MS60	MS63	MS65
1975	1,560,000	—	—	0.50	1.00	5.00
1976	1,321,000	—	—	0.50	1.00	5.00
1977	190,000	—	1.00	2.00	5.00	10.00

KM# 906 5 KURUS
0.91 g., Aluminum, 17 mm. **Series:** F.A.O. **Obv:** Anatolic bride's head left **Rev:** Oak branch divides date and value **Mint:** Istanbul

Date	Mintage	VF20	XF40	MS60	MS63	MS65
1975	1,019,000	—	—	1.00	2.00	4.00

KM# 907 5 KURUS
Aluminum **Series:** F.A.O. **Obv:** Mother breastfeading infant **Rev:** Oak branch divides value and date **Mint:** Istanbul

Date	Mintage	VF20	XF40	MS60	MS63	MS65
1976	17,000	—	1.00	1.50	3.00	5.00

KM# 934 5 KURUS
Bronze **Series:** F.A.O. **Obv:** Fisherman within flounder **Rev:** Oak branch divides value and date **Mint:** Istanbul

Date	Mintage	VF20	XF40	MS60	MS63	MS65
1980	13,000	—	1.50	3.00	5.00	7.50

KM# 863 10 KURUS
5.80 g., Copper-Nickel, 25.5 mm. **Obv:** Star within crescent **Rev:** Star above value and date within designed sprigs **Mint:** Istanbul

Date	Mintage	VF20	XF40	MS60	MS63	MS65
1935	60,000	8.00	15.00	45.00	75.00	—
1936	3,580,000	5.00	10.00	35.00	50.00	—
1937	3,020,000	4.00	8.00	25.00	40.00	—
1938	6,610,000	4.00	8.00	25.00	40.00	—
1939	4,610,000	2.50	5.00	20.00	35.00	—
1940	6,960,000	2.50	5.00	20.00	35.00	—

KM# 888 10 KURUS
2.60 g., Brass, 18 mm. **Obv:** Star, crescent and date **Rev:** Value within wreath **Edge Lettering:** TURMITE CUMHURITETI **Mint:** Istanbul

Date	Mintage	VF20	XF40	MS60	MS63	MS65
1949	27,000,000	0.25	0.75	1.50	3.00	8.00
1951	6,200,000	0.25	0.75	1.50	3.00	8.00
1955	10,090,000	0.25	0.75	1.50	3.00	8.00
1956	9,910,000	0.25	0.75	1.50	3.00	8.00

KM# 891.1 10 KURUS
4.00 g., Bronze, 21.3 mm. **Obv:** Star and crescent **Rev:** Oat stalks divide date and value **Mint:** Istanbul

Date	Mintage	VF20	XF40	MS60	MS63	MS65
1958	14,770,000	—	0.25	4.00	10.00	25.00
1959	11,160,000	—	0.10	4.00	10.00	25.00
1960	9,450,000	—	0.10	2.00	5.00	10.00
1961	5,370,000	—	0.10	2.00	5.00	10.00
1962	9,250,000	—	0.10	1.00	3.00	8.00
1963	10,390,000	—	0.10	0.50	2.00	3.00
1964	9,890,000	—	0.10	0.50	2.00	3.00
1965	10,480,000	—	0.10	0.50	2.00	3.00
1966	12,200,000	—	0.10	0.50	2.00	3.00
1967	11,410,000	—	0.10	0.50	2.00	3.00
1968	1,862,000	—	0.10	0.50	2.00	5.00

KM# 891.2 10 KURUS
3.50 g., Bronze **Obv:** Star and crescent **Rev:** Oat stalks divide date and value **Mint:** Istanbul **Note:** Reduced weight.

Date	Mintage	VF20	XF40	MS60	MS63	MS65
1969	21,190,000	—	0.10	0.50	1.00	3.00
1970	19,930,000	—	0.10	0.50	1.00	3.00
1971	14,780,000	—	0.10	0.50	1.00	3.00
1972	17,960,000	—	0.10	0.50	1.00	3.00
1973	11,930,000	—	0.10	0.50	1.00	3.00

KM# 891.3 10 KURUS
2.50 g., Bronze **Obv:** Star and crescent **Rev:** Oat stalks divide date and value **Mint:** Istanbul **Note:** Varieties exist.

Date	Mintage	VF20	XF40	MS60	MS63	MS65
1974	9,280,000	—	0.50	1.00	3.00	8.00
1974 Open 4	Inc. above	—	12.00	15.00	25.00	45.00

KM# 891a 10 KURUS
1.38 g., Aluminum **Obv:** Star and crescent **Rev:** Oat stalks divide date and value **Mint:** Istanbul

Date	Mintage	VF20	XF40	MS60	MS63	MS65
1975	2,165,000	—	0.10	0.50	1.00	3.00
1976	559,000	—	0.50	0.50	1.00	5.00
1977	106,000	—	0.50	1.00	3.00	10.00

KM# 898.1 10 KURUS
3.50 g., Bronze **Series:** F.A.O. **Obv:** Atatürk driving a tractor **Rev:** Oat stalks divide value and date **Mint:** Istanbul

Date	Mintage	VF20	XF40	MS60	MS63	MS65
1971	1,140,000	—	0.50	1.00	2.00	8.00
1972	500,000	—	1.00	2.00	4.00	15.00
1973	10,000	25.00	50.00	150	250	300

KM# 898.2 10 KURUS
2.50 g., Bronze **Obv:** Atatürk driving tractor **Rev:** Oat stalks divide date and value **Mint:** Istanbul

Date	Mintage	VF20	XF40	MS60	MS63	MS65
1974	605,000	—	0.50	1.50	3.00	10.00

KM# 898a 10 KURUS
1.40 g., Aluminum, 21.1 mm. **Obv:** Atatürk driving tractor **Rev:** Oat stalks divide date and value **Mint:** Istanbul

Date	Mintage	VF20	XF40	MS60	MS63	MS65
1975	517,000	—	0.50	1.50	3.00	10.00

KM# 908 10 KURUS
Aluminum **Series:** F.A.O. **Obv:** Mother breastfeading infant **Rev;** Oat stalks divide value and date **Mint:** Istanbul

Date	Mintage	VF20	XF40	MS60	MS63	MS65
1976	17,000	—	1.00	3.00	8.00	12.00

KM# 935 10 KURUS
Bronze **Series:** F.A.O. **Obv:** Anatolic bride's head left **Rev:** Oat stalks divide date and value **Mint:** Istanbul

Date	Mintage	VF20	XF40	MS60	MS63	MS65
1980	13,000	—	1.00	2.00	5.00	10.00

KM# 864 25 KURUS
3.00 g., 0.830 Silver 0.0801 oz. ASW, 19 mm. **Obv:** Head of Kemal Atatürk left **Rev:** Oat sprig divides date, value at left **Mint:** Istanbul

Date	Mintage	VF20	XF40	MS60	MS63	MS65
1935	888,000	8.00	15.00	35.00	50.00	—
1936	10,576,000	4.00	10.00	20.00	35.00	—
1937	8,536,000	5.00	12.50	25.00	45.00	—

KM# 880 25 KURUS
3.00 g., Nickel-Bronze, 19 mm. **Obv:** Crescent and star **Rev:** Oat sprig divides date, value at left **Mint:** Istanbul

Date	Mintage	VF20	XF40	MS60	MS63	MS65
1944	20,000,000	0.50	1.00	5.00	15.00	—
1945	5,328,000	1.00	1.50	5.00	15.00	—
1946	2,672,000	1.00	2.50	10.00	20.00	—

Note: Varieties exist

KM# 886 25 KURUS
4.25 g., Brass, 22.5 mm. **Obv:** Crescent and star **Rev:** Value within wreath **Mint:** Istanbul

Date	Mintage	VF20	XF40	MS60	MS63	MS65
1948	18,000,000	—	0.50	1.00	3.00	5.00
1949	21,000,000	—	0.50	1.00	3.00	5.00
1951	2,000,000	1.00	3.00	10.00	20.00	40.00
1955	9,624,000	—	0.50	1.00	3.00	5.00
1956	14,376,000	—	0.50	1.00	3.00	5.00

KM# 886a 25 KURUS
10.00 g., 0.916 Gold 0.2945 oz. AGW, 22.5 mm. **Series:** Nostalgia **Obv:** Crescent and star **Rev:** Value within wreath **Edge:** Plain **Mint:** Istanbul

Date	Mintage	VF20	XF40	MS60	MS63	MS65
1951	441	—	—	—	—	575

KM# 892.1 25 KURUS
5.00 g., Stainless Steel, 22.5 mm. **Obv:** Smooth ground under standing figure facing **Rev:** Value within wreath **Mint:** Istanbul

Date	Mintage	VF20	XF40	MS60	MS63	MS65
1959	21,864,000	0.15	0.30	1.00	3.00	8.00

KM# 892.2 25 KURUS
5.00 g., Stainless Steel, 22.5 mm. **Obv:** Rough ground under standing figure facing **Rev:** Value within wreath **Mint:** Istanbul

Date	Mintage	VF20	XF40	MS60	MS63	MS65
1960	14,778,000	0.10	0.15	1.00	3.00	8.00
1961	7,248,000	0.10	0.15	2.00	5.00	10.00
1962	10,722,000	0.10	0.15	1.00	3.00	8.00
1963	11,016,000	0.10	0.15	1.00	3.00	8.00
1964	13,962,000	0.10	0.15	1.00	3.00	5.00
1965	9,816,000	0.10	0.15	0.50	1.50	3.00
1966	2,424,000	0.10	0.15	0.50	1.50	3.00

KM# 892.3 25 KURUS
4.00 g., Stainless Steel **Obv:** Standing figure facing **Rev:** Value within wreath **Mint:** Istanbul **Note:** Reduced weight

Date	Mintage	VF20	XF40	MS60	MS63	MS65
1966	7,596,000	—	0.10	1.00	2.00	5.00
1967	17,022,000	—	0.10	0.50	1.50	3.00
1968	31,482,000	—	0.10	0.25	0.75	2.00
1969	34,566,000	—	0.10	0.25	0.75	2.00
1970	32,960,000	—	0.10	0.25	0.75	2.00
1973	20,496,000	—	0.10	0.25	0.75	2.00
1974	16,602,000	—	0.10	0.20	0.50	1.00
1977	10,204,000	—	0.10	0.20	0.50	1.00
1978	185,000	—	0.25	0.50	1.00	3.00

KM# 865 50 KURUS
6.00 g., 0.830 Silver 0.1601 oz. ASW, 24 mm. **Obv:** Head of Kemal Atatürk left **Rev:** Oat sprig divides date, value at left **Mint:** Istanbul

Date	Mintage	VF20	XF40	MS60	MS63	MS65
1935	630,000	5.00	25.00	45.00	75.00	—
1936	5,082,000	5.00	20.00	30.00	50.00	—
1937	4,270,000	15.00	40.00	65.00	125	—

KM# 882 50 KURUS
4.00 g., 0.600 Silver 0.0772 oz. ASW, 20 mm. **Obv:** Crescent, star and date **Rev:** Value within wreath **Mint:** Istanbul **Note:** Edge varieties exist.

Date	Mintage	VF20	XF40	MS60	MS63	MS65
1947	9,296,000	2.00	5.00	7.00	20.00	—
1948	12,704,000	2.00	5.00	7.00	20.00	—

KM# 899 50 KURUS
6.00 g., Stainless Steel, 24 mm. **Obv:** Anatolic bride's head left **Rev:** Value within wreath **Edge:** Reeded **Mint:** Istanbul

Date	Mintage	VF20	XF40	MS60	MS63	MS65
1971	16,756,000	0.10	0.15	0.25	0.50	1.00
1972	22,152,000	0.10	0.15	0.25	0.50	1.00
1973	18,928,000	0.10	0.15	0.25	0.50	1.00
1974	14,480,000	0.10	0.15	0.25	0.50	1.00
1975	27,714,000	0.10	0.15	0.25	0.50	1.00
1976	27,476,000	0.10	0.15	0.25	0.50	1.00
1977	5,062,000	0.10	0.15	0.25	0.50	1.00
1979	3,714,000	0.10	0.15	0.25	0.50	1.00

KM# 913 50 KURUS
Stainless Steel, 24 mm. **Series:** F.A.O. **Obv:** Mother breastfeeding child **Rev:** Value and date within wreath **Mint:** Istanbul

Date	Mintage	VF20	XF40	MS60	MS63	MS65
1978	10,000	0.50	1.00	3.00	5.00	8.00

KM# 925 50 KURUS
Stainless Steel, 24 mm. **Series:** F.A.O. **Obv:** Atatürk driving tractor **Rev:** Value and date within wreath **Mint:** Istanbul

Date	Mintage	VF20	XF40	MS60	MS63	MS65
1979	20,000	0.25	0.50	1.00	3.00	5.00

KM# 936 50 KURUS
Stainless Steel, 24 mm. **Series:** F.A.O. **Obv:** Anatolic bride's head left **Rev:** Value and date within wreath **Mint:** Istanbul

Date	Mintage	VF20	XF40	MS60	MS63	MS65
1980	13,000	0.25	0.50	1.00	3.00	5.00

KM# 860.1 100 KURUS (Lira)
12.00 g., 0.830 Silver 0.3202 oz. ASW **Obv:** Head of Kemal Atatürk left **Rev:** High star above value within crescent, date below **Mint:** Istanbul

Date	Mintage	VF20	XF40	MS60	MS63	MS65
1934	718,000	40.00	75.00	150	250	—

KM# 860.1a 100 KURUS (Lira)
13.50 g., 0.925 Silver 0.4015 oz. ASW, 29.5 mm. **Series:** Nostalgia **Obv:** Head of Kemal Atatürk left **Rev:** High star above value within crescent, date below **Edge:** Plain **Mint:** Istanbul

Date	Mintage	VF20	XF40	MS60	MS63	MS65
1934 Matte	684	—	—	—	—	40.00

KM# 860.2 100 KURUS (Lira)
12.00 g., 0.830 Silver 0.3202 oz. ASW **Obv:** Head of Kemal Atatürk left **Rev:** Low star above value within crescent, date below **Mint:** Istanbul

Date	Mintage	VF20	XF40	MS60	MS63	MS65
1934	Inc. above	30.00	75.00	100	175	—

KM# 941 1/2 LIRA
7.86 g., 0.925 Silver 0.2338 oz. ASW **Subject:** 100th Anniversary of Atatürk's Birth **Obv:** Crescent and star at top of mountain, signature above globe below **Rev:** Head of Kemal Atatürk right **Mint:** Istanbul

Date	Mintage	VF20	XF40	MS60	MS63	MS65
ND(1981)	7,555	—	—	—	10.00	15.00

KM# 941a 1/2 LIRA
8.00 g., 0.917 Gold 0.2359 oz. AGW **Subject:** 100th Anniversary of Atatürk's Birth **Obv:** Crescent and star at top of mountain, signature above globe below **Rev:** Head of Kemal Atatürk right **Mint:** Istanbul

Date	Mintage	VF20	XF40	MS60	MS63	MS65
ND(1981)	25,000	—	—	—	425	500

KM# 866 LIRA
12.00 g., 0.830 Silver 0.3202 oz. ASW, 29 mm. **Obv:** Head of Kemal Atatürk left **Rev:** Value and date within crescent below star **Mint:** Istanbul

Date	Mintage	VF20	XF40	MS60	MS63	MS65
1937	1,624,000	15.00	25.00	60.00	75.00	—
1938	8,282,000	50.00	75.00	150	225	—
1939	376,000	15.00	25.00	60.00	75.00	—

KM# 869 LIRA
12.00 g., 0.830 Silver 0.3202 oz. ASW, 29 mm. **Obv:** Head of Ismet Inonu left **Rev:** Star above value and date within crescent **Mint:** Istanbul

Date	Mintage	VF20	XF40	MS60	MS63	MS65
1940	253,000	—	6.25	25.00	75.00	—
1941	6,167,000	—	6.25	18.00	60.00	—

KM# 883 LIRA
7.50 g., 0.600 Silver 0.1447 oz. ASW, 25 mm. **Obv:** Crescent, star and date **Rev:** Value within wreath **Mint:** Istanbul **Note:** Edge varieties exist.

Date	Mintage	VF20	XF40	MS60	MS63	MS65
1947	11,104,000	2.75	5.50	12.00	20.00	—
1948	16,896,000	2.75	4.50	10.00	18.00	—

KM# 889 LIRA
7.50 g., Copper-Nickel, 27 mm. **Obv:** Head of Kemal Atatürk left **Rev:** Value and date within wreath **Edge:** Reeded **Mint:** Istanbul

Date	Mintage	VF20	XF40	MS60	MS63	MS65
1957	25,000,000	0.50	1.00	3.00	5.00	—

KM# 889a.1 LIRA
8.00 g., Stainless Steel, 27 mm. **Obv:** Head of Kemal Atat?rk left **Rev:** Value and date within wreath **Mint:** Istanbul

Date	Mintage	VF20	XF40	MS60	MS63	MS65
1959	7,452,000	0.10	0.20	5.00	10.00	18.00
1960	11,436,000	0.10	0.20	5.00	10.00	18.00
1961	2,100,000	0.10	0.20	10.00	20.00	35.00
1962	4,228,000	0.10	0.20	4.00	8.00	15.00
1963	4,316,000	0.10	0.20	4.00	8.00	15.00
1964	4,976,000	0.10	0.20	2.50	5.00	12.00
1965	5,348,000	0.10	0.20	1.50	3.00	5.00
1966	8,040,000	0.10	0.20	1.50	3.00	5.00
1967	—	5.00	8.00	15.00	25.00	50.00

KM# 889a.2 LIRA
7.00 g., Stainless Steel, 27 mm. **Obv:** Head of Kemal Atatürk left **Rev:** Value and date within wreath **Mint:** Istanbul **Note:** Reduced weight.

Date	Mintage	VF20	XF40	MS60	MS63	MS65
1967	10,444,000	0.10	0.20	1.50	3.00	8.00
1968	12,728,000	0.10	0.20	1.00	2.00	5.00
1969	6,612,000	0.10	0.20	1.00	2.00	5.00
1970	8,652,000	0.10	0.20	0.50	1.00	2.00
1971	10,504,000	0.10	0.20	0.50	1.00	2.00
1972	26,512,000	0.10	0.20	0.50	1.00	2.00
1973	12,596,000	0.10	0.20	0.50	1.00	2.00
1974	11,596,000	0.10	0.20	0.50	1.00	2.00
1975	20,348,000	0.10	0.20	0.30	0.50	1.00
1976	23,144,000	0.10	0.20	0.30	0.50	1.00
1977	30,244,000	0.10	0.20	0.30	0.50	1.00
1978	22,156,000	0.10	0.20	0.30	0.50	1.00
1979	9,289,000	0.10	0.20	0.30	0.50	1.00
1980	3,585,000	0.10	0.20	0.30	0.50	1.00

KM# 914 LIRA
8.00 g., Stainless Steel **Series:** F.A.O. **Obv:** Mother breastfeeding infant **Rev:** Value and date within wreath **Mint:** Istanbul

Date	Mintage	VF20	XF40	MS60	MS63	MS65
1978	20,000	0.50	1.00	3.00	5.00	8.00

KM# 926 LIRA
8.00 g., Stainless Steel **Series:** F.A.O. **Obv:** Atatürk driving tractor **Rev:** Value and date within wreath **Mint:** Istanbul

Date	Mintage	VF20	XF40	MS60	MS63	MS65
1979	20,000	0.50	1.00	3.00	5.00	8.00

KM# 937 LIRA
8.00 g., Stainless Steel **Series:** F.A.O. **Obv:** Anatolic bride's head left **Rev:** Value and date within wreath **Mint:** Istanbul

Date	Mintage	VF20	XF40	MS60	MS63	MS65
1980	13,000	0.50	1.00	3.00	5.00	8.00

KM# 942 LIRA
16.00 g., 0.925 Silver 0.4758 oz. ASW **Subject:** 100th Anniversary of Ataturk's Birth **Obv:** Crescent and star at top of mountain, signature above globe below **Rev:** Head of Kemal Atatürk right **Mint:** Istanbul

Date	Mintage	VF20	XF40	MS60	MS63	MS65
ND(1981)	7,580	—	—	—	12.00	15.00

KM# 942a LIRA
16.00 g., 0.917 Gold 0.4717 oz. AGW **Subject:** 100th Anniversary of Atatürk's Birth **Obv:** Crescent and star at top of mountain, signature above globe below **Rev:** Head of Kemal Atatürk right **Mint:** Istanbul

Date	Mintage	VF20	XF40	MS60	MS63	MS65
ND(1981)	25,000	—	—	—	900	1,000

KM# 943 LIRA
1.10 g., Aluminum, 17 mm. **Obv:** Head of Kemal Atatürk left **Rev:** Value and date within wreath **Mint:** Istanbul

Date	Mintage	VF20	XF40	MS60	MS63	MS65
1981	14,432,000	—	0.10	0.25	0.50	0.75

KM# 990 LIRA
1.10 g., Aluminum, 17 mm. **Obv:** Head of Kemal Atatürk left **Rev:** Crescent opens right with thin "1" **Mint:** Istanbul

Date	Mintage	VF20	XF40	MS60	MS63	MS65
1982	799,000	—	0.25	0.25	0.50	1.00

KM# 962.1 LIRA
1.10 g., Aluminum, 17 mm. **Obv:** Head of Kemal Atatürk left **Rev:** Large (5mm) "1" **Mint:** Istanbul

Date	Mintage	VF20	XF40	MS60	MS63	MS65
1984	498,000	—	0.10	0.25	0.50	0.75

KM# 962.2 LIRA
1.10 g., Aluminum, 17 mm. **Obv:** Head of Kemal Atatürk left **Rev:** Small (3.5mm) "1" **Mint:** Istanbul **Note:** Varieties exist.

Date	Mintage	VF20	XF40	MS60	MS63	MS65
1985	712,000	—	0.10	0.25	0.50	0.75
1986	504,000	—	0.10	0.25	0.50	0.75
1987	500,000	—	0.10	0.25	0.50	0.75
1988	75,000	—	0.10	0.25	0.50	0.75
1989	10,000	—	0.10	0.50	1.00	1.50

KM# 893.1 2-1/2 LIRA
12.00 g., Stainless Steel, 30 mm. **Obv:** Standing figure facing right **Rev:** Value and date within wreath **Mint:** Istanbul

Date	Mintage	VF20	XF40	MS60	MS63	MS65
1960	4,015,000	0.25	1.00	10.00	25.00	75.00
1961	1,222,000	0.25	1.00	15.00	35.00	100
1962	3,636,000	0.25	1.00	15.00	35.00	100
1963	3,108,000	0.25	1.00	10.00	25.00	75.00
1964	2,710,000	0.25	1.00	7.00	20.00	45.00
1965	1,246,000	0.25	1.00	2.00	5.00	8.00
1966	1,788,000	0.25	1.00	5.00	12.00	25.00
1967	5,333,000	0.25	1.00	4.00	10.00	15.00
1968	2,707,000	0.25	1.00	2.00	5.00	8.00

KM# 893.1a 2-1/2 LIRA
11.80 g., 0.925 Silver 0.3509 oz. ASW, 30 mm. **Series:** Nostalgia **Obv:** Standing figure facing right **Rev:** Value and date within wreath **Edge:** Plain **Mint:** Istanbul

Date	Mintage	VF20	XF40	MS60	MS63	MS65
1965	684	—	—	—	30.00	50.00

KM# 893.2 2-1/2 LIRA
9.00 g., Stainless Steel, 30 mm. **Obv:** Standing figure facing right **Rev:** Value and date within wreath **Mint:** Istanbul **Note:** Reduced weight. Varieties exist with landscape and number of beads in laurel.

Date	Mintage	VF20	XF40	MS60	MS63	MS65
1969	1,378,000	0.15	0.50	1.00	3.00	10.00
1970	3,777,000	0.15	0.50	1.00	3.00	5.00
1971	2,170,000	0.15	0.50	0.75	1.50	4.00
1972	9,147,000	0.15	0.50	0.75	1.50	4.00
1973	4,348,000	0.15	0.50	0.75	1.50	4.00
1974	3,816,000	0.15	0.50	0.75	1.50	4.00
1975	9,811,000	0.15	0.25	0.50	1.00	3.00
1976	3,952,000	0.15	0.25	0.50	1.00	3.00
1977	21,473,000	0.10	0.20	0.35	0.75	2.00
1978	15,738,000	0.10	0.20	0.35	0.75	2.00
1979	6,074,000	0.10	0.20	0.35	0.75	2.00
1980	2,621,000	0.10	0.20	0.35	0.75	2.00

KM# 896 2-1/2 LIRA
9.00 g., Stainless Steel, 30 mm. **Series:** F.A.O. **Obv:** Atatürk driving tractor **Rev:** Value and date within wreath **Mint:** Istanbul

Date	Mintage	VF20	XF40	MS60	MS63	MS65
1970	200,000	—	0.20	0.50	1.00	1.50

KM# 910 2-1/2 LIRA
Stainless Steel, 30 mm. **Series:** F.A.O. **Obv:** Stylized standing figures **Rev:** Value and date within wreath **Mint:** Istanbul

Date	Mintage	VF20	XF40	MS60	MS63	MS65
1977	25,000	0.50	1.00	1.50	3.00	5.00

KM# 915 2-1/2 LIRA
Stainless Steel, 30 mm. **Series:** F.A.O. **Obv:** Mother breastfeeding infant **Rev:** Value and date within wreath **Mint:** Istanbul

Date	Mintage	VF20	XF40	MS60	MS63	MS65
1978	10,000	0.50	1.00	3.00	5.00	8.00

KM# 927 2-1/2 LIRA
Stainless Steel, 30 mm. **Series:** F.A.O. **Obv:** Head of Kemal Atatürk left **Rev:** Value and date within wreath **Mint:** Istanbul

Date	Mintage	VF20	XF40	MS60	MS63	MS65
1979	20,000	—	1.00	2.00	3.00	5.00

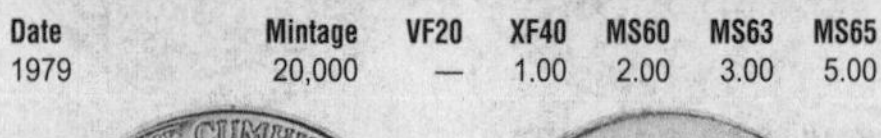

KM# 938 2-1/2 LIRA
Stainless Steel, 30 mm. **Series:** F.A.O. **Obv:** Fisherman within flounder **Rev:** Value and date within wreath **Mint:** Istanbul

Date	Mintage	VF20	XF40	MS60	MS63	MS65
1980	13,000	1.00	2.00	3.00	5.00	8.00

KM# 905 5 LIRA
11.10 g., Stainless Steel, 32.5 mm. **Obv:** Atatürk on horseback **Rev:** Value and date within wreath **Mint:** Istanbul

Date	Mintage	VF20	XF40	MS60	MS63	MS65
1974	2,842,000	0.15	0.25	1.00	2.00	5.00
1975	10,855,000	0.15	0.25	0.50	1.00	1.50
1976	17,532,000	0.15	0.25	0.50	1.00	1.50
1977	6,172,000	0.15	0.25	0.50	1.00	1.50
1978	76,000	0.25	0.50	2.00	4.00	8.00
1979	6,054,000	0.15	0.25	0.50	1.00	1.50

KM# 905a 5 LIRA
14.70 g., 0.925 Silver 0.4372 oz. ASW, 32.5 mm. **Series:** Nostalgia **Obv:** Atatürk on horseback **Rev:** Value and date within wreath **Edge:** Plain **Mint:** Istanbul

Date	Mintage	VF20	XF40	MS60	MS63	MS65
1975	684	—	—	—	30.00	50.00

KM# 909 5 LIRA
Stainless Steel **Series:** International Women's Year; F.A.O. **Obv:** Mother breastfeeding infant **Rev:** Value and date within wreath **Mint:** Istanbul

Date	Mintage	VF20	XF40	MS60	MS63	MS65
1976	17,000	—	1.00	2.00	3.00	5.00

KM# 911 5 LIRA
Stainless Steel **Series:** F.A.O. **Obv:** Stylized standing figures **Rev:** Value and date within wreath **Mint:** Istanbul

Date	Mintage	VF20	XF40	MS60	MS63	MS65
1977	25,000	—	1.00	2.00	3.00	5.00

KM# 916 5 LIRA
Stainless Steel **Series:** F.A.O. **Obv:** Atatürk driving tractor **Rev:** Value and date within wreath **Mint:** Istanbul

Date	Mintage	VF20	XF40	MS60	MS63	MS65
1978	10,000	1.00	2.00	3.00	5.00	8.00

KM# 928 5 LIRA
Stainless Steel **Series:** F.A.O. **Obv:** Anatolic bride's head left **Rev:** Value and date within wreath **Mint:** Istanbul

Date	Mintage	VF20	XF40	MS60	MS63	MS65
1979	20,000	—	1.00	2.00	3.00	5.00

KM# 939 5 LIRA
Stainless Steel **Series:** F.A.O. **Obv:** Fisherman within flounder **Rev:** Value and date within wreath **Mint:** Istanbul

Date	Mintage	VF20	XF40	MS60	MS63	MS65
1980	13,000	—	1.00	2.00	3.00	5.00

KM# 944 5 LIRA
Aluminum, 21 mm. **Obv:** Atatürk on horseback **Rev:** Crescent opens left **Edge:** Reeded **Mint:** Istanbul

Date	Mintage	VF20	XF40	MS60	MS63	MS65
1981	61,605,000	—	—	0.25	0.50	1.00

KM# 949.1 5 LIRA
1.70 g., Aluminum, 19.42 mm. **Obv:** Atatürk on horseback **Rev:** Crescent opens right **Edge:** Reeded **Mint:** Istanbul

Date	Mintage	VF20	XF40	MS60	MS63	MS65
1982	69,975,000	—	0.15	0.25	0.50	1.00

KM# 949.2 5 LIRA
Aluminum **Obv:** Atatürk on horseback **Rev:** Smaller, bolder "5" **Mint:** Istanbul

Date	Mintage	VF20	XF40	MS60	MS63	MS65
1983	90,310,000	—	0.15	0.25	0.50	1.00

KM# 963 5 LIRA
1.67 g., Aluminum, 19.46 mm. **Obv:** Head left **Rev:** Value and date within wreath **Edge:** Reeded **Mint:** Istanbul **Note:** Varieties exist.

Date	Mintage	VF20	XF40	MS60	MS63	MS65
1984	17,316,000	—	0.15	0.25	0.50	1.00
1985	9,405,000	—	0.15	0.25	0.50	1.00
1986	9,575,000	—	0.20	0.25	0.50	1.00
1987	500,000	—	0.20	0.25	0.50	1.00
1988	100,000	—	0.20	0.25	0.50	1.00
1989	10,000	—	0.20	0.50	1.00	3.00

KM# 894 10 LIRA
15.00 g., 0.830 Silver 0.4003 oz. ASW, 34 mm. **Subject:** 27th May Revolution **Obv:** Head of Atatürk left **Rev:** Radiant crescent and star above torch, balance scales, crossed flag and wing **Mint:** Istanbul

Date	Mintage	VF20	XF40	MS60	MS63	MS65
ND-1960	4,000,000	—	7.75	11.00	13.00	16.00
ND-1960 Prooflike	—	—	—	—	—	20.00

KM# 945 10 LIRA
Aluminum **Obv:** Half-length figure right **Rev:** Value and date within wreath, crescent opens left **Mint:** Istanbul

Date	Mintage	VF20	XF40	MS60	MS63	MS65
1981	25,520,000	—	0.25	0.35	0.50	0.75

KM# 950.1 10 LIRA
Aluminum **Obv:** Half-length figure right **Rev:** Value and date within wreath, crescent opens right **Mint:** Istanbul

Date	Mintage	VF20	XF40	MS60	MS63	MS65
1982	17,092,000	—	0.50	0.75	1.00	1.50

KM# 950.2 10 LIRA
Aluminum **Obv:** Half-length figure right **Rev:** Value and date within wreath **Mint:** Istanbul

Date	Mintage	VF20	XF40	MS60	MS63	MS65
1983	2,228,000	0.10	0.20	1.00	2.00	4.00

KM# 964 10 LIRA
2.30 g., Aluminum, 25 mm. **Obv:** Head of Atatürk left **Rev:** Value and date within wreath **Edge:** Reeded **Mint:** Istanbul **Note:** Varieties exist.

Date	Mintage	VF20	XF40	MS60	MS63	MS65
1984	23,360,000	—	0.15	0.25	0.50	0.75
1985	41,736,000	—	0.15	0.25	0.50	0.75
1986	78,224,000	—	0.15	0.25	0.50	0.75
1987	62,340,000	—	0.15	0.25	0.50	0.75
1988	17,620,000	—	0.15	0.25	0.50	0.75
1989	10,000	—	0.15	0.45	1.00	1.50

KM# 946 20 LIRA
Aluminum **Series:** World Food Day **Obv:** Value and date within wreath **Rev:** Stylized design below sprig **Mint:** Istanbul

Date	Mintage	VF20	XF40	MS60	MS63	MS65
1981	10,000	—	1.00	1.50	2.50	3.00

KM# 965 20 LIRA
7.20 g., Copper-Nickel **Obv:** Head of Atatürk left **Rev;** Value and date within wreath **Mint:** Istanbul

Date	Mintage	VF20	XF40	MS60	MS63	MS65
1984	1,644,000	—	0.25	0.35	0.50	1.00
1989	—	—	0.25	0.35	0.50	1.00

KM# 897 25 LIRA
14.60 g., 0.830 Silver 0.3896 oz. ASW **Subject:** 50th Anniversary of National Assembly in Ankara **Obv:** Bust facing **Rev:** Building above value **Mint:** Istanbul

Date	Mintage	VF20	XF40	MS60	MS63	MS65
ND-1970	23,000	—	—	11.00	13.00	16.00
ND-1970	Inc. above	PF65 14.00				

KM# 975 25 LIRA
2.85 g., Aluminum, 27 mm. **Obv:** Head of Atatürk left **Rev:** Value and date within wreath **Edge:** Reeded **Mint:** Istanbul **Note:** Varieties exist.

Date	Mintage	VF20	XF40	MS60	MS63	MS65
1985	37,014,000	—	0.15	0.25	0.50	1.00
1986	49,611,000	—	0.15	0.25	0.50	1.00
1987	61,335,000	—	0.15	0.25	0.50	1.00
1988	39,540,000	—	0.15	0.25	0.50	1.00
1989	10,000	—	0.15	0.25	0.50	1.00

KM# 900 50 LIRA
19.00 g., 0.830 Silver 0.507 oz. ASW, 34 mm. **Subject:** 900th Anniversary - Battle of Malazgirt, Alparslan **Obv:** Armored bust 1/4 left **Rev:** Map of Turkey **Mint:** Istanbul

Date	Mintage	VF20	XF40	MS60	MS63	MS65
ND-1971	33,000	—	9.75	12.50	15.00	17.00
ND-1971	Inc. above	PF65 12.00				

KM# 901 50 LIRA
20.10 g., 0.830 Silver 0.5364 oz. ASW, 34 mm. **Subject:** Kemal Atatürk's Entry into Smyrna **Obv:** Atatürk on horse left **Rev:** Uniformed figures in battle **Mint:** Istanbul

Date	Mintage	VF20	XF40	MS60	MS63	MS65
ND-1972	172,000	—	10.50	12.50	15.00	17.00
ND-1972	—	PF65 12.00				

KM# 902 50 LIRA
13.00 g., 0.900 Silver 0.3762 oz. ASW **Subject:** 50th Anniversary of Republic **Obv:** Radiant head on torch facing divides profiles **Rev:** Cascading star within flower at upper right of inscription **Mint:** Istanbul

Date	Mintage	VF20	XF40	MS60	MS63	MS65
ND-1973	70,000	—	7.25	11.00	13.00	16.00
ND-1973	Inc. above	PF65 12.00				

KM# 912 50 LIRA
8.85 g., 0.830 Silver 0.2362 oz. ASW **Series:** F.A.O. **Obv:** Stylized standing figures **Rev:** Value and date within wreath **Mint:** Istanbul

Date	Mintage	VF20	XF40	MS60	MS63	MS65
1977	25,000	4.50	6.00	8.00	10.00	12.00

KM# 966 50 LIRA
9.00 g., Copper-Nickel-Zinc, 26.8 mm. **Obv:** Head of Atatürk left **Rev:** Value and date within wreath **Edge:** Reeded **Mint:** Istanbul **Note:** Varieties exist.

Date	Mintage	VF20	XF40	MS60	MS63	MS65
1984	14,731,000	—	0.25	0.40	0.60	0.75

Date	Mintage	VF20	XF40	MS60	MS63	MS65
1985	52,658,000	—	0.20	0.35	0.50	0.75
1986	80,656,000	—	0.20	0.35	0.50	0.75
1987	32,078,000	—	0.20	0.35	0.50	0.75

KM# 987 50 LIRA
3.25 g., Aluminum-Bronze, 18.7 mm. **Obv:** Head of Atatürk left **Rev:** Value and date within wreath **Edge:** Reeded **Mint:** Istanbul **Note:** Varieties exist.

Date	Mintage	VF20	XF40	MS60	MS63	MS65
1988	3,396,000	—	—	—	0.15	0.50
1989	25,463,000	—	—	—	0.15	0.50
1990	500,000	—	—	—	0.15	0.50
1991	10,000	—	—	—	0.15	1.00
1992	10,000	—	—	—	0.15	1.00
1993	5,000	—	—	0.15	0.35	1.50
1994	2,500	—	—	0.25	0.50	1.50

KM# 903 100 LIRA
22.00 g., 0.900 Silver 0.6366 oz. ASW **Subject:** 50th Anniversary of Republic **Obv:** Radiant head on torch facing divides profiles **Rev:** Cascading star within flower to upper right of inscription **Mint:** Istanbul

Date	Mintage	VF20	XF40	MS60	MS63	MS65
1973	65,000	—	—	14.00	16.50	18.50
1973 Prooflike	—	—	—	—	18.50	20.50

KM# 951 100 LIRA
Copper-Nickel, 38.5 mm. **Subject:** World Championship Soccer - Madrid **Obv:** Soccer player **Rev:** Date within soccer ball **Mint:** Istanbul

Date	Mintage	VF20	XF40	MS60	MS63	MS65
1982	100,000	—	—	1.00	2.00	3.50

KM# 967 100 LIRA
11.05 g., Copper-Nickel-Zinc, 29.65 mm. **Obv:** Head of Atatürk left **Rev:** Value and date within wreath **Edge:** Reeded **Mint:** Istanbul **Note:** Varieties exist.

Date	Mintage	VF20	XF40	MS60	MS63	MS65
1984	758,000	—	0.40	0.60	0.85	1.00
1985	866,000	—	0.40	0.60	0.85	1.00
1986	12,064,000	—	0.40	0.60	0.85	1.00
1987	91,400,000	—	0.25	0.45	0.65	1.00
1988	16,184,000	—	0.25	0.45	0.65	1.00

KM# 988 100 LIRA
4.15 g., Aluminum-Bronze, 21 mm. **Obv:** Head of Atatürk left **Rev:** Value and date within wreath **Edge:** Reeded **Mint:** Istanbul **Note:** Varieties exist.

Date	Mintage	VF20	XF40	MS60	MS63	MS65
1988	10,000,000	—	—	0.20	0.50	0.75
1989	233,750,000	—	—	0.20	0.50	0.75
1990	152,230,000	—	—	0.20	0.50	0.75
1991	49,160,000	—	—	0.20	0.50	0.75
1992	22,930,000	—	—	0.20	0.50	0.75
1993	3,700,000	—	—	0.20	0.50	0.75
1994	2,500	—	—	0.50	1.50	2.00

KM# 988a 100 LIRA
5.10 g., 0.925 Silver 0.1517 oz. ASW, 21 mm. **Obv:** Head of Atatürk left **Rev:** Value and date within wreath **Edge:** Reeded **Mint:** Mexico City

Date	Mintage	VF20	XF40	MS60	MS63	MS65
1988	998	PF65 30.00				

KM# 917 150 LIRA
9.00 g., 0.800 Silver 0.2315 oz. ASW **Subject:** World Cup Soccer Championship **Obv:** Soccer player and net **Rev:** Various maps divide emblem and value **Mint:** Istanbul

Date	Mintage	VF20	XF40	MS60	MS63	MS65
1978	5,000	—	—	10.00	12.00	14.00

KM# 918.1 150 LIRA
9.00 g., 0.800 Silver 0.2315 oz. ASW **Series:** F.A.O. **Obv:** Atatürk driving tractor **Rev:** Value and date within wreath **Edge:** Reeded **Mint:** Istanbul

Date	Mintage	VF20	XF40	MS60	MS63	MS65
1978	10,000	—	12.50	14.00	18.00	20.00

KM# 918.2 150 LIRA
9.00 g., 0.800 Silver 0.2315 oz. ASW **Series:** F.A.O. **Obv:** Atatürk driving tractor **Rev:** Value and date within wreath **Edge:** Lettered **Mint:** Istanbul

Date	Mintage	VF20	XF40	MS60	MS63	MS65
1978	2,500	PF65 45.00				

KM# 929.1 150 LIRA
9.00 g., 0.800 Silver 0.2315 oz. ASW **Series:** F.A.O. **Obv:** Anatolic bride's head left **Rev:** Value and date within wreath **Edge:** Reeded **Mint:** Istanbul

Date	Mintage	VF20	XF40	MS60	MS63	MS65
1979	10,000	—	5.00	8.00	12.00	14.00

KM# 929.2 150 LIRA
9.00 g., 0.800 Silver 0.2315 oz. ASW **Series:** F.A.O. **Obv:** Anatolic bride's head left **Rev:** Value and date within wreath **Edge:** Lettered **Mint:** Istanbul

Date	Mintage	VF20	XF40	MS60	MS63	MS65
1979	2,500	PF65 25.00				

KM# 919 200 LIRA
9.00 g., 0.830 Silver 0.2402 oz. ASW **Subject:** 705th Anniversary - Death of Jalaladdin Rumi, Poet **Obv:** Bust with headdress facing 1/4 left **Rev:** Steepled and dome buildings **Mint:** Istanbul

Date	Mintage	VF20	XF40	MS60	MS63	MS65
1978	10,000	—	—	10.00	12.00	15.00
1978	1,000	PF65 20.00				

KM# 904 500 LIRA
6.00 g., 0.917 Gold 0.1769 oz. AGW **Subject:** 50th Anniversary of Republic **Obv:** Bust facing **Rev:** Cascading star within flower to upper right of inscription **Mint:** Istanbul

Date	Mintage	VF20	XF40	MS60	MS63	MS65
1973	30,000	—	—	—	350	375

KM# 920 500 LIRA
8.00 g., 0.917 Gold 0.2359 oz. AGW **Series:** F.A.O. **Obv:** Mother breastfeeding infant **Rev:** Value and date within wreath **Mint:** Istanbul

Date	Mintage	VF20	XF40	MS60	MS63	MS65
1978	650	PF65 850				

KM# 921 500 LIRA
8.00 g., 0.917 Gold 0.2359 oz. AGW **Subject:** 705th Anniversary - Death of Jalaladdin Rumi, Poet **Mint:** Istanbul

Date	Mintage	VF20	XF40	MS60	MS63	MS65
1978	900	PF65 950				

KM# 930 500 LIRA
8.00 g., 0.917 Gold 0.2359 oz. AGW **Series:** F.A.O. **Mint:** Istanbul

Date	Mintage	VF20	XF40	MS60	MS63	MS65
1979	783	PF65 1,100				

KM# 931 500 LIRA
23.33 g., 0.925 Silver 0.6938 oz. ASW **Subject:** UNICEF and I.Y.C. **Obv:** Value within wreath **Rev:** Multiracial children dancing, city view above, logos and date below **Mint:** Istanbul

Date	Mintage	VF20	XF40	MS60	MS63	MS65
1979(1981)	10,000	PF65 20.00				

KM# 940.1 500 LIRA
9.00 g., 0.900 Silver 0.2604 oz. ASW **Series:** F.A.O. **Obv:** Mother breastfeeding infant **Rev:** Value and date within wreath **Edge:** Reeded **Mint:** Istanbul

Date	Mintage	VF20	XF40	MS60	MS63	MS65
1980	13,000	—	6.00	9.00	12.00	14.00

KM# 940.2 500 LIRA
9.00 g., 0.900 Silver 0.2604 oz. ASW **Obv:** Mother breastfeeding infant **Rev:** Value and date within wreath **Edge:** Lettered **Mint:** Istanbul

Date	Mintage	VF20	XF40	MS60	MS63	MS65
1980	4,000	PF65 20.00				

KM# 952 500 LIRA
23.33 g., 0.925 Silver 0.6938 oz. ASW **Subject:** World Championship Soccer - Madrid **Obv:** Soccer player **Rev:** Soccer ball and map in front of lined globe design **Mint:** Istanbul

Date	Mintage	VF20	XF40	MS60	MS63	MS65
1982	12,000	PF65 17.00				

KM# 953 500 LIRA
23.33 g., 0.925 Silver 0.6938 oz. ASW **Subject:** World Championship Soccer - Madrid **Obv:** Soccer ball in inner circle **Rev:** Goalie blocking shot **Mint:** Istanbul

Date	Mintage	VF20	XF40	MS60	MS63	MS65
1982	12,000	PF65 17.00				

KM# 957 500 LIRA
Copper-Nickel **Subject:** Lydia - First Coin in the World **Obv:** Value and date within oat sprigs **Rev:** Animal heads at center of circular inscriptions **Mint:** Istanbul

Date	Mintage	VF20	XF40	MS60	MS63	MS65
1983	3,542	—	—	3.00	5.00	8.00

KM# 968 500 LIRA
Copper-Nickel **Series:** F.A.O. **Subject:** World Fisheries Conference **Obv:** Value **Rev:** Turbot fish **Mint:** Istanbul

Date	Mintage	VF20	XF40	MS60	MS63	MS65
ND(1984)	3,000	—	—	4.00	10.00	15.00

KM# 968a 500 LIRA
28.28 g., 0.925 Silver 0.841 oz. ASW **Series:** World Fisheries Conference **Obv:** Value **Rev:** Turbot fish **Mint:** Istanbul

Date	Mintage	VF20	XF40	MS60	MS63	MS65
ND-1984	763	PF65 40.00				

KM# 968b 500 LIRA
47.54 g., 0.917 Gold 1.4016 oz. AGW **Subject:** World Fisheries Conference **Obv:** Value **Rev:** Turbot fish **Mint:** Istanbul

Date	Mintage	VF20	XF40	MS60	MS63	MS65
ND-1984	74	PF65 2,600				

KM# 979 500 LIRA
Copper-Nickel **Subject:** 40th Anniversary of F.A.O. **Obv:** Value within wreath **Rev:** Leafy produce in bowl in front of FAO logo, dates on bottom **Mint:** Istanbul

Date	Mintage	VF20	XF40	MS60	MS63	MS65
ND-1986	3,000	PF65 8.00				

KM# 989 500 LIRA
6.15 g., Aluminum-Bronze, 24 mm. **Obv:** Head of Atatürk left **Rev:** Value and date within wreath **Edge:** Reeded **Mint:** Istanbul **Note:** Varieties exist.

Date	Mintage	VF20	XF40	MS60	MS63	MS65
1989	141,813,000	—	—	0.40	0.60	0.75
1990	100,114,000	—	—	0.40	0.60	0.75
1991	30,006,000	—	—	0.40	0.60	0.75
1992	10,000	—	—	0.40	0.60	1.00
1993	5,000	—	—	0.45	0.75	1.00
1994	2,500	—	—	0.50	0.85	1.00
1995	2,500	—	—	0.50	0.85	1.00
1996	10,000	—	—	0.40	0.60	1.00
1997	—	—	—	0.40	0.60	1.00

KM# 989a 500 LIRA
7.60 g., 0.925 Silver 0.226 oz. ASW, 24 mm. **Obv:** Head of Atatürk left **Rev:** Value and date within wreath **Edge:** Reeded **Mint:** Mexico City

Date	Mintage	VF20	XF40	MS60	MS63	MS65
1989	998	PF65 30.00				

KM# 922 1000 LIRA
16.00 g., 0.917 Gold 0.4717 oz. AGW **Series:** F.A.O. **Obv:** Anatolic bride's head left **Rev:** Value and date within wreath **Mint:** Istanbul

Date	Mintage	VF20	XF40	MS60	MS63	MS65
1978	650	PF65 1,250				

KM# 923 1000 LIRA
16.00 g., 0.917 Gold 0.4717 oz. AGW **Subject:** 705th Anniversary - Death of Jalaladdin Rumi, Poet **Mint:** Istanbul

Date	Mintage	VF20	XF40	MS60	MS63	MS65
1978	450	PF65 1,450				

KM# 932 1000 LIRA
16.00 g., 0.917 Gold 0.4717 oz. AGW **Series:** F.A.O. **Mint:** Istanbul

Date	Mintage	VF20	XF40	MS60	MS63	MS65
1979	900	PF65 1,200				

KM# 985 1000 LIRA
Nickel-Bronze **Subject:** Peace **Obv:** Value within wreath **Rev:** Doves within diamond shape **Mint:** Istanbul

Date	Mintage	VF20	XF40	MS60	MS63	MS65
1986	—	PF65 8.00				

KM# 980 1000 LIRA
Copper-Nickel **Subject:** Shelter for the Homeless **Obv:** Value within wreath **Rev:** Emblem within center of window design **Mint:** Istanbul

Date	Mintage	VF20	XF40	MS60	MS63	MS65
ND-1987	—	PF65 8.00				

KM# 991 1000 LIRA
Copper-Nickel **Subject:** 400th Anniversary - Death of Architect Sinan **Obv:** Value within wreath **Rev:** Arched city view **Mint:** Istanbul

Date	Mintage	VF20	XF40	MS60	MS63	MS65
ND-1988	—	PF65 10.00				

KM# 996 1000 LIRA
Copper-Nickel-Zinc, 25.8 mm. **Subject:** Environmental Protection **Obv:** Value and date within oat sprigs **Rev:** Fence surrounds tree trunk **Mint:** Istanbul

Date	Mintage	VF20	XF40	MS60	MS63	MS65
1990	500,000	—	—	0.75	1.50	3.00

KM# 997 1000 LIRA
8.00 g., Nickel-Brass, 26 mm. **Obv:** Head of Atatürk left **Rev:** Value and date within oat sprigs **Edge:** Reeded **Mint:** Istanbul

Date	Mintage	VF20	XF40	MS60	MS63	MS65
1990	136,480,000	—	0.25	0.35	0.50	0.75
1991	110,245,000	—	0.25	0.35	0.50	0.75
1992	15,820,000	—	0.25	0.35	0.50	0.75
1993	11,675,000	—	0.25	0.35	0.50	0.75
1994	61,515,000	—	0.25	0.35	0.50	0.75

KM# 1028 1000 LIRA
3.07 g., Bronze Clad Brass, 16.93 mm. **Obv:** Head of Atatürk left **Rev:** Value and date within oat sprigs **Mint:** Istanbul

Date	Mintage	VF20	XF40	MS60	MS63	MS65
1995	36,820,000	—	—	0.15	0.25	0.50
1996	3,900,000	—	—	0.15	0.25	0.50
1997	—	—	—	0.15	0.25	0.50

KM# 947 1500 LIRA
16.00 g., 0.925 Silver 0.4758 oz. ASW **Series:** F.A.O. **Obv:** Value and date within wreath **Rev:** Stylized design below sprig **Mint:** Istanbul

Date	Mintage	VF20	XF40	MS60	MS63	MS65
1981	6,000	—	—	9.50	12.50	17.50
1982	500	—	—	—	35.00	50.00

KM# 958 1500 LIRA
16.00 g., 0.925 Silver 0.4758 oz. ASW **Series:** World Food Day **Obv:** Value and date within wreath **Rev:** Nursing goat within designed wreath **Mint:** Istanbul

Date	Mintage	VF20	XF40	MS60	MS63	MS65
1983	2,914	—	—	10.00	15.00	20.00
1983	1,552					

KM# 1015 2500 LIRA
Nickel-Bronze, 26.5 mm. **Obv:** Head of Atatürk left **Rev:** Value to lower right of oak leaf branch **Edge Lettering:** TURKIYE CUMHURIYETI **Mint:** Istanbul

Date	Mintage	VF20	XF40	MS60	MS63	MS65
1991	22,938,000	—	0.25	0.35	0.50	0.75
1992	48,784,000	—	0.25	0.35	0.50	0.75
1993	2,310,000	—	0.25	0.35	0.50	0.75
1994	2,500	0.25	0.35	0.50	1.00	3.00
1995	2,500	0.25	0.35	0.50	1.00	3.00
1996	10,000	—	0.25	0.35	0.50	1.00
1997	—	—	0.25	0.35	0.50	1.00

KM# 948 3000 LIRA
28.28 g., 0.925 Silver 0.841 oz. ASW **Series:** International Year of Disabled Persons **Obv:** Stylized design divides top and bottom emblems **Rev:** Value within wreath **Mint:** Istanbul

Date	Mintage	VF20	XF40	MS60	MS63	MS65
1981	14,000	—	—	—	28.00	35.00
1981	16,000	PF65 32.00				

KM# 959 3000 LIRA
28.28 g., 0.925 Silver 0.841 oz. ASW **Series:** International Year of the Scout **Obv:** Value within wreath **Rev:** Mountain campsite scene **Mint:** Istanbul

Date	Mintage	VF20	XF40	MS60	MS63	MS65
ND-1982	12,000	—	—	—	28.00	35.00
ND-1982	14,000	PF65 32.00				

KM# 960 3000 LIRA
16.00 g., 0.925 Silver 0.4758 oz. ASW **Subject:** 60th Anniversary of the Republic **Obv:** Head of Atatürk left within circle **Rev:** Stylized reaching and standing figures within circle **Mint:** Istanbul

Date	Mintage	VF20	XF40	MS60	MS63	MS65
ND-1983	4,000	PF65 25.00				

KM# 954 5000 LIRA
7.13 g., 0.500 Gold 0.1146 oz. AGW **Subject:** World Championship Soccer - Madrid **Obv:** Soccer player kicking the ball **Rev:** Soccer ball as world globe with SPANYA'82 across middle **Mint:** Istanbul

Date	Mintage	VF20	XF40	MS60	MS63	MS65
ND(1982)	2,400	PF65 275				

KM# 969 5000 LIRA
23.33 g., 0.925 Silver 0.6938 oz. ASW **Subject:** Decade for Women **Obv:** Value and date within wreath **Rev:** Stylized woman holding dove **Mint:** Istanbul

Date	Mintage	VF20	XF40	MS60	MS63	MS65
1984	20,000	PF65 18.50				

KM# 970 5000 LIRA
23.33 g., 0.925 Silver 0.6938 oz. ASW **Series:** 1984 Summer Olympics **Obv:** Value within wreath **Rev:** Olympic athletes around center circle with stylized flame **Mint:** Istanbul

Date	Mintage	VF20	XF40	MS60	MS63	MS65
ND-1984	5,343	PF65 19.50				

KM# 971 5000 LIRA
23.33 g., 0.925 Silver 0.6938 oz. ASW **Series:** 1984 Winter Olympics **Obv:** Value within wreath **Rev:** Stylized slalom, bobsledder, ski jumper, and figure skater in inner circle, legend around **Mint:** Istanbul

Date	Mintage	VF20	XF40	MS60	MS63	MS65
1984	4,657	PF65 19.50				

KM# 972 5000 LIRA
23.33 g., 0.925 Silver 0.6938 oz. ASW **Subject:** 50th Anniversary of Women's Suffrage **Obv:** Value within wreath **Rev:** Three standing women facing in front of building **Mint:** Istanbul

Date	Mintage	VF20	XF40	MS60	MS63	MS65
ND-1984	1,000	PF65 35.00				

KM# 976 5000 LIRA
23.33 g., 0.925 Silver 0.6938 oz. ASW **Subject:** 500th Anniversary of Turkish Navy **Obv:** Value within wreath **Rev:** Bust with Turkish headdress at right, fleet of masted ships at left **Mint:** Istanbul

Date	Mintage	VF20	XF40	MS60	MS63	MS65
ND-1985	1,000	PF65 35.00				

KM# 977 5000 LIRA
23.33 g., 0.925 Silver 0.6938 oz. ASW **Subject:** Forestry Conference - Mexico **Obv:** Value within wreath **Rev:** Trees **Mint:** Istanbul

Date	Mintage	VF20	XF40	MS60	MS63	MS65
1985	3,088	PF65 19.50				

KM# 978 5000 LIRA
23.33 g., 0.925 Silver 0.6938 oz. ASW **Subject:** Youth Year **Obv:** Value within wreath **Rev:** Stylized head facing **Mint:** Istanbul

Date	Mintage	VF20	XF40	MS60	MS63	MS65
1985	2,000	PF65 25.00				

KM# 1011 5000 LIRA
23.33 g., 0.925 Silver 0.6938 oz. ASW **Subject:** Architect - Sinan **Mint:** Istanbul

Date	Mintage	VF20	XF40	MS60	MS63	MS65
ND-1988	—	PF65 25.00				

KM# 1005 5000 LIRA
Copper-Nickel **Subject:** Yunus Emre Sevgi Yili **Obv:** Value within wreath **Rev:** Inscription and arched design **Mint:** Istanbul

Date	Mintage	VF20	XF40	MS60	MS63	MS65
1991	—	PF65 5.00				

KM# 1018 5000 LIRA
Copper-Nickel **Subject:** Turkish Jews **Obv:** Value within wreath **Rev:** Standing figures below ship **Mint:** Istanbul

Date	Mintage	VF20	XF40	MS60	MS63	MS65
ND-1992	—	PF65 5.00				

KM# 1025 5000 LIRA
10.00 g., Nickel-Bronze, 28.5 mm. **Obv:** Head of Atatürk left **Rev:** Flower sprigs to left of value and date **Edge Lettering:** TURKIYE CUMHURIYETI **Mint:** Istanbul

Date	Mintage	VF20	XF40	MS60	MS63	MS65
1992	24,904,000	0.25	0.35	0.50	0.75	1.00
1992	—	PF65 6.50				
1993	15,872,000	0.25	0.35	0.50	0.75	1.00
1994	69,504,000	0.25	0.35	0.50	0.75	1.00

KM# 1029.1 5000 LIRA
5.98 g., Brass, 19.5 mm. **Obv:** Head of Atatürk left **Rev:** Flower sprigs to left of value and date **Edge:** Reeded **Mint:** Istanbul

Date	Mintage	VF20	XF40	MS60	MS63	MS65
1995 Large date	69,550,000	—	—	0.25	0.50	0.75

Date	Mintage	VF20	XF40	MS60	MS63	MS65
1995 Small date	Inc. above	—	—	0.25	0.50	0.75
1996	80,506,000	—	—	0.25	0.50	0.75
1997	—	—	—	0.25	0.50	0.75
1998	—	—	—	0.25	0.50	0.75

KM# 1029.2 5000 LIRA
3.48 g., Brass, 19.5 mm. **Obv:** Head of Atatürk left **Rev:** Flower sprigs to left of value and date **Edge:** Reeded **Mint:** Istanbul **Note:** Reduced weight version of KM#1029.1

Date	Mintage	VF20	XF40	MS60	MS63	MS65
1998	—	—	—	0.25	0.50	0.75
1999	—	—	—	0.25	0.50	0.75

KM# 933 10000 LIRA (10 Bin Lira)
17.17 g., 0.900 Gold 0.4968 oz. AGW **Subject:** UNICEF and I.Y.C. **Obv:** Value within wreath **Rev:** Multiracial children dancing, city view above, logos and date below **Mint:** Istanbul **Note:** Similar to 500 Lira, KM#931

Date	Mintage	VF20	XF40	MS60	MS63	MS65
1979	4,450	PF65 950				

KM# 986 10000 LIRA (10 Bin Lira)
23.33 g., 0.925 Silver 0.6938 oz. ASW **Subject:** 1986 World Cup Soccer - Mexico **Rev:** Soccer player in center of soccer ball **Mint:** Istanbul

Date	Mintage	VF20	XF40	MS60	MS63	MS65
1986	5,000	PF65 18.50				

KM# 1009 10000 LIRA (10 Bin Lira)
23.33 g., 0.925 Silver 0.6938 oz. ASW **Subject:** 1986 World Cup Soccer **Rev:** Cactus **Mint:** Istanbul

Date	Mintage	VF20	XF40	MS60	MS63	MS65
1986	7,000	PF65 18.50				

KM# 1010 10000 LIRA (10 Bin Lira)
23.33 g., 0.925 Silver 0.6938 oz. ASW **Subject:** A. Ersoy - Poet **Mint:** Istanbul

Date	Mintage	VF20	XF40	MS60	MS63	MS65
1986	—	PF65 18.50				

KM# 1022 10000 LIRA (10 Bin Lira)
23.33 g., 0.925 Silver 0.6938 oz. ASW **Subject:** World Peace **Obv:** Value within wreath **Rev:** Doves within diamond shape **Mint:** Istanbul

Date	Mintage	VF20	XF40	MS60	MS63	MS65
1986	Est. 1200	PF65 24.50				

KM# 981 10000 LIRA (10 Bin Lira)
22.97 g., 0.925 Silver 0.6831 oz. ASW **Subject:** Shelter for the Homeless **Obv:** Value within wreath **Rev:** Emblem within center of window design **Mint:** Istanbul

Date	Mintage	VF20	XF40	MS60	MS63	MS65
ND-1987	—	PF65 18.50				

KM# 982 10000 LIRA (10 Bin Lira)
22.97 g., 0.925 Silver 0.6831 oz. ASW **Subject:** 130 Years of Turkish Forestry **Obv:** Value within wreath **Rev:** Bird on top of globe design above pine trees **Mint:** Istanbul

Date	Mintage	VF20	XF40	MS60	MS63	MS65
ND-1987	5,000	PF65 18.50				

KM# 983 10000 LIRA (10 Bin Lira)
23.33 g., 0.925 Silver 0.6938 oz. ASW **Series:** Winter Olympics **Obv:** Value within wreath **Rev:** Stylized upright bear holding torch at left of totem pole **Mint:** Istanbul

Date	Mintage	VF20	XF40	MS60	MS63	MS65
1988	Est. 10000	PF65 18.50				

KM# 984 10000 LIRA (10 Bin Lira)
23.33 g., 0.925 Silver 0.6938 oz. ASW **Series:** 1988 Summer Olympics **Obv:** Value within wreath **Rev:** Stylized torch and designs **Mint:** Istanbul

Date	Mintage	VF20	XF40	MS60	MS63	MS65
1988	1,000	—	—	18.50	22.00	—
1988	Est. 10000	PF65 18.50				

KM# 1027.1 10000 LIRA (10 Bin Lira)
9.75 g., Copper-Nickel-Zinc, 23.5 mm. **Obv:** Head of Kemal Atat?rk left **Rev:** Value to left of flower sprig, large lettering **Edge:** Reeded with legend **Edge Lettering:** TURKIYE CUMHURIYETI, dates 1994 and 1995 **Mint:** Istanbul

Date	Mintage	VF20	XF40	MS60	MS63	MS65
1994	17,319,000	—	0.25	0.35	0.50	1.00
1995	56,584,000	—	0.25	0.35	0.50	1.00
1996	119,572,000	—	0.25	0.35	0.50	1.00
1997	—	—	0.25	0.35	0.50	1.00

KM# 1042 10000 LIRA (10 Bin Lira)
9.75 g., Copper-Nickel-Zinc, 23.5 mm. **Series:** 1994 Olympics **Obv:** Value to left of flower sprig **Rev:** Radiant Olympic rings **Mint:** Istanbul

Date	Mintage	VF20	XF40	MS60	MS63	MS65
1994	500,000	—	—	0.75	1.50	3.00

KM# 1027.2 10000 LIRA (10 Bin Lira)
9.75 g., Copper-Nickel-Zinc, 23.5 mm. **Obv:** Head of Kemal Atatürk left **Rev:** Value to left of flower sprig, small lettering **Edge:** Reeded with incuse legend **Edge Lettering:** TURKIYE CUMHURIYETI, dates 1996 and 1997 **Mint:** Istanbul **Note:** Thin planchet. Edge varieties exist.

Date	Mintage	VF20	XF40	MS60	MS63	MS65
1997	—	—	0.25	0.35	0.50	1.00
1998	—	—	0.25	0.35	0.50	1.00
1999	—	—	0.25	0.35	0.50	1.00

KM# 1027.3 10000 LIRA (10 Bin Lira)
6.75 g., Copper-Nickel-Zinc, 23.5 mm. **Obv:** Head of Kemal Atatürk left **Rev:** Value to left of flower sprig, small lettering **Edge:** "T.C." 6 times separated by vertical line pattern **Mint:** Istanbul **Note:** Thinner planchet, edge varieties exist,

Date	Mintage	VF20	XF40	MS60	MS63	MS65
1997	—	—	0.25	0.35	0.50	1.00
1998	—	—	0.25	0.35	0.50	1.00
1999	—	—	0.25	0.35	0.50	1.00

KM# 998 20000 LIRA (20 Bin Lira)
23.32 g., 0.925 Silver 0.6935 oz. ASW **Subject:** Environmental Protection **Obv:** Value within wreath **Rev:** Designs **Mint:** Istanbul

Date	Mintage	VF20	XF40	MS60	MS63	MS65
1988	—	PF65 18.50				

KM# 1001 20000 LIRA (20 Bin Lira)
23.32 g., 0.925 Silver 0.6935 oz. ASW **Subject:** 400th Anniversary - Death of Architect Sinan **Obv:** Value within wreath **Rev:** City view **Mint:** Istanbul

Date	Mintage	VF20	XF40	MS60	MS63	MS65
ND-1988	1,239	PF65 22.50				

KM# 1003 20000 LIRA (20 Bin Lira)
23.32 g., 0.925 Silver 0.6935 oz. ASW **Subject:** Teacher's Day **Obv:** Value within wreath **Rev:** Stylized design divides date below **Mint:** Istanbul

Date	Mintage	VF20	XF40	MS60	MS63	MS65
1989	1,013	PF65 22.50				

KM# 1013 20000 LIRA (20 Bin Lira)
23.32 g., 0.925 Silver 0.6935 oz. ASW **Subject:** Istanbul Metro **Obv:** Value within wreath **Rev:** City view **Mint:** Istanbul

Date	Mintage	VF20	XF40	MS60	MS63	MS65
ND-1989	Est. 5000	PF65 19.50				

KM# 992 20000 LIRA (20 Bin Lira)
23.32 g., 0.925 Silver 0.6935 oz. ASW **Subject:** 1990 World Cup Soccer **Obv:** Value within wreath **Rev:** Stylized football player kicking ball **Rev. Legend:** 1990 DUNYA FUTBOL SAMPIYONASI ITALYA **Mint:** Istanbul

Date	Mintage	VF20	XF40	MS60	MS63	MS65
1990	12,959	PF65 18.50				

KM# 993 20000 LIRA (20 Bin Lira)
23.32 g., 0.925 Silver 0.6935 oz. ASW **Subject:** 75th Anniversary - Battle of Gallipoli **Obv:** Value within wreath **Rev:** Armored figure facing, holding flag and weapon in front of monument **Mint:** Istanbul

Date	Mintage	VF20	XF40	MS60	MS63	MS65
ND-1990	1,963	PF65 21.50				

KM# 995 20000 LIRA (20 Bin Lira)
23.32 g., 0.925 Silver 0.6935 oz. ASW **Subject:** Soccer **Obv:** Value within wreath **Rev:** Soccer ball above stylized wolf **Mint:** Istanbul

Date	Mintage	VF20	XF40	MS60	MS63	MS65
1990	8,796	PF65 18.50				

KM# 1014 20000 LIRA (20 Bin Lira)
23.32 g., 0.925 Silver 0.6935 oz. ASW **Subject:** 70th Anniversary of Parliament **Rev:** Parliament building **Mint:** Istanbul

Date	Mintage	VF20	XF40	MS60	MS63	MS65
1990	1,163	PF65 22.50				

KM# 1057 20000 LIRA (20 Bin Lira)
23.32 g., 0.925 Silver 0.6935 oz. ASW **Series:** Summer Olympics **Obv:** Value within wreath **Rev:** Bicyclist **Mint:** Istanbul

Date	Mintage	VF20	XF40	MS60	MS63	MS65
ND(1990)	—	PF65 18.50				

KM# 1077 20000 LIRA (20 Bin Lira)
23.42 g., 0.925 Silver 0.6965 oz. ASW **Series:** Olympics **Subject:** Speed Skating **Obv:** Value within wreath **Rev:** Speed skater **Mint:** Istanbul

Date	Mintage	VF20	XF40	MS60	MS63	MS65
ND-1990	—	PF65 18.50				

KM# 1041 25000 LIRA (25 Bin Lira)
11.00 g., Copper-Nickel-Zinc, 26.5 mm. **Obv:** Head of Atatürk left **Rev:** Value to left of rose **Edge:** Lettered TC and flower five times **Mint:** Istanbul

Date	Mintage	VF20	XF40	MS60	MS63	MS65
1995	13,740,000	0.25	0.35	0.50	0.75	1.00
1996	59,742,000	0.25	0.35	0.50	0.75	1.00
1997	—	0.25	0.35	0.50	0.75	1.00
1998	—	0.25	0.35	0.50	0.75	1.00
1999	—	0.25	0.35	0.50	0.75	1.00
2000	—	0.25	0.35	0.50	0.75	1.00

KM# 1043 25000 LIRA (25 Bin Lira)
11.00 g., Copper-Nickel-Zinc, 26.5 mm. **Series:** Environmental Protection **Obv:** Small head facing divides profiles with birds and nest on top of heads **Rev:** Value to left of rose **Mint:** Istanbul

Date	Mintage	VF20	XF40	MS60	MS63	MS65
1995	500,000	—	—	0.75	1.50	3.00

KM# 955 30000 LIRA
15.98 g., 0.917 Gold 0.4711 oz. AGW **Series:** International Year of Disabled Persons **Obv:** Value within wreath **Rev:** Stylized seated figure missing legs and globe design **Mint:** Istanbul

Date	Mintage	VF20	XF40	MS60	MS63	MS65
1981	140	—	—	—	—	925
1981	3,000	PF65 900				

KM# 961 30000 LIRA
15.98 g., 0.917 Gold 0.4711 oz. AGW **Series:** International Year of the Scout **Obv:** Value within wreath **Rev:** Emblems within circle **Mint:** Istanbul

Date	Mintage	VF20	XF40	MS60	MS63	MS65
ND-1983	2,000	—	—	—	—	900
ND-1983	2,000	PF65 900				

KM# 973 50000 LIRA (50 Bin Lira)
7.13 g., 0.900 Gold 0.2063 oz. AGW **Series:** Decade for Women **Obv:** Value and date within wreath **Rev:** Half-figure of female facing **Mint:** Istanbul

Date	Mintage	VF20	XF40	MS60	MS63	MS65
1984	800	PF65 420				

KM# 999 50000 LIRA (50 Bin Lira)
28.28 g., 0.925 Silver 0.841 oz. ASW **Series:** Winter Olympics **Obv:** Value within wreath **Rev:** Speed skater **Mint:** Istanbul

Date	Mintage	VF20	XF40	MS60	MS63	MS65
ND-1990	15,000	PF65 22.50				

KM# 1000 50000 LIRA (50 Bin Lira)
28.28 g., 0.925 Silver 0.841 oz. ASW **Series:** 1990 Summer Olympics **Obv:** Value within wreath **Rev:** Bicyclist **Mint:** Istanbul

Date	Mintage	VF20	XF40	MS60	MS63	MS65
ND-1990	15,000	PF65 22.50				

KM# 1006 50000 LIRA (50 Bin Lira)
22.87 g., 0.925 Silver 0.6801 oz. ASW **Subject:** Yunus Emre Sevgi Yili **Obv:** Value within wreath **Rev:** Inscription and arched brick facade **Mint:** Istanbul

Date	Mintage	VF20	XF40	MS60	MS63	MS65
1991	1,578	PF65 24.00				

KM# 1007 50000 LIRA (50 Bin Lira)
22.87 g., 0.925 Silver 0.6801 oz. ASW **Subject:** Mozart Opera **Obv:** Value within wreath **Rev:** Cameo within curtains above theater, circle surrounds all **Mint:** Istanbul

Date	Mintage	VF20	XF40	MS60	MS63	MS65
ND-1991	1,614	PF65 24.00				

KM# 1019 50000 LIRA (50 Bin Lira)
22.77 g., 0.925 Silver 0.6772 oz. ASW **Subject:** Ahmet Adnan Saygun - Musician **Obv:** Value within wreath **Rev:** Bust facing in front of music sheet **Mint:** Istanbul

Date	Mintage	VF20	XF40	MS60	MS63	MS65
ND-1991	1,021	PF65 24.00				

KM# 1016 50000 LIRA (50 Bin Lira)
23.33 g., 0.925 Silver 0.6938 oz. ASW **Subject:** Turkish Jews **Obv:** Value within wreath **Rev:** Similar to 5000 Lira, KM#1018 **Mint:** Istanbul

Date	Mintage	VF20	XF40	MS60	MS63	MS65
ND-1992	—	PF65 22.50				

KM# 1023 50000 LIRA (50 Bin Lira)
23.08 g., 0.925 Silver 0.6864 oz. ASW **Subject:** 200th Birthday of Rossini **Obv:** Value within wreath **Rev:** Bust 1/4 right to left of building within circle **Mint:** Istanbul

Date	Mintage	VF20	XF40	MS60	MS63	MS65
ND-1992	—	PF65 27.00				

KM# 1136 50000 LIRA (50 Bin Lira)
23.16 g., 0.925 Silver 0.6888 oz. ASW, 38.6 mm. **Subject:** 30th Anniversary - Constitution **Obv:** Value within wreath **Rev:** Flame above open book within circle **Edge:** Reeded **Mint:** Istanbul

Date	Mintage	VF20	XF40	MS60	MS63	MS65
ND(1992)	1,134	PF65 42.00				

KM# 1020 50000 LIRA (50 Bin Lira)
23.08 g., 0.925 Silver 0.6864 oz. ASW **Subject:** 1994 World Cup Soccer **Obv:** Value within wreath **Rev:** Soccer ball on top of torch **Mint:** Istanbul

Date	Mintage	VF20	XF40	MS60	MS63	MS65
ND-1993	—	PF65 19.50				

KM# 1021.1 50000 LIRA (50 Bin Lira)
23.08 g., 0.925 Silver 0.6864 oz. ASW **Subject:** 1994 World Cup Soccer **Obv:** Value within wreath **Rev:** Bridge behind soccer player, fuzzy looking rock under bridge **Mint:** Istanbul

Date	Mintage	VF20	XF40	MS60	MS63	MS65
ND-1993	6,038	—	—	—	18.00	22.00
ND-1993	—	PF65 16.00				

KM# 1021.2 50000 LIRA (50 Bin Lira)
23.08 g., 0.925 Silver 0.6864 oz. ASW **Subject:** 1994 World Cup Soccer **Obv:** Value within wreath **Rev:** Sharp looking rock under bridge **Mint:** Istanbul

Date	Mintage	VF20	XF40	MS60	MS63	MS65
ND-1993	550	PF65 40.00				

KM# 1024 50000 LIRA (50 Bin Lira)
23.08 g., 0.925 Silver 0.6864 oz. ASW **Subject:** 25th Anniversary of Turkish Red Crescent **Obv:** Value within wreath **Rev:** Aerial country view below world globe **Mint:** Istanbul

Date	Mintage	VF20	XF40	MS60	MS63	MS65
ND-1993	938	PF65 35.00				

KM# 1044 50000 LIRA (50 Bin Lira)
23.08 g., 0.925 Silver 0.6864 oz. ASW **Subject:** 125 Years - Turkish Supreme Court **Obv:** Value within wreath **Rev:** Balance scales within circle **Mint:** Istanbul

Date	Mintage	VF20	XF40	MS60	MS63	MS65
ND-1993	1,052	PF65 30.00				

KM# 1026 50000 LIRA (50 Bin Lira)
22.84 g., 0.925 Silver 0.6792 oz. ASW **Series:** Olympics **Obv:** Value within wreath **Rev:** Flag and Olympic rings **Mint:** Istanbul

Date	Mintage	VF20	XF40	MS60	MS63	MS65
ND-1994	1,821	PF65 20.00				

KM# 1030 50000 LIRA (50 Bin Lira)
31.47 g., 0.925 Silver 0.9359 oz. ASW **Series:** Endangered Wildlife **Obv:** Value within wreath **Rev:** Bald Ibis **Mint:** Istanbul

Date	Mintage	VF20	XF40	MS60	MS63	MS65
ND-1994	6,807	PF65 26.50				

KM# 1031 50000 LIRA (50 Bin Lira)
23.33 g., 0.925 Silver 0.6938 oz. ASW **Subject:** Tschaikovsky **Obv:** Value within wreath **Rev:** Head facing at upper right of ballet scene **Mint:** Istanbul

Date	Mintage	VF20	XF40	MS60	MS63	MS65
ND-1994	1,237	PF65 35.00				

KM# 1033 50000 LIRA (50 Bin Lira)
23.33 g., 0.925 Silver 0.6938 oz. ASW **Subject:** 75th Anniversary - Turkish National Assembly **Obv:** Value within wreath **Rev:** Upright designs above building **Mint:** Istanbul

Date	Mintage	VF20	XF40	MS60	MS63	MS65
1995	3,000	PF65 18.00				

KM# 1035 50000 LIRA (50 Bin Lira)
23.33 g., 0.925 Silver 0.6938 oz. ASW **Subject:** 150th Anniversary - National Police **Obv:** Value within wreath **Rev:** Police badge above dates **Mint:** Istanbul

Date	Mintage	VF20	XF40	MS60	MS63	MS65
1995	1,262	PF65 20.50				

KM# 1037 50000 LIRA (50 Bin Lira)
Brass **Obv:** Value within wreath **Rev:** Swimming sea turtle **Mint:** Istanbul **Note:** Oxidized finish.

Date	Mintage	VF20	XF40	MS60	MS63	MS65
1995	1,235	—	—	7.00	12.00	15.00

KM# 1037a 50000 LIRA (50 Bin Lira)
23.33 g., 0.925 Silver 0.6938 oz. ASW **Obv:** Value within wreath **Rev:** Swimming sea turtle **Mint:** Istanbul

Date	Mintage	VF20	XF40	MS60	MS63	MS65
1995	2,961	PF65 25.00				

KM# 1038 50000 LIRA (50 Bin Lira)
23.33 g., 0.925 Silver 0.6938 oz. ASW **Obv:** Value within wreath **Rev:** Sailing ship - "Piri Reis" **Mint:** Istanbul

Date	Mintage	VF20	XF40	MS60	MS63	MS65
1995	13,923	PF65 18.00				

KM# 1040 50000 LIRA (50 Bin Lira)
23.33 g., 0.925 Silver 0.6938 oz. ASW **Series:** 50th Anniversary - F.A.O. **Obv:** Value within wreath **Rev:** Anniversary date above logo within design **Mint:** Istanbul

Date	Mintage	VF20	XF40	MS60	MS63	MS65
1995	2,845	PF65 20.50				

KM# 1045 50000 LIRA (50 Bin Lira)
31.47 g., 0.925 Silver 0.9359 oz. ASW **Series:** Summer Olympics **Obv:** Value and date within wreath **Rev:** Wrestlers **Mint:** Istanbul

Date	Mintage	VF20	XF40	MS60	MS63	MS65
1995	12,476	PF65 22.00				

KM# 1050 50000 LIRA (50 Bin Lira)
11.78 g., Copper-Nickel-Zinc, 28 mm. **Series:** F.A.O. **Obv:** Globe within center of designs, single sprig at left **Rev:** Value **Edge:** "T.C." and four fleur-de-lis repeated four times **Mint:** Istanbul

Date	Mintage	VF20	XF40	MS60	MS63	MS65
ND-1996	500,000	—	—	0.75	1.50	3.00

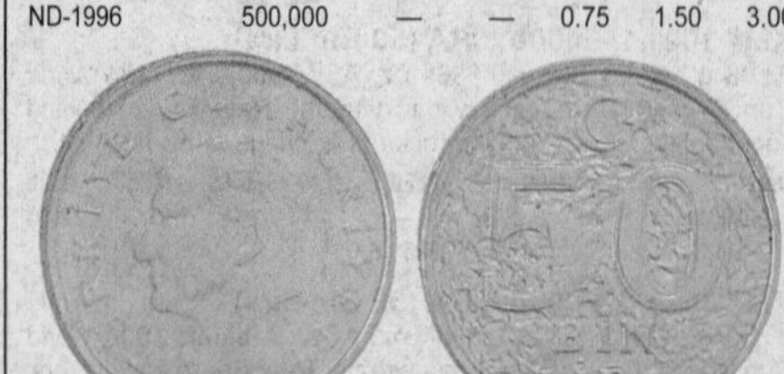

KM# 1056 50000 LIRA (50 Bin Lira)
11.60 g., Copper-Nickel-Zinc, 28 mm. **Obv:** Head of Atatürk left **Rev:** Value **Mint:** Istanbul

Date	Mintage	VF20	XF40	MS60	MS63	MS65
1996	11,916,000	—	—	0.45	0.75	1.00
1997	—	—	—	0.45	0.75	1.00
1998	—	—	—	0.45	0.75	1.00
1999	—	—	—	0.45	0.75	1.00
2000	—	—	—	0.45	0.75	1.00

KM# 1103 50000 LIRA (50 Bin Lira)
1.50 g., Aluminum, 20 mm. **Series:** F.A.O **Obv:** Value and date within wreath **Rev:** Ancient vintner **Edge:** Plain **Mint:** Istanbul

Date	Mintage	VF20	XF40	MS60	MS63	MS65
1999	—	—	0.25	0.45	0.75	1.00

KM# 956 100000 LIRA (100 Bin Lira)
33.82 g., 0.917 Gold 0.9971 oz. AGW **Subject:** Islamic World 15th Century **Rev:** City view above value within circle **Mint:** Istanbul

Date	Mintage	VF20	XF40	MS60	MS63	MS65
1982	12,000	PF65 1,900				

KM# 1078 100000 LIRA (100 Bin Lira)
7.50 g., Nickel-Brass **Subject:** 75th Anniversary of Republic **Obv:** Value below crescent and star **Rev:** Bust of Mustafa Kemal Atatürk left **Mint:** Istanbul

Date	Mintage	VF20	XF40	MS60	MS63	MS65
1999	—	—	—	0.25	0.50	1.00
2000	—	—	—	0.25	0.50	1.00

KM# 1079 100000 LIRA (100 Bin Lira)
7.50 g., Nickel-Brass **Subject:** 75th Anniversary of Republic **Obv:** Value below crescent and star **Rev:** Anniversary logo and dates **Mint:** Istanbul

Date	Mintage	VF20	XF40	MS60	MS63	MS65
1999	—	—	—	0.25	0.50	1.00
2000	—	—	—	0.25	0.50	1.00

KM# 974 200000 LIRA
33.82 g., 0.917 Gold 0.9971 oz. AGW **Subject:** 50th Anniversary of Women's Suffrage **Mint:** Istanbul

Date	Mintage	VF20	XF40	MS60	MS63	MS65
ND-1984	62	PF65 2,150				

KM# 1002 200000 LIRA
7.22 g., 0.917 Gold 0.2127 oz. AGW **Subject:** 400th Anniversary - Death of Architect Sinan **Obv:** Value within wreath **Rev:** Arched city view **Mint:** Istanbul

Date	Mintage	VF20	XF40	MS60	MS63	MS65
ND-1988	244	PF65 450				

KM# 1004 200000 LIRA
7.22 g., 0.917 Gold 0.2127 oz. AGW **Subject:** Teacher's Day **Obv:** Value within wreath **Rev:** Stylized design divides date **Mint:** Istanbul

Date	Mintage	VF20	XF40	MS60	MS63	MS65
1989	197	PF65 450				

KM# 994 200000 LIRA
7.22 g., 0.917 Gold 0.2127 oz. AGW **Subject:** 75th Anniversary - Battle of Gallipoli **Mint:** Istanbul

Date	Mintage	VF20	XF40	MS60	MS63	MS65
ND-1990	Est. 494	PF65 450				

KM# 1051 400000 LIRA
Bronze **Subject:** Habitat II **Obv:** City view **Rev:** Conference logo **Mint:** Istanbul

Date	Mintage	VF20	XF40	MS60	MS63	MS65
1996	2,402	—	—	2.00	3.00	5.00

KM# 1008 500000 LIRA
7.13 g., 0.900 Gold 0.2063 oz. AGW **Subject:** Yunus Emre **Obv:** Value within wreath **Rev:** Inscription and arched brick facade **Mint:** Istanbul

Date	Mintage	VF20	XF40	MS60	MS63	MS65
1991	288	PF65 435				

KM# 1017 500000 LIRA
7.14 g., 0.900 Gold 0.2066 oz. AGW **Subject:** 100 Years of Peace and Harmony - Turkish Jews **Obv:** Value within wreath **Rev:** Standing figures next to ship **Mint:** Istanbul

Date	Mintage	VF20	XF40	MS60	MS63	MS65
ND-1992	485	PF65 425				

KM# 1032 500000 LIRA
7.22 g., 0.9166 Gold 0.2127 oz. AGW **Subject:** Southeast Anatolian Project **Obv:** Value within wreath **Rev:** Design within wreath **Mint:** Istanbul

Date	Mintage	VF20	XF40	MS60	MS63	MS65
ND-1994	950	PF65 425				

KM# 1034 500000 LIRA
7.22 g., 0.9166 Gold 0.2127 oz. AGW **Subject:** 75th Anniversary - Turkish National Assembly **Obv:** Value and date within wreath **Rev:** Building in front of upright designs **Mint:** Istanbul

Date	Mintage	VF20	XF40	MS60	MS63	MS65
1995	255	PF65 435				

KM# 1036 500000 LIRA
7.22 g., 0.9166 Gold 0.2127 oz. AGW **Subject:** Istanbul Gold Exchange **Obv:** Value and date within wreath **Rev:** AR above inscription and date **Mint:** Istanbul

Date	Mintage	VF20	XF40	MS60	MS63	MS65
1995	271	PF65 435				

KM# 1039 500000 LIRA
7.22 g., 0.9166 Gold 0.2127 oz. AGW **Obv:** Value and date within wreath **Rev:** Sailing ship - "Piri Reis" **Mint:** Istanbul

Date	Mintage	VF20	XF40	MS60	MS63	MS65
1995	1,904	PF65 425				

KM# 1138 500000 LIRA
12.10 g., Copper-Nickel, 32 mm. **Subject:** Lira to Euro Transition **Obv:** Value and date within wreath **Rev:** Head of Atatürk left **Edge:** Reeded **Mint:** Istanbul **Note:** Dual denomination: 500,000 lira-2 euro

Date	Mintage	VF20	XF40	MS60	MS63	MS65
1998	12,660	—	—	2.00	3.00	5.00

KM# 1081 500000 LIRA
11.91 g., Copper-Nickel **Subject:** Trojan Horse **Obv:** Value and date within wreath **Rev:** Ancient Greek soldier and wooden horse **Edge:** Reeded **Mint:** Istanbul **Note:** Struck at Istanbul.

Date	Mintage	VF20	XF40	MS60	MS63	MS65
1999	6,243	—	—	3.00	5.00	8.00

KM# 1046 750000 LIRA
31.47 g., 0.925 Silver 0.9359 oz. ASW **Subject:** Europa **Obv:** Value and date within wreath **Rev:** Various landmarks **Mint:** Istanbul

Date	Mintage	VF20	XF40	MS60	MS63	MS65
1996	Est. 35000	PF65 30.00				

KM# 1048.1 750000 LIRA
23.20 g., 0.925 Silver 0.690 oz. ASW **Series:** F.A.O. **Obv:** Value within wreath **Rev:** World globe with corn stalks at left **Mint:** Istanbul

Date	Mintage	F12	VF20	XF40	MS60	MS63
1996	5,000	PF65 17.50				

KM# 1048.2 750000 LIRA
23.20 g., 0.925 Silver 0.690 oz. ASW **Series:** F.A.O. **Obv:** Value within wreath **Rev:** World globe with corn stalks at right **Mint:** Istanbul

Date	Mintage	VF20	XF40	MS60	MS63	MS65
1996	2,010	PF65 17.50				

KM# 1049 750000 LIRA
23.41 g., 0.925 Silver 0.6962 oz. ASW **Subject:** Turkish European Customs Union **Obv:** Flying plane and hills **Rev:** Clasped hands divide circle of stars **Mint:** Istanbul

Date	Mintage	VF20	XF40	MS60	MS63	MS65
1996	3,947	PF65 19.00				

KM# 1052 750000 LIRA
23.37 g., 0.925 Silver 0.695 oz. ASW **Subject:** Nasreddin Hoca **Obv:** Stylized figure with headdress on donkey facing **Rev:** Stylized figure with headdress on donkey walking away **Mint:** Istanbul

Date	Mintage	VF20	XF40	MS60	MS63	MS65
1996	4,300	PF65 19.00				

KM# 1063 750000 LIRA
31.47 g., 0.925 Silver 0.9359 oz. ASW **Subject:** World Cup Soccer **Obv:** Value and date within wreath **Rev:** Goalie catching ball **Mint:** Istanbul

Date	Mintage	VF20	XF40	MS60	MS63	MS65
1996	6,848	PF65 24.50				

KM# 1058 750000 LIRA
Bronze **Subject:** First World Air Games - Manned Flight **Obv:** Value within wreath **Rev:** Figure with bat-like wings flying over city, all within circle **Edge:** Reeded **Mint:** Istanbul

Date	Mintage	VF20	XF40	MS60	MS63	MS65
1997 Antique patina	1,733	—	—	2.00	3.00	5.00

KM# 1059 750000 LIRA
Bronze **Subject:** XI World Forestry Congress **Obv:** Value within wreath **Rev:** Stylized dove left below tree **Mint:** Istanbul

Date	Mintage	VF20	XF40	MS60	MS63	MS65
1997	1,778	—	—	2.00	3.00	5.00

KM# 1068 750000 LIRA
Bronze **Subject:** Forestry - "TEMA" **Obv:** Value within wreath **Rev:** Wheel of trees design **Edge:** Reeded **Mint:** Istanbul

Date	Mintage	VF20	XF40	MS60	MS63	MS65
1998	1,950	—	—	2.00	3.00	5.00

KM# 1047 1000000 LIRA
31.72 g., 0.925 Silver 0.9433 oz. ASW **Series:** Endangered Wildlife **Obv:** Ocean view within circle **Rev:** Mediterranean seal **Mint:** Istanbul

Date	Mintage	VF20	XF40	MS60	MS63	MS65
1996	3,594	PF65 25.00				

KM# 1053 1000000 LIRA
31.46 g., 0.925 Silver 0.9356 oz. ASW **Series:** Endangered Wildlife **Obv:** Value and date within wreath **Rev:** Galathus Elwesii flowers **Mint:** Istanbul

Date	Mintage	VF20	XF40	MS60	MS63	MS65
1996	3,100	PF65 24.50				

KM# 1054 1000000 LIRA
31.46 g., 0.925 Silver 0.9356 oz. ASW **Subject:** Habitat II **Obv:** Steepled buildings **Rev:** Conference logo **Mint:** Istanbul

Date	Mintage	VF20	XF40	MS60	MS63	MS65
1996	3,968	PF65 24.50				

KM# 1055 1000000 LIRA
31.77 g., 0.925 Silver 0.9448 oz. ASW **Obv:** Value and date within oat sprigs **Rev:** Bust of Hulusi Behcet facing **Mint:** Istanbul

Date	Mintage	VF20	XF40	MS60	MS63	MS65
1996	2,250	PF65 25.00				

KM# 1060 1000000 LIRA
31.57 g., 0.925 Silver 0.9389 oz. ASW **Subject:** Chinese History - Excavation of the Terra Cotta Army **Obv:** Great Wall of China **Rev:** Excavation site **Mint:** Istanbul

Date	Mintage	VF20	XF40	MS60	MS63	MS65
1997	4,273	—	—	—	—	24.50

Note: This coin does not have any national identification other than the mintmark and denomination

KM# 1066 1000000 LIRA
1.24 g., 0.999 Gold 0.040 oz. AGW **Obv:** Value in wreath **Rev:** Head of King Croesus of Lydia right **Edge:** Reeded **Mint:** Istanbul

Date	Mintage	VF20	XF40	MS60	MS63	MS65
1997	10,465	PF65 75.00				

KM# 1067 1000000 LIRA
1.24 g., 0.999 Gold 0.040 oz. AGW **Obv:** Value and date within wreath **Rev:** Ancient Lydian coin portraying lion **Mint:** Istanbul

Date	Mintage	VF20	XF40	MS60	MS63	MS65
1997	—	PF65 75.00				

KM# 1069 1000000 LIRA
31.44 g., 0.925 Silver 0.935 oz. ASW **Subject:** Mehmed Akif Ersoy **Obv:** Spiral inscription **Rev:** Bust facing **Mint:** Istanbul

Date	Mintage	VF20	XF40	MS60	MS63	MS65
1997	Est. 2250	PF65 24.50				

KM# 1098 1000000 LIRA
1.22 g., 0.999 Gold 0.0392 oz. AGW, 13.9 mm. **Obv:** Value and date within wreath **Rev:** Sailing ship - "Piri Reis" **Edge:** Reeded **Mint:** Istanbul

Date	Mintage	VF20	XF40	MS60	MS63	MS65
1997	10,655	PF65 75.00				

KM# 1061 1500000 LIRA
31.44 g., 0.925 Silver 0.935 oz. ASW **Subject:** First World Air Games - Manned Flight **Obv:** Value and date within wreath **Rev:** Figure with bat-like wings flying over city **Mint:** Istanbul

Date	Mintage	VF20	XF40	MS60	MS63	MS65
1997	2,300	PF65 24.50				

KM# 1062 1500000 LIRA
31.44 g., 0.925 Silver 0.935 oz. ASW **Subject:** XI World Forestry Conference **Obv:** Value within wreath **Rev:** Stylized dove left below tree **Mint:** Istanbul

Date	Mintage	VF20	XF40	MS60	MS63	MS65
1997	2,255	PF65 24.50				

KM# 1082 1500000 LIRA
31.33 g., 0.925 Silver 0.9317 oz. ASW **Subject:** Barbaros Hayreddin **Obv:** Value and date within wreath **Rev:** Two war ships **Edge:** Reeded **Mint:** Istanbul

Date	Mintage	VF20	XF40	MS60	MS63	MS65
1997	7,062	PF65 24.50				

KM# 1100 1500000 LIRA
31.37 g., 0.925 Silver 0.9329 oz. ASW, 38.6 mm. **Subject:** Myra'li Aziz Noel Baba and Euro **Obv:** Value and date within wreath **Rev:** Statue and tower within 1/2 star wreath **Edge:** Reeded **Mint:** Istanbul

Date	Mintage	VF20	XF40	MS60	MS63	MS65
1997	10,492	PF65 24.50				

KM# 1064 2500000 LIRA
31.15 g., 0.925 Silver 0.9264 oz. ASW **Obv:** Value and date within wreath **Rev:** Bust of Hasan-Ali Yücel 1/4 right **Mint:** Istanbul

Date	Mintage	VF20	XF40	MS60	MS63	MS65
1998	—	PF65 24.50				

KM# 1065 2500000 LIRA
31.58 g., 0.925 Silver 0.9392 oz. ASW **Subject:** Forestry - "TEMA" **Obv:** Value and date within wreath **Rev:** Wheel of trees design, similar to 750000 Lira, KM#1068 **Mint:** Istanbul

Date	Mintage	VF20	XF40	MS60	MS63	MS65
1998	Est. 4537	PF65 24.50				

KM# 1070 2500000 LIRA
31.44 g., 0.925 Silver 0.935 oz. ASW **Subject:** 75 Years of Peace **Obv:** Value and date within wreath **Rev:** Doves, treaty, and radiant sun **Mint:** Istanbul

Date	Mintage	VF20	XF40	MS60	MS63	MS65
1998	—	PF65 24.50				

KM# 1083 2500000 LIRA
31.35 g., 0.925 Silver 0.9323 oz. ASW **Series:** 2000 Olympics **Obv:** Value and date within wreath **Rev:** Weight lifter and mosque **Edge:** Reeded **Mint:** Istanbul **Note:** Struck at Istanbul.

Date	Mintage	VF20	XF40	MS60	MS63	MS65
1998	—	PF65 24.50				

KM# 1084 2500000 LIRA
23.30 g., 0.925 Silver 0.6929 oz. ASW **Obv:** Value and date within wreath **Rev:** Head of Atatürk left **Edge:** Reeded **Mint:** Istanbul

Date	Mintage	VF20	XF40	MS60	MS63	MS65
1998	—	PF65 19.00				

KM# 1071 3000000 LIRA
31.32 g., 0.925 Silver 0.9315 oz. ASW **Subject:** 75 Years of Peace **Obv:** 75th Anniversary logo above inscription, value below flanked by sprigs **Rev:** Doves, treaty, and radiant sun **Mint:** Istanbul

Date	Mintage	VF20	XF40	MS60	MS63	MS65
ND-1998	—	PF65 24.50				

KM# 1072 3000000 LIRA
31.32 g., 0.925 Silver 0.9315 oz. ASW **Subject:** 75th Anniversary Republic **Obv:** 75th Anniversary logo **Rev:** Atatürk's revolution **Mint:** Istanbul

Date	Mintage	VF20	XF40	MS60	MS63	MS65
ND-1998	—	PF65 24.50				

KM# 1073 3000000 LIRA
31.32 g., 0.925 Silver 0.9315 oz. ASW **Subject:** 75th Anniversary of Republic **Obv:** 75th Anniversary logo **Rev:** Couple dancing, people in background **Mint:** Istanbul

Date	Mintage	VF20	XF40	MS60	MS63	MS65
ND-1998	—	PF65 24.50				

KM# 1074 3000000 LIRA
31.32 g., 0.925 Silver 0.9315 oz. ASW **Obv:** 75th Anniversary logo **Rev:** Ataturk with children **Mint:** Istanbul

Date	Mintage	VF20	XF40	MS60	MS63	MS65
ND-1998	—	PF65 24.50				

KM# 1075 3000000 LIRA
31.32 g., 0.925 Silver 0.9315 oz. ASW **Obv:** 75th Anniversary logo **Rev:** Atatürk with cane before crowd **Mint:** Istanbul

Date	Mintage	VF20	XF40	MS60	MS63	MS65
ND-1998	—	PF65 24.50				

KM# 1076 3000000 LIRA
31.32 g., 0.925 Silver 0.9315 oz. ASW **Obv:** 75th Anniversary logo **Rev:** Depictions of arts and sciences in Turkey **Mint:** Istanbul

Date	Mintage	VF20	XF40	MS60	MS63	MS65
ND-1998	—	PF65 24.50				

KM# 1080 3000000 LIRA
31.36 g., 0.925 Silver 0.9326 oz. ASW **Subject:** Dolmabahce Sarayi Palace **Obv:** Value within wreath **Rev:** Building above "EURO" with stars above **Edge:** Reeded **Mint:** Istanbul **Note:** Struck at Istanbul.

Date	Mintage	VF20	XF40	MS60	MS63	MS65
1998	1,710	PF65 24.50				

KM# 1086 3000000 LIRA
31.36 g., 0.925 Silver 0.9326 oz. ASW **Subject:** Galata Kulesi **Obv:** Value and date within wreath **Rev:** Tower and city view above "EURO" **Mint:** Istanbul

Date	Mintage	VF20	XF40	MS60	MS63	MS65
1998	—	PF65 24.50				

KM# 1107 3000000 LIRA
31.47 g., 0.925 Silver 0.9359 oz. ASW, 38.6 mm. **Series:** Olympics **Obv:** Value and date within wreath **Rev:** Long jumper and logo **Edge:** Reeded **Mint:** Istanbul

Date	Mintage	VF20	XF40	MS60	MS63	MS65
1999	31,000	PF65 25.00				

KM# 1087 4000000 LIRA
31.40 g., 0.925 Silver 0.9338 oz. ASW **Subject:** Fethiye **Obv:** Value within wreath **Rev:** Two sailing ships **Edge:** Reeded **Mint:** Istanbul

Date	Mintage	VF20	XF40	MS60	MS63	MS65
1999	—	PF65 31.00				

KM# 1088 4000000 LIRA
31.40 g., 0.925 Silver 0.9338 oz. ASW **Subject:** 80th Anniversary - Atatürk's Landing at Samsun **Obv:** Value and date within wreath **Rev:** Bust right above steamship **Mint:** Istanbul

Date	Mintage	VF20	XF40	MS60	MS63	MS65
1999	1,632	PF65 24.50				

KM# 1089 4000000 LIRA
31.40 g., 0.925 Silver 0.9338 oz. ASW **Subject:** Istanbul Culture Capital **Obv:** Value and date within wreath **Rev:** Capital building **Mint:** Istanbul

Date	Mintage	VF20	XF40	MS60	MS63	MS65
1999	1,180	PF65 24.50				

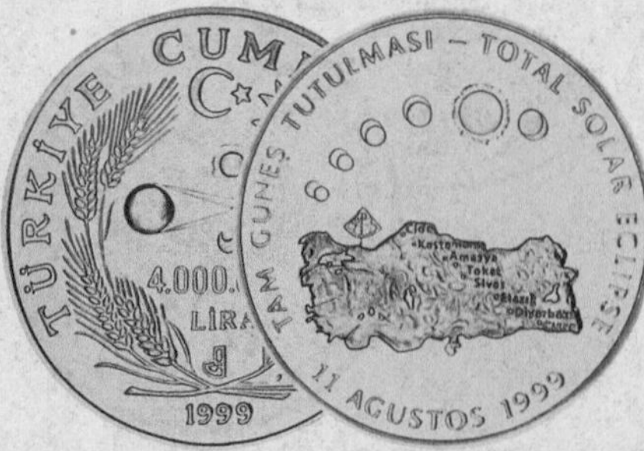

KM# 1090 4000000 LIRA
31.40 g., 0.925 Silver 0.9338 oz. ASW **Subject:** Solar Eclipse **Obv:** Value within wreath **Rev:** Eclipse stages above map **Mint:** Istanbul

Date	Mintage	VF20	XF40	MS60	MS63	MS65
1999	—	PF65 24.50				

KM# 1091 4000000 LIRA
31.40 g., 0.925 Silver 0.9338 oz. ASW **Subject:** Solar Eclipse **Obv:** Value and date within wreath **Rev:** People watching eclipse **Mint:** Istanbul

Date	Mintage	VF20	XF40	MS60	MS63	MS65
1999	—	PF65 24.50				

KM# 1092 4000000 LIRA
31.40 g., 0.925 Silver 0.9338 oz. ASW **Subject:** Silk Road **Obv:** Scroll design with landmarks **Rev:** Mounted archer hunting lion **Mint:** Istanbul **Note:** Antiqued finish.

Date	Mintage	VF20	XF40	MS60	MS63	MS65
1999	1,263	PF65 24.50				

KM# 1093 4000000 LIRA
31.40 g., 0.925 Silver 0.9338 oz. ASW **Subject:** Osman Gazi **Obv:** Value within wreath **Rev:** Turbaned 1/2-length bust facing **Mint:** Istanbul

Date	Mintage	VF20	XF40	MS60	MS63	MS65
1999	—	PF65 24.50				

KM# 1094 4000000 LIRA
31.40 g., 0.925 Silver 0.9338 oz. ASW **Obv:** Value within wreath **Rev:** Gazi leading mounted troops **Mint:** Istanbul

Date	Mintage	VF20	XF40	MS60	MS63	MS65
1999	—	PF65 24.50				

KM# 1095 4000000 LIRA
31.40 g., 0.925 Silver 0.9338 oz. ASW **Obv:** Value within wreath **Rev:** Mounted archers and prey **Mint:** Istanbul

Date	Mintage	VF20	XF40	MS60	MS63	MS65
1999	—	PF65 28.50				

KM# 1096 4000000 LIRA
31.40 g., 0.925 Silver 0.9338 oz. ASW **Obv:** Value within wreath **Rev:** 700-year-old Islamic coin design **Mint:** Istanbul

Date	Mintage	VF20	XF40	MS60	MS63	MS65
1999	—	PF65 24.50				

KM# 1099 4000000 LIRA
31.41 g., 0.925 Silver 0.9341 oz. ASW, 38.6 mm. **Subject:** Lacerta Clarkorum **Obv:** Value and date within wreath **Rev:** Two Clark's lizards **Edge:** Reeded **Mint:** Istanbul

Date	Mintage	VF20	XF40	MS60	MS63	MS65
1999	—	PF65 24.50				

KM# 1108 4000000 LIRA
31.47 g., 0.925 Silver 0.9359 oz. ASW, 38.6 mm. **Subject:** Ataturk **Obv:** Value and date within wreath **Rev:** Half length bust right below "EURO" flanked by stars **Edge:** Reeded **Mint:** Istanbul

Date	Mintage	VF20	XF40	MS60	MS63	MS65
1999	4,596	PF65 24.50				

KM# 1109 4000000 LIRA
31.47 g., 0.925 Silver 0.9359 oz. ASW, 38.6 mm. **Subject:** "Bogazici" (Bosphorus) **Obv:** Value within wreath **Rev:** Water front mosque above "EURO" **Edge:** Reeded **Mint:** Istanbul

Date	Mintage	VF20	XF40	MS60	MS63	MS65
1999	5,692	PF65 24.50				

KM# 1097 60000000 LIRA
15.00 g., 0.9167 Gold 0.4421 oz. AGW **Subject:** 700th Anniversary - The Ottoman Empire **Obv:** Value within wreath **Rev:** Ottoman coat of arms **Edge:** Reeded **Mint:** Istanbul

Date	Mintage	VF20	XF40	MS60	MS63	MS65
1999	1,904	PF65 850				

KM# 1187 7500000 LIRA
1.24 g., 0.9999 Gold 0.0399 oz. AGW, 13.91 mm. **Obv:** Value within sprays **Rev:** Trojan Horse **Edge:** Reeded **Mint:** Istanbul

Date	Mintage	VF20	XF40	MS60	MS63	MS65
1999	7,889	PF65 75.00				

KM# 1101 7500000 LIRA
31.40 g., 0.925 Silver 0.9338 oz. ASW, 38.6 mm. **Subject:** 34th World Chess Olympiad **Obv:** World globe with chess pieces within circle **Rev:** Logo and horse head **Edge:** Reeded **Mint:** Istanbul

Date	Mintage	VF20	XF40	MS60	MS63	MS65
2000	1,318	PF65 30.50				

KM# 1102 7500000 LIRA
23.33 g., 0.925 Silver 0.6938 oz. ASW, 38.6 mm. **Subject:** UNICEF **Obv:** Value within wreath **Rev:** Two children candle dancing **Edge:** Reeded **Mint:** Istanbul

Date	Mintage	VF20	XF40	MS60	MS63	MS65
2000	—	PF65 18.00				

KM# 1111 7500000 LIRA
31.47 g., 0.925 Silver 0.9359 oz. ASW, 38.6 mm. **Subject:** Ephesus' Celcius Library **Obv:** Mint logo and value within circle **Rev:** Building **Edge:** Reeded **Mint:** Istanbul

Date	Mintage	VF20	XF40	MS60	MS63	MS65
2000 Matte	1,042	—	—	—	25.00	—
2000	1,171	PF65 25.00				

KM# 1112 7500000 LIRA
31.47 g., 0.925 Silver 0.9359 oz. ASW **Subject:** Traditional Turkish Theater **Obv:** Mint logo and value within circle **Rev:** Marionette theater scene **Mint:** Istanbul

Date	Mintage	VF20	XF40	MS60	MS63	MS65
2000	1,183	PF65 25.00				

KM# 1113 7500000 LIRA
31.47 g., 0.925 Silver 0.9359 oz. ASW **Subject:** United Nations Summit **Obv:** Coiled rope design within circle **Rev:** UN logo and stylized 2000 **Mint:** Istanbul

Date	Mintage	VF20	XF40	MS60	MS63	MS65
2000	1,026	PF65 25.00				

KM# 1114 7500000 LIRA
31.47 g., 0.925 Silver 0.9359 oz. ASW **Subject:** Turkish European Union Candidacy **Obv:** Inscription within circular design **Rev:** Cluster of flags behind star and crescent within star border **Mint:** Istanbul

Date	Mintage	VF20	XF40	MS60	MS63	MS65
2000	1,202	PF65 25.00				

KM# 1115 7500000 LIRA

31.47 g., 0.925 Silver 0.9359 oz. ASW **Subject:** First Female Pilots **Obv:** Turkish pilot's badge within circle **Rev:** Early female pilot saluting **Mint:** Istanbul

Date	Mintage	VF20	XF40	MS60	MS63	MS65
2000	1,148	PF65 25.00				

KM# 1116 7500000 LIRA

31.47 g., 0.999 Silver 1.0108 oz. ASW **Subject:** President Clinton's Turkish Visit **Obv:** Mint logo within circle **Rev:** Clinton holding baby **Mint:** Istanbul

Date	Mintage	VF20	XF40	MS60	MS63	MS65
2000	1,490	PF65 25.00				

KM# 1186 10000000 LIRA

1.24 g., 0.999 Gold 0.0398 oz. AGW, 14.03 mm. **Subject:** Turkey in Europe **Obv:** Value within sprays **Rev:** Statue of Nikolas von Myra with children at center, tower at right **Edge:** Reeded **Mint:** Istanbul

Date	Mintage	VF20	XF40	MS60	MS63	MS65
2000	3,147	PF65 75.00				

KM# 1119 150000000 LIRA

Bi-Metallic 0.916 Gold center in 0.925 Silver ring, 38.6 mm. **Subject:** President Clinton's Turkish Visit **Obv:** Mint logo **Rev:** Clinton holding baby **Edge:** Reeded **Mint:** Istanbul

Date	Mintage	VF20	XF40	MS60	MS63	MS65
2000	444	PF65 700				

GOLD BULLION COINAGE

Since 1943, the Turkish government has issued regular and deluxe gold coins in five denominations corresponding to the old traditional 25, 50, 100, 250, and 500 Kurus of the Ottoman period. The regular coins are all dated 1923, plus the year of the republic (e.g. 1923/40 = 1963), de Luxe coins bear actual AD dates. For a few years, 1944-1950, the bust of Ismet Inonu replaced that of Kemal Ataturk.

KM# 850 25 KURUSH

1.80 g., 0.917 Gold 0.0532 oz. AGW, 15 mm. **Obv:** Head of Ismet Inonu **Mint:** Istanbul

Date	Mintage	VF20	XF40	MS60	MS63	MS65
1923/20	—	75.00	100	120	—	—
1923/22	3,228	75.00	100	140	—	—
1923/23	2,757	75.00	100	140	—	—
1923/24	46,000	75.00	100	120	—	—
1923/25	20,000	75.00	100	130	—	—
1923/26	11,000	75.00	100	130	—	—

KM# 851 25 KURUSH

1.80 g., 0.917 Gold 0.0532 oz. AGW **Obv:** Head of Atatürk left **Rev:** Legend and date within wreath **Mint:** Istanbul

Date	Mintage	VF20	XF40	MS60	MS63	MS65
1923/20	14,000	—	75.00	105	120	—
1923/27	18,000	—	75.00	105	120	—
1923/28	15,000	—	75.00	105	120	—
1923/29	15,000	—	75.00	105	120	—
1923/30	17,000	—	75.00	105	120	—
1923/31	19,000	—	75.00	105	120	—
1923/32	5,455	—	75.00	105	120	—
1923/33	11,000	—	75.00	105	120	—
1923/34	20,000	—	75.00	105	120	—
1923/35	25,000	—	75.00	105	120	—
1923/36	34,000	—	75.00	105	120	—
1923/37	31,000	—	75.00	105	120	—
1923/38	35,000	—	75.00	105	120	—
1923/39	46,000	—	75.00	105	120	—
1923/40	49,000	—	75.00	105	120	—
1923/41	59,000	—	75.00	105	120	—
1923/42	74,000	—	75.00	105	120	—
1923/43	90,000	—	75.00	105	120	—
1923/44	85,000	—	75.00	105	120	—
1923/45	73,000	—	75.00	105	120	—
1923/46	89,000	—	75.00	105	120	—
1923/47	119,000	—	75.00	105	120	—
1923/48	112,000	—	75.00	105	120	—
1923/49	112,000	—	75.00	105	120	—
1923/50	67,000	—	75.00	105	120	—
1923/51	40,000	—	75.00	105	120	—
1923/52	71,000	—	75.00	105	120	—
1923/53	124,000	—	75.00	105	120	—
1923/54	196	—	75.00	105	120	—
1923/55	112,000	—	75.00	105	120	—
1923/56	—	—	75.00	105	120	—
1923/57	—	—	75.00	105	120	—
1923/60	—	—	75.00	105	120	—
1923/64	—	—	75.00	105	120	—
1923/65	—	—	75.00	105	120	—
1923/66	—	—	75.00	105	120	—
1923/67	—	—	75.00	105	120	—
1923/68	—	—	75.00	105	120	—
1923/69	—	—	75.00	105	120	—
1923/70	—	—	75.00	105	120	—
1923/71	—	—	75.00	105	120	—
1923/72	—	—	75.00	105	120	—
1923/73	—	—	75.00	105	120	—
1923/74	—	—	75.00	105	120	—
1923/75	—	—	75.00	105	120	—
1923/76	—	—	75.00	105	120	—
1923/77	—	—	75.00	105	120	—

KM# 870 25 KURUSH

1.75 g., 0.917 Gold 0.0517 oz. AGW **Series:** Monnaie de Luxe **Obv:** Head of Atatürk left **Rev:** Country name and date in ornate monogram within circle of stars, floral border surrounds **Mint:** Istanbul

Date	Mintage	VF20	XF40	MS60	MS63	MS65
1942	138	78.00	120	170	—	—
1943	386	78.00	120	145	—	—
1944	811	78.00	120	145	—	—
1946	235	78.00	120	170	—	—
1950	2,053	—	73.00	105	120	—
1951	2,035	—	73.00	105	120	—
1952	3,374	—	73.00	105	120	—
1953	1,944	—	73.00	105	120	—
1954	2,244	—	73.00	105	120	—
1955	2,573	—	73.00	105	120	—
1956	4,004	—	73.00	105	120	—
1957	8,842	—	73.00	105	120	—
1958	9,546	—	73.00	105	120	—
1959	17,000	—	73.00	105	120	—
1960	19,000	—	73.00	105	120	—
1961	35,000	—	73.00	105	120	—
1962	31,000	—	73.00	105	120	—
1963	47,000	—	73.00	105	120	—
1964	57,000	—	73.00	105	120	—
1965	78,000	—	73.00	105	120	—
1966	106,000	—	73.00	105	120	—
1967	114,000	—	73.00	105	120	—
1968	152,000	—	73.00	105	120	—
1969	163,000	—	73.00	105	120	—
1970	224,000	—	73.00	105	120	—
1971	306,000	—	73.00	105	120	—
1972	271,000	—	73.00	105	120	—
1973	162,000	—	73.00	105	120	—
1974	141,000	—	73.00	105	120	—
1975	202,000	—	73.00	105	120	—
1976	583,000	—	73.00	105	120	—
1977	1,089,000	—	73.00	105	120	—
1978	238,000	—	73.00	105	120	—
1980	—	—	73.00	105	120	—
1981	—	—	73.00	105	120	—
1982	—	—	73.00	105	120	—
1983	—	—	73.00	105	120	—
1984	—	—	73.00	105	120	—
1985	—	—	73.00	105	120	—
1986	—	—	73.00	105	120	—
1987	—	—	73.00	105	120	—
1988	—	—	73.00	105	120	—
1989	—	—	73.00	105	120	—
1990	—	—	73.00	105	120	—
1991	—	—	73.00	105	120	—
1992	—	—	73.00	105	120	—
1993	—	—	73.00	105	120	—
1994	—	—	73.00	105	120	—
1995	—	—	73.00	105	120	—
1996	—	—	73.00	105	120	—
1997	—	—	73.00	105	120	—
1998	—	—	73.00	105	120	—
1999	—	—	73.00	105	120	—
2000	—	—	73.00	105	120	—

KM# 875 25 KURUSH

1.75 g., 0.917 Gold 0.0517 oz. AGW **Series:** Monnaie de Luxe **Obv:** Head of Ismet Inonu left **Mint:** Istanbul

Date	Mintage	VF20	XF40	MS60	MS63	MS65
1943	—	120	150	210	—	—
Note: Mintage included in KM#870						
1944	—	120	150	210	—	—
Note: Mintage included in KM#870						
1945	592	120	150	210	—	—
1946	—	120	150	210	—	—
Note: Mintage included in KM#870						
1947	3,443	120	135	195	—	—
1948	714	120	150	210	—	—
1949	552	120	150	210	—	—

KM# 852 50 KURUSH

3.61 g., 0.917 Gold 0.1064 oz. AGW, 18 mm. **Obv:** Head of Ismet Inonu left **Mint:** Istanbul

Date	Mintage	VF20	XF40	MS60	MS63	MS65
1923/20	—	150	200	225	—	—
1923/22	1,093	150	200	225	—	—
1923/23	897	150	200	225	—	—
1923/24	11,000	150	200	225	—	—
1923/25	3,004	150	200	225	—	—
1923/26	817	150	200	225	—	—
1923/27	5,228	150	200	225	—	—

KM# 853 50 KURUSH

3.61 g., 0.917 Gold 0.1064 oz. AGW **Obv:** Head of Atatürk left **Rev:** Legend and date within wreath **Mint:** Istanbul

Date	Mintage	VF20	XF40	MS60	MS63	MS65
1923/20	12,000	—	150	200	225	—
1923/27	Inc. above	—	150	200	225	—
1923/28	3,300	—	150	200	225	—
1923/29	6,384	—	150	200	225	—
1923/30	4,590	—	150	200	225	—
1923/31	9,068	—	150	200	225	—
1923/32	4,344	—	150	200	225	—
1923/33	3,958	—	150	200	225	—
1923/34	9,499	—	150	200	225	—
1923/35	9,307	—	150	200	225	—
1923/36	12,000	—	150	200	225	—
1923/37	9,049	—	150	200	225	—
1923/38	9,854	—	150	200	225	—
1923/39	11,000	—	150	200	225	—
1923/40	13,000	—	150	200	225	—
1923/41	13,000	—	150	200	225	—
1923/42	18,000	—	150	200	225	—
1923/43	26,000	—	150	200	225	—
1923/44	26,000	—	150	200	225	—
1923/45	25,000	—	150	200	225	—
1923/46	28,000	—	150	200	225	—
1923/47	38,000	—	150	200	225	—
1923/48	35,000	—	150	200	225	—
1923/49	28,000	—	150	200	225	—
1923/50	16,000	—	150	200	225	—
1923/51	8,000	—	150	200	225	—
1923/52	14,000	—	150	200	225	—
1923/53	28,000	—	150	200	225	—
1923/54	54,000	—	150	200	225	—
1923/55	16,000	—	150	200	225	—
1923/57	—	—	150	200	225	—
1923/64	—	—	150	200	225	—
1923/65	—	—	150	200	225	—
1923/66	—	—	150	200	225	—
1923/67	—	—	150	200	225	—

Date	Mintage	VF20	XF40	MS60	MS63	MS65
1923/68	—	—	150	200	225	—
1923/69	—	—	150	200	225	—
1923/70	—	—	150	200	225	—
1923/71	—	—	150	200	225	—
1923/72	—	—	150	200	225	—
1923/73	—	—	150	200	225	—
1923/74	—	—	150	200	225	—
1923/75	—	—	150	200	225	—
1923/76	—	—	150	200	225	—
1923/77	—	—	150	200	225	—

KM# 871 50 KURUSH

3.51 g., 0.917 Gold 0.1034 oz. AGW **Series:** Monnaie de Luxe **Obv:** Head of Kemal Atatürk left within circle of stars, wreath surrounds **Rev:** Country name and date in ornate monogram within circle of stars, floral border surrounds **Mint:** Istanbul

Date	Mintage	VF20	XF40	MS60	MS63	MS65
1942	115	150	235	285	—	—
1943	91	150	235	285	—	—
1944	950	145	200	225	—	—
1946	565	145	200	225	—	—
1950	1,971	145	200	225	—	—
1951	1,780	145	200	225	—	—
1952	2,557	145	200	225	—	—
1953	2,392	145	200	225	—	—
1954	1,714	145	200	225	—	—
1955	4,143	145	200	225	—	—
1956	2,956	145	200	225	—	—
1957	6,855	145	200	225	—	—
1958	6,381	145	200	225	—	—
1959	12,000	—	145	200	225	—
1960	12,000	—	145	200	225	—
1961	15,000	—	145	200	225	—
1962	22,000	—	145	200	225	—
1963	29,000	—	145	200	225	—
1964	34,000	—	145	200	225	—
1965	44,000	—	145	200	225	—
1966	58,000	—	145	200	225	—
1967	64,000	—	145	200	225	—
1968	82,000	—	145	200	225	—
1969	79,000	—	145	200	225	—
1970	109,000	—	145	200	225	—
1971	154,000	—	145	200	225	—
1972	110,000	—	145	200	225	—
1973	73,000	—	145	200	225	—
1974	45,000	—	145	200	225	—
1975	72,000	—	145	200	225	—
1976	196,000	—	145	200	225	—
1977	361,000	—	145	200	225	—
1978	161,000	—	145	200	225	—
1979	—	—	145	200	225	—
1980	—	—	145	200	225	—
1981	—	—	145	200	225	—
1982	—	—	145	200	225	—
1983	—	—	145	200	225	—
1984	—	—	145	200	225	—
1985	—	—	145	200	225	—
1986	—	—	145	200	225	—
1987	—	—	145	200	225	—
1988	—	—	145	200	225	—
1989	—	—	145	200	225	—
1990	—	—	145	200	225	—
1991	—	—	145	200	225	—
1992	—	—	145	200	225	—
1993	—	—	145	200	225	—
1994	—	—	145	200	225	—
1995	—	—	145	200	225	—
1996	—	—	145	200	225	—
1997	—	—	145	200	225	—
1998	—	—	145	200	225	—
1999	—	—	145	200	225	—
2000	—	—	145	200	225	—

KM# 876 50 KURUSH

3.51 g., 0.917 Gold 0.1034 oz. AGW **Series:** Monnaie de Luxe **Obv:** Head of Ismet Inonu left **Mint:** Istanbul

Date	Mintage	VF20	XF40	MS60	MS63	MS65
1943	—	150	230	280	—	—
Note: Mintage included in KM#871						
1944	—	150	225	250	—	—
Note: Mintage included in KM#871						
1946	—	145	200	220	—	—
Note: Mintage included in KM#871						
1947	3,481	145	200	220	—	—
1948	773	145	200	220	—	—
1949	582	145	200	220	—	—

KM# 872 100 KURUSH

7.02 g., 0.917 Gold 0.2068 oz. AGW **Series:** Monnaie de Luxe **Obv:** Head of Atatürk left within circle of stars, wreath surrounds **Rev:** Country name and date in ornate monogram within circle of stars, floral border surrounds **Mint:** Istanbul

Date	Mintage	VF20	XF40	MS60	MS63	MS65
1942	8,659	—	275	400	—	—
1943	6,594	—	275	400	—	—
1944	7,160	—	275	400	—	—
1948	14,000	—	275	400	—	—
1950	25,000	—	275	400	—	—
1951	35,000	—	275	400	—	—
1952	41,000	—	275	400	—	—
1953	32,000	—	275	400	—	—
1954	24,000	—	275	400	—	—
1955	4,881	—	275	400	—	—
1956	11,000	—	—	275	400	—
1957	49,000	—	—	275	400	—
1958	67,000	—	—	275	400	—
1959	89,000	—	—	275	400	—
1960	57,000	—	—	275	400	—
1961	77,000	—	—	275	400	—
1962	108,000	—	—	275	400	—
1963	146,000	—	—	275	400	—
1964	128,000	—	—	275	400	—
1965	157,000	—	—	275	400	—
1966	190,000	—	—	275	400	—
1967	177,000	—	—	275	400	—
1968	143,000	—	—	275	400	—
1969	206,000	—	—	275	400	—
1970	253,000	—	—	275	400	—
1971	293,000	—	—	275	400	—
1972	222,000	—	—	275	400	—
1973	140,000	—	—	275	400	—
1974	82,000	—	—	275	400	—
1975	142,000	—	—	275	400	—
1976	265,000	—	—	275	400	—
1977	277,000	—	—	275	400	—
1978	86,000	—	—	275	400	—
1979	—	—	—	275	400	—
1980	—	—	—	275	400	—
1981	—	—	—	275	400	—
1982	—	—	—	275	400	—
1983	—	—	—	275	400	—
1984	—	—	—	275	400	—
1985	—	—	—	275	400	—
1986	—	—	—	275	400	—
1987	—	—	—	275	400	—
1988	—	—	—	275	400	—
1989	—	—	—	275	400	—
1990	—	—	—	275	400	—
1991	—	—	—	275	400	—
1992	—	—	—	275	400	—
1993	—	—	—	275	400	—
1994	—	—	—	275	400	—
1995	—	—	—	275	400	—
1996	—	—	—	275	400	—
1997	—	—	—	275	400	—
1998	—	—	—	275	400	—
1999	—	—	—	275	400	—
2000	—	—	—	275	400	—

KM# 854 100 KURUSH

7.22 g., 0.917 Gold 0.2127 oz. AGW **Obv:** Head of Ismet Inonu left **Rev:** legend and date within wreath **Mint:** Istanbul

Date	Mintage	VF20	XF40	MS60	MS63	MS65
1923/20	—	—	285	400	425	—
1923/22 Rare	3	—	—	—	—	—
1923/23	381,000	—	285	400	425	—
1923/24	2,274	—	290	420	440	—
1923/25	28,000	—	285	400	425	—
1923/26	2,097	—	290	420	440	—
1923/27	17,000	—	285	400	425	—

KM# 855 100 KURUSH

7.22 g., 0.917 Gold 0.2127 oz. AGW **Obv:** Head of Atatürk left **Rev:** Legend and date within wreath **Mint:** Istanbul

Date	Mintage	VF20	XF40	MS60	MS63	MS65
1923/20	29,000	—	285	400	425	—
1923/27	Inc. above	—	285	400	425	—
1923/28 Rare	3	—	—	—	—	—
1923/29	2,111	—	290	420	440	—
1923/30	13,000	—	285	400	425	—
1923/31	109,000	—	285	400	425	—
1923/32	134,000	—	285	400	335	—
1923/33	216,000	—	285	400	425	—
1923/34	463,000	—	285	400	425	—
1923/35	405,000	—	285	400	425	—
1923/36	25,000	—	285	400	425	—
1923/37	131,000	—	285	400	425	—
1923/38	159,000	—	285	400	425	—
1923/39	85,000	—	285	400	425	—
1923/40	10,000	—	285	400	425	—
1923/41	164,000	—	285	400	425	—
1923/42	63,000	—	285	400	425	—
1923/43	56,000	—	285	400	425	—
1923/44	198,000	—	285	400	425	—
1923/45	176,000	—	285	400	425	—
1923/46	1,290,000	—	285	400	425	—
1923/47	513,000	—	285	400	425	—
1923/48	600	—	285	425	450	—
1923/49	1,300	—	285	420	440	—
1923/50	47,000	—	285	400	425	—
1923/51	240,000	—	285	400	425	—
1923/52	1,046,999	—	285	400	425	—
1923/53	550,000	—	285	400	425	—
1923/54	18,000	—	285	400	425	—
1923/55	309,000	—	285	400	425	—
1923/57	—	—	285	400	335	—
1923/58	—	—	285	400	425	—
1923/59	—	—	285	400	425	—
1923/60	—	—	285	400	425	—
1923/61	—	—	285	400	425	—
1923/62	—	—	285	400	425	—
1923/63	—	—	285	400	425	—
1923/64	—	—	285	400	425	—
1923/65	—	—	285	400	425	—
1923/66	—	—	285	400	425	—
1923/67	—	—	285	400	425	—
1923/68	—	—	285	400	425	—
1923/69	—	—	285	400	425	—
1923/70	—	—	285	400	425	—
1923/71	—	—	285	400	425	—
1923/72	—	—	285	400	425	—
1923/73	—	—	285	400	425	—
1923/74	—	—	285	400	425	—
1923/75	—	—	285	400	425	—
1923/76	—	—	285	400	425	—
1923/77	—	—	285	400	425	—

KM# 877 100 KURUSH

7.02 g., 0.917 Gold 0.2068 oz. AGW, 22 mm. **Series:** Monnaie de Luxe **Obv:** Head of Ismet Inonu left **Mint:** Istanbul

Date	Mintage	VF20	XF40	MS60	MS63	MS65
1943	—	275	400	425	—	—
Note: Mintage included in KM#872						
1944	—	275	400	425	—	—
Note: Mintage included in KM#872						
1945	2,202	275	400	450	—	—
1946	8,863	275	400	425	—	—
1947	28,000	275	400	425	—	—
1948	—	275	400	425	—	—
Note: Mintage included in KM#872						
1949	6,578	275	400	425	—	—
1950	—	275	400	425	—	—
Note: Mintage included in KM#872						

KM# 873 250 KURUSH
17.54 g., 0.917 Gold 0.5171 oz. AGW **Series:** Monnaie de Luxe **Obv:** Head of Atatürk left within circle of stars, wreath surrounds **Rev:** Country name and date in ornate monogram within circle of stars, floral border surrounds **Mint:** Istanbul

Date	Mintage	VF20	XF40	MS60	MS63	MS65
1942	10,000	—	680	1,000	—	—
1943	11,000	—	680	1,000	—	—
1944	15,000	—	680	1,000	—	—
1946	16,000	—	680	1,000	—	—
1947	42,000	—	680	1,000	—	—
1948	13,000	—	680	1,000	—	—
1950	45,000	—	680	1,000	—	—
1951	41,000	—	680	1,000	1,050	—
1952	59,000	—	680	1,000	1,050	—
1953	45,000	—	680	1,000	1,050	—
1954	40,000	—	680	1,000	1,050	—
1955	7,067	—	680	1,000	1,050	—
1956	14,000	—	680	1,000	1,050	—
1957	47,000	—	680	1,000	1,050	—
1958	75,000	—	680	1,000	1,050	—
1959	93,000	—	680	1,000	1,050	—
1960	50,000	—	680	1,000	1,050	—
1961	65,000	—	680	1,000	1,050	—
1962	99,000	—	680	1,000	1,050	—
1963	137,000	—	680	1,000	1,050	—
1964	152,000	—	680	1,000	1,050	—
1965	194,000	—	680	1,000	1,050	—
1966	218,000	—	680	1,000	1,050	—
1967	201,000	—	680	1,000	1,050	—
1968	150,000	—	680	1,000	1,050	—
1969	262,000	—	680	1,000	1,050	—
1970	301,000	—	680	1,000	1,050	—
1971	356,000	—	680	1,000	1,050	—
1972	305,000	—	680	1,000	1,050	—
1973	198,000	—	680	1,000	1,050	—
1974	142,000	—	680	1,000	1,050	—
1975	223,000	—	680	1,000	1,050	—
1976	345,000	—	680	1,000	1,050	—
1977	227,000	—	680	1,000	1,050	—
1978	311,000	—	680	1,000	1,050	—
1979	—	—	680	1,000	1,050	—
1980	—	—	680	1,000	1,050	—
1981	—	—	680	1,000	1,050	—
1982	—	—	680	1,000	1,050	—
1983	—	—	680	1,000	1,050	—
1984	—	—	680	1,000	1,050	—
1985	—	—	680	1,000	1,050	—
1986	—	—	680	1,000	1,050	—
1987	—	—	680	1,000	1,050	—
1988	—	—	680	1,000	1,050	—
1989	—	—	680	1,000	1,050	—
1990	—	—	680	1,000	1,050	—
1991	—	—	680	1,000	1,050	—
1992	—	—	680	1,000	1,050	—
1993	—	—	680	1,000	1,050	—
1994	—	—	680	1,000	1,050	—
1995	—	—	680	1,000	1,050	—
1996	—	—	680	1,000	1,050	—
1997	—	—	680	1,000	1,050	—
1998	—	—	680	1,000	1,050	—
1999	—	—	680	1,000	1,050	—
2000	—	—	680	1,000	1,050	—

KM# 856 250 KURUSH
18.04 g., 0.917 Gold 0.5319 oz. AGW **Obv:** Head of Ismet Inonu left **Mint:** Istanbul

Date	Mintage	VF20	XF40	MS60	MS63	MS65
1923/20	—	—	700	1,025	1,075	—
1923/23	14,000	—	700	1,025	1,075	—
1923/24	60	—	710	1,050	1,100	—

KM# 857 250 KURUSH
18.04 g., 0.917 Gold 0.5319 oz. AGW **Obv:** Head of Atatürk left **Rev:** Legend and date within wreath **Mint:** Istanbul

Date	Mintage	VF20	XF40	MS60	MS63	MS65
1923/20	10,000	—	700	1,025	1,075	—
1923/29 Rare	3	—	—	—	—	—
1923/30	130	—	710	1,075	—	—
1923/31	—	—	710	1,075	—	—
1923/38	245	—	710	1,075	—	—
1923/39	389	—	710	1,075	—	—
1923/40	435	—	710	1,075	—	—
1923/41	349	—	710	1,075	—	—
1923/42	460	—	710	1,075	—	—
1923/43	1,008	—	700	1,025	1,075	—
1923/44	712	—	710	1,050	1,100	—
1923/45	1,034	—	700	1,025	1,075	—
1923/46	1,035	—	700	1,025	1,075	—
1923/47	1,408	—	700	1,025	1,075	—
1923/48	904	—	710	1,050	1,100	—
1923/49	1,066	—	700	1,025	1,075	—
1923/50	975	—	710	1,050	1,100	—
1923/51	298	—	710	1,050	1,100	—
1923/52	610	—	710	1,050	1,100	—
1923/53	586	—	710	1,050	1,100	—
1923/54	289	—	710	1,050	1,100	—
1923/55	267	—	710	1,050	1,100	—
1923/57	—	—	700	1,025	1,075	—
1923/58	—	—	700	1,025	1,075	—
1923/59	—	—	700	1,025	1,075	—
1923/60	—	—	700	1,025	1,075	—
1923/61	—	—	700	1,025	1,075	—
1923/62	—	—	700	1,025	1,075	—
1923/63	—	—	700	1,025	1,075	—
1923/64	—	—	700	1,025	1,075	—
1923/65	—	—	700	1,025	1,075	—
1923/66	—	—	700	1,025	1,075	—
1923/67	—	—	700	1,025	1,075	—
1923/68	—	—	700	1,025	1,075	—
1923/69	—	—	700	1,025	1,075	—
1923/70	—	—	700	1,025	1,075	—
1923/71	—	—	700	1,025	1,075	—
1923/72	—	—	700	1,025	1,075	—
1923/73	—	—	700	1,025	1,075	—
1923/74	—	—	700	1,025	1,075	—
1923/75	—	—	700	1,025	1,075	—
1923/76	—	—	700	1,025	1,075	—
1923/77	—	—	700	1,025	1,075	—

KM# 878 250 KURUSH
17.54 g., 0.917 Gold 0.5171 oz. AGW, 27 mm. **Series:** Monnaie de Luxe **Obv:** Head of Ismet Inonu left **Mint:** Istanbul

Date	Mintage	VF20	XF40	MS60	MS63	MS65
1943	—	—	680	1,000	1,050	—
Note: Mintage included in KM#873						
1944	—	—	680	1,000	1,050	—
Note: Mintage included in KM#873						
1945	4,135	—	680	1,000	1,050	—
1946	—	—	680	1,000	1,050	—
Note: Mintage included in KM#873						
1947	—	—	680	1,000	1,050	—
Note: Mintage included in KM#873						
1948	—	—	680	1,000	1,050	—
Note: Mintage included in KM#873						
1949	11,000	—	680	1,000	1,050	—
1950	—	—	680	1,000	1,050	—
Note: Mintage included in KM#873						

KM# 858 500 KURUSH
36.08 g., 0.917 Gold 1.0637 oz. AGW, 35 mm. **Obv:** Head of Ismet Inonu left **Rev:** Legend and date within wreath **Mint:** Istanbul

Date	Mintage	VF20	XF40	MS60	MS63	MS65
1923/20	—	—	1,375	1,950	—	—
1923/23	9,006	—	1,375	1,950	—	—
1923/24	7,923	—	1,375	1,950	—	—
1923/25	272	—	1,400	2,000	—	—

KM# 859 500 KURUSH
36.08 g., 0.917 Gold 1.0637 oz. AGW **Obv:** Head of Atatürk left **Rev:** Legend and date within wreath **Mint:** Istanbul

Date	Mintage	VF20	XF40	MS60	MS63	MS65
1923/20	12,000	—	1,375	1,950	2,000	—
1923/27	615	—	1,400	2,000	—	—
1923/28	34	—	1,400	2,100	—	—
1923/29	137	—	1,400	2,050	—	—
1923/30	45	—	1,400	2,100	—	—
1923/31	100	—	1,400	2,050	—	—
1923/32	74	—	1,400	2,100	—	—
1923/33	268	—	1,400	2,000	—	—
1923/34	758	—	1,400	2,000	—	—
1923/35	1,586	—	1,375	1,950	2,000	—
1923/36	765	—	1,400	2,000	2,050	—
1923/37	983	—	1,400	2,000	2,050	—
1923/38	1,738	—	1,375	1,950	2,000	—
1923/39	2,629	—	1,375	1,950	2,000	—
1923/40	2,763	—	1,375	1,950	2,000	—
1923/41	3,440	—	1,375	1,950	2,000	—
1923/42	3,335	—	1,375	1,950	2,000	—
1923/43	4,914	—	1,375	1,950	2,000	—
1923/44	4,308	—	1,375	1,950	2,000	—
1923/45	3,488	—	1,375	1,950	2,000	—
1923/46	5,636	—	1,375	1,950	2,000	—
1923/47	7,588	—	1,375	1,950	2,000	—
1923/48	6,060	—	1,375	1,950	2,000	—
1923/49	4,235	—	1,375	1,950	2,000	—
1923/50	4,733	—	1,375	1,950	2,000	—
1923/51	2,757	—	1,375	1,950	2,000	—
1923/52	2,041	—	1,375	1,950	2,000	—
1923/53	4,819	—	1,375	1,950	2,000	—
1923/54	1,401	—	1,375	1,950	2,000	—
1923/55	1,484	—	1,375	1,950	2,000	—
1923/57	—	—	1,375	1,950	2,000	—
1923/58	—	—	1,375	1,950	2,000	—
1923/59	—	—	1,375	1,950	2,000	—
1923/60	—	—	1,375	1,950	2,000	—
1923/61	—	—	1,375	1,950	2,000	—
1923/62	—	—	1,375	1,950	2,000	—
1923/63	—	—	1,375	1,950	2,000	—
1923/64	—	—	1,375	1,950	2,000	—
1923/65	—	—	1,375	1,950	2,000	—
1923/66	—	—	1,375	1,950	2,000	—
1923/67	—	—	1,375	1,950	2,000	—
1923/68	—	—	1,375	1,950	2,000	—
1923/69	—	—	1,375	1,950	2,000	—
1923/70	—	—	1,375	1,950	2,000	—
1923/71	—	—	1,375	1,950	2,000	—
1923/72	—	—	1,375	1,950	2,000	—
1923/73	—	—	1,375	1,950	2,000	—
1923/74	—	—	1,375	1,950	2,000	—
1923/75	—	—	1,375	1,950	2,000	—
1923/76	—	—	1,375	1,950	2,000	—
1923/77	—	—	1,375	1,950	2,000	—

KM# 874 500 KURUSH

35.08 g., 0.917 Gold 1.0342 oz. AGW **Series:** Monnaie de Luxe **Obv:** Head of Atatürk left within circle of stars, wreath surrounds **Rev:** Country name and date in ornate monogram within circle of stars, floral border surrounds **Mint:** Istanbul

Date	Mintage	VF20	XF40	MS60	MS63	MS65
1942	2,949	—	1,350	1,950	2,000	—
1943	1,210	—	1,350	1,950	2,000	—
1944	1,254	—	1,350	1,950	2,000	—
1947	3,699	—	1,350	1,950	2,000	—
1950	59	—	1,350	2,050	2,100	—
1951	21	—	1,350	2,050	2,100	—
1952	26	—	1,350	2,050	2,100	—
1953	35	—	1,350	2,050	2,100	—
1954	182	—	1,350	2,000	2,050	—
1955	14	—	1,350	2,100	2,150	—
1956	13	—	1,350	2,100	2,150	—
1957	68	—	1,350	2,050	2,100	—
1958	121	—	1,350	2,000	2,050	—
1959	294	—	1,350	2,000	2,050	—
1960	208	—	1,350	2,000	2,050	—
1961	619	—	1,350	1,950	2,000	—
1962	1,228	—	1,350	1,950	2,000	—
1963	1,985	—	1,350	1,950	2,000	—
1964	2,787	—	1,350	1,950	2,000	—
1965	4,631	—	1,350	1,950	2,000	—
1966	5,572	—	1,350	1,950	2,000	—
1967	6,637	—	1,350	1,950	2,000	—
1968	5,983	—	1,350	1,950	2,000	—
1969	7,152	—	1,350	1,950	2,000	—
1970	11,000	—	1,350	1,950	2,000	—
1971	15,000	—	1,350	1,950	2,000	—
1972	15,000	—	1,350	1,950	2,000	—
1973	7,939	—	1,350	1,950	2,000	—
1974	5,412	—	1,350	1,950	2,000	—
1975	6,205	—	1,350	1,950	2,000	—
1976	11,000	—	1,350	1,950	2,000	—
1977	6,931	—	1,350	1,950	2,000	—
1978	5,740	—	1,350	1,950	2,000	—
1979	—	—	1,350	1,950	2,000	—
1980	—	—	1,350	1,950	2,000	—
1981	—	—	1,350	1,950	2,000	—
1982	—	—	1,350	1,950	2,000	—
1983	—	—	1,350	1,950	2,000	—
1984	—	—	1,350	1,950	2,000	—
1985	—	—	1,350	1,950	2,000	—
1986	—	—	1,350	1,950	2,000	—
1987	—	—	1,350	1,950	2,000	—
1988	—	—	1,350	1,950	2,000	—
1989	—	—	1,350	1,950	2,000	—
1990	—	—	1,350	1,950	2,000	—
1991	—	—	1,350	1,950	2,000	—
1992	—	—	1,350	1,950	2,000	—
1993	—	—	1,350	1,950	2,000	—
1994	—	—	1,350	1,950	2,000	—
1995	—	—	1,350	1,950	2,000	—
1996	—	—	1,350	1,950	2,000	—
1997	—	—	1,350	1,950	2,000	—
1998	—	—	1,350	1,950	2,000	—
1999	—	—	1,350	1,950	2,000	—
2000	—	—	1,350	1,950	2,000	—

KM# 879 500 KURUSH

35.08 g., 0.917 Gold 1.0342 oz. AGW **Series:** Monnaie de Luxe **Obv:** Head of Ismet Inonu left within circle of stars **Rev:** Country name and date in ornate monogram within circle of stars, floral border surrounds **Mint:** Istanbul

Date	Mintage	VF20	XF40	MS60	MS63	MS65
1943	—	—	1,350	1,950	2,000	—
Note: Mintage included in KM#874						
1944	—	—	1,350	1,950	2,000	—
Note: Mintage included in KM#874						
1945	115	—	1,350	1,950	2,000	—
1946	298	—	1,350	1,950	2,000	—
1947	—	—	1,350	1,950	2,000	—
Note: Mintage included in KM#874						
1948	40	—	1,350	2,000	2,050	—

PATTERNS

Including off metal strikes

KM#	Date	Mintage	Identification	Mkt Val
Pn9	1948	—	5 Kurus. Brass. KM#887. Prev. KM#Pn2.	700
Pn10	1948	—	10 Kurus. Brass. KM#888. Prev. KM#Pn3.	700

PIEDFORT

KM#	Date	Mintage	Identification	Mkt Val
P1	1981	2,500	500 Lira. 0.925. Silver. KM#931.	250
P2	1981	1,200	3000 Lira. 0.925. Silver. KM#948.	275
P3	1981	—	30000 Lira. Gold. KM#955.	1,850
P4	1982	600	3000 Lira. 0.925. Silver. KM#959.	175

MINT SETS

KM#	Date	Mintage	Identification	Issue Price	Mkt Val
MSA1	1949 (5)	—	KM#881-888	—	15.00
MS1	1962 (7)	—	KM#889a.1, 890.1, 891.1, 892.2, 893.1, 894 (1960), 895	—	225
MSA2	1963 (6)	—	KM#889a.1, 890.1, 891.1, 892.2, 893.1, 895a	—	150
MS2	1964 (6)	—	KM#889a.1, 890.1, 891.1, 892.2, 893.1, 895a	—	85.00
MS3	1965 (6)	—	KM#889a.1, 890.1, 891.1, 892.2, 893.1, 895a	—	32.50
MS4	1966 (6)	—	KM#889a.1, 890.1, 891.1, 892.2, 893.1, 895a	—	62.50
MSA5	1967 (6)	—	KM#889a.2, 890.1, 891.1, 892.3, 893.1, 895a	—	40.00
MS5	1968 (6)	—	KM#889a.2, 890.1, 891.1, 892.3, 893.1, 895a	—	25.00
MS6	1969 (6)	—	KM#889a.2, 890.2, 891.2, 892.3, 893.2, 895a	—	25.00
MS7	1970 (5)	—	KM#889a.2, 890.2, 891.2, 892.3, 893.2, 895a	—	12.50
MS8	1971 (6)	—	KM#889a.2, 890.2, 891.2, 893.2, 895a, 899	—	12.50
MS9	1972 (6)	—	KM#889a.2, 890.2, 891.2, 893.2, 895a, 899	—	12.50
MS10	1973 (7)	—	KM#889a.2, 890.2, 891.2, 892.3, 893.2, 895a, 899	—	13.50
MS11	1974 (7)	—	KM#889a.2, 890.3-892.3, 893.2, 895a, 899	—	13.50
MS12	1975 (7)	—	KM#889a.2, 890a, 891a, 893.2, 895b, 899, 905	—	12.50
MS13	1976 (7)	—	KM#889a.2, 890a, 891a, 893.2, 895b, 899, 905	—	10.00
MS14	1977 (8)	—	KM#889a.2, 890a, 891a, 892.3, 893.2, 895b, 899, 905	—	27.50
MS15	1978 (4)	—	KM#889a.2, 892.3, 893.2, 905	—	14.00
MS16	1979 (4)	—	KM#889a.2, 893.2, 899, 905	—	5.00
MS17	1980 (2)	—	KM#889a.2, 893.2	—	3.00
MS18	1981 (3)	—	KM#943-945	—	3.00
MS19	1982 (2)	—	KM#943, 949.1, 950.1	—	5.00
MS20	1983 (2)	—	KM#949.2, 950.2	—	5.00
MS21	1984 (6)	—	KM#962-967	—	5.50
MS22	1985 (6)	—	KM#962-964, 966, 967, 975	—	5.00
MS23	1986 (4)	—	KM#963-967	—	4.00
MS24	1989 (6)	9,350	KM#962.2, 963-964, 975, 987, 988, and medal	2.00	18.00
MS25	1990 (5)	5,300	KM#987-989, 996, 997, and medal	4.00	12.50
MS26	1991 (5)	2,250	KM#987-989, 997, 1015, and mint medal	—	20.00
MS27	1992 (6)	2,240	KM#987-989, 997, 1015, 1025, and mint medal	—	20.00
MS28	1993 (6)	1,750	KM#987-989, 997, 1015, 1025, and mint medal	—	20.00
MS29	1994 (8)	2,500	KM#987-989, 997, 1015, 1025, 1027, 1042, plus mint medal	—	20.00
MS30	1995 (7)	2,500	KM#989, 1015, 1027-1029, 1041, 1043, plus mint medal	—	15.00
MS31	1996 (8)	10,000	KM#989, 1015, 1027-1029, 1041, 1050, 1056, plus mint medal	—	20.00
MS32	1997 (7)	—	KM#989, 1015, 1027.1, 1028, 1029.1, 1041, 1056, plus silver mint medal	—	20.00
MS33	2000 (3)	10,000	KM#860.1a, 893.1a, 905a Mixed dates; Silver Coin Nostalgia Set	60.00	100
MS34	2000 (4)	25,000	KM#881a, 884a, 885a, 886a Mixed dates; Gold Coin Nostalgia Set	325	1,475
MS35	2000 (7)	10,000	KM#860.1a, 881a, 884a, 885a, 886a, 893.1a, 905a Mixed dates; Silver and Gold Nostalgia Set	350	1,575

Turkmenistan, (formerly the Turkmen Soviet Socialist Republic) covers the territory of the Trans-Caspian Region of Turkestan, the Charjiui Vilayet of Bukhara and the part of Khiva located on the right bank of the Oxus. Bordered on the north by the Autonomous Kara-Kalpak Republic (a constituent of Uzbekistan), by Iran and Afghanistan on the south, by the Usbek Republic on the east and the Caspian Sea on the west. It has an area of 186,400 sq. mi. (488,100 sq. km.) and a population of 3.5 million. Capital: Ashkhabad (formerly Poltoratsk). Main occupation is agricultural products including cotton and maize. It is rich in minerals, oil, coal, sulphur and salt and is also famous for its carpets, Turkoman horses and Karakui sheep.

The Turkomans arrived in Trancaspia as nomadic Seluk Turks in the 11th century. It often became subjected to one of the neighboring states. Late in the 19th century the Czarist Russians invaded with their first victory at Kyzyl Arvat in 1877, arriving in Ashkhabad in 1882 resulting in submission of the Turkmen tribes. By March 18,1884 the Transcaspian province of Russian Turkestan was formed. During WW I the Czarist government tried to conscript the Turkmen; this led to a revolt in Oct. 1916 under the leadership of Aziz Chapykov. In 1918 the Turks captured Baku from the Red army and the British sent a contingent to Merv to prevent a German-Turkish offensive toward Afghanistan and India. In mid-1919 a Bureau of Turkestan Moslem Communist Organization was formed in Moscow hoping to develop one large republic including all surrounding Turkic areas within a Soviet federation. A Turkestan Autonomous Soviet Socialist Republic was formed and plans to partition Turkestan into five republics according to the principle of nationalities was quickly implemented by Joseph Stalin. On Oct. 27, 1924 Turkmenistan became a Soviet Socialist Republic and was accepted as a member of the U.S.S.R. on Jan. 29, 1925. The Bureau of T.M.C.O. was disbanded in 1934. In Aug. 1990 the Turkmen Supreme Soviet adopted a declaration of sovereignty followed by a declaration of independence in Oct. 1991 joining the Commonwealth of Independent States in Dec. A new constitution was adopted in 1992 providing for an executive presidency.

REPUBLIC

STANDARD COINAGE

100 Tenge = 1 Manat

KM# 1 TENGE

1.90 g., Copper Plated Steel, 16 mm. **Obv:** Value in center of flower-like design within circle **Rev:** Head of President Saparmyrat Nyyazow left **Edge:** Plain

Date	Mintage	VF20	XF40	MS60	MS63	MS65
1993	—	—	—	0.25	0.35	0.50

KM# 2 5 TENGE

3.00 g., Copper Plated Steel, 19.5 mm. **Obv:** Value in center of flower-like design within circle **Rev:** Head of President Saparmyrat Nyyazow left **Edge:** Plain

Date	Mintage	VF20	XF40	MS60	MS63	MS65
1993	—	—	—	0.35	0.45	0.65

KM# 3 10 TENGE

4.50 g., Copper Plated Steel, 22.5 mm. **Obv:** Value in center of designs within circle **Rev:** Head of President Saparmyrat Nyyazow left **Edge:** Plain

Date	Mintage	VF20	XF40	MS60	MS63	MS65
1993	—	—	—	0.60	0.75	1.00

KM# 4 20 TENGE

3.60 g., Nickel Plated Steel, 20.9 mm. **Obv:** Value within ornate circle **Rev:** Head of President Saparmyrat Nyyazow left **Edge:** Plain

Date	Mintage	VF20	XF40	MS60	MS63	MS65
1993	—	—	—	1.25	1.50	1.75

KM# 5 50 TENGE

4.90 g., Nickel Plated Steel, 24 mm. **Obv:** Value above animal leaning on horn at right **Rev:** Head of President Saparmyrat Nyyazow left **Edge:** Plain

Date	Mintage	VF20	XF40	MS60	MS63	MS65
1993	—	—	—	2.75	3.00	3.50

KM# 6 500 MANAT

28.28 g., 0.925 Silver 0.841 oz. ASW **Series:** Endangered Wildlife **Obv:** Head of President Saparmyrat Nyyazow left **Rev:** Goitered gazelle

Date	Mintage	VF20	XF40	MS60	MS63	MS65
1996	Est. 5000	PF63 35.00	PF65 45.00	PF67 65.00		

KM# 7 500 MANAT

28.28 g., 0.925 Silver 0.841 oz. ASW **Series:** Endangered Wildlife **Obv:** Head of President Saparmyrat Nyyazow left **Rev:** Purple Swamphen

Date	Mintage	VF20	XF40	MS60	MS63	MS65
1996	Est. 5000	PF63 35.00	PF65 45.00	PF67 65.00		

KM# 8 500 MANAT

28.28 g., 0.925 Silver 0.841 oz. ASW **Series:** Endangered Wildlife **Subject:** Kaspi Ular **Obv:** Head of President Saparmyrat Nyyazow left **Rev:** Pair of Caspian Ular snowcock

Date	Mintage	VF20	XF40	MS60	MS63	MS65
1996	Est. 5000	PF63 35.00	PF65 45.00	PF67 65.00		

KM# 9 500 MANAT

28.28 g., 0.925 Silver 0.841 oz. ASW **Series:** Endangered Wildlife **Subject:** Manul **Obv:** Head of President Saparmyrat Nyyazow left **Rev:** Pallas' cat

Date	Mintage	VF20	XF40	MS60	MS63	MS65
1996	—	PF63 45.00	PF65 55.00	PF67 75.00		

KM# 10 500 MANAT

28.28 g., 0.925 Silver 0.841 oz. ASW **Series:** Endangered Wildlife **Subject:** Gulan **Obv:** Head of President Saparmyrat Nyyazow left **Rev:** Asian wild ass

Date	Mintage	VF20	XF40	MS60	MS63	MS65
1996	—	PF63 40.00	PF65 50.00	PF67 70.00		

KM# 11 500 MANAT

28.28 g., 0.925 Silver 0.841 oz. ASW **Series:** Endangered Wildlife **Obv:** Head of President Saparmyrat Nyyazow left **Rev:** Turkmenistan Gecko

Date	Mintage	VF20	XF40	MS60	MS63	MS65
1996	—	PF63 40.00	PF65 50.00	PF67 70.00		

KM# 12 500 MANAT

Nickel Clad Steel **Obv:** Head of President Saparmyrat Nyyazow left **Rev:** Crown and value within circle **Edge:** Reeded

Date	Mintage	VF20	XF40	MS60	MS63	MS65
1999	Est. 5000	—	—	1.25	1.50	1.75

KM# 14 500 MANAT

28.28 g., 0.925 Silver 0.841 oz. ASW **Series:** Wildlife Series **Subject:** Jaculus Turkmenicus **Obv:** Head of President Saparmyrat Nyyazow left **Rev:** Two Turkmenic Jerboa **Edge:** Reeded

Date	Mintage	VF20	XF40	MS60	MS63	MS65
1999	—	PF63 35.00	PF65 45.00	PF67 65.00		

KM# 15 500 MANAT

28.28 g., 0.925 Silver 0.841 oz. ASW **Series:** Wildlife Series **Subject:** Chlamydotis Undulata **Obv:** Head of President Saparmyrat Nyyazow left **Rev:** Two Houbara Bustards

Date	Mintage	VF20	XF40	MS60	MS63	MS65
1999	Est. 5000	PF63 35.00	PF65 45.00	PF67 65.00		

KM# 16 500 MANAT

28.28 g., 0.925 Silver 0.841 oz. ASW **Series:** Wildlife Series **Subject:** Falco cherrug **Obv:** Head of President Saparmyrat Nyyazow left **Rev:** Saker falcon on branch and falconer at left

Date	Mintage	VF20	XF40	MS60	MS63	MS65
1999	Est. 5000	PF63 35.00	PF65 45.00	PF67 65.00		

KM# 17 500 MANAT
28.28 g., 0.925 Silver 0.841 oz. ASW **Series:** Wildlife Series **Subject:** Naja Oxiana **Obv:** Head of President Saparmyrat Nyyazow left **Rev:** Central Asia Cobra

Date	Mintage	VF20	XF40	MS60	MS63	MS65
1999	—	PF63 40.00		PF65 50.00		PF67 70.00

KM# 18 500 MANAT
28.28 g., 0.925 Silver 0.841 oz. ASW **Series:** Wildlife Series **Subject:** Felis Caracal **Obv:** Head of President Saparmyrat Nyyazow left **Rev:** Seated caracal

Date	Mintage	VF20	XF40	MS60	MS63	MS65
1999	Est. 5000	PF63 40.00		PF65 50.00		PF67 70.00

KM# 19 500 MANAT
28.28 g., 0.925 Silver 0.841 oz. ASW **Series:** Wildlife Series **Subject:** Panthera tigris **Obv:** Head of President Saparmyrat Nyyazow left **Rev:** Tiger

Date	Mintage	VF20	XF40	MS60	MS63	MS65
1999	Est. 5000	PF63 40.00		PF65 50.00		PF67 70.00

KM# 20 500 MANAT
28.28 g., 0.925 Silver 0.841 oz. ASW, 38.5 mm. **Subject:** 5th Anniversary of Neutrality **Obv:** Head of President Saparmyrat Nyyazow left within circle **Rev:** Map and monument within sprigs and circle **Edge:** Reeded

Date	Mintage	VF20	XF40	MS60	MS63	MS65
ND (2000)	5,000	PF63 45.00		PF65 55.00		PF67 75.00

KM# 21 500 MANAT
28.28 g., 0.925 Silver 0.841 oz. ASW, 38.5 mm. **Subject:** 5th Anniversary of Neutrality **Obv:** Head of President Saparmyrat Nyyazow left within circle **Rev:** Astanbaba Mausoleum within circle **Edge:** Reeded

Date	Mintage	VF20	XF40	MS60	MS63	MS65
2000	5,000	PF63 50.00		PF65 60.00		PF67 80.00

KM# 22 500 MANAT
28.28 g., 0.925 Silver 0.841 oz. ASW, 38.5 mm. **Obv:** Head of President Saparmyrat Nyyazow left within circle **Rev:** Square based Soltan Sanjar Mausoleum within circle **Edge:** Reeded

Date	Mintage	VF20	XF40	MS60	MS63	MS65
2000	5,000	PF63 50.00		PF65 60.00		PF67 80.00

KM# 23 500 MANAT
28.28 g., 0.925 Silver 0.841 oz. ASW, 38.5 mm. **Obv:** Head of President Saparmyrat Nyyazow left within circle **Rev:** Shirkebir Mausoleum - Mosque within circle **Edge:** Reeded

Date	Mintage	VF20	XF40	MS60	MS63	MS65
2000	5,000	PF63 50.00		PF65 60.00		PF67 80.00

KM# 24 500 MANAT
28.28 g., 0.925 Silver 0.841 oz. ASW, 38.5 mm. **Obv:** Head left within circle **Rev:** Nisa Fortress, statue with mountaintop in background **Edge:** Reeded

Date	Mintage	VF20	XF40	MS60	MS63	MS65
2000	5,000	PF63 50.00		PF65 60.00		PF67 80.00

KM# 37 500 MANAT
28.28 g., 0.925 Silver 0.841 oz. ASW **Subject:** Architecture **Rev:** Ahal

Date	Mintage	XF40	MS60	MS63	MS65	MS66
2000	5,000	—	—	—	60.00	75.00

KM# 38 500 MANAT
28.28 g., 0.925 Silver 0.841 oz. ASW

Date	Mintage	XF40	MS60	MS63	MS65	MS66
2000	—	—	—	—	50.00	65.00

KM# 26 1000 MANAT
15.55 g., 0.999 Gold 0.4994 oz. AGW, 29 mm. **Obv:** Nyyazow bust left **Rev:** Horn tankard

Date	Mintage	XF40	MS60	MS63	MS65	MS66
1994	10,000	—	—	—	900	950

KM# 27 1000 MANAT
7.98 g., 0.916 Gold 0.235 oz. AGW **Rev:** National flag

Date	Mintage	XF40	MS60	MS63	MS65	MS66
1994	5,000	—	—	—	400	450

KM# 28 1000 MANAT
7.98 g., 0.916 Gold 0.235 oz. AGW **Subject:** 5th Anniversary

Date	Mintage	XF40	MS60	MS63	MS65	MS66
1996	5,000	—	—	—	400	450

KM# 29 1000 MANAT
7.98 g., 0.916 Gold 0.235 oz. AGW

Date	Mintage	XF40	MS60	MS63	MS65	MS66
1998	—	—	—	—	450	500

KM# 13 1000 MANAT
Nickel Clad Steel **Obv:** Head of President Saparmyrat Nyyazow left within circle **Rev:** Value within circle **Edge:** Reeded

Date	Mintage	VF20	XF40	MS60	MS63	MS65
1999 0	—	—	—	1.25	2.50	3.00

KM# 30 1000 MANAT
7.98 g., 0.916 Gold 0.235 oz. AGW **Subject:** 60th Birthday of President **Obv:** Bust facing **Rev:** 5 stars and crescent

Date	Mintage	XF40	MS60	MS63	MS65	MS66
2000	1,000	—	—	—	450	500

KM# 31 1000 MANAT
7.98 g., 0.916 Gold 0.235 oz. AGW **Subject:** Mother of the President **Rev:** 5 satrs and crescent

Date	Mintage	XF40	MS60	MS63	MS65	MS66
2000	—	—	—	—	450	500

KM# 32 1000 MANAT
7.98 g., 0.916 Gold 0.235 oz. AGW **Subject:** Younger brother of President **Rev:** 5 stars and crescent

Date	Mintage	XF40	MS60	MS63	MS65	MS66
2000	—	—	—	—	450	500

KM# 33 1000 MANAT
7.98 g., 0.916 Gold 0.235 oz. AGW **Subject:** Younger brother of President

Date	Mintage	XF40	MS60	MS63	MS65	MS66
2000	—	—	—	—	450	500

KM# 34 1000 MANAT
7.98 g., 0.916 Gold 0.235 oz. AGW **Subject:** Fine portraits **Rev:** Five stars - Crescent

Date	Mintage	XF40	MS60	MS63	MS65	MS66
2000	1,000	—	—	—	450	500

KM# 35 1000 MANAT
47.54 g., 0.916 Gold 1.4001 oz. AGW **Obv:** Five portraits **Rev:** Five stars - crescent

Date	Mintage	XF40	MS60	MS63	MS65	MS66
2000	1,000	—	—	—	2,600	2,900

KM# 36 1000 MANAT
7.98 g., 0.916 Gold 0.235 oz. AGW **Subject:** 5th Anniversary of Split **Obv:** President Nyyazov **Rev:** Monument for the Split of the Republics

Date	Mintage	XF40	MS60	MS63	MS65	MS66
2000	—	—	—	—	1,500	1,750

PROOF SETS

KM#	Date	Mintage	Identification	Issue Price	Mkt Val
PS1	1996 (6)	5,000	KM#6-11	—	260

TURKS & CAICOS ISLANDS

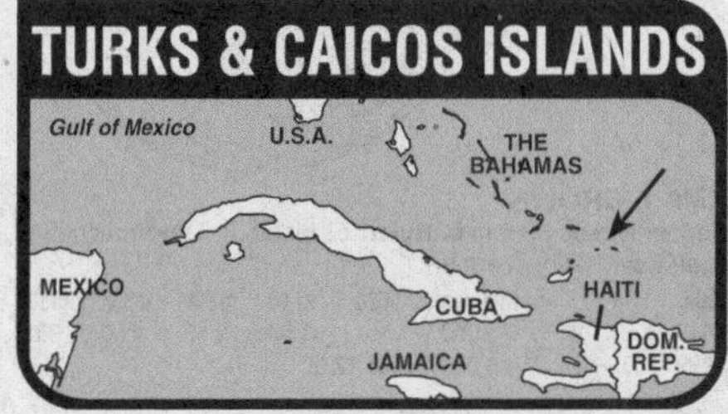

The Colony of the Turks and Caicos Islands, a British colony situated in the West Indies at the eastern end of the Bahama Islands, has an area of 166 sq. mi. (430 sq.km.) and a population of *10,000. Capital: Cockburn Town, on Grand Turk. The principal industry of the colony is the production of salt, which is gathered by raking. Salt, crayfish, and conch shells are exported.

The Turks and Caicos Islands were discovered by Juan Ponce de Leon in 1512, but were not settled until 1678 when Bermudians arrived to rake salt from the salt ponds. The Spanish drove the British settlers from the island in 1710, during the long War of the Spanish Succession. They returned and throughout the remaining years of the war repulsed repeated attacks by France and Spain. In 1799 the islands were granted representation in the Bahamian assembly, but in 1848, on petition of the inhabitants, they were made a separate colony under Jamaica. They were annexed by Jamaica in 1873 and remained a dependency until 1959 when they became a unit territory of the Federation of the West Indies. When the Federation was dissolved in 1962, the Turks and Caicos Islands became a separate Crown Colony.

RULER
British

MONETARY SYSTEM
100 Cents = 1 East Caribbean Dollar
1 Crown = 1 Dollar U.S.A.

BRITISH COLONY

STANDARD COINAGE

KM# 51 1/4 CROWN
Copper-Nickel, 24.3 mm. **Ruler:** Elizabeth II **Obv:** Young bust right **Rev:** Spiny Lobster

Date	Mintage	VF20	XF40	MS60	MS63	MS65
1981	—	0.50	1.00	2.00	4.00	6.00

KM# 52 1/2 CROWN
11.35 g., Copper-Nickel, 30.65 mm. **Ruler:** Elizabeth II **Obv:** Young bust right **Rev:** Windmill

Date	Mintage	VF20	XF40	MS60	MS63	MS65
1981	—	0.50	1.00	1.75	3.50	5.00

KM# 1 CROWN
Copper-Nickel, 38.5 mm. **Ruler:** Elizabeth II **Obv:** Young bust right **Rev:** National arms

Date	Mintage	VF20	XF40	MS60	MS63	MS65
1969	50,000	—	1.50	2.50	4.50	7.00
1969	6,000	PF65 12.50				

KM# 5 CROWN
Copper-Nickel, 36 mm. **Ruler:** Elizabeth II **Obv:** Young bust right **Rev:** Map **Edge Lettering:** REDEEMABLE AT TURKS AND CAICOS FOR US CURRENCY

Date	Mintage	VF20	XF40	MS60	MS63	MS65
1975 Matte	590	—	—	8.00	12.00	14.00
1975	1,370	PF65 13.50				
1976	1,960	—	—	3.00	6.00	8.00
1976	2,270	PF65 13.50				
1977	1,420	PF65 13.50				

KM# 60 CROWN
Copper-Nickel, 38.5 mm. **Ruler:** Elizabeth II **Subject:** Prince Andrew's Marriage **Obv:** Young bust right **Rev:** Conjoined heads right

Date	Mintage	VF20	XF40	MS60	MS63	MS65
1986	20,000	—	—	1.50	2.50	4.50

KM# 60a CROWN
28.28 g., 0.925 Silver 0.841 oz. ASW, 38.5 mm. **Ruler:** Elizabeth II **Subject:** Prince Andrew's Marriage **Obv:** Young bust right **Rev:** Conjoined heads right

Date	Mintage	VF20	XF40	MS60	MS63	MS65
1986	5,000	PF63 21.00	PF65 23.50			

KM# 122 CROWN
Copper-Nickel, 38.5 mm. **Ruler:** Elizabeth II **Obv:** Young bust right **Rev:** National arms

Date	Mintage	VF20	XF40	MS60	MS63	MS65
1986	—	—	—	1.50	2.50	4.50

KM# 64 CROWN
Copper-Nickel, 38.5 mm. **Ruler:** Elizabeth II **Series:** World Wildlife Fund **Obv:** Young bust right **Rev:** Turk's Rock Iguana within circle

Date	Mintage	VF20	XF40	MS60	MS63	MS65
1988	—	—	—	3.00	5.00	9.00

KM# 64a CROWN
28.28 g., 0.925 Silver 0.841 oz. ASW, 38.5 mm. **Ruler:** Elizabeth II **Series:** World Wildlife Fund **Obv:** Young bust right **Rev:** Turk's Rock Iguana within circle

Date	Mintage	VF20	XF40	MS60	MS63	MS65
1988	Est. 25000	PF63 23.00	PF65 25.50			

KM# 66 CROWN
Copper-Nickel, 38.5 mm. **Ruler:** Elizabeth II **Subject:** Queen Mother's 90th Birthday **Obv:** Crowned head right **Rev:** Crowned monogram flanked by thistle stems

Date	Mintage	VF20	XF40	MS60	MS63	MS65
ND-1990	—	—	—	2.00	3.50	5.50

KM# 66a CROWN
28.28 g., 0.925 Silver 0.841 oz. ASW, 38.5 mm. **Ruler:** Elizabeth II **Subject:** Queen Mother's 90th Birthday **Obv:** Crowned head right **Rev:** Crowned monogram flanked by thistle stems

Date	Mintage	VF20	XF40	MS60	MS63	MS65
ND-1990	Est. 10000	PF63 25.00	PF65 28.50			

KM# 74 CROWN
Copper-Nickel **Ruler:** Elizabeth II **Subject:** Royal Birthdays **Obv:** Crowned head right **Rev:** Conjoined heads of Queen Elizabeth II and Prince Philip facing

Date	Mintage	VF20	XF40	MS60	MS63	MS65
1991	—	—	—	2.00	3.50	5.50

KM# 74a CROWN
31.12 g., 0.999 Silver 0.9995 oz. ASW, 39.1 mm. **Ruler:** Elizabeth II **Subject:** Royal Birthdays **Obv:** Crowned head right **Rev:** Conjoined heads of Queen Elizabeth II and Prince Philip facing **Edge:** Reeded with plain section containing fineness

Date	Mintage	VF20	XF40	MS60	MS63	MS65
1991	—	PF63 26.50	PF65 29.00			

KM# 76 CROWN
Copper-Nickel, 39.25 mm. **Ruler:** Elizabeth II **Subject:** 10th Wedding Anniversary - Prince and Princess of Wales **Obv:** Crowned head right **Rev:** Head of Princess Diana facing **Edge:** Reeded

Date	Mintage	VF20	XF40	MS60	MS63	MS65
1991	—	—	—	2.00	3.00	5.00

KM# 76a CROWN
31.12 g., 0.999 Silver 0.9995 oz. ASW, 39.1 mm. **Ruler:** Elizabeth II **Subject:** 10th Wedding Anniversary - Prince Charles and Princess Diana **Obv:** Crowned head right **Rev:** Head of Princess Diana facing **Edge:** Reeded with plain section containing fineness

Date	Mintage	VF20	XF40	MS60	MS63	MS65
1991	—	PF63 27.50	PF65 30.00			

KM# 121 CROWN

Copper-Nickel, 39.25 mm. **Ruler:** Elizabeth II **Subject:** 10th Wedding Anniversary - Prince and Princess of Wales **Obv:** Crowned head right **Rev:** Head of Prince Charles facing **Edge:** Reeded

Date	Mintage	VF20	XF40	MS60	MS63	MS65
1991	—	—	—	2.00	3.00	5.00

KM# 121a CROWN

31.21 g., 0.925 Silver 0.9282 oz. ASW **Ruler:** Elizabeth II **Subject:** 10th Wedding Anniversary of Prince Charles and Princess Diana **Obv:** Crowned head right **Rev:** Head of Prince Charles facing

Date	Mintage	VF20	XF40	MS60	MS63	MS65
1991	—	PF63 24.50	PF65 27.50			

KM# 143 DOLLAR

Copper-Nickel **Ruler:** Elizabeth II **Series:** Steam Locomotive **Subject:** City of Truro **Obv:** Crowned head right **Rev:** Locomotive train **Note:** Similar to 20 Dollars, KM#145.

Date	Mintage	VF20	XF40	MS60	MS63	MS65
1996	—	—	—	2.50	4.00	6.50

KM# 146 DOLLAR

Copper-Nickel **Ruler:** Elizabeth II **Series:** Steam Locomotive **Subject:** Flying Scotsman **Obv:** Crowned head right **Rev:** Locomotive train **Note:** Similar to 20 Dollars, KM#148.

Date	Mintage	VF20	XF40	MS60	MS63	MS65
1996	—	—	—	2.50	4.00	6.50

KM# 149 DOLLAR

Copper-Nickel **Ruler:** Elizabeth II **Series:** Steam Locomotive **Subject:** Rocket **Obv:** Crowned head right **Rev:** Locomotive train **Note:** Similar to 20 Dollars, KM#151.

Date	Mintage	VF20	XF40	MS60	MS63	MS65
1996	—	—	—	2.50	4.00	6.50

KM# 152 DOLLAR

Copper-Nickel **Ruler:** Elizabeth II **Series:** Steam Locomotive **Subject:** Evening Star **Obv:** Crowned head right **Rev:** Locomotive train **Note:** Similar to 20 Dollars, KM#154.

Date	Mintage	VF20	XF40	MS60	MS63	MS65
1996	—	—	—	2.50	4.00	6.50

KM# 155 DOLLAR

Copper-Nickel **Ruler:** Elizabeth II **Series:** Steam Locomotive **Subject:** Mallard **Obv:** Crowned head right **Rev:** Locomotive train **Note:** Similar to 20 Dollars, KM#157.

Date	Mintage	VF20	XF40	MS60	MS63	MS65
1996	—	—	—	2.50	4.00	6.50

KM# 158 DOLLAR

Copper-Nickel **Ruler:** Elizabeth II **Series:** Steam Locomotive **Subject:** Princess Elizabeth **Obv:** Crowned head right **Rev:** Locomotive train **Note:** Similar to 20 Dollars, KM#160.

Date	Mintage	VF20	XF40	MS60	MS63	MS65
1996	—	—	—	2.50	4.00	6.50

KM# 161 DOLLAR

Copper-Nickel **Ruler:** Elizabeth II **Series:** Steam Locomotive **Subject:** Southern Pacific Lines - Class GS4 **Obv:** Crowned head right **Rev:** Locomotive train **Note:** Similar to 20 Dollars, KM#163.

Date	Mintage	VF20	XF40	MS60	MS63	MS65
1996	—	—	—	2.50	4.00	6.50

KM# 164 DOLLAR

Copper-Nickel **Ruler:** Elizabeth II **Series:** Steam Locomotive **Subject:** German States Railway Class 05 **Obv:** Crowned head right **Rev:** Locomotive train **Note:** Similar to 20 Dollars, KM#166.

Date	Mintage	VF20	XF40	MS60	MS63	MS65
1996	—	—	—	2.50	4.00	6.50

KM# 167 DOLLAR

Copper-Nickel **Ruler:** Elizabeth II **Series:** Steam Locomotive **Subject:** Japanese National Railways Class 62 **Obv:** Crowned head right **Rev:** Locomotive train **Note:** Similar to 20 Dollars, KM#169.

Date	Mintage	VF20	XF40	MS60	MS63	MS65
1996	—	—	—	2.50	4.00	6.50

KM# 170 DOLLAR

Copper-Nickel **Ruler:** Elizabeth II **Series:** Steam Locomotive **Subject:** Chinese State Railways Class RM **Obv:** Crowned head right **Rev:** Locomotive train **Note:** Similar to 20 Dollars, KM#171.

Date	Mintage	VF20	XF40	MS60	MS63	MS65
1996	—	—	—	2.50	4.00	6.50

KM# 258 4 CROWNS

1.24 g., 0.999 Gold 0.0398 oz. AGW, 13.92 mm. **Ruler:** Elizabeth II **Subject:** Hummingbirds

Date	Mintage	VF20	XF40	MS60	MS63	MS65
1995	—	PF65 80.00				

KM# 6 5 CROWNS

24.24 g., 0.500 Silver 0.3897 oz. ASW **Ruler:** Elizabeth II **Obv:** Young bust right **Rev:** Turks-head cactus

Date	Mintage	VF20	XF40	MS60	MS63	MS65
1975 Matte	440	—	—	14.00	20.00	22.50
1975	1,320	PF65 18.00				
1976	1,760	—	—	10.00	12.00	15.00
1976	2,220	PF65 16.00				
1977	1,370	PF65 18.00				

KM# 47 5 CROWNS

14.58 g., 0.500 Silver 0.2344 oz. ASW **Ruler:** Elizabeth II **Subject:** Lord Mountbatten **Obv:** Young bust right **Rev:** Uniformed head left above crossed flag and sword

Date	Mintage	VF20	XF40	MS60	MS63	MS65
1980	—	PF63 10.00	PF65 12.00			

KM# 75 5 CROWNS

Copper-Nickel **Ruler:** Elizabeth II **Subject:** Discovery of America **Obv:** Young bust right **Rev:** Columbus before Ferdinand and Isabella

Date	Mintage	VF20	XF40	MS60	MS63	MS65
1991	—	—	—	1.50	2.50	4.00

KM# 68 5 CROWNS

Copper-Nickel **Ruler:** Elizabeth II **Series:** Olympics **Obv:** National arms **Rev:** Equestrian and 3 events

Date	Mintage	VF20	XF40	MS60	MS63	MS65
1992	—	—	—	1.00	2.00	3.50

KM# 69 5 CROWNS

Copper-Nickel **Ruler:** Elizabeth II **Series:** Olympics **Obv:** National arms **Rev:** Gymnast on rings and 5 events

Date	Mintage	VF20	XF40	MS60	MS63	MS65
1992	—	—	—	1.00	2.00	3.50

KM# 70 5 CROWNS

Copper-Nickel **Ruler:** Elizabeth II **Series:** Olympics **Obv:** National arms **Rev:** Weightlifting and 3 events

Date	Mintage	VF20	XF40	MS60	MS63	MS65
1992	—	—	—	1.00	2.00	3.50

KM# 71 5 CROWNS

Copper-Nickel **Ruler:** Elizabeth II **Series:** Olympics **Obv:** National arms **Rev:** Rifle shooting and 3 events

Date	Mintage	VF20	XF40	MS60	MS63	MS65
1992	—	—	—	1.00	2.00	3.50

KM# 72 5 CROWNS

Copper-Nickel **Ruler:** Elizabeth II **Series:** Olympics **Obv:** National arms **Rev:** Sail boarding and 3 events

Date	Mintage	VF20	XF40	MS60	MS63	MS65
1992	—	—	—	1.00	2.00	3.50

KM# 73 5 CROWNS
Copper-Nickel **Ruler:** Elizabeth II **Series:** Olympics **Obv:** National arms **Rev:** Ski jumper and 4 events

Date	Mintage	VF20	XF40	MS60	MS63	MS65
1992	—	—	—	1.00	2.00	3.50

KM# 77 5 CROWNS
Copper-Nickel **Ruler:** Elizabeth II **Subject:** 40th Anniversary - Reign of Elizabeth II **Obv:** National arms **Rev:** Crowned bust facing

Date	Mintage	VF20	XF40	MS60	MS63	MS65
1992	—	—	—	2.50	4.00	6.50

KM# 77a 5 CROWNS
28.04 g., 0.925 Silver 0.8339 oz. ASW **Ruler:** Elizabeth II **Subject:** 40th Anniversary - Reign of Elizabeth II **Obv:** National arms **Rev:** Crowned bust facing

Date	Mintage	VF20	XF40	MS60	MS63	MS65
1992	—	PF63 21.50	PF65 24.50			

KM# 84 5 CROWNS
Copper-Nickel **Ruler:** Elizabeth II **Subject:** 40th Anniversary - Reign of Elizabeth II **Obv:** Crowned head right **Rev:** Conjoined busts of Queen Elizabeth II and Prince Philip facing

Date	Mintage	VF20	XF40	MS60	MS63	MS65
1992	—	—	—	2.50	4.00	6.50

KM# 84a 5 CROWNS
28.04 g., 0.925 Silver 0.8339 oz. ASW **Ruler:** Elizabeth II **Subject:** 40th Anniversary - Reign of Elizabeth II **Obv:** Crowned head right **Rev:** Conjoined busts of Queen Elizabeth II and Prince Philip facing

Date	Mintage	VF20	XF40	MS60	MS63	MS65
1992	—	PF63 21.50	PF65 24.50			

KM# 85 5 CROWNS
Copper-Nickel **Ruler:** Elizabeth II **Subject:** 40th Anniversary - Reign of Elizabeth II **Obv:** Crowned head right **Rev:** Head of King George VI facing

Date	Mintage	VF20	XF40	MS60	MS63	MS65
1992	—	—	—	2.50	4.00	6.50

KM# 85a 5 CROWNS
28.04 g., 0.925 Silver 0.8339 oz. ASW **Ruler:** Elizabeth II **Subject:** 40th Anniversary - Reign of Elizabeth II **Obv:** Crowned head right **Rev:** Head of King George VI facing

Date	Mintage	VF20	XF40	MS60	MS63	MS65
1992	—	PF63 21.50	PF65 24.50			

KM# 86 5 CROWNS
Copper-Nickel **Ruler:** Elizabeth II **Subject:** 40th Anniversary - Reign of Elizabeth II **Obv:** Crowned head right **Rev:** Windsor Castle

Date	Mintage	VF20	XF40	MS60	MS63	MS65
1992	—	—	—	2.50	4.00	6.50

KM# 86a 5 CROWNS
28.28 g., 0.925 Silver 0.841 oz. ASW **Ruler:** Elizabeth II **Subject:** 40th Anniversary - Reign of Elizabeth II **Obv:** Crowned head right **Rev:** Windsor Castle

Date	Mintage	VF20	XF40	MS60	MS63	MS65
1992	—	PF63 22.00	PF65 24.50			

KM# 87 5 CROWNS
Copper-Nickel **Ruler:** Elizabeth II **Subject:** World Cup '94 **Obv:** Crowned head right **Rev:** Jules Rimet and trophy

Date	Mintage	VF20	XF40	MS60	MS63	MS65
ND-1993	—	—	—	2.00	3.00	5.00

KM# 88 5 CROWNS
Copper-Nickel **Ruler:** Elizabeth II **Subject:** World Cup '94 - Uruguay Winners **Obv:** Crowned head right **Rev:** Soccer players shaking hands

Date	Mintage	VF20	XF40	MS60	MS63	MS65
ND-1993	—	—	—	2.00	3.00	5.00

KM# 89 5 CROWNS
Copper-Nickel **Ruler:** Elizabeth II **Subject:** World Cup '94 - Italy Winners **Obv:** Crowned head right **Rev:** Dino Zoff holding trophy

Date	Mintage	VF20	XF40	MS60	MS63	MS65
ND-1993	—	—	—	2.00	3.00	5.00

KM# 90 5 CROWNS
Copper-Nickel **Ruler:** Elizabeth II **Subject:** World Cup '94 - West Germany winners **Obv:** Crowned head right **Rev:** Franz Beckenbauer

Date	Mintage	VF20	XF40	MS60	MS63	MS65
ND-1993	—	—	—	2.00	3.00	5.00

KM# 91 5 CROWNS
Copper-Nickel **Ruler:** Elizabeth II **Subject:** World Cup '94 - Brazil Winners **Obv:** Crowned head right **Rev:** Pelé with arm raised

Date	Mintage	VF20	XF40	MS60	MS63	MS65
ND-1993	—	—	—	2.00	3.00	5.00

KM# 92 5 CROWNS
Copper-Nickel **Ruler:** Elizabeth II **Subject:** World Cup '94 - England Winners **Obv:** Crowned head right **Rev:** Bobby Moore with trophy on teammates shoulders

Date	Mintage	VF20	XF40	MS60	MS63	MS65
ND-1993	—	—	—	2.00	3.00	5.00

KM# 93 5 CROWNS
Copper-Nickel **Ruler:** Elizabeth II **Subject:** World Cup '94 - Argentina winners **Obv:** Crowned head right **Rev:** Mario Kempes running right

Date	Mintage	VF20	XF40	MS60	MS63	MS65
ND-1993	—	—	—	2.00	3.00	5.00

KM# 94 5 CROWNS
Copper-Nickel **Ruler:** Elizabeth II **Subject:** World Cup '94 - USA Host **Obv:** Crowned head right **Rev:** Stylized flag and trophy

Date	Mintage	VF20	XF40	MS60	MS63	MS65
ND-1993	—	—	—	2.00	3.00	5.00

KM# 103 5 CROWNS
Copper-Nickel **Ruler:** Elizabeth II **Subject:** 40th Anniversary of Coronation **Obv:** Crowned head right **Rev:** Westminster Abbey

Date	Mintage	VF20	XF40	MS60	MS63	MS65
ND-1993	—	—	—	1.50	2.50	4.50

KM# 104 5 CROWNS
Copper-Nickel **Ruler:** Elizabeth II **Subject:** 40th Anniversary of Coronation **Obv:** Crowned head right **Rev:** Crown jewels

Date	Mintage	VF20	XF40	MS60	MS63	MS65
ND-1993	—	—	—	1.50	2.50	4.50

KM# 105 5 CROWNS
Copper-Nickel **Ruler:** Elizabeth II **Subject:** 40th Anniversary of Coronation **Obv:** Crowned head right **Rev:** Queen, clergy and maids of honor

Date	Mintage	VF20	XF40	MS60	MS63	MS65
ND-1993	—	—	—	1.50	2.50	4.50

KM# 106 5 CROWNS
Copper-Nickel **Ruler:** Elizabeth II **Subject:** 40th Anniversary of Coronation **Obv:** Crowned head right **Rev:** Consort's Homage

Date	Mintage	VF20	XF40	MS60	MS63	MS65
ND-1993	—	—	—	1.50	2.50	4.50

KM# 107 5 CROWNS
Copper-Nickel **Ruler:** Elizabeth II **Subject:** 40th Anniversary of Coronation **Obv:** Crowned head right **Rev:** Enthroned Queen

Date	Mintage	VF20	XF40	MS60	MS63	MS65
ND-1993	—	—	—	1.50	2.50	4.50

KM# 108 5 CROWNS
Copper-Nickel **Ruler:** Elizabeth II **Subject:** 40th Anniversary of Coronation **Obv:** Crowned head right **Rev:** Queen in coach

Date	Mintage	VF20	XF40	MS60	MS63	MS65
ND-1993	—	—	—	1.50	2.50	4.50

KM# 123 5 CROWNS
Copper-Nickel **Ruler:** Elizabeth II **Series:** 1994 Winter Olympics - Lillehammer **Obv:** Crowned head right **Rev:** Speed skater within circle

Date	Mintage	VF20	XF40	MS60	MS63	MS65
1993 Prooflike	—	—	—	2.00	3.50	5.50

KM# 124 5 CROWNS
Copper-Nickel **Ruler:** Elizabeth II **Series:** 1994 Winter Olympics - Lillehammer **Obv:** Crowned head right **Rev:** Figure skater

Date	Mintage	VF20	XF40	MS60	MS63	MS65
1993 Prooflike	—	—	—	2.00	3.50	5.50

KM# 125 5 CROWNS
Copper-Nickel **Ruler:** Elizabeth II **Series:** 1994 Winter Olympics - Lillehammer **Obv:** Arms with supporters **Rev:** Hockey player within circle

Date	Mintage	VF20	XF40	MS60	MS63	MS65
1993 Prooflike	—	—	—	2.00	3.50	5.50

KM# 126 5 CROWNS
Copper-Nickel **Ruler:** Elizabeth II **Series:** 1994 Winter Olympics - Lillehammer **Obv:** Crowned head right **Rev:** Slalom skier within circle

Date	Mintage	VF20	XF40	MS60	MS63	MS65
1993 Prooflike	—	—	—	2.00	3.50	5.50

KM# 127 5 CROWNS
Copper-Nickel **Ruler:** Elizabeth II **Series:** 1994 Winter Olympics - Lillehammer **Obv:** Crowned head right **Rev:** Ski jumper

Date	Mintage	VF20	XF40	MS60	MS63	MS65
1993 Prooflike	—	—	—	2.00	3.50	5.50

KM# 128 5 CROWNS
Copper-Nickel **Ruler:** Elizabeth II **Series:** 1994 Winter Olympics - Lillehammer **Obv:** Crowned head right **Rev:** Bobsled and team within circle

Date	Mintage	VF20	XF40	MS60	MS63	MS65
1993 Prooflike	—	—	—	2.00	3.50	5.50

KM# 177 5 CROWNS
Copper-Nickel **Ruler:** Elizabeth II **Subject:** 25th Anniversary 1969-1994 - Apollo 11 **Obv:** Crowned head right **Rev:** Launching rocket

Date	Mintage	VF20	XF40	MS60	MS63	MS65
1993	—	—	—	2.50	4.00	6.00

KM# 178 5 CROWNS
Copper-Nickel **Ruler:** Elizabeth II **Subject:** 25th Anniversary 1969-1994 - Apollo 11 **Obv:** Crowned head right **Rev:** Lunar landing

Date	Mintage	VF20	XF40	MS60	MS63	MS65
1993	—	—	—	2.50	4.00	6.00

KM# 179 5 CROWNS
Copper-Nickel **Ruler:** Elizabeth II **Subject:** 25th Anniversary 1969-1994 - Apollo 11 **Obv:** Crowned head right **Rev:** Astronaut descending ladder

Date	Mintage	VF20	XF40	MS60	MS63	MS65
1993	—	—	—	2.50	4.00	6.00

KM# 181 5 CROWNS
Copper-Nickel **Ruler:** Elizabeth II **Subject:** 25th Anniversary 1969-1994 - Apollo 11 **Obv:** Crowned head right **Rev:** Astronaut walking on moon

Date	Mintage	VF20	XF40	MS60	MS63	MS65
1993	—	—	—	2.50	4.00	6.00

KM# 182 5 CROWNS
Copper-Nickel **Ruler:** Elizabeth II **Subject:** 25th Anniversary 1969-1994 - Apollo 11 **Obv:** Crowned head right **Rev:** Ocean recovery

Date	Mintage	VF20	XF40	MS60	MS63	MS65
1993	—	—	—	2.50	4.00	6.00

KM# 132 5 CROWNS
Copper-Nickel **Ruler:** Elizabeth II **Subject:** 25th Anniversary 1969-1994 - Apollo 11 **Obv:** Crowned head right **Rev:** Salute to ANA and coin collecting **Edge Lettering:** PEACE on a smooth section of alternating smooth and reeded

Date	Mintage	VF20	XF40	MS60	MS63	MS65
1994 Prooflike	10,000	—	—	4.00	8.00	12.00

KM# 173 5 CROWNS
Copper-Nickel **Ruler:** Elizabeth II **Subject:** 50th Anniversary - Normandy Landing **Obv:** Crowned head right **Rev:** Bust of Sir Bertram II Ramsay left

Date	Mintage	VF20	XF40	MS60	MS63	MS65
1994	—	—	—	3.00	5.00	7.00

KM# 174 5 CROWNS
Copper-Nickel **Ruler:** Elizabeth II **Subject:** 50th Aniversary - Normandy Landing **Obv:** Crowned head right **Rev:** Bust of Bernard L. Montgomery left

Date	Mintage	VF20	XF40	MS60	MS63	MS65
1994	—	—	—	3.00	5.00	7.00

KM# 175 5 CROWNS
Copper-Nickel **Ruler:** Elizabeth II **Subject:** 50th Anniversary - Normandy Landing **Obv:** Crowned head right **Rev:** Bust of Omar N. Bradley right

Date	Mintage	VF20	XF40	MS60	MS63	MS65
1994	—	—	—	3.00	5.00	7.00

KM# 176 5 CROWNS
Copper-Nickel **Ruler:** Elizabeth II **Subject:** 50th Anniversary - Normandy Landing **Obv:** Crowned head right **Rev:** Bust of Dwight D. Eisenhower right

Date	Mintage	VF20	XF40	MS60	MS63	MS65
1994	—	—	—	3.00	5.00	7.00

KM# 180 5 CROWNS
Copper-Nickel **Ruler:** Elizabeth II **Subject:** 25th Anniversary 1969-1994 - Apollo 11 **Obv:** Crowned head right **Rev:** Astronauts raising flag on moon

Date	Mintage	VF20	XF40	MS60	MS63	MS65
1993	—	—	—	2.50	4.00	6.00

KM# 234 5 CROWNS
3.11 g., 0.9995 Platinum 0.100 oz. APW, 16.5 mm. **Ruler:** Elizabeth II **Subject:** ANA Salute to Coin Collecting **Obv:** Crowned head right **Rev:** Astronaut on the moon **Edge:** Reeded

Date	Mintage	VF20	XF40	MS60	MS63	MS65
1994	200	PF63 225	PF65 245			

KM# 254 5 CROWNS
1.55 g., 0.9999 Gold 0.0498 oz. AGW, 13.85 mm. **Ruler:** Elizabeth II **Subject:** Wildlife of the Sea - Scarlet Flamingo

Date	Mintage	VF20	XF40	MS60	MS63	MS65
1994	Est. 5000	PF65 95.00	PF67 115			

KM# 133 5 CROWNS
27.20 g., Copper-Nickel, 39.14 mm. **Ruler:** Elizabeth II **Subject:** 50th Anniversary - VE Day **Obv:** National arms **Rev:** Heads of Churchill, Roosevelt and Stalin facing **Edge:** Reeded

Date	Mintage	VF20	XF40	MS60	MS63	MS65
1995	—	—	—	3.00	5.00	7.00

KM# 134 5 CROWNS
27.20 g., Copper-Nickel, 39.14 mm. **Ruler:** Elizabeth II **Subject:** 50th Anniversary - VE Day **Obv:** National arms **Rev:** Planes **Edge:** Reeded

Date	Mintage	VF20	XF40	MS60	MS63	MS65
1995	—	—	—	2.50	4.00	6.00

KM# 135 5 CROWNS
27.20 g., Copper-Nickel, 39.14 mm. **Ruler:** Elizabeth II **Subject:** 50th Anniversary - VE Day **Obv:** National arms **Rev:** U.S. and Soviet troops meet **Edge:** Reeded

Date	Mintage	VF20	XF40	MS60	MS63	MS65
1995	—	—	—	2.50	4.00	6.00

KM# 136 5 CROWNS
27.20 g., Copper-Nickel, 39.14 mm. **Ruler:** Elizabeth II **Subject:** 50th Anniversary - VE Day **Obv:** National arms **Rev:** Famous buildings of the capitals of the Allies--London, Washington, Moscow and Paris **Edge:** Reeded

Date	Mintage	VF20	XF40	MS60	MS63	MS65
1995	—	—	—	2.50	4.00	6.00

KM# 188 5 CROWNS
10.00 g., 0.999 Silver 0.3212 oz. ASW **Ruler:** Elizabeth II **Series:** XXVI Summer Olympics **Obv:** Crowned head right **Rev:** Hurdlers

Date	Mintage	VF20	XF40	MS60	MS63	MS65
1995	—	PF65 17.50				

KM# 190 5 CROWNS
10.00 g., 0.999 Silver 0.3212 oz. ASW **Ruler:** Elizabeth II **Series:** XXVI Summer Olympics **Obv:** Crowned head right **Rev:** Cyclist

Date	Mintage	VF20	XF40	MS60	MS63	MS65
1995	—	PF65 17.50				

KM# 192 5 CROWNS
10.00 g., 0.999 Silver 0.3212 oz. ASW **Ruler:** Elizabeth II **Series:** XXVI Summer Olympics **Obv:** Crowned head right **Rev:** Fencers

Date	Mintage	VF20	XF40	MS60	MS63	MS65
1995	—	PF65 17.50				

KM# 194 5 CROWNS
10.00 g., 0.999 Silver 0.3212 oz. ASW **Ruler:** Elizabeth II **Series:** XXVI Summer Olympics **Obv:** Crowned head right **Rev:** Equestrian

Date	Mintage	VF20	XF40	MS60	MS63	MS65
1995	—	PF65 17.50				

KM# 196 5 CROWNS
10.00 g., 0.999 Silver 0.3212 oz. ASW **Ruler:** George VI **Series:** XXVI Summer Olympics **Obv:** Crowned head right **Rev:** Pole vaulter

Date	Mintage	VF20	XF40	MS60	MS63	MS65
1995	—	PF65 17.50				

KM# 198 5 CROWNS
10.00 g., 0.999 Silver 0.3212 oz. ASW **Ruler:** Elizabeth II **Series:** XXVI Summer Olympics **Obv:** Crowned head right **Rev:** Runners

Date	Mintage	VF20	XF40	MS60	MS63	MS65
1995	—	PF65 17.50				

KM# 200 5 CROWNS
10.00 g., 0.999 Silver 0.3212 oz. ASW **Ruler:** Elizabeth II **Series:** XXVI Summer Olympics **Obv:** Crowned head right **Rev:** Gymnast

Date	Mintage	VF20	XF40	MS60	MS63	MS65
1995	—	PF65 17.50				

KM# 202 5 CROWNS
10.00 g., 0.999 Silver 0.3212 oz. ASW **Ruler:** Elizabeth II **Series:** XXVI Summer Olympics **Obv:** Crowned head right **Rev:** Swimmer

Date	Mintage	VF20	XF40	MS60	MS63	MS65
1995	—	PF65 17.50				

KM# 204 5 CROWNS
10.00 g., 0.999 Silver 0.3212 oz. ASW **Ruler:** Elizabeth II **Series:** XXVI Summer Olympics **Obv:** Crowned head right **Rev:** Diver

Date	Mintage	VF20	XF40	MS60	MS63	MS65
1995	—	PF65 17.50				

KM# 206 5 CROWNS
10.00 g., 0.999 Silver 0.3212 oz. ASW **Ruler:** Elizabeth II **Series:** XXVI Summer Olympics **Obv:** Crowned head right **Rev:** Sprinter within circle

Date	Mintage	VF20	XF40	MS60	MS63	MS65
1995	—	PF65 15.00				

KM# 225 5 CROWNS
26.20 g., Brass, 39.1 mm. **Ruler:** Elizabeth II **Subject:** Mother Theresa **Obv:** National arms **Rev:** Bust 1/4 left and star design within globe **Edge:** Reeded

Date	Mintage	VF20	XF40	MS60	MS63	MS65
1997	—	—	—	1.50	3.00	5.00

KM# 249 5 CROWNS
Copper-Nickel Plated Bronze **Ruler:** Elizabeth II **Subject:** 50th Wedding Anniversary **Rev:** Conjoined heads of Elizabeth and Prince Philip right

Date	Mintage	VF20	XF40	MS60	MS63	MS65
1997	—	—	—	2.50	4.00	6.00

KM# 259 5 CROWNS
10.00 g., 0.999 Silver 0.3212 oz. ASW, 31 mm. **Ruler:** Elizabeth II **Subject:** Birthday of Queen Elizabeth II

Date	Mintage	VF20	XF40	MS60	MS63	MS65
1997	—	PF65 25.00				

KM# 261 5 CROWNS
26.50 g., Copper-Nickel, 39 mm. **Ruler:** Elizabeth II **Subject:** Mother Teresa of Calcutta, Death

Date	Mintage	VF20	XF40	MS60	MS63	MS65
1997	—	PF65 8.00				

KM# 262 5 CROWNS
26.50 g., Copper-Nickel, 39 mm. **Ruler:** Elizabeth II **Subject:** 50th Wedding Anniversary of Queen Elizabeth II and Prince Phillip

Date	Mintage	VF20	XF40	MS60	MS63	MS65
1997	—	PF65 8.00				

KM# 232 5 CROWNS
26.43 g., Copper-Nickel, 39.2 mm. **Ruler:** Elizabeth II **Subject:** Year of the Tiger **Obv:** Crowned head right **Rev:** Stylized tiger within circle **Edge:** Reeded

Date	Mintage	VF20	XF40	MS60	MS63	MS65
1998	—	—	—	2.00	3.50	5.50

KM# 238 5 CROWNS
1.56 g., 0.9999 Gold 0.0502 oz. AGW, 13.7 mm. **Ruler:** Elizabeth II **Obv:** Crowned head right **Rev:** Two Bottle-nosed Dolphins **Edge:** Reeded

Date	Mintage	VF20	XF40	MS60	MS63	MS65
1998	—	PF63 80.00	PF65 90.00			

KM# 144 5 DOLLARS
10.00 g., 0.999 Silver 0.3212 oz. ASW **Ruler:** Elizabeth II **Series:** Steam Locomotive **Subject:** City of Truro **Obv:** Crowned head right **Rev:** Locomotive train **Note:** Similar to 20 Dollars, KM#145.

Date	Mintage	VF20	XF40	MS60	MS63	MS65
1996	—	PF65 17.50				

KM# 147 5 DOLLARS
10.00 g., 0.999 Silver 0.3212 oz. ASW **Ruler:** Elizabeth II **Series:** Steam Locomotive **Subject:** Flying Scotsman **Obv:** Crowned head right **Rev:** Locomotive train **Note:** Similar to 20 Dollars, KM#148.

Date	Mintage	VF20	XF40	MS60	MS63	MS65
1996	—	PF65 17.50				

KM# 150 5 DOLLARS
10.00 g., 0.999 Silver 0.3212 oz. ASW **Ruler:** Elizabeth II **Series:** Steam Locomotive **Subject:** Rocket **Obv:** Crowned head right **Rev:** Locomotive train **Note:** Similar to 20 Dollars, KM#151.

Date	Mintage	VF20	XF40	MS60	MS63	MS65
1996	—	PF65 17.50				

KM# 153 5 DOLLARS

10.00 g., 0.999 Silver 0.3212 oz. ASW **Ruler:** Elizabeth II **Series:** Steam Locomotive **Subject:** Evening Star **Obv:** Crowned head right **Rev:** Locomotive train **Note:** Similar to 20 Dollars, KM#154.

Date	Mintage	VF20	XF40	MS60	MS63	MS65
1996	Est. 25000	PF65 17.50				

KM# 156 5 DOLLARS

10.00 g., 0.999 Silver 0.3212 oz. ASW **Ruler:** Elizabeth II **Series:** Steam Locomotive **Subject:** Mallard **Obv:** Crowned head right **Rev:** Locomotive train **Note:** Similar to 20 Dollars, KM#157.

Date	Mintage	VF20	XF40	MS60	MS63	MS65
1996	—	PF65 17.50				

KM# 159 5 DOLLARS

10.00 g., 0.999 Silver 0.3212 oz. ASW **Ruler:** Elizabeth II **Series:** Steam Locomotive **Subject:** Princess Elizabeth **Obv:** Crowned head right **Rev:** Locomotive train **Note:** Similar to 20 Dollars, KM#160.

Date	Mintage	VF20	XF40	MS60	MS63	MS65
1996	Est. 25000	PF65 17.50				

KM# 162 5 DOLLARS

10.00 g., 0.999 Silver 0.3212 oz. ASW **Ruler:** Elizabeth II **Series:** Steam Locomotive **Subject:** Southern Pacific Lines - Class GS4 **Obv:** Crowned head right **Rev:** Locomotive train **Note:** Similar to 20 Dollars, KM#163.

Date	Mintage	VF20	XF40	MS60	MS63	MS65
1996	Est. 25000	PF65 17.50				

KM# 165 5 DOLLARS

10.00 g., 0.999 Silver 0.3212 oz. ASW **Ruler:** Elizabeth II **Series:** Steam Locomotive **Subject:** German States Railway - Class 05 **Obv:** Crowned head right **Rev:** Locomotive train **Note:** Similar to 20 Dollars, KM#166.

Date	Mintage	VF20	XF40	MS60	MS63	MS65
1996	Est. 25000	PF65 17.50				

KM# 168 5 DOLLARS

10.00 g., 0.999 Silver 0.3212 oz. ASW **Ruler:** Elizabeth II **Series:** Steam Locomotive **Subject:** Japanese National Railways - Class 62 **Obv:** Crowned head right **Rev:** Locomotive train **Note:** Similar to 20 Dollars, KM#169.

Date	Mintage	VF20	XF40	MS60	MS63	MS65
1996	—	PF65 17.50				

KM# 171 5 DOLLARS

10.00 g., 0.999 Silver 0.3212 oz. ASW **Ruler:** Elizabeth II **Series:** Steam Locomotive **Subject:** Chinese State Railways - Class RM **Obv:** Crowned head right **Rev:** Locomotive train **Note:** Similar to 20 Dollars, KM#172.

Date	Mintage	VF20	XF40	MS60	MS63	MS65
1996	Est. 25000	PF65 17.50				

KM# 7 10 CROWNS

29.98 g., 0.925 Silver 0.8916 oz. ASW **Ruler:** Elizabeth II **Subject:** Age of Exploration **Obv:** Young bust right **Rev:** Spacecraft's orbital paths

Date	Mintage	VF20	XF40	MS60	MS63	MS65
1975 Matte	1,250	—	—	—	32.00	37.00
1975	2,935	PF63 30.00	PF65 35.00			

KM# 12 10 CROWNS

29.98 g., 0.925 Silver 0.8916 oz. ASW **Ruler:** Elizabeth II **Obv:** Young bust right **Rev:** Salt windmill

Date	Mintage	VF20	XF40	MS60	MS63	MS65
1976	4,185	—	—	—	30.00	35.00
1976	2,220	PF63 32.00	PF65 37.00			
1977	1,370	PF63 35.00	PF65 40.00			

KM# 45 10 CROWNS

29.70 g., 0.925 Silver 0.8833 oz. ASW **Ruler:** Elizabeth II **Subject:** 10th Anniversary - Prince Charles' Investiture **Obv:** Young bust right **Rev:** Head of Prince Charles left above crossed scepter and sword, with crown and ring

Date	Mintage	VF20	XF40	MS60	MS63	MS65
1979	25,000	PF65 24.50				

KM# 48 10 CROWNS

23.33 g., 0.500 Silver 0.375 oz. ASW **Ruler:** Elizabeth II **Subject:** Lord Mountbatten **Obv:** Young bust right **Rev:** Uniformed bust right and crowned shield

Date	Mintage	VF20	XF40	MS60	MS63	MS65
1980	—	PF63 15.00	PF65 18.00			

KM# 53 10 CROWNS

29.70 g., 0.925 Silver 0.8833 oz. ASW **Ruler:** Elizabeth II **Subject:** Wedding of Prince Charles and Lady Diana **Obv:** Young bust right **Rev:** Conjoined busts 1/4 left **Note:** Similar to 100 Crowns, KM#54.

Date	Mintage	VF20	XF40	MS60	MS63	MS65
1981	40,000	PF63 21.00	PF65 24.50			

KM# 55 10 CROWNS

23.28 g., 0.925 Silver 0.6923 oz. ASW **Ruler:** Elizabeth II **Series:** International Year of the Child **Obv:** Young bust right **Rev:** Child holding shell, palm trees at left and right

Date	Mintage	VF20	XF40	MS60	MS63	MS65
1982	7,928	PF63 17.50	PF65 21.00			

KM# 56 10 CROWNS

23.28 g., 0.925 Silver 0.6923 oz. ASW **Ruler:** Elizabeth II **Subject:** World Football Championship **Obv:** Young bust right **Rev:** Soccer player

Date	Mintage	VF20	XF40	MS60	MS63	MS65
1982	7,865	PF63 17.50	PF65 21.00			

KM# 57 10 CROWNS

23.28 g., 0.925 Silver 0.6923 oz. ASW **Ruler:** Elizabeth II **Subject:** World Football Championship **Obv:** Young bust right **Rev:** Two players

Date	Mintage	VF20	XF40	MS60	MS63	MS65
1982	7,165	PF63 17.50	PF65 21.00			

KM# 58 10 CROWNS

23.28 g., 0.925 Silver 0.6923 oz. ASW **Ruler:** Elizabeth II **Series:** Summer Olympics **Obv:** Young bust right **Rev:** Javelin thrower

Date	Mintage	VF20	XF40	MS60	MS63	MS65
1984	2,160	PF63 32.00	PF65 38.00			

KM# 63 10 CROWNS

23.28 g., 0.925 Silver 0.6923 oz. ASW **Ruler:** Elizabeth II **Series:** Decade for Women **Obv:** Young bust right **Rev:** Female figure facing holding shell and stylized dove within circle

Date	Mintage	VF20	XF40	MS60	MS63	MS65
1985	1,001	PF63 30.00	PF65 35.00			

KM# 255 10 CROWNS

3.11 g., 0.9999 Gold 0.100 oz. AGW, 16.51 mm. **Ruler:** Elizabeth II **Subject:** Wildlife of the Sea - Scarlet Flamingo

Date	Mintage	VF20	XF40	MS60	MS63	MS65
1994	Est. 5000	PF65 200				

KM# 256 10 CROWNS
Gold **Ruler:** Elizabeth II **Series:** Wildlife of the Sea - Scarlet Flamingo

Date	Mintage	VF20	XF40	MS60	MS63	MS65
1994	—	PF65 200				

KM# 2 20 CROWNS
38.70 g., 0.925 Silver 1.1509 oz. ASW, 45 mm. **Ruler:** Elizabeth II **Subject:** Centenary - Birth of Winston Churchill **Obv:** National arms **Rev:** Bust 1/4 left

Date	Mintage	VF20	XF40	MS60	MS63	MS65
1974 Matte	268,000	—	—	30.00	32.00	35.00
1974	8,400	PF63 37.00	PF65 42.00			

Note: 4,100 issued individually; 4,300 issued in binational sets with Cayman Islands 25 Dollars, KM#10.

KM# 8 20 CROWNS
38.70 g., 0.925 Silver 1.1509 oz. ASW, 45 mm. **Ruler:** Elizabeth II **Subject:** Age of Exploration **Obv:** Young bust right **Rev:** Bust of Christopher Columbus right and three ships

Date	Mintage	VF20	XF40	MS60	MS63	MS65
1975 Matte	1,037	—	—	32.00	35.00	40.00
1975	2,769	PF63 35.00	PF65 40.00			

KM# 13 20 CROWNS
38.70 g., 0.925 Silver 1.1509 oz. ASW, 45 mm. **Ruler:** Elizabeth II **Subject:** U.S. Bicentennial **Obv:** Young bust right **Rev:** Two cameos facing each other below flags and crossed scepters

Date	Mintage	VF20	XF40	MS60	MS63	MS65
1976 Matte	5,022	—	—	30.00	32.00	35.00
1976	4,474	PF63 40.00	PF65 45.00			

KM# 14 20 CROWNS
38.70 g., 0.925 Silver 1.1509 oz. ASW, 45 mm. **Ruler:** Elizabeth II **Obv:** Young bust right **Rev:** 4 Victoria cameos left

Date	Mintage	VF20	XF40	MS60	MS63	MS65
1976	25,000	—	—	30.00	32.00	35.00
1976	22,000	PF63 35.00	PF65 40.00			
1977	1,934	PF63 40.00	PF65 45.00			

KM# 18 20 CROWNS
38.70 g., 0.925 Silver 1.1509 oz. ASW, 45 mm. **Ruler:** Elizabeth II **Obv:** Bust with tiara right **Rev:** 4 George III cameos right **Edge:** Plain

Date	Mintage	VF20	XF40	MS60	MS63	MS65
1977	—	—	—	32.00	35.00	40.00
1977	1,973	PF63 45.00	PF65 50.00			

KM# 23 20 CROWNS
38.70 g., 0.925 Silver 1.1509 oz. ASW, 45 mm. **Ruler:** Elizabeth II **Subject:** XI Commonwealth Games **Obv:** Young bust right **Rev:** Javelin thrower and runner

Date	Mintage	VF20	XF40	MS60	MS63	MS65
1978	10,000	PF63 35.00	PF65 40.00			

KM# 49 20 CROWNS
29.81 g., 0.500 Silver 0.4792 oz. ASW, 40.02 mm. **Ruler:** Elizabeth II **Subject:** Lord Mountbatten **Obv:** Bust with tiara right **Rev:** Uniformed bust 1/4 right divides dates **Edge:** Plain

Date	Mintage	VF20	XF40	MS60	MS63	MS65
1980	—	PF63 18.00	PF65 22.00			

KM# 67.1 20 CROWNS
28.04 g., 0.925 Silver 0.8339 oz. ASW **Ruler:** Elizabeth II **Subject:** 500th Anniversary - Discovery of America **Obv:** Crude young bust right **Rev:** Sailing ship - Santa Maria

Date	Mintage	VF20	XF40	MS60	MS63	MS65
1989	—	PF65 21.50				

KM# 67.2 20 CROWNS
28.04 g., 0.925 Silver 0.8339 oz. ASW **Ruler:** Elizabeth II **Subject:** 500th Anniversary - Discovery of America **Obv:** Refined young bust right **Rev:** Sailing ship - Santa Maria

Date	Mintage	VF20	XF40	MS60	MS63	MS65
1991	—	PF65 21.50				

KM# 67.3 20 CROWNS
28.04 g., 0.925 Silver 0.8339 oz. ASW **Ruler:** Elizabeth II **Subject:** 500th Anniversary - Discovery of America **Obv:** Refined young bust right #2 **Rev:** Sailing ship - Santa Maria

Date	Mintage	VF20	XF40	MS60	MS63	MS65
1992	—	PF65 21.50				

KM# 115.1 20 CROWNS
28.04 g., 0.925 Silver 0.8339 oz. ASW **Ruler:** Elizabeth II **Subject:** 500th Anniversary - Discovery of America **Obv:** Crude young bust right **Rev:** Ship - The Nina

Date	Mintage	VF20	XF40	MS60	MS63	MS65
1989	—	PF65 21.50				

KM# 115.2 20 CROWNS
28.04 g., 0.925 Silver 0.8339 oz. ASW **Ruler:** Elizabeth II **Subject:** 500th Anniversary - Discovery of America **Obv:** Refined young bust right **Rev:** Ship - The Nina

Date	Mintage	VF20	XF40	MS60	MS63	MS65
1991	—	PF65 21.50				

KM# 115.3 20 CROWNS
28.04 g., 0.925 Silver 0.8339 oz. ASW **Ruler:** Elizabeth II **Subject:** 500th Anniversary - Discovery of America **Obv:** Refined young bust #2 right **Rev:** Ship - The Nina

Date	Mintage	VF20	XF40	MS60	MS63	MS65
1992	—	PF65 21.50				

KM# 116.1 20 CROWNS
28.04 g., 0.925 Silver 0.8339 oz. ASW **Ruler:** Elizabeth II **Subject:** 500th Anniversary - Discovery of America **Obv:** Crude young bust right **Rev:** The Pinta

Date	Mintage	VF20	XF40	MS60	MS63	MS65
1989	—	PF65 21.50				

KM# 116.2 20 CROWNS
28.04 g., 0.925 Silver 0.8339 oz. ASW **Ruler:** Elizabeth II **Subject:** 500th Anniversary - Discovery of America **Obv:** Refined young bust right **Rev:** The Pinta

Date	Mintage	VF20	XF40	MS60	MS63	MS65
1991	—	PF65 21.50				

KM# 116.3 20 CROWNS
28.04 g., 0.925 Silver 0.8339 oz. ASW **Ruler:** Elizabeth II **Subject:** 500th Anniversary - Discovery of America **Obv:** Refined young bust right #2 **Rev:** The Pinta

Date	Mintage	VF20	XF40	MS60	MS63	MS65
1992	—	PF65 21.50				

KM# 117.1 20 CROWNS
28.04 g., 0.925 Silver 0.8339 oz. ASW **Ruler:** Elizabeth II **Subject:** 500th Anniversary - Discovery of America **Obv:** Crude young bust right **Rev:** Ships set sail

Date	Mintage	VF20	XF40	MS60	MS63	MS65
1989	—	PF65 21.50				

KM# 117.2 20 CROWNS
28.04 g., 0.925 Silver 0.8339 oz. ASW **Ruler:** Elizabeth II **Subject:** 500th Anniversary - Discovery of America **Obv:** Refined young bust right **Rev:** Ships set sail

Date	Mintage	VF20	XF40	MS60	MS63	MS65
1991	—	PF65 21.50				

KM# 117.3 20 CROWNS
28.04 g., 0.925 Silver 0.8339 oz. ASW **Ruler:** Elizabeth II **Subject:** 500th Anniversary - Discovery of America **Obv:** Refined young bust #2 right **Rev:** Ships set sail

Date	Mintage	VF20	XF40	MS60	MS63	MS65
1992	—	PF65 21.50				

KM# 118.1 20 CROWNS
28.04 g., 0.925 Silver 0.8339 oz. ASW **Ruler:** Elizabeth II **Subject:** 500th Anniversary-Discovery of America **Obv:** Crude young bust right **Rev:** Ships crossing the Atlantic

Date	Mintage	VF20	XF40	MS60	MS63	MS65
1989	—	PF65 21.50				

KM# 118.2 20 CROWNS
28.04 g., 0.925 Silver 0.8339 oz. ASW **Ruler:** Elizabeth II **Subject:** 500th Anniversary - Discovery of America **Obv:** Refined young bust right **Rev:** Ships crossing the Atlantic

Date	Mintage	VF20	XF40	MS60	MS63	MS65
1991	—	PF65 21.50				

KM# 118.3 20 CROWNS
28.04 g., 0.925 Silver 0.8339 oz. ASW **Ruler:** Elizabeth II **Subject:** 500th Anniversary - Discovery of America **Obv:** Refined young bust #2 right **Rev:** Ships crossing the Atlantic

Date	Mintage	VF20	XF40	MS60	MS63	MS65
1992	—	PF65 21.50				

KM# 119.1 20 CROWNS
28.04 g., 0.925 Silver 0.8339 oz. ASW **Ruler:** Elizabeth II **Subject:** 500th Anniversary - Discovery of America **Obv:** Crude young bust right **Rev:** Sighting land

Date	Mintage	VF20	XF40	MS60	MS63	MS65
1989	—	PF65 21.50				

KM# 119.2 20 CROWNS
28.04 g., 0.925 Silver 0.8339 oz. ASW **Ruler:** Elizabeth II **Subject:** 500th Anniversary - Discovery of America **Obv:** Refined young bust right **Rev:** Sighting land

Date	Mintage	VF20	XF40	MS60	MS63	MS65
1991	—	PF65 21.50				

KM# 119.3 20 CROWNS
28.04 g., 0.925 Silver 0.8339 oz. ASW **Ruler:** Elizabeth II **Subject:** 500th Anniversary - Discovery of America **Obv:** Refined young bust #2 right **Rev:** Sighting land

Date	Mintage	VF20	XF40	MS60	MS63	MS65
1992	—	PF65 21.50				

KM# 120.1 20 CROWNS
28.04 g., 0.925 Silver 0.8339 oz. ASW **Ruler:** Elizabeth II **Subject:** 500th Anniversary - Discovery of America **Obv:** Crude young bust right **Rev:** Columbus explores the Caribbean

Date	Mintage	VF20	XF40	MS60	MS63	MS65
1989	—	PF65 21.50				

KM# 120.2 20 CROWNS
28.04 g., 0.925 Silver 0.8339 oz. ASW **Ruler:** Elizabeth II **Subject:** 500th Anniversary - Discovery of America **Obv:** Refined young bust right **Rev:** Columbus explores the Caribbean

Date	Mintage	VF20	XF40	MS60	MS63	MS65
1991	—	PF65 21.50				

KM# 120.3 20 CROWNS

28.04 g., 0.925 Silver 0.8339 oz. ASW **Ruler:** Elizabeth II **Subject:** 500th Anniversary - Discovery of America **Obv:** Refined young bust #2 right **Rev:** Columbus explores the Caribbean

Date	Mintage	VF20	XF40	MS60	MS63	MS65
1992	—	PF65 21.50				

KM# 129.1 20 CROWNS

28.04 g., 0.925 Silver 0.8339 oz. ASW **Ruler:** Elizabeth II **Subject:** 500th Anniversary - Discovery of America **Obv:** Crude bust right **Rev:** Columbus sights New World

Date	Mintage	VF20	XF40	MS60	MS63	MS65
1989	—	PF65 21.50				

KM# 129.2 20 CROWNS

28.04 g., 0.925 Silver 0.8339 oz. ASW **Ruler:** Elizabeth II **Subject:** 500th Anniversary - Discovery of America **Obv:** Refined bust right **Rev:** Columbus sights New World

Date	Mintage	VF20	XF40	MS60	MS63	MS65
1991	—	PF65 21.50				

KM# 129.3 20 CROWNS

28.04 g., 0.925 Silver 0.8339 oz. ASW **Ruler:** Elizabeth II **Subject:** 500th Anniversary - Discovery of America **Obv:** Refined bust #2 right **Rev:** Columbus sights New World

Date	Mintage	VF20	XF40	MS60	MS63	MS65
1992	—	PF65 21.50				

KM# 130.1 20 CROWNS

28.04 g., 0.925 Silver 0.8339 oz. ASW **Ruler:** Elizabeth II **Subject:** 500th Anniversary - Discovery of America **Obv:** Crude bust right **Rev:** Columbus claims land for Spain

Date	Mintage	VF20	XF40	MS60	MS63	MS65
1989	—	PF65 21.50				

KM# 130.2 20 CROWNS

28.04 g., 0.925 Silver 0.8339 oz. ASW **Ruler:** Elizabeth II **Subject:** 500th Anniversary - Discovery of America **Obv:** Refined bust right **Rev:** Columbus claims land for Spain

Date	Mintage	VF20	XF40	MS60	MS63	MS65
1991	—	PF65 21.50				

KM# 130.3 20 CROWNS

28.04 g., 0.925 Silver 0.8339 oz. ASW **Ruler:** Elizabeth II **Subject:** 500th Anniversary - Discovery of America **Obv:** Refined bust #2 right **Rev:** Columbus claims land for Spain

Date	Mintage	VF20	XF40	MS60	MS63	MS65
1992	—	PF65 21.50				

KM# 131.1 20 CROWNS

28.04 g., 0.925 Silver 0.8339 oz. ASW **Ruler:** Elizabeth II **Subject:** 500th Anniversary - Discovery of America **Obv:** Crude bust right **Rev:** Columbus and Indians exchange gifts

Date	Mintage	VF20	XF40	MS60	MS63	MS65
1989	—	PF65 21.50				

KM# 131.2 20 CROWNS

28.04 g., 0.925 Silver 0.8339 oz. ASW **Ruler:** Elizabeth II **Subject:** 500th Anniversary - Discovery of America **Obv:** Refined bust right **Rev:** Columbus and Indians exchange gifts

Date	Mintage	VF20	XF40	MS60	MS63	MS65
1991	—	PF65 21.50				

KM# 78 20 CROWNS

31.10 g., 0.999 Silver 0.9989 oz. ASW, 38.95 mm. **Ruler:** Elizabeth II **Series:** Olympics **Obv:** National arms **Rev:** Equestrian and 3 events **Edge:** Reeded

Date	Mintage	VF20	XF40	MS60	MS63	MS65
1992	20,000	PF65 24.50				

KM# 79 20 CROWNS

31.10 g., 0.999 Silver 0.9989 oz. ASW, 38.95 mm. **Ruler:** Elizabeth II **Series:** Olympics **Obv:** National arms **Rev:** Gymnast on rings and 5 events **Edge:** Reeded

Date	Mintage	VF20	XF40	MS60	MS63	MS65
1992	—	PF65 24.50				

KM# 80 20 CROWNS

31.10 g., 0.999 Silver 0.9989 oz. ASW, 38.95 mm. **Ruler:** Elizabeth II **Series:** Olympics **Obv:** National arms **Rev:** Weightlifting and 3 events **Edge:** Reeded

Date	Mintage	VF20	XF40	MS60	MS63	MS65
1992	—	PF65 24.50				

KM# 81 20 CROWNS

31.10 g., 0.999 Silver 0.9989 oz. ASW, 38.95 mm. **Ruler:** Elizabeth II **Series:** Olympics **Obv:** National arms **Rev:** Rifle shooting and 3 events **Edge:** Reeded

Date	Mintage	VF20	XF40	MS60	MS63	MS65
1992	Est. 20000	PF65 24.50				

KM# 82 20 CROWNS

31.10 g., 0.999 Silver 0.9989 oz. ASW, 38.95 mm. **Ruler:** Elizabeth II **Series:** Olympics **Obv:** National arms **Rev:** Sail boarding and 3 events **Edge:** Reeded

Date	Mintage	VF20	XF40	MS60	MS63	MS65
1992	Est. 20000	PF65 24.50				

KM# 83 20 CROWNS

31.10 g., 0.999 Silver 0.9989 oz. ASW, 38.95 mm. **Ruler:** Elizabeth II **Series:** Olympics **Obv:** National arms **Rev:** Ski jumper and 4 events **Edge:** Reeded

Date	Mintage	VF20	XF40	MS60	MS63	MS65
1992	Est. 20000	PF65 24.50				

KM# 131.3 20 CROWNS
28.04 g., 0.925 Silver 0.8339 oz. ASW **Ruler:** Elizabeth II **Subject:** 500th Anniversary - Discovery of America **Obv:** Refined bust #2 right **Rev:** Columbus and Indians exchange gifts

Date	Mintage	VF20	XF40	MS60	MS63	MS65
1992	—	PF65 21.50				

KM# 226 20 CROWNS
31.17 g., 0.999 Silver 1.0011 oz. ASW, 38.9 mm. **Ruler:** Elizabeth II **Subject:** 40th Anniversary of Accession **Obv:** National arms **Rev:** Crowned bust facing **Edge:** Reeded

Date	Mintage	VF20	XF40	MS60	MS63	MS65
ND(1992)	—	PF63 25.00	PF65 30.00			
1993	—	PF63 25.00	PF65 30.00			

KM# 227.1 20 CROWNS
31.17 g., 0.999 Silver 1.0011 oz. ASW, 38.9 mm. **Ruler:** Elizabeth II **Subject:** 40th Anniversary of the Accession **Obv:** Crowned head right with wavy truncation **Rev:** Head of H.M. King George VI facing **Edge:** Reeded

Date	Mintage	VF20	XF40	MS60	MS63	MS65
ND(1992)	—	PF65 25.00				

KM# 228.1 20 CROWNS
31.17 g., 0.999 Silver 1.0011 oz. ASW, 38.9 mm. **Ruler:** Elizabeth II **Subject:** 40th Anniversary of the Accession **Obv:** Crowned head right with wavy truncation **Rev:** Windsor castle **Edge:** Reeded

Date	Mintage	VF20	XF40	MS60	MS63	MS65
ND(1992)	—	PF65 30.00				

KM# 229.1 20 CROWNS
31.17 g., 0.999 Silver 1.0011 oz. ASW, 38.9 mm. **Ruler:** Elizabeth II **Subject:** 40th Anniversary of the Accession **Obv:** Crowned head right with wavy truncation **Rev:** Conjoined busts of the Queen and Prince Philip facing **Edge:** Reeded

Date	Mintage	VF20	XF40	MS60	MS63	MS65
ND(1992)	—	PF65 25.00				

KM# 229.2 20 CROWNS
31.17 g., 0.999 Silver 1.0011 oz. ASW, 38.9 mm. **Ruler:** Elizabeth II **Subject:** 40th Anniversary of the Accession **Obv:** Crowned head right with smooth truncation **Rev:** Conjoined busts of the Queen and Prince Philip facing **Edge:** Reeded

Date	Mintage	VF20	XF40	MS60	MS63	MS65
ND(1992)	—	PF65 25.00				

KM# 95 20 CROWNS
31.10 g., 0.999 Silver 0.9989 oz. ASW **Ruler:** Elizabeth II **Subject:** World Cup '94 **Obv:** Crowned bust right **Rev:** Bust of Jules Rimet right and trophy

Date	Mintage	VF20	XF40	MS60	MS63	MS65
ND-1993	Est. 10000	PF65 34.00				

KM# 96 20 CROWNS
31.10 g., 0.999 Silver 0.9989 oz. ASW **Ruler:** Elizabeth II **Subject:** World Cup '94 - Uruguay Winners **Obv:** Crowned head right **Rev:** Two players

Date	Mintage	VF20	XF40	MS60	MS63	MS65
ND-1993	Est. 10000	PF65 34.00				

KM# 97 20 CROWNS
31.10 g., 0.999 Silver 0.9989 oz. ASW **Ruler:** Elizabeth II **Subject:** World Cup '94 - Italy Winners **Obv:** Crowned head right **Rev:** Dino Zoff

Date	Mintage	VF20	XF40	MS60	MS63	MS65
ND-1993	Est. 10000	PF65 34.00				

KM# 98 20 CROWNS
31.10 g., 0.999 Silver 0.9989 oz. ASW **Ruler:** Elizabeth II **Subject:** World Cup '94 - West German Winners **Obv:** Crowned head right **Rev:** Franz Breckenbauer

Date	Mintage	VF20	XF40	MS60	MS63	MS65
ND-1993	Est. 10000	PF65 34.00				

KM# 99 20 CROWNS
31.10 g., 0.999 Silver 0.9989 oz. ASW **Ruler:** Elizabeth II **Subject:** World Cup '94 - Brazil Winners **Obv:** Crowned head right **Rev:** Pelé

Date	Mintage	VF20	XF40	MS60	MS63	MS65
ND-1993	Est. 10000	PF65 34.00				

KM# 100 20 CROWNS
31.10 g., 0.999 Silver 0.9989 oz. ASW **Ruler:** Elizabeth II **Subject:** World Cup '94 - England Winners **Obv:** Crowned head right **Rev:** Bobby Moore

Date	Mintage	VF20	XF40	MS60	MS63	MS65
ND-1993	Est. 10000	PF65 34.00				

KM# 101 20 CROWNS
31.10 g., 0.999 Silver 0.9989 oz. ASW **Ruler:** Elizabeth II **Subject:** World Cup '94 - Argentina Winners **Obv:** Crowned head right **Rev:** Mario Kempes

Date	Mintage	VF20	XF40	MS60	MS63	MS65
ND-1993	Est. 10000	PF65 27.00				

KM# 102 20 CROWNS
31.10 g., 0.999 Silver 0.9989 oz. ASW **Ruler:** Elizabeth II **Subject:** World Cup '94 - USA Host **Obv:** Crowned head right **Rev:** Trophy and flag

Date	Mintage	VF20	XF40	MS60	MS63	MS65
ND-1993	Est. 10000	PF65 27.00				

KM# 109 20 CROWNS
31.10 g., 0.999 Silver 0.9989 oz. ASW **Ruler:** Elizabeth II **Subject:** 40th Anniversary of Coronation **Obv:** Crowned head right **Rev:** Westminster Abbey

Date	Mintage	VF20	XF40	MS60	MS63	MS65
ND-1993	Est. 10000	PF65 27.00				

KM# 110.1 20 CROWNS
31.10 g., 0.999 Silver 0.9989 oz. ASW **Ruler:** Elizabeth II **Subject:** 40th Anniversary of Coronation **Obv:** Crowned head right with wavy truncation **Rev:** Crown jewels

Date	Mintage	VF20	XF40	MS60	MS63	MS65
ND-1993	Est. 10000	PF65 27.00				

KM# 110.2 20 CROWNS
31.17 g., 0.999 Silver 1.0011 oz. ASW, 38.9 mm. **Ruler:** Elizabeth II **Subject:** 40th Anniversary of Coronation **Obv:** Crowned head right with smooth truncation **Rev:** Crown jewels **Edge:** Reeded

Date	Mintage	VF20	XF40	MS60	MS63	MS65
1993	—	PF65 27.00				

KM# 111.1 20 CROWNS
31.10 g., 0.999 Silver 0.9989 oz. ASW **Ruler:** Elizabeth II **Subject:** 40th Anniversary of Coronation **Obv:** Crowned head right with wavy truncation **Rev:** Queen, clergy and maids of honor

Date	Mintage	VF20	XF40	MS60	MS63	MS65
ND-1993	Est. 10000	PF65 27.00				

KM# 111.2 20 CROWNS
31.17 g., 0.999 Silver 1.0011 oz. ASW, 38.9 mm. **Ruler:** Elizabeth II **Subject:** 40th Anniversary of Coronation **Obv:** Crowned head right with smooth truncation **Rev:** Queen, clergy and maids of honor **Edge:** Reeded

Date	Mintage	VF20	XF40	MS60	MS63	MS65
1993	—	PF65 27.00				

KM# 112.1 20 CROWNS
31.10 g., 0.999 Silver 0.9989 oz. ASW **Ruler:** Elizabeth II **Subject:** 40th Anniversary of Coronation **Obv:** Crowned head right with wavy truncation **Rev:** Consort's homage

Date	Mintage	VF20	XF40	MS60	MS63	MS65
ND-1993	Est. 10000	PF65 27.00				

KM# 112.2 20 CROWNS
31.17 g., 0.999 Silver 1.0011 oz. ASW, 38.9 mm. **Ruler:** Elizabeth II **Subject:** Coronation Anniversary **Obv:** Crowned head right with smooth truncation **Rev:** Consort's homage **Edge:** Reeded

Date	Mintage	VF20	XF40	MS60	MS63	MS65
1993	—	PF65 27.00				

KM# 113.1 20 CROWNS
31.10 g., 0.999 Silver 0.9989 oz. ASW **Ruler:** Elizabeth II **Subject:** 40th Anniversary of Coronation **Obv:** Crowned head right with wavy truncation **Rev:** Enthroned Queen seated left facing

Date	Mintage	VF20	XF40	MS60	MS63	MS65
ND-1993	Est. 10000	PF65 27.00				

KM# 113.2 20 CROWNS
31.17 g., 0.999 Silver 1.0011 oz. ASW, 38.9 mm. **Ruler:** Elizabeth II **Subject:** Coronation Anniversary **Obv:** Crowned head right with smooth truncation **Rev:** Enthroned Queen seated left facing **Edge:** Reeded

Date	Mintage	VF20	XF40	MS60	MS63	MS65
1993	—	PF65 27.00				

KM# 114.1 20 CROWNS
31.10 g., 0.999 Silver 0.9989 oz. ASW **Ruler:** Elizabeth II **Subject:** 40th Anniversary of Coronation **Obv:** Crowned head right with wavy truncation **Rev:** Queen in coach

Date	Mintage	VF20	XF40	MS60	MS63	MS65
ND-1993	Est. 10000	PF65 27.00				

KM# 114.2 20 CROWNS
31.17 g., 0.999 Silver 1.0011 oz. ASW, 38.9 mm. **Ruler:** Elizabeth II **Subject:** Coronation Anniversary **Obv:** Crowned head right with smooth truncation **Rev:** Queen in coach **Edge:** Reeded

Date	Mintage	VF20	XF40	MS60	MS63	MS65
1993	—	PF65 27.00				

KM# 141 20 CROWNS
31.10 g., 0.999 Silver 0.9989 oz. ASW **Ruler:** Elizabeth II **Series:** 1994 Olympics **Obv:** Crowned head right **Rev:** Bobsled and team within circle

Date	Mintage	VF20	XF40	MS60	MS63	MS65
1993	—	PF65 30.00				

KM# 142 20 CROWNS
31.10 g., 0.999 Silver 0.9989 oz. ASW **Ruler:** Elizabeth II **Subject:** 25th Anniversary - Apollo 11 Moon Landing **Obv:** Crowned head right **Rev:** Astronaut descending ladder on moon

Date	Mintage	VF20	XF40	MS60	MS63	MS65
1993	—	PF65 30.00				

KM# 183 20 CROWNS
28.04 g., 0.925 Silver 0.8339 oz. ASW **Ruler:** Elizabeth II **Series:** Apollo II **Obv:** Crowned head right **Rev:** Rocket launch scene **Note:** Similar to 5 Crowns, KM#177.

Date	Mintage	VF20	XF40	MS60	MS63	MS65
1993	—	PF65 30.00				

KM# 184 20 CROWNS
28.04 g., 0.925 Silver 0.8339 oz. ASW **Ruler:** Elizabeth II **Series:** Apollo II **Obv:** Crowned head right **Rev:** Lunar landing scene

Date	Mintage	VF20	XF40	MS60	MS63	MS65
1993	—	PF65 22.00				
1994 Mule?	—	—	—	—	—	—

Note: Re-engraved number 4 in date

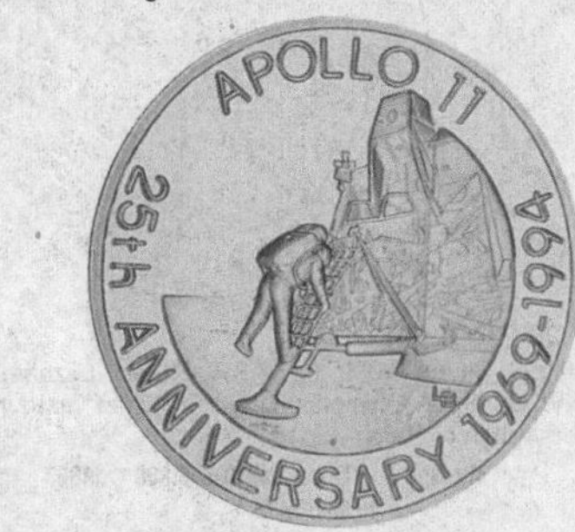

KM# 185 20 CROWNS
28.04 g., 0.925 Silver 0.8339 oz. ASW **Ruler:** Elizabeth II **Series:** Apollo II - Leaving Lunar Landing Module **Obv:** Crowned head right **Rev:** Astronaut descending ladder

Date	Mintage	VF20	XF40	MS60	MS63	MS65
1993	—	PF65 30.00				

KM# 186 20 CROWNS
28.04 g., 0.925 Silver 0.8339 oz. ASW **Ruler:** Elizabeth II **Series:** Apollo II **Obv:** Crowned head right **Rev:** Astronauts planting flag on moon

Date	Mintage	VF20	XF40	MS60	MS63	MS65
1993	—	PF65 30.00				

KM# 187 20 CROWNS
28.04 g., 0.925 Silver 0.8339 oz. ASW, 38.9 mm. **Ruler:** Elizabeth II **Series:** Apollo 11 **Obv:** Crowned head right **Rev:** Astronaut walking on the moon **Edge:** Reeded

Date	Mintage	VF20	XF40	MS60	MS63	MS65
1993	—	PF65 22.00				

KM# 227.2 20 CROWNS
31.17 g., 0.999 Silver 1.0011 oz. ASW, 38.9 mm. **Ruler:** Elizabeth II **Subject:** 40th Anniversary of the Accession **Obv:** Crowned head right with smooth truncation **Rev:** Head of H.M. King George VI facing **Edge:** Reeded

Date	Mintage	VF20	XF40	MS60	MS63	MS65
1993	—	PF65 35.00				

KM# 228.2 20 CROWNS
31.17 g., 0.999 Silver 1.0011 oz. ASW, 38.9 mm. **Ruler:** Elizabeth II **Subject:** 40th Anniversary of the Accession **Obv:** Crowned head right with smooth truncation **Rev:** Windsor Castle **Edge:** Reeded

Date	Mintage	VF20	XF40	MS60	MS63	MS65
1993	—	PF65 30.00				

KM# 239 20 CROWNS
28.04 g., 0.925 Silver 0.8339 oz. ASW **Ruler:** Elizabeth II **Series:** Lillehamer Winter Olympics **Obv:** Crowned head right **Rev:** Olympic skier

Date	Mintage	VF20	XF40	MS60	MS63	MS65
1993	—	PF65 22.00				

KM# 250 20 CROWNS
31.10 g., 0.999 Silver 0.9989 oz. ASW, 39 mm. **Ruler:** Elizabeth II **Subject:** Portrait of Luigi Badia with date

Date	Mintage	VF20	XF40	MS60	MS63	MS65
1993	Est. 10000	PF65 75.00				

KM# 251 20 CROWNS
31.10 g., 0.925 Silver 0.9249 oz. ASW, 39 mm. **Ruler:** Elizabeth II **Subject:** Portrait of Luigi Badia with date

Date	Mintage	VF20	XF40	MS60	MS63	MS65
1993	Est. 10000	PF65 75.00				

KM# 252 20 CROWNS
31.10 g., 0.925 Silver 0.9249 oz. ASW, 39 mm. **Ruler:** Elizabeth II **Subject:** Portrait of Luigi Badia with date

Date	Mintage	VF20	XF40	MS60	MS63	MS65
1993	Est. 10000	PF65 75.00				

KM# 253 20 CROWNS
Silver **Ruler:** Elizabeth II **Subject:** 25 Year Anniversary of the Apollo 11 Moon Landing **Rev:** Craft landing in the ocean

Date	Mintage	VF20	XF40	MS60	MS63	MS65
1993	—	PF65 45.00				

KM# 208 20 CROWNS
21.13 g., 0.999 Silver 0.6787 oz. ASW **Ruler:** Elizabeth II **Series:** XVII Winter Olympics **Obv:** Crowned head right **Rev:** Figure skater within circle **Note:** Reportedly a mule or pattern.

Date	Mintage	VF20	XF40	MS60	MS63	MS65
1994	—	PF63 110	PF65 125			

KM# 218 20 CROWNS
31.16 g., 0.999 Silver 1.0008 oz. ASW, 39 mm. **Ruler:** Elizabeth II **Series:** 50th Anniversary D-Day **Subject:** General Omar Bradley **Obv:** Crowned head right **Rev:** Helmeted bust 1/4 right **Edge:** Reeded

Date	Mintage	VF20	XF40	MS60	MS63	MS65
1994	—	PF65 27.50				

KM# 219 20 CROWNS
31.16 g., 0.999 Silver 1.0008 oz. ASW, 39 mm. **Ruler:** Elizabeth II **Series:** 50th Anniversary D-Day **Subject:** General Montgomery **Obv:** Crowned head right **Rev:** Uniformed bust left **Edge:** Reeded **Note:** Obverse date in error.

Date	Mintage	VF20	XF40	MS60	MS63	MS65
1994	—	PF65 27.50				

Note: The 4 in the date often looks like a 1

KM# 220 20 CROWNS
31.16 g., 0.999 Silver 1.0008 oz. ASW, 39 mm. **Ruler:** Elizabeth II **Series:** 50th Anniversary D-Day **Subject:** Normandy Landing **Obv:** Crowned head right **Rev:** Sir Bertram Ramsay left **Edge:** Reeded

Date	Mintage	VF20	XF40	MS60	MS63	MS65
1994	—	PF65 27.50				

KM# 221 20 CROWNS
31.16 g., 0.999 Silver 1.0008 oz. ASW, 39 mm. **Ruler:** Elizabeth II **Series:** 50th Anniversary D-Day **Subject:** Normandy Landing **Obv:** Crowned head right **Rev:** General Dwight Eisenhower right **Edge:** Reeded

Date	Mintage	VF20	XF40	MS60	MS63	MS65
1994	—	PF65 27.50				

KM# 137 20 CROWNS
31.10 g., 0.999 Silver 0.999 oz. ASW **Ruler:** Elizabeth II **Subject:** 50th Anniversary - VE Day **Obv:** Arms with supporters **Rev:** Heads of Churchill, Roosevelt and Stalin facing

Date	Mintage	VF20	XF40	MS60	MS63	MS65
1995	15,000	PF65 25.00				

KM# 138 20 CROWNS
31.10 g., 0.999 Silver 0.999 oz. ASW **Ruler:** Elizabeth II **Subject:** 50th Anniversary - VE Day **Obv:** Arms with supporters **Rev:** Three fighter planes

Date	Mintage	VF20	XF40	MS60	MS63	MS65
1995	15,000	PF65 25.00				

KM# 139 20 CROWNS
31.10 g., 0.999 Silver 0.999 oz. ASW **Ruler:** Elizabeth II **Subject:** 50th Anniversary - VE Day **Obv:** Arms with supporters **Rev:** U.S. and Soviet troops meet

Date	Mintage	VF20	XF40	MS60	MS63	MS65
1995	15,000	PF65 25.00				

KM# 140 20 CROWNS
31.10 g., 0.999 Silver 0.999 oz. ASW **Ruler:** Elizabeth II **Subject:** 50th Anniversary - VE Day **Obv:** Arms with supporters **Rev:** London, Washington, Moscow and Paris

Date	Mintage	VF20	XF40	MS60	MS63	MS65
1995	15,000	PF65 25.00				

KM# 189 20 CROWNS
31.10 g., 0.999 Silver 0.999 oz. ASW **Ruler:** Elizabeth II **Series:** XXVI Summer Olympics **Obv:** Crowned head right **Rev:** Hurdlers within circle

Date	Mintage	VF20	XF40	MS60	MS63	MS65
1995	—	PF65 30.00				

KM# 191 20 CROWNS
31.10 g., 0.999 Silver 0.999 oz. ASW **Ruler:** Elizabeth II **Series:** XXVI Summer Olympics **Obv:** Crowned head right **Rev:** Cyclist within circle

Date	Mintage	VF20	XF40	MS60	MS63	MS65
1995	—	PF65 30.00				

KM# 193 20 CROWNS
31.10 g., 0.999 Silver 0.999 oz. ASW **Ruler:** Elizabeth II **Series:** XXVI Summer Olympics **Obv:** Crowned head right **Rev:** Fencers within circle

Date	Mintage	VF20	XF40	MS60	MS63	MS65
1995	—	PF65 30.00				

KM# 195 20 CROWNS
31.10 g., 0.999 Silver 0.999 oz. ASW **Ruler:** Elizabeth II **Series:** XXVI Summer Olympics **Obv:** Crowned head right **Rev:** Equestrian

Date	Mintage	VF20	XF40	MS60	MS63	MS65
1995	—	PF65 30.00				

KM# 197 20 CROWNS
31.10 g., 0.999 Silver 0.999 oz. ASW **Ruler:** Elizabeth II **Series:** XXVI Summer Olympics **Obv:** Crowned head right **Rev:** Pole vaulter

Date	Mintage	VF20	XF40	MS60	MS63	MS65
1995	—	PF65 30.00				

KM# 199 20 CROWNS
31.10 g., 0.999 Silver 0.999 oz. ASW **Ruler:** Elizabeth II **Series:** XXVI Summer Olympics **Obv:** Crowned head right **Rev:** Runners within circle

Date	Mintage	VF20	XF40	MS60	MS63	MS65
1995	—	PF65 30.00				

KM# 201 20 CROWNS
31.10 g., 0.999 Silver 0.999 oz. ASW **Ruler:** Elizabeth II **Series:** XXVI Summer Olympics **Obv:** Crowned head right **Rev:** Gymnast

Date	Mintage	VF20	XF40	MS60	MS63	MS65
1995	—	PF65 30.00				

KM# 203 20 CROWNS
31.10 g., 0.999 Silver 0.999 oz. ASW **Ruler:** Elizabeth II **Series:** XXVI Summer Olympics **Obv:** Crowned head right **Rev:** Swimmer within circle

Date	Mintage	VF20	XF40	MS60	MS63	MS65
1995	—	PF65 30.00				

KM# 205 20 CROWNS
31.10 g., 0.999 Silver 0.999 oz. ASW **Ruler:** Elizabeth II **Series:** XXVI Summer Olympics **Obv:** Crowned head right **Rev:** Diver

Date	Mintage	VF20	XF40	MS60	MS63	MS65
1995	—	PF65 30.00				

KM# 207 20 CROWNS
31.10 g., 0.999 Silver 0.999 oz. ASW **Ruler:** Elizabeth II **Series:** XXVI Summer Olympics **Obv:** Crowned head right **Rev:** Sprinter within circle

Date	Mintage	VF20	XF40	MS60	MS63	MS65
1995	—	PF65 30.00				

KM# 230 20 CROWNS
31.17 g., 0.999 Silver 1.0011 oz. ASW, 38.9 mm. **Ruler:** Elizabeth II **Subject:** The Lady of the Century - The Queen Mother **Obv:** Crowned head right with smooth truncation **Rev:** Bust 1/4 right **Edge:** Reeded

Date	Mintage	VF20	XF40	MS60	MS63	MS65
1995	—	PF65 30.00				

KM# 231 20 CROWNS
31.11 g., 0.999 Silver 0.9992 oz. ASW, 38.9 mm. **Ruler:** Elizabeth II **Subject:** The 70th Birthday of H. M. Queen Elizabeth II **Obv:** National arms **Rev:** Seated Queen with her pet Corgi's on either side **Edge:** Reeded

Date	Mintage	VF20	XF40	MS60	MS63	MS65
1996	—	PF65 30.00				

KM# 222 20 CROWNS
31.10 g., 0.999 Silver 0.999 oz. ASW, 38.9 mm. **Ruler:** Elizabeth II **Subject:** Hong Kong's Return to China **Obv:** Crowned head right **Rev:** City view below flower design **Edge:** Reeded

Date	Mintage	VF20	XF40	MS60	MS63	MS65
1997	—	PF65 30.00				

KM# 243 20 CROWNS
31.16 g., 0.999 Silver 1.0008 oz. ASW, 39 mm. **Ruler:** Elizabeth II **Subject:** Return of Hong Kong **Obv:** Crowned head right **Rev:** Sailing junk in harbor **Edge:** Reeded

Date	Mintage	VF20	XF40	MS60	MS63	MS65
1997	—	PF65 35.00				

KM# 260 20 CROWNS
31.10 g., 0.999 Silver 0.9989 oz. ASW, 39 mm. **Ruler:** Elizabeth II **Subject:** Birthday of Queen Elizabeth II

Date	Mintage	VF20	XF40	MS60	MS63	MS65
1997	—	PF65 42.00				

KM# 263 20 CROWNS
31.10 g., 0.999 Silver 0.9989 oz. ASW, 39 mm. **Ruler:** Elizabeth II **Subject:** 50th Wedding Anniversary of Queen Elizabeth II and Prince Philip

Date	Mintage	VF20	XF40	MS60	MS63	MS65
1997	Est. 30000	PF65 42.00				

KM# 264 20 CROWNS
Gold Plated Silver **Ruler:** Elizabeth II **Subject:** 50th Wedding Anniversary of Queen Elizabeth II and Prince Philip

Date	Mintage	VF20	XF40	MS60	MS63	MS65
1997	—	PF65 42.00				

KM# 217 20 CROWNS
31.24 g., 0.999 Silver 1.0034 oz. ASW, 39 mm. **Ruler:** Elizabeth II **Obv:** Crowned head right **Rev:** Dolphins **Edge:** Reeded

Date	Mintage	VF20	XF40	MS60	MS63	MS65
1998	—	PF63 30.00	PF65 35.00			

KM# 240 20 CROWNS
31.23 g., 0.999 Silver 1.0031 oz. ASW, 38.9 mm. **Ruler:** Elizabeth II **Obv:** Crowned head right **Rev:** Ship - R.M.S. Titanic **Edge:** Reeded

Date	Mintage	VF20	XF40	MS60	MS63	MS65
1998	—	PF65 30.00				

KM# 241 20 CROWNS
31.23 g., 0.999 Silver 1.0031 oz. ASW **Ruler:** Elizabeth II **Subject:** 80th Anniversary of the British Royal Air Force **Obv:** Crowned head right **Rev:** Spitfire in flight **Edge:** Reeded

Date	Mintage	VF20	XF40	MS60	MS63	MS65
1998	—	PF65 30.00				

KM# 265 20 CROWNS
31.10 g., 0.999 Silver 0.9989 oz. ASW, 39 mm. **Ruler:** Elizabeth II **Subject:** Chinese Lunar Year of the Tiger

Date	Mintage	VF20	XF40	MS60	MS63	MS65
1998	—	PF65 40.00				

KM# 266 20 CROWNS
31.10 g., 0.999 Silver 0.9989 oz. ASW, 39 mm. **Ruler:** Elizabeth II **Subject:** 80 Years of the Royal Air Force

Date	Mintage	VF20	XF40	MS60	MS63	MS65
1998	—	PF65 45.00				

KM# 267 20 CROWNS
31.10 g., 0.999 Silver 0.9989 oz. ASW, 39 mm. **Ruler:** Elizabeth II **Subject:** Death of Lady Diana Princess of Wales

Date	Mintage	VF20	XF40	MS60	MS63	MS65
1998	—	PF65 45.00				

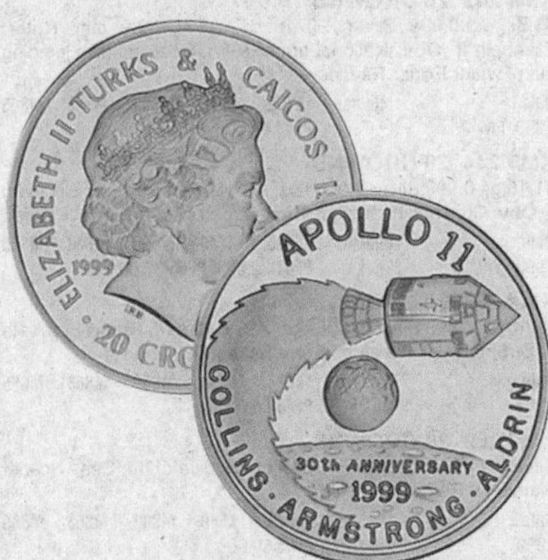

KM# 223 20 CROWNS
31.10 g., 0.999 Silver 0.999 oz. ASW, 39.02 mm. **Ruler:** Elizabeth II **Subject:** Apollo 11 **Obv:** Head with tiara right **Rev:** Spacecraft in flight above world globe **Edge:** Reeded

Date	Mintage	VF20	XF40	MS60	MS63	MS65
1999	—	PF63 25.00	PF65 30.00			

KM# 224 20 CROWNS

31.10 g., 0.999 Silver 0.999 oz. ASW, 39.02 mm. **Ruler:** Elizabeth II **Subject:** Apollo 11 **Obv:** Head with tiara right **Rev:** Heads of Collins, Armstrong and Aldrin left **Edge:** Reeded

Date	Mintage	VF20	XF40	MS60	MS63	MS65
1999	—	PF63 25.00	PF65 30.00			

KM# 235 20 CROWNS

31.20 g., 0.999 Silver 1.0021 oz. ASW, 38.9 mm. **Ruler:** Elizabeth II **Subject:** Prince Edward's Wedding **Obv:** Head with tiara right **Rev:** Conjoined busts of Edward and Sophie facing **Edge:** Reeded

Date	Mintage	VF20	XF40	MS60	MS63	MS65
1999	—	PF63 30.00	PF65 35.00			

KM# 242 20 CROWNS

33.37 g., 0.999 Silver 1.0718 oz. ASW, 39.9 mm. **Ruler:** Elizabeth II **Obv:** National arms **Rev:** Three marlins jumping out of water **Edge:** Reeded

Date	Mintage	VF20	XF40	MS60	MS63	MS65
1999 FM	—	PF63 40.00	PF65 45.00			

KM# 244 20 CROWNS

31.16 g., 0.999 Silver 1.0008 oz. ASW, 39 mm. **Ruler:** Elizabeth II **Obv:** Crowned head right **Rev:** Queen Mother **Edge:** Reeded

Date	Mintage	VF20	XF40	MS60	MS63	MS65
1999	—	PF63 32.00	PF65 37.00			

KM# 268 20 CROWNS

31.10 g., 0.999 Silver 0.9989 oz. ASW, 40 mm. **Ruler:** Elizabeth II **Subject:** Wildlife of the Sea - Scarlet Flamingo

Date	Mintage	VF20	XF40	MS60	MS63	MS65
1999	—	PF65 60.00				

KM# 269 20 CROWNS

Silver **Ruler:** Elizabeth II **Subject:** Wildlife of the Sea - Scarlet Flamingo **Rev:** Angler King

Date	Mintage	VF20	XF40	MS60	MS63	MS65
1999	—	PF65 60.00				

KM# 270 20 CROWNS

31.10 g., 0.999 Silver 0.9989 oz. ASW, 40 mm. **Ruler:** Elizabeth II **Subject:** Caribbean Flowers - Passion Flower

Date	Mintage	VF20	XF40	MS60	MS63	MS65
1999	—	PF65 60.00				

KM# 271 20 CROWNS

31.10 g., 0.999 Silver 0.9989 oz. ASW, 40 mm. **Ruler:** Elizabeth II **Subject:** Caribbean Flowers - Daffodils

Date	Mintage	VF20	XF40	MS60	MS63	MS65
1999	—	PF65 60.00				

KM# 273 20 CROWNS

31.10 g., 0.999 Silver 0.9989 oz. ASW, 39 mm. **Ruler:** Elizabeth II **Subject:** 2000 Summer Olympics in Sydney

Date	Mintage	VF20	XF40	MS60	MS63	MS65
2000	—	PF65 40.00				

KM# 145 20 DOLLARS

31.10 g., 0.999 Silver 0.999 oz. ASW **Ruler:** Elizabeth II **Subject:** Steam Locomotive **Obv:** Crowned head right **Rev:** City of Truro

Date	Mintage	VF20	XF40	MS60	MS63	MS65
1996	Est. 20000	PF65 25.00				

KM# 148 20 DOLLARS

31.10 g., 0.999 Silver 0.999 oz. ASW, 38.97 mm. **Ruler:** Elizabeth II **Subject:** Steam Locomotive **Obv:** Crowned head right **Rev:** Flying Scotsman **Edge:** Reeded

Date	Mintage	VF20	XF40	MS60	MS63	MS65
1996	Est. 20000	PF65 25.00				

KM# 151 20 DOLLARS

31.10 g., 0.999 Silver 0.999 oz. ASW, 38.97 mm. **Ruler:** Elizabeth II **Subject:** Steam Locomotive **Obv:** Crowned head right **Rev:** Rocket **Edge:** Reeded

Date	Mintage	VF20	XF40	MS60	MS63	MS65
1996	Est. 20000	PF65 27.50				

KM# 154 20 DOLLARS

31.10 g., 0.999 Silver 0.999 oz. ASW, 38.97 mm. **Ruler:** Elizabeth II **Subject:** Steam Locomotive **Obv:** Crowned head right **Rev:** Evening Star **Edge:** Reeded

Date	Mintage	VF20	XF40	MS60	MS63	MS65
1996	Est. 20000	PF65 27.50				

KM# 157 20 DOLLARS

31.10 g., 0.999 Silver 0.999 oz. ASW, 38.97 mm. **Ruler:** Elizabeth II **Subject:** Steam Locomotive **Obv:** Crowned head right **Rev:** Mallard **Edge:** Reeded

Date	Mintage	VF20	XF40	MS60	MS63	MS65
1996	—	PF65 27.50				

KM# 160 20 DOLLARS

31.10 g., 0.999 Silver 0.999 oz. ASW, 38.97 mm. **Ruler:** Elizabeth II **Subject:** Steam Locomotive **Obv:** Crowned head right **Rev:** Princess Elizabeth **Edge:** Reeded

Date	Mintage	VF20	XF40	MS60	MS63	MS65
1996	Est. 20000	PF65 25.00				

KM# 163 20 DOLLARS

31.10 g., 0.999 Silver 0.999 oz. ASW, 38.97 mm. **Ruler:** Elizabeth II **Subject:** Steam Locomotive **Obv:** Crowned head right **Rev:** Southern Pacific Lines - Class GS4 **Edge:** Reeded

Date	Mintage	VF20	XF40	MS60	MS63	MS65
1996	Est. 20000	PF65 27.50				

KM# 166 20 DOLLARS

31.10 g., 0.999 Silver 0.999 oz. ASW, 38.97 mm. **Ruler:** Elizabeth II **Subject:** Steam Locomotive **Obv:** Crowned head right **Rev:** German State railway - Class 05 **Edge:** Reeded

Date	Mintage	VF20	XF40	MS60	MS63	MS65
1996	Est. 20000	PF65 25.00				

KM# 169 20 DOLLARS
31.10 g., 0.999 Silver 0.999 oz. ASW, 38.97 mm. **Ruler:** Elizabeth II **Subject:** Steam Locomotive **Obv:** Crowned head right **Rev:** Japanese Railway - Class 62 **Edge:** Reeded

Date	Mintage	VF20	XF40	MS60	MS63	MS65
1996	Est. 20000	PF65 27.50				

KM# 172 20 DOLLARS
31.10 g., 0.999 Silver 0.999 oz. ASW, 38.97 mm. **Ruler:** Elizabeth II **Subject:** Steam Locomotive **Obv:** Crowned head right **Rev:** Chinese State Railways Class RM **Edge:** Reeded

Date	Mintage	VF20	XF40	MS60	MS63	MS65
1996	—	PF65 27.50				

KM# 9.1 25 CROWNS
3.11 g., 0.500 Gold 0.050 oz. AGW **Ruler:** Elizabeth II **Obv:** Young bust right **Rev:** National arms

Date	Mintage	XF40	MS60	MS63	MS65	MS66
1975	1,272	—	—	80.00	90.00	110
1975	2,096	PF65 100	PF67 120			

KM# 9.2 25 CROWNS
4.50 g., 0.500 Gold 0.0723 oz. AGW, 19 mm. **Ruler:** Elizabeth II **Obv:** Young bust right **Rev:** National arms

Date	Mintage	XF40	MS60	MS63	MS65	MS66
1976	—	—	—	115	125	145
1976	2,185	PF65 135	PF67 150			
1977	2,125	PF65 135	PF67 150			

KM# 19 25 CROWNS
43.75 g., 0.925 Silver 1.3011 oz. ASW **Ruler:** Elizabeth II **Subject:** Queen's Silver Jubilee **Obv:** Young bust right **Rev:** Crown and date within sprigs above banner

Date	Mintage	VF20	XF40	MS60	MS63	MS65
1977 Matte	—	—	—	—	33.00	37.50
1977	13,000	PF63 37.50	PF65 39.50			

KM# 24 25 CROWNS
43.75 g., 0.925 Silver 1.3011 oz. ASW **Ruler:** Elizabeth II **Subject:** 25th Anniversary of Coronation **Obv:** Young bust right **Rev:** Lion of England

Date	Mintage	VF20	XF40	MS60	MS63	MS65
1978	—	PF63 45.00	PF65 50.00			

KM# 25 25 CROWNS
43.75 g., 0.925 Silver 1.3011 oz. ASW **Ruler:** Elizabeth II **Obv:** Young bust right **Rev:** Griffin of Edward III left

Date	Mintage	VF20	XF40	MS60	MS63	MS65
1978	—	PF63 45.00	PF65 50.00			

KM# 26 25 CROWNS
43.75 g., 0.925 Silver 1.3011 oz. ASW **Ruler:** Elizabeth II **Obv:** Young bust right **Rev:** Red Dragon of Wales left

Date	Mintage	VF20	XF40	MS60	MS63	MS65
1978	—	PF63 45.00	PF65 50.00			

KM# 27 25 CROWNS
43.75 g., 0.925 Silver 1.3011 oz. ASW **Ruler:** Elizabeth II **Obv:** Young bust right **Rev:** White Greyhound of Richmond left

Date	Mintage	VF20	XF40	MS60	MS63	MS65
1978	—	PF63 45.00	PF65 50.00			

KM# 28 25 CROWNS
43.75 g., 0.925 Silver 1.3011 oz. ASW **Ruler:** Elizabeth II **Obv:** Young bust right **Rev:** Unicorn of Scotland right

Date	Mintage	VF20	XF40	MS60	MS63	MS65
1978	—	PF63 45.00	PF65 50.00			

KM# 29 25 CROWNS
43.75 g., 0.925 Silver 1.3011 oz. ASW **Ruler:** Elizabeth II **Obv:** Young bust right **Rev:** The White Horse of Hannover

Date	Mintage	VF20	XF40	MS60	MS63	MS65
1978	—	PF63 45.00	PF65 50.00			

KM# 30 25 CROWNS
43.75 g., 0.925 Silver 1.3011 oz. ASW **Ruler:** Elizabeth II **Obv:** Young bust right **Rev:** Black Bull of Clarence left

Date	Mintage	VF20	XF40	MS60	MS63	MS65
1978	—	PF63 45.00	PF65 50.00			

KM# 31 25 CROWNS
43.75 g., 0.925 Silver 1.3011 oz. ASW **Ruler:** Elizabeth II **Obv:** Young bust right **Rev:** Yale of Beaufort left

Date	Mintage	VF20	XF40	MS60	MS63	MS65
1978	—	PF63 45.00	PF65 50.00			

KM# 32 25 CROWNS
43.75 g., 0.925 Silver 1.3011 oz. ASW **Ruler:** Elizabeth II **Obv:** Young bust right **Rev:** Falcon of the Plantagenets right

Date	Mintage	VF20	XF40	MS60	MS63	MS65
1978	—	PF63 45.00	PF65 50.00			

KM# 33 25 CROWNS
43.75 g., 0.925 Silver 1.3011 oz. ASW **Ruler:** Elizabeth II **Obv:** Young bust right **Rev:** White Lion of Mortimer left

Date	Mintage	VF20	XF40	MS60	MS63	MS65
1978	—	PF63 45.00	PF65 50.00			

KM# 209 25 CROWNS
155.44 g., 0.999 Silver 4.9925 oz. ASW, 63 mm. **Ruler:** Elizabeth II **Obv:** Crowned bust right **Rev:** Multicolor purple-throated Carib bird within flowers **Note:** Illustration reduced.

Date	Mintage	VF20	XF40	MS60	MS63	MS65
1995 Matte	—	—	—	—	180	—
1995	—	PF63 150	PF65 175			

KM# 210 25 CROWNS
155.44 g., 0.999 Silver 4.9925 oz. ASW, 63 mm. **Ruler:** Elizabeth II **Obv:** Crowned bust right **Rev:** Multicolor Streamertail bird **Edge:** Reeded **Note:** Illustration reduced.

Date	Mintage	VF20	XF40	MS60	MS63	MS65
1995 Matte	—	—	—	—	180	—
1995	—	PF63 150	PF65 175			

KM# 211 25 CROWNS
155.44 g., 0.999 Silver 4.9925 oz. ASW, 63 mm. **Ruler:** Elizabeth II **Obv:** Crowned bust right **Rev:** Multicolor Woodstar bird **Edge:** Reeded **Note:** Illustration reduced.

Date	Mintage	VF20	XF40	MS60	MS63	MS65
1995 Matte	—	—	—	—	180	—
1995	—	PF63 150	PF65 175			

KM# 257 25 CROWNS
7.78 g., 0.9999 Gold 0.2501 oz. AGW, 25.5 mm. **Ruler:** Elizabeth II **Subject:** 50 Years of the Sieges of the Allied Forces in Europe

Date	Mintage	VF20	XF40	MS60	MS63	MS65
1995	Est. 1500	PF65 525				

KM# 272 25 CROWNS
Gold Plated Silver **Ruler:** Elizabeth II **Subject:** Christian Millenium Year 2000

Date	Mintage	VF20	XF40	MS60	MS63	MS65
2000	—	PF65 35.00				

KM# 3 50 CROWNS
9.00 g., 0.500 Gold 0.1447 oz. AGW **Ruler:** Elizabeth II **Subject:** Centenary - Birth of Churchill **Obv:** National arms **Rev:** Bust 1/4 left **Edge Lettering:** REDEEMABLE AT TURKS AND CAICOS FOR U.S. CURRENCY

Date	Mintage	XF40	MS60	MS63	MS65	MS66
1974 Matte	30,000	—	—	—	230	245
1974	4,000	PF65 265	PF67 285			

KM# 10 50 CROWNS
6.22 g., 0.500 Gold 0.100 oz. AGW **Ruler:** Elizabeth II **Subject:** Age of Exploration **Obv:** Young bust right **Rev:** Head of Christopher Columbus right and 3 ships

Date	Mintage	XF40	MS60	MS63	MS65	MS66
1975	2,863	—	—	—	160	190
1975	1,577	PF65 165	PF67 200			

KM# 15 50 CROWNS
6.22 g., 0.500 Gold 0.100 oz. AGW **Ruler:** Elizabeth II **Subject:** U.S. Bicentennial **Obv:** Young bust right **Rev:** Cameos facing each other below flags and crossed scepter and sword

Date	Mintage	XF40	MS60	MS63	MS65	MS66
1976	905	—	—	—	175	200
1976	2,421	PF65 180	PF67 200			

KM# 16 50 CROWNS
55.18 g., 0.925 Silver 1.641 oz. ASW **Ruler:** Elizabeth II **Obv:** Young bust right **Rev:** 4 Victoria cameos left

Date	Mintage	VF20	XF40	MS60	MS63	MS65
1976 Matte	3,500	—	—	—	60.00	65.00
1976	2,908	PF63 65.00	PF65 75.00			
1977	940	PF63 70.00	PF65 80.00			

KM# 20 50 CROWNS
9.00 g., 0.500 Gold 0.1447 oz. AGW **Ruler:** Elizabeth II **Subject:** Queen's Silver Jubilee **Obv:** Young bust right **Rev:** Crown and date within sprigs above banner

Date	Mintage	XF40	MS60	MS63	MS65	MS66
1977	—	—	—	—	250	270
1977	2,903	PF65 260	PF67 280			

KM# 21 50 CROWNS

55.18 g., 0.925 Silver 1.641 oz. ASW **Ruler:** Elizabeth II **Obv:** Young bust right **Rev:** 4 George III cameos right

Date	Mintage	VF20	XF40	MS60	MS63	MS65
1977	—	—	—	—	60.00	70.00
1977	958	PF63 70.00	PF65 80.00			

KM# 34 50 CROWNS

9.00 g., 0.500 Gold 0.1447 oz. AGW **Ruler:** Elizabeth II **Subject:** 25th Anniversary of Coronation **Obv:** Young bust right **Rev:** Lion of England right

Date	Mintage	VF20	XF40	MS60	MS63	MS65
1978	261	PF65 275	PF67 295			

KM# 35 50 CROWNS

9.00 g., 0.500 Gold 0.1447 oz. AGW **Ruler:** Elizabeth II **Obv:** Young bust right **Rev:** Griffin of Edward III left

Date	Mintage	VF20	XF40	MS60	MS63	MS65
1978	266	PF65 275	PF67 295			

KM# 36 50 CROWNS

9.00 g., 0.500 Gold 0.1447 oz. AGW **Ruler:** Elizabeth II **Obv:** Young bust right **Rev:** Red Dragon of Wales left

Date	Mintage	VF20	XF40	MS60	MS63	MS65
1978	266	PF65 275	PF67 295			

KM# 37 50 CROWNS

9.00 g., 0.500 Gold 0.1447 oz. AGW **Ruler:** Elizabeth II **Obv:** Young bust right **Rev:** White Greyhound of Richmond

Date	Mintage	VF20	XF40	MS60	MS63	MS65
1978	270	PF65 275	PF67 295			

KM# 38 50 CROWNS

9.00 g., 0.500 Gold 0.1447 oz. AGW **Ruler:** Elizabeth II **Obv:** Young bust right **Rev:** The Unicorn of Scotland right

Date	Mintage	VF20	XF40	MS60	MS63	MS65
1978	268	PF65 275	PF67 295			

KM# 39 50 CROWNS

9.00 g., 0.500 Gold 0.1447 oz. AGW **Ruler:** Elizabeth II **Obv:** Young bust right **Rev:** White Horse of Hannover left

Date	Mintage	VF20	XF40	MS60	MS63	MS65
1978	266	PF65 275	PF67 295			

KM# 40 50 CROWNS

9.00 g., 0.500 Gold 0.1447 oz. AGW **Ruler:** Elizabeth II **Obv:** Young bust right **Rev:** Black Bull of Clarence Left

Date	Mintage	VF20	XF40	MS60	MS63	MS65
1978	269	PF65 275	PF67 295			

KM# 41 50 CROWNS

9.00 g., 0.500 Gold 0.1447 oz. AGW **Ruler:** Elizabeth II **Obv:** Young bust right **Rev:** Yale of Beaufort left

Date	Mintage	VF20	XF40	MS60	MS63	MS65
1978	254	PF65 275	PF67 295			

KM# 42 50 CROWNS

9.00 g., 0.500 Gold 0.1447 oz. AGW **Ruler:** Elizabeth II **Obv:** Young bust right **Rev:** Falcon of the Plantagenets right

Date	Mintage	VF20	XF40	MS60	MS63	MS65
1978	265	PF65 275	PF67 295			

KM# 43 50 CROWNS

9.00 g., 0.500 Gold 0.1447 oz. AGW **Ruler:** Elizabeth II **Obv:** Young bust right **Rev:** White Lion of Mortimer left

Date	Mintage	VF20	XF40	MS60	MS63	MS65
1978	265	PF65 275	PF67 295			

KM# 61 50 CROWNS

136.08 g., 0.925 Silver 4.0469 oz. ASW, 63 mm. **Ruler:** Elizabeth II **Subject:** Columbus proposes Atlantic voyage to Ferdinand and Isabella **Obv:** Young bust right **Rev:** 3 Wreathed cameos and ship **Note:** Illustration reduced.

Date	Mintage	VF20	XF40	MS60	MS63	MS65
1986	20,000	PF63 125	PF65 150			

KM# 4 100 CROWNS

18.02 g., 0.500 Gold 0.2896 oz. AGW **Ruler:** Elizabeth II **Subject:** Birth of Churchill Centenary **Obv:** National arms **Rev:** Bust 1/4 left

Date	Mintage	XF40	MS60	MS63	MS65	MS66
1974	4,500	—	—	—	500	525
1974	5,100	PF65 525	PF67 550			

KM# 11 100 CROWNS

12.44 g., 0.500 Gold 0.200 oz. AGW **Ruler:** Elizabeth II **Subject:** Age of Exploration **Obv:** Young bust right **Rev:** Spacecraft flying around globe

Date	Mintage	XF40	MS60	MS63	MS65	MS66
1975	756	—	—	—	350	375
1975	1,508	PF65 360	PF67 385			

KM# 17 100 CROWNS

18.02 g., 0.500 Gold 0.2896 oz. AGW **Ruler:** Elizabeth II **Obv:** Young bust right **Rev:** 4 Victoria coin obverses

Date	Mintage	XF40	MS60	MS63	MS65	MS66
1976	250	—	—	—	525	550
1976	350	PF65 550	PF67 575			
1977	1,655	—	—	—	500	525
1977	2,648	PF65 525	PF67 550			

KM# 22 100 CROWNS

18.02 g., 0.500 Gold 0.2896 oz. AGW **Ruler:** Elizabeth II **Obv:** Young bust right **Rev:** 4 George III coin obverses

Date	Mintage	XF40	MS60	MS63	MS65	MS66
1977	—	—	—	—	500	525
1977	844	PF65 525	PF67 550			

KM# 44 100 CROWNS

18.02 g., 0.500 Gold 0.2896 oz. AGW **Ruler:** Elizabeth II **Subject:** XI Commonwealth Games

Date	Mintage	XF40	MS60	MS63	MS65	MS66
1978	540	PF65 550	PF67 575			

KM# 46 100 CROWNS

18.02 g., 0.500 Gold 0.2896 oz. AGW **Ruler:** Elizabeth II **Subject:** 10th Anniversary - Prince Charles' Investiture **Obv:** Young bust right **Rev:** Head of Prince Charles facing left at right with crown, crossed sword and sceptre at left

Date	Mintage	XF40	MS60	MS63	MS65	MS66
1979	10,000	—	—	—	500	525
1979	—	PF65 525	PF67 550			

KM# 50 100 CROWNS

12.96 g., 0.500 Gold 0.2083 oz. AGW **Ruler:** Elizabeth II **Subject:** Lord Mountbatten **Obv:** Crowned bust right **Rev:** Bust 1/4 right flanked by dates

Date	Mintage	XF40	MS60	MS63	MS65	MS66
1980	—	PF67 335	PF69 385			

KM# 54 100 CROWNS

6.48 g., 0.900 Gold 0.1875 oz. AGW **Ruler:** Elizabeth II **Subject:** Wedding of Princes Charles and Lady Diana **Rev:** Conjoined busts left

Date	Mintage	XF40	MS60	MS63	MS65	MS66
1981	1,205	PF67 285	PF69 335			

KM# 59 100 CROWNS

6.48 g., 0.900 Gold 0.1875 oz. AGW **Ruler:** Elizabeth II **Subject:** World Football Championship **Obv:** Young bust right **Rev:** Football players

Date	Mintage	XF40	MS60	MS63	MS65	MS66
1982	565	PF67 300	PF69 350			

KM# 62 100 CROWNS

7.13 g., 0.900 Gold 0.2063 oz. AGW **Ruler:** Elizabeth II **Series:** Decade for Women **Rev:** Half-length figure right

Date	Mintage	XF40	MS60	MS63	MS65	MS66
1985	313	PF67 325	PF69 375			

KM# 65 100 CROWNS

10.00 g., 0.917 Gold 0.2948 oz. AGW **Ruler:** Elizabeth II **Series:** World Wildlife Fund **Obv:** Crowned bust right **Rev:** Spiny lobster

Date	Mintage	VF20	XF40	MS60	MS63	MS65
1988	Est. 5000	PF65 500	PF67 525			

KM# 248 100 CROWNS

Silver **Ruler:** Elizabeth II **Subject:** 50th Anniversary Normandy Landings **Obv:** Crowned bust right **Obv. Legend:** ELIZABETH II - TURKS AND CAICOS ISLANDS **Rev:** Field Marshall Montgomery with planes and paratroopers in background **Rev. Legend:** D-DAY 6 JUNE '44 **Edge:** Reeded

Date	Mintage	VF20	XF40	MS60	MS63	MS65
1994	—	PF63 150	PF65 175			

KM# 237 100 CROWNS

155.52 g., 0.999 Silver Gilt 4.995 oz., 63.7 mm. **Ruler:** Elizabeth II **Subject:** Queen's Golden Wedding Anniversary **Obv:** National arms **Rev:** Wedding portrait of Queen and Prince Philip **Edge:** Reeded and numbered **Note:** Illustration reduced.

Date	Mintage	VF20	XF40	MS60	MS63	MS65
1997	—	PF63 160	PF65 195			

PATTERNS

Standard metals unless noted otherwise

KM#	Date	Mintage	Identification	Mkt Val
Pn1	ND-1993	50	20 Crowns. Silver. Bobsledders.	125
Pn2	ND-1993	50	20 Crowns. Silver. Skier.	125
Pn3	ND-1993	50	20 Crowns. Silver. Ski jumper.	125
Pn4	ND-1993	50	20 Crowns. Silver. Figure skater.	125
Pn5	ND-1993	50	20 Crowns. Silver. Hockey player.	125
Pn6	ND-1993	50	20 Crowns. Silver. Speed skater.	125

PIEDFORT

KM#	Date	Mintage	Identification	Mkt Val
P1	1980	500	5 Crowns. Silver. KM47.	42.00
P2	1980	400	10 Crowns. Silver. KM48.	48.00
P3	1980	300	20 Crowns. Silver. KM49.	50.00
P4	1980	250	100 Crowns. Gold. KM50.	600
P5	1982	80	10 Crowns. Silver. KM55.	325
P6	1991	—	Crown. Silver. 61.93 g, KM76.	50.00
P7	1991	400	Crown. Silver. 62.08 g, KM121.	40.00

MINT SETS

KM#	Date	Mintage	Identification	Issue Price	Mkt Val
MS1	1975 (7)	440	KM5-11	214	775
MS2	ND(1993) (8)	—	KM87-94	67.20	60.00
MS3	ND(1993) (6)	—	KM103-108	49.95	52.50
MS4	1995 (4)	—	KM133-136	33.50	37.50
MS5	1996 (10)	—	KM143, 146, 149, 152, 155, 158, 161, 164, 167, 170	33.50	65.00

PROOF SETS

KM#	Date	Mintage	Identification	Issue Price	Mkt Val
PS1	1974 (2)	1,600	KM2, 4	—	625
PS2	1975 (7)	1,270	KM5-8, 9.1, 10-11	313	820
PS3	1976 (4)	2,185	KM5, 6, 9.2, 12	78.00	210
PS4	1976 (3)	—	KM14, 16, 17	280	720
PS5	1976 (2)	1,951	KM13, 15	108	245
PS6	1977 (4)	1,370	KM5, 6, 9.2, 12	87.50	220
PS7	1977 (3)	—	KM18, 21, 22	280	710
PS8	1977 (2)	—	KM14, 18	62.00	115
PS9	1978 (10)	—	KM24-33	560	500
PS10	1978 (10)	—	KM34-43	1,120	2,800
PS11	1979 (2)	—	KM45, 46	227	610
PS12	1980 (4)	—	KM47-50	457	455
PS13	1980 (3)	—	KM47-49	107	55.00
PS15	ND(1993) (8)	—	KM95-102	319	325
PS17	ND(1993) (6)	—	KM109-114	234	240
PS18	1995 (4)	15,000	KM137-140	160	155
PS19	1996 (10)	20,000	KM144, 147, 150, 153, 156, 159, 162, 165, 168, 171	220	220
PS20	1996 (10)	20,000	KM145, 148, 151, 154, 157, 160, 163, 166, 169, 172	350	400

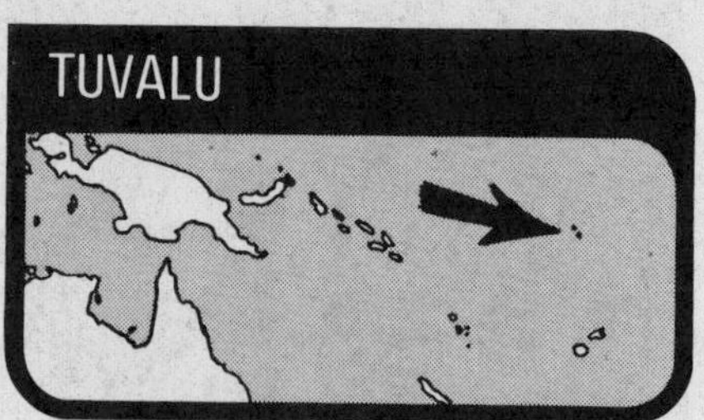

Tuvalu (formerly the Ellice or Lagoon Islands of the Gilbert and Ellice Islands), located in the South Pacific north of the Fiji Islands, has an area of 10 sq. mi. (26 sq.km.) and a population of *9,000. Capital: Funafuti. The independent state includes the islands of Nanumanga, Nanumea, Nui, Niutao, Viatupa, Funafuti, Nukufetau, Nukulailai and Nurakita. The latter four islands were claimed by the United States until relinquished by the Feb. 7, 1979, Treaty of Friendship signed by the United States and Tuvalu. The principal industries are copra production and phosphate mining.

The islands were discovered in 1764 by John Byron, a British navigator, and annexed by Britain in 1892. In 1915 they became part of the crown colony of the Gilbert and Ellice Islands. In 1974 the islanders voted to separate from the Gilberts, becoming on Jan. 1, 1976, the separate constitutional dependency of Tuvalu. Full independence was attained on Oct. 1, 1978. Tuvalu is a member of the Commonwealth of Nations. Elizabeth II is Head of State as Queen of Tuvalu.

RULER

British, until 1978

MONETARY SYSTEM

100 Cents = 1 Dollar

CONSTITUTIONAL MONARCHY WITHIN THE COMMONWEALTH

STANDARD COINAGE

KM# 1 CENT

2.60 g., Bronze, 17.5 mm. **Ruler:** Elizabeth II **Obv:** Young bust right **Rev:** Lambis shell and value

Date	Mintage	VF20	XF40	MS60	MS63	MS65
1976	93,000	—	0.10	0.25	0.50	1.00
1976	20,000	PF65 1.00				
1981	—	—	0.10	0.25	0.50	1.00
1981	—	PF65 1.00				
1985	—	—	0.25	0.50	1.00	1.50

KM# 26 CENT

2.60 g., Bronze, 17.5 mm. **Ruler:** Elizabeth II **Obv:** Crowned head right **Rev:** Sea shell and value

Date	Mintage	VF20	XF40	MS60	MS63	MS65
1994	—	—	—	0.25	0.50	1.00

KM# 2 2 CENTS

5.20 g., Bronze, 21.6 mm. **Ruler:** Elizabeth II **Obv:** Young bust right **Rev:** Stingray and value

Date	Mintage	VF20	XF40	MS60	MS63	MS65
1976	51,000	0.10	0.15	0.50	1.00	2.50
1976	—	PF65 2.00				
1981	—	0.10	0.15	0.50	1.00	2.50
1981	—	PF65 2.00				
1985	—	0.10	0.15	0.50	1.00	2.50

KM# 30 2 CENTS

5.20 g., Bronze, 21.6 mm. **Ruler:** Elizabeth II **Obv:** Crowned head right

Date	Mintage	VF20	XF40	MS60	MS63	MS65
1994	—	—	—	0.50	1.00	2.00

KM# 3 5 CENTS

2.80 g., Copper-Nickel, 19.4 mm. **Ruler:** Elizabeth II **Obv:** Young bust right **Rev:** Tiger shark and value

Date	Mintage	VF20	XF40	MS60	MS63	MS65
1976	26,000	0.10	0.25	0.75	1.50	3.50
1976	—	PF65 4.00				
1981	—	0.10	0.25	0.75	1.50	3.50
1981	—	PF65 4.00				
1985	—	0.10	0.25	0.75	1.50	3.50

KM# 31 5 CENTS

2.80 g., Copper-Nickel, 19.4 mm. **Ruler:** Elizabeth II **Obv:** Crowned head right

Date	Mintage	VF20	XF40	MS60	MS63	MS65
1994	—	—	—	0.75	1.50	3.00

KM# 4 10 CENTS

5.60 g., Copper-Nickel, 23.5 mm. **Ruler:** Elizabeth II **Obv:** Young bust right **Rev:** Crab and value

Date	Mintage	VF20	XF40	MS60	MS63	MS65
1976	26,000	0.20	0.35	0.75	1.50	3.00
1976	20,000	PF65 4.00				
1981	—	0.20	0.35	0.75	1.50	3.00
1981	—	PF65 4.00				
1985	—	0.20	0.35	0.75	1.50	3.00

KM# 32 10 CENTS

5.60 g., Copper-Nickel, 23.5 mm. **Ruler:** Elizabeth II **Obv:** Crowned head right

Date	Mintage	VF20	XF40	MS60	MS63	MS65
1994	—	—	—	0.75	1.50	3.00

KM# 5 20 CENTS

11.25 g., Copper-Nickel, 28.45 mm. **Ruler:** Elizabeth II **Obv:** Young bust right **Rev:** Flying fish and value

Date	Mintage	VF20	XF40	MS60	MS63	MS65
1976	36,000	0.40	0.60	1.25	2.50	4.00
1976	20,000	PF65 7.00				
1981	—	0.40	0.60	1.25	2.50	4.00
1981	—	PF65 7.00				
1985	—	0.40	0.60	1.25	2.50	4.00

KM# 33 20 CENTS

11.25 g., Copper-Nickel, 28.45 mm. **Ruler:** Elizabeth II **Obv:** Crowned head right

Date	Mintage	VF20	XF40	MS60	MS63	MS65
1994	—	—	—	1.00	2.00	3.50

KM# 6 50 CENTS

15.50 g., Copper-Nickel, 31.65 mm. **Ruler:** Elizabeth II **Obv:** Young bust right **Rev:** Octopus and value

Date	Mintage	VF20	XF40	MS60	MS63	MS65
1976	19,000	0.75	1.50	2.50	4.00	7.00
1976	20,000	PF65 9.00				
1981	—	0.75	1.50	2.50	4.00	7.00
1981	—	PF65 9.00				
1985	—	0.75	1.50	2.50	4.00	7.00

KM# 34 50 CENTS

15.50 g., Copper-Nickel, 31.65 mm. **Ruler:** Elizabeth II **Obv:** Crowned head right

Date	Mintage	VF20	XF40	MS60	MS63	MS65
1994	—	—	—	2.00	3.50	6.50

KM# 7 DOLLAR

16.00 g., Copper-Nickel, 33 mm. **Ruler:** Elizabeth II **Obv:** Young bust right **Rev:** Sea turtle and value **Shape:** 9-sided

Date	Mintage	VF20	XF40	MS60	MS63	MS65
1976	21,000	1.50	2.00	3.00	5.00	8.00
1976	20,000	PF65 12.50				
1981	—	1.50	2.00	3.00	5.00	8.00
1981	—	PF65 12.50				
1985	—	1.50	2.00	3.00	5.00	8.00

KM# 35 DOLLAR

16.00 g., Copper-Nickel, 33 mm. **Ruler:** Elizabeth II **Obv:** Crowned head right

Date	Mintage	VF20	XF40	MS60	MS63	MS65
1994	—	—	—	2.50	4.50	7.50

KM# 37 2 DOLLARS

10.00 g., 0.500 Silver 0.1608 oz. ASW, 30 mm. **Ruler:** Elizabeth II **Series:** Olympics **Obv:** Crowned head right **Rev:** Swimmer **Edge:** Reeded

Date	Mintage	VF20	XF40	MS60	MS63	MS65
1996	—	PF63 7.00	PF65 9.00			

KM# 48 2 DOLLARS

15.85 g., 0.925 Silver 0.4714 oz. ASW, 28.3 mm. **Ruler:** Elizabeth II **Obv:** Crowned head right **Rev:** Queen Mother receiving honorary Doctor of Music degree **Edge:** Reeded

Date	Mintage	VF20	XF40	MS60	MS63	MS65
1997	—	PF63 16.00	PF65 18.00			

KM# 216 3 DOLLARS

1.24 g., 0.9999 Gold 0.0399 oz. AGW, 13.92 mm. **Ruler:** Elizabeth II **Rev:** Horse galloping left

Date	Mintage	VF20	XF40	MS60	MS63	MS65
1996	Est. 60000	PF65 75.00				

KM# 8 5 DOLLARS

28.28 g., 0.925 Silver 0.841 oz. ASW **Ruler:** Elizabeth II **Obv:** Young bust right **Rev:** Outrigger canoe

Date	Mintage	VF20	XF40	MS60	MS63	MS65
1976	20,000	PF63 25.00	PF65 30.00			

KM# 12 5 DOLLARS

Copper-Nickel **Ruler:** Elizabeth II **Subject:** Wedding of Prince Charles and Lady Diana **Obv:** Young bust right **Rev:** Three plumes within crown, value at right

Date	Mintage	VF20	XF40	MS60	MS63	MS65
1981	—	—	—	—	3.50	5.50

KM# 12a 5 DOLLARS

28.28 g., 0.925 Silver 0.841 oz. ASW **Ruler:** Elizabeth II **Subject:** Wedding of Prince Charles and Lady Diana **Obv:** Young bust right **Rev:** Three plumes within crown, value at right

Date	Mintage	VF20	XF40	MS60	MS63	MS65
1981	35,000	PF63 22.00	PF65 25.00			

KM# 38 5 DOLLARS

31.64 g., 0.925 Silver 0.941 oz. ASW, 38.6 mm. **Ruler:** Elizabeth II **Subject:** Victorian Age **Obv:** Crowned head right **Rev:** 3/4 Standing figure at left, SS Great Britain in back at right **Edge:** Reeded

Date	Mintage	VF20	XF40	MS60	MS63	MS65
1997	—	PF65 27.00	PF67 32.00			

KM# 45 5 DOLLARS

31.55 g., 0.925 Silver 0.9383 oz. ASW, 38.6 mm. **Ruler:** Elizabeth II **Subject:** Queen Mother - Opening of the Federal Parliament at Canberra **Obv:** Crowned head right **Rev:** Cameo of the Queen Mother and King George VI above the Australian Parliament building **Edge:** Reeded

Date	Mintage	VF20	XF40	MS60	MS63	MS65
1997	—	PF65 27.00	PF67 32.00			

KM# 46 5 DOLLARS
31.55 g., 0.925 Silver 0.9383 oz. ASW, 38.6 mm. **Ruler:** Elizabeth II **Subject:** Queen Mother **Obv:** Crowned head right **Rev:** Queen Mother being granted an Honorary Doctor of Music degree **Edge:** Reeded

Date	Mintage	VF20	XF40	MS60	MS63	MS65
1997	—	PF65 27.00	PF67 32.00			

KM# 36 5 DOLLARS
31.22 g., 0.925 Silver 0.9285 oz. ASW, 30.2 mm. **Ruler:** Elizabeth II **Subject:** Millennium 2000 **Obv:** Crowned head right **Rev:** Seashell, stars and stylized waves above value **Edge:** Reeded, square

Date	Mintage	VF20	XF40	MS60	MS63	MS65
1998	—	PF65 32.00	PF67 37.00			

KM# 47 5 DOLLARS
31.52 g., 0.925 Silver 0.9374 oz. ASW, 38.7 mm. **Ruler:** Elizabeth II **Subject:** Princess Diana **Obv:** Crowned head right **Rev:** Diana **Edge:** Reeded

Date	Mintage	VF20	XF40	MS60	MS63	MS65
1998	—	PF65 27.00	PF67 32.00			

KM# 56 5 DOLLARS
31.06 g., Silver, 38.74 mm. **Ruler:** Elizabeth II **Obv:** Bust right **Obv. Legend:** • QUEEN ELIZABETH II • TUVALU • **Rev:** Early Spanish sailing ship - La Princesa **Rev. Legend:** * NANUMAGA - ISLA DEL COCAL * FRANCISCO MOURELLE * PRINCESA * **Edge:** Reeded

Date	Mintage	VF20	XF40	MS60	MS63	MS65
1999	—	PF63 35.00	PF65 40.00			

KM# 44 5 DOLLARS
31.20 g., 0.925 Silver 0.9279 oz. ASW, 30.2 mm. **Ruler:** Elizabeth II **Subject:** Millennium **Obv:** Crowned head right **Rev:** Seashell and value **Edge:** Reeded

Date	Mintage	VF20	XF40	MS60	MS63	MS65
2000	—	PF65 27.00	PF67 32.00			

KM# 10 10 DOLLARS
35.00 g., 0.500 Silver 0.5626 oz. ASW **Ruler:** Elizabeth II **Subject:** 1st Anniversary of Independence **Obv:** Young bust right **Rev:** Brigantine "Rebecca"

Date	Mintage	VF20	XF40	MS60	MS63	MS65
1979	5,000	—	—	—	15.00	20.00

KM# 10a 10 DOLLARS
35.00 g., 0.925 Silver 1.0409 oz. ASW **Ruler:** Elizabeth II **Obv:** Young bust right **Rev:** Brigantine "Rebecca"

Date	Mintage	VF20	XF40	MS60	MS63	MS65
1979	2,500	PF63 25.00	PF65 30.00			

KM# 11 10 DOLLARS
35.00 g., 0.500 Silver 0.5626 oz. ASW **Ruler:** Elizabeth II **Subject:** 80th Birthday of Queen Mother **Obv:** Young bust right **Rev:** Crowned bust of the Queen Mother left

Date	Mintage	VF20	XF40	MS60	MS63	MS65
1980	—	—	—	—	15.00	20.00

KM# 11a 10 DOLLARS
35.00 g., 0.925 Silver 1.0409 oz. ASW **Ruler:** Elizabeth II **Obv:** Young bust right **Rev:** Crowned bust of the Queen Mother left

Date	Mintage	VF20	XF40	MS60	MS63	MS65
1980	—	PF63 25.00	PF65 30.00			

KM# 13 10 DOLLARS
35.00 g., 0.500 Silver 0.5626 oz. ASW **Ruler:** Elizabeth II **Subject:** Duke of Edinburgh Award **Obv:** Young bust right **Rev:** Head left

Date	Mintage	VF20	XF40	MS60	MS63	MS65
1981	5,000	—	—	—	15.00	20.00

KM# 13a 10 DOLLARS
35.00 g., 0.925 Silver 1.0409 oz. ASW **Ruler:** Elizabeth II **Subject:** Duke of Edinburgh Award **Obv:** Young bust right **Rev:** Head left

Date	Mintage	VF20	XF40	MS60	MS63	MS65
1981	3,000	PF63 25.00	PF65 30.00			

KM# 15 10 DOLLARS
35.00 g., 0.500 Silver 0.5626 oz. ASW **Ruler:** Elizabeth II **Subject:** Royal Visit **Obv:** Young bust right **Rev:** Conjoined busts of the Queen and Prince Philip right within circle

Date	Mintage	VF20	XF40	MS60	MS63	MS65
1982	2,500	—	—	—	15.00	20.00

KM# 15a 10 DOLLARS
35.00 g., 0.925 Silver 1.0409 oz. ASW **Ruler:** Elizabeth II **Subject:** Royal Visit **Obv:** Young bust right **Rev:** Conjoined busts of the Queen and Prince Philip right within circle

Date	Mintage	VF20	XF40	MS60	MS63	MS65
1982	2,500	PF63 27.00	PF65 32.00			

KM# 16 20 DOLLARS
31.47 g., 0.925 Silver 0.9359 oz. ASW **Ruler:** Elizabeth II **Subject:** 40th Anniversary of Coronation **Obv:** Crowned head right **Rev:** Coronation scene

Date	Mintage	VF20	XF40	MS60	MS63	MS65
1993	10,000	PF63 22.00	PF65 28.00	PF67 35.00		

KM# 17 20 DOLLARS
31.47 g., 0.925 Silver 0.9359 oz. ASW **Ruler:** Elizabeth II **Subject:** Sir Isaac Newton **Obv:** Crowned head right

Date	Mintage	VF20	XF40	MS60	MS63	MS65
1993	10,000	PF63 22.00	PF65 28.00	PF67 35.00		

KM# 18 20 DOLLARS
31.47 g., 0.925 Silver 0.9359 oz. ASW **Ruler:** Elizabeth II **Obv:** Crowned head right **Rev:** HMS Royalist

Date	Mintage	VF20	XF40	MS60	MS63	MS65
1993	15,000	PF63 22.00	PF65 28.00	PF67 35.00		

KM# 19 20 DOLLARS
31.47 g., 0.925 Silver 0.9359 oz. ASW **Ruler:** Elizabeth II **Obv:** Crowned head right **Rev:** Leatherback Turtle

Date	Mintage	VF20	XF40	MS60	MS63	MS65
1993	Est. 10000	PF63 28.00	PF65 32.00	PF67 38.00		

KM# 20 20 DOLLARS
31.47 g., 0.925 Silver 0.9359 oz. ASW **Ruler:** Elizabeth II **Obv:** Crowned head right **Rev:** Dugong - Manatee-like animal

Date	Mintage	VF20	XF40	MS60	MS63	MS65
1994	Est. 10000	**PF63** 28.00	**PF65** 32.00	**PF67** 38.00		

KM# 22 20 DOLLARS
31.47 g., 0.925 Silver 0.9359 oz. ASW **Ruler:** Elizabeth II **Subject:** 1994 World Cup Soccer **Obv:** Crowned head right **Rev:** Soccer ball within circles of world flags

Date	Mintage	VF20	XF40	MS60	MS63	MS65
1994	Est. 30000	**PF63** 22.00	**PF65** 25.00	**PF67** 30.00		

KM# 24 20 DOLLARS
31.47 g., 0.925 Silver 0.9359 oz. ASW **Ruler:** Elizabeth II **Series:** Olympics **Obv:** Crowned head right **Rev:** Swimming event

Date	Mintage	VF20	XF40	MS60	MS63	MS65
1994	Est. 50000	**PF63** 22.00	**PF65** 25.00	**PF67** 30.00		

KM# 25 20 DOLLARS
31.47 g., 0.925 Silver 0.9359 oz. ASW **Ruler:** Elizabeth II **Series:** Olympics **Obv:** Crowned head right **Rev:** Javelin thrower

Date	Mintage	VF20	XF40	MS60	MS63	MS65
1994	Est. 50000	**PF63** 22.00	**PF65** 25.00	**PF67** 30.00		

KM# 27 20 DOLLARS
31.70 g., 0.925 Silver 0.9427 oz. ASW **Ruler:** Elizabeth II **Series:** Protect Our World **Obv:** Crowned head right **Rev:** Blue Coral seascape

Date	Mintage	VF20	XF40	MS60	MS63	MS65
1994	—	**PF63** 22.00	**PF65** 25.00	**PF67** 30.00		

KM# 39 20 DOLLARS
155.50 g., 0.999 Silver 4.9944 oz. ASW, 65 mm. **Ruler:** Elizabeth II **Subject:** Birthday of Queen Elizabeth - The Queen Mother **Obv:** Crowned head right **Rev:** Queen Mother and grandchildren **Edge:** Reeded **Note:** Illustration reduced.

Date	Mintage	VF20	XF40	MS60	MS63	MS65
1996	3,000	**PF65** 125	**PF67** 145			

KM# 70 20 DOLLARS
1.24 g., 0.999 Gold 0.0398 oz. AGW, 13.80 mm. **Ruler:** Elizabeth II **Subject:** Death of Princess Diana **Obv:** Crowned head right **Rev:** 1/2 length figure of Diana slightly right **Edge:** Reeded

Date	Mintage	VF20	XF40	MS60	MS63	MS65
1997	—	**PF63** 65.00	**PF65** 70.00			

KM# 9 50 DOLLARS
15.98 g., 0.917 Gold 0.4711 oz. AGW **Ruler:** Elizabeth II **Obv:** Young bust right **Rev:** Native meeting hut

Date	Mintage	XF40	MS60	MS63	MS65	MS66
1976	2,074	**PF67** 700	**PF69** 750			

KM# 14 50 DOLLARS
15.98 g., 0.917 Gold 0.4711 oz. AGW **Ruler:** Elizabeth II **Subject:** Wedding of Prince Charles and Lady Diana **Obv:** Young bust right **Rev:** Three plumes within crown, value at right

Date	Mintage	VF20	XF40	MS60	MS63	MS65
1981	5,000	**PF67** 675				

KM# 29 100 DOLLARS
7.78 g., 0.5833 Gold 0.1458 oz. AGW **Ruler:** Elizabeth II **Subject:** 40th Anniversary of Coronation **Obv:** Crowned head right **Rev:** Coronation scene

Date	Mintage	VF20	XF40	MS60	MS63	MS65
1993	—	**PF65** 350	**PF67** 500			

KM# 21 100 DOLLARS
7.78 g., 0.5833 Gold 0.1458 oz. AGW **Ruler:** Elizabeth II **Subject:** Todos Los Santos

Date	Mintage	VF20	XF40	MS60	MS63	MS65
1994	3,000	**PF67** 215				

KM# 23 100 DOLLARS
7.78 g., 0.5833 Gold 0.1458 oz. AGW **Ruler:** Elizabeth II **Subject:** 1994 World Cup Soccer **Obv:** Crowned head right **Rev:** Soccer ball to upper left of eagle head and wing

Date	Mintage	VF20	XF40	MS60	MS63	MS65
1994	3,000	**PF67** 215				

MINT SETS

KM#	Date	Mintage	Identification	Issue Price	Mkt Val
MS1	1985 (7)	—	KM#1-7	10.00	15.00

PROOF SETS

KM#	Date	Mintage	Identification	Issue Price	Mkt Val
PS1	1976 (7)	20,000	KM#1-7	13.00	20.00
PS2	1981 (7)	—	KM#1-7	—	20.00

UGANDA

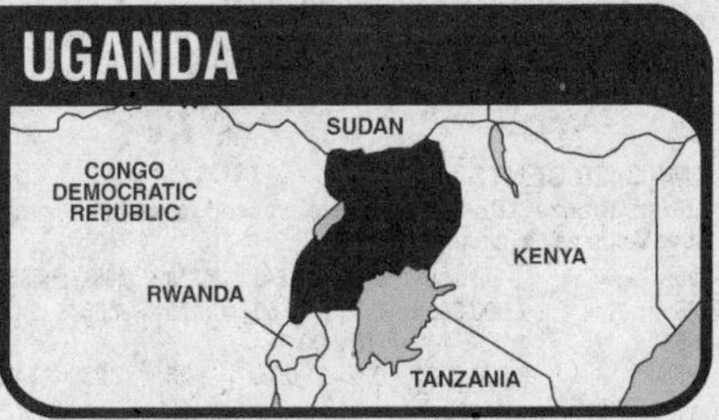

The Republic of Uganda, a former British protectorate located astride the equator in east-central Africa, has an area of 91,134 sq. mi. (236,040 sq. km.) and a population of *17 million. Capital: Kampala. Agriculture, including livestock, is the basis of the economy; there is some mining of copper, tin, gold and lead. Coffee, cotton, copper and tea are exported.

Uganda was first visited by Arab slavers in the 1830s. They were followed in the 1860s by British explorers searching for the headwaters of the Nile. The explorers, and the missionaries who followed them into the Lake Victoria region of south central Africa in 1877-79, found well-developed African kingdoms dating back several centuries. In 1894 the local native Kingdom of Buganda was established as a British protectorate that was extended in 1896 to encompass an area substantially the same as the present Republic of Uganda. The protectorate was given a ministerial form of government in 1955, full internal self-government on March 1, 1962, and complete independence on Oct. 9, 1962. Uganda is a member of the Commonwealth of Nations. The president is Chief of State and Head of Government.

For earlier coinage refer to East Africa.

RULER
British, until 1962

MONETARY SYSTEM
100 Cents = 1 Shilling

REPUBLIC

STANDARD COINAGE

KM# 1 5 CENTS

3.21 g., Bronze, 20 mm. **Obv:** Value above crossed tusks within circle **Rev:** Value within circular sprig **Edge:** Plain

Date	Mintage	VF20	XF40	MS60	MS63	MS65
1966	41,000,000	0.10	0.15	0.30	0.50	1.00
1966	—	PF65 1.00				
1974	8,624,000	0.20	0.30	0.45	0.75	1.00
1975	14,784,000	0.20	0.30	0.45	0.75	1.00

KM# 1a 5 CENTS

Copper Plated Steel **Obv:** Value above crossed tusks within circle **Rev:** Value within circular sprig

Date	Mintage	VF20	XF40	MS60	MS63	MS65
1976	10,000,000	0.20	0.30	0.45	0.75	1.00

KM# 2 10 CENTS

5.00 g., Bronze, 24.5 mm. **Obv:** Value above crossed tusks within circle **Rev:** Value within circular sprig

Date	Mintage	VF20	XF40	MS60	MS63	MS65
1966	19,100,000	0.10	0.15	0.30	0.50	1.00
1966	—	PF65 1.00				
1968	20,000,000	0.10	0.15	0.30	0.50	1.00
1970	6,000,000	0.20	0.30	0.45	0.75	1.00
1972	6,000,000	0.20	0.30	0.45	0.75	1.00
1974	4,110,000	0.20	0.30	0.45	0.75	1.25
1975	14,000,000	0.20	0.30	0.45	0.75	1.25

KM# 2a 10 CENTS

Copper Plated Steel **Obv:** Value above crossed tusks within circle **Rev:** Value within circular sprig

Date	Mintage	VF20	XF40	MS60	MS63	MS65
1976	10,000,000	0.20	0.30	0.45	0.75	1.25

KM# 3 20 CENTS

9.60 g., Bronze **Obv:** Value above crossed tusks within circle **Rev:** Value within circular sprig

Date	Mintage	VF20	XF40	MS60	MS63	MS65
1966	7,000,000	0.30	0.50	0.75	1.65	2.00
1966	—	PF65 2.00				
1974	2,000,000	0.50	0.75	1.25	2.25	3.00

KM# 4 50 CENTS

Copper-Nickel **Obv:** National arms **Rev:** East African crowned crane, mountains and value

Date	Mintage	VF20	XF40	MS60	MS63	MS65
1966	16,000,000	0.20	0.40	1.00	2.00	3.50
1966	—	PF65 3.50				
1970	3,000,000	0.25	0.75	1.50	3.00	3.50
1974	10,000,000	0.25	0.65	1.25	2.25	3.50

KM# 4a 50 CENTS

Copper-Nickel Plated Steel **Obv:** National arms **Rev:** East African crowned crane within circular sprig above value and date

Date	Mintage	VF20	XF40	MS60	MS63	MS65
1976	10,000,000	0.25	0.65	1.25	2.25	3.50

KM# 5 SHILLING

6.40 g., Copper-Nickel, 26 mm. **Obv:** National arms **Rev:** East African crowned crane within circular sprig above date and value

Date	Mintage	VF20	XF40	MS60	MS63	MS65
1966	24,500,000	0.25	0.50	1.25	2.50	4.50
1966	—	PF65 4.50				
1968	10,000,000	0.35	0.85	1.65	2.75	4.50
1972	4,040,000	0.35	0.85	1.65	2.75	4.50
1975	15,500,000	0.35	0.85	1.50	2.50	4.50

KM# 5a SHILLING

Copper-Nickel Plated Steel **Obv:** National arms **Rev:** East African crowned crane within circular sprig above date and value

Date	Mintage	VF20	XF40	MS60	MS63	MS65
1976	10,000,000	0.35	0.85	1.50	2.50	4.50

KM# 27 SHILLING

4.30 g., Copper Plated Steel, 19.85 mm. **Obv:** National arms **Rev:** Flowers 3/4 surround value within center circle, sack below above date **Edge:** Plain **Shape:** 12-sided

Date	Mintage	VF20	XF40	MS60	MS63	MS65
1987	—	—	—	—	0.25	0.40
1987	—	PF65 2.50				

KM# 6 2 SHILLINGS

Copper-Nickel **Obv:** National arms **Rev:** East African crowned crane within circular sprig above date and value

Date	Mintage	VF20	XF40	MS60	MS63	MS65
1966	4,000,000	—	1.00	2.00	3.00	5.00
1966	—	PF65 9.00				

KM# 8 2 SHILLINGS

4.00 g., 0.999 Silver 0.1285 oz. ASW **Subject:** Visit of Pope Paul VI **Obv:** National arms **Rev:** Head right

Date	Mintage	VF20	XF40	MS60	MS63	MS65
1969	8,170	PF65 7.50	PF67 12.50			
1970	Inc. above	PF65 7.50	PF67 12.50			

KM# 28 2 SHILLINGS

8.10 g., Copper Plated Steel, 24.37 mm. **Obv:** National arms **Rev:** Value in center circle of flowered sprigs **Edge:** Plain **Shape:** 12-sided

Date	Mintage	VF20	XF40	MS60	MS63	MS65
1987	—	—	—	—	1.00	1.50
1987	—	PF65 4.00				

KM# 7 5 SHILLINGS

Copper-Nickel, 37.8 mm. **Series:** F.A.O. **Obv:** National arms **Rev:** Cow and calf

Date	Mintage	VF20	XF40	MS60	MS63	MS65
ND-1968	100,000	1.00	2.00	3.00	5.00	7.00
ND-1968	5,000	PF65 20.00				

KM# 9 5 SHILLINGS

10.00 g., 0.999 Silver 0.3212 oz. ASW **Subject:** Visit of Pope Paul VI **Obv:** National arms **Rev:** Crested cranes within circle

Date	Mintage	VF20	XF40	MS60	MS63	MS65
1969	7,670	PF65 10.00	PF67 15.00			
1970	Inc. above	PF65 10.00	PF67 15.00			

KM# 18 5 SHILLINGS

Copper-Nickel, 30 mm. **Obv:** National arms **Rev:** East African crowned crane within circular sprig **Edge:** Plain **Shape:** 7-sided **Note:** Withdrawn from circulation. Almost entire mintage was melted.

Date	Mintage	VF20	XF40	MS60	MS63	MS65
1972	Est. 8000000	—	40.00	60.00	90.00	125

KM# 29 5 SHILLINGS

3.50 g., Nickel Plated Steel, 20.23 mm. **Obv:** National arms **Rev:** Value within center circle of sprigs **Edge:** Plain **Shape:** 7-sided

Date	Mintage	VF20	XF40	MS60	MS63	MS65
1987	—	—	—	—	1.00	2.00
1987	—	PF65 6.50				

KM# 10 10 SHILLINGS
20.00 g., 0.999 Silver 0.6424 oz. ASW, 40 mm. **Subject:** Visit of Pope Paul VI **Obv:** National arms **Rev:** Martyrs' shrine within circle

Date	Mintage	VF20	XF40	MS60	MS63	MS65
1969	6,720	PF65 22.00	PF67 27.00			
1970	Inc. above	PF65 22.00	PF67 27.00			

KM# 21 10 SHILLINGS
Copper-Nickel **Subject:** Wedding of Prince Charles and Lady Diana **Obv:** National arms **Rev:** Conjoined heads right

Date	Mintage	VF20	XF40	MS60	MS63	MS65
1981	10,000	—	—	—	3.00	5.00

KM# 30 10 SHILLINGS
5.80 g., Nickel Plated Steel, 25.91 mm. **Obv:** National arms **Rev:** Value in center circle of sprigs **Edge:** Plain **Shape:** 7-sided

Date	Mintage	VF20	XF40	MS60	MS63	MS65
1987	—	—	—	—	1.50	3.00
1987	—	PF65 12.50				

KM# 11 20 SHILLINGS
40.00 g., 0.999 Silver 1.2847 oz. ASW, 50 mm. **Subject:** Visit of Pope Paul VI **Obv:** National arms **Rev:** Bust right within map and circle

Date	Mintage	VF20	XF40	MS60	MS63	MS65
1969	6,670	PF65 32.50	PF67 40.00			
1970	Inc. above	PF65 32.50	PF67 40.00			

KM# 12 25 SHILLINGS
50.00 g., 0.999 Silver 1.6059 oz. ASW, 55 mm. **Subject:** Visit of Pope Paul VI **Obv:** National arms **Rev:** Half-length figure facing, right arm raised in blessing superimposed on world globe

Date	Mintage	VF20	XF40	MS60	MS63	MS65
1969	6,070	PF65 41.00	PF67 50.00			
1970	Inc. above	PF65 41.00	PF67 50.00			

KM# 13 30 SHILLINGS
60.00 g., 0.999 Silver 1.9271 oz. ASW, 60 mm. **Subject:** Visit of Pope Paul VI **Obv:** National arms **Rev:** Head right **Note:** Illustration reduced.

Date	Mintage	VF20	XF40	MS60	MS63	MS65
1969	6,720	PF65 49.50	PF67 60.00			
1970	Inc. above	PF65 49.50	PF67 60.00			

KM# 14 50 SHILLINGS
6.91 g., 0.900 Gold 0.1999 oz. AGW **Subject:** Visit of Pope Paul VI **Obv:** National arms **Rev:** Martyrs' shrine within circle

Date	Mintage	VF20	XF40	MS60	MS63	MS65
1969	4,390	PF65 300	PF67 350			
1970	Inc. above	PF65 300	PF67 350			

KM# 66 50 SHILLINGS
4.00 g., Nickel Plated Steel **Obv:** National arms **Rev:** Antelope head facing

Date	Mintage	VF20	XF40	MS60	MS63	MS65
1998	—	—	—	—	1.00	1.25

KM# 15 100 SHILLINGS
13.82 g., 0.900 Gold 0.3999 oz. AGW **Subject:** Visit of Pope Paul VI **Obv:** National arms **Rev:** Bust right within map and circle

Date	Mintage	VF20	XF40	MS60	MS63	MS65
1969	4,190	PF65 600	PF67 700			
1970	Inc. above	PF65 600	PF67 700			

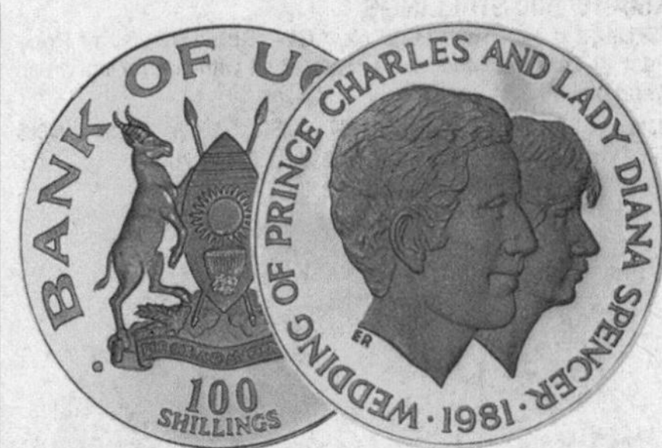

KM# 22 100 SHILLINGS
31.47 g., 0.925 Silver 0.9359 oz. ASW **Subject:** Wedding of Prince Charles and Lady Diana **Obv:** National arms

Date	Mintage	VF20	XF40	MS60	MS63	MS65
1981	5,000	PF63 25.00	PF65 30.00			

KM# 67 100 SHILLINGS
7.00 g., Copper-Nickel, 26.9 mm. **Obv:** National arms **Rev:** African bull **Edge:** Reeded

Date	Mintage	VF20	XF40	MS60	MS63	MS65
1998	—	—	—	1.00	1.50	1.75

KM# 26 200 SHILLINGS
28.28 g., 0.925 Silver 0.841 oz. ASW **Series:** International Year of Disabled Persons **Obv:** National arms **Rev:** Wooden cane divides emblem within wreath

Date	Mintage	VF20	XF40	MS60	MS63	MS65
1981	10,000	—	—	—	25.00	30.00
1981	10,000	PF63 30.00	PF65 35.00			

KM# 148 200 SHILLINGS
7.60 g., Aluminum-Bronze, 27 mm. **Series:** Food For All **Subject:** 50 Years - FAO **Obv:** National arms **Obv. Legend:** BANK OF UGANDA **Rev:** Fish

Date	Mintage	VF20	XF40	MS60	MS63	MS65
1995	—	1.50	3.00	6.50	9.50	12.50

KM# 68 200 SHILLINGS
8.05 g., Copper-Nickel, 24.9 mm. **Obv:** National arms **Rev:** Cichlid fish above value and date **Edge:** Plain

Date	Mintage	VF20	XF40	MS60	MS63	MS65
1998	—	—	—	0.75	1.50	2.50

KM# 16 500 SHILLINGS

69.12 g., 0.900 Gold 2.000 oz. AGW **Subject:** Visit of Pope Paul VI **Obv:** National arms **Rev:** Bust with hat facing within world globe

Date	Mintage	VF20	XF40	MS60	MS63	MS65
1969	1,680	PF65 3,200	PF67 3,700			
1970	Inc. above	PF65 3,200	PF67 3,700			

KM# 23 500 SHILLINGS

136.00 g., 0.500 Silver 2.1862 oz. ASW **Series:** Wildlife **Obv:** Bust of Dr. Milton Obote facing **Rev:** Elephants

Date	Mintage	VF20	XF40	MS60	MS63	MS65
1981	700	—	—	—	110	130

KM# 23a 500 SHILLINGS

136.00 g., 0.925 Silver 4.0446 oz. ASW **Series:** Wildlife **Obv:** Bust of Dr. Milton Obote facing **Rev:** Elephants

Date	Mintage	VF20	XF40	MS60	MS63	MS65
1981	700	PF63 130	PF65 150			

KM# 69 500 SHILLINGS

9.00 g., Nickel-Brass, 23.5 mm. **Obv:** National arms **Rev:** East African crowned crane head left **Edge:** Reeded

Date	Mintage	VF20	XF40	MS60	MS63	MS65
1998	—	—	—	1.00	2.00	3.00

KM# 149 500 SHILLINGS

20.00 g., Silver **Obv:** National arms **Obv. Legend:** BANK OF UGANDA **Rev:** Galao Matschiei animal sitting on tree branch

Date	Mintage	VF20	XF40	MS60	MS63	MS65
1999	—	PF63 30.00	PF65 35.00			

KM# 17 1000 SHILLINGS

138.24 g., 0.900 Gold 4.0001 oz. AGW **Subject:** Visit of Pope John Paul VI **Obv:** National arms **Rev:** Head right

Date	Mintage	VF20	XF40	MS60	MS63	MS65
1969	1,390	PF65 6,000	PF67 6,800			
1970	Inc. above	PF65 6,000	PF67 6,800			

KM# 24 1000 SHILLINGS

10.00 g., 0.500 Gold 0.1608 oz. AGW **Subject:** Wedding of Prince Charles and Lady Diana **Obv:** National arms **Rev:** Conjoined busts right

Date	Mintage	VF20	XF40	MS60	MS63	MS65
1981	1,500	PF63 300	PF65 325			

KM# 35 1000 SHILLINGS

Copper-Nickel **Series:** Famous Places **Subject:** Matterhorn Mountain **Obv:** National arms **Rev:** Multicolor plastic applique

Date	Mintage	VF20	XF40	MS60	MS63	MS65
1993	15,000	—	—	—	—	10.00

KM# 35a 1000 SHILLINGS

Silver **Series:** Famous Places **Subject:** Matterhorn Mountain **Obv:** National Arms

Date	Mintage	VF20	XF40	MS60	MS63	MS65
1993	—	PF63 30.00	PF65 35.00			

KM# 49 1000 SHILLINGS

Copper-Nickel **Series:** Famous Places **Subject:** Munich **Obv:** National arms

Date	Mintage	VF20	XF40	MS60	MS63	MS65
1994	—	PF65 10.00				

KM# 40 1000 SHILLINGS

Copper-Nickel **Series:** 50th Anniversary - United Nations **Obv:** National arms **Rev:** Monument divides sprigs within circle

Date	Mintage	VF20	XF40	MS60	MS63	MS65
1995	—	PF65 15.00				

KM# 50 1000 SHILLINGS

Copper-Nickel **Subject:** Year of the Pig **Obv:** Sow and piglets left **Rev:** Stylized pig left

Date	Mintage	VF20	XF40	MS60	MS63	MS65
1995	—	PF65 12.00				

KM# 41 1000 SHILLINGS

Copper-Nickel **Series:** Endangered Wildlife **Obv:** National arms **Rev:** Multicolor zebra applique

Date	Mintage	VF20	XF40	MS60	MS63	MS65
1996	—	PF65 15.00				

KM# 44 1000 SHILLINGS

Copper-Nickel **Series:** Endangered Wildlife **Obv:** National arms **Rev:** Rhinoceros

Date	Mintage	VF20	XF40	MS60	MS63	MS65
1996	15,000	PF65 12.50				

KM# 45 1000 SHILLINGS

Copper-Nickel **Series:** Endangered Wildlife **Obv:** National arms **Rev:** Lion

Date	Mintage	VF20	XF40	MS60	MS63	MS65
1996	15,000	PF65 12.50				

KM# 52 1000 SHILLINGS

Copper-Nickel **Subject:** Hong Kong's return to China **Obv:** National arms **Rev:** City view

Date	Mintage	VF20	XF40	MS60	MS63	MS65
1996	—	—	—	—	7.00	10.00

KM# 54 1000 SHILLINGS

Copper-Nickel **Subject:** Year of the rat **Obv:** Pair of rats flanking Chinese symbol **Rev:** Multicolor rat applique

Date	Mintage	VF20	XF40	MS60	MS63	MS65
1996	—	—	—	—	10.00	12.50

KM# 55 1000 SHILLINGS
Copper-Nickel **Subject:** Africa - Protection of Endangered Wildlife **Obv:** National arms **Rev:** Multicolor elephant applique

Date	Mintage	VF20	XF40	MS60	MS63	MS65
1996	—	PF65 10.00				

KM# 56 1000 SHILLINGS
Copper-Nickel **Subject:** Michael Schumacher **Obv:** National arms **Rev:** Multicolor applique head facing, car and flags

Date	Mintage	VF20	XF40	MS60	MS63	MS65
1996	—	PF65 12.50				
1997	—	PF65 10.00				

KM# 74 1000 SHILLINGS
28.52 g., Copper-Nickel, 38.15 mm. **Subject:** Birth of Jesus and the Modern Dating System **Obv:** National arms **Rev:** Head of Jesus facing **Edge:** Reeded

Date	Mintage	VF20	XF40	MS60	MS63	MS65
1996	—	PF65 10.00				

KM# 57 1000 SHILLINGS
Copper-Nickel **Subject:** Princess Diana - Queen of Hearts **Obv:** National arms **Rev:** Multicolor applique of Princess Diana

Date	Mintage	VF20	XF40	MS60	MS63	MS65
1997	—	PF65 12.50				

KM# 119 1000 SHILLINGS
28.74 g., Copper-Nickel, 38 mm. **Obv:** National arms **Rev:** Princess Diana hugging child **Edge:** Reeded

Date	Mintage	VF20	XF40	MS60	MS63	MS65
1998	—	—	—	—	7.50	10.00

KM# 120 1000 SHILLINGS
28.74 g., Copper-Nickel, 38 mm. **Obv:** National arms **Rev:** Diana holding one-legged child's crutch **Edge:** Reeded

Date	Mintage	VF20	XF40	MS60	MS63	MS65
1998	—	—	—	—	7.50	10.00

KM# 70 1000 SHILLINGS
14.97 g., 0.999 Silver 0.4808 oz. ASW **Series:** XXVII Olympic Games **Obv:** National arms **Rev:** Javelin thrower

Date	Mintage	VF20	XF40	MS60	MS63	MS65
1999	—	PF63 9.00	PF65 15.00			

KM# 116 1000 SHILLINGS
22.13 g., Copper-Nickel, 38.6 mm. **Subject:** Euro Currency **Obv:** National arms **Rev:** European map with paper applique illustrating the Netherlands 10 Euro cent coin KM-237 **Edge:** Reeded

Date	Mintage	VF20	XF40	MS60	MS63	MS65
1999	—	—	—	—	5.00	8.00

KM# 118 1000 SHILLINGS
31.56 g., 0.925 Silver 0.9386 oz. ASW, 38.7 mm. **Subject:** Princess Diana **Obv:** National arms **Rev:** Charles and Diana engagement portrait **Edge:** Reeded

Date	Mintage	VF20	XF40	MS60	MS63	MS65
1999	—	PF63 30.00	PF65 35.00			

KM# 146 1000 SHILLINGS
19.95 g., 0.999 Silver 0.6408 oz. ASW, 38.3 mm. **Obv:** National arms **Rev:** Lord Nelson and HMS Victory **Edge:** Plain

Date	Mintage	VF20	XF40	MS60	MS63	MS65
1999	—	PF63 27.00	PF65 32.00			

KM# 147 1000 SHILLINGS
19.95 g., 0.999 Silver 0.6408 oz. ASW, 38.3 mm. **Obv:** National arms **Rev:** Albert Einstein **Edge:** Plain

Date	Mintage	VF20	XF40	MS60	MS63	MS65
1999	—	PF63 27.00	PF65 32.00			

KM# 243 1000 SHILLINGS
22.13 g., Copper-Nickel, 38.6 mm. **Subject:** Euro Currency **Obv:** Arms **Rev:** European map with paper applique of Austria 1 Euro cent KM-3082

Date	Mintage	VF20	XF40	MS60	MS63	MS65
1999	—	—	—	—	4.00	6.00

KM# 244 1000 SHILLINGS
22.13 g., Copper-Nickel, 38.6 mm. **Obv:** Arms **Rev:** European map with paper applique of Belgium 1 Euro cent KM-224

Date	Mintage	VF20	XF40	MS60	MS63	MS65
1999	—	—	—	—	4.00	6.00

KM# 245 1000 SHILLINGS
22.13 g., Copper-Nickel, 38.6 mm. **Subject:** Euro Currency **Obv:** National arms **Rev:** European map with paper applique of Germany 1 Euro cent KM-207

Date	Mintage	VF20	XF40	MS60	MS63	MS65
1999	—	—	—	—	4.00	6.00

KM# 246 1000 SHILLINGS
22.13 g., Copper-Nickel, 38.6 mm. **Subject:** Euro currency **Obv:** National arms **Rev:** European map with paper applique of Netherlands 1 Euro cent KM-234

Date	Mintage	VF20	XF40	MS60	MS63	MS65
1999	—	—	—	—	4.00	6.00

KM# 247 1000 SHILLINGS
22.13 g., Copper-Nickel, 38.6 mm. **Subject:** Euro currency **Obv:** National arms **Rev:** European map with paper applique of Austrian 2 Euro cent KM-3083

Date	Mintage	VF20	XF40	MS60	MS63	MS65
1999	—	—	—	—	4.00	6.00

KM# 248 1000 SHILLINGS
22.13 g., Copper-Nickel, 38.6 mm. **Obv:** National arms **Rev:** European map with paper applique of Belgium 2 Euro cent KM-225

Date	Mintage	VF20	XF40	MS60	MS63	MS65
1999	—	—	—	—	4.00	6.00

KM# 249 1000 SHILLINGS
22.13 g., Copper-Nickel, 38.6 mm. **Subject:** Euro currency **Obv:** National arms **Rev:** European map with paper applique of German 2 Euro cent KM-208

Date	Mintage	VF20	XF40	MS60	MS63	MS65
1999	—	—	—	—	4.00	6.00

KM# 250 1000 SHILLINGS
22.13 g., Copper-Nickel **Subject:** Euro currency **Obv:** National Arms **Rev:** European map with paper applique of Netherlands 2 Euro cent KM-235 **Shape:** 38.6

Date	Mintage	VF20	XF40	MS60	MS63	MS65
1999	—	—	—	—	4.00	6.00

KM# 251 1000 SHILLINGS
22.13 g., Copper-Nickel, 38.6 mm. **Subject:** Euro currency **Obv:** National arms **Rev:** European map with paper applique of Austria 5 Euro cent KM-3084

Date	Mintage	VF20	XF40	MS60	MS63	MS65
1999	—	—	—	—	4.00	6.00

KM# 252 1000 SHILLINGS
22.13 g., Copper-Nickel, 38.6 mm. **Subject:** Euro currency **Obv:** National arms **Rev:** European map with paper applique of Belgium 5 Euro cent KM-226

Date	Mintage	VF20	XF40	MS60	MS63	MS65
1999	—	—	—	—	4.00	6.00

KM# 253 1000 SHILLINGS
22.13 g., Copper-Nickel, 38.6 mm. **Subject:** Euro currency **Obv:** National arms **Rev:** European map with paper applique of German 5 Euro cent KM-209

Date	Mintage	VF20	XF40	MS60	MS63	MS65
1999	—	—	—	—	4.00	6.00

KM# 254 1000 SHILLINGS
22.13 g., Copper-Nickel, 38.6 mm. **Subject:** Euro currency **Obv:** National Arms **Rev:** European map with paper applique of Netherlands 5 Euro cent KM-236

Date	Mintage	VF20	XF40	MS60	MS63	MS65
1999	—	—	—	—	4.00	6.00

KM# 255 1000 SHILLINGS
22.13 g., Copper-Nickel, 38.6 mm. **Subject:** Euro currency **Obv:** National arms **Rev:** European map with paper applique of Austria 10 Euro cent KM-3085

Date	Mintage	VF20	XF40	MS60	MS63	MS65
1999	—	—	—	—	4.00	6.00

KM# 256 1000 SHILLINGS
22.13 g., Copper-Nickel, 38.6 mm. **Subject:** Euro currency **Obv:** National arms **Rev:** European map with paper applique of Belgium 10 Euro cent KM-227

Date	Mintage	VF20	XF40	MS60	MS63	MS65
1999	—	—	—	—	4.00	6.00

KM# 257 1000 SHILLINGS
22.13 g., Copper-Nickel, 38.6 mm. **Subject:** Euro currency **Obv:** National arms **Rev:** European map with paper applique of German 10 Euro cent KM-210

Date	Mintage	VF20	XF40	MS60	MS63	MS65
1999	—	—	—	—	4.00	6.00

KM# 258 1000 SHILLINGS
22.13 g., Copper-Nickel, 38.6 mm. **Subject:** Euro currency **Obv:** National arms **Rev:** European map with paper applique of Austrian 20 Euro cent KM-3086

Date	Mintage	VF20	XF40	MS60	MS63	MS65
1999	—	—	—	—	4.00	6.00

KM# 260 1000 SHILLINGS
22.13 g., Copper-Nickel, 38.6 mm. **Subject:** Euro currency **Obv:** National arms **Rev:** European map with paper applique of Germany 20 Euro cent KM-211

Date	Mintage	VF20	XF40	MS60	MS63	MS65
1999	—	—	—	—	4.00	6.00

KM# 261 1000 SHILLINGS
22.13 g., Copper-Nickel, 38.6 mm. **Subject:** Euro currency **Obv:** National arms **Rev:** European map with paper applique of Netherlands 20 Euro cent KM-238

Date	Mintage	VF20	XF40	MS60	MS63	MS65
1999	—	—	—	—	4.00	6.00

KM# 262 1000 SHILLINGS
22.13 g., Copper-Nickel, 38.6 mm. **Subject:** Euro currency **Obv:** National arms **Rev:** European map with paper applique of Austrian 50 Euro cent KM-3087

Date	Mintage	VF20	XF40	MS60	MS63	MS65
1999	—	—	—	—	4.00	6.00

KM# 263 1000 SHILLINGS
22.13 g., Copper-Nickel, 38.6 mm. **Subject:** Euro currency **Obv:** National arms **Rev:** European map with paper applique of Belgium 50 Euro cent KM-229

Date	Mintage	VF20	XF40	MS60	MS63	MS65
1999	—	—	—	—	4.00	6.00

KM# 264 1000 SHILLINGS
22.13 g., Copper-Nickel, 38.6 mm. **Subject:** Euro currency **Obv:** National arms **Rev:** European map with paper applique of German 50 Euro cent KM-212

Date	Mintage	VF20	XF40	MS60	MS63	MS65
1999	—	—	—	—	4.00	6.00

KM# 265 1000 SHILLINGS
22.13 g., Copper-Nickel, 38.6 mm. **Subject:** Euro currency **Obv:** National arms **Rev:** European map with paper applique of Netherlands 50 Euro cent KM-239

Date	Mintage	VF20	XF40	MS60	MS63	MS65
1999	—	—	—	—	4.00	6.00

KM# 266 1000 SHILLINGS
22.13 g., Copper-Nickel, 38.6 mm. **Subject:** Euro currency **Obv:** National arms **Rev:** European map with paper applique of Austrian 1 Euro KM-3088

Date	Mintage	VF20	XF40	MS60	MS63	MS65
1999	—	—	—	—	4.00	6.00

KM# 267 1000 SHILLINGS
22.13 g., Copper-Nickel, 38.6 mm. **Subject:** Euro currency **Obv:** National arms **Rev:** European map with paper applique of Belgium 1 Euro KM-230

Date	Mintage	VF20	XF40	MS60	MS63	MS65
1999	—	—	—	—	4.00	6.00

KM# 268 1000 SHILLINGS
22.13 g., Copper-Nickel, 38.6 mm. **Subject:** Euro currency **Obv:** National arms **Rev:** European map with paper applique of German 1 Euro KM-213

Date	Mintage	VF20	XF40	MS60	MS63	MS65
1999	—	—	—	—	4.00	6.00

KM# 269 1000 SHILLINGS
22.13 g., Copper-Nickel, 38.6 mm. **Subject:** Euro currency **Obv:** National arms **Rev:** European map with paper applique of Netherland 1 Euro KM-240

Date	Mintage	VF20	XF40	MS60	MS63	MS65
1999	—	—	—	—	4.00	6.00

KM# 270 1000 SHILLINGS
22.13 g., Copper-Nickel, 38.6 mm. **Subject:** Euro currency **Obv:** National arms **Rev:** European map with paper applique of Austrian 2 Euro KM-3089

Date	Mintage	VF20	XF40	MS60	MS63	MS65
1999	—	—	—	—	4.00	6.00

KM# 271 1000 SHILLINGS
22.13 g., Copper-Nickel, 38.6 mm. **Subject:** Euro currency **Obv:** National arms **Rev:** European map with paper applique of Belgium 2 Euro KM-231

Date	Mintage	VF20	XF40	MS60	MS63	MS65
1999	—	—	—	—	4.00	6.00

KM# 272 1000 SHILLINGS
22.13 g., Copper-Nickel, 38.6 mm. **Subject:** Euro currency **Obv:** National arms **Rev:** European map with paper applique of Germany 2 Euro KM-214

Date	Mintage	VF20	XF40	MS60	MS63	MS65
1999	—	—	—	—	4.00	6.00

KM# 273 1000 SHILLINGS
22.13 g., Copper-Nickel, 38.6 mm. **Subject:** Euro currency **Obv:** National arms **Rev:** European map with paper applique of Netherlands 2 Euro KM-241

Date	Mintage	VF20	XF40	MS60	MS63	MS65
1999	—	—	—	—	4.00	6.00

KM# 31 2000 SHILLINGS
15.98 g., 0.917 Gold 0.4711 oz. AGW **Series:** International Year of Disabled Persons **Obv:** National arms **Rev:** Stylized standing figure with cane

Date	Mintage	XF40	MS60	MS63	MS65	MS66
1981	2,005	—	—	775	875	925
1981	2,005	PF65 900	PF67 950			

KM# 38 2000 SHILLINGS
19.80 g., 0.999 Silver 0.6359 oz. ASW **Subject:** World Cup Soccer **Obv:** Arms with supporters **Rev:** Soccer player

Date	Mintage	VF20	XF40	MS60	MS63	MS65
1993	—	PF63 20.00	PF65 25.00			

KM# 39 2000 SHILLINGS
19.80 g., 0.999 Silver 0.6359 oz. ASW **Subject:** World Cup Soccer **Obv:** National arms **Rev:** Player kicking ball down field

Date	Mintage	VF20	XF40	MS60	MS63	MS65
1993	—	PF63 20.00	PF65 25.00			

KM# 42 2000 SHILLINGS
19.92 g., 0.999 Silver 0.6398 oz. ASW **Series:** Famous Places **Subject:** Matterhorn Mountain **Note:** With multicolor applique.

Date	Mintage	VF20	XF40	MS60	MS63	MS65
1993	10,000	PF63 15.00	PF65 20.00			

KM# 64 2000 SHILLINGS
30.46 g., 0.999 Silver 0.9783 oz. ASW **Subject:** Protection of the African elephant **Obv:** National arms **Rev:** Elephant head facing

Date	Mintage	VF20	XF40	MS60	MS63	MS65
1993	—	PF63 30.00	PF65 35.00			

KM# 43 2000 SHILLINGS
19.92 g., 0.999 Silver 0.6398 oz. ASW **Series:** Famous Places **Subject:** Munich's Frauen Kirche **Obv:** National arms **Rev:** Towers

Date	Mintage	VF20	XF40	MS60	MS63	MS65
1994	10,000	PF63 15.00	PF65 20.00			

KM# 53 2000 SHILLINGS
Copper-Nickel **Subject:** Nations United for Peace **Obv:** National arms **Rev:** United Nations 50th Anniversary

Date	Mintage	VF20	XF40	MS60	MS63	MS65
ND-1995	—	—	—	—	7.50	9.00

KM# 58 2000 SHILLINGS
30.84 g., 0.999 Silver 0.9905 oz. ASW **Obv:** Sow and piglets **Rev:** Multicolor pig applique

Date	Mintage	VF20	XF40	MS60	MS63	MS65
1995	—	PF63 20.00	PF65 25.00			

KM# 46 2000 SHILLINGS
19.92 g., 0.999 Silver 0.6398 oz. ASW **Series:** Endangered Wildlife **Obv:** National arms **Rev:** Zebra

Date	Mintage	VF20	XF40	MS60	MS63	MS65
1996	10,000	PF63 25.00	PF65 30.00			

KM# 47 2000 SHILLINGS
19.92 g., 0.999 Silver 0.6398 oz. ASW **Series:** Endangered Wildlife **Obv:** National arms **Rev:** Rhinocerous within circle

Date	Mintage	VF20	XF40	MS60	MS63	MS65
1996	10,000	PF63 30.00	PF65 35.00			

KM# 48 2000 SHILLINGS
19.92 g., 0.999 Silver 0.6398 oz. ASW **Series:** Endangered Wildlife **Obv:** National arms **Rev:** Lion

Date	Mintage	VF20	XF40	MS60	MS63	MS65
1996	10,000	PF63 30.00	PF65 35.00			

KM# 59 2000 SHILLINGS
30.84 g., 0.999 Silver 0.9905 oz. ASW **Obv:** Pair of rats flanking Chinese symbols **Rev:** Multicolor rat applique

Date	Mintage	VF20	XF40	MS60	MS63	MS65
1996	—	PF63 20.00	PF65 25.00			

KM# 60 2000 SHILLINGS
7.10 g., 0.999 Silver 0.228 oz. ASW **Subject:** 1998 World Championship Football **Obv:** National arms **Rev:** Soccer player and Eiffel Tower within circle

Date	Mintage	VF20	XF40	MS60	MS63	MS65
1996	—	PF63 16.00	PF65 20.00			

KM# 61 2000 SHILLINGS
Copper-Nickel **Series:** XXVI Summer Olympic Games **Obv:** National arms **Rev:** German Olympic stamp

Date	Mintage	VF20	XF40	MS60	MS63	MS65
1996	—	PF65 10.00				

KM# 62 2000 SHILLINGS
Copper-Nickel **Series:** Olympics **Obv:** National arms **Rev:** Spanish postal stamp design

Date	Mintage	VF20	XF40	MS60	MS63	MS65
1996	—	PF65 10.00				

KM# 65 2000 SHILLINGS
20.26 g., 0.999 Silver 0.6507 oz. ASW **Series:** Endangered Wildlife **Obv:** National arms **Rev:** Multicolor elephant

Date	Mintage	VF20	XF40	MS60	MS63	MS65
1996	—	PF65 25.00				

KM# 93 2000 SHILLINGS
19.92 g., 0.999 Silver 0.6398 oz. ASW **Obv:** National arms **Rev:** Multicolor leaning Tower of Pisa

Date	Mintage	VF20	XF40	MS60	MS63	MS65
1996	10,000	PF63 17.50	PF65 22.50			

KM# 94 2000 SHILLINGS
19.90 g., 0.999 Silver 0.6392 oz. ASW, 37.9 mm. **Subject:** Christian Dating System **Obv:** National arms **Rev:** Head of Jesus facing **Edge:** Reeded

Date	Mintage	VF20	XF40	MS60	MS63	MS65
1996	—	PF63 20.00	PF65 25.00			

KM# 122 2000 SHILLINGS
31.02 g., 0.999 Silver 0.9963 oz. ASW, 38.5 mm. **Subject:** Wonders of the World - Leaning Tower of Pisa **Obv:** National arms **Rev:** Leaning tower within circle **Edge:** Reeded

Date	Mintage	VF20	XF40	MS60	MS63	MS65
1996	—	PF63 35.00	PF65 40.00			

KM# 123 2000 SHILLINGS
31.02 g., 0.999 Silver 0.9963 oz. ASW, 38.5 mm. **Subject:** Wonders of the World - The Pyramids **Obv:** National arms **Rev:** Sphinx within circle **Edge:** Reeded

Date	Mintage	VF20	XF40	MS60	MS63	MS65
1996	—	PF63 35.00	PF65 40.00			

KM# 124 2000 SHILLINGS
31.02 g., 0.999 Silver 0.9963 oz. ASW, 38.5 mm. **Subject:** Wonders of the World - The Parthenon **Obv:** National arms **Rev:** Building within circle **Edge:** Reeded

Date	Mintage	VF20	XF40	MS60	MS63	MS65
1996	—	PF63 35.00	PF65 40.00			

KM# 125 2000 SHILLINGS
31.02 g., 0.999 Silver 0.9963 oz. ASW, 38.5 mm. **Subject:** Rome Colosseum **Obv:** National arms **Rev:** Colosseum within circle **Edge:** Reeded

Date	Mintage	VF20	XF40	MS60	MS63	MS65
1996	—	PF63 35.00	PF65 40.00			

KM# 126 2000 SHILLINGS

31.02 g., 0.999 Silver 0.9963 oz. ASW, 38.5 mm. **Subject:** Wonders of the World - Taj Mahal **Obv:** National arms **Rev:** Taj Mahal within circle **Edge:** Reeded

Date	Mintage	VF20	XF40	MS60	MS63	MS65
1996	—	PF63 35.00	PF65 40.00			

KM# 127 2000 SHILLINGS

31.02 g., 0.999 Silver 0.9963 oz. ASW, 38.5 mm. **Subject:** Wonders of the World - Yungang Grottoes **Obv:** National arms **Rev:** Half figures facing in front of mountain **Edge:** Reeded

Date	Mintage	VF20	XF40	MS60	MS63	MS65
1996	—	PF63 35.00	PF65 40.00			

KM# 274 2000 SHILLINGS

31.11 g., 0.999 Silver 0.999 oz. ASW, 38.6 mm. **Subject:** Famous places of the World **Obv:** Arms **Rev:** Kreuzberge and Swiss stamp

Date	Mintage	VF20	XF40	MS60	MS63	MS65
1996	—	PF65 30.00				

KM# 275 2000 SHILLINGS

31.11 g., 0.999 Silver 0.999 oz. ASW, 38.6 mm. **Obv:** Arms **Rev:** Monch and Swiss stamp

Date	Mintage	VF20	XF40	MS60	MS63	MS65
1996	—	PF65 30.00				

KM# 276 2000 SHILLINGS

31.11 g., 0.999 Silver 0.999 oz. ASW, 38.6 mm. **Obv:** Arms **Rev:** Finesteraarhorn and Swiss stamp

Date	Mintage	VF20	XF40	MS60	MS63	MS65
1996	—	PF65 30.00				

KM# 277 2000 SHILLINGS

31.11 g., 0.999 Silver 0.999 oz. ASW, 38.6 mm. **Obv:** Arms **Rev:** Matterhorn and Swiss stamp

Date	Mintage	VF20	XF40	MS60	MS63	MS65
1996	—	PF65 30.00				

KM# 51 2000 SHILLINGS

19.74 g., 0.999 Silver 0.634 oz. ASW **Subject:** Hong Kong's return to China **Obv:** National arms **Rev:** City view below head left

Date	Mintage	VF20	XF40	MS60	MS63	MS65
1997	—	PF63 20.00	PF65 25.00			

KM# 63 2000 SHILLINGS

Copper-Nickel **Subject:** Queen's Golden Wedding Anniversary **Obv:** National arms **Rev:** Queen Elizabeth and Prince Philip on horseback

Date	Mintage	VF20	XF40	MS60	MS63	MS65
ND-1997	—	—	—	—	5.00	8.00

KM# 150 2000 SHILLINGS

6.88 g., Silver, 30 mm. **Subject:** Death of Mother Teresa **Obv:** National arms **Obv. Legend:** BANK OF UGANDA **Rev:** Bust of Mother Teresa with child **Rev. Legend:** THE ANGEL OF THE POOR **Edge:** Reeded

Date	Mintage	VF20	XF40	MS60	MS63	MS65
1997	—	PF63 20.00	PF65 25.00			

KM# 95 2000 SHILLINGS

31.32 g., 0.999 Silver 1.006 oz. ASW, 38.8 mm. **Subject:** Zebras **Obv:** National arms **Rev:** Zebra and nursing colt **Edge:** Reeded

Date	Mintage	VF20	XF40	MS60	MS63	MS65
1999	—	PF63 25.00	PF65 30.00			

KM# 71 2000 SHILLINGS

26.00 g., 0.999 Silver 0.8351 oz. ASW, 40.1 mm. **Series:** Olympics 2000 **Obv:** Crowned head right above national arms **Rev:** Hurdler **Edge:** Reeded

Date	Mintage	VF20	XF40	MS60	MS63	MS65
2000	—	PF63 20.00	PF65 25.00			

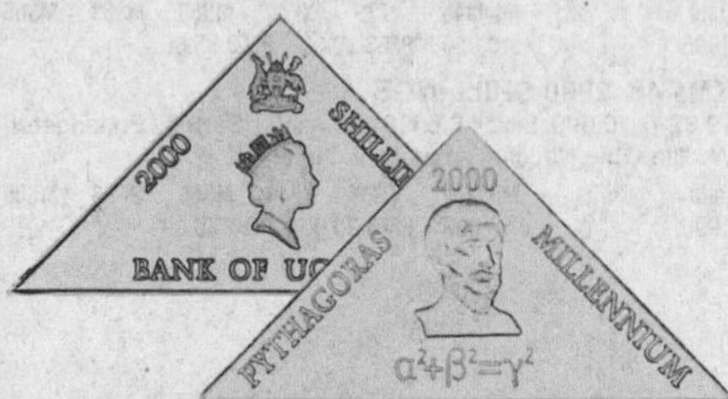

KM# 72 2000 SHILLINGS

15.75 g., 0.925 Silver 0.4684 oz. ASW, 45.2x23.2 mm. **Series:** Millennium **Obv:** National arms above crowned head right **Rev:** Pythagoras **Edge:** Plain **Shape:** Triangular

Date	Mintage	VF20	XF40	MS60	MS63	MS65
2000	10,000	PF65 40.00				

KM# 73 2000 SHILLINGS

25.00 g., 0.925 Silver 0.7435 oz. ASW, 37.9 mm. **Subject:** Wildlife protection **Obv:** National arms below crowned head right **Rev:** Three zebras drinking in reflective water **Edge:** Reeded

Date	Mintage	VF20	XF40	MS60	MS63	MS65
2000	—	PF63 25.00	PF65 30.00			

KM# 117 4000 SHILLINGS

1.53 g., 0.999 Gold 0.0491 oz. AGW, 16 mm. **Subject:** Famous Places **Obv:** Arms with supporters **Rev:** Matterhorn Mountain within circle **Edge:** Plain

Date	Mintage	VF20	XF40	MS60	MS63	MS65
ND-1997	—	PF63 85.00	PF65 100			

KM# 25 5000 SHILLINGS
33.93 g., 0.917 Gold 1.0003 oz. AGW **Subject:** Wildlife **Obv:** Bust of Dr. Milton Obote facing **Rev:** East African crowned crane

Date	Mintage	XF40	MS60	MS63	MS65	MS66
1981	100	—	—	1,600	1,700	1,800
1981	100	PF65 1,650	PF67 1,750	PF69 1,850		

KM# 32 5000 SHILLINGS
12.00 g., 0.999 Silver 0.3854 oz. ASW **Subject:** Soccer **Obv:** National arms **Rev:** Soccer ball and net

Date	Mintage	VF20	XF40	MS60	MS63	MS65
1992	Est. 10000	—	—	12.00	15.00	18.00

KM# 36 5000 SHILLINGS
500.00 g., 0.999 Silver 16.0593 oz. ASW **Series:** Endangered Wildlife **Obv:** African map **Rev:** 2 Leopards on branches

Date	Mintage	VF20	XF40	MS60	MS63	MS65
1993	2,500	PF65 320				

Note: Underweight coins exist

KM# 36.1 5000 SHILLINGS
10.48 g., 0.999 Silver 0.3366 oz. ASW, 38 mm. **Subject:** Reduced Size **Obv:** African map **Rev:** Two lions in tree **Edge:** Reeded

Date	Mintage	VF20	XF40	MS60	MS63	MS65
1993	—	PF63 15.00	PF65 18.00			

KM# 128 5000 SHILLINGS
28.20 g., Silver, 38 mm. **Subject:** FAO - Food for All **Obv:** National arms **Rev:** Bananas

Date	Mintage	VF20	XF40	MS60	MS63	MS65
1995	2,000	PF63 75.00	PF65 85.00			

KM# 33 10000 SHILLINGS
20.00 g., 0.999 Silver 0.6424 oz. ASW **Subject:** Soccer **Obv:** National arms **Rev:** Mount Rushmore behind soccer players

Date	Mintage	VF20	XF40	MS60	MS63	MS65
ND-1992	Est. 10000	PF63 25.00	PF65 30.00			

KM# 34 10000 SHILLINGS
20.00 g., 0.999 Silver 0.6424 oz. ASW **Subject:** Papal visit **Obv:** National arms **Rev:** Half-length figure facing

Date	Mintage	VF20	XF40	MS60	MS63	MS65
1993	—	PF63 20.00	PF65 25.00			

KM# 37.1 10000 SHILLINGS
12.94 g., 0.999 Silver 0.4157 oz. ASW, 38 mm. **Subject:** Reduced Size **Obv:** African map **Rev:** Two rhinos **Edge:** Reeded

Date	Mintage	VF20	XF40	MS60	MS63	MS65
1993	—	PF63 18.00	PF65 22.00			

KM# 37 10000 SHILLINGS
1000.00 g., 0.999 Silver 32.1186 oz. ASW **Series:** Endangered Wildlife **Obv:** African map **Rev:** Rhinoceros

Date	Mintage	VF20	XF40	MS60	MS63	MS65
1993	2,000	PF65 630				

Note: Underweight coins exist

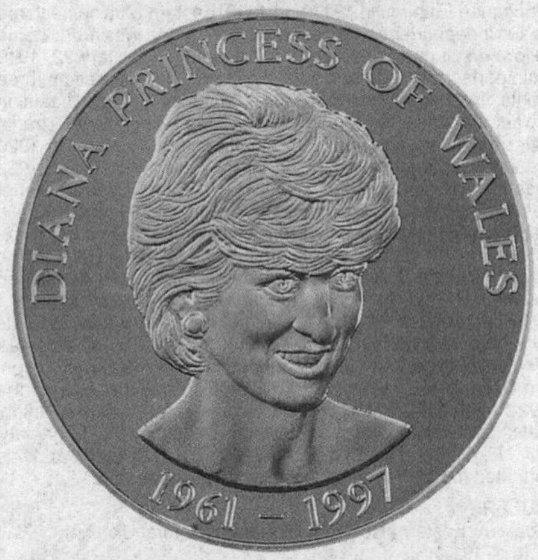

KM# 92 10000 SHILLINGS
155.50 g., 0.999 Silver 4.9944 oz. ASW, 65 mm. **Subject:** Diana Princess of Wales **Obv:** National arms **Rev:** Head 1/4 right **Edge:** Reeded **Note:** Illustration reduced.

Date	Mintage	VF20	XF40	MS60	MS63	MS65
1998	2,500	PF63 100	PF65 125			

PATTERNS

Including off metal strikes

KM#	Date	Mintage	Identification	Mkt Val
Pn1	1994	—	1000 Shillings. Copper-Nickel. Soccer player, 999.	—
Pn2	1994	—	1000 Shillings. Copper-Nickel. 3 soccer players, 999 CuNi.	—
Pn3	1994	—	1000 Shillings. Copper-Nickel. 4 soccer players, 999.	—
Pn4	1996	—	1000 Shillings. Bronze Gilt. Surinam. 100 Guilders.	—

PIEDFORT

KM#	Date	Mintage	Identification	Mkt Val
P1	1981	—	200 Shillings. 0.925. Silver. KM26.	100
P2	1981	505	2000 Shillings. 0.917. Gold. KM31.	1,650

TRIAL STRIKES

KM#	Date	Mintage	Identification	Mkt Val
TS1	1969	—	500 Shillings. Goldine. KM16.	100
TS2	1970	—	1000 Shillings. Goldine. National arms. KM17.	125

MINT SETS

KM#	Date	Mintage	Identification	Issue Price	Mkt Val
MS1	1987 (4)	—	KM27-30	10.50	7.50

PROOF SETS

KM#	Date	Mintage	Identification	Issue Price	Mkt Val
PS1	1966 (6)	8,250	KM1-6	7.75	12.50
PS2	1969 (10)	1,390	KM8-17	790	12,600
PS3	1969 (6)	6,070	KM8-13	78.50	200
PS4	1970 (10)	Inc. above	KM8-17, mintage included in KM-PS2	790	12,600
PS5	1970 (6)	Inc. above	KM8-13, mintage included in KM-PS3	78.50	200
PS6	1987 (4)	2,500	KM27-30	25.00	22.00

Ukraine (formerly the Ukrainian Soviet Socialist Republic) is bordered by Russia to the east, Russia and Belarus to the north, Poland, Slovakia and Hungary to the west, Romania and Moldova to the southwest and in the south by the Black Sea and the Sea of Azov. It has an area of 233,088 sq. mi. (603,700 sq. km.) and a population of 51.9 million. Capital: Kyiv (Kiev). Coal, grain, vegetables and heavy industrial machinery are major exports.

With the disintegration of the Russian and Austro-Hungarian Empires in 1917 and 1918. Eastern Ukraine declared its full independence on January 22,1918 and Western Ukraine followed suit on November 1 of that year. On January 22, 1919 both parts united into one state that had to defend itself on three fronts: from the "Red Bolsheviks"and their puppet Ukrainian Soviet Republic formed in Kharkiv, from the "White" czarist Russian forces, and from Poland. Ukraine lost the war. In 1920 Eastern Ukraine was occupied by the Bolsheviks and in 1922 was incorporated into the Soviet Union. There followed a brief resurgence of Ukrainian language and culture which Stalin suppressed in 1928. The artificial famine-genocide of 1932-33 killed 7-10 million Ukrainians, and Stalinist purges in the mid-1930s took a heavy toll. Western Ukraine was partitioned between Poland, Romania, Hungary and Czechoslovakia.

On August 24, 1991 Ukraine once again declared its independence. On December 1, 1991 over 90% of Ukraine's electorate approved full independence from the Soviet Union. On December 5, 1991 the Ukrainian Parliament abrogated the 1922 treaty which incorporated Ukraine into the Soviet Union. Later, Leonid Kravchuk was elected president by a 65% majority.

Ukraine is a charter member of the United Nations and has inherited the third largest nuclear arsenal in the world.

RULERS

Russian (Eastern, Northern, Southern, Central Ukraine), 1654-1917

Austrian (Western Ukraine),1774-1918

MINT

Without mm - Lugansk; Kiev (1997-1998)

MONETARY SYSTEM

(1) Kopiyka
(2) Kopiyky KOKH
(5 and up) Kopiyok KOIOK
100 Kopiyok = 1 Hrynia PBEH
100,000 Karbovanetsiv = 1 Hryni or Hryven)

REPUBLIC

STANDARD COINAGE

KM# 9 200000 KARBOVANTSIV

14.35 g., Copper-Nickel, 33 mm. **Obv:** National arms **Rev:** Bohdan Khmelnytsky Monument **Edge:** Reeded

Date	Mintage	XF40	MS60	MS63	MS65	MS66
1995 Prooflike	250,000	—	3.00	5.00	9.00	—

KM# 10.1 200000 KARBOVANTSIV

14.35 g., Copper-Nickel, 33 mm. **Subject:** 50th Anniversary - End of World War II **Rev:** Ukranian letter "Y" looks similar to "X" **Edge:** Reeded

Date	Mintage	XF40	MS60	MS63	MS65	MS66
1995 Prooflike	10,000	—	—	35.00	40.00	—

KM# 10.2 200000 KARBOVANTSIV

14.35 g., Copper-Nickel, 33 mm. **Subject:** 50th Anniversary - End of World War II **Rev:** Ukranian letter "Y" like "Y/2" in legends **Edge:** Reeded

Date	Mintage	XF40	MS60	MS63	MS65	MS66
1995 Prooflike	240,000	—	2.00	4.00	6.50	—

KM# 11 200000 KARBOVANTSIV

14.35 g., Copper-Nickel, 33 mm. **Subject:** World War II - Monument at Kerch **Obv:** National arms **Rev:** Monument and ship **Edge:** Reeded

Date	Mintage	XF40	MS60	MS63	MS65	MS66
1995 Prooflike	50,000	—	15.00	25.00	40.00	—

KM# 12 200000 KARBOVANTSIV

14.35 g., Copper-Nickel, 33 mm. **Subject:** World War II - Monument at Odessa **Obv:** National arms **Rev:** Monument divides ship and lighthouse **Edge:** Reeded

Date	Mintage	XF40	MS60	MS63	MS65	MS66
1995 Prooflike	75,000	—	5.00	9.00	17.00	—

KM# 13 200000 KARBOVANTSIV

14.35 g., Copper-Nickel, 33 mm. **Subject:** World War II - Monument at Kiev **Obv:** National arms **Rev:** Monument and city scene **Edge:** Reeded

Date	Mintage	XF40	MS60	MS63	MS65	MS66
1995 Prooflike	100,000	—	3.00	6.00	9.00	—

KM# 14 200000 KARBOVANTSIV

14.35 g., Copper-Nickel, 33 mm. **Subject:** World War II - Monument at Sevastopol **Obv:** National arms **Rev:** Monuments and ship **Edge:** Reeded

Date	Mintage	XF40	MS60	MS63	MS65	MS66
1995 Prooflike	75,000	—	3.00	6.00	9.00	—

KM# 15 200000 KARBOVANTSIV

28.28 g., Copper-Nickel, 38.61 mm. **Series:** 50th Anniversary - United Nations **Obv:** National arms **Rev:** Numeral 50 and emblem on top of assorted flag globe **Edge:** Reeded **Note:** Issued in March 1996

Date	Mintage	XF40	MS60	MS63	MS65	MS66
1995	100,000	—	5.00	9.00	17.00	—

KM# 17 200000 KARBOVANTSIV

14.35 g., Copper-Nickel, 33 mm. **Subject:** Lesya Ukrainka **Obv:** National arms **Rev:** Half-length Poetess facing **Edge:** Reeded

Date	Mintage	XF40	MS60	MS63	MS65	MS66
1996 Prooflike	100,000	—	3.00	6.00	9.00	—

KM# 21 200000 KARBOVANTSIV

14.35 g., Copper-Nickel, 33 mm. **Subject:** 10th Anniversary - Chernobyl Disaster **Obv:** National arms **Rev:** Bell with cross at top **Edge:** Reeded

Date	Mintage	XF40	MS60	MS63	MS65	MS66
1996 Prooflike	250,000	—	2.00	4.00	6.00	—

KM# 23 200000 KARBOVANTSIV

14.35 g., Copper-Nickel, 33 mm. **Series:** 1st Participation in Summer Olympics **Obv:** National arms **Rev:** Athletes around octagon **Edge:** Reeded

Date	Mintage	XF40	MS60	MS63	MS65	MS66
1996 Prooflike	100,000	—	3.00	5.00	7.00	—

KM# 24 200000 KARBOVANTSIV

14.35 g., Copper-Nickel, 33 mm. **Series:** Centennial of Modern Olympics **Obv:** National arms **Rev:** Flame and logo **Edge:** Reeded

Date	Mintage	XF40	MS60	MS63	MS65	MS66
1996 Prooflike	100,000	—	3.00	5.00	7.00	—

KM# 27 200000 KARBOVANTSIV

14.35 g., Copper-Nickel-Zinc, 33 mm. **Subject:** Mikhailo Hrushevsky - 1866-1934 **Obv:** National arms **Rev:** Half-length figure facing **Edge:** Reeded

Date	Mintage	XF40	MS60	MS63	MS65	MS66
1996 Prooflike	75,000	—	6.00	10.00	15.00	—

KM# 16 1000000 KARBOVANETS

16.81 g., 0.925 Silver 0.4999 oz. ASW, 33 mm. **Obv:** National arms **Rev:** Bohdan Khmelnytsky Monument **Edge:** Reeded

Date	Mintage	XF40	MS60	MS63	MS65	MS66
1996	10,000	PF65 120				

KM# 18 1000000 KARBOVANETS

16.81 g., 0.925 Silver 0.4999 oz. ASW, 33 mm. **Subject:** Lesya Ukrainka **Obv:** National arms **Rev:** Half-length Poetess facing **Edge:** Reeded

Date	Mintage	XF40	MS60	MS63	MS65	MS66
1996	10,000	PF65 95.00				

KM# 20 1000000 KARBOVANETS

16.81 g., 0.925 Silver 0.4999 oz. ASW, 33 mm. **Subject:** Hryhoriy Skovoroda **Obv:** National arms **Rev:** Bust facing **Edge:** Reeded

Date	Mintage	XF40	MS60	MS63	MS65	MS66
1996	10,000	PF65 75.00				

KM# 32 1000000 KARBOVANETS

16.81 g., 0.925 Silver 0.4999 oz. ASW, 33 mm. **Subject:** Mykhaylo Hrushevsky **Obv:** National arms **Rev:** Half-length figure facing **Edge:** Reeded

Date	Mintage	XF40	MS60	MS63	MS65	MS66
1996	10,000	PF65 65.00				

KM# 19 2000000 KARBOVANETS

33.63 g., 0.925 Silver 1.0001 oz. ASW, 33.63 mm. **Series:** 50 Years - United Nations **Obv:** National arms **Rev:** Numeral 50 and emblem on top of assorted flag globe **Edge:** Reeded **Note:** Minted in 1995, issued on March 7, 1996.

Date	Mintage	XF40	MS60	MS63	MS65	MS66
1996	10,000	PF65 35.00				

KM# 22 2000000 KARBOVANETS

33.63 g., 0.925 Silver 1.0001 oz. ASW, 33.63 mm. **Subject:** 10th Anniversary - Chernobyl Disaster **Obv:** National arms **Rev:** Bell with cross at top **Edge:** Reeded

Date	Mintage	XF40	MS60	MS63	MS65	MS66
1996	10,000	PF65 80.00				

KM# 25 2000000 KARBOVANETS

33.63 g., 0.925 Silver 1.0001 oz. ASW, 33.63 mm. **Series:** 1st Participation in Summer Olympics **Obv:** National arms **Rev:** Head right within octagon surrounded by athletes **Edge:** Reeded

Date	Mintage	XF40	MS60	MS63	MS65	MS66
1996	10,000	PF65 70.00				

KM# 26 2000000 KARBOVANETS

33.63 g., 0.925 Silver 1.0001 oz. ASW, 38.61 mm. **Series:** Centennial of Modern Olympics **Obv:** National arms **Rev:** Olympic flame and logo **Edge:** Reeded

Date	Mintage	XF40	MS60	MS63	MS65	MS66
1996	10,000	PF65 60.00				

KM# 33 2000000 KARBOVANETS

33.63 g., 0.925 Silver 1.0001 oz. ASW, 33.63 mm. **Subject:** Independence **Obv:** National arms **Rev:** Standing female figure holding sprig and wreath to left of flag and map **Edge:** Reeded

Date	Mintage	XF40	MS60	MS63	MS65	MS66
1996	10,000	PF65 200				

REFORM COINAGE

September 2, 1996

100,000 Karbovanets = 1 Hryvnia

100 Kopiyok = 1 Hryvnia

KM# 6 KOPIYKA

1.50 g., Stainless Steel, 16 mm. **Obv:** National arms **Rev:** Value within wreath **Edge:** Plain

Date	Mintage	XF40	MS60	MS63	MS65	MS66
1992	—	0.15	0.25	0.35	1.00	—
1994	—	2.00	3.00	5.00	8.00	—
1996	—	1.00	2.00	3.00	5.00	—
2000	—	0.25	0.35	0.75	1.25	—

KM# 4a 2 KOPIYKY

0.64 g., Aluminum, 17.3 mm. **Obv:** National arms **Rev:** Value within wreath **Edge:** Plain **Note:** Prev. KM#4.

Date	Mintage	XF40	MS60	MS63	MS65	MS66
1992	—	—	—	300	—	—
1993	—	0.30	0.50	1.00	1.50	—
1994	—	0.30	0.50	1.00	1.50	—
1996	—	1.00	2.00	3.00	—	—

KM# 7 5 KOPIYOK

4.30 g., Stainless Steel, 23.91 mm. **Obv:** National arms **Rev:** Value within wreath **Edge:** Reeded

Date	Mintage	XF40	MS60	MS63	MS65	MS66
1992	—	0.25	0.35	0.65	1.25	—
1994	—	—	—	100	—	—

KM# 1.1a 10 KOPIYOK

1.70 g., Brass, 16.3 mm. **Obv:** National arms **Rev:** Five dots right of final "K" in value **Edge:** Reeded **Note:** Fine or coarse reeded edge varieties exist. Prev. KM#1.1.

Date	Mintage	XF40	MS60	MS63	MS65	MS66
1992	—	0.50	1.00	1.50	2.25	—
1994	—	0.50	1.00	1.50	2.25	—
1996	—	0.60	1.25	1.75	2.50	—

KM# 1.2 10 KOPIYOK
1.70 g., Brass, 16.3 mm. **Obv:** National arms **Rev:** Six dots right of "K" **Edge:** Reeded

Date	Mintage	XF40	MS60	MS63	MS65	MS66
1992	—	0.50	1.00	1.50	2.25	—

KM# 2.1a 25 KOPIYOK
2.90 g., Brass, 20.8 mm. **Obv:** National arms **Rev:** Value within wreath, berries in wreath are solid **Edge:** Segmented reeding **Note:** Prev. KM#2.1.

Date	Mintage	XF40	MS60	MS63	MS65	MS66
1992	—	0.60	1.25	1.75	2.50	—
1994	—	0.60	1.25	1.75	2.50	—
1995	—	1.50	3.00	4.50	6.00	—
1996	—	0.80	1.75	2.25	4.00	—

KM# 2.2 25 KOPIYOK
2.90 g., Aluminum-Bronze, 20.8 mm. **Obv:** National arms **Rev:** Value within wreath, berries with center hole **Edge:** Segmented reeding

Date	Mintage	XF40	MS60	MS63	MS65	MS66
1992	—	0.60	1.25	1.75	2.50	—

KM# 3.1 50 KOPIYOK
4.20 g., Brass, 23 mm. **Obv:** National arms **Rev:** Five dots grouped in wreath to right of final letter "K" in value **Edge:** Reeded sections of 16 grooves each

Date	Mintage	XF40	MS60	MS63	MS65	MS66
1992	—	1.75	2.25	3.50	5.00	—
1994	—	1.75	2.25	3.50	5.00	—

KM# 3.2 50 KOPIYOK
4.20 g., Brass, 23 mm. **Obv:** National arms **Rev:** Four dots grouped in wreath to right of final letter "K" in value **Edge:** Reeded sections of 7 grooves each

Date	Mintage	XF40	MS60	MS63	MS65	MS66
1992	—	1.75	2.25	3.50	5.00	—

KM# 3.3a 50 KOPIYOK
4.20 g., Brass, 23 mm. **Obv:** National arms **Rev:** Five dots grouped in wreath to right of final letter "K" in value **Edge:** Segmented reeding **Note:** Prev. KM#3.3.

Date	Mintage	XF40	MS60	MS63	MS65	MS66
1992	—	1.75	2.25	3.50	5.00	—
1994	—	1.75	2.25	3.50	5.00	—
1995	—	5.00	7.00	10.00	12.00	—
1996	—	10.00	15.00	30.00	40.00	—

KM# 8a HRYVNIA
7.10 g., Brass, 26 mm. **Obv:** National arms **Rev:** Value, sprigs and designs **Edge:** Lettered **Note:** Prev. KM#8.

Date	Mintage	XF40	MS60	MS63	MS65	MS66
1992	—	35.00	75.00	125	200	—
1995	—	3.00	5.00	8.00	12.00	—
1996	—	2.50	3.50	4.50	6.50	—

KM# 28 2 HRYVNI
14.35 g., Copper-Nickel, 33 mm. **Subject:** 200th Anniversary - Sophiyivka Dendrological Park **Obv:** National arms **Rev:** Partially overgrown stone face **Edge:** Reeded

Date	Mintage	XF40	MS60	MS63	MS65	MS66
1996 Prooflike	30,000	—	—	—	45.00	50.00

KM# 29 2 HRYVNI
14.35 g., Copper-Nickel, 33 mm. **Subject:** Desiatynna Church **Obv:** National arms above Madonna and child, vines surround **Rev:** Church **Edge:** Reeded

Date	Mintage	XF40	MS60	MS63	MS65	MS66
1996 Prooflike	30,000	—	—	—	75.00	80.00

KM# 30 2 HRYVNI
Copper-Nickel-Zinc, 31 mm. **Subject:** Modern Ukrainian coinage **Obv:** National arms within beaded circle **Rev:** Assorted coins **Edge:** Reeded

Date	Mintage	XF40	MS60	MS63	MS65	MS66
1997 Prooflike	250,000	—	6.00	8.00	—	—

Note: 200,000 minted at Lugansk Mint in 1997 with an additional 50,000 struck at Kiev Mint in 1998

KM# 39 2 HRYVNI
14.35 g., Copper-Nickel, 33 mm. **Subject:** Yuri Kondratiuk **Obv:** National arms on astrological design **Rev:** Scientific drawing to right of bust facing **Edge:** Reeded

Date	Mintage	XF40	MS60	MS63	MS65	MS66
1997 Prooflike	20,000	—	—	—	90.00	100

KM# 40 2 HRYVNI
14.35 g., Copper-Nickel, 33 mm. **Subject:** 1st Anniversary of the Constitution **Obv:** National arms **Rev:** Scroll below design within beaded circle **Edge:** Reeded

Date	Mintage	XF40	MS60	MS63	MS65	MS66
1997 Prooflike	20,000	—	—	—	145	160

KM# 41 2 HRYVNI
14.35 g., Copper-Nickel, 33 mm. **Subject:** Solomiya Krushelnytska - 1872-1952 **Obv:** National arms within beaded circle **Rev:** Bust with hat left **Edge:** Reeded

Date	Mintage	XF40	MS60	MS63	MS65	MS66
1997 Prooflike	20,000	—	—	—	85.00	95.00

KM# 42 2 HRYVNI
12.80 g., Copper-Nickel-Zinc, 31 mm. **Subject:** 80 Years of Nationhood **Obv:** National arms and people above value **Rev:** Outreached arm with army on forearm to right of Cossacks **Edge:** Reeded

Date	Mintage	XF40	MS60	MS63	MS65	MS66
ND-1998	150,000	—	—	6.00	—	—
ND-1998 Prooflike	50,000	—	—	—	10.00	12.00

KM# 43 2 HRYVNI
12.80 g., Copper-Nickel-Zinc, 31 mm. **Subject:** Volodymyr Sosyura - 1898-1965 **Obv:** National arms within beaded circle **Rev:** Head facing 1/4 left **Edge:** Reeded

Date	Mintage	XF40	MS60	MS63	MS65	MS66
1998 Prooflike	20,000	—	—	—	55.00	65.00

KM# 47 2 HRYVNI
12.80 g., Copper-Nickel-Zinc, 31 mm. **Subject:** The 80th Anniversary of the Battle of Kruty **Obv:** National arms and family group **Rev:** Soldiers on guard **Edge:** Reeded

Date	Mintage	XF40	MS60	MS63	MS65	MS66
1998	150,000	—	—	6.00	—	—
1998 Prooflike	50,000	—	—	—	10.00	12.00

KM# 48 2 HRYVNI
12.80 g., Copper-Nickel-Zinc, 31 mm. **Subject:** European Bank of Reconstruction and Development **Obv:** National arms and value **Rev:** Legendary founders at Kiev monument, emblem of the ERRD **Edge:** Reeded

Date	Mintage	XF40	MS60	MS63	MS65	MS66
1998	10,000	—	—	—	245	275

KM# 49 2 HRYVNI
12.80 g., Copper-Nickel-Zinc, 31 mm. **Subject:** 100th Anniversary - Askania-Nova Wildlife Preserve **Obv:** National arms, value, wild animals and plants **Rev:** Standing half-length figure to lower left of animals running right **Edge:** Reeded

Date	Mintage	XF40	MS60	MS63	MS65	MS66
1998	90,000	—	—	20.00	—	—
1998 Prooflike	10,000	—	—	—	—	45.00

KM# 51 2 HRYVNI
12.80 g., Copper-Nickel-Zinc, 31 mm. **Subject:** 100th Anniversary - Kiev Polytechnical Institute **Obv:** National arms in circular design **Rev:** Building within circle **Edge:** Reeded

Date	Mintage	XF40	MS60	MS63	MS65	MS66
1998	40,000	—	—	30.00	—	—
1998 Prooflike	10,000	—	—	—	—	50.00

KM# 72 2 HRYVNI
12.80 g., Copper-Nickel-Zinc, 31 mm. **Subject:** 50 Years - United Nations Human Rights Declaration **Obv:** National arms and value **Rev:** Logo on globe within circle **Edge:** Reeded

Date	Mintage	XF40	MS60	MS63	MS65	MS66
1998	100,000	—	—	—	12.00	15.00

KM# 73 2 HRYVNI
12.80 g., Copper-Nickel-Zinc, 31 mm. **Subject:** Steppe Eagle **Obv:** National arms and date divide wreath, value in center **Rev:** Eagle in flight **Edge:** Reeded

Date	Mintage	XF40	MS60	MS63	MS65	MS66
1999	50,000	—	—	—	30.00	35.00

KM# 75 2 HRYVNI
12.80 g., Copper-Nickel-Zinc, 31 mm. **Subject:** 80th Anniversary - Ukranian State **Obv:** National arms divides date **Rev:** Seated woman in front of two shields **Edge:** Reeded

Date	Mintage	XF40	MS60	MS63	MS65	MS66
1999	50,000	—	—	—	8.00	10.00

KM# 76 2 HRYVNI
12.80 g., Copper-Nickel-Zinc, 31 mm. **Subject:** Panas Myrny, (P.Y. Rudchenko, 1849-1920), writer **Obv:** National arms within beaded circle **Rev:** Half length figure facing divides dates divides beaded circle **Edge:** Reeded

Date	Mintage	XF40	MS60	MS63	MS65	MS66
1999 Prooflike	50,000	—	—	—	8.00	10.00

KM# 78 2 HRYVNI
12.80 g., Copper-Nickel-Zinc, 31 mm. **Subject:** Anatoliy Solovianenko (opera singer) **Obv:** National arms within beaded circle **Rev:** Head left **Edge:** Reeded

Date	Mintage	XF40	MS60	MS63	MS65	MS66
1999 Prooflike	25,000	—	—	—	13.00	15.00

KM# 79 2 HRYVNI
12.80 g., Copper-Nickel-Zinc, 31 mm. **Subject:** 55th Annivesary - Freedom From Nazi Occupation **Obv:** National arms divides date at center of grain sprig wreath **Rev:** Stylized sword design **Edge:** Reeded

Date	Mintage	XF40	MS60	MS63	MS65	MS66
1999	50,000	—	—	—	18.00	20.00

KM# 81 2 HRYVNI
12.80 g., Copper-Nickel-Zinc, 31 mm. **Subject:** Platanthera Bifolia **Obv:** National arms and date divide wreath, value in center **Rev:** Flower **Edge:** Reeded

Date	Mintage	XF40	MS60	MS63	MS65	MS66
1999	50,000	—	—	—	22.00	25.00

KM# 82 2 HRYVNI
12.80 g., Copper-Nickel-Zinc, 31 mm. **Subject:** 100 Years - Ukraine's National Mining Academy **Obv:** National arms within beaded circle **Rev:** Building within circle **Edge:** Reeded

Date	Mintage	XF40	MS60	MS63	MS65	MS66
1999	20,000	—	—	—	32.00	35.00

KM# 83 2 HRYVNI
12.80 g., Copper-Nickel-Zinc, 31 mm. **Obv:** National arms and date divide wreath, value in center **Rev:** Mouse **Edge:** Reeded

Date	Mintage	XF40	MS60	MS63	MS65	MS66
1999	50,000	—	—	—	22.00	25.00

KM# 91 2 HRYVNI
12.80 g., Copper-Nickel-Zinc, 31 mm. **Subject:** 55th Annivesary - Victory in World War II **Obv:** National arms and ribbon divide wreath, value and date within **Rev:** Symbolic "Peace" figure **Edge:** Reeded

Date	Mintage	XF40	MS60	MS63	MS65	MS66
2000	50,000	—	—	—	10.00	12.00

KM# 92 2 HRYVNI
12.80 g., Copper-Nickel-Zinc, 31 mm. **Subject:** Archaeologist V. Hvoika **Obv:** National arms within circles and artifacts **Rev:** Head facing **Edge:** Reeded

Date	Mintage	XF40	MS60	MS63	MS65	MS66
2000	20,000	—	—	—	10.00	12.00

KM# 93 2 HRYVNI
12.80 g., Copper-Nickel-Zinc, 31 mm. **Series:** Sydney 2000 Olympics **Obv:** Horizontal stylized figures divides arms and value **Rev:** Stylized broad jumper **Edge:** Reeded

Date	Mintage	XF40	MS60	MS63	MS65	MS66
2000	50,000	—	—	—	10.00	12.00

KM# 94 2 HRYVNI

12.80 g., Copper-Nickel-Zinc, 31 mm. **Series:** Sydney 2000 Olympics **Obv:** Horizontal stylized figures divide arms and value **Rev:** Stylized gymnast on parallel bars **Edge:** Reeded

Date	Mintage	XF40	MS60	MS63	MS65	MS66
2000	50,000	—	—	—	10.00	12.00

KM# 96 2 HRYVNI

12.80 g., Copper-Nickel-Zinc, 31 mm. **Subject:** Musician Ivan Kozlovsky **Obv:** Head left **Rev:** Value within lyre, shield at top divides date, all within cluster of sprigs **Edge:** Reeded

Date	Mintage	XF40	MS60	MS63	MS65	MS66
2000	20,000	—	—	—	10.00	12.00

KM# 97 2 HRYVNI

12.80 g., Copper-Nickel-Zinc, 31 mm. **Series:** Sydney 2000 Olympics **Obv:** Horizontal stylized sports figures divide arms and value **Rev:** Stylized sailing scene **Edge:** Reeded

Date	Mintage	XF40	MS60	MS63	MS65	MS66
2000	50,000	—	—	—	10.00	12.00

KM# 98 2 HRYVNI

12.80 g., Copper-Nickel-Zinc, 31 mm. **Subject:** Oles' Honchar (writer) **Obv:** National arms, flowers and value **Rev:** Head facing to right of stylized buildings, dates below **Edge:** Reeded

Date	Mintage	XF40	MS60	MS63	MS65	MS66
2000	20,000	—	—	—	10.00	12.00

KM# 99 2 HRYVNI

12.80 g., Copper-Nickel-Zinc, 31 mm. **Obv:** Arms and date divide wreath, value within **Rev:** Crab **Edge:** Reeded

Date	Mintage	XF40	MS60	MS63	MS65	MS66
2000	50,000	—	—	—	25.00	28.00

KM# 100 2 HRYVNI

12.80 g., Copper-Nickel-Zinc, 31 mm. **Subject:** Chernivtsi National University, 125th Anniversary **Obv:** Arms divide circular designs **Rev:** University viewed through arch **Edge:** Reeded

Date	Mintage	XF40	MS60	MS63	MS65	MS66
2000	50,000	—	—	—	12.00	15.00

KM# 101 2 HRYVNI

12.80 g., Copper-Nickel-Zinc, 31 mm. **Series:** Sydney 2000 Olympics **Obv:** National arms, athletes and value **Rev:** Gymnast doing floor exercise **Edge:** Reeded

Date	Mintage	XF40	MS60	MS63	MS65	MS66
2000	50,000	—	—	—	12.00	15.00

KM# 110 2 HRYVNI

12.80 g., Copper-Nickel-Zinc, 31 mm. **Subject:** Kateryna Bilokour (People's Artist of Ukraine) **Obv:** Shield divides date above flowers and value **Rev:** Half-figure facing right **Edge:** Reeded

Date	Mintage	XF40	MS60	MS63	MS65	MS66
2000	30,000	—	—	—	32.00	35.00

KM# 66 5 HRYVEN

16.54 g., Copper-Nickel-Zinc, 35 mm. **Subject:** St. Michaels Cathedral **Obv:** Arms, value and date within beaded star **Rev:** Cathedral behind human silhouettes **Edge:** Reeded

Date	Mintage	XF40	MS60	MS63	MS65	MS66
1998	200,000	—	—	—	10.00	12.00

KM# 69 5 HRYVEN

16.54 g., Copper-Nickel-Zinc, 35 mm. **Subject:** Kiev-Pechersk Assumption Cathedral **Obv:** Shield, value and date within beaded star **Rev:** Cathedral behind carved ruins **Edge:** Reeded

Date	Mintage	XF40	MS60	MS63	MS65	MS66
1998	200,000	—	—	—	10.00	12.00

KM# 74 5 HRYVEN

16.54 g., Copper-Nickel-Zinc, 35 mm. **Subject:** 900th Anniversary - Novgorod-Siversky Principality **Obv:** Value in center of stylized sun with doves left and right **Rev:** Armored horsemen **Edge:** Reeded

Date	Mintage	XF40	MS60	MS63	MS65	MS66
1999	50,000	—	—	—	45.00	55.00

KM# 80 5 HRYVEN

16.54 g., Copper-Nickel-Zinc, 35 mm. **Subject:** 500th Anniversary - Kiev Magdeburg Law **Obv:** Arms above value and date in center of design **Rev:** Monument to the Law **Edge:** Reeded

Date	Mintage	XF40	MS60	MS63	MS65	MS66
1999	50,000	—	—	—	18.00	20.00

KM# 84 5 HRYVEN

16.54 g., Copper-Nickel-Zinc, 35 mm. **Subject:** Birth of Jesus **Obv:** National arms, value and angels **Rev:** Nativity scene **Edge:** Reeded

Date	Mintage	XF40	MS60	MS63	MS65	MS66
1999	100,000	—	—	—	13.00	15.00

KM# 95 5 HRYVEN

16.54 g., Copper-Nickel-Zinc, 35 mm. **Subject:** 2,500 Years - Bilgorod-Dnestrovski **Obv:** Arms above value and date within design **Rev:** Castle above city arms and ancient coins **Edge:** Reeded

Date	Mintage	XF40	MS60	MS63	MS65	MS66
2000	50,000	—	—	—	13.00	15.00

KM# 102 5 HRYVEN
16.54 g., Copper-Nickel-Zinc, 35 mm. **Subject:** Christening of Russ (Kyiv's Russ) **Obv:** National arms and angels **Rev:** Standing bearded figure facing and crowd **Edge:** Reeded

Date	Mintage	XF40	MS60	MS63	MS65	MS66
2000	100,000	—	—	—	13.00	15.00

KM# 103 5 HRYVEN
16.54 g., Copper-Nickel-Zinc, 35 mm. **Subject:** Centennial - Lviv's Opera House **Obv:** Vase divides seated figures below shield **Rev:** Opera house **Edge:** Reeded

Date	Mintage	XF40	MS60	MS63	MS65	MS66
2000	50,000	—	—	—	13.00	15.00

KM# 104 5 HRYVEN
9.40 g., Bi-Metallic Brass center in Copper-Nickel ring, 28 mm. **Subject:** Third Millennium **Obv:** National arms **Rev:** Figure sowing seeds within circle **Edge:** Reeded and plain sections

Date	Mintage	XF40	MS60	MS63	MS65	MS66
2000	50,000	—	—	—	23.00	25.00

KM# 105 5 HRYVEN
16.54 g., Copper-Nickel-Zinc, 35 mm. **Subject:** 2600th Anniversary - City of Kerch's **Obv:** National arms above value and bracelet **Rev:** Ancient coins above pillar **Edge:** Reeded

Date	Mintage	XF40	MS60	MS63	MS65	MS66
2000	50,000	—	—	—	23.00	25.00

KM# 34 10 HRYVEN
16.81 g., 0.925 Silver 0.4999 oz. ASW, 33 mm. **Subject:** Petro Mohyla, 1596-1647 **Obv:** National arms, people and building **Rev:** Bust1/4n right holding scepter **Edge:** Reeded

Date	Mintage	XF40	MS60	MS63	MS65	MS66
1996	5,000	PF67 850				

KM# 44 10 HRYVEN
33.62 g., 0.925 Silver 0.9999 oz. ASW, 38.61 mm. **Series:** Nagano Olympics **Obv:** National arms divide large snow flake designs **Rev:** Cross-country skier **Edge:** Reeded

Date	Mintage	XF40	MS60	MS63	MS65	MS66
1998	7,500	PF65 35.00	PF67 45.00			

KM# 45 10 HRYVEN
33.62 g., 0.925 Silver 0.9999 oz. ASW, 38.61 mm. **Series:** Nagano Olympics **Obv:** National arms divide larg snowflake designs **Rev:** Biathlon shooter **Edge:** Reeded

Date	Mintage	XF40	MS60	MS63	MS65	MS66
1998	7,500	PF65 35.00	PF67 45.00			

KM# 50 10 HRYVEN
33.62 g., 0.925 Silver 0.9999 oz. ASW, 38.61 mm. **Subject:** 100th Anniversary - Ascania National Park **Obv:** National arms within cluster of plants and animals above value **Rev:** Standing half length figure to lower left of animals running right **Edge:** Reeded

Date	Mintage	XF40	MS60	MS63	MS65	MS66
1998	10,000	PF65 70.00	PF67 80.00			

KM# 52 10 HRYVEN
33.62 g., 0.925 Silver 0.9999 oz. ASW, 38.61 mm. **Series:** Nagano Olympics **Obv:** National arms and value **Rev:** Figure skater **Edge:** Reeded

Date	Mintage	XF40	MS60	MS63	MS65	MS66
1998	7,500	PF65 35.00	PF67 45.00			

KM# 53 10 HRYVEN
33.62 g., 0.925 Silver 0.9999 oz. ASW, 38.61 mm. **Subject:** Prince Kiy - Founder of Kyiv or Kiev **Obv:** Value and arms within ornamental frame **Rev:** Head facing and armored equestrians **Edge:** Reeded

Date	Mintage	XF40	MS60	MS63	MS65	MS66
1998	10,000	PF65 65.00	PF67 75.00			

KM# 64 10 HRYVEN
33.62 g., 0.925 Silver 0.9999 oz. ASW, 38.61 mm. **Subject:** Prince Danylo of Halych **Obv:** National arms and value within ornamental frame **Rev:** Half-length bust holding sword, castle at left and army at right **Edge:** Reeded

Date	Mintage	XF40	MS60	MS63	MS65	MS66
1998	10,000	PF65 65.00	PF67 75.00			

KM# 67 10 HRYVEN
33.62 g., 0.925 Silver 0.9999 oz. ASW, 38.61 mm. **Subject:** St. Michael's Golden-Domed Cathedral **Obv:** Arms, value and date within ornamental frame **Rev:** Human silhouettes in front of cathedral **Edge:** Reeded

Date	Mintage	XF40	MS60	MS63	MS65	MS66
1998	10,000	PF65 80.00	PF67 90.00			

KM# 70 10 HRYVEN
33.62 g., 0.925 Silver 0.9999 oz. ASW, 38.61 mm. **Subject:** The Kyiv-Pechersk Assumption Cathedral **Obv:** Arms, value and date within beaded star **Rev:** Cathedral behind carved ruins **Edge:** Reeded

Date	Mintage	XF40	MS60	MS63	MS65	MS66
1998	10,000	PF65 80.00	PF67 90.00			

KM# 77 10 HRYVEN
33.62 g., 0.925 Silver 0.9999 oz. ASW, 38.61 mm. **Subject:** Dmytro Vyshnevetsky - BAYDA (Cossack leader) **Obv:** National arms with angel and crowned lion within beaded circle **Rev:** 3/4-length figure facing with bow and arrow **Edge:** Reeded

Date	Mintage	XF40	MS60	MS63	MS65	MS66
1999	10,000	PF65 65.00	PF67 75.00			

KM# 85 10 HRYVEN
33.90 g., 0.925 Silver 1.0082 oz. ASW, 38.6 mm. **Subject:** Birth of Jesus **Obv:** National arms, value and angels **Rev:** Nativity scene **Edge:** Reeded

Date	Mintage	XF40	MS60	MS63	MS65	MS66
1999	10,000	PF65 125	PF67 175			

KM# 86 10 HRYVEN
33.90 g., 0.925 Silver 1.0082 oz. ASW, 38.61 mm. **Subject:** Prince Askold **Obv:** Shield and value within Viking carvings **Rev:** Viking and ships **Edge:** Reeded

Date	Mintage	XF40	MS60	MS63	MS65	MS66
1999	10,000	PF65 70.00	PF67 80.00			

KM# 87 10 HRYVEN
33.62 g., 0.925 Silver 0.9998 oz. ASW, 38.61 mm. **Subject:** 500th Anniversary - Magdeburg Law **Obv:** National arms, value and date within design **Rev:** Monument **Edge:** Reeded

Date	Mintage	XF40	MS60	MS63	MS65	MS66
1999	5,000	PF65 70.00	PF67 80.00			

KM# 88 10 HRYVEN
33.62 g., 0.925 Silver 0.9998 oz. ASW, 38.61 mm. **Subject:** Petro Doroshenko (Cossack leader) **Obv:** National arms, angel and crowned lion within beaded circle **Rev:** Armored equestrian divides beaded circle **Edge:** Reeded

Date	Mintage	XF40	MS60	MS63	MS65	MS66
1999	10,000	PF65 70.00	PF67 80.00			

KM# 89 10 HRYVEN
33.62 g., 0.925 Silver 0.9998 oz. ASW, 38.6 mm. **Obv:** Arms and date divide wreath with bird, value within **Rev:** Dormouse **Edge:** Reeded

Date	Mintage	XF40	MS60	MS63	MS65	MS66
1999	5,000	PF65 90.00	PF67 100			

KM# 90 10 HRYVEN
33.62 g., 0.925 Silver 0.9998 oz. ASW, 38.61 mm. **Obv:** Arms and date divide wreath with bird, value within **Rev:** Eagle in flight **Edge:** Reeded

Date	Mintage	XF40	MS60	MS63	MS65	MS66
1999	—	PF65 150	PF67 200			

KM# 116 10 HRYVEN
33.62 g., 0.925 Silver 0.9999 oz. ASW, 38.61 mm. **Series:** Olympics **Obv:** National arms, value and Olympic motto **Rev:** Stylized broad jumper **Edge:** Reeded

Date	Mintage	XF40	MS60	MS63	MS65	MS66
1999	15,000	PF65 32.00	PF67 42.00			

KM# 117 10 HRYVEN
33.62 g., 0.925 Silver 0.9999 oz. ASW, 38.61 mm. **Series:** Olympics **Obv:** National arms, value and Olympic motto **Rev:** Stylized gymnast on parallel bars **Edge:** Reeded

Date	Mintage	XF40	MS60	MS63	MS65	MS66
1999	15,000	PF65 40.00	PF67 50.00			

KM# 118 10 HRYVEN
33.62 g., 0.925 Silver 0.9999 oz. ASW, 38.61 mm. **Subject:** Platanthera Bifolia **Obv:** Arms and date divide wreath, value within **Rev:** Flower **Edge:** Reeded

Date	Mintage	XF40	MS60	MS63	MS65	MS66
1999	5,000	PF65 100	PF67 125			

KM# 108 10 HRYVEN
33.62 g., 0.925 Silver 0.9999 oz. ASW, 38.61 mm. **Subject:** 55th Anniversary - End of WWII **Obv:** Arms and ribbon divide wreath, value and date within **Rev:** Standing figure holding palm branch above head in front of globe within 1/2 wreath **Edge:** Reeded

Date	Mintage	XF40	MS60	MS63	MS65	MS66
2000	3,000	PF65 450	PF67 500			

KM# 109 10 HRYVEN
33.62 g., 0.925 Silver 0.9999 oz. ASW, 38.61 mm. **Subject:** Conversion of the Russ to Christianity **Obv:** Arms and value divide angels **Rev:** Mass baptism scene **Edge:** Reeded

Date	Mintage	XF40	MS60	MS63	MS65	MS66
2000	10,000	PF65 65.00	PF67 75.00			

KM# 119 10 HRYVEN
33.62 g., 0.925 Silver 0.9999 oz. ASW, 38.61 mm. **Subject:** Princess Olga **Obv:** Arms, date and value within ornamental frame **Rev:** Princess and court scene **Edge:** Reeded

Date	Mintage	XF40	MS60	MS63	MS65	MS66
2000	10,000	PF65 90.00	PF67 100			

KM# 120 10 HRYVEN
33.62 g., 0.925 Silver 0.9999 oz. ASW, 38.61 mm. **Subject:** Petro Sahaidachny (Cossack leader) **Obv:** National arms, angel and crowned lion within beaded circle **Rev:** Cameo to upper right of ship within beaded circle **Edge:** Reeded

Date	Mintage	XF40	MS60	MS63	MS65	MS66
2000	10,000	PF65 65.00	PF67 75.00			

KM# 121 10 HRYVEN
33.62 g., 0.925 Silver 0.9999 oz. ASW, 38.61 mm. **Obv:** Arms and date divide wreath with bird, value within **Rev:** Freshwater crab **Edge:** Reeded

Date	Mintage	XF40	MS60	MS63	MS65	MS66
2000	5,000	PF65 125	PF67 175			

KM# 122 10 HRYVEN
33.62 g., 0.925 Silver 0.9999 oz. ASW, 38.61 mm. **Subject:** Prince Volodymyr the Great **Obv:** Arms divide ornamental frame, value within **Rev:** Crowned bust with raised hands

Date	Mintage	XF40	MS60	MS63	MS65	MS66
2000	5,000	PF65 400	PF67 450			

KM# 123 10 HRYVEN
33.62 g., 0.925 Silver 0.9999 oz. ASW, 38.61 mm. **Subject:** 100 Years of L'viv Opera and Ballet Theatre **Obv:** Vase divides seated figures below shield **Rev:** Opera House **Edge:** Reeded

Date	Mintage	XF40	MS60	MS63	MS65	MS66
2000	3,000	PF65 150	PF67 200			

KM# 35 20 HRYVEN
33.62 g., 0.925 Silver 0.9999 oz. ASW, 38.61 mm. **Subject:** The Tithe Church **Obv:** Madonna and child in center circle, vines surround **Rev:** Church **Edge:** Reeded

Date	Mintage	XF40	MS60	MS63	MS65	MS66
1996	5,000	PF65 650	PF67 750			

KM# 36 20 HRYVEN
33.62 g., 0.925 Silver 0.9999 oz. ASW, 38.61 mm. **Subject:** The Savior Cathedral in Chernihiv **Obv:** Arms above Madonna and child **Rev:** Cathedral **Edge:** Reeded

Date	Mintage	XF40	MS60	MS63	MS65	MS66
1997	5,000	PF65 450	PF67 550			

KM# 46 20 HRYVEN
33.62 g., 0.925 Silver 0.9999 oz. ASW, 38.61 mm. **Subject:** Severyn Nalyvaiko **Obv:** National arms **Rev:** Cossacks in revolt **Note:** Issued Jan. 10, 1998.

Date	Mintage	XF40	MS60	MS63	MS65	MS66
1997	5,000	PF65 200	PF67 300			

KM# 54 20 HRYVEN
33.62 g., 0.925 Silver 0.9999 oz. ASW, 38.61 mm. **Subject:** Cossack Mamay **Obv:** National arms supported by St. Michael and lion **Rev:** Cossack playing a bandre in center of assorted designs **Edge:** Reeded

Date	Mintage	XF40	MS60	MS63	MS65	MS66
1997	5,000	PF65 650	PF67 750			

KM# 57 20 HRYVEN
33.62 g., 0.925 Silver 0.9999 oz. ASW, 38.61 mm. **Subject:** 200th Anniversary - Kiev Commodity Futures Market **Obv:** National arms within center of scrolls **Rev:** Steepled building, sailboat and balance scale **Edge:** Reeded

Date	Mintage	XF40	MS60	MS63	MS65	MS66
1997	5,000	PF65 250	PF67 350			

KM# 58 20 HRYVEN
33.62 g., 0.925 Silver 0.9999 oz. ASW, 38.61 mm. **Subject:** 350th Anniversary - Cossack Revolt **Obv:** National arms supported by St. Michael and lion **Rev:** Cossacks attacking Polish cavalryman **Edge:** Reeded

Date	Mintage	XF40	MS60	MS63	MS65	MS66
1998	10,000	PF65 55.00	PF67 65.00			

KM# 126 20 HRYVEN
Bi-Metallic Gold center in silver ring, 31 mm. **Subject:** Paleolithic Age **Obv:** Eagle on captains wheel **Rev:** Pottery and petroglyphs **Edge:** Reeded and plain sections

Date	Mintage	XF40	MS60	MS63	MS65	MS66
2000	3,000	PF67 550				

KM# 127 20 HRYVEN
Bi-Metallic Gold center in silver ring **Subject:** Trypolean Culture **Obv:** Eagle on captains wheel **Rev:** Ancient sculptures **Edge:** Reeded and plain alternating

Date	Mintage	XF40	MS60	MS63	MS65	MS66
2000	3,000	PF67 550				

KM# 128 20 HRYVEN
Bi-Metallic Gold center in silver ring **Subject:** The Olbian City State **Obv:** Eagle on captains wheel **Rev:** Ancient coin in center circle of Greek figures

Date	Mintage	XF40	MS60	MS63	MS65	MS66
2000	3,000	PF67 550				

KM# 59 50 HRYVEN
3.11 g., 0.9999 Gold 0.100 oz. AGW, 16 mm. **Subject:** St. Sophia Cathedral in Kiev **Obv:** Cathedral **Rev:** Mother of God Mossaic **Edge:** Segmented reeding **Note:** Minted in 1996, issued on July 28, 1997.

Date	Mintage	XF40	MS60	MS63	MS65	MS66
1996	2,000	—	—	—	—	4,000

KM# 124 50 HRYVEN
17.63 g., 0.900 Gold 0.5101 oz. AGW, 25 mm. **Subject:** Birth of Jesus **Obv:** Two angels, arms and value **Rev:** Nativity scene **Edge:** Plain

Date	Mintage	XF40	MS60	MS63	MS65	MS66
1999	3,000	PF67 4,000				

KM# 125 50 HRYVEN
17.63 g., 0.900 Gold 0.5101 oz. AGW, 25 mm. **Subject:** Conversion of the Russ to Christianity **Obv:** National arms, angels and value **Rev:** Baptism scene **Edge:** Plain

Date	Mintage	XF40	MS60	MS63	MS65	MS66
2000	3,000	PF67 2,500				

KM# 63 100 HRYVEN
17.28 g., 0.900 Gold 0.500 oz. AGW, 25 mm. **Subject:** Kyiv Psalm book **Obv:** Open book divides shield and value **Rev:** Monk writing book **Edge:** Plain **Note:** Minted in 1997, issued in January 1998.

Date	Mintage	XF40	MS60	MS63	MS65	MS66
1997	2,000	PF67 4,700				

KM# 65 100 HRYVEN
17.28 g., 0.900 Gold 0.500 oz. AGW **Subject:** Poem "Eneida" by Ivan P. Kotlyarevsky **Obv:** Helmet and musical instruments divide shield and value **Rev:** Seated helmeted figure playing a bandre

Date	Mintage	XF40	MS60	MS63	MS65	MS66
1998	2,000	PF67 4,700				

KM# 68 100 HRYVEN
17.28 g., 0.900 Gold 0.500 oz. AGW, 25 mm. **Subject:** St. Michael's Cathedral **Obv:** Arms, value and date in center of design **Rev:** Cathedral behind human silhouettes **Edge:** Plain

Date	Mintage	XF40	MS60	MS63	MS65	MS66
1998	3,000	PF67 3,500				

KM# 71 100 HRYVEN
17.28 g., 0.900 Gold 0.500 oz. AGW, 25 mm. **Subject:** Kyiv-Pechersk Assumption Cathedral **Obv:** Arms, value and date within beaded star **Rev:** Cathedral behind carved ruins **Edge:** Plain

Date	Mintage	XF40	MS60	MS63	MS65	MS66
1998	3,000	PF65 1,550				

KM# 60 125 HRYVEN
7.78 g., 0.9999 Gold 0.250 oz. AGW, 20 mm. **Obv:** St. Sophia Cathedral in Kiev **Rev:** Ornate Mosaic of the Mother of God - "Oranta" **Edge:** Segmented reeding **Note:** Minted in 1996, issued on July 28, 1997.

Date	Mintage	XF40	MS60	MS63	MS65	MS66
1996	4,000	—	—	—	—	1,200

KM# 37 200 HRYVEN
17.50 g., 0.900 Gold 0.5064 oz. AGW, 25 mm. **Obv:** National arms within beaded circle **Rev:** Bust of Taras G. Shevchenko facing **Edge:** Plain **Note:** Minted in 1996, issued on March 12, 1997.

Date	Mintage	XF40	MS60	MS63	MS65	MS66
1996	10,000	PF65 675	PF67 800			

KM# 38 200 HRYVEN
17.50 g., 0.900 Gold 0.5064 oz. AGW, 25 mm. **Subject:** Pecherska Lavra **Obv:** Church above date and value within beaded circle **Rev:** Standing angelic figure with radiant dove within cloud-like wings **Edge:** Plain **Note:** Minted in 1996, issued on April 10, 1997.

Date	Mintage	XF40	MS60	MS63	MS65	MS66
1996	20,000	PF65 750	PF67 950			

KM# 61 250 HRYVEN
15.55 g., 0.9999 Gold 0.500 oz. AGW, 25 mm. **Obv:** St. Sophia Cathedral in Kiev **Rev:** St. Sophia **Edge:** Segmented reeding **Note:** Minted in 1996, issued on July 28, 1997.

Date	Mintage	XF40	MS60	MS63	MS65	MS66
1996	3,000	—	—	—	—	3,000

KM# 62 500 HRYVEN
31.10 g., 0.9999 Gold 0.9999 oz. AGW, 32 mm. **Obv:** St. Sophia Cathedral in Kiev **Rev:** St. Sophia **Edge:** Segmented reeding **Note:** Minted in 1996, issued on July 28, 1997.

Date	Mintage	XF40	MS60	MS63	MS65	MS66
1996	1,000	—	—	—	—	14,000

PATTERNS

Including off metal strikes

KM#	Date	Mintage	Identification	Mkt Val
PnA1	1992	—	Hryvnia. Brass. 26mm. KM#8a.	80.00
Pn1	1992	—	Kopiyka. Aluminum.	—
Pn2	1992	—	2 Kopiyky. Aluminum.	—
Pn3	1992	—	5 Kopiyok. White Brass.	—
Pn4	1992	—	10 Kopiyok. Brass. Incuse shield.	200
Pn5	1992	—	15 Kopiyok. Brass.	120
Pn6	1992	—	15 Kopiyok. Bronze.	120
Pn7	1992	—	25 Kopiyok. Brass. Incuse shield.	90.00
Pn8	1992	—	50 Kopiyok. Copper-Nickel.	—
Pn9	1992	—	50 Kopiyok. Brass. Incuse shield.	80.00
Pn10	1992	—	50 Kopiyok. Brass Clad Steel.	—
Pn11	1993	—	2 Kopiyky. Brass.	—
Pn12	1993	—	2 Kopiyky. Aluminum-Zinc.	—
Pn13	1993	—	15 Kopiyok. Aluminum.	120
Pn14	1994	—	Kopiyka. 0.600. Silver. Specific gravity: 9.8.	—
Pn15	1994	—	2 Kopiyky. Bronze. Piefort.	—
Pn16	1996	—	Kopiyka. 0.350. Silver. Specific gravity: 9.43.	—
Pn17	1996	—	25 Kopiyok. Aluminum.	—
Pn18	1998	—	100 Hryven. Brass.	—
Pn19	ND-1998	—	100 Hryven. Brass.	—
Pn20	1998	—	100 Hryven. Brass.	—
Pn21	ND-1998	—	100 Hryven. Brass.	—
Pn22	1998	—	100 Hryven. Brass.	—
Pn23	ND-1998	—	100 Hryven. Brass.	—

MINT SETS

KM#	Date	Mintage	Identification	Issue Price	Mkt Val
MS1	1996 (8)	—	KM#1, 2, 3.3, 4, 6, 7, 8, 30	—	200

UMM AL QAIWAIN - U.A.E.

This emirate, one of the original members of the United Arab Emirates, is the second smallest, least developed and lowest in population. The area is 300 sq. mi. (800 sq. km.) and the population is 5,000. The first recognition by the West was in 1820. Most of the emirate is uninhabited desert. Native boat building is an important activity.

TITLES

ام القيوين

Umm al Qaiwain

RULERS

Ahmad Bin Abdullah al-Mualla, 1872-1904
Rashid Bin Ahmad al-Mualla, 1904-1929
Ahmad Bin Rashid al-Mualla, 1929-1981
Rashid Bin Ahmad al-Mualla, 1981-

EMIRATE

NON-CIRCULATING LEGAL TENDER COINAGE

KM# 1 RIYAL
3.00 g., 1.000 Silver 0.0965 oz. ASW **Ruler:** Ahmad bin Rashid al-Mualla **Obv:** Dates within crossed flags, sprigs within circle **Rev:** Old cannon within wreath

Date	Mintage	XF40	MS60	MS63	MS65	MS66
AH1389	2,050	PF65 45.00		PF67 60.00	PF69 75.00	

KM# 2 2 RIYALS
6.00 g., 1.000 Silver 0.1929 oz. ASW **Ruler:** Ahmad bin Rashid al-Mualla **Obv:** Dates within crossed flags, sprigs at left and right within circle **Rev:** Fort of the 19th Century

Date	Mintage	XF40	MS60	MS63	MS65	MS66
AH1389	2,050	PF65 85.00		PF67 110	PF69 150	

KM# 3 5 RIYALS
15.00 g., 1.000 Silver 0.4823 oz. ASW **Ruler:** Ahmad bin Rashid al-Mualla **Obv:** Dates within crossed flags, sprigs at left and right within circle **Rev:** Two gazelles

Date	Mintage	XF40	MS60	MS63	MS65	MS66
AH1389	2,100	PF65 275		PF67 350	PF69 450	

KM# 4 10 RIYALS
30.00 g., 1.000 Silver 0.9645 oz. ASW, 45 mm. **Ruler:** Ahmad bin Rashid al-Mualla **Obv:** Dates within crossed flags, sprigs at left and right within circle **Rev:** Facade of the great Rock Temple

Date	Mintage	XF40	MS60	MS63	MS65	MS66
AH1389	2,000	PF65 450		PF67 600	PF69 750	

KM# 6 25 RIYALS
5.18 g., 0.900 Gold 0.1499 oz. AGW **Ruler:** Ahmad bin Rashid al-Mualla **Obv:** Dates within crossed flags, sprigs at left and right within circle **Rev:** Old cannon within wreath

Date	Mintage	XF40	MS60	MS63	MS65	MS66
AH1389	500	PF65 375		PF67 650	PF69 950	

KM# 7 50 RIYALS
10.36 g., 0.900 Gold 0.2998 oz. AGW **Ruler:** Ahmad bin Rashid al-Mualla **Obv:** Dates within crossed flags, sprigs at left and right within circle **Rev:** Fort of the 19th Century

Date	Mintage	XF40	MS60	MS63	MS65	MS66
AH1389	420	PF65 750		PF67 1,000	PF69 1,400	

KM# 8 100 RIYALS
20.73 g., 0.900 Gold 0.5998 oz. AGW **Ruler:** Ahmad bin Rashid al-Mualla **Obv:** Dates within crossed flags, sprigs at left and right within circle **Rev:** Gazelles

Date	Mintage	XF40	MS60	MS63	MS65	MS66
AH1389	300	PF65 1,250		PF67 2,150	PF69 2,800	

KM# 9 200 RIYALS
41.46 g., 0.900 Gold 1.1997 oz. AGW **Ruler:** Ahmad bin Rashid al-Mualla **Obv:** Dates within crossed flags, sprigs at left and right within circle **Rev:** Head of Sheik Ahmed Ben Rashid as Moalia left

Date	Mintage	XF40	MS60	MS63	MS65	MS66
AH1389	230	PF65 2,250		PF67 3,850	PF69 4,500	

PROOF SETS

KM#	Date	Mintage	Identification	Issue Price	Mkt Val
PS1	1970 (4)	2,000	KM#1-4	26.30	1,275
PS2	1970 (4)	230	KM#6-9	—	8,750
PS3	1970 (8)	—	KM#1-4, 6-9	—	11,000

The seven United Arab Emirates (formerly known as the Trucial Sheikhdoms or States), located along the southern shore of the Persian Gulf, are comprised of the Sheikhdoms of Abu Dhabi, Dubai, al-Sharjah, Ajman, Umm al Qaiwain, Ras al-Khaimah and al-Fujairah. They have a combined area of about 32,000 sq. mi. (83,600 sq. km.) and a population of *2.1 million. Capital: Abu Zaby (Abu Dhabi). Since the oil strikes of 1958-60, the economy has centered about petroleum.

The Trucial States came under direct British influence in1892 when the Maritime Truce Treaty enacted after the supression of pirate activity along the Trucial Coast was enlarged to enjoin the states from disposing of any territory, or entering into any foreign agreements, without British consent in return for British protection from external aggression. In March of 1971 Britain reaffirmed its decision to terminate its treaty relationships with the Trucial Sheikhdoms, whereupon the seven states joined with Bahrain and Qatar in an effort to form a union of Arab Emirates under British protection. When the prospective members failed to agree on terms of union, Bahrain and Qatar declared their respective independence, Aug. and Sept. of 1971. Six of the sheikhdoms united to form the United Arab Emirates on Dec. 2, 1971.Ras al-Khaimah joined a few weeks later.

TITLES

الامارات العربية المتحدة

al-Imara(t) al-Arabiya(t) al-Muttahida(t)

MONETARY SYSTEM

 فلس 

Falus, Fulus — Fals, Fils — Falsan

100 Fils = 1 Dirham

UNITED EMIRATES

STANDARD COINAGE

KM# 1 FILS
1.50 g., Bronze, 15 mm. **Series:** F.A.O. **Obv:** Value **Rev:** Date palms above dates **Edge:** Plain

Date	Mintage	VF20	XF40	MS60	MS63	MS65
AH1393-1973	4,000,000	—	0.50	0.75	1.50	2.00
AH1395-1975	—	—	0.50	0.75	1.50	2.00
AH1408-1988	—	—	0.50	0.75	1.50	2.00
AH1409-1989	—	—	0.50	0.75	1.50	2.00
AH1418-1997	—	—	0.40	0.60	1.00	2.00

KM# 2.1 5 FILS
3.75 g., Bronze, 22 mm. **Series:** F.A.O. **Obv:** Value **Rev:** Fish above dates **Edge:** Plain

Date	Mintage	VF20	XF40	MS60	MS63	MS65
AH1393-1973	11,400,000	0.25	1.00	0.75	1.50	1.75
AH1402-1982	—	0.25	0.45	0.65	1.25	1.50
AH1407-1987	—	0.25	0.45	0.65	1.25	1.50
AH1408-1988	—	0.20	0.30	0.50	0.80	1.50
AH1409-1989	—	0.20	0.30	0.40	0.60	1.50

KM# 2.2 5 FILS
Bronze **Series:** F.A.O. **Obv:** Value **Rev:** Fish above dates **Note:** Reduced size.

Date	Mintage	VF20	XF40	MS60	MS63	MS65
AH1416-1996	—	0.20	0.25	0.35	0.50	1.50
AH1417-1997	—	0.10	0.25	0.35	0.50	1.50

KM# 3.1 10 FILS

7.50 g., Bronze, 27 mm. **Obv:** Value **Rev:** Arab dhow above dates

Date	Mintage	VF20	XF40	MS60	MS63	MS65
AH1393-1973	6,400,000	0.40	0.60	1.00	2.00	2.50
AH1402-1982	—	0.40	0.60	1.00	2.00	2.50
AH1404-1984	—	0.40	0.60	1.00	2.00	2.50
AH1407-1987	—	0.25	0.45	0.60	1.00	1.50
AH1408-1988	—	0.25	0.45	0.60	1.00	1.50
AH1409-1989	—	0.25	0.45	0.60	1.00	1.50

KM# 3.2 10 FILS

Bronze, 19 mm. **Obv:** Value **Rev:** Arab dhow above dates **Note:** Reduced size.

Date	Mintage	VF20	XF40	MS60	MS63	MS65
AH1416-1996	—	0.30	0.50	0.70	1.25	1.75

KM# 4 25 FILS

3.50 g., Copper-Nickel, 20 mm. **Obv:** Value **Rev:** Gazelle above dates **Edge:** Reeded

Date	Mintage	VF20	XF40	MS60	MS63	MS65
AH1393-1973	10,400,000	0.30	0.70	1.00	1.50	2.00
AH1402-1982	—	0.30	0.70	1.00	1.50	2.00
AH1403-1983	—	0.30	0.70	1.00	1.50	2.00
AH1404-1984	—	0.30	0.70	1.00	1.50	2.00
AH1406-1986	—	0.30	0.70	1.00	1.50	2.00
AH1407-1987	—	0.20	0.40	0.60	1.00	2.00
AH1408-1988	—	0.20	0.40	0.60	1.00	2.00
AH1409-1989	—	0.20	0.40	0.60	1.00	2.00
AH1410-1990	—	0.20	0.40	0.60	1.00	2.00
AH1415-1995	—	0.20	0.40	0.60	1.00	2.00
AH1416-1996	—	0.20	0.40	0.60	1.00	1.50
AH1419-1998	—	0.20	0.40	0.60	1.00	1.50

KM# 5 50 FILS

6.25 g., Copper-Nickel, 24.8 mm. **Obv:** Value **Rev:** Oil derricks above dates **Edge:** Reeded

Date	Mintage	VF20	XF40	MS60	MS63	MS65
AH1393-1973	8,400,000	0.60	1.00	1.50	2.50	3.00
AH1402-1982	—	0.60	0.80	1.25	2.00	3.00
AH1404-1984	—	0.60	0.80	1.25	2.00	3.00
AH1407-1987	—	0.50	0.80	1.25	2.00	3.00
AH1408-1988	—	0.50	0.80	1.25	2.00	3.00
Note: Coarser edge reeding						
AH1409-1989	—	0.60	0.80	1.25	2.00	3.00

KM# 16 50 FILS

4.30 g., Copper-Nickel, 21 mm. **Obv:** Value **Rev:** Oil derricks above dates **Shape:** 7-sided **Note:** Reduced size.

Date	Mintage	VF20	XF40	MS60	MS63	MS65
AH1415-1995	—	—	0.70	1.25	2.00	2.50
AH1419-1998	—	—	0.70	1.25	2.00	2.50

KM# 6.1 DIRHAM

11.30 g., Copper-Nickel, 28.5 mm. **Obv:** Value **Rev:** Jug above dates **Edge:** Reeded

Date	Mintage	VF20	XF40	MS60	MS63	MS65
AH1393-1973	13,000,000	1.00	1.50	2.50	3.50	4.50
AH1402-1982	—	1.00	1.50	2.00	3.00	4.00
AH1404-1984	—	1.00	1.50	2.00	3.00	4.00
AH1406-1986	—	1.00	1.50	2.00	3.00	4.00
AH1407-1987	—	1.00	1.50	2.00	3.00	4.00
AH1408-1988	—	0.50	0.80	1.50	2.50	4.00
AH1409-1989	—	0.50	0.80	1.50	2.50	4.00

KM# 6.2 DIRHAM

6.40 g., Copper-Nickel, 24 mm. **Obv:** Value **Rev:** Jug above dates **Edge:** Reeded **Note:** Reduced size.

Date	Mintage	VF20	XF40	MS60	MS63	MS65
AH1415-1995	—	0.35	0.65	1.25	2.50	4.50
AH1419-1998	—	0.35	0.65	1.25	2.50	4.00

KM# 10 DIRHAM

11.31 g., Copper-Nickel, 28.5 mm. **Subject:** 27th Chess Olympiad in Dubai **Obv:** Value **Rev:** Chess pieces and olympic rings

Date	Mintage	VF20	XF40	MS60	MS63	MS65
ND-1986	200,000	2.00	5.00	10.00	12.00	15.00

KM# 11 DIRHAM

Copper-Nickel, 28.5 mm. **Subject:** 25th Anniversary - Offshore Oil Drilling **Obv:** Value **Rev:** Offshore oil drilling rig

Date	Mintage	VF20	XF40	MS60	MS63	MS65
ND-1987	300,000	2.50	5.00	10.00	12.00	15.00

KM# 14 DIRHAM

11.31 g., Copper-Nickel, 28.5 mm. **Subject:** 10th Anniversary - al-Ain University **Obv:** Value **Rev:** Emblem above map and book within radiant design

Date	Mintage	VF20	XF40	MS60	MS63	MS65
ND-1987	200,000	3.00	5.00	9.00	11.00	13.00

KM# 15 DIRHAM

11.31 g., Copper-Nickel, 28.5 mm. **Subject:** U.A.E. Soccer Team - Qualification for WC - 1990 **Obv:** Value **Rev:** Stylized winged soccer player

Date	Mintage	VF20	XF40	MS60	MS63	MS65
ND-1991	250,000	2.50	3.50	6.00	10.00	12.00

KM# 32 DIRHAM

6.50 g., Copper-Nickel, 24 mm. **Subject:** Bank of Dubai 35th Anniversary **Obv:** Value **Rev:** Towered bank building divides dates

Date	Mintage	VF20	XF40	MS60	MS63	MS65
ND-1998	500,000	—	1.00	2.00	4.00	6.00

KM# 35 DIRHAM

6.40 g., Copper-Nickel, 24 mm. **Subject:** 10th Anniversary - College of Technology **Obv:** Value **Rev:** Bird viewed through window frame

Date	Mintage	VF20	XF40	MS60	MS63	MS65
ND-1998	250,000	—	1.00	2.00	4.00	6.00

KM# 38 DIRHAM

6.40 g., Copper-Nickel, 24 mm. **Subject:** 15th Anniversary - Rashid bin Humaid Award for Culture **Obv:** Value **Rev:** Logo within circle

Date	Mintage	VF20	XF40	MS60	MS63	MS65
ND-1998	250,000	—	1.00	2.50	5.00	7.00

KM# 39 DIRHAM

6.40 g., Copper-Nickel, 24 mm. **Subject:** Sharjah Cultural City **Obv:** Value **Rev:** Stylized flame within beaded circle

Date	Mintage	VF20	XF40	MS60	MS63	MS65
ND-1998	200,000	—	1.00	2.50	5.00	7.00

KM# 40 DIRHAM

6.40 g., Copper-Nickel, 24 mm. **Subject:** 25 Years - Oil Production on Abu Al Bukhoosh Oil Field **Obv:** Value **Rev:** Offshore oil drilling rig **Edge:** Reeded

Date	Mintage	VF20	XF40	MS60	MS63	MS65
ND-1999	200,000	—	1.00	2.50	5.50	7.50

KM# 41 DIRHAM
6.40 g., Copper-Nickel, 24 mm. **Subject:** Islamic Personality of 1999 - Sheikh Zayed **Obv:** Value **Rev:** Square design

Date	Mintage	VF20	XF40	MS60	MS63	MS65
ND-1999	500,000	—	1.00	2.00	4.00	6.00

KM# 43 DIRHAM
6.40 g., Copper-Nickel, 24 mm. **Subject:** 25th Anniversary - Dubai Islamic Bank **Obv:** Value **Rev:** Bank name within circle

Date	Mintage	VF20	XF40	MS60	MS63	MS65
ND-1999	250,000	—	1.00	2.00	4.00	6.00

KM# 46 DIRHAM
6.40 g., Copper-Nickel, 24 mm. **Subject:** 25th Anniversary - General Women's Union (1975-2000) **Obv:** Value **Rev:** Stylized gazelle

Date	Mintage	VF20	XF40	MS60	MS63	MS65
ND-2000	500,000	—	1.00	2.00	4.00	6.00

KM# 9 5 DIRHAMS
14.25 g., Copper-Nickel **Subject:** 1500th Anniversary - al-Hegira **Obv:** Value flanked by dates **Rev:** Perched eagle **Shape:** 15-sided

Date	Mintage	VF20	XF40	MS60	MS63	MS65
AH1401-1981	2,000,000	3.00	5.00	12.00	20.00	25.00

KM# 33 25 DIRHAMS
20.00 g., 0.925 Silver 0.5948 oz. ASW **Subject:** Dubai National Bank - 35 Years **Obv:** Value **Rev:** Towered bank building divides dates

Date	Mintage	VF20	XF40	MS60	MS63	MS65
ND-1998	5,000	PF65 75.00				

KM# 55 25 DIRHAMS
20.00 g., 0.925 Silver 0.5948 oz. ASW **Subject:** 25th Anniversary - Al Bukhoosh Oil Field's Production

Date	Mintage	VF20	XF40	MS60	MS63	MS65
ND-1999	2,000	PF65 400				

KM# 44 25 DIRHAMS
20.00 g., 0.925 Silver 0.5948 oz. ASW, 27.9 mm. **Subject:** 25th Anniversary - Dubai Islamic Bank **Obv:** Value **Rev:** Bank name within circle **Edge:** Reeded

Date	Mintage	VF20	XF40	MS60	MS63	MS65
ND-2000	1,000	PF65 400				

KM# 7 50 DIRHAMS
27.22 g., 0.925 Silver 0.8095 oz. ASW **Subject:** IYC and UNICEF **Obv:** Value **Rev:** Conjoined standing figures, emblems at sides

Date	Mintage	VF20	XF40	MS60	MS63	MS65
AH1400-1980	8,031	PF63 35.00	PF65 50.00	PF67 100		

KM# 17 50 DIRHAMS
40.00 g., 0.925 Silver 1.1896 oz. ASW, 40 mm. **Subject:** Death of Shaikh Rashid Bin Saeed Al-Maktoum **Obv:** Bust facing **Rev:** International Trade Center **Edge:** Reeded

Date	Mintage	VF20	XF40	MS60	MS63	MS65
1990	4,000	PF65 350				

KM# 18 50 DIRHAMS
40.00 g., 0.925 Silver 1.1896 oz. ASW, 40 mm. **Subject:** 10th Anniversary - UAE Central Bank **Obv:** Bust of Shaikh Zayed Bin Sultan Al-Nahyan right **Rev:** Bank **Edge:** Reeded

Date	Mintage	VF20	XF40	MS60	MS63	MS65
1990	2,000	PF65 400				

KM# 19 50 DIRHAMS
40.00 g., 0.925 Silver 1.1896 oz. ASW, 40 mm. **Subject:** 50th Anniversary of the Arab League **Obv:** Eagle **Rev:** Inscription in center circle of wreath **Edge:** Reeded

Date	Mintage	VF20	XF40	MS60	MS63	MS65
1995	2,000	PF65 300				

KM# 21 50 DIRHAMS
40.00 g., 0.925 Silver 1.1896 oz. ASW, 40 mm. **Subject:** 25th Anniversary of the UAE - National Day Issue **Obv:** Bust of Shaikh Zayed Bin Sultan Al-Nahyan right **Rev:** Eagle within circle **Edge:** Reeded

Date	Mintage	VF20	XF40	MS60	MS63	MS65
1996	8,000	PF65 180				

KM# 22 50 DIRHAMS
40.00 g., 0.925 Silver 1.1896 oz. ASW, 40 mm. **Subject:** 30th Anniversary - Reign of Shaikh Zayed **Obv:** Bust of Shaikh Zayed Bin Sultan Al-Nahyan right **Rev:** Circular design of Arabic lettering **Edge:** Reeded

Date	Mintage	VF20	XF40	MS60	MS63	MS65
1996	8,000	PF65 140				

KM# 34 50 DIRHAMS

40.00 g., 0.925 Silver 1.1896 oz. ASW, 40 mm. **Subject:** Dubai National Bank - 35 Years **Obv:** Value **Rev:** Towered bank building divides dates **Edge:** Reeded

Date	Mintage	VF20	XF40	MS60	MS63	MS65
ND-1998	5,000	PF65 160				

KM# 36 50 DIRHAMS

40.00 g., 0.925 Silver 1.1896 oz. ASW, 40 mm. **Subject:** Colleges of Technology: 10 Years **Obv:** Bust of Shaikh Zayed Bin Sultan Al-Nahyan right **Rev:** Bird viewed through window frame **Edge:** Reeded

Date	Mintage	VF20	XF40	MS60	MS63	MS65
ND-1998	6,000	PF65 300				

KM# 37 50 DIRHAMS

27.50 g., 0.925 Silver 0.8178 oz. ASW **Series:** UNICEF **Obv:** Value **Rev:** Two children, dates at left and right

Date	Mintage	VF20	XF40	MS60	MS63	MS65
AH1419-1998	25,000	PF63 40.00	PF65 55.00	PF67 110		

KM# 57 50 DIRHAMS

40.00 g., 0.925 Silver 1.1896 oz. ASW, 40 mm. **Subject:** Sharjah - Cultural Capital **Obv:** Large value at center **Obv. Legend:** UNITED ARAB EMIRATES **Rev:** Large flame-like logo **Edge:** Reeded

Date	Mintage	VF20	XF40	MS60	MS63	MS65
1998	4,000	PF65 110				

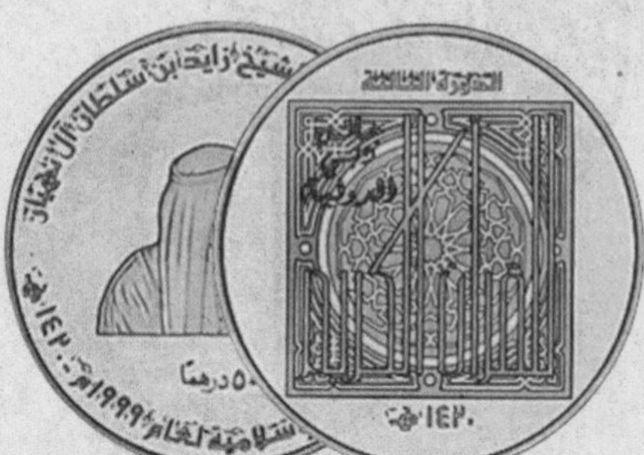

KM# 42 50 DIRHAMS

40.22 g., 0.925 Silver 1.1961 oz. ASW, 40 mm. **Subject:** Islamic Personality of 1999 - Sheikh Zayed **Obv:** Bust of Shaikh Zayed Bin Sultan Al-Nahyan right **Rev:** Square design **Edge:** Reeded

Date	Mintage	VF20	XF40	MS60	MS63	MS65
1999	—	PF65 120				

KM# 89 50 DIRHAMS

40.00 g., 0.925 Silver 1.1896 oz. ASW, 40 mm. **Subject:** 30th Anniversary Abu Dhabi Chamber of Commerce and Industry **Obv:** Bust of President H. H. Sheikh Zayed bin Sultan Al Hahyan 3/4 right **Rev:** Arabic "30" / 30th

Date	Mintage	VF20	XF40	MS60	MS63	MS65
ND-1999	5,000	PF65 100				

KM# 45 50 DIRHAMS

40.22 g., 0.925 Silver 1.1961 oz. ASW, 40 mm. **Subject:** 25th Anniversary - Dubai Islamic Bank **Obv:** Value **Rev:** Bank name within circle **Edge:** Reeded

Date	Mintage	VF20	XF40	MS60	MS63	MS65
ND-2000	—	PF65 200				

KM# 48 50 DIRHAMS

40.00 g., 0.925 Silver 1.1896 oz. ASW, 40 mm. **Subject:** Dubai Airport - Sheikh Rashid Terminal **Obv:** Bust facing **Rev:** Airport scene **Edge:** Reeded

Date	Mintage	VF20	XF40	MS60	MS63	MS65
2000	5,000	PF65 110				

KM# 58 100 DIRHAMS

40.00 g., 0.925 Silver 1.1896 oz. ASW **Subject:** 100th Anniversary - Dubai Dept. of Ports & Customs **Edge:** Reeded

Date	Mintage	VF20	XF40	MS60	MS63	MS65
1999	—	PF65 125				

KM# 12 500 DIRHAMS

19.97 g., 0.917 Gold 0.5888 oz. AGW, 25 mm. **Subject:** 5th Anniversary - United Arab Emirates **Obv:** Head /4 right, inscription above **Rev:** Dates

Date	Mintage	XF40	MS60	MS63	MS65	MS66
ND-1976	13,450	PF67 850	PF69 1,150			

KM# 23 500 DIRHAMS

19.97 g., 0.917 Gold 0.5888 oz. AGW, 25 mm. **Subject:** Commemoration - Death of Sheikh Rashid Bin Saeed Al Maktoum **Obv:** Bust right **Rev:** Dubai International Trade Center **Note:** Similar to 50 Dirhams, KM#17.

Date	Mintage	XF40	MS60	MS63	MS65	MS66
1990	2,000	PF67 950	PF69 1,250			

KM# 24 500 DIRHAMS

19.97 g., 0.917 Gold 0.5888 oz. AGW, 25 mm. **Subject:** 10th Anniversary - U.A.E. Central Bank **Obv:** Bust of Shaikh Zayed Bin Sultan Al-Nahyan right **Rev:** Bank building **Note:** Similar to 50 Dirhams, KM#18.

Date	Mintage	XF40	MS60	MS63	MS65	MS66
ND-1992	1,000	PF67 950	PF69 1,250			

KM# 25 500 DIRHAMS

19.97 g., 0.917 Gold 0.5888 oz. AGW, 25 mm. **Subject:** 20th Anniversary - Women's Union **Obv:** Heraldic eagle **Rev:** Seal in wreath **Note:** Similar to 1000 Dirhams, KM#28.

Date	Mintage	XF40	MS60	MS63	MS65	MS66
1995	1,000	PF67 950	PF69 1,250			

KM# 8 750 DIRHAMS

17.17 g., 0.900 Gold 0.4968 oz. AGW, 25 mm. **Subject:** IYC and UNICEF **Obv:** Value **Rev:** Armored horseman divides emblems

Date	Mintage	XF40	MS60	MS63	MS65	MS66
AH1400-1980	3,063	PF67 750	PF69 1,000			

KM# 13 1000 DIRHAMS

39.94 g., 0.917 Gold 1.1775 oz. AGW, 40 mm. **Subject:** 5th Anniversary - United Arab Emirates **Obv:** Head 1/4 right **Rev:** Dates

Date	Mintage	XF40	MS60	MS63	MS65	MS66
ND-1976	12,500	PF67 2,000	PF69 3,000			

KM# 26 1000 DIRHAMS

39.94 g., 0.917 Gold 1.1775 oz. AGW, 40 mm. **Subject:** Death of Shaikh Rashid Bin Saeed Al Maktoum **Obv:** Bust right **Rev:** Dubai International Trade Center **Note:** Similar to 50 Dirhams, KM#17.

Date	Mintage	XF40	MS60	MS63	MS65	MS66
1990	2,000	PF67 2,250	PF69 3,250			

KM# 27 1000 DIRHAMS

39.94 g., 0.917 Gold 1.1775 oz. AGW, 40 mm. **Subject:** 10th Anniversary - U.A.E. Central Bank **Obv:** Bust half right **Rev:** Bank building **Note:** Similar to 50 Dirhams, KM#18.

Date	Mintage	XF40	MS60	MS63	MS65	MS66
ND-1992	1,000	PF67 2,500	PF69 3,500			

KM# 28 1000 DIRHAMS

39.94 g., 0.917 Gold 1.1775 oz. AGW, 40 mm. **Subject:** 20th Anniversary - General Women's Union **Obv:** Bust right **Rev:** Seal in wreath

Date	Mintage	XF40	MS60	MS63	MS65	MS66
1995	1,000	PF67 2,500	PF69 3,500			

KM# 29 1000 DIRHAMS

39.94 g., 0.917 Gold 1.1775 oz. AGW, 40 mm. **Subject:** 30th Anniversary - Reign of Shaikh Zayed **Obv:** Bust of Shaikh Zayed Bin Sultan Al-Nahyan right **Rev:** Circular design of Arabic lettering

Date	Mintage	XF40	MS60	MS63	MS65	MS66
1996	—	PF67 2,250	PF69 3,250			

PIEDFORT

KM#	Date	Mintage	Identification	Mkt Val
P1	1980	75	50 Dirhams. 0.925. Silver. KM#7.	8,500
P2	1981	100	750 Dirhams. 0.900. Gold. KM#8.	5,500

MINT SETS

KM#	Date	Mintage	Identification	Issue Price	Mkt Val
MS1	AH1409/1989 (6)	—	KM#1, 2.1-3.1, 4-5, 6.1	—	20.00
MS2	Mixed dates (5)	—	KM#10-11 1987, KM#14 1988, KM#15 1991, KM#9 1981	—	65.00

UNITED STATES OF AMERICA

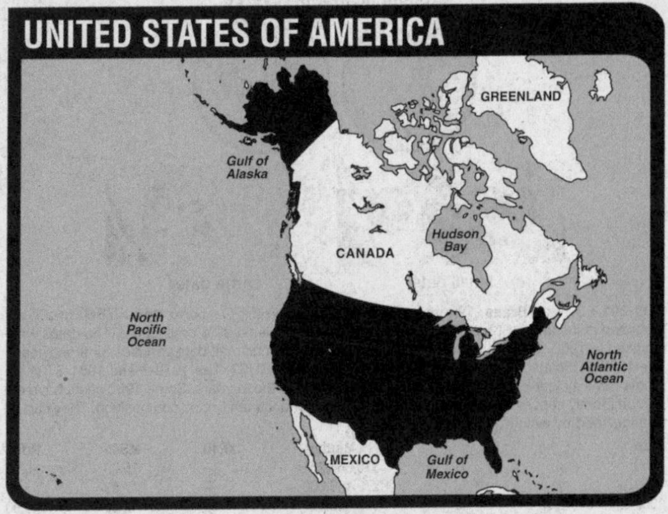

The United States of America as politically organized, under the Articles of Confederation consisted of the 13 original British-American colonies; New Hampshire, Massachusetts, Rhode Island, Connecticut, New York, New Jersey, Pennsylvania, Delaware, Virginia, North Carolina, South Carolina, Georgia and Maryland. Clustered along the eastern seaboard of North America between the forests of Maine and the marshes of Georgia. Under the Article of Confederation, the United States had no national capital: Philadelphia, where the "United States in Congress Assembled", was the "seat of government". The population during this political phase of America's history (1781-1789) was about 3 million, most of whom lived on self-sufficient family farms. Fishing, lumbering and the production of grains for export were major economic endeavors. Rapid strides were also being made in industry and manufacturing by 1775, the (then) colonies were accounting for one-seventh of the world's production of raw iron.

On the basis of the voyage of John Cabot to the North American mainland in 1497, England claimed the entire continent. The first permanent English settlement was established at Jamestown, Virginia, in 1607. France and Spain also claimed extensive territory in North America. At the end of the French and Indian Wars (1763), England acquired all of the territory east of the Mississippi River, including East and West Florida. From 1776 to 1781, the States were governed by the Continental Congress. From 1781 to 1789, they were organized under the Articles of Confederation, during which period the individual States had the right to issue money. Independence from Great Britain was attained with the American Revolution in 1776. The Constitution organized and governs the present United States. It was ratified on Nov. 21, 1788.

MINT MARKS

C – Charlotte, N.C., 1838-61
CC – Carson City, NV, 1870-93
D – Dahlonega, GA, 1838-61
D – Denver, CO, 1906-present
O – New Orleans, LA, 1838-1909
P – Philadelphia, PA, 1793-present
S – San Francisco, CA, 1854-present
W – West Point, NY, 1984-present

MONETARY SYSTEM

Trime = 3 Cents
Nickel = 5 Cents
Dime = 10 Cents
Quarter = 25 Cents
Half Dollar = 50 Cents
Dollar = 100 Cents
Quarter Eagle = $2.50 Gold
Stella = $4.00 Gold
Half Eagle = $5.00 Gold
Eagle = $10.00 Gold
Double Eagle = $20.00 Gold

BULLION COINS

Silver Eagle = $1.00
Gold 1/10 Ounce = $5.00
Gold ¼ Ounce = $10.00
Gold ½ Ounce = $25.00
Gold Ounce = $50.00
Platinum 1/10 Ounce = $10.00
Platinum ¼ Ounce = $25.00
Platinum ½ Ounce = $50.00
Platinum Ounce = $100.00

CIRCULATION COINAGE

CENT

Indian Head Cent

Indian head with headdress left above date obverse
Value within wreath, shield above reverse

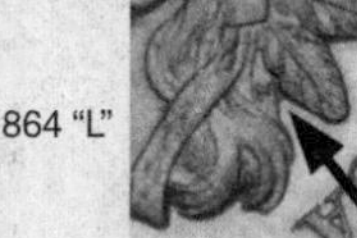

1864 "L"

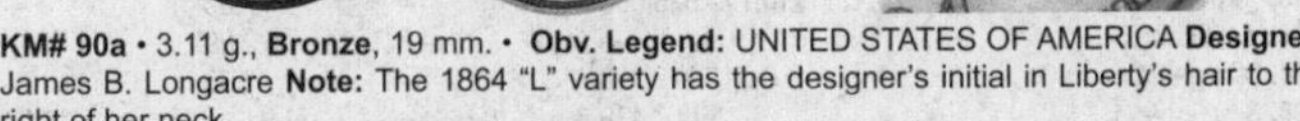

KM# 90a • 3.11 g., **Bronze**, 19 mm. • **Obv. Legend:** UNITED STATES OF AMERICA **Designer:** James B. Longacre **Note:** The 1864 "L" variety has the designer's initial in Liberty's hair to the right of her neck.

Date	Mintage	G4	VG8	F12	VF20	XF40	AU50	MS60	MS65	Prf65
1901	79,611,143	1.35	1.80	2.00	3.00	8.00	18.00	38.00	125	375
1902	87,376,722	1.35	1.80	2.00	3.00	8.00	18.00	38.00	125	375
1903	85,094,493	1.35	1.80	2.00	3.00	8.00	18.00	38.00	125	375
1904	61,328,015	1.35	1.80	2.00	3.00	8.00	18.00	38.00	125	375
1905	80,719,163	1.35	1.80	2.00	3.00	8.00	18.00	38.00	125	375
1906	96,022,255	1.35	1.80	2.00	3.00	8.00	18.00	38.00	125	375
1907	108,138,618	1.35	1.80	2.00	3.00	8.00	18.00	38.00	125	375
1908	32,327,987	1.35	1.80	2.00	3.00	8.00	18.00	38.00	125	375
1908S	1,115,000	80.00	85.00	90.00	110	145	180	225	1,250	—
1909	14,370,645	10.00	12.00	13.00	14.00	18.00	26.00	43.00	125	375
1909S	309,000	435	445	480	550	600	750	1,050	2,100	—

Lincoln Cent

Wheat Ears reverse

KM# 132 • 3.11 g., **Bronze**, 19 mm. • **Designer:** Victor D. Brenner **Note:** The 1909 "VDB" varieties have the designer's initials inscribed at the 6 o'clock position on the reverse. The initials were removed until 1918, when they were restored on the obverse • MS60 and MS63 prices are for brown coins and MS65 prices are for coins that are at least 90% original red.

Date	Mintage	G4	VG8	F12	VF20	XF40	AU50	MS60	MS65	Prf65
1909 VDB	27,995,000	10.00	11.00	12.00	13.00	14.00	15.00	20.00	125	27,000
1909 VDB Doubled Die Obverse	Inc. above	—	—	45.00	65.00	90.00	110	180	1,400	—
1909S VDB	484,000	660	725	850	900	1,000	1,100	1,500	4,600	—
1909	72,702,618	2.75	3.00	3.50	12.00	14.00	16.00	22.00	100	900
1909S	1,825,000	70.00	80.00	95.00	125	140	250	325	1,175	—
1909S/S S over horizontal S	Inc. above	110	125	135	180	250	280	235	750	—
1910	146,801,218	0.30	0.40	0.50	0.60	4.00	8.00	16.00	210	850
1910S	6,045,000	12.00	17.00	18.00	20.00	45.00	65.00	90.00	650	—
1911	101,177,787	0.35	0.45	1.25	1.75	6.00	9.00	16.00	360	1,100
1911D	12,672,000	4.25	5.00	8.00	20.00	45.00	65.00	80.00	1,100	—
1911S	4,026,000	40.00	45.00	48.00	50.00	65.00	90.00	160	1,850	—
1912	68,153,060	1.20	1.40	2.00	4.50	12.00	23.00	30.00	500	1,200
1912D	10,411,000	6.00	8.00	9.00	24.00	65.00	95.00	145	1,900	—
1912S	4,431,000	18.00	20.00	25.00	40.00	60.00	95.00	155	1,650	—
1913	76,532,352	0.65	0.75	1.25	3.00	16.00	25.00	30.00	440	1,000
1913D	15,804,000	2.35	2.60	3.00	9.00	45.00	55.00	90.00	1,600	—
1913S	6,101,000	9.00	13.00	17.00	25.00	50.00	95.00	170	3,200	—
1914	75,238,432	0.40	0.55	2.00	5.00	16.00	35.00	50.00	475	1,100
1914D	1,193,000	130	135	180	250	625	1,200	1,800	15,000	—
1914S	4,137,000	20.00	23.00	25.00	35.00	75.00	115	275	4,800	—
1915	29,092,120	1.35	2.50	3.30	16.00	55.00	65.00	75.00	850	1,800
1915D	22,050,000	1.35	2.50	3.50	6.00	21.00	4.00	65.00	1,000	—
1915S	4,833,000	16.00	20.00	23.00	25.00	60.00	85.00	1,654	8,500	—
1916	131,833,677	0.30	0.35	0.65	2.00	7.00	12.00	17.00	330	4,000
1916D	35,956,000	1.00	1.65	3.00	5.00	16.00	33.00	80.00	1,850	—
1916S	22,510,000	1.35	2.75	4.00	8.00	24.00	42.00	95.00	7,700	—
1917	196,429,785	0.25	0.30	0.35	1.50	4.00	12.00	14.00	325	—
1917 Doubled Die Obverse	Inc. above	125	195	240	300	1,000	1,500	2,500	13,000	—
1917D	55,120,000	0.85	1.00	2.50	4.25	33.00	40.00	65.00	1,800	—
1917S	32,620,000	0.40	0.65	1.00	2.00	10.00	25.00	65.00	8,500	—
1918	288,104,634	0.25	0.30	0.35	0.55	4.00	8.00	11.00	330	—
1918D	47,830,000	0.75	1.00	2.00	4.00	14.00	31.00	70.00	2,500	—
1918S	34,680,000	0.25	0.75	1.00	3.00	9.00	30.00	60.00	10,000	—
1919	392,021,000	0.25	0.30	0.35	0.40	1.00	5.00	7.00	125	—
1919D	57,154,000	0.65	0.90	1.25	4.00	11.00	32.00	55.00	1,400	—
1919S	139,760,000	0.20	0.35	1.25	2.00	5.00	15.00	45.00	4,700	—
1920	310,165,000	0.15	0.20	0.45	1.00	2.50	7.00	13.00	225	—
1920D	49,280,000	1.00	1.25	2.50	6.00	17.00	35.00	65.00	1,200	—
1920S	46,220,000	0.45	0.50	1.25	2.25	11.00	31.00	95.00	11,000	—
1921	39,157,000	0.40	0.50	0.75	2.50	9.50	20.00	37.00	360	—
1921S	15,274,000	1.20	1.75	3.00	6.00	33.00	60.00	95.00	10,000	—
1922D	7,160,000	16.00	18.00	19.00	20.00	33.00	60.00	90.00	1,600	—
1922D Weak Rev	Inc. above	22.00	23.00	24.00	25.50	34.00	65.00	95.00	400	—
1922D Weak D	Inc. above	20.00	30.00	40.00	50.00	105	150	225	1,500	—
1922 No D Die 2 Strong Rev	Inc. above	425	475	535	650	1,600	2,600	8,000	130,000	—
1922 No D Die 3 Weak Rev	Inc. above	75.00	100	125	175	400	600	1,000	-	—
1923	74,723,000	0.30	0.40	0.50	1.00	5.00	10.00	12.00	330	—
1923S	8,700,000	5.85	7.00	8.50	12.50	38.00	90.00	165	16,000	—
1924	75,178,000	0.25	0.35	0.45	1.00	4.50	9.00	16.00	440	—
1924D	2,520,000	30.00	33.00	37.00	45.00	105	160	260	11,250	—
1924S	11,696,000	1.25	1.50	2.75	5.35	30.00	60.00	100	16,500	—
1925	139,949,000	0.25	0.35	0.45	0.70	3.00	6.50	8.00	95.00	—
1925D	22,580,000	1.00	1.65	3.10	6.25	13.00	26.00	55.00	3,000	—
1925S	26,380,000	0.80	1.20	1.85	2.75	10.00	25.00	75.00	15,500	—
1926	157,088,000	0.25	0.35	0.45	0.60	1.65	5.00	6.00	50.00	—
1926D	28,020,000	1.50	1.70	3.40	5.25	13.00	28.00	75.00	2,000	—
1926S	4,550,000	9.00	10.00	11.75	16.50	30.00	60.00	120	85,000	—
1927	144,440,000	0.20	0.25	0.35	0.60	1.60	5.25	7.50	80.00	—
1927D	27,170,000	1.15	1.70	2.25	3.35	7.50	25.00	50.00	2,000	—
1927S	14,276,000	1.40	1.85	2.65	5.25	13.00	36.00	55.00	8,000	—
1928	134,116,000	0.20	0.25	0.35	0.60	1.45	4.00	7.50	95.00	—
1928D	31,170,000	0.90	1.40	2.15	3.65	6.75	17.00	32.00	815	—
1928S Small S	17,266,000	1.00	1.65	2.60	4.00	8.00	27.00	60.00	2,500	—
1928S Large S	Inc. above	1.65	2.85	4.25	7.50	15.00	45.00	110	1,000	—
1929	185,262,000	0.20	0.25	0.35	0.55	2.75	4.50	5.50	85.00	—

Date	Mintage	G4	VG8	F12	VF20	XF40	AU50	MS60	MS65	Prf65
1929D	41,730,000	0.50	1.00	1.40	2.75	5.00	12.00	21.00	445	—
1929S	50,148,000	0.60	1.10	1.85	2.80	6.00	13.00	17.00	345	—
1930	157,415,000	0.20	0.25	0.35	0.60	1.25	2.75	4.00	35.00	—
1930D	40,100,000	0.25	0.35	0.60	0.90	2.00	5.50	9.00	140	—
1930S	24,286,000	0.25	0.35	0.55	0.80	1.50	6.50	9.50	85.00	—
1931	19,396,000	0.65	0.75	1.10	2.00	4.00	9.50	17.00	120	—
1931D	4,480,000	5.00	5.85	6.50	8.00	13.00	33.50	45.00	860	—
1931S	866,000	60.00	65.00	70.00	75.00	80.00	85.00	145	560	—
1932	9,062,000	1.60	1.95	2.85	3.50	6.75	11.00	15.00	90.00	—
1932D	10,500,000	1.50	1.90	2.50	2.85	4.15	9.00	16.00	140	—
1933	14,360,000	1.50	1.80	2.65	2.85	6.50	10.00	14.00	77.00	—
1933D	6,200,000	3.50	4.25	5.65	7.50	12.00	17.00	21.00	110	—
1934	219,080,000	0.15	0.25	0.30	0.45	1.25	4.00	9.00	25.00	—
1934D	28,446,000	0.35	0.50	0.80	1.25	5.50	9.00	20.00	30.00	—
1935	245,338,000	0.15	0.20	0.25	0.40	0.90	1.50	5.00	20.00	—
1935D	47,000,000	0.20	0.30	0.40	0.55	0.95	2.50	5.50	20.00	—
1935S	38,702,000	0.25	0.35	0.60	1.75	3.00	5.00	11.00	44.00	—
1936 (Proof in Satin Finish)	309,637,569	0.15	0.20	0.30	0.40	0.85	1.40	1.90	10.00	2,500
1936 Brilliant Proof	Inc. above	—	—	—	—	—	—	—	—	2,300
1936 DDO	Inc. above	—	—	25.00	50.00	80.00	125	175	1,000	—
1936D	40,620,000	0.20	0.30	0.40	0.55	0.90	1.50	4.00	15.00	—
1936S	29,130,000	0.20	0.30	0.45	0.60	1.50	2.25	5.00	18.00	—
1937	309,179,320	0.15	0.20	0.30	0.40	0.50	0.75	1.75	13.50	300
1937D	50,430,000	0.20	0.30	0.40	0.60	0.80	1.20	2.65	15.00	—
1937S	34,500,000	0.20	0.30	0.40	0.55	0.90	1.25	2.75	16.50	—
1938	156,696,734	0.15	0.20	0.30	0.40	0.50	1.20	2.25	18.00	185
1938D	20,010,000	0.20	0.30	0.45	0.60	1.00	1.50	3.50	20.00	—
1938S	15,180,000	0.30	0.40	0.50	0.70	1.00	1.75	3.00	15.00	—
1939	316,479,520	0.15	0.20	0.30	0.40	0.45	0.75	1.00	16.00	165
1939D	15,160,000	0.35	0.45	0.50	0.60	0.95	1.75	3.00	18.00	—
1939S	52,070,000	0.30	0.40	0.50	0.60	0.80	1.20	2.50	16.00	—
1940	586,825,872	0.10	0.20	0.30	0.35	0.45	0.75	1.00	12.00	130
1940D	81,390,000	0.20	0.30	0.40	0.55	0.75	1.10	2.00	11.00	—
1940S	112,940,000	0.20	0.30	0.40	0.55	0.70	1.25	2.50	12.50	—
1941	887,039,100	0.10	0.20	0.30	0.35	0.45	0.60	1.25	10.00	170
1941 Doubled Die Obv	Inc. above	35.00	50.00	70.00	80.00	95.00	135	200	1,000	—
1941D	128,700,000	0.20	0.30	0.40	0.55	0.90	1.35	2.20	12.50	—
1941S	92,360,000	0.20	0.30	0.40	0.55	0.95	1.75	2.50	15.00	—
1942	657,828,600	0.10	0.20	0.30	0.35	0.40	0.55	0.85	11.00	170
1942D	206,698,000	0.20	0.25	0.30	0.35	0.45	0.60	1.00	12.00	—
1942S	85,590,000	0.25	0.35	0.45	0.85	1.25	2.50	5.00	18.00	—
1943 Copper planchet error	—	—	—	35,000	42,000	45,000	80,000	155,000	—	—
1943S Copper planchet error	—	—	—	125,000	150,000	185,000	275,000	—	—	—

KM# 132a • 2.70 g., **Zinc Coated Steel**, 19 mm. • **Designer:** Victor D. Brenner

Date	Mintage	G4	VG8	F12	VF20	XF40	AU50	MS60	MS65	Prf65
1943	684,628,670	0.20	0.30	0.35	0.45	0.60	0.85	1.25	18.00	—
1943D	217,660,000	0.35	0.40	0.45	0.50	0.70	1.00	1.50	—	—
1943D/D RPM	Inc. above	30.00	38.00	50.00	65.00	90.00	125	200	—	—
1943S	191,550,000	0.40	0.45	0.50	0.65	0.90	1.40	4.00	28.00	—

KM# A132 • 3.11 g., **Brass**, 19 mm. • **Designer:** Victor D. Brenner **Note:** KM#132 design and composition resumed • MS60 prices are for brown coins and MS65 prices are for coins that are at least 90% original red.

Date	Mintage	XF40	MS65	Prf65
1944	1,435,400,000	0.30	8.00	—
1944D	430,578,000	0.40	14.00	—
1944D/S Type 1	Inc. above	115	3,300	—
1944D/S Type 2	Inc. above	115	2,500	—
1944S	282,760,000	0.35	8.00	—
1945	1,040,515,000	0.40	13.50	—
1945D	226,268,000	0.40	8.00	—
1945S	181,770,000	0.40	7.50	—
1946	991,655,000	0.25	13.50	—
1946D	315,690,000	0.30	10.00	—
1946S	198,100,000	0.30	13.50	—
1946S/D	—	70.00	650	—
1947	190,555,000	0.45	18.50	—
1947D	194,750,000	0.35	7.50	—
1947S	99,000,000	0.35	8.00	—
1948	317,570,000	0.35	18.50	—
1948D	172,637,000	0.40	12.00	—
1948S	81,735,000	0.40	12.00	—
1949	217,775,000	0.40	18.00	—
1949D	153,132,000	0.40	15.00	—
1949S	64,290,000	0.50	10.00	—
1950	272,686,386	0.35	16.50	85.00
1950D	334,950,000	0.35	12.50	—
1950S	118,505,000	0.30	9.00	—

Date	Mintage	XF40	MS65	Prf65
1951	295,633,500	0.40	16.50	80.00
1951D	625,355,000	0.30	8.50	—
1951S	136,010,000	0.40	9.00	—
1952	186,856,980	0.40	16.00	50.00
1952D	746,130,000	0.30	8.50	—
1952S	137,800,004	0.60	12.00	—
1953	256,883,800	0.25	18.00	40.00
1953D	700,515,000	0.25	8.50	—
1953S	181,835,000	0.40	8.00	—
1954	71,873,350	0.25	20.00	19.00
1954D	251,552,500	0.25	8.50	—
1954S	96,190,000	0.25	10.00	—
1955	330,958,000	0.25	9.00	20.00
1955 Doubled Die	Inc. above	1,450	35,000	—

Note: The 1955 "doubled die" has distinct doubling of the date and lettering on the obverse.

Date	Mintage	XF40	MS65	Prf65
1955D	563,257,500	0.20	8.00	—
1955S	44,610,000	0.35	7.50	—
1956	421,414,384	0.20	12.00	5.00
1956D	1,098,201,100	0.20	7.00	—
1957	283,787,952	0.20	7.50	4.00
1957D	1,051,342,000	0.20	6.00	—
1958	253,400,652	0.20	9.00	6.50
1958D	800,953,300	0.20	7.00	—

Lincoln Memorial reverse

Small date

Large date

KM# 201 • 3.11 g., **Brass**, 19 mm. • **Rev. Designer:** Frank Gasparro **Note:** MS60 prices are for brown coins and MS65 prices are for coins that are at least 90% original red. The dates were modified in 1960, 1970 and 1982, resulting in large-date and small-date varieties for those years. The 1972 "doubled die" shows doubling of IN GOD WE TRUST. The 1979-S and 1981-S Type II proofs have a clearer mint mark than the Type I proofs of those years. Some 1982 cents have the predominantly copper composition; others have the predominantly zinc composition. They can be distinguished by weight.

Date	Mintage	XF40	MS65	Prf65
1959	610,864,291	—	15.00	6.50
1959D	1,279,760,000	—	7.50	—
1960 small date, low 9	588,096,602	1.85	12.00	16.00
1960 large date, high 9	Inc. above	—	8.00	7.50
1960 small over large date	Inc. above	—	—	600
1960D small date, low 9	1,580,884,000	—	10.00	—
1960D large date, high 9	Inc. above	—	8.00	—
1960D/D small over large date	Inc. above	—	300	—
1961	756,373,244	—	8.50	9.00
1961D	1,753,266,700	—	18.00	—
1962	609,263,019	—	8.00	8.00
1962D	1,793,148,400	—	14.00	—
1963	757,185,645	—	10.00	6.00
1963D	1,774,020,400	—	12.00	—
1964	2,652,525,762	—	8.50	6.00
1964D	3,799,071,500	—	10.00	—
1965	1,497,224,900	—	10.00	—
1965 SMS	Inc. above	—	7.50	—
1966	2,188,147,783	—	10.00	—
1966 SMS	Inc. above	—	8.00	—
1967	3,048,667,100	—	12.00	—
1967 SMS	Inc. above	—	8.00	—
1968	1,707,880,970	—	12.00	—
1968D	2,886,269,600	—	12.50	—
1968S	261,311,510	—	10.00	4.50
1969	1,136,910,000	—	7.00	—
1969D	4,002,832,200	—	10.00	—
1969S	547,309,631	—	15.00	5.50
1969S Doubled Die Obverse	Inc. above	10,000	125,000	100,000
1970	1,898,315,000	—	8.00	—
1970D	2,891,438,900	—	6.00	—
1970S small date, level 7	Inc. above	30.00	65.00	60.00
1970S large date, low 7	Inc. above	—	15.00	5.00
1970S Doubled Die Obverse	Inc. above	—	20,000	15,000
1971	1,919,490,000	—	20.00	—
1971D	2,911,045,600	—	6.50	—
1971S	528,354,192	—	7.50	5.50
1971S Doubled Die Obverse	Inc. above	—	—	400
1972	2,933,255,000	—	6.00	—
1972 Doubled Die Obverse	Inc. above	240	625	—
1972D	2,665,071,400	—	12.00	—
1972S	380,200,104	—	26.50	5.50
1973	3,728,245,000	—	8.00	—
1973D	3,549,576,588	—	11.00	—
1973S	319,937,634	—	10.00	5.50
1974	4,232,140,523	—	12.00	—
1974D	4,235,098,000	—	9.00	—
1974S	412,039,228	—	12.00	5.00
1975	5,451,476,142	—	8.00	—
1975D	4,505,245,300	—	13.50	—
1975S	2,845,450	—	—	5.00
1976	4,674,292,426	—	14.00	—
1976D	4,221,592,455	—	16.00	—
1976S	4,149,730	—	—	6.00
1977	4,469,930,000	—	16.00	—
1977D	4,149,062,300	—	16.00	—
1977S	3,251,152	—	—	5.00
1978	5,558,605,000	—	16.00	—
1978D	4,280,233,400	—	14.00	—
1978S	3,127,781	—	—	5.00
1979	6,018,515,000	—	12.00	—
1979D	4,139,357,254	—	8.00	—
1979S type I, proof	3,677,175	—	—	5.00
1979S type II, proof	—	—	—	10.00
1980	7,414,705,000	—	6.50	—
1980D	5,140,098,660	—	12.00	—
1980S	3,554,806	—	—	5.00
1981	7,491,750,000	—	8.50	—
1981D	5,373,235,677	—	9.00	—
1981S type I, proof	4,063,083	—	—	5.00
1981S type II, proof	—	—	—	42.00
1982 large date	10,712,525,000	—	7.00	—
1982 small date	Inc. above	—	9.00	—
1982D large date	6,012,979,368	—	7.50	—
1982S	3,857,479	—	—	5.00

KM# 201a • 2.50 g., **Copper Plated Zinc**, 19 mm. • **Note:** MS60 prices are for brown coins and MS65 prices are for coins that are at least 90% original red.

Date	Mintage	XF40	MS65	Prf65
1982 large date	—	—	6.00	—
1982 small date	—	—	9.00	—
1982D large date	—	—	8.00	—
1982D small date	—	—	6.00	—

KM# 201b • **Copper Plated Zinc**, 19 mm. • **Note:** MS60 prices are for brown coins and MS65 prices are for coins that are at least 90% original red.

Date	Mintage	XF40	MS65	Prf65
1983	7,752,355,000	—	7.00	—
1983 Doubled Die	Inc. above	135	450	—
1983D	6,467,199,428	—	5.50	—
1983S	3,279,126	—	—	3.50
1984	8,151,079,000	—	7.50	—
1984 Doubled Die	Inc. above	90.00	300	—
1984D	5,569,238,906	—	6.50	—
1984S	3,065,110	—	—	3.50
1985	5,648,489,887	—	4.50	—
1985D	5,287,399,926	—	4.50	—
1985S	3,362,821	—	—	3.50
1986	4,491,395,493	—	5.00	—
1986D	4,442,866,698	—	8.00	—
1986S	3,010,497	—	—	3.50
1987	4,682,466,931	—	7.50	—
1987D	4,879,389,514	—	5.50	—
1987S	4,227,728	—	—	3.50
1988	6,092,810,000	—	10.00	—
1988D	5,253,740,443	—	6.00	—
1988S	3,262,948	—	—	3.50
1989	7,261,535,000	—	6.50	—
1989D	5,345,467,111	—	6.50	—
1989S	3,220,194	—	—	5.00
1990	6,851,765,000	—	5.00	—
1990D	4,922,894,533	—	5.50	—
1990S	3,299,559	—	—	3.50
1990 no S, Proof only	Inc. above	—	—	4,650
1991	5,165,940,000	—	6.50	—
1991D	4,158,442,076	—	5.50	—
1991S	2,867,787	—	—	3.50
1992	4,648,905,000	—	5.50	—
1992D	4,448,673,300	—	5.50	—
1992D Close AM, Proof Reverse Die	Inc. above	—	—	—

Date	Mintage	XF40	MS65	Prf65
1992S	4,176,560	—	—	3.50
1993	5,684,705,000	—	5.00	—
1993D	6,426,650,571	—	4.50	—
1993S	3,394,792	—	—	3.50
1994	6,500,850,000	—	6.00	—
1994D	7,131,765,000	—	4.50	—
1994S	3,269,923	—	—	3.50
1995	6,411,440,000	—	5.00	—
1995 Doubled Die Obverse	Inc. above	20.00	60.00	—
1995D	7,128,560,000	—	4.50	—
1995S	2,707,481	—	—	3.50
1996	6,612,465,000	—	4.50	—
1996D	6,510,795,000	—	4.50	—
1996S	2,915,212	—	—	3.50
1997	4,622,800,000	—	3.00	—
1997D	4,576,555,000	—	3.50	—
1997S	2,796,678	—	—	4.00
1998	5,032,155,000	—	3.00	—
1998 Wide AM, reverse from proof die	Inc. above	—	110	—
1998D	5,255,353,500	—	3.00	—
1998S	2,957,286	—	—	4.00
1999	5,237,600,000	—	3.00	—
1999 Wide AM, reverse from proof die	Inc. above	—	450	—
1999D	6,360,065,000	—	3.00	—
1999S	3,362,462	—	—	3.50
2000 Wide AM, reverse from proof die	Inc. above	—	45.00	—
2000	5,503,200,000	—	3.00	—
2000D	8,774,220,000	—	3.00	—
2000S	4,063,361	—	—	3.50

5 CENTS

Liberty Nickel

Liberty head left, within circle of stars, date below obverse
Roman numeral value within wreath, CENTS below reverse

KM# 112 • 5.00 g., **Copper-Nickel**, 21.2 mm. • **Rev. Legend:** UNITED STATES OF AMERICA

Date	Mintage	G4	VG8	F12	VF20	XF40	AU50	MS60	MS65	Prf65
1901	26,480,213	3.00	6.00	14.00	25.00	35.00	60.00	82.00	425	580
1902	31,480,579	3.00	6.00	14.00	25.00	35.00	60.00	82.00	425	580
1903	28,006,725	3.00	6.00	14.00	25.00	35.00	60.00	82.00	425	580
1904	21,404,984	3.00	6.00	14.00	25.00	35.00	60.00	82.00	425	580
1905	29,827,276	3.00	6.00	14.00	25.00	35.00	60.00	82.00	425	580
1906	38,613,725	3.00	6.00	14.00	25.00	35.00	60.00	82.00	475	580
1907	39,214,800	3.00	6.00	14.00	25.00	35.00	60.00	82.00	700	580
1908	22,686,177	3.00	6.00	14.00	25.00	35.00	60.00	82.00	675	580
1909	11,590,526	4.00	6.00	7.00	14.00	35.00	78.00	100	550	580
1910	30,169,353	3.00	6.00	14.00	25.00	35.00	60.00	82.00	425	580
1911	39,559,372	3.00	6.00	14.00	25.00	35.00	60.00	82.00	425	580
1912	26,236,714	3.00	6.00	14.00	25.00	35.00	60.00	82.00	425	580
1912D	8,474,000	4.00	5.00	16.00	38.00	105	200	260	1,750	—
1912S	238,000	135	175	200	425	850	1,225	1,350	2,800	—
1913 5 known	—	—	—	—	—	—	—	—	—	—

Note: 1913, Heritage Sale, January 2010, Proof-64 (Olsen), $3,737,500. Private treaty, 2007, (Eliasburg) Proof-66 $5 million.

Buffalo Nickel

American Bison standing on a mound reverse

KM# 133 • 5.00 g., **Copper-Nickel**, 21.2 mm. • **Designer:** James Earle Fraser

Date	Mintage	G4	VG8	F12	VF20	XF40	AU50	MS60	MS65	Prf65
1913	30,993,520	20.00	21.00	22.00	23.00	27.00	40.00	48.00	150	3,150
1913D	5,337,000	23.00	25.00	26.00	28.00	30.00	55.00	67.00	400	—
1913S	2,105,000	44.00	46.00	50.00	60.00	65.00	92.00	160	675	—

American Bison standing on a line reverse

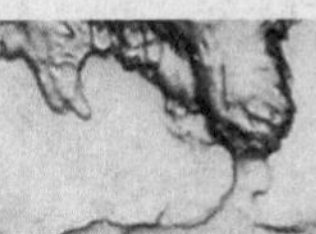
1937D 3-legged

1918/17D

KM# 134 • 5.00 g., **Copper-Nickel**, 21.2 mm. • **Designer:** James Earle Fraser **Note:** In 1913 the reverse design was modified so the ground under the buffalo was represented as a line rather than a mound. On the 1937D 3-legged variety, the buffalo's right front leg is missing, the result of a damaged die.

Date	Mintage	G4	VG8	F12	VF20	XF40	AU50	MS60	MS65	Prf65
1913	29,858,700	21.00	22.00	23.00	24.00	26.00	32.00	50.00	340	2,500
1913D	4,156,000	195	225	250	260	310	300	355	1,100	—
1913S	1,209,000	300	340	370	445	500	700	850	3,200	—
1914	20,665,738	27.00	28.00	29.00	30.00	31.00	38.00	70.00	425	2,250
1914/3	Inc. above	110	250	400	500	600	825	1,800	30,000	—
1914D	3,912,000	80.00	100	130	190	300	400	430	1,150	—
1914/3D	Inc. above	90.00	200	300	400	590	800	3,200	—	—
1914S	3,470,000	29.00	37.00	43.00	55.00	90.00	165	205	1,825	—
1914/3S	Inc. above	210	400	650	900	1,300	2,000	4,100	—	—
1915	20,987,270	10.00	12.00	14.00	16.00	25.00	46.00	70.00	400	2,100
1915D	7,569,500	18.00	25.00	35.00	50.00	105	140	245	1,400	—
1915S	1,505,000	50.00	60.00	88.00	155	300	500	600	3,500	—
1916	63,498,066	10.00	11.00	12.00	14.00	18.00	25.00	60.00	305	3,250
1916 2 Feathers	Inc. above	40.00	—	65.00	—	—	—	—	200	—
1916/16	Inc. above	3,400	4,400	8,500	10,500	16,000	29,000	55,000	—	—
1916D	13,333,000	18.00	25.00	28.00	32.00	80.00	105	160	1,150	—
1916S	11,860,000	12.00	16.00	22.00	32.00	80.00	140	200	1,900	—
1917	51,424,029	10.00	14.00	15.00	17.00	20.00	40.00	64.00	505	—
1917 2 Feathers	Inc. above	30.00	—	40.00	—	—	—	—	145	—
1917D	9,910,800	20.00	30.00	46.00	67.00	135	255	325	1,975	—
1917S	4,193,000	17.50	40.00	70.00	87.00	160	270	475	3,650	—
1917S 2 Feathers	Inc. above	40.00	60.00	85.00	—	—	—	—	255	—
1918	32,086,314	7.00	8.50	9.00	15.00	35.00	55.00	110	1,175	—
1918/17D	8,362,314	825	1,400	2,100	4,700	8,000	10,500	32,000	250,000	—
1918D	Inc. above	21.00	33.00	55.00	105	205	315	450	3,400	—
1918 2 Feathers	Inc. above	40.00	—	85.00	—	—	—	—	275	—
1918S	4,882,000	13.00	23.00	47.00	90.00	160	295	455	13,250	—
1919	60,868,000	3.00	3.75	4.25	6.50	12.00	27.00	51.00	415	—
1919D	8,006,000	14.50	25.00	56.00	100	215	320	610	5,500	—
1919S	7,521,000	7.00	17.00	42.00	82.00	200	330	610	10,500	—
1920	63,093,000	1.50	3.00	3.25	6.50	13.50	26.00	54.00	575	—
1920D	9,418,000	8.50	17.50	31.00	93.00	260	320	485	4,500	—
1920S	9,689,000	4.00	12.50	25.50	95.00	185	255	465	14,000	—
1921	10,663,000	6.00	9.00	12.00	30.00	50.00	100	120	790	—
1921S	1,557,000	60.00	90.00	155	410	800	1,000	1,525	6,600	—
1923	35,715,000	1.75	2.75	4.50	7.00	13.00	35.00	54.00	480	—
1923S	6,142,000	7.00	9.50	21.00	95.00	250	325	550	6,250	—
1924	21,620,000	2.25	3.00	6.00	13.00	30.00	50.00	69.00	770	—
1924D	5,258,000	6.75	10.00	30.00	55.00	160	300	380	3,300	—
1924S	1,437,000	15.00	27.00	80.00	455	1,000	1,550	2,325	9,600	—
1925	35,565,100	3.50	4.25	5.00	8.00	20.00	28.00	39.00	325	—
1925D	4,450,000	9.25	17.50	31.00	62.00	145	270	410	4,500	—
1925S	6,256,000	3.75	8.25	13.50	61.00	170	245	405	17,500	—
1926	44,693,000	1.50	2.50	4.00	6.00	12.00	20.00	29.00	185	—
1926D	5,638,000	10.50	17.00	26.00	100	185	290	335	3,950	—
1926S	970,000	20.00	39.00	80.00	375	750	2,200	4,100	90,000	—
1927	37,981,000	1.00	1.50	3.00	5.00	13.00	21.00	31.00	250	—
1927D	5,730,000	3.50	7.00	10.00	50.00	120	160	180	5,800	—
1927S	3,430,000	1.75	3.00	4.75	45.00	80.00	165	725	13,500	—
1928	23,411,000	2.00	2.25	2.50	4.00	11.00	21.00	40.00	110	—
1928D	6,436,000	2.00	3.00	5.00	14.00	38.00	51.00	80.00	600	—
1928S	6,936,000	2.00	3.00	5.00	14.00	38.00	130	245	2,800	—
1929	36,446,000	1.00	1.50	2.00	4.25	13.00	21.00	33.00	265	—
1929D	8,370,000	1.00	1.50	3.00	6.00	30.00	43.00	60.00	900	—
1929S	7,754,000	1.00	1.50	1.90	2.00	16.00	26.00	45.00	400	—
1930	22,849,000	2.00	2.25	2.50	4.00	16.00	21.00	30.00	245	—
1930S	5,435,000	2.00	2.25	2.50	4.00	16.00	35.00	65.00	375	—
1931S	1,200,000	15.00	18.00	21.00	23.00	34.00	45.00	63.00	310	—
1934	20,213,003	1.75	2.00	2.50	4.00	9.50	24.00	41.00	215	—
1934D	7,480,000	1.75	3.00	4.00	9.00	19.00	41.00	70.00	400	—
1935	58,264,000	1.00	1.25	1.60	2.00	3.00	12.00	28.00	120	—
1935 Double Die Rev.	Inc. above	80.00	100	125	185	600	1,100	2,900	22,000	—
1935D	12,092,000	2.00	2.50	3.00	8.00	18.00	40.00	70.00	370	—
1935S	10,300,000	1.00	1.50	1.60	2.00	4.00	21.00	42.00	175	—
1936	119,001,420	1.00	1.50	1.60	2.00	4.00	10.00	25.00	65.00	1,650
1936 Brilliant	Inc. above	—	—	—	—	—	—	—	—	2,300

Date	Mintage	G4	VG8	F12	VF20	XF40	AU50	MS60	MS65	Prf65
1936D	24,814,000	1.00	1.50	1.60	2.00	4.00	21.00	32.00	105	—
1936D 3-1/2 leg	Inc. above	400	600	1,000	1,400	3,900	3,375	12,000	—	—
1936D/S	Inc. above	—	—	10.00	16.00	25.00	—	—	—	—
1936S	14,930,000	1.00	1.50	1.60	2.00	4.00	12.00	31.00	105	—
1937	79,485,769	1.00	1.50	1.60	2.00	4.00	10.00	31.00	72.00	1,600
1937D	17,826,000	1.00	1.50	1.60	2.00	4.00	10.00	31.00	70.00	—
1937D 3-legged	Inc. above	425	485	500	565	700	760	2,000	29,000	—
1937S	5,635,000	1.00	1.50	1.60	2.00	4.00	11.00	28.00	60.00	—
1938D	7,020,000	3.50	3.75	4.00	4.25	4.50	9.25	25.00	45.00	—
1938D/D	Inc. above	6.00	7.00	8.00	10.00	12.00	22.00	40.00	85.00	—
1938D/S	Inc. above	6.50	8.00	10.00	11.00	18.00	33.00	50.00	100	—

Jefferson Nickel

Monticello, mintmark to right side reverse

KM# 192 • 5.00 g., **Copper-Nickel**, 21.2 mm. • **Designer:** Felix Schlag **Note:** Some 1939 strikes have doubling of the word MONTICELLO on the reverse.

Date	Mintage	VG8	F12	VF20	XF40	MS60	MS65	65FS	Prf65
1938	19,515,365	0.50	0.75	1.00	2.25	7.50	18.00	125	105
1938D	5,376,000	1.00	1.25	1.50	2.00	4.00	15.00	95.00	—
1938S	4,105,000	1.75	2.00	2.50	3.00	5.25	12.00	165	—
1939 T I, wavy steps, Rev. of 1939	120,627,535	—	—	—	—	3.00	30.00	300	125
1939 T II, even steps, Rev. of 1940	Inc. above	—	0.20	0.25	0.30	4.00	45.00	50.00	130
1939 doubled MONTICELLO T II	Inc. above	40.00	60.00	90.00	165	375	1,250	2,000	—
1939D T IT I, wavy steps, Rev. of 1939	3,514,000	—	—	10.00	17.50	75.00	160	275	—
1939D T IIT II, even steps, Rev. of 1940	Inc. above	4.00	5.00	8.00	14.00	55.00	105	400	—
1939S T IT I, wavy steps, Rev. of 1939	6,630,000	0.45	0.60	1.50	4.00	17.00	45.00	250	—
1939S T IIT II, even steps, Rev. of 1940	Inc. above	—	—	—	5.00	24.00	250	275	—
1940	176,499,158	—	—	—	0.25	1.00	12.00	60.00	125
1940D	43,540,000	—	0.20	0.30	0.40	1.50	2.75	25.00	—
1940S	39,690,000	0.25	0.40	0.50	1.25	4.50	20.00	55.00	—
1941	203,283,720	—	—	—	0.20	0.75	20.00	55.00	65.00
1941D	53,432,000	—	0.20	0.30	0.50	2.25	7.50	25.00	—
1941S	43,445,000	0.25	0.40	0.50	1.35	5.00	14.00	60.00	—
1942	49,818,600	—	—	—	0.40	5.00	22.00	75.00	68.00
1942D	13,938,000	1.00	1.75	3.00	5.00	38.00	65.00	85.00	—
1942D D over horizontal D	Inc. above	35.00	60.00	100	165	750	10,000	25,000	—

Note: Fully Struck Full Step nickels command higher prices. Bright, Fully Struck coins command even higher prices. 1938 thru 1989 - 5 Full Steps. 1990 to date - 6 Full Steps. Without bag marks or nicks on steps.

Monticello, mint mark above reverse

1943/2P

KM# 192a • 0.350 **Copper-Silver-Manganese**, 21.2 mm. • **Designer:** Felix Schlag **Note:** War-time composition nickels have the mint mark above MONTICELLO on the reverse.

Date	Mintage	VG8	F12	VF20	XF40	MS60	MS65	65FS	Prf65
1942P	57,900,600	1.87	1.93	2.13	2.00	9.00	20.00	75.00	150
1942S	32,900,000	1.87	1.93	2.13	2.45	8.00	19.00	170	—
1943P	271,165,000	1.87	1.93	2.13	2.00	5.00	20.00	40.00	—
1943P DDO	Inc. above	—	—	32.00	54.00	125	575	1,100	—
1943/2P	Inc. above	35.00	50.00	75.00	110	300	775	1,000	—
1943D	15,294,000	2.12	2.18	2.38	2.05	4.00	18.00	40.00	—
1943S	104,060,000	1.87	1.93	2.13	2.15	6.75	18.50	48.00	—
1944P	119,150,000	1.87	1.93	2.13	2.15	10.00	28.00	75.00	—
1944D	32,309,000	1.92	1.98	2.18	2.25	10.00	22.50	65.00	—
1944S	21,640,000	1.92	1.98	2.18	2.15	8.50	20.00	185	—
1945P	119,408,100	1.87	1.93	2.13	2.15	6.00	28.00	120	—
1945D	37,158,000	1.97	2.03	2.28	2.30	5.50	20.00	40.00	—
1945S	58,939,000	1.87	1.93	2.13	2.15	5.00	18.00	250	—

Note: Fully Struck Full Step nickels command higher prices. Bright, Fully Struck coins command even higher prices. 1938 thru 1989 - 5 Full Steps. 1990 to date - 6 Full Steps. Without bag marks or nicks on steps.

Pre-war design resumed reverse

KM# A192 • 5.00 g., **Copper-Nickel**, 21.2 mm. • **Edge:** Plain **Designer:** Felix Schlag

Date	Mintage	XF40	MS65	Prf65
1946	161,116,000	0.25	35.00	—
1946D	45,292,200	0.35	22.00	—
1946D/D	Inc. above	—	1,750	—
1946S	13,560,000	0.40	15.00	—
1947	95,000,000	0.25	18.00	—
1947D	37,822,000	0.30	18.00	—
1947S	24,720,000	0.25	20.00	—
1948	89,348,000	0.25	25.00	—
1948D	44,734,000	0.35	19.00	—
1948S	11,300,000	0.50	15.00	—
1949	60,652,000	0.30	40.00	—
1949D	36,498,000	0.40	18.00	—
1949D/S	Inc. above	65.00	550	—
1949S	9,716,000	0.90	25.00	—
1950	9,847,386	0.75	25.00	75.00
1950D	2,630,030	10.00	28.00	—
1951	28,609,500	0.50	35.00	70.00
1951D	20,460,000	0.50	22.00	—
1951S	7,776,000	1.10	28.00	—
1952	64,069,980	0.25	35.00	42.00
1952D	30,638,000	0.45	30.00	—
1952S	20,572,000	0.25	30.00	—
1953	46,772,800	0.25	26.00	45.00
1953D	59,878,600	0.25	25.00	—
1953S	19,210,900	0.25	35.00	—
1954	47,917,350	—	37.50	20.00
1954D	117,136,560	—	40.00	—
1954S	29,384,000	0.20	35.00	—
1954S/D	Inc. above	20.00	350	—
1955	8,266,200	0.45	25.00	17.00
1955D	74,464,100	—	25.00	—
1955D/S	Inc. above	25.00	300	—
1956	35,885,384	—	16.00	3.00
1956D	67,222,940	—	26.00	—
1957	39,655,952	—	35.00	2.50
1957D	136,828,900	—	22.00	—
1958	17,963,652	0.20	36.00	8.00
1958D	168,249,120	—	13.00	—

Note: Fully Struck Full Step nickels command higher prices. Bright, Fully Struck coins command even higher prices. 1938 thru 1989 - 5 Full Steps. 1990 to date - 6 Full Steps. Without bag marks or nicks on steps.

Date	Mintage	XF40	MS65	Prf65
1959	28,397,291	—	22.00	1.40
1959D	160,738,240	—	22.00	—
1960	57,107,602	—	30.00	1.25
1960D	192,582,180	—	25.00	—
1961	76,668,244	—	40.00	1.00
1961D	229,342,760	—	35.00	—
1962	100,602,019	—	24.00	1.00
1962D	280,195,720	—	110	—
1963	178,851,645	—	4.00	1.00
1963D	276,829,460	—	100	—
1964	1,028,622,762	—	5.00	1.00
1964D	1,787,297,160	—	12.00	—
1965	136,131,380	—	12.00	—
1965SMS	2,360,000	—	12.00	—
1966	156,208,283	—	10.00	—
1966SMS	2,261,583	—	15.00	—
1967	107,325,800	—	8.00	—
1967SMS	1,863,344	—	12.00	—
1968 none minted	—	—	—	—
1968D	91,227,880	—	6.00	—
1968S	103,437,510	—	5.00	0.75
1969 none minted	—	—	—	—
1969D	202,807,500	—	5.00	—
1969S	123,099,631	—	7.50	0.75
1970 none minted	—	—	—	—
1970D	515,485,380	—	12.00	—
1970S	241,464,814	—	30.00	0.75
1971	106,884,000	—	9.00	—
1971D	316,144,800	—	4.50	—
1971S	3,220,733	—	—	1.00
1972	202,036,000	—	4.00	—
1972D	351,694,600	—	3.00	—
1972S	3,260,996	—	—	1.00
1973	384,396,000	—	5.00	—
1973D	261,405,000	—	4.00	—
1973S	2,760,339	—	—	0.75
1974	601,752,000	—	12.00	—
1974D	277,373,000	—	5.00	—
1974S	2,612,568	—	—	0.75
1975	181,772,000	—	6.00	—
1975D	401,875,300	—	6.00	—
1975S	2,845,450	—	—	0.75
1976	367,124,000	—	8.00	—
1976D	563,964,147	—	6.00	—
1976S	4,149,730	—	—	0.75
1977	585,376,000	—	8.50	—
1977D	297,313,460	—	6.50	—
1977S	3,251,152	—	—	0.75
1978	391,308,000	—	7.00	—
1978D	313,092,780	—	5.00	—
1978S	3,127,781	—	—	0.75
1979	463,188,000	—	8.50	—
1979D	325,867,672	—	5.50	—
1979S type I, proof	3,677,175	—	—	0.75
1979S type II, proof	—	—	—	2.00
1980P	593,004,000	—	6.50	—
1980D	502,323,448	—	5.50	—
1980S	3,554,806	—	—	0.75
1981P	657,504,000	—	5.00	—
1981D	364,801,843	—	6.00	—
1981S type I, proof	4,063,083	—	—	2.00
1981S type II, proof	—	—	—	2.50
1982P	292,355,000	—	15.00	—
1982D	373,726,544	—	14.00	—
1982S	3,857,479	—	—	1.50
1983P	561,615,000	—	9.00	—
1983D	536,726,276	—	6.00	—
1983S	3,279,126	—	—	1.50
1984P	746,769,000	—	5.00	—
1984D	517,675,146	—	4.75	—
1984S	3,065,110	—	—	1.50
1985P	647,114,962	—	4.75	—
1985D	459,747,446	—	4.75	—
1985S	3,362,821	—	—	1.50
1986P	536,883,483	—	5.00	—
1986D	361,819,140	—	4.75	—
1986S	3,010,497	—	—	3.00
1987P	371,499,481	—	5.00	—
1987D	410,590,604	—	4.50	—
1987S	4,227,728	—	—	1.25
1988P	771,360,000	—	4.50	—
1988D	663,771,652	—	5.00	—
1988S	3,262,948	—	—	1.75
1989P	898,812,000	—	4.50	—
1989D	570,842,474	—	6.00	—
1989S	3,220,194	—	—	1.50
1990P	661,636,000	—	4.50	—
1990D	663,938,503	—	5.50	—
1990S	3,299,559	—	—	1.50
1991P	614,104,000	—	4.50	—
1991D	436,496,678	—	4.50	—
1991S	2,867,787	—	—	1.50
1992P	399,552,000	—	5.00	—
1992D	450,565,113	—	4.00	—
1992S	4,176,560	—	—	1.00
1993P	412,076,000	—	4.00	—
1993D	406,084,135	—	4.00	—
1993S	3,394,792	—	—	1.00
1994P	722,160,000	—	4.00	—
1994P Special Uncirculated matte finish	167,703	—	—	—
1994D	715,762,110	—	4.00	—
1994S	3,269,923	—	—	1.00
1995P	774,156,000	—	4.00	—
1995D	888,112,000	—	4.50	—
1995S	2,707,481	—	—	1.50
1996P	829,332,000	—	4.00	—
1996D	817,736,000	—	4.00	—
1996S	2,915,212	—	—	1.50
1997P	470,972,000	—	4.75	—
1997P Special Uncirculated matte finish	25,000	—	—	—
1997D	466,640,000	—	4.50	—
1997S	1,975,000	—	—	1.50
1998P	688,272,000	—	3.75	—
1998D	635,360,000	—	3.75	—
1998S	2,957,286	—	—	1.25
1999P	1,212,000,000	—	3.75	—
1999D	1,066,720,000	—	3.75	—
1999S	3,362,462	—	—	1.25
2000P	846,240,000	—	3.75	—
2000D	1,509,520,000	—	3.75	—
2000S	4,063,361	—	—	1.00

DIME

Barber Dime

Laureate head right, date at angle below obverse Value within wreath reverse

KM# 113 • 2.50 g., 0.900 **Silver** 0.0723 oz. ASW, 17.9 mm. • **Obv. Legend:** UNITED STATES OF AMERICA **Designer:** Charles E. Barber

Date	Mintage	G4	VG8	F12	VF20	XF40	AU50	MS60	MS65	Prf65
1901	18,860,478	3.75	4.05	4.50	11.00	32.00	72.00	120	475	1,050
1901O	5,620,000	5.00	7.00	15.00	27.00	85.00	185	525	2,100	—
1901S	593,022	85.00	135	350	415	525	700	1,200	4,600	—
1902	21,380,777	5.00	7.00	8.00	10.00	32.00	72.00	120	600	1,050
1902O	4,500,000	5.00	7.00	15.00	35.00	65.00	175	400	3,300	—
1902S	2,070,000	11.00	25.00	56.00	85.00	135	185	380	3,125	—
1903	19,500,755	3.75	4.05	4.50	8.50	32.00	72.00	140	945	1,050
1903O	8,180,000	4.75	5.50	16.00	23.00	51.00	95.00	205	2,625	—
1903S	613,300	85.00	120	315	460	600	670	925	2,200	—
1904	14,601,027	3.75	4.05	4.50	8.50	32.00	72.00	120	800	1,050
1904S	800,000	45.00	60.00	145	205	270	450	675	3,400	—
1905	14,552,350	3.75	4.05	4.50	11.00	32.00	72.00	120	550	1,050
1905O	3,400,000	5.00	9.00	36.00	54.00	100	135	275	1,100	—
1905O micro O	Inc. above	75.00	105	155	300	700	1,050	2,325	8,800	—
1905S	6,855,199	4.00	6.00	10.00	22.00	43.00	100	190	900	—
1906	19,958,406	3.75	4.05	4.55	8.50	32.00	72.00	120	430	1,050
1906D	4,060,000	3.75	4.05	4.55	18.00	37.00	70.00	145	1,300	—
1906O	2,610,000	6.00	15.00	50.00	74.00	95.00	125	200	950	—
1906S	3,136,640	3.75	5.05	15.00	23.00	48.00	135	250	900	—
1907	22,220,575	3.75	4.05	4.55	8.50	32.00	72.00	230	450	1,050
1907D	4,080,000	3.75	4.05	14.00	20.00	43.00	105	240	1,500	—
1907O	5,058,000	3.75	7.75	42.00	55.00	65.00	95.00	195	1,025	—
1907S	3,178,470	3.75	4.05	18.00	29.00	65.00	130	340	1,750	—
1908	10,600,545	3.75	4.05	4.55	8.50	32.00	72.00	230	430	1,050
1908D	7,490,000	3.75	4.05	4.55	16.00	34.00	65.00	125	625	—
1908O	1,789,000	4.25	12.00	47.00	65.00	90.00	135	260	960	—
1908S	3,220,000	5.00	6.25	13.00	24.00	48.00	155	285	1,550	—
1909	10,240,650	3.75	4.05	4.55	8.50	32.00	72.00	230	430	1,050
1909D	954,000	7.00	19.00	60.00	95.00	135	200	440	1,575	—
1909O	2,287,000	3.75	8.75	12.75	24.00	60.00	170	275	1,425	—
1909S	1,000,000	11.00	22.00	83.00	125	190	280	490	2,100	—
1910	11,520,551	3.75	4.05	4.55	8.50	32.00	72.00	230	440	1,050
1910D	3,490,000	3.75	3.75	11.00	20.00	48.00	100	195	1,275	—
1910S	1,240,000	6.00	13.00	52.00	75.00	105	200	370	1,700	—
1911	18,870,543	3.75	8.05	8.55	7.50	32.00	72.00	230	430	1,050
1911D	11,209,000	3.75	4.05	4.55	8.50	32.00	72.00	230	475	—
1911S	3,520,000	4.50	6.00	9.00	25.00	40.00	105	200	800	—
1912	19,350,700	3.75	4.05	4.55	8.50	32.00	72.00	230	430	1,050
1912D	11,760,000	3.75	4.05	4.55	8.50	32.00	72.00	230	615	—
1912S	3,420,000	3.75	4.05	4.55	16.00	35.00	85.00	165	975	—
1913	19,760,622	3.75	4.05	4.55	8.50	32.00	72.00	230	430	1,050
1913S	510,000	35.00	65.00	125	185	220	300	600	2,500	—
1914	17,360,655	3.75	4.05	4.55	8.00	32.00	72.00	230	430	1,050
1914D	11,908,000	3.75	5.75	8.75	12.75	32.00	72.00	230	430	—
1914S	2,100,000	3.75	5.25	6.75	21.00	45.00	80.00	130	1,000	—
1915	5,620,450	3.75	4.05	4.55	8.00	32.00	72.00	230	430	1,050
1915S	960,000	7.00	11.00	35.00	50.00	75.00	125	205	1,300	—
1916	18,490,000	3.75	4.05	4.55	4.85	32.00	72.00	230	430	—
1916S	5,820,000	3.75	4.05	4.55	6.50	32.00	72.00	230	430	—

Mercury Dime

Mint mark

1942/41

Full split bands

KM# 140 • 2.50 g., 0.900 **Silver** 0.0723 oz. ASW, 17.8 mm. • **Designer:** Adolph A. Weinman
Note: All specimens listed as -65FSB are for fully struck MS-65 coins with fully split and rounded horizontal bands on the fasces.

Date	Mintage	G4	VG8	F12	VF20	XF40	MS60	MS65	MS65FSB	PF65
1916	22,180,080	3.50	6.50	7.00	8.50	10.50	40.00	105	165	—
1916D	264,000	625	1,300	2,115	3,600	5,700	10,400	24,000	48,500	—
1916S	10,450,000	3.50	6.50	7.85	12.00	19.00	55.00	205	800	—
1917	55,230,000	3.50	6.50	7.00	8.50	9.50	31.00	170	375	—
1917D	9,402,000	3.50	6.50	13.00	23.00	46.00	125	925	5,650	—
1917S	27,330,000	3.50	6.50	7.00	8.00	12.00	68.00	400	1,265	—
1918	26,680,000	3.50	6.50	7.00	10.00	28.00	85.00	355	1,325	—
1918D	22,674,800	3.50	6.50	7.00	11.00	26.00	110	725	27,500	—
1918S	19,300,000	3.50	6.50	7.00	9.00	20.00	115	800	7,450	—
1919	35,740,000	3.50	6.50	7.00	8.50	9.00	48.00	325	685	—
1919D	9,939,000	3.50	6.50	12.00	27.00	38.00	157	1,200	38,500	—
1919S	8,850,000	3.50	6.50	10.00	17.00	35.00	157	1,550	14,350	—
1920	59,030,000	3.50	6.50	7.00	8.50	9.50	42.00	240	540	—
1920D	19,171,000	3.50	6.50	7.00	8.00	20.00	120	700	4,750	—
1920S	13,820,000	3.50	6.50	9.00	9.00	17.00	120	11,225	8,250	—
1921	1,230,000	40.00	63.00	90.00	220	450	1,000	2,900	4,350	—
1921D	1,080,000	50.00	100	160	320	570	1,250	3,050	5,200	—
1923	50,130,000	3.50	6.50	7.00	8.50	9.50	35.00	125	340	—
1923S	6,440,000	3.50	6.50	8.50	18.00	63.00	190	1,200	7,450	—
1924	24,010,000	3.50	6.50	7.00	8.50	11.00	52.00	181	500	—
1924D	6,810,000	3.50	6.50	8.00	20.00	60.00	180	900	1,365	—
1924S	7,120,000	3.50	6.50	7.00	10.00	50.00	240	1,300	16,750	—
1925	25,610,000	3.50	6.50	7.00	8.50	9.50	41.00	275	990	—
1925D	5,117,000	3.00	4.50	11.00	42.00	110	350	1,520	3,500	—
1925S	5,850,000	3.00	3.40	7.75	16.50	77.00	185	1,050	4,650	—
1926	32,160,000	3.50	6.50	7.00	8.50	9.50	24.00	205	525	—
1926D	6,828,000	3.50	6.50	7.00	11.00	26.00	110	450	2,500	—
1926S	1,520,000	10.00	12.00	25.00	55.00	210	900	3,000	6,750	—
1927	28,080,000	3.50	6.50	7.00	8.50	9.50	28.00	145	350	—
1927D	4,812,000	3.50	6.50	8.50	24.00	77.00	185	1,150	8,500	—
1927S	4,770,000	3.50	6.50	7.00	11.00	25.00	295	1,200	7,600	—
1928	19,480,000	3.50	6.50	7.00	8.50	9.50	28.00	135	345	—
1928D	4,161,000	3.50	6.50	11.50	24.00	52.00	170	750	2,750	—
1928S Large S	7,400,000	3.50	6.50	7.00	7.00	16.50	160	410	6,500	—
1928S Small S	Inc. above	3.50	6.50	7.00	9.50	17.00	205	440	2,000	—
1929	25,970,000	3.50	6.50	7.00	8.50	9.50	24.00	72.00	175	—
1929D	5,034,000	3.50	6.50	7.00	10.50	13.50	28.00	73.00	225	—
1929S	4,730,000	3.50	6.50	7.00	9.50	11.50	33.00	125	560	—
1929S Doubled Die Obv	Inc. above	8.00	11.00	16.00	25.00	40.00	95.00	335	1,150	—
1930	6,770,000	3.50	6.50	7.00	9.50	11.50	28.00	115	575	—
1930S	1,843,000	3.50	6.50	7.00	8.50	15.00	75.00	195	685	—
1931	3,150,000	3.50	6.50	7.00	8.50	10.00	36.00	175	800	—
1931D	1,260,000	6.75	8.00	13.00	18.00	42.50	105	285	375	—
1931 Doubled Die Obv & Rev	Inc. above	—	20.00	27.50	50.00	70.00	135	485	650	—
1931S	1,800,000	3.50	6.50	7.00	9.00	20.00	105	280	2,500	—
1931S Doubled Die Obv	Inc. above	7.50	10.00	13.00	25.00	35.00	140	425	3,850	—
1934	24,080,000	3.00	3.30	3.80	4.10	5.60	32.00	53.00	130	—
1934D	6,772,000	3.00	3.30	3.80	7.50	14.00	54.00	80.00	320	—
1935	58,830,000	3.00	3.30	3.80	4.10	5.60	12.00	32.00	68.00	—
1935D	10,477,000	3.00	3.30	3.80	6.50	13.00	36.00	85.00	500	—
1935S	15,840,000	3.00	3.30	3.80	4.10	5.60	26.00	37.00	360	—
1936	87,504,130	3.00	3.30	3.80	4.10	5.60	9.50	28.00	84.00	1,000
1936 Doubled Die Obv	Inc. above	—	—	8.00	15.00	25.00	50.00	165	—	—
1936D	16,132,000	3.00	3.30	3.80	4.10	8.50	30.00	55.00	290	—
1936S	9,210,000	3.00	3.30	3.80	4.10	5.60	28.00	36.00	88.00	—
1937	56,865,756	3.00	3.30	3.80	4.10	5.60	11.00	25.00	52.00	500
1937 Doubled Die Obv	Inc. above	—	—	—	6.00	9.00	30.00	105	175	—
1937D	14,146,000	3.00	3.30	3.80	4.10	5.60	21.50	40.00	105	—
1937S	9,740,000	3.00	3.30	3.80	4.10	5.60	21.00	33.00	190	—
1937S Doubled Die Obv	Inc. above	—	—	—	5.00	8.00	38.00	135	275	—
1938	22,198,728	3.00	3.30	3.80	4.10	5.60	14.00	28.00	80.00	275
1938D	5,537,000	3.00	3.30	3.80	4.10	5.60	17.50	32.00	62.00	—
1938S	8,090,000	3.00	3.30	3.80	4.10	5.60	21.00	40.00	160	—
1939	67,749,321	3.00	3.30	3.80	4.10	5.60	9.00	28.00	170	235
1939 Doubled Die Obv	Inc. above	—	—	—	4.00	6.00	20.00	45.00	450	—
1939D	24,394,000	3.00	3.30	3.80	4.10	5.60	9.00	28.00	49.00	—
1939S	10,540,000	3.00	7.30	7.80	8.10	9.60	26.00	37.00	765	—
1940	65,361,827	3.00	3.30	3.80	4.10	5.60	9.00	30.00	48.00	200
1940D	21,198,000	3.00	3.30	3.80	4.10	5.60	9.50	32.00	48.00	—
1940S	21,560,000	3.00	3.30	3.80	4.10	5.60	9.50	32.00	95.00	—
1941	175,106,557	3.00	3.30	3.80	4.10	5.60	9.00	30.00	46.00	200
1941 Doubled Die Obv	Inc. above	—	—	—	10.00	16.00	65.00	175	295	—
1941D	45,634,000	3.00	3.30	3.80	4.10	5.60	11.00	24.00	46.00	—
1941D Doubled Die Obv	Inc. above	—	—	—	9.00	14.00	40.00	135	250	—
1941S Small S	43,090,000	3.00	3.30	3.80	4.10	5.60	10.00	30.00	46.00	—
1941S Large S	Inc. above	4.00	5.00	8.00	15.00	25.00	120	265	425	—
1941S Doubled Die Rev	Inc. above	4.00	4.50	5.00	5.50	6.00	20.00	70.00	85.00	—
1942	205,432,329	3.00	3.30	3.80	4.10	5.60	9.00	24.00	46.00	200
1942/41	Inc. above	325	340	375	430	500	2,500	12,000	35,000	—
1942D	60,740,000	3.00	3.30	3.80	4.10	5.60	12.00	27.00	46.00	—
1942/41D	Inc. above	310	330	350	410	500	2,750	12,000	26,500	—
1942S	49,300,000	3.00	3.30	3.80	4.10	5.60	19.00	26.00	145	—
1943	191,710,000	3.00	3.30	3.80	4.10	5.60	9.00	28.00	50.00	—
1943D	71,949,000	3.00	3.30	3.80	4.10	5.60	13.00	28.00	47.00	—

Date	Mintage	G4	VG8	F12	VF20	XF40	MS60	MS65	MS65FSB	PF65
1943S	60,400,000	3.00	3.30	3.80	4.10	5.60	13.00	27.00	66.00	—
1944	231,410,000	3.00	3.30	3.80	4.10	5.60	9.00	25.00	75.00	—
1944D	62,224,000	3.00	3.30	3.80	4.10	5.60	13.00	25.00	46.00	—
1944S	49,490,000	3.00	3.30	3.80	4.10	5.60	14.00	30.00	50.00	—
1945	159,130,000	3.00	3.30	3.80	4.10	5.60	9.00	26.00	97.50	—
1945D	40,245,000	3.00	3.30	3.80	4.10	5.60	11.00	26.00	46.50	—
1945S	41,920,000	3.00	3.30	3.80	4.10	5.60	12.00	26.00	105	—
1945S micro S	Inc. above	3.25	4.00	6.00	9.00	13.00	30.00	90.00	685	—

Roosevelt Dime

Mint mark 1946-64

KM# 195 • 2.50 g., 0.900 **Silver** 0.0723 oz. ASW, 17.9 mm. • **Designer:** John R. Sinnock

Date	Mintage	G4	VG8	F12	VF20	XF40	AU50	MS60	MS65	Prf65
1946	225,250,000	—	—	—	—	$3.00	$3.30	$3.80	9.00	—
1946D	61,043,500	—	—	—	—	$3.00	$3.30	$3.80	10.00	—
1946S	27,900,000	—	—	—	—	$3.00	$3.30	$3.80	10.00	—
1947	121,520,000	—	—	—	—	$3.00	$3.30	$3.80	12.00	—
1947D	46,835,000	—	—	—	—	$3.00	$3.30	4.00	16.00	—
1947S	34,840,000	—	—	—	—	$3.00	$3.30	3.50	12.00	—
1948	74,950,000	—	—	—	—	$3.00	$3.30	3.25	10.00	—
1948D	52,841,000	—	—	—	—	$3.00	$3.30	5.00	14.00	—
1948S	35,520,000	—	—	—	—	$3.00	$3.30	4.50	15.00	—
1949	30,940,000	—	—	$3.00	$3.30	$5.00	8.50	12.00	25.00	—
1949D	26,034,000	—	—	$3.00	3.30	5.00	5.50	7.00	20.00	—
1949S	13,510,000	—	—	$3.00	3.30	8.00	15.00	35.00	60.00	—
1950	50,181,500	—	—	—	$3.30	3.60	5.30	6.00	12.00	60.00
1950D	46,803,000	—	—	—	—	—	1.63	3.25	10.00	—
1950S	20,440,000	—	—	$3.00	3.30	5.00	9.00	23.00	35.00	—
1951	102,937,602	—	—	—	—	—	$3.00	3.30	13.00	60.00
1951D	56,529,000	—	—	—	—	—	1.73	2.80	12.00	—
1951S	31,630,000	—	—	—	$3.00	3.30	5.00	10.00	18.00	—
1952	99,122,073	—	—	—	—	—	$3.00	3.30	20.00	45.00
1952D	122,100,000	—	—	—	—	—	$3.00	3.30	10.00	—
1952S	44,419,500	—	—	—	$3.00	3.30	5.00	5.50	16.00	—
1953	53,618,920	—	—	—	—	—	$3.00	3.30	12.00	40.00
1953D	136,433,000	—	—	—	—	—	$3.00	3.30	11.00	—
1953S	39,180,000	—	—	—	—	—	$3.70	3.00	12.50	—
1954	114,243,503	—	—	—	—	—	$3.00	3.30	10.00	24.00
1954D	106,397,000	—	—	—	—	—	$3.00	3.30	15.00	—
1954S	22,860,000	—	—	—	—	—	$3.00	3.30	10.00	—
1955	12,828,381	—	—	—	$3.00	$3.30	$3.80	$4.10	8.50	20.00
1955D	13,959,000	—	—	—	$3.00	$3.30	$3.80	$4.10	8.50	—
1955S	18,510,000	—	—	—	$3.00	$3.30	$3.80	$4.10	8.00	—
1956	109,309,384	—	—	—	—	—	$3.00	$3.30	9.50	12.00
1956D	108,015,100	—	—	—	—	—	$3.00	$3.30	9.00	—
1957	161,407,952	—	—	—	—	—	$3.00	$3.30	8.50	10.00
1957D	113,354,330	—	—	—	—	—	$3.00	$3.30	7.50	—
1958	32,785,652	—	—	—	—	—	$3.00	$3.30	11.00	10.00
1958D	136,564,600	—	—	—	—	—	$3.00	$3.30	10.00	—
1959	86,929,291	—	—	—	—	—	$3.00	$3.30	8.00	10.00
1959D	164,919,790	—	—	—	—	—	$3.00	$3.30	8.50	—
1960	72,081,602	—	—	—	—	—	$3.00	$3.30	8.50	10.00
1960D	200,160,400	—	—	—	—	—	$3.00	$3.30	7.50	—
1961	96,758,244	—	—	—	—	—	$3.00	$3.30	8.00	10.00
1961D	209,146,550	—	—	—	—	—	$3.00	$3.30	6.50	—
1962	75,668,019	—	—	—	—	—	$3.00	$3.30	6.50	10.00
1962D	334,948,380	—	—	—	—	—	$3.00	$3.30	7.00	—
1963	126,725,645	—	—	—	—	—	$3.00	$3.30	7.50	10.00
1963D	421,476,530	—	—	—	—	—	$3.00	$3.30	7.00	—
1964	933,310,762	—	—	—	—	—	$3.00	$3.30	7.50	10.00
1964D	1,357,517,180	—	—	—	—	—	$3.00	$3.30	7.00	—

Mint mark 1968- present Mint mark 1968- present

KM# 195a • 2.27 g., **Copper-Nickel Clad Copper**, 17.91 mm. • **Designer:** John R. Sinnock **Note:** The 1979-S and 1981-S Type II proofs have clearer mint marks than the Type I proofs of those years. On the 1982 no-mint-mark variety, the mint mark was inadvertently left off.

Date	Mintage	MS65	Prf65
1965	1,652,140,570	6.00	—
1965SMS	—	2.00	—
1966	1,382,734,540	6.50	—
1966SMS	—	2.25	—
1967	2,244,007,320	7.00	—
1967SMS	—	3.50	—
1968	424,470,000	6.50	—
1968D	480,748,280	6.50	—
1968S	3,041,506	—	4.00
1968 no S error	—	—	7,500
1969	145,790,000	7.00	—
1969D	563,323,870	6.00	—
1969S	2,934,631	—	4.00
1970	345,570,000	5.50	—
1970D	754,942,100	5.00	—
1970S	2,632,810	—	4.00
1970S No S	—	—	1,300
1971	162,690,000	10.00	—
1971D	377,914,240	8.00	—
1971S	3,220,733	—	4.00
1972	431,540,000	7.50	—
1972D	330,290,000	8.50	—
1972S	3,260,996	—	4.00
1973	315,670,000	6.00	—
1973D	455,032,426	5.50	—
1973S	2,760,339	—	4.00
1974	470,248,000	5.50	—
1974D	571,083,000	4.50	—
1974S	2,612,568	—	4.00
1975	585,673,900	4.50	—
1975D	313,705,300	4.50	—
1975S	2,845,450	—	4.00
1976	568,760,000	4.50	—
1976D	695,222,774	4.50	—
1976S	4,149,730	—	4.00
1977	796,930,000	4.50	—
1977D	376,607,228	8.00	—
1977S	3,251,152	—	4.00
1978	663,980,000	5.00	—
1978D	282,847,540	4.50	—
1978S	3,127,781	—	4.00
1979	315,440,000	5.50	—
1979D	390,921,184	5.00	—
1979S type I	3,677,175	—	5.00
1979S type II	—	—	2.00
1980P	735,170,000	6.00	—
1980D	719,354,321	5.00	—
1980S	3,554,806	—	4.00
1981P	676,650,000	4.00	—
1981D	712,284,143	4.00	—
1981S type I	—	—	4.00
1981S type II	—	—	6.50
1982P	519,475,000	8.50	—
1982 no mint mark	Inc. above	200	—
1982D	542,713,584	3.20	—
1982S	3,857,479	—	4.00
1983P	647,025,000	6.00	—
1983D	730,129,224	4.00	—
1983S	3,279,126	—	4.00
1984P	856,669,000	4.00	—
1984D	704,803,976	3.50	—
1984S	3,065,110	—	4.00
1985P	705,200,962	5.00	—
1985D	587,979,970	3.50	—
1985S	3,362,821	—	4.00
1986P	682,649,693	3.50	—
1986D	473,326,970	3.50	—
1986S	3,010,497	—	4.00
1987P	762,709,481	4.50	—
1987D	653,203,402	4.50	—
1987S	4,227,728	—	4.00
1988P	1,030,550,000	5.50	—
1988D	962,385,488	5.50	—
1988S	3,262,948	—	3.00
1989P	1,298,400,000	4.00	—
1989D	896,535,597	5.00	—
1989S	3,220,194	—	4.00
1990P	1,034,340,000	4.50	—
1990D	839,995,824	5.50	—
1990S	3,299,559	—	4.00
1991P	927,220,000	5.00	—
1991D	601,241,114	5.00	—
1991S	2,867,787	—	3.00
1992P	593,500,000	4.50	—
1992D	616,273,932	4.50	—
1992S	2,858,981	—	4.00
1993P	766,180,000	3.50	—
1993D	750,110,166	4.50	—
1993S	2,633,439	—	7.00
1994P	1,189,000,000	4.00	—
1994D	1,303,268,110	5.50	—
1994S	2,484,594	—	5.00
1995P	1,125,500,000	4.00	—
1995D	1,274,890,000	4.50	—
1995S	2,010,384	—	20.00
1996P	1,421,163,000	3.00	—
1996D	1,400,300,000	5.00	—
1996W	1,457,949	24.00	—
1996S	2,085,191	—	3.50
1997P	991,640,000	4.00	—
1997D	979,810,000	3.00	—
1997S	1,975,000	—	14.00
1998P	1,163,000,000	2.75	—
1998D	1,172,250,000	2.75	—
1998S	2,078,494	—	4.00
1999P	2,164,000,000	2.75	—
1999D	1,397,750,000	2.75	—
1999S	2,557,897	—	4.00
2000P	1,842,500,000	2.75	—
2000D	1,818,700,000	2.75	—
2000S	3,097,440	—	1.00

KM# 195b • 2.50 g., 0.900 **Silver** 0.0723 oz. ASW, 17.9 mm. • **Designer:** John R. Sinnock

Date	Mintage	Prf65
1992S	1,317,579	5.00
1993S	761,353	7.00
1994S	785,329	7.00
1995S	838,953	8.00
1996S	830,021	7.00
1997S	821,678	14.00
1998S	878,792	7.00
1999S	804,565	7.00
1999S	1,317,579	7.00
1999S	761,353	7.00
1999S	785,329	7.00
1999S	838,953	7.00
2000S	965,921	5.50

QUARTER

Barber Quarter

Laureate head right, flanked by stars, date below obverse Heraldic eagle reverse

KM# 114 • 6.25 g., 0.900 **Silver** 0.1808 oz. ASW, 24.3 mm. • **Obv. Legend:** IN GOD WE TRUST **Rev. Legend:** UNITED STATES OF AMERICA **Designer:** Charles E. Barber

Date	Mintage	G4	VG8	F12	VF20	XF40	AU50	MS60	MS65	Prf65
1901	8,892,813	27.00	31.00	39.00	63.00	76.00	115	275	1,050	1,450
1901O	1,612,000	63.00	95.00	185	400	880	1,200	1,725	6,600	—
1901S	72,664	4,000	7,000	15,000	18,500	25,500	34,500	37,500	65,000	—
1902	12,197,744	8.00	9.00	16.00	27.00	55.00	125	245	740	1,450
1902O	4,748,000	10.00	13.00	44.00	72.00	120	220	500	2,900	—
1902S	1,524,612	12.00	19.00	44.00	77.00	140	275	500	2,750	—
1903	9,670,064	8.00	9.00	17.00	29.00	61.00	125	245	1,600	1,450
1903O	3,500,000	10.00	11.00	33.00	55.00	105	210	440	3,300	—
1903S	1,036,000	13.00	21.00	37.00	77.00	125	230	440	1,800	—
1904	9,588,813	8.00	11.00	17.00	30.00	58.00	110	220	1,300	1,450
1904O	2,456,000	27.00	37.00	78.00	140	190	440	875	4,000	—
1905	4,968,250	27.00	31.00	42.00	55.00	60.00	115	220	850	1,450
1905O	1,230,000	39.00	55.00	110	210	220	300	550	4,800	—
1905S	1,884,000	29.00	37.00	62.00	90.00	95.00	180	500	3,300	—
1906	3,656,435	8.00	9.00	16.00	27.00	55.00	125	245	740	1,450
1906D	3,280,000	8.00	16.00	20.00	35.00	57.00	125	220	1,500	—
1906O	2,056,000	10.00	14.00	33.00	51.00	95.00	165	240	1,250	—
1907	7,192,575	8.00	9.00	14.00	27.00	53.00	125	245	740	1,450
1907D	2,484,000	8.00	9.00	22.00	42.00	65.00	200	330	2,200	—
1907O	4,560,000	10.00	11.00	16.00	33.00	55.00	115	220	1,550	—
1907S	1,360,000	10.00	15.00	38.00	60.00	110	220	500	3,450	—
1908	4,232,545	8.00	9.00	16.00	27.00	55.00	125	245	740	1,450
1908D	5,788,000	8.00	9.00	14.00	30.00	55.00	125	245	740	—
1908O	6,244,000	8.00	9.00	14.00	30.00	55.00	125	220	360	—
1908S	784,000	28.00	60.00	120	140	300	525	725	3,700	—
1909	9,268,650	8.00	9.00	14.00	30.00	55.00	125	245	740	1,450
1909D	5,114,000	8.00	9.00	14.00	30.00	55.00	125	245	740	—
1909O	712,000	50.00	175	500	815	2,000	3,100	4,000	7,250	—
1909S	1,348,000	10.00	11.00	30.00	46.00	77.00	200	330	1,550	—
1910	2,244,551	8.00	9.00	14.00	30.00	55.00	125	245	740	1,450
1910D	1,500,000	8.00	9.00	38.00	60.00	105	210	375	1,325	—
1911	3,720,543	8.00	9.00	14.00	30.00	55.00	125	220	740	1,450
1911D	933,600	27.00	37.00	140	275	400	575	800	4,500	—

Date	Mintage	G4	VG8	F12	VF20	XF40	AU50	MS60	MS65	Prf65
1911S	988,000	10.00	13.00	46.00	82.00	150	240	320	1,350	—
1912	4,400,700	8.00	9.00	14.00	27.00	46.00	125	245	740	1,450
1912S	708,000	22.00	28.00	65.00	90.00	110	185	350	1,700	—
1913	484,613	26.00	41.00	100	160	330	440	725	2,100	1,450
1913D	1,450,800	12.00	15.00	38.00	53.00	85.00	170	350	1,050	—
1913S	40,000	1,250	1,775	4,200	7,000	9,550	12,000	14,250	31,000	—
1914	6,244,610	8.00	9.00	14.00	27.00	46.00	125	245	740	1,450
1914D	3,046,000	8.00	9.00	14.00	27.00	46.00	125	245	740	—
1914S	264,000	125	165	375	550	800	1,100	1,550	7,000	—
1915	3,480,450	8.00	9.00	14.00	27.00	46.00	125	245	740	1,450
1915D	3,694,000	8.00	9.00	14.00	27.00	46.00	125	245	740	—
1915S	704,000	22.00	37.00	55.00	82.00	88.00	175	250	990	—
1916	1,788,000	8.00	9.00	14.00	27.00	46.00	125	245	740	—
1916D	6,540,800	8.00	9.00	14.00	27.00	46.00	125	245	740	—
1916D/D	Inc. above	12.00	16.00	21.00	32.00	59.00	148	280	—	—

Standing Liberty Quarter

Right breast exposed; Type 1 obverse

Right breast exposed

KM# 141 • 6.25 g., 0.900 **Silver** 0.1808 oz. ASW, 24.3 mm. • **Designer:** Hermon A. MacNeil

Date	Mintage	G4	VG8	F12	VF20	XF40	AU50	MS60	MS65	65FH
1916	52,000	2,650	4,100	5,500	6,300	9,000	10,000	13,000	31,000	36,500
1917	8,792,000	18.00	38.00	55.00	80.00	110	165	205	330	850
1917D	1,509,200	19.00	55.00	80.00	115	175	210	275	750	1,650
1917S	1,952,000	22.00	62.00	95.00	130	180	250	300	1,000	3,200

Right breast covered; Type 2 obverse Three stars below eagle reverse

Right breast covered

Right breast covered

KM# 145 • 6.25 g., 0.900 **Silver** 0.1808 oz. ASW, 24.3 mm. • **Designer:** Hermon A. MacNeil

Date	Mintage	G4	VG8	F12	VF20	XF40	AU50	MS60	MS65	65FH
1917	13,880,000	16.00	35.00	46.00	55.00	88.00	115	175	515	900
1917D	6,224,400	32.00	35.00	77.00	100	135	180	235	1,400	3,350
1917S	5,522,000	29.00	36.00	80.00	100	130	175	225	950	3,650
1918	14,240,000	12.00	18.00	24.00	25.00	35.00	70.00	110	440	1,750
1918D	7,380,000	18.00	32.00	62.00	65.00	120	165	240	1,350	4,850
1918S	11,072,000	13.00	15.00	25.00	28.00	44.00	72.00	145	1,050	10,500
1918/17S	Inc. above	1,400	1,750	3,400	4,500	7,000	10,500	16,750	83,000	320,000
1919	11,324,000	26.00	40.00	53.00	60.00	71.00	100	150	440	1,275
1919D	1,944,000	60.00	80.00	180	345	530	685	900	4,000	37,500
1919S	1,836,000	55.00	80.00	145	325	450	650	1,030	6,500	31,500
1920	27,860,000	11.00	13.00	20.00	31.00	44.00	77.00	125	260	1,850
1920D	3,586,400	125	135	170	205	245	300	500	1,900	6,850
1920S	6,380,000	13.00	18.00	23.00	30.00	50.00	150	325	2,150	24,000
1921	1,916,000	130	150	330	560	700	975	1,450	2,900	5,500
1923	9,716,000	11.00	12.00	28.00	33.00	46.00	82.00	130	400	3,850
1923S	1,360,000	200	300	575	875	1,300	1,750	2,300	4,000	7,500
1924	10,920,000	11.00	13.00	19.00	30.00	40.00	95.00	160	300	1,550
1924D	3,112,000	40.00	50.00	88.00	115	160	200	255	440	4,350
1924S	2,860,000	20.00	25.00	37.00	50.00	105	190	260	1,800	5,650
1925	12,280,000	5.00	6.00	9.00	16.00	38.00	77.00	125	440	950
1926	11,316,000	5.00	6.00	9.00	16.00	38.00	77.00	125	425	1,650
1926D	1,716,000	5.00	15.00	21.00	40.00	80.00	115	150	425	25,000
1926S	2,700,000	5.00	6.00	10.00	16.00	80.00	175	400	2,750	26,000
1927	11,912,000	5.00	6.00	9.00	16.00	38.00	77.00	125	440	1,150
1927D	976,400	15.00	18.00	26.00	66.00	130	185	220	500	2,450
1927S	396,000	40.00	50.00	100	265	775	2,100	4,500	11,500	185,000
1928	6,336,000	5.00	6.00	9.00	16.00	38.00	77.00	125	440	1,850
1928D	1,627,600	5.00	6.00	9.00	16.00	38.00	77.00	125	440	4,950
1928S Large S	2,644,000	5.00	6.00	9.00	16.00	38.00	77.00	125	440	—
1928S Small S	Inc. above	5.00	6.00	9.00	16.00	38.00	77.00	125	440	900
1929	11,140,000	5.00	6.00	9.00	16.00	38.00	77.00	125	440	795
1929D	1,358,000	5.00	6.00	9.00	16.00	38.00	77.00	125	440	5,850
1929S	1,764,000	5.00	6.00	9.00	16.00	38.00	77.00	125	440	795
1930	5,632,000	5.00	6.00	9.00	16.00	38.00	77.00	125	440	795
1930S	1,556,000	5.00	6.00	9.00	16.00	38.00	77.00	125	440	845

Washington Quarter

Mint mark 1932-64

KM# 164 • 6.25 g., 0.900 **Silver** 0.1808 oz. ASW, 24.3 mm. • **Designer:** John Flanagan

Date	Mintage	G4	VG8	F12	VF20	XF40	AU50	MS60	MS65	Prf65
1932	5,404,000	6.00	7.00	8.00	9.00	10.50	16.00	27.00	200	—
1932D	436,800	80.00	95.00	115	130	160	350	1,025	11,000	—
1932S	408,000	80.00	90.00	105	120	155	240	400	2,800	—
1934 Medium Motto	31,912,052	5.00	6.00	7.00	8.00	8.50	9.00	20.00	90.00	—
1934 Heavy Motto	Inc. Above	6.00	7.00	9.00	12.50	15.00	25.00	45.00	225	—
1934 Light motto	Inc. Above	6.00	7.00	10.00	13.00	17.00	25.00	45.00	290	—
1934 Doubled Die Obverse	Inc. Above	60.00	80.00	140	180	290	410	800	3,000	—
1934D Medium Motto	3,527,200	5.00	6.00	10.00	17.00	25.00	90.00	200	500	—
1934D Heavy Motto	Inc. Above	5.00	7.50	12.50	20.00	30.00	100	240	1,000	—
1935	32,484,000	5.00	6.00	7.00	8.00	8.50	9.00	17.00	70.00	—
1935D	5,780,000	5.00	6.00	9.00	14.00	35.00	125	260	500	—
1935S	5,660,000	5.00	6.00	7.00	8.00	13.00	30.00	82.00	275	—
1936	41,303,837	5.00	6.00	7.00	8.00	8.50	10.00	22.00	85.00	1,550
1936D	5,374,000	5.00	8.00	9.00	31.00	60.00	285	530	870	—
1936S	3,828,000	5.00	6.00	7.00	15.00	20.00	48.00	92.00	245	—
1937	19,701,542	5.00	6.00	7.00	12.00	20.00	45.00	75.00	175	475
1937 Double Die Obverse	Inc. Above	95.00	140	250	350	600	800	1,650	8,000	—
1937D	7,189,600	5.00	6.00	7.00	9.00	14.00	40.00	60.00	135	—
1937S	1,652,000	5.00	6.00	8.00	19.00	38.00	125	195	405	—
1938	9,480,045	5.00	6.00	7.00	8.00	24.00	55.00	100	225	350
1938S	2,832,000	5.00	6.00	7.00	11.00	32.00	60.00	105	200	—
1939	33,548,795	5.00	6.00	7.00	12.00	14.00	15.00	22.00	65.00	250
1939D	7,092,000	5.00	6.00	7.00	12.00	18.00	24.00	41.00	115	—
1939S	2,628,000	5.00	6.00	7.00	10.00	30.00	55.00	105	275	—
1940	35,715,246	5.00	6.00	7.00	8.00	9.00	12.00	15.00	45.00	160
1940D	2,797,600	5.00	6.00	8.00	11.00	22.00	55.00	110	220	—
1940S	8,244,000	5.00	6.00	7.00	8.00	9.00	15.00	25.00	36.00	—
1941	79,047,287	—	—	—	—	—	8.00	9.00	30.00	175
1941 Double Die Obv.	Inc. Above	—	—	—	20.00	30.00	50.00	65.00	120	—
1941D	16,714,800	—	—	—	—	—	12.00	28.00	58.00	—
1941S	16,080,000	—	—	—	—	—	10.00	25.00	55.00	—
1941 Lg S	Inc. Above	—	4.00	8.00	10.00	15.00	40.00	85.00	300	—
1942	102,117,123	—	—	—	—	—	8.00	8.50	25.00	135
1942D	17,487,200	—	—	—	—	—	9.00	16.00	33.00	—
1942D Double Die Obv.	Inc. Above	—	75.00	190	390	575	1,000	1,800	4,000	—
1942D Double Die Rev.	Inc. Above	—	18.00	35.00	50.00	65.00	120	300	1,550	—
1942S	19,384,000	—	—	—	—	—	19.00	63.00	110	—
1943	99,700,000	—	—	—	—	—	8.00	8.50	35.00	—
1943 Double Die Obv.	Inc. Above	—	7.00	15.00	25.00	40.00	60.00	145	380	—
1943D	16,095,600	—	—	—	—	—	14.00	25.00	44.00	—
1943S	21,700,000	—	—	—	—	—	11.00	23.00	45.00	—
1943S Double Die Obv.	Inc. Above	20.00	45.00	65.00	90.00	120	200	300	1,000	—
1943 Trumpet tail S	Inc. Above	6.00	12.00	18.00	30.00	45.00	80.00	140	500	—
1944	104,956,000	—	—	—	—	—	8.00	8.50	25.00	—
1944D	14,600,800	—	—	—	—	—	9.00	16.00	34.00	—
1944S	12,560,000	—	—	—	—	—	9.00	13.00	27.00	—
1945	74,372,000	—	—	—	—	—	8.00	8.50	30.00	—
1945D	12,341,600	—	—	—	—	—	11.00	16.00	33.00	—
1945S	17,004,001	—	—	—	—	—	8.00	9.00	28.00	—
1946	53,436,000	—	—	—	—	—	8.00	8.50	34.00	—
1946D	9,072,800	—	—	—	—	—	8.00	9.00	35.00	—
1946S	4,204,000	—	—	—	—	—	8.00	8.50	26.00	—
1947	22,556,000	—	—	—	—	—	8.00	9.00	28.00	—
1947D	15,338,400	—	—	—	—	—	8.00	9.00	32.00	—
1947S	5,532,000	—	—	—	—	—	8.00	9.00	20.00	—
1948	35,196,000	—	—	—	—	—	8.00	8.50	20.00	—
1948D	16,766,800	—	—	—	—	—	8.00	11.00	45.00	—
1948S	15,960,000	—	—	—	—	—	8.00	9.00	36.00	—
1949	9,312,000	—	—	—	—	—	13.00	31.00	60.00	—
1949D	10,068,400	—	—	—	—	—	10.00	15.00	33.00	—
1950	24,971,512	—	—	—	—	—	8.00	8.50	26.00	65.00
1950D	21,075,600	—	—	—	—	—	8.00	8.50	26.00	—
1950D/S	Inc. Above	18.00	21.00	30.00	49.00	120	185	215	3,300	—
1950S	10,284,004	—	—	—	—	—	8.00	8.50	26.00	—
1950S/D	Inc. Above	18.00	21.00	30.00	49.00	155	260	325	680	—
1950S/S	Inc. Above	6.00	7.00	8.00	10.00	—	18.00	35.00	135	—
1951	43,505,602	—	—	—	—	—	8.00	8.50	26.00	60.00
1951D	35,354,800	—	—	—	—	—	8.00	8.50	26.00	—
1951S	9,048,000	—	—	—	—	—	8.00	8.50	26.00	—
1952	38,862,073	—	—	—	—	—	8.00	8.50	26.00	46.00
1952D	49,795,200	—	—	—	—	—	8.00	8.50	26.00	—
1952S	13,707,800	—	—	—	—	—	8.00	8.50	26.00	—
1953	18,664,920	—	—	—	—	—	8.00	8.50	26.00	44.00
1953D	56,112,400	—	—	—	—	—	8.00	8.50	26.00	—
1953S	14,016,000	—	—	—	—	—	8.00	8.50	26.00	—
1954	54,645,503	—	—	—	—	—	8.00	8.50	26.00	18.00
1954D	42,305,500	—	—	—	—	—	8.00	8.50	26.00	—
1954S	11,834,722	—	—	—	—	—	8.00	8.50	26.00	—
1955	18,558,381	—	—	—	—	—	8.00	8.50	26.00	22.00
1955D	3,182,400	—	—	—	—	—	8.00	8.50	26.00	—
1956	44,813,384	—	—	—	—	—	8.00	8.50	26.00	15.00
1956 Double Bar 5	Inc. Above	—	5.60	5.70	5.80	6.50	9.00	20.00	125	—
1956 Type B rev, proof rev die	Inc. Above	—	—	8.00	12.00	18.00	25.00	35.00	275	—

Date	Mintage	G4	VG8	F12	VF20	XF40	AU50	MS60	MS65	Prf65
1956D	32,334,500	—	—	—	—	—	8.00	8.50	26.00	—
1957	47,779,952	—	—	—	—	—	8.00	8.50	26.00	15.00
1957 Type B rev, proof rev die	Inc. Above	—	—	—	5.60	10.00	20.00	40.00	125	—
1957D	77,924,160	—	—	—	—	—	8.00	8.50	26.00	—
1958	7,235,652	—	—	—	—	—	8.00	8.50	26.00	15.00
1958 Type B rev, proof rev die	Inc. Above	—	—	—	5.60	10.00	16.00	24.00	90.00	—
1958D	78,124,900	—	—	—	—	—	8.00	8.50	26.00	—
1959	25,533,291	—	—	—	—	—	8.00	8.50	26.00	15.00
1959 Type B rev, proof rev die	Inc. Above	—	—	—	5.80	8.00	12.00	18.00	65.00	—
1959D	62,054,232	—	—	—	—	—	8.00	8.50	26.00	—
1960	30,855,602	—	—	—	—	—	8.00	8.50	26.00	15.00
1960 Type B rev, proof rev die	Inc. Above	—	—	—	5.10	10.00	16.00	24.00	90.00	—
1960D	63,000,324	—	—	—	—	—	8.00	8.50	26.00	—
1961	40,064,244	—	—	—	—	—	8.00	8.50	26.00	15.00
1961 Type B rev, proof rev die	Inc. Above	—	—	—	5.80	10.00	14.00	20.00	200	—
1961D	83,656,928	—	—	—	—	—	8.00	8.50	26.00	—
1962	39,374,019	—	—	—	—	—	8.00	8.50	26.00	15.00
1962 Type B rev, proof rev die	Inc. Above	—	—	—	8.00	12.00	15.00	30.00	175	—
1962D	127,554,756	—	—	—	—	—	8.00	8.50	26.00	—
1963	77,391,645	—	—	—	—	—	8.00	8.50	26.00	15.00
1963 Type B rev, proof rev die	Inc. Above	—	—	—	5.80	5.90	8.00	15.00	50.00	—
1963D	135,288,184	—	—	—	—	—	8.00	8.50	26.00	—
1964	564,341,347	—	—	—	—	—	8.00	8.50	26.00	15.00
1964 Type B rev, proof rev die	Inc. Above	—	—	—	5.80	9.00	10.00	18.00	75.00	—
1964 SMS	Inc. Above	—	—	—	—	—	250	750	1,400	—
1964D	704,135,528	—	—	—	—	—	8.00	8.50	26.00	—
1964D Type C rev, clad rev die	Inc. Above	—	—	—	40.00	55.00	75.00	125	450	—

KM# 164a • 5.67 g., **Copper-Nickel Clad Copper**, 24.3 mm. • **Designer:** John Flanagan

Date	Mintage	MS65	Prf65	Date	Mintage	MS65	Prf65
1965	1,819,717,540	10.00	—	1971	109,284,000	12.00	—
1965 SMS	2,360,000	9.00	—	1971D	258,634,428	6.00	—
1966	821,101,500	7.50	—	1971S	3,220,733	—	2.00
1966 SMS	2,261,583	9.00	—	1972	215,048,000	7.50	—
1967	1,524,031,848	10.00	—	1972D	311,067,732	6.00	—
1967 SMS	1,863,344	9.00	—	1972S	3,260,996	—	2.00
1968	220,731,500	10.00	—	1973	346,924,000	8.00	—
1968D	101,534,000	7.00	—	1973D	232,977,400	7.00	—
1968S	3,041,506	—	2.00	1973S	2,760,339	—	1.75
1969	176,212,000	14.00	—	1974	801,456,000	6.00	—
1969D	114,372,000	8.00	—	1974D	353,160,300	8.00	—
1969S	2,934,631	—	2.25	1974S	2,612,568	—	2.10
1970	136,420,000	12.00	—	1975 none minted	—	—	—
1970D	417,341,364	6.00	—	1975D none minted	—	—	—
1970S	2,632,810	—	2.00	1975S none minted	—	—	—

Colonial drummer, torch at top left within ring of stars reverse

KM# 204 • 5.67 g., **Copper-Nickel Clad Copper**, 24.3 mm. • **Rev. Designer:** Jack L. Ahr

Date	Mintage	MS60	MS65	PF65	Date	Mintage	MS60	MS65	PF65
1976	809,784,016	0.50	7.00	—	1976S	4,149,730	—	—	3.25
1976D	860,118,839	0.50	8.00	—					

Bicentennial design, drummer boy reverse

KM# 204a • 5.75 g., **Silver Clad**, 24.3 mm. • **Rev. Designer:** Jack L. Ahr

Date	Mintage	MS60	MS65	PF65	Date	Mintage	MS60	MS65	PF65
1976S	4,908,319	1.85	6.00	—	1976S	3,998,621	1.85	6.00	4.50

Eagle, regular design resumed reverse

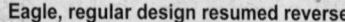

KM# A164a • 5.67 g., **Copper-Nickel Clad Copper**, 24.3 mm. • **Edge:** Reeded **Note:** KM#164 design and composition resumed. The 1979-S and 1981 Type II proofs have clearer mint marks than the Type I proofs for those years.

Date	Mintage	MS65	Prf65	Date	Mintage	MS65	Prf65
1977	468,556,000	7.50	—	1977S	3,251,152	—	2.75
1977D	256,524,978	8.00	—	1978	521,452,000	6.00	—

Date	Mintage	MS65	Prf65	Date	Mintage	MS65	Prf65
1978D	287,373,152	7.00	—	1988D	596,810,688	7.50	—
1978S	3,127,781	—	2.75	1988S	3,262,948	—	3.00
1979	515,708,000	8.00	—	1989P	512,868,000	16.00	—
1979D	489,789,780	7.00	—	1989D	896,535,597	7.50	—
1979S T-I	3,677,175	—	2.50	1989S	3,220,194	—	3.00
1979S T-II	Inc. above	—	4.00	1990P	613,792,000	12.00	—
1980P	635,832,000	8.00	—	1990D	927,638,181	6.00	—
1980D	518,327,487	8.50	—	1990S	3,299,559	—	4.50
1980S	3,554,806	—	2.75	1991P	570,968,000	10.00	—
1981P	601,716,000	7.50	—	1991D	630,966,693	12.00	—
1981D	575,722,833	6.50	—	1991S	2,867,787	—	3.00
1981S T-I	4,063,083	—	2.75	1992P	384,764,000	20.00	—
1981S T-II	Inc. above	—	7.50	1992D	389,777,107	12.00	—
1982P	500,931,000	28.00	—	1992S	2,858,981	—	3.00
1982D	480,042,788	15.00	—	1993P	639,276,000	7.50	—
1982S	3,857,479	—	4.00	1993D	645,476,128	8.50	—
1983P	673,535,000	50.00	—	1993S	2,633,439	—	3.00
1983D	617,806,446	30.00	—	1994P	825,600,000	8.00	—
1983S	3,279,126	—	3.00	1994D	880,034,110	8.00	—
1984P	676,545,000	14.50	—	1994S	2,484,594	—	3.00
1984D	546,483,064	12.50	—	1995P	1,004,336,000	7.50	—
1984S	3,065,110	—	3.00	1995D	1,103,216,000	6.50	—
1985P	775,818,962	12.50	—	1995S	2,117,496	—	6.00
1985D	519,962,888	10.00	—	1996P	925,040,000	7.50	—
1985S	3,362,821	—	3.00	1996D	906,868,000	11.00	—
1986P	551,199,333	11.00	—	1996S	1,750,244	—	4.00
1986D	504,298,660	15.00	—	1997P	595,740,000	22.50	—
1986S	3,010,497	—	3.00	1997D	599,680,000	17.00	—
1987P	582,499,481	10.50	—	1997S	2,055,000	—	9.00
1987D	655,594,696	8.50	—	1998P	896,268,000	14.00	—
1987S	4,227,728	—	3.00	1998D	821,000,000	18.00	—
1988P	562,052,000	10.00	—	1998S	2,086,507	—	9.00

KM# A164b • 6.25 g., 0.900 **Silver** 0.1808 oz. ASW, 24.3 mm. •

Date	Mintage	MS65	Prf65	Date	Mintage	MS65	Prf65
1992S	1,317,579	—	6.80	1996S	775,021	—	—
1993S	761,353	6.80	—	1997S	741,678	—	8.00
1994S	785,329	8.00	—	1998S	878,792	—	6.80
1995S	838,953	—	8.00				

50 STATE QUARTERS

Connecticut

KM# 297 • 5.67 g., **Copper-Nickel Clad Copper**, 24.3 mm.

Date	Mintage	MS63	MS65	Prf65
1999P	688,744,000	0.80	6.00	—
1999D	657,480,000	0.80	5.00	—
1999S	3,713,359	—	—	3.50

KM# 297a • 6.25 g., 0.900 **Silver**, 0.1808 oz. ASW 24.3 mm.

Date	Mintage	MS63	MS65	Prf65
1999S	804,565	—	—	20.00

Delaware

KM# 293 • 5.67 g., **Copper-Nickel Clad Copper**, 24.3 mm.

Date	Mintage	MS63	MS65	Prf65
1999P	373,400,000	1.00	5.00	—
1999D	401,424,000	1.00	7.00	—
1999S	3,713,359	—	—	3.50

KM# 293a • 6.25 g., 0.900 **Silver**, 0.1808 oz. ASW 24.3 mm.

Date	Mintage	MS63	MS65	Prf65
1999S	804,565	—	—	20.00

Georgia

KM# 296 • 5.67 g., **Copper-Nickel Clad Copper**, 24.3 mm.

Date	Mintage	MS63	MS65	Prf65
1999P	451,188,000	1.00	4.50	—
1999D	488,744,000	1.00	4.50	—
1999S	3,713,359	—	—	3.50

KM# 296a • 6.25 g., 0.900 **Silver**, 0.1808 oz. ASW 24.3 mm.

Date	Mintage	MS63	MS65	Prf65
1999S	804,565	—	—	20.00

New Jersey

KM# 295 • 5.67 g., **Copper-Nickel Clad Copper**, 24.3 mm.

Date	Mintage	MS63	MS65	Prf65
1999P	363,200,000	1.00	5.00	—
1999D	299,028,000	1.00	4.00	—
1999S	3,713,359	—	—	3.50

KM# 295a • 6.25 g., 0.900 **Silver**, 0.1808 oz. ASW 24.3 mm.

Date	Mintage	MS63	MS65	Prf65
1999S	804,565	—	—	20.00

Pennsylvania

KM# 294 • 5.67 g., **Copper-Nickel Clad Copper**, 24.3 mm.

Date	Mintage	MS63	MS65	Prf65
1999P	349,000,000	1.00	5.00	—
1999D	358,332,000	1.00	4.00	—
1999S	3,713,359	—	—	3.50

KM# 294a • 6.25 g., 0.900 **Silver**, 0.1808 oz. ASW 24.3 mm.

Date	Mintage	MS63	MS65	Prf65
1999S	804,565	—	—	20.00

Maryland

KM# 306 • 5.67 g., **Copper-Nickel Clad Copper**, 24.3 mm.

Date	Mintage	MS63	MS65	Prf65
2000P	678,200,000	0.80	6.00	—
2000D	556,526,000	0.80	6.00	—
2000S	4,078,747	—	—	3.00

KM# 306a • 6.25 g., 0.900 **Silver**, 0.1808 oz. ASW 24.3 mm.

Date	Mintage	MS63	MS65	Prf65
2000S	965,921	—	—	9.00

Massachusetts

KM# 305 • 5.67 g., **Copper-Nickel Clad Copper**, 24.3 mm.

Date	Mintage	MS63	MS65	Prf65
2000P	629,800,000	0.80	7.00	—
2000D	535,184,000	0.80	8.00	—
2000S	4,078,747	—	—	3.00

KM# 305a • 6.25 g., 0.900 **Silver**, 0.1808 oz. ASW 24.3 mm.

Date	Mintage	MS63	MS65	Prf65
2000S	965,921	—	—	9.00

New Hampshire

KM# 308 • 5.67 g., **Copper-Nickel Clad Copper**, 24.3 mm.

Date	Mintage	MS63	MS65	Prf65
2000P	673,040,000	0.80	8.00	—
2000D	495,976,000	0.80	9.00	—
2000S	4,078,747	—	—	3.00

KM# 308a • 6.25 g., 0.900 **Silver**, 0.1808 oz. ASW 24.3 mm.

Date	Mintage	MS63	MS65	Prf65
2000S	965,921	—	—	9.00

South Carolina

KM# 307 • 5.67 g., **Copper-Nickel Clad Copper**, 24.3 mm.

Date	Mintage	MS63	MS65	Prf65
2000P	742,756,000	0.80	6.00	—
2000D	566,208,000	0.80	9.00	—
2000S	4,078,747	—	—	3.00

KM# 307a • 6.25 g., 0.900 **Silver**, 0.1808 oz. ASW 24.3 mm.

Date	Mintage	MS63	MS65	Prf65
2000S	965,921	—	—	9.00

Virginia

KM# 309 • 5.67 g., **Copper-Nickel Clad Copper**, 24.3 mm.

Date	Mintage	MS63	MS65	Prf65
2000P	943,000,000	0.80	6.50	—
2000D	651,616,000	0.80	6.50	—
2000S	4,078,747	—	—	3.00

KM# 309a • 6.25 g., 0.900 **Silver**, 0.1808 oz. ASW 24.3 mm.

Date	Mintage	MS63	MS65	Prf65
2000S	965,921	—	—	9.50

HALF DOLLAR

Barber Half Dollar

Laureate head right, flanked by stars, date below obverse

Heraldic eagle reverse

KM# 116 • 12.50 g., 0.900 **Silver** 0.3617 oz. ASW, 30.6 mm. • **Obv. Legend:** IN GOD WE TRUST **Rev. Legend:** UNITED STATES OF AMERICA **Designer:** Charles E. Barber

Date	Mintage	G4	VG8	F12	VF20	XF40	AU50	MS60	MS65	Prf65
1901	4,268,813	24.00	35.00	55.00	135	195	360	530	2,400	2,200
1901O	1,124,000	24.00	35.00	70.00	195	1,100	1,500	2,200	12,500	—
1901S	847,044	27.00	44.00	145	425	1,200	1,575	3,750	12,000	—
1902	4,922,777	24.00	35.00	55.00	135	200	375	600	2,400	2,200
1902O	2,526,000	24.00	35.00	55.00	145	265	475	900	7,500	—
1902S	1,460,670	24.00	35.00	80.00	155	310	440	880	4,500	—
1903	2,278,755	24.00	35.00	55.00	135	195	360	550	7,000	2,200
1903O	2,100,000	24.00	35.00	55.00	135	195	415	770	4,900	—
1903S	1,920,772	24.00	35.00	55.00	135	225	440	900	3,500	—
1904	2,992,670	24.00	35.00	55.00	135	195	360	630	3,600	2,200
1904O	1,117,600	24.00	35.00	70.00	200	510	865	1,525	10,400	—
1904S	553,038	100	175	375	820	3,300	7,000	12,500	36,000	—
1905	662,727	24.00	38.00	80.00	165	225	425	700	4,700	2,200
1905O	505,000	26.00	40.00	140	220	350	550	850	4,000	—
1905S	2,494,000	24.00	35.00	55.00	135	235	410	660	6,800	—
1906	2,638,675	24.00	35.00	55.00	135	195	360	530	2,000	2,200
1906D	4,028,000	24.00	35.00	55.00	135	195	330	530	2,450	—
1906O	2,446,000	24.00	35.00	55.00	135	195	410	850	5,100	—
1906S	1,740,154	24.00	35.00	55.00	135	195	330	575	3,100	—
1907	2,598,575	24.00	35.00	55.00	135	195	330	530	2,000	2,200
1907D	3,856,000	24.00	35.00	55.00	135	195	330	530	2,000	—
1907O	3,946,000	24.00	35.00	55.00	135	195	360	530	2,000	—
1907S	1,250,000	24.00	35.00	90.00	200	425	700	2,500	9,300	—
1908	1,354,545	24.00	35.00	55.00	135	195	330	530	2,000	2,200
1908D	3,280,000	24.00	35.00	55.00	135	195	330	530	2,350	—
1908O	5,360,000	24.00	35.00	55.00	135	195	330	530	2,000	—
1908S	1,644,828	24.00	35.00	55.00	135	400	625	990	4,400	—
1909	2,368,650	24.00	35.00	55.00	135	195	330	530	2,000	2,200
1909O	925,400	24.00	35.00	55.00	135	480	675	990	4,200	—

Date	Mintage	G4	VG8	F12	VF20	XF40	AU50	MS60	MS65	Prf65
1909S	1,764,000	24.00	35.00	55.00	135	275	440	660	3,300	—
1910	418,551	24.00	35.00	75.00	185	315	340	535	3,200	2,200
1910S	1,948,000	24.00	35.00	55.00	135	220	400	660	4,700	—
1911	1,406,543	24.00	35.00	55.00	135	195	330	530	2,000	2,200
1911D	695,080	24.00	35.00	55.00	135	195	330	530	2,000	—
1911S	1,272,000	24.00	35.00	55.00	135	220	400	700	3,500	—
1912	1,550,700	24.00	35.00	55.00	135	195	330	530	2,000	2,200
1912D	2,300,800	24.00	35.00	55.00	135	195	330	530	2,000	—
1912S	1,370,000	24.00	35.00	55.00	135	195	360	550	3,100	—
1913	188,627	65.00	75.00	185	385	770	1,250	1,600	3,900	2,200
1913D	534,000	24.00	35.00	55.00	135	175	330	530	3,500	—
1913S	604,000	24.00	35.00	55.00	135	220	400	660	3,750	—
1914	124,610	120	145	260	500	880	1,100	1,425	5,800	2,200
1914S	992,000	24.00	35.00	55.00	135	220	400	585	3,300	—
1915	138,450	75.00	115	245	325	600	975	1,300	5,500	2,200
1915D	1,170,400	24.00	35.00	55.00	135	195	330	530	2,000	—
1915S	1,604,000	24.00	35.00	55.00	135	195	330	530	2,000	—

Walking Liberty Half Dollar

Liberty walking left wearing U.S. flag gown, sunrise at left obverse

Eagle advancing left reverse

Obverse mint mark 1916-1917

Reverse mint mark 1917-1947

KM# 142 • 12.50 g., 0.900 **Silver** 0.3617 oz. ASW, 30.6 mm. • **Designer:** Adolph A. Weinman **Note:** The mint mark appears on the obverse below the word "Trust" on 1916 and some 1917 issues. Starting with some 1917 issues and continuing through the remainder of the series, the mint mark was changed to the reverse, at about the 8 o'clock position near the rim.

Date	Mintage	G4	VG8	F12	VF20	XF40	AU50	MS60	MS65	Prf65
1916	608,000	44.00	75.00	130	180	170	300	375	2,400	—
1916D	1,014,400	44.00	75.00	130	180	170	225	375	2,600	—
1916S	508,000	80.00	110	220	350	495	750	1,600	6,400	—
1917	12,292,000	14.00	15.00	21.00	23.00	35.00	85.00	150	1,000	—
1917D obv. mint mark	765,400	21.00	30.00	68.00	130	350	400	600	7,800	—
1917S obv. mint mark	952,000	23.00	37.00	160	300	625	1,100	3,000	24,750	—
1917D rev. mint mark	1,940,000	15.00	16.00	38.00	110	240	460	1,125	16,000	—
1917S rev. mint mark	5,554,000	14.00	15.00	16.00	27.00	52.00	275	700	14,000	—
1918	6,634,000	15.00	16.00	17.00	60.00	100	275	600	5,000	—
1918D	3,853,040	15.00	22.00	38.00	77.00	190	460	1,350	27,500	—
1918S	10,282,000	14.00	15.00	16.00	28.00	65.00	225	600	18,000	—
1919	962,000	21.00	27.00	65.00	210	440	1,000	2,200	8,000	—
1919D	1,165,000	22.00	32.00	85.00	260	660	2,000	4,500	210,000	—
1919S	1,552,000	16.00	24.00	60.00	300	700	1,500	3,650	25,500	—
1920	6,372,000	15.00	16.00	18.00	35.00	60.00	190	425	4,000	—
1920D	1,551,000	15.00	17.00	55.00	200	400	800	2,600	17,750	—
1920S	4,624,000	14.00	16.00	20.00	85.00	200	700	1,100	16,500	—
1921	246,000	130	175	280	675	1,900	3,000	5,750	20,000	—
1921D	208,000	205	320	500	775	2,625	5,050	8,500	38,500	—
1921S	548,000	38.00	52.00	205	680	3,200	7,900	20,000	104,000	—
1923S	2,178,000	16.00	21.00	41.00	130	500	1,450	2,400	16,250	—
1927S	2,392,000	13.00	14.00	16.00	44.00	140	500	1,200	12,000	—
1928S Large S	1,940,000	19.50	22.00	28.00	90.00	290	950	1,700	10,000	—
1928S Small S	Inc. above	13.00	14.00	15.00	55.00	170	550	1,200	11,000	—
1929D	1,001,200	12.00	14.00	16.00	35.00	80.00	200	450	3,100	—
1929S	1,902,000	12.00	13.00	15.00	25.00	90.00	220	500	3,300	—
1933S	1,786,000	11.00	12.00	13.00	20.00	50.00	310	700	3,100	—
1934	6,964,000	10.00	11.00	13.00	18.00	19.00	30.00	80.00	400	—
1934D	2,361,400	10.00	11.00	13.00	18.00	19.00	105	155	1,100	—
1934S	3,652,000	10.00	11.00	13.00	18.00	19.00	125	345	3,000	—
1935	9,162,000	10.00	11.00	13.00	18.00	19.00	30.00	60.00	275	—
1935D	3,003,800	10.00	11.00	13.00	18.00	19.00	75.00	155	2,000	—
1935S	3,854,000	10.00	11.00	13.00	18.00	19.00	140	265	2,000	—
1936	12,617,901	10.00	11.00	13.00	18.00	19.00	30.00	42.00	210	3,100
1936D	4,252,400	10.00	11.00	13.00	18.00	19.00	65.00	95.00	380	—
1936S	3,884,000	10.00	11.00	13.00	18.00	19.00	75.00	165	575	—
1937	9,527,728	10.00	11.00	13.00	18.00	19.00	30.00	64.00	200	825
1937D	1,676,000	10.00	11.00	13.00	18.00	19.00	120	205	710	—
1937S	2,090,000	10.00	11.00	13.00	18.00	19.00	75.00	180	540	—
1938	4,118,152	10.00	11.00	13.00	18.00	19.00	50.00	100	300	785
1938D	491,600	65.00	75.00	90.00	105	185	290	485	1,400	—
1939	6,820,808	10.00	11.00	13.00	18.00	19.00	40.00	57.00	200	710
1939D	4,267,800	10.00	11.00	13.00	18.00	19.00	30.00	57.00	200	—
1939S	2,552,000	10.00	11.00	13.00	18.00	19.00	100	175	245	—
1940	9,167,279	10.00	11.00	13.00	18.00	19.00	30.00	50.00	145	575
1940S	4,550,000	10.00	11.00	13.00	18.00	19.00	50.00	65.00	370	—
1941	24,207,412	10.00	11.00	13.00	18.00	19.00	30.00	45.00	135	580
1941D	11,248,400	10.00	11.00	13.00	18.00	19.00	30.00	52.00	150	—
1941S Small S	8,098,000	10.00	11.00	13.00	18.00	19.00	43.00	85.00	610	—
1941S Large S	Inc. above	10.00	11.00	13.00	18.00	19.00	30.00	80.00	625	—
1942	47,839,120	10.00	11.00	13.00	18.00	19.00	30.00	47.00	130	605
1942D	10,973,800	10.00	11.00	13.00	18.00	19.00	30.00	52.00	215	—
1942S	12,708,000	10.00	11.00	13.00	18.00	19.00	30.00	52.00	375	—
1943	53,190,000	10.00	11.00	13.00	18.00	19.00	30.00	57.00	130	—
1943D	11,346,000	10.00	11.00	13.00	18.00	19.00	30.00	55.00	225	—
1943D Double Die Obverse	Inc. above	10.00	11.00	13.00	18.00	19.00	50.00	78.00	500	—
1943S	13,450,000	10.00	11.00	13.00	18.00	19.00	30.00	65.00	280	—
1944	28,206,000	10.00	11.00	13.00	18.00	19.00	30.00	62.00	135	—
1944D	9,769,000	10.00	11.00	13.00	18.00	19.00	30.00	62.00	135	—
1944S	8,904,000	10.00	11.00	13.00	18.00	19.00	57.00	67.00	340	—
1945	31,502,000	10.00	11.00	13.00	18.00	19.00	30.00	57.00	130	—
1945D	9,966,800	10.00	11.00	13.00	18.00	19.00	30.00	62.00	155	—
1945S	10,156,000	10.00	11.00	13.00	18.00	19.00	52.00	67.00	140	—
1946	12,118,000	10.00	11.00	13.00	18.00	19.00	30.00	57.00	145	—
1946 Double Die Reverse	Inc. above	—	—	65.00	85.00	105	155	400	2,000	—
1946D	2,151,000	10.00	11.00	13.00	18.00	19.00	65.00	70.00	140	—
1946S	3,724,000	10.00	11.00	13.00	18.00	19.00	65.00	80.00	130	—
1947	4,094,000	10.00	11.00	13.00	18.00	19.00	30.00	58.00	130	—
1947D	3,900,600	10.00	11.00	13.00	18.00	19.00	58.00	68.00	130	—

Franklin Half Dollar

Franklin bust right obverse Liberty Bell, small eagle at right reverse

Mint mark

KM# 199 • 12.50 g., 0.900 **Silver** 0.3617 oz. ASW, 30.6 mm. • **Designer:** John R. Sinnock **Note:** The type I reverse is distinguished by the eagle having four full feathers on the wing closest the bell, whereas the type II reverse eagle has three full feathers.

Date	Mintage	VG8	F12	VF20	XF40	AU50	MS60	MS65	65FBL	65CAM
1948	3,006,814	—	—	—	—	12.00	18.00	66.00	190	—
1948D	4,028,600	—	—	—	—	12.00	18.00	90.00	260	—
1949	5,614,000	—	—	—	—	15.00	33.00	100	250	—
1949D	4,120,600	—	—	—	—	24.00	48.00	350	1,750	—
1949S	3,744,000	—	—	—	—	33.00	70.00	115	700	—
1950	7,793,509	—	—	—	—	14.00	23.00	75.00	285	2,000
1950D	8,031,600	—	—	—	—	13.00	24.00	200	900	—
1951	16,859,602	—	—	—	—	12.00	15.00	44.00	340	1,500
1951D	9,475,200	—	—	—	—	22.00	33.00	125	540	—
1951S	13,696,000	—	—	—	—	15.00	22.00	48.00	750	—
1952	21,274,073	—	—	—	—	12.00	15.00	44.00	210	775
1952D	25,395,600	—	—	—	—	12.00	16.00	95.00	450	—
1952S	5,526,000	—	—	—	—	44.00	60.00	90.00	1,500	—
1953	2,796,920	—	—	—	—	20.00	22.00	63.00	1,000	475
1953D	20,900,400	—	—	—	—	13.00	16.00	88.00	400	—
1953S	4,148,000	—	—	—	—	22.00	28.00	40.00	160	—
1954	13,421,503	—	—	—	—	12.00	14.00	35.00	225	175
1954D	25,445,580	—	—	—	—	13.00	13.00	65.00	235	—
1954S	4,993,400	—	—	—	—	14.00	15.00	30.00	440	—
1955	2,876,381	—	—	—	—	14.00	17.00	37.00	140	120
1955 Bugs Bunny	Inc. above	15.00	17.00	19.00	21.00	22.00	25.00	95.00	750	—
1956 Type 1 rev.	4,701,384	—	—	—	—	12.00	15.00	25.00	125	300
1956 Type 2 rev.	Inc. above	—	—	—	—	—	—	—	—	40.00
1957 Type 1 rev.	6,361,952	—	—	—	—	13.00	14.00	28.00	95.00	—
1957 Type 2 rev.	Inc. above	—	—	—	—	—	—	—	—	55.00
1957D	19,966,850	—	—	—	—	13.00	14.00	30.00	100	—
1958 Type 1 rev.	4,917,652	—	—	—	—	11.00	13.00	26.00	110	—
1958 Type 2 rev.	Inc. above	—	—	—	—	15.00	20.00	—	—	60.00
1958D	23,962,412	—	—	—	—	11.00	13.00	26.00	80.00	—
1959 Type 1 rev.	7,349,291	—	—	—	—	11.00	13.00	44.00	250	—
1959 Type 2 rev.	Inc. above	—	—	—	—	16.00	25.00	90.00	—	75.00
1959D	13,053,750	—	—	—	—	11.00	14.00	55.00	215	—
1960 Type 1 rev.	7,715,602	—	—	—	—	11.00	14.00	72.00	340	—
1960 Type 2 rev.	Inc. above	—	—	—	—	—	—	—	—	45.00
1960D	18,215,812	—	—	—	—	11.00	14.00	170	1,350	—
1961 Type 1 rev.	11,318,244	—	—	—	—	11.00	14.00	36.00	1,300	—
1961 Type 2 rev.	Inc. above	—	—	—	20.00	—	—	—	—	40.00
1961 Double die rev.	Inc. above	—	—	—	—	—	—	—	—	3,500
1961D	20,276,442	—	—	—	—	11.00	14.00	90.00	875	—
1962 Type 1 rev.	12,932,019	—	—	—	—	11.00	14.00	66.00	1,850	—
1962 Type 2 rev.	Inc. above	—	—	—	—	—	—	—	—	35.00
1962D	35,473,281	—	—	—	—	11.00	13.00	60.00	800	—
1963 Type 1 rev.	25,239,645	—	—	—	—	11.00	13.00	25.00	1,200	—
1963 Type 2 rev.	Inc. above	—	—	—	—	—	—	—	—	35.00
1963D	67,069,292	—	—	—	—	11.00	13.00	26.00	165	—

Kennedy Half Dollar

Mint mark 1964

KM# 202 • 12.50 g., 0.900 **Silver** 0.3617 oz. ASW, 30.6 mm. • **Obv. Designer:** Gilroy Roberts **Rev. Designer:** Frank Gasparro **Edge:** Reeded

Date	Mintage	MS60	MS65	PF65
1964	277,254,766	13.00	19.00	32.00
1964 Accented Hair	Inc. above	—	—	40.00
1964D	156,205,446	13.00	19.00	—

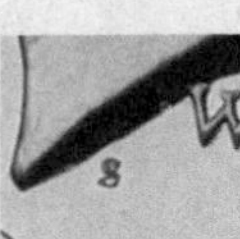

Mint mark 1968 - present

KM# 202a • 11.50 g., 0.400 **Silver** 0.1479 oz. ASW, 30.6 mm. • **Obv. Designer:** Gilroy Roberts **Rev. Designer:** Frank Gasparro **Edge:** Reeded

Date	Mintage	MS60	MS65	PF65
1965	65,879,366	6.10	14.50	—
1965 SMS	2,360,000	—	15.00	—
1966	108,984,932	6.10	22.50	—
1966 SMS	2,261,583	—	17.00	—
1967	295,046,978	6.10	18.50	—
1967 SMS	1,863,344	—	18.00	—
1968D	246,951,930	6.10	16.50	—
1968S	3,041,506	—	—	8.56
1969D	129,881,800	6.10	20.00	—
1969S	2,934,631	—	—	8.56
1970D	2,150,000	8.50	40.00	—
1970S	2,632,810	—	—	12.00

KM# 202b • 11.34 g., **Copper-Nickel Clad Copper**, 30.6 mm. • **Obv. Designer:** Gilroy Roberts **Rev. Designer:** Frank Gasparro

Date	Mintage	MS60	MS65	PF65
1971	155,640,000	1.00	17.50	—
1971D	302,097,424	1.00	12.00	—
1971S	3,244,183	—	—	5.00
1972	153,180,000	1.00	15.50	—
1972D	141,890,000	1.00	14.50	—
1972S	3,267,667	—	—	5.00
1973	64,964,000	1.00	20.00	—
1973D	83,171,400	—	12.00	—
1973S	2,769,624	—	—	5.00
1974	201,596,000	1.00	25.00	—
1974D	79,066,300	1.00	17.00	—
1974D DDO	Inc. above	32.00	165	—
1974S	2,617,350	—	—	5.00
1975 none minted	—	—	—	—
1975D none minted	—	—	—	—
1975S none minted	—	—	—	—

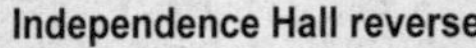

Independence Hall reverse

KM# 205 • 11.20 g., **Copper-Nickel**, 30.6 mm. • **Obv. Designer:** Gilroy Roberts **Rev. Designer:** Seth Huntington

Date	Mintage	MS60	MS65	PF65
1976	234,308,000	1.00	16.50	—
1976D	287,565,248	1.00	14.00	—
1976S	7,059,099	—	—	5.00

Bicentennial design, Independence Hall reverse

KM# 205a • 11.50 g., 0.400 **Silver** 0.1479 oz. ASW, 30.6 mm. • **Rev. Designer:** Seth Huntington

Date	Mintage	MS60	MS65	PF65
1976S	4,908,319	—	12.00	8.70
1976S	3,998,621	—	—	8.70

Regular design resumed reverse

KM# A202b • 11.34 g., **Copper-Nickel Clad Copper**, 30.61 mm. • **Edge:** Reeded **Note:** KM#202b design and composition resumed. The 1979-S and 1981-S Type II proofs have clearer mint marks than the Type I proofs of those years.

Date	Mintage	MS65	Prf65
1977	43,598,000	12.50	—
1977D	31,449,106	16.50	—
1977S	3,251,152	—	4.50
1978	14,350,000	12.00	—
1978D	13,765,799	15.00	—
1978S	3,127,788	—	5.00
1979	68,312,000	13.50	—
1979D	15,815,422	13.50	—
1979S Type I	3,677,175	—	5.00
1979S Type II	Inc. above	—	18.00
1980P	44,134,000	12.50	—
1980D	33,456,449	17.50	—
1980S	3,547,030	—	5.00
1981P	29,544,000	9.00	—
1981D	27,839,533	12.00	—
1981S Type I	4,063,083	—	5.00
1981S Type II	Inc. above	—	18.50
1982P	10,819,000	18.50	—
1982P no initials FG	Inc. above	110	—
1982D	13,140,102	20.00	—
1982S	38,957,479	—	5.00
1983P	34,139,000	22.50	—
1983D	32,472,244	12.50	—
1983S	3,279,126	—	5.00
1984P	26,029,000	12.00	—
1984D	26,262,158	18.00	—
1984S	3,065,110	—	6.00
1985P	18,706,962	16.50	—
1985D	19,814,034	12.50	—
1985S	3,962,138	—	5.00
1986P	13,107,633	17.50	—
1986D	15,336,145	14.00	—
1986S	2,411,180	—	6.00
1987P	2,890,758	16.50	—
1987D	2,890,758	12.50	—
1987S	4,407,728	—	5.00
1988P	13,626,000	16.50	—
1988D	12,000,096	10.00	—

Date	Mintage	MS65	Prf65
1988S	3,262,948	—	5.00
1989P	24,542,000	13.00	—
1989D	23,000,216	13.00	—
1989S	3,220,194	—	5.00
1990P	22,780,000	17.50	—
1990D	20,096,242	20.00	—
1990S	3,299,559	—	5.00
1991P	14,874,000	12.50	—
1991D	15,054,678	16.00	—
1991S	2,867,787	—	5.00
1992P	17,628,000	10.00	—
1992D	17,000,106	10.00	—
1992S	2,858,981	—	5.00
1993P	15,510,000	12.00	—
1993D	15,000,006	10.00	—
1993S	2,633,439	—	5.00
1994P	23,718,000	12.00	—
1994D	23,828,110	8.50	—
1994S	2,484,594	—	5.00
1995P	26,496,000	10.00	—
1995D	26,288,000	8.00	—
1995S	2,010,384	—	12.00
1996P	24,442,000	10.00	—
1996D	24,744,000	10.00	—
1996S	2,085,191	—	9.00
1997P	20,882,000	14.00	—
1997D	19,876,000	13.50	—
1997S	1,975,000	—	10.00
1998P	15,646,000	12.50	—
1998D	15,064,000	12.50	—
1998S	2,078,494	—	7.00
1999P	8,900,000	11.00	—
1999D	10,682,000	10.00	—
1999S	2,557,897	—	8.00
2000P	22,600,000	12.00	—
2000D	19,466,000	12.00	—
2000S	3,082,944	—	5.00

KM# A202c • 12.50 g., 0.900 **Silver** 0.3617 oz. ASW, 30.6 mm. • **Designer:** Gilroy Roberts

Date	Mintage	Prf65
1992S	1,317,579	13.20
1993S	761,353	15.20
1994S	785,329	13.20
1995S	838,953	46.00
1996S	830,021	15.20

Date	Mintage	Prf65
1997S	821,678	35.00
1998S Matte Finish	62,350	—
1998S	878,792	13.20
1999S	804,565	15.20
2000S	965,921	13.20

DOLLAR

Morgan Dollar

Laureate head left, date below flanked by stars obverse
Eagle within 1/2 wreath reverse

7 Tail feathers

7/8 Tail feathers

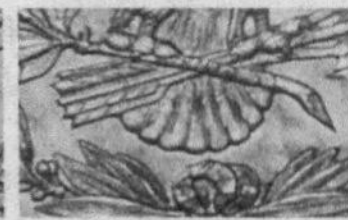
8 Tail feathers

KM# 110 • 26.73 g., 0.900 **Silver** 0.7734 oz. ASW, 38.1 mm. • **Obv. Legend:** E • PLURIBUS • UNUM **Rev. Legend:** UNITED STATES OF AMERICA **Designer:** George T. Morgan **Note:** "65DMPL" values are for coins grading MS-65 deep-mirror prooflike. The 1878 "8 tail feathers" and "7 tail feathers" varieties are distinguished by the number of feathers in the eagle's tail. On the "reverse of 1878" varieties, the top of the top feather in the arrows held by the eagle is straight across and the eagle's breast is concave. On the "reverse of 1879 varieties," the top feather in the arrows held by the eagle is slanted and the eagle's breast is convex. The 1890-CC "tail-bar" variety has a bar extending from the arrow feathers to the wreath on the reverse, the result of a die gouge. The Pittman Act of 1918 authorized the melting of 270 Million pieces of various dates. They were not individually recorded.

Date	Mintage	VG8	F12	VF20	XF40	AU50	MS60	MS63	MS64	MS65	65DMPL	Prf65
1901	6,962,813	47.00	48.00	55.00	85.00	250	3,300	15,000	48,000	450,000	—	4,800
1901 doubled die reverse	—	275	450	900	2,000	3,850	—	—	—	—	—	—
1901O	13,320,000	50.00	53.00	53.00	54.00	59.00	71.00	82.00	95.00	225	9,000	—
1901S	2,284,000	45.00	50.00	51.00	60.00	185	550	825	1,250	3,000	23,000	—
1902	7,994,777	42.00	46.00	47.00	50.00	56.00	100	170	210	490	17,500	5,000
1902O	8,636,000	43.00	44.00	47.00	—	59.00	65.00	85.00	95.00	230	14,000	—
1902S	1,530,000	102	105	140	160	250	415	615	810	2,350	12,000	—
1903	4,652,755	50.00	51.00	53.00	54.00	55.00	85.00	105	155	340	23,000	4,800
1903O	4,450,000	330	350	375	385	420	470	485	500	675	6,800	—
1903S	1,241,000	80.00	105	195	300	1,600	5,500	7,000	8,000	10,400	32,500	—
1903S Micro S	—	155	245	500	1,250	—	—	—	—	—	—	—
1904	2,788,650	43.00	44.00	45.00	47.00	60.00	135	275	600	2,050	65,000	5,000
1904O	3,720,000	43.00	44.00	45.00	50.00	58.00	70.00	85.00	95.00	205	1,125	—
1904S	2,304,000	45.00	50.00	80.00	110	475	2,550	4,550	6,000	10,500	20,000	—
1921	44,690,000	16.05	25.05	50.00	—	56.00	60.00	66.00	85.00	200	16,500	10,000
1921D	20,345,000	16.05	25.05	50.00	—	56.00	60.00	85.00	135	305	—	—
1921S	21,695,000	19.05	50.00	50.00	—	56.00	60.00	88.00	180	1,790	—	—

Peace Dollar

Liberty Head left obverse Eagle facing right perched on rock reverse

KM# 150 • 26.73 g., 0.900 **Silver** 0.7734 oz. ASW, 38.1 mm. • **Designer:** Anthony DeFrancisci **Note:** Prices with a letter after them mean, e=estimated, a=auction realization, h=historical record over 5 years old.

Date	Mintage	G4	VG8	F12	VF20	XF40	AU50	MS60	MS63	MS64	MS65
1921	1,006,473	70.00	95.00	100	110	115	150	285	500	800	1,950
1921 rev ray over first L in DOLLAR Vam 3	—	—	—	—	—	200	250	475	—	—	—
1922	51,737,000	23.00	24.00	25.00	27.00	30.00	34.00	37.00	43.00	55.00	140
1922D	15,063,000	23.00	24.00	25.00	27.00	30.00	34.00	66.00	100	135	625
1922S	17,475,000	23.00	—	25.00	27.00	30.00	34.00	64.00	105	265	2,000
1923	30,800,000	23.00	24.00	25.00	27.00	30.00	34.00	40.00	45.00	55.00	135
1923D	6,811,000	23.00	24.00	25.00	27.00	33.00	45.00	76.00	180	365	1,250
1923S	19,020,000	23.00	24.00	25.00	27.00	32.00	44.00	62.00	105	390	4,200
1924	11,811,000	23.00	24.00	25.00	27.00	30.00	33.00	50.00	58.00	70.00	130
1924S	1,728,000	23.00	24.00	25.00	37.00	47.00	80.00	265	500	1,075	9,000
1925	10,198,000	23.00	24.00	25.00	27.00	32.00	33.00	40.00	45.50	60.00	130
1925S	1,610,000	23.00	24.00	25.00	30.00	37.00	48.00	80.00	275	735	25,500
1926	1,939,000	23.00	24.00	25.00	30.00	37.00	45.00	65.00	110	160	475
1926D	2,348,700	23.00	24.00	25.00	27.00	37.00	60.00	100	260	400	1,050
1926S	6,980,000	23.00	24.00	25.00	27.00	35.00	45.00	70.00	105	275	1,025
1927	848,000	23.00	33.00	34.00	35.00	45.00	55.00	98.00	200	600	2,200
1927D	1,268,900	23.00	31.00	32.00	43.00	46.00	100	165	425	1,125	4,425
1927S	866,000	23.00	33.00	34.00	43.00	56.00	81.00	230	575	1,160	8,550
1928	360,649	185	260	270	280	295	320	480	725	1,020	4,000
1928S	1,632,000	23.00	35.00	40.00	42.00	49.00	70.00	250	510	950	17,000
1934	954,057	25.00	32.00	45.00	47.00	50.00	55.00	125	215	400	725
1934D Large D	1,569,500	25.00	42.00	45.00	47.00	52.00	55.00	175	400	575	1,575
1934D Small D	—	25.00	40.00	45.00	50.00	52.00	55.00	160	410	575	1,550
1934S	1,011,000	—	42.00	42.00	65.00	150	500	2,300	4,250	6,500	8,200
1935	1,576,000	25.00	42.00	44.00	46.00	48.00	65.00	95.00	145	245	730
1935S 3 Rays	1,964,000	25.00	42.00	44.00	47.00	50.00	95.00	285	420	650	1,320
1935S 4 Rays	—	25.00	42.00	44.00	52.00	54.00	100	275	465	660	1,550

Eisenhower Dollar

KM# 203 • 22.80 g., **Copper-Nickel Clad Copper**, 38 mm. • **Designer:** Frank Gasparro

Date	Mintage	MS63	MS65	Prf65
1971	47,799,000	—	5.00	—
1971D	68,587,424	—	4.00	—
1972 Low Relief	75,890,000	—	18.00	—
1972 High Relief	Inc. above	—	100	—
1972 Modified High Relief	Inc. above	—	25.00	—
1972D	92,548,511	—	8.00	—
1973	2,000,056	—	12.00	—
1973D	2,000,000	—	12.00	—
1973S	2,769,624	7.00	—	12.00
1974	27,366,000	—	9.00	—
1974D	35,466,000	—	7.50	—
1974S	2,617,350	6.00	—	11.00

KM# 203a • 24.59 g., 0.400 **Silver** 0.3162 oz. ASW, 38.1 mm. • **Designer:** Frank Gasparro

Date	Mintage	MS63	MS65	Prf65
1971S	6,868,530	6.50	7.50	11.00
1971S	4,265,234	—	—	—
1971S Peg Leg "R" Variety	Inc. above	8.00	—	17.00
1971S Partial Peg Leg "R" Variety	Inc. above	9.00	—	18.00
1972S	2,193,056	—	7.50	—
1972S	1,811,631	6.50	—	9.00
1973S	1,833,140	—	7.50	—
1973S	1,005,617	30.00	—	45.00
1974S	1,720,000	—	7.50	—
1974S	1,306,579	6.50	—	11.00

Moon behind Liberty Bell reverse

Type I
Squared "T"

Type II
Slant-top "T"

KM# 206 • 22.68 g., **Copper-Nickel Clad Copper**, 38.1 mm. • **Rev. Designer:** Dennis R. Williams **Note:** In 1976 the lettering on the reverse was changed to thinner letters, resulting in the Type II variety for that year. The Type I variety was minted 1975 and dated 1976.

Date	Mintage	MS63	MS65	Prf65
1976 type I	117,337,000	—	12.00	—
1976 type II	Inc. above	—	7.50	—
1976D type I	103,228,274	—	10.00	—
1976D type II	Inc. above	—	7.00	—
1976S type I	2,909,369	5.00	—	10.00
1976S type II	4,149,730	5.00	—	9.00

Bicentennial design, moon behind Liberty Bell reverse

KM# 206a • 24.59 g., 0.400 **Silver** 0.3162 oz. ASW **Rev. Designer:** Dennis R. Williams

Date	Mintage	MS63	MS65	Prf65
1976S	4,908,319	11.50	7.50	14.00
1976S	3,998,621	—	—	—

Regular design resumed reverse

KM# A203 • **Copper-Nickel Clad Copper**, 38.1 mm. • **Designer:** Frank Gasparro

Date	Mintage	MS63	MS65	Prf65
1977	12,596,000	—	5.50	—
1977D	32,983,006	—	8.00	—
1977S	3,251,152	5.00	—	9.00
1978	25,702,000	—	6.50	—
1978D	33,012,890	—	6.50	—
1978S	3,127,788	5.50	—	9.00

Susan B. Anthony Dollar

Susan B. Anthony bust right obverse

Eagle landing on moon, symbolic of Apollo manned moon landing reverse

KM# 207 • 8.10 g., **Copper-Nickel Clad Copper**, 26.5 mm. • **Edge:** Reeded **Designer:** Frank Gasparro **Note:** The 1979-S and 1981-S Type II coins have a clearer mint mark than the Type I varieties for those years.

Date	Mintage	MS63	MS65	Prf65
1979P Near date	360,222,000	30.00	90.00	—
1979P	Inc. above	2.50	12.50	—
1979D	288,015,744	2.50	12.50	—
1979S Proof, Type I	3,677,175	—	—	6.00
1979S Proof, Type II	Inc. above	—	—	85.00
1979S	109,576,000	2.50	13.50	—
1980P	27,610,000	2.50	12.00	—
1980D	41,628,708	2.50	12.00	—
1980S	20,422,000	5.00	20.00	—
1980S Proof	3,547,030	—	—	5.00
1981P	3,000,000	5.00	18.00	—
1981D	3,250,000	5.00	13.50	—
1981S	3,492,000	5.00	30.00	—
1981S Proof, Type I	4,063,083	—	—	7.00
1981S Proof, Type II	Inc. above	—	—	225
1999P	29,592,000	3.00	10.00	—
1999P Proof	Est. 750000	—	—	22.00
1999D	11,776,000	3.00	10.00	—

Sacagawea Dollar

Sacagawea bust right, with baby on back obverse

Eagle in flight left reverse

KM# 310 • 8.07 g., **Copper-Zinc-Manganese-Nickel Clad Copper**, 26.5 mm. • **Obv. Designer:** Glenda Goodacre **Rev. Designer:** Thomas D. Rodgers

Date	Mintage	MS63	MS65	Prf65
2000P	767,140,000	2.00	7.50	—
2000P Goodacre Presentation	5,000	—	575	—
2000D	518,916,000	2.00	11.00	—
2000D from Millennium Set	5,500	10.00	50.00	—
2000S	4,048,000	—	—	5.00

GOLD

$2.50 (QUARTER EAGLE)

Coronet Head

Coronet head left within circle of stars obverse

No motto above eagle reverse

1848 "Cal." reverse

KM# 72 • 4.18 g., 0.900 **Gold** 0.121 oz. AGW, 18 mm. • **Rev. Legend:** UNITED STATES OF AMERICA **Designer:** Christian Gobrecht

Date	Mintage	F12	VF20	XF40	AU50	MS60	PF65
1901	91,322	240	285	325	345	435	15,000
1902	133,733	240	285	325	345	435	15,000
1903	201,257	240	285	325	345	435	15,000
1904	160,960	240	285	325	345	435	15,000
1905	217,944	240	285	325	345	435	15,000
1906	176,490	240	285	325	345	435	15,000
1907	336,448	240	285	325	345	435	15,000

Indian Head

KM# 128 • 4.18 g., 0.900 Gold 0.121 oz. AGW, 18 mm. • **Designer:** Bela Lyon Pratt

Date	Mintage	VF20	XF40	AU50	MS60	MS63	MS65	Prf65
1908	565,057	—	285	295	310	850	2,500	23,000
1909	441,899	—	285	295	310	1,300	4,000	29,000
1910	492,682	—	285	295	310	950	3,000	26,500
1911	704,191	—	285	295	310	725	4,400	23,000
1911D D strong D	55,680	2,600	2,950	3,775	7,200	12,500	55,000	—
1911D 1D weak D	Inc. above	—	1,800	2,600	4,500	—	—	—
1912	616,197	—	285	295	310	485	13,500	23,000
1913	722,165	—	285	295	310	485	4,300	23,000
1914	240,117	—	285	330	525	2,400	19,000	23,000
1914D	448,000	—	285	295	310	1,250	16,000	—
1915	606,100	—	285	295	310	650	3,300	29,250
1925D	578,000	—	285	295	310	420	1,280	—
1926	446,000	—	285	295	310	420	1,280	—
1927	388,000	—	285	295	310	420	1,280	—
1928	416,000	—	285	295	310	420	1,280	—
1929	532,000	—	285	295	310	420	3,700	—

$5 (HALF EAGLE)

Coronet Head

Coronet head, left, within circle of stars obverse

IN GOD WE TRUST above eagle reverse

KM# 101 • 8.36 g., 0.900 Gold 0.2419 oz. AGW, 21.6 mm. • **Rev. Legend:** UNITED STATES OF AMERICA **Designer:** Christian Gobrecht

Date	Mintage	VF20	XF40	AU50	MS60	MS63	MS65	Prf65
1901	616,040	420	435	440	465	550	2,300	25,000
1901S	3,648,000	420	435	440	465	550	2,300	—
1902	172,562	420	435	440	465	725	2,300	25,000
1902S	939,000	420	435	440	465	550	2,300	—
1903	227,024	420	435	440	465	925	2,300	25,000
1903S	1,855,000	420	435	440	465	550	2,300	—
1904	392,136	420	435	440	465	675	2,300	25,000
1904S	97,000	420	435	440	825	3,000	10,500	—
1905	302,308	420	435	440	465	650	2,300	27,500
1905S	880,700	420	435	440	625	1,350	7,150	—
1906	348,820	420	435	440	465	550	2,300	25,000
1906D	320,000	420	435	440	465	550	2,300	—
1906S	598,000	420	435	440	480	900	4,450	—
1907	626,192	420	435	440	465	550	2,300	25,000
1907D	888,000	420	435	440	465	550	2,300	—
1908	421,874	420	435	440	465	550	2,300	—

Indian Head

KM# 129 • 8.36 g., 0.900 Gold 0.2419 oz. AGW, 21.6 mm. • **Designer:** Bela Lyon Pratt

Date	Mintage	VF20	XF40	AU50	MS60	MS63	MS65	Prf65
1908	578,012	365	385	405	450	1,025	7,500	33,000
1908D	148,000	365	385	405	520	1,150	27,000	—
1908S	82,000	365	385	900	2,200	7,000	20,000	—
1909	627,138	365	385	405	465	1,000	7,500	42,000
1909D	3,423,560	365	385	405	450	760	7,500	—
1909O	34,200	4,200	5,600	9,500	32,000	85,000	450,000	—
1909S	297,200	390	400	475	1,800	11,000	55,000	—
1910	604,250	365	385	405	465	950	7,500	37,000
1910D	193,600	365	385	405	525	2,600	28,500	—
1910S	770,200	365	385	405	1,100	8,000	65,000	—
1911	915,139	365	385	405	645	1,100	7,500	38,000
1911D	72,500	600	800	1,600	7,500	37,000	225,000	—
1911S	1,416,000	365	385	525	700	4,000	50,000	—
1912	790,144	365	385	405	465	1,000	7,500	38,000
1912S	392,000	425	440	525	1,600	14,500	165,000	—
1913	916,099	365	385	405	465	1,025	7,500	38,000
1913S	408,000	400	440	470	1,600	15,000	130,000	—
1914	247,125	365	385	405	500	2,000	13,500	33,000
1914D	247,000	365	385	405	500	2,200	20,000	—
1914S	263,000	390	415	435	1,600	8,000	105,000	—
1915	588,075	365	385	405	465	1,100	7,500	46,000

Date	Mintage	VF20	XF40	AU50	MS60	MS63	MS65	Prf65
1915S	164,000	365	385	405	2,000	15,000	120,000	—
1916S	240,000	395	415	435	900	4,350	40,000	—
1929	662,000	—	15,000	17,000	27,000	45,000	110,000	—

$10 (EAGLE)

Coronet Head

New-style head, left, within circle of stars obverse
IN GOD WE TRUST above eagle reverse

KM# 102 • 16.72 g., 0.900 Gold 0.4837 oz. AGW, 27 mm. • **Rev. Legend:** UNITED STATES OF AMERICA **Designer:** Christian Gobrecht

Date	Mintage	VF20	XF40	AU50	MS60	MS63	MS65	Prf65
1901	1,718,825	670	680	685	725	1,000	3,500	34,000
1901O	72,041	670	680	685	1,050	3,000	—	—
1901S	2,812,750	670	680	685	725	1,000	3,500	—
1902	82,513	670	680	685	725	1,550	8,650	34,000
1902S	469,500	670	680	685	725	1,000	3,500	—
1903	125,926	670	680	685	725	1,000	6,750	34,000
1903O	112,771	670	680	685	1,025	2,500	20,500	—
1903S	538,000	670	680	685	725	1,000	3,500	—
1904	162,038	670	680	685	725	1,500	6,150	37,000
1904O	108,950	670	680	685	900	2,800	2,000	—
1905	201,078	670	680	685	725	1,000	6,750	34,000
1905S	369,250	670	680	685	925	4,400	—	—
1906	165,497	670	680	685	725	1,175	6,500	34,000
1906D	981,000	670	680	685	725	1,000	7,100	—
1906O	86,895	670	680	710	1,225	4,350	23,000	—
1906S	457,000	670	680	685	725	2,300	15,750	—
1907	1,203,973	670	680	685	725	1,000	3,500	37,000
1907D	1,030,000	670	680	685	725	1,550	12,000	—
1907S	210,500	670	680	685	875	3,550	—	—

Indian Head

No motto to left of eagle reverse

KM# 125 • 16.72 g., 0.900 Gold 0.4837 oz. AGW, 27 mm. • **Designer:** Augustus Saint-Gaudens **Note:** 1907 varieties are distinguished by whether the edge is rolled or wired, and whether the legend E PLURIBUS UNUM has periods between each word.

Date	Mintage	VF20	XF40	AU50	MS60	MS63	MS65	Prf65
1907 wire edge, periods before and after legend	500	11,000	16,500	19,000	24,000	37,000	70,000	—
1907 same, without stars on edge, unique	—	—	—	—	—	—	—	—
1907 rolled edge, periods	42	24,500	38,000	48,000	73,000	115,000	275,000	—
1907 without periods	239,406	—	710	740	1,200	3,000	8,500	—
1908 without motto	33,500	—	710	760	1,200	4,600	15,000	—
1908D without motto	210,000	—	710	760	1,200	6,275	33,000	—

IN GOD WE TRUST left of eagle reverse

KM# 130 • 16.72 g., 0.900 Gold 0.4837 oz. AGW, 27 mm. • **Designer:** Augustus Saint-Gaudens

Date	Mintage	VF20	XF40	AU50	MS60	MS63	MS65	Prf65
1908	341,486	—	880	900	950	1,625	9,000	55,000
1908D	836,500	—	685	745	1,225	6,600	24,000	
1908S	59,850	900	975	1,250	3,600	12,000	23,000	
1909	184,863	—	685	745	750	2,800	20,500	68,000
1909D	121,540	—	685	745	1,200	4,000	28,000	—
1909S	292,350	—	675	880	1,800	5,500	19,000	—
1910	318,704	—	685	745	705	1,000	8,500	55,000
1910D	2,356,640	—	685	745	705	975	8,500	—
1910S	811,000	—	685	745	1,050	7,600	49,000	—
1911	505,595	—	685	745	705	1,300	7,500	55,000
1911D	30,100	900	1,250	2,550	8,500	29,000	220,000	—
1911S	51,000	950	1,100	1,200	2,900	11,000	23,000	—
1912	405,083	—	685	745	705	1,125	9,000	55,000
1912S	300,000	—	685	745	1,425	6,000	39,000	—

Date	Mintage	VF20	XF40	AU50	MS60	MS63	MS65	Prf65
1913	442,071	—	685	745	705	975	8,500	55,000
1913S	66,000	840	950	1,200	5,500	25,000	170,000	—
1914	151,050	—	685	745	705	2,000	11,000	60,000
1914D	343,500	—	685	745	705	1,700	12,500	—
1914S	208,000	850	975	1,125	1,800	5,500	30,500	—
1915	351,075	—	685	745	705	1,450	9,000	55,000
1915S	59,000	840	1,100	1,400	5,500	17,500	69,000	—
1916S	138,500	—	740	750	1,750	5,600	24,000	—
1920S	126,500	16,500	23,000	26,000	38,000	93,000	275,000	—
1926	1,014,000	—	685	745	740	970	2,975	—
1930S	96,000	9,000	16,500	19,750	27,000	44,000	93,000	—
1932	4,463,000	—	685	745	730	975	2,975	—
1933	312,500	130,000	140,000	145,000	165,000	225,000	600,000	—

$20 (DOUBLE EAGLE)

Liberty Head

Coronet head, left, within circle of stars obverse
TWENTY DOLLARS below eagle reverse

KM# 74.3 • 33.44 g., 0.900 Gold 0.9675 oz. AGW **Rev. Legend:** UNITED STATES OF AMERICA

Date	Mintage	VF20	XF40	AU50	MS60	MS63	MS65	Prf65
1901	111,526	1,290	1,300	1,310	1,450	1,800	4,000	84,000
1901S	1,596,000	1,290	1,300	1,310	1,450	3,500	17,000	—
1902	31,254	1,290	1,300	1,310	1,450	11,000	—	84,000
1902S	1,753,625	1,290	1,300	1,310	1,450	2,900	29,000	—
1903	287,428	1,290	1,300	1,310	1,450	1,725	3,900	84,000
1903S	954,000	1,290	1,300	1,310	1,450	1,800	12,000	—
1904	6,256,797	1,290	1,300	1,310	1,450	1,725	4,000	84,000
1904S	5,134,175	1,290	1,300	1,310	1,450	1,725	4,000	—
1905	59,011	1,290	1,300	1,600	2,450	13,000	85,000	84,000
1905S	1,813,000	1,290	1,300	1,310	1,260	3,000	18,000	—
1906	69,690	1,290	1,300	1,600	2,100	6,700	29,000	84,000
1906D	620,250	1,290	1,300	1,310	1,450	3,400	18,000	—
1906S	2,065,750	1,290	1,300	1,310	1,450	1,950	22,000	—
1907	1,451,864	1,290	1,300	1,310	1,450	1,725	7,000	84,000
1907D	842,250	1,290	1,300	1,310	1,450	2,900	7,000	—
1907S	2,165,800	1,290	1,300	1,310	1,450	2,100	22,000	—

Saint-Gaudens High Relief

Roman numerals in date obverse No motto below eagle reverse

KM# 126 • 33.44 g., 0.900 Gold 0.9675 oz. AGW, 34 mm. • **Edge:** Plain. **Designer:** Augustus Saint-Gaudens

Date	Mintage	VF20	XF40	AU50	MS60	MS63	MS65	Prf65
MCMVII (1907) high relief, unique, AU-55, 150,000	—	—	—	—	—	—	—	—
MCMVII (1907) high relief, wire rim	11,250	6,000	8,300	9,800	13,500	23,500	42,000	—
MCMVII (1907) high relief, flat rim	Inc. above	7,000	8,500	11,000	14,000	24,000	45,500	—

Saint-Gaudens

Arabic numerals in date obverse No motto below eagle reverse

KM# 127 • 33.44 g., 0.900 Gold 0.9675 oz. AGW, 34 mm. • **Edge:** Lettered; large letters. **Designer:** Augustus Saint-Gaudens

Date	Mintage	VF20	XF40	AU50	MS60	MS63	MS65	Prf65
1907 large letters on edge, unique	—	—	—	—	—	—	—	—
1907 small letters on edge	361,667	1,210	1,260	1,270	1,300	1,600	3,500	—
1908	4,271,551	1,210	1,260	1,270	1,300	1,360	2,000	—
1908D	663,750	1,210	1,260	1,270	1,300	1,360	7,000	—

IN GOD WE TRUST below eagle reverse

KM# 131 • 33.44 g., 0.900 Gold 0.9675 oz. AGW, 34 mm. • **Designer:** Augustus Saint-Gaudens

Date	Mintage	VF20	XF40	AU50	MS60	MS63	MS65	Prf65
1908	156,359	1,210	1,260	1,270	1,400	1,800	20,000	75,000
1908 Roman finish; Prf64 Rare								
Note: Rare								
1908D	349,500	1,210	1,260	1,270	1,300	1,600	5,500	—
1908S	22,000	1,800	3,000	4,250	9,500	20,000	42,000	
1909/8	161,282	1,400	1,600	1,650	2,000	3,800	38,000	—
1909	Inc. Above	1,210	1,260	1,270	1,300	2,300	34,000	75,000
1909D	52,500	1,300	1,260	1,270	2,800	5,000	35,000	—
1909S	2,774,925	1,210	1,260	1,270	1,300	1,400	5,100	—
1910	482,167	1,210	1,260	1,270	1,300	1,360	7,000	80,000
1910D	429,000	1,210	1,260	1,270	1,300	1,360	3,100	—
1910S	2,128,250	1,210	1,260	1,270	1,300	2,000	7,300	—
1911	197,350	1,210	1,260	1,270	1,300	2,300	17,000	74,000
1911D	846,500	1,210	1,260	1,270	1,300	1,360	2,300	—
1911S	775,750	1,210	1,260	1,270	1,300	1,360	5,100	—
1912	149,824	1,210	1,260	1,270	1,300	2,200	24,000	74,000
1913	168,838	1,210	1,260	1,270	1,300	2,300	45,000	79,000
1913D	393,500	1,210	1,260	1,270	1,300	1,750	5,300	—
1913S	34,000	1,210	1,260	1,800	2,200	3,500	29,000	—
1914	95,320	1,210	1,260	1,270	1,300	2,600	20,000	79,000
1914D	453,000	1,210	1,260	1,270	1,300	1,360	3,100	—
1914S	1,498,000	1,210	1,260	1,270	1,300	1,360	2,400	—
1915	152,050	1,210	1,260	1,270	1,300	1,800	22,000	90,000
1915S	567,500	1,210	1,260	1,270	1,300	1,360	2,300	—
1916S	796,000	1,210	1,260	1,270	1,300	1,500	2,900	—
1920	228,250	1,210	1,260	1,270	1,300	1,700	85,000	—
1920S	558,000	11,000	15,500	24,000	42,000	75,000	250,000	—
1921	528,500	—	38,000	48,000	90,000	225,000	585,000	—
1922	1,375,500	1,210	1,260	1,270	1,300	1,360	6,500	—
1922S	2,658,000	1,210	1,260	2,000	2,300	4,600	38,000	—
1923	566,000	1,210	1,260	1,270	1,300	1,360	6,500	—
1923D	1,702,250	1,210	1,260	1,270	1,300	1,360	2,225	—
1924	4,323,500	1,210	1,260	1,270	1,300	1,360	2,225	—
1924D	3,049,500	1,210	1,260	1,270	4,000	6,800	73,000	—
1924S	2,927,500	1,215	1,300	1,750	3,800	9,000	140,000	—
1925	2,831,750	1,210	1,260	1,270	1,300	1,360	2,225	—
1925D	2,938,500	1,600	1,900	2,500	4,000	8,500	85,000	—
1925S	3,776,500	1,900	2,300	3,300	8,000	1,360	150,000	—
1926	816,750	1,210	1,260	1,270	1,300	1,360	2,225	—
1926D	481,000	8,000	9,000	10,000	13,000	19,000	195,000	—
1926S	2,041,500	1,650	1,760	1,900	3,000	5,000	32,000	—
1927	2,946,750	1,210	1,260	1,270	1,300	1,360	2,225	—
1927D	180,000	240,000	300,000	500,000	750,000	1,000,000	1,600,000	—
1927S	3,107,000	7,500	10,000	13,000	22,000	35,000	110,000	—
1928	8,816,000	1,210	1,260	1,270	1,175	1,360	2,225	—
1929	1,779,750	9,000	11,000	13,000	17,000	30,000	75,000	—
1930S	74,000	33,000	37,000	42,000	60,000	84,000	165,000	—
1931	2,938,250	13,000	16,000	20,000	30,000	50,000	95,000	—
1931D	106,500	13,000	16,000	26,000	36,000	60,000	105,000	—
1932	1,101,750	13,000	16,000	20,000	25,000	70,000	97,500	—
1933	445,500	—	—	—	—	—	9,000,000	—

Note: Sotheby/Stack's Sale, July 2002. Thirteen known, only one currently available.

COMMEMORATIVE COINAGE 1892-1954

All commemorative half dollars of 1892-1954 have the following specifications: diameter — 30.6 millimeters; weight — 12.500 grams; composition — 0.900 silver, 0.3617 ounces actual silver weight. Values for PDS sets contain one example each from the Philadelphia, Denver and San Francisco mints. Type coin prices are the most inexpensive single coin available from the date and mint mark combinations listed.

HALF DOLLAR

PANAMA-PACIFIC EXPOSITION. KM# 135 Designer: Charles E. Barber **Obv.** Columbia standing, sunset in background **Rev:** Eagle standing on shield

Date	Mintage	AU50	MS60	MS63	MS64	MS65
1915 S	27,134	360	475	725	875	1,300

ILLINOIS CENTENNIAL-LINCOLN. KM# 143 Obv. Designer: George T. Morgan **Obv.** Abraham Lincon bust right **Rev. Designer:** John R. Sinnock **Rev:** Eagle standing left

Date	Mintage	AU50	MS60	MS63	MS64	MS65
1918	100,058	155	170	180	210	345

MAINE CENTENNIAL. KM# 146 Designer: Anthony de Francisci **Obv.** Arms of the State of Maine **Rev:** Legend within wreath

Date	Mintage	AU50	MS60	MS63	MS64	MS65
1920	50,028	135	160	165	195	370

PILGRIM TERCENTENARY. KM# 147.1 Designer: Cyrus E. Dallin **Obv.** William Bradford half-length left **Rev:** Mayflower sailing left

Date	Mintage	AU50	MS60	MS63	MS64	MS65
1920	152,112	88.00	105	110	130	210

PILGRIM TERCENTENARY. KM# 147.2 Designer: Cyrus E. Dallin **Obv.** William Bradford half-length left, 1921 added at left **Rev:** Mayflower sailing left

Date	Mintage	AU50	MS60	MS63	MS64	MS65
1921	20,053	215	220	230	240	300

2x2

ALABAMA CENTENNIAL. **KM# 148.1 Designer:** Laura G. Fraser **Obv.** William W. Bibb and T.E. Kilby conjoint busts left. "2x2" at right above stars **Rev:** Ealge left on shield **Note:** Fake 2x2" counterstamps exist.

Date	Mintage	AU50	MS60	MS63	MS64	MS65
1921	6,006	300	320	465	550	1,300

ALABAMA CENTENNIAL. **KM# 148.2 Obv. Designer:** Laura G. Fraser **Obv.** William W. Bibb and T.E. Kilby conjoint busts left **Rev:** Eagle standing left on shield

Date	Mintage	AU50	MS60	MS63	MS64	MS65
1921	59,038	160	210	420	450	1,050

MISSOURI CENTENNIAL. **KM# 149.1 Designer:** Robert Aitken **Obv.** Frontiersman in coonskin cap left **Rev:** Frontiersman and Native American standing left

Date	Mintage	AU50	MS60	MS63	MS64	MS65
1921	15,428	375	475	550	850	2,020

2x4

MISSOURI CENTENNIAL. **KM# 149.2 Designer:** Robert Aitken **Obv.** Frontiersman in coonskin cap left, 2(star)4 in field at left **Rev:** Frontiersman and Native American standing left **Note:** Fake "2(star)4" counterstamps exist.

Date	Mintage	AU50	MS60	MS63	MS64	MS65
1921	5,000	600	675	985	1,050	1,600

GRANT MEMORIAL. **KM# 151.1 Designer:** Laura G. Fraser **Obv.** Grant bust right **Rev:** Birthplace in Point Pleasant, Ohio

Date	Mintage	AU50	MS60	MS63	MS64	MS65
1922	67,405	110	125	160	275	600

GRANT MEMORIAL. **KM# 151.2 Designer:** Laura G. Fraser **Obv.** Grant bust left, star above the word GRANT **Rev:** Birthplace in Point Pleasant, Ohio **Note:** Fake "star" counterstamps exist.

Date	Mintage	AU50	MS60	MS63	MS64	MS65
1922	4,256	840	1,150	1,580	2,450	5,100

MONROE DOCTRINE CENTENNIAL. **KM# 153 Designer:** Chester Beach **Obv.** James Monroe and John Quincy Adams conjoint busts left **Rev:** Western Hemisphere portraied by two female figures

Date	Mintage	AU50	MS60	MS63	MS64	MS65
1923 S	274,077	55.00	80.00	130	210	900

HUGUENOT-WALLOON TERCENTENARY. **KM# 154 Designer:** George T. Morgan **Obv.** Huguenot leader Gaspard de Coligny and William I of Orange conjoint busts right **Rev:** Nieuw Nederland sailing left

Date	Mintage	AU50	MS60	MS63	MS64	MS65
1924	142,080	135	140	175	205	300

CALIFORNIA DIAMOND JUBILEE. **KM# 155 Designer:** Jo Mora **Obv.** Fourty-Niner kneeling panning for gold **Rev:** Grizzly bear walking left

Date	Mintage	AU50	MS60	MS63	MS64	MS65
1925 S	86,594	200	205	215	375	450

LEXINGTON-CONCORD SESQUICENTENNIAL. **KM# 156 Designer:** Chester Beach **Obv.** Concord's Minute Man statue **Rev:** Old Belfry at Lexington

Date	Mintage	AU50	MS60	MS63	MS64	MS65
1925	162,013	80.00	95.00	105	135	375

STONE MOUNTAIN MEMORIAL. KM# 157 Designer: Gutzon Borglum **Obv.** Generals Robert E. Lee and Thomas "Stonewall" Jackson mounted left. **Rev:** Eagle on rock at right

Date	Mintage	AU50	MS60	MS63	MS64	MS65
1925	1,314,709	60.00	70.00	80.00	140	195

FORT VANCOUVER CENTENNIAL. KM# 158 Designer: Laura G. Fraser **Obv.** John McLoughlin bust left **Rev:** Frontiersmen standing with musket, Ft. Vancouver in background

Date	Mintage	AU50	MS60	MS63	MS64	MS65
1925	14,994	325	380	425	480	625

OREGON TRAIL MEMORIAL. KM# 159 Designer: James E. and Laura G. Fraser **Obv.** Native American standing in full headdress and holding bow, US Map in background **Rev:** Conestoga wagon pulled by oxen left towards sunset

Date	Mintage	AU50	MS60	MS63	MS64	MS65
1926	47,955	145	170	190	215	265
1926 S	83,055	145	170	190	215	265
1928	6,028	155	180	200	260	325
1933 D	5,008	350	365	380	390	425
1934 D	7,006	200	205	215	225	325
1936	10,006	170	200	215	250	300
1936 S	5,006	175	200	215	260	300
1937 D	12,008	175	210	215	260	275
1938	6,006	185	220	225	260	325
1938 D	6,005	185	220	225	260	325
1938 S	6,006	185	220	225	260	325
1939	3,004	460	500	525	600	700
1939 D	3,004	460	500	525	600	700
1939 S	3,005	460	500	525	600	700

U.S. SESQUICENTENNIAL. KM# 160 Designer: John R. Sinnock **Obv.** George Washington and Calvin Coolidge conjoint busts right **Rev:** Liberty Bell

Date	Mintage	AU50	MS60	MS63	MS64	MS65
1926	141,120	85.00	95.00	125	210	1,850

VERMONT SESQUICENTENNIAL. KM# 162 Obv. Designer: Charles Keck **Obv.** Ira Allen bust right **Rev:** Catamount advancing left

Date	Mintage	AU50	MS60	MS63	MS64	MS65
1927	28,142	270	285	300	315	500

HAWAIIAN SESQUICENTENNIAL. KM# 163 Designer: Juliette May Fraser and Chester Beach **Obv.** Captain James Cook bust left **Rev:** Native Hawaiian standing over view of Diamond Head **Note:** Counterfeits exist.

Date	Mintage	AU50	MS60	MS63	MS64	MS65
1928	10,008	1,700	2,100	2,100	2,500	3,400

DANIEL BOONE BICENTENNIAL. KM# 165.1 Designer: Augustus Lukeman **Obv.** Daniel Boone bust left **Rev:** Daniel Boone and Native American standing

Date	Mintage	AU50	MS60	MS63	MS64	MS65
1934	10,007	145	160	185	200	250
1935	10,010	145	160	185	200	250
1935 D	5,005	260	275	300	400	775
1935 S	5,005	260	275	300	375	660

DANIEL BOONE BICENTENNIAL. KM# 165.2 Designer: Augustus Lukeman **Obv.** Daniel Boone bust left **Rev:** Daniel Boone and Native American standing, "1934" added above the word "PIONEER."

Date	Mintage	AU50	MS60	MS63	MS64	MS65
1935	10,008	160	170	185	200	220
1935 D	2,003	160	170	185	200	220
1935 S	2,004	160	170	185	190	200
1936	12,012	165	180	200	225	290
1936 D	5,005	165	180	200	225	290
1936 S	5,006	155	170	190	215	280
1937	9,810	150	160	180	205	260
1937 D	2,506	225	235	280	310	375
1937 S	2,506	225	235	280	310	380
1938	2,100	290	310	345	390	480
1938 D	2,100	290	310	345	390	460
1938 S	2,100	290	310	345	390	460

MARYLAND TERCENTENARY. KM# 166 Designer: Hans Schuler **Obv.** Lord Baltimore, Cecil Calvert bust right **Rev:** Maryland state arms

Date	Mintage	AU50	MS60	MS63	MS64	MS65
1934	25,015	155	160	170	190	210

TEXAS CENTENNIAL. KM# 167 Designer: Pompeo Coppini **Obv.** Eagle standing left, large star in background **Rev:** Winged Victory kneeling beside Alamo Mission, small busts of Sam Houston and Stephen Austin at sides

Date	Mintage	AU50	MS60	MS63	MS64	MS65
1934	61,463	130	140	155	165	200

Date	Mintage	AU50	MS60	MS63	MS64	MS65
1935	9,994	130	140	155	165	200
1935 D	10,007	130	140	155	165	200
1935 S	10,008	130	140	155	165	200
1936	8,911	130	140	155	165	200
1936 D	9,039	130	140	155	165	200
1936 S	9,055	130	140	155	165	200
1937	6,571	130	140	155	165	200
1937 D	6,605	130	140	155	165	200
1937 S	6,637	130	140	155	165	200
1938	3,780	260	270	275	285	500
1938 D	3,775	260	270	275	285	500
1938 S	3,814	260	270	275	285	500

ARKANSAS CENTENNIAL. KM# 168 Designer: Edward E. Burr **Obv.** Liberty and Indian Chief's conjoint heads left **Rev:** Eagle with outstretched wings and flag of Arkansas in background

Date	Mintage	AU50	MS60	MS63	MS64	MS65
1935	13,012	105	110	120	145	180
1935 D	5,505	105	110	120	145	180
1935 S	5,506	105	110	120	145	225
1936	9,660	105	110	120	145	185
1936 D	9,660	105	110	120	145	200
1936 S	9,662	105	110	120	145	225
1937	5,505	105	110	120	145	180
1937 D	5,505	105	110	120	145	180
1937 S	5,506	105	110	120	145	400
1938	3,156	135	140	190	225	425
1938 D	3,155	135	140	170	225	275
1938 S	3,156	135	140	170	225	375
1939	2,104	220	240	250	280	580
1939 D	2,104	220	240	250	280	800
1939 S	2,105	220	240	250	280	910

CONNECTICUT TERCENTENARY. KM# 169 Designer: Henry Kreiss **Obv.** Eagle standing left **Rev:** Charter oak tree

Date	Mintage	AU50	MS60	MS63	MS64	MS65
1935	25,018	205	210	220	245	375

HUDSON, N.Y., SESQUICENTENNIAL. KM# 170 Designer: Chester Beach **Obv.** Hudson's ship, the Half Moon sailing right **Rev:** Seal of the City of Hudson

Date	Mintage	AU50	MS60	MS63	MS64	MS65
1935	10,008	700	725	800	875	1,025

SAN DIEGO-PACIFIC INTERNATIONAL EXPOSITION. KM# 171 Designer: Robert Aitken **Obv.** Seated female with bear at her side **Rev:** State of California exposition building

Date	Mintage	AU50	MS60	MS63	MS64	MS65
1935 S	70,132	105	110	115	120	160
1936 D	30,092	105	110	115	120	160

OLD SPANISH TRAIL. KM# 172 Designer: L.W. Hoffecker **Obv.** Long-horn cow's head facing **Rev:** The 1535 route of Cabeza de Vaca's expedition and a yucca tree **Note:** Counterfeits exist.

Date	Mintage	AU50	MS60	MS63	MS64	MS65
1935	10,008	1,050	1,075	1,100	1,200	1,425

ALBANY, N.Y., CHARTER ANNIVERSARY. KM# 173 Designer: Gertrude K. Lathrop **Obv.** Beaver knawing on maple branch **Rev:** Standing figures of Thomas Dongan, Peter Schyuyler and Robert Livingston

Date	Mintage	AU50	MS60	MS63	MS64	MS65
1936	17,671	210	220	235	245	300

SAN FRANCISCO-OAKLAND BAY BRIDGE. KM# 174 Designer: Jacques Schnier **Obv.** Grizzly bear facing **Rev:** Oakland Bay Bridge

Date	Mintage	AU50	MS60	MS63	MS64	MS65
1936	71,424	150	175	180	190	220

BRIDGEPORT, CONN., CENTENNIAL. KM# 175 Designer: Henry Kreiss **Obv.** P.T. Barnum bust left **Rev:** Eagle standing right

Date	Mintage	AU50	MS60	MS63	MS64	MS65
1936	25,015	130	135	145	150	185

CINCINNATI MUSIC CENTER. KM# 176 Designer: Constance Ortmayer **Obv.** Stephen Foster bust right **Rev:** Kneeling female with lyre

Date	Mintage	AU50	MS60	MS63	MS64	MS65
1936	5,005	280	300	350	375	425
1936 D	5,005	280	300	350	375	425
1936 S	5,006	280	300	350	375	475

CLEVELAND-GREAT LAKES EXPOSITION. KM# 177 Designer: Brenda Putnam **Obv.** Moses Cleaveland bust left **Rev:** Dividers and map of the Great Lakes

Date	Mintage	AU50	MS60	MS63	MS64	MS65
1936	50,030	110	120	130	145	180

COLUMBIA, S.C., SESQUICENTENNIAL. KM# 178 Designer: A. Wolfe Davidson **Obv.** Figure of Justice between capitols of 1786 and 1936 **Rev:** Palmetto tree

Date	Mintage	AU50	MS60	MS63	MS64	MS65
1936	9,007	200	225	240	260	300
1936 D	8,009	200	225	240	260	300
1936 S	8,007	200	225	240	260	300

DELAWARE TERCENTENARY. KM# 179 Designer: Carl L. Schmitz **Obv.** Old Swedes Church in Wilmington **Rev:** Kalmar Nyckel sailing left

Date	Mintage	AU50	MS60	MS63	MS64	MS65
1936	20,993	220	230	245	260	285

ELGIN, ILL., CENTENNIAL. KM# 180 Designer: Trygve Rovelstad **Obv.** Pioneer head left **Rev:** Statue group

Date	Mintage	AU50	MS60	MS63	MS64	MS65
1936	20,015	185	190	195	210	275

BATTLE OF GETTYSBURG 75TH ANNIVERSARY. KM# 181 Designer: Frank Vittor **Obv.** Union and Confederate veteran conjoint busts right **Rev:** Double bladed fasces seperating two shields

Date	Mintage	AU50	MS60	MS63	MS64	MS65
1936	26,928	475	485	500	600	825

LONG ISLAND TERCENTENARY. KM# 182 Designer: Howard K. Weinman **Obv.** Dutch settler and Native American conjoint head right **Rev:** Dutch sailing vessel

Date	Mintage	AU50	MS60	MS63	MS64	MS65
1936	81,826	95.00	105	110	120	200

LYNCHBURG, VA., SESQUICENTENNIAL. KM# 183 Designer: Charles Keck **Obv.** Sen. Carter Glass bust left **Rev:** Liberty standing, old Lynchburg courthouse at right

Date	Mintage	AU50	MS60	MS63	MS64	MS65
1936	20,013	225	235	250	265	300

NORFOLK, VA., BICENTENNIAL. KM# 184 Designer: William M. and Marjorie E. Simpson **Obv.** Seal of the City of Norfolk **Rev:** Royal Mace of Norfolk

Date	Mintage	AU50	MS60	MS63	MS64	MS65
1936	16,936	300	305	325	350	380

RHODE ISLAND TERCENTENARY. KM# 185 Designer: Arthur G. Carey and John H. Benson **Obv.** Roger Williams in canoe hailing Native American **Rev:** Shield with anchor

Date	Mintage	AU50	MS60	MS63	MS64	MS65
1936	20,013	110	125	130	140	170
1936 D	15,010	110	125	130	140	170
1936 S	15,011	110	125	130	160	225

ROANOKE ISLAND, N.C.. KM# 186 Designer: William M. Simpson **Obv.** Sir Walter Raleigh bust left **Rev:** Ellinor Dare holding baby Virginia, two small ships flanking

Date	Mintage	AU50	MS60	MS63	MS64	MS65
1937	29,030	180	185	195	210	275

ARKANSAS CENTENNIAL. KM# 187 Obv. Designer: Henry Kreiss **Obv.** Eagle with wings outstreatched, Arkansas flag in backgorund **Rev. Designer:** Edward E. Burr **Rev:** Sen. Joseph T. Robinson bust right

Date	Mintage	AU50	MS60	MS63	MS64	MS65
1936	25,265	115	135	145	155	210

WISCONSIN TERRITORIAL CENTENNIAL. KM# 188 Designer: David Parsons **Obv.** Badger from the Territorial seal **Rev:** Pick axe and mound of lead ore

Date	Mintage	AU50	MS60	MS63	MS64	MS65
1936	25,015	195	200	210	225	275

YORK COUNTY, MAINE, TERCENTENARY. KM# 189 Designer: Walter H. Rich **Obv.** Stockade **Rev:** York County seal

Date	Mintage	AU50	MS60	MS63	MS64	MS65
1936	25,015	160	170	180	195	205

BATTLE OF ANTIETAM 75TH ANNIVERSARY. KM# 190 Designer: William M. Simpson **Obv.** Generals Robert E. Lee and George McClellan conjoint busts left **Rev:** Burnside Bridge

Date	Mintage	AU50	MS60	MS63	MS64	MS65
1937	18,028	530	550	570	590	625

NEW ROCHELLE, N.Y.. KM# 191 Designer: Gertrude K. Lathrop **Obv.** John Pell and a calf **Rev:** Fleur-de-lis from the seal of the city

Date	Mintage	AU50	MS60	MS63	MS64	MS65
1938	15,266	300	320	340	350	390

Iowa Statehood Centennial. KM# 197 Designer: Adam Pietz Obv. First Capitol building at Iowa City Rev: Iowa state seal

Date	Mintage	AU50	MS60	MS63	MS64	MS65
1946	100,057	92.00	100	120	130	155

BOOKER T. WASHINGTON. KM# 198 Designer: Isaac S. Hathaway **Obv.** Booker T. Washington bust right **Rev:** Cabin and NYU's Hall of Fame **Note:** Actual mintages are higher, but unsold issues were melted to produce Washington Carver issues.

Date	Mintage	AU50	MS60	MS63	MS64	MS65
1946	1,000,546	22.00	28.00	32.00	45.00	65.00
1946 D	200,113	22.00	28.00	32.00	45.00	65.00
1946 S	500,729	22.00	28.00	32.00	45.00	65.00
1947	100,017	22.00	28.00	60.00	75.00	85.00
1947 D	100,017	22.00	28.00	60.00	75.00	85.00
1947 S	100,017	22.00	28.00	60.00	75.00	85.00
1948	8,005	22.00	28.00	60.00	75.00	85.00
1948 D	8,005	22.00	28.00	60.00	75.00	85.00
1948 S	8,005	22.00	28.00	60.00	75.00	110
1949	6,004	22.00	35.00	45.00	60.00	175
1949 D	6,004	32.00	50.00	60.00	70.00	150
1949 S	6,004	32.00	50.00	60.00	70.00	140
1950	6,004	30.00	40.00	60.00	70.00	100
1950 D	6,004	22.00	28.00	60.00	65.00	105
1950 S	512,091	22.00	28.00	45.00	55.00	95.00
1951	51,082	22.00	28.00	40.00	55.00	75.00
1951 D	7,004	22.00	40.00	60.00	75.00	100
1951 S	7,004	22.00	35.00	60.00	75.00	100

BOOKER T. WASHINGTON AND GEORGE WASHINGTON CARVER. KM# 200 Designer: Isaac S. Hathaway **Obv.** Booker T. Washington and George Washington Carver conjoint busts right **Rev:** Map of the United States

Date	Mintage	AU50	MS60	MS63	MS64	MS65
1951	110,018	22.00	28.00	40.00	75.00	225
1951 D	10,004	22.00	30.00	40.00	50.00	90.00
1951 S	10,004	22.00	28.00	55.00	60.00	95.00
1952	2,006,292	22.00	28.00	42.00	55.00	75.00
1952 D	8,006	30.00	35.00	45.00	70.00	160
1952 S	8,006	22.00	28.00	40.00	55.00	105
1953	8,003	22.00	28.00	40.00	55.00	110
1953 D	8,003	22.00	28.00	40.00	65.00	120
1953 S	108,020	22.00	28.00	40.00	50.00	75.00
1954	12,006	22.00	28.00	40.00	55.00	75.00
1954 D	12,006	22.00	28.00	40.00	55.00	100
1954 S	122,024	22.00	28.00	40.00	45.00	75.00

DOLLAR

LOUISIANA PURCHASE EXPOSITION - JEFFERSON BUST. KM# 119 Designer: Charles E. Barber **Obv.** Jefferson bust left **Rev:** Legend and laurel branch

Date	Mintage	AU50	MS60	MS63	MS64	MS65
1903	17,500	570	635	875	900	1,400

LOUISIANA PURCHASE EXPOSITION - MCKINLEY BUST. KM# 120 Obv. Designer: Charles E. Barber **Obv.** William McKinley bust left **Rev:** Legend and laurel branch

Date	Mintage	AU50	MS60	MS63	MS64	MS65
1903	17,500	560	575	725	875	1,300

LEWIS AND CLARK EXPOSITION. KM# 121 Obv. Designer: Charles E. Barber **Obv.** Lewis bust left **Rev:** Clark bust left

Date	Mintage	AU50	MS60	MS63	MS64	MS65
1904	10,025	900	1,000	1,525	2,300	4,500
1905	10,041	850	1,300	1,725	3,000	8,200

PANAMA-PACIFIC EXPOSITION. **KM# 136** **Obv. Designer:** Charles Keck **Obv.** Canal laborer bust left **Rev:** Value within two dolphins

Date	Mintage	AU50	MS60	MS63	MS64	MS65
1915 S	15,000	530	600	725	850	1,250

MCKINLEY MEMORIAL. **KM# 144** **Obv. Designer:** Charles E. Barber **Obv.** William McKinley head left **Rev. Designer:** George T. Morgan **Rev:** Memorial building at Niles, Ohio

Date	Mintage	AU50	MS60	MS63	MS64	MS65
1916	9,977	520	550	585	695	1,200
1917	10,000	550	700	800	925	1,425

GRANT MEMORIAL. **KM# 152.1** **Obv. Designer:** Laura G. Fraser **Obv.** U.S. Grant bust right **Rev:** Birthplace **Note:** Without an incuse "star" above the word GRANT on the obverse.

Date	Mintage	AU50	MS60	MS63	MS64	MS65
1922	5,000	1,200	1,300	1,400	1,600	2,350

Star

GRANT MEMORIAL. **KM# 152.2** **Obv. Designer:** Laura G. Fraser **Obv.** U.S. Grant bust right **Rev:** Birthplace **Note:** Variety with an incuse "star" above the word GRANT on the obverse.

Date	Mintage	AU50	MS60	MS63	MS64	MS65
1922	5,016	1,400	1,500	1,650	1,785	1,925

$2.50 (QUARTER EAGLE)

PANAMA-PACIFIC EXPOSITION. **KM# 137** **Obv. Designer:** Charles E. Barber **Obv.** Columbia holding cadueus while seated on a hippocamp **Rev. Designer:** George T. Morgan **Rev:** Eagle standing left

Date	Mintage	AU50	MS60	MS63	MS64	MS65
1915 S	6,749	295	310	420	4,500	1,280

U.S. SESQUICENTENNIAL. **KM# 161** **Obv. Designer:** John R. Sinnock **Obv.** Liberty standing holding torch and scroll **Rev:** Independence Hall

Date	Mintage	AU50	MS60	MS63	MS64	MS65
1926	46,019	295	310	420	875	1,280

$50

PANAMA-PACIFIC EXPOSITION OCTAGONAL. **KM# 139** **Obv. Designer:** Robert Aitken **Obv.** Minerva bust helmeted left **Rev:** Owl perched on California pine branch **Shape:** Octagon

Date	Mintage	AU50	MS60	MS63	MS64	MS65
1915 S	645	50,000	65,500	85,000	110,000	200,000

PANAMA-PACIFIC EXPOSITION ROUND. **KM# 138** **Obv. Designer:** Robert Aitken **Obv.** Minerva bust helmeted left **Rev:** Owl perched on California pin branch **Shape:** Round

Date	Mintage	AU50	MS60	MS63	MS64	MS65
1915 S	483	50,000	65,500	85,000	110,000	210,000

COMMEMORATIVE COINAGE 1982-2000

All commemorative silver dollar coins of 1982-present have the following specifications: diameter — 38.1 millimeters; weight — 26.730 grams; composition — 0.900 silver, 0.7736 ounces actual silver weight. All commemorative $5 coins of 1982-present have the following specificiations: diameter — 21.6 millimeters; weight — 8.359 grams; composition: 0.900 gold, 0.242 ounces actual gold weight.

Note: In 1982, after a hiatus of nearly 30 years, coinage of commemorative half dollars resumed. Those designated with a 'W' were struck at the West Point Mint. Some issues were struck in copper-nickel. Those struck in silver have the same size, weight and composition as the prior commemorative half-dollar series.

HALF DOLLAR

GEORGE WASHINGTON, 250TH BIRTH ANNIVERSARY. **KM# 208** **Obv. Designer:** Elizabeth Jones **Obv.** George Washington on horseback facing **Rev. Designer:** Matthew Peloso **Rev:** Mount Vernon

Date	Mintage	MS63	MS65	Prf65
1982D	2,210,458	—	10.00	—
1982S	4,894,044	—	—	11.00

STATUE OF LIBERTY CENTENNIAL. **KM# 212** **Obv. Designer:** Edgar Z. Steever **Obv.** Statue of Liberty and sunrise **Rev. Designer:** Sherl Joseph Winter **Rev:** Immigrant family looking toward mainland

Date	Mintage	MS63	MS65	Prf65
1986D	928,008	—	5.00	—
1986S	6,925,627	—	—	3.50

CONGRESS BICENTENNIAL. **KM# 224** **Obv. Designer:** Patricia L. Verani **Obv.** Statue of Freedom head **Rev. Designer:** William Woodward and Edgar Z. Steever **Rev:** Capitol building

Date	Mintage	MS63	MS65	Prf65
1989D	163,753	—	7.00	—
1989S	762,198	—	—	6.00

MOUNT RUSHMORE 50TH ANNIVERSARY. KM# 228 Obv. Designer: Marcel Jovine **Rev. Designer:** T. James Ferrell **Rev:** Mount Rushmore portraits **Edge:** Bison standing left

Date	Mintage	MS63	MS65	Prf65
1991D	172,754	—	13.00	—
1991S	753,257	—	—	10.00

1992 OLYMPICS. KM# 233 Obv. Designer: William Cousins **Obv.** Torch and laurel **Rev. Designer:** Steven M. Bieda **Rev:** Female gymnast and large flag

Date	Mintage	MS63	MS65	Prf65
1992P	161,607	—	8.00	—
1992S	519,645	—	—	7.00

COLUMBUS VOYAGE - 500TH ANNIVERSARY. KM# 237 Obv. Designer: T. James Ferrell **Obv.** Columbus standing on shore **Rev. Designer:** Thomas D. Rogers, Sr. **Rev:** Nina, Pinta and Santa Maria sailing right

Date	Mintage	MS63	MS65	Prf65
1992D	135,702	—	9.00	—
1992S	390,154	—	—	6.50

JAMES MADISON - BILL OF RIGHTS. KM# 240 Obv. Designer: T. James Ferrell **Obv.** James Madison writing, Montpelier in background **Rev. Designer:** Dean McMullen **Rev:** Statue of Liberty torch

Date	Mintage	MS63	MS65	Prf65
1993W	193,346	—	18.00	—
1993S	586,315	—	—	15.00

WORLD WAR II 50TH ANNIVERSARY. KM# 243 Obv. Designer: George Klauba and T. James Ferrell **Obv.** Three portraits, plane above, large V in backgound **Rev. Designer:** William J. Leftwich and T. James Ferrell **Rev:** Pacific island battle scene

Date	Mintage	MS63	MS65	Prf65
ND-1993P	317,396	—	—	14.00
ND-1993P	197,072	—	13.00	—

1994 WORLD CUP SOCCER. KM# 246 Obv. Designer: Richard T. LaRoche **Obv.** Soccer player with ball **Rev. Designer:** Dean McMullen **Rev:** World Cup 94 logo

Date	Mintage	MS63	MS65	Prf65
1994D	168,208	—	9.00	—
1994P	609,354	—	—	9.00

1996 ATLANTA OLYMPICS - BASEBALL. KM# 262 Obv. Designer: Edgar Z. Steever **Obv.** Baseball batter at plate, catcher and umpire **Rev. Designer:** T. James Ferrell **Rev:** Hemisphere and Atlanta Olympics logo

Date	Mintage	MS63	MS65	Prf65
1995S	164,605	—	16.00	—
1995S	118,087	—	—	17.00

1996 ATLANTA OLYMPICS - BASKETBALL. KM# 257 Obv. Designer: Clint Hansen and Al Maletsky **Obv.** Three players, one jumping for a shot **Rev. Designer:** T. James Ferrell **Rev:** Hemisphere and Atlanta Olympics logo

Date	Mintage	MS63	MS65	Prf65
1995S	171,001	—	15.00	—
1995S	169,655	—	—	15.00

CIVIL WAR BATTLEFIELD PRESERVATION. KM# 254 Obv. Designer: Don Troiani **Obv.** Drummer and fenceline **Rev. Designer:** T. James Ferrell **Rev:** Canon overlooking battlefield

Date	Mintage	MS63	MS65	Prf65
1995S	119,510	—	30.00	—
1995S	330,099	—	—	30.00

1996 ATLANTA OLYMPICS - SOCCER. KM# 271 Obv. Two female soccer players **Rev:** Atlanta Olympics logo

Date	Mintage	MS63	MS65	Prf65
1996S	52,836	—	90.00	—
1996S	122,412	—	—	75.00

1996 ATLANTA OLYMPICS - SWIMMING. **KM# 267** **Obv. Designer:** William J. Krawczewicz and Edgar Z. Steever **Obv.** Swimmer right in butterfly stroke **Rev. Designer:** Malcolm Farley and Thomas D. Rogers, Sr. **Rev:** Atlanta Olympics logo

Date	Mintage	MS63	MS65	Prf65
1996S	49,533	—	90.00	—
1996S	114,315	—	—	28.00

DOLLAR

1984 LOS ANGELES OLYMPICS - DISCUS. **KM# 209** **Obv. Designer:** Elizabeth Jones **Obv.** Trippled discus thrower and five star logo **Rev:** Eagle bust left

Date	Mintage	MS63	MS65	Prf65
1983P	294,543	—	23.00	—
1983D	174,014	—	23.00	—
1983S	174,014	—	23.00	—
1983S	1,577,025	—	—	25.00

1984 LOS ANGELES OLYMPICS - STADIUM STATUES. **KM# 210** **Obv. Designer:** Robert Graham **Obv.** Statues at exterior of Los Angeles Memorial Coliseum **Rev:** Eagle standing on rock

Date	Mintage	MS63	MS65	Prf65
1984P	217,954	—	21.00	—
1984D	116,675	—	21.00	—
1984S	116,675	—	21.00	—
1984S	1,801,210	—	—	25.00

STATUE OF LIBERTY CENTENNIAL. **KM# 214** **Obv. Designer:** John Mercanti **Obv.** Statue of Liberty and Ellis Island great hall **Rev. Designer:** John Mercanti and Matthew Peloso **Rev:** Statue of Liberty torch

Date	Mintage	MS63	MS65	Prf65
1986P	723,635	—	21.00	—
1986S	6,414,638	—	—	21.00

CONSTITUTION BICENTENNIAL. **KM# 220** **Obv. Designer:** Patricia L. Verani **Obv.** Feather pen and document **Rev:** Group of people

Date	Mintage	MS63	MS65	Prf65
1987P	451,629	—	21.00	—
1987S	2,747,116	—	—	21.00

1988 OLYMPICS. **KM# 222** **Obv. Designer:** Patricia L. Verani **Obv.** Olympic torch and Statue of Liberty torch within laurel wreath **Rev. Designer:** Sherl Joseph Winter **Rev:** Olympic rights within olive wreath

Date	Mintage	MS63	MS65	Prf65
1988D	191,368	—	21.50	—
1988S	1,359,366	—	—	22.00

CONGRESS BICENTENNIAL. **KM# 225** **Designer:** William Woodward and Chester Y. Martin **Obv.** Statue of Freedom in clouds and sunburst **Rev:** Mace from the House of Represenatives

Date	Mintage	MS63	MS65	Prf65
1989D	135,203	—	22.00	—
1989S	762,198	—	—	25.00

EISENHOWER CENTENNIAL. **KM# 227** **Obv. Designer:** John Mercanti **Obv.** Two Eisenhower profiles, as general, left, as President, right **Rev. Designer:** Marcel Jovine and John Mercanti **Rev:** Eisenhower home at Gettysburg

Date	Mintage	MS63	MS65	Prf65
1990W	241,669	—	29.00	—
1990P	1,144,461	—	—	25.00

MOUNT RUSHMORE 50TH ANNIVERSARY. KM# 229 Obv. Designer: Marika Somogyi and Chester Martin **Obv.** Mount Rushmore portraits, wreath below **Rev. Designer:** Frank Gasparro **Rev:** Great seal in rays, United States map in background

Date	Mintage	MS63	MS65	Prf65
1991P	133,139	—	36.00	—
1991S	738,419	—	—	30.00

KOREAN WAR - 38TH ANNIVERSARY. KM# 231 Obv. Designer: John Mercanti **Obv.** Soldier advancing right up a hill; planes above, ships below **Rev. Designer:** T. James Ferrell **Rev:** Map of Korean peninsula, eagle's head at right

Date	Mintage	MS63	MS65	Prf65
1991D	213,049	—	30.00	—
1991P	618,488	—	—	25.00

USO 50TH ANNIVERSARY. KM# 232 Obv. Designer: Robert Lamb **Obv.** USO banner **Rev. Designer:** John Mercanti **Rev:** Eagle perched right atop globe

Date	Mintage	MS63	MS65	Prf65
1991D	124,958	—	30.00	—
1991S	321,275	—	—	25.00

1992 OLYMPICS - BASEBALL. KM# 234 Obv. Designer: John R. Deecken and Chester Y. Martin **Obv.** Baseball pitcher, Nolan Ryan as depicted on card **Rev. Designer:** Marcel Jovine **Rev:** Shield flanked by stylized wreath, olympic rings above

Date	Mintage	MS63	MS65	Prf65
1992D	187,552	—	34.00	—
1992S	504,505	—	—	33.00

COLUMBUS DISCOVERY - 500TH ANNIVERSARY. KM# 238 Obv. Designer: John Mercanti **Obv.** Columbus standing with banner, three ships in background **Rev. Designer:** Thomas D. Rogers, Sr. **Rev:** Half view of Santa Maria on left, Space Shuttle Discovery on right

Date	Mintage	MS63	MS65	Prf65
1992D	106,949	—	35.00	—
1992P	385,241	—	—	30.00

WHITE HOUSE BICENTENNIAL. KM# 236 Obv. Designer: Edgar Z. Steever **Obv.** White House's north portico **Rev. Designer:** Chester Y. Martin **Rev:** John Hoban bust left, main entrance doorway

Date	Mintage	MS63	MS65	Prf65
1992D	123,803	—	26.00	—
1992W	375,851	—	—	28.00

1994 WORLD CUP SOCCER. KM# 247 Obv. Designer: Dean McMullen and T. James Ferrell **Obv.** Two players with ball **Rev. Designer:** Dean McMullen **Rev:** World Cup 94 logo

Date	Mintage	MS63	MS65	Prf65
1994D	81,698	—	40.00	—
1994S	576,978	—	—	33.00

JAMES MADISON - BILL OF RIGHTS. KM# 241 Obv. Designer: William Krawczewicz and Thomas D. Rogers, Sr. **Obv.** James Madison bust right, at left **Rev. Designer:** Dean McMullen and Thomas D. Rogers, Sr. **Rev:** Montpelier home

Date	Mintage	MS63	MS65	Prf65
1993D	98,383	—	35.00	—
1993S	534,001	—	—	33.00

THOMAS JEFFERSON 250TH BIRTH ANNIVERSARY. KM# 249 Designer: T. James Ferrell **Obv.** Jefferson's head left **Rev:** Monticello home

Date	Mintage	MS63	MS65	Prf65
1993P	266,927	—	26.00	—
1993S	332,891	—	—	28.00

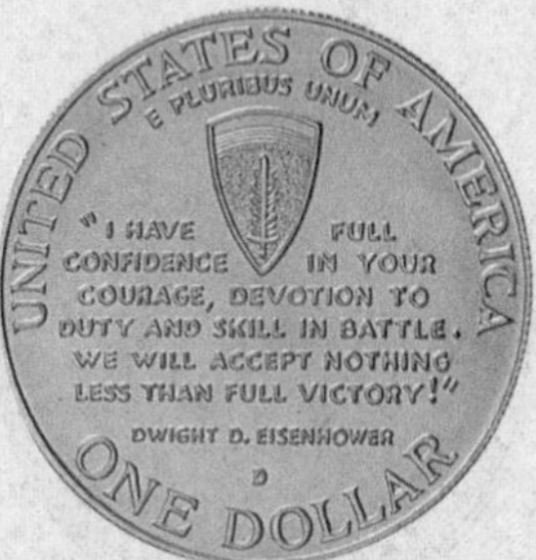

WORLD WAR II 50TH ANNIVERSARY. KM# 244 Designer: Thomas D. Rogers, Sr. **Obv.** Soldier on Normandy beach **Rev:** Insignia of the Supreme Headquarters of the AEF above Eisenhower quote

Date	Mintage	MS63	MS65	Prf65
1993D	94,708	—	40.00	—
1993W	342,041	—	—	40.00

NATIONAL PRISONER OF WAR MUSEUM. KM# 251 Obv. Designer: Thomas Nielson and Alfred Maletsky **Obv.** Eagle in flight left within circle of barbed wire **Rev. Designer:** Edgar Z. Steever **Rev:** National Prisoner of War Museum

Date	Mintage	MS63	MS65	Prf65
1994W	54,790	—	65.00	—
1994P	220,100	—	—	42.00

U.S. CAPITOL BICENTENNIAL. KM# 253 Obv. Designer: William C. Cousins **Obv.** Capitol dome, Statue fo Freedom surrounded by stars **Rev. Designer:** John Mercanti **Rev:** Eagle on shield, flags flanking

Date	Mintage	MS63	MS65	Prf65
1994D	68,352	—	35.00	—
1994S	279,416	—	—	38.00

VIETNAM VETERANS MEMORIAL. KM# 250 Obv. Designer: John Mercanti **Obv.** Outstretched hand touching names on the Wall, Washington Monument in background **Rev. Designer:** Thomas D. Rogers, Sr. **Rev:** Service Medals

Date	Mintage	MS63	MS65	Prf65
1994W	57,317	—	65.00	—
1994P	226,262	—	—	57.00

WOMEN IN MILITARY SERVICE MEMORIAL. KM# 252 Obv. Designer: T. James Ferrell **Obv.** Five uniformed women left **Rev. Designer:** Thomas D. Rogers, Sr. **Rev:** Memorial at Arlington National Cemetery

Date	Mintage	MS63	MS65	Prf65
1994W	53,054	—	32.00	—
1994P	213,201	—	—	37.00

1996 ATLANTA OLYMPICS - CYCLING. KM# 263 Obv. Designer: John Mercanti **Obv.** Three cyclists approaching **Rev. Designer:** William J. Krawczewicz and T. James Ferrell **Rev:** Two clasped hands, Atlanta Olympic logo above

Date	Mintage	MS63	MS65	Prf65
1995D	19,662	—	115	—
1995P	118,795	—	—	45.00

1996 ATLANTA OLYMPICS - GYMNASTICS. KM# 260 Obv. Designer: James C. Sharpe and Thomas D. Rogers, Sr. **Obv.** Two gymnasts, female on floor exercise and male on rings **Rev. Designer:** William J. Krawczewicz and T. James Ferrell **Rev:** Two clasped hands, Atlanta Olympic logo above

Date	Mintage	MS63	MS65	Prf65
1995D	42,497	—	41.00	—
1995P	182,676	—	—	33.00

1996 ATLANTA OLYMPICS - TRACK AND FIELD. KM# 264 Obv. Designer: John Mercanti **Obv.** Two runners on a track, one crossing finish line **Rev. Designer:** William J. Krawczewicz and T. James Ferrell **Rev:** Two clasped hands, Atlanta Olympic logo above

Date	Mintage	MS63	MS65	Prf65
1995D	24,796	—	65.00	—
1995P	136,935	—	—	38.00

1996 ATLANTA PARALYMPICS - BLIND RUNNER. KM# 259 Obv. Designer: Jim C. Sharpe and Thomas D. Rogers, Sr. **Obv.** Blind runner **Rev. Designer:** William J. Krawczewicz and T. James Ferrell **Rev:** Two clasped hands, Atlanta Olympic logo above

Date	Mintage	MS63	MS65	Prf65
1995D	28,649	—	58.00	—
1995P	138,337	—	—	40.00

CIVIL WAR. KM# 255 Obv. Designer: Don Troiani and Edgar Z. Steever **Obv.** Soldier giving water to wounded soldier **Rev. Designer:** John Mercanti **Rev:** Chamberlain quote and battlefield monument

Date	Mintage	MS63	MS65	Prf65
1995P	45,866	—	53.00	—
1995S	437,114	—	—	45.00

SPECIAL OLYMPICS WORLD GAMES. KM# 266 Obv. Designer: Jamie Wyeth and T. James Ferrell **Obv.** Eunice Schriver head left; founder of the Special Olympics **Rev. Designer:** Thomas D. Rogers, Sr. **Rev:** Special Olympics Logo on an award medal, rose, quote from Schriver

Date	Mintage	MS63	MS65	Prf65
1995W	89,301	—	33.00	—
1995P	351,764	—	—	33.00

1996 ATLANTA OLYMPICS - HIGH JUMP. KM# A272 Obv. Designer: T. James Ferrell **Obv.** High jumper **Rev. Designer:** Thomas D. Rogers, Sr.

Date	Mintage	MS63	MS65	Prf65
1996D	15,697	—	190	—
1996P	124,502	—	—	46.00

1996 ATLANTA OLYMPICS - ROWING. KM# 272 Obv. Designer: Bart Forbes and T. James Ferrell **Obv.** Four man crew rowing left **Rev. Designer:** Thomas D. Rogers, Sr. **Rev:** Atlanta Olympic logo

Date	Mintage	MS63	MS65	Prf65
1996D	16,258	—	165	—
1996P	151,890	—	—	62.00

1996 ATLANTA OLYMPICS - TENNIS. KM# 269 Obv. Designer: James C. Sharpe and T. James Ferrell **Obv.** Female tennis player **Rev. Designer:** Thomas D. Rogers, Sr. **Rev:** Atlanta Olympics logo

Date	Mintage	MS63	MS65	Prf65
1996D	15,983	—	165	—
1996P	92,016	—	—	70.00

1996 ATLANTA PARALYMPICS - WHEELCHAIR RACER. KM# 268 Obv. Designer: James C. Sharpe and Alfred F. Maletsky **Obv.** Wheelchair racer approaching with uplifted arms **Rev. Designer:** Thomas D. Rogers, Sr. **Rev:** Atlanta Olympics logo

Date	Mintage	MS63	MS65	Prf65
1996D	14,497	—	185	—
1996P	84,280	—	—	65.00

NATIONAL COMMUNITY SERVICE. KM# 275 Obv. Designer: Thomas D. Rogers, Sr. **Obv.** Female standing with lamp and shield **Rev. Designer:** William C. Cousins **Rev:** Legend within wreath

Date	Mintage	MS63	MS65	Prf65
1996S	101,543	—	—	32.00
1996S	23,500	—	95.00	—

SMITHSONIAN INSTITUTION 150TH ANNIVERSARY. KM# 276 Obv. Designer: Thomas D. Rogers, Sr. **Obv.** Original Smithsonian building, the "Castle" designed by James Renwick **Rev. Designer:** John Mercanti **Rev:** Female seated with torch and scroll on globe

Date	Mintage	MS63	MS65	Prf65
1996D	31,230	—	65.00	—
1996P	129,152	—	—	40.00

JACKIE ROBINSON. KM# 279 Obv. Designer: Alfred Maletsky **Obv.** Jackie Robinson sliding into base **Rev. Designer:** T. James Ferrell **Rev:** Anniversary logo

Date	Mintage	MS63	MS65	Prf65
1997S	30,007	—	65.00	—
1997S	110,495	—	—	53.00

NATIONAL LAW ENFORCEMENT OFFICERS MEMORIAL. KM# 281 Designer: Alfred F. Maletsky **Obv.** Male and female officer admiring name on monument **Rev:** Rose on a plain shield

Date	Mintage	MS63	MS65	Prf65
1997P	28,575	—	115	—
1997P	110,428	—	—	65.00

U.S. BOTANIC GARDENS 175TH ANNIVERSARY. KM# 278 Obv. Designer: Edgar Z. Steever **Obv.** National Botanic Gardens Conservatory building **Rev. Designer:** William C. Cousins **Rev:** Rose

Date	Mintage	MS63	MS65	Prf65
1997P	57,272	—	28.00	—
1997P	264,528	—	—	40.00

BLACK REVOLUTIONARY WAR PATRIOTS. KM# 288 Obv. Designer: John Mercanti **Obv.** Crispus Attucks bust right **Rev. Designer:** Edward Dwight and Thomas D. Rogers, Sr. **Rev:** Family standing

Date	Mintage	MS63	MS65	Prf65
1998S	37,210	—	75.00	—
1998S	75,070	—	—	50.00

ROBERT F. KENNEDY. KM# 287 Obv. Designer: Thomas D. Rogers, Sr. **Obv.** Kennedy bust facing **Rev. Designer:** James M. Peed and Thomas D. Rogers, Sr. **Rev:** Eagle on shield, Senate Seal

Date	Mintage	MS63	MS65	Prf65
1998S	106,422	—	40.00	—
1998S	99,020	—	—	60.00

DOLLEY MADISON. KM# 298 Obv. Designer: Tiffany & Co. and T. James Ferrell **Obv.** Madison bust right, at left **Rev. Designer:** Tiffany & Co. and Thomas D. Rogers, Sr. **Rev:** Montpelier home

Date	Mintage	MS63	MS65	Prf65
1999P	22,948	—	33.00	—
1999P	158,247	—	—	32.00

YELLOWSTONE. KM# 299 Obv. Designer: Edgar Z. Steever **Obv.** Old Faithful gyser erupting **Rev. Designer:** William C. Cousins **Rev:** Bison and vista as on National Parks shield

Date	Mintage	MS63	MS65	Prf65
1999P	82,563	—	45.00	—
1999P	187,595	—	—	43.00

LEIF ERICSON. KM# 313 Obv. Designer: John Mercanti **Obv.** Ericson bust helmeted right **Rev. Designer:** T. James Ferrell **Rev:** Viking ship sailing left

Date	Mintage	MS63	MS65	Prf65
2000P	28,150	—	65.00	—
2000P	58,612	—	—	45.00
2000 Iceland	15,947	—	—	23.00

LIBRARY OF CONGRESS BICENTENNIAL. KM# 311 Obv. Designer: Thomas D. Rogers, Sr. **Obv.** Open and closed book, torch in background **Rev. Designer:** John Mercanti **Rev:** Skylight dome above the main reading room

Date	Mintage	MS63	MS65	Prf65
2000P	52,771	—	26.00	—
2000P	196,900	—	—	22.00

$5 (HALF EAGLE)

STATUE OF LIBERTY CENTENNIAL. KM# 215 Designer: Elizabeth Jones **Obv.** Statue of Liberty head right **Rev:** Eagle in flight left

Date	Mintage	MS63	MS65	Prf65
1986W	95,248	—	345	—
1986W	404,013	—	—	345

CONSTITUTION BICENTENNIAL. KM# 221 Designer: Marcel Jovine **Obv.** Eagle left with quill pen in talon **Rev:** Upright quill pen

Date	Mintage	MS63	MS65	Prf65
1987W	214,225	—	345	—
1987W	651,659	—	—	345

1988 OLYMPICS. KM# 223 Obv. Designer: Elizabeth Jones **Obv.** Nike head wearing olive wreath **Rev. Designer:** Marcel Jovine **Rev:** Stylized Olympic cauldron

Date	Mintage	MS63	MS65	Prf65
1988W	62,913	—	345	—
1988W	281,456	—	—	345

CONGRESS BICENTENNIAL. KM# 226 Designer: John Mercanti **Obv.** Capitol dome **Rev:** Eagle atop of the canopy from the Old Senate Chamber

Date	Mintage	MS63	MS65	Prf65
1989W	46,899	—	345	—
1989W	164,690	—	—	345

MOUNT RUSHMORE 50TH ANNIVERSARY. KM# 230 Obv. Designer: John Mercanti **Obv.** Eagle in flight towards Mount Rushmore **Rev. Designer:** Robert Lamb and William C. Cousins **Rev:** Legend at center

Date	Mintage	MS63	MS65	Prf65
1991W	31,959	—	345	—
1991W	111,991	—	—	345

1992 OLYMPICS. KM# 235 Obv. Designer: James C. Sharpe and T. James Ferrell **Obv.** Sprinter, U.S. Flag in background **Rev. Designer:** James M. Peed **Rev:** Heraldic eagle, Olympic rings above

Date	Mintage	MS63	MS65	Prf65
1992W	27,732	—	345	—
1992W	77,313	—	—	345

COLUMBUS QUINCENTENARY. KM# 239 Obv. Designer: T. James Ferrell **Obv.** Columbus' profile left, at right, map of Western Hemisphere at left **Rev. Designer:** Thomas D. Rogers, Sr. **Rev:** Arms of Spain, and parchment map

Date	Mintage	MS63	MS65	Prf65
1992W	24,329	—	345	—
1992W	79,730	—	—	345

JAMES MADISON - BILL OF RIGHTS. KM# 242 Obv. Designer: Scott R. Blazek **Obv.** Madison at left holding document **Rev. Designer:** Joseph D. Peña **Rev:** Eagle above legend, torch and laurel at sides

Date	Mintage	MS63	MS65	Prf65
1993W	22,266	—	345	—
1993W	78,651	—	—	345

WORLD WAR II 50TH ANNIVERSARY. KM# 245 Obv. Designer: Charles J. Madsen and T. James Ferrell **Obv.** Soldier with expression of victory **Rev. Designer:** Edward S. Fisher and T. James Ferrell **Rev:** Morse code dot-dot-dot-dash for V, large in background; V for Victory

Date	Mintage	MS63	MS65	Prf65
1993W	23,089	—	345	—
1993W	65,461	—	—	325

1994 WORLD CUP SOCCER. KM# 248 Obv. Designer: William J. Krawczewicz **Obv.** World Cup trophy **Rev. Designer:** Dean McMullen **Rev:** World Cup 94 logo

Date	Mintage	MS63	MS65	Prf65
1994W	22,464	—	325	—
1994W	89,619	—	—	325

1996 OLYMPICS - STADIUM. KM# 265 Obv. Designer: Marvel Jovine and William C. Cousins **Obv.** Atlanta Stadium and logo **Rev. Designer:** Frank Gasparro **Rev:** Eagle advancing right

Date	Mintage	MS63	MS65	Prf65
1995W	10,579	—	800	—
1995W	43,124	—	—	345

1996 OLYMPICS - TORCH RUNNER. KM# 261 Designer: Frank Gasparro **Obv.** Torch runner, Atlanta skyline and logo in background **Rev:** Eagle advancing right

Date	Mintage	MS63	MS65	Prf65
1995W	14,675	—	450	—
1995W	57,442	—	—	345

CIVIL WAR. KM# 256 Designer: Don Troiani and Alfred F. Maletsky **Obv.** Bugler on horseback right **Rev:** Eagle on shield

Date	Mintage	MS63	MS65	Prf65
1995W	55,246	—	—	325
1995W	12,735	—	350	—

1996 OLYMPICS - CAULDRON. KM# 270 Obv. Designer: Frank Gasparro and T. James Ferrell **Obv.** Torch bearer lighting cauldron **Rev. Designer:** William J. Krawczewicz and Thomas D. Rogers, Sr. **Rev:** Atlanta Olympics logo flanked by laurel

Date	Mintage	MS63	MS65	Prf65
1996W	9,210	—	900	—
1996W	38,555	—	—	345

1996 OLYMPICS - FLAG BEARER. KM# 274 Obv. Designer: Patricia Verani and John Mercanti **Obv.** Flag bearer advancing **Rev. Designer:** William J. Krawczewicz and Thomas D. Rogers, Sr. **Rev:** Atlanta Olympic logo flanked by laurel

Date	Mintage	MS63	MS65	Prf65
1996W	9,174	—	400	—
1996W	32,886	—	—	345

SMITHSONIAN INSTITUTION 150TH ANNIVERSARY. KM# 277 Obv. Designer: Alfred Maletsky **Obv.** Smithson bust left **Rev. Designer:** T. James Ferrell **Rev:** Sunburst museum logo

Date	Mintage	MS63	MS65	Prf65
1996W	9,068	—	345	—
1996W	29,474	—	—	345

FRANKLIN DELANO ROOSEVELT. KM# 282 Obv. Designer: T. James Ferrell **Obv.** Roosevelt bust right **Rev. Designer:** James M. Peed and Thomas D. Rogers, Sr. **Rev:** Eagle shield

Date	Mintage	MS63	MS65	Prf65
1997W	11,894	—	350	—
1997W	29,474	—	—	345

JACKIE ROBINSON. KM# 280 Obv. Designer: William C. Cousins **Obv.** Robinson head right **Rev. Designer:** James M. Peed **Rev:** Legend on baseball

Date	Mintage	MS63	MS65	Prf65
1997W	5,202	—	1,100	—
1997W	24,072	—	—	400

GEORGE WASHINGTON DEATH BICENTENNIAL. KM# 300 Designer: Laura G. Fraser **Obv.** Washington's head right **Rev:** Eagle with wings outstretched

Date	Mintage	MS63	MS65	Prf65
1999W	22,511	—	345	—
1999W	41,693	—	—	345

$10 (EAGLE)

1984 OLYMPICS. KM# 211 Obv. Designer: James M. Peed and John Mercanti **Obv.** Male and female runner with torch **Rev. Designer:** John Mercanti **Rev:** Heraldic eagle

Date	Mintage	MS63	MS65	Prf65
1984W	75,886	—	670	—
1984W	381,085	—	—	670
1984P	33,309	—	—	670
1984D	34,533	—	—	670
1984S	48,551	—	—	670

LIBRARY OF CONGRESS. **KM# 312** **Obv. Designer:** John Mercanti **Obv.** Torch and partial facade **Rev. Designer:** Thomas D. Rogers, Sr. **Rev:** Stylized eagle within laurel wreath

Date	Mintage	MS63	MS65	Prf65
2000W	6,683	—	1,000	—
2000W	27,167	—	—	800

AMERICAN EAGLE SILVER BULLION COINS

SILVER DOLLAR

KM# 273 • **ObvDesc:** Liberty walking left • **RevDesc:** Eagle with shield • 31.11 g., 0.9993 **Silver** 0.9993 oz. ASW, 40.6 • **Obv. Designer:** Adolph A. Weinman • **Rev. Designer:** John Mercanti

Date	Mintage	MS65	Prf65
1986	5,393,005	36.20	—
1986S	1,446,778	—	48.00
1987	11,442,335	19.20	—
1987S	904,732	—	48.00
1988	5,004,646	21.20	—
1988S	557,370	—	48.00
1989	5,203,327	21.20	—
1989S	617,694	—	48.00
1990	5,840,110	21.20	—
1990S	695,510	—	48.00
1991	7,191,066	21.20	—
1991S	511,924	—	48.00
1992	5,540,068	23.20	—
1992S	498,543	—	48.00
1993	6,763,762	23.20	—
1993P	405,913	—	69.20

Date	Mintage	MS65	Prf65
1994	4,227,319	34.20	—
1994P	372,168	—	150
1995W	4,672,051	30.20	—
1995	407,822	—	55.00
1995P 10th Anniversary	30,102	4,000	—
1996P	3,603,386	55.00	—
1996	498,293	—	69.20
1997P	4,295,004	19.20	—
1997	440,315	—	48.00
1998P	4,847,547	19.20	—
1998	450,728	—	48.00
1999P	7,408,640	19.20	—
1999	549,330	—	48.00
2000	9,239,132	19.20	—
2000P	600,743	—	48.00

GOLD $5

KM# 216 • 3.39 g., 0.9167 **Gold** 0.100 oz. AGW, 16.5 • **Obv. Designer:** Augustus Saint-Gaudens • **Rev. Designer:** Miley Busiek

Date	Mintage	MS65	Prf65
MCMLXXXVI 1986	912,609	160	—
MCMLXXXVII 1987	580,266	140	—
MCMLXXXVIII 1988	159,500	140	—
MCMLXXXVIII (1988)P	143,881	—	138
MCMLXXXIX 1989	264,790	150	—
MCMLXXXIX (1989)P	84,647	—	138
MCMXC 1990	210,210	165	—
MCMXC (1990)P	99,349	—	138
MCMXCI 1991	165,200	170	—
MCMXCI (1991)P	70,334	—	138
1992	209,300	110	—
1992P	64,874	—	138
1993	210,709	110	—
1993P	45,960	—	138
1994W	206,380	140	—
1994	62,849	—	138

Date	Mintage	MS65	Prf65
1995	223,025	110	—
1995W	62,667	—	205
1996	401,964	110	—
1996W	57,047	—	138
1997	528,515	110	—
1997W	34,977	—	138
1998	1,344,520	110	—
1998W	39,395	—	138
1999W	2,750,338	160	—
1999W	48,428	—	138
1999 Unfinished Proof die	Est. 6000	825	—
Note: The 1999 W issues are standard matte finished gold that were struck with unfinished proof dies.			
2000W	569,153	110	—
2000	49,971	—	138

GOLD $10

KM# 217 • 8.48 g., 0.9167 **Gold** 0.250 oz. AGW, 22 • **Obv. Designer:** Augustus Saint-Gaudens • **Rev. Designer:** Miley Busiek

Date	Mintage	MS65	Prf65
MCMLXXXVI 1986	726,031	376	—
MCMLXXXVII 1987	269,255	391	—
MCMLXXXVIII 1988	49,000	—	341
MCMLXXXVIII (1988)P	98,028	562	—
MCMLXXXIX 1989	81,789	562	—
MCMLXXXIX (1989)P	54,170	—	341
MCMXC 1990	41,000	—	341
MCMXC (1990)P	62,674	678	—
MCMXCI 1991	36,100	—	341
MCMXCI (1991)P	50,839	678	—
1992	59,546	—	341
1992P	46,269	497	—
1993	71,864	497	—
1993P	33,775	—	341
1994	72,650	497	—
1994W	47,172	—	341

Date	Mintage	MS65	Prf65
1995	83,752	497	—
1995W	47,526	—	341
1996	60,318	497	—
1996W	38,219	—	341
1997	108,805	—	341
1997W	29,805	276	—
1998	309,829	—	341
1998W	29,503	276	—
1999	564,232	276	—
1999W	34,417	—	341
1999W Unfinished Proof die	Est. 6000	1,500	—
Note: The 1999 W issues are standard matte finished gold that were struck with unfinished proof dies.			
2000	128,964	276	—
2000W	36,036	—	341

GOLD $25

KM# 218 • 16.97 g., 0.9167 **Gold** 0.500 oz. AGW, 27 • **Obv. Designer:** Augustus Saint-Gaudens • **Rev. Designer:** Miley Busiek

Date	Mintage	MS65	Prf65
MCMLXXXVI 1986	599,566	1,105	—
MCMLXXXVII 1987	131,255	—	1,236
MCMLXXXVII (1987)P	143,398	1,105	—
MCMLXXXVIII 1988	45,000	—	1,235
MCMLXXXVIII (1988)P	76,528	1,105	—
MCMLXXXIX 1989	44,829	1,105	—
MCMLXXXIX (1989)P	44,798	—	1,235
MCMXC 1990	31,000	1,105	—
MCMXC (1990)P	51,636	—	1,495
MCMXCI 1991	24,100	—	1,535
MCMXCI (1991)P	53,125	1,105	—
1992	54,404	—	1,200
1992P	40,976	1,105	—
1993	73,324	—	1,650
1993P	31,130	1,105	—

Date	Mintage	MS65	Prf65
1994	62,400	—	1,300
1994W	44,584	1,105	—
1995	53,474	—	1,300
1995W	45,388	1,105	—
1996	39,287	1,105	—
1996W	35,058	—	1,300
1997	79,605	—	1,300
1997W	26,344	1,105	—
1998	169,029	—	1,300
1998W	25,374	1,105	—
1999	263,013	1,105	—
1999W	30,427	—	1,500
2000	79,287	1,105	—
2000W	32,028	—	1,235

GOLD $50

KM# 219 • 33.93 g., 0.9167 **Gold** 1.000 oz. AGW, 32.7 • **Obv. Designer:** Augustus Saint-Gaudens • **Rev. Designer:** Miley Busiek

Date	Mintage	MS65	Prf65
MCMLXXXVI (1986)W	446,290	—	1,330
MCMLXXXVI -1986	1,362,650	1,273	—
MCMLXXXVII (1987)W	147,498	—	1,330
MCMLXXXVII -1987	1,045,500	1,273	—
MCMLXXXVIII (1988)W	87,133	—	1,330
MCMLXXXVIII -1988	465,000	1,273	—
MCMLXXXIX (1989)W	54,570	—	1,330
MCMLXXXIX -1989	415,790	1,273	—
MCMXC (1990)W	62,401	—	1,590
MCMXC -1990	373,219	1,273	—
MCMXCI (1991)W	50,411	—	1,630
MCMXCI -1991	243,100	1,273	—
1992W	275,000	1,273	—

Date	Mintage	MS65	Prf65
1992	44,826	—	1,295
1993W	480,192	1,273	—
1993	34,369	—	1,745
1994W	221,663	1,273	—
1994	46,674	—	1,395
1995W	200,636	1,273	—
1995	46,368	—	1,395
1995W 10th Anniversary	30,125	—	—
1996W	189,148	1,273	—
1996	36,153	—	1,395
1997	664,508	1,273	—
1997W	28,034	—	1,395
1998	1,468,530	1,273	—
1998W	25,886	—	1,395
1999	1,505,026	1,273	—

Date	Mintage	MS65	Prf65	Date	Mintage	MS65	Prf65
1999W	31,427	—	1,595	2000W	33,007	—	1,295
2000	433,319	1,273	—				

AMERICAN EAGLE BULLION COINS

PLATINUM $10

KM# 283 • RevDesc: Eagle flying right over sunrise • 3.11 g., 0.9995 **Platinum** 0.0999 oz. APW, 17 • **Obv. Designer:** John Mercanti • **Rev. Designer:** Thomas D. Rogers Sr

Date	Mintage	MS65	Prf65	Date	Mintage	MS65	Prf65
1997	70,250	120	180	1999	55,955	120	—
1997W	36,996	—	—	2000	34,027	120	—
1998	39,525	120	—				

KM# 289 • RevDesc: Eagle in flight over New England costal lighthouse • 3.11 g., 0.9995 **Platinum** 0.0999 oz. APW, 17 • **Obv. Designer:** John Mercanti

Date	Mintage	MS65	Prf65
1998W	19,847	—	110

KM# 301 • RevDesc: Eagle in flight over Southeastern Wetlands • 3.11 g., 0.9995 **Platinum** 0.0999 oz. APW, 17 • **Obv. Designer:** John Mercanti

Date	Mintage	MS65	Prf65
1999W	19,133	—	110

KM# 314 • RevDesc: Eagle in flight over Heartland • 3.11 g., 0.9995 **Platinum** 0.0999 oz. APW, 17 • **Obv. Designer:** John Mercanti

Date	Mintage	MS65	Prf65
2000W	15,651	—	110

PLATINUM $25

KM# 284 • RevDesc: Eagle in flight over sunrise • 7.79 g., 0.9995 **Platinum** 0.2502 oz. APW, 22 • **Obv. Designer:** John Mercanti • **Rev. Designer:** Thomas D. Rogers Sr

Date	Mintage	MS65	Prf65	Date	Mintage	MS65	Prf65
1997	27,100	364	—	1999	39,734	364	—
1997W	18,628	—	368	2000	20,054	364	—
1998	38,887	364	—				

KM# 290 • RevDesc: Eagle in flight over New England costal lighthouse • 7.79 g., 0.9995 **Platinum** 0.2502 oz. APW, 22 • **Obv. Designer:** John Mercanti

Date	Mintage	MS65	Prf65
1998W	14,873	—	368

KM# 302 • RevDesc: Eagle in flight over Southeastern Wetlands • 7.79 g., 0.9995 **Platinum** 0.2502 oz. APW, 22 • **Obv. Designer:** John Mercanti

Date	Mintage	MS65	Prf65
1999W	13,507	—	368

KM# 315 • RevDesc: Eagle in flight over Heartland • 7.79 g., 0.9995 **Platinum** 0.2502 oz. APW, 22 • **Obv. Designer:** John Mercanti

Date	Mintage	MS65	Prf65
2000W	11,995	—	368

PLATINUM $50

KM# 285 • RevDesc: Eagle flying right over sunrise • 15.55 g., 0.9995 **Platinum** 0.4998 oz. APW, 27 • **Obv. Designer:** John Mercanti • **Rev. Designer:** Thomas D. Rogers Sr

Date	Mintage	MS65	Prf65	Date	Mintage	MS65	Prf65
1997W	20,500	478	—	1999	32,309	478	—
1997	15,432	—	541	2000	18,892	478	—
1998	32,419	478	—				

KM# 291 • RevDesc: Eagle in flight over New England costal lighthouse • 15.55 g., 0.9995 **Platinum** 0.4998 oz. APW, 27 • **Obv. Designer:** John Mercanti

Date	Mintage	MS65	Prf65
1998W	13,836	—	541

KM# 303 • RevDesc: Eagle in flight over Southeastern Wetlands • 15.55 g., 0.9995 **Platinum** 0.4998 oz. APW, 27 • **Obv. Designer:** John Mercanti

Date	Mintage	MS65	Prf65
1999W	11,103	—	541

KM# 316 • RevDesc: Eagle in flight over Heartland • 15.55 g., 0.9995 **Platinum** 0.4998 oz. APW, 27 • **Obv. Designer:** John Mercanti

Date	Mintage	MS65	Prf65
2000W	11,049	—	541

PLATINUM $100

KM# 286 • ObvDesc: Statue of Liberty • **RevDesc:** Eagle in flight over sunrise • 31.11 g., 0.9995 **Platinum** 0.9995 oz. APW, 33 • **Obv. Designer:** John Mercanti • **Rev. Designer:** Thomas D. Rogers Sr

Date	Mintage	MS65	Prf65	Date	Mintage	MS65	Prf65
1997W	15,885	—	1,275	1999	56,707	1,003	—
1997	56,000	1,003	—	2000	10,003	1,003	—
1998	133,002	1,003	—				

KM# 292 • RevDesc: Eagle in flight over New England costal lighthouse • 31.11 g., 0.9995 **Platinum** 0.9995 oz. APW, 33 • **Obv. Designer:** John Mercanti

Date	Mintage	MS65	Prf65
1998W	14,912	—	1,275

KM# 304 • RevDesc: Eagle in flight over Southeastern Wetlands • 31.11 g., 0.9995 **Platinum** 0.9995 oz. APW, 33 • **Obv. Designer:** John Mercanti

Date	Mintage	MS65	Prf65
1999W	12,363	—	1,275

KM# 317 • RevDesc: Eagle in flight over Heartland • 31.11 g., 0.9995 **Platinum** 0.9995 oz. APW • **Obv. Designer:** John Mercanti

Date	Mintage	MS65	Prf65
2000W	12,453	—	1,275

UNCIRCULATED ROLLS

Listings are for rolls containing uncirculated coins. Large date and small date varieties for 1960 and 1970 apply to the one cent coins.

Date	Cents	Nickels	Dimes	Quarters	Halves
1934	585	3,500	2,350	1,650	2,350
1934D	2,650	4,350	2,950	9,000	—
1934S	—	—	—	—	—
1935	885	1,700	1,450	1,725	1,250
1935D	750	3,150	2,950	8,850	4,000
1935S	2,500	1,725	1,950	4,650	6,500
1936	285	1,450	885	1,300	1,750
1936D	400	1,450	1,700	—	2,750
1936S	885	1,800	1,675	6,250	3,500
1937	250	1,100	710	1,250	1,150
1937D	250	1,200	1,550	3,450	5,000
1937S	335	1,285	1,650	4,850	3,450
1938	665	535	1,100	3,100	1,850
1938D Buffalo	—	1,065	—	—	—
1938D	710	485	1,000	—	—
1938S	440	355	1,350	3,250	—
1939	180	160	630	1,040	1,250
1939D	535	3,850	610	1,875	1,975
1939S	265	2,750	1,900	3,200	2,350
1940	225	145	535	1,850	975
1940D	265	120	780	5,350	—
1940S	300	265	675	1,275	1,200
1941	170	215	430	475	750
1941D	335	330	710	2,750	1,200
1941S	360	295	535	2,450	3,000
1942	140	315	465	450	690
1942P	—	600	—	—	—
1942D	140	2,550	740	1,060	1,350
1942S	585	525	1,050	5,350	1,475
1943	60.00	275	470	365	725
1943D	170	210	610	2,000	1,775
1943S	310	325	650	2,100	1,365
1944	30.00	720	460	280	715
1944D	38.00	680	635	725	1,250
1944S	120	565	660	950	1,300
1945	125	375	410	325	730
1945D	110	315	500	1,000	1,000
1945S	80.00	270	525	575	950
1946	39.00	80.00	140	365	1,025
1946D	36.50	75.00	140	380	900
1946S	185	50.00	140	275	900
1947	220	58.00	215	735	1,000
1947D	46.50	72.00	275	385	1,000
1947S	39.00	72.00	210	415	—
1948	72.50	55.00	188	270	450
1948D	175	155	325	645	425
1948S	165	80.00	255	475	—
1949	180	330	1,200	2,350	1,300
1949D	125	215	550	1,285	1,475
1949S	140	138	2,350	—	2,250
1950	115	120	525	395	750
1950D	42.00	385	200	440	875
1950S	78.00	—	1,550	850	—
1951	165	230	140	435	390
1951D	26.50	285	140	325	800
1951S	60.00	265	690	1,350	750
1952	165	145	140	535	385
1952D	26.50	260	140	300	230
1952S	300	42.00	290	1,000	1,585
1953	42.00	24.50	140	635	490
1953D	22.50	17.00	140	280	280
1953S	35.00	39.00	140	280	850
1954	39.00	57.50	140	280	280
1954D	22.50	24.00	140	280	280
1954S	22.50	39.50	140	280	400
1955	24.50	19.00	140	280	300
1955D	19.00	7.00	170	280	—
1955S	27.50	—	140	—	—
1956	10.50	7.50	140	280	280
1956D	12.50	9.25	140	280	—
1957	10.00	12.50	140	280	280
1957D	9.50	4.75	140	280	280
1958	10.50	6.50	140	280	280
1958D	9.75	5.50	140	280	280
1959	2.50	5.00	140	280	280
1959D	2.10	5.25	140	280	280
1960 large date	1.60	4.40	140	280	280
1960 small date	220	—	—	—	—
1960D large date	1.60	5.00	140	280	280
1960D small date	2.85	—	—	—	—
1961	1.60	4.25	140	280	280
1961D	1.90	4.50	140	280	280
1962	1.65	5.25	140	280	280
1962D	1.65	5.50	140	280	280
1963	1.50	4.25	140	280	280
1963D	1.65	4.75	140	280	280
1964	1.50	3.50	140	280	280
1964D	1.60	3.50	140	280	280
1965	2.25	8.75	8.00	25.00	120
1966	3.75	6.00	10.00	53.00	120
1967	4.50	9.75	8.50	25.00	120
1968	1.75	—	8.50	25.00	—
1968D	1.70	6.00	9.50	33.00	120
1968S	1.90	6.25	—	—	—
1969	7.75	—	44.00	100	—
1969D	2.00	6.25	21.50	82.00	120
1969S	3.75	6.75	—	—	—
1970	2.10	—	8.00	26.00	—
1970D	2.10	4.00	7.75	16.00	235
1970S	3.00	4.50	—	—	—
1970S small date	2,650	—	—	—	—
1971	17.00	26.50	16.00	50.00	26.00
1971D	3.00	7.50	9.50	19.50	15.50
1971S	4.00	—	—	—	—
1972	2.00	6.50	11.00	23.00	32.00
1972D	6.00	5.75	10.00	21.50	23.00
1972S	4.75	—	—	—	—
1973	1.75	6.25	10.50	22.00	25.50
1973D	1.75	6.25	9.00	23.00	18.00
1973S	3.00	—	—	—	—
1974	1.75	4.50	7.50	18.50	15.00
1974D	1.75	5.75	7.75	17.50	21.00
1974S	3.50	—	—	—	—
1975	3.75	12.50	8.75	—	—
1975D	1.75	5.25	15.50	—	—
1976	1.75	13.50	21.00	17.50	18.00
1976D	2.50	11.00	18.00	17.50	15.50
1977	1.75	6.25	9.75	16.50	21.50
1977D	2.85	5.75	8.50	17.50	24.00
1978	3.00	4.50	7.25	16.00	32.00
1978D	10.00	5.00	8.00	16.50	46.50
1979	1.75	4.75	8.75	17.00	22.50
1979D	3.00	5.75	8.00	22.50	22.50
1980	1.75	4.25	8.00	16.50	20.50
1980D	2.50	4.50	7.50	16.50	20.50
1981	1.75	4.25	7.50	16.50	16.50
1981D	1.85	4.25	8.00	16.50	19.00
1982 Large date	2.50	—	—	—	—
1982 Small date	25.00	325	270	250	98.00
1982D Large date	4.00	54.00	66.00	165	80.00
1982 Copper plated Zinc	8.00	—	—	—	—
1982 Small date, copper plated zinc	3.00	—	—	—	—
1982D Large date, copper plated zinc	35.00	—	—	—	—
1982D Small date, copper plated zinc	2.50	—	—	—	—
1983	7.50	90.00	235	945	80.00
1983D	17.50	39.00	39.00	410	120
1984	5.50	22.00	8.50	17.00	26.00
1984D	14.50	6.50	21.00	29.00	37.00
1985	4.25	10.00	9.75	31.00	76.00

1985D	9.75	8.00	9.25	22.00	44.00
1986	20.00	8.75	25.00	85.00	75.00
1986D	31.50	24.50	22.50	210	90.00
1987	6.50	6.00	7.75	15.50	52.00
1987D	13.50	4.50	8.75	15.50	52.00
1988	6.25	5.50	9.75	39.00	75.00
1988D	12.50	9.00	9.25	22.50	45.00
1989	3.25	5.50	12.00	19.50	42.00
1989D	3.50	8.75	12.50	17.00	25.00
1990	4.00	11.50	14.50	20.00	39.00
1990D	5.85	13.75	10.00	25.00	52.00
1991	2.60	12.00	10.00	29.00	37.50
1991D	11.50	12.00	11.00	31.00	33.00
1992	3.00	46.00	8.00	42.00	21.00
1992D	5.00	9.00	8.00	27.50	50.00
1993	3.25	13.50	9.50	39.00	64.00
1993D	7.50	17.50	13.00	36.00	17.00
1994	2.00	7.75	12.00	42.00	15.00
1994D	2.00	8.00	12.00	47.50	20.00
1995	1.85	10.50	16.50	45.00	17.00
1995D	2.00	20.00	19.50	53.00	40.00
1996	2.25	8.75	11.00	19.00	17.00
1996D	2.85	8.25	11.50	27.50	19.00
1997	2.75	14.50	29.00	22.50	20.00
1997D	3.35	60.00	11.00	39.00	16.50
1998	2.00	13.75	9.75	17.00	20.00
1998D	1.85	14.00	12.00	18.00	16.50
1999P	2.35	5.50	8.50	—	20.00
1999D	2.25	6.25	8.50	—	19.00
2000P	2.50	6.25	7.75	—	15.00
2000D	1.75	4.75	7.00	—	17.00

MINT SETS

Date	Sets Sold	Issue Price	Value
1947 Est. 5,000	—	4.87	2,300
1948 Est. 6,000	—	4.92	1,350
1949 Est. 5,200	—	5.45	1,800
1950 None issued	—	—	—
1951	8,654	6.75	1,500
1952	11,499	6.14	1,250
1953	15,538	6.14	1,000
1954	25,599	6.19	560
1955 flat pack	49,656	3.57	350
1956	45,475	3.34	400
1957	32,324	24.50	620
1958	50,314	4.43	385
1959	187,000	2.40	46.00
1960 large date	260,485	2.40	40.00
1961	223,704	2.40	38.00
1962	385,285	2.40	37.50
1963	606,612	2.40	32.00
1964	1,008,108	2.40	32.00
1965 Special Mint Set	2,360,000	4.00	8.50
1966 Special Mint Set	2,261,583	4.00	8.00
1967 Special Mint Set	1,863,344	4.00	9.00
1968	2,105,128	2.50	6.25
1969	1,817,392	2.50	5.50
1970 large date	2,038,134	2.50	16.00
1970 small date	Inc. above	2.50	44.00
1971	2,193,396	3.50	350
1972	2,750,000	3.50	3.00
1973	1,767,691	8.00	10.50
1974	1,975,981	6.75	5.00
1975	1,921,488	6.00	7.50
1976 3 coins	4,908,319	9.00	15.50
1976	1,892,513	6.00	8.00
1977	2,006,869	7.00	5.00
1978	2,162,609	7.00	5.50
1979 Type I	2,526,000	8.00	5.00
1979 Susan B Anthony PDS Souvenir Set	—	—	6.50
1980	2,815,066	9.00	6.00
1981 Type I	2,908,145	11.00	8.00
1981 Susan B. Anthony PDS Souvenir Set	—	—	22.00
1982 & 1983 None issued	—	—	—
1982 Souvenir set	—	—	55.00
1983 Souvenir set	—	—	60.00
1984	1,832,857	7.00	3.00
1985	1,710,571	7.00	3.50
1986	1,153,536	7.50	6.00
1987	2,890,758	7.00	3.50
1988	1,646,204	7.00	3.50
1989	1,987,915	7.00	3.50
1990	1,809,184	7.00	3.50
1991	1,352,101	7.00	4.00
1992	1,500,143	7.00	3.50
1993	1,297,094	8.00	3.75
1994	1,234,813	8.00	3.00
1995	1,038,787	8.00	4.00
1996	1,457,949	8.00	14.00
1997	950,473	8.00	4.00
1998	1,187,325	8.00	4.50
1999 9 piece	1,421,625	14.95	7.00
2000	1,490,160	14.95	7.00

MODERN COMMEMORATIVE COIN SETS

Olympic, 1983-1984

Date		Price
1983	1983 collectors 3 coin set: 1983 PDS uncirculated dollars; KM209.	104
1983	1983 & 1984 3 coin set: 1983 and one 1984 uncirculated dollar and 1984W uncirculated gold $10; KM209, 210, 211.	952
1983	1983S & 1984S 3 coin set: proof 1983 and 1984 dollar and 1984W gold $10; KM209, 210, 211.	956
1983	1983 & 1984 6 coin set in a cherrywood box: 1983S and 1984S uncirculated and proof dollars, 1984W uncirculated and proof gold $10; KM209, 210, 211.	1,909
1983	1983S & 1984S 2 coin set: proof dollars.	74.00
1984	1984 collectors 3 coin set: 1984 PDS uncirculated dollars; KM210.	105

Statue of Liberty

Date		Price
1986	1986 2 coin set: uncirculated silver dollar and clad half dollar; KM212, 214.	38.00
1986	1986 2 coin set: proof silver dollar and clad half dollar; KM212, 214.	40.00
1986	1986 3 coin set: uncirculated silver dollar, clad half dollar and gold $5; KM212, 214, 215.	480
1986	1986 3 coin set: proof silver dollar, clad half dollar and gold $5; KM212, 214, 215.	483
1986	1986 6 coin set: 1 each of the proof and uncirculated issues; KM212, 214, 215.	963

Constitution

Date		Price
1987	1987 2 coin set: uncirculated silver dollar and gold $5; KM220, 221.	477
1987	1987 2 coin set: proof silver dollar and gold $5; KM220, 221.	479
1987	1987 4 coin set: silver dollar and $5 gold proof and uncirculated issues; KM220, 221.	958

Olympic, 1988

Date		Price
1988	1988 2 coin set: uncirculated silver dollar and gold $5; KM222, 223.	477
1988	1988 2 coin set: proof silver dollar and gold $5; KM222, 223.	479
1988	1988 4 coin set: silver dollar and $5 gold proof and uncirculated issues; KM222, 223.	958

Congress

Date		Price
1989	1989 2 coin set: uncirculated silver dollar and clad half dollar; KM224, 225.	42.00
1989	1989 2 coin set: proof silver dollar and clad half dollar; KM224, 225.	44.00
1989	1989 3 coin set: uncirculated silver dollar, clad half and gold $5; KM224, 225, 226.	485
1989	1989 3 coin set: proof silver dollar, clad half and gold $5; KM224, 225, 226.	487
1989	1989 6 coin set: 1 each of the proof and uncirculated issues; KM224, 225, 226.	973

Mt. Rushmore

Date		Price
1991	1991 2 coin set: uncirculated half dollar and silver dollar; KM228, 229.	57.00
1991	1991 2 coin set: proof half dollar and silver dollar; KM228, 229.	60.00
1991	1991 3 coin set: uncirculated half dollar, silver dollar and gold $5; KM228, 229, 230.	500
1991	1991 3 coin set: proof half dollar, silver dollar and gold $5; KM228, 229, 230.	502
1991	1991 6 coin set: 1 each of proof and uncirculated issues; KM228, 229, 230.	1,004

Olympic, 1992

Date		Price
1992	1992 2 coin set: uncirculated half dollar and silver dollar; KM233, 234.	46.00
1992	1992 2 coin set: proof half dollar and silver dollar; KM233, 234.	47.00
1992	1992 3 coin set: uncirculated half dollar, silver dollar and gold $5; KM233, 234, 235.	489
1992	1992 3 coin set: proof half dollar, silver dollar and gold $5; KM233, 234, 235.	490
1992	1992 6 coin set: 1 each of proof and uncirculated issues; KM233, 234, 235.	978

Columbus Quincentenary

Date		Price
1992	1992 2 coin set: uncirculated half dollar and silver dollar; KM237, 238.	52.00
1992	1992 2 coin set: proof half dollar and silver dollar; KM237, 238.	47.00
1992	1992 3 coin set: uncirculated half dollar, silver dollar and gold $5; KM237, 238, 239.	495
1992	1992 3 coin set: proof half dollar, silver dollar and gold $5; KM237, 238, 239.	489
1992	1992 6 coin set: 1 each of proof and uncirculated issues; KM237, 238, 239.	985

Jefferson

Date		Price
1993	1993 Jefferson: dollar, 1994 matte proof nickel and $2 note; KM249, 192.	109

Madison / Bill of Rights

Date		Price
1993	1993 2 coin set: uncirculated half dollar and silver dollar; KM240, 241.	57.00
1993	1993 2 coin set: proof half dollar and silver dollar; KM240, 241.	58.00
1993	1993 3 coin set: uncirculated half dollar, silver dollar and gold $5; KM240, 241, 242.	499
1993	1993 3 coin set: proof half dollar, silver dollar and gold $5; KM240, 241, 242.	500
1993	1993 6 coin set: 1 each of proof and uncirculated issues; KM240, 241, 242.	999
1993	Coin and stamp set; KM#240 and 20c stamp	21.00

World War II

Date		Price
1993	1993 2 coin set: uncirculated half dollar and silver dollar; KM243, 244.	54.00
1993	1993 2 coin set: proof half dollar and silver dollar; KM243, 244.	57.00
1993	1993 3 coin set: uncirculated half dollar, silver dollar and gold $5; KM243, 244, 245.	496
1993	1993 3 coin set: proof half dollar, silver dollar and gold $5; KM243, 244, 245.	500
1993	1993 6 coin set: 1 each of proof and uncirculated issues; KM243, 244, 245.	1,000

U.S. Veterans

Date		Price
1994	1994 3 coin set: uncirculated POW, Vietnam, Women dollars; KM250, 251, 252.	202
1994	1994 3 coin set: proof POW, Vietnam, Women dollars; KM250, 251, 252.	142

World Cup

Date		Price
1994	1994 2 coin set: uncirculated half dollar and silver dollar; KM246, 247.	48.00
1994	1994 2 coin set: proof half dollar and silver dollar; KM246, 247.	45.00
1994	1994 3 coin set: uncirculated half dollar, silver dollar and gold $5; KM246, 247, 248.	490
1994	1994 3 coin set: proof half dollar, silver dollar and gold $5; KM246, 247, 248.	487
1994	1994 6 coin set: 1 each of proof and uncirculated issues; KM246, 247, 248.	983

Olympic, 1995-96

Date		Price
1995	1995 4 coin set: uncirculated basketball half, $1 gymnast & blind runner, $5 torch runner; KM257, 259, 260, 261.	1,024

1995 1995 4 coin set: proof basketball half, $1 gymnast & blind runner, $5 torch runner; KM257, 259, 260, 261.	533
1995 1995P 2 coin set: proof $1 gymnast & blind runner; KM259, 260.	82.00
1995 1995P 2 coin set: proof $1 track & field, cycling; KM263, 264.	84.00
1995 1995-96 4 coin set: proof halves, basketball, baseball, swimming, soccer; KM257, 262, 267, 271.	75.00
1995 1995 & 96 16 coins in cherry wood case: bu and proof silver dollars: blind runner, gymnast, cycling, track & field, wheelchair, tennis, rowing, high jump; KM259, 260, 263, 264, 268, 269, 272, 272A.	10,400
1995 1995 & 96 16 coins in cherry wood case: proof half dollars: basketball, baseball, swimming, soccer, KM257, 262, 267, 271. Proof silver dollars: blind runner, gymnast, cycling, track & field, wheelchair, tennis, rowing, high jump, KM259, 260, 263, 264, 268, 269, 272, 272A. Proof $5 gold: torch runner, stadium, cauldron, flag bearer, KM 261, 265, 270, 274.	2,370
1995 1995 & 96 32 coins in cherry wood case: bu & proof half dollars: basketball, baseball, swimming, soccer, KM257, 262, 267, 271. BU & proof silver dollars: blind runner, gymnast, cycling, track & field, wheelchair, tennis, rowing, high jump, KM259, 260, 263, 264, 268, 269, 272, 272A. BU & proof $5 gold: torch runner, stadium, cauldron, flag bearer, KM261, 265, 270, 274.	12,800
1996 1996P 2 coin set: proof $1 wheelchair & tennis; KM268, 269.	154
1996 1996P 2 coin set: proof $1 rowing & high jump; KM272, 272A.	105
1996 Young collector 4 coin set; Half dollars: KM#257, 262, 267, 271	205

Civil War

Date	Price
1995 1995 2 coin set: uncirculated half and dollar; KM254, 255.	102
1995 1995 2 coin set: proof half and dollar; KM254, 255.	88.00
1995 1995 3 coin set: uncirculated half, dollar and gold $5; KM254, 255, 256.	1,055
1995 1995 3 coin set: proof half, dollar and gold $5; KM254, 255, 256.	530
1995 1995 6 coin set: 1 each of proof and uncirculated issues; KM254, 255, 256.	1,585
1995 Civil War Young Collectors set KM#245	37.50

Smithsonian

Date	Price
1996 1996 2 coin set: proof dollar and $5 gold; KM276, 277.	495
1996 1996 4 coin set: proof and B.U. ; KM276, 277.	1,465

Franklin Delano Roosevelt

Date	Price
1997 1997W 2 coin set: uncirculated and proof; KM282.	3,500

Jackie Robinson

Date	Price
1997 1997 2 coin set: proof dollar & $5 gold; KM279, 280.	680
1997 1997 4 coin set: proof & BU; KM279, 280.	3,660
1997 1997 legacy set.	650

Botanic Garden

Date	Price
1997 1997 2 coin set: dollar, Jefferson nickel and $1 note; KM278, 192.	220

Black Patriots

Date	Price
1998 1998S 2 coin set: uncirculated and proof; KM288.	220

Kennedy

Date	Price
1998 1998 2 coin set: proof; KM287.	88.00
1998 1998 2 coin collectors set: Robert Kennedy dollar and John Kennedy half dollar; KM287, 202b. Matte finished.	225

Dolley Madison

Date	Price
1999 1999 2 coin set: proof and uncirculated silver dollars; KM298.	76.00

Yellowstone National Park

Date	Price
1999 1999 2 coin set: proof and uncirculated silver dollars; KM299.	84.00

George Washington

Date	Price
1999 1999 2 coin set: proof and uncirculated gold $5; KM300.	900

Millennium Coin & Currency

Date	Price
2000 2000 2 coin set: uncirculated Sacagewea $1, silver Eagle & $1 note.	67.50

Leif Ericson

Date	Price
2000 2000 2 coin set: proof and uncirculated silver dollars; KM313.	85.00

PROOF SETS

Date	Sets Sold	Issue Price	Value
1936	3,837	1.89	7,500
1937	5,542	1.89	2,800
1938	8,045	1.89	1,135
1939	8,795	—	1,150
1940	11,246	—	900
1941	15,287	—	850
1942 6 coins	21,120	1.89	900
1942 5 coins	Inc. above	1.89	800
1950	51,386	2.10	500
1951	57,500	2.10	500
1952	81,980	2.10	210
1953	128,800	2.10	175
1954	233,300	2.10	90.00
1955 box	378,200	2.10	115
1955 flat pack	Inc. above	2.10	95.00
1956	669,384	2.10	58.00
1957	1,247,952	2.10	27.00
1958	875,652	2.10	29.00
1959	1,149,291	2.10	26.00
1960 large date	1,691,602	2.10	27.00
1960 small date	Inc. above	2.10	28.00
1961	3,028,244	2.10	23.00
1962	3,218,019	2.10	23.00
1963	3,075,645	2.10	16.00
1964	3,950,762	2.10	23.00
1968S	3,041,509	5.00	7.00
1968S no mint mark dime	Inc. above	5.00	13,000
1969S	2,934,631	5.00	6.50
1970S large date	2,632,810	5.00	10.00
1970S small date	Inc. above	5.00	77.00
1970S no mint mark dime	Inc. above	5.00	750
1971S	3,224,138	5.00	3.25
1971S no mint mark nickel Est. 1,655	1,655	5.00	1,100
1972S	3,267,667	5.00	3.75
1973S	2,769,624	7.00	7.50
1974S	2,617,350	7.00	9.50
1975S	2,909,369	7.00	9.00
1975S no mint mark dime	Inc. above	7.00	220,000
1976S 3 coins	3,998,621	13.00	21.00
1976S	4,149,730	7.00	8.00
1977S	3,251,152	9.00	6.00
1978S	3,127,788	9.00	5.25
1979S Type I	3,677,175	9.00	7.50
1979S Type II	Inc. above	9.00	45.00
1981S Type II	Inc. above	11.00	250
1982S	3,857,479	11.00	4.50
1983S	3,138,765	11.00	4.00
1983S Prestige Set	140,361	59.00	38.50
1983S no mint mark dime	Inc. above	11.00	650
1984S	2,748,430	11.00	5.00
1984S Prestige Set	316,680	59.00	22.00
1985S	3,362,821	11.00	3.00
1986S	2,411,180	11.00	5.00
1986S Prestige Set	599,317	48.50	26.00
1987S	3,972,233	11.00	3.50
1987S Prestige Set	435,495	45.00	23.00
1988S	3,031,287	11.00	4.00
1988S Prestige Set	231,661	45.00	27.00
1989S	3,009,107	11.00	3.75
1989S Prestige Set	211,087	45.00	26.50
1990S	2,793,433	11.00	4.00
1990S no S 1¢	3,555	11.00	4,100
1990S Prestige Set	506,126	45.00	24.00
1990S Prestige Set, no S 1¢	Inc. above	45.00	4,300
1991S	2,610,833	11.00	3.50
1991S Prestige Set	256,954	59.00	42.00
1992S	2,675,618	12.00	3.50
1992S Prestige Set	183,285	59.00	46.00
1992S Silver	1,009,585	21.00	19.00
1992S Silver premier	308,055	37.00	21.00
1993S	2,337,819	12.50	4.75
1993S Prestige Set	224,045	57.00	31.00
1993S Silver	570,213	21.00	24.00
1993S Silver premier	191,140	37.00	30.00
1994S	2,308,701	13.00	4.50
1994S Prestige Set	175,893	57.00	31.00
1994S Silver	636,009	21.00	22.00
1994S Silver premier	149,320	37.50	30.00
1995S	2,010,384	12.50	9.00
1995S Prestige Set	107,112	57.00	72.00
1995S Silver	549,878	21.00	48.00
1995S Silver premier	130,107	37.50	48.00
1996S	2,085,191	16.00	7.00
1996S Prestige Set	55,000	57.00	285
1996S Silver	623,655	21.00	24.00
1996S Silver premier	151,366	37.50	27.50
1997S	1,975,000	12.50	7.00
1997S Prestige Set	80,000	57.00	53.00
1997S Silver	605,473	21.00	30.00
1997S Silver premier	136,205	37.50	34.00
1998S	2,078,494	12.50	9.00
1998S Silver	638,134	21.00	20.00
1998S Silver premier	240,658	26.50	26.00
1999S 9 piece	2,557,899	19.95	7.50
1999S 5 quarter set	1,169,958	13.95	3.25
1999S Silver	804,565	31.95	83.00
2000S 10 piece	3,097,442	19.95	5.00
2000S 5 quarter set	995,803	13.95	2.50
2000S Silver	965,421	31.95	34.00

The Oriental Republic of Uruguay (so called because of its location on the east bank of the Uruguay River) is situated on the Atlantic coast of South America between Argentina and Brazil. This South American country has an area of 68,536 sq. mi. (176,220 sq. km.) and a population of *3 million. Capital: Montevideo. Uruguay's chief economic assets are the rich, rolling grassy plains. Meat, wool, hides and skins are exported.

Uruguay was discovered in 1516 by Juan Diaz de Solis, a Spaniard, but settled by the Portuguese who founded Colony in 1680. Spain contested Portuguese possession and, after a long struggle, gained control of the country in 1778. During the general South American struggle for independence, Uruguay 's first attempt was led by Gaucho soldier Jose Gervasio Artigas leading, the Banda Oriental. It was quelled by Spanish and Portuguese forces in 1811. The armistice was soon broken and Argentine force from Buenos Aires cast off the Spanish bond in the Plata region in 1814 only to be conquered again by the Portuguese from Brazil in the struggle of 1816-20. Revolt flared anew in 1825 and independence was reasserted in 1828 with the help of Argentina. The Uruguayan Republic was established in 1830.

MINT MARKS

A – Aron Hirsch and Son, Berlin (1901)
A, (v) – Vienna (A - 1909 and 1936); (no mint mark 1984)
(a) – Paris; privy marks - torch & cornucopia 1930; no marks 1989 and 1998
(ba) – Buenos Aires
(br) – Acunaciones Espanolas S.A., Barcelona
(k) – Kremnica (Slovakia)
(l) – London (1953 and 1959-1961); Llantrisant (1984 and 1995) (British Royal Mint)
(m) - Madrid
Mo, (mo) and Mx - Mexico City
(p) – thunderbolt: Poissy, France
(rcm) – Royal Canadian Mint
(rj) – Rio de Janeiro
(sa) – Pretoria, South Africa
So, (so) – Santiago (Small o above S); (except 2007 2 Pesos Uruguayos)
(u) – Utrecht (Netherlands); caduceus 1954; no mint mark 2006

MONETARY SYSTEM

100 Centesimo = 1 Peso
1975-1993
1000 Old Pesos = 1 Nuevo (New) Peso
Commencing 1994
1000 Nuevos Pesos = 1 Peso Uruguayo

REPUBLIC

DECIMAL COINAGE

KM# 19 CENTESIMO

2.00 g., Copper-Nickel, 20 mm. **Obv:** Radiant sun design **Rev:** Value within wreath **Edge:** Plain

Date	Mintage	F12	VF20	XF40	MS60	MS63
1901 A	6,000,000	1.00	5.00	20.00	35.00	75.00
1901 A	—	PF63 225				
1909 A	5,000,000	0.50	2.00	6.00	20.00	35.00
1924 (p)	3,000,000	0.50	2.00	8.00	15.00	20.00
1936 A	2,000,000	0.50	2.00	8.00	15.00	20.00

KM# 32 CENTESIMO

1.50 g., Copper-Nickel, 15 mm. **Obv:** Artigas bust right, 'HP' below **Rev:** Value within wreath **Note:** Medal rotation.

Date	Mintage	VF20	XF40	MS60	MS63	MS65
1953 (l)	5,000,000	0.25	0.50	1.00	1.50	3.00
1953	—	PF63 150				

KM# 20 2 CENTESIMOS

3.50 g., Copper-Nickel, 20 mm. **Obv:** Radiant sun design **Rev:** Value within wreath **Edge:** Plain

Date	Mintage	F12	VF20	XF40	MS60	MS63
1901 A	7,500,000	1.00	4.00	12.00	30.00	75.00
1909 A	10,000,000	1.00	2.00	9.00	20.00	35.00
1924 (p)	11,000,000	1.00	2.00	7.00	15.00	25.00
1936 A	6,500,000	1.00	2.00	7.00	15.00	25.00
1941 So	10,000,000	1.00	2.00	7.00	15.00	25.00

KM# 20a 2 CENTESIMOS

3.50 g., Copper-Tin-Zinc, 20 mm. **Obv:** Radiant sun design **Rev:** Value within wreath

Date	Mintage	F12	VF20	XF40	MS60	MS63
1943 So	5,000,000	0.25	1.00	3.00	5.00	10.00
1944 So	3,500,000	0.25	1.00	3.00	5.00	10.00
1945 So	2,500,000	0.25	1.00	3.00	5.00	10.00
1946 So	2,500,000	0.25	0.50	3.00	5.00	10.00
1947 So	5,000,000	0.25	0.50	1.50	3.50	7.50
1948 So	7,500,000	0.25	0.50	1.00	3.00	7.50
1949 So	7,400,000	0.25	0.50	1.00	3.00	5.00
1951 So	12,500,000	0.25	0.50	1.00	3.00	5.00

KM# 33 2 CENTESIMOS

2.50 g., Copper-Nickel, 17 mm. **Obv:** Artigas, 'HP' below **Rev:** Value within wreath **Note:** Medal rotation.

Date	Mintage	VF20	XF40	MS60	MS63	MS65
1953 (l)	50,000,000	0.15	0.30	1.00	3.00	5.00
1953	—	PF63 65.00				

KM# 37 2 CENTESIMOS

2.00 g., Nickel-Brass, 16 mm. **Obv:** Artigas, 'HP' below **Rev:** Value within wreath **Note:** Medal rotation.

Date	Mintage	VF20	XF40	MS60	MS63	MS65
1960 (l)	17,500,000	—	0.15	0.25	1.00	1.50
1960	—	PF63 40.00				

KM# 21 5 CENTESIMOS

5.00 g., Copper-Nickel, 23 mm. **Obv:** Radiant sun design **Rev:** Value within wreath **Edge:** Plain

Date	Mintage	F12	VF20	XF40	MS60	MS63
1901 A	6,000,000	1.00	4.00	12.00	30.00	50.00
1901 A	—	PF63 325				
1909 A	5,000,000	1.00	3.00	10.00	22.00	35.00
1909 A	—	PF63 175				
1924 (p)	5,000,000	0.50	2.00	6.00	10.00	15.00
1936 A	3,000,000	0.50	2.00	6.00	10.00	15.00
1941 So	2,400,000	0.25	1.00	4.00	7.00	10.00
1941 So	—	PF63 200				

KM# 21a 5 CENTESIMOS

5.00 g., Copper, 23 mm. **Obv:** Radiant sun design **Rev:** Value within wreath

Date	Mintage	F12	VF20	XF40	MS60	MS63
1944 So	4,000,000	0.25	1.00	3.00	5.00	10.00
1946 So	2,000,000	0.20	1.00	4.00	6.00	12.00
1947 So	2,000,000	0.20	1.00	4.00	6.00	12.00
1948 So	3,000,000	0.20	0.75	3.00	5.00	10.00
1949 So	2,800,000	0.20	0.75	3.00	5.00	10.00
1951 So	15,000,000	0.20	0.50	2.00	3.00	5.00

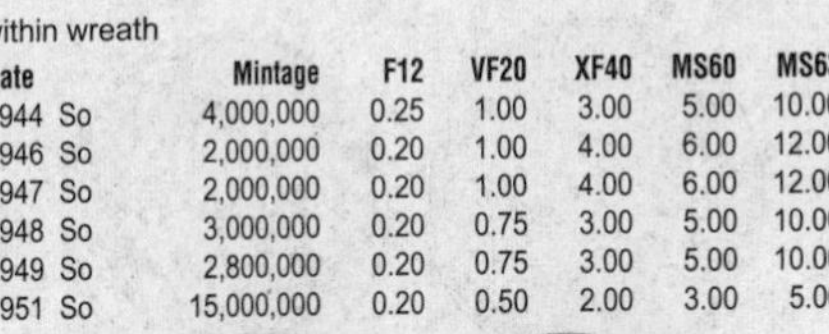

KM# 34 5 CENTESIMOS

3.50 g., Copper-Nickel, 20 mm. **Obv:** Artigas, 'HP' below **Rev:** Value within wreath **Note:** Medal rotation.

Date	Mintage	F12	VF20	XF40	MS60	MS63
1953 (l)	17,500,000	0.20	0.30	0.50	1.00	1.50
1953	—	PF63 75.00				

KM# 38 5 CENTESIMOS

3.50 g., Nickel-Brass, 20 mm. **Obv:** Artigas, 'HP' below **Rev:** Value within wreath **Note:** Medal rotation.

Date	Mintage	VF20	XF40	MS60	MS63	MS65
1960 (l)	88,000,000	—	0.15	0.25	1.00	1.50
1960	—	PF63 75.00				

KM# 25 10 CENTESIMOS

8.00 g., Aluminum-Bronze, 27 mm. **Subject:** Constitutional Centennial **Obv:** MORLON behind neck **Rev:** Puma walking left in front of sun rays above value

Date	Mintage	F12	VF20	XF40	MS60	MS63
1930 (a)	5,000,000	2.00	4.00	12.00	30.00	—
1930 (a)	—	PF63 375				

KM# 28 10 CENTESIMOS

6.00 g., Aluminum-Bronze, 25 mm. **Obv:** Head laureate right **Rev:** Puma walking left in front of sunrays above value

Date	Mintage	F12	VF20	XF40	MS60	MS63
1936 A	2,000,000	1.50	3.50	10.00	25.00	65.00
1936 A	—	PF63 375				

KM# 35 10 CENTESIMOS

4.50 g., Copper-Nickel, 22 mm. **Obv:** Artigas, 'HP' below **Rev:** Value within wreath **Note:** Medal rotation.

Date	Mintage	F12	VF20	XF40	MS60	MS63
1953 (l)	28,250,000	0.15	0.20	0.30	1.00	1.50
1953	—	PF63 75.00				
1959 (l)	10,000,000	0.20	0.30	1.00	3.00	5.00

KM# 39 10 CENTESIMOS

4.50 g., Nickel-Brass, 24 mm. **Obv:** Artigas, 'HP' below **Rev:** Value within wreath **Note:** Medal rotation.

Date	Mintage	VF20	XF40	MS60	MS63	MS65
1960 (l)	72,500,000	0.15	0.20	0.30	1.00	1.50
1960	—	PF63 100				

KM# 24 20 CENTESIMOS

5.00 g., 0.800 Silver 0.1286 oz. ASW, 25 mm. **Obv:** Radiant sun peeks out over arms within wreath **Rev:** Head left

Date	Mintage	F12	VF20	XF40	MS60	MS63
1920 (So)	2,500,000	5.00	7.00	15.00	35.00	50.00

KM# 26 20 CENTESIMOS

5.00 g., 0.800 Silver 0.1286 oz. ASW, 25 mm. **Subject:** Constitutional Centennial **Obv:** Seated figure left above date **Rev:** Wheat stalks divide value, mint marks flank stems

Date	Mintage	F12	VF20	XF40	MS60	MS63
1930 (a)	2,500,000	3.00	5.00	9.00	20.00	35.00

KM# 29 20 CENTESIMOS

3.00 g., 0.720 Silver 0.0694 oz. ASW, 18.5 mm. **Obv:** Head laureate right **Rev:** Wheat stalks divide value

Date	Mintage	F12	VF20	XF40	MS60	MS63
1942 So	18,000,000	3.00	4.00	6.00	10.00	15.00

KM# 36 20 CENTESIMOS

3.00 g., 0.720 Silver 0.0694 oz. ASW, 18.5 mm. **Obv:** Head right **Rev:** Wheat stalks divide value

Date	Mintage	F12	VF20	XF40	MS60	MS63
1954 (u)	10,000,000	1.30	2.75	3.50	7.50	10.00

KM# 44 20 CENTESIMOS

1.50 g., Aluminum, 20.5 mm. **Obv:** Head right **Rev:** Value within wreath **Note:** Medal rotation.

Date	Mintage	VF20	XF40	MS60	MS63	MS65
1965 So	40,000,000	0.15	0.20	0.35	1.00	1.50

KM# 40 25 CENTESIMOS

3.00 g., Copper-Nickel, 18 mm. **Obv:** 'HP' below bust **Rev:** Radiant sun peeking out above arms within wreath, value divides circle of stars **Note:** Medal rotation.

Date	Mintage	VF20	XF40	MS60	MS63	MS65
1960 (l)	48,000,000	0.20	0.35	0.50	1.00	1.50
1960	—	PF63 80.00				

KM# 22 50 CENTESIMOS

12.50 g., 0.900 Silver 0.3617 oz. ASW, 30 mm.

Date	Mintage	F12	VF20	XF40	MS60	MS63
1916 (ba)	400,000	13.00	20.00	50.00	200	350
1917 (ba)	5,600,000	13.00	15.00	35.00	100	175

KM# 31 50 CENTESIMOS

7.00 g., 0.720 Silver 0.162 oz. ASW, 24 mm. **Obv:** Head right **Rev:** Date below value

Date	Mintage	VF20	XF40	MS60	MS63	MS65
1943 So	10,800,000	3.25	6.00	7.50	15.00	25.00

KM# 41 50 CENTESIMOS

4.50 g., Copper-Nickel, 22 mm. **Obv:** Artigas bust right, 'HP' below **Rev:** Radiant sun peeking out above arms within wreath, value divides circle of stars **Note:** Medal rotation.

Date	Mintage	VF20	XF40	MS60	MS63	MS65
1960 (l)	18,000,000	0.20	0.50	1.00	1.25	1.75
1960	—	PF63 80.00				

KM# 45 50 CENTESIMOS

2.00 g., Aluminum, 23.5 mm. **Obv:** Artigas head right **Rev:** Value within wreath **Note:** Medal rotation.

Date	Mintage	VF20	XF40	MS60	MS63	MS65
1965 So	50,000,000	0.15	0.25	0.40	1.00	1.50

KM# 23 PESO

25.00 g., 0.900 Silver 0.7234 oz. ASW, 37 mm. **Obv:** Radiant sun peeking out above arms within wreath **Rev:** Bust left

Date	Mintage	F12	VF20	XF40	MS60	MS63
1917 (ba)	2,000,000	15.00	27.50	60.00	150	275

KM# 30 PESO

9.00 g., 0.720 Silver 0.2083 oz. ASW, 27 mm. **Obv:** Artigas head right **Rev:** Puma walking left, sunrays behind

Date	Mintage	F12	VF20	XF40	MS60	MS63
1942 So	9,000,000	4.25	7.50	12.50	40.00	65.00

KM# 42 PESO

6.00 g., Copper-Nickel, 26 mm. **Obv:** Artigas head right, 'HP' below **Rev:** Radiant sun peeking out above arms within wreath, value divides circle of stars **Note:** Medal rotation.

Date	Mintage	VF20	XF40	MS60	MS63	MS65
1960 (l)	8,000,000	0.25	0.50	0.75	1.00	1.50
1960	—	PF63 75.00				

KM# 46 PESO

5.00 g., Aluminum-Bronze, 22 mm. **Obv:** Artigas head right **Rev:** Radiant sun peeking out above arms within wreath, value divides circle of stars **Note:** Medal rotation.

Date	Mintage	VF20	XF40	MS60	MS63	MS65
1965 So	60,000,000	—	0.15	0.35	1.00	1.50
1965 So	25	PF65 65.00				

KM# 49 PESO

2.00 g., Nickel-Brass, 17 mm. **Obv:** Artigas head right **Rev:** Flower and value **Note:** Medal rotation.

Date	Mintage	VF20	XF40	MS60	MS63	MS65
1968 So	103,200,000	—	—	0.15	0.75	1.00
1968 So	50	PF65 50.00				

KM# 52 PESO

2.00 g., Aluminum-Brass, 17 mm. **Obv:** Radiant sun with face **Rev:** Flower and value **Note:** Medal rotation.

Date	Mintage	VF20	XF40	MS60	MS63	MS65
1969 So	51,800,000	—	—	0.15	0.75	1.00

KM# 27 5 PESOS

8.49 g., 0.917 Gold 0.2502 oz. AGW, 22' mm. **Subject:** Constitution Centennial **Obv:** Artigas head right, L. BAZOR in left field behind neck **Rev:** Date flanked by sprigs below value

Date	Mintage	VF20	XF40	MS60	MS63	MS65
1930 (a)	100,000	335	375	450	525	600

Note: Only 14,415 were released; Remainder withheld

KM# 47 5 PESOS

7.00 g., Aluminum-Bronze, 25 mm. **Obv:** Artigas head right **Rev:** Radiant sun peeking out above arms within wreath, value divides circle of stars **Note:** Medal rotation.

Date	Mintage	VF20	XF40	MS60	MS63	MS65
1965 So	18,000,000	0.20	0.30	0.50	1.00	1.50
1965 So	25	PF65 75.00				

KM# 50 5 PESOS

3.00 g., Nickel-Brass, 20 mm. **Obv:** Artigas head right **Rev:** Flower and value **Note:** Medal rotation.

Date	Mintage	VF20	XF40	MS60	MS63	MS65
1968 So	42,680,000	0.10	0.20	0.30	0.40	1.00
1968 So	50	PF65 65.00				

KM# 53 5 PESOS

3.00 g., Aluminum-Bronze, 20 mm. **Obv:** Radiant sun with face **Rev:** Flower and value **Note:** Medal rotation.

Date	Mintage	VF20	XF40	MS60	MS63	MS65
1969 So	42,320,000	—	—	0.10	0.30	1.00

KM# 43 10 PESOS

12.50 g., 0.900 Silver 0.3617 oz. ASW, 33 mm. **Subject:** Sesquicentennial of Revolution Against Spain **Obv:** M.G. Rizzello bust right with hat **Rev:** Value within wreath **Edge:** Reeded

Date	Mintage	VF20	XF40	MS60	MS63	MS65
1961 (l)	3,000,000	—	7.00	10.00	12.00	15.00
1961	—	PF63 600	PF65 700			

KM# 48 10 PESOS

9.00 g., Aluminum-Bronze, 28 mm. **Obv:** Artigas head right **Rev:** Radiant sun peeking out above arms within wreath, value divides circle of stars **Note:** Medal rotation.

Date	Mintage	VF20	XF40	MS60	MS63	MS65
1965 So	18,000,000	0.20	0.35	—	0.50	1.00

KM# 51 10 PESOS

4.00 g., Nickel-Brass, 23 mm. **Obv:** Artigas head right **Rev:** Flower and value **Note:** Medal rotation.

Date	Mintage	VF20	XF40	MS60	MS63	MS65
1968 So	90,000,000	0.20	0.35	—	0.50	1.00
1968 So	50	PF65 80.00				

KM# 54 10 PESOS

4.00 g., Aluminum-Bronze, 23 mm. **Obv:** Radiant sun with face **Rev:** Flower and value **Note:** Medal rotation.

Date	Mintage	VF20	XF40	MS60	MS63	MS65
1969 So	10,000,000	0.20	0.35	—	0.50	1.00

KM# 56 20 PESOS

3.75 g., Copper-Nickel-Zinc, 21.5 mm. **Obv:** Radiant sun peeking out above arms within wreath **Rev:** Spears of wheat and value **Note:** Medal rotation.

Date	Mintage	VF20	XF40	MS60	MS63	MS65
1970 So	50,000,000	0.15	0.25	—	0.40	0.75
1970 So	—	PF65 80.00				

KM# 57 50 PESOS

5.25 g., Copper-Nickel-Zinc, 24.5 mm. **Obv:** Radiant sun peeking out above arms within wreath **Rev:** Spears of wheat and value **Note:** Medal rotation.

Date	Mintage	VF20	XF40	MS60	MS63	MS65
1970 So	20,000,000	0.35	0.50	—	0.75	1.50
1970 So	—	PF65 80.00				

KM# 58 50 PESOS

5.25 g., Nickel-Brass, 24.5 mm. **Subject:** Centennial - Birth of Rodo **Obv:** Rodo facing **Rev:** Feather, value and date **Note:** Medal rotation.

Date	Mintage	VF20	XF40	MS60	MS63	MS65
1971 So	15,000,000	0.35	0.50	—	0.75	1.50

KM# 58a 50 PESOS

6.02 g., 0.900 Silver 0.1742 oz. ASW **Subject:** Centennial - Birth of Rodo **Obv:** Rodo facing **Rev:** Feather, value and date

Date	Mintage	VF20	XF40	MS60	MS63	MS65
1971 So	1,000	PF63 18.00	PF65 20.00			

KM# 58b 50 PESOS

Gold **Subject:** Centennial - Birth of Rodo **Obv:** Rodo facing **Rev:** Feather, value and date

Date	Mintage	VF20	XF40	MS60	MS63	MS65
1971 So	100	PF63 550	PF65 650			

KM# 59 100 PESOS

8.00 g., Copper-Nickel-Zinc, 27.5 mm. **Obv:** Artigas head 1/4 left **Rev:** Value, date and sprig **Note:** Coin rotation.

Date	Mintage	VF20	XF40	MS60	MS63	MS65
1973 Mx	20,000,000	—	0.25	0.50	1.00	1.50

KM# 55 1000 PESOS

25.00 g., 0.900 Silver 0.7234 oz. ASW, 37 mm. **Series:** F.A.O. **Obv:** Stylized radiant sun with face **Rev:** Assorted stylized designs within circle **Edge Lettering:** REPUBLICA ORIENTAL DEL URUGUAY **Note:** Medal rotation.

Date	Mintage	VF20	XF40	MS60	MS63	MS65
1969 So	500,000	—	14.00	16.50	22.00	30.00
1969 So	350	PF63 200	PF65 250			

KM# 55a 1000 PESOS

25.00 g., Copper, 37 mm. **Series:** F.A.O. **Obv:** Stylized radiant sun with face **Rev:** Assorted stylized designs within circle **Edge:** Lettered **Edge Lettering:** REPUBLICA ORIENTAL DEL URUGUAY **Note:** 'So' mintmark also appears on edge.

Date	Mintage	VF20	XF40	MS60	MS63	MS65
1969 So	11,000	—	14.00	22.00	27.00	35.00

KM# 55b 1000 PESOS

Gold **Series:** F.A.O. **Obv:** Stylized radiant sun with face **Rev:** Assorted stylized designs within circle

Date	Mintage	VF20	XF40	MS60	MS63	MS65
1969 So	450	—	—	1,600	1,800	2,000

KM# 55c 1000 PESOS

25.00 g., 0.900 Silver 0.7234 oz. ASW, 37 mm. **Subject:** F.A.O., Central Bank 20th Anniversary **Obv:** Countermark: BANCO CENTRAL DEL URUGUAY 1967-1987

Date	Mintage	VF20	XF40	MS60	MS63	MS65
1987 So	2,000	—	—	—	300	—

KM# 55d 1000 PESOS

25.00 g., 0.900 Silver 0.7234 oz. ASW, 37 mm. **Subject:** F.A.O. and Central Bank 30th Anniversary **Obv:** Countermark: BANCO CENTRAL DEL URUGUAY 1967-1997

Date	Mintage	VF20	XF40	MS60	MS63	MS65
1997 So	500	—	—	—	—	—

REFORM COINAGE

1000 Old Pesos = 1 Nuevo (New) Peso

KM# 71 CENTESIMO

1.00 g., Aluminum, 18 mm. **Obv:** Radiant sun with face **Rev:** Value in front of supine wheat stalk **Shape:** 12-sided **Note:** Medal rotation.

Date	Mintage	VF20	XF40	MS60	MS63	MS65
1977 So	10,000,000	—	—	0.15	0.25	0.75

KM# 71a CENTESIMO

3.70 g., 0.900 Silver 0.1071 oz. ASW, 19 mm. **Obv:** Radiant sun with face **Rev:** Value in front of supine wheat stalk

Date	Mintage	VF20	XF40	MS60	MS63	MS65
1979 So	202	PF63 15.00	PF65 17.00			

KM# 71b CENTESIMO

6.26 g., 0.900 Gold 0.1811 oz. AGW, 19 mm. **Obv:** Radiant sun with face **Rev:** Value in front of supine wheat stalk

Date	Mintage	VF20	XF40	MS60	MS63	MS65
1979 So	50	PF63 350	PF65 375			

KM# 72 2 CENTESIMOS

1.50 g., Aluminum, 20 mm. **Obv:** Radiant sun with face **Rev:** Value in front of supine wheat stalk **Shape:** 12-sided **Note:** Medal rotation.

Date	Mintage	VF20	XF40	MS60	MS63	MS65
1977 So	17,000,000	—	—	0.15	0.25	0.75
1978 So	3,000,000	—	—	0.15	0.25	0.75

KM# 72a 2 CENTESIMOS
5.20 g., 0.900 Silver 0.1505 oz. ASW, 21 mm. **Obv:** Radiant sun with face **Rev:** Value in front of supine wheat stalk

Date	Mintage	VF20	XF40	MS60	MS63	MS65
1979 So	202	PF63 20.00	PF65 22.00			

KM# 72b 2 CENTESIMOS
9.25 g., 0.900 Gold 0.2677 oz. AGW, 21 mm. **Obv:** Radiant sun with face **Rev:** Value in front of supine wheat stalk

Date	Mintage	VF20	XF40	MS60	MS63	MS65
1979 So	52	PF63 475	PF65 500			

KM# 73 5 CENTESIMOS
2.00 g., Aluminum, 22 mm. **Obv:** Steer left **Rev:** Value in front of supine wheat stalk **Shape:** 12-sided **Note:** Medal rotation.

Date	Mintage	VF20	XF40	MS60	MS63	MS65
1977 So	11,000,000	—	—	0.15	0.50	1.00
1978 So	19,000,000	—	—	0.15	0.50	1.00

KM# 73a 5 CENTESIMOS
7.40 g., 0.900 Silver 0.2141 oz. ASW, 23 mm. **Obv:** Steer left **Rev:** Value in front of supine wheat stalk

Date	Mintage	VF20	XF40	MS60	MS63	MS65
1979 So	202	PF63 22.00	PF65 25.00			

KM# 73b 5 CENTESIMOS
12.55 g., 0.900 Gold 0.3631 oz. AGW, 23 mm. **Obv:** Steer left **Rev:** Value in front of supine wheat stalk

Date	Mintage	VF20	XF40	MS60	MS63	MS65
1979 So	52	PF63 675	PF65 700			

KM# 66 10 CENTESIMOS
3.00 g., Aluminum-Bronze, 18.5 mm. **Obv:** Horse left **Rev:** Value flanked by sprigs **Shape:** 12-sided **Note:** Medal rotation.

Date	Mintage	VF20	XF40	MS60	MS63	MS65
1976 So	50,000,000	—	—	0.30	0.80	1.50
1976 So Proof	—	—	—	—	—	—
1977 So	12,700,000	—	—	0.35	0.85	1.50
1978 So	19,900,000	—	—	0.35	0.85	1.50
1981 So	—	—	—	0.35	0.85	1.50

KM# 66a 10 CENTESIMOS
3.80 g., 0.900 Silver 0.110 oz. ASW, 19 mm. **Obv:** Horse left **Rev:** Value flanked by sprigs

Date	Mintage	VF20	XF40	MS60	MS63	MS65
1976 So	200	PF63 20.00	PF65 22.00			
1977 So	200	PF63 20.00	PF65 22.00			

KM# 66b 10 CENTESIMOS
6.00 g., 0.900 Gold 0.1736 oz. AGW, 19 mm. **Obv:** Horse left **Rev:** Value flanked by sprigs

Date	Mintage	VF20	XF40	MS60	MS63	MS65
1976 So	50	PF63 325	PF65 350			

KM# 67 20 CENTESIMOS
5.00 g., Aluminum-Bronze, 21.5 mm. **Obv:** Small building on top of hill **Rev:** Value flanked by sprigs **Shape:** 12-sided **Note:** Medal rotation.

Date	Mintage	VF20	XF40	MS60	MS63	MS65
1976 So	40,000,000	—	—	0.20	0.45	0.85
1976 So Proof	—	—	—	—	—	—
1977 So	4,700,000	—	—	0.20	0.60	1.00
1978 So	15,300,000	—	—	0.20	0.45	0.85
1981 So	—	—	—	0.20	0.45	0.85

KM# 67a 20 CENTESIMOS
6.40 g., 0.900 Silver 0.1852 oz. ASW, 22 mm. **Obv:** Small building on top of hill **Rev:** Value flanked by sprigs

Date	Mintage	VF20	XF40	MS60	MS63	MS65
1976 So	200	PF63 22.00	PF65 25.00			
1977 So	200	PF63 22.00	PF65 25.00			

KM# 67b 20 CENTESIMOS
10.50 g., 0.900 Gold 0.3038 oz. AGW, 22 mm. **Obv:** Small building on top of hill **Rev:** Value flanked by sprigs

Date	Mintage	VF20	XF40	MS60	MS63	MS65
1976 So	50	PF63 575	PF65 600			

KM# 68 50 CENTESIMOS
7.00 g., Aluminum-Bronze, 25 mm. **Obv:** Scale **Rev:** Value flanked by sprigs **Shape:** 12-sided

Date	Mintage	VF20	XF40	MS60	MS63	MS65
1976 So	30,000,000	—	—	0.20	0.50	1.00
1976 So Proof	—	—	—	—	—	—
1977 So	9,800,000	—	—	0.20	0.50	1.00
1981 So	200,000	—	—	0.25	0.60	1.25

KM# 68a 50 CENTESIMOS
9.00 g., 0.900 Silver 0.2604 oz. ASW, 25.5 mm. **Obv:** Scale **Rev:** Value flanked by sprigs

Date	Mintage	VF20	XF40	MS60	MS63	MS65
1976 So	200	PF63 32.00	PF65 35.00			
1977 So	200	PF63 32.00	PF65 35.00			

KM# 68b 50 CENTESIMOS
15.00 g., 0.900 Gold 0.434 oz. AGW, 25.5 mm. **Obv:** Scale **Rev:** Value flanked by sprigs

Date	Mintage	VF20	XF40	MS60	MS63	MS65
1976 So	50	PF63 775	PF65 800			

KM# 69 NUEVO PESO
9.00 g., Aluminum-Bronze, 29 mm. **Obv:** Head of Jose Gervasio Artigas left **Rev:** Value in front of supine wheat stalk **Edge:** Plain **Shape:** 12-sided **Note:** Medal rotation.

Date	Mintage	VF20	XF40	MS60	MS63	MS65
1976 So	65,540,000	—	—	0.30	0.60	1.25
1976 So Proof	—	—	—	—	—	—
1977 So	7,360,000	—	—	0.30	0.65	1.45
1978 So	27,100,000	—	—	0.30	0.65	1.45

KM# 69a NUEVO PESO
13.50 g., 0.900 Silver 0.3906 oz. ASW, 30 mm. **Obv:** Head of Jose Gervasio Artigas left **Rev:** Value in front of supine wheat stalk

Date	Mintage	VF20	XF40	MS60	MS63	MS65
1976 So	200	PF63 35.00	PF65 38.00			

KM# 69b NUEVO PESO
23.00 g., 0.900 Gold 0.6655 oz. AGW, 30 mm. **Obv:** Head of Jose Gervasio Artigas left **Rev:** Value in front of supine wheat stalk

Date	Mintage	VF20	XF40	MS60	MS63	MS65
1976 So	50	PF63 1,250	PF65 1,300			

KM# 74 NUEVO PESO
6.00 g., Copper-Nickel, 24 mm. **Obv:** Radiant sun peeking over arms within wreath **Rev:** Flower and value **Note:** Medal rotation.

Date	Mintage	VF20	XF40	MS60	MS63	MS65
1980 So	50,000,000	0.20	0.25	0.35	0.65	1.00

KM# 74a NUEVO PESO
7.00 g., 0.900 Silver 0.2025 oz. ASW, 24 mm. **Obv:** Radiant sun peeking over arms within wreath **Rev:** Flower and value

Date	Mintage	VF20	XF40	MS60	MS63	MS65
1980 So	300	PF63 22.00	PF65 25.00			

KM# 74b NUEVO PESO
11.65 g., 0.900 Gold 0.3371 oz. AGW, 24 mm. **Obv:** Radiant sun peeking over arms within wreath **Rev:** Flower and value

Date	Mintage	VF20	XF40	MS60	MS63	MS65
1980 So	100	PF63 625	PF65 650			

KM# 76 NUEVO PESO
6.94 g., 0.900 Silver 0.2008 oz. ASW **Obv:** National flag

Date	Mintage	VF20	XF40	MS60	MS63	MS65
1981	100	PF63 25.00	PF65 30.00			

KM# 95 NUEVO PESO
0.87 g., Stainless Steel, 12 mm. **Obv:** Radiant sun **Rev:** Value within wreath **Note:** Medal rotation.

Date	Mintage	VF20	XF40	MS60	MS63	MS65
1989 (a)	500,000	—	0.50	0.75	1.50	2.00

KM# 77 2 NUEVOS PESOS
7.00 g., Copper-Nickel-Zinc, 25 mm. **Subject:** World Food Day **Obv:** Wheat stalks divide date and country name **Rev:** Value **Edge:** Plain **Shape:** 12-sided

Date	Mintage	VF20	XF40	MS60	MS63	MS65
1981	95,000,000	0.25	0.35	0.50	1.00	1.50

KM# 77a 2 NUEVOS PESOS
14.53 g., 0.900 Gold 0.4204 oz. AGW, 25 mm. **Subject:** World Food Day **Obv:** Wheat stalks divide date country name **Rev:** Value

Date	Mintage	VF20	XF40	MS60	MS63	MS65
1981	100	PF63 775	PF65 800			

KM# 65 5 NUEVOS PESOS
14.50 g., Copper-Nickel-Aluminum, 33 mm. **Subject:** 150th Anniversary - Revolutionary Movement **Obv:** Artigas head facing within square above inscription **Rev:** Upright design **Note:** Medal rotation.

Date	Mintage	VF20	XF40	MS60	MS63	MS65
ND-1975 So	3,000,000	0.50	0.75	1.25	3.50	5.00

KM# 65a 5 NUEVOS PESOS
18.43 g., 0.900 Silver 0.5333 oz. ASW, 33 mm. **Subject:** 150th Anniversary - Revolutionary Movement **Obv:** Artigas head facing within square above inscription **Rev:** Upright design

Date	Mintage	VF20	XF40	MS60	MS63	MS65
ND-1975 So	2,000	PF63 22.00	PF65 25.00			

KM# 65b 5 NUEVOS PESOS
14.50 g., 0.900 Gold 0.4196 oz. AGW, 33 mm. **Subject:** 150th Anniversary - Revolutionary Movement **Obv:** Artigas head facing within square above inscription **Rev:** Upright design

Date	Mintage	VF20	XF40	MS60	MS63	MS65
ND-1975 So	1,000	PF63 800	PF65 825			

Note: 50 pieces each in aluminum, alpaca and copper are reported to have been struck

KM# 70 5 NUEVOS PESOS
14.50 g., Copper-Nickel-Aluminum, 33 mm. **Subject:** 250th Anniversary - Founding of Montevideo **Obv:** Head facing to left of value **Rev:** Crowned shield within wreath **Note:** Medal rotation.

Date	Mintage	VF20	XF40	MS60	MS63	MS65
1976 So	300,000	0.75	1.00	1.50	4.00	5.50

KM# 70a 5 NUEVOS PESOS
30.00 g., 0.900 Gold 0.8681 oz. AGW **Subject:** 250th Anniversary - Founding of Montevideo **Obv:** Head facing to left of value **Rev:** Crowned shield within wreath

Date	Mintage	VF20	XF40	MS60	MS63	MS65
1976 So	100	PF63 1,650	PF65 1,750			

KM# 70b 5 NUEVOS PESOS

Silver **Subject:** 250th Anniversary - Founding of Montevideo **Obv:** Head facing to left of value **Rev:** Crowned shield within wreath

Date	Mintage	VF20	XF40	MS60	MS63	MS65
1976 So	300	—	—	—	150	175

KM# 75 5 NUEVOS PESOS

8.00 g., Copper-Nickel-Zinc, 26 mm. **Obv:** National flag **Rev:** Flower and value **Note:** Medal rotation.

Date	Mintage	VF20	XF40	MS60	MS63	MS65
1980 So	50,000,000	0.20	0.40	0.75	1.50	2.00
1981 So	—	0.20	0.40	0.75	1.50	2.00

KM# 75a 5 NUEVOS PESOS

9.30 g., 0.900 Silver 0.2691 oz. ASW, 26.15 mm. **Obv:** National flag **Rev:** Flower and value

Date	Mintage	VF20	XF40	MS60	MS63	MS65
1980 So	300	PF63 28.00	PF65 30.00			

KM# 75b 5 NUEVOS PESOS

15.60 g., 0.900 Gold 0.4514 oz. AGW, 26.15 mm. **Obv:** National flag **Rev:** Flower and value

Date	Mintage	VF20	XF40	MS60	MS63	MS65
1980 So	100	PF63 800	PF65 825			

KM# 78 5 NUEVOS PESOS

9.30 g., 0.900 Silver 0.2691 oz. ASW **Obv:** Coat of arms

Date	Mintage	VF20	XF40	MS60	MS63	MS65
1981	100	PF63 28.00	PF65 30.00			

KM# 92 5 NUEVOS PESOS

1.36 g., Stainless Steel, 15 mm. **Obv:** Radiant sun **Rev:** Value and date within wreath **Note:** Medal rotation.

Date	Mintage	VF20	XF40	MS60	MS63	MS65
1989 (a)	65,000,000	—	0.15	0.25	0.35	0.65

KM# 79 10 NUEVOS PESOS

10.00 g., Copper-Nickel, 28 mm. **Obv:** Bust of Jose Gervasio Artigas half left **Rev:** Flower and value **Note:** Medal rotation.

Date	Mintage	VF20	XF40	MS60	MS63	MS65
1981 So	3,000,000	0.20	0.50	0.75	1.75	2.25

KM# 79a 10 NUEVOS PESOS

11.63 g., 0.900 Silver 0.3365 oz. ASW, 28 mm. **Obv:** Bust of Jose Gervasio Artigas half left **Rev:** Flower and value

Date	Mintage	VF20	XF40	MS60	MS63	MS65
1981 So	100	PF63 32.00	PF65 35.00			

KM# 79b 10 NUEVOS PESOS

19.48 g., 0.900 Gold 0.5637 oz. AGW, 28 mm. **Obv:** Bust of Jose Gervasio Artigas half left **Rev:** Flower and value

Date	Mintage	VF20	XF40	MS60	MS63	MS65
1981 So	100	PF63 1,000	PF65 1,100			

KM# 93 10 NUEVOS PESOS

2.94 g., Stainless Steel, 18 mm. **Obv:** Radiant sun **Rev:** Value and date within wreath **Note:** Medal rotation.

Date	Mintage	VF20	XF40	MS60	MS63	MS65
1989 (a)	75,000,000	—	0.20	0.30	0.45	0.75

KM# 86 20 NUEVOS PESOS

Copper-Nickel, 30 mm. **Subject:** World Fisheries Conference **Obv:** Radiant sun peeking out above arms within wreath **Rev:** Fish **Edge:** Reeded **Note:** Medal rotation.

Date	Mintage	VF20	XF40	MS60	MS63	MS65
1984 (l)	3,771	—	—	12.00	20.00	30.00

KM# 86a 20 NUEVOS PESOS

11.66 g., 0.925 Silver 0.3468 oz. ASW, 30 mm. **Subject:** World Fisheries Conference **Obv:** Radiant sun peeking out above arms within wreath **Rev:** Fish

Date	Mintage	VF20	XF40	MS60	MS63	MS65
1984	25,000	PF63 10.00	PF65 15.00			

KM# 86b 20 NUEVOS PESOS

19.60 g., 0.917 Gold 0.5779 oz. AGW, 30 mm. **Subject:** World Fisheries Conference **Obv:** Radiant sun peeking out above arms within wreath **Rev:** Fish

Date	Mintage	VF20	XF40	MS60	MS63	MS65
1984	100	PF63 1,000	PF65 1,100			

KM# 94 50 NUEVOS PESOS

4.80 g., Stainless Steel, 23 mm. **Obv:** Radiant sun **Rev:** Value and date within wreath **Note:** Medal rotation.

Date	Mintage	VF20	XF40	MS60	MS63	MS65
1989 (a)	42,000,000	—	0.20	0.35	0.50	0.85

KM# 80 100 NUEVOS PESOS

12.00 g., 0.900 Silver 0.3472 oz. ASW, 33 mm. **Obv:** Hydroelectric dam **Rev:** Conjoined arms with radiant sun peeking out above arms within wreath

Date	Mintage	VF20	XF40	MS60	MS63	MS65
1981 So	25,000	—	—	6.75	9.00	12.50

KM# 96 100 NUEVOS PESOS

7.56 g., Stainless Steel, 25 mm. **Obv:** Gaucho with hat right **Rev:** Value and date within wreath **Note:** Medal rotation.

Date	Mintage	VF20	XF40	MS60	MS63	MS65
1989 (a)	35,000,000	—	0.35	0.50	0.75	1.50

KM# 97 200 NUEVOS PESOS

10.00 g., Copper-Nickel-Zinc, 27 mm. **Obv:** Unchained Liberty **Rev:** Value and date within wreath **Edge:** Segmented reeding **Note:** Medal rotation.

Date	Mintage	VF20	XF40	MS60	MS63	MS65
1989 (a)	15,000,000	—	—	0.75	1.00	1.50

KM# 82 500 NUEVOS PESOS

12.00 g., 0.900 Silver 0.3472 oz. ASW, 33 mm. **Obv:** Hydroelectric dam **Rev:** Radiant sun peeking out above arms within wreath above date and legend **Rev. Legend:** REPRESA 9 DE FEBRERO DE 1973

Date	Mintage	VF20	XF40	MS60	MS63	MS65
1983 So	15,000	—	—	6.75	9.00	12.50

KM# 90 500 NUEVOS PESOS

12.00 g., 0.900 Silver 0.3472 oz. ASW, 33 mm. **Obv:** Head of General Leandro Gomez half left **Rev:** Building above value and date

Date	Mintage	VF20	XF40	MS60	MS63	MS65
1986 Mo	6,000	PF63 15.00	PF65 20.00			

KM# 98 500 NUEVOS PESOS

11.80 g., Copper-Nickel, 29 mm. **Obv:** Bust of Jose Gervasio Artigas half right **Rev:** Value and date within wreath **Note:** Medal rotation.

Date	Mintage	VF20	XF40	MS60	MS63	MS65
1989 (a)	22,000,000	—	—	1.50	2.50	4.50

KM# 131 2000 NUEVOS PESOS

65.00 g., 0.900 Silver 1.8808 oz. ASW, 50 mm. **Subject:** Visit of King and Queen of Spain **Obv:** Uruguay and Spanish arms **Rev:** Conjoined busts of King and Queen **Rev. Legend:** VISITA DE LOS REYES DE ESPANA A LA R.O. DEL URUGUAY MAYO 1983 **Edge:** Reeded

Date	Mintage	VF20	XF40	MS60	MS63	MS65
1983	20,000	PF63 55.00	PF65 65.00			

KM# 87 2000 NUEVOS PESOS

25.00 g., 0.900 Silver 0.7234 oz. ASW, 40 mm. **Subject:** 140th Anniversary of Silver Coinage and 25th Meeting of Inter-American Bank Governors **Obv:** Radiant sun peeking over arms in wreath within beaded circle (1844 coin) **Rev:** Map within U-shaped auditorium seating design below inscription **Note:** Coin rotation.

Date	Mintage	VF20	XF40	MS60	MS63	MS65
1984 (v)	15,000	PF63 22.00	PF65 25.00			

KM# 88 2000 NUEVOS PESOS

25.00 g., 0.900 Silver 0.7234 oz. ASW, 40 mm. **Subject:** 25th Meeting of Inter-American Bank Governors **Obv:** Radiant sun peeking over arms within wreath **Rev:** Map within U-shaped auditorium seating design below inscription **Note:** Coin rotation.

Date	Mintage	VF20	XF40	MS60	MS63	MS65
1984 (v)	15,000	PF63 22.00	PF65 25.00			

KM# 81 5000 NUEVOS PESOS

20.00 g., 0.900 Gold 0.5787 oz. AGW, 33 mm. **Obv:** Hydroelectric dam **Rev:** Conjoined arms with radiant sun peeking out above arms within wreath

Date	Mintage	VF20	XF40	MS60	MS63	MS65
1981 So	3,000	PF63 1,000	PF65 1,100			

KM# 91 5000 NUEVOS PESOS

25.00 g., 0.900 Silver 0.7234 oz. ASW, 37 mm. **Subject:** 20th Anniversary of Central Bank **Obv:** National arms, sun face **Rev:** Triangular wheel design

Date	Mintage	VF20	XF40	MS60	MS63	MS65
1987 So	20,000	PF63 22.00	PF65 25.00			

Note: Two varieties: A in AG900 is larger than the others, the second variety the A is the same size.

KM# 91a 5000 NUEVOS PESOS

42.76 g., Gold **Obv:** Double wheel design **Rev:** Snowflake design

Date	Mintage	VF20	XF40	MS60	MS63	MS65
1987 So	—	PF63 2,350	PF65 2,500			

KM# 99 5000 NUEVOS PESOS

25.00 g., 0.900 Silver 0.7234 oz. ASW, 37 mm. **Subject:** Latin America Presidents' Assembly **Obv:** Value and date within circle **Rev:** Assorted arms

Date	Mintage	VF20	XF40	MS60	MS63	MS65
1988 (So)	—	PF63 22.00	PF65 25.00			

KM# 85 20000 NUEVOS PESOS

20.00 g., 0.900 Gold 0.5787 oz. AGW, 33 mm. **Obv:** Hydroelectric dam **Rev:** Radiant sun peeking out above arms within wreath and legend **Rev. Legend:** REPRESA 9 DE FEBRERO DE 1973 **Edge:** Reeded

Date	Mintage	VF20	XF40	MS60	MS63	MS65
1983 So	1,500	PF63 925	PF65 1,000			

KM# 132 20000 NUEVOS PESOS

20.00 g., 0.900 Gold 0.5787 oz. AGW, 33 mm. **Subject:** Visit of King and Queen of Spain **Obv:** Arms of Uruguay and Spain **Rev:** Conjoined busts left **Rev. Legend:** VISITA DE LOS REYES DE ESPANA A LA R.O. DEL URUGUAY MAY 1983 **Edge:** Reeded

Date	Mintage	VF20	XF40	MS60	MS63	MS65
1983	1,500	PF63 950	PF65 1,050			

KM# 89 20000 NUEVOS PESOS

20.00 g., 0.900 Gold 0.5787 oz. AGW, 33 mm. **Subject:** 130th Anniversary of Gold Coinage and 25th Meeting of Inter-American Bank Governors **Obv:** Radiant sun peeking out above arms within wreath of assorted flags **Rev:** Map within U-shaped auditorium seating area design below value and inscription **Edge:** Reeded

Date	Mintage	VF20	XF40	MS60	MS63	MS65
1984 (v)	1,500	PF63 925	PF65 1,000			

KM# 101 25000 NUEVOS PESOS

12.50 g., 0.900 Silver 0.3617 oz. ASW, 33 mm. **Subject:** 25th Anniversary of Central Bank **Obv:** Bell design above value **Rev:** Towered bank building to lower right of arms

Date	Mintage	VF20	XF40	MS60	MS63	MS65
1992 (So)	50,000	—	—	7.00	9.00	12.50

KM# 100 50000 NUEVOS PESOS

27.00 g., 0.925 Silver 0.803 oz. ASW, 40 mm. **Subject:** Ibero - American Series **Obv:** Arms within center circle of value, country name and assorted arms **Rev:** Crossed flags and crowned shield divides dates **Note:** Coin rotation.

Date	Mintage	VF20	XF40	MS60	MS63	MS65
1991 (So)	40,000	PF63 40.00	PF65 45.00			

REFORM COINAGE

1,000 Nuevos Pesos = 1 Uruguayan Peso;
100 Centesimos = 1 Uruguayan Peso (UYP)
March 1993

KM# 102 10 CENTESIMOS

1.60 g., Stainless Steel, 15 mm. **Obv:** Artigas head right **Rev:** Value, date and sprig **Edge:** Plain **Note:** Coin rotation.

Date	Mintage	VF20	XF40	MS60	MS63	MS65
1994 (rj)	40,000,000	—	—	0.25	0.50	0.65

KM# 105 20 CENTESIMOS

2.25 g., Stainless Steel, 18 mm. **Obv:** Artigas head right **Rev:** Value, date and sprig **Note:** Coin rotation.

Date	Mintage	VF20	XF40	MS60	MS63	MS65
1994 (rj)	40,000,000	—	—	0.30	0.60	0.75

KM# 106 50 CENTESIMOS

3.00 g., Stainless Steel, 21 mm. **Obv:** Bust of Artigas right **Obv. Legend:** REPUBLICA ORIENTAL DEL URUGUAY **Rev:** Value, date and sprig **Edge:** Plain **Note:** Coin rotation.

Date	Mintage	VF20	XF40	MS60	MS63	MS65
1994 (rj)	40,000,000	—	—	0.30	0.70	0.80
1998 (a)	40,000,000	—	—	0.30	0.70	0.80

KM# 103.1 UN PESO URUGUAYO

3.50 g., Aluminum-Bronze, 20 mm. **Obv:** Artigas head right **Rev:** Value and date **Note:** Left point of bust shoulder points at "U" in Republic.

Date	Mintage	VF20	XF40	MS60	MS63	MS65
1994 (ba)	50,000,000	—	—	0.25	0.50	0.75

KM# 103.2 UN PESO URUGUAYO

3.50 g., Aluminum-Bronze, 20 mm. **Obv:** Bust of Artigas right **Obv. Legend:** REPUBLICA ORIENTAL DEL URUGUAY **Rev:** Value and date **Edge:** Plain **Note:** Medal rotation; left point of bust shoulder points at "P" in Republic.

Date	Mintage	VF20	XF40	MS60	MS63	MS65
1998 So	60,000,000	—	—	0.20	0.40	0.60

KM# 104.1 2 PESOS URUGUAYOS

4.50 g., Aluminum-Bronze, 23 mm. **Obv:** Artigas head right **Rev:** Value and date **Note:** Medal rotation. Left point of bust shoulder points at "U" in "Republic".

Date	Mintage	VF20	XF40	MS60	MS63	MS65
1994 (ba)	60,000,000	—	—	0.60	1.00	1.50

KM# 104.2 2 PESOS URUGUAYOS
4.50 g., Aluminum-Bronze, 23 mm. **Obv:** Bust of Artigas right **Obv. Legend:** REPUBLICA ORIENTAL DEL URUGUAY **Rev:** Value and date **Edge:** Plain **Note:** Medal rotation. Left point of bust shoulder points at "P" in "Republic".

Date	Mintage	VF20	XF40	MS60	MS63	MS65
1998 So	20,000,000	—	—	0.50	0.75	1.00

KM# 121 10 PESOS URUGUAYOS
10.40 g., Bi-Metallic Aluminum-Bronze center in Stainless Steel ring, 28 mm. **Obv:** Artigas head right within circle **Rev:** Value above signature within circle **Edge:** Plain

Date	Mintage	VF20	XF40	MS60	MS63	MS65
2000 (ba)	10,000,000	—	—	1.50	1.75	3.00

Note: Issued 2004

KM# 113 50 PESOS URUGUAYOS
12.50 g., 0.900 Silver 0.3617 oz. ASW, 33 mm. **Subject:** Bicentennial - City of Melo **Obv:** Map and date **Rev:** City arms, value and date

Date	Mintage	VF20	XF40	MS60	MS63	MS65
1996 So	10,000	PF63 12.00	PF65 16.00	PF67 18.00		

KM# 111 100 PESOS URUGUAYOS
25.00 g., 0.900 Silver 0.7234 oz. ASW, 37 mm. **Subject:** 50th Anniversary - F.A.O. **Obv:** Wheat stalks divide value **Rev:** F.A.O logo and dates within circle

Date	Mintage	VF20	XF40	MS60	MS63	MS65
ND1995 (Mo)	3,000	PF63 32.00	PF65 37.00	PF67 42.00		

KM# 112 100 PESOS URUGUAYOS
25.00 g., 0.900 Silver 0.7234 oz. ASW, 37 mm. **Subject:** Centennial - Central Bank **Obv:** Radiant sun face **Rev:** Central Bank building

Date	Mintage	VF20	XF40	MS60	MS63	MS65
1996 (Mo)	50,000	PF63 17.00	PF65 22.00	PF67 25.00		

KM# 107 200 PESOS URUGUAYOS
27.00 g., 0.925 Silver 0.803 oz. ASW, 40 mm. **Subject:** Environmental Protection **Obv:** Arms in wreath within center circle of assorted arms **Rev:** Pampas deer right

Date	Mintage	VF20	XF40	MS60	MS63	MS65
1994 (Mo)	13,000	PF63 30.00	PF65 35.00	PF67 40.00		

KM# 116 200 PESOS URUGUAYOS
28.28 g., 0.925 Silver 0.841 oz. ASW, 38.61 mm. **Subject:** 50th Anniversary - United Nations

Date	Mintage	VF20	XF40	MS60	MS63	MS65
1995 (l)	8,251	PF63 50.00	PF65 60.00	PF67 70.00		

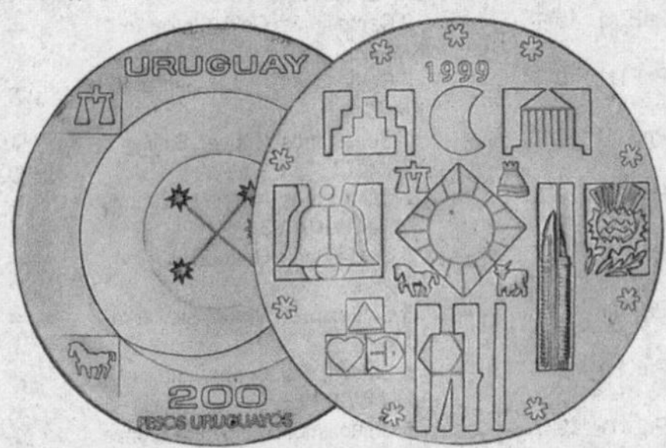

KM# 115 200 PESOS URUGUAYOS
25.00 g., 0.900 Silver 0.7234 oz. ASW, 37 mm. **Subject:** Millennium Change **Obv:** Southern Cross stars within design **Rev:** Stylized symbols of mankinds connection to the stars **Edge Lettering:** CAMBIO DE MILENIO twice

Date	Mintage	VF20	XF40	MS60	MS63	MS65
1999 (Mo)	50,000	—	—	22.00	32.00	45.00

KM# 114 250 PESOS URUGUAYOS
27.00 g., 0.925 Silver 0.803 oz. ASW, 40 mm. **Subject:** Ibero - American Series **Obv:** Arms in wreath within center circle of assorted arms **Rev:** Standing figures leaning on wooden gate

Date	Mintage	VF20	XF40	MS60	MS63	MS65
1997 (Mo)	11,000	PF63 40.00	PF65 45.00	PF67 50.00		

KM# 117 250 PESOS URUGUAYOS
27.00 g., 0.925 Silver 0.803 oz. ASW, 40 mm. **Series:** Ibero-American **Obv:** Arms in wreath within center circle of assorted arms **Rev:** Man and woman on horseback **Edge:** Reeded

Date	Mintage	VF20	XF40	MS60	MS63	MS65
2000 (Mo)	8,000	PF63 45.00	PF65 50.00	PF67 55.00		

GOLD BULLION COINAGE

KM# 108 1/4 GAUCHO
8.64 g., 0.900 Gold 0.250 oz. AGW, 18 mm. **Obv:** Head of Gaucho right **Rev:** Value within wreath **Edge:** Reeded

Date	Mintage	VF20	XF40	MS60	MS63	MS65
1992 So	500	PF63 365	PF65 385	PF67 415		

KM# 109 1/2 GAUCHO
17.28 g., 0.900 Gold 0.500 oz. AGW, 23 mm. **Obv:** Head of Gaucho right **Rev:** 1/2 within wreath **Edge:** Reeded

Date	Mintage	VF20	XF40	MS60	MS63	MS65
1992 So	375	PF63 710	PF65 740	PF67 800		

KM# 110 GAUCHO
34.56 g., 0.900 Gold 1.000 oz. AGW, 31 mm. **Obv:** Head of Gaucho right **Rev:** Value within wreath **Edge:** Reeded

Date	Mintage	VF20	XF40	MS60	MS63	MS65
1992 So	250	PF63 1,400	PF65 1,450	PF67 1,525		

ESSAIS

KM#	Date	Mintage	Identification	Mkt Val
E5	1924(p)	12	Centesimo. Nickel. KM19.	500
E6	1924(p)	12	2 Centesimos. Nickel. KM20.	600
E7	1924(p)	12	5 Centesimos. Nickel. KM21.	700
E8	1930(a)	70	10 Centesimos. Aluminum-Bronze. KM25.	100
E10	1930(a)	60	10 Centesimos. Gold. Head laureate right. Puma walking left in front of sun rays. KM25.	4,500
E11	1930(a)	—	20 Centesimos. Aluminum-Bronze. Seated figure left above date. Wheat stalks divides value. KM24.	100
EA12	1930	—	20 Centesimos. Silver.	—
E12	1930(a)	60	20 Centesimos. Gold. KM24.	5,000
E13	1930(a)	70	5 Pesos. Aluminum-Bronze. KM27.	225
E14	1930(a)	60	5 Pesos. Gold. KM27.	4,500
E15	1983	100	500 Pesos. Gold. ENSAYO, KM82.	425
E16	1983	200	2000 Pesos. Copper. KM83.	95.00
E17	1983	20	2000 Pesos. Gold. KM83.	2,750
E18	1983	200	20000 Pesos. Silver. ENSAYO, KM85.	65.00
E19	1983	1,500	20000 Pesos. Gold. ENSAYO, KM85.	475
E20	1984	20,500	20 Pesos. Silver. ENSAYO, KM86a.	22.50
E21	1984	600	20 Pesos. Gold. ENSAYO, KM86b.	375
E22	1984	1,500	20000 Pesos. Gold. ENSAYO, KM89.	425

PATTERNS

Including off metal strikes

KM#	Date	Mintage	Identification	Mkt Val
Pn38	ND-1904	—	4 Centesimos. Copper-Nickel. Radiant sun face. Value below banner in center.	275
PnA39	1916	—	50 Centesimos. Silver.	—
Pn39	1916	45	50 Centesimos. Silver.	—
Pn40	1917	20	Peso. Silver.	—
PnA41	1920	—	20 Centesimos. Copper-Nickel. Similar to KM#24.	—
Pn41	1942	10	20 Centesimos. Copper Gilt.	—
PnA42	1942	20	20 Centesimos. Silver Gilt.	—
Pn42	1942	—	20 Centesimos. Gold. KM29.	575
Pn43	1942So	—	Peso. Gold. KM30.	1,400
Pn44	1943So	—	2 Centesimos. Gold. KM20a.	1,000
Pn45	1943So	—	50 Centesimos. Gold. KM31.	1,400

KM#	Date	Mintage	Identification	Mkt Val
Pn46	1953	100	Centesimo. 0.916. Gold. KM32.	—
Pn47	1953	—	2 Centesimos. Aluminum. KM33.	—
Pn48	1953	100	2 Centesimos. 0.916. Gold. KM33.	—
Pn49	1953	100	5 Centesimos. 0.916. Gold. KM34.	650
Pn50	1953	100	10 Centesimos. 0.916. Gold. KM35.	1,000
PnB51	1953	—	Peso. Brass. Similar to PNA51.	—
PnC51	1953	—	Peso. Copper-Nickel. Similar to PNA51.	—
PnD51	1953	—	Peso. Silver. Similar to PNA51.	—
Pn51	1954	100	20 Centesimos. 0.983. Gold. KM36.	650
Pn52	1959	—	10 Centesimos. 0.916. Gold. KM35.	—
Pn53	1960	100	2 Centesimos. Gold. KM37.	—
PnA54	ND-1960	—	5 Centesimos. Nickel. Similar to KM#34 and KM#38 reverses. WIth a "Z" inside the base of the 5.	135
PnB54	ND-1960	—	5 Centesimos. Aluminum. Similar to KM#34 and KM#38 reverses. With "HA" in the base of the 5 and "MBL" above the 5.	135
Pn54	1960	100	5 Centesimos. Gold. KM38.	—
Pn55	1960	100	10 Centesimos. Gold. KM39.	—
Pn56	1960	100	25 Centesimos. Gold. KM40.	—
Pn57	1960	100	50 Centesimos. Gold. KM41.	—
Pn58	1960	—	Peso. Gold. KM42.	1,350
Pn59	1960	—	10 Pesos. Gold.	—
PnA60	1961	—	10 Pesos. Gold. KM43.	—
Pn60	1965So	10	20 Centesimos. Copper. KM44.	—
Pn61	1965So	—	20 Centesimos. Silver. KM44.	—
Pn62	1965So	—	20 Centesimos. Gold. KM44.	—
Pn63	1965So	25	50 Centesimos. Aluminum-Bronze. KM45.	—
Pn64	1965So	10	50 Centesimos. Copper. KM45.	—
Pn65	1965So	25	50 Centesimos. Copper-Nickel. KM45.	—
Pn66	1965So	—	50 Centesimos. Silver. KM45.	—
Pn67	1965So	—	50 Centesimos. Gold. KM45.	—
Pn68	1965So	10	Peso. Copper. KM46.	—
PnA69	1965	—	Peso. Aluminum-Bronze. Similar to KM#46. Planchet is 5 Pesos.	—
Pn69	1965So	25	Peso. Copper-Nickel. KM46.	—
Pn70	1965So	—	Peso. Silver. KM46.	—
Pn71	1965So	—	Peso. Gold. KM46.	—
Pn72	1965So	10	5 Pesos. Copper. KM47.	—
PnA73	1965	—	5 Pesos. Copper-Nickel. Similar to KM#47. Planchet is 10 Pesos.	—
Pn73	1965So	25	5 Pesos. Copper-Nickel. KM47.	—
Pn74	1965So	—	5 Pesos. Silver. KM47.	—
Pn75	1965So	—	5 Pesos. Gold. KM47.	—
Pn76	1965So	10	10 Pesos. Copper. KM48.	—
Pn77	1965So	—	10 Pesos. Silver. KM48.	—
Pn78	1968So	100	Peso. Copper-Nickel. KM49.	35.00
Pn79	1968So	1,000	Peso. Silver. KM49.	25.00
Pn80	1968So	100	5 Pesos. Copper-Nickel. KM50.	40.00
Pn81	1968So	1,000	5 Pesos. Silver. KM50.	30.00
Pn82	1968So	100	10 Pesos. Copper-Nickel. KM51.	40.00
Pn83	1968So	1,000	10 Pesos. Silver. KM51.	35.00
PnA84	1968S	—	20 Pesos. Yellow Metal.	—
PnB84	1968	—	20 Pesos. Copper-Nickel. Similar to KM#56; Proof.	—
PnC84	1968	—	20 Pesos. Silver. Star. Similar to KM#56.	—
Pn84	1968So	1,000	20 Pesos. Silver.	30.00
PnA85	1968S	—	50 Pesos. Yellow Metal.	—
PnB85	1968	—	50 Pesos. Copper-Nickel. Similar to KM#57; Proof.	—
PnC85	1968	—	50 Pesos. Silver. Star. Similar to KM#57.	—
Pn85	1968So	1,000	50 Pesos. Silver.	35.00
Pn86	1969So	50	Peso. Copper-Nickel. KM52.	40.00
Pn87	1969So	1,000	Peso. 0.900. Silver. KM52.	25.00
PnA88	1969So	—	Peso. 0.750. Gold. KM52.	500
Pn88	1969So	50	5 Pesos. Copper-Nickel. KM53.	40.00
Pn89	1969So	1,000	5 Pesos. 0.900. Silver. KM53.	20.00
PnA90	1969So	—	5 Pesos. 0.750. Gold. KM53.	650
Pn90	1969So	50	10 Pesos. Copper-Nickel. KM54.	40.00
Pn91	1969So	1,000	10 Pesos. 0.900. Silver. KM54.	25.00
PnA92	1969	—	10 Pesos. 0.750. Gold. Similar to KM#54; Proof.	750
Pn92	1969	20,000	1000 Pesos. Copper.	30.00
Pn93	1969	250	1000 Pesos. Silver.	45.00
Pn95	1970So	—	20 Pesos. Silver. Star on reverse. KM56.	—
Pn96	1970So	—	20 Pesos. Silver. No star on reverse. KM56.	25.00
Pn97	1970So	1,000	20 Pesos. Gold. KM56.	400
Pn98	1970So	—	50 Pesos. Silver. KM57.	25.00
Pn99	1970So	1,000	50 Pesos. Gold. KM57.	450
Pn100	1971So	—	50 Pesos. Copper-Nickel. KM58.	75.00
Pn101	1971So	80	50 Pesos. Copper-Nickel. With F. ORRELLANA, P., KM58.	125
Pn102	1971So	2,000	50 Pesos. Silver. KM58.	30.00
Pn103	1971So	200	50 Pesos. Gold. KM58.	475
Pn104	1972So	3	100 Pesos.	—
Pn105	1972So	12	100 Pesos. Alpaca.	350
Pn106	1973	—	100 Pesos. Silver. KM59.	35.00
PnA107	1973	—	100 Pesos. Gold. Similar to KM#59.	—
PnB107	1973	50	100 Pesos. Aluminum.	—
PnD107	1973	50	100 Pesos. Copper.	—
PnC107	1975	50	5 Pesos. Alpaca. Similar to KM#65.	1,850
Pn107	1976	—	5 Nuevos Pesos. Aluminum. KM70.	125
PnA108	1976	—	10 Centesimos. Copper. Similar to KM#66.	—
PnB108	1976	—	10 Centesimos. Aluminum. Similar to KM#66.	—
PnC108	1976	—	20 Centesimos. Copper. Similar to KM#67.	—
PnD108	1976	—	20 Centesimos. Aluminum. Similar to KM#67.	—
PnE108	1976	—	50 Centesimos. Copper. Similar to KM#68.	—
PnF108	1976	—	50 Centesimos. Aluminum. Similar to KM#68.	—
PnG108	1976	—	Nuevo Peso. Copper. Similar to KM#69.	—
PnH108	1976	—	Nuevo Peso. Aluminum. Similar to KM#69.	—
Pn108	1976	—	5 Nuevos Pesos. Copper-Aluminum. KM70.	125
Pn109	1976	—	5 Nuevos Pesos. Copper-Nickel. KM70.	200
Pn110	1976	—	5 Nuevos Pesos. Silver. KM70.	300
PnA111	1977	—	Centesimo. Gold. Similar to KM#71.	—
PnB111	1977	—	Centesimo. Nickel. Similar to KM#71.	—
PnC111	1977	—	Centesimo. Copper. Similar to KM#71.	—
PnD111	1977	—	Centesimo. Aluminum-Bronze. Similar to KM#71.	—
PnE111	1977	—	2 Centesimos. Gold. Similar to KM#72.	—
PnF111	1977	—	2 Centesimos. Nickel. Similar to KM#72.	—
PnG111	1977	—	2 Centesimos. Copper. Similar to KM#72.	—
PnH111	1977	—	2 Centesimos. Aluminum-Bronze. Similar to KM#72.	—
PnI111	1977	—	5 Centesimos. Gold. Similar to KM#73.	—
PnJ111	1977	—	5 Centesimos. Nickel. Similar to KM#73.	—
PnK111	1977	—	5 Centesimos. Copper. Similar to KM#73.	—
PnL111	1977	—	5 Centesimos. Aluminum-Bronze. Similar to KM#73.	—
PnM111	1980	—	Nuevo Peso. Aluminum. Similar to KM#74.	—
PnN111	1980	—	Nuevo Peso. Copper. Similar to KM#74.	—
Pn111	1980	—	Peso. Brass. KM74.	—
PnA112	1980	—	5 Nuevos Pesos. Aluminum. Similar to KM#75.	—
PnB112	1980	—	5 Nuevos Pesos. Copper. Similar to KM#75.	—
Pn112	1980	—	5 Pesos. Brass. KM75.	—
PnA113	1981	—	2 Nuevos Pesos. Silver, Similar to KM#77; Proof.	—
PnB113	1981	—	2 Nuevos Pesos. Aluminum-Bronze. Similar to KM#77; Proof.	—
PnC113	1981	—	10 Nuevos Pesos. Copper. Similar to KM#79.	—
PnD113	1981	—	10 Nuevos Pesos. Aluminum. Similar to KM#79.	—
Pn113	1981	—	10 Pesos. Brass. KM79.	—
PnA114	1981So	—	100 Nuevos Pesos. 0.900. Gold. KM80.	1,300
PnB114	1981So	—	5000 Nuevos Pesos. 0.900. Gold. KM81.	1,500
PnC114	1983So	—	500 Nuevos Pesos. 0.900. Gold. KM82.	1,300
Pn114	1984	—	2000 Nuevos Pesos. Copper. Thick reeded. KM87.	—
Pn115	1984	—	2000 Nuevos Pesos. Aluminum. Thick reeded. KM87.	—
Pn116	1984	—	2000 Nuevos Pesos. Aluminum. Thick reeded. KM88.	—
Pn117	1984	—	2000 Nuevos Pesos. Aluminum. Thick reeded. KM88.	—
PnA118	1984	40	2000 Nuevos Pesos. Silver. Similar to KM#88. Different obverse and reverse; Proof.	—
Pn118	1984	—	20000 Nuevos Pesos. Aluminum. KM89.	—
PnA119	1984	—	20000 Nuevos Pesos. Silver. Similar to KM#89.	—
PnB119	1984	—	20000 Nuevos Pesos. Copper. Similar to KM#89.	—
PnC119	1984	—	20000 Nuevos Pesos. Brass. Similar to KM#89.	—
Pn119	1984	—	20000 Nuevos Pesos. Gold. KM89.	—
Pn120	1987	—	5000 Pesos. Alpaca. KM91; Alpaca.	—
Pn121	1987	—	5000 Pesos. Copper. KM91.	—
Pn122	1987	—	5000 Pesos. Bronze. KM91.	—
Pn123	1988	—	5000 Nuevos Pesos. Copper. Similar to KM#99.	—
Pn124	1988	—	5000 Nuevos Pesos. Alpaca. Similar to KM#99.	—

TRIAL STRIKES

KM#	Date	Mintage	Identification	Mkt Val
TS9	1984	—	20000 Nuevos Pesos. Silver. Radiant sun peeking over shield of arms in wreath within inner circle. PRUEBA.	125
TS10	1984	—	2000 Nuevos Pesos. Silver. PRUEBA. Map of Uruguay at right, map of North and South America above rising sun at lower left.	125
TS11	1984	—	2000 Nuevos Pesos. Copper. Radiant sun peeking over shield of arms in wreath within inner circle. PRUEBA.	85.00
TS12	1984	—	2000 Nuevos Pesos. Copper. PRUEBA. Map of Uruguay at right, map of North and South America above rising sun at lower left.	85.00
TS13	1984	—	2000 Nuevos Pesos. Copper Gilt. Radiant sun peeking over shield of arms in wreath within inner circle. PRUEBA.	100
TS14	1984	—	2000 Nuevos Pesos. Copper Gilt. PRUEBA. Map of Uruguay at right, map of North and South America above rising sun at lower left.	100
TS15	1984	—	2000 Nuevos Pesos. Aluminum. Radiant sun peeking over shield of arms in wreath within inner circle. PRUEBA.	85.00
TS16	1984	—	2000 Nuevos Pesos. Aluminum. PRUEBA. Map of Uruguay at right, map of North and South America above rising sun.	85.00
TS17	1984	—	2000 Nuevos Pesos. Silver. Radiant sun peeking over shield of arms within wreath. PRUEBA.	125
TS18	1984	—	2000 Nuevos Pesos. Silver. PRUEBA. Map of Uruguay at right, map of North and South America above rising sun.	125
TS19	1984	—	2000 Nuevos Pesos. Copper. Radiant sun peeking over arms within wreath. Winged Liberty divides value.	85.00
TS20	1984	—	2000 Nuevos Pesos. Copper. PRUEBA. Map of Uruguay at right, map of North and South America above rising sun at lower left.	85.00
TS21	1984	—	2000 Nuevos Pesos. Copper Gilt. Radiant sun peeking over shield of arms within wreath. PRUEBA.	100
TS22	1984	—	2000 Nuevos Pesos. Copper Gilt. PRUEBA. Map of Uruguay at right, map of North and South America above rising sun at lower left.	100
TS23	1984	—	2000 Nuevos Pesos. Aluminum. Radiant sun peeking over shield of arms within wreath. PRUEBA.	85.00
TS24	1984	—	2000 Nuevos Pesos. Aluminum. PRUEBA. Map of Uruguay at right, map of North and South America above rising sun at lower left.	85.00
TS25	1984	—	20000 Nuevos Pesos. Silver. Shield of arms flanked by flags in inner circle. PRUEBA.	135
TS26	1984	—	20000 Nuevos Pesos. Silver. PRUEBA. Map of Uruguay at right, map of North and South America above rising sun at lower left.	135
TS27	1984	—	20000 Nuevos Pesos. Copper. Shield of arms flanked by flags in inner circle. PRUEBA.	80.00
TS28	1984	—	20000 Nuevos Pesos. Copper. PRUEBA. Map of Uruguay at right, map of North and South America above rising sun at lower left.	80.00
TS29	1984	—	20000 Nuevos Pesos. Copper Gilt. Shield of arms flanked by flags in inner circle. PRUEBA.	90.00
TS30	1984	—	20000 Nuevos Pesos. Copper Gilt. PRUEBA. Map of Uruguay at right, map of North and South America above rising sun at lower left.	90.00

PIEDFORT

Double Thickness

KM#	Date	Mintage	Identification	Mkt Val
P6	1984	600	20 Pesos. Silver. KM86a.	90.00
P7	1984	—	2000 Nuevos Pesos. Silver. Plain. KM87.	200

KM#	Date	Mintage	Identification	Mkt Val
P8	1984	—	2000 Nuevos Pesos. Copper. Thick plain. KM87.	65.00
P9	1984	—	2000 Nuevos Pesos. Copper Gilt. Thick plain. KM87.	75.00
P10	1984	—	2000 Nuevos Pesos. Silver. Plain. KM88.	150
P11	1984	—	2000 Nuevos Pesos. Copper. Thick plain. KM88.	65.00
P12	1984	—	2000 Nuevos Pesos. Copper Gilt. Thick plain. KM88.	75.00
P13	1984	—	20000 Nuevos Pesos. Silver. Reeded. KM89.	150
P14	1984	—	20000 Nuevos Pesos. Silver. Reeded. KM89.	250
P15	1984	—	20000 Nuevos Pesos. Silver. Plain. KM89.	250
P16	1984	—	20000 Nuevos Pesos. Copper. Thick reeded. KM89.	80.00
P17	1984	—	20000 Nuevos Pesos. Copper. Reeded. KM89.	80.00
P18	1984	—	20000 Nuevos Pesos. Copper Gilt. KM89.	100

MINT SETS

KM#	Date	Mintage	Identification	Issue Price	Mkt Val
MS1	1969/70 (5)	—	KM52-54, 56-57 KM#MS1 was issued under the law no. 13,637 of December 21, 1967.	—	5.00
MS2	1969/70 (5)	—	KM52-54, 56-57 KM#MS2 was issued for the 11th Assembly of the Interamerica Bank.	—	5.00
MS3	1976 (4)	—	KM66-69	—	5.00
MS4	1976 (4)	—	KM#Pn107-110	—	400
MS5	1994-2003 (7)	—	KM#102, 105 (1994), 103.2, 104.2 (1998), 106 (2002), 120.1 (2003), 121 (2000) (ba)	—	15.00

PROOF SETS

KM#	Date	Mintage	Identification	Issue Price	Mkt Val
PS1	1953 (4)	100	KM32-35	—	365
PS2	1968 (5)	1,000	KM#Pn79, Pn81, Pn83-85	—	155
PS3	1968 (3)	50	KM49-51	—	200
PS4	1968 (3)	100	KM#Pn78, Pn80, Pn82	—	115
PS5	1969 (3)	50	KM#Pn86, Pn88, Pn90	—	120
PS6	1969 (3)	1,000	KM#Pn87, Pn89, Pn91	—	70.00
PS7	1969/70 (5)	1,000	KM#Pn87, Pn89, Pn91, Pn96, Pn98	—	120
PS8	1976 (4)	—	KM#66a-69a	—	125

The Republic of Uzbekistan (formerly the Uzbek S.S.R.), is bordered on the north by Kazakhstan, to the east by Kirghizia and Tajikistan, on the south by Afghanistan and on the west by Turkmenistan. The republic is comprised of the regions of Andizhan, Bukhara, Dzhizak, Ferghana, Kashkadar, Khorezm (Khiva), Namangan, Navoi, Samarkand, Surkhan-Darya, Syr-Darya, Tashkent and the Karakalpak Autonomous Republic. It has an area of 172,741 sq. mi. (447,400 sq. km.) and a population of 20.3 million. Capital: Tashkent.

Crude oil, natural gas, coal, copper, and gold deposits make up the chief resources, while intensive farming, based on artificial irrigation, provides an abundance of cotton.

On June 20, 1990 the Uzbek Supreme Soviet adopted a declaration of sovereignty, and in Aug. 1991, following an unsuccessful coup, declared itself independent as the "Republic of Uzbekistan", which was confirmed by referendum in Dec. That same month Uzbekistan became a member of the CIS.

MONETARY SYSTEM
100 Tiyin = 1 Som

REPUBLIC

STANDARD COINAGE

KM# 1.1 TIYIN
1.75 g., Brass Clad Steel, 16.9 mm. **Obv:** Arms within wreath below stars **Rev:** Tall thin 1 and date flanked by sprigs **Edge:** Plain

Date	Mintage	VF20	XF40	MS60	MS63	MS65
1994	—	—	—	1.50	3.00	5.50

KM# 1.2 TIYIN
1.75 g., Brass Clad Steel, 16.9 mm. **Obv:** Arms within wreath below stars **Rev:** Short thick 1 and date flanked by sprigs **Edge:** Plain

Date	Mintage	VF20	XF40	MS60	MS63	MS65
1994	—	—	—	0.15	0.25	0.35

KM# 2.1 3 TIYIN
2.70 g., Brass Plated Steel, 19.9 mm. **Obv:** Arms within wreath below stars **Rev:** Small 3 and date flanked by sprigs **Edge:** Reeded

Date	Mintage	VF20	XF40	MS60	MS63	MS65
1994	—	—	—	1.00	2.00	3.50

KM# 2.2 3 TIYIN
2.70 g., Brass Plated Steel, 19.9 mm. **Obv:** Arms within wreath below stars **Rev:** Large 3 and date flanked by sprigs **Edge:** Reeded

Date	Mintage	VF20	XF40	MS60	MS63	MS65
1994	—	—	—	0.25	0.35	0.50

KM# 3.1 5 TIYIN
3.40 g., Brass Plated Steel, 21.4 mm. **Obv:** Arms within wreath below stars **Rev:** Small 5 and date flanked by sprigs **Edge:** Reeded

Date	Mintage	VF20	XF40	MS60	MS63	MS65
1994	—	—	—	0.75	1.25	2.50

KM# 3.2 5 TIYIN
3.40 g., Brass Plated Steel, 21.4 mm. **Obv:** Arms within wreath below stars **Rev:** Large 5 and date flanked by sprigs **Edge:** Reeded

Date	Mintage	VF20	XF40	MS60	MS63	MS65
1994	—	—	—	0.30	0.45	0.65

KM# 4.1 10 TIYIN
2.85 g., Nickel Clad Steel, 18.7 mm. **Obv:** Arms within wreath below stars, without beaded rim **Rev:** Value and date flanked by sprigs **Edge:** Reeded **Note:** Two varieties of sunray arrangements exist; die varieties exist with slightly larger or smaller denomination, plain rim.

Date	Mintage	VF20	XF40	MS60	MS63	MS65
1994	—	—	—	0.35	0.50	0.75

KM# 4.2 10 TIYIN
2.85 g., Nickel Clad Steel, 18.7 mm. **Obv:** Arms within wreath below stars, with beaded rim **Rev:** Value and date flanked by sprigs **Edge:** Reeded

Date	Mintage	VF20	XF40	MS60	MS63	MS65
1994 PM	—	—	—	—	45.00	90.00
1994	—	—	—	0.45	0.65	1.00

KM# 5.1 20 TIYIN
4.00 g., Nickel Clad Steel, 22 mm. **Obv:** Arms within wreath below stars, without beaded rim **Rev:** Value and date flanked by sprigs **Edge Lettering:** Cyrillic denomination twice

Date	Mintage	VF20	XF40	MS60	MS63	MS65
1994	—	—	—	0.50	0.75	1.25

KM# 5.2 20 TIYIN
4.00 g., Nickel Clad Steel, 22 mm. **Obv:** Arms within wreath below stars, with beaded rim **Rev:** Value and date flanked by sprigs **Note:** Two sun ray varieties exist, varieties exist with wide and narrow edge lettering.

Date	Mintage	VF20	XF40	MS60	MS63	MS65
1994 PM	—	—	—	—	275	550
1994	—	—	—	0.60	0.85	1.50

KM# 6.1 50 TIYIN
4.80 g., Nickel Clad Steel, 23.9 mm. **Obv:** Arms within wreath below stars, without beaded rim **Rev:** Value and date flanked by sprigs **Edge:** Lettering in Cyrillic **Note:** 2 varieties of sunray arrangements exist; all coins show orthographic error in 1st letter of "ellik" within edge inscription.

Date	Mintage	VF20	XF40	MS60	MS63	MS65
1994	—	—	—	0.75	1.00	1.50

KM# 6.2 50 TIYIN
4.80 g., Nickel Clad Steel, 23.9 mm. **Obv:** Arms within wreath below stars, with beaded rim **Rev:** Value and date flanked by sprigs **Edge:** Lettering in Cyrillic **Note:** All coins show orthographic error in 1st letter of "ellik" within edge inscription.

Date	Mintage	VF20	XF40	MS60	MS63	MS65
1994 PM	—	—	—	—	20.00	35.00
1994	—	—	—	3.00	5.00	9.00

KM# 8 SOM
2.80 g., Nickel Clad Steel, 19 mm. **Obv:** Arms within wreath below stars **Rev:** Value and date flanked by sprigs **Edge:** plain **Note:** Edge varieties exist.

Date	Mintage	VF20	XF40	MS60	MS63	MS65
1997	—	—	—	0.75	1.35	1.50
1998 Rare	—	—	—	—	—	—
1999 Rare	—	—	—	—	—	—
2000	—	—	—	0.75	1.35	1.50

KM# 12 SOM
2.83 g., Nickel Clad Steel, 18.8 mm. **Obv:** National arms **Rev:** Value and map **Edge:** Reeded

Date	Mintage	VF20	XF40	MS60	MS63	MS65
2000	—	—	—	0.60	1.00	1.25

KM# 9 5 SOM
4.00 g., Nickel Clad Steel **Obv:** Arms within wreath below stars **Rev:** Value and date flanked by sprigs

Date	Mintage	VF20	XF40	MS60	MS63	MS65
1997	—	—	—	1.00	1.50	1.75
Note: Edge varieties exist						
1998 Rare	—	—	—	—	—	—
1999	—	—	—	1.00	1.50	1.75

KM# 7 10 SOM
31.10 g., 0.999 Silver 0.9989 oz. ASW **Subject:** 3rd Anniversary of Independence **Obv:** Arms within wreath **Rev:** Equestrian above value

Date	Mintage	VF20	XF40	MS60	MS63	MS65
1994	Est. 1000	PF63 165	PF65 185			

KM# 10 10 SOM
4.70 g., Nickel Clad Steel **Obv:** Arms within wreath below stars **Rev:** Value and date flanked by sprigs

Date	Mintage	VF20	XF40	MS60	MS63	MS65
1997	—	—	—	1.00	1.50	2.50
Note: Edge varieties exist						
1998 Rare	—	—	—	—	—	—
1999	—	—	—	1.00	1.50	2.50
2000	—	—	—	1.00	1.50	2.50

KM# 11 25 SOM
Nickel Clad Steel, 27 mm. **Subject:** Jaloliddin Manguberdi **Obv:** Arms within wreath **Rev:** Bust with headdress facing 1/4 right **Edge:** Plain

Date	Mintage	VF20	XF40	MS60	MS63	MS65
1999	—	—	—	2.00	3.00	5.00

PATTERNS

Including off metal strikes

KM#	Date	Mintage	Identification	Mkt Val
Pn1	1994	—	Som. Bronze Gilt. National arms. Muhammad Taragay Ulugbek (1394-1449). Reeded. Proof.	100
Pn2	1994	—	10 Som. Bronze Gilt. National arms. as KM#7, Tamerlane Statue. Reeded. Proof.	300
Pn3	1995	—	100 Som. Bronze Gilt. National arms. Samarkand - Tamerlane's Mausoleum. Reeded. Proof.	200
Pn4	1995	—	Tiyin. 0.800. Silver Gilt. National arms. Samarkand building. Reeded. Proof.	200

VANUATU

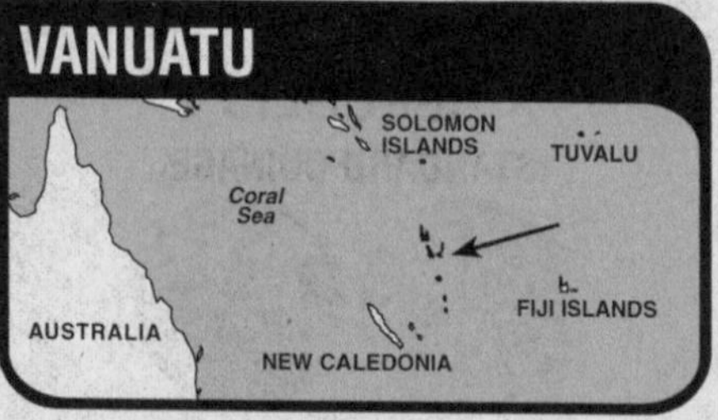

The Republic of Vanuatu, formerly New Hebrides Condominium, a group of islands located in the South Pacific 500 miles (800 km.) west of Fiji, were under the joint sovereignty of Great Britain and France. The islands have an area of 5,700 sq. mi. (14,760 sq. km.) and a population of 165,000, mainly Melanesians of mixed blood. Capital: Port-Vila. The volcanic and coral islands, while malarial land subject to frequent earthquakes, are extremely fertile, and produce copra, coffee, tropical fruits and timber for export.

The New Hebrides were discovered by Portuguese navigator Pedro de Quiros (sailing under orders by the King of Spain) in 1606, visited by French explorer Bougainville in 1768, and named by British navigator Capt. James Cook in 1774. Ships of all nations converged on the islands to trade for sandalwood, prompting France and Britain to relinquish their individual claims and declare the islands a neutral zone in 1878. The New Hebrides were placed under the control of a mixed Anglo-French commission of naval officers during the native uprisings of 1887, and established as a condominium under the joint sovereignty of France and Great Britain in 1906.

Vanuatu became an independent republic within the Commonwealth in July 1980. A president is Head of State and the Prime Minister is Head of Government.

MONETARY SYSTEM
Vatu to Present

REPUBLIC

STANDARD COINAGE

KM# 3 VATU
1.99 g., Nickel-Brass, 16.95 mm. **Obv:** National arms **Rev:** Shell and value **Edge:** Plain

Date	Mintage	VF20	XF40	MS60	MS63	MS65
1983	—	—	0.15	0.25	0.50	0.75
1983	—	PF65 2.50				
1990	—	—	0.15	0.25	0.50	0.75
1999	—	—	0.15	0.25	0.50	0.75

KM# 4 2 VATU
3.00 g., Nickel-Brass, 20 mm. **Obv:** National arms **Rev:** Shell and value **Edge:** Plain

Date	Mintage	VF20	XF40	MS60	MS63	MS65
1983	—	—	0.25	0.45	0.85	1.50
1983	—	PF65 3.50				
1990	—	—	0.25	0.45	0.85	1.50
1995	—	—	0.25	0.45	0.85	1.50
1999	—	—	0.25	0.45	0.85	1.50

KM# 5 5 VATU
4.10 g., Nickel-Brass, 23.5 mm. **Obv:** National arms **Rev:** Shell and value **Edge:** Plain

Date	Mintage	VF20	XF40	MS60	MS63	MS65
1983	—	—	0.30	0.50	1.00	1.75
1983	—	PF65 4.00				
1990	—	—	0.30	0.50	1.00	1.75
1995	—	—	0.30	0.50	1.00	1.75
1999	—	—	0.30	0.50	1.00	1.75

KM# 6 10 VATU
6.10 g., Copper-Nickel, 23.95 mm. **Obv:** National arms **Rev:** Crab and value, palm trees **Edge:** Plain

Date	Mintage	VF20	XF40	MS60	MS63	MS65
1983	—	—	0.35	0.65	1.25	2.00
1983	—	PF65 7.50				
1990	—	—	0.35	0.65	1.25	2.00
1995	—	—	0.35	0.65	1.25	2.00
1999	—	—	0.35	0.65	1.25	2.00

KM# 25 10 VATU
Copper-Nickel **Subject:** End of Victorian Era - Queen Victoria **Obv:** Arms **Rev:** Seated half figure of Queen Mother left within beaded circle

Date	Mintage	VF20	XF40	MS60	MS63	MS65
1995	Est. 30000	—	—	1.00	1.50	2.50

KM# 28 10 VATU
10.00 g., 0.500 Silver 0.1608 oz. ASW **Series:** Olympics **Obv:** Arms **Rev:** Gymnast

Date	Mintage	VF20	XF40	MS60	MS63	MS65
1996	Est. 10000	—	—	—	5.00	8.00

KM# 7 20 VATU
10.00 g., Copper-Nickel, 28.45 mm. **Obv:** National arms **Rev:** Crab, value, palm trees **Edge:** Reeded **Note:** Similar 10 Vatu, KM#6.

Date	Mintage	VF20	XF40	MS60	MS63	MS65
1983	—	—	0.45	0.75	1.50	2.50
1983	—	PF65 10.00				
1990	—	—	0.45	0.75	1.50	2.50
1995	—	—	0.45	0.75	1.50	2.50
1999	—	—	0.45	0.75	1.50	2.50

KM# 19 20 VATU
20.00 g., 0.500 Silver 0.3215 oz. ASW **Subject:** Captain James Cook **Obv:** National arms **Rev:** Seated half figure facing right

Date	Mintage	VF20	XF40	MS60	MS63	MS65
1994	Est. 25000	PF63 9.00	PF65 12.00			

KM# 20 20 VATU
20.00 g., 0.925 Silver 0.5948 oz. ASW **Series:** Endangered Wildlife **Obv:** National arms **Rev:** Kingfisher

Date	Mintage	VF20	XF40	MS60	MS63	MS65
1994	Est. 25000	PF63 17.00	PF65 20.00			

KM# 1 50 VATU
15.00 g., Nickel, 32.9 mm. **Subject:** 1st Anniversary of Independence **Obv:** National arms **Rev:** Figures working in fields

Date	Mintage	VF20	XF40	MS60	MS63	MS65
1981	—	—	0.75	1.25	2.00	3.00

KM# 1a 50 VATU
15.00 g., 0.925 Silver 0.4461 oz. ASW **Obv:** National arms **Rev:** Figures working in field

Date	Mintage	VF20	XF40	MS60	MS63	MS65
1981	846	PF63 35.00	PF65 50.00			

KM# 8 50 VATU
15.00 g., Copper-Nickel, 32.9 mm. **Series:** F.A.O. **Obv:** National arms **Rev:** Tubers encircled by leafy vines, value above

Date	Mintage	VF20	XF40	MS60	MS63	MS65
1983	—	—	0.75	1.25	2.00	3.00
1983	—	PF65 12.00				
1990	—	—	0.75	1.25	2.00	3.00
1995	—	—	1.00	1.50	2.50	4.50
1999	—	—	0.75	1.25	2.00	3.00

KM# 10 50 VATU
34.00 g., 0.925 Silver 1.0111 oz. ASW **Series:** Seoul Olympics **Subject:** Boxing **Obv:** National arms **Rev:** Boxers

Date	Mintage	VF20	XF40	MS60	MS63	MS65
1988	15,000	PF63 25.00	PF65 28.00			

KM# 11 50 VATU
31.47 g., 0.925 Silver 0.9359 oz. ASW **Subject:** Voyager I **Obv:** National arms **Rev:** Space shuttle and planets

Date	Mintage	VF20	XF40	MS60	MS63	MS65
1992	10,000	PF63 22.00	PF65 24.00			

KM# 12 50 VATU
31.47 g., 0.925 Silver 0.9359 oz. ASW **Subject:** Pedro Fernandez De Quiros **Obv:** National arms **Rev:** Kneeling figure facing, boat and ship

Date	Mintage	VF20	XF40	MS60	MS63	MS65
1992	—	PF63 25.00	PF65 28.00			

KM# 13 50 VATU
31.47 g., 0.925 Silver 0.9359 oz. ASW **Series:** Endangered Wildlife **Subject:** Earth Pigeons **Obv:** National arms **Rev:** Birds

Date	Mintage	VF20	XF40	MS60	MS63	MS65
1992	—	PF63 25.00	PF65 28.00			

KM# 14 50 VATU
31.47 g., 0.925 Silver 0.9359 oz. ASW **Series:** Olympics **Subject:** Canoes **Obv:** National arms **Rev:** Canoers

Date	Mintage	VF20	XF40	MS60	MS63	MS65
1992	Est. 40000	PF63 27.00	PF65 30.00			

KM# 15 50 VATU
31.47 g., 0.925 Silver 0.9359 oz. ASW **Subject:** 40th Anniversary of Coronation **Obv:** National arms

Date	Mintage	VF20	XF40	MS60	MS63	MS65
1993	Est. 10000	PF63 25.00	PF65 28.00			

KM# 16 50 VATU
31.47 g., 0.925 Silver 0.9359 oz. ASW **Subject:** The Boudeuse **Obv:** National arms **Rev:** Ship to left of half figure right

Date	Mintage	VF20	XF40	MS60	MS63	MS65
1993	Est. 15000	PF63 22.00	PF65 24.00			

KM# 17 50 VATU
31.47 g., 0.925 Silver 0.9359 oz. ASW **Subject:** Protect Our World **Obv:** National arms **Rev:** Whale and ship

Date	Mintage	VF20	XF40	MS60	MS63	MS65
1993	Est. 10000	PF63 22.00	PF65 24.00			

KM# 18 50 VATU
31.47 g., 0.925 Silver 0.9359 oz. ASW **Subject:** World Cup Soccer **Obv:** National arms **Rev:** Soccer player

Date	Mintage	VF20	XF40	MS60	MS63	MS65
1994	Est. 10000	PF63 25.00	PF65 28.00			

KM# 21 50 VATU
31.47 g., 0.925 Silver 0.9359 oz. ASW **Subject:** De Bougainville **Obv:** National arms **Rev:** Bust facing at left of book, globe and ship

Date	Mintage	VF20	XF40	MS60	MS63	MS65
1994	Est. 10000	PF63 25.00	PF65 28.00			

KM# 22 50 VATU
31.47 g., 0.925 Silver 0.9359 oz. ASW **Subject:** Queen Victoria **Obv:** National arms **Rev:** Seated half figure of Queen Mother right within beaded circle

Date	Mintage	VF20	XF40	MS60	MS63	MS65
1994	—	PF63 22.00	PF65 24.00			

KM# 24 50 VATU
31.47 g., 0.925 Silver 0.9359 oz. ASW **Series:** Olympics **Obv:** National arms **Rev:** Swimmers

Date	Mintage	VF20	XF40	MS60	MS63	MS65
1994	Est. 40000	PF63 25.00	PF65 28.00			

KM# 30 50 VATU
31.47 g., 0.925 Silver 0.9359 oz. ASW **Series:** Olympic Games 1996 **Obv:** National arms **Rev:** Gymnast

Date	Mintage	VF20	XF40	MS60	MS63	MS65
1994	40,000	PF63 22.00	PF65 24.00			

KM# 26 50 VATU
31.47 g., 0.925 Silver 0.9359 oz. ASW **Subject:** Birth of Great Grandson Prince William **Obv:** National arms **Rev:** Conjoined busts facing holding infant within beaded circle

Date	Mintage	VF20	XF40	MS60	MS63	MS65
1995	Est. 30000	PF63 27.00	PF65 30.00			

KM# 29 50 VATU
31.47 g., 0.925 Silver 0.9359 oz. ASW **Subject:** Queen Victoria and Prince Albert **Obv:** National arms **Rev:** Conjoined standing figures in front of building within circle

Date	Mintage	VF20	XF40	MS60	MS63	MS65
1996	Est. 10000	PF63 25.00	PF65 28.00			

KM# 35 50 VATU
28.31 g., Silver, 38.5 mm. **Subject:** 50th Anniversary - Elizabeth and Philip **Obv:** National arms **Rev:** Family members gazing at baby Prince Andrew **Edge:** Reeded **Note:** Gold-plated shield on reverse reads: Prince Andrew 1960

Date	Mintage	VF20	XF40	MS60	MS63	MS65
1997	—	PF63 25.00	PF65 27.00			

KM# 44 50 VATU
1.25 g., 0.999 Gold 0.0401 oz. AGW, 13.87 mm. **Subject:** 1996 Summer Olympics - Atlanta **Obv:** National arms **Obv. Legend:** RIPABLIK BLONG VANUATU **Rev:** Gymnast **Edge:** Reeded

Date	Mintage	VF20	XF40	MS60	MS63	MS65
1997	—	PF63 60.00	PF65 70.00			

KM# 31 50 VATU
1.24 g., 0.999 Gold 0.040 oz. AGW **Obv:** National arms **Rev:** Spanish 1704 gold coin design

Date	Mintage	VF20	XF40	MS60	MS63	MS65
1998	—	PF63 60.00	PF65 70.00			

KM# 32 50 VATU
1.24 g., 0.999 Gold 0.040 oz. AGW **Obv:** National arms **Rev:** Boar tusk necklace

Date	Mintage	VF20	XF40	MS60	MS63	MS65
1998	—	PF63 60.00	PF65 70.00			

KM# 33 50 VATU
30.97 g., 0.925 Silver 0.921 oz. ASW **Subject:** Millennium 2000 **Obv:** National arms **Rev:** Gold-plated shell

Date	Mintage	VF20	XF40	MS60	MS63	MS65
1998	—	PF63 32.00	PF65 42.00			

KM# 36 50 VATU
31.47 g., 0.925 Silver 0.9359 oz. ASW, 37 mm. **Obv:** Standing native **Rev:** Three-masted corvette Zelee **Edge:** Reeded **Shape:** Octagonal

Date	Mintage	VF20	XF40	MS60	MS63	MS65
1999	—	PF63 32.00	PF65 35.00			

KM# 37 50 VATU
31.47 g., 0.925 Silver 0.9359 oz. ASW, 37 mm. **Obv:** Standing native **Rev:** Three-masted corvette Astrolabe **Edge:** Reeded **Shape:** Octagonal

Date	Mintage	VF20	XF40	MS60	MS63	MS65
1999	—	PF63 32.00	PF65 35.00			

KM# 40 50 VATU
3.11 g., 0.585 Gold 0.0585 oz. AGW **Subject:** XXVII Summer Olympics - Sydney 2000 **Obv:** National arms **Rev:** Sprinter

Date	Mintage	VF20	XF40	MS60	MS63	MS65
1999	—	PF63 100	PF65 110			

KM# 9 100 VATU
9.55 g., Nickel-Brass, 23.9 mm. **Obv:** National arms **Rev:** Sprouting bulbs

Date	Mintage	VF20	XF40	MS60	MS63	MS65
1988	—	—	—	1.50	2.50	4.00
1995	—	—	—	1.50	2.50	4.00

KM# 23 100 VATU
7.78 g., 0.583 Gold 0.1458 oz. AGW **Series:** Endangered Wildlife **Obv:** National arms **Rev:** Kingfisher

Date	Mintage	VF20	XF40	MS60	MS63	MS65
1994	Est. 2000	PF65 250	PF67 290			

KM# 27 100 VATU
155.50 g., 0.925 Silver 4.6245 oz. ASW, 65 mm. **Obv:** National arms **Rev:** Crowned standing figures facing within beaded circle **Note:** Illustration reduced.

Date	Mintage	VF20	XF40	MS60	MS63	MS65
1995	Est. 2000	PF63 100	PF65 120			

KM# 34 100 VATU
155.50 g., 0.925 Silver 4.6245 oz. ASW, 65.7 mm. **Subject:** H.M.S. Resolution **Obv:** National arms **Rev:** Sailing ship and carvings **Edge:** Reeded **Note:** Illustration reduced.

Date	Mintage	VF20	XF40	MS60	MS63	MS65
1996	—	PF63 100	PF65 120			

KM# 39 100 VATU
7.78 g., 0.5833 Gold 0.1459 oz. AGW **Subject:** Queen Mother Elizabeth - Birth of Prince William **Obv:** National arms

Date	Mintage	VF20	XF40	MS60	MS63	MS65
1997	Est. 25000	PF65 225	PF67 275			

KM# 2 10000 VATU
15.98 g., 0.917 Gold 0.4711 oz. AGW **Subject:** 1st Anniversary of Independence **Obv:** National arms **Rev:** Crab flanked by palm trees

Date	Mintage	XF40	MS60	MS63	MS65	MS66
1981	538	—	—	—	825	900
1981	1,054	PF65 825	PF67 900			

PROOF SETS

KM#	Date	Mintage	Identification	Issue Price	Mkt Val
PS1	1983 (6)	—	KM#3-8	—	40.00

VATICAN CITY

The State of the Vatican City, a papal state on the right bank of the Tiber River within the boundaries of Rome, has an area of 0.17 sq. mi. (0.44 sq. km.) and a population of *775. Capital: Vatican City.

Vatican City State, comprising the Vatican, St. Peter's, extra-territorial right to Castel Gandolfo and 13 buildings throughout Rome, is all that remains of the extensive Papal States over which the Pope exercised temporal power in central Italy. During the struggle for Italian unification, the Papal States, including Rome, were forcibly incorporated into the Kingdom of Italy in 1870. The resultant confrontation of crozier and sword remained unresolved until the signing of the Lateran Treaty, Feb. 11, 1929, between the Vatican and the Kingdom of Italy which recognized the independence and sovereignty of the State of the Vatican City, defined the relationship between the government and the church within Italy, and financially compensated the Holy See for the territorial losses from 1870.

Today the Pope exercises supreme legislative, executive and judicial power within the Vatican City, and the State of the Vatican City is recognized by many nations as an independent sovereign state under the temporal jurisdiction of the Pope, even to the extent of ambassadorial exchange. The Pope, is of course, the head of the Roman Catholic Church.

PONTIFFS
Pius XI, 1922-1939
Sede Vacante, Feb. 10 - Mar. 2, 1939
Pius XII, 1939-1958
Sede Vacante, Oct. 9 - 28, 1958
John XXIII, 1958-1963
Sede Vacante, June 3 - 21,1963
Paul VI, 1963-1978
Sede Vacante, Aug. 6 - 26, 1978
John Paul I, Aug. 26 - Sept. 28, 1978
Sede Vacante, Sept. 28 - Oct. 16, 1978
John Paul II, 1978-2005
Sede Vacante, April 2 - 19, 2005
Benedict XVI, 2005-2013

MINT MARK
Commencing 1981
R – Rome

MONETARY SYSTEM
100 Centesimi = 1 Lira (thru 2002)
100 Euro Cent = 1 Euro

DATING
Most Vatican coins indicate the regnal year of the pope preceded by the word *Anno* (or an abbreviation), even if the *anno domini* date is omitted.

CITY STATE

Pius XI

DECIMAL COINAGE

100 Centesimi = 1 Lira

KM# 1 5 CENTESIMI
Bronze, 20 mm. **Obv:** Crowned shield divides date **Rev:** Olive branch divides value

Date	Mintage	F12	VF20	XF40	MS60	MS63
1929/VIII	10,000	—	10.00	17.50	40.00	50.00
1930/IX	100,000	—	5.00	7.50	15.00	25.00
1931/X	100,000	—	5.00	7.50	15.00	25.00
1932/XI	100,000	—	5.00	7.50	15.00	25.00
1934/XIII	100,000	—	5.00	7.50	15.00	25.00
1935/XIV	44,000	—	7.50	12.50	30.00	35.00
1936/XV	62,000	—	5.00	7.50	15.00	25.00
1937/XVI	62,000	—	5.00	7.50	15.00	25.00
1938/XVII Rare	—	—	—	—	—	—

KM# 11 5 CENTESIMI
Bronze, 20 mm. **Subject:** Jubilee **Obv:** Crowned shield flanked by date **Rev:** Olive branch divides value

Date	Mintage	F12	VF20	XF40	MS60	MS63
1933-34	100,000	—	7.50	12.50	28.00	35.00

KM# 2 10 CENTESIMI
Bronze **Obv:** Crowned shield divides date **Rev:** St. Peter bust right

Date	Mintage	F12	VF20	XF40	MS60	MS63
1929/VIII	10,000	—	10.00	17.50	40.00	50.00
1930/IX	90,000	—	5.00	7.50	15.00	25.00
1931/X	90,000	—	5.00	7.50	15.00	25.00
1932/XI	90,000	—	5.00	7.50	15.00	25.00
1934/XIII	90,000	—	5.00	7.50	15.00	25.00
1935/XIV	90,000	—	5.00	7.50	15.00	25.00
1936/XV	81,000	—	5.00	7.50	15.00	25.00
1937/XVI	81,000	—	5.00	7.50	15.00	25.00
1938/XVII	—	—	450	900	1,500	—

KM# 12 10 CENTESIMI
Bronze, 22 mm. **Subject:** Jubilee **Obv:** Crowned shield flanked by dates **Rev:** St. Peter bust right

Date	Mintage	F12	VF20	XF40	MS60	MS63
1933-34	90,000	—	7.50	12.50	30.00	35.00

KM# 3 20 CENTESIMI
Nickel **Obv:** Crowned Arms **Rev:** St. Paul bust left

Date	Mintage	F12	VF20	XF40	MS60	MS63
1929/VIII	10,000	—	10.00	17.50	40.00	45.00
1930/IX	80,000	—	5.00	7.50	15.00	18.00
1931/X	80,000	—	5.00	7.50	15.00	18.00
1932/XI	80,000	—	5.00	7.50	15.00	18.00
1934/XIII	80,000	—	5.00	7.50	15.00	18.00
1935/XIV	11,000	—	25.00	60.00	90.00	120
1936/XV	64,000	—	5.00	7.50	15.00	18.00
1937/XVI	64,000	—	5.00	7.50	15.00	18.00

KM# 13 20 CENTESIMI
Nickel, 21 mm. **Subject:** Jubilee **Obv:** Crowned Arms **Rev:** St. Paul bust left

Date	Mintage	F12	VF20	XF40	MS60	MS63
1933-34	80,000	—	7.50	12.50	28.00	35.00

KM# 4 50 CENTESIMI
Nickel, 24 mm. **Obv:** Crowned Arms **Rev:** Archangel Michael divides value

Date	Mintage	F12	VF20	XF40	MS60	MS63
1929/VIII	10,000	—	10.00	17.50	40.00	—
1930/IX	80,000	—	5.00	7.50	15.00	—
1931/X	80,000	—	5.00	7.50	15.00	—
1932/XI	80,000	—	5.00	7.50	15.00	—
1934/XIII	80,000	—	5.00	7.50	15.00	—
1935/XIV	14,000	—	7.50	15.00	30.00	—
1936/XV	52,000	—	5.00	7.50	15.00	—
1937/XVI	52,000	—	5.00	7.50	15.00	—

KM# 14 50 CENTESIMI
Nickel, 24 mm. **Subject:** Jubilee **Obv:** Crowned Arms **Rev:** Archangel Michael divides value

Date	Mintage	F12	VF20	XF40	MS60	MS63
1933-34	80,000	—	6.00	12.00	22.00	25.00

KM# 5 LIRA

Nickel **Obv:** Crowned Arms **Rev:** Virgin Mary standing on globe and crescent

Date	Mintage	F12	VF20	XF40	MS60	MS63
1929/VIII	10,000	—	10.00	17.50	40.00	45.00
1930/IX	80,000	—	5.00	7.50	15.00	18.00
1931/X	80,000	—	5.00	7.50	15.00	18.00
1932/XI	80,000	—	5.00	7.50	15.00	18.00
1934/XIII	80,000	—	5.00	7.50	15.00	18.00
1935/XIV	40,000	—	5.00	7.50	15.00	18.00
1936/XV	40,000	—	5.00	7.50	15.00	18.00
1937/XVI	70,000	—	5.00	7.50	15.00	18.00

KM# 15 LIRA

Nickel, 27 mm. **Subject:** Jubilee **Obv:** Crowned Arms **Rev:** Virgin Mary standing on globe and crescent **Note:** Enlargement of date area.

Date	Mintage	F12	VF20	XF40	MS60	MS63
1933-34	80,000	—	7.50	15.00	30.00	35.00

KM# 6 2 LIRE

Nickel, 29 mm. **Obv:** Crowned Arms **Rev:** Lamb on shoulders of young shepherd

Date	Mintage	F12	VF20	XF40	MS60	MS63
1929/VIII	10,000	—	10.00	17.50	40.00	45.00
1930/IX	50,000	—	5.00	7.50	15.00	18.00
1931/X	50,000	—	5.00	7.50	15.00	18.00
1932/XI	50,000	—	5.00	7.50	15.00	18.00
1934/XIII	50,000	—	5.00	7.50	15.00	18.00
1935/XIV	70,000	—	5.00	7.50	15.00	18.00
1936/XV	40,000	—	5.00	7.50	15.00	18.00
1937/XVI	70,000	—	5.00	7.50	15.00	18.00

KM# 16 2 LIRE

Nickel, 30 mm. **Subject:** Jubilee **Obv:** Crowned Arms **Rev:** Lamb on shoulders of young shepherd

Date	Mintage	F12	VF20	XF40	MS60	MS63
1933-34	50,000	—	5.00	7.50	15.00	18.00

KM# 7 5 LIRE

5.00 g., 0.835 Silver 0.1342 oz. ASW, 23 mm. **Obv:** Bust left **Rev:** St. Peter in a boat

Date	Mintage	F12	VF20	XF40	MS60	MS63
1929/VIII	10,000	—	15.00	30.00	45.00	55.00
1930/IX	50,000	—	7.50	15.00	30.00	36.00
1931/X	50,000	—	7.50	15.00	30.00	36.00
1932/XI	50,000	—	7.50	15.00	30.00	36.00
1934/XIII	30,000	—	7.50	15.00	30.00	36.00
1935/XIV	20,000	—	10.00	20.00	40.00	45.00
1936/XV	40,000	—	7.50	15.00	30.00	36.00
1937/XVI	40,000	—	7.50	15.00	30.00	36.00

KM# 17 5 LIRE

5.00 g., 0.835 Silver 0.1342 oz. ASW, 23 mm. **Subject:** Jubilee **Obv:** Bust left **Rev:** St. Peter in a boat

Date	Mintage	F12	VF20	XF40	MS60	MS63
1933-34	50,000	—	10.00	20.00	40.00	45.00

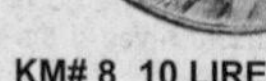

KM# 8 10 LIRE

10.00 g., 0.835 Silver 0.2685 oz. ASW, 27 mm. **Obv:** Bust left **Rev:** Mary, Queen of Peace holding infant

Date	Mintage	F12	VF20	XF40	MS60	MS63
1929/VIII	10,000	—	20.00	35.00	50.00	60.00
1930/IX	50,000	—	10.00	20.00	40.00	45.00
1931/X	50,000	—	10.00	20.00	40.00	45.00
1932/XI	50,000	—	10.00	20.00	40.00	45.00
1934/XIII	60,000	—	10.00	20.00	40.00	45.00
1935/XIV	50,000	—	10.00	20.00	40.00	45.00
1936/XV	40,000	—	10.00	20.00	40.00	45.00
1937/XVI	40,000	—	10.00	20.00	40.00	45.00

KM# 18 10 LIRE

10.00 g., 0.835 Silver 0.2685 oz. ASW, 27 mm. **Subject:** Jubilee **Obv:** Bust left **Rev:** Seated crowned figure of Mary, Queen of peace facing holding infant

Date	Mintage	F12	VF20	XF40	MS60	MS63
1933-34	50,000	—	10.00	20.00	40.00	45.00

KM# 9 100 LIRE

8.80 g., 0.900 Gold 0.2546 oz. AGW, 23.5 mm. **Obv:** Bust right **Rev:** Standing Jesus facing with child at feet

Date	Mintage	F12	VF20	XF40	MS60	MS63
1929/VIII	10,000	—	—	400	550	700
1930/IX	2,621	—	—	400	550	700
1931/X	3,343	—	—	400	550	700
1932/XI	5,073	—	—	400	550	700
1934/XIII	2,533	—	—	400	550	700
1935/XIV	2,015	—	—	400	550	700

KM# 19 100 LIRE

8.80 g., 0.900 Gold 0.2546 oz. AGW, 23.5 mm. **Subject:** Jubilee **Obv:** Bust right **Rev:** Standing Jesus facing with child at feet

Date	Mintage	F12	VF20	XF40	MS60	MS63
1933-34	23,000	—	—	350	500	675

KM# 10 100 LIRE

5.19 g., 0.900 Gold 0.1502 oz. AGW, 20.5 mm. **Obv:** Bust right **Rev:** Standing Jesus facing with child at feet

Date	Mintage	F12	VF20	XF40	MS60	MS63
1936/XV	8,239	—	—	450	650	800
1937/XVI	2,000	—	—	—	2,500	3,500
1938 Rare	6	—	—	—	—	—

Sede Vacante

KM# 20 5 LIRE

5.00 g., 0.835 Silver 0.1342 oz. ASW, 23 mm. **Subject:** Sede Vacante **Obv:** Arms of Cardinal Pacelli **Rev:** Dove within 1/2 sun

Date	Mintage	F12	VF20	XF40	MS60	MS63
1939	40,000	—	20.00	35.00	45.00	50.00

KM# 21 10 LIRE

10.00 g., 0.835 Silver 0.2685 oz. ASW, 27 mm. **Obv:** Arms of Cardinal Eugenio Pacelli **Rev:** Dove within 1/2 sun

Date	Mintage	F12	VF20	XF40	MS60	MS63
1939	30,000	—	25.00	40.00	55.00	—

Pius XII

KM# 22 5 CENTESIMI

Aluminum-Bronze **Obv:** Crowned shield divides date

Date	Mintage	F12	VF20	XF40	MS60	MS63
1939/I	62,000	—	5.00	7.50	15.00	18.00
1940/II	62,000	—	5.00	7.50	15.00	18.00
1941/III	5,000	—	10.00	17.50	40.00	45.00

KM# 31 5 CENTESIMI

Brass **Obv:** Bust left **Rev:** Dove

Date	Mintage	F12	VF20	XF40	MS60	MS63
1942/IV	5,000	—	30.00	50.00	75.00	85.00
1943/V	1,000	—	45.00	65.00	110	125
1944/VI	1,000	—	45.00	65.00	110	125
1945/VII	1,000	—	45.00	65.00	110	125
1946/VIII	1,000	—	45.00	65.00	110	125

KM# 23 10 CENTESIMI

Aluminum-Bronze **Obv:** Crowned shield divides date **Rev:** St. Peter bust right

Date	Mintage	F12	VF20	XF40	MS60	MS63
1939/I	81,000	—	5.00	7.50	15.00	18.00
1940/II	81,000	—	5.00	7.50	15.00	18.00
1941/III	7,500	—	20.00	35.00	50.00	60.00

KM# 32 10 CENTESIMI

Brass **Obv:** Bust left **Rev:** Dove

Date	Mintage	F12	VF20	XF40	MS60	MS63
1942/IV	7,500	—	35.00	50.00	75.00	85.00
1943/V	1,000	—	50.00	75.00	125	135
1944/VI	1,000	—	50.00	75.00	125	135
1945/VII	1,000	—	50.00	75.00	125	135
1946/VIII	1,000	—	50.00	75.00	125	135

KM# 24 20 CENTESIMI

Nickel **Obv:** Crowned Arms **Rev:** St. Paul bust left

Date	Mintage	F12	VF20	XF40	MS60	MS63
1939/I	64,000	—	2.00	4.00	6.00	7.00

KM# 24a 20 CENTESIMI

Stainless Steel **Obv:** Crowned Arms **Rev:** St. Paul bust left

Date	Mintage	F12	VF20	XF40	MS60	MS63
1940/II	64,000	—	2.00	4.00	5.25	6.00
1941/III	125,000	—	2.00	4.00	5.25	6.00

KM# 33 20 CENTESIMI

Stainless Steel **Obv:** Crowned shield divides date and beaded circle **Rev:** Justice seated with tablets of the Law

Date	Mintage	F12	VF20	XF40	MS60	MS63
1942/IV	125,000	—	2.00	4.00	5.25	6.00
1943/V	1,000	—	50.00	75.00	100	125
1944/VI	1,000	—	50.00	75.00	100	125
1945/VII	1,000	—	50.00	75.00	100	125
1946/VIII	1,000	—	50.00	75.00	100	125

KM# 25 50 CENTESIMI

Nickel, 24 mm. **Obv:** Crowned Arms **Rev:** Archangel Michael facing, divides value

Date	Mintage	F12	VF20	XF40	MS60	MS63
1939/I	52,000	—	2.50	4.00	6.00	7.00

KM# 25a 50 CENTESIMI

Stainless Steel, 24 mm. **Obv:** Crowned Arms **Rev:** Archangel Michael facing, divides value

Date	Mintage	F12	VF20	XF40	MS60	MS63
1940/II	52,000	—	2.00	4.00	5.25	6.00
1941/III	180,000	—	2.00	4.00	5.25	6.00

KM# 34 50 CENTESIMI

Stainless Steel, 24 mm. **Obv:** Crowned shield divides date and beaded circle **Rev:** Justice seated with tablets of the Law

Date	Mintage	F12	VF20	XF40	MS60	MS63
1942/IV	180,000	—	2.00	4.00	5.25	6.00
1943/V	1,000	—	50.00	75.00	100	125
1944/VI	1,000	—	50.00	75.00	100	125

Date	Mintage	F12	VF20	XF40	MS60	MS63
1945/VII	1,000	—	50.00	75.00	100	125
1946/VIII	1,000	—	50.00	75.00	100	125

KM# 26 LIRA

Nickel **Rev:** Virgin Mary standing on globe and crescent

Date	Mintage	F12	VF20	XF40	MS60	MS63
1939/I	70,000	—	5.00	10.00	17.50	20.00

KM# 26a LIRA

7.86 g., Stainless Steel, 26.65 mm. **Obv:** Papal arms **Rev:** Virgin Mary standing on globe and crescent **Edge:** Reeded

Date	Mintage	F12	VF20	XF40	MS60	MS63
1940/II	70,000	—	3.00	5.00	7.50	7.50
1941/III	284,000	—	1.00	2.00	4.00	4.50

KM# 35 LIRA

Stainless Steel **Obv:** Crowned shield divides date and beaded circle **Rev:** Justice seated with tablets of the Law

Date	Mintage	F12	VF20	XF40	MS60	MS63
1942/IV	284,000	—	1.00	2.00	4.00	4.50
1943/V	1,000	—	50.00	75.00	100	125
1944/VI	1,000	—	50.00	75.00	100	125
1945/VII	1,000	—	50.00	75.00	100	125
1946/VIII	1,000	—	50.00	75.00	100	125

KM# 40 LIRA

Aluminum, 21.5 mm. **Obv:** Crowned shield divides date and beaded circle **Rev:** Justice seated with tablet of the Law

Date	Mintage	F12	VF20	XF40	MS60	MS63
1947/IX	120,000	—	1.00	2.00	3.25	4.00
1948/X	10,000	—	2.00	4.00	6.25	7.00
1949/XI	10,000	—	2.00	4.00	6.25	7.00

KM# 44 LIRA

Aluminum, 21.5 mm. **Subject:** Holy Year **Obv:** Crowned shield **Rev:** Holy Year Door

Date	Mintage	F12	VF20	XF40	MS60	MS63
1950	50,000	—	1.00	2.00	4.00	5.00

KM# 49.1 LIRA

0.62 g., Aluminum, 17 mm. **Obv:** Crowned shield **Obv. Legend:** ANNO **Rev:** Temperance standing pouring libation in bowl **Edge:** Plain

Date	Mintage	F12	VF20	XF40	MS60	MS63
1951/XIII	400,000	—	0.25	0.50	1.25	1.50
1952/XIV	400,000	—	0.25	0.50	1.25	1.50
1953/XV	400,000	—	0.25	0.50	1.25	1.50
1955/XVII	10,000	—	1.50	3.00	5.25	6.00
1957/XIX	30,000	—	0.75	2.00	3.00	3.50
1958/XX	30,000	—	0.75	2.00	3.00	3.50

KM# 49.2 LIRA

Aluminum, 17 mm. **Obv:** Crowned shield **Obv. Legend:** A **Edge:** Plain

Date	Mintage	F12	VF20	XF40	MS60	MS63
1956/XVIII	10,000	—	1.50	3.00	5.25	6.00

KM# 27 2 LIRE

Nickel, 29 mm. **Obv:** Crowned Arms **Rev:** Lamb on shoulders of shepherd

Date	Mintage	F12	VF20	XF40	MS60	MS63
1939/I	40,000	—	4.00	6.00	10.00	12.50

KM# 27a 2 LIRE

10.00 g., Stainless Steel, 29 mm. **Obv:** Crowned Arms **Rev:** Lamb on shoulders of shepherd **Edge:** Reeded

Date	Mintage	F12	VF20	XF40	MS60	MS63
1940/II	40,000	—	0.75	2.00	3.25	4.00
1941/III	270,000	—	0.50	1.00	2.50	3.00

KM# 36 2 LIRE

Stainless Steel, 29 mm. **Obv:** Crowned shield divides date and beaded circle **Rev:** Justice seated with tablets of the Law

Date	Mintage	F12	VF20	XF40	MS60	MS63
1942/IV	270,000	—	0.50	1.00	2.50	3.00
1943/V	1,000	—	50.00	75.00	100	125
1944/VI	1,000	—	50.00	75.00	100	125
1945/VII	1,000	—	50.00	75.00	100	125
1946/VIII	1,000	—	50.00	75.00	100	125

KM# 41 2 LIRE

Aluminum **Obv:** Crowned shield divides date and beaded circle **Rev:** Justice seated with tablets of the Law

Date	Mintage	F12	VF20	XF40	MS60	MS63
1947/IX	65,000	—	2.00	4.00	8.00	10.00
1948/X	110,000	—	1.50	3.50	6.00	8.00
1949/XI	10,000	—	4.00	8.00	18.00	20.00

KM# 45 2 LIRE

Aluminum **Subject:** Holy Year **Obv:** Bust right **Rev:** Dove and St. Peter's Basilica Dome

Date	Mintage	F12	VF20	XF40	MS60	MS63
1950	50,000	—	1.25	2.50	7.50	10.00

KM# 50 2 LIRE

0.80 g., Aluminum, 18 mm. **Obv:** Crowned shield **Rev:** Fortude standing with lion at feet **Edge:** Reeded

Date	Mintage	F12	VF20	XF40	MS60	MS63
1951/XIII	400,000	—	0.25	0.50	1.25	1.50
1952/XIV	400,000	—	0.25	0.50	1.25	1.50
1953/XV	400,000	—	0.25	0.50	1.25	1.50

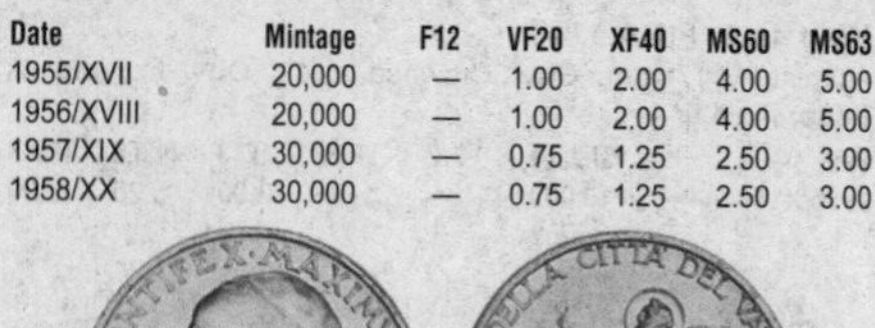

Date	Mintage	F12	VF20	XF40	MS60	MS63
1955/XVII	20,000	—	1.00	2.00	4.00	5.00
1956/XVIII	20,000	—	1.00	2.00	4.00	5.00
1957/XIX	30,000	—	0.75	1.25	2.50	3.00
1958/XX	30,000	—	0.75	1.25	2.50	3.00

KM# 28 5 LIRE

5.00 g., 0.835 Silver 0.1342 oz. ASW, 23 mm. **Obv:** Bust left **Rev:** St. Peter in a boat

Date	Mintage	F12	VF20	XF40	MS60	MS63
1939/I	100,000	—	5.00	10.00	20.00	25.00
1940/II	100,000	—	5.00	10.00	20.00	25.00
1941/III	4,000	—	25.00	40.00	65.00	70.00

KM# 37 5 LIRE

5.00 g., 0.835 Silver 0.1342 oz. ASW, 23 mm. **Obv:** Bust left **Rev:** Caritas figure facing flanked by children

Date	Mintage	F12	VF20	XF40	MS60	MS63
1942/IV	4,000	—	25.00	40.00	60.00	70.00
1943/V	1,000	—	60.00	90.00	135	150
1944/VI	1,000	—	60.00	90.00	135	150
1945/VII	1,000	—	60.00	90.00	135	150
1946/VIII	1,000	—	60.00	90.00	135	150

KM# 42 5 LIRE

Aluminum, 26.5 mm. **Obv:** Bust left **Rev:** Caritas figure facing flanked by children

Date	Mintage	F12	VF20	XF40	MS60	MS63
1947/IX	50,000	—	2.00	4.00	7.50	10.00
1948/X	74,000	—	2.00	4.00	7.50	10.00
1949/XI	74,000	—	2.00	4.00	7.50	10.00

KM# 46 5 LIRE

Aluminum, 26.5 mm. **Subject:** Holy Year **Obv:** Bust left **Rev:** Standing Pope with staff flanked by figures within Holy Year Door

Date	Mintage	F12	VF20	XF40	MS60	MS63
1950	50,000	—	3.00	5.00	8.00	10.00

KM# 51.1 5 LIRE

1.00 g., Aluminum, 20 mm. **Obv:** Bust right **Obv. Legend:** AN **Rev:** Justice standing with sword and scales

Date	Mintage	F12	VF20	XF40	MS60	MS63
1951/XIII	1,500,000	—	0.25	0.50	1.25	1.50
1952/XIV	1,500,000	—	0.25	0.50	1.25	1.50
1953/XV	1,500,000	—	0.25	0.50	1.25	1.50
1955/XVII	30,000	—	0.50	0.75	2.25	3.00
1956/XVIII	60,000	—	0.50	0.75	2.00	2.50
1957/XIX	30,000	—	0.50	0.75	2.25	3.00
1958/XX	30,000	—	0.50	0.75	2.25	3.00

KM# 51.2 5 LIRE

Aluminum, 20 mm. **Obv:** Bust right **Obv. Legend:** A

Date	Mintage	F12	VF20	XF40	MS60	MS63
1956/XVIII	30,000	—	0.50	1.00	2.50	3.00
1957/XIX	30,000	—	0.50	1.00	2.50	3.00
1958/XX	30,000	—	0.50	1.00	2.50	3.00

KM# 29 10 LIRE

10.00 g., 0.835 Silver 0.2685 oz. ASW, 27 mm. **Obv:** Bust left **Rev:** Mary, Queen of Peace holding child

Date	Mintage	F12	VF20	XF40	MS60	MS63
1939/I	10,000	—	15.00	25.00	45.00	50.00
1940/II	10,000	—	15.00	25.00	45.00	50.00
1941/III	4,000	—	20.00	40.00	60.00	75.00

KM# 38 10 LIRE

10.00 g., 0.835 Silver 0.2685 oz. ASW, 27 mm. **Obv:** Bust left **Rev:** Caritas figure facing flanked by children

Date	Mintage	F12	VF20	XF40	MS60	MS63
1942/IV	4,000	—	25.00	50.00	80.00	90.00
1943/V	1,000	—	60.00	85.00	125	135
1944/VI	1,000	—	60.00	85.00	125	135
1945/VII	1,000	—	60.00	85.00	125	135
1946/VIII	1,000	—	60.00	85.00	125	135

KM# 43 10 LIRE

Aluminum, 29 mm. **Obv:** Bust left **Rev:** Caritas figure facing flanked by children

Date	Mintage	F12	VF20	XF40	MS60	MS63
1947/IX	50,000	—	3.00	5.00	8.00	10.00
1948/X	60,000	—	3.00	5.00	8.00	10.00
1949/XI	60,000	—	3.00	5.00	8.00	10.00

KM# 47 10 LIRE

Aluminum, 29 mm. **Subject:** Holy Year **Obv:** Bust right **Rev:** Procession thru Holy Year door

Date	Mintage	F12	VF20	XF40	MS60	MS63
1950	60,000	—	3.00	5.00	8.00	10.00

KM# 52.1 10 LIRE

1.00 g., Aluminum, 23 mm. **Obv:** Bust left **Obv. Legend:** AN **Rev:** Prudence standing and date divides value

Date	Mintage	F12	VF20	XF40	MS60	MS63
1951/XIII	1,130,000	—	0.50	0.75	1.25	1.50
1952/XIV	1,130,000	—	0.50	0.75	1.25	1.50
1953/XV	1,130,000	—	0.50	0.75	1.25	1.50

Date	Mintage	F12	VF20	XF40	MS60	MS63
1955/XVII	80,000	—	0.75	1.50	2.50	3.00
1957/XIX	—	—	0.75	1.50	2.50	3.00
1958/XX	—	—	0.75	1.50	2.50	3.00

KM# 52.2 10 LIRE

Aluminum, 23 mm. **Obv:** Bust left **Obv. Legend:** A **Rev:** Prudence standing date divides value

Date	Mintage	F12	VF20	XF40	MS60	MS63
1956/XVIII	80,000	—	0.75	1.50	2.50	3.00

KM# A52.1 20 LIRE

3.60 g., Aluminum-Bronze, 21.25 mm. **Obv:** Bust left **Obv. Legend:** A **Rev:** Caritas standing holding child with another at feet

Date	Mintage	F12	VF20	XF40	MS60	MS63
1957/XIX	20,000	—	0.75	1.25	2.50	3.00

KM# A52.2 20 LIRE

5.60 g., Aluminum-Bronze, 21.25 mm. **Obv:** Bust left **Obv. Legend:** AN **Rev:** Caritas standing holding child with another at feet

Date	Mintage	F12	VF20	XF40	MS60	MS63
1958/XX	60,000	—	0.75	1.25	2.50	3.00

KM# 54.1 50 LIRE

6.20 g., Stainless Steel, 24.8 mm. **Obv:** Bust right **Obv. Legend:** AN **Rev:** Spes standing with large anchor which divides date and value

Date	Mintage	F12	VF20	XF40	MS60	MS63
1955/XVII	180,000	—	1.00	1.50	3.00	—
1956/XVIII	—	—	1.00	1.50	3.00	—
1957/XIX	—	—	1.00	1.50	3.00	—
1958/XX	—	—	1.00	1.50	3.00	—

KM# 54.2 50 LIRE

6.20 g., Stainless Steel, 24.8 mm. **Obv:** Bust right **Obv. Legend:** A **Rev:** Spes standing facing with large anchor which divides date and value

Date	Mintage	F12	VF20	XF40	MS60	MS63
1956/XVIII	180,000	—	1.00	1.50	2.50	3.00
1957/XIX	180,000	—	1.00	1.50	2.50	3.00
1958/XX	60,000	—	1.00	1.50	2.50	3.00

KM# 30.1 100 LIRE

5.19 g., 0.900 Gold 0.1502 oz. AGW **Obv:** Head right **Obv. Legend:** AN **Rev:** Standing Jesus divides value

Date	Mintage	XF40	MS60	MS63	MS65	MS66
1939/I	2,700	400	600	750	900	1,150
1940/II	2,000	400	600	750	900	1,150

KM# 30.2 100 LIRE

5.19 g., 0.900 Gold 0.1502 oz. AGW **Obv:** Head right **Obv. Legend:** A **Rev:** Standing Jesus divides value

Date	Mintage	XF40	MS60	MS63	MS65	MS66
1941/III	2,000	400	600	750	900	1,150

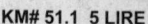

KM# 39 100 LIRE

5.19 g., 0.900 Gold 0.1502 oz. AGW **Obv:** Head right **Rev:** Caritas seated facing flanked by children

Date	Mintage	XF40	MS60	MS63	MS65	MS66
1942/IV	2,000	350	550	700	800	1,000
1943/V	1,000	—	650	950	1,150	—
1944/VI	1,000	—	650	950	1,150	—
1945/VII	1,000	—	650	950	1,150	—
1946/VIII	1,000	—	650	950	1,150	—
1947/IX	1,000	—	650	950	1,150	—
1948/X	5,000	350	550	700	800	1,000
1949/XI	1,000	400	600	750	900	1,200

KM# 48 100 LIRE

5.19 g., 0.900 Gold 0.1502 oz. AGW **Subject:** Holy Year **Obv:** Crowned bust left **Rev:** Opening of the Holy Year Door

Date	Mintage	XF40	MS60	MS63	MS65	MS66
MCML (1950)	20,000	300	400	500	650	775

KM# 53.1 100 LIRE

5.19 g., 0.900 Gold 0.1502 oz. AGW **Obv:** Bust right **Obv. Legend:** AN **Rev:** Caritas standing facing holding child with another at feet

Date	Mintage	XF40	MS60	MS63	MS65	MS66
1951/XIII	1,000	400	600	750	900	1,200
1952/XIV	1,000	400	600	750	900	1,200
1953/XV	1,000	400	600	750	900	1,200
1954/XVI	1,000	400	600	750	900	1,200
1955/XVII	1,000	400	600	750	900	1,200

KM# 53.2 100 LIRE

5.19 g., 0.900 Gold 0.1502 oz. AGW **Obv:** Bust right **Obv. Legend:** A **Rev:** Caritas standing facing holding child with another at feet

Date	Mintage	XF40	MS60	MS63	MS65	MS66
1956/XVIII	1,000	400	650	800	1,000	—

KM# 55 100 LIRE

8.00 g., Stainless Steel, 27.75 mm. **Obv:** Bust left **Rev:** Fides standing with large cross divides value and date **Edge:** Reeded

Date	Mintage	F12	VF20	XF40	MS60	MS63
1955/XVII	1,300,000	—	0.50	1.00	2.00	2.50
1956/XVII	1,400,000	—	0.50	1.00	2.00	2.50
1957/XIX	900,000	—	0.50	1.00	2.00	2.50
1958/XX	852,000	—	0.50	1.00	2.00	2.50

KM# A53 100 LIRE

5.19 g., 0.900 Gold 0.1502 oz. AGW **Obv:** Bust right **Rev:** Crowned shield divides value

Date	Mintage	XF40	MS60	MS63	MS65	MS66
1957/XIX	2,000	350	550	700	800	1,000
1958/XX	3,000	350	550	700	800	1,000

KM# 56 500 LIRE

11.00 g., 0.835 Silver 0.2953 oz. ASW, 29 mm. **Obv:** Bust left **Rev:** Crowned shield divides value

Date	Mintage	F12	VF20	XF40	MS60	MS63
1958/XX	20,000	—	8.00	16.00	25.00	35.00

Sede Vacante

KM# 57 500 LIRE

11.00 g., 0.835 Silver 0.2953 oz. ASW, 29.3 mm. **Obv:** Descending dove divides sun above value **Rev:** Arms of Cardinal Benedetto Aloisi-Masella

Date	Mintage	F12	VF20	XF40	MS60	MS63
1958	100,000	—	10.00	18.00	30.00	40.00

John XXIII

KM# 58.1 LIRA

Aluminum, 17 mm. **Obv:** Crowned shield **Obv. Legend:** AN **Rev:** Temperance kneeling pouring libation into bowl **Edge:** Plain

Date	Mintage	F12	VF20	XF40	MS60	MS63
1959/I	25,000	—	1.00	3.00	5.25	6.00
1960/II	25,000	—	1.00	2.00	3.50	4.00

KM# 58.2 LIRA

Aluminum, 17 mm. **Obv:** Crowned shield **Obv. Legend:** A **Rev:** Temperance kneeling pouring libation into bowl **Edge:** Plain

Date	Mintage	F12	VF20	XF40	MS60	MS63
1961/III	25,000	—	1.00	2.00	3.25	4.00
1962/IV	25,000	—	1.00	2.00	3.25	4.00

KM# 67 LIRA

Aluminum, 17 mm. **Subject:** Second Ecumenical Council **Obv:** Crowned shield **Rev:** Radiant dove in rays **Edge:** Plain

Date	Mintage	F12	VF20	XF40	MS60	MS63
1962/IV	50,000	—	1.00	1.50	2.50	3.00

KM# 59.1 2 LIRE

0.80 g., Aluminum, 18 mm. **Obv:** Crowned shield **Obv. Legend:** AN **Rev:** Fortude seated facing and lion divides value and date **Edge:** Reeded

Date	Mintage	F12	VF20	XF40	MS60	MS63
1959/I	25,000	—	1.50	4.00	5.25	6.00
1960/II	25,000	—	1.50	4.00	5.25	6.00

KM# 59.2 2 LIRE

0.80 g., Aluminum, 18 mm. **Obv:** Crowned shield **Obv. Legend:** A **Rev:** Fortude seated facing and lion divides value and date **Edge:** Reeded

Date	Mintage	F12	VF20	XF40	MS60	MS63
1961/III	25,000	—	1.50	4.00	5.25	6.00
1962/IV	25,000	—	1.50	4.00	5.25	6.00

KM# 68 2 LIRE

Aluminum, 18 mm. **Subject:** Second Ecumenical Council **Obv:** Crowned shield **Rev:** Radiant dove in rays

Date	Mintage	F12	VF20	XF40	MS60	MS63
1962/IV	50,000	—	1.00	1.50	2.50	3.00

KM# 60.1 5 LIRE

Aluminum, 20 mm. **Obv:** Bust right **Obv. Legend:** AN **Rev:** Kneeling figure holding sword and scales divides value and date

Date	Mintage	F12	VF20	XF40	MS60	MS63
1959/I	25,000	—	1.50	4.00	6.25	7.00

KM# 60.2 5 LIRE

Aluminum, 20 mm. **Obv:** Bust right **Obv. Legend:** A **Rev:** Kneeling figure holding sword and scales divides date and value

Date	Mintage	F12	VF20	XF40	MS60	MS63
1960/II	25,000	—	1.50	4.00	6.25	7.00
1961/III	25,000	—	1.50	4.00	6.25	7.00
1962/IV	25,000	—	1.00	2.00	3.50	4.00

KM# 69 5 LIRE

Aluminum, 20 mm. **Subject:** Second Ecumenical Council **Obv:** Bust right **Rev:** Radiant dove

Date	Mintage	F12	VF20	XF40	MS60	MS63
1962/IV	50,000	—	0.40	0.75	2.00	2.50

KM# 61.1 10 LIRE

Aluminum, 23 mm. **Obv:** Bust left **Obv. Legend:** AN **Rev:** Prudence kneeling holding snake and object divides value and date

Date	Mintage	F12	VF20	XF40	MS60	MS63
1959/I	50,000	—	1.00	3.00	5.25	6.00

KM# 61.2 10 LIRE

Aluminum, 23 mm. **Obv:** Bust left **Obv. Legend:** A **Rev:** Prudence kneeling

Date	Mintage	F12	VF20	XF40	MS60	MS63
1960/II	50,000	—	1.00	3.00	5.25	6.00
1961/III	50,000	—	1.00	3.00	5.25	6.00
1962/IV	50,000	—	1.00	2.00	3.25	4.00

KM# 70 10 LIRE

Aluminum, 23 mm. **Subject:** Second Ecumenical Council **Obv:** Bust left **Rev:** Radiant dove

Date	Mintage	F12	VF20	XF40	MS60	MS63
1962/IV	100,000	—	1.00	2.00	3.25	4.00

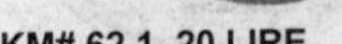

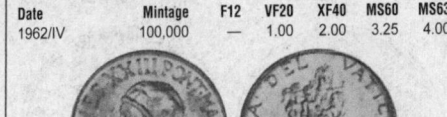

KM# 62.1 20 LIRE

3.60 g., Aluminum-Bronze, 21.25 mm. **Obv:** Helmeted bust

left **Obv. Legend:** AN **Rev:** Caritas seated facing flanked by children

Date	Mintage	F12	VF20	XF40	MS60	MS63
1959/I	50,000	—	0.75	1.25	2.50	3.00

KM# 62.2 20 LIRE
3.60 g., Aluminum-Bronze, 21.25 mm. **Obv:** Capped bust left **Obv. Legend:** A **Rev:** Seated figure with children

Date	Mintage	F12	VF20	XF40	MS60	MS63
1960/II	50,000	—	0.75	1.25	2.50	3.00
1961/III	50,000	—	0.75	1.00	2.50	3.00
1962/IV	50,000	—	0.75	1.00	2.50	3.00

KM# 71 20 LIRE
3.60 g., Aluminum-Bronze, 21.25 mm. **Subject:** Second Ecumenical Council **Obv:** Capped bust left **Rev:** Radiant dove

Date	Mintage	F12	VF20	XF40	MS60	MS63
1962/IV	100,000	—	0.75	1.00	2.00	2.50

KM# 63.1 50 LIRE
6.20 g., Stainless Steel, 24.8 mm. **Obv:** Bust right **Rev:** Spes standing facing with large anchor divides date and value

Date	Mintage	F12	VF20	XF40	MS60	MS63
1959/I	100,000	—	1.00	2.50	5.75	6.50

KM# 63.2 50 LIRE
6.20 g., Stainless Steel, 24.8 mm. **Obv:** Bust right **Rev:** Spes standing facing and large anchor divides date and value **Edge:** Reeded

Date	Mintage	F12	VF20	XF40	MS60	MS63
1960/II	100,000	—	1.00	2.50	5.00	5.50
1961/III	100,000	—	1.00	2.00	4.00	4.50
1962/IV	100,000	—	1.00	2.00	4.00	4.50

KM# 72 50 LIRE
6.20 g., Stainless Steel, 24.8 mm. **Subject:** Second Ecumenical Council **Obv:** Bust right **Rev:** Bishops at council meeting with radiant dove above

Date	Mintage	F12	VF20	XF40	MS60	MS63
1962/IV	200,000	—	0.50	1.25	2.50	3.00

KM# 64.1 100 LIRE
8.00 g., Stainless Steel, 27.75 mm. **Obv:** Bust left **Rev:** Fides standing, cross divides value and date

Date	Mintage	F12	VF20	XF40	MS60	MS63
1959/I	783,000	—	1.25	2.00	3.50	4.00

KM# 66 100 LIRE
5.19 g., 0.900 Gold 0.1502 oz. AGW **Obv:** Bust right **Rev:** Crowned shield divides value

Date	Mintage	F12	VF20	XF40	MS60	MS63
1959/I	3,000	—	—	1,250	1,550	1,850

KM# 64.2 100 LIRE
8.00 g., Stainless Steel, 27.75 mm. **Obv:** Regnal year under bust facing left **Rev:** Fides standing, cross divides value and date

Date	Mintage	F12	VF20	XF40	MS60	MS63
1960/II	783,000	—	1.75	3.00	5.75	6.50
1961/III	783,000	—	0.75	1.00	2.50	3.00
1962/IV	783,000	—	0.75	1.00	2.50	3.00

KM# 73 100 LIRE
8.00 g., Stainless Steel, 27.75 mm. **Subject:** Second Ecumenical Council **Obv:** Bust left **Rev:** Bishops at council meeting with radiant doves

Date	Mintage	F12	VF20	XF40	MS60	MS63
1962/IV	1,566,000	—	0.40	1.00	2.25	3.00

KM# 65.1 500 LIRE
11.00 g., 0.835 Silver 0.2953 oz. ASW, 29.3 mm. **Obv:** Bust left with continuous legend **Rev:** Crowned shield divides value

Date	Mintage	F12	VF20	XF40	MS60	MS63
1959/I	30,000	—	9.00	16.00	27.00	32.00

KM# 65.2 500 LIRE
11.00 g., 0.835 Silver 0.2953 oz. ASW, 29.3 mm. **Obv:** Regnal year under bust facing left **Rev:** Crowned shield divides value

Date	Mintage	F12	VF20	XF40	MS60	MS63
1960/II	30,000	—	9.00	16.00	27.00	32.00
1961/III	30,000	—	9.00	16.00	27.00	32.00
1962/IV	30,000	—	9.00	16.00	27.00	32.00

KM# 74 500 LIRE
11.00 g., 0.835 Silver 0.2953 oz. ASW, 29.3 mm. **Subject:** Second Ecumenical Council **Obv:** Crowned bust left **Rev:** Bishops at council meeting with radiant doves

Date	Mintage	F12	VF20	XF40	MS60	MS63
1962/IV	60,000	—	9.00	16.00	27.00	32.00

Sede Vacante

KM# 75 500 LIRE
11.00 g., 0.835 Silver 0.2953 oz. ASW, 29.3 mm. **Obv:** Descending dove divides sun above value **Rev:** Arms of Cardinal Benedetto Aloisi-Masella

Date	Mintage	F12	VF20	XF40	MS60	MS63
1963	200,000	—	8.00	15.00	25.00	30.00

Paul VI

KM# 76.1 LIRA
Aluminum, 17 mm. **Obv:** Crowned shield **Obv. Legend:** AN **Rev:** Temperance seated pouring libation divides value and date **Edge:** Plain

Date	Mintage	F12	VF20	XF40	MS60	MS63
1963/I	60,000	—	—	2.00	3.00	3.50

KM# 76.2 LIRA
Aluminum, 17 mm. **Obv:** Crowned shield **Obv. Legend:** A **Rev:** Temperance seated pouring libation divides value and date **Edge:** Plain

Date	Mintage	F12	VF20	XF40	MS60	MS63
1964/II	60,000	—	—	1.00	1.50	2.00
1965/III	60,000	—	—	1.00	1.50	2.00

KM# 84 LIRA
Aluminum, 17 mm. **Obv:** Crowned head left **Rev:** Sheep on shoulders of shepherd **Edge:** Plain

Date	Mintage	F12	VF20	XF40	MS60	MS63
1966/IV	90,000	—	—	0.75	1.00	1.25

KM# 92 LIRA
Aluminum, 17 mm. **Obv:** Crowned shield **Rev:** Crossed keys within radiant sword **Edge:** Plain

Date	Mintage	F12	VF20	XF40	MS60	MS63
1967/V	100,000	—	—	0.75	1.00	1.25

KM# 100 LIRA
Aluminum, 17 mm. **Series:** F.A.O. **Obv:** Bust left **Rev:** Wheat ears forming radiant cross **Edge:** Plain

Date	Mintage	F12	VF20	XF40	MS60	MS63
ND(1968)/VI	100,000	—	—	0.75	1.00	1.25

KM# 108 LIRA
Aluminum, 17 mm. **Series:** F.A.O. **Obv:** Crowned head 1/4 left divides inscription **Rev:** Stylized angel in flight **Edge:** Plain

Date	Mintage	F12	VF20	XF40	MS60	MS63
1969/VII	100,000	—	—	0.75	1.00	1.25

KM# 116 LIRA
Aluminum, 17 mm. **Series:** F.A.O. **Obv:** Crowned shield **Rev:** Palm sprigs

Date	Mintage	F12	VF20	XF40	MS60	MS63
1970/VIII	100,000	—	—	0.50	0.80	1.00
1971/IX	110,000	—	—	0.50	0.80	1.00
1972/X	110,000	—	—	0.50	0.80	1.00
1973/XI	132,000	—	—	0.50	0.80	1.00
1974/XII	132,000	—	—	0.50	0.80	1.00
1975/XIII	150,000	—	—	0.50	0.80	1.00
1976/XIV	150,000	—	—	0.50	0.80	1.00
1977/XV	135,000	—	—	0.50	0.80	1.00

KM# 124 LIRA
Aluminum, 17 mm. **Subject:** Holy Year - Faith in the Lord on Part of Man Afflicted by Evil **Obv:** Crowned shield **Rev:** Mother and child playing

Date	Mintage	F12	VF20	XF40	MS60	MS63
1975	170,000	—	—	0.50	0.80	1.00

KM# 77.1 2 LIRE
0.80 g., Aluminum, 18 mm. **Obv:** Crowned shield **Obv. Legend:** AN **Rev:** Fortude standing with shield, lion at side, value **Edge:** Reeded

Date	Mintage	F12	VF20	XF40	MS60	MS63
1963/I	60,000	—	—	2.00	2.75	3.00

KM# 77.2 2 LIRE
0.80 g., Aluminum, 18 mm. **Obv:** Crowned shield **Obv. Legend:** A **Rev:** Fortude standing with shield, lion at side, value **Edge:** Reeded

Date	Mintage	F12	VF20	XF40	MS60	MS63
1964/II	60,000	—	—	2.00	2.75	3.00
1965/III	60,000	—	—	2.00	2.75	3.00

KM# 85 2 LIRE
0.80 g., Aluminum, 18 mm. **Obv:** Crowned head left **Rev:** Sheep on shoulder of shepherd **Edge:** Reeded

Date	Mintage	F12	VF20	XF40	MS60	MS63
1966/IV	90,000	—	—	0.75	1.00	1.25

KM# 93 2 LIRE
0.80 g., Aluminum, 18 mm. **Obv:** Crowned shield **Rev:** Papal tiara above inverted cross, keys flanking **Edge:** Reeded

Date	Mintage	F12	VF20	XF40	MS60	MS63
1967/V	100,000	—	—	0.75	1.00	1.25

KM# 101 2 LIRE
0.80 g., Aluminum, 18 mm. **Series:** F.A.O. **Subject:** Feeding of the 5,000 **Obv:** Bust right **Rev:** Standing figure flanked by others **Edge:** Reeded

Date	Mintage	F12	VF20	XF40	MS60	MS63
ND(1968)/VI	100,000	—	—	0.75	1.00	1.25

KM# 109 2 LIRE
0.80 g., Aluminum, 18 mm. **Obv:** Crowned head 1/4 left divides inscription **Rev:** Stylized angel in flight **Edge:** Reeded

Date	Mintage	F12	VF20	XF40	MS60	MS63
1969/VII	100,000	—	—	0.75	1.00	1.25

KM# 117 2 LIRE
0.80 g., Aluminum, 18 mm. **Obv:** Crowned shield **Rev:** Lamb standing **Edge:** Reeded

Date	Mintage	F12	VF20	XF40	MS60	MS63
1970/VIII	100,000	—	—	0.50	0.80	1.00
1971/IX	110,000	—	—	0.50	0.80	1.00
1972/X	110,000	—	—	0.50	0.80	1.00
1973/XI	132,000	—	—	0.50	0.80	1.00
1974/XII	132,000	—	—	0.50	0.80	1.00
1975/XIII	150,000	—	—	0.50	0.80	1.00
1976/XIV	150,000	—	—	0.50	0.80	1.00
1977/XV	135,000	—	—	0.50	0.80	1.00

KM# 125 2 LIRE
0.80 g., Aluminum, 18 mm. **Subject:** Holy Year - Reconciliation among brothers **Obv:** Crowned shield **Rev:** Two men embracing **Edge:** Reeded

Date	Mintage	F12	VF20	XF40	MS60	MS63
1975	180,000	—	—	0.50	0.80	1.00

KM# 78.1 5 LIRE
Aluminum, 20 mm. **Obv:** Bust right **Obv. Legend:** AN **Rev:** Justice seated with sword and scales

Date	Mintage	F12	VF20	XF40	MS60	MS63
1963/I	60,000	—	—	2.00	3.50	4.00

KM# 78.2 5 LIRE
Aluminum, 20 mm. **Obv:** Bust right **Obv. Legend:** A **Rev:** Justice seated with sword and scales

Date	Mintage	F12	VF20	XF40	MS60	MS63
1964/II	60,000	—	—	4.00	5.25	6.00
1965/III	60,000	—	—	4.00	5.25	6.00

KM# 86 5 LIRE
Aluminum, 20 mm. **Obv:** Crowned head left **Rev:** Sheep on shoulder of shepherd

Date	Mintage	F12	VF20	XF40	MS60	MS63
1966/IV	90,000	—	—	0.50	1.00	1.25

KM# 94 5 LIRE
Aluminum, 20 mm. **Obv:** Bust right **Rev:** Crossed keys within radiant sword

Date	Mintage	F12	VF20	XF40	MS60	MS63
1967/V	100,000	—	—	0.50	1.00	1.25

KM# 102 5 LIRE
Aluminum, 20 mm. **Series:** F.A.O. **Subject:** Lady of the Harvest **Obv:** Bust right **Rev:** Our Lady of the Harvest within wheat sprigs

Date	Mintage	F12	VF20	XF40	MS60	MS63
ND(1968)/VI	100,000	—	—	0.50	1.00	1.25

KM# 110 5 LIRE
Aluminum, 20 mm. **Obv:** Crowned head 1/4 left divides inscription **Rev:** Stylized angel in flight

Date	Mintage	F12	VF20	XF40	MS60	MS63
1969/VII	100,000	—	—	0.50	1.00	1.25

KM# 118 5 LIRE
Aluminum, 20 mm. **Obv:** Crowned shield **Rev:** Pelican feeding young

Date	Mintage	F12	VF20	XF40	MS60	MS63
1970/VIII	100,000	—	—	0.50	1.00	1.25
1971/IX	110,000	—	—	0.50	1.00	1.25
1972/X	110,000	—	—	0.50	1.00	1.25
1973/XI	132,000	—	—	0.50	1.00	1.25
1974/XII	132,000	—	—	0.50	1.00	1.25
1975/XIII	150,000	—	—	0.50	1.00	1.25
1976/XIV	150,000	—	—	0.50	1.00	1.25
1977/XV	135,000	—	—	0.50	1.00	1.25

KM# 126 5 LIRE
Aluminum, 20 mm. **Subject:** Holy Year - Redemption of the Woman of Bethany **Obv:** Crowned shield **Rev:** Female kneeling receiving blessing from seated figure

Date	Mintage	F12	VF20	XF40	MS60	MS63
1975	380,000	—	—	0.50	1.00	1.25

KM# 133 5 LIRE
Aluminum, 20 mm. **Obv:** Crowned shield **Rev:** Stylized standing figure divides value

Date	Mintage	F12	VF20	XF40	MS60	MS63
1978/XVI	120,000	—	—	0.50	1.00	1.25

KM# 79.1 10 LIRE
Aluminum, 23 mm. **Obv:** Bust left **Obv. Legend:** AN **Rev:** Prudence standing dividing date and value

Date	Mintage	F12	VF20	XF40	MS60	MS63
1963/I	90,000	—	—	1.50	2.50	3.00

KM# 79.2 10 LIRE
Aluminum, 23 mm. **Obv:** Bust left **Obv. Legend:** A **Rev:** Prudence standing dividing date and value

Date	Mintage	F12	VF20	XF40	MS60	MS63
1964/II	90,000	—	—	1.50	2.50	3.00
1965/III	90,000	—	—	1.50	2.50	3.00

KM# 87 10 LIRE
Aluminum, 23 mm. **Obv:** Crowned head left **Rev:** Shepard with sheep on his shoulders

Date	Mintage	F12	VF20	XF40	MS60	MS63
1966/IV	100,000	—	—	1.00	1.75	2.00

KM# 95 10 LIRE
Aluminum, 23 mm. **Obv:** Bust left **Rev:** Papal taira above inverted cross, keys flanking

Date	Mintage	F12	VF20	XF40	MS60	MS63
ND(1967)/V	110,000	—	—	0.75	1.00	1.25

KM# 103 10 LIRE
Aluminum, 23 mm. **Series:** F.A.O. **Obv:** Bust left **Rev:** Feeding of the 5,000

Date	Mintage	F12	VF20	XF40	MS60	MS63
ND(1968)/VI	110,000	—	—	0.75	1.25	1.50

KM# 111 10 LIRE
Aluminum, 23 mm. **Obv:** Crowned head 1/4 left divides inscription **Rev:** Stylized angel in flight

Date	Mintage	F12	VF20	XF40	MS60	MS63
1969/VII	110,000	—	—	0.50	1.00	1.25

KM# 119 10 LIRE
Aluminum, 23 mm. **Obv:** Crowned shield **Rev:** Fish

Date	Mintage	F12	VF20	XF40	MS60	MS63
1970/VIII	110,000	—	—	0.50	1.00	1.25
1971/IX	160,000	—	—	0.50	1.00	1.25
1972/X	160,000	—	—	0.50	1.00	1.25
1973/XI	170,000	—	—	0.50	1.00	1.25
1974/XII	170,000	—	—	0.50	1.00	1.25
1975/XIII	200,000	—	—	0.50	1.00	1.25
1976/XIV	200,000	—	—	0.50	1.00	1.25
1977/XV	200,000	—	—	0.50	1.00	1.25

KM# 127 10 LIRE
Aluminum, 23 mm. **Subject:** Holy Year - Reconciliation between God and man **Obv:** Crowned shield **Rev:** Noah's ark

Date	Mintage	F12	VF20	XF40	MS60	MS63
1975	400,000	—	—	0.75	1.25	1.50

KM# 134 10 LIRE
Aluminum, 23 mm. **Obv:** Crowned shield **Rev:** Figure kneeling left

Date	Mintage	F12	VF20	XF40	MS60	MS63
1978/XVI	250,000	—	—	0.50	0.80	1.00

KM# 80.1 20 LIRE
3.60 g., Aluminum-Bronze, 21.25 mm. **Obv:** Bust left **Obv. Legend:** AN **Rev:** Caritas seated flanked by children

Date	Mintage	F12	VF20	XF40	MS60	MS63
1963/I	90,000	—	—	2.00	3.50	4.00
1964/II	90,000	—	—	2.00	3.50	4.00

KM# 80.2 20 LIRE
3.60 g., Aluminum-Bronze, 21.25 mm. **Obv:** Bust left **Obv. Legend:** A **Rev:** Caritas seated flanked by children

Date	Mintage	F12	VF20	XF40	MS60	MS63
1965/III	90,000	—	—	1.00	1.75	2.00

KM# 88 20 LIRE
3.60 g., Aluminum-Bronze, 21.25 mm. **Obv:** Crowned head left **Rev:** Shepard with sheep on his shoulders

Date	Mintage	F12	VF20	XF40	MS60	MS63
1966/IV	100,000	—	—	0.75	1.00	1.25

KM# 96 20 LIRE
3.60 g., Aluminum-Bronze, 21.25 mm. **Obv:** Bust right **Rev:** Saints Peter and Paul, sword between

Date	Mintage	F12	VF20	XF40	MS60	MS63
ND(1967)/V	105,000	—	—	0.75	1.25	1.50

KM# 104 20 LIRE
3.60 g., Aluminum-Bronze, 21.25 mm. **Series:** F.A.O. **Obv:** Bust right **Rev:** Wheat ears forming radiant cross

Date	Mintage	F12	VF20	XF40	MS60	MS63
ND(1968)/VI	105,000	—	—	0.75	1.25	2.00

KM# 112 20 LIRE
3.60 g., Aluminum-Bronze, 21.25 mm. **Obv:** Crowned head 1/4 left divides inscription **Rev:** Stylized angel in flight

Date	Mintage	F12	VF20	XF40	MS60	MS63
1969/VII	105,000	—	—	0.60	1.25	2.00

KM# 120 20 LIRE
3.60 g., Aluminum-Bronze, 21.3 mm. **Obv:** Crowned shield **Rev:** Red deer

Date	Mintage	F12	VF20	XF40	MS60	MS63
1970/VIII	105,000	—	—	0.50	1.25	2.00
1971/IX	170,000	—	—	0.50	1.25	2.00
1972/X	170,000	—	—	0.50	1.25	2.00
1973/XI	—	—	—	0.50	1.25	2.00
1974/XII	—	—	—	0.50	1.25	2.00
1975/XIII	250,000	—	—	0.50	1.25	2.00
1976/XIV	250,000	—	—	0.50	1.25	2.00
1977/XV	250,000	—	—	0.50	1.25	2.00

KM# 128 20 LIRE
3.60 g., Aluminum-Bronze, 21.25 mm. **Subject:** Holy Year - Man's Confidence in the Lord **Obv:** Crowned shield **Rev:** Standing figure facing right and value

Date	Mintage	F12	VF20	XF40	MS60	MS63
1975	400,000	—	—	0.50	1.25	2.00

KM# 135 20 LIRE
3.60 g., Aluminum-Bronze, 21.25 mm. **Subject:** Prodigal Son Parable **Obv:** Crowned shield **Rev:** Standing figures facing each other above value

Date	Mintage	F12	VF20	XF40	MS60	MS63
1978/XVI	120,000	—	—	0.50	1.25	2.00

KM# 81.1 50 LIRE
6.20 g., Stainless Steel, 24.8 mm. **Obv:** Bust right **Obv. Legend:** AN **Rev:** Spes standing with anchor, date and value are divided

Date	Mintage	F12	VF20	XF40	MS60	MS63
1963/I	120,000	—	—	2.00	3.25	4.00
1964/II	120,000	—	—	1.50	2.75	3.00

KM# 81.2 50 LIRE
6.20 g., Stainless Steel, 24.8 mm. **Obv:** Bust right **Obv. Legend:** A **Rev:** Spes standing with anchor, date and value divided

Date	Mintage	F12	VF20	XF40	MS60	MS63
1965/III	120,000	—	—	1.00	1.75	2.00

KM# 89 50 LIRE

6.20 g., Stainless Steel, 24.8 mm. **Obv:** Crowned head left **Rev:** Shepard with sheep on shoulders

Date	Mintage	F12	VF20	XF40	MS60	MS63
1966/IV	150,000	—	—	1.00	1.75	2.00

KM# 97 50 LIRE

6.20 g., Stainless Steel, 24.8 mm. **Subject:** Conversion of Saint Paul **Obv:** Bust right **Rev:** Rearing equestrian

Date	Mintage	F12	VF20	XF40	MS60	MS63
1967/V	190,000	—	—	1.00	1.75	2.00

KM# 105 50 LIRE

6.20 g., Stainless Steel, 24.8 mm. **Series:** F.A.O. **Obv:** Bust right **Rev:** Our Lady of Harvest standing within wheat sprigs

Date	Mintage	F12	VF20	XF40	MS60	MS63
ND(1968)/VI	190,000	—	—	1.00	1.75	2.00

KM# 113 50 LIRE

6.20 g., Stainless Steel, 24.8 mm. **Obv:** Crowned head 1/4 left divides inscription **Rev:** Stylized angel

Date	Mintage	F12	VF20	XF40	MS60	MS63
1969/VII	190,000	—	—	1.00	1.75	2.00

KM# 121 50 LIRE

6.20 g., Stainless Steel, 24.9 mm. **Obv:** Crowned shield **Rev:** Olive branch

Date	Mintage	F12	VF20	XF40	MS60	MS63
1970/VIII	190,000	—	—	0.75	1.50	1.75
1971/IX	700,000	—	—	0.75	1.25	1.50
1972/X	700,000	—	—	0.75	1.25	1.50
1973/XI	750,000	—	—	0.75	1.25	1.50
1974/XII	750,000	—	—	0.75	1.25	1.50
1975/XIII	600,000	—	—	0.75	1.25	1.50
1976/XIV	600,000	—	—	0.75	1.25	1.50

KM# 129 50 LIRE

6.20 g., Stainless Steel, 24.8 mm. **Subject:** Holy Year - The Peace of the Lord **Obv:** Crowned shield **Rev:** Stylized figure in fetal position within design with hand above **Edge:** Reeded

Date	Mintage	F12	VF20	XF40	MS60	MS63
1975	500,000	—	—	0.75	1.25	1.50

KM# A121 50 LIRE

6.20 g., Stainless Steel, 24.8 mm. **Obv:** Crowned shield **Rev:** Wheat and grapes

Date	Mintage	F12	VF20	XF40	MS60	MS63
1977/XV	600,000	—	—	0.40	1.25	1.50

KM# 136 50 LIRE

6.20 g., Stainless Steel, 24.8 mm. **Obv:** Crowned shield **Rev:** Child and kneeling adult

Date	Mintage	F12	VF20	XF40	MS60	MS63
1978/XVI	223,000	—	—	0.75	1.25	1.50

KM# 82.1 100 LIRE

8.00 g., Stainless Steel, 27.75 mm. **Obv:** Bust left **Obv. Legend:** AN **Rev:** Fides standing figure divides value and date

Date	Mintage	F12	VF20	XF40	MS60	MS63
1963/I	558,000	—	—	2.00	3.25	3.75

KM# 82.2 100 LIRE

8.00 g., Stainless Steel, 27.75 mm. **Obv:** Bust left **Obv. Legend:** A **Rev:** Fides standing figure divides value and date

Date	Mintage	F12	VF20	XF40	MS60	MS63
1964/II	558,000	—	—	1.00	2.50	3.00
1965/III	558,000	—	—	1.00	2.50	3.00

KM# 90 100 LIRE

8.00 g., Stainless Steel, 27.75 mm. **Obv:** Crowned head left **Rev:** Shepard with sheep on shoulders

Date	Mintage	F12	VF20	XF40	MS60	MS63
1966/IV	388,000	—	—	1.00	2.00	2.50

KM# 98 100 LIRE

8.00 g., Stainless Steel, 27.75 mm. **Obv:** Bust left **Rev:** St. Peter seated on throne facing **Edge:** Reeded

Date	Mintage	F12	VF20	XF40	MS60	MS63
1967/V	315,000	—	—	1.00	2.25	2.50

KM# 106 100 LIRE

8.00 g., Stainless Steel, 27.75 mm. **Series:** F.A.O. **Obv:** Bust left **Rev:** Feeding of the 5,000

Date	Mintage	F12	VF20	XF40	MS60	MS63
ND(1968)/VI	315,000	—	—	1.00	2.25	2.50

KM# 114 100 LIRE

8.00 g., Stainless Steel, 27.75 mm. **Obv:** Crowned head 1/4 left divides inscription **Rev:** Stylized angel in flight

Date	Mintage	F12	VF20	XF40	MS60	MS63
1969/VII	315,000	—	—	1.00	2.25	2.50

KM# 122 100 LIRE

8.10 g., Stainless Steel, 27.9 mm. **Obv:** Crowned shield **Rev:** Dove in flight with olive branch

Date	Mintage	F12	VF20	XF40	MS60	MS63
1970/VIII	315,000	—	—	1.00	2.00	2.50
1971/IX	966,000	—	—	0.75	1.25	1.50
1972/X	966,000	—	—	0.75	1.25	1.50
1973/XI	830,000	—	—	0.75	1.25	1.50
1974/XII	830,000	—	—	0.75	1.25	1.50
1975/XIII	808,000	—	—	0.75	1.25	1.50
1976/XIV	808,000	—	—	0.75	1.25	1.50
1977/XV	819,000	—	—	0.75	1.25	1.50

KM# 130 100 LIRE

8.00 g., Stainless Steel, 27.75 mm. **Subject:** Holy Year - Symbolic Baptism of Man **Obv:** Crowned shield **Rev:** Hands pulling up net filled with fish

Date	Mintage	F12	VF20	XF40	MS60	MS63
1975	605,000	—	—	1.50	3.25	3.50

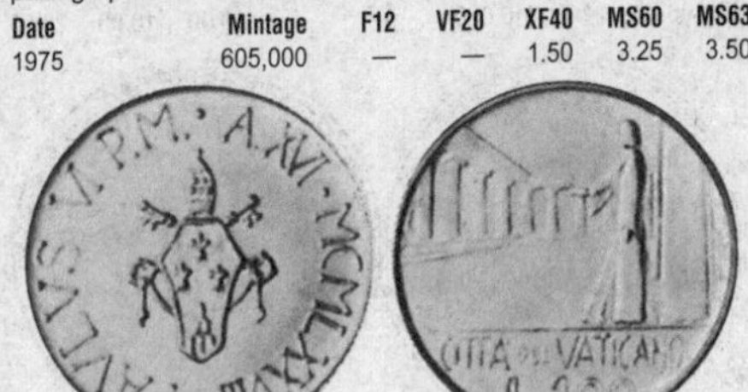

KM# 137 100 LIRE

8.00 g., Stainless Steel, 27.75 mm. **Obv:** Crowned shield **Rev:** Stylized figure standing in courtyard

Date	Mintage	F12	VF20	XF40	MS60	MS63
1978/XVI	399,000	—	—	1.00	2.25	2.50

KM# 138 200 LIRE
5.00 g., Aluminum-Bronze, 24 mm. **Obv:** Crowned shield **Rev:** Stylized figure above value

Date	Mintage	F12	VF20	XF40	MS60	MS63
1978/XVI	355,000	—	—	1.00	2.00	2.50

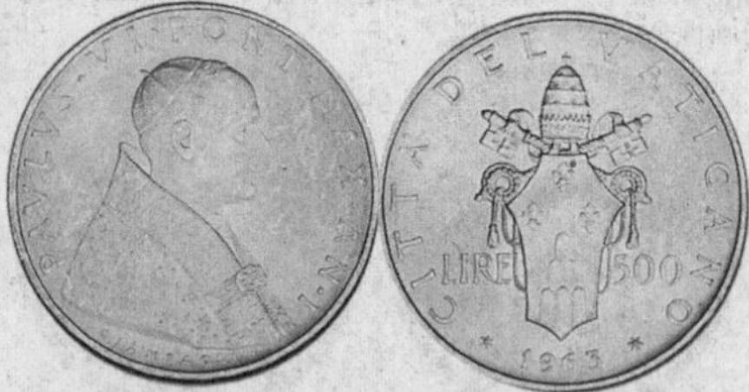

KM# 83.1 500 LIRE
11.00 g., 0.835 Silver 0.2953 oz. ASW, 29.3 mm. **Obv:** Bust right **Obv. Legend:** AN **Rev:** Crowned shield divides value

Date	Mintage	F12	VF20	XF40	MS60	MS63
1963/I	70,000	—	—	12.00	20.00	30.00

KM# 83.2 500 LIRE
11.00 g., 0.835 Silver 0.2953 oz. ASW, 29.3 mm. **Obv:** Bust right **Obv. Legend:** A **Rev:** Crowned shield divides value

Date	Mintage	F12	VF20	XF40	MS60	MS63
1964/II	70,000	—	—	12.00	20.00	30.00
1965/III	70,000	—	—	12.00	20.00	30.00

KM# 91 500 LIRE
11.00 g., 0.835 Silver 0.2953 oz. ASW, 29.3 mm. **Obv:** Crowned head left **Rev:** Shepard with sheep on shoulders

Date	Mintage	F12	VF20	XF40	MS60	MS63
1966/IV	100,000	—	—	10.00	18.00	28.00

KM# 99 500 LIRE
11.00 g., 0.835 Silver 0.2953 oz. ASW, 29.3 mm. **Obv:** Bust left **Rev:** Saint Peter and Paul, cross between, keys below

Date	Mintage	F12	VF20	XF40	MS60	MS63
ND(1967)/V	110,000	—	—	10.00	18.00	28.00

KM# 107 500 LIRE
11.00 g., 0.835 Silver 0.2953 oz. ASW, 29.3 mm. **Series:** F.A.O. **Obv:** Bust left **Rev:** Wheat ears forming radiant cross

Date	Mintage	F12	VF20	XF40	MS60	MS63
ND(1968)/VI	110,000	—	—	10.00	18.00	28.00

KM# 115 500 LIRE
11.00 g., 0.835 Silver 0.2953 oz. ASW, 29.3 mm. **Obv:** Crowned head 1/4 left divides inscription **Rev:** Stylized angel in flight

Date	Mintage	F12	VF20	XF40	MS60	MS63
1969/VII	110,000	—	—	10.00	18.00	28.00

KM# 123 500 LIRE
11.00 g., 0.835 Silver 0.2953 oz. ASW, 29.3 mm. **Obv:** Crowned shield **Rev:** Wheat and grapes

Date	Mintage	F12	VF20	XF40	MS60	MS63
1970/VIII	110,000	—	—	9.00	15.00	20.00
1971/IX	125,000	—	—	9.00	15.00	20.00
1972/X	125,000	—	—	9.00	15.00	20.00
1973/XI	145,000	—	—	9.00	15.00	20.00
1974/XII	145,000	—	—	9.00	15.00	20.00
1975/XIII	162,000	—	—	9.00	15.00	20.00
1976/XIV	162,000	—	—	9.00	15.00	20.00

KM# 131 500 LIRE
11.00 g., 0.835 Silver 0.2953 oz. ASW, 29.3 mm. **Subject:** Holy Year - Forgiveness **Obv:** Crowned shield **Rev:** Stylized father embracing son

Date	Mintage	F12	VF20	XF40	MS60	MS63
1975	200,000	—	—	9.00	15.00	20.00

KM# 132 500 LIRE
11.00 g., 0.835 Silver 0.2953 oz. ASW, 29.3 mm. **Subject:** Book of the Evangelists **Obv:** Crowned shield **Rev:** Assorted animal heads within cross window frame

Date	Mintage	F12	VF20	XF40	MS60	MS63
1977/XV	160,000	—	—	9.00	15.00	20.00

KM# 139 500 LIRE
11.00 g., 0.835 Silver 0.2953 oz. ASW, 29.3 mm. **Obv:** Crowned shield **Rev:** Stylized Jesus walking on water reaching for figure in boat

Date	Mintage	F12	VF20	XF40	MS60	MS63
1978/XVI	145,000	—	—	9.00	15.00	20.00

John Paul I

KM# 142 1000 LIRE
14.60 g., 0.835 Silver 0.3919 oz. ASW **Obv:** Bust left **Rev:** Crowned shield

Date	Mintage	VF20	XF40	MS60	MS63	MS65
1978	200,000	—	17.00	22.00	30.00	35.00

Sede Vacante

KM# 140 500 LIRE
11.00 g., 0.835 Silver 0.2953 oz. ASW, 29.3 mm. **Obv:** Descending stylized dove above value **Rev:** Arms of Cardinal Jean Villot **Rev. Legend:** SEDE VACANTE MCMLXXVIII **Note:** First 1978 Sede Vacante issue

Date	Mintage	VF20	XF40	MS60	MS63	MS65
1978	500,000	—	15.00	20.00	28.00	32.00

KM# 141 500 LIRE
11.00 g., 0.835 Silver 0.2953 oz. ASW **Obv:** Descending radiant dove **Rev:** Arms of Cardinal Jean Villot **Rev. Legend:** SEDE VACANTE SEPTEMBER MCMLXXVIII **Note:** Second 1978 Sede Vacante issue

Date	Mintage	VF20	XF40	MS60	MS63	MS65
1978	—	—	17.00	22.00	30.00	35.00

Note: Mintage included with KM#140

John Paul II

KM# 143 10 LIRE
Aluminum, 23 mm. **Obv:** Bust left **Rev:** Cardinal Virtues - Temperance

Date	Mintage	VF20	XF40	MS60	MS63	MS65
1979/I	250,000	—	1.00	2.00	2.50	—
1980/II	170,000	—	1.00	2.00	2.50	—

KM# 155 10 LIRE
Aluminum, 23 mm. **Obv:** Head left **Rev:** Jesus given water at the well

Date	Mintage	VF20	XF40	MS60	MS63	MS65
1981/III R	170,000	—	1.00	2.00	2.50	—

KM# 161 10 LIRE
Aluminum, 23 mm. **Subject:** Creation of Woman **Obv:** Bust right **Rev:** Standing figure facing to right of value

Date	Mintage	VF20	XF40	MS60	MS63	MS65
1982/IV R	220,000	—	1.00	2.00	2.50	—

KM# 170 10 LIRE
Aluminum, 23 mm. **Subject:** Work and Teaching **Obv:** Head left at lower right of cross **Rev:** Teacher, student and value

Date	Mintage	VF20	XF40	MS60	MS63	MS65
1983/V R	110,000	—	1.00	2.00	2.50	—

KM# 177 10 LIRE
Aluminum, 23 mm. **Subject:** Year of Peace **Obv:** Bust left **Rev:** Hand holding bouquet

Date	Mintage	VF20	XF40	MS60	MS63	MS65
1984/VI R	110,000	—	1.00	2.00	2.50	—

KM# 185 10 LIRE
Aluminum, 23 mm. **Obv:** Head left **Rev:** Angel with gospel of St. Matthew

Date	Mintage	VF20	XF40	MS60	MS63	MS65
1985/VII	90,000	—	1.00	2.00	2.50	—

KM# 192 10 LIRE
Aluminum, 23 mm. **Rev:** Mary seated, value

Date	Mintage	VF20	XF40	MS60	MS63	MS65
1986/VIII	90,000	—	1.00	2.00	2.50	—

KM# 199 10 LIRE
Aluminum, 23 mm. **Obv:** Bust right **Rev:** Basilica behind Pieta Statue

Date	Mintage	VF20	XF40	MS60	MS63	MS65
1987/IX	—	—	1.00	2.00	2.50	—

KM# 206 10 LIRE
Aluminum, 23 mm. **Subject:** Temptation of Adam and Eve **Obv:** Bust right **Rev:** Tree with snake divides standing figures

Date	Mintage	VF20	XF40	MS60	MS63	MS65
1988/X	—	—	1.00	2.00	2.50	—

KM# 213 10 LIRE
Aluminum, 23 mm. **Subject:** Jesus the Teacher **Rev:** Seated figure facing standing figure

Date	Mintage	VF20	XF40	MS60	MS63	MS65
1989/XI	—	—	1.00	2.00	2.50	—

KM# 220 10 LIRE
Aluminum, 23 mm. **Subject:** Saints Peter and Paul **Obv:** Bust 3/4 left **Rev:** Saints Peter and Paul facing

Date	Mintage	VF20	XF40	MS60	MS63	MS65
1990/XII	—	—	1.00	2.00	2.50	—

KM# 228 10 LIRE
Aluminum, 23 mm. **Obv:** Head left **Rev:** Standing figure with book to right of value

Date	Mintage	VF20	XF40	MS60	MS63	MS65
1991/XIII	—	—	1.00	2.00	2.50	—

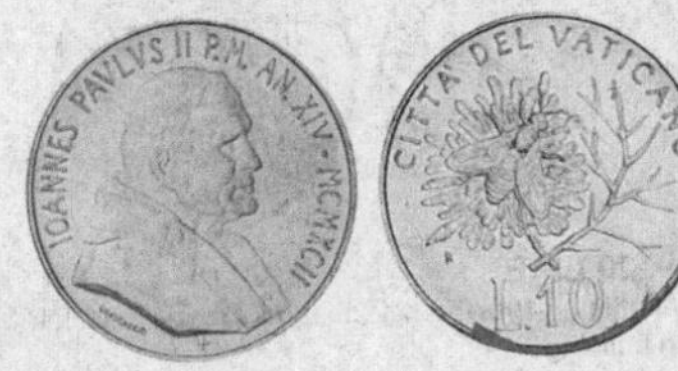

KM# 236 10 LIRE
Aluminum, 23 mm. **Obv:** Bust right **Rev:** Bee on flower

Date	Mintage	VF20	XF40	MS60	MS63	MS65
1992/XIV	—	—	1.00	2.00	2.50	—

KM# 244 10 LIRE
Aluminum, 23 mm. **Obv:** Head facing **Rev:** Sailboat divides inscription

Date	Mintage	VF20	XF40	MS60	MS63	MS65
1993/XV	—	—	1.00	2.00	2.50	—

KM# 252 10 LIRE
Aluminum, 23 mm. **Obv:** Bust left **Rev:** Figures planting trees

Date	Mintage	VF20	XF40	MS60	MS63	MS65
1994/XVI	—	—	1.00	2.00	2.50	—

KM# 262 10 LIRE
Aluminum, 23 mm. **Rev:** Preaching

Date	Mintage	VF20	XF40	MS60	MS63	MS65
1995/XVII	—	—	1.00	2.00	2.50	—

KM# 272 10 LIRE
Aluminum, 23 mm. **Subject:** Child Carried to Peace **Obv:** Head left **Rev:** Stylized standing figure holding infant walking left

Date	Mintage	VF20	XF40	MS60	MS63	MS65
1996/XVIII	—	—	1.00	2.50	3.00	—

KM# 280 10 LIRE
Aluminum, 23 mm. **Obv:** Head right **Rev:** Angel blowing horn to upper right of man sowing seeds

Date	Mintage	VF20	XF40	MS60	MS63	MS65
1997/XIX	—	—	1.00	2.50	3.00	—

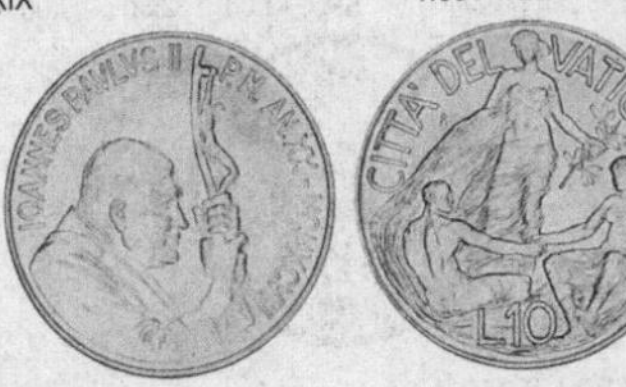

KM# 293 10 LIRE
1.60 g., Aluminum, 23 mm. **Obv:** Bust right holding crucifix **Rev:** Standing figure flanked by seated figures

Date	Mintage	VF20	XF40	MS60	MS63	MS65
1998/XX	—	—	1.00	2.50	3.00	—

KM# 305 10 LIRE
1.60 g., Aluminum, 23.3 mm. **Subject:** Right to Life - Motherhood **Obv:** Bust right **Rev:** Mother with baby and child below tree **Edge:** Plain

Date	Mintage	VF20	XF40	MS60	MS63	MS65
1999/XXI	—	—	1.00	2.50	3.00	—

KM# 323 10 LIRE
1.60 g., Aluminum, 23.2 mm. **Obv:** Papal arms within circle **Rev:** Pope lifting child **Edge:** Plain

Date	Mintage	VF20	XF40	MS60	MS63	MS65
2000/XXII	—	—	1.00	2.50	3.00	—

KM# 144 20 LIRE
3.60 g., Aluminum-Bronze, 21.25 mm. **Rev:** Fortitude

Date	Mintage	VF20	XF40	MS60	MS63	MS65
1979/I	120,000	—	1.00	2.50	3.00	—
1980/II	265,000	—	1.00	2.50	3.00	—

KM# 156 20 LIRE
3.60 g., Aluminum-Bronze, 21.25 mm. **Obv:** Head left **Rev:** Open door flanked by standing figures

Date	Mintage	VF20	XF40	MS60	MS63	MS65
1981/III	265,000	—	1.00	2.50	3.00	—

KM# 162 20 LIRE
3.60 g., Aluminum-Bronze, 21.25 mm. **Subject:** Marriage **Obv:** Bust right **Rev:** Standing figures shaking hands

Date	Mintage	VF20	XF40	MS60	MS63	MS65
1982/IV	360,000	—	1.00	2.50	3.00	—

KM# 171 20 LIRE
3.60 g., Aluminum-Bronze, 21.25 mm. **Subject:** Incarnation of the Word **Obv:** Head left to lower right of cross **Rev:** Radiant dove above stylized kneeling figures within triangle shape

Date	Mintage	VF20	XF40	MS60	MS63	MS65
1983/V	170,000	—	1.00	2.50	3.00	—

KM# 178 20 LIRE
3.60 g., Aluminum-Bronze, 21.25 mm. **Subject:** Year of Peace **Obv:** Bust left **Rev:** Child and sheep

Date	Mintage	VF20	XF40	MS60	MS63	MS65
1984/VI	170,000	—	1.00	2.50	3.00	—

KM# 186 20 LIRE
3.60 g., Aluminum-Bronze, 21.25 mm. **Obv:** Head left **Rev:** Stylized eagle holding gospel of St. John

Date	Mintage	VF20	XF40	MS60	MS63	MS65
1985/VII	255,000	—	1.00	2.50	3.00	—

KM# 193 20 LIRE
3.60 g., Aluminum-Bronze, 21.25 mm. **Obv:** Bust right **Rev:** Stylized standing angel

Date	Mintage	VF20	XF40	MS60	MS63	MS65
1986/VIII	100,000	—	1.00	2.50	3.00	—

KM# 200 20 LIRE
3.60 g., Aluminum-Bronze, 21.25 mm. **Obv:** Bust right **Rev:** Assumption of Mother Mary into heaven

Date	Mintage	VF20	XF40	MS60	MS63	MS65
1987/IX	—	—	1.00	2.50	3.00	—

KM# 207 20 LIRE
3.60 g., Aluminum-Bronze, 21.25 mm. **Subject:** Temptation of Adam and Eve **Rev:** Apple tree flanked by standing figures and pair of hands **Note:** Similar to 200 Lire, KM#210.

Date	Mintage	VF20	XF40	MS60	MS63	MS65
1988/X	—	—	1.00	2.50	3.00	—

KM# 214 20 LIRE
3.60 g., Aluminum-Bronze, 21.25 mm. **Subject:** The Harvest **Rev:** Standing and kneeling figures

Date	Mintage	VF20	XF40	MS60	MS63	MS65
1989/XI	—	—	1.00	2.50	3.00	—

KM# 221 20 LIRE
3.60 g., Aluminum-Bronze, 21.25 mm. **Obv:** Bust 3/4 left **Rev:** Pope John Paul II and Eastern Rite Bishop

Date	Mintage	VF20	XF40	MS60	MS63	MS65
1990/XII	—	—	1.00	2.50	3.00	—

KM# 229 20 LIRE
3.60 g., Aluminum-Bronze, 21.25 mm. **Obv:** Head left **Rev:** Crane and buildings

Date	Mintage	VF20	XF40	MS60	MS63	MS65
1991/XIII	—	—	1.00	2.50	3.00	—

KM# 237 20 LIRE
3.60 g., Aluminum-Bronze, 21.25 mm. **Obv:** Bust right **Rev:** Three children above value

Date	Mintage	VF20	XF40	MS60	MS63	MS65
1992/XIV	—	—	1.00	2.50	3.00	—

KM# 245 20 LIRE
3.60 g., Aluminum-Bronze, 21.25 mm. **Obv:** Head facing **Rev:** Crucifix, as on papal croizer

Date	Mintage	VF20	XF40	MS60	MS63	MS65
1993/XV	—	—	1.00	2.50	3.00	—

KM# 253 20 LIRE
3.60 g., Aluminum-Bronze, 21.25 mm. **Obv:** Bust left **Rev:** Hospital patient with visitors

Date	Mintage	VF20	XF40	MS60	MS63	MS65
1994/XVI	—	—	1.00	2.50	3.00	—

KM# 263 20 LIRE
3.60 g., Aluminum-Bronze, 21.25 mm. **Subject:** Euthanasia

Date	Mintage	VF20	XF40	MS60	MS63	MS65
1995/XVII	—	—	1.00	2.50	3.00	—

KM# 273 20 LIRE
3.60 g., Aluminum-Bronze, 21.25 mm. **Obv:** Head left **Rev:** Parents praising child

Date	Mintage	VF20	XF40	MS60	MS63	MS65
1996/XVIII	—	—	1.00	2.50	3.00	—

KM# 281 20 LIRE
3.60 g., Aluminum-Bronze, 21.25 mm. **Obv:** Bust right **Rev:** Jesus teaching with book

Date	Mintage	VF20	XF40	MS60	MS63	MS65
1997/XIX	—	—	1.00	2.50	3.00	—

KM# 294 20 LIRE
3.60 g., Aluminum-Bronze, 21.25 mm. **Obv:** Bust right holding crucifix **Rev:** Family and sun

Date	Mintage	VF20	XF40	MS60	MS63	MS65
1998/XX	—	—	1.00	2.50	3.00	—

KM# 306 20 LIRE
3.60 g., Aluminum-Bronze, 21.3 mm. **Subject:** Work - The Right to Fulfill One's Potential **Obv:** Bust right **Rev:** Workers **Edge:** Plain

Date	Mintage	VF20	XF40	MS60	MS63	MS65
1999/XXI	—	—	1.00	2.50	3.00	—

KM# 324 20 LIRE
3.57 g., Brass, 21.2 mm. **Obv:** Papal arms within circle **Rev:** Head of Pope stargazing **Edge:** Plain

Date	Mintage	VF20	XF40	MS60	MS63	MS65
2000/XXII	—	—	1.00	2.50	3.00	—

KM# 145 50 LIRE
6.20 g., Stainless Steel, 24.8 mm. **Obv:** Bust left **Rev:** Justice seated right with sword and scales

Date	Mintage	VF20	XF40	MS60	MS63	MS65
1979/I	223,000	0.50	1.00	3.00	—	—
1980/II	250,000	0.50	1.00	3.00	—	—

KM# 157 50 LIRE

6.20 g., Stainless Steel, 24.8 mm. **Obv:** Head left **Rev:** Upright design flanked by standing figures

Date	Mintage	VF20	XF40	MS60	MS63	MS65
1981/III	240,000	—	1.00	2.50	3.00	—

KM# 163 50 LIRE

6.20 g., Stainless Steel, 24.8 mm. **Subject:** Motherhood **Obv:** Bust right **Rev:** Seated figure with infant on lap

Date	Mintage	VF20	XF40	MS60	MS63	MS65
1982/IV	400,000	—	1.00	2.50	3.00	—

KM# 172 50 LIRE

6.20 g., Stainless Steel, 24.8 mm. **Subject:** Banishment of Adam and Eve **Obv:** Head left to lower right of cross **Rev:** Stylized figure

Date	Mintage	VF20	XF40	MS60	MS63	MS65
1983/V	300,000	—	1.00	2.50	3.00	—

KM# 179 50 LIRE

6.20 g., Stainless Steel, 24.8 mm. **Subject:** Year of Peace **Obv:** Bust left **Rev:** Doves

Date	Mintage	VF20	XF40	MS60	MS63	MS65
1984/VI	300,000	—	1.00	2.50	3.00	—

KM# 187 50 LIRE

6.20 g., Stainless Steel, 24.8 mm. **Obv:** Head left **Rev:** Winged lion holding gospel of St. Mark

Date	Mintage	VF20	XF40	MS60	MS63	MS65
1985/VII	360,000	—	1.00	2.50	3.00	—

KM# 194 50 LIRE

6.20 g., Stainless Steel, 24.8 mm. **Obv:** Bust right **Rev:** Moses seated on rock

Date	Mintage	VF20	XF40	MS60	MS63	MS65
1986/VIII	100,000	—	1.00	2.50	3.00	—

KM# 201 50 LIRE

6.20 g., Stainless Steel, 24.8 mm. **Obv:** Bust right **Rev:** Mother Mary protecting kneeling sinners

Date	Mintage	VF20	XF40	MS60	MS63	MS65
1987/IX	—	—	1.00	2.50	3.00	—

KM# 208 50 LIRE

6.20 g., Stainless Steel, 24.8 mm. **Subject:** Creation of Eve From Adam's Rib **Obv:** Bust right **Rev:** Face profile to right of female figure rising out of male figure on ground

Date	Mintage	VF20	XF40	MS60	MS63	MS65
1988/X	—	—	1.00	2.50	3.00	—

KM# 215 50 LIRE

6.20 g., Stainless Steel, 24.8 mm. **Subject:** Human Solidarity **Rev:** Standing figures

Date	Mintage	VF20	XF40	MS60	MS63	MS65
1989/XI	—	—	1.00	2.50	3.00	—

KM# 222 50 LIRE

Stainless Steel, 16.3 mm. **Obv:** Bust 3/4 left **Rev:** Radiant cross in open door

Date	Mintage	VF20	XF40	MS60	MS63	MS65
1990/XII	—	—	1.00	2.50	3.00	—

KM# 230 50 LIRE

Stainless Steel, 16.3 mm. **Obv:** Head left **Rev:** Baptism scene

Date	Mintage	VF20	XF40	MS60	MS63	MS65
1991/XIII	—	—	1.00	2.50	3.00	—

KM# 238 50 LIRE

Stainless Steel, 16.3 mm. **Obv:** Bust right **Rev:** Cross as balance scale between agriculture and industry

Date	Mintage	VF20	XF40	MS60	MS63	MS65
1992/XIV	—	—	1.00	2.50	3.00	—

KM# 246 50 LIRE

Stainless Steel, 16.3 mm. **Obv:** Head facing **Rev:** Chalice divides inscription

Date	Mintage	VF20	XF40	MS60	MS63	MS65
1993/XV	—	—	1.00	2.50	3.00	—

KM# 254 50 LIRE

Stainless Steel, 16.3 mm. **Obv:** Bust left **Rev:** Hands and prison bars

Date	Mintage	VF20	XF40	MS60	MS63	MS65
1994/XVI	—	—	1.00	2.50	3.00	—

KM# 264 50 LIRE

Stainless Steel, 16.3 mm. **Rev:** Dragon on Prone Woman (Abortion)

Date	Mintage	VF20	XF40	MS60	MS63	MS65
1995/XVII	—	—	1.00	2.50	3.00	—

KM# 274 50 LIRE

Copper-Nickel, 19.2 mm. **Obv:** Head left **Rev:** Guardian angel protecting child

Date	Mintage	VF20	XF40	MS60	MS63	MS65
1996/XVIII	—	—	1.00	2.50	3.00	—

KM# 282 50 LIRE

Copper-Nickel, 19.2 mm. **Obv:** Head right **Rev:** One man with lowered sword, the other with dove

Date	Mintage	VF20	XF40	MS60	MS63	MS65
1997/XIX	—	—	1.00	2.50	3.00	—

KM# 295 50 LIRE

Copper-Nickel, 19.2 mm. **Obv:** Pope with crucifix croizer **Rev:** Two figures and hand

Date	Mintage	VF20	XF40	MS60	MS63	MS65
1998/XX	—	—	1.00	2.50	3.00	—

KM# 307 50 LIRE

4.46 g., Copper-Nickel, 19.2 mm. **Subject:** Ecosystem - Agriculture **Obv:** Bust right **Rev:** Agricultural workers **Edge:** Plain

Date	Mintage	VF20	XF40	MS60	MS63	MS65
1999/XXI	—	—	1.00	2.50	3.00	—

KM# 325 50 LIRE

4.50 g., Copper-Nickel, 19.2 mm. **Obv:** Papal arms within circle **Rev:** Pope about to kiss ground **Edge:** Plain

Date	Mintage	VF20	XF40	MS60	MS63	MS65
2000/XXII	—	—	1.00	2.50	3.00	—

KM# 146 100 LIRE
8.00 g., Stainless Steel, 27.75 mm. **Obv:** Bust left **Rev:** Prudence seated

Date	Mintage	VF20	XF40	MS60	MS63	MS65
1979/I	399,000	—	1.50	3.00	3.50	—
1980/II	485,000	—	1.50	3.00	3.50	—

KM# 158 100 LIRE
8.00 g., Stainless Steel, 27.75 mm. **Obv:** Head left **Rev:** Angel offering food to seated figure

Date	Mintage	VF20	XF40	MS60	MS63	MS65
1981/III	550,000	—	1.50	3.00	3.50	—

KM# 164 100 LIRE
8.00 g., Stainless Steel, 27.75 mm. **Subject:** Family Unit **Obv:** Bust right **Rev:** Standing and seated figure divides value

Date	Mintage	VF20	XF40	MS60	MS63	MS65
1982/IV	656,000	—	1.50	3.00	3.50	—

KM# 173 100 LIRE
8.00 g., Stainless Steel, 27.75 mm. **Subject:** God Gives World to Mankind **Obv:** Head left to lower right of cross **Rev:** Design flanked by hand and kneeling figure

Date	Mintage	VF20	XF40	MS60	MS63	MS65
1983/V	455,000	—	1.50	3.00	3.50	—

KM# 180 100 LIRE
8.00 g., Stainless Steel, 27.75 mm. **Subject:** Year of Peace **Obv:** Bust left **Rev:** Cross divides lamb and value

Date	Mintage	VF20	XF40	MS60	MS63	MS65
1984/VI	400,000	—	1.50	3.00	3.50	—

KM# 188 100 LIRE
8.00 g., Stainless Steel, 27.75 mm. **Obv:** Head left **Rev:** Small airplane in flight over map

Date	Mintage	VF20	XF40	MS60	MS63	MS65
1985/VII	800,000	—	1.50	3.00	3.50	—

KM# 195 100 LIRE
8.00 g., Stainless Steel, 27.75 mm. **Obv:** Bust right **Rev:** Christ seated on rocks

Date	Mintage	VF20	XF40	MS60	MS63	MS65
1986/VIII	100,000	—	1.50	3.00	3.50	—

KM# 202 100 LIRE
8.00 g., Stainless Steel, 27.75 mm. **Subject:** Angel and Mary, The Annunciation **Obv:** Bust right **Rev:** Dove above angel and seated figure

Date	Mintage	VF20	XF40	MS60	MS63	MS65
1987/IX	—	—	1.50	3.00	3.50	—

KM# 209 100 LIRE
8.00 g., Stainless Steel, 27.75 mm. **Subject:** Adam naming the Animals **Obv:** Bust right **Rev:** Standing figure in palm of hand to left of assorted animals

Date	Mintage	VF20	XF40	MS60	MS63	MS65
1988/X	—	—	1.50	3.00	3.50	—

KM# 216 100 LIRE
8.00 g., Stainless Steel, 27.75 mm. **Rev:** Pelican feeding young

Date	Mintage	VF20	XF40	MS60	MS63	MS65
1989/XI	—	—	1.50	3.00	3.50	—

KM# 223 100 LIRE
Stainless Steel, 18 mm. **Subject:** Early Bishop **Obv:** Bust 3/4 left **Rev:** Hooded half-figure facing

Date	Mintage	VF20	XF40	MS60	MS63	MS65
1990/XII	—	—	1.50	3.00	3.50	—

KM# 231 100 LIRE
Stainless Steel, 18 mm. **Obv:** Head left **Rev:** Depiction of the risen Christ

Date	Mintage	VF20	XF40	MS60	MS63	MS65
1991/XIII	—	—	1.50	3.00	3.50	—

KM# 239 100 LIRE
Stainless Steel, 18 mm. **Obv:** Bust right **Rev:** Open book above value

Date	Mintage	VF20	XF40	MS60	MS63	MS65
1992/XIV	—	—	1.50	3.00	3.50	—

KM# 247 100 LIRE
Copper-Nickel, 21.8 mm. **Obv:** Head facing **Rev:** Portrait of Jesus facing divides inscription above value

Date	Mintage	VF20	XF40	MS60	MS63	MS65
1993/XV	—	—	1.50	3.00	3.50	—

KM# 255 100 LIRE
Copper-Nickel, 21.8 mm. **Obv:** Bust left **Rev:** Basketball players with one in wheelchair

Date	Mintage	VF20	XF40	MS60	MS63	MS65
1994/XVI	—	—	1.50	3.00	3.50	—

KM# 265 100 LIRE
Copper-Nickel, 21.8 mm. **Rev:** Guard and prisoners

Date	Mintage	VF20	XF40	MS60	MS63	MS65
1995/XVII	—	—	1.50	3.00	3.50	—

KM# 275 100 LIRE
Copper-Nickel, 21.8 mm. **Obv:** Head left **Rev:** Women helping children

Date	Mintage	VF20	XF40	MS60	MS63	MS65
1996/XVIII	—	—	1.50	3.00	3.50	—

KM# 283 100 LIRE
Copper-Nickel, 21.8 mm. **Obv:** Bust right **Rev:** Woman filling birdbath and doves

Date	Mintage	VF20	XF40	MS60	MS63	MS65
1997/XIX	—	—	1.25	3.00	3.50	—

KM# 296 100 LIRE
Copper-Nickel, 21.8 mm. **Obv:** Pope with crucifix croizer **Rev:** Female figure in front of globe

Date	Mintage	VF20	XF40	MS60	MS63	MS65
1998/XX	—	—	1.50	3.00	3.50	—

KM# 308 100 LIRE
4.50 g., Copper-Nickel, 22 mm. **Subject:** The Right to Peace **Obv:** Bust right within circle **Rev:** Children of the world gathered in peace **Edge:** Reeded and plain sections

Date	Mintage	VF20	XF40	MS60	MS63	MS65
1999/XXI	—	—	1.50	3.00	3.50	—

KM# 326 100 LIRE
4.50 g., Copper-Nickel, 22 mm. **Obv:** Papal arms within circle **Rev:** Pope resting head on hand within window frame design **Edge:** Plain and reeded sections

Date	Mintage	VF20	XF40	MS60	MS63	MS65
2000/XXII	—	—	1.50	3.00	3.50	—

KM# 147 200 LIRE
5.00 g., Aluminum-Bronze, 24 mm. **Obv:** Bust left **Rev:** Peace seated flanked by value and sprig

Date	Mintage	VF20	XF40	MS60	MS63	MS65
1979/I	355,000	—	1.00	2.50	3.00	—
1980/II	200,000	—	1.00	2.50	3.00	—

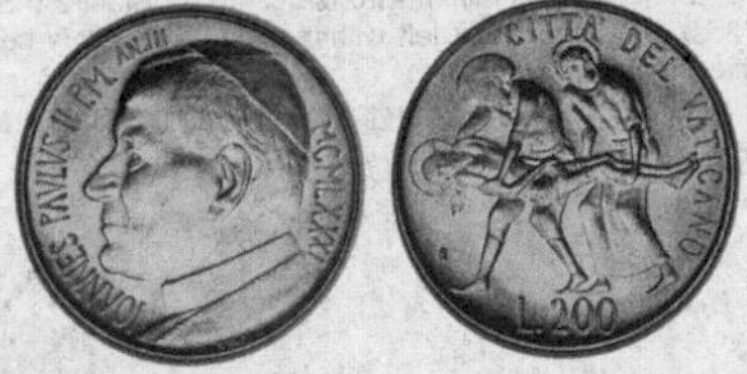

KM# 159 200 LIRE
5.00 g., Aluminum-Bronze, 24 mm. **Subject:** Corporal acts of Mercy - Bury the dead **Obv:** Head left **Rev:** Standing figures carrying supine figure

Date	Mintage	VF20	XF40	MS60	MS63	MS65
1981/III	170,000	—	1.00	2.50	3.00	—

KM# 165 200 LIRE
5.00 g., Aluminum-Bronze, 24 mm. **Subject:** Farm labor **Obv:** Bust right **Rev:** Workers and ox

Date	Mintage	VF20	XF40	MS60	MS63	MS65
1982/IV	500,000	—	1.00	2.50	3.00	—

KM# 174 200 LIRE
5.00 g., Aluminum-Bronze, 24 mm. **Subject:** Creation of Man **Obv:** Head left to lower right of cross **Rev:** Stylized figure above hands

Date	Mintage	VF20	XF40	MS60	MS63	MS65
1983/V	300,000	—	1.00	2.50	3.00	—

KM# 181 200 LIRE
5.00 g., Aluminum-Bronze, 24 mm. **Subject:** Year of Peace **Obv:** Bust left **Rev:** Sailboat and cross

Date	Mintage	VF20	XF40	MS60	MS63	MS65
1984/VI	250,000	—	1.00	2.50	3.00	—

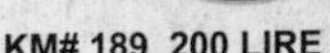

KM# 189 200 LIRE
5.00 g., Aluminum-Bronze, 24 mm. **Obv:** Head left **Rev:** Winged Ox holding gospel

Date	Mintage	VF20	XF40	MS60	MS63	MS65
1985/VII	300,000	—	1.00	2.50	3.00	—

KM# 196 200 LIRE
5.00 g., Aluminum-Bronze, 24 mm. **Obv:** Bust right **Rev:** Archangel Michael and value

Date	Mintage	VF20	XF40	MS60	MS63	MS65
1986/VIII	100,000	—	1.00	2.50	3.00	—

KM# 203 200 LIRE
5.00 g., Aluminum-Bronze, 24 mm. **Subject:** Mary, Queen of Peace **Obv:** Bust right **Rev:** Seated figure in front of trees

Date	Mintage	VF20	XF40	MS60	MS63	MS65
1987/IX	—	—	1.00	2.50	3.00	—

KM# 210 200 LIRE
5.00 g., Aluminum-Bronze, 24 mm. **Subject:** Creation of Adam **Obv:** Bust right **Rev:** Face profile at left of figure within palm of hand

Date	Mintage	VF20	XF40	MS60	MS63	MS65
1988/X	—	—	1.00	2.50	3.00	—

KM# 217 200 LIRE
5.00 g., Aluminum-Bronze, 24 mm. **Obv:** Bust 3/4 right **Rev:** Group of standing figures

Date	Mintage	VF20	XF40	MS60	MS63	MS65
1989/XI	—	—	1.00	2.50	3.00	—

KM# 224 200 LIRE
5.00 g., Aluminum-Bronze, 24 mm. **Subject:** Blessed Virgin Mary **Obv:** Bust 3/4 left **Rev:** Standing figure facing and value

Date	Mintage	VF20	XF40	MS60	MS63	MS65
1990/XII	—	—	1.00	2.50	3.00	—

KM# 232 200 LIRE
5.00 g., Aluminum-Bronze, 24 mm. **Obv:** Head left **Rev:** Stylized figure to left of city

Date	Mintage	VF20	XF40	MS60	MS63	MS65
1991/XIII	—	—	1.00	2.50	3.00	—

KM# 240 200 LIRE
5.00 g., Aluminum-Bronze, 24 mm. **Obv:** Bust right **Rev:** Mother nursing child

Date	Mintage	VF20	XF40	MS60	MS63	MS65
1992/XIV	—	—	1.00	2.50	3.00	—

KM# 248 200 LIRE
5.00 g., Aluminum-Bronze, 24 mm. **Subject:** Ten Commandments **Obv:** Head facing **Rev:** 10 commandment stone divides name above value

Date	Mintage	VF20	XF40	MS60	MS63	MS65
1993/XV	—	—	1.00	2.50	3.00	—

KM# 256 200 LIRE
5.00 g., Aluminum-Bronze, 24 mm. **Subject:** Helping Victims of Drug Abuse **Obv:** Bust left **Rev:** Group of standing figures

Date	Mintage	VF20	XF40	MS60	MS63	MS65
1994/XVI	—	—	1.00	2.50	3.00	—

KM# 266 200 LIRE
5.00 g., Aluminum-Bronze, 24 mm. **Rev:** Family and farming scene

Date	Mintage	VF20	XF40	MS60	MS63	MS65
1995/XVII	—	—	1.00	2.50	3.00	—

KM# 276 200 LIRE
5.00 g., Aluminum-Bronze, 24 mm. **Obv:** Head left **Rev:** Display of family togetherness

Date	Mintage	VF20	XF40	MS60	MS63	MS65
1996/XVIII	—	—	1.00	2.50	3.00	—

KM# 284 200 LIRE
5.00 g., Aluminum-Bronze, 24 mm. **Obv:** Bust right **Rev:** Angel guiding two people

Date	Mintage	VF20	XF40	MS60	MS63	MS65
1997/XIX	—	—	1.00	2.50	3.00	—

KM# 297 200 LIRE
5.00 g., Aluminum-Bronze, 24 mm. **Obv:** Bust left **Rev:** Group of standing figures

Date	Mintage	VF20	XF40	MS60	MS63	MS65
1998/XX	—	—	1.00	2.50	3.00	—

KM# 309 200 LIRE
5.00 g., Aluminum-Bronze, 24 mm. **Obv:** Bust right **Rev:** Christ among the poor and outcast **Edge:** Reeded

Date	Mintage	VF20	XF40	MS60	MS63	MS65
1999/XXI	—	—	1.00	2.50	3.00	—

KM# 327 200 LIRE
5.00 g., Brass, 22 mm. **Obv:** Papal arms within circle **Rev:** Pope praying **Edge:** Reeded

Date	Mintage	VF20	XF40	MS60	MS63	MS65
2000/XXII	—	—	1.00	2.50	3.00	—

KM# 148 500 LIRE
11.00 g., 0.835 Silver 0.2953 oz. ASW, 29.3 mm. **Obv:** Head left **Rev:** Crowned shield

Date	Mintage	VF20	XF40	MS60	MS63	MS65
1979/I	145,000	—	15.00	20.00	25.00	35.00
1980/II	184,000	—	15.00	20.00	25.00	35.00

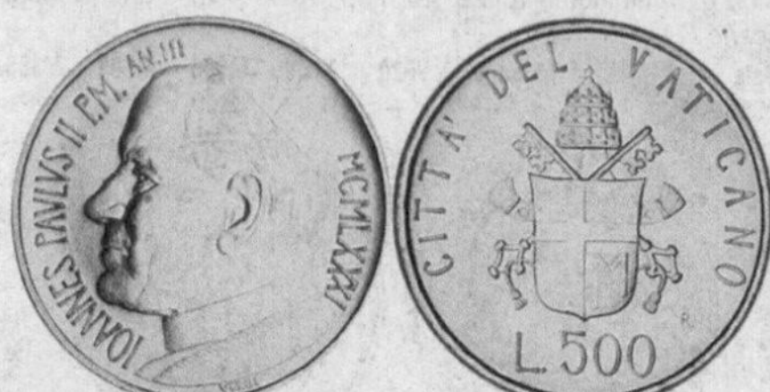

KM# 160 500 LIRE
11.00 g., 0.835 Silver 0.2953 oz. ASW, 29.3 mm. **Obv:** Head left **Rev:** Crowned shield

Date	Mintage	VF20	XF40	MS60	MS63	MS65
1981/III	184,000	—	15.00	20.00	25.00	35.00

KM# 166 500 LIRE
6.80 g., Bi-Metallic Aluminum-Bronze center in Stainless Steel ring, 25.8 mm. **Subject:** Education **Obv:** Bust right within circle **Rev:** Seated figure flanked by children within circle

Date	Mintage	VF20	XF40	MS60	MS63	MS65
1982/IV	1,852,000	—	4.50	5.50	7.50	8.50

KM# 168 500 LIRE
11.00 g., 0.835 Silver 0.2953 oz. ASW, 29.3 mm. **Subject:** Extraordinary Holy Year **Obv:** Crowned shield **Rev:** Kneeling figure facing, people and buildings in background

Date	Mintage	VF20	XF40	MS60	MS63	MS65
1983-84	130,000	—	15.00	20.00	25.00	35.00

KM# 175 500 LIRE
6.80 g., Bi-Metallic Aluminum-Bronze center in Stainless Steel ring, 25.8 mm. **Subject:** Creation of the Universe **Obv:** Head left to lower right of cross within circle **Rev:** Hand reaching in globe within circle

Date	Mintage	VF20	XF40	MS60	MS63	MS65
1983/V	—	—	4.50	5.50	7.50	8.50

KM# 182 500 LIRE
6.80 g., Bi-Metallic Aluminum-Bronze center in Stainless Steel ring, 25.8 mm. **Subject:** Year of Peace **Obv:** Head left within circle **Rev:** Sprig within clasped hands within circle

Date	Mintage	VF20	XF40	MS60	MS63	MS65
1984/VI	270,000	—	4.50	5.50	7.50	8.50

KM# 184 500 LIRE
11.00 g., 0.835 Silver 0.2953 oz. ASW, 29.3 mm. **Subject:** 2000th Anniversary - Birth of Blessed Virgin Mary **Obv:** Crowned shield **Rev:** Standing and kneeling figures, crosses and domed building

Date	Mintage	VF20	XF40	MS60	MS63	MS65
1984/VI	105,000	PF65 40.00				

KM# 190 500 LIRE
6.80 g., Bi-Metallic Aluminum-Bronze center in Stainless Steel ring, 25.8 mm. **Obv:** Head left within circle **Rev:** St. Paul in boat within circle

Date	Mintage	VF20	XF40	MS60	MS63	MS65
1985/VII	300,000	—	4.50	5.50	7.50	8.50

KM# 197 500 LIRE
6.80 g., Bi-Metallic Aluminum-Bronze center in Stainless Steel ring, 25.8 mm. **Obv:** Bust right within circle **Rev:** Seated Mary and Jesus within circle

Date	Mintage	VF20	XF40	MS60	MS63	MS65
1986/VIII	300,000	—	4.50	5.50	7.50	8.50

KM# 204 500 LIRE
6.80 g., Bi-Metallic Aluminum-Bronze center in Stainless Steel ring, 25.8 mm. **Obv:** Bust left within circle **Rev:** Mary before Crucified Jesus within circle

Date	Mintage	VF20	XF40	MS60	MS63	MS65
1987/IX	—	—	4.50	5.50	7.50	8.50

KM# 211 500 LIRE
6.80 g., Bi-Metallic Aluminum-Bronze center in Stainless Steel ring, 25.8 mm. **Obv:** Head right within circle **Rev:** Dove at center, conjoined busts within circle

Date	Mintage	VF20	XF40	MS60	MS63	MS65
1988/X	—	—	4.50	5.50	7.50	8.50

KM# 218 500 LIRE
6.80 g., Bi-Metallic Aluminum-Bronze center in Stainless Steel ring, 25.8 mm. **Obv:** Bust right within circle **Rev:** Grapevine within circle

Date	Mintage	VF20	XF40	MS60	MS63	MS65
1989/XI	—	—	4.50	5.50	7.50	8.50

KM# 225 500 LIRE
6.80 g., Bi-Metallic Aluminum-Bronze center in Stainless Steel ring, 25.8 mm. **Obv:** Bust left within circle **Rev:** Jesus flanked by kneeling figures within circle

Date	Mintage	VF20	XF40	MS60	MS63	MS65
1990/XII	—	—	4.50	5.50	7.50	8.50

KM# 227 500 LIRE
11.00 g., 0.835 Silver 0.2953 oz. ASW, 29.3 mm. **Subject:** Social doctrine **Obv:** Bust right **Rev:** Stylized figures within circle

Date	Mintage	VF20	XF40	MS60	MS63	MS65
1991/XIII	—	—	15.00	20.00	25.00	35.00

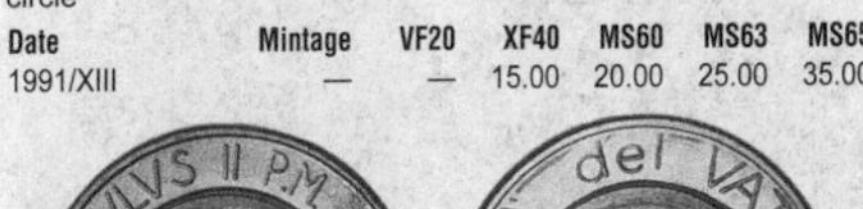

KM# 233 500 LIRE
6.80 g., Bi-Metallic Aluminum-Bronze center in Stainless Steel ring, 25.8 mm. **Obv:** Head left within circle **Rev:** Redeemer sending out missionaries within circle

Date	Mintage	VF20	XF40	MS60	MS63	MS65
1991/XIII	—	—	3.50	5.50	7.50	8.50

KM# 235 500 LIRE
11.00 g., 0.835 Silver 0.2953 oz. ASW, 29.3 mm. **Subject:** Evangelization of America **Obv:** Crowned bust left to right of world globe **Rev:** Three ships in center of map

Date	Mintage	VF20	XF40	MS60	MS63	MS65
1992/XIV	—	—	15.00	20.00	25.00	35.00

KM# 241 500 LIRE
6.80 g., Bi-Metallic Aluminum-Bronze center in Stainless Steel ring, 25.8 mm. **Obv:** Bust right within circle **Rev:** Hands holding loaf of bread within globe

Date	Mintage	VF20	XF40	MS60	MS63	MS65
1992/XIV	—	—	3.50	5.00	7.00	8.00

KM# 243 500 LIRE
11.00 g., 0.835 Silver 0.2953 oz. ASW, 29.3 mm. **Subject:** World Peace **Rev:** Seated figure with infant

Date	Mintage	VF20	XF40	MS60	MS63	MS65
1993/XV	—	—	15.00	20.00	25.00	35.00

KM# 249 500 LIRE
6.80 g., Bi-Metallic Aluminum-Bronze center in Stainless Steel ring, 25.8 mm. **Rev:** Thurible

Date	Mintage	VF20	XF40	MS60	MS63	MS65
1993/XV	—	—	3.50	5.00	7.00	8.00

KM# 251 500 LIRE
11.00 g., 0.835 Silver 0.2953 oz. ASW, 29.3 mm. **Subject:** Veritatis Splendor **Obv:** Sunrays above bust right holding crucifix **Rev:** Sunrays divide circle with standing figure within map

Date	Mintage	VF20	XF40	MS60	MS63	MS65
1994/XVI	—	—	15.00	20.00	25.00	35.00
1994/XVI	—	PF65 40.00				

KM# 257 500 LIRE
6.80 g., Bi-Metallic Aluminum-Bronze center in Stainless Steel ring, 25.8 mm. **Obv:** Bust left within circle **Rev:** People meeting, Golgotha in background

Date	Mintage	VF20	XF40	MS60	MS63	MS65
1994/XVI	—	—	3.50	5.00	7.00	8.00

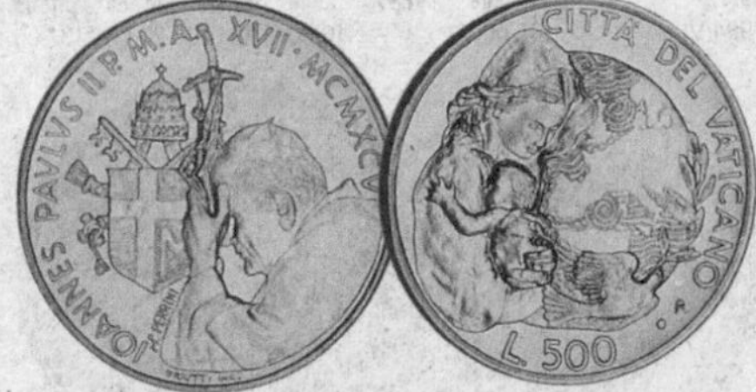

KM# 259 500 LIRE
11.00 g., 0.835 Silver 0.2953 oz. ASW, 29.3 mm. **Series:** International Women's Year **Obv:** Pope resting head on hand with crucifix to right of crowned shield **Rev:** 1/2-length figure holding infant to left of 1/2 designed globe **Edge Lettering:** INTERNATIONALIS ANNUS MELIEREI DICATUS

Date	Mintage	VF20	XF40	MS60	MS63	MS65
1995/XVII	20,000	—	15.00	20.00	25.00	35.00
1995/XVII	7,000	PF65 65.00				

KM# 267 500 LIRE
6.80 g., Bi-Metallic, 25.8 mm. **Rev:** Cain slaying Abel within circle

Date	Mintage	VF20	XF40	MS60	MS63	MS65
1995/XVII	460,000	—	3.50	5.00	7.00	8.00

KM# 269 500 LIRE
11.00 g., 0.835 Silver 0.2953 oz. ASW, 29.3 mm. **Subject:** 50th Anniversary - Ordination of Pope John Paul II **Obv:** Bust right **Rev:** Sheep, lamb on shepherds shoulder and flying figure holding infant

Date	Mintage	VF20	XF40	MS60	MS63	MS65
1996/XVIII	33,000	—	15.00	20.00	25.00	35.00
1996/XVIII	7,000	PF65 70.00				

KM# 277 500 LIRE
6.80 g., Bi-Metallic Aluminum-Bronze center in Stainless Steel ring, 25.8 mm. **Obv:** Head left within circle **Rev:** Seated figures within circle, serpent at left of circle

Date	Mintage	VF20	XF40	MS60	MS63	MS65
1996/XVIII	100,000	—	3.50	5.00	7.00	8.00

KM# 279 500 LIRE
11.00 g., 0.835 Silver 0.2953 oz. ASW, 29.3 mm. **Subject:** XII World Youth Conference **Obv:** Bust right **Rev:** Six children with Jesus **Edge Lettering:** IUVENTUTIS XII UNIVERSALIS DIES PARISIIS

Date	Mintage	VF20	XF40	MS60	MS63	MS65
1997/XIX	18,000	—	18.00	22.00	28.00	40.00
1997/XIX	—	PF65 65.00				

KM# 285 500 LIRE
6.80 g., Bi-Metallic Aluminum-Bronze center in Stainless Steel ring, 25.8 mm. **Obv:** Head right within circle **Rev:** One man freeing another from thorns

Date	Mintage	VF20	XF40	MS60	MS63	MS65
1997/XIX	160,000	—	3.50	5.00	7.00	8.00

KM# 292 500 LIRE
11.00 g., 0.835 Silver 0.2953 oz. ASW, 29.3 mm. **Obv:** Crowned bust right **Rev:** Shroud of Turin, head facing **Edge Lettering:** SACRA SINDON OSTENTATUR AVG. TAVR. MCMXCVIII

Date	Mintage	VF20	XF40	MS60	MS63	MS65
1998/XX	23,000	—	18.00	22.00	28.00	40.00
1998 R	—	PF65 65.00				

KM# 298 500 LIRE
6.80 g., Bi-Metallic Aluminum-Bronze center in Stainless Steel ring, 25.8 mm. **Obv:** Bust right holding crucifix within circle **Rev:** Two figures within circle

Date	Mintage	VF20	XF40	MS60	MS63	MS65
1998/XX	103,500	—	3.50	5.00	7.00	8.00

KM# 310 500 LIRE
6.70 g., Bi-Metallic Aluminum-Bronze center in Stainless Steel ring, 25.9 mm. **Subject:** Time of Choices, Time of Hope **Obv:** Bust right within circle **Rev:** God's hand above young parent's with baby **Edge:** Reeded

Date	Mintage	VF20	XF40	MS60	MS63	MS65
1999/XXI	161,000	—	3.50	5.00	7.00	8.00

KM# 322 500 LIRE
11.00 g., 0.835 Silver 0.2953 oz. ASW, 29.3 mm. **Subject:** 70th Anniversary - Vatican City Arms of Six Popes **Obv:** Bust right **Rev:** Dates in center of assorted crowned shields

Date	Mintage	VF20	XF40	MS60	MS63	MS65
1999/XXI	—	—	18.00	22.00	28.00	40.00
1999/XXI	—	PF65 65.00				

KM# 328 500 LIRE
6.77 g., Bi-Metallic Aluminum-Bronze center in Stainless Steel ring, 25.7 mm. **Obv:** Papal arms within circle **Rev:** Bust right turning a page within circle **Edge:** Reeded and plain sections

Date	Mintage	VF20	XF40	MS60	MS63	MS65
2000/XXII	—	—	3.50	5.00	7.00	8.00

KM# 167 1000 LIRE
14.60 g., 0.835 Silver 0.3919 oz. ASW **Obv:** Bust right **Rev:** Crowned shield divides value

Date	Mintage	VF20	XF40	MS60	MS63	MS65
1982/IV	210,000	—	16.00	22.00	27.00	37.00

KM# 169 1000 LIRE
14.60 g., 0.835 Silver 0.3919 oz. ASW **Subject:** Extraordinary Holy Year **Obv:** Crowned half figure left **Rev:** Crowned shield divides value

Date	Mintage	VF20	XF40	MS60	MS63	MS65
1983-84	130,000	—	16.00	22.00	27.00	37.00

KM# 176 1000 LIRE
14.60 g., 0.835 Silver 0.3919 oz. ASW **Subject:** Prayer **Obv:** Crowned bust left holding crucifix **Rev:** Crowned shield

Date	Mintage	VF20	XF40	MS60	MS63	MS65
1983/V	110,000	—	16.00	22.00	27.00	37.00

KM# 183 1000 LIRE
14.60 g., 0.835 Silver 0.3919 oz. ASW **Subject:** Year of Peace **Obv:** Bust left **Rev:** Crowned shield

Date	Mintage	VF20	XF40	MS60	MS63	MS65
1984/VI	105,000	—	16.00	22.00	27.00	37.00

KM# 191 1000 LIRE
14.60 g., 0.835 Silver 0.3919 oz. ASW **Obv:** Pope standing, vestments blowing in the wind **Rev:** Crowned shield

Date	Mintage	VF20	XF40	MS60	MS63	MS65
1985/VII	86,000	—	16.00	22.00	27.00	37.00

KM# 198 1000 LIRE
14.60 g., 0.835 Silver 0.3919 oz. ASW **Obv:** Crowned shield **Rev:** Pope seated at microphone

Date	Mintage	VF20	XF40	MS60	MS63	MS65
1986/VIII	80,000	—	16.00	22.00	27.00	37.00

KM# 205 1000 LIRE
14.60 g., 0.835 Silver 0.3919 oz. ASW **Obv:** Crowned shield **Rev:** Pope in prayer and seated figure with infant

Date	Mintage	VF20	XF40	MS60	MS63	MS65
1987/IX	—	—	16.00	22.00	27.00	37.00

KM# 212 1000 LIRE
14.60 g., 0.835 Silver 0.3919 oz. ASW **Rev:** Pope seated at desk

Date	Mintage	VF20	XF40	MS60	MS63	MS65
1988/X	—	—	16.00	22.00	27.00	37.00

KM# 219 1000 LIRE
14.60 g., 0.835 Silver 0.3919 oz. ASW **Obv:** Crowned shield **Rev:** Pope with Prelates and worshippers

Date	Mintage	VF20	XF40	MS60	MS63	MS65
1989/XI	—	—	16.00	22.00	27.00	37.00

KM# 226 1000 LIRE
14.60 g., 0.835 Silver 0.3919 oz. ASW **Obv:** Crowned shield **Rev:** Pope walking over destroyed barbed-wire fence

Date	Mintage	VF20	XF40	MS60	MS63	MS65
1990/XII	—	—	16.00	22.00	27.00	37.00

KM# 234 1000 LIRE
14.60 g., 0.835 Silver 0.3919 oz. ASW **Obv:** Crowned shield **Rev:** Pope handing missionary cross to two young people

Date	Mintage	VF20	XF40	MS60	MS63	MS65
1991/XIII	—	—	16.00	22.00	27.00	37.00

KM# 242 1000 LIRE
14.60 g., 0.835 Silver 0.3919 oz. ASW **Obv:** Bust right **Rev:** Pope's coat-of-arms

Date	Mintage	VF20	XF40	MS60	MS63	MS65
1992/XIV	—	—	16.00	22.00	27.00	37.00

KM# 250 1000 LIRE
14.60 g., 0.835 Silver 0.3919 oz. ASW **Obv:** Head facing **Rev:** Papal coat-of-arms divides inscription

Date	Mintage	VF20	XF40	MS60	MS63	MS65
1993/XV	—	—	16.00	22.00	27.00	37.00

KM# 258 1000 LIRE
14.60 g., 0.835 Silver 0.3919 oz. ASW **Subject:** The Good Samaritan **Obv:** Kneeling figure reaching for standing Pope **Rev:** Horse behind figures

Date	Mintage	VF20	XF40	MS60	MS63	MS65
1994/XVI	—	—	16.00	22.00	27.00	37.00

KM# 268 1000 LIRE
14.60 g., 0.835 Silver 0.3919 oz. ASW **Obv:** Head left **Rev:** Radiant Virgin Mary within stylized dragon

Date	Mintage	VF20	XF40	MS60	MS63	MS65
1995/XVII	—	—	16.00	22.00	27.00	37.00

KM# 278 1000 LIRE
14.60 g., 0.835 Silver 0.3919 oz. ASW **Obv:** John Paul II releasing doves from balcony **Rev:** Jesus welcomes the little children

Date	Mintage	VF20	XF40	MS60	MS63	MS65
1996/XVIII	—	—	16.00	22.00	27.00	37.00

KM# 286 1000 LIRE
Bi-Metallic Stainless Steel center in Aluminum-Bronze ring, 26.9 mm. **Obv:** Head right within circle **Rev:** Crowned shield within circle

Date	Mintage	VF20	XF40	MS60	MS63	MS65
1997/XIX	270,000	—	3.50	5.00	7.00	8.50

KM# 287 1000 LIRE
14.00 g., 0.835 Silver 0.3758 oz. ASW **Obv:** John Paul II teaching people **Rev:** Saint cradling ill man **Edge Lettering:** TOTVS TVVS MCMXCVII

Date	Mintage	VF20	XF40	MS60	MS63	MS65
1997/XIX	—	—	16.00	22.00	27.00	37.00

KM# 299 1000 LIRE
Bi-Metallic Stainless Steel center in Aluminum-Bronze ring, 26.9 mm. **Obv:** Head left within circle **Rev:** Papal coat-of-arms within circle

Date	Mintage	VF20	XF40	MS60	MS63	MS65
1998/XX	306,500	—	4.00	5.00	7.00	8.50

KM# 300 1000 LIRE
14.00 g., 0.835 Silver 0.3758 oz. ASW **Obv:** Pope with crucifix croizer within sun rays **Rev:** Jesus on globe **Edge Lettering:** TOTVS TVVS MCMXCVIII

Date	Mintage	VF20	XF40	MS60	MS63	MS65
1998/XX	—	—	16.00	22.00	27.00	37.00

KM# 311 1000 LIRE
8.85 g., Bi-Metallic Stainless Steel center in Aluminum-Bronze ring, 26.9 mm. **Obv:** Pope's arms within circle **Rev:** Couple at base of Christ on cross within circle **Edge:** Reeded and plain sections

Date	Mintage	VF20	XF40	MS60	MS63	MS65
1999/XXI	126,100	—	4.00	5.00	7.00	8.50

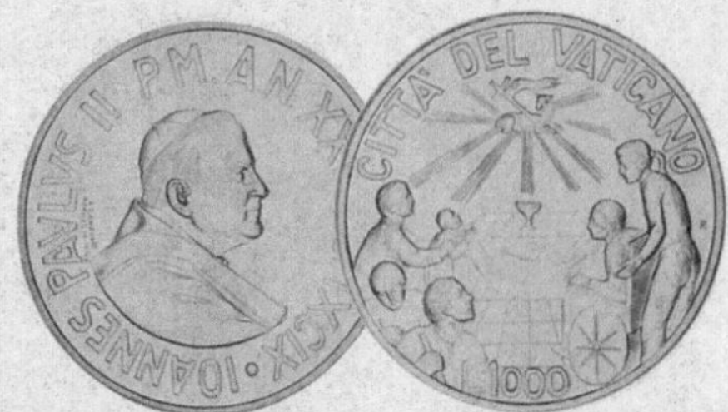

KM# 312 1000 LIRE
14.00 g., 0.835 Silver 0.3758 oz. ASW **Subject:** The Right to Religous Freedom **Obv:** Bust right **Rev:** Family at altar **Edge:** TOTVS TVVS ++ ++ ++ ++ MCMXCIX ++ ++ ++ ++

Date	Mintage	VF20	XF40	MS60	MS63	MS65
1999/XXI	—	—	16.00	22.00	27.00	37.00

KM# 329 1000 LIRE
8.85 g., Bi-Metallic Stainless Steel center in Aluminum-Bronze ring, 26.9 mm. **Obv:** Papal arms within circle **Rev:** Pope and Eastern Orthodox Patriarch within circle **Edge:** Reeded and plain sections

Date	Mintage	VF20	XF40	MS60	MS63	MS65
2000/XXII	—	—	4.00	5.00	7.00	8.50

KM# 330 1000 LIRE
14.60 g., 0.835 Silver 0.3919 oz. ASW, 31.4 mm. **Obv:** Papal arms within circle **Rev:** Praying Pope divides assorted figures within circle **Edge Lettering:** TOTVS TVVS +++MM+++

Date	Mintage	VF20	XF40	MS60	MS63	MS65
2000/XXII	—	—	16.00	22.00	27.00	37.00

KM# 313 2000 LIRE
16.00 g., 0.835 Silver 0.4295 oz. ASW **Subject:** Holy Year **Obv:** Pope standing by open door **Rev:** Three seated figures **Edge:** Reeded

Date	Mintage	VF20	XF40	MS60	MS63	MS65
2000	60,000	—	16.00	22.00	27.00	37.00
2000	10,000	PF63 200				

KM# 353 2000 LIRE
16.00 g., 0.835 Silver 0.4295 oz. ASW, 31.4 mm. **Subject:** 2000th Birthday of Jesus **Obv:** Bust of Pope in prayer **Rev:** Baby divides value **Edge:** Reeded

Date	Mintage	VF20	XF40	MS60	MS63	MS65
2000	—	—	16.00	22.00	28.00	40.00
2000 R	8,000	PF63 100				

KM# 260 10000 LIRE
22.00 g., 0.835 Silver 0.5906 oz. ASW **Subject:** The Annunciation **Obv:** Bust right **Rev:** Angel and seated figure below radiant dove

Date	Mintage	VF20	XF40	MS60	MS63	MS65
1995	—	—	—	—	100	110
1995	30,000	PF65 80.00				

KM# 261 10000 LIRE
22.00 g., 0.835 Silver 0.5906 oz. ASW **Subject:** The Nativity **Obv:** Bust right **Rev:** Donkey heads and baby at center, standing figures at sides

Date	Mintage	VF20	XF40	MS60	MS63	MS65
1995	—	—	—	—	40.00	45.00
1995	30,000	PF65 80.00				

KM# 270 10000 LIRE
22.00 g., 0.835 Silver 0.5906 oz. ASW **Subject:** Holy Year 2000 **Obv:** Bust right **Rev:** Baptism in River Jordan

Date	Mintage	VF20	XF40	MS60	MS63	MS65
1996	—	—	—	—	40.00	45.00
1996	30,000	PF65 80.00				

KM# 271 10000 LIRE
22.00 g., 0.835 Silver 0.5906 oz. ASW **Subject:** Holy Year 2000 **Obv:** Bust right **Rev:** Jesus seated teaching above group of people

Date	Mintage	VF20	XF40	MS60	MS63	MS65
1996	—	—	—	—	40.00	45.00
1996	30,000	PF65 80.00				

KM# 318 10000 LIRE
22.00 g., 0.835 Silver 0.5906 oz. ASW **Subject:** Cure of the Paralytic **Obv:** Bust left **Rev:** Two kneeling figures on roof above figure helping ill person

Date	Mintage	VF20	XF40	MS60	MS63	MS65
1997	—	—	—	—	—	110
1997	—	PF65 80.00				

KM# 319 10000 LIRE
22.00 g., 0.835 Silver 0.5906 oz. ASW **Subject:** Calming of the Storm **Obv:** Bust left **Rev:** Figures in boat

Date	Mintage	VF20	XF40	MS60	MS63	MS65
1997	—	—	—	—	—	110
1997	—	PF65 80.00				

KM# 290 10000 LIRE
22.00 g., 0.835 Silver 0.5906 oz. ASW **Obv:** Bust left **Rev:** Seated figures at long table, Last Supper

Date	Mintage	VF20	XF40	MS60	MS63	MS65
1998	—	—	—	—	40.00	45.00
1998	30,000	PF65 80.00				

KM# 291 10000 LIRE
22.00 g., 0.835 Silver 0.5906 oz. ASW **Obv:** Bust left **Rev:** Jesus on cross flanked by standing figures

Date	Mintage	VF20	XF40	MS60	MS63	MS65
1998	—	—	—	—	40.00	45.00
1998	30,000	PF65 80.00				

KM# 303 10000 LIRE
22.00 g., 0.835 Silver 0.5906 oz. ASW, 34 mm. **Obv:** Bust right **Rev:** Group with flames above head

Date	Mintage	VF20	XF40	MS60	MS63	MS65
1999	—	—	—	—	—	110
1999	30,000	PF65 80.00				

KM# 304 10000 LIRE
22.00 g., 0.835 Silver 0.5906 oz. ASW **Rev:** Jesus rising from his tomb

Date	Mintage	VF20	XF40	MS60	MS63	MS65
1999	—	—	—	—	—	110
1999	30,000	PF65 80.00				

KM# 314 10000 LIRE
22.00 g., 0.835 Silver 0.5906 oz. ASW **Obv:** Bust right **Rev:** Seated angel holding church above "GERUSALEMME"

Date	Mintage	VF20	XF40	MS60	MS63	MS65
2000	—	—	—	—	—	110
2000	30,000	PF65 80.00				

KM# 315 10000 LIRE
22.00 g., 0.835 Silver 0.5906 oz. ASW **Obv:** Bust right **Rev:** Seated angel holding church above "ROMA"

Date	Mintage	VF20	XF40	MS60	MS63	MS65
2000	—	—	—	—	—	110
2000	30,000	PF65 80.00				

KM# 356 50000 LIRE
7.50 g., 0.917 Gold 0.2211 oz. AGW **Obv:** Pope and Holy Year Door **Rev:** John the Baptist and St. John the Evangelist facing each other

Date	Mintage	VF20	XF40	MS60	MS63	MS65
1996/XVIII R	6,000	PF65 1,250	PF67 1,800			

KM# 288 50000 LIRE
7.50 g., 0.917 Gold 0.2211 oz. AGW **Obv:** Pope and Holy Year Door **Rev:** St. Paul facing

Date	Mintage	VF20	XF40	MS60	MS63	MS65
1997/XIX	6,000	PF65 1,250	PF67 1,800			

KM# 301 50000 LIRE
7.50 g., 0.917 Gold 0.2211 oz. AGW, 23 mm. **Obv:** Pope and Holy Year Door **Rev:** Madonna and child **Edge:** Reeded

Date	Mintage	VF20	XF40	MS60	MS63	MS65
1998/XX	6,000	PF65 1,250	PF67 1,800			

KM# 320 50000 LIRE
7.50 g., 0.917 Gold 0.2211 oz. AGW **Obv:** Pope and Holy Year Door **Rev:** Statue of St. Peter

Date	Mintage	VF20	XF40	MS60	MS63	MS65
1999/XXI	—	PF65 1,250	PF67 1,800			

KM# 316 50000 LIRE
7.50 g., 0.917 Gold 0.2211 oz. AGW **Subject:** Crucifixion **Obv:** Bust right **Rev:** Jesus on cross, standing figures at sides

Date	Mintage	VF20	XF40	MS60	MS63	MS65
2000/XXII	6,000	PF65 1,250	PF67 1,800			

KM# 357 100000 LIRE
15.00 g., 0.917 Gold 0.4422 oz. AGW **Obv:** Pope and Holy Year Door **Rev:** Basilica of St. John Lateran

Date	Mintage	VF20	XF40	MS60	MS63	MS65
1996/XVIII R	6,000	PF65 1,750	PF67 2,750			

KM# 289 100000 LIRE
15.00 g., 0.917 Gold 0.4422 oz. AGW **Obv:** Pope and Holy Year Door **Rev:** Basilica of St. Paul outside the walls

Date	Mintage	VF20	XF40	MS60	MS63	MS65
1997/XIX	6,000	PF65 1,750	PF67 2,750			

KM# 302 100000 LIRE
15.00 g., 0.917 Gold 0.4422 oz. AGW, 28 mm. **Obv:** Pope and Holy Year Door **Rev:** Basilica of St. Mary Major **Edge:** Reeded

Date	Mintage	VF20	XF40	MS60	MS63	MS65
1998/XX	6,000	PF65 1,750	PF67 2,750			

KM# 321 100000 LIRE
15.00 g., 0.917 Gold 0.4422 oz. AGW **Obv:** Pope and Holy Year Door **Rev:** St. Peter's Basilica

Date	Mintage	VF20	XF40	MS60	MS63	MS65
1999/XXI	—	PF65 1,750	PF67 2,750			

KM# 317 100000 LIRE
15.00 g., 0.917 Gold 0.4422 oz. AGW **Obv:** Bust right **Rev:** Prodigal son embraced by father

Date	Mintage	VF20	XF40	MS60	MS63	MS65
2000/XXII R	6,000	PF65 1,750	PF67 2,750			

PROVAS

KM#	Date	Mintage	Identification	Mkt Val
Pr1	1951	103	Lira. Silver. Y#49.	75.00
Pr2	1951	103	2 Lire. Silver. Y#50.	75.00
Pr3	1951	103	5 Lire. Silver. Y#51.	110
Pr4	1951	103	10 Lire. Silver. Y#52.	125
Pr5	1952	103	Lira. Silver. Y#49.	75.00
Pr6	1952	103	2 Lire. Silver. Y#50.	75.00
Pr7	1952	103	5 Lire. Silver. Y#51.	110
Pr8	1952	103	10 Lire. Silver. Y#52.	125
Pr9	1953	103	Lira. Silver. Y#49.	75.00
Pr10	1953	103	2 Lire. Silver. Y#50.	75.00
Pr11	1953	103	5 Lire. Silver. Y#51.	110
Pr12	1953	103	10 Lire. Silver. Y#52.	125
Pr13	1955	103	Lira. Silver. Y#49.	75.00
Pr14	1955	103	2 Lire. Silver. Y#50.	75.00
Pr15	1955	103	5 Lire. Silver. Y#51.	75.00
Pr16	1955	103	10 Lire. Silver. Y#52.	95.00
Pr17	1955	103	50 Lire. Silver. Y#54.	115
Pr18	1955	103	100 Lire. Silver. Y#55.	125
Pr19	1956	103	Lira. Silver. Y#49.	75.00
Pr20	1956	103	2 Lire. Silver. Y#50.	75.00
Pr21	1956	103	5 Lire. Silver. Y#51.	75.00
Pr22	1956	103	10 Lire. Silver. Y#52.	95.00
Pr23	1956	103	50 Lire. Silver. Y#54.	115
Pr24	1956	103	100 Lire. Silver. Y#55.	125
Pr25	1957	103	Lira. Silver. Y#49.	75.00
Pr26	1957	103	2 Lire. Silver. Y#50.	75.00
Pr27	1957	103	5 Lire. Silver. Y#51.	75.00
Pr28	1957	103	10 Lire. Silver. Y#52.	75.00
Pr29	1957	103	20 Lire. Silver. Y-A52.	100
Pr30	1957	103	50 Lire. Silver. Y#54.	115
Pr31	1957	103	100 Lire. Silver. Y#55.	125
Pr32	1958	103	Lira. Silver. Y#49.	75.00
Pr33	1958	103	2 Lire. Silver. Y#50.	75.00
Pr34	1958	103	5 Lire. Silver. Y#51.	75.00
Pr35	1958	103	10 Lire. Silver. Y#52.	75.00
Pr36	1958	103	20 Lire. Silver. Y-A52.	100
Pr37	1958	103	50 Lire. Silver. Y#54.	115
Pr38	1958	103	100 Lire. Silver. Y#55.	125
Pr39	1958	103	500 Lire. Silver. Y#56.	155
Pr40	1959	103	Lira. Silver. Y#58.	75.00
Pr41	1959	103	2 Lire. Silver. Y#59.	75.00
Pr42	1959	103	5 Lire. Silver. Y#60.	75.00
Pr43	1959	103	10 Lire. Silver. Y#61.	75.00
Pr44	1959	103	20 Lire. Silver. Y#62.	100
Pr45	1959	103	50 Lire. Silver. Y#63.	115
Pr46	1959	103	100 Lire. Silver. Y#64.	125
Pr47	1959	103	500 Lire. Silver. Y#65.	155
Pr48	1960	103	Lira. Silver. Y#58.	75.00
Pr49	1960	103	2 Lire. Silver. Y#59.	75.00
Pr50	1960	103	5 Lire. Silver. Y#60.	75.00
Pr51	1960	103	10 Lire. Silver. Y#61.	75.00
Pr52	1960	103	20 Lire. Silver. Y#62.	100
Pr53	1960	103	50 Lire. Silver. Y#63.1.	115
Pr54	1960	103	100 Lire. Silver. Y#64.1.	125
Pr55	1960	103	500 Lire. Silver. Y#65.1.	155
Pr56	1961	103	Lira. Silver. Y#58.	75.00
Pr57	1961	103	2 Lire. Silver. Y#59.	75.00
Pr58	1961	103	5 Lire. Silver. Y#60.	75.00
Pr59	1961	103	10 Lire. Silver. Y#61.	75.00
Pr60	1961	103	20 Lire. Silver. Y#62.	100
Pr61	1961	103	50 Lire. Silver. Y#63.1.	115
Pr62	1961	103	100 Lire. Silver. Y#64.1.	125
Pr63	1961	103	500 Lire. Silver. Y#65.1.	155
Pr64	1962	103	Lira. Silver. Y#58.	75.00
Pr65	1962	103	2 Lire. Silver. Y#59.	75.00
Pr66	1962	103	5 Lire. Silver. Y#60.	75.00
Pr67	1962	103	10 Lire. Silver. Y#61.	75.00
Pr68	1962	103	20 Lire. Silver. Y#62.	100
Pr69	1962	103	50 Lire. Silver. Y#63.1.	115
Pr70	1962	103	100 Lire. Silver. Y#64.1.	125
Pr71	1962	103	500 Lire. Silver. Y#65.1.	155
Pr72	1962	103	Lira. Silver. Y#67.	75.00
Pr73	1962	103	2 Lire. Silver. Y#68.	75.00
Pr74	1962	103	5 Lire. Silver. Y#69.	75.00
Pr75	1962	103	10 Lire. Silver. Y#70.	75.00
Pr76	1962	103	20 Lire. Silver. Y#71.	100
Pr77	1962	103	50 Lire. Silver. Y#72.	115
Pr78	1962	103	100 Lire. Silver. Y#73.	125
Pr79	1962	103	500 Lire. Silver. Y#74.	155
Pr80	1963	103	Lira. Silver. Y#76.	75.00
Pr81	1963	103	2 Lire. Silver. Y#77.	75.00
Pr82	1963	103	5 Lire. Silver. Y#78.	75.00
Pr83	1963	103	10 Lire. Silver. Y#79.	75.00
Pr84	1963	103	20 Lire. Silver. Y#80.	100
Pr85	1963	103	50 Lire. Silver. Y#81.	115
Pr86	1963	103	100 Lire. Silver. Y#82.	125
Pr87	1963	103	500 Lire. Silver. Y#83.	155
Pr88	1964	103	Lira. Silver. Y#76.	75.00
Pr89	1964	103	2 Lire. Silver. Y#77.	75.00
Pr90	1964	103	5 Lire. Silver. Y#78.	75.00
Pr91	1964	103	10 Lire. Silver. Y#79.	75.00
Pr92	1964	103	20 Lire. Silver. Y#80.	100
Pr93	1964	103	50 Lire. Silver. Y#81.	115
Pr94	1964	103	100 Lire. Silver. Y#82.	125
Pr95	1964	103	500 Lire. Silver. Y#83.	155
Pr96	1965	103	Lira. Silver. Y#76.	75.00
Pr97	1965	103	2 Lire. Silver. Y#77.	75.00
Pr98	1965	103	5 Lire. Silver. Y#78.	75.00
Pr99	1965	103	10 Lire. Silver. Y#79.	75.00
Pr100	1965	103	20 Lire. Silver. Y#80.	100
Pr101	1965	103	50 Lire. Silver. Y#81.	115
Pr102	1965	103	100 Lire. Silver. Y#82.	125
Pr103	1965	103	500 Lire. Silver. Y#83.	155
Pr104	1966	103	Lira. Silver. Y#84.	75.00
Pr105	1966	103	2 Lire. Silver. Y#85.	75.00
Pr106	1966	103	5 Lire. Silver. Y#86.	75.00
Pr107	1966	103	10 Lire. Silver. Y#87.	75.00
Pr108	1966	103	20 Lire. Silver. Y#88.	100
Pr109	1966	103	50 Lire. Silver. Y#89.	115
Pr110	1966	103	100 Lire. Silver. Y#90.	125
Pr111	1966	103	500 Lire. Silver. Y#91.	155
Pr112	ND-1967	103	Lira. Silver. Y#92.	75.00
Pr113	ND-1967	103	2 Lire. Silver. Y#93.	75.00
Pr114	ND-1967	103	5 Lire. Silver. Y#94.	75.00
Pr115	ND-1967	103	10 Lire. Silver. Y#95.	75.00
Pr116	ND-1967	103	20 Lire. Silver. Y#96.	100
Pr117	1967	103	50 Lire. Silver. Y#97.	115
Pr118	1967	103	100 Lire. Silver. Y#98.	125
Pr119	1967	103	500 Lire. Silver. Y#99.	155
Pr120	ND-1968	103	Lira. Silver. Y#100.	75.00
Pr121	ND-1968	103	2 Lire. Silver. Y#101.	75.00
Pr122	ND-1968	103	5 Lire. Silver. Y#102.	75.00
Pr123	ND-1968	103	10 Lire. Silver. Y#103.	75.00
Pr124	ND-1968	103	20 Lire. Silver. Y#104.	100
Pr125	ND-1968	103	50 Lire. Silver. Y#105.	115
Pr126	ND-1968	103	100 Lire. Silver. Y#106.	125
Pr127	ND-1968	103	500 Lire. Silver. Y#107.	155
Pr128	1969	103	Lira. Silver. Y#108.	75.00
Pr129	1969	103	2 Lire. Silver. Y#109.	75.00
Pr130	1969	103	5 Lire. Silver. Y#110.	75.00
Pr131	1969	103	10 Lire. Silver. Y#111.	75.00
Pr132	1969	103	20 Lire. Silver. Y#112.	100
Pr133	1969	103	50 Lire. Silver. Y#113.	115
Pr134	1969	103	100 Lire. Silver. Y#114.	125
Pr135	1969	103	500 Lire. Silver. Y#115.	155
Pr136	1970	103	Lira. Silver. Y#116.	75.00
Pr137	1970	103	2 Lire. Silver. Y#117.	75.00
Pr138	1970	103	5 Lire. Silver. Y#118.	75.00
Pr139	1970	103	10 Lire. Silver. Y#119.	75.00
Pr140	1970	103	20 Lire. Silver. Y#120.	100
Pr141	1970	103	50 Lire. Silver. Y#121.	115
Pr142	1970	103	100 Lire. Silver. Y#122.	125
Pr143	1970	103	500 Lire. Silver. Y#123.	155
Pr144	1971	103	Lira. Silver. Y#116.	75.00
Pr145	1971	103	2 Lire. Silver. Y#117.	75.00
Pr146	1971	103	5 Lire. Silver. Y#118.	75.00
Pr147	1971	103	10 Lire. Silver. Y#119.	75.00
Pr148	1971	103	20 Lire. Silver. Y#120.	100
Pr149	1971	103	50 Lire. Silver. Y#121.	115
Pr150	1971	103	100 Lire. Silver. Y#122.	125
Pr151	1971	103	500 Lire. Silver. Y#123.	150
Pr152	1972	103	Lira. Silver. Y#116.	75.00
Pr153	1972	103	2 Lire. Silver. Y#117.	75.00
Pr154	1972	103	5 Lire. Silver. Y#118.	75.00
Pr155	1972	103	10 Lire. Silver. Y#119.	75.00
Pr156	1972	103	20 Lire. Silver. Y#120.	100
Pr157	1972	103	50 Lire. Silver. Y#121.	115
Pr158	1972	103	100 Lire. Silver. Y#122.	125
Pr159	1972	103	500 Lire. Silver. Y#123.	155
Pr160	1973	103	Lira. Silver. Y#116.	75.00
Pr161	1973	103	2 Lire. Silver. Y#117.	75.00
Pr162	1973	103	5 Lire. Silver. Y#118.	75.00
Pr163	1973	103	10 Lire. Silver. Y#119.	75.00
Pr164	1973	103	20 Lire. Silver. Y#120.	100
Pr165	1973	103	50 Lire. Silver. Y#121.	115
Pr166	1973	103	100 Lire. Silver. Y#122.	125
Pr167	1973	103	500 Lire. Silver. Y#123.	155
Pr168	1974	103	Lira. Silver. Y#116.	75.00
Pr169	1974	103	2 Lire. Silver. Y#117.	75.00
Pr170	1974	103	5 Lire. Silver. Y#118.	75.00
Pr171	1974	103	10 Lire. Silver. Y#119.	75.00
Pr172	1974	103	20 Lire. Silver. Y#120.	100
Pr173	1974	103	50 Lire. Silver. Y#121.	115
Pr174	1974	103	100 Lire. Silver. Y#122.	125
Pr175	1974	103	500 Lire. Silver. Y#123.	155
Pr176	1975	103	Lira. Silver. Y#116.	75.00
Pr177	1975	103	2 Lire. Silver. Y#117.	75.00
Pr178	1975	103	5 Lire. Silver. Y#118.	75.00
Pr179	1975	103	10 Lire. Silver. Y#119.	75.00
Pr180	1975	103	20 Lire. Silver. Y#120.	100
Pr181	1975	103	50 Lire. Silver. Y#121.	115
Pr182	1975	103	100 Lire. Silver. Y#122.	125
Pr183	1975	103	500 Lire. Silver. Y#123.	155
Pr184	1975	103	Lira. Silver. Y#124.	75.00
Pr185	1975	103	2 Lire. Silver. Y#125.	75.00
Pr186	1975	103	5 Lire. Silver. Y#126.	75.00
Pr187	1975	103	10 Lire. Silver. Y#127.	75.00
Pr188	1975	103	20 Lire. Silver. Y#128.	100
Pr189	1975	103	50 Lire. Silver. Y#129.	115
Pr190	1975	103	100 Lire. Silver. Y#130.	125
Pr191	1975	103	500 Lire. Silver. Y#131.	155

MINT SETS

KM#	Date	Mintage	Identification	Issue Price	Mkt Val
MS1	1929 (9)	10,000	KM#1-9	—	2,400
MS2	1929 (8)	10,000	KM#1-8	—	280
MS3	1930 (9)	2,621	KM#1-9	—	2,300
MS4	1930 (8)	50,000	KM#1-8	—	125
MS5	1931 (9)	3,343	KM#1-9	—	2,300
MS6	1931 (8)	50,000	KM#1-8	—	125
MS7	1932 (9)	5,073	KM#1-9	—	2,300
MS8	1932 (8)	50,000	KM#1-8	—	125
MS9	1933-34 (9)	23,235	KM#11-19	—	2,000
MS10	1933-34 (8)	50,000	KM#11-18	—	235
MS11	1934 (9)	2,533	KM#1-9	—	2,300
MS12	1934 (8)	30,000	KM#1-8	—	125
MS13	1935 (9)	2,105	KM#1-9	—	2,400
MS14	1935 (8)	9,000	KM#1-8	—	200
MS15	1936 (9)	8,239	KM#1-8, 10	—	2,300
MS16	1936 (8)	40,000	KM#1-8	—	125
MS17	1937 (9)	2,000	KM#1-8, 10	—	3,500
MS18	1937 (8)	20,000	KM#1-8	—	125
MS19	1938 (3)	—	KM#1-2, 10 Rare	—	—
MS20	1939 (9)	2,700	KM#22-30.1	—	2,300
MS21	1939 (8)	10,000	KM#22-29	—	110
MS22	1939 (2)	30,000	KM#20, 21	—	85.00
MS23	1940 (9)	2,000	KM#22, 23, 24a-27a, 28-30.1	—	2,300
MS24	1940 (8)	10,000	KM#22, 23, 24a-27a, 28-29	—	95.00
MS25	1941 (9)	2,000	KM#22, 23, 24a-27a, 28-30.2	—	2,400
MS26	1941 (8)	4,000	KM#22, 23, 24a-27a, 28-29	—	195
MS27	1942 (9)	2,000	KM#31-39	—	2,400
MS28	1942 (8)	4,000	KM#31-38	—	260
MSA29	1942 (4)	—	KM#33-36	—	16.00
MS29	1943 (9)	1,000	KM#31-39	—	3,000
MS30	1943 (8)	1,000	KM#31-38	—	800

MS31	1944 (9)	1,000	KM#31-39	—	3,000
MS32	1944 (8)	1,000	KM#31-38	—	800
MS33	1945 (9)	1,000	KM#31-39	—	3,000
MS34	1945 (8)	1,000	KM#31-38	—	800
MS35	1946 (9)	1,000	KM#31-39	—	3,000
MS36	1946 (8)	1,000	KM#31-38	—	800
MS37	1947 (5)	1,000	KM#39-43	—	2,200
MS38	1947 (4)	50,000	KM#40-43	—	22.00
MS39	1947 (2)	—	KM#42-43	—	12.00
MS40	1948 (5)	5,000	KM#39-43	—	2,200
MS41	1948 (4)	10,000	KM#40-43	—	22.00
MS42	1949 (5)	1,000	KM#39-43	—	2,200
MS43	1949 (4)	10,000	KM#40-43	—	32.00
MS44	1950 (5)	20,000	KM#44-48	—	2,200
MS45	1950 (4)	50,000	KM#44-47	—	22.00
MS46	1951 (4)	1,000	KM#49.1-53.1	—	2,200
MS47	1951 (4)	400,000	KM#49.1, 50, 51.1-52.1	—	6.00
MS48	1952 (5)	1,000	KM#49.1-52.1, 53.1	—	2,200
MS49	1952 (4)	400,000	KM#49.1-52.1	—	6.00
MS50	1953 (5)	1,000	KM#49.1-52.1, 53.1	—	2,200
MS51	1953 (4)	400,000	KM#49.1-52.1	—	6.00
MS52	1955 (7)	1,000	KM#49.1-55	—	2,200
MS53	1955 (6)	10,000	KM#49.1-52.1, 54.1, 55	—	15.00
MS54	1956 (7)	1,000	KM#49.2-55	—	2,200
MS55	1956 (6)	10,000	KM#49.2-52.2, 54.2, 55	—	18.00
MS56	1957 (8)	2,000	KM#49.1-52.2, A53, 54.2, 55	—	2,200
MS57	1957 (6)	20,000	KM#49.1-52.2, 54.2, 55	—	14.00
MS58	1958 (8)	3,000	KM#49.1-52.2, 54.2-57	—	100
MS59	1958 (7)	20,000	KM#49.1-52.2, 54.2-56	—	40.00
MS60	1959 (9)	3,000	KM#58.1-64.1, 65.1, 66	—	3,000
MS61	1959 (8)	25,000	KM#58.1-64.1, 65	—	65.00
MS62	1960 (8)	25,000	KM#58.1-59.1, 60.2-64.2, 65.1	—	65.00
MS63	1961 (8)	25,000	KM#58.2-62.2, 63.2-64.2, 65.1	—	60.00
MS64	1962 (8)	25,000	KM#58.2-64.2, 65.1	—	55.00
MS65	1962 (8)	50,000	KM#67-74	—	48.00
MS66	1963 (8)	60,000	KM#76.1-83.1	—	55.00
MS68	1964 (8)	60,000	KM#76.2-79.2, 80.1-81.1, 82.2-83.2	—	70.00
MS69	1965 (8)	60,000	KM#76.2-83.2	—	70.00
MS70	1966 (8)	90,000	KM#84-91	—	40.00
MS71	1967 (8)	100,000	KM#92-99	3.25	40.00
MS72	1968 (8)	100,000	KM#100-107	4.20	40.00
MS73	1969 (8)	100,000	KM#108-115	4.20	40.00
MS74	1970 (8)	100,000	KM#116-123	5.00	22.00
MS75	1971 (8)	110,000	KM#116-123	—	22.00
MS76	1972 (8)	110,000	KM#116-123	6.00	22.00
MS77	1973 (8)	120,000	KM#116-123	6.75	22.00
MS78	1974 (8)	120,000	KM#116-123	7.25	22.00
MS79	1975 (8)	132,000	KM#116-123	9.00	22.00
MSA80	1975 (5)	—	KM#126-130	—	10.00
MS80	1975 (8)	170,000	KM#124-131	—	40.00
MS81	1976 (8)	180,000	KM#116-123	—	22.00
MS82	1977 (7)	180,000	KM#116-120, 122, 132	—	20.00
MS83	1978 (7)	180,000	KM#133-139	—	22.00
MS84	1979 (6)	156,000	KM#143-148	—	42.00
MS85	1980 (6)	—	KM#143-148	18.00	42.00
MS86	1981 (6)	—	KM#155-160	—	42.00
MS87	1982 (7)	120,000	KM#161-167	—	50.00
MS88	1983 (7)	120,000	KM#170-176	—	50.00
MS89	1984 (7)	—	KM#177-183	—	50.00
MS90	1985 (7)	—	KM#185-191	—	50.00
MS91	1986 (7)	—	KM#192-198	23.50	50.00
MS92	1987 (7)	—	KM#199-205	27.00	50.00
MSA93	1987 (5)	—	KM#200-204	—	18.00
MS94	1988 (7)	—	KM#206-212	—	50.00
MS95	1989 (7)	—	KM#213-219	30.00	50.00
MS96	1990 (7)	—	KM#220-226	33.00	50.00
MS97	1991 (7)	—	KM#228-234	25.00	50.00
MS98	1992 (7)	—	KM#236-242	25.00	50.00
MS99	1993 (7)	—	KM#244-250	—	50.00
MS100	1994 (7)	—	KM#252-258	—	50.00
MS101	1995 (7)	—	KM#262-268	32.50	50.00
MS102	1996 (7)	—	KM#272-278	33.00	50.00
MS103	1997 (8)	—	KM#280-287	—	55.00
MS104	1998 (8)	—	KM#293-300	—	55.00
MS105	1999 (8)	—	KM#205-312	—	55.00
MS106	2000 (8)	—	KM#323-330	37.50	85.00

PROOF SETS

KM#	Date	Mintage	Identification	Issue Price	Mkt Val
PS1	1995 (2)	30,000	KM#260-261	70.00	135
PS2	1996 (2)	30,000	KM#270-271	75.00	135
PS3	1996 (2)	—	KM#356, 357	—	1,000
PS4	1997 (2)	6,000	KM#288-289	547	2,600
PS5	1997 (2)	—	KM#318, 319	—	135
PS6	1998 (2)	30,000	KM#290-291	—	135
PS7	1998 (2)	—	KM#301, 302	—	1,000
PS8	1999 (2)	—	KM#303, 304	—	135
PS9	1999 (2)	—	KM#320, 321	—	1,120
PS10	2000 (2)	—	KM#314, 315	—	130
PS11	2000 (10)	30,000	KM#288, 289, 301, 302, 316, 317, 320, 321, 356, 357 Anticipation of the Holy Year 2000	—	5,000
PS12	2000 (2)	—	KM#316, 317	—	1,120

PROVA SETS

KM#	Date	Mintage	Identification	Issue Price	Mkt Val
PrS1	1951 (4)	103	Pr1-Pr4	—	375
PrS2	1952 (4)	103	Pr5-Pr8	—	375
PrS3	1953 (4)	103	Pr9-Pr12	—	375
PrS4	1955 (6)	103	Pr13-Pr18	—	550
PrS5	1956 (6)	103	Pr19-Pr24	—	550
PrS6	1957 (7)	103	Pr25-31	—	625
PrS7	1958 (8)	103	Pr32-Pr39	—	750
PrS8	1959 (8)	103	Pr40-Pr47	—	750
PrS9	1960 (8)	103	Pr48-Pr55	—	750
PrS10	1961 (8)	103	Pr56-Pr63	—	750
PrS11	1962 (8)	103	Pr64-Pr71	—	750
PrS12	1962 (8)	103	Pr72-Pr79	—	750
PrS13	1963 (8)	103	Pr80-Pr87	—	750
PrS14	1964 (8)	103	Pr88-Pr95	—	750
PrS15	1965 (8)	103	Pr96-103	—	750
PrS16	1966 (8)	103	Pr104-Pr111	—	750
PrS17	1967 (8)	103	Pr112-Pr119	—	750
PrS18	1968 (8)	103	Pr120-Pr127	—	750
PrS19	1969 (8)	103	Pr128-Pr135	—	750
PrS20	1970 (8)	103	Pr136-Pr143	—	750
PrS21	1971 (8)	103	Pr144-Pr151	—	750
PrS22	1972 (8)	103	Pr152-Pr159	—	750
PrS23	1973 (8)	103	Pr160-Pr167	—	750
PrS24	1974 (8)	103	Pr168-Pr175	—	750
PrS25	1975 (8)	103	Pr176-Pr183	—	750
PrS26	1975 (8)	103	Pr184-Pr191	—	750

VENEZUELA

The Bolivarian Republic of Venezuela ("Little Venice"), located on the northern coast of South America between Colombia and Guyana, has an area of 352,145 sq. mi. (912,050 sq. km.) and a population of 20 million. Capital: Caracas. Petroleum and mining provide a significant portion of Venezuela's exports. Coffee, grown on 60,000 plantations, is the chief crop. Metalurgy, refining, oil, iron and steel production are the main employment industries.

Columbus discovered Venezuela on his third voyage in 1498. Initial exploration did not reveal Venezuela to be a land of great wealth. An active pearl trade operated on the offshore islands and slavers raided the interior in search of Indians to be sold into slavery, but no significant mainland settlements were made before 1567 when Caracas was founded. Venezuela, the home of Bolivar, was among the first South American colonies to rebel against Spain in 1810. The declaration of Independence of Venezuela was signed by seven provinces which are represented by the seven stars of the Venezuelan flag. Coinage of Caracas and Margarita use the seven stars in their designs. These original provinces were: Barcelona, Barinas, Caracas, Cumana, Margarita, Merida and Trujillo. The Provinces of Coro, Guyana and Maracaibo were added to Venezuela during the Independence War. Independence was attained in 1821 but not recognized by Spain until 1845. Together with Ecuador, Panama and Colombia, Venezuela was part of "Gran Colombia" until 1830, when it became a sovereign and independent state.

RULER

Republic, 1823-2000
Republic Bolivarian, 2000-

MINT MARKS

A - Paris
(a) - Paris, privy marks only
(aa) - Altena
(b) - Berlin
(bb) - Brussels
(cc) – Canada
(c) - Caracas
(d) - Denver
H, Heaton - Heaton, Birmingham
(l) - London
(m) – Madrid
(mm) - Mexico
(o) - Ontario
(p) - Philadelphia
(s) - San Francisco
(sc) - Schwerte - Vereinigte Deutsche Nickelwerke
(w) - Werdohl - Vereinigte Deutsche Metalwerke

MONETARY SYSTEM

100 Centimos = 1 Bolivar

REPUBLIC

REFORM COINAGE

1896
100 Centimos = 1 Bolivar

Y# 27 5 CENTIMOS

2.30 g., Copper-Nickel **Obv:** National arms, stars above **Obv. Legend:** ESTADOS UNIDOS DE VENEZUELA **Rev:** Value within wreath

Date	Mintage	F12	VF20	XF40	MS60	MS63
1915 (p)	2,000,000	1.00	4.00	60.00	150	300
1921 (p)	2,000,000	0.50	4.00	80.00	200	400
1925 (p)	2,000,000	0.30	1.00	10.00	40.00	80.00
1927 (p)	2,000,000	0.30	1.00	10.00	30.00	60.00
1929 (p)	2,000,000	0.25	1.00	10.00	30.00	60.00
1936 (p)	5,000,000	0.15	0.50	4.00	20.00	35.00
1938 (p)	6,000,000	0.10	0.20	4.00	20.00	35.00

Y# 29 5 CENTIMOS

2.43 g., Brass **Obv:** National arms, stars above **Rev:** Denomination within wreath

Date	Mintage	F12	VF20	XF40	MS60	MS63
1944 (d)	4,000,000	0.50	1.00	6.00	25.00	60.00

Y# 29a 5 CENTIMOS

2.40 g., Copper-Nickel, 19.1 mm. **Obv:** National arms, stars above **Rev:** Denomination within wreath

Date	Mintage	F12	VF20	XF40	MS60	MS63
1945 (p)	12,000,000	0.10	0.20	0.50	5.00	7.00
1946 (p)	12,000,000	0.10	0.20	0.50	5.00	7.00
1948 (p)	18,000,000	0.10	0.20	0.50	4.00	6.00

Y# 38.1 5 CENTIMOS

Copper-Nickel **Obv:** National arms, stars above **Rev:** Denomination within wreath

Date	Mintage	VF20	XF40	MS60	MS63	MS65
1958 (p)	25,000,000	—	—	0.75	1.25	1.75

Y# 38.2 5 CENTIMOS

2.50 g., Copper-Nickel, 19.8 mm. **Obv:** National arms, stars above **Rev:** Denomination within wreath

Date	Mintage	VF20	XF40	MS60	MS63	MS65
1964 (m)	40,000,000	—	—	0.50	1.00	1.50
1965 (m)	60,000,000	—	—	0.50	1.00	1.50

Y# 38.3 5 CENTIMOS

Copper-Nickel **Obv:** National arms, stars above **Rev:** Denomination within wreath

Date	Mintage	VF20	XF40	MS60	MS63	MS65
1971 (o)	40,000,000	—	—	0.50	1.00	1.50

Y# 49 5 CENTIMOS

Copper Clad Steel **Obv:** National arms, stars above **Rev:** Denomination below spray

Date	Mintage	VF20	XF40	MS60	MS63	MS65
1974 (w)	200,000,000	—	—	1.50	4.00	15.00
1976 (w)	200,000,000	—	—	1.00	3.00	10.00
1977 (l)	600,000,000	—	—	0.50	1.00	2.00

Y# 49a 5 CENTIMOS

Nickel Clad Steel **Obv:** National arms, stars above **Rev:** Denomination below spray

Date	Mintage	VF20	XF40	MS60	MS63	MS65
1983 (w)	600,000,000	—	—	0.25	0.35	0.50

Y# 49b 5 CENTIMOS

2.00 g., Copper-Nickel Clad Steel **Obv:** National arms, stars above **Rev:** Denomination below spray

Date	Mintage	VF20	XF40	MS60	MS63	MS65
1986 (w)	500,000,000	—	—	0.25	0.35	0.50

Y# A40 10 CENTIMOS

Copper-Nickel **Obv:** National arms, stars above **Rev:** Denomination within wreath

Date	Mintage	VF20	XF40	MS60	MS63	MS65
1971 (o)	60,000,000	—	—	0.10	0.25	0.50

Y# 28 12-1/2 CENTIMOS

Copper-Nickel, 23 mm. **Obv:** National arms, stars above **Obv. Legend:** ESTADOS UNIDOS DE VENEZUELA **Rev:** Value within wreath **Note:** Varieties exist.

Date	Mintage	F12	VF20	XF40	MS60	MS63
1925 (p)	800,000	2.50	10.00	55.00	300	600
1927 (p)	800,000	1.00	3.00	20.00	150	250
1929 (p)	800,000	0.15	1.00	15.00	125	175
1936 (p)	1,200,000	0.15	1.00	10.00	75.00	150
1938 (p)	1,600,000	0.15	1.00	5.00	60.00	100

Y# 30 12-1/2 CENTIMOS

Brass, 23 mm. **Obv:** National arms, stars above **Rev:** Denomination within wreath

Date	Mintage	F12	VF20	XF40	MS60	MS63
1944 (d)	800,000	2.50	4.50	15.00	75.00	150

Y# 30a 12-1/2 CENTIMOS

Copper-Nickel, 23 mm. **Obv:** National arms, stars above **Rev:** Denomination within wreath

Date	Mintage	F12	VF20	XF40	MS60	MS63
1945 (p)	11,200,000	0.10	0.20	1.00	10.00	20.00
1946 (p)	9,200,000	0.10	0.20	1.00	15.00	25.00
1948 (s)	6,000,000	0.10	0.20	1.00	15.00	25.00

Y# 39 12-1/2 CENTIMOS

Copper-Nickel, 23 mm. **Obv:** National arms, stars above **Rev:** Denomination within wreath, knobbed 2

Date	Mintage	VF20	XF40	MS60	MS63	MS65
1958 (p)	10,000,000	—	0.20	1.00	2.00	4.00

Y# A39.1 12-1/2 CENTIMOS

Copper-Nickel **Obv:** National arms, flat stars **Rev:** Denomination within wreath, plain 2

Date	Mintage	VF20	XF40	MS60	MS63	MS65
1969 (m)	2,000,000	—	—	100	125	—

Y# A39.2 12-1/2 CENTIMOS

Copper-Nickel **Obv:** National arms, raised stars **Rev:** Denomination within wreath, outlined stem ends

Date	Mintage	VF20	XF40	MS60	MS63	MS65
1969 (m)	Inc. above	—	—	100	200	—

Y# A39.3 12-1/2 CENTIMOS

Copper-Nickel **Obv:** National arms, stars above **Rev:** Denomination within wreath, solid stem ends

Date	Mintage	VF20	XF40	MS60	MS63	MS65
1969 (m)	Inc. above	—	—	100	200	—

Note: 1969 dated strikes were not released into circulation, but the Central Bank has been selling limited quantities on occasion

Y# 20 25 CENTIMOS

1.25 g., 0.835 Silver 0.0336 oz. ASW, 20 mm. **Obv:** National arms **Obv. Legend:** ESTADOS UNIDOS DE VENEZUELA. **Rev:** Head left **Rev. Legend:** BOLIVAR LIBERTADOR **Edge:** Reeded

Date	Mintage	F12	VF20	XF40	MS60	MS63
1901	393,000	7.00	25.00	55.00	500	600
1903 (p)	400,000	6.00	30.00	60.00	250	450
1911	600,000	2.50	5.00	15.00	75.00	150
1912	800,000	3.00	6.00	20.00	125	225
1919 (p)	400,000	2.50	5.00	15.00	150	375
1921 (p) High 2	800,000	2.00	4.00	15.00	85.00	175
1921 (p) Low 2	Inc. above	1.50	3.00	15.00	85.00	175
1924 (p)	400,000	1.50	3.00	12.00	75.00	125
1929 (p)	1,200,000	—	0.70	2.00	8.00	17.00
1935 (p)	3,400,000	—	0.70	1.50	4.00	12.00
1936 (p)	2,800,000	—	0.70	1.50	4.00	12.00
1944 (p)	1,800,000	—	0.70	1.50	2.00	5.00
1945 (p)	8,000,000	—	—	0.70	1.50	2.50
1946 (p)	8,000,000	—	—	0.70	2.00	2.00
1948 (s)	8,638,000	—	—	0.70	2.00	2.00

Y# 35 25 CENTIMOS

1.25 g., 0.835 Silver 0.0336 oz. ASW, 16 mm. **Obv:** National arms **Rev:** Head of Bolivar left

Date	Mintage	F12	VF20	XF40	MS60	MS63
1954	36,000,000	—	—	0.70	1.50	1.75

Y# 35a 25 CENTIMOS

1.25 g., 0.835 Silver 0.0336 oz. ASW, 16 mm. **Obv:** National arms **Rev:** Head of Bolivar left

Date	Mintage	VF20	XF40	MS60	MS63	MS65
1960	48,000,000	—	0.70	1.25	1.50	1.75

Y# 40 25 CENTIMOS

1.25 g., Nickel, 17 mm. **Obv:** National arms **Rev:** Head of Bolivar left **Edge:** Reeded

Date	Mintage	VF20	XF40	MS60	MS63	MS65
1965 (l)	240,000,000	—	0.10	0.35	0.60	1.00

Y# 50.1 25 CENTIMOS

1.75 g., Nickel, 17 mm. **Obv:** National arms **Rev:** Head of Bolivar left **Edge:** Reeded **Note:** 1.18mm thick.

Date	Mintage	VF20	XF40	MS60	MS63	MS65
1977 (w)	240,000,000	—	0.10	0.20	0.35	0.50
1978	—	—	0.10	0.20	0.35	0.50

Y# 50.2 25 CENTIMOS

1.75 g., Nickel, 17 mm. **Obv:** National arms **Rev:** Head of Bolivar left **Edge:** Reeded **Note:** Dies vary for each date; thin.

Date	Mintage	VF20	XF40	MS60	MS63	MS65
1977 (w)	Inc. above	—	0.10	0.20	0.35	0.50
1978 (w)	200,000,000	—	0.10	0.20	0.35	0.50
1987	150,000,000	—	0.10	0.20	0.35	0.50

Y# 50a 25 CENTIMOS

1.50 g., Nickel Clad Steel, 16.06 mm. **Obv:** National arms **Rev:** Head of Bolivar left **Edge:** Reeded **Note:** Varieties exist.

Date	Mintage	VF20	XF40	MS60	MS63	MS65
1989 (sc)	510,000,000	—	0.10	0.20	0.35	0.50
1990 (mm)	400,000,000	—	0.10	0.20	0.35	0.50

Y# 21 50 CENTIMOS (Gr 2.500)

2.50 g., 0.835 Silver 0.0671 oz. ASW, 18 mm. **Obv:** Arms within sprigs above banner, cornucopias above **Obv. Legend:** ESTADOS UNIDOS DE VENEZUELA **Rev:** Head of Bolivar left **Rev. Legend:** BOLIVAR LIBERTADOR **Edge:** Reeded

Date	Mintage	F12	VF20	XF40	MS60	MS63
1901	600,000	20.00	50.00	175	1,100	1,900
Note: Privy mark placement varies with 1901						
1903 (p)	200,000	80.00	225	700	2,200	3,750
1911	300,000	35.00	70.00	220	700	1,300
Note: Privy mark placement varies with 1911						
1912	1,920,000	5.00	15.00	50.00	300	600
1919 (p)	400,000	6.00	20.00	80.00	300	800
1921 (p) Normal date	600,000	2.75	7.00	16.00	150	300
1921 (p) Narrow date	Inc. above	3.50	9.00	27.50	150	300
1921 (p) Wide date	Inc. above	3.50	9.00	27.50	150	300
1924 (p)	800,000	2.50	7.00	16.00	85.00	200
1929 (p)	400,000	2.50	3.50	6.00	55.00	135
1935 (p)	1,000,000	—	1.30	2.50	12.00	30.00
1936 (p)	600,000	1.30	2.50	5.00	60.00	150

Y# 21a 50 CENTIMOS (Gr 2.500)

2.50 g., 0.835 Silver 0.0671 oz. ASW, 18 mm. **Obv:** National arms above ribbon, plants flank, cornucopias above **Rev:** Head of Bolivar left

Date	Mintage	F12	VF20	XF40	MS60	MS63
1944 (d)	500,000	2.50	3.00	5.00	17.00	35.00
Note: Accent in Bolivar						
1944 (d)	Inc. above	2.50	6.00	10.00	25.00	50.00
Note: Without accent in Bolivar						
1945 (p)	4,000,000	—	1.30	2.25	6.00	12.00
1946 (p)	2,500,000	—	1.30	2.25	6.00	12.00

Y# 36 50 CENTIMOS

2.50 g., 0.835 Silver 0.0671 oz. ASW, 18 mm. **Obv:** National arms **Rev:** Head of Bolivar left

Date	Mintage	F12	VF20	XF40	MS60	MS63
1954 (p)	15,000,000	—	—	1.30	2.00	3.00

Y# 36a 50 CENTIMOS

2.50 g., 0.835 Silver 0.0671 oz. ASW, 18 mm. **Obv:** National arms **Rev:** Head of Bolivar left

Date	Mintage	VF20	XF40	MS60	MS63	MS65
1960 (a)	20,000,000	—	1.30	1.75	2.50	4.00

Y# 41 50 CENTIMOS

3.50 g., Nickel, 20 mm. **Obv:** National arms **Rev:** Head of Bolivar left **Edge:** Reeded

Date	Mintage	VF20	XF40	MS60	MS63	MS65
1965 (l)	180,000,000	0.10	0.15	0.35	0.50	1.00
1985 (o)	50,000,000	0.10	0.15	0.35	0.50	1.00

Y# 41a 50 CENTIMOS

3.00 g., Nickel Clad Steel, 20 mm. **Obv:** National arms **Rev:** Head of Bolivar left **Edge:** Reeded

Date	Mintage	VF20	XF40	MS60	MS63	MS65
1988 (w)	80,000,000	0.10	0.15	0.25	0.40	0.60
1989 (w)	260,000,000	0.10	0.15	0.25	0.40	0.60
1990 (l)	300,000,000	0.10	0.15	0.25	0.40	0.60
Note: Die varieties exist for 1990 dated strikes						

Y# 22 BOLIVAR (Gram 5)

5.00 g., 0.835 Silver 0.1342 oz. ASW, 23 mm. **Obv:** Arms within sprigs above banner, cornucopias above **Obv. Legend:** ESTADOS UNIDOS DE VENEZUELA. **Rev:** Head of Bolivar left **Rev. Legend:** BOLIVAR LIBERTADOR

Date	Mintage	F12	VF20	XF40	MS60	MS63
1901	323,000	20.00	55.00	150	850	1,000
1903 (p)	800,000	5.00	15.00	100	550	900
1911	1,500,000	5.00	7.50	50.00	225	700
1912 Wide date	820,000	6.00	16.50	85.00	325	850
1912 Narrow date	Inc. above	6.00	16.50	85.00	325	850
1919 (p)	1,000,000	5.00	6.00	15.00	85.00	225
1921 (p)	1,000,000	5.00	6.00	15.00	150	225
1924 (p)	1,500,000	2.50	4.75	8.00	85.00	225
1926 (p)	1,000,000	2.50	4.75	8.00	85.00	225
1929 (p)	2,500,000	—	2.50	5.50	10.00	30.00
1935 (p)	5,000,000	—	2.50	5.00	6.00	12.50
1936 (p)	5,000,000	—	2.50	5.00	6.00	12.50

Y# 22a BOLIVAR (Gram 5)

5.00 g., 0.835 Silver 0.1342 oz. ASW, 23 mm. **Obv:** National arms above ribbon, plants flank, cornucopias above **Rev:** Head of Bolivar left

Date	Mintage	F12	VF20	XF40	MS60	MS63
1945 (p)	8,000,000	—	—	2.50	3.50	4.50

Y# 37 BOLIVAR

5.00 g., 0.835 Silver 0.1342 oz. ASW, 23 mm. **Obv:** National arms above ribbon, plants flank, cornucopias above **Rev:** Head of Bolivar left

Date	Mintage	F12	VF20	XF40	MS60	MS63
1954 (p)	13,500,000	—	—	2.50	3.00	4.00

Y# 37a BOLIVAR

5.00 g., 0.835 Silver 0.1342 oz. ASW, 23 mm. **Obv:** National arms above ribbon, plants flank, cornucopias above **Rev:** Head of Bolivar left

Date	Mintage	VF20	XF40	MS60	MS63	MS65
1960	30,000,000	—	2.50	3.00	4.00	5.50
Note: Thin letters						
1960	Inc. above	—	2.50	3.00	4.00	5.50
Note: Thick letters						
1965 (l)	20,000,000	—	2.50	3.00	4.00	5.50

Y# 42 BOLIVAR

5.00 g., Nickel, 23 mm. **Obv:** National arms above ribbon, plants flank, cornucopias above **Rev:** Head of Bolivar left **Edge:** Reeded

Date	Mintage	VF20	XF40	MS60	MS63	MS65
1967 (l)	180,000,000	0.10	0.15	0.75	1.25	2.00

Y# 52 BOLIVAR

5.00 g., Nickel, 23 mm. **Obv:** National arms above ribbon, plants flank, cornucopias above **Rev:** Head of Bolivar left **Edge:** Reeded **Note:** Dies vary for each date.

Date	Mintage	VF20	XF40	MS60	MS63	MS65
1977 (l)	200,000,000	0.10	0.15	0.50	1.00	2.00
1986 (w)	200,000,000	0.10	0.15	0.50	1.00	2.00
1986 (w) Prooflike	50,000,000	—	—	—	—	25.00

Y# 52a.1 BOLIVAR

4.20 g., Nickel Clad Steel, 23 mm. **Obv:** National arms above ribbon, plants flank, cornucopias above **Rev:** Head of Bolivar left **Note:** Both sides of coin have small letters and date

Date	Mintage	VF20	XF40	MS60	MS63	MS65
1989 (w)	370,000,000	0.10	0.15	0.25	0.45	1.00

Y# 52a.2 BOLIVAR

4.20 g., Nickel Clad Steel, 23 mm. **Obv:** National arms above ribbon, plants flank, cornucopias above **Rev:** Head of Bolivar left **Note:** Dies vary for each date. Obverse has large letters and date

Date	Mintage	VF20	XF40	MS60	MS63	MS65
1989 (sc)	600,000,000	0.10	0.15	0.25	0.45	1.00
1990 (mm)	600,000,000	0.10	0.15	0.25	0.45	1.00

Knobbed 6 Pointed 6

Y# 23 2 BOLIVARES (Gram 10)

10.00 g., 0.835 Silver 0.2685 oz. ASW, 27 mm. **Obv:** Arms within sprigs above banner, cornucopias above **Obv. Legend:** ESTADOS UNIDOS DE VENEZUELA **Rev:** Head of Bolivar left **Rev. Legend:** BOLIVAR LIBERTADOR

Date	Mintage	F12	VF20	XF40	MS60	MS63
1902 (p)	500,000	13.50	45.00	200	550	1,000
1903 (p)	500,000	15.00	50.00	250	600	1,100
1904 Large 0, small 4	550,000	13.50	40.00	175	550	1,000
1904 Large 0, large 4	Inc. above	13.50	40.00	175	550	1,000
1904 Small 0, large 4	Inc. above	13.50	45.00	185	550	1,000
1904 Small 0, large slant 4	Inc. above	13.50	45.00	185	550	1,000
1904 Small 0, small 4	Inc. above	20.00	55.00	200	550	1,000
1905 Upright 5	750,000	9.75	17.50	100	450	900
1905 Slant 5	Inc. above	9.75	17.50	100	450	900
1911	750,000	9.75	17.50	60.00	275	650
1912	500,000	9.75	17.50	140	400	1,000
1913 Normal date	210,000	40.00	250	500	1,000	2,000
1913 Raised 3	Inc. above	40.00	250	500	1,000	2,000
1919 (p)	1,000,000	5.25	9.75	13.50	175	400
1922 (p) Narrow date	1,000,000	5.25	9.75	13.50	150	275
1922 (p) Wide date	Inc. above	5.25	9.75	13.50	150	275
1922 (p) Low first 2	Inc. above	5.25	9.75	13.50	150	275
1924 (p)	1,250,000	5.25	9.75	13.50	150	200
1926 (p)	1,000,000	5.25	9.75	13.50	130	250
1929 (p)	1,500,000	—	5.25	10.00	20.00	50.00
1930 (p)	425,000	5.25	10.00	25.00	130	300
1935 (p)	3,000,000	—	5.25	9.75	12.50	25.00
1936 (p)	2,500,000	—	5.25	9.75	12.50	25.00

Y# 23a 2 BOLIVARES (Gram 10)

10.00 g., 0.835 Silver 0.2685 oz. ASW, 27 mm. **Obv:** National arms above ribbon, plants flank, cornucopias above **Rev:** Head of Bolivar left

Date	Mintage	F12	VF20	XF40	MS60	MS63
1945 (p)	3,000,000	—	—	5.25	9.00	10.00

Y# A37 2 BOLIVARES

10.00 g., 0.835 Silver 0.2685 oz. ASW, 27 mm. **Obv:** National arms above ribbon, plants flank, cornucopias above **Rev:** Head of Bolivar left

Date	Mintage	VF20	XF40	MS60	MS63	MS65
1960	4,000,000	—	5.25	9.00	10.00	12.00
1965 (l)	7,170,000	—	5.25	9.00	10.00	12.00

Y# 43 2 BOLIVARES
10.00 g., Nickel, 27 mm. **Obv:** National arms above ribbon, plants flank, cornucopias above **Rev:** Head of Bolivar left **Edge:** Reeded **Note:** Dies vary for each date.

Date	Mintage	VF20	XF40	MS60	MS63	MS65
1967 (l)	50,000,000	—	0.25	0.50	1.00	2.00
1986 (w)	50,000,000	—	0.25	0.50	1.00	2.00
Note: Die varieties exist for 1986 strikes						
1986 (w) Prooflike	—	—	—	—	—	30.00
Note: Die varieties exist for 1986 strikes						
1988 (c)	80,000,000	—	0.25	0.50	1.00	2.00

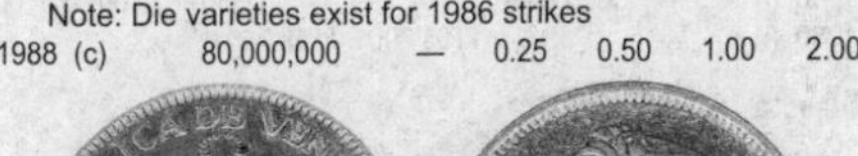

Y# 43a.1 2 BOLIVARES
7.50 g., Nickel Clad Steel, 27 mm. **Obv:** Small letters in legend, raised motto in ribbon, lines beneath horse, "R" in 'Libertador' 2mm away from truncation **Rev:** Head of Bolivar left, small letters **Edge:** Reeded

Date	Mintage	VF20	XF40	MS60	MS63	MS65
1989 (sc)	200,000,000	—	0.20	0.50	1.00	2.00
1990 (c)	400,000,000	—	0.20	0.50	1.00	2.00
Note: Two varieties of 1990 exist						

Y# 43a.2 2 BOLIVARES
7.50 g., Nickel Clad Steel, 27 mm. **Obv:** Large letters in legend, no lines beneath horse, "R" in 'Libertador' touching truncation **Rev:** Head of Bolivar left, large letters **Edge:** Reeded

Date	Mintage	VF20	XF40	MS60	MS63	MS65
1989 (w)	100,000,000	—	0.20	0.50	1.00	2.00
1989 (c)	95,000,000	—	0.20	0.50	1.00	2.00

Y# 24.2 5 BOLIVARES (Gram 25)
25.00 g., 0.900 Silver 0.7234 oz. ASW, 37 mm. **Obv:** Date on ribbon right of arms 13 DE APRIL DE 1864, cornucopias above **Obv. Legend:** ESTADOS UNIDOS DE VENEZUELA **Rev:** Head of Bolivar left **Rev. Legend:** BOLIVAR LIBERTADOR

Date	Mintage	F12	VF20	XF40	MS60	MS63
1901	90,000	30.00	100	375	1,500	3,000
1902 (p) Wide date	500,000	24.00	28.00	120	900	1,300
1902 (p) Narrow date	Inc. above	24.00	28.00	120	900	1,300
1903 (p)	200,000	24.00	28.00	120	900	1,300
1904	200,000	24.00	28.00	150	1,300	3,200
1905	300,000	24.00	28.00	120	900	1,300
1910 Oval 0	400,000	24.00	28.00	85.00	550	900
1910 Round 0	Inc. above	24.00	28.00	100	550	900
1911 Normal date	1,104,000	14.00	26.00	45.00	300	600
1911 Wide date	Inc. above	14.00	26.00	45.00	300	600
1911 Narrow date	Inc. above	14.00	26.00	45.00	300	600
1912 Normal date	696,000	14.00	26.00	45.00	300	600
1912 Wide date	Inc. above	14.00	26.00	45.00	300	600
1912 Narrow date	Inc. above	14.00	26.00	45.00	300	600
1919 (p)	400,000	14.00	26.00	40.00	225	500
1921 (p) Wide date	500,000	14.00	25.00	30.00	125	250
1921 (p) Narrow date	Inc. above	14.00	25.00	30.00	125	250
1924 (p) Wide date	500,000	14.00	25.00	30.00	125	250
1924 (p) Narrow date	Inc. above	14.00	25.00	30.00	125	250
1924 (p) Low 9	Inc. above	14.00	25.00	30.00	125	250
1926 (p)	800,000	14.00	24.00	28.00	100	175
1929 (p) High 9	800,000	14.00	24.00	28.00	70.00	150
1929 (p) Low 9	Inc. above	14.00	24.00	28.00	70.00	150
1935 (p)	1,600,000	14.00	24.00	27.00	40.00	75.00
1936 (p) Normal date	2,000,000	14.00	24.00	27.00	40.00	75.00
1936 (p) High 3	Inc. above	14.00	24.00	27.00	40.00	75.00
1936 (p) Low 3	Inc. above	14.00	24.00	27.00	40.00	75.00

Y# 44 5 BOLIVARES
15.00 g., Nickel, 31 mm. **Obv:** National arms above ribbon, plants flank, cornucopias above **Rev:** Head of Bolivar left **Edge:** Reeded

Date	Mintage	VF20	XF40	MS60	MS63	MS65
1973	20,000,000	0.45	0.75	1.75	3.00	12.00

Y# 53.1 5 BOLIVARES
15.00 g., Nickel, 31 mm. **Obv:** National arms above ribbon, plants flank, cornucopias above, date and denomination below, six-pointed stars **Rev:** Head of Bolivar left **Edge:** Reeded

Date	Mintage	VF20	XF40	MS60	MS63	MS65
1977 (m)	60,000,000	—	0.50	0.75	1.50	3.00

Y# 53.2 5 BOLIVARES
15.00 g., Nickel, 31 mm. **Obv:** National arms above ribbon, plants flank, cornucopias above, date and denomination below, five-pointed stars **Rev:** Head of Bolivar left **Edge:** Reeded

Date	Mintage	VF20	XF40	MS60	MS63	MS65
1987 (c)	25,000,000	—	0.50	0.75	1.50	3.00
1987 (c) Prooflike	Inc. above	—	—	—	—	35.00
1988 (w)	20,000,000	—	0.50	1.00	3.00	6.00

Y# 53a.1 5 BOLIVARES
13.30 g., Nickel Clad Steel, 31 mm. **Obv:** National arms above ribbon, plants flank, cornucopias above, small letters **Rev:** Head of Bolivar left, large letters **Edge:** Reeded

Date	Mintage	VF20	XF40	MS60	MS63	MS65
1989	55,000,000	—	0.50	0.75	1.25	2.50
1989 Prooflike	26,000,000	—	—	—	—	30.00

Y# 53a.2 5 BOLIVARES
13.30 g., Nickel Clad Steel, 31 mm. **Obv:** National arms, large letters **Rev:** Head of Bolivar left, small letters **Edge:** Reeded

Date	Mintage	VF20	XF40	MS60	MS63	MS65
1989 (sc)	100,000,000	—	0.50	0.75	1.50	3.00
1990 (c)	200,000,000	—	0.50	0.75	1.50	3.00

Y# 53a.3 5 BOLIVARES
13.30 g., Nickel Clad Steel, 31 mm. **Obv:** National arms above ribbon, plants flank, cornucopias above, large letters **Rev:** Head of Bolivar left, large letters **Edge:** Reeded

Date	Mintage	VF20	XF40	MS60	MS63	MS65
1990	—	—	0.50	0.75	1.25	2.50

Y# 31 10 BOLIVARES (Gr 3.2258)
3.23 g., 0.900 Gold 0.0933 oz. AGW **Obv:** National arms above ribbon, plants flank, cornucopias above **Rev:** Head of Bolivar right

Date	Mintage	F12	VF20	XF40	MS60	MS63
1930 (p)	Est. 500000	—	125	175	225	275
Note: Only 10% of the total mintage was released; the balance remaining as part of the nation's gold reserve						

Y# 45 10 BOLIVARES
30.00 g., 0.900 Silver 0.8681 oz. ASW, 39 mm. **Obv:** Arms within inset at left, inscription at right **Rev:** Head of Bolivar within inset at right, inscription at left **Edge Lettering:** CENTENARIO DE LA EFIGLE DEL LIBERTADOR EN EL MONEDA

Date	Mintage	VF20	XF40	MS60	MS63	MS65
1973	2,000,000	—	—	18.50	21.00	24.00
1973	200	PF63 400	PF65 450			

Y# 75 10 BOLIVARES
2.40 g., Nickel Clad Steel, 17 mm. **Obv:** National arms **Rev:** Head of Bolivar left within 7-sided outline **Edge:** Reeded **Note:** Struck at Ceska Mincova and Budapest mints.

Date	Mintage	VF20	XF40	MS60	MS63	MS65
1998	—	—	—	0.15	0.25	0.50

Y# 32 20 BOLIVARES (Gr 6.4516)
6.45 g., 0.900 Gold 0.1867 oz. AGW **Obv:** Arms within sprigs above banner, cornucopias above **Obv. Legend:** ESTADOS UNIDOS DE VENEZUELA **Rev:** Head of Bolivar right **Rev. Legend:** BOLIVAR LIBERTADOR

Date	Mintage	F12	VF20	XF40	MS60	MS63
1904	100,000	—	250	425	450	500
1905	100,000	—	250	425	450	500
1910	70,000	—	250	425	450	500
Note: Die varieties exist in the placement of dot between date and Lei, Type 1 is evenly spaced, Type 2 had dot closer to L of Lei						

Date	Mintage	F12	VF20	XF40	MS60	MS63
1911	80,000	—	250	425	450	500

Note: Die varieties exist in the placement of dot between date and Lei, Type 1 is evenly spaced, Type 2 had dot closer to L of Lei

Date	Mintage	F12	VF20	XF40	MS60	MS63
1912	150,000	—	250	425	450	500

Note: Die varieties exist in the placement of the torch privy mark in relation to bust truncation; Type 1 is well below truncation, Type 2 is slightly below truncation and Type 3 is in line with the truncation

Y# 76.1 20 BOLIVARES

Nickel Clad Steel, 20 mm. **Obv:** National arms **Rev:** Head of Bolivar left within 7-sided outline **Note:** Struck at Ceska Mincova and Budapest mints.

Date	Mintage	VF20	XF40	MS60	MS63	MS65
1998	—	—	—	0.15	0.25	0.50

Y# 76.2 20 BOLIVARES

4.32 g., Nickel Clad Steel, 20 mm. **Obv:** National arms **Rev:** Head of Bolivar left within 7-sided outline **Edge:** Plain

Date	Mintage	VF20	XF40	MS60	MS63	MS65
1999	—	—	0.25	0.35	0.50	0.75

Y# 46 25 BOLIVARES

28.28 g., 0.925 Silver 0.841 oz. ASW **Subject:** Conservation **Obv:** National arms above ribbon, plants flank, cornucopias above **Rev:** Jaguar, denomination below

Date	Mintage	VF20	XF40	MS60	MS63	MS65
1975 (l)	38,000	—	—	22.00	30.00	35.00
1975 (l)	Est. 8000	PF63 40.00	PF65 45.00	PF67 55.00		

Y# 47 50 BOLIVARES

35.00 g., 0.925 Silver 1.0409 oz. ASW **Subject:** Conservation **Obv:** National arms above ribbon, plants flank, cornucopias above **Rev:** Giant Armadillo

Date	Mintage	VF20	XF40	MS60	MS63	MS65
1975 (l)	39,000	—	—	27.00	45.00	50.00
1975 (l)	Est. 8000	PF63 50.00	PF65 55.00	PF67 65.00		

Y# 66 50 BOLIVARES

31.10 g., 0.900 Silver 0.8999 oz. ASW **Subject:** 50th Anniversary of Central Bank **Obv:** Flag design with initials in circle at right **Rev:** Building facade

Date	Mintage	VF20	XF40	MS60	MS63	MS65
1990	10,000	PF63 50.00	PF65 55.00			

Y# 67 50 BOLIVARES

15.55 g., 0.900 Gold 0.4499 oz. AGW **Subject:** 50th Anniversary of Central Bank **Obv:** Flag design with initials in circle at right **Rev:** Building facade

Date	Mintage	VF20	XF40	MS60	MS63	MS65
1990	5,000	PF63 750	PF65 800			

Y# 77.1 50 BOLIVARES

6.60 g., Nickel Clad Steel **Obv:** National arms **Rev:** Head of Bolivar left within 7-sided outline **Note:** Struck at Ceska Mincova and Budapest mints.

Date	Mintage	VF20	XF40	MS60	MS63	MS65
1998	—	—	—	0.35	0.50	0.75

Y# 77.2 50 BOLIVARES

6.65 g., Nickel Clad Steel, 23 mm. **Obv:** National arms **Rev:** Head of Bolívar left and mint mark, in 7-sided outline **Edge:** Reeded

Date	Mintage	VF20	XF40	MS60	MS63	MS65
1999	—	—	0.35	0.50	0.75	1.00

Y# 55 75 BOLIVARES

17.00 g., 0.900 Silver 0.4919 oz. ASW **Subject:** 50th Anniversary - Sucre's Death **Obv:** Body on ground at right, mountains in background, horse at left **Rev:** Head of Bolivar 3/4 facing divides dates

Date	Mintage	VF20	XF40	MS60	MS63	MS65
1980 (l)	500,000	—	—	12.50	15.00	18.00
1980 (l)	200	PF63 700	PF65 750			

Y# 56 100 BOLIVARES

22.00 g., 0.900 Silver 0.6366 oz. ASW **Subject:** 150th Anniversary - Bolivar's Death **Obv:** Monument **Rev:** Bust of Bolivar facing divides dates

Date	Mintage	VF20	XF40	MS60	MS63	MS65
1980 (l)	500,000	—	—	17.50	20.00	25.00
1980 (l)	—	PF63 700	PF65 750			

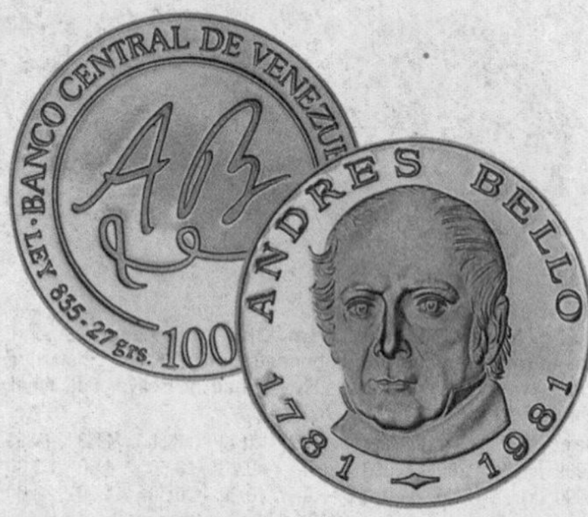

Y# 57 100 BOLIVARES

27.00 g., 0.835 Silver 0.7248 oz. ASW **Subject:** 200th Anniversary - Birth of Andres Bello **Obv:** Initials within circle **Rev:** Head of Bolivar facing, dates below

Date	Mintage	VF20	XF40	MS60	MS63	MS65
ND (1981) (w)	200	—	—	—	350	400
ND (1981) (w)	—	PF63 20.00	PF65 23.00			

Y# 58 100 BOLIVARES

31.00 g., 0.900 Silver 0.897 oz. ASW **Subject:** 200th Anniversary - Birth of Simon Bolivar **Obv:** Building **Rev:** Bookshselves back of 3/4 figure looking left

Date	Mintage	VF20	XF40	MS60	MS63	MS65
ND (1983) (w)	300,000	PF63 22.00	PF65 25.00			

Y# 60 100 BOLIVARES

31.00 g., 0.900 Silver 0.897 oz. ASW, 35 mm. **Subject:** 200th Anniversary - Birth of Jose M. Vargas **Obv:** Steepled building within circle **Rev:** Bust of Jose Vargas facing within circle

Date	Mintage	VF20	XF40	MS60	MS63	MS65
ND (1986) (l)	500,000	—	—	20.00	25.00	30.00
ND (1986) (l)	—	PF63 325	PF65 350			

Note: Beware of some altered circulation coins to look like proofs

Y# 78.1 100 BOLIVARES

6.80 g., Nickel Clad Steel, 25 mm. **Obv:** National arms **Rev:** Head of Bolívar left in 7-sided outline **Note:** Struck at Ceska Mincova and Budapest mints.

Date	Mintage	VF20	XF40	MS60	MS63	MS65
1998	—	—	—	0.50	0.75	1.00

Y# 78.2 100 BOLIVARES

6.82 g., Nickel Clad Steel, 25 mm. **Obv:** National arms **Rev:** Head of Bolívar right in 7-sided outline **Edge:** Plain

Date	Mintage	VF20	XF40	MS60	MS63	MS65
1999	—	—	0.50	0.75	1.20	1.50

Y# 54 500 BOLIVARES

18.00 g., 0.900 Gold 0.5208 oz. AGW, 30 mm. **Subject:** Nationalization of Oil Industry **Obv:** Oil derricks within inset at left **Rev:** Head of Bolivar left within inset

Date	Mintage	VF20	XF40	MS60	MS63	MS65
1975 (c)	100	PF65 20,000				

Y# 64 500 BOLIVARES

31.10 g., 0.900 Silver 0.8999 oz. ASW **Obv:** National arms above ribbon, plants flank, cornucopias above **Rev:** Head of Paez left, dates below

Date	Mintage	VF20	XF40	MS60	MS63	MS65
1990 (mm)	30,000	PF63 35.00	PF65 40.00			

Y# 69 500 BOLIVARES

31.10 g., 0.900 Silver 0.8999 oz. ASW **Subject:** Battle of Matasiete **Obv:** National arms above ribbon, plants flank, cornucopias above **Rev:** Monument divides dates below mountains

Date	Mintage	VF20	XF40	MS60	MS63	MS65
1992 (w)	10,000	PF63 40.00	PF65 45.00			

Y# 71 500 BOLIVARES

31.10 g., 0.900 Silver 0.8999 oz. ASW **Subject:** 50th Anniversary - United Nations **Obv:** National arms above ribbon, plants flank, cornucopias above **Rev:** UN logo within wreath

Date	Mintage	VF20	XF40	MS60	MS63	MS65
1995	10,000	PF63 40.00	PF65 45.00			

Y# 72 500 BOLIVARES

31.10 g., 0.900 Silver 0.8999 oz. ASW **Subject:** 200th Anniversary - Sucre's Birth **Obv:** National arms above ribbon, plants flank, cornucopias above **Rev:** Bust of Sucre facing, dates below

Date	Mintage	VF20	XF40	MS60	MS63	MS65
1995	15,000	PF63 40.00	PF65 45.00			

Y# 74 500 BOLIVARES

31.10 g., 0.900 Silver 0.8999 oz. ASW **Subject:** Manuel Gual and Jose Maria Espana **Obv:** National arms above ribbon, plants flank, cornucopias above **Rev:** Two busts above dates **Edge:** Reeded

Date	Mintage	VF20	XF40	MS60	MS63	MS65
1997 A	10,000	PF63 40.00	PF65 45.00			

Y# 79.1 500 BOLIVARES

8.40 g., Nickel Clad Steel, 28.5 mm. **Obv:** National arms **Rev:** Head of Bolívar left in 7-sided outline **Edge:** Segmented reeding **Note:** Struck at Ceska Mincova and Budapest mints.

Date	Mintage	VF20	XF40	MS60	MS63	MS65
1998	—	—	0.50	0.75	1.25	1.75

Y# 79.2 500 BOLIVARES

8.40 g., Nickel Clad Steel, 28.5 mm. **Obv:** National arms **Obv. Legend:** REPUBLICA DE VENEZUELA **Rev:** Head of Bolívar left in 7-sided outline **Rev. Legend:** BOLÍVAR - LIBERTADOR **Edge:** Segmented reeding **Note:** Prev. KM# 84.

Date	Mintage	VF20	XF40	MS60	MS63	MS65
1999	—	—	0.60	1.00	1.50	2.00

Y# 48.1 1000 BOLIVARES

33.44 g., 0.900 Gold 0.9675 oz. AGW, 34 mm. **Subject:** Conservation Series - Cock of the Rocks **Obv:** National arms above ribbon, plants flank, cornucopias above **Rev:** Bird on branch

Date	Mintage	VF20	XF40	MS60	MS63	MS65
1975 (l)	5,047	—	—	1,600	2,000	2,500
1975 (l)	483	PF65 4,500	PF67 5,500			

Y# 48.2 1000 BOLIVARES

33.44 g., 0.900 Gold 0.9675 oz. AGW, 34 mm. **Subject:** Conservation Series - Cock of the Rocks **Obv:** National arms above ribbon, plants flank, cornucopias above **Rev:** Bird on branch with smooth wings

Date	Mintage	VF20	XF40	MS60	MS63	MS65
1975 (l)	Inc. above	—	—	1,700	2,100	2,700
1975 (l)	2 known	PF65 12,000				

Y# 68 1100 BOLIVARES

27.00 g., 0.925 Silver 0.803 oz. ASW **Subject:** Ibero - American Series **Obv:** Arms at center within legend, 13 shields surround **Rev:** Statue

Date	Mintage	VF20	XF40	MS60	MS63	MS65
1991 (mm)	30,000	PF63 60.00	PF65 85.00			

Y# 59 3000 BOLIVARES

31.10 g., 0.900 Gold 0.8999 oz. AGW **Subject:** 200th Anniversary - Birth of Simon Bolivar **Obv:** Building **Rev:** Bookshelves back of 3/4 figure looking left

Date	Mintage	XF40	MS60	MS63	MS65	MS66
ND (1983) (w)	10,000	PF67 1,650	PF69 1,750			

Y# 62 5000 BOLIVARES
15.55 g., 0.900 Gold 0.4499 oz. AGW, 27 mm. **Obv:** National arms above ribbon, plants flank, cornucopias above **Rev:** Bust of Urdaneta 3/4 left, dates below

Date	Mintage	XF40	MS60	MS63	MS65	MS66
1988	25,000	PF67 675	PF69 750			

Y# 63 5000 BOLIVARES
15.55 g., 0.900 Gold 0.4499 oz. AGW, 27 mm. **Obv:** National arms above ribbon, plants flank, cornucopias above **Rev:** Bust of Marino facing, dates below

Date	Mintage	XF40	MS60	MS63	MS65	MS66
1988	25,000	PF67 675	PF69 750			

Y# 65 5000 BOLIVARES
15.55 g., 0.900 Gold 0.4499 oz. AGW, 27 mm. **Obv:** National arms above ribbon, plants flank, cornucopias above **Rev:** Head of Paez right, dates below

Date	Mintage	XF40	MS60	MS63	MS65	MS66
1990 (mm)	10,000	PF67 750	PF69 850			

Y# 73 5000 BOLIVARES
15.55 g., 0.900 Gold 0.4499 oz. AGW, 27 mm. **Subject:** 200th Anniversary - Sucre's Birth **Obv:** National arms above ribbon, plants flank, cornucopias above **Rev:** Bust of Sucre facing, dates below

Date	Mintage	XF40	MS60	MS63	MS65	MS66
1995	10,000	PF67 750	PF69 850			

Y# 86 6000 BOLIVARES
28.00 g., 0.900 Silver 0.8102 oz. ASW, 35 mm. **Subject:** Founding of Maracay Mint **Obv:** Central Bank Building **Obv. Legend:** BANCO CENTRAL DE VENEZUELA **Rev:** Mint building complex **Rev. Legend:** CASA DE LA MONEDA VENEZUELA - MARACAY **Rev. Inscription:** FUNDADA/1999

Date	Mintage	VF20	XF40	MS60	MS63	MS65
1999	5,000	—	—	—	55.00	60.00

Y# 61 10000 BOLIVARES
31.10 g., 0.900 Gold 0.8999 oz. AGW, 35 mm. **Obv:** National arms above ribbon, plants flank, cornucopias above **Rev:** Head of Bolivar right

Date	Mintage	XF40	MS60	MS63	MS65	MS66
1987 (c)	50,000	PF65 1,350	PF67 1,550	PF69 1,750		

REPUBLIC

REFORM COINAGE

1998

100 Centimos = 1 Bolivar (1600 Bolivares = $1 U.S.)

Y# 80 10 BOLIVARES
2.33 g., Nickel Clad Steel, 17 mm. **Obv:** National arms left of denomination **Obv. Legend:** REPÚBLICA BOLIVARIANA DE VENEZUELA **Rev:** Head of Bolívar left in 7-sided outline **Rev. Legend:** BOLÍVAR - LIBERTADOR **Edge:** Reeded

Date	Mintage	VF20	XF40	MS60	MS63	MS65
2000	—	—	—	0.15	0.25	0.50

Y# 81 20 BOLIVARES
4.32 g., Nickel Clad Steel, 20 mm. **Obv:** National arms left of denomination **Obv. Legend:** REPÚBLICA BOLIVARIANA DE VENEZUELA **Rev:** Head of Bolivar left in 7-sided outline **Rev. Legend:** BOLÍVAR - LIBERTADOR **Edge:** Plain

Date	Mintage	VF20	XF40	MS60	MS63	MS65
2000	—	—	—	0.15	0.25	0.50

Y# 82 50 BOLIVARES
6.58 g., Nickel Clad Steel, 23 mm. **Obv:** National arms left of denomination **Obv. Legend:** REPÚBLICA BOLIVARIANA DE VENEZUELA **Rev:** Head of Bolivar left in 7-sided outline **Rev. Legend:** BOLÍVAR - LIBERTADOR **Edge:** Reeded

Date	Mintage	VF20	XF40	MS60	MS63	MS65
2000	—	—	0.30	0.45	0.75	1.00

ESSAIS

KM#	Date	Mintage	Identification	Mkt Val
E18	1991(c)	—	1300 Bolivares. 0.900. Copper. M1, thick planchet.	—
E26	1991(c)	—	1300 Bolivares. Copper. M1, thin planchet.	—
E27	1991(c)	—	1300 Bolivares. Copper. M1, thick planchet.	—

PATTERNS

Including off metal strikes

KM#	Date	Mintage	Identification	Mkt Val
Pn47	1973(m)	—	5 Bolivares. Nickel.	1,500
Note: Without engraver's name "Barre"				
Pn48	1977(w)	—	25 Centimos. Nickel.	200
Pn49	1977(m)	—	5 Bolivares. Nickel.	300
Pn50	1981(w)	—	100 Bolivares. Silver. Y57, with LEY.	500
Pn51	1990(c)	—	50 Bolivares. Lead.	500
Pn52	1990(c)	—	50 Bolivares. Silver.	800
Pn53	1990(c)	—	50 Bolivares. Gold. Medal rotation.	950
Pn54	1990(c)	—	50 Bolivares. Gold. Coin rotation.	950
Pn55	1990(c)	—	50 Bolivares. Gold.	1,250
Pn56	1990	—	5000 Bolivares. Copper-Nickel. Y65.	2,500

TRIAL STRIKES

KM#	Date	Mintage	Identification	Mkt Val
TS10	1973(c)	—	10 Bolivares. Silver. 2 obverses.	400
TS12	1975(c)	—	500 Bolivares. Gold plated; Uniface reverse.	17,500
TS9	1977	—	10 Bolivares. 0.900. Silver. Uniface reverse.	1,300
TS13	1977(m)	—	5 Bolivares. Nickel. Uniface obverse.	300
TS11	1975 (1990)(c)	—	500 Bolivares. Gold plated; Uniface obverse.	17,500
TS14	1990(c)	—	50 Bolivares. Copper. Y66, uniface obverse.	600
TS15	1990(c)	—	50 Bolivares. Copper. Y66, uniface reverse.	600
TS16	1990(c)	—	50 Bolivares. Bronze. Y66, uniface obverse.	600
TS17	1990(c)	—	50 Bolivares. Bronze. Y66, uniface reverse.	600
TS18	1990(c)	—	50 Bolivares. Silver. Y66, uniface obverse.	1,000
TS19	1990(c)	—	50 Bolivares. Silver. Y#66. Uniface.	600
TS20	1990(d)	—	50 Bolivares. Copper. Y67, uniface obverse.	600
TS21	1990(c)	—	50 Bolivares. Copper. Y67, uniface reverse.	600
TS22	1991	—	1100 Bolivares. Silver. Arms at center within legend, 13 shields surround. Y68, uniface obverse.	2,500
TS23	ND (1991)	—	1100 Bolivares. Silver. Statue, two dates at right. Y68, uniface reverse.	2,500
TS24	1991(c)	—	1300 Bolivares. Copper. Numbers on and below shield, text below. Y79, uniface obverse.	350
TS25	1991(c)	—	1300 Bolivares. Copper. Two busts facing. Y79, uniface reverse.	350
TS26	1991(c)	—	1300 Bolivares. Silver. Y79, uniface obverse.	450
TS27	1991(c)	—	1300 Bolivares. Silver. Y79, uniface reverse.	450

PRIVATE PATTERNS

KM#	Date	Mintage	Identification	Mkt Val
PPn2	1973(c)	—	10 Bolivares. Silver. Arms within inset at left, legend and denomination at right. Head left within inset, name below, dates at left.	1,000
PPn3	1973(c)	—	10 Bolivares. Silver. Double obverse similar to KM45.	600

PRIVATE TRIAL STRIKES

KM#	Date	Mintage	Identification	Mkt Val
PTS1	1973	—	10 Bolivares. Copper Gilt. Uniface obverse similar to KM45. (TS2).	300
PTS2	1973	—	10 Bolivares. Copper Gilt. Uniface reverse similar to KM45. (TS3).	500

MINT SETS

KM#	Date	Mintage	Identification	Issue Price	Mkt Val
MS1	1975 (3)	—	Y46-48	250	2,400

PROOF SETS

KM#	Date	Mintage	Identification	Issue Price	Mkt Val
PS1	1975 (3)	—	Y46-48	—	4,000

LEPER COLONIES

In the late 1600s the Hospital de Lazarinos was built in Hoyada, outside of Caracas for the care and confinement of those suffering from leprosy. Early in the 1900s this hospital was relocated to Maiquetia, also near Caracas and became known as Cabo Blanco. The hospital remained in use until the early 1970s and coins were struck in 1936 for patient use within the confines of this institution.

CABO BLANCO

LEPROSARIUM COINAGE

KM# L11 0.05 BOLIVAR (5 Centimos)
Brass **Note:** Prev. KM#10.

Date	Mintage	VG8	F12	VF20	XF40	MS60
1936	—	3.00	6.00	10.00	20.00	45.00

KM# L12 0.12-1/2 BOLIVAR (12-1/2 Centimos)
Brass **Note:** Prev. KM#L11.

Date	Mintage	VG8	F12	VF20	XF40	MS60
1936	—	20.00	40.00	60.00	100	200

KM# L13 0.50 BOLIVAR (50 Centimos)
Brass **Note:** Prev. KM#L12.

Date	Mintage	VG8	F12	VF20	XF40	MS60
1936	—	30.00	50.00	90.00	120	—

KM# L14 BOLIVAR
Brass **Note:** Prev. KM#L13.

Date	Mintage	VG8	F12	VF20	XF40	MS60
1936	—	50.00	85.00	150	250	500

KM# L15 2 BOLIVARES
Brass **Note:** Prev. KM#L14.

Date	Mintage	VG8	F12	VF20	XF40	MS60
1936	—	60.00	100	165	270	—

KM# L16 5 BOLIVARES
Brass **Note:** Prev. KM#L15.

Date	Mintage	VG8	F12	VF20	XF40	MS60
1936	—	80.00	140	220	375	750

KM# L17 10 BOLIVARES
Brass **Note:** Prev. KM#L16.

Date	Mintage	VG8	F12	VF20	XF40	MS60
1936	—	120	200	320	500	—

KM# L18 20 BOLIVARES
Brass **Note:** Prev. KM#L17.

Date	Mintage	VG8	F12	VF20	XF40	MS60
1936	—	175	300	500	900	—

ISLA DE PROVIDENCIA

KM# L19 0.05 BOLIVAR (5 Centimos)
Brass **Note:** Prev. KM#L20.

Date	Mintage	VG8	F12	VF20	XF40	MS60
1939	—	2.00	4.00	8.00	16.00	35.00

KM# L20 0.12-1/2 BOLIVAR (12-1/2 Centimos)
Brass **Note:** Prev. KM#L21.

Date	Mintage	VG8	F12	VF20	XF40	MS60
1939	—	2.50	5.00	8.00	16.00	—

KM# L20a 0.12-1/2 BOLIVAR (12-1/2 Centimos)
Copper-Nickel **Note:** Prev. KM#L21a.

Date	Mintage	VG8	F12	VF20	XF40	MS60
1939 Rare	—	—	—	—	—	—

KM# L21 0.50 BOLIVAR (50 Centimos)
Brass **Note:** Prev. KM#L22.

Date	Mintage	VG8	F12	VF20	XF40	MS60
1939	—	20.00	40.00	75.00	125	—

KM# L22 BOLIVAR
Brass **Note:** Prev. KM#L23.

Date	Mintage	VG8	F12	VF20	XF40	MS60
1939	—	25.00	50.00	90.00	150	—

KM# L23 2 BOLIVARES
Brass **Note:** Prev. KM#L24.

Date	Mintage	VG8	F12	VF20	XF40	MS60
1939	—	30.00	60.00	110	185	—

KM# L24 5 BOLIVARES
Brass **Note:** Prev. KM#L25.

Date	Mintage	VG8	F12	VF20	XF40	MS60
1939	—	40.00	85.00	165	275	—

KM# L25 10 BOLIVARES
Brass **Note:** Prev. KM#L26.

Date	Mintage	VG8	F12	VF20	XF40	MS60
1939	—	—	—	—	—	—

Note: Requires Confirmation; According to records, coins with the 10 Bolivares denomination were authorized to be struck, but at present none are known to exist in the numismatic community

MARACAIBO LAZARETO NACIONAL

KM# L10 5 CENTIMOS
Brass **Note:** Prev. KM#L8.

Date	Mintage	VG8	F12	VF20	XF40	MS60
1916	—	3.00	6.00	10.00	20.00	—

KM# L3 1/8 BOLIVAR
Brass **Note:** Prev. KM#L1.

Date	Mintage	VG8	F12	VF20	XF40	MS60
1913	—	3.50	7.00	12.00	25.00	—
1916	—	20.00	40.00	80.00	145	—

KM# L3a 1/8 BOLIVAR
Copper-Nickel **Note:** Prev. KM#L1a.

Date	Mintage	VG8	F12	VF20	XF40	MS60
1913	—	7.00	15.00	25.00	50.00	—

KM# L4 1/2 BOLIVAR
Brass **Note:** Similar to 1/8 Bolivar KM#L5. Prev. KM#L2.

Date	Mintage	VG8	F12	VF20	XF40	MS60
1913	—	20.00	35.00	75.00	135	—
1916	—	35.00	65.00	140	260	—

KM# L5 BOLIVAR
Brass **Note:** Prev. KM#L3.

Date	Mintage	VG8	F12	VF20	XF40	MS60
1913	—	20.00	30.00	45.00	80.00	—
1916	—	25.00	40.00	55.00	95.00	—

KM# L6 2 BOLIVARES
Brass **Obv:** Similar to 20 Bolivares, KM#L9 **Note:** Prev. KM#L4.

Date	Mintage	VG8	F12	VF20	XF40	MS60
1913	—	25.00	40.00	60.00	100	—
1916	—	35.00	60.00	100	200	800

KM# L7 5 BOLIVARES
Brass **Note:** Similar to 1/8 Bolivar, KM#L3. Prev. KM#L5.

Date	Mintage	VG8	F12	VF20	XF40	MS60
1913	—	55.00	100	175	275	—
1916	—	85.00	120	200	350	—

KM# L8 10 BOLIVARES
Brass **Note:** Similar to 1/8 Bolivar, KM#L3. Prev. KM#L6.

Date	Mintage	VG8	F12	VF20	XF40	MS60
1913	—	60.00	120	200	350	—
1916	—	90.00	180	300	500	—

KM# L9 20 BOLIVARES

Brass **Rev:** Similar to 2 Bolivares, KM#L6 **Note:** Prev. KM#L7.

Date	Mintage	VG8	F12	VF20	XF40	MS60
1913	—	175	400	700	1,200	—
1916	—	250	350	600	1,000	—

VIET NAM

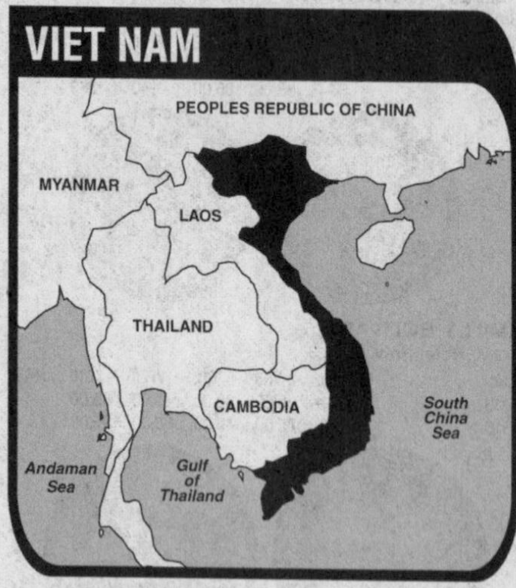

In 207 B.C. a Chinese general set up the Kingdom of Nam-Viet on the Red River. This kingdom was over-thrown by the Chinese under the Han Dynasty in 111 B.C., where upon the country became a Chinese province under the name of Giao-Chi, which was later changed to Annam or peaceful or pacified South. Chinese rule was maintained until 968, when the Vietnamese became independent until 1407 when China again invaded Viet Nam. The Chinese were driven out in 1428 and the country became independent and named Dai-Viet. Gia Long united the North and South as Dai Nam in 1802.

After the French conquered Dai Nam, they split the country into three parts. The South became the Colony of Cochin China; the North became the Protectorate of Tonkin; and the central became the Protectorate of Annam. The emperors were permitted to have their capital in Hue and to produce small quantities of their coins, presentation pieces, and bullion bars. Annam had an area of 57,840 sq. mi. (141,806 sq. km.) and a population of about 6 million. Chief products of the area are silk, cinnamon and rice. There are important mineral deposits in the mountainous inland.

EMPERORS

成泰

Thanh Thai, 1888-1907

維新

Duy Tan, 1907-1916

啓定

Khai Dinh, 1916-1925

保大

Bao Dai, 1926-1945

IDENTIFICATION

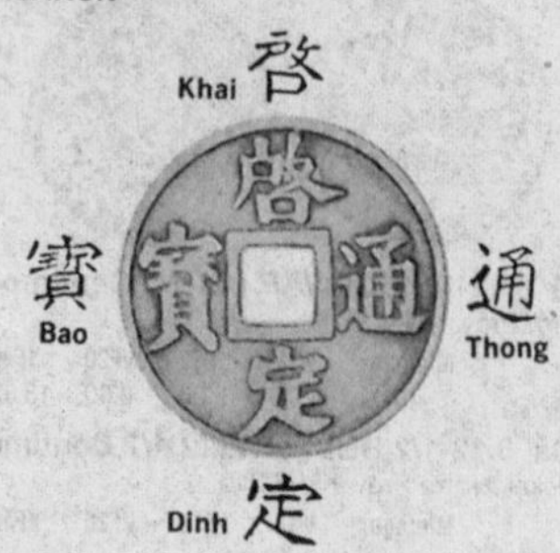

CYCLICAL DATES

	庚	辛	壬	癸	甲	乙	丙	丁	戊	己
戌	1850 1910		1862 1922		1874 1934		1886 1946		1838 1898	
亥		1851 1911		1863 1923		1875 1935		1887 1947		1839 1899
子	1840 1900		1852 1912		1864 1924		1876 1936		1888 1948	
丑		1841 1901		1853 1913		1865 1925		1877 1937		1889 1949
寅	1830 1890		1842 1902		1854 1914		1866 1926		1878 1938	
卯		1831 1891		1843 1903		1855 1915		1867 1927		1879 1939
辰	1880 1940		1832 1892		1844 1904		1856 1916		1868 1928	
巳		1881 1941		1833 1893		1845 1905		1857 1917		1869 1929
午	1870 1930		1882 1942		1834 1894		1846 1906		1858 1918	
未		1871 1931		1883 1943		1835 1895		1847 1907		1859 1919
申	1860 1920		1872 1932		1884 1944		1836 1896		1848 1908	
酉		1861 1921		1873 1933		1885 1945		1837 1897		1849 1909

NOTE: This table has been adapted from *Chinese Bank Notes* by Ward Smith and Brian Matravers.

Cyclical dates consist of a pair of characters one of which indicates the animal associated with that year. Every 60 years, this pair of characters is repeated. The first character of a cyclical date corresponds to a character in the first row of the chart above. The second character is taken from the column at left. In this catalog where a cyclical date is used, the abbreviation CD appears before the A.D. date.

Annamese silver and gold coins were sometimes dated according to the year of the emperor's reign. In this case, simply add the year of reign to the year in which the reign would be 1849 (1847 plus 3 = 1850 -1 = 1849 or 1847 = 1; 1848 = 2; 1849 = 3). In this catalog the A.D. date appears in parenthesis followed by the year of reign.

NUMERALS

NUMBER	CONVENTIONAL	FORMAL	COMMERCIAL
1	一 元	壹 弌	〡
2	二	弍 貳	〢
3	三	叁 弎	〣
4	四	肆	〤
5	五	伍	〥
6	六	陸	〦
7	七	柒	〧
8	八	捌	〨
9	九	玖	〩
10	十	拾 什	十
20	十 二 or 廿	拾貳	〢十
25	五 十 二 or 五廿	伍拾貳	〢十〥
30	十 三 or 卅	拾叁	〣十
100	百 一	佰壹	〡百
1,000	千 一	仟壹	〡千
10,000	萬 一	萬壹	〡万
100,000	萬十 億一	萬拾 億壹	十万
1,000,000	萬百一	萬佰壹	〡百万

NOTE: This table has been adapted from Chinese Bank Notes by Ward Smith and Brian Matravers.

MONETARY SYSTEM

10 Dong (zinc) = 1 Dong (copper)
600 Dong (zinc) = 1 Quan (string of cash)
Approx. 2600 Dong (zinc) = 1 Piastre

NOTE: Ratios between metals changed frequently, therefore the above is given as an approximate relationship.

SILVER and GOLD

2-1/2 Quan = 1 Lang
10 Tien (Mace) = 1 Lang (Tael)
14 to 17 Piastres (silver) = 1 Piastre (gold)
14 to 17 Lang (silver) = 1 Lang (gold)

The real currency of Dai Nam and An Nam consisted of copper and zinc coins similar to Chinese cash-style coins and were called sapeques and dongs by the French.

The smaller gold pieces saw a limited circulation, mainly among the local merchants and foreign traders. The larger gold pieces were used mainly for hoarding, while most of these were intended as rewards and gifts. Many of these gold pieces appear to have been struck from silver coin dies or vice-versa.

NOTE: Sch# are in reference to Albert Schroeder's *Annam, Etudes Numismatiques* or to the same numbering system used in *Gold and Silver Coins of Annam*, by Bernard Permar and John Novak.

CHARACTER IDENTIFICATION

The Vietnamese used Chinese-style characters for official documents and coins and bars. Some were modified to their liking and will sometimes not match the Chinese character for the same word. The above identification and this table will translate most of the Vietnamese characters (Chinese-style) on their coins and bars described herein.

Chinese/French
Vietnamese/English

安南

An Nam = name of the French protectorate

大南

Dai Nam = name of the country under Gia Long's Nguyen dynasty

越南

Viet Nam = name used briefly during Minh Mang's reign and became the modern name of the country

河內

Ha Noi = city and province in north Dai NamTonkin

內帑

Noi Thang = court treasury in the capital of Hue

年

Nien = year

造

Tao = made

銀

Ngan = silver

金

Kim = gold

錢

Tien = a weight of about 3.78 grams

兩

Lang = a weight of about 37.78 grams

貫

Quan = a string of cash-style coins

分

Phan = a weight of about .38 grams

文

Van = cash-style coins

中平

Trung Binh = a name of weight standard

FRENCH PROTECTORATE OF ANNAM

CAST COINAGE

KM# 626 PHAN
Cast Copper Alloys **Ruler:** Thanh Thai **Obv. Inscription:** Thanh Thai Thong Bao **Rev:** Plain **Note:** Y#1.

Date	Mintage	G4	VG8	F12	VF20	XF40
ND(1888-1907)	—	2.50	4.00	7.00	12.00	—

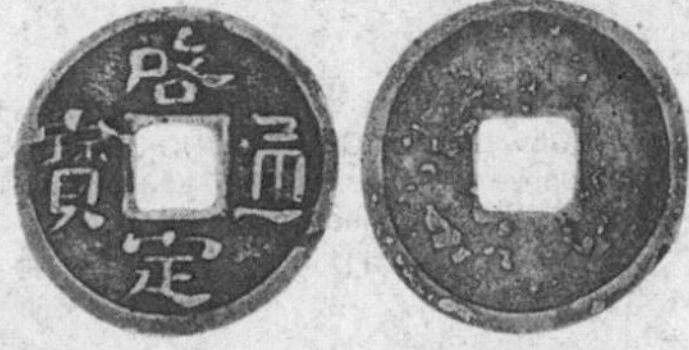

KM# 654 PHAN
Cast Copper Alloys **Ruler:** Khai Dinh **Obv. Inscription:** Khai Dinh Thong Bao **Note:** Prev. Y#4.

Date	Mintage	Good	VG	F	VF	XF
ND(1916-25)	—	5.50	9.00	15.00	25.00	—

KM# 661 PHAN
Cast Brass **Ruler:** Bao Dai **Obv. Inscription:** Bao-dai Thong bao **Note:** Prev. Y#6a.

Date	Mintage	Good	VG	F	VF	XF
ND(1926-45)	—	2.50	5.00	7.50	12.50	—

KM# 628 10 VAN
Cast Copper Alloys **Ruler:** Thanh Thai **Obv. Inscription:** Thanh Thai Thong Bao **Rev. Inscription:** Thap Van **Note:** Y#2.

Date	Mintage	G4	VG8	F12	VF20	XF40
ND(1888-1907)	—	0.60	0.90	1.50	3.00	—

KM# 652 10 VAN
Cast Brass **Ruler:** Duy Tan **Obv. Inscription:** Duy Tan Thong Bao **Rev. Inscription:** 10 Van **Note:** Prev. Y#3.

Date	Mintage	G4	VG8	F12	VF20	XF40
ND(1907-16)	—	0.50	0.75	1.25	2.50	—

KM# 664 10 VAN
Copper Alloys **Ruler:** Bao Dai **Obv. Inscription:** Bao Dai Thong Bao **Rev. Inscription:** 10 Van **Note:** Prev. Y#7.

Date	Mintage	Good	VG	F	VF	XF
ND(1926-45)	—	2.00	3.50	7.50	12.50	—

MILLED COINAGE

Brass

KM# 655 PHAN
Brass **Ruler:** Khai Dinh **Obv. Inscription:** Khai Dinh Thong Bao **Note:** Uniface. Prev. Y#5.1.

Date	Mintage	Good	VG	F	VF	XF
ND(1916-25)	—	1.75	2.75	4.50	7.50	—

KM# 656 PHAN
Brass **Ruler:** Khai Dinh **Obv:** Characters slightly different **Obv. Inscription:** Khai Dinh Thong Bao **Note:** Prev. Y#5.2.

Date	Mintage	Good	VG	F	VF	XF
ND(1916-25)	—	2.00	3.50	6.00	10.00	—

KM# 662 PHAN
Copper Alloys, 18 mm. **Ruler:** Bao Dai **Obv. Inscription:** Bao Dai Thong Bao **Note:** Prev. Y#6.

Date	Mintage	Good	VG	F	VF	XF
ND(1926-45)	—	2.50	5.00	7.50	12.50	—

SILVER MILLED COINAGE

The silver dragon coins with crude oblique milled edges are considered to be those in imitation of the Mexican/ Spanish Colonial 8 Reales (Dollar/Piastre) coins and its minor denominations. The smooth edge silver dragon coins and those with square center holes are considered presentation pieces. Each coin is compared to the Weight System table in the introduction and assigned the respective Tien or Lang designation corresponding to its actual weight in grams.

VIRTUES
1 Tien - Viet Tu (benignity)
2 Tien - Viet Hein (gratitude)
3 Tien - Viet lang (kindness)
4 Tien - Viet De (respect)
5 Tien - Viet Ngai (justice)
6 Tien - Viet Thinh (obedience)
7 Tien - Viet Hue (benevolence)
8 Tien - Viet Thuan (submissiveness)
9 Tien - Viet Nhan (humanity)
1 Lang - Viet Trung (faithfulness)

KM# 630 3 TIEN
Silver **Ruler:** Thanh Thai **Obv. Inscription:** Thanh Thai Thong Bao **Rev:** Dragon **Note:** Schroeder #428.

Date	Mintage	VG8	F12	VF20	XF40	MS60
ND(1888-1907)	—	170	325	550	950	1,750

BULLION SILVER BARS

All of the bars described here are inscribed with their weight, except the 10 Lang banana bars, and many contain a date or the name of the province in which they were made.

KM# 632 LANG
Silver, 65 mm. **Ruler:** Thanh Thai **Obv. Inscription:** Than Thai Thong Bao **Rev. Inscription:** Van The Vinh Lai **Note:** Schroeder #431. Weight unknown.

Date	Mintage	VG8	F12	VF20	XF40	MS60
ND(1888-1907)	—	265	525	900	1,500	—

KM# 658 LANG
Silver **Ruler:** Khai Dinh **Note:** Date on edge. Weight unknown.

Date	Mintage	VG8	F12	VF20	XF40	MS60
CD1919	—	75.00	125	185	275	—

KM# 659 LANG
Silver **Ruler:** Khai Dinh **Note:** Date on edge. Weight unknown.

Date	Mintage	VG8	F12	VF20	XF40	MS60
CD1922	—	75.00	125	185	275	—

GOLD MILLED COINAGE

KM# 634 TIEN
3.90 g., Gold **Ruler:** Thanh Thai **Obv. Inscription:** Thanh Thai Thong Bao **Rev. Inscription:** Nhat Nguyen **Note:** Schroeder #432.

Date	Mintage	VG8	F12	VF20	XF40	MS60
ND(1888-1907)	—	800	1,450	2,550	4,350	—

KM# 636 1-1/2 TIEN
6.60 g., Gold **Ruler:** Thanh Thai **Obv. Inscription:** Thanh Thai Thong Bao **Rev:** Inscription between moon and sun **Rev. Inscription:** Nhi Nghi **Note:** Schroeder #435.

Date	Mintage	VG8	F12	VF20	XF40	MS60
ND(1888-1907)	—	650	1,100	2,150	3,500	—

KM# 638 3 TIEN
Gold **Ruler:** Thanh Thai **Obv. Inscription:** Thanh Thai Thong Bao **Rev:** Dragon **Note:** Weight varies: 10.50-12.40 grams. Schroeder #433.

Date	Mintage	VG8	F12	VF20	XF40	MS60
ND(1888-1907)	—	2,700	5,300	9,800	15,000	—

KM# 639 3 TIEN
Gold **Ruler:** Thanh Thai **Obv. Inscription:** Thanh Thai Thong Bao **Rev:** Dragon above three Longevities **Rev. Inscription:** Tam Tho **Note:** Weight varies: 10.00-10.50 grams. Schroeder #436.

Date	Mintage	VG8	F12	VF20	XF40	MS60
ND(1888-1907)	—	1,350	2,250	4,600	7,800	—

KM# 641 4 TIEN
14.50 g., Gold **Ruler:** Thanh Thai **Obv. Inscription:** Thanh Thai Thong Bao **Rev:** Inscription between Four Perfections **Note:** Schroeder #437.

Date	Mintage	VG8	F12	VF20	XF40	MS60
ND(1888-1907)	—	1,250	2,250	4,750	8,500	—

KM# 643 5 TIEN
15.48 g., Gold **Ruler:** Thanh Thai **Obv. Legend:** Than Thai Thong Bao **Rev:** Dragon

Date	Mintage	VG8	F12	VF20	XF40	MS60
ND(1888-1907)	—	1,150	2,150	4,500	8,000	—

KM# 645 6 TIEN
23.00 g., Gold **Ruler:** Thanh Thai **Obv. Inscription:** Thanh Thai Thong Bao **Rev:** Large dragon **Note:** Schroeder #382A.

Date	Mintage	VG8	F12	XF40	MS60
ND(1888-1907)	—	—	—	10,000	20,000	—

KM# 647 LANG
Gold **Ruler:** Thanh Thai **Obv. Inscription:** Thanh-thai Thong-bao at right, "Van The Vinh Lai" at left **Note:** Weight unknown. Schroeder #431.

Date	Mintage	VG8	F12	VF20	XF40	MS60
ND(1888-1907)	—	—	20,000	32,000	50,000	—

BULLION GOLD BARS

KM# 649 LANG
0.850 Gold **Ruler:** Thanh Thai **Issuer:** Court Treasury **Obv. Inscription:** Thanh-thai Nien-tao **Rev. Inscription:** Noi Thang Kim Nhat Lang **Note:** Fineness on edge; weight varies: 36.10-36.70 grams; Schroeder#429.

Date	Mintage	VG8	F12	VF20	XF40	MS60
ND(1888-1907)	—	—	—	6,500	8,500	12,000

KM# 650 LANG
0.800 Gold **Ruler:** Thanh Thai **Issuer:** Court Treasury **Obv. Inscription:** Thanh-thai Nien-tao **Rev. Inscription:** Noi Thang Kim Nhat Lang **Note:** Fineness on edge; Schroeder #430.

Date	Mintage	VG8	F12	VF20	XF40	MS60
ND(1888-1907)	—	—	—	6,500	8,500	12,000

DEMOCRATIC REPUBLIC

MILLED COINAGE

KM# 1 20 XU
Aluminum **Ruler:** Bao Dai **Obv:** Star, date below **Obv. Legend:** VIET NAM DAN CHU CHONG HOA **Rev:** Denomination **Rev. Inscription:** 20 XU

Date	Mintage	F12	VF20	XF40	MS60	MS63
1945 (v)	—	40.00	125	250	350	450

KM# 2.1 5 HAO
Aluminum **Obv:** Ceremonial pot **Obv. Legend:** VIET-NAM DAN-CHU CONG-HOA **Rev:** Value incused in star **Rev. Inscription:** 5 HAO

Date	Mintage	F12	VF20	XF40	MS60	MS63
1946 (v)	—	4.00	10.00	20.00	60.00	125

Note: Commonly encountered with rotated dies

KM# 2.2 5 HAO
Aluminum **Obv:** Ceremonial pot **Obv. Legend:** VIET-NAM DAN-CHU CONG-HOA **Rev:** Value raised in star

Date	Mintage	F12	VF20	XF40	MS60	MS63
1946 (v)	—	—	—	65.00	125	250

KM# 3 DONG
Aluminum **Obv:** Head right **Obv. Legend:** VIET-NAM DAN-CHU CONG-HOA **Rev:** Value to right of spray **Rev. Inscription:** 1 DONG

Date	Mintage	F12	VF20	XF40	MS60	MS63
1946 (v)	—	15.00	25.00	50.00	100	200

KM# 4 2 DONG
Bronze **Obv:** Bust of Ho Chi Minh 3/4 facing **Obv. Legend:** CHU TICH HO MIHN **Rev:** Value above and below in wreath, Nam II at bottom **Rev. Legend:** VIET-NAM DAN CHU CONG HOA **Rev. Inscription:** HAI DONG **Note:** Varieties exist.

Date	Mintage	F12	VF20	XF40	MS60	MS63
1946 (v)	—	7.50	15.00	50.00	150	400

NORTH VIET NAM

DEMOCRATIC REPUBLIC

PRESENTATION COINAGE

KM# A5 10 VIET
4.16 g., 0.900 Gold 0.1204 oz. AGW, 17 mm. **Obv:** Head of Ho Chi Minh right **Obv. Legend:** CHU-TICH HO-CHI-MINH **Rev:** Denomination above grain sheaves **Rev. Legend:** VIET-NAM DAN-CHU CONG-HOA **Rev. Inscription:** 10 Viet

Date	Mintage	F12	VF20	XF40	MS60	MS63
1948 (v)	—	—	—	275	375	450

KM# B5 20 VIET
8.33 g., 0.900 Gold 0.2409 oz. AGW, 21 mm. **Obv:** Head of Ho Chi Minh right **Obv. Legend:** CHU-TICH HO-CHI-MINH **Rev:** Denomination above grain sheaves **Rev. Legend:** VIET-NAM DAN-CHU CONG-HOA **Rev. Inscription:** 20 VIET

Date	Mintage	F12	VF20	XF40	MS60	MS63
1948 (v)	—	—	—	450	550	600

KM# C5 50 VIET
16.65 g., 0.900 Gold 0.4818 oz. AGW, 29 mm. **Obv:** Head of Ho Chi Minh right **Obv. Legend:** CHU-TICH HO-CHI-MINH **Rev:** Denomination above grain sheaves **Rev. Legend:** VIET-NAM DAN-CHU CONG-HOA **Rev. Inscription:** 50 VIET

Date	Mintage	F12	VF20	XF40	MS60	MS63
1948 (v)	—	—	—	900	950	1,000

REFORM COINAGE

KM# 5 XU
Aluminum **Obv:** Center hole within arms **Obv. Legend:** NUOC VIET NAM DAN CHU CONG HOA **Rev:** Center hole divides date and denomination **Rev. Legend:** NGAN HANG QUOC GIA VIET NAM **Rev. Inscription:** Value: "MOT XU"

Date	Mintage	F12	VF20	XF40	MS60	MS63
1958 (s)	—	1.25	2.50	3.50	5.50	8.00

KM# 6 2 XU
Aluminum **Obv:** Center hole within arms **Obv. Legend:** NUOC VIET NAM DAN CHU CONG HOA **Rev:** Center hole divides denomination and date **Rev. Legend:** NGAN HANG QUOC GIA VIET NAM **Rev. Inscription:** Value: "HAI XU"

Date	Mintage	F12	VF20	XF40	MS60	MS63
1958 (s)	—	1.50	3.00	4.50	7.00	10.00

KM# A11 2 XU
0.90 g., Aluminum, 18 mm. **Obv:** Center hole divides denomination **Obv. Legend:** NGAN HANG NHA NUOC VIET NAM **Rev:** Lotus arround center hole, denomination above and below, date at bottom **Rev. Legend:** NUOC VIET NAM DAN CHU CONG HOA **Note:** Issued very briefly, prior to unification

Date	Mintage	F12	VF20	XF40	MS60	MS63
1975	—	50.00	80.00	100	150	200

KM# 7 5 XU
Aluminum **Obv:** Center hole within arms **Obv. Legend:** NUOC VIET NAM DAN CHU CONG HOA **Rev:** Center hole divides denomination and date **Rev. Legend:** NGAN HANG QUOC GIA VIET NAM **Rev. Inscription:** Value: "NAM XU"

Date	Mintage	F12	VF20	XF40	MS60	MS63
1958 (s)	—	2.00	4.00	6.00	8.00	15.00

PATTERNS

Including off metal strikes

KM#	Date	Mintage	Identification	Mkt Val
Pn1	1946(v)	—	5 Dong. Bronze.	—

SOCIALIST REPUBLIC

The Socialist Republic of Viet Nam, located in Southeast Asia west of the South China Sea, has an area of 127,300 sq. mi. (329,560 sq. km.) and a population of *66.8 million. Capital: Hanoi. Agricultural products, coal, and mineral ores are exported.

At the start of World War II, Vietnamese Communists fled to China's Kwangsi provinces where Ho Chi Minh organized the Revolution to free Viet Nam of French rule. The Japanese occupied Viet Nam during World War II. As the end of the war drew near, they ousted the Vichy French administration and granted Viet Nam independence under a puppet government headed by Bao Dai, Emperor of Annam. The Bao Dai government collapsed at the end of the war, and on Sept. 2, 1945, Ho Chi Minh proclaimed the existence of an independent Viet Nam consisting of Cochin-China, Annam, and Tonkin, and set up a Communist government. France recognized the new government as a free state, but reneged and in 1949 reinstalled Bao Dai as ruler of Viet Nam and extended the regime independence within the French Union. Ho Chi Minh led a guerrilla war, in the first Indochina war, against the French which raged on to the disastrous defeat of the French at Dien Bien Phu on May 7,1954.

An agreement signed at Geneva on July 21, 1954, provided for a temporary division of Viet Nam at the 17th parallel of latitude, between a Communist-supported North and a U.S.-supported South. In Oct. 1955, South Viet Nam deposed Bao Dai by referendum and authorized the establishment of a republic with Ngo Dinh Diem as president. The Republic of South Viet Nam was proclaimed on Oct. 26, 1955, and was immediately recognized by some Western Powers.

The activities of Communists in South Viet Nam led to the second Indochina war which came to a brief halt in 1973 (when a cease-fire was arranged and U.S. forces withdrew), but it didn't end until April 30, 1975 when South Viet Nam surrendered unconditionally. The two Viet Nams were reunited as the Socialist Republic of Viet Nam on July 2, 1976.

NOTE: For earlier coinage refer to French Indo-China or Tonkin.

MONETARY SYSTEM
10 Xu = 1 Hao
10 Hao = 1 Dong

SOCIALIST REPUBLIC

STANDARD COINAGE

KM# 11 HAO
Aluminum **Obv:** Arms **Rev:** Spray divides denomination **Rev. Legend:** NGAN HANG NHA NUOC VIET NAM **Rev. Inscription:** 1 HAO

Date	Mintage	VF20	XF40	MS60	MS63	MS65
1976 (s)	—	2.50	5.00	7.50	10.00	—

KM# 12 2 HAO
1.41 g., Aluminum **Obv:** Arms **Rev:** Spray divides denomination **Rev. Legend:** NGAN HANG NHA HUOC VIET NAM **Rev. Inscription:** 2 HOA

Date	Mintage	VF20	XF40	MS60	MS63	MS65
1976 (s)	—	2.50	5.00	7.50	10.00	—

KM# 13 5 HAO
Aluminum **Obv:** Arms **Rev:** Denomination above ornament

Date	Mintage	VF20	XF40	MS60	MS63	MS65
1976	—	3.00	6.00	9.00	12.00	—

KM# 14 DONG
Aluminum **Obv:** Arms **Rev:** Ornaments flank thick denomination **Rev. Legend:** NGAN HANG NHA NUOC VIET NAM **Rev. Inscription:** 1 DONG

Date	Mintage	VF20	XF40	MS60	MS63	MS65
1976 (s)	—	8.00	15.00	22.00	35.00	—

KM# 36 5 DONG
Brass **Obv:** Arms **Obv. Legend:** CONG HOA XA HOI CHU NGHIA VIET NAM **Obv. Inscription:** 5 DONG **Rev:** Mythological bird - Phoenix flying right **Rev. Legend:** CHIM PHUONG **Note:** KM#36 and 36a were minted in the Leningrad (St. Petersburg) Mint (L) as gifts to the Vietnamese government and were not circulated. KM#36a was available in boxed sets of three, with KM#38a and 40a, and KM#36 and 36a were also available as encapsulated individual pieces.

Date	Mintage	VF20	XF40	MS60	MS63	MS65
1989 (L)	—	PF63 14.00	PF65 17.00			

KM# 36a 5 DONG
8.77 g., 0.900 Silver 0.2538 oz. ASW **Obv:** Arms **Obv. Legend:** CONG HOA XA HOI CHU NGHIA VIET NAM **Obv. Inscription:** 5 DONG **Rev:** Mythological bird - Phoenix flying right **Rev. Inscription:** CHIM PHUONG

Date	Mintage	VF20	XF40	MS60	MS63	MS65
1989 (L)	—	PF63 20.00	PF65 22.00			

KM# 15 10 DONG
Copper-Nickel **Subject:** Nature **Obv:** Arms **Obv. Legend:** CONG HOA XA HOI CHU NGHIA VIET NAM **Rev:** Water buffalo head left, "TRAU" below **Rev. Legend:** BAO VE THIEN NHIEM

Date	Mintage	VF20	XF40	MS60	MS63	MS65
1986	5,000	—	—	7.50	12.50	25.00

KM# 16 10 DONG
Copper-Nickel **Subject:** Nature **Obv:** Arms **Obv. Legend:** CONG HOA XA HOI CHU NGHIA VIET NAM **Rev:** Peacock head right, "CONG" below **Rev. Legend:** BAO VE THIEN NHIEN

Date	Mintage	VF20	XF40	MS60	MS63	MS65
1986	5,000	—	—	7.50	12.50	25.00

KM# 17 10 DONG
Copper-Nickel **Subject:** Nature **Obv:** Arms **Obv. Legend:** CONG HOA XA HOI CHU NGHIA VIET NAM **Rev:** Elephant head left, "VOI" below **Rev. Legend:** BAO VE THIEM NHIEN

Date	Mintage	VF20	XF40	MS60	MS63	MS65
1986	5,000	—	—	12.00	20.00	35.00

KM# 28 10 DONG
Copper-Nickel **Subject:** Wildlife Preservation **Obv:** Arms **Obv. Legend:** CONG HOA XA HOI CHU NGHIA VIET NAM **Rev:** Orangutan with logo **Rev. Legend:** BAO VE THIEM NHIEN, DUOI UOI

Date	Mintage	VF20	XF40	MS60	MS63	MS65
1987	22,000	—	—	10.00	18.00	30.00

KM# 37.1 10 DONG
11.31 g., Copper-Nickel, 30 mm. **Obv:** Arms **Obv. Legend:** CONG HOA XA HOI CHU NGHIA VIET NAM **Rev:** Dragon ship **Rev. Legend:** THUYEN CO. **Edge:** Plain

Date	Mintage	VF20	XF40	MS60	MS63	MS65
1988	—	—	—	3.50	6.00	10.00

KM# 37.2 10 DONG
29.75 g., Copper, 38 mm. **Obv:** State emblem **Rev:** Asian Dragon Ship **Edge:** Plain

Date	Mintage	VF20	XF40	MS60	MS63	MS65
1988	—	—	—	4.50	7.50	12.00

KM# 27 10 DONG
Copper-Nickel **Subject:** Soccer - Italy **Obv:** Arms **Obv. Legend:** CONG HOA XA HOI CHU NGHIA VIET NAM **Rev:** Soccer player **Rev. Legend:** GIAI BONGDA THE GIOI

Date	Mintage	VF20	XF40	MS60	MS63	MS65
1989	—	—	—	4.50	7.50	12.00

KM# 38 10 DONG
Brass **Obv:** Arms **Obv. Legend:** CONG HOA XA HOI CHU NGHIA VIET NAM **Rev:** One-pillar Pagoda above water and legend **Rev. Legend:** CHUA MOT COT-HANOI **Note:** KM#38 and 38a were minted in the Leningrad (St. Petersburg) Mint (L) as gifts to the Vietnamese government and were not circulated. KM#38a was available in boxed sets of three, with KM#36a and 40a, and KM#38 and 38a were also available as encapsulated individual pieces.

Date	Mintage	VF20	XF40	MS60	MS63	MS65
1989 (L)	—	PF63 7.00	PF65 9.00			

KM# 38a 10 DONG
0.900 Silver **Obv:** Arms **Obv. Legend:** CONG HOA XA HOI CHU NGHIA VIET NAM **Rev:** One-pillar Pagoda above water and legend **Rev. Legend:** CHUA MOT COT-HANOI

Date	Mintage	VF20	XF40	MS60	MS63	MS65
1989 (L)	—	PF63 28.00	PF65 32.00			

KM# 33 10 DONG
Copper-Nickel **Obv:** Arms **Obv. Legend:** CONG HOA XA HOI CHU NGHIA VIET NAM **Rev:** Crested Gibbons **Rev. Legend:** BAO VE THIEM NHIEN, DUOI UOI

Date	Mintage	VF20	XF40	MS60	MS63	MS65
1990	20,000	—	—	15.00	25.00	40.00

KM# 39 10 DONG
Copper-Nickel **Obv:** Arms **Obv. Legend:** CONG HOA XA HOI CHU NGHIA VIET NAM **Rev:** Steam and sailship - Savannah **Rev. Legend:** THUYEN CO SAVANNAH

Date	Mintage	VF20	XF40	MS60	MS63	MS65
1991	—	—	—	3.50	6.00	10.00

KM# 46 10 DONG
Copper **Series:** World Cup Soccer **Obv:** Arms **Obv. Legend:** CONG HOA XA HOI CHU NGHIA VIET NAM **Rev:** Soccer player and U.S. Capitol **Rev. Legend:** CUP BONG DA THE GIOI LAN THU XV, HOA KY

Date	Mintage	VF20	XF40	MS60	MS63	MS65
1992	—	—	—	3.50	5.50	9.00

KM# 44 10 DONG
Copper-Nickel **Series:** Prehistoric Animals **Obv:** Arms **Obv. Legend:** CONG HOA XA HOI CHU NGHIA VIET NAM **Rev:** Diplodocus **Rev. Legend:** DONG VAT CO DAI

Date	Mintage	VF20	XF40	MS60	MS63	MS65
1993	—	—	—	12.00	20.00	35.00

KM# 49 10 DONG
Copper-Nickel **Subject:** World Food Summit **Obv:** Arms **Obv. Legend:** CONG HOA XA HOI CHU NGHIA VIET NAM **Rev:** Rice harvesting scene, logo above **Rev. Legend:** MOI NGHI THUONG DINH THE GIOI VE LUOIN THUC

Date	Mintage	VF20	XF40	MS60	MS63	MS65
1996	10,000	—	—	5.50	9.00	15.00

KM# 40 20 DONG
Brass **Subject:** 100th Anniversary - Birth of Ho Chi Minh **Obv:** Arms **Obv. Legend:** CONG HOA XA HOI CHU NGHIA VIET NAM **Rev:** Head left, dates at right **Rev. Legend:** HO CHI MINH **Edge:** Nikolay Nosov **Note:** KM#40 and 40a were minted in the Leningrad (St. Petersburg) Mint (L) as gifts to the Vietnamese government and were not circulated. KM#40a was available in boxed sets of three, with KM#36a and 38a, and KM#40 and 40a were also available as encapsulated individual pieces.

Date	Mintage	VF20	XF40	MS60	MS63	MS65
1989 (L)	—	PF63 11.00	PF65 16.50			

KM# 40a 20 DONG
0.900 Silver **Obv:** Arms **Obv. Legend:** CONG HOA XA HOI CHU NGHIA VIET NAM **Rev:** Head left, dates at right **Rev. Legend:** HO CHI MINH

Date	Mintage	VF20	XF40	MS60	MS63	MS65
1989 (L)	—	PF63 45.00	PF65 50.00			

KM# 18 100 DONG
12.00 g., 0.999 Silver 0.3854 oz. ASW **Obv:** Arms **Obv. Legend:** CONG HOA XA HOI CHU NGHIA VIET NAM **Rev:** Junk under sail **Rev. Legend:** VIETNAM, THUYEN BUOM

Date	Mintage	VF20	XF40	MS60	MS63	MS65
1986	2,000	—	—	18.00	30.00	50.00

KM# 19 100 DONG
12.00 g., 0.999 Silver 0.3854 oz. ASW **Subject:** Wildlife **Obv:** Arms **Obv. Legend:** CONG HOA XA HOI CHU NGHIA VIET NAM **Rev:** Water buffalo right looking left **Rev. Legend:** BAO VE THIEN KHIEN, TRAU

Date	Mintage	VF20	XF40	MS60	MS63	MS65
1986	5,000	—	—	16.00	27.00	45.00

KM# 20 100 DONG
12.00 g., 0.999 Silver 0.3854 oz. ASW **Subject:** Wildlife **Obv:** Arms **Obv. Legend:** CONG HOA XA HOI CHU NGHIA VIET NAM **Rev:** Peacock left **Rev. Legend:** BAO VE THIEN NHIEN, CONG

Date	Mintage	VF20	XF40	MS60	MS63	MS65
1986	5,000	—	—	14.00	24.00	40.00

KM# 21 100 DONG
12.00 g., 0.999 Silver 0.3854 oz. ASW **Subject:** Wildlife **Obv:** Arms **Obv. Legend:** CONG HOA XA HOI CHU NGHIA VIET NAM **Rev:** Elephant walking right **Rev. Legend:** BAO VI THIEN NHIEN, VOI

Date	Mintage	VF20	XF40	MS60	MS63	MS65
1986	5,000	—	—	20.00	35.00	60.00

KM# 22 100 DONG
12.00 g., 0.999 Silver 0.3854 oz. ASW **Subject:** 100 Years of the Automobile **Obv:** Arms **Obv. Legend:** CONG HOA XA HOI CHU NGHIA VIET NAM **Rev:** Jaguar 3/4 left **Rev. Legend:** 100 NAN XE O TO A DOI, 1886-1986

Date	Mintage	VF20	XF40	MS60	MS63	MS65
1986	2,000	—	—	18.00	30.00	50.00

KM# 23.1 100 DONG
6.00 g., 0.999 Silver 0.1927 oz. ASW, 29.5 mm. **Series:** Calgary Olympics **Obv:** Arms **Obv. Legend:** CONG HOA XA HOI CHU NGHIA VIET NAM **Rev:** Skier **Rev. Legend:** THE VAN HOI O-LIM-PIC MUA DONG XV, GAN-GA-RAY 1986 **Edge:** Plain

Date	Mintage	VF20	XF40	MS60	MS63	MS65
1986	5,000	—	—	12.00	20.00	35.00

KM# 23.2 100 DONG
6.00 g., 0.999 Silver 0.1927 oz. ASW, 29.7 mm. **Series:** Calgary Olympics **Obv:** Arms, large letters **Obv. Legend:** CONG HOA XA HOI CHUNGHIA VIET NAM **Rev:** Skier **Rev. Legend:** THE VAN HOI OLIM-PIC MUA DONG XV, GAN-GA-RAY 1986 **Edge:** Reeded

Date	Mintage	VF20	XF40	MS60	MS63	MS65
1986	Inc. above	—	—	10.00	18.00	30.00

KM# 24.1 100 DONG
6.00 g., 0.999 Silver 0.1927 oz. ASW, 30 mm. **Series:** Seoul Olympics - Fencer **Obv:** Small letters and design **Obv. Legend:** CONG HOA XA HOI CHU NGHIA VIET NAM **Rev:** Reverse legend close to rim, fencer en garde **Edge:** Reeded

Date	Mintage	VF20	XF40	MS60	MS63	MS65
1986	5,000	—	—	7.50	10.00	15.00

KM# 24.2 100 DONG
12.00 g., 0.999 Silver 0.3854 oz. ASW, 30 mm. **Series:** Seoul Olympics - Fencer **Obv:** Arms, large letters and design **Obv. Legend:** CONG HOA XA HOI CHU NGHIA VIET NAM **Rev:** Fencer, reverse legend far from rim **Rev. Legend:** THE VAN HOI O LIM PIC MUA HE **Edge:** Reeded

Date	Mintage	VF20	XF40	MS60	MS63	MS65
1986	Inc. above	—	—	8.50	12.00	20.00

KM# 29.1 100 DONG
12.00 g., 0.999 Silver 0.3854 oz. ASW, 30 mm. **Subject:** Soccer - Mexico **Obv:** Arms, small letters **Obv. Legend:** CONG HOA XA HOI CHU NGHIA VIET NAM **Rev:** Soccer player **Rev. Legend:** GIAI VO DICH BONG DA THE GIOI LAM THU XIII, ME HI CO **Edge:** Reeded

Date	Mintage	VF20	XF40	MS60	MS63	MS65
1986	5,000	—	—	12.00	20.00	35.00

KM# 29.2 100 DONG
6.00 g., 0.999 Silver 0.1927 oz. ASW, 30 mm. **Subject:** Mexico Olympics - Soccer **Obv:** Arms, large letters **Obv. Legend:** CONG HOA XA HOI CHU NGHIA VIET NAM **Rev:** Soccer player **Rev. Legend:** GIAI VO DICH BONG DA THE GIOI LAM THU XIII, ME HI CO **Edge:** Reeded

Date	Mintage	VF20	XF40	MS60	MS63	MS65
1986	Inc. above	—	—	12.00	20.00	35.00

KM# 25.1 100 DONG
15.99 g., 0.980 Silver 0.5038 oz. ASW **Obv:** Arms large 100 **Obv. Legend:** CONG HOA XA HOI CHU NGHIA VIET NAM **Rev:** Suphanna hong (dragon ship) **Rev. Legend:** THUYEN CO

Date	Mintage	VF20	XF40	MS60	MS63	MS65
1988	3,000	—	—	10.00	15.00	25.00
1988	—	PF65 28.00				

KM# 25.2 100 DONG
15.99 g., 0.980 Silver 0.5038 oz. ASW **Obv:** Arms small 100 **Obv. Legend:** CONG HOA XA HOI CHU NGHIA VIET NAM **Rev:** Dragon ship **Rev. Legend:** THUYEN CO

Date	Mintage	VF20	XF40	MS60	MS63	MS65
1988	—	PF65 37.50				

KM# 26 100 DONG
12.00 g., 0.999 Silver 0.3854 oz. ASW **Subject:** Soccer - 1988 **Obv:** Arms **Obv. Legend:** CONG HOA XA HOI CHU NGHIA VIET NAM **Rev:** Soccer players **Rev. Legend:** GIAI BONG DA CHAU AU, CONG HOA LIEN BANG DUCTHUYENCO.

Date	Mintage	VF20	XF40	MS60	MS63	MS65
1988	1,500	—	—	12.00	20.00	35.00

KM# 30 100 DONG
16.00 g., 0.999 Silver 0.5139 oz. ASW **Subject:** Soccer - Italy **Obv:** Arms **Obv. Legend:** CONG HOA XA HOI CHU NGHIA VIET NAM **Rev:** Soccer player **Rev. Legend:** GIAI BONG DA THE GIOI, I-TA-LI-A

Date	Mintage	VF20	XF40	MS60	MS63	MS65
1989	10,000	PF65 32.00				

KM# 31 100 DONG
16.00 g., 0.999 Silver 0.5139 oz. ASW **Series:** Summer Olympics **Subject:** Rowing **Obv:** Arms **Obv. Legend:** CONG HOA XA HOI CHU NGHIA VIET NAM **Rev:** Six people rowing **Rev. Legend:** THE VAN HOI LAN THU XXV, BARCELONA 1992

Date	Mintage	VF20	XF40	MS60	MS63	MS65
1989	10,000	PF65 30.00				

KM# 32 100 DONG
16.00 g., 0.999 Silver 0.5139 oz. ASW **Series:** Winter Olympics **Subject:** Hockey **Obv:** Arms **Obv. Legend:** CONG HOA XA HOI CHU NGHIA VIET NAM **Rev:** Hockey players **Rev. Legend:** THE VAN HOI MUA DONG XVI, ALBERTVILLE 1992

Date	Mintage	VF20	XF40	MS60	MS63	MS65
1990	10,000	PF65 40.00				

KM# 34 100 DONG
12.00 g., 0.999 Silver 0.3854 oz. ASW **Subject:** Soccer **Obv:** Arms **Obv. Legend:** CONG HOA XA HOI CHU NGHIA VIET NAM **Rev:** Soccer players within design **Rev. Legend:** CUP BONG DA THE FIOI LAN THU XV, HOA KY 1994

Date	Mintage	VF20	XF40	MS60	MS63	MS65
1991	—	—	—	9.00	15.00	25.00

KM# 35 100 DONG
16.00 g., 0.999 Silver 0.5139 oz. ASW **Obv:** Arms **Obv. Legend:** CONG HOA XA HOI CHU NGHIA VIET NAM **Rev:** Steamship Savannah **Rev. Legend:** THUYEN CO SAVANNAH

Date	Mintage	VF20	XF40	MS60	MS63	MS65
1991	—	PF65 40.00				

KM# 70 100 DONG
19.90 g., 0.999 Silver 0.6392 oz. ASW, 38.1 mm. **Obv:** Arms **Rev:** Soccer player with U.S. Capital building in background **Edge:** Reeded

Date	Mintage	VF20	XF40	MS60	MS63	MS65
1992	—	PF65 35.00				

KM# 42 100 DONG
16.00 g., 0.999 Silver 0.5139 oz. ASW **Series:** Prehistoric Animals **Obv:** Arms **Obv. Legend:** CONG HOA XA HOI CHU NGHIA VIET NAM **Rev:** Rhamphorhynchus **Rev. Legend:** DONG VAT CO DAI

Date	Mintage	VF20	XF40	MS60	MS63	MS65
1993	—	PF65 60.00				

KM# 43 100 DONG
16.00 g., 0.999 Silver 0.5139 oz. ASW **Obv:** Arms **Obv. Legend:** CONG HOA XA HOI CHU NGHIA VIET NAM **Rev:** Elephants **Rev. Legend:** BAO VI THIEN NHIEN - VOI

Date	Mintage	VF20	XF40	MS60	MS63	MS65
1993	—	PF65 45.00				

KM# 45 100 DONG
16.00 g., 0.999 Silver 0.5139 oz. ASW **Series:** Prehistoric Animals **Obv:** Arms **Obv. Legend:** CONG HOA XA HOI CHU NGHIA VIET NAM **Rev:** Edaphosaurus **Rev. Legend:** DONG VAT CO DAI

Date	Mintage	VF20	XF40	MS60	MS63	MS65
1994	—	PF65 50.00				

KM# 78 100 DONG
16.00 g., 0.999 Silver 0.5139 oz. ASW **Obv:** National arms, value below **Rev:** Gallimimus dynosaur **Edge:** Plain

Date	Mintage	VF20	XF40	MS60	MS63	MS65
1994	—	PF65 50.00				

KM# 47 100 DONG
20.00 g., 0.999 Silver 0.6424 oz. ASW **Series:** Olympics **Obv:** Arms **Obv. Legend:** CONG HOA XA HOI CHU NGHIA VIET NAM **Rev:** Gymnast on pommel horse **Rev. Legend:** TU ATEN DEN ATLANTA

Date	Mintage	VF20	XF40	MS60	MS63	MS65
1995	15,000	PF63 35.00	PF65 40.00			

KM# 48 100 DONG
20.00 g., 0.999 Silver 0.6424 oz. ASW enameled **Obv:** Arms **Obv. Legend:** CONG HOA XA HOI CHU NGHIA VIET NAM **Rev:** Caracal **Rev. Legend:** THU AN THIT/CARACAL CARACAL

Date	Mintage	VF20	XF40	MS60	MS63	MS65
1996	—	PF65 85.00				

KM# 50 100 DONG
20.00 g., 0.999 Silver 0.6424 oz. ASW enameled **Subject:** World Food Summit **Obv:** Arms **Obv. Legend:** CONG HOA XA HOI CHU NGHIA VIET NAM **Rev:** Rice harvesting scene, logo above **Rev. Legend:** HOI NGHI THUONG DINH THE GIOI VE LUONG THUC

Date	Mintage	VF20	XF40	MS60	MS63	MS65
1996	2,000	PF65 85.00				

KM# 60 100 DONG
16.00 g., 0.999 Silver 0.5139 oz. ASW, 38 mm. **Subject:** UNICEF **Obv:** Arms **Rev:** Child on water buffalo **Edge:** Reeded

Date	Mintage	VF20	XF40	MS60	MS63	MS65
1997	25,000	PF65 25.00				

KM# 77 100 DONG
16.00 g., 0.999 Silver 0.5139 oz. ASW, 35 mm. **Subject:** 2000 XXIV Olympics **Obv:** Arms **Obv. Legend:** CONG HOA XA HOI CHU NGHIA VIET NAM **Rev:** Multicolored Steeple chase horse and rider **Rev. Legend:** O – LIM – PIC XXVII **Edge:** Plain

Date	Mintage	VF20	XF40	MS60	MS63	MS65
1998	—	—	—	—	—	55.00

KM# 79 100 DONG
Silver, 39 mm. **Obv:** National arms **Rev:** Discus thrower **Edge:** Plain

Date	Mintage	VF20	XF40	MS60	MS63	MS65
2000	—	PF65 30.00				

KM# 41 500 DONG
3.10 g., 0.999 Gold 0.0997 oz. AGW **Subject:** 100th Anniversary - Birth of Ho Chi Minh **Obv:** Bust facing 1890-1969 at sides. **Obv. Legend:** CONG HOA XA HOI CHU NGHIA VIET NAM **Note:** KM#41 were minted at the Havana Mint (h) as "Gift Coins"

Date	Mintage	VF20	XF40	MS60	MS63	MS65
ND-1989 (L)	—	—	—	—	500	800

KM# 54 5000 DONG
1.24 g., 0.9999 Gold 0.040 oz. AGW, 13.92 mm. **Subject:** Year of the Dragon **Obv:** Arms **Obv. Legend:** CONG HOA XA HOI CHU NGHIA VIET NAM **Rev:** Dragon with radiant sun **Rev. Legend:** RONG VIET NAM **Edge:** Reeded

Date	Mintage	VF20	XF40	MS60	MS63	MS65
2000 (S)	10,000	PF63 75.00	PF65 125	PF67 150		

KM# 51 10000 DONG
20.00 g., 0.925 Silver 0.5948 oz. ASW, 38.7 mm. **Subject:** Year of the Dragon **Obv:** Arms **Obv. Legend:** CONG HOA XA HOI CHU NGHIA VIET NAM **Rev:** Dragon with radiant sun **Edge:** Reeded

Date	Mintage	VF20	XF40	MS60	MS63	MS65
2000 (S)	10,000	PF63 50.00	PF65 60.00			

KM# 52 10000 DONG
20.00 g., 0.925 Silver 0.5948 oz. ASW, 38.7 mm. **Subject:** Year of the Dragon **Obv:** Arms **Obv. Legend:** CONG HOA XA HOI CHU NGHIA VIET NAM **Rev:** Multicolor dragon **Rev. Legend:** RONG VIET NAM **Edge:** Reeded

Date	Mintage	VF20	XF40	MS60	MS63	MS65
2000 (S)	10,000	PF63 50.00	PF65 60.00			

KM# 53 10000 DONG
20.00 g., 0.925 Silver 0.5948 oz. ASW, 38.7 mm. **Subject:** Year of the Dragon **Obv:** Arms **Obv. Legend:** CONG HOA XA HOI CHU NGHIA VIET NAM **Rev:** Two dragons **Edge:** Reeded

Date	Mintage	VF20	XF40	MS60	MS63	MS65
2000 (S)	10,000	PF63 50.00	PF65 60.00			

KM# 55 20000 DONG
7.77 g., 0.9999 Gold 0.2499 oz. AGW, 22 mm. **Subject:** Year of the Dragon **Obv:** Arms **Obv. Legend:** CONG HOA XA HOI CHU NGHIA VIET NAM **Rev:** Dragon and clouds **Rev. Legend:** RONG VIET NAM **Edge:** Reeded

Date	Mintage	VF20	XF40	MS60	MS63	MS65
2000 (S)	1,800	PF63 400	PF65 450	PF67 500		

KM# 56 50000 DONG
15.55 g., 0.9999 Gold 0.500 oz. AGW, 27 mm. **Subject:** Year of the Dragon **Obv:** Arms **Obv. Legend:** CONG HOA XA HOI CHU NGHIA VIET NAM **Rev:** Dragon before radiant sun **Rev. Legend:** RONG VIET NAM **Edge:** Reeded

Date	Mintage	VF20	XF40	MS60	MS63	MS65
2000 (S)	—	PF63 800	PF65 900	PF67 950		

PATTERNS

KM#	Date	Mintage	Identification	Mkt Val
Pn1	1976(s)	—	Hao. Silver. Arms. KM#11.	—
Pn2	1976(s)	—	Dong. Silver. Arms. KM#14.	—

PIEDFORT

KM#	Date	Mintage	Identification	Mkt Val
PE1	1990	110	100 Dong. Silver. KM#32.	175

MINT SETS

KM#	Date	Mintage	Identification	Issue Price	Mkt Val
MS1	1958-1976 (s) (7)	—	KM#5-7, Democratic Republic; KM#11-14, Socialist Republic	—	85.00

MS2	1975/1976 (s) (4)	—	KM#8-14 NOTE: Created and sold by the Bank for Foreign Trade of Viet Nam to tourists and collectors.	—	70.00

PROOF SETS

KM#	Date	Mintage	Identification	Issue Price	Mkt Val
PS1	1989(L) (3)	—	KM#36a, 38a, 40a	—	85.00
PS2	2000(S) (3)	2,000	KM#51-53	—	120
PS3	2000(S) (2)	800	KM#55-56	—	1,450

STATE OF SOUTH VIET NAM

South Viet Nam (the former Republic of Viet Nam), located in the Southeast Asia, bounded by North Viet Nam on the north, Laos and Cambodia on the west, and the South China Sea on the east and south, had an area of 66,280 sq. mi. (171,665 sq. km.) and a population of 20 million. Capital: Saigon (now Ho Chi Minh City). The economy of the area is predominantly agricultural.

South Viet Nam, the direct successor of the French-dominated Emperor Bao Dai regime (also known as the State of Viet Nam), was created after the first Indo-China War (between the French and the Viet-Minh) by the Geneva agreement of 1954 which divided Viet Nam at the 17th parallel of latitude. The National Bank of Viet Nam, with headquarters in the old Bank of Indochina building in Saigon, came into being on Dec. 31, 1954. Elections which would have reunified North and South Viet Nam in 1956 never took place, and the North continued the war for unification of Viet Nam under the communist government of the Democratic Republic of Viet Nam begun at the close of World War II. South Viet Nam surrendered unconditionally on April 30, 1975. There followed a short period of coexistence of the two Vietnamese states, but the south was governed by the North through the Peoples' Revolutionary Government (PRG). On July 2, 1976, South and North Viet Nam joined to form the Socialist Republic of Viet Nam.

MINT MARK

(a)- Paris, privy marks only

MONETARY SYSTEM

100 Xu (Su) = 1 Dong

DEMOCRATIC STATE

STANDARD COINAGE

KM# 1 10 SU

Aluminum **Obv:** Three conjoined busts left **Obv. Legend:** QUOC-GIA VIET-NAM **Rev:** Rice plant (oryza sativa - Gramineae) dividing value **Rev. Legend:** VIET-NAM

Date	Mintage	VF20	XF40	MS60	MS63	MS65
1953 (a)	20,000,000	1.00	1.50	2.00	3.00	4.50

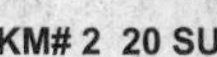

KM# 2 20 SU

Aluminum **Obv:** Three conjoined busts left **Obv. Legend:** QUOC-GIA VIET-NAM **Rev:** Rice plant dividing value **Rev. Legend:** VIET-NAM

Date	Mintage	VF20	XF40	MS60	MS63	MS65
1953 (a)	15,000,000	0.75	1.25	1.75	2.75	4.00

KM# 3 50 XU

Aluminum **Obv:** Three busts; 3/4 left, facing and 3/4 right **Obv. Legend:** QUOC-GIA VIET-NAM **Rev:** Dragons flank denomination **Rev. Legend:** VIET-NAM

Date	Mintage	VF20	XF40	MS60	MS63	MS65
1953 (a)	15,000,000	3.00	5.00	7.00	14.00	28.00

REPUBLIC OF VIET NAM

KM# 4 50 SU

Aluminum **Obv:** Bust of Ngo Dihn Diem left **Obv. Legend:** VIET-NAM CONG-HOA **Rev:** Bamboo plants divide denomination **Note:** The 1960 50 Su coin was minted by the Paris Mint with the French spelling Su for Xu. The coin was restruck with the correct Xu, a new date of 1963, and is cataloged as KM#6.

Date	Mintage	VF20	XF40	MS60	MS63	MS65
1960 (a)	10,000,000	2.00	3.00	5.00	7.00	10.00
1960 (a)	—	PF63 80.00	PF65 120			

KM# 6 50 XU

2.94 g., Aluminum **Obv:** Bust of Ngo Dihn Diem left **Obv. Legend:** VIET-NAM CONG-HOA **Rev:** Bamboo plants divide denomination

Date	Mintage	VF20	XF40	MS60	MS63	MS65
1963	20,000,000	0.80	1.50	2.50	4.00	6.00
1963	—	PF63 80.00	PF65 120			

KM# 5 DONG

4.00 g., Copper-Nickel, 22 mm. **Obv:** Bust of Ngo Dihn Diem left **Obv. Legend:** VIET-NAM CONG-HOA **Rev:** Bamboo plants divide denomination **Edge:** Reeded

Date	Mintage	VF20	XF40	MS60	MS63	MS65
1960 (a)	105,000,000	0.50	1.25	2.00	3.00	5.00
1960 (a)	—	PF63 80.00	PF65 120			

KM# 7 DONG

3.95 g., Copper-Nickel, 22.3 mm. **Obv:** Denomination **Obv. Legend:** VIET-NAM CONG-HOA **Rev:** Rice stalks **Edge:** Reeded

Date	Mintage	VF20	XF40	MS60	MS63	MS65
1964	190,000,000	0.35	0.75	1.50	2.00	3.50
1964 Proof	—	—	—	—	—	—

KM# 12 DONG

1.20 g., Aluminum, 22.40 mm. **Series:** F.A.O. **Obv:** Denomination **Obv. Legend:** VIET-NAM CONG-HOA **Rev:** Rice stalks **Rev. Legend:** TANG-GIA SAN-NUAT LUONG-THUC

Date	Mintage	VF20	XF40	MS60	MS63	MS65
1971	30,000,000	0.50	1.00	1.75	2.75	5.50

KM# 7a DONG

3.60 g., Nickel Clad Steel **Obv:** Denomination **Obv. Legend:** VIET-NAM CONG-HOA **Rev:** Rice stalks

Date	Mintage	VF20	XF40	MS60	MS63	MS65
1971	—	0.15	0.35	0.65	1.25	3.00

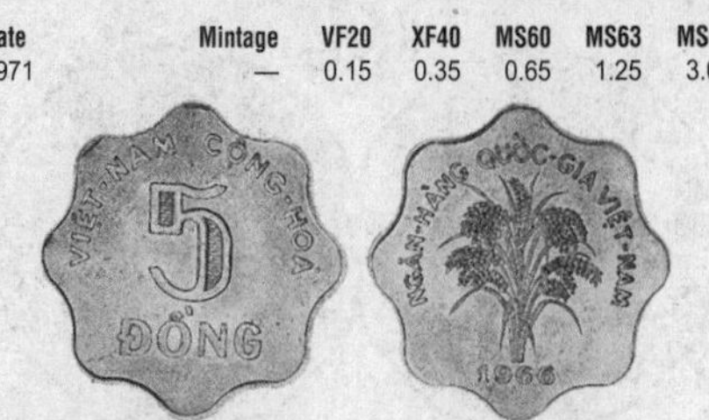

KM# 9 5 DONG

4.00 g., Copper-Nickel **Obv:** Denomination **Obv. Legend:** VIET-NAM CONG-HOA **Rev:** Rice stalks **Rev. Legend:** NGAN-HANG VIET-NAM CONG-HOA **Shape:** Scalloped

Date	Mintage	VF20	XF40	MS60	MS63	MS65
1966	100,000,000	0.50	1.00	1.50	2.50	4.00

KM# 9a 5 DONG

Nickel Clad Steel **Obv:** Denomination **Obv. Legend:** VIET-NAM CONG-HAO **Rev:** Rice stalks **Rev. Legend:** NGAN-HANG VIET-NAM CONG-HOA

Date	Mintage	VF20	XF40	MS60	MS63	MS65
1971	15,000,000	0.75	1.50	2.50	4.00	7.50

KM# 8 10 DONG

5.50 g., Copper-Nickel, 25.5 mm. **Obv:** Denomination **Obv. Legend:** VIET-NAM CONG-HOA **Rev:** Rice stalks **Edge:** Reeded

Date	Mintage	VF20	XF40	MS60	MS63	MS65
1964	45,000,000	0.50	1.00	1.50	2.50	5.00

KM# 8a 10 DONG

Nickel Clad Steel **Obv:** Denomination **Obv. Legend:** VIET-NAM CONG-HOA **Rev:** Rice stalks

Date	Mintage	VF20	XF40	MS60	MS63	MS65
1968	30,000,000	0.50	1.00	1.50	2.50	5.00
1970	50,000,000	0.50	1.00	1.50	2.50	5.00

KM# 13 10 DONG

4.39 g., Brass Clad Steel, 24 mm. **Series:** F.A.O. **Obv:** Denomination **Obv. Legend:** VIET-NAM CONG-HAO, NGAN-HUAN QUOC-GIA VIET-NAM **Rev:** Farmers in rice paddy **Rev. Legend:** TANG-GIA SAM-XUAT NONG-PHAN

Date	Mintage	VF20	XF40	MS60	MS63	MS65
1974	30,000,000	0.50	1.00	1.50	2.50	4.00

KM# 10 20 DONG

9.00 g., Nickel Clad Steel **Obv:** Denomination **Obv. Legend:** VIET-NAM CONG-HOA **Rev:** Farmer in rice paddy **Rev. Legend:** NGAN-HANG QUOC-GIA VIET-NAM **Shape:** 12-sided

Date	Mintage	VF20	XF40	MS60	MS63	MS65
1968	14,500,000	1.25	2.50	4.00	6.00	10.00

KM# 11 20 DONG

9.00 g., Nickel Clad Steel, 29.6 mm. **Series:** F.A.O. **Obv:** Denomination **Obv. Legend:** VIET-NAM CONG-HOA **Rev:** Farmer in rice paddy **Rev. Legend:** CHIEN-TICH THE-GIOI CHONG NAM DOI **Shape:** 12-sided

Date	Mintage	VF20	XF40	MS60	MS63	MS65
1968	500,000	1.50	3.00	5.00	7.00	12.00

KM# 14 50 DONG

Nickel Clad Steel **Series:** F.A.O. **Obv:** Denomination **Obv. Legend:** VIET-NAM CONG-HAO, NGAN-HANG QUOC-GIA VIET-NAM **Rev:** Farmers in rice paddy **Rev. Legend:** TANG-GIA SAM-XUAT NONG-PHAN

Date	Mintage	VF20	XF40	MS60	MS63	MS65
1975	1,010,000	—	350	500	750	1,000

Note: It is reported that all but a few examples were disposed of as scrap metal

PEOPLE'S REVOLUTIONARY GOVERNMENT

KM# A8 XU

Aluminum **Obv:** Star above center hole, spray below **Obv. Legend:** NGAN HANG VIET NAM **Rev:** 1 above center hole, MOT XU below, grain stalks flank

Date	Mintage	VF20	XF40	MS60	MS63	MS65
ND-1975	—	2.00	3.00	5.00	7.00	12.00

KM# A9 2 XU

Aluminum **Obv:** Wreath surrounds center hole, HAI XU below **Obv. Legend:** NGAN HANG VIET NAM **Rev:** Ornaments surround center hole, 2 above, XU below ornamentation

Date	Mintage	VF20	XF40	MS60	MS63	MS65
1975	—	3.00	5.00	7.00	12.00	20.00

KM# A10 5 XU

Aluminum **Obv:** Denomination below center hole **Obv. Legend:** NGAN HANG VIET NAM **Rev:** "NAM XU" above, 5 below in stylized sprays

Date	Mintage	VF20	XF40	MS60	MS63	MS65
ND-1975	—	4.00	6.00	9.00	15.00	25.00

ESSAIS

Standard metals unless otherwise noted

KM#	Date	Mintage	Identification	Mkt Val
E1	1953	1,200	10 Su. Aluminum. KM#1.	100
E2	1953(a)	1,200	20 Su. Aluminum. KM#2.	125
E3	1953(a)	1,200	50 Su. Aluminum. KM#3.	150

PATTERNS

Including off metal strikes

KM#	Date	Mintage	Identification	Mkt Val
Pn1	1963	—	50 Xu. Aluminum-Bronze.	500
Pn2	1963	—	50 Xu. Copper-Nickel.	500

PIEDFORT WITH ESSAI

Standard metals unless otherwise noted

KM#	Date	Mintage	Identification	Mkt Val
PE1	1953(a)	104	10 Su. Aluminum. KM#1.	325
PE2	1953(a)	104	20 Su. Aluminum. KM#2.	350
PE3	1953(a)	104	50 Xu. Aluminum. KM#3.	375

WEST AFRICAN STATES

The West African States, a former federation of eight French colonial territories on the northwest coast of Africa, has an area of 1,831,079 sq. mi. (4,742,495 sq. km.) and a population of about 17 million. Capital: Dakar. The constituent territories were Mauritania, Senegal, Dahomey, French Sudan, Ivory Coast, Upper Volta, Niger and French Guinea.

The members of the federation were overseas territories within the French Union until Sept. of 1958 when all but French Guinea approved the constitution of the Fifth French Republic, thereby electing to become autonomous members of the new French Community. French Guinea voted to become the fully independent Republic of Guinea. The other seven attained independence in 1960. The French West Africa territories were provided with a common currency, a practice which was continued as the monetary union of the West African States which provides a common currency to the autonomous republics of Dahomey (now Benin), Senegal, Upper Volta (now Burkina Faso), Ivory Coast, Mali, Togo, Niger, and Guinea-Bissau.

For earlier coinage refer to Togo, and French West Africa.

MINT MARK

(a)- Paris, privy marks only

MONETARY SYSTEM

100 Centimes = 1 Franc

FEDERATION

STANDARD COINAGE

KM# 3.1 FRANC

1.30 g., Aluminum, 23 mm. **Obv:** Taku symbol divides denomination **Rev:** Gazelle head facing (gazella leptoceros - bovidae)

Date	Mintage	F12	VF20	XF40	MS60	MS63
1961 (a)	3,000,000	—	0.15	0.30	0.60	0.85
1964 (a)	10,500,000	—	0.15	0.30	0.60	0.85
1965 (a)	6,000,000	—	0.15	0.30	0.60	0.85
1967 (a)	2,500,000	—	0.15	0.30	0.60	0.85
1971 (a)	8,000,000	—	0.15	0.30	0.60	0.85
1972 (a)	4,000,000	—	0.15	0.30	0.60	0.85
1973 (a)	4,500,000	—	0.15	0.30	0.60	0.85
1974 (a)	4,500,000	—	0.15	0.30	0.60	0.85
1975 (a)	18,000,000	—	0.15	0.30	0.60	0.85

KM# 3.2 FRANC

Aluminum, 23 mm. **Obv:** Taku symbol divides denomination **Rev:** Engraver general's name

Date	Mintage	F12	VF20	XF40	MS60	MS63
1962 (a)	2,000,000	—	2.00	5.00	10.00	12.00
1963 (a)	4,500,000	—	1.50	4.00	7.00	9.00

KM# 8 FRANC

1.60 g., Steel **Obv:** Taku - Ashanti gold weight **Rev:** Value and date

Date	Mintage	F12	VF20	XF40	MS60	MS63
1976 (a)	8,000,000	—	—	0.10	0.35	0.60
1977 (a)	14,700,000	—	—	0.10	0.35	0.60
1978 (a)	21,800,000	—	—	0.10	0.35	0.60
1979 (a)	16,600,000	—	—	0.10	0.35	0.60
1980 (a)	13,000,000	—	—	0.10	0.35	0.60
1981 (a)	2,000,000	—	—	0.10	0.35	0.60
1982 (a)	6,000,000	—	—	0.10	0.35	0.60
1984 (a)	33,400,000	—	—	0.10	0.35	0.60
1985 (a)	26,900,000	—	—	0.10	0.35	0.60
1988 (a)	—	—	—	0.10	0.35	0.60
1990 (a)	10,000,000	—	—	0.10	0.35	0.60
1991 (a)	3,500,000	—	—	0.10	0.35	0.60
1992 (a)	6,000,000	—	—	0.10	0.35	0.60
1995 (a)	3,000,000	—	—	0.10	0.35	0.60
1996 (a)	3,000,000	—	—	0.10	0.35	0.60
1997 (a)	1,500,000	—	—	0.10	0.35	0.60
1999 (a)	1,000,000	—	—	0.10	0.35	0.60
2000 (a)	—	—	—	0.10	0.35	0.60

KM# 2 5 FRANCS

2.94 g., Aluminum-Bronze, 20.2 mm. **Obv:** Taku symbol divides denomination **Rev:** Gazelle head facing

Date	Mintage	F12	VF20	XF40	MS60	MS63
1960 (a)	5,000,000	—	0.20	0.40	0.70	1.00

KM# 2a 5 FRANCS

3.00 g., Aluminum-Nickel-Bronze, 20 mm. **Obv:** Taku - Ashanti gold weight divides value **Rev:** Gazelle head facing

Date	Mintage	F12	VF20	XF40	MS60	MS63
1965 (a)	12,500,000	—	0.20	0.40	0.70	1.00
1967 (a)	6,500,000	—	0.20	0.40	0.70	1.00
1968 (a)	6,000,000	—	0.20	0.45	0.75	1.10
1969 (a)	8,000,000	—	0.20	0.40	0.70	1.00
1970 (a)	10,005,000	—	0.20	0.40	0.70	1.00
1971 (a)	10,000,000	—	0.20	0.40	0.70	1.00
1972 (a)	5,000,000	—	0.20	0.40	0.70	1.00
1973 (a)	6,000,000	—	0.20	0.45	0.75	1.10
1974 (a)	13,326,000	—	0.10	0.15	0.30	0.50
1975 (a)	16,840,000	—	0.20	0.40	0.70	1.00
1976 (a)	20,010,000	—	0.20	0.30	0.60	0.85
1977 (a)	22,000,000	—	0.20	0.30	0.60	0.85
1978 (a)	40,000,000	—	0.20	0.30	0.60	0.85
1979 (a)	11,000,000	—	0.10	0.20	0.40	0.60
1980 (a)	18,000,000	—	0.10	0.20	0.40	0.60
1981 (a)	18,000,000	—	0.10	0.20	0.40	0.60
1982 (a)	25,000,000	—	0.10	0.20	0.40	0.60
1984 (a)	31,700,000	—	0.10	0.20	0.40	0.60
1985 (a)	16,000,000	—	0.10	0.20	0.40	0.60
1986 (a)	8,000,000	—	0.10	0.20	0.40	0.60
1987 (a)	26,500,000	—	0.10	0.20	0.40	0.60
1989 (a)	44,500,000	—	0.10	0.20	0.40	0.60
1990 (a)	—	—	0.10	0.20	0.40	0.60
1991 (a)	19,000,000	—	0.10	0.20	0.40	0.60
1992 (a)	—	—	0.10	0.20	0.40	0.60
1993 (a)	—	—	0.10	0.20	0.40	0.60
1994 (a)	20,000,000	—	0.10	0.20	0.40	0.60
1995 (a)	—	—	0.10	0.20	0.40	0.60
1996 (a)	21,500,000	—	0.10	0.20	0.40	0.60
1997 (a)	18,000,000	—	0.10	0.20	0.40	0.60
1999 (a)	36,900,000	—	0.10	0.20	0.40	0.60
2000 (a)	—	—	0.10	0.20	0.40	0.60

KM# 1 10 FRANCS

Aluminum-Bronze **Obv:** Taku symbol divides denomination

Date	Mintage	F12	VF20	XF40	MS60	MS63
1959 (a)	10,000,000	—	0.15	0.30	0.60	0.85
1964 (a)	10,000,000	—	0.20	0.40	0.70	1.00

KM# 1a 10 FRANCS
Aluminum-Nickel-Bronze **Obv:** Taku symbol divides denomination **Rev:** Gazelle head facing

Date	Mintage	F12	VF20	XF40	MS60	MS63
1966 (a)	6,000,000	—	0.20	0.40	0.70	1.00
1967 (a)	3,500,000	—	0.25	0.50	0.90	1.25
1968 (a)	6,000,000	—	0.20	0.40	0.70	1.00
1969 (a)	7,000,000	—	0.25	0.50	0.90	1.25
1970 (a)	7,000,000	—	0.15	0.30	0.60	0.85
1971 (a)	8,000,000	—	0.15	0.30	0.60	0.85
1972 (a)	5,500,000	—	0.20	0.40	0.70	1.00
1973 (a)	3,000,000	—	0.20	0.40	0.70	1.00
1974 (a)	10,000,000	—	0.15	0.30	0.60	0.85
1975 (a)	17,000,000	—	0.15	0.30	0.60	0.85
1976 (a)	18,000,000	—	0.15	0.30	0.60	0.85
1977 (a)	11,000,000	—	0.15	0.25	0.50	0.75
1978 (a)	21,000,000	—	0.15	0.25	0.50	0.75
1979 (a)	11,000,000	—	0.15	0.25	0.50	0.75
1980 (a)	16,000,000	—	0.15	0.25	0.50	0.75
1981 (a)	12,000,000	—	0.15	0.25	0.50	0.75

KM# 10 10 FRANCS
4.00 g., Aluminum-Bronze, 23.4 mm. **Series:** F.A.O. **Obv:** Taku - Ashanti gold weight divides value **Rev:** People getting water

Date	Mintage	F12	VF20	XF40	MS60	MS63
1981 (a)	2,000,000	—	0.25	0.50	1.25	1.50
1982 (a)	23,000,000	—	0.25	0.50	1.25	1.50
1983 (a)	6,000,000	—	0.50	1.00	2.50	3.00
1984 (a)	10,000,000	—	0.25	0.50	1.25	1.50
1985 (a)	5,000,000	—	0.50	1.00	2.50	3.00
1986 (a)	7,500,000	—	0.25	0.50	1.25	1.50
1987 (a)	28,000,000	—	0.25	0.50	1.25	1.50
1989 (a)	40,500,000	—	0.25	0.50	1.25	1.50
1990 (a)	18,000,000	—	0.25	0.50	1.25	1.50
1991 (a)	18,000,000	—	0.25	0.50	1.25	1.50
1992 (a)	5,000,000	—	0.50	1.00	2.50	3.00
1993 (a)	4,400,000	—	0.50	1.00	2.50	3.00
1994 (a)	19,900,000	—	0.25	0.50	1.25	1.50
1995 (a)	3,700,000	—	0.50	1.00	2.50	3.00
1996 (a)	33,300,000	—	0.25	0.50	1.25	1.50
1997 (a)	38,200,000	—	0.25	0.50	1.25	1.50
1999 (a)	33,000,000	—	0.25	0.50	1.25	1.50
2000 (a)	6,500,000	—	0.50	1.00	2.50	3.00

KM# 5 25 FRANCS
Aluminum-Bronze, 27 mm. **Obv:** Taku divides denomination **Rev:** Gazelle head facing

Date	Mintage	F12	VF20	XF40	MS60	MS63
1970 (a)	7,000,000	—	0.25	0.45	1.00	1.25
1971 (a)	7,000,000	—	0.50	0.75	1.25	1.50
1972 (a)	2,000,000	—	1.50	2.50	4.50	6.00
1975 (a)	5,035,000	—	0.25	0.45	1.00	1.25
1976 (a)	3,365,000	—	0.25	0.45	1.00	1.25
1977 (a)	3,288,000	—	0.25	0.45	1.00	1.25
1978 (a)	6,800,000	—	0.25	0.45	1.00	1.25
1979 (a)	5,200,000	—	0.25	0.45	1.00	1.25

KM# 9 25 FRANCS
7.95 g., Aluminum-Bronze, 27 mm. **Series:** F.A.O. **Obv:** Taku - Ashanti gold weight divides value **Rev:** Figure filling tube **Note:** Mint mark position varieties exist.

Date	Mintage	F12	VF20	XF40	MS60	MS63
1980 (a)	7,800,000	—	0.25	0.75	1.75	2.00
1981 (a)	4,000,000	—	0.50	1.50	4.00	4.00
1982 (a)	8,000,000	—	0.25	0.75	1.75	2.00
1984 (a)	15,300,000	—	0.25	0.75	1.75	2.00
1985 (a)	8,587,000	—	0.25	0.75	1.75	2.00
1987 (a)	9,000,000	—	0.25	0.75	1.75	2.00
1989 (a)	17,600,000	—	0.25	0.75	1.75	2.00
1990 (a)	6,000,000	—	0.25	0.75	1.75	2.00
1991 (a)	1,700,000	—	0.50	1.50	4.00	4.00
1992 (a)	6,000,000	—	0.25	0.75	1.75	2.00
1994 (a)	8,200,000	—	0.25	0.75	1.75	2.00
1995 (a)	—	—	0.25	0.75	1.75	2.00
1996 (a)	18,300,000	—	0.25	0.75	1.75	2.00
1997 (a)	22,000,000	—	0.25	0.75	1.75	2.00
1999 (a)	16,700,000	—	0.25	0.75	1.75	2.00
2000 (a)	16,800,000	—	0.25	0.75	1.75	2.00

KM# 6 50 FRANCS
5.00 g., Copper-Nickel, 22 mm. **Series:** F.A.O. **Obv:** Taku - Ashanti gold weight **Rev:** Value within mixed beans, grains and nuts

Date	Mintage	F12	VF20	XF40	MS60	MS63
1972 (a)	20,000,000	—	0.35	0.50	1.25	1.50
1974 (a)	3,000,000	—	1.00	1.50	3.00	4.00
1975 (a)	9,000,000	—	0.25	0.40	1.00	1.25
1976 (a)	6,002,000	—	0.35	0.50	1.25	1.50
1977 (a)	4,832,000	—	0.70	1.00	2.50	3.00
1978 (a)	7,200,000	—	0.35	0.50	1.25	1.50
1979 (a)	4,200,000	—	0.70	1.00	2.50	3.00
1980 (a)	7,200,000	—	0.35	0.50	1.25	1.50
1981 (a)	6,000,000	—	0.70	1.00	2.50	3.00
1982 (a)	12,000,000	—	0.35	0.50	1.25	1.50
1984 (a)	25,500,000	—	0.35	0.50	1.25	1.50
1985 (a)	4,120,000	—	0.70	1.00	2.50	3.00
1986 (a)	—	—	0.35	0.50	1.25	1.50
1987 (a)	10,000,000	—	0.35	0.50	1.25	1.50
1989 (a)	17,000,000	—	0.35	0.50	1.25	1.50
1990 (a)	7,500,000	—	0.35	0.50	1.25	1.50
1991 (a)	5,600,000	—	0.50	0.70	2.00	2.25
1992 (a)	7,000,000	—	0.35	0.50	1.25	1.50
1993 (a)	2,800,000	—	0.70	1.00	2.50	3.00
1995 (a)	40,000,000	—	0.35	0.50	1.25	1.50
1996 (a)	20,500,000	—	0.35	0.50	1.25	1.50
1997 (a)	25,800,000	—	0.35	0.50	1.25	1.50
1999 (a)	25,200,000	—	0.35	0.50	1.25	1.50
2000 (a)	14,400,000	—	0.35	0.50	1.25	1.50

KM# 4 100 FRANCS
7.07 g., Nickel, 26 mm. **Obv:** Taku - Ashanti gold weight **Rev:** Value within flowers **Edge:** Reeded

Date	Mintage	F12	VF20	XF40	MS60	MS63
1967 (a)	—	—	0.75	1.00	2.50	3.00
1968 (a)	25,000,000	—	0.75	1.00	2.50	3.00
1969 (a)	25,000,000	—	0.75	1.00	2.50	3.00
1970 (a)	4,510,000	—	0.80	1.50	3.50	7.00
1971 (a)	12,000,000	—	0.50	0.75	1.85	2.25
1972 (a)	5,000,000	—	0.60	0.85	2.00	2.50
1973 (a)	5,000,000	—	0.60	0.85	2.00	2.50
1974 (a)	8,500,000	—	0.60	0.75	1.85	2.25
1975 (a)	16,000,000	—	0.60	0.75	1.85	2.25
1976 (a)	11,575,000	—	0.60	0.75	1.85	2.25
1977 (a)	6,200,000	—	0.60	0.75	1.85	2.25
1978 (a)	12,000,000	—	0.60	0.75	1.85	2.25
1979 (a)	12,400,000	—	0.60	0.85	2.00	2.50
1980 (a)	13,000,000	—	0.60	0.75	2.00	2.50
1981 (a)	8,000,000	—	0.60	0.75	2.00	2.50
1982 (a)	18,000,000	—	0.60	0.75	2.00	2.50
1984 (a)	2,500,000	—	0.65	0.85	2.25	2.75
1985 (a)	1,460,000	—	0.65	0.85	2.25	2.75
1987 (a)	9,000,000	—	0.65	0.85	2.25	2.75
1989 (a)	16,500,000	—	0.65	0.85	2.25	2.75
1990 (a)	6,500,000	—	0.65	0.85	2.25	2.75
1991 (a)	1,000,000	—	0.65	0.85	2.25	2.75
1992 (a)	4,000,000	—	0.65	0.85	2.25	2.75
1996 (a)	24,000,000	—	0.65	0.85	2.25	2.75
1997 (a)	69,000,000	—	0.65	0.85	2.25	2.75
2000 (a)	1,800,000	—	0.60	0.85	2.25	2.75

KM# 13 250 FRANCS
Bi-Metallic Brass center in Copper-Nickel ring **Obv:** Map on globe, Taku symbol at top **Rev:** Stalks behind denomination, circle surrounds

Date	Mintage	VF20	XF40	MS60	MS63	MS65
1992 (a)	9,000,000	1.75	2.75	4.50	6.00	8.00
1993 (a)	10,000,000	1.75	2.75	4.50	6.00	8.00
1996 (a)	7,500,000	2.00	3.00	5.00	7.00	9.00

KM# 7 500 FRANCS
25.00 g., 0.900 Silver 0.7234 oz. ASW, 37 mm. **Subject:** 10th Anniversary of Monetary Union **Obv:** Gold weight in the shape of a fish, "Taku", a symbol of prosperity **Rev:** Shields of seven states and script form circle around denomination and date

Date	Mintage	XF40	MS60	MS63	MS65	MS66
1972 (a)	100,000	20.00	30.00	50.00	70.00	85.00
1972 (a) Prooflike	2,000	—	—	95.00	125	145

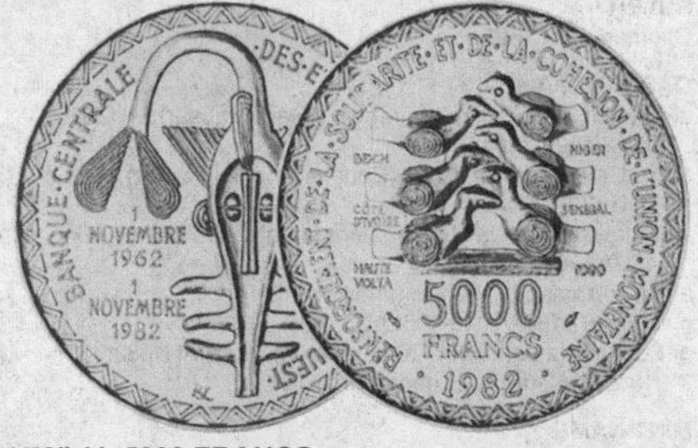

KM# 11 5000 FRANCS
24.95 g., 0.900 Silver 0.7219 oz. ASW **Subject:** 20th Anniversary of Monetary Union **Obv:** Gold weight in the shape of a fish, "Taku", a symbol of prosperity **Rev:** Six interlaced birds symbolizing states

Date	Mintage	XF40	MS60	MS63	MS65	MS66
1982 (a)	200,000	20.00	30.00	45.00	65.00	75.00

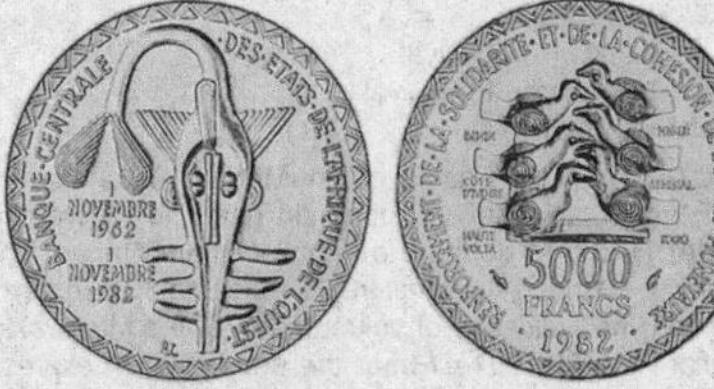

KM# 12 5000 FRANCS
14.49 g., 0.900 Gold 0.4193 oz. AGW **Subject:** 20th Anniversary of Monetary Union **Obv:** Gold weight in the shape of a fish, "Taku", a symbol of prosperity **Rev:** Six interlaced birds symbolizing states

Date	Mintage	XF40	MS60	MS63	MS65	MS66
1982 (a)	—	—	—	1,800	2,700	2,900

ESSAIS

KM#	Date	Mintage	Identification	Mkt Val
E1	1959(a)	—	10 Francs. Aluminum-Bronze. KM1.	17.00
E2	1960(a)	—	5 Francs. Aluminum-Bronze. KM2.	15.00
E3	1961(a)	—	Franc. Aluminum. KM3.	15.00
E4	1967(a)	1,600	100 Francs. Nickel. KM4.	20.00
E4a	1967(a)	100	100 Francs. Silver. KM4.	200

KM#	Date	Mintage	Identification	Mkt Val
E4b	1967(a)	21	100 Francs. Gold. KM4.	2,500
E5	1970(a)	1,450	25 Francs. Aluminum-Bronze. KM5.	17.00
E6	1972(a)	1,750	50 Francs. Copper-Nickel. KM6.	15.00
E6a	1972(a)	120	50 Francs. Silver. KM6.	225
E6b	1972(a)	17	50 Francs. Gold. KM6.	2,200
E7	1972(a)	1,300	500 Francs. Silver. KM7.	250
E8	1976(a)	1,900	Franc. Steel. KM8.	15.00
E9	1980(a)	3,000	25 Francs. Aluminum-Bronze. Figure filling tube, date above. KM9.	50.00
E10	1980(a)	5	25 Francs. Gold.	2,750
E11	1980(a)	1,700	500 Francs.	40.00
E12	1981(a)	1,950	10 Francs. Brass. KM10.	45.00
E13	1982(a)	1,700	5000 Francs. Silver. KM11.	225
E14	1982(a)	12	5000 Francs. Gold. KM11.	4,000

FDC SETS

KM#	Date	Mintage	Identification	Issue Price	Mkt Val
SS1	1968(a) (3)	—	KM1a, 2a, 4	—	12.50

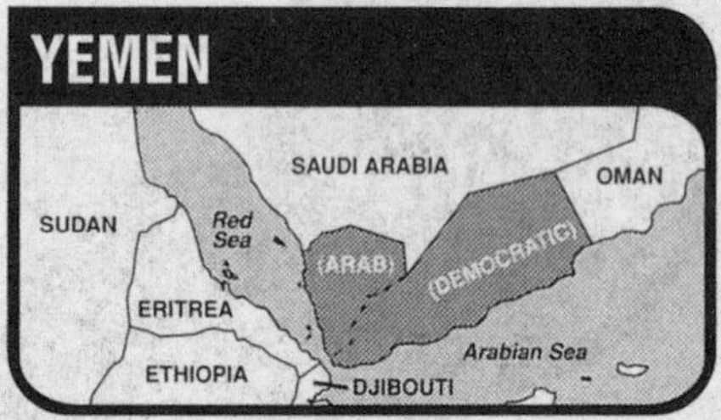

One of the oldest centers of civilization in the Middle East, Yemen was once part of the Minaean Kingdom and of the ancient Kingdom of Sheba, after which it was captured successively by Egyptians, Ethiopians and Romans. It was converted to Islam in 628 A.D. and administered as a caliphate until 1538, when it came under Ottoman occupation in 1849. The second Ottoman occupation which began in 1872 was maintained until 1918 when autonomy was achieved through revolution.

TITLE

المتوكلية اليمنية

al-Mamlaka(t) al-Mutawakkiliya(t) al-Yamaniya(t)

RULER

Ottoman, until 1625

QASIMID IMAMS

al-Mansur Muhammad bin Yahya, (Imam Mansur) AH1307-1322/1890-1904AD

al Hadi al-Hasan bin Yahya (Counter Imam, in Sa'da) AH1322/1904AD

al-Mutawakkil Yahya bin Muhammad (Imam Yahya) AH1322-1367/1904-1948AD

al-Nasir Ahmad bin Yahya, (Imam Ahmad) AH1367-1382/1948-1962AD

al-Badr Muhammad bin Ahmad, (Imam Badr) AH1382-1388/1962-1968AD (mostly in exile)

MINT NAME

المملكة

Sania

MONETARY SYSTEM

After Accession of Iman Yahya AH1322/1904AD

1 Zalat = 1/160 Riyal
2 Zalat = 1 Halala = 1/80 Riyal
2 Halala = 1 Buqsha = 1/40 Riyal
40 Buqsha = 1 Riyal

NOTE: The Riyal was called an IMADI (RIYAL) during the reign of Imam Yahya "Imadi" honorific name for Yahyawi and an AHMADI (RIYAL) during the reign of Imam Ahmad. The 1 Zalat, Y#2.1, D1, A3, A4 and all Imam Yahya gold strikes except Y#F10, bear no indication of value. Many of the Mutawakkilite coins after AH1322/1904AD bear the denomination expressed as fraction of the Riyal as follows.

BRONZE and ALUMINUM

Thumn ushr = 1/80 Riyal = 1/2 Buqsha = 1 Halala
Rub ushr = 1/40 Riyal = 1 Buqsha
Nisf ushr = 1/20 Riyal = 2 Buqsha = 1/2 Bawlah
Nisf thumn = 1/16 Riyal = 2-1/2 Buqsha
Ushr = 1/10 Riyal = 4 Buqsha = 1 Bawlah
Thumn = 1/8 Riyal = 5 Buqsha
Rub = 1/4 Riyal = 10 Buqsha
Nisf = 1/2 Riyal = 20 Buqsha
1 Riyal (Imadi, Ahmadi) = 40 Buqsha

DATING

All coins of Imam Yahya have accession date AH1322 on obverse and actual date of issue on reverse. All coins of Imam Ahmad bear accession date AH1367 on obverse and actual date on reverse.

If not otherwise noted, all coins of Imam Yahya and Imam Ahad as well as the early issues of the Republic (Y#20 through Y#A25 and Y#32), were struck at the mint in Sana'a. The Sana'a Mint was essentially a medieval mint, using hand-cut dies and crudely machined blanks. There is a large amount of variation from one die to the next in arrangement of legends and ornaments, form of crescents, number of stars, size of the circle, etc., and literally hundreds of subtypes could be identified. Types are divided only when there are changes in the inscriptions, or major variations in the basic type, such as the presence or absence of "Rabb al-Alamin" in the legend or the position of the word Sana (= year) in relation to the year.

NOTE: All "ZALAT" coins are without mint name or denomination.

KINGDOM

al-Mansur Muhammad bin Yahya (Imam Mansur)

AH1307-1322 / 1890-1904AD

HAMMERED COINAGE

KM# 403 HARF
Bronze **Note:** Similar to 1 Kabir, KM#410.

Date	Mintage	G4	VG8	F12	VF20	XF40
AH1320	—	—	—	—	—	—

KM# 410 KABIR
Silver, 15-16 mm. **Obv:** Similar to KM#409 **Rev:** "Allah/Abd/" date, divided by ornament, wtih four circular segments **Note:** Weight varies: 0.60-1.00 gram. Size varies. Varieties with three and four stars on reverse exist. Varieties of planchet thickness exist.

Date	Mintage	G4	VG8	F12	VF20	XF40
AH1319	—	20.00	30.00	70.00	150	—
AH1320	—	20.00	30.00	70.00	150	—
AH1321	—	20.00	30.00	70.00	150	—

al-Hadi al-Hasan

AH1322 / 1904AD

MILLED COINAGE

Y# C1 HALALA
1.93 g., Bronze **Obv:** Al-Hasan/bin Yahya/Sana 1322 **Rev:** Al-Hadi/Li-din Allah

Date	Mintage	G4	VG8	F12	VF20	XF40
AH1322	—	—	—	—	—	—

al-Mutawakkil Yahya bin Muhammad (Imam Yahya)

AH1322-1367 / 1904-1948AD

Y# 1.1 ZALAT
Bronze **Obv:** Inscription in three lines above accession date AH1322 **Edge:** Plain **Note:** Weight varies: 0.90-1.60 grams. Obverse varieties with no stars or two stars. Reverse with eight stars. Size of inner circle varies, various planchet thicknesses.

Date	Mintage	G4	VG8	F12	VF20	XF40
AH1341	—	15.00	30.00	100	160	—
AH1342	—	5.00	12.00	30.00	50.00	—
AH1343	—	4.00	10.00	20.00	40.00	—
Note: 1343 also known with seven stars						
AH1344	—	5.00	12.00	30.00	50.00	—
Note: 1344 also exists with traces of reeded edges						
AH1345	—	10.00	25.00	75.00	125	—
AH1346	—	4.00	10.00	20.00	40.00	—

Y# 1.2 ZALAT
Bronze **Obv:** Inscription in two lines above accession date AH1322

Date	Mintage	G4	VG8	F12	VF20	XF40
AH1342	—	5.00	12.00	30.00	50.00	—

Note: Obverse varieties with 1, 2, and 4 stars, and reverse with 8, 11, 12, 13, 14, 15, 16, 17, 20, and 22 stars exist; Some specimens show traces of reeded edges; Various planchet thicknesses exist

Y# 1.4 ZALAT
Bronze **Obv:** Crescent below accession date AH1322

Date	Mintage	G4	VG8	F12	VF20	XF40
AH1342	—	300	425	650	1,000	—

Note: Varieties exist with 11, 14, 15, 16, and 17 stars on reverse and with 1, 2, and 4 stars on obverse; Various planchet thicknesses

Y# 1.7 ZALAT
Bronze **Obv:** Inscription in two lines above accession date AH1322 **Rev:** Date in margin at bottom

Date	Mintage	G4	VG8	F12	VF20	XF40
AH1342 Rare	—	—	—	—	—	—

Note: Obverse varieties with 1 and 2 stars, Reverse with 11 stars, various planchet thicknesses

Y# B1 ZALAT
Bronze **Obv:** Inscription in two lines above accession date AH1322 **Note:** Probably struck at Shaharah about 1925. Dies were reportedly prepared in Italy. For silver strikes, see Y#A4.

Date	Mintage	G4	VG8	F12	VF20	XF40
ND(ca.1925)	—	30.00	60.00	125	200	—

Note: Possibly a pattern

Y# D1 1/80 RIYAL (1/2 Buqsha)
Bronze **Obv:** Crescent below accession date AH1322 **Obv. Inscription:** Rabb al-Alamin **Rev:** Toughra **Note:** Without denomination or mint name.

Date	Mintage	G4	VG8	F12	VF20	XF40
ND(ca.1911) Rare; Accessional date only	—	—	—	—	—	—

Y# 2.1 1/80 RIYAL (1/2 Buqsha)
Bronze **Note:** Accession date AH1322 above crescent on obverse and within crescent on reverse.

Date	Mintage	G4	VG8	F12	VF20	XF40
ND(ca.1911)	—	25.00	50.00	100	200	—

Note: Probably struck at Shaharah

Y# 2.2 1/80 RIYAL (1/2 Buqsha)

Bronze **Obv:** Crescent below accession date AH1322 **Note:** Thin flan, 1.50-3.00 grams. The number and arrangement of stars and the size of the circle on the reverse vary as well as the exact arrangement of the legends which sometimes vary within each year. The reverse exists with 10, 12, 14, 20, 22, 24, 28, and 34 stars. Obverse varieties exist with 1, 2, 3 or 4 stars and without stars. Accession date: AH(1)322 or 1322. Struck at Shaharah.

Date	Mintage	G4	VG8	F12	VF20	XF40
AH1330	—	20.00	35.00	60.00	100	—
AH1331	—	20.00	35.00	75.00	150	—
AH1332	—	10.00	15.00	25.00	40.00	—
AH1333	—	10.00	15.00	25.00	40.00	—
AH1337	—	10.00	15.00	25.00	40.00	—
AH1338	—	10.00	15.00	25.00	40.00	—
AH1339	—	10.00	15.00	25.00	40.00	—

Y# 2.3 1/80 RIYAL (1/2 Buqsha)

Bronze **Rev:** "Duriba Bi Sana'a" added

Date	Mintage	G4	VG8	F12	VF20	XF40
AH1340	—	10.00	20.00	40.00	75.00	—
Note: AH1340 exists with 4 and 8 stars on reverse						
AH1341	—	10.00	20.00	40.00	75.00	—
Note: AH1341 exists with 4 stars on reverse						

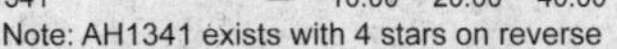

Y# 2.4 1/80 RIYAL (1/2 Buqsha)

Bronze **Obv:** Without "Rabb al-Alamin" with crescent below accession date AH1322 **Note:** Weight and diameter varies.

Date	Mintage	G4	VG8	F12	VF20	XF40
AH1341	—	12.00	25.00	50.00	85.00	—
Note: AH1341 exists with 4 stars on reverse						
AH1342	—	12.00	25.00	50.00	85.00	—
Note: AH1342 coins exist with 4 and 6 stars on reverse						

Y# 2.5 1/80 RIYAL (1/2 Buqsha)

Bronze (Red to Yellow) **Obv:** Crescent below accession date AH1332 **Obv. Inscription:** Rabb al-alamin **Rev:** "Sana" above date **Note:** Number and arrangement of stars on reverse (4, 5, 6, 7, or 8) as well as the size of the inner circle vary. Varieties exist in the form of crescent and arrangement of legends and planchet thicknesses.

Date	Mintage	G4	VG8	F12	VF20	XF40
AH1339	—	7.00	12.00	25.00	40.00	—
AH1341	—	7.00	12.00	25.00	40.00	—
AH1342	—	2.00	5.00	12.00	20.00	—
AH1343	—	2.00	5.00	12.00	20.00	—
AH1344	—	2.00	5.00	12.00	20.00	—
AH1345	—	1.50	4.00	8.00	15.00	—
AH1346	—	1.50	3.00	6.00	12.00	—
Note: Some examples of AH1346 show the 6 re-engraved over low I						
AH1347	—	1.50	4.00	8.00	15.00	—
AH1348	—	1.50	4.00	8.00	15.00	—
AH1349	—	1.50	4.00	8.00	15.00	—
AH1350	—	1.50	4.00	8.00	15.00	—
AH135x	—	1.50	4.00	8.00	15.00	—
AH1351	—	2.00	6.00	12.00	20.00	—
AH1352	—	2.00	6.00	12.00	20.00	—
AH1353	—	2.00	6.00	12.00	20.00	—
AH1358	—	—	—	—	—	—
Note: Requires Confirmation						
AH1359	—	2.50	6.00	12.00	20.00	—
AH1360	—	2.50	4.00	8.00	15.00	—
AH1361	—	4.00	8.00	15.00	25.00	—

Y# 2.6 1/80 RIYAL (1/2 Buqsha)

3.00 g., Bronze **Rev:** "Sana" below date **Note:** Thin flan. Struck at Shaharah.

Date	Mintage	G4	VG8	F12	VF20	XF40
AH1333	—	80.00	100	200	300	—

Y# 2.7 1/80 RIYAL (1/2 Buqsha)

Bronze **Note:** Thick flan. Weight varies: 4-5.4 grams. Varieties with 10 and 14 stars on reverse. Obverse with 1, 2, 3, 4, or no stars. Varieties of legend distribution. Some coins occur with light silver wash. Struck at Shaharah.

Date	Mintage	G4	VG8	F12	VF20	XF40
AH1332	—	10.00	15.00	25.00	40.00	—
AH1333	—	10.00	15.00	25.00	40.00	—
AH1338	—	10.00	15.00	25.00	40.00	—

Y# 2.8 1/80 RIYAL (1/2 Buqsha)

Bronze **Note:** Mule, two obverses.

Date	Mintage	G4	VG8	F12	VF20	XF40
ND(ca.1911-21)	—	20.00	30.00	60.00	100	—

Y# A3 1/40 RIYAL (1 Buqsha)

Billon **Note:** Weight varies: 0.65-1.25 grams. Size varies: 15-16 mm. Accession date: AH1322.

Date	Mintage	VG8	F12	VF20	XF40	MS60
ND(ca.1911-21)	—	275	550	1,100	1,650	—
Note: Minted at Qaflat Idhar, without mint name or denomination						

Y# 3.1 1/40 RIYAL (1 Buqsha)

Bronze **Obv:** Without "Rabb al-Alamin", with crescent below accession date AH1322 **Rev:** "Sana" below date

Date	Mintage	VG8	F12	VF20	XF40	MS60
AH1341	—	10.00	20.00	40.00	80.00	—
Note: Varieties of borders, arrangement of legends, and thickness of planchets exist						

Y# 3.2 1/40 RIYAL (1 Buqsha)

Bronze (Red to Yellow) **Obv:** Crescent below accession date AH1322 **Obv. Inscription:** Rabb al-Alamin **Rev:** "Sana" above date, small "Sana'a" and three leaf ornaments plus star in border legend

Date	Mintage	VG8	F12	VF20	XF40	MS60
AH1342	—	4.00	10.00	20.00	60.00	—
Note: AH1342 exists with 4 leaf ornaments and without star in border legend						
AH13442	—	65.00	125	—	—	—
AH1343	—	4.00	10.00	20.00	60.00	—
AH1344	—	15.00	30.00	50.00	75.00	—

Y# 3.3 1/40 RIYAL (1 Buqsha)

Bronze (Red to Yellow) **Obv:** Crescent below accession date AH1322 **Rev:** Large "Sana'a" in legend **Note:** Varieties in arrangement of legends, ornaments, form of the crescent, and size of the circle on reverse exist; weight varies.

Date	Mintage	VG8	F12	VF20	XF40	MS60
AH1344	—	12.00	20.00	35.00	100	—
AH1345	—	12.00	20.00	35.00	100	—
AH1349	—	1.50	3.50	10.00	25.00	—
AH1353	—	—	—	—	—	—
Note: Requires Confirmation						
AH1358	—	2.00	4.00	10.00	25.00	—
AH1359	—	2.00	4.00	10.00	25.00	—
AH1360	—	2.00	4.00	10.00	25.00	—
AH1361/0	—	10.00	20.00	50.00	75.00	—
AH1362/0	—	2.50	5.00	10.00	35.00	—
AH1362	—	1.50	3.50	10.00	30.00	—
AH1363	—	1.50	5.00	12.00	35.00	—
AH1364	—	1.50	5.00	12.00	35.00	—
AH1365/4	—	2.25	5.00	12.00	35.00	—
AH1365	—	2.50	5.00	12.00	35.00	—
AH1366	—	1.50	3.50	12.00	30.00	—
AH1366/x	—	2.50	5.00	12.00	35.00	—
AH1367	—	10.00	20.00	50.00	75.00	—

Y# A4 1/20 IMADI RIYAL

Silver **Obv:** Inscription in two lines above

Date	Mintage	VG8	F12	VF20	XF40	MS60
ND(1911-21)	—	125	250	600	1,500	—
Note: Dated accessionally on obverse without mint name or denomination; Probably struck at Shaharah about 1925; dies were reportedly prepared in Italy; Strikes in nickel reported; See Y#B1;This issue is believed to be a pattern						

Y# B4 1/20 IMADI RIYAL

Silver **Obv:** Crescent below accession date AH1322 **Rev:** Without "Sana"

Date	Mintage	VG8	F12	VF20	XF40	MS60
AH1337 Rare	—	—	—	—	—	—
Note: Three stars on reverse						

Y# 4.1 1/20 IMADI RIYAL

Silver **Obv:** Without "Rabb al-Alamin", with crescent below accession date AH1322 **Note:** Varieties in arrangement of legends, size of circle, and with 3 and 4 stars on reverse exist. Variety of Y#4 dated with 2 digits AH(13)22 of the accessional year are considered local contemporary counterfeits by leading authorities. They are reported having been produced by the Zaraing tribe at Bait Al-Faqih.

Date	Mintage	VG8	F12	VF20	XF40	MS60
AH1337	—	40.00	80.00	150	250	—
AH1338 Rare	—	—	—	—	—	—
AH1339	—	40.00	80.00	150	250	—
Note: Some strikes show accessional year as 322 only						
AH1340	—	20.00	30.00	60.00	100	—
Note: Some strikes show accessional year as 322 only						
AH1342	—	6.00	12.00	30.00	60.00	—
AH1343	—	5.00	10.00	25.00	50.00	—
AH1344	—	5.00	10.00	25.00	50.00	—
AH1345/2	—	5.00	10.00	25.00	50.00	—
AH1345	—	5.00	10.00	25.00	50.00	—
AH1347	—	6.00	12.00	30.00	60.00	—
AH1348	—	5.00	10.00	25.00	50.00	—
AH1349	—	5.00	10.00	25.00	50.00	—
AH1350	—	5.00	12.00	30.00	60.00	—
AH1351	—	6.00	15.00	35.00	75.00	—
AH1352	—	5.00	12.00	30.00	60.00	—
AH1353	—	5.00	12.00	30.00	60.00	—
AH1358	—	4.00	8.00	20.00	40.00	—
AH1359	—	4.00	8.00	20.00	40.00	—
AH1362/58	—	6.00	15.00	30.00	60.00	—
AH1362/59	—	6.00	15.00	30.00	60.00	—
AH1363	—	5.00	10.00	30.00	60.00	—
AH1364/46	—	4.00	8.00	20.00	40.00	—
AH1364	—	4.00	8.00	20.00	40.00	—
AHx364	—	4.00	8.00	20.00	40.00	—
AH1365	—	4.00	10.00	25.00	50.00	—
AH1366/44	—	5.00	12.00	30.00	60.00	—
AH1366	—	5.00	12.00	30.00	60.00	—

Y# 4.4 1/20 IMADI RIYAL

Silver **Rev:** Border legend shifted to left **Note:** Accession date AH1322.

Date	Mintage	VG8	F12	VF20	XF40	MS60
AH1340 Rare	—	—	—	—	—	—
Note: Three stars on reverse						

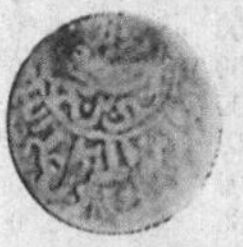

Y# 4.2 1/20 IMADI RIYAL

Silver **Obv:** Crescent **Rev:** "Sana" below date, normal legend position **Note:** Four stars on reverse.

Date	Mintage	VG8	F12	VF20	XF40	MS60
AH1341	—	40.00	80.00	150	250	—
AHx341	—	40.00	80.00	150	250	—

Y# 5.1 1/10 IMADI RIYAL

Silver **Obv:** Crescent below accession date AH1322 **Obv. Inscription:** Rabb al-Alamin **Rev:** Without "Sana"

Date	Mintage	VG8	F12	VF20	XF40	MS60
AH1337	—	30.00	60.00	100	175	—

Note: Reverse varieties with 3, 4, and 5 stars. Size of circle and form of crescent varies

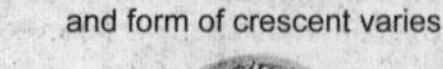

Y# 5.2 1/10 IMADI RIYAL

Silver **Obv:** Without "Rabb al-Alamin", with crescent below accession date AH1322

Date	Mintage	VG8	F12	VF20	XF40	MS60
AH1339	—	20.00	40.00	75.00	150	—
Note: Some AH1339 strikes show accession date as 322						
AH1340	—	20.00	40.00	75.00	150	—
Note: AH1340 also exists with three stars, others with six stars on reverse						
AH1341	—	20.00	40.00	75.00	150	—
AH1348	—	100	150	350	500	—

Y# 5.3 1/10 IMADI RIYAL

Silver **Obv:** Crescent below accession date AH1322 **Rev:** "Sana" above date **Note:** Varieties with three and six stars on the reverse exist.

Date	Mintage	VG8	F12	VF20	XF40	MS60
AH1341	—	20.00	40.00	75.00	150	—
AH1342	—	20.00	40.00	75.00	150	—

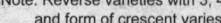

Y# 5.5 1/10 IMADI RIYAL

Silver **Obv:** Without "Rabb al-Alamin" **Rev:** "Sana" above date **Note:** Form of crescent, size of circle on reverse, and arrangement of legends vary. Normal reverse contains 6 stars though varieties with 7, 8, 9, 10, and 12 stars on reverse exist. Some earlier dates show varying amounts of edge reeding.

Date	Mintage	VG8	F12	VF20	XF40	MS60
AH1342	—	5.00	10.00	25.00	50.00	—
AH1343	—	5.00	10.00	25.00	50.00	—
AH1344	—	4.00	8.00	20.00	40.00	—
AH1345	—	4.00	8.00	20.00	40.00	—
AH1347	—	4.00	8.00	20.00	40.00	—
AH1348	—	4.00	8.00	20.00	35.00	—
AH1349	—	4.00	6.00	15.00	30.00	—
AH1350	—	—	—	—	—	—
Note: Requires Confirmation						
AH1351	—	5.00	10.00	25.00	40.00	—
AH1352	—	5.00	10.00	25.00	40.00	—
AH1358/49	—	4.00	8.00	15.00	30.00	—
AH1358	—	4.00	8.00	15.00	30.00	—
AH1359/3	—	4.00	8.00	15.00	30.00	—
AH1359/49	—	4.00	8.00	15.00	30.00	—
AH1362/44	—	5.00	10.00	25.00	40.00	—
AH1362/59	—	5.00	10.00	25.00	40.00	—
AH1363	—	4.00	8.00	25.00	45.00	—
AH1364/43	—	4.00	8.00	20.00	40.00	—
AH1364/3	—	4.00	8.00	25.00	45.00	—
AH1364/52	—	4.00	8.00	25.00	45.00	—
AH1364	—	4.00	8.00	15.00	35.00	—
AH1365	—	4.00	8.00	15.00	35.00	—
AH1366/5	—	4.00	10.00	20.00	50.00	—
AH1366/5x	—	4.00	10.00	20.00	50.00	—

Y# 5.4 1/10 IMADI RIYAL

Silver **Obv:** Crescent below accession date AH1322 **Obv. Inscription:** Rabb al-Alamin **Rev:** "Sana" above date **Note:** Varieties with 8, 9, and 10 stars on reverse exist.

Date	Mintage	VG8	F12	VF20	XF40	MS60
AH1342	—	20.00	40.00	75.00	150	—

Y# 8 1/8 IMADI RIYAL

Silver **Obv:** One or no stars in crescent below accession date AH1322 **Rev:** "Thumn" in place of "Ushr" below date, 6 stars

Date	Mintage	VG8	F12	VF20	XF40	MS60
AH1339	—	325	550	1,100	1,650	—

Y# 6.1 1/4 IMADI RIYAL

Silver **Obv:** Without "Rabb al-Alamin", with crescent below accession date AH1322 **Rev:** "Sana" below date

Date	Mintage	VG8	F12	VF20	XF40	MS60
AH1341	—	20.00	45.00	75.00	150	—
Note: AH1341 with 4 stars on reverse						
AH1342	—	25.00	50.00	100	175	—
Note: AH1342 with 4 stars on reverse and 2 stars flanking date						

Y# 6.2 1/4 IMADI RIYAL

Silver **Obv:** Crescent below accession date AH1322 **Obv. Inscription:** Rabb al-Alamin **Rev:** "Sana" above date, two stars and two ornaments in border

Date	Mintage	VG8	F12	VF20	XF40	MS60
AH1342	—	70.00	100	300	450	—

Y# 6.5 1/4 IMADI RIYAL

Silver **Obv:** Crescent below accession date AH1322 **Rev:** "Sana" below date, eight stars in border

Date	Mintage	VG8	F12	VF20	XF40	MS60
AH1342	—	100	150	300	500	—

Y# 6.6 1/4 IMADI RIYAL

Silver **Obv:** Crescent below accession date AH1322 **Rev:** "Sana" below date, one star in border

Date	Mintage	VG8	F12	VF20	XF40	MS60
AH1342	—	100	150	300	500	—
Note: Obverse varieties with one and two stars exist						

Y# 10 1/4 IMADI RIYAL

Silver **Obv:** Crescent below accession date AH1322 **Rev:** Redesigned, date moved to margin **Edge:** Plain, traces of reeding to full reeding known **Note:** The size of the reverse inner circle varies, 12 to 16 crescents on obverse.

Date	Mintage	VG8	F12	VF20	XF40	MS60
AH1342	—	20.00	40.00	75.00	150	—
AH1343	—	20.00	60.00	100	175	—
AH1344	—	7.50	12.50	25.00	75.00	—
AH1345	—	7.50	12.50	25.00	60.00	—
AH1349	—	—	—	—	—	—
Note: Requires Confirmation						
AH1351	—	20.00	30.00	50.00	100	—
AH1352	—	8.00	12.00	22.00	45.00	—
AH1358	—	6.50	8.00	15.00	35.00	—
AH1359	—	6.50	8.00	15.00	35.00	—
AH1363	—	6.50	10.00	22.00	45.00	—
AH1364/3	—	7.50	10.00	22.00	45.00	—
AH1364	—	6.50	8.00	20.00	40.00	—
AH1365/4	—	7.50	10.00	22.00	45.00	—
AH1365	—	6.50	8.00	20.00	40.00	—
AH1366	—	6.50	8.00	20.00	40.00	—

Y# 7 IMADI RIYAL

28.07 g., Silver **Obv:** Double crescent below accession date AH1322 **Note:** Several die varieties exist, possibly struck over a number of years with frozen date AH1344. Edge varieties exist.

Date	Mintage	VG8	F12	VF20	XF40	MS60
AH1342	—	—	—	—	—	—
Note: Requires Confirmation						
AH1344	—	27.00	30.00	35.00	45.00	60.00
Note: Copper trial strikes dated AH1344 reported						
AH1365 Two known	—	—	—	—	—	2,000

GOLD PRESENTATION COINAGE

All Imam Yahya gold strikes are considered presentation issues which were based on the gold standard of the Turkish Lira.

Y# A10 1/8 LIRA (1/40 Riyal)

0.92 g., Gold **Note:** Accession date: AH1322.

Date	Mintage	VG8	F12	VF20	XF40	MS60
AH(13)44	—	—	—	—	1,350	—

Y# B10 1/4 LIRA (1/20 Riyal)

1.70 g., Gold **Note:** Accession date: AH1322.

Date	Mintage	VG8	F12	VF20	XF40	MS60
AH(13)44	—	—	—	—	1,500	—

Y# C10 1/2 LIRA (1/10 Riyal)

3.31 g., Gold **Note:** Accession date: AH1322.

Date	Mintage	VG8	F12	VF20	XF40	MS60
AH(13)44	—	—	—	—	1,650	—

Y# D10 LIRA (1/5 Riyal)

6.80 g., Gold **Obv:** Crescent below accession date AH1322

Date	Mintage	VG8	F12	VF20	XF40	MS60
AH(13)44	—	—	—	—	2,000	—

Y# E10 2-1/2 LIRA (1/2 Riyal)

17.70 g., Gold **Obv:** Crescent below accession date AH1322

Date	Mintage	VG8	F12	VF20	XF40	MS60
AH(13)44	—	—	—	—	3,500	—

Y# K10 2-1/2 LIRA (1/2 Riyal)

Gold **Note:** Weight varies: 17.44-17.82 grams. Accession date: AH1322.

Date	Mintage	VG8	F12	VF20	XF40	MS60
AH1352 Rare	—	—	—	—	—	—

Y# F10 5 LIRA (1 Riyal)
35.50 g., Gold **Note:** Similar to 1 Imadi Riyal, Y#7.

Date	Mintage	VG8	F12	VF20	XF40	MS60
AH1344 Rare	—	—	—	—	—	—

Note: Dies of AH1344 Riyal silver and gold strikes are not identical

Y# P10 5 LIRA (1 Riyal)
34.24 g., Gold **Note:** Thin planchet strike of 10 Lira (2 Riyal), Y#N10.

Date	Mintage	VG8	F12	VF20	XF40	MS60
AH1358 2 known	—	—	—	—	3,250	—

Y# M10 10 LIRA (2 Riyal)
69.83 g., Gold **Obv:** Similar to Gold 2-1/2 Lira, Y#K10 **Note:** Accession date: AH1322.

Date	Mintage	VG8	F12	VF20	XF40	MS60
AH1352	—	—	—	—	6,500	—

Y# N10 10 LIRA (2 Riyal)
69.83 g., Gold **Obv:** Crescent below accession date AH1322 **Rev:** Two crossed flags in center **Rev. Legend:** Duriba bi-dar al-khilafa al-mutawakkiliya bi Sana'a 'asimat al-Yamam sana 1358

Date	Mintage	VG8	F12	VF20	XF40	MS60
AH1358 4 known	—	—	—	—	5,500	—

al-Nasir Ahmad bin Yahya (Imam Ahmad)

AH1367-1382 / 1948-1962AD

MILLED COINAGE

Y# 11.1 1/80 RIYAL (1 Halala = 1/2 Buqsha)
Bronze (Red to Yellow) **Obv:** Crescent below accession date AH1367 which may vary as 1367/1267, 1367/1777, etc. **Rev:** "Sana" above date **Note:** There is a variation in the number of stars on reverse, as follows: AH1368 - 8 stars; AH1371-74 and some AH1381 (not overdate) - 7 stars; AH1375-81 including some AH1381, some AH1382, and all AH1381 overdates - 8 stars. Varieties of arrangement of legends, form of crescent, and size of circle on reverse exist. Some earlier dates exist on thinner planchets.

Date	Mintage	VG8	F12	VF20	XF40	MS60
AH1368	—	1.00	2.00	4.00	7.00	10.00
AH1371	—	0.30	1.00	3.00	5.00	8.00
AH1372	—	0.30	1.00	3.00	5.00	8.00
AH1373	—	0.30	0.60	1.00	2.00	3.00
AH1374	—	0.30	1.00	3.00	5.00	8.00
AH1275 Error for 1375	—	1.00	2.00	5.00	8.00	12.00
AH1375	—	—	—	—	—	—
AH1376	—	—	—	—	—	—
AH1376/86 Error	—	—	—	—	—	—
AH1278 Error for 1378	—	1.00	2.00	5.00	8.00	12.00
AH1378	—	—	—	—	—	—
AHx379	—	1.00	2.00	5.00	8.00	12.00
AH1379	—	0.50	1.00	2.00	3.50	5.00
AH1380/1	—	1.00	2.00	5.00	8.00	12.00
AH1380/79	—	0.50	1.00	2.00	3.50	5.00
AH1380/9	—	0.50	1.00	2.00	3.50	5.00
AH1380	—	0.50	1.00	2.00	3.50	5.00
AH1381/80/79	—	0.40	0.85	1.50	2.00	3.00
AH1381/79	—	0.40	0.85	1.50	2.00	3.00
AH1381	—	0.20	0.40	0.75	1.25	2.00
AH1382	—	5.00	7.00	12.00	15.00	20.00

Y# 11.2 1/80 RIYAL (1 Halala = 1/2 Buqsha)
Bronze **Rev:** Without "Sana"

Date	Mintage	VG8	F12	VF20	XF40	MS60
AH1373 Rare	—	—	—	—	—	—

Y# 11a 1/80 RIYAL (1 Halala = 1/2 Buqsha)
Aluminum **Obv:** Crescent below accession date AH1367 **Rev:** "Sana" above date **Note:** AH1374 and some AH1380 have 7 stars, the rest have 8 stars on reverse. Dies of 1/80 Riyal, Y#11.1, were used.

Date	Mintage	VG8	F12	VF20	XF40	MS60
AH1374	—	0.25	1.00	2.00	3.50	5.00
AH1375	—	0.75	2.50	5.00	7.00	10.00
AH1376	—	0.25	1.50	3.00	6.00	9.00
AH1377	—	0.75	2.50	5.00	7.00	10.00
AH1378	—	0.25	1.00	2.00	3.50	5.00
AH1378/6	—	0.25	1.00	2.00	3.50	5.00
AH1379	—	0.25	1.00	2.00	3.50	5.00
AH1379/5	—	0.75	2.50	5.00	7.00	10.00
AH1379/8	—	0.75	2.50	5.00	7.00	10.00
AH1380	—	0.25	1.00	2.00	3.50	5.00

Y# 18 1/80 RIYAL (1 Halala = 1/2 Buqsha)
Aluminum **Note:** Accession date: AH1367.

Date	Mintage	F12	VF20	XF40	MS60	MS63
ND (1956)	—	0.25	0.50	0.75	1.00	3.00

Note: Struck privately in Lebanon in 1955 and 1956 and released into circulation in 1956

Y# 11.3 1/80 RIYAL (1 Halala = 1/2 Buqsha)
Bronze **Obv:** Crescent below accession date AH1367 **Note:** Struck with dies of 1/4 Ahmadi Riyal, Y#15 on 1/80 Riyal planchet.

Date	Mintage	VG8	F12	VF20	XF40	MS60
AH(13)80 Rare	—	—	—	—	—	—

Y# 12.1 1/40 RIYAL (1 Buqsha)
Bronze (Red to Yellow) **Obv:** Crescent below accession date AH1367 **Rev:** "Sana" above date, large "Sana'a" in border legend **Note:** Some dates exist on thinner planchets and weight varies.

Date	Mintage	VG8	F12	VF20	XF40	MS60
AH1368	—	0.50	1.00	3.50	7.00	12.00

Note: AH1368 also exists with accession date 13776 (error) known

Date	Mintage	VG8	F12	VF20	XF40	MS60
AH1369	—	0.75	1.25	4.50	9.00	15.00
AH1370	—	0.35	0.75	2.00	4.00	6.00
AH1371	—	0.35	0.75	2.00	4.00	6.00
AH1372	—	0.35	0.75	1.50	2.50	4.00
AH1373/1	—	—	—	—	—	—
AH1373/2	—	0.85	1.80	3.00	5.00	9.00
AH1373	—	0.35	0.75	1.50	2.50	4.00
AH1374	—	0.35	0.75	1.50	2.50	4.00
AH1375/4	—	0.50	1.00	2.00	4.00	6.00
AH1377	—	—	—	—	—	—

Note: Requires Confirmation

Y# 12.2 1/40 RIYAL (1 Buqsha)
Bronze (Red to Yellow) **Obv:** Crescent below accession date AH1367 **Rev:** Small "Sana'a" in legend **Note:** Varieties of arrangement of legends, form of crescent, and size of circle exist.

Date	Mintage	VG8	F12	VF20	XF40	MS60
AH1371	—	0.35	0.75	1.50	3.50	6.00
AH1374	—	0.35	0.75	1.50	2.50	4.00
AH1375	—	0.35	0.75	1.50	2.50	4.00
AH1376	—	0.50	1.00	5.00	7.00	12.00

Note: Exists with accession date 1376 instead of 1367 on obverse

Date	Mintage	VG8	F12	VF20	XF40	MS60
AH1377/6	—	0.85	1.75	3.50	5.50	8.00

Note: Exists with accession date 1376 instead of 1367 on obverse

Date	Mintage	VG8	F12	VF20	XF40	MS60
AH1377	—	0.85	1.75	4.50	6.50	10.00
AH1378/5	—	—	—	—	—	—
AH1379/7	—	0.85	1.75	3.50	5.50	8.00
AH1380/79	—	0.85	1.75	3.50	5.50	8.00
AH1380	—	10.00	20.00	40.00	55.00	75.00

Y# 12.3 1/40 RIYAL (1 Buqsha)
Bronze (Red to Yellow) **Obv:** Crescent below accession date AH1367 **Rev:** Large "Sana'a" in legend, without "Sana" above date

Date	Mintage	VG8	F12	VF20	XF40	MS60
AH1371	—	0.50	1.00	4.00	7.00	12.00

Y# 12a.1 1/40 RIYAL (1 Buqsha)
Aluminum **Obv:** Crescent below accession date AH1367 **Rev:** "Sana" above date, large "Sana'a" in border legend **Note:** Dies of 1/40 Riyal, Y#12.1, were used.

Date	Mintage	VG8	F12	VF20	XF40	MS60
AH1371	—	0.50	1.00	4.00	6.00	10.00
AH1373	—	0.50	1.00	4.00	6.00	10.00
AH1374	—	0.50	1.00	4.00	6.00	10.00
AH1375	—	0.50	1.00	4.00	6.00	10.00
AH1377	—	15.00	30.00	45.00	60.00	90.00

Y# 12a.2 1/40 RIYAL (1 Buqsha)
Aluminum **Obv:** Crescent below accession date AH1367 **Rev:** Small "Sana'a" in legend **Note:** Dies of 1/40 Riyal, Y#12.2, were used. AH1376 and AH1377 plain dates also exist with accession date AH1376 instead of AH1367 on obverse. Varieties exist.

Date	Mintage	VG8	F12	VF20	XF40	MS60
AH1375	—	0.50	1.00	4.00	6.00	10.00
AH1376	—	0.50	1.00	4.00	6.00	10.00
AH1377/6	—	10.00	20.00	40.00	55.00	75.00
AH1377	—	15.00	30.00	45.00	60.00	90.00

Y# 19 1/40 RIYAL (1 Buqsha)

Aluminum **Note:** Accession date: AH1367 at bottom.

Date	Mintage	F12	VF20	XF40	MS60	MS63
ND (1956)	—	0.45	0.65	1.00	2.00	3.00

Note: Struck privately in Lebanon in 1955 and 1956 and released into circulation in 1956

Y# 13 1/16 AHMADI RIYAL

Silver **Obv:** Crescent below accession date AH1367 **Obv. Inscription:** Amir al-Mu'minin **Shape:** 5-sided **Note:** Arrangement of legends and size of inner circle on reverse vary.

Date	Mintage	VG8	F12	VF20	XF40	MS60
AH1367	—	1.75	2.50	5.00	7.00	12.00
AH1368	—	1.75	2.25	4.50	6.00	10.00
AH1371	—	1.75	2.25	4.50	6.00	10.00
AH1374	—	1.75	2.00	3.50	5.00	9.00

Y# 13.1 1/16 AHMADI RIYAL

Silver **Obv:** Crescent below accession date AH1367, 1/8 Ahmadi Riyal, Y#14 **Rev:** Y#13 **Shape:** 5-sided **Note:** Mule. Ends of crescents cut off on reverse.

Date	Mintage	VG8	F12	VF20	XF40	MS60
AH1374	—	20.00	40.00	60.00	100	150

Y# A14 1/10 AHMADI RIYAL

Silver **Obv:** Crescent below accession date AH1367

Date	Mintage	VG8	F12	VF20	XF40	MS60
AH1370	—	400	750	1,250	1,500	—

Y# 14 1/8 AHMADI RIYAL

Silver **Obv:** Crescent below accession date AH1367 **Note:** Pentagonal planchet. Arrangement of legends and size of inner circle on reverse vary.

Date	Mintage	F12	VF20	XF40	MS60	MS63
AH1367	—	2.50	5.00	9.00	15.00	30.00
AH1368	—	2.00	4.00	5.00	9.00	20.00
AH1370	—	2.00	4.00	5.00	9.00	20.00
AH1371	—	2.00	3.50	4.50	7.00	15.00
AH1372	—	2.00	3.50	4.00	6.00	12.00
AH1373	—	2.00	3.50	4.00	6.00	12.00
AH1374	—	2.00	3.50	4.00	6.50	15.00
AH1375/1	—	2.50	5.00	10.00	40.00	80.00
AH1379/x	—	2.00	3.50	4.00	6.50	15.00
AH1379/5	—	2.00	3.50	4.00	6.50	15.00
AH1379	—	2.00	3.50	4.00	7.00	15.00
AH1380	—	2.00	3.50	4.50	8.50	20.00

Y# 14a 1/8 AHMADI RIYAL

Silver **Shape:** Hexagonal

Date	Mintage	F12	VF20	XF40	MS60	MS63
AH1368	—	200	350	650	1,250	1,850

Y# 15 1/4 AHMADI RIYAL

Silver **Obv:** Crescent below accession date AH1367 **Edge:** Reeded **Note:** The size of inner circle as well as the arrangement of legends on reverse vary. All dates have only the final 2 digits on the coin.

Date	Mintage	F12	VF20	XF40	MS60	MS63
AH(13)67	—	4.00	7.00	9.00	13.00	20.00
AH(13)68	—	4.00	7.00	9.00	13.00	20.00
AH(13)70	—	3.00	6.50	8.00	12.00	18.00
AH(13)71/68	—	5.00	8.00	12.00	17.00	28.00
AH(13)71/0	—	5.00	8.00	12.00	15.00	25.00
AH(13)71	—	3.00	6.50	8.00	10.00	17.00
AH(13)72	—	3.00	6.50	8.00	10.00	17.00
AH(13)74	—	3.00	6.50	8.00	10.00	17.00
AH(13)75/3	—	5.00	8.00	12.00	15.00	25.00
AH(13)75	—	3.00	6.50	8.00	10.00	17.00
AH(13)77/5	—	5.00	8.00	12.00	15.00	25.00
AH(13)80	—	20.00	30.00	60.00	100	175

Y# 15a 1/4 AHMADI RIYAL

Copper

Date	Mintage	F12	VF20	XF40	MS60	MS63
AH(13)81d Rare	—	—	—	—	—	—

Note: This issue is considered a pattern

Y# 16.1 1/2 AHMADI RIYAL

Silver **Obv:** Double crescent below accession date AH1367 **Rev:** Full dates; denomination and mint name read inward

Date	Mintage	F12	VF20	XF40	MS60	MS63
AH1367	—	7.50	13.50	15.00	20.00	38.00
AH1368	—	7.50	13.50	15.00	20.00	38.00
AH1369	—	7.00	12.50	14.50	18.00	25.00
AH1370	—	8.00	15.00	18.00	25.00	45.00
AH1371	—	8.00	15.00	18.00	25.00	45.00
AH1372/68	—	7.50	13.50	15.00	20.00	38.00
AH1373	—	10.00	17.00	20.00	28.00	48.00
AH1375	—	—	—	—	—	—
Note: Requires Confirmation						
AH(13)75	—	20.00	30.00	50.00	80.00	100
AH1377	—	—	—	—	—	—

Y# 16.2 1/2 AHMADI RIYAL

Silver **Obv:** Double crescent below accession date AH1367 **Rev:** Full dates; denomination and mint name read outward **Edge:** Reeded **Note:** Arrangement of legends and size of circle on reverse vary. These coins were struck over blanks punched from Maria Theresa Thalers. The outer rings are reported to have circulated as currency, but this is doubtful, as they are found only counterstamped "Void" in Arabic.

Date	Mintage	F12	VF20	XF40	MS60	MS63
AH1377	—	7.00	12.50	13.50	17.50	25.00
AH1378	—	7.50	13.50	15.00	20.00	30.00
AH1379	—	7.00	12.50	13.50	17.50	25.00
AH1380	—	12.00	20.00	32.00	42.00	75.00
AH1381	—	9.00	15.00	25.00	32.00	50.00
AH1382	—	8.00	14.50	16.00	27.50	42.00

Y# 16a 1/2 AHMADI RIYAL

Copper

Date	Mintage	F12	VF20	XF40	MS60	MS63
AH1381 Rare	—	—	—	—	—	—

Note: This issue is considered a pattern

Y# 17 AHMADI RIYAL

Silver, 39.5 mm. **Obv:** Double crescent below accession date AH1367 **Note:** These are usually found struck over Austrian Maria Theresa Talers and occasionally over other foreign crowns. All Y-17s have 1367 in the center obverse. The date for each piece is located in the lower left of the reverse. Varieties exist.

Date	Mintage	VF20	XF40	MS60	MS63	MS65
AH1367	—	28.00	45.00	60.00	95.00	125
AH1370	—	27.50	32.50	45.00	70.00	100
AH1371	—	27.50	32.50	45.00	70.00	100
AH1372/68	—	—	—	—	—	—
Note: Requires Confirmation						
AH1373	—	26.00	28.00	37.50	50.00	75.00
Note: Most AH1373 Riyals appear to be weakly struck from recut AH1372 dies, and the dates are easily confused						
AH1374	—	26.50	28.50	40.00	60.00	85.00
AH1375	—	26.50	28.50	40.00	60.00	85.00
AH1377	—	26.50	28.50	40.00	60.00	85.00
AH1378	—	26.50	28.50	40.00	60.00	85.00
AH1380	—	26.50	28.50	40.00	60.00	85.00
AH1381	—	26.50	28.50	40.00	60.00	85.00

GOLD COINAGE

Imam Ahmad gold strikes were based on the gold standard of the Turkish Lira (7.2164 g gold). Strikes on the British Gold Standard can have an additional countermark of an Arabic 1, 2, or 4, probably indicating the equivalence to 1, 2, or 4 British Sovereigns.

Y# G15 GOLD 1/4 RIYAL (1 Lira - Sovereign)

Gold **Obv:** Crescent below accession date AH1367 **Note:** Weight varies: 6.30-8.90 grams. Dies of silver 1/4 Ahmadi riyal, (Y#15) were used.

Date	Mintage	F12	VF20	XF40	MS60	MS63
AH(13)71	—	—	1,200	1,500	2,250	3,000
AH(13)75/3	—	—	1,200	1,500	2,250	3,000
AH(13)75	—	—	1,200	1,500	2,250	3,000
AH(13)77/5	—	—	1,200	1,500	2,250	3,000

Y# G16.1 GOLD 1/2 RIYAL (2-1/2 Lira - 2 Sovereigns)

Gold **Obv:** Double crescent below accession date AH1367 **Rev:** Full dates; denomination and mint name read inward **Note:** Weight varies: 15.57-17.99 grams.

Date	Mintage	F12	VF20	XF40	MS60	MS63
AH1369 Rare	—	—	—	—	—	—
Note: Currently, one known						
AH1370	—	—	1,350	1,750	2,500	3,500
AH1371	—	—	1,350	1,750	2,500	3,500
AH1375	—	—	1,350	1,750	2,500	3,500
AH(13)75	—	—	1,350	1,750	2,500	3,500
AH1377	—	—	1,350	1,750	2,500	3,500

Y# G16.2 GOLD 1/2 RIYAL (2-1/2 Lira - 2 Sovereigns)
Gold **Obv:** Double crescent below accession date AH1367 **Rev:** Full date; denomination and mint name read outward **Note:** Dies of silver 1/2 Ahmadi Riyal, (Y#16) were used.

Date	Mintage	F12	VF20	XF40	MS60	MS63
AH1377	—	—	1,350	1,750	2,500	3,500
AH1378	—	—	1,350	1,750	2,500	3,500
AH1379	—	—	1,350	1,750	2,500	3,500
AH1380	—	—	1,350	1,750	2,500	3,500
AH1381	—	—	1,350	1,750	2,500	3,500

Y# G17.1 GOLD RIYAL (5 Lira - 4 Sovereigns)
32.49 g., 0.900 Gold 0.940 oz. AGW, 40 mm. **Obv:** Double crescent below accession date AH1367 with incuse Arabic number four above sword handles **Rev:** Arabic legend and inscription

Date	Mintage	F12	VF20	XF40	MS60	MS63
AH1371 Rare	—	—	—	—	—	—
AH1372 Rare	—	—	—	—	—	—

Y# G17.2 GOLD RIYAL (5 Lira - 4 Sovereigns)
32.49 g., 0.900 Gold 0.940 oz. AGW, 40 mm. **Obv:** Double crescent below accession date AH1367 without incuse Arabic number four above sword handles **Rev:** Arabic legend and inscription **Note:** Weight varies: 30.46-39.06 grams. Dies of silver Ahmadi Riyal (Y#17) were used.

Date	Mintage	F12	VF20	XF40	MS60	MS63
AH1373	—	—	1,750	2,250	3,250	4,000
AH1374	—	—	1,750	2,250	3,250	4,000
AH1375	—	—	1,750	2,250	3,250	4,000
AH1377	—	—	1,750	2,250	3,250	4,000
AH1378	—	—	1,750	2,250	3,250	4,000
AH1381	—	—	1,750	2,250	3,250	4,000

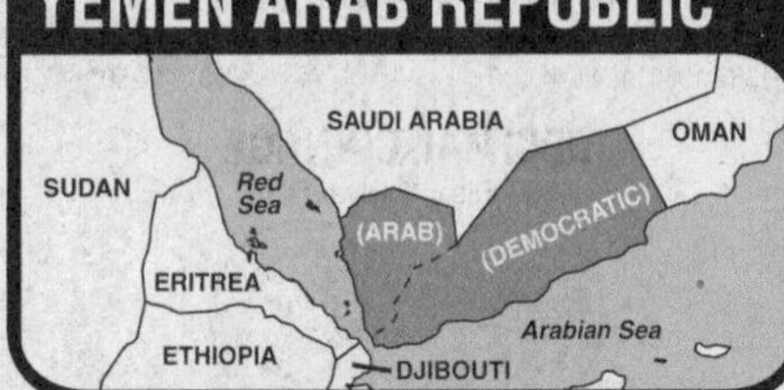

The northwestern region of present day Yemen was dominated by Ottoman Turks until 1918. Formal boundaries were established in 1934 and a Republic was formed in 1962 leading to an eight year civil war between royalist imam and new republican forces.

REPUBLIC

MILLED COINAGE

Y# 20 1/80 RIYAL (1/2 Buqsha)
Bronze **Obv:** Denomination within circle **Rev:** Hand holding torch within circle **Note:** Varieties exist.

Date	Mintage	F12	VF20	XF40	MS60	MS63
AH1382	—	—	0.50	1.00	3.00	5.00

Y# 21.1 1/80 RIYAL (1/2 Buqsha)
Bronze **Obv:** Denomination within circle **Rev:** Full star between lines within circle

Date	Mintage	F12	VF20	XF40	MS60	MS63
AH1382	—	—	1.00	3.00	5.00	15.00

Y# 21.2 1/80 RIYAL (1/2 Buqsha)
Bronze **Obv:** Denomination within circle **Rev:** Outlined star between lines within circle **Note:** Varieties exist.

Date	Mintage	F12	VF20	XF40	MS60	MS63
AH13882 (sic)	—	—	—	—	—	—
AH1382	—	—	1.00	3.00	5.00	15.00

Y# 26 1/2 BUQSHA
Copper-Aluminum **Obv:** Denomination within circle **Rev:** Leafy branch within wreath **Mint:** Cairo **Note:** Varieties exist.

Date	Mintage	F12	VF20	XF40	MS60	MS63
AH1382-1963	10,000,000	—	—	—	0.25	0.50

Y# 32 1/2 BUQSHA
Bronze **Obv:** Denomination within circle **Rev:** Full star between lines within circle **Note:** Varieties exist.

Date	Mintage	F12	VF20	XF40	MS60	MS63
AH1382	—	—	1.00	1.50	3.00	5.00

Y# 22 1/40 RIYAL (1 Buqsha)
Brass or Bronze **Obv:** Denomination within circle **Rev:** Hand holding torch within circle **Note:** Dated both sides; AH1382, AH1383 and AH1384/3 are dated AH1382 on obverse, actual date on reverse; AH1384 and AH1384/284 dated AH1384 on both sides. There are varieties of date size and design.

Date	Mintage	F12	VF20	XF40	MS60	MS63
AH1382	—	—	0.50	1.00	2.25	5.00
AH1383/282	—	—	0.50	1.00	2.25	5.00
AH1383	—	—	0.50	1.00	3.50	7.00
AH1384/284	—	—	0.50	1.00	2.25	5.00
AH1384/3	—	—	0.50	1.00	2.25	5.00
AH1384	—	—	0.50	2.00	5.00	10.00

Y# 27 BUQSHA
Copper-Aluminum **Obv:** Denomination within circle **Rev:** Leafy branch within wreath **Mint:** Cairo

Date	Mintage	F12	VF20	XF40	MS60	MS63
AH1382-1963	10,377,000	—	—	0.25	0.50	1.00

Y# 23.1 1/20 RIYAL (2 Buqsha)
0.720 Silver **Obv:** Denomination within circle **Rev:** Three stones on top row of wall within circle **Note:** Thick variety, 1.10-1.60 grams

Date	Mintage	F12	VF20	XF40	MS60	MS63
AH1382	—	20.00	35.00	60.00	100	125

Y# 23.2 1/20 RIYAL (2 Buqsha)
0.720 Silver **Obv:** Denomination within circle **Rev:** Two stones on top row of wall within circle **Note:** Thin variety, 0.60-0.90 grams

Date	Mintage	F12	VF20	XF40	MS60	MS63
AH1382	—	10.00	20.00	45.00	75.00	100

Y# A27 2 BUQSHA
4.91 g., Copper-Aluminum, 23 mm. **Obv:** Denomination within circle **Rev:** Leafy branch within wreath

Date	Mintage	F12	VF20	XF40	MS60	MS63
AH1382-1963	—	—	—	0.35	0.50	1.00

Y# 24.1 1/10 RIYAL (4 Buqsha)
0.720 Silver **Rev:** Three or four stones in top row of wall within circle **Note:** Thick variety, 2.40-3.00 grams

Date	Mintage	F12	VF20	XF40	MS60	MS63
AH1382	—	3.00	10.00	20.00	35.00	50.00

Y# 24.2 1/10 RIYAL (4 Buqsha)
0.720 Silver **Obv:** Denomination within circle **Rev:** Four stones in top row of wall within circle **Note:** Thin variety, 1.40-1.80 grams. Edge varieties, varying number of stones in wall, exist.

Date	Mintage	F12	VF20	XF40	MS60	MS63
AH1382	—	—	2.50	6.00	10.00	15.00

Y# 28 5 BUQSHA
0.720 Silver **Obv:** Denomination within circle **Rev:** Leafy branch within wreath, dates below **Mint:** Cairo

Date	Mintage	F12	VF20	XF40	MS60	MS63
AH1382-1963	1,600,000	—	—	0.50	1.00	1.50

Y# 25.1 2/10 RIYAL (8 Buqsha)

0.720 Silver **Obv:** Denomination within circle **Rev:** Tree and wall within circle **Note:** Thick variety, 5.80-6.50 grams.

Date	Mintage	F12	VF20	XF40	MS60	MS63
AH1382	—	10.00	20.00	35.00	70.00	125

Y# 25.2 2/10 RIYAL (8 Buqsha)

0.720 Silver **Obv:** Denomination within circle **Rev:** Tree and wall within circle **Note:** Thin variety, 4.90-5.10 grams.

Date	Mintage	F12	VF20	XF40	MS60	MS63
AH1382	—	—	60.00	125	200	250

Y# A25.1 1/4 RIYAL (10 Buqsha)

0.720 Silver **Obv:** Denomination within circle **Rev:** Tree and wall within circle **Note:** Thick variety, 6.00-7.30 grams.

Date	Mintage	F12	VF20	XF40	MS60	MS63
AH1382	—	250	500	900	1,250	1,750

Y# A25.2 1/4 RIYAL (10 Buqsha)

0.720 Silver **Obv:** Denomination within circle **Rev:** Tree and wall within circle **Note:** Thin variety, 4.00-4.60 grams. Overstrikes over earlier 1/4 Riyal coins exist.

Date	Mintage	F12	VF20	XF40	MS60	MS63
AH1382	—	250	500	900	1,250	1,750

Y# 29 10 BUQSHA

5.00 g., 0.720 Silver 0.1157 oz. ASW **Obv:** Denomination within circle **Rev:** Leafy branch within wreath

Date	Mintage	F12	VF20	XF40	MS60	MS63
AH1382-1963	1,024,000	—	—	2.50	3.00	4.50

Y# 30 20 BUQSHA

9.85 g., 0.720 Silver 0.228 oz. ASW **Obv:** Denomination within circle **Rev:** Leafy branch within wreath

Date	Mintage	F12	VF20	XF40	MS60	MS63
AH1382-1963	1,016,000	—	—	4.50	7.50	10.00

Y# 31 RIYAL

19.75 g., 0.720 Silver 0.4572 oz. ASW **Obv:** Denomination within wreath **Rev:** Leafy branch within wreath

Date	Mintage	F12	VF20	XF40	MS60	MS63
AH1382-1963	4,614,000	—	—	9.00	12.50	17.50

DECIMAL COINAGE

100 Fils = 1 Riyal/Rial

Y# 33 FILS

Aluminum **Obv:** National arms **Rev:** Denomination within circle

Date	Mintage	VF20	XF40	MS60	MS63	MS65
AH1394-1974	Est. 1000000	—	1.50	3.00	5.00	7.50
Note: It is doubtful that the entire mintage was released for circulation						
AH1394-1974	—	PF65 1.50				
AH1400-1980	10,000	PF65 1.50				

Y# 43 FILS

Aluminum **Series:** F.A.O. **Obv:** National arms **Rev:** Denomination within circle

Date	Mintage	VF20	XF40	MS60	MS63	MS65
AH1398-1978	7,050	—	1.00	1.50	3.00	5.00

Y# 34 5 FILS

2.75 g., Brass, 21 mm. **Obv:** National arms **Rev:** Denomination within circle

Date	Mintage	VF20	XF40	MS60	MS63	MS65
AH1394-1974	10,000,000	—	0.50	1.00	1.50	2.50
AH1394-1974	—	PF65 2.50				
AH1400-1980	—	PF65 2.00				

Y# 38 5 FILS

2.75 g., Brass, 21 mm. **Series:** F.A.O. **Obv:** National arms **Rev:** Denomination within circle

Date	Mintage	VF20	XF40	MS60	MS63	MS65
AH1394-1974	500,000	—	0.25	0.75	1.50	2.50

Y# 35 10 FILS

4.25 g., Brass, 23 mm. **Obv:** National arms **Rev:** Denomination within circle

Date	Mintage	VF20	XF40	MS60	MS63	MS65
AH1394-1974	20,000,000	—	0.25	0.50	1.00	1.50
AH1394-1974	—	PF65 2.50				
AH1400-1980	10,000	PF65 2.00				

Y# 39 10 FILS

4.25 g., Brass, 23 mm. **Series:** F.A.O. **Obv:** National arms **Rev:** Denomination within circle

Date	Mintage	VF20	XF40	MS60	MS63	MS65
AH1394-1974	200,000	—	0.25	0.75	1.50	2.50

Y# 36 25 FILS

3.00 g., Copper-Nickel, 20 mm. **Obv:** National arms **Rev:** Denomination within circle

Date	Mintage	VF20	XF40	MS60	MS63	MS65
AH1394-1974	15,000,000	—	0.25	0.50	1.00	1.50
AH1394-1974	—	PF65 3.00				
AH1399-1979	11,000,000	—	0.25	0.50	1.00	1.50
AH1400-1980	10,000	PF65 2.25				

Y# 40 25 FILS

3.00 g., Copper-Nickel, 20 mm. **Series:** F.A.O. **Obv:** National arms **Rev:** Denomination within circle

Date	Mintage	VF20	XF40	MS60	MS63	MS65
AH1394-1974	40,000	—	0.50	1.00	1.50	3.00

Y# 37 50 FILS

5.30 g., Copper-Nickel, 24 mm. **Obv:** National arms **Rev:** Denomination within circle

Date	Mintage	VF20	XF40	MS60	MS63	MS65
AH1394-1974	10,000,000	—	—	0.25	1.00	1.50
AH1394-1974	—	PF65 3.50				
AH1399-1979	4,000,000	—	—	0.25	1.00	1.50
AH1400-1980	10,000	PF65 2.50				
AH1405-1985	—	—	—	0.25	1.00	1.50

Y# 41 50 FILS

5.30 g., Copper-Nickel, 24 mm. **Series:** F.A.O. **Obv:** National arms **Rev:** Denomination within circle

Date	Mintage	VF20	XF40	MS60	MS63	MS65
AH1394-1974	25,000	—	0.50	1.00	1.50	3.00

KM# 1 RIYAL

12.00 g., 0.925 Silver 0.3569 oz. ASW **Subject:** Qadhi Mohammed Mahmud Azzubairi Memorial **Obv:** National arms **Rev:** Figure on camel right

Date	Mintage	VF20	XF40	MS60	MS63	MS65
1969	3,200	PF63 15.00	PF65 20.00			

KM# 1a RIYAL

20.48 g., 0.900 Gold 0.5926 oz. AGW **Subject:** Qadhi Mohammed Mahmud Azzubairi Memorial **Obv:** National arms **Rev:** Figure on camel right

Date	Mintage	F12	VF20	XF40	MS60	MS63
1969	100	PF65 1,125				

Y# 42 RIYAL
8.00 g., Copper-Nickel, 28 mm. **Obv:** National arms **Rev:** Denomination within circle

Date	Mintage	VF20	XF40	MS60	MS63	MS65
AH1396-1976	7,800,000	—	—	0.50	1.00	1.50
AH1400-1980	—	PF60 5.00				
AH1405-1985	—	—	—	0.50	1.00	1.50
AH1414-1993	—	—	—	0.50	1.00	1.50

Y# 44 RIYAL
8.00 g., Copper-Nickel, 28 mm. **Series:** F.A.O. **Obv:** National arms **Rev:** Denomination within circle

Date	Mintage	VF20	XF40	MS60	MS63	MS65
AH1398-1978	7,050	—	—	1.00	1.50	3.00

KM# 2.1 2 RIYALS
25.00 g., 0.925 Silver 0.7435 oz. ASW, 37 mm. **Subject:** Apollo II - Cape Kennedy **Obv:** Eagle with shield on breast and flags on legs **Rev:** Space shuttle and launch pad **Note:** Dotted border.

Date	Mintage	VF20	XF40	MS60	MS63	MS65
1969	7,583	—	—	20.00	25.00	27.00
1969	200	PF60 27.00	PF63 37.00	PF65 50.00		

KM# 2.2 2 RIYALS
25.00 g., 0.925 Silver 0.7435 oz. ASW, 37 mm. **Obv:** Eagle with shield on breast and flags on legs **Rev:** Space shuttle and launch pad **Note:** Border of dots near rim.

Date	Mintage	VF20	XF40	MS60	MS63	MS65
1969 Proof; restrike	1,000	PF60 17.00	PF63 22.00	PF65 27.00		

KM# 3.1 2 RIYALS
25.00 g., 0.925 Silver 0.7435 oz. ASW, 37 mm. **Subject:** Apollo II - Moon Landing **Obv:** Eagle with shield on breast and flags on legs **Rev:** Moon landing scene **Note:** Dotted border.

Date	Mintage	VF20	XF40	MS60	MS63	MS65
1969	7,583	—	—	17.00	22.00	27.00
1969	200	PF60 27.00	PF63 37.00	PF65 50.00		

KM# 3.2 2 RIYALS
25.00 g., 0.925 Silver 0.7435 oz. ASW, 37 mm. **Obv:** Eagle with shield on breast and flags on legs **Rev:** Moon landing scene **Note:** Border of dots near rim.

Date	Mintage	VF20	XF40	MS60	MS63	MS65
1969 Proof; restrike	1,000	PF60 17.00	PF63 22.00	PF65 27.00		

KM# 4 2 RIYALS
25.00 g., 0.925 Silver 0.7435 oz. ASW, 37 mm. **Subject:** Qadhi Mohammed Mahmud Azzubairi Memorial **Obv:** National arms **Rev:** Roaring lion's head 3/4 left

Date	Mintage	VF20	XF40	MS60	MS63	MS65
1969	4,200	PF60 20.00	PF63 30.00	PF65 35.00		

KM# 4a 2 RIYALS
42.29 g., 0.900 Gold 1.2237 oz. AGW, 37 mm. **Subject:** Qadhi Mohammed Mahmud Azzubairi Memorial **Obv:** National arms **Rev:** Roaring lion's head 3/4 left

Date	Mintage	F12	VF20	XF40	MS60	MS63
1969	100	PF65 2,250				

KM# 14 2-1/2 RIYALS
9.00 g., 0.925 Silver 0.2677 oz. ASW **Subject:** Oil Exploration **Obv:** National arms **Rev:** Oil derricks in field

Date	Mintage	VF20	XF40	MS60	MS63	MS65
AH1395-1975	Est. 205000	—	—	10.00	12.00	15.00
AH1395-1975	Est. 5000	PF60 15.00	PF63 18.00	PF65 22.00		

KM# 6 5 RIYALS/RIALS
4.90 g., 0.900 Gold 0.1418 oz. AGW **Subject:** Qadhi Mohammed Mahmud Azzubairi Memorial **Obv:** Monument **Rev:** Denomination within circle

Date	Mintage	VF20	XF40	MS60	MS63	MS65
1969	—	PF63 260	PF65 280			

KM# 15 5 RIYALS/RIALS
18.00 g., 0.925 Silver 0.5353 oz. ASW **Subject:** Mona Lisa **Rev:** Mona Lisa within center box, chain with ornaments surrounds

Date	Mintage	VF20	XF40	MS60	MS63	MS65
AH1395-1975	235,000	—	—	12.00	15.00	20.00
AH1395-1975	5,000	PF60 20.00	PF63 25.00	PF65 35.00		

KM# 7 10 RIYALS/RIALS
9.80 g., 0.900 Gold 0.2836 oz. AGW **Subject:** Qadhi Mohammed Mahmud Azzubairi Memorial **Obv:** National arms **Rev:** Three gazelles leaping right

Date	Mintage	VF20	XF40	MS60	MS63	MS65
1969	—	PF63 500	PF65 550			

KM# 23 10 RIYALS/RIALS
12.08 g., 0.925 Silver 0.3593 oz. ASW **Obv:** Camel with rider right **Rev:** National arms **Note:** Mule.

Date	Mintage	VF20	XF40	MS60	MS63	MS65
1969	—	PF60 25.00	PF63 35.00	PF65 45.00		

KM# 16 10 RIYALS/RIALS
36.00 g., 0.925 Silver 1.0706 oz. ASW **Series:** Montreal Olympics **Obv:** National arms **Rev:** Olympic events surround central flame

Date	Mintage	VF20	XF40	MS60	MS63	MS65
AH1395-1975	8,000	—	—	30.00	50.00	70.00
AH1395-1975	4,000	PF60 65.00	PF63 110	PF65 140		

KM# 28 10 RIYALS/RIALS
35.90 g., 0.925 Silver 1.0676 oz. ASW, 45.6 mm. **Subject:** Montreal Olympics **Obv:** National arms **Rev:** Olympic events surround central flame **Edge:** Plain **Mint:** Numismatica Italiana

Date	Mintage	VF20	XF40	MS60	MS63	MS65
AH1395-1975	100	PF63 200	PF65 300			

KM# 17 15 RIALS
54.00 g., 0.925 Silver 1.6059 oz. ASW **Subject:** Jerusalem **Rev:** Domed buildings

Date	Mintage	VF20	XF40	MS60	MS63	MS65
AH1395-1975	70,000	—	—	30.00	40.00	55.00
AH1395-1975	5,000	PF60 70.00	PF63 90.00	PF65 120		

KM# 8 20 RIYALS/RIALS
19.60 g., 0.900 Gold 0.5671 oz. AGW **Subject:** Apollo II - Moon Landing **Obv:** Eagle with shield on breast and flags on legs **Rev:** Capsule above astronauts on moon's surface

Date	Mintage	VF20	XF40	MS60	MS63	MS65
1969	—	PF63 1,000	PF65 1,100			

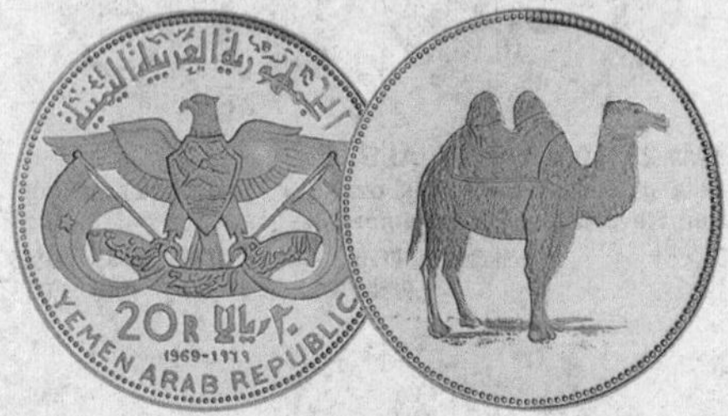

KM# 9 20 RIYALS/RIALS
19.60 g., 0.900 Gold 0.5671 oz. AGW **Subject:** Qadhi Mohammed Mahmud Azzubairi Memorial **Obv:** National arms **Rev:** Camel facing right

Date	Mintage	VF20	XF40	MS60	MS63	MS65
1969	—	PF63 1,000	PF65 1,100			

KM# 18 20 RIYALS/RIALS
0.900 Gold **Subject:** Albakiriah Mosque **Rev:** Mosque within oval **Shape:** Octagon

Date	Mintage	VF20	XF40	MS60	MS63	MS65
AH1395-1975	—	—	—	—	450	475
AH1395-1975	3,500	PF63 500	PF65 525			

KM# 19 25 RIYALS/RIALS
0.900 Gold **Subject:** Oil Exploration **Obv:** National arms within rounded square **Rev:** Oil derricks in field, rounded square surrounds

Date	Mintage	VF20	XF40	MS60	MS63	MS65
AH1395-1975	—	—	—	—	450	475
AH1395-1975	3,500	PF63 500	PF65 525			

Y# 46 25 RIYALS/RIALS
28.28 g., 0.925 Silver 0.841 oz. ASW **Series:** International Year of the Disabled Person **Obv:** National arms **Rev:** Head right

Date	Mintage	VF20	XF40	MS60	MS63	MS65
AH1401-1981	10,000	—	—	25.00	30.00	35.00
AH1401-1981	Est. 10000	PF60 25.00	PF63 35.00	PF65 45.00		

Y# 47 25 RIYALS/RIALS
28.28 g., 0.925 Silver 0.841 oz. ASW **Subject:** 20th Anniversary of the Revolution

Date	Mintage	VF20	XF40	MS60	MS63	MS65
AH1402-1982	2,000	PF60 35.00	PF63 45.00	PF65 55.00		

Y# 45 25 RIYALS/RIALS
28.25 g., 0.925 Silver 0.8401 oz. ASW **Series:** International Year of the Child **Obv:** National arms within wreath of leaves **Rev:** Children dancing, logos flank

Date	Mintage	VF20	XF40	MS60	MS63	MS65
AH1403-1983	6,604	PF60 22.00	PF63 25.00	PF65 30.00		

Y# 49 25 RIYALS/RIALS
28.25 g., 0.925 Silver 0.8401 oz. ASW **Series:** Decade for Women **Obv:** National arms within wreath of leaves **Rev:** Three half-figures of women looking left, ankh on dove cutout at left

Date	Mintage	VF20	XF40	MS60	MS63	MS65
AH1405-1985	1,000	PF60 30.00	PF63 40.00	PF65 55.00		

KM# 10 30 RIYALS
29.40 g., 0.900 Gold 0.8507 oz. AGW **Subject:** Qadhi Mohammed Mahmud Azzubairi Memorial **Obv:** National arms **Rev:** Head 3/4 right

Date	Mintage	VF20	XF40	MS60	MS63	MS65
1969	—	PF63 1,450	PF65 1,600			

KM# 11 50 RIYALS/RIALS
49.97 g., Silver **Subject:** Qadhi Mohammed Mahmud Azzubairi Memorial **Obv:** National arms **Rev:** Lion standing right, facing front

Date	Mintage	VF20	XF40	MS60	MS63	MS65
1969 Proof; restrike	—	PF60 35.00	PF63 50.00	PF65 65.00		

KM# 11a 50 RIYALS/RIALS
49.00 g., 0.900 Gold 1.4178 oz. AGW **Subject:** Qadhi Mohammed Mahmud Azzubairi Memorial **Obv:** National arms above dates and denomination **Rev:** Lion standing right, facing front

Date	Mintage	F12	VF20	XF40	MS60	MS63
1969	—	PF63 2,400	PF65 2,600			

KM# 20 50 RIYALS/RIALS
9.10 g., 0.900 Gold 0.2633 oz. AGW **Subject:** Mona Lisa **Rev:** Mona Lisa within box, chain with ornaments surrounds

Date	Mintage	VF20	XF40	MS60	MS63	MS65
AH1395-1975	—	—	—	—	500	525
AH1395-1975	3,500	PF63 525	PF65 550			

KM# 21 75 RIYALS
13.65 g., 0.900 Gold 0.395 oz. AGW **Series:** Montreal Olympics **Obv:** Arms **Rev:** XXI Olympiad

Date	Mintage	VF20	XF40	MS60	MS63	MS65
AH1395-1975	—	—	—	—	780	800
AH1395-1975	3,500	PF63 800	PF65 820			

KM# 22 100 RIALS
18.20 g., 0.900 Gold 0.5266 oz. AGW **Obv:** National arms **Rev:** Domed buildings

Date	Mintage	VF20	XF40	MS60	MS63	MS65
AH1395-1975	—	—	—	—	1,000	1,100
AH1395-1975	3,500	PF63 1,100	PF65 1,200			

KM# 24 500 RIYALS/RIALS
15.98 g., 0.917 Gold 0.4711 oz. AGW **Series:** International Year of the Disabled Person **Obv:** National arms **Rev:** Head of Bolivar facing, tiny logos flank below

Date	Mintage	VF20	XF40	MS60	MS63	MS65
AH1401-1981	—	—	—	—	1,000	1,100
AH1401-1981	—	PF63 1,100	PF65 1,200			

Y# 48 500 RIYALS/RIALS
15.90 g., 0.917 Gold 0.4688 oz. AGW **Subject:** 20th Anniversary of the Revolution **Rev:** Ship within small center circle, figures above, oil derrick at left, grain sprig at right, circle surrounds all

Date	Mintage	VF20	XF40	MS60	MS63	MS65
AH1402-1982	1,000	PF60 850	PF63 950	PF65 1,000		

ESSAIS

KM#	Date	Mintage	Identification	Mkt Val
E1	AH1385 (1965)	500	Rial. 0.720. Silver.	60.00

PIEDFORT

KM#	Date	Mintage	Identification	Mkt Val
P1	1981	1,150	25 Riyals/Rials. Silver. I.Y.D.P.; Y#46.	150
P2	1981	—	500 Riyals/Rials. Gold. I.Y.P.D.; KM#24.	1,750
P3	1983	—	25 Riyals/Rials. 0.925. Silver. Arms, legend, date. Children. I.Y.C.; Y#45.	200

TRIAL STRIKES

KM#	Date	Mintage	Identification	Mkt Val
TS1	1975	—	100 Rials. Goldine. Uniface; national arms divide dates, denomination below.	—

MINT SETS

KM#	Date	Mintage	Identification	Issue Price	Mkt Val
MS1	1975 (4)	—	KM#14-17	50.00	150
MS2	1975 (5)	—	KM#18-22	360	3,375

PROOF SETS

KM#	Date	Mintage	Identification	Issue Price	Mkt Val
PS1	1969 (7)	2,000	KM#1, 4, 6, 7, 9-10, 11a	375	6,200
PS2	1969 (4)	1,500	KM#1, 2.1-3.1, 4	—	85.00
PS4	1969 (3)	—	KM#2.1, 3.1, 6	78.00	410
PS5	1974 (5)	5,024	Y#33-37	15.00	10.00
PS6	1975 (5)	3,500	KM#18-22	485	3,375
PS7	1975 (4)	5,000	KM#14-17	75.00	125
PS8	1980 (6)	10,000	Y#33-37, 42	31.00	15.00

YEMEN EASTERN ADEN PROTECTORATE

Between 1200 B.C. and the 6th century A.D., what is now the Peoples Democratic Republic of Yemen was part of the Minaean kingdom. In subsequent years it was controlled by Persians, Egyptians and Turks. Aden, one of the cities mentioned in the Bible, had been a port for trade between the East and West for 2,000 years. British rule began in 1839 when the British East India Co. seized control to put an end to the piracy threatening trade with India. To protect their foothold in Aden, the British found it necessary to extend their control into the area known historically as the Hadhramaut, and to sign protection treaties with the sheiks of the hinterland.

QUATI STATE OF HADRAMAUT

GHURFAH

A city sultanate of Eastern Aden Protectorate was an oasis settlement located in the Hadhramaut Wadi region of southern Arabia.

TITLES
al-Gurfah

RULERS
Saleh 'Ubayd bin Abdat, AH1339-1358/1920-1939AD
Ubayd bin Saleh bin Abdat, AH1358-1365/1939-1945AD

NOTE: The Arabic *129* in the obv. legend is an anagram for Saleh.

MINT

الغرفه

Ghurfah

Saleh 'Ubayd bin Abdat
AH1339-1358 / 1920-1939AD

STANDARD COINAGE

KM# 101 4 KHUMSI
0.65 g., 0.900 Silver 0.0188 oz. ASW, 11.5 mm. **Obv:** Legend within circle and wreath **Rev:** Value within circle and wreath **Note:** Prev. KM#1.

Date	Mintage	F12	VF20	XF40	MS60	MS63
AH1344	5,000	50.00	100	200	350	400

KM# 102 8 KHUMSI
1.10 g., 0.900 Silver 0.0318 oz. ASW, 14 mm. **Obv:** Legend within circle and wreath **Rev:** Value within circle and wreath **Note:** Prev. KM#2.

Date	Mintage	F12	VF20	XF40	MS60	MS63
AH1344	5,000	27.50	37.50	75.00	150	200

KM# 103 15 KHUMSI
2.00 g., 0.900 Silver 0.0579 oz. ASW, 18 mm. **Obv:** Legend within circle and wreath **Rev:** Value within circle and wreath **Note:** Prev. KM#3.

Date	Mintage	F12	VF20	XF40	MS60	MS63
AH1344	10,000	10.00	15.00	60.00	125	175

KM# 104 30 KHUMSI
3.95 g., 0.900 Silver 0.1143 oz. ASW, 22 mm. **Obv:** Legend within circle and wreath **Rev:** Value within circle and wreath **Note:** Prev. KM#4.

Date	Mintage	F12	VF20	XF40	MS60	MS63
AH1344	10,000	15.00	22.50	90.00	175	250

KM# 105 45 KHUMSI
5.90 g., 0.900 Silver 0.1707 oz. ASW, 24.5 mm. **Obv:** Legend within circle and wreath **Rev:** Value within circle and wreath **Note:** Prev. KM#5.

Date	Mintage	F12	VF20	XF40	MS60	MS63
AH1344	10,000	175	350	750	1,250	1,600

KM# 106 60 KHUMSI
7.80 g., 0.900 Silver 0.2257 oz. ASW, 27 mm. **Obv:** Legend within circle and wreath **Rev:** Value within circle and wreath **Note:** Prev. KM#6.

Date	Mintage	F12	VF20	XF40	MS60	MS63
AH1344	10,000	37.50	55.00	225	425	500

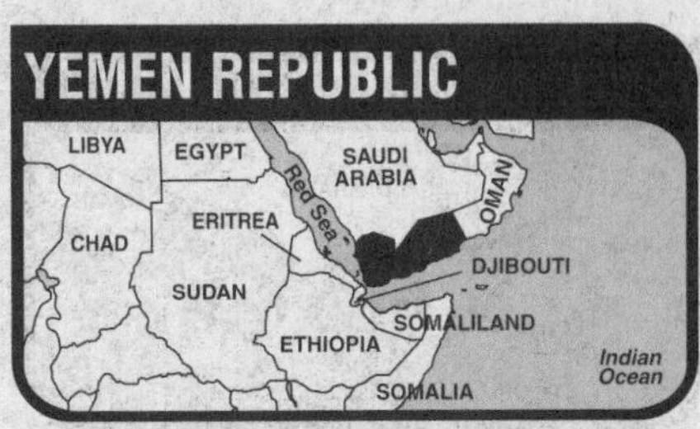

The Republic of Yemen, formerly Yemen Arab Republic and Peoples Democratic Republic of Yemen, is located on the southern coast of the Arabian Peninsula. It has an area of 205,020 sq. mi. (531,000 sq. km.) and a population of 12 million. Capital: San'a. The port of Aden is the main commercial center and the area's most valuable natural resource. Recent oil and gas finds and a developing petroleum industry have improved their economic prospects. Agriculture and local handicrafts are the main industries. Cotton, fish, coffee, rock salt and hides are exported.

On May 22, 1990, the Yemen Arab Republic (North Yemen) and Peoples Democratic Republic of Yemen (South Yemen) merged into a unified Republic of Yemen. Disagreements between the two former governments simmered until civil war erupted in 1994, with the northern forces of the old Yemen Arab Republic eventually prevailing.

TITLE

دار الخلافة

Dar al-Khilafa(t)

REPUBLIC

MILLED COINAGE

KM# 25 RIYAL
2.65 g., Stainless Steel, 19.95 mm. **Obv:** Denomination within circle **Rev:** National arms **Edge:** Multi-sided **Shape:** 21-sided

Date	Mintage	VF20	XF40	MS60	MS63	MS65
AH1414-1993	—	—	—	0.35	0.75	1.00

KM# 26 5 RIYALS
4.50 g., Stainless Steel, 22.9 mm. **Obv:** Denomination within circle **Rev:** Building **Shape:** 21-sided

Date	Mintage	VF20	XF40	MS60	MS63	MS65
AH1414-1993	—	—	—	0.35	0.75	1.00
AH1420-2000	—	—	—	0.35	0.75	1.00

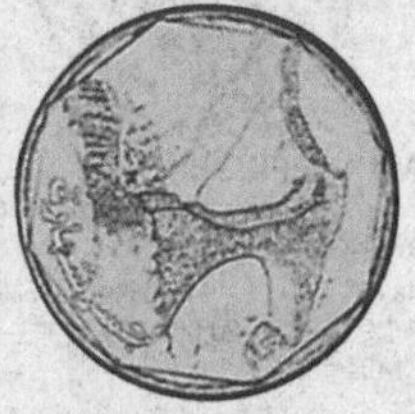

KM# 27 10 RIYALS
6.05 g., Stainless Steel, 26 mm. **Obv:** Denomination within circle **Rev:** Bridge at Shaharah

Date	Mintage	VF20	XF40	MS60	MS63	MS65
AH1416-1995	—	—	—	0.50	1.00	1.50

YEMEN, DEMOCRATIC REPUBLIC

SAUDI ARABIA
OMAN
SUDAN
Red Sea
(ARAB)
(DEMOCRATIC)
ERITREA
Arabian Sea
ETHIOPIA
DJIBOUTI

The southeast region of present day Yemen was predominately controlled by the British since their occupation of Aden in 1839. Independence was declared November 30, 1967 after the collapse of the Federation of South Arabia and the withdrawal of the British.

TITLES

Al-Jumhuriya(t) al-Yamaniya(t)
ad-Dimiqratiya(t) ash-Sha'biya(t)

MONETARY SYSTEM

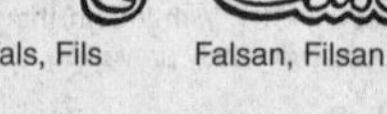

Falus, Fulus — Fals, Fils — Falsan, Filsan

1000 Fils = 1 Dinar

PEOPLES DEMOCRATIC REPUBLIC

DECIMAL COINAGE

KM# 3 2-1/2 FILS
0.65 g., Aluminum, 17 mm. **Obv:** Denomination and dates **Rev:** Cotton plant

Date	Mintage	VF20	XF40	MS60	MS63	MS65
AH1393-1973	20,000,000	—	0.25	0.35	0.50	1.00

KM# 2 5 FILS
1.35 g., Bronze, 23.1 mm. **Obv:** 8-sided star design **Rev:** Crossed daggers

Date	Mintage	VF20	XF40	MS60	MS63	MS65
1971	2,000,000	—	0.25	0.35	0.50	1.00

KM# 4 5 FILS
1.35 g., Aluminum, 23.1 mm. **Obv:** Denomination and dates **Rev:** Spiny lobster

Date	Mintage	VF20	XF40	MS60	MS63	MS65
AH1393-1973	20,000,000	—	0.25	0.35	0.50	1.00
AH1404-1984	—	—	0.25	0.35	0.50	1.00

KM# 9 10 FILS
2.20 g., Aluminum, 25.6 mm. **Obv:** Monument **Rev:** Denomination within circle **Shape:** Scallop

Date	Mintage	VF20	XF40	MS60	MS63	MS65
1981	—	—	0.25	0.50	1.00	2.00

KM# 5 25 FILS
4.55 g., Copper-Nickel, 20 mm. **Obv:** 8-sided star design **Rev:** Dhow

Date	Mintage	VF20	XF40	MS60	MS63	MS65
1976	2,000,000	—	0.25	0.50	1.00	2.00
1977	1,000,000	—	0.25	0.50	1.00	2.00
1979	—	—	0.25	0.50	1.00	2.00
1982	—	—	0.25	0.50	1.00	2.00
1984	—	—	0.25	0.50	1.00	2.00

KM# 6 50 FILS
9.10 g., Copper-Nickel, 27.8 mm. **Obv:** 8-sided star design **Rev:** Dhow

Date	Mintage	VF20	XF40	MS60	MS63	MS65
1976	2,000,000	—	0.45	0.65	1.25	3.00
1977	2,000,000	—	0.45	0.65	1.25	3.00
1979	—	—	0.45	0.65	1.25	3.00
1984	—	—	0.45	0.65	1.25	3.00

KM# 10 100 FILS
10.00 g., Copper-Nickel, 23.1 mm. **Obv:** Monument **Rev:** Denomination within circle **Shape:** 8-sided

Date	Mintage	VF20	XF40	MS60	MS63	MS65
1981	—	—	0.25	0.75	1.50	3.50

KM# 7 250 FILS
11.20 g., Copper-Nickel, 31 mm. **Subject:** 10th Anniversary of Independence **Obv:** Monument **Rev:** Ship at sea with date below

Date	Mintage	VF20	XF40	MS60	MS63	MS65
1977	30,000	1.50	2.50	4.50	7.50	12.00

KM# 11 250 FILS
11.20 g., Copper-Nickel, 31 mm. **Obv:** Monument **Rev:** Denomination within circle

Date	Mintage	VF20	XF40	MS60	MS63	MS65
1981	—	0.50	1.00	2.00	3.50	5.00

KM# 12 2 DINARS
28.28 g., 0.925 Silver 0.841 oz. ASW **Subject:** International Year of Disabled Persons - Abdulla Baradoni **Obv:** Head right **Rev:** Triangular design within wreath divides date

Date	Mintage	VF20	XF40	MS60	MS63	MS65
1981	10,000	—	—	—	30.00	35.00
1981	10,000	PF65 30.00				

KM# 8 5 DINARS
12.50 g., 0.925 Silver 0.3717 oz. ASW **Subject:** 10th Anniversary of Independence **Obv:** Monument **Rev:** Ship at sea with date below

Date	Mintage	VF20	XF40	MS60	MS63	MS65
1977	6,000	PF65 40.00				

KM# 13 50 DINARS
15.98 g., 0.917 Gold 0.4711 oz. AGW **Series:** International Year of Disabled Persons **Obv:** National arms **Rev:** Triangular design within wreath divides date

Date	Mintage	VF20	XF40	MS60	MS63	MS65
1981	2,100	—	—	—	900	925
1981	1,100	PF65 950				

PIEDFORT

KM#	Date	Mintage	Identification	Mkt Val
P1	1981	1,050	2 Dinars. Silver. KM#12..	200
P1	1981	500	50 Dinars. Gold. KM#13..	1,850

The Federal Republic of Yugoslavia, formerly the Socialist Federal Republic of Yugoslavia, a Balkan country located on the east shore of the Adriatic Sea, has an area of 39,450 sq. mi. (102,173 sq. km.) and a population of 10.5 million. Capital: Belgrade. The chief industries area agriculture, mining, manufacturing and tourism. Machinery, nonferrous metals, meat and fabrics are exported.

Yugoslavia was proclaimed on Dec. 1, 1918, after the union of the Kingdom of Serbia, Montenegro and the South Slav territories of Austria-Hungary; and changed its official name from the Kingdom of the Serbs, Croats and Slovenes to the Kingdom of Yugoslavia on Oct. 3, 1929.The republic was composed of six autonomous republics -Serbia, Croatia, Slovenia, Bosnia-Herzegovina, Macedonia and Montenegro - and two autonomous provinces within Serbia: Kosovo-Melohija and Vojvodina. The government of Yugoslavia attempted to remain neutral in World War II but, yielding to German pressure, aligned itself with the Axis powers in March of 1941; a few days later it was overthrown by revolutionary forces and its neutrality reasserted. The Nazis occupied the country on April 6, and throughout the remaining war years were resisted by a number of guerrilla armies, notably that of Marshal Josip Broz Tito. After the defeat of the Axis powers, a leftist coalition headed by Tito abolished the monarchy and, on Jan. 31, 1946, established a "People's Republic". The collapse of the Federal Republic during 1991-1992 has resulted in the autonomous republics of Croatia, Slovenia, Bosnia-Herzegovina and Macedonia declaring their respective independence. Bosnia-Herzegovina is under military contest with the Serbian, Croat and Muslim populace opposing each other. Besides the remainder of the older Serbian sectors, a Serbian enclave in Knin located in southern Croatia has emerged called REPUBLIKE SRPSKEKRAJINE or Serbian Republic - Krajina whose capital is Knin and has also declared its independence in1992 when the former Republics of Serbia and Montenegro became the Federal Republic of Yugoslavia.

The name Yugoslavia appears on the coinage in letters of the Cyrillic alphabet alone until formation of the Federated Peoples Republic of Yugoslavia in 1953, after which both the Cyrillic and Latin alphabets are employed. From 1965, the coin denomination appears in the 4 different languages of the federated republics in letters of both the Cyrillic and Latin alphabets.

DENOMINATIONS

Para ÏÀÐÀ
Dinar, ÄÈÍÀÐ, Dinara ÄÈÍÀÐÀ
Dinari ÄÈÍÀÐÈ, Dinarjev

RULERS

Petar I, 1918-1921
Alexander I, 1921-1934
Petar II, 1934-1945

MINT MARKS

(a) - Paris, privy marks only
(b) - Brussels
(k) - Kovnica, A.D.
(Akcionarno Drustvo) Belgrade
(l) - London
(p) - Poissy (thunderbolt)
(v) – Vienna

MONETARY SYSTEM

100 Para = 1 Dinar

KINGDOM OF THE SERBS, CROATS AND SLOVENES

STANDARD COINAGE

KM# 1 5 PARA
Zinc, 18.8 mm. **Ruler:** Petar I **Obv:** Crowned and mantled arms on shield **Rev:** Denomination above date **Edge:** Plain

Date	Mintage	F12	VF20	XF40	MS60	MS63
1920 (v)	3,825,514	2.00	4.00	7.00	22.00	45.00

KM# 2 10 PARA
Zinc, 20.85 mm. **Ruler:** Petar I **Obv:** Crowned and mantled arms on shield **Rev:** Denomination above date **Edge:** Plain

Date	Mintage	F12	VF20	XF40	MS60	MS63
1920 (v)	58,946,122	1.50	3.50	5.00	15.00	25.00

KM# 3 25 PARA
Nickel-Bronze, 24 mm. **Ruler:** Petar I **Obv:** Crowned and mantled arms on shield **Rev:** Denomination above date **Edge:** Plain

Date	Mintage	F12	VF20	XF40	MS60	MS63
1920 (v)	48,173,138	1.50	3.50	5.00	15.00	35.00

KM# 4 50 PARA
Nickel-Bronze, 18 mm. **Ruler:** Alexander I **Obv:** Head left **Rev:** Denomination and date within crowned wreath **Edge:** Milled **Note:** Mint mark: lightning bolt.

Date	Mintage	VF20	XF40	MS60	MS63	MS65
1925 (b)	24,500,000	1.00	2.00	4.00	8.00	12.00
1925 (p)	25,000,000	1.50	3.00	5.00	10.00	15.00

KM# 5 DINAR
4.92 g., Nickel-Bronze, 23 mm. **Ruler:** Alexander I **Obv:** Head left **Rev:** Denomination and date within crowned wreath **Edge:** Milled **Note:** Mint mark: lightning bolt.

Date	Mintage	VF20	XF40	MS60	MS63	MS65
1925	37,000,000	1.00	2.50	4.50	9.00	14.00
1925	37,500,410	1.50	3.00	5.00	10.00	15.00

KM# 6 2 DINARA
Nickel-Bronze, 27 mm. **Ruler:** Alexander I **Obv:** Head left **Rev:** Denomination and date within crowned wreath **Edge:** Milled **Note:** Mint mark: lightning bolt.

Date	Mintage	VF20	XF40	MS60	MS63	MS65
1925 (b)	29,500,000	2.00	5.00	8.00	16.00	22.00
1925 (p)	25,004,177	2.50	6.00	9.00	18.00	25.00

KM# 7 20 DINARA
6.45 g., 0.900 Gold 0.1867 oz. AGW, 21 mm. **Ruler:** Alexander I **Obv:** Head left **Rev:** Denomination and date within crowned wreath **Edge:** Milled

Date	Mintage	VF20	XF40	MS60	MS63	MS65
1925	1,000,000	260	285	335	425	495
1925 Proof	—	—	—	—	—	—

KINGDOM OF YUGOSLAVIA

KM# 17 25 PARA
Bronze, 20 mm. **Ruler:** Petar II **Obv:** Center hole within crowned wreath **Rev:** Center hole divides denomination **Edge:** Plain **Note:** 4 mm hole in center of coin.

Date	Mintage	VF20	XF40	MS60	MS63	MS65
1938	40,000,000	2.50	5.50	8.00	12.00	14.00
1938 Proof	—	—	—	—	—	—

KM# 18 50 PARA
Aluminum-Bronze, 18 mm. **Ruler:** Petar II **Obv:** Crown **Rev:** Denomination above date **Edge:** Plain

Date	Mintage	VF20	XF40	MS60	MS63	MS65
1938	100,000,000	1.00	2.00	3.50	5.00	7.50

KM# 19 DINAR
Aluminum-Bronze, 21 mm. **Ruler:** Petar II **Obv:** Crown **Rev:** Denomination above date **Edge:** Plain

Date	Mintage	VF20	XF40	MS60	MS63	MS65
1938	100,000,000	0.75	1.25	2.00	4.00	6.00
1938 Proof	—	—	—	—	—	—

KM# 20 2 DINARA
5.10 g., Aluminum-Bronze, 24.5 mm. **Ruler:** Petar II **Obv:** Crown **Rev:** Denomination above date, large numeral **Edge:** Plain

Date	Mintage	VF20	XF40	MS60	MS63	MS65
1938	74,250,000	1.00	2.00	3.50	5.00	9.00
1938 Proof	—	—	—	—	—	—

KM# 21 2 DINARA
Aluminum-Bronze, 24.5 mm. **Ruler:** Petar II **Obv:** 12 mm crown **Rev:** Denomination above date, large numeral **Edge:** Plain

Date	Mintage	VF20	XF40	MS60	MS63	MS65
1938	750,000	6.00	10.00	15.00	22.00	38.00
1938 Proof	—	—	—	—	—	—

KM# 10 10 DINARA
7.00 g., 0.500 Silver 0.1125 oz. ASW, 25 mm. **Ruler:** Alexander I **Obv:** Head left **Rev:** Crowned double eagle with shield on breast **Edge:** Reeded

Date	Mintage	VF20	XF40	MS60	MS63	MS65
1931 (l)	19,000,000	6.50	9.00	12.00	16.00	22.00
1931 (l) Proof	—	—	—	—	—	—
1931 (a)	4,000,000	7.00	10.00	14.00	20.00	35.00
1931 (a) Proof	—	—	—	—	—	—

KM# 22 10 DINARA
5.00 g., Nickel, 23 mm. **Ruler:** Petar II **Obv:** Head right **Rev:** Denomination and date within crowned wreath **Edge:** Reeded

Date	Mintage	VF20	XF40	MS60	MS63	MS65
1938	25,000,000	0.75	1.00	1.50	2.50	5.00

KM# 11 20 DINARA
14.00 g., 0.500 Silver 0.2251 oz. ASW, 31 mm. **Ruler:** Alexander I **Obv:** Head left **Rev:** Crowned double eagle with shield on breast **Edge:** Milled

Date	Mintage	VF20	XF40	MS60	MS63	MS65
1931 (k)	12,500,000	7.00	10.00	14.00	20.00	35.00
1931 (k) Proof	—	—	—	—	—	—

KM# 23 20 DINARA
9.00 g., 0.750 Silver 0.217 oz. ASW, 27 mm. **Ruler:** Petar II **Obv:** Head left **Rev:** Crowned double eagle with shield on breast **Edge Lettering:** BOG CUVA JUGOSLAVIJU ***

Date	Mintage	VF20	XF40	MS60	MS63	MS65
1938	15,000,000	5.00	8.00	10.00	15.00	20.00

KM# 16 50 DINARA
23.33 g., 0.750 Silver 0.5626 oz. ASW, 36 mm. **Ruler:** Alexander I **Obv:** Head left **Rev:** Crowned double eagle with shield on breast **Edge Lettering:** BOG CUVA JUGOSLAVIJU **Note:** Also known without the signature under the head.

Date	Mintage	VF20	XF40	MS60	MS63	MS65
1932 (k)	5,500,000	25.00	35.00	55.00	100	175
1932 (l)	5,500,000	27.50	40.00	60.00	125	200
1932 (l)	—	PF63 2,200				

KM# 24 50 DINARA
15.00 g., 0.750 Silver 0.3617 oz. ASW, 31 mm. **Ruler:** Petar II **Obv:** Head right **Rev:** Crowned double eagle with shield on breast

Date	Mintage	VF20	XF40	MS60	MS63	MS65
1938	10,000,000	7.00	12.50	15.00	20.00	30.00

TRADE COINAGE

Trade-coinage countermarks were applied by the Yugoslav Control Office for Noble Metals to confirm gold purity. The initial countermark displayed a sword, but part way through the first production year, this was retired and the second countermark, showing an ear of corn, was used.

KM# 12.1 DUKAT
3.49 g., 0.986 Gold 0.1106 oz. AGW **Ruler:** Alexander I **Obv:** Head left, small legend with КОВНИА, А.Д. below head **Rev:** Crowned double eagle with shield on breast **Edge:** Milled **Countermark:** Birds

CM Date	Host Date	F12	VF20	XF40	MS60	MS63
(k)	1931	—	—	200	245	320
(k)	1932 Rare	—	—	—	—	—

Note: The 1932(k) examples with sword countermark are believed to be mint sports

KM# 12.2 DUKAT
3.49 g., 0.986 Gold 0.1106 oz. AGW **Ruler:** Alexander I **Obv:** Head left **Rev:** Crowned double eagle with shield on breast **Countermark:** Ear of corn **Note:** Forgeries bearing no countermark exist for 1932 and possibly other dates. Small legend on both sides

CM Date	Host Date	F12	VF20	XF40	MS60	MS63
(k)	1931	—	—	200	245	320
(k)	1932	—	—	200	245	320
(k)	1933	—	—	—	350	550
(k)	1934	—	—	1,500	2,000	3,200

KM# 12.3 DUKAT
3.49 g., 0.986 Gold 0.1106 oz. AGW **Ruler:** Alexander I **Obv:** Head left **Rev:** Crowned double eagle with shield on breast **Countermark:** Sword **Note:** Mule.

CM Date	Host Date	F12	VF20	XF40	MS60	MS63
(k)	1931	—	—	—	3,000	5,500

KM# 13.1 DUKAT
3.49 g., 0.986 Gold 0.1106 oz. AGW **Ruler:** Alexander I **Obv:** Head left **Rev:** Crowned double eagle with shield on breast **Note:** Large legend on both sides.

Date	Mintage	F12	VF20	XF40	MS60	MS63
1931 (k)	2,869	—	—	—	3,500	6,000

KM# 13.2 DUKAT
3.49 g., 0.986 Gold 0.1106 oz. AGW **Ruler:** Alexander I **Obv:** Head left **Rev:** Crowned double eagle with shield on breast **Countermark:** Sword **Note:** Large-letter varieties bear the Kovnica, A.D. mint mark but were actually struck in Vienna.

CM Date	Host Date	F12	VF20	XF40	MS60	MS63
(k)	1931	—	—	—	4,000	6,500

KM# 14.1 4 DUKATA
13.96 g., 0.986 Gold 0.4425 oz. AGW **Ruler:** Alexander I **Obv:** Conjoined busts of royal couple left **Rev:** Crowned double eagle with shield on breast **Edge:** Milled **Countermark:** Sword **Note:** Small legend on both sides. The 1932(k) examples with birds countermark are believed to be mint sports.

CM Date	Host Date	F12	VF20	XF40	MS60	MS63
(k)	1931	—	—	850	1,250	1,750
(k)	1932 Rare	—	—	—	—	—

KM# 14.2 4 DUKATA
13.96 g., 0.986 Gold 0.4425 oz. AGW **Ruler:** Alexander I **Obv:** Conjoined busts of royal couple left **Rev:** Crowned double eagle with shield on breast **Countermark:** Ear of corn

CM Date	Host Date	F12	VF20	XF40	MS60	MS63
(k)	1931	—	—	850	1,250	1,750
(k)	1932	—	—	850	1,350	1,950
(k)	1933	—	—	2,500	5,000	7,000

KM# 14.3 4 DUKATA
13.96 g., 0.986 Gold 0.4425 oz. AGW **Ruler:** Alexander I **Obv:** Conjoined busts of royal couple left **Rev:** Crowned double eagle with shield on breast **Note:** Without countermark on either side. Only one genuine piece has been reported.

Date	Mintage	F12	VF20	XF40	MS60	MS63
1931 (k) Rare	—	—	—	—	—	—

KM# A15.1 4 DUKATA
13.96 g., 0.986 Gold 0.4425 oz. AGW **Ruler:** Alexander I **Obv:** Conjoined busts of royal couple left **Rev:** Crowned double eagle with shield on breast **Note:** Large legend on both sides. Sword Countermark.

Date	Mintage	F12	VF20	XF40	MS60	MS63
1931 (k) Rare	51	—	—	—	—	—

KM# A15.2 4 DUKATA
13.96 g., 0.986 Gold 0.4425 oz. AGW **Ruler:** Alexander I **Obv:** Conjoined busts of royal couple left, large legend **Rev:** Crowned double eagle with shield on breast, large legend **Countermark:** Sword **Note:** Large-letter varieties bear the Kovnica, A.D. mint mark but were actually struck in Vienna.

Date	Mintage	F12	VF20	XF40	MS60	MS63
1931 (k)	Inc. above	—	—	—	—	—

POST WAR COINAGE

KM# 25 50 PARA
2.00 g., Zinc, 18 mm. **Obv:** State emblem, nine stars below **Rev:** Denomination surrounded by stars **Edge:** Reeded

Date	Mintage	F12	VF20	XF40	MS60	MS63
1945	40,000,000	0.50	1.00	3.00	5.00	9.00

KM# 26 DINAR
Zinc, 20 mm. **Obv:** State emblem, nine stars below **Rev:** Stars surround denomination **Edge:** Reeded

Date	Mintage	F12	VF20	XF40	MS60	MS63
1945	90,000,000	0.50	1.00	2.50	4.50	7.50

KM# 27 2 DINARA
Zinc, 22 mm. **Obv:** State emblem, nine stars below **Rev:** Stars surround denomination **Edge:** Reeded

Date	Mintage	F12	VF20	XF40	MS60	MS63
1945	70,000,000	0.50	1.25	3.00	5.00	9.00

KM# 28 5 DINARA
Zinc, 26.5 mm. **Obv:** State emblem, nine stars below **Rev:** Stars surround denomination **Edge:** Reeded

Date	Mintage	F12	VF20	XF40	MS60	MS63
1945	50,000,000	1.00	2.00	4.00	7.50	12.00

FEDERAL PEOPLE'S REPUBLIC

STANDARD COINAGE

KM# 29 50 PARA
0.60 g., Aluminum, 17.4 mm. **Obv:** State emblem **Rev:** Denomination divides date, seven stars above **Edge:** Plain

Date	Mintage	VF20	XF40	MS60	MS63	MS65
1953	—	—	0.10	0.25	0.50	1.00

KM# 30 DINAR
0.90 g., Aluminum, 19.8 mm. **Obv:** State emblem **Rev:** Denomination divides date, seven stars above **Edge:** Plain

Date	Mintage	VF20	XF40	MS60	MS63	MS65
1953	—	0.10	0.15	0.25	0.50	1.00

KM# 31 2 DINARA
1.20 g., Aluminum, 22.2 mm. **Obv:** State emblem **Rev:** Denomination divides date, seven stars above **Edge:** Plain

Date	Mintage	VF20	XF40	MS60	MS63	MS65
1953	—	0.10	0.25	0.45	0.75	1.50

KM# 32 5 DINARA
1.60 g., Aluminum, 24.6 mm. **Obv:** State emblem **Rev:** Denomination divides date, seven stars above **Edge:** Plain

Date	Mintage	VF20	XF40	MS60	MS63	MS65
1953	—	0.25	0.35	0.50	1.00	2.00

KM# 33 10 DINARA
Aluminum-Bronze, 21 mm. **Obv:** State emblem **Rev:** Hand holding grain stalks below head left **Edge:** Reeded

Date	Mintage	VF20	XF40	MS60	MS63	MS65
1955	—	0.25	0.45	0.75	1.50	3.00

KM# 34 20 DINARA
Aluminum-Bronze, 23 mm. **Obv:** State emblem **Rev:** Head at left looking right, cogwheel lower right **Edge:** Reeded

Date	Mintage	VF20	XF40	MS60	MS63	MS65
1955	—	0.45	0.65	1.00	2.00	3.50

KM# 35 50 DINARA
6.00 g., Aluminum-Bronze, 25.5 mm. **Obv:** State emblem **Rev:** Two jugate heads right, cogwheel below **Edge:** Reeded

Date	Mintage	VF20	XF40	MS60	MS63	MS65
1955	—	0.75	1.50	2.50	4.50	7.50

SOCIALIST FEDERAL REPUBLIC

KM# 42 5 PARA
1.50 g., Brass, 16 mm. **Obv:** State emblem **Rev:** Denomination above date within wreath, six stars above **Edge:** Reeded

Date	Mintage	VF20	XF40	MS60	MS63	MS65
1965	23,839,900	0.10	0.20	0.40	1.00	—

KM# 43 5 PARA
1.50 g., Brass, 16 mm. **Obv:** State emblem **Rev:** Denomination divides date **Edge:** Reeded

Date	Mintage	VF20	XF40	MS60	MS63	MS65
1965	16,200,000	—	0.10	0.20	0.50	—
1973	36,384,000	—	0.10	0.15	0.50	—
1974	3,628,000	—	0.10	0.25	0.50	—
1975	20,272,000	—	0.10	0.15	0.50	—
1976	30,490,000	—	0.10	0.15	0.50	—
1977	10,270,000	—	0.10	0.15	0.50	—
1978	12,000,000	—	0.10	0.15	0.50	—
1979	20,414,000	—	0.10	0.15	0.50	—
1980	22,412,000	—	0.10	0.15	0.50	—
1981	630,000	0.10	0.25	0.50	1.00	—

KM# 44 10 PARA
3.00 g., Brass, 21 mm. **Obv:** State emblem **Rev:** Denomination divides date **Edge:** Reeded

Date	Mintage	VF20	XF40	MS60	MS63	MS65
1965	15,400,000	—	0.10	0.20	0.50	—
1973	15,647,000	—	0.10	0.20	0.50	—
1974	60,139,000	—	0.10	0.20	0.50	—
1975	36,139,000	—	0.10	0.15	0.50	—
1976	36,111,000	—	0.10	0.15	0.50	—
1977	40,451,000	—	0.10	0.15	0.50	—
1978	50,129,000	—	0.10	0.15	0.50	—
Note: Two varieties of "7" exist						
1979	89,738,000	—	0.10	0.15	0.50	—
1980	90,111,000	—	0.10	0.15	0.50	—
1981	14,090,000	—	0.10	0.15	0.50	—

KM# 139 10 PARA
3.00 g., Brass, 18 mm. **Obv:** State emblem **Rev:** Denomination **Edge:** Plain

Date	Mintage	VF20	XF40	MS60	MS63	MS65
1990	174,028,000	—	0.10	0.15	0.50	—
1991	60,828,000	—	0.15	0.35	0.75	—

KM# 45 20 PARA
4.00 g., Brass, 23.2 mm. **Obv:** State emblem **Rev:** Denomination divides date **Edge:** Reeded **Note:** Thickness varies: 1.3-1.5 mm.

Date	Mintage	VF20	XF40	MS60	MS63	MS65
1965	—	—	0.10	0.30	1.00	—
1973	30,448,000	—	0.10	0.30	1.00	—
1974	31,364,000	—	0.10	0.30	1.00	—
1975	44,683,000	—	0.10	0.30	1.00	—
1976	33,312,000	—	0.10	0.30	1.00	—
1977	40,782,000	—	0.10	0.30	1.00	—
1978	39,999,000	—	0.10	0.30	1.00	—
1979	49,121,000	—	0.10	0.30	1.00	—
1980	73,757,000	—	0.10	0.30	1.00	—
1981	96,144,000	—	0.10	0.30	1.00	—

KM# 140 20 PARA
3.80 g., Brass **Obv:** State emblem **Rev:** Denomination above date

Date	Mintage	VF20	XF40	MS60	MS63	MS65
1990	174,028,500	—	—	0.10	0.20	0.50
1991	60,828,000	—	—	0.10	0.20	0.50

KM# 84 25 PARA
2.25 g., Bronze, 17 mm. **Obv:** State emblem **Rev:** Denomination above date **Edge:** Plain

Date	Mintage	VF20	XF40	MS60	MS63	MS65
1982	185,316,000	—	—	0.10	0.25	0.50
1983	65,290,000	—	—	0.15	0.30	0.60

KM# 46.1 50 PARA
6.00 g., Brass, 25.5 mm. **Obv:** State emblem **Rev:** Denomination divides date **Edge:** Reeded

Date	Mintage	VF20	XF40	MS60	MS63	MS65
1965	—	0.10	0.20	0.65	1.00	—
1973	23,739,000	0.10	0.20	0.65	1.00	—
1974	33,000	1.50	2.50	5.00	7.50	—
1975	10,220,000	0.10	0.20	0.80	1.25	—
1976	8,438,000	0.10	0.20	1.00	1.50	—
1977	17,864,000	0.10	0.20	0.75	1.25	—
1978	40,177,000	0.10	0.20	0.65	1.00	—
Note: Two varieties of "7" exist						
1979	3,021,000	1.00	2.00	3.00	5.00	—

KM# 46.2 50 PARA
6.00 g., Brass, 25.5 mm. **Obv:** State emblem **Rev:** Denomination divides date **Edge:** Reeded

Date	Mintage	VF20	XF40	MS60	MS63	MS65
1979	12,278,000	0.50	1.00	2.50	3.50	—
1980	24,974,000	0.10	0.20	0.65	1.00	—
1981	40,319,000	0.10	0.20	0.65	1.00	—

KM# 85 50 PARA
2.85 g., Bronze, 19 mm. **Obv:** State emblem **Rev:** Denomination above date **Edge:** Plain

Date	Mintage	VF20	XF40	MS60	MS63	MS65
1982	79,584,000	—	0.10	0.15	0.25	0.50
1983	72,100,000	—	0.10	0.15	0.25	0.50
1984	59,642,000	—	0.25	0.50	0.75	1.00

KM# 141 50 PARA
Brass **Obv:** State emblem **Rev:** Denomination

Date	Mintage	VF20	XF40	MS60	MS63	MS65
1990	137,873,000	—	0.10	0.20	0.40	1.00
1991	42,152,000	—	0.20	0.40	0.75	1.25

KM# 36 DINAR
0.90 g., Aluminum, 19.8 mm. **Obv:** State emblem **Rev:** Denomination divides date, seven stars above **Edge:** Plain

Date	Mintage	VF20	XF40	MS60	MS63	MS65
1963	—	0.10	0.15	0.25	0.75	—

KM# 47 DINAR
4.00 g., Copper-Nickel, 21.8 mm. **Obv:** State emblem **Rev:** Denomination and date within wreath, six stars above **Edge:** Reeded

Date	Mintage	VF20	XF40	MS60	MS63	MS65
1965	75,822,000	0.15	0.20	0.30	0.60	1.00

KM# 48 DINAR
4.00 g., Copper-Nickel, 21.8 mm. **Obv:** State emblem **Rev:** Denomination above date within wreath, six stars above **Edge:** Reeded

Date	Mintage	VF20	XF40	MS60	MS63	MS65
1968	35,497,000	0.15	0.25	0.40	0.80	1.25

KM# 59 DINAR
4.00 g., Copper-Nickel-Zinc, 21.8 mm. **Obv:** State emblem **Rev:** Text surrounds denomination within wreath, six stars above **Edge:** Reeded

Date	Mintage	VF20	XF40	MS60	MS63	MS65
1973	18,974,000	—	0.10	0.15	0.40	1.00
1974	42,724,000	—	0.10	0.15	0.35	1.00
1975	30,260,000	—	0.10	0.15	0.35	1.00
1976	21,849,000	—	0.10	0.15	0.35	1.00
1977	30,468,000	—	0.10	0.15	0.35	1.00
Note: Two varieties of wreath						
1977	—	PF65 40.00				
1978	35,032,000	—	0.10	0.15	0.35	1.00
1979	39,844,000	—	0.10	0.15	0.35	1.00
1980	60,630,000	—	0.10	0.15	0.35	1.00
1981	56,650,000	—	0.10	0.15	0.35	1.00

KM# 61 DINAR
4.00 g., Copper-Nickel-Zinc, 21.8 mm. **Series:** F.A.O. **Obv:** State emblem **Rev:** Text surrounds denomination, stylized grain stalks at sides **Edge:** Reeded

Date	Mintage	VF20	XF40	MS60	MS63	MS65
1976	500,000	—	0.10	0.30	1.00	1.50

KM# 86 DINAR
3.60 g., Nickel-Brass, 20 mm. **Obv:** State emblem **Rev:** Text surrounds denomination **Edge:** Reeded

Date	Mintage	VF20	XF40	MS60	MS63	MS65
1982	70,105,000	—	—	0.10	0.30	1.00
1983	114,180,000	—	—	0.10	0.20	1.00
1984	172,185,000	—	—	0.10	0.20	1.00
1985	64,436,000	—	—	0.10	0.25	1.00
1986	122,643,000	—	—	0.10	0.20	1.00

KM# 142 DINAR
6.00 g., Copper-Nickel-Zinc **Obv:** State emblem **Rev:** Text surrounds denomination **Edge:** Reeded

Date	Mintage	VF20	XF40	MS60	MS63	MS65
1990	172,105,000	—	—	0.10	0.25	0.75
1991	79,549,000	—	0.15	0.25	0.75	1.25

KM# 37 2 DINARA
1.20 g., Aluminum, 22.2 mm. **Obv:** State emblem **Rev:** Denomination divides date, seven stars above **Edge:** Plain

Date	Mintage	VF20	XF40	MS60	MS63	MS65
1963	—	—	0.10	0.15	0.25	0.75

KM# 55 2 DINARA
Copper-Nickel-Zinc, 24.5 mm. **Series:** F.A.O. **Obv:** State emblem **Rev:** Text surrounds denomination, grain stalks at sides **Edge:** Milled

Date	Mintage	VF20	XF40	MS60	MS63	MS65
1970	500,000	—	0.20	0.40	0.75	1.25

KM# 57 2 DINARA
5.00 g., Copper-Nickel-Zinc, 24.5 mm. **Obv:** State emblem **Rev:** Text encircles denomination, wreath surrounds, six stars above **Edge:** Reeded

Date	Mintage	VF20	XF40	MS60	MS63	MS65
1971	10,413,000	—	0.10	0.30	0.70	1.20
1972	18,446,000	—	0.10	0.20	0.50	1.00
1973	31,848,000	—	0.10	0.20	0.45	1.00
1974	10,989,000	—	0.10	0.20	0.50	1.00
1975	92,000	2.00	4.00	7.50	10.00	15.00
1976	6,092,000	—	0.10	0.20	0.50	1.00
1977	19,335,000	—	0.10	0.20	0.50	1.00
1978	13,035,000	—	0.10	0.20	0.50	1.00
1979	20,069,000	—	0.10	0.20	0.45	1.00
1980	36,088,000	—	0.10	0.20	0.45	1.00
1981	42,599,000	—	0.10	0.20	0.45	1.00

KM# 87 2 DINARA
4.40 g., Nickel-Brass, 22 mm. **Obv:** State emblem **Rev:** Text surrounds denomination **Edge:** Milled

Date	Mintage	VF20	XF40	MS60	MS63	MS65
1982	40,632,000	—	0.10	0.15	0.35	1.00
1983	35,468,000	—	0.10	0.15	0.35	1.00
1984	51,500,000	—	0.10	0.15	0.35	1.00
1985	81,100,000	—	0.10	0.15	0.35	1.00
1986	50,453,000	—	0.10	0.15	0.35	1.00

KM# 143 2 DINARA
Copper-Nickel-Zinc **Obv:** State emblem **Rev:** Text surrounds denomination

Date	Mintage	VF20	XF40	MS60	MS63	MS65
1990	15,936,000	0.15	0.30	0.60	2.00	3.00
1991	32,836,000	0.10	0.20	0.40	1.00	1.50
1992	14,155,000	2.50	3.50	5.00	7.50	12.50

KM# 38 5 DINARA
1.60 g., Aluminum, 24.6 mm. **Obv:** State emblem **Rev:** Denomination divides date, seven stars above **Edge:** Plain

Date	Mintage	VF20	XF40	MS60	MS63	MS65
1963	—	0.10	0.20	0.35	0.50	1.00

KM# 56 5 DINARA
Copper-Nickel-Zinc, 27.5 mm. **Series:** F.A.O. **Obv:** State emblem **Rev:** Text surrounds denomination, grain stalks at sides **Edge:** Milled

Date	Mintage	VF20	XF40	MS60	MS63	MS65
1970	500,000	0.20	0.50	1.00	2.50	3.50

KM# 58 5 DINARA
6.90 g., Copper-Nickel-Zinc, 27.5 mm. **Obv:** State emblem **Rev:** Text encircles denomination, wreath surrounds, six stars above **Edge:** Milled **Note:** Regular issue.

Date	Mintage	VF20	XF40	MS60	MS63	MS65
1971	10,224,000	0.20	0.40	0.60	1.00	1.50
Note: Two varieties of wreath						
1972	27,974,000	0.10	0.20	0.35	0.60	1.20
Note: Two varieties of 2 in date						
1973	12,705,000	0.20	0.40	0.60	1.00	1.50
1974	6,054,000	0.25	0.50	1.00	2.00	2.50
1975	13,533,000	0.10	0.20	0.35	0.60	1.00
1976	4,965,383	0.10	0.25	0.40	0.80	1.25
1977	922,000	0.30	0.60	1.20	2.50	3.00
1978	1,000,000	0.10	0.25	0.50	1.50	2.00
1979	3,000,000	0.10	0.25	0.40	0.80	1.25
1980	9,977,000	0.10	0.20	0.35	0.60	1.00
1981	15,450,000	0.10	0.20	0.35	0.60	1.00

KM# 60 5 DINARA
Copper-Nickel-Zinc, 27.5 mm. **Subject:** 30th Anniversary of Nazi Defeat **Obv:** State emblem **Rev:** Denomination, six stars

Date	Mintage	VF20	XF40	MS60	MS63	MS65
1975	1,020,000	0.25	0.50	1.00	1.50	2.50

KM# 88 5 DINARA
5.50 g., Nickel-Brass, 24 mm. **Obv:** State emblem **Rev:** Denomination **Edge:** Milled

Date	Mintage	VF20	XF40	MS60	MS63	MS65
1982	40,956,000	—	0.10	0.15	0.50	1.00
1983	40,156,000	—	0.10	0.15	0.50	1.00
1984	33,023,000	—	0.10	0.15	0.50	1.00
1985	94,422,000	—	0.10	0.15	0.50	1.00
1986	37,199,000	—	0.10	0.15	0.50	1.00

KM# 144 5 DINARA
Copper-Nickel-Zinc **Obv:** State emblem **Rev:** Denomination

Date	Mintage	VF20	XF40	MS60	MS63	MS65
1990	9,354,000	0.25	0.45	1.00	1.50	2.50
1991	113,420,000	—	0.25	0.50	1.25	2.00
1992	15,970,000	0.50	1.00	2.00	3.50	5.00

KM# 145 5 DINARA
Copper-Nickel-Zinc **Subject:** 1990 Chess Olympiad **Obv:** State emblem within flat bottom circle **Rev:** Logo

Date	Mintage	VF20	XF40	MS60	MS63	MS65
1990	20,000	PF63 7.00	PF65 10.00			

KM# 39 10 DINARA
Aluminum-Bronze, 21 mm. **Obv:** State emblem **Rev:** Hand holding grain stalks below head left **Edge:** Milled

Date	Mintage	VF20	XF40	MS60	MS63	MS65
1963	—	0.15	0.30	0.75	1.50	3.00

KM# 62 10 DINARA
9.80 g., Copper-Nickel, 30 mm. **Obv:** State emblem **Rev:** Text encircles denomination, wreath surrounds, six stars above **Edge:** Milled

Date	Mintage	VF20	XF40	MS60	MS63	MS65
1976	10,549,500	0.30	0.60	0.75	1.50	2.50
1977	39,645,000	0.30	0.60	0.75	1.25	2.00
Note: Two varieties of wreath						
1978	29,834,000	0.30	0.60	0.75	1.25	2.00
1979	4,969,000	0.35	0.75	1.25	2.00	3.00
1980	10,139,000	0.30	0.60	0.75	1.25	2.00
1981	20,166,000	0.30	0.60	0.75	1.25	2.00

KM# 63 10 DINARA
Copper-Nickel-Zinc, 30 mm. **Series:** F.A.O. **Obv:** State emblem **Rev:** Text surrounds denomination, grain stalks at sides, six stars above

Date	Mintage	VF20	XF40	MS60	MS63	MS65
1976	500,000	0.50	0.75	1.00	1.50	2.50

KM# 89 10 DINARA
5.20 g., Copper-Nickel, 23 mm. **Obv:** State emblem **Rev:** Text surrounds denomination **Edge:** Milled

Date	Mintage	VF20	XF40	MS60	MS63	MS65
1982	8,862,000	—	0.10	0.20	0.80	1.20
1983	42,400,000	—	0.10	0.20	0.75	1.00
1984	30,900,000	—	0.10	0.20	0.75	1.00
1985	31,647,000	—	0.10	0.20	0.75	1.00
1986	40,739,000	—	0.10	0.20	0.75	1.00
1987	104,988,000	—	0.10	0.20	0.75	1.00
1988	27,614,000	—	0.10	0.20	0.75	1.00

KM# 96 10 DINARA
Copper-Nickel, 30 mm. **Subject:** 40th Anniversary - Battle of Neretva River **Obv:** State emblem within flat bottomed circle **Rev:** Bridge over the River Neretva **Edge:** Milled

Date	Mintage	VF20	XF40	MS60	MS63	MS65
ND-1983	900,000	—	1.00	1.50	3.50	5.00
ND-1983	100,000	PF63 8.00	PF65 12.00			

KM# 97.1 10 DINARA
Copper-Nickel, 30 mm. **Subject:** 40th Anniversary - Battle of Sutjeska River **Obv:** State emblem within flat bottom circle **Rev:** Pathway divides monument **Edge:** Milled

Date	Mintage	VF20	XF40	MS60	MS63	MS65
ND-1983	900,000	—	1.00	1.50	3.50	5.00
ND-1983	100,000	PF63 8.00	PF65 12.00			

KM# 97.2 10 DINARA
Copper-Nickel, 30 mm. **Subject:** 40th Anniversary - Battle of Sutjeska River **Obv:** State emblem within flat bottom circle **Rev:** Without pathway in front of monument

Date	Mintage	VF20	XF40	MS60	MS63	MS65
ND-1983	—	—	—	7.00	9.00	13.00

KM# 131 10 DINARA
2.50 g., Brass **Obv:** Text surrounds state emblem within square **Rev:** Denomination within square, text on four sides **Edge:** Plain

Date	Mintage	VF20	XF40	MS60	MS63	MS65
1988	35,992,000	—	0.10	0.15	0.25	0.35
1989	75,000,000	—	0.10	0.15	0.25	0.35

KM# 40 20 DINARA
3.70 g., Aluminum-Bronze, 23.2 mm. **Obv:** State emblem **Rev:** Head at left looking right, cogwheel below **Edge:** Milled

Date	Mintage	VF20	XF40	MS60	MS63	MS65
1963	—	1.00	1.50	2.00	3.50	5.00

KM# 49 20 DINARA
9.00 g., 0.925 Silver 0.2677 oz. ASW, 28 mm. **Subject:** 25th Anniversary of Republic **Obv:** State emblem within circle **Rev:** Figures with arms raised, large rock in background **Edge:** Milled **Note:** Mint mark: NI (Numismatica Italiana, Milano, Italy).

Date	Mintage	VF20	XF40	MS60	MS63	MS65
1968	100,000	PF63 12.00	PF65 17.00			
1968 NI	—	PF63 12.00	PF65 17.00			

KM# 112 20 DINARA
Copper-Nickel-Zinc, 25 mm. **Obv:** State emblem **Rev:** Denomination **Edge:** Milled

Date	Mintage	VF20	XF40	MS60	MS63	MS65
1985	5,000,000	—	0.10	0.20	0.50	1.00
1986	20,235,000	—	0.10	0.15	0.35	0.75
1987	39,514,000	—	0.10	0.15	0.35	0.75

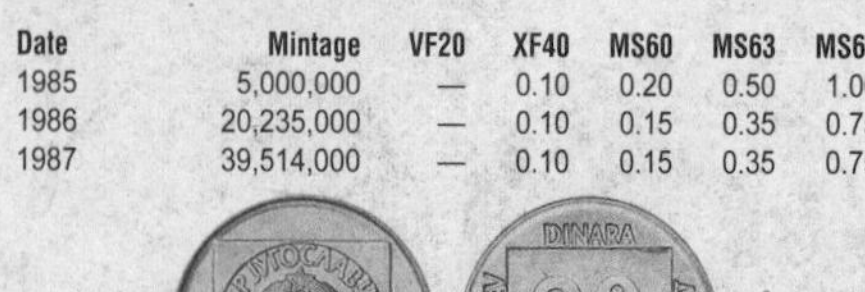

KM# 132 20 DINARA

Brass **Obv:** Text surrounds state emblem within square **Rev:** Denomination within square, text on four sides **Edge:** Plain

Date	Mintage	VF20	XF40	MS60	MS63	MS65
1988	29,775,000	—	—	0.10	0.25	0.35
1989	12,994,000	—	—	0.10	0.25	0.35

KM# 41 50 DINARA

Aluminum-Bronze, 25.5 mm. **Obv:** State emblem **Rev:** Conjoined heads looking right, cogwheel below **Edge:** Milled **Note:** Exists with filled letter in denomination. Two varieties of the letter "P" in ANHAPA.

Date	Mintage	VF20	XF40	MS60	MS63	MS65
1963	—	2.00	3.50	6.00	9.00	15.00

KM# 50 50 DINARA

20.00 g., 0.925 Silver 0.5948 oz. ASW, 34 mm. **Subject:** 25th Anniversary of Republic **Obv:** State emblem within circle **Rev:** Head left within circle **Note:** Mint mark: NI.

Date	Mintage	VF20	XF40	MS60	MS63	MS65
ND-1968	100,000	PF63 25.00	PF65 30.00			
ND-1968 NI	Inc. above	PF63 25.00	PF65 30.00			

KM# 113 50 DINARA

Copper-Nickel-Zinc, 27 mm. **Obv:** State emblem **Rev:** Denomination **Edge:** Milled

Date	Mintage	VF20	XF40	MS60	MS63	MS65
1985	25,488,000	—	0.10	0.25	0.75	1.25
1986	20,353,000	—	0.10	0.25	0.75	1.25
1987	21,792,000	—	0.10	0.25	0.75	1.25
1988	28,370,000	—	0.10	0.25	0.75	1.25

KM# 133 50 DINARA

Brass **Obv:** Text surrounds state emblem within square **Rev:** Denomination within square, text on four sides

Date	Mintage	VF20	XF40	MS60	MS63	MS65
1988	46,973,000	—	—	0.10	0.25	0.35
1989	2,999,000	—	0.50	1.00	2.00	3.50

Note: Not issued

KM# 51 100 DINARA

7.82 g., 0.900 Gold 0.2263 oz. AGW, 24 mm. **Subject:** 25th Anniversary of Republic **Obv:** State emblem within circle **Rev:** Figures with arms raised, large rock in background

Date	Mintage	VF20	XF40	MS60	MS63	MS65
ND-1968	10,000	PF63 375	PF65 425	PF67 475		
ND-1968 NI	Inc. above	PF63 375	PF65 425	PF67 475		

KM# 65 100 DINARA

10.00 g., 0.925 Silver 0.2974 oz. ASW, 28 mm. **Subject:** 8th Mediterranean Games at Split **Obv:** Map of Split left of emblem **Rev:** Bust left

Date	Mintage	VF20	XF40	MS60	MS63	MS65
1978	71,000	PF63 16.00	PF65 18.00			

KM# 90 100 DINARA

13.00 g., 0.925 Silver 0.3866 oz. ASW, 30 mm. **Series:** 1984 Winter Olympics **Subject:** Ice Hockey **Obv:** Emblem and Olympic logo on separate shields within flat bottom circle **Rev:** Hockey players **Edge:** Milled

Date	Mintage	VF20	XF40	MS60	MS63	MS65
1982	110,000	PF63 12.00	PF65 15.00			

KM# 98 100 DINARA

13.00 g., 0.925 Silver 0.3866 oz. ASW, 30 mm. **Series:** 1984 Winter Olympics **Subject:** Figure Skating **Obv:** Emblem and Olympic logo on separate shields within flat bottom circle **Rev:** Figure skater

Date	Mintage	VF20	XF40	MS60	MS63	MS65
1983	110,000	PF63 12.00	PF65 15.00			

KM# 99 100 DINARA

13.00 g., 0.925 Silver 0.3866 oz. ASW, 30 mm. **Series:** 1984 Winter Olympics **Subject:** Bobsledding **Obv:** Emblem and Olympic logo on separate shields within flat bottom circle **Rev:** Bobsledders

Date	Mintage	VF20	XF40	MS60	MS63	MS65
1983	110,000	PF63 12.00	PF65 15.00			

KM# 105 100 DINARA

13.00 g., 0.925 Silver 0.3866 oz. ASW, 30 mm. **Series:** 1984 Winter Olympics **Subject:** Speed Skating **Obv:** Emblem and Olympic logo on separate shields within flat bottom circle **Rev:** Skater

Date	Mintage	VF20	XF40	MS60	MS63	MS65
1984	110,000	PF63 12.00	PF65 15.00			

KM# 106 100 DINARA

13.00 g., 0.925 Silver 0.3866 oz. ASW, 30 mm. **Series:** 1984 Winter Olympics **Subject:** Pairs Figure Skating **Obv:** Emblem and Olympic logo on separate shields within flat bottom circle **Rev:** Figure skaters

Date	Mintage	VF20	XF40	MS60	MS63	MS65
1984	110,000	PF63 12.00	PF65 15.00			

KM# 114 100 DINARA

8.70 g., Copper-Nickel-Zinc, 29 mm. **Obv:** State emblem **Rev:** Denomination **Edge:** Reeded

Date	Mintage	VF20	XF40	MS60	MS63	MS65
1985	18,684,000	—	0.30	0.65	1.50	2.50
1986	17,905,000	—	0.25	0.50	1.00	1.50
1987	94,069,000	—	0.20	0.40	0.80	1.25
1988	50,294,000	—	0.20	0.40	0.80	1.25

KM# 115 100 DINARA

Copper-Nickel-Zinc **Subject:** 40th Anniversary - Liberation From Fascism **Obv:** State emblem within flat bottom circle **Rev:** Head left within circle of design

Date	Mintage	VF20	XF40	MS60	MS63	MS65
ND-1985	200,000	PF63 3.50	PF65 6.00			

KM# 127.1 100 DINARA

Copper-Nickel **Subject:** 200th Anniversary - Birth of Karajich **Obv:** State emblem **Rev:** Squared head right

Date	Mintage	VF20	XF40	MS60	MS63	MS65
1987	Est. 200000	PF63 3.50	PF65 6.00			

KM# 127.2 100 DINARA
Copper-Nickel **Subject:** 200th Anniversary - Birth of Karajich **Obv:** State emblem within flat bottom circle **Rev:** Squared head right

Date	Mintage	VF20	XF40	MS60	MS63	MS65
1987	Inc. above	PF63 15.00	PF65 20.00			

KM# 134 100 DINARA
5.50 g., Brass **Obv:** Text surrounds state emblem within square **Rev:** Denomination within square, text on four sides

Date	Mintage	VF20	XF40	MS60	MS63	MS65
1988	12,610,000	—	0.15	0.25	0.35	0.50
1989	124,260,000	—	0.15	0.25	0.35	0.50

KM# 146 100 DINARA
13.00 g., 0.925 Silver 0.3866 oz. ASW **Subject:** 1990 Chess Olympiad **Obv:** State emblem within flat bottom circle **Rev:** Petrovaradin clock tower, chessboard background

Date	Mintage	VF20	XF40	MS60	MS63	MS65
1990	10,000	PF63 28.00	PF65 32.00			

KM# 66 150 DINARA
12.50 g., 0.925 Silver 0.3717 oz. ASW, 30 mm. **Subject:** 8th Mediterranean Games at Split **Obv:** State emblem above boats **Rev:** Head left

Date	Mintage	VF20	XF40	MS60	MS63	MS65
1978	70,000	PF63 18.00	PF65 20.00			

KM# 147 150 DINARA
17.00 g., 0.925 Silver 0.5056 oz. ASW **Subject:** 1990 Chess Olympiad **Obv:** State emblem within flat bottom circle **Rev:** Globe, chessboard design at right

Date	Mintage	VF20	XF40	MS60	MS63	MS65
1990	10,000	PF63 25.00	PF65 30.00			

KM# 52 200 DINARA
15.64 g., 0.900 Gold 0.4526 oz. AGW, 30 mm. **Subject:** 25th Anniversary of Republic **Obv:** State emblem within circle **Rev:** Head left

Date	Mintage	VF20	XF40	MS60	MS63	MS65
ND-1968	10,000	PF63 650	PF65 750	PF67 850		
ND-1968 NI	Inc. above	PF63 650	PF65 750	PF67 850		

KM# 64 200 DINARA
15.00 g., 0.750 Silver 0.3617 oz. ASW, 32 mm. **Subject:** Tito's 85th Birthday **Obv:** State emblem at left, dates at right, denomination below, fan background **Rev:** Head left **Edge:** Lettered **Note:** Edge varieties with inscription in Cyrillic, Western and alternating Cyrillic-Western exist.

Date	Mintage	VF20	XF40	MS60	MS63	MS65
1977	300,000	—	—	7.00	10.00	12.00

KM# 64a 200 DINARA
15.00 g., 0.750 Silver 0.3617 oz. ASW **Subject:** Tito's 85th Birthday **Obv:** State emblem at left, dates at right, denomination below, fan background **Rev:** Head left

Date	Mintage	VF20	XF40	MS60	MS63	MS65
1977	500,000	PF63 12.00	PF65 14.00			

KM# 67 200 DINARA
15.00 g., 0.925 Silver 0.4461 oz. ASW **Subject:** 8th Mediterranean Games at Split **Obv:** State emblem at left, ancient urn at right **Rev:** Head left

Date	Mintage	VF20	XF40	MS60	MS63	MS65
1978	58,000	PF63 18.00	PF65 23.00			

KM# 68 250 DINARA
17.50 g., 0.925 Silver 0.5204 oz. ASW, 34 mm. **Subject:** 8th Mediterranean Games at Split **Obv:** Basilica of St. Donat in Zadar **Rev:** Head left

Date	Mintage	VF20	XF40	MS60	MS63	MS65
1979	48,000	PF63 23.00	PF65 28.00			

KM# 91 250 DINARA
17.00 g., 0.925 Silver 0.5056 oz. ASW, 34 mm. **Series:** 1984 Winter Olympics **Obv:** Emblem and Olympic logo on separate shields within flat bottom circle **Rev:** Sarajevo view within circle

Date	Mintage	VF20	XF40	MS60	MS63	MS65
1982	110,000	PF63 14.00	PF65 16.00			

KM# 100 250 DINARA
17.00 g., 0.925 Silver 0.5056 oz. ASW, 34 mm. **Series:** 1984 Winter Olympics **Obv:** Emblem and Olympic logo on separate shields within flat bottom circle **Rev:** Artifact within circle

Date	Mintage	VF20	XF40	MS60	MS63	MS65
1983	110,000	PF63 14.00	PF65 16.00			

KM# 101 250 DINARA
17.00 g., 0.925 Silver 0.5056 oz. ASW, 34 mm. **Series:** 1984 Winter Olympics **Obv:** Emblem and Olympic logo on separate shields within flat bottom circle **Rev:** Radimlja tombs

Date	Mintage	VF20	XF40	MS60	MS63	MS65
1983	110,000	PF63 14.00	PF65 16.00			

KM# 107 250 DINARA
17.00 g., 0.925 Silver 0.5056 oz. ASW, 34 mm. **Series:** 1984 Winter Olympics **Obv:** Emblem and Olympic logo on separate shields within flat bottom circle **Rev:** Jajce village

Date	Mintage	VF20	XF40	MS60	MS63	MS65
1984	110,000	PF63 14.00	PF65 16.00			

KM# 108 250 DINARA
17.00 g., 0.925 Silver 0.5056 oz. ASW, 34 mm. **Series:** 1984 Winter Olympics **Obv:** Emblem and Olympic logo on separate shields within flat bottom circle **Rev:** Head of Tito left

Date	Mintage	VF20	XF40	MS60	MS63	MS65
1984	110,000	PF63 14.00	PF65 16.00			

KM# 69 300 DINARA
20.00 g., 0.925 Silver 0.5948 oz. ASW, 36 mm. **Subject:** Eighth Mediterranean Games at Split **Obv:** State emblem and date above church **Rev:** Bust left

Date	Mintage	VF20	XF40	MS60	MS63	MS65
1978	36,000	PF63 22.00	PF65 27.00			

KM# 70 350 DINARA
22.50 g., 0.925 Silver 0.6691 oz. ASW, 36 mm. **Subject:** 8th Mediterranean Games at Split **Obv:** Statue divides emblem and denomination **Rev:** Head left

Date	Mintage	VF20	XF40	MS60	MS63	MS65
1978	24,000	PF63 25.00	PF65 30.00			

KM# 71 400 DINARA
25.00 g., 0.925 Silver 0.7435 oz. ASW, 40 mm. **Subject:** 8th Mediterranean Games at Split **Obv:** State emblem above pillared building **Rev:** Head left

Date	Mintage	VF20	XF40	MS60	MS63	MS65
1978	24,000	PF63 30.00	PF65 35.00			

KM# 53 500 DINARA
39.10 g., 0.900 Gold 1.1314 oz. AGW, 45 mm. **Subject:** 25th Anniversary of Republic **Obv:** State emblem **Rev:** Figures with arms raised, large rock in background

Date	Mintage	VF20	XF40	MS60	MS63	MS65
ND-1968	10,000	PF63 1,650	PF65 1,850	PF67 2,150		
ND-1968 NI	Inc. above	PF63 1,650	PF65 1,850	PF67 2,150		

KM# 76 500 DINARA
8.00 g., 0.925 Silver 0.2379 oz. ASW, 27 mm. **Subject:** Vukovar Congress **Obv:** State emblem above city hall of Vukovar **Rev:** Bust 3/4 left

Date	Mintage	VF20	XF40	MS60	MS63	MS65
1980	18,000	PF63 13.00	PF65 16.00			

KM# 80 500 DINARA
8.00 g., 0.750 Silver 0.1929 oz. ASW, 27 mm. **Subject:** World Table Tennis Championship Games **Obv:** State emblem above town Novi Sad **Rev:** Geometric array of four table tennis paddles with ball at center.

Date	Mintage	VF20	XF40	MS60	MS63	MS65
1981	18,000	PF63 16.00	PF65 18.00			

KM# 92 500 DINARA
23.00 g., 0.925 Silver 0.684 oz. ASW **Series:** 1984 Winter Olympics **Subject:** Downhill Skiing **Obv:** Emblem and Olympic logo on separate shields within flat bottom circle **Rev:** Downhill Skier

Date	Mintage	VF20	XF40	MS60	MS63	MS65
1982	110,000	PF63 22.00	PF65 25.00			

KM# 102 500 DINARA
23.00 g., 0.925 Silver 0.684 oz. ASW, 38 mm. **Series:** 1984 Winter Olympics **Subject:** Ski Jumping **Obv:** Emblem and Olympic logo on separate shields within flat bottom circle **Rev:** Ski jumper

Date	Mintage	VF20	XF40	MS60	MS63	MS65
1983	110,000	PF63 22.00	PF65 25.00			

KM# 103 500 DINARA
23.00 g., 0.925 Silver 0.684 oz. ASW, 38 mm. **Series:** 1984 Winter Olympics **Subject:** Biathalon **Obv:** Emblem and Olympic logo on separate shields within flat bottom circle **Rev:** Cross country skier and shooter

Date	Mintage	VF20	XF40	MS60	MS63	MS65
1983	110,000	PF63 22.00	PF65 25.00			

KM# 109 500 DINARA
23.00 g., 0.925 Silver 0.684 oz. ASW, 38 mm. **Series:** 1984 Winter Olympics **Subject:** Cross-country Skiing **Obv:** Emblem and Olympic logo on separate shields within flat bottom circle **Rev:** Cross-country skier

Date	Mintage	VF20	XF40	MS60	MS63	MS65
1984	110,000	PF63 22.00	PF65 25.00			

KM# 110 500 DINARA
23.00 g., 0.925 Silver 0.684 oz. ASW, 38 mm. **Series:** 1984 Winter Olympics **Subject:** Slalom Skiing **Obv:** Emblem and Olympic logo on separate shields within flat bottom circle **Rev:** Slalom skier

Date	Mintage	VF20	XF40	MS60	MS63	MS65
1984	110,000	PF63 22.00	PF65 25.00			

KM# 116 500 DINARA
13.00 g., 0.925 Silver 0.3866 oz. ASW **Subject:** Ski Jumping Championship **Obv:** Similar to 10,000 Dinara, KM#123 **Rev:** Herons

Date	Mintage	VF20	XF40	MS60	MS63	MS65
1985	50,000	PF63 17.00	PF65 22.00			

KM# 54 1000 DINARA
78.20 g., 0.900 Gold 2.2628 oz. AGW, 55 mm. **Subject:** 25th Anniversary of Republic **Obv:** State emblem **Rev:** Bust of Tito left

Date	Mintage	VF20	XF40	MS60	MS63	MS65
ND-1968	10,000	PF63 3,000	PF65 3,500	PF67 3,750		
ND-1968 NI	Inc. above	PF63 3,000	PF65 3,500	PF67 3,750		

KM# 77 1000 DINARA
14.00 g., 0.925 Silver 0.4164 oz. ASW, 30 mm. **Subject:** Vukovar Congress **Obv:** State emblem above city hall in Vukovar **Rev:** Bust 3/4 left

Date	Mintage	VF20	XF40	MS60	MS63	MS65
1980	16,000	PF63 22.00	PF65 27.00			

KM# 78 1000 DINARA
25.90 g., 0.750 Silver 0.6245 oz. ASW **Subject:** Tito's Death **Obv:** State emblem on map of Yugoslavia, globe background **Rev:** Bust 3/4 left **Note:** Eyes with and without pupils.

Date	Mintage	VF20	XF40	MS60	MS63	MS65
1980	800,000	—	—	22.00	25.00	28.00

KM# 78a 1000 DINARA
26.00 g., 0.925 Silver 0.7732 oz. ASW **Subject:** Tito's Death **Obv:** State emblem on map of Yugoslavia, globe background **Rev:** Bust 3/4 left

Date	Mintage	VF20	XF40	MS60	MS63	MS65
1980	200,000	PF63 27.00	PF65 30.00			
1980 ZM	Inc. above	PF63 27.00	PF65 30.00			

KM# 81 1000 DINARA
14.00 g., 0.750 Silver 0.3376 oz. ASW, 30 mm. **Subject:** World Table Tennis Championship Games **Obv:** State emblem above town Novi Sad **Rev:** Hand with paddle hitting ball

Date	Mintage	VF20	XF40	MS60	MS63	MS65
1981	16,000	PF63 30.00	PF65 40.00			

KM# 82 1000 DINARA
14.00 g., 0.750 Silver 0.3376 oz. ASW, 30 mm. **Subject:** 40th Anniversary of Uprising and Revolution **Obv:** State emblem **Rev:** Bust and dates left, stars in background

Date	Mintage	VF20	XF40	MS60	MS63	MS65
1981	100,000	PF63 15.00	PF65 20.00			

KM# 93 1000 DINARA
18.00 g., 0.925 Silver 0.5353 oz. ASW **Subject:** International Canoeing Championships **Obv:** State emblem left of statue **Rev:** City views, bird on left

Date	Mintage	VF20	XF40	MS60	MS63	MS65
1982	46,000	PF63 25.00	PF65 30.00			

KM# 117 1000 DINARA
23.00 g., 0.925 Silver 0.684 oz. ASW, 38 mm. **Subject:** Ski Jumping Championship **Obv:** State emblem on shield within flat bottom circle, denomination below **Rev:** Bloudek

Date	Mintage	VF20	XF40	MS60	MS63	MS65
1985	20,000	PF63 40.00	PF65 45.00			

KM# 118 1000 DINARA
23.00 g., 0.925 Silver 0.684 oz. ASW, 38 mm. **Subject:** Ski Jumping Championship **Obv:** Similar to 10,000 Dinara, KM#123 **Rev:** Slovenian cradle

Date	Mintage	VF20	XF40	MS60	MS63	MS65
1985	20,000	PF63 40.00	PF65 45.00			

KM# 119 1000 DINARA
6.00 g., 0.925 Silver 0.1784 oz. ASW **Subject:** Sinjska Alka **Obv:** State emblem at left of map outline **Rev:** Figures with pack horse

Date	Mintage	VF20	XF40	MS60	MS63	MS65
ND-1985	60,000	PF63 12.00	PF65 15.00			

KM# 148 1000 DINARA
3.50 g., 0.900 Gold 0.1013 oz. AGW **Subject:** 1990 Chess Olympiad **Obv:** State emblem above denomination **Rev:** Logo

Date	Mintage	VF20	XF40	MS60	MS63	MS65
1990	2,000	PF63 250	PF65 300	PF67 350		

KM# 72 1500 DINARA
8.80 g., 0.900 Gold 0.2546 oz. AGW, 24 mm. **Subject:** 8th Mediterranean Games at Split **Obv:** State emblem above rings **Rev:** Head left

Date	Mintage	VF20	XF40	MS60	MS63	MS65
1978	35,000	PF63 400	PF65 450	PF67 500		

KM# 79 1500 DINARA
22.00 g., 0.925 Silver 0.6543 oz. ASW, 34 mm. **Subject:** Vukovar Congress **Obv:** State emblem above city hall in Vukovar **Rev:** Bust 3/4 left

Date	Mintage	VF20	XF40	MS60	MS63	MS65
1980	16,000	PF63 23.00	PF65 28.00			

KM# 83 1500 DINARA
22.00 g., 0.750 Silver 0.5305 oz. ASW, 34 mm. **Subject:** World Table Tennis Championship Games **Obv:** State emblem over town view **Rev:** Stylized design of city

Date	Mintage	VF20	XF40	MS60	MS63	MS65
1981	16,000	PF63 25.00	PF65 30.00			

KM# 94 1500 DINARA
22.00 g., 0.925 Silver 0.6543 oz. ASW, 36 mm. **Subject:** International Canoeing Championships **Rev:** Tito

Date	Mintage	VF20	XF40	MS60	MS63	MS65
1982	36,000	PF63 32.00	PF65 35.00			

KM# 73 2000 DINARA
11.80 g., 0.900 Gold 0.3414 oz. AGW, 27 mm. **Subject:** 8th Mediterranean Games at Split **Obv:** State emblem above city view **Rev:** Head left

Date	Mintage	VF20	XF40	MS60	MS63	MS65
1978	35,000	PF63 550	PF65 600	PF67 650		

KM# 120 2000 DINARA
14.00 g., 0.925 Silver 0.4164 oz. ASW **Subject:** Sinska Alka **Obv:** State emblem left of map outline **Rev:** Three figures on horseback

Date	Mintage	VF20	XF40	MS60	MS63	MS65
ND-1985	20,000	PF63 22.00	PF65 27.00			

KM# 74 2500 DINARA
14.70 g., 0.900 Gold 0.4254 oz. AGW **Subject:** 8th Mediterranean Games at Split **Obv:** State emblem above stadium **Rev:** Bust left

Date	Mintage	VF20	XF40	MS60	MS63	MS65
1978	35,000	PF63 700	PF65 775	PF67 850		

KM# 121 3000 DINARA
26.00 g., 0.925 Silver 0.7732 oz. ASW **Subject:** Sinkska Alka **Obv:** State emblem left of map outline **Rev:** Armored figures

Date	Mintage	VF20	XF40	MS60	MS63	MS65
ND-1985	20,000	PF63 37.00	PF65 42.00			

KM# 128 3000 DINARA
13.00 g., 0.925 Silver 0.3866 oz. ASW **Subject:** 200th Anniversary - Birth of Krajich **Obv:** State emblem on shield within flat bottom circle **Rev:** Squared head right

Date	Mintage	VF20	XF40	MS60	MS63	MS65
1987	50,000	PF63 18.00	PF65 22.00			

KM# 75 5000 DINARA
29.50 g., 0.900 Gold 0.8536 oz. AGW, 38 mm. **Subject:** 8th Mediterranean Games at Split **Obv:** State emblem above palace of Diocletian in Split **Rev:** Bust left

Date	Mintage	VF20	XF40	MS60	MS63	MS65
1978	12,000	PF63 1,300	PF65 1,450	PF67 1,550		

KM# 95 5000 DINARA
8.00 g., 0.900 Gold 0.2315 oz. AGW, 24 mm. **Series:** 1984 Winter Olympics **Obv:** Emblem and Olympic logo on separate shields within flat bottom circle **Rev:** Olympic emblem within circle

Date	Mintage	VF20	XF40	MS60	MS63	MS65
1982	55,000	PF63 325	PF65 350	PF67 400		

KM# 104 5000 DINARA
8.00 g., 0.900 Gold 0.2315 oz. AGW, 24 mm. **Series:** 1984 Winter Olympics **Obv:** Emblem and Olympic logo on separate shields within flat bottom circle **Rev:** Bust 3/4 left within circle

Date	Mintage	VF20	XF40	MS60	MS63	MS65
1983	55,000	PF63 325	PF65 350	PF67 400		

KM# 111 5000 DINARA
8.00 g., 0.900 Gold 0.2315 oz. AGW, 24 mm. **Series:** 1984 Winter Olympics **Obv:** Emblem and Olympic logo on separate shields within flat bottom circle **Rev:** Olympic torch within circle

Date	Mintage	VF20	XF40	MS60	MS63	MS65
1984	55,000	PF63 325	PF65 350	PF67 400		

KM# 122 5000 DINARA
23.50 g., 0.925 Silver 0.6989 oz. ASW **Subject:** 400th Anniversary - Liberation from Fascism **Note:** Similar to 100 Dinara, KM#115.

Date	Mintage	VF20	XF40	MS60	MS63	MS65
1985	100,000	PF63 40.00	PF65 50.00			

KM# 129 5000 DINARA
17.00 g., 0.925 Silver 0.5056 oz. ASW **Subject:** 200th Anniversary - Birth of Karajich **Obv:** State emblem on shield within flat bottom circle **Rev:** Squared head right

Date	Mintage	VF20	XF40	MS60	MS63	MS65
1987	Est. 50000	PF63 22.00	PF65 25.00			

KM# 135 5000 DINARA
Copper-Nickel-Zinc **Subject:** Non-aligned Summit **Obv:** State emblem **Rev:** Symbols within circle

Date	Mintage	VF20	XF40	MS60	MS63	MS65
ND-1989	50,000	PF63 3.50	PF65 6.00			

KM# 123 10000 DINARA
8.00 g., 0.900 Gold 0.2315 oz. AGW, 24 mm. **Subject:** World Ski Jumping Championship

Date	Mintage	VF20	XF40	MS60	MS63	MS65
1985	10,000	PF63 350	PF65 400	PF67 450		

KM# 124 10000 DINARA
5.00 g., 0.900 Gold 0.1447 oz. AGW **Subject:** Sinjska Alka

Date	Mintage	VF20	XF40	MS60	MS63	MS65
ND-1985	12,000	PF63 200	PF65 235	PF67 285		

KM# 125 20000 DINARA
8.00 g., 0.900 Gold 0.2315 oz. AGW **Subject:** Sinjska Alka

Date	Mintage	VF20	XF40	MS60	MS63	MS65
ND-1985	8,000	PF63 325	PF65 375	PF67 425		

KM# 126 40000 DINARA
14.00 g., 0.900 Gold 0.4051 oz. AGW **Subject:** Sinjska Alka **Obv:** State emblem left of map outline **Rev:** Three figures on horseback

Date	Mintage	VF20	XF40	MS60	MS63	MS65
ND-1985	5,000	PF63 600	PF65 650	PF67 700		

KM# 130 50000 DINARA
8.00 g., 0.900 Gold 0.2315 oz. AGW **Subject:** 200th Anniversary - Birth of Karajich **Obv:** State emblem on shield within flat bottom circle **Rev:** Squared head right

Date	Mintage	VF20	XF40	MS60	MS63	MS65
1987	Est. 10000	PF63 350	PF65 400	PF67 450		

KM# 136 50000 DINARA
13.00 g., 0.925 Silver 0.3866 oz. ASW **Subject:** Non-aligned Summit **Obv:** State emblem above denomination **Rev:** Statue left divides dates within circle

Date	Mintage	VF20	XF40	MS60	MS63	MS65
ND-1989	15,000	PF63 20.00	PF65 25.00			

KM# 137 100000 DINARA
17.00 g., 0.925 Silver 0.5056 oz. ASW **Subject:** Non-aligned Summit **Obv:** State emblem above denomination **Rev:** Building above dates within circle

Date	Mintage	VF20	XF40	MS60	MS63	MS65
ND-1989	10,000	PF63 35.00	PF65 40.00			

KM# 138 2000000 DINARA
8.00 g., 0.900 Gold 0.2315 oz. AGW **Subject:** Non-aligned Summit **Obv:** State emblem above denomination **Rev:** Symbols within circle

Date	Mintage	VF20	XF40	MS60	MS63	MS65
ND-1989	5,000	PF63 350	PF65 400	PF67 450		

FEDERAL REPUBLIC

KM# 161 PARA
Brass **Obv:** Monogram on shield **Rev:** Denomination and date

Date	Mintage	VF20	XF40	MS60	MS63	MS65
1994	25,350,000	—	—	0.35	0.50	0.80

KM# 164.1 5 PARA
Brass **Obv:** Monogram on shield **Rev:** Denomination and date

Date	Mintage	VF20	XF40	MS60	MS63	MS65
1994	30,408,000	—	—	0.50	0.65	1.00
1995	3,400,000	—	—	0.60	0.85	1.25

KM# 164.2 5 PARA
2.72 g., Brass, 17 mm. **Obv:** Monogram on shield **Rev:** Denomination and date **Note:** Reduced size.

Date	Mintage	VF20	XF40	MS60	MS63	MS65
1996	9,951,000	—	—	0.50	0.70	1.00

KM# 162.1 10 PARA
Copper-Nickel-Zinc **Obv:** Monogram on shield **Rev:** Denomination and date

Date	Mintage	VF20	XF40	MS60	MS63	MS65
1994	52,161,000	—	—	0.50	0.65	1.00

KM# 162.2 10 PARA
Brass **Obv:** Monogram on shield **Rev:** Denomination and date **Note:** Reduced size.

Date	Mintage	VF20	XF40	MS60	MS63	MS65
1995	31,041,000	—	—	0.65	0.85	1.25

KM# 173 10 PARA
3.36 g., Brass **Obv:** National arms **Rev:** Denomination and date

Date	Mintage	VF20	XF40	MS60	MS63	MS65
1996	18,129,000	—	—	0.50	0.65	1.00
1997	21,384,000	—	—	0.50	0.65	1.00
1998	5,153,000	—	—	0.50	0.70	1.00

KM# 163 50 PARA
Copper-Nickel-Zinc **Obv:** Monogram on shield **Rev:** Date and denomination

Date	Mintage	VF20	XF40	MS60	MS63	MS65
1994	45,013,000	—	—	0.75	0.90	1.25

KM# 163a 50 PARA
Brass **Obv:** Monogram on shield **Rev:** Date and denomination

Date	Mintage	VF20	XF40	MS60	MS63	MS65
1995	19,193,000	—	—	1.00	1.20	1.50

KM# 174 50 PARA
Brass **Obv:** National arms **Rev:** Date and denomination

Date	Mintage	VF20	XF40	MS60	MS63	MS65
1996	3,520,000	—	—	1.00	1.25	1.75
1997	14,742,000	—	—	1.00	1.20	1.50
1998	20,050,000	—	—	1.00	1.20	1.50
1999	18,140,000	—	—	1.00	1.20	1.50

KM# 179 50 PARA
3.30 g., Brass, 18 mm. **Obv:** Head 3/4 facing **Rev:** National arms above denomination **Edge:** Plain

Date	Mintage	VF20	XF40	MS60	MS63	MS65
2000	23,821,000	—	—	0.25	0.45	0.75

KM# 165 NOVI DINAR
Copper-Nickel-Zinc **Obv:** Monogram on shield **Rev:** Date and denomination

Date	Mintage	VF20	XF40	MS60	MS63	MS65
1994	47,755,000	—	—	1.00	1.20	1.50
1995	10,359,000	—	—	1.25	1.50	2.00

KM# 168 NOVI DINAR
4.00 g., Copper-Nickel-Zinc **Obv:** National arms **Rev:** Date and denomination **Note:** Reduced size.

Date	Mintage	VF20	XF40	MS60	MS63	MS65
1996	80,122,000	—	—	1.00	1.20	1.50
1999	21,686,000	—	—	1.00	1.20	1.50

KM# 149 DINAR
Brass **Obv:** Monogram on shield **Rev:** Date and denomination

Date	Mintage	VF20	XF40	MS60	MS63	MS65
1992	49,269,000	0.10	0.30	0.60	0.75	1.25

KM# 154 DINAR
3.10 g., Copper-Nickel-Zinc **Obv:** Monogram on shield **Rev:** Date and denomination

Date	Mintage	VF20	XF40	MS60	MS63	MS65
1993	20,249,000	0.10	0.20	0.50	0.65	1.00

KM# 160 DINAR
Copper-Nickel-Zinc **Obv:** Monogram on shield **Rev:** Date and denomination

Date	Mintage	VF20	XF40	MS60	MS63	MS65
1994	10,747,000	—	—	1.00	1.20	1.50

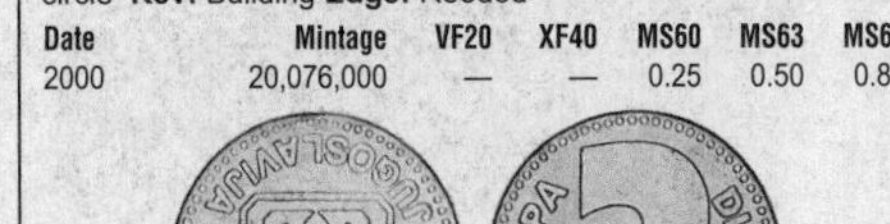

KM# 180 DINAR
4.40 g., Copper-Nickel-Zinc, 20 mm. **Obv:** National arms within circle **Rev:** Building **Edge:** Reeded

Date	Mintage	VF20	XF40	MS60	MS63	MS65
2000	20,076,000	—	—	0.25	0.50	0.80

KM# 150 2 DINARA
4.18 g., Brass **Obv:** Monogram on shield **Rev:** Large, thick denomination, date below

Date	Mintage	VF20	XF40	MS60	MS63	MS65
1992	10,571,000	0.20	0.40	1.00	1.25	1.50

KM# 155 2 DINARA
3.80 g., Copper-Nickel-Zinc **Obv:** Monogram on shield **Rev:** Denomination and date

Date	Mintage	VF20	XF40	MS60	MS63	MS65
1993	10,263,000	0.10	0.20	0.50	0.70	1.25

KM# 181 2 DINARA
5.20 g., Copper-Nickel-Zinc, 21.9 mm. **Obv:** National arms within circle **Rev:** Church **Edge:** Reeded

Date	Mintage	VF20	XF40	MS60	MS63	MS65
2000	10,071,000	—	—	0.25	0.50	0.80

KM# 151 5 DINARA
5.00 g., Brass **Obv:** Monogram on shield **Rev:** Large, thick denomination, date below

Date	Mintage	VF20	XF40	MS60	MS63	MS65
1992	26,658,000	0.15	0.30	0.75	0.90	1.25

KM# 156 5 DINARA
Copper-Nickel-Zinc **Obv:** Monogram on shield **Rev:** Denomination and date

Date	Mintage	VF20	XF40	MS60	MS63	MS65
1993	10,135,000	0.10	0.20	0.50	0.65	1.00

KM# 182 5 DINARA
6.30 g., Copper-Nickel-Zinc, 24 mm. **Obv:** National arms **Rev:** Domed building, denomination and date at left **Edge:** Reeded

Date	Mintage	VF20	XF40	MS60	MS63	MS65
2000	32,762,500	—	—	1.25	1.50	2.00

KM# 152 10 DINARA
Copper-Nickel-Zinc **Obv:** Monogram on shield **Rev:** Large, thick denomination, date below

Date	Mintage	VF20	XF40	MS60	MS63	MS65
1992	76,607,000	0.10	0.25	0.60	0.75	1.25

KM# 157 10 DINARA

6.00 g., Copper-Nickel-Zinc **Obv:** Monogram on shield **Rev:** Large denomination, date below

Date	Mintage	VF20	XF40	MS60	MS63	MS65
1993	20,461,000	0.15	0.30	0.70	1.00	1.50

KM# 169 20 NOVIH DINARA

Copper-Nickel-Zinc **Subject:** Nikola Tesla **Obv:** National arms **Rev:** Head 3/4 left

Date	Mintage	VF20	XF40	MS60	MS63	MS65
1996	—	PF65 37.50				

KM# 153 50 DINARA

Copper-Nickel-Zinc **Obv:** Monogram on shield **Rev:** Large, thick denomination, date below

Date	Mintage	VF20	XF40	MS60	MS63	MS65
1992	50,571,000	0.25	0.50	1.00	1.25	1.75

KM# 158 50 DINARA

7.00 g., Copper-Nickel-Zinc **Obv:** Monogram on shield **Rev:** Large denomination, date below

Date	Mintage	VF20	XF40	MS60	MS63	MS65
1993	10,823,000	0.20	0.40	0.80	1.00	1.50

KM# 159 100 DINARA

Brass **Obv:** Monogram on shield **Rev:** Denomination and date

Date	Mintage	VF20	XF40	MS60	MS63	MS65
1993	14,294,500	0.25	0.50	1.00	1.25	1.75

KM# 166 150 NOVIH DINARA

7.80 g., 0.900 Gold 0.2257 oz. AGW **Subject:** 110th Anniversary - National Bank **Obv:** National arms, building at left **Rev:** Peace dove in flight

Date	Mintage	VF20	XF40	MS60	MS63	MS65
ND-1995	100,000	PF63 325	PF65 375	PF67 425		

KM# 170 200 NOVIH DINARA

13.00 g., 0.925 Silver 0.3866 oz. ASW **Subject:** Nikola Tesla **Obv:** National arms **Rev:** Head 3/4 left

Date	Mintage	VF20	XF40	MS60	MS63	MS65
1996	—	PF63 20.00	PF65 25.00			

KM# 171 300 NOVIH DINARA

26.00 g., 0.925 Silver 0.7732 oz. ASW **Subject:** Nikola Tesla **Obv:** National arms **Rev:** Head 3/4 left

Date	Mintage	VF20	XF40	MS60	MS63	MS65
1996	—	PF63 30.00	PF65 40.00			

KM# 167 500 DINARA

Brass **Obv:** Monogram on shield **Rev:** Denomination and date **Note:** All but 1,000 reported melted. Not released for circulation.

Date	Mintage	VF20	XF40	MS60	MS63	MS65
1993	—	—	—	3.00	5.00	7.00

KM# 175 600 NOVIH DINARA

3.46 g., 0.900 Gold 0.100 oz. AGW **Subject:** Chilander Monastery **Obv:** Monastery **Rev:** Portraits of SS Simon and Sava

Date	Mintage	XF40	MS60	MS63	MS65	MS66
1998(1999)	10,000	—	—	175	200	250

KM# 172 1000 NOVIH DINARA

8.64 g., 0.900 Gold 0.250 oz. AGW **Subject:** Nikola Tesla **Obv:** National arms **Rev:** Head 3/4 left

Date	Mintage	VF20	XF40	MS60	MS63	MS65
1996	—	PF63 425	PF65 475	PF67 550		

KM# 176 1500 NOVIH DINARA

8.64 g., 0.900 Gold 0.250 oz. AGW **Subject:** Chilander Monastery **Obv:** Monastery **Rev:** Portraits of SS Simon and Sava

Date	Mintage	XF40	MS60	MS63	MS65	MS66
1998(1999)	—	—	—	400	450	500

KM# 177 3000 NOVIH DINARA

17.28 g., 0.900 Gold 0.4999 oz. AGW **Subject:** Chilander Monastery **Obv:** Monastery **Rev:** Portraits of SS Simon and Sava

Date	Mintage	VF20	XF40	MS60	MS63	MS65
1998	—	PF63 800	PF65 850	PF67 950		
1999	—	PF63 800	PF65 850	PF67 950		

KM# 178 6000 NOVIH DINARA

34.56 g., 0.900 Gold 0.9999 oz. AGW **Subject:** Chilander Monastery **Obv:** Monastery **Rev:** Portraits of SS Simon and Sava

Date	Mintage	VF20	XF40	MS60	MS63	MS65
1998	—	PF63 1,550	PF65 1,650	PF67 1,850		
1999	—	PF63 1,550	PF65 1,650	PF67 1,850		

PATTERNS

Including off metal strikes

KM#	Date	Mintage	Identification	Mkt Val
Pn9	1925	—	50 Para. Nickel. KM4. By Pattey.	900
Pn9a	1925	1	50 Para. Silver. KM4. By Pattey.	650
Pn10	1925	—	Dinar. Nickel. KM5. By Pattey.	525
Pn10a	1925	—	Dinar. Copper. KM5. By Pattey.	525
PnA11	1925	—	Dinar. Aluminum. By Pattey.	500
Pn11	1925	—	Dinar. Nickel. KM5.	525
Pn12	1925	—	2 Dinara. Nickel-Bronze. KM6. ESSAI.	1,250
Pn12a	1925	—	2 Dinara. Copper-Nickel. KM6. ESSAI. 3 millimeters thick.	1,250
Pn13	1925	—	2 Dinara. Nickel. KM6.	775
Pn14	1925(a)	—	10 Dinara. Gold.	—
Pn15	1926(k)	—	Dukat. Gold.	—
Pn16	1926	—	4 Dukata. Silver. River scene.	—
Pn17	1926(k)	—	4 Dukata. Gold. River scene.	—
Pn19	1931	—	4 Dukata. Gold. ESSAI.	—
Pn20	ND (1931)	—	4 Dukata. Silver.	—
Pn21	1932	—	50 Dinara. Bronze. Milled.	525
Pn21a	1932	—	50 Dinara. Copper.	525
Pn22	1938	—	10 Dinara. Copper.	275
Pn23	1938	—	20 Dinara. Copper.	350
Pn24	1938	—	50 Dinara. Copper.	400
Pn25	1953	—	25 Para. Aluminum. Hole in center.	525
Pn26	1978	20	25 Para. Aluminum.	—
Pn27	1978	19	Dinar. Copper-Nickel.	—
Pn28	1978	15	10 Dinara. Copper-Nickel.	—

PIEDFORT

KM#	Date	Mintage	Identification	Mkt Val
P1	ND(1931-1934)	—	4 Dukata. Gold. Conjoined busts.	—

TRIAL STRIKES

KM#	Date	Mintage	Identification	Mkt Val
TS1	1931(a)	—	Dukat. Gold. Uniface. ESSAI Paris/1931.	—
TS2	1931(a)	—	4 Dukata. Gold. Uniface. ESSAI Paris/1931.	—
TS3	1931	—	4 Dukata. Bronze. Uniface.	—
TS4	ND-1931(k)	—	4 Dukata. 0.9167. Gold. Uniface obverse. KM#14 (hallmarked 22K on edge).	—
TS5	1931(k)	—	4 Dukata. Platinum. Uniface.	—
TS6	1931(k)	—	8 Dukata. Gold. Uniface.	—
TS7	1931	—	8 Dukata. 0.900. Gold. Uniface. ESSAI/PARIS/1931.	—
TS8	1931	2	12 Dukata. 0.900. Gold. Uniface. ESSAI/PARIS/1931. 45.875-46.45 grams.	—

MINT SETS

KM#	Date	Mintage	Identification	Issue Price	Mkt Val
MS1	1953/1955 (7)	—	KM29-35	—	12.00
MS2	1963 (6)	—	KM36-41	—	22.00
MS3	1965 (5)	—	KM42, 44-47	—	4.00
MS4	1965 (5)	—	KM43-47	—	4.00
MSA5	1976 (4)	—	KM#55-56, 62, 63	—	8.00
MS5	1982 (6)	—	KM84-89	—	3.00
MS6	1983 (6)	—	KM84-89	—	3.00
MS7	1983 (2)	—	KM96-97. Blue plastic wallet.	—	12.50
MS8	1984 (5)	—	KM85-89	—	4.00
MS9	1985 (7)	—	KM86-89, 112-114	—	5.00
MS10	1986 (7)	—	KM86-89, 112-114	—	4.00
MS11	1987 (4)	—	KM89, 112-114	—	3.00
MS12	1988 (7)	—	KM89, 113-114, 131-134	—	3.50
MS13	1989 (4)	—	KM131-134	—	6.50
MS14	1990 (6)	—	KM139-144	—	6.50
MS15	1991 (6)	—	KM139-144	—	5.00
MS16	1992 (2)	—	KM143-144	—	25.00
MS17	2000 (4)	—	KM#179-182	—	3.50

PROOF SETS

KM#	Date	Mintage	Identification	Issue Price	Mkt Val
PS1	1968 (6)	10,000	KM49-54	—	7,750
PS2	1968 (4)	10,000	KM51-54	—	7,650
PS3	1968 (2)	10,000	KM49-50	15.00	65.00
PS4	1978 (7)	6,000	KM65-71	—	200
PS5	1978 (11)	12,000	KM65-75	—	3,750
PS6	1980 (3)	—	KM76-77, 79	—	85.00
PS7	1981 (3)	—	KM80-81, 83	—	90.00
PS8	1982 (3)	—	KM90-92	—	50.00
PS9	1982 (2)	—	KM93-94	—	70.00
PS10	1983 (3)	—	KM98, 100, 102	—	50.00
PS11	1983 (3)	—	KM99, 101, 103	—	50.00
PS12	1983 (2)	100,000	KM96-97	—	20.00
PS13	1984 (3)	—	KM105, 107, 109	—	50.00
PS14	1984 (3)	—	KM106, 108, 110	—	50.00
PS15	Mixed dates (3)	—	KM95, 104, 111	—	1,250
PS16	1985 (6)	—	KM119-121, 124-126	—	1,500
PS17	1985 (4)	—	KM116-118, 123	—	550

PS18	1985 (3)	—	KM116-118	—	100
PS19	1985 (3)	—	KM119-121	—	85.00
PS20	1987 (3)	—	KM128-130	—	500
PS21	1987 (2)	—	KM128-129	—	60.00
PS22	1989 (3)	—	KM136-138	—	500
PS23	1989 (2)	—	KM136-137	—	60.00
PS24	1990 (3)	—	KM146-148	—	300
PS25	1990 (2)	10,000	KM146-147	—	55.00
PS26	1998-1999 (4)	—	KM#175-176 dated 1998; KM#177-178 dated 1999	—	3,250

ZAÏRE

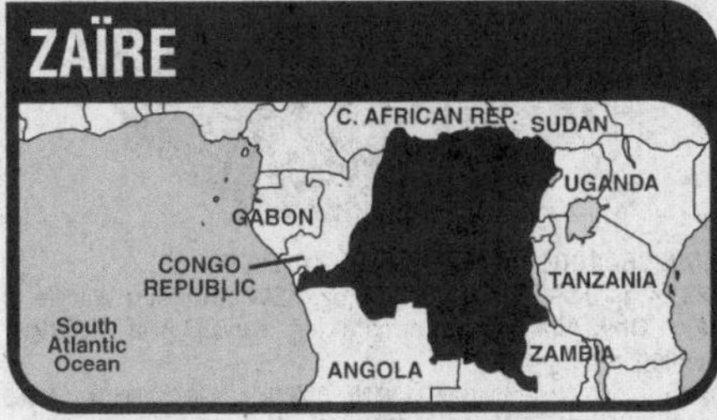

Democratic Republic of the Congo achieved independence on June 30, 1960. It followed the same monetary system as when under the Belgians. Monetary Reform of 1967 introduced new denominations and coins. The name of the country was changed to **Zaire** in 1971.

Under the command of Laurent Kabila, rebel forces overthrew ruler Sese Seko Mobutu in May of 1997. Self appointed President Kabila has officially renamed the country the Democratic Republic of Congo.

MONETARY SYSTEM

100 Makuta = 1 Zaire

1993 -

3,000,000 old Zaires = 1 Nouveau Zaire

REPUBLIC

DECIMAL COINAGE

KM# 12 5 MAKUTA

Copper-Nickel **Obv:** Denomination **Rev:** Mobuto bust left

Date	Mintage	VF20	XF40	MS60	MS63	MS65
1977	8,000,000	1.00	3.00	6.00	12.00	20.00

KM# 7 10 MAKUTA

8.95 g., Copper-Nickel **Obv:** Mobuto bust 1/4 right **Rev:** Arms below denomination

Date	Mintage	VF20	XF40	MS60	MS63	MS65
1973	5,000,000	1.25	2.00	4.00	6.00	10.00
1975	—	1.25	2.00	4.00	6.00	10.00
1976	—	1.50	2.50	5.00	9.00	15.00
1978	—	1.25	2.25	4.50	7.50	12.00

KM# 8 20 MAKUTA

Copper-Nickel **Obv:** Mobuto bust right **Rev:** Hand with torch

Date	Mintage	VF20	XF40	MS60	MS63	MS65
1973	—	1.75	3.00	5.00	7.50	12.00
1976	—	2.00	3.50	6.00	9.00	15.00

KM# 13 ZAIRE

Brass **Obv:** Denomination **Rev:** Bust facing

Date	Mintage	VF20	XF40	MS60	MS63	MS65
1987	—	0.35	0.75	1.25	2.00	3.50

KM# 9 2-1/2 ZAIRES

28.28 g., 0.925 Silver 0.841 oz. ASW **Subject:** Conservation **Obv:** Mobuto bust 1/4 right **Rev:** Mountain gorillas

Date	Mintage	XF40	MS60	MS63	MS65	MS66
1975	5,735	—	—	25.00	30.00	35.00
1975	6,629	PF65 37.00	PF67 45.00	PF69 65.00		

KM# 1 5 ZAIRES

27.84 g., 0.925 Silver 0.8279 oz. ASW **Obv:** Mobuto bust left **Rev:** Hotel Intercontinental

Date	Mintage	VF20	XF40	MS60	MS63	MS65
1971	—	PF63 50.00	PF65 55.00	PF67 65.00		

KM# 10 5 ZAIRES

35.00 g., 0.925 Silver 1.0409 oz. ASW **Subject:** Conservation **Obv:** Mobuto bust 1/4 right **Rev:** Okapi right

Date	Mintage	XF40	MS60	MS63	MS65	MS66
1975	5,734	—	—	30.00	35.00	40.00
1975	6,431	PF65 45.00	PF67 55.00	PF69 75.00		

KM# 14 5 ZAIRES

Brass, 24 mm. **Obv:** Denomination **Rev:** Mobuto bust facing

Date	Mintage	VF20	XF40	MS60	MS63	MS65
1987	—	0.50	1.00	1.50	2.50	3.75

KM# 2 10 ZAIRES

9.96 g., 0.900 Gold 0.2882 oz. AGW **Obv:** Mobuto bust left **Rev:** Hotel Intercontinental

Date	Mintage	VF20	XF40	MS60	MS63	MS65
1971	—	PF63 475	PF65 525	PF67 550		

KM# 3 10 ZAIRES

6.04 g., 0.999 Platinum 0.194 oz. APW **Obv:** Mobuto bust left **Rev:** Hotel Intercontinental

Date	Mintage	VF20	XF40	MS60	MS63	MS65
1971	—	PF63 375	PF65 425	PF67 475		

KM# 19 10 ZAIRES

7.92 g., Brass **Obv:** Denomination **Rev:** Mobuto bust facing

Date	Mintage	VF20	XF40	MS60	MS63	MS65
1988	—	1.00	2.00	3.00	5.00	7.00

KM# 4 20 ZAIRES

20.90 g., 0.900 Gold 0.6048 oz. AGW **Obv:** Mobuto bust left **Rev:** Hotel Intercontinental

Date	Mintage	VF20	XF40	MS60	MS63	MS65
1971	—	PF63 950	PF65 1,100	PF67 1,250		

KM# 5 20 ZAIRES

3.89 g., 0.999 Platinum 0.1249 oz. APW **Obv:** Mobuto bust left **Rev:** Hotel Intercontinental

Date	Mintage	VF20	XF40	MS60	MS63	MS65
1971	—	PF63 225	PF65 265	PF67 295		

KM# 6 50 ZAIRES

46.96 g., 0.900 Gold 1.3588 oz. AGW **Obv:** Mobuto bust 3/4 left **Rev:** Hotel Intercontinental

Date	Mintage	VF20	XF40	MS60	MS63	MS65
1971	—	PF63 2,200	PF65 2,400	PF67 2,700		

KM# 11 100 ZAIRES
33.44 g., 0.900 Gold 0.9675 oz. AGW **Subject:** Conservation **Obv:** Mobuto bust 1/4 right **Rev:** Leopard right

Date	Mintage	XF40	MS60	MS63	MS65	MS66
1975	1,415	—	—	1,500	1,650	1,800
1975	279	PF65 2,000	PF67 2,500	PF69 3,200		

KM# 20 500 NOUVEAUX ZAIRES
20.00 g., 0.500 Silver 0.3215 oz. ASW **Subject:** Wildlife of Africa **Obv:** African map, arms at left **Rev:** Leopard on branch

Date	Mintage	VF20	XF40	MS60	MS63	MS65
1996	10,000	PF63 22.00	PF65 27.00	PF67 32.00		

KM# 21 500 NOUVEAUX ZAIRES
20.00 g., 0.500 Silver 0.3215 oz. ASW **Subject:** Wildlife of Africa **Obv:** African map, arms at left **Rev:** Gorilla left

Date	Mintage	VF20	XF40	MS60	MS63	MS65
1996	Est. 10000	PF63 22.00	PF65 27.00	PF67 32.00		

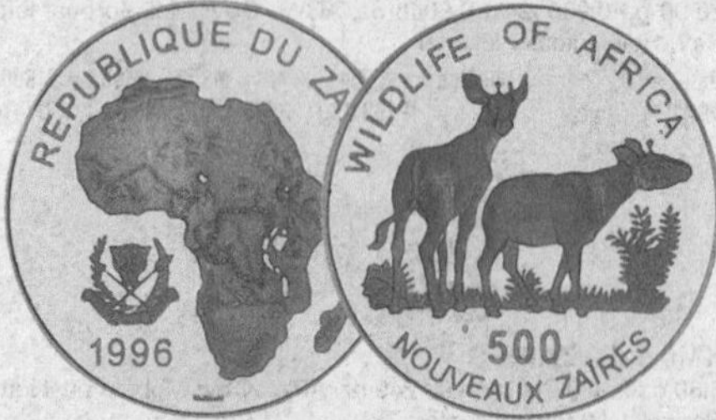

KM# 22 500 NOUVEAUX ZAIRES
20.00 g., 0.500 Silver 0.3215 oz. ASW **Subject:** Wildlife of Africa **Obv:** African map, arms at left **Rev:** Two okapi

Date	Mintage	VF20	XF40	MS60	MS63	MS65
1996	Est. 10000	PF63 22.00	PF65 27.00	PF67 32.00		

KM# 23 1000 NOUVEAUX ZAIRES
29.63 g., 0.925 Silver 0.8812 oz. ASW **Subject:** Wildlife of Africa **Obv:** African map, arms at left **Rev:** Common hippopotamus left

Date	Mintage	VF20	XF40	MS60	MS63	MS65
1997	Est. 20000	PF63 28.00	PF65 32.00	PF67 37.00		

KM# 24 1000 NOUVEAUX ZAIRES
30.09 g., 0.925 Silver 0.8949 oz. ASW **Subject:** Wildlife of Africa **Obv:** African map, arms at left **Rev:** Sailing ship "Portuguese Caravel"

Date	Mintage	VF20	XF40	MS60	MS63	MS65
1997	Est. 20000	PF63 30.00	PF65 35.00	PF67 40.00		

KM# 28 1000 NOUVEAUX ZAIRES
Silver, 39 mm. **Subject:** World Cup, France, 1998 **Obv:** Map of Africa, National arms at lower left **Rev:** Soccer field, ball, globe and Eifle tower

Date	Mintage	VF20	XF40	MS60	MS63	MS65
1997	—	PF63 32.00	PF65 37.00	PF67 42.00		

KM# 25 5000 NOUVEAUX ZAIRES
411.42 g., 0.999 Silver 13.2143 oz. ASW **Subject:** Wildlife of Africa **Obv:** African map, arms at left **Rev:** Leopard on branch **Edge:** Reeded

Date	Mintage	VF20	XF40	MS60	MS63	MS65
1996	1,000	PF65 300	PF67 350			

KM# 26 10000 NOUVEAUX ZAIRES
822.84 g., 0.999 Silver 26.4286 oz. ASW **Subject:** Wildlife of Africa **Obv:** African map, arms at left **Rev:** Gorilla left **Edge:** Reeded

Date	Mintage	VF20	XF40	MS60	MS63	MS65
1996	1,000	PF65 550	PF67 600			

KM# 27 10000 NOUVEAUX ZAIRES
155.50 g., 0.999 Gold 4.9944 oz. AGW, 62 mm. **Rev:** Leopard in tree

Date	Mintage	XF40	MS60	MS63	MS65	MS66
1996	—	—	—	7,000	8,000	9,000

PATTERNS

Including off metal strikes

KM#	Date	Mintage	Identification	Mkt Val
Pn1	1987	—	Zaire. KM#13; coin rotation.	300
Pn2	1987	—	Zaire. KM#13; medal rotation.	300

PROOF SETS

KM#	Date	Mintage	Identification	Issue Price	Mkt Val
PS1	1971 (6)	—	KM1-6	—	5,350
PS2	1975 (2)	500	KM9-10	60.00	100

ZAMBIA

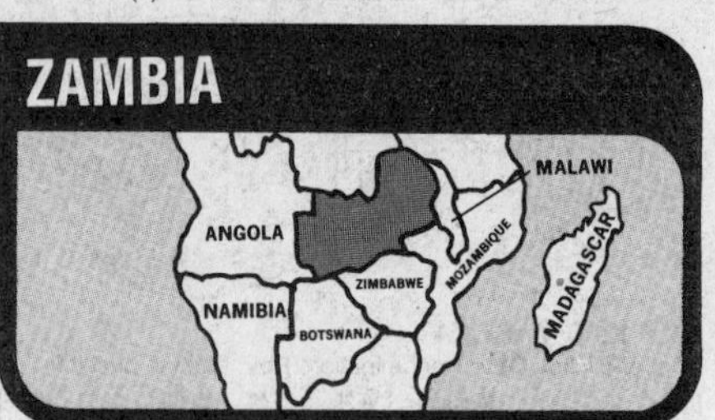

The Republic of Zambia (formerly Northern Rhodesia), a landlocked country in south-central Africa, has an area of 290,586 sq. mi. (752,610 sq. km.) and a population of*7.9 million. Capital: Lusaka. The economy of Zambia is based principally on copper, of which Zambia is the world's third largest producer. Copper, zinc, lead, cobalt and tobacco are exported.

The area that is now Zambia was brought within the British sphere of influence in 1888 by empire builder Cecil Rhodes, who obtained mining concessions in south-central Africa from indigenous chiefs. The territory was ruled by the British South Africa Company, which Rhodes established, until 1924 when its administration was transferred to the British government as a protectorate. In1953, Northern Rhodesia was joined with Nyasaland and the colony of Southern Rhodesia to form the Federation of Rhodesia and Nyasaland. Northern Rhodesia seceded from the Federation on Oct. 24, 1964, and became the independent Republic of Zambia. Zambia is a member of the Commonwealth of Nations. The president is Chief of State.

Zambia converted to a decimal coinage on January 16, 1969.

For earlier coinage refer to Rhodesia and Nyasaland.

RULER
British, until 1964

MONETARY SYSTEM
12 Pence = 1 Shilling
20 Shillings = 1 Pound

REPUBLIC

STANDARD COINAGE

KM# 58 100 KWACHA

28.28 g., Copper-Nickel **Obv:** National arms with supporters, date below **Rev:** Rhinoceros running right, denomination above **Edge:** Reeded

Date	Mintage	VF20	XF40	MS60	MS63	MS65
1998	Est. 100000	—	—	4.00	7.00	10.00

KM# 58a 100 KWACHA

28.28 g., 0.999 Silver 0.9083 oz. ASW **Obv:** National arms with supporters, date below **Rev:** Black Rhinoceros running right, denomination above

Date	Mintage	VF20	XF40	MS60	MS63	MS65
1998	Est. 25000	**PF63** 45.00		**PF65** 50.00	**PF67** 60.00	

KM# 59 100 KWACHA

28.28 g., Copper-Nickel **Obv:** National arms with supporters, date below **Rev:** Hippopotamus and calf, denomination above **Edge:** Reeded

Date	Mintage	VF20	XF40	MS60	MS63	MS65
1998	Est. 100000	—	—	4.00	7.00	10.00

KM# 59a 100 KWACHA

28.28 g., 0.999 Silver 0.9083 oz. ASW **Obv:** National arms with supporters, date below **Rev:** Hippopotamus and calf, denomination above

Date	Mintage	VF20	XF40	MS60	MS63	MS65
1998	Est. 25000	**PF63** 45.00		**PF65** 50.00	**PF67** 60.00	

KM# 60 100 KWACHA

28.28 g., Copper-Nickel **Obv:** National arms with supporters, date below **Rev:** Antelopes jumping over denomination **Edge:** Reeded

Date	Mintage	VF20	XF40	MS60	MS63	MS65
1998	Est. 100000	—	—	4.00	7.00	10.00

KM# 60a 100 KWACHA

28.28 g., 0.999 Silver 0.9083 oz. ASW **Obv:** National arms with supporters, date below **Rev:** Antelopes jumping over denomination

Date	Mintage	VF20	XF40	MS60	MS63	MS65
1998	Est. 25000	**PF63** 40.00		**PF65** 45.00	**PF67** 55.00	

KM# 61 100 KWACHA

28.28 g., Copper-Nickel **Obv:** National arms with supporters, date below **Rev:** Pelican on branch, denomination at right **Edge:** Reeded

Date	Mintage	VF20	XF40	MS60	MS63	MS65
1998	Est. 100000	—	—	4.00	7.00	10.00

KM# 61a 100 KWACHA

28.28 g., 0.999 Silver 0.9083 oz. ASW **Obv:** National arms with supporters, date below **Rev:** Pelican on branch, denomination at right

Date	Mintage	VF20	XF40	MS60	MS63	MS65
1998	Est. 25000	**PF63** 50.00		**PF65** 55.00	**PF67** 65.00	

KM# 62 100 KWACHA

28.28 g., Copper-Nickel **Obv:** National arms with supporters, date below **Rev:** Storks left and right, denomination at right **Edge:** Reeded

Date	Mintage	VF20	XF40	MS60	MS63	MS65
1998	Est. 100000	—	—	4.00	7.00	10.00

KM# 62a 100 KWACHA

28.28 g., 0.999 Silver 0.9083 oz. ASW **Obv:** National arms with supporters, date below **Rev:** Storks left and right, denomination at right

Date	Mintage	VF20	XF40	MS60	MS63	MS65
1998	—	**PF63** 40.00		**PF65** 45.00	**PF67** 55.00	

KM# 63 100 KWACHA

28.28 g., Copper-Nickel **Obv:** National arms with supporters, date below **Rev:** Zebra right, denomination at right **Edge:** Reeded

Date	Mintage	VF20	XF40	MS60	MS63	MS65
1998	Est. 100000	—	—	4.00	7.00	10.00

KM# 63a 100 KWACHA

28.28 g., 0.999 Silver 0.9083 oz. ASW **Obv:** National arms with supporters, date below **Rev:** Burchell's Zebra right, denomination at right

Date	Mintage	VF20	XF40	MS60	MS63	MS65
1998	Est. 25000	**PF63** 40.00		**PF65** 45.00	**PF67** 55.00	

KM# 64 100 KWACHA

28.28 g., Copper-Nickel **Obv:** National arms with supporters, date below **Rev:** Flamingo, denomination at left **Edge:** Reeded

Date	Mintage	VF20	XF40	MS60	MS63	MS65
1998	Est. 100000	—	—	4.00	7.00	10.00

KM# 64a 100 KWACHA

28.28 g., 0.999 Silver 0.9083 oz. ASW **Obv:** National arms with supporters, date below **Rev:** Flamingos, denomination at left

Date	Mintage	VF20	XF40	MS60	MS63	MS65
1998	Est. 25000	**PF63** 40.00		**PF65** 45.00	**PF67** 55.00	

KM# 65 100 KWACHA

28.28 g., Copper-Nickel **Obv:** National arms with supporters, date below **Rev:** Giraffes, denomination at left **Edge:** Reeded

Date	Mintage	VF20	XF40	MS60	MS63	MS65
1998	Est. 100000	—	—	4.00	7.00	10.00

KM# 65a 100 KWACHA

28.28 g., 0.999 Silver 0.9083 oz. ASW **Obv:** National arms with supporters, date below **Rev:** Giraffes, denomination at left

Date	Mintage	VF20	XF40	MS60	MS63	MS65
1998	Est. 25000	**PF63** 45.00		**PF65** 50.00	**PF67** 60.00	

KM# 66 100 KWACHA

28.28 g., Copper-Nickel **Obv:** National arms with supporters, date below **Rev:** Lion facing, denomination at left **Edge:** Reeded

Date	Mintage	VF20	XF40	MS60	MS63	MS65
1998	Est. 100000	—	—	4.00	7.00	10.00

KM# 66a 100 KWACHA

28.28 g., 0.999 Silver 0.9083 oz. ASW **Obv:** National arms with supporters, date below **Rev:** Lion facing, denomination at left

Date	Mintage	VF20	XF40	MS60	MS63	MS65
1998	—	**PF63** 45.00		**PF65** 50.00	**PF67** 60.00	

KM# 67 100 KWACHA

28.28 g., Copper-Nickel **Obv:** National arms with supporters, date below **Rev:** Gazelle, denomination above **Edge:** Reeded

Date	Mintage	VF20	XF40	MS60	MS63	MS65
1998	Est. 100000	—	—	4.00	7.00	10.00

Note: Please note that the copper-nickel versions were offered to the market almost two months after the silver version

KM# 67a 100 KWACHA

28.28 g., 0.999 Silver 0.9083 oz. ASW **Obv:** National arms with supporters, date below **Rev:** Two gazelles, denomination above

Date	Mintage	VF20	XF40	MS60	MS63	MS65
1998	Est. 25000	**PF63** 40.00		**PF65** 45.00	**PF67** 55.00	

KM# 5 PENNY

Bronze, 27 mm. **Obv:** Date below center hole **Rev:** Denomination below center hole

Date	Mintage	F12	VF20	XF40	MS60	MS63
1966	7,200,000	0.25	0.45	0.85	1.75	2.75
1966 Proof	60	—	—	—	—	—

KM# 1 6 PENCE

Copper-Nickel-Zinc, 19.4 mm. **Obv:** National arms divide date **Rev:** Morning Glory (Ipomoea sp. convolvulaceae), denomination below

Date	Mintage	VF20	XF40	MS60	MS63	MS65
1964	3,500,000	0.30	0.60	1.00	1.20	1.50
1964	5,000	**PF65** 1.75				

KM# 6 6 PENCE

Copper-Nickel-Zinc, 19.4 mm. **Obv:** Head of K.D. Kaunda right, date below **Rev:** Morning glory, denomination below

Date	Mintage	VF20	XF40	MS60	MS63	MS65
1966	7,200,000	0.50	1.00	1.25	2.00	2.50
1966 Proof	60	—	—	—	—	—

KM# 2 SHILLING

Copper-Nickel, 23.6 mm. **Obv:** National arms divides date **Rev:** Crowned Hornbill, oribi and denomination

Date	Mintage	VF20	XF40	MS60	MS63	MS65
1964	3,510,000	0.50	1.00	1.25	2.00	2.50
1964	5,000	**PF65** 3.50				

KM# 7 SHILLING

Copper-Nickel, 23.6 mm. **Obv:** Head of K.D. Kaunda right, date below **Rev:** Crowned hornbill and denomination

Date	Mintage	VF20	XF40	MS60	MS63	MS65
1966	5,000,000	0.75	1.50	2.25	3.25	4.00
1966 Proof	60	—	—	—	—	—

KM# 3 2 SHILLINGS

Copper-Nickel, 28.5 mm. **Obv:** National arms divides date **Rev:** Bohor Reedbuck right and denomination

Date	Mintage	VF20	XF40	MS60	MS63	MS65
1964	3,770,000	0.75	1.50	2.00	3.00	5.00
1964	5,000	**PF65** 6.00				

KM# 8 2 SHILLINGS

Copper-Nickel, 28.5 mm. **Obv:** Head of K.D. Kaunda right, date below **Rev:** Bohor Reedbuck right and denomination

Date	Mintage	VF20	XF40	MS60	MS63	MS65
1966	5,000,000	1.00	1.50	2.25	4.50	5.00
1966 Proof	60	—	—	—	—	—

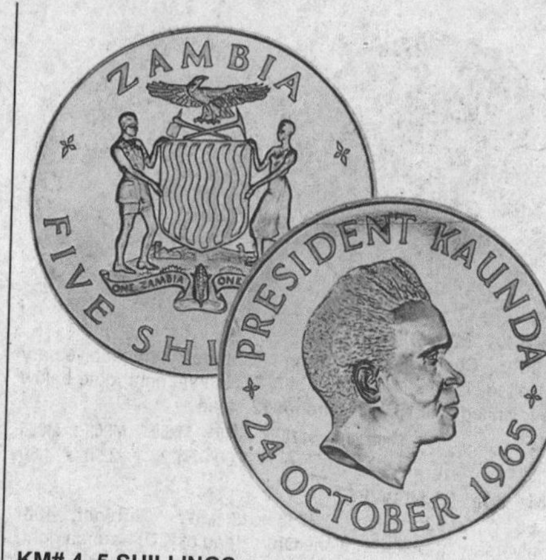

KM# 4 5 SHILLINGS

Copper-Nickel, 38.8 mm. **Subject:** 1st Anniversary of Independence **Obv:** National arms with supporters, denomination below **Rev:** Head of K.D. Kaunda right, date below **Edge Lettering:** ONE ZAMBIA ONE NATION * 24.10.1964 * **Note:** Two edge ltter varieties.

Date	Mintage	VF20	XF40	MS60	MS63	MS65
1965	10,000	2.50	3.50	5.00	7.50	9.00
1965	20,000	**PF63** 10.00	**PF65** 14.00			

DECIMAL COINAGE

100 Ngwee = 1 Kwacha

KM# 9 NGWEE

2.30 g., Bronze, 17.6 mm. **Obv:** Head of K.D. Kaunda right, date below **Rev:** Aardvark left, denomination below

Date	Mintage	VF20	XF40	MS60	MS63	MS65
1968	8,000,000	0.10	0.30	0.75	1.50	2.50
1968	4,000	**PF65** 2.50				
1969	16,000,000	0.10	0.20	0.50	1.00	2.00
1972	21,000,000	0.10	0.20	0.50	1.00	2.00
1978	23,976,000	0.10	0.20	0.50	1.00	2.00
1978	24,000	**PF65** 1.50				

KM# 9a NGWEE

2.10 g., Copper Clad Steel, 16.47 mm. **Obv:** Head of K.D. Kaunda right, date below **Rev:** Aardvark left, denomination below **Edge:** Plain

Date	Mintage	VF20	XF40	MS60	MS63	MS65
1982	10,000,000	0.10	0.20	0.50	1.00	1.50
1983	60,000,000	0.10	0.20	0.50	1.00	1.50

KM# 10 2 NGWEE

4.20 g., Bronze, 21 mm. **Obv:** Head of K.D. Kaunda right, date below **Rev:** Martial Eagle, denomination at right

Date	Mintage	VF20	XF40	MS60	MS63	MS65
1968	19,000,000	0.10	0.20	0.50	1.00	1.50
1968	4,000	**PF65** 3.50				
1978	—	0.15	0.25	0.60	1.25	2.00
1978	24,000	**PF65** 2.00				

KM# 10a 2 NGWEE

4.19 g., Copper Clad Steel, 19.39 mm. **Obv:** Head of K.D. Kaunda right, date below **Rev:** Martial Eagle, denomination at right **Edge:** Plain

Date	Mintage	VF20	XF40	MS60	MS63	MS65
1982	7,500,000	0.10	0.20	0.50	1.00	1.75
1983	60,000,000	0.10	0.15	0.35	0.75	1.50

KM# 11 5 NGWEE

2.80 g., Copper-Nickel, 19.4 mm. **Obv:** Head of K.D. Kaunda right, date below **Rev:** Morning Glory, denomination below

Date	Mintage	VF20	XF40	MS60	MS63	MS65
1968	12,000,000	0.15	0.25	0.30	0.60	1.50
1968	4,000	**PF65** 3.50				
1972	9,000,000	0.15	0.25	0.30	0.60	1.50
1978	1,976,000	0.15	0.25	0.30	0.60	1.50
1978	24,000	**PF65** 2.00				
1982	12,000,000	0.15	0.25	0.30	0.60	1.50
1987	10,000,000	0.15	0.25	0.30	0.60	1.50

KM# 12 10 NGWEE

5.65 g., Copper-Nickel-Zinc, 23.6 mm. **Obv:** K.D. Kaunda head right **Rev:** Crowned Hornbill and denomination

Date	Mintage	VF20	XF40	MS60	MS63	MS65
1968	1,000,000	0.40	0.85	1.25	1.75	2.50
1968	4,000	**PF65** 3.75				
1972	1,000,000	0.30	0.50	0.75	1.00	1.75
1978	1,976,000	0.30	0.50	0.75	1.00	1.75
1978	24,000	**PF65** 2.25				
1982	8,000,000	0.30	0.50	0.75	1.00	1.75
1983	2,500	0.30	0.50	0.75	1.00	1.75
1987	6,000,000	0.30	0.50	0.75	1.00	1.75

KM# 13 20 NGWEE

11.30 g., Copper-Nickel, 28.5 mm. **Obv:** Head of K.D. Kaunda right, date below **Rev:** Bohur Reedbuck right and denomination

Date	Mintage	VF20	XF40	MS60	MS63	MS65
1968	1,500,000	0.75	1.50	2.00	2.50	3.75
1968	4,000	**PF65** 4.00				
1972	7,500,000	0.50	1.00	1.50	2.00	3.00
1978	24,000	**PF65** 3.00				
1983	998,000	0.75	1.50	2.00	2.50	3.75
1987	—	0.50	1.00	1.50	2.00	3.00
1988	3,000,000	0.50	1.00	1.50	2.00	3.00

KM# 22 20 NGWEE

11.30 g., Copper-Nickel, 28.5 mm. **Series:** F.A.O. - World Food Day **Obv:** Head of K.D. Kaunda right, date below **Rev:** Corn plant, date and denomination within inner circle

Date	Mintage	VF20	XF40	MS60	MS63	MS65
1981	970,000	0.75	1.50	2.00	2.75	5.00

KM# 23 20 NGWEE

11.30 g., Copper-Nickel, 28.5 mm. **Subject:** 20th Anniversary

- Bank of Zambia **Obv:** Head of K.D. Kaunda right, date below **Rev:** Bank building divides dates, denomination above

Date	Mintage	VF20	XF40	MS60	MS63	MS65
1985	—	0.65	1.25	1.75	2.25	3.50

KM# 23a 20 NGWEE

11.31 g., 0.925 Silver 0.3364 oz. ASW, 28.5 mm. **Subject:** 20th Anniversary - Bank of Zambia **Obv:** Head of K.D. Kaunda right, date below **Rev:** Bank building divides dates, denominaton above

Date	Mintage	VF20	XF40	MS60	MS63	MS65
1985	—	PF63 16.00		PF65 18.00		

KM# 29 25 NGWEE

2.51 g., Nickel Plated Steel, 19.93 mm. **Obv:** National arms with supporters, date below **Rev:** Crowned Hornbill and denomination **Edge:** Plain

Date	Mintage	VF20	XF40	MS60	MS63	MS65
1992	—	—	—	0.50	1.00	1.50

KM# 14 50 NGWEE

11.60 g., Copper-Nickel, 30 mm. **Series:** F.A.O. **Obv:** Head of K.D. Kaunda right, date below **Rev:** Ear of corn divides denomination **Shape:** 12-sided

Date	Mintage	VF20	XF40	MS60	MS63	MS65
ND-1969	70,000	2.00	3.00	4.00	6.00	7.50

KM# 15 50 NGWEE

11.60 g., Copper-Nickel, 30 mm. **Series:** F.A.O. **Obv:** Head of K.D. Kaunda right, date below **Rev:** Ear of corn divides denomination **Shape:** 12-sided

Date	Mintage	VF20	XF40	MS60	MS63	MS65
1972	510,000	1.25	2.50	3.50	5.00	6.50

KM# 16 50 NGWEE

11.60 g., Copper-Nickel, 30 mm. **Subject:** Second Republic, 13 December 1972 **Obv:** Head of K.D. Kaunda right, date below **Rev:** National arms with supporters, denomination below **Shape:** 12-sided

Date	Mintage	VF20	XF40	MS60	MS63	MS65
1972	6,000,000	1.00	2.00	2.50	3.00	5.00
1972	2,000	PF65 14.00				
1978	24,000	PF65 8.00				
1983	998,000	—	1.00	2.00	3.00	5.00

KM# 24 50 NGWEE

11.60 g., Copper-Nickel, 30 mm. **Subject:** 40th Anniversary of United Nations **Obv:** Head of K.D. Kaunda right, date below **Rev:** United Nations logo **Shape:** 12-sided

Date	Mintage	VF20	XF40	MS60	MS63	MS65
1985	—	—	1.00	1.25	2.50	4.50

KM# 24a 50 NGWEE

11.66 g., 0.925 Silver 0.3468 oz. ASW **Subject:** 40th Anniversary of United Nations **Obv:** Head of K.D. Kaunda right, date below **Rev:** United Nations logo **Shape:** 12-sided

Date	Mintage	VF20	XF40	MS60	MS63	MS65
1985	—	PF63 17.00		PF65 20.00		

KM# 30 50 NGWEE

4.05 g., Nickel Plated Steel, 22.55 mm. **Obv:** National arms with supporters, date below **Rev:** Kafue Lechwe and denomination **Edge:** Plain

Date	Mintage	VF20	XF40	MS60	MS63	MS65
1992	—	—	—	1.00	1.50	2.00

KM# 17 KWACHA

Copper-Nickel **Subject:** 10th Anniversary of Independence **Obv:** Head of K.D. Kaunda right, date below **Rev:** National arms with supporters, denomination below

Date	Mintage	VF20	XF40	MS60	MS63	MS65
ND(1974)	4,000	—	—	—	35.00	45.00
ND(1974)	1,500	PF63 65.00		PF65 75.00		

KM# 26 KWACHA

Nickel-Brass **Obv:** Head of K.D. Kaunda right, date below **Rev:** Two falcons on branch divided by denomination

Date	Mintage	VF20	XF40	MS60	MS63	MS65
1989	8,000,000	0.75	1.50	2.50	3.50	5.00

KM# 38 KWACHA

3.00 g., Brass, 19.2 mm. **Obv:** National arms with supporters, date below **Rev:** Two falcons on branch divided by denomination

Date	Mintage	VF20	XF40	MS60	MS63	MS65
1992	—	—	—	0.75	1.50	2.50

KM# 18 5 KWACHA

25.31 g., 0.925 Silver 0.7527 oz. ASW **Subject:** Conservation **Obv:** Head of K.D. Kaunda right, date below **Rev:** Kafue Lechwe right, denomination below

Date	Mintage	XF40	MS60	MS63	MS65	MS66
1979	3,250	—	25.00	35.00	40.00	45.00

KM# 18a 5 KWACHA

28.28 g., 0.925 Silver 0.841 oz. ASW **Subject:** Conservation **Obv:** Head of K.D. Kaunda right, date below **Rev:** Kafue Lechwe right, denomination below

Date	Mintage	XF40	MS60	MS63	MS65	MS66
1979	3,407	PF65 42.00		PF67 50.00	PF69 60.00	

KM# 31 5 KWACHA

3.50 g., Brass, 21 mm. **Obv:** National arms with supporters, date below **Rev:** Oryx right and denomination **Edge:** Reeded

Date	Mintage	VF20	XF40	MS60	MS63	MS65
1992	—	—	—	1.00	2.00	3.00

KM# 19 10 KWACHA

31.65 g., 0.925 Silver 0.9413 oz. ASW **Subject:** Conservation **Obv:** Head of K.D. Kaunda right, date below **Rev:** Taita Falcon flying right, denomination below

Date	Mintage	XF40	MS60	MS63	MS65	MS66
1979	3,250	—	30.00	40.00	45.00	50.00

KM# 19a 10 KWACHA

35.00 g., 0.925 Silver 1.0409 oz. ASW **Subject:** Conservation **Obv:** Head of K.D. Kaunda right, date below **Rev:** Taita Falcon flying right, denomination below

Date	Mintage	XF40	MS60	MS63	MS65	MS66
1979	3,256	PF65 47.00		PF67 55.00	PF69 65.00	

KM# 21 10 KWACHA

27.22 g., 0.925 Silver 0.8095 oz. ASW **Series:** International Year of the Child **Obv:** Head of K.D. Kaunda right, date below **Rev:** 3 children on playground equipment

Date	Mintage	VF20	XF40	MS60	MS63	MS65
1980	12,000	PF63 18.00		PF65 22.00	PF67 27.00	

KM# 25 10 KWACHA

27.22 g., 0.925 Silver 0.8095 oz. ASW **Series:** World Wildlife Fund **Obv:** Head of K.D. Kaunda right, date below **Rev:** White-winged Flufftail, denomination below

Date	Mintage	VF20	XF40	MS60	MS63	MS65
1986	25,000	PF63 18.00		PF65 22.00	PF67 27.00	

KM# 27 10 KWACHA

27.22 g., 0.925 Silver 0.8095 oz. ASW **Subject:** 70th Anniversary - Save the Children Fund **Obv:** Head of K.D. Kaunda right, date below **Rev:** Child holding up corn cob, denomination below

Date	Mintage	VF20	XF40	MS60	MS63	MS65
1989	Est. 20000	PF63 18.00		PF65 22.00	PF67 27.00	

KM# 32 10 KWACHA

5.10 g., Brass, 24 mm. **Obv:** National arms, date below **Rev:** Rhinoceros facing and denomination **Edge:** Reeded

Date	Mintage	VF20	XF40	MS60	MS63	MS65
1992	—	—	—	1.25	2.50	3.50

KM# 39 10 KWACHA

20.00 g., 0.999 Silver 0.6424 oz. ASW **Subject:** World Cup Soccer **Obv:** National arms with supporters divide date, denomination below **Rev:** Player kicking ball; .999 in field

Date	Mintage	VF20	XF40	MS60	MS63	MS65
1994	—	PF63 25.00		PF65 30.00	PF67 40.00	

KM# 119 10 KWACHA

27.34 g., Copper-Nickel, 40.1 mm. **Subject:** UNICEF **Obv:** National arms with supporters divide date, denomination below **Rev:** Three boys playing soccer **Edge:** Reeded

Date	Mintage	VF20	XF40	MS60	MS63	MS65
2000 Matte	—	—	—	3.50	5.00	7.50

KM# 119a 10 KWACHA

27.22 g., 0.925 Silver 0.8095 oz. ASW, 40.1 mm. **Subject:** UNICEF **Obv:** National arms with supporters divide date, denomination below **Rev:** Three boys playing soccer **Edge:** Reeded

Date	Mintage	VF20	XF40	MS60	MS63	MS65
2000	25,000	PF63 22.00		PF65 27.00		

KM# 33 20 KWACHA

10.17 g., 0.999 Silver 0.3266 oz. ASW **Series:** 1994 Olympics **Obv:** National arms **Rev:** Slalom skier

Date	Mintage	VF20	XF40	MS60	MS63	MS65
1994	25,000	PF63 17.00		PF65 20.00	PF67 30.00	

KM# 213 20 KWACHA

10.00 g., 0.999 Silver 0.3212 oz. ASW **Subject:** XVII Winter Olympics, Lillehammer **Rev:** Salom

Date	Mintage	VF20	XF40	MS60	MS63	MS65
1994	1,700	PF65 45.00		PF67 55.00		

KM# 215 75 KWACHA

31.10 g., 0.999 Gold 0.9989 oz. AGW **Subject:** Equality

Date	Mintage	VF20	XF40	MS60	MS63	MS65
1994	—	PF65 1,500		PF67 1,700		

KM# 51 75 KWACHA

5.00 g., 0.999 Silver 0.1606 oz. ASW, 22 mm. **Subject:** Diana - The People's Princess **Obv:** National arms with supporters divide date **Rev:** Bust facing

Date	Mintage	VF20	XF40	MS60	MS63	MS65
1997	—	PF63 12.00		PF65 15.00		

KM# 28 100 KWACHA

28.28 g., 0.925 Silver 0.841 oz. ASW **Series:** Barcelona Summer Olympics **Subject:** Boxing **Obv:** National arms with supporters, date below **Rev:** 2 boxers in ring fighting, denomination above

Date	Mintage	VF20	XF40	MS60	MS63	MS65
1992	Est. 50000	PF63 25.00		PF65 30.00	PF67 40.00	

KM# 50 100 KWACHA

Copper-Nickel **Obv:** National arms with supporters **Rev:** Charging bull elephant, denomination at right

Date	Mintage	VF20	XF40	MS60	MS63	MS65
1997	—	—	—	10.00	12.00	15.00

KM# 56 100 KWACHA

28.28 g., Copper-Nickel **Obv:** National arms with supporters, date below **Rev:** Crocodile, denomination at right **Edge:** Reeded

Date	Mintage	VF20	XF40	MS60	MS63	MS65
1998	Est. 100000	—	—	4.00	7.00	10.00

KM# 56a 100 KWACHA

28.28 g., 0.999 Silver 0.9083 oz. ASW **Obv:** National arms with supporters, date below **Rev:** Crocodile, denomination at right

Date	Mintage	VF20	XF40	MS60	MS63	MS65
1998	Est. 25000	PF63 40.00		PF65 45.00	PF67 55.00	

KM# 57 100 KWACHA

28.28 g., Copper-Nickel **Obv:** National arms with supporters, date below **Rev:** Leopard on branch left, denomination below **Edge:** Reeded

Date	Mintage	VF20	XF40	MS60	MS63	MS65
1998	Est. 100000	—	—	4.00	7.00	10.00

KM# 57a 100 KWACHA

28.28 g., 0.999 Silver 0.9083 oz. ASW **Obv:** National arms with supporters, date below **Rev:** Leopard on branch left, denomination below

Date	Mintage	VF20	XF40	MS60	MS63	MS65
1998	Est. 25000	PF63 45.00		PF65 50.00	PF67 60.00	

KM# 52 200 KWACHA
Copper-Nickel **Subject:** Diana - The People's Princess **Obv:** National arms with supporters divide date, denomination below **Rev:** Head facing

Date	Mintage	VF20	XF40	MS60	MS63	MS65
1997	—	PF63 7.00	PF65 9.00			

KM# 52a 200 KWACHA
31.13 g., 0.999 Silver 0.9999 oz. ASW, 35 mm. **Obv:** National arms with supporters divide date, denomination below **Rev:** Head facing **Edge:** Partially reeded with metal content from 5-7 o'clock

Date	Mintage	VF20	XF40	MS60	MS63	MS65
1997	197	PF65 50.00	PF67 60.00			

KM# 20 250 KWACHA
33.63 g., 0.900 Gold 0.9731 oz. AGW **Subject:** Conservation **Obv:** Head of K.D. Kaunda right, date below **Rev:** African wild dog right, denomination below

Date	Mintage	XF40	MS60	MS63	MS65	MS66
1979	455	—	—	1,750	1,950	2,200
1979	245	PF65 2,400	PF67 2,800	PF69 3,600		

KM# 34 250 KWACHA
136.08 g., 0.925 Silver 4.0469 oz. ASW, 63 mm. **Obv:** National arms with supporters, date below **Rev:** African fish eagles, one on branch and one in flight, denomination below **Note:** Illustration reduced.

Date	Mintage	XF40	MS60	MS63	MS65	MS66
1993	400	—	—	175	200	225
1993	5,000	PF65 150	PF67 175	PF69 200		

KM# 35 250 KWACHA
136.08 g., 0.925 Silver 4.0469 oz. ASW, 63 mm. **Obv:** National arms with supporters, date below **Rev:** Saddle-billed stork drinking, denomination below **Note:** Illustration reduced.

Date	Mintage	XF40	MS60	MS63	MS65	MS66
1993	400	—	—	175	200	225
1993	5,000	PF65 150	PF67 175	PF69 200		

KM# 36 250 KWACHA
136.08 g., 0.925 Silver 4.0469 oz. ASW, 63 mm. **Obv:** National arms with supporters, date below **Rev:** Paradise Flycatchers on branch, denomination below **Note:** Illustration reduced.

Date	Mintage	XF40	MS60	MS63	MS65	MS66
1993	400	—	—	175	200	225
1993	5,000	PF65 150	PF67 175	PF69 200		

KM# 37 250 KWACHA
136.08 g., 0.925 Silver 4.0469 oz. ASW, 63 mm. **Obv:** National arms with supporters, date below **Rev:** Red-breasted Swallows facing each other on branches, denomination below **Note:** Illustration reduced.

Date	Mintage	XF40	MS60	MS63	MS65	MS66
1993	400	—	—	175	200	225
1993	5,000	PF65 150	PF67 175	PF69 200		

KM# 173 250 KWACHA
136.08 g., 0.925 Silver 4.0469 oz. ASW, 62.9 mm. **Subject:** Birds **Obv:** National arms with supporters, date below **Rev:** Two Lizard Buzzards, denomination below **Edge:** Reeded **Note:** Illustration reduced.

Date	Mintage	XF40	MS60	MS63	MS65	MS66
1994	—	PF65 150	PF67 175	PF69 200		

KM# 210 250 KWACHA
136.08 g., 0.925 Silver 4.0469 oz. ASW, 63 mm. **Rev:** Secretary Bird

Date	Mintage	XF40	MS60	MS63	MS65	MS66
1994	400	—	—	175	200	225
1994	5,000	PF65 150	PF67 175	PF69 200		

KM# 211 250 KWACHA
136.08 g., 0.925 Silver 4.0469 oz. ASW, 63 mm. **Rev:** African Scops Owl

Date	Mintage	XF40	MS60	MS63	MS65	MS66
1994	400	—	—	175	200	225
1994	5,000	PF65 150	PF67 175	PF69 200		

KM# 212 250 KWACHA
136.08 g., 0.925 Silver 4.0469 oz. ASW, 63 mm. **Rev:** African Jacana

Date	Mintage	XF40	MS60	MS63	MS65	MS66
1994	400	—	—	175	200	225
1994	5,000	PF65 150	PF67 175	PF69 200		

KM# 266 250 KWACHA
Silver **Rev:** Giraffe

Date	Mintage	VF20	XF40	MS60	MS63	MS65
1999	—	PF63 25.00	PF65 30.00	PF67 35.00		

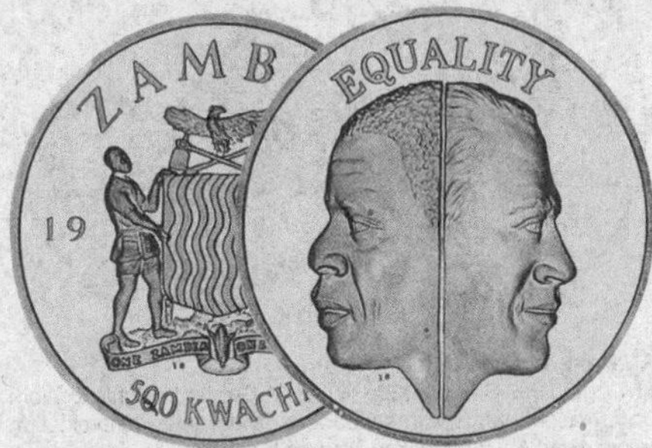

KM# 40 500 KWACHA
31.77 g., 0.999 Silver 1.0205 oz. ASW **Subject:** Equality **Obv:** National arms with supporters divide date, denomination below **Rev:** Black and white face profiles

Date	Mintage	VF20	XF40	MS60	MS63	MS65
1994	—	PF63 25.00	PF65 30.00	PF67 35.00		

KM# 41 500 KWACHA
31.77 g., 0.999 Silver 1.0205 oz. ASW **Subject:** Freedom of Speech **Obv:** National arms with supporters divide date, denomination below **Rev:** Perched African Fish Eagle

Date	Mintage	VF20	XF40	MS60	MS63	MS65
1994	—	PF63 25.00	PF65 30.00	PF67 35.00		

KM# 42 500 KWACHA
31.77 g., 0.999 Silver 1.0205 oz. ASW **Subject:** Rights of Religion and Culture **Obv:** National arms with supporters divide date, denomination below **Rev:** Books, scroll, and mask

Date	Mintage	VF20	XF40	MS60	MS63	MS65
1994	—	PF63 25.00	PF65 30.00	PF67 35.00		

KM# 43 500 KWACHA
31.77 g., 0.999 Silver 1.0205 oz. ASW **Subject:** Rights of Association **Obv:** National arms with supporters divide date, denomination below **Rev:** Lion cub and lamb

Date	Mintage	VF20	XF40	MS60	MS63	MS65
1994	—	PF63 30.00	PF65 35.00	PF67 40.00		

KM# 44 500 KWACHA
31.77 g., 0.999 Silver 1.0205 oz. ASW **Subject:** Rights to Work **Obv:** National arms with supporters divide date, denomination below **Rev:** African Masked Weaver building nest

Date	Mintage	VF20	XF40	MS60	MS63	MS65
1994	—	PF63 30.00	PF65 35.00	PF67 40.00		

KM# 45 500 KWACHA
31.77 g., 0.999 Silver 1.0205 oz. ASW **Subject:** Rights to Health **Obv:** National arms with supporters divide date, denomination below **Rev:** Shaman and Caduceus

Date	Mintage	VF20	XF40	MS60	MS63	MS65
1994	—	PF63 25.00	PF65 30.00	PF67 35.00		

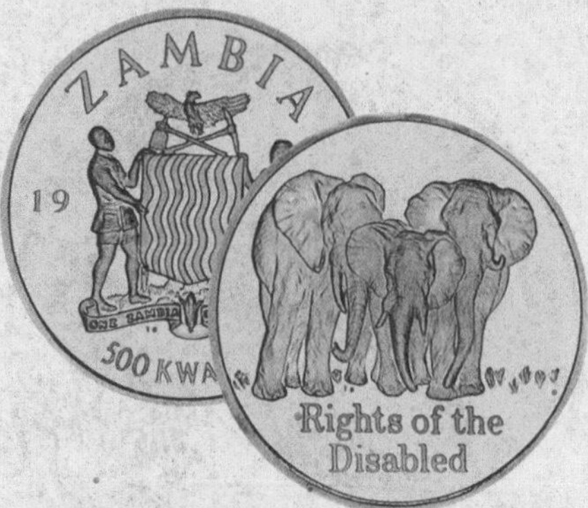

KM# 46 500 KWACHA
31.77 g., 0.999 Silver 1.0205 oz. ASW **Subject:** Rights of the Disabled **Obv:** National arms divide date, denomination below **Rev:** Three elephants

Date	Mintage	VF20	XF40	MS60	MS63	MS65
1994	—	PF63 30.00	PF65 35.00	PF67 40.00		

KM# 47 500 KWACHA
31.77 g., 0.999 Silver 1.0205 oz. ASW **Subject:** Rights to a Clean Environment **Obv:** National arms divide date, denomination below **Rev:** Two South African Shelducks

Date	Mintage	VF20	XF40	MS60	MS63	MS65
1994	—	PF63 30.00	PF65 35.00	PF67 40.00		

KM# 48 500 KWACHA
31.77 g., 0.999 Silver 1.0205 oz. ASW **Subject:** Children's Rights **Obv:** National arms divide date, denomination below **Rev:** Fawn

Date	Mintage	VF20	XF40	MS60	MS63	MS65
1994	—	PF63 30.00	PF65 35.00	PF67 40.00		

KM# 49 500 KWACHA
31.77 g., 0.999 Silver 1.0205 oz. ASW **Subject:** Women's Rights **Obv:** National arms divide date, denomination below **Rev:** Women with firewood

Date	Mintage	VF20	XF40	MS60	MS63	MS65
1994	—	PF63 25.00	PF65 30.00	PF67 35.00		

KM# 214 500 KWACHA
31.10 g., 0.999 Silver 0.9989 oz. ASW **Subject:** Woman's Rights

Date	Mintage	VF20	XF40	MS60	MS63	MS65
1994	—	PF65 50.00	PF67 60.00			

KM# 136 500 KWACHA
223.00 g., 0.999 Silver 7.1624 oz. ASW, 75.15 mm. **Subject:** Equality **Obv:** National arms divide date, denomination below **Rev:** Black and white facial profiles **Edge:** Reeded **Note:** Illustration reduced.

Date	Mintage	VF20	XF40	MS60	MS63	MS65
1995	—	PF63 175	PF65 200	PF67 225		

KM# 225 500 KWACHA
155.50 g., 0.999 Silver 4.9944 oz. ASW **Rev:** Freedom of Speech

Date	Mintage	VF20	XF40	MS60	MS63	MS65
1995	2,000	PF67 175				

KM# 226 500 KWACHA
155.50 g., 0.999 Silver 4.9944 oz. ASW **Subject:** Women's Rights

Date	Mintage	VF20	XF40	MS60	MS63	MS65
1995	2,000	PF67 175				

KM# 227 500 KWACHA
155.50 g., 0.999 Silver 4.9944 oz. ASW **Subject:** Rights of Association

Date	Mintage	VF20	XF40	MS60	MS63	MS65
1995	2,000	PF67 175				

KM# 228 500 KWACHA
155.50 g., 0.999 Silver 4.9944 oz. ASW **Subject:** Right to Work

Date	Mintage	VF20	XF40	MS60	MS63	MS65
1995	2,000	PF67 175				

KM# 229 500 KWACHA
155.50 g., 0.999 Silver 4.9944 oz. ASW **Subject:** Right to Health

Date	Mintage	VF20	XF40	MS60	MS63	MS65
1995	2,000	PF67 175				

KM# 230 500 KWACHA
155.50 g., 0.999 Silver 4.9944 oz. ASW **Subject:** Right to a Clean Environment

Date	Mintage	VF20	XF40	MS60	MS63	MS65
1995	2,000	PF67 175				

KM# 231 500 KWACHA
155.50 g., 0.999 Silver 4.9944 oz. ASW **Subject:** Children's Rights

Date	Mintage	VF20	XF40	MS60	MS63	MS65
1995	2,000	PF67 175				

KM# 232 500 KWACHA
155.50 g., 0.999 Silver 4.9944 oz. ASW **Subject:** Rights of Religion and Culture

Date	Mintage	VF20	XF40	MS60	MS63	MS65
1995	2,000	PF67 175				

KM# 233 500 KWACHA
155.50 g., 0.999 Silver 4.9944 oz. ASW **Subject:** Rights for the Disabled

Date	Mintage	VF20	XF40	MS60	MS63	MS65
1995	2,000	PF67 175				

KM# 53 500 KWACHA
31.10 g., 0.999 Silver 0.999 oz. ASW, 38 mm. **Subject:** Diana - The People's Princess **Obv:** National arms divide date, denomination below **Rev:** Diana facing **Edge:** Reeded with plain section for serial number

Date	Mintage	VF20	XF40	MS60	MS63	MS65
1997	Est. 13211	PF63 22.00	PF65 25.00	PF67 30.00		

KM# 182 500 KWACHA
1.22 g., 0.9999 Gold 0.0392 oz. AGW, 13.9 mm. **Obv:** National arms **Obv. Legend:** BANK OF ZAMBIA **Rev:** Bust of Dr. David Livingstone at lower left in front of wall **Edge:** Reeded

Date	Mintage	VF20	XF40	MS60	MS63	MS65
1999	—	PF63 60.00	PF65 70.00			

KM# 216 750 KWACHA
31.10 g., 0.999 Gold 0.9989 oz. AGW **Subject:** Freedom of Speech

Date	Mintage	VF20	XF40	MS60	MS63	MS65
1994	—	PF67 1,400				

KM# 217 750 KWACHA
31.10 g., 0.999 Gold 0.9989 oz. AGW **Subject:** Women's Rights

Date	Mintage	VF20	XF40	MS60	MS63	MS65
1994	—	PF67 1,400				

KM# 218 750 KWACHA
31.10 g., 0.999 Gold 0.9989 oz. AGW **Subject:** Rights of Association

Date	Mintage	VF20	XF40	MS60	MS63	MS65
1994	—	PF67 1,400				

KM# 219 750 KWACHA
31.10 g., 0.999 Gold 0.9989 oz. AGW **Subject:** Right to Work

Date	Mintage	VF20	XF40	MS60	MS63	MS65
1994	—	PF67 1,400				

KM# 220 750 KWACHA
31.100 Gold .999 **Rev:** Rights to Health

Date	Mintage	VF20	XF40	MS60	MS63	MS65
1994	—	PF67 1,400				

KM# 221 750 KWACHA
31.10 g., 0.999 Gold 0.9989 oz. AGW **Subject:** Right to a Clean Environment

Date	Mintage	VF20	XF40	MS60	MS63	MS65
1994	—	PF67 1,400				

KM# 222 750 KWACHA
31.10 g., 0.999 Gold 0.9989 oz. AGW **Subject:** Children's Rights

Date	Mintage	VF20	XF40	MS60	MS63	MS65
1994	—	PF67 1,400				

KM# 223 750 KWACHA
31.10 g., 0.999 Gold 0.9989 oz. AGW **Subject:** Rights of Religion & Culture

Date	Mintage	VF20	XF40	MS60	MS63	MS65
1994	—	PF67 1,400				

KM# 224 750 KWACHA
31.10 g., 0.999 Gold 0.9989 oz. AGW **Subject:** Rights of the Disabled

Date	Mintage	VF20	XF40	MS60	MS63	MS65
1994	—	PF67 1,400				

KM# 179 1000 KWACHA
28.30 g., Silver with gilt cameo, 27 mm. **Subject:** Silver Jubilee, Elizabeth II and Prince Philip **Obv:** National arms **Rev:** Royal couple

Date	Mintage	VF20	XF40	MS60	MS63	MS65
1997	30,000	PF65 55.00	PF67 65.00			

KM# 237 1000 KWACHA
7.78 g., 0.9999 Gold 0.2501 oz. AGW **Obv:** National arms **Rev:** Screaming eagle

Date	Mintage	VF20	XF40	MS60	MS63	MS65
1997	5,000	PF65 500	PF67 550			

KM# 238 1000 KWACHA
7.78 g., 0.9999 Gold 0.2501 oz. AGW **Obv:** National arms **Rev:** Lion family

Date	Mintage	VF20	XF40	MS60	MS63	MS65
1997	5,000	PF65 450	PF67 500			

KM# 241 1000 KWACHA
28.28 g., 0.925 Silver 0.841 oz. ASW partially gilt **Subject:** Elizabeth II and Prince Philip, 50th Wedding Anniversary

Date	Mintage	VF20	XF40	MS60	MS63	MS65
1997	30,000	PF65 35.00				

KM# 120 1000 KWACHA
28.50 g., Silver Plated Copper-Nickel, 38 mm. **Subject:** European Unity - One Currency **Obv:** National arms divide date, denomination below **Rev:** Multicolor 5 Euro note face design **Edge:** Reeded

Date	Mintage	VF20	XF40	MS60	MS63	MS65
1998	—	PF65 9.00				

KM# 121 1000 KWACHA
28.50 g., Silver Plated Copper-Nickel, 38 mm. **Subject:** European Unity - One Currency **Obv:** National arms divide date, denomination below **Rev:** Multicolor 5 Euro note back design **Edge:** Reeded

Date	Mintage	VF20	XF40	MS60	MS63	MS65
1998	—	PF65 9.00				

KM# 122 1000 KWACHA
28.50 g., Silver Plated Copper-Nickel, 38 mm. **Subject:** European Unity - One Currency **Obv:** National arms divide date, denomination below **Rev:** Multicolor 10 Euro note face design **Edge:** Reeded

Date	Mintage	VF20	XF40	MS60	MS63	MS65
1998	—	PF65 9.00				

KM# 123 1000 KWACHA
28.50 g., Silver Plated Copper-Nickel, 38 mm. **Subject:** European Unity - One Currency **Obv:** National arms divide date, denomination below **Rev:** Multicolor 10 Euro note back design **Edge:** Reeded

Date	Mintage	VF20	XF40	MS60	MS63	MS65
1998	—	PF65 9.00				

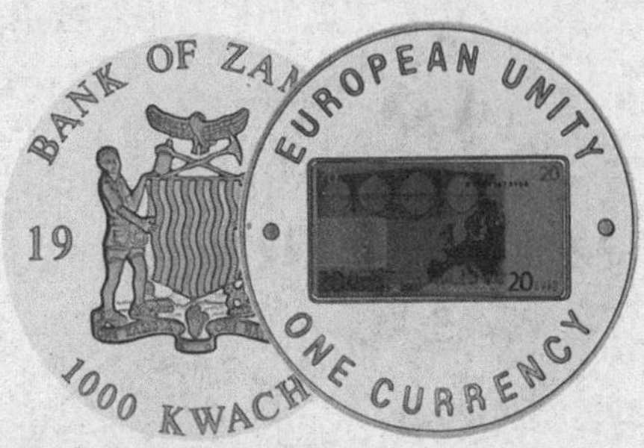

KM# 125 1000 KWACHA
28.50 g., Silver Plated Copper-Nickel, 38 mm. **Subject:** European Unity - One Currency **Obv:** National arms divide date, denomination below **Rev:** Multicolor 20 Euro note back design **Edge:** Reeded

Date	Mintage	VF20	XF40	MS60	MS63	MS65
1998	—	PF65 9.00				

KM# 126 1000 KWACHA
28.50 g., Silver Plated Copper-Nickel, 38 mm. **Subject:** European Unity - One Currency **Obv:** National arms divide date, denomination below **Rev:** Multicolor 50 Euro note face design **Edge:** Reeded

Date	Mintage	VF20	XF40	MS60	MS63	MS65
1998	—	PF65 10.00				

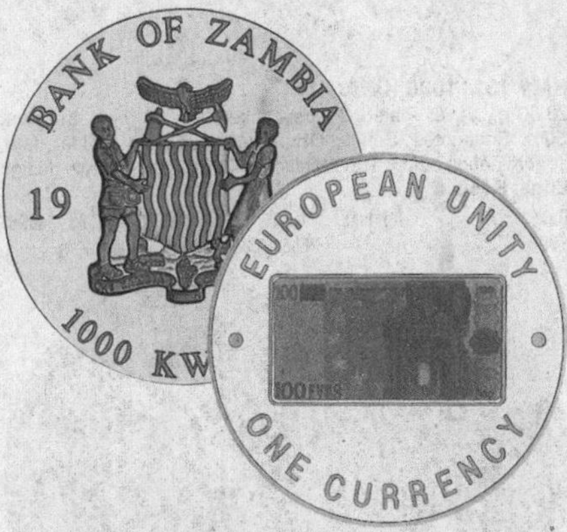

KM# 128 1000 KWACHA
28.50 g., Silver Plated Copper-Nickel-Zinc, 38 mm. **Subject:** Euro Banknotes Series **Obv:** National arms divide date, denomination below **Rev:** Multicolor 100 Euro note face design **Edge:** Reeded

Date	Mintage	VF20	XF40	MS60	MS63	MS65
1998	—	PF65 10.00				

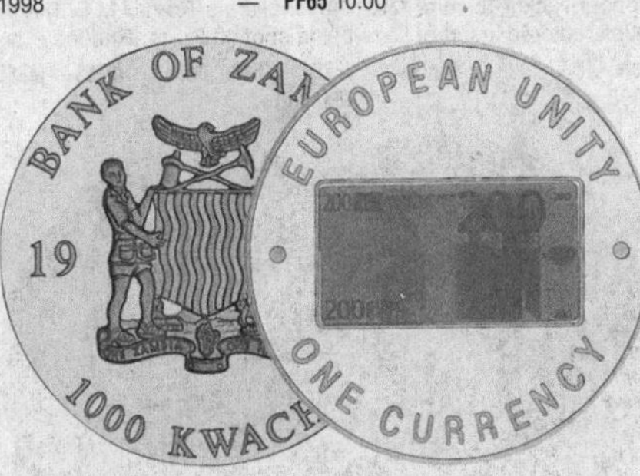

KM# 130 1000 KWACHA
28.50 g., Silver Plated Copper-Nickel-Zinc, 38 mm. **Subject:** Euro Banknotes Series **Obv:** National arms divide date, denomination below **Rev:** Multicolor 200 Euro note face design **Edge:** Reeded

Date	Mintage	VF20	XF40	MS60	MS63	MS65
1998	—	PF65 10.00				

KM# 131 1000 KWACHA
28.50 g., Silver Plated Copper-Nickel-Zinc, 38 mm. **Subject:** Euro Banknotes Series **Obv:** National arms divide date, denomination below **Rev:** Multicolor 200 Euro note back design **Edge:** Reeded

Date	Mintage	VF20	XF40	MS60	MS63	MS65
1998	—	PF65 10.00				

KM# 132 1000 KWACHA
28.50 g., Silver Plated Copper-Nickel-Zinc, 38 mm. **Subject:** Euro Banknotes Series **Obv:** National arms divide date, denomination below **Rev:** Multicolor 500 Euro note face design **Edge:** Reeded

Date	Mintage	VF20	XF40	MS60	MS63	MS65
1998	—	PF65 10.00				

KM# 197 1000 KWACHA
Copper-Nickel, 39 mm. **Obv:** National arms **Rev:** H.M.S. Titanic at left, colored insert of flairs being shot off **Edge:** Reeded

Date	Mintage	VF20	XF40	MS60	MS63	MS65
1998	—	PF65 7.00				

KM# 198 1000 KWACHA
Copper-Nickel, 39 mm. **Obv:** National arms **Rev:** R.M.S. Titanic at left, color insert of sinking ship at right

Date	Mintage	VF20	XF40	MS60	MS63	MS65
1998	—	PF65 7.00				

KM# 91 1000 KWACHA
28.72 g., Copper-Nickel, 38 mm. **Subject:** European Unity **Obv:** National arms divide date, denomination below **Rev:** Multicolor 20 euro note **Edge:** Plain **Note:** Deleted per contributor

Date	Mintage	VF20	XF40	MS60	MS63	MS65
1999	—	PF65 9.00				

KM# 109 1000 KWACHA
20.00 g., 0.925 Silver 0.5948 oz. ASW, 38.6 mm. **Series:** Sydney Olympics **Obv:** Crowned head right within circle, divides date above arms and denomination **Rev:** Discus thrower **Edge:** Plain

Date	Mintage	VF20	XF40	MS60	MS63	MS65
1999	—	PF63 22.00	PF65 25.00			

KM# 124 1000 KWACHA
28.50 g., Silver Plated Copper-Nickel, 38 mm. **Subject:** European Unity - One Currency **Obv:** National arms divide date, denomination below **Rev:** Multicolor 20 Euro note face design **Edge:** Reeded

Date	Mintage	VF20	XF40	MS60	MS63	MS65
1999	—	PF65 9.00				

KM# 127 1000 KWACHA
28.50 g., Silver Plated Copper-Nickel, 38 mm. **Subject:** European Unity - One Currency **Obv:** National arms divide date, denomination below **Rev:** Multicolor 50 Euro note back design **Edge:** Reeded

Date	Mintage	VF20	XF40	MS60	MS63	MS65
1999	—	PF65 20.00				

KM# 129 1000 KWACHA
28.50 g., Silver Plated Copper-Nickel-Zinc, 38 mm. **Subject:** Euro Banknotes Series **Obv:** National arms divide date, denomination below **Rev:** Multicolor 100 Euro note back design **Edge:** Reeded

Date	Mintage	VF20	XF40	MS60	MS63	MS65
1999	—	PF65 20.00				

KM# 133 1000 KWACHA
28.50 g., Silver Plated Copper-Nickel-Zinc, 38 mm. **Subject:** Euro Banknotes Series **Obv:** National arms divide date, denomination below **Rev:** Multicolor 500 Euro note back design **Edge:** Reeded

Date	Mintage	VF20	XF40	MS60	MS63	MS65
1999	—	PF65 20.00				

KM# 176 1000 KWACHA
19.92 g., 0.925 Silver 0.5924 oz. ASW, 38.4 mm. **Obv:** British Queen Elizabeth II above Zambian arms **Rev:** 1st Man on the Moon **Edge:** Plain

Date	Mintage	VF20	XF40	MS60	MS63	MS65
1999	—	PF63 27.00	PF65 30.00			

KM# 180 1000 KWACHA
28.00 g., Copper-Nickel, 27.00 mm. **Subject:** !st Anniversary Death of Princess Diana **Obv:** National arms **Rev:** Bust of Diana and her memorial

Date	Mintage	VF20	XF40	MS60	MS63	MS65
1999	—	PF65 35.00				

KM# 191 1000 KWACHA
28.00 g., Copper-Nickel, 38 mm. **Obv:** National Arms **Rev:** Montage of all seven Euro bank notes

Date	Mintage	VF20	XF40	MS60	MS63	MS65
1999	—	—	—	—	12.50	—

KM# 192 1000 KWACHA
28.00 g., Copper-Nickel, 38 mm. **Obv:** National Arms **Rev:** European Commission HQ building

Date	Mintage	VF20	XF40	MS60	MS63	MS65
1999	—	—	—	—	12.50	—

KM# 193 1000 KWACHA
28.00 g., Copper-Nickel, 38 mm. **Obv:** National Arms **Rev:** Europa riding bull

Date	Mintage	VF20	XF40	MS60	MS63	MS65
1999	—	—	—	—	12.50	—

KM# 194 1000 KWACHA
28.00 g., Copper-Nickel, 38 mm. **Obv:** National arms **Rev:** Portraits of Adenauer, Schuman and deGasperi

Date	Mintage	VF20	XF40	MS60	MS63	MS65
1999	—	—	—	—	12.50	—

KM# 74 1000 KWACHA
29.00 g., Copper-Nickel, 40 mm. **Obv:** Crowned head right above arms with supporters divides date **Rev:** Dated calendar within circular design **Shape:** 7-sided

Date	Mintage	VF20	XF40	MS60	MS63	MS65
2000	—	PF65 18.00				

KM# 75 1000 KWACHA
20.00 g., Copper-Nickel, 48x30 mm. **Subject:** 100th Birthday - Queen Mother **Obv:** Head with tiara right divides date above arms **Rev:** Shaded bust facing **Edge:** Reeded **Shape:** Oval

Date	Mintage	VF20	XF40	MS60	MS63	MS65
2000	—	PF65 13.50				

KM# 76 1000 KWACHA
20.00 g., Copper-Nickel, 48x30 mm. **Subject:** 100th Birthday - Queen Mother **Obv:** Head with tiara right divides date above arms **Rev:** Black and white photo of Queen Mother seated on throne at 1937 coronation

Date	Mintage	VF20	XF40	MS60	MS63	MS65
2000	—	PF65 13.50				

KM# 77 1000 KWACHA
20.00 g., Copper-Nickel, 48x30 mm. **Subject:** 100th Birthday - Queen Mother **Obv:** Head with tiara right divides date above arms **Rev:** Black and white photo of Queen Mother as an elderly lady

Date	Mintage	VF20	XF40	MS60	MS63	MS65
2000	—	PF65 13.50				

KM# 95 1000 KWACHA
Copper-Nickel, 48 x 30.1 mm. **Series:** 1,000 Years of Exploration **Obv:** Head with tiara right divides date above arms **Rev:** Multicolor portrait of Leif Ericksson and Viking ship **Edge:** Reeded

Date	Mintage	VF20	XF40	MS60	MS63	MS65
2000	15,000	PF65 12.00				

KM# 96 1000 KWACHA
Copper-Nickel **Series:** 1,000 Years of Exploration **Obv:** Head with tiara right divides date above arms **Rev:** Multicolor portrait of Marco Polo and ship

Date	Mintage	VF20	XF40	MS60	MS63	MS65
2000	15,000	PF65 12.00				

KM# 97 1000 KWACHA
Copper-Nickel **Series:** 1,000 Years of Exploration **Obv:** Head with tiara right divides date above arms **Rev:** Multicolor portrait of Columbus and ship

Date	Mintage	VF20	XF40	MS60	MS63	MS65
2000	15,000	PF65 12.00				

KM# 98 1000 KWACHA
Copper-Nickel **Series:** 1,000 Years of Exploration **Obv:** Head with tiara right divides date above arms **Rev:** Multicolor portrait of Sir Francis Drake and ship

Date	Mintage	VF20	XF40	MS60	MS63	MS65
2000	15,000	PF65 12.00				

KM# 99 1000 KWACHA
Copper-Nickel **Series:** 1,000 Years of Exploration **Obv:** Head with tiara right divides date above arms **Rev:** Multicolor portrait of Captain Cook and ship

Date	Mintage	VF20	XF40	MS60	MS63	MS65
2000	15,000	PF65 12.00				

KM# 100 1000 KWACHA
Copper-Nickel **Series:** 1,000 Years of Exploration **Obv:** Head with tiara right divides date above arms **Rev:** Multicolor portrait of Amundsen and ship

Date	Mintage	VF20	XF40	MS60	MS63	MS65
2000	15,000	PF65 12.00				

KM# 147 1000 KWACHA
28.90 g., 0.925 Silver 0.8595 oz. ASW, 40.3 mm. **Subject:** African Wildlife **Obv:** Head with tiara right divides date above arms **Rev:** Multicolor snarling leopard under protective acrylic, denomination below **Edge:** Reeded

Date	Mintage	VF20	XF40	MS60	MS63	MS65
2000	—	PF63 35.00	PF65 40.00			

KM# 148 1000 KWACHA
28.90 g., 0.925 Silver 0.8595 oz. ASW, 40.3 mm. **Subject:** African Wildlife **Obv:** Head with tiara right divides date above national arms **Rev:** Multicolor white stork under protective acrylic, denomination below **Edge:** Reeded

Date	Mintage	VF20	XF40	MS60	MS63	MS65
2000	—	PF63 35.00	PF65 40.00			

KM# 149 1000 KWACHA
28.90 g., 0.925 Silver 0.8595 oz. ASW, 40.3 mm. **Subject:** African Wildlife **Obv:** Head with tiara right divides date above national arms **Rev:** Multicolor cheetah under protective acrylic, denomination below **Edge:** Reeded

Date	Mintage	VF20	XF40	MS60	MS63	MS65
2000	—	PF63 35.00	PF65 40.00			

KM# 190 1000 KWACHA
Silver **Obv:** Head above arms **Rev:** Multicolor image of Lief Ericksson in Canada **Shape:** Vertical oval

Date	Mintage	VF20	XF40	MS60	MS63	MS65
2000	—	PF63 30.00	PF65 35.00			

KM# 272 1000 KWACHA
Silver **Rev:** Hippopotamus in color

Date	Mintage	VF20	XF40	MS60	MS63	MS65
2000	—	PF65 45.00				

KM# 137 2000 KWACHA
22.50 g., Copper-Nickel, 38 mm. **Subject:** World Cup Soccer **Obv:** National arms with supporters divide date, denomination below **Rev:** Player kicking ball **Edge:** Reeded

Date	Mintage	VF20	XF40	MS60	MS63	MS65
1994	—	PF65 15.00	PF67 20.00			

KM# 138 2000 KWACHA
22.50 g., Copper-Nickel, 38 mm. **Subject:** World Cup Soccer **Obv:** National arms with supporters divide date, denomination below **Rev:** Two players in action **Edge:** Reeded

Date	Mintage	VF20	XF40	MS60	MS63	MS65
1994	—	PF65 15.00	PF67 20.00			

KM# 139 2000 KWACHA
22.50 g., Copper-Nickel, 38 mm. **Subject:** World Cup Soccer **Obv:** National arms with supporters divide date, denomination below **Rev:** Three players and "Winner Brazil" **Edge:** Reeded

Date	Mintage	VF20	XF40	MS60	MS63	MS65
1994	—	PF65 15.00	PF67 20.00			

KM# 54 2000 KWACHA
3.11 g., 0.9999 Gold 0.100 oz. AGW **Subject:** Diana - The People's Princess **Obv:** National arms with supporters divide date, denomination below **Rev:** Head facing **Note:** Similar to 200 Kwacha, KM#52.

Date	Mintage	VF20	XF40	MS60	MS63	MS65
1997	—	PF65 180	PF67 200			

KM# 152 2000 KWACHA
20.22 g., 0.9999 Silver 0.650 oz. ASW, 38 mm. **Subject:** World History **Obv:** National arms with supporters divide date, denomination below **Rev:** Human figure study **Edge:** Reeded

Date	Mintage	VF20	XF40	MS60	MS63	MS65
1997	—	PF63 25.00	PF65 27.00			

KM# 68 2000 KWACHA
15.55 g., 0.999 Silver 0.4995 oz. ASW **Subject:** Taipai Subway **Obv:** National arms **Rev:** Train with inset diamond headlight **Note:** Struck at Singapore Mint.

Date	Mintage	VF20	XF40	MS60	MS63	MS65
1998	9,999	PF63 40.00	PF65 45.00	PF67 50.00		

KM# 146 2000 KWACHA/100 GUILDERS
26.00 g., Copper-Nickel, 38 mm. **Subject:** World Cup Soccer **Obv:** National arms with supporters divide date, denomination below **Rev:** Two soccer players of Suriname **Edge:** Reeded **Note:** Zambia/Suriname muled dies error. Obverse is Zambia and the reverse is Suriname. Not in silver although it says so.

Date	Mintage	VF20	XF40	MS60	MS63	MS65
1994	—	PF63 75.00	PF65 95.00			

KM# 55 2500 KWACHA
15.55 g., 0.4995 Silver 0.2497 oz. ASW **Subject:** Diana - The People's Princess **Obv:** National arms with supporters divide date, denomination below **Rev:** With sons, William and Harry

Date	Mintage	VF20	XF40	MS60	MS63	MS65
1997	Est. 1997	PF63 60.00	PF65 70.00			

KM# 107 2500 KWACHA
15.55 g., 0.925 Silver 0.4626 oz. ASW, 36 mm. **Series:** World Health Organization **Obv:** National arms with supporters divide date, denomination below **Rev:** Bust at left facing right, logo at right **Edge:** Reeded

Date	Mintage	VF20	XF40	MS60	MS63	MS65
1998	—	PF63 27.00	PF65 30.00			

KM# 134 4000 KWACHA
31.10 g., 0.999 Silver 0.999 oz. ASW, 38.5 mm. **Subject:** Year of the Tiger **Obv:** National arms with supporters divide date, denomination below **Rev:** Gold bat disc mounted above tiger **Edge:** Reeded

Date	Mintage	VF20	XF40	MS60	MS63	MS65
1997	—	PF65 110	PF67 125			

KM# 69 4000 KWACHA
31.10 g., 0.999 Silver 0.999 oz. ASW **Subject:** Taipai Subway **Obv:** National arms **Rev:** Train with inset diamond headlight **Note:** Struck at Singapore Mint.

Date	Mintage	VF20	XF40	MS60	MS63	MS65
1998	9,999	PF63 60.00	PF65 70.00			

KM# 155 4000 KWACHA
30.33 g., 0.999 Silver 0.9742 oz. ASW, 38 mm. **Subject:** King of Peace - King Hussein of Jordan **Obv:** National arms with supporters divide date, denomination below **Rev:** Bust at left looking right, multicolor view of Petra at right **Edge:** Reeded

Date	Mintage	VF20	XF40	MS60	MS63	MS65
1998	—	PF63 45.00	PF65 50.00	PF67 60.00		

KM# 161 4000 KWACHA
28.95 g., Copper-Nickel, 37.9 mm. **Subject:** Patrons of the Ocean **Obv:** National arms divide date above "999", denomination below **Rev:** Sea Turtle and fish **Edge:** Reeded

Date	Mintage	VF20	XF40	MS60	MS63	MS65
1998	—	PF63 12.00	PF65 15.00			

KM# 162 4000 KWACHA
28.95 g., Copper-Nickel, 37.9 mm. **Subject:** Patrons of the Ocean **Obv:** National arms divide date above "999", denomination below **Rev:** Seahorse and fish **Edge:** Reeded

Date	Mintage	VF20	XF40	MS60	MS63	MS65
1998	—	PF63 12.00	PF65 15.00			

KM# 163 4000 KWACHA
28.95 g., Copper-Nickel, 37.9 mm. **Subject:** Patrons of the Ocean **Obv:** National arms divide date above "999", denomination below **Rev:** Two dolphins **Edge:** Reeded

Date	Mintage	VF20	XF40	MS60	MS63	MS65
1998	—	PF63 12.00	PF65 15.00			

KM# 164 4000 KWACHA
28.95 g., Copper-Nickel, 37.9 mm. **Subject:** Patrons of the Ocean **Obv:** National arms divide date above "999", denomination below **Rev:** Coelacanth **Edge:** Reeded

Date	Mintage	VF20	XF40	MS60	MS63	MS65
1998	—	PF63 12.00	PF65 15.00			

KM# 195 4000 KWACHA
31.11 g., 0.999 Silver 0.999 oz. ASW, 38.6 mm. **Obv:** Arms **Rev:** Mother and baby elephant

Date	Mintage	VF20	XF40	MS60	MS63	MS65
1998	—	—	—	—	35.00	40.00

KM# 196 4000 KWACHA
31.11 g., 0.999 Silver 0.999 oz. ASW, 38.6 mm. **Obv:** Arms **Rev:** Elephant

Date	Mintage	VF20	XF40	MS60	MS63	MS65
1998	—	—	—	—	35.00	40.00

KM# 261 4000 KWACHA
0.999 Silver **Subject:** Lady Diana, 1st Anniversary of Death

Date	Mintage	VF20	XF40	MS60	MS63	MS65
1998	—	PF65 45.00				

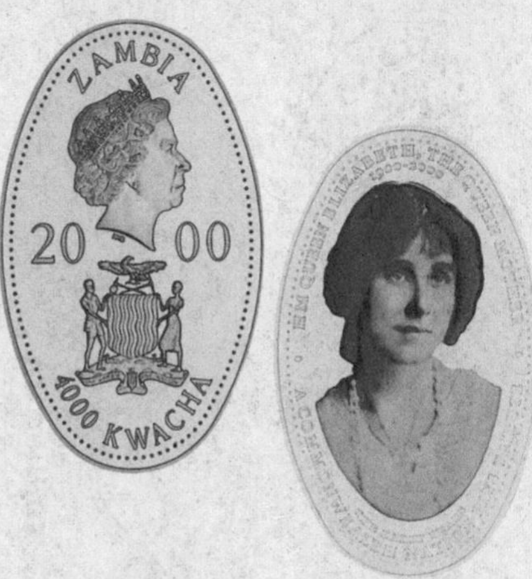

KM# 78 4000 KWACHA
20.00 g., 0.925 Silver 0.5948 oz. ASW, 48x30 mm. **Subject:** 100th Birthday - Queen Mother **Obv:** Head with tiara right divides date above arms **Rev:** Black and white photo of the Queen Mother as a young lady **Edge:** Reeded **Shape:** Oval

Date	Mintage	VF20	XF40	MS60	MS63	MS65
2000	—	PF63 15.00	PF65 18.00			

KM# 79 4000 KWACHA
20.00 g., 0.925 Silver 0.5948 oz. ASW, 48x30 mm. **Subject:** 100th Birthday - Queen Mother **Obv:** Head with tiara right divides date above arms **Rev:** Black and white photo of Queen Mother on throne at 1937 coronation **Shape:** Oval

Date	Mintage	VF20	XF40	MS60	MS63	MS65
2000	—	PF63 15.00	PF65 18.00			

KM# 80 4000 KWACHA
20.00 g., 0.925 Silver 0.5948 oz. ASW, 48x30 mm. **Subject:** 100th Birthday - Queen Mother **Obv:** Head with tiara right divides date above arms **Rev:** Black and white photo of an elderly Queen Mother **Shape:** Oval

Date	Mintage	VF20	XF40	MS60	MS63	MS65
2000	—	PF63 15.00	PF65 18.00			

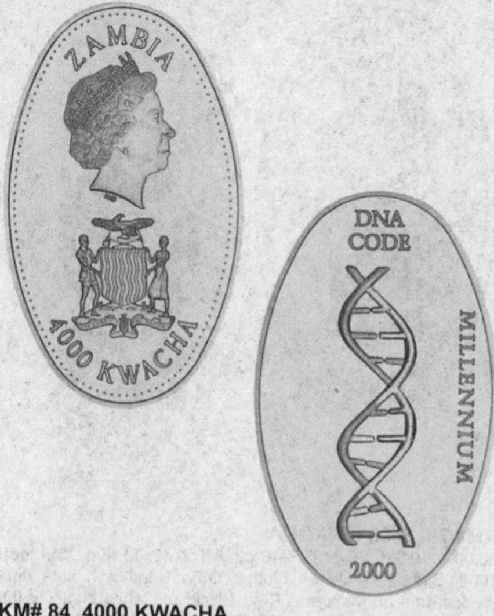

KM# 84 4000 KWACHA

20.00 g., 0.925 Silver 0.5948 oz. ASW, 30.1x48 mm. **Subject:** Millennium - DNA Code **Obv:** Head with tiara right above arms and denomination **Rev:** DNA chain, date below **Edge:** Reeded

Date	Mintage	VF20	XF40	MS60	MS63	MS65
2000	—	PF65 50.00	PF67 60.00			

KM# 85 4000 KWACHA

25.10 g., 0.925 Silver 0.7465 oz. ASW, 37.9 mm. **Series:** Wildlife Protection **Obv:** Crowned head right below arms **Rev:** Lion head hologram **Edge:** Reeded **Note:** Lighter weight and smaller diameter than official specifications

Date	Mintage	VF20	XF40	MS60	MS63	MS65
2000	—	PF63 35.00	PF65 40.00			

KM# 101 4000 KWACHA

20.00 g., 0.925 Silver 0.5948 oz. ASW, 48x30.1 mm. **Series:** 1000 Years of Exploration **Obv:** Head with tiara right divides date above arms **Rev:** Multicolor portrait of Leif Eriksson and ship **Edge:** Reeded **Shape:** Oval

Date	Mintage	VF20	XF40	MS60	MS63	MS65
2000	—	PF63 15.00	PF65 18.00			

KM# 102 4000 KWACHA

20.00 g., 0.925 Silver 0.5948 oz. ASW **Subject:** 1000 Years of Exploration **Obv:** Head with tiara right divides date above arms **Rev:** Multicolor portrait of Marco Polo and ship **Shape:** Oval

Date	Mintage	VF20	XF40	MS60	MS63	MS65
2000	—	PF63 15.00	PF65 18.00			

KM# 103 4000 KWACHA

20.00 g., 0.925 Silver 0.5948 oz. ASW **Subject:** 1000 Years of Exploration **Obv:** Head with tiara right divides date above arms **Rev:** Multicolor portrait of Columbus and ship **Shape:** Oval

Date	Mintage	VF20	XF40	MS60	MS63	MS65
2000	—	PF63 15.00	PF65 18.00			

KM# 104 4000 KWACHA

20.00 g., 0.925 Silver 0.5948 oz. ASW **Subject:** 1000 Years of Exploration **Obv:** Head with tiara right divides date above arms **Rev:** Multicolor portrait of Sir Francis Drake and ship

Date	Mintage	VF20	XF40	MS60	MS63	MS65
2000	—	PF63 15.00	PF65 18.00			

KM# 105 4000 KWACHA

20.00 g., 0.925 Silver 0.5948 oz. ASW **Subject:** 1000 Years of Exploration **Obv:** Head with tiara right divides date above arms **Rev:** Multicolor portrait of Captain Cook and ship **Shape:** Oval

Date	Mintage	VF20	XF40	MS60	MS63	MS65
2000	—	PF63 15.00	PF65 18.00			

KM# 106 4000 KWACHA

20.00 g., 0.925 Silver 0.5948 oz. ASW **Subject:** 1000 Years of Exploration **Obv:** Head with tiara right divides date above arms **Rev:** Multicolor portrait of Amundsen and ship **Shape:** Oval

Date	Mintage	VF20	XF40	MS60	MS63	MS65
2000	—	PF63 15.00	PF65 18.00			

KM# 158 4000 KWACHA

31.00 g., 0.999 Silver 0.9957 oz. ASW, 38.8 mm. **Subject:** African Wildlife **Obv:** Head with tiara right divides date above arms **Rev:** Leopard and two cubs, denomination below **Edge:** Reeded

Date	Mintage	VF20	XF40	MS60	MS63	MS65
2000	—	PF63 38.00	PF65 42.00			

KM# 175 4000 KWACHA

23.00 g., 0.999 Silver 0.7387 oz. ASW, 40 mm. **Obv:** Head with tiara right divides date above arms **Rev:** Dated calendar **Shape:** Seven-sided

Date	Mintage	VF20	XF40	MS60	MS63	MS65
2000 Prooflike	—	—	—	—	40.00	45.00